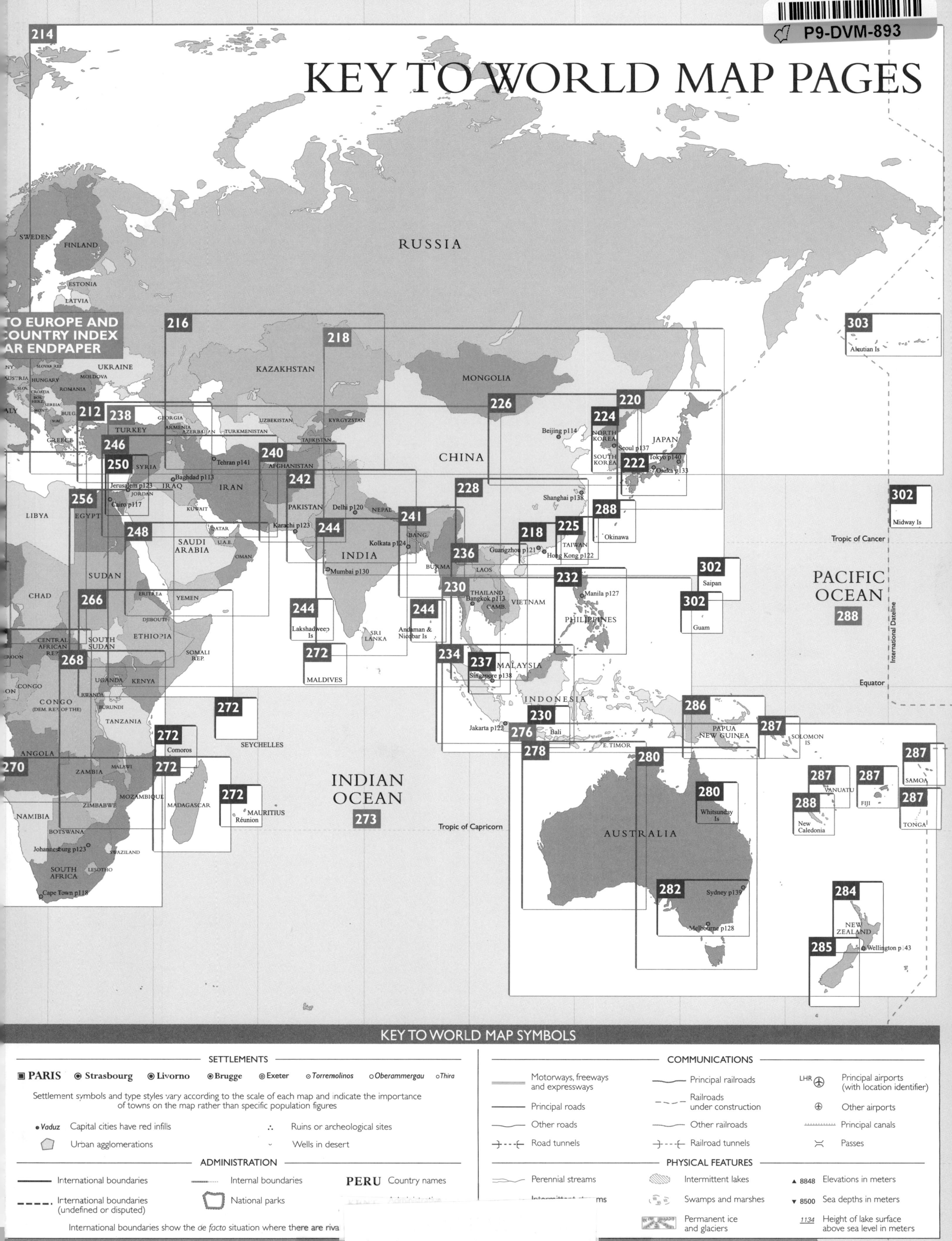

P9-DVM-893

KEY TO WORLD MAP PAGES

KEY TO WORLD MAP SYMBOLS

SETTLEMENTS

■ **PARIS**   ◉ **Strasbourg**   ◉ **Livorno**   ◉ **Brugge**   ◉ **Exeter**   ⊙ **Torremolinos**   ○ *Oberammergau*   ○ *Thira*

Settlement symbols and type styles vary according to the scale of each map and indicate the importance
of towns on the map rather than specific population figures

● *Vaduz*   Capital cities have red infills

Urban agglomerations

∴ Ruins or archeological sites

Wells in desert

ADMINISTRATION

International boundaries

Internal boundaries

PERU   Country names

National parks

International boundaries
(undefined or disputed)

International boundaries show the *de facto* situation where there are riva

COMMUNICATIONS

Motorways, freeways
and expressways

Principal roads

Other roads

Road tunnels

Principal railroads

Railroads
under construction

Other railroads

Railroad tunnels

LHR ⊕ Principal airports
(with location identifier)

⊕ Other airports

Principal canals

✕ Passes

PHYSICAL FEATURES

Perennial streams

Intermittent streams

Intermittent lakes

Swamps and marshes

Permanent ice
and glaciers

▲ 8848 Elevations in meters

▼ 8500 Sea depths in meters

1134 Height of lake surface
above sea level in meters

OXFORD

ATLAS

OF THE

WORLD

EIGHTEENTH EDITION

FOREWORD

GAZETTEER OF NATIONS
TEXT Keith Lye

PHOTOGRAPHIC ACKNOWLEDGEMENTS
Alamy /Peter Barritt 10 (right), /Cultura 13 (top),
/David R. Frazier Photolibrary, Inc. 12 (left);
Corbis /William Caram 103, /P. Deliss 10 (left),
/Nigel J. Dennis/Gallo Images 86, /Jay Dickman 109
(bottom left), /Paulo Fridman 8–9, /Yang Liu 91,
/Gideon Mendel 13 (centre), /Radius Images 11, /Royalty-Free
97, /Liba Taylor 104, /David Turnley 109 (bottom right);
© Crown copyright 2007. Published by the Met Office,
UK 82;
Fugro NPA Ltd 14–31, 32–33, 66–67, 84, 110–111,
144–145, 156–157, 208–209, 252–253, 274–275, 290–291,
324–325 /Image provided by the USGS EROS Data Center
Satellite Systems Branch 87;
Galaxy Picture Library /Robin Scagell 73;
iStockphoto.com 101;
Javier Méndez (ING)/Nik Szymanek (Univ. Herts) 68;
NASA/GSFC 83 (top and bottom), 98, /Jacques
Descloitres, MODIS Rapid Response Team 81;
Plantagon International 13 (bottom);
Science Photo Library /Lawrence Migdale 12 (right).

STAR CHARTS (PAGE 69)
Wil Tirion

CARTOGRAPHY BY PHILIP'S

WORLD CITIES
PAGE 120, DUBLIN: The town plan of Dublin is based on
Ordnance Survey Ireland by permission of the Government
Permit Number 8704. © Ordnance Survey Ireland and
Government of Ireland.

Ordnance Survey®   PAGE 121, EDINBURGH,
and PAGE 125, LONDON:
This product includes mapping data licensed from
Ordnance Survey® with the permission of the Controller
of Her Majesty's Stationery Office. © Crown copyright
2011. All rights reserved. Licence number 100011710.

Copyright © 2011 Philip's
www.philips-maps.co.uk

Philip's, a division of Octopus Publishing Group Limited
(www.octopusbooks.co.uk)
Endeavour House, 189 Shaftesbury Avenue, London WC2H 8JY
An Hachette UK Company (www.hachette.co.uk)

Published in North America by
Oxford University Press, Inc.
198 Madison Avenue
New York, NY 10016

www.oup.com/us

OXFORD   Oxford is a registered trademark
UNIVERSITY PRESS   of Oxford University Press

All rights reserved. No part of this publication may be reproduced,
stored in a retrieval system, or transmitted in any form or by
any means, electronic, electrical, chemical, mechanical, optical,
photocopying, recording, or otherwise, without the prior permission
of the Publisher.

Library of Congress Cataloging-in-Publication Data available

ISBN 978–0–19–982995–8

Printing (last digit): 9 8 7 6 5 4 3 2 1

Printed in Malaysia for Imago

AN AUTHORITATIVE AND SERIOUS REFERENCE WORK, the Oxford *Atlas of the World* is one of the finest atlases available anywhere in the world. The atlas incorporates computer-derived maps that have been produced using the very latest in digital cartographic techniques. Country names are shown in conventional English form and are those that are in common usage. They are the forms used by publications such as *Newsweek* and *The Washington Post*, and by the BBC and the British Foreign Office. Alternative country names appear in parentheses on the maps where space permits – for example, Burma (Myanmar) – and are cross-referenced in the index, for example, Côte d'Ivoire = Ivory Coast.

HOW TO USE THE ATLAS
The atlas is divided into a number of sections which are explained below.

WORLD STATISTICS AND "WILL THE WORLD RUN OUT OF FOOD?"
World statistics on topics such as area and population for every country in the world. Also included in this section is a listing of the world's largest cities by population, arranged in country alphabetical order. This section is followed by the highly topical "Will the World Run Out of Food?" feature, which examines the issues and possible solutions to the world's most pressing problem.

IMAGES OF EARTH
A beautifully illustrated satellite section showing 16 of the world's major regions and cities in the Americas, Europe, Africa, Asia, and Australasia.

GAZETTEER OF NATIONS
A comprehensive A–Z reference providing concise profiles of every country's geography, climate, history, politics, and economy, together with ready-reference tables, and illustrated with flags and locator maps.

WORLD GEOGRAPHY
A richly informative section comprising 42 pages of maps, charts, graphs, and diagrams that explain key themes about the world in which we live. The topics covered include the Solar System, oceans, climate, the natural world, energy, and trade. Explanatory text on each spread describes the patterns shown by the data.

CITY MAPS
A detailed selection of maps for 69 urban areas around the world. These are useful for planning trips abroad as well as for comparative studies of cities worldwide.

WORLD MAPS
An outstanding collection of 179 pages of distinctive Philip's cartography. The highly acclaimed physical world maps combine relief shading with layer-colored contours to give a striking visual picture of the Earth's surface. Roads, railroads, canals, and airports are accurately depicted on the maps, and towns and cities are clearly marked. More information on the key features employed in the construction and presentation of the maps is given on the facing page.

GEOGRAPHICAL GLOSSARY AND INDEX
The 84,000-name index to the world maps includes geographical features as well as towns and cities, with both latitude/longitude and letter/figure grid references. Preceding the index is a list of geographical terms from various foreign languages that may be found in the place names on the maps and also in the index, together with their meanings.

SPECIALIST GEOGRAPHY CONSULTANTS

WILL THE WORLD RUN OUT OF FOOD?
The specialist consultant for the
"Will the World Run Out of Food?"
section is Professor Keith W. T.
Goulding, President of the
British Society of Soil Science
and Head of the Department of
Soil Science, Rothamsted Research,
Harpenden, UK
(www.rothamsted.ac.uk).

BRITISH
SOCIETY
OF SOIL
SCIENCE

ROTHAMSTED
RESEARCH

Rothamsted Research
is an institute of the
Biotechnology and Biological
Sciences Research Council.

BBSRC
bioscience for the future

THE EDITORS are especially grateful to
Professor Goulding and Dr Sharon Hall
of Rothamsted Research for their invaluable
assistance in preparing this section.

THE EDITORS are grateful to the following
for their contributions to the "World
Geography" section in this atlas:

Dr Dibyesh Anand
John Burden
Peter Grego
Keith Lye
Garrett Nagle
Ross Reynolds
Robin Scagell
John Woodruff

THE EDITORS would also like to thank
Richard Chiles and the staff at
Fugro NPA Ltd, Edenbridge, Kent, UK
(www.satmaps.com) for sourcing and
processing the satellite imagery that appears
in the atlas.

USER GUIDE

The reference maps which form the main body of this atlas have been prepared in accordance with the highest standards of international cartography to provide an accurate and detailed representation of the Earth. The scales and projections used have been carefully chosen to give balanced coverage of the world, while emphasizing the most densely populated and economically significant regions. A hallmark of Philip's mapping is the use of hill shading and relief coloring to create a graphic impression of landforms: this makes the maps exceptionally easy to read. However, knowledge of the key features employed in the construction and presentation of the maps will enable the reader to derive the fullest benefit from the atlas.

MAP SEQUENCE

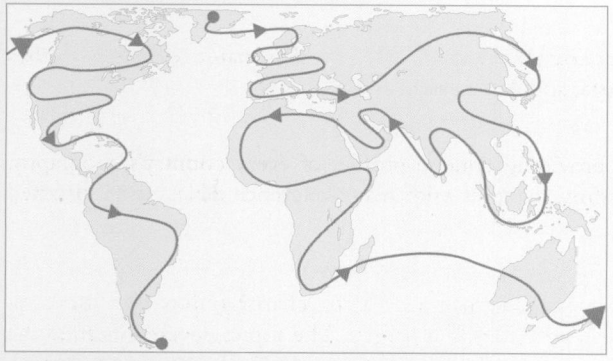

The atlas covers the Earth continent by continent: first Europe; then its land neighbor Asia (mapped north before south, in a clockwise sequence), then Africa, Australia and Oceania, North America, and South America. This is the classic arrangement adopted by most cartographers since the 16th century. For each continent, there are maps at a variety of scales. First, physical relief and political maps of the whole continent; then a series of larger-scale maps of the regions within the continent, each followed, where required, by still larger-scale maps of the most important or densely populated areas. The governing principle is that by turning the pages of the atlas, the reader moves steadily from north to south through each continent, with each map overlapping its neighbors.

MAP PRESENTATION

With very few exceptions (for example, for the Arctic and Antarctica), the maps are drawn with north at the top, regardless of whether they are presented upright or sideways on the page. In the borders will be found the map title; a locator diagram showing the area covered; continuation arrows showing the page numbers for maps of adjacent areas; the scale; the projection used; the degrees of latitude and longitude; and the letters and figures used in the index for locating place names and geographical features. Physical relief maps also have a height reference panel identifying the colors used for each layer of contouring.

MAP SYMBOLS

Each map contains a vast amount of detail which can only be conveyed clearly and accurately by the use of symbols. Points and circles of varying sizes locate and identify the relative importance of towns and cities; different styles of type are employed for administrative, geographical, and regional place names to aid identification. A variety of pictorial symbols denote landforms such as glaciers, marshes, and coral reefs, and man-made structures including roads, railroads, airports, and canals. International borders are shown by red lines. Where neighboring countries are in dispute, for example in parts of the Middle East, the maps show the *de facto* boundary between nations, regardless of the legal or historical situation.

The symbols are explained on the front endpapers of the atlas.

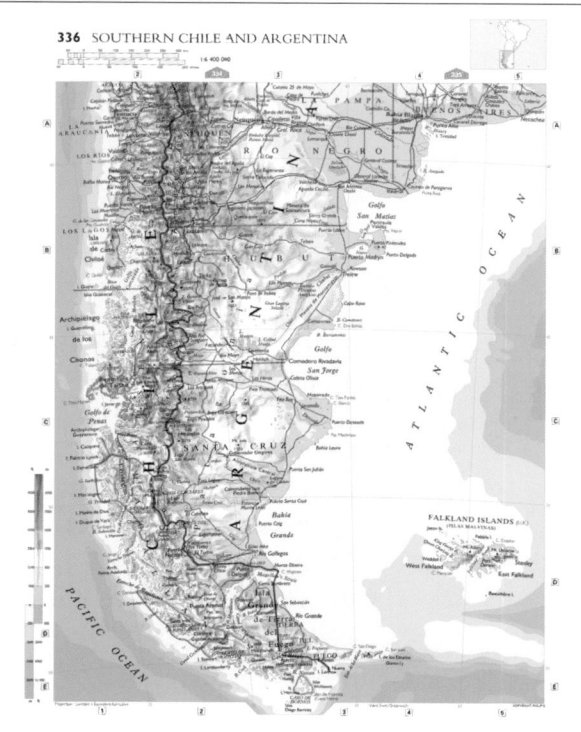

MAP SCALES

1:16 000 000
1 inch = 252 statute miles

The scale of each map is given in the numerical form known as the "representative fraction." The first figure is always one, signifying one unit of distance on the map; the second figure, usually in millions, is the number by which the map unit must be multiplied to give the equivalent distance on the Earth's surface. Calculations can easily be made in centimeters and kilometers, by dividing the Earth units figure by 100 000 (i.e. deleting the last five 0s). Thus 1:1 000 000 means 1 cm = 10 km. The calculation for inches and miles is more laborious, but 1 000 000 divided by 63 360 (the number of inches in a mile) shows that 1:1 000 000 means approximately 1 inch = 16 miles. The table below provides distance equivalents for scales down to 1:50 000 000.

LARGE SCALE		
1:1 000 000	1 cm = 10 km	1 inch = 16 miles
1:2 500 000	1 cm = 25 km	1 inch = 39.5 miles
1:5 000 000	1 cm = 50 km	1 inch = 79 miles
1:6 000 000	1 cm = 60 km	1 inch = 95 miles
1:8 000 000	1 cm = 80 km	1 inch = 126 miles
1:10 000 000	1 cm = 100 km	1 inch = 158 miles
1:15 000 000	1 cm = 150 km	1 inch = 237 miles
1:20 000 000	1 cm = 200 km	1 inch = 316 miles
1:50 000 000	1 cm = 500 km	1 inch = 790 miles
SMALL SCALE		

MEASURING DISTANCES

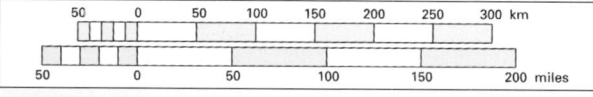

Although each map is accompanied by a scale bar, distances cannot always be measured with confidence because of the distortions involved in portraying the curved surface of the Earth on a flat page. As a general rule, the larger the map scale, the more accurate and reliable will be the distance measured. On small-scale maps such as those of the world and of entire continents, measurement may only be accurate along the "standard parallels," or central axes, and should not be attempted without considering the map projection.

MAP PROJECTIONS

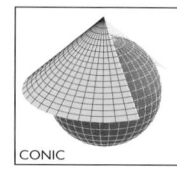
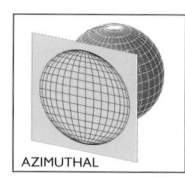
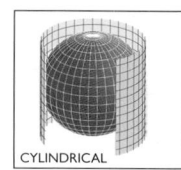

Unlike a globe, no flat map can give a true scale representation of the world in terms of area, shape, and position of every region. Each of the numerous systems that have been devised for projecting the curved surface of the Earth on to a flat page involves the sacrifice of accuracy in one or more of these elements. The variations in shape and position of land masses such as Alaska, Greenland, and Australia, for example, can be quite dramatic when different projections are compared.

For this atlas, the guiding principle has been to select projections that involve the least distortion of size and distance. The projection used for each map is noted in the border. Most fall into one of three categories – conic, azimuthal, or cylindrical – whose basic concepts are shown above. Each involves plotting the forms of the Earth's surface on a grid of latitude and longitude lines, which may be shown as parallels, curves, or radiating spokes.

LATITUDE AND LONGITUDE

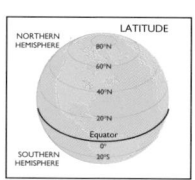
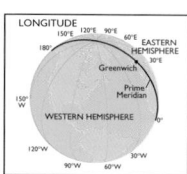
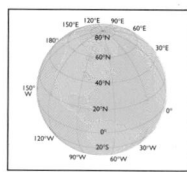

Accurate positioning of individual points on the Earth's surface is made possible by reference to the geometrical system of latitude and longitude. Latitude *parallels* are drawn west–east around the Earth and numbered by degrees north and south of the Equator, which is designated 0° of latitude. Longitude *meridians* are drawn north–south and numbered by degrees east and west of the *prime meridian*, 0° of longitude, which passes through Greenwich in England. By referring to these co-ordinates and their subdivisions of minutes (1/60th of a degree) and seconds (1/60th of a minute), any place on Earth can be located to within a few hundred meters. Latitude and longitude are indicated by blue lines on the maps; they are straight or curved according to the projection employed. Reference to these lines is the easiest way of determining the relative positions of places on different maps, and for plotting compass directions.

NAME FORMS

For ease of reference, both English and local name forms appear in the atlas. Oceans, seas, and countries are shown in English throughout the atlas; country names may be abbreviated to their commonly accepted form (for example, Germany, not The Federal Republic of Germany). Conventional English forms are also used for place names on the smaller-scale maps of the continents. However, local name forms are used on all large-scale and regional maps, with the English form given in brackets only for important cities – the large-scale map of Russia and Northern Asia thus shows Moskva (Moscow). For countries which do not use a Roman script, place names have been transcribed according to the systems adopted by the British and US Geographic Names Authorities. For China, the Pin Yin system has been used, with some more widely known forms appearing in brackets, as with Beijing (Peking). Both English and local names appear in the index, the English form being cross-referenced to the local form.

CONTENTS

WORLD STATISTICS

COUNTRIES 6
CITIES 7

WILL THE WORLD RUN OUT OF FOOD?

THE ISSUES 10–11
THE SOLUTIONS 12–13

IMAGES OF EARTH

ICELAND 14–15
LONDON, UK 16
ROME, ITALY 17
ATHENS, GREECE 18
BAKU, AZERBAIJAN 19
SANA', YEMEN 20
SHANGHAI, CHINA 21
JUBA, SOUTH SUDAN 22
BRAZZAVILLE AND KINSHASA, AFRICA 23
THE CAPE PENINSULA, SOUTH AFRICA 24
SYDNEY, AUSTRALIA 25
CHRISTCHURCH, NEW ZEALAND 26
QUÉBEC, CANADA 27
NEW YORK, USA 28
LAS VEGAS, USA 29
MEXICO CITY, MEXICO 30
LIMA, PERU 31

GAZETTEER OF NATIONS

AN A–Z GAZETTEER OF COUNTRIES 34–65

WORLD GEOGRAPHY

THE UNIVERSE 68–69
THE SOLAR SYSTEM 70–71
SEASONS, TIME AND MOTION 72–73
GEOLOGY OF THE EARTH 74–75
OCEANS 76–77
THE ATMOSPHERE 78–79
CLIMATE 80–81
CLIMATE CHANGE AND GLOBAL WARMING 82–83
WATER AND VEGETATION 84–85
BIODIVERSITY AND THE NATURAL WORLD 86–87
POPULATION 88–89
CITIES 90–91
THE HUMAN FAMILY 92–93
CONFLICT AND COOPERATION 94–95
ENERGY 96–97
MINERALS 98–99
EMPLOYMENT AND INDUSTRY 100–101
TRADE 102–103
HEALTH 104–105
WEALTH 106–107
STANDARDS OF LIVING 108–109

WORLD CITIES

AMSTERDAM 112
ATHENS 112
ATLANTA 113
BAGHDAD 113
BANGKOK 113
BARCELONA 114
BEIJING 114
BERLIN 115
BOSTON 116
BRUSSELS 116
BUDAPEST 117
BUENOS AIRES 117
CAIRO 117
CAPE TOWN 118
COPENHAGEN 118
CHICAGO 119
DELHI 120
DUBLIN 120
EDINBURGH 121
GUANGZHOU (CANTON) 121
HELSINKI 121
HONG KONG 122
ISTANBUL 122
JAKARTA 122
JERUSALEM 123
JOHANNESBURG 123
KARACHI 123
KOLKATA (CALCUTTA) 124
LAGOS 124
LAS VEGAS 124
LIMA 124
LONDON 125
LISBON 126
LOS ANGELES 126
MADRID 127
MANILA 127
MELBOURNE 128
MEXICO CITY 128
MIAMI 128
MILAN 129
MOSCOW 129
MONTREAL 130
MUMBAI (BOMBAY) 130
MUNICH 131
NEW ORLEANS 131
NEW YORK 132
ORLANDO 133
OSAKA 133
OSLO 133
PARIS 134
PRAGUE 135
RIO DE JANEIRO 135
ROME 136
SAN FRANCISCO 136
ST PETERSBURG 137
SANTIAGO 137
SÃO PAULO 137
SEOUL 137
SHANGHAI 138
SINGAPORE 138
STOCKHOLM 139
SYDNEY 139
TOKYO 140
TEHRAN 141
TORONTO 141
VIENNA 142
WARSAW 142
WASHINGTON 143
WELLINGTON 143

WORLD MAPS

THE WORLD

MAP SYMBOLS FRONT ENDPAPER

THE WORLD: PHYSICAL 146–147
1:76 000 000

THE WORLD: POLITICAL 148–149
1:76 000 000

ARCTIC OCEAN 150
1:28 000 000

ANTARCTICA 151
1:28 000 000

ATLANTIC OCEAN 152
1:41 000 000

ISLANDS OF THE ATLANTIC 153
BERMUDA 1:400 000
NEW PROVIDENCE ISLAND 1:400 000
MADEIRA 1:800 000
AZORES 1:1 600 000
CANARY ISLANDS 1:1 600 000
FALKLAND ISLANDS 1:6 400 000
ASCENSION ISLAND 1:400 000
ST HELENA 1:400 000
CAPE VERDE ISLANDS 1:8 000 000

GREENLAND 154
1:10 000 000

ICELAND 155
1:2 000 000

EUROPE

EUROPE: PHYSICAL 158
1:16 000 000

EUROPE: POLITICAL 159
1:16 000 000

SCANDINAVIA 160–161
1:4 800 000
ICELAND 1:4 800 000
FÆROE ISLANDS 1:4 800 000

DENMARK AND SOUTHERN SWEDEN 162–163
1:2 000 000

SOUTHERN NORWAY 164
1:2 000 000

BRITISH ISLES 165
1:4 000 000

IRELAND 166
1:1 600 000

SCOTLAND 167
1:1 600 000

ENGLAND AND WALES 168–169
1:1 600 000

NETHERLANDS, BELGIUM AND LUXEMBOURG 170
1:2 000 000

FRANCE 171
1:4 000 000

NORTHERN FRANCE 172–173
1:2 000 000

SOUTHERN FRANCE 174–175
1:2 000 000

CENTRAL EUROPE 176–177
1:4 000 000

GERMANY AND SWITZERLAND 178–179
1:2 000 000

AUSTRIA, CZECH REPUBLIC AND SLOVAK REPUBLIC 180–181
1:2 000 000

HUNGARY, ROMANIA AND THE LOWER DANUBE 182–183
1:2 000 000

POLAND AND THE SOUTHERN BALTIC 184–185
1:2 000 000

EASTERN EUROPE 186–187
1:8 000 000

BALTIC STATES, BELARUS AND UKRAINE 188–189
1:4 000 000

THE VOLGA BASIN AND THE CAUCASUS 190–191
1:4 000 000

SOUTHERN EUROPE 192–193
1:8 000 000

WESTERN SPAIN AND PORTUGAL 194–195
1:2 000 000

EASTERN SPAIN 196–197
1:2 000 000

NORTHERN ITALY, SLOVENIA AND CROATIA 198–199
1:2 000 000

SOUTHERN ITALY 200–201
1:2 000 000

THE BALKANS 202–203
1:2 000 000

SOUTHERN GREECE AND WESTERN TURKEY 204–205
1:2 000 000

MEDITERRANEAN ISLANDS 206–207
IBIZA, MAJORCA, MINORCA 1:800 000
MALTA 1:400 000
CORFU 1:800 000
RHODES 1:800 000
LEVKAS, ZANTE, CEPHALONIA 1:800 000
CRETE 1:1 000 000
CYPRUS 1:1 000 000

ASIA

ASIA: PHYSICAL 210
1:40 000 000

ASIA: POLITICAL 211
1:40 000 000

TURKEY AND TRANSCAUCASIA 212–213
1:4 000 000

CONTENTS

RUSSIA AND
NORTHERN ASIA   214–215
1:16 000 000

KAZAKHSTAN
AND CENTRAL ASIA 216–127
1:8 000 000

CHINA
AND THE FAR EAST 218–219
1:12 000 000
HONG KONG AND MACAU 1:800 000

JAPAN   220–221
1:4 000 000
RYUKYU ISLANDS 1:4 000 000

SOUTHERN JAPAN   222–223
1:2 000 000

KOREA   224
1:3 100 000

TAIWAN   225
1:1 400 000

NORTHERN CHINA
AND KOREA   226–227
1:4 800 000

SOUTHERN CHINA   228–229
1:4 800 000

SOUTHEAST ASIA   230–231
1:10 000 000
JAVA AND MADURA 1:6 000 000
BALI 1:1 600 000

PHILIPPINES   232–233
1:3 200 000

WESTERN INDONESIA 234–235
1:5 600 000

MAINLAND
SOUTHEAST ASIA   236–237
1:4 800 000
KO PHUKET 1:800 000
KO SAMUI 1:800 000
PINANG 1:800 000
SINGAPORE 1:800 000

SOUTHERN ASIA AND
THE MIDDLE EAST   238–239
1:14 000 000

AFGHANISTAN
AND PAKISTAN   240
1:5 600 000

BANGLADESH,
NORTHEASTERN INDIA
AND BURMA   241
1:4 800 000

NORTHERN INDIA,
PAKISTAN AND
NEPAL   242–243
1:4 800 000

SOUTHERN INDIA AND
SRI LANKA   244–245
1:4 800 000
LAKSHADWEEP ISLANDS 1:4 800 000
ANDAMAN AND
NICOBAR ISLANDS 1:4 800 000

THE MIDDLE EAST   246–247
1:5 600 000

SOUTHERN ARABIAN
PENINSULA   248–249
1:5 600 000

EASTERN
MEDITERRANEAN   250–251
1:2 000 000

AFRICA

AFRICA: PHYSICAL 254
1:33 600 000

AFRICA: POLITICAL 255
1:33 600 000

THE NILE VALLEY   256–257
1:6 400 000
THE NILE DELTA 1:3 200 000

CENTRAL NORTH
AFRICA   258–259
1:6 400 000

NORTHWEST AFRICA 260–261
1:6 400 000

WEST AFRICA   262–263
1:6 400 000

CENTRAL AFRICA   264–265
1:6 400 000
SÃO TOMÉ AND PRÍNCIPE 1:6 400 000

ETHIOPIA AND THE
HORN OF AFRICA   266–267
1:6 400 000

EAST AFRICA   268–269
1:6 400 000

SOUTHERN AFRICA   270–271
1:6 400 000

MADAGASCAR   272
1:6 400 000
COMOROS 1:2 000 000
MAYOTTE 1:800 000
SEYCHELLES 1:2 000 000
RÉUNION 1:800 000
MAURITIUS 1:800 000
MALDIVES 1:6 400 000

INDIAN OCEAN   273
1:40 000 000

AUSTRALIA
AND OCEANIA

AUSTRALIA AND OCEANIA:
PHYSICAL
AND POLITICAL   276–277
1:16 000 000

WESTERN AUSTRALIA 278–279
1:6 400 000

EASTERN AUSTRALIA 280–281
1:6 400 000
WHITSUNDAY GROUP 1:2 000 000
TASMANIA 1:6 400 000
TORRES STRAIT 1:6 400 000

SOUTHEAST
AUSTRALIA   282–283
1:3 200 000

NEW ZEALAND –
NORTH ISLAND   284
1:2 800 000

NEW ZEALAND –
SOUTH ISLAND   285
1:2 800 000
CHATHAM ISLANDS 1:2 800 000

PAPUA NEW GUINEA 286
1:5 200 000

ISLANDS OF THE
SOUTHWEST PACIFIC 287
FIJI 1:4 000 000
VANUATU 1:4 000 000
SOLOMON ISLANDS 1:4 000 000
TONGA 1:4 000 000
YAP 1:830 000
CHUUK 1:830 000
SAMOAN ISLANDS 1:4 000 000

PACIFIC OCEAN   288–289
1:43 200 000
OKINAWA 1:1 550 000
IWO JIMA 1:200 000
PALAU 1:1 550 000
NEW CALEDONIA 1:5 750 000
TAHITI 1:1 150 000
FRENCH POLYNESIA 1:26 000 000
NIUE 1:830 000
RAROTONGA 1:415 000

NORTH
AMERICA

NORTH AMERICA:
PHYSICAL   292
1:28 000 000

NORTH AMERICA:
POLITICAL   293
1:28 000 000

CANADA   294–295
1:12 000 000

WESTERN CANADA   296–297
1:5 600 000

EASTERN CANADA   298–299
1:5 600 000

UNITED STATES   300–301
1:12 000 000
ALASKA 1:12 000 000
HAWAI'I 1:12 000 000

HAWAI'I   302
1:2 500 000
OAHU 1:500 000
NORTHERN MARIANAS 1:12 800 000
WAKE ISLAND 1:200 000
MIDWAY ISLANDS 1:200 000
GUAM 1:800 000
SAIPAN AND TINIAN 1:800 000
TUTUILA 1:640 000
MANUA ISLANDS 1:640 000

ALASKA   303
1:8 000 000

UNITED STATES –
WEST   304–305
1:5 360 000

CENTRAL AND SOUTHERN
CALIFORNIA AND WESTERN
WASHINGTON   306–307
1:2 000 000

UNITED STATES – MIDWEST
AND NORTHEAST   308–309
1:5 360 000

CHICAGO AND
THE MIDWEST   310–311
1:2 000 000

NORTHEASTERN
UNITED STATES   312–313
1:2 000 000

UNITED STATES –
SOUTH   314–315
1:5 360 000

SOUTHEASTERN
UNITED STATES   316–317
1:2 000 000

MEXICO   318–319
1:6 400 000

CENTRAL AMERICA AND
THE WEST INDIES   320–321
1:6 400 000
PUERTO RICO AND THE
VIRGIN ISLANDS 1:1 600 000
JAMAICA 1:1 600 000
PANAMA CANAL 1:800 000

LESSER ANTILLES   322–323
NORTHERN LEEWARDS 1:600 000
ANTIGUA AND BARBUDA 1:600 000
ST KITTS AND NEVIS 1:600 000
GUADELOUPE 1:600 000
ARUBA 1:600 000
BONAIRE AND CURAÇAO 1:600 000
MARTINIQUE 1:600 000
DOMINICA 1:600 000
ST LUCIA 1:600 000
ST VINCENT AND
THE GRENADINES 1:600 000
MONTSERRAT 1:600 000
GRENADA 1:600 000
BARBADOS 1:600 000
TRINIDAD AND TOBAGO 1:600 000

SOUTH
AMERICA

SOUTH AMERICA:
PHYSICAL   326
1:28 000 000

SOUTH AMERICA:
POLITICAL   327
1:28 000 000

SOUTH AMERICA –
NORTHWEST   328–329
1:6 400 000

SOUTH AMERICA –
WEST   330–331
1:6 400 000
GALAPAGOS ISLANDS 1:3 200 000
EASTER ISLAND 1:400 000
ROBINSON CRUSOE ISLAND 1:400 000

EASTERN BRAZIL   332–333
1:6 400 000

CENTRAL
SOUTH AMERICA   334–335
1:6 400 000

SOUTHERN CHILE AND
ARGENTINA   336
1:6 400 000

GEOGRAPHICAL
GLOSSARY   337–338

INDEX TO
WORLD MAPS   339–448

WORLD STATISTICS: COUNTRIES

This alphabetical list includes the principal countries and territories of the world. If a territory is not completely independent, the country it is associated with is named. The area figures give the total area of land, inland water, and ice. The population figures are 2010 estimates where available. The annual income is the Gross Domestic Product per capita in US dollars; the figures are the latest available, usually 2010 estimates.

Country/Territory	Area km^2 *Thousands*	Area miles^2 *Thousands*	Population *Thousands*	Capital	Annual Income US $
Afghanistan	652	252	29,121	Kabul	1,000
Albania	28.7	11.1	2,987	Tirana	6,400
Algeria	2,382	920	34,586	Algiers	7,100
American Samoa (US)	0.20	0.08	66	Pago Pago	8,000
Andorra	0.47	0.18	85	Andorra La Vella	44,900
Angola	1,247	481	13,068	Luanda	8,400
Anguilla (UK)	0.10	0.04	15	The Valley	12,200
Antigua & Barbuda	0.44	0.17	87	St John's	17,800
Argentina	2,780	1,074	41,343	Buenos Aires	13,400
Armenia	29.8	11.5	2,967	Yerevan	5,500
Aruba (Netherlands)	0.19	0.07	105	Oranjestad	21,800
Australia	7,741	2,989	21,516	Canberra	40,000
Austria	83.9	32.4	8,214	Vienna	39,200
Azerbaijan	86.6	33.4	8,304	Baku	10,400
Azores (Portugal)	2.2	0.86	236	Ponta Delgada	15,000
Bahamas	13.9	5.4	310	Nassau	29,700
Bahrain	0.69	0.27	738	Manama	38,800
Bangladesh	144	55.6	156,118	Dhaka	1,500
Barbados	0.43	0.17	286	Bridgetown	17,700
Belarus	208	80.2	9,613	Minsk	12,500
Belgium	30.5	11.8	10,423	Brussels	36,800
Belize	23.0	8.9	315	Belmopan	8,300
Benin	113	43.5	9,056	Porto-Novo	1,500
Bermuda (UK)	0.05	0.02	68	Hamilton	69,900
Bhutan	47.0	18.1	700	Thimphu	4,700
Bolivia	1,099	424	9,947	La Paz/Sucre	4,700
Bosnia-Herzegovina	51.2	19.8	4,622	Sarajevo	6,400
Botswana	582	225	2,029	Gaborone	12,800
Brazil	8,514	3,287	201,103	Brasília	10,100
Brunei	5.8	2.2	395	Bandar Seri Begawan	51,200
Bulgaria	111	42.8	7,149	Sofia	12,500
Burkina Faso	274	106	16,242	Ouagadougou	1,200
Burma (Myanmar)	677	261	53,414	Rangoon/Naypyidaw	1,100
Burundi	27.8	10.7	9,863	Bujumbura	300
Cambodia	181	69.9	14,454	Phnom Penh	1,900
Cameroon	475	184	19,194	Yaoundé	2,300
Canada	9,971	3,850	33,760	Ottawa	38,200
Canary Is. (Spain)	7.2	2.8	1,682	Las Palmas/Santa Cruz	19,900
Cape Verde Is.	4.0	1.6	509	Praia	3,600
Cayman Is. (UK)	0.26	0.10	50	George Town	43,800
Central African Republic	623	241	4,845	Bangui	700
Chad	1,284	496	10,543	Ndjaména	1,900
Chile	757	292	16,746	Santiago	14,600
China	9,597	3,705	1,330,141	Beijing	6,600
Colombia	1,139	440	44,205	Bogotá	9,200
Comoros	2.2	0.86	773	Moroni	1,000
Congo	342	132	4,126	Brazzaville	3,900
Congo (Dem. Rep. of the)	2,345	905	70,916	Kinshasa	300
Cook Is. (NZ)	0.24	0.09	11	Avarua	9,100
Costa Rica	51.1	19.7	4,516	San José	10,900
Croatia	56.5	21.8	4,487	Zagreb	17,500
Cuba	111	42.8	11,477	Havana	9,700
Curaçao (Netherlands)	0.44	0.17	142	Willemstad	15,000
Cyprus	9.3	3.6	1,103	Nicosia	21,000
Czech Republic	78.9	30.5	10,202	Prague	24,900
Denmark	43.1	16.6	5,516	Copenhagen	36,000
Djibouti	23.2	9.0	741	Djibouti	2,700
Dominica	0.75	0.29	73	Roseau	10,200
Dominican Republic	48.5	18.7	9,824	Santo Domingo	8,300
East Timor	14.9	5.7	1,155	Dili	2,400
Ecuador	284	109	14,791	Quito	7,500
Egypt	1,001	387	80,472	Cairo	6,000
El Salvador	21.0	8.1	6,052	San Salvador	7,200
Equatorial Guinea	28.1	10.8	651	Malabo	37,500
Eritrea	118	45.4	5,793	Asmara	700
Estonia	45.1	17.4	1,291	Tallinn	18,500
Ethiopia	1,104	426	88,013	Addis Ababa	900
Falkland Is. (UK)	12.2	4.7	3	Stanley	35,400
Faroe Is. (Denmark)	1.4	0.54	49	Tórshavn	48,200
Fiji	18.3	7.1	876	Suva	3,900
Finland	338	131	5,255	Helsinki	34,100
France	552	213	64,768	Paris	32,600
French Guiana (France)	90.0	34.7	203	Cayenne	8,300
French Polynesia (France)	4.0	1.5	291	Papeete	18,000
Gabon	268	103	1,545	Libreville	14,000
Gambia, The	11.3	4.4	1,824	Banjul	1,400
Gaza Strip (OPT)*	0.36	0.14	1,604	–	2,900
Georgia	69.7	26.9	4,601	Tbilisi	4,400
Germany	357	138	82,283	Berlin	34,100
Ghana	239	92.1	24,340	Accra	1,500
Gibraltar (UK)	0.006	0.002	29	Gibraltar Town	38,400
Greece	132	50.9	10,750	Athens	31,000
Greenland (Denmark)	2,176	840	58	Nuuk	35,900
Grenada	0.34	0.13	108	St George's	10,300
Guadeloupe (France)	1.7	0.66	453	Basse-Terre	7,900
Guam (US)	0.55	0.21	181	Agana	15,000
Guatemala	109	42.0	13,550	Guatemala City	5,100
Guinea	246	94.9	10,324	Conakry	1,000
Guinea-Bissau	36.1	13.9	1,565	Bissau	1,100
Guyana	215	83.0	748	Georgetown	6,500
Haiti	27.8	10.7	9,649	Port-au-Prince	1,300
Honduras	112	43.3	7,989	Tegucigalpa	4,100
Hungary	93.0	35.9	9,992	Budapest	18,800
Iceland	103	39.8	309	Reykjavik	39,600
India	3,287	1,269	1,173,108	New Delhi	3,100
Indonesia	1,905	735	242,968	Jakarta	4,000
Iran	1,648	636	76,923	Tehran	12,500
Iraq	438	169	29,672	Baghdad	3,800
Ireland	70.3	27.1	4,623	Dublin	41,000
Israel	20.6	8.0	7,354	Jerusalem	28,400
Italy	301	116	58,091	Rome	29,900
Ivory Coast (Côte d'Ivoire)	322	125	21,059	Yamoussoukro	1,700
Jamaica	11.0	4.2	2,847	Kingston	8,400
Japan	378	146	126,804	Tokyo	32,700
Jordan	89.3	34.5	6,407	Amman	5,200
Kazakhstan	2,725	1,052	15,460	Astana	11,800
Kenya	580	224	40,047	Nairobi	1,600
Kiribati	0.73	0.28	99	Tarawa	6,100
Korea, North	121	46.5	22,757	Pyŏngyang	1,900
Korea, South	99.3	38.3	48,636	Seoul	28,100
Kosovo	10.9	4.2	1,815	Pristina	2,500
Kuwait	17.8	6.9	2,789	Kuwait City	52,800
Kyrgyzstan	200	77.2	5,509	Bishkek	2,200
Laos	237	91.4	6,368	Vientiane	2,100
Latvia	64.6	24.9	2,218	Riga	14,400
Lebanon	10.4	4.0	4,125	Beirut	13,200
Lesotho	30.4	11.7	1,920	Maseru	1,600
Liberia	111	43.0	3,685	Monrovia	400
Libya	1,760	679	6,461	Tripoli	13,400
Liechtenstein	0.16	0.06	35	Vaduz	122,100
Lithuania	65.2	25.2	3,545	Vilnius	15,500
Luxembourg	2.6	1.0	498	Luxembourg	79,600
Macedonia (FYROM)	25.7	9.9	2,072	Skopje	9,100
Madagascar	587	227	21,282	Antananarivo	1,000
Madeira (Portugal)	0.78	0.30	241	Funchal	22,700
Malawi	118	45.7	15,448	Lilongwe	800
Malaysia	330	127	28,275	Kuala Lumpur/Putrajaya	14,900
Maldives	0.30	0.12	396	Malé	4,300
Mali	1,240	479	13,796	Bamako	1,200
Malta	0.32	0.12	407	Valletta	24,300
Marshall Is.	0.18	0.07	66	Majuro	2,500
Martinique (France)	1.1	0.43	436	Fort-de-France	14,400
Mauritania	1,026	396	3,205	Nouakchott	2,000
Mauritius	2.0	0.79	1,294	Port Louis	13,000
Mayotte (France)	0.37	0.14	231	Mamoudzou	4,900
Mexico	1,958	756	112,469	Mexico City	13,200
Micronesia, Fed. States of	0.70	0.27	107	Palikir	2,200
Moldova	33.9	13.1	4,317	Kishinev	2,300
Monaco	0.001	0.0004	31	Monaco	30,000
Mongolia	1,567	605	3,087	Ulan Bator	3,100
Montenegro	14.0	5.4	667	Podgorica	9,800
Montserrat (UK)	0.10	0.39	5	Brades	3,400
Morocco	447	172	31,627	Rabat	4,700
Mozambique	802	309	22,061	Maputo	900
Namibia	824	318	2,128	Windhoek	6,600
Nauru	0.02	0.008	9	Yaren	5,000
Nepal	147	56.8	28,952	Katmandu	1,200
Netherlands	41.5	16.0	16,783	Amsterdam/The Hague	39,500
New Caledonia (France)	18.6	7.2	252	Nouméa	15,000
New Zealand	271	104	4,252	Wellington	27,400
Nicaragua	130	50.2	5,996	Managua	2,800
Niger	1,267	489	15,878	Niamey	700
Nigeria	924	357	152,217	Abuja	2,300
Northern Mariana Is. (US)	0.46	0.18	48	Saipan	12,500
Norway	324	125	4,676	Oslo	57,400
Oman	310	119	2,968	Muscat	25,000
Pakistan	796	307	184,405	Islamabad	2,500
Palau	0.46	0.18	21	Melekeok	8,100
Panama	75.5	29.2	3,411	Panamá	12,100
Papua New Guinea	463	179	6,065	Port Moresby	2,300
Paraguay	407	157	6,376	Asunción	4,600
Peru	1,285	496	29,907	Lima	8,500
Philippines	300	116	99,900	Manila	3,300
Poland	323	125	38,464	Warsaw	17,900
Portugal	88.8	34.3	10,736	Lisbon	21,700
Puerto Rico (US)	8.9	3.4	3,979	San Juan	17,100
Qatar	11.0	4.2	841	Doha	119,500
Réunion (France)	2.5	0.97	788	St-Denis	6,200
Romania	238	92.0	21,959	Bucharest	11,500
Russia	17,075	6,593	139,390	Moscow	15,100
Rwanda	26.3	10.2	11,056	Kigali	1,000
St Kitts & Nevis	0.26	0.10	50	Basseterre	14,700
St Lucia	0.54	0.21	161	Castries	10,900
St Maarten (Netherlands)	0.03	0.01	37	Philipsburg	15,400
St Vincent & Grenadines	0.39	0.15	104	Kingstown	10,200
Samoa	2.8	1.1	192	Apia	5,400
San Marino	0.06	0.02	31	San Marino	41,900
São Tomé & Príncipe	0.96	0.37	176	São Tomé	1,700
Saudi Arabia	2,150	830	25,732	Riyadh	20,600
Senegal	197	76.0	12,323	Dakar	1,600
Serbia	77.5	29.9	7,345	Belgrade	10,600
Seychelles	0.46	0.18	88	Victoria	20,800
Sierra Leone	71.7	27.7	5,246	Freetown	900
Singapore	0.68	0.26	4,701	Singapore City	52,200
Slovak Republic	49.0	18.9	5,470	Bratislava	21,100
Slovenia	20.3	7.8	2,003	Ljubljana	27,700
Solomon Is.	28.9	11.2	559	Honiara	2,500
Somalia	638	246	10,112	Mogadishu	600
South Africa	1,221	471	49,109	Cape Town/Pretoria	10,300
Spain	498	192	46,506	Madrid	33,600
Sri Lanka	65.6	25.3	21,514	Colombo	4,500
Sudan	1,886	728	35,680	Khartoum	2,300
Sudan, South	620	239	8,260	Juba	1,900
Suriname	163	63.0	487	Paramaribo	9,500
Swaziland	17.4	6.7	1,354	Mbabane	4,400
Sweden	450	174	9,074	Stockholm	36,600
Switzerland	41.3	15.9	7,623	Bern	41,400
Syria	185	71.5	22,198	Damascus	4,600
Taiwan	36.0	13.9	23,025	Taipei	32,000
Tajikistan	143	55.3	7,487	Dushanbe	1,900
Tanzania	945	365	41,893	Dodoma	1,400
Thailand	513	198	67,090	Bangkok	8,200
Togo	56.8	21.9	6,587	Lomé	900
Tonga	0.65	0.25	123	Nuku'alofa	6,300
Trinidad & Tobago	5.1	2.0	1,229	Port of Spain	21,300
Tunisia	164	63.2	10,589	Tunis	8,200
Turkey	775	299	77,804	Ankara	11,400
Turkmenistan	488	188	4,941	Ashkhabad	6,700
Turks & Caicos Is. (UK)	0.43	0.17	24	Cockburn Town	11,500
Tuvalu	0.03	0.01	10	Fongafale	1,600
Uganda	241	93.1	33,399	Kampala	1,200
Ukraine	604	233	45,416	Kiev	6,300
United Arab Emirates	83.6	32.3	4,976	Abu Dhabi	38,900
United Kingdom	242	93.4	62,348	London	34,800
United States of America	9,629	3,718	310,233	Washington, DC	46,000
Uruguay	175	67.6	3,510	Montevideo	12,600
Uzbekistan	447	173	27,866	Tashkent	2,800
Vanuatu	12.2	4.7	222	Port-Vila	5,300
Venezuela	912	352	27,223	Caracas	13,000
Vietnam	332	128	89,571	Hanoi	2,900
Virgin Is. (UK)	0.15	0.06	25	Road Town	38,500
Virgin Is. (US)	0.35	0.13	110	Charlotte Amalie	14,500
Wallis & Futuna Is. (France)	0.20	0.08	15	Mata-Utu	3,800
West Bank (OPT)*	5.9	2.3	2,515	–	2,900
Western Sahara	266	103	492	El Aaiún	2,500
Yemen	528	204	23,495	Sana'	2,500
Zambia	753	291	13,460	Lusaka	1,600
Zimbabwe	391	151	11,652	Harare	100

*OPT = Occupied Palestinian Territory

This list shows the principal cities with more than 800,000 inhabitants. The figures are taken from the most recent census or estimate available, usually 2010, and as far as possible are the population of the metropolitan area or urban agglomeration. The list includes Metropolitan Statistical Areas from the United States 2010 Census. All the figures are in thousands. Local name forms have been used for the smaller cities (for example, Thessaloniki).

AFGHANISTAN
Kabul 3,731
ALGERIA
Algiers 3,260
ANGOLA
Luanda 4,772
Huambo 1,034
ARGENTINA
Buenos Aires 13,349
Córdoba 1,592
Rosario 1,312
Mendoza 1,072
San Miguel de
 Tucumán 837
ARMENIA
Yerevan 1,112
AUSTRALIA
Sydney 4,429
Melbourne 3,853
Brisbane 1,970
Perth 1,599
Adelaide 1,168
AUSTRIA
Vienna 1,706
AZERBAIJAN
Baku 1,972
BANGLADESH
Dhaka 14,648
Chittagong 4,962
Khulna 1,682
Rajshahi 878
BELARUS
Minsk 1,852
BELGIUM
Brussels 1,904
Antwerpen 965
BENIN
Cotonou 844
BOLIVIA
La Paz 1,673
Santa Cruz 1,649
BRAZIL
São Paulo 20,262
Rio de Janeiro 11,950
Belo Horizonte 5,852
Pôrto Alegre 4,092
Salvador 3,918
Brasília 3,905
Recife 3,871
Fortaleza 3,719
Curitiba 3,462
Campinas 2,818
Belém 2,191
Goiânia 2,146
Vitória 1,848
Manaus 1,775
Natal 1,316
São Luís 1,283
Maceió 1,192
Florianópolis 1,049
João Pessoa 1,015
Teresina 900
Londrina 814
BULGARIA
Sofia 1,196
BURKINA FASO
Ouagadougou 1,908
BURMA (MYANMAR)
Rangoon 4,350
Mandalay 1,034
Naypyidaw 1,024
CAMBODIA
Phnom Penh 1,562
CAMEROON
Douala 2,125
Yaoundé 1,801
CANADA
Toronto 5,449
Montréal 3,783
Vancouver 2,187
Ottawa 1,182
Calgary 1,182
Edmonton 1,113
CHAD
Ndjamena 829
CHILE
Santiago 5,952
Valparaiso 873
CHINA
Shanghai 16,575
Beijing 12,385
Chongqing 9,401
Shenzhen 9,005
Guangzhou, Guangdong 8,884
Tianjin 7,884
Wuhan 7,681
Hong Kong 7,069
Dongguan, Guangdong 5,347
Shenyang 5,166
Foshan 4,969
Chengdu 4,961
Xi'an, Shaanxi 4,747
Nanjing, Jiangsu 4,519
Harbin 4,251
Hangzhou 3,860
Changchun 3,597
Shantou 3,502
Guiyang 3,447
Qingdao 3,323
Dalian 3,306
Jinan, Shandong 3,237
Taiyuan, Shanxi 3,154
Kunming 3,116
Zibo 2,982
Zhengzhou 2,966
Fuzhou, Fujian 2,787
Nanchang 2,701
Wuxi, Jiangsu 2,682
Wenzhou 2,659
Shijiazhuang 2,487
Changsha 2,451
Lanzhou 2,411
Hefei 2,404
Suzhou, Jiangsu 2,398
Ürümqi (Wulumuchi) 2,398
Xiamen 2,371
Jinxi 2,268
Jilin 2,255
Ningbo 2,217
Zhongshan 2,211
Xuzhou 2,142
Nanning 2,096
Zaozhuang 2,096
Changzhou, Jiangsu 2,062
Nanchong 2,046
Linyi 2,035
Yantai 1,991
Wanxian 1,963
Baotou 1,920
Nanyang 1,830
Tangshan 1,825
Datong 1,763
Yancheng 1,678
Tianmen 1,676
Shangqiu 1,650
Lu'an 1,647
Luoyang 1,644
Hohhot 1,644
Anshan 1,611
Qiqihar 1,607
Tai'an 1,598
Daqing 1,594
Xinghua 1,587
Pingxiang 1,562
Handan 1,535
Xiantao 1,528
Zhanjiang 1,514
Weifang 1,498
Fushun 1,456
Xianyang 1,450
Luzhou 1,447
Neijiang 1,441
Changde 1,429
Huainan 1,420
Liuzhou 1,409
Suining, Sichuan 1,401
Quanzhou 1,377
Xintai 1,334
Mianyang 1,322
Heze 1,318
Yiyang 1,318
Yueyang 1,286
Suqian 1,258
Huai'an 1,243
Chifeng 1,238
Jingmen 1,228
Yuzhou 1,226
Zaoyang 1,210
Huzhou 1,203
Tianshui 1,199
Yongzhou 1,182
Mudanjiang 1,171
Liupanshui 1,149
Leshan 1,143
Jining, Shandong 1,143
Xiaoshan 1,130
Yixing 1,129
Zigong 1,087
Fuyu 1,068
Yulin 1,060
Baoding 1,042
Xinyi, Jiangsu 1,022
Zhuzhou 1,016
Jixi 1,012
Linqing 1,009
Jiamusi 1,006
Xiangfan 1,006
Zhangjiakou 1,001
Benxi 967
Xiangxiang 936
Zhangjiagang 936
Xinyu 932
Yichun, Heilongjiang 916
Yichun, Jiangxi 890
Jinzhou 888
Zhaotong 879
Yuyao 876
Anshun 864
Hengyang 853
Xuanzhou 851
Tongliao 847
Huaibei 830
Jiaxing 817
Kaifeng 810
Fuxin 807
COLOMBIA
Bogotá 7,594
Medellín 3,236
Cali 2,583
Barranquilla 1,918
Bucaramanga 1,069
Cartagena 1,002
Cúcuta 883
CONGO
Brazzaville 1,323
CONGO (DEM. REP. OF THE)
Kinshasa 8,754
Lubumbashi 1,543
Mbuji-Mayi 1,488
Kolwezi 1,207
Kananga 878
Kisangani 812
COSTA RICA
San José 1,461
CROATIA
Zagreb 1,067
CUBA
Havana 2,192
CZECH REPUBLIC
Prague 1,162
DENMARK
Copenhagen 1,186
DOMINICAN REPUBLIC
Santo Domingo 2,563
Santiago de los Caballeros 804
ECUADOR
Guayaquil 2,690
Quito 1,846
EGYPT
Cairo 11,146
Alexandria 3,760
Shubrâ el Kheima 937
EL SALVADOR
San Salvador 1,565
ETHIOPIA
Addis Ababa 2,930
FINLAND
Helsinki 1,117
FRANCE
Paris 10,485
Marseilles 1,469
Lyons 1,468
Lille 1,033
Nice 977
Toulouse 912
Bordeaux 838
GEORGIA
Tbilisi 1,406
GERMANY
Berlin 3,450
Hamburg 1,786
Munich 1,349
Cologne 1,001
GHANA
Accra 2,342
Kumasi 1,834
GREECE
Athens 3,257
Thessaloniki 837
GUATEMALA
Guatemala City 3,242
GUINEA
Conakry 1,653
HAITI
Port-au-Prince 2,143
HONDURAS
Tegucigalpa 1,061
HUNGARY
Budapest 1,706
INDIA
Delhi 22,157
Mumbai 20,041
Kolkata 15,552
Chennai 7,549
Bangalore 7,218
Hyderabad 5,761
Ahmedabad 5,717
Pune 5,002
Surat 4,168
Kanpur 3,364
Jaipur 3,131
Lucknow 2,873
Nagpur 2,607
Patna 2,321
Indore 2,173
Vadodara 1,872
Bhopal 1,843
Coimbatore 1,807
Ludhiana 1,760
Agra 1,703
Vishakhapatnam 1,625
Cochin 1,610
Nashik 1,588
Meerut 1,494
Varanasi 1,432
Asansol 1,423
Jamshedpur 1,387
Jabalpur 1,367
Madurai 1,365
Rajkot 1,357
Dharbad 1,328
Amritsar 1,297
Allahabad 1,277
Srinagar 1,216
Vijayawada 1,207
Aurangabad 1,193
Bhilainagar-Durg 1,172
Solapur 1,133
Ranchi 1,119
Jodhpur 1,061
Guwahati 1,053
Chandigarh 1,049
Gwalior 1,039
Trivandrum 1,010
Calicut 1,007
Tiruchchirapalli 1,006
Hubli-Dharwad 946
Mysore 943
Raipur 942
Salem 932
Jalandhar 917
Bhubaneswar 912
Kota 884
Bareilly 868
Aligarh 863
Bhiwandi 859
Jammu 857
Moradabad 845
INDONESIA
Jakarta 13,215
Bandung 4,126
Surabaya 2,992
Medan 2,287
Palembang 1,733
Ujung Pandang 1,284
Bandar Lampung 915
Malang 898
Tegal 898
Semarang 816
IRAN
Tehran 7,352
Mashhad 2,652
Esfahan 1,742
Karaj 1,584
Tabriz 1,483
Shiraz 1,299
Ahvaz 1,060
Qom 1,042
Kermanshah 837
IRAQ
Baghdad 5,910
Mosul 1,236
Basra 1,187
Irbil 840
IRELAND
Dublin 1,099
ISRAEL
Tel Aviv-Yafo 3,272
Haifa 1,036
ITALY
Rome 3,362
Milan 2,967
Naples 2,276
Turin 1,665
Palermo 875
Genoa 803
IVORY COAST (CÔTE D'IVOIRE)
Abidjan 4,125
Yamoussoukro 885
JAPAN
Tokyo 12,064
Yokohama 6,427
Osaka 2,599
Nagoya 2,172
Sapporo 1,922
Kobe 1,493
Kyoto 1,468
Fukuoka 1,341
Kawasaki 1,250
Hiroshima 1,126
Kitakyushu 1,011
Sendai 1,008
Chiba 887
JORDAN
Amman 1,292
KAZAKHSTAN
Almaty 1,383
KENYA
Nairobi 3,523
Mombasa 1,003
KOREA, NORTH
Pyŏngyang 3,351
Namp'o 1,102
Hamhung 821
KOREA, SOUTH
Seoul 9,888
Busan 3,830
Incheon 2,884
Daegu 2,675
Daejeon 1,522
Gwangju 1,379
Seognam 1,353
Ulsan 1,340
Ansan 984
Bucheon 900
Suwon 876
KUWAIT
Kuwait City 2,305
KYRGYZSTAN
Bishkek 864
LAOS
Vientiane 831
LEBANON
Beirut 2,070
LIBERIA
Monrovia 827
LIBYA
Tripoli 2,098
Benghazi 1,114
MADAGASCAR
Antananarivo 1,879
MALAWI
Lilongwe 865
Blantyre 856
MALAYSIA
Kuala Lumpur 1,519
Klang 1,128
Johore Bharu 999
MALI
Bamako 1,699
MEXICO
Mexico City 19,460
Guadalajara 4,402
Monterrey 3,896
Puebla 2,315
Tijuana 1,664
Toluca 1,582
León 1,571
Ciudad Juárez 1,394
Torreón 1,199
San Luis Potosí 1,049
Querétaro 1,031
Mérida 1,015
Mexicali 934
Aguascalientes 926
Chihuahua 840
Culiacán 836
Saltillo 801
MONGOLIA
Ulan Bator 966
MOROCCO
Casablanca 3,743
Rabat 1,859
Fès 1,032
Marrakesh 951
MOZAMBIQUE
Maputo 1,655
NEPAL
Katmandu 1,176
NETHERLANDS
Amsterdam 1,157
Rotterdam 1,112
NEW ZEALAND
Auckland 1,404
NICARAGUA
Managua 1,165
NIGER
Niamey 1,048
NIGERIA
Lagos 11,135
Kano 3,395
Ibadan 2,837
Abuja 1,995
Kaduna 1,561
Benin City 1,302
Port Harcourt 1,104
Ogbomosho 1,032
Maiduguri 970
Zaria 963
Ilorin 835
Jos 802
NORWAY
Oslo 888
PAKISTAN
Karachi 14,818
Lahore 8,087
Faisalabad 2,849
Rawalpindi 2,026
Multan 1,659
Gujranwala 1,652
Hyderabad 1,590
Peshawar 1,422
Islamabad 856
Quetta 841
PANAMA
Panamá 1,378
PARAGUAY
Asunción 2,030
PERU
Lima 8,941
PHILIPPINES
Manila 11,628
Davao 1,519
Cebu 860
Zamboanga 854
POLAND
Warsaw 1,712
Lódz 815
PORTUGAL
Lisbon 2,824
Porto 1,355
PUERTO RICO
San Juan 2,743
ROMANIA
Bucharest 1,934
RUSSIA
Moscow 10,550
St Petersburg 4,575
Novosibirsk 1,397
Yekaterinburg 1,344
Nizhniy Novgorod 1,267
Kazan 1,140
Samara 1,131
Omsk 1,124
Chelyabinsk 1,094
Rostov 1,046
Ufa 1,023
Perm 982
Volgograd 977
Krasnoyarsk 961
Voronezh 842
Saratov 822
RWANDA
Kigali 939
SAUDI ARABIA
Riyadh 5,514
Jedda 3,807
Mecca 1,529
Medina 1,044
Dammam 920
SENEGAL
Dakar 2,863
SERBIA
Belgrade 1,117
SIERRA LEONE
Freetown 1,007
SINGAPORE
Singapore City 4,837
SOMALIA
Mogadishu 1,320
SOUTH AFRICA
Johannesburg 3,670
Cape Town 3,405
Durban 2,879
Pretoria 1,429
Vereeniging 1,143
Port Elizabeth 1,068
SPAIN
Madrid 5,851
Barcelona 5,083
Valencia 814
SRI LANKA
Colombo 1,699
SUDAN
Khartoum 5,172
SWEDEN
Stockholm 1,729
Gothenburg 829
SWITZERLAND
Zürich 1,150
SYRIA
Aleppo 3,087
Damascus 2,597
Homs 1,328
Hamah 897
TAIWAN
Taipei 2,633
Kaohsiung 1,611
T'aichung 1,251
TANZANIA
Dar es Salaam 3,349
THAILAND
Bangkok 6,976
TOGO
Lomé 1,667
TUNISIA
Tunis 2,063
TURKEY
Istanbul 10,525
Ankara 3,906
Izmir 2,723
Bursa 1,588
Adana 1,361
Gaziantep 1,109
Konya 978
Antalya 909
UGANDA
Kampala 1,598
UKRAINE
Kiev 2,805
Kharkov 1,453
Odessa 1,009
Dnepropetrovsk 1,004
Donetsk 966
UNITED ARAB EMIRATES
Dubai 1,567
Abu Dhabi 928
Sharjah 809
UNITED KINGDOM
London 8,631
Birmingham 2,302
Manchester 2,253
Liverpool 1,519
Glasgow 1,170
Newcastle-upon-Tyne 891
UNITED STATES OF AMERICA
New York 18,897
Los Angeles 12,829
Chicago 9,461
Dallas–Fort Worth 6,372
Philadelphia 5,965
Houston 5,947
Washington, DC 5,582
Miami 5,565
Atlanta 5,269
Boston 4,552
San Francisco 4,335
Detroit 4,296
Phoenix–Mesa 4,193
Seattle 3,440
Minneapolis–St Paul 3,280
San Diego 3,095
St Louis 2,813
Tampa–St Petersburg 2,783
Baltimore 2,710
Denver 2,543
Portland 2,356
Pittsburgh 2,356
Sacramento 2,149
San Antonio 2,143
Orlando 2,134
Cincinnati 2,130
Cleveland 2,077
Kansas City 2,035
Las Vegas 1,951
Columbus 1,337
San Jose 1,836
San Bernadino 1,807
Charlotte 1,758
Indianapolis 1,756
Austin 1,716
Norfolk–Virginia Beach 1,672
Providence 1,601
Nashville 1,590
Milwaukee 1,556
Jacksonville 1,346
Memphis 1,316
Louisville 1,284
Richmond 1,258
Oklahoma 1,253
Hartford 1,212
New Orleans 1,168
Buffalo 1,136
Raleigh 1,130
Birmingham 1,128
Salt Lake City 1,124
Rochester 1,054
Tucson 980
Honolulu 953
Tulsa 937
Fresno 930
Stamford 917
Albuquerque 887
Albany 870
Omaha 865
New Haven 862
Dayton 841
Bakersfield 839
Baton Rouge 832
El Paso 801
URUGUAY
Montevideo 1,635
UZBEKISTAN
Tashkent 2,210
VENEZUELA
Caracas 3,276
Valencia 2,330
Maracaibo 2,182
Maracay 1,138
Barquisimeto 1,180
Ciudad Guayana 966
VIETNAM
Ho Chi Minh City 6,167
Hanoi 2,814
Haiphong 1,970
Da Nang 838
YEMEN
Sana' 2,342
ZAMBIA
Lusaka 1,451
ZIMBABWE
Harare 1,632
Bulawayo 824

In many ways this image represents 21st-century world farming and how it may develop. It shows 25 combine harvesters on a huge farm in Mato Grosso state, western Brazil. They are harvesting soybeans (or soya beans), a crop where much of the world's production is from GM seed. Brazil is the second largest world producer and exporter after the US, followed by Argentina and Paraguay. This crop requires a hot summer to grow well and much land has been cleared in South America in order to grow it on a massive scale. Soybeans contain twice the protein of any other vegetable crop and there is a high demand from Asia as well as the food-processing industry, where it is used as a protein "extender" in pre-prepared meals. But is this type of large-scale farming desirable or sustainable?

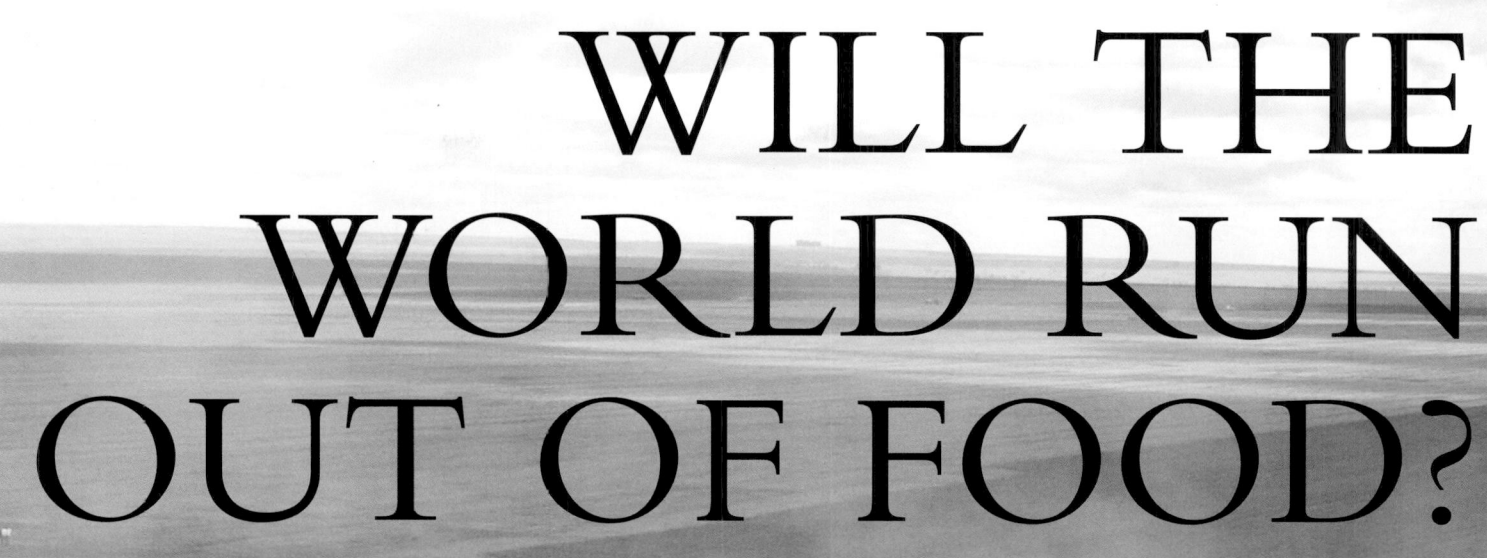

WILL THE WORLD RUN OUT OF FOOD?

For more information:

80 Temperature
   and precipitation
82 Climate change
   and global warming
84 Water
   distribution
88 Population
98 Minerals

▼ Supermarkets in the developed world carry a huge variety of fresh foods from all over the world, much of it out of season. A modern supermarket can often stock in excess of 130 varieties of vegetables and fruit for sale at any one time, much of it flown in chilled from abroad. As well as being extremely costly, these flights produce CO_2 emissions and, because of the high water content of fruit and vegetables, effectively export water and nutrients from countries that can often ill afford to do so. However, they do provide much needed income and employment for the producing country. By comparison, the market in the photograph (below right) only sells produce which can be grown locally and carried there, with no consequent CO_2 cost.

At current rates of growth, the world's population will increase to 9 billion people by 2050, from just over 6.5 billion today. To sustain this population there will have to be a 40% increase in food production which, as now, will have to be grown on the fertile soils irregularly distributed across just 11% of the Earth's surface. In addition, the fast growing and increasingly better-off economies of countries such as China and India are demanding a wider variety and better food in their diets, with many people eating more meat. However, the global trend in population is for people to move off the land toward the cities, resulting in fewer people to produce the food.

Similar conditions have been faced before: in 1898, the eminent Victorian scientist Sir William Crookes predicted that "England and all the civilized nations stand in deadly peril of not having enough to eat." But by 1909 the process to make synthetic nitrogen fertilizer from ammonia (the Haber-Bosch method) had been developed in Germany and Crookes' concerns were forgotten. Artificial nitrogen fixation has been a major factor in enabling the world's population to grow to today's levels. The process uses about 2% of the world's total energy demand to produce more than 100 million tonnes of nitrogen fertilizer, which helps feed about 30% of the world's population.

The issues in the developed world revolve around the quality and quantity of what we eat. The range of food available to consumers in a modern supermarket shows the extent to which food products are transported from around the world to satisfy the perceived need for such a wide variety of choice. There are also huge economic pressures from parts of the processed food industry to entice people in the developed world to eat more than is actually good for them. By comparison, in the developing world many struggle to achieve the minimum food intake to sustain life. Globally, about 1 billion people are malnourished and 1 billion are overweight. One of the biggest problems society faces is balancing this inequality of distribution, not only of food, but also of wealth.

Without the application of fertilizers, we would have been unable to sustain our historic growth rates of agricultural production. Yet the production of these is under pressure. The supply of phosphate rock, which occurs naturally and is currently the major source of phosphorus fertilizer (an essential plant nutrient), is predicted to peak in the 2030s and could be exhausted within 50 years or so, at the current rate of use. More phosphate rock is available but it would cost more to extract and contains cadmium and other contaminants, further increasing the cost of converting it into fertilizer. Nitrogen fertilizer currently uses expensive fossil fuels for its production, although an alternative production process using renewable hydroelectricity has been developed.

At the same time as the demand for food has increased, in recent years the demand for so-called "green" biofuels, derived from plant products, has also had an inflationary effect on prices by reducing the amount of land on which food can be grown.

In addition, because of the increase in the global demand for meat, more agricultural land is being used to grow crops to feed livestock, again pushing up the price of staple foods. This rise in prices disproportionately affects poorer developing economies, where a much higher proportion of family income is spent on food, perhaps as high as 50–70%.

SOIL FERTILITY

The map shows all soils, whether currently used for agriculture or covered by forest, grassland etc.

As much as 90% of all food is grown in soil, but fertile soil irregularly covers only 11% of the global land surface and is a non-renewable asset. Some soils are naturally fertile, such as the Black Earths of Russia and Ukraine. Natural soil fertility results from a combination of a temperate climate and nutrient-rich rocks that slowly weather. Those soils which are not naturally fertile, or which have been degraded by erosion or over-exploitation, require the incorporation of manures and fertilizers to improve soil fertility and maximize production.

This fragile asset is under threat from effects such as erosion and desertification, acidification, salinization, pollution and compaction (modern farm machinery gets heavier each year as its size increases).

Source: US Dept. of Agriculture Natural Resources Conservation Service – inherent land quality assessment map

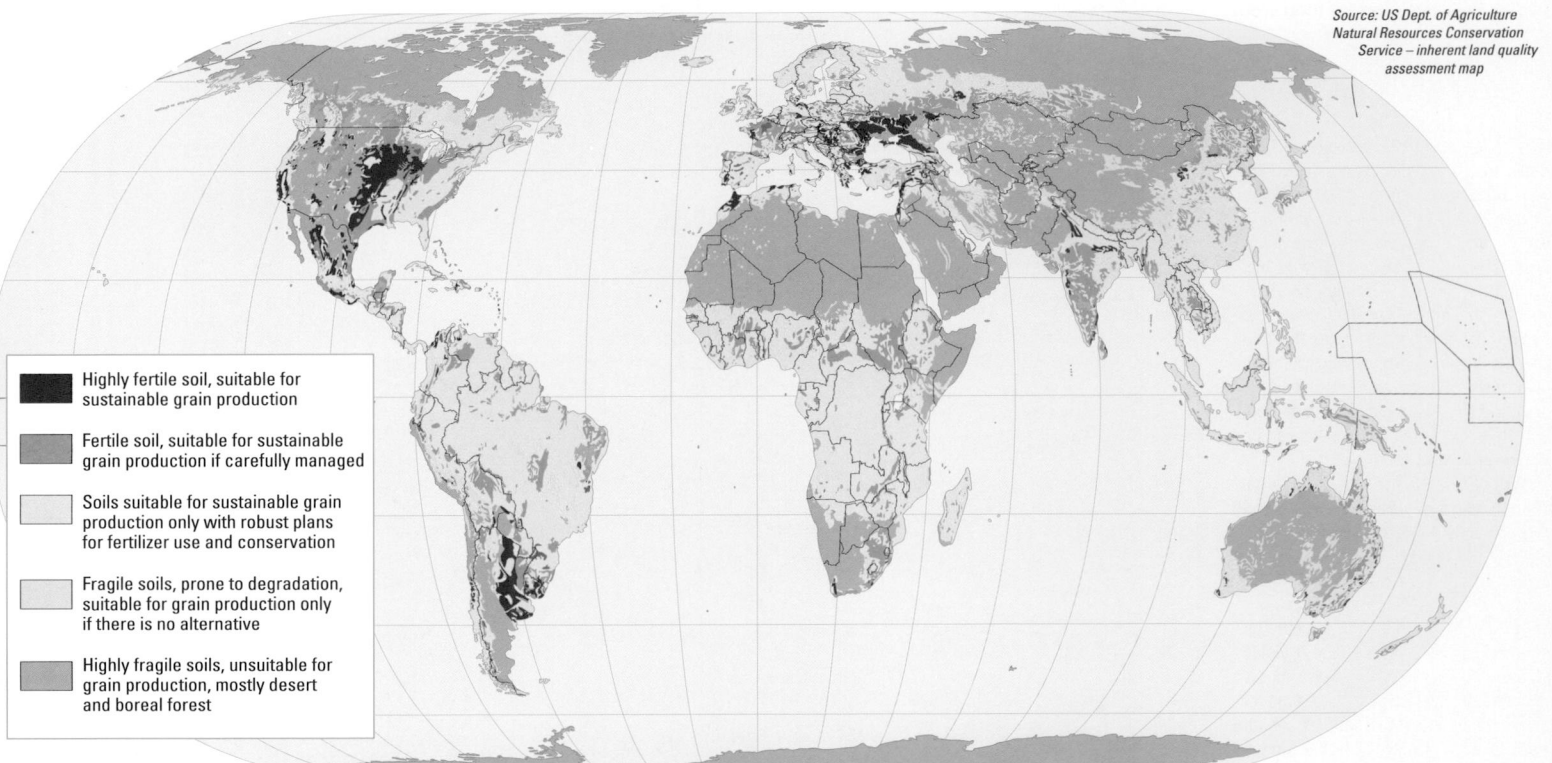

- Highly fertile soil, suitable for sustainable grain production
- Fertile soil, suitable for sustainable grain production if carefully managed
- Soils suitable for sustainable grain production only with robust plans for fertilizer use and conservation
- Fragile soils, prone to degradation, suitable for grain production only if there is no alternative
- Highly fragile soils, unsuitable for grain production, mostly desert and boreal forest

SOIL DEGRADATION

Areas of concern

- Areas of serious concern
- Areas of some concern
- Stable terrain
- Non-vegetated land

Causes of soil degradation (by region)

- Grazing practices
- Other agricultural practices
- Industrialization
- Deforestation
- Fuelwood collection

An estimated 75 billion tonnes of soil comprising 10 million hectares of potentially usable arable land are annually degraded or lost due to erosion. Current rates of loss in China are 57 times the rate of soil creation; in Europe the rate is 17 times and in the US 10 times. There have been frightening predictions of the loss of all fertile soil within 60 years.

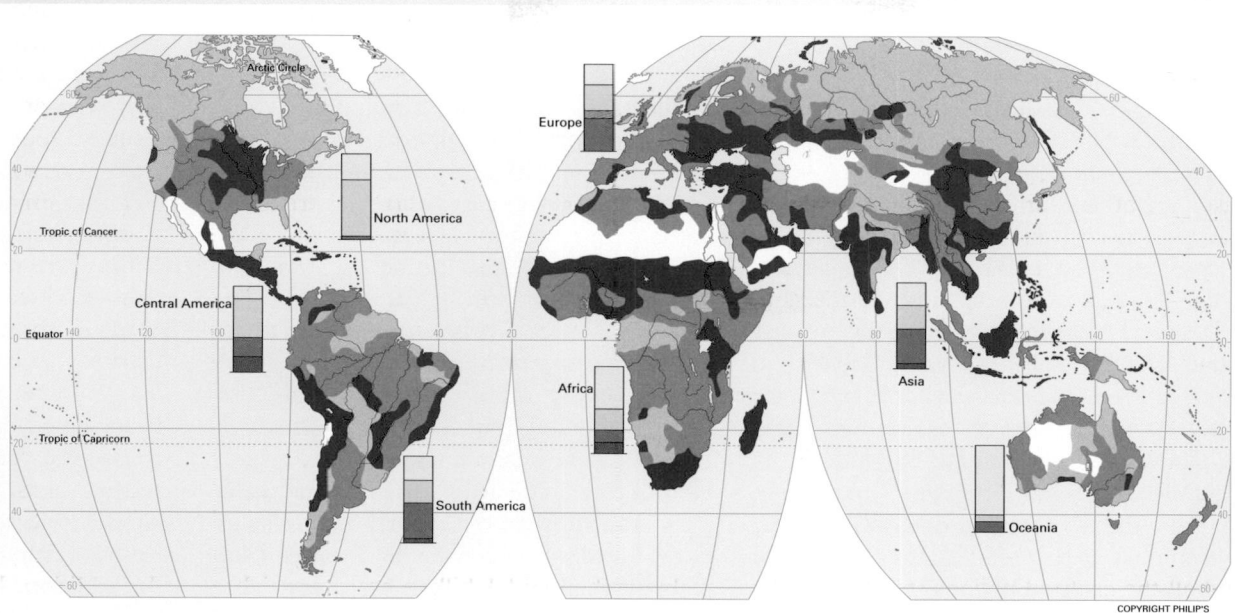

COPYRIGHT PHILIP'S

WORLD CROP PRODUCTION

ROOTS AND TUBERS

- Yams 7.1%
- Other 2.8%
- Sweet potatoes 15.1%
- Potatoes 43.1%
- Cassava 31.9%

World total (2008): 729.6 million tonnes

OIL CROPS

- Olives 2.4%
- Other 3.5%
- Sunflower seeds 4.8%
- Groundnuts 5.2%
- Rapeseed 7.8%
- Coconuts 8.3%
- Seed cotton 8.9%
- Soybeans 31.3%
- Oil palm fruit 27.8%

World total (2008): 738.8 million tonnes

CEREALS

- Rye 0.7%
- Oats 1.0%
- Millet 1.4%
- Sorghum 2.6%
- Barley 6.2%
- Triticale 0.6%
- Other 0.4%
- Maize 32.6%
- Rice paddy 27.1%
- Wheat 27.3%

World total (2008): 2,252.0 million tonnes

BIOFUELS

Industrialized countries, looking to reduce their reliance on fossil fuels such as oil and gas, are setting targets for "bioenergy" production, i.e. energy from renewable sources such as maize, sugarcane, potatoes, or manioc. The EU has decided that 10% of its fuel for transport should be from these sources – mostly bioethanol – by 2020. This demand is resulting in both developed and developing countries converting food crops into bioethanol, jeopardizing food supplies. A major push by the US for bioethanol, coupled with poor harvests in Europe, Australia and the other grain-exporting countries, pushed grain prices up to unusually high levels in late 2007 and 2008; the poor suffered as a result.

This may be overcome as "first generation" biofuels – arable crops, which need fertilizers so the energy balance is not good – are replaced by "second generation" bioenergy crops such as willow and miscanthus grass, which need little if any fertilizer and can be grown on poorer soils not used for food crops.

GLOBAL LAND USAGE

Most suitable land for agriculture is already in use and much is lost to development and erosion each year. The amount of extra land for agriculture is very limited unless we cut down forests or plow up old grasslands, which results in the release of CO_2 into the atmosphere.

- Desert, mountain & ice 31.8%
- Forest 30.3%
- Meadows & pastures 26.0%
- Cereals 4.6%
- Other arable & permanent crops 7.3%

World total (2008): 13,009.1 million hectares

THE GREEN REVOLUTION

Fifty years ago there was a food crisis in the developing world, which was tackled by the so-called "Green Revolution." This combined the breeding of sturdy disease-resistant dwarf crop varieties with the use of irrigation, synthetic fertilizers, and chemical pesticides. Productivity per acre increased by up to 300%. Thus, countries that had only been able to grow enough for their own needs drove down the cost of food and became net exporters of food. Currently, 30–50% of crop yields can be attributed to fertilizer use.

Without fertilizer, under an ideal climate and with adequate pest and disease control, a wheat grain yield of 2–3 tonnes per hectare can be achieved; however, without good pest and disease control, 1 tonne per hectare is more likely. This can be compared with average wheat yields of about 8 tonnes per hectare in the UK, and the current (at the time of going to press) world record wheat yield in New Zealand of 15.6 tonnes per hectare.

The benefits of the Green Revolution plateaued out in the 1990s. There is now the need for a new phase to reinvigorate production to feed 9 billion people.

Using the latest technology to increase the worst yields to match the average, and the average to match the best, would transform food supplies.

YIELDS OF WHEAT GRAIN GROWN IN BROADBALK, ROTHAMSTED, FROM 1852 TO 2005

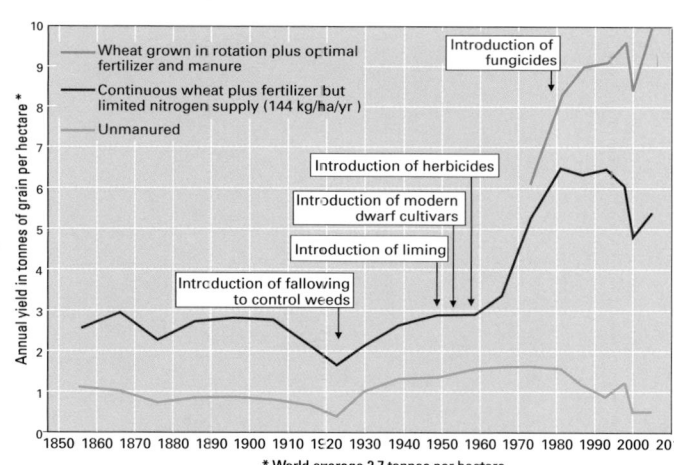

- Wheat grown in rotation plus optimal fertilizer and manure
- Continuous wheat plus fertilizer but limited nitrogen supply (144 kg/ha/yr)
- Unmanured

Introduction of fungicides
Introduction of herbicides
Introduction of modern dwarf cultivars
Introduction of liming
Introduction of fallowing to control weeds

Annual yield in tonnes of grain per hectare *

* World average 2.7 tonnes per hectare

LIVESTOCK

As can be seen on the graph below, world livestock production has increased dramatically over the last half century. Currently, over a third of the world's grain is fed to livestock for intensive stock raising, rising to 70% in developed countries where there is higher meat consumption per person.

Animals (and humans) are very inefficient in their utilization of nutrients – generally less than 20% of the nitrogen in their food is used; the rest is excreted, causing problems for recycling and the risk of environmental impact. Methane emissions from cattle are also a major contributor to greenhouse gases in the atmosphere. Additionally, meat is very expensive in terms of water consumption; for example, 1 lb [0.5 kg] of beef requires 1,857 gallons [8,442 liters] of water to produce it, taking account of the water used to grow feed, etc.

The adoption of vegetarianism has been suggested as a possible solution to some of these problems. However, even if this proved acceptable to the majority population, land in many parts of the world is suitable only for livestock production by extensive grazing. In any case, developing countries, which were previously predominantly vegetarian, are demanding more meat, regarded in some societies as a measurement of status. For example, Chinese meat consumption has risen from 9 lb [4 kg] per person in 1960 to 119 lb [54 kg] today. This compares with a figure of 176 lb [80 kg] in the UK and 254 lb [115 kg] in the United States.

WORLD LIVESTOCK PRODUCTION

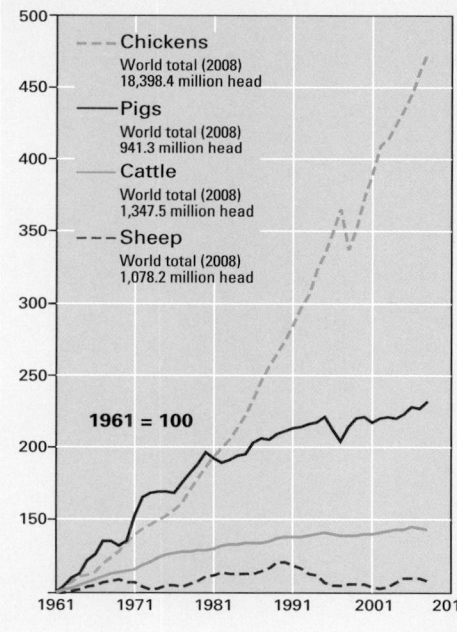

- Chickens — World total (2008) 18,398.4 million head
- Pigs — World total (2008) 941.3 million head
- Cattle — World total (2008) 1,347.5 million head
- Sheep — World total (2008) 1,078.2 million head

1961 = 100

◄ The top lines on the graph show the effects of fertilizers and other developments in agricultural practice on wheat production over time, in the longest running trial of this type. The Broadbalk Wheat Experiment at Rothamsted Research in the UK has been running on the same field since 1843. The lower line represents the same crop grown in the same conditions, but with none of these inputs applied – the equivalent of yields in many parts of the developing world.

FOOD & POPULATION

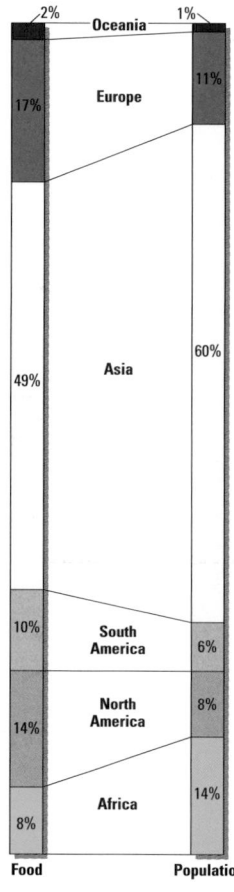

	Food	Population
Oceania	2%	1%
Europe	17%	11%
Asia	49%	60%
South America	10%	6%
North America	14%	8%
Africa	8%	14%

Comparison of food production and population by continent
The left column indicates the proportion of world food production and the right shows population in proportion.

IRRIGATION

By 2030 there will be a 30% increase in water demand to support the world's population and its value will soar, so more efficient methods of collection and delivery will have to be developed.

China currently has 23% of the world's population, but only 11% of its water. The country is therefore building new reservoirs to catch runoff from Himalayan glaciers. Their efforts have, however, already resulted in a conference of the countries downstream on the Mekong River to discuss how to tackle the resultant reduced water flow.

Since over 71% of the Earth's surface is covered in water, it can hardly be said to be in short supply. However, less than 3% of this is fresh water and, of that, over two-thirds is frozen in ice caps and glaciers. The world, therefore, will never run out of water as such, but its over-exploitation in developed areas and availability in regions where it is scarce are major problems.

For more information:

84 Water distribution

85 Natural vegetation

86 Biodiversity and the natural world

▼ If the ever-increasing world demand for food continues, it is likely that more intensive livestock production units will have to be adopted. Pictured below, this battery farm for chickens is in the US. In the past, these units have been synonymous in many people's minds with cruelty to the animals and issues associated with the spread of disease.

The growth of food crops in a protected environment without the use of soil as the growing medium will also become more widespread. In hydroponics the plants grow in nutrient-enriched water, as can be seen in the picture below right, taken at a research establishment in California.

How can we feed 9 billion people adequately and sustainably? There are some simple solutions that we should note before looking at more complicated and technological "fixes." Most agree that we should not be taking more land from forest and other uncropped areas into production because of the release of CO_2 that this would cause and the adverse impacts on predicted climate change and biodiversity. As already noted on page 11, enabling those producing the lowest yields to produce national average yields, and those producing average yields to equal the best, would transform food production. This is likely to involve better pest and disease control, and more widespread and effective use of fertilizers. The Alliance for the Green Revolution in Africa (AGRA), with initial support from the Rockefeller Foundation and the Bill and Melinda Gates Foundation, is looking to achieve this.

It is important to control pests and diseases in growing crops, but post-harvest crop losses from molds, insects, rodents, and birds are 10–40% of the total, according to the FAO. Again, the application of existing technologies could avoid these and make a significant impact on food supplies. Finally, the avoidance of waste would also make an important contribution in developed countries.

But if this is not sufficient, what then? The UK's Royal Society published a report in 2009 entitled "Reaping the benefits. Science and the sustainable intensification of global agriculture." It suggested that we will need to increase crop production but without cultivating more land, while sustaining the environment, preserving natural resources, and supporting farmers' livelihoods: that is, produce more using less and with less of an impact. The Royal Society saw good soil management, maintaining or enhancing crop genetic diversity, and introducing pest and disease resistance, as well as better nitrogen-use efficiency through GM technologies, as key to this.

Research is in progress now at such centers as the International Rice Research Institute in the Philippines and the John Innes Centre in the UK to develop cereals (rice and wheat, for example) that fix their own nitrogen and so do not need nitrogen fertilizer. Possible problems here are the carbon/energy cost to the plant of accommodating the nitrogen-fixing organisms or traits, and the consequent likely reductions in yield. In the longer-term, and even more aspirational, there is the idea of perennial cereals such as wheat, maize, and rice that would not need to be replanted each year, but would regrow and yield each year in the same way as a fruit tree.

However, some reject such technological approaches, saying that reliance on chemical fertilizers and pesticides is a threat to sustainability. They advocate extensive systems that could be viewed as "organic," "biodynamic" or "ecological." But these mostly involve mixed systems rather than the specialist crop or livestock production systems that dominate most developed countries, crop rotations to control pests and diseases, and legumes to supply nitrogen.

Finally, we must note the increasing interest in healthy eating and the efforts of many governments to promote this, mostly with a view to reducing obesity and other diet-induced health problems. This may well drive food production in a particular direction.

NITROGEN – THE KEY TO CROP GROWTH

In most countries, nitrogen is the main yield-determining plant nutrient; exceptions are areas where degraded soils are deficient in phosphorus, such as in parts of Africa and Australia. Adequate inputs of nitrogen are therefore essential for food security.

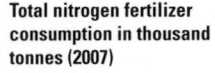

Total nitrogen fertilizer consumption in thousand tonnes (2007)

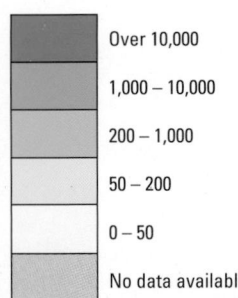

Over 10,000

1,000 – 10,000

200 – 1,000

50 – 200

0 – 50

No data available

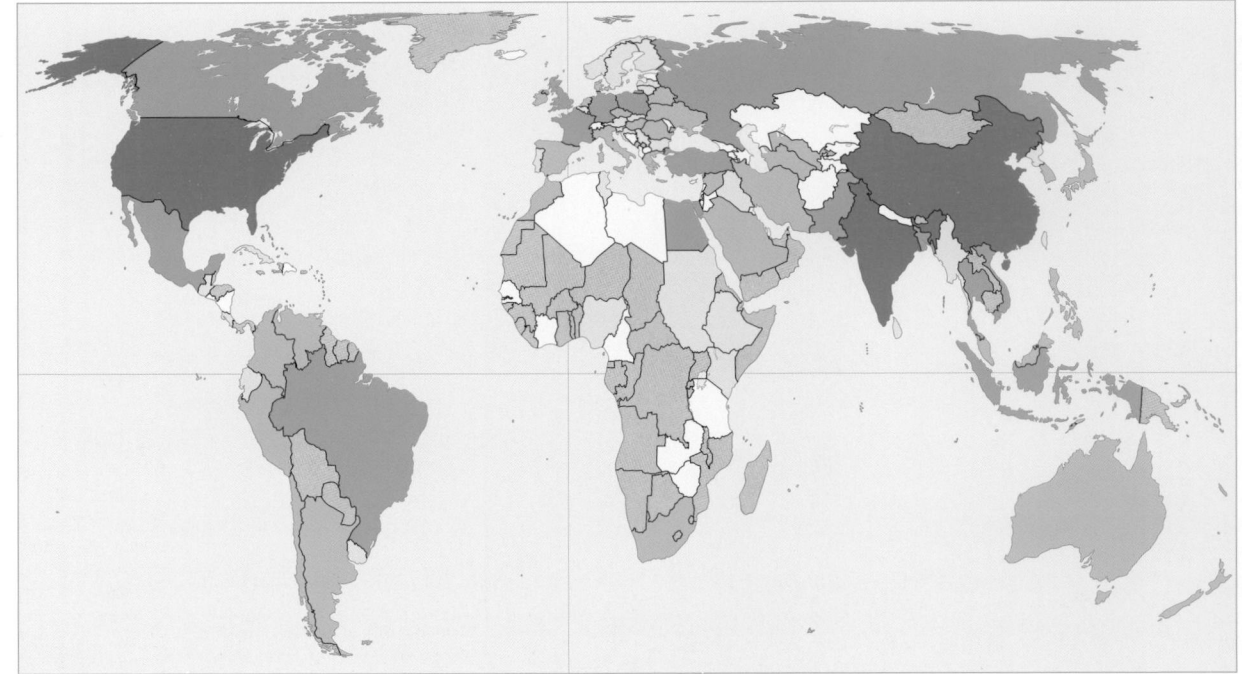

The map shows nitrogen fertilizer inputs across the world. This, in a very real sense, is an index of food production. However, producing nitrogen fertilizer requires energy, so many see a system in which the nitrogen is brought in (or fixed) by legumes such as clover and alfalfa (lucerne) as being more sustainable. However, the problem with such systems is that, in general, while the legume is being grown, a food crop is not being produced (apart from livestock that may graze the legume). In addition, pollution in the form of nitrogen losses to air and water from legume-based systems can be as large as those from fertilizers, and the energy needed to produce fertilizers could be obtained from renewable sources.

PESTS, DISEASES AND WEEDS

Currently, 30% of the world's crop yield is lost because of the effects of pests, diseases, and weeds. Chemical controls (such as herbicides and fungicides) continue to be effective but are disliked by many.

REACH is a new EU regulation on chemicals and their safe use. It deals with the Registration, Evaluation, Authorization and restriction of CHemical substances, and severely limits those chemicals that growers can use.

Because of this, research is focusing on isolating pest and disease resistance genes or traits using molecular methods. Breeding for resistance, transferring these identified traits into crop plants and animals, can be done using conventional plant breeding methods but is much quicker using GM methods (see below right).

Crop rotations can be used to control pests, diseases and weeds, as can mechanical methods, cultivations, and inter-cropping (that is, mixing crops) and trap crops (which protect the main crop from pests).

Although climate change is not accepted by some, whatever happens in the future, changing weather patterns have already caused the movement of pests and diseases around the world.

One example of this is "bluetongue," which has been monitored and action taken to prevent serious impact on food production in Europe. This disease, which affects livestock, has been spread by a species of tiny biting midge from sub-Saharan Africa into northwest Europe since 2006, before which it was never recorded in Europe.

A sustained research program, vector surveillance, restrictions on animal movements, and a vaccination program have helped limit the spread of the disease in the UK.

This map shows the spread of the disease between 2006 and 2009 in Europe as a whole.

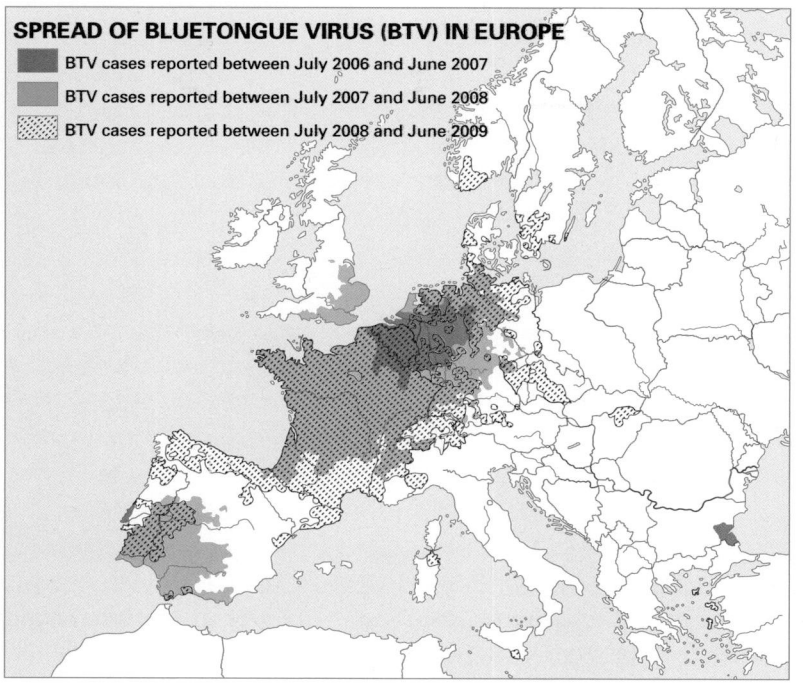

SPREAD OF BLUETONGUE VIRUS (BTV) IN EUROPE

- BTV cases reported between July 2006 and June 2007
- BTV cases reported between July 2007 and June 2008
- BTV cases reported between July 2008 and June 2009

AQUACULTURE

With a greater demand in some western countries for increased fish content in their diets, at the same time as fish stocks in the oceans are becoming depleted from overfishing, fish farming or "aquaculture" has become more important.

The term covers both salt and freshwater fish, and shellfish, but has the same inherent issues as livestock farming in relation to pollution and pest and disease problems. It contributes about a third of the total world fish catch, with carp, oysters, clams, salmon, mussels, and scallops forming some of the major varieties. China, India, and Southeast Asia, where it has always been important for local consumption, are the biggest producers.

It is estimated that 90% of the USA's consumption of shrimps are farmed and imported.

CUTTING BACK ON FOOD WASTE

Major retailers can be fussy because they know that their customers are fussy. Over 30 years ago, the singer Joni Mitchell wrote "Give me spots on my apples, but leave me the birds and bees," but not much has changed. The US Government has estimated that currently 60 million tonnes of food worth $5 billion is left in the fields because it is regarded as being of poor quality and unsaleable. More is left unsold in shops and discarded: in the UK it is estimated that 8.3 million tonnes of food worth £20 billion is sent to landfill each year, and some people now live on the food shops' throwaway ("Dumpster Diving" in the US; "Skipping" in the UK). A further fraction is bought but never consumed. It is estimated that food wasted by the US and Europe could feed the world three times over. Food waste now accounts for more than a quarter of the total freshwater consumption and 300 million barrels of oil per year. Clearly using this waste would make a big impact and must be part of sustainable food supply.

GENETIC MODIFICATION (GM)

Mankind has undertaken selective breeding of crops and livestock for thousands of years, to maintain and improve their most desirable characteristics. In the past 20–30 years, molecular genetics has increasingly been used to guide crop breeding. Biotechnological tools, such as molecular markers and genetic modification (GM), can complement conventional breeding processes to improve almost all important traits, including yield potential, plant structure, tolerance to abiotic stress (that is, salinity, cold, acidity), disease resistances, food and nutritional quality, and market preference.

GM critics suggest that there may be unforeseen effects on human health and the environment. However, in Europe and elsewhere, detailed risk analysis of potential effects of GM crops is made before licences to release the technology are granted. For example, UK Farm Scale Evaluations compared the effects on farmland biodiversity of growing conventional and GM (herbicide-resistant) sugar beet, maize, and oilseed rape. It was found that the species of crop grown (that is, beet, maize or rape) had a greater impact on biodiversity than whether the crop was GM or conventional.

Some would claim proven benefits and GM crops are currently grown in more than 23 countries, on over 114 million hectares worldwide, equivalent to about 5% of global cultivated land. These include eight EU states: Spain, France, Czech Republic, Portugal, Poland, Germany, Slovak Republic, and Romania. In addition, eight countries now grow more than 1 million hectares of GM crops: USA, Canada, China, India, South Africa, Paraguay, Argentina, and Brazil.

A major obstacle for GM acceptance is public perception of the technology. Biotechnology is only part of the solution; research in sustainable agriculture will provide new methods of crop and soil management, and support the development of improved varieties by both conventional breeding and GM.

IMPROVED LAND MANAGEMENT

Improved land management has a large part to play in improving food production. Many soils have been compacted through the use of heavy machinery or by regular plowing, which causes a "plow pan" (a thin compacted layer of soil) to develop just below the bottom of the plow. Other soils have been allowed to become acid or saline through acid rain, the inappropriate use of fertilizers or other amendments, or polluted by toxic metals such as cadmium, nickel, and copper, or by organic pollutants through the use of human and animal "wastes."

Conservation agriculture that includes "no-till" and "min-till" has many benefits in terms of allowing a stable and good soil structure to develop, retaining organic matter, nutrients and moisture. But perennial weeds can be a problem on "heavy" clay soils, requiring a greater use of herbicides.

Strip tillage (cultivating only a narrow strip in which the crop is planted) saves energy use, maintains a soil cover (preventing erosion), and generally carries the benefits of conservation tillage.

In the longer-term, "controlled traffic" in which tractors and other equipment travel along fixed paths, or in which equipment is run from gantries, all linked to GPS, are precision farming systems that would contribute to a high-tech solution to food security.

One matter still to be resolved is the importance of the biodiversity of soil organisms and micro-organisms (for example, earthworms, mycorrhizal fungi, bacteria) to soil fertility and thus sustainable food production. Plants can be grown in sand culture or hydroponics, suggesting that organisms, let alone biodiversity, are not essential. However, for many this is the key to a truly sustainable system based on soil.

THE FUTURE

If we adopt and develop appropriate techniques and practices, and modify our behavior, we stand a good chance of feeding the future, predominantly urban, world population. The image at bottom left shows one of several proposals for a new development currently under discussion: the "vertical farm," this from Plantagon International. Theoretically, this would consist of a giant self-contained production unit, enabling crop production to take place in a controlled environment, regardless of climatic variations, and situated within urban regions, the main areas of consumption.

Its proponents also claim that crops will be able to be grown throughout the year, making one acre in the controlled environment the equivalent of many times more acres grown outdoors. They also say that the units would grow the crops organically, would reduce runoff pollution, and would also ease the pressure on water demand by recycling the water used from evapotranspiration.

However, whether or not we can afford proposals such as these, it still seems likely that parts of the world will still be using subsistence agriculture to feed themselves (such as in the photograph at upper left, taken in southern Africa). Brazil, though, has developed from primarily subsistence agriculture to "modern" intensive methods, and China and India are currently undergoing a similar process. As people move away from the land to live in the growing urban centers, farm sizes can grow and opportunities, created by economies of scale, may evolve to improve the lifestyle of the subsistence farmer.

Whatever develops, it will be our choices that will influence it. What is your concept of a sustainable system of food supply that can feed 9 billion people and provide a livelihood for producers?

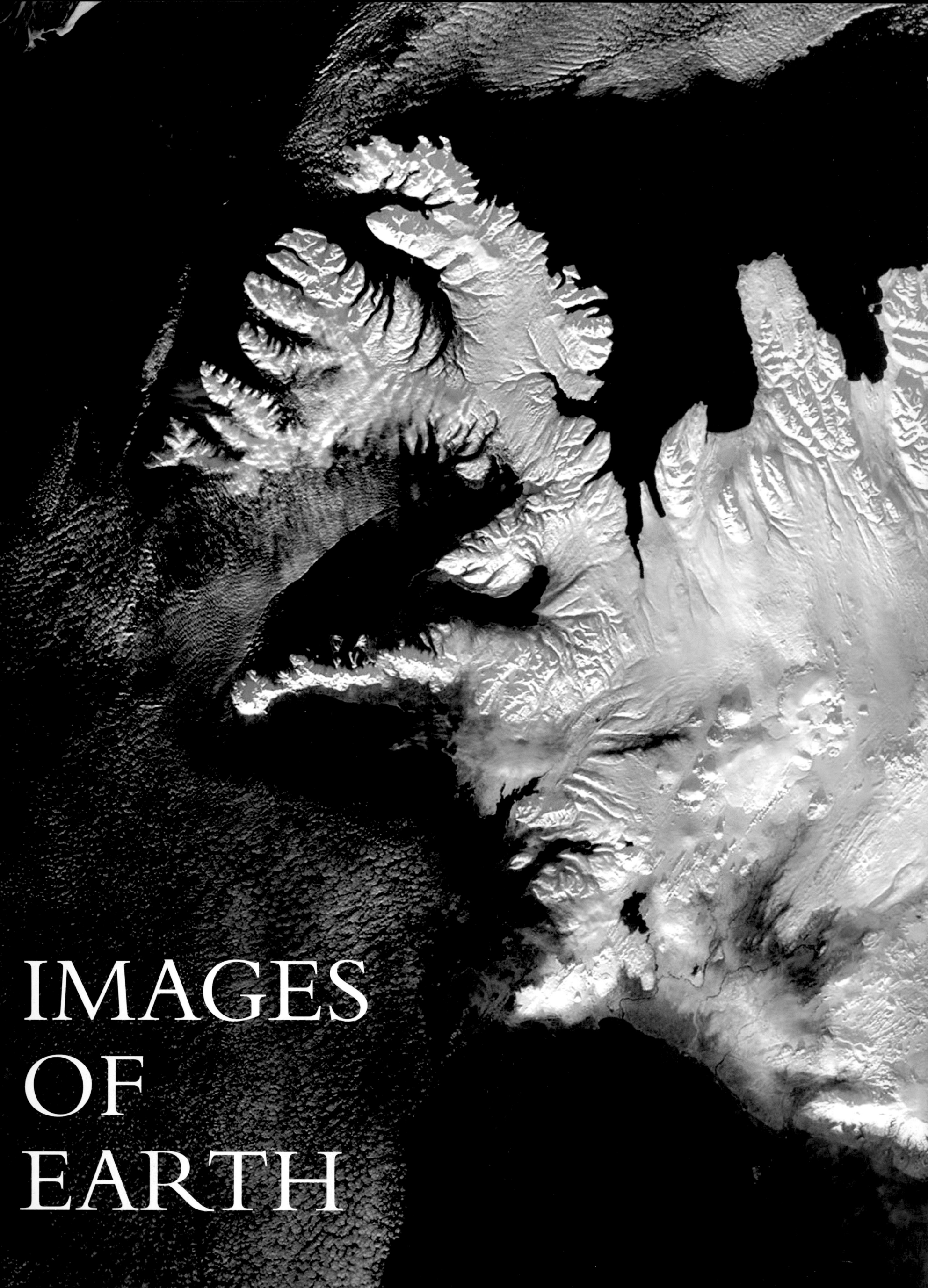

IMAGES
OF
EARTH

This winter image, captured in January, shows Iceland cloaked in snow, covering its four permanent ice caps. The island sits astride the fault line between the North American and Eurasian tectonic plates. These plates are moving away from each other, resulting in a high level of volcanic activity, with much of the land covered in lava flows. Although situated just below the Arctic Circle, Iceland's climate in the south is modified by the relatively warm waters of the North Atlantic Drift current. [Map page 155]

The River Thames snakes from Chelsea Bridge in the west to Tower Bridge in the east in this image covering both the West End and the City of London. Despite having a population in excess of 8 million people, there are still many parks and open spaces around the city center. St James's Park, Green Park, and part of Hyde Park, together with Buckingham Palace and its gardens, can be seen center left of the image, and farther north the eastern edge of Regent's Park can be seen. Just below the title, the newly developing area around St Pancras, the terminus of the direct high-speed rail link to Europe, can be seen. *(Satellite image courtesy of Digital Globe)* [Map page 125]

One of the great cultural centers of the
world, the city of Rome (in the center
of this image) lies on the west coast of
the Italian Peninsula, 15 miles (24 km)
inland from the Tyrrhenian Sea. It was
established at the lowest crossing point
of the River Tiber and was the center of
an extensive European and North African
empire as early as the 1st century BC. The
importance of the city was maintained by
the establishment of the city as the center
of the Catholic Church and the home of
the Pope in the Vatican City, to the west
of the river. The capital of Italy, with a
population of over 3 million people,
Rome retains its place as a major
tourist destination. [Map page 136]

The metropolitan area of Athens, including its port of Piraeus, is home to nearly a third of the total population of Greece. The capital of the country, it was a powerful city state in the era of Ancient Greece, some 2,500 years ago. At the bottom left of the image is part of the Peloponnese Peninsula, connected to the mainland by the Isthmus of Corinth. To shorten the sailing time around the peninsula, the Corinth Canal was excavated at the end of the 19th century and can be seen here as a fine blue line. [Map page 112]

Baku (or Baki) sits on the southern shore of the distinctive hook-shaped Absheron Peninsula on the west coast of the Caspian Sea. Lying 92 ft (28 m) below sea level, it is the capital and largest town in Azerbaijan, with a population of nearly 2 million, and is a major port. Parts of the old city were designated a UNESCO World Heritage site in 2000. The town has been associated with the commercial oil industry since the early 19th century and, with extensive foreign investment, the area was producing almost half of the world's oil at the beginning of the 20th century. Oil production has since moved offshore, but it remains the major part of the city's and country's economy. [Map page 191]

The capital of Yemen, with a population of over 2 million, the city is one of the world's oldest continuously inhabited sites, believed to have been in existence in the 6th century BC. It is situated in a highland area in the west of the country at an altitude of 7,382 ft (2,250 m), which moderates what would otherwise be a desert climate. The city, seen in this view at the bottom center, is surrounded by a series of extinct volcanic cones, which are shown here in a reddish-brown color. The distinctive architecture of the city, with decorated clay walls and wooden windows, led to Sana' being designated a UNESCO World Heritage site in 1986. [Map page 248]

This image shows Shanghai, lower left, in its setting on the south bank of the mouth of the Chang Jiang (Yangtse) river. Since it sits at the gateway to one of China's richest regions and the river is navigable for ocean-going vessels up to Hankou, a further 600 miles (1,000 km) inland, it has developed to become the world's largest cargo port. It has grown rapidly with the booming Chinese economy to become the largest city in China, with a population of over 16 million. Much new development has taken place, including the newly expanded airport, which can be seen on the coast at Pudong and which is linked to the city by high-speed Maglev train. [Map page 138]

The light purple area on the western bank of the White Nile River (Bahr el Jebel) in this image is the newest capital city in the world. Juba is the capital of the Republic of South Sudan, which gained its independence on July 9, 2011. Its population is approximately 163,000 and the town is situated deep in the south of the country, near to the borders with the Democratic Republic of the Congo, Uganda and Kenya. South Sudan has a less arid climate than Sudan to the north, and contains a wide variety of wildlife. Most of the oilfields in the former Sudan are situated in the new state and timber is another important part of the economy. However, civil war has destroyed much of the transportation infrastructure, and the links between Juba and its neighboring countries have yet to be re-established. [Map page 266]

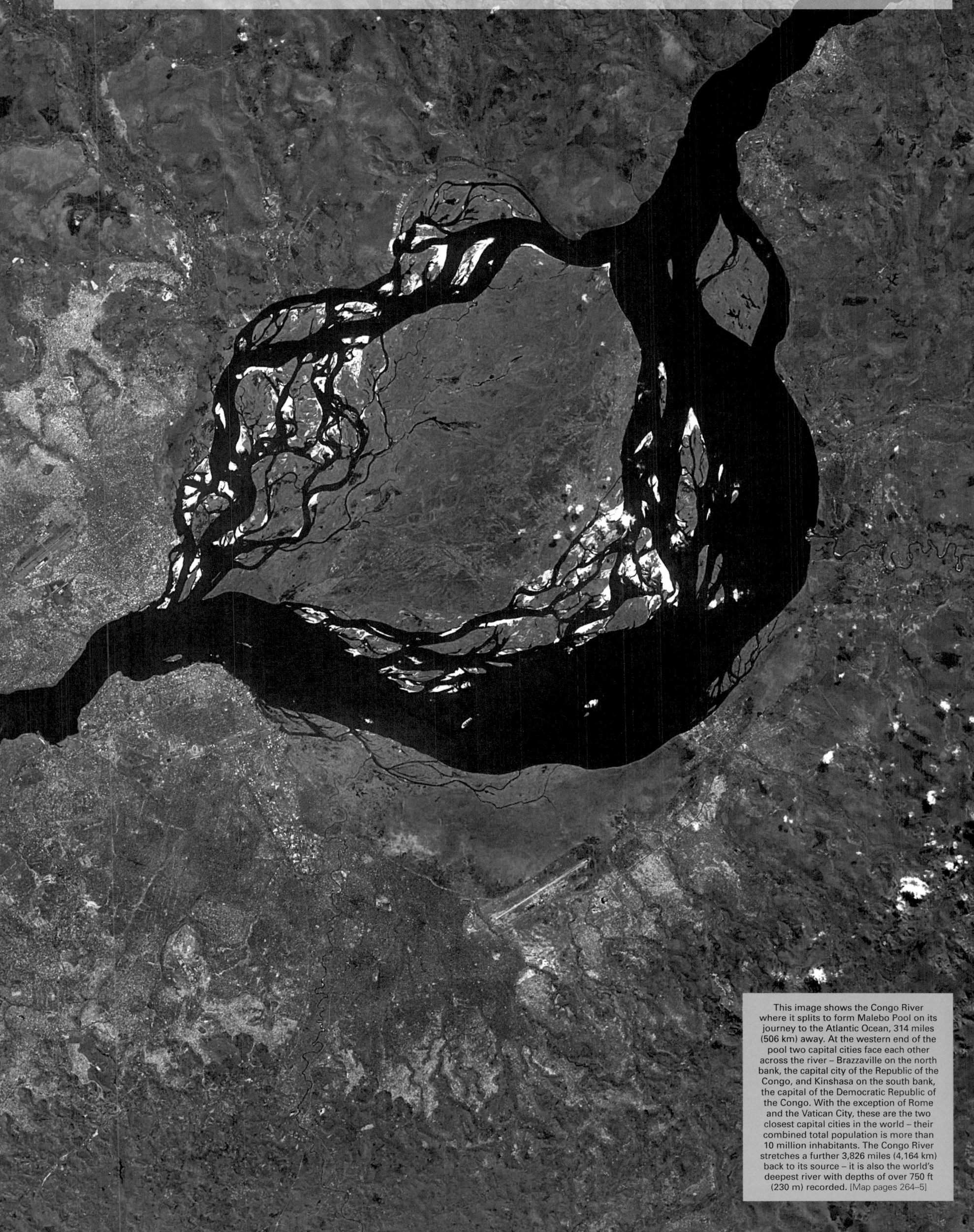

This image shows the Congo River where it splits to form Malebo Pool on its journey to the Atlantic Ocean, 314 miles (506 km) away. At the western end of the pool two capital cities face each other across the river – Brazzaville on the north bank, the capital city of the Republic of the Congo, and Kinshasa on the south bank, the capital of the Democratic Republic of the Congo. With the exception of Rome and the Vatican City, these are the two closest capital cities in the world – their combined total population is more than 10 million inhabitants. The Congo River stretches a further 3,826 miles (4,164 km) back to its source – it is also the world's deepest river with depths of over 750 ft (230 m) recorded. [Map pages 264–5]

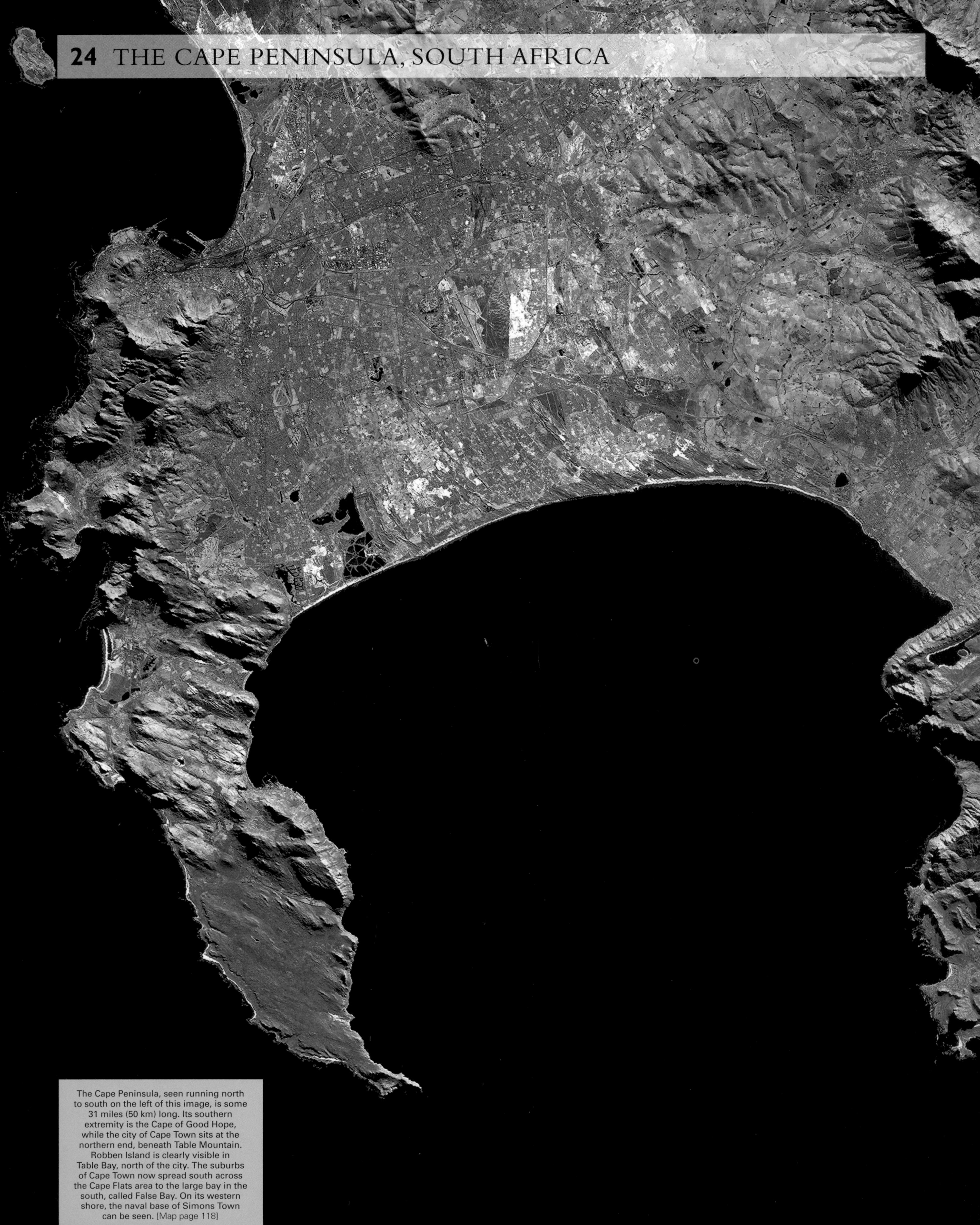

The Cape Peninsula, seen running north to south on the left of this image, is some 31 miles (50 km) long. Its southern extremity is the Cape of Good Hope, while the city of Cape Town sits at the northern end, beneath Table Mountain. Robben Island is clearly visible in Table Bay, north of the city. The suburbs of Cape Town now spread south across the Cape Flats area to the large bay in the south, called False Bay. On its western shore, the naval base of Simons Town can be seen. [Map page 118]

The largest city in Australia, Sydney was founded at the end of the 18th century on the north shore of Botany Bay. It has since spread inland along the valley of the Parramatta River, but is constrained by the Blue Mountains National Park in the west (the green area in this image). Within this area the reservoir Lake Burragong can be seen, which supplies 80% of the city's water. The runways of Australia's busiest airport are also visible, projecting from the north shore of Botany Bay. [Map page 139]

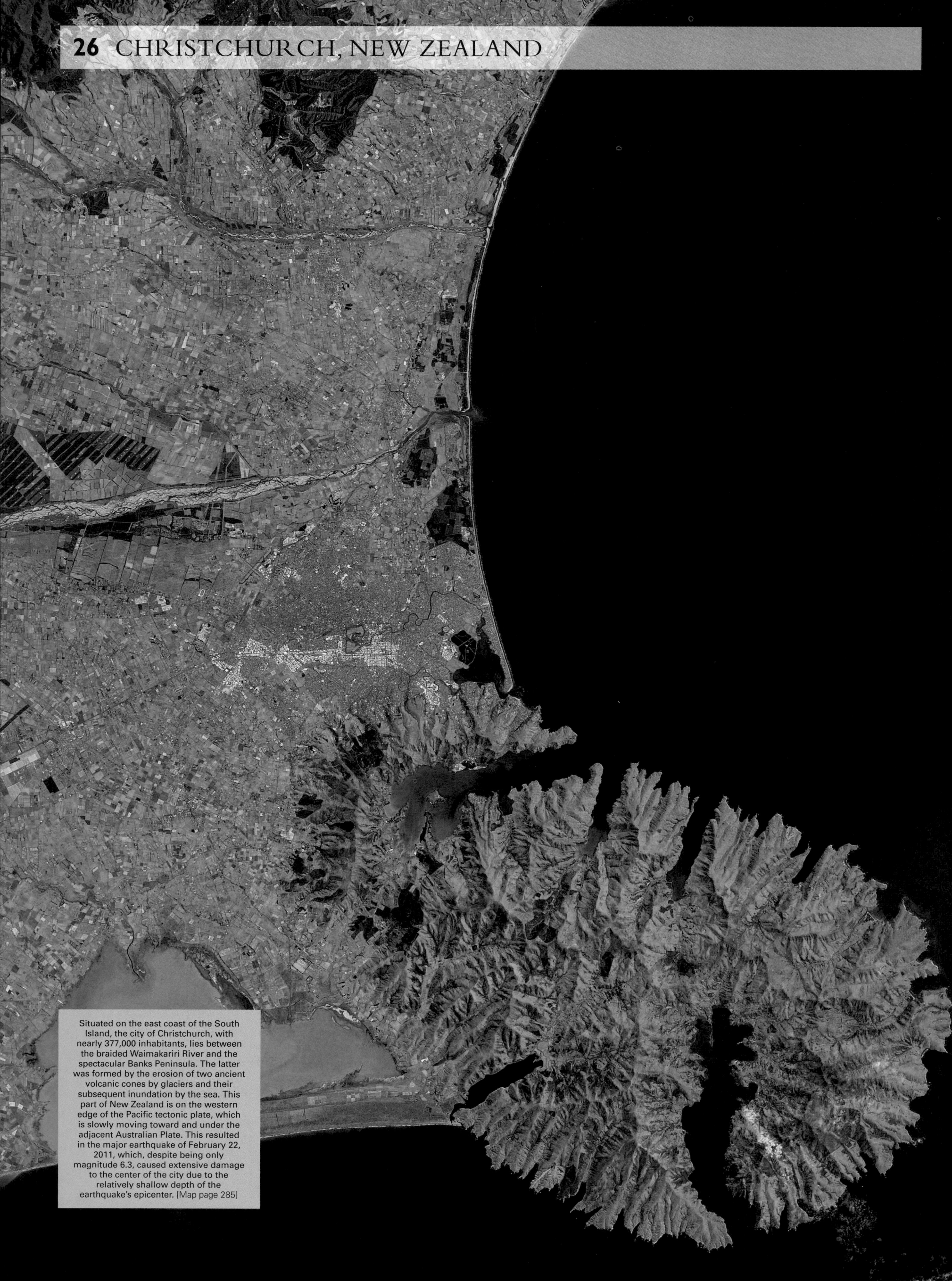

Situated on the east coast of the South Island, the city of Christchurch, with nearly 377,000 inhabitants, lies between the braided Waimakariri River and the spectacular Banks Peninsula. The latter was formed by the erosion of two ancient volcanic cones by glaciers and their subsequent inundation by the sea. This part of New Zealand is on the western edge of the Pacific tectonic plate, which is slowly moving toward and under the adjacent Australian Plate. This resulted in the major earthquake of February 22, 2011, which, despite being only magnitude 6.3, caused extensive damage to the center of the city due to the relatively shallow depth of the earthquake's epicenter. [Map page 285]

Québec was founded as a trading post in 1608, at the narrowest point of the St Lawrence River, just to the southwest of the Île d'Orléans, and is one of the oldest cities in North America. Strategically, the city controlled the movement of shipping between the Atlantic Ocean and the Great Lakes, and consequently developed fortifications on the cliffs of Cape Diamond, 320 ft (97 m) above the river. The port is 850 miles (1,370 km) from the Atlantic, 1,495 miles (2,404 km) from Duluth, and 1,400 miles (2,252 km) from Chicago. It has a population of over 491,000 people and is the capital city of the province of the same name. [Map page 299]

This image covers the largest urban area in the USA, which has a population of nearly 19 million people. Flowing from the north, the Hudson River divides the two cities of New York (to the east) and New Jersey (to the west). Toward its mouth on the east bank lies Manhattan Island, with Central Park. Below this is Long Island, with its distinctive offshore spits. At its western end lie the urban areas of Brooklyn and Queens, but further southeast are resorts such as Long Beach and the Fire Islands National Seashore. [Map page 132]

The city is situated in a basin within the
Mojave Desert in Nevada, and is one of
the fastest growing areas in the country.
Known worldwide for its night life and
gambling, Las Vegas has also become
a popular destination for retired people
and families. The population of the
metropolitan area is now almost 2 million
people. To the east of the grid-pattern
layout of the town lies the Hoover Dam,
which was built across the Colorado
River in 1935. The lake behind the dam
is known as Lake Mead, the largest
man-made reservoir in the United States.
It is used for flood control, irrigation, and
hydroelectric power generation in the
region, but recent dry years have resulted
in reduced water levels. [Map page 124]

With a population of over 19 million people, Mexico City is one of North America's most important commercial centers. The city lies in a valley some 7,350 ft (2,240 m) above sea level, and was originally founded by the Aztecs in 1325 on an island in Lake Texcoco, which has dried up over time. The relentless growth of the urban area has resulted in both air pollution and water supply problems. To the southeast of the city can be seen three towering snow-covered volcanic peaks – the southernmost of these is Popocatépetl, an active volcano 17,887 ft (5,452 m) high, which has two glaciers near its summit. [Map page 128]

Peru's largest city and its capital, Lima was founded in the 16th century by the Spanish. Situated at the mouth of the Rimac river, it became one of the pre-eminent cities of the Spanish Empire. On the coast to the north of the distinct Isla San Lorenzo is its port of Callao, a major South American fishing port, whilst behind it lie the foothills of the Andes. With its thriving financial and commercial districts, it is now the major city of the Andean region in South America, and some believe that its current population of nearly 9 million could reach 10 million by 2015, with people being attracted there from all over the region. [Map page 124]

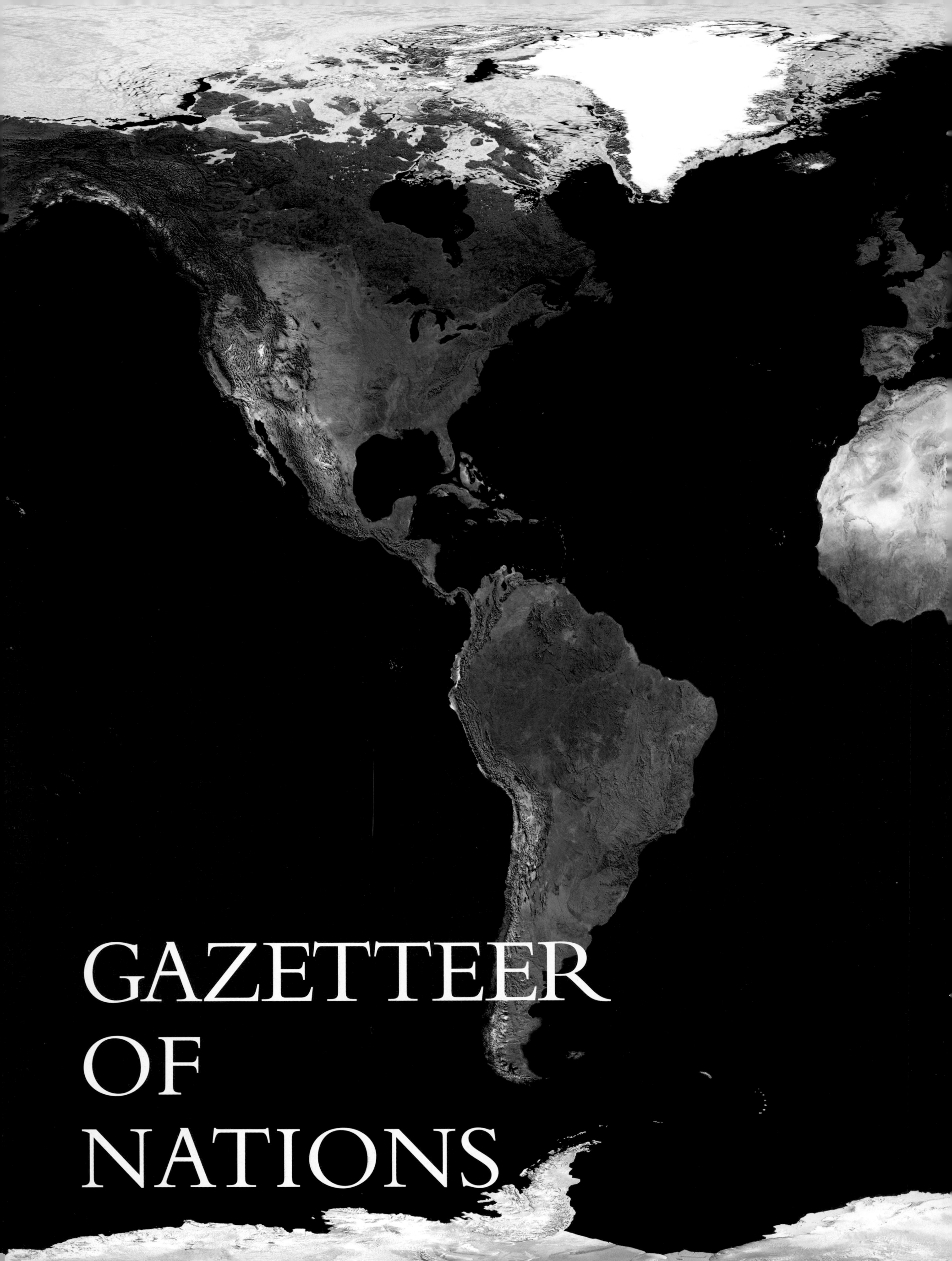

GAZETTEER
OF
NATIONS

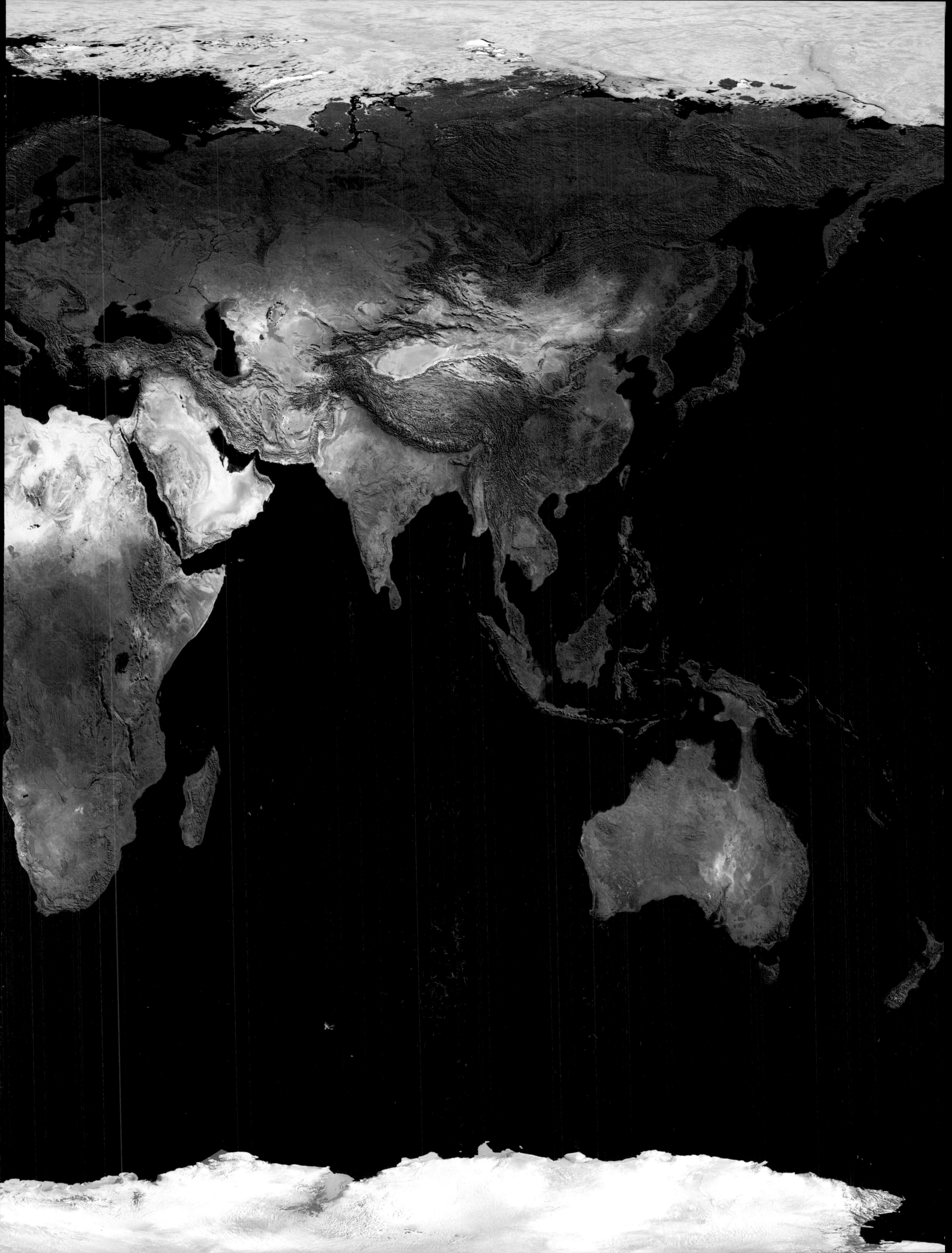

AFGHANISTAN

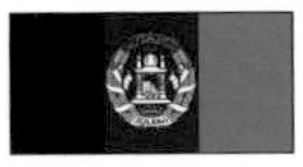

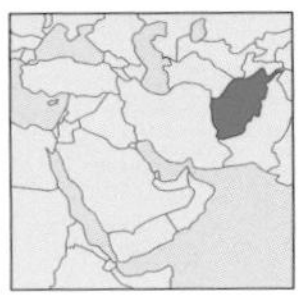

GEOGRAPHY The Republic of Afghanistan is a landlocked, mountainous country in southern Asia. The central highlands reach a height of more than 22,966 ft [7,000 m] in the east and make up nearly three-quarters of Afghanistan. The main range is the Hindu Kush, which is cut by deep, fertile valleys.

In winter, northerly winds bring cold, snowy weather to the mountains, but summers are hot and dry.

POLITICS & ECONOMY The modern history of Afghanistan began in 1747, when the various tribes in the area united for the first time. In the 19th century, Russia and Britain struggled for control of the country. Following Britain's withdrawal in 1919, Afghanistan became fully independent. Soviet troops invaded in 1979 to support a socialist regime in Kabul, but they withdrew in 1989. By 2001, a group called the Taliban ("Islamic students") controlled 90% of the country. In 2001, following the refusal of the Taliban to hand over the terrorist leader Osama bin Laden, an international force invaded Afghanistan. In 2002, a coalition government was set up under Hamid Karzai, who was elected president in 2004 and 2009. Parliamentary elections in 2010 were marred by Taliban violence and charges of fraud.

Afghanistan is a poor country and nearly 70% of its people are farmers or nomadic herders. Natural gas is produced, together with some coal, copper, gold, precious stones, and salt.

AREA 251,772 sq mi [652,090 sq km]
POPULATION 29,121,000 **CAPITAL** Kabul
GOVERNMENT Islamic Republic **ETHNIC GROUPS** Pashtun (Pathan) 44%, Tajik 25%, Hazara 10%, Uzbek 8%, others 13%
LANGUAGES Pashtu, Dari/Persian (both official), Uzbek
RELIGIONS Islam (Sunni Muslim 84%, Shi'ite Muslim 15%), others 1%
CURRENCY Afghani = 100 puls

ALBANIA

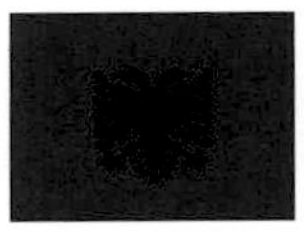

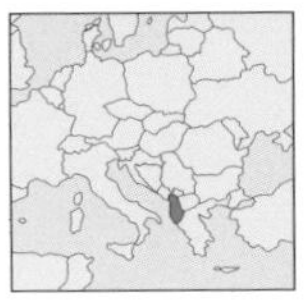

GEOGRAPHY The Republic of Albania lies in the Balkan peninsula, facing the Adriatic Sea. About 70% of the land is mountainous, but most Albanians live in the west on the coastal lowlands.

The coastal areas of Albania experience a typical Mediterranean climate, with fairly dry, sunny summers and cool, moist winters. The mountains have a severe climate, with heavy winter snowfalls.

POLITICS & ECONOMY Albania is one of Europe's poorest nations. A former Communist country, Albania adopted a multi-party system in the early 1990s. The change proved difficult. But after elections in 1997, a socialist government committed to a market system took office. The transition to democracy has been difficult. Elections were held in 2005, and again in 2009 amid accusations of vote-rigging. Violent anti-government demonstrations occurred in January 2011.

In 2006, agriculture employed about 50% of the people. Since 1991, private ownership of land has been encouraged, replacing the former state farm and collective system. Albania has some minerals. Chromite, copper, and nickel are exported.

AREA 11,100 sq mi [28,748 sq km] **POPULATION** 2,987,000
CAPITAL Tirana **GOVERNMENT** Multiparty republic
ETHNIC GROUPS Albanian 95%, Greek 3%, Macedonian, Vlachs, Gypsy **LANGUAGES** Albanian (official) **RELIGIONS** Many people say they are non-believers; of the believers, 70% follow Islam and 30% follow Christianity (Orthodox 20%, Roman Catholic 10%)
CURRENCY Lek = 100 qindars

ALGERIA

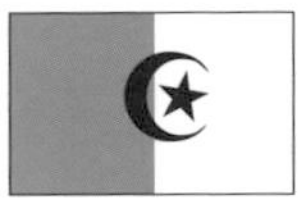

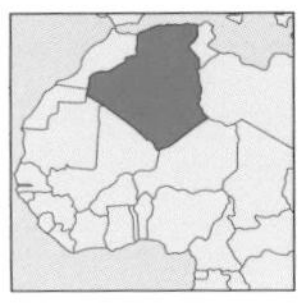

GEOGRAPHY The People's Democratic Republic of Algeria is Africa's second largest country after Sudan. Most Algerians live in the north, on the fertile coastal plains and hill country bordering the Mediterranean Sea. Four-fifths of Algeria is in the Sahara. The coast has a Mediterranean climate, but the arid Sahara is hot by day and cool at night.

POLITICS & ECONOMY France ruled Algeria from 1830 until 1962, when the socialist FLN (National Liberation Front) formed a one-party government. Following the recognition of opposition parties in 1989, a Muslim group, the FIS (Islamic Salvation Front), won an election in 1991. The FLN canceled the elections and civil conflict broke out. About 100,000 people were killed in the 1990s. Abdelaziz Bouteflika was elected president in 1999 and 2004. Constitutional changes enabled Bouteflika to stand for a third term and he was re-elected in 2009. The scale of violence was reduced under his leadership. However, in early 2011, protests broke out over food prices and unemployment.

Algeria is a developing country, whose chief resources are oil and natural gas, which were discovered in the Sahara in 1956. The natural gas reserves are among the world's largest, and gas and oil account for more than 90% of the exports. Cement, iron and steel, textiles, and vehicles are manufactured. Barley, citrus fruits, dates, potatoes, and wheat are major crops.

AREA 919,590 sq mi [2,381,741 sq km]
POPULATION 34,586,000 **CAPITAL** Algiers
GOVERNMENT Socialist republic **ETHNIC GROUPS** Arab-Berber 99%
LANGUAGES Arabic and Berber (official), French **RELIGIONS** Sunni Muslim 99% **CURRENCY** Algerian dinar = 100 centimes

AMERICAN SAMOA

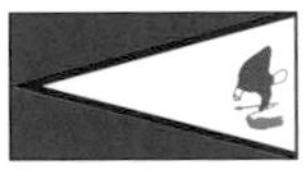

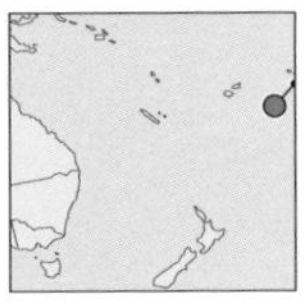

An "unincorporated territory" of the United States, American Samoa lies in the south-central Pacific Ocean.

AREA 77 sq mi [199 sq km]
POPULATION 66,000 **CAPITAL** Pago Pago

ANDORRA

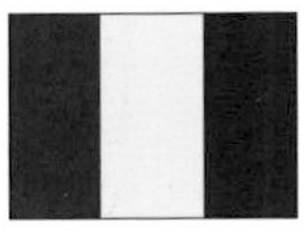

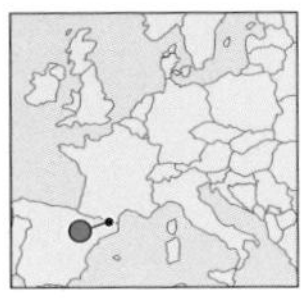

A mini-state situated in the Pyrenees Mountains, Andorra is a coprincipality whose main activity is tourism. Most Andorrans live in the six valleys (the Valls) that drain into the River Valira.

AREA 181 sq mi [468 sq km]
POPULATION 85,000 **CAPITAL** Andorra La Vella

ANGOLA

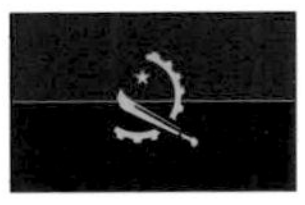

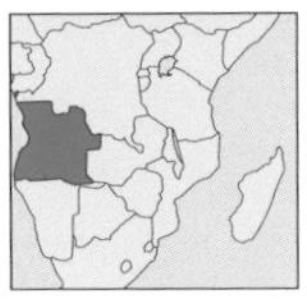

GEOGRAPHY The Republic of Angola is a large country in southwestern Africa. Much of the country is part of the plateau that forms most of southern Africa, with a narrow coastal plain in the west.

Angola has a tropical climate, with temperatures of over 68°F [20°C] throughout the year, though the highest areas are cooler. The coast is dry, but the rainfall increases to the north and east.

POLITICS & ECONOMY Bantu-speaking people settled in Angola in the 13th century and later founded large kingdoms, such as the Kongo and Mbundu. Portugal controlled the coastal slave trade from the 17th century and extended their control inland in the 19th century. Angola became independent from Portugal in 1975, after which rival nationalist groups struggled for power. Despite a ceasefire in the mid-1990s, conflict finally ended in 2002, when the rebel leader, Jonas Savimbi, was killed. Successful parliamentary elections were held in 2008.

Angola is a developing country, where 70% of the people are poor farmers. The main food crops are cassava and maize. Coffee is exported. Angola has important oil reserves and oil is exported. Angola also produces diamonds and has reserves of copper, manganese, and phosphates.

AREA 481,351 sq mi [1,246,700 sq km]
POPULATION 13,068,000 **CAPITAL** Luanda
GOVERNMENT Multiparty republic
ETHNIC GROUPS Ovimbundu 37%, Kimbundu 25%, Bakongo 13%, others 25% **LANGUAGES** Portuguese (official), many others
RELIGIONS Traditional beliefs 47%, Roman Catholic 38%, Protestant 15%
CURRENCY Kwanza = 100 lwei

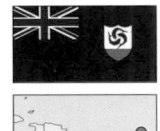

ANGUILLA

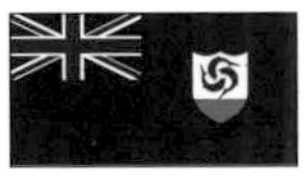

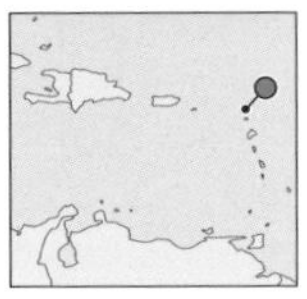

Formerly part of St Kitts and Nevis, Anguilla, the most northerly of the Leeward Islands, became a British dependency (now a British overseas territory) in 1980. The main source of revenue is now tourism, although lobster still accounts for half the island's exports.

AREA 37 sq mi [96 sq km]
POPULATION 15,000 **CAPITAL** The Valley

ANTIGUA & BARBUDA

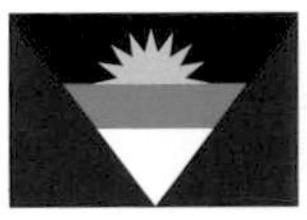

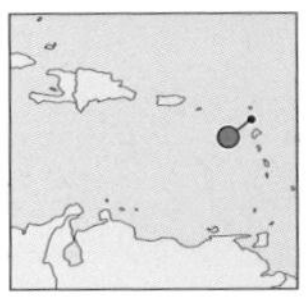

A former British dependency in the Caribbean, Antigua and Barbuda became independent in 1981. Tourism is the main industry, though sugar is an important product.

AREA 171 sq mi [442 sq km]
POPULATION 87,000 **CAPITAL** St John's

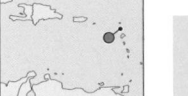

ARGENTINA

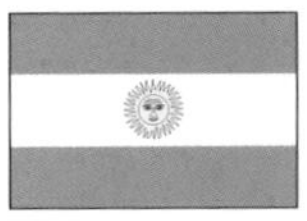

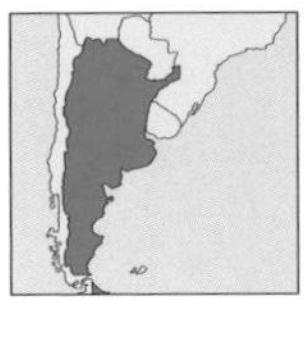

GEOGRAPHY The Argentine Republic is South America's second largest and the world's eighth largest country. The high Andes range in the west contains Mount Aconcagua, the highest peak in the Americas. In southern Argentina, the Andes Mountains overlook Patagonia, a plateau region. In east-central Argentina lies a fertile plain called the pampas.

The climate varies from subtropical in the north to temperate in the south. Rainfall is abundant in the north-east but lower to the west and south. Patagonia is largely desert.

POLITICS & ECONOMY The earliest people were American Indians, but 86% of the people are now of European ancestry. Spain took control in the 16th century and ruled until 1816. Argentina later suffered from instability and periods of military rule. In 1982, Argentina's military regime invaded the Falkland (Malvinas) Islands, but Britain regained the islands later that year. Argentina restored civilian rule in 1983. In 2007, Christina Fernández de Kirchner was elected president, succeeding her husband, Néstor Carlos Kirchner, who had served as president from 2003. She was the first woman to be Argentina's directly elected president. The dispute over the Falklands resurfaced in 2010, when drilling for oil began around the islands.

The World Bank classifies Argentina as an "upper-middle-income" developing country. About 90% of the people live in urban areas. Manufactures include food products, cars, electrical equipment, and textiles. Oil is the main resource and the chief farm products are beef, maize, and wheat. Exports include oil, meat, wheat, maize, vegetable oils, hides and skins, and wool. In 1991, Argentina, Brazil, Paraguay, and Uruguay set up an alliance, Mercosur, aimed at creating a common market.

AREA 1,073,512 sq mi [2,780,400 sq km]
POPULATION 41,343,000 **CAPITAL** Buenos Aires
GOVERNMENT Federal republic **ETHNIC GROUPS** European 97%, Mestizo, Amerindian **LANGUAGES** Spanish (official)
RELIGIONS Roman Catholic 92%, Protestant 2%, Jewish 2%, others **CURRENCY** Argentine peso = 10,000 australs

ARMENIA

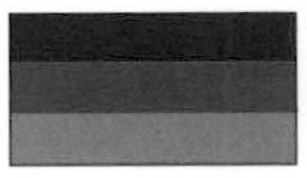

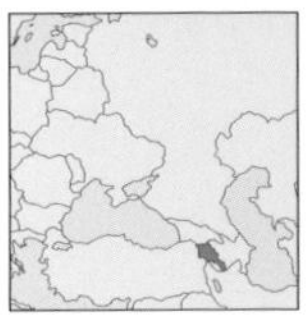

GEOGRAPHY The Republic of Armenia is a landlocked country in southwestern Asia. Most of Armenia consists of a rugged plateau, crisscrossed by long faults (cracks). Movements along the faults cause earthquakes. The highest point is Mount Aragats, at 13,419 ft [4,090 m] above sea level.

The height of the land, which averages 4,920 ft [1,500 m] above sea level gives rise to severe winters and cool summers. The highest peaks are snow-capped, but the total yearly rainfall is generally low.

POLITICS & ECONOMY In 1920, Armenia became a Communist republic and, in 1922, it became, with Azerbaijan and Georgia, part of the Transcaucasian Republic within the Soviet Union. But the three territories became separate Soviet Socialist Republics in 1936. After the breakup of the Soviet Union in 1991, Armenia became an independent republic. Fighting broke out over Nagorno-Karabakh, an area enclosed by Azerbaijan where most people are Armenians. In 1992, Armenia occupied the land between it and Nagorno-Karabakh. A ceasefire in 1994 left Armenia in control of about 20% of Azerbaijan's land area. In 2010, Armenia and Azerbaijan agreed to exchange prisoners taken during the Nagorno-Karabakh conflict.

Armenia's economy has suffered because of its former dependency on a centrally planned Soviet system.

AREA 11,506 sq mi [29,800 sq km]
POPULATION 2,967,000 **CAPITAL** Yerevan
GOVERNMENT Multiparty republic **ETHNIC GROUPS** Armenian 93%, Russian 2%, Azeri 1%, others (mostly Kurds) 4%
LANGUAGES Armenian (official) **RELIGIONS** Armenian Apostolic 94%
CURRENCY Dram = 100 couma

NOTE: This alphabetical list includes the principal countries and territories of the world. The area figures give the total area of land, inland water, and ice. The population figures are 2010 estimates where available.

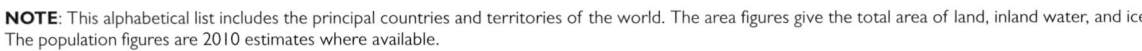

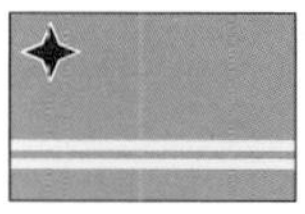
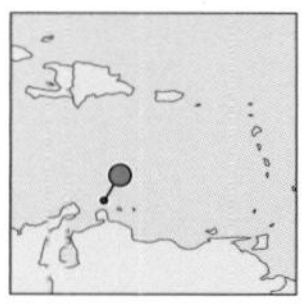

ARUBA

Formerly part of the Netherlands Antilles, Aruba (the most western of the Lesser Antilles) became a separate self-governing Dutch territory in 1986.

AREA 75 sq mi [193 sq km]
POPULATION 105,000 **CAPITAL** Oranjestad

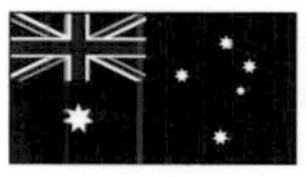
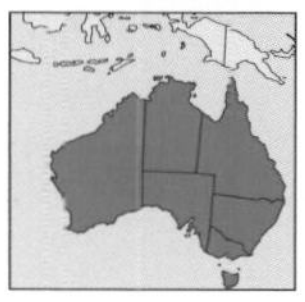

AUSTRALIA

GEOGRAPHY The Commonwealth of Australia, the world's sixth largest country, is also a continent. Australia is the flattest of the continents and the main highland area is in the east. Here the Great Dividing Range separates the eastern coastal plains from the Central Plains. This range extends from the Cape York Peninsula to Victoria in the far south. The longest rivers, the Murray and Darling, drain the southeastern part of the Central Plains. The Western Plateau makes up two-thirds of Australia. A few mountain ranges break the monotony of the generally flat landscape. Only 10% of Australia, notably the tropical north, the northeast coast and the southeast, has an average annual rainfall of more than 39 inches [1,000 mm]. But extreme weather events, including a prolonged drought in the Murray–Darling basin in the early 21st century and severe flooding in Queensland in 2010–11, cause periodic problems.

POLITICS & ECONOMY The Aboriginal people of Australia entered the continent from Southeast Asia more than 50,000 years ago. The first European explorers were Dutch in the 17th century, but they did not settle. In 1770, the British Captain Cook explored the east coast and, in 1788, the first British settlement was established for convicts on the site of what is now Sydney. Australia has strong ties with the British Isles. But in the last 50 years, people from other parts of Europe and, most recently, from Asia have settled in Australia. Ties with Britain were also weakened by Britain's membership of the European Union. Many Australians believe that they should become more involved with the nations of eastern Asia and the Americas rather than with Europe. In 1999, Australians voted to retain the country's status as a monarchy. In 2003, Australian troops joined in the invasion of Iraq. The Labor Party won the 2007 elections. The prime minister, Kevin Rudd, was succeeded in 2010 by Julia Gillard.

Australia is a prosperous country. Crops can be grown on only 6% of the land, but dry pasture covers another 58%. Yet the country remains a major producer and exporter of farm products, particularly cattle, wheat, and wool. Grapes grown for wine-making are also important. The country is a major producer of minerals, including bauxite, coal, copper, diamonds, gold, iron ore, manganese, nickel, silver, tin, tungsten, and zinc. Australia also produces oil and natural gas. Metals, minerals, and farm products account for the bulk of exports. Australia's imports are mostly manufactured goods, especially machinery, though industry is now important, especially the manufacture of consumer goods.

AREA 2,988,885 sq mi [7,741,220 sq km] **POPULATION** 21,516,000
CAPITAL Canberra **GOVERNMENT** Federal constitutional monarchy
ETHNIC GROUPS Caucasian 92%, Asian 7%, Aboriginal 1%
LANGUAGES English (official) **RELIGIONS** Roman Catholic 26%, Anglican 26%, other Christian 24%, non-Christian 24%
CURRENCY Australian dollar = 100 cents

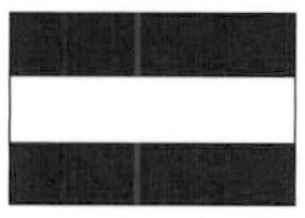
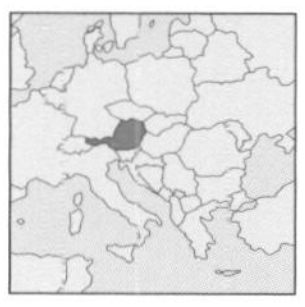

AUSTRIA

GEOGRAPHY Austria is a landlocked country in Europe. Northern Austria contains the valley of the River Danube, which flows from Germany to the Black Sea, and the Vienna basin. Southern Austria contains ranges of the Alps, their highest point at Grossglockner, 12,457 ft [3,797 m] above sea level.

The climate is temperate in the west and more continental in the east. Winters are cold and snowy. Summers are warm and dry in the east.

POLITICS & ECONOMY Formerly part of the monarchy of Austria–Hungary, which collapsed in 1918, Austria was annexed by Germany in 1938. After World War II, the Allies partitioned and occupied the country. In 1955, Austria became a neutral federal republic. It joined the European Union in 1995. In 2000, a coalition government was formed by the right-wing People's Party and the extreme right-wing Freedom Party, which lost much of its support in 2002. In 2008, the Social Democratic/People's Party coalition (formed in 2007) collapsed, but the same parties formed another government after elections, in which far right parties won nearly 29% of the vote.

Austria has a highly developed economy, with plenty of hydroelectric power and some oil, gas, and coal reserves. The country's leading economic activity is manufacturing metals and metal products. Crops are grown on 18% of the land, and another 24% is pasture. Dairy and livestock farming are the leading activities. Major crops include barley, potatoes, rye, sugar beet, and wheat. Tourism is a major activity in this scenic country.

AREA 32,378 sq mi [83,859 sq km] **POPULATION** 8,214,000
CAPITAL Vienna **GOVERNMENT** Federal republic
ETHNIC GROUPS Austrian 90%, Croatian, Slovene, others
LANGUAGES German (official) **RELIGIONS** Roman Catholic 78%, Protestant 5%, Islam and others 17% **CURRENCY** Euro = 100 cents

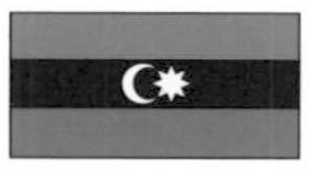
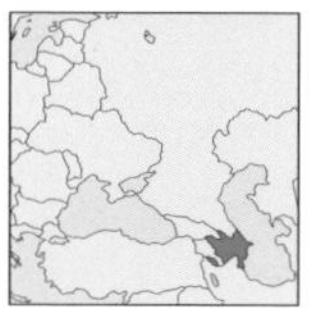

AZERBAIJAN

GEOGRAPHY The Azerbaijani Republic is a country in the southwest of Asia, facing the Caspian Sea to the east. It includes an area called the Naxçivan Autonomous Republic, which is completely cut off from the rest of Azerbaijan by Armenian territory. The Caucasus Mountains border Russia in the north.

Azerbaijan has hot summers and cool winters. The plains are fairly dry, but the mountains are rainy.

POLITICS & ECONOMY After the Russian Revolution of 1917, attempts were made to form a Transcaucasian Federation made up of Armenia, Azerbaijan, and Georgia. When this failed, Azerbaijanis set up an independent state. But Russian forces occupied the area in 1920. In 1922, the Communists set up a Transcaucasian Republic consisting of Armenia, Azerbaijan, and Georgia under Russian control. In 1936, the three areas became separate Soviet Socialist Republics within the Soviet Union. In 1991, following the breakup of the Soviet Union, Azerbaijan became an independent nation. After independence, Azerbaijan clashed with Armenia over the enclave of Nagorno-Karabakh, a region in Azerbaijan where the majority of the people are Armenian. A ceasefire in 1994 left Armenia in control of 20% of Azerbaijan's area, including Nagorno-Karabakh.

Azerbaijan has huge oil reserves. Oil extraction and manufacturing, including oil refining and the production of chemicals, machinery, and textiles are important.

AREA 33,436 sq mi [86,600 sq km] **POPULATION** 8,304,000
CAPITAL Baku **GOVERNMENT** Federal multiparty republic
ETHNIC GROUPS Azeri 90%, Dagestani 3%, Russian, Armenian, others **LANGUAGES** Azerbaijan (official), Russian, Armenian
RELIGIONS Islam 93%, Russian Orthodox 2%, Armenian Orthodox 2%
CURRENCY Azerbaijani manat = 100 gopik

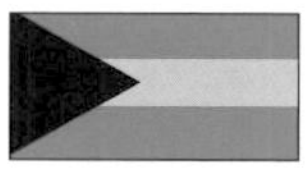
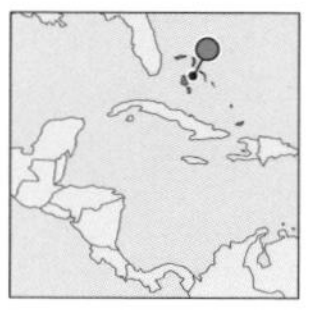

BAHAMAS

A coral-limestone archipelago off the coast of Florida, the Bahamas became independent from Britain in 1973, and has since developed strong ties with the United States. Tourism and banking are major activities.

AREA 5,358 sq mi [13,878 sq km]
POPULATION 310,000 **CAPITAL** Nassau

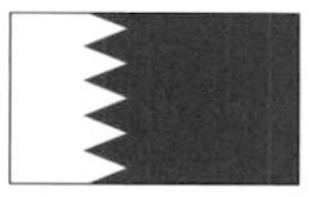
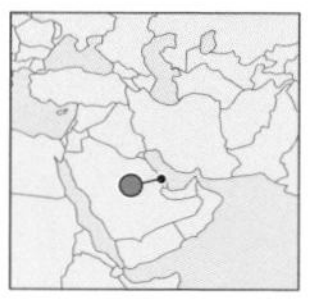

BAHRAIN

The Kingdom of Bahrain, an island nation in the Persian Gulf, became independent from the UK in 1971. Oil accounts for 80% of its exports.

In early 2011, demonstrators called for reform. Violence occurred and the king declared a state of emergency. Troops from nearby Gulf states arrived to help control the situation.

AREA 268 sq mi [694 sq km] **POPULATION** 738,000 **CAPITAL** Manama

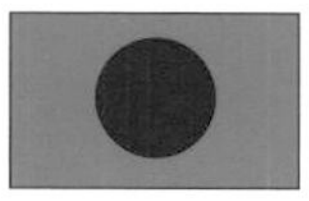
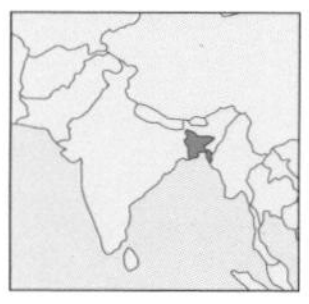

BANGLADESH

GEOGRAPHY The People's Republic of Bangladesh is one of the world's most densely populated countries. Apart from hilly regions in the far northeast and southeast, most of the land is flat and covered by fertile alluvium spread over the land by the Ganges, Brahmaputra and Meghna rivers. These rivers overflow when they are swollen by the annual monsoon rains. Floods also occur along the coast, 357 mi [575 km] long, when cyclones (hurricanes) drive seawater inland. Bangladesh has a tropical monsoon climate. Dry northerly winds blow in winter, but moist southerly winds bring heavy rain in summer.

POLITICS & ECONOMY In 1947, British India was partitioned between the mainly Hindu India and the Muslim Pakistan. Pakistan consisted of two parts, West and East Pakistan, which were separated by about 1,000 mi [1,600 km] of Indian territory. Differences developed between West and East Pakistan. In 1971, the East Pakistanis rebeled. After a nine-month civil war, they declared East Pakistan to be a new nation named Bangladesh. A famine in 1974 and a coup in 1975 were followed by political upheavals. The army seized power in 2007, but elections in 2008 returned Sheikh Hasina's Awami League to power.

Bangladesh is one of the world's poorest countries. Its economy depends mainly on agriculture, which employs nearly half the population. Bangladesh is the world's fourth largest producer of rice.

AREA 55,598 sq mi [143,998 sq km]
POPULATION 156,118,000 **CAPITAL** Dhaka
GOVERNMENT Multiparty republic **ETHNIC GROUPS** Bengali 98%, tribal groups **LANGUAGES** Bengali (official), English
RELIGIONS Islam 83%, Hinduism 16% **CURRENCY** Taka = 100 paisas

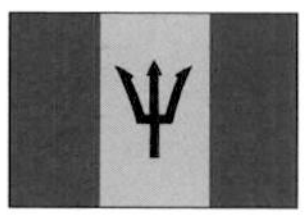
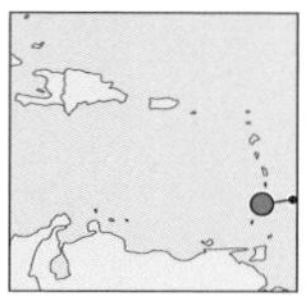

BARBADOS

The most easterly Caribbean country, Barbados became independent from the UK in 1960. A densely populated island, Barbados is prosperous by comparison with most Caribbean countries.

AREA 166 sq mi [430 sq km]
POPULATION 286,000 **CAPITAL** Bridgetown

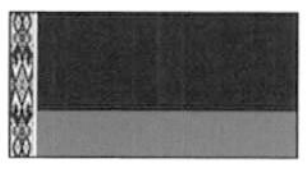
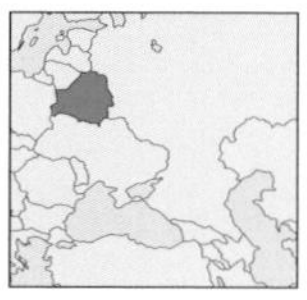

BELARUS

GEOGRAPHY The Republic of Belarus is a landlocked country in Eastern Europe. The land is low-lying and mostly flat. In the south, much of the land is marshy and this area contains Europe's largest marsh and peat bog, the Pripet Marshes. The climate is affected by both the moderating influence of the Baltic Sea and continental conditions to the east. The winters are cold and the summers warm.

POLITICS & ECONOMY In 1918, Belarus (White Russia) became an independent republic, but Russia invaded the country and, in 1919, a Communist state was set up. In 1922, Belarus became a founder republic of the Soviet Union. In 1991, Belarus again became an independent republic, and although Belarus continued to support reunification with Russia, any surrender of sovereignty was not expected. President Alexander Lukashenko, who was elected in flawed elections in 1994, 2001, 2006, and 2010, when he won nearly 80% of the vote amid opposition protests, has been criticized for his autocratic rule, his poor record on human rights, and his disregard for freedom of speech.

According to the World Bank, Belarus has an "upper-middle-income" economy. Most economic activities remain under government control and, in the 1990s, the economy declined. Mining and manufacturing are the most valuable activities.

AREA 80,154 sq mi [207,600 sq km]
POPULATION 9,613,000 **CAPITAL** Minsk
GOVERNMENT Multiparty republic **ETHNIC GROUPS** Belarusian 81%, Russian 11%, Polish, Ukrainian, others **LANGUAGES** Belarusian, Russian (both official) **RELIGIONS** Eastern Orthodox 80%, others 20% **CURRENCY** Belarusian rouble = 100 kopecks

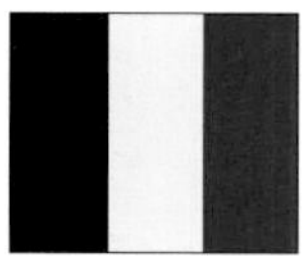
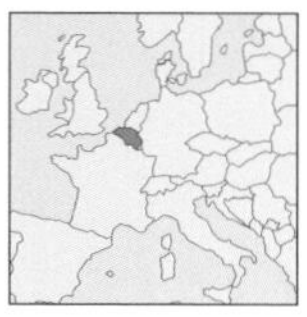

BELGIUM

GEOGRAPHY The Kingdom of Belgium is a densely populated country in western Europe. Behind the coastline on the North Sea, which is 39 mi [63 km] long, lie its coastal plains. Central Belgium consists of low plateaux and the only highland region is the Ardennes in the southeast.

Belgium has a cool, temperate climate. Moist winds from the Atlantic Ocean bring fairly heavy rain, especially in the Ardennes. In January and February much snow falls on the Ardennes.

POLITICS & ECONOMY In 1815, Belgium and the Netherlands united as the "low countries," but Belgium became independent in 1830. Belgium's economy was weakened by the two World

Wars, but, from 1945, the country recovered quickly, first through collaboration with the Netherlands and Luxembourg, which formed a customs union called Benelux, and later through its membership of the European Union.

A central political problem in Belgium has been the tension between the Dutch-speaking Flemings and the French-speaking Walloons. In the 1970s, the government divided the country into three economic regions: Dutch-speaking Flanders, French-speaking Wallonia, and bilingual Brussels. In 1993, Belgium adopted a federal constitution, giving each region its own parliament. In 2010, a coalition government set up in 2009 collapsed because of deep differences between the Flemish- and French-speaking parties. By early 2011, Belgium had achieved a world record period of a country without a national government.

Belgium is a major trading nation, though most materials used in manufacturing are imported. Major products include chemicals, processed food, and steel. The textile industry has existed since medieval times in Flanders. Agriculture employs less than 2% of the people, but farmers produce most of the food the country needs. Barley and wheat are major crops, followed by flax, hops, potatoes, and sugar beet. But the most valuable agricultural activities are dairy farming and livestock rearing.

AREA 11,787 sq mi [30,528 sq km]
POPULATION 10,423,000
CAPITAL Brussels
GOVERNMENT Federal constitutional monarchy
ETHNIC GROUPS Belgian 89% (Fleming 58%, Walloon 31%), others 11% **LANGUAGES** Dutch, French, German (all official)
RELIGIONS Roman Catholic 75%, others 25%
CURRENCY Euro = 100 cents

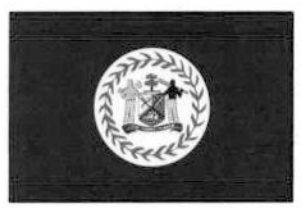

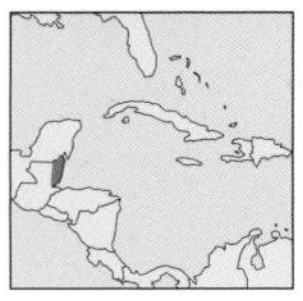

BELIZE

GEOGRAPHY Behind the southern coastal plain, the land rises to the Maya Mountains, which reach 3,674 ft [1,120 m] at Victoria Peak. The north is mostly low-lying and swampy. Temperatures are high all year round, while the average annual rainfall ranges from 51 inches [1,300 mm] in the north to over 150 inches [3,800 mm] in the south. Hurricanes caused much damage in the 1990s and 2000s, but tourist numbers have continued to increase.

POLITICS & ECONOMY From 1862, Belize (then called British Honduras) was a British colony. Full independence was achieved in 1981, but Guatemala, which had claimed the area since the early 19th century, opposed Belize's independence and British troops remained to prevent a possible invasion. In 1983, Guatemala reduced its claim to the southern fifth of Belize. Improved relations in the early 1990s led Guatemala to recognize Belize's independence and, in 1992, Britain agreed to withdraw its troops from the country.

The World Bank classifies Belize as a "lower-middle-income" developing country. Its economy is based on agriculture and sugarcane is the chief commercial crop and export. Other crops include bananas, beans, citrus fruits, maize, and rice. Forestry, fishing, and tourism are other important activities.

AREA 8,867 sq mi [22,966 sq km]
POPULATION 315,000 **CAPITAL** Belmopan
GOVERNMENT Constitutional monarchy **ETHNIC GROUPS** Mestizo 49%, Creole 25%, Mayan Indian 11%, Garifuna 6%, others 9%
LANGUAGES English (official), Spanish, Creole
RELIGIONS Roman Catholic 50%, Protestant 27%, others
CURRENCY Belizean dollar = 100 cents

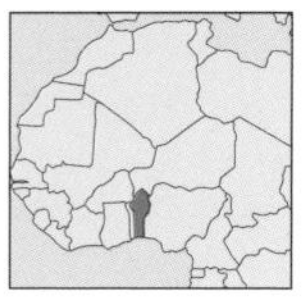

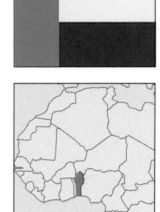

BENIN

GEOGRAPHY The Republic of Benin is one of Africa's smallest countries. It extends north–south for about 390 mi [620 km]. Lagoons line the short coastline, and the country has no natural harbors.

Benin has a hot, wet climate. The average annual temperature on the coast is about 77°F [25°C], and the average rainfall is about 52 inches [1,330 mm]. The inland plains are wetter than the coast.

POLITICS & ECONOMY After slavery was ended in the 19th century, the French began to gain influence in the area. Benin became self-governing in 1958 and fully independent in 1960. After much instability and many changes of government, a military group took over in 1972. The country, renamed Benin in 1975, became a one-party socialist state. Socialism was abandoned in 1989. Former coup leader Mathieu Kérékou served as president until 2006, when a former banker, Yayi Boni, was elected president. He was re-elected in 2011.

Benin is a poor developing country. About half of the people live by farming, mainly at subsistence level. Exports include cotton, petroleum, and palm products. Cocoa, coffee, groundnuts (peanuts), tobacco, and shea nuts are also grown for export.

AREA 43,483 sq mi [112,622 sq km]
POPULATION 9,056,000 **CAPITAL** Porto-Novo
GOVERNMENT Multiparty republic **ETHNIC GROUPS** Fon, Adja, Bariba, Yoruba, Fulani **LANGUAGES** French (official), Fon, Adja, Yoruba
RELIGIONS Traditional beliefs 50%, Christianity 30%, Islam 20%
CURRENCY CFA franc = 100 centimes

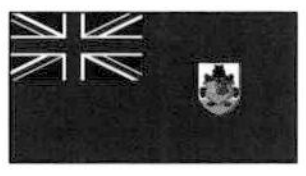

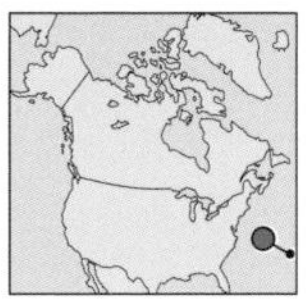

BERMUDA

A group of about 150 small islands situated 570 mi [920 km] east of the USA. Bermuda remains Britain's oldest overseas territory, but it has a long tradition of self-government.

AREA 21 sq mi [53 sq km]
POPULATION 68,000 **CAPITAL** Hamilton

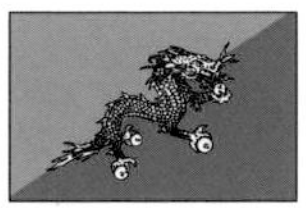

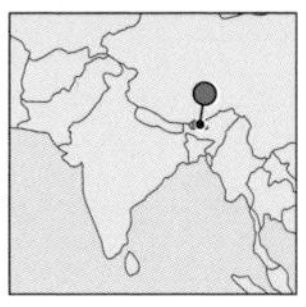

BHUTAN

GEOGRAPHY A mountainous, isolated Himalayan country located between India and Tibet. The climate is similar to that of Nepal, being dependent on altitude and affected by monsoonal winds.

POLITICS & ECONOMY The monarch of Bhutan is head of both state and government, and this predominantly Buddhist country remains, even in the Asian context, both conservative and poor. In 2008, Bhutan held its first ever democratic elections, ending over a century of absolute royal rule and turning Bhutan into a constitutional monarchy.

AREA 18,147 sq mi [47,000 sq km] **POPULATION** 700,000
CAPITAL Thimphu **GOVERNMENT** Constitutional monarchy
ETHNIC GROUPS Bhutanese 50%, Nepalese 35%
LANGUAGES Dzongkha (official) **RELIGIONS** Buddhism 75%, Hinduism 25% **CURRENCY** Ngultrum = 100 chetrum

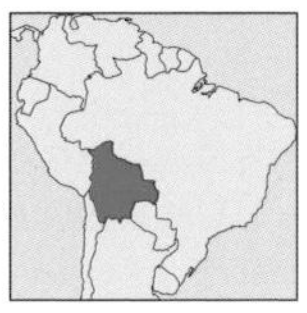

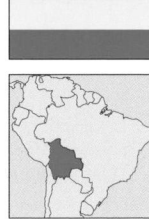

BOLIVIA

GEOGRAPHY The Republic of Bolivia is a landlocked country which straddles the Andes Mountains in central South America. The Andes rise to a height of 21,391 ft [6,520 m] at Nevado Sajama in the west.

About 40% of Bolivians live on a high plateau called the Altiplano in the Andean region, while the sparsely populated east is essentially a vast lowland plain.

The Bolivian climate is greatly affected by altitude, with the Andean peaks permanently snow-covered, and the eastern plains remaining hot and humid.

POLITICS & ECONOMY American Indians have lived in Bolivia for at least 10,000 years. The main groups today are the Aymara and Quechua people.

In the last 50 years, Bolivia, an independent country since 1825, has been ruled by a succession of civilian and military governments, which violated human rights. Democracy was restored in 1982. Economic problems led a widening of the gap between rich and poor and, in 2005, Evo Morales, a left-wing Aymara farmer, was elected president. His policies of nationalization and redistributing wealth to peasants aroused opposition especially in the richer east. In 2009, Morales was re-elected president, but his popularity declined in 2010–11 because of food shortages and price rises.

Bolivia is one of South America's poorest countries. Resources include natural gas, silver, tin, and zinc, but the main activity is agriculture. Soybeans and soybean products are exported.

AREA 424,162 sq mi [1,098,581 sq km]
POPULATION 9,947,000 **CAPITAL** La Paz (seat of government); Sucre (legal capital/seat of judiciary)
GOVERNMENT Multiparty republic **ETHNIC GROUPS** Mestizo 30%, Quechua 30%, Aymara 25%, White 15% **LANGUAGES** Spanish, Aymara, Quechua (all official) **RELIGIONS** Roman Catholic 95%
CURRENCY Boliviano = 100 centavos

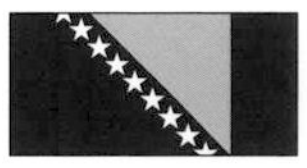

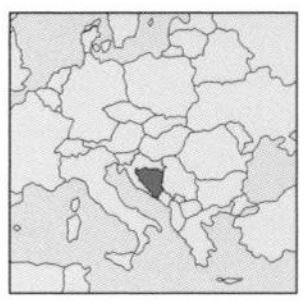

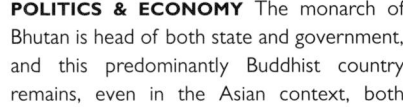

BOSNIA-HERZEGOVINA

GEOGRAPHY The Republic of Bosnia-Herzegovina is one of the five republics to emerge from the former Federal People's Republic of Yugoslavia. Much of the country is mountainous or hilly, with an arid limestone plateau in the southwest. The River Sava, which forms most of the northern border with Croatia, is a tributary of the River Danube. Because of the country's odd shape, the coastline is limited to a short stretch of 13 mi [20 km] on the Adriatic coast.

A Mediterranean climate, with dry, sunny summers and moist, mild winters, prevails only near the coast. Inland, the weather is more severe, with hot, dry summers and bitterly cold, snowy winters.

POLITICS & ECONOMY In 1918, Bosnia-Herzegovina became part of the Kingdom of the Serbs, Croats, and Slovenes, which was renamed Yugoslavia in 1929. Germany occupied the area during World War II (1939–45). From 1945, Communist governments ruled Yugoslavia as a federation containing six republics, one of which was Bosnia-Herzegovina. In the 1980s, the country faced problems as Communist policies proved unsuccessful.

In 1990, free elections were held in Bosnia-Herzegovina and the non-Communists won a majority. A Muslim, Alija Izetbegovic, was elected president. In 1991, Croatia and Slovenia, other parts of the former Yugoslavia, declared themselves independent. In 1992, Bosnia-Herzegovina held a vote on independence. Most Bosnian Serbs boycotted the vote, while the Muslims and Bosnian Croats voted in favor. Many Bosnian Serbs, opposed to independence, started a war against the non-Serbs. They soon occupied more than two-thirds of the land. The Bosnian Serbs were accused of "ethnic cleansing" – that is, the killing or expulsion of other ethnic groups from Serb-occupied areas. The war was later extended when Croat forces seized other parts of the country.

In 1995, the conflict was resolved. Under an agreement, the country's boundaries were maintained, but the territory was divided into two self-governing provinces, one Bosnian-Serb and the other Muslim-Croat, under a central government. Stability was restored with the help of NATO. In 2010, the Serb nationalist Alliance of Independent Social Democrats and the multi-ethnic Social Democratic Party emerged as the leading parties.

The economy of Bosnia-Herzegovina, the least developed of the six republics of the former Yugoslavia apart from Macedonia, was shattered by the war in the early 1990s. Before the war, manufactures were the main exports, including electrical, machinery and transport equipment, and textiles. Farm products include fruits, maize, tobacco, vegetables, and wheat, but food has to be imported.

AREA 19,767 sq mi [51,197 sq km]
POPULATION 4,622,000 **CAPITAL** Sarajevo
GOVERNMENT Federal republic **ETHNIC GROUPS** Bosnian 48%, Serb 37%, Croat 14% **LANGUAGES** Bosnian, Serbian, Croatian
RELIGIONS Islam 40%, Serbian Orthodox 31%, Roman Catholic 15%, others 14% **CURRENCY** Convertible marka = 100 convertible pfenniga

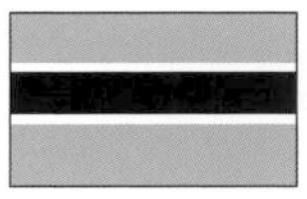

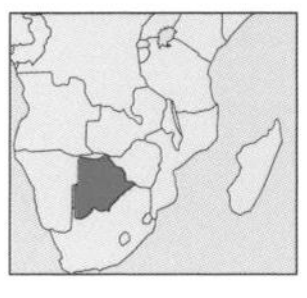

BOTSWANA

GEOGRAPHY The Republic of Botswana is a landlocked country in southern Africa. The Kalahari, a semidesert area covered mostly by grasses and thorn scrub, covers much of the country. Most of the south has no permanent streams. But large depressions in the north are inland drainage basins. In one of them, the Okavango River, which rises in Angola, forms a large, swampy delta.

Temperatures are high in the summer months (October to April), but the winter months are much cooler. In winter, night-time temperatures sometimes drop below freezing point. The average annual rainfall ranges from over 16 inches [400 mm] in the east to less than 8 inches [200 mm] in the southwest.

POLITICS & ECONOMY The earliest inhabitants of the region were the San, who are also called Bushmen. They had a nomadic way of life, hunting wild animals and collecting wild plant foods.

Britain ruled the area as the Bechuanaland Protectorate between 1885 and 1966. When the country became independent, it was renamed Botswana. Since then, the country has been a stable, multiparty democracy. However, a major setback occurred in the early 21st century, when health officials announced that around 25% of the people were infected with HIV/AIDS.

In 1966, Botswana was extremely poor, depending on meat and live cattle for its exports. But the discovery of minerals, including coal, cobalt, copper, diamonds, and nickel, has boosted the economy. About 16% of the people now depend on agriculture, raising cattle, and growing crops. Industries include the processing of farm products.

AREA 224,606 sq mi [581,730 sq km]
POPULATION 2,029,000 **CAPITAL** Gaborone
GOVERNMENT Multiparty republic **ETHNIC GROUPS** Tswana (or Setswana) 79%, Kalanga 11%, Basarwa 3%, others
LANGUAGES English (official), Setswana **RELIGIONS** Traditional beliefs 85%, Christianity 15% **CURRENCY** Pula = 100 thebe

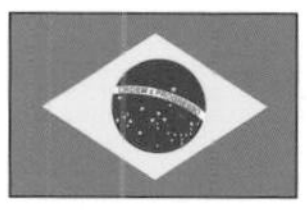

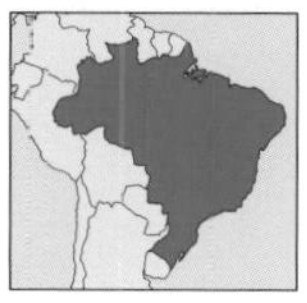

BRAZIL

GEOGRAPHY The Federative Republic of Brazil is the world's fifth largest country. It contains three main regions. The Amazon basin in the north covers more than half of Brazil. The Amazon, the world's second longest river, has a far greater volume than any other river. The second region, the north-east, consists of a coastal plain and the *sertão*, which is the name for the inland plateaux and hill country. The main river in this region is the São Francisco.

The third region is made up of the plateaux in the southeast. This region, which covers about a quarter of the country, is the most developed and densely populated part of Brazil. Its main river is the Paraná, which flows south through Argentina.

Manaus has high temperatures all through the year. The rainfall is heavy, though the period from June to September is drier than the rest of the year. The capital, Brasília, and the city Rio de Janeiro also have tropical climates, with much more marked dry seasons than Manaus. The far south has a temperate climate. The north-eastern interior is the driest region, with an average annual rainfall of only 10 inches [250 mm] in places. The rainfall is also unreliable and severe droughts are common in this region.

POLITICS & ECONOMY The Portuguese explorer Pedro Alvarez Cabral claimed Brazil for Portugal in 1500. With Spain occupied in western South America, the Portuguese began to develop their colony, which was more than 90 times as big as Portugal. To do this, they enslaved many local Amerindian people and introduced about 4 million African slaves. Brazil declared itself an independent empire in 1822 and a republic in 1889. From the 1930s, Brazil faced periods of military rule and widespread corruption. Civilian rule was restored in 1985. Brazil adopted a new constitution in 1988.

The United Nations has described Brazil as a "Rapidly Industrializing Country," or RIC. Its total volume of production is one of the largest in the world. But many people, including poor farmers and residents of the *favelas* (city slums), do not share in the country's fast economic growth. Poverty led to the election of President Luiz Inácio Lula da Silva (generally called "Lula") in 2002. His economic policies proved popular. In 2010, he was succeeded by Dilma Rousseff, also of Lula's Workers Party. She was Brazil's first female president.

Industry is the most important economic sector. Brazil is among the world's top producers of bauxite, chrome, diamonds, gold, iron ore, manganese, and tin. It is also a major manufacturing country. Its products include aircraft, cars, chemicals, processed food, iron and steel, paper, and textiles. The discovery of a major offshore oilfield was announced in 2007. Brazil is a major farming nation and agriculture employs 18% of the people. Coffee is a leading export. Other products include bananas, citrus fruits, cocoa, maize, rice, soybeans, and sugarcane. Brazil is also South America's top producer of eggs, meat, and milk.

Forestry is a major industry, though many people fear that the destruction of the rain forests, which may accelerate global warming, is an impending disaster for the entire world.

AREA 3,287,338 sq mi [8,514,215 sq km]
POPULATION 201,103,000 **CAPITAL** Brasília
GOVERNMENT Federal republic
ETHNIC GROUPS White 55%, Mulatto 38%, Black 6%, others 1% **LANGUAGES** Portuguese (official)
RELIGIONS Roman Catholic 80%
CURRENCY Real = 100 centavos

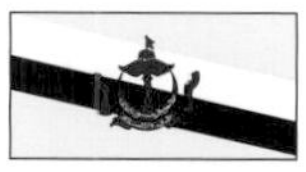

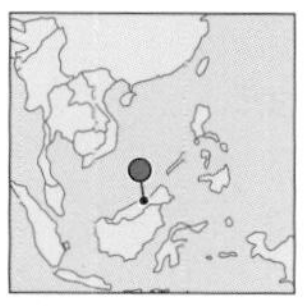

BRUNEI

The Islamic Sultanate of Brunei, a British protectorate until 1984, lies on the north coast of Borneo. The climate is tropical and rain forests cover large areas. Brunei is a prosperous country because of its oil and natural gas production, and the Sultan is said to be among the world's richest men.

AREA 2,226 sq mi [5,765 sq km]
POPULATION 395,000 **CAPITAL** Bandar Seri Begawan

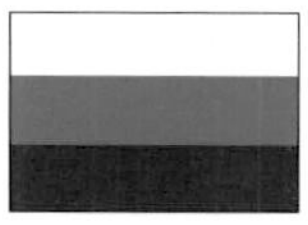

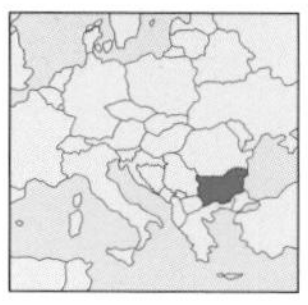

BULGARIA

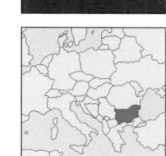

GEOGRAPHY The Republic of Bulgaria is a country in the Balkan peninsula, facing the Black Sea in the east. The heart of Bulgaria is mountainous. The main ranges are the Balkan Mountains in the center and the Rhodope (or Rhodopi) Mountains in the south.

Summers are hot and winters are cold, though seldom severe. The rainfall is moderate.

POLITICS & ECONOMY Ottoman Turks ruled Bulgaria from 1396 and ethnic Turks still form a sizable minority in the country. In 1879, Bulgaria became a monarchy, and in 1908 it became fully independent. Bulgaria was an ally of Germany in World War I (1914–18) and again in World War II (1939–45). In 1944, Soviet troops invaded Bulgaria and, after the war, the monarchy was abolished and the country became a Communist ally of the Soviet Union. In the late 1980s, reforms in the Soviet Union led Bulgaria's government to introduce a multi-party system in 1990. A non-Communist government was elected in 1991, the first free elections in 44 years. Throughout the 1990s, Bulgaria faced many problems and it sought to become aligned to the West. Bulgaria became a member of NATO in 2004 and a member of the European Union in 2007. In 2009, the center-right GERB party, led by Boiko Borisov, who promised to tackle corruption and the economic crisis, won the parliamentary elections.

Bulgaria has a "lower-middle economy." It has some mineral deposits, including brown coal, manganese, and iron ore. But manufacturing is the leading activity, though, in the early 1990s, much of its industrial plant was out of date. Leading products include chemicals, processed foods, metal products, machinery, and textiles. Manufactures are the leading exports.

AREA 42,823 sq mi [110,912 sq km] **POPULATION** 7,149,000
CAPITAL Sofia **GOVERNMENT** Multiparty republic
ETHNIC GROUPS Bulgarian 84%, Turkish 9%, Gypsy 5%, Macedonian, Armenian, others **LANGUAGES** Bulgarian (official), Turkish **RELIGIONS** Bulgarian Orthodox 83%, Islam 12%, Roman Catholic 2%, others **CURRENCY** Lev = 100 stotinki

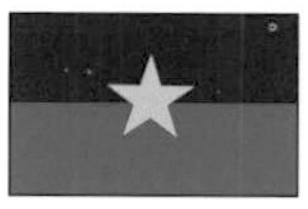

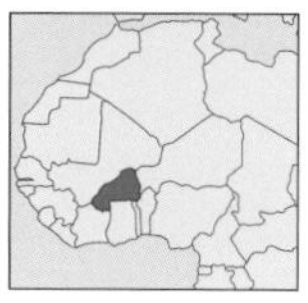

BURKINA FASO

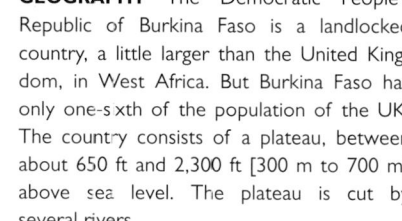

GEOGRAPHY The Democratic People's Republic of Burkina Faso is a landlocked country, a little larger than the United Kingdom, in West Africa. But Burkina Faso has only one-sixth of the population of the UK. The country consists of a plateau, between about 650 ft and 2,300 ft [300 m to 700 m] above sea level. The plateau is cut by several rivers.

The capital city, Ouagadougou, in central Burkina Faso, has high temperatures throughout the year. Most of the rain falls between May and September, but the rainfall is erratic and droughts are common.

POLITICS & ECONOMY The people of Burkina Faso are divided into two main groups. The Voltaic group includes the Mossi, who form the largest single group, and the Bobo. The French conquered the Mossi capital of Ouagadougou in 1897 and they made the area a protectorate. In 1919, the area became a French colony called Upper Volta. After independence in 1960, Upper Volta became a one-party state. But it was unstable – military groups seized power several times and political killings took place. In 1984, the country's name was changed to Burkina Faso. In 1991, 1998, 2005, and 2010, the former coup leader, Captain Blaise Compaoré, was elected president.

Burkina Faso is one of the world's 20 poorest countries and has become very dependent on foreign aid. Most of Burkina Faso is dry with thin soils. The country's main food crops are beans, maize, millet, rice, and sorghum. Cotton, groundnuts, and shea nuts, whose seeds produce a fat used to make cooking oil and soap, are grown for sale abroad. Livestock are also an important export.

The country has few resources and manufacturing is on a small scale. There are some deposits of manganese, zinc, lead, and nickel in the north of the country, but there is not yet a good enough transport system there. Many young men seek jobs abroad in Ghana and Ivory Coast. The money they send home to their families is important to the country's economy.

AREA 105,791 sq mi [274,000 sq km]
POPULATION 16,242,000 **CAPITAL** Ouagadougou
GOVERNMENT Multiparty republic **ETHNIC GROUPS** Mossi 40%, Gurunsi, Senufo, Lobi, Bobo, Mande, Fulani **LANGUAGES** French (official), Mossi, Fulani **RELIGIONS** Islam 50%, traditional beliefs 40%, Christianity 10% **CURRENCY** CFA franc = 100 centimes

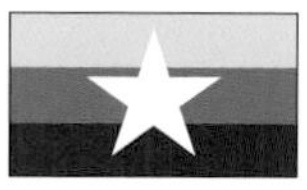

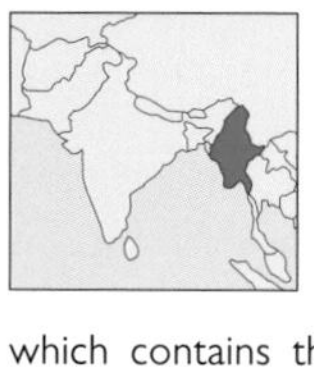

BURMA (MYANMAR)

GEOGRAPHY The Union of Burma has been officially known as the Union of Myanmar since 1989. However, it is more usually referred to as Burma. Mountains border the country in the east and west, with the highest mountains in the north. Burma's highest mountain is Hkakabo Razi, which is 19,294 ft [5,881 m] high. Between these ranges is central Burma, which contains the fertile valleys of the Irrawaddy and Sittang rivers. The Irrawaddy delta is a leading rice-growing area.

Burma has a tropical monsoon climate with three seasons. The rainy season runs from late May to mid-October. A cool, dry season follows, between late October and the middle part of February. The hot season lasts from late February to mid-May. In May 2008, a typhoon devastated the south, including the Irrawaddy delta. More than 80,000 people were reported killed and another 50,000 were missing.

POLITICS & ECONOMY Many groups settled in Burma in ancient times. Some, called the hill peoples, live in remote mountain areas where they have retained their own cultures. The ancestors of the country's main ethnic group today, the Burmese, arrived in the 9th century AD. Britain conquered Burma in the 19th century and made it a province of British India. But, in 1937, the British granted Burma limited self-government. Japan conquered Burma in 1942, but the Japanese were driven out in 1945. Burma became a fully independent country in 1948.

Revolts by Communists and various hill people led to instability in the 1950s. In 1962, Burma became a military dictatorship and, in 1974, a one-party state. Attempts to control minority liberation movements and the opium trade led to repressive rule. The National League for Democracy led by Aung San Suu Kyi won the elections in 1990, but the military continued their repressive rule, earning Burma the reputation for having one of the world's worst human rights records. In 2005, the government announced that a new capital, Naypyidaw ("Abode of Kings"), was being built north of Rangoon (Yangon). In 2010, the military released Aung San Suu Kyi from house arrest, but said she would not be allowed to participate in elections. A military-backed party was victorious in elections in 2010 and, in 2011, a civilian government backed by the military took power.

Agriculture is the main activity, employing 66% of the people. The chief crop is rice. Maize, pulses, oilseeds, and sugarcane are other major products. Forestry is important. Teak and rice together make up about two-thirds of the total value of the exports. Burma has many mineral resources, though they are mostly undeveloped, but the country is famous for its precious stones, especially rubies. Manufacturing is mostly on a small scale.

AREA 261,227 sq mi [676,578 sq km] **POPULATION** 53,414,000
CAPITAL Rangoon (Yangon); Naypyidaw (administrative capital)
GOVERNMENT Military regime **ETHNIC GROUPS** Burman 68%, Shan 9%, Karen 7%, Rakhine 4%, Chinese, Indian, Mon
LANGUAGES Burmese (official); minority ethnic groups have their own languages **RELIGIONS** Buddhism 89%, Christianity, Islam
CURRENCY Kyat = 100 pyas

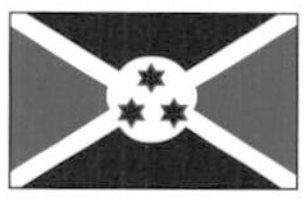

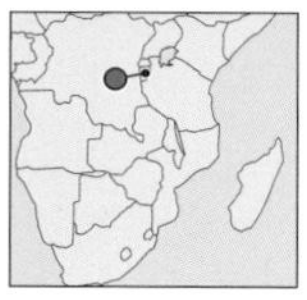

BURUNDI

GEOGRAPHY The Republic of Burundi is the fifth smallest country in mainland Africa. It is also the second most densely populated after its northern neighbor, Rwanda. Part of the Great African Rift Valley, which runs throughout eastern Africa into southwestern Asia, lies in western Burundi. It includes part of Lake Tanganyika. Bujumbura, the capital city, lies on the shore of Lake Tanganyika and has a warm climate. A dry season occurs from June to September, but the other months are fairly rainy. The mountains and plateaux to the east are cooler and wetter, but the rainfall generally decreases to the east.

POLITICS & ECONOMY The Twa, a pygmy people, were the first known inhabitants of Burundi. About 1,000 years ago, the Hutu, a people who speak a Bantu language, gradually began to settle the area, pushing the Twa into remote areas.

From the 15th century, the Tutsi, a cattle-owning people from the northeast, gradually took over the country. The Hutu, though greatly outnumbering the Tutsi, were forced to serve the Tutsi overlords.

Germany conquered the area that is now Burundi and Rwanda in the late 1890s. The area, called Ruanda-Urundi, was taken by Belgium during World War I (1914–18). In 1961, the people of Urundi voted to become a monarchy, while the people of Ruanda voted to become a republic. The two territories became fully independent as Burundi and Rwanda in 1962. After 1962, the rivalries between the Hutu and Tutsi led to periodic outbreaks of

fighting. The Tutsi monarchy was ended in 1966 and Burundi became a republic. Instability continued with coups and massacres as Tutsis and Hutus fought against each other. A power-sharing agreement was reached in 2001, though conflict continued in places. Elections were held in 2005 under a new constitution and the last major rebel group disarmed in 2009.

Burundi is one of the world's poorest countries. About 93% of the people live by farming, mostly at subsistence level. Food crops include beans, cassava, maize, and sweet potatoes. Livestock are raised and fishing is important. But Burundi has to import food.

AREA 10,747 SQ MI [27,834 SQ KM]
POPULATION 9,863,000 **CAPITAL** BUJUMBURA
GOVERNMENT REPUBLIC **ETHNIC GROUPS** HUTU 85%, TUTSI 14%, TWA (PYGMY) 1% **LANGUAGES** FRENCH AND KIRUNDI (BOTH OFFICIAL)
RELIGIONS ROMAN CATHOLIC 62%, TRADITIONAL BELIEFS 23%, ISLAM 10%, PROTESTANT 5% **CURRENCY** BURUNDI FRANC = 100 CENTIMES

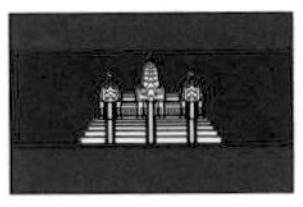
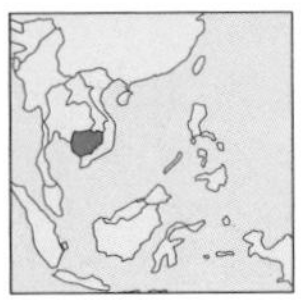

CAMBODIA

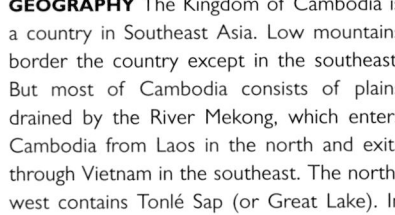

GEOGRAPHY The Kingdom of Cambodia is a country in Southeast Asia. Low mountains border the country except in the southeast. But most of Cambodia consists of plains drained by the River Mekong, which enters Cambodia from Laos in the north and exits through Vietnam in the southeast. The northwest contains Tonlé Sap (or Great Lake). In the dry season, this lake drains into the River Mekong. But in the wet season, the level of the Mekong rises and water flows in the opposite direction from the river into Tonlé Sap – the lake then becomes the largest freshwater lake in Asia.

Cambodia has a tropical monsoon climate, with high temperatures throughout the year. The dry season, when winds blow from the north or northeast, runs from November to April. During the rainy season (May to October), moist winds blow from the south or southeast. The high humidity and heat often make conditions unpleasant. Rainfall is heaviest near the coast, and rather lower inland.

POLITICS & ECONOMY From 802 to 1432, the Khmer people ruled a great empire, which reached its peak in the 12th century. The Khmer capital was at Angkor. The Hindu stone temples built there and at nearby Angkor Wat form the world's largest group of religious buildings. France ruled the country between 1863 and 1954, when the country became an independent monarchy. But the monarchy was abolished in 1970 and Cambodia became a republic.

In 1970, US and South Vietnamese troops entered Cambodia but left after destroying North Vietnamese Communist camps in the east. The country became involved in the Vietnamese War, and then in a civil war as Cambodian Communists of the Khmer Rouge organization fought for power. The Khmer Rouge took over Cambodia in 1975 and launched a reign of terror in which between 1 million and 2.5 million people were killed. In 1979, Vietnamese and Cambodian troops overthrew the Khmer Rouge government. But fighting continued between factions. Vietnam withdrew in 1989, and in 1991 Prince Sihanouk was recognized as head of state. Elections were held in May 1993, and in September 1993 the monarchy was restored. Elections were held in 1998, 2003, and 2008. In 2004, King Sihanouk abdicated because of ill health and his son, Prince Norodom Sihamoni, became king. Between 2008 and 2011, Cambodia and Thailand clashed periodically over a border dispute involving an area near the ancient Preah Vihear temple, which had been declared a World Heritage site.

Cambodia is a poor country whose economy has been wrecked by war. Farming is the main activity and rice, rubber, and maize are leading products. Manufacturing is on a small scale, but the discovery of oil reserves and an increase in tourism have recently boosted the economy.

AREA 69,898 SQ MI [181,035 SQ KM] **POPULATION** 14,454,000
CAPITAL PHNOM PENH **GOVERNMENT** CONSTITUTIONAL MONARCHY
ETHNIC GROUPS KHMER 90%, VIETNAMESE 5%, CHINESE 1%, OTHERS
LANGUAGES KHMER (OFFICIAL), FRENCH, ENGLISH
RELIGIONS BUDDHISM 95%, OTHERS 5% **CURRENCY** RIEL = 100 SEN

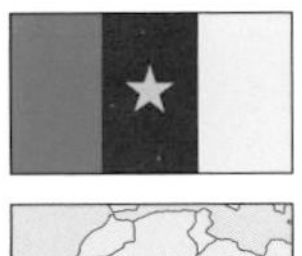
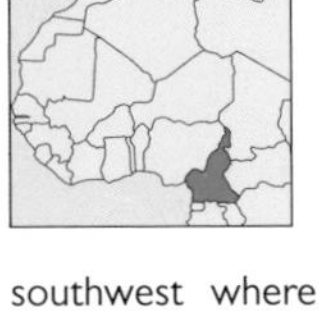

CAMEROON

GEOGRAPHY The Republic of Cameroon in West Africa derived its name from the Portuguese word *camarões*, or prawns. This name was used by Portuguese explorers who fished for prawns along the coast. Behind the narrow coastal plains on the Gulf of Guinea, the land rises to a series of plateaux, with a mountainous region in the southwest where the volcano Mount Cameroun is situated. In the north, the land slopes down toward the Lake Chad basin.

The rainfall is heavy, especially in the highlands, but it becomes drier to the north. Temperatures are high on the coast, while the inland plateaux are cooler.

POLITICS & ECONOMY Germany lost Cameroon during World War I (1914–18). The country was then divided into two parts, one ruled by Britain and the other by France. In 1960, French Cameroon became the independent Cameroon Republic. In 1961, after a vote in British Cameroon, part of the territory joined the Cameroon Republic to become the Federal Republic of Cameroon – the other part joined Nigeria. In 1972, Cameroon became a unitary state called the United Republic of Cameroon. It adopted the name Republic of Cameroon in 1984, but the country had two official languages. In 1995, partly to placate the English-speaking people, Cameroon became the 52nd member of the Commonwealth. In 2008, parliament passed a controversial amendment enabling President Paul Biya, who had assumed office in 1982, to run for a third term in 2011.

Like most countries in tropical Africa, Cameroon's economy is based on agriculture, which employs 54% of the people. The chief food crops include cassava, maize, millet, sweet potatoes, and yams. Cocoa and coffee are exported, along with oil and bauxite. In 2002, Cameroon's claim over the disputed oil-rich Bakassi peninsula was upheld and the handover by Nigeria was finally completed in 2008. Cameroon has few manufacturing industries, but it is self-sufficient in food.

AREA 183,568 SQ MI [475,442 SQ KM] **POPULATION** 19,194,000
CAPITAL YAOUNDÉ **GOVERNMENT** MULTIPARTY REPUBLIC
ETHNIC GROUPS CAMEROON HIGHLANDERS 31%, BANTU 27%, KIRDI 11%, FULANI 10%, OTHERS **LANGUAGES** FRENCH AND ENGLISH (BOTH OFFICIAL)
RELIGIONS CHRISTIANITY 40%, TRADITIONAL BELIEFS 40%, ISLAM 20%
CURRENCY CFA FRANC = 100 CENTIMES

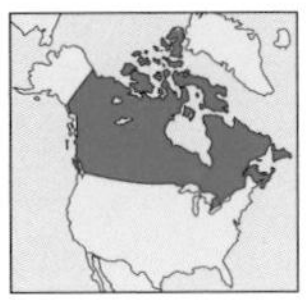

CANADA

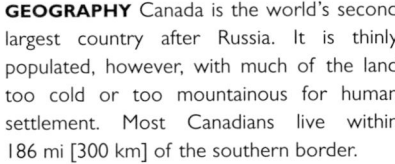

GEOGRAPHY Canada is the world's second largest country after Russia. It is thinly populated, however, with much of the land too cold or too mountainous for human settlement. Most Canadians live within 186 mi [300 km] of the southern border.

Western Canada is rugged. It includes the Pacific ranges and the mighty Rocky Mountains. East of the Rockies are the interior plains. In the north lie the bleak Arctic islands, while to the south lie the densely populated lowlands around lakes Erie and Ontario and in the St Lawrence River valley. The melting of Arctic ice, attributed to global warming, has led to concern about international rights over the Arctic waters off northern Canada.

Canada has a cold climate. In winter, temperatures fall below freezing point throughout most of Canada. But the southwestern coast has a relatively mild climate. Along the Arctic Circle, mean temperatures are below freezing for seven months a year. The west and southeast have high rainfall, but the prairies are dry with 10 inches to 20 inches [250 mm to 500 mm] of rain every year.

POLITICS & ECONOMY Canada's first people, the ancestors of the Native Americans, or Indians, arrived in North America from Asia around 40,000 years ago. The Inuit (Eskimos) were later arrivals from Asia. Europeans first reached Canada in 1497 and soon Britain and France began to compete for control.

France gained an initial advantage, and the French founded Québec in 1608. But the British later occupied eastern Canada. In 1867, Britain passed the British North America Act, which set up the Dominion of Canada, which was made up of Québec, Ontario, Nova Scotia, and New Brunswick. Other areas were added, the last being Newfoundland in 1949. Canada fought alongside Britain in both World Wars and many Canadians feel close ties with Britain. Canada is a constitutional monarchy, and the British monarch is Canada's head of state.

In 1995, the people of Québec voted narrowly against a move to make Québec a sovereign state. In 2006, the national parliament voted to recognize Québec as a nation within a united Canada – a symbolic act of reconciliation. Another major issue concerns the rights of Aboriginal minorities. In 1999, Canada created the territory of Nunavut for the Inuit population. Nunavut covers 64% of what was formerly the eastern part of the Northwest Territories. In 2006, the Conservative Party, led by Stephen Harper, was returned to power, ending 12 years of Liberal Party rule. Stephen Harper was re-elected in 2008 and 2011.

Canada is a highly developed and prosperous country. Although farmland covers only 8% of the country, Canadian farms are highly productive. Canada is one of the world's leading producers of barley, wheat, meat, and milk. Forestry and fishing are other important industries. It is rich in natural resources, especially oil and natural gas, and is a major exporter of minerals. The country also produces copper, gold, iron ore, uranium, and zinc. Manufacturing is important in the cities, where 80% of the people live. Manufactures include processed mineral and farm products, cars, chemicals, electronic goods, machinery, paper, and timber products.

AREA 3,849,653 SQ MI [9,970,610 SQ KM]
POPULATION 33,760,000 **CAPITAL** OTTAWA
GOVERNMENT FEDERAL MULTIPARTY CONSTITUTIONAL MONARCHY
ETHNIC GROUPS BRITISH ORIGIN 28%, FRENCH ORIGIN 23%, OTHER EUROPEAN 15%, AMERINDIAN/INUIT 2%, OTHERS
LANGUAGES ENGLISH AND FRENCH (BOTH OFFICIAL)
RELIGIONS ROMAN CATHOLIC 46%, PROTESTANT 36%, JUDAISM, ISLAM, HINDUISM **CURRENCY** CANADIAN DOLLAR = 100 CENTS

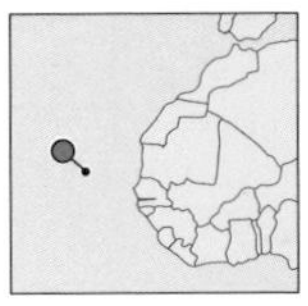

CAPE VERDE

Cape Verde consists of ten large and five small islands, and is situated 350 mi [560 km] west of Dakar in Senegal. The islands have a tropical climate, with high temperatures all year round. Cape Verde became independent from Portugal in 1975 and is rated as a "low-income" developing country by the World Bank.

AREA 1,557 SQ MI [4,033 SQ KM]
POPULATION 509,000 **CAPITAL** PRAIA

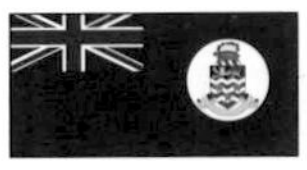
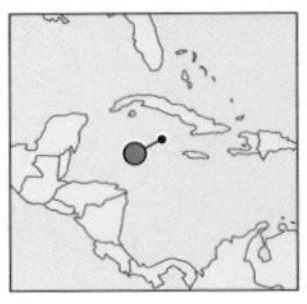

CAYMAN ISLANDS

The Cayman Islands are an overseas territory of the UK, consisting of three low-lying islands. Financial services are the main economic activity and the islands offer a secret tax haven to many companies and banks.

AREA 102 SQ MI [264 SQ KM]
POPULATION 50,000 **CAPITAL** GEORGE TOWN

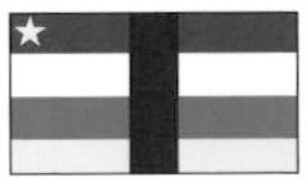
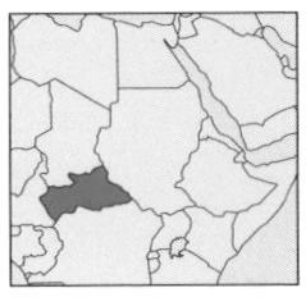

CENTRAL AFRICAN REPUBLIC

GEOGRAPHY The Central African Republic is a remote, landlocked country in the heart of Africa. It consists mostly of a plateau lying between 1,970 ft and 2,620 ft [600 m to 800 m] above sea level. The Ubangi drains the south, while the Chari (or Shari) River flows from the north to the Lake Chad basin. The climate is warm throughout the year, while the annual average rainfall in the capital Bangui totals 62 inches [1,574 mm]. The north is drier, with an average annual rainfall of about 31 inches [800 mm].

POLITICS & ECONOMY France set up an outpost at Bangui in 1899 and ruled the country as a colony from 1894. Known as Ubangi-Shari, the country was ruled by France as part of French Equatorial Africa until it gained independence in 1960.

Central African Republic became a one-party state in 1962, but army officers seized power in 1966. The head of the army, Jean-Bedel Bokassa, made himself emperor in 1976. The country was renamed the Central African Empire, but Bokassa was removed by a military coup in 1979. The country again became a republic.

The republic adopted a new multiparty constitution in 1991, and elections were held in 1993 and 1998. An army uprising in 2002 ended in the overthrow of the government in 2003. General François Bozize took power. He was elected president in 2005 and 2010. In 2006–7, rebel activities led thousands of refugees to flee into Chad and Cameroon, and in 2009 the US-based Fund for Peace classified the country as a "failed state."

The World Bank classifies Central African Republic as a "low-income" developing country. Over 80% of the people are farmers, and most of them produce little more than they need to feed their families. The main crops are bananas, maize, manioc, millet, and yams. Coffee, cotton, timber, and tobacco are produced for export. Development has been impeded by the country's remote position, its poor transport system, and its untrained work force. The country depends heavily on aid from France.

AREA 240,534 SQ MI [622,984 SQ KM] **POPULATION** 4,845,000
CAPITAL BANGUI **GOVERNMENT** MULTIPARTY REPUBLIC
ETHNIC GROUPS BAYA 33%, BANDA 27%, MANDJIA 13%, SARA 10%, MBOUM 7%, MBAKA 4%, OTHERS **LANGUAGES** FRENCH (OFFICIAL), SANGHO
RELIGIONS TRADITIONAL BELIEFS 35%, PROTESTANT 25%, ROMAN CATHOLIC 25%, ISLAM 15% **CURRENCY** CFA FRANC = 100 CENTIMES

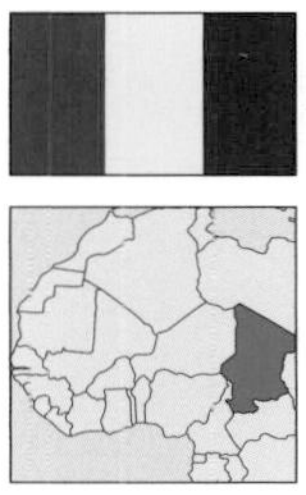

CHAD

GEOGRAPHY The Republic of Chad is a landlocked country in north-central Africa. It is Africa's fifth largest country and is over twice the size of France, the country which once ruled it as a colony.

Ndjamena in central Chad has a hot tropical climate, with a marked dry season from November to April. The south of the country is wetter, with an average yearly rainfall of around 39 inches [1,000 mm]. The burning-hot desert in the north has an average yearly rainfall of less than 5 inches [130 mm].

POLITICS & ECONOMY Chad straddles two worlds. The north is populated by Muslim Arab and Berber peoples, while black Africans, who follow traditional beliefs or who have converted to Christianity, live in the south. French explorers were active in the area in the late 19th century. France made Chad a colony in 1902.

Chad became independent in 1960, but the 1970s were marked by ethnic conflict that led to civil wars, coups and conflict with Libya, which supported rebel factions. Chad and Libya agreed a truce in 1987 and, in 1994, the International Court of Justice ruled against Libya's claim on the Aozou Strip. From 2004, Chad forces clashed with pro-Sudanese militias as the conflict in Sudan's Darfur province spilled over the border. In 2010, talks between Chad and Sudan led to hopes of normalization along the border.

Chad is one of the world's poorest countries. Farming and fishing employ 83% of the people. Food crops include groundnuts, millet, rice and sorghum, but cotton is the chief export crop. Chad has few manufacturing industries, but its oil reserves hold out hope for development. Oil production began in 2003.

AREA 495,752 SQ MI [1,284,000 SQ KM]
POPULATION 10,543,000 **CAPITAL** NDJAMENA
GOVERNMENT MULTIPARTY REPUBLIC **ETHNIC GROUPS** 200 DISTINCT GROUPS: MOSTLY MUSLIM IN THE NORTH AND CENTER; MOSTLY CHRISTIAN OR ANIMIST IN THE SOUTH **LANGUAGES** FRENCH AND ARABIC (BOTH OFFICIAL), MANY OTHERS **RELIGIONS** ISLAM 51%, CHRISTIANITY 35%, ANIMIST 7%
CURRENCY CFA FRANC = 100 CENTIMES

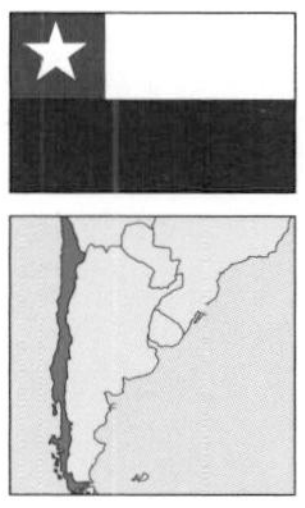

CHILE

GEOGRAPHY The Republic of Chile stretches about 2,650 mi [4,260 km] from north to south, although the maximum east–west distance is only about 267 mi [430 km]. The high Andes Mountains form Chile's eastern borders with Argentina and Bolivia. To the west are basins and valleys, with coastal uplands overlooking the shore. Most people live in the central valley, where Santiago is situated. Earthquakes are common. In February 2010, an earthquake with a magnitude of 8.8 (the biggest in 50 years) struck central Chile, killing more than 400 people.

Santiago has a Mediterranean climate with hot, dry summers and mild, moist winters. The Atacama Desert in the north is extremely arid, while the south is cold and stormy.

POLITICS & ECONOMY Amerindian people reached the southern tip of South America 8,000 years ago. In 1520, Portuguese navigator Ferdinand Magellan was the first European to sight Chile. The country became a Spanish colony in the 1540s. Chile became independent in 1818. During a war (1879–83), it gained mineral-rich areas from Peru and Bolivia.

In 1970, Salvador Allende became the first Communist leader to be elected democratically. He was overthrown in 1973 by army officers, who were supported by the CIA. General Augusto Pinochet then ruled as a dictator. A new constitution was introduced in 1981. Pinochet remained in power until 1989. In 2006, Michelle Bachelet, a center-left former torture victim under the Pinochet regime, became president. She was succeeded in 2010 by a right-winger, Sebastian Pinera.

According to the World Bank, Chile has a "lower-middle-income" economy. Mining, especially copper, is important and minerals dominate the exports. But manufacturing is the most valuable activity. Products include processed foods, metals, iron and steel, transport equipment, and textiles. The chief crop is wheat, while beans, fruits, maize, and livestock products are also important. Chile's fishing industry is one of the world's largest.

AREA 292,133 SQ MI [756,626 SQ KM]
POPULATION 16,746,000 **CAPITAL** SANTIAGO
GOVERNMENT MULTIPARTY REPUBLIC **ETHNIC GROUPS** MESTIZO 95%, AMERINDIAN 3% **LANGUAGES** SPANISH (OFFICIAL)
RELIGIONS ROMAN CATHOLIC 89%, PROTESTANT 11%
CURRENCY CHILEAN PESO = 100 CENTAVOS

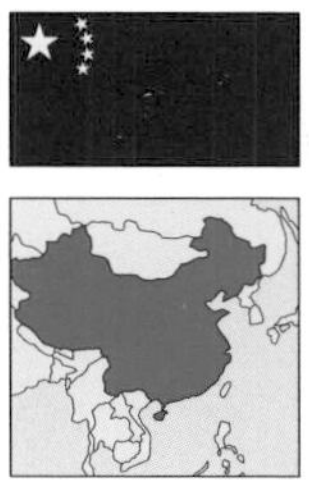

CHINA

GEOGRAPHY The People's Republic of China is the world's third largest country. Most people live in the east – on the coastal plains or in the fertile valleys of the Huang He (Hwang Ho or Yellow River), the Chang Jiang (Yangtze Kiang), which is Asia's longest river at 3,960 mi [6,380 km], and the Xi Jiang (Si Kiang). Western China is thinly populated. It includes the bleak Tibetan plateau which is bounded by the Himalaya, the world's highest mountain range. Deserts include the Gobi Desert along the Mongolian border and the Taklamakan Desert in the far west. Earthquakes are common. In May 2008, a major earthquake in the southwest killed more than 69,000 people and made millions homeless.

Beijing has cold winters and warm summers with moderate rainfall. To the south, Shanghai has milder winters and more rain. The southeast has a wet, subtropical climate, but the west has a severe climate. Lhasa has very cold winters and a low rainfall.

POLITICS & ECONOMY China is one of the world's oldest civilizations, going back 3,500 years. Under the Han dynasty (202 BC to AD 220), the Chinese empire was as large as the Roman empire. Mongols conquered China in the 13th century, but Chinese rule was restored in 1368. The Manchu people of Mongolia ruled the country from 1644 to 1912, when the country became a republic.

War with Japan (1937–45) was followed by civil war between the nationalists and the Communists. The Communists triumphed in 1949, setting up the People's Republic of China. In the 1980s, following the death of the revolutionary leader Mao Zedong (Mao Tse-tung) in 1976, China encouraged formerly forbidden policies, namely private enterprise and foreign investment. But the Communist leaders have not permitted political freedom. Opponents are still harshly treated, while attempts to negotiate some degree of autonomy for Tibet have been rejected.

China's economy has expanded greatly since the 1970s and many new industries have been set up in the east. Between 1989 and 2008, the economy grew by around 9% per year and China is now one of the world's four largest economies. China has benefited from the return of Hong Kong in 1997 and its admission to the World Trade Organization in 2001. The global financial crisis in 2008 slowed the economic growth rate, though China's grew faster than any other major economy. In early 2011, China overtook Japan to become the world's second largest economy after the United States.

Despite its recent success, China remains a poor country. In 2002, agriculture employed 43% of the work force, although only 10% of the land is farmed. In 2006, plans were announced to help the people living in the countryside catch up economically with people in the cities.

Farm products include rice, sweet potatoes, tea, and wheat, and many fruits and vegetables. Livestock farming is important, and China has more than a third of the world's pigs. Resources include coal, iron ore, and other metals. Manufactures include cement, chemicals, fertilizers, machinery, telecommunications and recording equipment, and textiles. China is now a major producer of consumer goods, including cameras, computer products, refrigerators, and television sets.

AREA 3,705,387 SQ MI [9,596,961 SQ KM]
POPULATION 1,330,141,000 **CAPITAL** BEIJING
GOVERNMENT SINGLE-PARTY COMMUNIST REPUBLIC
ETHNIC GROUPS HAN CHINESE 92%, MANY OTHERS
LANGUAGES MANDARIN CHINESE (OFFICIAL) **RELIGIONS** ATHEIST (OFFICIAL)
CURRENCY RENMINBI YUAN = 10 JIAO = 100 FEN

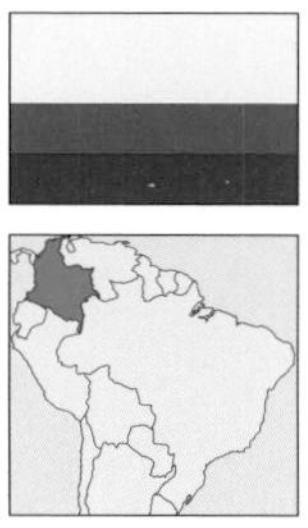

COLOMBIA

GEOGRAPHY The Republic of Colombia, in northeastern South America, is the only country in the continent to have coastlines on both the Pacific and the Caribbean Sea. Colombia also contains the northernmost ranges of the Andes Mountains.

There is a tropical climate in the lowlands, but the altitude greatly affects the climate of the Andes. The capital, Bogotá, which stands on a plateau in the eastern Andes at about 9,200 ft [2,800 m] above sea level, has mild temperatures throughout the year. The rainfall is heavy, especially on the Pacific coast.

POLITICS & ECONOMY Amerindian people have lived in Colombia for thousands of years. But today, only a small proportion of the people are of unmixed Amerindian ancestry. Mestizos (people of mixed white and Amerindian ancestry) form the largest group, followed by whites and mulattos (people of mixed European and African ancestry). Spaniards opened up the area in the early 16th century. They set up a territory known as the Viceroyalty of the New Kingdom of Granada, including Colombia, Ecuador, Panama, and Venezuela. In 1819, the area became independent, but Ecuador and Venezuela soon split away, followed by Panama in 1903.

Instability has marked its recent history. Colombia faces economic and security problems, notably combating left-wing guerrillas and right-wing paramilitaries, while controlling the illicit drugs industry. Andrés Pastrana, president in 1998–2002, tried to end the guerrilla war, but peace talks collapsed and conflict resumed. His successors, Alvaro Uribe and, from 2010, Juan Manuel Santos, pursued tough policies against the rebels.

Colombia has a "lower-middle-income" economy. It exports oil, coffee, and chemicals.

AREA 439,735 SQ MI [1,138,914 SQ KM] **POPULATION** 44,205,000
CAPITAL BOGOTÁ **GOVERNMENT** MULTIPARTY REPUBLIC
ETHNIC GROUPS MESTIZO 58%, WHITE 20%, MULATTO 14%, BLACK 4%
LANGUAGES SPANISH (OFFICIAL) **RELIGIONS** ROMAN CATHOLIC 90%
CURRENCY COLOMBIAN PESO = 100 CENTAVOS

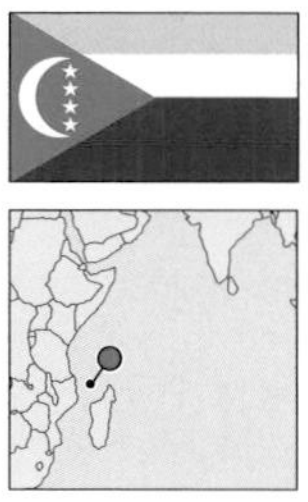

COMOROS

The Union des Isles Comores, as the Comoros is officially called, consists of three large volcanic islands and some smaller ones, lying at the north end of the Mozambique Channel in the Indian Ocean. France took over one of the islands, Mayotte, in 1843, and, in 1886, the other islands came under French protection. The Comoros became independent in 1974, but Mayotte remained French, becoming fully integrated with France in 2009. In the 1990s, the islands of Anjouan and Mohéli tried to secede, but, in 2004, the large islands were granted autonomy. In 2008, an illegal regime on Anjouan was overthrown. Exports include cloves, perfume oil, and vanilla.

AREA 863 SQ MI [2,235 SQ KM] **POPULATION** 773,000 **CAPITAL** MORONI

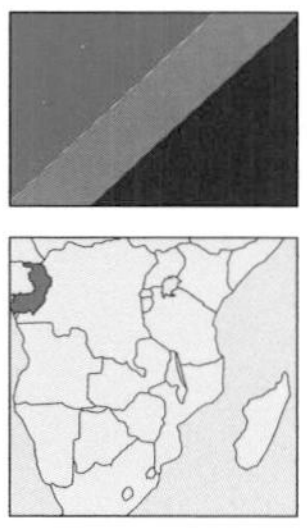

CONGO

GEOGRAPHY The Republic of the Congo is a country on the River Congo in west-central Africa. The Equator runs through the center of the country. Congo has a narrow coastal plain on which its main port, Pointe Noire, stands. Behind the plain are uplands through which the River Niari has carved a fertile valley. Central Congo consists of high plains. The north contains large swampy areas in the valleys of the tributaries of the River Congo.

Congo has a hot, wet equatorial climate. Brazzaville has a dry season between June and September. The coast is drier and cooler than the rest of Congo, because of the cold offshore Benguela ocean current.

POLITICS & ECONOMY Part of the huge Kongo kingdom between the 15th and 18th centuries, the coast of the Congo later became a center of the European slave trade. The area came under French protection in 1880. It was later governed as part of a larger region called French Equatorial Africa. The country remained under French control until 1960.

Congo became a one-party state in 1964 and a military group took over the government in 1968. In 1970, Congo declared itself a Communist country, though it continued to seek aid from Western countries. The government officially abandoned its Communist policies in 1990. Multiparty elections were held in 1992, but the elected president, Pascal Lissouba, was overthrown in 1997 by former president Denis Sassou-Nguesso. Civil war broke out in 1999 but peace was restored in 2002. Sassou-Nguesso was elected president. He was re-elected in 2009.

The World Bank classifies Congo as a "lower-middle-income" developing country. Agriculture is the most important activity, employing about 38% of the people. But many farmers produce little more than they need to feed their families. Major food crops include bananas, cassava, maize, and rice, while the leading cash crops are coffee and cocoa. Congo's main exports are oil (which makes up more than 90% of the total) and timber. Manufacturing is relatively unimportant at the moment, still hampered by poor transport links, but it is gradually being developed.

AREA 132,046 SQ MI [342,000 SQ KM]
POPULATION 4,126,000 **CAPITAL** BRAZZAVILLE
GOVERNMENT MILITARY REGIME **ETHNIC GROUPS** KONGO 48%, SANGHA 20%, TEKE 17%, M'BOCHI 12% **LANGUAGES** FRENCH (OFFICIAL), MANY OTHERS **RELIGIONS** CHRISTIANITY 50%, ANIMIST 48%, ISLAM 2%
CURRENCY CFA FRANC = 100 CENTIMES

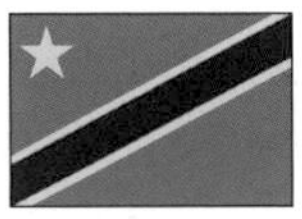
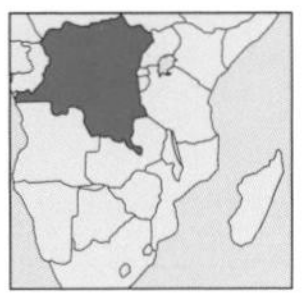

CONGO (DEMOCRATIC REPUBLIC OF THE)

GEOGRAPHY The Democratic Republic of the Congo, formerly known as Zaïre, is the world's 12th largest country. Much of the country lies within the drainage basin of the huge River Congo. The river reaches the sea along the country's coastline, which is 25 mi [40 km] long. Mountains rise in the east, where the country's borders run through lakes Tanganyika, Kivu, Edward, and Albert. The equatorial region has high temperatures and heavy rainfall throughout the year.

POLITICS & ECONOMY Pygmies were the first inhabitants of the region, with Portuguese navigators not reaching the coast until 1482, but the interior was not explored until the late 19th century. In 1885, the country, called Congo Free State, became the personal property of King Léopold II of Belgium. In 1908, the country became a Belgian colony.

The Belgian Congo became independent in 1960 and was renamed Zaïre in 1971. Ethnic rivalries caused instability until 1965, when the country became a one-party state, ruled by President Mobutu. The government allowed the formation of political parties in 1990, but elections were repeatedly postponed. In 1996, fighting broke out in eastern Zaïre, as the Tutsi–Hutu conflict in Burundi and Rwanda spilled over. The rebel leader Laurent Kabila took power in 1997, ousting Mobutu and renaming the country. A rebellion against Kabila broke out in 1998. Rwanda and Uganda supported the rebels, while Angola, Chad, Namibia, and Zimbabwe assisted Kabila. A peace treaty was signed in 1999, but fighting continued. Kabila was assassinated in 2001. His son, Major-General Joseph Kabila, became president. But instability continued into 2011 as various militias, including Tutsi, Hutu, and Ugandan rebels clashed with government forces in the east.

The World Bank classifies the Democratic Republic of the Congo as a "low-income" developing country, despite its reserves of copper, the main export, and other minerals. Agriculture, mainly at subsistence level, employs 62% of the people.

AREA 905,350 SQ MI [2,344,858 SQ KM]
POPULATION 70,916,000 **CAPITAL** KINSHASA
GOVERNMENT SINGLE-PARTY REPUBLIC
ETHNIC GROUPS OVER 200; THE LARGEST ARE MONGO, LUBA, KONGO, MANGBETU-AZANDE
LANGUAGES FRENCH (OFFICIAL), TRIBAL LANGUAGES
RELIGIONS ROMAN CATHOLIC 50%, PROTESTANT 20%, ISLAM 10%, OTHERS
CURRENCY CONGOLESE FRANC = 100 CENTIMES

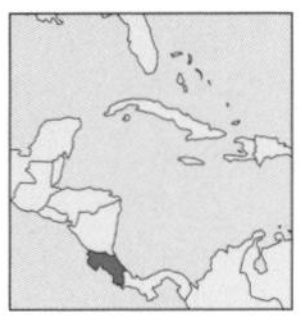

COSTA RICA

GEOGRAPHY The Republic of Costa Rica in Central America has coastlines on both the Pacific Ocean and also on the Caribbean Sea. Central Costa Rica consists of mountain ranges and plateaux with many volcanoes.

The coolest months are December and January. The northeast trade winds bring heavy rain to the Caribbean coast. There is less rainfall in the highlands and on the Pacific coastlands.

POLITICS & ECONOMY Christopher Columbus reached the Caribbean coast in 1502 and rumors of treasure soon attracted many Spaniards to settle in the country. Spain ruled the country until 1821, when Spain's Central American colonies broke away to join Mexico in 1822. In 1823, the Central American states broke with Mexico and set up the Central American Federation. Later, this large union broke up and Costa Rica became fully independent in 1838.

From the late 19th century, Costa Rica experienced a number of revolutions, with periods of dictatorship and periods of democracy. In 1948, following a revolt, the armed forces were abolished. Since 1948, Costa Rica has enjoyed a long period of stable democracy. In 2010, Costa Ricans elected their first woman president, Laura Chinchilla.

Costa Rica is classified by the World Bank as a "lower-middle-income" developing country and one of the most prosperous countries in Central America. There are high educational standards and a high average life expectancy (about 77 years for men and 81 years for women). Agriculture employs 12% of the people. Costa Rica's natural resources include its forests, but it lacks minerals apart from some bauxite and manganese. Manufacturing is increasing. The United States is Costa Rica's main trading partner. Tourism is a fast-growing industry.

AREA 19,730 SQ MI [51,100 SQ KM] **POPULATION** 4,516,000
CAPITAL SAN JOSÉ **GOVERNMENT** MULTIPARTY REPUBLIC
ETHNIC GROUPS WHITE (INCLUDING MESTIZO) 94%, BLACK 3%, AMERINDIAN 1%, CHINESE 1%, OTHERS **LANGUAGES** SPANISH (OFFICIAL), ENGLISH **RELIGIONS** ROMAN CATHOLIC 76%, EVANGELICAL 14%
CURRENCY COSTA RICAN COLÓN = 100 CÉNTIMOS

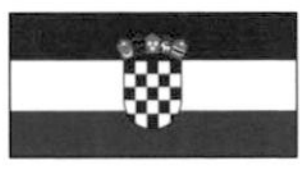
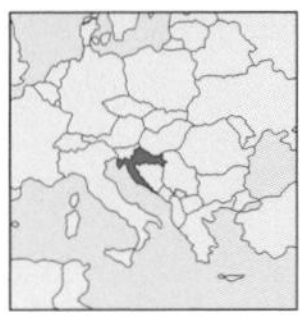

CROATIA

GEOGRAPHY The Republic of Croatia was one of the six republics that made up the former Communist country of Yugoslavia until it became independent in 1991. The region bordering the Adriatic Sea is called Dalmatia. It includes the coastal ranges, which contain large areas of bare limestone. Most of the rest of the country consists of the fertile Pannonian plains.

The coastal area has a typical Mediterranean climate, with hot, dry summers and mild, moist winters. Inland, the climate becomes more continental. Winters are cold, while temperatures often soar to 100°F [38°C] in the summer months.

POLITICS & ECONOMY Slav people settled in the area around 1,400 years ago. In 803, Croatia became part of the Holy Roman empire and the Croats soon adopted Christianity. Croatia was an independent kingdom in the 10th and 11th centuries. In 1102, the king of Hungary also became king of Croatia, creating a union that lasted 800 years. In 1526, part of Croatia came under the Turkish Ottoman empire, while the rest came under the Austrian Habsburgs.

After Austria–Hungary was defeated in World War I (1914–18), Croatia became part of the new Kingdom of the Serbs, Croats, and Slovenes. This kingdom was renamed Yugoslavia in 1929. Germany occupied Yugoslavia during World War II (1939–45). Croatia was proclaimed independent, but it was really ruled by the invaders.

After the war, Communists took power with Josip Broz Tito as the country's leader. Despite ethnic differences between the people, Tito held Yugoslavia together until his death in 1980. In the 1980s, economic and ethnic problems, including a deterioration in relations with Serbia, threatened stability. In the 1990s, Yugoslavia split into five nations, one of which was Croatia, which declared itself independent in 1991.

After Serbia supplied arms to Serbs living in Croatia, war broke out between the two republics, causing great damage. Croatia lost more than 30% of its territory. But in 1992, the United Nations sent a peacekeeping force to Croatia, which effectively ended the war with Serbia.

In 1992, when war broke out in Bosnia-Herzegovina, Bosnian Croats occupied parts of the country. But in 1994, Croatia helped to end Croat–Muslim conflict in Bosnia-Herzegovina and, in 1995, after retaking some areas occupied by Serbs, it helped to draw up the Dayton Peace Accord, ending the civil war. The conflict in the early 1990s disrupted the economy. In 2009, Slovenia lifted its block on Croatia's membership talks with the European Union following the resolution of a border dispute. In 2010, Social Democrat Ivo Josipovic was elected president. Croatia's main exports are manufactures.

AREA 21,829 SQ MI [56,538 SQ KM] **POPULATION** 4,487,000
CAPITAL ZAGREB **GOVERNMENT** MULTIPARTY REPUBLIC
ETHNIC GROUPS CROAT 90%, SERB 5%, OTHERS
LANGUAGES CROATIAN 96% **RELIGIONS** ROMAN CATHOLIC 88%, ORTHODOX 4%, ISLAM 1%, OTHERS **CURRENCY** KUNA = 100 LIPAS

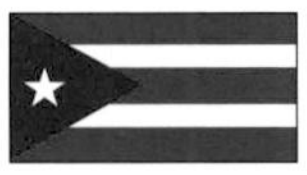
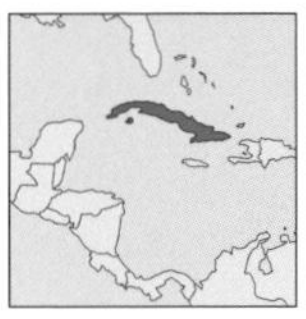

CUBA

GEOGRAPHY The Republic of Cuba is the largest island country in the Caribbean Sea. It consists of one large island, Cuba, the Isle of Youth (Isla de la Juventud), and about 1,600 small islets. Mountains and hills cover about a quarter of Cuba. The highest mountain range, the Sierra Maestra in the southeast, reaches 6,562 ft [2,000 m] above sea level. The rest of the land consists of gently rolling country or coastal plains, crossed by fertile valleys carved by the short, mostly shallow and narrow rivers.

Cuba lies in the tropics. But sea breezes moderate the temperature, warming the land in winter and cooling it in summer.

POLITICS & ECONOMY Christopher Columbus discovered the island in 1492 and Spaniards began to settle there from 1511. Spanish rule ended in 1898, when the United States defeated Spain in the Spanish–American War. American influence in Cuba remained strong until 1959, when revolutionary forces under Fidel Castro overthrew the dictatorial government of Fulgencio Batista.

The United States opposed Castro's policies, when he turned to the Soviet Union for assistance. In 1962, a world crisis occurred when, under intense US pressure, the Soviet Union withdrew missile sites that could have been used to launch nuclear strikes against the United States. The breakup of the Soviet Union in 1991 damaged Cuba's economy. Fidel Castro's brother, Raul, took over the leadership in 2008. He introduced reforms in 2009–11, including the overhaul of the state-run economy and the release of political prisoners.

The government runs Cuba's economy and owns 70% of the farmland. Agriculture is important and sugar is the chief export, followed by refined nickel ore. Other exports include cigars, citrus fruits, fish, medical products, and rum.

Before 1959, US companies owned most of Cuba's manufacturing industries. But under Fidel Castro, they became government property. After the collapse of Communist governments in the Soviet Union and its allies, Cuba worked to increase its trade with Latin America and China.

AREA 42,803 SQ MI [110,861 SQ KM]
POPULATION 11,477,000 **CAPITAL** HAVANA
GOVERNMENT SOCIALIST REPUBLIC
ETHNIC GROUPS MULATTO 51%, WHITE 37%, BLACK 11%
LANGUAGES SPANISH (OFFICIAL) **RELIGIONS** CHRISTIANITY
CURRENCY CUBAN PESO = 100 CENTAVOS

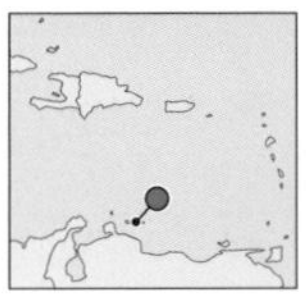

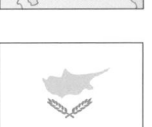

CURAÇAO

Part of the Netherlands Antilles until 2010, Curaçao is a self-governing territory within the Kingdom of the Netherlands. Oil refining, tourism, and trade are important.

AREA 171 SQ MI [444 SQ KM]
POPULATION 142,000 **CAPITAL** WILLEMSTAD

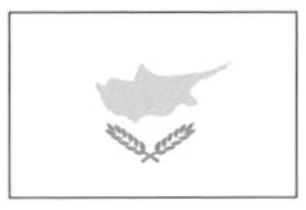
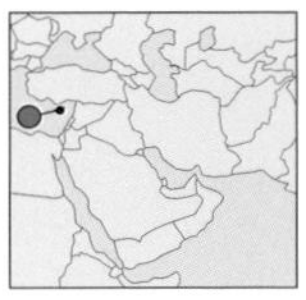

CYPRUS

GEOGRAPHY The Republic of Cyprus is an island nation in the northeastern Mediterranean Sea. Geographers regard it as part of Asia, but it resembles southern Europe in many ways. Its scenic mountain ranges include the southern Troodos Mountains, which reach 6,401 ft [1,951 m] at Mount Olympus, and the Kyrenia range in the north. Between them lies the Mesaoria plain. The climate is Mediterranean, with hot, dry summers and mild, moist winters.

POLITICS & ECONOMY Greeks settled on Cyprus around 3,200 years ago. From AD 330, the island was part of the Byzantine empire. In the 1570s, Cyprus became part of the Turkish Ottoman empire. Turkish rule continued until 1878 when Cyprus was leased to Britain. Britain annexed the island in 1914 and proclaimed it a colony in 1925. In the 1950s, Greek Cypriots, who made up four-fifths of the population, began a campaign for *enosis* (union) with Greece. Their leader was the Greek Orthodox Archbishop Makarios. A secret guerrilla force called EOKA attacked the British, who exiled Makarios in 1956; he returned to Cyprus in 1959.

Cyprus became an independent country in 1960, although Britain retained two military bases. Independent Cyprus had a constitution which provided for power-sharing between the Greek and Turkish Cypriots. But the constitution proved unworkable and fighting broke out between the two communities. In 1964, the United Nations sent in a peacekeeping force, but communal clashes recurred in 1967.

In 1974, Makarios was overthrown by Greek officers and Turkey invaded northern Cyprus. In 1979, the north was proclaimed the Turkish Republic of Northern Cyprus. The only country to recognize this state was Turkey. In 2002, the European Union invited Cyprus to become a member in 2004. In 2004, the people voted on a UN plan to reunify Cyprus. The Turkish-Cypriots voted in favor, but the Greek-Cypriots voted against. As a result, only the south was admitted to EU membership on May 1, 2004. Talks on reunification began in 2008.

Cyprus got its name from the Greek word *kypros*, meaning copper. But little copper remains and the chief minerals today are asbestos and chromium. However, the most valuable activity in Cyprus is tourism. Manufactures include cement, clothes, footwear, tiles, and wine.

In the early 1990s. the United Nations reclassified Cyprus as a developed rather than a developing country, reflecting the rapid economic progress in the south. But the north lagged far behind the prosperous Greek-Cypriot south.

AREA 3,572 SQ MI [9,251 SQ KM]
POPULATION 1,103,000 **CAPITAL** NICOSIA
GOVERNMENT MULTIPARTY REPUBLIC **ETHNIC GROUPS** GREEK CYPRIOT 77%, TURKISH CYPRIOT 18%, OTHERS **LANGUAGES** GREEK AND TURKISH (BOTH OFFICIAL), ENGLISH **RELIGIONS** GREEK ORTHODOX 78%, ISLAM 18%
CURRENCY EURO = 100 CENTS

CZECH REPUBLIC

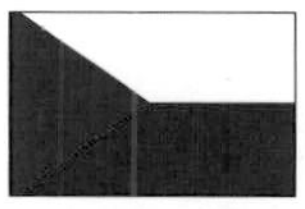

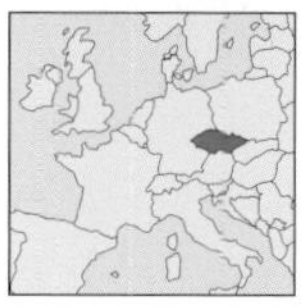

GEOGRAPHY The Czech Republic is the western three-fifths of the former country of Czechoslovakia. It contains two regions: Bohemia in the west and Moravia in the east. Mountains border much of the country in the west. The Bohemian basin in the north-center is a fertile lowland region, with Prague, the capital city, as its main center. Highlands cover much of the center of the country, with lowlands in the southeast.

The climate is influenced by its landlocked position in east-central Europe. Summers are warm and winters cold. The rainfall is moderate.

POLITICS & ECONOMY After World War I (1914–18), Czechoslovakia was created. Germany seized the country in World War II (1939–45). In 1948, Communist leaders took power and Czechoslovakia was allied to the Soviet Union. When democratic reforms were introduced in the Soviet Union in the late 1980s, the Czechs also demanded reforms. Free elections were held in 1990, but differences between the Czechs and Slovaks led to the partitioning of the country on January 1, 1993. The Czech Republic became a member of NATO in 1999 and a member of the European Union on May 1, 2004. Following elections in 2010, Petr Necas, leader of the conservative Civic Democratic Party, became prime minister.

Under Communist rule the Czech Republic became one of the most industrialized parts of Eastern Europe. The country has deposits of coal, uranium, iron ore, magnesite, tin, and zinc. Manufacturing employs about 25% of the Czech Republic's entire work force. Farming is also important. The main crops include barley, fruit, hops for beer-making, maize, potatoes, sugar beet, vegetables, and wheat.

AREA 30,450 SQ MI [78,866 SQ KM]
POPULATION 10,202,000 **CAPITAL** PRAGUE
GOVERNMENT MULTIPARTY REPUBLIC **ETHNIC GROUPS** CZECH 81%, MORAVIAN 13%, SLOVAK 3%, POLISH, GERMAN, SILESIAN, GYPSY, HUNGARIAN, UKRAINIAN **LANGUAGES** CZECH (OFFICIAL) **RELIGIONS** ATHEIST 40%, ROMAN CATHOLIC 39%, PROTESTANT 4%, ORTHODOX 3%, OTHERS
CURRENCY CZECH KORUNA = 100 HALER

DENMARK

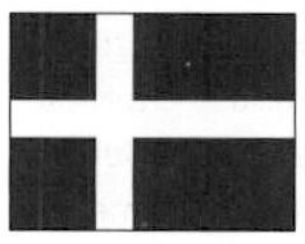

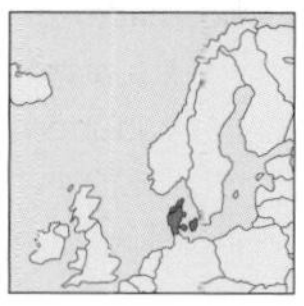

GEOGRAPHY The Kingdom of Denmark is the smallest country in Scandinavia. It consists of a peninsula, called Jutland (or Jylland), which is joined to Germany, and more than 400 islands, 89 of which are inhabited. The land is flat and mostly covered by rocks dropped there by huge ice sheets during the last Ice Age. The highest point in Denmark is on Jutland. It is only 568 ft [173 m] above sea level. Denmark has a mild, moist climate, except during cold spells in winter when The Sound between Sjælland and Sweden may freeze over.

POLITICS & ECONOMY Danish Vikings terrorized much of Western Europe for about 300 years after AD 800. In the late 14th century, Denmark formed a union with Norway and Sweden (which included Finland). Sweden broke away in 1523, while Denmark lost Norway to Sweden in 1814. After 1945, Denmark joined NATO and it became a member of the European Union in 1973. The people of Greenland, a former Danish territory, voted in 2008 for a greater degree of autonomy, and in 2010 it became a self-governing territory. Also in 2010, potentially important oil deposits were confirmed off Greenland's coast.

Denmark is a prosperous country. Reources include some oil and gas. Manufacturing employs 15% of the people. Products include furniture, processed food, machinery, television sets, and textiles. Farming employs 3% of the people, but it is highly scientific. Meat and dairy farming are the chief activities.

AREA 16,639 SQ MI [43,094 SQ KM] **POPULATION** 5,516,000
CAPITAL COPENHAGEN **GOVERNMENT** PARLIAMENTARY MONARCHY
ETHNIC GROUPS SCANDINAVIAN, INUIT, FÆROESE **LANGUAGES** DANISH (OFFICIAL), GREENLANDIC, ENGLISH, FÆROESE **RELIGIONS** EVANGELICAL LUTHERAN 95% **CURRENCY** DANISH KRONE = 100 ØRE

DJIBOUTI

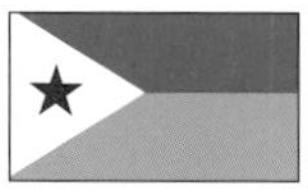

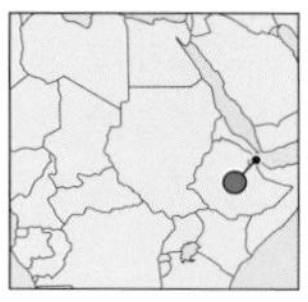

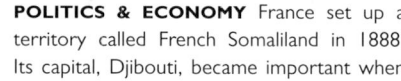

GEOGRAPHY The Republic of Djibouti in eastern Africa occupies a strategic position where the Red Sea meets the Gulf of Aden. Djibouti has one of the world's hottest and driest climates.

POLITICS & ECONOMY France set up a territory called French Somaliland in 1888. Its capital, Djibouti, became important when a railroad was built to Addis Ababa and Djibouti became the main outlet for Ethiopian trade. In 1967, France renamed the dependency the French Territory of the Afars and Issas, but it was renamed Djibouti on independence in 1977. It became a one-party state in 1981, but a new constitution (1992) permitted four parties which had to maintain a balance between the country's ethnic groups. In 2008, a border dispute led to clashes between Djiboutian and Eritrean troops.

Djibouti is a poor country. Its economy is based largely on the revenue it gets from its port and the railroad to Addis Ababa.

AREA 8,958 SQ MI [23,200 SQ KM] **POPULATION** 741,000
CAPITAL DJIBOUTI **GOVERNMENT** MULTIPARTY REPUBLIC
ETHNIC GROUPS SOMALI 60%, AFAR 35% **LANGUAGES** ARABIC AND FRENCH (BOTH OFFICIAL) **RELIGIONS** ISLAM 94%, CHRISTIANITY 6%
CURRENCY DJIBOUTIAN FRANC = 100 CENTIMES

DOMINICA

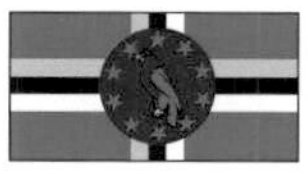

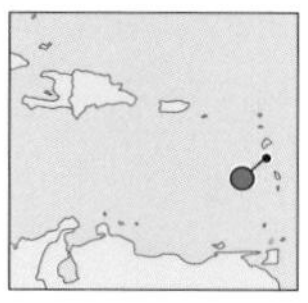

The Commonwealth of Dominica, a former British colony, became independent in 1978. The island has a mountainous spine and less than 10% of the land is cultivated. But agriculture employs 18% of the people. The manufacture of coconut-based soap is important, while tourism and mining are other economic activities.

AREA 290 SQ MI [751 SQ KM] **POPULATION** 73,000 **CAPITAL** ROSEAU

DOMINICAN REPUBLIC

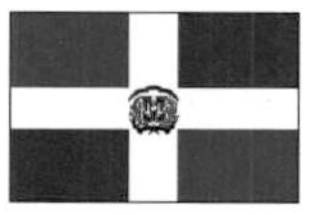

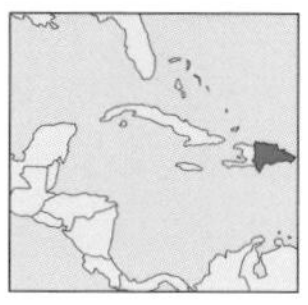

GEOGRAPHY Second largest of the Caribbean nations in both area and population, the Dominican Republic shares the island of Hispaniola with Haiti, with the Dominican Republic occupying the eastern two-thirds. The country is mountainous, and the generally hot and humid climate eases with altitude.

POLITICS & ECONOMY In 1492, Christopher Columbus landed on Hispaniola and Spaniards soon settled the island, followed by the French who occupied the western third of the island (which is now Haiti). The island was held by Haitians from 1822 until 1844, when the Dominican Republic was established. Civil war broke out in 1966 but US intervention ended the conflict. Since 1966, the young democracy has survived violent elections under the watchful eye of the United States.

The Dominican Republic is a developing country and agriculture is the chief activity. Sugarcane, rice, bananas, and cocoa are leading crops. Food processing is also important and some ferronickel is produced.

AREA 18,730 SQ MI [48,511 SQ KM] **POPULATION** 9,824,000
CAPITAL SANTO DOMINGO **GOVERNMENT** MULTIPARTY REPUBLIC
ETHNIC GROUPS MULATTO 73%, WHITE 16%, BLACK 11%
LANGUAGES SPANISH (OFFICIAL) **RELIGIONS** ROMAN CATHOLIC 95%
CURRENCY DOMINICAN PESO = 100 CENTAVOS

EAST TIMOR

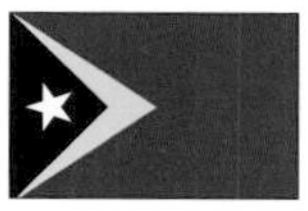

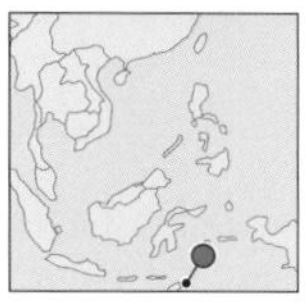

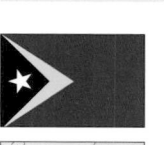

The Republic of East Timor became fully independent on May 20, 2002. The land is mainly rugged. Temperatures are generally high and the rainfall is moderate. Portugal ruled the area from the late 19th century, when it was called Portuguese Timor. Portugal withdrew in 1975 and Indonesia seized the area. Guerrilla activity mounted under Indonesian rule and, in 1999, the people voted for independence. Agriculture is the main activity and East Timor is the poorest country in Southeast Asia. But, in 2006, East Timor and Australia signed a deal to share the revenue from the oil and natural gas deposits under the Timor Sea.

AREA 5,743 SQ MI [14,874 SQ KM] **POPULATION** 1,155,000 **CAPITAL** DILI

ECUADOR

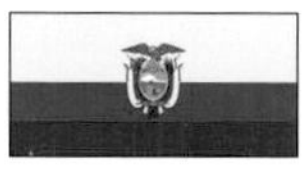

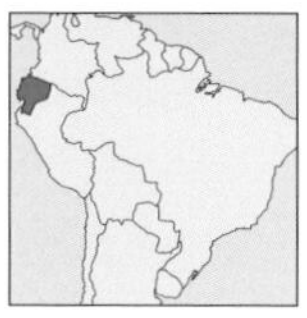

GEOGRAPHY The Republic of Ecuador straddles the Equator on the west coast of South America. Three ranges of the high Andes Mountains form the backbone of the country. Between the towering, snow-capped peaks of the mountains, some of which are volcanoes, lie a series of high plateaux, or basins. Nearly half of Ecuador's population lives on these plateaux. The coast has a warm tropical climate, despite the cold offshore Peruvian Current. Inland, the altitude gives the plateaux spring-like weather throughout the year.

POLITICS & ECONOMY The Inca people of Peru conquered much of what is now Ecuador in the late 15th century. They introduced their language, Quechua, which is widely spoken today. Spanish forces defeated the Incas in 1533 and took control of Ecuador. The country became independent in 1822, following the defeat of a Spanish force in a battle near Quito.

In the 19th and 20th centuries, Ecuador suffered from political instability, while successive governments failed to tackle the country's social and economic problems. A war with Peru in 1941 led to a loss of territory. Disputes continued until 1995, but a border agreement was signed in January 1998. Economic crises in the early 21st century led to the adoption of the US dollar as the official currency. Political instability marred progress. A coup in 2000 was led by Colonel Lucio Gutiérrez, who was elected president in 2002. He was overthrown in 2005. In 2006, the leftist Rafael Correa was elected president. In 2010, a state of emergency was declared following a coup attempt.

The World Bank classifies Ecuador as a "lower-middle-income" developing country. Agriculture employs 8% of the people and bananas, cocoa, and coffee are all important crops. Fishing, forestry, mining, and manufacturing are other activities.

AREA 109,483 SQ MI [283,561 SQ KM]
POPULATION 14,791,000 **CAPITAL** QUITO
GOVERNMENT MULTIPARTY REPUBLIC
ETHNIC GROUPS MESTIZO (MIXED WHITE/AMERINDIAN) 65%, AMERINDIAN 25%, WHITE 7%, BLACK 3%
LANGUAGES SPANISH (OFFICIAL), QUECHUA
RELIGIONS ROMAN CATHOLIC 95%
CURRENCY US DOLLAR = 100 CENTS

EGYPT

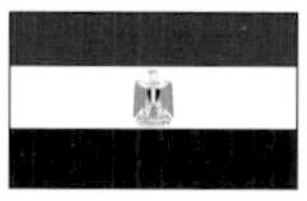

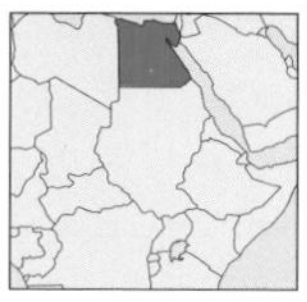

GEOGRAPHY The Arab Republic of Egypt is Africa's second largest country by population after Nigeria, though it ranks 13th in area. Most of Egypt is desert. Almost all the people live either in the Nile Valley and its fertile delta or along the Suez Canal, the artificial waterway between the Mediterranean and Red seas. This canal shortens the sea journey between the United Kingdom and India by 6,027 mi [9,700 km]. Recent attempts have been made to irrigate parts of the western desert and thus redistribute the rapidly growing Egyptian population into previously uninhabited regions.

Apart from the Nile Valley, Egypt has three other main regions. The Western and Eastern deserts are parts of the Sahara. The Sinai peninsula (Es Sina), to the east of the Suez Canal, is a mountainous desert region, geographically within Asia. It contains Egypt's highest peak, Gebel Katherina (8,650 ft [2,637 m]); few people live in this area.

Egypt is a dry country. The low rainfall occurs, if at all, in winter and the country is one of the sunniest places on Earth.

POLITICS & ECONOMY Ancient Egypt, which was founded about 5,000 years ago, was one of the great early civilizations. Throughout the country, pyramids, temples and richly decorated tombs are memorials to its great achievements.

After Ancient Egypt declined, the country came under successive foreign rulers. Arabs occupied Egypt in AD 639–42. They introduced the Arabic language and Islam. Their influence was so great that most Egyptians now regard themselves as Arabs.

Egypt came under British rule in 1882, but it gained partial independence in 1922, becoming a monarchy. The monarchy was abolished in 1952, when Egypt became a republic. The creation of Israel in 1948 led Egypt into a series of wars in 1948–9, 1956, 1967, and 1973. Since the late 1970s, Egypt has sought for peace. In 1979, Egypt signed a peace treaty with Israel and regained the Sinai region which it had lost in a war in 1967. Extremists opposed contacts with Israel and, in 1981, President Sadat, who had signed the treaty, was assassinated.

While Egypt plays a major part in Arab affairs, most of its people are poor. Some Islamic fundamentalists, who dislike Western influences on their way of life, have resorted to violence.

In the 1990s, attacks on foreign visitors caused a decline in the valuable tourist industry. Hosni Mubarak, president since 1981, was forced out of office in February 2011, following huge popular demonstrations. Parliament was dissolved and a Supreme Military Council took power in the run-up to constitutional reform and national elections.

Egypt is Africa's second most industrialized country after South Africa, but most people are poor. Oil and textiles are the country's main exports. In 2007, the government announced plans to build several nuclear power stations to generate electricity.

AREA 386,659 SQ MI [1,001,449 SQ KM] **POPULATION** 80,472,000
CAPITAL Cairo **GOVERNMENT** Republic
ETHNIC GROUPS Egyptians/Bedouins/Berbers 99%
LANGUAGES Arabic (official), French, English
RELIGIONS Islam (mainly Sunni Muslim) 94%, Christianity (mainly Coptic Christian) and others 6%
CURRENCY Egyptian pound = 100 piastres

EL SALVADOR

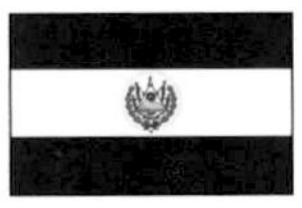

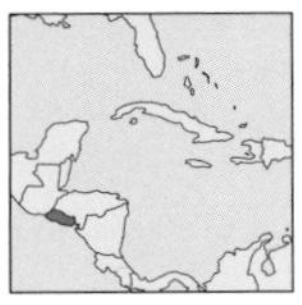

GEOGRAPHY The Republic of El Salvador is the only country in Central America which does not have a coast on the Caribbean Sea. El Salvador has a narrow coastal plain along the Pacific Ocean. Behind the coastal plain, the coastal range is a zone of rugged mountains, including volcanoes, which overlooks a densely populated inland plateau. Beyond the plateau, the land rises to the sparsely populated interior highlands. The coast has a hot, tropical climate. Inland the climate is moderated by the altitude. Rain falls on practically every afternoon between May and October.

POLITICS & ECONOMY Amerindians have lived in El Salvador for thousands of years. The ruins of Mayan pyramids built between AD 100 and 1000 are still found in the western part of the country. Spanish soldiers conquered the area in 1524 and 1525, and Spain ruled until 1821. In 1823, all the Central American countries, except for Panama, set up a Central American Federation. But El Salvador withdrew in 1840 and declared its independence in 1841. El Salvador suffered from instability throughout the 19th century. The 20th century saw a more stable government, but from 1931 military dictatorships alternated with elected governments.

The country remained poor. In the 1970s, protesters demanded that the government introduce reforms to help the poor. Kidnappings and murders committed by left- and right-wing groups caused instability. A civil war broke out in 1979 between the US-backed government forces and left-wing guerrillas. A ceasefire was agreed in 1992. In 2009, Mauricio Funes, a former Marxist rebel and leader of the Farabundo Marti National Liberation Front (FMLN), won the presidential election.

The World Bank classifies El Salvador as a "lower-middle-income" economy. About three-quarters of the country is farmed. Coffee, grown in the highlands, is the main export, followed by sugar and cotton, which grow on the coastal lowlands. Fishing for lobsters and shrimps is important, but manufacturing is on a small scale.

AREA 8,124 SQ MI [21,041 SQ KM]
POPULATION 6,052,000 **CAPITAL** San Salvador
GOVERNMENT Republic **ETHNIC GROUPS** Mestizo (mixed White and Amerindian) 90%, White 9%, Amerindian 1%
LANGUAGES Spanish (official) **RELIGIONS** Roman Catholic 83%
CURRENCY US dollar = 100 cents

EQUATORIAL GUINEA

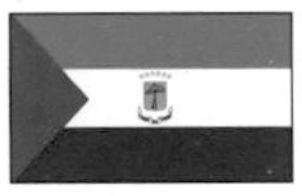

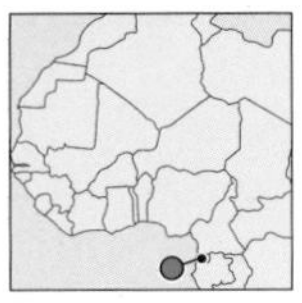

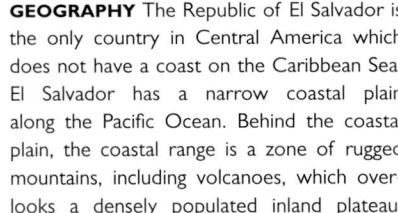

GEOGRAPHY The Republic of Equatorial Guinea is a small republic in west-central Africa. It consists of a mainland territory which makes up 90% of the land area, called Rio Muni, between Cameroon and Gabon, and five offshore islands in the Bight of Bonny, the largest of which is Bioko. The island of Annobon lies 350 mi [560 km] southwest of Rio Muni. Rio Muni consists mainly of hills and plateaux behind the coastal plains.

The climate is hot and humid. Bioko is mountainous, with the land rising to 9,869 ft [3,008 m], and hence it is particularly rainy. However, there is a marked dry season between the months of December and February. Mainland Rio Muni has a similar climate, though the rainfall diminishes inland.

POLITICS & ECONOMY Portuguese navigators reached the area in 1471. In 1778, Portugal granted Bioko, together with rights over Rio Muni, to Spain.

In 1959, Spain made Bioko and Rio Muni provinces of overseas Spain and, in 1963, it gave the provinces a degree of self-government. Equatorial Guinea became independent in 1968.

The first president of Equatorial Guinea, Francisco Macias Nguema, proved to be a tyrant. He was overthrown in 1979 and a group of officers, led by Lieutenant-Colonel Teodoro Obiang Nguema Mbasogo, set up a Supreme Military Council to rule the country. In 1991, a democratic system was restored, but alleged human rights abuses continued. In 2004, a coup attempt was foiled. In 2008, one of its leaders, the Briton Simon Mann, was sentenced to 34 years in prison, but he was pardoned in 2009.

Agriculture employs two-thirds of the people. The most valuable crop is coffee. Oil, which has been produced since 1966, accounts for most of the export revenue.

AREA 10,830 SQ MI [28,051 SQ KM] **POPULATION** 651,000
CAPITAL Malabo **GOVERNMENT** Multiparty republic (transitional)
ETHNIC GROUPS Bubi (on Bioko), Fang (in Rio Muni)
LANGUAGES Spanish and French (both official)
RELIGIONS Christianity **CURRENCY** CFA franc = 100 centimes

ERITREA

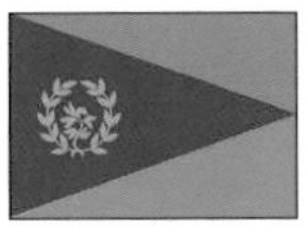

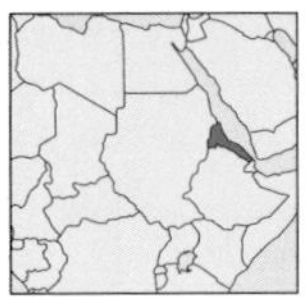

GEOGRAPHY The State of Eritrea consists of a hot, dry coastal plain facing the Red Sea, with a fairly mountainous area in the center. Most people live in the cooler highland area.

POLITICS & ECONOMY From the 1st century AD, Eritrea was part of the ancient Kingdom of Axum, which adopted Christianity in the 4th century AD. It began to decline in the 7th century. The Ottoman Turks took over the area in the 16th century and it became an Italian colony in the 1880s. The Italians were driven out in 1941 and, in 1952, it became part of Ethiopia.

A guerrilla struggle launched in 1961 ended in 1993, when Eritrea became independent. Economic recovery was hampered by conflict with Yemen over three islands in the Red Sea. In 1988–9, clashes occurred along the border with Ethiopia. A peace agreement was signed in 2000, but problems continued. In 2007–8, Eritrea was accused of supporting Islamist forces in Somalia and, in 2008, Eritrean troops clashed with Djiboutian forces over a border dispute, but the countries resolved their disagreement in 2010.

The main economic activities are farming and livestock rearing. The few manufacturing industries are based mainly in Asmara.

AREA 45,405 SQ MI [117,600 SQ KM] **POPULATION** 5,793,000
CAPITAL Asmara **GOVERNMENT** Transitional government
ETHNIC GROUPS Tigrinya 50%, Tigre and Kunama 40%, Afar 4%, Saho 3%, others **LANGUAGES** Afar, Arabic, Tigre, Kunama, Tigrinya **RELIGIONS** Islam, Coptic Christian, Roman Catholic
CURRENCY Nakfa = 100 cents

ESTONIA

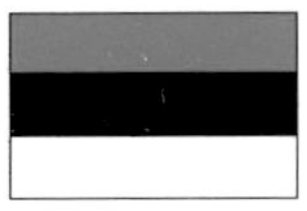

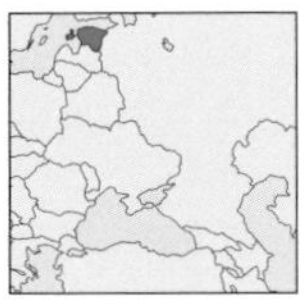

GEOGRAPHY The Republic of Estonia is the smallest of the three states on the Baltic Sea, which were formerly part of the Soviet Union, but which became independent in the early 1990s. Estonia consists of a generally flat plain which was covered by ice sheets during the Ice Age. The land is strewn with moraine (rocks deposited by the ice).

The country is dotted with more than 1,500 small lakes. The large Lake Peipus (Chudskoye Ozero) and the River Narva together make up much of Estonia's eastern border with Russia. The largest of the islands is Saaremaa (Sarema). The climate is fairly mild because of the moderating effects of the sea.

POLITICS & ECONOMY The ancestors of the Estonians, who are related to the Finns, settled in the area several thousand years ago. German crusaders, known as the Teutonic Knights, introduced Christianity in the early 13th century. By the 16th century, German noblemen owned much of the land in Estonia. In 1561, Sweden took the northern part of the country and Poland the south. From 1625, Sweden controlled the entire country until Sweden handed it over to Russia in 1721.

Estonian nationalists campaigned for their independence from around the mid-19th century. Finally, Estonia was proclaimed independent in 1918. In 1919, the government began to break up the large estates and distribute land among the peasants.

In 1939, Germany and the Soviet Union agreed to take over parts of Eastern Europe. In 1940, Soviet forces occupied Estonia, but they were driven out by the Germans in 1941. Soviet troops returned in 1944 and Estonia became one of the 15 Soviet Socialist Republics of the Soviet Union. The Estonians strongly opposed Soviet rule. Many of them were deported to Siberia.

Political changes in the Soviet Union in the late 1980s led to renewed demands for freedom. In 1990, the Estonian government declared the country independent and, finally, the Soviet Union recognized this act in September 1991, shortly before the Soviet Union was dissolved. Estonia adopted a new constitution in 1992, and elections were held. In 1994, Russian troops withdrew, but anti-Russian sentiment continued. On January 1, 2011, Estonia became the 17th member of the eurozone.

Under Soviet rule, Estonia was the most prosperous of the three Baltic states. Since 1988, Estonia has worked to restructure its economy. Turning increasingly to the West, it became a member of both the North Atlantic Treaty Organization and the European Union in 2004. Estonia's resources include oil shale and its forests. Industries produce fertilizers, processed food, machinery, petrochemical products, wood products, and textiles. Agriculture and fishing are also important activities.

AREA 17,413 SQ MI [45,100 SQ KM] **POPULATION** 1,291,000
CAPITAL Tallinn **GOVERNMENT** Multiparty republic
ETHNIC GROUPS Estonian 65%, Russian 28%, Ukrainian 3%, Belarusian 2%, Finnish 1% **LANGUAGES** Estonian (official), Russian
RELIGIONS Lutheran, Russian and Estonian Orthodox, Methodist, Baptist, Roman Catholic **CURRENCY** Euro = 100 cents

ETHIOPIA

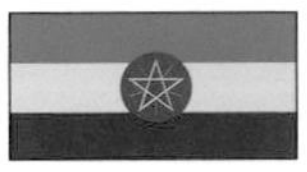

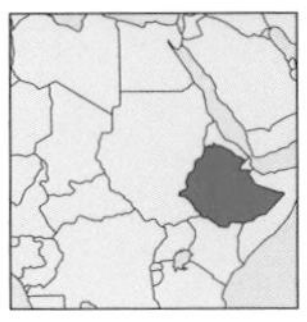

GEOGRAPHY Ethiopia is a landlocked country in northeastern Africa. The land is mainly mountainous, though there are extensive plains in the east, bordering southern Eritrea, and in the south, bordering Somalia. The highlands are divided into two blocks by an arm of the Great Rift Valley which runs throughout eastern Africa. North of the Rift Valley, the land is especially rugged, rising to 15,157 ft [4,620 m] at Ras Dashen. Southeast of Ras Dashen is Lake Tana, source of the River Abay (Blue Nile). The climate is affected by the altitude. The rainfall in the highlands is generally more than 39 inches [1,000 mm]. The lowlands are hot and arid.

POLITICS & ECONOMY Ethiopia was the home of an ancient monarchy, which became Christian in the 4th century. In the 7th century, Muslims gained control of the lowlands, but Christianity survived in the highlands. Ethiopia resisted attempts to colonize it, but Italy invaded the country in 1935. The Italians were driven out in 1941 during World War II.

In 1952, Eritrea, on the Red Sea coast, was federated with Ethiopia. But in 1961, Eritrean nationalists demanded their freedom and began a struggle that ended in their independence in 1993. In 1995, because of Ethiopia's great ethnic diversity, the country was divided into nine provinces, each with its own regional assembly. In 1998, boundary disputes with Eritrea led to conflict. A peace agreement was reached in 2001, but tensions mounted in 2005–6 when Ethiopia failed to accept an international ruling over Badme, a border settlement. In 2006, Ethiopian troops intervened in Somalia on behalf of its provisional government. Ethiopian troops defeated the Islamists, who had taken control of Mogadishu. Ethiopia withdrew its forces in 2009. In 2010, fighting occurred in Ogaden, Ethiopia's Somali region, against militants demanding self-determination.

Ethiopia is one of the world poorest countries. It is heavily dependent on aid. Agriculture is the main activity. Coffee and the drug khat are leading exports.

AREA 426,370 SQ MI [1,104,300 SQ KM]
POPULATION 88,013,000 **CAPITAL** Addis Ababa
GOVERNMENT Federation of nine provinces
ETHNIC GROUPS Oromo 40%, Amhara and Tigre 32%, Sidamo 9%, Shankella 6%, Somali 6%, others **LANGUAGES** Amharic (official), many others **RELIGIONS** Islam 47%, Ethiopian Orthodox 40%, traditional beliefs 12% **CURRENCY** Birr = 100 cents

FALKLAND ISLANDS

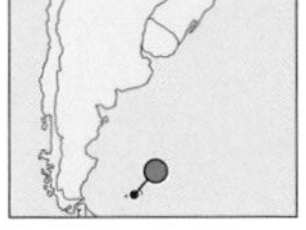

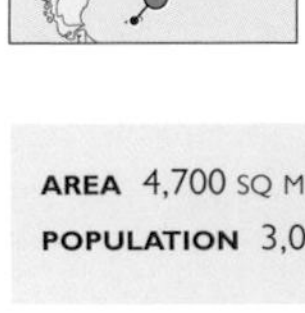

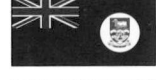

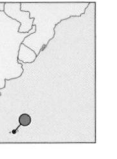

Comprising two main islands and over 200 small islands, the Falkland Islands (or the Islas Malvinas, as they are called in Argentina) lie 300 mi [480 km] from South America. Sheep farming is the main activity, though the search for oil and diamonds holds out hope for the future of this harsh and virtually treeless environment.

AREA 4,700 SQ MI [12,173 SQ KM]
POPULATION 3,000 **CAPITAL** Stanley

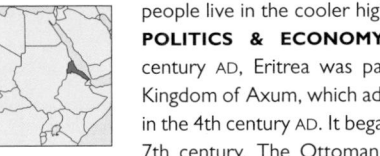

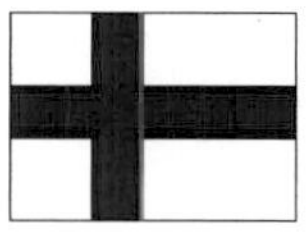

FÆROE ISLANDS

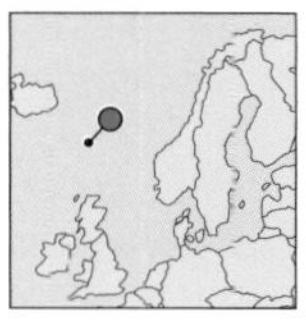

The Færoe Islands are a group of 18 volcanic islands and some reefs in the North Atlantic Ocean. The islands have been Danish since the 1380s, but they became largely self-governing in 1948. In 2001, a referendum on independence was called off after Denmark said that subsidies would end soon after independence.

AREA 540 SQ MI [1,399 SQ KM]
POPULATION 49,000 **CAPITAL** TÓRSHAVN

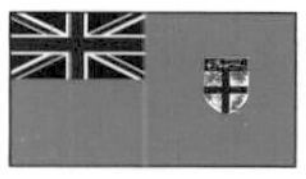

FIJI ISLANDS

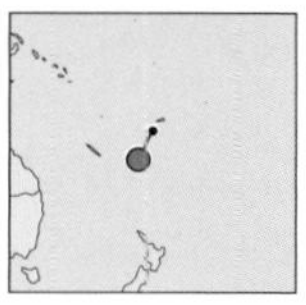

The Fiji Islands (the official name of Fiji since 1998) is a republic consisting of more than 800 Melanesian islands, the biggest being Viti Levu and Vanua Levu. The climate is tropical. A former British colony, Fiji became independent in 1970. Its recent history has been marred by efforts by ethnic Fijians to impose their rule, stopping members of the ethnic Indian community from holding senior cabinet posts. Coups have occurred in 1987, 2000, and 2006.

AREA 7,056 SQ MI [18,274 SQ KM] **POPULATION** 876,000 **CAPITAL** SUVA

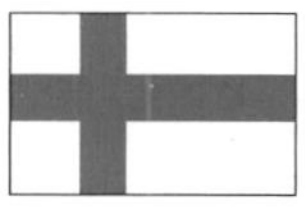

FINLAND

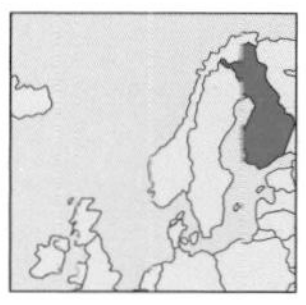

GEOGRAPHY The Republic of Finland is a beautiful country in northern Europe. In the south, behind the coastal lowlands where most Finns live, lies a region of sparkling lakes worn out by ice sheets in the Ice Age. The thinly populated northern uplands cover about two-fifths of the country.

Helsinki, the capital city, has warm summers, but the average temperatures between the months of December and March are below freezing point. Snow covers the land in winter. The north has less precipitation than the south, but it is much colder.

POLITICS & ECONOMY Between 1150 and 1809, Finland was under Swedish rule. The close links between the countries continue today. Swedish remains an official language in Finland and many towns have Swedish as well as Finnish names.

In 1809, Finland became a grand duchy of the Russian empire. It finally declared itself independent in 1917, after the Russian Revolution and the collapse of the Russian empire. But during World War II (1939–45), the Soviet Union declared war on Finland and took part of Finland's territory. Finland allied itself with Germany, but it lost more land to the Soviet Union at the end of the war.

After World War II, Finland became a neutral country and negotiated peace treaties with the Soviet Union. Finland also strengthened its relations with other northern European countries and became an associate member of the European Free Trade Association (EFTA) in 1961. Finland became a full member of EFTA in 1986, but it became a member of the European Union on January 1, 1995. It adopted the euro as its currency in 2002. In 2000 and 2006, the Social Democrat Tarja Halonen was elected Finland's first woman president, while in 2010, Mari Kiviniemi became its second woman prime minister.

Forests are the chief resource and wood, wood products, and paper once dominated the economy. They still make up about a quarter of the exports, but, since World War II, Finland has set up many new industries, producing machinery and transport equipment. The economy has expanded quickly and machinery and apparatus now account for more than a third of the exports.

AREA 130,558 SQ MI [338,145 SQ KM]
POPULATION 5,255,000 **CAPITAL** HELSINKI
GOVERNMENT MULTIPARTY REPUBLIC **ETHNIC GROUPS** FINNISH 93%, SWEDISH 6% **LANGUAGES** FINNISH AND SWEDISH (BOTH OFFICIAL)
RELIGIONS EVANGELICAL LUTHERAN 89% **CURRENCY** EURO = 100 CENTS

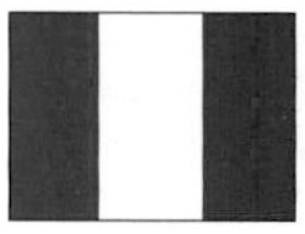

FRANCE

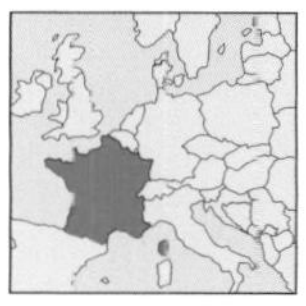

GEOGRAPHY The Republic of France is the largest country in Western Europe. The scenery is extremely varied. The Vosges Mountains overlook the Rhine valley in the northeast, the Jura Mountains and the Alps form the borders with Switzerland and Italy in the southeast, while the Pyrenees straddle France's border with Spain. The only large highland area entirely within France is the Massif Central between the Rhône-Saône valley and the basin of Aquitaine in southern France.

Brittany (Bretagne) and Normandy (Normande) form a scenic hill region. Fertile lowlands cover most of northern France, including the densely populated Paris basin. Another major lowland area, the Aquitanian basin, is in the southwest, while the Rhône-Saône valley and the Mediterranean lowlands are in the southeast.

The climate of France varies from west to east and from north to south. The west comes under the moderating influence of the Atlantic Ocean, giving generally mild weather. To the east, summers are warmer and winters colder. The climate also becomes warmer as one travels from north to south. The Mediterranean Sea coast has hot, dry summers and mild, moist winters. The Alps, Jura, and Pyrenees mountains have snowy winters. Winter sports centers are found in all three areas. Large glaciers occupy high valleys in the Alps.

POLITICS & ECONOMY The Romans conquered France (then called Gaul) in the 50s BC. Roman rule began to decline in the 5th century AD and, in 486, the Frankish realm (as France was called) became independent under a Christian king, Clovis. In 800, Charlemagne, who had been king since 768, became emperor of the Romans. He extended France's boundaries, but, in 843, his empire was divided into three parts and the area of France contracted. After the Norman invasion of England in 1066, large areas of France came under English rule, but this was finally ended in 1453.

France later became a powerful monarchy. But the French Revolution (1789–99) ended absolute rule by French kings. In 1799, Napoleon Bonaparte took power and fought a series of brilliant military campaigns before his final defeat in 1815. The monarchy was restored until 1848, when the Second Republic was founded. In 1852, Napoleon's nephew became Napoleon III, but the Third Republic was established in 1875. France was the scene of much fighting during World War I (1914–18) and World War II (1939–45), causing great loss of life and much damage to the economy.

In 1946, France adopted a new constitution, establishing the Fourth Republic. But political instability and costly colonial wars slowed France's post-war recovery. In 1958, Charles de Gaulle was elected president and he introduced a new constitution, giving the president extra powers and inaugurating the Fifth Republic.

Since the 1960s, France has made rapid economic progress, becoming one of the most prosperous nations in the European Union. But France's government faced a number of problems, including unemployment, pollution, and the growing number of elderly people, who find it difficult to live when inflation rates are high. One social problem concerns the presence in France of large numbers of immigrants from Africa and southern Europe, many of whom live in poor areas.

In 2002, the euro became France's sole unit of currency, replacing the franc. In 2005, France was rocked by inter-ethnic violence and, in 2007, the right-wing Nicolas Sarkozy was elected president. In 2009, he announced that France would rejoin NATO, from which President de Gaulle had withdrawn in 1966.

France is one of the world's most developed countries. Its natural resources include its fertile soil, together with deposits of bauxite, coal, iron ore, oil and natural gas, and potash. France is also one of the world's top manufacturing nations, and it has often innovated in bold and imaginative ways. The TGV and hypermarkets are typical examples. Paris is a world center of fashion industries, but France has many other industrial towns and cities. Major manufactures include aircraft, cars, chemicals, electronic and metal products, machinery, processed food, steel, and textiles.

Agriculture employs about 3% of the people, but France is the largest producer of farm products in Western Europe, producing most of the food it needs. Wheat is the leading crop and livestock farming is of major importance. Fishing and forestry are leading industries, while tourism is a major activity.

AREA 212,934 SQ MI [551,500 SQ KM] **POPULATION** 64,768,000
CAPITAL PARIS **GOVERNMENT** MULTIPARTY REPUBLIC
ETHNIC GROUPS CELTIC, LATIN, ARAB, TEUTONIC, SLAVIC
LANGUAGES FRENCH (OFFICIAL) **RELIGIONS** ROMAN CATHOLIC 85%, ISLAM 8%, OTHERS **CURRENCY** EURO = 100 CENTS

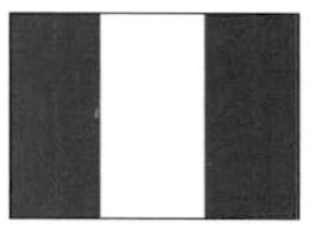

FRENCH GUIANA

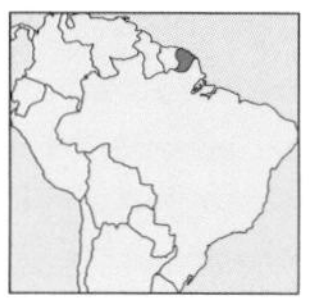

GEOGRAPHY French Guiana is the smallest country in mainland South America. The coastal plain is swampy in places, but some dry areas are cultivated. Inland lies a plateau, with the low Tumachumac Mountains in the south. Most of the rivers run north toward the Atlantic Ocean.

French Guiana has a hot, equatorial climate, with high temperatures throughout the year. The rainfall is heavy, especially between December and June, but it is dry between August and October. The northeast trade winds blow constantly across the country.

POLITICS & ECONOMY The first people to live in what is now French Guiana were Amerindians. Today, only a few of them survive in the interior. The first Europeans to explore the coast arrived in 1500, and they were followed by adventurers seeking El Dorado, the mythical city of gold. Cayenne was founded in 1637 by a group of French merchants. The area became a French colony in the late 17th century.

France used the colony as a penal settlement for political prisoners from the times of the French Revolution in the 1790s. From the 1850s to 1945, the country became notorious as a place where prisoners were harshly treated. Many of them died, unable to survive in the tropical conditions.

In 1946, French Guiana became an overseas department of France, and in 1974 it also became an administrative region. An independence movement developed in the 1980s, but most people want to retain their links with France. In 2010, the people voted in a referendum to reject plans for increased autonomy.

Although it has rich forest and mineral resources, such as bauxite (aluminum ore), French Guiana is a developing country. It depends greatly on France for money to run its services and the government is the country's biggest employer. Since 1968, Kourou in French Guiana, the European Space Agency's rocket-launching site, has earned money for France by sending communications satellites into space.

AREA 34,749 SQ MI [90,000 SQ KM]
POPULATION 203,000 **CAPITAL** CAYENNE
GOVERNMENT OVERSEAS DEPARTMENT OF FRANCE
ETHNIC GROUPS BLACK OR MULATTO 66%, EAST INDIAN/CHINESE AND AMERINDIAN 12%, WHITE 12%, OTHERS 10% **LANGUAGES** FRENCH (OFFICIAL) **RELIGIONS** ROMAN CATHOLIC **CURRENCY** EURO = 100 CENTS

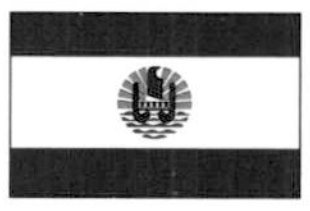

FRENCH POLYNESIA

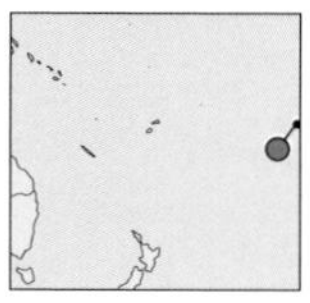

French Polynesia consists of 130 islands, scattered over 1 million sq mi [2.5 million sq km] of the Pacific Ocean. Tribal chiefs in the area agreed to a French protectorate in 1843. They gained increased autonomy in 1984, but the links with France ensure a high standard of living.

AREA 1,544 SQ MI [4,000 SQ KM]
POPULATION 291,000 **CAPITAL** PAPEETE

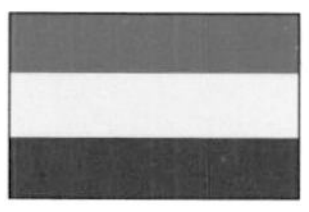

GABON

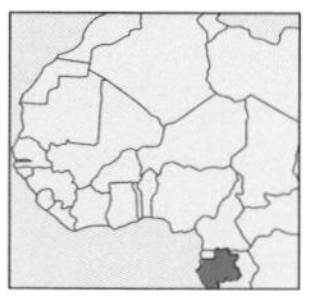

GEOGRAPHY The Gabonese Republic lies on the Equator in west-central Africa. In area, it is a little larger than the United Kingdom, with a coastline 500 mi [800 km] long. Behind the narrow, partly lagoon-lined coastal plain, the land rises to hills, plateaux and mountains divided by deep valleys carved by the River Ogooué and its tributaries.

Most of Gabon has an equatorial climate, with high temperatures and humidity throughout the year. The rainfall is heavy and the skies are often cloudy.

POLITICS & ECONOMY Gabon became a French colony in the 1880s, but it achieved full independence in 1960. In 1964, an attempted coup was put down when French troops intervened and crushed the revolt. In 1967, Bernard-Albert Bongo, who later renamed himself El Hadj Omar Bongo, became president. He declared Gabon a one-party state in 1968. Opposition parties were legalized in 1991, but Bongo was re-elected president in 1993. Following his death in 2008, he was succeeded by his son Ali Ben Bongo, who was elected in 2009.

Gabon's natural resources include its forests, oil and gas deposits, manganese, and uranium. Its mineral deposits make it one of Africa's better-off countries. But agriculture still employs about one-third of the people and many farmers produce little more than they need to support their families.

AREA 103,347 SQ MI [267,668 SQ KM]
POPULATION 1,545,000 **CAPITAL** LIBREVILLE
GOVERNMENT MULTIPARTY REPUBLIC
ETHNIC GROUPS FOUR MAJOR BANTU TRIBES: FANG, BAPOUNOU, NZEBI AND OBAMBA **LANGUAGES** FRENCH (OFFICIAL), FANG, MYENE, NZEBI, BAPOUNOU/ESCHIRA, BANDJABI
RELIGIONS CHRISTIANITY 75%, ANIMIST, ISLAM
CURRENCY CFA FRANC = 100 CENTIMES

GAMBIA, THE

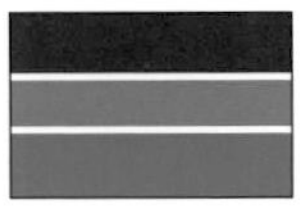

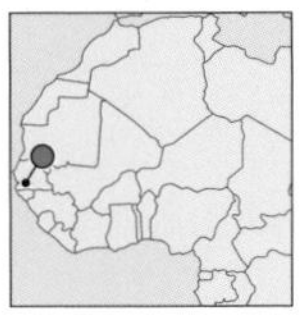

GEOGRAPHY The Republic of The Gambia is the smallest country in mainland Africa. It consists of a narrow strip of land bordering the River Gambia. The Gambia is almost entirely enclosed by Senegal, except along the short Atlantic coastline.

The Gambia has hot and humid summers, but the winter temperatures (November to May) drop to around 61°F [16°C]. In the summer, moist southwesterlies bring rain, which is heaviest on the coast.

POLITICS & ECONOMY English traders bought rights to trade on the River Gambia in 1588, and in 1664 the English established a settlement on an island in the river estuary. In 1765, the British founded Senegambia, which included parts of The Gambia and Senegal. In 1783, Britain handed this colony over to France. In the 19th century, Britain and France discussed the exchange of The Gambia for some other French territory, but an agreement was reached and Britain made The Gambia a British colony in 1888.

The Gambia achieved independence in 1965 and it became a republic in 1970. In 1981, an attempted coup in The Gambia was put down with the help of Senegalese troops. In 1982, The Gambia and Senegal set up a defense alliance, called the Confederation of Senegambia. But this alliance was dissolved in 1989. In 1994, a military group led by Captain Yahya Jammeh overthrew the government of Sir Dawda Jawara. Jammeh became president and was re-elected in 1996, 2001, and 2006.

Agriculture is the chief activity. Food crops include cassava, millet, and sorghum, but groundnuts and groundnut products are the main exports. Tourism is growing and offshore oilfields were discovered in 2004. In the early 21st century, Gambia became a transit point for drugs from Latin America.

AREA 4,361 sq mi [11,295 sq km]
POPULATION 1,824,000 **CAPITAL** Banjul
GOVERNMENT Military regime
ETHNIC GROUPS Mandinka 42%, Fula 18%, Wolof 16%, Jola 10%, Serahuli 9%, others
LANGUAGES English (official), Mandinka, Wolof, Fula
RELIGIONS Islam 90%, Christianity 9%, traditional beliefs 1%
CURRENCY Dalasi = 100 butut

GEORGIA

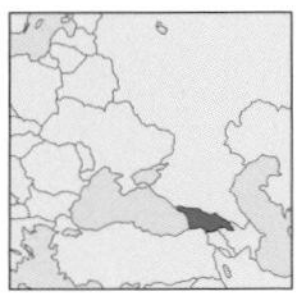

GEOGRAPHY Georgia is a country on the borders of Europe and Asia, facing the Black Sea. The land is rugged with the Caucasus Mountains forming its northern border. The highest mountain in this range, Mount Elbrus (18,510 ft [5,642 m]), lies over the border in Russia. The Black Sea plains have hot summers and mild winters. The rainfall is heavy, though inland areas are drier.

POLITICS & ECONOMY The first Georgian state was set up nearly 2,500 years ago. But for much of its history, the area was ruled by various conquerors. Christianity was introduced in AD 330. Georgia freed itself of foreign rule in the 11th and 12th centuries, but Mongol armies attacked in the 13th century. From the 16th to the 18th centuries, Iran and the Turkish Ottoman empire struggled for control of the area, and in the late 18th century Georgia sought the protection of Russia, and by the early 19th century Georgia was part of the Russian empire. After the Russian Revolution of 1917, Georgia declared its independence, but Russia invaded, making the country part of the Soviet regime. Georgia declared itself independent in 1991. It became a separate country when the Soviet Union was dissolved in December 1991.

Georgia contains three regions containing minority peoples: Abkhazia in the northwest, South Ossetia in north-central Georgia, and Adjaria (also spelled Adzharia) in the southwest. Civil war broke out in South Ossetia in the early 1990s, while fierce fighting continued in Abkhazia until the late 1990s. In 2000, Georgia agreed to recognize Adjaria's autonomy in the country's constitution. In 2003, the pro-Western Mikhail Saakashvili was elected president following the "Rose Revolution." Following Saakashvili's re-election in 2008, relations with Russia deteriorated. In August 2008, Georgia tried to retake South Ossetia by force. Russian troops counter-attacked and drove Georgian troops out of South Ossetia and Abkhazia. Despite Georgian and Western protests, Russia recognized both of these breakaway regions as independent nations.

Georgia is a developing country. Agriculture, food processing, and perfume-making are important activities. Products include barley, citrus fruits, grapes for wine-making, maize, tea, tobacco, and vegetables. Sheep and cattle are reared.

AREA 26,911 sq mi [69,700 sq km]
POPULATION 4,601,000 **CAPITAL** Tbilisi
GOVERNMENT Multiparty republic
ETHNIC GROUPS Georgian 70%, Armenian 8%, Russian 6%, Azeri 6%, Ossetian 3%, Greek 2%, Abkhaz 2%, others 3%
LANGUAGES Georgian (official), Russian
RELIGIONS Georgian Orthodox 65%, Islam 11%, Russian Orthodox 10%, Armenian Apostolic 8% **CURRENCY** Lari = 100 tetri

GERMANY

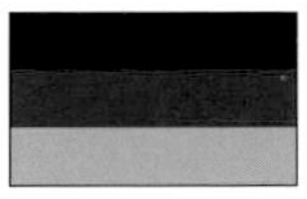

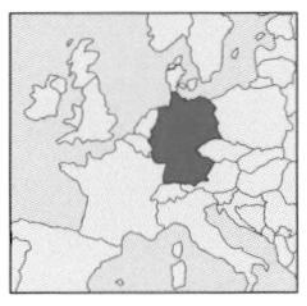

GEOGRAPHY The Federal Republic of Germany is the fourth largest country in Western Europe, after France, Spain, and Sweden. The North German plain borders the North Sea in the northwest and the Baltic Sea in the northeast. Major rivers draining the plain include the Weser, Elbe, and Oder.

The central highlands include the Harz Mountains, the Thuringian Forest (Thüringer Wald), the Ore Mountains (Erzgebirge), and the Bohemian Forest (Böhmerwald) on the Czech border. The Bavarian Alps in the south contain Germany's highest peak, Zugspitze, at 9,718 ft [2,962 m] above sea level. The Black Forest (Schwarzwald) in the southwest overlooks the River Rhine. Northwestern Germany has a mild climate, but the Baltic coasts are cooler. To the south, the climate becomes more continental, especially in the highlands. The precipitation is greatest on the uplands, with snow in winter.

POLITICS & ECONOMY Germany and its allies were defeated in World War I (1914–18) and the country became a republic. Adolf Hitler came to power in 1933 and ruled as a dictator. His order to invade Poland led to the start of World War II (1939–45), which ended with Germany in ruins.

In 1945, Germany was divided into four military zones. In 1949, the American, British, and French zones were amalgamated to form the Federal Republic of Germany (West Germany), while the Soviet zone became the German Democratic Republic (East Germany), a Communist state. Berlin, which had also been partitioned, became a divided city. West Berlin was part of West Germany, while East Berlin became the capital of East Germany. Bonn was the capital of West Germany.

Tension between East and West mounted during the Cold War, but West Germany rebuilt its economy quickly. In East Germany, the recovery was less rapid. In the late 1980s, reforms in the Soviet Union led to unrest in East Germany. Free elections were held in East Germany in 1990 and, on October 3, 1990, Germany was reunited.

The united Germany adopted West Germany's official name, the Federal Republic of Germany. In the 1990s, the government faced many problems, especially those arising from reunification. In 1999, the parliament moved from Bonn to a reconstructed Reichstag building in Berlin. In 2005, Angela Merkel became Germany's first female Chancellor. She was swept back into power in elections in 2009.

West Germany's "economic miracle" after World War II was greatly helped by foreign aid. Today, Germany is one of the world's top economic powers. Manufacturing is the mainstay of the economy and manufactured goods are the chief exports. Cars and other vehicles, cement, chemicals, computers, electrical equipment, processed food, machinery, scientific instruments, ships, steel, textiles, and tools are manufactured. Germany has some coal, potash, and rock salt deposits, but it imports many industrial raw materials. Germany also imports food. Leading products include fruits, grapes for wine-making, potatoes, sugar beet, and vegetables. Livestock include beef and dairy cattle.

AREA 137,846 sq mi [357,022 sq km]
POPULATION 82,283,000 **CAPITAL** Berlin
GOVERNMENT Federal multiparty republic
ETHNIC GROUPS German 92%, Turkish 3%, Serbo-Croatian, Italian, Greek, Polish, Spanish **LANGUAGES** German (official)
RELIGIONS Protestant (mainly Lutheran) 34%, Roman Catholic 34%, Islam 4%, others **CURRENCY** Euro = 100 cents

GHANA

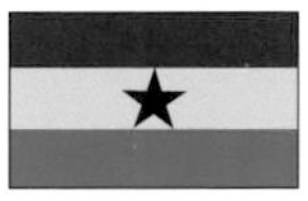

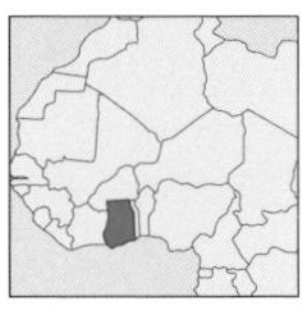

GEOGRAPHY The Republic of Ghana faces the Gulf of Guinea in West Africa. This hot country, just north of the Equator, was formerly called the Gold Coast. Behind the thickly populated southern coastal plains, which are lined with lagoons, lies a plateau region in the southwest.

Accra has a hot, tropical climate. Rain occurs all through the year, though Accra is drier than areas inland.

POLITICS & ECONOMY Portuguese explorers reached the area in 1471 and named it the Gold Coast. The area became a center of the slave trade in the 17th century. The slave trade was ended in the 1860s and, gradually, the British took control of the area. After independence in 1957, attempts were made to develop the economy by creating large state-owned manufacturing industries. But debt and corruption, together with falls in the price of cocoa, the chief export, caused economic problems. This led to instability and frequent coups. In 1981, power was invested in a Provisional National Defense Council, led by Flight-Lieutenant Jerry Rawlings.

The government steadied the economy and introduced reforms. In 1992, a new constitution, allowing for multiparty elections was adopted. Rawlings was elected president in 1992 and 1996. He retired in 2002 and was succeeded as president by John Ageykum Kufuor. In 2008, opposition leader John Atta-Mills was narrowly elected president. The World Bank classifies Ghana as a "low-income" developing country. Most people are poor and farming employs 50% of the population.

AREA 92,098 sq mi [238,533 sq km] **POPULATION** 24,340,000
CAPITAL Accra **GOVERNMENT** Republic
ETHNIC GROUPS Akan 44%, Moshi-Dagomba 16%, Ewe 13%, Ga 8%, Gurma 3%, Yoruba 1% **LANGUAGES** English (official), Akan, Moshi-Dagomba, Ewe, Ga **RELIGIONS** Christianity 63%, traditional beliefs 21%, Islam 16% **CURRENCY** Cedi = 100 pesewas

GIBRALTAR

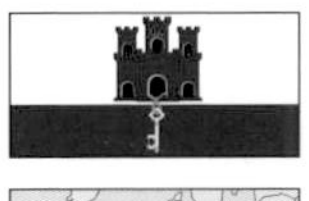

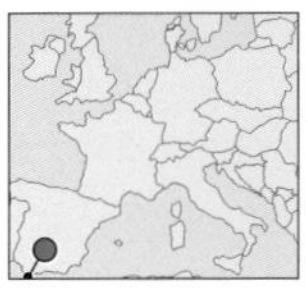

Gibraltar occupies a strategic position on the south coast of Spain where the Mediterranean meets the Atlantic. It was recognized as a British possession in 1713 and, despite Spanish claims, its population has consistently voted to retain its contacts with Britain.

AREA 2.3 sq mi [6 sq km]
POPULATION 29,000 **CAPITAL** Gibraltar Town

GREECE

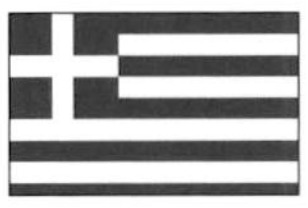

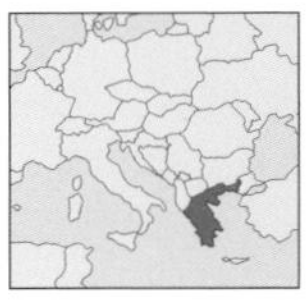

GEOGRAPHY The Hellenic Republic, as Greece is officially called, is a rugged country situated at the southern end of the Balkan peninsula. Olympus, at 9,570 ft [2,917 m] is the highest peak. Islands make up about a fifth of the land.

Low-lying areas in Greece have mild, moist winters and hot, dry summers. The east coast has more than 2,700 hours of sunshine a year and only about half of the rainfall of the west. The mountains have a much more severe climate, with snow on the higher slopes in winter.

POLITICS & ECONOMY Around 2,500 years ago, Greece became the birthplace of Western civilization, and Ancient Greek ruins and art still attract millions of tourists to the country. The first civilization, the Minoan, was centered on Crete. It flourished between about 3000 and 1400 BC. Following the end of the related Mycaenean period on the mainland (1580–1100 BC), a "dark age" lasted until about 800 BC. But from 750 BC, Greeks became rich traders and the city-state of Athens reached its peak in 461–431 BC. Greece became a Roman province in 146 BC and, in AD 365, it became part of the Byzantine Empire.

The Byzantine empire fell to the Turks in 1453. But Greece became an independent monarchy in 1830. After World War II (1939–45), when Germany ruled Greece, a civil war broke out between Greek Communists and nationalists. It ended in 1949 and a military dictatorship seized power in 1967. The monarchy was abolished in 1973 and democracy was restored in 1974. Greece joined the European Community (now the European Union) in 1981 and, on January 1, 2002, the euro became the sole unit of currency in Greece. In 2010, its government faced a debt crisis and was forced to take drastic emergency measures.

Greece is one of the EU's less economically developed members. Manufactured products include processed food, cement, chemicals, metal products, textiles, and tobacco. Greece also mines lignite (brown coal), bauxite, and chromite. Farmland covers about a third of the country and pasture 40%. Crops include barley, grapes, dried fruits, olives, potatoes, sugar beet, and wheat. Livestock farming is important and tourism is a major industry.

AREA 50,949 sq mi [131,957 sq km]
POPULATION 10,750,000 **CAPITAL** Athens
GOVERNMENT Multiparty republic **ETHNIC GROUPS** Greek 98%
LANGUAGES Greek (official) **RELIGIONS** Greek Orthodox 98%
CURRENCY Euro = 100 cents

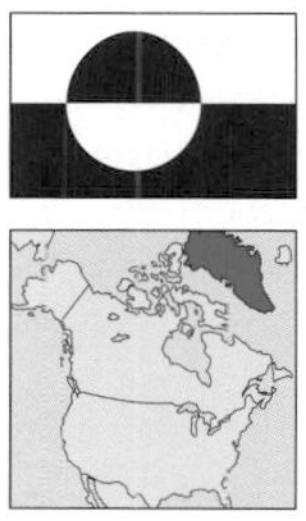

GREENLAND

Greenland is the world's largest island. Settlements are confined to the coast, because an ice sheet covers four-fifths of the land. Greenland became a Danish possession in 1380. Full internal self-government was granted in 1981 and, in 2009, Greenland became a self-governing territory, though it remains dependent on Danish subsidies.

AREA 838,999 sq mi [2,175,600 sq km]
POPULATION 58,000 **CAPITAL** Nuuk

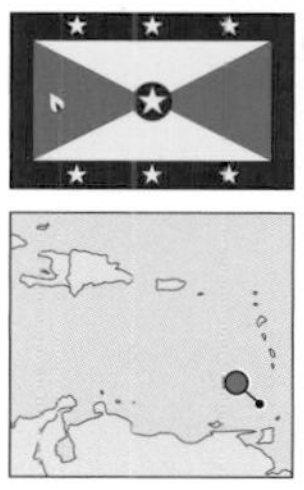

GRENADA

The most southerly of the Windward Islands in the Caribbean Sea, Grenada became independent from the UK in 1974. A military group seized power in 1983, when the prime minister was killed. US troops intervened and restored order and constitutional government.

AREA 133 sq mi [344 sq km]
POPULATION 108,000 **CAPITAL** St George's

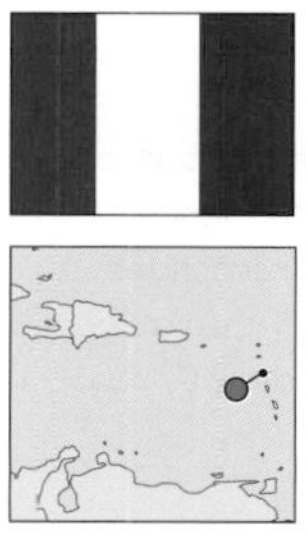

GUADELOUPE

Guadeloupe is a French overseas department which includes seven Caribbean islands, the largest of which is Basse-Terre. French aid has helped to mantain a reasonable standard of living for the people.

AREA 658 sq mi [1,705 sq km]
POPULATION 453,000 **CAPITAL** Basse-Terre

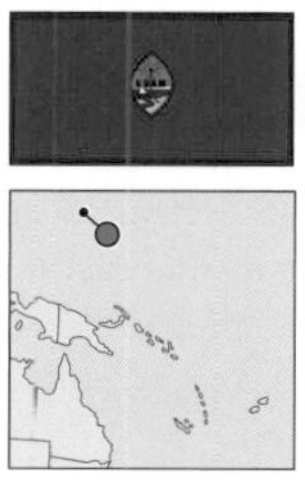

GUAM

Guam, a strategically important "unincorporated territory" of the USA, is the largest of the Mariana Islands in the Pacific Ocean. It is composed of a coralline limestone plateau.

AREA 212 sq mi [549 sq km]
POPULATION 181,000 **CAPITAL** Agana

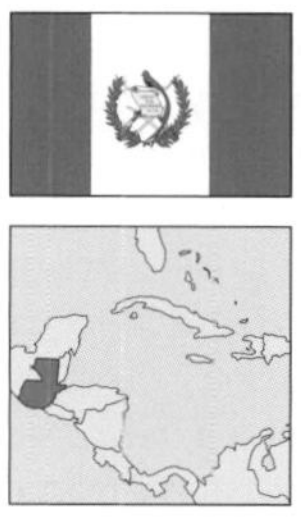

GUATEMALA

GEOGRAPHY The Republic of Guatemala in Central America contains a thickly populated mountain region, with fertile soils. The mountains, which run in an east–west direction, contain many volcanoes, some of which are active. Volcanic eruptions and earthquakes are common in the highlands. South of the mountains lie the thinly populated Pacific coastlands, while a large inland plain occupies the north.

The lowlands of Guatemala are hot and rainy, but the central highlands are cooler and drier. Guatemala City has a pleasant, warm climate with a dry season between November and April.

POLITICS & ECONOMY Much of what is now Guatemala was part of the Maya empire which thrived between AD 300 and 900. Spain ruled the area from the 1520s until 1821. In 1823, Guatemala joined the Central American Federation. But it became fully independent in 1839. Instability and periodic violence have marred its progress. Guatemala has a long-standing claim over Belize, but this was reduced in 1983 to the southern fifth of the country. Between 1960 and 1996, civil war occurred between left-wing groups, including many Amerindians, and government forces. The war claimed perhaps 200,000 lives. In 2004, the government paid US$3.5 million to victims of state-sponsored oppression. In 2007, Alvaro Colom, a center-left politician, became president.

Guatemala is ranked as a "lower-middle-income" economy. Agriculture employs 38% of the population. Coffee, sugar, bananas, and beef are exported, and the spice cardamom and cotton are also important. Maize is the main food crop.

AREA 42,042 sq mi [108,889 sq km]
POPULATION 13,550,000 **CAPITAL** Guatemala City
GOVERNMENT Republic **ETHNIC GROUPS** Ladino (mixed Hispanic and Amerindian) 55%, Amerindian 43%, others 2%
LANGUAGES Spanish (official), Amerindian languages
RELIGIONS Christianity, indigenous Mayan beliefs
CURRENCY US dollar; Quetzal = 100 centavos

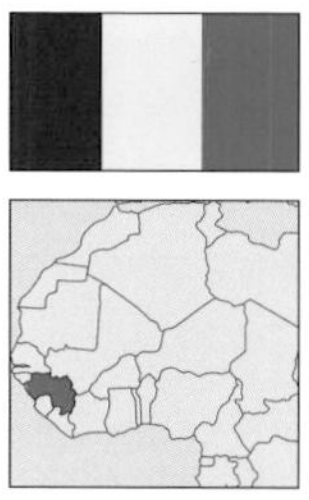

GUINEA

GEOGRAPHY The Republic of Guinea faces the Atlantic Ocean in West Africa. A flat, swampy plain borders the coast. Behind this plain, the land rises to a plateau region called Fouta Djalon. The Upper Niger plains, named after one of Africa's longest rivers, the Niger, which rises there, are in the northeast.

Guinea has a tropical climate and Conakry has its rainy period between May and November, the coolest season. In the dry season, hot harmattan winds blow from the Sahara.

POLITICS & ECONOMY Guinea came under the influence of several medieval African states, including Ancient Ghana and Ancient Mali. France began to control the area in the late 19th century. Guinea became independent in 1958. Its leaders pursued socialist policies but resorted to repressive measures to hold on to power. A military regime under Lansana Conté took over in 1984, but a multiparty system was restored in 1992. Conté was elected president in 1993, 1998, and 2002. But following Conté's death in 2008, an army group led by Captain Mousa Dadis Camara seized power. But in 2010, Alpha Condé was elected president in Guinea's first democratic election since independence.

Guinea is a "low-income" developing country. Its resources include bauxite (aluminum ore), diamonds, gold, iron ore, and uranium. Bauxite and alumina (processed bauxite) account for more than half of the exports. Agriculture employs more than 70% of the people, but most farmers are poor. Manufactures include alumina, processed food, and textiles.

AREA 94,925 sq mi [245,857 sq km]
POPULATION 10,324,000 **CAPITAL** Conakry
GOVERNMENT Multiparty republic
ETHNIC GROUPS Peuhl 40%, Malinke 30%, Soussou 20%, others 10% **LANGUAGES** French (official)
RELIGIONS Islam 85%, Christianity 8%, traditional beliefs 7%
CURRENCY Guinean franc = 100 cauris

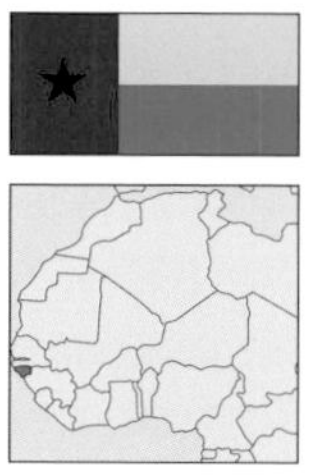

GUINEA-BISSAU

GEOGRAPHY The Republic of Guinea-Bissau, formerly known as Portuguese Guinea, is a small country in West Africa. The land is mostly low-lying, with a broad, swampy coastal plain and many flat offshore islands. The country has a tropical climate, with a dry season (December to May) and a wet season (June to November).

POLITICS & ECONOMY Portuguese explorers reached Guinea-Bissau in 1446 and the area became a center of the slave trade. From 1836, Portugal administered Guinea-Bissau with the Cape Verde Islands but, in 1879, the territories were separated. Guinea-Bissau became a separate colony called Portuguese Guinea. But economic development in the colony was slow.

In 1956, African nationalists in Portuguese Guinea and Cape Verde founded the African Party for the Independence of Guinea and Cape Verde (PAIGC). The PAIGC began a guerrilla war in 1963 and, by 1968, it held two-thirds of the country. In 1972, a rebel National Assembly, elected by the people in the PAIGC-controlled area, voted to make the country independent as Guinea-Bissau.

In 1974, newly independent Guinea-Bissau faced many problems arising from its underdeveloped economy and its lack of trained people to work in the administration. One objective of the leaders of Guinea-Bissau was to unite their country with Cape Verde. But, in 1980, army leaders overthrew Guinea-Bissau's government. The Revolutionary Council, which took over, opposed unification with Cape Verde. Guinea-Bissau ceased to be a one-party state in 1991 and multiparty elections were held in 1994. Civil war broke out in 1998 and a military coup occurred in 1999. Elections were held in 2000. Another coup occurred in 2003, but civilian government was restored in 2004. In 2005, a former military leader, Joao Bernardo Vieira, became president but he was assassinated in 2009. A former president, Malam Bacai Sanha, was elected president in July 2009.

Agriculture employs 76% of the people. Crops include coconuts, groundnuts, maize, and rice. The country is a major hub for drug trafficking between Latin America and Europe.

AREA 13,948 sq mi [36,125 sq km]
POPULATION 1,565,000 **CAPITAL** Bissau
GOVERNMENT "Interim" government
ETHNIC GROUPS Balanta 30%, Fula 20%, Manjaca 14%, Mandinga 13%, Papel 7% **LANGUAGES** Portuguese (official), Crioulo
RELIGIONS Traditional beliefs 50%, Islam 45%, Christianity 5%
CURRENCY CFA franc = 100 centimes

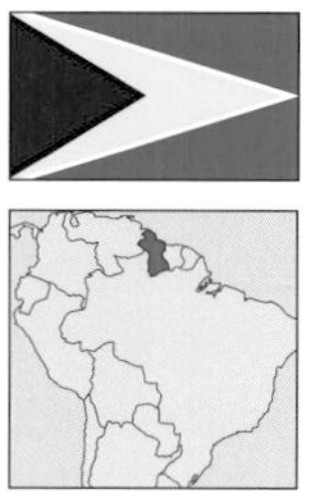

GUYANA

GEOGRAPHY The Cooperative Republic of Guyana is a country facing the Atlantic Ocean in northeastern South America. The coastal plain is flat and much of it is below sea level.

The climate is hot and humid, though the interior highlands are cooler than the coast. The rainfall is heavy, occurring on more than 200 days a year.

POLITICS & ECONOMY Britain gained control of the area in 1814 and ruled British Guiana until it became independent as Guyana in 1966. A black lawyer, Forbes Burnham, was the first prime minister. Under a new constitution adopted in 1980, the president's powers were increased. Burnham became president and served in this post until he died in 1985. He was succeeded by Hugh Desmond Hoyte, who was defeated in 1993 by an ethnic Indian, Cheddi Jagan. Jagan died in 1997 and was succeeded by his wife, Janet. In 1999, Bharrat Jagdeo was elected president. He was re-elected in 2001 and again in 2006.

Guyana is a poor country. Its resources include gold, bauxite (aluminum ore) and other minerals, forests, and fertile soils. Sugarcane and rice are leading crops. Guyana has potential for producing hydroelectricity from its many rivers.

AREA 83,000 sq mi [214,969 sq km]
POPULATION 748,000 **CAPITAL** Georgetown
GOVERNMENT Multiparty republic
ETHNIC GROUPS East Indian 50%, Black 36%, Amerindian 7%, others 7% **LANGUAGES** English (official), Creole, Hindi, Urdu
RELIGIONS Christianity 50%, Hinduism 35%, Islam 10%, others 5%
CURRENCY Guyanese dollar = 100 cents

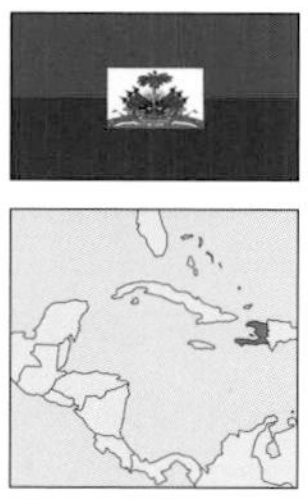

HAITI

GEOGRAPHY The Republic of Haiti occupies the western third of Hispaniola in the Caribbean. The land is mainly mountainous. The climate is hot and humid, though the northern highlands, with about 79 inches [200 mm], have more than twice as much rainfall as the southern coast.

POLITICS & ECONOMY Visited by Christopher Columbus in 1492, Haiti was later developed by the French. The African slaves revolted in 1791 and the country became independent in 1804. Haiti subsequently suffered from instability, violence, and dictatorial rule. Elections in 1990 returned Jean-Bertrand Aristide as president, but he was overthrown in 1991. In 1995, René Préval was elected president, but Aristide was again elected president in 2000. In 2004, rebel activity forced Aristide to flee the country. A US-backed government was set up to restore order and, in 2006, René Préval was re-elected president. In January 2010, an earthquake hit Port-au-Prince, killing about 230,000 people and devastating the economy.

AREA 10,714 sq mi [27,750 sq km]
POPULATION 9,649,000 **CAPITAL** Port-au-Prince
GOVERNMENT Multiparty republic **ETHNIC GROUPS** Black 95%, Mulatto/White 5% **LANGUAGES** French and Creole (both official)
RELIGIONS Roman Catholic 80%, Voodoo
CURRENCY Gourde = 100 centimes

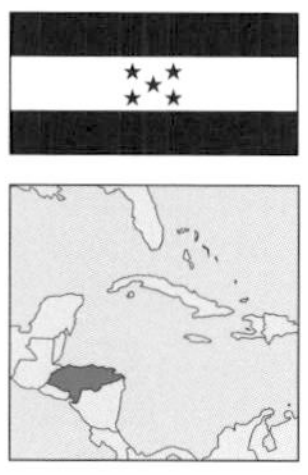

HONDURAS

GEOGRAPHY The Republic of Honduras is the second largest country in Central America. The northern coast on the Caribbean Sea extends more than 373 mi [600 km], but the Pacific coast in the southeast is only about 50 mi [80 km] long. Honduras has a tropical climate, but the highlands are cooler. The rainiest months are between May and November. Hurricanes often hit the north coast. Hurricane Mitch in 1998 caused the worst destruction in modern times.

POLITICS & ECONOMY Western Honduras was part of the Maya empire which flourished between AD 300 and 900. Christopher Columbus claimed the area for Spain in 1502 and Spain ruled from 1625 until 1821. Honduras became part of the Central American Federation but withdrew in 1838.

In the 1890s, American companies developed plantations to grow bananas and Honduras became known as a "banana state." But instability slowed economic progress. Since 1980, civilian governments friendly toward the United States have ruled Honduras, but in 2008 Honduras joined the "Bolivarian Alternative to the Americas," a left-wing alliance headed by Venezuelan President Hugo Chavez. A military coup in 2009 removed

President Manuel Zelaya from office. In elections in November 2009, Porfiro Lobo was elected president.

Honduras is a developing country. Its few resources include silver, lead, and zinc. Agriculture is the main activity. Bananas and coffee are exported and maize is the chief food crop. Honduras is one of Central America's least industrialized countries. Products include processed food, textiles, and wood products.

AREA 43,277 sq mi [112,088 sq km]
POPULATION 7,989,000 **CAPITAL** Tegucigalpa
GOVERNMENT Republic **ETHNIC GROUPS** Mestizo 90%, Amerindian 7%, Black (including Black Carib) 2%, White 1% **LANGUAGES** Spanish (official), Amerindian dialects **RELIGIONS** Roman Catholic 97%
CURRENCY Honduran lempira = 100 centavos

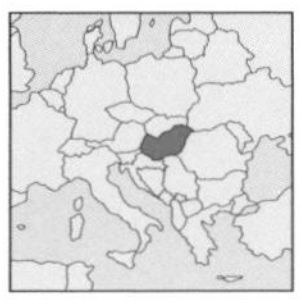

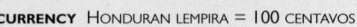

HUNGARY

GEOGRAPHY The Hungarian Republic is a landlocked country in central Europe. The land is mostly low-lying and drained by the Danube (Duna) and its tributary, the Tisza. Most of the land east of the Danube belongs to a region called the Great Plain (Nagyalföld), which covers about half of Hungary.

Hungary lies far from the moderating influence of the sea. As a result, summers are warmer and sunnier, and the winters colder than in Western Europe.

POLITICS & ECONOMY Hungary entered World War II (1939–45) in 1941, as an ally of Germany, but the Germans occupied the country in 1944. The Soviet Union invaded Hungary in 1944 and, in 1946, the country became a republic. The Communists gradually took over the government, taking complete control in 1949. From 1949, Hungary was an ally of the Soviet Union. In 1956, Soviet troops crushed an anti-Communist revolt. But in the 1980s, reforms in the Soviet Union led to the growth of anti-Communist groups in Hungary. In 1989, Hungary adopted a new constitution making it a multiparty state. Elections held in 1990 led to a victory for the non-Communist Democratic Forum. In 2002, the Hungarian Socialist Party, in alliance with the liberal Free Democrats, won a majority in parliament. In 2004, Hungary became a member of both the North Atlantic Treaty Organization and the European Union.

Before World War II, Hungary's economy was based mainly on agriculture. But the Communists set up many manufacturing industries. From the late 1980s, private ownership increased. This caused problems, including inflation and high rates of unemployment. Elections in 2010 resulted in victory for the center-right Fidezs Party led by Viktor Oban, though 17% of voters supported the far-right Jobbik Party. Leading manufactures include aluminum, chemicals, electrical and electronic goods, and telecommunications equipment.

AREA 35,920 sq mi [93,032 sq km]
POPULATION 9,992,000 **CAPITAL** Budapest
GOVERNMENT Multiparty republic
ETHNIC GROUPS Magyar 90%, Gypsy, German, Serb, Romanian, Slovak **LANGUAGES** Hungarian (official)
RELIGIONS Roman Catholic 68%, Calvinist 20%, Lutheran 5%, others **CURRENCY** Forint = 100 fillér

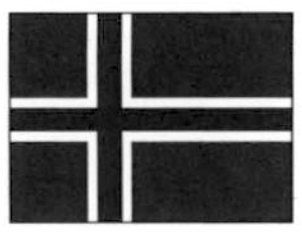

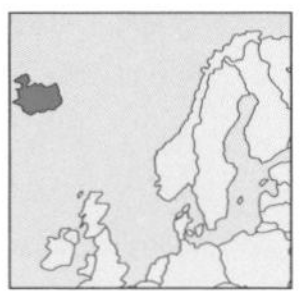

ICELAND

GEOGRAPHY The Republic of Iceland, in the North Atlantic Ocean, is closer to Greenland than Scotland. Iceland sits astride the Mid-Atlantic Ridge. It is slowly getting wider as the ocean is being stretched apart by continental drift.

Iceland has around 200 volcanoes, and eruptions are frequent. An eruption under the Vatnajökull ice cap in 1996 created a subglacial lake which subsequently burst, causing severe flooding. Geysers and hot springs are common, and in 2010 a volcanic eruption and its resulting ash cloud disrupted international air services. Ice caps and glaciers cover about an eighth of the land. The only habitable regions are the coastal lowlands. Despite its northerly position, Iceland's climate is moderated by the warm waters of the Gulf Stream. The port of Reykjavik is ice-free all year round.

POLITICS & ECONOMY Norwegian Vikings colonized Iceland in AD 874, and in 930 the settlers founded the world's oldest parliament, the Althing.

Iceland united with Norway in 1262. But when Norway united with Denmark in 1380, Iceland came under Danish rule. Iceland became a self-governing kingdom, united with Denmark, in 1918. It became a fully independent republic in 1944, following a referendum in which 97% of the people voted to break their country's ties with Denmark. Iceland has played a leading part in European affairs and is a member of the North Atlantic Treaty Organization. But it has been involved in fishing and whaling disputes. Iceland has few resources besides its fishing grounds, and fishing and fish processing dominate Iceland's overseas trade. Barely 1% of the land is used to grow crops, but 23% of the country can be used for grazing sheep and cattle. Vegetables and fruit are grown in greenhouses, heated by water from the hot springs. Iceland's economy was hit by the global financial crisis of 2008–9, causing the collapse of its currency and banking system. In 2009, Johanna Sigurdardottir became Iceland's first female prime minister and Iceland applied for membership of the European Union.

AREA 39,768 sq mi [103,000 sq km]
POPULATION 309,000 **CAPITAL** Reykjavik
GOVERNMENT Multiparty republic
ETHNIC GROUPS Icelandic 97%, Danish 1%
LANGUAGES Icelandic (official) **RELIGIONS** Evangelical Lutheran 87%, other Protestant 4%, Roman Catholic 2%, others
CURRENCY Icelandic króna = 100 aurar

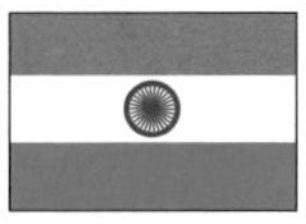

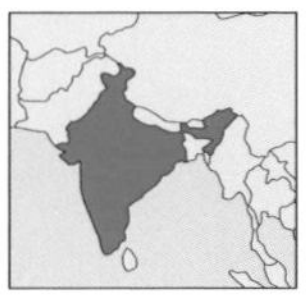

INDIA

GEOGRAPHY The Republic of India is the world's seventh largest country. In population, it ranks second only to China. The north is mountainous, with mountains and foothills of the Himalayan range. Rivers, such as the Brahmaputra and Ganges (Ganga), rise in the Himalaya and flow across the fertile northern plains. Southern India consists of a large plateau, called the Deccan. The Deccan is bordered by two mountain ranges, the Western Ghats and the Eastern Ghats.

India has three main seasons. The cool season runs from October to February. The hot season runs from March to June. The rainy monsoon season starts in the middle of June and continues into September. Delhi has a moderate rainfall, with about 25 inches [640 mm] a year. The southwestern coast and the northeast have far more rain. Darjeeling in the northeast has an average annual rainfall of 120 inches [3,040 mm]. But parts of the Thar Desert in the northwest have only 2 inches [50 mm] of rain per year.

POLITICS & ECONOMY In southern India, most of the people are descendants of the dark-skinned Dravidians, who were among India's earliest people. Most northerners are descendants of lighter-skinned Aryans who arrived around 3,500 years ago.

India was the birthplace of several major religions, including Hinduism, Buddhism, and Sikhism. Islam was introduced from about AD 1000. The Muslim Mughal empire was founded in 1526. From the 17th century, Britain began to gain influence. From 1858 to 1947, India was ruled as part of the British empire. An independence movement began after the Sepoy Rebellion (1857–9), and in 1885 the Indian National Congress was formed. In 1920, Mohandas K. Gandhi became its leader and it soon became a mass movement. When independence was finally achieved in 1947, British India was divided into modern India and Muslim Pakistan. Partition was marred by mass slaughter as Hindus and Sikhs fled from Pakistan, and Indian Muslims poured into Pakistan. In the ensuing disputes, some 1 million people were killed.

Although India has 15 major languages and hundreds of minor ones, together with many religions, the country remains the world's largest democracy. It has faced many problems, especially with Pakistan, over the disputed territory of Jammu and Kashmir. Two wars in 1965 and 1972 failed to alter greatly the 1948 ceasefire lines. In the late 1980s, Kashmiri nationalists in the Indian-controlled area waged a campaign, demanding either integration into Pakistan or independence. India sent in troops and accused Pakistan of intervention. In the 1990s, Pakistani-backed guerrillas fought to break India's hold on the Srinagar valley, Kashmir's most populous region. Tension mounted following the testing of nuclear devices by both countries in 1998. Relations improved, but an attack on buildings in Mumbai in 2008, allegedly by Pakistanis, caused tension. In 2009–11, the dispute with Maoists in central and eastern India flared up again.

The World Bank classifies India as a developing country and a large number of people are poor. However, since 2004, under a government led by the United Progressive Alliance, led by Manmohan Singh, the national economy developed rapidly. By 2010–11, India's economy was the world's second fastest growing after China.

Agriculture employs 52% of the people. Crops include rice, wheat, millet, sorghum, peas, and beans. India has more cattle than any other country. Milk is produced, but Hindus do not eat beef. Resources include coal, iron ore, and oil. Manufacturing has expanded greatly since 1947. Iron and steel, machinery, refined petroleum, textiles, and transport equipment are major products.

AREA 1,269,212 sq mi [3,287,263 sq km]
POPULATION 1,173,108,000 **CAPITAL** New Delhi
GOVERNMENT Multiparty federal republic
ETHNIC GROUPS Indo-Aryan (Caucasoid) 72%, Dravidian (Aboriginal) 25%, others (mainly Mongoloid) 3%
LANGUAGES Hindi, English, Telugu, Bengali, Marathi, Tamil, Urdu, Gujarati, Malayalam, Kannada, Oriya, Punjabi, Assamese, Kashmiri, Sindhi, and Sanskrit are all official languages
RELIGIONS Hinduism 82%, Islam 12%, Christianity 2%, Sikhism 2%, Buddhism, and others **CURRENCY** Indian rupee = 100 paisa

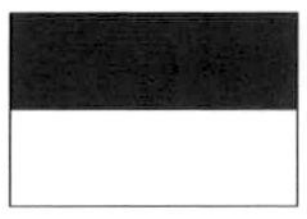

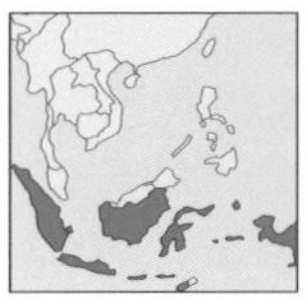

INDONESIA

GEOGRAPHY The Republic of Indonesia is an island nation in Southeast Asia. In all, Indonesia contains about 13,600 islands, less than 6,000 of which are inhabited. Three-quarters of the country is made up of five main areas: the islands of Sumatra, Java and Sulawesi (Celebes), together with Kalimantan (southern Borneo) and Irian Jaya (western New Guinea). The islands are generally mountainous and volcanic. The larger islands have extensive coastal lowlands. The climate is hot and humid, with a high rainfall. Only Java and the Sunda Islands have relatively dry seasons.

POLITICS & ECONOMY Indonesia is the world's most populous Muslim nation, though Islam was introduced as recently as the 15th century. The Dutch became active in the area in the early 17th century and Indonesia became a Dutch colony in 1799. After a long struggle, the Netherlands recognized Indonesia's independence in 1949. The economy has expanded, but ethnic and religious conflict have slowed down economic progress.

In the early 21st century, Indonesia was facing many problems, arising from widespread corruption in the government and the army. Separatists were operating in Aceh province in northern Sumatra and in West Papua (formerly Irian Jaya), Christian-Muslim clashes led to loss of life in the Moluccas, and East (formerly Portuguese) Timor became an independent country. Terrorist incidents occurred in the early 21st century. In December 2004, a tsunami killed more than 100,000 people. Worst hit was Aceh, but the tragedy was followed by the granting of autonomy for Aceh province in 2006. Indonesia is a democratic, developing country with a growing industrial sector. It exports oil and natural gas, and also mines tin and other minerals. Timber, textiles, rubber, coffee, and tea are also exported. Rice is the main food crop.

AREA 735,354 sq mi [1,904,569 sq km]
POPULATION 242,968,000 **CAPITAL** Jakarta
GOVERNMENT Multiparty republic
ETHNIC GROUPS Javanese 45%, Sundanese 14%, Madurese 7%, coastal Malays 7%, approximately 300 others
LANGUAGES Bahasa Indonesian (official), many others
RELIGIONS Islam 88%, Roman Catholic 3%, Hinduism 2%, Buddhism 1%
CURRENCY Indonesian rupiah = 100 sen

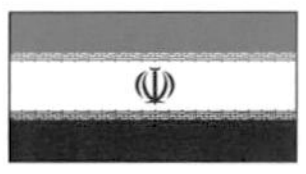

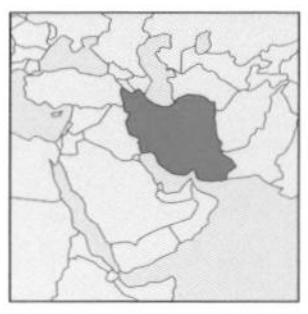

IRAN

GEOGRAPHY The Republic of Iran contains a barren central plateau which covers about half of the country. It includes the Dasht-e-Kavir (Great Salt Desert) and the Dasht-e-Lut (Great Sand Desert). The Elburz Mountains north of the plateau contain Iran's highest peak, Damavand, while narrow lowlands lie between the mountains and the Caspian Sea. West of the plateau are the Zagros Mountains, beyond which the land descends to the plains bordering the Persian Gulf.

Much of Iran has a severe, dry climate, with hot summers and cold winters. In Tehran, rain falls on only about 30 days in the year and the annual temperature range is more than 45°F [25°C]. The climate in the lowlands, however, is generally milder.

POLITICS & ECONOMY Iran was called Persia until 1935. The empire of Ancient Persia flourished between 550 and 350 BC, when it fell to Alexander the Great. Islam was introduced in AD 641.

Britain and Russia competed for influence in the area in the 19th century, and in the early 20th century the British began to develop the country's oil resources. In 1925, the Pahlavi family took power.

Reza Khan became shah (king) and worked to modernize the country. The Pahlavi dynasty was ended in 1979 when a religious leader, Ayatollah Ruhollah Khomeini, made Iran an Islamic republic. In 1980–8, Iran and Iraq fought a war over disputed borders. Khomeini died in 1989, but his fundamentalist views and anti-Western attitudes continued to dominate politics. In 2005, a hardliner, Mahmoud Ahmadinejad, was elected president. Iran's nuclear policies, which many in the West considered were to develop nuclear weapons, led to the application of international sanctions against Iran in 2009–11.

Iran's prosperity is based on its oil production and oil accounts for more than 70% of the country's exports. However, the economy was severely damaged by the Iran–Iraq war in the 1980s. Oil revenues have been used to develop a growing manufacturing sector. Agriculture is important even though farms cover only a tenth of the land. The main crops are wheat and barley. Livestock farming and fishing are other important activities, although Iran has to import much of the food it needs.

AREA 636,368 SQ MI [1,648,195 SQ KM]
POPULATION 76,923,000 **CAPITAL** TEHRAN
GOVERNMENT ISLAMIC REPUBLIC **ETHNIC GROUPS** PERSIAN 51%, AZERI 24%, GILAKI AND MAZANDARANI 8%, KURD 7%, ARAB 3%, LUR 2%, BALUCHI 2%, TURKMEN 2% **LANGUAGES** PERSIAN 58%, TURKIC 26%, KURDISH **RELIGIONS** ISLAM (SHI'ITE MUSLIM 89%)
CURRENCY IRANIAN RIAL = 100 DINARS

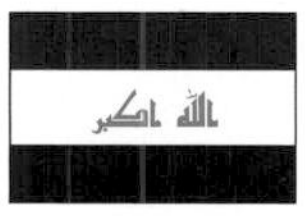

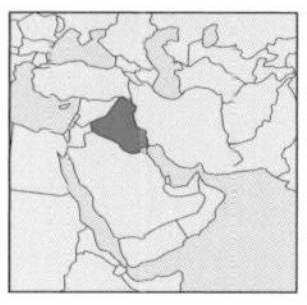

IRAQ

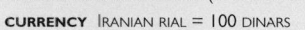

GEOGRAPHY The Republic of Iraq is a southwest Asian country at the head of the Persian Gulf. Rolling deserts cover western and southwestern Iraq, with part of the Zagros Mountains in the northeast, where farming can be practised without irrigation. The northern plains, across which flow the rivers Euphrates (Nahr al Furat) and Tigris (Nahr Dijlah), are dry. But the southern plains, including Mesopotamia and the delta of the Shatt al Arab, contain irrigated farmland, together with marshland.

The climate of Iraq ranges from temperate in the north to subtropical in the south. Baghdad, in central Iraq, has cool winters, with occasional frosts, and hot summers. The rainfall is generally low.

POLITICS & ECONOMY Mesopotamia was the home of several great civilizations, including Sumer, Babylon, and Assyria. It later became part of the Persian empire. Islam was introduced in AD 637 and Baghdad became the brilliant capital of the powerful Arab empire. But Mesopotamia declined after the Mongols invaded it in 1258. From 1534, Mesopotamia became part of the Turkish Ottoman empire. Britain invaded the area in 1916. In 1921, Britain renamed the country Iraq and set up an Arab monarchy. Iraq finally became independent in 1932.

By the 1950s, oil dominated Iraq's economy. In 1952, Iraq agreed to take 50% of the profits of the foreign oil companies. This revenue enabled the government to pay for welfare services and development projects. But many Iraqis felt that they should benefit more from their oil. Since 1958, when army officers killed the king and made Iraq a republic, Iraq has undergone turbulent times. In the 1960s, the Kurds, who live in northern Iraq and also in Iran, Turkey, Syria, and Armenia, asked for self-rule. The government rejected their demands and war broke out. A peace treaty was signed in 1975, but conflict has continued.

In 1979, Saddam Hussein became Iraq's president. Under his leadership, Iraq invaded Iran in 1980, starting an eight-year war. Iraqi Kurds supported Iran and the Iraqi government attacked Kurdish villages with poison gas. In 1990, Iraqi troops occupied Kuwait, but an international force drove them out in 1991. Since 1991, Iraqi troops have attacked Shi'ite Marsh Arabs and Kurds. In 1998, Iraq's failure to permit UN inspectors, charged with disposing of Iraq's deadliest weapons, access to suspect sites led to the Western bombardment of Iraqi military sites. Another major offensive occurred in 2001. In 2002–3, pressure mounted on Iraq to dispose of its alleged weapons of mass destruction. In March–April 2003, a coalition force headed by the United States invaded Iraq, overthrowing Saddam Hussein's regime. Despite ongoing violence, elections were held in 2005, and again in 2010 when deadlock followed the elections in March. Finally, a settlement was agreed in November, with Nouri al-Maliki remaining as prime minister.

Civil war, war damage, mismanagement, and UN sanctions have damaged the economy. Oil remains the main resource. Farmland, including pasture, covers about a fifth of the land. Products include barley, cotton, dates, fruit, livestock, wheat, and wool. But Iraq still has to import food. Manufactures include refined oil, petrochemicals, and consumer goods.

AREA 169,672 SQ MI [438,317 SQ KM]
POPULATION 29,672,000 **CAPITAL** BAGHDAD
GOVERNMENT PARLIAMENTARY DEMOCRACY **ETHNIC GROUPS** ARAB 77%, KURDISH 19%, ASSYRIAN, AND OTHERS **LANGUAGES** ARABIC (OFFICIAL), KURDISH (OFFICIAL IN KURDISH AREAS), ASSYRIAN, ARMENIAN **RELIGIONS** ISLAM 97%, CHRISTIANITY, AND OTHERS **CURRENCY** NEW IRAQI DINAR

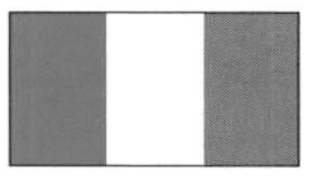

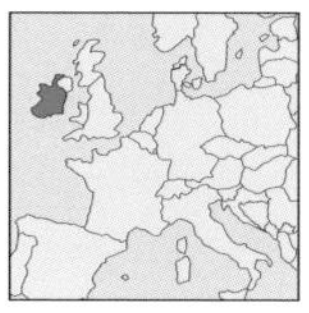

IRELAND

GEOGRAPHY The Republic of Ireland occupies five-sixths of the island of Ireland. The country consists of a large lowland region surrounded by a broken rim of low mountains. The uplands include the Mountains of Kerry where Carrauntoohill, Ireland's highest peak at 3,415 ft [1,041 m], is situated. The River Shannon is the longest in Ireland, flowing through three large lakes, loughs Allen, Ree, and Derg.

Ireland has a mild, rainy climate influenced by the warm Gulf Stream current, whose effects are greatest in the west. However, Dublin in the east is cooler than places on the west coast.

POLITICS & ECONOMY In 1801, the Act of Union created the United Kingdom of Great Britain and Ireland. But Irish discontent intensified in the 1840s when a potato blight caused a famine in which a million people died and nearly a million emigrated. Britain was blamed for not having done enough to help. In 1916, an uprising in Dublin was crushed, but between 1919 and 1922 civil war occurred. In 1922, the Irish Free State was created as a Dominion in the British Commonwealth. But Northern Ireland remained part of the UK.

Ireland became a republic in 1949. In 1973, Ireland became a member of the European Community (now the European Union) and, until the global financial crisis of 2008–9, it prospered. In 1998, Ireland took part in the negotiations to produce a constitutional settlement in Northern Ireland. Ireland agreed to give up its claim on Northern Ireland and, in 2007, a power-sharing government was set up in the north.

Major farm products in Ireland include barley, cattle and dairy products, pigs, potatoes, poultry, sheep, sugar beet, and wheat, while fishing is also important. But manufacturing is the leading activity. In 2010, the economy worsened and Ireland sought assistance from the EU and the IMF. Following elections in 2011, a coalition government was set up by two opposition parties, Fine Gael and the center-left Labour Party.

AREA 27,132 SQ MI [70,273 SQ KM]
POPULATION 4,623,000 **CAPITAL** DUBLIN
GOVERNMENT MULTIPARTY REPUBLIC **ETHNIC GROUPS** IRISH 94%
LANGUAGES IRISH (GAELIC) AND ENGLISH (BOTH OFFICIAL)
RELIGIONS ROMAN CATHOLIC 92%, PROTESTANT 3%
CURRENCY EURO = 100 CENTS

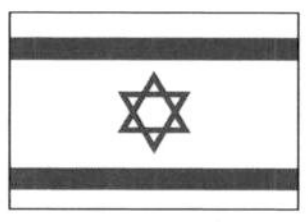

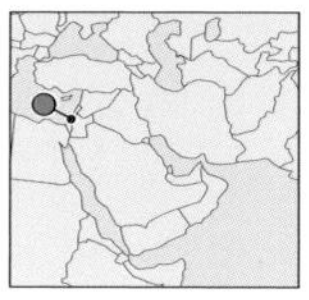

ISRAEL

GEOGRAPHY The State of Israel is a small country in the eastern Mediterranean. It includes a fertile coastal plain, where Israel's main industrial cities, Haifa (Hefa) and Tel Aviv-Jaffa, are situated. Inland lie the Judaeo-Galilean highlands, which run from northern Israel to the northern tip of the Negev Desert. To the east lies part of the Great Rift Valley which contains the River Jordan, the Sea of Galilee, and the Dead Sea. Summers are hot and dry. Winters on the coast are mild and moist, but the rainfall decreases from west to east and from north to south.

POLITICS & ECONOMY Israel is part of a region called Palestine. Some Jews have always lived in the area, though most modern Israelis are descendants of immigrants who began to settle there from the 1880s. Britain ruled Palestine from 1917. Large numbers of Jews escaping Nazi persecution arrived in the 1930s, provoking an Arab uprising against British rule. In 1947, the UN agreed to partition Palestine into an Arab and a Jewish state. Fighting broke out after Arabs rejected the plan. The State of Israel came into being in May 1948, but fighting continued into 1949. Other Arab-Israeli wars in 1956, 1967, and 1973 led to land gains for Israel.

In 1978, Israel signed a treaty with Egypt which led to the return of the occupied Sinai peninsula to Egypt in 1979. But conflict continued between Israel and the PLO (Palestine Liberation Organization). In 1993, the PLO and Israel agreed to establish Palestinian self-rule in two areas: the occupied Gaza Strip, and in the town of Jericho in the occupied West Bank. The agreement was extended in 1995 to include more than 30% of the West Bank. Israel's prime minister, Yitzhak Rabin, was assassinated in 1995. In 1996, Benjamin Netanyahu was elected prime minister. The peace process stalled until Ehud Barak defeated Netanyahu in 1999. In 2001, Ariel Sharon became prime minister. In 2005, he handed over the Gaza Strip to the Palestinian Authority. Sharon formed a new political party, Kadima. After Sharon suffered a stroke, Ehud Olmert became leader of Kadima and prime minister. Between 2005 and 2009, Israeli forces clashed with Palestinians in southern Lebanon and Gaza. In 2009, elections led to the return of the right-wing Benjamin Netanyahu. In 2010, talks between Israel and the Palestinian Authority collapsed.

Manufacturing is the most valuable activity. Products include chemicals, electronic equipment, plastics, processed food, scientific instruments, and textiles. Fruit and vegetables are major exports.

AREA 7,954 SQ MI [20,600 SQ KM] **POPULATION** 7,354,000
CAPITAL JERUSALEM **GOVERNMENT** MULTIPARTY REPUBLIC
ETHNIC GROUPS JEWISH 80%, ARAB AND OTHERS 20%
LANGUAGES HEBREW AND ARABIC (BOTH OFFICIAL)
RELIGIONS JUDAISM 80%, ISLAM (MOSTLY SUNNI) 14%, CHRISTIANITY 2%, DRUZE AND OTHERS 2% **CURRENCY** NEW ISRAELI SHEKEL = 100 AGORAT

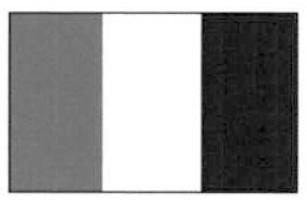

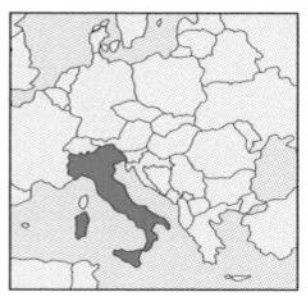

ITALY

GEOGRAPHY The Republic of Italy is famous for its history and traditions, its art and culture, and its beautiful scenery. Northern Italy is bordered in the north by the high Alps, with their many climbing and skiing resorts. The Alps overlook the northern plains – Italy's most fertile and densely populated region – drained by the River Po. The rugged Apennines form the backbone of southern Italy. Bordering the range are scenic hilly areas and coastal plains. Southern Italy contains a string of volcanoes, stretching from Vesuvius, through the Lipari Islands, to Etna on Sicily, the largest Mediterranean island. Northern Italy has cold, often snowy, winters, but the summer months are warm and sunny, with brief summer thunderstorms. Rainfall is abundant. The south has mild, moist winters and warm, dry summers.

POLITICS & ECONOMY Magnificent ruins throughout Italy testify to the glories of the ancient Roman Empire, which was founded, according to legend, in 753 BC. It reached its peak in the AD 100s. It finally collapsed in the 400s, although the Eastern Roman Empire, also called the Byzantine Empire, survived for another 1,000 years.

In the Middle Ages, Italy was split into many tiny states. These states made a great contribution to the revival of art and learning, called the Renaissance, in the 14th to 16th centuries. Beautiful cities, such as Florence (Firenze) and Venice (Venézia), testify to the artistic achievements of this period.

Italy finally became a united kingdom in 1861, although the Papal Territories (a large area ruled by the Roman Catholic Church) was not added until 1870. The Pope and his successors disputed the takeover of the Papal Territories. The dispute was finally resolved in 1929, when the Vatican City was set up in Rome as a fully independent state.

Italy fought in World War I (1914–18) alongside the Allies – Britain, France, and Russia. In 1922, the dictator Benito Mussolini, leader of the Fascist Party, took power. Under Mussolini, Italy conquered Ethiopia. During World War II (1939–45), Italy at first fought on Germany's side against the Allies. But in late 1943, Italy declared war on Germany. Italy became a republic in 1946. It has played an important part in European affairs. It was a founder member of the North Atlantic Treaty Organization (NATO) in 1949 and also, in 1958, of what has since become the European Union.

After the setting up of the European Union, Italy's economy developed quickly. But the country faced many problems. For example, much of the economic development was in the north. This forced many people to leave the poor south to find jobs in the north or abroad. Social problems, corruption at high levels of society, and a succession of weak coalition governments all contributed to instability. From 1998, power shifted between center-left coalitions led by Romano Prodi and center-right coalitions led by media tycoon Silvio Berlusconi. Berlusconi won elections in 2008, and in 2009 he formed a new, broad center-right coalition called People of Freedom, which included his own party, Forza Italia.

Only 50 years ago, Italy was a mainly agricultural society. But today it is a leading industrial power. It lacks mineral resources, and imports most of the raw materials used in industry. Manufactures include textiles and clothing, processed food, machinery, cars, and chemicals. The chief industrial region is in the northwest.

Farmland covers around 42% of the land, pasture 17%, and forest and woodland 22%. Major crops include citrus fruits, grapes which are used to make wine, olive oil, sugar beet, and vegetables. Livestock farming is important, though meat is imported.

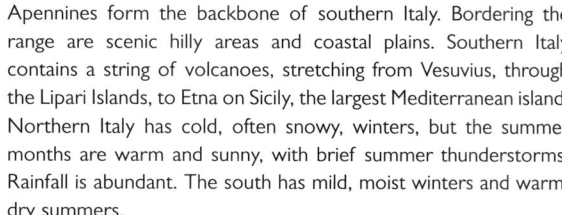

AREA 116,339 sq mi [301,318 sq km]
POPULATION 58,091,000 **CAPITAL** Rome
GOVERNMENT Multiparty republic **ETHNIC GROUPS** Italian 94%, German, French, Albanian, Slovene, Greek **LANGUAGES** Italian (official), German, French, Slovene **RELIGIONS** Predominantly Roman Catholic **CURRENCY** Euro = 100 cents

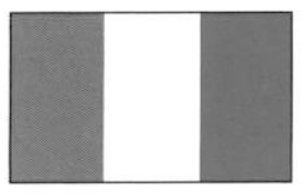
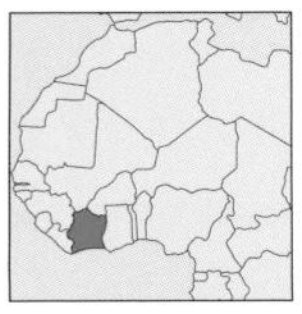

IVORY COAST

GEOGRAPHY The Republic of the Ivory Coast, in West Africa, is officially known as Côte d'Ivoire. The southeast coast is bordered by sand bars that enclose lagoons. The southwest coast is lined by rocky cliffs.

Ivory Coast has a hot and humid tropical climate, with high temperatures all year. The south has two rainy seasons: between May and July, and from October to November. Inland, the rainfall decreases and the north has one dry and one rainy season.

POLITICS & ECONOMY From 1895, Ivory Coast was governed as part of French West Africa, which also included what are now Benin, Burkina Faso, Guinea, Mali, Mauritania, Niger, and Senegal. In 1946, Ivory Coast became a territory in the French Union.

Ivory Coast became fully independent in 1960. Its first president, Félix Houphouët-Boigny, became the longest serving head of state in Africa with an uninterrupted period in office which ended with his death in 1993. Houphouët-Boigny, a pro-Western leader, made Ivory Coast a one-party state. In 1983, the National Assembly voted to make Yamoussoukro, the president's birthplace, the new capital. In 1999, a military coup occurred, but civilian rule was restored in 2000, when Laurent Gbagbo was elected president. An army rebellion began in 2002. By 2004, the government held the south, while mainly Muslim rebels held the north. A peace deal was agreed in 2007. Elections held in 2010 were won by opposition leader Alassane Ouattara, but President Laurent Gbagbo refused to stand down. After much fighting, Gbagbo was finally arrested in April 2011.

Agriculture employs 45% of the people. Cocoa beans, farm products, and petroleum products are exported.

AREA 124,503 sq mi [322,463 sq km]
POPULATION 21,059,000 **CAPITAL** Yamoussoukro
GOVERNMENT Multiparty republic **ETHNIC GROUPS** Akan 42%, Voltaiques 18%, Northern Mandes 16%, Krous 11%, Southern Mandes 10% **LANGUAGES** French (official), many native dialects **RELIGIONS** Islam 40%, Christianity 30%, traditional beliefs 30%
CURRENCY CFA franc = 100 centimes

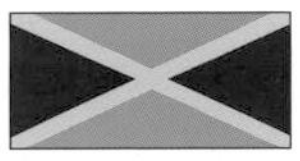
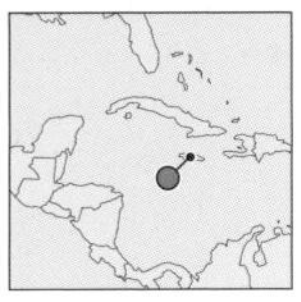

JAMAICA

GEOGRAPHY Third largest of the Caribbean islands, half of Jamaica lies above 1,000 ft [300 m] and moist southeast trade winds bring rain to the central mountain range.

The "cockpit country" in the northwest of the island is an inaccessible limestone area of steep broken ridges and isolated basins.

POLITICS & ECONOMY Britain took Jamaica from Spain in the 17th century, and the island did not gain its independence until 1962. Power has alternated between the People's National Party (PNP) and Jamaica Labor Party. In 2006, Portia Simpson Miller succeeded Percival Patterson as prime minister. In 2007 she was succeeded by Bruce Golding after elections. Tourism and sugarcane farming are important, but alumina and bauxite make up half of the exports.

AREA 4,244 sq mi [10,991 sq km]
POPULATION 2,847,000 **CAPITAL** Kingston
GOVERNMENT Constitutional monarchy
ETHNIC GROUPS Black 91%, Mixed 7%, East Indian 1%
LANGUAGES English (official), patois English
RELIGIONS Protestant 61%, Roman Catholic 4%
CURRENCY Jamaican dollar = 100 cents

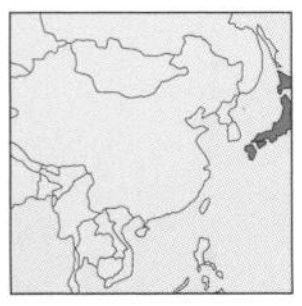

JAPAN

GEOGRAPHY Japan's four largest islands – Honshu, Hokkaido, Kyushu, and Shikoku – make up 98% of the country. But Japan contains thousands of small islands. The four largest islands are mainly mountainous, while many of the small islands are the tips of volcanoes. Japan has more than 150 volcanoes, about 60 of which are active. Volcanic eruptions, earthquakes, and tsunamis (destructive sea waves triggered by earthquakes and eruptions). In March 2011, an earthquake, the most powerful ever recorded in Japan (magnitude 9.0), struck northeast Japan. The tremors and the ensuing tsunami caused enormous damage and loss of life.

The climate of Japan varies greatly from north to south. Hokkaido in the north has cold, snowy winters. At Sapporo, temperatures below 4°F [–20°C] have been recorded between December and March. But summers are warm, with temperatures sometimes exceeding 86°F [30°C]. Rain falls throughout the year, though Hokkaido is one of the driest parts of Japan. Tokyo has higher rainfall and temperatures, while the southern islands of Shikoku and Kyushu have warm temperate climates. Summers are long and hot. Winters are cold.

POLITICS & ECONOMY In the late 19th century, Japan began a program of modernization. Under its new imperial leaders, it began to look for lands to conquer. In 1894–5, it fought a war with China and, in 1904–5, it defeated Russia. Soon its overseas empire included Korea and Taiwan. In 1930, Japan invaded Manchuria (northeast China), and in 1937 it began a war against China. In 1941, Japan launched an attack on the US base at Pearl Harbor in Hawai'i. This drew both Japan and the United States into World War II.

Japan surrendered in 1945 when the Americans dropped atomic bombs on two cities, Hiroshima and Nagasaki. The United States occupied Japan until 1952. During this period, Japan adopted a democratic constitution. The emperor, who had previously been regarded as a god, became a constitutional monarch. Power was vested in the prime minister and cabinet, who are chosen from the Diet (elected parliament).

From the 1960s, Japan experienced many changes as the country rapidly built up new industries. By the early 1990s, Japan had become the world's second richest economic power after the US. But economic success has brought problems. For example, the rapid growth of cities has led to housing shortages and pollution. Another problem is that the proportion of people over 65 years of age is steadily increasing.

In 2011, China overtook Japan as the world's second largest economy after the United States. Japan had held second place since 1968, and, although its economy grew by 3.9% in 2010, it was insufficient to keep it in second place.

The leading activity is manufacturing. Japan imports most of the materials and fuels it needs, and its success has been based on its use of the latest technology, its skilled work force, its vigorous export policies, and the relatively low expenditure on defense. Exports include machinery, electrical and electronic equipment, iron and steel, chemicals, textiles, and ships. Japan's economy suffered a stagnation in the 1990s. Signs of recovery from 2005 were shattered by the global financial crisis in 2008–9, when exports greatly declined.

Japan is one of the world's top fishing nations and fish is an important source of protein. Because the land is so rugged, only 15% of the country can be farmed. Yet Japan produces about 70% of the food it needs. Rice is the chief crop, taking up about half of the total farmland. Other major products include fruits, sugar beet, tea, and vegetables. Livestock farming has increased since the 1950s.

AREA 145,880 sq mi [377,829 sq km]
POPULATION 126,804,000 **CAPITAL** Tokyo
GOVERNMENT Constitutional monarchy
ETHNIC GROUPS Japanese 99%, Chinese, Korean, Brazilian, and others
LANGUAGES Japanese (official) **RELIGIONS** Shintoism and Buddhism 84% (most Japanese consider themselves to be both Shinto and Buddhist), others **CURRENCY** Yen = 100 sen

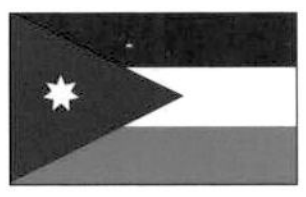
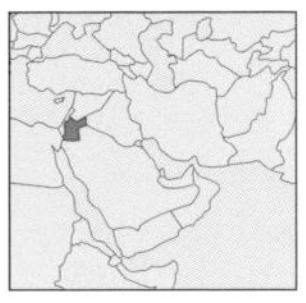

JORDAN

GEOGRAPHY The Hashemite Kingdom of Jordan is an Arab country in southwestern Asia. The Great Rift Valley in the west contains the River Jordan and the Dead Sea, which Jordan shares with Israel. East of the Rift Valley is the Transjordan plateau, where most Jordanians live. To the east and south lie vast areas of desert.

Amman has a much lower rainfall and longer dry season than the Mediterranean lands to the west. The Transjordan plateau, on which Amman stands, is a transition zone between the Mediterranean climate zone and the desert climate to the east.

POLITICS & ECONOMY In 1921, Britain created a territory called Transjordan east of the River Jordan. In 1923, Transjordan became self-governing, but Britain retained control of its defenses, finances, and foreign affairs. This territory became fully independent as Jordan in 1946. Jordan has suffered from instability arising from the Arab–Israeli conflict since the creation of the State of Israel in 1948. After the first Arab–Israeli War in 1948–9, Jordan acquired East Jerusalem and a fertile area called the West Bank. In 1967, Israel occupied this area. In Jordan, the presence of Palestinian refugees led to civil war in 1970–1.

In 1974, Arab leaders declared that the PLO (Palestine Liberation Organization) was the sole representative of the Palestinian people. In 1988, King Hussein of Jordan renounced Jordan's claims to the West Bank and passed responsibility for it to the PLO. Opposition parties were legalized in 1991 and elections were held in 1993. In October 1994, Jordan and Israel signed a peace treaty, ending a state of war that had lasted more than 40 years. Jordan's King Hussein commanded respect for his role in Middle Eastern affairs until his death in 1999. He was succeeded by his eldest son, who became Abdullah II. Jordan supported the US-led war on terrorism. In 2005, suicide bombings on hotels in Amman damaged Jordan's reputation as a stable country. In 2009, the king dissolved parliament. Elections were held in 2010, but anti-government protests occurred in early 2011.

Jordan has a "lower-middle-income" economy. It lacks natural resources, apart from phosphates and potash, and depends on substantial aid. Less than 6% of the land is farmed or used as pasture. Jordan has an oil refinery and manufactures include cement, pharmaceuticals, processed food, fertilizers, and textiles.

AREA 34,495 sq mi [89,342 sq km]
POPULATION 6,407,000 **CAPITAL** Amman
GOVERNMENT Constitutional monarchy **ETHNIC GROUPS** Arab 98%, of which Palestinians make up roughly half **LANGUAGES** Arabic (official) **RELIGIONS** Islam (mostly Sunni) 94%, Christianity (mostly Greek Orthodox) 6% **CURRENCY** Jordanian dinar = 1,000 fils

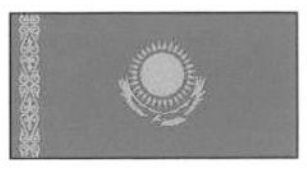
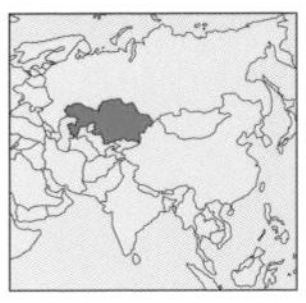

KAZAKHSTAN

GEOGRAPHY Kazakhstan is a large country in west-central Asia. In the west, the Caspian Sea lowlands include the Karagiye depression, which reaches 433 ft [132 m] below sea level. The lowlands extend eastward through the Aral Sea area. The north contains high plains, but the highest land is along the eastern and southern borders. These areas include parts of the Altai and Tian Shan mountain ranges. Eastern Kazakhstan contains several freshwater lakes, the largest of which is Lake Balkhash. The water in the rivers has been used for irrigation, causing ecological problems. For example, the Aral Sea, deprived of water, shrank from 25,830 sq mi [66,900 sq km] in 1960 to 12,989 sq mi [33,642 sq km] in 1993. Large areas are now barren desert.

Kazakhstan has an extreme climate. Winters are cold and snowy. The rainfall is generally low.

POLITICS & ECONOMY After the Russian Revolution of 1917, many Kazakhs wanted to make their country independent. But the Communists prevailed and in 1936 Kazakhstan became a republic of the Soviet Union, called the Kazakh Soviet Socialist Republic. During World War II and also after the war, the Soviet government moved many people from the west into Kazakhstan. From the 1950s, people were encouraged to work on a "Virgin Lands" project, which involved bringing large areas of grassland under cultivation.

Reforms in the Soviet Union in the 1980s led to its breakup in December 1991. Kazakhstan maintained contacts with Russia through the Commonwealth of Independent States (CIS). In 1997, the government moved its capital from Almaty to Aqmola (later renamed Astana), a town in the north. By the mid-2000s, the economy was in better shape than the other ex-Soviet republics in Central Asia. But President Nursultan Nazarbaev was criticized for his authoritarian rule. In 2007, constitutional changes enabled Nazarbaev to stand for the presidency as many times as he wished. In 2011, he was re-elected, despite opposition protests that he had given them no time to prepare.

The World Bank classifies Kazakhstan as a "lower-middle-income" developing country. Livestock farming, especially sheep and cattle, is an important activity, and major crops include barley, cotton, rice, and wheat. The country is rich in mineral resources, including coal and oil reserves, together with bauxite, copper, lead, tungsten, and zinc. Manufactures include chemicals, food products, machinery, and textiles. Oil is exported via a pipeline through Russia. However, to reduce the country's dependence on Russia, another pipeline to China was inaugurated in 2009. Other exports include metals, chemicals, grain, wool, and meat.

AREA 1,052,084 sq mi [2,724,900 sq km] **POPULATION** 15,460,000
CAPITAL Astana **GOVERNMENT** Multiparty republic
ETHNIC GROUPS Kazakh 53%, Russian 30%, Ukrainian 4%, German 2%, Uzbek 2% **LANGUAGES** Kazakh (official); Russian, the former official language, is widely spoken **RELIGIONS** Islam 47%, Russian Orthodox 44% **CURRENCY** Tenge = 100 tiyn

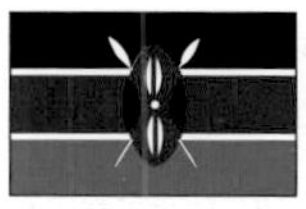
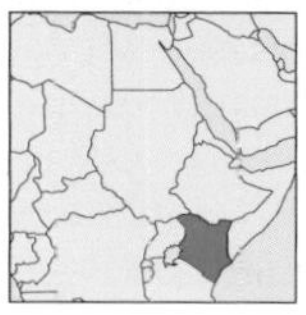

KENYA

GEOGRAPHY The Republic of Kenya is a country in East Africa which straddles the Equator. Behind the narrow coastal plain on the Indian Ocean, the land rises to high plains and highlands, broken by volcanic mountains, including Mount Kenya, the country's highest peak at 17,057 ft [5,199 m]. Crossing the country is an arm of the Great Rift Valley, on the floor of which are several lakes, including Baringo, Magadi, Naivasha, Nakuru and, on the northern frontier, Lake Turkana (formerly Lake Rudolf).

The climate is moderated by the terrain. Nairobi, in the southwestern highlands, has summer temperatures which are 18°C [10°F] lower than humid Mombasa. Only about 15% of Kenya has a reliable annual rainfall of 31 inches [800 mm].

POLITICS & ECONOMY The Kenyan coast has been a trading center for more than 2,000 years. Britain took over the coast in 1895 and soon extended its influence inland. In the 1950s, a secret movement, called Mau Mau, launched an armed struggle against British rule. Although Mau Mau was eventually defeated, Kenya became independent in 1963.

Kenya was a one-party state for much of the time after 1963. Democracy was restored in 1992. Elections in 2007 led to inter-ethnic violence when the opposition refused to accept the declared results. A deal agreed by President Mwai Kibaki and opposition leader Raila Odinga, who became prime minister, restored peace, but charges of corruption persisted. Kenya adopted a new constitution in 2010.

Kenya remains a "low-income" developing country. Many Kenyans are subsistence farmers. The chief food crop is maize. The main cash crops and the leading exports are coffee and tea. Manufactures include chemicals, leather and footwear, processed food, petroleum products, and textiles.

AREA 224,080 sq mi [580,367 sq km]
POPULATION 40,047,000 **CAPITAL** Nairobi
GOVERNMENT Multiparty republic **ETHNIC GROUPS** Kikuyu 22%, Luhya 14%, Luo 13%, Kalenjin 12%, Kamba 11%, others
LANGUAGES Kiswahili and English (both official)
RELIGIONS Protestant 45%, Roman Catholic 33%, traditional beliefs 10%, Islam 10% **CURRENCY** Kenyan shilling = 100 cents

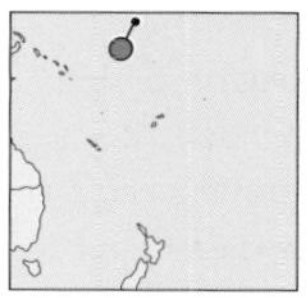

KIRIBATI

The Republic of Kiribati comprises three groups of coral atolls scattered over about 2 million sq mi [5 million sq km]. Kiribati straddles the equator and temperatures are high and the rainfall is abundant.

Formerly part of the British Gilbert and Ellice Islands, Kiribati became independent in 1979. The main export is copra and the country depends heavily on foreign aid.

AREA 280 sq mi [726 sq km] **POPULATION** 99,000 **CAPITAL** Tarawa

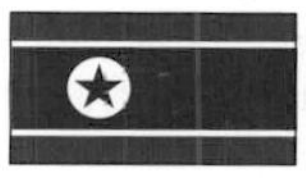
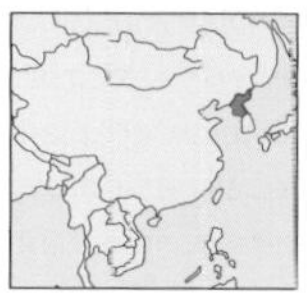

KOREA, NORTH

GEOGRAPHY The Democratic People's Republic of Korea occupies the northern part of the Korean peninsula which extends south from northeastern China. Mountains form the heart of the country, with the highest peak, Paektu-san, reaching 9,003 ft [2,744 m] on the northern border.

North Korea has a fairly severe climate, with cold, snowy winters. In summer, moist winds from the oceans bring rain.

POLITICS & ECONOMY North Korea was created in 1945, when the peninsula, which had been a Japanese colony since 1910, was divided into two parts. Soviet forces occupied the north, with US forces in the south. Soviet occupation led to a Communist government being established in 1948 under the leadership of Kim Il Sung, who effectively became a dictator.

The Korean War began in June 1950 when North Korean troops invaded the south. North Korea, aided by China and the Soviet Union, fought with South Korea, which was supported by troops from the United States and other UN members. The war ended in July 1953. An armistice was signed but no permanent peace treaty was agreed. The end of the Cold War in the late 1990s eased the situation. North and South Korea joined the United Nations in 1991, although North Korea remained isolated from most other countries. In 1993, North Korea withdrew from the Nuclear Non-Proliferation Treaty, arousing suspicions that it was developing nuclear weapons. Kim Il Sung died in 1994 and was succeeded by his son, Kim Jong Il. From 2003, the United States accused North Korea of developing nuclear weapons and, in 2006, it conducted its first nuclear test. Tensions mounted in 2010 when North Korea shelled a South Korean island.

North Korea's resources include coal, copper, iron ore, lead, tin, tungsten, and zinc. Under Communism, the country developed heavy, state-owned industries. Manufactures include chemicals, iron and steel, machinery, processed food, and textiles. Agriculture employs 27% of the people. Rice is the chief food crop, but food shortages have occurred in recent years.

AREA 46,540 sq mi [120,538 sq km]
POPULATION 22,757,000 **CAPITAL** Pyŏngyang
GOVERNMENT Single-party people's republic
ETHNIC GROUPS Korean 99%
LANGUAGES Korean (official)
RELIGIONS Buddhism and Confucianism
CURRENCY North Korean won = 100 chon

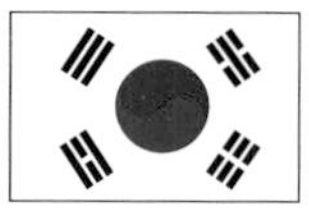
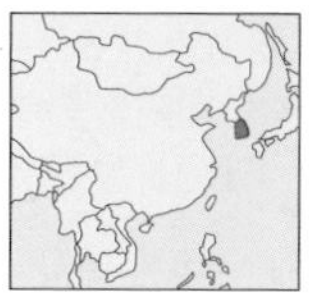

KOREA, SOUTH

GEOGRAPHY The Republic of Korea, as South Korea is officially known, occupies the southern part of the Korean peninsula. Mountains cover much of the country. The southern and western coasts are major farming regions. Many islands are found along the west and south coasts. The largest of these is Cheju-do, which contains South Korea's highest peak, Halla-San, which rises to 6,398 ft [1,950 m].

Like North Korea, South Korea is chilled in winter by cold, dry winds from central Asia. Summers are hot and wet, especially in July and August.

POLITICS & ECONOMY After Japan's defeat in World War II (1939–45), North Korea was occupied by troops from the Soviet Union, while South Korea was occupied by United States forces. A National Assembly elected in 1948 in South Korea created the Republic of Korea, while North Korea became a Communist state. North Korea invaded the South in June 1950, sparking off the Korean War (1950–3). Despite the destruction caused by the war, South Korea under a series of rather authoritarian governments began to industrialize the economy between the 1960s and 1980s. In 1987, a new constitution permitted the election of presidents every five years. In the 2000s, South Korea worked for closer contacts with the North, but relations deteriorated in 2008–10.

Until the onset of the global financial crisis in 2008, South Korea had one of the world's fastest growing economies. Its main manufactures are processed food and textiles. Heavy industries produce chemicals, fertilizers, and iron and steel, together with a wide range of consumer products, such as computers, cars, and television sets.

Farming remains important in South Korea. Rice is the chief crop, together with fruits, grains, and vegetables, while fishing provides a major source of protein.

AREA 38,327 sq mi [99,268 sq km]
POPULATION 48,636,000 **CAPITAL** Seoul
GOVERNMENT Multiparty republic **ETHNIC GROUPS** Korean 99%
LANGUAGES Korean (official) **RELIGIONS** No affiliation 46%, Christianity 26%, Buddhism 26%, Confucianism 1%
CURRENCY South Korean won = 100 chon

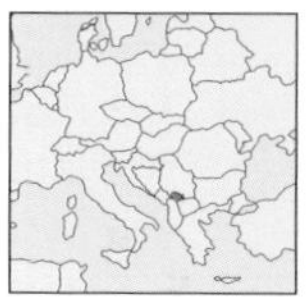

KOSOVO

GEOGRAPHY The Republic of Kosovo, formerly part of Serbia and, before 2003, part of Yugoslavia, declared its independence in February 2008. Its independence was recognized by the United States and major EU countries. But Serbia and its ally Russia refused recognition. It is a landlocked country, consisting of a river basin bounded by uplands in the north and southwest. It has cold, snowy winters and hot, dry summers.

POLITICS & ECONOMY Most people are Albanian-speakers who are Muslims, but there is an important Christian Serb minority. In the early 13th century, Kosovo was part of the Serbian empire but, after 1389, it came under Muslim Turkish Ottoman rule. Serbia regained control of Kosovo in 1912 and, in 1918, it became part of the Kingdom of Serbia. In 1946, it became part of the Socialist Federal Republic of Yugoslavia, becoming an autonomous province within the Republic of Serbia. In 1989, Serbia curtailed Kosovo's autonomy, while Albanian speakers declared their province independent. In 1995, the Albanian speakers set up the Kosovo Liberation Army, which launched an uprising against Serbia. In 1998, Serbia began repressive measures against Kosovo, resulting in massacres and ethnic cleansing of Albanian-speaking Kosovars. In 1999, NATO forces bombed Serbia and placed Kosovo under a temporary administration, pending agreement on Kosovo's future status. Finally, the Kosovo Assembly declared its independence on February 17, 2008. Local elections were held in 2009.

Kosovo is a poor country, with the lowest per capita income in Europe. Many people are subsistence farmers and its industries have declined because of lack of investment. The economy is highly dependent on international aid.

AREA 4,203 sq mi [10,887 sq km]
POPULATION 1,815,000 **CAPITAL** Pristina
GOVERNMENT Republic
ETHNIC GROUPS Albanian 88%, Serb 7%, others 5%
LANGUAGES Albanian and Serbian (both official), Turkish
RELIGIONS Islam, Serbian Orthodox, Roman Catholic
CURRENCY Euro = 100 cents

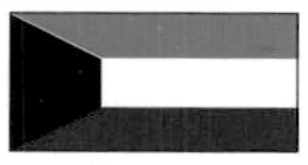
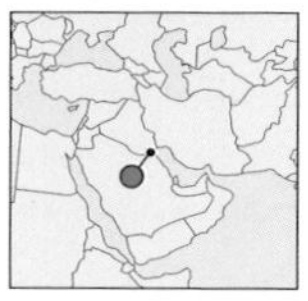

KUWAIT

GEOGRAPHY The State of Kuwait at the north end of the Persian Gulf is an emirate (ruled by an emir, or amir). The land is low-lying and largely desert. Summer temperatures are high but winters are cooler. The rainfall is low.

POLITICS & ECONOMY British influence began in 1775 and, in 1899, the local ruler concluded a treaty with Britain, agreeing to support British interests in return for British protection. Kuwait became independent in 1961. Its revenue from its oil exports made it highly prosperous. Iraq invaded Kuwait in 1990, but it was liberated in 1991 by a coalition force. In 2004, the government announced legislation for women to vote and stand for parliament. Women stood in the 2008 elections, but none was elected.

AREA 6,880 sq mi [17,818 sq km]
POPULATION 2,789,000 **CAPITAL** Kuwait City

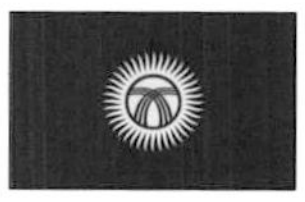
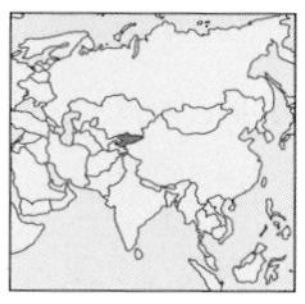

KYRGYZSTAN

GEOGRAPHY The Republic of Kyrgyzstan is a landlocked country between China, Tajikistan, Uzbekistan, and Kazakhstan. The country is mountainous, with spectacular scenery. The highest mountain, Pik Pobedy in the Tian Shan range, reaches 24,406 ft [7,439 m] in the east. The lowlands have warm summers and cold winters. But January temperatures in the mountains plummet to –18°F [–28°C]. Kyrgyzstan has a low annual rainfall.

POLITICS & ECONOMY In 1876, Kyrgyzstan became a province of Russia and Russian settlement in the area began. In 1916, Russia crushed a rebellion among the Kyrgyz, and many subsequently fled to China. In 1922, the area became an autonomous oblast (self-governing region) of the newly formed Soviet Union, but in 1936 it became one of the Soviet Socialist Republics. Under Communist rule, local customs and religious worship were suppressed, but education and health services were greatly improved.

In 1991, Kyrgyzstan became an independent country following the breakup of the Soviet Union. The Communist Party was dissolved, but the country maintained ties with Russia through an organization called the Commonwealth of Independent States. Elections were held under a new constitution adopted in 1994. Massive protests followed elections in 2005. President Askar Akayev fled the country. His successor, Kurmanbek Bakiyev, faced huge protests in 2010 and he also fled. Elections in 2010 led to opposition leader Roza Otunbayeva becoming president.

In the 1990s, Kyrgyzstan sought to reform its Soviet-style economy. Now classified as a "lower-middle income" developing country, agriculture is the main activity. Major products include cotton, eggs, fruits, grain, tobacco, vegetables, and wool. But food is imported. Most industries are concentrated around the capital Bishkek.

AREA 77,181 sq mi [199,900 sq km]
POPULATION 5,509,000 **CAPITAL** Bishkek
GOVERNMENT Multiparty republic
ETHNIC GROUPS Kyrgyz 65%, Russian 13%, Uzbek 13%
LANGUAGES Kyrgyz and Russian (both official)
RELIGIONS Islam 75%, Russian Orthodox 20%
CURRENCY Kyrgyzstani som = 100 tyiyn

LAOS

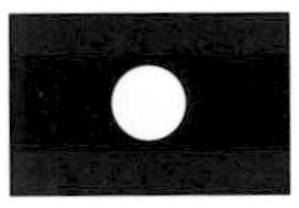

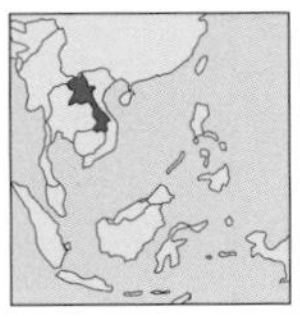

GEOGRAPHY The Lao People's Democratic Republic is a landlocked country in Southeast Asia. Mountains and plateaux cover much of the country. Most people live on the plains bordering the River Mekong and its tributaries. This river, one of Asia's longest, forms much of the country's northwestern and southwestern borders.

Laos has a tropical monsoon climate. Winters are dry and sunny with winds blowing from the northeast. From April, the monsoon season starts with the arrival of moist southwesterly winds.

POLITICS & ECONOMY France made Laos a protectorate in the late 19th century and ruled it, with Cambodia and Vietnam, as part of French Indochina. Laos became an independent kingdom in 1954. After independence, a power struggle between royalist government forces and a pro-Communist group called Pathet Lao caused instability. A civil war broke out and continued into the 1970s. The Pathet Lao took control in 1975 and the king abdicated. In the 1990s, Laos started to open to the world and began tentative reforms. In 2011, a stock exchange was opened in Vientiane, as part of a gradual move toward capitalism.

Laos is one of the world's poorest countries. Agriculture employs nearly 80% of the population and accounts for 31% of the gross domestic product. Rice is the main crop. Timber and coffee are exported. But the most valuable export is electricity, which is produced at hydroelectric power stations on the River Mekong and is exported to Thailand. Laos also produces opium.

AREA 91,428 sq mi [236,800 sq km]
POPULATION 6,368,000 **CAPITAL** Vientiane
GOVERNMENT Single-party republic
ETHNIC GROUPS Lao Loum 68%, Lao Theung 22%, Lao Soung 9%
LANGUAGES Lao (official), French, English **RELIGIONS** Buddhism 60%, traditional beliefs and others 40% **CURRENCY** Kip = 100 at

LATVIA

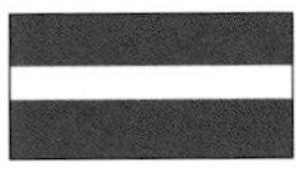

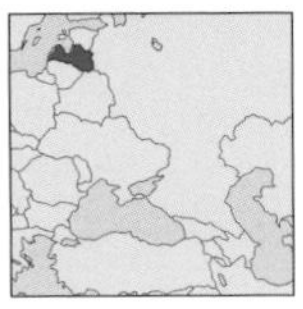

GEOGRAPHY The Republic of Latvia is one of three states on the southeastern corner of the Baltic Sea which were ruled as parts of the Soviet Union between 1940 and 1991. Latvia consists mainly of flat plains separated by low hills, composed of moraine (ice-worn rocks).

Riga has warm summers, but the winter months are subzero. The rainfall is moderate.

POLITICS & ECONOMY In 1800, Russia was in control of Latvia, but Latvians declared their independence after World War I. In 1940, under a German-Soviet pact, Soviet troops occupied Latvia, but they were driven out by the Germans in 1941. Soviet troops returned in 1944 and Latvia became part of the Soviet Union. Under Soviet rule, many Russian immigrants settled in Latvia and many Latvians feared that the Russians would become the dominant ethnic group.

In the late 1980s, when reforms were being introduced in the Soviet Union, Latvia's government ended absolute Communist rule and made Latvian the official language. In 1990, it declared the country to be independent, an act which was finally recognized by the Soviet Union in September 1991.

Latvia held its first free elections to its parliament (the Saeima) in 1993. Voting was limited only to citizens of Latvia on June 17, 1940, and their descendants. This meant that about 34% of Latvian residents were unable to vote. In 1994, Latvia restricted the naturalization of non-Latvians, including many Russian settlers, who were not allowed to vote or own land. However, in 1998, the government agreed that all children born since independence should have automatic citizenship. In 2004, Latvia became a member of the North Atlantic Treaty Organization and the European Union. Latvia was hit hard by the global financial crisis in 2009. In 2010, when Latvia had Europe's highest unemployment rate, a center-right coalition was elected.

The World Bank classifies Latvia as a "lower-middle-income" country. Manufactures include electronic goods, farm machinery, fertilizers, processed food, plastics, radios, and vehicles. Latvia produces only about a tenth of the electricity it needs. It imports the rest from Belarus, Russia, and Ukraine.

AREA 24,942 sq mi [64,600 sq km]
POPULATION 2,218,000 **CAPITAL** Riga
GOVERNMENT Multiparty republic
ETHNIC GROUPS Latvian 58%, Russian 30%, Belarusian, Ukrainian, Polish, Lithuanian **LANGUAGES** Latvian (official), Lithuanian, Russian **RELIGIONS** Lutheran, Roman Catholic, Russian Orthodox
CURRENCY Latvian lats = 10 santimi

LEBANON

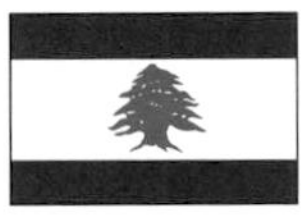

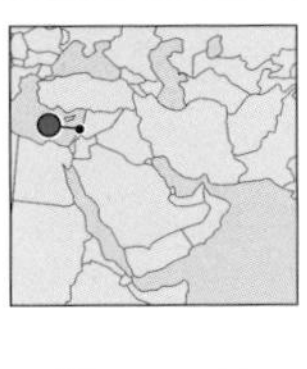

GEOGRAPHY The Republic of Lebanon is a country on the eastern shores of the Mediterranean Sea. Behind the coastal plain are the rugged Lebanon Mountains (Jabal Lubnan), which rise to 10,131 ft [3,088 m]. Another range, the Anti-Lebanon Mountains (Al Jabal Ash Sharqi), form the eastern border with Syria. Between the two ranges is the Bekaa (Beqaa) Valley, a fertile farming region.

The coast has hot, dry summers and mild, wet winters. Heavy rain falls on the mountains, with snow at high altitudes.

POLITICS & ECONOMY Lebanon was ruled by Turkey from 1516 until World War I. France ruled the country from 1923, but Lebanon became independent in 1946. After independence, the Muslims and Christians agreed to share power, and Lebanon made rapid economic progress. But from the late 1950s, development was slowed by periodic conflict between Sunni and Shia Muslims, Druze, and Christians. The situation was further complicated by the presence of Palestinian refugees who used bases in Lebanon to attack Israel.

In 1975, civil war broke out as private armies representing the many factions struggled for power. This led to intervention by Israel in the south and Syria in the north. UN peacekeeping forces arrived in 1978, but violence continued in the 1980s. Peace was restored in the 1990s, but, in 2005, the assassination of Rafik Hariri, former prime minister, was blamed on Syria. Under pressure, Syria withdrew its forces from Lebanon. In 2006, a 34-day conflict between Israeli troops and Hezbollah guerrillas caused devastation in southern Lebanon. In 2008–9, relations with Syria improved. In early 2011, the government fell when the militant Shia group, Hezbollah, withdrew its support.

Lebanon's civil war almost destroyed valuable trade and financial services that had been Lebanon's chief source of income, together with tourism. Manufacturing, formerly a major activity, was badly hit.

AREA 4,015 sq mi [10,400 sq km]
POPULATION 4,125,000 **CAPITAL** Beirut
GOVERNMENT Multiparty republic **ETHNIC GROUPS** Arab 95%, Armenian 4%, others **LANGUAGES** Arabic (official), French, English, Armenian **RELIGIONS** Islam 70%, Christianity 30%
CURRENCY Lebanese pound = 100 piastres

LESOTHO

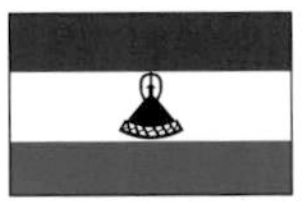

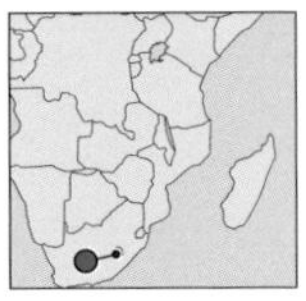

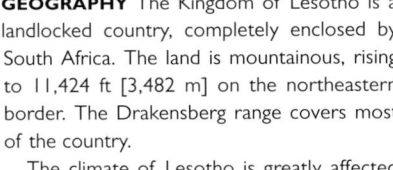

GEOGRAPHY The Kingdom of Lesotho is a landlocked country, completely enclosed by South Africa. The land is mountainous, rising to 11,424 ft [3,482 m] on the northeastern border. The Drakensberg range covers most of the country.

The climate of Lesotho is greatly affected by the altitude, because most of the country lies above 4,920 ft [1,500 m]. Summers are warm but winters are cold. The rainfall averages about 28 inches [700 mm].

POLITICS & ECONOMY The Basotho nation was founded in the 1820s by King Moshoeshoe I, who united various groups fleeing from tribal wars in southern Africa. Britain made the area a protectorate in 1868 and, in 1871, placed it under the British Cape Colony in South Africa. But in 1884, Basutoland, as the area was called, was reconstituted as a British protectorate, where whites were not allowed to own land.

The country finally became independent in 1966 as the Kingdom of Lesotho, with Moshoeshoe II, great-grandson of Moshoeshoe I, as its king. Since independence, Lesotho has suffered instability. The military seized power in 1986 and stripped Moshoeshoe II of his powers in 1990, installing his son, Letsie III, as monarch. After elections in 1993, Moshoeshoe II was restored to office in 1995. But after his death in a car crash in 1996, Letsie III again became king. In 1998, an army revolt, following an election in which the ruling party won 79 out of the 80 seats, caused much damage to the economy. Lesotho has faced many problems, including drought, while 23.2% of the people were reported to be infected with the HIV virus in 2008.

Lesotho lacks natural resources, and the UN has stated that 40% of the people are "ultra-poor." Agriculture employs 18% of the people, mostly at subsistence level. Remittances sent home by Basotho working abroad are important to the economy.

AREA 11,720 sq mi [30,355 sq km]
POPULATION 1,920,000 **CAPITAL** Maseru
GOVERNMENT Constitutional monarchy
ETHNIC GROUPS Sotho 99% **LANGUAGES** Sesotho and English (both official) **RELIGIONS** Christianity 80%, traditional beliefs 20%
CURRENCY Loti = 100 lisente

LIBERIA

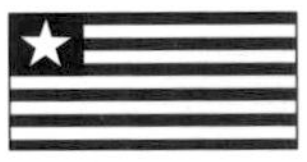

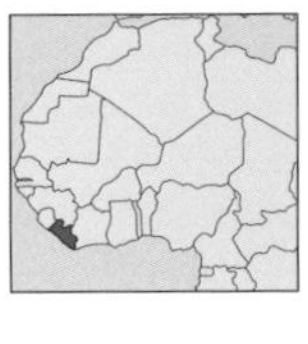

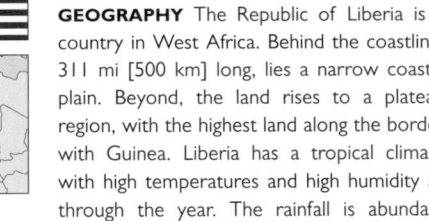

GEOGRAPHY The Republic of Liberia is a country in West Africa. Behind the coastline, 311 mi [500 km] long, lies a narrow coastal plain. Beyond, the land rises to a plateau region, with the highest land along the border with Guinea. Liberia has a tropical climate with high temperatures and high humidity all through the year. The rainfall is abundant all year round, but there is a particularly wet period from June to November. The rainfall generally increases from east to west.

POLITICS & ECONOMY In the late 18th century, some white Americans in the United States wanted to help freed black slaves to return to Africa. In 1816, they set up the American Colonization Society, which bought land in what is now Liberia.

In 1822, the Society landed former slaves at a settlement on the coast which they named Monrovia. In 1847, Liberia became a fully independent republic with a constitution much like that of the United States. For many years, the Americo-Liberians controlled the country's government. US influence remained strong and the American Firestone Company, which ran Liberia's rubber plantations, was especially influential. Foreign companies were also involved in exploiting Liberia's mineral resources, including its huge iron-ore deposits.

In 1980, a military group composed of people from the local population killed the Americo-Liberian president, William R. Tolbert. An army sergeant, Samuel K. Doe, was made president of Liberia. Elections held in 1985 resulted in victory for Doe. From 1989, the country was plunged into civil war between various ethnic groups. Doe was assassinated in 1990 and the struggle with rebel groups continued. West African peacekeeping forces arrived in Liberia and, in 1995, a ceasefire was agreed. A council of state, composed of former warlords, was set up in 1997 and Charles Taylor became president. Taylor fled the country in 2003, and in 2006 he was extradited and charged with war crimes. Following elections in 2005, Ellen Sirleaf-Johnson was elected president. She became Africa's first woman president.

Liberia's economy was devastated by the civil war. Agriculture is important, but most farmers live at subsistence level. Food crops include cassava, rice, and sugarcane, while rubber, cocoa, and coffee are exported. The most valuable export is rubber.

Liberia also obtains revenue from its "flag of convenience," which is used by about one-sixth of the world's commercial shipping, exploiting low taxes.

AREA 43,000 sq mi [111,369 sq km]
POPULATION 3,685,000 **CAPITAL** Monrovia
GOVERNMENT Multiparty republic **ETHNIC GROUPS** Indigenous African tribes 95% (including Kpelle, Bassa, Grebo, Gio, Kru, Mano)
LANGUAGES English (official), ethnic languages
RELIGIONS Christianity 40%, Islam 20%, traditional beliefs and others 40% **CURRENCY** Liberian dollar = 100 cents

LIBYA

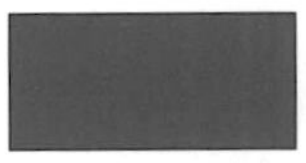

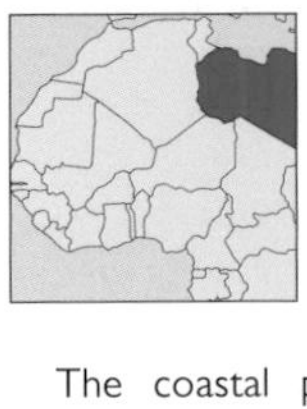

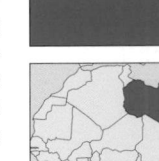

GEOGRAPHY The Socialist People's Libyan Arab Jamahiriya, as Libya is officially called, is a large country in North Africa. Most people live on the coastal plains in the northeast and northwest. The Sahara, the world's largest desert which occupies 95% of Libya, reaches the Mediterranean coast along the Gulf of Sidra (Khalij Surt).

The coastal plains in the northeast and northwest have Mediterranean climates, with hot, dry summers and mild, sometimes wet winters. Hot desert conditions prevail inland.

POLITICS & ECONOMY Italy took over Libya in 1911, but lost it during World War II. Britain and France jointly ruled Libya until 1951, when the country became an independent kingdom.

In 1969, a military group headed by Colonel Muammar Gaddafi deposed the king and set up a military government. Under Gaddafi, the government took control of the economy and used money from oil exports to finance welfare services and development projects. Gaddafi was criticized for supporting terrorist groups around the world, and Libya became isolated from the mid-1980s.

From 2004, relations with the West improved and diplomatic relations were restored with many nations, including the United States. However, in February 2011, the arrest of a human rights campaigner sparked off protests in Benghazi. The protests rapidly spread to other cities in the east and west. Pro-Gaddafi forces clashed with protesters, while Gaddafi insisted that he would remain in Libya. Sanctions were imposed on Libya. In March, as Gaddafi's forces continued to attack the protesters, the UN Security Council sanctioned Western governments to impose a no-fly zone over Libya.

The discovery of oil and natural gas in 1959 led to a transformation of Libya's economy. This formerly poor country soon became Africa's richest in terms of its per capita income. But it remains a developing country, because oil accounts for nearly all its export revenues. Agriculture is important, although Libya imports food. Crops include barley, citrus fruits, dates, olives, potatoes, and wheat, while cattle, sheep, and poultry are raised. Libya has oil refineries and petrochemical plants. Other manufactures include cement and steel.

AREA 679,358 SQ MI [1,759,540 SQ KM] **POPULATION** 6,461,000
CAPITAL TRIPOLI **GOVERNMENT** SINGLE-PARTY SOCIALIST STATE
ETHNIC GROUPS LIBYAN ARAB AND BERBER 97%
LANGUAGES ARABIC (OFFICIAL), BERBER **RELIGIONS** ISLAM (SUNNI MUSLIM) 97% **CURRENCY** LIBYAN DINAR = 1,000 DIRHAMS

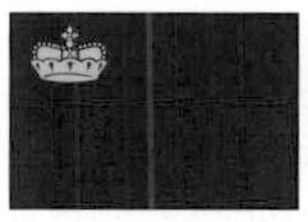
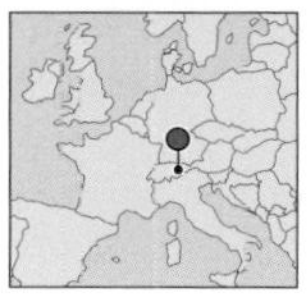

LIECHTENSTEIN

The tiny Principality of Liechtenstein is sandwiched between Switzerland and Austria. The River Rhine flows along its western border, while Alpine peaks rise in the east and south. The climate is relatively mild. Since 1924, Liechtenstein has been in a customs union with Switzerland. Taxation is low and the country is a haven for foreign companies. In 2004, the head of state Prince Hans-Adam II handed over the running of the country to his son, Prince Alois, though he remained titular head of state. In 2009, Liechtenstein agreed to share tax information with a number of countries, including Germany, the UK, and the US.

AREA 62 SQ MI [160 SQ KM] **POPULATION** 35,000 **CAPITAL** VADUZ

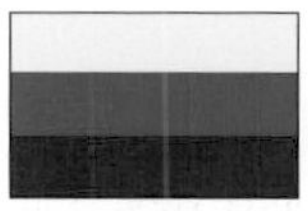
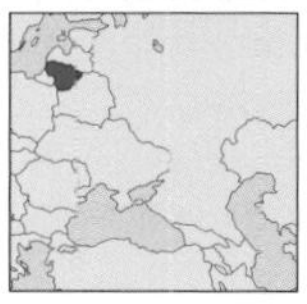

LITHUANIA

GEOGRAPHY The Republic of Lithuania is the southernmost of the three Baltic states which were ruled as part of the Soviet Union between 1940 and 1991. Much of the land is flat or gently rolling, with the highest land in the southeast.

Winters are cold and summers warm. The annual rainfall in the west is about 25 inches [630 mm]. Eastern areas are drier.

POLITICS & ECONOMY The Lithuanian people were united into a single nation in the 12th century, and later joined a union with Poland. In 1795, Lithuania came under Russian rule. After World War I (1914–18), Lithuania declared itself independent, and in 1920 it signed a peace treaty with the Russians, though Poland held Vilnius until 1939. In 1940, the Soviet Union occupied Lithuania, but the Germans invaded in 1941. Soviet forces returned in 1944, and Lithuania was integrated into the Soviet Union. In 1988, when the Soviet Union was introducing reforms, the Lithuanians demanded independence. Their language is one of the oldest in the world, and the country was always the most homogenous of the Baltic states, staunchly Catholic and resistant of attempts to suppress their culture. Pro-independence groups won the national elections in 1990 and, in 1991, the Soviet Union recognized Lithuania's independence.

Since 1991, Lithuania has sought to reform its economy and introduce a private enterprise system. Lithuania has also drawn closer to the West and, in 2004, it became a member of both the North Atlantic Treaty Organization and the European Union.

The World Bank classifies Lithuania as a "lower-middle-income" developing country. Lithuania lacks natural resources, but manufacturing, based on imported materials, is the most valuable activity.

AREA 25,174 SQ MI [65,200 SQ KM]
POPULATION 3,545,000 **CAPITAL** VILNIUS
GOVERNMENT MULTIPARTY REPUBLIC
ETHNIC GROUPS LITHUANIAN 80%, RUSSIAN 9%, POLISH 7%, BELARUSIAN 2% **LANGUAGES** LITHUANIAN (OFFICIAL), RUSSIAN, POLISH
RELIGIONS MAINLY ROMAN CATHOLIC **CURRENCY** LITAS = 100 CENTAI

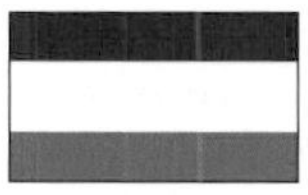
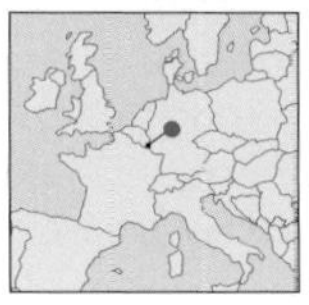

LUXEMBOURG

GEOGRAPHY The Grand Duchy of Luxembourg is one of the smallest and oldest countries in Europe. The north belongs to an upland region which includes the Ardenne in Belgium and Luxembourg, and the Eifel highlands in Germany.

Luxembourg has a temperate climate. The south has warm summers and falls, when grapes ripen in sheltered southeastern valleys. Winters are sometimes severe, especially in upland areas.

POLITICS & ECONOMY Germany occupied Luxembourg in World Wars I and II. In 1944–5, northern Luxembourg was the scene of the Battle of the Bulge. In 1948, Luxembourg joined Belgium and the Netherlands in a union called Benelux. In the 1950s, it was one of the six founders of what is now the European Union. Its capital is a major financial center and contains several international agencies. In 2008, parliament restricted the monarch to a ceremonial role following the grand duke's refusal to sign a law allowing for euthanasia.

Luxembourg has iron-ore reserves and is a major steel producer. It also has many high-technology industries, producing electronic goods and computers. Steel and other manufactures, including chemicals, rubber products, glass, and aluminum, dominate the country's exports. Other major activities include tourism and financial services.

AREA 998 SQ MI [2,586 SQ KM]
POPULATION 498,000 **CAPITAL** LUXEMBOURG
GOVERNMENT CONSTITUTIONAL MONARCHY (GRAND DUCHY)
ETHNIC GROUPS LUXEMBOURGER 71%, PORTUGUESE, ITALIAN, FRENCH, BELGIAN, SLAVS **LANGUAGES** LUXEMBOURGISH (OFFICIAL), FRENCH, GERMAN **RELIGIONS** ROMAN CATHOLIC 87%, OTHERS 13%
CURRENCY EURO = 100 CENTS

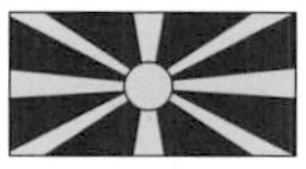
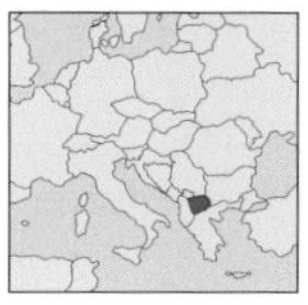

MACEDONIA (FYROM)

GEOGRAPHY The Republic of Macedonia is a country in southeastern Europe, which was once one of the six republics that made up the former Federal People's Republic of Yugoslavia. This landlocked country is largely mountainous or hilly. Macedonia has hot summers, though highland areas are cooler. Winters are cold and snowfalls are often heavy. The climate is fairly continental in character and rain occurs throughout the year.

POLITICS & ECONOMY Until the 20th century, Macedonia's history was closely tied to a larger area, also called Macedonia, which included parts of northern Greece and southwestern Bulgaria. This region reached its peak in power at the time of Philip II (382–336 BC) and his son Alexander the Great (336–323 BC). After Alexander's death, his empire was split up and it gradually declined. The area became a Roman province in the 140s BC and part of the Byzantine Empire from AD 395. In the 6th century, Slavs from eastern Europe settled in the area, followed by Bulgars from central Asia in the 9th century. The Byzantine Empire regained control in 1018, but Serbia took Macedonia in the early 14th century. In 1371, the Ottoman Turks conquered the area and ruled it for more than 500 years.

In 1913, at the end of the Balkan Wars, the area was divided between Serbia, Bulgaria, and Greece. At the end of World War I, Serbian Macedonia became part of the Kingdom of the Serbs, Croats, and Slovenes, which was renamed Yugoslavia in 1929. After World War II, Yugoslavia became a Communist country under ex-partisan leader Josip Broz Tito.

Tito died in 1980 and, in the early 1990s, the country broke up into five separate republics. Macedonia declared its independence in September 1991. Greece objected to this territory using the name Macedonia, which it considered to be a Greek name. It also objected to a symbol on Macedonia's flag and a reference in the constitution to the desire to reunite the three parts of the old Macedonia.

Macedonia adopted a new clause in its constitution rejecting any Macedonian claims on Greek territory and, in 1993, the United Nations accepted the new republic as a member under the name of The Former Yugoslav Republic of Macedonia (FYROM). By the end of 1993, all the countries of the EU, except Greece, were establishing diplomatic relations with the FYROM. In 1995, Greece lifted its trade ban, when Macedonia agreed to redesign its flag and remove territorial claims from its constitution. In 2001, fighting along the Kosovo border was attributed to people who wanted to create a Greater Albania. The uprising ended when Macedonia granted its Albanian-speakers increased rights. In 2009, Macedonia applied to the International Court of Justice for a ruling on its dispute with Greece over its name.

The World Bank describes Macedonia as a "lower-middle-income" economy. Manufactures dominate the country's exports. Coal is mined, but oil and natural gas are imported. The country is self-sufficient in its basic food needs.

AREA 9,928 SQ MI [25,713 SQ KM] **POPULATION** 2,072,000
CAPITAL SKOPJE **GOVERNMENT** MULTIPARTY REPUBLIC
ETHNIC GROUPS MACEDONIAN 64%, ALBANIAN 25%, TURKISH 4%, ROMANIAN 3%, SERB 2% **LANGUAGES** MACEDONIAN AND ALBANIAN (OFFICIAL) **RELIGIONS** MACEDONIAN ORTHODOX 70%, ISLAM 29%
CURRENCY MACEDONIAN DENAR = 100 PARAS

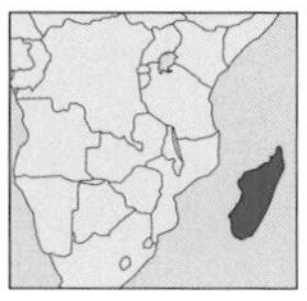

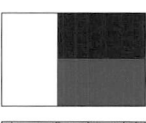

MADAGASCAR

GEOGRAPHY The Democratic Republic of Madagascar, in southeastern Africa, is an island nation, which has a larger area than France. Behind the narrow coastal plains in the east lies a highland zone, mostly between 2,000 ft and 4,000 ft [610 m to 1,220 m] above sea level. Broad plains border the Mozambique Channel in the west.

Temperatures in the highlands are moderated by the altitude. The winters (from April to September) are dry, but heavy rains occur in summer. The eastern coastlands are warm and humid. The west is drier, and the south and southwest are hot and dry.

POLITICS & ECONOMY People from Southeast Asia began to settle on Madagascar around 2,000 years ago. Subsequent influxes from Africa and Arabia added to the island's diverse heritage, culture, and language.

French troops defeated a Malagasy army in 1895 and Madagascar became a French colony. In 1960, it achieved full independence as the Malagasy Republic. In 1972, army officers seized control and, in 1975, under the leadership of Lieutenant-Commander Didier Ratsiraka, the country was renamed Madagascar. In 2002, the country came close to civil war when Ratsiraka and his opponent Marc Ravalomanana both claimed victory in presidential elections. Ravalomanana became president, but he was deposed by Andry Rajoelina in 2009, who became *de facto* president. In 2010, a new constitution was adopted in a referendum, enabling Rajoelina to run for president.

Madagascar is a poor country. Poverty and population growth impose pressure on the dwindling forests and the unique wildlife, as well as causing severe soil erosion. Farming, fishing, and forestry employ about 80% of the people. Food crops include bananas, cassava, rice, and sweet potatoes. Coffee is exported.

AREA 226,657 SQ MI [587,041 SQ KM]
POPULATION 21,282,000 **CAPITAL** ANTANANARIVO
GOVERNMENT REPUBLIC **ETHNIC GROUPS** MERINA, BETSIMISARAKA, BETSILEO, TSIMIHETY, SAKALAVA, AND OTHERS
LANGUAGES MALAGASY AND FRENCH (BOTH OFFICIAL)
RELIGIONS TRADITIONAL BELIEFS 52%, CHRISTIANITY 41%, ISLAM 7%
CURRENCY MALAGASY FRANC = 100 CENTIMES

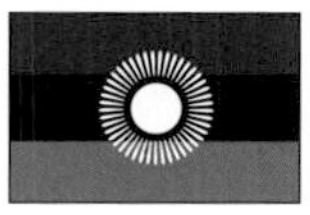
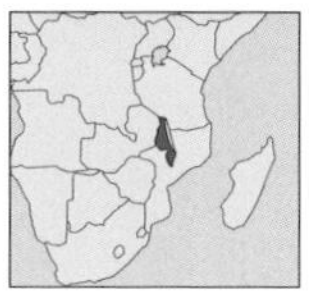

MALAWI

GEOGRAPHY The Republic of Malawi includes part of Lake Malawi, which is drained by the River Shire, a tributary of the River Zambezi. The land is mostly mountainous. The highest peak, Mulanje, reaches 9,843 ft [3,000 m] in the southeast.

While the low-lying areas of Malawi are hot and humid all year round, the uplands have a pleasant climate. Lilongwe has a warm and sunny climate. Frosts sometimes occur in July and August, in the middle of the long dry season.

POLITICS & ECONOMY Malawi, then called Nyasaland, became a British protectorate in 1891. In 1953, Britain established the Federation of Rhodesia and Nyasaland, which also included what are now Zambia and Zimbabwe. Black African opposition, led in Nyasaland by Dr Hastings Kamuzu Banda, led to the dissolution of the federation in 1963. In 1964, Nyasaland became independent as Malawi, with Banda as prime minister. Banda became president when the country became a republic in 1966, and in 1971 he was made president for life. Banda was an autocrat, ruling through the only party, the Malawi Congress Party. But a multiparty system was restored in 1993. Bakili Muluzi became president, and in 2004 he was succeeded by Bingu wa Mutharika, leader of the United Democratic Front (UDF). In 2005, he resigned from the UDF and set up a new Democratic Progressive Party. Mutharika was re-elected president in 2009.

Malawi is one of the world's poorest countries. More than 80% of the people are farmers, but many grow little more than they need to feed their families.

AREA 45,747 SQ MI [118,484 SQ KM]
POPULATION 15,448,000 **CAPITAL** LILONGWE
GOVERNMENT MULTIPARTY REPUBLIC
ETHNIC GROUPS CHEWA, NYANJA, TONGA, TUMBUKA, LOMWE, YAO, NGONI, AND OTHERS
LANGUAGES CHICHEWA AND ENGLISH (BOTH OFFICIAL)
RELIGIONS PROTESTANT 55%, ROMAN CATHOLIC 20%, ISLAM 20%
CURRENCY MALAWIAN KWACHA = 100 TAMBALA

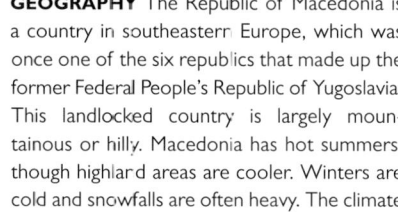

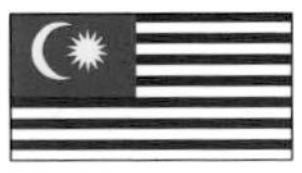
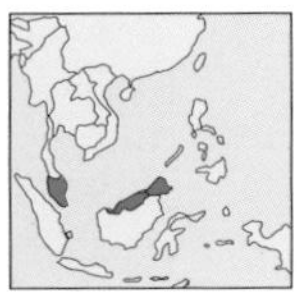

MALAYSIA

GEOGRAPHY The Federation of Malaysia consists of two main parts. Peninsular Malaysia, which is joined to mainland Asia, contains about 80% of the population. The other main regions, Sabah and Sarawak, are in northern Borneo, an island which Malaysia shares with Indonesia. Behind the coastal lowlands, the interior is mountainous.

Malaysia has a hot equatorial climate. The temperatures are high all through the year, though the mountains are much cooler than the lowland areas. The rainfall is heavy throughout the year.

POLITICS & ECONOMY Around 1,200 years ago, Indian traders introduced Hinduism and Buddhism into the Malay peninsula, while Arabs introduced Islam in the 15th century. Portuguese traders reached Melaka in 1509, but the Dutch took over in 1641. Britain became established in the area in 1786.

Japan occupied the area during World War II (1939–45), but the area reverted to British rule in 1945. In the 1940s and 1950s, Communist guerrillas battled unsuccessfully for power. Malaya (Peninsular Malaysia) became independent in 1957. Malaysia was created in 1963, when Malaya, Singapore, Sabah, and Sarawak agreed to unite, but Singapore withdrew in 1965.

From 1981, under the leadership of Dr Mahathir bin Mohamad, Malaysia achieved rapid economic progress. However, together with other countries in eastern Asia, it experienced an economic recession in 1997. The government initiated measures aimed at restoring confidence. In 2003 Mahathir bin Mohamad was succeeded by Abdullah Ahmad Badawi, who stood down in 2009, following poor parliamentary election results in 2008. His deputy, Najib Razak, took over as prime minister. He faced many economic problems caused by the global financial crisis.

The World Bank classifies Malaysia as an "upper-middle-income" developing country. Palm oil, rubber, and tin are major products. Manufactures include cars, chemicals, a wide range of electronic goods, plastics, textiles, rubber, and wood products.

AREA 127,320 SQ MI [329,758 SQ KM] **POPULATION** 28,275,000
CAPITAL KUALA LUMPUR; PUTRAJAYA (ADMINISTRATIVE CAPITAL AWAITING COMPLETION)
GOVERNMENT FEDERAL CONSTITUTIONAL MONARCHY
ETHNIC GROUPS MALAY AND OTHER INDIGENOUS GROUPS 58%, CHINESE 24%, INDIAN 8%, OTHERS **LANGUAGES** MALAY (OFFICIAL), CHINESE, ENGLISH **RELIGIONS** ISLAM, BUDDHISM, DAOISM, HINDUISM, CHRISTIANITY, SIKHISM **CURRENCY** RINGGIT = 100 CENTS

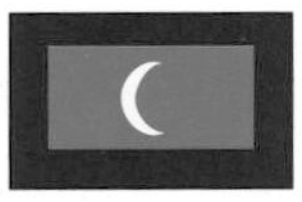
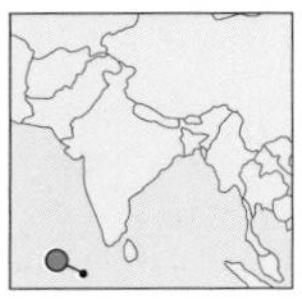

MALDIVES

The Republic of the Maldives consists of about 1,200 low-lying coral islands, south of India. The highest point is 79 ft [24 m], but most of the land is only 6 ft [1.8 m] above sea level. The islands became a British territory in 1887 and independence was achieved in 1965. Tourism and fishing are the main industries.

AREA 115 SQ MI [298 SQ KM] **POPULATION** 396,000 **CAPITAL** MALÉ

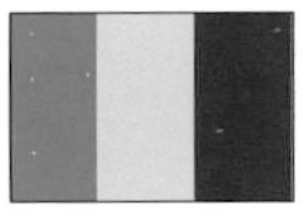
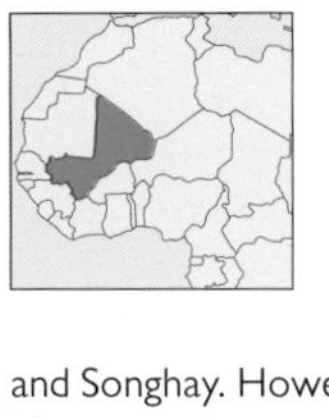

MALI

GEOGRAPHY The Republic of Mali is a landlocked country in northern Africa. The land is generally flat, with the highest land in the north. Northern Mali is hot and practically rainless. The south has enough rain for farming.

POLITICS & ECONOMY Between the 4th and 16th centuries, Mali was part of three African empires – ancient Ghana, ancient Mali, and Songhay. However, after 1591, when Songhay was defeated by Morocco, the area was divided into small kingdoms. France ruled the area, then known as French Sudan, from 1893 until the country became independent as Mali in 1960.

The first socialist government was overthrown in 1968 by an army group led by Moussa Traoré, but he was ousted in 1991. Multiparty democracy was restored in 1992 and Alpha Oumar Konaré was elected president. Konaré stood down in 2002 and Ahmadou Toure, who had restored democracy in 1992, was elected president. He was re-elected in 2007.

Mali is one of the world's poorest countries and 70% of the land is desert or semidesert. Only about 2% of the land is used for growing crops, while 25% is used for grazing animals. Agriculture employs more than one-third of the people, many of whom subsist by nomadic livestock rearing.

AREA 478,838 SQ MI [1,240,192 SQ KM]
POPULATION 13,796,000 **CAPITAL** BAMAKO
GOVERNMENT MULTIPARTY REPUBLIC **ETHNIC GROUPS** MANDE 50% (BAMBARA, MALINKE, SONINKE), PEUL 17%, VOLTAIC 12%, SONGHAI 6%, TUAREG AND MOOR 10%, OTHERS **LANGUAGES** FRENCH (OFFICIAL), MANY AFRICAN LANGUAGES **RELIGIONS** ISLAM 90%, TRADITIONAL BELIEFS 9%, CHRISTIANITY 1% **CURRENCY** CFA FRANC = 100 CENTIMES

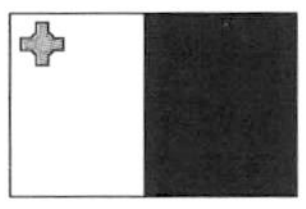
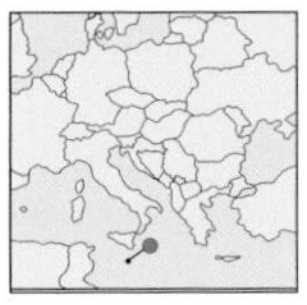

MALTA

GEOGRAPHY The Republic of Malta consists of two main islands, Malta and Gozo, with a third, much smaller island called Comino lying between the two large islands and two islets. The climate is typically Mediterranean, with hot, dry summers and mild, moist winters.

POLITICS & ECONOMY Malta has fascinating Stone and Bronze age remains. The islands later came under Phoenician, Greek, Carthaginian, Roman, and Arab rule. In about 1090, Malta came under the Norman kings of Sicily and, from 1530, the Knights Hospitallers (also called the Knights of St John of Jerusalem). France took the islands in 1798, but the British drove them out in 1800. British rule was officially recognized in 1815.

During World War I (1914–18), Malta was an important naval base. In World War II (1939–45), Italian and German aircraft bombed the islands. In recognition of the islanders' bravery, the British King George VI awarded the George Cross to Malta in 1942. In 1953, Malta became a base for NATO (North Atlantic Treaty Organization). Malta became independent in 1964 and a republic in 1974. In 1979, Malta ceased to be a British military base. Malta was declared a neutral country in the 1980s. It became a member of the European Union on May 1, 2004, and adopted the euro as its official currency in 2008.

The World Bank classifies Malta as an "upper-middle-income" developing country. It lacks natural resources, and most people work in the former naval dockyards, which are now used for commercial shipbuilding and repair, in manufacturing industries, and in the tourist industry.

Manufactures include processed food and chemicals. Farming is difficult, because of the rocky soils. Crops include barley, fruits, potatoes, and wheat. Malta also has a small fishing industry.

AREA 122 SQ MI [316 SQ KM] **POPULATION** 407,000
CAPITAL VALLETTA **GOVERNMENT** MULTIPARTY REPUBLIC
ETHNIC GROUPS MALTESE 96%, BRITISH 2% **LANGUAGES** MALTESE AND ENGLISH (BOTH OFFICIAL) **RELIGIONS** ROMAN CATHOLIC 98%
CURRENCY EURO = 100 CENTS

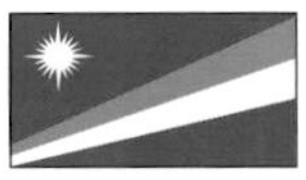
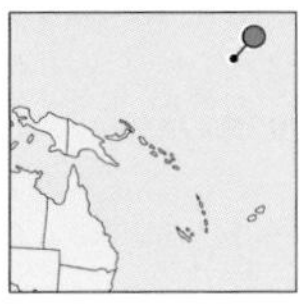

MARSHALL ISLANDS

The Republic of the Marshall Islands, a former US territory, became fully independent in 1991. This island nation, lying north of Kiribati in a region known as Micronesia, is heavily dependent on US aid. The main activities are agriculture and tourism.

AREA 70 SQ MI [181 SQ KM]
POPULATION 66,000 **CAPITAL** MAJURO

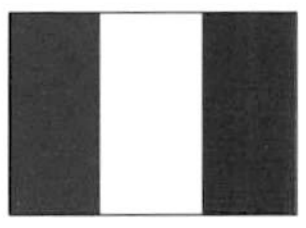
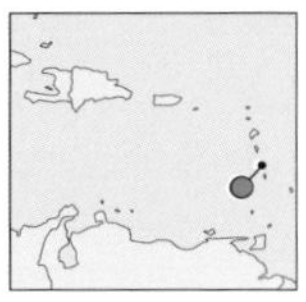

MARTINIQUE

Martinique, a volcanic island nation in the Caribbean, was colonized by France in 1635. It became a French overseas department in 1946. Tourism and agriculture are major activities. About 70% of Martinique's gross domestic product is provided by the French government, allowing for a good standard of living.

AREA 425 SQ MI [1,102 SQ KM]
POPULATION 436,000 **CAPITAL** FORT-DE-FRANCE

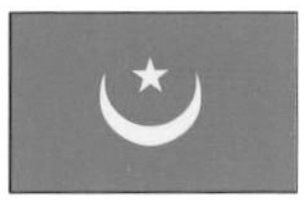
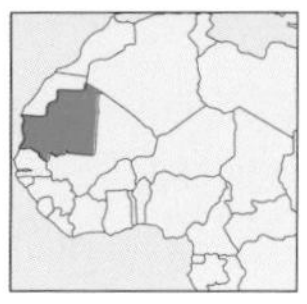

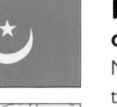

MAURITANIA

GEOGRAPHY The Islamic Republic of Mauritania in northwestern Africa is nearly twice the size of France. But France has more than 28 times as many people. Part of the world's largest desert, the Sahara, covers northern Mauritania and most Mauritanians live in the southwest. The amount of rainfall and the length of the rainy season increase from north to south. Much of the land is desert, but southwesterly winds bring summer rain to the south.

POLITICS & ECONOMY Originally part of the great African empires of Ghana and Mali, France set up a protectorate in Mauritania in 1903, attempting to exploit the trade in gum arabic. The country became a territory of French West Africa and a French colony in 1920. French West Africa was a huge territory, which included present-day Benin, Burkina Faso, Guinea, Ivory Coast, Mali, Niger, and Senegal, as well as Mauritania. Mauritania became independent in 1960.

In 1976, Spain withdrew from Spanish (now Western) Sahara, a territory bordering Mauritania to the north. Morocco occupied the northern two-thirds of this territory, while Mauritania took the rest. But Saharan guerrillas belonging to POLISARIO (the Popular Front for the Liberation of Saharan Territories) began an armed struggle for independence. In 1979, Mauritania withdrew from the southern part of Western Sahara, which was then occupied by Morocco. Democracy was restored after a new constitution was adopted in 1991. A military group seized power in 2005, but democratic elections were held in 2007. The military again seized control in 2008, and in 2009 its leader, Mohamad Ould Abdelaziz, was elected president.

Mauritania is a "low-income" developing country. Nearly half of the people are engaged in agriculture. In 2006, Mauritania became Africa's newest oil producer, when an offshore platform came online for the first time.

AREA 395,953 SQ MI [1,025,520 SQ KM]
POPULATION 3,205,000 **CAPITAL** NOUAKCHOTT
GOVERNMENT MULTIPARTY ISLAMIC REPUBLIC
ETHNIC GROUPS MIXED MOOR/BLACK 40%, MOOR 30%, BLACK 30%
LANGUAGES ARABIC AND WOLOF (BOTH OFFICIAL), FRENCH
RELIGIONS ISLAM
CURRENCY OUGUIYA = 5 KHOUMS

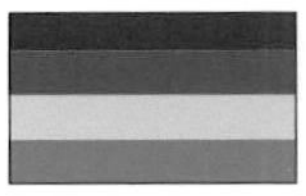
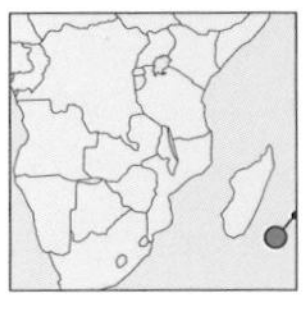

MAURITIUS

The Republic of Mauritius, an Indian Ocean nation lying east of Madagascar, was previously ruled by France and Britain until it achieved independence in 1968. It became a republic in 1992. Sugar production is in decline but tourism is vital to the economy.

AREA 788 SQ MI [2,040 SQ KM]
POPULATION 1,294,000 **CAPITAL** PORT LOUIS

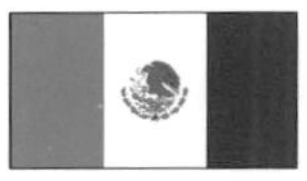
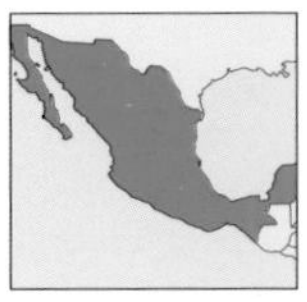

MEXICO

GEOGRAPHY The United Mexican States, as Mexico is officially named, is the world's most populous Spanish-speaking country. Much of the land is mountainous, although most people live on the central plateau. Mexico contains two large peninsulas, Lower (or Baja) California in the northwest and the flat Yucatán peninsula in the southeast.

The climate varies according to the altitude. The resort of Acapulco on the southwest coast has a dry and sunny climate. Mexico City, at about 7,546 ft [2,300 m] above sea level, is much cooler. Most rain occurs between June and September. The rainfall decreases north of Mexico City and northern Mexico is mainly arid.

POLITICS & ECONOMY In the mid-19th century, Mexico lost land to the United States, and between 1910 and 1921 violent revolutions created chaos. Reforms were introduced in the 1920s and, in 1929, the Institutional Revolutionary Party (PRI) was formed. The PRI ruled Mexico effectively as a one-party state until it was finally defeated in 2001. The new president, Vicente Fox, faced many problems. He was succeeded by Felipe Calderón. In 2008–9, killings associated with the illegal drug traffic increased, spreading over the border into the United States.

The World Bank classifies Mexico as an "upper-middle-income" developing country. Agriculture is important. Food crops include beans, maize, rice, and wheat, while cash crops include coffee, cotton, fruits, and vegetables. Beef cattle, dairy cattle, and other livestock are raised and fishing is also important.

But oil and oil products are the chief exports, while manufacturing is the most valuable activity. Mexico is the world's leading silver producer, and it also mines copper, gold, lead, zinc, and other minerals. Many factories near the northern border assemble goods, such as car parts and electrical products, for US companies.

Hopes for the future lie in increasing cooperation with the USA and Canada. However, problems with the United States mounted

from 2008 as drug cartels carried out large numbers of killings, mostly along the US border.

AREA 756,061 SQ MI [1,958,201 SQ KM]
POPULATION 112,469,000 **CAPITAL** MEXICO CITY
GOVERNMENT FEDERAL REPUBLIC
ETHNIC GROUPS MESTIZO 60%, AMERINDIAN 30%, WHITE 9%
LANGUAGES SPANISH (OFFICIAL)
RELIGIONS ROMAN CATHOLIC 90%, PROTESTANT 6%
CURRENCY MEXICAN PESO = 100 CENTAVOS

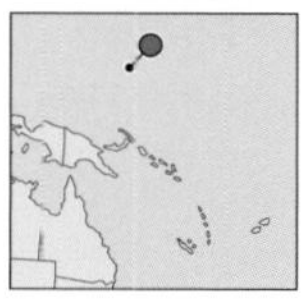

MICRONESIA

The Federated States of Micronesia, a former US territory covering a vast area in the western Pacific Ocean, became fully independent in 1991. The main export is copra. Fishing and tourism are also important.

AREA 271 SQ MI [702 SQ KM]
POPULATION 107,000 **CAPITAL** PALIKIR

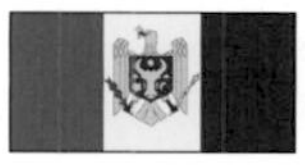
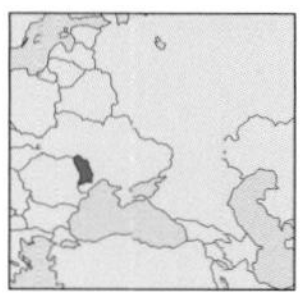

MOLDOVA

GEOGRAPHY The Republic of Moldova is a small country sandwiched between Ukraine and Romania. It was formerly one of the 15 republics that made up the Soviet Union. Much of the land is hilly and the highest areas are near the center of the country.

Moldova has a moderately continental climate, with warm summers and fairly cold winters when temperatures dip below freezing point. Most of the rain comes in the warmer months.

POLITICS & ECONOMY In the 14th century, the Moldavians formed a state called Moldavia. It included part of Romania and Bessarabia (now the modern country of Moldova). The Ottoman Turks took the area in the 16th century, but in 1812 Russia took over Bessarabia. In 1861, Moldavia and Walachia united to form Romania. Russia retook southern Bessarabia in 1878.

After World War I (1914–18), all of Bessarabia was returned to Romania, but the Soviet Union did not recognize this act. From 1944, the Moldovan Soviet Socialist Republic was part of the Soviet Union.

In 1989, the Moldovans asserted their independence and ethnicity by making Romanian the official language and, at the end of 1991, Moldova became an independent nation. But Trans-Dniester, an area east of the River Dniester, has sought autonomy. In 2006, its people voted for independence and union with Russia. This vote was not recognized internationally.

In 2001, Moldovans returned the Communist Party to power in a general election. Under President Vladimir Voronin, Moldova enjoyed a period of economic growth. The Communist Party was re-elected in 2005 and 2009. Following allegations of fraud, further inconclusive elections were held in 2010.

In terms of its GNP per capita, Moldova is one of Europe's poorest countries. Agriculture is the leading activity and products include fruits, maize, tobacco, and wine. Moldova has few natural resources and it imports materials and fuels for its industries. Light industries, such as food processing and factories making household appliances, are increasing.

AREA 13,070 SQ MI [33,851 SQ KM]
POPULATION 4,317,000 **CAPITAL** KISHINEV
GOVERNMENT MULTIPARTY REPUBLIC
ETHNIC GROUPS MOLDOVAN/ROMANIAN 65%, UKRAINIAN 14%, RUSSIAN 13%, OTHERS
LANGUAGES MOLDOVAN/ROMANIAN AND RUSSIAN (OFFICIAL)
RELIGIONS EASTERN ORTHODOX 98%
CURRENCY MOLDOVAN LEU = 100 BANI

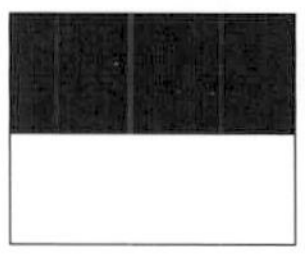
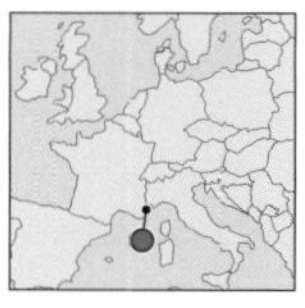

MONACO

The tiny Principality of Monaco consists of a narrow strip of coastline and a rocky peninsula on the French Riviera. Its considerable wealth is derived largely from banking, finance, gambling, and tourism. Monaco's citizens do not pay any state tax. The reigning prince is Albert II. In 2008, plans to extend the area of Monaco by reclaiming land from under the sea were shelved.

AREA 0.4 SQ MI [1 SQ KM] **POPULATION** 31,000 **CAPITAL** MONACO

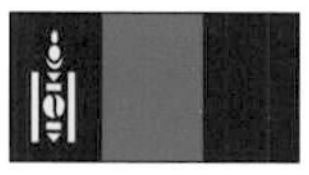
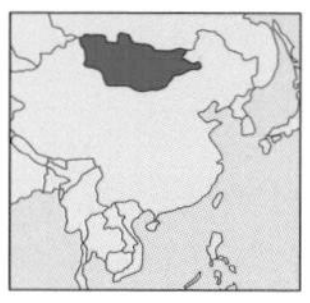

MONGOLIA

GEOGRAPHY The State of Mongolia is the world's largest landlocked country. It consists mainly of high plateaux, with the Gobi Desert in the southeast.

Ulan Bator lies on the northern edge of a desert plateau. It has bitterly cold winters. Summer temperatures are moderated by the altitude.

POLITICS & ECONOMY In the 13th century, Genghis Khan united the Mongolian peoples and built up a great empire. Under his grandson, Kublai Khan, the Mongol empire extended from Korea and China to eastern Europe and present-day Iraq.

The Mongol empire broke up in the late 14th century. In the early 17th century, Inner Mongolia came under Chinese control, and by the late 17th century Outer Mongolia had become a Chinese province. In 1911, the Mongolians drove the Chinese out of Outer Mongolia and made the area a Buddhist kingdom. But in 1924, under Russian influence, the Communist Mongolian People's Republic was set up. From the 1950s, Mongolia supported the Soviet Union in its disputes with China. In 1990, the people demonstrated for more freedom, and free elections in June 1990 were won by the Communist Mongolian People's Revolutionary Party (MPRP). The Democratic Union coalition won power in 1996, but the MPRP regained power in 2000. In 2004, after disputed elections, a coalition government was set up. In 2009, the Democratic Union candidate, Tsakhiagiin Elbegdorj, was elected president.

The World Bank classifies Mongolia as a "lower-middle-income" developing country. Most people were once nomads, who moved around with their herds of sheep, cattle, goats, and horses. Under Communist rule, most people were moved into permanent homes on government-owned farms. Livestock and animal products remain important, but minerals and fuels now account for more than three-fifths of Mongolia's exports.

AREA 604,826 SQ MI [1,566,500 SQ KM]
POPULATION 3,087,000 **CAPITAL** ULAN BATOR
GOVERNMENT MULTIPARTY REPUBLIC **ETHNIC GROUPS** KHALKHA MONGOL 85%, KAZAKH 6% **LANGUAGES** KHALKHA MONGOLIAN (OFFICIAL), TURKIC, RUSSIAN **RELIGIONS** TIBETAN BUDDHIST LAMAISM 96%
CURRENCY TUGRIK = 100 MÖNGÖS

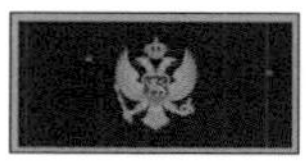
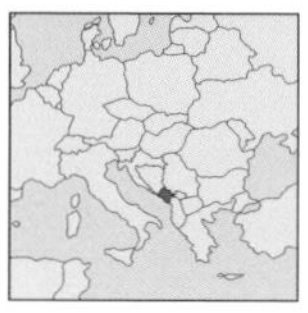

MONTENEGRO

The Republic of Montenegro became a fully independent nation in 2006. It was formerly part of the Union of Serbia and Montenegro and, before 2003, part of Yugoslavia.

The coastal region has a Mediterranean climate. However, inland, the Dinaric Alps, which reach a height of 8,274 ft [2,522 m], have a more severe climate.

Serbia fell under Turkish rule in the 14th century, but Montenegro remained Christian. Montenegro was absorbed into Serbia in 1918. It became part of the Kingdom of the Serbs, Croats, and Slovenes, which was renamed Yugoslavia in 1929. After World War II, Montenegro was recognized as one of the six republics in the Federal Republic of Yugoslavia.

Elections were held in 2009, and in 2010 Igor Luksic became prime minister, following the retirement of Milo Djukanovic.

Manufacturing is the leading activity, and steel and aluminum are major products. But farming remains important. Forests cover more than half of the land.

AREA 5,415 SQ MI [14,026 SQ KM]
POPULATION 667,000 **CAPITAL** PODGORICA
GOVERNMENT REPUBLIC **ETHNIC GROUPS** MONTENEGRIN 43%, SERB 32%, BOSNIAN 8%, ALBANIAN 5%, OTHERS
LANGUAGES SERBIAN (OFFICIAL), BOSNIAN, ALBANIAN, CROATIAN
RELIGIONS ORTHODOX, ISLAM, ROMAN CATHOLIC
CURRENCY EURO = 100 CENTS

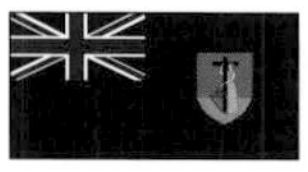
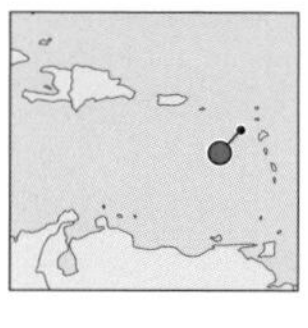

MONTSERRAT

Montserrat is a British overseas territory in the Caribbean Sea. The climate is tropical and hurricanes often cause much damage. Intermittent eruptions of the Soufrière Hills volcano between 1995 and 1998, and again in 2003, led to the emigration of many people and the virtual destruction of Plymouth, the then capital. A new airport was opened in 2005.

AREA 39 SQ MI [102 SQ KM] **POPULATION** 5,000 **CAPITAL** BRADES

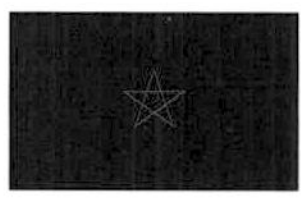
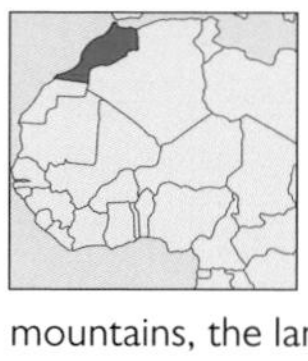

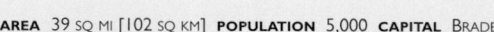

MOROCCO

GEOGRAPHY The Kingdom of Morocco lies in northwestern Africa. Its name comes from the Arabic Maghreb-el-Aksa, meaning "the farthest west." Behind the western coastal plain the land rises to a broad plateau and ranges of the Atlas Mountains. The High (Haut) Atlas contains the highest peak, Djebel Toubkal, at 13,665 ft [4,165 m]. East of the mountains, the land descends to the Sahara. The Canaries Current cools the Atlantic coast. Inland, summers are hot and dry. Winters are mild, with moderate rainfall. Snow often falls on the High Atlas Mountains.

POLITICS & ECONOMY The original people of Morocco were the Berbers. But in the 680s, Arab invaders introduced Islam and the Arabic language. By the early 20th century, France and Spain controlled Morocco, which became an independent kingdom in 1956. Although Morocco is a constitutional monarchy, King Hassan II ruled the country in a generally authoritarian way from the time of his accession to the throne in 1961 to his death in 1999. His successor, Mohamed VI, faced several problems, including that of Western Sahara, which he claimed for Morocco, and the activities of Islamic extremists. In 2009, the alleged al Qaida leader in Morocco was sentenced to imprisonment for life.

Morocco is classified as a "lower-middle-income" developing country. It is the world's third largest producer of phosphate rock, which is used to make fertilizer. One of the reasons why Morocco wants to keep Western Sahara is that it, too, has large phosphate reserves. Farming employs about 40% of Moroccans. Chief crops include barley, beans, citrus fruits, maize, olives, sugar beet, and wheat. Processed phosphates are exported, but most of Morocco's manufactures are for home consumption. Fishing and tourism are also important.

AREA 172,413 SQ MI [446,550 SQ KM]
POPULATION 31,627,000 **CAPITAL** RABAT
GOVERNMENT CONSTITUTIONAL MONARCHY
ETHNIC GROUPS ARAB-BERBER 99%
LANGUAGES ARABIC (OFFICIAL), BERBER DIALECTS, FRENCH
RELIGIONS ISLAM 99% **CURRENCY** MOROCCAN DIRHAM = 100 CENTIMES

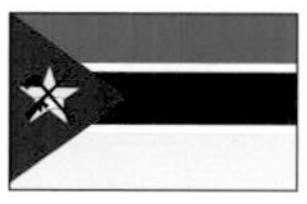
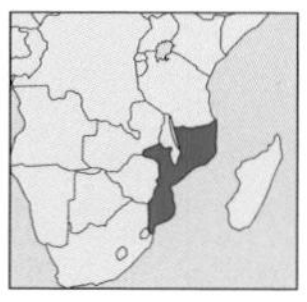

MOZAMBIQUE

GEOGRAPHY The Republic of Mozambique borders the Indian Ocean in southeastern Africa. The coastal plains are narrow in the north but broaden in the south. Inland lie plateaux and hills, which make up another two-fifths of the country. Mozambique has a mostly tropical climate. The capital Maputo, which lies outside the tropics, has hot and humid summers, though the winters are mild and fairly dry.

POLITICS & ECONOMY In 1885, when the European powers divided Africa, Mozambique was recognized as a Portuguese colony. But black African opposition to European rule gradually increased. In 1961, the Front for the Liberation of Mozambique (FRELIMO) was founded to oppose Portuguese rule. In 1964, FRELIMO launched a guerrilla war, which continued for ten years. Mozambique became independent in 1975.

After independence, Mozambique became a one-party state. Its government aided African nationalists in Rhodesia (now Zimbabwe) and South Africa. But the white governments of these countries helped an opposition group, the Mozambique National Resistance Movement (RENAMO) to lead an armed struggle against Mozambique's government. Civil war, combined with droughts, caused much suffering in the 1980s. In 1989, FRELIMO ended one-party rule. The war ended in 1992 and multiparty elections were held in 1994. In 1995 Mozambique became the 53rd member of the Commonwealth. In 2004, and again in 2009, FRELIMO leader Antonio Guebuza was elected president.

In the early 1990s, the UN rated Mozambique as one of the world's poorest countries. The second half of the 1990s saw the start of renewed economic growth, but floods in 2000–1, 2007, and 2008, and prolonged droughts in the mid-2000s and 2008, were major setbacks. About 80% of the people are poor farmers. Crops include cassava, cotton, maize, rice, and tea.

AREA 309,494 SQ MI [801,590 SQ KM]
POPULATION 22,061,000 **CAPITAL** MAPUTO
GOVERNMENT MULTIPARTY REPUBLIC **ETHNIC GROUPS** INDIGENOUS TRIBAL GROUPS (SHANGAAN, CHOKWE, MANYIKA, SENA, MAKUA, OTHERS) 99%
LANGUAGES PORTUGUESE (OFFICIAL), MANY OTHERS
RELIGIONS TRADITIONAL BELIEFS 50%, CHRISTIANITY 30%, ISLAM 20%
CURRENCY METICAL = 100 CENTAVOS

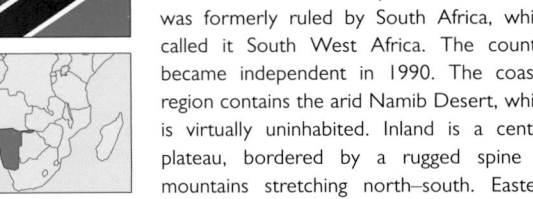

NAMIBIA

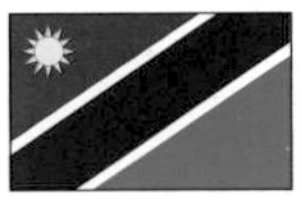

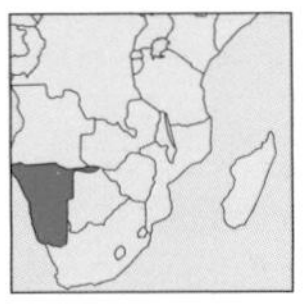

GEOGRAPHY The Republic of Namibia was formerly ruled by South Africa, which called it South West Africa. The country became independent in 1990. The coastal region contains the arid Namib Desert, which is virtually uninhabited. Inland is a central plateau, bordered by a rugged spine of mountains stretching north–south. Eastern Namibia contains part of the Kalahari Desert, a semidesert area extending into Botswana. Namibia has a warm and arid climate. Windhoek has an average annual rainfall of 15 inches [370 mm], which often occurs in thunderstorms during the hot summer.

POLITICS & ECONOMY During World War I, South African troops defeated the Germans who ruled what is now Namibia. After World War II, many people challenged South Africa's right to govern the territory and a civil war began in the 1960s between African guerrillas and South African troops. A ceasefire was agreed in 1989 and Namibia became independent in 1990. In the 1990s, the government pursued a policy of "national reconciliation." An enclave on the coast, called Walvis Bay (Walvisbaai), remained part of South Africa until 1994, when it was transferred to Namibia. In 2004, the nationalist leader, Sam Nujoma, president since 1990, retired. He was succeeded by Hifikepunye Pohamba, who was re-elected in 2009.

Namibia has reserves of diamonds, uranium, zinc, and copper. Minerals make up the bulk of the exports, though agriculture employs 20% of the people. Sea fishing is also important. Namibia has few industries, but tourism is expanding.

AREA 318,259 SQ MI [824,292 SQ KM]
POPULATION 2,128,000 **CAPITAL** WINDHOEK
GOVERNMENT MULTIPARTY REPUBLIC **ETHNIC GROUPS** OVAMBO 50%, KAVANGO 9%, HERERO 7%, DAMARA 7%, WHITE 6%, NAMA 5%
LANGUAGES ENGLISH (OFFICIAL), AFRIKAANS, GERMAN, INDIGENOUS DIALECTS **RELIGIONS** CHRISTIANITY 90% (LUTHERAN 51%)
CURRENCY NAMIBIAN DOLLAR = 100 CENTS

NAURU

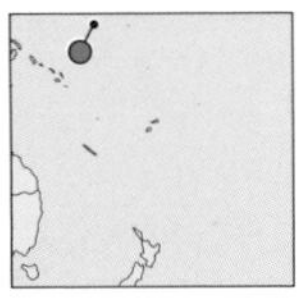

Nauru is the world's smallest republic, located in the western Pacific Ocean, close to the equator. Independent since 1968, Nauru's prosperity is based on phosphate mining, but the reserves are running out.

AREA 8 SQ MI [21 SQ KM]
POPULATION 9,000 **CAPITAL** YAREN

NEPAL

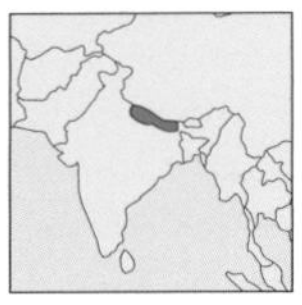

GEOGRAPHY Over three-quarters of Nepal lies in the Himalayan region, culminating in the world's highest peak (Mount Everest, or Chomolongma in Nepali) at 29,035 ft [8,850 m]. As a result, climatic conditions vary widely according to the altitude.

POLITICS & ECONOMY Nepal was united in the late 18th century, although its complex topography has ensured that it remains a diverse patchwork of peoples. From the mid-19th century to 1951, power was held by the royal Rana family. The first democratic elections in 32 years were held in 1991, but, by the early 21st century, Nepal faced many problems, including an uprising of Maoist guerrillas. In 2005, King Gyanendra seized power but failed to stop the conflict. In 2006, the Maoists joined a provisional coalition government. In elections in April 2008, the Maoists became the largest single party. In May, Nepal became a republic and the Maoist leader, named Prachanda, became prime minister in August. He resigned in 2009. In 2010, Jhalnath Khanal became prime minister, ending a seven-month stalemate.

Agriculture is the main activity in this overwhelmingly rural country, and Nepal is heavily dependent on aid. Tourism, based on the attractions of the high Himalaya, is growing in importance. There are also ambitious plans to exploit the hydroelectric potential offered by the ferocious Himalayan rivers.

AREA 56,827 SQ MI [147,181 SQ KM] **POPULATION** 28,952,000
CAPITAL KATMANDU **GOVERNMENT** MULTIPARTY REPUBLIC
ETHNIC GROUPS BRAHMAN, CHETRI, NEWAR, GURUNG, MAGAR, TAMANG, SHERPA, AND OTHERS
LANGUAGES NEPALI (OFFICIAL), LOCAL LANGUAGES
RELIGIONS HINDUISM 86%, BUDDHISM 8%, ISLAM 4%
CURRENCY NEPALESE RUPEE = 100 PAISA

NETHERLANDS

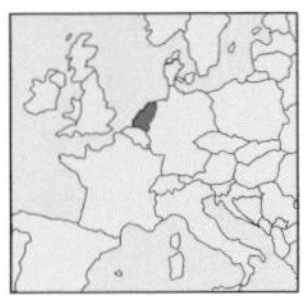

GEOGRAPHY The Netherlands lies at the western end of the North European Plain, which extends to the Ural Mountains in Russia. Except for the far southeastern corner, the Netherlands is flat and about 40% lies below sea level at high tide. To prevent flooding, the Dutch have built dykes (sea walls) to hold back the waves. Large areas which were once under the sea, but which have been reclaimed, are called polders. Because of its position on the North Sea, the Netherlands has a temperate climate, with mild, rainy winters.

POLITICS & ECONOMY Before the 16th century, the area that is now the Netherlands was under a succession of foreign rulers, including the Romans, the Germanic Franks, the French, and the Spanish. The Dutch declared their independence from Spain in 1581 and their status was finally recognized by Spain in 1648. In the 17th century, the Dutch built up a great overseas empire, especially in Southeast Asia. But in the early 18th century, the Dutch lost control of the seas to England.

France controlled the Netherlands from 1795 to 1813. In 1815, the Netherlands, then containing Belgium and Luxembourg, became an independent kingdom. Belgium broke away in 1830 and Luxembourg followed in 1890.

The Netherlands was neutral in World War I (1914–18), but was occupied by Germany in World War II (1939–45). After the war, the Netherlands Indies became independent as Indonesia. The Netherlands became active in West European affairs. With Belgium and Luxembourg, it formed a customs union called Benelux in 1948. In 1949, it joined NATO (the North Atlantic Treaty Organization), and the European Coal and Steel Community (ECSC) in 1953. In 1957, it became a founder member of the European Economic Community (now the European Union), and in 2002 it adopted the euro as its sole unit of currency.

Since 2002, four coalition governments, under Prime Minister Jan Peter Balkenende, have collapsed. Following elections in 2010, a Liberal–Christian coalition was set up, with parliamentary support from the right-wing Freedom Party. Also, in 2010, the Netherlands Antilles, an island territory in the Caribbean, was dissolved. Curaçao and St Maarten became nations in the Kingdom of the Netherlands. The small islands of Bonaire, St Eustatius, and Saba became special municipalities of the Netherlands.

The Netherlands is a highly industrialized country, and industry and commerce are the most valuable activities. Its resources include natural gas, some oil, salt, and china clay. But the Netherlands imports many of the materials needed by its industries and it is, therefore, a major trading country. Industrial products are wide-ranging, including aircraft, chemicals, electronic equipment, machinery, textiles, and vehicles. Farming is scientific and yields are high. Dairy farming is the leading farming activity. Major products include barley, flowers and bulbs, potatoes, sugar beet, and wheat.

AREA 16,033 SQ MI [41,526 SQ KM]
POPULATION 16,783,000
CAPITAL AMSTERDAM; THE HAGUE (SEAT OF GOVERNMENT)
GOVERNMENT CONSTITUTIONAL MONARCHY
ETHNIC GROUPS DUTCH 83%, INDONESIAN, TURKISH, MOROCCAN, AND OTHERS **LANGUAGES** DUTCH (OFFICIAL), FRISIAN
RELIGIONS ROMAN CATHOLIC 31%, PROTESTANT 21%, ISLAM 4%, OTHERS
CURRENCY EURO = 100 CENTS

NEW CALEDONIA

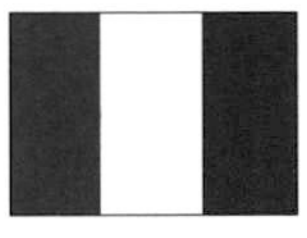

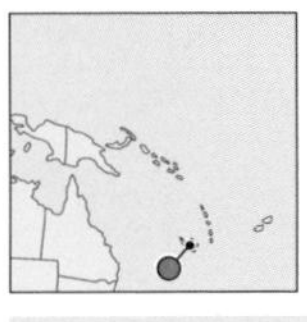

New Caledonia is the most southerly of the Melanesian countries in the Pacific. It has been a French possession since 1853 and an Overseas Territory since 1958. In 1998, France announced an agreement with local Melanesians that a vote on independence would be postponed until 2014. The country is rich in mineral resources, especially nickel.

AREA 7,172 SQ MI [18,575 SQ KM] **POPULATION** 252,000 **CAPITAL** NOUMÉA

NEW ZEALAND

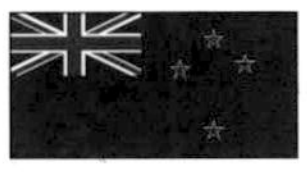

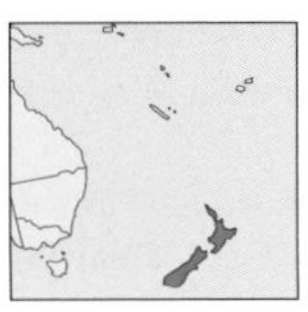

GEOGRAPHY New Zealand lies about 994 mi [1,600 km] southeast of Australia. It consists of two main islands and several other small ones. Much of North Island is volcanic. Active volcanoes include Ngauruhoe and Ruapehu. Hot springs and geysers are common, and steam from the ground is used to produce electricity. The Southern Alps, which contain the country's highest peak, Aoraki Mount Cook, at 12,313 ft [3,753 m], form the backbone of South Island. The island also has some large, fertile plains.

New Zealand lies on the geologically active "Pacific ring of fire." Most of the 14,000 earthquakes that occur every year have a magnitude of less than 5.0. But, in 2010 and 2011, two earthquakes, with magnitudes of 7.0 and 6.3 respectively, struck Christchurch on South Island, causing great damage. The 2011 earthquake resulted in a death toll of more than 180.

Auckland in the north has a warm, humid climate throughout the year. Wellington has cooler summers, while in Dunedin, in the southeast, temperatures sometimes dip below freezing in winter. The rainfall is heaviest on the western highlands.

POLITICS & ECONOMY Evidence suggests that early Maori settlers arrived in New Zealand more than 1,000 years ago. The Dutch navigator Abel Tasman reached New Zealand in 1642, but his discovery was not followed up. In 1769, the British Captain James Cook rediscovered the islands. In the early 19th century, British settlers arrived and, in 1840, under the Treaty of Waitangi, Britain took possession of the islands. From the 1870s, the Maoris were gradually integrated into colonial society.

In 1907, New Zealand became a self-governing dominion in the British Commonwealth. The country's economy developed quickly and the people became increasingly prosperous. However, after Britain joined the European Economic Community in 1973, New Zealand's exports to Britain shrank and the country had to reassess its economic and defense strategies and seek new markets. The world recession led the government to cut back on welfare spending in the 1990s. The preservation of Maori culture and Maori rights are major issues. The Maoris, a Polynesian people, make up about 13% of the population. Other mainly Polynesian Pacific people make up another 6%. Ties with Britain have been reduced. Helen Clark, leader of the Labor Party and prime minister from 1999–2008, has expressed the view that New Zealand will eventually abolish the monarchy and become a republic. In November 2008, the center-right National Party defeated the Labor Party in elections. John Key became prime minister.

The economy once depended on agriculture, but manufacturing now employs twice as many people as farming. Meat and dairy products are leading commodities. Sheep rearing has declined as the area under cattle, deer, and vines has expanded. Crops include barley, fruits, potatoes and other vegetables, and wheat. In 2008–9, New Zealand's economy entered a period of recession. The economy grew by 2.1% in 2010, but full recovery was expected to be slow.

AREA 104,453 SQ MI [270,534 SQ KM]
POPULATION 4,252,000 **CAPITAL** WELLINGTON
GOVERNMENT CONSTITUTIONAL MONARCHY
ETHNIC GROUPS NEW ZEALAND EUROPEAN 74%, NEW ZEALAND MAORI 13%, POLYNESIAN 6% **LANGUAGES** ENGLISH AND MAORI (BOTH OFFICIAL) **RELIGIONS** ANGLICAN 24%, PRESBYTERIAN 18%, ROMAN CATHOLIC 15%, OTHERS
CURRENCY NEW ZEALAND DOLLAR = 100 CENTS

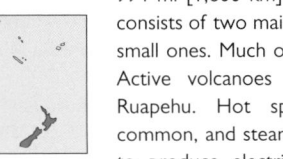

NICARAGUA

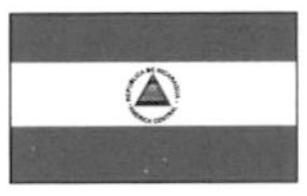

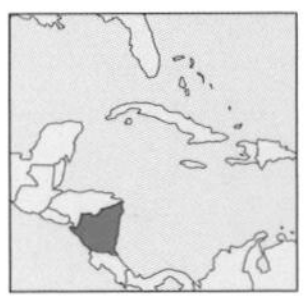

GEOGRAPHY The Republic of Nicaragua is a large country in Central America. In the east is a broad plain bordering the Caribbean Sea. The plain is drained by rivers that flow from the Central Highlands. The fertile western Pacific region contains about 40 volcanoes, many of which are active, and earthquakes are common.

Nicaragua has a tropical climate. Managua is hot throughout the year and there is a marked rainy season from May to October. In October 1998, Hurricane Mitch caused great devastation in Nicaragua. The Central Highlands and Caribbean region are cooler and wetter. The wettest region is the humid Caribbean plain.

POLITICS & ECONOMY In 1502, Christopher Columbus claimed the area for Spain, which ruled Nicaragua until 1821. By the early 20th century, the United States had considerable influence in the country and, in 1912, US forces entered Nicaragua to protect US interests. From 1927 to 1933, rebels under General Augusto César Sandino tried to drive US forces out of the country. In 1933, US marines set up a Nicaraguan army, the National Guard, to help to defeat the rebels. Its leader, Anastasio Somoza Garcia, had Sandino murdered in 1934, and from 1937 Somoza ruled as a dictator.

In the mid-1970s, many people began to protest against Somoza's rule. Many joined a guerrilla force, called the Sandinista National Liberation Front, named after General Sandino. The rebels defeated the Somoza regime in 1979. In the 1980s, the US-supported forces, called the "Contras," launched a campaign

against the Sandinista government. The US government opposed the Sandinista regime, under Daniel José Ortega Saavedra, claiming that it was a Communist dictatorship. A coalition, the National Opposition Union, defeated the Sandinistas in 1990. In 2001, the Sandinista candidate, Daniel Ortega, was defeated in presidential elections, but he was re-elected president of Nicaragua in 2006. In 2009, he announced plans to change the constitution so that he could stand for another term.

In the early 1990s, Nicaragua faced many problems in rebuilding its shattered economy. Agriculture employs about 28% of the people. Coffee, cotton, sugar, and bananas are grown for export, while rice is the main food crop.

AREA 50,193 sq mi [130,000 sq km]
POPULATION 5,996,000 **CAPITAL** Managua
GOVERNMENT Multiparty republic
ETHNIC GROUPS Mestizo 69%, White 17%, Black 9%, Amerindian 5%
LANGUAGES Spanish (official)
RELIGIONS Roman Catholic 85%, Protestant
CURRENCY Córdoba oro (gold córdoba) = 100 centavos

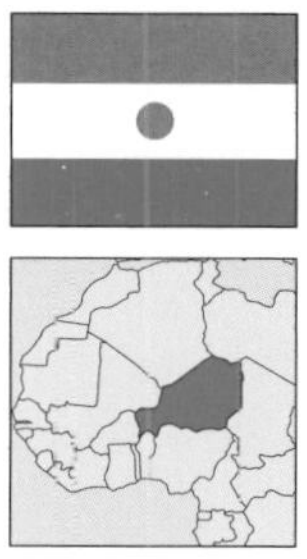

NIGER

GEOGRAPHY The Republic of Niger is a landlocked nation in north-central Africa. The northern plateaux lie in the Sahara Desert, while Central Niger contains the rugged Aïr Mountains. The most fertile, densely populated region is the Niger valley in the southwest.

Niger has a tropical climate and the south has a rainy season between June and September. The north is practically rainless.

POLITICS & ECONOMY Since independence in 1960, Niger, a French territory from 1900, has suffered severe droughts. Food shortages and the collapse of the traditional nomadic way of life of some of Niger's people have caused political instability. After a period of military rule, a multiparty constitution was adopted in 1992, but the military again seized power in 1996. Later that year, the coup leader, Colonel Ibrahim Barre Mainassara, was elected president. He was assassinated in 1999, but parliamentary rule was restored and Mamadou Tandja was elected president. He was overthrown in a coup in 2010 and a military regime took power. But democratic elections took place in 2011.

Niger's chief resource is uranium and the country is the world's fourth largest producer. Some tin and tungsten are also mined, though other mineral reserves are largely untouched. Despite its considerable resources, Niger remains one of the world's poorest countries. Only 3% of the land can be used for growing crops.

AREA 489,189 sq mi [1,267,000 sq km]
POPULATION 15,878,000 **CAPITAL** Niamey
GOVERNMENT Multiparty republic **ETHNIC GROUPS** Hausa 56%, Djerma 22%, Tuareg 8%, Fula 8%, others **LANGUAGES** French (official), Hausa, Djerma **RELIGIONS** Islam 80%, indigenous beliefs, Christianity **CURRENCY** CFA franc = 100 centimes

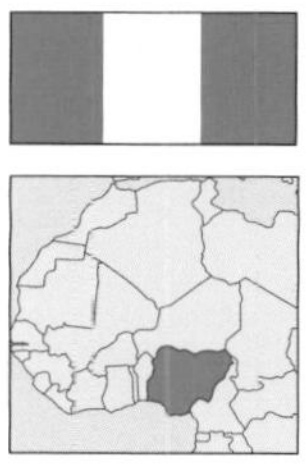

NIGERIA

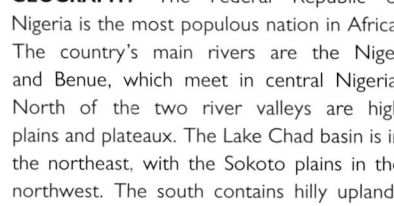

GEOGRAPHY The Federal Republic of Nigeria is the most populous nation in Africa. The country's main rivers are the Niger and Benue, which meet in central Nigeria. North of the two river valleys are high plains and plateaux. The Lake Chad basin is in the northeast, with the Sokoto plains in the northwest. The south contains hilly uplands and plains. The south has a hot, rainy climate. The north is drier and often hotter than the south.

POLITICS & ECONOMY Nigeria has a long artistic tradition. Major cultures include the Nok (500 BC to AD 200), the Ife, a major Yoruba culture which developed about 1,000 years ago, and the Benin (15th to 17th centuries). Britain gradually extended its influence over the area in the second half of the 19th century.

Nigeria became independent in 1960 and a federal republic in 1963. A federal constitution dividing the country into regions was necessary because Nigeria contains more than 250 ethnic and linguistic groups, as well as several religious ones. Local rivalries have long been a threat to national unity, and six new states were created in 1996 in an attempt to overcome this. Civil war occurred between 1967 and 1970, when the people of the southeast attempted unsuccessfully to secede during the Biafran War. Between 1960 and 1998, Nigeria had only nine years of civilian government.

In 1998–9, civilian rule was restored and Olusegun Obasanjo became president. Nigeria faced many problems, including violence in the Niger delta region and religious conflict. In 2007, Umar Yar'Adua, a northerner, was elected president. However, he died in 2010, and was replaced as head of state by the vice president, Goodluck Johnson, a southerner, who was formally elected president in 2011.

Nigeria is a developing country with great potential. Its chief natural resource is oil, which accounts for most of its exports. Agriculture employs 59% of the people and the country is a major producer of cocoa, palm oil and palm kernels, groundnuts (peanuts), and rubber. Industry is increasing and manufactures include cement, chemicals, fertilizers, textiles, and timber.

AREA 356,667 sq mi [923,768 sq km] **POPULATION** 152,217,000
CAPITAL Abuja **GOVERNMENT** Federal multiparty republic
ETHNIC GROUPS Hausa and Fulani 29%, Yoruba 21%, Ibo (or Igbo) 18%, Ijaw 10%, Kanuri 4%, many others
LANGUAGES English (official), Hausa, Yoruba, Ibo
RELIGIONS Islam 50%, Christianity 40%, traditional beliefs 10%
CURRENCY Naira = 100 kobo

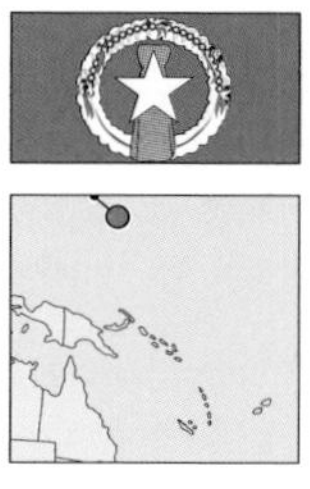

NORTHERN MARIANA ISLANDS

The Commonwealth of the Northern Mariana Islands contains 16 mountainous islands north of Guam in the western Pacific Ocean. In a 1975 plebiscite, the islanders voted for Commonwealth status in union with the United States, and in 1986 they were granted US citizenship.

AREA 179 sq mi [464 sq km] **POPULATION** 48,000 **CAPITAL** Saipan

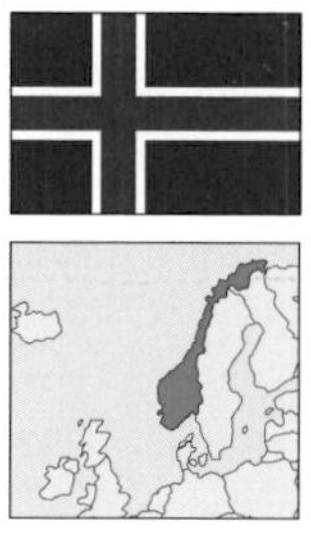

NORWAY

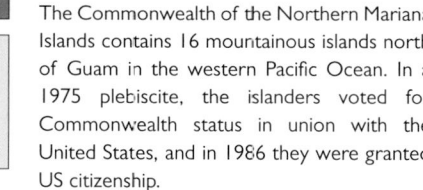

GEOGRAPHY The Kingdom of Norway forms the western part of the rugged Scandinavian peninsula. The deep inlets along the highly indented coastline were worn out by glaciers during the Ice Age. The warm North Atlantic Drift off the coast of Norway moderates the climate, with mild winters and cool summers. Nearly all the ports are ice-free throughout the year. Inland, winters are colder and snow cover lasts for at least three months a year.

POLITICS & ECONOMY Between about AD 800 and 1100, Norwegian Vikings ravaged western Europe. In 1380, Norway was united with Denmark. But in 1814, Denmark handed Norway over to Sweden, though it kept Norway's colonies – Greenland, Iceland, and the Færoe Islands. Norway briefly became independent, but Swedish forces defeated the Norwegians and Norway had to accept Sweden's king as its ruler. The union with Sweden ended in 1903. Germany occupied Norway during World War II (1939–45). Norway recovered quickly after the war and it now has one of the world's highest standards of living. In 1960, Norway and six other countries formed the European Free Trade Association (EFTA). But, in 1994, Norway voted against joining the European Union. In 2009, the center-left coalition led by Prime Minister Jens Stoltenberg was narrowly re-elected.

Norway's chief resources and exports are oil and natural gas which come from wells under the North Sea. Farmland covers only 3% of the land. Dairy farming and meat production are important, but Norway has to import food. Norway has many industries powered by cheap hydroelectricity.

AREA 125,049 sq mi [323,877 sq km]
POPULATION 4,676,000 **CAPITAL** Oslo
GOVERNMENT Constitutional monarchy
ETHNIC GROUPS Norwegian 97%
LANGUAGES Norwegian (official)
RELIGIONS Evangelical Lutheran 86%
CURRENCY Norwegian krone = 100 ore

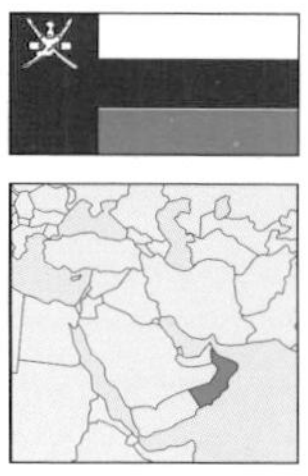

OMAN

GEOGRAPHY The Sultanate of Oman occupies the southeastern corner of the Arabian peninsula. It also includes the tip of the Musandam peninsula, overlooking the strategic Strait of Hormuz.

Oman has a hot tropical climate. In Muscat, temperatures may reach 117°F [47°C] in the summer months.

POLITICS & ECONOMY British influence in Oman dates back to the end of the 18th century, but the country became fully independent in 1971. Since then, using revenue from oil, which was discovered in 1964, the absolute ruler, Qaboos ibn Said, and his government have sought to modernize Oman. In 2000, Oman held elections to its consultative parliament. In 2004, the Sultan appointed Oman's first woman minister without portfolio. In 2001, following anti-government demonstrations, Sultan Qaboos ibn Said promised jobs and benefits.

Oil and natural gas make up about 80% of Oman's exports. Agriculture and fishing remain important. Crops include alfalfa, bananas, coconuts, dates, limes, tobacco, vegetables, and wheat. However, Oman has to import food.

AREA 119,498 sq mi [309,500 sq km]
POPULATION 2,968,000 **CAPITAL** Muscat
GOVERNMENT Monarchy with consultative council
ETHNIC GROUPS Arab, Baluchi, Indian, Pakistani
LANGUAGES Arabic (official), Baluchi, English
RELIGIONS Islam (mainly Ibadhi), Hinduism
CURRENCY Omani rial = 1,000 baizas

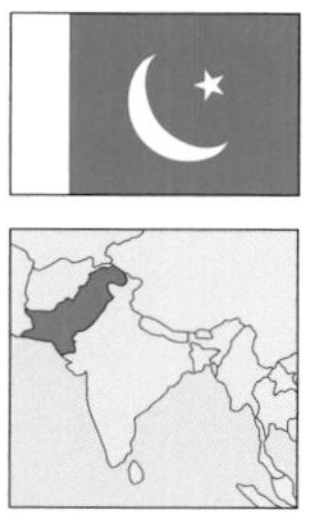

PAKISTAN

GEOGRAPHY The Islamic Republic of Pakistan contains high mountains, fertile plains and rocky deserts. The Karakoram range, which contains K2, the world's second highest peak, lies in the northern part of Jammu and Kashmir, which is occupied by Pakistan but claimed by India. Other mountains rise in the west. Plains, drained by the River Indus and its tributaries, occupy much of eastern Pakistan. Arid areas include the Thar Desert and the Baluchistan plateau. Most of Pakistan has hot summers and mild winters, though the mountains have cold winters. The rainfall is generally sparse.

POLITICS & ECONOMY Pakistan was the site of the Indus Valley civilization which developed about 4,500 years ago. But Pakistan's modern history dates from 1947, when British India was divided into India and Pakistan. Muslim Pakistan was divided into two parts: East and West Pakistan, but East Pakistan broke away in 1971 to become Bangladesh. In 1948–9, 1965, and 1971, Pakistan and India clashed over Kashmir. In 1998, Pakistan responded in kind to India's nuclear weapons tests, but, in 2003–7, Pakistan and India launched a series of initiatives aimed at achieving peace.

Pakistan has been subject to several periods of military rule, but elections in 1988 led to Benazir Bhutto becoming prime minister. She was removed from office in 1990, but she returned as prime minister between 1993 and 1996. In 1997, Narwaz Sharif was elected prime minister, but a military coup in 1999 brought General Pervez Musharraf to power. The security situation deteriorated in 2006–7. In 2007, in the run-up to elections in February 2008, Benazir Bhutto was assassinated, but in the elections, the opposition parties heavily defeated Musharraf's supporters. Musharraf resigned in August 2008 and was succeeded as president by Benazir Bhutto's widower, Asif Ali Zardari. The security situation in the border regions of the northwest worsened. In 2010, parliament approved measures to reduce the powers of the presidency.

According to the World Bank, Pakistan is a "low-income" developing country. The economy is based on farming or rearing goats and sheep. Agriculture employs 40% of the people. Major crops include cotton, fruits, rice, sugarcane, and wheat.

AREA 307,372 sq mi [796,095 sq km]
POPULATION 184,405,000 **CAPITAL** Islamabad
GOVERNMENT Military regime **ETHNIC GROUPS** Punjabi, Sindhi, Pashtun (Pathan), Baluchi, Muhajir
LANGUAGES Urdu (official), many others
RELIGIONS Islam 97%, Christianity, Hinduism
CURRENCY Pakistani rupee = 100 paisa

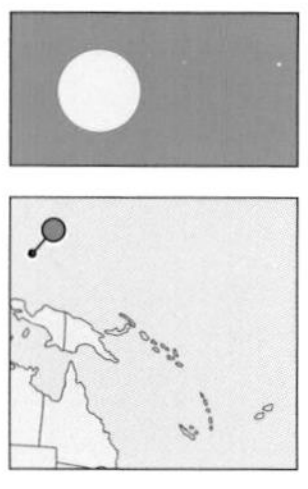

PALAU

The Republic of Palau became fully independent in 1994, after the USA refused to accede to a 1979 referendum that declared this island nation a nuclear-free zone. In December 1994 Palau joined the United Nations. The economy relies heavily on US aid, tourism, fishing, and subsistence agriculture. The main crops include cassava, coconuts, and copra.

AREA 177 sq mi [459 sq km] **POPULATION** 21,000 **CAPITAL** Melekeok

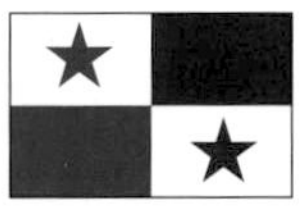
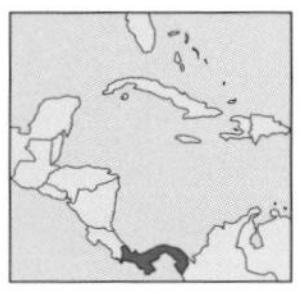

PANAMA

GEOGRAPHY The Republic of Panama forms an isthmus linking Central America to South America. The Panama Canal, which is 50.7 mi [81.6 km] long, cuts across the isthmus. It has made the country a major transport center.

Panama has a tropical climate. Temperatures are high, though the mountains are much cooler than the coastal plains. The main rainy season is between May and December.

POLITICS & ECONOMY Christopher Columbus landed in Panama in 1502 and Spain soon took the area. In 1821, Panama became independent from Spain and a province of Colombia.

In 1903, Colombia refused a request by the United States to build a canal. Panama then revolted against Colombia, and became independent. The United States then began to build the canal, which was opened in 1914. The United States administered the Panama Canal Zone, a strip of land along the canal. But many Panamanians resented US influence and, in 1979, the Canal Zone was returned to Panama. Control of the canal itself was handed over by the USA to Panama on December 31, 1999.

Panama's government has changed many times since independence, and there have been periods of military dictatorships, including that of General Manuel Antonio Noriega in the 1980s. He was finally convicted of drug offences in the United States in 1992. Noriega was released from a Florida prison in 2009. In May 2009, Ricardo Martinelli of the conservative Alliance for Change coalition was elected president.

The World Bank classifies Panama as a "lower-middle-income" developing country. The Panama Canal is an important source of revenue and, in 2006, work began on widening the canal to take giant container ships. Away from the canal, the main activity is agriculture, which employs 14% of the people.

AREA 29,157 sq mi [75,517 sq km] **POPULATION** 3,411,000
CAPITAL Panamá **GOVERNMENT** Multiparty republic
ETHNIC GROUPS Mestizo 70%, Black and Mulatto 14%, White 10%, Amerindian 6% **LANGUAGES** Spanish (official), English **RELIGIONS** Roman Catholic 85%, Protestant 15%
CURRENCY US dollar; Balboa = 100 centésimos

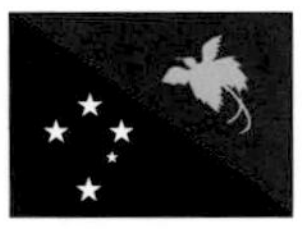
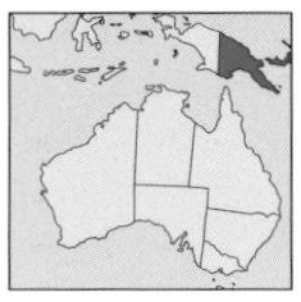

PAPUA NEW GUINEA

GEOGRAPHY Papua New Guinea is an independent country in the Pacific Ocean, north of Australia. It is part of a Pacific island region called Melanesia. Papua New Guinea includes the eastern part of New Guinea, the Bismarck Archipelago, the northern Solomon Islands, the D'Entrecasteaux Islands, and the Louisiade Archipelago. The land is largely mountainous.

Papua New Guinea has a tropical climate, with high temperatures throughout the year. Most of the rain occurs during the monsoon season (from December to April), when the northwesterly winds blow. Winds blow from the southeast during the dry season.

POLITICS & ECONOMY The Dutch took western New Guinea (now part of Indonesia) in 1828, but it was not until 1884 that Germany took northeastern New Guinea and Britain took the southeast. In 1906, Britain handed the southeast over to Australia. It then became known as the Territory of Papua. When World War I broke out in 1914, Australia took German New Guinea and, in 1921, the League of Nations gave Australia a mandate to rule the area, which was named the Territory of New Guinea. Japan invaded New Guinea in 1942, but the Allies reconquered the area in 1944. In 1949, Papua and New Guinea were combined into the Territory of Papua and New Guinea. Papua New Guinea became fully independent in 1975.

Mining is important. An important mine was on Bougainville, where a secessionist group declared the island independent. Under a peace treaty in 2001, Bougainville became autonomous and held elections in 2005. In 2004, Australia sent police to Papua New Guinea to help fight crime. They were withdrawn in 2005, following a Supreme Court ruling that their presence was unconstitutional.

The country has a "lower-middle-income" economy. Agriculture employs 70% of the people, mostly at subsistence level. Petroleum and minerals, notably copper, are major exports.

AREA 178,703 sq mi [462,840 sq km] **POPULATION** 6,065,000
CAPITAL Port Moresby **GOVERNMENT** Constitutional monarchy
ETHNIC GROUPS Papuan, Melanesian, Micronesian **LANGUAGES** English (official), Melanesian Pidgin; more than 700 indigenous languages **RELIGIONS** Traditional beliefs 34%, Roman Catholic 22%, Lutheran 16% **CURRENCY** Kina = 100 toea

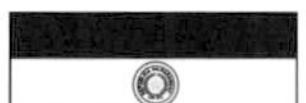
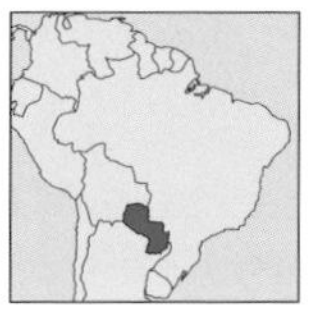

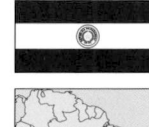

PARAGUAY

GEOGRAPHY The Republic of Paraguay is a landlocked country and rivers, notably the Paraná, Pilcomayo (Brazo Sur), and Paraguay, form most of its borders. A flat region called the Gran Chaco lies in the northwest, while the southeast contains plains, hills, and plateaux. Northern Paraguay lies in the tropics, while the south is subtropical. Most of the country has a warm, humid climate.

POLITICS & ECONOMY In 1776, Paraguay became part of a large colony called the Viceroyalty of La Plata, with Buenos Aires as the capital. Paraguayans opposed this move and the country declared its independence in 1811.

For many years, Paraguay was torn by internal strife and conflict with its neighbors. A war against Brazil, Argentina, and Uruguay (1865–70) led to the deaths of more than half of Paraguay's population, and a great loss of territory.

General Alfredo Stroessner took power in 1954 and ruled as a dictator. His government imprisoned many opponents. Stroessner was overthrown in 1989 (he died in exile in Brazil in 2006). However, the return of democracy in the years that followed often seemed precarious, because of rivalries between politicians and army leaders, together with economic problems arising partly from the severe problems experienced in neighboring Argentina and Brazil in 1999. In 2008, a former Roman Catholic bishop, Fernando Lugo, who was regarded as a champion of the poor, was elected president. His victory ended more than six decades of rule by the Colorado Party.

The World Bank classifies Paraguay as a "lower-middle-income" developing country. Agriculture and forestry, employing about a third of the population, are important. Paraguay produces hydroelectricity and exports power to its neighbors.

AREA 157,047 sq mi [406,752 sq km]
POPULATION 6,376,000 **CAPITAL** Asunción
GOVERNMENT Multiparty republic **ETHNIC GROUPS** Mestizo 95%
LANGUAGES Spanish and Guaraní (both official)
RELIGIONS Roman Catholic 90%, Protestant
CURRENCY Guaraní = 100 céntimos

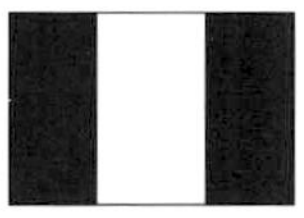
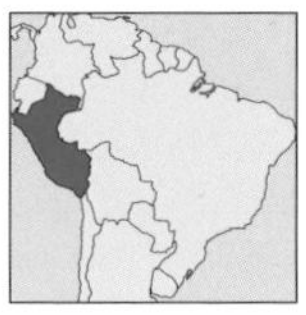

PERU

GEOGRAPHY The Republic of Peru lies in the tropics in western South America. A narrow coastal plain borders the Pacific Ocean in the west. Inland are ranges of the Andes Mountains, which rise to 22,205 ft [6,768 m] at Mount Huascarán, an extinct volcano. East of the Andes lies the Amazon basin.

Lima, on the coastal plain, has an arid climate. The coastal region is chilled by the cold, offshore Humboldt Current. The rainfall increases inland and many mountains in the high Andes are snow-capped.

POLITICS & ECONOMY Spanish *conquistadores* conquered Peru in the 1530s. In 1820, an Argentinian, José de San Martín, led an army into Peru and declared it independent. But Spain still held large areas. In 1823, the Venezuelan Simon Bolívar led another army into Peru and, in 1824, one of his generals defeated the Spaniards at Ayacucho. The Spaniards surrendered in 1826. Peru suffered much instability throughout the 19th century.

Instability continued in the 20th century. In 1980, when civilian rule was restored, a left-wing group called the Sendero Luminoso, or the "Shining Path," began guerrilla warfare against the government. In 1990, Alberto Fujimori, son of Japanese immigrants, became president. In 1992, he suspended the constitution and dismissed the legislature. The guerrilla leader, Abimael Guzmán, was arrested in 1992 and, in 2006, he was sentenced to life imprisonment. Fujimori left Peru but was later extradited, and in 2009 he was found guilty of ordering killings and kidnapping during the conflict and sentenced to 25 years in jail. In 2006, Alan Garcia was elected president. In 2009, tension arose with Chile over a disputed border.

The World Bank classifies Peru as a "lower-middle-income" developing country. Major food crops include beans, maize, potatoes, and rice. Fish products are exported, but the most valuable export is copper. Peru also produces lead, silver, zinc, and iron ore.

AREA 496,222 sq mi [1,285,216 sq km]
POPULATION 29,907,000 **CAPITAL** Lima
GOVERNMENT Constitutional republic **ETHNIC GROUPS** Amerindian 45%, Mestizo 37%, White 15% **LANGUAGES** Spanish and Quechua (both official), Aymara, other Amazonian languages **RELIGIONS** Roman Catholic 90% **CURRENCY** New sol = 100 centavos

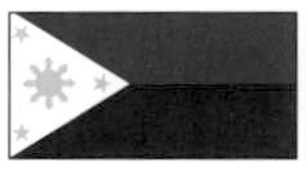
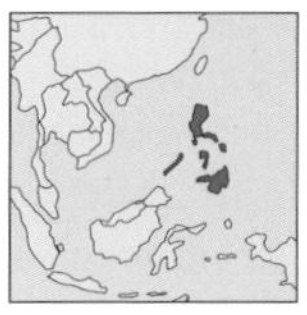

PHILIPPINES

GEOGRAPHY The Republic of the Philippines is an island country in southeastern Asia. It includes about 7,100 islands, of which 2,770 are named and about 1,000 are inhabited. Luzon and Mindanao, the two largest islands, make up more than two-thirds of the country. The land is mainly mountainous.

The country has a hot tropical climate. The dry season runs from December to April. The rest of the year is wet. Much of the rainfall comes from the typhoons which periodically strike the east coast. In November 2006, a powerful typhoon struck Luzon in the Philippines. The typhoon triggered mudslides on the slopes of Mount Mayon, one of the country's many volcanoes. The mudslides destroyed several villages and killed around 1,000 people.

POLITICS & ECONOMY The first European to reach the Philippines was the Portuguese navigator Ferdinand Magellan in 1521. Spanish explorers claimed the region in 1565 when they established a settlement on Cebu. The Spaniards ruled the country until 1898, when the United States took over at the end of the Spanish–American War. Japan invaded the Philippines in 1941, but US forces returned in 1944. The country became fully independent as the Republic of the Philippines in 1946.

Since independence, the country's problems have included armed uprisings by left-wing guerrillas demanding land reform, and Muslim separatist groups, crime, corruption, and unemployment. The dominant figure in recent times was Ferdinand Marcos, who ruled in a dictatorial manner from 1965 to 1986. His successors were Corazon Aquino (1986–92), Fidel Ramos (1992–8), and Joseph Estrada, who resigned following accusations of corruption. He was succeeded by Vice President Gloria Arroyo, who was re-elected president in 2004. In 2010, Benigno Aquino was elected president. Fighting, killings, and kidnappings continued throughout the 2000s, while the government attempted to agree a peace settlement with rebel groups.

The Philippines is a developing country. Agriculture employs around 30% of the people. The main foods are rice and maize, while bananas, cocoa, coffee, sugarcane, and tobacco are grown commercially. Shellfish and sea fishing in coastal waters are also important, while manufacturing plays an increasingly significant part in the economy.

AREA 115,830 sq mi [300,000 sq km]
POPULATION 99,900,000 **CAPITAL** Manila
GOVERNMENT Multiparty republic
ETHNIC GROUPS Christian Malay 92%, Muslim Malay 4%, Chinese, and others **LANGUAGES** Filipino (Tagalog) and English (both official), Spanish, many others
RELIGIONS Roman Catholic 83%, Protestant 9%, Islam 5%
CURRENCY Philippine peso = 100 centavos

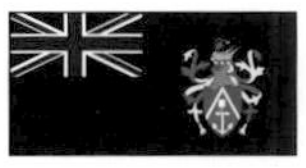
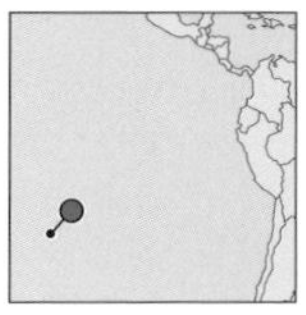

PITCAIRN

Pitcairn Island is a British overseas territory in the Pacific Ocean. Its inhabitants are descendants of the original settlers – nine mutineers from HMS *Bounty* and 18 Tahitians who arrived in 1790.

AREA 21 sq mi [55 sq km]
POPULATION 48 **CAPITAL** Adamstown

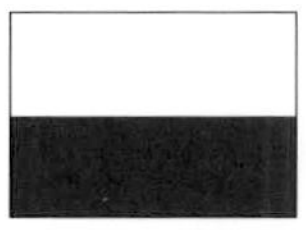
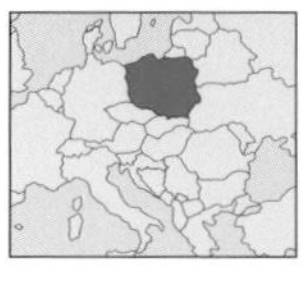

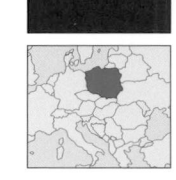

POLAND

GEOGRAPHY The Republic of Poland faces the Baltic Sea and behind its lagoon-fringed coast lies a broad plain. A plateau lies in the southeast, while the Sudeten Highlands straddle part of the border with the Czech Republic. Part of the Carpathian Range (the Tatra) lies in the southeast.

Poland's climate is influenced by its position in Europe. Warm, moist air masses come from the west, while cold air masses come from the north and east. Summers are warm, but winters are cold and snowy.

POLITICS & ECONOMY Poland's boundaries have changed several times in the last 200 years, partly as a result of its geographical location between the powers of Germany and Russia. It disappeared from the map in the late 18th century, when a Polish state called the Grand Duchy of Warsaw was set up. But in 1815, the country was partitioned between Austria, Prussia, and Russia. Poland became independent in 1918, but in 1939 it was divided between Germany and the Soviet Union. The country again became independent in 1945, when it lost land to Russia

but gained some from Germany. Communists took power in 1948, but opposition mounted and eventually became focused through an organization called Solidarity.

Solidarity was led by a trade unionist, Lech Walesa. A coalition government was formed between Solidarity and the Communists in 1989. In 1990, the Communist Party was dissolved and Walesa became president. But Walesa faced many problems in turning Poland toward a market economy, and he was defeated in presidential elections in 1995. But his successor followed westward-looking policies. Poland joined NATO in 1999 and the European Union in 2004. In 2005, a nationalist, Lech Kaczynski, was elected president. But, along with other prominent Poles, he was killed in a plane crash in Russia in 2010. In July 2010, Bronislaw Komorowski was elected president.

Poland has large reserves of coal and deposits of various minerals which are used in its factories. Manufactures include chemicals, processed food, machinery, ships, steel, and textiles.

AREA 124,807 SQ MI [323,250 SQ KM]
POPULATION 38,464,000 **CAPITAL** WARSAW
GOVERNMENT MULTIPARTY REPUBLIC
ETHNIC GROUPS POLISH 97%, BELARUSIAN, UKRAINIAN, GERMAN
LANGUAGES POLISH (OFFICIAL) **RELIGIONS** ROMAN CATHOLIC 95%, EASTERN ORTHODOX **CURRENCY** ZLOTY = 100 GROSZY

PORTUGAL

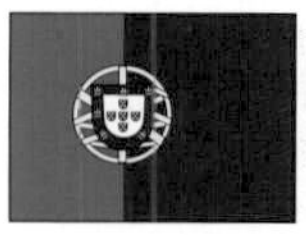

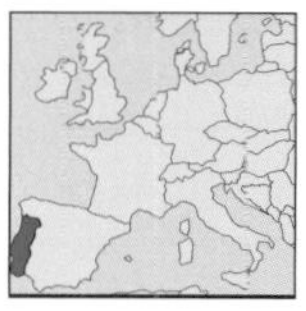

GEOGRAPHY The Republic of Portugal is the most westerly of Europe's mainland countries. The land rises from the coastal plains on the Atlantic Ocean to the western edge of the huge plateau, or Meseta, which occupies most of the Iberian peninsula. The climate is moderated by winds blowing from the Atlantic Ocean. Summers are cooler and winters are milder than in other Mediterranean lands. Portugal also contains two autonomous regions, the Azores and Madeira island groups.

POLITICS & ECONOMY Portugal became a separate country, independent of Spain, in 1143. In the 15th century, Portugal led the "Age of European Exploration." This led to the growth of a large Portuguese empire, with colonies in Africa, Asia and, most valuable of all, Brazil in South America. Portuguese power began to decline in the 16th century and, between 1580 and 1640, Portugal was ruled by Spain. Portugal lost Brazil in 1822, and in 1910 Portugal became a republic. Instability hampered progress and army officers seized power in 1926. In 1928, they chose Antonio de Salazar to be minister of finance.

Salazar became prime minister in 1932 and ruled as a dictator from 1933 until 1968. In 1974, army officers mounted a coup. The new regime made most of Portugal's colonies independent and held free elections in 1978. Portugal joined the European Community (now the European Union) in 1986, and in 2002 the euro became the sole unit of currency. In 2011, the socialist prime minister, José Sócrates, resigned after parliament rejected his government's austerity budget, which was aimed at reducing the country's budget deficit.

Agriculture and fishing were the mainstays of the economy until the mid-20th century, when manufacturing became the most valuable activity.

AREA 34,285 SQ MI [88,797 SQ KM]
POPULATION 10,736,000 **CAPITAL** LISBON
GOVERNMENT MULTIPARTY REPUBLIC **ETHNIC GROUPS** PORTUGUESE 99%
LANGUAGES PORTUGUESE (OFFICIAL) **RELIGIONS** ROMAN CATHOLIC 94%, PROTESTANT **CURRENCY** EURO = 100 CENTS

PUERTO RICO

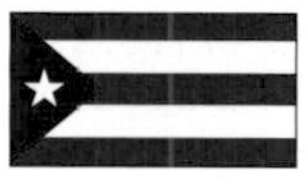

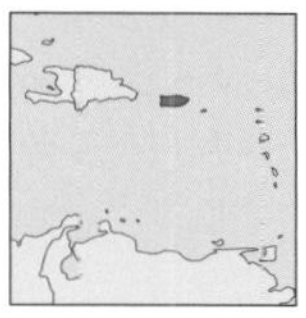

The Commonwealth of Puerto Rico, a mainly mountainous island, is the easternmost of the Greater Antilles chain. The climate is hot and wet. Puerto Rico is a dependent territory of the USA and the people are US citizens. In 1998, 50.2% of the population voted in a referendum on possible statehood to maintain the status quo.

Puerto Rico is the most industrialized country in the Caribbean. Tax exemptions attract US companies to the island and manufacturing is expanding. The chief exports are chemicals and chemical products, machinery, and food.

AREA 3,427 SQ MI [8,875 SQ KM]
POPULATION 3,979,000 **CAPITAL** SAN JUAN

QATAR

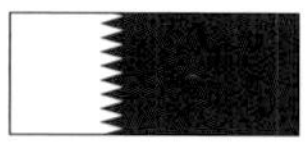

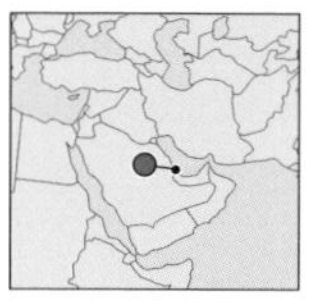

The State of Qatar occupies a low, barren peninsula that extends northward from the Arabian peninsula into the Persian Gulf. The climate is hot and dry. Qatar became a British protectorate in 1916, but it became fully independent in 1971. Oil, first discovered in 1939, is the mainstay of the economy of this prosperous nation.

AREA 4,247 SQ MI [11,000 SQ KM] **POPULATION** 841,000 **CAPITAL** DOHA

RÉUNION

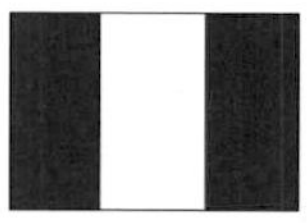

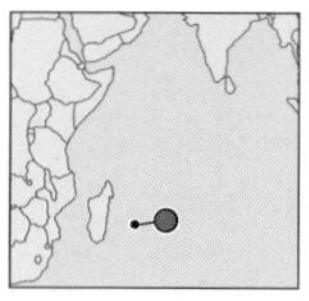

Réunion is a French overseas department in the Indian Ocean. The land is mainly mountainous, though the lowlands are intensely cultivated. Sugar and sugar products are the main exports, but French aid, given to the island in return for its use as a military base, is important to the economy.

AREA 969 SQ MI [2,510 SQ KM]
POPULATION 788,000 **CAPITAL** ST-DENIS

ROMANIA

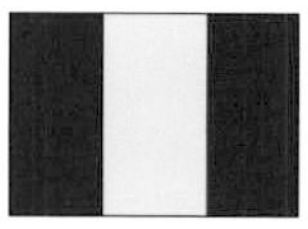

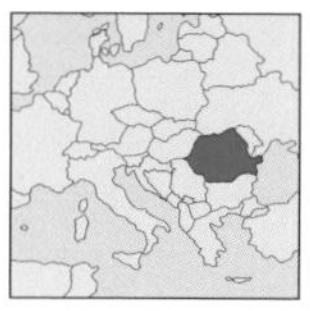

GEOGRAPHY Romania is a country on the Black Sea in eastern Europe. Eastern and southern Romania form part of the Danube river basin. The delta region, near the mouths of the Danube, where the river flows into the Black Sea, is one of Europe's finest wetlands. The southern part of the coast contains several resorts. The heart of the country is called Transylvania. It is ringed in the east, south, and west by scenic mountains which are part of the Carpathian mountain system. Romania has hot summers and cold winters. The rainfall is heaviest in spring and early summer.

POLITICS & ECONOMY From the late 18th century, the Turkish empire began to break up. The modern history of Romania began in 1861 when Walachia and Moldavia united. After World War I (1914–18), Romania, which had fought on the side of the victorious Allies, obtained large areas, including Transylvania, where most people were Romanians. This almost doubled the country's size and population. In 1939, Romania lost territory to Bulgaria, Hungary, and the Soviet Union. Romania fought alongside Germany in World War II, and Soviet troops occupied the country in 1944. Hungary returned northern Transylvania to Romania in 1945, but Bulgaria and the Soviet Union kept former Romanian territory. In 1947, Romania officially became a Communist country.

In 1990, Romania held its first free elections since the end of World War II. The National Salvation Front, led by Ion Iliescu and containing many former Communist leaders, won a large majority. A new constitution, approved in 1991, made the country a democratic republic. Elections held under this constitution in 1992 again resulted in victory for Ion Iliescu, whose party was renamed the Party of Social Democracy in 1993. Iliescu was defeated in 1996, but he served again as president in 2000–4. Romania joined NATO in 2004 and the European Union in 2007. In 2010, the European Union called on Romania to take urgent action to combat crime and corruption.

Romania has a "lower-middle-income" economy. Under Communist rule, industry, including mining and manufacturing, became more important than farming.

AREA 92,043 SQ MI [238,391 SQ KM]
POPULATION 21,959,000 **CAPITAL** BUCHAREST
GOVERNMENT MULTIPARTY REPUBLIC
ETHNIC GROUPS ROMANIAN 89%, HUNGARIAN 7%, ROMA 2%, UKRAINIAN **LANGUAGES** ROMANIAN (OFFICIAL), HUNGARIAN, GERMAN **RELIGIONS** EASTERN ORTHODOX 87%, PROTESTANT 7%, ROMAN CATHOLIC 5% **CURRENCY** LEU = 100 BANI

RUSSIA

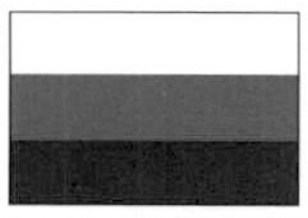

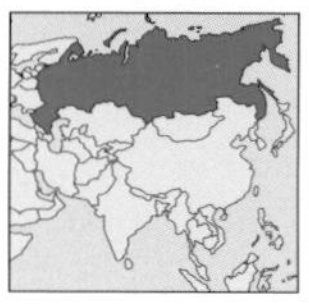

GEOGRAPHY Russia is the world's largest country. About 25% lies west of the Ural Mountains in European Russia, where 80% of the population lives. It is mostly flat or undulating, but the land rises to the Caucasus Mountains in the south, where Russia's highest peak, Elbrus, at 18,481 ft [5,633 m], is found. Asian Russia, or Siberia, contains vast plains and plateaux, with mountains in the east and south. The Kamchatka peninsula in the far east has many active volcanoes. Russia contains several of the world's longest rivers. It also includes part of the world's largest inland body of water, the Caspian Sea, and Lake Baikal, the world's deepest lake.

Moscow has a continental climate, with cold, snowy winters and hot summers. Siberia has a harsher, drier climate. In 2010, during a long heat wave, devastating wildfires swept over large areas.

POLITICS & ECONOMY In the 9th century AD, a state called Kievan Rus was formed by a group of people called the East Slavs. Kiev, now capital of Ukraine, became a major trading center, but, in 1237, Mongol armies conquered Russia and destroyed Kiev. Russia was part of the Mongol empire until the late 15th century. Under Mongol rule, Moscow became the leading Russian city.

In the 16th century, Moscow's grand prince was retitled "tsar." The first tsar, Ivan the Terrible, expanded Russian territory. In 1613, after a period of civil war, Michael Romanov became tsar, founding a dynasty which ruled until 1917. In the early 18th century, Tsar Peter the Great began to westernize Russia and, by 1812, when Napoleon failed to conquer the country, Russia was a major European power. But during the 19th century, many Russians demanded reforms and discontent was widespread.

In World War I (1914–18), the Russian people suffered great hardships and, in 1917, Tsar Nicholas II was forced to abdicate. In November 1917, the Bolsheviks seized power under Vladimir Lenin. The Bolsheviks set up the Union of Soviet Socialist Republics (also called the USSR or the Soviet Union).

From 1924, Joseph Stalin introduced a socialist economic program, suppressing all opposition. In 1939, the Soviet Union and Germany signed a non-aggression pact, but Germany invaded the Soviet Union in 1941. Soviet forces pushed the Germans back, occupying eastern Europe. They reached Berlin in May 1945. From the late 1940s, tension between the Soviet Union and its allies and Western nations developed into a "Cold War." This continued until 1991, when the Soviet Union was dissolved.

The Soviet Union collapsed because of the failure of its economic policies. From 1991, President Boris Yeltsin introduced democratic and economic reforms. Yeltsin retired in 1999 and, in 2000, was succeeded by Vladimir Putin. Putin, who was re-elected in 2004, sought to develop contacts with the West. He supported the US-declared "war on terrorism," though he opposed the invasion of Iraq in 2003. The secessionist conflict in Chechenia, including the occupation of a school by Muslim extremists in 2004, causing more than 330 deaths, provoked outrage. In 2005, violent incidents in the republics of Dagestan, Ingushetia, and Kabardino-Balkaria further confirmed that Russia's size and diversity make national unity hard to achieve. From 2006, relations with the West appeared to deteriorate, with Russia criticizing the expansion of NATO in Eastern Europe. In 2008, Putin, having served two terms as president, was replaced by his ally Dmitry Medvedev. But Putin took the post of prime minister. In August 2008, Russia fought a short war against Georgia, which had attacked South Ossetia, one of Georgia's secessionist regions. In 2010, Muslim militants from the North Caucasus were accused of bomb attacks on Moscow's Metro. Also in 2010, Russia and the US signed a strategic arms agreement, reducing their nuclear warheads.

Russia's economy was thrown into disarray after the collapse of the Soviet Union, and in the early 1990s the World Bank described Russia as a "lower-middle-income" economy. Russia was admitted to the Council of Europe in 1997 and was also invited to attend the G7 summit in 1997. Industry is Russia's leading economic activity. Resources include oil and natural gas, coal, timber, metal ores, and hydroelectric power.

Russia is a major producer of farm products, though it imports grains. Major crops include barley, flax, fruits, oats, rye, potatoes, sugar beet, sunflower seeds, vegetables, and wheat.

AREA 6,592,812 SQ MI [17,075,400 SQ KM]
POPULATION 139,390,000 **CAPITAL** MOSCOW
GOVERNMENT FEDERAL MULTIPARTY REPUBLIC
ETHNIC GROUPS RUSSIAN 82%, TATAR 4%, UKRAINIAN 3%, CHUVASH 1%, MORE THAN 100 OTHERS **LANGUAGES** RUSSIAN (OFFICIAL), MANY OTHERS
RELIGIONS MAINLY RUSSIAN ORTHODOX, ISLAM, JUDAISM
CURRENCY RUSSIAN RUBLE = 100 KOPEKS

RWANDA

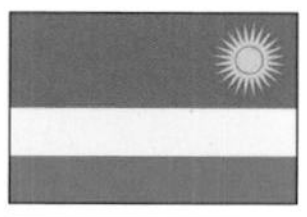

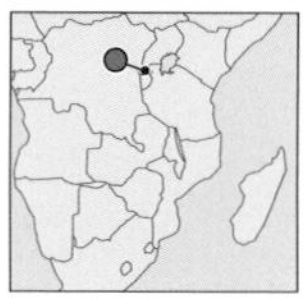

GEOGRAPHY The Republic of Rwanda is a small, landlocked country in east-central Africa. Lake Kivu and the River Ruzizi in the Great African Rift Valley form the country's western border.

Kigali stands on the central plateau of Rwanda. Here, temperatures are moderated by the altitude. The rainfall is abundant, but much

heavier rain falls on the western uplands, while the Rift Valley floor is drier and warmer than the rest of Rwanda.

POLITICS & ECONOMY Germany conquered the area, called Ruanda-Urundi, in the 1890s. However, Belgium occupied the region during World War I (1914–18) and ruled it until 1961, when the people of Ruanda voted for their country to become a republic, called Rwanda. This decision followed a rebellion by the majority Hutu people against the Tutsi monarchy. About 150,000 deaths resulted from this conflict. Many Tutsis fled to Uganda, where they formed a rebel army. Relations between Hutus and Tutsis deteriorated and, in 1994, between 500,000 and 800,000 people were massacred in Rwanda. After the Tutsis had restored order, Hutu rebels fled into the Democratic Republic of the Congo. Rwanda intervened in the Congo in 1996, 2002, and again in 2009. In 2009, Rwanda became the 54th member of the Commonwealth.

According to the World Bank, Rwanda is a "low-income" developing country. Most people are poor farmers. Food crops include bananas, beans, cassava, and sorghum. Some cattle are raised.

AREA 10,169 SQ MI [26,338 SQ KM]
POPULATION 11,056,000 **CAPITAL** KIGALI
GOVERNMENT REPUBLIC **ETHNIC GROUPS** HUTU 84%, TUTSI 15%, TWA 1% **LANGUAGES** FRENCH, ENGLISH AND KINYARWANDA (ALL OFFICIAL) **RELIGIONS** ROMAN CATHOLIC 57%, PROTESTANT 26%, ADVENTIST 11%, ISLAM 5% **CURRENCY** RWANDAN FRANC = 100 CENTIMES

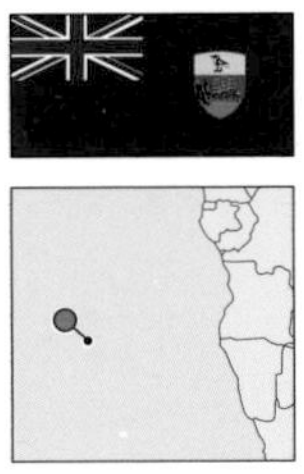

ST HELENA

St Helena, which became a British colony in 1834, is an isolated volcanic island in the south Atlantic Ocean. Now a British overseas territory, it is also the administrative center of Ascension and Tristan da Cunha.

AREA 47 SQ MI [122 SQ KM]
POPULATION 4,000 **CAPITAL** JAMESTOWN

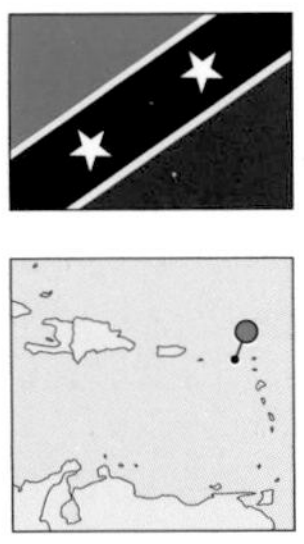

ST KITTS AND NEVIS

The Federation of St Kitts and Nevis comprises two well-watered volcanic islands, with mountains rising to around 3,300 ft [1,000 m]. The islands were the first in the Caribbean to be colonized by Britain (in 1623 and 1628), and they became an independent country in 1983. In 1998, a vote for the secession of Nevis fell short of the two-thirds majority required. Tourism has replaced sugar as the principal earner.

AREA 101 SQ MI [261 SQ KM]
POPULATION 50,000 **CAPITAL** BASSETERRE

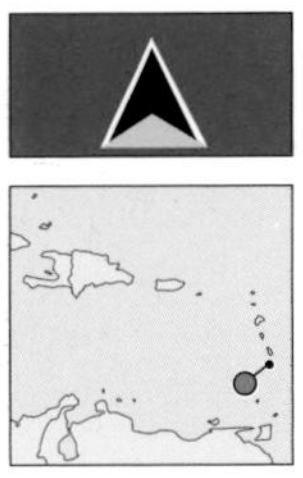

ST LUCIA

St Lucia, which became independent from Britain in 1979, is a mountainous, forested island of extinct volcanoes. It exports bananas and coconuts, and now attracts many tourists.

AREA 208 SQ MI [539 SQ KM]
POPULATION 161,000 **CAPITAL** CASTRIES

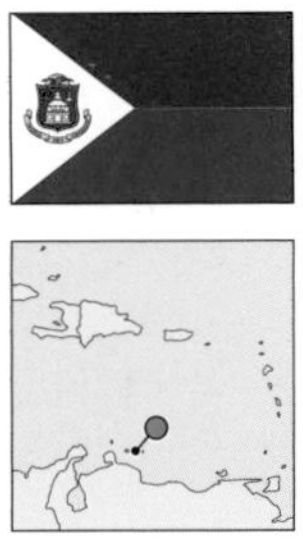

ST MAARTEN

Part of the Netherlands Antilles until 2010, the southern part of the island of St Maarten (called Sint Maarten in Dutch) is a self-governing territory within the Kingdom of the Netherlands.

AREA 13 SQ MI [34 SQ KM]
POPULATION 37,000 **CAPITAL** PHILIPSBURG

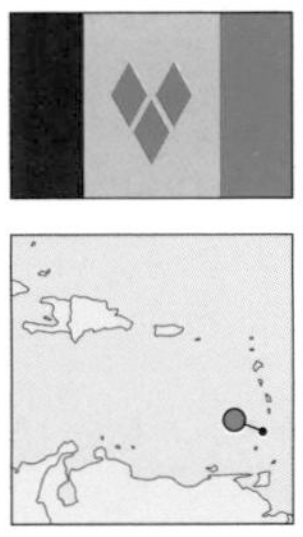

ST VINCENT AND THE GRENADINES

St Vincent and the Grenadines achieved its independence from Britain in 1979. Tourism is growing, but the territory is less prosperous than its neighbors.

AREA 150 SQ MI [388 SQ KM]
POPULATION 104,000 **CAPITAL** KINGSTOWN

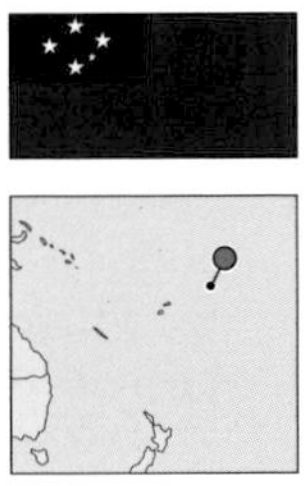

SAMOA

The Independent State of Samoa (formerly Western Samoa) comprises two islands in the South Pacific Ocean. Governed by New Zealand from 1920, the territory became independent in 1962. Exports include coconut cream and beer.

AREA 1,093 SQ MI [2,831 SQ KM]
POPULATION 192,000 **CAPITAL** APIA

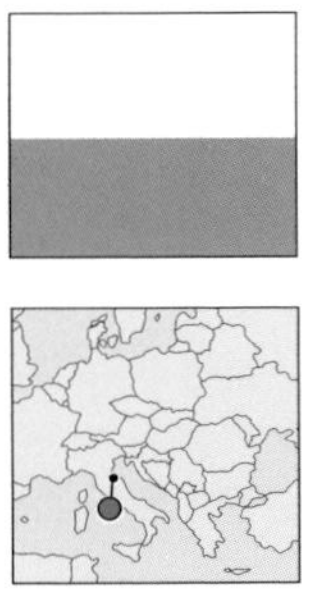

SAN MARINO

San Marino in northern Italy has been independent since 885 and a republic since the 14th century. It is the world's oldest republic. It has a friendship and cooperation treaty with Italy dating back to 1862. The state is governed by an elected council and has its own legal system. It has no armed forces and the police are "hired" from the Italian constabulary. The chief occupations are tourism, limestone quarrying, textiles, and wine-making.

AREA 24 SQ MI [61 SQ KM] **POPULATION** 31,000 **CAPITAL** SAN MARINO

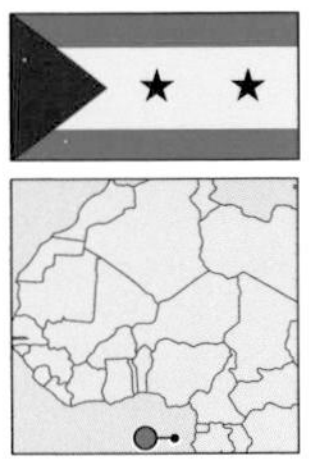

SÃO TOMÉ AND PRÍNCIPE

The Democratic Republic of São Tomé and Príncipe, a mountainous island territory west of Gabon, became a Portuguese colony in 1522. Following independence in 1975, the islands became a one-party Marxist state, but multiparty elections were held from 1991.

AREA 372 SQ MI [964 SQ KM] **POPULATION** 176,000 **CAPITAL** SÃO TOMÉ

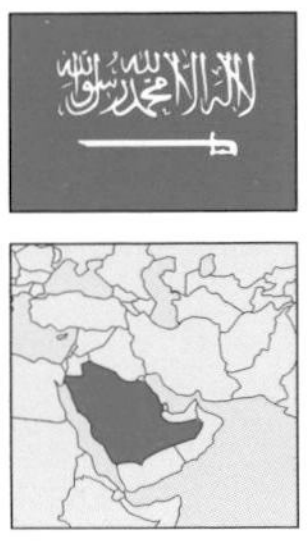

SAUDI ARABIA

GEOGRAPHY The Kingdom of Saudi Arabia occupies about three-quarters of the Arabian peninsula in southwest Asia. Deserts cover most of the land. Mountains border the Red Sea plains in the west. In the north is the sandy Nafud Desert (An Nafud). In the south is the Rub' al Khali (the "Empty Quarter"), one of the world's bleakest deserts.

Saudi Arabia has a hot dry climate. Summer temperatures in Riyadh often exceed 104°F [40°C]. The nights are cool.

POLITICS & ECONOMY Saudi Arabia contains the two holiest places in Islam – Mecca (or Makka), the birthplace of the Prophet Muhammad in AD 570, and Medina (Al Madinah) where Muhammad went in 622. These places are visited by many pilgrims.

Since 1933, oil has been the mainstay of the economy. The monarch has supreme authority. Many of the alleged terrorists involved in attacks on the US on September 11, 2001, were Saudi nationals. Saudi Arabia condemned the violence and, from 2003, Islamists launched attacks in Saudi Arabia. In 2010, 149 militants were arrested, most of them allegedly members of al Qaida.

Saudi Arabia has about 25% of the world's known oil reserves and oil products make up about 90% of the exports. Irrigation and desalination projects have increased crop production.

AREA 829,995 SQ MI [2,149,690 SQ KM]
POPULATION 25,732,000 **CAPITAL** RIYADH
GOVERNMENT ABSOLUTE MONARCHY WITH CONSULTATIVE ASSEMBLY
ETHNIC GROUPS ARAB 90%, AFRO-ASIAN 10%
LANGUAGES ARABIC (OFFICIAL)
RELIGIONS ISLAM 100%
CURRENCY SAUDI RIYAL = 100 HALALAS

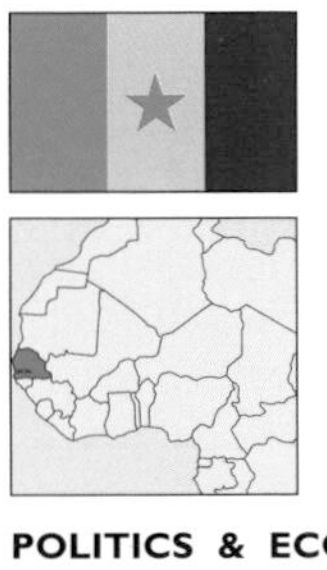

SENEGAL

GEOGRAPHY The Republic of Senegal is on the northwest coast of Africa. The volcanic Cape Verde (Cap Vert), on which Dakar stands, is the most westerly point in Africa. Plains cover most of Senegal, though the land rises gently in the southeast.

Dakar has a tropical climate, with a short rainy season between July and October.

POLITICS & ECONOMY In 1882, Senegal became a French colony, and from 1895 it was ruled as part of French West Africa, the capital of which, Dakar, developed as a major port and city.

In 1959, Senegal joined French Sudan (now Mali) to form the Federation of Mali. But Senegal withdrew in 1960 and became the separate Republic of Senegal. Its first president, Léopold Sédar Senghor, served until 1981, when he was succeeded by Abdou Diouf. However, in 2000, Diouf was defeated in elections by Abdoulaye Wade. In 2001, the government signed a peace treaty with separatist rebels in the southern Casamance province, but sporadic violence continued throughout the 2000s.

According to the World Bank, Senegal is a "lower-middle-income" developing country. It was badly hit in the 1960s and 1970s by droughts, which caused starvation. Agriculture still employs 30% of the population, though many farmers produce little more than they need to feed their families. Food crops include groundnuts, millet, and rice. Phosphates are the country's chief resource, but Senegal also refines oil, which it imports from Gabon and Nigeria. Dakar is a busy port and has many industries.

AREA 75,954 SQ MI [196,722 SQ KM]
POPULATION 12,323,000 **CAPITAL** DAKAR
GOVERNMENT MULTIPARTY REPUBLIC
ETHNIC GROUPS WOLOF 44%, PULAR 24%, SERER 15%
LANGUAGES FRENCH (OFFICIAL), TRIBAL LANGUAGES
RELIGIONS ISLAM 94%, CHRISTIANITY (MAINLY ROMAN CATHOLIC) 5%, TRADITIONAL BELIEFS 1%
CURRENCY CFA FRANC = 100 CENTIMES

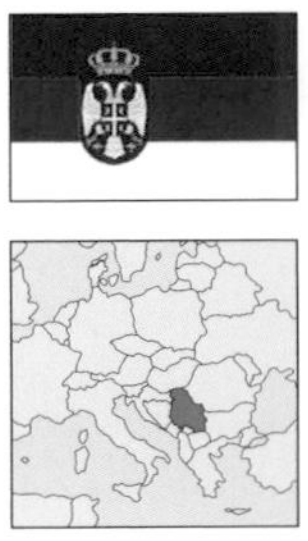

SERBIA

GEOGRAPHY The Republic of Serbia lies in the central Balkan peninsula. A landlocked country, it contains large, fertile lowlands drained by the River Danube and its tributaries, with uplands in the south. Most of Serbia has a continental climate, with cold, snowy winters and hot, dry summers. Heavy rains fall in the spring and the fall.

POLITICS & ECONOMY Around 1,500 years ago, South Slavs moved into the Balkan peninsula, and each group founded its own state. Serbia came under the Turkish Ottoman Empire in the 15th century. In the 19th century, many Slavs worked for independence and Slavic unity. In 1914, Austria–Hungary declared war on Serbia, blaming it for the assassination of Archduke Franz Ferdinand of Austria–Hungary. In 1918, the South Slavs united in the Kingdom of the Serbs, Croats, and Slovenes, which was renamed Yugoslavia in 1929. Germany invaded in 1941, but Communist partisans, led by Josip Broz Tito, took power in 1945.

From 1945, the country became the Federal People's Republic of Yugoslavia. In 1991–2, the country split apart, with Bosnia-Herzegovina, Croatia, Macedonia, and Slovenia proclaiming their independence. The remaining republics, Serbia and Montenegro, retained the name Yugoslavia. In 2003, these two republics agreed to form the loose Union of Serbia and Montenegro. In 2006, the Montenegrins voted for full independence, and Serbia and Montenegro became separate republics. In 2008, the province of Kosovo, which had been under a NATO administration since 1999, declared itself independent. Its new status was widely recognized, though not by Serbia and Russia. In 2009, Serbia formally applied to join the European Union.

Serbia's resources include bauxite, coal, copper and other metals, together with oil and natural gas. Manufactured products include aluminum, machinery, plastics, steel, textiles, and vehicles. Crops include fruits, maize, potatoes, tobacco, and wheat. Livestock include cattle, pigs, and sheep.

AREA 29,913 SQ MI [77,474 SQ KM]
POPULATION 7,345,000 **CAPITAL** BELGRADE
GOVERNMENT REPUBLIC
ETHNIC GROUPS SERB 83%, HUNGARIAN 4%, OTHERS
LANGUAGES SERBIAN (OFFICIAL), HUNGARIAN
RELIGIONS SERBIAN ORTHODOX, ROMAN CATHOLIC, ISLAM, PROTESTANT
CURRENCY NEW DINAR = 100 PARAS

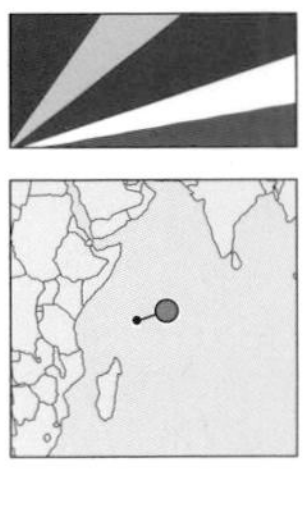

SEYCHELLES

The Republic of Seychelles in the western Indian Ocean achieved independence from Britain in 1976. Coconuts are the main cash crop, and fishing and tourism are important to the country's economy.

AREA 176 SQ MI [455 SQ KM]
POPULATION 88,000 **CAPITAL** VICTORIA

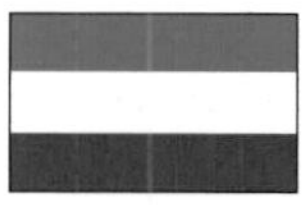

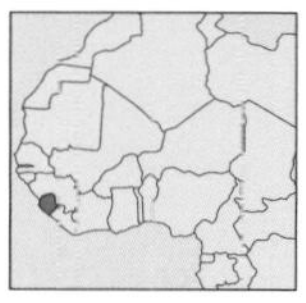

SIERRA LEONE

GEOGRAPHY The Republic of Sierra Leone in West Africa is about the same size as the Republic of Ireland. The coast contains several deep estuaries in the north, with lagoons in the south. The most prominent feature is the mountainous Freetown (or Sierra Leone) peninsula.

Sierra Leone has a tropical climate, with heavy rainfall between April and November.

POLITICS & ECONOMY A former British territory, Sierra Leone became independent in 1961 and a republic in 1971. It became a one-party state in 1978, but, in 1991, the people voted for the restoration of democracy. The military seized power in 1992 and a civil war caused much destruction in 1994–5. Elections in 1996 were followed by another military coup. In 1998, the West African Peace Force restored the deposed President Ahmed Tejan Kabbah. In 1999, a peace agreement followed further conflict. As part of this agreement, Foday Sankoh, one of the rebel leaders, became vice president. However, he was arrested in 2000 and charged with war crimes. Another ceasefire was agreed in 2004. The last of the UN troops left the country in 2005, and national elections were held in 2007. In 2010, the UN Security Council lifted the last remaining sanctions against Sierra Leone.

Sierra Leone has a "low-income" economy. About 58% of the people live by farming, mainly at subsistence level. The leading exports are minerals, including diamonds, bauxite, and rutile (titanium ore). The country has few manufacturing industries.

AREA 27,699 SQ MI [71,740 SQ KM]
POPULATION 5,246,000 **CAPITAL** FREETOWN
GOVERNMENT SINGLE-PARTY REPUBLIC **ETHNIC GROUPS** NATIVE AFRICAN TRIBES 90% **LANGUAGES** ENGLISH (OFFICIAL), MENDE, TEMNE, KRIO
RELIGIONS ISLAM 60%, TRADITIONAL BELIEFS 30%, CHRISTIANITY 10%
CURRENCY LEONE = 100 CENTS

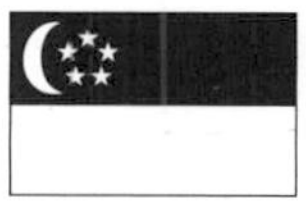

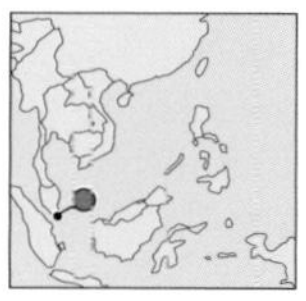

SINGAPORE

GEOGRAPHY The Republic of Singapore is an island country at the southern tip of the Malay peninsula. It consists of the large Singapore Island and 58 small islands, 20 of which are inhabited. The climate is hot and humid. Temperatures are high and rainfall is heavy throughout the year.

POLITICS & ECONOMY In 1819, Sir Thomas Stamford Raffles (1781–1826), agent of the British East India Company, made a treaty with the Sultan of Johor allowing the British to build a settlement on Singapore Island. Singapore soon became the leading British trading center in Southeast Asia and it later became a naval base. Japanese forces seized the island in 1942, but British rule was restored in 1945.

In 1963, Singapore became part of the Federation of Malaysia, which also included Malaya and the territories of Sabah and Sarawak on Borneo. In 1965, Singapore broke away and became independent.

The People's Action Party (PAP) has ruled Singapore since 1959. Its leader, Lee Kuan Yew, served as prime minister from 1959 until 1990, when he resigned and was succeeded by Goh Chok Tong. In 2004, Lee Hsien Loong, son of Lee Kuan Yew, became prime minister.

The World Bank classifies Singapore as a "high-income" economy, where a skilled work force has created a fast-growing economy. Trade and finance are major activities. The global financial crisis in 2008–9 caused great concern, but recovery was rapid. Manufactures include electronic products, machinery, scientific instruments, textiles, and ships. Petroleum products and manufactures are the main exports.

AREA 264 SQ MI [683 SQ KM]
POPULATION 4,701,000 **CAPITAL** SINGAPORE CITY
GOVERNMENT MULTIPARTY REPUBLIC
ETHNIC GROUPS CHINESE 77%, MALAY 14%, INDIAN 8%
LANGUAGES CHINESE, MALAY, TAMIL AND ENGLISH (ALL OFFICIAL)
RELIGIONS BUDDHISM, ISLAM, CHRISTIANITY, HINDUISM
CURRENCY SINGAPORE DOLLAR = 100 CENTS

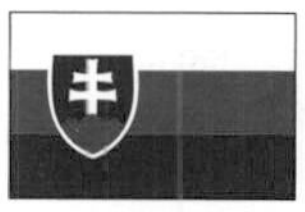

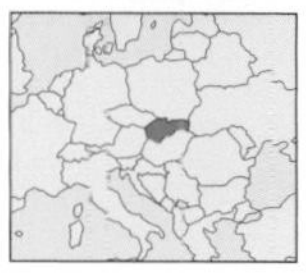

SLOVAK REPUBLIC

GEOGRAPHY The Slovak Republic is a predominantly mountainous country, consisting of part of the Carpathian range. The highest peak is Gerlachovsky in the Tatra Mountains, which reaches 8,711 ft [2,655 m]. The south is a fertile lowland. The Slovak Republic has cold winters and warm summers. Kosice, in the east, has average temperatures ranging from 27°F [–3°C] in January to 68°F [20°C] in July. The highland areas are much colder. Snow or rain falls throughout the year. Kosice has an average annual rainfall of 24 inches [600 mm], the wettest months being July and August.

POLITICS & ECONOMY Slavic peoples settled in the region in the 5th century AD. They were subsequently conquered by Hungary, beginning a millennium of Hungarian rule and suppression of Slovak culture.

In 1867, Hungary and Austria united to form Austria–Hungary, of which the present-day Slovak Republic was a part. Austria–Hungary collapsed at the end of World War I (1914–18). The Czech and Slovak people then united to form a new nation, Czechoslovakia. But Czech domination led to resentment by many Slovaks. In 1939, the Slovak Republic declared itself independent, but Germany occupied the country. At the end of World War II, the Slovak Republic again became part of Czechoslovakia.

The Communist Party took control in 1948. In the 1960s, many people sought reform, but they were crushed by the Russians. In the late 1980s, demands for democracy mounted and a non-Communist government took office in 1990. Elections in 1992 led to victory for the Movement for a Democratic Slovakia headed by a former Communist and nationalist, Vladimir Meciar, and the independent Slovak Republic came into existence on January 1, 1993.

Independence raised national aspirations among Slovakia's Magyar-speaking community, but relations with Hungary deteriorated when the Magyars felt that administrative changes under-represented them politically. The government also made Slovak the only official language. The government's autocratic rule and human rights record provoked international criticism. But the government continued to strengthen its ties with the West, gaining membership of NATO and the European Union in 2004. On January 1, 2009, Slovakia became the 16th country to adopt the euro as its official currency.

Before 1948, the Slovak Republic's economy was based on farming, but Communist governments developed manufacturing industries, producing such things as chemicals, machinery, steel, and weapons. Since the late 1980s, many state-run businesses have been handed over to private owners.

AREA 18,924 SQ MI [49,012 SQ KM]
POPULATION 5,470,000 **CAPITAL** BRATISLAVA
GOVERNMENT MULTIPARTY REPUBLIC
ETHNIC GROUPS SLOVAK 86%, HUNGARIAN 11%
LANGUAGES SLOVAK (OFFICIAL), HUNGARIAN
RELIGIONS ROMAN CATHOLIC 60%, PROTESTANT 8%, ORTHODOX 4%, OTHERS **CURRENCY** EURO = 100 CENTS

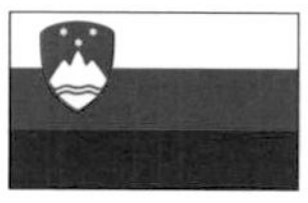

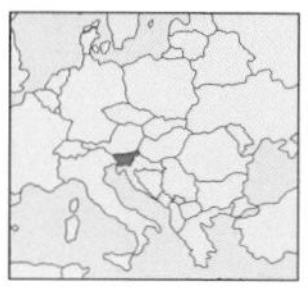

SLOVENIA

GEOGRAPHY The Republic of Slovenia was one of the six republics which made up the former Yugoslavia. Much of the land is mountainous, rising to 9,393 ft [2,863 m] at Mount Triglav in the Julian Alps (Julijske Alpe) in the northwest. Central Slovenia contains the limestone Karst region. The Postojna caves near Ljubljana are among the largest in Europe.

The coast has a mild Mediterranean climate, but inland the climate is more continental. The mountains are snow-capped in winter.

POLITICS & ECONOMY In the last 2,000 years, the Slovene people have been independent as a nation for less than 50 years. The Austrian Habsburgs ruled over the region from the 13th century until World War I. Slovenia became part of the Kingdom of the Serbs, Croats, and Slovenes (later called Yugoslavia) in 1918. During World War II, Slovenia was invaded and partitioned between Italy, Germany, and Hungary, but, after the war, Slovenia again became part of Yugoslavia.

From the late 1960s, some Slovenes demanded independence, but the central government opposed the breakup of the country. In 1990, when Communist governments had collapsed throughout Eastern Europe, elections were held and a non-Communist coalition government was set up. Slovenia then declared itself independent. This led to fighting between Slovenes and the federal army, but Slovenia did not become a battlefield. Slovenia's independence was recognized in 1992 and a coalition led by the Liberal Democrats was elected in 1992, 1996, and 2000. In 2004, Slovenia became a member of the North Atlantic Treaty Organization and the European Union. In 2009, Slovenia became the first former Communist country to assume the presidency of the European Union.

The reform of the formerly state-run economy caused problems for Slovenia. However, it has enjoyed considerable economic progress, with one of Europe's fastest growing economies. In 1992, the World Bank classified Slovenia's economy as "upper-middle-income."

Manufacturing is the leading activity and manufactures are the main exports. Manufactures include chemicals, machinery and transport equipment, metal goods, and textiles. Slovenia mines some iron ore, lead, lignite, and mercury. Agriculture and forestry employ 9% of the people. Fruits, maize, potatoes, and wheat are major crops, and many farmers raise animals.

AREA 7,821 SQ MI [20,256 SQ KM]
POPULATION 2,003,000 **CAPITAL** LJUBLJANA
GOVERNMENT MULTIPARTY REPUBLIC
ETHNIC GROUPS SLOVENE 92%, CROAT 1%, SERB, HUNGARIAN, BOSNIAK
LANGUAGES SLOVENIAN (OFFICIAL), SERBO-CROATIAN
RELIGIONS MAINLY ROMAN CATHOLIC
CURRENCY EURO = 100 CENTS

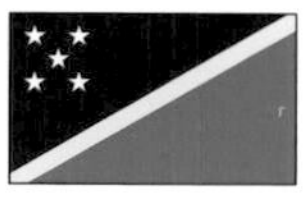

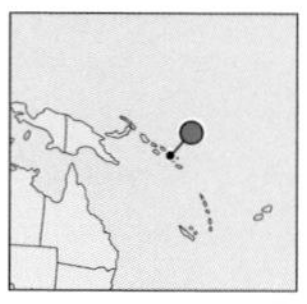

SOLOMON ISLANDS

The Solomon Islands, a chain of mainly volcanic islands in the Pacific Ocean, were a British territory between 1893 and 1978. The chain extends for some 1,400 mi [2,250 km]. They were the scene of fierce fighting during World War II. Most people are Melanesians, and the islands have a young population profile, with 40% of the people aged under 15. Fish, coconuts, and cocoa are leading products, though development is hampered by mountainous, forested terrain.

AREA 11,157 SQ MI [28,896 SQ KM]
POPULATION 559,000 **CAPITAL** HONIARA

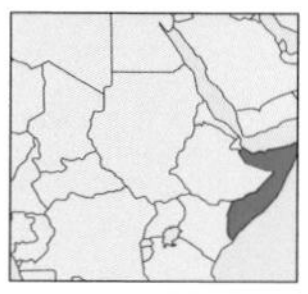

SOMALIA

GEOGRAPHY The Somali Democratic Republic, or Somalia, is in a region known as the "Horn of Africa." It is more than twice the size of Italy, the country which once ruled the southern part of Somalia. The most mountainous part of the country is in the north, behind the narrow coastal plains that border the Gulf of Aden. Rainfall is sparse, with the wettest regions in the south and northern mountains. Droughts are common and temperatures are generally high.

POLITICS & ECONOMY European powers became interested in the Horn of Africa in the 19th century. In 1884, Britain made the northern part of what is now Somalia a protectorate, while Italy took the south in 1905. The new boundaries divided the Somalis into five areas: the two Somalilands, Djibouti (which was taken by France in the 1880s), Ethiopia, and Kenya. Since then, many Somalis have wanted to create a Greater Somalia. Italy invaded British Somaliland in 1940, but was defeated in 1941. Britain ruled both Somalilands until 1950, when the United Nations asked Italy to take over the former Italian Somaliland for ten years. In 1960, the two Somalilands united to become Somalia.

Somalia has faced many problems. Economic difficulties led a military group to seize power in 1969. In the 1970s, Somalia supported an uprising of Somali-speaking people in the Ogaden region of Ethiopia. But, in 1988, Somalia and Ethiopia signed a peace treaty. In the 1990s, Somalia gradually broke apart. In 1991, the people in what was once British Somaliland set up the "Somaliland Republic," but it failed to get international recognition. The northeast, called Puntland, also seceded, while the south was riven by clan warfare. In 2004–5, a Somali parliament was set up in Kenya. In 2006, it moved to Baidoa, in Somalia (Mogadishu was regarded as unsafe). In 2006, Mogadishu was taken over by the Islamist Union of Islamic Courts, but government forces backed by Ethiopian troops defeated the Islamists. Ethiopia finally withdrew all its troops in January 2009. By 2011, the militant group al-Shabab controlled much of central and southern Somalia, while Somali pirates were a major threat to international shipping.

Somalia's economy has been shattered by war, droughts, and periodic floods. Many Somalis are nomads, who raise livestock. Live animals, meat, and hides and skins are exported. Crops include bananas, citrus fruits, cotton, maize, and sugarcane. Mining and manufacturing are relatively unimportant.

AREA 246,199 SQ MI [637,657 SQ KM] **POPULATION** 10,112,000
CAPITAL MOGADISHU **GOVERNMENT** SINGLE-PARTY REPUBLIC, MILITARY DOMINATED **ETHNIC GROUPS** SOMALI 85%, BANTU, ARAB
LANGUAGES SOMALI (OFFICIAL), ARABIC **RELIGIONS** ISLAM (SUNNI MUSLIM)
CURRENCY SOMALI SHILLING = 100 CENTS

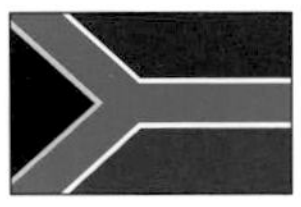
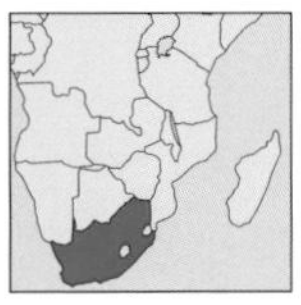

SOUTH AFRICA

GEOGRAPHY The Republic of South Africa is made up largely of the southern part of the huge plateau which makes up most of southern Africa. The highest peaks are in the Drakensberg range. Part of the Namib Desert is in the northwest. The area around Cape Town has a sunny climate with mild, rainy winters. Inland, large areas of the plateau are arid.

POLITICS & ECONOMY Early inhabitants in South Africa were the Khoisan. In the last 2,000 years, Bantu-speaking people moved into the area. Their descendants include the Zulu, Xhosa, Sotho, and Tswana. The Dutch founded a settlement at the Cape in 1652, but Britain took over in the early 19th century, making the area a colony. The Dutch, called Boers or Afrikaners, resented British rule and moved inland. Rivalry between the groups led to Anglo-Boer Wars in 1880–1 and 1899–1902.

In 1910, the country was united as the Union of South Africa. In 1948, the National Party won power and introduced a policy known as apartheid, under which non-whites had no votes and their human rights were strictly limited. In 1990, Nelson Mandela, leader of the African National Congress (ANC), was released from prison. Multi-racial elections were held in 1994 and Mandela became president. After Mandela retired, the ANC won elections in 1999 and 2004, led by Thabo Mbeki, and in 2009 when Jacob Zuma became president. The government has faced many problems, including a health crisis – South Africa has more people infected with the HIV virus than any other country.

South Africa is Africa's most developed country. However, most of the black people are poor, with low standards of living. Natural resources include diamonds, gold, and many other metals. Mining and manufacturing are the most valuable activities.

AREA 471,442 SQ MI [1,221,037 SQ KM] **POPULATION** 49,109,000
CAPITAL CAPE TOWN (LEGISLATIVE); PRETORIA/TSHWANE (ADMINISTRATIVE); BLOEMFONTEIN (JUDICIARY) **GOVERNMENT** MULTIPARTY REPUBLIC
ETHNIC GROUPS BLACK 76%, WHITE 13%, COLORED 9%, ASIAN 2%
LANGUAGES AFRIKAANS, ENGLISH, NDEBELE, PEDI, SOTHO, SWAZI, TSONGA, TSWANA, VENDA, XHOSA, AND ZULU (ALL OFFICIAL)
RELIGIONS CHRISTIANITY 68%, ISLAM 2%, HINDUISM 1%
CURRENCY RAND = 100 CENTS

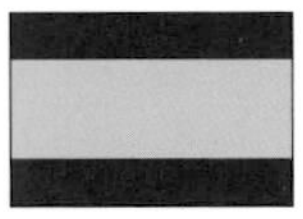
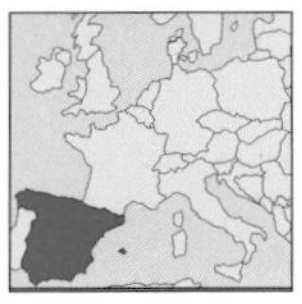

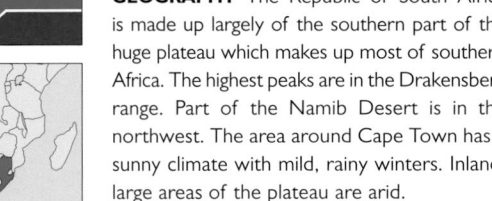

SPAIN

GEOGRAPHY The Kingdom of Spain is the second largest country in Western Europe after France. It shares the Iberian peninsula with Portugal. A large plateau, called the Meseta, covers most of Spain. Much of the Meseta is flat, but it is crossed by several mountain ranges, called sierras.

The northern highlands include the Cantabrian Mountains (Cordillera Cantabrica) and the high Pyrenees, which form Spain's border with France. But Mulhacén, the highest peak on the Spanish mainland, is in the Sierra Nevada in the southeast. Spain also contains fertile coastal plains. Other major lowlands are the Ebro river basin in the northeast and the Guadalquivir river basin in the southwest. Spain also includes the Balearic Islands in the Mediterranean Sea and the Canary Islands off the northwest coast of Africa.

The Meseta has a continental climate, with hot summers and cold winters, when temperatures often fall below freezing point. Snow frequently covers the mountain ranges on the Meseta. The Mediterranean coasts have hot, dry summers and mild winters.

POLITICS & ECONOMY In the 16th century, Spain became a world power. At its peak, it controlled much of Central and South America, parts of Africa, and the Philippines in Asia. Spain began to decline in the late 16th century. Its sea power was destroyed by a British fleet in the Battle of Trafalgar (1805). By the 20th century, it was a poor country.

Spain became a republic in 1931, but the republicans were defeated in the Spanish Civil War (1936–9). General Francisco Franco became the country's dictator, though technically Spain remained a monarchy. After Franco died in 1975, Prince Juan Carlos became king.

Spain has several groups with their own languages and cultures. Some of these people want to run their own regional affairs. In the northern Basque region, some nationalists have waged a terrorist campaign. A truce in 1998 was ended in 1999 when talks failed to produce results.

Since the 1970s, regional parliaments with a large degree of autonomy have been set up in the Basque Country, in Catalonia in the northeast, and in Galicia in the northwest. From the 1960s, ETA, a Basque terrorist group, waged a violent campaign for the secession of the Basque Country. Despite temporary ceasefires, the conflict continued.

In the last 50 years, Spain has changed from one of Europe's poorest countries into a prosperous nation and major holiday destination. Agriculture employs 4% of the people, as compared with 14% in mining and manufacturing. Farmland makes up two-thirds of Spain, with forests covering most of the rest. Crops include barley, citrus fruits, grapes for wine-making, olives, potatoes, and wheat. Spain lacks natural resources apart from some high-grade iron ore in the north. Manufactures include cars, chemicals, electronic goods, food, metal goods, and textiles.

AREA 192,103 SQ MI [497,548 SQ KM] **POPULATION** 46,506,000
CAPITAL MADRID **GOVERNMENT** CONSTITUTIONAL MONARCHY
ETHNIC GROUPS COMPOSITE OF MEDITERRANEAN AND NORDIC TYPES
LANGUAGES CASTILIAN SPANISH (OFFICIAL) 74%, CATALAN 17%, GALICIAN 7%, BASQUE 2%
RELIGIONS ROMAN CATHOLIC 94%, OTHERS
CURRENCY EURO = 100 CENTS

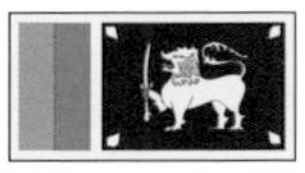
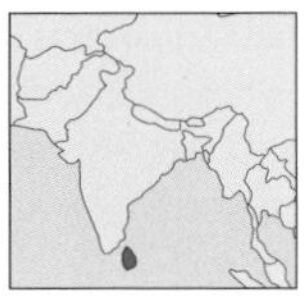

SRI LANKA

GEOGRAPHY The Democratic Socialist Republic of Sri Lanka is an island nation, separated from the southeast coast of India by the Palk Strait. The land is mostly low-lying, but a mountain region dominates the south-central part of the country.

The western part of Sri Lanka has a wet equatorial climate. Temperatures are high and the rainfall is heavy.

POLITICS & ECONOMY From the early 16th century, Ceylon (as Sri Lanka was then known) was ruled successively by the Portuguese, Dutch, and British. Independence was achieved in 1948 and the country was renamed Sri Lanka in 1972.

After independence, rivalries between the two main ethnic groups, the Sinhalese and Tamils, marred progress. In the 1950s, the government made Sinhala the official language. Following protests, the prime minister made provisions for Tamil to be used in some areas. In 1959, the prime minister was assassinated by a Sinhalese extremist and he was succeeded by Sirimavo Bandanaraike, the world's first woman prime minister.

Conflict between Tamils and Sinhalese continued in the 1970s and 1980s. In 1987, India helped to engineer a ceasefire. Indian troops arrived to enforce the agreement, but withdrew in 1990 after failing to subdue the main guerrilla group, the Tamil Tigers, who wanted to set up an independent Tamil homeland in northern Sri Lanka. The Tamil Tigers were finally defeated in May 2009 and, in 2010, Mahinda Rajapaksa was re-elected president of Sri Lanka.

In late 2004, a natural disaster occurred when a tsunami, caused by a sudden movement of the plates underlying the eastern Indian Ocean, struck parts of the coast of Sri Lanka. killing more than 30,000 people.

Sri Lanka is classed as a "low-income" economy. Agriculture employs about 28% of the people. Coconuts, rubber, and tea are exported, but rice is the main food crop. Factories process farm products and manufacture textiles.

AREA 25,332 SQ MI [65,610 SQ KM]
POPULATION 21,514,000 **CAPITAL** COLOMBO
GOVERNMENT MULTIPARTY REPUBLIC
ETHNIC GROUPS SINHALESE 74%, TAMIL 18%, MOOR 7%
LANGUAGES SINHALA AND TAMIL (BOTH OFFICIAL)
RELIGIONS BUDDHISM 70%, HINDUISM 15%, CHRISTIANITY 8%, ISLAM 7%
CURRENCY SRI LANKAN RUPEE = 100 CENTS

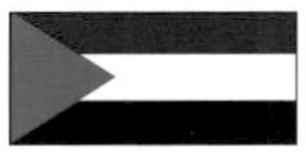
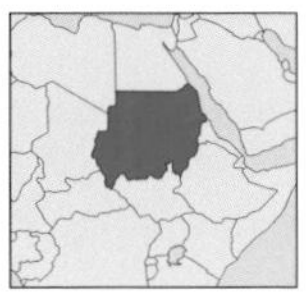

SUDAN

GEOGRAPHY The Republic of Sudan was Africa's largest country until 2011, when the people in the south voted to secede and set up a new nation called South Sudan. Sudan is mainly arid, with part of the vast Sahara in the north. The main feature is the fertile River Nile valley, where most people live.

POLITICS & ECONOMY In the 19th century, Egypt gradually took over Sudan. In 1881, a Muslim religious teacher, the Mahdi ("divinely appointed guide"), led an uprising. Britain and Egypt put the rebellion down in 1898. In 1899, they agreed to rule Sudan jointly as a condominium. After independence in 1952, the black Africans in the south, who were either Christians or followers of traditional religions, feared domination by the Muslim north. They objected to Arabic becoming the sole official language and, in 1964, civil war broke out. The war ended in 1972, when the south was granted regional self-government.

In 1983, the announcement that Islamic law would apply throughout Sudan sparked off further resistance from the rebel Sudan People's Liberation Army (SPLA) in the south. In 1998, Sudan's government announced that it accepted the idea of a referendum in the south. In 2005, a peace agreement was signed, bringing peace to the south. The referendum took place in January 2011, when around 99% of the people in the south voted to set up their own country, South Sudan.

Since 2003, another conflict has raged in the western province of Darfur, where government-backed militias battled with local rebel forces. In 2008, the International Criminal Court charged President al-Bashir with war crimes, but he was re-elected president in national elections in 2010.

Cotton is the chief crop in Sudan. Cotton, gum arabic, and sesame seeds are exported, but the most valuable exports are oil and oil products. More than 80% of the oil is produced in South Sudan, but Sudan has the infrastructure to exploit and export it. Manufacturing industries produce various items mainly for home consumption.

AREA 728,222 SQ MI [1,886,086 SQ KM] **POPULATION** 35,680,000
CAPITAL KHARTOUM **GOVERNMENT** FEDERAL PRESIDENTIAL DEMOCRATIC REPUBLIC **ETHNIC GROUPS** ARAB, BLACK, BEJA, OTHERS
LANGUAGES ARABIC, NUBIAN, BEJA, ENGLISH
RELIGIONS ISLAM, TRADITIONAL BELIEFS
CURRENCY SUDANESE POUND

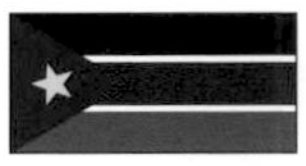
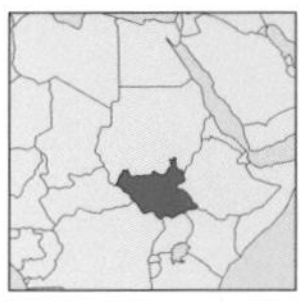

SUDAN, SOUTH

GEOGRAPHY The Republic of South Sudan is a landlocked country in northeastern Africa. Much of the land is low-lying and drained by the White Nile and its tributaries. Mountains lie in the far south. The country has a wet tropical climate. Forests, swamps, and grasslands cover large areas.

POLITICS & ECONOMY South Sudan has about 200 ethnic groups, including the Dinka and Nuer. Each group has its own traditional beliefs and languages. The South's deep cultural differences with the mainly Arab-Muslim north led to civil war (1964–1972 and 1983–2005). In January 2011, as part of the peace agreement, a referendum was held in which the vast majority of the people in the south voted for independence on July 9, 2011.

Most people depend on agriculture and forestry, but South Sudan has many mineral resources, including oil.

AREA 239,285 SQ MI [619,745 SQ KM] **POPULATION** 8,260,000
CAPITAL JUBA **GOVERNMENT** TRANSITIONAL
ETHNIC GROUPS DINKA, NUER, OTHERS
LANGUAGES LOCAL LANGUAGES
RELIGIONS TRADITIONAL BELIEFS, CHRISTIANITY
CURRENCY SUDANESE POUND

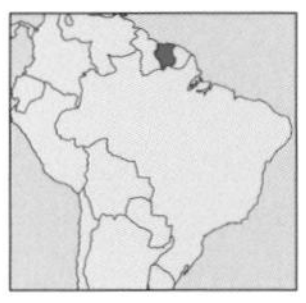

SURINAME

GEOGRAPHY The Republic of Suriname is sandwiched between French Guiana and Guyana in northeastern South America. The narrow coastal plain was once swampy, but it has been drained and now consists mainly of farmland. Inland lie hills and low mountains, which rise to 4,199 ft [1,280 m].

Suriname has a hot, wet and humid climate. Temperatures are high throughout the year.

POLITICS & ECONOMY In 1667, the British handed Suriname to the Dutch in return for New Amsterdam, an area that is now the state of New York. Slave revolts and Dutch neglect hampered development. In the early 19th century, Britain and the Netherlands disputed the ownership of the area. The British gave up their claims in 1813. Slavery was abolished in 1863 and, soon afterward, Indian and Indonesian laborers were introduced to work on the plantations.

Suriname became fully independent in 1975, but the economy was weakened when thousands of skilled people emigrated from Suriname to the Netherlands. Following a coup in 1980, Suriname was ruled by a military dictator, Dési Bouterse. The adoption of a new constitution led to the restoration of democracy in 1988, though another military coup occurred in 1990. Ronald Venetiaan was elected president in 2000 and his government replaced the guilder with the Surinamese dollar in 2004. Venetiaan was re-elected in 2005, when his New Front coalition won a narrow majority in elections.

The World Bank classifies Suriname as an "upper-middle-income" developing country. Its economy is based on mining and metal processing. Suriname is a leading producer of bauxite, from which the metal aluminum is made.

AREA 63,037 sq mi [163,265 sq km]
POPULATION 487,000 **CAPITAL** Paramaribo
GOVERNMENT Multiparty republic
ETHNIC GROUPS Hindustani/East Indian 37%, Creole (mixed White and Black) 31%, Javanese 15%, Black 10%, Amerindian 2%, Chinese 2%, others **LANGUAGES** Dutch (official), Sranang Tonga
RELIGIONS Hinduism 27%, Protestant 25%, Roman Catholic 23%, Islam 20% **CURRENCY** Surinamese dollar= 100 cents

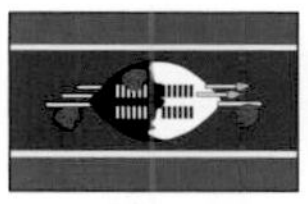
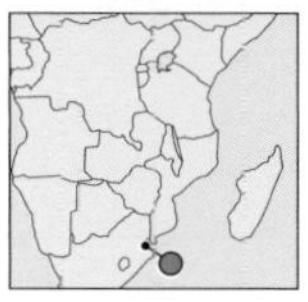

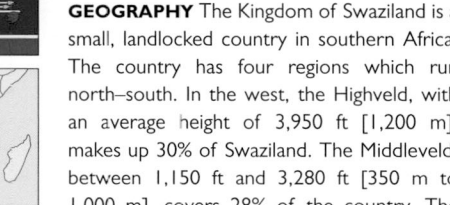

SWAZILAND

GEOGRAPHY The Kingdom of Swaziland is a small, landlocked country in southern Africa. The country has four regions which run north–south. In the west, the Highveld, with an average height of 3,950 ft [1,200 m], makes up 30% of Swaziland. The Middleveld, between 1,150 ft and 3,280 ft [350 m to 1,000 m], covers 28% of the country. The Lowveld, with an average height of 886 ft [270 m], covers another 33%. Finally, the Lebombo Mountains reach 2,600 ft [800 m] along the eastern border. The Lowveld is almost tropical, with average temperatures of 72°F [22°C] and low rainfall.

POLITICS & ECONOMY In 1894, Britain and the Boers of South Africa agreed to put Swaziland under the control of the South African Republic (the Transvaal). But at the end of the Anglo–Boer War (1899–1902), Britain took control of the country. In 1968, when Swaziland became fully independent as a constitutional monarchy, the head of state was King Sobhuza II. Sobhuza died in 1982 and was succeeded by his son, who, in 1986, became King Mswati III. Political parties were banned in elections in 1993 and 1998. Mswati ruled by decree. In 2005, Mswati signed a new constitution, but Swaziland remained an absolute monarchy.

Swaziland is a developing country. Farm products and processed food and drink, sugar, wood pulp, citrus fruits, and canned fruit are the leading exports. Many farmers live at subsistence level. Swaziland is heavily dependent on South Africa and it shares two problems with its large neighbor – widespread poverty and the high incidence of HIV/AIDS.

AREA 6,704 sq mi [17,364 sq km]
POPULATION 1,354,000 **CAPITAL** Mbabane
GOVERNMENT Monarchy **ETHNIC GROUPS** African 97%, European 3% **LANGUAGES** Siswati and English (both official)
RELIGIONS Zionist (a mix of Christianity and traditional beliefs) 40%, Roman Catholic 20%, Islam 10% **CURRENCY** Lilangeni = 100 cents

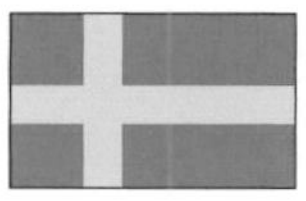
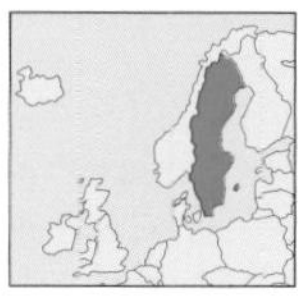

SWEDEN

GEOGRAPHY The Kingdom of Sweden is the largest of the countries of Scandinavia in both area and population. It shares the Scandinavian peninsula with Norway. The western part of the country, along the border with Norway, is mountainous. The highest point is Kebnekaise, which reaches 6,946 ft [2,117 m] in the northwest. The climate becomes increasingly severe from south to north.

POLITICS & ECONOMY Swedish Vikings plundered areas to the south and east between the 9th and 11th centuries. Sweden, Denmark, and Norway were united in 1397, but Sweden regained its independence in 1523. In 1809, Sweden lost Finland to Russia, but, in 1814, it gained Norway from Denmark. The union between Sweden and Norway was dissolved in 1905. Sweden was neutral in World Wars I and II. Since 1945, Sweden has become a prosperous country. In 1995, it joined the European Union. However, it did not adopt the euro in 1999.

Sweden has wide-ranging welfare services. But many people are concerned about the high cost of these services and the high taxes they must pay. In 2006, a center-right alliance defeated the Social Democrats, who had ruled Sweden for 65 of the previous 74 years. Fredrik Reinfeldt replaced Göran Persson as prime minister.

Sweden is a highly developed industrial country. Major products include steel and steel goods. Steel is used in the engineering industry to manufacture aircraft, cars, machinery, and ships. Sweden has some of the world's richest iron ore deposits. They are located near Kiruna in the far north. But most of this ore is exported, and Sweden imports most of the materials needed by its industries. Forestry is also important and hydroelectricity is a major source of energy. In 1996, Sweden announced the decommissioning of its nuclear power stations. The first reactor closed in 1999, followed by a second in 2005. But in 2009, the government, under pressure to diversify from fossil fuels, reversed this policy.

AREA 173,731 sq mi [449,964 sq km]
POPULATION 9,074,000 **CAPITAL** Stockholm
GOVERNMENT Constitutional monarchy **ETHNIC GROUPS** Swedish 91%, Finnish, Sami **LANGUAGES** Swedish (official), Finnish, Sami
RELIGIONS Lutheran 87%, Roman Catholic, Orthodox
CURRENCY Swedish krona = 100 öre

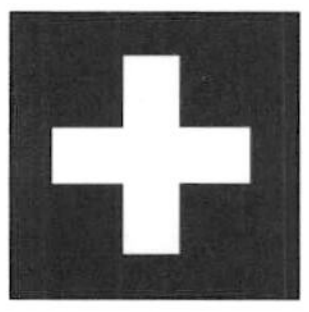
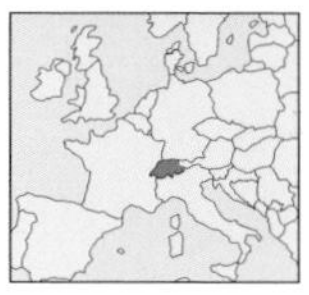

SWITZERLAND

GEOGRAPHY The Swiss Confederation is a landlocked country in Western Europe. Much of the land is mountainous. The Jura Mountains lie along Switzerland's western border with France, while the Swiss Alps make up about 60% of the country in the south and east. Four-fifths of the people of Switzerland live on the fertile Swiss plateau, which contains most of Switzerland's large cities.

The climate of Switzerland varies greatly according to the altitude. The plateau has warm summers and cold, snowy winters. Rain occurs throughout the year.

POLITICS & ECONOMY In 1291, three small cantons (states) united to defend their freedom against the Habsburg rulers of the Holy Roman Empire. They were Schwyz, Uri, and Unterwalden, and they called the confederation they formed "Switzerland." Switzerland expanded and, in the 14th century, defeated Austria in three wars of independence. After a defeat by the French in 1515, the Swiss adopted a policy of neutrality, which they still follow. In 1815, the Congress of Vienna expanded Switzerland to 22 cantons and guaranteed its neutrality. Switzerland's 23rd canton, Jura, was created in 1979 from part of Bern.

Neutrality combined with the vigor and independence of its people have made Switzerland prosperous. In 2002, Switzerland became a member of the United Nations, though it still maintained its tradition of neutrality. In 2010, a fourth female minister was elected by the Federal Assembly to the seven-member Federal Council. For the first time, women were in the majority in the country's cabinet.

Although lacking in natural resources, Switzerland is a wealthy, industrialized country. Products include chemicals, electrical equipment, machinery and machine tools, precision instruments, processed food, watches, and textiles. Farmers produce about three-fifths of the country's food – the rest is imported. Crops include fruits, potatoes, and wheat. Tourism and banking are also important. Swiss banks attract investors from all over the world.

AREA 15,940 sq mi [41,284 sq km] **POPULATION** 7,623,000
CAPITAL Bern **GOVERNMENT** Federal republic
ETHNIC GROUPS German 65%, French 18%, Italian 10%, Romansch 1%, others **LANGUAGES** French, German, Italian, and Romansch (all official) **RELIGIONS** Roman Catholic 46%, Protestant 40% **CURRENCY** Swiss franc = 100 centimes

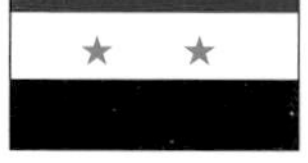
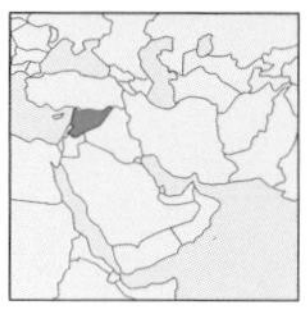

SYRIA

GEOGRAPHY The Syrian Arab Republic is a country in southwestern Asia. The narrow coastal plain is overlooked by a low mountain range which runs north–south. Another range, the Jabal ash Sharqi, runs along the border with Lebanon. South of this range is the Golan Heights, which Israel has occupied since 1967.

The coast has a Mediterranean climate, with dry, warm summers and wet, mild winters. The low mountains cut off Damascus from the sea. It has less rainfall than the coastal areas. To the east, the land becomes drier.

POLITICS & ECONOMY After the collapse of the Turkish Ottoman empire in World War I, Syria was ruled by France. Since independence in 1946, Syria has been involved in the Arab–Israeli wars, and in 1967 it lost a strategic border area, the Golan Heights, to Israel. In 1970, Lieutenant-General Hafez al-Assad took power, establishing a stable but repressive regime. Syria sent troops into Lebanon in 1976 in an effort to halt the civil war there, but, in 2005, following demonstrations, Syria withdrew its troops. Hafez al-Assad died in 2000 and was succeeded by his son, Bashar al-Assad. Anti-government demonstrations in 2011, the most serious internal unrest for decades, led to the resignation of the government.

The World Bank classifies Syria as a "lower-middle-income" developing country. But it has great potential for development. Its main resources are oil, hydroelectricity from the dam at Lake Assad, and fertile land. Oil is the main export; farm products, textiles, and phosphates are also important. Agriculture employs about 17% of the work force.

AREA 71,498 sq mi [185,180 sq km]
POPULATION 22,198,000 **CAPITAL** Damascus
GOVERNMENT Multiparty republic **ETHNIC GROUPS** Arab 90%, Kurdish, Armenian, others **LANGUAGES** Arabic (official), Kurdish, Armenian **RELIGIONS** Sunni Muslim 74%, other Islam 16%
CURRENCY Syrian pound = 100 piastres

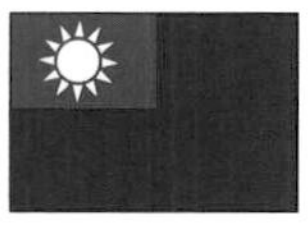
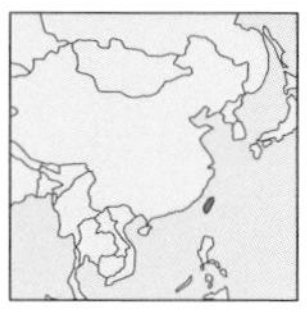

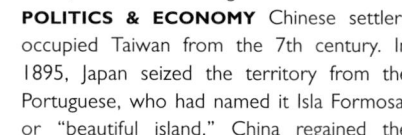

TAIWAN

GEOGRAPHY High mountain ranges run down the length of the island, with dense forest in many areas. The climate is warm, moist, and suitable for agriculture.

POLITICS & ECONOMY Chinese settlers occupied Taiwan from the 7th century. In 1895, Japan seized the territory from the Portuguese, who had named it Isla Formosa, or "beautiful island." China regained the island after World War II. In 1949, it became the refuge of the Nationalists who had been driven out of China by the Communists. They set up the Republic of China, which, with US help, began to expand its economy. Today, it produces a wide range of manufactured goods.

In the early 21st century, the Taiwanese declared full nationhood for Taiwan. But the government of mainland China threatened to attack the territory if it did not accept the fact that it was a self-governing province of China. However, in 2010, Taiwan and China signed a free-trade pact.

AREA 13,900 sq mi [36,000 sq km]
POPULATION 23,025,000 **CAPITAL** Taipei
GOVERNMENT Unitary multiparty republic
ETHNIC GROUPS Taiwanese 84%, mainland Chinese 14%
LANGUAGES Mandarin Chinese (official), Min, Hakka
RELIGIONS Buddhism, Taoism, Confucianism
CURRENCY New Taiwan dollar = 100 cents

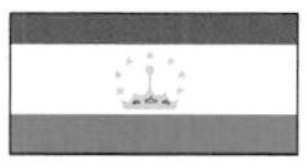
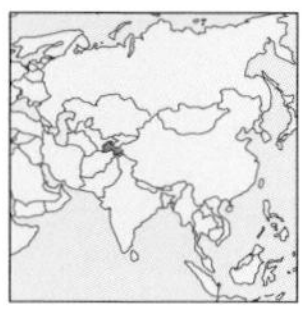

TAJIKISTAN

GEOGRAPHY The Republic of Tajikistan is one of the five central Asian republics that formed part of the former Soviet Union. Only 7% of the land is below 3,280 ft [1,000 m], while almost all of eastern Tajikistan is above 9,840 ft [3,000 m]. The highest point is Pik Imeni Ismail Samani (formerly known as Communism Peak or Pik Kommunizma), which reaches 24,590 ft [7,495 m]. The main ranges are the westward extension of the Tian Shan Range in the north and the snow-capped Pamirs in the southeast. Earthquakes are common throughout the country. The climate is continental, with hot, dry summers in the lower valleys and bitterly cold winters, especially in the mountains.

POLITICS & ECONOMY Russia conquered parts of Tajikistan in the late 19th century and, by 1920, Russia took complete control. In 1924, Tajikistan became part of the Uzbek Soviet Socialist Republic, but, in 1929, it was expanded, taking in some areas populated by Uzbeks, becoming the Tajik Soviet Socialist Republic.

While the Soviet Union began to introduce reforms during the 1980s, many Tajiks demanded freedom. In 1989, the Tajik government made Tajik the official language instead of Russian and, in 1990, it stated that its local laws overruled Soviet laws. Tajikistan became fully independent in 1991, following the breakup of the Soviet Union. In 1992, civil war broke out between the government, which was run by former Communists, and an alliance of democrats and Islamic forces. A ceasefire was agreed in 1996. In 2006, President Emomali Rahmon, president since 1994, was re-elected. In 2010, his party won parliamentary elections amid accusations of fraud.

The World Bank classifies Tajikistan as a "low-income" developing country and, in 2009, an international think tank warned that it risked becoming a failed state, with 70% of its people living in abject poverty. Agriculture, mainly on irrigated land, is the main activity and cotton is the chief product. Other crops include fruits, grains, and vegetables. The country has large hydroelectric resources and it produces aluminum.

AREA 55,521 sq mi [143,100 sq km]
POPULATION 7,487,000 **CAPITAL** Dushanbe
GOVERNMENT Transitional democracy
ETHNIC GROUPS Tajik 65%, Uzbek 25%, Russian
LANGUAGES Tajik (official), Russian
RELIGIONS Islam (Sunni Muslim 85%)
CURRENCY Somoni = 100 dirams

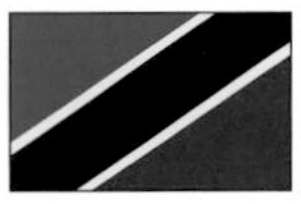
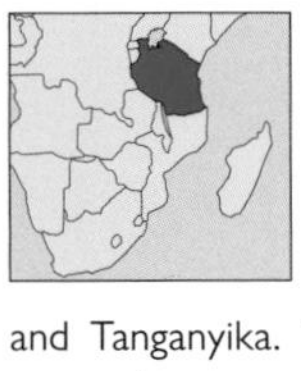

TANZANIA

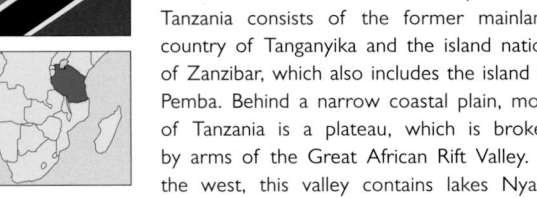

GEOGRAPHY The United Republic of Tanzania consists of the former mainland country of Tanganyika and the island nation of Zanzibar, which also includes the island of Pemba. Behind a narrow coastal plain, most of Tanzania is a plateau, which is broken by arms of the Great African Rift Valley. In the west, this valley contains lakes Nyasa and Tanganyika. The highest peak is Kilimanjaro, Africa's tallest mountain.

The coast has a hot and humid climate, with the greatest rainfall in April and May. The inland plateaux and mountains are cooler and less humid.

POLITICS & ECONOMY Mainland Tanganyika became a German territory in the 1880s, while Zanzibar and Pemba became a British protectorate in 1890. Following Germany's defeat in World War I, Britain took over Tanganyika, which remained a British territory until its independence in 1961. In 1964, Tanganyika and Zanzibar united to form the United Republic of Tanzania. The country's president, Julius Nyerere, pursued socialist policies of self-help (*ujamaa*) and egalitarianism. Many of its social reforms were successful, though the country failed to make economic progress. Nyerere resigned as president in 1985. His successors followed more liberal economic policies. In 2009, Tanzania joined with Burundi, Kenya, Rwanda, and Uganda in a common market agreement, allowing free movement of goods and people between them.

Tanzania is a poor country. Crops are grown on only 4.2% of the land, yet agriculture employs nearly 80% of the people. Food crops include bananas, cassava, maize, millet, and rice. Minerals, including gold, as well as cashews, tobacco, coffee, and tea are exported.

AREA 364,899 sq mi [945,090 sq km]
POPULATION 41,893,000 **CAPITAL** Dodoma
GOVERNMENT Multiparty republic
ETHNIC GROUPS Native African 99% (of whch 95% are Bantu consisting of more than 130 tribes)
LANGUAGES Swahili (Kiswahili) and English (both official)
RELIGIONS Islam 35% (99% in Zanzibar), traditional beliefs 35%, Christianity 30%
CURRENCY Tanzanian shilling = 100 cents

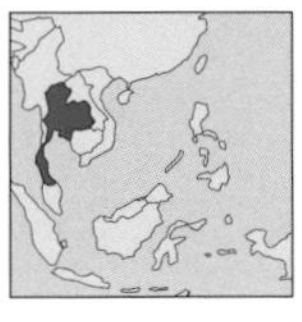

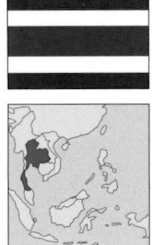

THAILAND

GEOGRAPHY The Kingdom of Thailand is one of the ten countries in Southeast Asia. The highest land is in the north, where Doi Inthanon, the highest peak, reaches 8,415 ft [2,565 m]. The Khorat plateau, in the north-east, makes up about 30% of the country and is the most heavily populated part of Thailand. In the south, Thailand shares the finger-like Malay peninsula with Burma and Malaysia.

Thailand has a tropical climate. Monsoon winds from the south-west bring heavy rains in May to October. Mountains shelter the central plains from the rain-bearing winds.

POLITICS & ECONOMY The first Thai state was set up in the 13th century. By 1350, it included most of what is now Thailand. European contact began in the early 16th century. But, in the late 17th century, the Thais, fearing interference in their affairs, forced all Europeans to leave. This policy continued for 150 years. In 1782, a Thai General, Chao Phraya Chakkri, became king, founding a dynasty which continues today. The country became known as Siam, and Bangkok became its capital. From the mid-19th century, contacts with the West were restored. In World War I, Siam supported the Allies against Germany and Austria–Hungary. But in 1941, the country was conquered by Japan and became its ally. After 1945, it became an ally of the United States.

After 1967, when Thailand became a member of ASEAN (Association of Southeast Asian Nations), its economy expanded rapidly, especially in manufacturing and service industries. In 1997, with other eastern Asian economies, it suffered an economic recession. Thailand has also faced conflict in southern Thailand, where the government has clashed with Muslim groups who feel that the government discriminates against them. In 2001, Thaksin Shinawatra, a businessman, became prime minister. In 2006, his party won a majority, the result of a boycott of opposition parties. Following mass protests, a military *junta* took power. Civilian rule was restored in 2007 and Thaksin was tried in his absence. Huge anti-government protests in 2010 showed that the people of Thailand remained deeply divided.

Agriculture employs 41% of the people and rice is the chief crop. Cassava, cotton, maize, rubber, sugarcane, and tobacco are also grown. Tin is mined, but the chief exports are manufactures and food products. Tourism is also important.

AREA 198,114 sq mi [513,115 sq km]
POPULATION 67,090,000 **CAPITAL** Bangkok
GOVERNMENT Constitutional monarchy
ETHNIC GROUPS Thai 75%, Chinese 14%, others 11%
LANGUAGES Thai (official), English, ethnic and regional dialects
RELIGIONS Buddhism 95%, Islam, Christianity
CURRENCY Baht = 100 satang

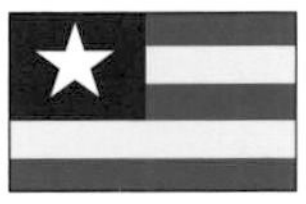
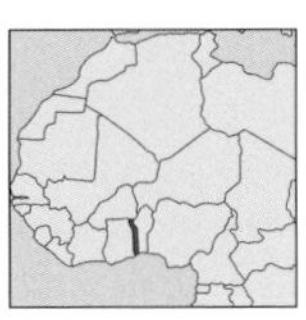

TOGO

GEOGRAPHY The Republic of Togo is a long, narrow country in West Africa. From north to south, it extends about 311 mi [500 km]. Its coastline on the Gulf of Guinea is only 40 mi [64 km] long and it is only 90 mi [145 km] at its widest point.

Togo has high temperatures all through the year. The main wet season is from March to July, with a minor wet season in October and November.

POLITICS & ECONOMY Togo became a German protectorate in 1884 but, in 1919, Britain took over the western third of the territory, while France took over the eastern two-thirds. In 1956, the people of British Togoland voted to join Ghana, while French Togoland became an independent republic in 1960.

A military regime took power in 1963. In 1967, General Gnassingbé Eyadéma became head of state and suspended the constitution. Under a new constitution adopted in 1992, multiparty elections were held in 1994. However, in 1998, the count in the presidential elections was stopped when it became clear that Eyadéma had been defeated. The opposition boycotted subsequent elections. Eyadéma died in 2005. His son, Faure Gnassingbé, took over as president, but international pressure forced him to step down. However, he was elected president in 2005 and 2010.

Togo is a poor, developing country dependent on agriculture. Major food crops include cassava, maize, millet, and yams. Phosphate rock is the leading export.

AREA 21,925 sq mi [56,785 sq km]
POPULATION 6,587,000 **CAPITAL** Lomé
GOVERNMENT Multiparty republic **ETHNIC GROUPS** Native African 99% (largest tribes are Ewe, Mina and Kabre) **LANGUAGES** French (official), African languages **RELIGIONS** Traditional beliefs 51%, Christianity 29%, Islam 20% **CURRENCY** CFA franc = 100 centimes

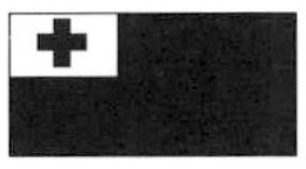
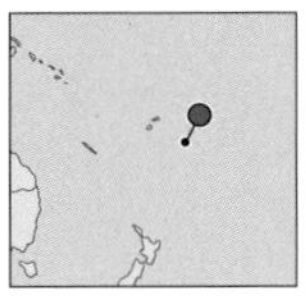

TONGA

The Kingdom of Tonga, a former British protectorate, became independent in 1970. Situated in the South Pacific Ocean, it contains more than 170 islands, 36 of which are inhabited. In 2009, a committee proposed that the Tongan monarchy should have a ceremonial role. Agriculture is the main activity.

AREA 251 sq mi [650 sq km] **POPULATION** 123,000 **CAPITAL** Nuku'alofa

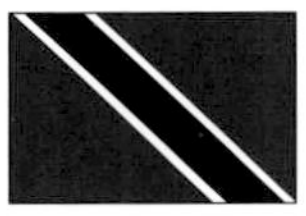
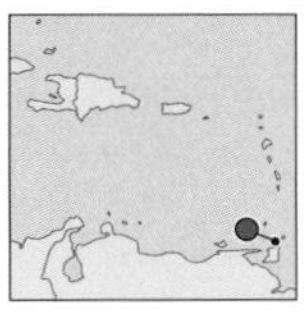

TRINIDAD AND TOBAGO

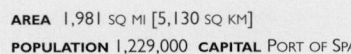

The Republic of Trinidad and Tobago became independent from Britain in 1962. These tropical islands, populated by people of African, Asian (mainly Indian) and European origin, are hilly and forested, though there are some fertile plains. Oil production is the mainstay of the economy.

AREA 1,981 sq mi [5,130 sq km]
POPULATION 1,229,000 **CAPITAL** Port of Spain

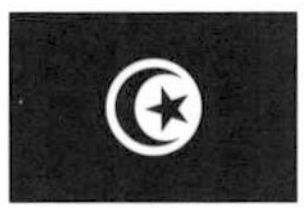
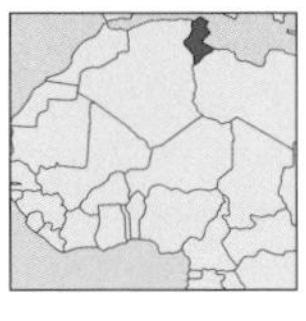

TUNISIA

GEOGRAPHY The Republic of Tunisia is the smallest country in North Africa. The mountains in the north are an eastward and comparatively low extension of the Atlas Mountains. To the north and east of the mountains lie fertile plains, especially between Sfax, Tunis, and Bizerte. In the south, low-lying regions contain a vast salt pan, called the Chott Djerid, and part of the Sahara Desert.

Northern Tunisia has a Mediterranean climate, with dry, sunny summers, and mild winters with a moderate rainfall. The average yearly rainfall decreases toward the south.

POLITICS & ECONOMY In 1881, France established a protectorate over Tunisia and ruled the country until 1956. The new parliament abolished the monarchy and declared Tunisia to be a republic in 1957, with the nationalist leader, Habib Bourguiba, as president. His government introduced many reforms, including votes for women, but various problems arose, including unemployment among the middle class and fears that Western values introduced by tourists might undermine Muslim values. In 1987, the prime minister, Zine el Abidine Ben Ali, removed Bourguiba, and became president. He was re-elected to a fifth term in 2009. In 2011, widespread anti-government demonstrations led the president to flee the county. An interim government promised new elections.

The World Bank classifies Tunisia as a "middle-income" developing country. The main resources and chief exports are phosphates and oil. Most industries are concerned with food processing. Barley, dates, grapes, olives, and wheat are major crops. Fishing is important, as also is tourism.

AREA 63,170 sq mi [163,610 sq km] **POPULATION** 10,589,000
CAPITAL Tunis **GOVERNMENT** Multiparty republic
ETHNIC GROUPS Arab 98%, European 1% **LANGUAGES** Arabic (official), French **RELIGIONS** Islam 98%, Christianity 1%, others
CURRENCY Tunisian dinar = 1,000 millimes

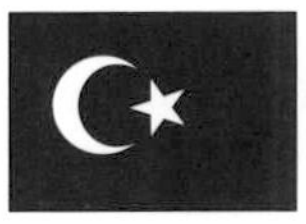
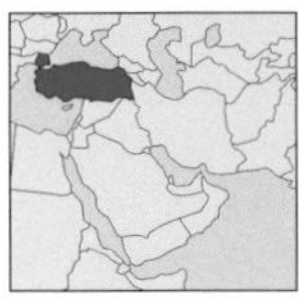

TURKEY

GEOGRAPHY The Republic of Turkey lies in two continents. European Turkey, also called Thrace, lies west of a waterway linking the Mediterranean and Black seas. Most of Asian Turkey consists of plateaux and mountains, which rise to 16,945 ft [5,165 m] at Mount Ararat (Agri Dagi) near the border with Armenia. Earthquakes are common. Central Turkey has a dry climate, with hot, sunny summers and cold winters. The west has a Mediterranean climate, but the Black Sea coast has cooler summers.

POLITICS & ECONOMY In AD 330, the Roman empire moved its capital to Byzantium, which it renamed Constantinople. Constantinople became capital of the East Roman (or Byzantine) empire in 395. Muslim Seljuk Turks from central Asia invaded Anatolia in the 11th century. In the 14th century, another group of Turks, the Ottomans, conquered the area. In 1453, the Ottoman Turks took Constantinople, which they called Istanbul. The Ottomans built up a vast empire which finally collapsed during World War I (1914–18). Turkey became a republic in 1923. Its leader, Mustafa Kemal, or Atatürk ("father of the Turks") began to modernize and secularize the country.

Since the 1940s, Turkey has sought to strengthen its ties with Western powers. It joined NATO (North Atlantic Treaty Organization) in 1951 and it applied to join the European Economic Community in 1987. But Turkey's conflict with Greece, together with its invasion of northern Cyprus in 1974, have led many Europeans to treat Turkey's aspirations with caution. Political instability, military coups, conflict with Kurdish nationalists in eastern Turkey, and concern about the country's record on human rights are other problems.

Turkey has enjoyed democracy since 1983, though, in 1998, the government banned the Islamist Welfare Party, which it accused of violating secular principles. In 1999, the Muslim Virtue Party (successor to Islamist Welfare Party) lost ground. The largest numbers of parliamentary seats were won by the ruling Democratic Left Party and the far-right National Action Party. However, in the elections in 2002, the moderate Islamic Justice and Development Party (AKP) won 362 of the 500 seats in parliament. Despite its Islamist roots, the AKP was re-elected in 2007. In 2007–8, the activities of the separatist Kurdish Workers Party (PKK) guerrillas provoked Turkey to bomb its bases in northern Iraq. In 2009–10, the government accused some military leaders of planning a coup.

Turkey came close to economic collapse in 2002, but its recovery enabled it to withstand the global financial crisis in 2008, and its economy bounced back in 2010–11. Agriculture employs 25% of the people. Barley, cotton, fruits, maize, tobacco, and wheat are major crops. But manufactures, including textiles, cars, machinery, and paper products, are among the leading exports.

AREA 299,156 sq mi [774,815 sq km]
POPULATION 77,804,000 **CAPITAL** Ankara
GOVERNMENT Multiparty republic **ETHNIC GROUPS** Turkish 80%, Kurdish 20% **LANGUAGES** Turkish (official), Kurdish, Arabic
RELIGIONS Islam (mainly Sunni Muslim) 99%
CURRENCY New Turkish lira = 100 kurus

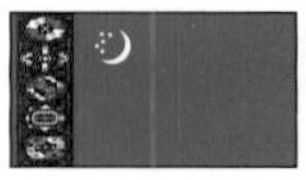
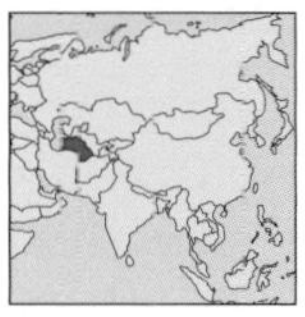

TURKMENISTAN

GEOGRAPHY The Republic of Turkmenistan is one of the five central Asian republics which once formed part of the former Soviet Union. Most of the land is low-lying, with mountains lying on the southern and southwestern borders. In the west lies the salty Caspian Sea. Most of Turkmenistan is arid and the Garagum, Asia's largest sand desert, covers about 80% of the country. Turkmenistan has a continental climate, with average annual rainfall varying from 3 inches [80 mm] in the desert to 12 inches [300 mm] in the mountains. Summer months are hot, but winter temperatures drop well below freezing point.

POLITICS & ECONOMY Just over 1,000 years ago, Turkic people settled in the lands east of the Caspian Sea and the name "Turkmen" comes from this time. Mongol armies conquered the area in the 13th century and Islam was introduced in the 14th century. Russia took over the area in the 1870s and 1880s. The area came under Communist rule in 1917 and, in 1924, it became the Turkmen Soviet Socialist Republic. The Communists controlled all aspects of life, but they raised living standards.

In the 1980s, when the Soviet Union began to introduce reforms, the Turkmen began to demand more freedom. In 1990, the Turkmen government stated that its laws overruled Soviet laws. In 1991, Turkmenistan became fully independent after the breakup of the Soviet Union. But the country kept ties with Russia through the Commonwealth of Independent States (CIS).

In 1992, Turkmenistan adopted a new constitution, allowing for the setting up of political parties, providing that they were not ethnic or religious in character. But, effectively, Turkmenistan remained a one-party state and, in 1992, Saparmurad Niyazov, the former Communist and now Democratic Party leader, was the only presidential candidate. In 1999, parliament declared Niyazov president for life. Niyazov died in 2006 and was succeeded by Gurbanguly Berdymukhammedov. He was formally elected (no opposition candidates were allowed to stand) and was sworn in as president in 2007.

Faced with many economic problems, Turkmenistan began to look south rather than to the CIS for support. As part of this policy, it joined the Economic Cooperation Organization, which had been set up in 1985 by Iran, Pakistan, and Turkey. In 1996, the completion of a rail link from Turkmenistan to the Iranian coast was an important step in the development of Central Asia. Oil and natural gas are the chief resources, and gas pipelines to China and Iran were opened in 2009 and 2010. But agriculture is the main activity. Cotton is the main commercial crop. Manufactures include cement, glass, petrochemicals, and textiles.

AREA 188,455 sq mi [488,100 sq km] **POPULATION** 4,941,000
CAPITAL Ashkhabad **GOVERNMENT** Single-party republic
ETHNIC GROUPS Turkmen 85%, Uzbek 5%, Russian 4%
LANGUAGES Turkmen (official), Russian, Uzbek **RELIGIONS** Islam 89%, Eastern Orthodox 9% **CURRENCY** Turkmen manat = 100 tenesi

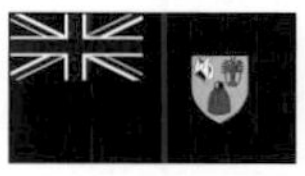
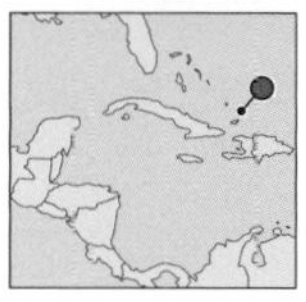

TURKS AND CAICOS ISLANDS

The Turks and Caicos Islands, a British territory in the Caribbean since 1776, are a group of about 30 islands. Fishing and tourism are major activities.

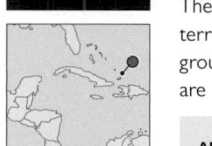

AREA 166 sq mi [430 sq km]
POPULATION 24,000 **CAPITAL** Cockburn Town

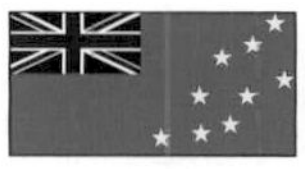
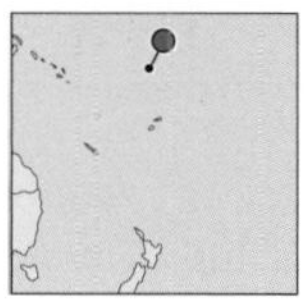

TUVALU

Tuvalu, formerly called the Ellice Islands, was a British territory from the 1890s until it became independent in 1978. It consists of nine low-lying coral atolls in the southern Pacific Ocean. Copra is the chief export.

AREA 10 sq mi [26 sq km]
POPULATION 10,000 **CAPITAL** Fongafale

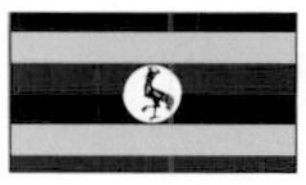
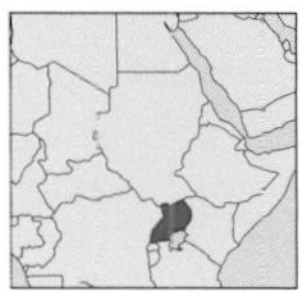

UGANDA

GEOGRAPHY The Republic of Uganda is a landlocked country on the East African plateau. It contains part of Lake Victoria, Africa's largest lake and a source of the River Nile, which occupies a shallow depression in the plateau.

The equator runs through Uganda and the country is warm throughout the year, though the high altitude moderates the temperature. The wettest regions are the lands to the north of Lake Victoria, where Kampala is situated, and the western mountains, especially the high Ruwenzori range.

POLITICS & ECONOMY Little is known of the early history of Uganda. When Europeans first reached the area in the 19th century, many of the people were organized in kingdoms, the most powerful of which was Buganda, the home of the Baganda people. Britain took over the country between 1894 and 1914, and ruled it until independence in 1962.

In 1967, Uganda became a republic and Buganda's Kabaka (king), Sir Edward Mutesa II, was made president. But tensions between the Kabaka and the prime minister, Apollo Milton Obote, led to the dismissal of the Kabaka in 1966. Obote also abolished the traditional kingdoms, including Buganda. Obote was overthrown in 1971 by an army group led by General Idi Amin Dada. Amin ruled as a dictator. He forced most of the Asians who lived in Uganda to leave the country and had many of his opponents killed.

In 1978, a border dispute between Uganda and Tanzania led Tanzanian troops to enter Uganda. With help from Ugandan opponents of Amin, they overthrew Amin's government. In 1980, Obote led his party to victory in national elections. But after charges of fraud, Obote's opponents began guerrilla warfare. A military group overthrew Obote in 1985, though strife continued until 1986, when Yoweri Museveni's National Resistance Movement seized power. In 1993, Museveni restored the traditional kingdoms. Elections were held in 1994, but political parties were forbidden. Museveni was elected in 1996, 2001, 2006, and 2011. In recent years, Uganda has faced the rebel Lord's Resistance Army (LRA) in the north. The LRA extended its activities into the Central African Republic, the Democratic Republic of Congo, and Sudan. In 2010, two bombings in Kampala, killing 74 people, were carried out by a Somali Islamist group, al-Shabab, which said it was a response to Uganda's role in supplying troops to the African Union mission in Somalia.

Agriculture dominates the economy, employing 66% of the people. The chief export is coffee.

AREA 93,065 sq mi [241,038 sq km]
POPULATION 33,399,000 **CAPITAL** Kampala
GOVERNMENT Republic
ETHNIC GROUPS Baganda 17%, Ankole 8%, Basogo 8%, Iteso 8%, Bakiga 7%, Langi 6%, Rwanda 6%, Bagisu 5%, Acholi 4%, Lugbara 4%, and others
LANGUAGES English and Swahili (both official), Ganda
RELIGIONS Roman Catholic 33%, Protestant 33%, traditional beliefs 18%, Islam 16%
CURRENCY Ugandan shilling = 100 cents

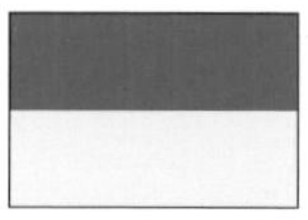
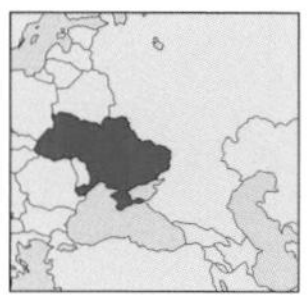

UKRAINE

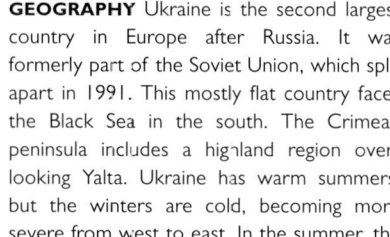

GEOGRAPHY Ukraine is the second largest country in Europe after Russia. It was formerly part of the Soviet Union, which split apart in 1991. This mostly flat country faces the Black Sea in the south. The Crimean peninsula includes a highland region overlooking Yalta. Ukraine has warm summers, but the winters are cold, becoming more severe from west to east. In the summer, the east is often warmer than the west. Most rain comes in summer.

POLITICS & ECONOMY Kiev was the original capital of the early Slavic civilization known as Kievan Rus. In the 17th and 18th centuries, parts of Ukraine came under Polish and Russian rule. But Russia gained most of Ukraine in the late 18th century. In 1918, Ukraine became independent, but in 1922 it became part of the Soviet Union.

In the 1980s, Ukrainian people demanded more say over their affairs. The country became independent in 1991. Leonid Kuchma, who became president in 1994, came under fire in the early 2000s for maladministration and for his alleged involvement in the murder of a journalist. In 2005, the pro-Western leader Viktor Yushchenko was elected president. Economic problems and political infighting led to a Russian-leaning party, led by Viktor Yanukovych, winning most seats in parliament in 2006. Yanukovych became prime minister, but an election in 2007 resulted in a pro-Western coalition government led by a former prime minister, Yulia Tymoshenko. In 2010, the pro-Russian Viktor Yanukovych was declared winner of the presidential election. Tymoshenko stood down and Yanukovych's ally Mykola Azarov was appointed prime minister.

The World Bank classifies Ukraine as a "lower-middle-income" economy. Agriculture is important. Wheat and sugar are exported. Barley, maize, potatoes, sunflowers, and tobacco are also grown. Livestock rearing and fishing are also important.

Manufacturing is the chief economic activity. Major manufactures include iron and steel, machinery, and vehicles. Ukraine has large coalfields. The country imports oil and natural gas, but it has hydroelectric and nuclear power stations.

AREA 233,089 sq mi [603,700 sq km]
POPULATION 45,416,000 **CAPITAL** Kiev
GOVERNMENT Multiparty republic
ETHNIC GROUPS Ukrainian 78%, Russian 17%, Belarusian, Moldovan, Bulgarian, Hungarian, Polish
LANGUAGES Ukrainian (official), Russian
RELIGIONS Mostly Ukrainian Orthodox
CURRENCY Hryvnia = 100 kopiykas

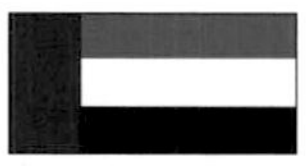
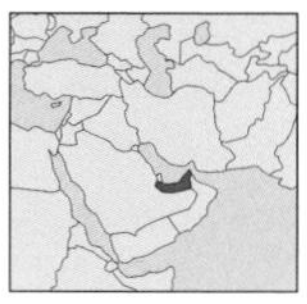

UNITED ARAB EMIRATES

The United Arab Emirates were formed in 1971 when the seven Trucial States of the Persian Gulf (Abu Dhabi, Dubai, Sharjah, Ajman, Umm al Qawayn, Ra's al Khaymah, and Al Fujayrah) opted to join together and form an independent country. The economy of this hot and dry country depends on oil production, and oil revenues give the United Arab Emirates one of the highest per capita GDPs in Asia.

AREA 32,278 sq mi [83,600 sq km]
POPULATION 4,976,000 **CAPITAL** Abu Dhabi

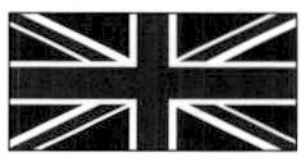
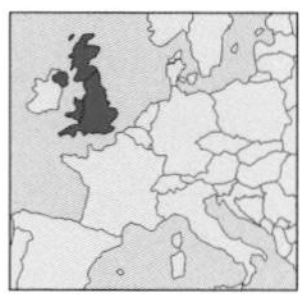

UNITED KINGDOM

GEOGRAPHY The United Kingdom (or UK) is a union of four countries. Three of them – England, Scotland, and Wales – make up Great Britain. The fourth country is Northern Ireland. The Isle of Man and the Channel Islands, including Jersey and Guernsey, are not part of the UK. They are self-governing British dependencies.

The land is highly varied. Much of Scotland and Wales is mountainous, and the highest peak is Scotland's Ben Nevis at 4,404 ft [1,342 m]. England has some highland areas, including the Cumbrian Mountains (or Lake District) and the Pennine range in the north. But England also has large areas of fertile lowland. Northern Ireland is also a mixture of lowlands and uplands. It contains the UK's largest lake, Lough Neagh.

The UK has a mild climate, influenced by the warm Gulf Stream which flows across the Atlantic from the Gulf of Mexico, then past the British Isles. Moist winds from the southwest bring rain, but the rainfall decreases from west to east. Winds from the east and north bring cold weather in winter.

POLITICS & ECONOMY In ancient times, Britain was invaded by many peoples, including Iberians, Celts, Romans, Angles, Saxons, Jutes, Norsemen, Danes, and Normans, who arrived in 1066. The evolution of the United Kingdom spanned hundreds of years. The Normans finally overcame Welsh resistance in 1282, when King Edward I annexed Wales and united it with England. Union with Scotland was achieved by the Act of Union of 1707. This created a country known as the United Kingdom of Great Britain.

Ireland came under Norman rule in the 11th century, and much of its later history was concerned with a struggle against English domination. In 1801, Ireland became part of the United Kingdom of Great Britain and Ireland. But in 1921, southern Ireland broke away to become the Irish Free State. Most of the people in the Irish Free State were Roman Catholics. In Northern Ireland, where the majority of the people were Protestants, most people wanted to remain citizens of the United Kingdom. As a result, the country's official name changed to the United Kingdom of Great Britain and Northern Ireland.

The modern history of the UK began in the 18th century when the British empire began to develop, despite the loss in 1783 of its 13 North American colonies which became the core of the modern United States. The other major event occurred in the late 18th century, when the UK became the first country to industrialize its economy.

The British empire broke up after World War II (1939–45), though the UK still administers many small, mainly island, territories around the world. The empire was transformed into the Commonwealth of Nations, a free association of independent countries which numbered 54 in 2011.

The UK has retained an important world role. For example, in 2001, it played a prominent role in creating a broad alliance to counter international terrorism following the attacks on the United

States. It was also a prominent member of the coalition force which invaded Iraq in 2003. However, the UK has recognized that its economic future lies within Europe. It became a member of the European Economic Community (now the European Union) in 1973. Membership of the EU has been important to the British economy, but some people fear a loss of British identity should the EU ever evolve into a political union. Another matter of public concern is large-scale immigration, both from the EU and outside.

The UK is a major industrial and trading nation. It lacks natural resources apart from coal, iron ore, oil, and natural gas, and has to import most of the materials it needs for its industries. The UK also has to import food, because it produces only about two-thirds of the food it needs. In the first half of the 20th century, Britain was a major exporter of cars, ships, steel, and textiles. But many industries have suffered from competition from other countries, with lower labor costs. In 2008–9, Britain's economy was hit by the global financial crisis, which led the country into recession.

The UK is one of the world's most urbanized countries, and agriculture employs only 1% of the people. Production is high because of the use of scientific methods and modern machinery. However, in the early 21st century, especially following the outbreak of foot-and-mouth disease in 2001, questions were raised about the future of rural industries. Major crops include barley, potatoes, sugar beet, and wheat. Sheep are the leading livestock, but beef and dairy cattle, pigs, and poultry are also important. Fishing is another major activity and the UK is one of the largest fishing countries in the EU. Important catches include cod, haddock, plaice, and mackerel.

Service industries play a major part in the UK's economy. Financial and insurance services bring in much-needed foreign exchange, while tourism has become a major earner.

AREA 93,381 SQ MI [241,857 SQ KM]
POPULATION 62,348,000 **CAPITAL** LONDON
GOVERNMENT CONSTITUTIONAL MONARCHY
ETHNIC GROUPS ENGLISH 82%, SCOTTISH 10%, IRISH 2%, WELSH 2%, ULSTER 2%, WEST INDIAN, INDIAN, PAKISTANI, AND OTHERS **LANGUAGES** ENGLISH (OFFICIAL), WELSH, GAELIC
RELIGIONS CHRISTIANITY (ANGLICAN, ROMAN CATHOLIC, PRESBYTERIAN, METHODIST), ISLAM, SIKHISM, HINDUISM, JUDAISM
CURRENCY POUND STERLING = 100 PENCE

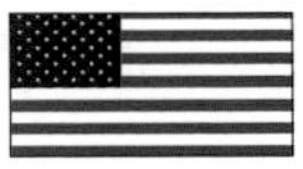

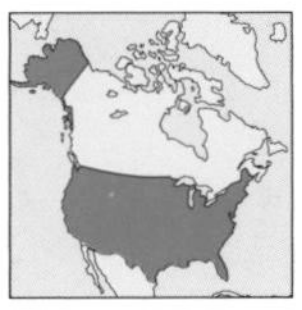

UNITED STATES OF AMERICA

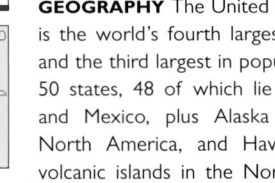

GEOGRAPHY The United States of America is the world's fourth largest country in area and the third largest in population. It contains 50 states, 48 of which lie between Canada and Mexico, plus Alaska in northwestern North America, and Hawai'i, a group of volcanic islands in the North Pacific Ocean. Densely populated coastal plains lie to the east and south of the Appalachian Mountains. The central lowlands, drained by the Mississippi–Missouri rivers, stretch from the Appalachians to the Rocky Mountains in the west. The Pacific region contains fertile valleys, separated by mountain ranges.

The climate varies greatly, ranging from the Arctic cold of Alaska to the intense heat of Death Valley, a bleak desert in California. Of the 48 states between Canada and Mexico, winters are cold and snowy in the north, but mild in the south, a region which is often called the "Sun Belt."

POLITICS & ECONOMY The first people in North America, the ancestors of the Native Americans (or American Indians) arrived perhaps 40,000 years ago from Asia. Although Vikings probably reached North America 1,000 years ago, European exploration proper did not begin until the late 15th century.

The first Europeans to settle in large numbers were the British, who founded settlements on the eastern coast in the early 17th century. British rule ended in the War of Independence (1775–83). The country expanded in 1803 when a vast territory in the south and west was acquired through the Louisiana Purchase, while the border with Mexico was fixed in the mid-19th century. The Civil War (1861–5) ended slavery and the serious threat that the nation might split into two parts. In the late 19th century, the West was opened up, while immigrants flooded in from Europe and elsewhere.

During the late 19th and early 20th centuries, industrialization led to the United States becoming the world's leading economic superpower and a pioneer in science and technology. It took on the mantle of the champion of Western democracy and, following the breakup of the former Soviet Union, it became the world's only superpower. But the attacks on the country on September 11, 2001, revealed its vulnerability to terrorists and rogue states. The response was vigorous. In 2001, it attacked the Taliban government in Afghanistan, which was protecting al Qaida terrorists. Then, in 2003, it led a coalition force to invade Iraq and overthrow Saddam Hussein. President George W. Bush was re-elected in 2004, but the conflicts in Afghanistan and Iraq continued. In 2008, the Democratic Party candidate, Barack Obama, defeated the Republican John McCain in the presidential elections. Obama, the first black president in US history, faced many challenges, including those arising from the global financial crisis and the conflicts in southwestern Asia.

The United States has the world's largest economy in terms of the total value of its production. Although agriculture employs only about 1.4% of the people, farming is highly mechanized and scientific, and the United States leads the world in farm production. Major products include beef and dairy cattle, together with such crops as cotton, fruits, groundnuts, maize, potatoes, soybeans, tobacco, and wheat.

Natural resources include oil, natural gas, coal, a wide range of metal ores, and timber, especially from the Pacific northwest. Manufacturing is the single most valuable activity, employing 10.7% of the people. Major products include vehicles, food products, chemicals, machinery, printed goods, metal products, and scientific instruments. California, with its high-tech electronics industries, is the top manufacturing state.

AREA 3,717,792 SQ MI [9,629,091 SQ KM]
POPULATION 310,233,000 **CAPITAL** WASHINGTON, DC
GOVERNMENT FEDERAL REPUBLIC
ETHNIC GROUPS WHITE 77%, AFRICAN AMERICAN 13%, ASIAN 4%, AMERINDIAN 2%, OTHERS **LANGUAGES** ENGLISH, SPANISH, MORE THAN 30 OTHERS **RELIGIONS** PROTESTANT 56%, ROMAN CATHOLIC 28%, ISLAM 2%, JUDAISM 2%
CURRENCY US DOLLAR = 100 CENTS

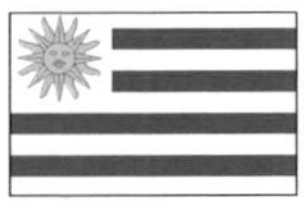

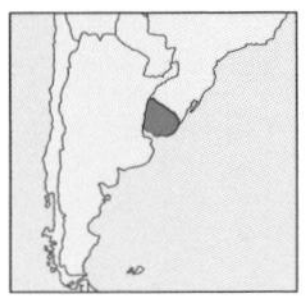

URUGUAY

GEOGRAPHY Uruguay is South America's second smallest independent country after Suriname. The land consists mainly of flat plains and hills. The River Uruguay, which forms the country's western border, flows into the Río de la Plata, a large estuary which leads into the South Atlantic Ocean.

Uruguay has a mild climate, with rain in every month, though droughts sometimes occur. Summers are pleasantly warm and winters relatively mild.

POLITICS & ECONOMY In 1726, Spanish settlers founded Montevideo in order to halt the Portuguese gaining influence in the area. By the late 18th century, Spaniards had settled in most of the country. Uruguay became part of a colony called the Viceroyalty of La Plata, which also included Argentina, Paraguay, and parts of Bolivia, Brazil, and Chile. In 1820 Brazil annexed Uruguay, ending Spanish rule. In 1825, Uruguayans, supported by Argentina, began a struggle for independence. Finally, in 1828, Brazil and Argentina recognized Uruguay as an independent republic. Social and economic developments were slow, but, from 1903, Uruguay became stable and democratic.

From the 1950s, economic problems caused unrest. Terrorist groups, notably the Tupumaros, carried out murders and kidnappings. The army crushed the Tupumaros in 1972, but the army took over the government in 1973. Military rule continued until 1984 when elections were held. In the early 21st century, Uruguay faced many economic problems, many of which were the result of the economic crisis in its neighbor, Argentina, and its imposition of banking controls. In 2009, the former left-wing rebel-turned-moderate Jose Mujica, of the governing Broad Front, was elected president.

The World Bank classifies Uruguay as an "upper-middle-income" developing country. Agriculture employs 10% of the people, but farm products, notably hides and leather goods, beef, and wool, are the main exports, while many manufacturing industries process farm products. Crops include maize, potatoes, wheat, and sugar beet. Uruguay depends largely on hydroelectric power for energy. In 2008, Uruguay announced the discovery of a natural gas field off the country's coast.

AREA 67,574 SQ MI [175,016 SQ KM]
POPULATION 3,510,000 **CAPITAL** MONTEVIDEO
GOVERNMENT MULTIPARTY REPUBLIC
ETHNIC GROUPS WHITE 88%, MESTIZO 8%, MULATTO OR BLACK 4%
LANGUAGES SPANISH (OFFICIAL)
RELIGIONS ROMAN CATHOLIC 66%, PROTESTANT 2%, JUDAISM 1%
CURRENCY URUGUAYAN PESO = 100 CENTÉSIMOS

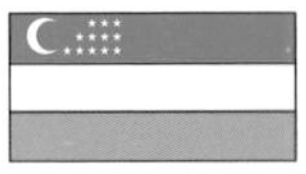

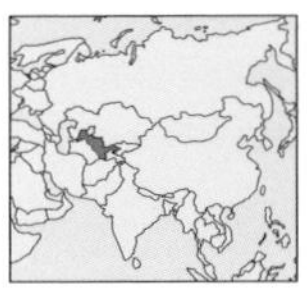

UZBEKISTAN

GEOGRAPHY The Republic of Uzbekistan is one of the five republics in Central Asia which were once part of the Soviet Union. Plains cover most of western Uzbekistan, with highlands in the east. The main rivers, the Amu (or Amu Darya) and Syr (or Syr Darya), drain into the Aral Sea. So much water has been taken from these rivers to irrigate the land that the Aral Sea has now shrunk to about a quarter of its size in 1960. The former lake area is now desert. Uzbekistan has cold winters and hot summers. The largely uninhabited Kyzyl Kum desert lies in central Uzbekistan.

POLITICS & ECONOMY Russia took the area in the 19th century. After the Russian Revolution of 1917, the Communists took over and, in 1924, they set up the Uzbek Soviet Socialist Republic. Under Communism, all aspects of Uzbek life were controlled and religious worship was discouraged. But education, health, housing, and transport were improved. In the late 1980s, the people demanded more freedom, and in 1990 the government stated that its laws overruled those of the Soviet Union. Uzbekistan became independent in 1991 when the Soviet Union broke up, but it retained links with Russia through the Commonwealth of Independent States. Islam Karimov, leader of the People's Democratic Party (formerly the Communist Party), was elected president in December 1991. In 1992–3, many opposition leaders were arrested because the government said that they threatened national stability. In 1994–5, the PDP was victorious in national elections. Karimov was re-elected in 2001 and 2007. Initially, his government allowed the US to use bases in Uzbekistan for its military campaign in Afghanistan. It asked US troops to leave in 2005, but, in 2009, it allowed the US to transport supplies through Uzbekistan to its troops in Afghanistan. In 2010, the United Nations called on Uzbekistan to improve its human rights record.

The World Bank classifies Uzbekistan as a "lower-middle-income" developing country and the government still controls most economic activity. The country produces coal, copper, gold, oil, and natural gas.

AREA 172,741 SQ MI [447,400 SQ KM]
POPULATION 27,866,000 **CAPITAL** TASHKENT
GOVERNMENT SOCIALIST REPUBLIC **ETHNIC GROUPS** UZBEK 80%, RUSSIAN 5%, TAJIK 5%, KAZAKH 3%, TATAR 2%, KARA-KALPAK 2%
LANGUAGES UZBEK (OFFICIAL), RUSSIAN **RELIGIONS** ISLAM 88%, EASTERN ORTHODOX 9% **CURRENCY** UZBEKISTANI SUM = 100 TYIYN

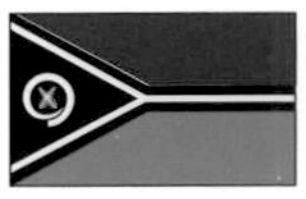

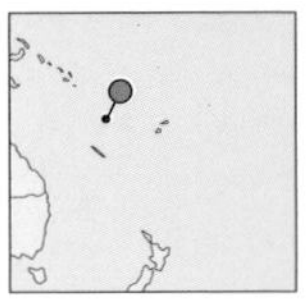

VANUATU

The Republic of Vanuatu, formerly the Anglo-French Condominium of the New Hebrides, became independent in 1980. It consists of a chain of 80 islands in the South Pacific Ocean. Its economy is based on agriculture and it exports copra, beef and veal, timber, and cocoa.

AREA 4,706 SQ MI [12,189 SQ KM]
POPULATION 222,000 **CAPITAL** PORT-VILA

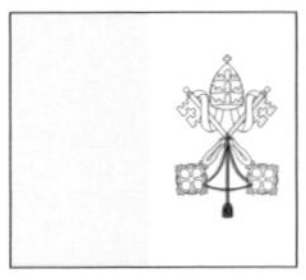

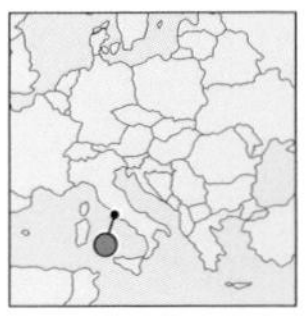

VATICAN CITY

Vatican City State, the world's smallest independent nation, is an enclave on the west bank of the River Tiber in Rome. It forms an independent base for the Holy See, the governing body of the Roman Catholic Church.

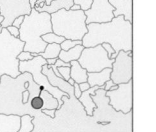

AREA 0.17 SQ MI [0.44 SQ KM]
POPULATION 832

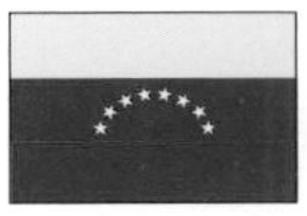

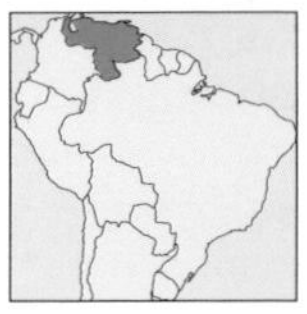

VENEZUELA

GEOGRAPHY The Bolivarian Republic of Venezuela, in northern South America, contains the Maracaibo lowlands around the oil-rich Lake Maracaibo in the west. Andean ranges enclose the lowlands and extend across most of northern Venezuela. The Orinoco river basin, containing tropical grasslands called *llanos*, lies between the northern highlands and the Guiana Highlands in the southeast. The Orinoco is Venezuela's longest river.

Venezuela has a tropical climate. Temperatures are high

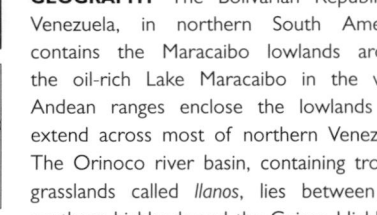

throughout the year on the lowlands, though the mountains are cooler. Rainfall is heaviest in the mountains. But much of the country has a dry season between December and April.

POLITICS & ECONOMY In the early 19th century, Venezuelans, such as Simón Bolívar and Francisco de Miranda, began a struggle against Spanish rule. Venezuela declared its independence in 1811. But it only became truly independent in 1821, when the Spanish were defeated in a battle near Valencia.

The development of Venezuela in the 19th and the first half of the 20th centuries was marred by instability, violence, and periods of harsh dictatorial rule. But Venezuela has had elected governments since 1958. The country has greatly benefited from its oil resources which were first exploited in 1917. In 1960, Venezuela helped to form OPEC (the Organization of Petroleum Exporting Countries) and, in 1976, the government of Venezuela took control of the entire oil industry. In 1999, Hugo Chavez, who had staged an unsuccessful coup in 1992, was elected president. In 2004, he won a majority in a referendum that had been intended by the opposition to remove him from office. He was re-elected in 2006, and his left-wing policies continued to arouse US hostility. In 2010, the opposition made gains in parliamentary elections and reduced the majority of Chavez's socialist party.

With oil accounting for about 90% of its exports, Venezuela has an "upper-middle-income" economy. Other exports include bauxite and aluminum, iron ore, and farm products. Beef cattle, dairy cattle, and poultry are raised. Crops include bananas, cassava, citrus fruits, coffee, and rice. The main industry is petroleum refining. Cement, steel, and textiles are also produced.

AREA 352,143 SQ MI [912,050 SQ KM] **POPULATION** 27,223,000
CAPITAL CARACAS **GOVERNMENT** FEDERAL REPUBLIC
ETHNIC GROUPS SPANISH, ITALIAN, PORTUGUESE, ARAB, GERMAN, AFRICAN, INDIGENOUS PEOPLE **LANGUAGES** SPANISH (OFFICIAL), INDIGENOUS DIALECTS **RELIGIONS** ROMAN CATHOLIC 96%
CURRENCY BOLÍVAR = 100 CÉNTIMOS

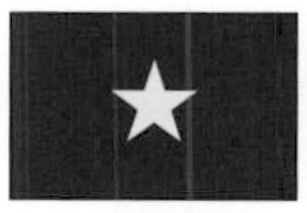
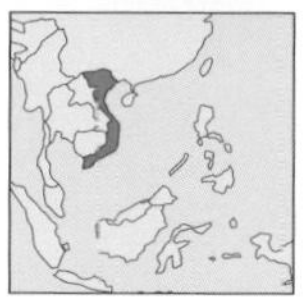

VIETNAM

GEOGRAPHY The Socialist Republic of Vietnam occupies an S-shaped strip of land facing the South China Sea in Southeast Asia. The coastal plains include two densely populated, fertile delta regions: the Red (Hong) delta facing the Gulf of Tonkin in the north, and the Mekong delta in the south.

Vietnam has a tropical climate, though the driest months of January to March are a little cooler than the wet, hot summer months, when monsoon winds blow from the southwest. Typhoons (cyclones or hurricanes) sometimes hit the coast, causing extensive flooding and much damage.

POLITICS & ECONOMY China dominated Vietnam for a thousand years before AD 939, when a Vietnamese state was founded. The French took over the area between the 1850s and 1880s. They ruled Vietnam as part of French Indochina, which also included Cambodia and Laos.

Japan conquered Vietnam during World War II (1939–45). In 1946, war broke out between a nationalist group, called the Vietminh, and the French colonial government. France withdrew in 1954 and Vietnam was divided into a Communist North Vietnam, led by the Vietminh leader, Ho Chi Minh, and a non-Communist South.

A force called the Viet Cong rebeled against South Vietnam's government in 1957 and a war began, which gradually increased in intensity. The United States aided the South, but after it withdrew in 1975, South Vietnam surrendered. In 1976, the united Vietnam became a socialist republic. Vietnamese troops intervened in Cambodia in 1978 to defeat the Khmer Rouge government, but it withdrew its troops in 1989. Following reforms in Vietnam, the US opened an embassy in Hanoi in 1995, and, in 2002, trade relations with the US were normalized. In 2007, Vietnam became a member of the World Trade Organization. By 2011, economic reforms were continuing, but Vietnam resisted calls for increased human rights.

Agriculture remains the main activity and rice the main food crop. Vietnam produces chromium, tin, and phosphates.

AREA 128,065 SQ MI [331,689 SQ KM]
POPULATION 89,571,000 **CAPITAL** HANOI
GOVERNMENT SOCIALIST REPUBLIC
ETHNIC GROUPS VIETNAMESE 87%, CHINESE, HMONG, THAI, KHMER, CHAM, MOUNTAIN GROUPS **LANGUAGES** VIETNAMESE (OFFICIAL), ENGLISH, CHINESE **RELIGIONS** BUDDHISM, CHRISTIANITY, INDIGENOUS BELIEFS
CURRENCY DONG = 10 HAO = 100 XU

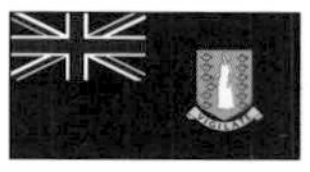
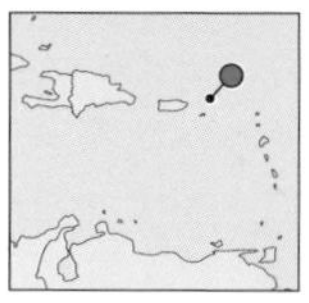

VIRGIN ISLANDS, BRITISH

The British Virgin Islands, the most northerly of the Lesser Antilles, are a British overseas territory, with a substantial measure of self-government.

AREA 58 SQ MI [151 SQ KM]
POPULATION 25,000 **CAPITAL** ROAD TOWN

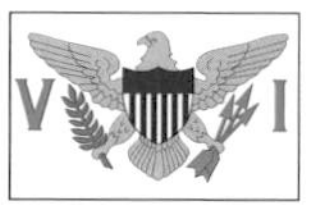
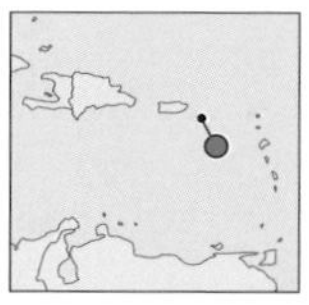

VIRGIN ISLANDS, US

The Virgin Islands of the United States, a group of three islands and 65 small islets, are a self-governing US territory. Purchased from Denmark in 1917, its residents are US citizens and they elect a non-voting delegate to the US House of Representatives.

AREA 134 SQ MI [347 SQ KM]
POPULATION 110,000 **CAPITAL** CHARLOTTE AMALIE

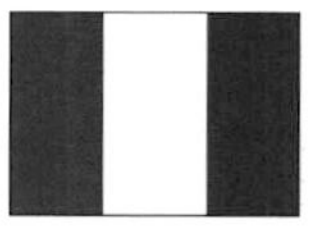
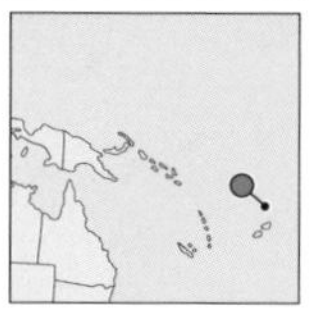

WALLIS AND FUTUNA

Wallis and Futuna, in the South Pacific Ocean, is the smallest and the poorest of France's overseas territories. French aid remains vital to an economy based on subsistence agriculture.

AREA 77 SQ MI [200 SQ KM]
POPULATION 15,000 **CAPITAL** MATA-UTU

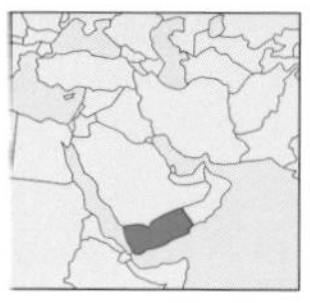

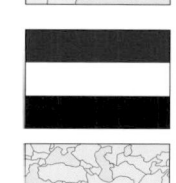

YEMEN

GEOGRAPHY The Republic of Yemen faces the Red Sea and the Gulf of Aden in the southwestern corner of the Arabian peninsula. Behind the narrow coastal plain along the Red Sea, the land rises to a mountain region called High Yemen. The climate ranges from hot and often humid conditions on the coast to the cooler highlands. Most of the country is arid. The south coasts are particularly hot and humid.

POLITICS & ECONOMY After World War I, northern Yemen, which had been ruled by Turkey, began to evolve into a separate state from the south, where Britain was in control. Britain withdrew in 1967 and a left-wing government took power in the south. In North Yemen, the monarchy was abolished in 1962 and the country became a republic.

Clashes occurred between the traditionalist Yemen Arab Republic in the north and the formerly British Marxist People's Democratic Republic of Yemen, but, in 1990, the two Yemens merged to form a single country. Further conflict occurred in 1994, when southern secessionists were defeated. However, in the 2000s, the government faced conflict with Shi'ite northern rebels, called Houthis, al Qaida supporters, and southern separatists. In 2011, protesters in the cities called on President Ali Abdullah Saleh to resign. He pledged not to run at the next election and to introduce constitutional reforms, including the introduction of a parliamentary system, but the increasingly violent protests continued. In June 2011, Saleh was seriously wounded in an attack on the presidential compound.

Yemen is a developing country and agriculture employs about half of the people. Sheep are reared and such crops as barley, fruits, wheat, and vegetables are grown in highland valleys and around oases. Cash crops include coffee and cotton. Since the 1980s, petroleum extraction has been important in the economy. Manufactures include handicrafts, leather goods, and textiles. Remittances from Yemenis abroad are a major source of revenue.

AREA 203,848 SQ MI [527,968 SQ KM] **POPULATION** 23,495,000
CAPITAL SANA' **GOVERNMENT** MULTIPARTY REPUBLIC
ETHNIC GROUPS PREDOMINANTLY ARAB **LANGUAGES** ARABIC (OFFICIAL)
RELIGIONS ISLAM **CURRENCY** YEMENI RIAL = 100 FILS

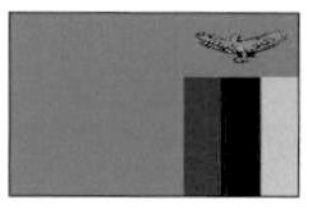
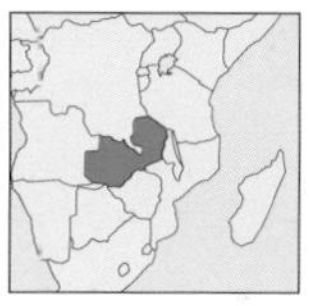

ZAMBIA

GEOGRAPHY The Republic of Zambia is a landlocked country in southern Africa. Zambia lies on the plateau that makes up most of southern Africa. Much of the land is between 2,950 ft and 4,920 ft [900 m to 1,500 m] above sea level. The Muchinga Mountains in the northeast rise above this flat land. Lakes include Bangweulu, which is entirely within Zambia, together with parts of lakes Mweru and Tanganyika in the north. Zambia lies in the tropics, but temperatures are moderated by the altitude.

POLITICS & ECONOMY European contact with Zambia began in the 19th century, when the explorer David Livingstone crossed the River Zambezi. In the 1890s, the British South Africa Company, set up by Cecil Rhodes (1853–1902), the British financier and statesman, made treaties with local chiefs and gradually took over the area. In 1911, the Company named the area Northern Rhodesia. In 1924, Britain took over the government of the country.

In 1953, Britain formed a federation of Northern Rhodesia, Southern Rhodesia (now Zimbabwe), and Nyasaland (now Malawi). Because of African opposition, the federation was dissolved in 1963 and Northern Rhodesia became independent as Zambia in 1964. Kenneth Kaunda became president and one-party rule was introduced in 1972. Under a new constitution, Frederick Chiluba was elected president in 1996. He stood down in 2001 and Levy Mwanawasa became president. But following his death in 2008, he was succeeded by his vice president, Rupiah Banda.

Copper, the main resource, accounts for about 70% of the country's exports. Zambia also produces cobalt, lead, zinc, and gemstones. Agriculture employs about 60% of the people, as compared with less than 4% in industry and mining. Food crops include cassava, fruits and vegetables, maize, millet, and sorghum. Cash crops include coffee, sugarcane, and tobacco.

AREA 290,586 SQ MI [752,618 SQ KM]
POPULATION 13,460,000 **CAPITAL** LUSAKA
GOVERNMENT MULTIPARTY REPUBLIC **ETHNIC GROUPS** NATIVE AFRICAN (BEMBA, TONGA, MARAVI/NYANJA) **LANGUAGES** ENGLISH (OFFICIAL), BEMBA, KAONDA, NYANJA, AND ABOUT 70 OTHERS **RELIGIONS** CHRISTIANITY 70%, ISLAM, HINDUISM **CURRENCY** ZAMBIAN KWACHA = 100 NGWEE

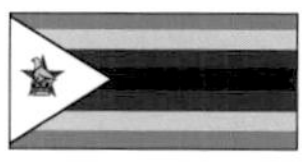
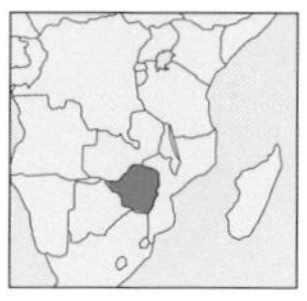

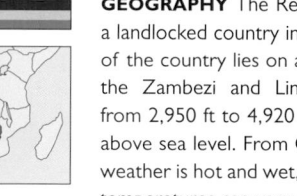

ZIMBABWE

GEOGRAPHY The Republic of Zimbabwe is a landlocked country in southern Africa. Most of the country lies on a high plateau between the Zambezi and Limpopo rivers, ranging from 2,950 ft to 4,920 ft [900 m to 1,500 m] above sea level. From October to March, the weather is hot and wet, but in the winter, daily temperatures can vary greatly.

POLITICS & ECONOMY The Shona people became dominant in the region about 1,000 years ago. The British South Africa Company, under the statesman Cecil Rhodes (1853–1902), occupied the area in the 1890s, after obtaining mineral rights from local chiefs. The area was named Rhodesia and later Southern Rhodesia. It became a self-governing British colony in 1923. Between 1953 and 1963, Southern and Northern Rhodesia (now Zambia) were joined to Nyasaland (Malawi) in the Central African Federation.

In 1965, the European government of Southern Rhodesia (then called Rhodesia) declared their country independent, but Britain refused to accept this. Finally, after a civil war, the country became legally independent in 1980, though rivalries between the Shona and Ndebele people threatened stability. Order was restored when the Shona prime minister, Robert Mugabe, brought his Ndebele rivals into his government. In 1987, Mugabe became the country's executive president, and in 1991 the government renounced its Marxist ideology. Mugabe was re-elected president in 1990 and 1996.

From the late 1990s, Mugabe's government seized white-owned farms and landless "war veterans" began to occupy them. In 2002, Mugabe was re-elected amid accusations of electoral irregularities. In elections in 2008, Mugabe's party was defeated and Mugabe lost to Morgan Tsvangirai in the presidential election. A presidential run-off was ordered, but intimidation of opposition supporters led Tsvangirai to withdraw. In September 2008, a power-sharing agreement was signed and a power-sharing government was set up, with Mugabe as president and Tsvangirai as prime minister. But relations between them proved difficult.

In the 2000s, the economy collapsed. Hyperinflation occurred and many people starved, while the breakdown of public services led to a cholera epidemic. Zimbabwe has valuable mineral reserves and minerals are important exports. Agriculture employs 56% of the people. Maize is the main food crop. Cash crops include cotton, sugar, and tobacco. Cattle ranching is also important.

AREA 150,871 SQ MI [390,757 SQ KM]
POPULATION 11,652,000 **CAPITAL** HARARE
GOVERNMENT MULTIPARTY REPUBLIC **ETHNIC GROUPS** SHONA 82%, NDEBELE 14%, OTHER AFRICAN GROUPS 2%, MIXED AND ASIAN 1%
LANGUAGES ENGLISH (OFFICIAL), SHONA, NDEBELE
RELIGIONS CHRISTIANITY, TRADITIONAL BELIEFS
CURRENCY ZIMBABWEAN NEW DOLLAR = 100 CENTS [SUSPENDED IN 2009]

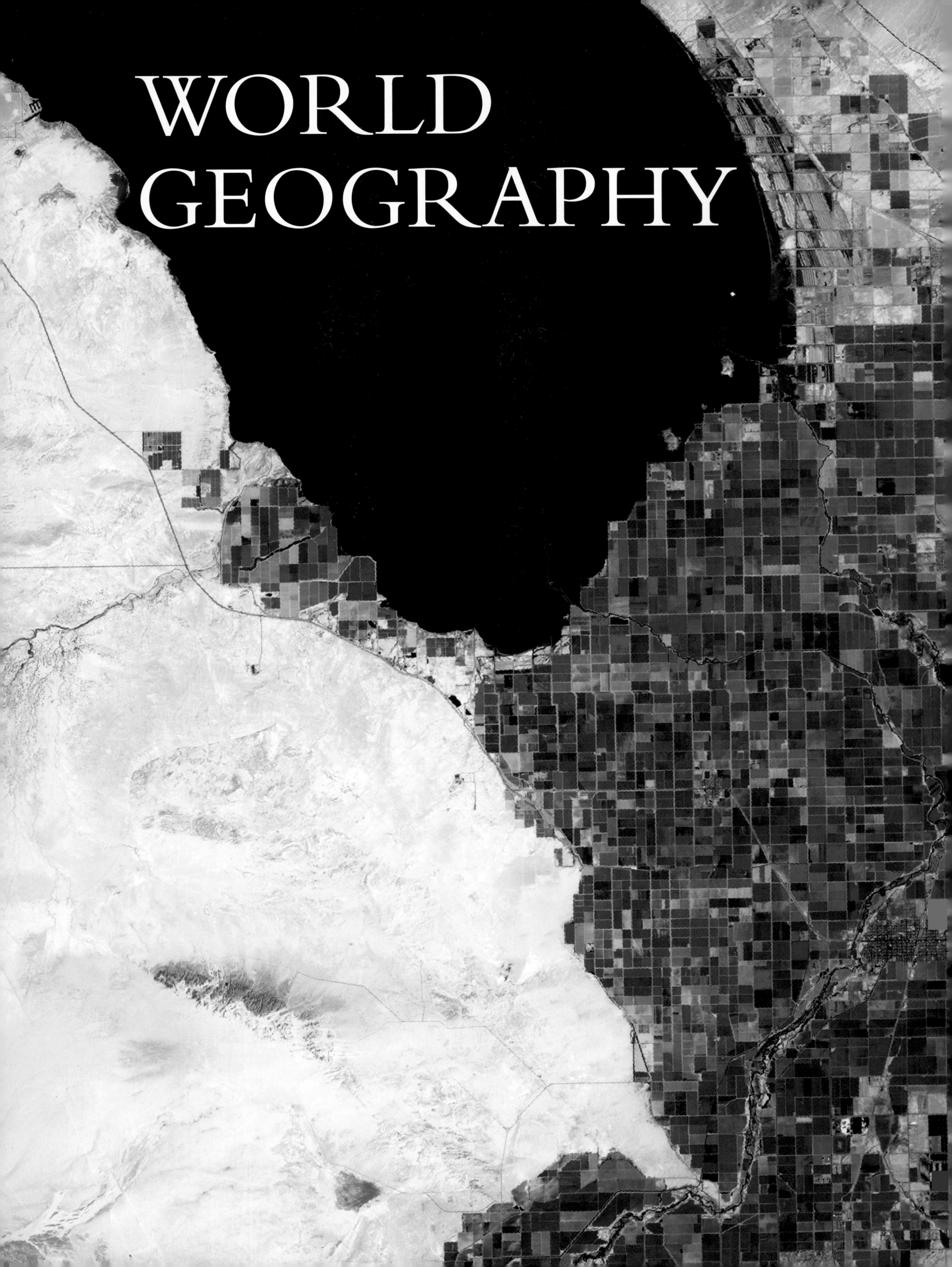

WORLD
GEOGRAPHY

– IMPERIAL VALLEY, USA/MEXICO –
The dark area at top left of this false-color image is the Salton Sea. It is the largest lake in California but was created inadvertently in 1905 during an attempt to divert the flow of the Colorado River for irrigation. The resultant floodwaters filled part of the Imperial Valley. It lies 236 ft (72 m) below sea level and is very saline. To the south is a large area of productive land, which uses irrigated water from the river. The vegetation appears bright red on this image. [Map page 307]

For more information:
70 Orbits of the planets
Planetary data

About 13.7 billion years ago, time and space began with the most colossal explosion in cosmic history: the so-called Big Bang that is believed to have initiated the Universe. According to current theory, in the first millionth of a second of its existence it expanded from a dimensionless point of infinite mass and density into a fireball about the size of our present Solar System – and it has been expanding ever since.

It took about 300,000 years for the primal fireball to cool enough for atoms to form. They were mostly hydrogen which is still the most abundant material in the Universe. The radiation from this era still pervades the Universe, though its subsequent expansion means that we see it at about 3° above absolute zero instead of its original 3,000°C. Observations of this faint background glow reveal slight fluctuations. It is these which appear to have become, over the next billion years or so, the large-scale structures in present Universe. As well as the matter which we can see, there is evidence of a much greater quantity of dark matter whose nature remains unknown. Within knots of this dark matter, the first stars and galaxies formed, probably within the first billion years of the life of the Universe. Our own Galaxy was among them.

There were several generations of stars, each feeding on the wreckage of its extinct predecessors as well as the original galactic gas swirls. With each new generation, pro-gressively larger atoms were forged in stellar furnaces, and the Galaxy's range of elements, once restricted to hydrogen and helium, grew larger. About 9 billion years after the Big Bang, a star formed on the outskirts of our Galaxy with enough matter left over to create a retinue of planets. Nearly 5 billion years after that, human beings evolved.

The Sun is one of more than 100 billion stars in the Home Galaxy alone. Our Galaxy, in turn, forms part of a local group consisting of approximately 30 similar structures, mostly small "dwarf" galaxies but a few large ones, and one – the Andromeda Galaxy – larger than our own. There are at least 100 billion galaxies in the Universe, many of which are members of huge galaxy clusters.

LIFE OF A STAR

For most of its existence, a star produces energy by the nuclear fusion of hydrogen into helium at its core. The duration of this hydrogen-burning period – known as the *main sequence* – depends on the star's mass; the greater the mass, the higher the core temperatures and the sooner the star's supply of hydrogen is exhausted. Dim, dwarf stars consume their hydrogen slowly, eking it out over billions of years. The Sun, like other stars of its mass, should spend about 10 billion years on the main sequence; since it was formed less than 5 billion years ago, it still has half its life left.

Once all of a star's core hydrogen has been fused into helium, nuclear activity moves outward into layers of unconsumed hydrogen. For a time, energy production sharply increases: the star grows hotter and expands enormously, turning into a so-called red giant. Its energy output will increase a thousandfold, and it will swell to a hundred times its former diameter.

After a few hundred million years, helium in the core will become sufficiently compressed to initiate a new cycle of nuclear fusion: from helium to carbon. The star will contract somewhat, before beginning its last expansion, in the Sun's case engulfing the Earth and perhaps Mars. In this bloated condition, the Sun's outer layers will break off into space, leaving a tiny inner core, mainly of carbon, that shrinks progressively under its own gravity. The white dwarf star thus formed can attain a density more than 10,000 times that of normal matter, with crushing surface gravity to match. Gradually, the nuclear fires will die down, and the Sun will reach its terminal stage: a black dwarf, emitting insignificant amounts of energy.

Black holes

However, stars more massive than the Sun may undergo a different transformation. The additional mass allows gravitational collapse to continue indefinitely: eventually, all the star's remaining matter shrinks to a point, and its density approaches infinity – a state that will not permit even subatomic structures to survive.

The star has become a *black hole*: an anomalous "singularity" in the fabric of space and time. Although vast coruscations of radiation will be emitted by any matter falling into its grasp, the singularity itself has an escape velocity that exceeds the speed of light, and nothing can ever be released from it. Within the boundaries of the black hole, the laws of physics are suspended.

GALACTIC STRUCTURES

Many of the Universe's 100 billion galaxies show clear structural patterns, originally classified by the American astronomer Edwin Hubble in 1925. Spiral galaxies like our own have a central, almost spherical bulge and a surrounding disk composed of spiral arms. Barred spirals have a central bar of stars across the nucleus, with spiral arms trailing from the ends of the bar. Elliptical galaxies have a more uniform appearance, ranging from a flattened disk to a near sphere.

▲ M51, the Whirlpool Nebula, comprises the large spiral galaxy NGC 5194 and its smaller, barred companion NGC 5195. M51 was the first astronomical object in which a spiral structure was identified, in 1845. Although smaller and less massive than our own Galaxy, M51 is much brighter, due to recent star formation.

Most galaxies, however, have no obvious structure at all. Galaxies also vary enormously in size, from dwarf galaxies only 2,000 light-years across to great assemblies of stars 80 or more times larger.

THE HOME GALAXY

The Sun and its planets are located in one of the spiral arms of the Galaxy, about 26,000 light-years from the galactic center and orbiting around it in a period of about 220 million years. The center is invisible from the Earth, masked by vast, light-absorbing clouds of interstellar dust.

The Galaxy is probably around 12 billion years old and, like other spiral galaxies, has three distinct regions. The central bulge is about 30,000 light-years in diameter. The disk in which the Sun is located is not much more than 1,000 light-years thick, but approximately 100,000 light-years from end to end. Around the Galaxy is the halo, a spherical zone 300,000 light-years across, studded with globular star clusters and sprinkled with individual suns.

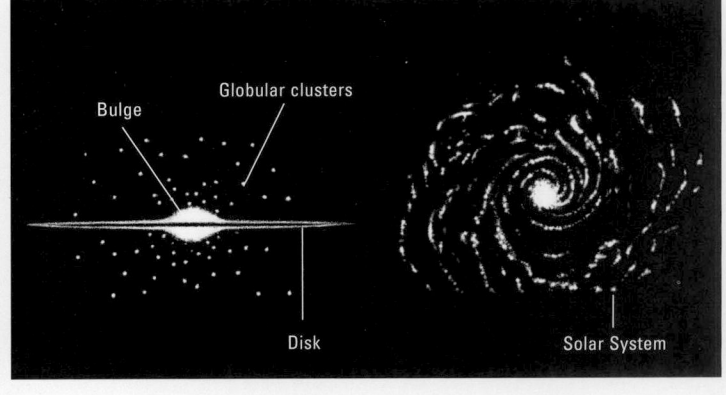

THE END OF THE UNIVERSE

The likely fate of the Universe is disputed. According to one theory (*top of diagram, below*), the expansion begun at the time of the Big Bang will continue "indefinitely," with aging galaxies moving further and further apart in an immense, dark graveyard.

Alternatively, gravity may overcome the expansion (*bottom of diagram*). Galaxies will fall back together until everything is again concentrated at a single point, followed by a new Big Bang and a new expansion, in an endlessly repeated cycle.

The first theory is supported by the amount of visible matter in the Universe; the second theory assumes that there is enough dark material in the Universe to bring about the gravitational collapse.

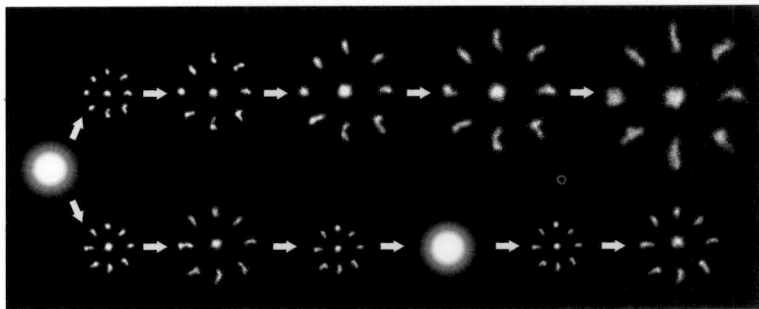

THE NEAREST STARS

The 22 nearest stars, excluding the Sun, with their distance from Earth in light-years*

Proxima Centauri	4.2	UV Ceti A	8.7	61 Cygni A	11.4
Alpha Centauri A	4.4	UV Ceti B	8.7	Procyon A	11.4
Alpha Centauri B	4.4	Ross 154	9.7	Procyon B	11.4
Barnard's Star	5.9	Ross 248	10.3	61 Cygni B	11.4
Wolf 359	7.8	Epsilon Eridani	10.5	HD 173740	11.5
Lalande 21185	8.3	HD 217987	10.7	HD 173739	11.7
Sirius A	8.6	Ross 128	10.9	* A light-year is about 5,900	
Sirius B	8.6	L789-6	11.2	billion miles [9,500 billion km]	

Many of the nearest stars, like Alpha Centauri A and B, are double stars, orbiting about their common center of gravity and to all intents and purposes equidistant from Earth. Many of them are dim objects, with no name other than the designation given to them by the astronomers who first investigated them.

However, they include Sirius, the brightest star in the sky, and Procyon, the seventh brightest. Both are larger than the Sun; of the nearest stars, only Epsilon Eridani is similar in size and luminosity. Most of the other bright stars in the sky are within 500 light-years of the Sun – a small fraction of the diameter of our Galaxy.

STAR CHARTS

NORTHERN HEMISPHERE SKY

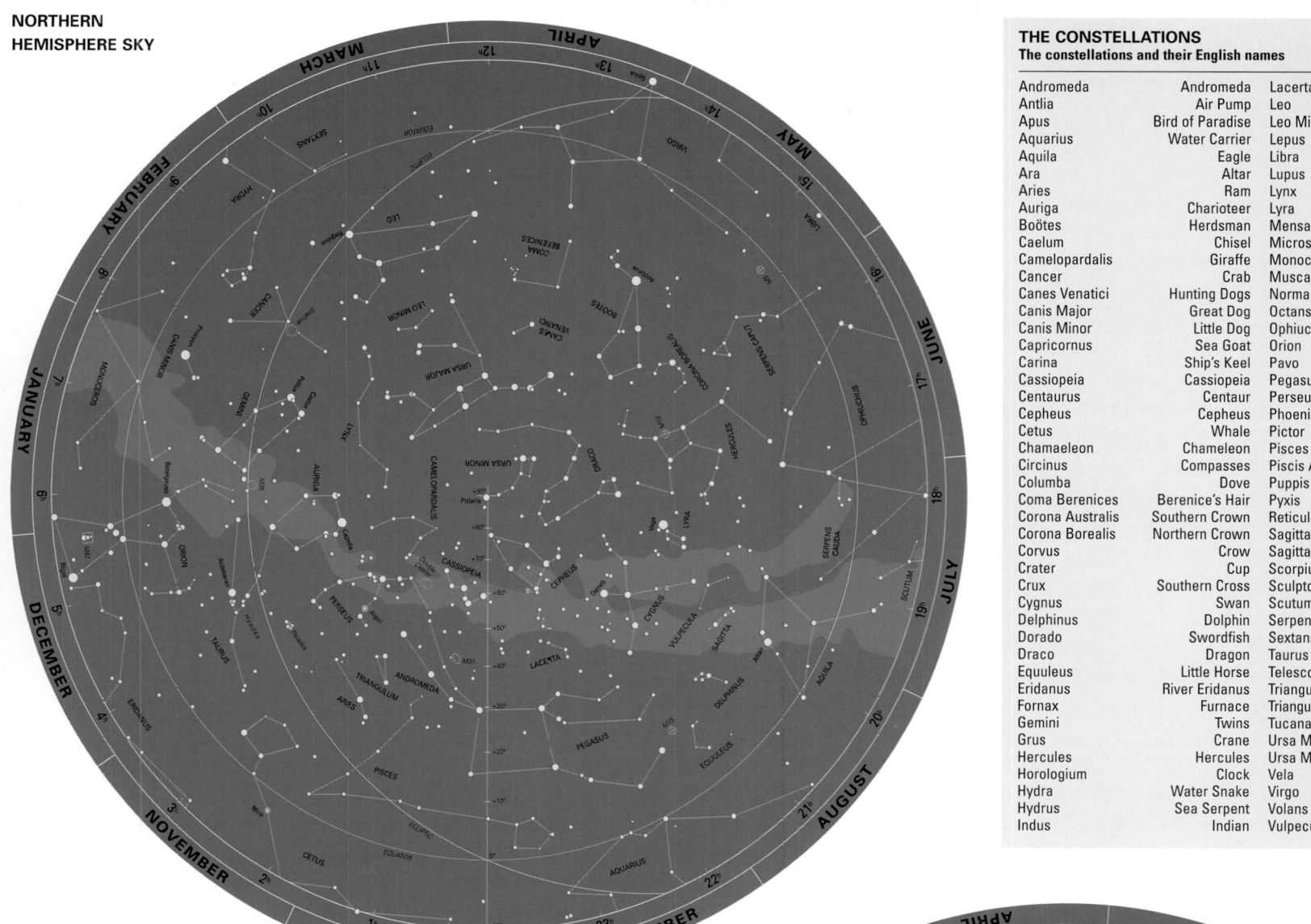

SOUTHERN HEMISPHERE SKY

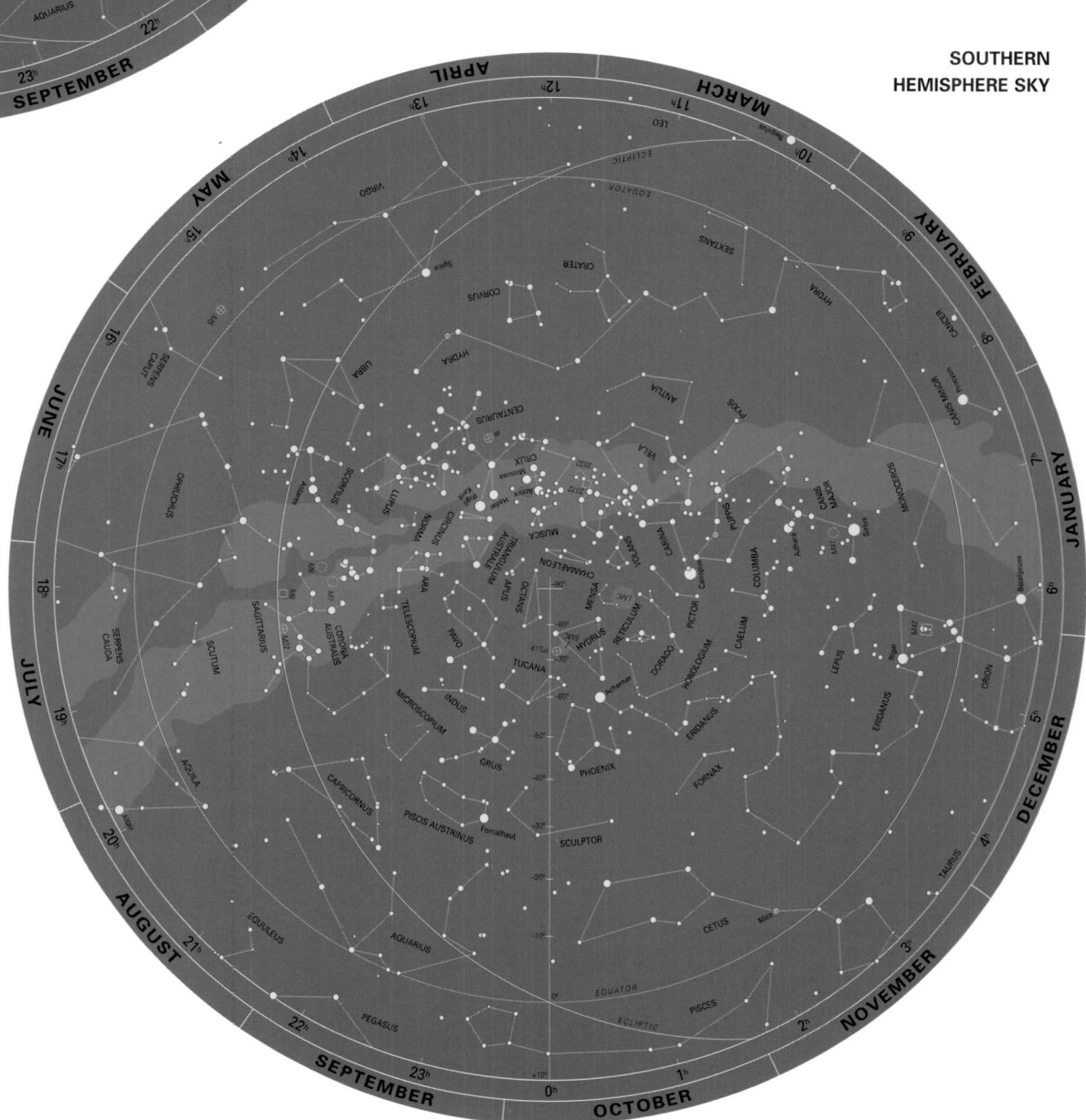

THE CONSTELLATIONS
The constellations and their English names

Andromeda	Andromeda	Lacerta	Lizard
Antlia	Air Pump	Leo	Lion
Apus	Bird of Paradise	Leo Minor	Little Lion
Aquarius	Water Carrier	Lepus	Hare
Aquila	Eagle	Libra	Scales
Ara	Altar	Lupus	Wolf
Aries	Ram	Lynx	Lynx
Auriga	Charioteer	Lyra	Lyre
Boötes	Herdsman	Mensa	Table Mountain
Caelum	Chisel	Microscopium	Microscope
Camelopardalis	Giraffe	Monoceros	Unicorn
Cancer	Crab	Musca	Fly
Canes Venatici	Hunting Dogs	Norma	Level
Canis Major	Great Dog	Octans	Octant
Canis Minor	Little Dog	Ophiuchus	Serpent Bearer
Capricornus	Sea Goat	Orion	Orion
Carina	Ship's Keel	Pavo	Peacock
Cassiopeia	Cassiopeia	Pegasus	Winged Horse
Centaurus	Centaur	Perseus	Perseus
Cepheus	Cepheus	Phoenix	Phoenix
Cetus	Whale	Pictor	Easel
Chamaeleon	Chameleon	Pisces	Fishes
Circinus	Compasses	Piscis Austrinus	Southern Fish
Columba	Dove	Puppis	Ship's Stern
Coma Berenices	Berenice's Hair	Pyxis	Mariner's Compass
Corona Australis	Southern Crown	Reticulum	Net
Corona Borealis	Northern Crown	Sagitta	Arrow
Corvus	Crow	Sagittarius	Archer
Crater	Cup	Scorpius	Scorpion
Crux	Southern Cross	Sculptor	Sculptor
Cygnus	Swan	Scutum	Shield
Delphinus	Dolphin	Serpens	Serpent
Dorado	Swordfish	Sextans	Sextant
Draco	Dragon	Taurus	Bull
Equuleus	Little Horse	Telescopium	Telescope
Eridanus	River Eridanus	Triangulum	Triangle
Fornax	Furnace	Triangulum Australe	Southern Triangle
Gemini	Twins	Tucana	Toucan
Grus	Crane	Ursa Major	Great Bear
Hercules	Hercules	Ursa Minor	Little Bear
Horologium	Clock	Vela	Ship's Sails
Hydra	Water Snake	Virgo	Virgin
Hydrus	Sea Serpent	Volans	Flying Fish
Indus	Indian	Vulpecula	Fox

The charts on this page show the entire heavens divided into northern and southern hemispheres, with 10° of overlap between them around the perimeter of each one. However, the view from any particular location on Earth will be different, and will change both hourly as the Earth turns, and throughout the year as the Earth goes around the Sun.

The Sun's annual path through the heavens is known as the "ecliptic," and is shown here by an orange line. When the Sun is in the sky its light drowns out our view of the stars, so only that part of the heavens opposite the Sun is visible at a particular time. The sky's equivalent of longitude is known as "right ascension." As the stars appear to rotate around the Earth once every 24 hours, right ascension is measured eastward in hours and minutes, and is marked around the edge of the maps. The equivalent of latitude is "declination," measured in degrees north or south of the celestial equator, and shown by the vertical line on each chart.

Using the charts

At any place and time you can see half of the whole sky, assuming a flat horizon. If you were at one of the poles your view would be shown as a circle centered on the middle of the map for the appropriate hemisphere, with the horizon marked by the celestial equator. From all other locations the center of your view (your overhead point) will be at some other point on the map whose location changes with time. The closer you are to Earth's equator, the closer the center will be to the edge of the map and more stars in the opposite hemisphere will be visible.

So first choose the appropriate chart for your hemisphere and hold it with the month at the bottom. At 11 p.m., not allowing for Daylight Saving Time (Summer Time), your overhead point will be at the same declination as your geographical latitude and stars lower on the map will be due south (or north in the southern hemisphere). From latitude 50° in mid August, for example, your overhead point will be close to the star Deneb in the constellation of Cygnus. Stars on the opposite side of the map will be below your northern horizon, while stars below Deneb will be due south.

STAR MAGNITUDES
Apparent visual magnitudes

The magnitude scale of star brightnesses is developed from the system used by the Ancient Greeks in which the brightest stars were first magnitude and the faintest visible to the naked eye were sixth. Today the scale has a mathematical basis and extends, at the brightest end, through to negative magnitudes.

The Milky Way is shown in light blue on these charts.

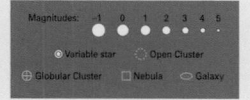

For more information:
68 The Home Galaxy
72 The seasons
   Day and night
73 The Moon

Lying about halfway from the center of one of billions of galaxies that populate the observable Universe, our Solar System contains eight planets and their moons, five dwarf planets, innumerable asteroids, comets and other icy bodies, and a miscellany of dust and gas, all tethered by the immense gravitational field of the Sun, the star whose thermonuclear furnaces provide them all with heat and light.

The Solar System was formed about 5 billion years ago, when a spinning cloud of gas, mostly hydrogen but seeded with other heavier elements, condensed enough to ignite a nuclear reaction and create a star. The Sun still accounts for almost 99.9% of the system's total mass.

By composition as well as distance, the planetary array divides quite neatly in two: an inner system of four small, solid planets, including the Earth, and an outer system, from Jupiter to Neptune, of four much larger planets composed of lighter materials, such as gas, liquid, and ice. Lying mostly between the two groups is a scattering of rocky asteroids, numbering perhaps a million or more. They may be debris left over from the formation of the inner Solar System. In 2006, Pluto was demoted from its former status as a planet and is now regarded as a member of the Kuiper Belt of icy bodies at the fringes of the Solar System.

Much of the early history of science is the story of people trying to make sense of

the wandering points of light that were all they knew of the planets. Now, men have themselves stood on the Earth's Moon, space probes have landed on Mars and Venus, and distant landscapes have been mapped with astonishing accuracy, transforming our knowledge of our celestial environment.

In the 1980s, the Voyager space probes skimmed all four major planets of the outer Solar System, bringing new revelations with each close approach. The Magellan (Venus), Galileo (Jupiter) and Cassini–Huygens (Saturn) missions have transformed our knowledge of those planets and the giants' moons, and a host of orbiters and landers have shown us Mars in a new light. A spacecraft is also on its way to visit Pluto.

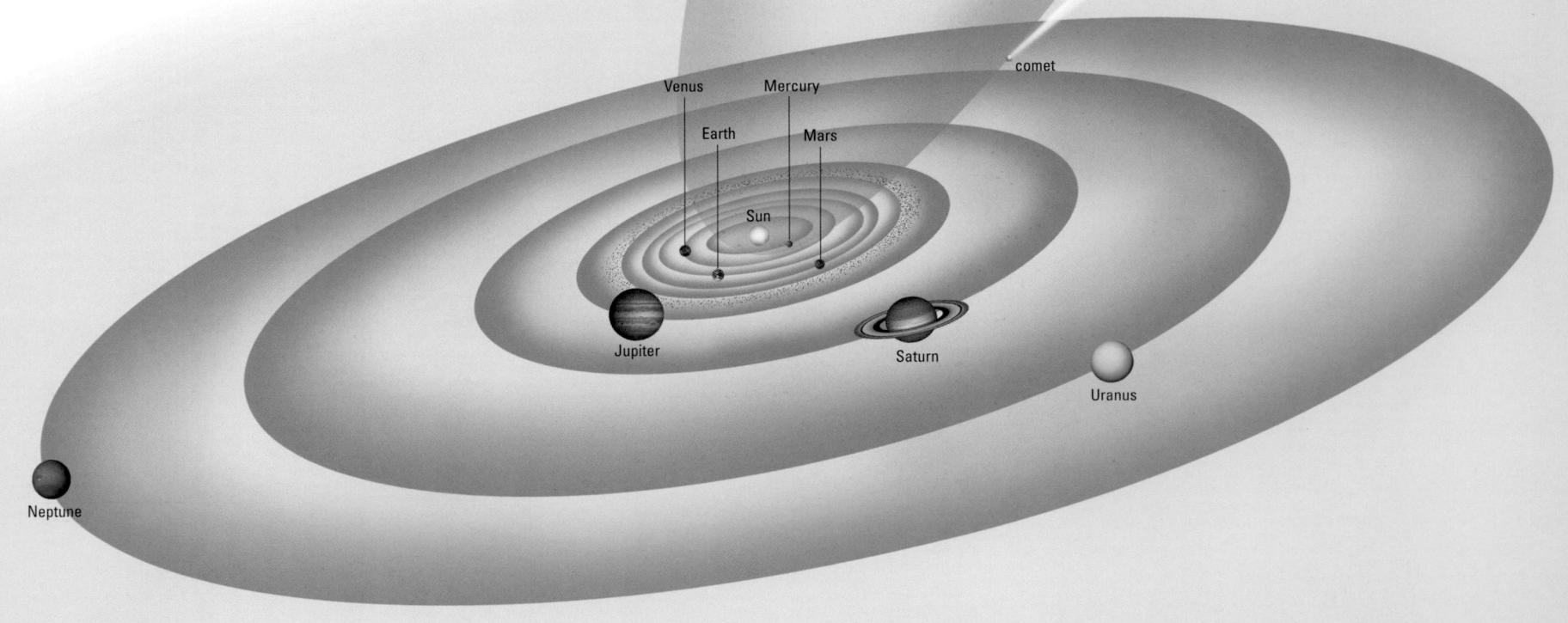

Diagram not drawn to scale

ORBITS OF THE PLANETS

The diagram above shows the Solar System as it might appear to an observer a few light-hours away in the direction of the constellation Hercules. Seen from such a position, above the plane of the ecliptic, all the planets revolve about the Sun in a counterclockwise direction. The perspective

view exaggerates the elliptical form of all the planetary orbits: only Mercury follows a path that deviates noticeably from circularity.

The diagram also shows the main swarm of asteroids between Mars and Jupiter, and the orbit of a comet. Comets reside in a vast spherical halo beyond the Solar System,

and are occasionally diverted toward the Sun on highly elliptical orbits which may take many thousands of years to complete. Most, therefore, still await discovery, though there are a number of shorter-period comets which return regularly, such as Halley's Comet.

PLANETARY DATA

	Mean distance from Sun (million miles)	Mass (Earth = 1)	Period of orbit (Earth days/years)	Period of rotation (Earth days)	Equatorial diameter (miles)	Average density (water = 1)	Surface gravity (Earth = 1)	Number of known satellites*
Sun	–	332,946	–	25.38	865,000	1.41	27.9	–
Mercury	36.0	0.06	87.97d	58.65	3,032	5.43	0.38	0
Venus	67.2	0.82	224.7d	243.02	7,521	5.24	0.91	0
Earth	93.0	1.00	365.3d	1.00	7,926	5.52	1.00	1
Mars	141.6	0.11	687.0d	1.029	4,220	3.94	0.38	2
Jupiter	483.7	317.8	11.86y	0.411	88,848	1.33	2.36	63
Saturn	886.6	95.2	29.45y	0.428	74,900	0.69	0.91	62
Uranus	1,784.0	14.5	84.02y	0.720	31,764	1.27	0.89	27
Neptune	2,795.2	17.2	164.8y	0.673	30,776	1.64	1.13	13

Planetary days are given in sidereal days – that is, with respect to the stars rather than the Sun. The difference is caused by the movement of the planet in its orbit, so the interval between successive noons is slightly different from that between the rising of a particular star. The Earth's own sidereal day is 23h 56m in solar time. The equatorial diameters of most planets differ from their polar diameters as a consequence of their rotation, which is most marked in the case of Jupiter and Saturn, which are very noticeably flattened at the poles. Strictly speaking, the figures for surface gravity apply to the four inner planets only, as the outer planets have no solid surfaces. In their case, the figure is given for an arbitrary point in the atmosphere where the pressure is 1 bar.

* Number of known satellites at mid-2011

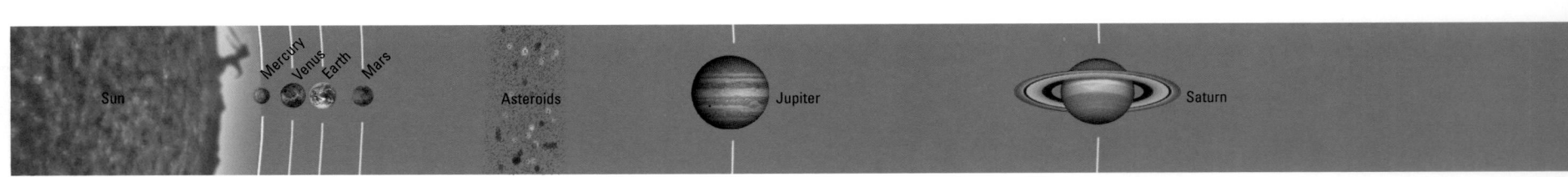

THE PLANETS

Mercury is the closest planet to the Sun and hence the fastest-moving. It is very hot, with a cratered, wrinkled surface very similar to that of Earth's Moon. It is small and has low gravity, so there is no significant atmosphere.

Venus has much the same physical dimensions as Earth. Its dense atmosphere is composed of 97% carbon dioxide resulting in a runaway greenhouse effect that makes the surface, at 890°F, the hottest of all the planets in the Solar System. Radar mapping revealed a terrain consisting of highland regions and vast, rolling plains crossed by volcanic flows and dotted with craters. Discharges from volcanic regions could explain the sulfuric-acid rain detected by spacecraft. Soft-landers last less than an hour in Venus's fierce climate.

Earth seen from space is easily the most beautiful of the inner planets; it is also, and more objectively, the largest, as well as the only known home of life. Living things are the main reason why the Earth is able to retain a substantial proportion of reactive oxygen in its atmosphere; the oxygen in turn supports the life that constantly regenerates it. The Earth's natural satellite, the Moon, is believed to have been created when an asteroid struck our planet in its infancy.

Mars, smaller and cooler than the Earth, is nevertheless the most likely planet other than Earth where life may have formed. The planet was until recently (in astronomical terms) a geologically active world with water on its surface: rivers, lakes, and even an ocean. Liquid water may well exist today, but trapped beneath its dusty, boulder-strewn surface. The Martian landscape features huge extinct volcanoes, a giant canyon system, craters, and sand dunes. Its thin atmosphere is mostly carbon dioxide, and its polar caps are of frozen carbon dioxide and water ice. It has two tiny moons, probably captured asteroids.

Jupiter has about three times the mass of all the other planets combined. The planet is mostly gas, under intense pressure in the lower atmosphere above a core of fiercely compressed hydrogen and helium. The upper layers form strikingly colored rotating belts, the outward sign of the intense storms created by Jupiter's rapid rotation. The Great Red Spot is a storm feature that has persisted for at least 170 years. Jupiter has at least 63 moons. Most are very small, but the four largest – Io, Europa, Ganymede, and Callisto – are fascinating worlds in their own right. Io is the most volcanically active world known, and Europa possesses an ocean deep below its icy surface. The planet also has a system of rings, though nowhere near as prominent as Saturn's.

Saturn is structurally similar to Jupiter, rotating fast enough to produce an obvious bulge at its equator. It is composed of 89% hydrogen and 11% helium, and has wind velocities in the outer atmosphere of 1,600 ft/sec. Ever since the invention of the telescope, Saturn's rings have been the feature that has most attracted observers. The rings consist of thousands of individual ringlets, composed of icy particles ranging in size from 30 feet down to microscopic. Titan, the largest of Saturn's 62 known moons, has a dense atmosphere.

Uranus was unknown to the ancients. Although it is faintly visible to the naked eye, it was not established as a planet until 1781. In its interior is probably a rocky core surrounded by frozen methane, water, and ammonia; the atmosphere is of hydrogen, helium, and some methane, which gives the planet its greenish-blue color. There is a system of thin, dark rings and a retinue of 27 moons, all but five of which are small.

Neptune is always more than 2.5 billion miles from Earth, and despite its diameter of over 31,000 miles, it can only be seen by telescope. Its discovery in 1846 was the result of mathematical predictions by astronomers seeking to explain irregularities in the orbit of Uranus. Like Uranus, it has a ring system; recent observations have revealed a total of 13 moons.

In 2006, following an increasing number of discoveries of objects orbiting the Sun of similar size to Pluto but at a greater distance, the International Astronomical Union issued for the first time a definition of a planet. A planet is defined as "a body orbiting the Sun, which is essentially round as a consequence of its gravity, and which does not share its orbital neighborhood with similar bodies." On this definition, Pluto is no longer classified as a planet, but is instead a member of a new category of "dwarf planet," which relaxes the last criterion but excludes bodies in orbit around another one.

Mean distance from the
Sun in millions of miles

Mercury	36.0 Mercury
Venus	67.2 Venus
Earth	93.0 Earth
Mars	141.6 Mars
Jupiter	483.7 Jupiter
Saturn	886.6 Saturn
Uranus	1,784.0 Uranus
Neptune	2,795.2 Neptune

Diagrams not drawn to scale

Uranus

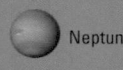

Neptune

For more information:

70 Orbits of the planets

77 Ocean currents

78 Circulation of the air

80 Climate

The basic units of time measurement are the day and the year. The day is one rotation of the Earth on its axis. Our present calendar is based on the solar year of 365.24 days, the time taken by the Earth to orbit the Sun. Calendars based on the movements of the Sun and Moon have been used since ancient times. The length of the year, reckoned by the Julian Calendar introduced by Julius Caesar, was about 11 minutes too long. The cumulative error was rectified in 1582 by the Gregorian Calendar, when Pope Gregory XIII decreed that the day following October 4 was October 15, and that century years did not count as leap years unless they were divisible by 400. England finally adopted the reformed calendar in 1752, when it was 11 days behind the European mainland.

The rotation of the Earth on its axis causes day and night. The Earth rotates through 360° every 24 hours, and the world is divided into 24 time zones centered on lines of longitude at 15° intervals.

The tilt of the Earth's axis, which is also called the "obliquity of the ecliptic," accounts for the seasons which are so familiar in the middle latitudes. However, geological evidence shows that, over long periods of time, climates change, and the advances and retreats of the ice during the Pleistocene Ice Age may have been caused by regular variations in the Earth's tilt, its orbit around the Sun, and changes in the season when it is closest to the Sun (perihelion).

THE SEASONS

Seasons occur because the Earth's axis is tilted at an angle of approximately 23½°. When the northern hemisphere is tilted to a maximum extent toward the Sun, on June 21, the Sun is overhead at the Tropic of Cancer (latitude 23½° North). This is midsummer, or the summer solstice, in the northern hemisphere.

On September 22 or 23, the Sun is overhead at the equator, and day and night are of equal length throughout the world. This is the autumnal equinox in the northern hemisphere.

On December 21 or 22, the Sun is overhead at the Tropic of Capricorn (23½° South), the winter solstice in the northern hemisphere. The overhead Sun then tracks north until, on March 21, it is overhead at the equator. This is the spring (vernal) equinox in the northern hemisphere.

In the southern hemisphere, the seasons are the reverse of those in the north.

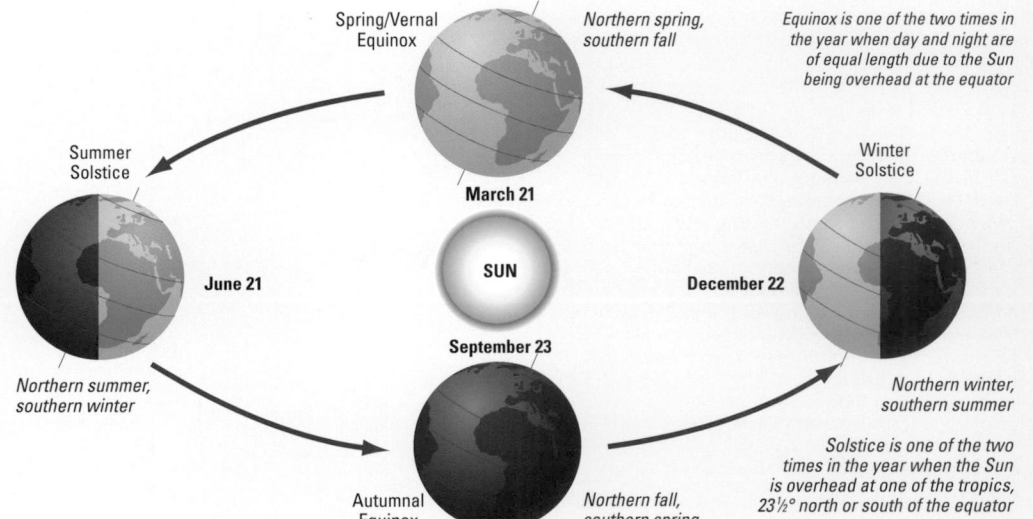

DAY AND NIGHT

The Sun appears to rise in the east, reach its highest point at noon, and then set in the west, to be followed by night. In reality, it is not the Sun that is moving but the Earth rotating from west to east. The moment when the Sun's upper limb first appears above the horizon is termed sunrise; the moment when the Sun's upper limb disappears below the horizon is sunset.

At the summer solstice in the northern hemisphere (June 21), the Arctic has total daylight and the Antarctic total darkness. The opposite occurs at the winter solstice (December 21 or 22). At the equator, the length of day and night are almost equal all year.

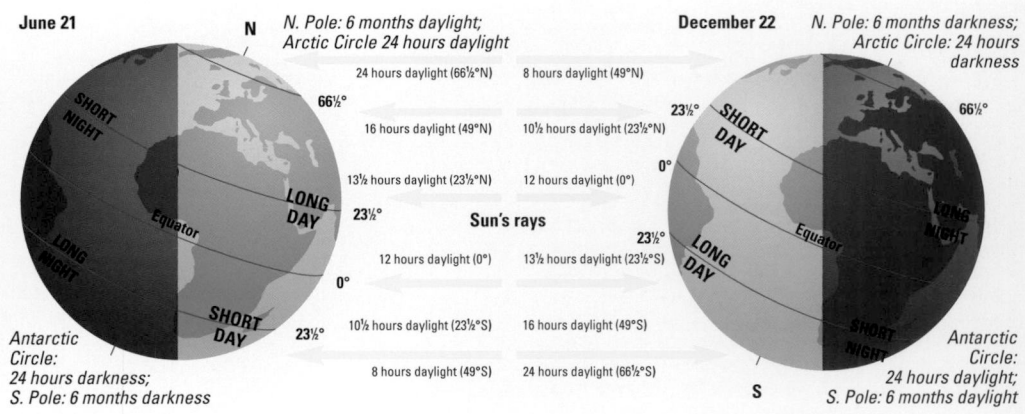

EARTH DATA

Aphelion (maximum distance from Sun):	94,508,166 miles	Length of year:	365 days, 5 hours, 48 minutes, 46 seconds of mean solar time	Polar circumference:	24,860 miles
				Equatorial diameter:	7,926 miles
Perihelion (minimum distance from Sun):	91,403,477 miles	Superficial area:	197,000,000 sq miles	Polar diameter:	7,900 miles
Angle of tilt (obliquity of the ecliptic):	23° 27' 08"	Land surface:	57,500,000 sq miles (29.2%)	Equatorial radius:	3,963 miles
		Water surface:	139,500,000 sq miles (70.8%)	Polar radius:	3,950 miles
Length of year – solar tropical (equinox to equinox):	365.24 days	Equatorial circumference:	24,901 miles	Volume of the Earth:	259,880 × 10⁶ cu miles
				Mass of the Earth:	5.97 × 10²⁴ kg

SUNRISE AND SUNSET

The term "equinox" comes from the Latin for "equal night." At the spring and autumnal equinoxes, the Sun is vertically overhead at midday at the equator and all places on Earth have 12 hours of darkness and 12 hours of daylight. The graphs of sunrise and sunset show that these occasions occur on March 21 and on September 22 or 23. The graphs also show that, because the Sun remains high in the sky at the equator throughout the year, the length of day and night there remains roughly the same throughout the year, with sunrise around 6 a.m. and sunset around 6 p.m.

The further north or south one travels, the greater the difference between the number of hours of daylight and darkness. For example, the graph (right) shows that at latitude 60°N sunrise varies from just after 9 a.m. in midwinter (on December 22 or 23) to about 2.30 a.m. in midsummer (around the summer solstice on June 21). By contrast, the second graph (far right) shows that sunset at latitude 60°N occurs at about 2.45 p.m. in midwinter and 9.20 p.m. in midsummer.

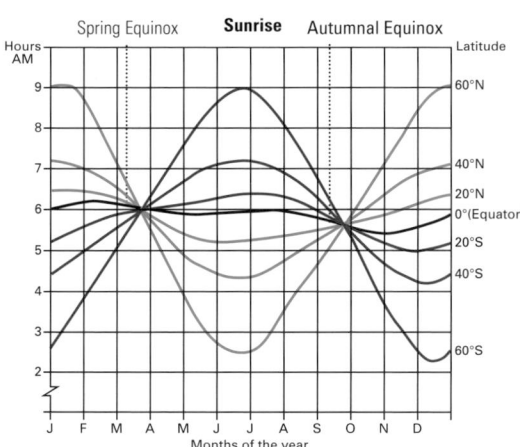

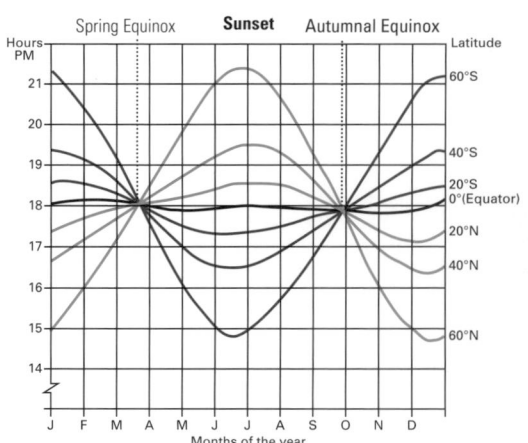

THE MOON

The Moon rotates more slowly than the Earth, taking just over 27 days to make one complete rotation on its axis. This corresponds to the Moon's orbital period around the Earth, and therefore the Moon always presents the same hemisphere toward us; some 41% of the Moon's far side is never visible from the Earth. The interval between one New Moon and the next is 29½ days – this is called a lunation, or lunar month. The Moon shines only by reflected sunlight, and emits no light of its own. During each lunation the Moon displays a complete cycle of phases, caused by the changing angle of illumination from the Sun.

PHASES OF THE MOON

Mean distance from Earth: 238,856 miles; Mean diameter: 2,159 miles;
Mass: approximately 1/80 that of Earth; Surface gravity: one-sixth of Earth's;
Daily range of temperature at lunar equator: 504°F; Average orbital speed: 2,287 mph

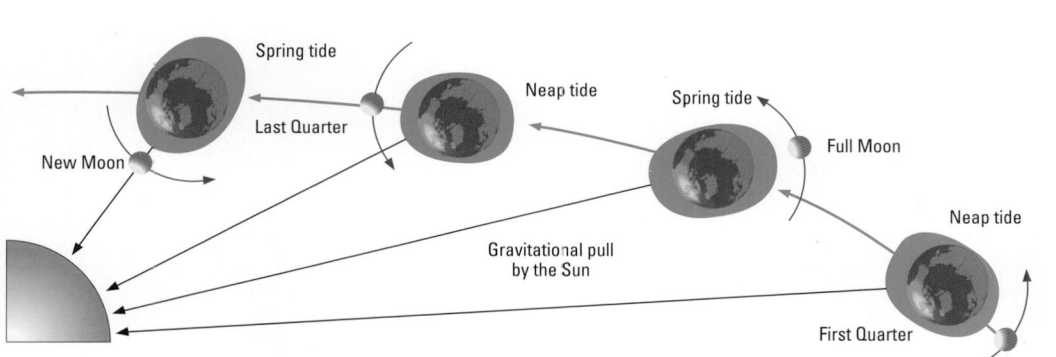

New Moon · Waxing Crescent · First Quarter · Waxing Gibbous · Full Moon · Waning Gibbous · Last Quarter · Waning Crescent · New Moon

MOON DATA

Distance from Earth
The Moon orbits at a mean distance of 238,856 miles, at an average speed of 2,287 mph in relation to the Earth.

Size and mass
The average diameter of the Moon is 2,159 miles. It is 400 times smaller than the Sun but is about 400 times closer to the Earth, so we see them as the same size. The Moon has a mass of 7.35×10^{22} kg, with a density 3.344 times that of water.

Visibility
Only 59% of the Moon's surface is visible from the Earth over time. Sunlight reflected from the Moon takes 1.3 seconds to reach the Earth (the Sun itself is around 8½ light-minutes away).

Temperature
With the Sun overhead, the temperature on the lunar equator can reach 243°F [117°C]. At night it can sink to −261°F [−163°C].

ECLIPSES

When the Moon passes between the Sun and the Earth, the Sun becomes partially eclipsed (1). A partial eclipse becomes a total eclipse if the Moon proceeds to cover the Sun completely (2) and the dark central part of the lunar shadow touches the Earth. The broad geographical zone covered by the Moon's outer shadow (P), has only a very small central area (often less than 62 miles wide) that experiences totality. Totality can never last for more than 7½ minutes at maximum, but is usually much briefer than this. Lunar eclipses take place when the Moon moves through the shadow of the Earth, and can be partial or total. Any single location on Earth can experience a maximum of four solar and three lunar eclipses in any single year, while a total solar eclipse occurs an average of once every 360 years for any given location.

Partial eclipse (1) · Solar eclipse · Lunar eclipse

Total eclipse (2)

TIDES

The daily rise and fall of the ocean's tides are the result of the gravitational pull of the Moon and that of the Sun, though the effect of the latter is not as strong as that of the Moon. This effect is greatest on the hemisphere facing the Moon and causes a tidal "bulge." Spring tides occur when the Sun, Earth, and Moon are aligned; high tides are at their highest, and low tides fall to their lowest. When the Moon and Sun are furthest out of line (near the Moon's First and Last Quarters), neap tides occur, producing the smallest range between high and low tides.

Spring tide · Neap tide · Spring tide · Full Moon · Last Quarter · New Moon · Neap tide · Gravitational pull by the Sun · First Quarter

TIME ZONES

The Earth rotates through 360° in 24 hours, and so moves 15° every hour. The world is divided into 24 standard time zones, each centered on lines of longitude at 15° intervals. At the center of the first zone is the prime meridian, or Greenwich meridian. All places to the west of Greenwich are one hour behind for every 15° of longitude; places to the east are ahead by one hour for every 15°.

International Date Line
When it is 12 noon on the Greenwich meridian, 180° east it is midnight of the same day – while 180° west the day is just beginning. To overcome this, the International Date Line was established, approximately following the 180° meridian. Thus, if you were to travel eastward from Japan (140°E) to Hawai'i (160°W), you would pass from Sunday night into Sunday morning.

10 Hours behind or ahead of UT or Coordinated Universal Time

- Zones using UT (GMT)
- Zones behind UT (GMT)
- International boundaries
- Zones ahead of UT (GMT)
- Half-hour zones
- Time-zone boundaries
- International Date Line
- Actual solar time when time at Greenwich is 12:00 (noon)

Note: Some of the above time zones are affected by the incidence of Daylight Saving Time in countries where it is adopted.

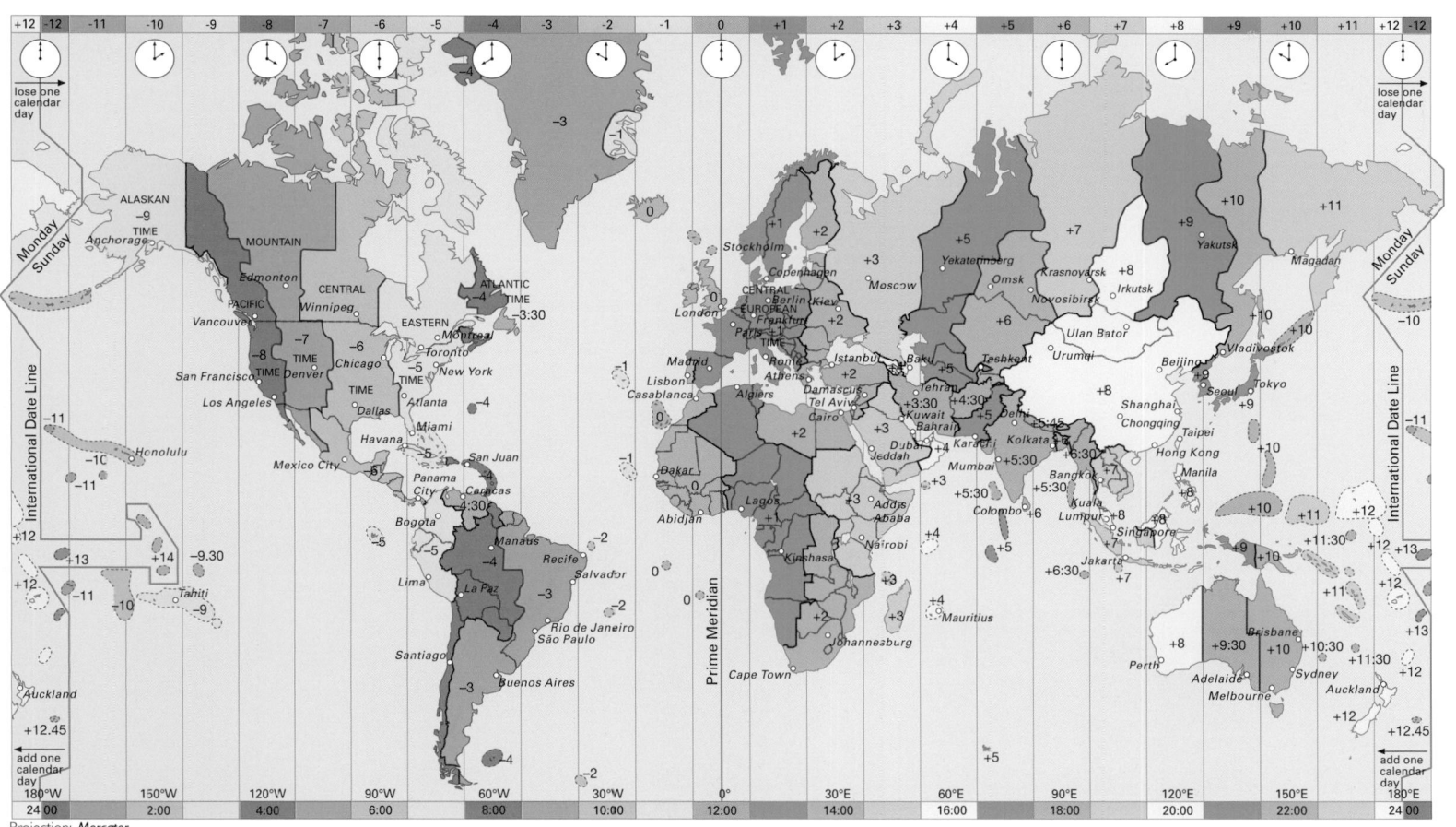

Projection: Mercator

For more information:
98 Minerals

Every year, earthquakes and volcanic eruptions cause much destruction throughout the world. Such phenomena were once thought to be unconnected, but since the late 1960s, scientists have understood that these events are surface manifestations of the tremendous forces operating in the Earth's interior that are slowly but constantly changing the face of our planet.

The Earth is divided into three zones. The crust, a brittle, low-density zone, overlies the dense mantle. Separating the crust from the mantle is a distinct boundary called the Mohorovičić (or Moho) discontinuity. Enclosed by the mantle is the Earth's core, which consists mainly of iron and nickel.

Temperatures inside the Earth range from about 1,600°F in the upper mantle to perhaps 9,000°F in the core. Heat creates convection currents in a semimolten part of the mantle called the asthenosphere. Above the asthenosphere is the lithosphere, a solid layer about 40 miles thick, consisting of the crust and part of the mantle. The lithosphere is divided into rigid plates, moved around by the currents in the asthenosphere, a process named plate tectonics.

The Earth was formed around 4.6 billion years ago. Lighter elements floated toward the surface, where they formed crustal rocks. The oldest rocks so far discovered are about 4 billion years old, while the oldest fossils occur in rocks formed around 3.5 billion years ago. An explosion of life occurred at the start of the Cambrian period, 570 million years ago. The fossil record since the start of the Cambrian has enabled scientists to piece together the story of life on Earth.

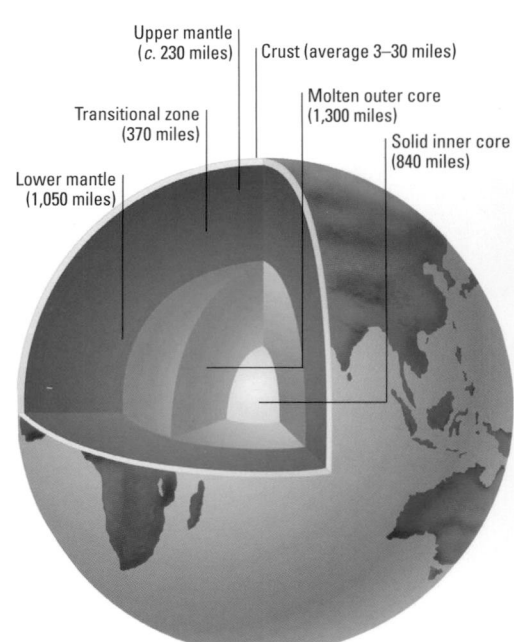

CONTINENTAL DRIFT

—— Trench
—— Rift
▱ New ocean floor
—— Zones of slippage

In 1915, Alfred Wegener produced a series of world maps proposing that, around 200 million years ago, the continents had been joined together in a supercontinent that he called Pangaea. This land mass started to break up about 180 million years ago and the parts drifted to their present positions. In the 1950s and 1960s, evidence from studies of the ocean floor suggested that the low-density continents rest on huge slow-moving plates. The arrows on the present-day world map (*below*) show that the continents are still on the move.

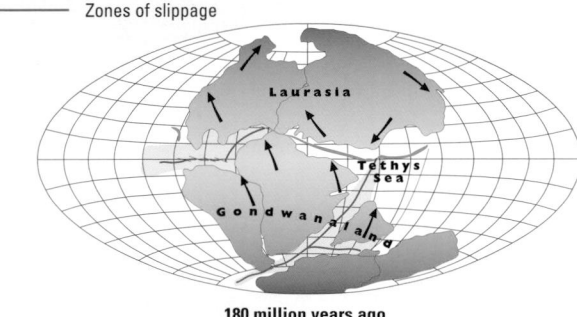

180 million years ago

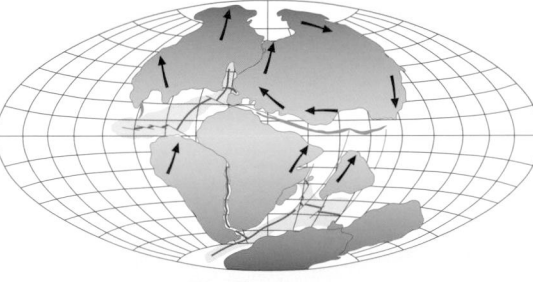

135 million years ago

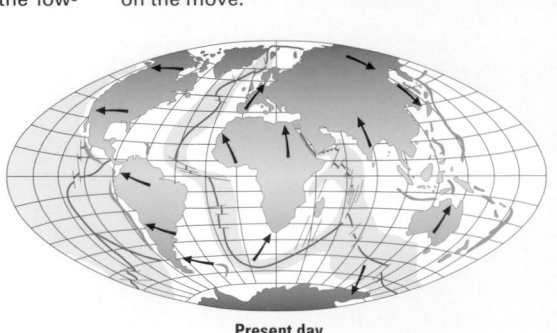

Present day

DISTRIBUTION OF VOLCANOES

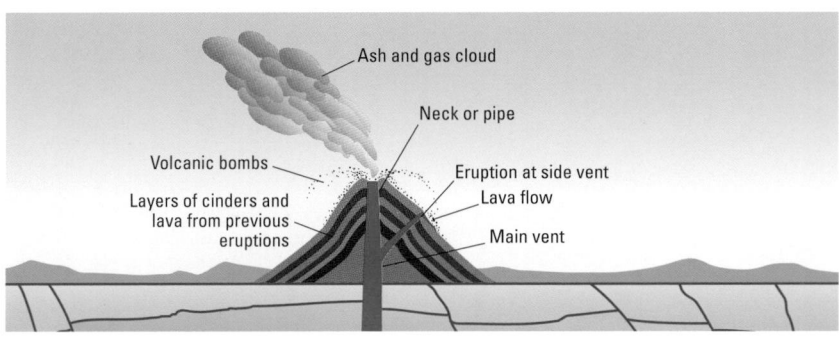

Volcanoes occur when hot liquefied rock beneath the Earth's crust is pushed up by pressure to the surface as molten lava. There are some 550 known active volcanoes, around 20 of which are erupting at any one time.

○ Submarine volcanoes
▲ Land volcanoes active since 1700
—— Boundaries of tectonic plates

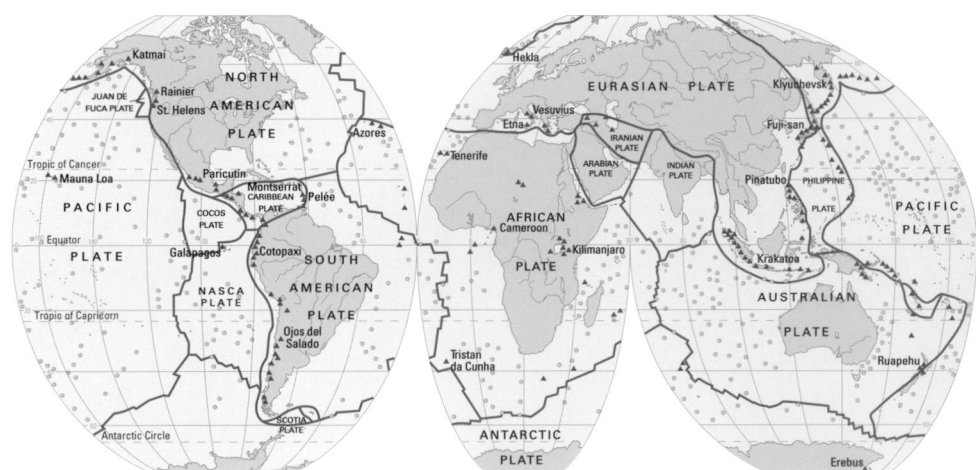

PLATE TECTONICS

The huge ridges that run through the oceans represent boundaries between plates. Here plates are diverging and molten magma from the mantle rises along a central rift valley to form new crustal rock. These ocean ridges, which are active zones where earthquakes and volcanic eruptions are common, are called constructive plate margins. Destructive plate margins, which occur when two contrasting plates converge, are marked by deep-ocean trenches as one plate is forced under the other. The descending plate is melted to produce the magma that fuels volcanoes alongside the trenches. Movements of descending plates are often sudden, triggering earthquakes in overlying continental areas.

Sea-floor spreading in the Atlantic Ocean and plate collision

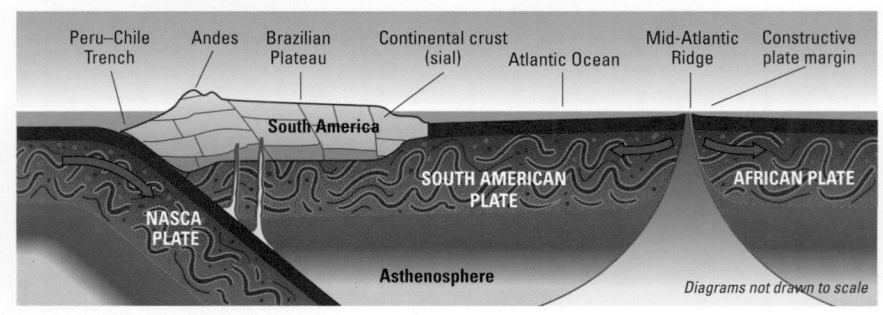

Sea-floor spreading in the Indian Ocean and continental plate collision

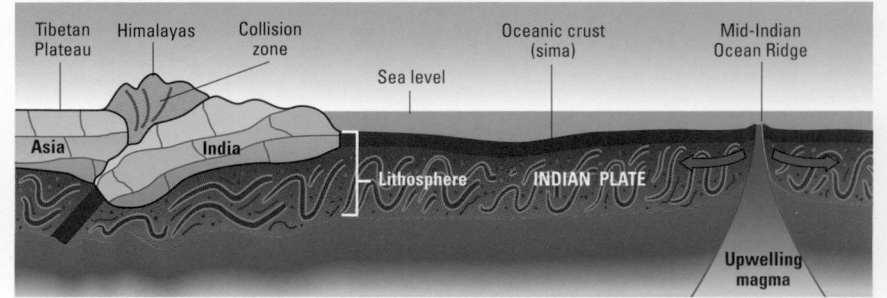

GEOLOGICAL TIME

Time, in millions of years before the present, is shown on a sliding scale, greatly compressed in the distant past.

ERA	PERIOD	EPOCH
PRE-CAMBRIAN		
PALEOZOIC	Cambrian 542	
	Ordovician 488.3	
	Silurian 443.7	
	Devonian 416	
	Carboniferous 359.2	
	Permian 299	
MESOZOIC	Triassic 251	
	Jurassic 199.6	
	Cretaceous 145.5	
CENOZOIC	Tertiary	Paleocene 65.5
		Eocene 55.8
		Oligocene 33.9
		Miocene 23.03
		Pliocene 5.33
	Quaternary	Pleistocene 1.81
		Holocene 10,000 BP to present

Geologists devised their timescale on the basis of relative, not calendar, ages. Accurate dating was impossible and estimates were often bitterly disputed, but the order in which the rocks were formed could be deduced from careful observation. The advent of radioactive dating – culminating in the 1950s with the development of a mass spectrometer capable of accurately measuring tiny quantities of isotopes – appears to have settled the arguments. The Earth is far older than geologists first imagined, but their painstakingly-created structure of geological time has withstood the advent of high technology.

The 4.6 billion (4,600 million) years since the formation of the Earth are divided into four great eras, further split into periods and, in the case of the most recent era, epochs. The present era is the Cenozoic ("new life"), extending backward through "middle life" and "ancient life" to the Pre-Cambrian, named after the Latin word for Wales, the location of some of the earliest known fossils. Most of the Earth's geological history is encompassed by the Pre-Cambrian: though traces of ancient life have since been found, it was largely the proliferation of fossils from the beginning of the Paleozoic era onward, some 570 million years ago, which first allowed precise subdivisions to be made.

Like the Cambrian, most are named after regions exemplifying a period's geology. Others – such as the Carboniferous ("coal-bearing") or the Cretaceous ("chalk-bearing") – are more directly descriptive.

- Pre-Cambrian shields
- Sedimentary cover on Pre-Cambrian shields
- Paleozoic (Caledonian and Hercynian) folding
- Sedimentary cover on Paleozoic folding
- Mesozoic folding
- Sedimentary cover on Mesozoic folding
- Cenozoic (Alpine) folding
- Sedimentary cover on Cenozoic folding
- Intensive Mesozoic and Cenozoic vulcanism
- Principal faults
- Oceanic marginal troughs
- Mid-oceanic ridges
- Overthrust faults

EARTHQUAKES

Earthquake magnitude is usually rated according to either the Richter scale or the Modified Mercalli scale, both devised by seismologists in the 1930s. The Richter scale measures absolute earthquake power with mathematical precision: each step upward represents a tenfold increase in the amplitude of the shockwave. Theoretically, there is no upper limit, but most of the largest earthquakes measured have been rated at between 8.8 and 8.9. The 12-point Mercalli scale, based on observed effects, is often more meaningful, ranging from I (earthquakes noticed only by seismographs) to XII (total destruction); intermediate points include V (people awakened at night; unstable objects overturned), VII (collapse of ordinary buildings; chimneys and monuments fall), and IX (conspicuous cracks in ground; serious damage to reservoirs).

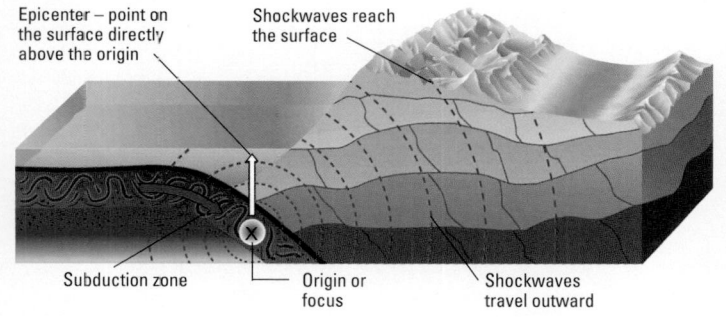

Epicenter – point on the surface directly above the origin
Shockwaves reach the surface
Subduction zone
Origin or focus
Shockwaves travel outward

- Mobile land areas
- Submarine zones of mobile land areas
- Stable land platforms
- Submarine extensions of land platforms
- Mid-oceanic volcanic ridges
- Oceanic platforms

1976 ○ Principal earthquakes and dates (since 1900)

Earthquakes are a series of rapid vibrations originating from the slipping or faulting of parts of the Earth's crust when stresses within build up to breaking point. They usually happen at depths varying from 5 to 20 miles. Severe earthquakes cause extensive damage when they take place in populated areas, destroying structures and severing communications. Most initial loss of life occurs due to secondary causes such as falling masonry, fires, and flooding.

Notable Earthquakes Since 1900

Year	Location	Mag.	Deaths
1906	San Francisco, USA	8.3	3,000
1906	Valparaiso, Chile	8.6	22,000
1908	Messina, Italy	7.5	83,000
1915	Avezzano, Italy	7.5	30,000
1920	Gansu (Kansu), China	8.6	180,000
1923	Yokohama, Japan	8.3	143,000
1927	Nan Shan, China	8.3	200,000
1932	Gansu (Kansu), China	7.6	70,000
1933	Sanriku, Japan	8.9	2,990
1934	Bihar, India/Nepal	8.4	10,700
1935	Quetta, India*	7.5	60,000
1939	Chillan, Chile	8.3	28,000
1939	Erzincan, Turkey	7.9	30,000
1960	S. W. Chile	9.5	2,200
1960	Agadir, Morocco	5.8	12,000
1962	Khorasan, Iran	7.1	12,230
1964	Anchorage, USA	9.2	125
1968	N. E. Iran	7.4	12,000
1970	N. Peru	7.8	70,000
1972	Managua, Nicaragua	6.2	5,000
1974	N. Pakistan	6.3	5,200
1976	Guatemala	7.5	22,500
1976	Tangshan, China	8.2	255,000
1978	Tabas, Iran	7.7	25,000
1980	El Asnam, Algeria	7.3	20,000
1980	S. Italy	7.2	4,800
1985	Mexico City, Mexico	8.1	4,200
1988	N.W. Armenia	6.8	55,000
1990	N. Iran	7.7	36,000
1993	Maharashtra, India	6.4	30,000
1994	Los Angeles, USA	6.6	51
1995	Kobe, Japan	7.2	5,000
1995	Sakhalin, Russia	7.5	2,000
1998	Takhar, Afghanistan	6.1	4,200
1998	Rostaq, Afghanistan	7.0	5,000
1999	Izmit, Turkey	7.4	15,000
1999	Taipei, Taiwan	7.6	1,700
2001	Gujarat, India	7.7	14,000
2003	Boumerdes, Algeria	6.8	2,200
2003	Bam, Iran	6.6	30,000
2004	Sumatra, Indonesia	9.0	250,000
2005	N. Pakistan	7.6	74,000
2006	Java, Indonesia	6.4	6,200
2007	S. Peru	8.0	600
2008	Sichuan, China	7.9	70,000
2010	Haiti	7.0	230,000
2011	Christchurch, NZ	6.3	182
2011	N. Japan	9.0	28,000

An earthquake off the coast of Sumatra on December 26, 2004, triggered a deadly tsunami that swept across the Indian Ocean, causing devastation in many countries, in particular Sri Lanka, India, Thailand, and Indonesia, where the loss of life was greatest.

* now Pakistan

For more information:

73 Tides
74 Plate tectonics
78 Atmosphere
84 Hydrological cycle
   Water distribution
85 Watersheds
103 World shipping

The last 40 years have been described as the "Space Age," but another exciting and perhaps even more important area of discovery, proceeding at the same time, has been the exploration of the oceans, which cover more than 70% of our planet. Studies of the ocean floor and oceanic islands have revealed features that help to explain how continents move, and how the movements are related to earthquakes and volcanic activity.

Manned submersibles have established that life exists even in the deepest trenches, where the pressure reaches 1,000 atmospheres, the equivalent of the force of 1 tonne bearing down on every square centimeter. Further exploration in the pitch-black environment of the ocean ridges has revealed strange forms of marine life around scalding hot vents. The creatures include giant tubeworms, blind shrimps, and bacteria, some of which are genetically very different from any other known life forms. In 1996, an analysis of one microorganism revealed that at least half of its 1,700 or so genes were hitherto unknown. This environment, which is based on chemicals, not sunlight, may resemble the places where life on Earth first began.

Another vital area of contemporary research concerns the interactions between the oceans and the atmosphere, as exemplified in the El Niño–Southern Oscillation (ENSO) cycle, and the bearing that these have on climatic change (see below).

Most geographers divide the world's ocean waters into five areas: the Pacific, Atlantic, Indian, Southern, and Arctic oceans. The most active zone in the oceans is the sunlit upper layer, where the water is moved around by wind-blown currents. It is the home of most sea life and acts as a membrane through which the ocean breathes,

ATOLL BUILDING

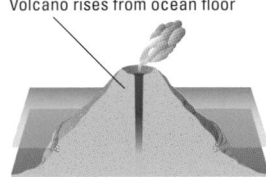

Volcano rises from ocean floor

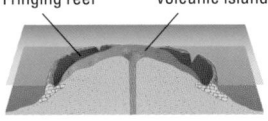

Fringing reef

Extinct, eroding volcanic island

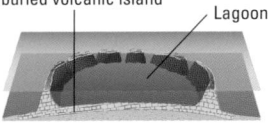

After subsidence, reef covers buried volcanic island

Lagoon

A coral atoll usually begins existence as a bare volcanic peak, thrusting above the surface of the ocean. A colony of coral – organisms with calcium carbonate skeletons – forms itself in the shallow water around the peak. The volcano is eroded and slowly sinks, leaving the coral forming a ring of hard limestone around its remnant. In time, the barrier reef of an atoll is all that remains.

LIFE IN THE OCEANS

An imaginary profile of the typical coastal and oceanic zones is shown, with a selection of the life forms that might occur in the waters off the Pacific Coast of Central America. The animals illustrated are not drawn to scale as the range of sizes is too great. Most marine life is confined to the first 650 feet, the upper sunlit (photic) zone, where sunlight can still penetrate. Plant and animal plankton, the basis of life in the oceans, occur in great quantities in all zones.

In the pelagic environment (open sea), vertical gradients, including those of light, temperature, and salinity, determine the distribution of organisms. From the tidal zone at the coastline, the continental shelf, geologically still part of the continental land mass, drops gently to about 650 feet – the sunlit zone. At the end of the shelf, the seabed falls away in the steeper angle of the continental slope. The subsequent descent to the deep-ocean floor, known as the "continental rise," is more gentle, with gradients between 1 in 100 and 1 in 700 until the abyssal plains and hills between 8,000 and 19,500 feet below the surface.

The deep-sea floor contains seamounts, some of which are capped by coral reefs, ocean ridges – the longest mountain chains on Earth – and deep-ocean trenches, especially in the Pacific Ocean where six trenches reach depths of more than 33,000 feet, including the Mariana Trench at 36,161 feet deep.

Each of these zones contains a distinctive community of species adapted to the different conditions of salinity, temperature, and light intensity. Indeed, a few organisms have been found even in the abyssal darkness of the great ocean trenches.

absorbing great quantities of carbon dioxide and partly exchanging it for oxygen.

As the depth increases, so light fades and temperatures fall until just before 3,000 feet where there is a marked temperature change at the thermocline, the boundary between the warm surface zone and the cold deep zone. Below the thermocline, slow currents are caused by density differences between bodies of water with varying temperatures and salinity.

Crab
Seaweed
Jellyfish
Anchovy
Green turtle
Dolphin
— SEA LEVEL

Marlin
Bonito
Snake eel
Blue Whale
— SUNLIT ZONE 650 feet

Phytoplankton and zooplankton
Lantern fish
— TWILIGHT ZONE 3,000 feet

Ray
Sperm whale

Deep-sea squid
— DARK ZONE 19,500 feet

Anglerfish

Halosaur

Sea cucumber
Sponge

— TRENCH ZONE 33,000 feet

Isopod

EL NIÑO PHENOMENON

Typical air and sea circulation pattern

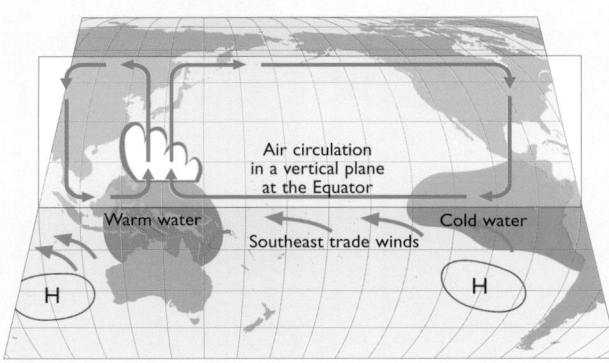

Air circulation in a vertical plane at the Equator

Warm water
Cold water
Southeast trade winds
H   H

El Niño air and sea circulation pattern

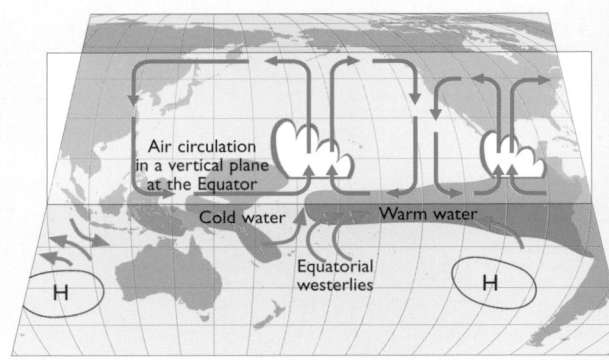

Air circulation in a vertical plane at the Equator

Cold water
Warm water
Equatorial westerlies
H   H

The importance of the ocean–atmosphere interaction is nowhere more dramatically demonstrated than in the El Niño phenomenon of the southern Pacific Ocean. Under normal conditions, called La Niña, cold, nutrient-rich water rises to the surface off South America and spreads westward. In the western Pacific, sea surface temperatures reach 82°F or more and warm air rises, creating a low-pressure air system and causing heavy rains. The rising air spreads out and some of it descends over South America and the eastern Pacific, creating a high-pressure air system from which winds blow westward.

An El Niño event is characterized by a reversal of currents. The upwelling of cold water is greatly reduced and surface water temperatures rise, causing a drastic reduction in fish life. The heaviest rainfall is over the eastern Pacific, while Southeast Asia is drier than usual. However, each El Niño event is unique in terms of its strength as well as its impact.

During an intense El Niño, the effects of the current and wind reversals affect the weather around the world. In the 1997 El Niño event there was a very suppressed hurricane season in the Caribbean but numerous super typhoons in the Pacific. Whilst South America and East Africa were much wetter than average, West Africa and parts of

Indonesia were much drier than normal. Algal blooms occurred in Australia's drought-stricken rivers and there were numerous bush fires in Indonesia.

Scientists have found evidence that the frequency of the El Niño event, which normally occurs every three to seven years, and lasts between 12–18 months, may have increased in recent years.

We do not fully understand the causes of the El Niño event, though some researchers are currently investigating possible connections between major volcanic eruptions in the tropical Pacific region, the El Niño Southern Oscillation (ENSO) cycle, and atmospheric circulation.

OCEAN CURRENTS

JANUARY CURRENTS
(Northern Hemisphere: winter)

Cold Warm Speed (knots)
— ← Less than 0.5
— ← 0.5 – 1.0
— ← Over 1.0

JULY CURRENTS
(Northern Hemisphere: summer)

Cold Warm Speed (knots)
— ← Less than 0.5
— ← 0.5 – 1.0
— ← Over 1.0

Moving immense quantities of energy as well as billions of tonnes of water every hour, the ocean currents are a vital part of the great heat engine that drives the Earth's climate. They themselves are produced by a twofold mechanism. At the surface, winds push huge masses of water before them; in the deep ocean below, an abrupt temperature gradient separates the churning surface waters from the still depths (see the ocean conveyor belt diagram, below left).

Coriolis effect
The pattern of circulation of the great surface currents is determined by the displacement known as the "Coriolis effect." As the Earth turns, the vast mass of ocean water is deflected to one side. The deflection is most obvious near the equator, where the Earth's surface is spinning eastward at 1,000 mph; currents moving poleward are curved clockwise in the northern hemisphere and counterclockwise in the southern hemisphere.

Ocean currents
The result is a system of spinning circles known as "gyres." Warm currents move constantly from the equator toward the poles, while cold water moves in the reverse direction. In this way, ocean currents act like a thermostat, helping to regulate temperatures around the world.
  Depending on the annual movements of the prevailing wind belts, some currents on or near the equator may reverse their direction in the course of the year, a variation on which Asia's monsoon rains depend and whose occasional failure has brought disaster to millions of people.

THE OCEAN CONVEYOR BELT

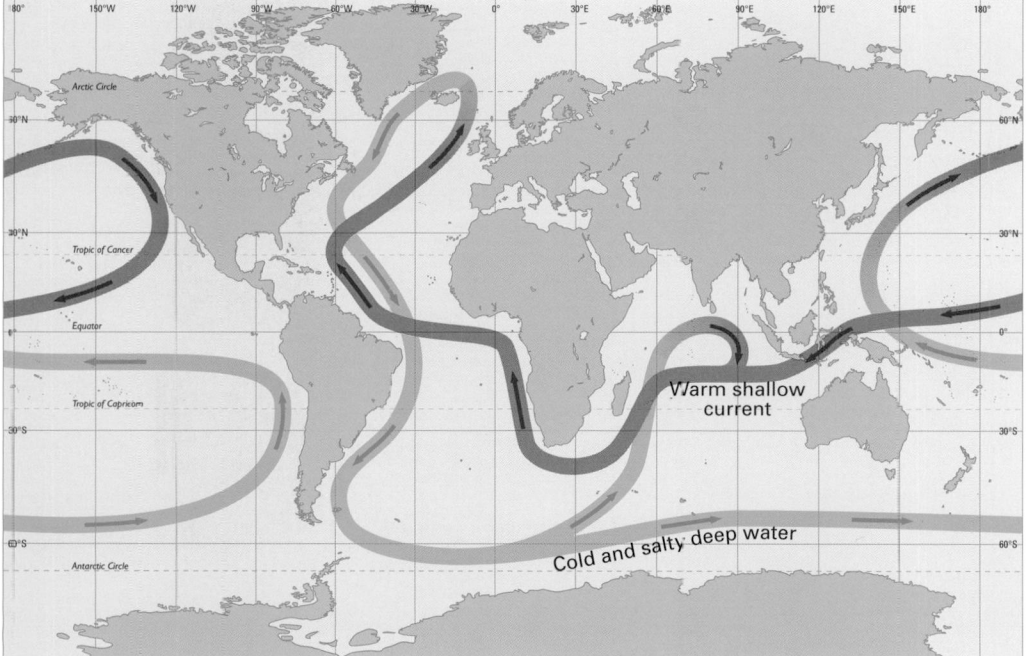

Thermohaline circulation, or the ocean conveyor belt, refers to the global, density-driven circulation of the oceans. The name comes from "thermo," for temperature, and "haline," for salt, which together determine the density of sea water.
  The cycle starts near the equator in the Pacific Ocean, where surface currents drive the water westward. This water is warm and not very salty, making it lightweight, so it travels along the surface of the ocean.

As the water progresses west it eventually works its way into the North Atlantic where it cools, increases in salinity and sinks. It slowly circulates southward then eastward toward the Antarctic, where it splits into two routes: one to the Indian Ocean and one into the Pacific.
  As the water recycles, it once again becomes warmer, less salty, lighter, and upwells in the Pacific to start the cycle all over again.

WORLD FISH CATCH

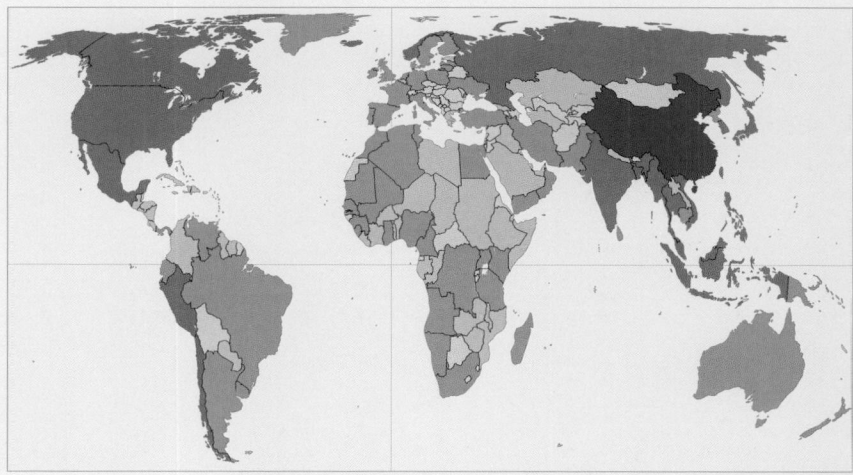

Total world fish catch in metric tonnes (2007)
(inland and marine fishing)

- Over 10 million
- 1 million – 10 million
- 100,000 – 1 million
- 10,000 – 100,000
- Under 10,000
- No data available

Leading fishing nations
(percentage of total world catch in 2007)

China 16.3%
Peru 9%
Indonesia 5.4%
USA 5.3%
Japan 4.7%
India 4.4%
Chile 4.2%

World total (2007): 90.1 million tonnes
(Marine catch 90.3% : Inland catch 9.7%)

With many marine stocks now fully exploited or over-exploited, future fish supplies are likely to be constrained by resource limits.

For more information:
76 El Niño phenomenon
77 Ocean currents
81 Beaufort wind scale
    Monsoon
82 Climate change
    Global warming

The atmosphere is a meteor shield, a radiation deflector, a thermal blanket, and a source of chemical energy for the Earth's diverse life forms. Five-sixths of its mass is in the lowest layer, the troposphere, which ranges in thickness from 11–6 miles between the equator and the poles. Powered by the Sun, the air is always on the move, flowing generally from high- to low-pressure areas. The troposphere is the layer where virtually all weather phenomena, including clouds, precipitation, and winds, occur. Above the troposphere is the stratosphere, which contains the important ozone layer and extends to about 30 miles above the Earth's surface. Beyond 60 miles, atmospheric density is lower than most laboratory vacuums.

STRUCTURE OF THE ATMOSPHERE

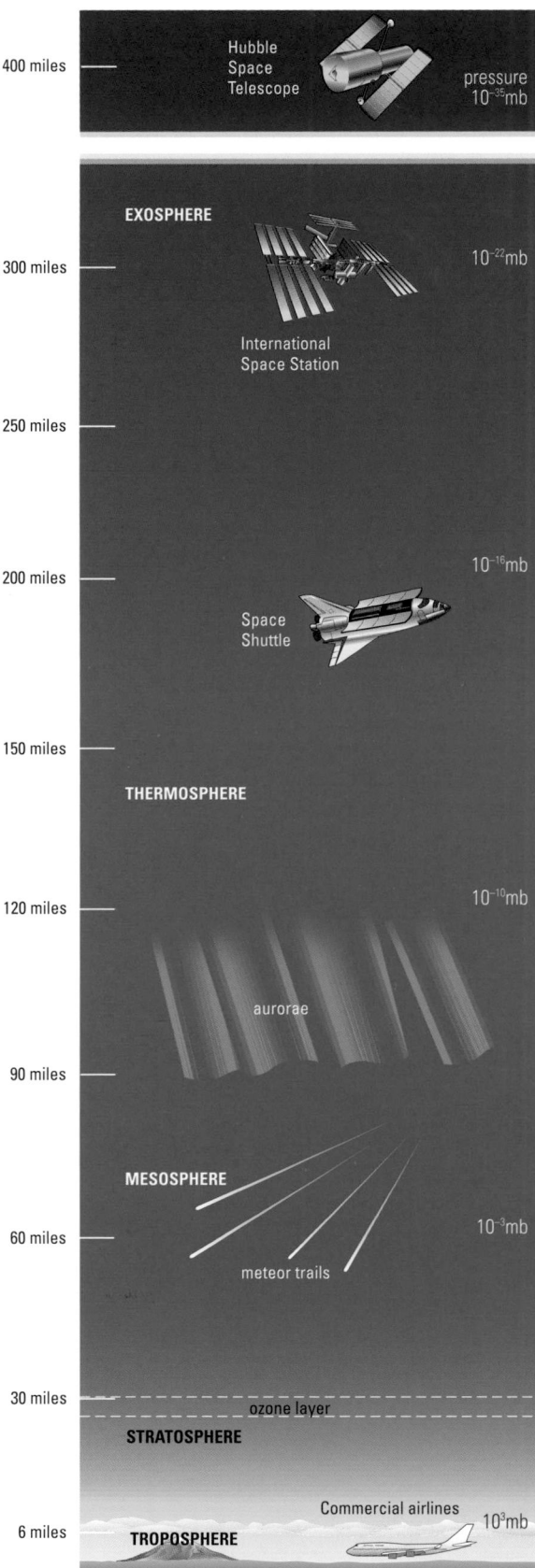

CIRCULATION OF THE AIR

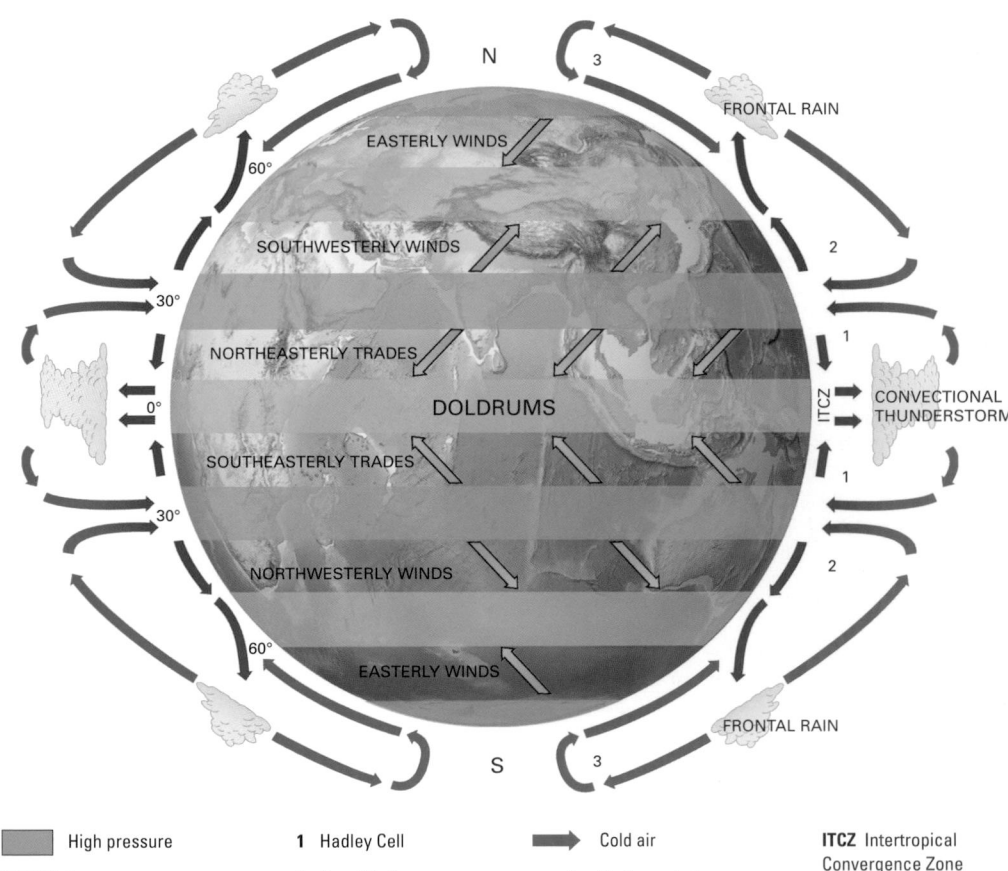

■ High pressure	**1** Hadley Cell	➡ Cold air
■ Low pressure	**2** Ferrel Cell	➡ Surface winds
➡ Warm air	**3** Polar Cell	☁ Clouds

ITCZ Intertropical Convergence Zone

FRONTAL SYSTEMS

Depressions, also known as cyclones or lows, form on the polar front where relatively cold and dry polar air flows alongside warmer, moister subtropical air. They occur when the flow high above the polar front generates a surface inward-swirling circulation that moves along the polar front as a wave.

The warm front is the leading edge of the subtropical air that glides up and over the cooler air ahead of it. This gently ascending flow produces a characteristic sequence of clouds ahead of the warm front and a band of precipitation a few hundred miles wide immediately in advance of it. Conditions within the warm sector are often overcast with layer cloud and generally light rain or drizzle. The cloud sometimes breaks up downwind of hills.

Another band of precipitation often occurs just ahead of the cold front that is the leading edge of the cooler polar air. Cumulus clouds tend to occur in the air behind the cold front, producing scattered showers. The changes of temperature, wind direction, and cloud, etc, are illustrated by the diagram below.

CHEMICAL COMPOSITION

Gaseous composition of the principal atmospheric layers

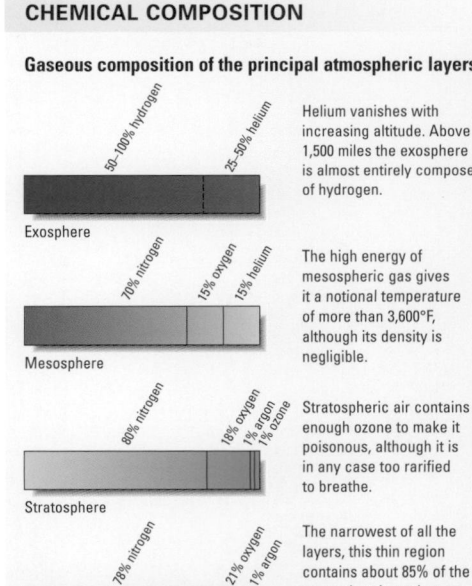

Helium vanishes with increasing altitude. Above 1,500 miles the exosphere is almost entirely composed of hydrogen.

The high energy of mesospheric gas gives it a notional temperature of more than 3,600°F, although its density is negligible.

Stratospheric air contains enough ozone to make it poisonous, although it is in any case too rarified to breathe.

The narrowest of all the layers, this thin region contains about 85% of the atmosphere's total mass and almost all of its water vapor. It is also the realm of the Earth's weather.

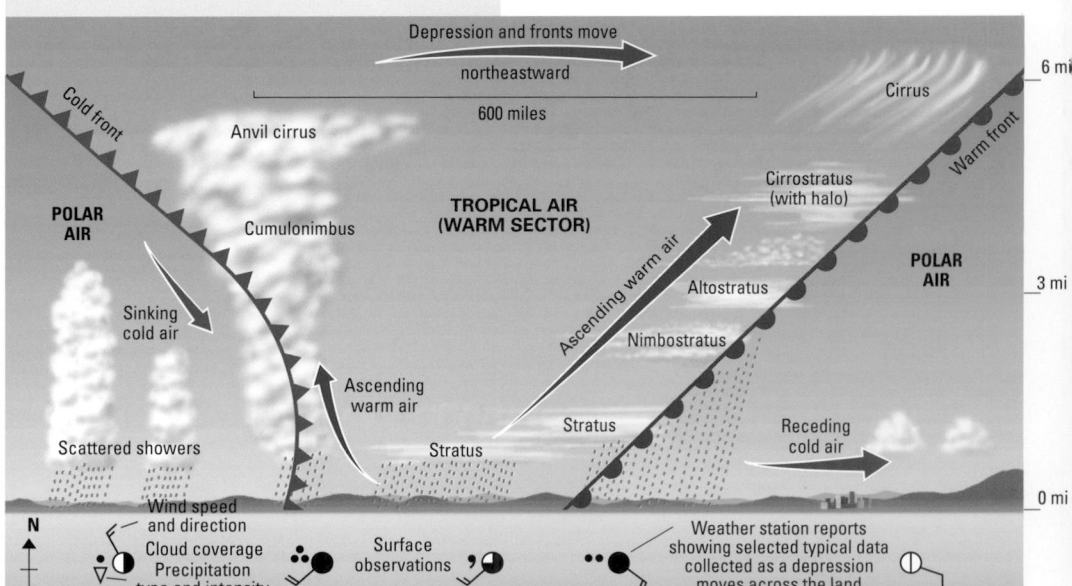

AIR MASSES

Air masses are extensive regions of air, typically a few thousand miles across, that have horizontally gently varying temperature and humidity characteristics produced by the underlying continental or maritime surfaces over which they occur. They can, for example, be warm and moist air or cold and dry air that spiral slowly out from their "source regions." These are the highs marked on the world maps below.

A particular location's weather associated with an air mass depends on the air's source region (for example, the North Atlantic subtropical high), the track it has taken (for example, long maritime or continental track), and the time of year (for example, across a cold or strongly heated continent). The polar front (and its frontal cyclones) is a gently sloping, troposphere-deep surface that separates two air masses – the North Atlantic subtropical high and the North American wintertime anticyclone. The warmer, damper subtropical air rides up and over the cooler, drier polar air to produce widespread frontal cloud and precipitation.

Air masses are classified as, amongst others, "polar continental," "polar maritime" or "tropical maritime." The massive Asian high in January is a source of polar continental, very cold, very dry air, while in contrast the extensive North Pacific and North Atlantic highs are sources of warm and very moist air throughout the year.

CLASSIFICATION OF CLOUDS

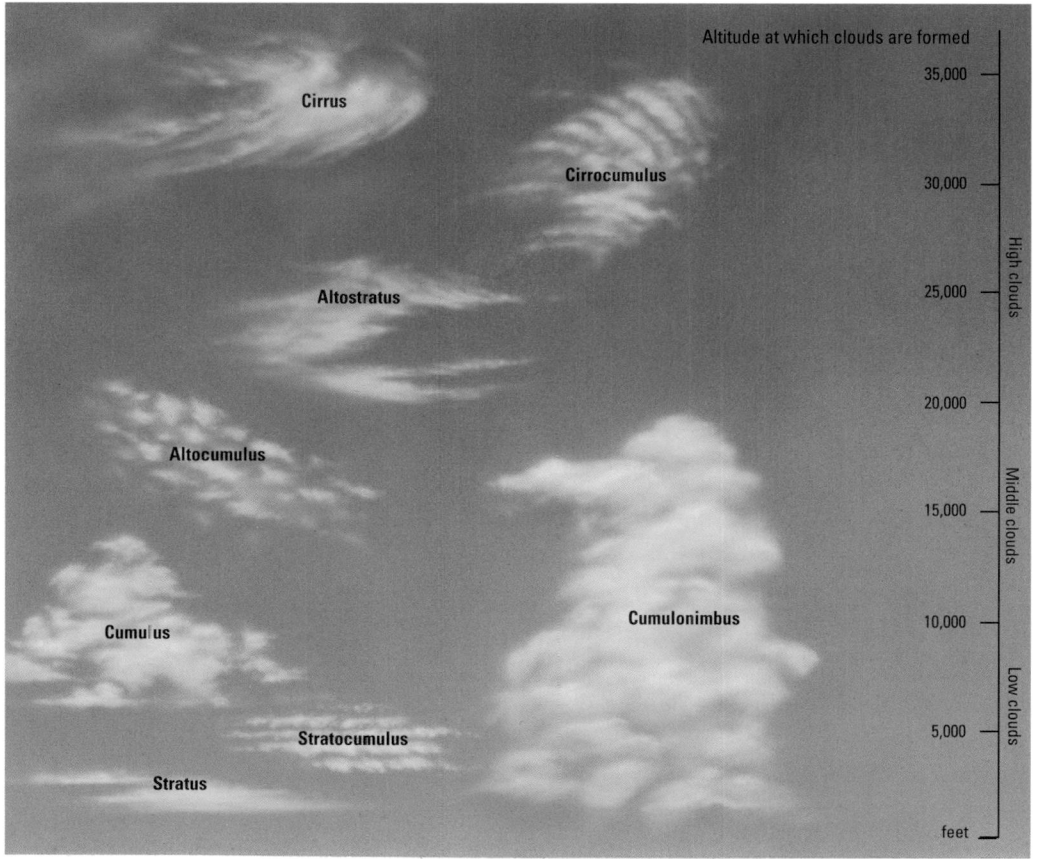

Clouds form when damp, usually rising, air is cooled. Thus they form when a wind rises to cross hills or mountains; when a mass of air rises over, or is pushed up by, another mass of denser air; or when local heating of the ground causes convection currents.

The first classification of clouds was developed by a London chemist, Luke Howard, in 1803, and it was later modified by the World Meteorological Organization. The types of clouds are classified according to altitude as high, middle, or low. The high ones, composed of ice crystals, are cirrus, cirrostratus, and cirrocumulus.

The middle clouds are altostratus – a gray or bluish striated, fibrous or uniform sheet producing light drizzle – and altocumulus, a thicker and fluffier version of cirrocumulus.

Low clouds include nimbostratus, a dark gray layer that brings rain or snow; cumulus, a detached heap, dark at the base; stratus, which forms dull, overcast skies at low levels; and stratocumulus, which consists of fluffy grayish-white layers.

Cumulonimbus, associated with storms and rains, heavy and dense with a flat base and a high, fluffy outline, can be tall enough to occupy middle as well as low altitudes.

PRESSURE AND SURFACE WINDS

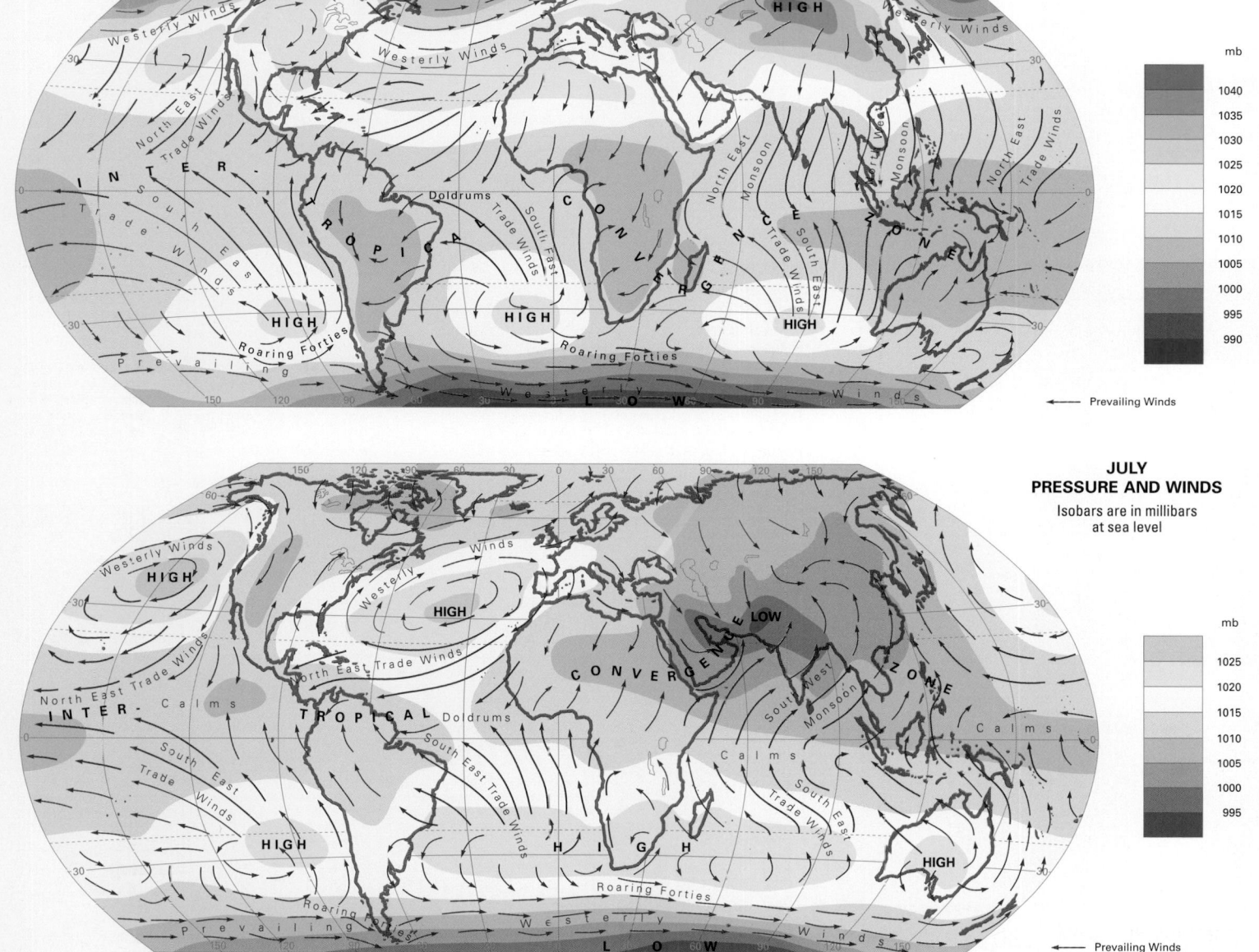

JANUARY PRESSURE AND WINDS
Isobars are in millibars at sea level

JULY PRESSURE AND WINDS
Isobars are in millibars at sea level

← Prevailing Winds

WEATHER RECORDS

Pressure and winds

Highest barometric pressure:
Agata, Siberia, 1,083.8 mb at altitude 862 ft [262 m], December 31, 1968.

Lowest barometric pressure:
Typhoon Tip, 300 mi [480 km] west of Guam, Pacific Ocean, 870 mb, October 12, 1979.

Highest recorded wind speed:
Bridge Creek, Oklahoma, USA, 318 mph [512 km/h], May 3, 1999. Measured by Doppler radar monitoring a tornado.

Windiest place:
Port Martin, Antarctica, where winds of more than 40 mph [64 km/h] occur for not less than 100 days a year.

Worst recorded storm:
Bangladesh (then East Pakistan) cyclone, November 13, 1970 – over 300,000 dead or missing. The 1991 cyclone, Bangladesh's and the world's second worst in terms of loss of life, killed an estimated 138,000 people.

Worst recorded tornado:
Tri-state tornado – Missouri/Illinois/ Indiana, USA, March 18, 1925 – 695 deaths, lasted 3 hours with 219 mi [352 km] path length. A suspected tornado in Bangladesh on April 26, 1989, killed approximately 1,300 people.

For more information:

77 Ocean currents
78 Circulation of the air
79 Classification of
   clouds
   Pressure and winds
82 Climate change
   Global warming
84 Hydrological cycle
85 Natural vegetation

Weather is the day-to-day or hour-to-hour condition of the air, while climate is weather in the long term – the seasonal pattern of hot and cold, wet and dry, averaged over a long period.

Most classifications of climate are based on a system developed in the early 19th century by Vladimir Köppen, a Russian meteorologist. Using a code based on letters and a classification centered on two main features, temperature and precipitation, he identified five main climatic types: tropical (A), dry (B), warm temperate (C), cold temperate (D), and polar (E). A highland mountain climate (H) was added later to account for the variety of altitudinal climatic zones on high mountains. Each of these main regions was then further subdivided.

Latitude is a major factor in determining climate, but other factors add to the complexity. These include the differential heating of land and sea, the distance from the sea, the effect of mountains on winds, and the influence of ocean currents. For example, New York City, Naples, and the Gobi Desert share almost the same latitude, but their climates are very different.

During the last Ice Age, the Earth underwent alternating cold periods, called glacials, separated by warm interglacials. The Milankovich theory suggests such cycles may be caused by variations in the Earth's path around the Sun, changing from almost circular to elliptical every 95,000 years, and variations in the Earth's tilt from 21.5° to 24.5° every 42,000 years. Another factor is that the Earth is now closest to the Sun in the middle of winter in the northern hemisphere and furthest away in summer. But 12,000 years ago, at the height of the last glacial period, the northern winter fell with the Sun at its most distant.

Studies of these cycles suggest that we are now in an interglacial with a new glacial period on the way. However, scientists believe that global warming, largely a result of burning fossil fuels and deforestation, may be occurring much faster than the great, slow cycles of the Solar System.

Tropical rainy climates
All mean monthly temperatures above 64°F.

Af Rain forest climate
Am Monsoon climate
Aw Savanna climate

Dry climates
Low rainfall combined with a wide range of temperatures

BS Steppe climate
BW Desert climate

Warm temperate rainy climates
The mean temperature is below 64°F but above 26°F and that of the warmest month is over 50°F.

Cw Dry winter climate
Cs Dry summer climate
Cf Climate with no dry season

Cold temperate rainy climates
The mean temperature of the coldest month is below 26°F but that of the warmest month is still over 50°F.

Dw Dry winter climate
Df Climate with no dry season

Polar climates
The mean temperature of the warmest month is below 50°F, giving permanently frozen subsoil.

ET Tundra climate

The mean temperature of the warmest month is below 32°F, giving permanent ice and snow.

EF Polar climate

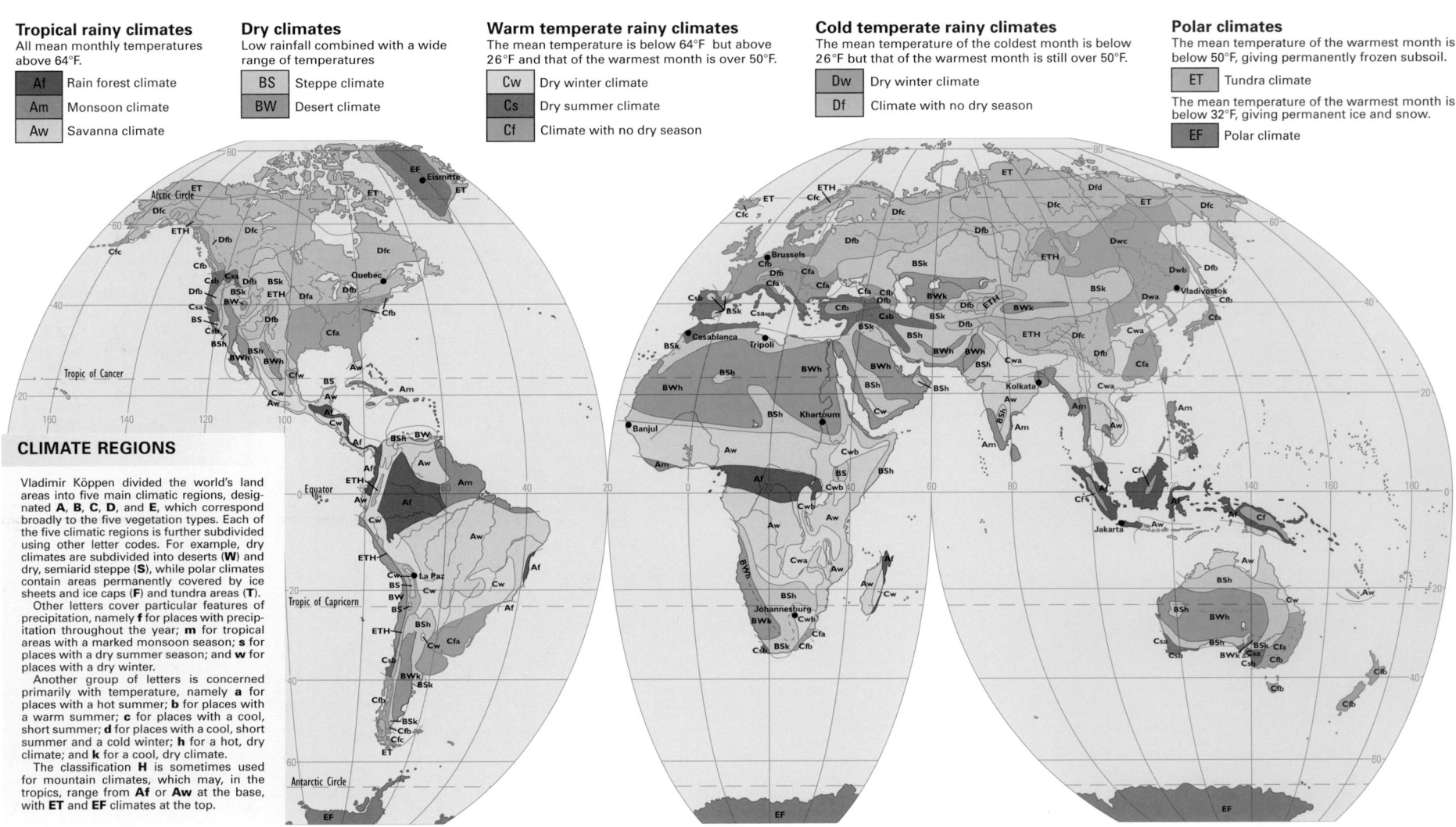

CLIMATE REGIONS

Vladimir Köppen divided the world's land areas into five main climatic regions, designated **A**, **B**, **C**, **D**, and **E**, which correspond broadly to the five vegetation types. Each of the five climatic regions is further subdivided using other letter codes. For example, dry climates are subdivided into deserts (**W**) and dry, semiarid steppe (**S**), while polar climates contain areas permanently covered by ice sheets and ice caps (**F**) and tundra areas (**T**).

Other letters cover particular features of precipitation, namely **f** for places with precipitation throughout the year; **m** for tropical areas with a marked monsoon season; **s** for places with a dry summer season; and **w** for places with a dry winter.

Another group of letters is concerned primarily with temperature, namely **a** for places with a hot summer; **b** for places with a warm summer; **c** for places with a cool, short summer; **d** for places with a cool, short summer and a cold winter; **h** for a hot, dry climate; and **k** for a cool, dry climate.

The classification **H** is sometimes used for mountain climates, which may, in the tropics, range from **Af** or **Aw** at the base, with **ET** and **EF** climates at the top.

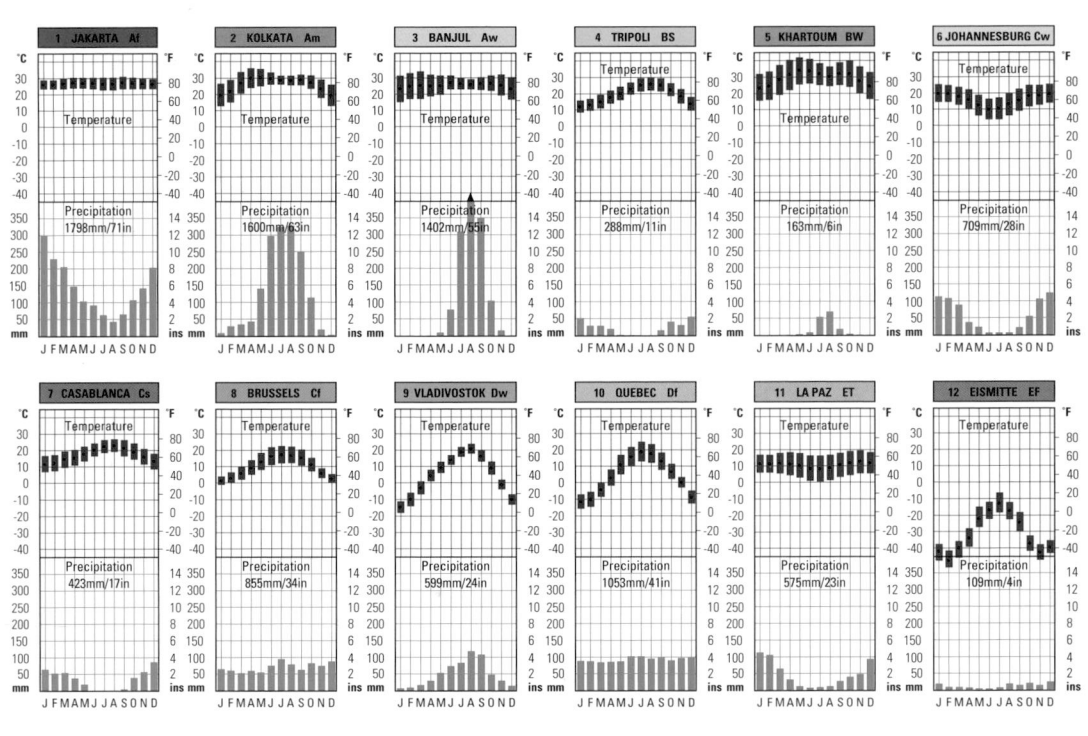

CLIMATE AND WEATHER TERMS

Anticyclone: area of high pressure with light winds and generally quiet weather.
Absolute humidity: mass of water vapor contained in a given volume of air.
Cloud cover: amount of cloud in the sky; measured in oktas (from 0–9), with 0 clear, and 9 "sky obscured."
Condensation: the conversion of water vapor into liquid.
Cyclone: violent storm resulting from counterclockwise rotation of winds in the northern hemisphere and clockwise in the southern; called hurricane in North America, typhoon in the Far East.
Depression: large area of low barometric pressure, a few thousand miles across.
Dew: deposition of small water droplets on the Earth's surface by direct condensation of water vapor.
Dew point: the temperature at which air becomes saturated by cooling at constant barometric pressure and absolute humidity.
Drizzle: precipitation drops between 0.01–0.02 inches [0.2 and 0.5 mm] in diameter.
Evaporation: conversion of water from liquid into vapor or moisture in the air.
Front: the dividing line between two air masses.
Frost: the surface deposition of water vapor as minute ice crystals, when temperature reaches the frost point.

Hail: variably-sized pieces of ice that fall in downdrafts from cumulonimbus clouds.
Humidity: amount of water vapor in the air.
Isobar: line joining places with the same barometric pressure.
Isotherm: line connecting places of equal temperature.
Lightning: massive electrical discharge released in thunderstorm from cloud to cloud or cloud to ground, the result of the top becoming positively charged and the bottom negatively charged.
Precipitation: measurable rain, snow, sleet, or hail.
Prevailing wind: most common direction of wind at a given location.
Rain: precipitation of liquid particles with diameter larger than 0.02 inches [0.5 mm].
Relative humidity: observed quantity of water vapor in a mass of air over the saturation value at a given temperature (as a percentage).
Snow: flake-like coagulations of ice crystals that fall from clouds in subzero temperatures.
Thunder: sound produced by the rapid expansion of air heated by lightning.
Tornado: rapidly-rotating funnel-shaped cloud or debris column that must reach the surface and be attached to a parent cumulonimbus cloud.

BEAUFORT WIND SCALE

Named after Admiral Sir Francis Beaufort, the 19th-century British naval officer who devised it, the Beaufort Scale assesses wind speed according to its effects. It was originally designed as an aid for sailors, but has since been adapted for use on the land. It is used internationally.

Scale	Wind speed		Effect
	mph	km/h	
0	0–1	0–1	**Calm**
			Smoke rises vertically
1	1–3	1–5	**Light air**
			Wind direction shown only by
			smoke drift
2	4–7	6–11	**Light breeze**
			Wind felt on face; leaves rustle;
			vanes moved by wind
3	8–12	12–19	**Gentle breeze**
			Leaves and small twigs in constant
			motion; wind extends small flag
4	13–18	20–28	**Moderate**
			Raises dust and loose paper;
			small branches move
5	19–24	29–38	**Fresh**
			Small trees in leaf sway; crested
			wavelets on inland waters
6	25–31	39–49	**Strong**
			Large branches move; difficult to
			use umbrellas; overhead wires
			whistle
7	32–38	50–61	**Near gale**
			Whole trees in motion; difficult
			to walk against wind
8	39–46	62–74	**Gale**
			Twigs break from trees; walking
			very difficult
9	47–54	75–88	**Strong gale**
			Slight structural damage
10	55–63	89–102	**Storm**
			Trees uprooted; serious structural
			damage
11	64–72	103–117	**Violent storm**
			Widespread damage
12	73+	118+	**Hurricane**

▲ On September 14, 2003, Hurricane Isabel was located over the Atlantic Ocean, 400 miles [640 km] north of Puerto Rico. It moved in a northwestward direction with maximum winds of 155 mph [250 km/h], making it a Category 5 hurricane.

THE MONSOON

Monsoon is the term given to the seasonal reversal of wind direction, most noticeably in Southeast Asia. It results from a combination of factors: the extreme heating and cooling of large land masses in relation to the less marked changes in temperature of the adjacent seas; the northward movement of the Intertropical Convergence Zone (ITCZ); and the effect of the Himalayas on the circulation of the air.

In March, winds blow outward from the mainland. But as the Sun and the ITCZ move northward, the land is intensely heated, and a low-pressure system develops. The southeast trade winds change direction and are sucked into the interior to become southwesterlies, bringing heavy rain. By November, the Sun and the ITCZ have again moved south and the wind directions are again reversed. Cool winds blow from the Asian interior to the sea, losing any moisture on the Himalayas before descending to the coast.

TEMPERATURE

Average temperature in January

Average temperature

- 86°F
- 68°F
- 50°F
- 32°F
- 14°F
- −4°F
- −22°F
- −40°F

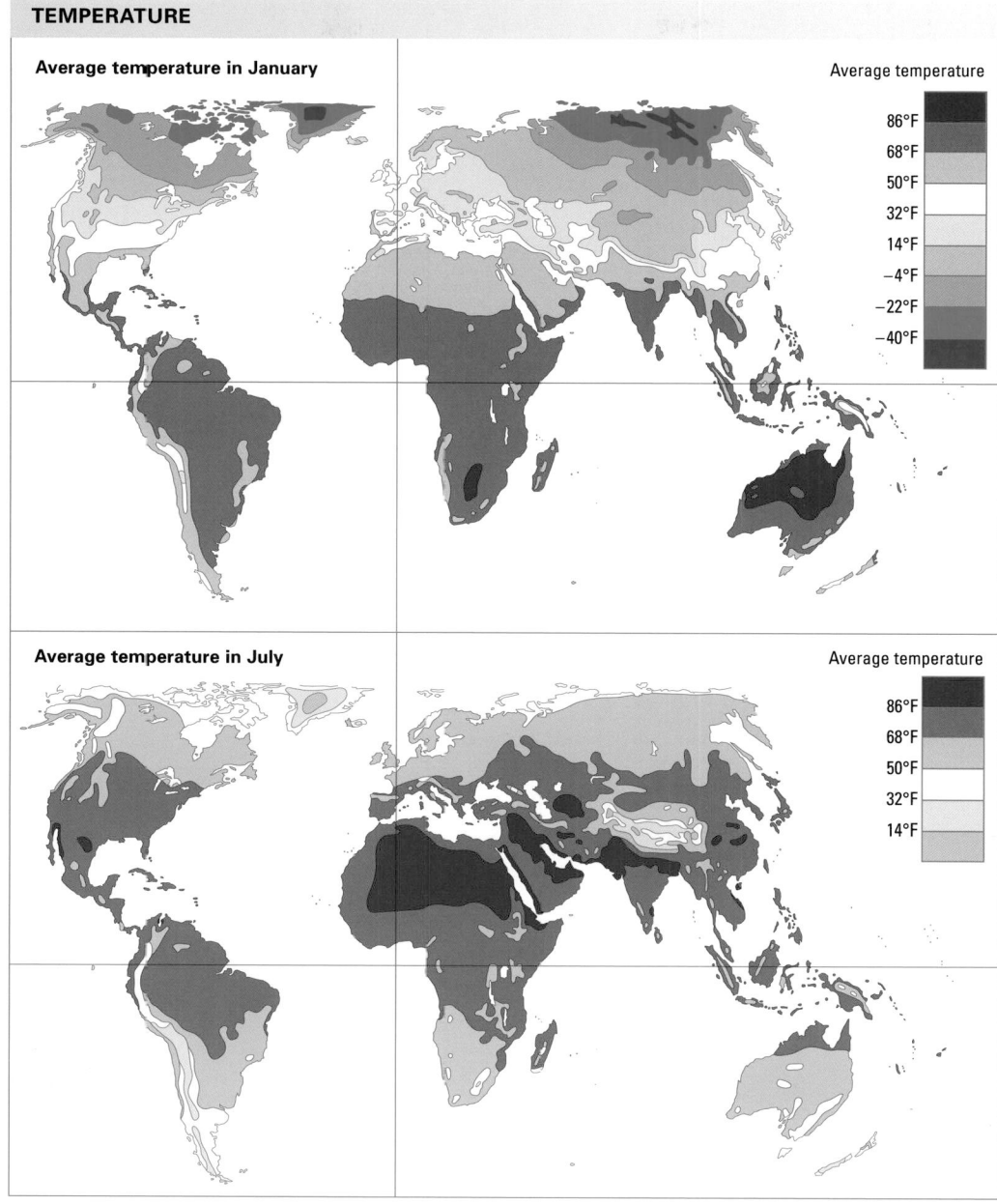

Average temperature in July

Average temperature

- 86°F
- 68°F
- 50°F
- 32°F
- 14°F

PRECIPITATION (RAINFALL AND SNOW)

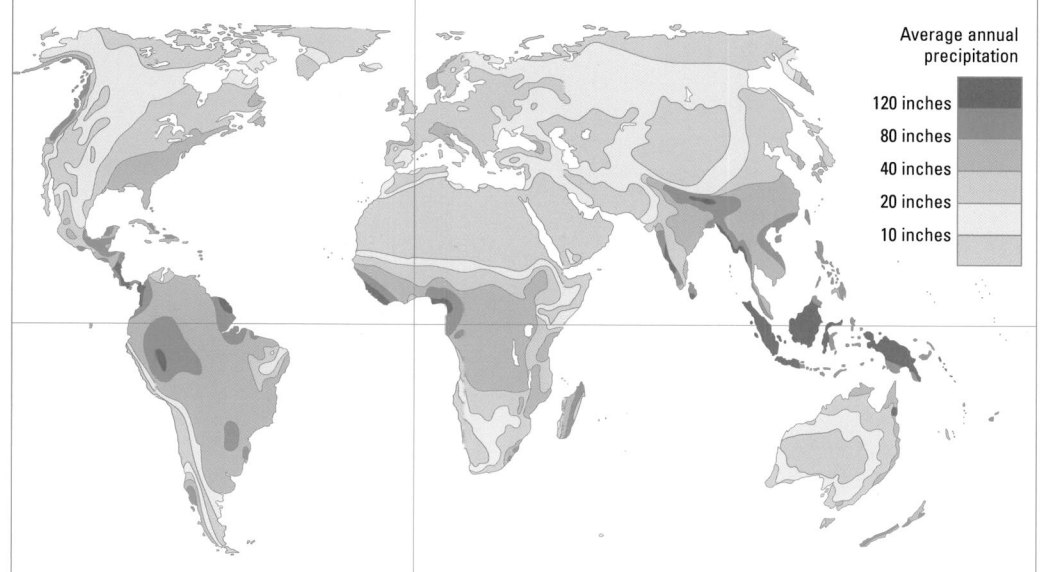

Average annual precipitation

- 120 inches
- 80 inches
- 40 inches
- 20 inches
- 10 inches

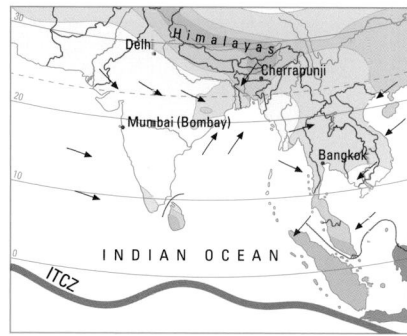

March – Start of the hot, dry season. The ITCZ is over the southern Indian Ocean.

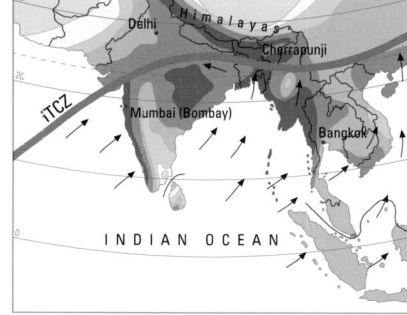

July – The rainy season. The ITCZ has migrated northward; winds blow onshore.

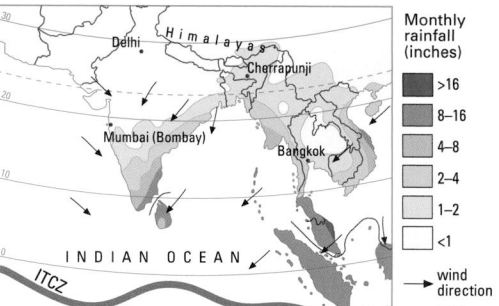

November – The ITCZ has returned south. The offshore winds are cool and dry.

Monthly rainfall (inches)

- >16
- 8–16
- 4–8
- 2–4
- 1–2
- <1

→ wind direction
— ITCZ

CLIMATE RECORDS

TEMPERATURE

Highest recorded temperature:
Al Aziziyah, Libya, 135.9°F [57.7°C], September 13, 1922.

Highest mean annual temperature:
Dallol, Ethiopia, 94°F [34.4°C], 1960–6.

Longest heatwave:
Marble Bar, W. Australia, 162 days over 100°F [38°C], October 23, 1923, to April 7, 1924.

Lowest recorded temperature (outside poles):
Verkhoyansk, Siberia, −93.6°F [−69.8°C], February 7, 1982. Verkhoyansk also registered the greatest annual range of temperature: −90°F to 98°F [−68°C to 37°C].

Lowest mean annual temperature:
Polus Nedostupnosti, Pole of Cold, Antarctica, −72°F [−57.8°C].

PRECIPITATION

Driest place:
Quillagua, N. Chile, mean annual rainfall 0.02 inches [0.5 mm], 1964–2001.

Wettest place (average):
Mt Wai'ale'ale, Hawai'i, USA, mean annual rainfall 459.8 inches [11,680 mm].

Wettest place (12 months):
Cherrapunji, Meghalaya, N.E. India, 1,042 inches [26,461 mm], August 1860 to August 1861. Cherrapunji also holds the record for rainfall in one month: 115 inches [2,930 mm], July 1861. (*See Monsoon maps below.*)

Wettest place (24 hours):
Fac Fac, Réunion, Indian Ocean, 71.9 inches [1,825 mm], March 15–16, 1952.

Heaviest hailstones:
Gopalganj, Bangladesh, up to 2.25 lb [1.02 kg], April 14, 1986 (killed 92 people).

Heaviest snowfall (continuous):
Bessans, Savoie, France, 68 inches [1,730 mm] in 19 hours, April 5–6. 1969.

Heaviest snowfall (season/year):
Mt Baker, Washington, USA, 1,140 inches [28,956 mm], June 1998 to June 1999.

For more information:

77 Ocean currents

78 Atmosphere

80 Climate

Ever since the Industrial Revolution began, the amount of carbon dioxide in the atmosphere has steadily increased. It is the result of burning fossil fuels – coal, oil, and natural gas, and also the destruction of forests which absorb carbon dioxide. In the late 18th century, carbon dioxide made up about 280 parts per million by volume (ppmv). Since 1958, regular measurements have been made at the Mauna Kea Observatory, Hawai'i, to avoid local pollution. It has since risen from 316 ppmv to 387 ppmv in 2008.

Carbon dioxide is one of the "greenhouse gases," which also include CFCs (which also cause ozone depletion in the upper atmosphere), methane, and nitrous oxides. Water vapor is another greenhouse gas. The volume of vapor in the atmosphere is not changing significantly, though it may increase if the atmosphere warms up, causing an increase in the evaporation of surface waters.

Greenhouse gases are so-called because they slow the escape of heat that is reradiated from the Earth's surface, in much the same way the glass walls and roof of a greenhouse block the escape of heat. The greenhouse effect is essential for life on Earth. Without it, our planet would be some 54°F [30°C] colder than it is. But the increase in the volume of carbon dioxide in particular has caused global temperatures to rise. These changes were detailed by the Intergovernmental Panel on Climate Change (IPCC) report in 2007. While computer projections are difficult to make, the IPCC report concluded that a rise in temperatures of 7°F [4°C] was likely by 2100. Global warming will almost certainly alter weather patterns, causing extreme food and water shortages in vulnerable parts of the world, massive floods, and a rise in sea levels of between 7 inches and 23 inches [18–59 cm].

While an international ban has been imposed on some greenhouse gases, their residence time in the atmosphere may have long-lasting consequences.

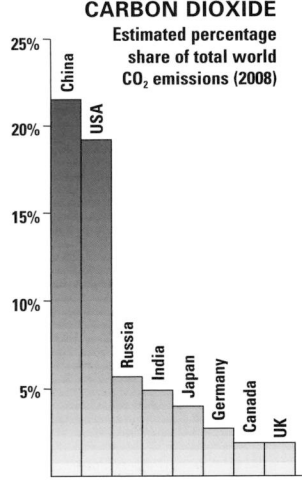

CARBON DIOXIDE

Estimated percentage share of total world CO_2 emissions (2008)

In 2007 it was estimated that China was building two coal-fired power stations every week to support its economic boom. It has since overtaken the USA to become the world's biggest producer of carbon dioxide.

GLOBAL WARMING

High atmospheric concentrations of heat-absorbing gases appear to be causing a rise in average temperatures worldwide – up by approximately 3°F [1.5°C] by the year 2020, according to some estimates. Global warming is also likely to bring about a rise in sea levels that may flood some of the world's densely populated coastal areas.

Evidence of global warming is attributed mainly to the "greenhouse effect," caused by the emission of certain gases, notably carbon dioxide, into the atmosphere. Despite international action to control emissions of some greenhouse gases, carbon dioxide levels are still rising.

Carbon dioxide emissions in tonnes per capita (2008)

Over 15

10 – 15

5 – 10

1 – 5

Under 1

No data available

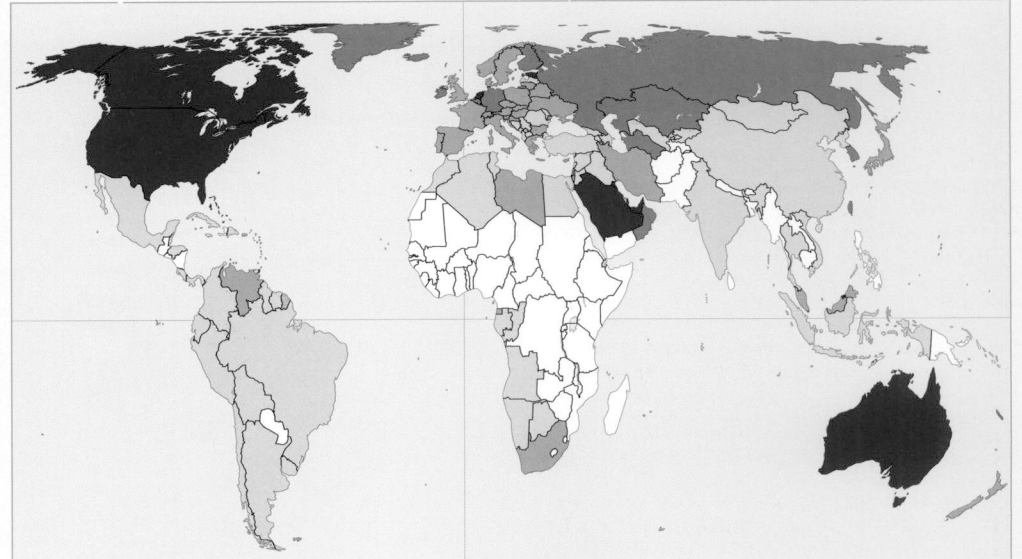

CLIMATE CHANGE

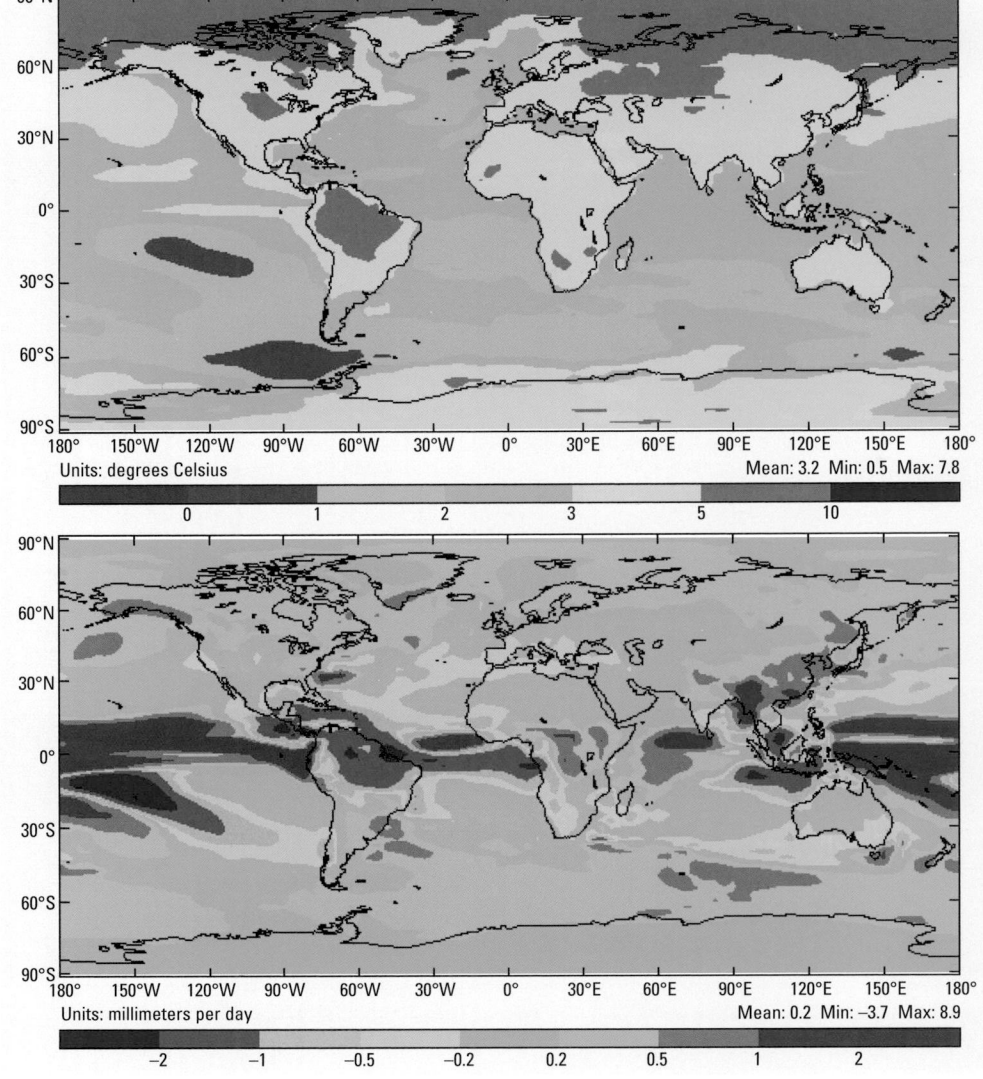

Units: degrees Celsius   Mean: 3.2 Min: 0.5 Max: 7.8

0   1   2   3   5   10

Units: millimeters per day   Mean: 0.2 Min: -3.7 Max: 8.9

-2   -1   -0.5 -0.2   0.2   0.5   1   2

Annual average surface air temperature

The map summarizes the change in long-term mean values between the predicted average for the period from 2070 to 2100, and the observed average for 1960 to 1990. The predictions are from a long-term "run" of a "coupled" atmosphere-ocean computer model that represents the complex processes in the Earth's climate system. It assumes that the atmospheric concentration of carbon dioxide will increase more than twofold during the 21st century, assuming "medium growth" of the global economy, and that no measures to combat the emission of greenhouse gases are taken. Note that the predicted increase in average surface temperature suggests a warming across Britain and Ireland of between 2°C [3.6°F] in the north and west to possibly 4°C [7.2°F] in the southeast. Very broadly, the oceans and some adjacent continental areas are likely to see the smaller increases.

Annual average precipitation

Predictions from climate models always involve some degree of uncertainty. This is because our understanding of the climate system and its complex workings are imperfect, as are the model representations of the physical system. Additionally, we are unsure quite how the world will evolve economically and politically over the coming decades – although different scenarios are used in this regard. The map of predicted precipitation change indicates broadly, for example, an increase across Britain and Ireland. The largest increases of some 0.01–0.02 inches [0.2–0.5 mm] a day are anticipated to be over northern and western areas. This equates to some 3–7 inches [75–180 mm] a year.

It should be noted that both these maps mask quite significant seasonal detail, which is also predicted by the models.

ANTARCTICA

► Between January and March 2002, the 1,255 sq mi [3,250 sq km] Larsen B ice shelf on the Antarctic Peninsula collapsed. The left-hand image shows its area (in blue) in December 2001 before the collapse, while the right-hand image shows the area fragmented in December 2002 after the collapse. The 656 ft [200 m] thick ice sheet had been retreating before this date, but over 500 billion tonnes of ice collapsed in under a month. This was due to rising temperatures of 0.9°F [0.5°C] per year in this part of Antarctica.

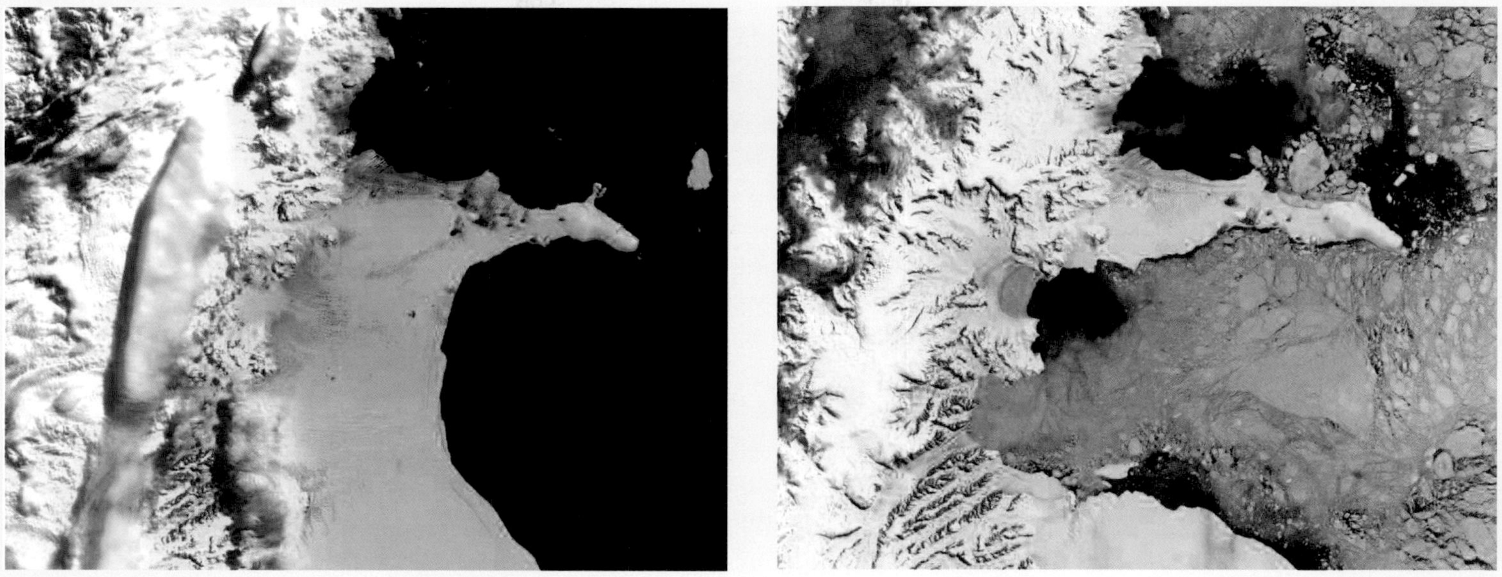

TEMPERATURE CHANGE

Climate modelers have produced simulations of global and continental surface temperature changes over the last century. This is done using only "natural forcing" by modeling the impact on atmospheric temperatures from known solar variability and volcanic eruptions. In addition, the same period of time is simulated by adding to natural forcing the impact of anthropogenic (human) influence due to measured changes in the concentration of greenhouse gases, particulate matter, etc.

The separate model "runs" are then compared with the observed temperature changes to illustrate which of the simulations matches the observations best.

This is a powerful means of verifying the relative roles of natural and human induced changes in atmospheric composition, and known solar output fluctuations on climate change.

► Climate model simulations for 1906 to 2005 using "natural forcings only" (blue bands) and "natural plus anthropogenic forcings" (pink bands). Regional decadal averages of observed temperature (black lines) are plotted as anomalies with respect to the 1901 to 1950 average. Blue and pink bands define the 5% to 95% range of possibilities for 19 runs produced by five models (natural forcing), and 58 simulations from 14 models (natural plus anthropogenic forcing).

Models using only natural forcings

Models using both natural and anthropogenic forcings

Observations
(dashed when spatial coverage is less than 50%)

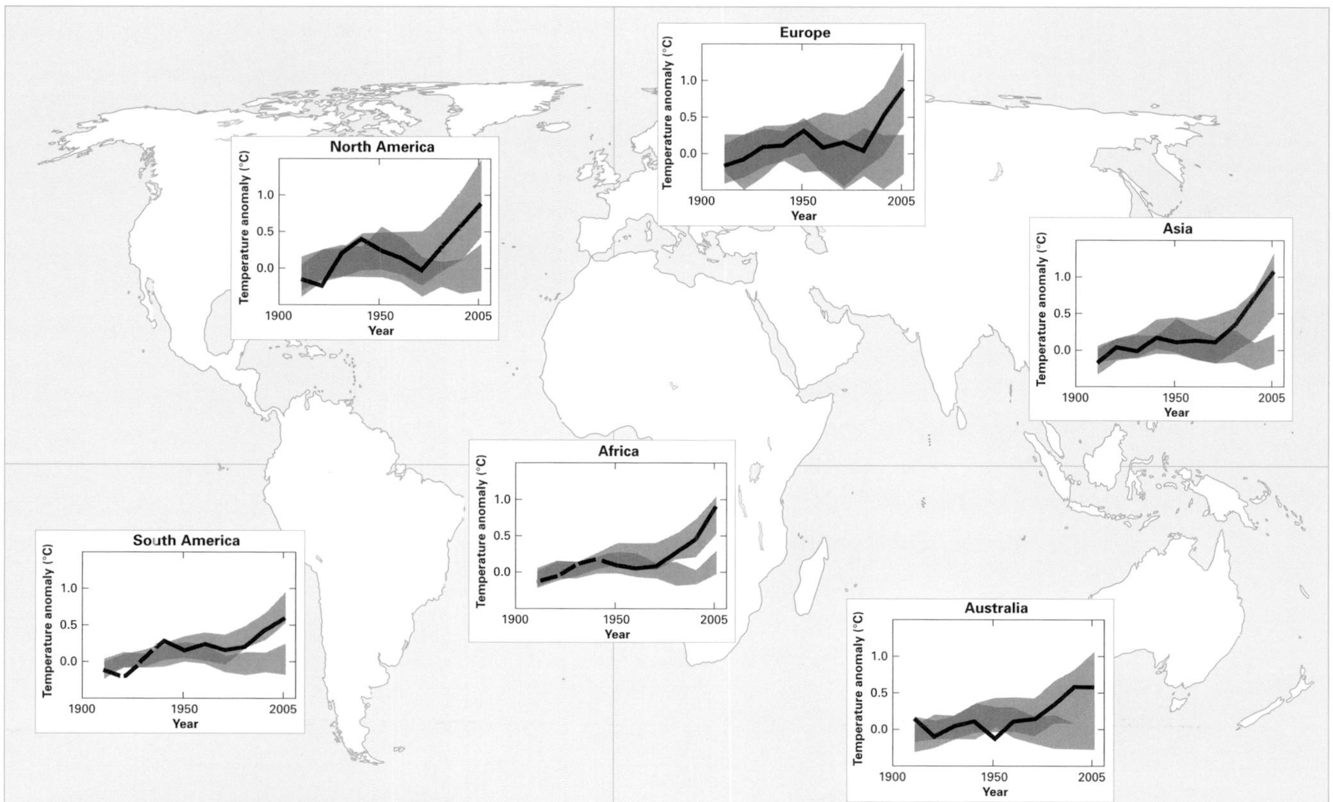

Europe
North America
Asia
Africa
South America
Australia
Temperature anomaly (°C)
1.0
0.5
0.0
1900
1950
2005
Year

Source: Intergovernmental Panel on Climate Change (IPCC)

PROJECTED CHANGE IN GLOBAL WARMING

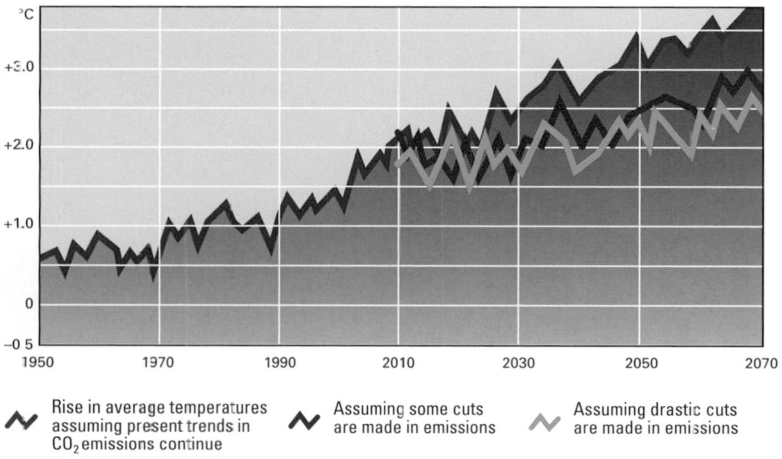

°C
+3.0
+2.0
+1.0
0
–0.5
1950
1970
1990
2010
2030
2050
2070
Rise in average temperatures assuming present trends in CO_2 emissions continue
Assuming some cuts are made in emissions
Assuming drastic cuts are made in emissions

Climate models are used to provide the best scientifically-based estimates of the future global climate. A typical method is to run the models for some decades ahead and then to compare the predicted average with a past 30-year period. A range of climate models are used, run with different scenarios that express the breadth of possibilities of, for example, industrial development and the degree of atmospheric pollution "clean-up" by industrial nations.

The diagram above shows global observed and predicted surface mean temperature change from 1950 to 2070 with three prediction scenarios. The first (red) assumes rapid economic growth and continued population increases. The second (blue) assumes some attempts are made to cut greenhouse gas emissions, while the green line involves the greater use of cleaner technologies, with global population peaking mid-century then declining.

THE OZONE LAYER

Total atmospheric ozone concentration in the southern hemisphere (2009)

In 1985, scientists working in Antarctica discovered a thinning of the ozone layer, resulting in what is commonly known as the "ozone hole." This caused immediate alarm because the ozone layer absorbs most of the Sun's dangerous ultraviolet radiation, which is believed to cause an increase in skin cancer, cataracts, and damage to the immune system.

Between 1985 and 2001 the ozone depletion increased and, by 2002, the ozone hole over the South Pole was estimated to be three times as large as the USA. This false-color image shows the total atmospheric ozone concentration in the southern hemisphere in October 2010, with the ozone hole clearly identifiable in purple and blue at the center. The data is from NASA's Aura satellite, ESA's ERS-2 satellite, and the NOAA-16 weather-forecasting satellite. The colors represent the ozone concentration in Dobson Units (DU).

Scientists agree that ozone depletion is caused by CFCs, a group of manufactured chemicals that were used in refrigerators and air-conditioning systems. In the Montreal Protocol in 1987, industrial nations agreed to phase out CFCs, and a complete ban on most CFCs was agreed after the end of 1995.

Since 2001 the amount of ozone in the atmosphere has stabilized and so too has the hole. While scientists believe that the chemicals may remain in the atmosphere for 50 to 100 years, if current trends are maintained it is possible that ozone levels may recover by 2050.

Southern hemisphere

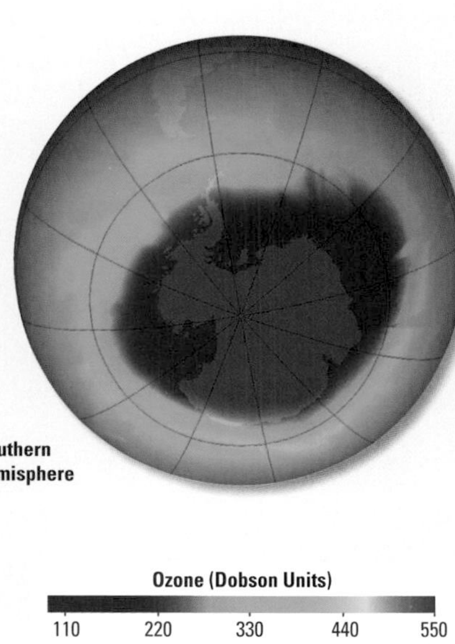

Ozone (Dobson Units)
110
220
330
440
550

For more information:
80 Climate regions
81 Precipitation
86 Biodiversity

Without the hydrological cycle, by which water is constantly recycled between the oceans, the atmosphere and the land, the continents would be barren. Precipitation enables plants to grow and soils to form, creating the world's natural vegetation regions and the ecosystems that support animal life.

Running water also plays a major role in shaping landforms. Yet in many parts of the world, people do not have safe water to drink and suffer from diseases caused by water-borne organisms and pollution. In 2008, an estimated 884 million people lacked access to safe water and 2.6 billion people lacked basic sanitation.

Experts argue that world demand for water is increasing at about twice the rate of population growth. It is predicted that, by 2025, half the world's population will face water shortages. This could lead to conflict and even boundary wars – 300 major rivers cross national frontiers and access to their water is likely to be disputed.

THE HYDROLOGICAL CYCLE

The world's water balance is regulated by the constant recycling of water between the oceans, the atmosphere and the land. The movement of water between these three reservoirs is known as the "hydrological cycle." The oceans play a vital role in the hydrological cycle: 74% of the total precipitation falls over the oceans and 84% of the total evaporation comes from the oceans. Water vapor in the atmosphere circulates around the planet, transporting energy as well as the water itself. When the vapor cools, it falls as rain or snow. The whole cycle is driven by the Sun.

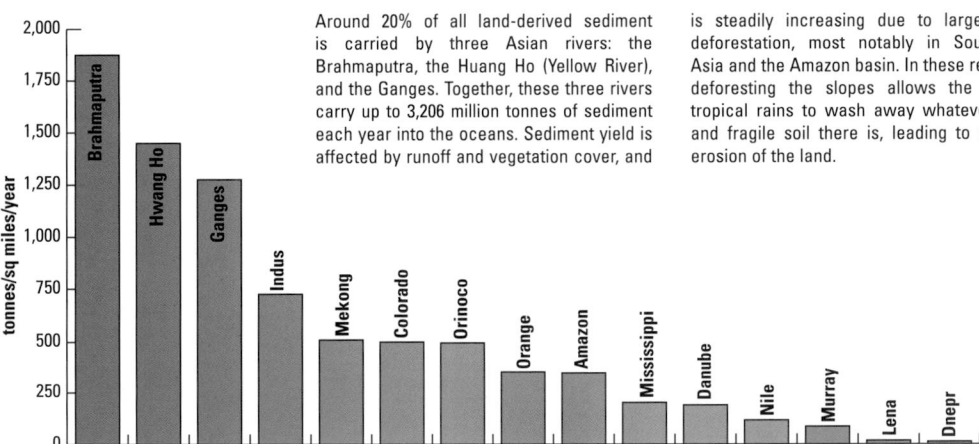

WATER DISTRIBUTION

The distribution of planetary water, by percentage. Oceans and ice caps together account for more than 99% of the total; the breakdown of the remainder is estimated.

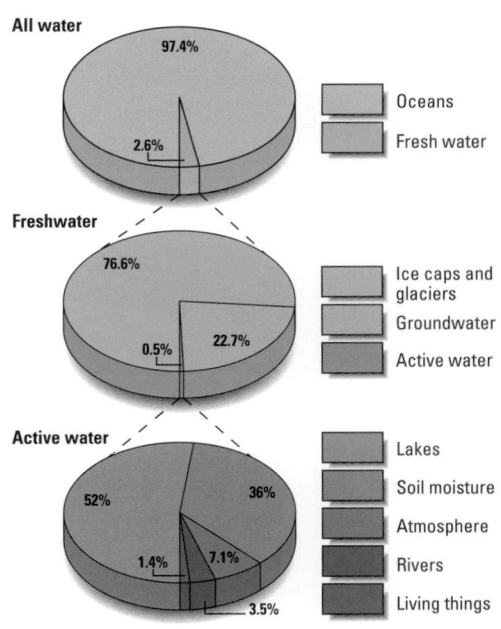

Almost all the world's water is 3,000 million years old, and all of it cycles endlessly through the hydrosphere, though at different rates. Water vapor circulates over days, even hours; deep-ocean water circulates over millennia; and ice-cap water remains solid for millions of years.

ANNUAL SEDIMENT YIELD

Around 20% of all land-derived sediment is carried by three Asian rivers: the Brahmaputra, the Huang Ho (Yellow River), and the Ganges. Together, these three rivers carry up to 3,206 million tonnes of sediment each year into the oceans. Sediment yield is affected by runoff and vegetation cover, and is steadily increasing due to large-scale deforestation, most notably in Southeast Asia and the Amazon basin. In these regions, deforesting the slopes allows the heavy tropical rains to wash away whatever thin and fragile soil there is, leading to severe erosion of the land.

WATER RUNOFF

Annual freshwater runoff by continent in cubic miles

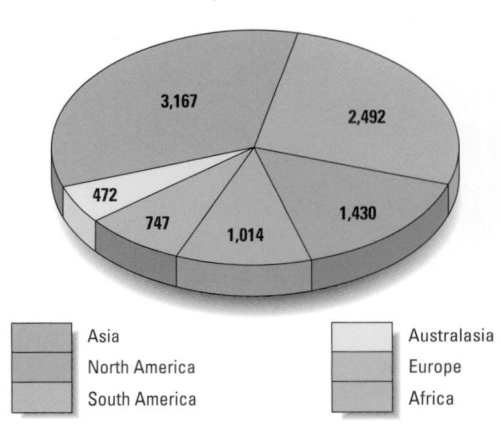

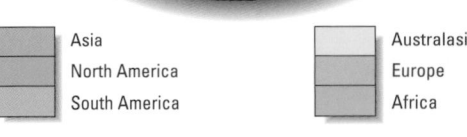

▶ The River Amazon is the world's second-longest river (after the River Nile), draining the vast rain forest basin of northern South America. The Amazon carries by far the greatest volume of water of any river in the world: the average rate of discharge is approximately 3,355,000 cu ft [95,000 cu m] per second, nearly three times as much as its nearest rival, the Congo. The flow is so great that its silt discolors the water up to 125 miles [200 km] into the Atlantic. At approximately 2.7 million sq miles [7 million sq km], the Amazon basin comprises nearly 40% of the whole of South America. Nevertheless, in 2005 large parts of the Amazon rain forest were at their driest in living memory, partly related to the severe hurricane season off the US Gulf coast. Rainfall was significantly below average, causing water levels to drop to record lows. At Tabatinga, 600 miles [970 km] west of Manaus, rainfall was almost 70% down from 2004. Rivers and lakes began to dry up, revealing huge sandbanks and making navigation difficult for boats.

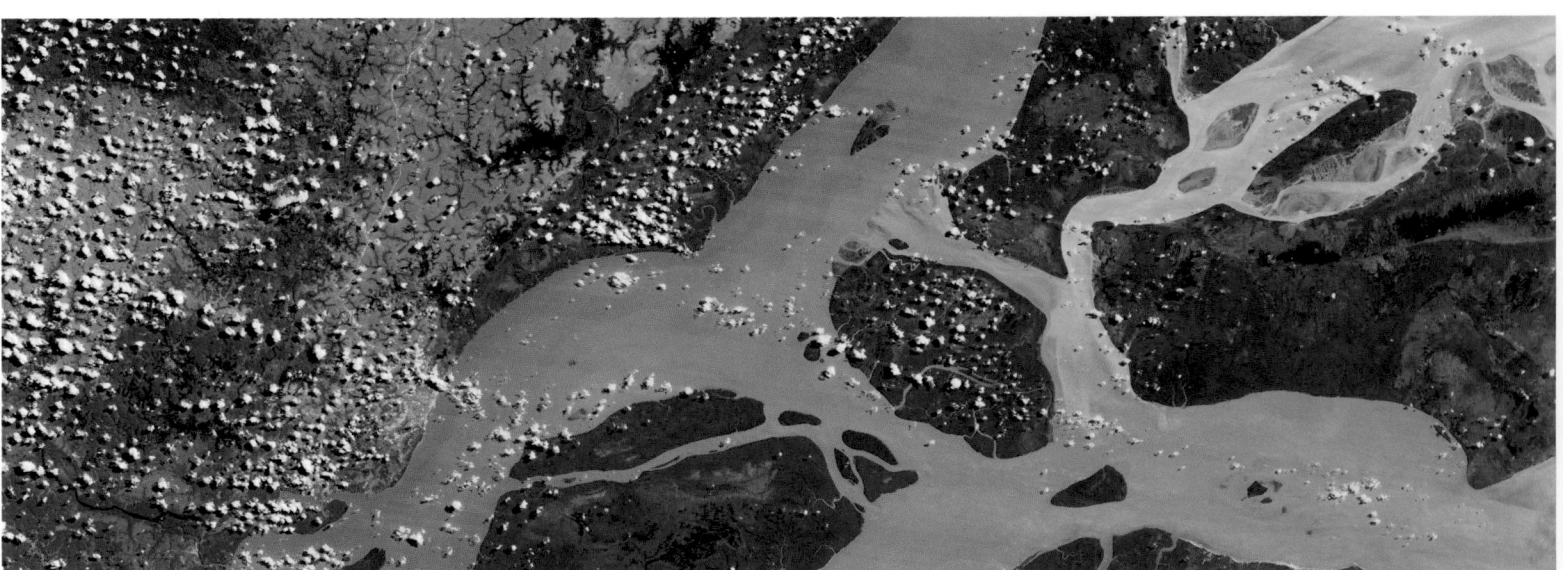

WATERSHEDS

The map below shows the world's major rivers, with the ranking of the 20 longest rivers shown in square brackets after their name, led by the Nile [1] and the Amazon [2].

The map shows the direction of freshwater flow on a continental scale, whereas the water runoff chart on the facing page indicates the quantities involved annually.

The rate of runoff varies seasonally and is affected by the surface vegetation and climate. Most of the world's major rivers discharge into the Atlantic Ocean.

Where the rivers run

- Pacific Ocean
- Indian Ocean
- Arctic Ocean
- Atlantic Ocean
- Caribbean Sea – Gulf of Mexico
- Mediterranean Sea
- Inland basins, ice caps, and deserts

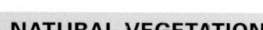

NATURAL VEGETATION

The map below illustrates the natural "climax vegetation" of a region, as dictated by its climate and topography. In most cases, human agricultural activity has drastically altered the pattern of the vegetation. The various vegetation regions support different kinds of animals and wildlife, and, in an undisturbed state, they are highly developed biological communities, or "biomes."

The blue line on the map represents the northern limit of tree growth, and the red lines indicate the northern and southern limits of palm growth. The majority of the numerous species are tropical or subtropical. Some, such as the coconut, date, sago, and oil palms, are important economically.

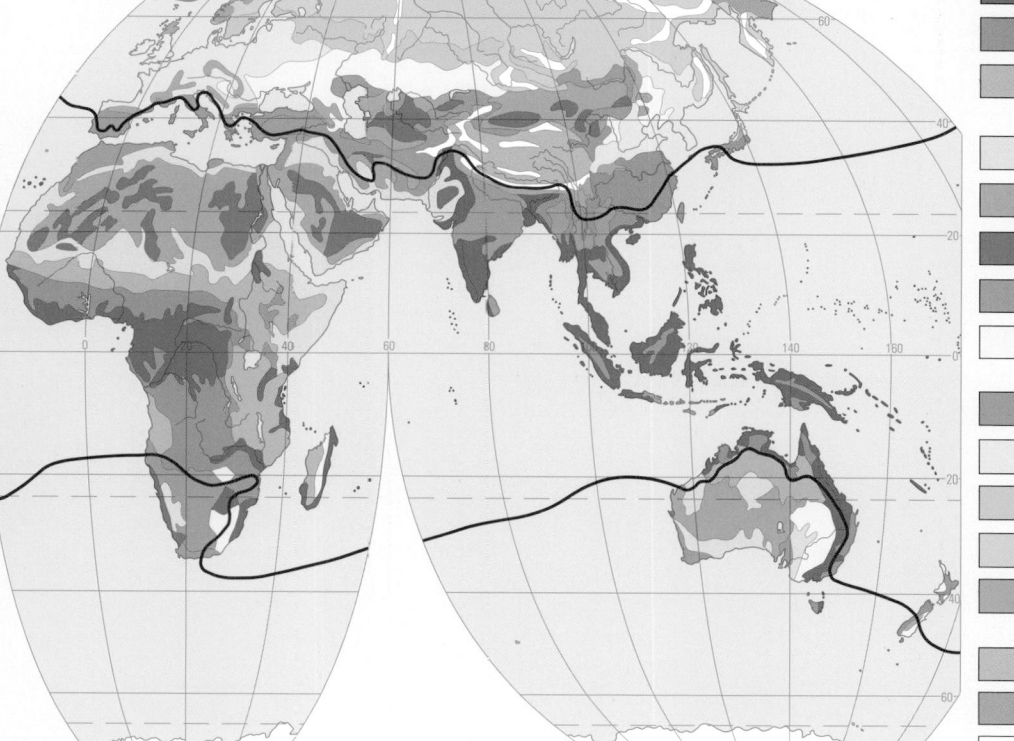

- Tropical rain forest
- Subtropical and temperate rain forest
- Monsoon woodland and open jungle
- Subtropical and temperate woodland, scrub, and bush
- Tropical savanna, with low trees and bush
- Tropical savanna and grasslands
- Dry semidesert, with shrub and grass
- Desert shrub
- Desert
- Dry steppe and shrub
- Temperate grasslands, prairie, and steppe
- Mediterranean hard-wood forest and scrub
- Temperate deciduous forest and meadow
- Temperate deciduous and coniferous forest
- Northern coniferous forest (taïga)
- Mountainous forest, mainly coniferous
- High plateau steppe and tundra
- Arctic tundra
- Polar and mountain-ous ice desert

For more information:
76 Life in the oceans
80 Climate
82 Climate change
    Global warming
85 Natural vegetation

Levels of endemism
Known endemic species per
100 sq miles, selected countries (2004)

- USA
- Congo (Dem. Rep.)
- Kenya
- Ethiopia
- India
- Burma (Myanmar)
- China
- Australia
- Italy
- Bulgaria
- Turkey
- Peru
- Greece
- Japan
- Mexico
- Venezuela
- Indonesia
- Malaysia
- Madagascar
- Colombia
- Ecuador
- Costa Rica 0.9

0.2   0.4   0.6

Biodiversity refers to the variety of living material. It includes the variety of species, the variety within the same species, and the variety of ecosystems within which species operate. Estimates of the number of species in the world vary from between 7 million and 80 million. The currently accepted total is about 14 million, yet only 2 million species have been formally identified.

Biodiversity is vital for human survival. It remains the basis for our food and most of our medicine. In less economically developed countries (LEDCs), over 20% of the food consumed is gathered from natural sources. At a global level, over 15% of animal protein consumed is from sea fish caught in the wild. More than 60% of the world's population rely on traditional medicines for their health care. In Mexico, the Popoluca Indians "farm" over 250 species of plant. Many medicines come from natural sources. Aspirin, for example, comes from an acid taken from the bark of willow trees. The anti-cancer drug "taxol" originates from the wild Pacific yew tree. It is estimated that

the pharmaceuticals industry gains US $32 billion per year in profits from traditional remedies.

However, the loss of biodiversity is increasing at an accelerating rate. Up to 27,000 species a year may be lost, and the United Nations Environment Program (UNEP) suggests that the current rate of extinction is 50–100 times greater than "normal," and believes that up to 25% of all the world's species may be lost by 2025. The main reasons for the decline are the introduction of alien species and habitat destruction. Human impact on biodiversity has brought about more extinctions than any other single factor since the extinction of the dinosaurs (65 million years ago).

Since 1600, 39% of animal extinctions have been due to the introduction of alien species, 36% from habitat destruction, and 23% from hunting or deliberate extermination. The introduction of rats, cats, and other species has led to the extinction of many flightless birds in Polynesia. Plantation crops, such as rubber, often thrive best when taken away from their natural homes, since in

the new lands there may not be the pests to control them. One noted example of extinction was caused by the introduction of the Nile perch into Lake Victoria, East Africa: introduced in the 1960s, it led to the extinction of some 50 species of cichlid fish within 20 years.

In 2007, a report by the International Union for the Conservation of Nature listed 16,306 organisms facing extinction. Up to 46% of primates are said to be at risk of extinction. Overall, some 25% of mammals are endangered – including "charismatic" species such as the tiger and the panda, but equally less recognizable species of bats, rodents, and marsupials. Up to one-fifth of reptiles, one-third of amphibians, and one-third of bird species are at risk of extinction. The most threatened group are fish (one-third are at risk), largely as a result of overfishing. The World Conservation Union reported that 8% of mammals were threatened in the US, compared with 32% in the Philippines and 44% in Madagascar, two countries where habitat destruction has been proceeding on a large scale.

THREATENED MAMMAL SPECIES

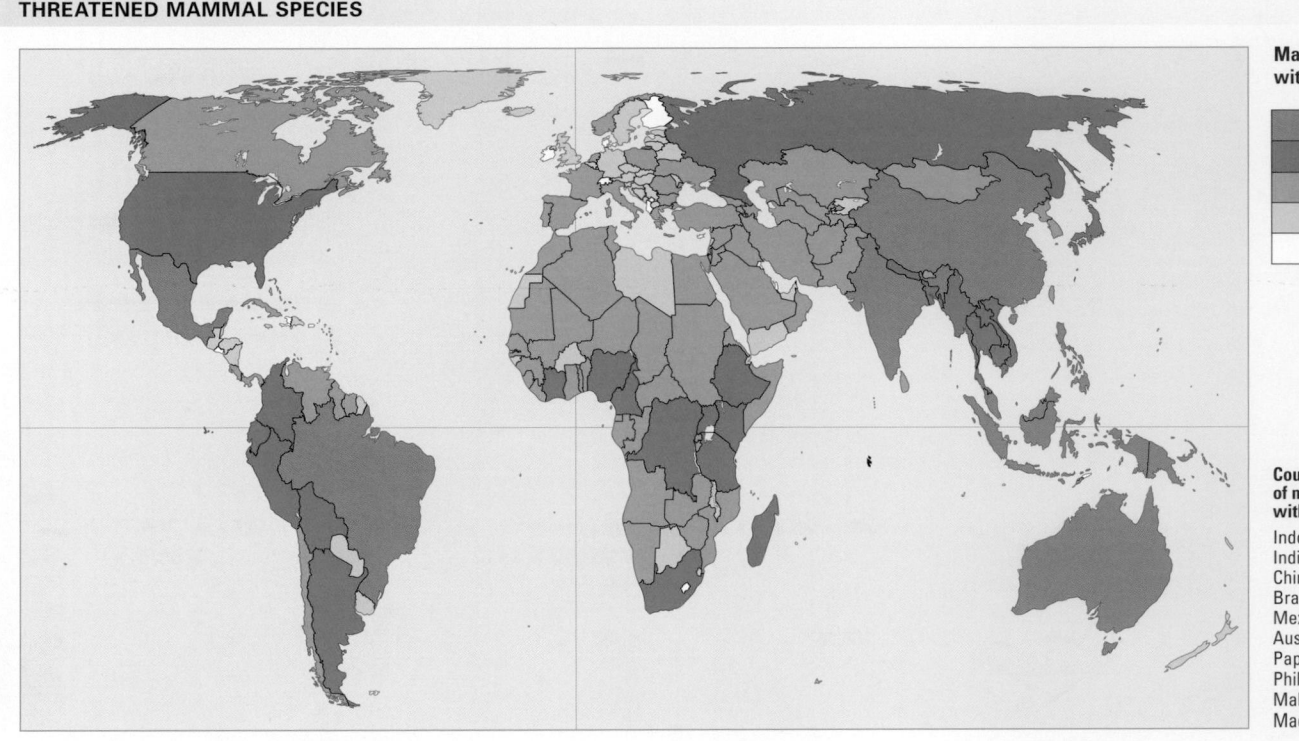

Mammal species threatened with extinction (2007)
- Over 50
- 25 – 50
- 10 – 25
- 5 – 10
- Under 5

Countries with the highest number of mammal species threatened with extinction (2007)

Indonesia	146
India	89
China	83
Brazil	73
Mexico	72
Australia	64
Papua New Guinea	58
Philippines	51
Malaysia	50
Madagascar	47

NATIVE ('ENDEMIC') SPECIES AS A PROPORTION OF TOTAL SPECIES (SELECTED COUNTRIES)

Country	Mammals (2004)		Birds (2004)		Higher Plants (2004)	
	Total	Endemic	Total	Endemic	Total	Endemic
Australia	376	225	851	387	15,638	14,074
Brazil	578	131	1,712	207	56,215	18,000
Burma (Myanmar)	288	4	1,047	24	7,000	1,071
China	502	78	1,221	92	32,200	18,000
Colombia	467	43	1,821	84	51,220	15,000
Congo (Dem. Rep.)	430	26	1,148	24	11,007	1,100
Ecuador	341	26	1,515	56	19,362	4,000
Ethiopia	288	34	839	24	6,603	1,000
India	422	44	1,180	70	18,664	5,000
Indonesia	667	216	1,604	443	29,375	17,500
Japan	171	43	592	55	5,565	2,000
Madagascar	165	102	262	111	9,505	6,500
Malaysia	337	35	746	26	15,500	3,600
Mexico	544	155	1,026	125	26,071	12,500
Peru	441	48	1,781	125	17,144	5,356
Philippines	222	106	590	205	8,931	3,500
South Africa	320	33	829	27	23,420	8,200
Turkey	145	4	436	3	8,650	2,675
USA	468	104	888	122	19,473	4,036
Venezuela	353	18	1,392	46	21,073	8,000

▲ Madagascar has developed in isolation since it split from Africa 150 million years ago. As a result of this isolation, a unique range of plants and animals have evolved, adapted to its own specific conditions. Over 95% of Madagascar's mammals, 90% of its reptiles, over 66% of its plants, and over 40% of its breeding birds do not exist anywhere else in the world.
Madagascar is home to all of the world's lemurs (all of which are endangered, such as the aye-aye pictured above) and two-thirds of the world's chameleons. Its plant species include pitcher plants, orchids, and the Madagascan rosy periwinkle (the most effective known treatment for childhood leukemia). However, large-scale deforestation since the 1970s has reduced Madagascar's cover of rain forest to less than 10% of the island's original forest cover.

ENVIRONMENTAL HOTSPOTS

Up to 75% of the world's most threatened mammals, birds and amphibians live in an area covering just 2.3% of the Earth's surface, and roughly half of all flowering plant species and 42% of land-based vertebrates exist in 34 biological hotspots.

Scientists argue that, with limited financial resources, governments and conservationists should prioritize by protecting the small total land areas that account for a very high percentage of global biodiversity. In 1999, scientists identified 25 such areas, mostly in the tropics, which were the center of global biodiversity.

By 2005, the number of hotspots had risen to 34. These include the mountains of central Asia, the whole of Japan, the Horn of Africa including the Ethiopian highlands, and the Himalayas region. The hotspots once covered 15.7% of the Earth's surface, an area roughly the size of Russia and Australia combined – now they cover only 2.3% of the Earth's surface, an area slightly larger than India.

Over 70% of all mammals, 86% of all birds, and 92% of all amphibians are crammed into this small area of the world's total land mass. Madagascar and the Indian Ocean Islands hotspot was found to have very high concentrations of plant and vertebrate families that are found nowhere else on the globe.

Global warming could have a devastating effect on biodiversity hotspots such as the Amazonian and Indonesian rain forests. By 2100, between 12% and 39% of the land surface of the Earth will have a new climate. There are numerous species that will be unable to move in order to stay within their preferred climate range. These species will either have to evolve rapidly or die out.

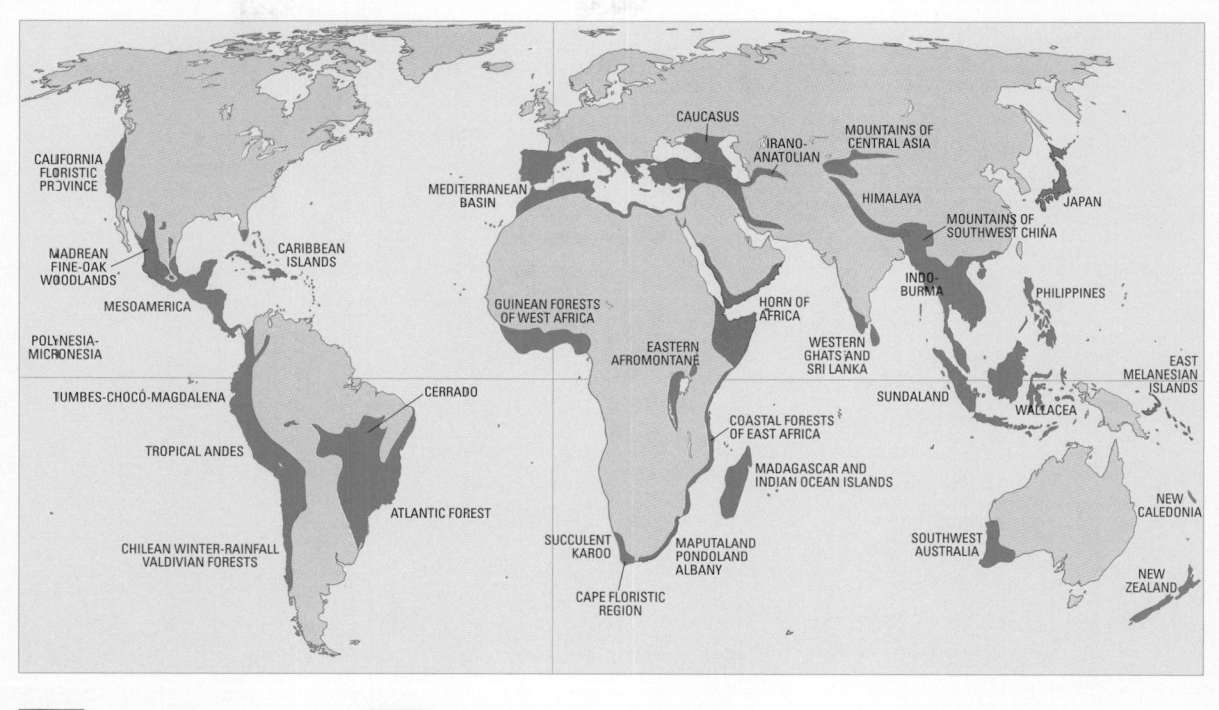

■ New hotspots   ■ Recognized environmental areas

AUSTRALIA'S INTRODUCED SPECIES

Australia's native plants and animals adapted to life on an isolated continent over millions of years. Since European settlement in the 18th century they have had to compete with a range of species introduced by the settlers, which impact on the native species by predation, competition for food and shelter, destroying habitat, and by spreading diseases. Introduced species typically have few predators or fatal diseases, and some have very high reproductive rates.

Management and the prevention of the introduction of new invasive species are key environmental and agricultural policy issues for the Australian federal and state governments.

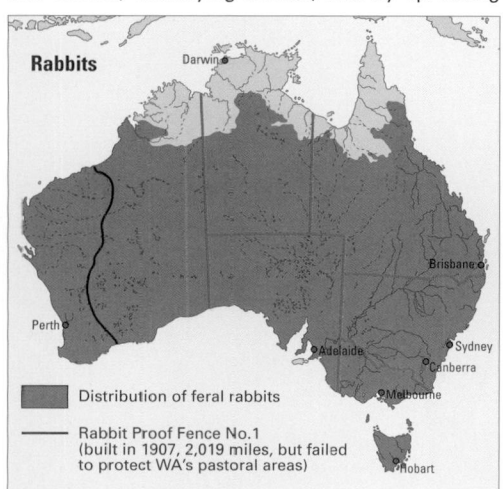

Rabbits

■ Distribution of feral rabbits

— Rabbit Proof Fence No.1 (built in 1907, 2,019 miles, but failed to protect WA's pastoral areas)

▲ Rabbits were introduced to Australia from England in 1859 for hunting, and quickly spread throughout the country. They are one of the most destructive introduced species in Australia, competing with native wildlife, damaging vegetation, and degrading the land.

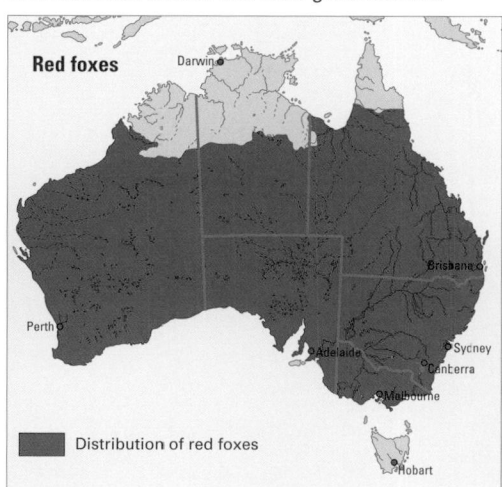

Red foxes

■ Distribution of red foxes

▲ The red fox was introduced from Europe for recreational hunting in 1855 and populations became established in the wild within 15 years. They prey on newborn lambs and have also been responsible for the decline of a number of native species.

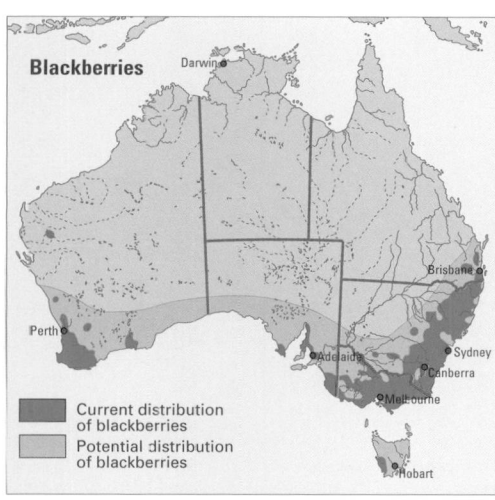

Blackberries

■ Current distribution of blackberries
■ Potential distribution of blackberries

▲ The blackberry was introduced from Europe as a source of fresh fruit. It is now regarded as one of the worst weeds in Australia because of its invasiveness, spreading through farmland, forests, and scrub. It out-competes many native plants, prevents light reaching the ground below, and provides food and shelter for pests.

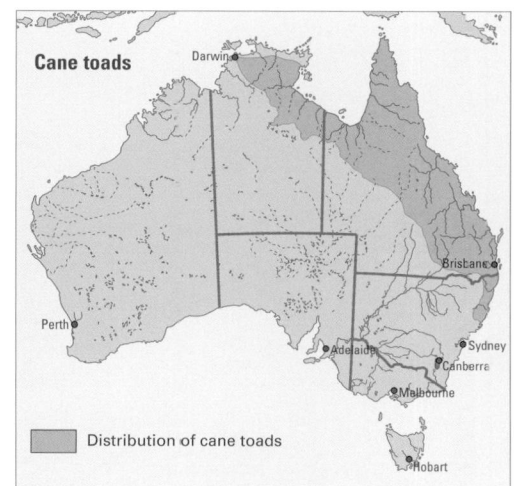

Cane toads

■ Distribution of cane toads

▲ Cane toads were introduced in 1935 to control beetles which were threatening the sugarcane industry. However, this was a failure and both the toad and the beetle are still thriving. They adapted well to the Australian environment and with no natural predators they quickly spread. They eat small native wildlife and poison any predators.

ESTIMATED VALUE OF WILD RESOURCES IN LESS ECONOMICALLY DEVELOPED COUNTRIES

Tropical non-coniferous forest product exports	US $11 billion per year
Fruit/latex harvesting, Peru	US $6,330 per hectare
Sustainable timber harvesting, Peru	US $490 per hectare
Buffalo range ranching, Zimbabwe	US $3.5–4.5 per hectare
Wetlands fish and fuelwood, Nigeria	US $38–59 per hectare
Viewing value of elephants, Kenya	US $25 million per year
Ecotourism, Costa Rica	US $1,250 per hectare
Tourism, Thailand	US $385,000–860,000 per year
Research/education, Thailand	US $38,000–77,000 per year
Tourism, Cameroon	US $10 per hectare
Genetic value, Cameroon	US $7 per hectare
Pharmaceutical prospecting, Costa Rica	US $4,981 million per product

▲ Bolivia has over 100,000 sq miles [250,000 sq km] of dry tropical forest, home to animals such as jaguars and ocelots. It is, however, being cleared at a rate of over 2% per annum.

This false-color image shows an area that has been almost completely cleared. The darkest areas are remnants of the original forest, some of which have been retained

as wind-breaks between newly created arable fields. The radial patterns are fields with new villages at their centers, part of a government resettlement scheme.

For more information:

11   Food and
      population
90   Urbanization of
      the Earth
      Urban population
91   Largest cities

LARGEST NATIONS

The world's most populous
nations, in millions (2010)

1.	China	1,330
2.	India	1,173
3.	USA	310
4.	Indonesia	243
5.	Brazil	201
6.	Pakistan	184
7.	Bangladesh	156
8.	Nigeria	152
9.	Russia	139
10.	Japan	127
11.	Mexico	112
12.	Philippines	100
13.	Vietnam	90
14.	Ethiopia	88
15.	Germany	82
16.	Egypt	80
17.	Turkey	78
18.	Iran	77
19.	Congo (Dem.Rep.)	71
20.	Thailand	67
21.	France	65
22.	UK	62
23.	Italy	58
24.	Burma (Myanmar)	53
25.	South Africa	49

MOST CROWDED NATIONS

Population per square mile
(2010)

1.	Monaco	77,500
2.	Singapore	18,081
3.	Gaza Strip (OPT)	11,457
4.	Maldives	3,300
5.	Malta	3,392
6.	Bangladesh	2,808
7.	Bahrain	2,733
8.	Barbados	1,682
9.	Mauritius	1,681
10.	Taiwan	1,656

LEAST CROWDED NATIONS

Population per square mile
(2010)

1.	Western Sahara	4.8
2.	Mongolia	5.1
3.	Namibia	6.7
4.	Australia	7.2
5.	Suriname	7.7
6.	Iceland	7.8
7.	Mauritania	8.1
8.	Canada	8.8
9.	Guyana	9.0
10.	Botswana	9.0

In 8000 BC, following the development of agriculture, the world had an estimated population of 8 million and by AD 1000 it was about 300 million. The onset of the Industrial Revolution in the late 18th century led to a population explosion. The 1,000 million mark was passed by 1850, it doubled by the 1920s, and doubled again to 4,000 million by 1975.

In the 1990s, demographers estimated that the world's population, which passed the 6 billion mark in 1999, would reach 9.3 billion by 2050 and only level out in 2200, at a peak of around 11 billion. However, in the early 21st century, after the rate of population growth had shown signs of decline, the Institute for Applied Systems Analysis suggested that the world's population might peak at about 9 billion in 2070. Whatever the global projections, everyone agreed that the greatest population growth would be in the developing countries.

The developing world includes what the World Bank (2010) describes as low-income economies (per capita GNI of US $995 or less), lower-middle-income economies (per capita GNI of US $996 to US $3,945), and upper-middle-income economies (per capita GNI of US $3,946 to US $12,195). Most developing countries are in Africa, Asia, and Latin America. The developed world, made up of high-income, industrialized economies (per capita GNI of US $12,196 or more), contains Australasia, most of Europe and North America, and Japan.

In developing countries, a high proportion of the population is young and so these countries face high expenditure on health and education. In developed countries, the population pyramids are becoming top-heavy, with increasingly aging populations.

POPULATION CHANGE

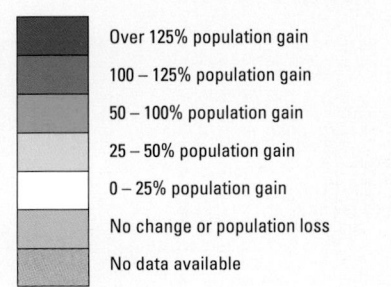

The projected population change for the years 2004–2050

- Over 125% population gain
- 100 – 125% population gain
- 50 – 100% population gain
- 25 – 50% population gain
- 0 – 25% population gain
- No change or population loss
- No data available

Based on estimates for the year 2050, below are listed the ten most populous nations in the world, in millions:

1.	India	1,628	6.	Pakistan	295
2.	China	1,437	7.	Bangladesh	280
3.	USA	420	8.	Brazil	221
4.	Indonesia	308	9.	Congo (Dem. Rep.)	181
5.	Nigeria	307	10.	Ethiopia	173

POPULATION DENSITY

The places marked on the map reflect the size of the urban agglomerations and conurbations, rather than the actual city limits. San Francisco itself, for example, has an official population of less than a million people.

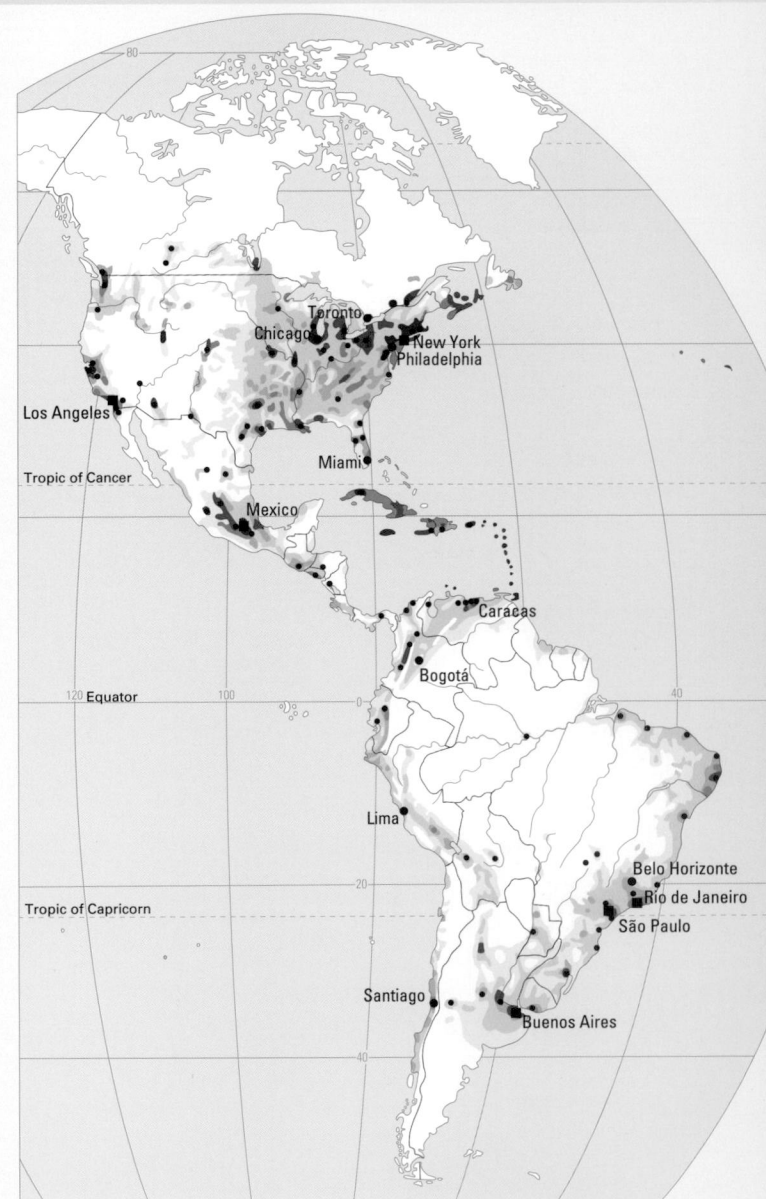

Inhabitants per square mile

- Over 500
- 250 – 500
- 125 – 250
- 65 – 125
- 15 – 65
- 8 – 15
- 3 – 8
- Under 3

Urban population

- ■ Over 10,000,000
- ● 5,000,000 – 10,000,000
- · 1,000,000 – 5,000,000

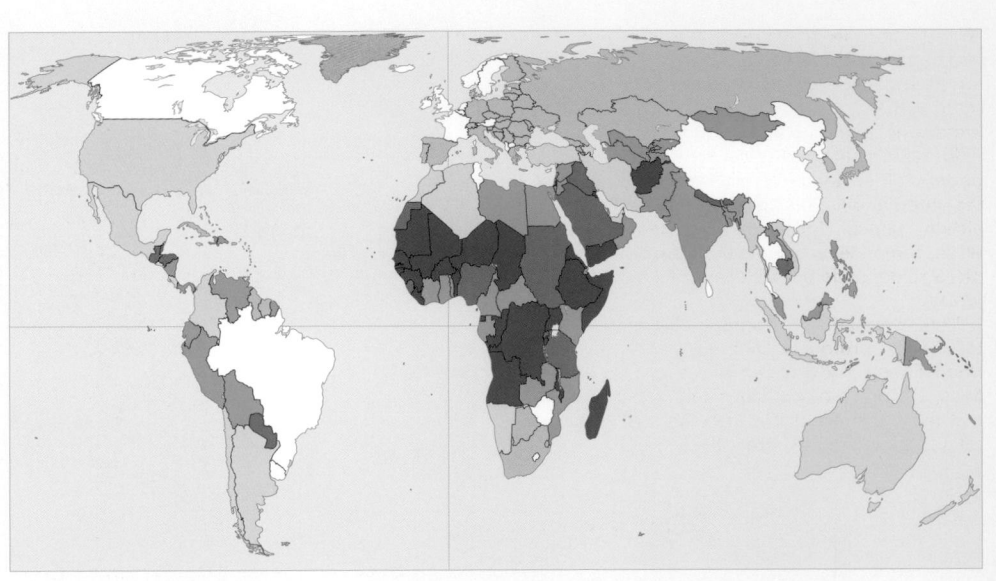

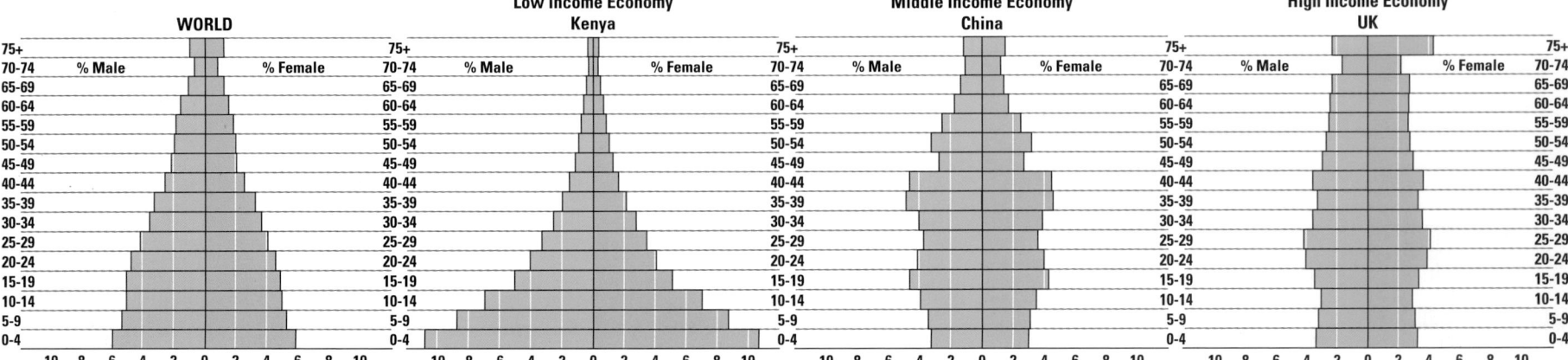

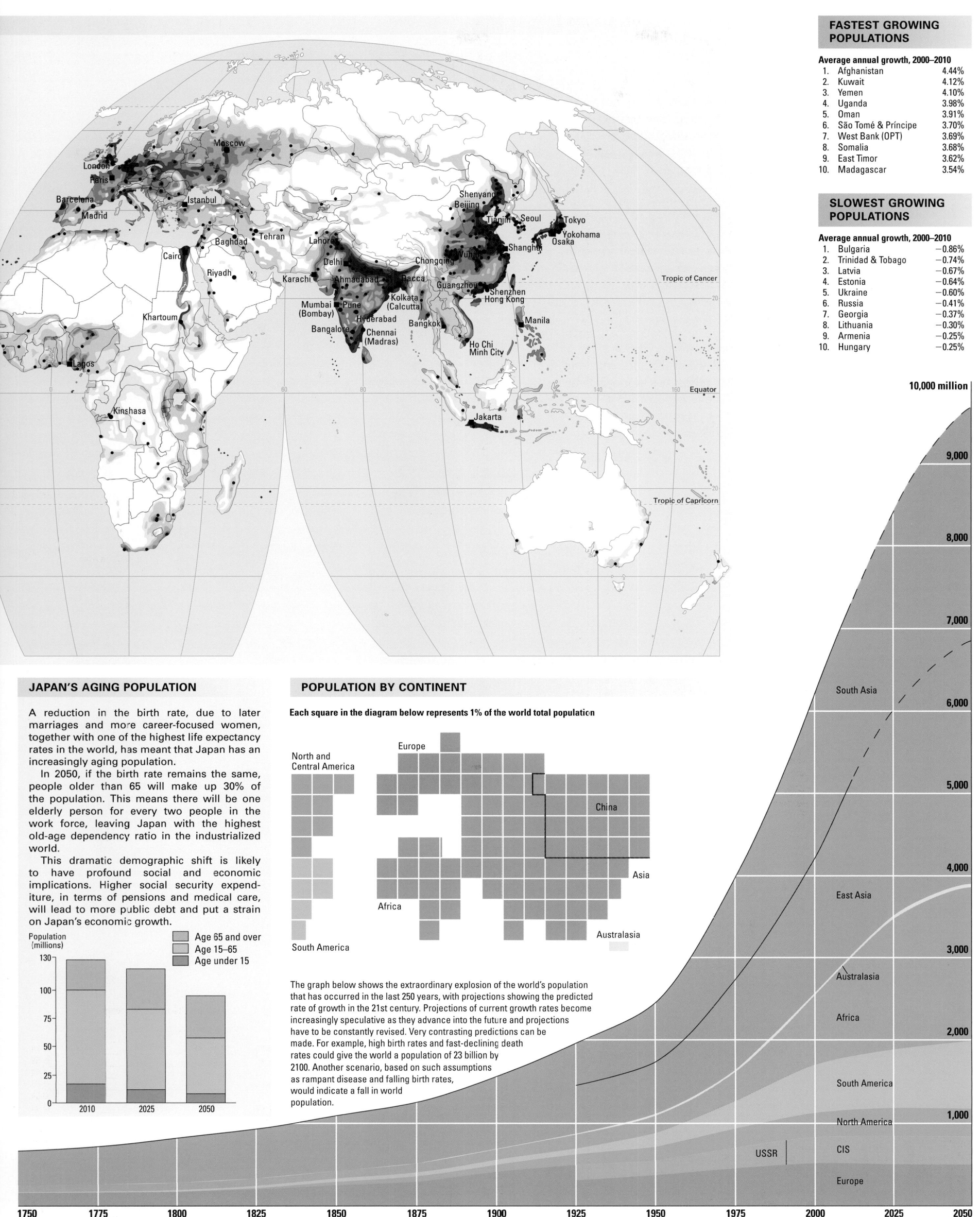

FASTEST GROWING POPULATIONS

Average annual growth, 2000–2010
1.	Afghanistan	4.44%
2.	Kuwait	4.12%
3.	Yemen	4.10%
4.	Uganda	3.98%
5.	Oman	3.91%
6.	São Tomé & Príncipe	3.70%
7.	West Bank (OPT)	3.69%
8.	Somalia	3.68%
9.	East Timor	3.62%
10.	Madagascar	3.54%

SLOWEST GROWING POPULATIONS

Average annual growth, 2000–2010
1.	Bulgaria	−0.86%
2.	Trinidad & Tobago	−0.74%
3.	Latvia	−0.67%
4.	Estonia	−0.64%
5.	Ukraine	−0.60%
6.	Russia	−0.41%
7.	Georgia	−0.37%
8.	Lithuania	−0.30%
9.	Armenia	−0.25%
10.	Hungary	−0.25%

JAPAN'S AGING POPULATION

A reduction in the birth rate, due to later marriages and more career-focused women, together with one of the highest life expectancy rates in the world, has meant that Japan has an increasingly aging population.

In 2050, if the birth rate remains the same, people older than 65 will make up 30% of the population. This means there will be one elderly person for every two people in the work force, leaving Japan with the highest old-age dependency ratio in the industrialized world.

This dramatic demographic shift is likely to have profound social and economic implications. Higher social security expenditure, in terms of pensions and medical care, will lead to more public debt and put a strain on Japan's economic growth.

POPULATION BY CONTINENT

Each square in the diagram below represents 1% of the world total population

The graph below shows the extraordinary explosion of the world's population that has occurred in the last 250 years, with projections showing the predicted rate of growth in the 21st century. Projections of current growth rates become increasingly speculative as they advance into the future and projections have to be constantly revised. Very contrasting predictions can be made. For example, high birth rates and fast-declining death rates could give the world a population of 23 billion by 2100. Another scenario, based on such assumptions as rampant disease and falling birth rates, would indicate a fall in world population.

For more information:
82 Greenhouse gases
84 Water distribution
88 Population density
102 World trade

Following the development of agriculture more than 10,000 years ago, people began to live in farming villages. Around 5,500 years ago, the world's first cities appeared in the lower Tigris and Euphrates valleys in Mesopotamia. Cities were founded in Ancient Egypt around 5,000 years ago and in China around 3,600 years ago.

By contrast with the villages, most people in the early cities were not engaged in farming. Instead, they worked in craft industries, in government services, in religion, and in trade. The cities became centres of early civilizations and, through trade, their influence spread far and wide. However, they were dependent on the surrounding farming communities for their food and other materials.

In 1750, prior to the start of the Industrial Revolution, barely 3% of the world's population lived in urban areas. By 1850, London and Paris had more than a million people, and, by 1900, 14% of the world's population lived in cities. By 1950, the world had 83 cities with more than a million people, and

by 1996 there were 280; by 2015, experts predict there will be more than 500.

New York City was the only city with a population in excess of 10 million in 1950; by 2015, experts predict there will be 26 such cities worldwide, the majority located in the developing world. In addition, many of the world's largest cities are now merging to form "mega regions," such as Hong Kong-Shenzhen-Guangzhou in China, and these are becoming major economic drivers, on a world scale.

In 2008, for the first time in history, more than half of the world's population lived in urban areas. By 2050, it is thought that 5.3 billion people in the developing world will be living in an urban environment, with Asia having over 60% of the world's urban population and Africa almost 25%.

Urbanization is greatest in industrialized countries. For example, in 2004, 81% of the people in the US lived in urban areas. However, in low-income countries, which had nearly 40% of the world's population in the early 21st century, only 31% lived in urban areas.

The rapid rate of urbanization has created many social problems, especially in cities that have been unable to provide enough jobs and services for the new arrivals. Many of the new city dwellers come from rural areas and take time to adjust to urban life and employment possibilities.

A typical city in a developing country contains millions of people living, often illegally, in shanty towns (or "informal settlements"), while thousands live on the streets. Yet many of these shanty towns are healthier than the industrial cities of 19th-century Europe and North America. Indeed, surveys have shown that migrants to cities in developing countries are less likely to face poverty than they are in rural areas, while benefiting from greater access to healthcare services and education.

Modern cities face many problems today, including pollution, unemployment, and crime. Yet, with competent government, they are capable of generating the wealth they need to solve them, as well as making a major contribution to the nation's economy.

URBAN POPULATION

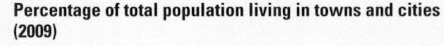

Percentage of total population living in towns and cities (2009)

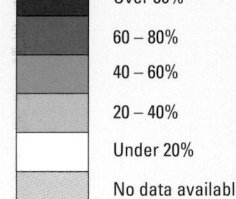

Over 80%
60 – 80%
40 – 60%
20 – 40%
Under 20%
No data available

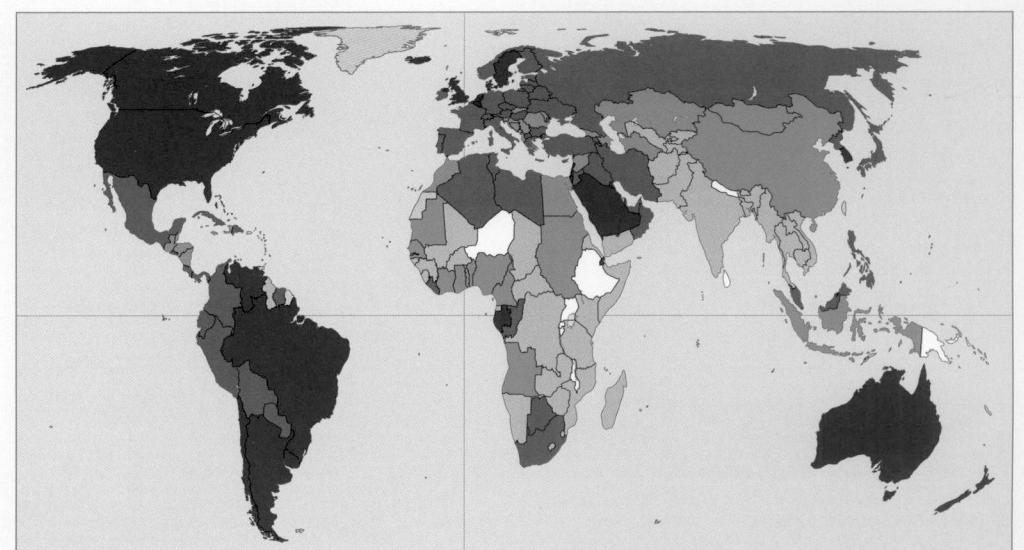

Most urbanized		Least urbanized	
Singapore	100%	Burundi	11%
Kuwait	98%	Papua New Guinea	13%
Belgium	97%	Uganda	13%
Qatar	96%	Trinidad & Tobago	14%
Malta	95%	Sri Lanka	15%

THE URBANIZATION OF THE EARTH

City-building, 1900–2005; each white spot represents a city of at least 1 million inhabitants

1900

1950

1975

2005

URBANIZATION

The urban population of 3.3 billion people in 2008 was larger than the entire global population in 1947, 61 years earlier. Cities and urban areas are gaining an estimated 60 million people per year – over 1 million every week.

Urbanization rates vary across the world; the US and UK have far lower rates of urbanization compared to less developed countries. This is because a high proportion of their populations already live in cities. The largest percentage increases in the urban population in the next decade will be in Africa and Asia. Dhaka in Bangladesh, for example, nearly doubled in population between 1990 and 2000.

Rapid urban growth reflects three factors:
1. Migration to cities from rural areas.
2. Natural population increases (births minus deaths).
3. Reclassification of previously rural areas as urban as they become built up and engulfed by urban sprawl.

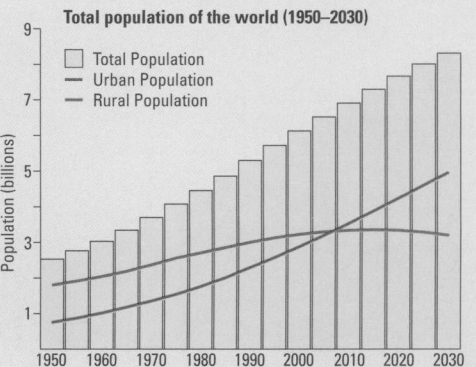

Total population of the world (1950–2030)

SLUM CITIES

The total number of slum dwellers in the world reached 1 billion in 2007, with one in every three city residents living in inadequate housing, with no or few basic services.

Urbanization in most developing countries has been proceeding so rapidly that local governments have been unable to provide the necessary services and housing to meet demand.

In some cities, many people make their homes in squatter settlements, or slums, which are frequently without basic services such as power, water, and sanitation. They are often on hazardous, dangerous or polluted land, and the building structures are inadequate and sometimes unsafe. Slum dwellers have limited access to credit and formal job markets due to stigmatization, discrimination, and geographical isolation.

Slums have a high concentration of poverty and social and economic deprivation, which may include broken families, unemployment, and economic, physical, and social exclusion. Yet these communities are often a dynamic part of the city's economy, keeping the wheels of the city turning in many different ways. Their inhabitants often take the initiative in setting up their own local government and self-help associations.

Some of the world's richest cities also have a homeless underclass, although calculating the numbers of people involved is problematic. Yet it is the case that homelessness and unemployment are currently affecting an increasing number of people in the developed world.

The locus of poverty is moving from the countryside to cities, in a process now recognized as the "urbanization of poverty."

Efforts to improve the living conditions of slum dwellers peaked during the 1980s. However, renewed concern about poverty has recently led governments to adopt specific targets on slums in the United Nations Millennium Declaration, which aims to improve the lives of at least 100 million slum dwellers by the year 2020.

CITIES IN DANGER

In mid-2002, a "brown haze," stretching 2 miles [3 km] high, covered much of southern Asia. Caused mainly by the burning of coal and biomass, it caused respiratory diseases and many deaths. Alarm concerning urban air pollution had been expressed much earlier, but controls since the 1980s had proved difficult to enforce and expensive to introduce.

Those cities taking part in the United Nation's Global Environment Monitoring System frequently show dangerous levels of pollutants, ranging from soot to sulfur dioxide and photochemical smog. Air in the majority of cities without such sampling equipment is likely to be at least as bad. Traffic, a major source of air pollution worldwide, loses Thailand's work force 44 working days each year. It was also a major cause for concern in the run-up to the 2008 Beijing Olympic Games.

URBAN ADVANTAGES

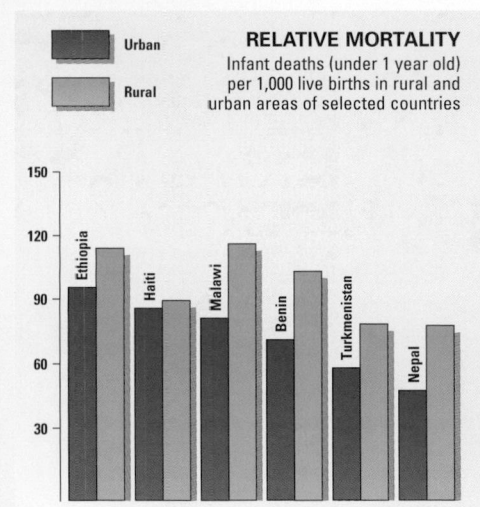

RELATIVE MORTALITY
Infant deaths (under 1 year old) per 1,000 live births in rural and urban areas of selected countries

Urban
Rural

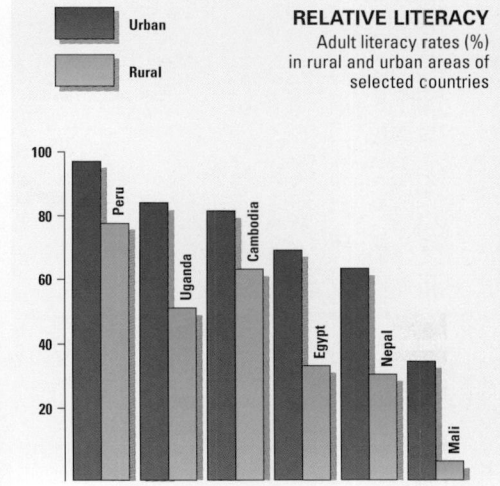

RELATIVE LITERACY
Adult literacy rates (%) in rural and urban areas of selected countries

Urban
Rural

SLUM FACTBOX

• 78% of the urban population in developing countries live in slums.

• The total number of slum dwellers in the world increased by about 36% during the 1990s.

• More than 41% of Kolkata's slum households have lived there for more than 30 years.

• In most African cities between 40% and 70% of the city's population live in slums or squatter settlements.

• Slum populations in some parts of the world (for example, Pune in India and Ibadan in Nigeria) quite often include university lecturers, students, civil servants, and formal private-sector employees.

• All slum households in Bangkok have a color television.

• Singapore is one of the few countries that successfully practises comprehensive public-sector housing development.

LARGEST CITIES

Despite overcrowding and poor housing, living standards in the developing world's cities are almost invariably better than in the surrounding countryside. Resources – financial, material, and administrative – are concentrated in the towns, which are usually also the centers of political activity and pressure. Governments – frequently unstable, and rarely established on a solid democratic base – are usually more responsive to urban discontent than to rural misery.

In many developing countries, especially in Africa, food prices are kept artificially low, thus appeasing the underemployed urban masses at the expense of agricultural development.

This imbalance encourages further cityward migration, helping to account for the astonishing rate of post-1950 urbanization and putting great strain on the ability of many nations to provide even modest improvements for their people.

CITY GROWTH

The growth of some of the world's largest cities in millions, 1950–2015
Comparisons of city populations over time are problematic due to changes in the definition of the city limits. These figures attempt to take such changes into consideration.

1950
2015

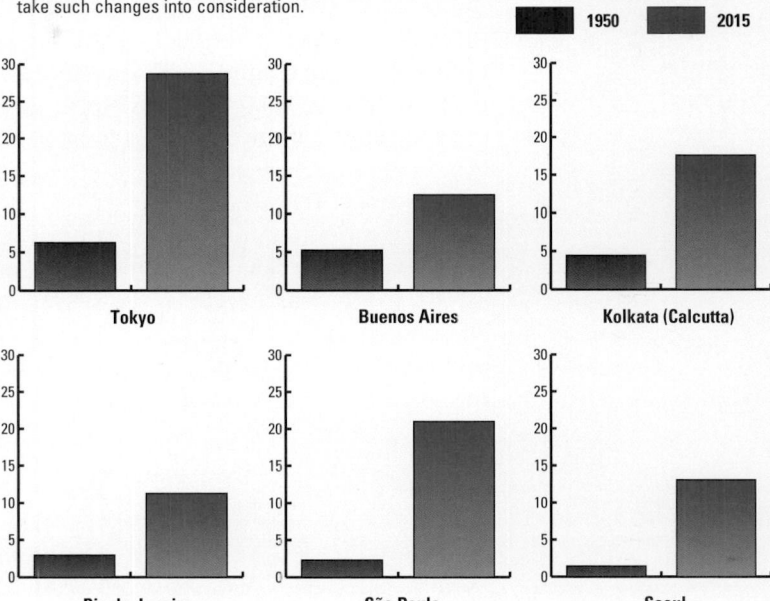

Tokyo   Buenos Aires   Kolkata (Calcutta)
Rio de Janeiro   São Paulo   Seoul

◄ Originally a fishing village, Shanghai's skyscrapers and modern lifestyle are often seen as representing China's recent economic development. It is now the sixth largest city in the world and home to many of Asia's tallest buildings, including the Jinmao Tower on the right of this image.

In 2008, for the first time in history, the majority of the world's population lived in cities. Below is a list of all the cities that are expected to have more than 10 million inhabitants by the year 2015, based on current estimates:

	City	
1.	Tokyo–Yokohama	28.7
2.	Mumbai (Bombay)	27.4
3.	Lagos	24.1
4.	Shanghai	23.2
5.	Jakarta	21.5
6.	São Paulo	21.0
7.	Karachi	20.6
8.	Beijing	19.6
9.	Dhaka	19.2
10.	Mexico City	19.1
11.	Kolkata (Calcutta)	17.6
12.	Delhi	17.5
13.	New York City	17.4
14.	Tianjin	17.1
15.	Manila	14.9
16.	Cairo	14.7
17.	Los Angeles	14.5
18.	Seoul	13.1
19.	Buenos Aires	12.5
20.	Istanbul	12.1
21.	Rio de Janeiro	11.3
22.	Lahore	10.9
23.	Hyderabad	10.6
24.	Bangkok	10.4
25.	Osaka	10.2
26.	Lima	10.1
27.	Tehran	10.0

The city populations above are based on urban agglomerations rather than legal city limits. In some cases, where two adjacent cities have merged into one concentration, such as Tokyo–Yokohama, they have been regarded as a single unit.

For more information:
88 Population density
94 The world's refugees
    War since 1945
95 United Nations
    International
    organizations

Racial, language, and religious differences have led to appalling acts of inhumanity throughout history. Yet, strictly speaking, all human beings belong to one species, *Homo sapiens*, which has no subspecies. The differences between the three racial types which most people identify – Caucasoid, Mongoloid, and Negroid – reflect not so much evolutionary differences as long periods of separation.

Migration has recently mingled the various groups to an unprecedented extent, and most nations now have some degree of racial mixing. For example, the USA has often been called a melting pot, because of the large numbers of people from various geographical locations that make up the population. The country has no official language but, until recently, English was spoken by the vast majority of the people. But in recent years, some of the immigrants from Mexico, Cuba, and other parts of Latin America have not learned English and speak only Spanish. This development disturbs those Americans who believe that the use of English binds the nation together, and several states have passed laws stating that English is their only official language.

Language is fundamental to human culture. Because definitions of languages vary, estimates of the total number range from 3,000 to 6,000, although most are spoken by only a few people. Chinese is spoken by more people as a first language than any other, while Spanish ranks second, but English is the leading international language, because so many people speak it as their second tongue.

Like language, religion encourages cohesion in single human groups and it satisfies a deep human need by assigning people a place in a divinely ordered world. Religion is a way in which a culture can express its individuality. For example, the rise of Islamic fundamentalism in the late 20th century was partly an expression of resentment that secular Western values were being imposed on Muslims.

WORLD MIGRATION

The greatest voluntary migration was the colonization of North America by 30–35 million European settlers during the 19th century. The greatest forced migration involved 9–11 million Africans taken as slaves to America between 1550 and 1860. The migrations shown on the map below are mostly international, as population movements within borders are not usually recorded. Many of the statistics are necessarily estimates as so many refugees and migrant workers enter countries illegally and unrecorded. Emigrants may have a variety of motives for leaving, thus making it difficult to distinguish between voluntary and involuntary migrations.

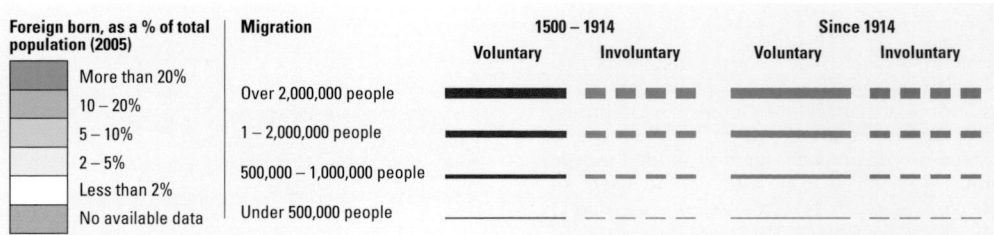

Foreign born, as a % of total population (2005)
- More than 20%
- 10 – 20%
- 5 – 10%
- 2 – 5%
- Less than 2%
- No available data

Migration
- Over 2,000,000 people
- 1 – 2,000,000 people
- 500,000 – 1,000,000 people
- Under 500,000 people

	1500 – 1914		Since 1914	
	Voluntary	Involuntary	Voluntary	Involuntary

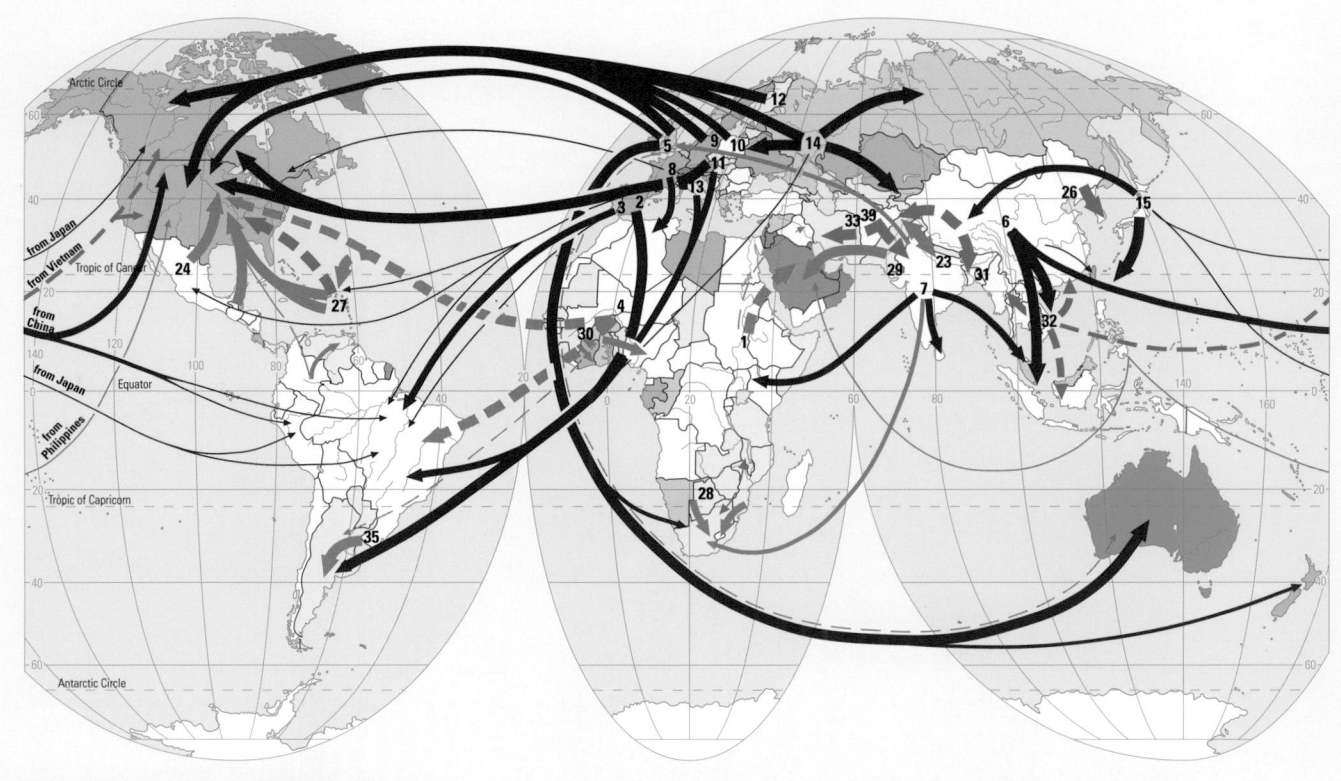

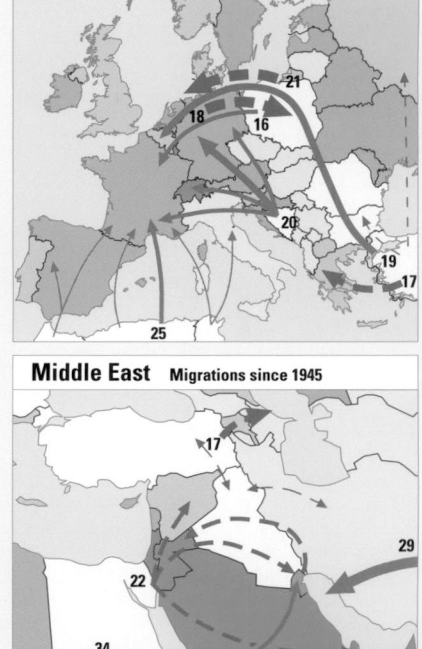

Europe Migrations since 1914

Middle East Migrations since 1945

Major world migrations since 1500 (over 1 million people)

1. North and East African slaves to Arabia (4.3m) 1500–1900
2. Spanish to South and Central America (2.3m) 1530–1914
3. Portuguese to Brazil (1.4m)..........................1530–1914
4. West African slaves to South America (4.6m) 1550–1860
   to Caribbean (4m) 1580–1860
   to North/Central America (1m) 1650–1820
5. British and Irish to North America (13.5m) 1620–1914
   to Australasia and South Africa (3m) 1790–1914
6. Chinese to Southeast Asia (22m) 1820–1914
   to North America (1m) 1880–1914
7. Indian migrant workers (3m) 1850–1914
8. French to North Africa (1.5m) 1850–1914
9. Germans to North America (5m)..........................1850–1914
10. Poles to North America (3.6m) 1850–1914
11. Austro-Hungarians to North America (3.2m) 1850–1914
    to Western Europe (3.4m)...........1850–1914
    to South America (1.8m) 1850–1914

12. Scandinavians to North America (2.7m) 1850–1914
13. Italians to North America (5m) 1860–1914
    to South America (3.7m)..............1860–1914
14. Russians to North America (2.2m) 1880–1914
    to Western Europe (2.2m)..............1880–1914
    to Siberia (6m) 1880–1914
    to Central Asia (4m)..................1880–1914
15. Japanese to Eastern Asia, Southeast Asia and America (8m) 1900–1914
16. Poles to Western Europe (1m) 1920–1940
17. Greeks and Armenians from Turkey (1.6m) 1922–1923
18. European Jews to extermination camps (5m) 1940–1944
19. Turks to Western Europe (1.9m) 1940–
20. Yugoslavs to Western Europe (2m) 1940–
21. Germans to Western Europe (9.8m) 1945–1947
22. Palestinian refugees (2m)............................1947–
23. Indian and Pakistani refugees (15m) 1947
24. Mexicans to North America (9m)........................1950–

25. North Africans to Western Europe (1.1m) 1950–
26. Korean refugees (5m)..............................1950–1954
27. Latin Americans and West Indians to North America (4.7m) 1960–
28. Migrant workers to South Africa (1.5m)...............1960–
29. Indians and Pakistanis to the Persian Gulf (2.4m) 1970–
30. Migrant workers to Nigeria and Ivory Coast (3m) 1970–
31. Bangladeshi and Pakistani refugees (2m) 1972
32. Vietnamese and Cambodian refugees (1.5m) 1975–
33. Afghan refugees (6.1m).............................1979–
34. Egyptians to the Persian Gulf and Libya (2.9m) 1980–
35. Migrant workers to Argentina (2m) 1980–
36. Mozambique refugees (1.7m)........................1985–
37. Yugoslav/Balkan refugees (1.7m) 1992–
38. Rwanda/Burundi refugees (2.6m) 1994–
39. Afghan refugees (2.1m)............................2001–

BUILDING THE USA

US Immigration, 1920 and 2009

For decades the USA was the magnet that attracted millions of immigrants, notably from Central and Eastern Europe, the flow peaking in the early years of the 20th century. By the mid-1990s the proportion of immigrants had increased again to pre-World War II rates, reaching over 12% by 2009. However, the balance of origin had swung from Europe to Latin America and Asia, as the graphs indicate.

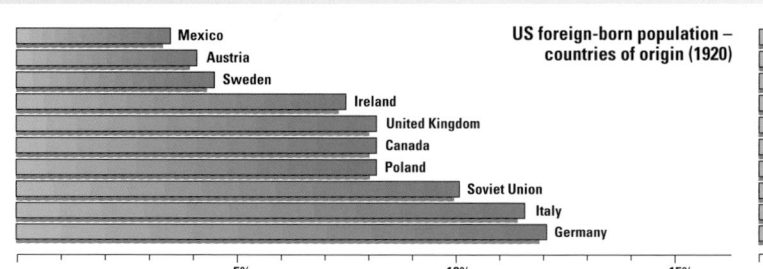

US foreign-born population – countries of origin (1920)

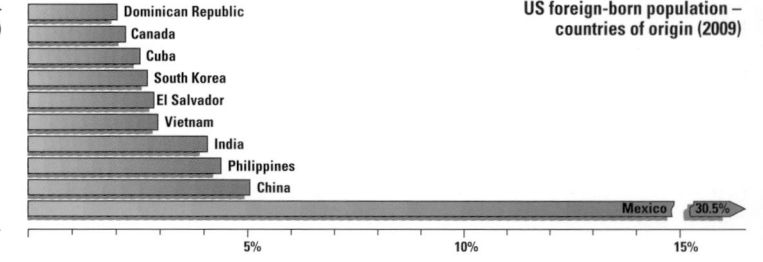

US foreign-born population – countries of origin (2009)

PREDOMINANT LANGUAGES

INDO-EUROPEAN FAMILY

1	Balto-Slavic group (incl. Russian, Ukrainian)
2	Germanic group (incl. English, German)
3	Celtic group
4	Greek
	Albanian
6	Iranian group
	Armenian
8	Romance group (incl. Spanish, Portuguese, French, Italian)
9	Indo-Aryan group (incl. Hindi, Bengali, Urdu, Punjabi, Marathi)

CAUCASIAN FAMILY

AFRO-ASIATIC FAMILY

11	Semitic group (incl. Arabic)
12	Kushitic group
13	Berber group

14	**KHOISAN FAMILY**
15	**NIGER-CONGO FAMILY**
16	**NILO-SAHARAN FAMILY**
17	**URALIC FAMILY**

ALTAIC FAMILY

18	Turkic group (incl. Turkish)
19	Mongolian group
20	Tungus-Manchu group
21	Japanese and Korean

SINO-TIBETAN FAMILY

22	Sinitic (Chinese) languages (incl. Mandarin, Wu, Yue)
23	Tibetic-Burmic languages

| 24 | **TAI FAMILY** |

AUSTRO-ASIATIC FAMILY

25	Mon-Khmer group
26	Munda group
27	Vietnamese

28	**DRAVIDIAN FAMILY** (incl. Telugu, Tamil)
29	**AUSTRONESIAN FAMILY** (incl. Malay-Indonesian, Javanese)
30	**OTHER LANGUAGES**

First-language speakers, in millions (2008)

Mandarin Chinese	845
Spanish	329
English	328
Arabic	221
Hindi	182
Bengali	181
Portuguese	178
Russian	144
Japanese	122
German	90
Javanese	85
Wu Chinese	77
Telugu	70
Vietnamese	69
Marathi	68
French	68
Korean	66
Tamil	66
Punjabi	63
Italian	62

Languages form a kind of tree of development, splitting from a few ancient proto-tongues into branches that have grown apart and further divided with the passage of time. English and Hindi, for example, both belong to the great Indo-European family, although the relationship is only apparent after much analysis and comparison with non-Indo-European languages such as Chinese or Arabic. Hindi is part of the Indo-Aryan subgroup, whereas English is a member of Indo-European's Germanic branch. French, another Indo-European tongue, traces its descent through the Latin, or Romance, branch. A few languages – Basque is one example – have no apparent links with any other, living or dead. Most modern languages, of course, have acquired enormous quantities of vocabulary from each other.

DISTRIBUTION OF LIVING LANGUAGES

The figures refer to the number of languages currently in use in the regions shown

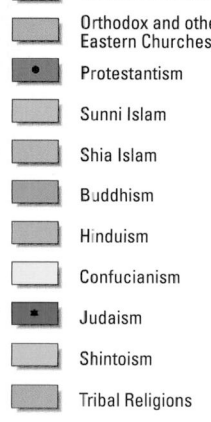

- Europe 234
- Americas 993
- Asia 2,322
- Pacific 1,250
- Africa 2,110

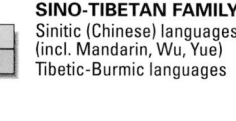

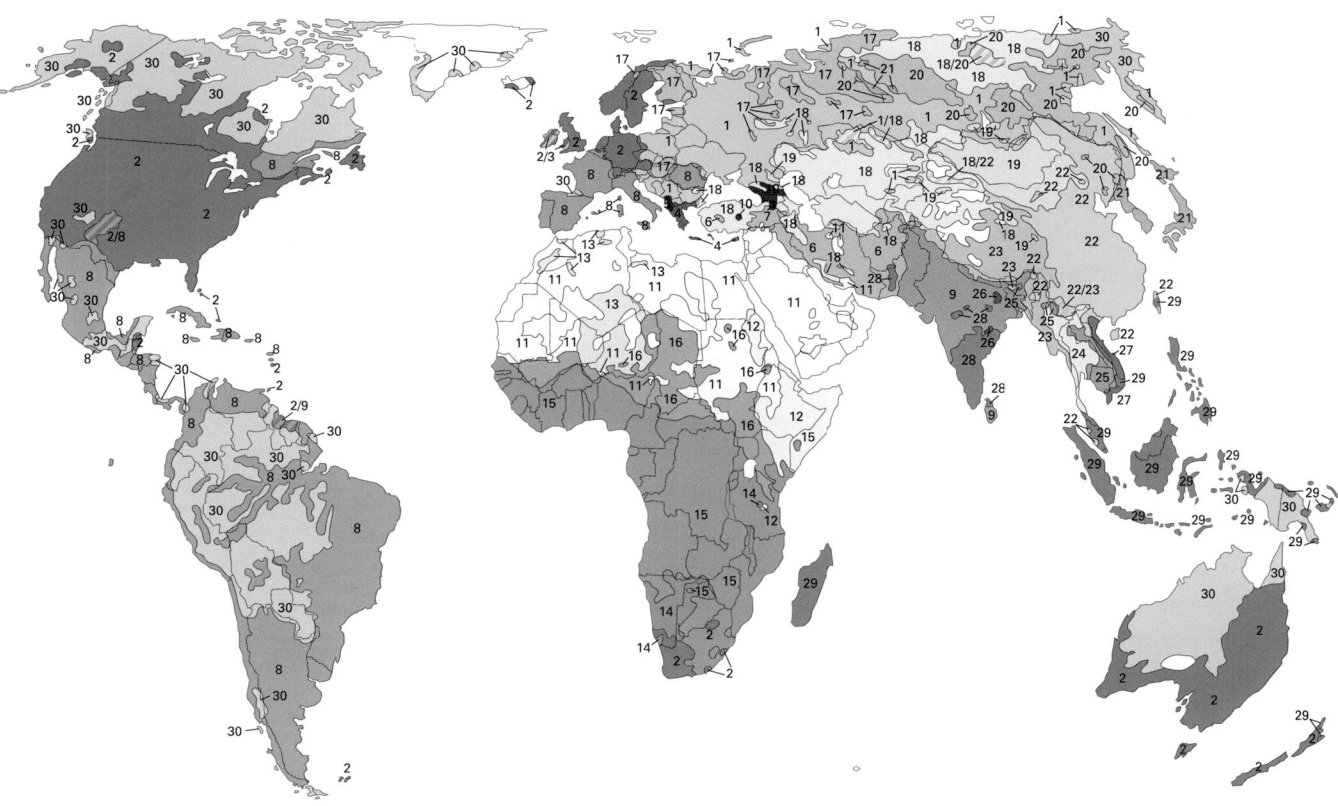

PREDOMINANT RELIGIONS

- Roman Catholicism
- Orthodox and other Eastern Churches
- Protestantism
- Sunni Islam
- Shia Islam
- Buddhism
- Hinduism
- Confucianism
- Judaism
- Shintoism
- Tribal Religions

Religions are not as easily mapped as the physical contours of the land. Divisions are often blurred and frequently overlapping: most nations include people of many different faiths – or no faith at all. Some religions, like Islam and Christianity, have proselytes worldwide; others, like Hinduism and Confucianism, are restricted to a particular area, though modern migrations have taken some Indians and Chinese very far from their cultural origins. It is also difficult to show the degree to which religion controls daily life: Christian Western Europe, for example, is now far less dominated by its religion than are the Islamic nations of the Middle East. Similarly, figures for the major faiths' adherents make no distinction between nominal believers enrolled at birth and those for whom religion is a vital part of their existence.

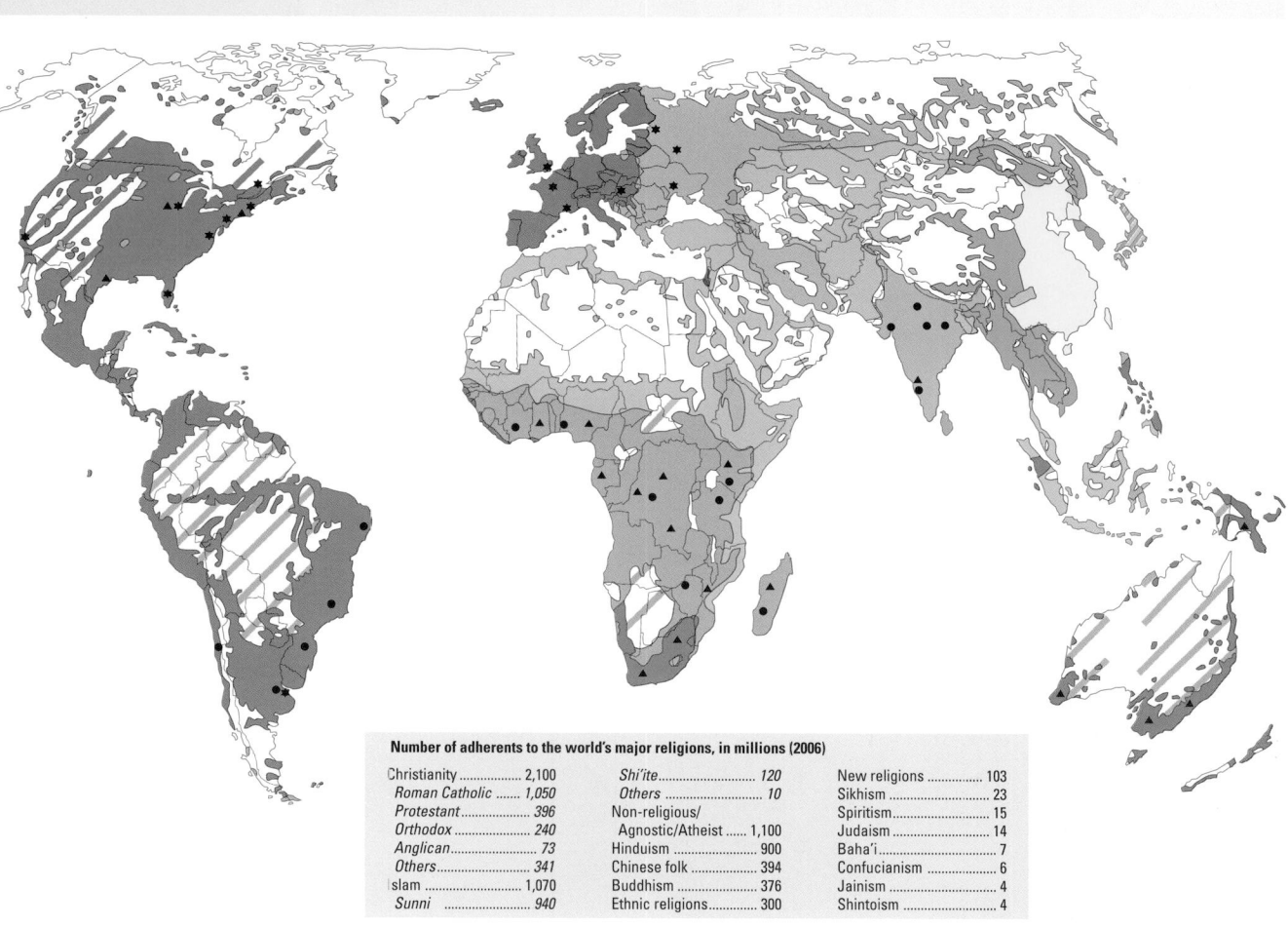

Number of adherents to the world's major religions, in millions (2006)

Christianity ... 2,100	Shi'ite ... 120	New religions ... 103
Roman Catholic ... 1,050	*Others ... 10*	Sikhism ... 23
Protestant ... 396	Non-religious/	Spiritism ... 15
Orthodox ... 240	Agnostic/Atheist ... 1,100	Judaism ... 14
Anglican ... 73	Hinduism ... 900	Baha'i ... 7
Others ... 341	Chinese folk ... 394	Confucianism ... 6
Islam ... 1,070	Buddhism ... 376	Jainism ... 4
Sunni ... 940	Ethnic religions ... 300	Shintoism ... 4

For more information:
92 Migration
93 Religion

The 20th century witnessed two world wars, followed by a Cold War which several times threatened to erupt into a third world war, fought with nuclear weapons. The Cold War was marked by a great number of conflicts. Some were colonial wars, as the empires of the first half of the century fell apart, some were border wars, and some were civil wars. All the wars have caused great suffering among civilians, many of whom were forced to join the ranks of the world's refugees.

In the late 1980s, many people hoped that the end of the Cold War, following the collapse of Communist regimes in the former Soviet Union and Eastern Europe, would herald a new era of international stability. Instead, old ethnic and religious antagonisms surfaced in many areas, leading to civil war in such places as Chechenia, in Russia, and the former Yugoslavia. Nationalist rivalries, suppressed under Communist rule, replaced ideological factors as the major cause of conflict.

War is a very human activity, with no real equivalent in any other species. Yet humans also function well when they cooperate – evolution has made this so. Hunter-gatherers in cooperative bands were far more effective than animals that prowled. Agriculture, urbanization, and industrialization all depend on the ability of humans to cooperate.

The creation of the United Nations in 1945 held out hope that the world's nations, tired of war, would have the means to control humanity's aggressive instincts. Although the UN lacks the power to halt conflicts, it has often helped to achieve negotiation. Economic pressures have led to another kind of cooperation, resulting in the creation of common markets and economic unions, such as ASEAN in Southeast Asia, the European Union, and NAFTA in North America.

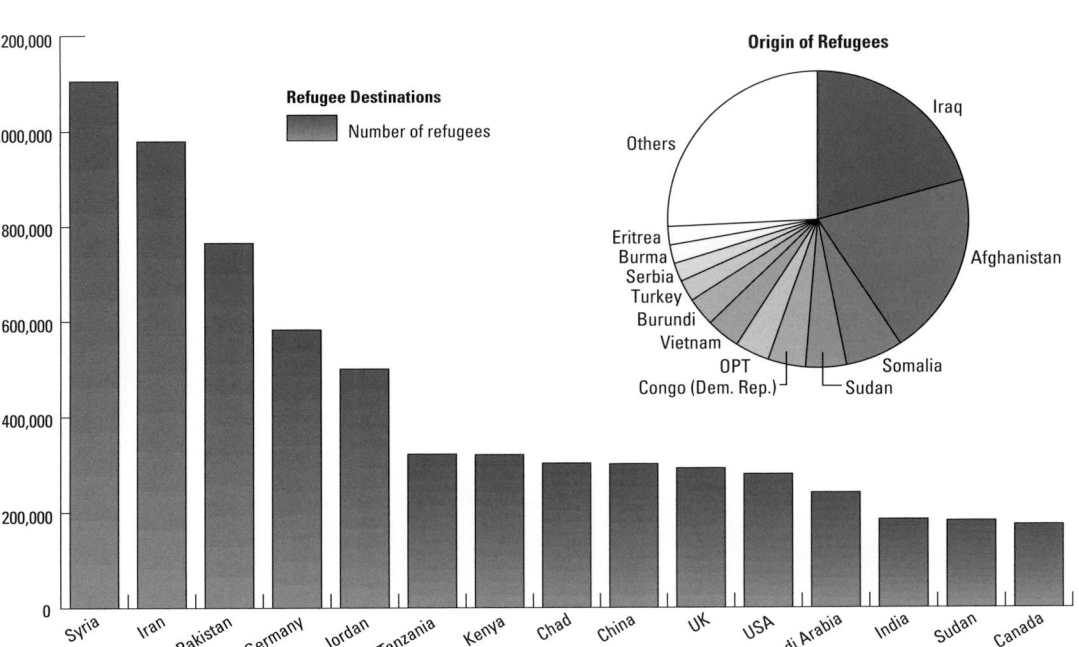

THE WORLD'S REFUGEES

Refugees by host nation (bar-chart, left) and by nation of origin (pie-chart, left) (2008). The source is the United Nations High Commission for Refugees (UNHCR).

The pie-chart shows the origins of the world's refugees, while the bar-chart below shows their destinations. According to the United Nations High Commission for Refugees (UNHCR) in 2009 there were 10.4 million refugees. However, the UNHCR definition of a refugee, "a person who has left or remains outside their own country because they have a well-founded fear of persecution, or because their safety is threatened by events seriously disturbing public order," does not include people who are in a refugee-like situation but who have not been formally recognized. In 2009, there were a further 15.6 million people who were internally displaced, and a total "population of concern" of 36.5 million people, worldwide.

All but a few who cross international boundaries seek asylum in neighboring countries, which are often the least equipped to deal with them. Lacking any rights or power, they frequently become an unwelcome burden to their hosts. Usually, the best any refugee can hope for is rudimentary food and shelter in temporary camps. Many Palestinians have been forced to live in camps since 1948.

WAR SINCE 1945

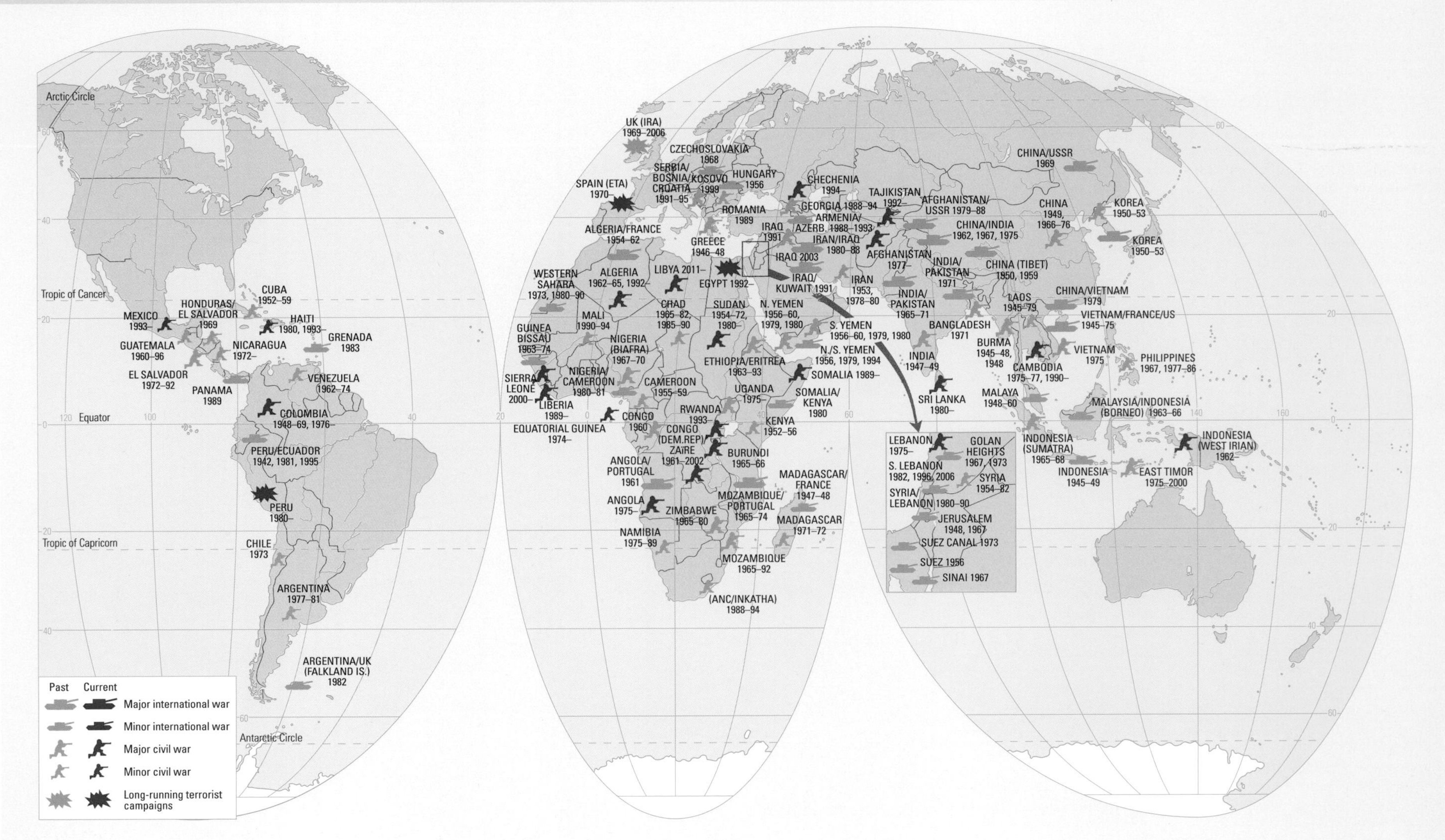

Past Current
- Major international war
- Minor international war
- Major civil war
- Minor civil war
- Long-running terrorist campaigns

UNITED NATIONS

The United Nations Organization was born as World War II drew to its conclusion. Six years of strife had strengthened the world's desire for peace, but an effective international organization was needed to help achieve it. That body would replace the League of Nations which, since its inception in 1920, had failed to curb the aggression of at least some of its member nations. At the United Nations Conference on International Organization held in San Francisco, the United Nations Charter was drawn up. Ratified by the Security Council and signed by the 51 original members, it came into effect on October 24, 1945.

The Charter set out the aims of the organization: to maintain peace and security, and to develop friendly relations between nations; to achieve international cooperation in solving economic, social, cultural, and humanitarian problems; to promote respect for human rights and fundamental freedoms; and to harmonize the activities of nations in order to achieve these common goals.

Membership From the original 51, membership of the UN has now grown to 192. Recent additions include East Timor, Switzerland, and Montenegro. There are only two independent states which are not members – Taiwan and the Vatican City. Official languages are Chinese, English, French, Russian, Spanish, and Arabic.

Funding The UN budget for 2008–9 was US $4.2 billion. Contributions are assessed by the members' ability to pay, with the maximum 22% of the total (the USA's share), and the minimum 0.001%. The 27-member EU pays nearly 39% of the budget.

Peacekeeping The UN has been involved in 64 peacekeeping operations worldwide since 1948.

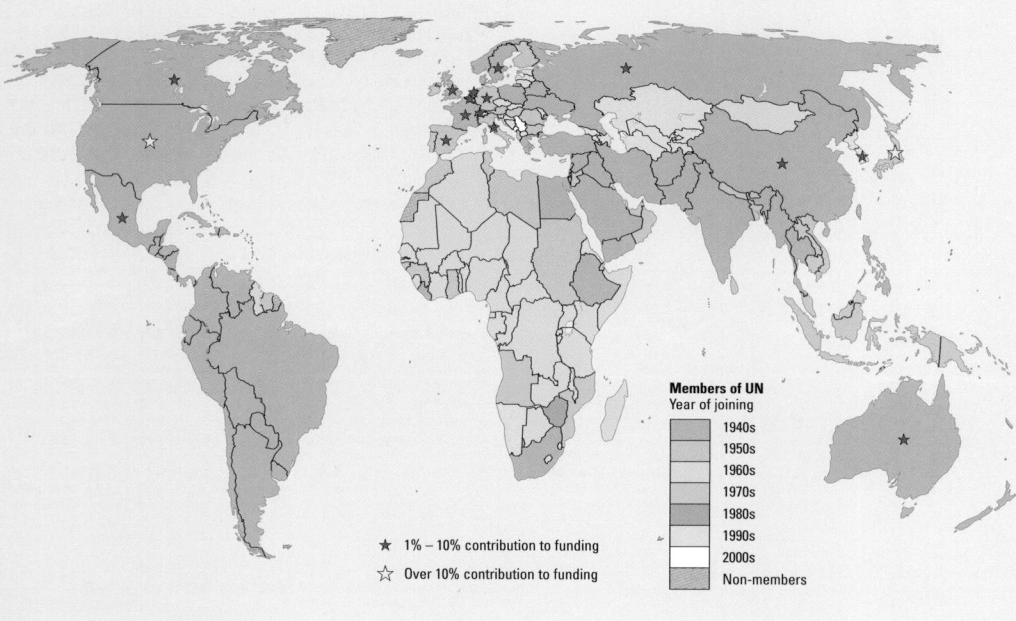

Members of UN
Year of joining

- 1940s
- 1950s
- 1960s
- 1970s
- 1980s
- 1990s
- 2000s
- Non-members

★ 1% – 10% contribution to funding
☆ Over 10% contribution to funding

OCEAN PIRACY

Piracy, or the robbing or hijacking of ships, their crews, and their cargoes, has been increasing steadily in certain parts of the world over recent years. In 2009, the International Maritime Bureau recorded 380 attacks on vessels worldwide, compared with 239 attacks in 2006. The most high-profile acts of piracy were off the coasts of Nigeria and Indonesia, and, most particularly, off the Somali coast in the Gulf of Aden (see map right).

Some of the ships involved have been large ocean-going tankers, bulk carriers, and container vessels, and the pirates have proved that they can sail these without the crew. Attacks have taken place up to 1,150 miles [1,852 km] off the Somali coast when larger "mother ships" are used, from which smaller vessels operate. Firearms and rocket-propelled grenades have been used by the hijackers and many millions of pounds paid in ransom by the ships' owners to release their vessels, much of which goes to support terrorist groups.

To counter this very real threat, both the United States and the European Union have introduced naval operations in the area to try to protect their shipping interests, with some success. However, with such a large area of ocean to cover, it is very difficult to police.

As a result of the pirate activity, insurance premiums have risen and, should this continue, shipping will start to avoid the Suez Canal and take the longer and more expensive route around the Cape of Good Hope.

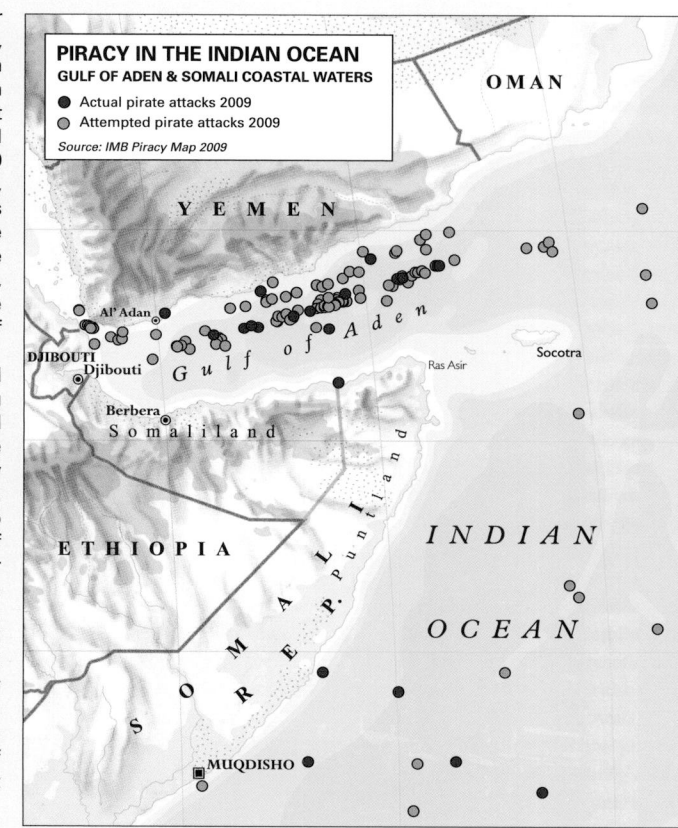

PIRACY IN THE INDIAN OCEAN
GULF OF ADEN & SOMALI COASTAL WATERS
● Actual pirate attacks 2009
● Attempted pirate attacks 2009
Source: IMB Piracy Map 2009

INTERNATIONAL ORGANIZATIONS

OAS Organization of American States (formed in 1948). It aims to promote social and economic cooperation between countries in the developed North America and developing Latin America.
EU European Union (evolved from the European Community in 1993). Cyprus, the Czech Republic, Estonia, Hungary, Latvia, Lithuania, Malta, Poland, the Slovak Republic, and Slovenia joined the EU in May 2004, Bulgaria and Romania joined in 2007. The other 15 members of the EU are Austria, Belgium, Denmark, Finland, France, Germany, Greece, Ireland, Italy, Luxembourg, Netherlands, Portugal, Spain, Sweden, and the UK. Together, the 27 members aim to integrate economies, coordinate social developments, and bring about political union.
AU The African Union was set up in 2002, taking over from the Organization of African Unity (1963). It has 53 members. Working languages are Arabic, English, French, and Portuguese.
COLOMBO PLAN (formed in 1951) Its 25 members aim to promote economic and social development in Asia and the Pacific.

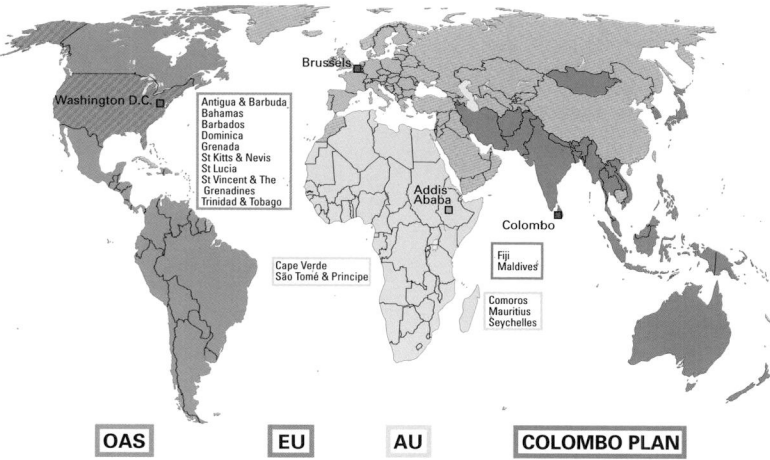

Antigua & Barbuda
Bahamas
Barbados
Dominica
Grenada
St Kitts & Nevis
St Lucia
St Vincent & The Grenadines
Trinidad & Tobago

Cape Verde
São Tomé & Principe

Fiji
Maldives

Comoros
Mauritius
Seychelles

| OAS | EU | AU | COLOMBO PLAN |

G8 Group of eight leading industrialized nations, comprising Canada, France, Germany, Italy, Japan, Russia, the UK, and the USA. Periodic meetings are held to discuss major world issues, such as world recessions.
APEC Asia-Pacific Economic Cooperation (formed in 1989). It aims to enhance economic growth and prosperity for the region and to strengthen the Asia-Pacific community. APEC is the only intergovernmental grouping in the world operating on the basis of non-binding commitments, open dialogue, and equal respect for the views of all participants. There are 21 member economies.
OECD Organization for Economic Cooperation and Development (formed in 1961). It comprises 30 major free-market economies. The "G8" is its "inner group" of leading industrial nations, comprising Canada, France, Germany, Italy, Japan, Russia, the UK, and the USA.
ACP African-Caribbean-Pacific (formed in 1963). Members enjoy economic ties with the EU.
OPEC Organization of Petroleum Exporting Countries (formed in 1960). It controls about three-quarters of the world's oil supply. Gabon formally withdrew from OPEC in August 1996.

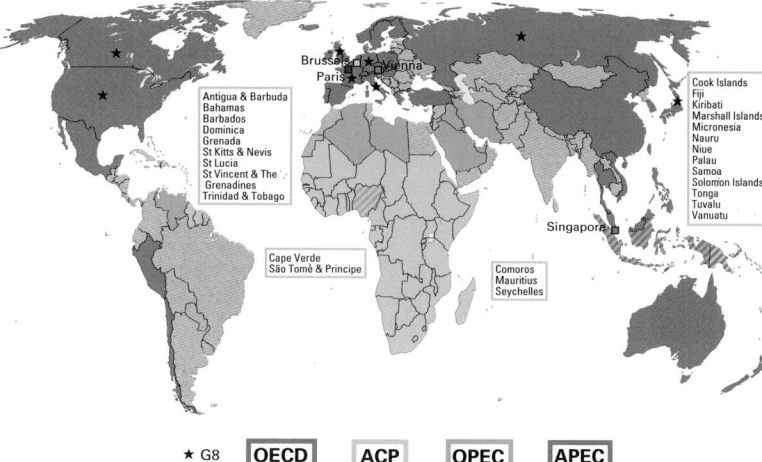

Antigua & Barbuda
Bahamas
Barbados
Dominica
Grenada
St Kitts & Nevis
St Lucia
St Vincent & The Grenadines
Trinidad & Tobago

Cook Islands
Fiji
Kiribati
Marshall Islands
Micronesia
Nauru
Niue
Palau
Samoa
Solomon Islands
Tonga
Tuvalu
Vanuatu

Cape Verde
São Tomé & Principe

Comoros
Mauritius
Seychelles

★ G8 | OECD | ACP | OPEC | APEC |

NATO North Atlantic Treaty Organization (formed in 1949). It continues despite the winding-up of the Warsaw Pact in 1991. Bulgaria, Estonia, Latvia, Lithuania, Romania, the Slovak Republic, and Slovenia became members in 2004.
LAIA The Latin American Integration Association (formed in 1980) superceded the Latin American Free Trade Association formed in 1961. Its aim is to promote freer regional trade.
ARAB LEAGUE (1945) Aims to promote economic, social, political, and military cooperation. There are 22 member nations.
COMMONWEALTH The Commonwealth of Nations evolved from the British Empire. Pakistan was suspended in 1999, but reinstated in 2004. Zimbabwe was suspended in 2002 and, in response to its continued suspension, Zimbabwe left the Commonwealth in 2003. Fiji Islands was suspended in 2006 following a military coup. Rwanda joined the Commonwealth in 2009, as the 54th member state, becoming only the second country which was not formerly a British colony to be admitted to the group.
ASEAN Association of Southeast Asian Nations (formed in 1967). Cambodia joined in 1999.

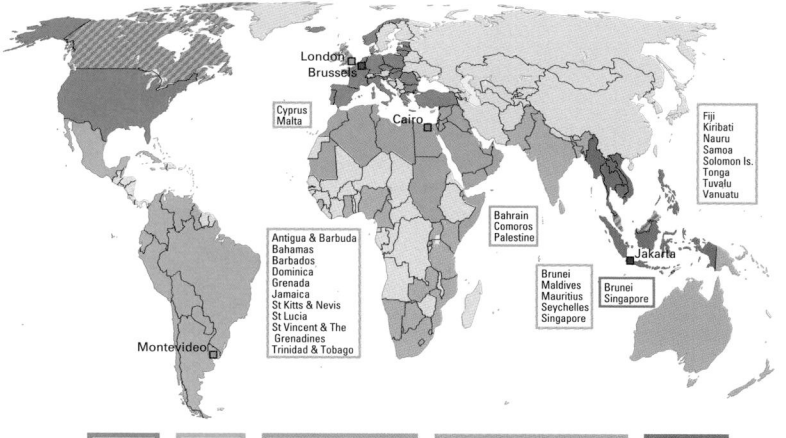

Cyprus
Malta

Fiji
Kiribati
Nauru
Samoa
Solomon Is.
Tonga
Tuvalu
Vanuatu

Bahrain
Comoros
Palestine

Antigua & Barbuda
Bahamas
Barbados
Dominica
Grenada
Jamaica
St Kitts & Nevis
St Lucia
St Vincent & The Grenadines
Trinidad & Tobago

Brunei
Maldives
Mauritius
Seychelles
Singapore

Brunei
Singapore

| NATO | LAIA | ARAB LEAGUE | COMMONWEALTH | ASEAN |

For more information:
82 Global warming
   Carbon dioxide
98 Minerals
103 World shipping

Every year, the world's energy consumption is about the equivalent of what would come from burning 10,000 million tonnes of oil (10,000 MtOe) – a 20-fold increase since 1850. Two-fifths of this total actually comes from burning oil and most of the rest comes from coal and natural gas.

The oil crises in the 1970s precipitated concern over dependence on finite fossil fuels as the primary source of energy, and growing environmental awareness has added impetus to the search for alternative energy resources. Fossil fuel combustion damages the environment through the release of gases and particulate matter, but two other major sources of energy, hydro-electricity and nuclear power, are also controversial. Hydroelectricity production involves flooding large areas to create reservoirs, while nuclear power stations generate dangerous radioactive wastes and can cause major disasters. Nuclear power is now a growing source of energy. By 2009, about 15% of the world's electricity was produced by nuclear plants, compared with 3.3% in 1973.

Alternative energy resources may soon provide a much larger proportion of the world's energy consumption. Solar and wind energy may become important in such countries as China and India, while tidal, wave, and geothermal energy all have potential in appropriate areas. Experts calculate that solar power could, in theory, supply between five and ten times the present electricity supply of developing countries.

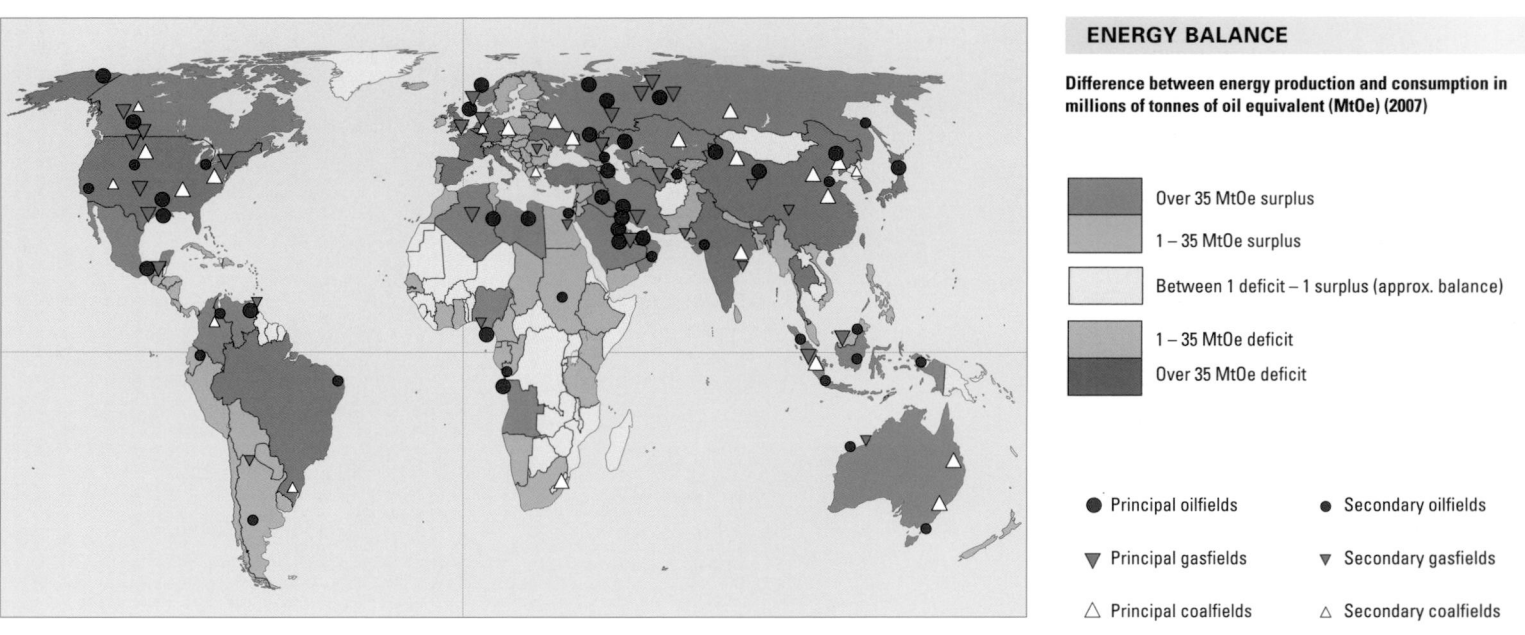

ENERGY BALANCE

Difference between energy production and consumption in millions of tonnes of oil equivalent (MtOe) (2007)

- Over 35 MtOe surplus
- 1 – 35 MtOe surplus
- Between 1 deficit – 1 surplus (approx. balance)
- 1 – 35 MtOe deficit
- Over 35 MtOe deficit

● Principal oilfields   ● Secondary oilfields
▼ Principal gasfields   ▼ Secondary gasfields
△ Principal coalfields   △ Secondary coalfields

ENERGY CONSUMPTION

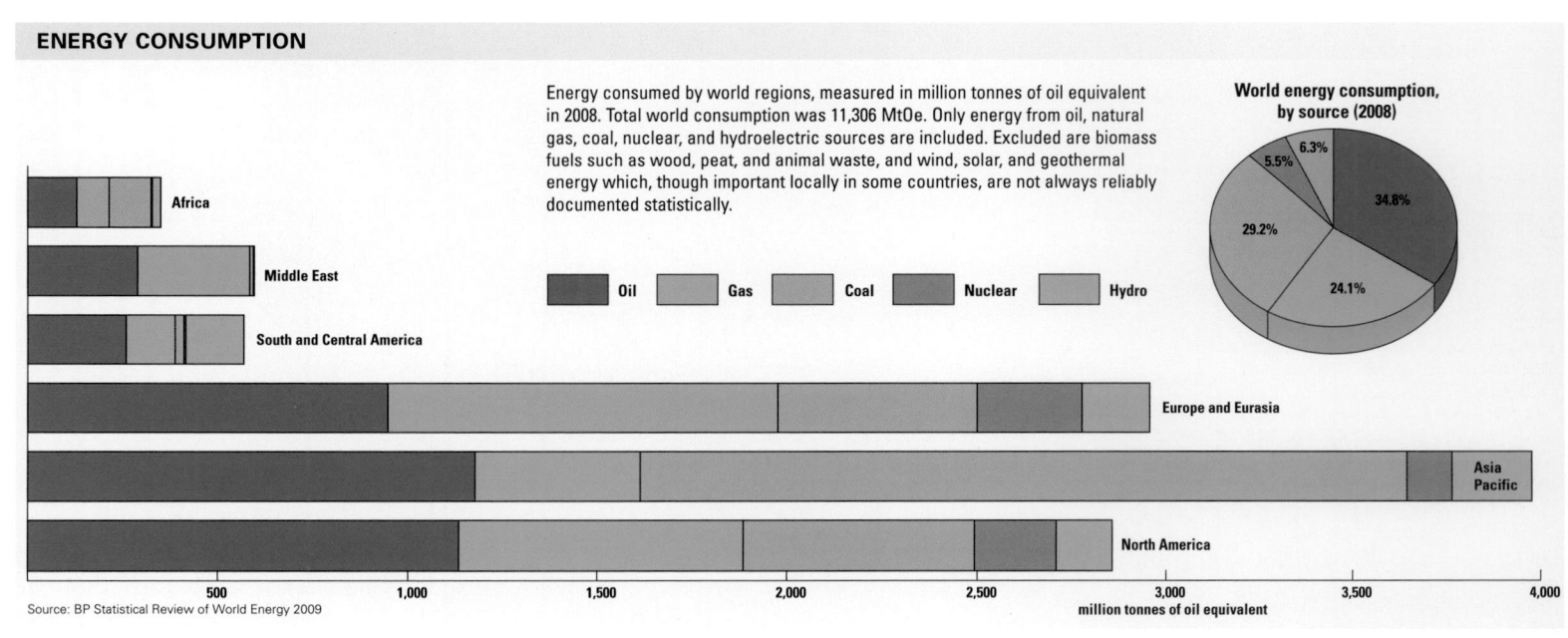

Energy consumed by world regions, measured in million tonnes of oil equivalent in 2008. Total world consumption was 11,306 MtOe. Only energy from oil, natural gas, coal, nuclear, and hydroelectric sources are included. Excluded are biomass fuels such as wood, peat, and animal waste, and wind, solar, and geothermal energy which, though important locally in some countries, are not always reliably documented statistically.

■ Oil   ■ Gas   ■ Coal   ■ Nuclear   ■ Hydro

World energy consumption, by source (2008)

34.8%
24.1%
29.2%
5.5%
6.3%

Africa
Middle East
South and Central America
Europe and Eurasia
Asia Pacific
North America

500 1,000 1,500 2,000 2,500 3,000 3,500 4,000
million tonnes of oil equivalent

Source: BP Statistical Review of World Energy 2009

ENERGY PRODUCTION

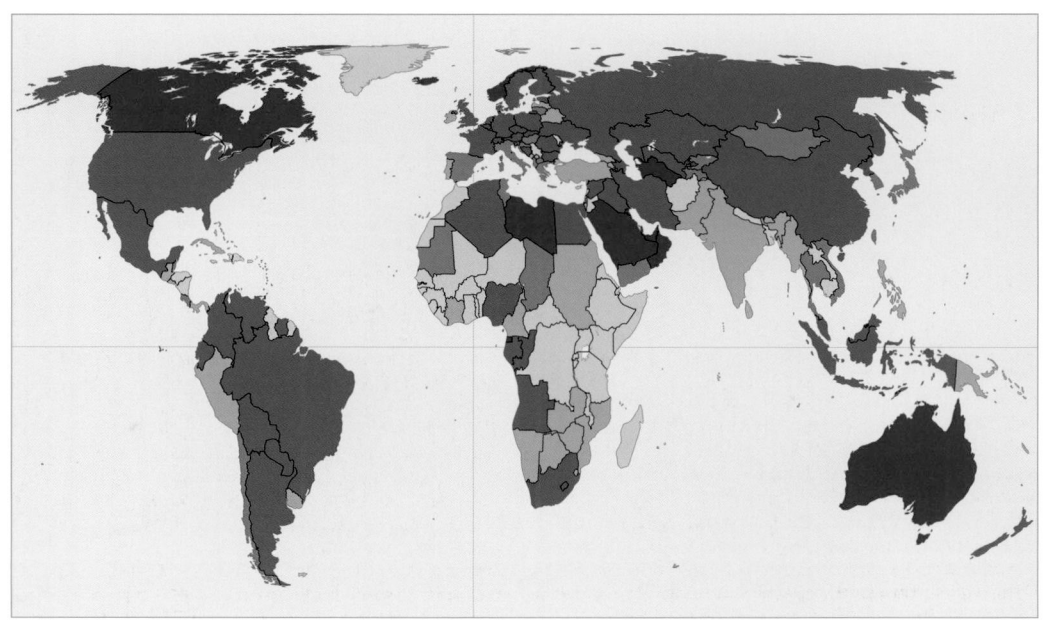

Energy production in tonnes of oil equivalent per capita (2007)

- Over 10
- 1 – 10
- 0.5 – 1
- 0.1 – 0.5
- Under 0.1
- No data available

Highest energy producers, tonnes of oil equivalent per capita

Qatar	111.7
Brunei	65.0
Kuwait	61.3
Norway	55.5
United Arab Emirates	44.3

OIL MOVEMENTS

Major world movements of oil in millions of tonnes (2008)

1.	Middle East to Asia (not China or Japan)	399.0
2.	Former Soviet Union to Europe	318.5
3.	Middle East to Japan	196.9
4.	Middle East to Europe	127.6
5.	Canada to USA	121.7
6.	Middle East to USA	119.7
7.	South and Central America to USA	119.4
8.	North Africa to Europe	101.3
9.	Middle East to China	92.0
10.	West Africa to USA	90.9
11.	Mexico to USA	64.7
	Total world imports	**2,697.8 million tonnes**

In 1990, China consumed 120 million tonnes of oil, leaving a surplus for export. In 2009 it consumed 405 million tonnes, of which it had to import around half. It is predicted that by 2030 China will be consuming over 800 million tonnes of oil, importing around three-quarters.

The majority of China's imported oil comes from the Middle East and Africa and has to pass through the narrow and crowded Singapore Strait. The Chinese government is pushing for alternative routes, such as a pipeline from Kazakhstan and a transit route from the Indian Ocean through Burma to Southern China.

◄ With many of the world's onshore oilfields reaching their maturity, exploration and production in ever-deeper ocean waters is taking place to try to satisfy demand. The "Deepwater Horizon" rig in the Gulf of Mexico drilled one of the world's deepest oil wells with a depth of 35,055 ft [10,685 m] before an explosion in April 2010 resulted in a massive oil spill.

ENERGY RESERVES

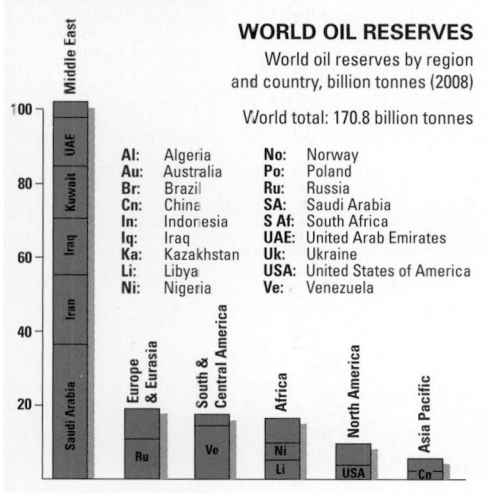

WORLD OIL RESERVES
World oil reserves by region and country, billion tonnes (2008)

World total: 170.8 billion tonnes

Al:	Algeria	No:	Norway
Au:	Australia	Po:	Poland
Br:	Brazil	Ru:	Russia
Cn:	China	SA:	Saudi Arabia
In:	Indonesia	S Af:	South Africa
Iq:	Iraq	UAE:	United Arab Emirates
Ka:	Kazakhstan	Uk:	Ukraine
Li:	Libya	USA:	United States of America
Ni:	Nigeria	Ve:	Venezuela

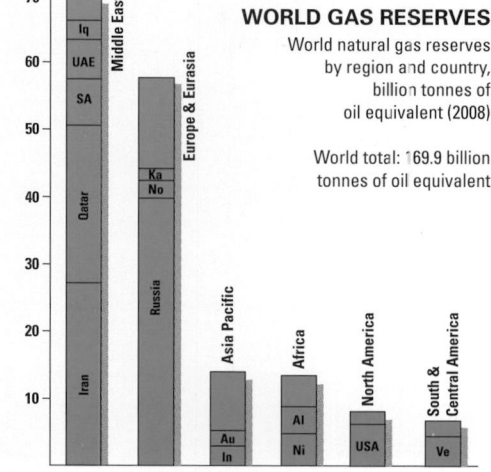

WORLD GAS RESERVES
World natural gas reserves by region and country, billion tonnes of oil equivalent (2008)

World total: 169.9 billion tonnes of oil equivalent

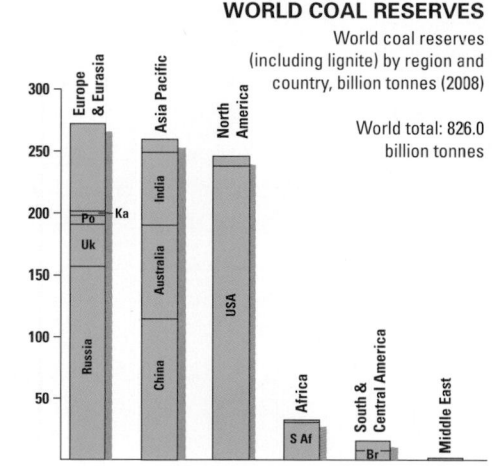

WORLD COAL RESERVES
World coal reserves (including lignite) by region and country, billion tonnes (2008)

World total: 826.0 billion tonnes

NUCLEAR POWER

Major producers by percentage of world total and by percentage of domestic electricity generation (2008)

Country	% of world total production	Country	% of nuclear as proportion of domestic electricity
1. USA	31.0%	1. France	77.5%
2. France	16.1%	2. Lithuania	75.6%
3. Japan	9.4%	3. Slovak Rep.	56.7%
4. Russia	5.9%	4. Belgium	55.4%
5. South Korea	5.5%	5. Ukraine	45.5%
6. Germany	5.4%	6. Slovenia	42.2%
7. Canada	3.4%	7. Sweden	41.9%
8. Ukraine	3.2%	8. Armenia	40.7%
9. China	2.5%	9. Switzerland	40.2%
10. Sweden	2.3%	10. Hungary	37.2%

Although the 1980s were a bad time for the nuclear power industry (fears of long-term environmental damage were heavily reinforced by the 1986 disaster at Chernobyl), the industry picked up in the early 1990s. Sixteen countries currently rely on nuclear power to supply over 25% of their total electricity requirements. There are over 400 operating nuclear power stations worldwide, with over 100 more planned or under construction.

ELECTRICITY PRODUCTION

Percentage of electricity generated by source (2007)

	Over 75% from thermal
	50 – 75% from thermal
	Over 75% from hydro
	50 – 75% from hydro
	Over 50% from nuclear
	Other (no dominant source)
	No data available
◉	Selected geothermal plants
◈	Selected hydroelectric plants

HYDROELECTRICITY

Major producers by percentage of world total and by percentage of domestic electricity generation (2007)

Country	% of world total production	Country	% of hydroelectric as proportion of domestic electricity
1. China	14.3%	1. Lesotho	100%
2. Brazil	12.3%	= Bhutan	100%
3. Canada	12.2%	= Paraguay	100%
4. USA	8.3%	4. Mozambique	99.9%
5. Russia	5.8%	5. Congo (Dem. Rep.)	99.7%
6. Norway	4.4%	6. Nepal	99.5%
7. India	4.1%	7. Zambia	99.4%
8. Venezuela	2.8%	8. Norway	98.7%
9. Japan	2.4%	9. Tajikistan	97.9%
10. Sweden	2.2%	10. Burundi	97.8%

Countries heavily reliant on hydroelectricity are usually small and non-industrial: a high proportion of hydroelectric power more often reflects a modest energy budget than vast hydroelectric resources. The USA, for instance, produces only 6% of its domestic power requirements from hydroelectricity; yet that 6% amounts to almost half the hydropower generated by the whole of Africa.

ALTERNATIVE ENERGY RESOURCES

Solar: Each year the Sun bestows upon the Earth almost a million times as much energy as is locked up in all the planet's oil reserves, but only an insignificant fraction is trapped and used commercially. In a few installations around the world, mirrors focus the Sun's rays on to boilers, whose steam generates electricity by spinning turbines.

Wind: Caused by uneven heating of the Earth, winds are themselves a form of solar energy. Windmills have been long used for wind power; recent models, often arranged in banks on wind-swept high ground or off coastlines, usually generate electricity. Wind-power figures are given in the table (*right*). Although it currently produces less than 1% of the world's electricity, wind power contributes 19% of all electricity generated in Denmark.

Tidal: The energy from tides is potentially enormous, although only a few installations have so far been built to exploit it. In theory, at least, waves and currents could also provide almost unimaginable power, and the thermal differences in the ocean depths are another huge well

of potential energy. But work on extracting it is still at the experimental stage.

Geothermal: The Earth's temperature rises by 1°F for every 50 feet descent, with much steeper temperature gradients in geologically active areas. El Salvador, for example, produces 25% of its electricity from geothermal power stations, whilst the USA is the world's leading producer. Some of the oldest and most successful applications are in Iceland, where 86% of all households are heated by geothermal energy.

Biomass: The oldest of human fuels ranges from animal dung, still burned in cooking fires in much of North Africa and elsewhere, to sugarcane plantations feeding high-technology distilleries to produce ethanol for motor-vehicle engines. In Brazil and South Africa, plant ethanol provides up to 25% of motor fuel. Throughout the developing world, most biomass energy comes from firewood: although accurate figures are impossible to obtain, it may yield as much as 10% of the world's total energy consumption.

WIND POWER

World wind energy generating capacity, in megawatts

1984	600
1986	1,270
1988	1,580
1990	1,930
1992	2,510
1994	3,710
1996	6,115
1998	9,600
1999	11,700
2000	17,800
2001	23,300
2002	31,000
2003	39,300
2004	47,671
2005	58,982
2006	74,151
2007	93,927
2008	121,188
2009	157,899

For more information:

74 Geology

101 Patterns of production

103 World shipping

The use of metals played a vital part in the evolving technologies of early peoples. Copper first came into use around 10,000 years ago, bronze about 5,000 years ago, and iron 3,300 years ago. In the early stages of the Industrial Revolution, the location of coal, iron ore, and water power usually determined the location of new industries. But due to continuing improvements in transport, including oil pipelines, industries can now be located almost anywhere.

Minerals are distributed unevenly and some industrial countries, lacking their own mineral resources, import most of the raw materials they need. Some imports come from mineral-rich countries, such as Australia, but others come from developing countries, especially in Africa and South America. Most developing countries export unprocessed ores, losing out on the higher revenues gained from exporting metals.

Most minerals come from land deposits, because undersea deposits, with the exception of oil reserves under the continental shelves, have been inaccessible. But shortages of terrestrial minerals may one day encourage exploitation of the ocean floor.

URANIUM

Uranium was first discovered by the German chemist Martin Klaproth in 1789. In its pure state, uranium is an immensely heavy, white metal. Its main use is as a fuel in nuclear reactors and in nuclear weaponry, although depleted uranium is employed as a projectile in anti-missile cannons, where its mass ensures a lethal punch.

Uranium is very scarce: the main source is the rare ore pitchblende, which itself contains only 0.2% uranium oxide. This blackish, lustrous ore occurs in quartz veins. Only a minute fraction of that is the radioactive U^{235} isotope, though so-called breeder reactors can transmute the more common U^{238} into highly radioactive plutonium.

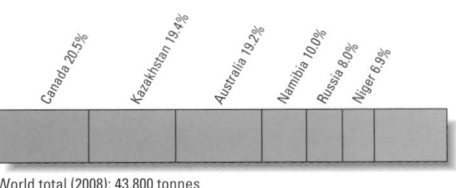

World total (2008): 43,800 tonnes

▶ Bingham Canyon Mine in Utah, USA, is one of the largest open-pit mines in the world. It measures over 2.5 miles [4 km] wide and 3,900 ft [1,200 m] deep. Copper-containing rocks are excavated from the surface downward in terraces. These terraces are 50–80 ft [15–25 m] high and provide access for equipment to work the rock face whilst maintaining stability of the sloping pit walls.

Today's copper market is booming due to global demands from construction, telecommunications, and electronics companies. Over 17 million tonnes of copper have been mined from Bingham Canyon Mine to date.

DIAMOND

Most of the world's diamond is found in kimberlite, or "blue ground," a basic peridotite rock; erosion may wash the diamond from its kimberlite matrix and deposit it with sand or gravel on river beds. Only a small proportion of the world's diamond, the most flawless, is cut into gemstones – "diamonds"; most are used in industry, where the material's remarkable hardness and abrasion resistance finds a use in cutting tools, drills, and dies. In 2008, the world's major producers were the Democratic Republic of the Congo (29.9%), Australia (23.4%), Russia (19.5%), South Africa (11.7%), and Botswana (10.4%). Natural diamonds now account for less than 10% of all industrial diamond output. Synthetic diamond production in centers such as Ireland, Japan, Russia, and the USA far exceeds it.

METALS

Figures refer to ore production unless otherwise specified after the world total figure.

The world's leading producers of aluminum ore (bauxite) in 2008 were as follows:

1. Australia 29.9%
2. China 17.1%
3. Brazil 10.7%
4. India 10.3%
5. Guinea 9.0%
6. Jamaica 6.8%
7. Russia 3.1%
8. Venezuela 2.7%
9. Suriname 2.6%
10. Kazakhstan 2.4%

The figures shown above are in stark contrast to the figures showing aluminum production (*see above right*). Australia, for example, produces 29.9% of the world's bauxite but only 5.1% of aluminum. Guinea and Jamaica account for almost 16% of the bauxite mined but have no smelters and export virtually all of it to countries like the USA and Canada.

Aluminum: Produced mainly from its oxide, bauxite, which yields 25% of its weight in aluminum. The cost of refining and production is often too high for producer-countries to bear, so bauxite is largely exported. Lightweight and corrosion resistant, aluminum alloys are widely used in aircraft, vehicles, cans, and packaging.

World total (2008): 39,000,000 tonnes

Lead: A soft metal, obtained mainly from galena (lead sulfide), which occurs in veins associated with iron, zinc, and silver sulfides. Its use in vehicle batteries accounts for the USA's prime consumer status; lead is also made into sheeting and piping. Its use as an additive to paints and petrol is decreasing.

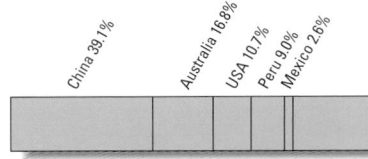

World total (2008): 3,840,000 tonnes

Tin: Soft, pliable and non-toxic, used to coat "tin" (tin-plated steel) cans, in the manufacture of foils and in alloys. The principal tin-bearing mineral is cassiterite (SnO_2), found in ore formed from molten rock. Producers and refiners were hit by a price collapse in 1991.

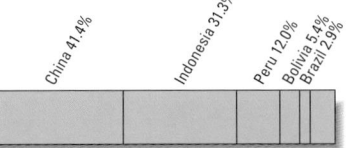

World total (2008): 326,000 tonnes

Gold: Regarded for centuries as the most valuable metal in the world and used to make coins, gold is still recognized as the monetary standard. A soft metal, it is alloyed to make jewelry; the electronics industry values its corrosion resistance and conductivity.

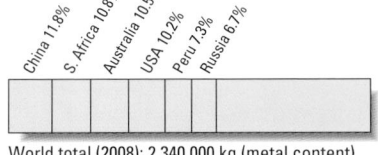

World total (2008): 2,340,000 kg (metal content)

Copper: Derived from low-yielding sulfide ores, copper is an important export for several developing countries. An excellent conductor of heat and electricity, it forms part of most electrical items, and is used in the manufacture of brass and bronze. Major importers include Japan and Germany.

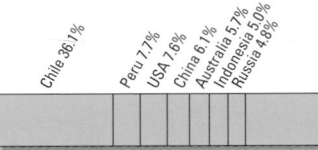

World total (2008): 15,400,000 tonnes

Mercury: The only metal that is liquid at normal temperatures, most is derived from its sulfide, cinnabar, found only in small quantities in volcanic areas. Apart from its value in thermometers and other instruments, most mercury production is used in anti-fungal and anti-fouling preparations, and to make detonators.

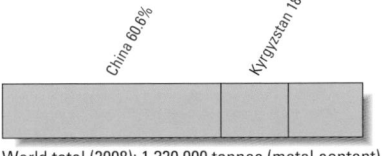

World total (2008): 1,320,000 tonnes (metal content)

Zinc: Often found in association with lead ores, zinc is highly resistant to corrosion, and about 40% of the refined metal is used to plate sheet steel, particularly vehicle bodies – a process known as galvanizing. Zinc is also used in dry batteries, paints, and dyes.

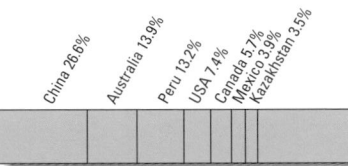

World total (2008): 10,900,000 tonnes

Silver: Most silver comes from ores mined and processed for other metals (including lead and copper). Pure or alloyed with harder metals, it is used for jewelry and ornaments. Industrial use includes dentistry, electronics, photography, and as a chemical catalyst.

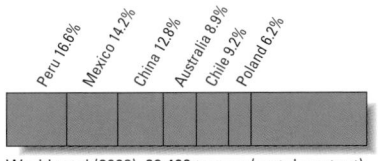

World total (2008): 20,400 tonnes (metal content)

DISTRIBUTION OF MINERALS

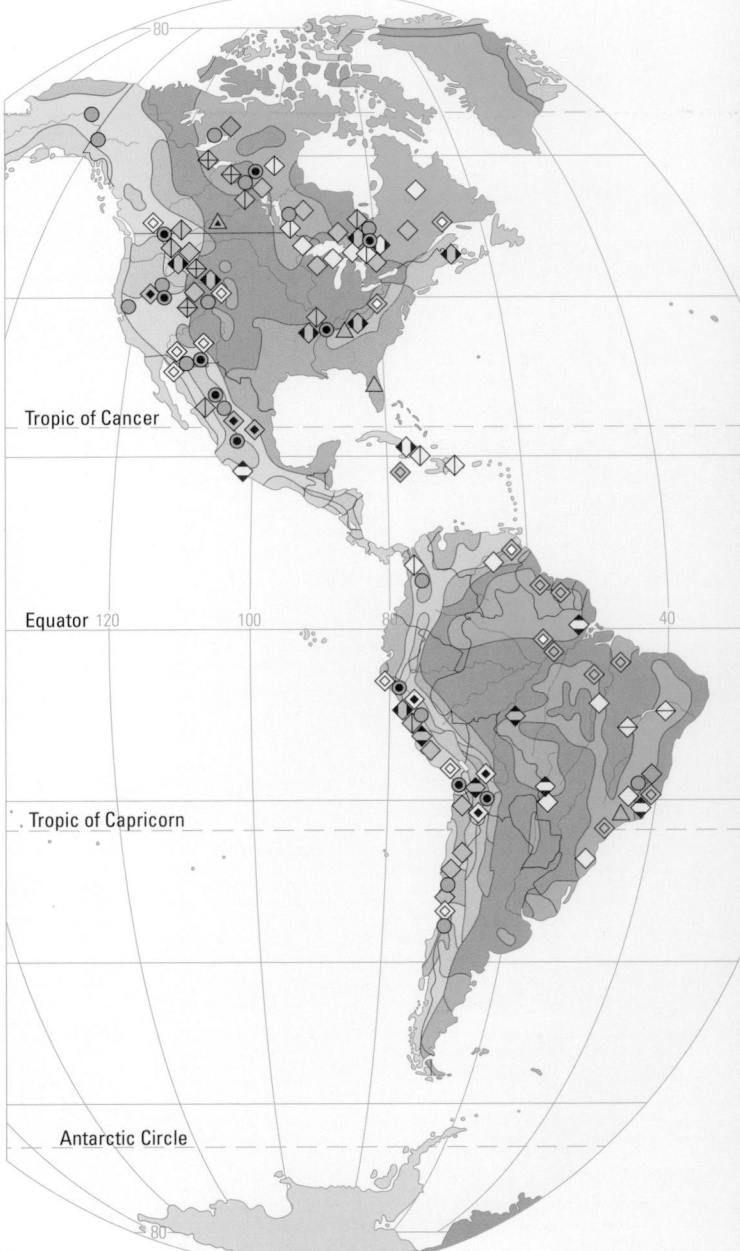

Tropic of Cancer

Equator

Tropic of Capricorn

Antarctic Circle

IRON ORE

Ever since the art of high-temperature smelting was discovered, some time in the second millennium BC, iron has been by far the most important metal known to man. The earliest iron plows transformed primitive agriculture and led to the first human population explosion, while iron weapons – or the lack of them – ensured the rise or fall of entire cultures.

Widely distributed around the world, iron ores usually contain 25–60% iron; blast furnaces process the raw product into pig-iron, which is then alloyed with carbon and other minerals to produce steels of various qualities. From the time of the Industrial Revolution, steel has been almost literally the backbone of modern civilization, the prime structural material on which all else is built.

Iron smelting usually developed close to the sources of ore and, later, to the coalfields that fueled the furnaces. Today, most ore comes from a few richly-endowed locations where large-scale mining is possible.

Iron and steel plants are generally built at coastal sites so that giant ore carriers, which account for a sizable proportion of the world's merchant fleet, can easily discharge their cargoes.

World production of pig-iron (2008)

Total world production:
10.9 million tonnes

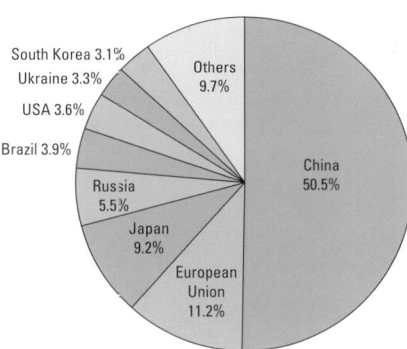

South Korea 3.1%
Ukraine 3.3%
USA 3.6%
Brazil 3.9%
Russia 5.5%
Japan 9.2%
European Union 11.2%
China 50.5%
Others 9.7%

Manganese: In its pure state, manganese is a hard, brittle metal. Alloyed with chromium, iron and nickel, it produces abrasion-resistant steels; manganese-aluminum alloys are light but tough. Found in batteries and inks, manganese is also used in glass production. Manganese ores are frequently found in the same location as sedimentary iron ores. Pyrolusite (MnO_2) and psilomelane are the main economically-exploitable sources.

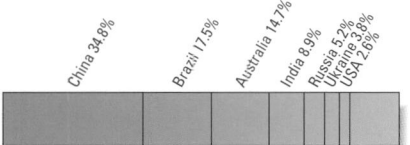

China 34.8%
Brazil 17.5%
Australia 14.7%
India 8.9%
Russia 5.2%
Ukraine 3.9%
USA 2.6%

World total (2008): 2,030,000,000 tonnes

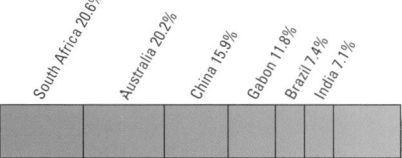

South Africa 20.6%
Australia 20.2%
China 15.9%
Gabon 11.8%
Brazil 7.4%
India 7.1%

World total (2008): 12,600,000 tonnes

Chromium: Most of the world's chromium production is alloyed with iron and other metals to produce steels with various different properties. Combined with iron, nickel, cobalt, and tungsten, chromium produces an exceptionally hard steel, which is resistant to heat; chrome steels are used for many household items where utility must be matched with appearance – cutlery, for example. Chromium is also used in the production of refractory bricks, and its salts for tanning and dyeing leather and cloth.

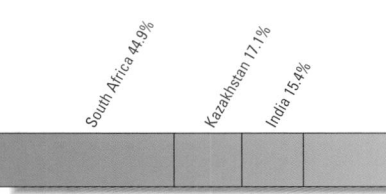

South Africa 44.9%
Kazakhstan 17.1%
India 15.4%

World total (2008): 21,500,000 tonnes

Nickel: Combined with chromium and iron, nickel produces stainless and high-strength steels; similar alloys go to make magnets and electrical heating elements. Nickel combined with copper is widely used to make coins; cupro-nickel alloy is very resistant to corrosion. Its ores yield only modest quantities of nickel – 0.5% to 3% – but also contain copper, iron, and small amounts of precious metals. Japan, USA, UK, Germany, and France are the principal importers.

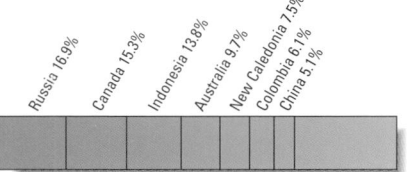

Russia 16.9%
Canada 15.3%
Indonesia 13.8%
Australia 9.7%
New Caledonia 7.5%
Colombia 6.1%
China 5.1%

World total (2008): 1,660,000 tonnes

SCRAP METAL

Scrap metal has been an important source material for the manufacturing industry in domestic markets for decades; its value fluctuating according to the state of the local economy. Recently, however, with growing concern for the global environment and the rapid development of the economies in the Far East, the industry has become far more globalized. Container loads of processed-metal scrap from time-expired machinery in the Western world are now being exported to the Far East to be recycled. Processed-steel scrap accounts for almost half of the requirements for "furnace feed" for the world's steelmakers, and 40% of the world's copper requirements are derived from scrap.

Two major advantages of using scrap rather than refining mined ore are the energy and raw material savings that can be made. If 1 tonne of steel scrap is recycled, it saves 120 lb [54 kg] of limestone, 2,500 lb [1,130 kg] of iron ore and 1,400 lb [635 kg] of coal, with a consequent 86% reduction in air pollution, 40% saving in water use, and 76% reduction in water pollution. Huge energy savings, with consequent cuts in greenhouse-gas emissions, can also be made by using scrap.

As well as bulk minerals, such as those quoted above, alloys using nickel, chromium, tungsten, molybdenum, cobalt, and titanium, which are often only available in limited supplies and are expensive to produce, can also be recycled. The techniques involved to do this work are often very sophisticated, involving X-ray spectrometry and other computer-controlled methods, in order to recover high-value but low-volume metals from devices such as computers and televisions.

With companies having to take increased responsibility for their products, from manufacturing to sale and thence to their ultimate disposal at the end of their useful life, recycling scrap metals will become a much more important method of conserving the world's raw materials and preserving the environment in the future.

STRUCTURAL REGIONS

Pre-Cambrian shields

Sedimentary cover on Pre-Cambrian shields

Paleozoic (Caledonian and Hercynian) folding

Sedimentary cover on Paleozoic folding

Mesozoic folding

Sedimentary cover on Mesozoic folding

Cenozoic (Alpine) folding

Sedimentary cover on Cenozoic folding

Intensive Mesozoic and Cenozoic vulcanism

DISTRIBUTION
Iron and ferro-alloys

Chromium
Cobalt
Iron ore
Manganese
Molybdenum
Nickel ore
Tungsten

Non-ferrous metals

Bauxite (Aluminum)
Copper
Lead
Mercury
Tin
Zinc
Uranium

Precious metals and stones

Diamonds
Gold
Silver

Fertilizers

Phosphates
Potash

For more information:
84 Water distribution
98 Minerals
99 Iron and ferro-alloys
102 Major exports
Traded products

The Industrial Revolution, which began in Britain in the late 18th century, represented a major technological advance in the evolution of human society. It enabled a group of countries to become prosperous by replacing expensive human labor with increasingly sophisticated machinery. In economic terms, manufacturing is the transformation of raw materials, energy, labor, and machines into finished goods, which have a higher value than the various elements used in production.

The economies of countries can be compared by reference to their per capita Gross Domestic Products (GDPs), namely, the total value of goods and services produced within a country in a year, divided by the population. The industrialized, or developed, countries accounted for 19% of the world's population in 2009 with an average per capita GDP of more than US $36,000. On the other hand, low-income developing countries, with small industrial sectors, accounted for 38% of the world's population. Their per capita GDPs are less than $2,100, with some as low as $500.

Kenya, with its low-income economy, had a per capita GDP in 2009 of US $1,600. Agriculture employs 75% of the people, while industry together with services employs 25%. The main industries are the processing of agricultural imports and import substitution (making such necessities as cement, footwear, and textiles). Heavy industry plays only a small part. By contrast, Germany had a per capita GDP in 2009 of $34,200. Agriculture employs only 2% of the population, with 30% in industry and 68% in services. Germany's industrial sector differs greatly from Kenya's, with its emphasis on vehicles, machinery, chemicals, and electronics.

Since the 1970s, some former developing countries in eastern Asia achieved rapid economic growth through industrialization. Despite setbacks in the late 1990s, they demonstrated that a developing industrial sector can transform an economy, which starts off with certain advantages, such as low labor costs. But economic success also depends on such factors as education to provide skills, and regulations that attract foreign investors. China, whose economy grew by more than 9% per year between 2001 and 2007, satisfies many of these criteria, though its record on human rights leaves much to be desired.

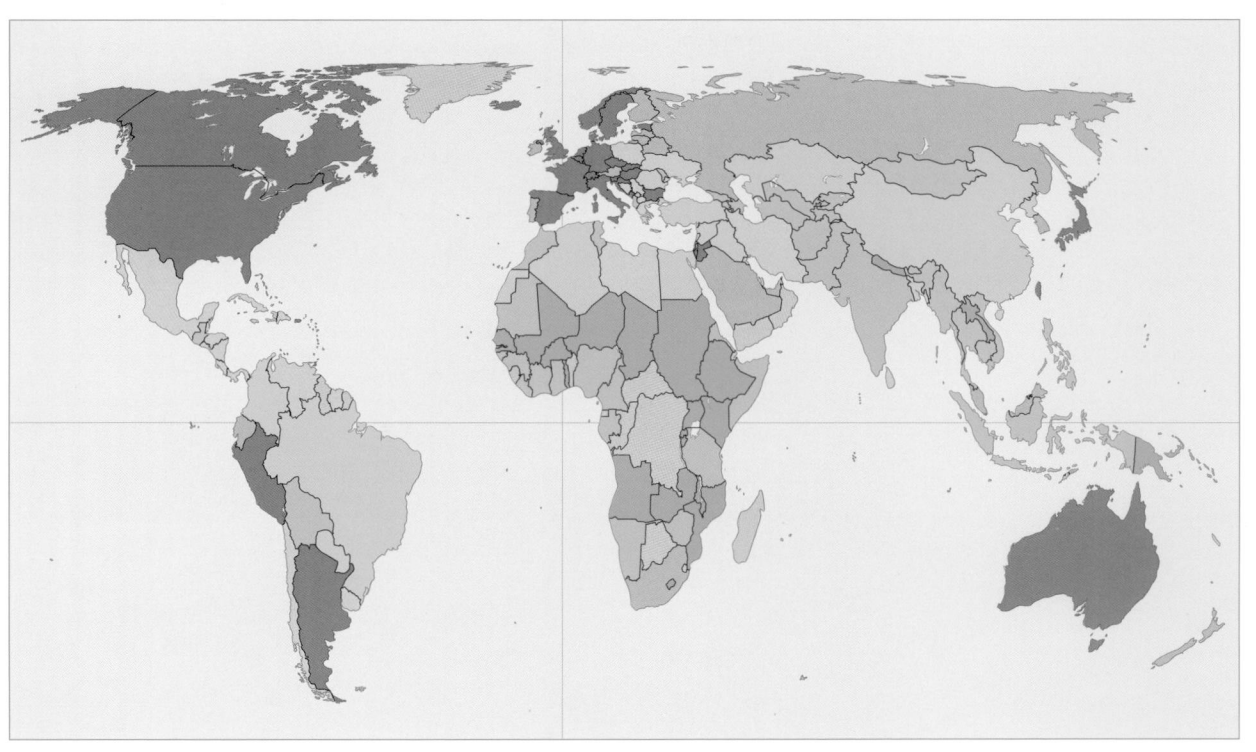

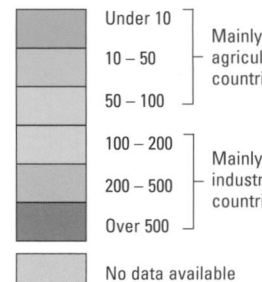

EMPLOYMENT

The number of workers employed in manufacturing for every 100 workers engaged in agriculture (2007)

Under 10	Mainly agricultural countries
10 – 50	
50 – 100	
100 – 200	Mainly industrial countries
200 – 500	
Over 500	
No data available	

Countries with the highest number of workers employed in manufacturing per 100 workers in agriculture (2007)

Bahrain	7,900
USA	3,800
San Marino	3,700
Micronesia, Fed. States of	3,400
Sweden	2,800
Peru	2,400
Argentina	2,300
Singapore	2,200
Liechtenstein	2,150
Andorra	2,000

DIVISION OF EMPLOYMENT

Distribution of workers between agriculture, industry and services, selected countries (2006)

The six countries selected illustrate the usual stages of economic development, from dependence on agriculture through industrial growth to the expansion of the service sector.

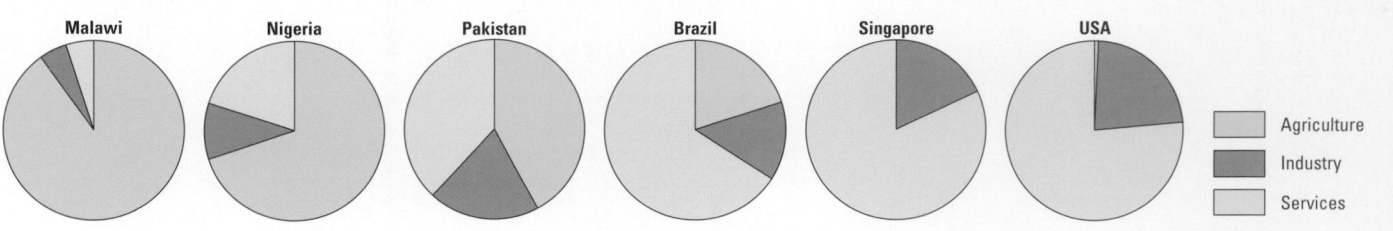

Malawi Nigeria Pakistan Brazil Singapore USA

- Agriculture
- Industry
- Services

THE WORK FORCE

Percentages of men and women between 15 and 64 in employment (selected countries)

The figures include employees and the self-employed, who in developing countries are often subsistence farmers. People in full-time education are excluded. Because of the population age structure in developing countries, the employed population has to support a far larger number of non-workers than its industrial equivalent. For example, more than 52% of Kenya's people are under 15, an age group that makes up less than a tenth of the UK population.

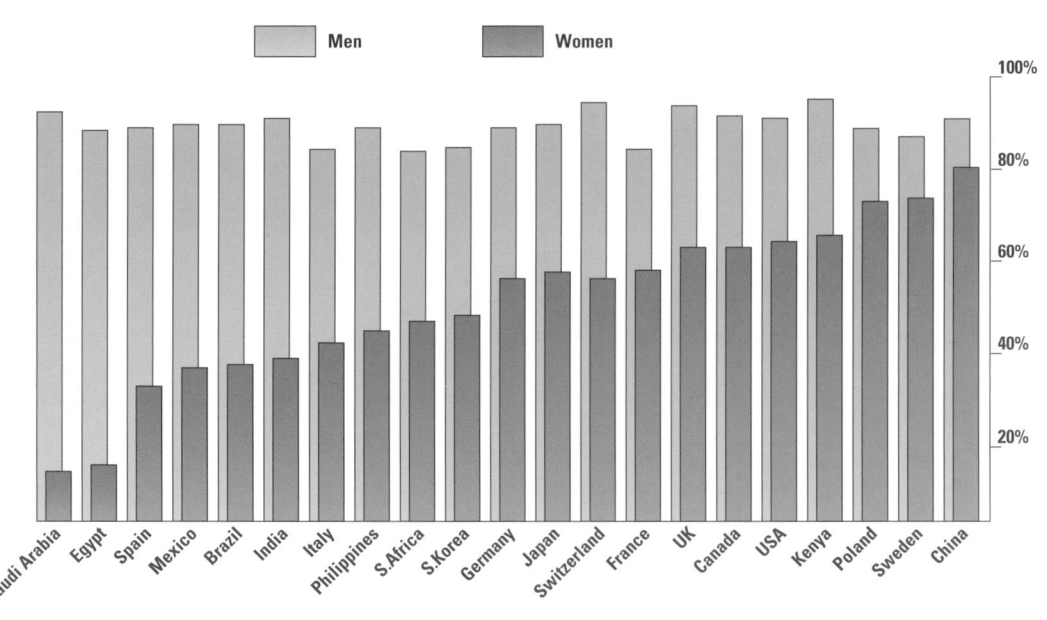

Men   Women

Saudi Arabia, Egypt, Spain, Mexico, Brazil, India, Italy, Philippines, S.Africa, S.Korea, Germany, Japan, Switzerland, France, UK, Canada, USA, Kenya, Poland, Sweden, China

WEALTH CREATION

The Gross National Income (GNI) of the world's largest economies, US $ million (2008)

1.	USA	14,466,100	21.	Indonesia	458,200
2.	Japan	4,879,200	22.	Poland	453,000
3.	China	3,899,300	23.	Norway	415,200
4.	Germany	3,485,700	24.	Austria	386,000
5.	UK	2,787,200	25.	Saudi Arabia	374,300
6.	France	2,702,200	26.	Denmark	325,100
7.	Italy	2,109,100	27.	Greece	322,000
8.	Spain	1,456,500	28.	Argentina	287,200
9.	Brazil	1,411,200	29.	South Africa	283,300
10.	Canada	1,390,000	30.	Venezuela	257,800
11.	Russia	1,364,500	31.	Finland	255,700
12.	India	1,215,500	32.	Iran	251,500
13.	Mexico	1,061,400	33.	Ireland	221,200
14.	South Korea	1,046,300	34.	Hong Kong	219,300
15.	Australia	862,500	35.	Portugal	218,400
16.	Netherlands	824,600	36.	Colombia	207,400
17.	Turkey	690,700	37.	Thailand	191,700
18.	Switzerland	498,500	38.	Malaysia	188,100
19.	Belgium	474,500	39.	Israel	180,500
20.	Sweden	469,700	40.	Nigeria	175,600

INDUSTRIAL OUTPUT

Largest industrial output (mining, manufacturing, construction, energy, and water production), US $ billion (2007)

1.	USA	2,634	22.	Switzerland	98
2.	Japan	1,355	23.	Sweden	97
3.	China	1,279	24.	Iran	96
4.	Germany	783	25.	Poland	94
5.	UK	508	26.	Thailand	92
6.	Italy	439	27.	Austria	89
7.	France	417	28.	Belgium	85
8.	Canada	371	29.	Malaysia	75
9.	Russia	332	30.	UAE	74
10.	Spain	324	31.	South Africa	70
11.	South Korea	313	=	Argentina	70
12.	Brazil	284	33.	Chile	66
13.	India	231	34.	Ireland	64
14.	Saudi Arabia	227	35.	Denmark	61
15.	Mexico	201	36.	Finland	59
16.	Australia	190	=	Algeria	59
17.	Indonesia	172	38.	Greece	58
18.	Netherlands	144	39.	Nigeria	55
19.	Norway	134	40.	Czech Rep.	50
20.	Turkey	103	41.	Colombia	49
21.	Taiwan	100	42.	Israel	48

INDUSTRY AND TRADE

Manufactured goods (including machinery and transport) as a percentage of total exports (2008)

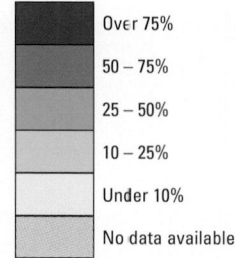

- Over 75%
- 50 – 75%
- 25 – 50%
- 10 – 25%
- Under 10%
- No data available

Countries most dependent on the export of manufactured goods

Cambodia	94%
China	93%
Israel	93%
Malta	90%
Slovenia	90%
Switzerland	89%

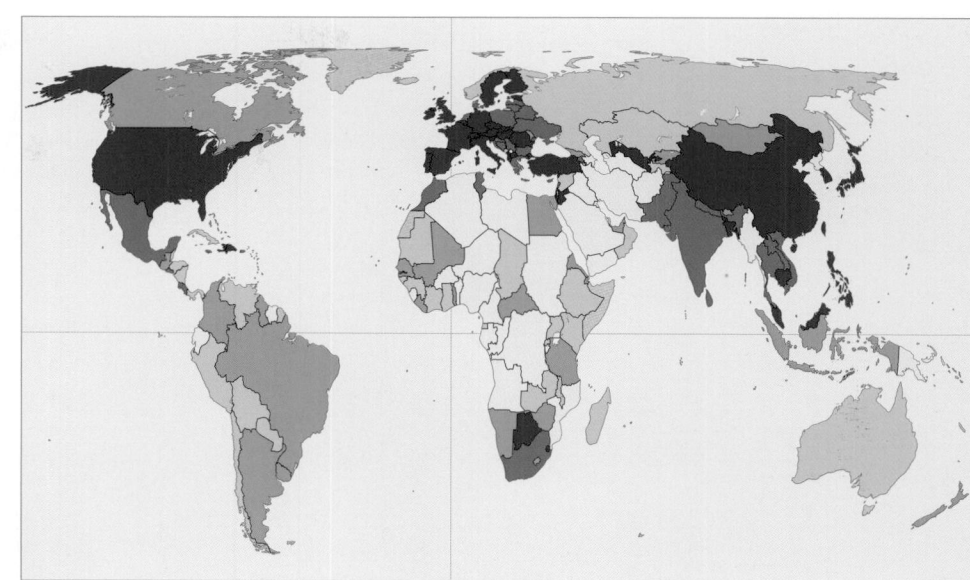

UNEMPLOYMENT

Highest rates of unemployment, percentage of the labor force (2008)

1.	Macedonia	36.0%
2.	Namibia	33.8%
3.	Réunion	29.1%
4.	Guadeloupe	27.3%
5.	Guinea-Bissau	26.3%
6.	South Africa	25.5%
7.	Martinique	25.2%
8.	West Bank and Gaza (OPT)	23.3%
9.	Serbia	20.9%
10.	Dominican Republic	17.9%
11.	Botswana	17.6%
12.	Ethiopia	16.7%
13.	Venezuela	15.8%
14.	Tunisia	14.2%
15.	Burundi	14.0%
16.	Albania	13.8%
=	Georgia	13.8%
=	Poland	13.8%
19.	Slovak Republic	13.3%
20.	Jordan	13.2%

◄ This photograph shows a cement-manufacturing plant in Vác, Hungary. Cement production figures are often an indicator of the relative prosperity of a country, since they show the construction of roads, dams, and other infrastructure projects (*see the graph below*). However, cement manufacture emits high levels of carbon dioxide into the atmosphere.

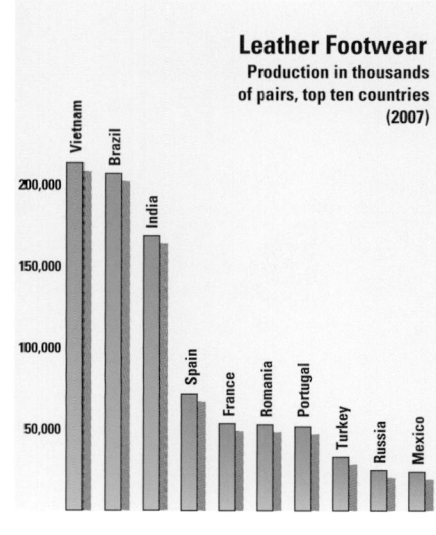

Leather Footwear
Production in thousands of pairs, top ten countries (2007)

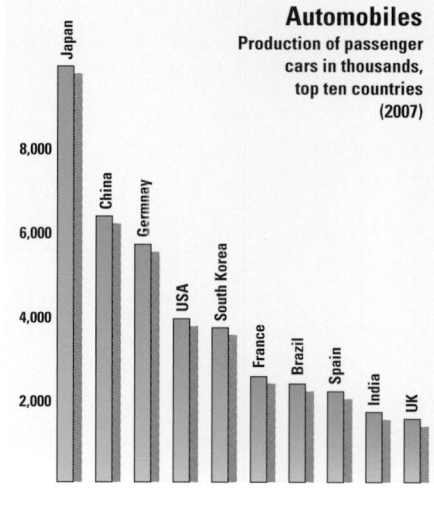

Automobiles
Production of passenger cars in thousands, top ten countries (2007)

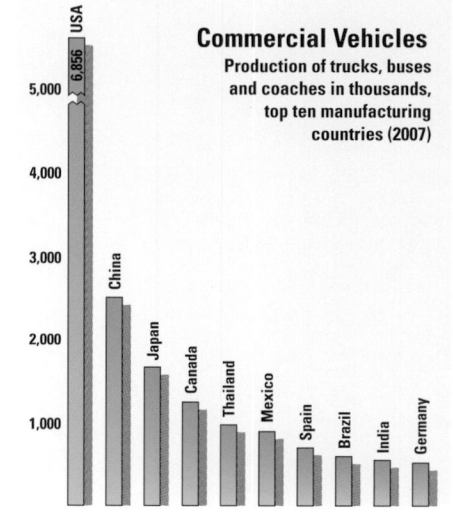

Commercial Vehicles
Production of trucks, buses and coaches in thousands, top ten manufacturing countries (2007)

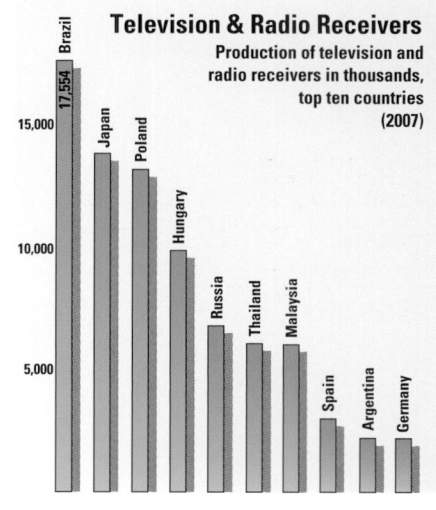

Television & Radio Receivers
Production of television and radio receivers in thousands, top ten countries (2007)

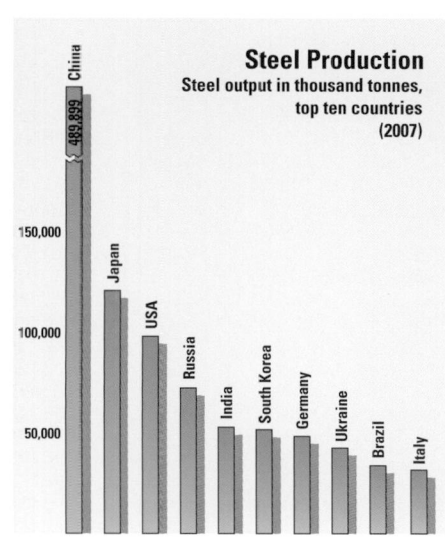

Steel Production
Steel output in thousand tonnes, top ten countries (2007)

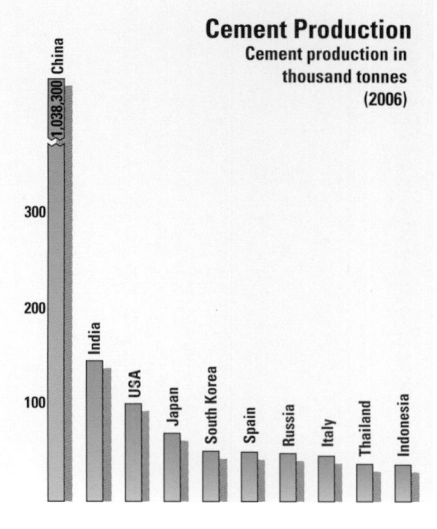

Cement Production
Cement production in thousand tonnes (2006)

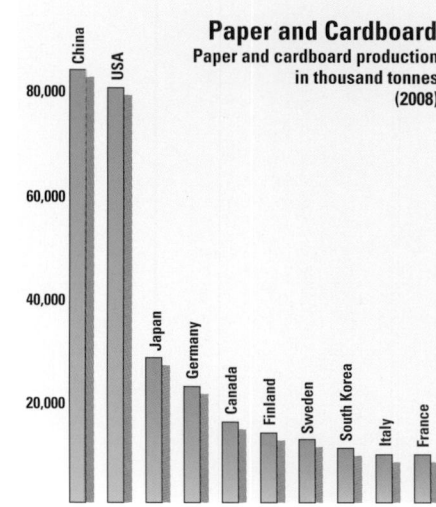

Paper and Cardboard
Paper and cardboard production in thousand tonnes (2008)

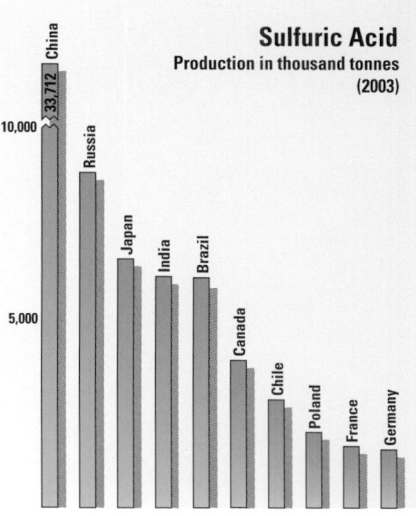

Sulfuric Acid
Production in thousand tonnes (2003)

For more information:

95 International organizations

97 Movements of oil

98 Minerals

100 Wealth creation

101 Industry and trade

107 Air travel and tourism

Inflation

Trade played a vital role in the growth of early civilizations and it was later a spur to European exploration and colonization. The colonial powers grew rich by exporting cheap manufactures, such as clothing and footwear, while obtaining primary products from their colonies.

From the late 19th century to the early 1950s, as transport technology improved, primary products, especially oil in the later stages of this period, dominated world trade. However, since that time, manufactures have become the chief commodities in world trade, which is dominated by the industrialized countries. Nearly half of all world trade flows between the developed market economies of the European Union, the United States, and Japan, although a number of Asian economies, notably China, Malaysia, Singapore, South Korea, Taiwan, and Thailand, increased their share since the 1990s.

China's remarkable growth means that it has rapidly overtaken countries such as Japan, Mexico, and Germany, to become the second biggest exporter to the United States. China's low production costs, especially its cheap labor, were estimated to be one-twentieth of those of Japan, making its high-quality exports highly competitive in price. Growth in world trade is regarded as a sign of economic health, as is a favorable balance of trade (or trade surplus) in any country.

WORLD TRADE

Percentage share of total world exports by value (2009)

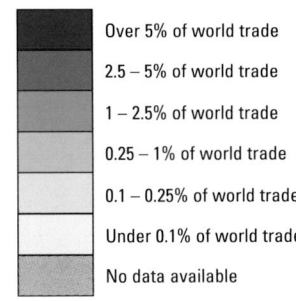

- Over 5% of world trade
- 2.5 – 5% of world trade
- 1 – 2.5% of world trade
- 0.25 – 1% of world trade
- 0.1 – 0.25% of world trade
- Under 0.1% of world trade
- No data available

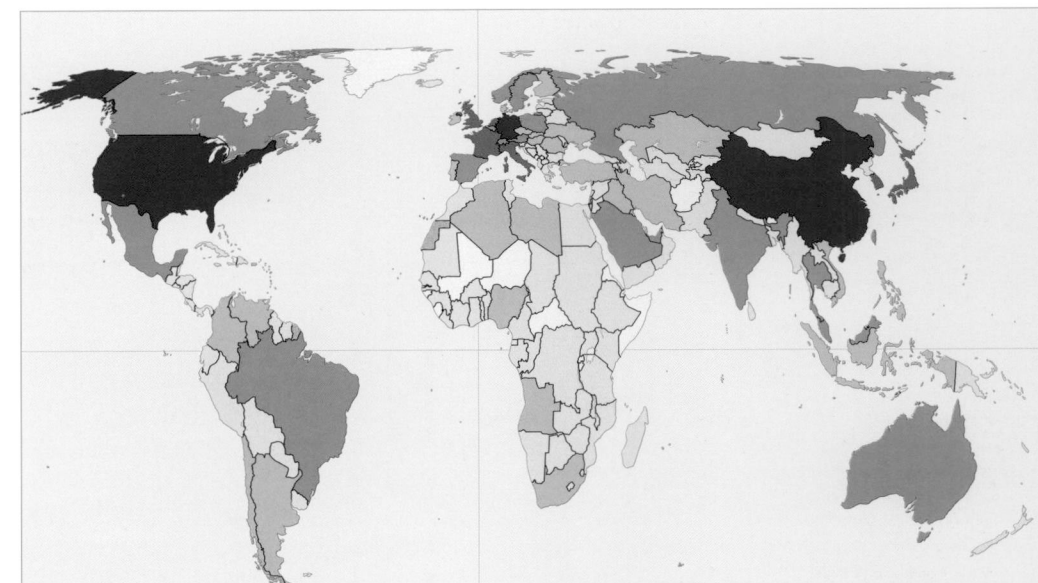

International trade is dominated by a handful of powerful maritime nations. The members of "G8" (Canada, France, Germany, Italy, Japan, Russia, the United Kingdom, and the United States) account for more than one-third of the total. The majority of nations contribute less than a quarter of 1% to the worldwide total of exports.

DEPENDENCE ON TRADE

Exports as a percentage of GDP (2009)

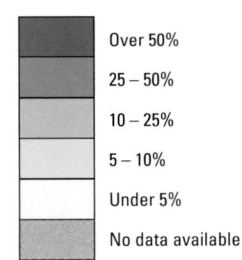

- Over 50%
- 25 – 50%
- 10 – 25%
- 5 – 10%
- Under 5%
- No data available

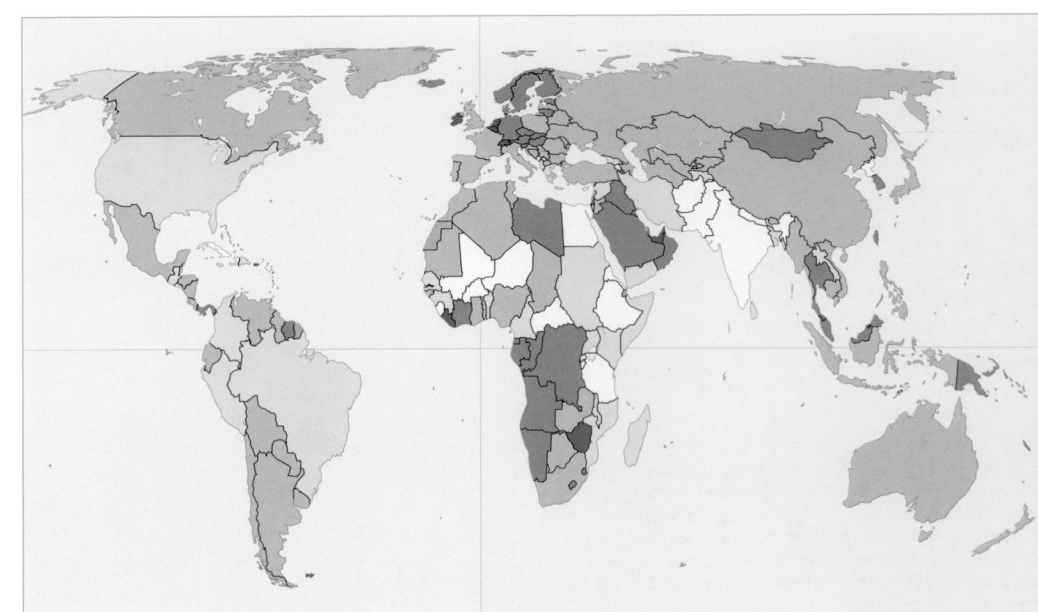

The character of world trade has changed a great deal in the last 50 years or so. While many developing countries still remain heavily dependent on exporting mineral ores, fossil fuels or farm products, such as coffee or cocoa, world trade is now dominated by manufactured goods. Since the 1980s, high-tech products, such as computer equipment, telecommunications gear, and transistors, have become increasingly important.

TRADED PRODUCTS

World merchandise exports by product, percentage of total value (2007)

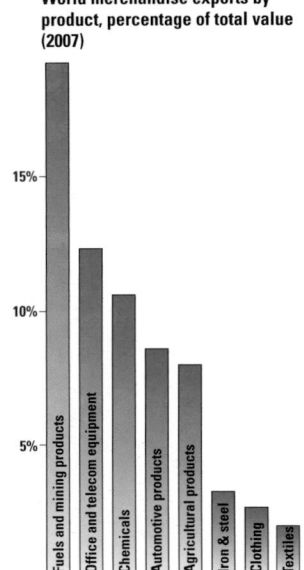

MAJOR EXPORTS

Leading manufactured items and their exporters

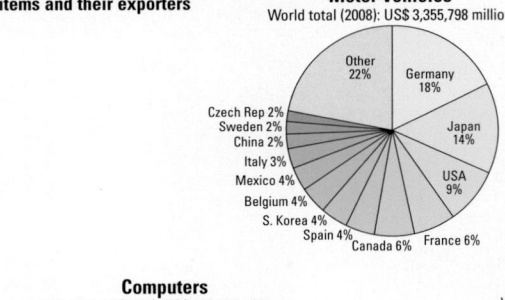

Motor Vehicles
World total (2008): US$ 3,355,798 million

Germany 18%, Japan 14%, USA 9%, France 6%, Canada 6%, Spain 4%, S. Korea 4%, Belgium 4%, Mexico 4%, Italy 3%, China 2%, Sweden 2%, Czech Rep 2%, Other 22%

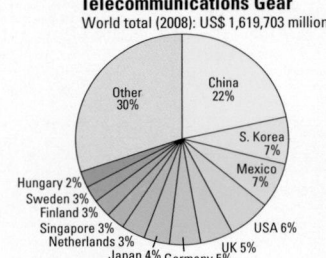

Telecommunications Gear
World total (2008): US$ 1,619,703 million

China 22%, S. Korea 7%, Mexico 7%, USA 6%, Germany 5%, Japan 4%, Netherlands 3%, Singapore 3%, Finland 3%, Sweden 3%, Hungary 2%, Other 30%, UK 5%

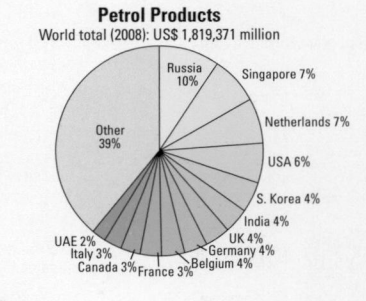

Petrol Products
World total (2008): US$ 1,819,371 million

Russia 10%, Singapore 7%, Netherlands 7%, USA 6%, S. Korea 4%, India 4%, UK 4%, Germany 4%, Belgium 4%, France 3%, Canada 3%, Italy 3%, UAE 2%, Other 39%

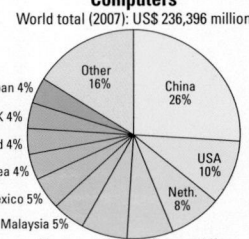

Computers
World total (2007): US$ 236,396 million

China 26%, USA 10%, Neth. 8%, Germany 7%, Singapore 7%, Malaysia 5%, Mexico 5%, S. Korea 4%, Ireland 4%, UK 4%, Japan 4%, Other 16%

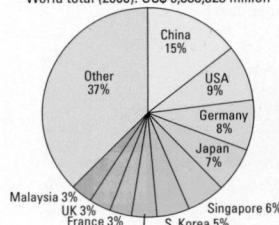

Electrical Components
World total (2008): US$ 5,333,323 million

China 15%, USA 9%, Germany 8%, Japan 7%, Singapore 6%, S. Korea 5%, Mexico 4%, France 3%, UK 3%, Malaysia 3%, Other 37%

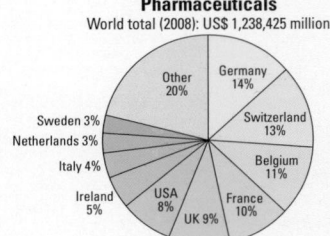

Pharmaceuticals
World total (2008): US$ 1,238,425 million

Germany 14%, Switzerland 13%, Belgium 11%, France 10%, UK 9%, USA 8%, Ireland 5%, Italy 4%, Netherlands 3%, Sweden 3%, Other 20%

WORLD SHIPPING

While ocean passenger traffic is relatively modest nowadays, sea transport still carries most of the world's trade. Oil and bulk carriers make up the majority of the world fleet, although the general cargo category is the fastest growing. Two innovations have revolutionized sea transport. The first is the development of the roll-on/roll-off (Ro-Ro) method where trucks or even trains loaded with freight are driven straight on to the ship, thus saving time. The second is containerization in which goods are packed into containers (the dimensions of which are fixed) at the factory, driven to the port, and loaded on board by specialist machinery.

Almost 30% of world shipping today sails under a "flag of convenience," whereby owners take advantage of low taxes by registering their vessels in a foreign country the ships will never see, notably Panama and Liberia.

TYPES OF VESSELS
World merchant fleet by type of vessel (2009)

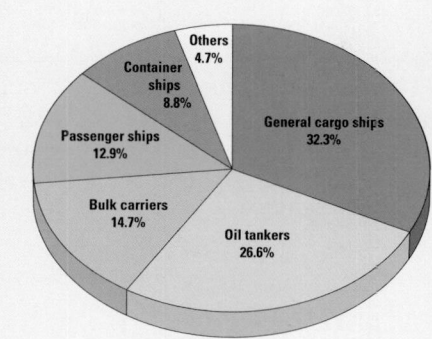

- Others 4.7%
- Container ships 8.8%
- Passenger ships 12.9%
- Bulk carriers 14.7%
- General cargo ships 32.3%
- Oil tankers 26.6%

MERCHANT FLEETS
Merchant fleets in thousand gross registered tonnage (2009). Although a large number of vessels are registered in Liberia and Panama, they are not part of the national fleet.

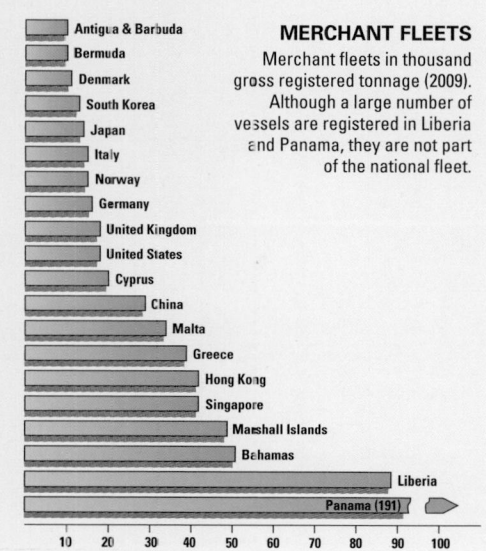

Antigua & Barbuda
Bermuda
Denmark
South Korea
Japan
Italy
Norway
Germany
United Kingdom
United States
Cyprus
China
Malta
Greece
Hong Kong
Singapore
Marshall Islands
Bahamas
Liberia
Panama (191)

10 20 30 40 50 60 70 80 90 100

TOP TEN PORTS
Total container traffic, in million TEU (2008)
("TEU" stands for Twenty-foot Equivalent Unit, the equivalent of a standard container)

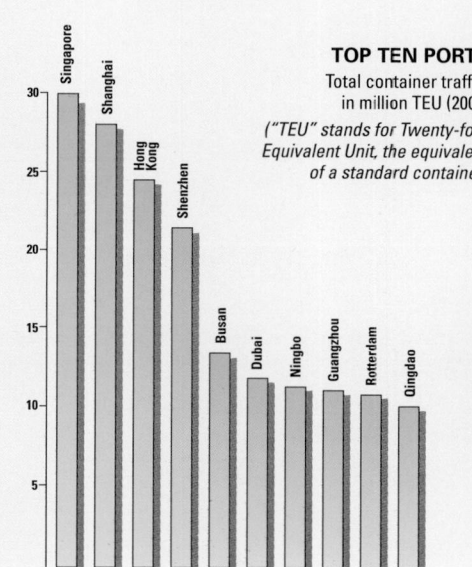

Singapore
Shanghai
Hong Kong
Shenzhen
Busan
Dubai
Ningbo
Guangzhou
Rotterdam
Qingdao

▲ A container ship being unloaded in the port of Melbourne, Australia. World trade depends on transport. Containerization, introduced in the 1950s, reduced the risk of damage to cargo and cut the time and cost of loading and unloading.

TRADE IN PRIMARY EXPORTS

Primary exports as a percentage of total export value (2008)

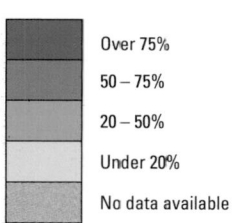

Over 75%
50 – 75%
20 – 50%
Under 20%
No data available

Primary exports are raw materials or partly processed products that form the basis for manufacturing. They are the necessary requirements of industries and include agricultural products, minerals, fuels, and timber, as well as many semimanufactured goods such as cotton, which has been spun but not woven, wood pulp, or flour. Many developed countries have few natural resources and rely on imports for the majority of their primary products. The countries of Southeast Asia export hardwoods to the rest of the world, while many South American countries are heavily dependent on coffee exports.

BALANCE OF TRADE

Value of exports in proportion to the value of imports (2009)

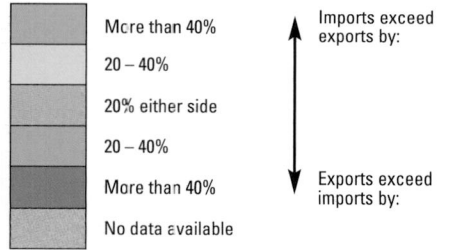

More than 40% — Imports exceed exports by:
20 – 40%
20% either side
20 – 40%
More than 40% — Exports exceed imports by:
No data available

The total world trade balance should amount to zero, since exports must equal imports on a global scale. In practice, though, at least US $100 billion in exports go unrecorded, leaving the world with an apparent deficit and many countries in a better position than public accounting reveals. However, a favorable trade balance is not necessarily a sign of prosperity: many poorer countries must maintain a high surplus in order to service debts, and do so by restricting imports below the levels needed to sustain successful economies.

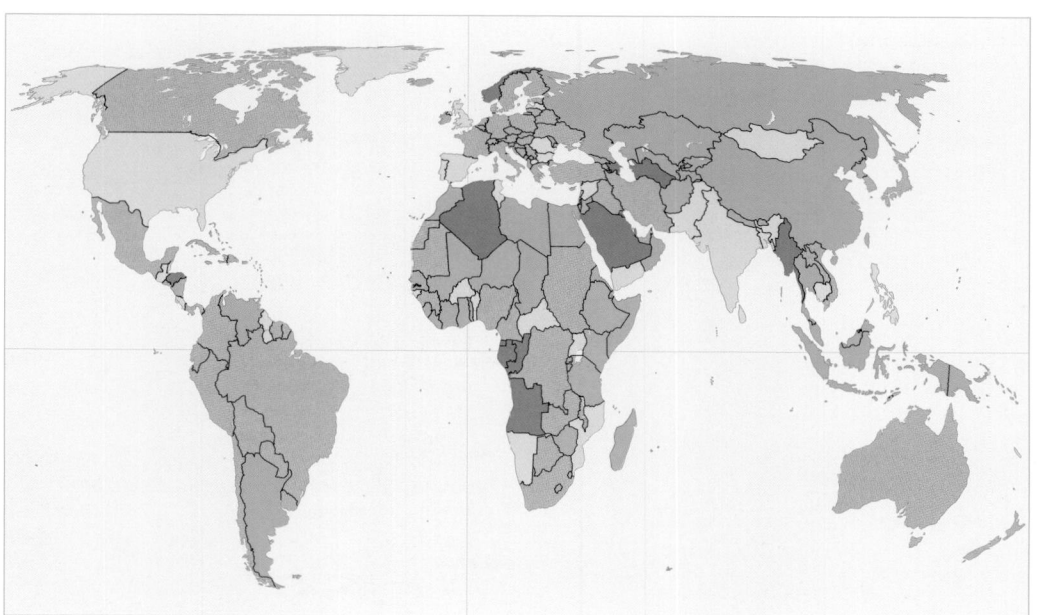

For more information:
84 Water distribution
91 Urban pollution
   Urban advantages
109 Distribution of
    spending

Until the late 1990s, when the full extent of the AIDS crisis emerged, average life expectancies at birth were rising almost everywhere. By 2005, they ranged from 78 years in high-income economies to 46 in sub-Saharan Africa. These figures represented an enormous advance on the situation in 1880, when citizens of Berlin had an estimated life expectancy of 30 years.

The ravages of AIDS have been greatest in southern Africa. One of the worst affected countries is Swaziland, where over 26% of the adult population were thought to be infected in 2007. Life expectancies had fallen to 31 years in 2008, instead of an original estimate of 57 years, and 10,000 people died from AIDS in 2007. However, in much of the world, average life expectancies are still increasing. The rises are attributed to improvements in agriculture and, hence, nutrition, as well as health education, improved sanitation and the quality of drinking water, together with advances in medicine.

Besides AIDS, the people of the developing world are subject to another affliction – malnutrition. The map below shows that in most of Africa, Asia, and Latin America, the average daily calorie supply per person is so low as to cause malnutrition. Malnutrition is a serious condition – among pregnant women it causes high rates of child mortality.

Deficiency diseases occur when people do not have a balanced diet. Protein deficiency causes stunting and kwashiorkor, which can be fatal, especially among young children, while vitamin deficiencies cause such illnesses as beri beri, pellagra, scurvy, and rickets. Iron deficiency causes anemia, while a lack of iodine causes mental retardation.

Infectious diseases, in association with deficient diets, continue to affect people in developing countries. Around the turn of the century, a WHO report stated that infectious diseases cause over 16 million deaths a year. Most of the victims are young and otherwise fit people in developing countries. The major killers are AIDS, cholera, dysentery, malaria, measles, pneumonia, respiratory infections, tuberculosis, and typhoid.

Infectious diseases are much less important as causes of death in developed countries, where cancer and circulatory diseases, such as atherosclerosis and hypertension, which cause strokes and heart attacks, are the most common causes of fatality. Because these diseases tend to kill older people, they are relatively less important in the developing countries where people have shorter lifespans.

Harmful habits are also generally practiced more by the rich than the poor. For example, smoking is an important cause of death in developed countries, while poor diet and high alcohol consumption can badly affect health.

▲ Almost 25% of the world's population does not have access to safe water (the diagram at the bottom left-hand corner of this page shows how this breaks down by continent). This places a huge strain on the millions of mainly women and children who have to walk, collect, and carry drinkable water in order to survive. UNICEF is dedicated to help improve this situation and to react swiftly in the case of emergencies such as civil war, as with the case of this man in Liberia.

FOOD CONSUMPTION

Average daily food intake in calories per person (2005)

- Over 3,500 calories
- 3,000 – 3,500 calories
- 2,500 – 3,000 calories
- 2,000 – 2,500 calories
- Under 2,000 calories
- No data available

The daily food intake rated adequate by the World Health Organization is between 2,300 and 2,500 calories per day. Approximately 6 million children under the age of 5 years die of starvation each year, the vast majority in Africa. In 2006, the FAO estimated that 854 million people were undernourished, contrasting sharply with the overconsumption of food in some Western cultures.

ACCESS TO SAFE WATER

- Urban
- Rural

Proportion of urban and rural population with access to safe water, by region (2006)

TOBACCO

Up to 1.3 billion people smoke worldwide (1 billion men and 0.3 billion women). According to the World Health Organization, tobacco claims 4.9 million lives each year. At the end of 2007, 29 countries had introduced smoking bans in public places.

Percentage of the population who smoke

	Men	Women
Africa	29%	4%
North America	35%	22%
Eastern Mediterranean	35%	4%
Europe	46%	26%
South-east Asia	44%	4%
Western Pacific	60%	8%

Countries with the highest annual consumption of cigarettes per person

1. Greece	4,313	5. South Korea	2,918
2. Hungary	3,265	6. Slovenia	2,917
3. Kuwait	3,062	7. Spain	2,779
4. Japan	3,023	8. Switzerland	2,720

ALCOHOL

The average Western European and North American drinks over a third more alcohol than the average person living in any other region. Globally, alcohol consumption has increased in recent decades, with all of that increase being found in developing countries. Alcohol consumption has health and social consequences, and is responsible for 1.8 millions deaths per year.

Liters of alcohol consumed per person per year

	1980	1990	2000	2007
Developed countries	11.1	9.5	8.9	8.7
Developing countries	2.0	2.4	2.9	3.1

Countries with the highest annual consumption of alcohol per person (liters)

1. Luxembourg	15.6	6. Croatia	12.3
2. Ireland	13.7	7. Germany	12.0
3. Hungary	13.6	8. UK	11.8
4. Moldova	13.2	9. Denmark	11.7
5. Czech Republic	13.0	= Spain	11.7

INFANT MORTALITY

Number of babies who died under the age of one, per 1,000 live births (2009)

- Over 100 deaths
- 50 – 100 deaths
- 20 – 50 deaths
- 10 – 20 deaths
- Under 10 deaths
- No data available

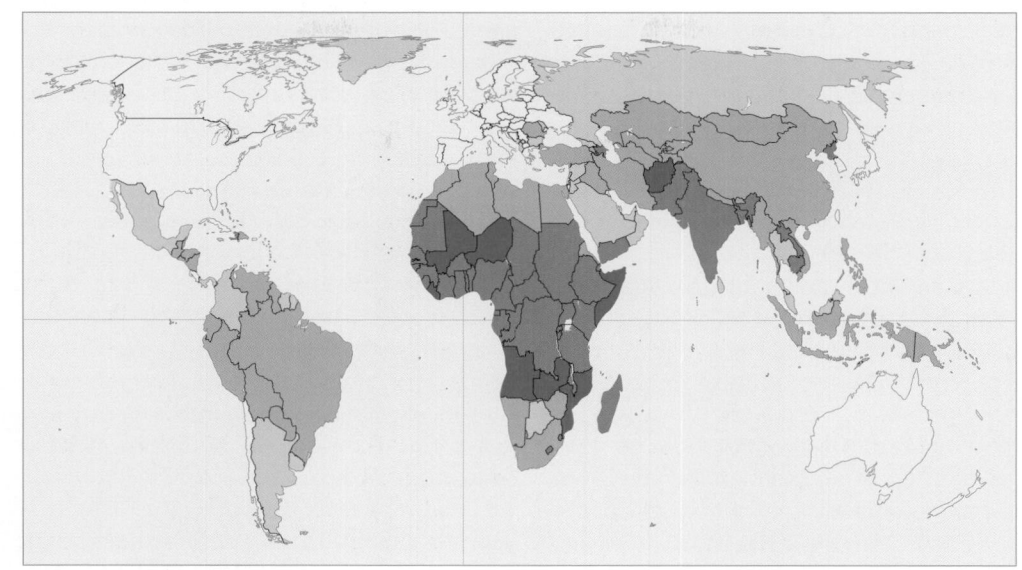

Highest infant mortality

Angola	180 deaths
Afghanistan	153 deaths
Liberia	138 deaths

Lowest infant mortality

Japan	3 deaths
Iceland	3 deaths
France	3 deaths

THE AIDS CRISIS

Number of children orphaned due to AIDS (2006)

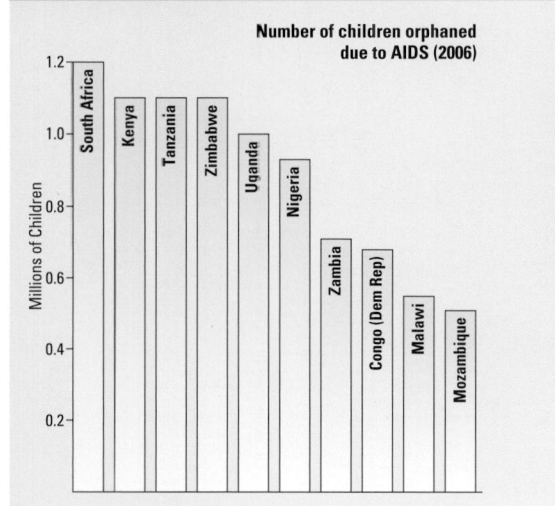

Millions of Children

South Africa, Kenya, Tanzania, Zimbabwe, Uganda, Nigeria, Zambia, Congo (Dem Rep), Malawi, Mozambique

Percentage of the population infected with HIV/AIDS (2007)

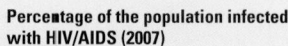
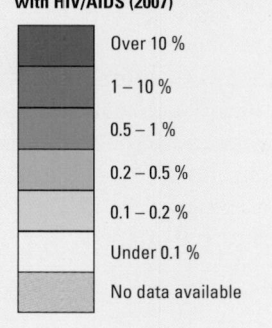

- Over 10 %
- 1 – 10 %
- 0.5 – 1 %
- 0.2 – 0.5 %
- 0.1 – 0.2 %
- Under 0.1 %
- No data available

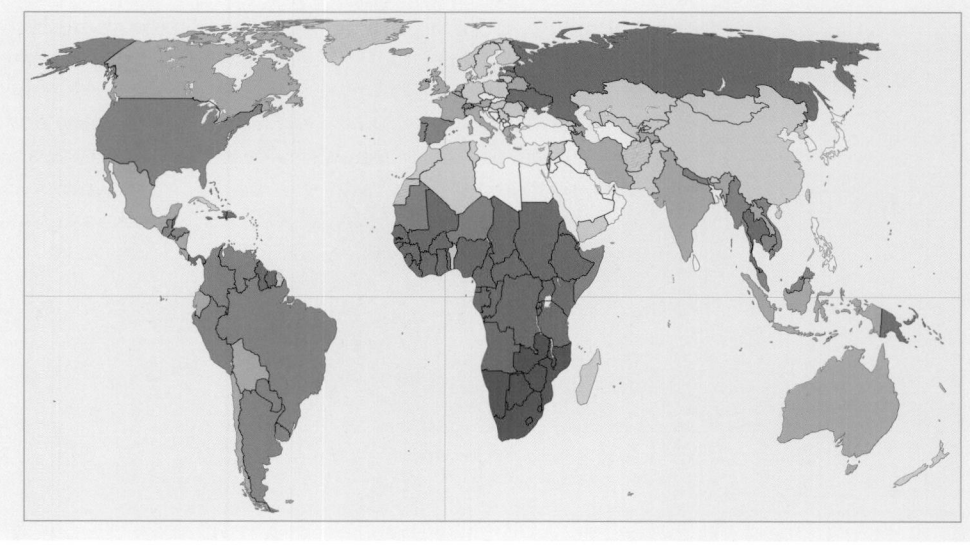

EXPENDITURE ON HEALTH

Public health expenditure per capita, in US $ (2006)

Countries with the highest spending		Countries with the lowest spending	
Monaco	$5,309	Burundi	$4
Luxembourg	$5,233	Congo (Dem. Rep.)	$7
Norway	$3,780	Burma (Myanmar)	$7
USA	$3,074	Somalia	$8
France	$2,833	Afghanistan	$8
Denmark	$2,812	Pakistan	$8
Netherlands	$2,768	Guinea-Bissau	$10
San Marino	$2,765	Eritrea	$10
Iceland	$2,758	Ethiopia	$13
Austria	$2,729	Congo	$13

The allocation of limited funds for health care in developing countries is rarely evenly spread – for example, the quality of treatment can vary enormously from place to place within the same country. Urban dwellers tend to have much better access to health provisions than those living in rural areas.

CAUSES OF DEATH

- Accidents, poisoning, and violence
- Respiratory and digestive diseases
- Nervous and circulatory diseases
- Metabolic disorders
- Cancers
- Infectious and parasitic diseases

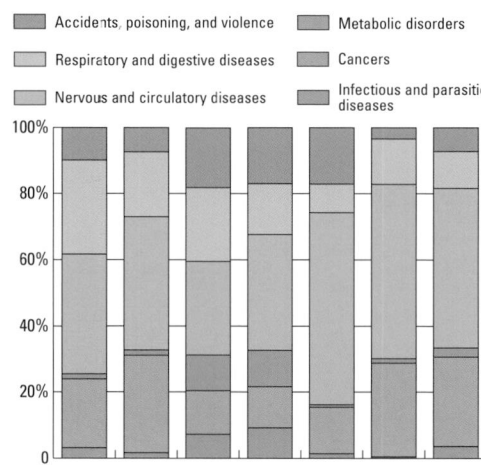

China, Japan, Mexico, Morocco, Russia, UK, USA

MEDICAL PROVISION

Doctors per 100,000 population, selected countries (2006)

Although the ratio of people to doctors gives a good approximation of a country's health provision, it is not an absolute indicator. Raw numbers may mask inefficiency and other weaknesses. The definition of a doctor also varies from nation to nation.

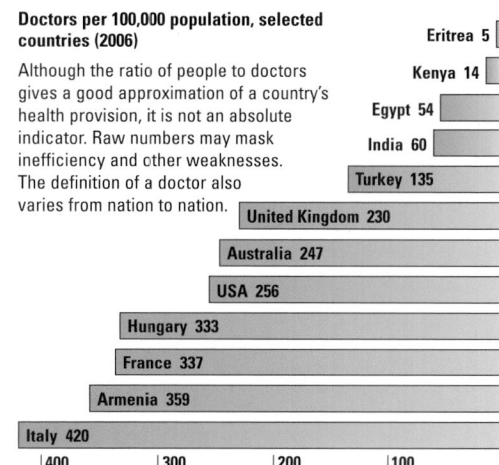

Eritrea	5
Kenya	14
Egypt	54
India	60
Turkey	135
United Kingdom	230
Australia	247
USA	256
Hungary	333
France	337
Armenia	359
Italy	420

OBESITY IN EUROPE

The percentage of adults who are obese (2005)

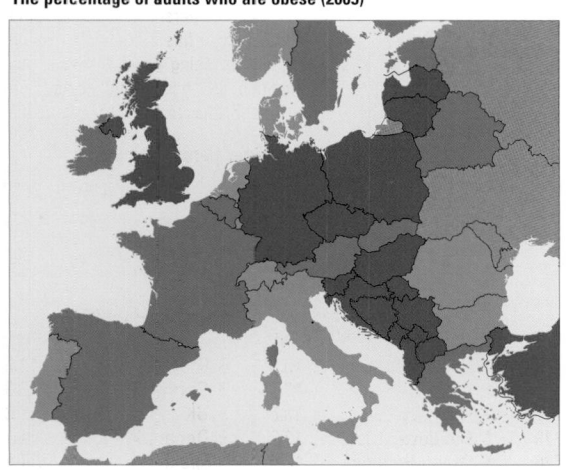

- Over 20%
- 15 – 20%
- 10 – 15%
- Under 10%
- No data available

By comparison, over 32% of people in the USA are obese.

The global epidemic of overweight and obesity is rapidly becoming a major public health problem in many parts of the world. It is associated with diet-related chronic diseases such as diabetes, strokes, cardiovascular disease, and certain cancers.

SANITATION

Percentage of population with access to sanitation services, selected countries (2006)

- Urban
- Rural

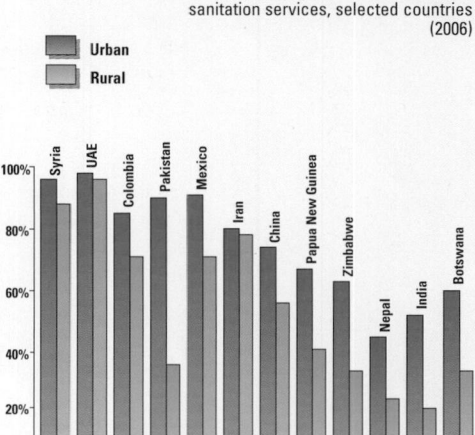

Syria, UAE, Colombia, Pakistan, Mexico, Iran, China, Papua New Guinea, Zimbabwe, Nepal, India, Botswana

MALARIA

Cases of malaria per 100,000 people exposed to malaria-infected environments (2007)

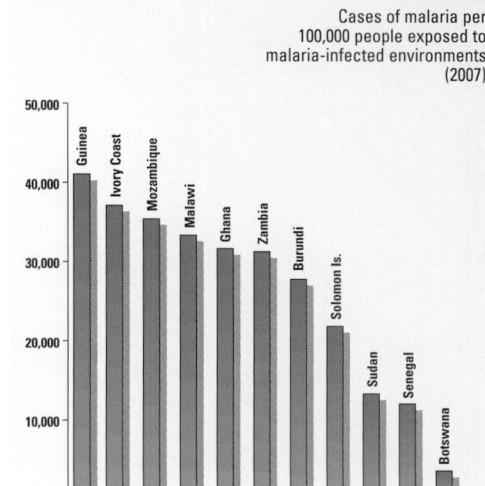

Guinea, Ivory Coast, Mozambique, Malawi, Ghana, Zambia, Burundi, Solomon Is., Sudan, Senegal, Botswana

For more information:
100 Wealth creation
101 Industrial output
102 World trade
     Major exports
103 Balance of trade
109 Distribution of
     spending

Perhaps the most glaring differences in the world today are those between the rich and the poor. The World Bank divides countries into three main groups based on average economic production expressed in terms of per capita GNI (Gross National Income). They are the low-income economies (most African countries and much of Asia), the middle-income economies (most of Latin America and most of the former USSR), and the high-income economies of Canada, the United States, Western Europe, Japan, and Australia.

Per capita GNIs are a measure of the total goods and services produced by a country divided by the population, and then converted into US dollars at official exchange rates. They are useful indicators of a country's prosperity, though, like all statistics, they must be treated with care. For example, the prices for goods and services in China are far cheaper than they are in the United States. China's per capita GNI in 2008 was $2,940 (as compared with $47,930 in the US), but the PPP (Purchasing Power Parity, which adjusts the figure for cost-of-living differences) estimate of China's per capita GNI was considerably higher at $6,010. Another problem with per capita GNIs is that they are averages, which often conceal wide internal variations.

The pattern of poverty varies from region to region. In Latin America, much progress has been made through industrialization, though startling inequalities still exist between rich and poor. China and other countries in eastern Asia, including South Korea and Taiwan, have followed Japan's example in pursuing export-led industrial policies. The success of China's Special Economic Zones, where foreign investment is encouraged, has led to a huge rise in China's per capita GNI.

In contrast to the dynamism of Asia, Africa lags behind as an impoverished continent. Corrupt governments, wasteful expenditures, civil wars, natural disasters, faulty national and international policy environments, high population growth, and the failure to break away from the neo-colonial trading patterns – all these contribute to keeping the majority of Africans impoverished. An initiative in some African countries has been to improve the infrastructure and develop tourism, creating employment and providing much-needed foreign currency. But the social and environmental cost of mass tourism needs to be taken seriously too.

The International Monetary Fund and the World Bank argue that real economic progress in Africa will be achieved only when African countries create market-friendly economies that encourage trade through export-led manufacturing, while at the same time strictly controlling public spending.

CONTINENTAL SHARES

Shares of population and of wealth (GNI) by continent

These generalized continental figures show the startling difference between rich and poor, but mask the successes or failures of individual countries. Japan, for example, with less than 4% of Asia's population, produces almost 40% of the continent's output. Within countries, the difference between rich and poor can also be startling. In Brazil, for example, the richest 20% of the population own 60% of the wealth.

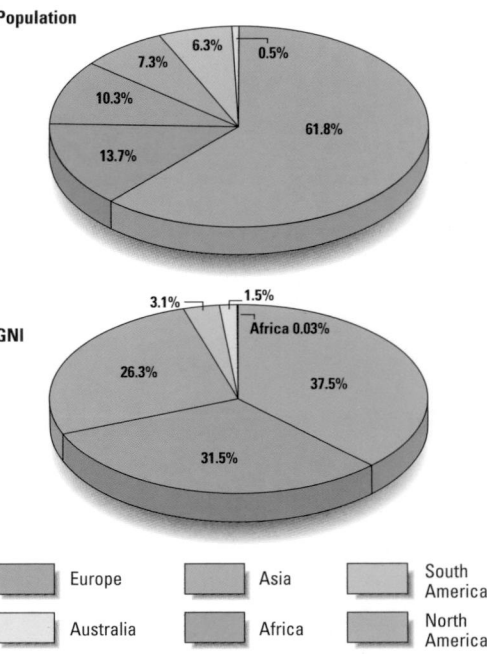

Population / GNI

Europe — Asia — South America — Australia — Africa — North America

LEVELS OF INCOME

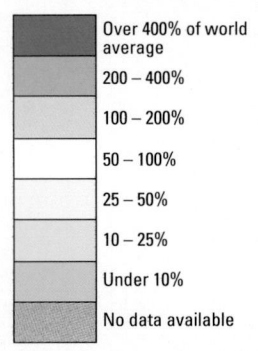

Gross National Income per capita: the value of total production divided by the population (2009)

- Over 400% of world average
- 200 – 400%
- 100 – 200%
- 50 – 100%
- 25 – 50%
- 10 – 25%
- Under 10%
- No data available

Richest countries (GNI per capita)
Luxembourg.....................US $64,320
Norway..............................US $58,500
Kuwait................................US $52,610
Brunei................................US $50,200
Singapore.........................US $47,940

Poorest countries (GNI per capita)
Congo (Dem. Rep.)...............US $290
Liberia....................................US $300
Burundi..................................US $380
Guinea-Bissau.......................US $530
Eritrea....................................US $630

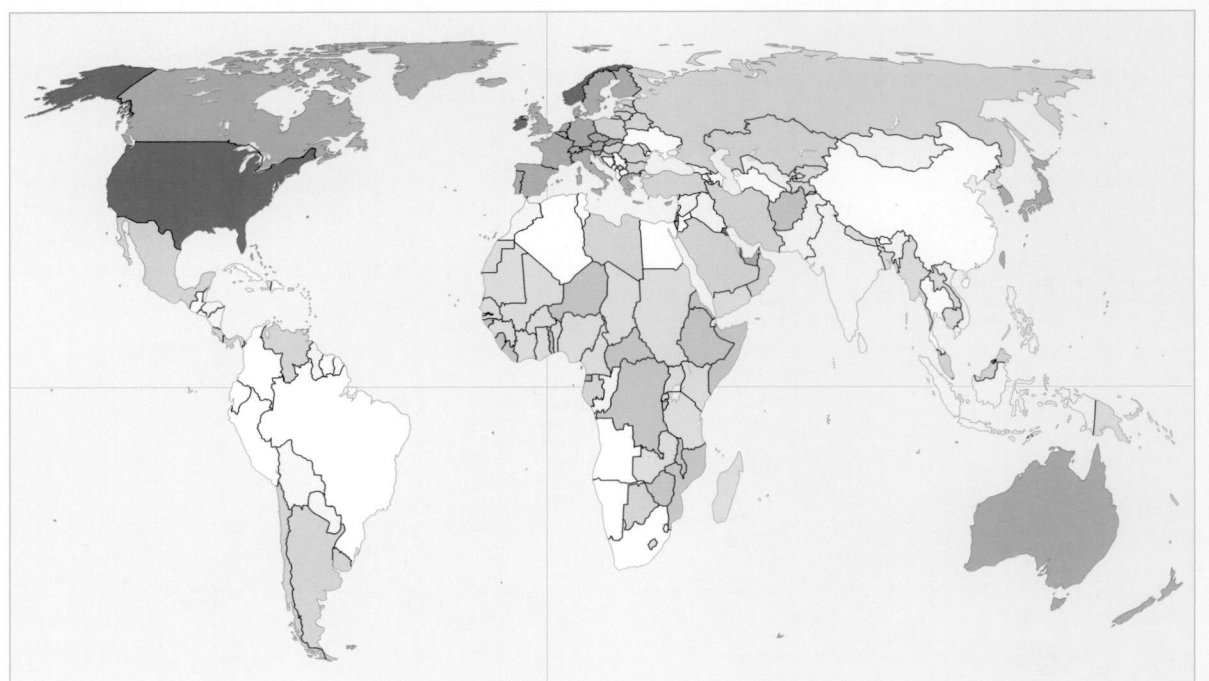

INDICATORS

The gap between the world's rich and poor is now so great that it is difficult to illustrate on a single graph. Within each income group (as defined by the World Bank), however, comparisons have some meaning. The wealth gap in many developing countries, though, is wide, with a small, rich class and a large, impoverished majority, while many high-income countries contain an underclass of unemployed and homeless people.

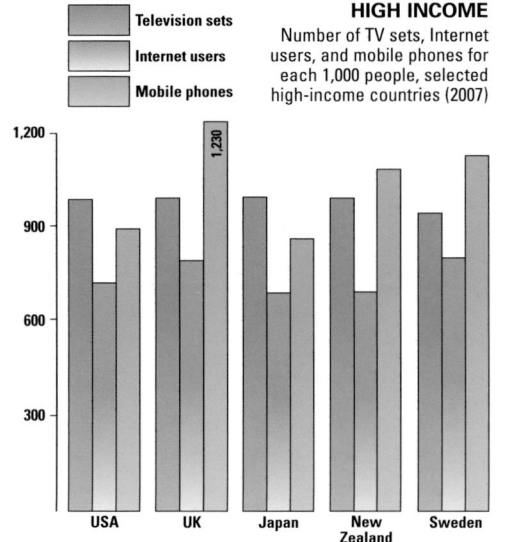

HIGH INCOME
Number of TV sets, Internet users, and mobile phones for each 1,000 people, selected high-income countries (2007)

Television sets / Internet users / Mobile phones

USA, UK, Japan, New Zealand, Sweden

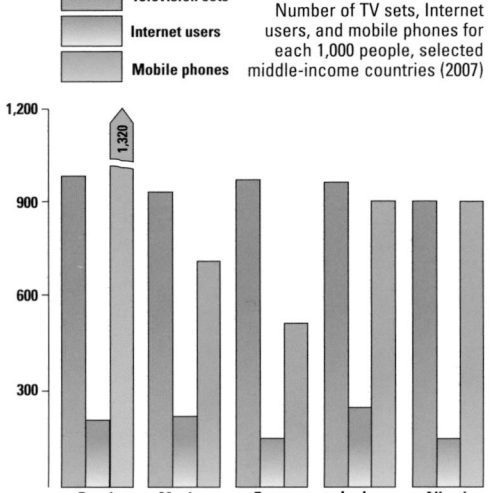

MIDDLE INCOME
Number of TV sets, Internet users, and mobile phones for each 1,000 people, selected middle-income countries (2007)

Television sets / Internet users / Mobile phones

Russia, Mexico, Egypt, Jordan, Albania

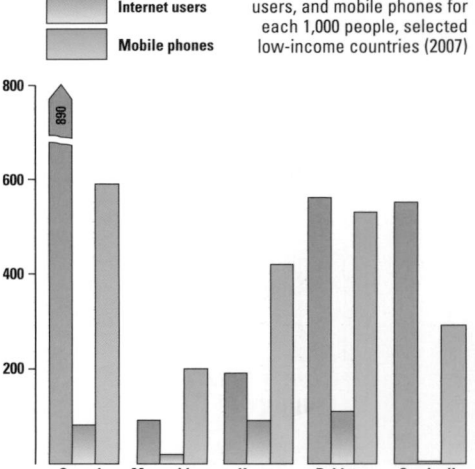

LOW INCOME
Number of TV sets, Internet users, and mobile phones for each 1,000 people, selected low-income countries (2007)

Television sets / Internet users / Mobile phones

Georgia, Mozambique, Kenya, Pakistan, Cambodia

STATE FINANCE

Inflation rates (*shown on the map, right*) are an indication of a country's financial stability and, usually, of its prosperity. Annual inflation rates above 20% are usually marked by slow or even negative growth of the GNI. Above 50%, it becomes hyperinflation and an economy is left reeling.

In the late 1980s and early 1990s, many high-income countries had to contend with annual inflation rates of 10% or more, while Japan, the growth leader, had an average inflation rate of just 1.3% between 1985 and 1994.

Market-friendly policies, including low taxes and state spending, liberal trade policies, and a warm welcome for foreign investors, are major factors in countries that have enjoyed rapid economic growth in the decades since 1980. For example, the setting-up of Special Economic Zones in eastern China has led to a spectacular rise in that country's per capita GNI. However, an effective state remains a crucial factor in economic growth in most countries.

Other successful countries include South Korea and Singapore, although an Asian market crash in 1997 temporarily halted the dramatic economic expansion of these countries.

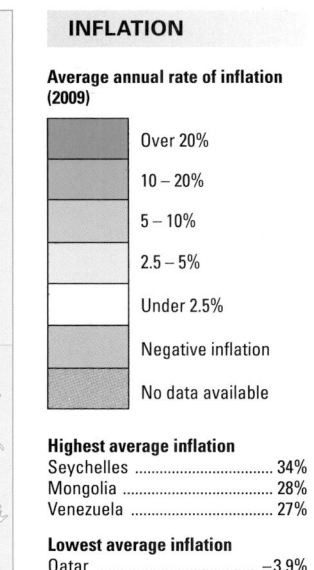

INFLATION

Average annual rate of inflation (2009)

- Over 20%
- 10 – 20%
- 5 – 10%
- 2.5 – 5%
- Under 2.5%
- Negative inflation
- No data available

Highest average inflation

Seychelles	34%
Mongolia	28%
Venezuela	27%

Lowest average inflation

Qatar	–3.9%
Ireland	–3.9%
San Marino	–3.5%

GROWTH IN GNI

GNI average annual change (1999–2008)

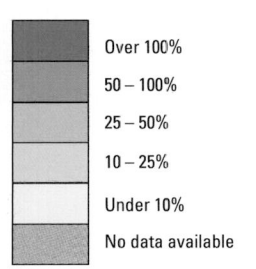

- Over 100%
- 50 – 100%
- 25 – 50%
- 10 – 25%
- Under 10%
- No data available

Countries with the highest rate of change

Equatorial Guinea	283%
Azerbaijan	140%
Angola	119%
Tajikistan	110%
Bhutan	104%

WORLD AIR TRAVEL

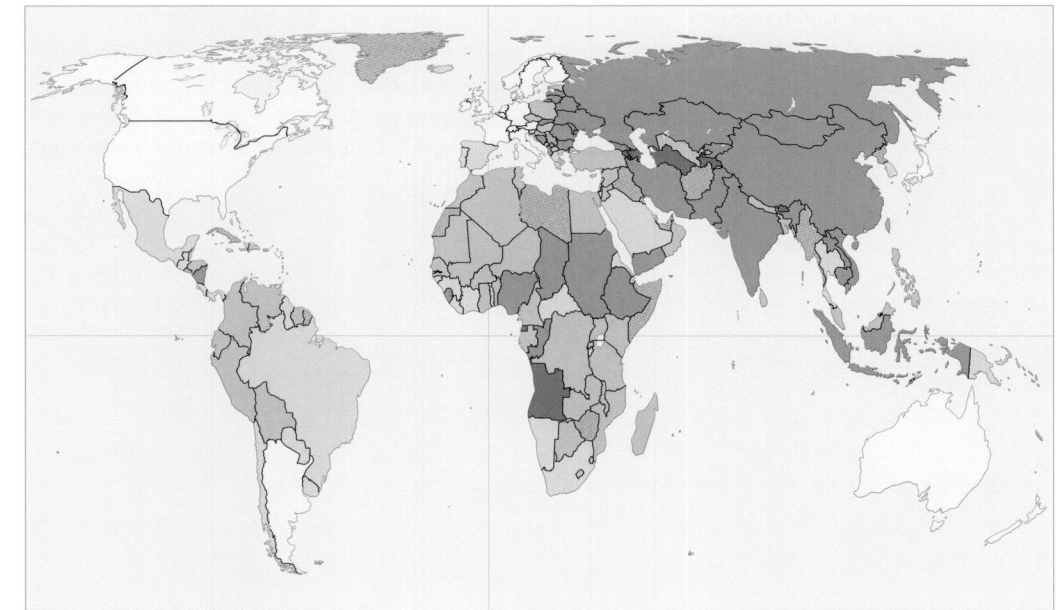

Total world air passenger traffic (2006)

Africa 3%
Middle East 2%
Latin America & Caribbean 6%
Asia Pacific 21%
North America 37%
Europe 31%

Major airports
Number of passengers (international and domestic) per year

- ● Over 25 million
- ● 15 – 25 million
- • 10 – 15 million

Major air routes
Number of international flights per year

- Over 50 million
- 10 – 50 million
- 5 – 10 million

Leisure and tourism is the world's second largest industry in terms of revenue generated. Small economies in attractive areas are often completely dominated by tourism: in some Caribbean islands, for example, tourist spending provides over 90% of the total income and is the biggest foreign-exchange earner.

In cash terms, the United States is the world leader: its 2006 earnings exceeded US $85 billion, although that sum amounted to approximately 0.6% of its total GNI. Of the 46 million visitors to the US, 29% came from Canada and 20% came from Mexico. Germany spends the most on overseas tourism; this amounts to nearly US $75,000 million. The next biggest spenders are the US, the UK, and France.

The world's travel and tourist industry was predicted to generate 74 million jobs in 2006. If the broader travel and tourist economy is considered, this total would increase to 215 million.

WORLD'S BUSIEST AIRPORTS
Total passengers in millions (2009)

1. Atlanta Hartsfield Intl. (ATL)	88.0
2. London Heathrow (LHR)	66.0
3. Beijing Capital Intl. (PEK)	65.3
4. Chicago O'Hare Intl. (ORD)	64.4
5. Tokyo Haneda (HND)	61.9
6. Paris Charles de Gaulle (CDG)	57.9
7. Los Angeles Intl. (LAX)	56.5
8. Dallas/Fort Worth Intl. (DFW)	56.0
9. Frankfurt Intl. (FRA)	50.9
10. Denver Intl. (DEN)	50.2

For more information:
84 Water supply
88 Population density
90 Urban population
91 Urban advantages
94 World's refugees
   War since 1945
100 Employment
   The work force
105 Infant mortality
106 Wealth

Wealth is a basic factor in determining standards of living. Everywhere, the rich have more of everything, including higher average life expectancies, while the poor have to spend most of their income on basic human needs, such as food and clothing. Yet poverty and wealth are relative terms: slum dwellers living on social security in an industrial society feel their poverty acutely, but have far more resources than an average African living in a rural area.

In 1990 the United Nations Development Program published its first Human Development Index (HDI), an attempt to construct a comparative scale by which a simplified form of well-being might be measured. The HDI, expressed as a value between 0 and 0.999, combines figures for life expectancy and literacy with a wealth scale, based on Purchasing Power Parity.

The world's countries are divided into three groups: those with a high HDI (0.8 and above); those with a medium HDI (0.5 to 0.799); and those with a low HDI (below 0.5). In 2007, Norway and Australia were top in the world rankings and Niger was bottom. In fact, 22 of the 24 countries with a low HDI were from Africa. Besides having low per capita GNIs, the average life expectancy in these

countries was 51 years, while the adult literacy rate was 48%. By comparison, the average life expectancy at birth in countries in the high HDI group was 72 years, while the literacy rate was 94%.

Comparisons between countries with similar per capita GNIs reveal the effects of government actions. For example, the World Bank classifies both India and China as low-income economies, but India's HDI at 0.612 is much lower than that of China, at 0.772. This reflects not only China's economic progress in the 1980s and 1990s, but also differences in average life expectancies (63 years in India and 72 years in China), and adult literacy rates (66% in India and 93% in China).

Disparities in standards of living exist not only between countries but also between individuals, groups, and regions within countries. For example, income distribution figures for 2007 show that, in the United States, the poorest 10% of households received less than 2% of the income.

Other contrasts exist in developing countries between rural communities, where incomes are low and basic services are often in short supply, and urban areas, where even those living in slums are

generally better off than their rural neighbors. Other striking differences exist between men and women. For example, while adult literacy rates for men and women living in developed countries are more or less the same, large differences exist in many developing countries. In 2007, in countries in the lowest HDI category, only 36% of women were literate, as compared with 58% of men.

Female education is a factor in population control, especially as women's fertility rates appear to fall in direct proportion to the amount of secondary education they receive. This point was acknowledged in 2004 by the UN Population Fund, which defined four main objectives relating to women and population control: the reduction of maternal, infant, and child mortality; better education, especially for girls; universal access to reproductive health services; and gender equality.

Statistical analysis presents many problems of interpretation, especially when trying to define such intangible factors as a sense of well-being. For example, education helps create wealth; but are rich countries wealthy because their people are well educated, or are they well educated because they are rich?

HUMAN DEVELOPMENT INDEX

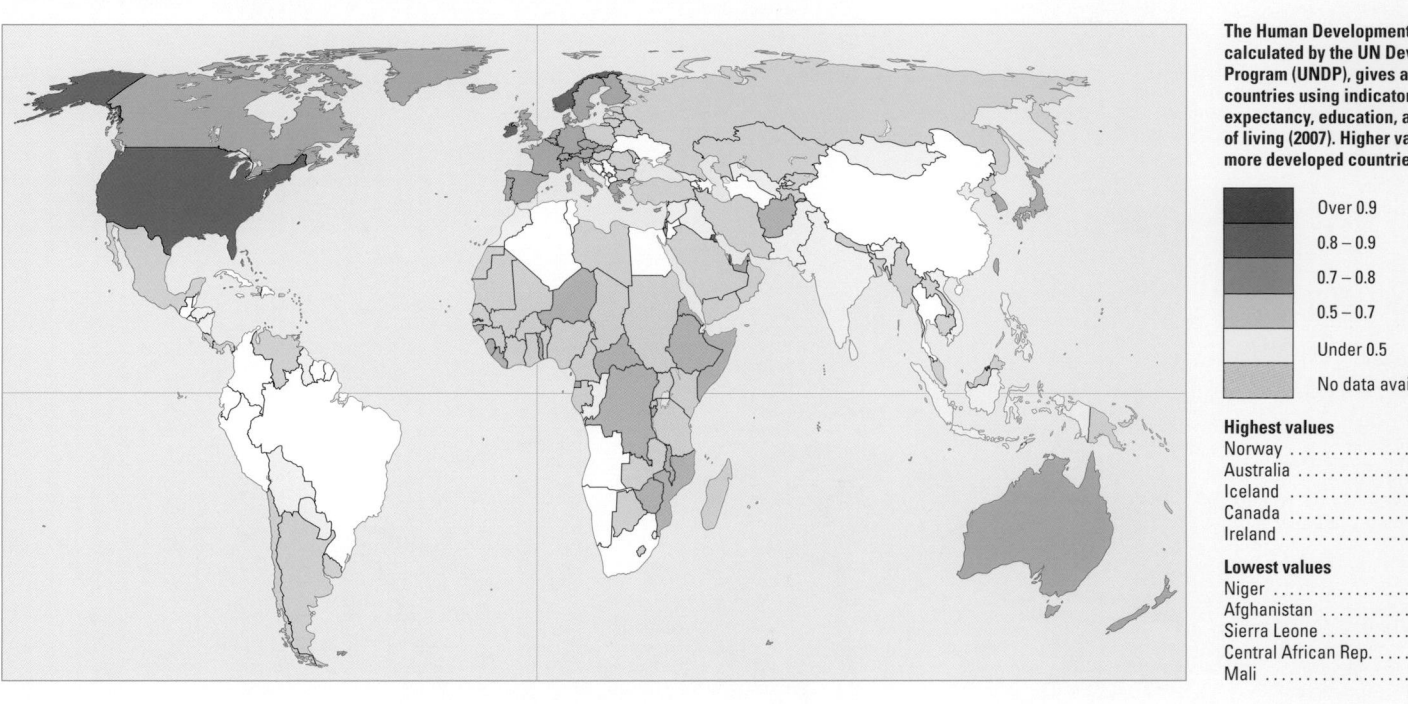

The Human Development Index (HDI), calculated by the UN Development Program (UNDP), gives a value to countries using indicators of life expectancy, education, and standards of living (2007). Higher values show more developed countries.

Over 0.9
0.8 – 0.9
0.7 – 0.8
0.5 – 0.7
Under 0.5
No data available

Highest values
Norway 0.971
Australia 0.970
Iceland 0.969
Canada 0.966
Ireland 0.965

Lowest values
Niger 0.340
Afghanistan 0.352
Sierra Leone 0.365
Central African Rep. 0.369
Mali 0.371

EDUCATION

The developing countries made great efforts in the 1970s and 1980s to bring at least a basic education to their people. In all but the poorest nations, primary school enrolments rose above 60%. However, figures often include teenagers or young adults, and there are still 300 million children worldwide who receive no schooling at all. A lack of resources has restricted the development of secondary and higher education. Most primary school education is free in the poorer countries, but fees are often paid for secondary and higher education, thus heightening the differences between rich and poor.

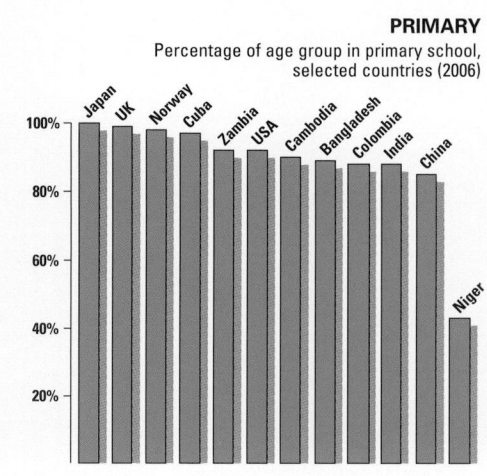

PRIMARY
Percentage of age group in primary school, selected countries (2006)

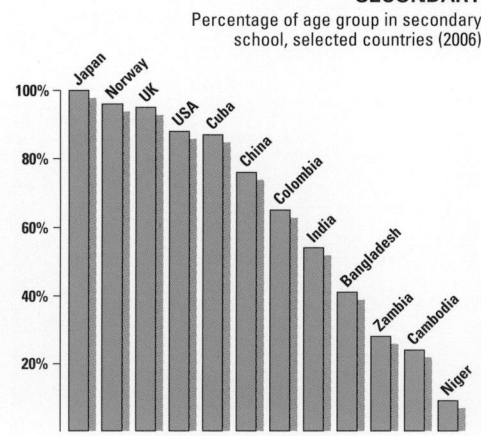

SECONDARY
Percentage of age group in secondary school, selected countries (2006)

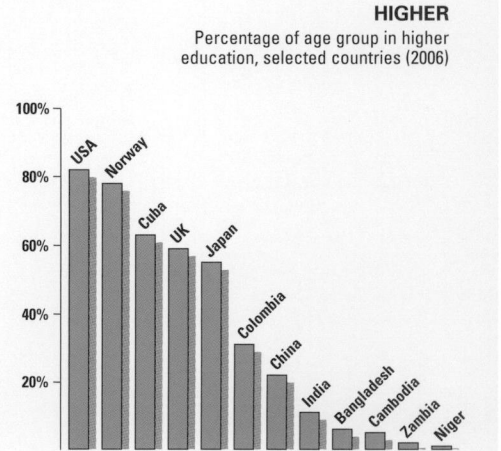

HIGHER
Percentage of age group in higher education, selected countries (2006)

DISTRIBUTION OF SPENDING

Percentage share of household spending

A high proportion of the average income of households in developing nations is spent on basic needs such as food and clothing. In most Western countries food and clothing account for less than 25% of expenditure.

- Food
- Medicine & Education
- Clothing
- Transport
- Energy & Housing
- Other

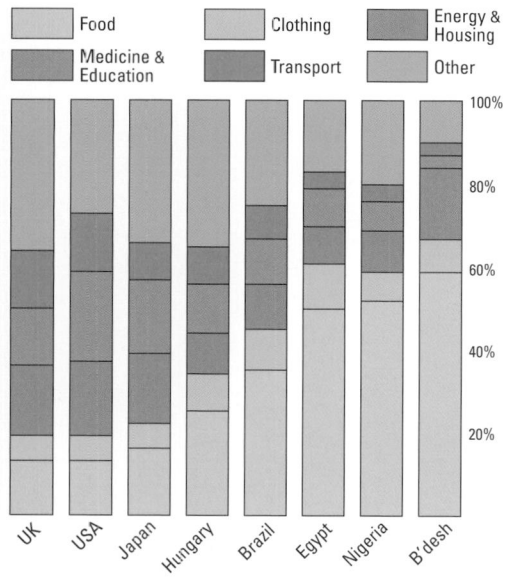

UK · USA · Japan · Hungary · Brazil · Egypt · Nigeria · B'desh

FERTILITY AND EDUCATION

Fertility rates compared with female education, selected countries (2008)

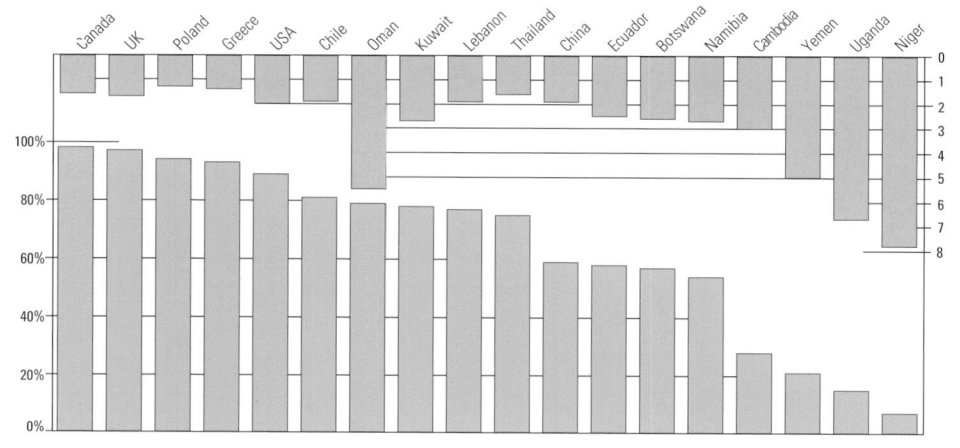

Canada · UK · Poland · Greece · USA · Chile · Oman · Kuwait · Lebanon · Thailand · China · Ecuador · Botswana · Namibia · Cambodia · Yemen · Uganda · Niger

There seems to be a strong link between access to secondary education and the fertility rate. In developed countries, young girls have a high access to education and a low fertility rate. In contrast, in many developing countries women have a high fertility rate but lack access to education. This can be for a complex mix of social, economic, and cultural reasons. Despite a few high-profile examples of female politicians in different parts of the world, all evidence points to the continuing marginalization of women from the political and economic processes of decision-making. Female wages are, on average, only two-thirds of those of men.

- Fertility rate: average number of children borne per woman
- Percentage of females aged 12–17 in secondary education

GENDER DEVELOPMENT INDEX

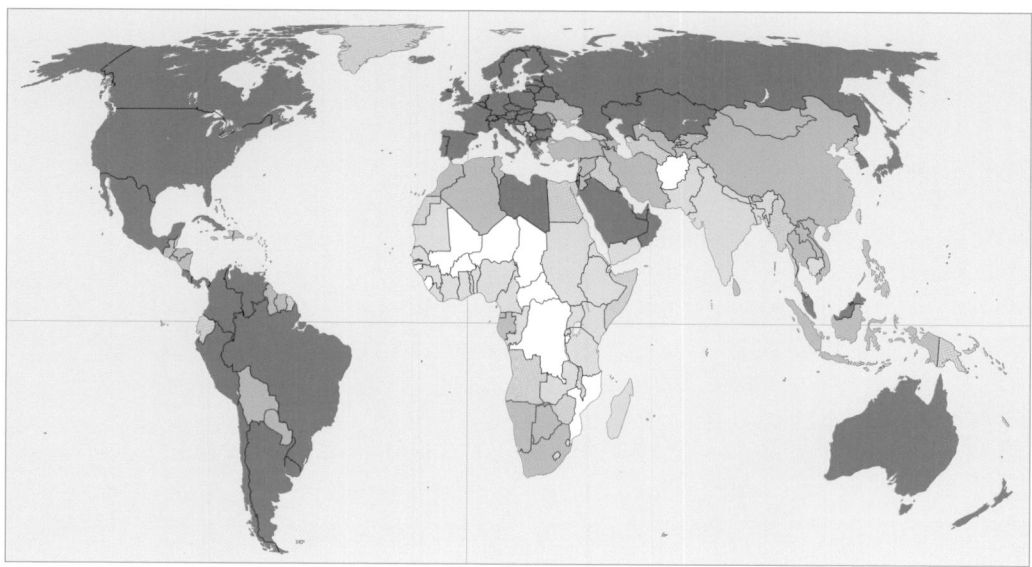
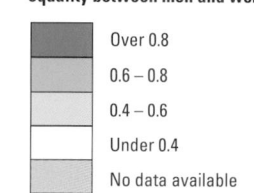

The Gender Development Index (GDI) shows economic and social differences between men and women by using various UNDP indicators (2007). Countries with higher values of GDI have more equality between men and women.

- Over 0.8
- 0.6 – 0.8
- 0.4 – 0.6
- Under 0.4
- No data available

Highest values

Australia	0.966
Norway	0.961
Canada	0.959
Iceland	0.959

Lowest values

Niger	0.308
Afghanistan	0.310
Mali	0.353
Sierra Leone	0.354

STANDARDS OF LIVING IN THE USA BY RACE, AGE AND REGION

A comparison of measures of income and education, by selected characteristics (2008)

Median income per household (US $), by age and region

15–24 years	27,235
25–44 years	57,154
45–64 years	64,040
65 years and over	33,055
Northeast	57,595
Midwest	50,780
South	48,046
West	56,837

Per capita income (US $), by race and Hispanic origin of householder

ALL RACES	27,466
White	30,299
Black	18,119
Asian and Pacific Is.	30,248
Hispanic (any race)	15,916

The poorest 20% of households received just 2.4% of the income, whereas the richest 20% received 55.4%.

Percentage of persons aged 25 and over who have completed High School, by race or origin

ALL RACES	1975	62.5
	2008	84.5
White	1975	64.5
	2008	86.9
Black	1975	42.5
	2008	80.0
Hispanic	1975	37.9
	2008	60.5

REGIONAL INEQUALITY IN ITALY

The southern part of Italy, known as the *Mezzogiorno*, has been described as one of the poorest parts of the European Union. It is identifiable on the map (*right*) as all the regions with a GDP per capita of less than US $30,000 (including the two islands of Sicily and Sardinia).

The *Mezzogiorno* region suffers from a lack of energy resources, minerals, industry, commerce, services, and skilled labor. As a result, standards of living in the region are well below the rest of Italy. Employment is predominantly agricultural and small-scale.

The north of Italy accounts for 60% of the population but 80% of the GDP, whereas the *Mezzogiorno* accounts for 40% of the population and only 20% of the GDP. Manpower surpluses in the south led to emigration to other parts of Europe and the Americas.

It has also led, especially in the last 50 years, to inter-regional migration from the islands and the southern mainland to the north. The main regions attracting migrants are the northwest (the prosperous Liguria–Piedmont–Lombardy triangle, with its great industrial cities of Genoa, Milan and Turin) and the Venetia region in the northeast.

As a result, the north has experienced much higher population growth rates than the rest of Italy.

Gross Domestic Product (GDP) per capita in Italy, by region (2007)

- Over US $40,000
- $35,000 – $40,000
- $30,000 – $35,000
- $25,000 – $30,000
- Under $25,000

The average GDP per capita for Italy is US $29,900. By comparison, the GDP for the UK is $35,200; for the USA $46,100; and for the EU $32,800.

The number of inhabitants per doctor, another social indicator, varies from less than 600 in the northwest of Italy to nearly 800 in the far south (the *Mezzogiorno*), with a national average of 628.

◄ These two images illustrate the reality of suburban life for people at either end of the economic scale. On the far left is part of a huge area of "tract housing" in California, where large houses of a similar design are laid out by a developer, complete with gardens, drives, and swimming pools. On the right is a much more haphazard arrangement of home-built, rudimentary shelters, many without sanitation and most with no electricity, in Crossroads Township, outside Cape Town in South Africa.

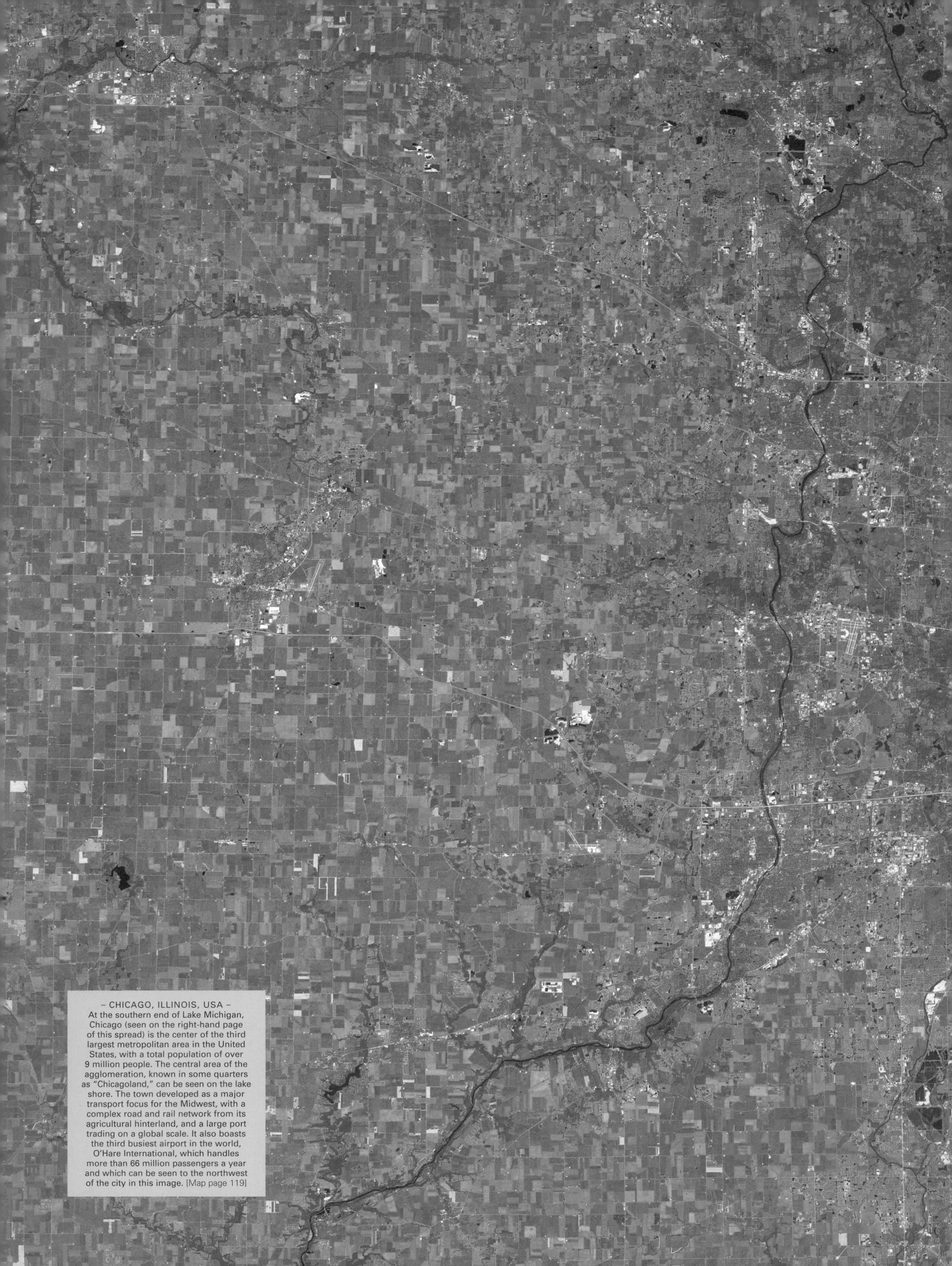

– CHICAGO, ILLINOIS, USA –
At the southern end of Lake Michigan, Chicago (seen on the right-hand page of this spread) is the center of the third largest metropolitan area in the United States, with a total population of over 9 million people. The central area of the agglomeration, known in some quarters as "Chicagoland," can be seen on the lake shore. The town developed as a major transport focus for the Midwest, with a complex road and rail network from its agricultural hinterland, and a large port trading on a global scale. It also boasts the third busiest airport in the world, O'Hare International, which handles more than 66 million passengers a year and which can be seen to the northwest of the city in this image. [Map page 119]

WORLD
CITIES

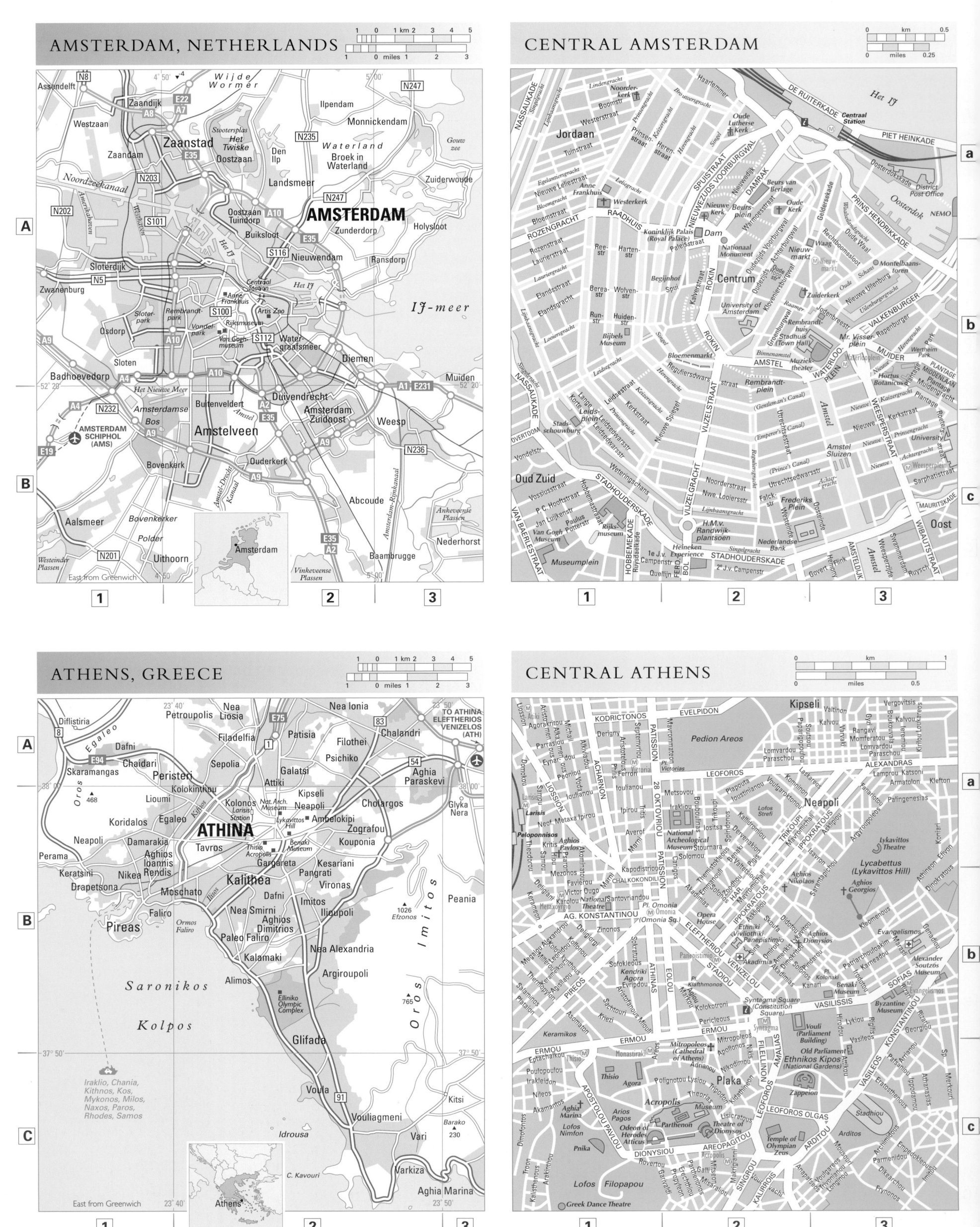

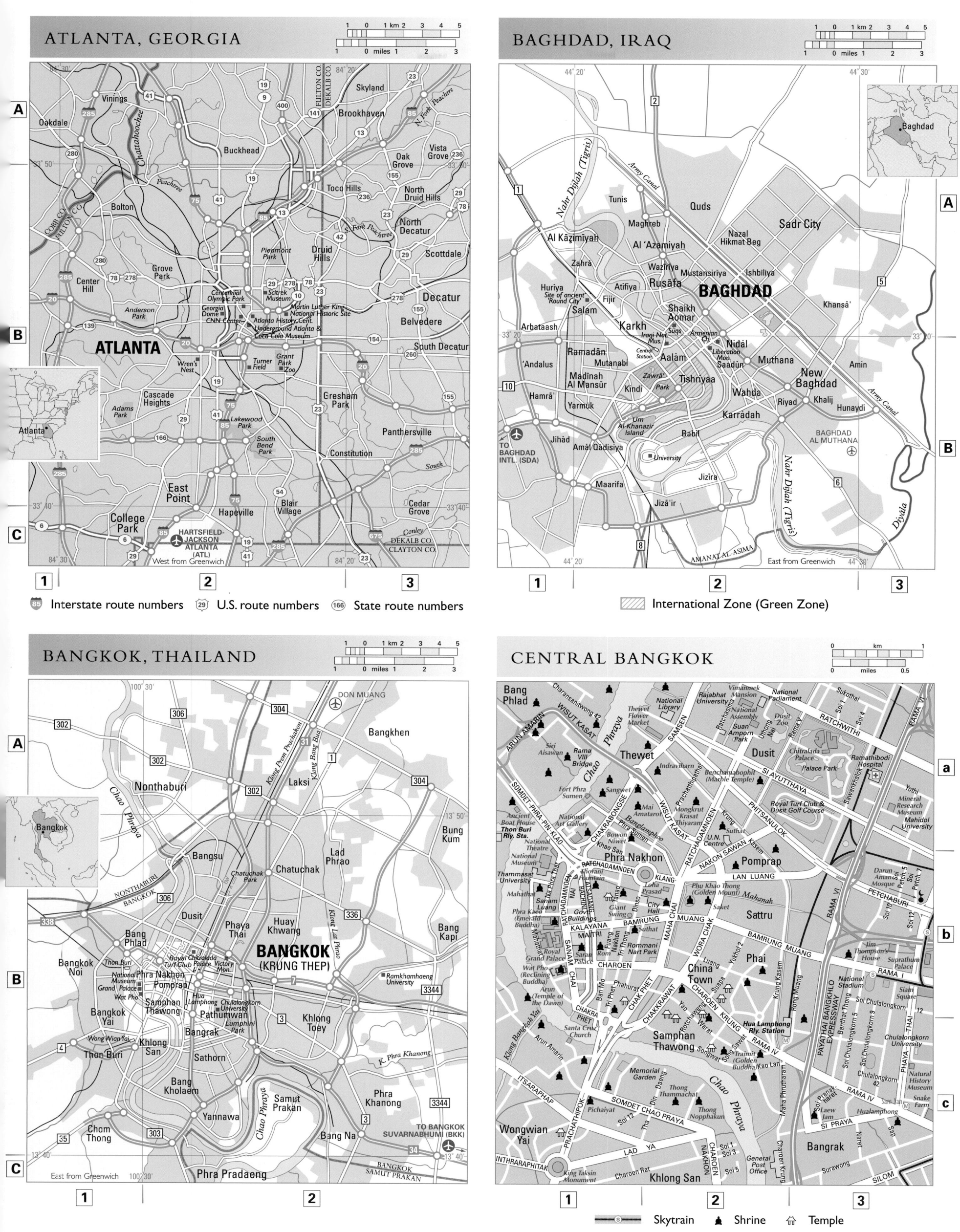

ATLANTA, GEORGIA

BAGHDAD, IRAQ

🛡85 Interstate route numbers   ㉙ U.S. route numbers   ⑯⑥ State route numbers

▨ International Zone (Green Zone)

BANGKOK, THAILAND

CENTRAL BANGKOK

━━Ⓢ━━ Skytrain   ▲ Shrine   ⌂ Temple

COPYRIGHT PHILIP'S

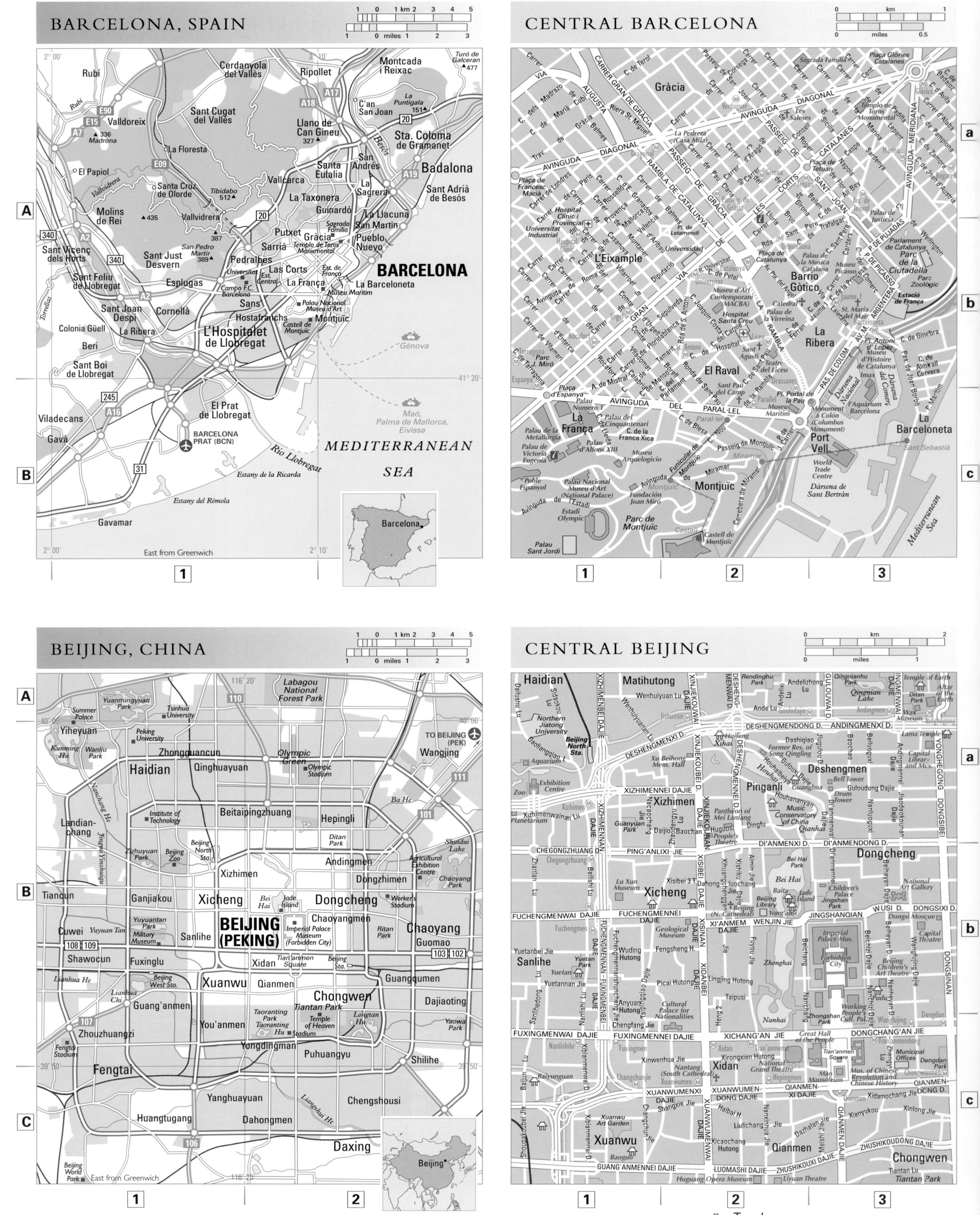

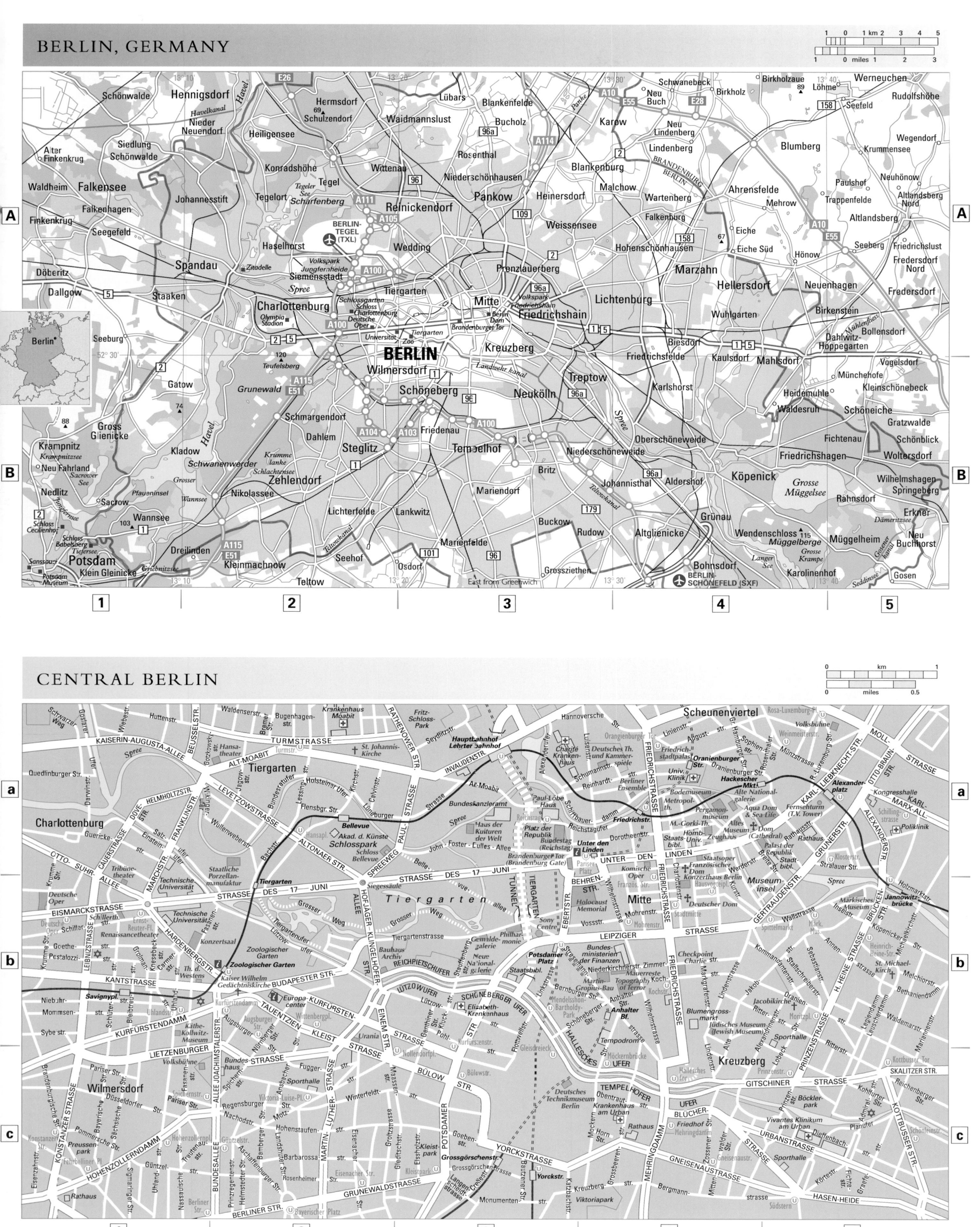

BERLIN, GERMANY

Schönwalde · Hennigsdorf · Lübars · Blankenfelde · Schwanebeck · Birkholzaue · Birkholz · 89 Löhme · Werneuchen · Rudolfshöhe

Waldheim · Falkensee · Alter Finkenkrug · Siedlung Schönwalde · Hermsdorf · 69 Schulzendorf · Waidmannslust · Bucholz · Karow · Neu Lindenberg · Lindenberg · Blumberg · Krummensee · Wegendorf

Havelkanal · Nieder Neuendorf · Heiligensee · Rosenthal · Niederschönhausen · Blankenburg · Wartenberg · Ahrensfelde · Paulshof · Neuhönow

Finkenkrug · Falkenhagen · Johannesstift · Konradshöhe · Tegel · Tegeler See · Scharfenberg · Pankow · Heinersdorf · Malchow · Falkenburg · 67 Eiche · Eiche Süd · Hönow · Trappenfelde · Altlandsberg Nord

Seegefeld · Spandau · Haselhorst · BERLIN-TEGEL (TXL) · Wedding · Prenzlauerberg · Hohenschönhausen · Mehrow · Seeberg · Friedrichslust · Altlandsberg

Döberitz · Dallgow · Staaken · Siemensstadt · Volkspark Jungfernheide · Tiergarten · Mitte · Berlin Dom · Volkspark Friedrichshain · Marzahn · Hellersdorf · Neuenhagen · Fredersdorf Nord

Gross Glienicke · Charlottenburg · Schlossgarten Charlottenburg · Schloss Charlottenburg · Deutsche Oper · Tiergarten · Zoo · Brandenburger Tor · Lichtenburg · Wuhlgarten · Birkenstein · Fredersdorf

Olympia Stadion · BERLIN · Kreuzberg · Friedrichshain · Biesdorf · Dahlwitz-Hoppegarten · Bollensdorf

Krampnitz · Krampnitzsee · Neu Fahrland · Sacrower See · Seeburg · 120 · Teufelsberg · Wilmersdorf · Schöneberg · Friedrichsfelde · Kaulsdorf · Mahlsdorf · Vogelsdorf

Nedlitz · Gatow · Grunewald · Schmargendorf · Neukölln · Karlshorst · Münchehofe · Kleinschönebeck

Pfaueninsel · Grosser Wannsee · Dahlem · Steglitz · Friedenau · Tempelhof · Niederschöneweide · Oberschöneweide · Heidemühle · Waldesruh · Schöneiche · Gratzwalde

Sacrow · Schloss Cecilienhof · Nikolassee · Krumme Lanke · Schlachtensee · Lichterfelde · Lankwitz · Britz · Johannisthal · Aldershof · Köpenick · Grosse Müggelsee · Schönblick · Fichtenau · Friedrichshagen · Wolterdorf

Potsdam · Klein Gleinicke · Griebnitzsee · Dreilinden · Kleinmachnow · Zehlendorf · Mariendorf · Buckow · Rudow · Altglienicke · Grünau · Wendenschloss · 115 Müggelberge · Müggelheim · Wilhelmshagen · Springeberg · Erkner · Dämeritzsee · Neu Buchhorst

Schloss Babelsberg · Tiefersee · Sanssouci · Potsdam Museum · 103 Wannsee · Schwanenwerder · Seehof · Osdorf · Grossziethen · Bohnsdorf · BERLIN-SCHÖNEFELD (SXF) · Karolinenhof · Gosen · Seddinsee

Teltow · East from Greenwich

CENTRAL BERLIN

Charlottenburg · Tiergarten · Scheunenviertel · Hauptbahnhof Lehrter Bahnhof · Oranienburger Str. · Hackescher Mkt. · Alexanderplatz

Deutsche Oper · Technische Universität · Zoologischer Garten · Zoologischer Garten · Bellevue · Schloss Bellevue · Haus der Kulturen der Welt · Bundeskanzleramt · Reichstag · Brandenburger Tor (Brandenburg Gate) · Unter den Linden · Dom (Cathedral) · Fernsehturm (T.V. Tower) · Museuminsel · Pergamon museum

Kaiser Wilhelm Gedächtniskirche · Europa-Center · Tiergarten · Siegessäule · Holocaust Memorial · Sony Centre · Philharmonie · Gemäldegalerie · Potsdamer Platz · Mitte · Deutscher Dom

Wilmersdorf · Kurfürstendamm · Savignypl. · Kreuzberg · Checkpoint Charlie · Topography of Terror · Anhalter Bf. · Jüdisches Museum (Jewish Museum) · Deutsches Technikmuseum Berlin · Tempodrom

Yorckstrasse · Viktoriapark · Hasen-Heide

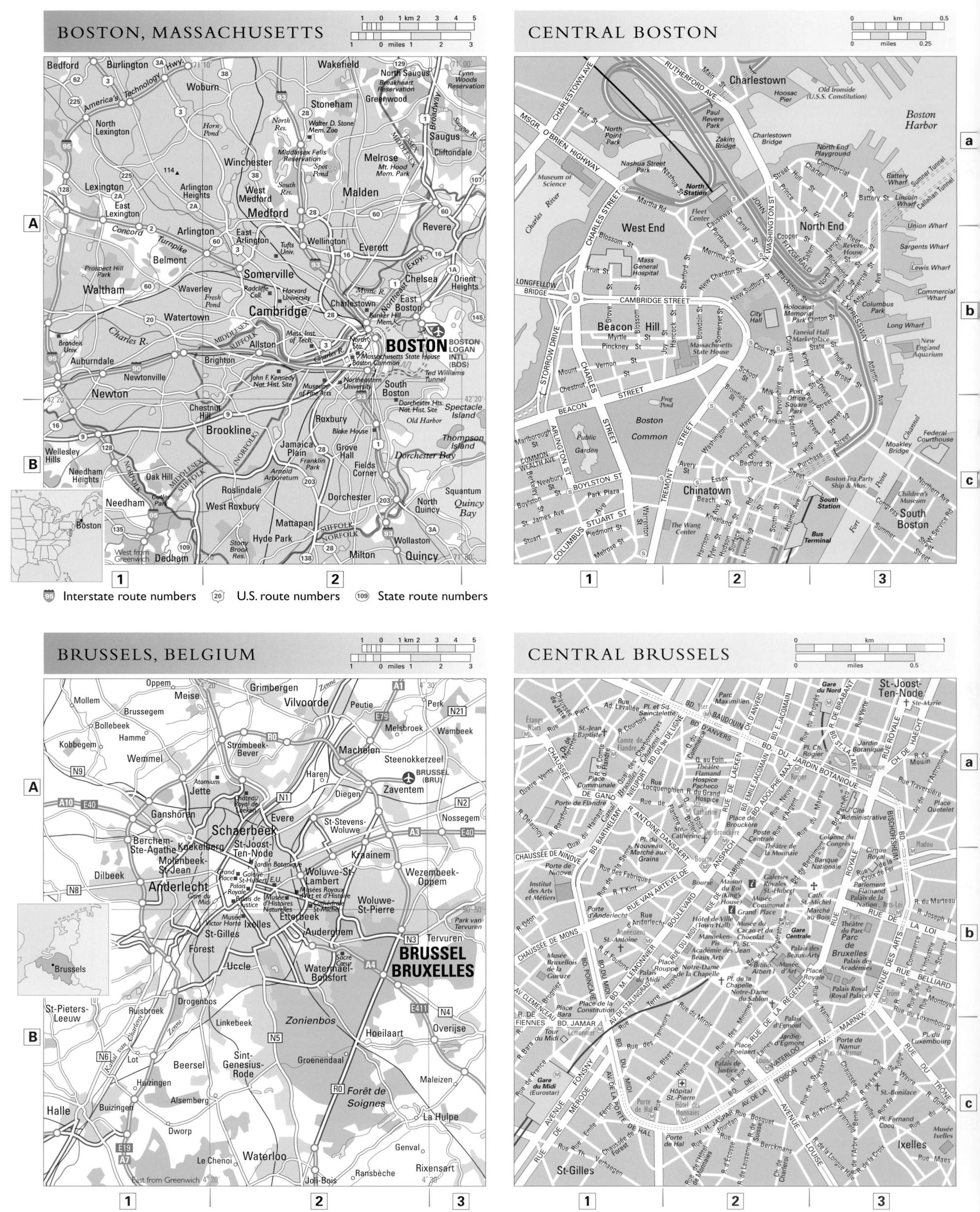

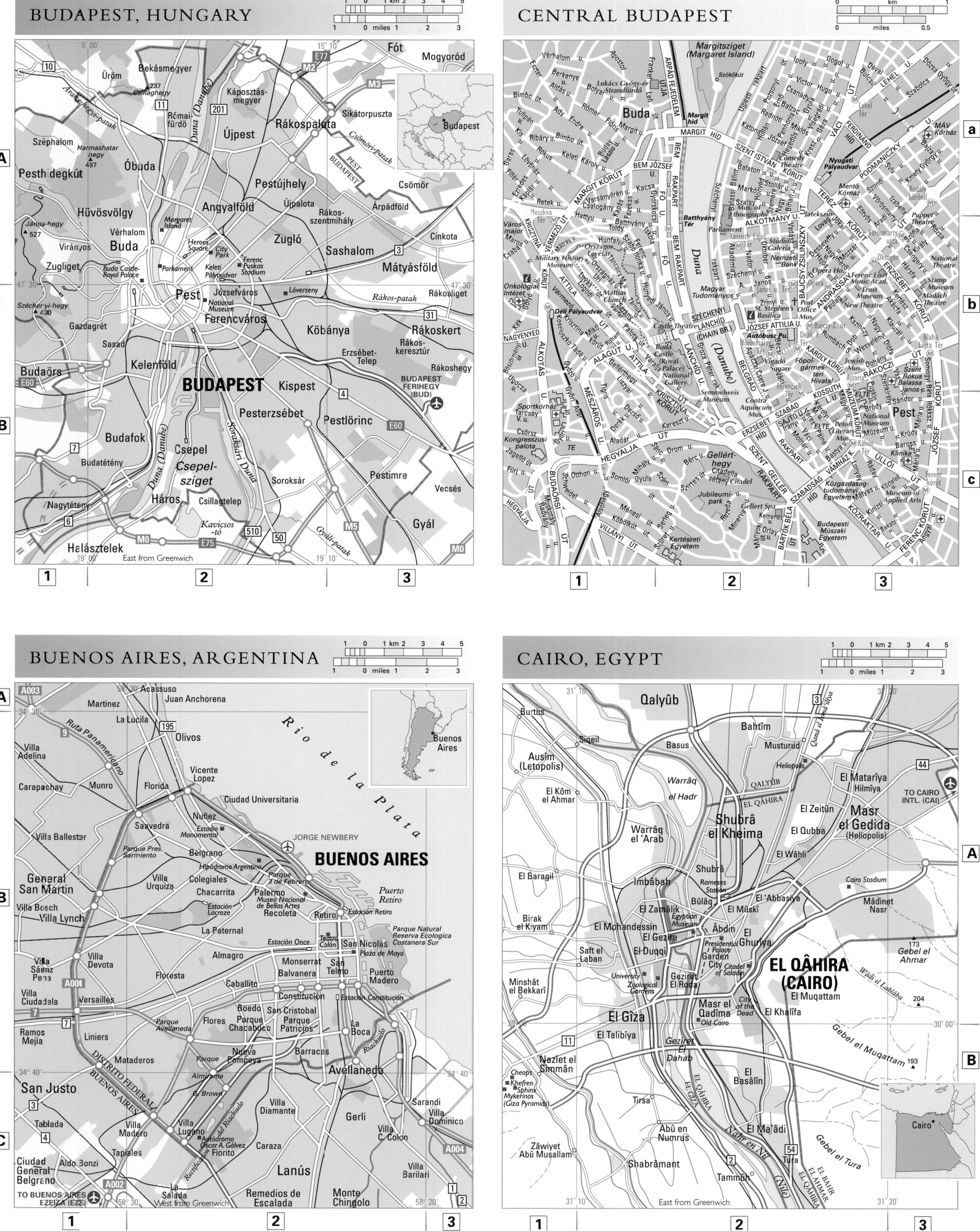

BUDAPEST, HUNGARY

CENTRAL BUDAPEST

BUENOS AIRES, ARGENTINA

CAIRO, EGYPT

COPYRIGHT PHILIP'S

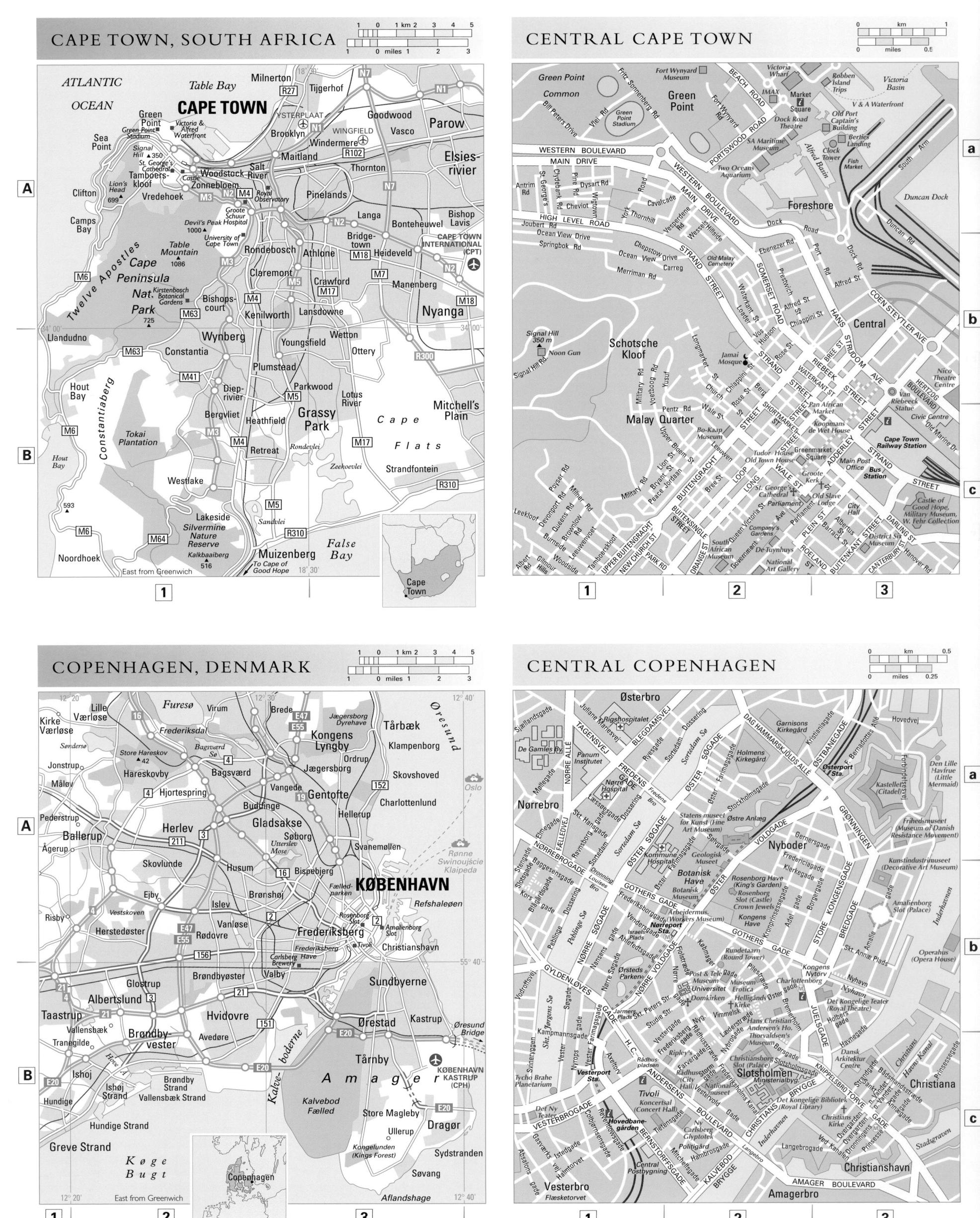

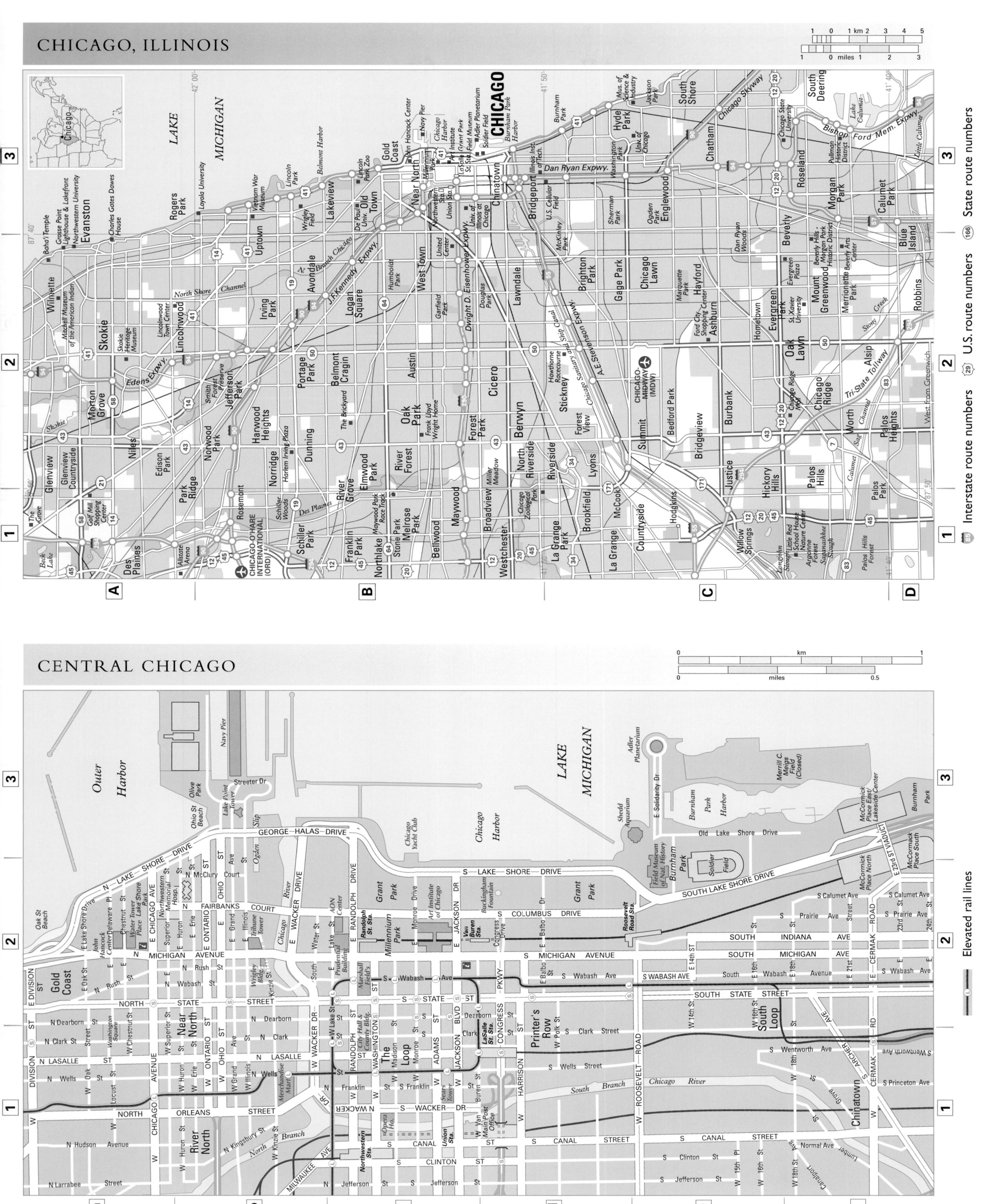

CHICAGO, ILLINOIS

CENTRAL CHICAGO

State route numbers

U.S. route numbers

Interstate route numbers

Elevated rail lines

COPYRIGHT PHILIP'S

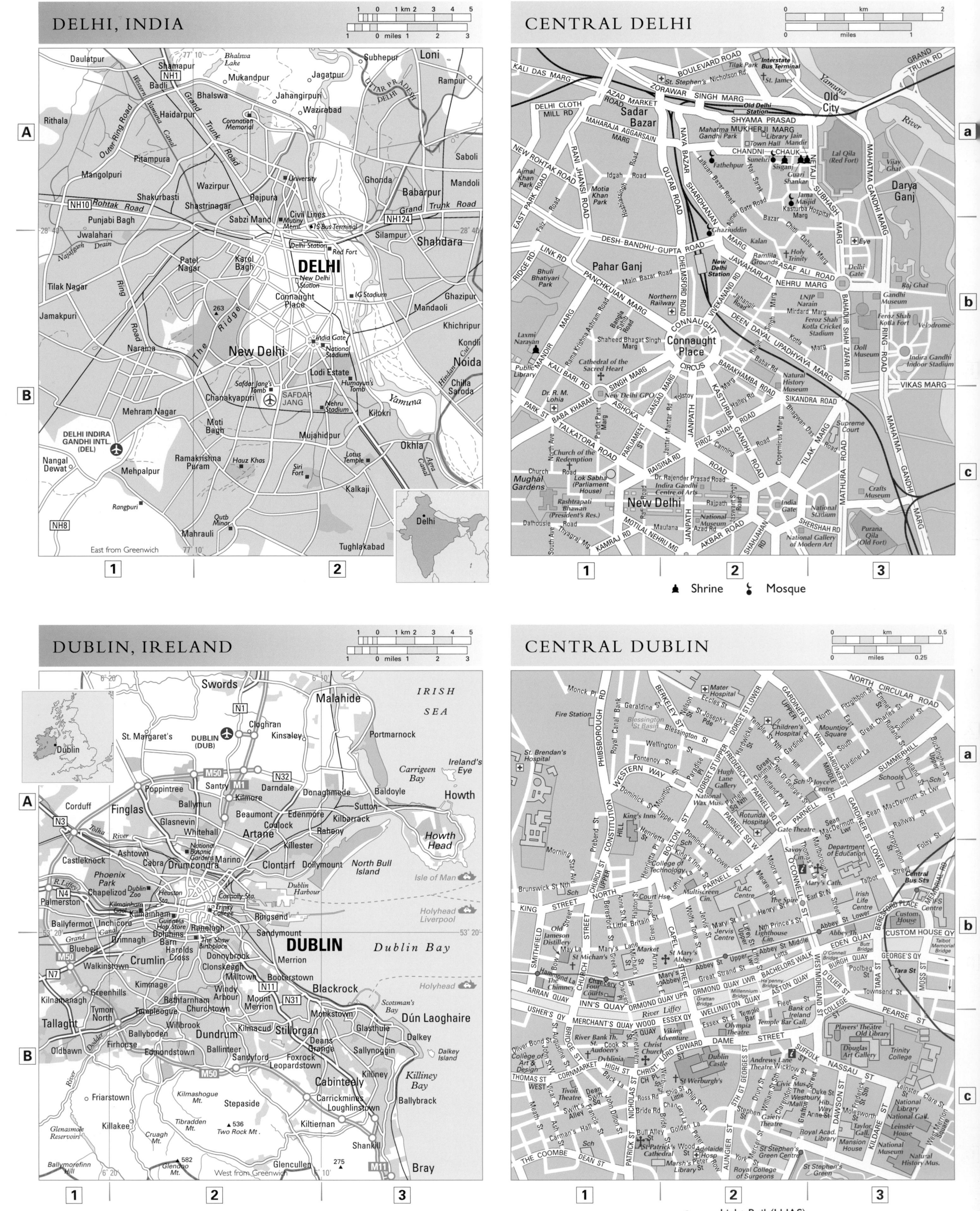

DELHI, INDIA

CENTRAL DELHI

▲ Shrine   ⚲ Mosque

DUBLIN, IRELAND

CENTRAL DUBLIN

— Light Rail (LUAS)

EDINBURGH, U.K.

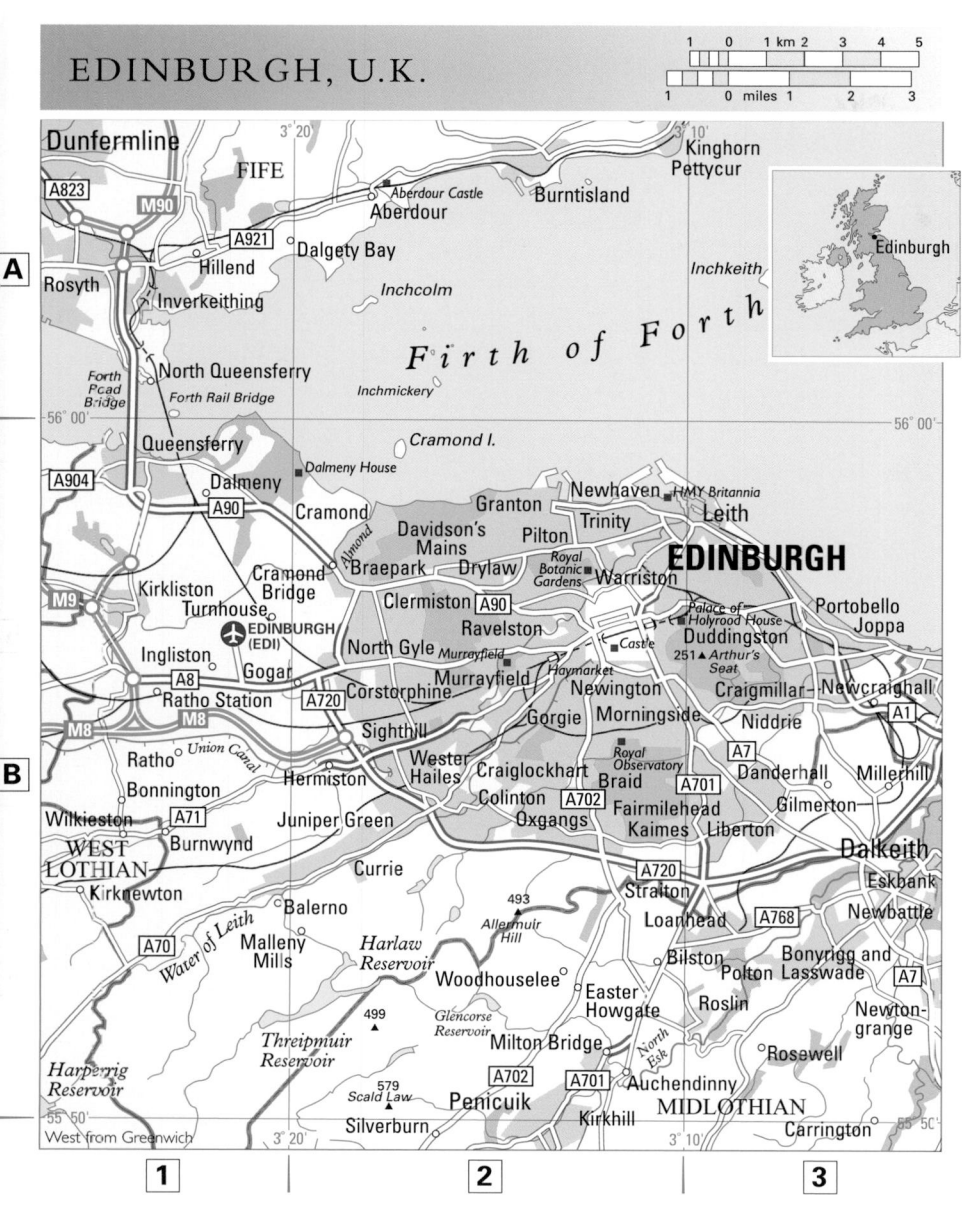

CENTRAL EDINBURGH

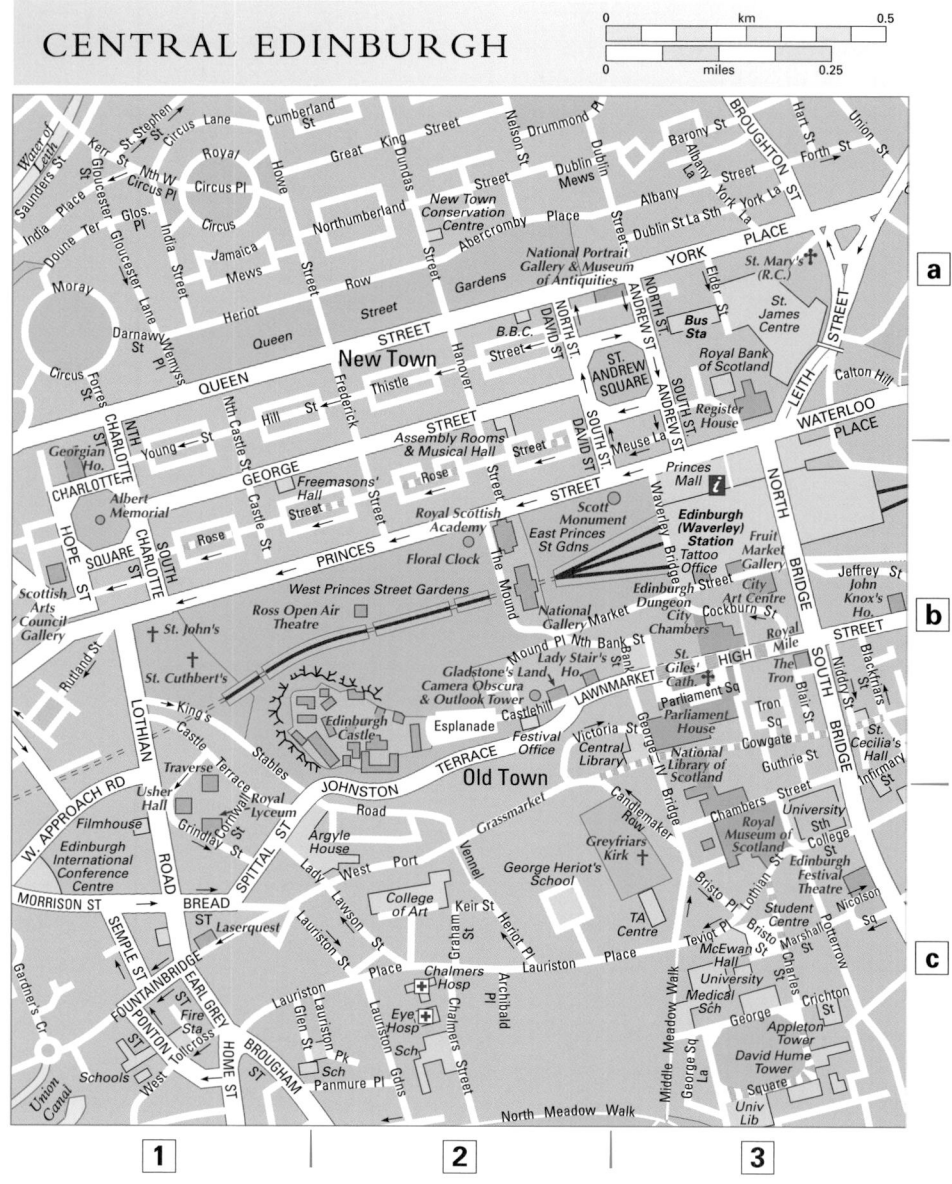

GUANGZHOU, CHINA

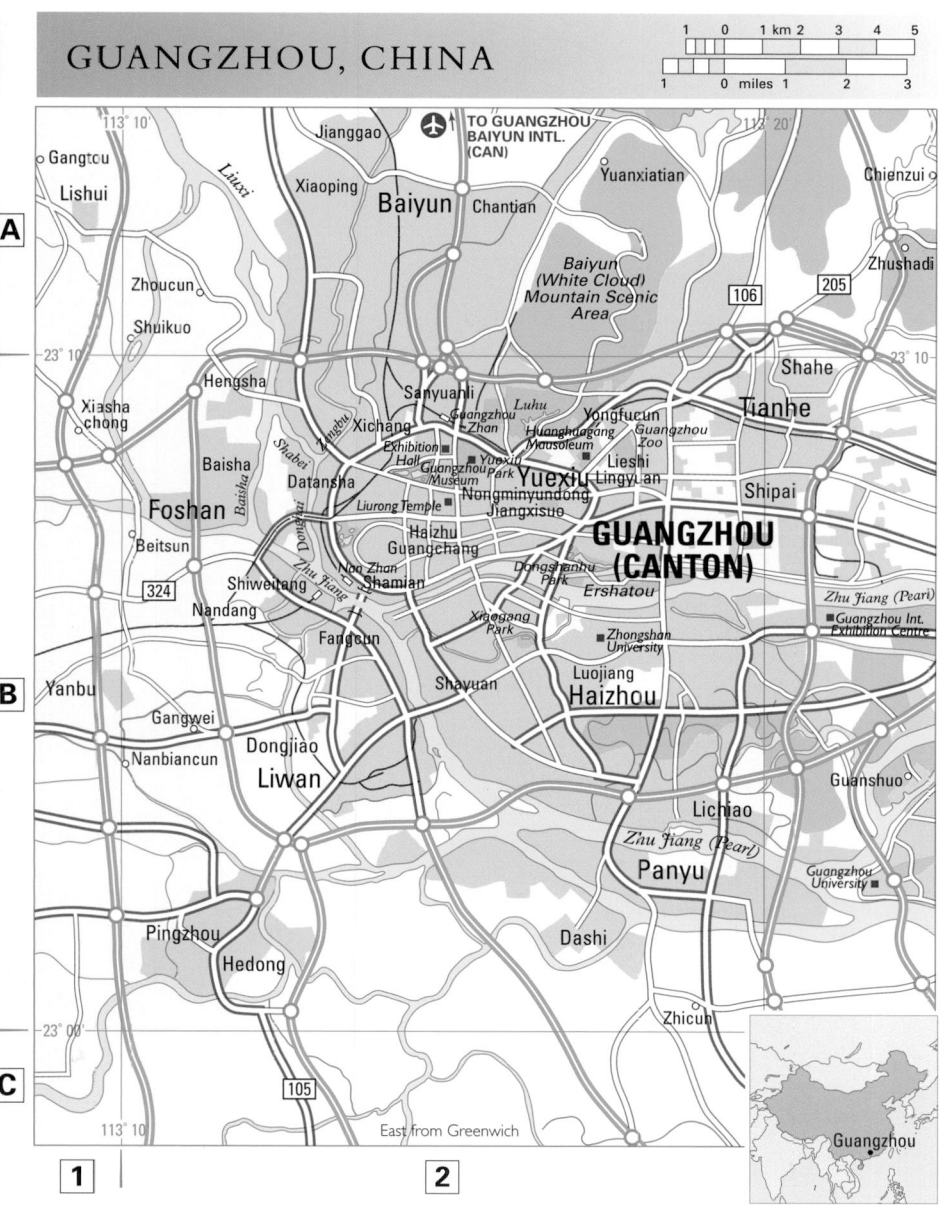

HELSINKI, FINLAND

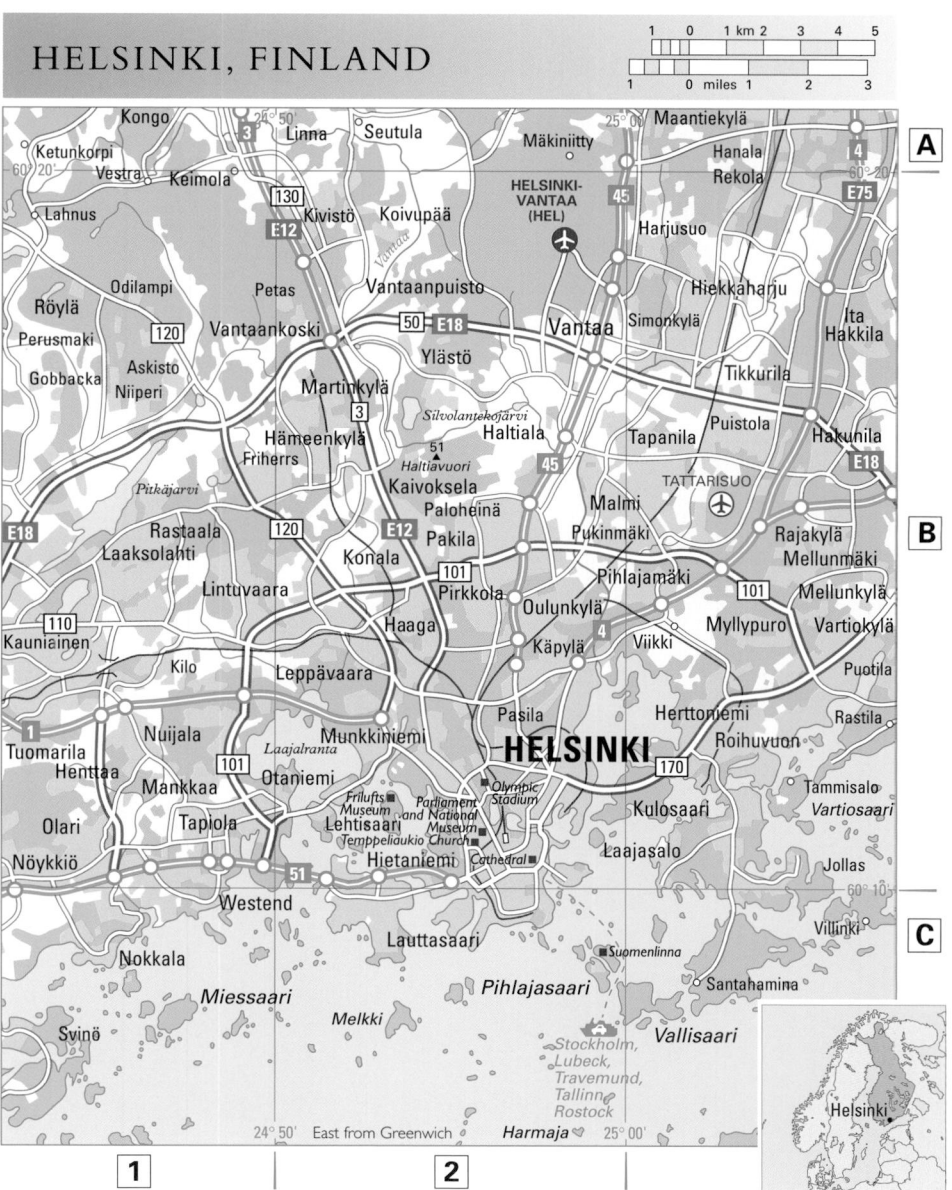

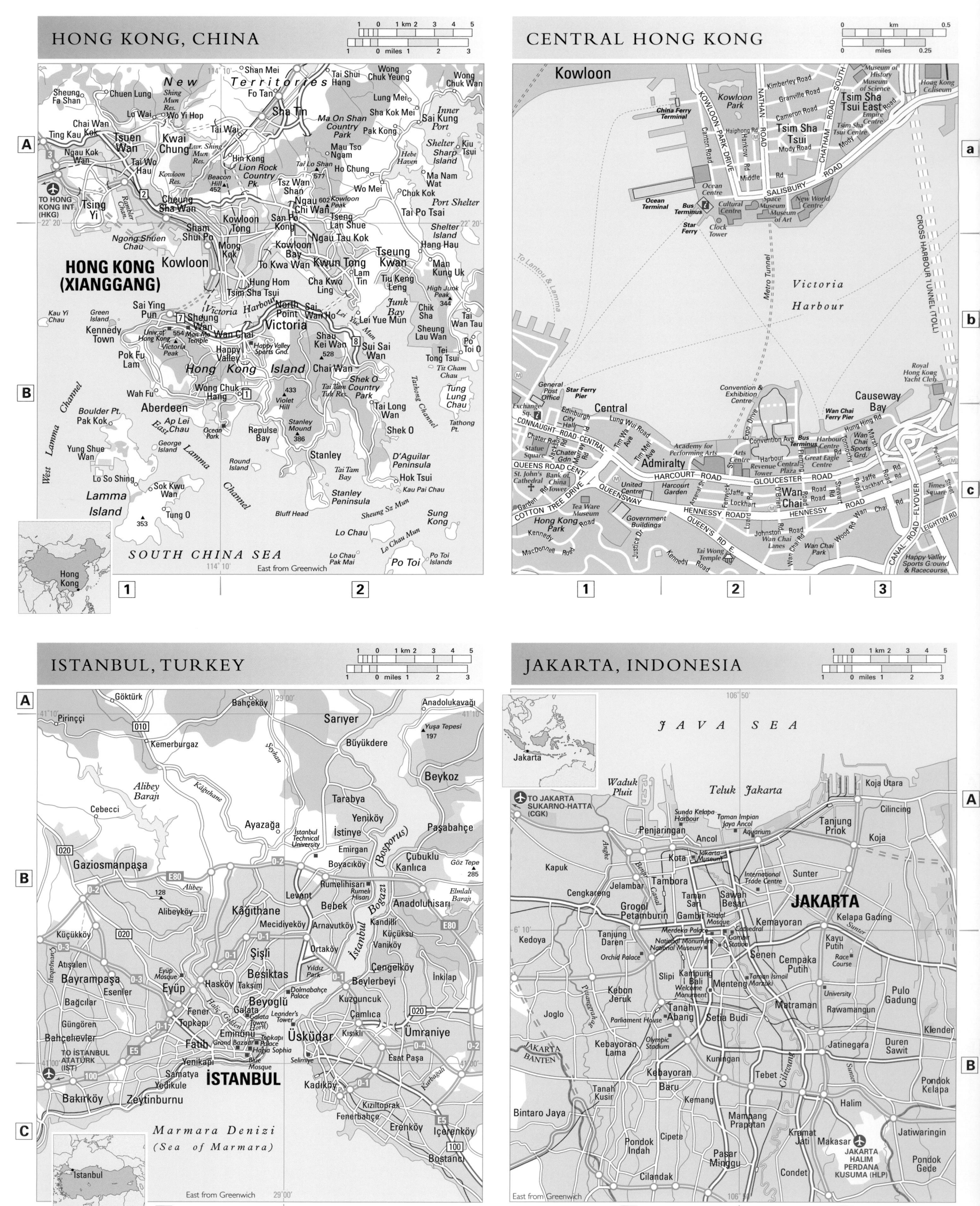

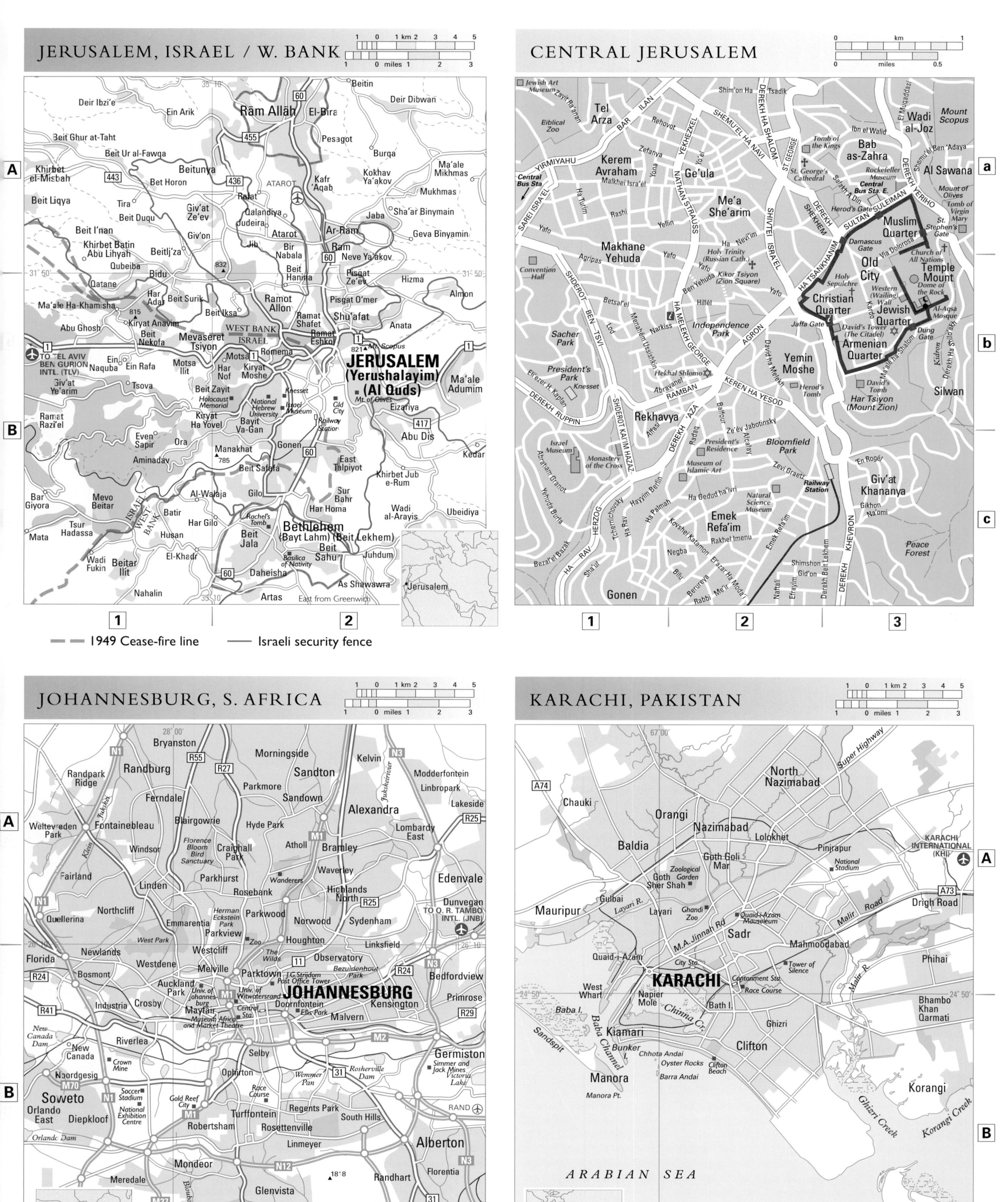

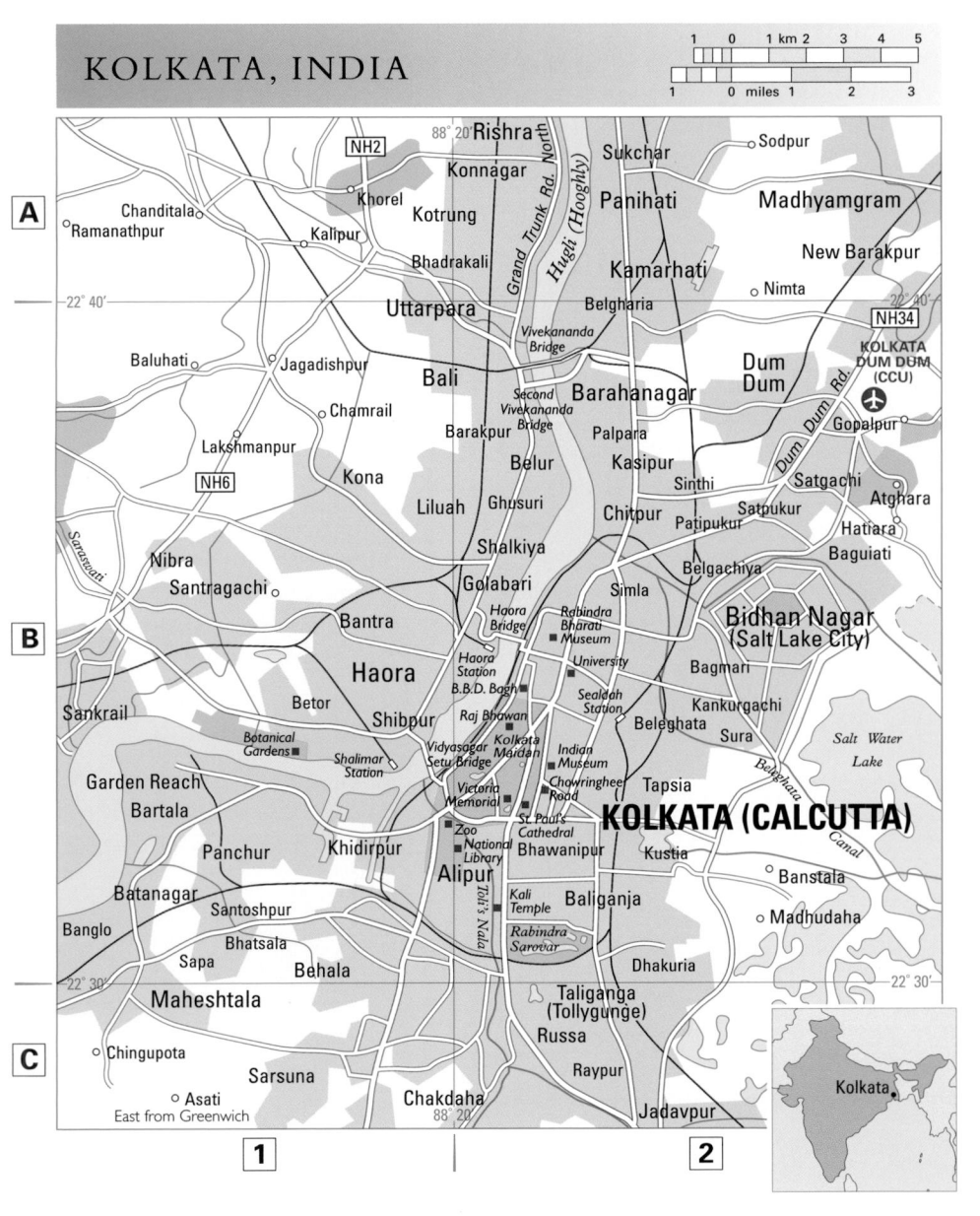

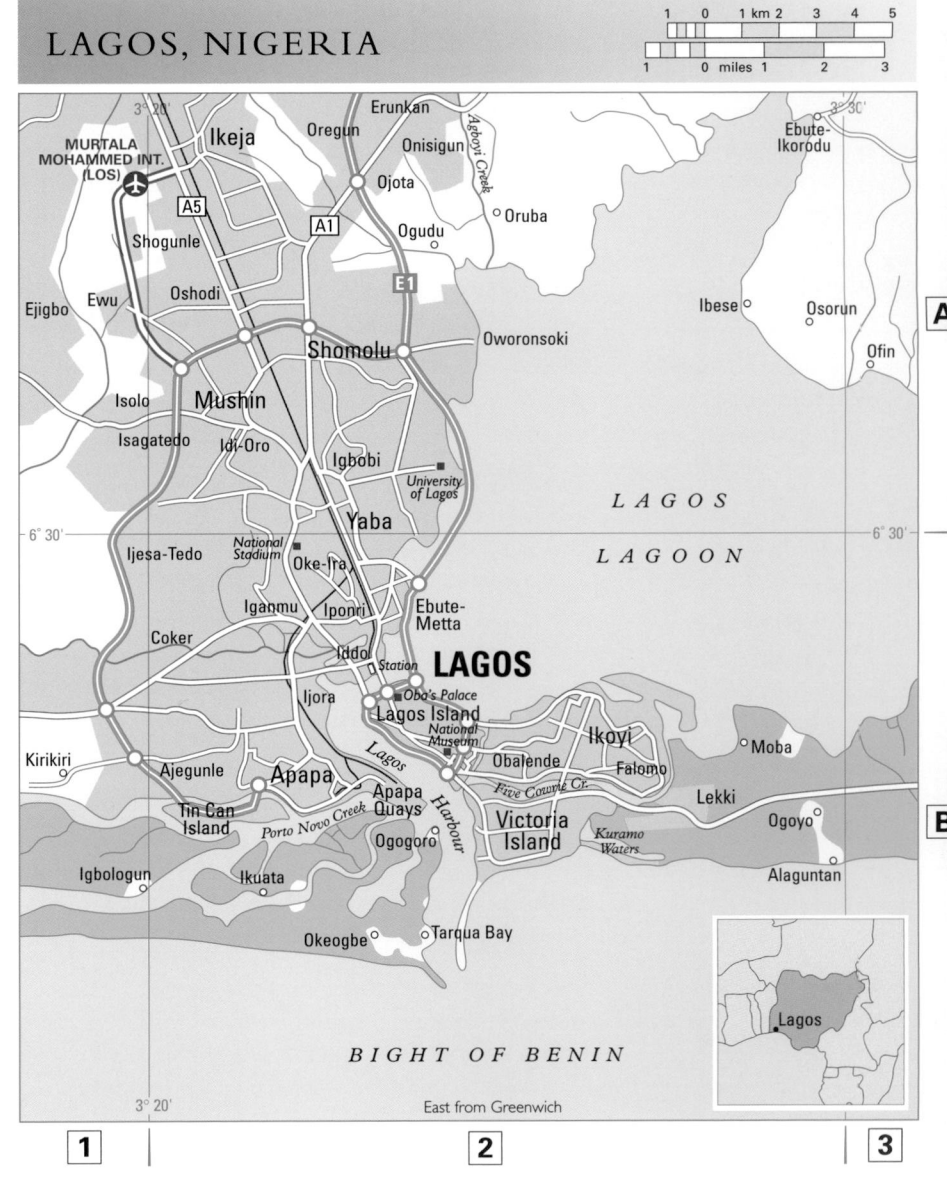

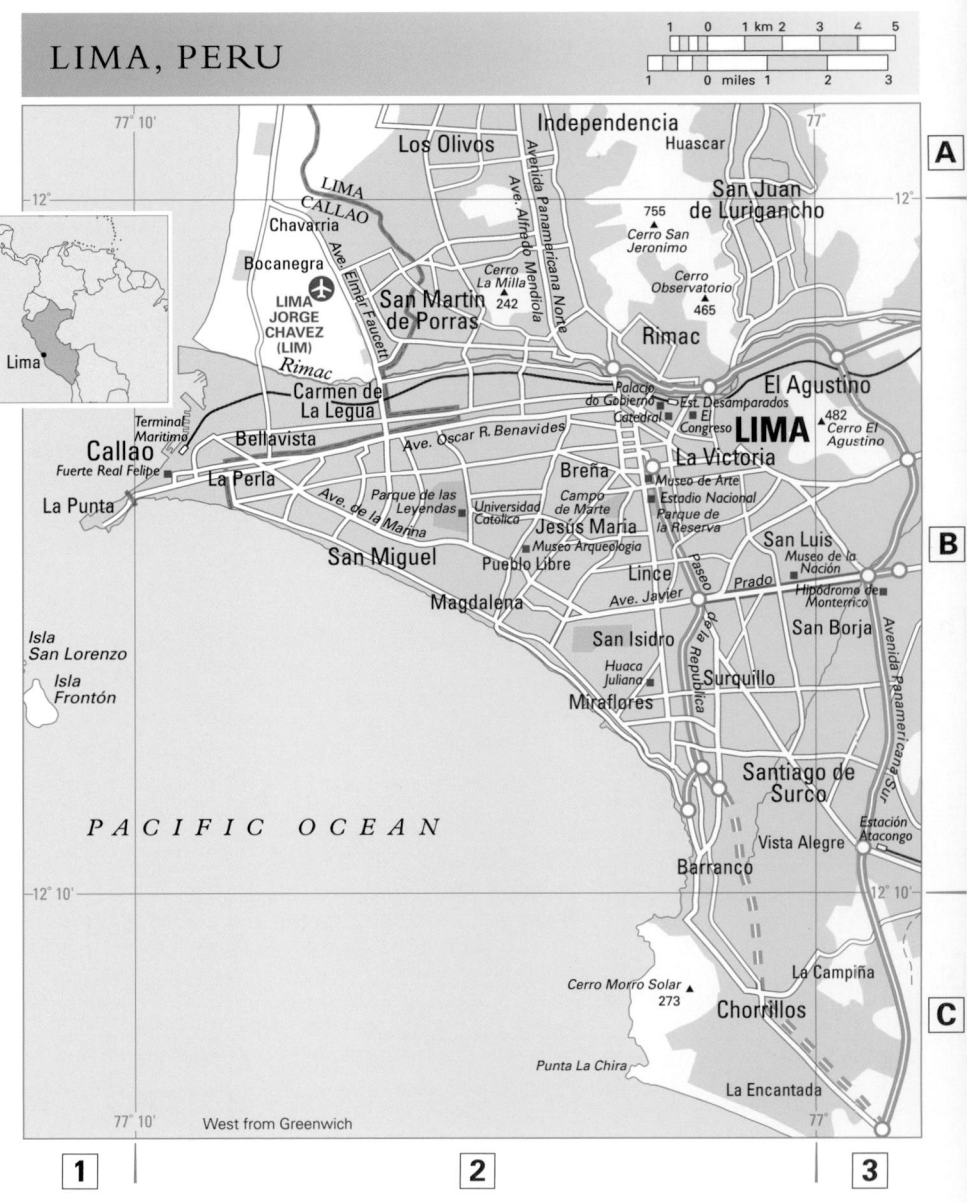

🛡15 Interstate route numbers   95 U.S. route numbers   147 State route numbers

COPYRIGHT PHILIP'S

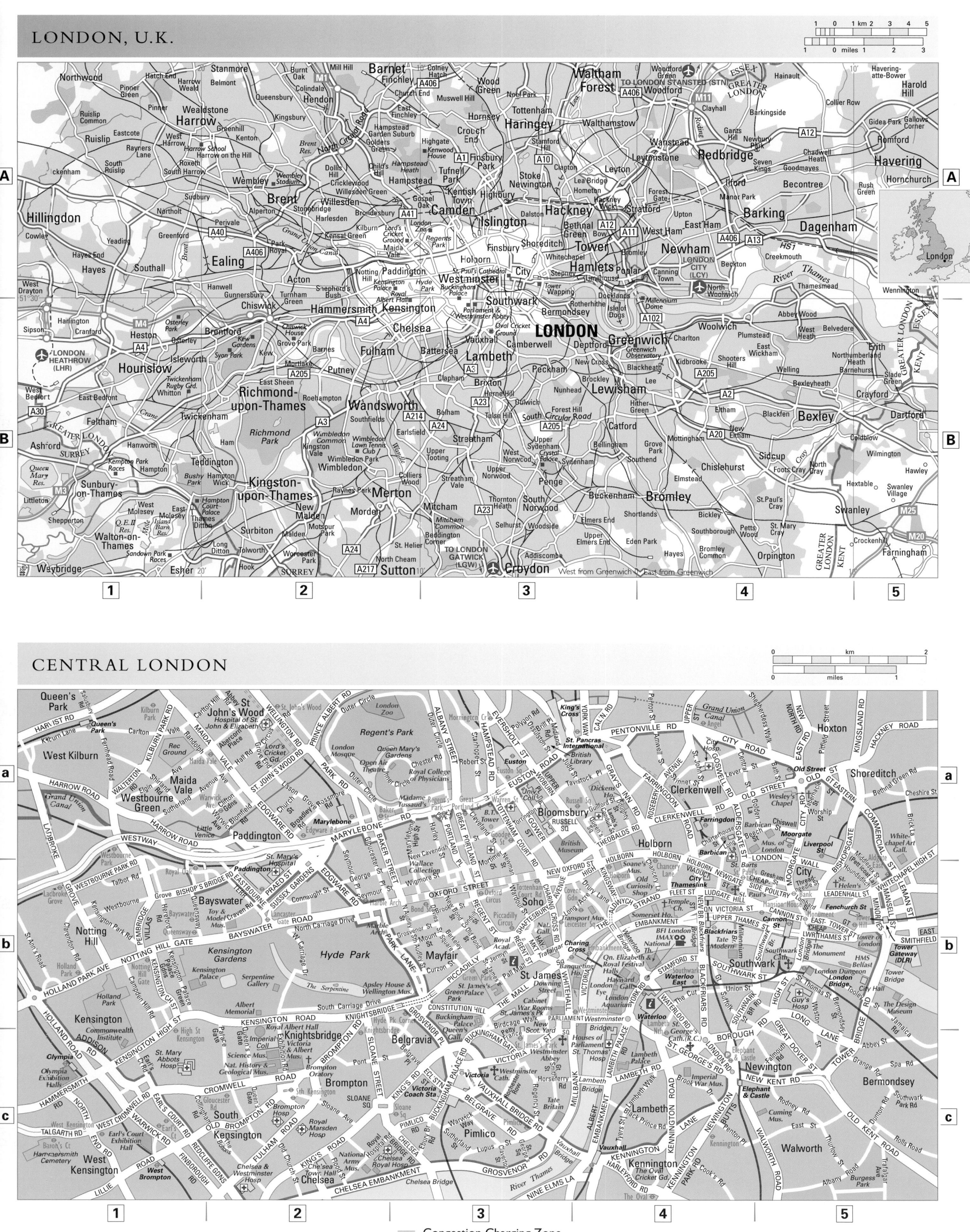

LONDON, U.K.

CENTRAL LONDON

— Congestion Charging Zone

COPYRIGHT PHILIP'S

LISBON, PORTUGAL

Almargem do Bispo
Botica Sete
São Julião do Tojal
Santo Antão do Tojal
Sabugo
Piedade
Tapada
Camarões
Montemor
Loures
Santa Iria da Azóia
Telhal
Caneças
Apelação
Povoa de Santo Adrião
Amoreira
Boavista
Camarate
Sacavém
Ponte Vasco da Gama
Venda Seca
Ada Beja
Odivelas
Charneca
Moscavide
Parque das Nações (Park of Nations)
Rio de Mouro
Belas
Agualva-Cacem
Massamá
Lumiar
Pontinha
Carnide
LISBOA PORTELA (LIS)
Olivais
Queluz
Amadora
Benfica
Campo Grande
University
Matinha
Damaia
Monsanto
Campo Pequeno
Alto do Pina
Beato
Barcarena
Carnaxide
Parque Florestal de Monsanto
Rato
Bairro Lopes
LISBOA
Linda-a-Pastora
Ajuda
Santo Amaro
Alcântara
Campolide
Castelo de S. Jorge
Estação Santa Apolónia
Leião
Terrugem
Caxias
Algés
Mosteiro dos Jerónimos (Hieronymos Monastery)
Estação do Rossio
Basílica da Estrela
Praça do Comércio
Estação Cais do Sodré
Oeiras
Paço de Arcos
Porto Brandão
Banática
Belém
Cacilhas
Almada
Lavradio
Torre de Belém (Tower of Belém)
Padrão dos Descobrimentos (Discoveries Monument)
Ponte 25 de Abril
ATLANTIC
Trafaria
Raposo
Cova de Piedade
OCEAN
Bugio
Caparica
Barreiro
Quinta de Santo António
Costa da Caparica
Sobreda
Laranjeiro
Corroios
Coina
Capuchos
Seixal
Santo André
Amora
Cruz de Pau
Palhais
Arrentela
Charneca

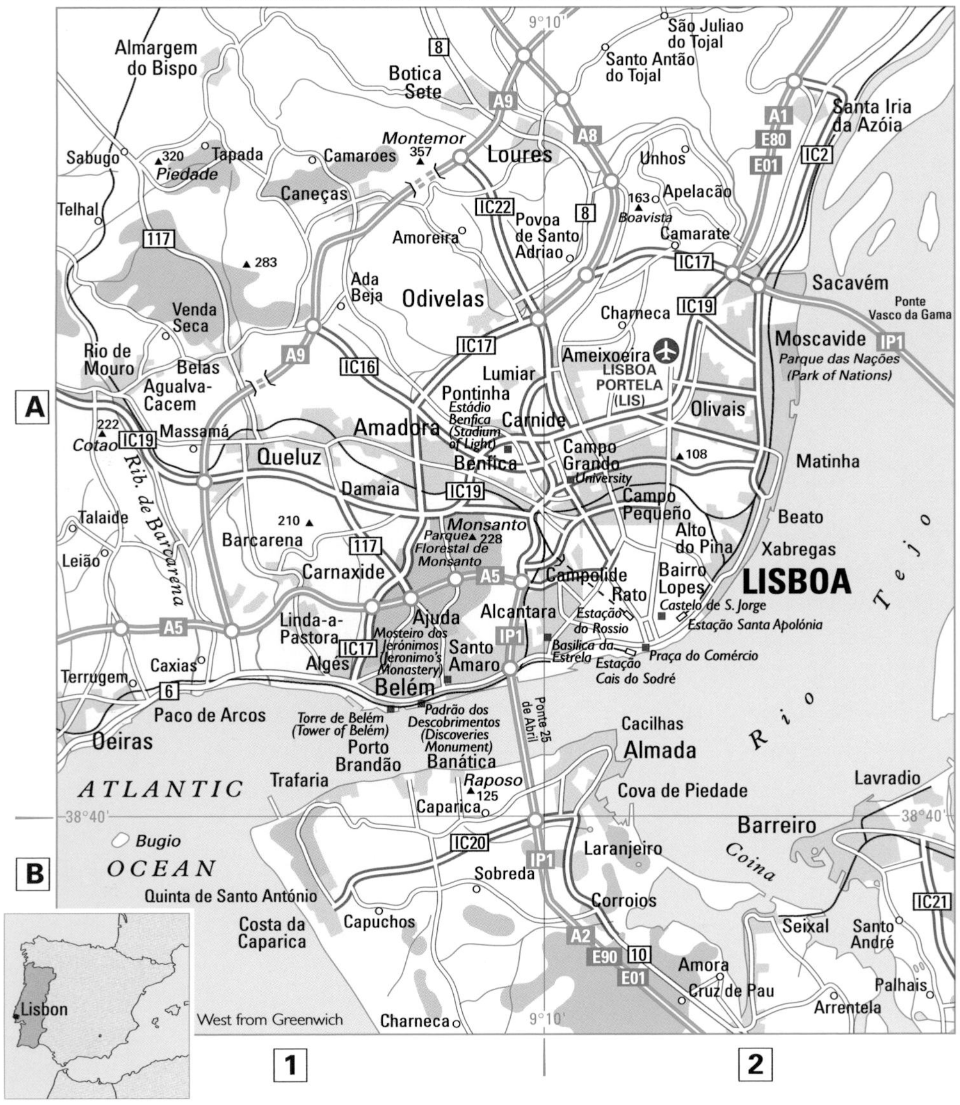

Lisbon

West from Greenwich

CENTRAL LISBON

Palacio de Penitenciária
Palácio de Justiça
Instituto Superior Técnico
Praça Duque Saldanha
Parque Eduardo VII
Pavilhão dos Desportos
Maternidade
Estefânia
Penha França
Amoreiros
Praça Marquês de Pombal
Anjos
Bairro Alto
Rato
Academia das Ciências
Jardim Botanico
Graça
Palácio de Assembleia Nacional
Bairro Alto
Praça dos Restauradores
Teatro Nac. de Dona Maria II
Estação do Rossio
Praça Rossio
Alfama
Baixa
Castelo de São Jorge (St. George's Castle)
Museu de Arte Decorativa
Sé Catedral
Military Museum
Praça do Comércio
Estação Santa Apolónia
AV. VINTE E QUATRO DE JULHO
RUA DO ARSENAL
Estação Cais do Sodré
AV. RIBEIRA DAS NAUS
Estação Fluvial
Rio Tejo (Tagus)
INFANTE DOM HENRIQUE

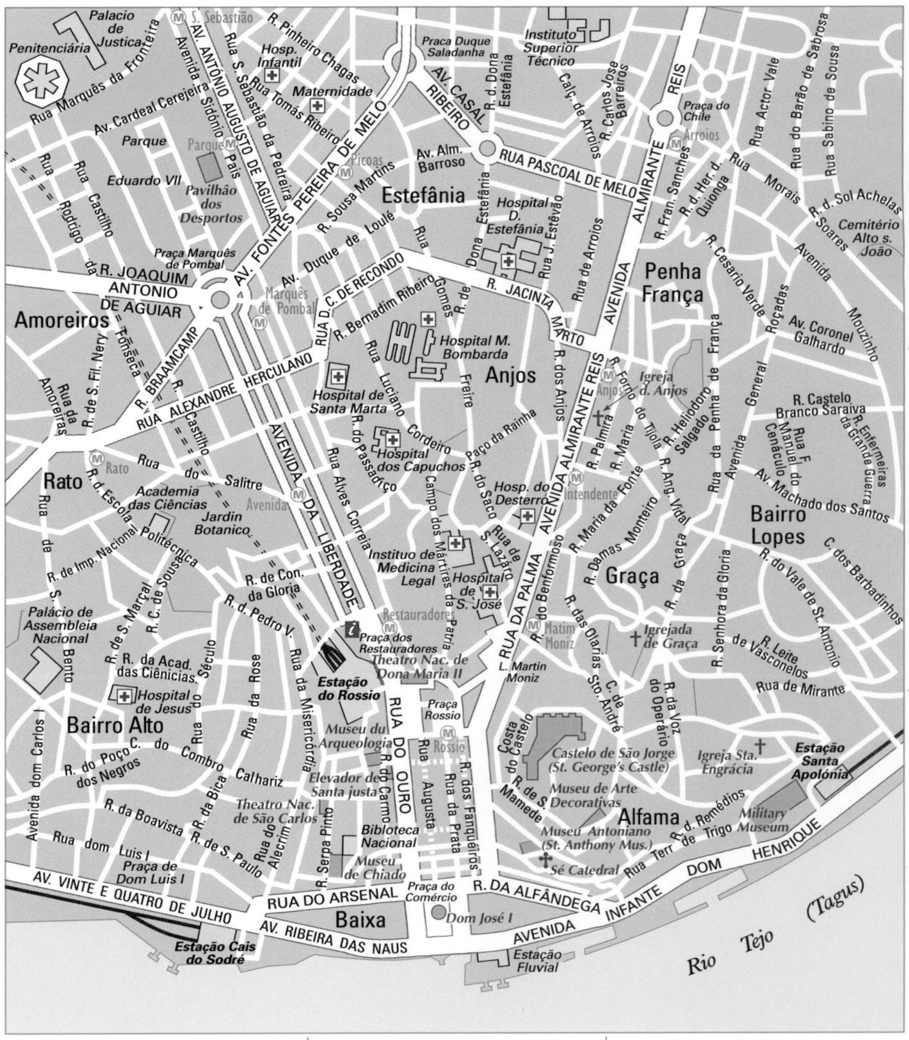

LOS ANGELES, CALIFORNIA

Tarzana
San Fernando Valley
Van Nuys
Burbank
Verdugo Mts.
Altadena
San Gabriel Mts.
Eaton Canyon Park
Encino
Sepulveda Dam Rec. Area
North Hollywood
N.&C. Studios
Disney Studios
Flint Peak 575
Rose Bowl
Pasadena
Sierra Madre
Monrovia
Encino Reservoir
Sherman Oaks
Studio City
C.B.S. Fox Studios
Warner Brothers Studios
Zoo
Cahuenga Peak 555
Glendale
Glendale Galleria
Norton Simon Museum
California Institute of Technology
L.A. State & County Arboretum
Santa Anita Park
Arcadia
Mulholland Dr.
Universal Studios
Griffith Park
Lake Hollywood
Griffith Observatory
Eagle Rock
Occidental Coll.
South Pasadena
The Huntington
San Marino
Santa Monica Mts.
Topanga State Park
Stone Canyon Reservoir
Beverly Glen
Mount Olympus
Hollywood Bowl
Hollywood
Los Feliz Blvd.
Highland Park
Southwest Museum
Garvanza
Mission San Gabriel Archángel
San Gabriel
Temple City
Nat. Rec. Area
Franklin Reservoir
Mann's Chinese Theatre
Walk of Fame
Sunset Blvd.
L.A. Municipal Art Gallery
Silver Lake Reservoir
Cypress Park
Monterey Hills
Alhambra
Rosemead
The Getty Center
Bel Air
Beverly Hills
West Hollywood
Santa Monica Blvd.
Paramount Studios
Silver Lake
Elysian Park
Echo Park
Dodger Stadium
Lincoln Heights
El Sereno
California State University
Brentwood
University of California Los Angeles
Farmers Market
L.A. County Art Museum
Beverly Blvd.
Getty Ho.
MacArthur Park
Westlake
Monterey Park
San Bernardino Fwy.
El Monte
Brentwood Park
Westwood Village
Century City
Petersen Automotive Museum
Wilshire Blvd.
LOS ANGELES
Civic Center
City Hall
City Terrace
South San Gabriel
South El Monte
Pacific Palisades
Sawtelle
Rancho Park
Cheviot Hills
Mid-City
Convention Center
Union Sta.
Boyle Heights
East Los Angeles
Montebello Town Center
Santa Monica
Museum of Art
20th Century Fox Studios
Santa Monica Fwy.
Jefferson Park
University of Southern California
California Space & Science Center
Vernon
Commerce
Pico Rivera
Pio Pico State Historic Park
Mus. of Flying
SANTA MONICA
Palms
Sony Picture Studio
Baldwin Hills Reservoir
View Park
Memorial Coliseum
Exposition Park
Maywood
Puente Hills
Santa Monica Pier
California Heritage Museum
Mar Vista
Culver City
Baldwin Hills
Windsor Hills
Huntington Park
Bicentennial Park
PACIFIC OCEAN
Venice
Del Rey
Ladera Heights
Hyde Park
Vermont Knolls
Florence
Bell
Bell Gardens
Los Nietos
Venice Boardwalk
Loyola Marymount University
Manchester Ave.
Slauson Ave.
Walnut Park
Cudahy
Whittier
Marina del Rey
Westchester
University of West Los Angeles
Great Western Forum
Inglewood
South Gate
Downey
Santa Fe Springs
LOS ANGELES INTERNATIONAL (LAX)
Lennox

West from Greenwich

Los Angeles

85 Interstate route numbers
166 State route numbers

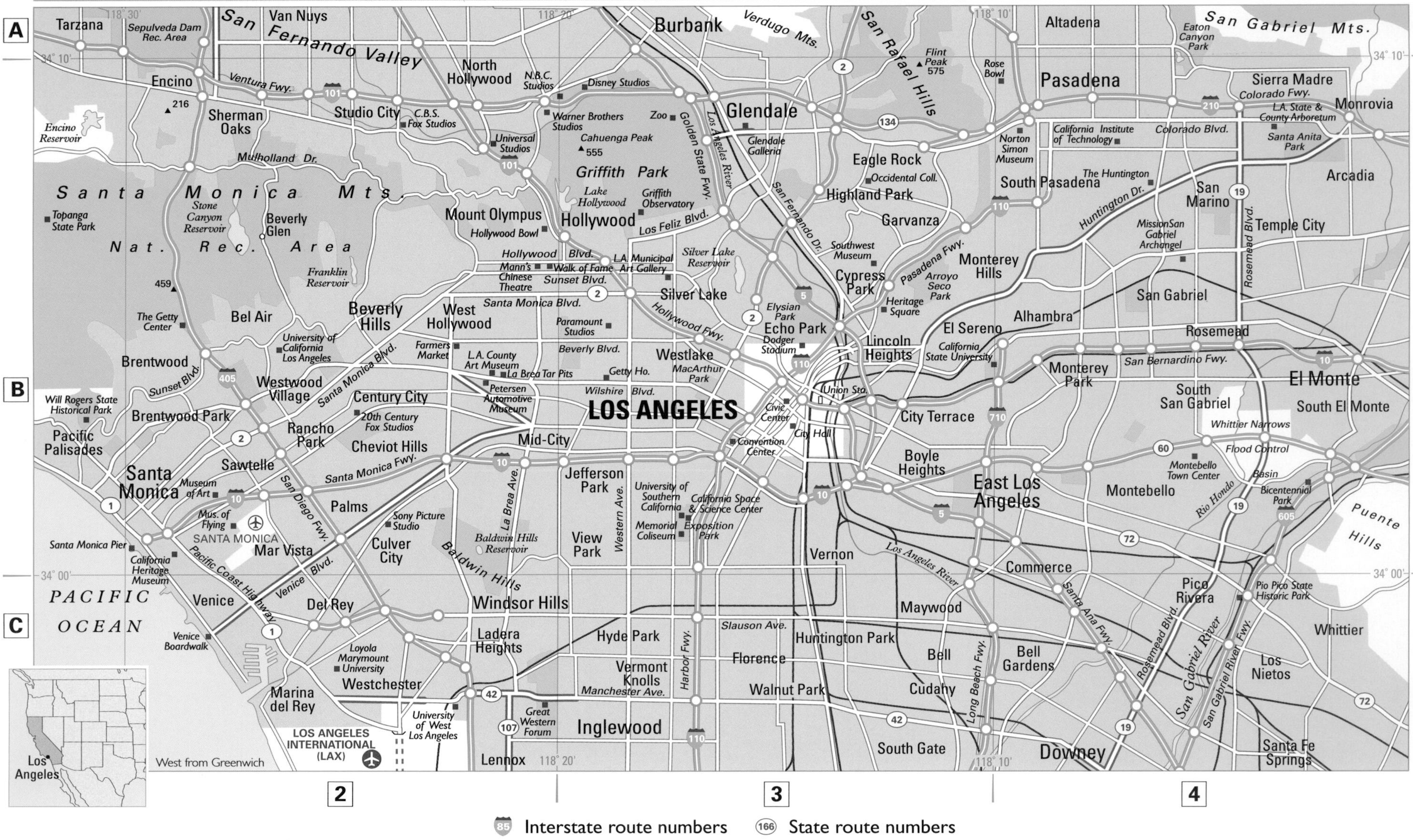

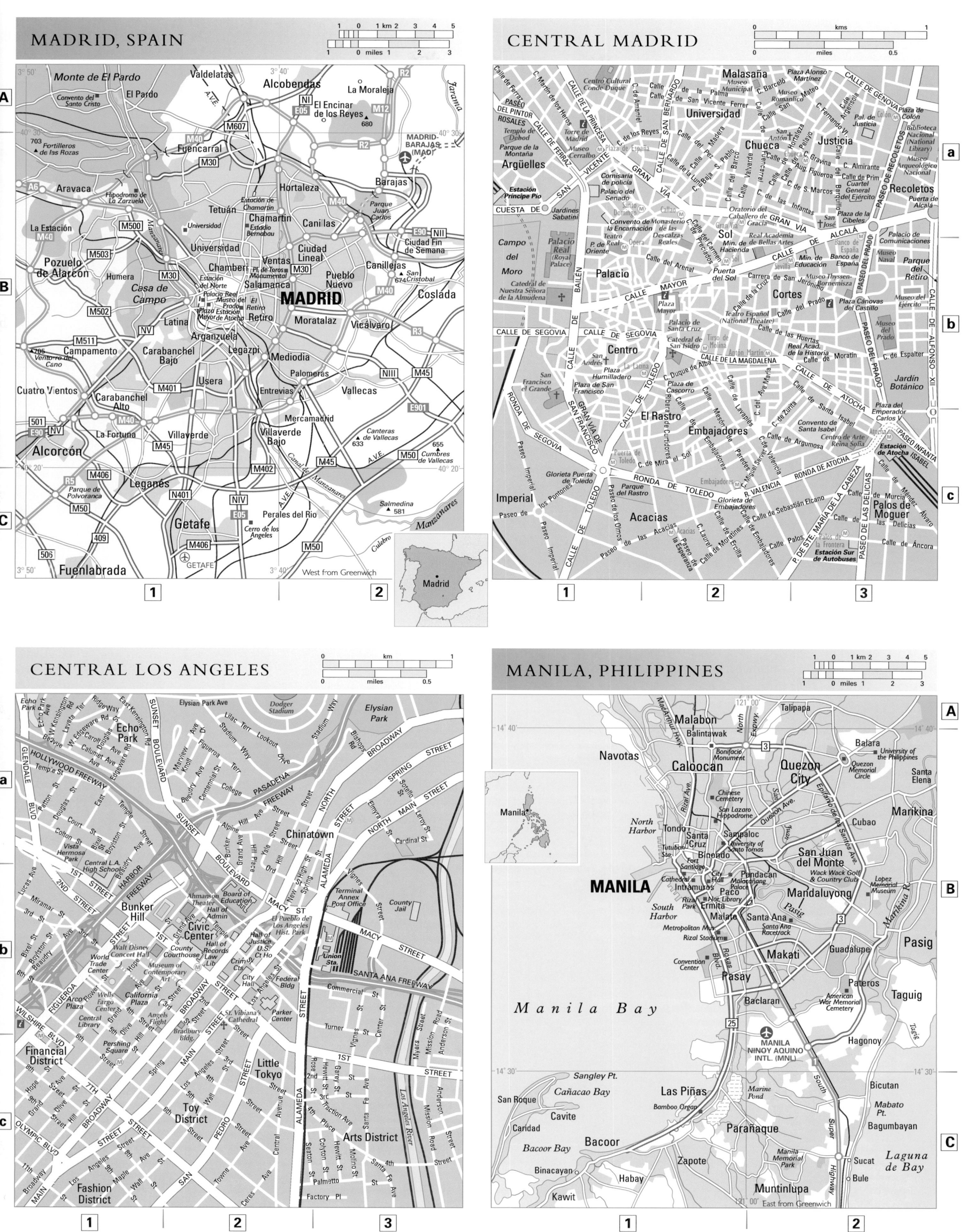

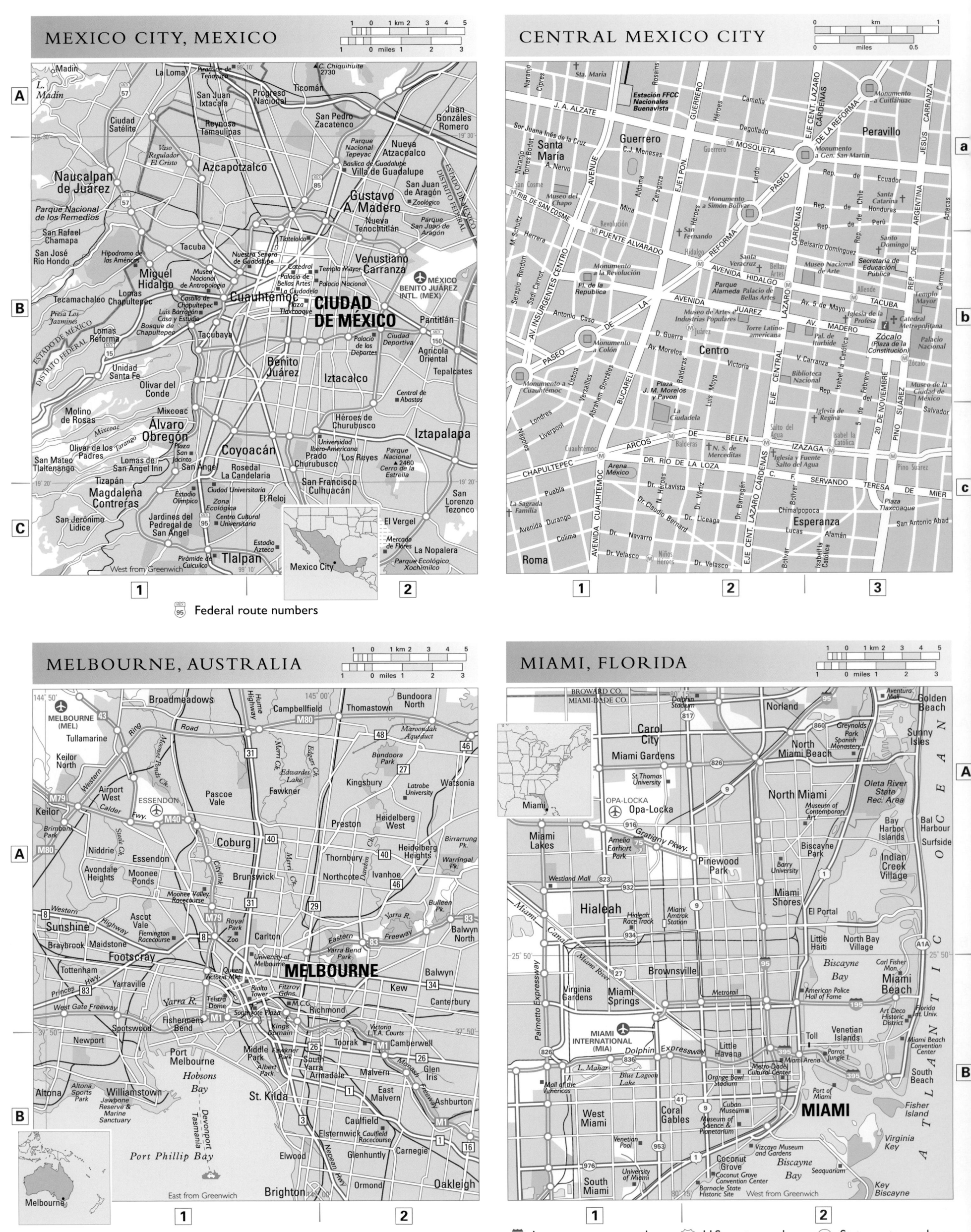

MEXICO CITY, MEXICO

Federal route numbers

CENTRAL MEXICO CITY

MELBOURNE, AUSTRALIA

MIAMI, FLORIDA

Interstate route numbers   U.S. route numbers   State route numbers

MILAN, ITALY

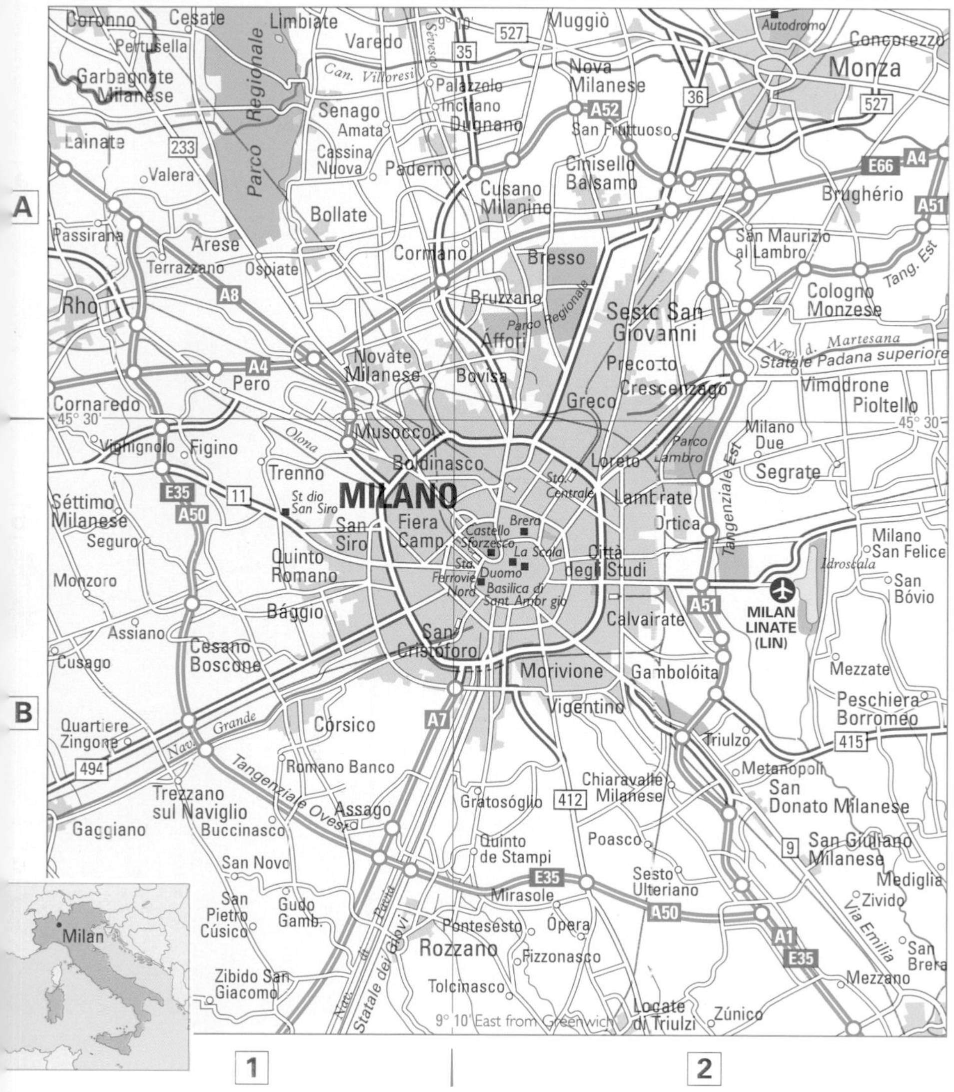

Coronno, Cesate, Limbiate, Varedo, Muggiò, Autodromo, Concorrezzo
Pertusella, Nova Milanese, Monza
Garbagnate Milanese, Senago, Amata, Paderno Dugnano, San Fruttuoso
Lainate, Valera, Cassina Nuova, Cusano Milanino, Brughério
Passirana, Arese, Ospiate, Cormano, Bresso, San Maurizio al Lambro, Cologno Monzese
Rho, Terrazzano, Bruzzano, Affori, Sesto San Giovanni, Tang. Est
Cornaredo, Novate Milanese, Pero, Musocco, Preco_to, Crescenzago, Vimodrone, Pioltello
Vighignolo, Figino, Trenno, Bodinasco, **MILANO**, Loreto, Milano Due, Segrate
Séttimo Milanese, Seguro, San Siro, Fiera Camp., Brera, Lambrate, Ortica, Milano San Felice
Monzoro, Quinto Romano, Castello Sforzesco, Duomo, degli Studi, San Bóvio
Bággio, Basilica di Sant' Ambrogio, Ferrovie Nord, Idrostala
Assiano, Cusago, Quartiere Zingone, San Cristoforo, Morivione, Gambolóita, Mezzate
Cesano Boscone, Corsico, Vigentino, Triulzo, Peschiera Borroméo
Trezzano sul Naviglio, Buccinasco, Assago, Romano Banco, Chiaravalle Milanese, Metanopoli San Donato Milanese
Gaggiano, Quinto de Stampi, Gratosóglio, Poasco, Zivido, San Giuliano Milanese
San Novo, Mirasole, Sesto Ulteriano, Mediglia
San Pietro Cúsico, Gudo Gamb., San Brea
Zibido San Giacomo, Rozzano, Opera, Pizzonasco, Mezzano
Tolcinasco, Locate di Triulzi, Zúnico

9° 10′ East from Greenwich

Milan (inset)

CENTRAL MOSCOW

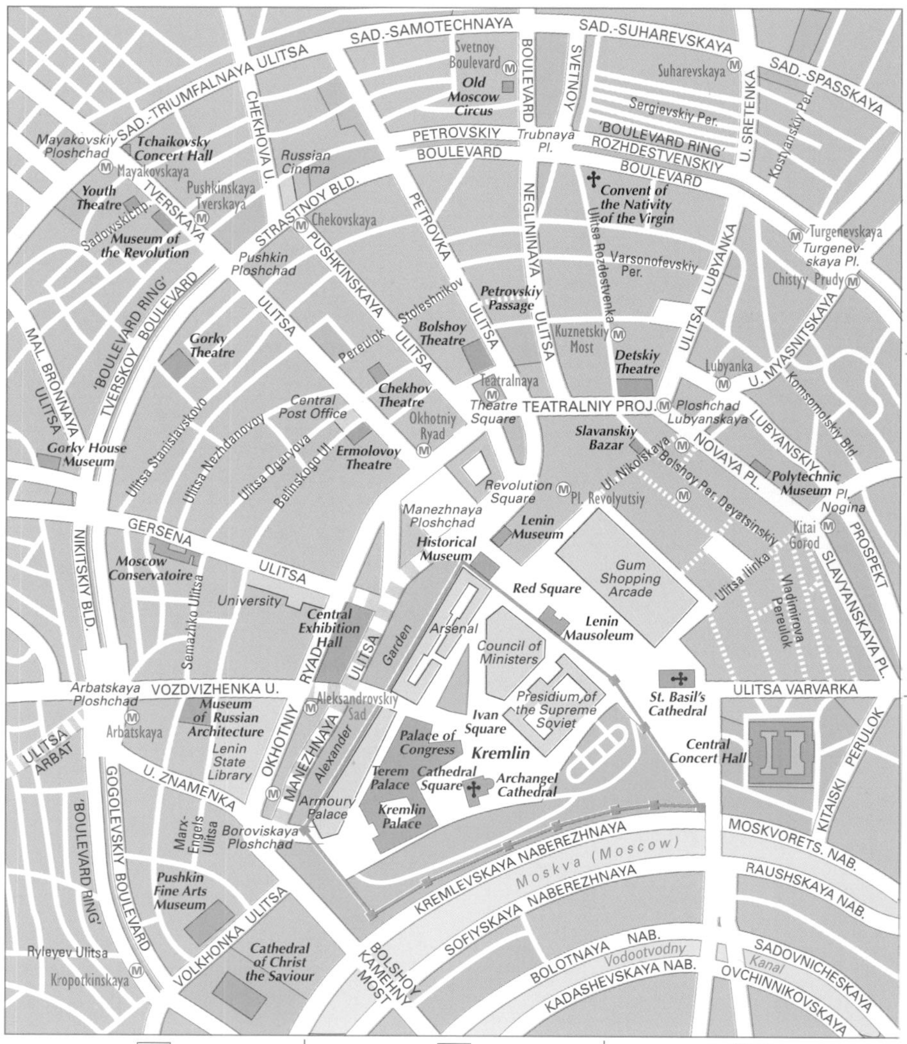

Svetnoy Boulevard, SAD.-SAMOTECHNAYA, Old Moscow Circus, SAD.-SUHAREVSKAYA, SAD.-SPASSKAYA
Mayakovskiy Ploshchad, SAD.-TRIUMFALNAYA ULITSA, CHEKHOVA UL., Suharevskaya, Sretenka
Tchaikovsky Concert Hall, Mayakovskaya, PETROVSKIY, Trubnaya Pl., Sergievskiy Per., Rozhdestvenskiy, BOULEVARD
Youth Theatre, TVERSKAYA, Pushkinskaya, Tverskaya, STRASTNOY BLD., Russian Cinema, BOULEVARD RING, Chistyy Prudy
Museum of the Revolution, Pushkin Ploshchad, Chekovskaya, PETROVKA, NEGLINNAYA, U. SRETENKA, Turgenevskaya, Turgenevskaya Pl.
Gorky Theatre, ULITSA, BOULEVARD RING, Petrovskiy Passage, Kuznetskiy Most, LUBYANKA, U. MYASNITSKAYA
Gorky House Museum, TVERSKOY BOULEVARD, Bolshoy Theatre, Detskiy Theatre, Lubyanka, Polytechnic Museum
Moscow Conservatoire, GERSENA ULITSA, Chekhov Theatre, Ermolovoy Theatre, Teatralnaya, Ploshchad Lubyanskaya, Kitai Gorod
Central Post Office, Okhotniy Ryad, TEATRALNIY PROJ., NOVAYA PL., Nogina
NIKITSKIY BLD., Revolution Square, Slavanskiy Bazar, Bolshoy Per., PROSPEKT
University, Manezhnaya Ploshchad, Historical Museum, Lenin Museum, Gum Shopping Arcade, SLAVYANSKAYA PL.
Central Exhibition Hall, Red Square, Lenin Mausoleum
Arbatskaya Ploshchad, VOZDVIZHENKA U., Museum of Russian Architecture, Arsenal, Council of Ministers, Central Concert Hall
ULITSA ARBAT, Arbatskaya, Lenin State Library, Aleksandrovsky Sad, Ivan Square, Presidium of the Supreme Soviet, St. Basil's Cathedral, ULITSA VARVARKA
GOGOLEVSKIY BOULEVARD, U. ZNAMENKA, Palace of Congress, Terem Palace, Cathedral Square, Archangel Cathedral
BOULEVARD RING, Armoury Palace, Kremlin Palace, Kremlin
Marx-Engels Ulitsa, Borovískaya Ploshchad, Moskva (Moscow), MOSKVORETS. NAB., RAUSHSKAYA NAB.
Ryleyev Ulitsa, Pushkin Fine Arts Museum, KREMLEVSKAYA NABEREZHNAYA, SOFIYSKAYA NABEREZHNAYA
Kropotkinskaya, VOLKHONKA ULITSA, Cathedral of Christ the Saviour, BOLSHOY KAMENNIY MOST, BOLOTNAYA NAB., Vodootvodny Kanal, OVCHINNIKOVSKAYA, SADOVNICHESKAYA
KADASHEVSKAYA NAB.

MOSCOW, RUSSIA

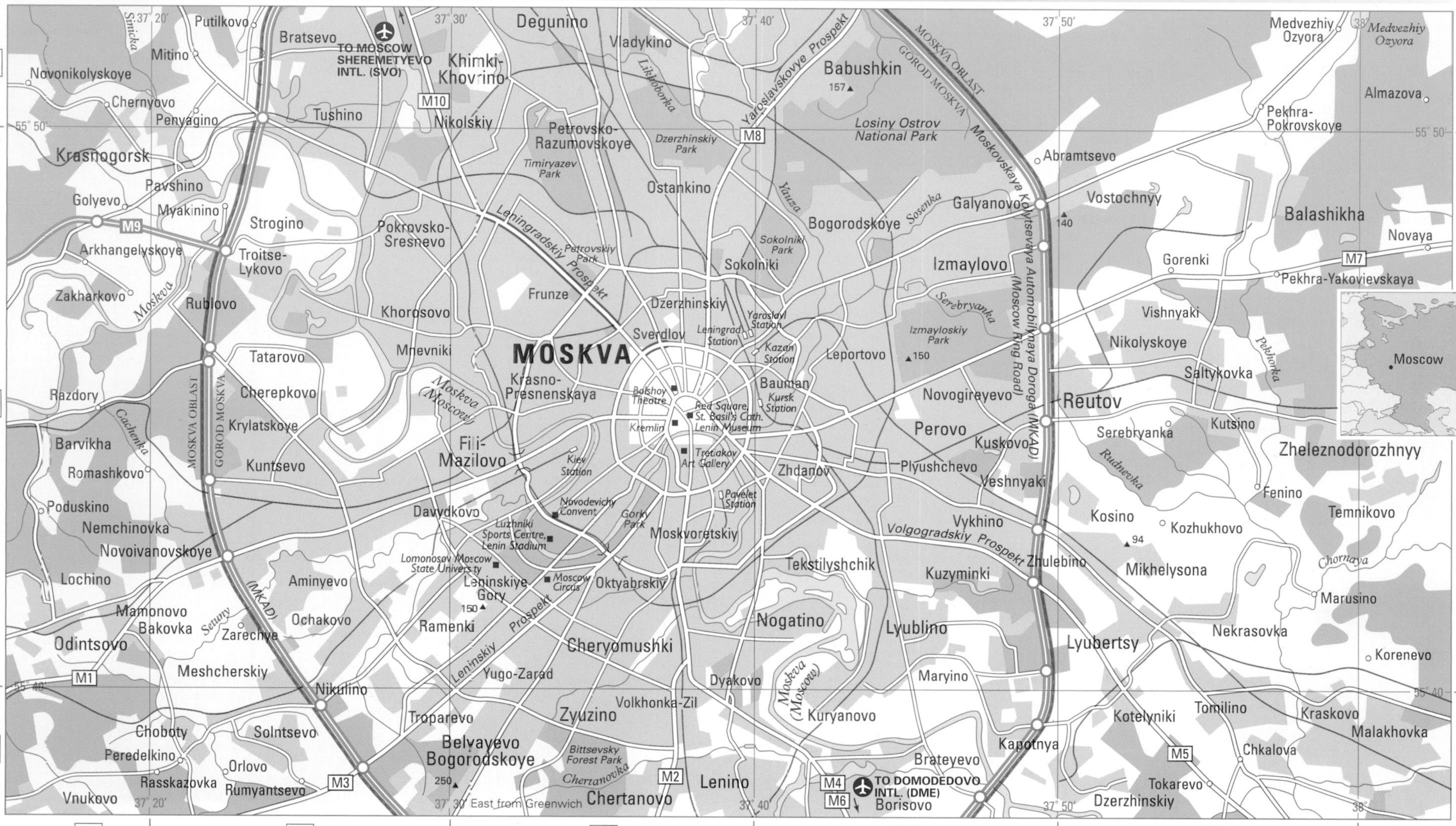

Novonikolyskoye, Putilkovo, Bratsevo, TO MOSCOW SHEREMETYEVO INTL. (SVO), Degunino, Babushkin, Medvezhiy Ozyora, Medvezhiy Ozyora
Mitino, Chernyovo, Khimki-Khovrino, Vladykino, Pekhra-Pokrovskoye, Almazova
Krasnogorsk, Penyagino, Tushino, Nikolskiy, Losiny Ostrov National Park
Pavshino, Myakinino, Petrovsko-Razumovskoye, Dzerzhinskiy Park, Abramtsevo, Gorod Moskva
Golyevo, Timiryazev Park, Ostankino, Bogorodskoye, Galyanovo, Vostochnyy, Balashikha
Arkhangelskoye, Troitse-Lykovo, Strogino, Pokrovsko-Sresnevo, Petrovskiy Park, Sokolniki, Izmaylovo, Gorenki, Novaya
Zakharkovo, Rublovo, Khorasovo, Frunze, Sokolniki, Dzerzhinskiy, Pekhra-Yakovievskaya
Razdory, Barvikha, Cherepkovo, Mnevniki, Sverdlov, **MOSKVA**, Yaroslavl Station, Kazan Station, Izmayloskiy Park, Vishnyaki, Nikolyskoye
Romashkovo, Krylatskoye, Krasno-Presnenskaya, Bolshoy Theatre, Bauman, Kursk Station, Novogireyevo, Reutov, Saltykovka
Poduskino, Nemchinovka, Fili-Mazilovo, Kiev Station, Red Square, St. Basil's Cath., Lenin Museum, Kremlin, Perovo, Kuskovo, Serebryanka, Zheleznodorozhnyy
Lochino, Kuntsevo, Davdkóvo, Novodevichy Convent, Zhdanov, Plyushchevo, Veshnyaki, Fenino
Mamonovo, Bakovka, Zarechye, Aminyevo, Leninskiye Gory, Gorky Park, Pavelet Station, Vykhino, Kosino, Kozhukhovo, Mikhelysona, Temnikovo
Odintsovo, Ochakovo, Lomonosov Moscow State University, Luzhniki Sports Centre Lenin Stadium, Moscow Circus, Oktyabrskiy, Vyorino, Volgogradskiy Prospekt, Zhulebino, Marusino
Meshcherskiy, Nikulino, Ramenki, Cheryomushki, Tekstilyshchik, Kuzyminki, Lyubertsy, Nekrasova, Koreneva
Choboty, Peredelkino, Rasskazovka, Troparevo, Zyuzino, Yugo-Zarad, Nogatino, Lyublino, Lyubertsy, Kraskovo, Malakhovka
Vnukovo, Rumyantsevo, Solntsevo, Zuzino, Volkhonka-Zil, Dyakovo, Maryino, Kúryanovo, Kotelniki, Tomilino
Orlovo, Belvayevo Bogorodskoye, Bittsevsky Forest Park, Chertanovo, Lenino, TO DOMODEDOVO INTL. (DME), Brateyevo, Kapotnya, Dzerzhinskiy, Chkalova

37° 30′ East from Greenwich

Moscow (inset)

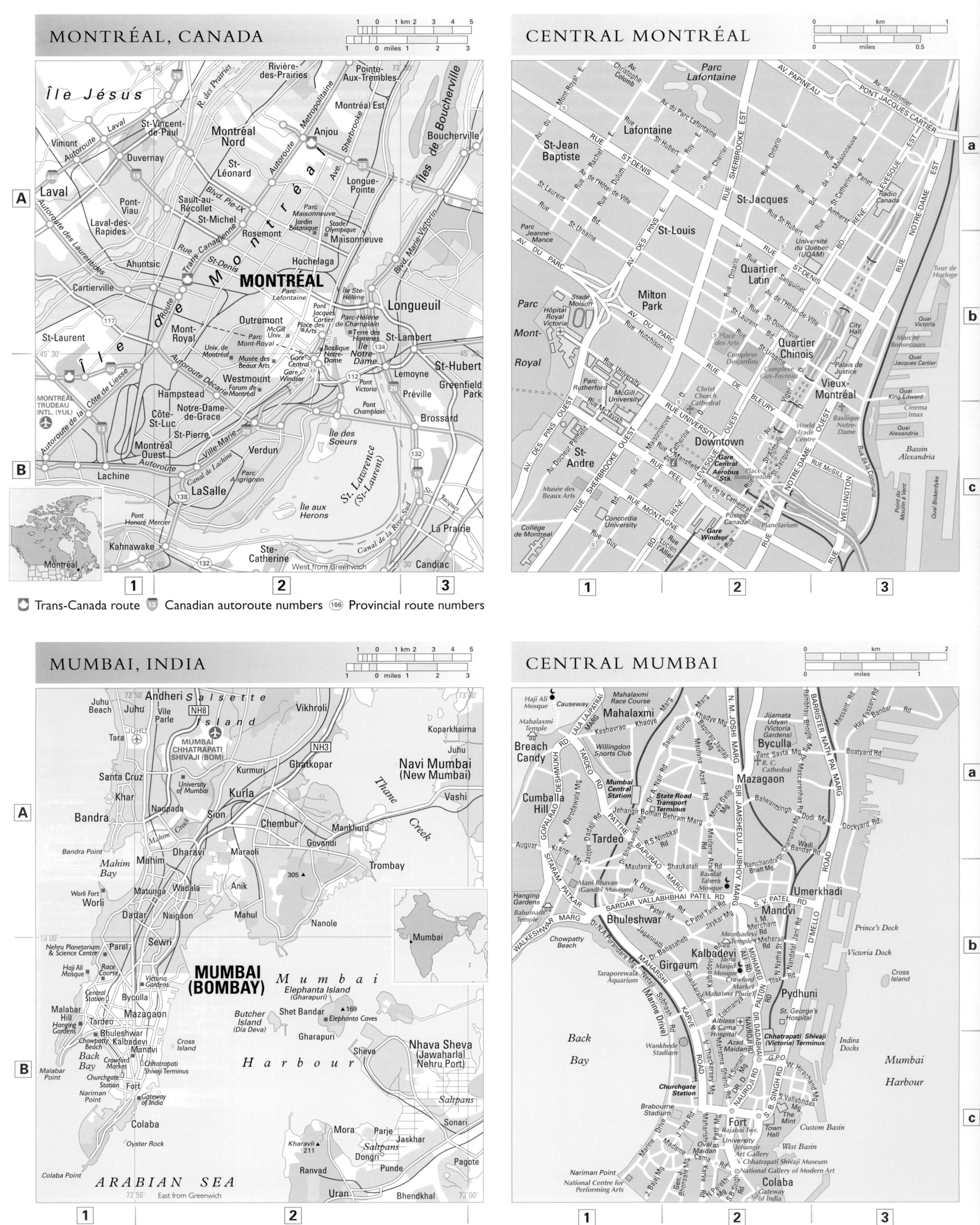

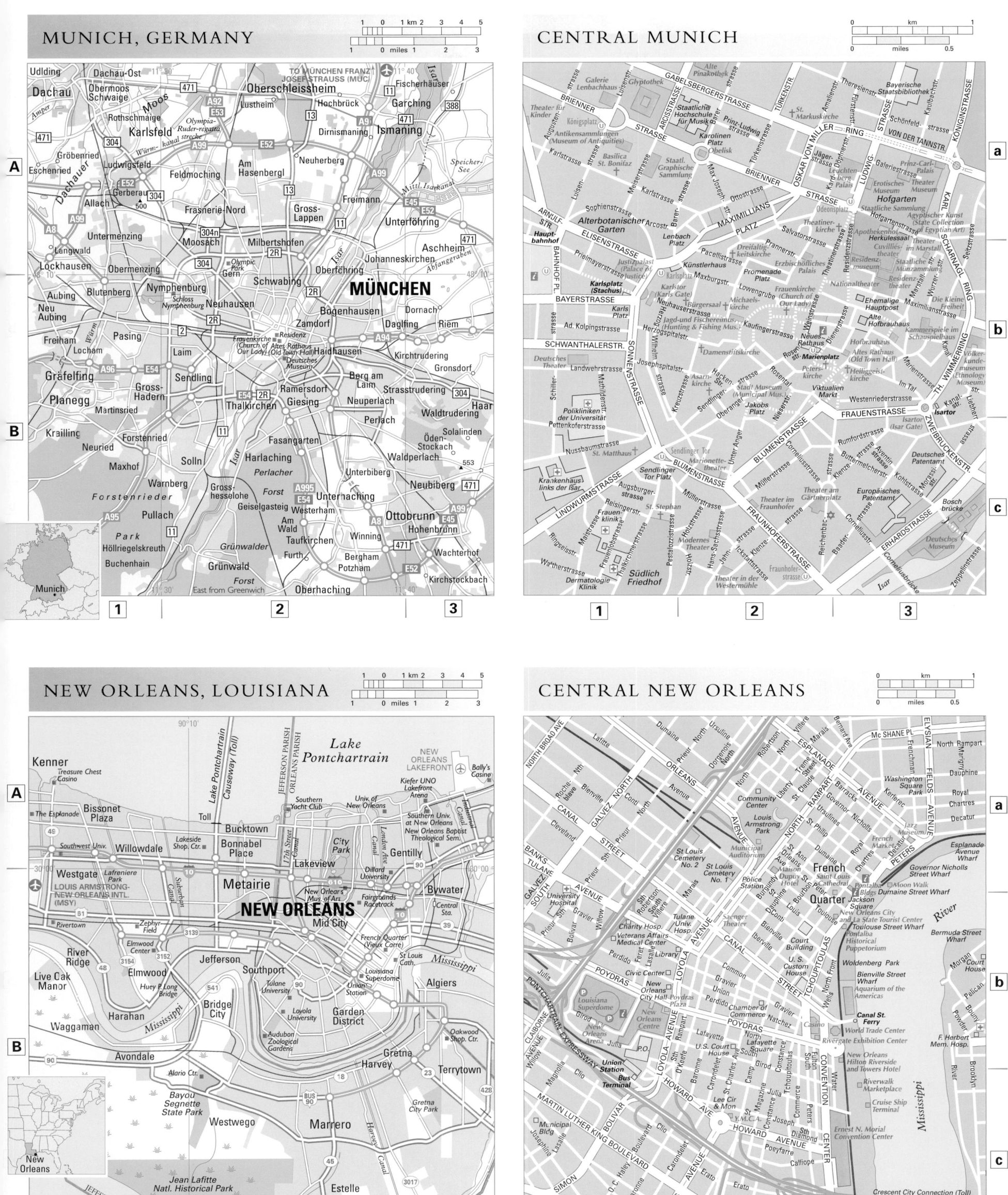

MUNICH, GERMANY

CENTRAL MUNICH

NEW ORLEANS, LOUISIANA

CENTRAL NEW ORLEANS

Interstate route numbers   U.S. route numbers   State route numbers

COPYRIGHT PHILIP'S

NEW YORK, NEW YORK

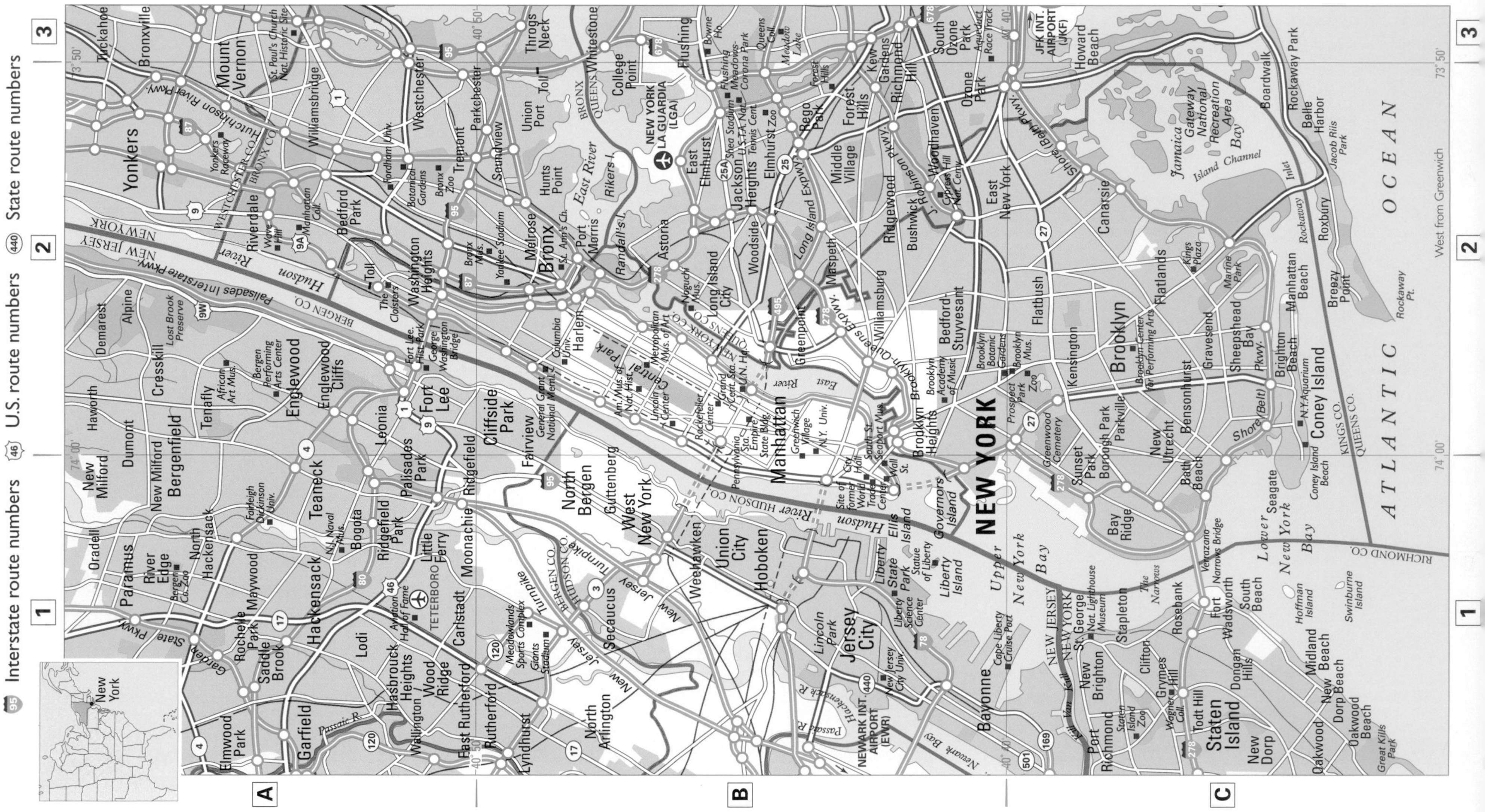

Interstate route numbers
U.S. route numbers
State route numbers

Map labels (upper map)

Pickahoe, Bronxville, Mount Vernon, Yonkers, Westchester, Throgs Neck, Whitestone, College Point, Flushing, Bowne, Queens, Corona Park, Riverdale, Bedford Park, Fordham Univ., Tremont, Sandyview, Jackson Heights, Elmhurst, Rego Park, Forest Hills, Middle Village, Richmond Hill, Ozone Park, JFK INT. AIRPORT (JFK), Howard Beach, Rockaway Park, Boardwalk, Belle Harbor, Jacob Riis Park, Breezy Point, Rockaway Pt.

Alpine, Demarest, Cresskill, Haworth, Englewood, Englewood Cliffs, Tenafly, Leonia, Fort Lee, Cliffside Park, Fairview, North Bergen, Guttenberg, West New York, Weehawken, Union City, Hoboken, Harlem, Bronx, Melrose, Morris, Hunts Point, Astoria, Long Island City, Greenpoint, Williamsburg, Bedford-Stuyvesant, Brooklyn, Kensington, Flatbush, Canarsie, Flatlands, Sheepshead Bay, Brighton Beach, Coney Island, Manhattan Beach

NEW YORK, Manhattan, Jersey City, Bayonne, Staten Island, Paramus, River Edge, Hackensack, Maywood, Lodi, Saddle Brook, Rochelle Park, Garfield, Elmwood Park, New Milford, Bergenfield, Teaneck, Bogota, Ridgefield Park, Little Ferry, Moonachie, Ridgefield, Carlstadt, East Rutherford, Rutherford, Lyndhurst, North Arlington, Secaucus, Kearny, Newark, NEWARK INT. AIRPORT (EWR), Port Richmond, New Brighton, Stapleton, Clifton, Grymes Hill, Dongan Hills, New Dorp, Oakwood, Midland Beach, South Beach, Fort Wadsworth

Hudson River, East River, Long Island Sound, Upper New York Bay, Lower New York Bay, ATLANTIC OCEAN, Jamaica Bay

BERGEN CO., HUDSON CO., RICHMOND CO., KINGS CO., QUEENS CO., NEW JERSEY, NEW YORK

Statue of Liberty, Ellis Island, Liberty Island, Governors Island, Randalls I., Rikers I., Verrazano Narrows Bridge, George Washington Bridge, Lincoln Tunnel, Holland Tunnel, Brooklyn Bridge

New York, Palisades Interstate Pkwy, Hutchinson River Pkwy, Garden State Pkwy, New Jersey Turnpike

CENTRAL NEW YORK

Map labels (lower map)

Harlem, Upper East Side, Upper West Side, Central Park, Midtown, Manhattan, Chelsea, Greenwich Village, East Village, Little Italy, China Town, Soho, Tribeca, Lower Manhattan, Lower East Side, West Village, Queens, Long Island City, Greenpoint, Williamsburg, Brooklyn, Fort Greene, Brooklyn Heights

West New York, Weehawken, Union City, Hoboken, Guttenberg

Hudson River, East River

Harlem Meer, The Lake, Central Park Zoo, Jacqueline Kennedy Onassis Res., The Reservoir

American Museum of Natural History, Metropolitan Museum of Art, Solomon R. Guggenheim Museum, Frick Collection, Jewish Museum, Lincoln Center for the Performing Arts, Columbus Circle, Carnegie Hall, MoMA, St. Patrick's Cathedral, Rockefeller Center, Grand Central Sta., Chrysler Building, United Nations Headquarters, Times Square, Port Authority Bus Terminal, Penn Sta., Macy's, G.P.O., Empire State Building, Flatiron Building, Madison Square, Bellevue Medical Center, N.Y. State Univ., University Place, Washington Square, N.Y. Univ., Bowery, Delancey, Criminal Ct. Bldg., Woolworth Building, City Hall, World Financial Center, Ground Zero Site of former World Trade Center, Trinity Church, N.Y. State Exch., Battery Park, Staten Island Ferry, Brooklyn-Battery Tunnel, Ellis & Statue of Liberty Ferry, South St. Seaport

Queensboro Bridge, Queens-Midtown Tunnel, Williamsburg Bridge, Manhattan Bridge, Brooklyn Bridge, Lincoln Tunnel, Holland Tunnel, Queens-Midtown Tunnel

FRANKLIN D. ROOSEVELT DRIVE, JOE DIMAGGIO HIGHWAY, HENRY HUDSON PARKWAY, J.F. KENNEDY BLVD., HILLSIDE RD., McGUINNESS BOULEVARD, BROOKLYN-QUEENS EXPRESSWAY, FLATBUSH AVE, ADAMS ST, TWELFTH AVENUE, ELEVENTH AVE, WEST STREET, CANAL ST

Intrepid Air & Space Museum, Passenger Ship Terminal, Chelsea Piers Sports and Entertainment Complex, Jacob Javits Convention Center, Madison Square Garden, U.S. Naval Reserve Center, Bryant Park, Main Library, Tompkins Sq Park

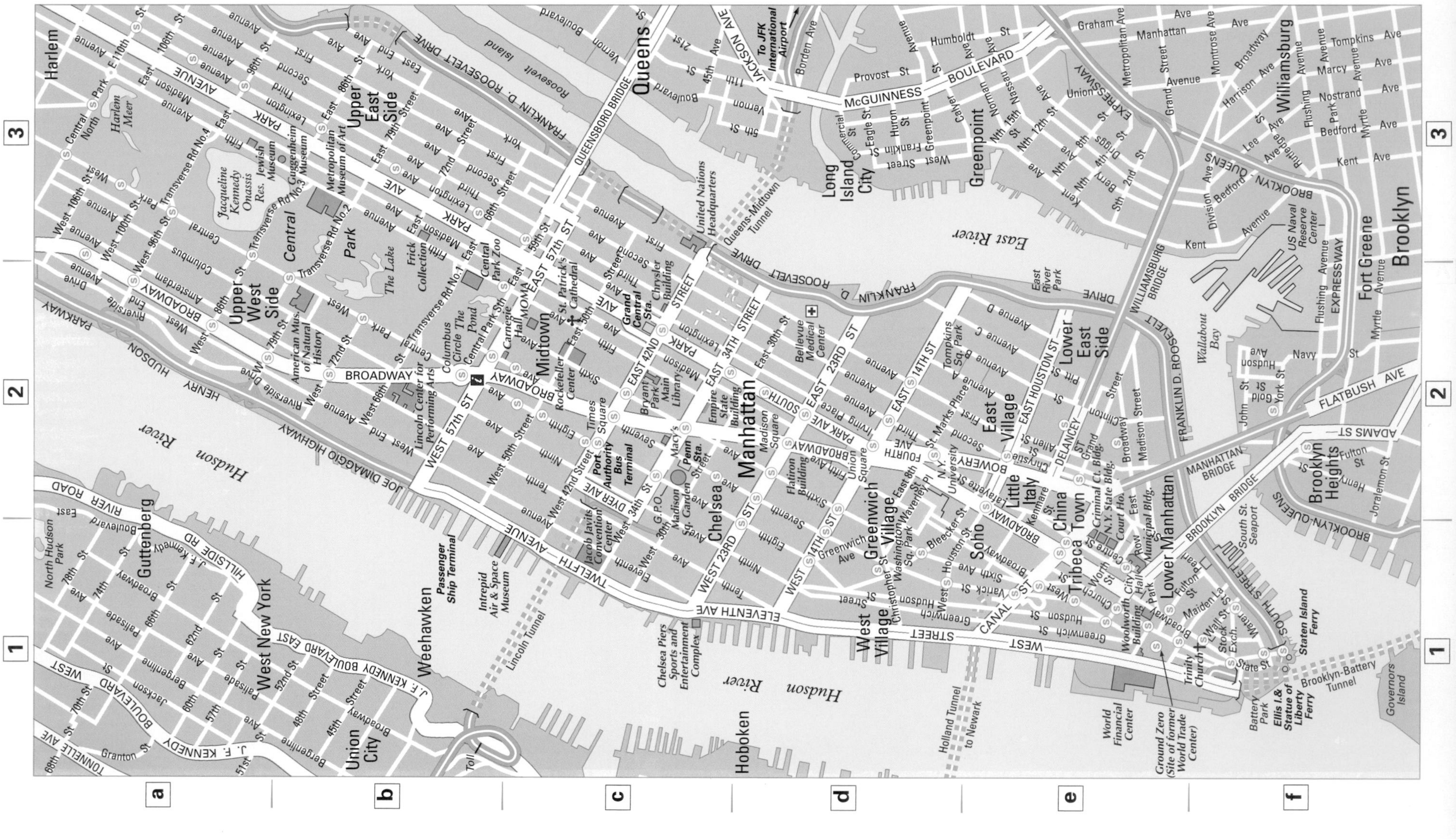

COPYRIGHT PHILIP'S

ORLANDO, FLORIDA

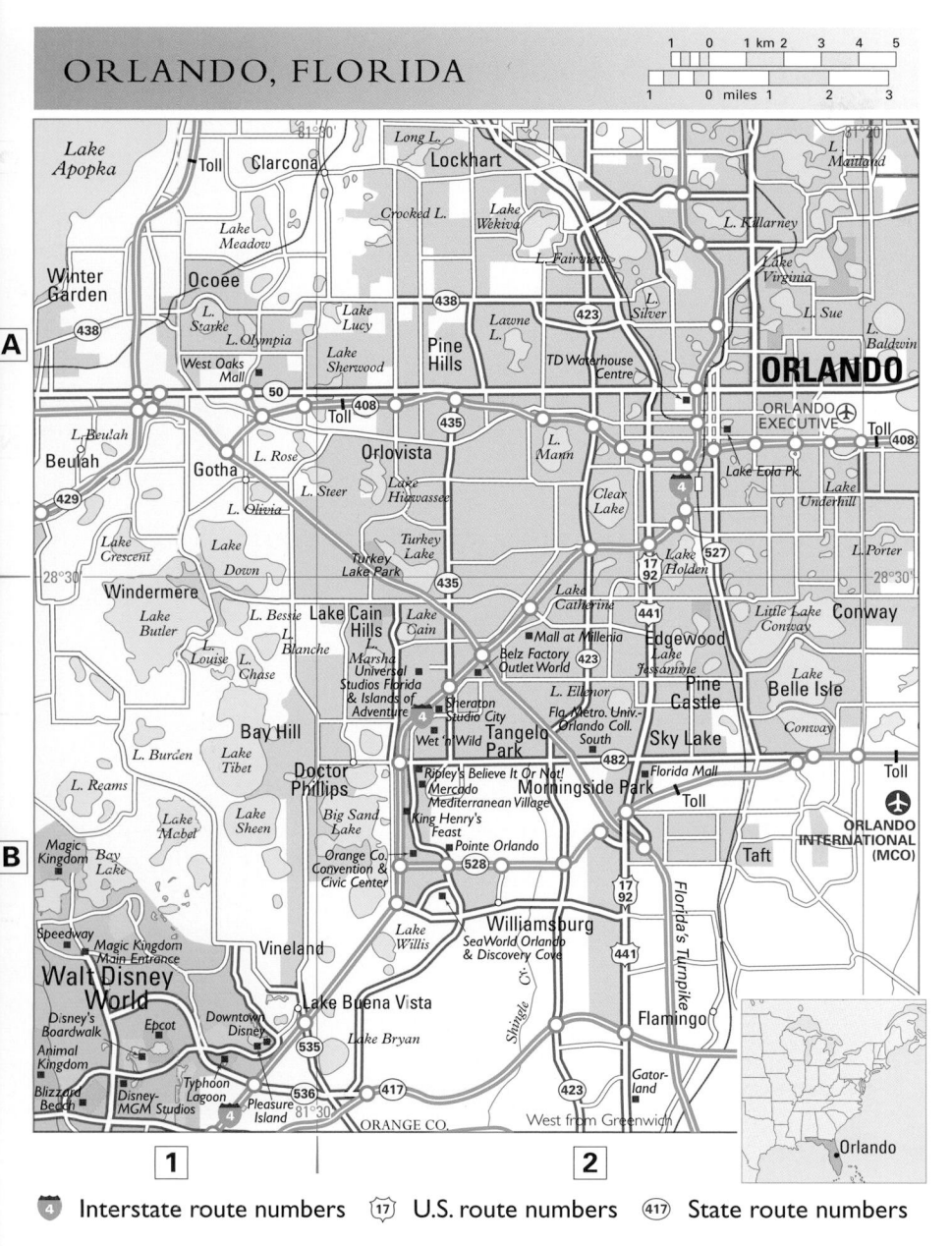

Interstate route numbers ④ · **U.S. route numbers** ⑰ · **State route numbers** ④₁₇

OSAKA, JAPAN

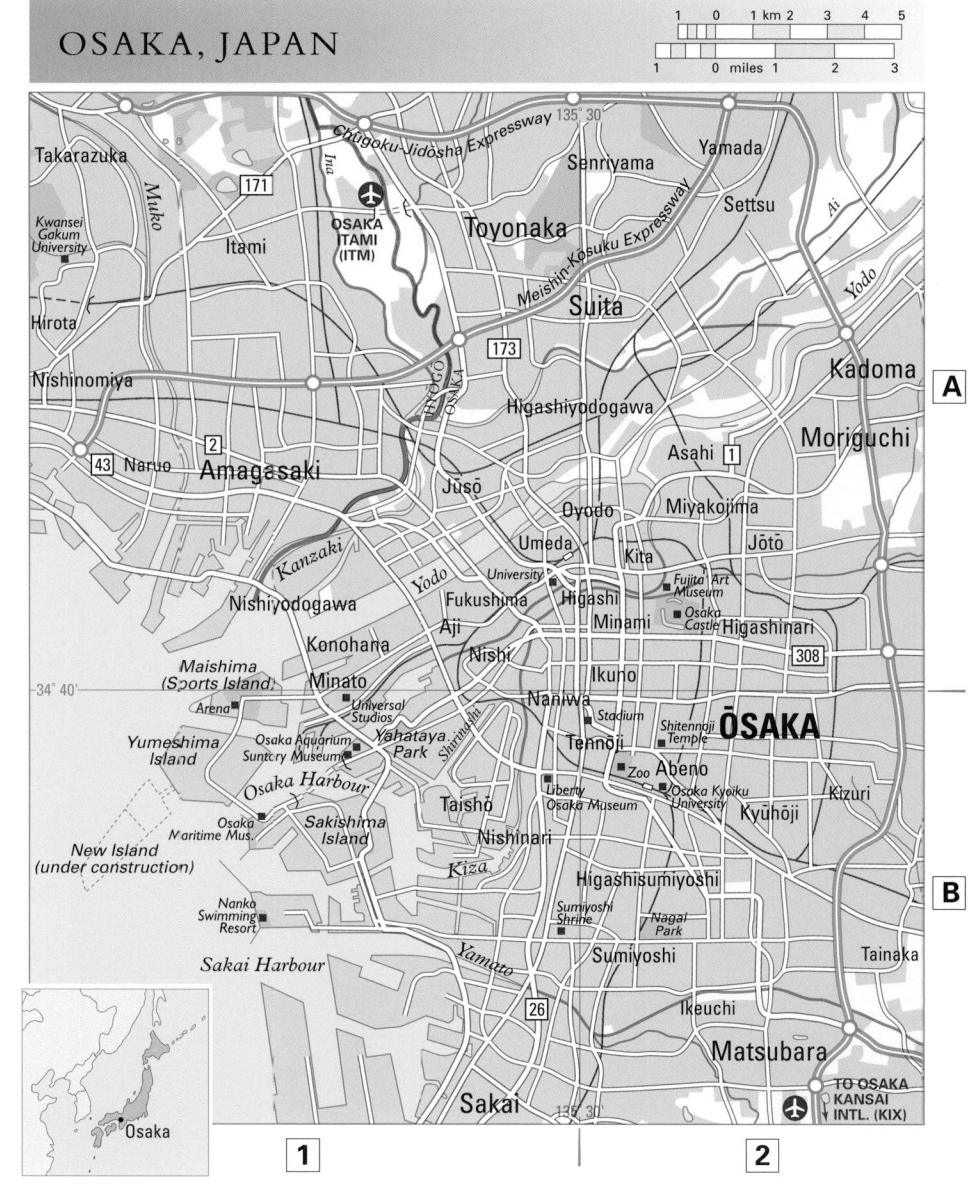

OSLO, NORWAY

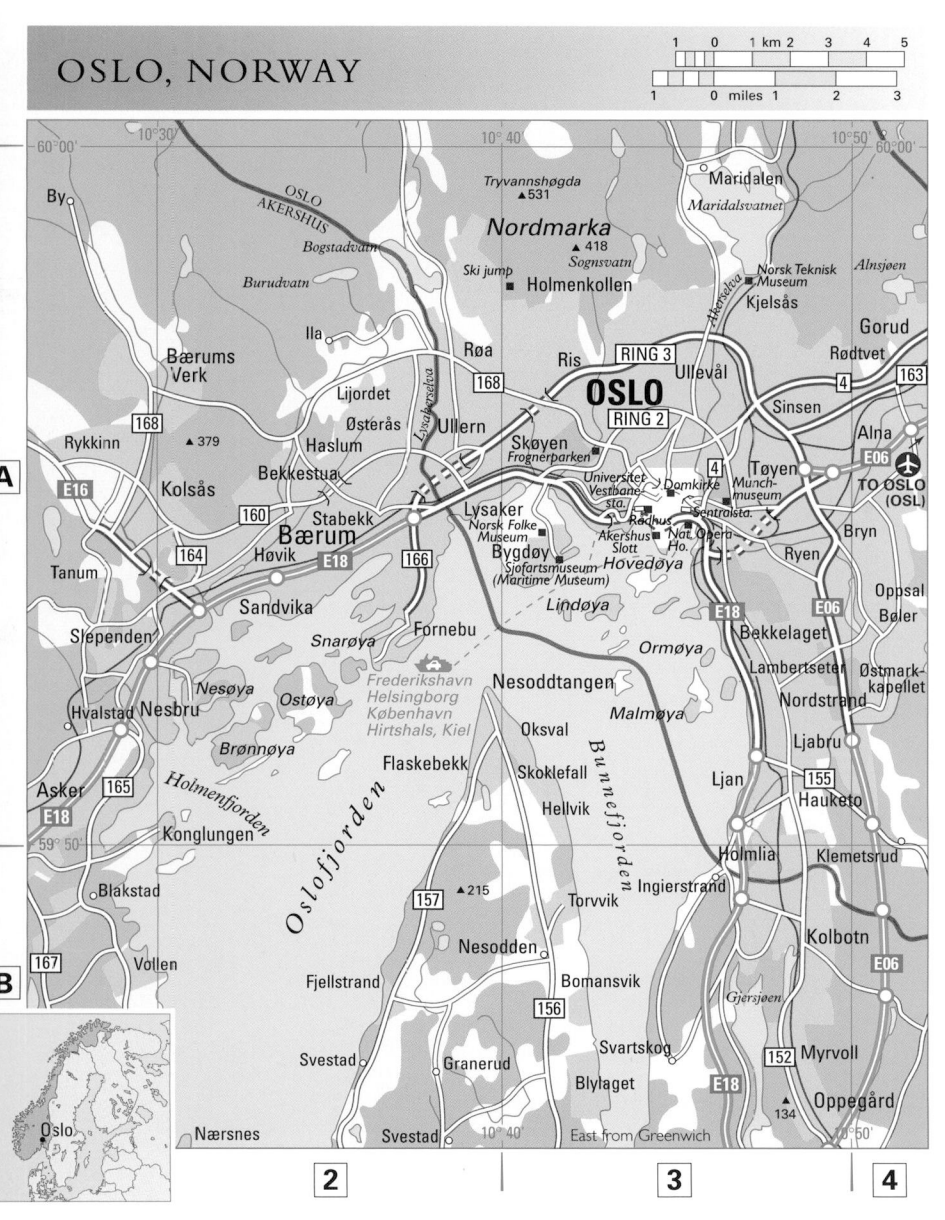

CENTRAL OSLO

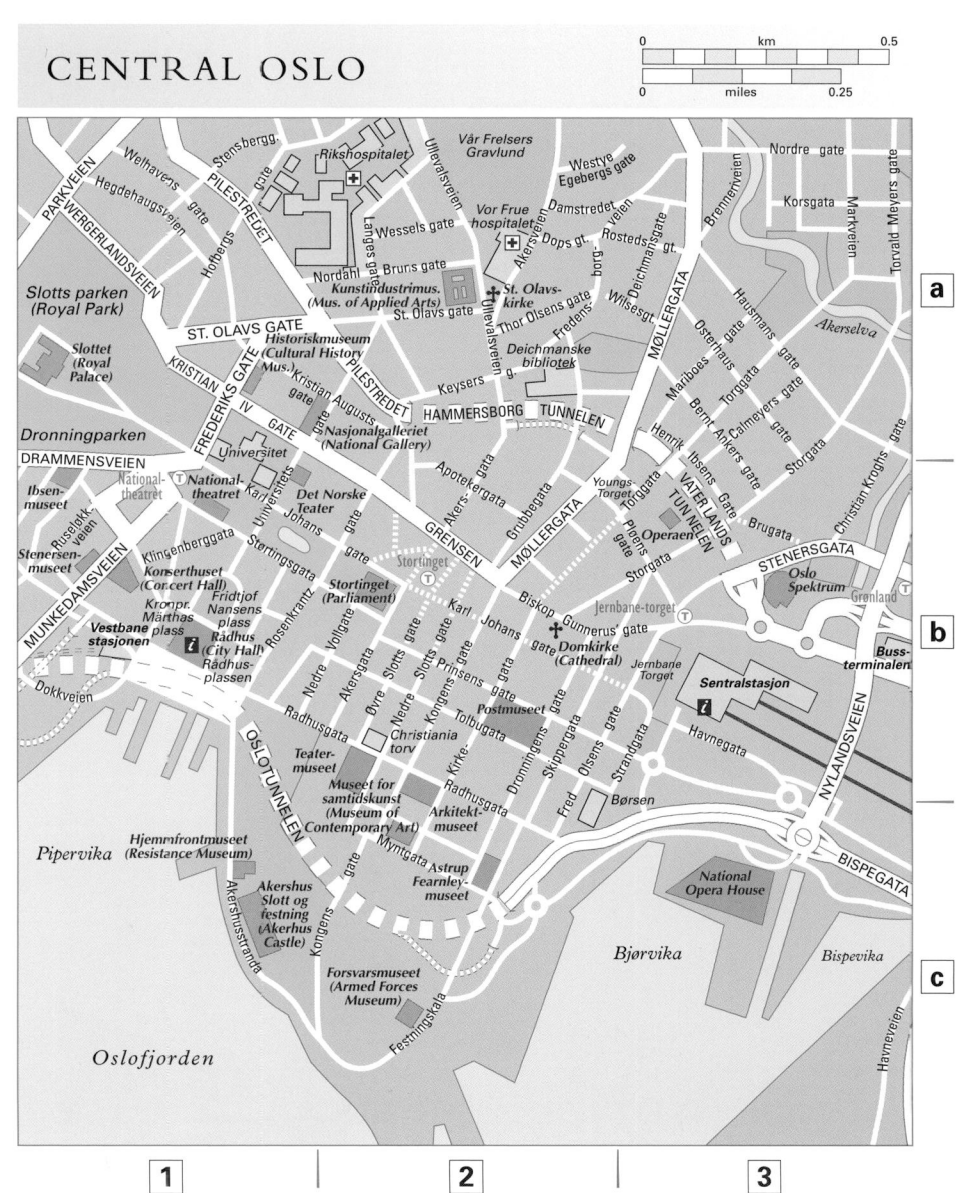

COPYRIGHT PHILIP'S

PARIS, FRANCE

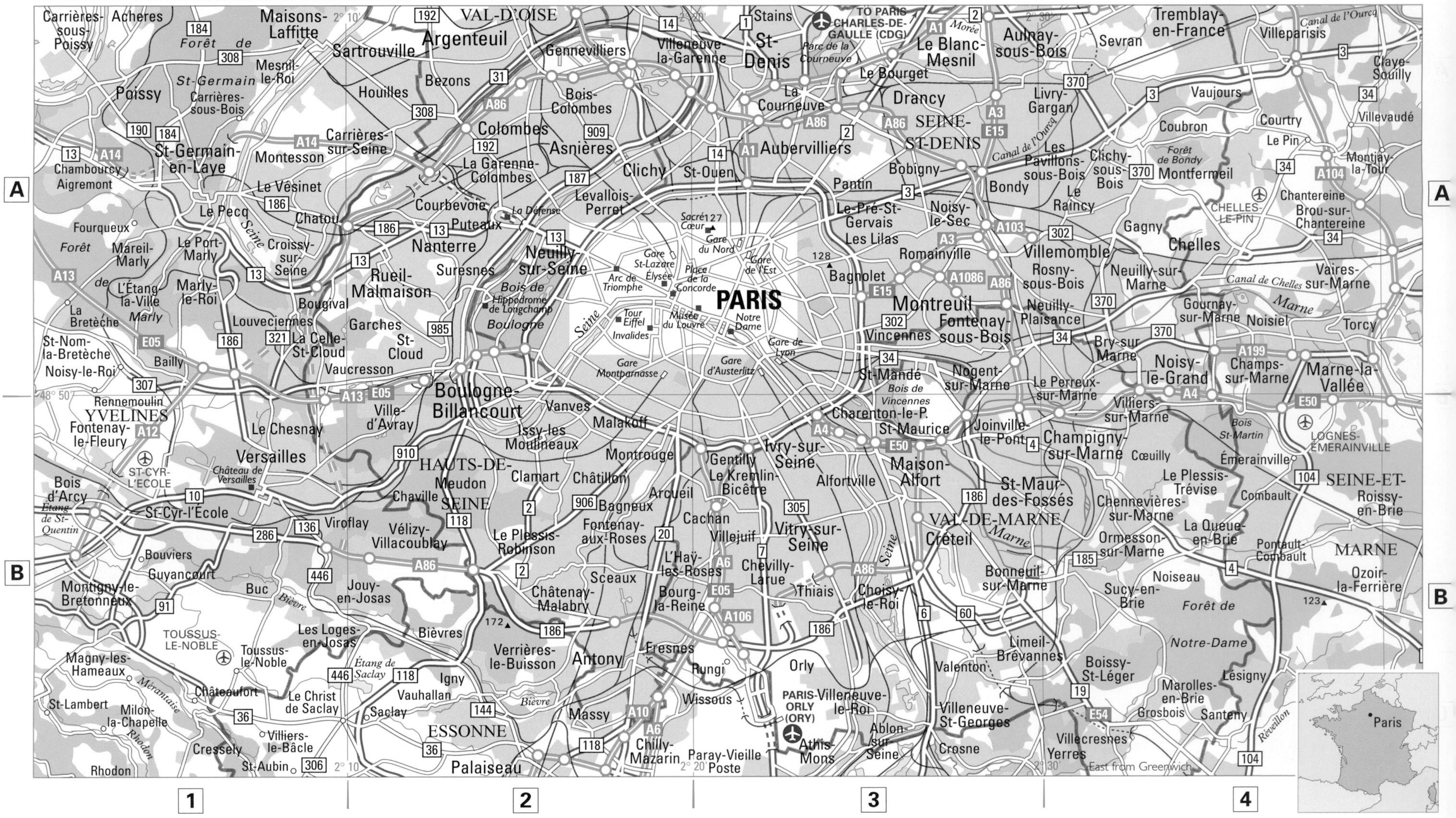

1 0 1 km 2 3 4 5
1 0 miles 1 2 3

Carrières-sous-Poissy · Achères · Maisons-Laffitte · VAL-D'OISE · Argenteuil · Gennevilliers · Villeneuve-la-Garenne · Stains · St-Denis · TO PARIS CHARLES-DE-GAULLE (CDG) · Le Blanc-Mesnil · Aulnay-sous-Bois · Sevran · Tremblay-en-France · Villeparisis

Forêt de St-Germain · Sartrouville · Houilles · Bois-Colombes · La Courneuve · Le Bourget · Drancy · Livry-Gargan · Vaujours · Coubron · Courtry · Villevaudé

Poissy · Mesnil-le-Roi · Carrières-sous-Bois · Colombes · Asnières · Aubervilliers · SEINE-ST-DENIS · Bobigny · Les Pavillons-sous-Bois · Montfermeil · Le Pin · Montjay-la-Tour

St-Germain-en-Laye · Montesson · Carrières-sur-Seine · La Garenne-Colombes · Clichy · St-Ouen · Pantin · Le Pré-St-Gervais · Les Lilas · Noisy-le-Sec · Le Raincy · Gagny · CHELLES-LE-PIN · Brou-sur-Chantereine

Chambourcy · Aigremont · Le Vésinet · Chatou · Courbevoie · Puteaux · Levallois-Perret · Sacré Cœur · Gare du Nord · Romainville · Villemomble · Rosny-sous-Bois · Neuilly-sur-Marne · Chelles · Vaires-sur-Marne

Fourqueux · Mareil-Marly · Le Pecq · Croissy-sur-Seine · Nanterre · Neuilly-sur-Seine · Arc de Triomphe · Place de la Concorde · **PARIS** · Notre Dame · Montreuil · Vincennes · Fontenay-sous-Bois · Neuilly-Plaisance · Gournay-sur-Marne · Noisiel · Torcy

Forêt · L'Étang-la-Ville · Le Port-Marly · Rueil-Malmaison · Suresnes · Bois de Boulogne · Tour Eiffel · Invalides · Gare de Lyon · Nogent-sur-Marne · Le Perreux-sur-Marne · Villiers-sur-Marne · Noisy-le-Grand · Champs-sur-Marne · Marne-la-Vallée

St-Nom-la-Bretèche · Marly · Louveciennes · Garches · La Celle-St-Cloud · St-Cloud · Gare Montparnasse · Gare d'Austerlitz · St-Mandé · Bry-sur-Marne · LOGNES-ÉMERAINVILLE

St-Cyr-l'École · YVELINES · Fontenay-le-Fleury · Le Chesnay · Vaucresson · Boulogne-Billancourt · Vanves · Charenton-le-Pont · St-Maurice · Joinville-le-Pont · Champigny-sur-Marne · Cœuilly · Émerainville

Bois d'Arcy · Étang de St-Quentin · Versailles · Château de Versailles · HAUTS-DE-SEINE · Meudon · Chaville · Clamart · Châtillon · Malakoff · Montrouge · Gentilly · Le Kremlin-Bicêtre · Ivry-sur-Seine · Maisons-Alfort · St-Maur-des-Fossés · Chennevières-sur-Marne · Ormesson-sur-Marne · La Queue-en-Brie · Pontault-Combault · SEINE-ET-MARNE

Rennemoulin · Bouviers · Viroflay · Vélizy-Villacoublay · Le Plessis-Robinson · Bagneux · Arcueil · Cachan · Villejuif · Vitry-sur-Seine · Créteil · VAL-DE-MARNE · Ormesson · Combault · Ozoir-la-Ferrière · MARNE

Montigny-le-Bretonneux · Guyancourt · Buc · Jouy-en-Josas · Châtenay-Malabry · Sceaux · Fontenay-aux-Roses · L'Haÿ-les-Roses · Bourg-la-Reine · Chevilly-Larue · Thiais · Choisy-le-Roi · Bonneuil-sur-Marne · Sucy-en-Brie · Noiseau · Forêt de Notre-Dame

TOUSSUS-LE-NOBLE · Les Loges-en-Josas · Bièvres · Verrières-le-Buisson · Antony · Fresnes · Rungis · Orly · Valenton · Limeil-Brévannes · Boissy-St-Léger · Marolles-en-Brie · Grosbois · Santeny

Magny-les-Hameaux · Châteaufort · Le Christ de Saclay · Saclay · Vauhallan · Igny · Massy · PARIS-VILLENEUVE-ORLY (ORY) · Paray-Vieille-Poste · Villeneuve-St-Georges · Villecresnes · Yerres · Lésigny

St-Lambert · Milon-la-Chapelle · Cresselly · Villiers-le-Bâcle · ESSONNE · Chilly-Mazarin · Athis-Mons · Ablon-sur-Seine · Crosne · Rhodon · St-Aubin · Palaiseau · Wissous

YVELINES · East from Greenwich · Paris

1 2 3 4

CENTRAL PARIS

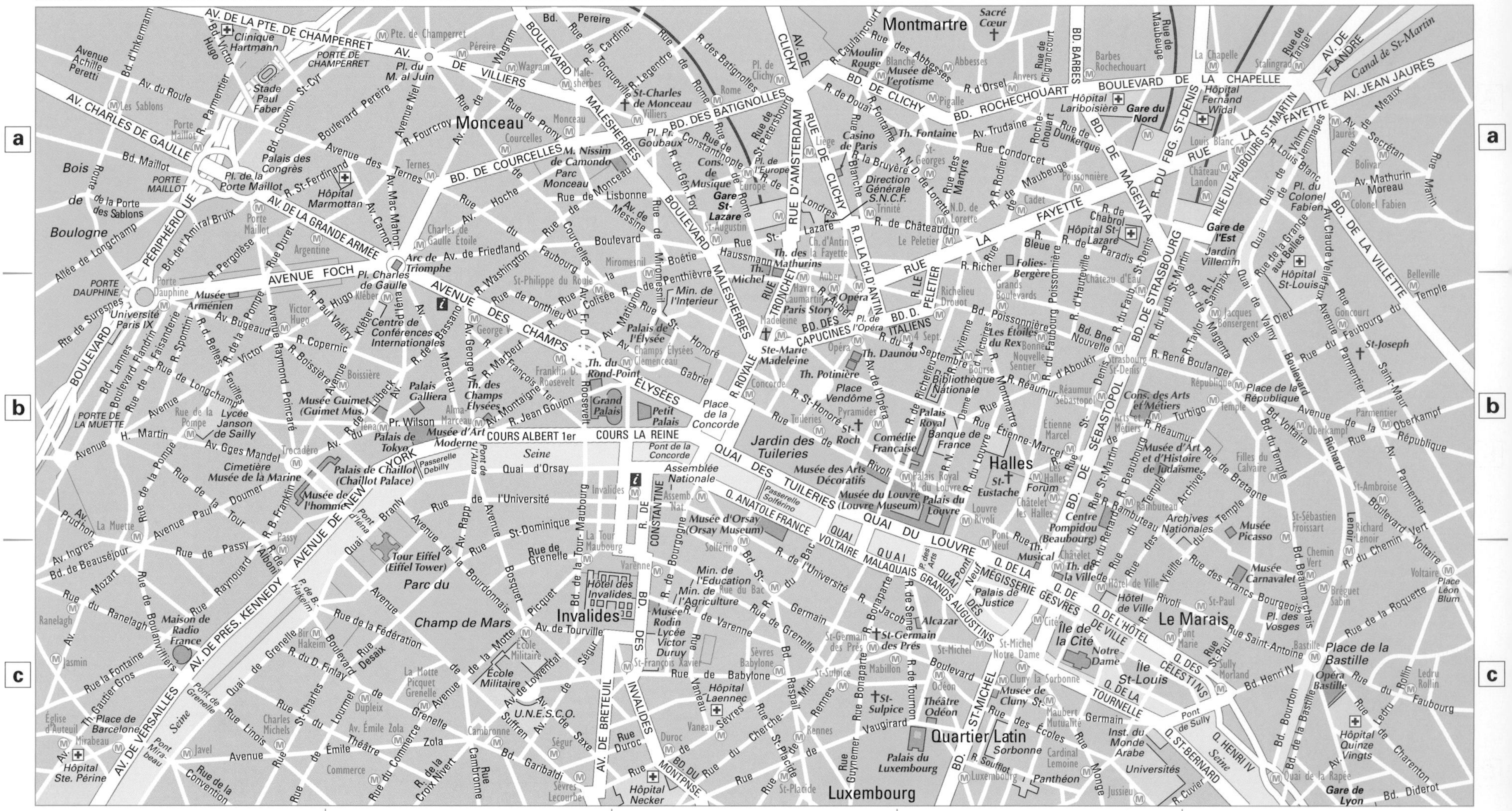

0 km 1
0 miles 0.5

AV. DE LA PTE. DE CHAMPERRET · PORTE DE CHAMPERRET · Montmartre · Sacré Cœur · Canal St-Martin

Monceau · Parc Monceau · Gare St-Lazare · Pl. de Clichy · Moulin Rouge · Gare du Nord · Gare de l'Est

PORTE MAILLOT · Bois de Boulogne · Av. de la Grande Armée · AVENUE FOCH · Pl. Charles de Gaulle · Arc de Triomphe · Opéra · BOULEVARD HAUSSMANN · Madeleine · Bibliothèque Nationale

PORTE DAUPHINE · AVENUE DES CHAMPS ÉLYSÉES · Palais de l'Élysée · Place de la Concorde · Jardin des Tuileries · Palais Royal · Halles · Centre Pompidou (Beaubourg) · Musée Picasso

Palais de Chaillot (Chaillot Palace) · Musée de la Marine · Musée de l'Homme · Seine · Assemblée Nationale · Musée d'Orsay (Orsay Museum) · Musée du Louvre (Louvre Museum) · Île de la Cité · Le Marais

Tour Eiffel (Eiffel Tower) · Parc du Champ de Mars · Invalides · Min. de l'Education · St-Germain des Prés · Notre Dame · Île St-Louis · Place de la Bastille · Opéra Bastille

Maison de Radio France · U.N.E.S.C.O. · École Militaire · Hôpital Laennec · Quartier Latin · Sorbonne · Panthéon · Gare de Lyon

Hôpital Ste. Périne · Place de Barcelone · Émile Zola · Théâtre · Hôpital Necker · Palais du Luxembourg · Luxembourg

1 2 3 4 5

PRAGUE, CZECH REPUBLIC

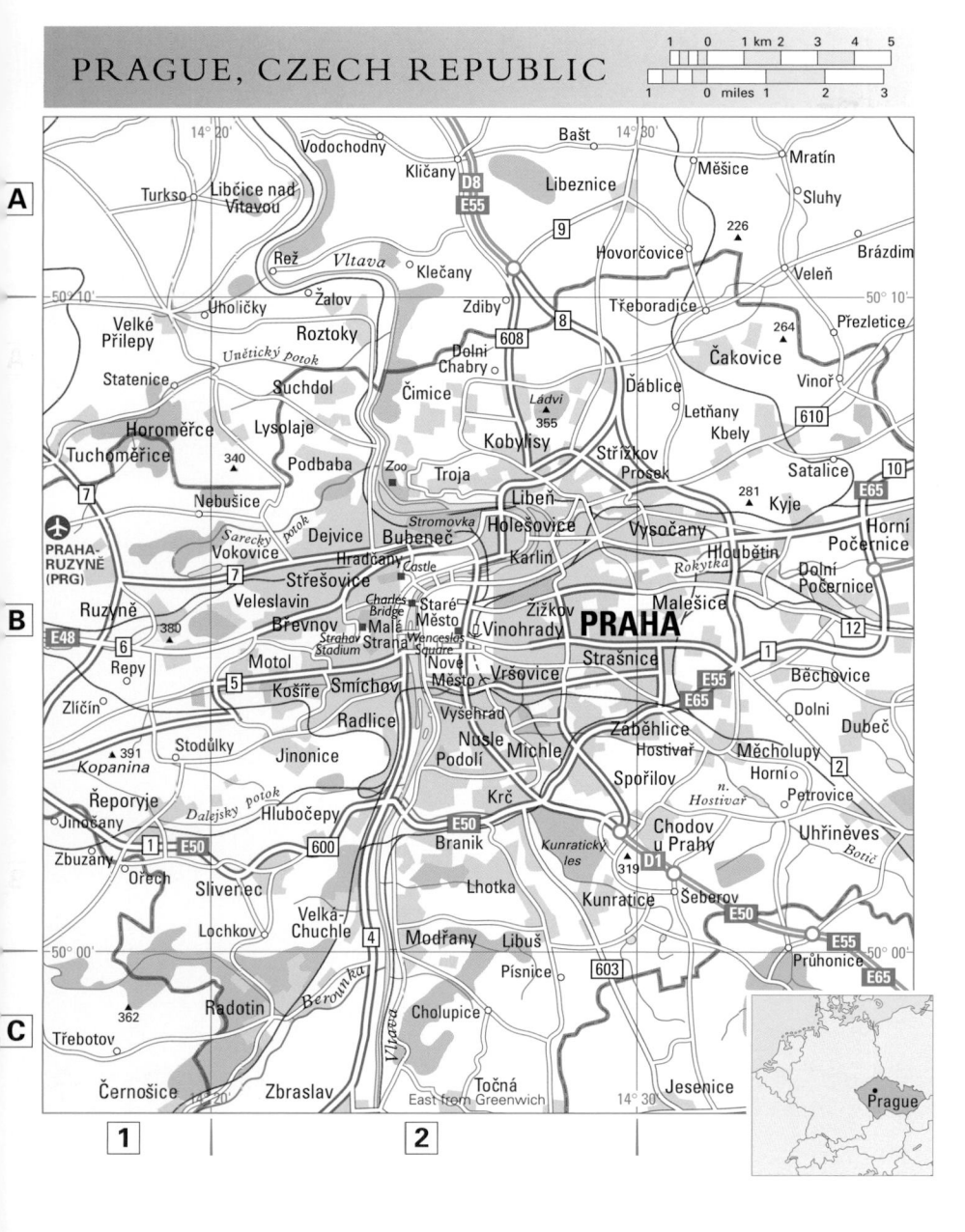

CENTRAL PRAGUE

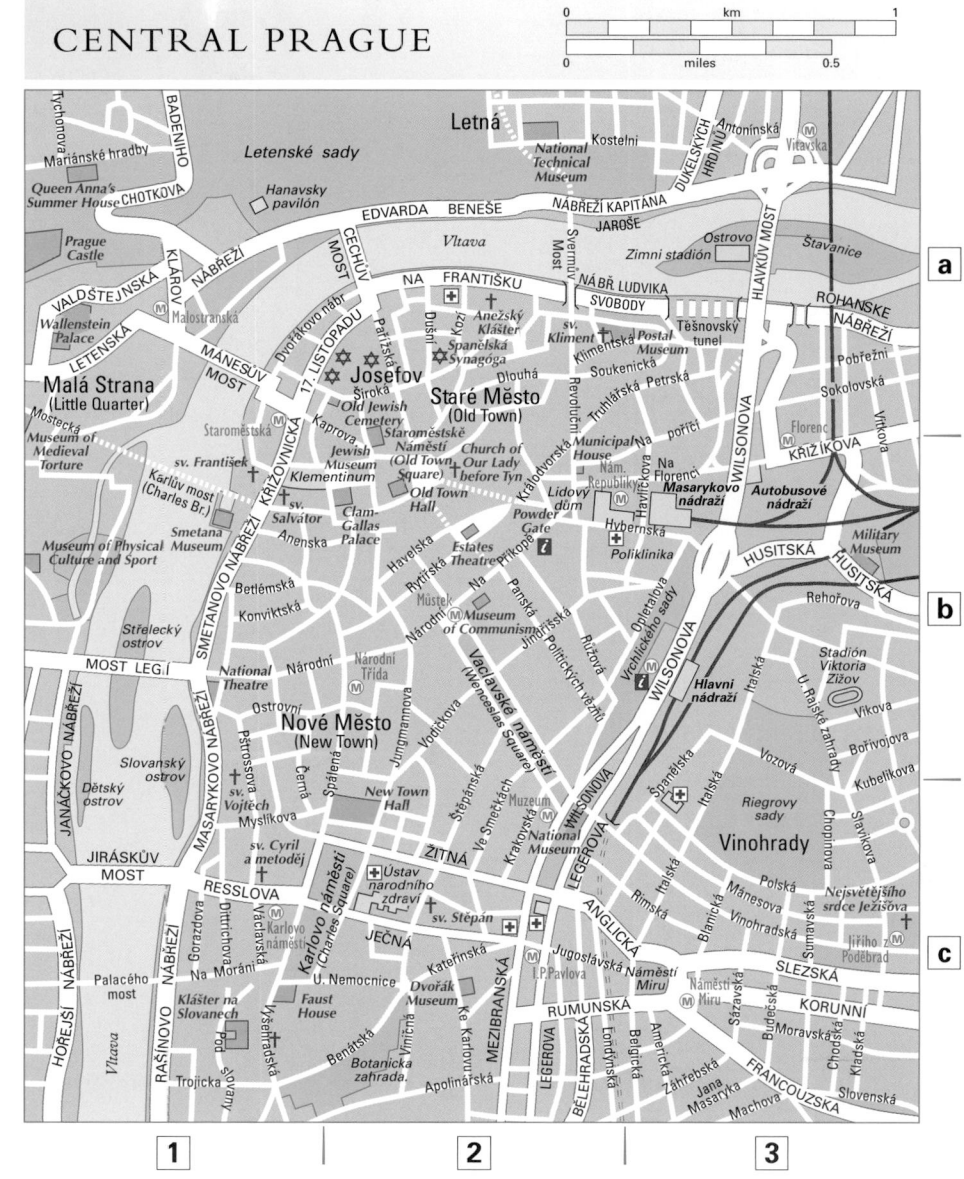

RIO DE JANEIRO, BRAZIL

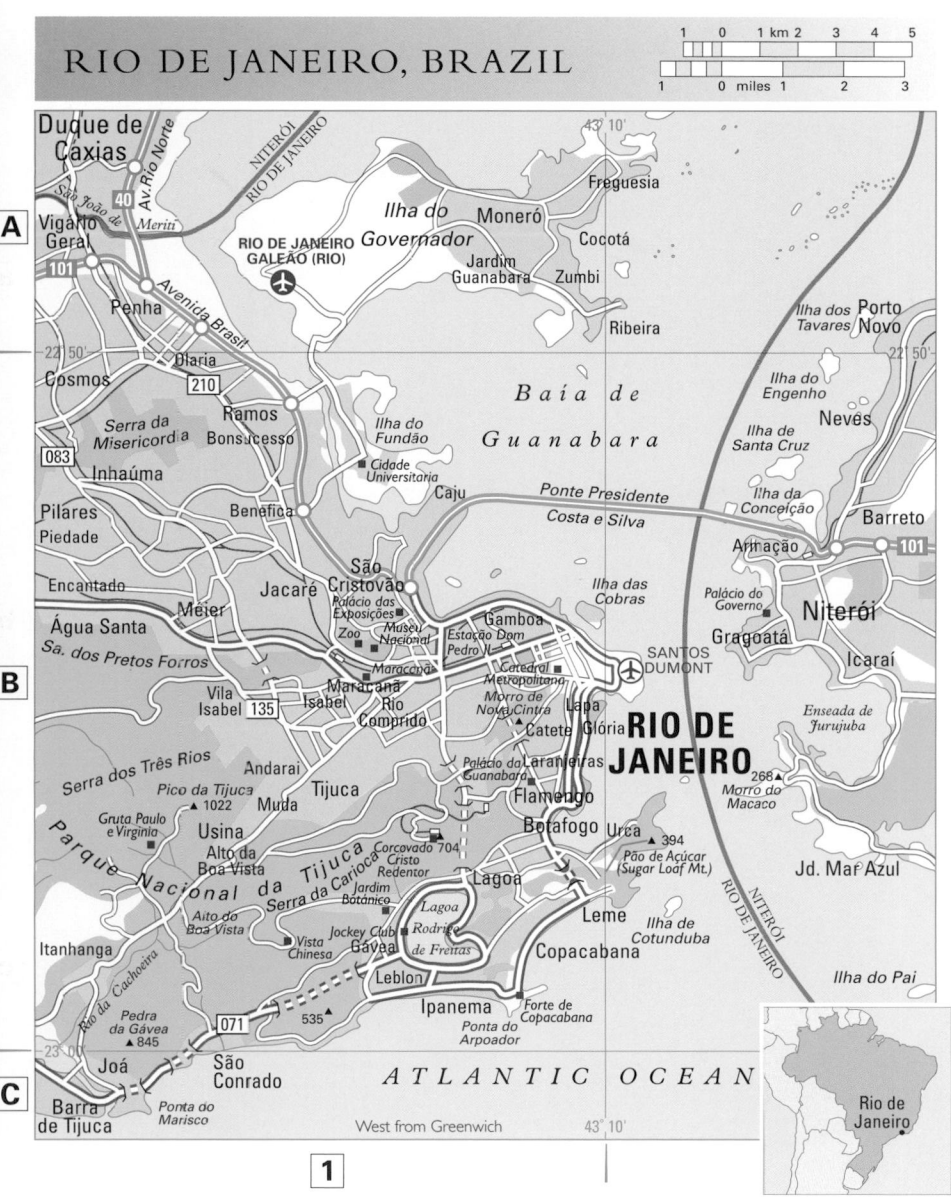

CENTRAL RIO DE JANEIRO

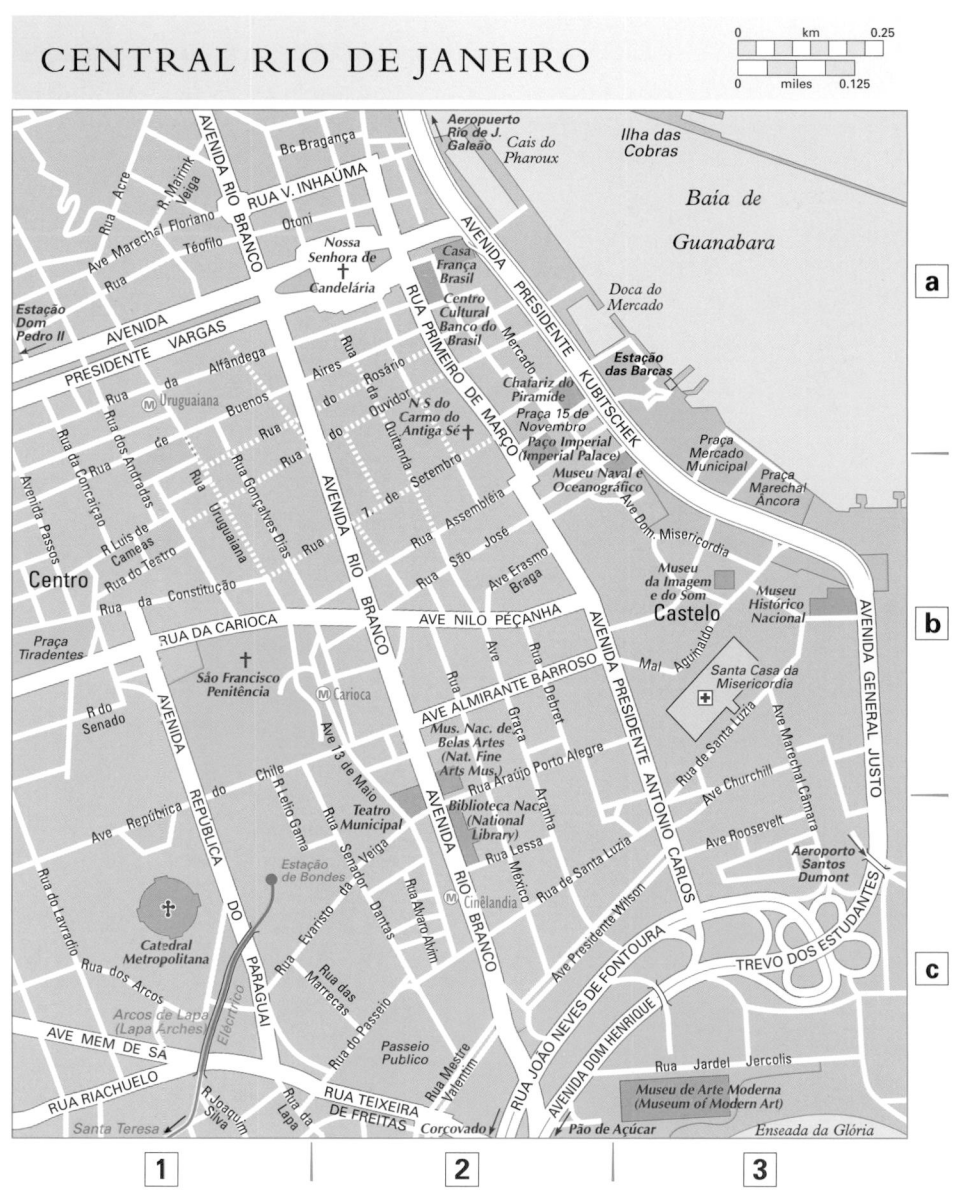

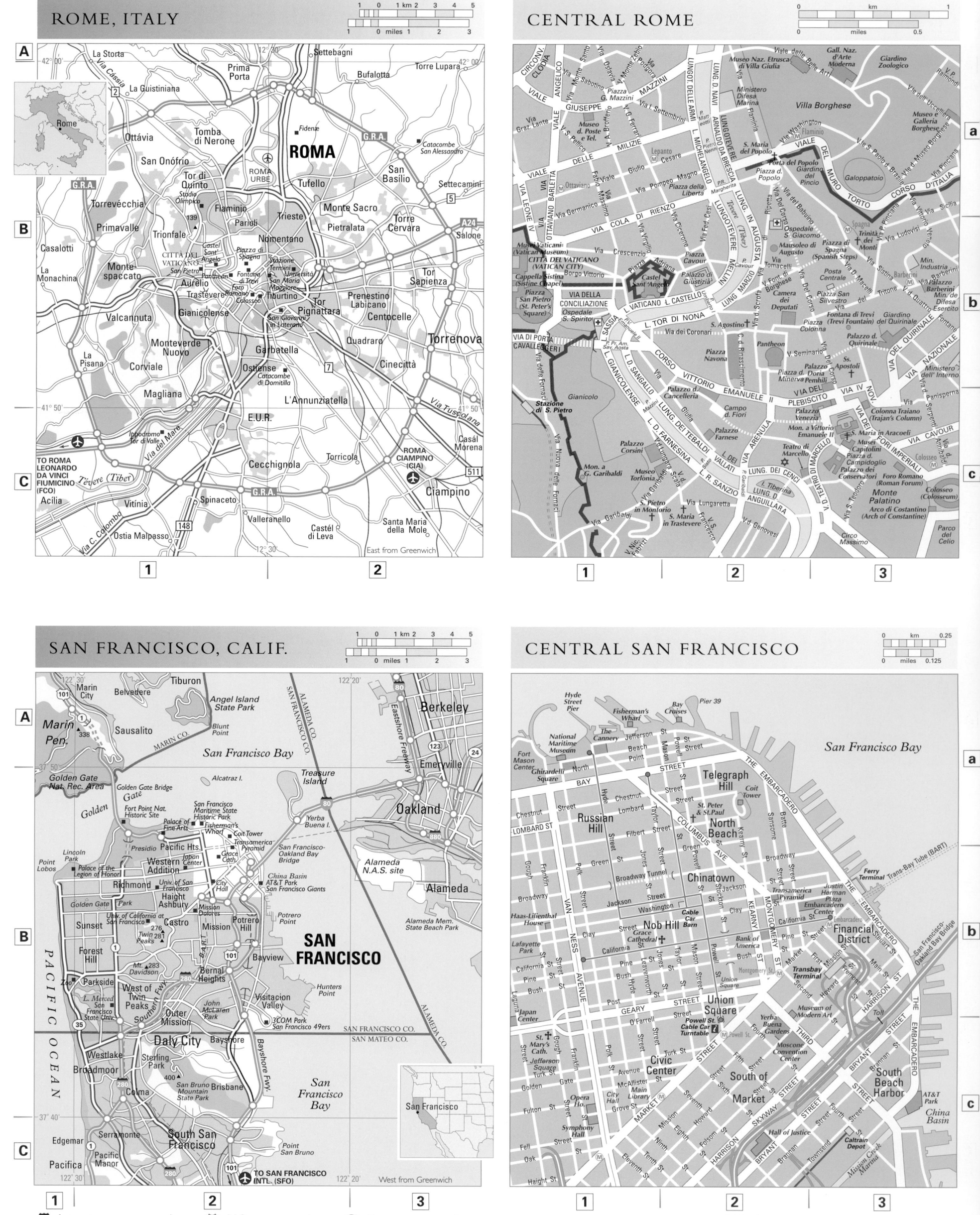

ROME, ITALY

CENTRAL ROME

SAN FRANCISCO, CALIF.

CENTRAL SAN FRANCISCO

🛡 Interstate route numbers   🛡 U.S. route numbers   🛡 State route numbers

— Cable Car route

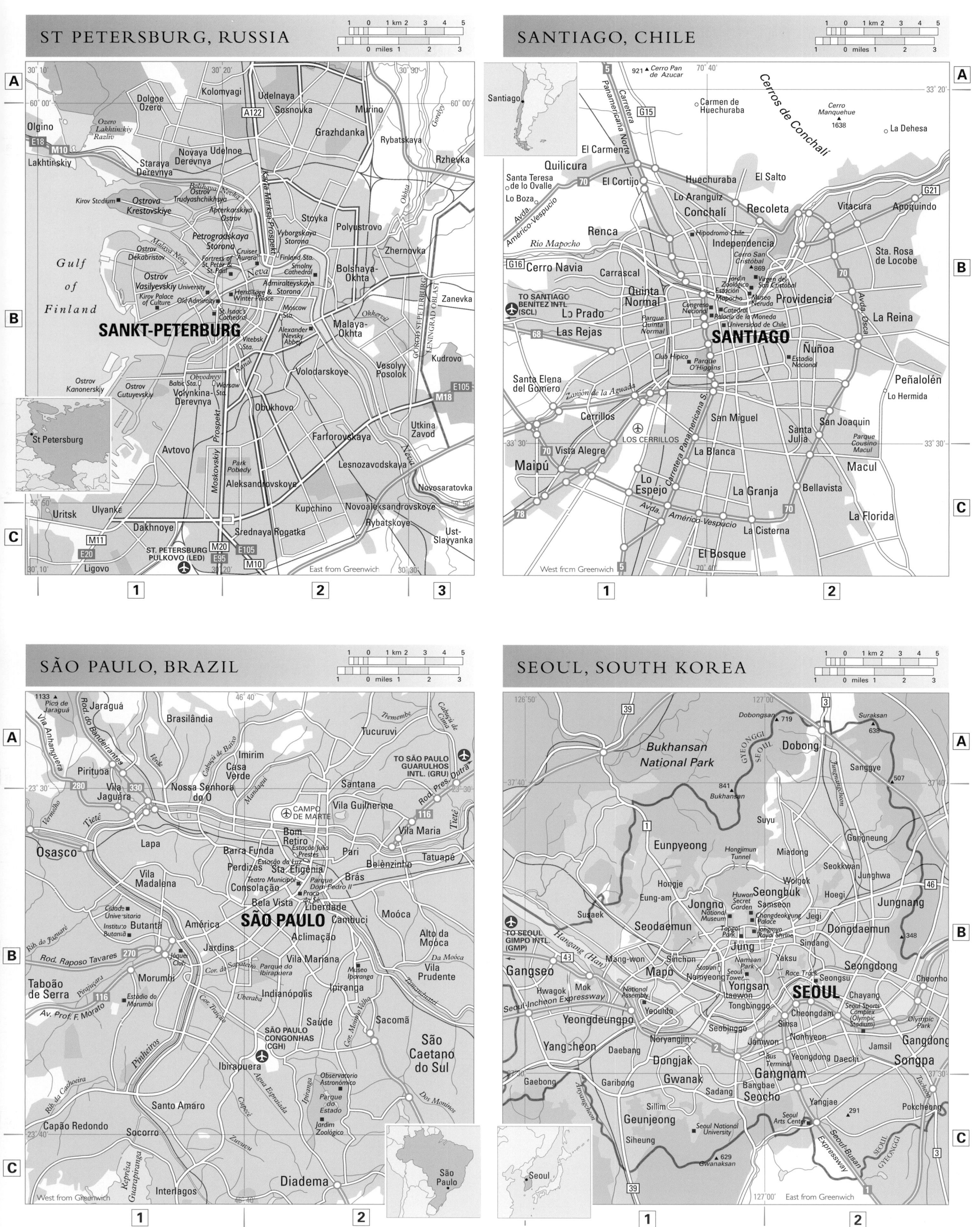

ST PETERSBURG, RUSSIA

SEAOUL, SOUTH KOREA

Gulf of Finland

SANKT-PETERBURG

SANTIAGO, CHILE

SANTIAGO

SÃO PAULO, BRAZIL

SÃO PAULO

SEOUL, SOUTH KOREA

SEOUL

COPYRIGHT PHILIP'S

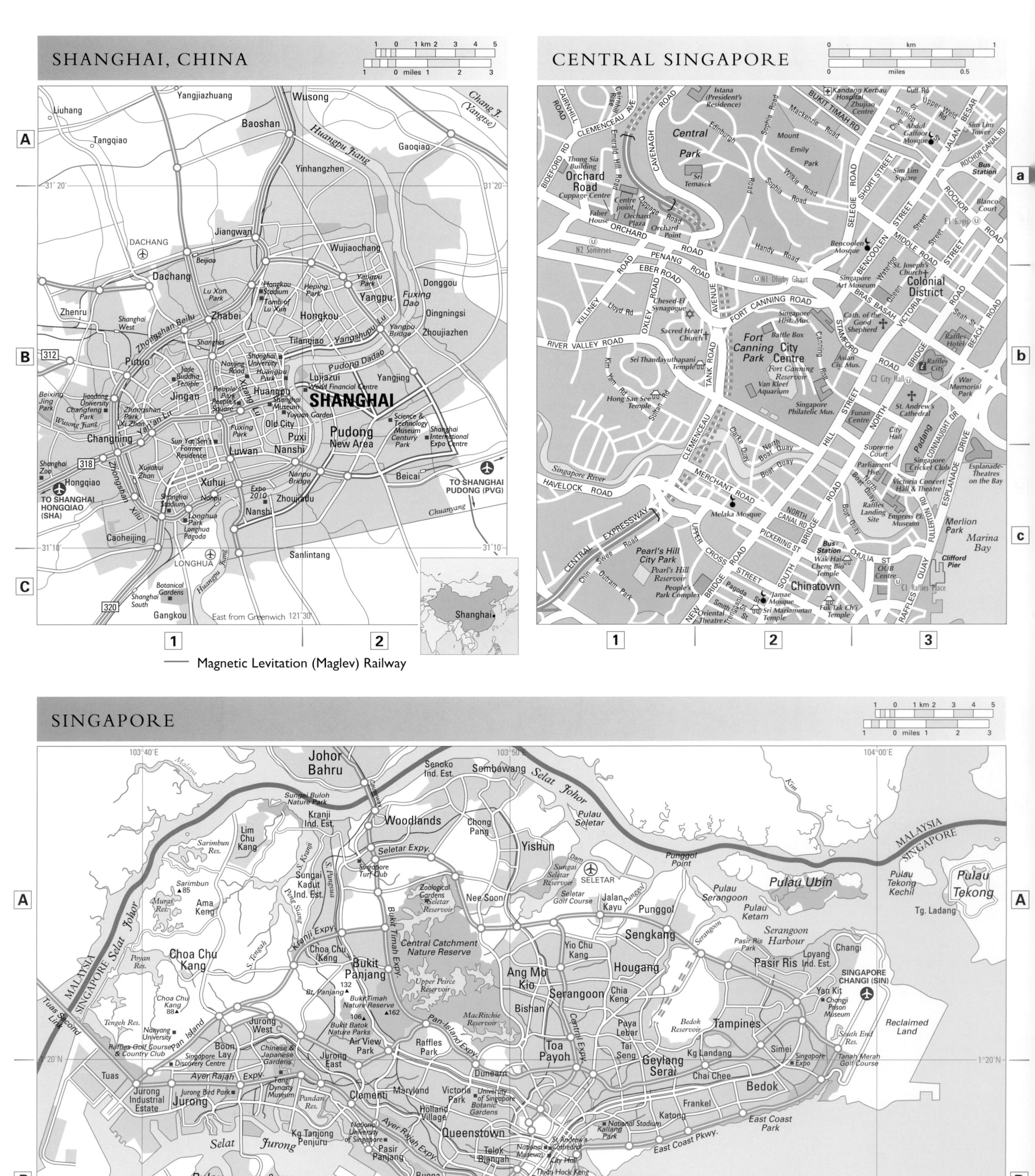

SHANGHAI, CHINA

Liuhang
Tangqiao
Yangjiazhuang
Baoshan
Wusong
Chang J. (Yangtze)
Huangpu Jiang
Gaoqiao
Yinhangzhen
A
31° 20'
31°20'
Jiangwan
DACHANG
Beijiao
Dachang
Wujiaochang
Yangpu
Donggou
Zhenru
Hongkou Stadium
Heping Park
Yangpu Park
Fuxing Dao
Lu Xun Park
Tomb of Lu Xun
Hongkou
Qingningsi
Putuo
Zhabei
Tilanqiao
Yangpu Bridge
Zhoujiazhen
312
Zhongshan Beilu
Shanghai
Nanjing Road
Huangpu Park
Yangjing
B
Shanghai West
Jade Buddha Temple
Shanghai University
Pudong Dadao
Lujiazui
World Financial Centre
Yangjing
b
Beixing Jing Park
Jingan
People's Park
People's Square
Huangpu
Shanghai Museum
SHANGHAI
Jiaotong University
Changfeng Park
Zhongshan Park
Xi Tian Lu
Old City
Yuyuan Garden
Pudong New Area
Science & Technology Museum
Changning
Sun Yat Sen's Former Residence
Fuxing Park
Puxi
Nanshi
Century Park
Shanghai International Expo Centre
318
Zhongshan Xilu
Xupujiang Zhan
Luwan
Nanpu Bridge
Beicai
Shanghai Zoo
Xuhui
Expo 2010
Zhoujiadu
TO SHANGHAI HONGQIAO (SHA)
Hongqiao
Shanghai Stadium
Nanpu
Nanshi
TO SHANGHAI PUDONG (PVG)
31° 10'
Caoheijing
Longhua Park
Longhua Pagoda
Sanlintang
31°10'
C
LONGHUA
Huangpu Kiang
Chuanyang
320
Botanical Gardens
Shanghai South
Gangkou
East from Greenwich 121°30'
Shanghai

— Magnetic Levitation (Maglev) Railway

CENTRAL SINGAPORE

CAIRNHILL ROAD
Cairnhill Rise
CLEMENCEAU ROAD
Istana (President's Residence)
Kandang Kerbau Hospital
Bukit Timah Rd
Zhujiao
Cuff Rd
Upper Weld
Dunlop
Clive
Abdul Gafoor Mosque
Sim Lim Rd
JALAN BESAR
A
a
CAVENAGH AVE
Emerald Hill Rd
Edinburgh Road
Central Park
Mount Emily
Mackenzie Road
Wilkie Road
Sophia Road
SELEGIE ROAD
SHORT STREET
Sim Lim Tower
Sim Lim Square
ROCHOR
Blanco Court
ROCHOR CANAL ROAD
Bideford Rd
Thong Sia Building
Orchard Road
Cuppage Centre
Sri Temasek
Emily
Handy Road
BRAS BASAH ROAD
Bencoolen Mosque
MIDDLE ROAD
St. Joseph's Church
Bugis
a
Faber House
Centre point
Cuppage Road
Orchard Plaza
ORCHARD
Penang Road
BENCOOLEN STREET
Singapore Art Museum
Colonial District
VICTORIA STREET
Raffles Hotel
b
N2 Somerset
Orchard Point
N1 Dhoby Ghaut
Singapore Hist. Mus.
Cath. of the Good Shepherd
Raffles City
KILLINEY ROAD
EBER ROAD
OXLEY ROAD
PENANG ROAD
Chesed-El Synagogue
FORT CANNING ROAD
Fort Canning Park
Fort Canning Reservoir
STAMFORD
CANNING
NORTH BRIDGE ROAD
BEACH ROAD
War Memorial Park
b
Lloyd Rd
RIVER VALLEY ROAD
Sacred Heart Church
Sri Thandayuthapani Temple
TANK ROAD
City Centre
Van Kleef Aquarium
Asian Civ. Mus.
HILL
C2 City Hall
St. Andrew's Cathedral
Hong San See Temple
Singapore Philatelic Mus.
Funan Centre
City Hall
Supreme Court
Padang
Singapore Cricket Club
CONNAUGHT DR
Esplanade-Theatres on the Bay
CLEMENCEAU
Clarke Quay
Parliament Hse
Singapore River
North Boat Quay
Boat Quay
Victoria Concert Hall & Theatre
ESPLANADE DRIVE
HAVELOCK ROAD
MERCHANT ROAD
Raffles Landing Site
Empress Pl. Museum
FULLERTON RD
Merlion Park
Marina Bay
c
Melaka Mosque
UPPER CROSS STREET
NORTH CANAL RD
SOUTH CANAL RD
PICKERING ST
Bus Station
Boat Quay
CENTRAL EXPRESSWAY
Pearl's Hill City Park
Pearl's Hill Reservoir
People's Park Complex
Chin Swee Road
NEW BRIDGE ROAD
SOUTH BRIDGE ROAD
Wak Hai Cheng Bio Temple
Raffles Place
OUB Centre
C1 Raffles Place
Clifford Pier
Outram Park
Pagoda
Smith
Temple
Oriental Theatre
Jamae Mosque
Sri Mariamman Temple
Chinatown
Fuk Tak Ch'i Temple
RAFFLES QUAY

SINGAPORE

103°40'E
Malaya
Johor Bahru
Senoko Ind. Est.
Sembawang
Selat Johor
103°50'E
104°00'E
MALAYSIA
SINGAPORE
Sungei Buloh Nature Park
Kranji Ind. Est.
Woodlands
Chong Pang
Pulau Seletar
Kim
Lim Chu Kang
Sarimbun Res.
S. Kranji
Seletar Expy.
Yishun
Punggol Point
Pulau Tekong Kechil
Pulau Tekong
A
Sarimbun 85
Murai Res.
Ama Keng
S. Tengah
Sungai Kadut Ind. Est.
Singapore Turf Club
Zoological Gardens
Neg Soon
Dam
Seletar Reservoir
Seletar Golf Course
Jalan Kayu
Punggol
Pulau Serangoon
Pulau Ketam
Pulau Ubin
Serangoon Harbour
Changi
Tg. Ladang
A
Poyan Res.
Choa Chu Kang
Choa Chu Kang
Bukit Panjang
Bt. Panjang 132
Central Catchment Nature Reserve
Upper Peirce Reservoir
Sengkang
Pasir Ris Park
Loyang Ind. Est.
Pasir Ris
Yan Kit
Chongi Prison Museum
SINGAPORE CHANGI (SIN)
Tengeh Res.
Choa Chu Kang 88
Bukit Batok Nature Parks
Bukit Timah Nature Reserve 162
Ang Mo Kio
Yio Chu Kang
Hougang
Chia Keng
Nanyang University
106
Air View Park
Pan Island Expy.
MacRitchie Reservoir
Serangoon
Bishan
Paya Lebar
Bedok Reservoir
Tampines
South End Res.
Reclaimed Land
1°20'N
Raffles Golf Course & Country Club
Jurong West
Jurong East
Raffles Park
Toa Payoh
Tai Seng
Simei
Singapore Expo
Tanah Merah Golf Course
Jurong Industrial Estate
Boon Lay
Chinese & Japanese Gardens
Tang Dynasty Museum
Dunearn
Geylang Serai
Chai Chee
Singapore Discovery Centre
Ayer Rajah Expy.
Clementi
Pandan Res.
Maryland
Victoria Park
Holland Village
University of Singapore Botanic Gardens
Bedok
Frankel
Katong
East Coast Park
Jurong
Ayer Rajah
Kg Tanjong Penjuru
National University of Singapore
Queenstown
Telok Blangah
National Museum
St. Andrew's Cathedral
Thian Hock Keng Temple
City Hall
National Stadium
Kallang Park
East Coast Pkwy.
B
Reclaimed Land
Selat Jurong
Pulau Jurong
Seraya
Pasir Panjang
Buona Vista Park
Mt 105 Faber
Cable Car
Underwater World
World Trade Centre P. Brani
Keppel Harbour
SINGAPORE
B
Sakra
Reclaimed Land
Selat Pandan
Pulau Busing
Pulau Bukum
Sentosa
Sentosa Golf Course
Tanjong Golf Course
Straits of Singapore
East from Greenwich
104°00'E
Singapore

STOCKHOLM, SWEDEN

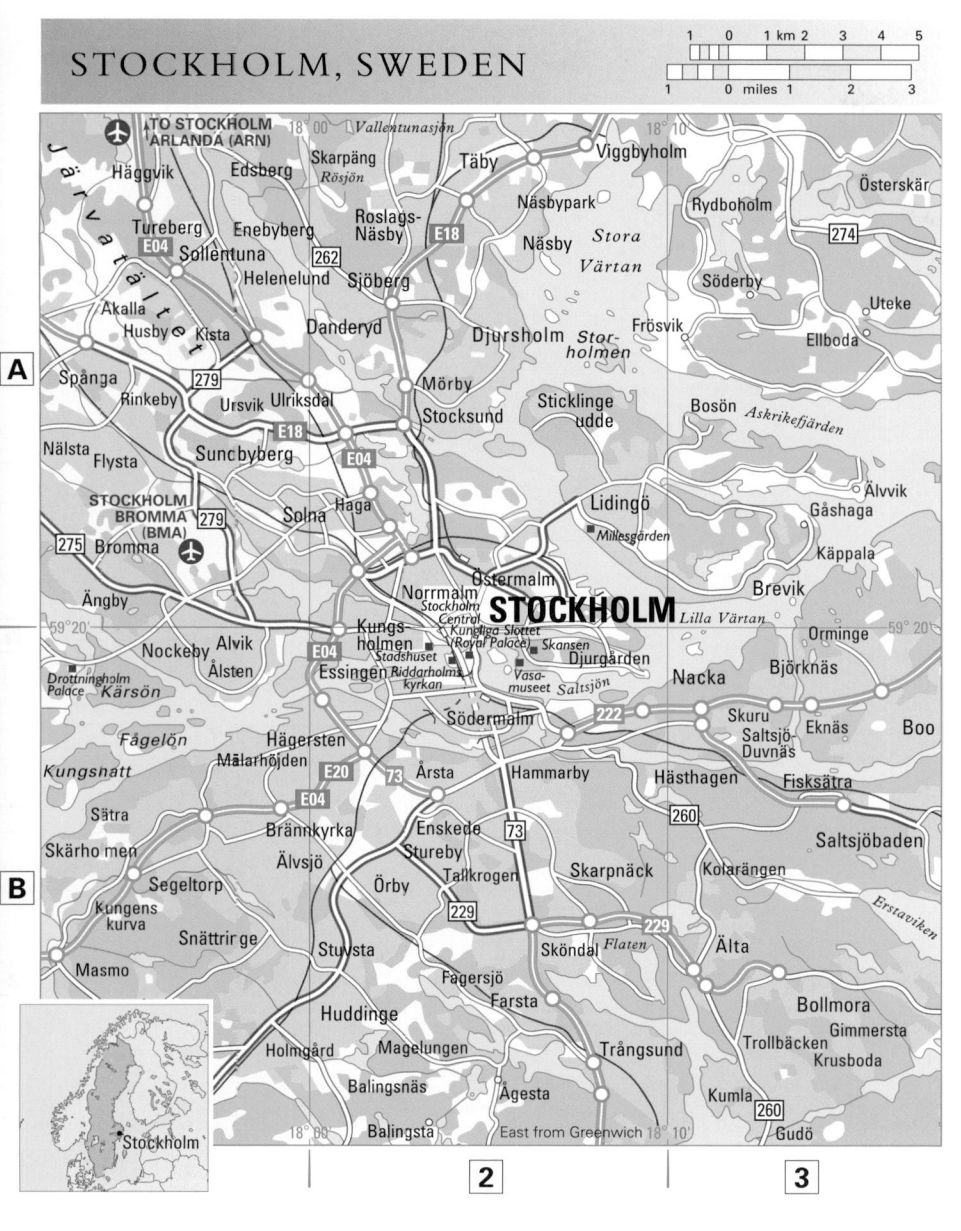

CENTRAL STOCKHOLM

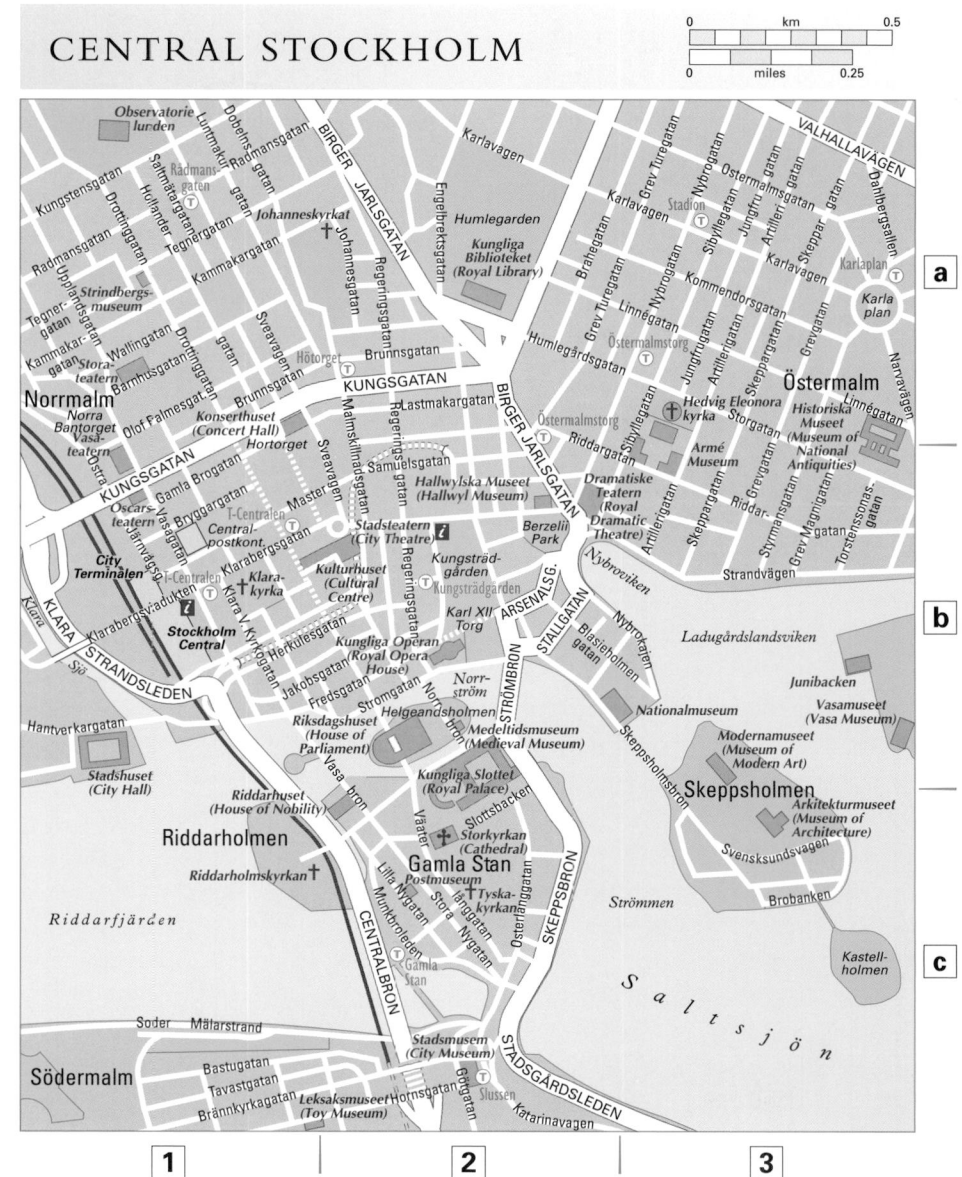

SYDNEY, AUSTRALIA

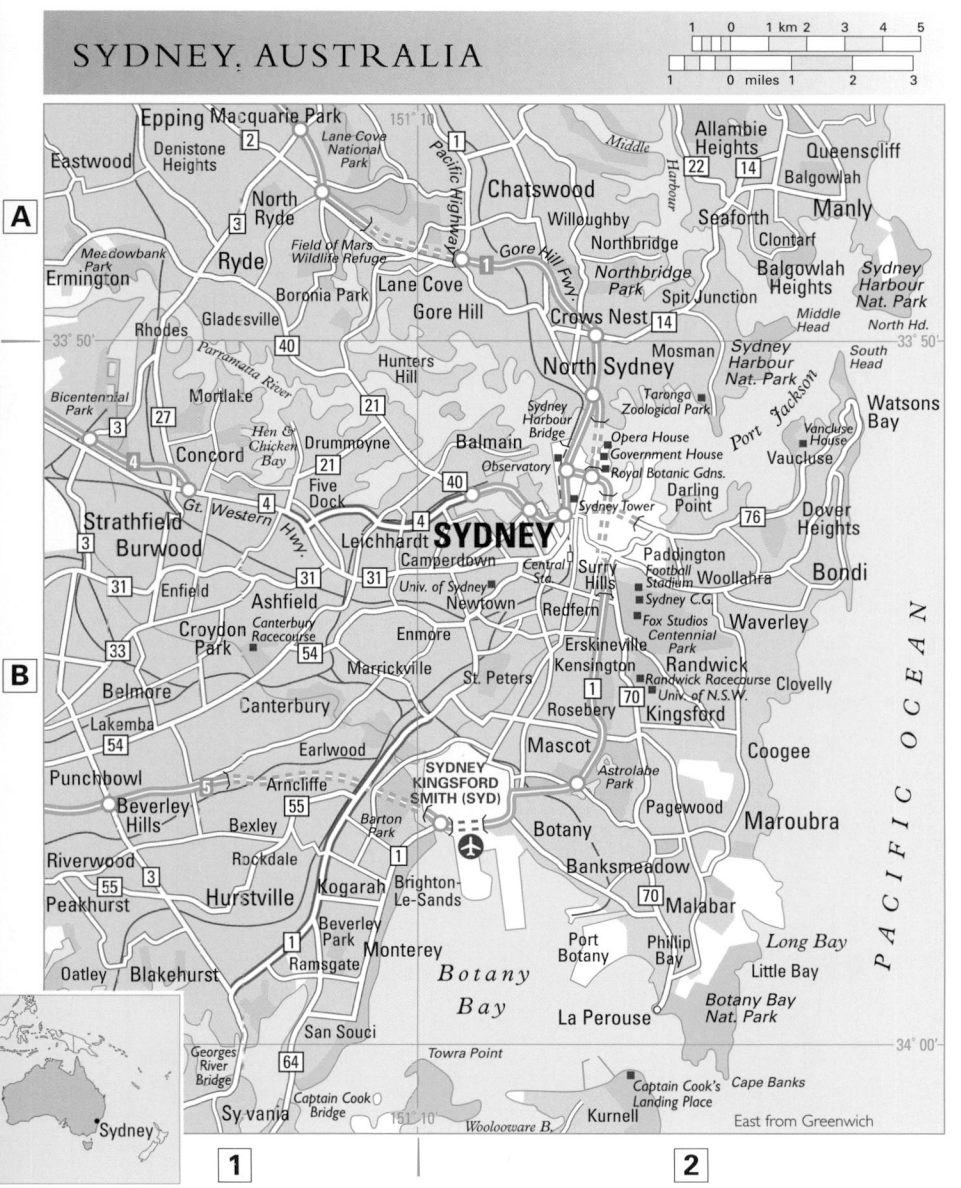

CENTRAL SYDNEY

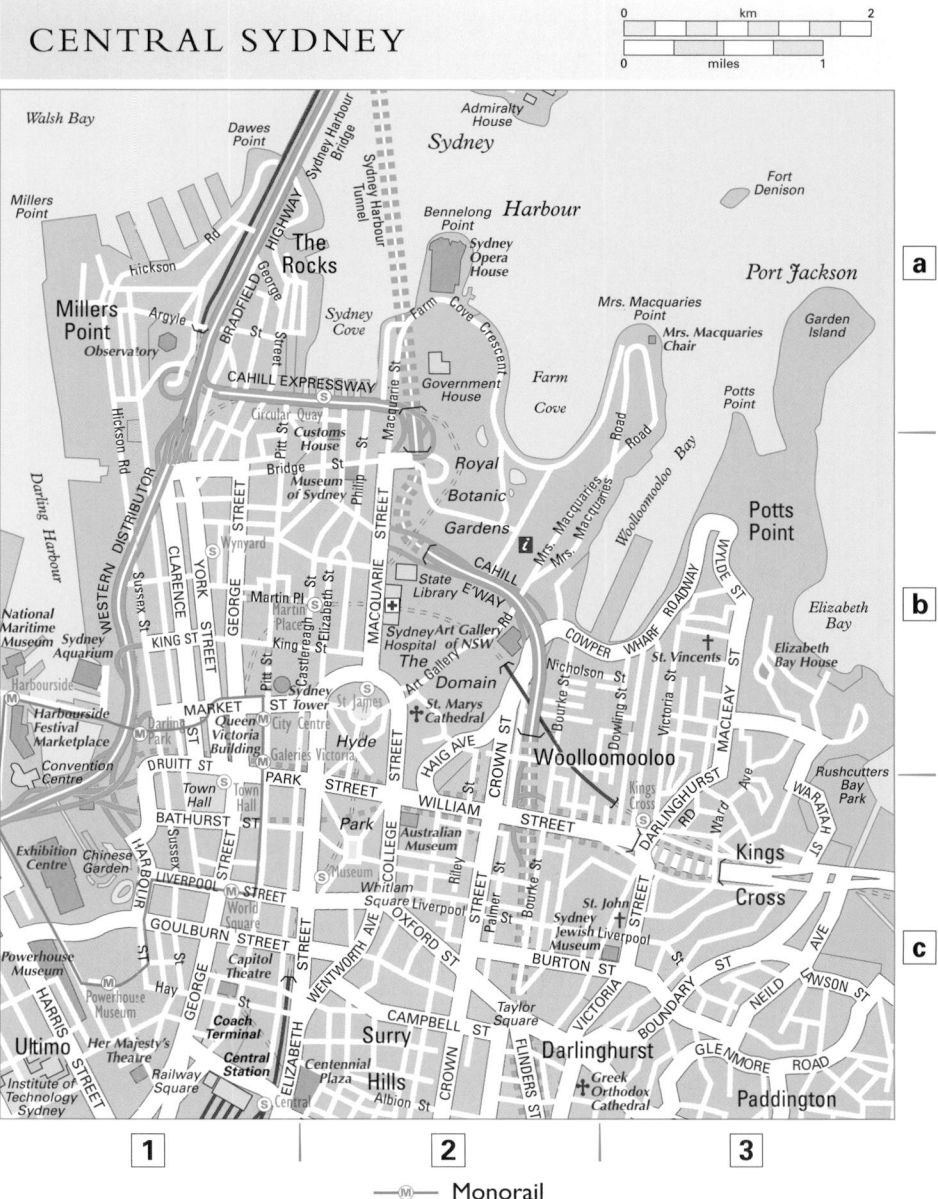

—Ⓜ— Monorail

TOKYO, JAPAN

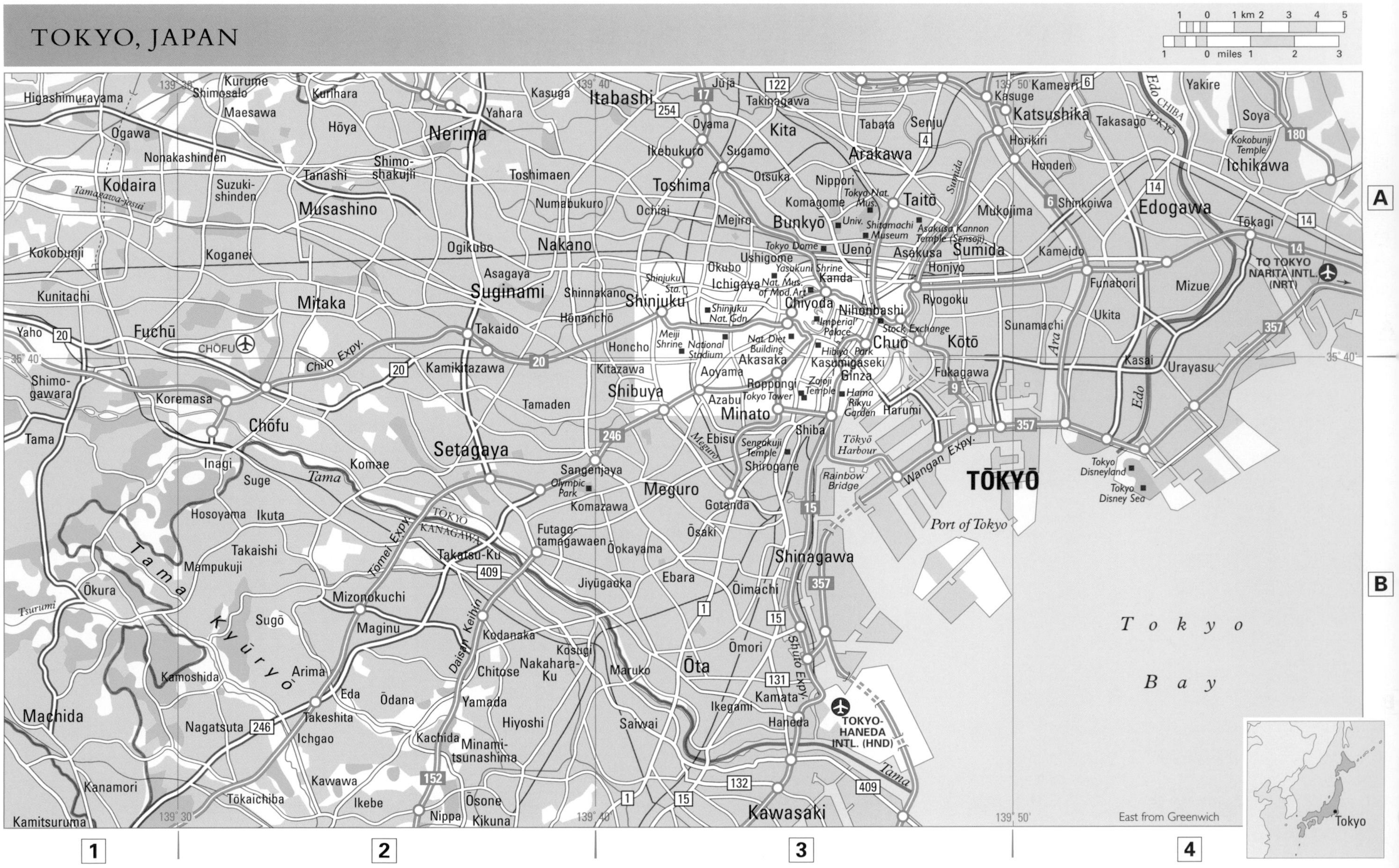

1 0 1 km 2 3 4 5
1 0 miles 1 2 3

Higashimurayama · Kurume · Shimosato · Kurihara · Kasuga · Jūjō · Takinogawa · Kameari · Yakire · Soya

Kodaira · Ogawa · Shimoshakuji · Yahara · Itabashi · 254 · 17 · Ōyama · Kita · Tabata · Senju · Katsushika · Takasago · Kokubunji Temple · Ichikawa

Nonakashinden · Nerima · Hōya · Ikebukuro · Sugamo · Arakawa · Horikiri · Honden · Shinkoiwa · Edogawa · Tōkagi

Musashino · Suzuki-shinden · Tanashi · Toshimaen · Toshima · Otsuka · Nippori · Tokyo Nat. Mus · Taitō · Mukōjima · Kameido · Mizue

Kokubunji · Koganei · Ogikubo · Nakano · Numabukuro · Ochiai · Mejiro · Komagome · Bunkyō · Univ. · Asakusa Kannon Temple (Sensōji) · Sumida · Funabori · Ukita

Kunitachi · Mitaka · Asagaya · Suginami · Honancho · Shinnakano · Shinjuku Sta. · Ushigome · Nat. Mus. of Mod. Art · Ichigaya · Kanda · Honjyo · Ryōgoku

Yaho · 20 · Fuchū · CHOFU · Takaido · Kamikitazawa · 20 · Meiji Shrine · National Stadium · Shinjuku Nat. Gdn · Nat. Diet Building · Imperial Palace · Stock Exchange · Chūō · Kōtō · Fukagawa · Kasai · Urayasu

Shimo-gawara · Koremasa · Chūō Expy. · Kitazawa · Shibuya · Aoyama · Akasaka · Roppongi · Kasumigaseki · Ginza · Hama Rikyū Garden · Harumi · 357

Tama · Inagi · Chōfu · Komae · Tamaden · Setagaya · Sangenjaya · Olympic Park · Ebisu · Azabu · Minato · Tokyo Tower · Shiba · Zōjō Temple · Tōkyō Harbour · Wangan Expy · TŌKYŌ

Hosoyama · Ikuta · Suge · Komazawa · Futago-tamagawaen · Meguro · Gotanda · Sengakuji Temple · Shirogane · Rainbow Bridge · Port of Tokyo · Tokyo Disneyland · Tokyo Disney Sea

Takaishi · Mampukuji · Mizonokuchi · Jiyūgaoka · Ōkayama · Ōsaki · Shinagawa · 15 · 357

Ōkura · Sugō · Maginu · Kodanaka · Chitose · Nakahara-Ku · Kosugi · Maruko · Ebara · Ōimachi · 1 · 15

Tsurumi · Arima · Eda · Ōdana · Yamada · Hiyoshi · Saiwai · Ōmori · Ōta · Kamata · Ikegami · Haneda · 131 · TOKYO-HANEDA INTL. (HND)

Machida · Kamoshida · Takeshita · Minami-tsunashima · Kawawa · 152 · Ōsone · Kikuna · Nippa · 132 · 409 · Kawasaki

Tokaichiba · Kamitsuruma · Kanamori · Nagatsuta · Ichgao · Kachida · Ikebe · Tokyo Bay

East from Greenwich

A · B · 1 · 2 · 3 · 4

CENTRAL TOKYO

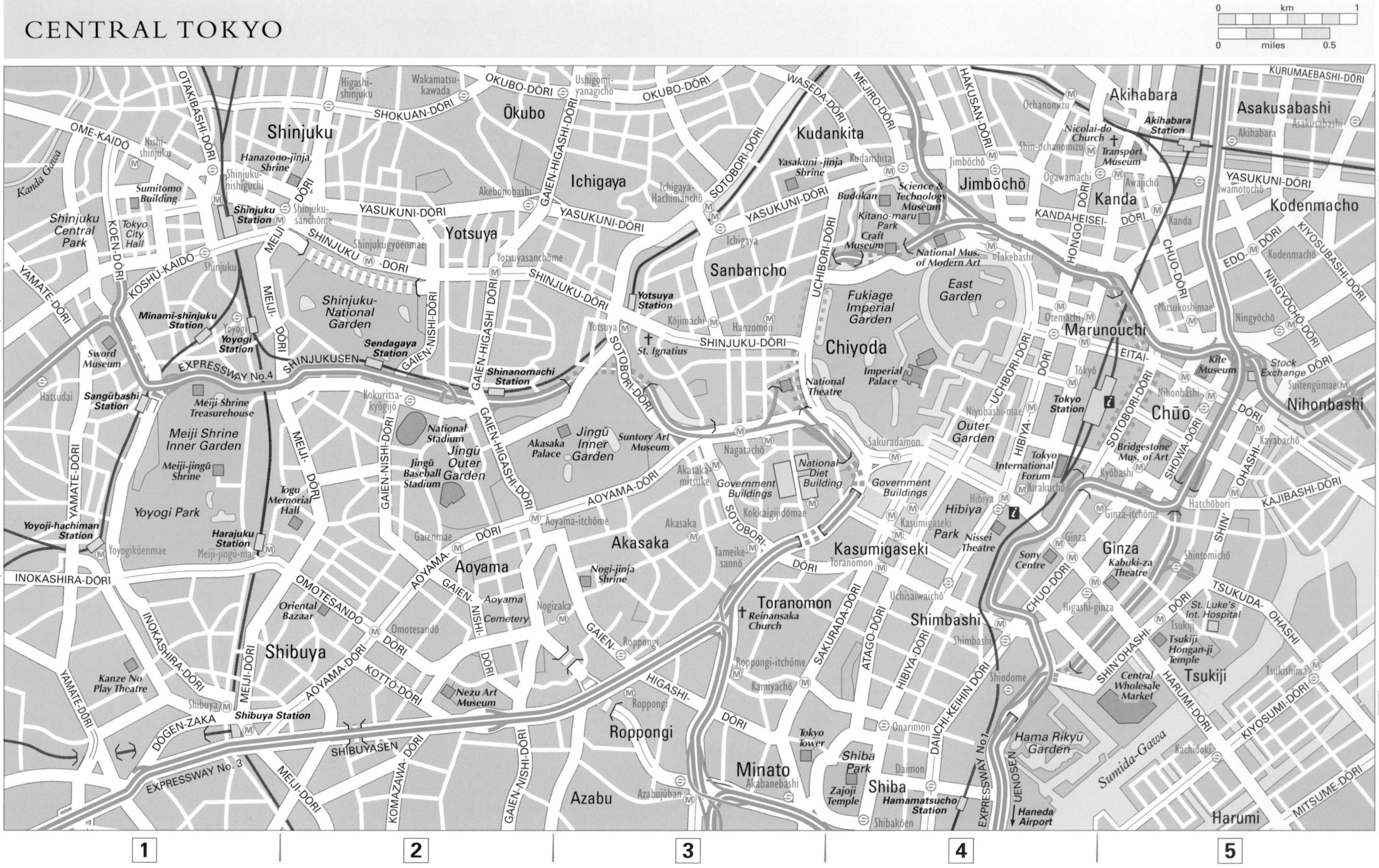

0 km 1
0 miles 0.5

Higashi-shinjuku · Wakamatsu-kawada · Ushigomi-yanagicho · Ochanomizu · Akihabara · Asakusabashi · KURUMEBASHI-DORI

Shinjuku · Ōkubo · OKUBO-DORI · Kudankita · Akihabara Station · Akihabara · YASUKUNI-DORI

OME-KAIDO · SHOKUAN-DORI · Hanazono-jinja Shrine · Ichigaya · Jimbōchō · Kanda · Kodenmacho

Shinjuku Central Park · Sumitomo Building · Shinjuku Station · Ichigaya Yotsuya · Sanbancho · National Mus. of Modern Art · Marunouchi · KANDAHEISEI-DORI

Tokyo City Hall · Minami-shinjuku Station · SHINJUKU-DORI · Yotsuya · Yotsuya Station · Kōjimachi · Fukiage Imperial Garden · East Garden · Chiyoda · Tokyo Station · Nihonbashi · Stock Exchange

Sword Museum · Sangūbashi Station · Meiji Shrine Treasurehouse · Shinanomachi Station · St. Ignatius · National Theatre · Imperial Palace · Outer Garden · Bridgestone Mus. of Art

Meiji Shrine Inner Garden · National Stadium · Jingū Outer Garden · Akasaka Palace · Jingū Inner Garden · Suntory Art Museum · National Diet Building · Government Buildings · Hibiya · Tokyo International Forum · Nihonbashi

Yoyogi-hachiman Station · Meiji-jingū Shrine · Yoyogi Park · Togu Memorial Hall · Jingū Baseball Stadium · AOYAMA-DORI · Akasaka · SOTOBORI · Kasumigaseki · Hibiya Park · Nissei Theatre · Sony Centre · Ginza · Kabuki-za Theatre

INOKASHIRA-DORI · Harajuku Station · Omotesando · Aoyama · Aoyama-itchōme · Nogi-jinja Shrine · Toranomon · Reinanzaka Church · Shimbashi · St. Luke's Int. Hospital · Tsukiji Hongan-ji Temple

Kanze No Play Theatre · Oriental Bazaar · Nezu Art Museum · Nogizaka · Aoyama Cemetery · HIGASHI-DORI · Roppongi-itchōme · Shimbashi · Shiodome · Tsukiji

Shibuya Station · DOGEN-ZAKA · Shibuya · KOTTO-DORI · Roppongi · Tokyo Tower · Shiba Park · Hamamatsucho Station · Central Wholesale Market

SHIBUYASEN · EXPRESSWAY No. 3 · Minato · Azabu · Shiba · Zajoji Temple · Damon · Haneda Airport · Hama Rikyū Garden · Harumi · KIYOSUMI-DORI · MITSUME-DORI

a · b · c · 1 · 2 · 3 · 4 · 5

Ⓣ Toei Subway   Ⓜ Tokyo Metro

TEHRAN, IRAN

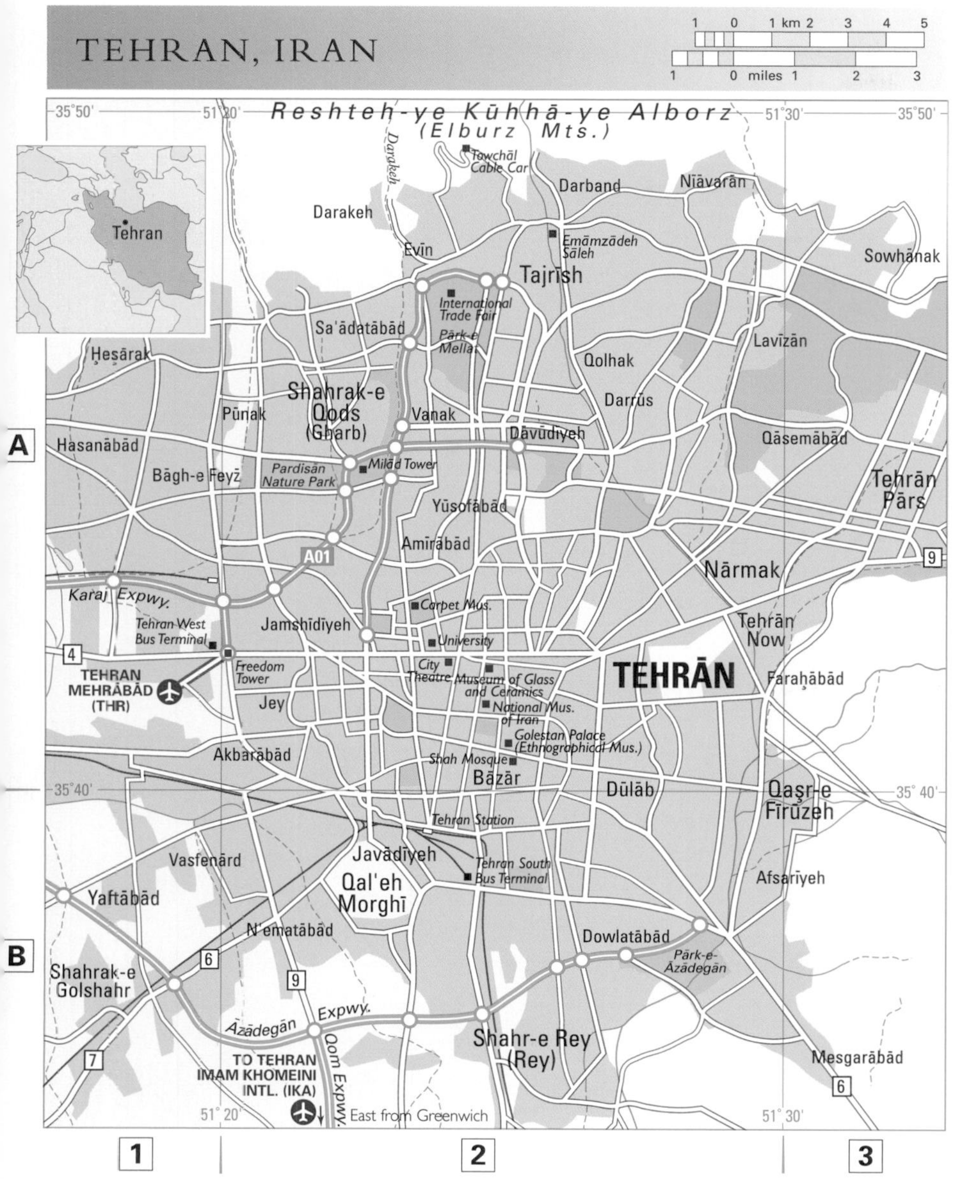

Reshteh-ye Kūhhā-ye Alborz
(Elburz Mts.)

1 0 1 km 2 3 4 5
0 miles 1 2 3

35°50' 51°20' 51°30' 35°50'

Tehran

Towchāl Cable Car
Darakeh
Darband
Niāvarān
Darabad
Sowhānak
Evin
Emāmzādeh Sāleh
Tajrīsh
International Trade Fair
Pārk-e Mellat
Sa'ādatābād
Qolhak
Lavīzān
Hesārak
Shahrak-e Qods (Sharb)
Vanak
Darrūs
Qāsemābād
Pūnak
Dāvūdiyeh
A
Hasanābād
Bāgh-e Feyż
Milād Tower
Pardisān Nature Park
Yūsofābād
Tehrān Pārs
A01
Amīrābād
Nārmak
Karaj Expwy.
Carpet Mus.
Tehrān West Bus Terminal
Jamshīdīyeh
University
Tehrān Now
9
4
TEHRAN MEHRĀBĀD (THR)
Freedom Tower
City Theatre
Museum of Glass and Ceramics
National Mus. of Iran
Farahābād
Jey
Golestan Palace (Ethnographical Mus.)
TEHRĀN
Akbarābād
Shah Mosque
Bāzār
Dūlāb
Qasr-e Fīrūzeh
35°40'
Tehran Station
35°40'
Vasfenārd
Javādiyeh
Afsārīyeh
Yaftābād
Qal'eh Morghī
Tehran South Bus Terminal
B
Shahrak-e Golshahr
6
9
Park-e Azādegān
Dowlatābād
7
Āzādegān Expwy.
Qom Expwy.
Shahr-e Rey (Rey)
Mesgarābād
6
TO TEHRAN IMAM KHOMEINI INTL. (IKA)
East from Greenwich
51°20'
51°30'

1 2 3

CENTRAL TORONTO

0 km 0.5
0 miles 0.25

Queen's Park
Galbraith Road
University of Toronto
COLLEGE STREET
Barbara Ann Scott Park
Granby Street
McGill Street
Gerrard Street East
Mintō Street
Allan Gdns
Glenholme Pl
Pembroke St
Sherbourne St
COLLEGE STREET
Toronto General Hospital
YONGE
Ryerson University
JARVIS
STREET
George St
a
Ross Street
Cecil Street
Orde Street
Princess Margaret Hospital
Mt Sinai Hospital
Hospital for Sick Children
Gould Street
D'Arcy St
Gerrard Street West
Elm St
Edward St
Baldwin Street
McCaul Street
Henry Street
Toronto Rehab Institute
Elm St
Coach Terminal
Dundas St WEST
St Michael's Cathedral
Armoury
Moss Park
Huron Street
DUNDAS
Edward Street
St Patrick's Church
Foster Pl
Trinity Sq
Toronto Eaton Centre
Massey Hall
Metro United Church
DUNDAS STREET WEST
The Art Gallery of Ontario
Grange Avenue
County Courthouse
City Hall
St Michael's Hospital
Theatre Centre
China Town
Grange Park
Old City Hall
QUEEN STREET EAST
Toronto's First P.O.
Sullivan Street
St Patrick Street
Osgoode Hall
Nathan Phillips Square
P.O.
Lombard Street
Phoebe Street
Stephanie St
Campbell Ho
RICHMOND STREET EAST
St James' Park
Bulwer Street
Renfrew Place
Bank of Canada
Richmond Adelaide Centre
St James' Cathedral
b
QUEEN
STREET
National Bank Bldg
King Street East
Colborne Street
RICHMOND
Nelson Street
Toronto Stock Exchange
Scotia Plaza
ADELAIDE
Peter St
Royal Pearl St
Commerce Court
FRONT STREET EAST
St Lawrence Market
Alexandra Theatre
Gallery of Inuit Art
Hockey Hall of Fame
Roy Thomson Hall
Toronto Dominion Centre
Hummingbird Centre
The Esplanade
KING
Mercer Street
Metro Hall
Wellington
Canada Trust Tower
Canada Custom Building
Wellington Street West
Simcoe Park
SPADINA
Clarence Square Park
CBC Broadcast Centre & Mus
Union Station
Bus Terminal
FRONT
STREET
Air Canada Centre
GARDINER
Isabella Valancy Crawford Park
Metro Toronto Conv. Cen. (Nth)
Convention Centre (Sth)
Simcoe Street
Police Station
EXPRESSWAY
LAKE SHORE BOULEVARD EAST
AVENUE
Rogers Centre (Sky Dome)
C.N. Tower
Roundhouse Park
HARBOUR ST
Queen's Quay East
Redpath Sugar Museum
c
City Core Golf & Driving Range
Bremner Boulevard
Roundhouse
Harbour Square Park
Toronto Island Ferry Terminal
GARDINER EXPRESSWAY
Queen's Quay
Harbourfront Park
Queen's Quay Terminal
Lake Ontario
LAKE SHORE BOULEVARD WEST

1 2 3

TORONTO, CANADA

1 0 1 km 2 3 4 5
1 0 miles 1 2 3

79°40' 79°30' 79°20' 79°10'

Boyd Conservation Area
7
407
Markham
Metro Toronto Zoo
Rouge
Little Rouge
401
Fairport
27
Humber
Vaughan
Thornhill
The Promenade
East Don
Brown
Glen Rouge Park
2
West Rouge
Rouge Hill
Woodbridge
7
Edgeley
Pine Grove
Concord
Newtonbrook
48
Highland Creek
Port Union
407
Fisherville
Willowdale
11
2A
Black Creek Pioneer Village
York University
G. Ross Lord Park
East Don Parkland
404
Fairview Mall
Scarborough Town Centre
Morningside Park
West Hill
Humber Summit
North York
Northmount
Malvern
Woburn
A
Beaumonte Heights
Black Northwood Park Creek
Lansing
401
Bendale
Eastpoint Park
Thistletown
400
Armour Heights
Highland
Claireville Reservoir
York Mills
Scarborough
Humberwood Park
Woodbine Centre
Downsview
Yorkdale Shopping Centre
Lawrence Heights
Don Mills
York Univ.
Wilket Creek Park
Cliffside
427
Kipling Heights
Rexdale
Humberlea
401
West Don
Sunnybrook Health Science Centre
Ontario Science Centre
Malton
Woodbine Race Track
Weston
11A
Forest Hill
Thorncliffe
Bluffers Park
27
Cedarvale Park
Leaside
Dentonia Park
Scarborough Bluffs
409
York
11
Don Valley Pkwy
East York
Birch Cliff
TORONTO LESTER B. PEARSON INTL. (YYZ)
401
Humber Valley Village
Mount Dennis
Casa Loma
Riverdale Park
5
Kew Gardens
43°40'
Royal Ontario Museum
2
Mimico Creek
Lambton Mills
University of Toronto
Parliament Buildings
Ashbridge's Bay Park
410
Hanlon
Etobicoke
Swansea
High Park
Old City Hall
C.N. Tower & Rogers Centre
Union Sta
Gardiner Expy
TORONTO
401
Islington
Kingsway
5
Parkdale
Old Fort York
Tommy Thompson Park
Markland Wood
Humber Bay
Humber
Exhibition Place
TORONTO CITY CENTRE (ISLAND)
B
Burnhamthorpe
427
Summerville
Way
Ontario Place
Island Airport
Toronto Harbour
10
5
Humber Bay Park
Toronto Islands
Elizabeth
Mimico
LAKE ONTARIO
403
Square One
2
Humber College
New Toronto
Gibraltar Point
Dixie Rd
Samuel Smith Park
Cooksville
Mississauga
Long Branch
West from Greenwich
79°40' 79°30' 79°20' 79°10'

1 2 3 4

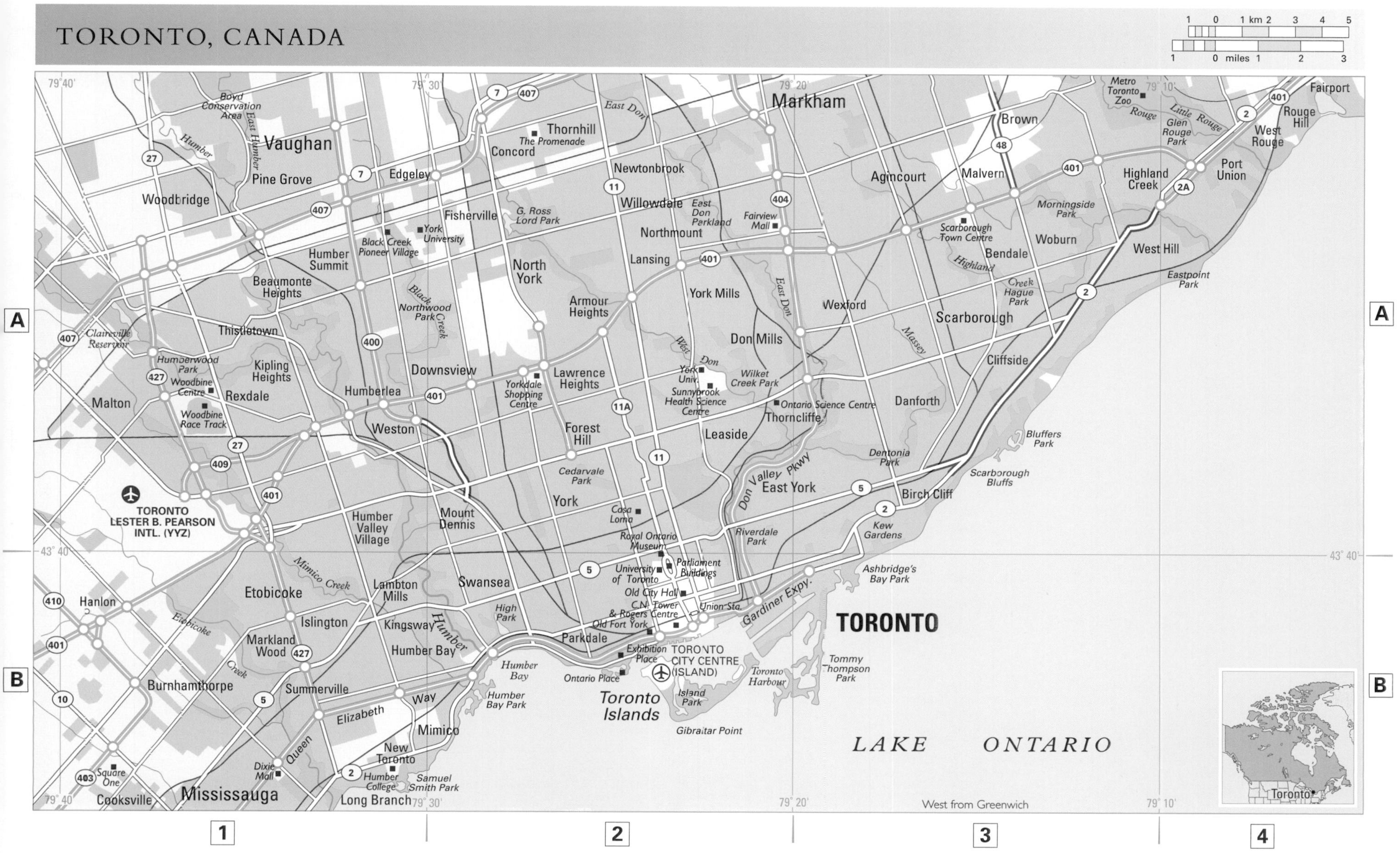

427 Provincial route numbers

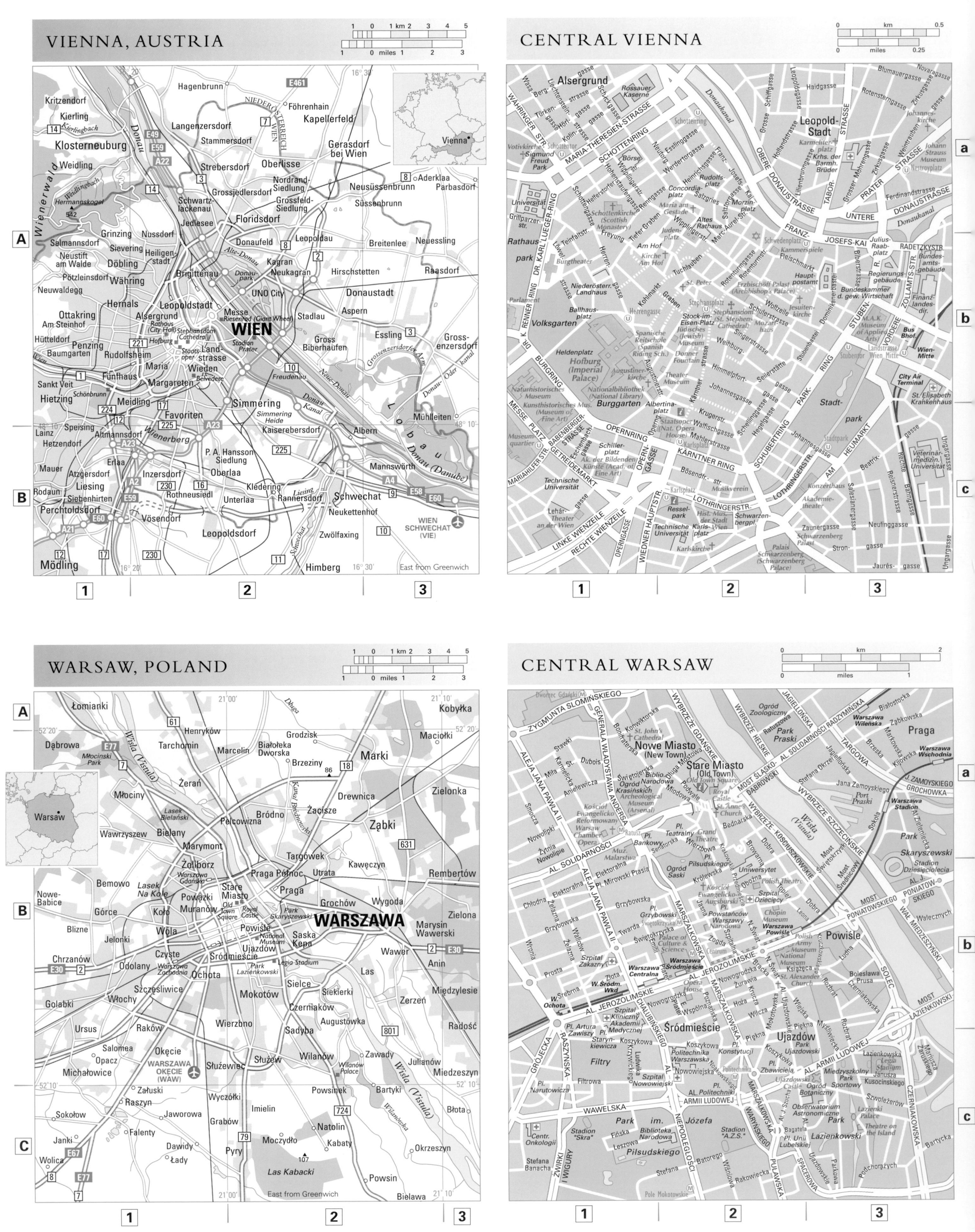

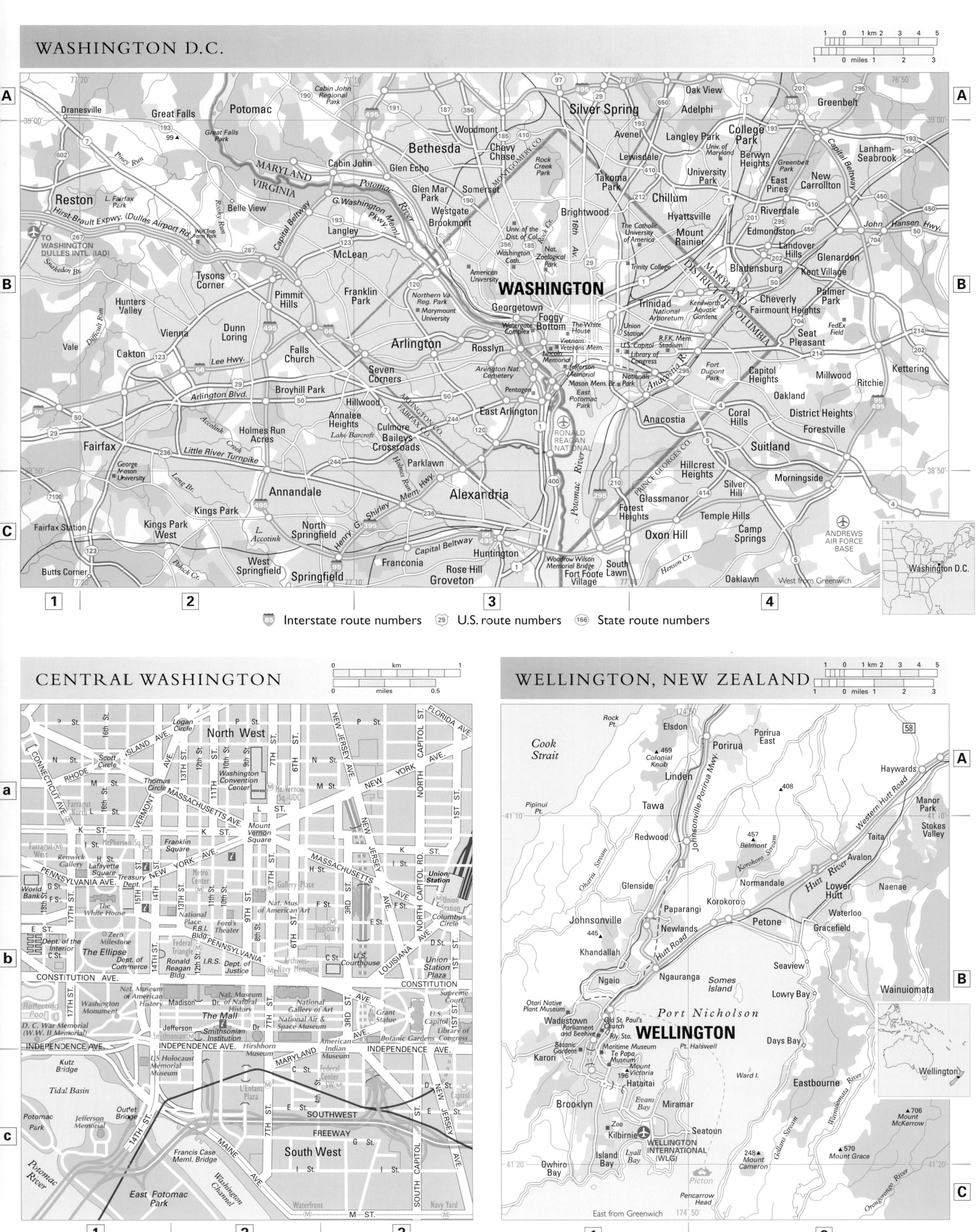

WASHINGTON D.C.

Interstate route numbers U.S. route numbers State route numbers

CENTRAL WASHINGTON

WELLINGTON, NEW ZEALAND

COPYRIGHT PHILIP'S

WORLD
MAPS

A B C D E F G H

1 2 3 4 5 6 7 8 9

Pt. Barrow
Beaufort Sea
Banks I.
Parry Is.
Queen Elizabeth Islands
North Magnetic Pole
Devon I.
Ellesmere I.
Greenland
Greenland Sea
Jan Mayen
Norwegian Sea
Alaska
Yukon
Mt. McKinley (Denali) 6194
Bering Str.
Bering Sea
Aleutian Is.
Gulf of Kodiak I. Alaska
Queen Charlotte Is.
Vancouver I.
Mackenzie
Gr. Bear L.
Gr. Slave L.
Baffin Island
Hudson Str.
Hudson Bay
Nelson
Place
L. Winnipeg
Arctic Circle 3360
Davis Str.
Denmark Str.
2116
Iceland
Faroe Is.
British Isles 1342
North Sea
North America
Great Lakes
Laurentian Plateau
St. Lawrence
Gulf of St. Lawrence
Newfoundland
C. Race
Nova Scotia
Labrador
Labrador Sea
C. Farewell
B. of Biscay
Mt. Blanc 4808
Pic d'Aneto 3404
Iberian Pen.
A 40
C. Mendocino
Mt. Elbert 4399
Great Basin
Sierra Nevada
Mt. Whitney 4418
Death Valley
Colorado
Rocky Mountains
Great Plains
Arkansas
Missouri
Mississippi
Ohio
Appalachian Mts.
Mt. Mitchell 2037
C. Cod
C. Hatteras
Bermuda
Azores
ATLANTIC OCEAN
Madeira
Canary Is. 3718
Atlas Mts.
J. Toubkal 4165
Maghreb
Tropic of Cancer
Sahara
A f r i c a
Rio Grande
Lower California
Sierra Madre
C. San Lucas
Revilla Gigedo Is.
Popocatepetl 5452
Pico de Orizaba 5610
Yucatan
Gulf of Mexico
Florida
Florida Str.
Cuba
Bahamas
Greater Antilles
Jamaica
3175
Milwaukee Deep 9200
Hispaniola
Puerto Rico
Sargasso Sea
Caribbean Sea
Lesser Antilles
C. Verde
C. Verde Is.
St. of Gibraltar
Senegal
1752
Gulf of Guinea
C. Palmas
Mt. Came
Hawaiian Is.
Mauna Kea 4205
P A C I F I C
O C E A N
4093
Central America
5775
Trinidad
Isthmus of Panama
Galapagos Is.
Line Is.
Kiritimati
P o l y n e s i a
Marquesas Is.
Llanos
Orinoco
Mt. Roraima 2810
Guiana Highlands
Negro 2994
Japurá
Amazon
Selvas
Chimborazo 6310
Marañón
Juruá
Purús
Madeira
Tapajós
Xingu
South America
Equator
C. de São Roque
Equator
Ascension
St. Helena
6768
8425
L. Titicaca
Bolivian Plateau
Plateau of Mato Grosso
Brazilian Highlands
2890
C. Frio
Trindade
Tropic of Capricorn
Society Is.
Tahiti
Tuamotu Is.
Cook Is.
Tubuai Is.
Pitcairn I.
Easter I.
Chile Trench 8050
Cerro Ojos del Salado 6863
Arch. de Juan Fernández
Cerro Aconcagua 6960
Gran Chaco
Pilcomayo
Paraguay
Paraná
Pampas
R. de la Plata
ATLANTIC OCEAN
Tristan da Cunha
Andes
Negro
Patagonia
4058
-40
-105
2937
S. Georgia
Falkland Is.
Scotia Sea
South Sandwich Is.
Magellan's Str.
Tierra del Fuego
C. Horn
Drake Passage
South Shetland Is.
South Orkney Is.
Antarctic Peninsula
Weddell Sea
Antarctic Circle
Bellingshausen Sea
Alexander I.
Palmer Land
Ronne Ice Shelf
Berkner I.
Caird Coast
Coats Land
Que
Amundsen Sea
Thurston I.
Ellsworth Land
Vinson Massif 4897
Marie Byrd Land
Roosevelt I.
Ross Sea
60

Projection: Winkel III
West from Greenwich

1 2 3 4 5 6 7 8 9

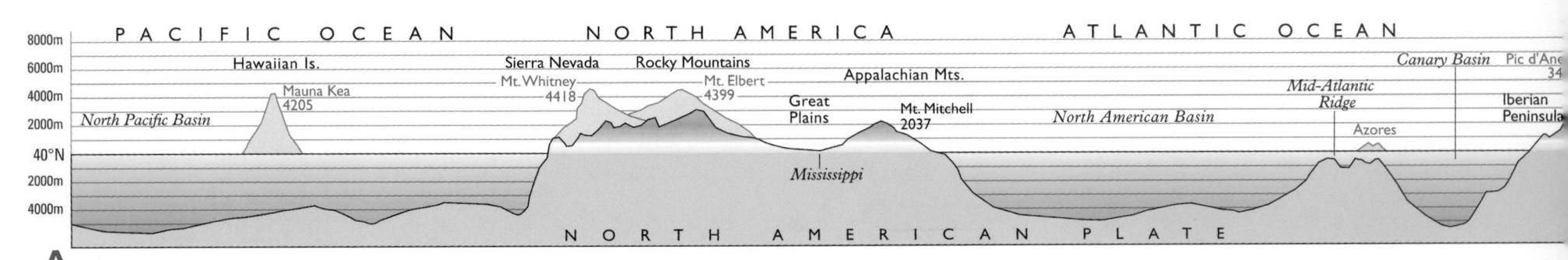

PACIFIC OCEAN   NORTH AMERICA   ATLANTIC OCEAN
8000m
6000m   Hawaiian Is.   Sierra Nevada   Rocky Mountains   Appalachian Mts.   Canary Basin   Pic d'Ane
4000m   Mauna Kea 4205   Mt. Whitney 4418   Mt. Elbert 4399   Mid-Atlantic Ridge   Iberian Peninsula
North Pacific Basin   Great Plains   Mt. Mitchell 2037   *North American Basin*   Azores
2000m
40°N
2000m   Mississippi
4000m
N O R T H   A M E R I C A N   P L A T E
A

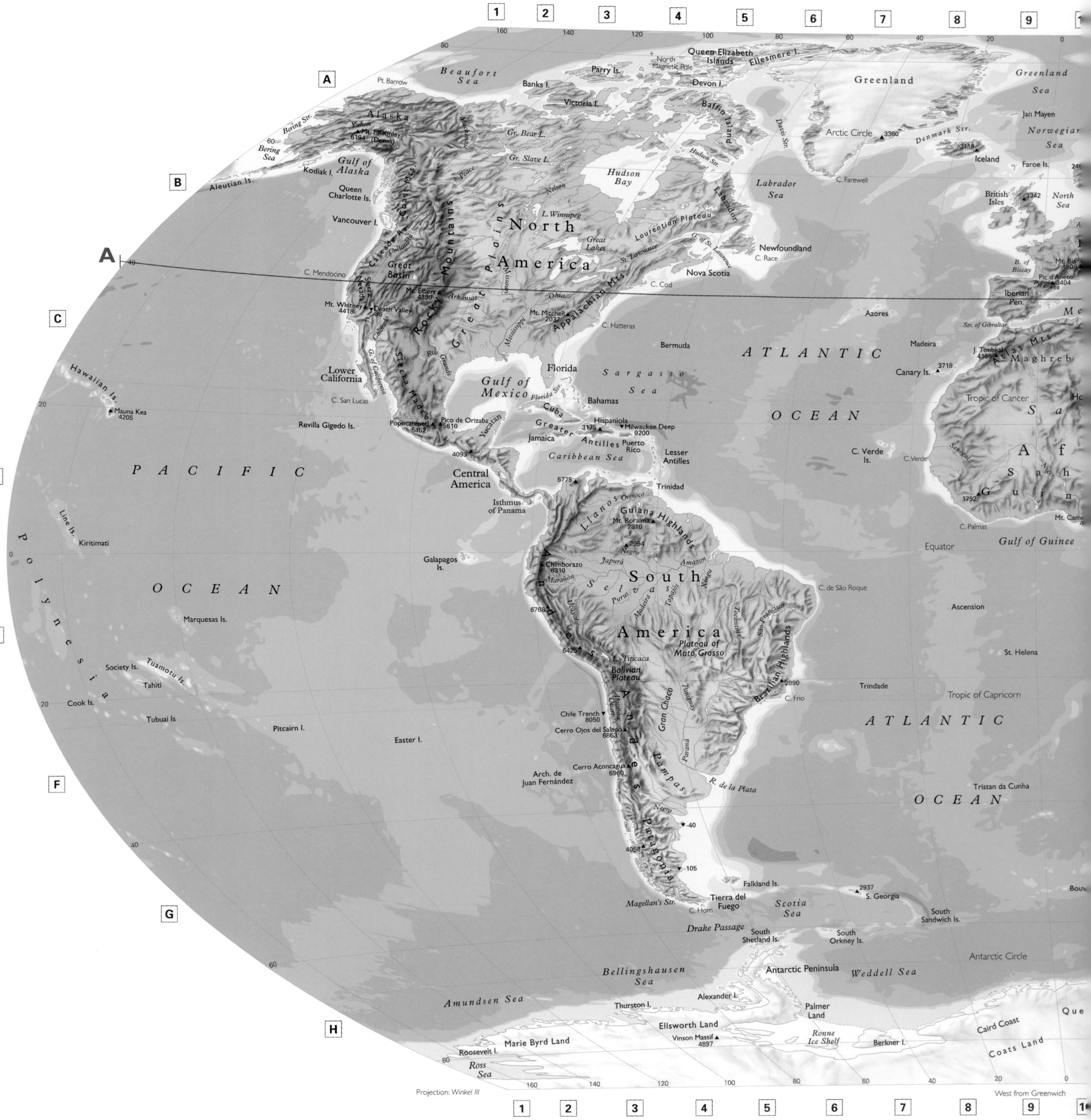

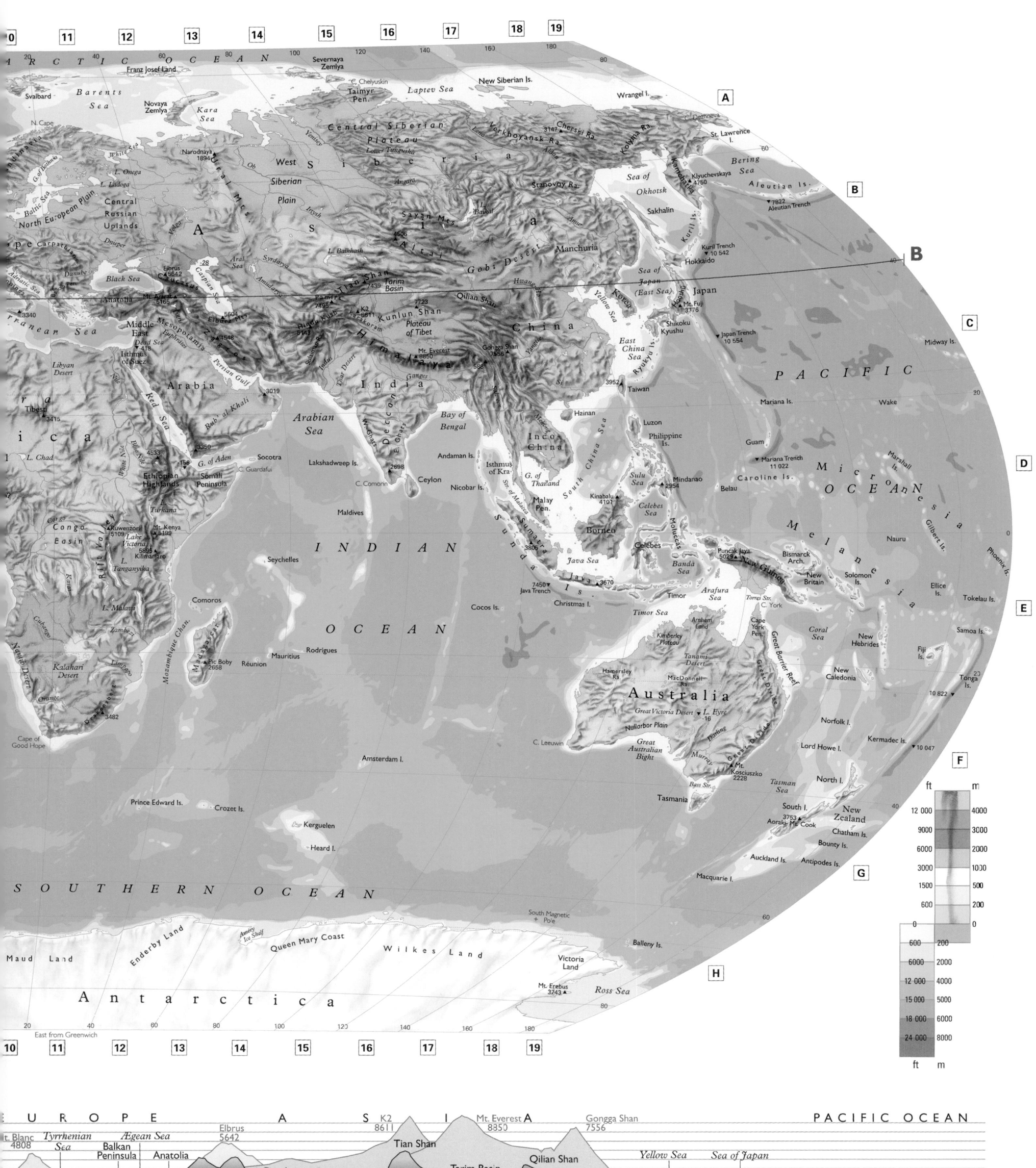

ARCTIC OCEAN

Franz Josef Land

Svalbard

N. Cape

Barents
Sea

Novaya
Zemlya

Kara
Sea

Severnaya
Zemlya

C. Chelyuskin

Taimyr
Pen.

Laptev Sea

New Siberian Is.

Wrangel I.

Dezhneva

L. Onega

Narodnaya
1894

Central Siberian
Plateau

Verkhoyansk Ra.

3147

Cherski Ra.

Kolyma Ra.

St. Lawrence I.

Kamchatka

Klyuchevskaya
4760

Bering
Sea

Aleutian Is.

7822
Aleutian Trench

White Sea

L. Ladoga

West
Siberian
Plain

Ob

Lower Tunguska

Yenisey

Angara

S

i

b

e

r

i

a

Stanovoy Ra.

Sea of
Okhotsk

Sakhalin

Kuril Is.

Kuril Trench
10 542

Hokkaido

Central
Russian
Uplands

Dnieper

Carpathians

Volga

Ural Mts.

Irtysh

L. Baikal

Sayan Mts.

Altai

4506

Gobi Desert

Manchuria

Amur

Sea of
Japan
(East Sea)

Japan

Hokkaido

Danube

Black Sea

Caspian Sea

Elbrus
5642

28

Aral
Sea

Syrdarya

Amudarya

L. Balkhash

Tian Shan
7439

Tarim
Basin

Pamirs
7495

K2
8611

Kunlun Shan

Qilian Shan

7723

Hwang-ho

Korea

Mt. Fuji
3776

Adriatic Sea

Mediterranean Sea

3340

Anatolia

Mt. Ararat
5165

Caucasus

Elbrus
5604

Mesopotamia

Euphrates

Hindu Kush
5143

4546

Karakoram

Plateau
of Tibet

Gongga Shan
7556

East
China
Sea

Shikoku
Kyushu

Japan Trench
10 554

Middle
East

Dead Sea

Isthmus
of Suez

Tigris

Persian Gulf

Thar Desert

Indus

Himalaya

Mt. Everest
8850

3952

Ryukyu Is.

Taiwan

PACIFIC

Midway Is.

Libyan
Desert

Tibesti
3415

Red Sea

Arabia

3019

India

Ganges

Deccan

Ghats

Si

Hainan

Arabian
Sea

Bay of
Bengal

Indo-
China

Luzon

Philippine
Is.

Mariana Is.

Wake

Mariana Trench
11 022

Guam

L. Chad

Bab el
Mandeb

G. of Aden

3350

Socotra

C. Guardafui

Lakshadweep Is.

2698

Andaman Is.

Isthmus
of Kra

G. of
Thailand

South China Sea

Sulu
Sea

Mindanao

Caroline Is.

Belau

MICRONESIA

OCEAN

Marshall
Is.

Nauru

Phoenix Is.

White Nile

Blue Nile

4533

Somali
Peninsula

C. Comorin

Ceylon

Nicobar Is.

Malay
Pen.

Kinabalu
4101

2954

Celebes
Sea

Moluccas

MELANESIA

Ethiopian
Highlands

Turkana

Ruwenzori
5109

Mt. Kenya
5199

Kilimanjaro
5895

Lake
Victoria

Maldives

Seychelles

INDIAN

Sumatra

3806

Borneo

Celebes

Java Sea

Banda
Sea

Puncak Jaya
5029

New Guinea

Bismarck
Arch.

New
Britain

Solomon
Is.

Ellice
Is.

Tokelau Is.

Congo
Basin

Kasai

L. Malawi

Zambezi

Comoros

Mozambique Chan.

Madagascar

Pic Boby
2658

Réunion

OCEAN

Java
7450

Java Trench

3670

Christmas I.

Timor

Arafura
Sea

Torres Str.

C. York

Coral
Sea

New
Hebrides

Fiji
Is.

Samoa Is.

Kalahari
Desert

Okavango

Limpopo

Orange

3482

Cape of
Good Hope

Amsterdam I.

Rodrigues

Mauritius

Cocos Is.

Timor Sea

Kimberley
Plateau

Arnhem
Land

Tanami
Desert

Hamersley
Ra.

MacDonnell
Ra.

Australia

Great Barrier Reef

Great Dividing Ra.

New
Caledonia

Tonga
Is.

10 822

Prince Edward Is.

Crozet Is.

Kerguelen

Heard I.

Great Victoria Desert

L. Eyre
-16

Nullarbor Plain

Great
Australian
Bight

C. Leeuwin

Murray

Darling

Mt.
Kosciuszko
2228

Norfolk I.

Lord Howe I.

Kermadec Is.

10 047

SOUTHERN

OCEAN

Bass Str.

Tasman
Sea

North I.

Macquarie I.

South Magnetic
Pole

Balleny Is.

Tasmania

South I.

Aoraki/Mt Cook
3753

Chatham Is.

Bounty Is.

New
Zealand

Auckland Is.

Antipodes Is.

Maud Land

Enderby Land

Amery
Ice Shelf

Queen Mary Coast

Wilkes Land

Victoria
Land

Antarctica

Mt. Erebus
3743

Ross Sea

East from Greenwich

EUROPE   ASIA   PACIFIC OCEAN

Mt. Blanc
4808

Tyrrhenian
Sea

Ægean Sea

Elbrus
5642

K2
8611

Mt. Everest
8350

Gongga Shan
7556

Apennines

Balkan
Peninsula

Anatolia

Tian Shan

Yellow Sea

Sea of Japan

Caucasus

Caspian
Sea

Pamirs

Tarim Basin

Qilian Shan

Korea

Honshū

40°N

Japan
Trench

Emperor
Seamount
Chain

E U R A S I A N   P L A T E

ft m
12 000 4000
9000 3000
6000 2000
3000 1000
1500 500
600 200
0 0
600 200
6000 2000
12 000 4000
15 000 5000
18 000 6000
24 000 8000
ft m

Equatorial Scale 1·76 000 000

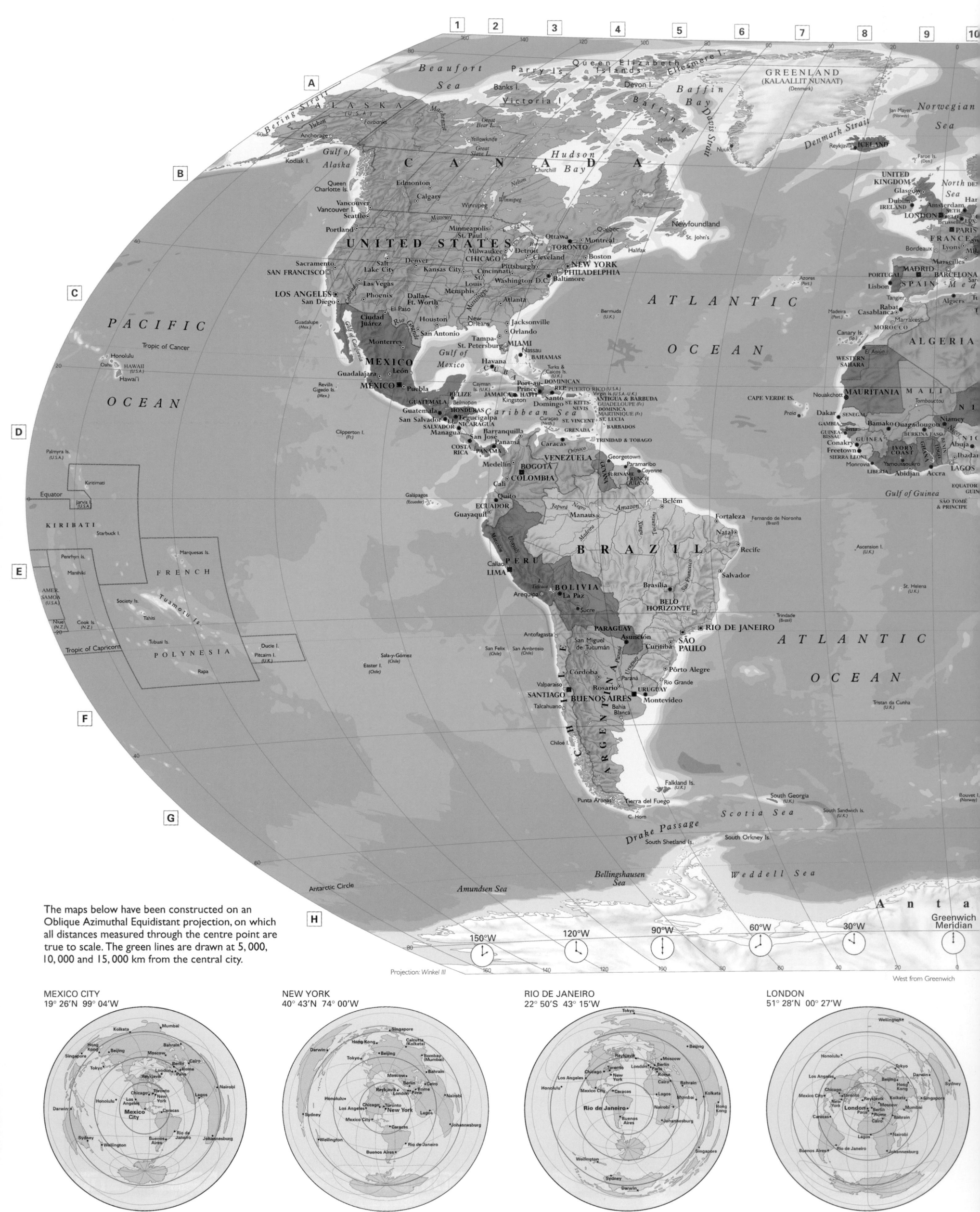

The maps below have been constructed on an Oblique Azimuthal Equidistant projection, on which all distances measured through the centre point are true to scale. The green lines are drawn at 5,000, 10,000 and 15,000 km from the central city.

Projection: Winkel III

West from Greenwich

MEXICO CITY
19° 26'N 99° 04'W

NEW YORK
40° 43'N 74° 00'W

RIO DE JANEIRO
22° 50'S 43° 15'W

LONDON
51° 28'N 00° 27'W

ARCTIC OCEAN

Barents Sea Franz Josef Land (Russia)   *Novaya Zemlya*   Severnaya Zemlya   *Laptev Sea*   New Siberian Is.   *East Siberian Sea*   Wrangel I.

Svalbard (Norway)   *Kara Sea*

A

NORWAY   SWEDEN   FINLAND   Murmansk   Arkhangelsk   Norilsk   Yenisey   Verkhoyansk   Arctic Circle   Yakutsk   Magadan   Okhotsk   *Bering Sea*

Helsinki   ST. PETERSBURG   R U S S I A   *Sea of Okhotsk*   Aleutian Is. (USA)   **B**

Stockholm   ESTONIA   Perm   Yekaterinburg   Tomsk   Krasnoyarsk   L. Baikal   Komsomolsk   Sakhalin   Petropavlovsk-Kamchatskiy

Copenhagen   LATVIA   MOSCOW   Volga   Kazan   Omsk   Novosibirsk   Irkutsk   Ulan Ude   Amur   Khabarovsk

LITHUANIA   Minsk   Samara   Chelyabinsk   Barnaul   Ulan Bator   Harbin   Vladivostok   Sapporo

POLAND   BELARUS   Saratov   Volgograd   KAZAKHSTAN   Astana   Changchun   SHENYANG   Sapporo

Berlin   Warsaw   Kiev   Astrakhan   Aral Sea   L. Balkhash   Almaty   Ürümqi   MONGOLIA   BEIJING   TIANJIN   Dalian   TŌKYŌ   *Japan*

Prague   UKRAINE   Odessa   Caspian Sea   UZBEKISTAN   Bishkek   KYRGYZSTAN   SINKIANG   NORTH KOREA   Pyongyang   SEOUL   ŌSAKA   PACIFIC

Budapest   ROMANIA   Black Sea   GEORGIA   Tbilisi   AZER.   Baku   TURKMENISTAN   Samarkand   Tashkent   TAJIKISTAN   Dushanbe   Taiyuan   SOUTH KOREA   Kitakyūshū

ISTANBUL   Bucharest   ARMENIA   Yerevan   Tabriz   Ashkhabad   CHINA   Lanzhou   Xi'an   Hwang He   Nanjing   SHANGHAI   **C**

BULGARIA   Sofia   Ankara   Baku   Mashhad   Kābul   TIBET   Chengdu   WUHAN   *East China Sea*

GREECE   TURKEY   Izmir   CYPRUS   SYRIA   Beirut   IRAQ   TEHRĀN   Eşfahān   AFGHANISTAN   Islamabad   JAMMU & KASHMIR   Lhasa   CHONGQING   Yangtze   Fuzhou   Ryukyu Is.

Athens   Crete   LEB.   Damascus   IRAN   LAHORE   DELHI   NEPAL   Kathmandu   Kunming   GUANGZHOU   TAIPEI

Tripoli   ISRAEL   Jerusalem   JORDAN   BAGHDAD   Shirāz   New Delhi   BHUTAN   Thimphu   BURMA   Hanoi   HONG KONG   TAIWAN

MALTA   KUWAIT   Kuwait   BAHRAIN   Abu Dhabi   PAKISTAN   Kanpur   Ganges   BANGLADESH   MYANMAR   Naypyidaw

LIBYA   Benghazi   Alexandria   CAIRO   EGYPT   SAUDI   Riyadh   QATAR   Doha   UNITED ARAB EMIRATES   Muscat   KARACHI   AHMADABAD   KOLKATA (Calcutta)   DHAKA   Hainan

Aswan   Nile   Red Sea   Mecca   ARABIA   OMAN   Abu Dhabi   INDIA   Nagpur   HYDERABAD   Rangoon   THAILAND   VIETNAM   Tropic of Cancer

CHAD   SUDAN   Omdurman   Khartoum   YEMEN   Sana'   Aden   Gulf of Aden   Socotra (Yemen)   MUMBAI (Bombay)   Bay of Bengal   BANGKOK   CAMBODIA   PHILIPPINES   **D**

N'Djamena   Addis Ababa   DJIBOUTI   BANGALORE (Bengaluru)   CHENNAI (Madras)   Andaman Is. (India)   Phnom Penh   HO CHI MINH CITY   MANILA

CENTRAL AFRICAN REP.   SOUTH SUDAN   Juba   ETHIOPIA   SOMALI REP.   Lakshadweep (India)   Nicobar Is. (India)   NORTHERN MARIANAS (USA)   GUAM (USA)

CAMEROON   Bangui   UGANDA   Kampala   KENYA   Nairobi   Mogadishu   SRI LANKA   Colombo   MALDIVES   MALAYSIA   Medan   BRUNEI   Caroline Is.   Yap   Truk   Pohnpei   MARSHALL IS.

CONGO   KINSHASA   RWANDA   BURUNDI   TANZANIA   Dodoma   Dar es Salaam   Zanzibar   SEYCHELLES   Kuala Lumpur   SINGAPORE   Borneo   Celebes   FED. STATES OF MICRONESIA   PALAU

ANGOLA   Lubumbashi   MALAWI   Amirante Is. (Seychelles)   Aldabra Is. (Seychelles)   Chagos Arch. (U.K.)   Palembang   Banjarmasin   INDONESIA   Makassar   Papua   PAPUA NEW GUINEA   New Ireland   New Britain   SOLOMON IS.   NAURU   KIRIBATI

ZAMBIA   Lusaka   Harare   MOZAMBIQUE   COMOROS   Mayotte   JAKARTA   Bandung   Java   Surabaya   Dili   EAST TIMOR   *Arafura Sea*   Port Moresby   TUVALU

NAMIBIA   ZIMBABWE   Bulawayo   MADAGASCAR   Antananarivo   MAURITIUS   Réunion (Fr.)   Cocos Is. (Austral.)   Christmas I. (Austral.)   C. York   Darwin   VANUATU   FIJI   Suva

BOTSWANA   Gaborone   Pretoria   Maputo   Cargados Carajos (Mauritius)   Rodrigues (Mauritius)   Port Hedland   Cairns   NEW CALEDONIA   Port Vila   TONGA

Windhoek   Johannesburg   SWAZ.   LES.   Alice Springs   Townsville   **E**

SOUTH AFRICA   Durban   AUSTRALIA   Brisbane   Norfolk I. (Austral.)   Lord Howe I. (Austral.)

Cape Town   C. of Good Hope   Port Elizabeth   *INDIAN OCEAN*   Prince Edward Is. (S. Africa)   Crozet Is. (Fr.)   Amsterdam I. (Fr.)   St. Paul I. (Fr.)   Geraldton   Kalgoorlie-Boulder   Perth   Fremantle   *Great Australian Bight*   Adelaide   Newcastle   Sydney   Kermadec Is. (N.Z.)   **F**

Kerguelen (Fr.)   McDonald Is. (Austral.)   Heard I. (Austral.)   Canberra   *Tasman Sea*   Auckland   North I.

Melbourne   Tasmania   Hobart   NEW ZEALAND   Wellington

South I.   Christchurch   Chatham Is. (N.Z.)

SOUTHERN OCEAN   Dunedin   Bounty Is. (N.Z.)   **G**

Antipodes Is. (N.Z.)

Macquarie I. (Austral.)   Campbell I. (N.Z.)

Arctica   Antarctic Circle   **H**

30°E   60°E   90°E   120°E   150°E   IDL   *Ross Sea*   30°W

East from Greenwich

The time at this longitude when it is 12.00 (noon) at Greenwich

CAPE TOWN
33° 55'S 18° 35'E

DELHI
28° 39'N 77° 13'E

TOKYO
35° 33'N 139° 46'E

SYDNEY
33° 56' S 151° 10'E

COPYRIGHT PHILIP'S

100 0 200 400 600 800 1000 1200 1400 km

1:28 000 000

100 0 200 400 600 800 1000 miles

Projection : Zenithal Equidistant

West from Greenwich   East from Greenwich

COPYRIGHT PHILIP'S

Maximum extent of sea ice

Minimum extent of sea ice (September 2007)

Ice caps and permanent ice shelf

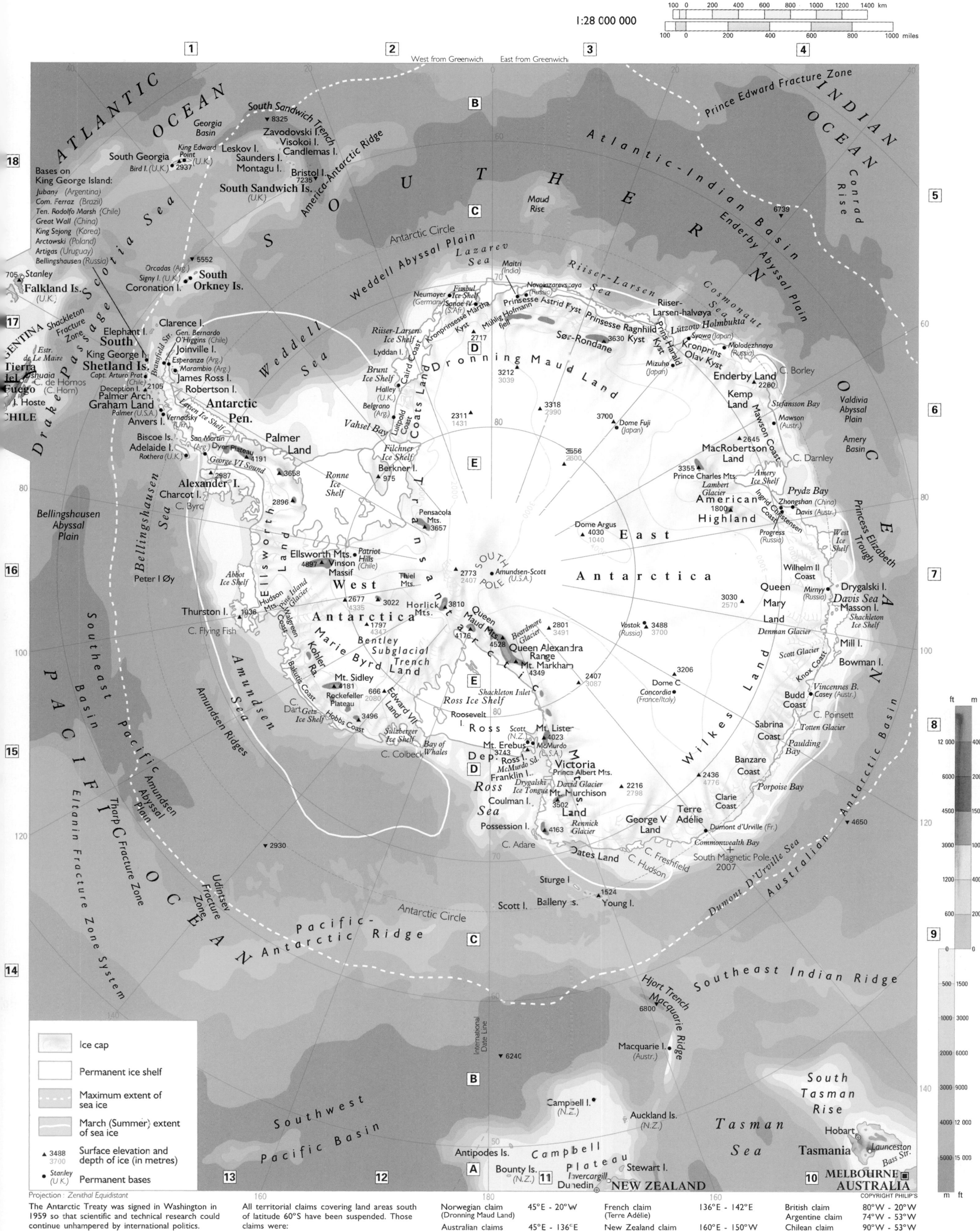

West from Greenwich
East from Greenwich

Ice cap

Permanent ice shelf

**Maximum extent of
sea ice**

**March (Summer) extent
of sea ice**

▲3488
3700   Surface elevation and
depth of ice (in metres)

• Stanley
(U.K.)   Permanent bases

Projection : Zenithal Equidistant

The Antarctic Treaty was signed in Washington in
1959 so that scientific and technical research could
continue unhampered by international politics.

All territorial claims covering land areas south
of latitude 60°S have been suspended. Those
claims are:

Norwegian claim (Dronning Maud Land)	45°E - 20°W
Australian claims	45°E - 136°E 142°E - 160°E
French claim (Terre Adélie)	136°E - 142°E
New Zealand claim (Ross Dependency)	160°E - 150°W
British claim	80°W - 20°W
Argentine claim	74°W - 53°W
Chilean claim	90°W - 53°W

COPYRIGHT PHILIP'S

Equatorial Scale 1:41 000 000

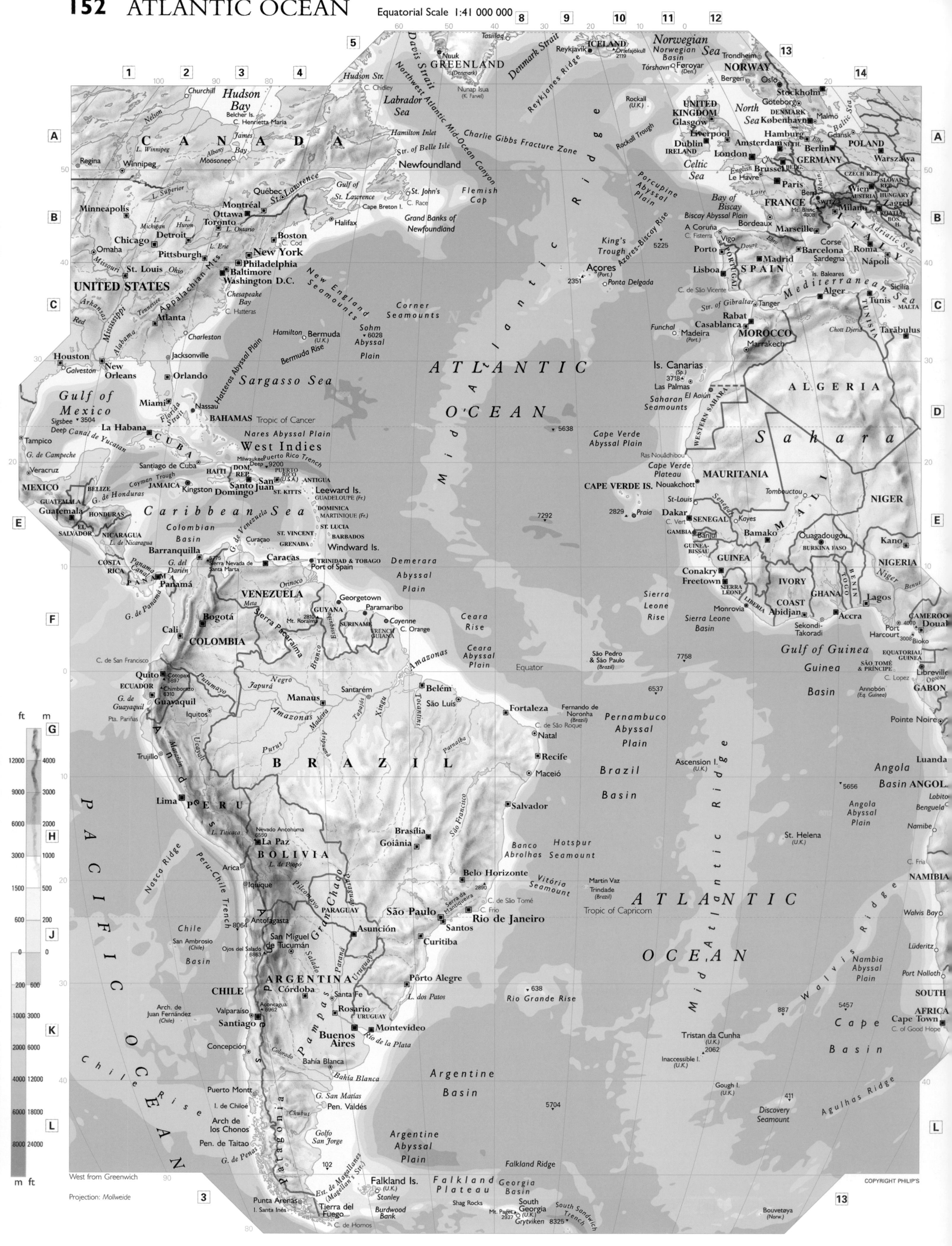

COPYRIGHT PHILIP'S

West from Greenwich

Projection: Mollweide

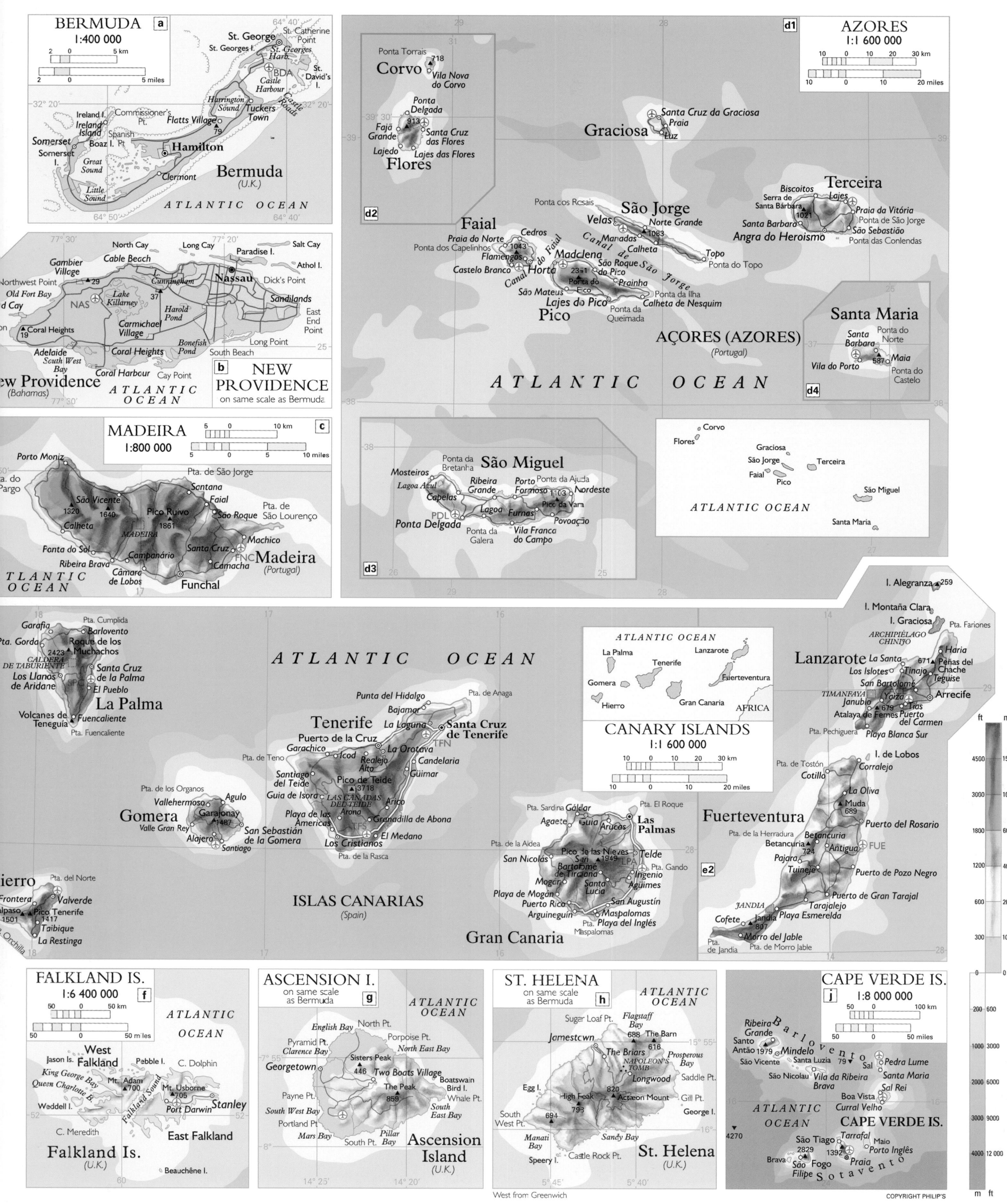

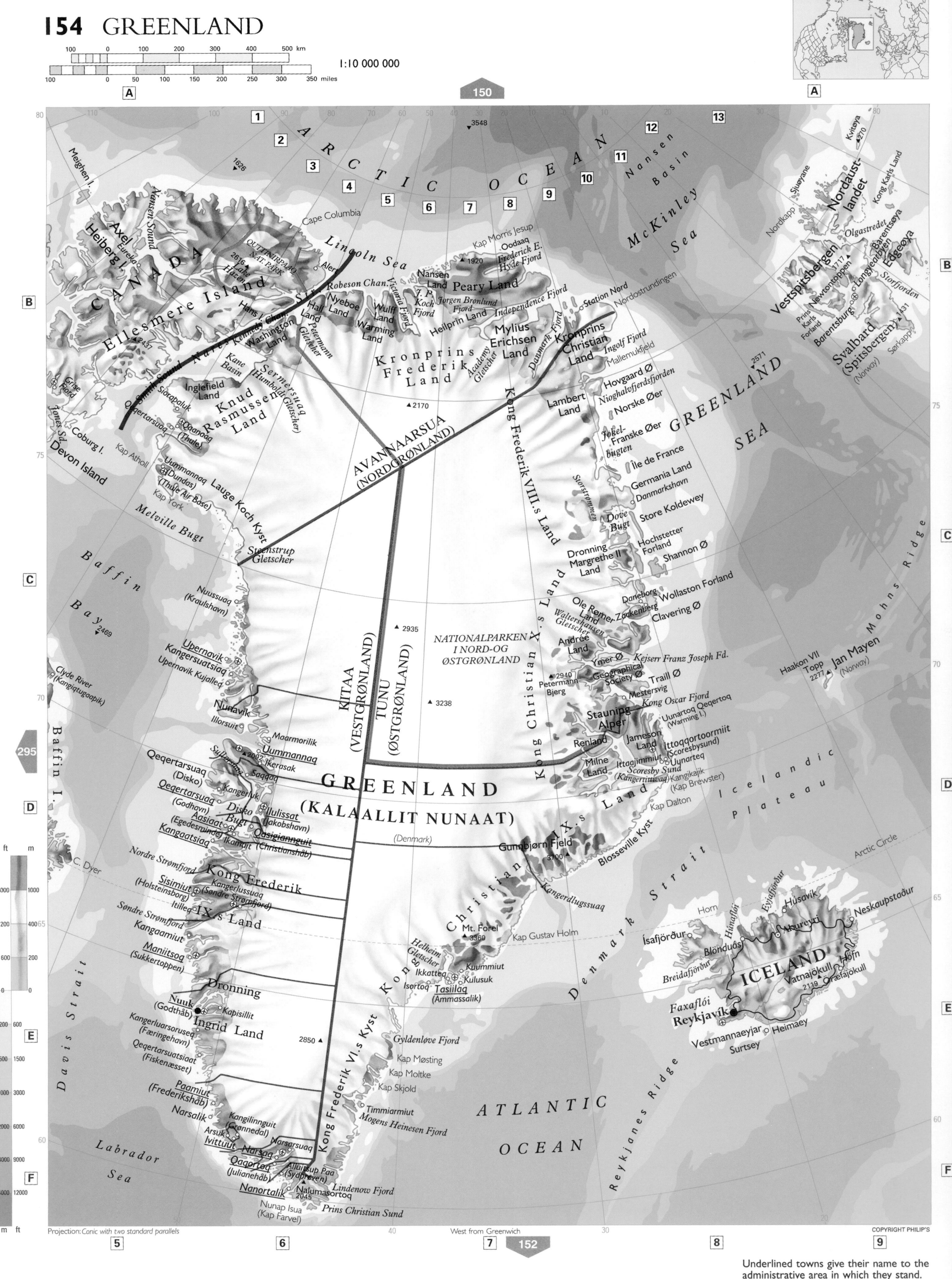

100 0 100 200 300 400 500 km
1:10 000 000
100 0 50 100 150 200 250 300 350 miles

Kvitøya

A

B

C

D

E

F

Projection: Conic with two standard parallels

West from Greenwich

COPYRIGHT PHILIP'S

Underlined towns give their name to the
administrative area in which they stand.

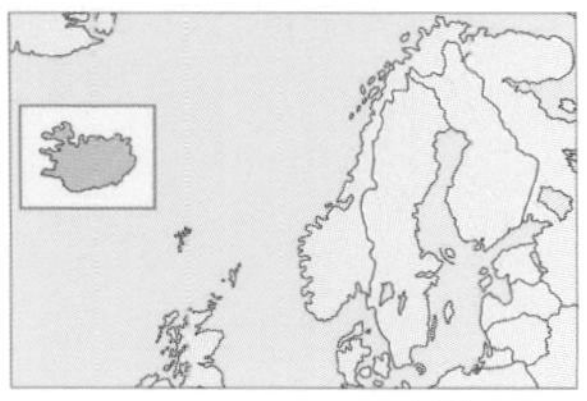

1:2 000 000

COPYRIGHT PHILIP'S

Projection: Polyconic

West from Greenwich

GREENLAND SEA

ATLANTIC OCEAN

DENMARK STRAIT

ICELAND

Arctic Circle

Breiðafjörður

Faxaflói

Húnaflói

Vatnajökull

Hofsjökull

Langjökull

Myrdalsjökull

Eyjafjörður

Skagafjörður

Reykjavík
Kópavogur
Hafnarfjörður
Garðabær
Mosfellsbær
Akranes
Borgarnes
Selfoss
Keflavík
Grindavík
Höfn
Egilsstaðir
Akureyri
Húsavík
Ísafjörður
Siglufjörður
Sauðárkrókur
Blönduós
Vestmannaeyjar

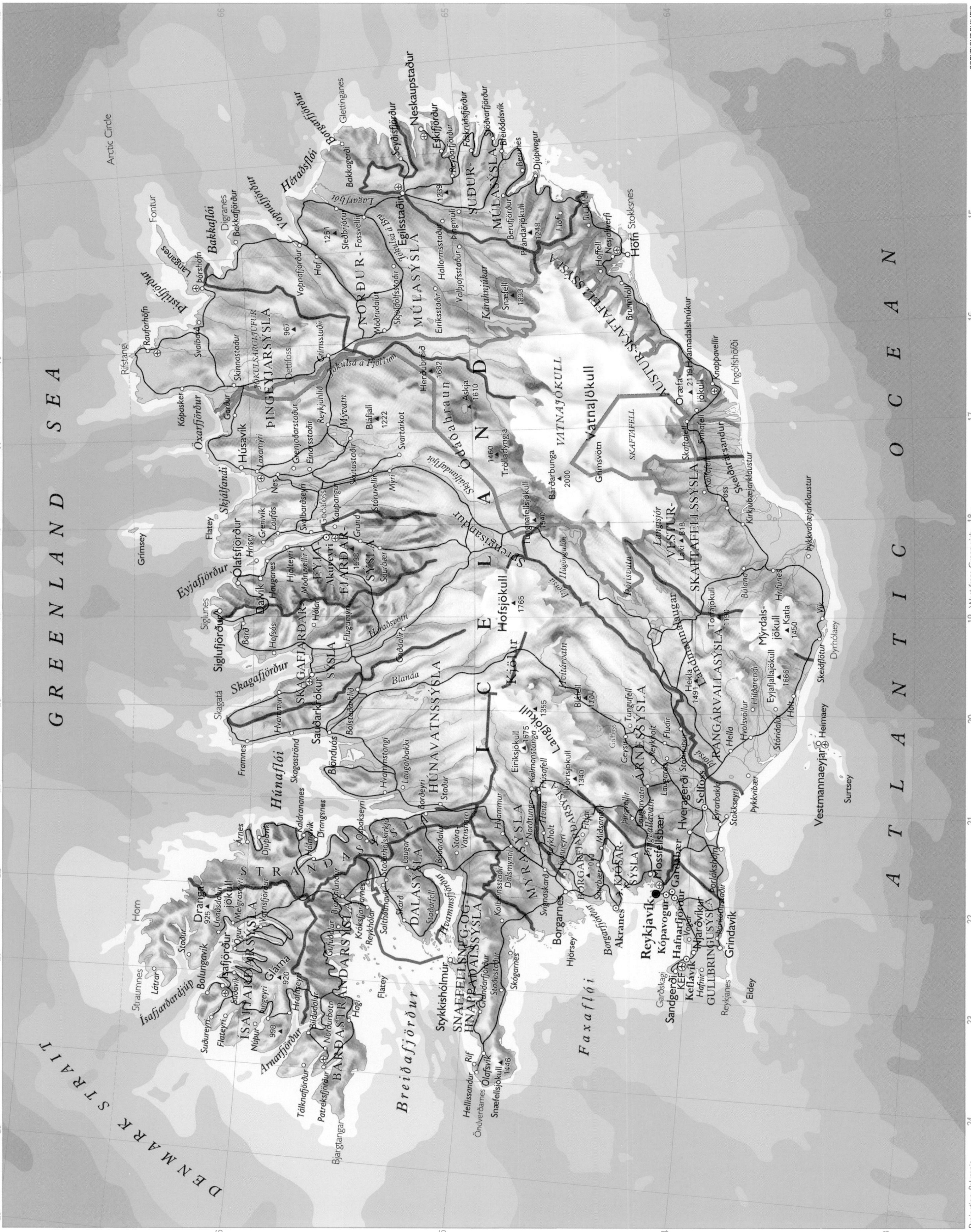

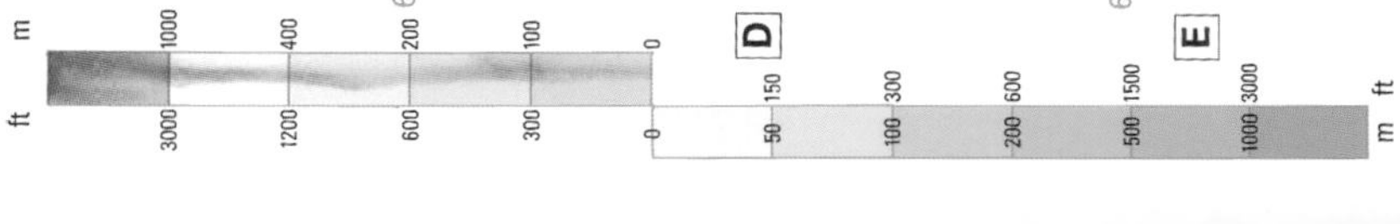

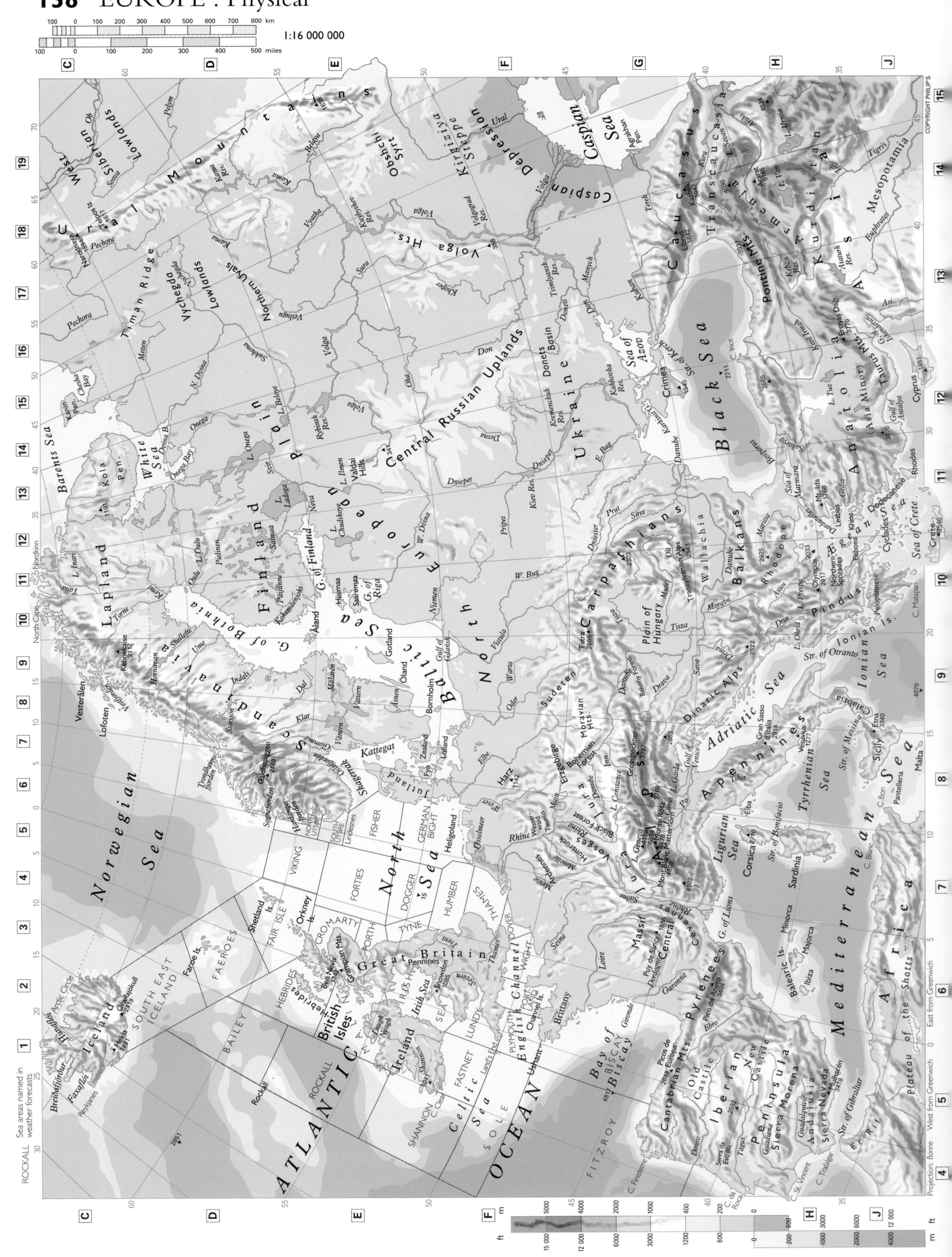

1:16 000 000

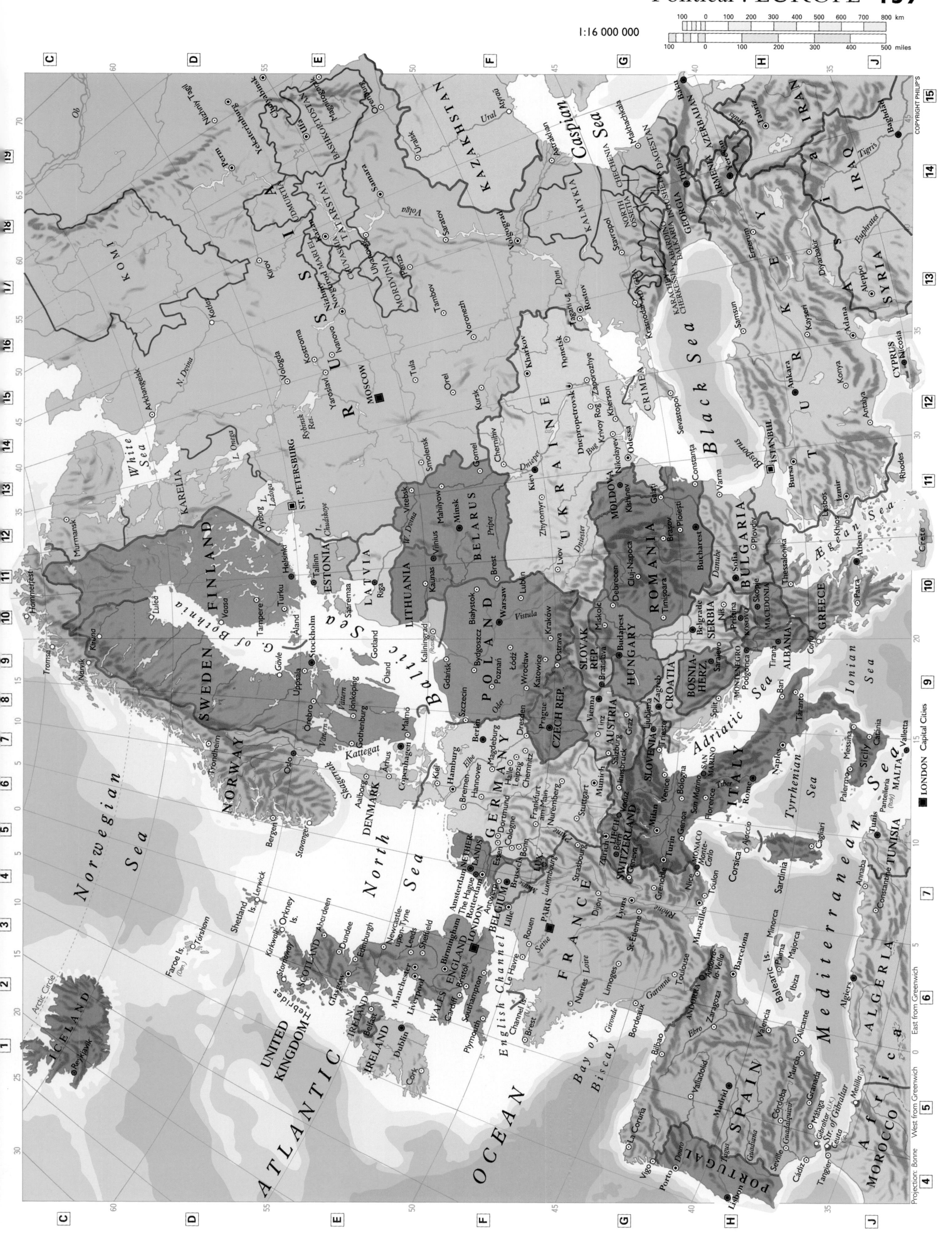

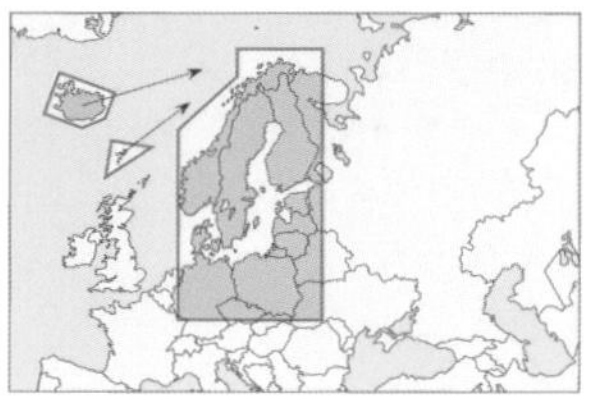

50 0 25 50 75 100 125 150 175 km

50 0 25 50 75 100 125 miles

1:4 800 000

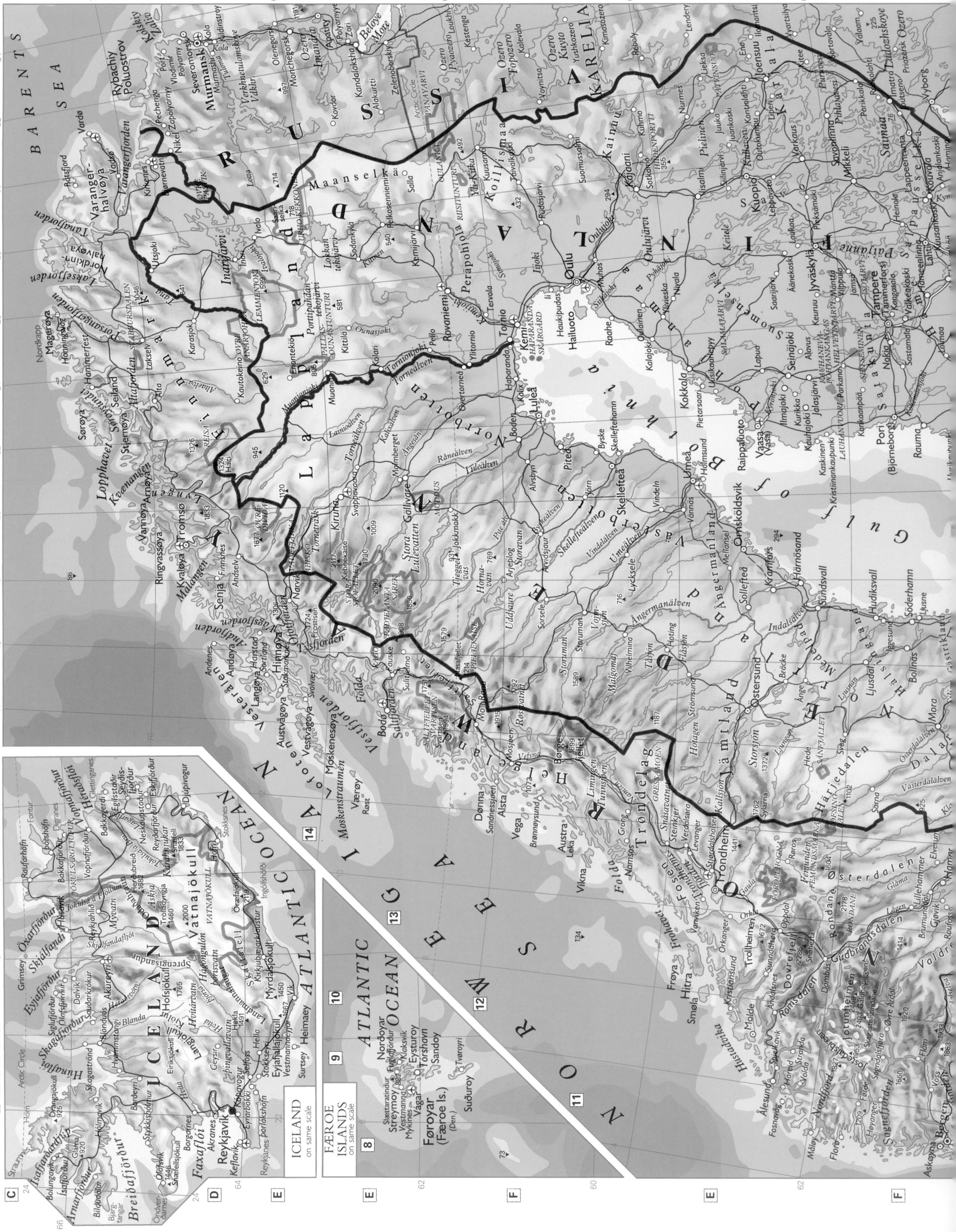
BARENTS SEA
RUSSIA
KARELIA
FINLAND
Lapland
Gulf of Bothnia
NORWEGIAN SEA
ATLANTIC OCEAN
ICELAND
Vatnajökull
Reykjavík
Akureyri
ICELAND on same scale
FÆROE ISLANDS on same scale
Føroyar (Færoe Is.) (Den.)
Tórshavn
Lofoten
Vesterålen
Tromsø
Narvik
Bodø
Trondheim
Ålesund
Bergen
Oulu
Luleå
Umeå
Vaasa
Tampere
Pori
Murmansk
Kiruna
Hammerfest
Arctic Circle
22 West from Greenwich

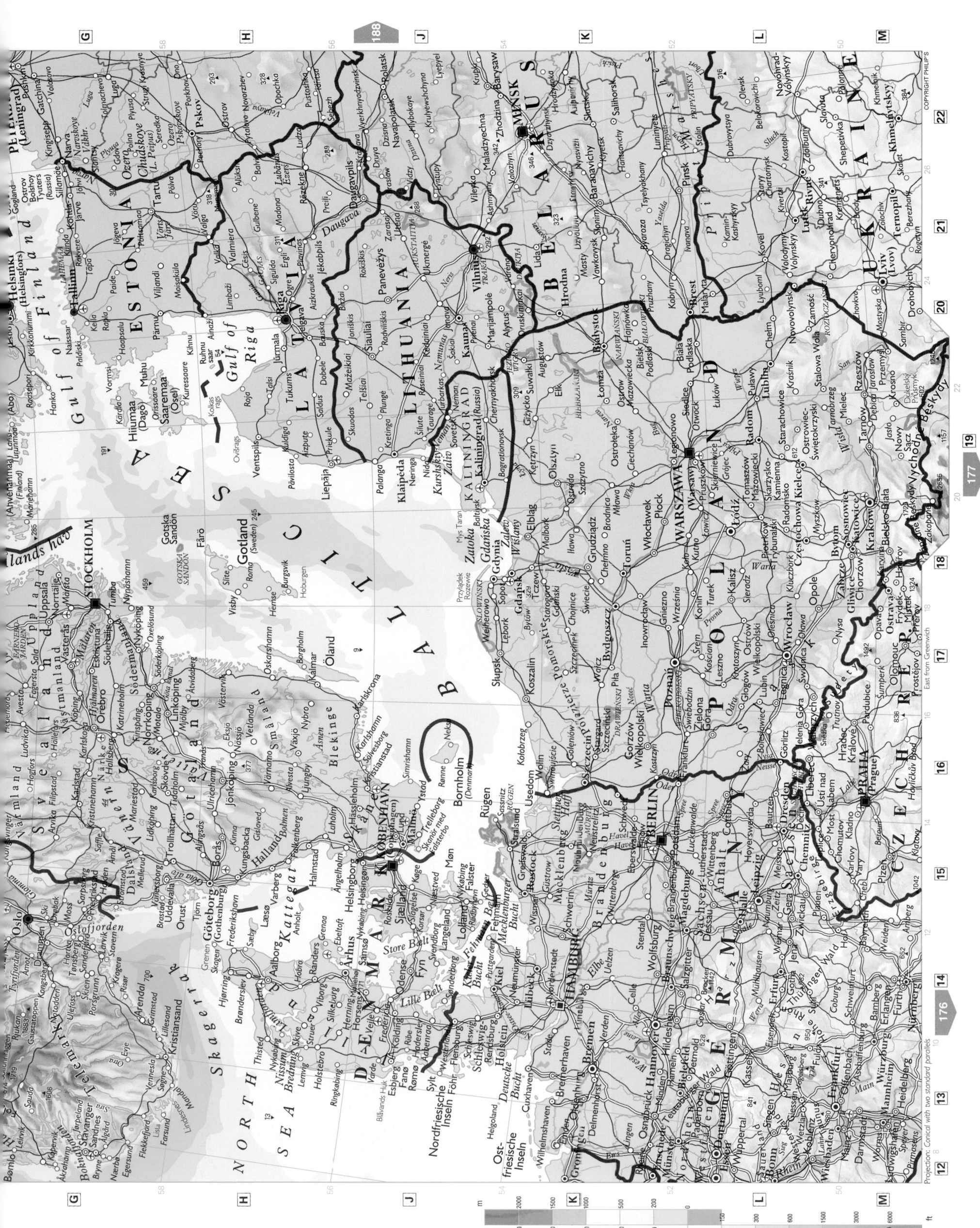

1:2 000 000

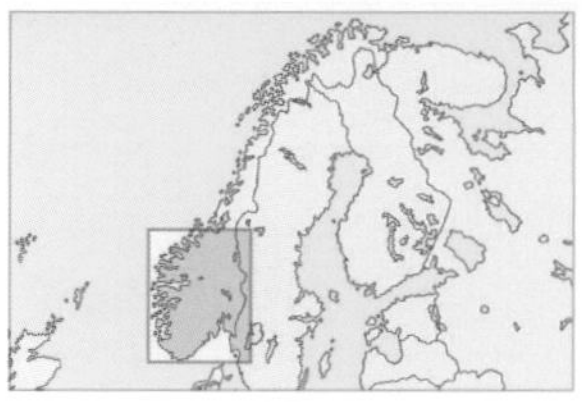

10 0 10 20 30 40 50 60 70 80 90 km
10 0 10 20 30 40 50 60 miles

NORWEGIAN SEA

Trondheim

SØR-TRØNDELAG

MØRE OG ROMSDAL

Ålesund
Molde
Kristiansund

Dovrefjell
DOVREFJELL-SUNNDALSFJELLA
Snøhetta 2286

REINHEIMEN

RONDANE
Rondslottet 2178

Jotunheimen
Galdhøpiggen 2452
Glittertind 2469

JOSTEDALSBREEN

OPPLAND

HEDMARK

SOGN OG FJORDANE

Sognefjorden

FJORDANE

Lillehammer

Gjøvik
Hamar
Elverum

Hardangerjøkulen

HALLINGSKARVET

HORDALAND

Bergen

BUSKERUD

Hardangervidda

AKERSHUS

Oslo

Drammen

TELEMARK

Gaustatoppen
1883

VESTFOLD

ØSTFOLD

Tønsberg
Sandefjord
Larvik

Fredrikstad

Stavanger
Sandnes

ROGALAND

Haugesund
Karmøy

Ryfylke

Jæren

VEST-AGDER

AUST-AGDER

Arendal

Kristiansand

Flekkefjord

Skagerrak

SWEDEN

Norskerenna

1:4 000 000

50 0 25 50 75 100 125 150 175 km
50 0 25 50 75 100 125 miles

ATLANTIC OCEAN

NORWAY
Askøyna
Bergen
Osøyro
Stord
Bømlo Leirvik
Haugesund
Kopervik
Åkrahamn
Boknafjorden
Stavanger
Sandnes
Bryne
Nærbø

Shetland Is.
(U.K.)
Yell
Unst
Fetlar
Foula
Mainland
Lerwick

Fair Isle

Orkney Is.
Westray Sanday
Stronsay
Mainland
Hoy Kirkwall
South Ronaldsay
Pentland Firth

C. Wrath
Thurso
Wick
Helmsdale
Golspie
Lairg
Tain
Ullapool Dingwall Elgin Buckie Banff Fraserburgh
North West Highlands
Lewis
Stornoway
Harris
North Uist
Benbecula
South Uist
Barra
St. Kilda (U.K.)
Outer Hebrides
Skye
Portree
Mallaig
Rhum Eigg
Coll
Tiree
Tobermory
Mull
Colonsay
Jura
Islay

SCOTLAND
Inverness Nairn Aviemore
CAIRNGORMS Mts.
Ben Nevis
Fort William
Grampian Mts.
Forfar
Montrose
Arbroath
Dundee
St. Andrews
Perth
Stirling
Glenrothes
Kirkcaldy
Dunbar
GLASGOW Edinburgh
Paisley Motherwell
Greenock East Kilbride Hamilton
Dumbarton
Oban
Loch Lomond
Loch Fyne
Loch Awe

NORTH SEA

Berwick-upon-Tweed
Galashiels
Jedburgh
Hawick
Cheviot Hills
Alnwick
Southern Uplands
Ayr
Kilmarnock
Irvine
Campbeltown
Arran
Girvan
Kirkcudbright
Dumfries
Annan
Carlisle
Stranraer
Workington
Whitehaven
Mull of Galloway

NORTHUMBERLAND
Newcastle-upon-Tyne
South Shields
Hexham Gateshead Sunderland
Durham
Darlington Hartlepool
Redcar
Middlesbrough
Stockton-on-Tees
Scarborough
N. YORK MOORS

Cumbrian Mts.
LAKE DISTRICT
Barrow-in-Furness
Pennines
Lancaster
YORKSHIRE DALES
Harrogate
Bridlington
York
Beverley
Kingston upon Hull
Humber

UNITED KINGDOM

NORTHERN IRELAND
Londonderry
Coleraine
Ballymena
Larne
Bangor
Belfast
Lisburn
Lurgan Portadown
Armagh Newry
Omagh
Enniskillen
Lough Neagh
Lough Erne

IRELAND
Letterkenny
Buncrana
Malin Hd.
Donegal
Sligo
Ballina
Achill I.
Westport
Castlebar
Lough Mask
Lough Corrib
Connemara
Galway
Galway B.
Aran Is.
BURREN
Ennis
Kilrush
Shannon
Limerick
Listowel
Tralee
Dingle
Killarney
Carrauntoohill
Macgillycuddy's Reeks
Mallow
Bantry
Kinsale
Bandon
Cork
Cobh
C. Clear
Youghal
Dungarvan
Waterford
Clonmel
Carrick-on-Suir
Tipperary
Thurles
Kilkenny
Carlow
Athy
Port Laoise
Tullamore
Athlone
Roscommon
Longford
Mullingar
Lough Ree
Lough Derg
Birr
Leitrim
Cavan
Ceanannus Mor
Navan
DUBLIN
Dun Laoghaire
Bray
Wicklow Mts.
Arklow
Wexford
Rosslare

Lough Gara

Drogheda
Dundalk
Castleblaney
Clones
Monaghan

IRISH SEA
Douglas
I. of Man
Blackpool
Preston
Blackburn Burnley
Bolton
Southport
MANCHESTER
LIVERPOOL Stockport
Warrington
Holyhead
Anglesey
Bangor
Colwyn Bay
Chester
Wrexham
Crewe
PEAK DISTRICT
Derby
Stoke-on-Trent
Pwllheli
Snowdon
SNOWDONIA
Cambrian Mts.
Welshpool
Shrewsbury
Telford
Cardigan Bay
Aberystwyth
Cardigan

Leeds
Bradford
Halifax Huddersfield
Barnsley
Sheffield Doncaster Rotherham
Chesterfield
Scunthorpe
Grimsby
Lincoln
Louth
Skegness
Boston
The Wash
Cromer
THE BROADS
Mansfield
Nottingham
King's Lynn
Norwich
Great Yarmouth
Lowestoft

ENGLAND

WALES
Llanelli
Swansea
Port Talbot
Neath
Merthyr Tydfil
Rhondda
Cwmbran
Newport
Cardiff
Barry
BRECON BEACONS
Carmarthen
Haverfordwest
Milford Haven
Pembroke
Fishguard
PEMBROKESHIRE COAST
St. George's Channel

BIRMINGHAM
WOLVERHAMPTON
Reddich
Worcester
Hereford
Gloucester
Cheltenham
Leamington Spa
Rugby
Coventry
Nuneaton
Leicester
Corby
Peterborough
Northampton
Bedford
Cambridge
Bury St. Edmunds
Thetford
Ipswich
Felixstowe
Harwich
Colchester
Chelmsford
COTSWOLD HILLS
Oxford
Swindon
Newbury
Reading
Milton Keynes
Stevenage
Luton
Hemel Hempstead
Harlow
Watford
Slough
LONDON
Basildon
Southend-on-Sea

Bristol Channel
Weston-super-Mare
EXMOOR
Barnstaple
Bude
Taunton
Yeovil
Bridgwater
Bath
Bristol
Chippenham
Salisbury
Basingstoke
Guildford
Woking
Reigate
Crawley
Maidstone
Canterbury
Margate
Dover
Folkestone
Hastings
Eastbourne
Brighton
Worthing
Chichester
Portsmouth
Southampton
Bournemouth
Poole
Weymouth
Isle of Wight
Newport
Winchester
Fareham
Havant
Newbury

DARTMOOR
Exeter
Exmouth
Torbay
Plymouth
St. Austell
Truro
Newquay
Falmouth
Penzance
Land's End
Isles of Scilly

CELTIC SEA

ENGLISH CHANNEL
Str. of Dover

NETHERLANDS
Texel
Den Helder
Alkmaar
Haarlem
's-Gravenhage (Den Haag)
Hoek van Holland
ROTTERDAM
Dordrecht
Vlissingen
Zeebrugge
Oostende
Brugge
Gent
Antwerpen
Mechelen
BELGIUM
BRUSSEL (Bruxelles)
LILLE
Tournai
Valenciennes
Cambrai

FRANCE
Dunkerque
Calais
St-Omer
Boulogne-sur-Mer
Le Touquet-Paris-Plage
Étaples
Béthune
Bruay-la-Buissière
Bruay-la-Buissière
C. Gris-Nez
Le Tréport
Abbeville
St. Quentin
Laon
Dieppe
Fécamp
Pays de Caux
Amiens
PICARDIE
Rouen
Le Havre
Alderney
C. de la Hague
Pte. de Barfleur
Cherbourg
Valognes
Bayeux
Caen
Lisieux
Elbeuf
Seine
Guernsey
St. Peter Port
Sark
Jersey
St. Helier
Channel Is. (U.K.)
Cotentin
COPYRIGHT PHILIP'S
East from Greenwich
West from Greenwich
Projection: Conical with two standard parallels

1:1 600 000

10 0 10 20 30 40 50 60 70 80 km
10 0 10 20 30 40 50 miles

SCOTLAND
Kintyre

A T L A N T I C   O C E A N

NORTHERN IRELAND

Londonderry
Belfast

DONEGAL
TYRONE
ANTRIM
DOWN
ARMAGH
FERMANAGH
MONAGHAN
LEITRIM
SLIGO
MAYO
CAVAN
LONGFORD
ROSCOMMON
LOUTH
MEATH
WESTMEATH
Connacht
GALWAY
I R E L A N D
Leinster
OFFALY
KILDARE
DUBLIN
Dublin
Dun Laoghaire
LAOIS
WICKLOW
CARLOW
CLARE
TIPPERARY
KILKENNY
WEXFORD
LIMERICK
Munster
Limerick
Golden Vale
KERRY
CORK
WATERFORD
Cork
Waterford
Killarney
Macgillycuddy's Reeks

I R I S H   S E A

St. George's Channel

WALES

C E L T I C   S E A

North Channel
Firth of Clyde

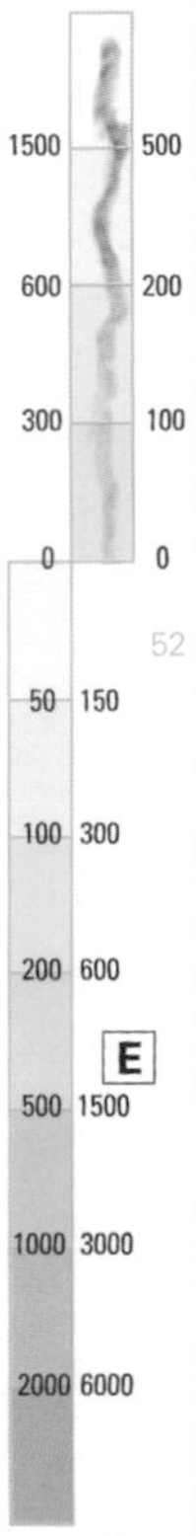

Projection : Lambert's Conformal Conic
West from Greenwich
COPYRIGHT PHILIP'S

ft m
1500 500
600 200
300 100
0 0
50 150
100 300
200 600
500 1500
1000 3000
2000 6000
m ft

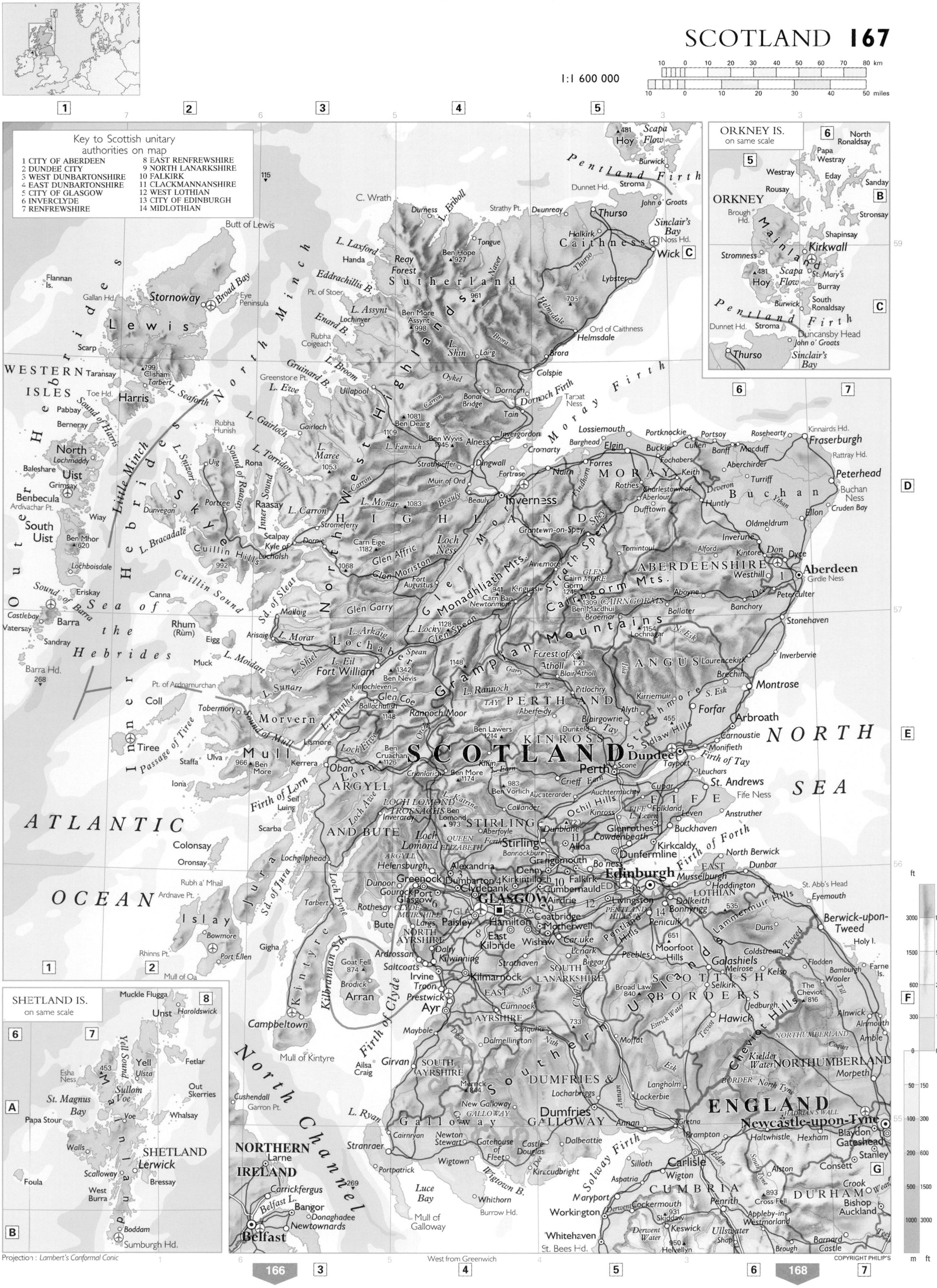
1:1 600 000
10 0 10 20 30 40 50 60 70 80 km
10 0 10 20 30 40 50 miles
Key to Scottish unitary authorities on map
1 CITY OF ABERDEEN
2 DUNDEE CITY
3 WEST DUNBARTONSHIRE
4 EAST DUNBARTONSHIRE
5 CITY OF GLASGOW
6 INVERCLYDE
7 RENFREWSHIRE
8 EAST RENFREWSHIRE
9 NORTH LANARKSHIRE
10 FALKIRK
11 CLACKMANNANSHIRE
12 WEST LOTHIAN
13 CITY OF EDINBURGH
14 MIDLOTHIAN
ORKNEY IS.
on same scale
SHETLAND IS.
on same scale
SCOTLAND
WESTERN ISLES
Outer Hebrides
Inner Hebrides
Lewis
Harris
North Uist
South Uist
Barra
Skye
Mull
Islay
Jura
Arran
Stornoway
Inverness
Aberdeen
Dundee
Perth
Stirling
Edinburgh
GLASGOW
Paisley
Ayr
Dumfries
Carlisle
Fort William
Oban
Thurso
Wick
Kirkwall
Lerwick
Belfast
Newcastle-upon-Tyne
HIGHLAND
MORAY
ABERDEENSHIRE
ANGUS
PERTH AND KINROSS
ARGYLL AND BUTE
STIRLING
FIFE
LOTHIAN
SCOTTISH BORDERS
DUMFRIES & GALLOWAY
SOUTH AYRSHIRE
NORTHUMBERLAND
CUMBRIA
DURHAM
ENGLAND
NORTHERN IRELAND
ORKNEY
SHETLAND
Grampian Mountains
Cairngorm Mts.
Monadhliath Mts.
Southern Uplands
Cheviot Hills
Glen More
North West Highlands
Sutherland
Caithness
Buchan
ATLANTIC OCEAN
NORTH SEA
Sea of the Hebrides
The Minch
Little Minch
North Channel
Pentland Firth
Moray Firth
Firth of Forth
Firth of Clyde
Firth of Lorn
Firth of Tay
Solway Firth
Ben Nevis 1342
Ben Macdhui 1309
Projection : Lambert's Conformal Conic
West from Greenwich
COPYRIGHT PHILIP'S

166
168

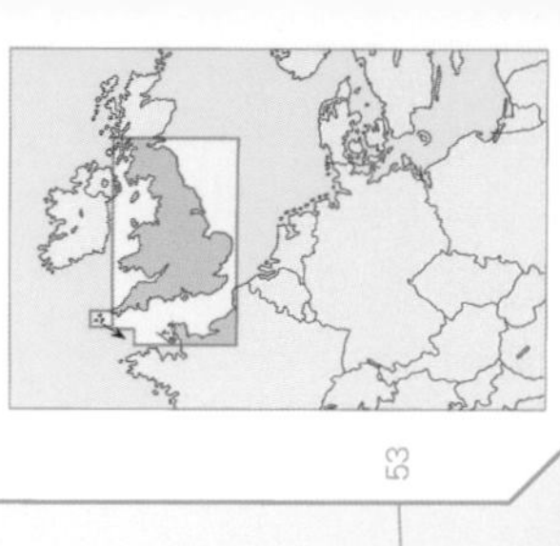

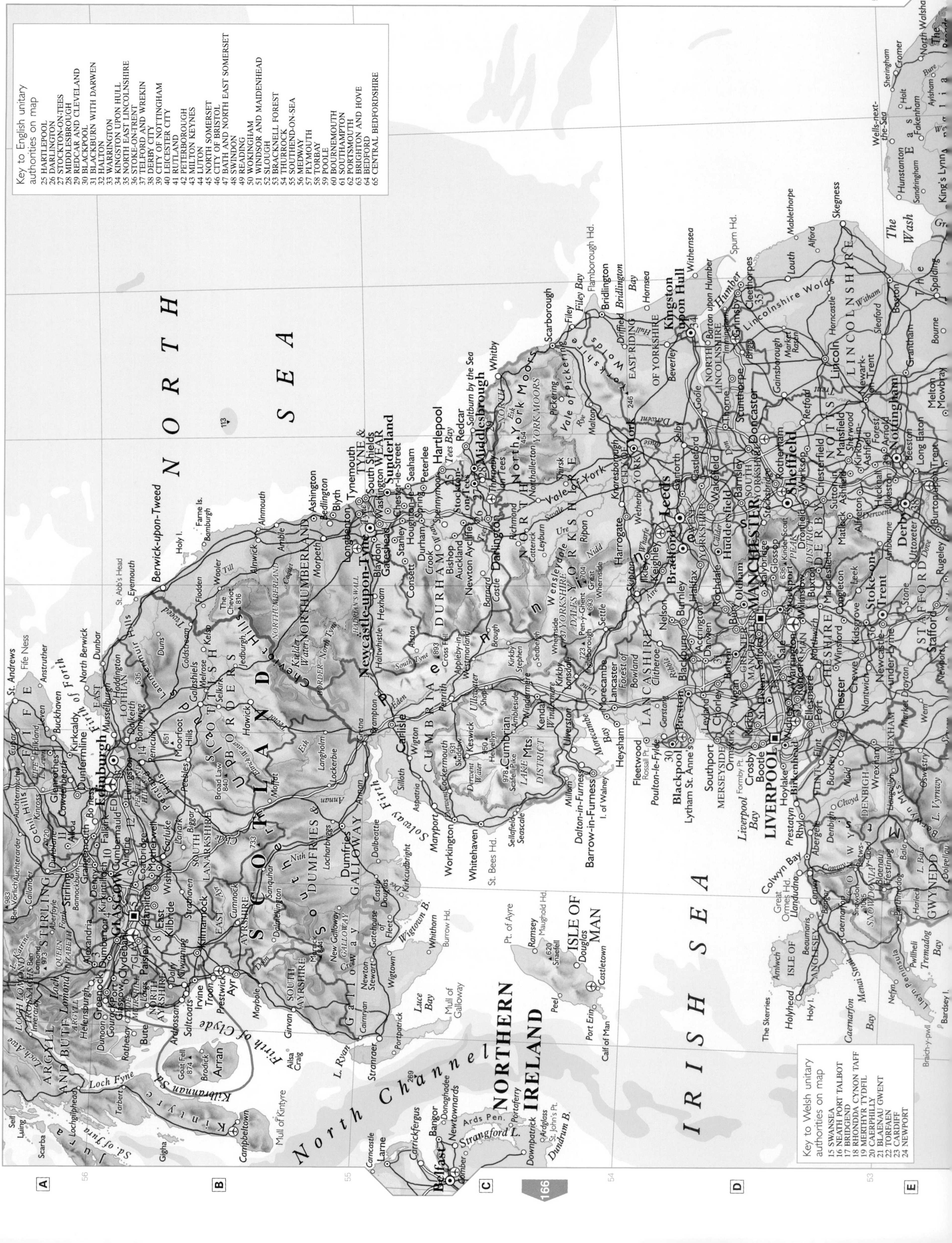

1:1 600 000
km
miles
Key to English unitary authorities on map
25 HARTLEPOOL
26 DARLINGTON
27 STOCKTON-ON-TEES
28 MIDDLESBROUGH
29 REDCAR AND CLEVELAND
30 BLACKPOOL
31 BLACKBURN WITH DARWEN
32 HALTON
33 WARRINGTON
34 KINGSTON UPON HULL
35 NORTH EAST LINCOLNSHIRE
36 STOKE-ON-TRENT
37 TELFORD AND WREKIN
38 DERBY CITY
39 CITY OF NOTTINGHAM
40 LEICESTER CITY
41 RUTLAND
42 PETERBOROUGH
43 MILTON KEYNES
44 LUTON
45 NORTH SOMERSET
46 CITY OF BRISTOL
47 BATH AND NORTH EAST SOMERSET
48 SWINDON
49 READING
50 WOKINGHAM
51 WINDSOR AND MAIDENHEAD
52 SLOUGH
53 BRACKNELL FOREST
54 THURROCK
55 SOUTHEND-ON-SEA
56 MEDWAY
57 PLYMOUTH
58 TORBAY
59 POOLE
60 BOURNEMOUTH
61 SOUTHAMPTON
62 PORTSMOUTH
63 BRIGHTON AND HOVE
64 BEDFORD
65 CENTRAL BEDFORDSHIRE
Key to Welsh unitary authorities on map
15 SWANSEA
16 NEATH PORT TALBOT
17 BRIDGEND
18 RHONDDA CYNON TAFF
19 MERTHYR TYDFIL
20 CAERPHILLY
21 BLAENAU GWENT
22 TORFAEN
23 CARDIFF
24 NEWPORT
NORTH SEA
IRISH SEA
North Channel
NORTHERN IRELAND
ISLE OF MAN
SCOTLAND
LIVERPOOL
MANCHESTER
Leeds
Sheffield
Newcastle-upon-Tyne
Edinburgh
GLASGOW
167
166

10 0 10 20 30 40 50 60 70 80 90 km

1:2 000 000

10 0 10 20 30 40 50 60 miles

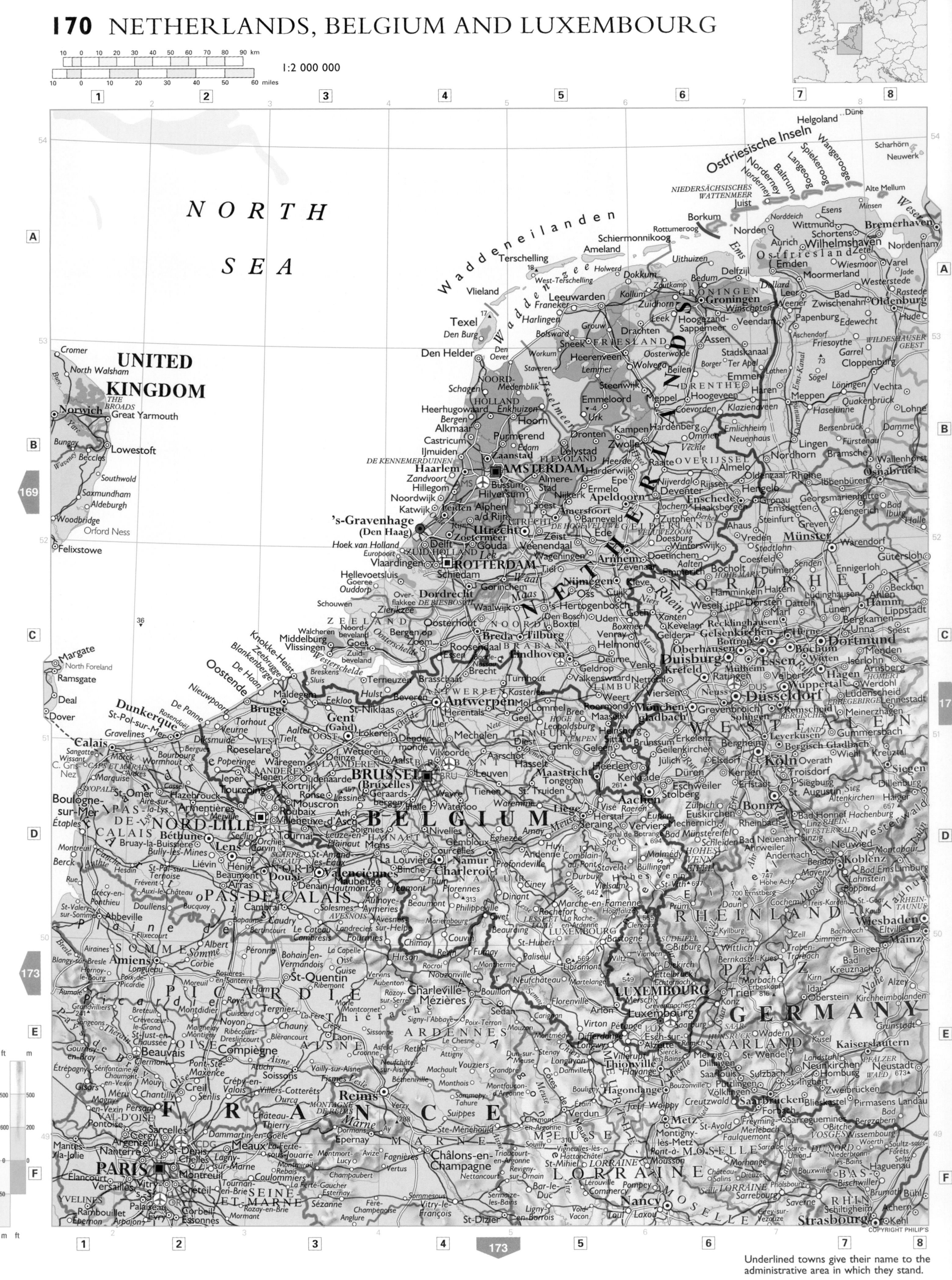

NORTH

SEA

**UNITED
KINGDOM**

NETHERLANDS

BELGIUM

FRANCE

GERMANY

LUXEMBOURG

ft m

1500 500

600 200

0

50

m ft

COPYRIGHT PHILIP'S

Underlined towns give their name to the
administrative area in which they stand.

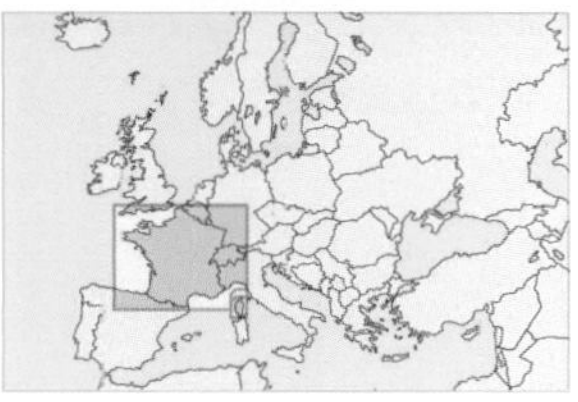

1:4 000 000

50   0   25   50   75   100   125   150   175 km
50   0   25   50   75   100   125 miles

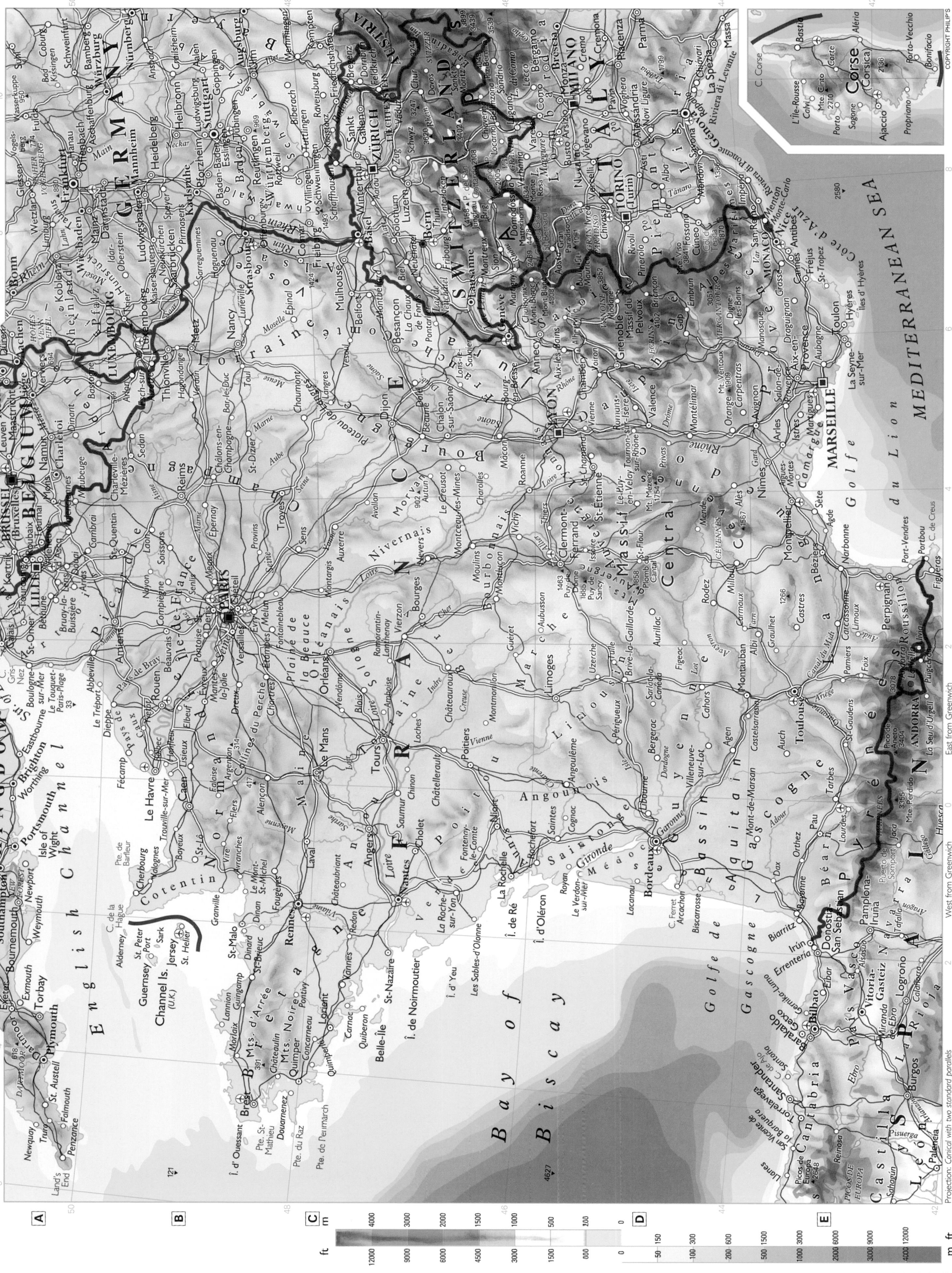

COPYRIGHT PHILIP'S

C. Corse
L'Île-Rousse
Calvi
Mte. Cinto
2710
Bastia
Corte
Corse
Corsica
2136
Porto-Vecchio
Bonifacio
Porto
Sagone
Ajaccio
Propriano

UNITED KINGDOM

GERMANY

BELGIUM

LUXEMBOURG

SWITZERLAND

ITALY

AUSTRIA

FRANCE

ANDORRA

MONACO

SPAIN

English Channel

Bay of Biscay

Golfe de Gascogne

MEDITERRANEAN SEA

Golfe du Lion

Côte d'Azur

Channel Is. (U.K.)
Guernsey
Jersey
St. Helier
St. Peter Port
Sark
Alderney

PARIS
MARSEILLE
LYON
TORINO (Turin)
MILANO
ZÜRICH
BRUXELLES
BRUSSEL
LILLE
Genève
Bern
Bordeaux
Nantes
Toulouse
Nice
Marseille

Pyrénées
Massif Central
Alpes
Jura
Vosges
Ardenne

West from Greenwich
East from Greenwich

Projection: Conical with two standard parallels

ft   12000   9000   6000   4500   3000   1500   600   300   150   0
m   4000   3000   2000   1500   1000   500   200   100   50   0   -50   -100   -200   -500   -1000   -2000   -3000   -4000   m

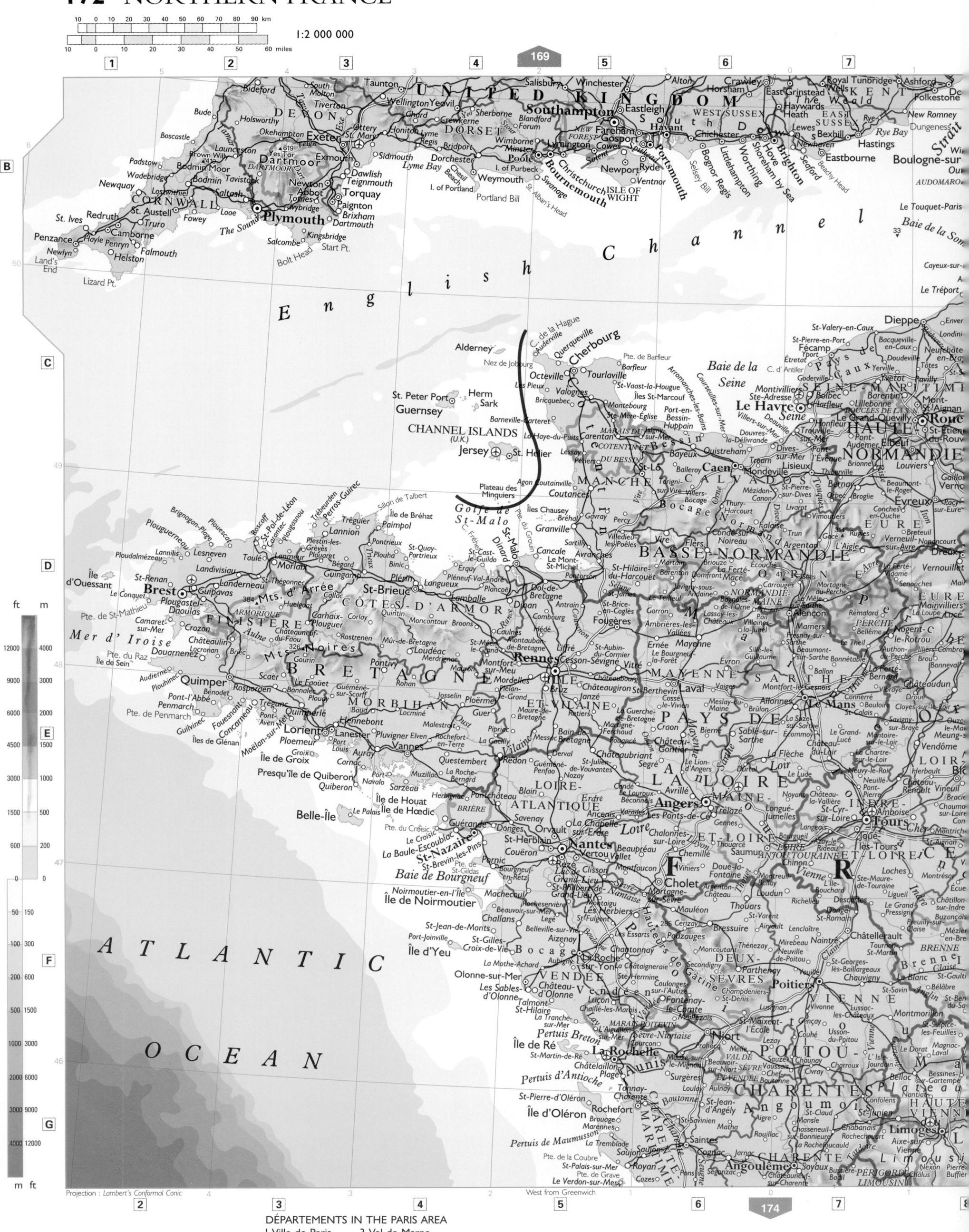

10 0 10 20 30 40 50 60 70 80 90 km

1:2 000 000

10 0 10 20 30 40 50 60 miles

169

B

C

D

E

F

G

ft m
12000 4000
9000 3000
6000 2000
4500 1500
3000 1000
1500 500
600 200
0 0
0 0
50 150
100 300
200 600
500 1500
1000 3000
2000 6000
3000 9000
4000 12000
m ft

1 2 3 4 5 6 7

UNITED KINGDOM

Bideford Taunton Salisbury Winchester Alton Crawley East Grinstead Royal Tunbridge Ashford
South Molton Wellington Yeovil Sherborne Southampton Eastleigh WEST SUSSEX Haywards Heath EAST SUSSEX Folkestone
Bude Holsworthy Chard Blandford Fareham Gosport Chichester New Romney
Okehampton DORSET Forum Lymington Havant Bognor Regis Worthing Brighton Hastings Dungeness
Exeter Dorchester Poole Bournemouth Isle of Wight Littlehampton Hove Seaford Eastbourne Boulogne-sur
Plymouth Torquay Weymouth

English Channel

CHANNEL ISLANDS (U.K.)

Cherbourg Dieppe

ATLANTIC OCEAN

Brest Rennes Le Mans Tours

Nantes Angers

Poitiers

La Rochelle

Angoulême Limoges

DÉPARTEMENTS IN THE PARIS AREA
1 Ville de Paris 3 Val-de-Marne
2 Seine-St-Denis 4 Hauts-de-Seine

Underlined towns give their name to the
administrative area in which they stand.

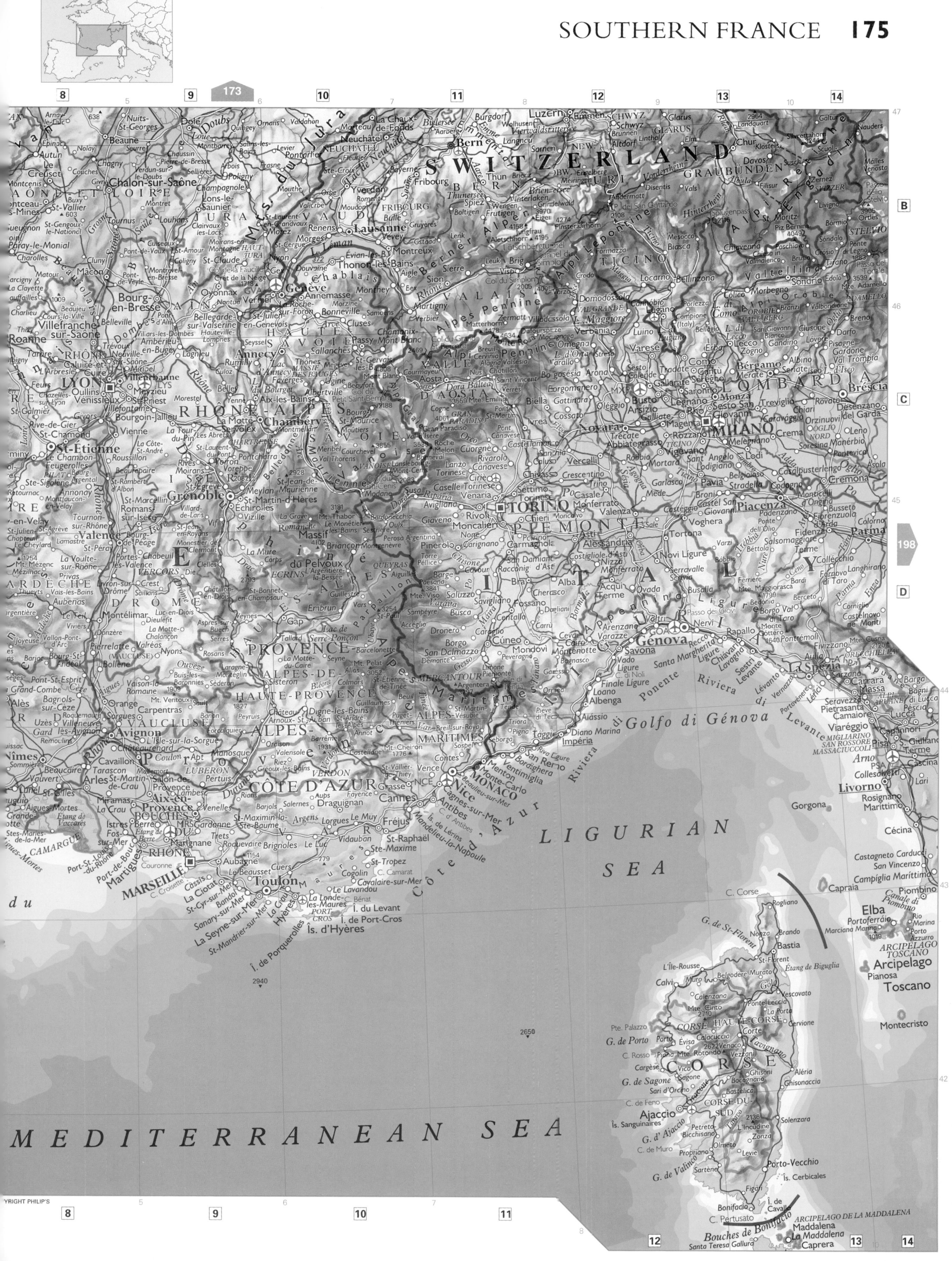

50 0 25 50 75 100 125 150 175 km
50 0 25 50 75 100 125 miles

1:4 000 000

Projection: Conical with two standard parallels

NORTH SEA

BALTIC SEA

ADRIATIC SEA

UNITED KINGDOM

NETHERLANDS

BELGIUM

LUXEMBOURG

FRANCE

GERMANY

DENMARK

SWITZERLAND

AUSTRIA

ITALY

CZECH

SLOVENIA

Selected place names: Norwich, Ipswich, Felixstowe, Harwich, Margate, Dover, Calais, Dunkerque, Lille, Amsterdam, 's-Gravenhage (Den Haag), Rotterdam, Utrecht, Groningen, Haarlem, Leiden, Antwerpen, Brussel (Bruxelles), Gent, Brugge, Liège, Namur, Charleroi, Luxembourg, Köln (Cologne), Bonn, Düsseldorf, Dortmund, Essen, Duisburg, Wuppertal, Aachen, Bremen, Hamburg, Hannover, Braunschweig, Magdeburg, Berlin, Potsdam, Leipzig, Dresden, Erfurt, Frankfurt, Mainz, Wiesbaden, Mannheim, Heidelberg, Karlsruhe, Stuttgart, Nürnberg, München (Munich), Augsburg, Kiel, Lübeck, Rostock, Schwerin, Szczecin, Praha (Prague), Plzeň, České Budějovice, Liberec, Linz, Salzburg, Innsbruck, Klagenfurt, Graz, Ljubljana, Zagreb, Trieste, Venézia (Venice), Milano, Torino (Turin), Genova, Monaco, Nice, Marseille, Paris, Reims, Metz, Nancy, Strasbourg, Dijon, Lyon, Grenoble, Genève, Lausanne, Bern, Zürich, Basel

ft m
12000 4000
9000 3000
6000 2000
4500 1500
3000 1000
1500 500
600 200
0 0
150
300
600
1500
3000
6000
m ft

161
165
171
192

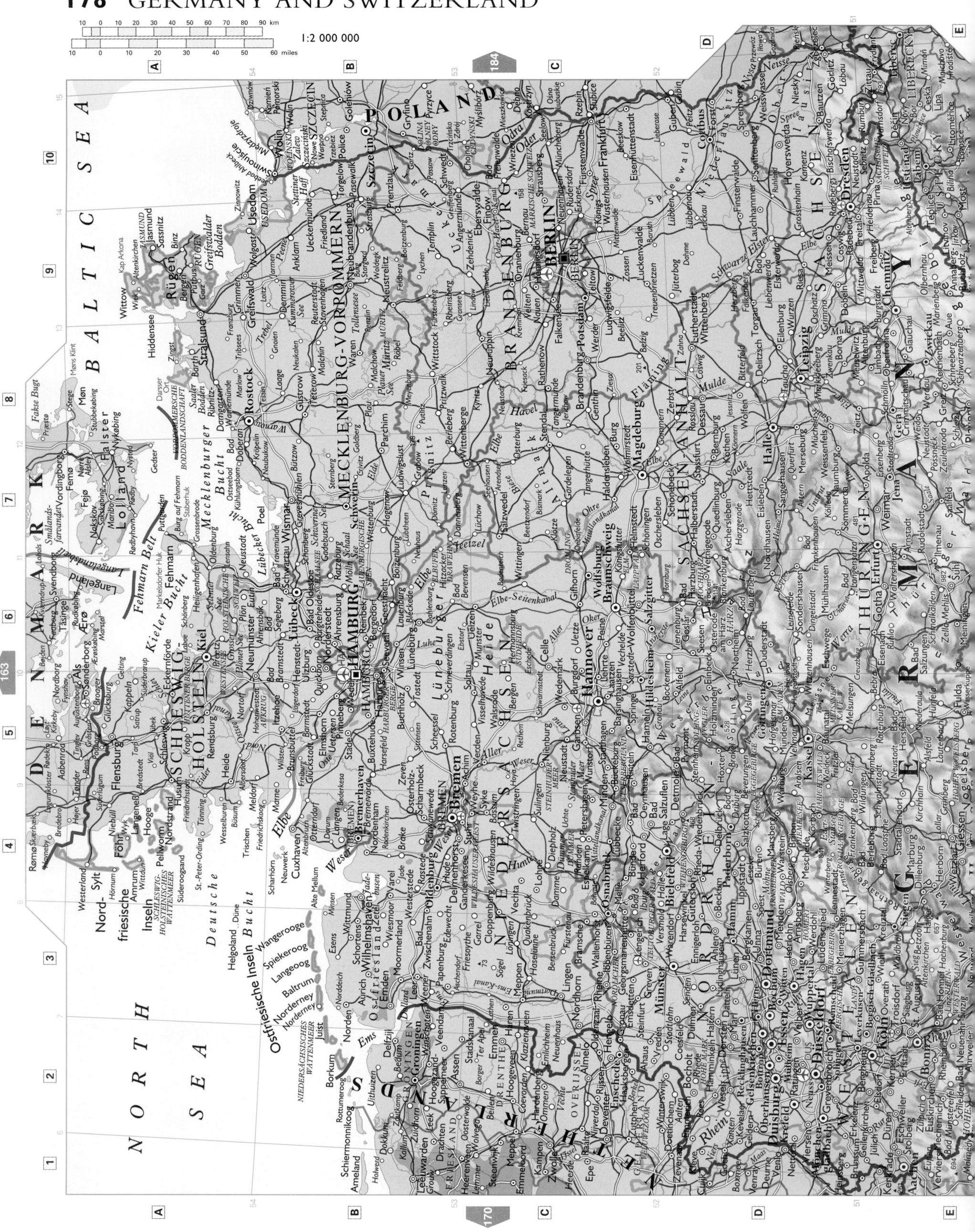

Projection: Lambert's Conformal Conic

Underlined towns give their name to the administrative area in which they stand.

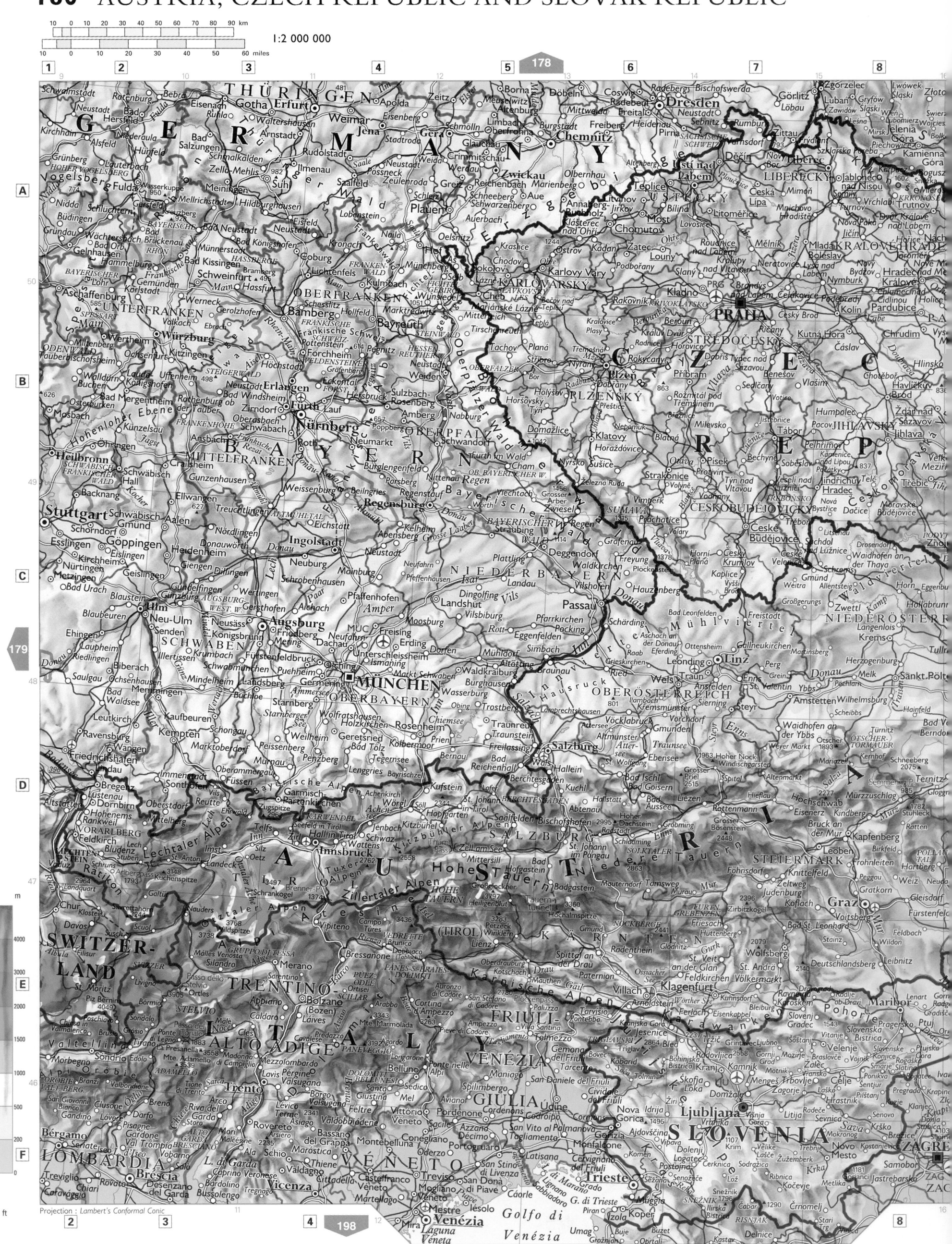

Underlined towns give their name to the
administrative area in which they stand.

10 0 10 20 30 40 50 60 70 80 90 km

1:2 000 000

10 0 10 20 30 40 50 60 miles

Projection : Lambert's Conformal Conic

East from Greenwich

Administrative divisions in Croatia:
1 Brodsko-Posavska   5 Osječko-Baranjska   9 Vukovarsko-Srijemska
2 Koprivničko-Križevačka   6 Požeško-Slavonska
4 Medimurska   8 Virovitičko-Podravska

Underlined towns give their name to the
administrative area in which they stand.

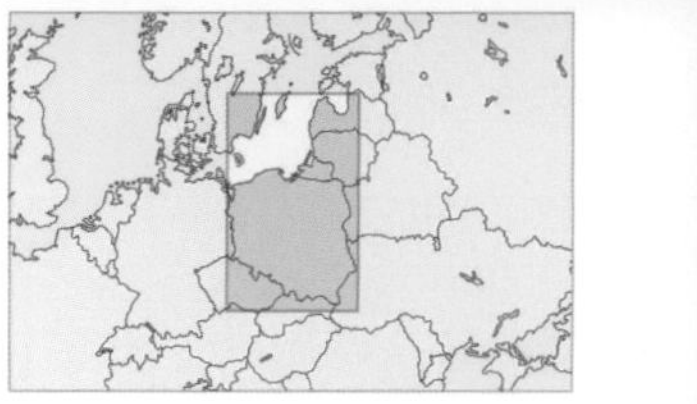

1:2 000 000

10 0 10 20 30 40 50 60 70 80 90 km
10 0 10 20 30 40 50 60 miles

188

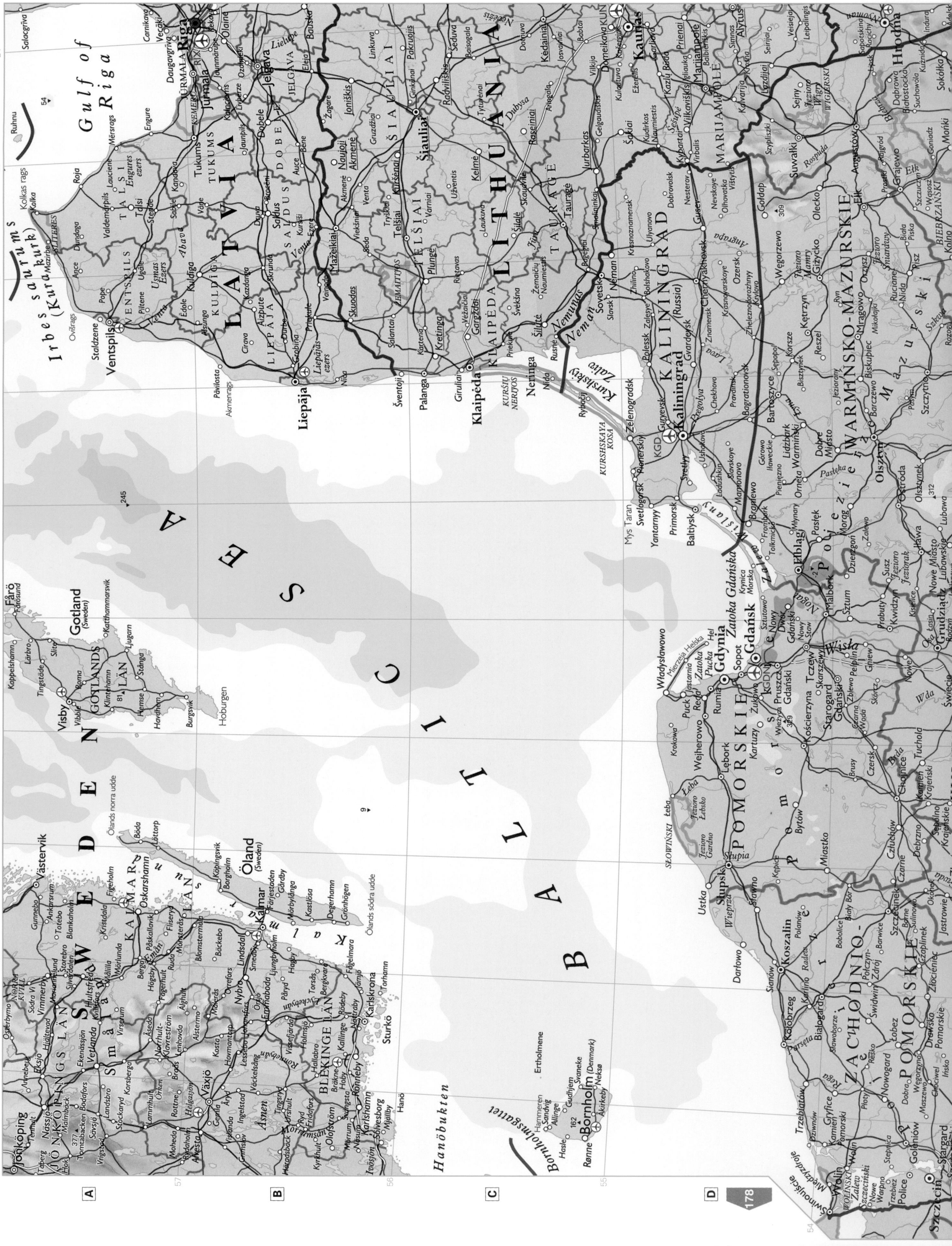

163

178

Gulf of Riga

BALTIC SEA

SWEDEN

Gotland (Sweden)

GOTLANDS LÄN

Öland (Sweden)

KALMAR LÄN

KRONOBERGS LÄN

BLEKINGE LÄN

Bornholm (Denmark)

Hanöbukten

LATVIA

VENTSPILS

TALSI

KULDĪGA

LIEPĀJA

SALDUS

DOBELE

TUKUMS

ŠIAULIAI

LITHUANIA

ŽEMAITIJA

KLAIPĖDA

TELŠIAI

PLUNGĖ

TAURAGĖ

MARIJAMPOLĖ

KALININGRAD (Russia)

WARMIŃSKO-MAZURSKIE

Mazury

POMORSKIE

ZACHODNIO-POMORSKIE

Pomorze

Riga

Jūrmala

Jelgava

Liepāja

Ventspils

Šiauliai

Klaipėda

Kaunas

Kaliningrad

Gdańsk

Gdynia

Sopot

Elbląg

Koszalin

Słupsk

Szczecin

Irbes šaurums (Kura kurk)

KURŠIŲ NERIJOS

Kuršský Zalv

KURSHSKAYA KOSA

Zatoka Gdańska

Nemunas / Neman

Wisła

Underlined towns give their name to the administrative area in which they stand.

Projection : Lambert's Conformal Conic

East from Greenwich

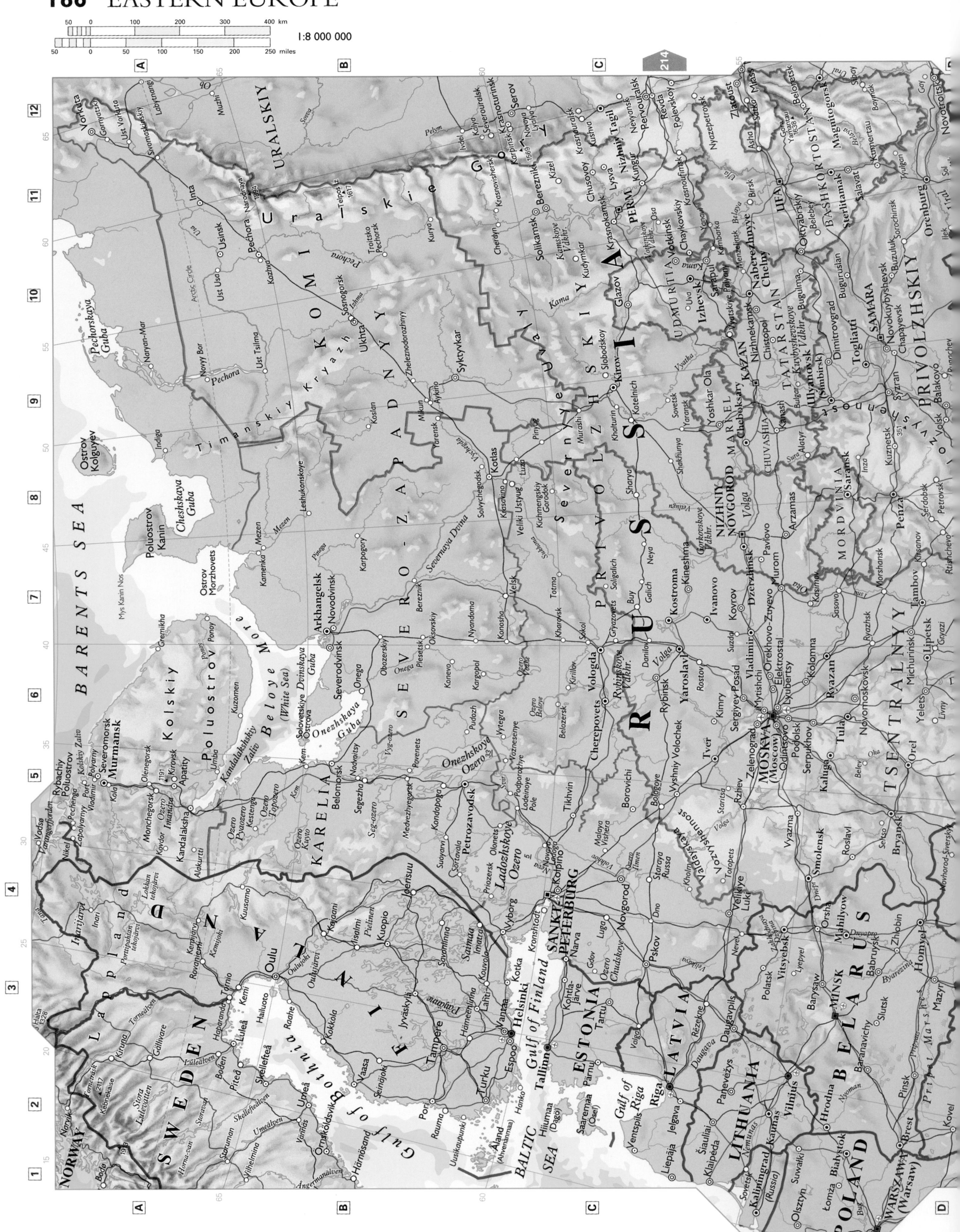

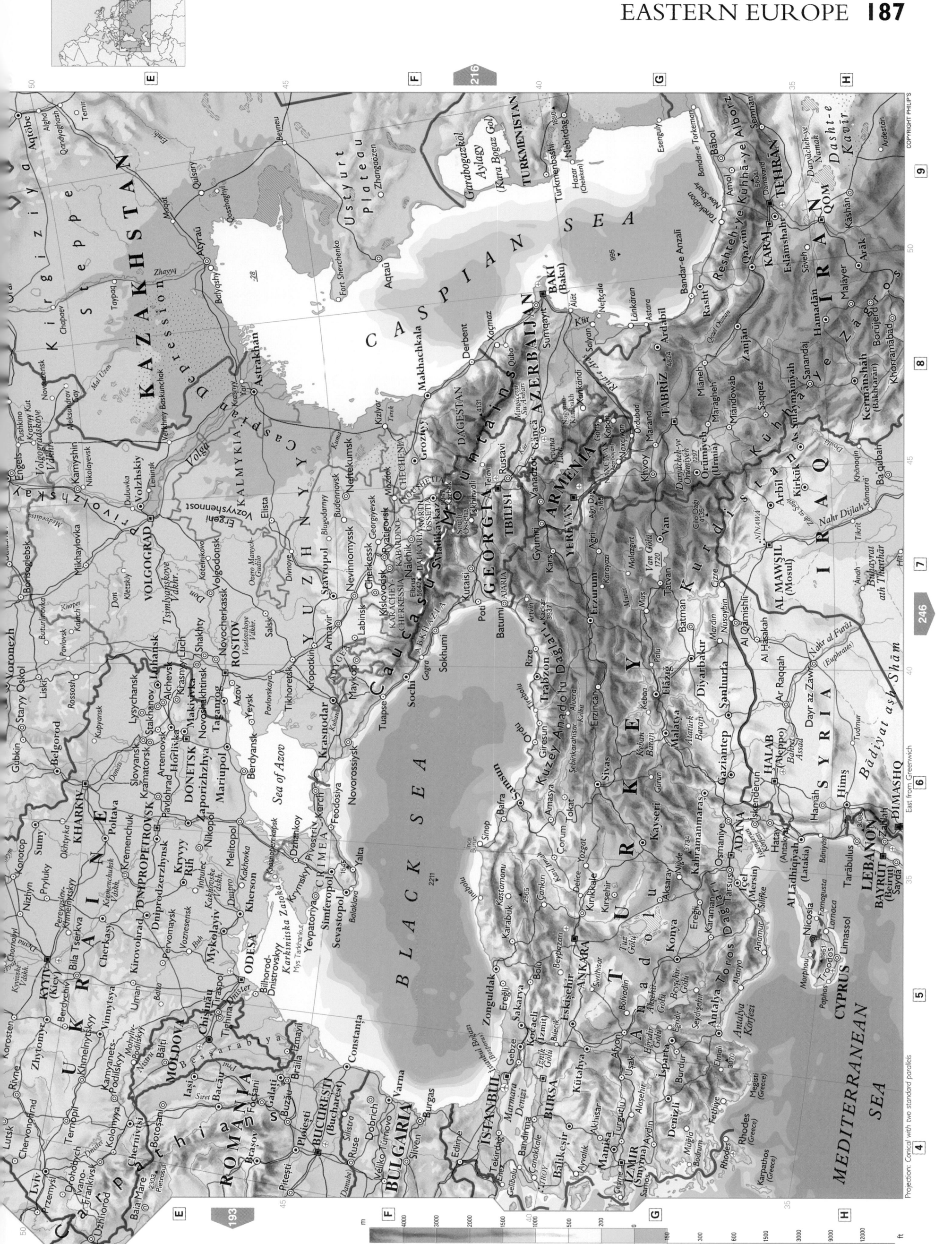

Projection: Conical with two standard parallels

East from Greenwich

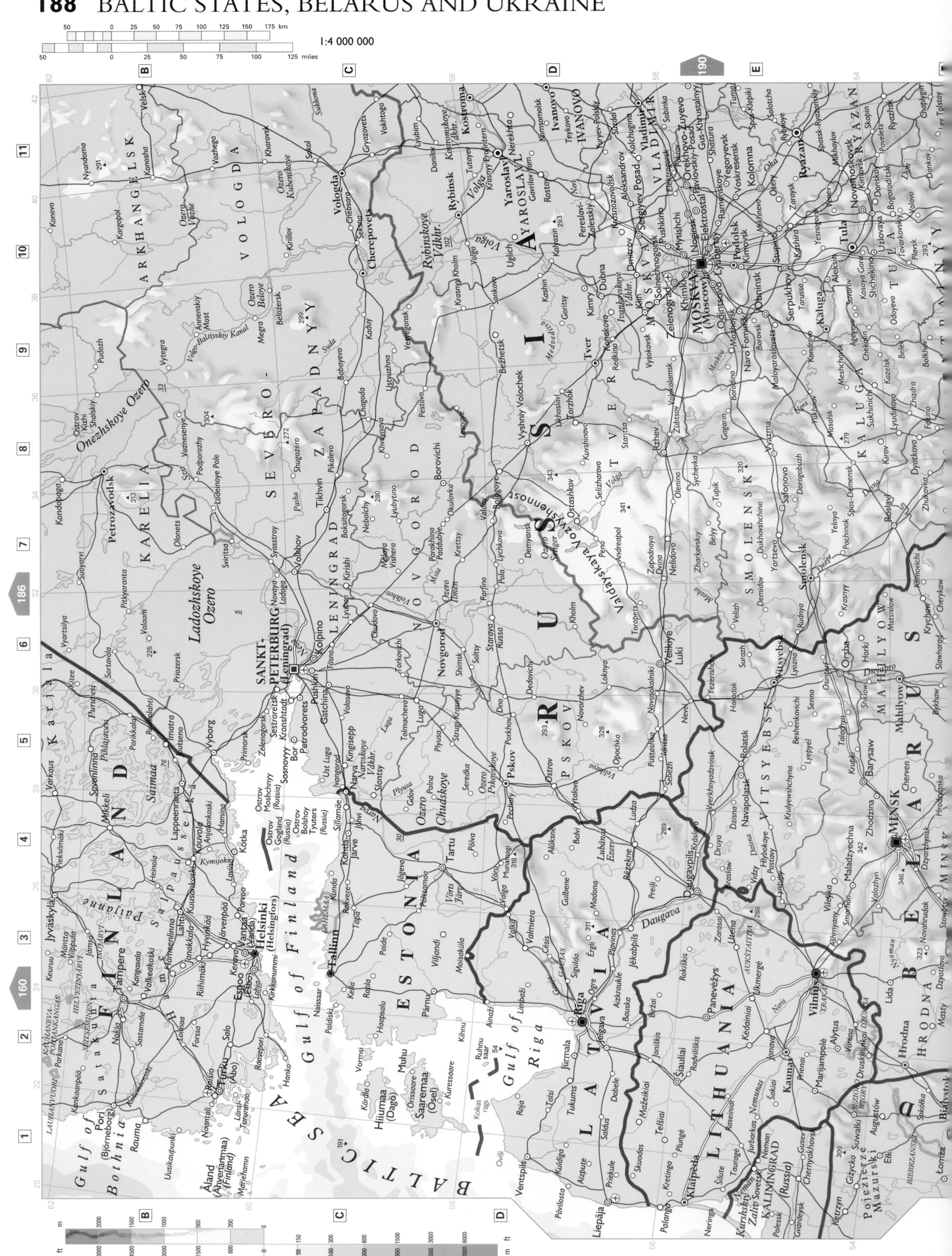

1:4 000 000

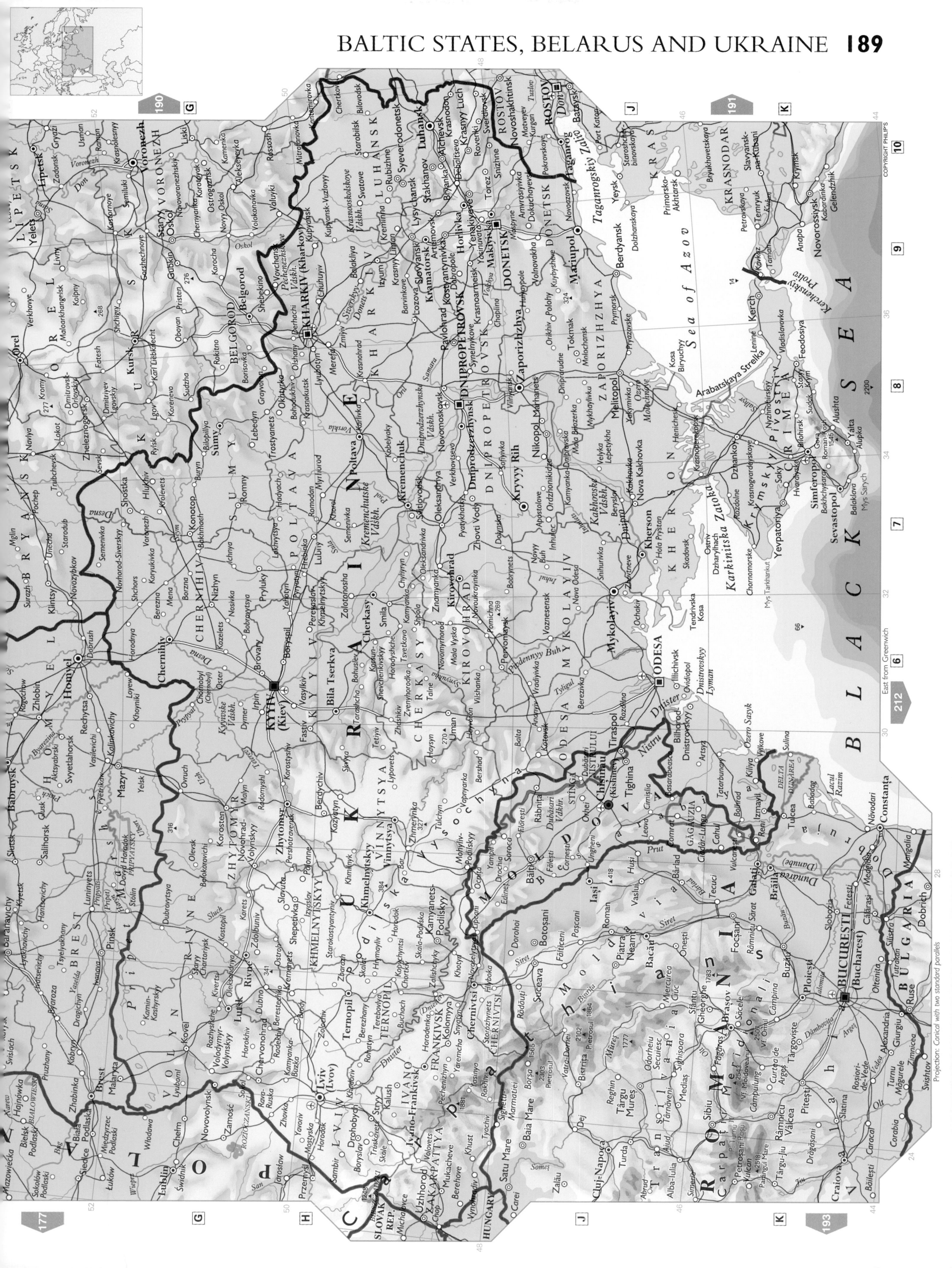

50 0 100 200 300 400 km

50 0 50 100 150 200 250 miles

1:8 000 000

ft **m**
9000 3000
6000 2000
4500 1500
3000 1000
1500 500
600 200
0 0
50 150
100 300
200 600
500 1500
260
1000 3000
2000 6000
3000 9000
4000 12000
m **ft**

ATLANTIC OCEAN

Bay of Biscay

English Channel

NETHERLANDS

GERMAN

BELGIUM

LUXEMBOURG

FRANCE

PARIS

SWITZERLAND

Golfe de Gascogne

PORTUGAL

SPAIN

MADRID

LISBOA

Pyrénées

ANDORRA

BARCELONA

Islas Baleares
(Spain)

Mallorca

MARSEILLE

Golfe du Lion

LIGURIAN SEA

Corse
(France)

Sardegna
(Italy)

TYRRHENIAN SEA

MEDITERRANEAN SEA

MOROCCO

RABAT

ALGERIA

ALGER
(Algiers)

TUNIS

TUNISIA

Haut Atlas

Moyen Atlas

Atlas Saharien

Hauts Plateaux

Sahara

Grand Erg Occidental

Grand Erg Oriental

TARĀBULUS
(Tripoli)

Tarābulus
(Tripolitania)

MILANO

TORINO

ROMA

NÁPOLI

Sicilia

MALT

Projection: Conical with two standard parallels   West from Greenwich   East from Greenwich

1:2 000 000

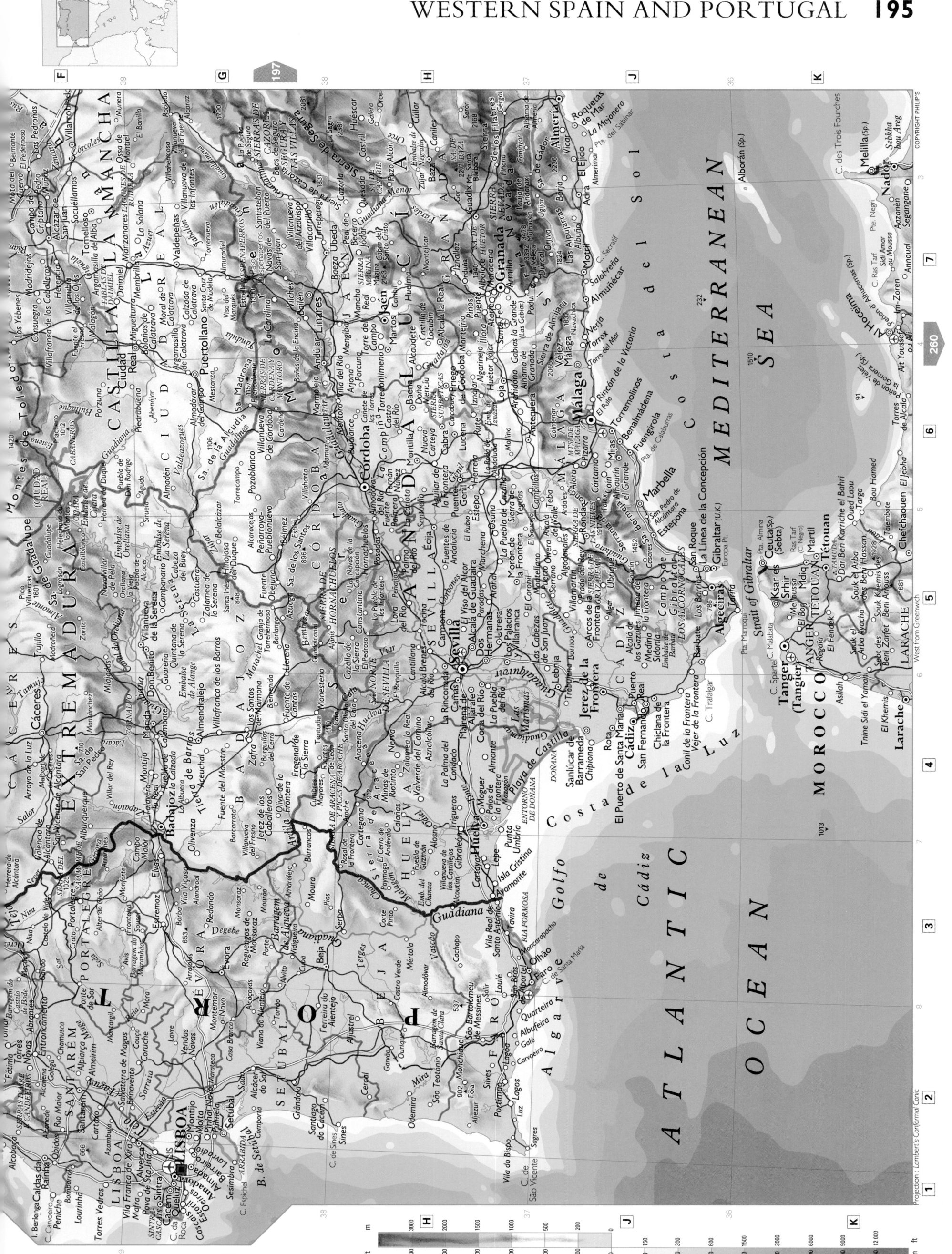

COPYRIGHT PHILIP'S

West from Greenwich

1:2 000 000

Projection: Lambert's Conformal Conic

Administrative divisions in Croatia:

Brodsko-Posavska	4 Medimurska	8 Virovitičko-Podravska
Koprivničko-Križevačka	6 Požeško-Slavonska	10 Zagreba čka
Krapinsko-Zagorska	7 Varaždinska	

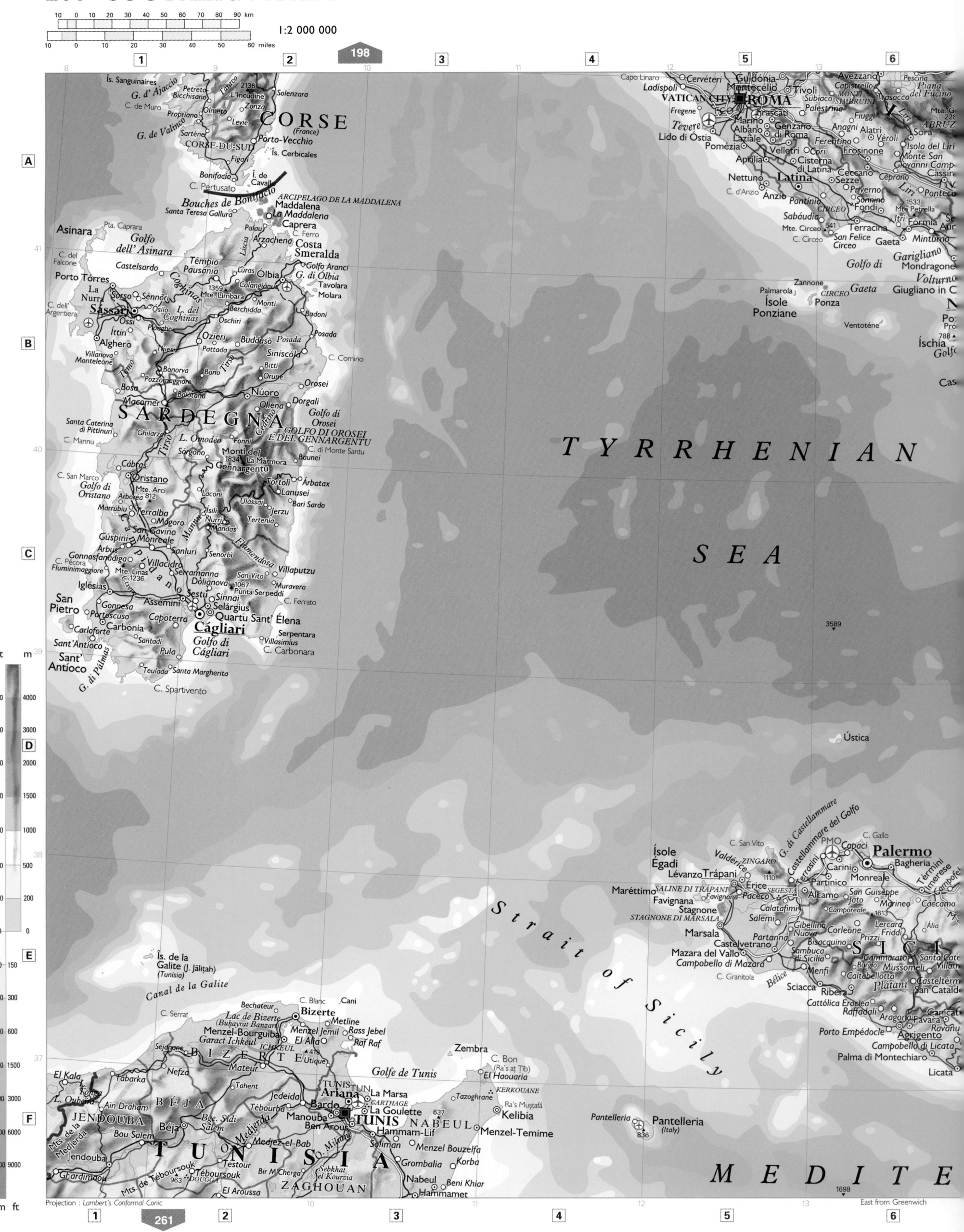

TYRRHENIAN

SEA

Strait of Sicily

MEDITE

THE BALKANS

ROMANIA

BULGARIA

TURKEY

BLACK SEA

Bucureşti (Bucharest)

Constanţa

Ploieşti

Pleven

Ruse

Varna

Burgas

Plovdiv

Stara Zagora

Sliven

Yambol

Istanbul

Üsküdar

Kartal

Bursa

Edirne

Kırklareli

Tekirdağ

Çanakkale

Marmara Denizi (Sea of Marmara)

Sea of Thrace

Kavala

ANATOLIKI MAKEDONIA

Samothraki

Thasos

Limnos

Gökçeada

Dunărea (Danube)

Galaţi

Brăila

Buzău

Tulcea

DELTA DUNĂREA

Dobrich

Şumen

Türgovishte

Razgrad

Veliko Türnovo

Gabrovo

Pazardzhik

Khaskovo

Kürdzhali

Mangalia

Underlined towns give their name to the
administrative area in which they stand.

COPYRIGHT PHILIP'S

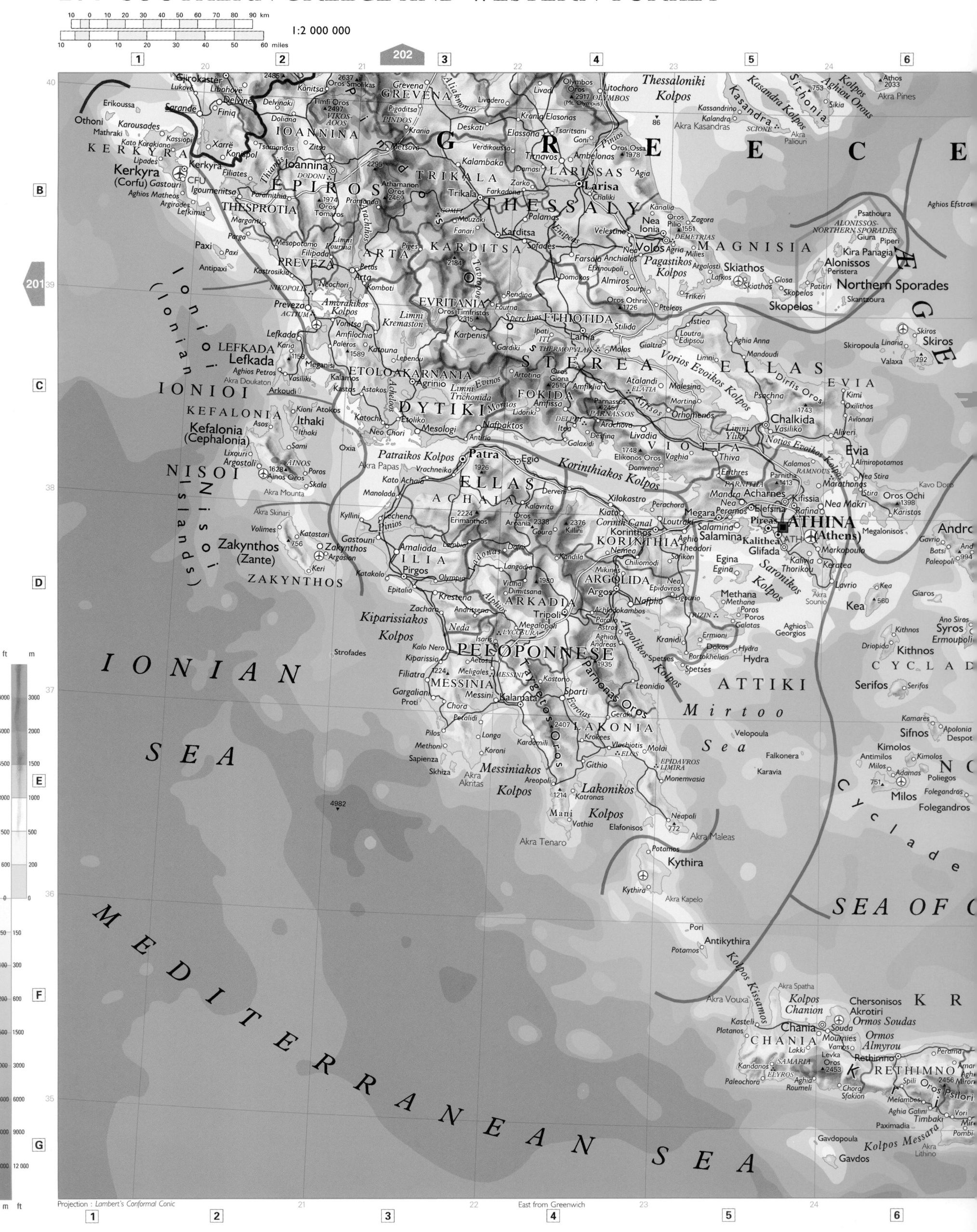

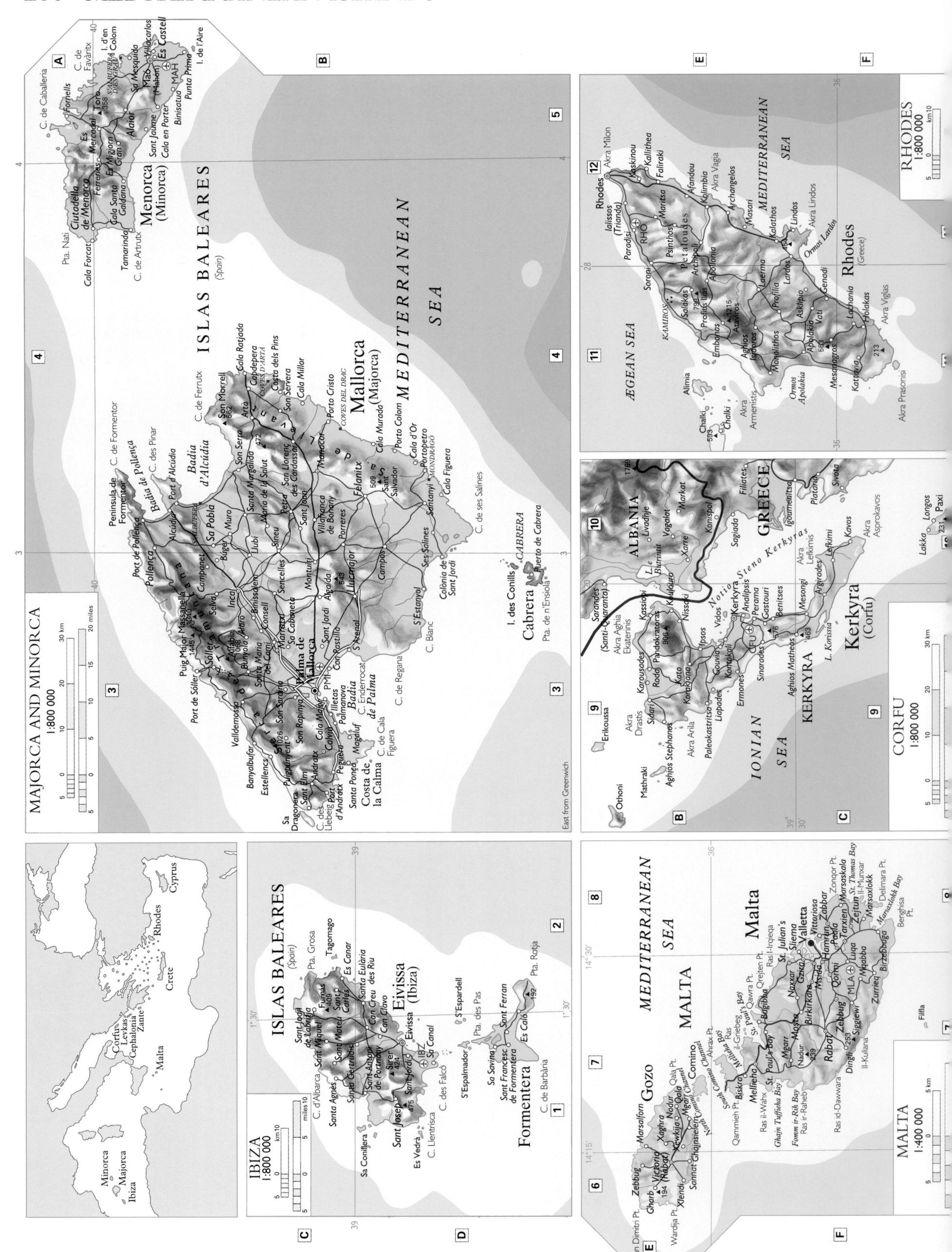

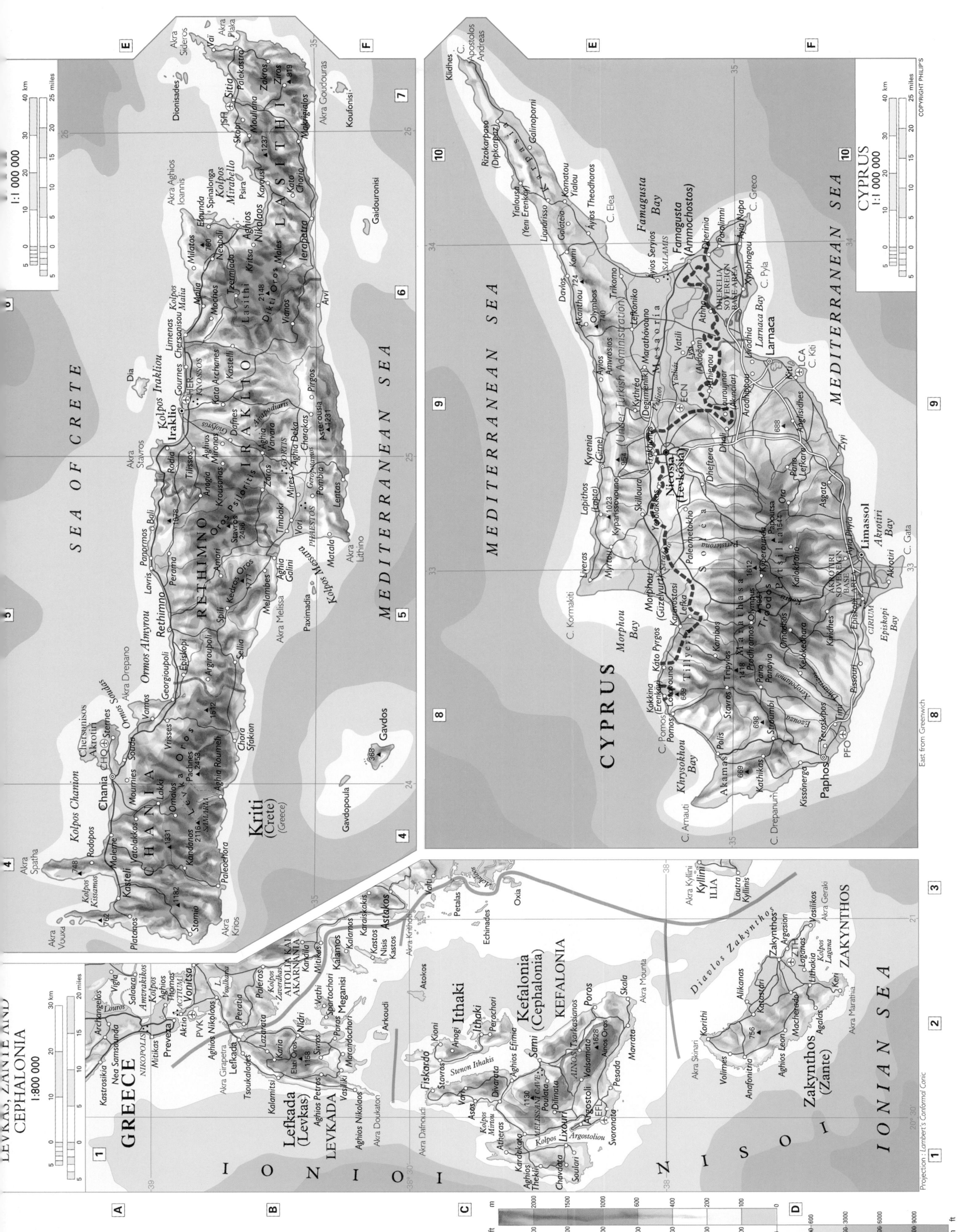

LEVKAS, ZANTE AND CEPHALONIA
1:800 000

GREECE

Lefkada (Levkas)
LEVKADA

Ithaki
Ithaki

Kefalonia (Cephalonia)
KEFALONIA

Zakynthos (Zante)
ZAKYNTHOS

IONIAN SEA

NISOI   IONIOI

SEA OF CRETE

Kriti
(Crete)
(Greece)

CHANIA

RETHIMNO

IRAKLIO

LASITHI

MEDITERRANEAN SEA

MEDITERRANEAN SEA

CYPRUS
1:1 000 000

CYPRUS

Under Turkish Administration

Nicosia (Levkosia)

Famagusta (Ammochostos)

Larnaca

Limassol

Paphos

MEDITERRANEAN SEA

MEDITERRANEAN SEA

East from Greenwich

Projection: Lambert's Conformal Conic

COPYRIGHT PHILIP'S

1:1 000 000

ASIA

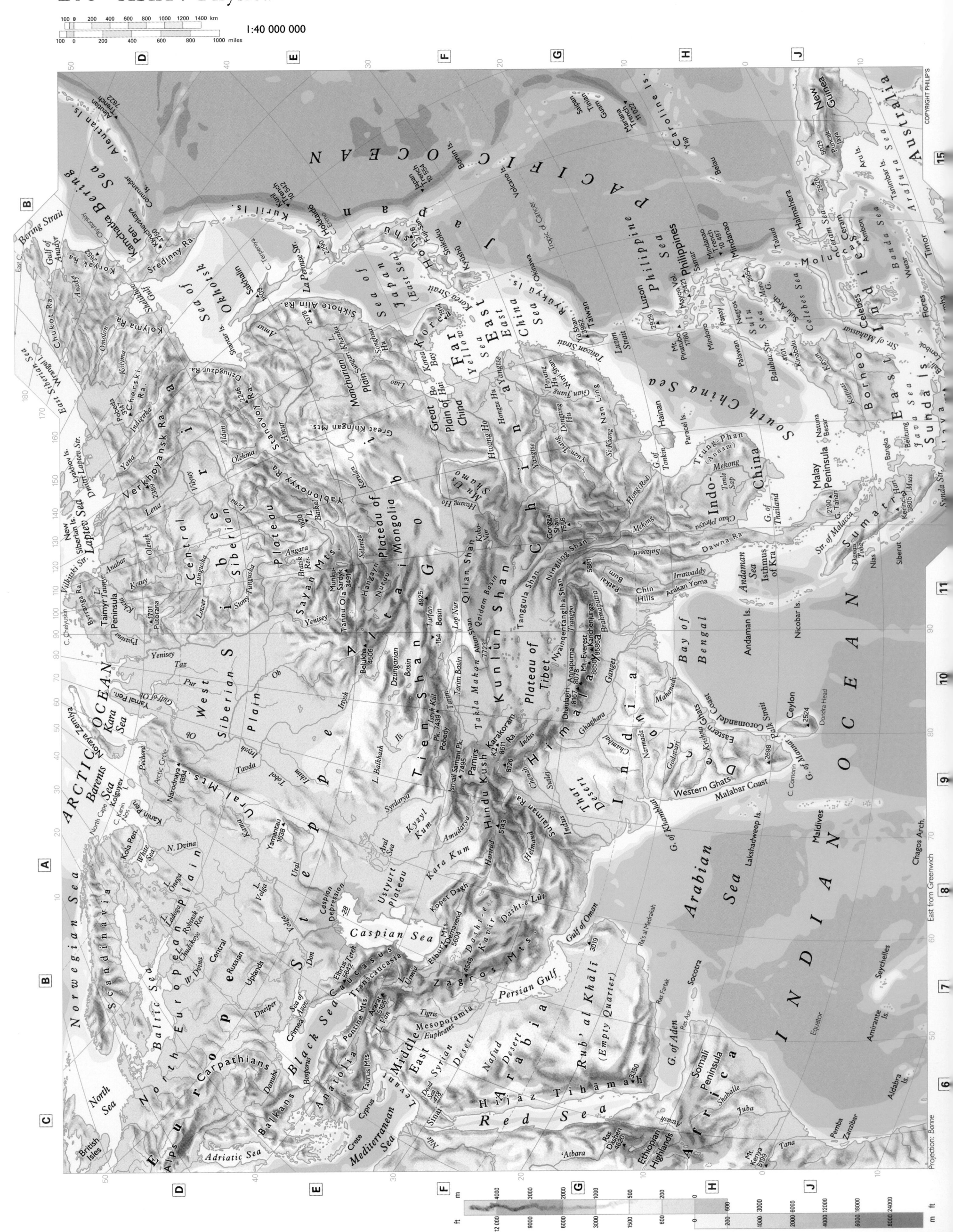

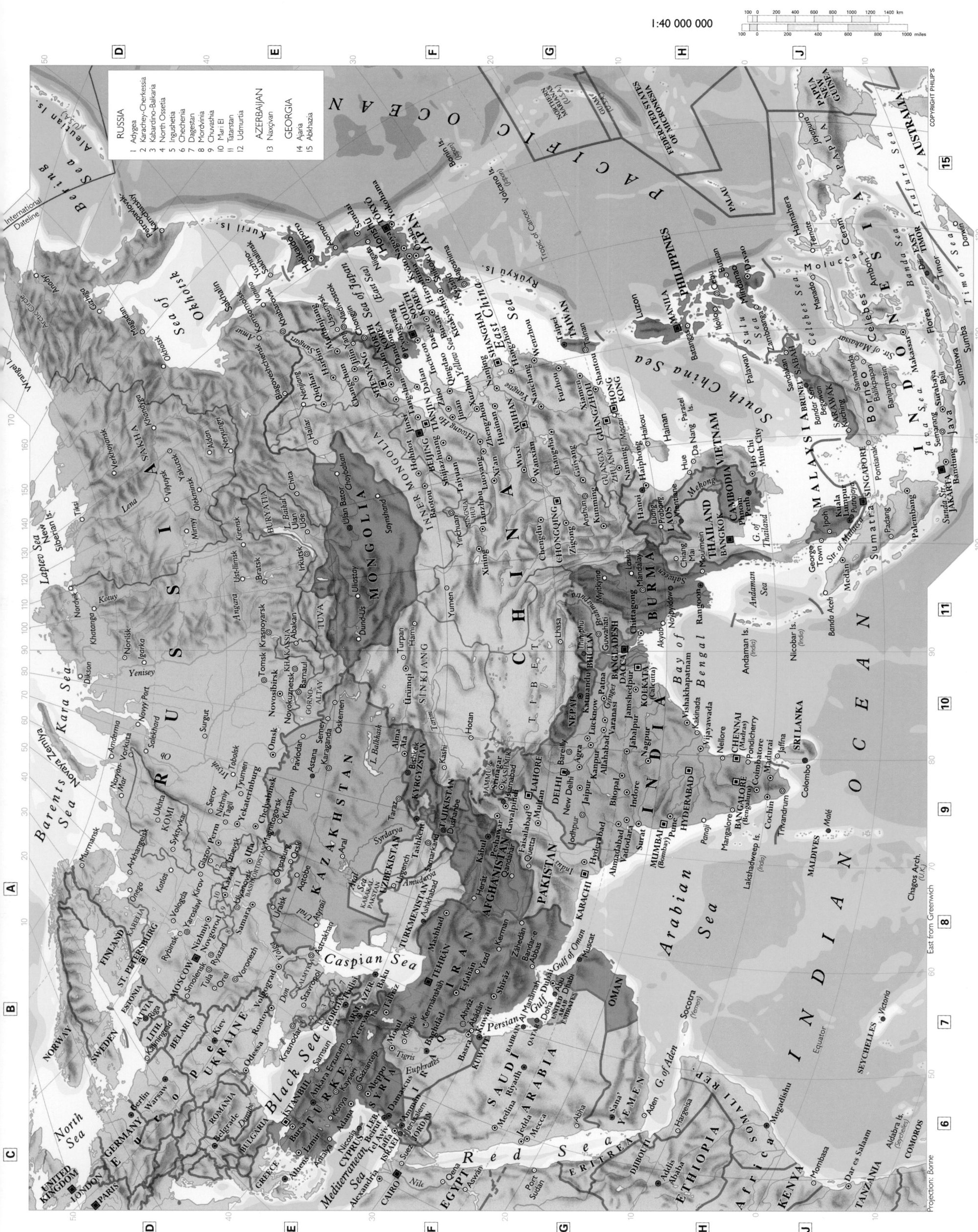

1:40 000 000

Projection: Bonne

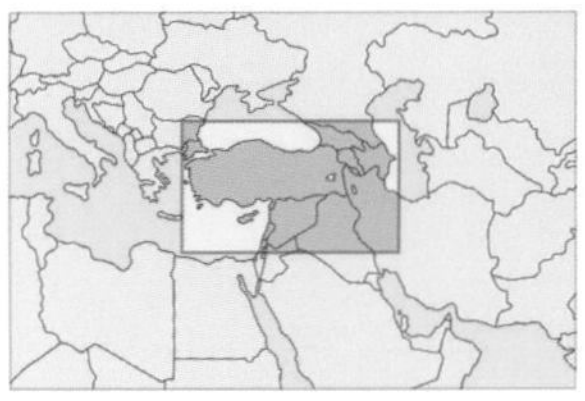

1 : 4 000 000

BULGARIA

BLACK SEA

Stara Zagora
Yambol
Burgas
Aytos
Nos Emine
Michurin
Elkhovo
Kırklareli
Demirköy
İğneada
İğneada Burnu
Edirne
Pınarhisar
Vize
Çerkezköy
Çatalca
İSTANBUL
İstanbul Boğazı (Bosporus)
Kocaeli (İzmit) (Adapazarı)
Kartal
Gebze
Darıca
Körfez
Sakarya
Zonguldak
Karadeniz Ereğli
Devrek
Bartın
Amasra
Kurucaşile
Cide
İnebolu
Abana
Çatalzeytin
Sinop
İnce Burun
Samsun
Bafra

Paphlagonia
Küre Dağları
Kastamonu
İlgaz Dağları
ÇANKIRI
ANKARA
Kırıkkale
ÇORUM
TOKAT
AMASYA

Marmara Denizi (Sea of Marmara)
BURSA
Uludağ
İznik Gölü
Eskişehir
KÜTAHYA
Anadolu
Afyon (Afyonkarahisar)
Phrygia
Tuz Gölü
AKSARAY
NEVŞEHİR
KAYSERİ
Cappadocia
SİVAS

İZMİR (Smyrna)
MANİSA
Lydia
Aydın
DENİZLİ
ISPARTA
Eğridir Gölü
Beyşehir Gölü
KONYA
Konya Ovası
Pisidia
NİĞDE
ADANA
KAHRAMANMARAŞ
GAZİANTEP

GREECE
Rhodes (Rhodes)
MUĞLA
Lycia
ANTALYA
Antalya Körfezi
Pamphylia
Toros Dağları
İÇEL
İçel (Mersin)
Tarsus
İskenderun
HATAY
HALAB (Aleppo)

CYPRUS
Nicosia
Famagusta
Kyrenia
Morphou
Larnaca
Limassol
Paphos
Troodos
Olympus 1951

Al Lādhiqīyah (Latakia)
Hamāh
Homs (Hims)
SYRIA

MEDITERRANEAN SEA

Tarābulus (Tripoli)
LEBANON
BAYRŪT (Beirut)
Saydā
DIMASHQ (Damascus)

ISRAEL
TEL AVIV-YAFO
Hefa (Haifa)
Nazerat
WEST BANK
Jerusalem
AMMĀN
JORDAN

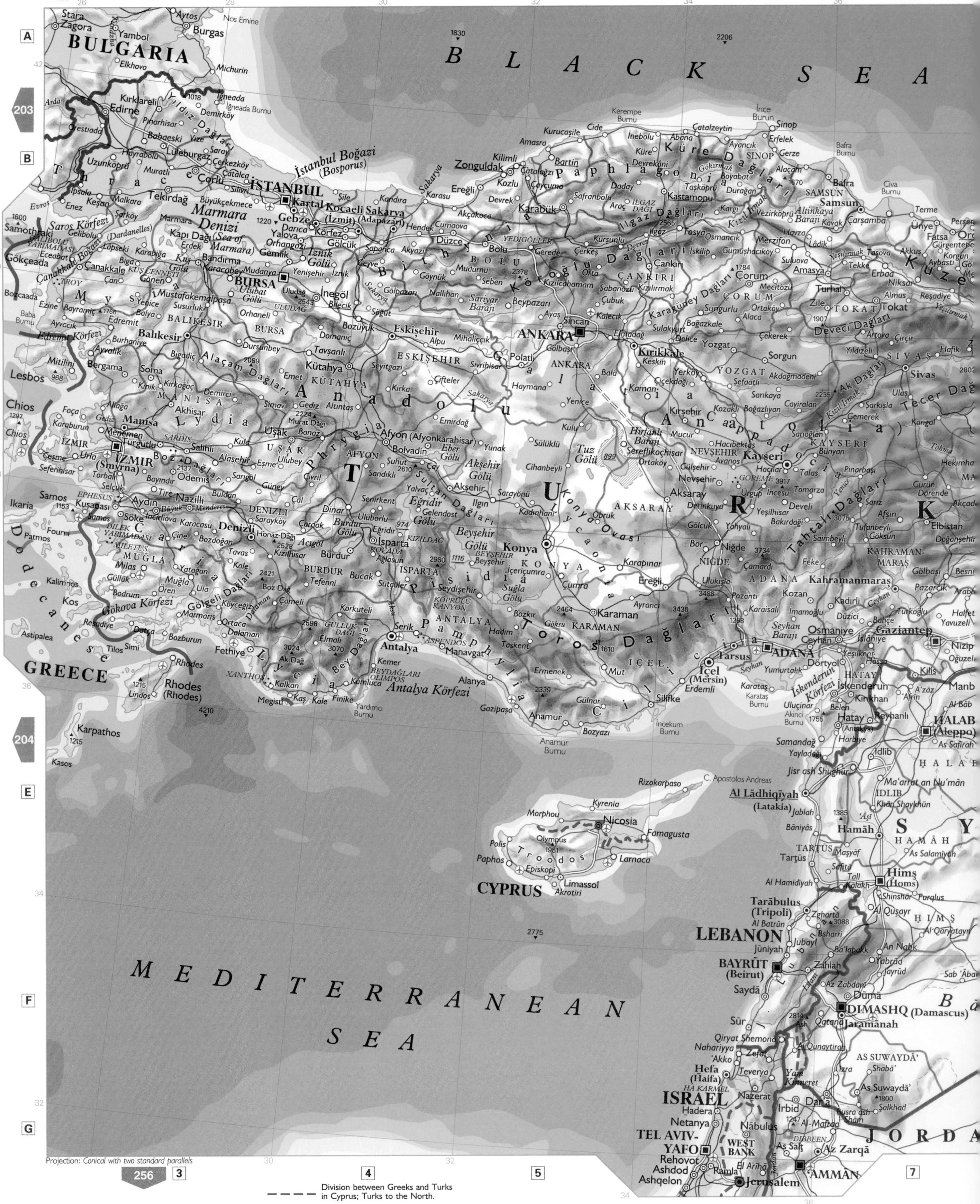

Projection: Conical with two standard parallels

- - - - - Division between Greeks and Turks in Cyprus; Turks to the North.

Underlined towns give their name
to the administrative area in which they stand

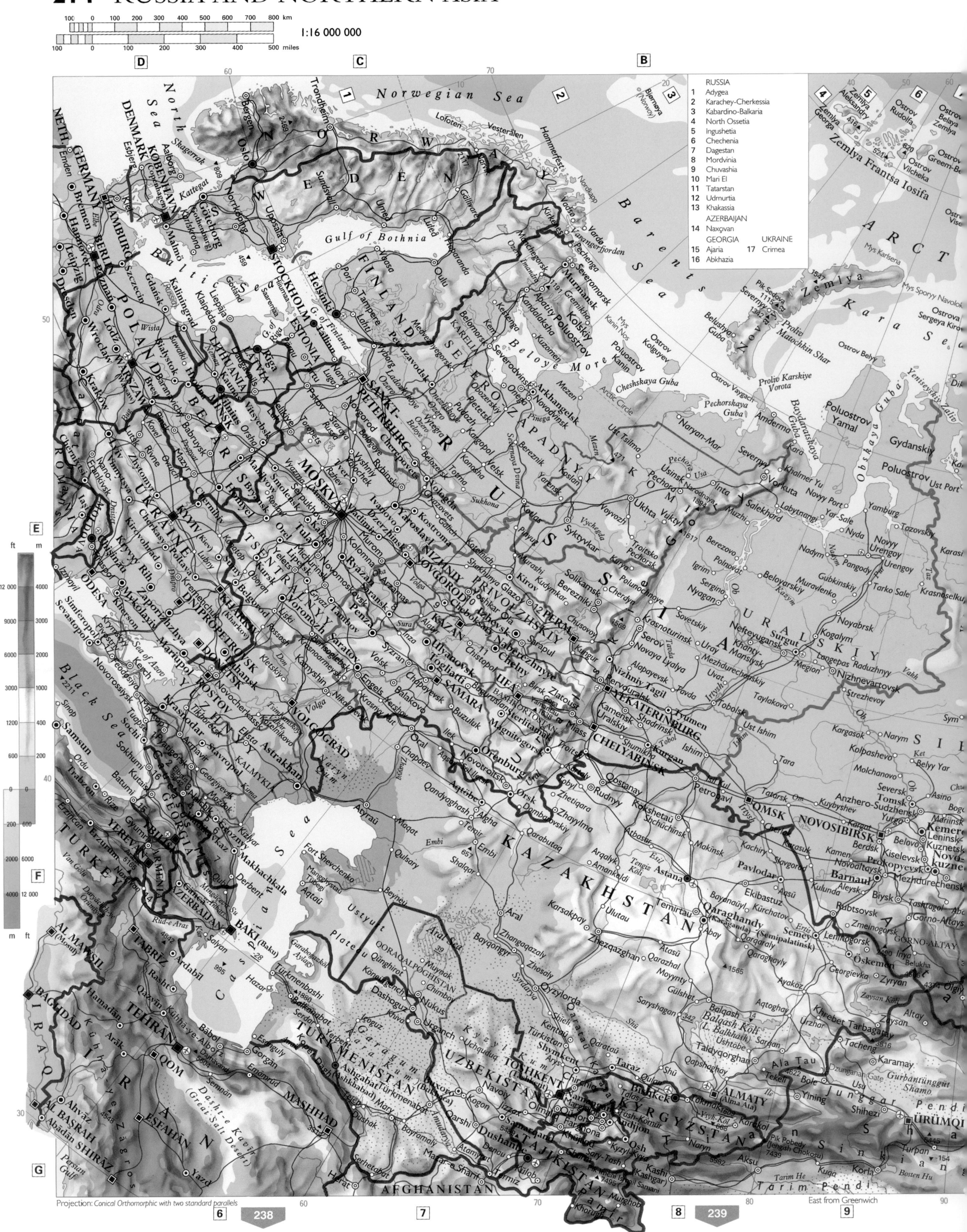

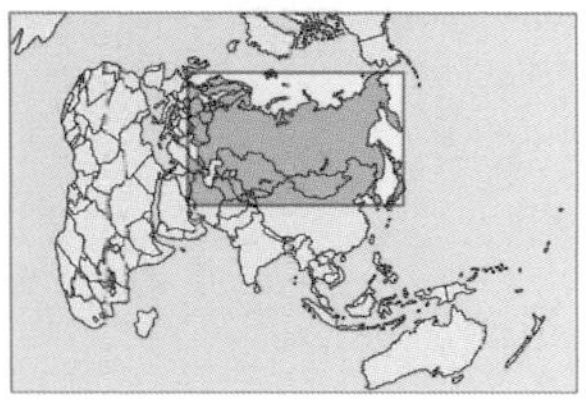

150

OCEAN

Laptev Sea

East Siberian Sea

Chukchi Sea

Bering Sea

Bering Str.

Sea of Okhotsk

Sea of Japan (East Sea)

Severnaya Zemlya

Poluostrov Gory Taymyr

Ostrov Shmidta
Ostrov Ushakova
Ostrova Sergeya Kirova
Novosibirskiye Ostrova
Ostrova Delonga
Mys Dezhneva (East C.)

Poluostrov Kamchatka
Sakhalin
Hokkaido
Honshū

R U S S I A

D A L N E V O S T O C H N Y

Verkhoyansk
Khrebet Cherskogo
Stanovoy Khrebet
Yablonovyy Khrebet
Sredinnyy Khrebet
Sikhote Alin
Kurilskiye Ostrova

M O N G O L I A
(Aerhtai Shan)
G o b i
C H I N A
Manchuria

Norilsk
Talnakh
Khatanga
Tiksi
Yakutsk
Lensk
Mirnyy
Bratsk
Krasnoyarsk
Irkutsk
Ulan Ude
Chita
Ulaanbaatar
Khabarovsk
Komsomolsk-na-Amur
Magadan
Petropavlovsk-Kamchatskiy
Vladivostok

QIQIHAR
HARBIN
DAQING
JIAMUSI
MUDANJIANG
JILIN
CHANGCHUN
FUSHUN
SHENYANG
ANSHAN
CHIFENG
BEIJING
HOHHOT
BAOTOU
ZHANGJIAKOU
TANGSHAN
DALIAN

NORTH KOREA
PYONGYANG
NAMPO
HAMHŬNG
WŎNSAN
CH'ŎNGJIN

SOUTH KOREA
SEOUL
INCHEON
DAEJEON
DAEGU
BUSAN
GWANGJU

JAPAN
SAPPORO
KYOTO
OSAKA
KOBE

218
219

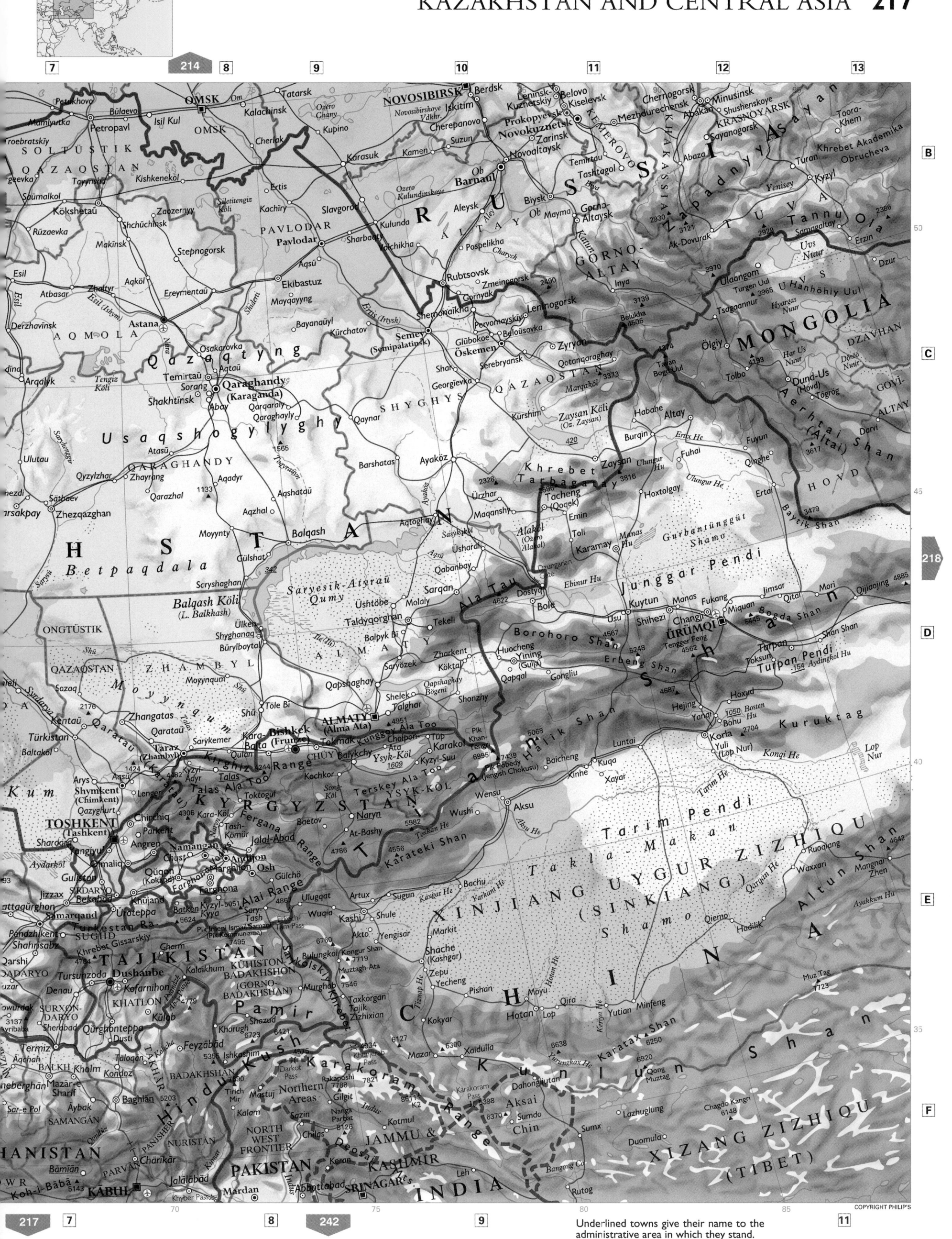

COPYRIGHT PHILIP'S

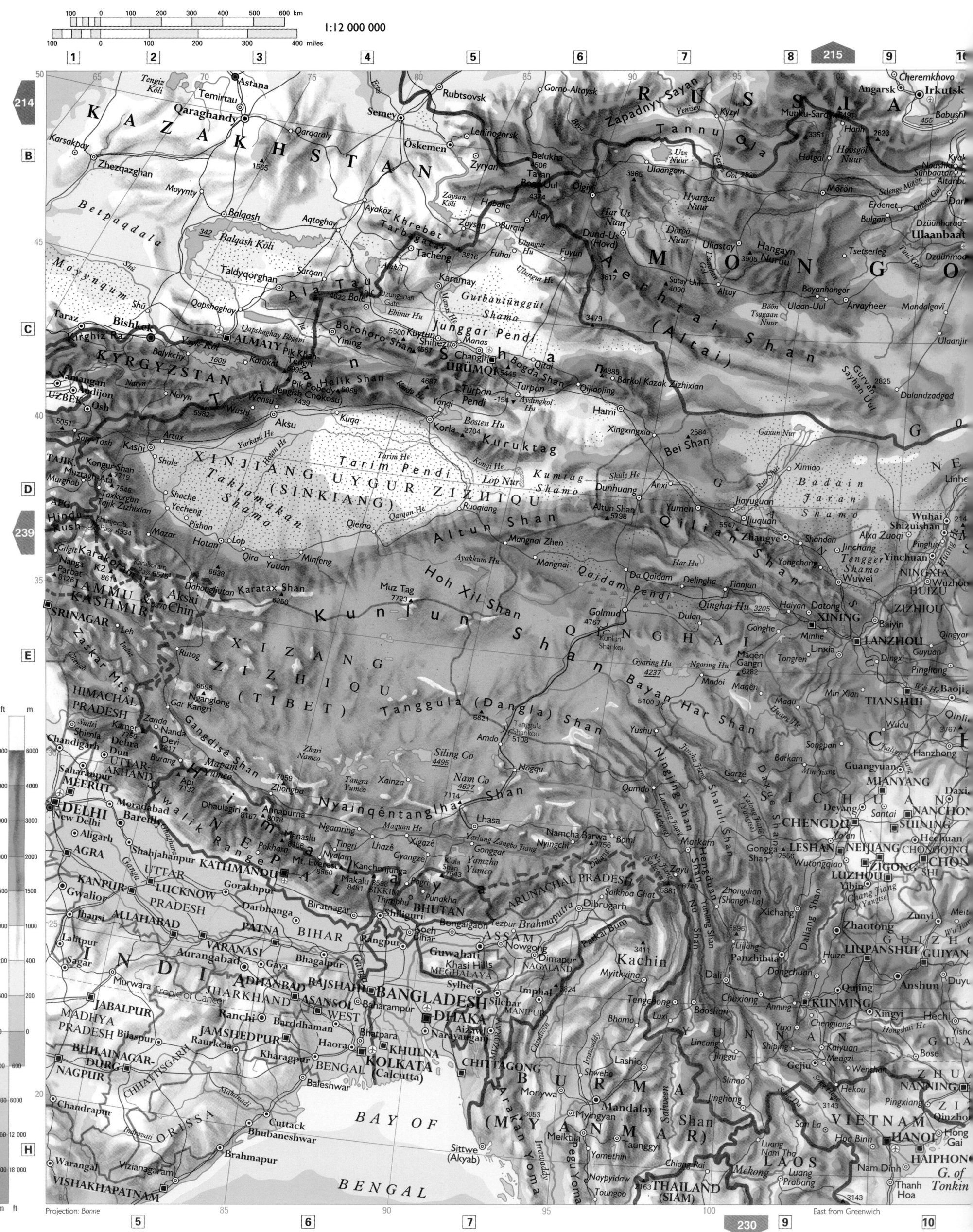

1:12 000 000

Projection: Bonne

East from Greenwich

HONG KONG, MACAU
AND SHENZHEN
1:800 000

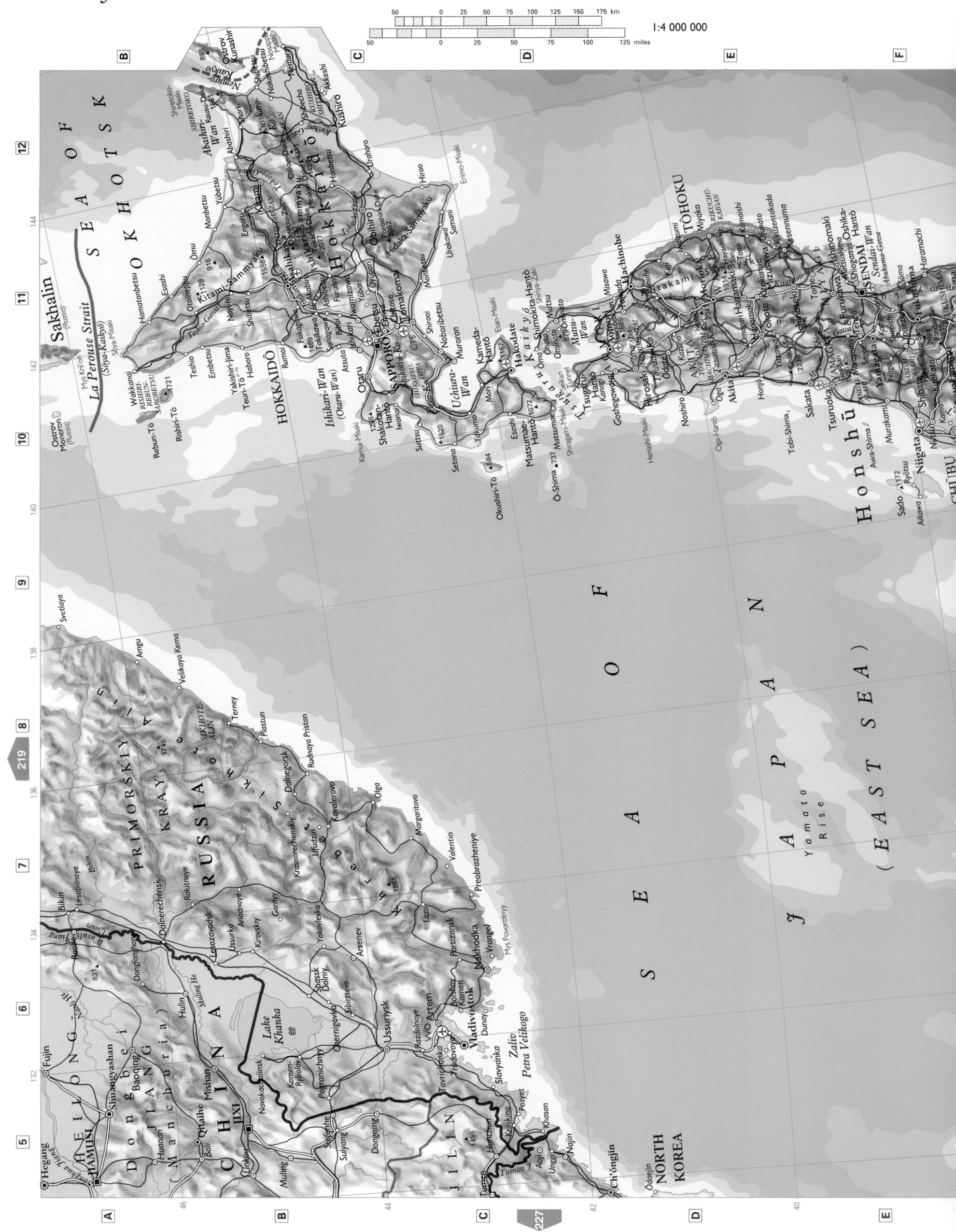

1:4 000 000

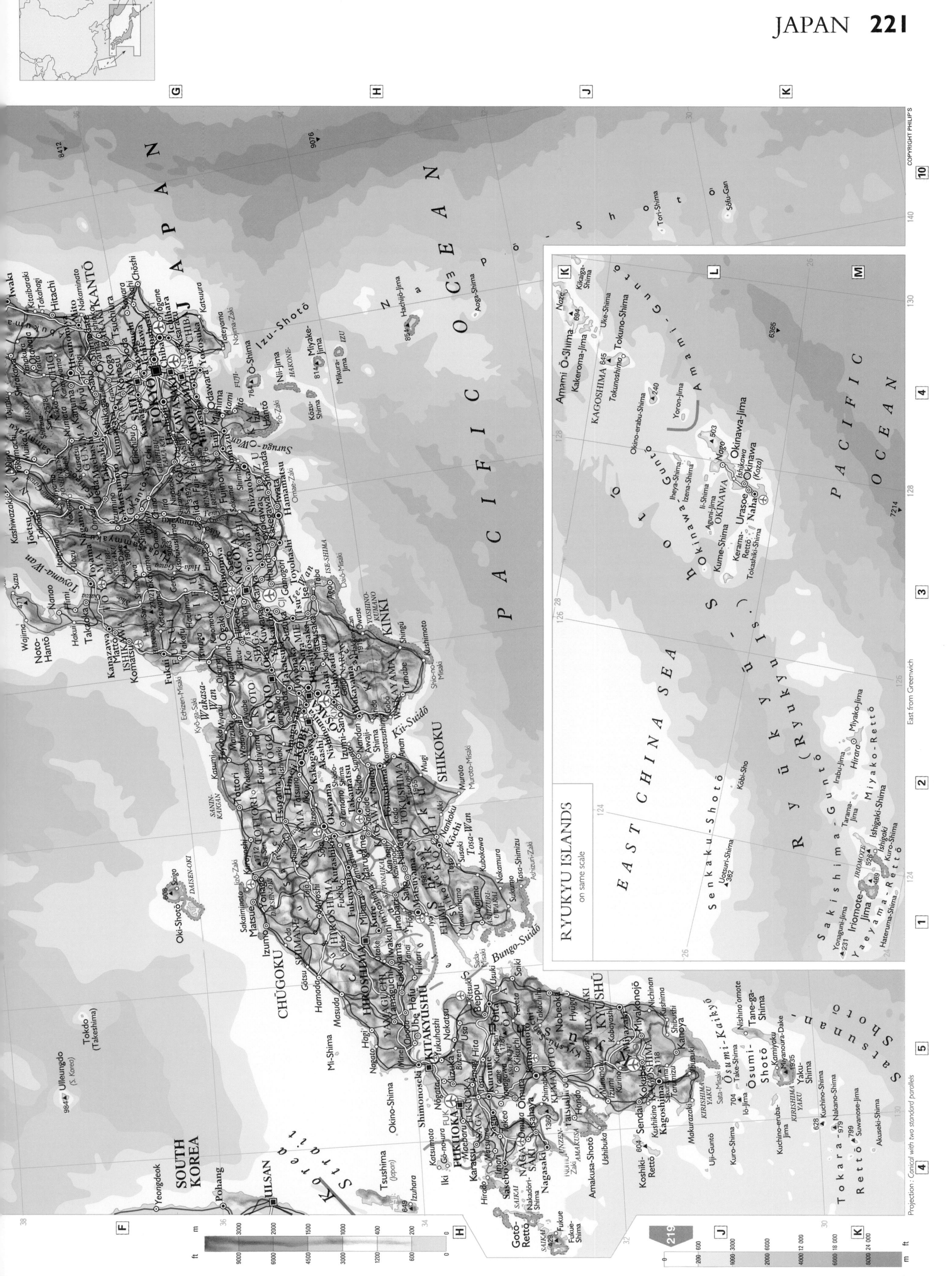

PACIFIC OCEAN

PACIFIC OCEAN

JAPAN

SOUTH KOREA

RYUKYU ISLANDS
on same scale

EAST CHINA SEA

Ryūkyū (Ryukyu) Islands

Projection: Conical with two standard parallels

East from Greenwich

SEA OF JAPAN (EAST SEA)

Oki-Shotō

Daimanji-San 608
Dōgo
Saigō
DAISEN-OKI

Dōzen

SOUTH KOREA

Yeongdeok

Heunghae

Pohang

Korea Strait

H o n s h u

SANIN-KAIGAN

Iwami

Kasumi

Toyooka

Hidaka

Suga-no-Sen 1510

CHŪGOKU-DISTRICT

DAISEN-OKI

Shimane-Hantō
Jizō-Zaki

Hi-no-Misaki
Taisha
Hirata
Matsue
Shinji-Ko
Yonago
Sakaiminato

TOTTORI
Tottori

Izumo
Shinji
Yasugi

Kurayoshi
Wakasa
Chizu
Wadayama

Ikuno

Dai-Sen 1729

S a n i n

Daitō
Tsuyama
Yamasaki

Ōda
Sanbe-San 1126

Dōgo-San 1209
Katsuyama
Ochiai

Yanahara
Sayo
Kasai

HYŌGO
Nishiwaki

IWAMI UNZAN

Yunotsu
Gōtsu

SHIMANE
Bingo-Ochiai
Tōjō

Niimi
Takahashi

OKAYAMA
Wake
Tatsuno
Himeji

Hamada
Gō-Gawa
Miyoshi
Shōbara

Ibara
Sōja

Bizen
Akō
Takasago
Kakogawa

Masuda
Chūgoku
Kake
Yoshida

Fuchū

Okayama
Kurashiki
Shōdo-Shima
Akashi

Aono-Yama 1339
Kanmuri-Yama

Higashi-Hiroshima
Konabe
Tamano

Ieshima-Shotō
Harima-Nada
Tsuna

Atō

HIROSHIMA
Saita

Mihara
Kasaoka
Sakaide

Ōmi-Shima
Hagi
Hatsukaichi
ITSUKUSHIMA SHIMA

Onomichi
In'noshima

Takamatsu
Awaji-Shima
Sumoto
608

Tsuno-Shima
Nagato
Ōta-Gawa

Kure
Takehara

KAGAWA
Miki
Shido

Naruto-Kaikyō
Naruto
Nandan

Mi-Shima

YAMAGUCHI
Yamaguchi
Mine
Ōgōri
Hōfu
Tokuji
Shin-Nan'yō
Iwakuni
Ōtake
Hiroshima-Wan

Ōmi-Shima
Aki-Nada
Marugame
Zentsūji
Kotohira

Sanuki-Sammyaku
Waki
Kamojima
Tokushima

Higashi-Suidō
Toyoura
Onoda
Ube
San'yō

Kudamatsu
Hikari
Yanai

Hōjō
Niihama
Ikeda

TOKUSHIMA
Komatsushima

Genkai-Nada

Shimonoseki
Ō-Shima
Nakama

Naga-Shima
Yashiro-Jima
Iwai-Jima
Matsuyama

Iyo-Mishima
Saijō
1981
Otoyo
Tsurugi-San 1955
Anan

Hibiki-Nada

KITAKYŪSHŪ
Suō-Nada

Heigun-Tō

Kan'onji
Kawanoe

Shikoku-Sanchi

Kii

Kamiagata
Kara-Saki
Kamitsushima
Gō-no-ura
Munakata
Fukuma
Koga
Yukuhashi

Naga-Shima
Hime-Shima

EHIME
Matsuyama
Iyo
Tōyō
Ishizuchi-Yama 1981
Kōchi-Sanchi
Nankoku
Tosa-Yamada

Tsushima
Iki
Iki-Kaikyō

Miyata
Nōgata
Nakatsu
Futago-Yama

Nagahama
Ōzu
Uchiko 1562
Ino

Noichi
Aki
Tōyō

Izuhara
Mitsushima
649
Kō-Saki

FUKUOKA
FUK
Maebaru
Dazaifu

Iizuka
Tagawa
Buzen

Usa
Bungotakada
Kitsuki

Iyo-Nada
Sada-Misaki-Hantō
Yawatahama

KŌCHI
Kōchi
Tosa

Shikoku
SHIKOKU-DISTRICT

Ō-Shima
Ikitsuki-Shima
Hirado
Matsuura

SAGA
Tosu
Ogōri
Amagi
Hita

Yufu-Dake 1584
Beppu
Sada-Misaki
Saganoseki

Uwa
Nishi-Tosa
Susaki

Tosa-Wan

Muroto

Hirado-Shima
674
SAIKAI
Saza

Takeo
Taku
Saga
Kurume
Chikugo
Kurogi
Kusu

Beppu-Wan
Tsurusaki

Uwajima
Hiromi
Tsushima

Kubokawa
Muroto-Misaki

Ōmura-Wan

Imari
Karatsu
Tsukushi-Sanchi
Sefuri-San 1055
Kashima
Setaka

ŌITA
Ōita
Usuki

Saga
Nakamura

865
Tosa-Shimizu

Hirado
Matsushima
Arita
Yanagawa
Iyama

Aso
Ichinomiya
Takeda
Mie

Saiki

ASHIZURI-UWAKAI
Ashizuri-Zaki

NAGASAKI
Ureshino
Ariake-Tara

Ōmuta
Yamaga
Aso-Zan
Sobo-Yama 1758

Tsurumi-Saki
Kamae

Oki-no-Shima

Tara-Dake 1076
Isahata
Arao
ASO-KUJŪ
Oguni
Kuju-San 1787

Takachiho

Sasebo
Nagayo
Kumamoto
1592
Kikuchi
Kōshi

Hinokage

Tachibana-Wan
Ōmura

KUMAMOTO
Aso
Mashiki

Ōzu
Sōyō
Yamato

Isahaya
Shimabara
Uto
Matsubase

Kunimi-Dake 1739
Nobeoka

Nagasaki
1360
Obama
UNZEN AMAKUSA

Misumi

Kyūshū-Sanchi

Nomo-Zaki
Kuchinotsu

Hondo
Matsushima
Kami
UNZEN AMAKUSA

Yatsushiro
Takachiho

Hyūga

Amakusa-Nada

Amakusa-Shotō
Shimo-Jima

Itsuki
Shiiba

Kyūshū
KYŪSHŪ-DISTRICT

Ushibuka
Naga-Shima
Yatsushiro-Kai
Taragi
Hitoyoshi

MIYAZAKI
Saito
Takanabe

Kyūshū Trench

Izumi
Minamata
Ebino
Kobayashi

Sadowara

Akune
Ōkuchi
Kurino

Miyazaki

Kami-Koshiki-Jima
Yoshimatsu
Kirishima-Yama 1700

604
Koshiki-Rettō
Miyanojō
KIRISHIMA YAKU
Miyakonojō
Nichinan

Shimo-Koshiki-Jima
Sendai
Aira
Kokubu

Kushikino
Hayato
On-Take 1118
Sueyoshi
Aburatsu

KAGOSHIMA
Kagoshima
Ijūin
Miyakonojō

Koshiki-Kaikyō
Fukiage
KAGOSHIMA
Sakurajima
Shibushi

Kaseda
Tarumizu
Kanoya
Kushima

Noma-Saki
Makurazaki
Kiire
Shibushi-Wan

Bō-no-Misaki
Ibusuki
Kōyama 968

Kawanabe
Kaimon-Dake 924
Yamagawa

KIRISHIMA YAKU
Ōsumi-Hantō

Sata-Misaki

5737

Shinkansen line

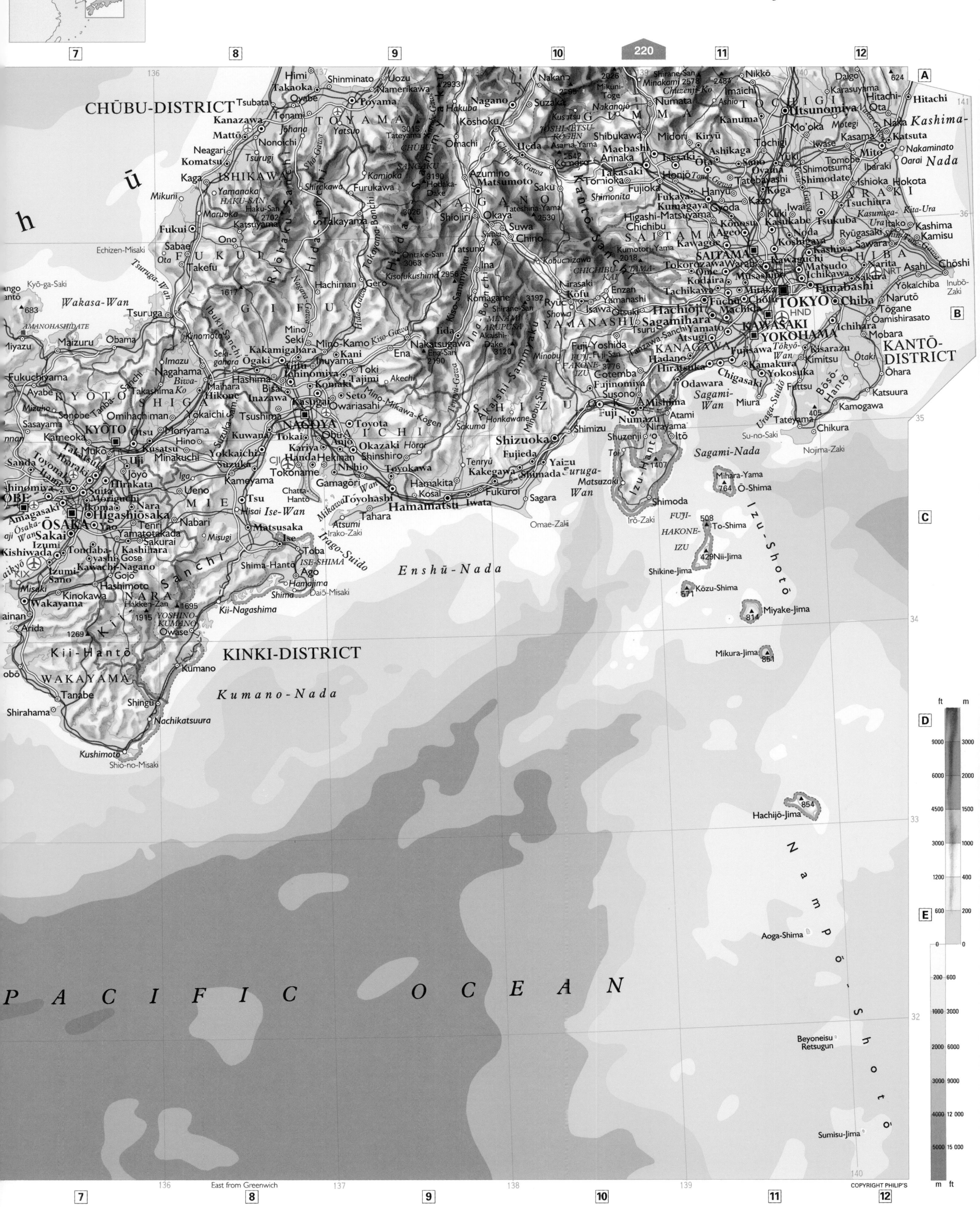

CHŪBU-DISTRICT

KANTŌ-DISTRICT

KINKI-DISTRICT

Enshū-Nada

Kumano-Nada

Sagami-Nada

Izu-Shotō

PACIFIC OCEAN

Nampo Shotō

East from Greenwich

COPYRIGHT PHILIP'S

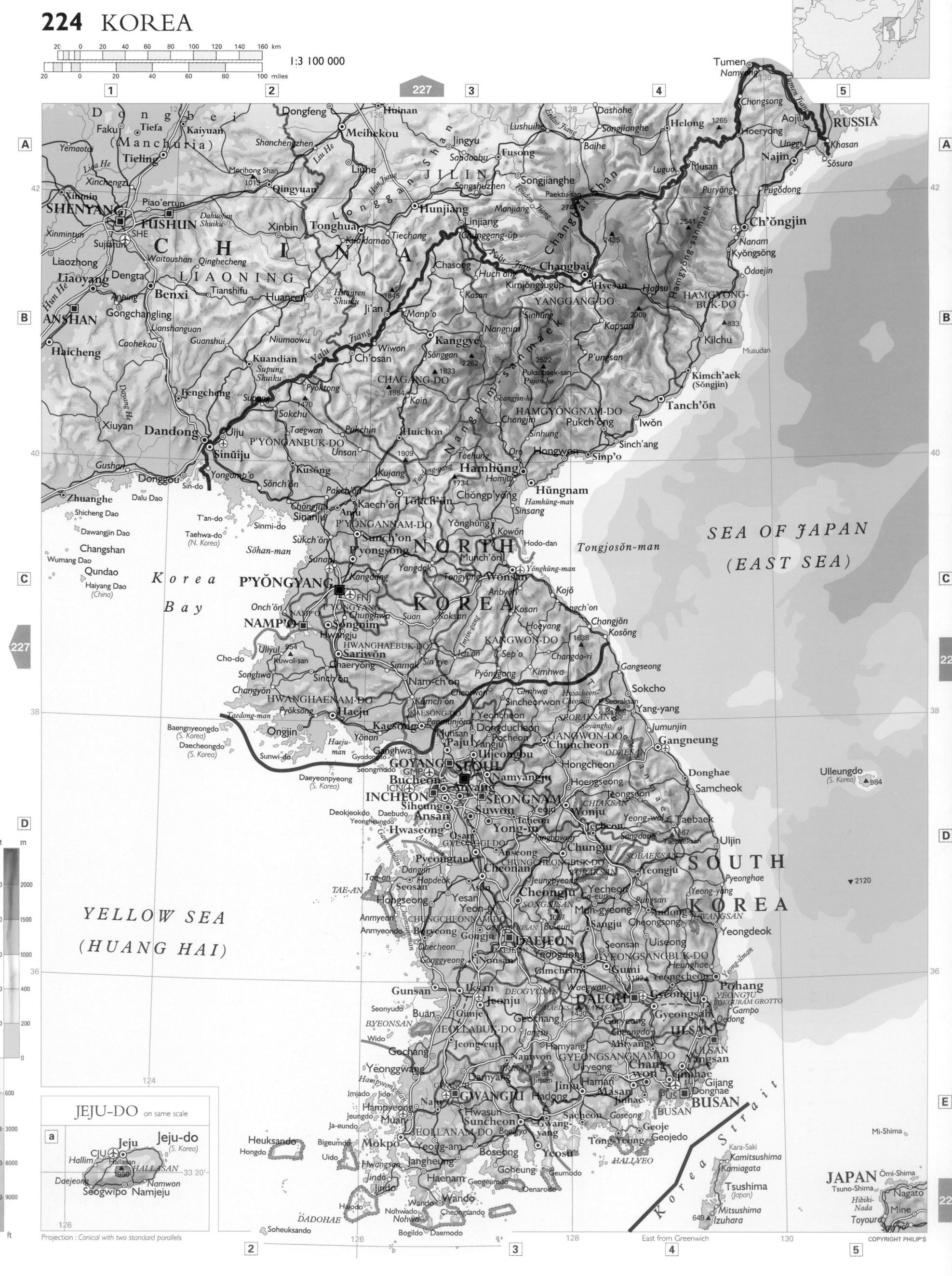

1:3 100 000

YELLOW SEA
(HUANG HAI)

SEA OF JAPAN
(EAST SEA)

Korea
Bay

RUSSIA

CHINA

LIAONING

JILIN

NORTH
KOREA

SOUTH
KOREA

JAPAN

Korea Strait

JEJU-DO on same scale

Jeju-do
(S. Korea)

Projection : Conical with two standard parallels

COPYRIGHT PHILIP'S

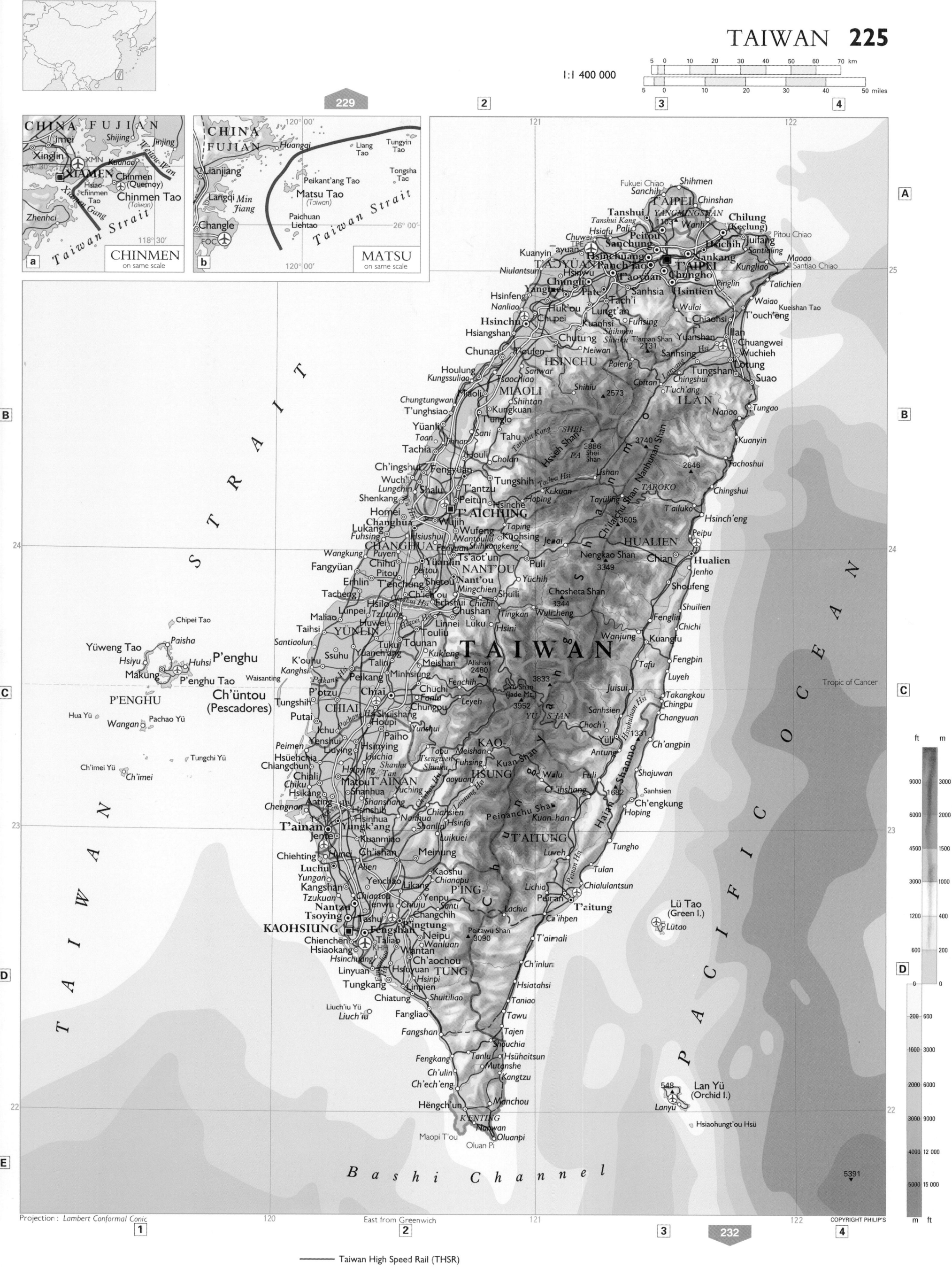

1:1 400 000

5   0   10   20   30   40   50   60   70 km
5   0   10   20   30   40   50 miles

CHINMEN
on same scale

CHINA FUJIAN

Il imei
Xinglin   Shijing   Jinjing
Kuanao   Chinmen
XIAMEN   (Quemoy)
XMN
Hsiao-   Chinmen Tao
Zhenhci   chinmen Tao   (Taiwan)
          Xiang Gang
                a   Taiwan Strait

MATSU
on same scale

CHINA
FUJIAN   120° 00'

Lianjiang   Huangqi   Liang   Tungyin
                        Tao   Tao
Langqi Min   Peikant'ang Tao   Tongsha
        Jiang   Tao
Changle   Matsu Tao
FOC   (Taiwan)   26° 00'
                Paichuan
                Liehtao
          b   Taiwan Strait
          120° 00'

229

2   **3**   **4**

121   122

Fukuei Chiao   Shihmen
Sanchih   **A**
              T'AIPEI Chinshan
Tanshui **Tanshui** YANGMINGSHAN Chilung
Tanshui Kang 1103 Wanli (Keelung)
Hsiafu Pali Peitou Hsichih Pitou Chiao
Kuanyin Chuwei Sanchung Nankang Santiaoling
TAO'Y'UAN   T'AIPEI   Kungliao
Niulantsun Panch'iao Chungho Maoao Santiao Chiao
Chungli Paoyuan Pinglin Talichien
TAOYUAN Hsinchuang **Hsintien**
Hsinfeng Yangmei Patu   25
Nanliao Huk'ou Lungt'an Wulai Waiao Kueishan Tao
Hsiangshan Chupei Kuanghsi Fuhsing Chiaohsi T'ouch'eng
Hsinchu Chutung Shihmen Yuanshan Ilan
Chunan Neiwan T'aman Shan Sanhsing Chuangwei
Houlung **HSINCHU** 2131 Hsi Wuchieh
Kungssuliao Tsaochiao Paleng Chingshui Lotung
Miaoli Shihtan Chitan T'uch'ang Tungshan Suao **B**
T'unghsiao **MIAOLI** 2573 **ILAN**
Y'uanli Sani Tahu Nanao
Taan Tunglo Kang SHEI- 3740 Tungao
Tachia Houli PA Nanhunan Shan
Ch'ingshui Fengyuan Hsueh Shan Kuanyin
Wuch'i Cholan 886 2646 Tachoshui
Lungching Shalu Tungshih shei Shan TAROKO
Shenkang Peitun Hsinche Ushan Chingshui
Homei **T'AICHUNG** Hoping Tayuling T'ailuko
Changhua Wujih Taping Shan 3605 Hsinch'eng
Lukang Wufeng Kuohsing Chilai Peipu
Fuhsing Hsiushui Wantouliu Shihkangkeng Jemai **HUALIEN**
CHANGHUA Ts'aot'un Chian Hualien 24
Wangkung Yuanlin Puli Nengkao Shan Jenho
Fangyuan Chihu Pitou Nant'ou 3349
Erhlin Shetou Yuchih Shoufeng
Tacheng T'enchiang **NANT'OU** Mingchien Shuili Shuilien
Maliao Hsilo Echshui Chushan Choshcta Shan Fenglin Chichi
Taihsi Lunpei Tzutung Linnei Luku 3344 Kuangfu
Santiaolun Tuku **YUNLIN** Tingkan Wuli-heng Fengpin
Huwei Yuanch'ang Hsini Wanjung Tafu
K'ouhu Ssuhu Kuk'eng Chichi
Kanghsi Talin Meishan **TAIWAN** Tafu
Waisanting Peikang Minhsiung Alishan Luyeh **C**
P'enghu P'tzu Chuchi 2480 Juisui Takangkou
Makung P'enghu Tao Chiai Fenchih Yu Shan Changyuan Chingpu
P'enghu Tungshih Fonla (Jade Mt.) Sanhsien Ch'angpin
Ch'untou Putai Chungpu 3952 3833 Choch'i
(Pescadores) Houpi Yunshui YU Yuli
Ichu Paiho Leyeh SHAN 1331 Antung
Peimen Yenshui Hsinying Meishan Kuan Shan Ch'angpin
Hsuehchia Liuying Iuchia Fuhsing Walu Ch'ihshang
Chiangchun KAO- Tapu Shajuwan
Chiali Hsinhua HSUNG Tsengwen Kuan-han Sanhsien
Chiku MatouT'AINAN Shanhua Shuiku Taoyuan 1682 Ch'engkung
Chengnan Anting Yuching Chiahsien Peinanchu Sha Hoping
Hsikang Hsinshih Shanshang Nankua Kuan- 23
Anping **T'AINAN** Hsinfa Hsinfa han
T'ainan Jente Yungk'ang Luikuei **T'AITUNG**
Chiehting Ch'ishan Shanlin Luyeh
Hunei Meinung Lichia Peinan Tungho
Luchu Alien Kaoshu Lulan Tulan
Yungan Chianapu P'ING- Peir'an Chialulantsun
Kangshan Yenchao Likang santi **T'aitung** Lü Tao
Tzukuan Chiatou Chuju Changchih HUNG (Green I.)
Nantzu Jenwu Neipu Peitawu Shan C'ihpen Lütao
Tsoying Tashu Changchih 3090
KAOHSIUNG Fengshan Pingtung Taliao T'aimali
Chienchen KHH Wantan Ch'inlun
Hsiaokang Taliao Ch'aochou Hsiatahsi
Hsinchuang Hsinyuan **TUNG** Taniao
Linyuan Hsinpi Tawu
Tungkang Limpien
Liuch'iu Yü Chiatung Shuitiliao
Liuch'iu Fangliao Tanlu **D**
Fangshan Tajen
Shouchia
Fengkang Tanlu Hsüheitsun
Ch'ulin Mutanshe 548 Lan Yü
Ch'ech'eng Kangtzu Lanyu (Orchid I.)
Hëngch'un Manchou Hsiaohungt'ou Hsü
K'ENTING
Maopi T'ou Nanwan
Oluanpi 22
Oluan Pi

Tropic of Cancer

PACIFIC OCEAN

TAIWAN STRAIT

Chipei Tao
Yüweng Tao Paisha
Hsiyu Huhsi
Makung P'enghu Tao
P'enghu Tao Waisanting
Hua Yü
Wangan Pachao Yü
Ch'imei Yü Tungchi Yü
Ch'imei

TAIWAN

Bashi Channel

5391

ft   m
9000 3000
6000 2000
4500 1500
3000 1000
1200   400
600   200
0   0
0   0
200   600
1000   3000
2000   6000
3000   9000
4000   12000
5000   15000
m   ft

Projection: Lambert Conformal Conic

1   East from Greenwich **2**   **3**   **4**

120   121   122

COPYRIGHT PHILIP'S

232

——— Taiwan High Speed Rail (THSR)

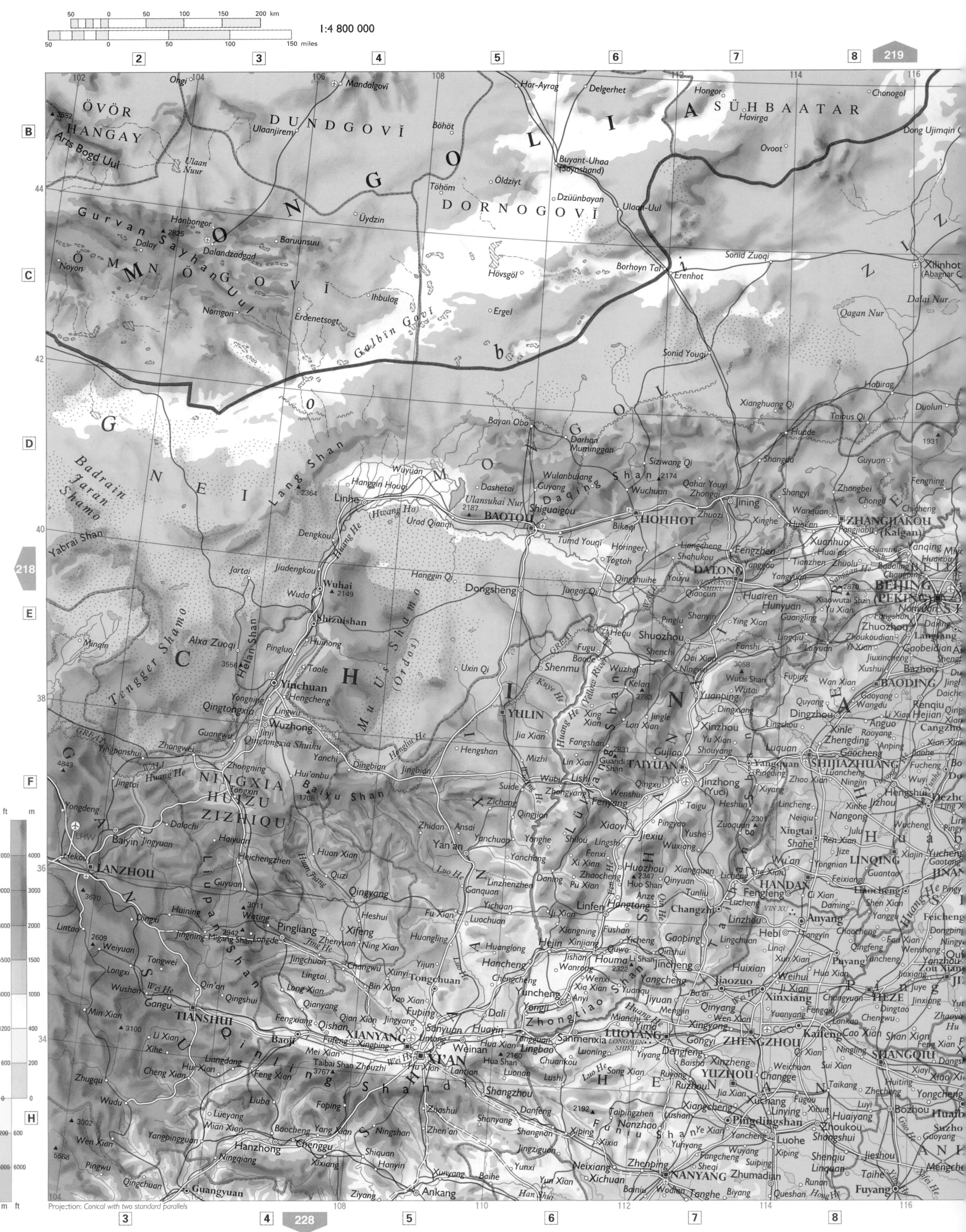

1:4 800 000

Projection: Conical with two standard parallels

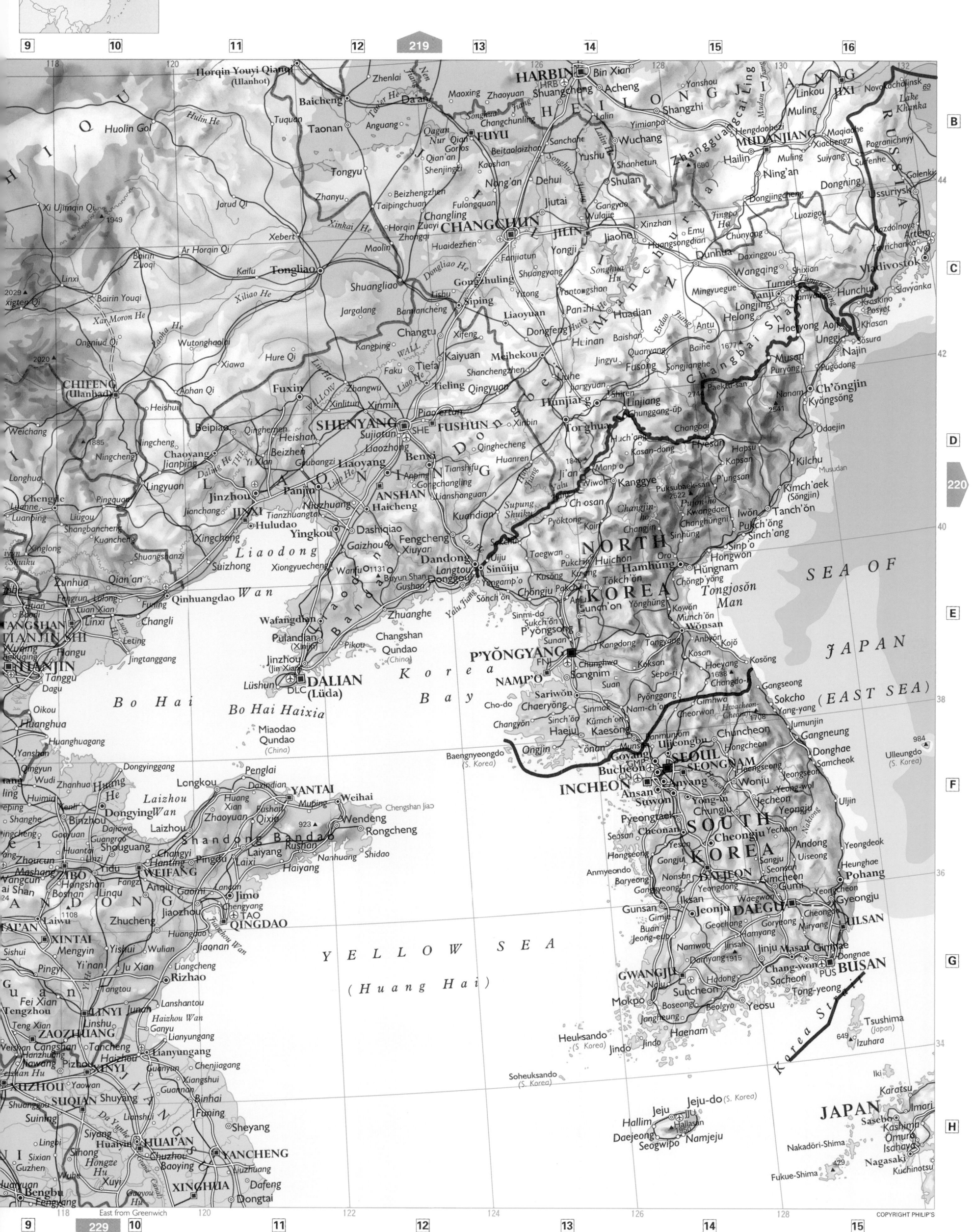

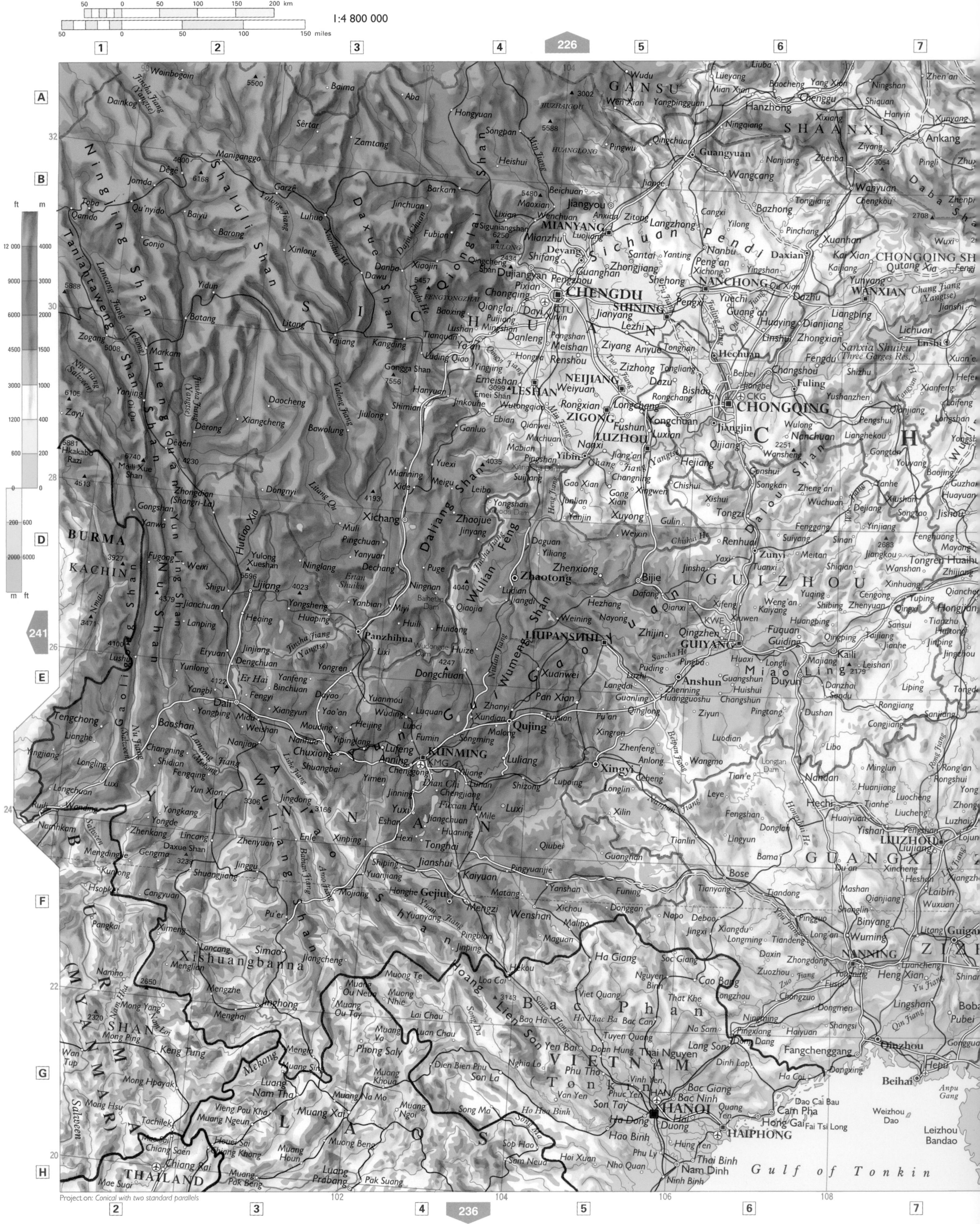

1:4 800 000

Projection: Conical with two standard parallels

East from Greenwich

SOUTH CHINA SEA

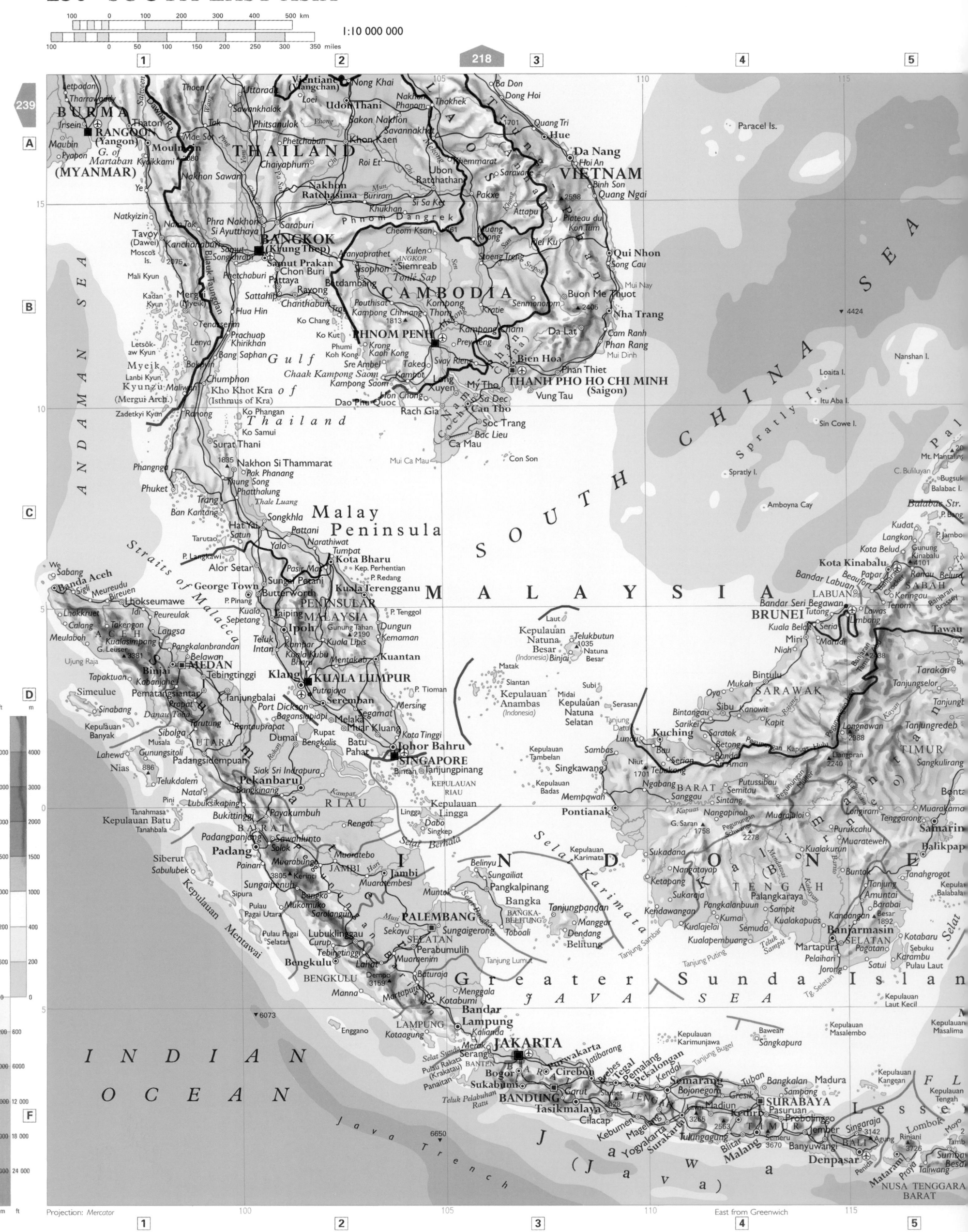

Projection: Mercator

East from Greenwich

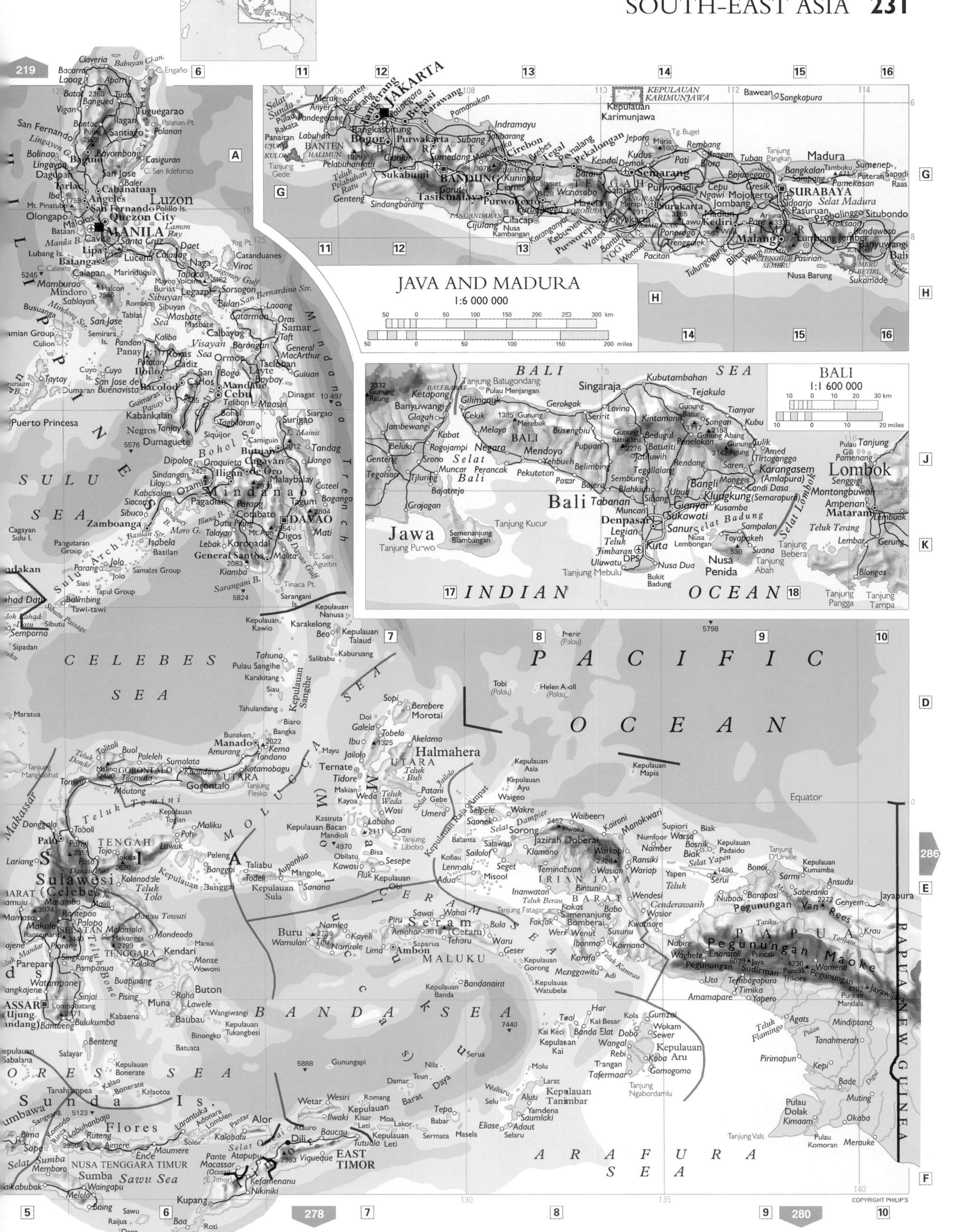

JAVA AND MADURA
1:6 000 000

BALI
1:1 600 000

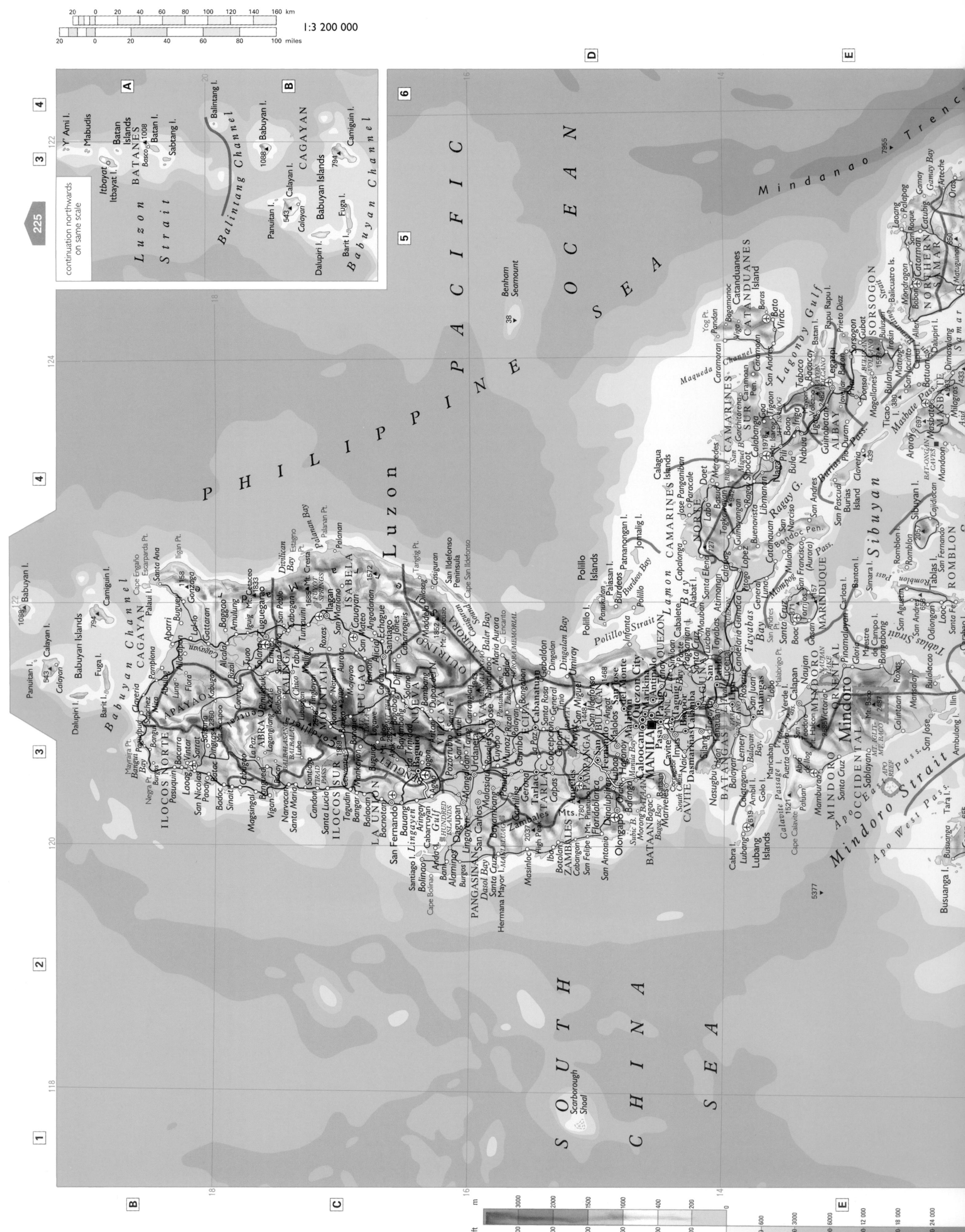

1:3 200 000

225

continuation northwards on same scale

A

Y' Ami I.
Mabudis
Itbayat I.
Itbayat I.
BATANES
Islands
Batan I.
Basco 1008
Batan I.
Sabtang I.
Balintang I.
Balintang Channel

Luzon Strait

B

Babuyan I.
1088
CAGAYAN
Camiguin I.
794
Calayan I.
Panutan I.
543
Calayan
Babuyan Islands
Dalupiri I.
Fuga I.
Barit I.
Babuyan Channel

PHILIPPINE PACIFIC OCEAN SEA

Mindanao Trench
7955

Benham Seamount
38

SOUTH CHINA SEA

Scarborough Shoal

Luzon

Mindoro

m 3000 2000 1500 1000 400 200 0
ft 9000 6000 4500 3000 1200 600 0

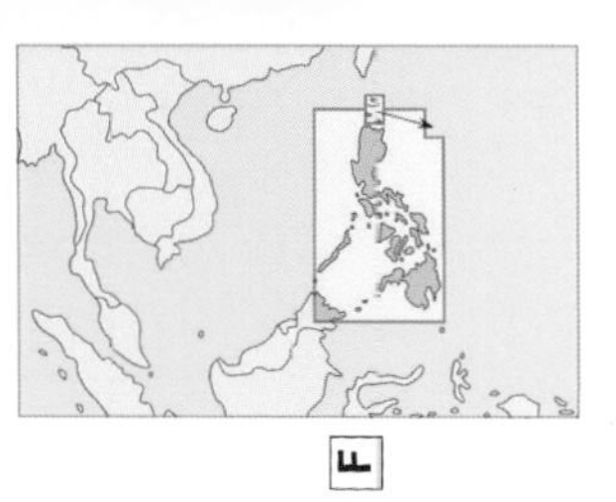

Projection: Lambert Conformal Conic

East from Greenwich

COPYRIGHT PHILIP'S

Major regions / provinces labelled:

EASTERN SAMAR
SAMAR
CARAGA
SURIGAO DEL NORTE
SURIGAO DEL SUR
DINAGAT
SOUTHERN LEYTE
LEYTE
BILIRAN
AGUSAN DEL NORTE
AGUSAN DEL SUR
DAVAO ORIENTAL
DAVAO
DAVAO DEL NORTE
DAVAO DEL SUR
BUKIDNON
MISAMIS ORIENTAL
MISAMIS OCCIDENTAL
CAMIGUIN
LANAO DEL NORTE
LANAO DEL SUR
NORTH COTABATO
SOUTH COTABATO
SULTAN KUDARAT
MAGUINDANAO
SHARIFF KABUNSUAN
ZAMBOANGA DEL NORTE
ZAMBOANGA DEL SUR
SOCCSKSARGEN
CEBU
BOHOL
SIQUIJOR
NEGROS ORIENTAL
NEGROS OCCIDENTAL
GUIMARAS
ILOILO
CAPIZ
AKLAN
ANTIQUE
PANAY
PALAWAN
BASILAN
SULU
TAWI-TAWI

MUSLIM MINDANAO (ARMM)

Mindanao

VISAYAS

Seas and water bodies:

Samar Sea
Visayan Sea
Camotes Sea
Sibuyan Sea
Bohol Sea
Mindanao Sea
SULU SEA
CELEBES SEA
Moro Gulf
Davao Gulf
Leyte Gulf
Panay Gulf
Cuyo West Pass
Cuyo East Pass
Palawan Passage
Balabac Strait
Basilan Strait
Sibutu Passage
Sibutu Passage
Sulu Archipelago

Malaysia / Borneo:

MALAYSIA
SABAH
Borneo
Sandakan
Lahad Datu
Turtle Islands

Selected towns:

Tacloban, Ormoc, Maasin, Surigao, Butuan, Cabadbaran, Davao, Digos, General Santos, Koronadal, Cotabato, Marawi, Iligan, Cagayan de Oro, Valencia, Malaybalay, Pagadian, Dipolog, Zamboanga, Jolo, Bongao, Cebu, Mandaue, Toledo, Dumaguete, Bacolod, Iloilo, Roxas, Kalibo, Puerto Princesa

Tubbataha Reefs
5207

1:5 600 000

Projection: Mercator

East from Greenw

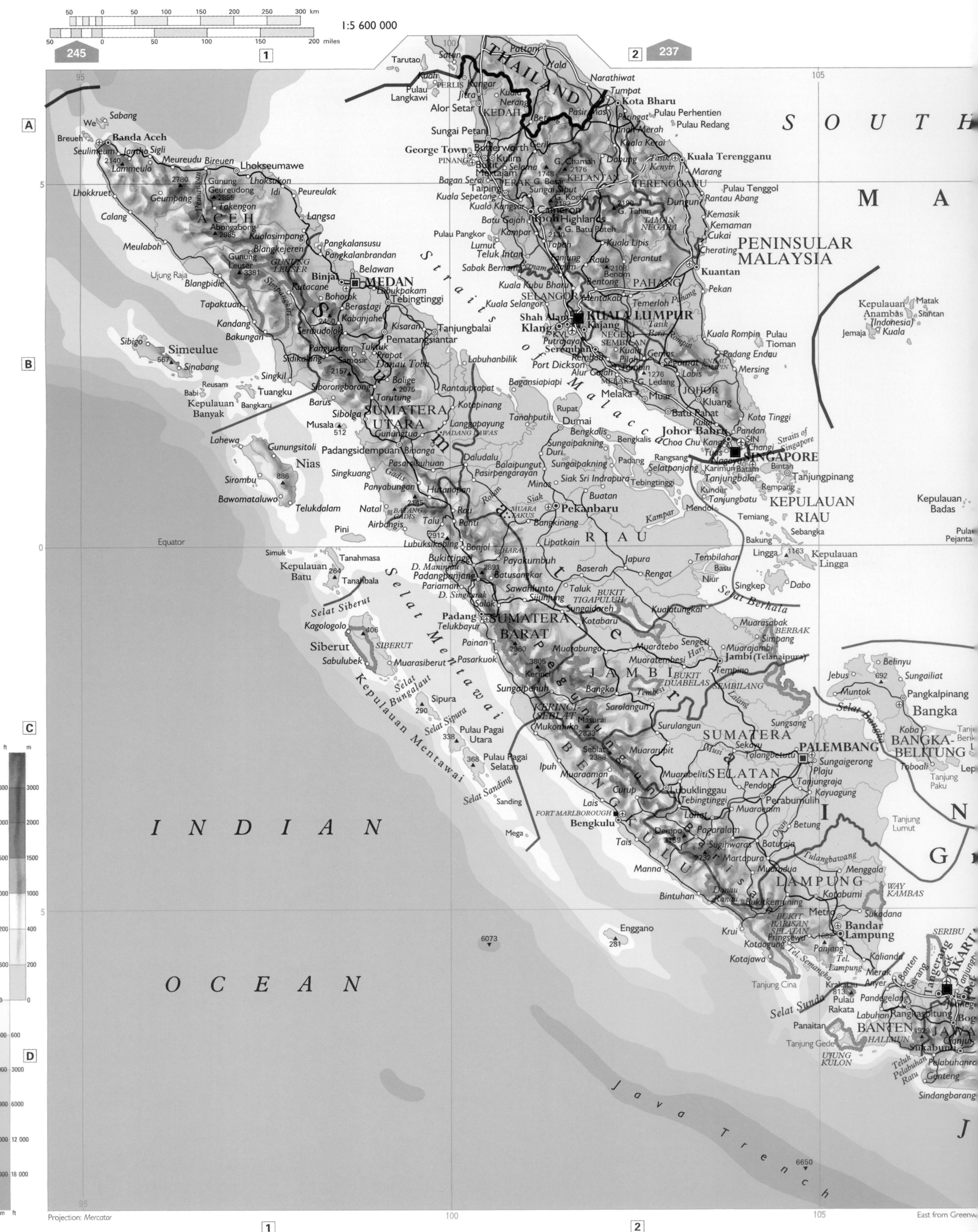

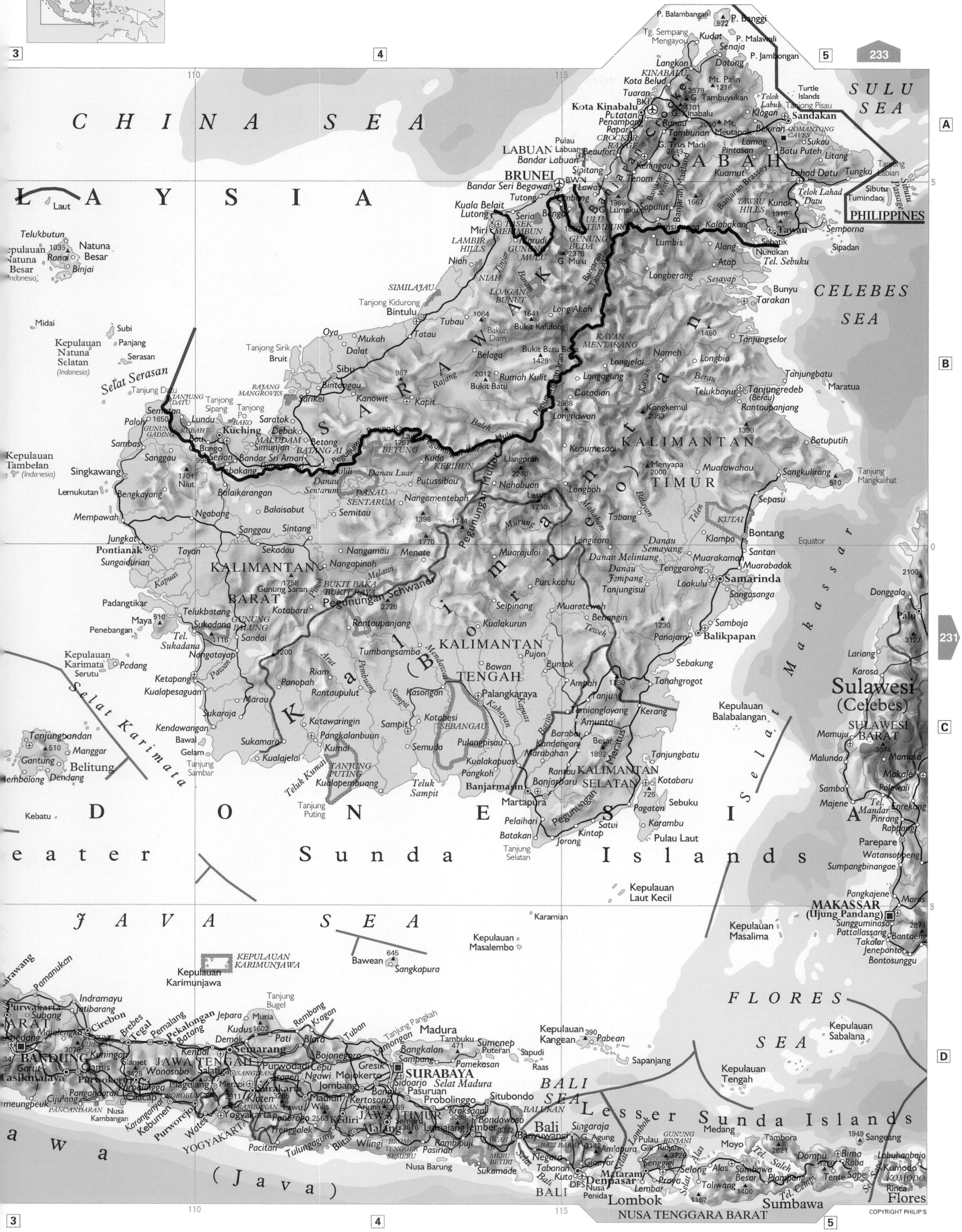

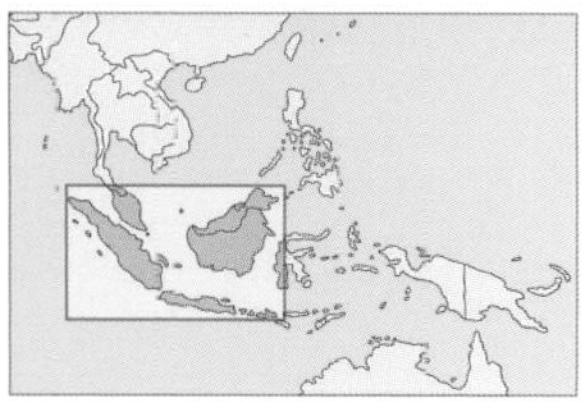

CHINA SEA

MALAYSIA

SULU SEA

CELEBES SEA

PHILIPPINES

BRUNEI
Bandar Seri Begawan
Kuala Belait
Lutong
Miri

SABAH
Kota Kinabalu
KINABALU
Sandakan
Labuan
Bandar Labuan
Lahad Datu
Tawau

SARAWAK

Kuching
Sibu
Bintulu
Sri Aman

KALIMANTAN BARAT
Pontianak
Singkawang
Sambas
Ketapang

KALIMANTAN TENGAH
Palangkaraya
Sampit
Pangkalanbuun

KALIMANTAN TIMUR
Samarinda
Balikpapan
Bontang
Tarakan

KALIMANTAN SELATAN
Banjarmasin
Banjarbaru
Martapura

Pegunungan Muller
Pegunungan Schwaner

Sulawesi (Celebes)
SULAWESI BARAT
Mamuju
MAKASSAR (Ujung Pandang)

Selat Makassar

Greater Sunda Islands

JAVA SEA

Kepulauan Karimunjawa

Madura
SURABAYA
Semarang
BANDUNG
Cirebon
YOGYAKARTA
JAWA TENGAH
JAWA TIMUR
Malang

FLORES SEA

BALI SEA
Bali
Denpasar
Mataram
Lombok
Sumbawa

Lesser Sunda Islands
NUSA TENGGARA BARAT

INDONESIA

Kepulauan Natuna
Natuna Besar
Ranai

Kepulauan Tambelan

Kepulauan Karimata
Belitung

Selat Karimata

(Java)

Equator

COPYRIGHT PHILIP'S

1:4 800 000

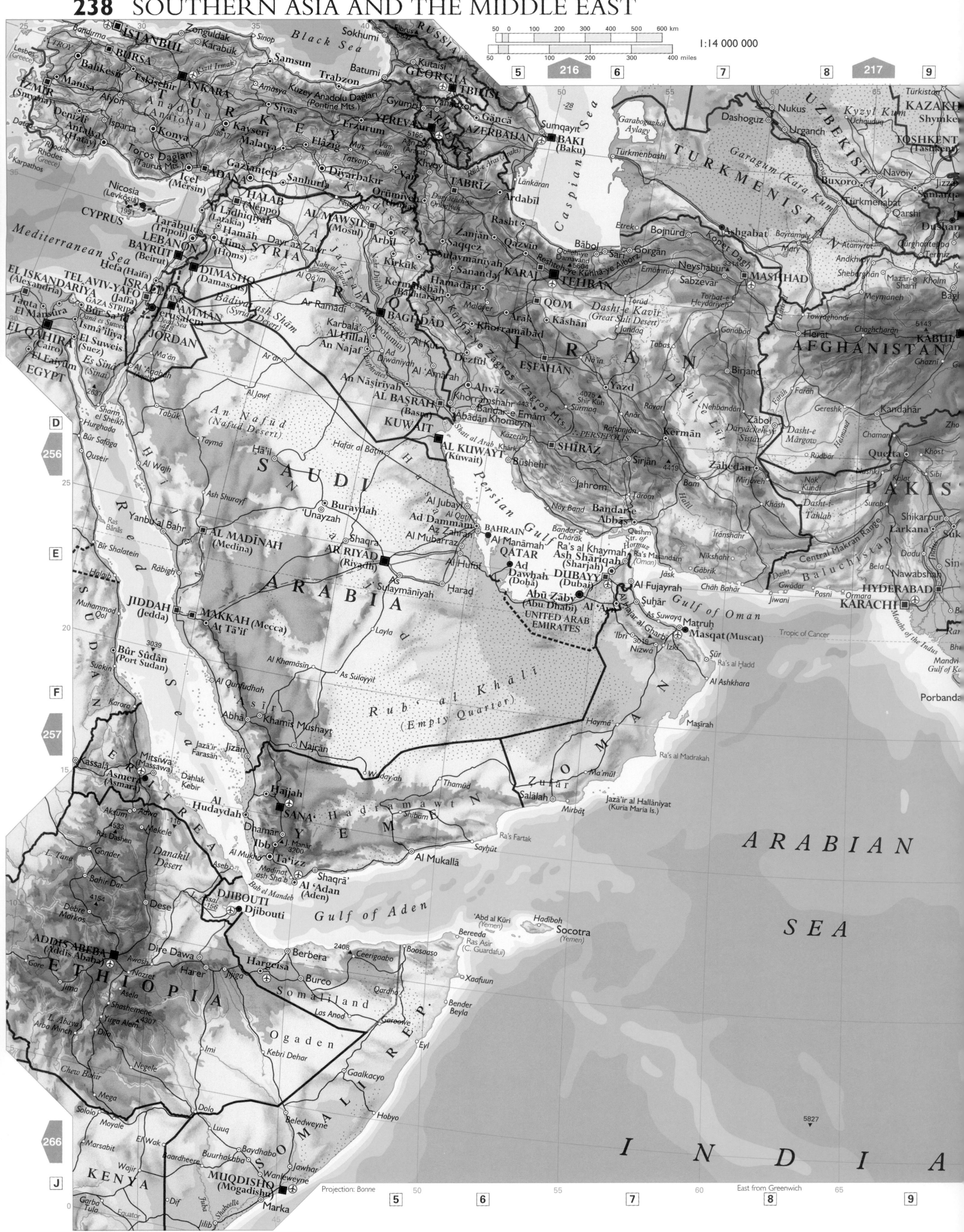

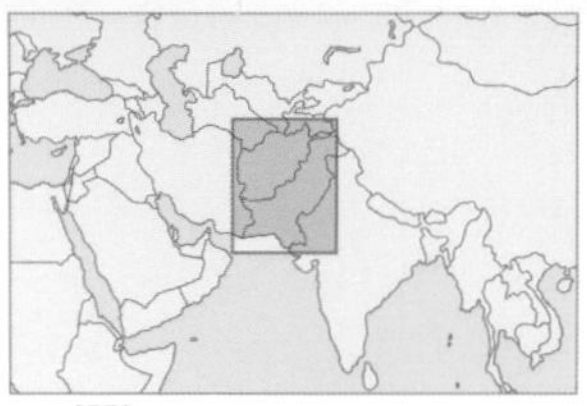

50 0 50 100 150 200 250 300 km
50 0 50 100 150 200 miles

1:5 600 000

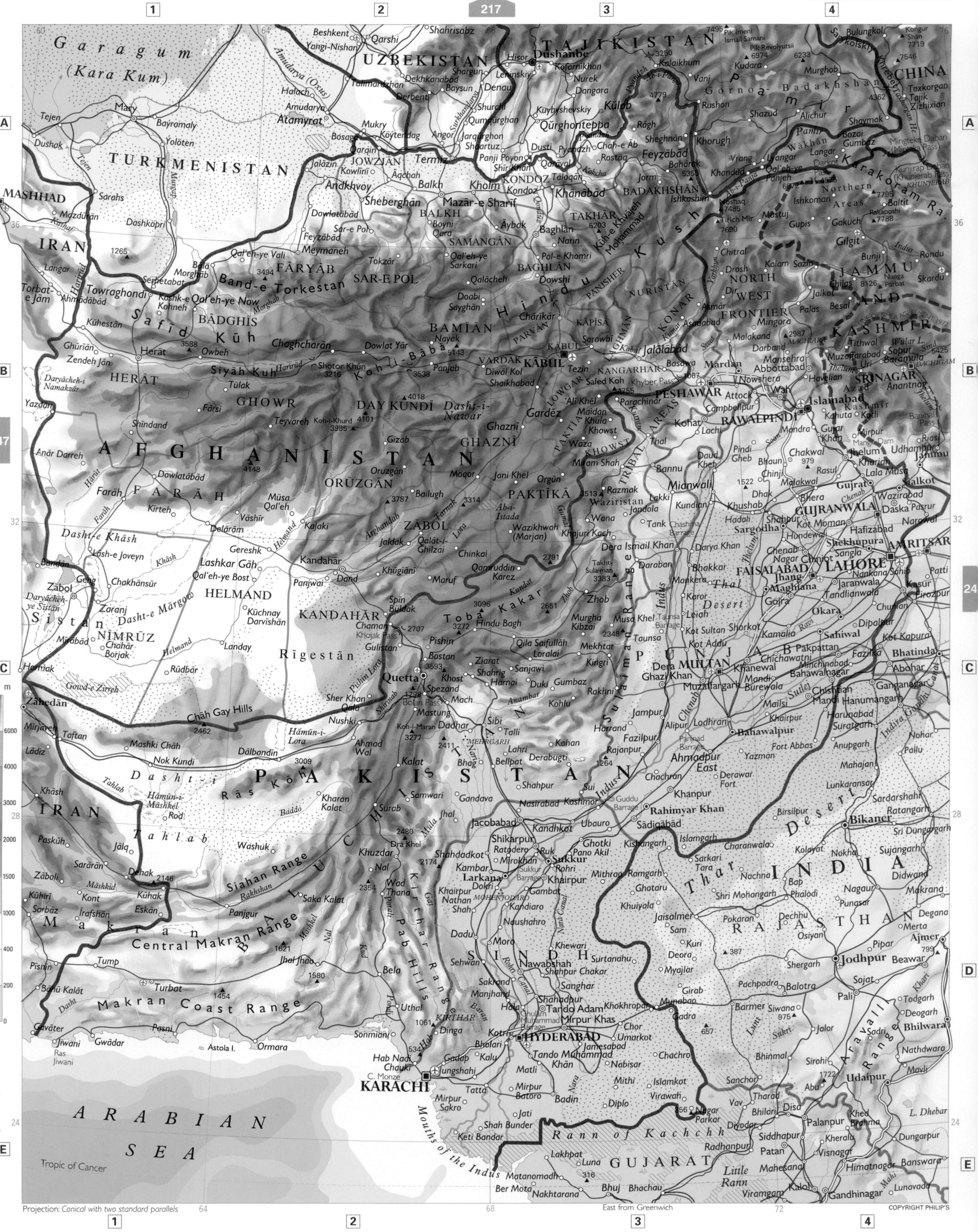

247

24

TURKMENISTAN

UZBEKISTAN

TAJIKISTAN

CHINA

Garagum
(Kara Kum)

IRAN

MASHHAD

Hindu Kush

AFGHANISTAN

HERĀT

GHOWR

BĀDGHĪS

FĀRYĀB

SAR-E POL

BALKH

SAMANGĀN

BAGHLĀN

TAKHĀR

BADAKHSHĀN

NURISTAN

KUNAR

NORTH
WEST
FRONTIER

JAMMU
AND
KASHMIR

SRĪNAGAR

KĀBUL

KĀPISA

PARVAN

VARDAK

LOWGAR

NANGARHĀR

PESHAWAR

RAWALPINDI

Islamabad

DAY KŪNDĪ

BĀMIĀN

GHAZNĪ

ORŪZGĀN

PAKTIĀ

KHOWST

TRIBAL
AREAS

ZĀBOL

PAKTĪKĀ

Waziristan

FARĀH

HELMAND

NĪMRŪZ

KANDAHĀR

Rīgestān

Khyber Pass

Kandahar

Quetta

B A L U C H I S T A N

P A K I S T A N

IRAN

Makran

Makran Coast Range

Central Makran Range

Siahan Range

SINDH

KARACHI

HYDERABAD

Mouths of the Indus

P U N J A B

LAHORE

AMRITSAR

FAISALABAD

GUJRANWALA

MULTAN

Bahawalpur

Thar Desert

INDIA

RAJASTHAN

Jodhpur

Bikaner

GUJARAT

Rann of Kachchh

Little
Rann

A R A B I A N
S E A

Tropic of Cancer

Projection: Conical with two standard parallels

East from Greenwich

COPYRIGHT PHILIP'S

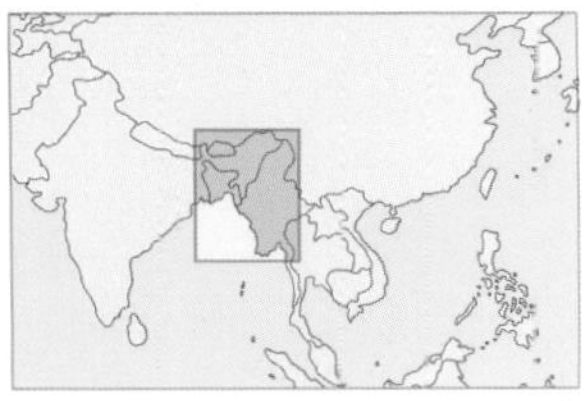

1:4 800 000

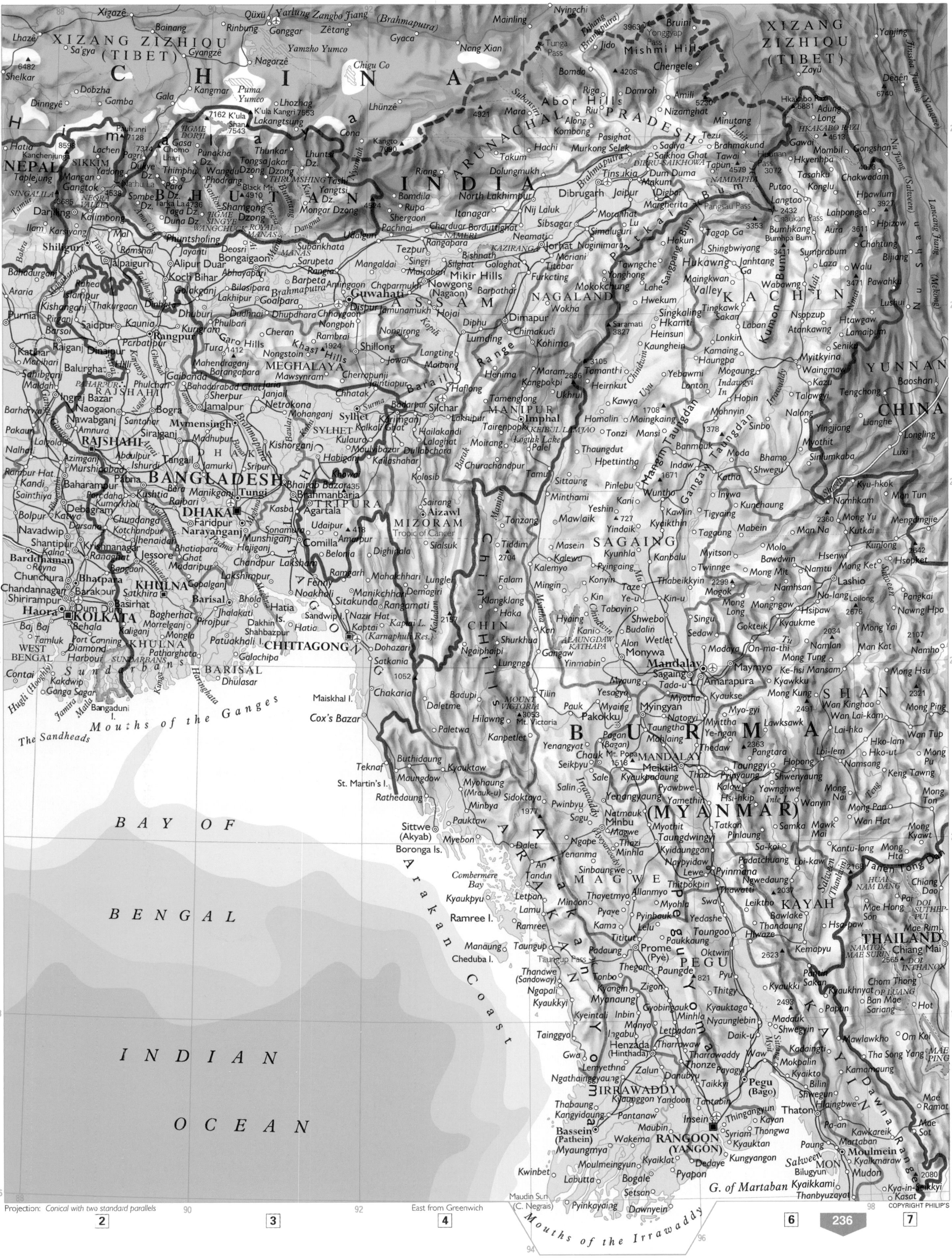

50   0   50   100   150   200 km
50   0   50   100   150 miles

1   2   3   4   218   5   6   7

CHINA

XIZANG ZIZHIQU (TIBET)

ARUNACHAL PRADESH

Abor Hills · Mishmi Hills

HKAKABO RAZI

NEPAL · SIKKIM · BHUTAN

INDIA

ASSAM · Guwahati · Brahmaputra

MEGHALAYA · Shillong

Garo Hills · Khasi Hills · Barail Range

NAGALAND · Dimapur · Kohima

KACHIN · Kawng Valley · YUNNAN · CHINA

BANGLADESH

RAJSHAHI · DHAKA · Narayanganj

KHULNA · Barisal · CHITTAGONG

WEST BENGAL · KOLKATA · Haora

Sundarbans · Mouths of the Ganges

The Sandheads

TRIPURA · Agartala · MIZORAM · Aizawl

MANIPUR · Imphal · Tropic of Cancer

Chin Hills · SAGAING · Mandalay

Sagaing · Amarapura · Monywa

BURMA (MYANMAR)

MAGWE · Pagan (Bagan) · Pakokku

ARAKAN · Arakan Coast · Sittwe (Akyab)

Ramree I. · Cheduba I.

MOUNT VICTORIA · Mt. Victoria

SHAN · Lashio · Taunggyi · Inle L.

KAYAH · Loikaw

PEGU · Prome (Pye) · Toungoo

IRRAWADDY · Bassein (Pathein)

Pegu (Bago) · RANGOON (YANGON)

Insein · Syriam · Thaton · MON

Moulmein · THAILAND · Chiang Mai

BAY OF BENGAL

INDIAN OCEAN

G. of Martaban · Mouths of the Irrawaddy

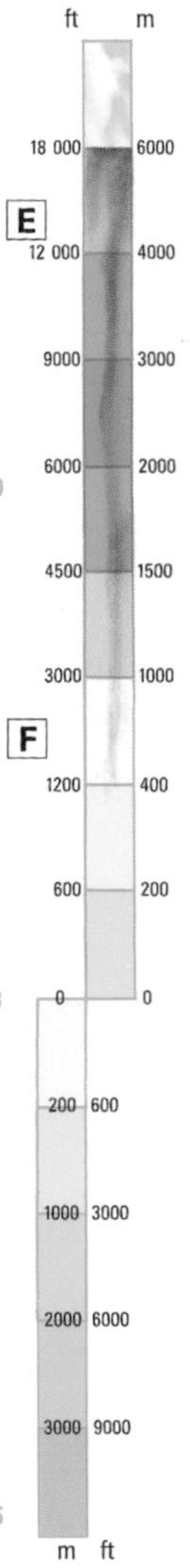

ft   m   18 000   6000 · 12 000   4000 · 9000   3000 · 6000   2000 · 4500   1500 · 3000   1000 · 1200   400 · 600   200 · 0 · 600   200 · 3000   2000 · 6000   3000 · 9000   m ft

Projection: Conical with two standard parallels

East from Greenwich

COPYRIGHT PHILIP'S

1:4 800 000

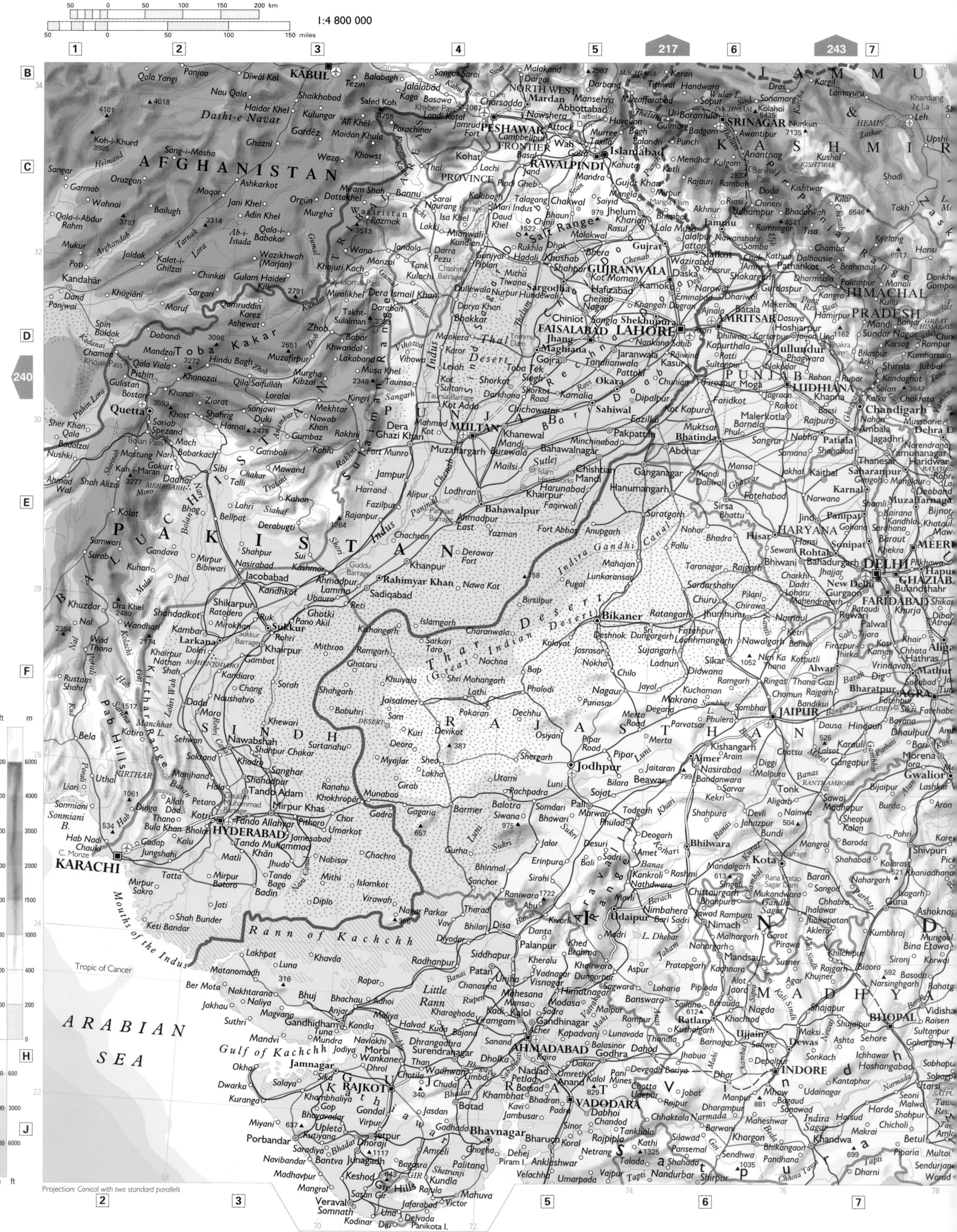

Projection: Conical with two standard parallels

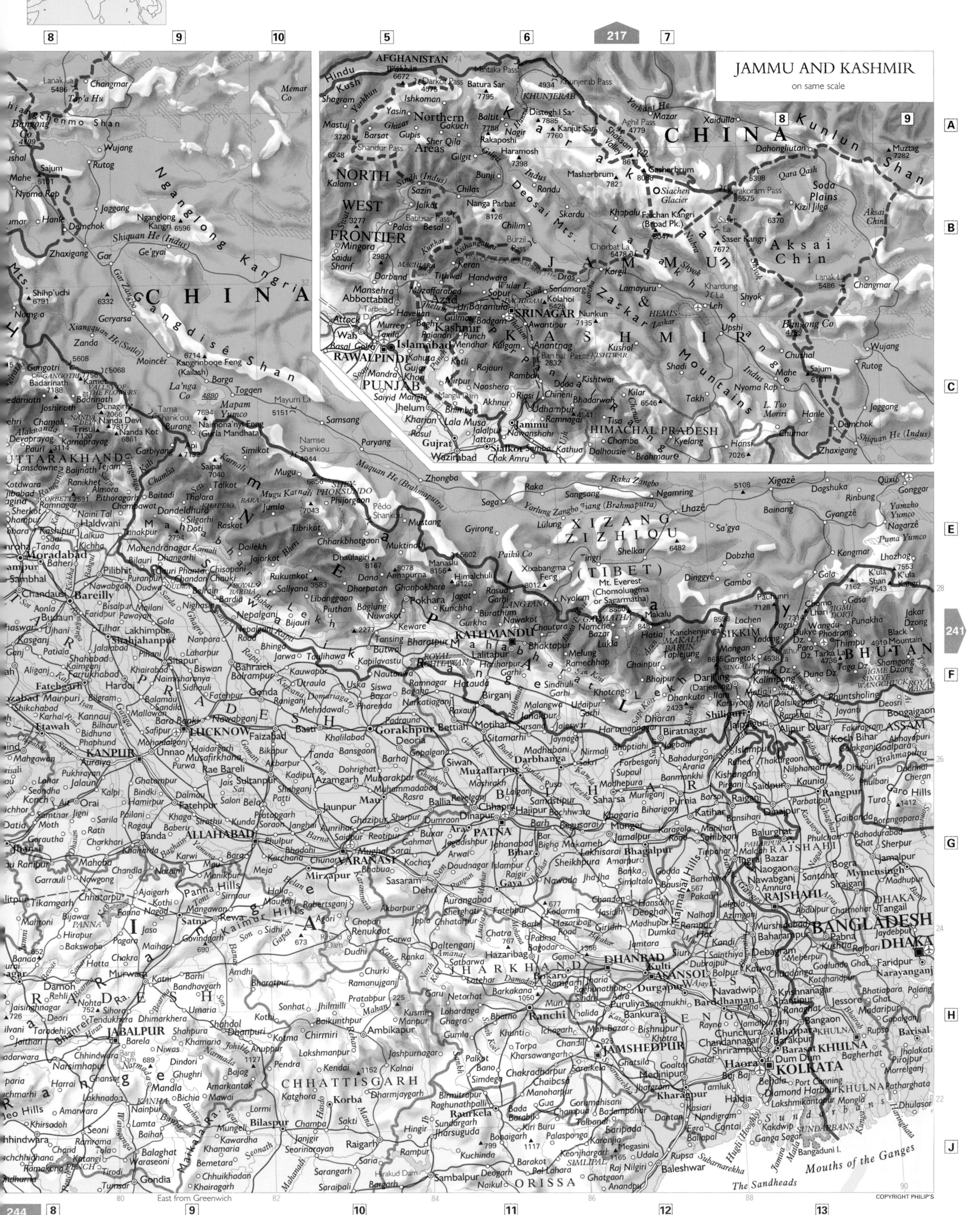

JAMMU AND KASHMIR
on same scale

COPYRIGHT PHILIP'S

East from Greenwich

Mouths of the Ganges

The Sandheads

1:4 800 000

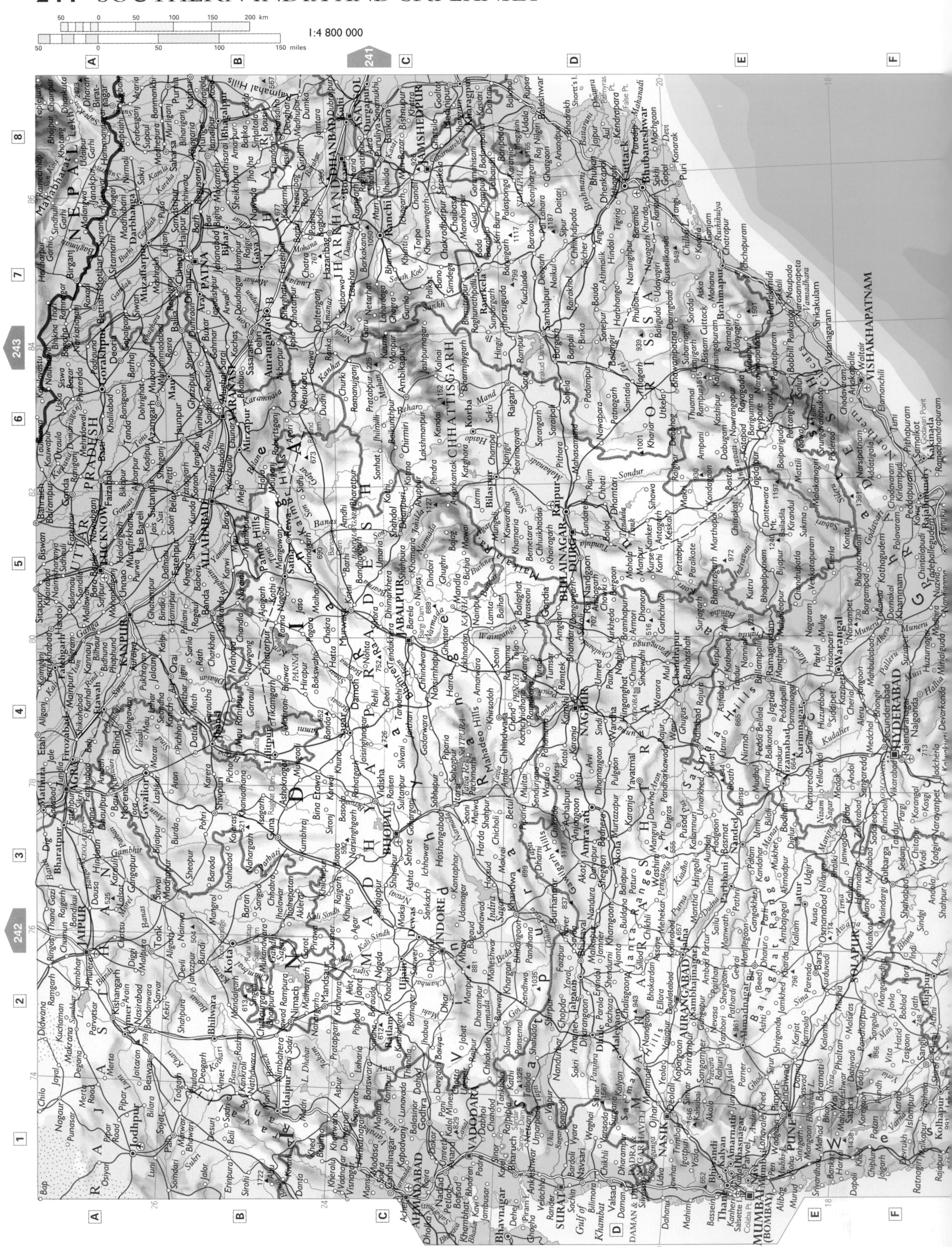

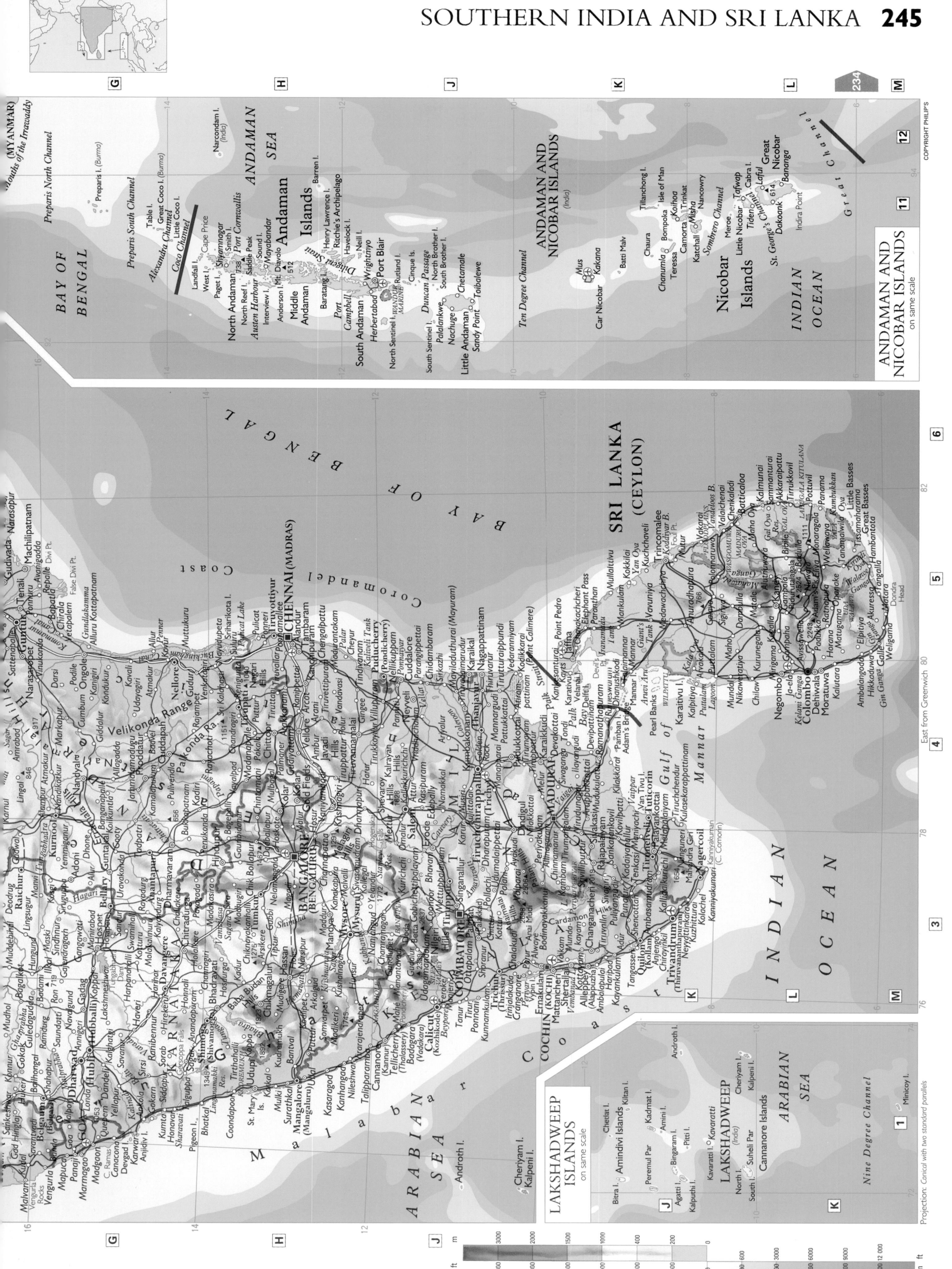

ANDAMAN SEA

BAY OF BENGAL

ANDAMAN
Islands

ANDAMAN AND
NICOBAR ISLANDS

ANDAMAN AND
NICOBAR ISLANDS
on same scale

Nicobar
Islands

INDIAN
OCEAN

BAY OF BENGAL

SRI LANKA
(CEYLON)

INDIAN

OCEAN

ARABIAN
SEA

LAKSHADWEEP
ISLANDS
on same scale

LAKSHADWEEP

ARABIAN
SEA

Nine Degree Channel

Projection: Conical with two standard parallels

East from Greenwich

1:5 600 000

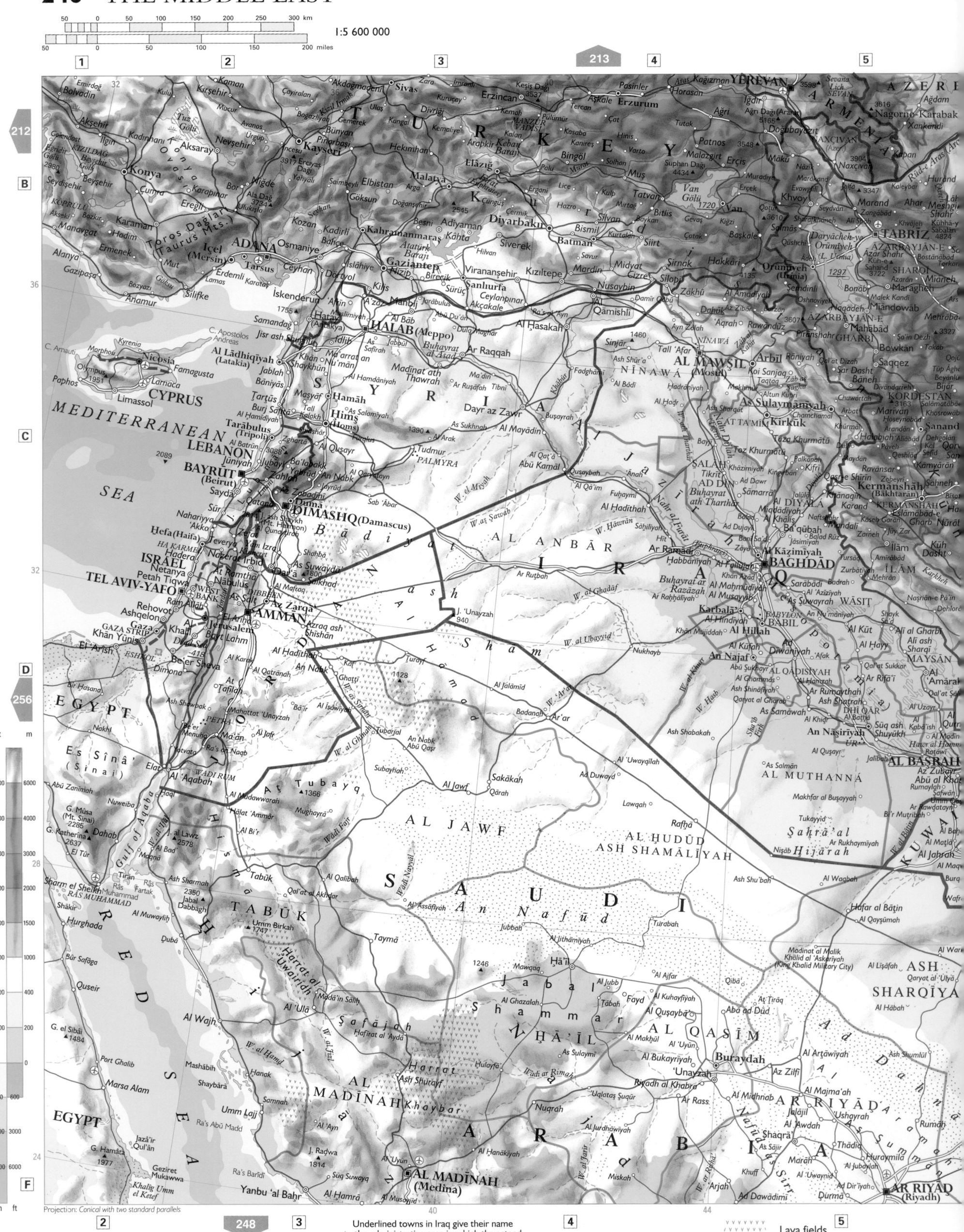

Underlined towns in Iraq give their name
to the administrative area in which they stand

v v v v v v
v v v v v v   Lava fields
v v v v v v

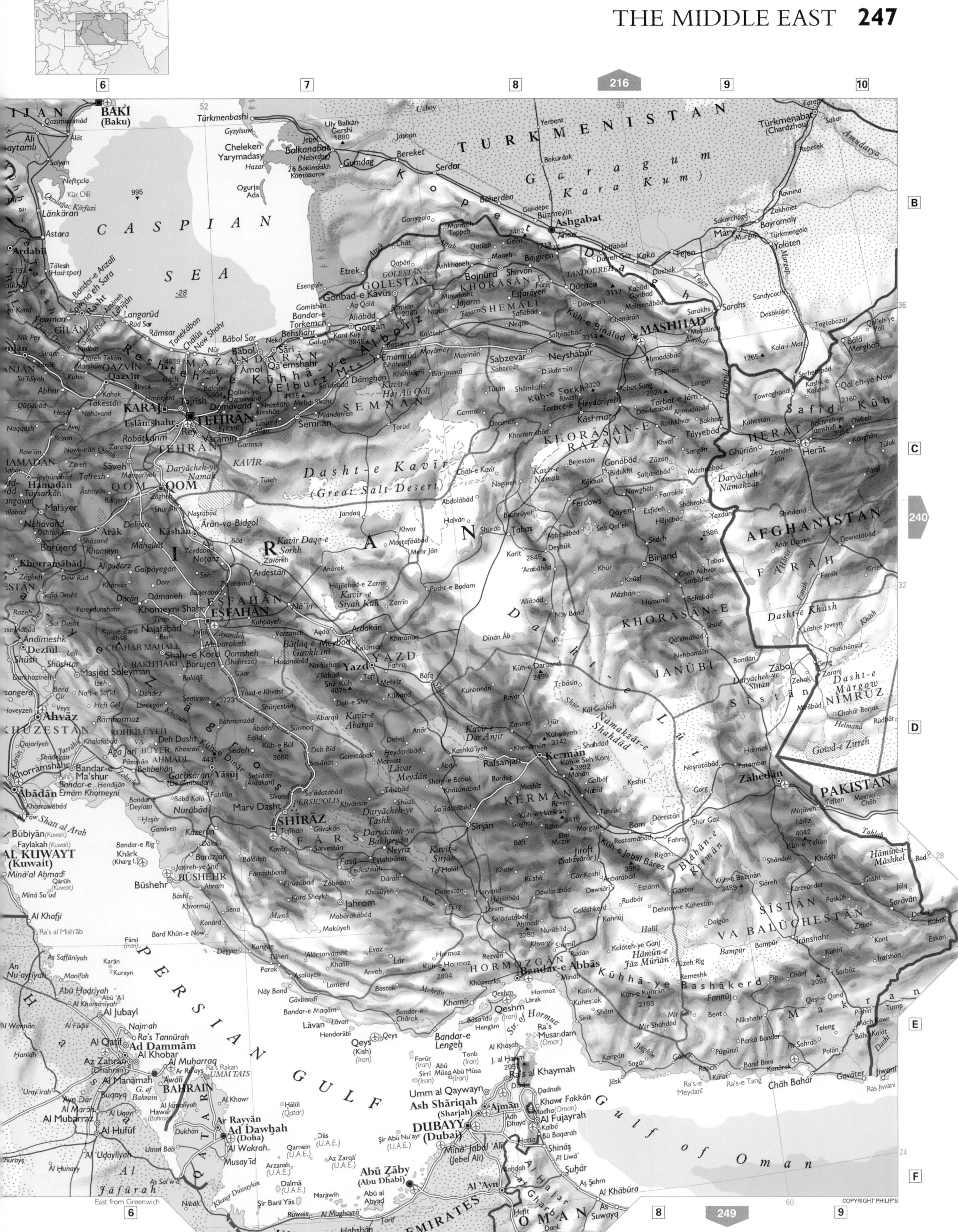

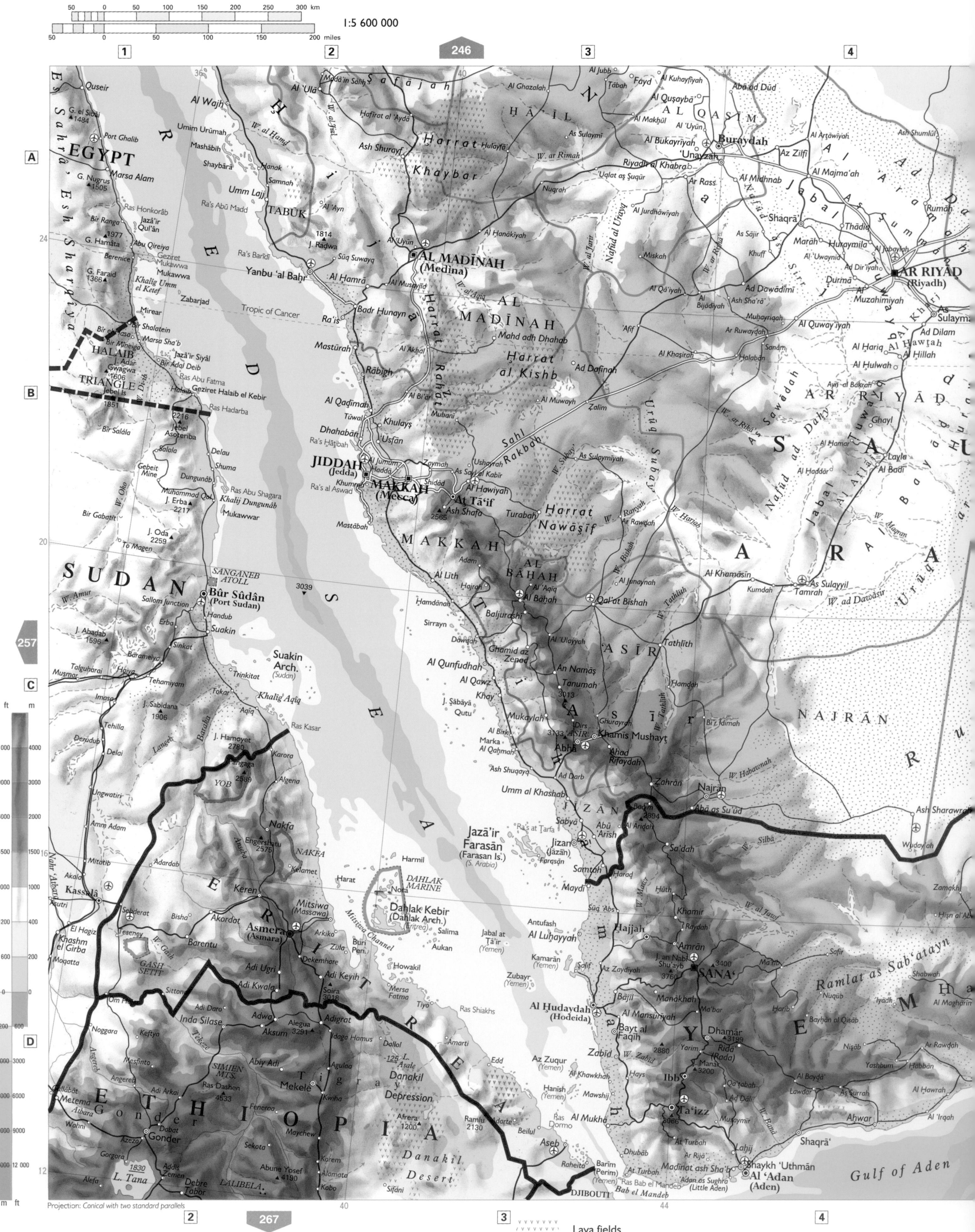

1:5 600 000

Projection: Conical with two standard parallels

Lava fields

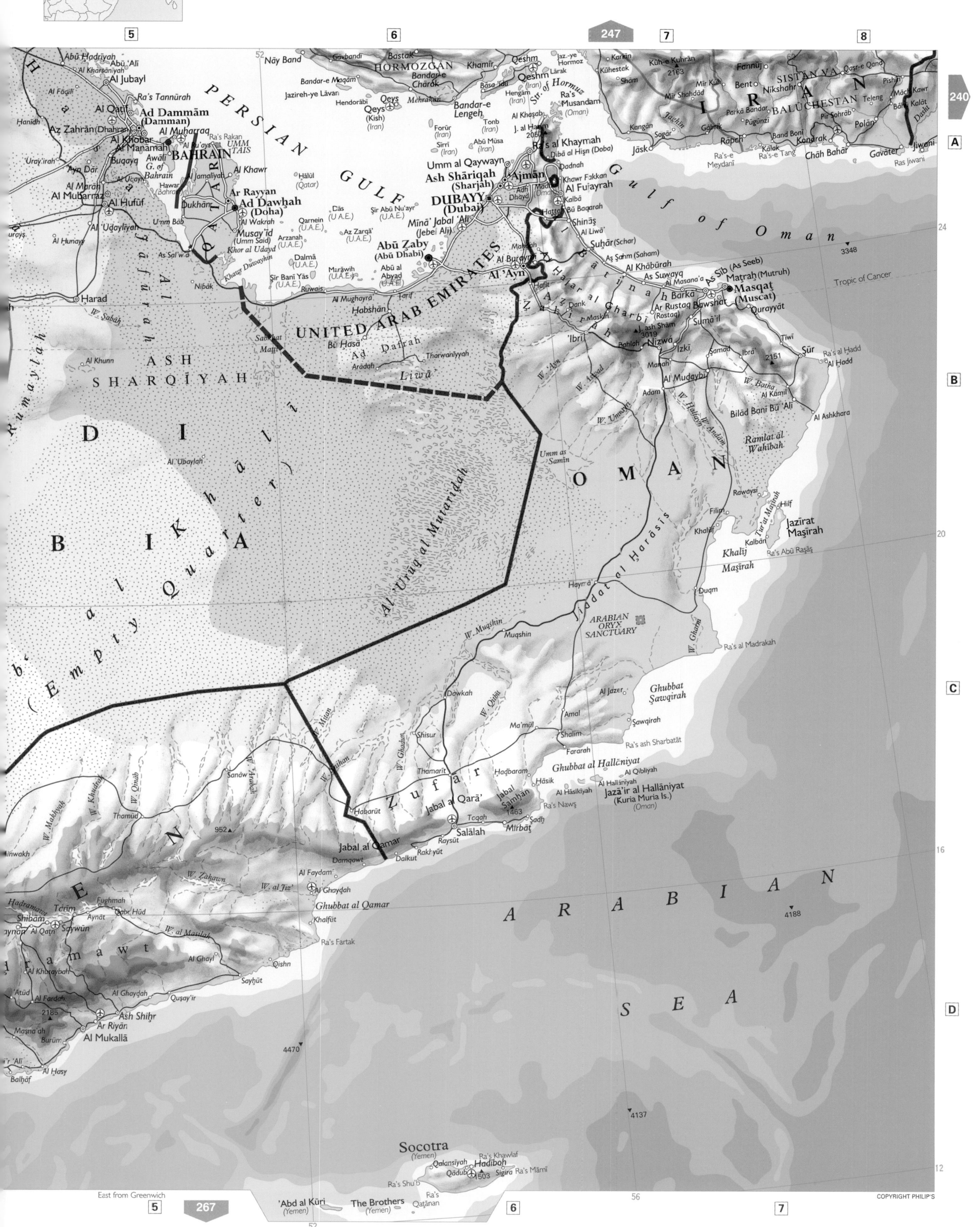

1:2 000 000

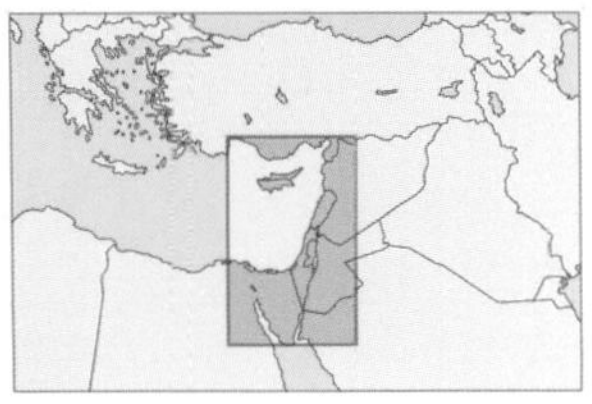

ISRAEL

JORDAN

SAUDI ARABIA

EGYPT

AL MAFRAQ

AMMĀN

AL BALQĀ'

WEST BANK

GAZA STRIP

HADAROM

Hanegev (Negev Desert)

SHAMĀL SĪNĪ

E T (Sînâ') J A N Ū B S Ī N Ī

Nile Delta

KAFR EL SHEIKH

DUMYÂT

EL QÂHIRA

EL GÎZA

EL BAHR EL AHMAR

Gulf of Suweis (Khalîg es Suweis)

Gulf of Aqaba

TEL AVIV-YAFO

Jerusalem (El Quds)

Al 'Aqabah

Bûr Sa'îd (Port Said)

Qanâ es Suweis (Suez Canal)

El Suweis (Suez)

Es Sahrâ' esh Sharqîya (Eastern Desert)

37 COPYRIGHT PHILIP'S

Projection : Polyconic

East from Greenwich

═══ 1974 Cease Fire Lines

AFRICA

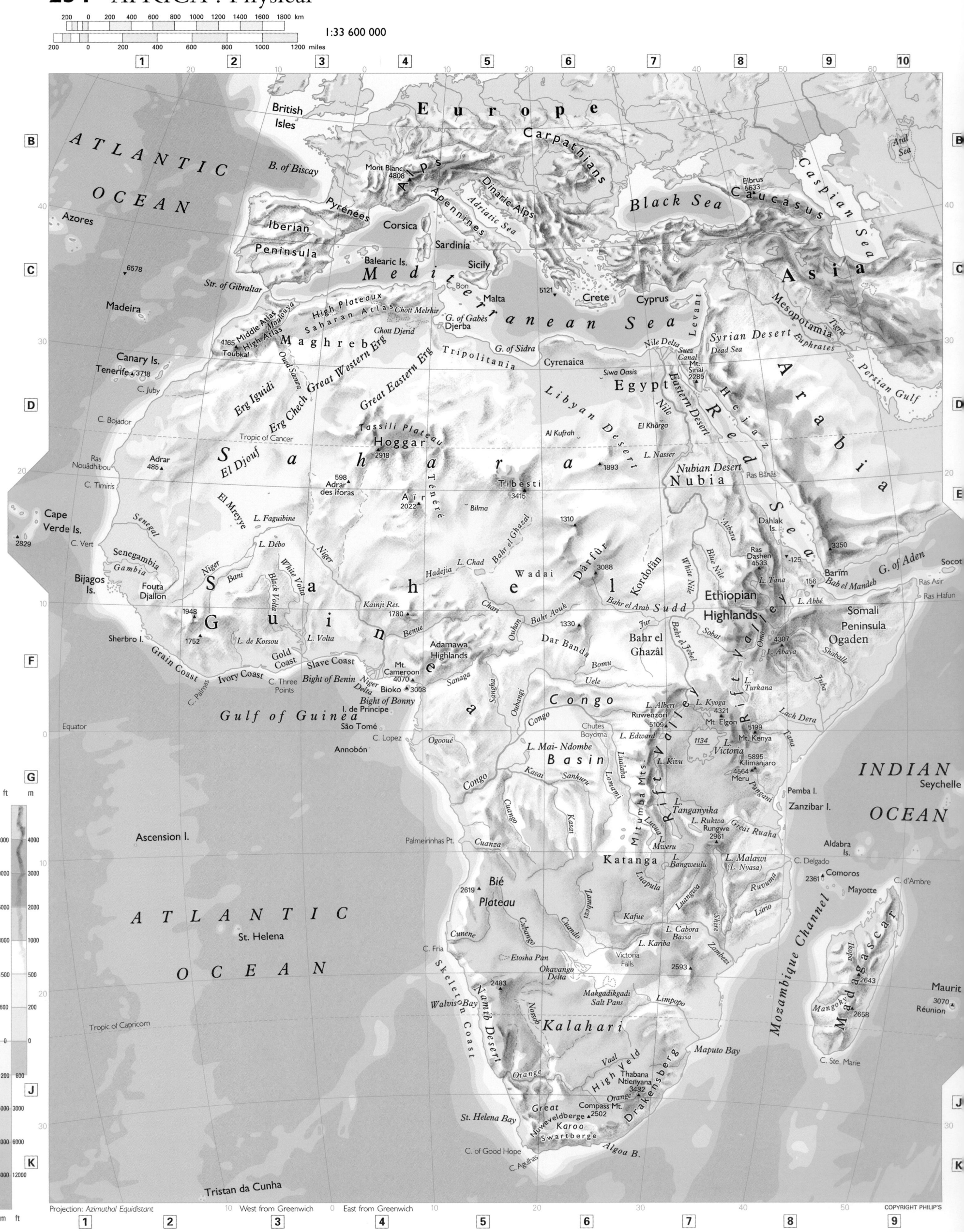

1:33 600 000

Projection: Azimuthal Equidistant

COPYRIGHT PHILIP'S

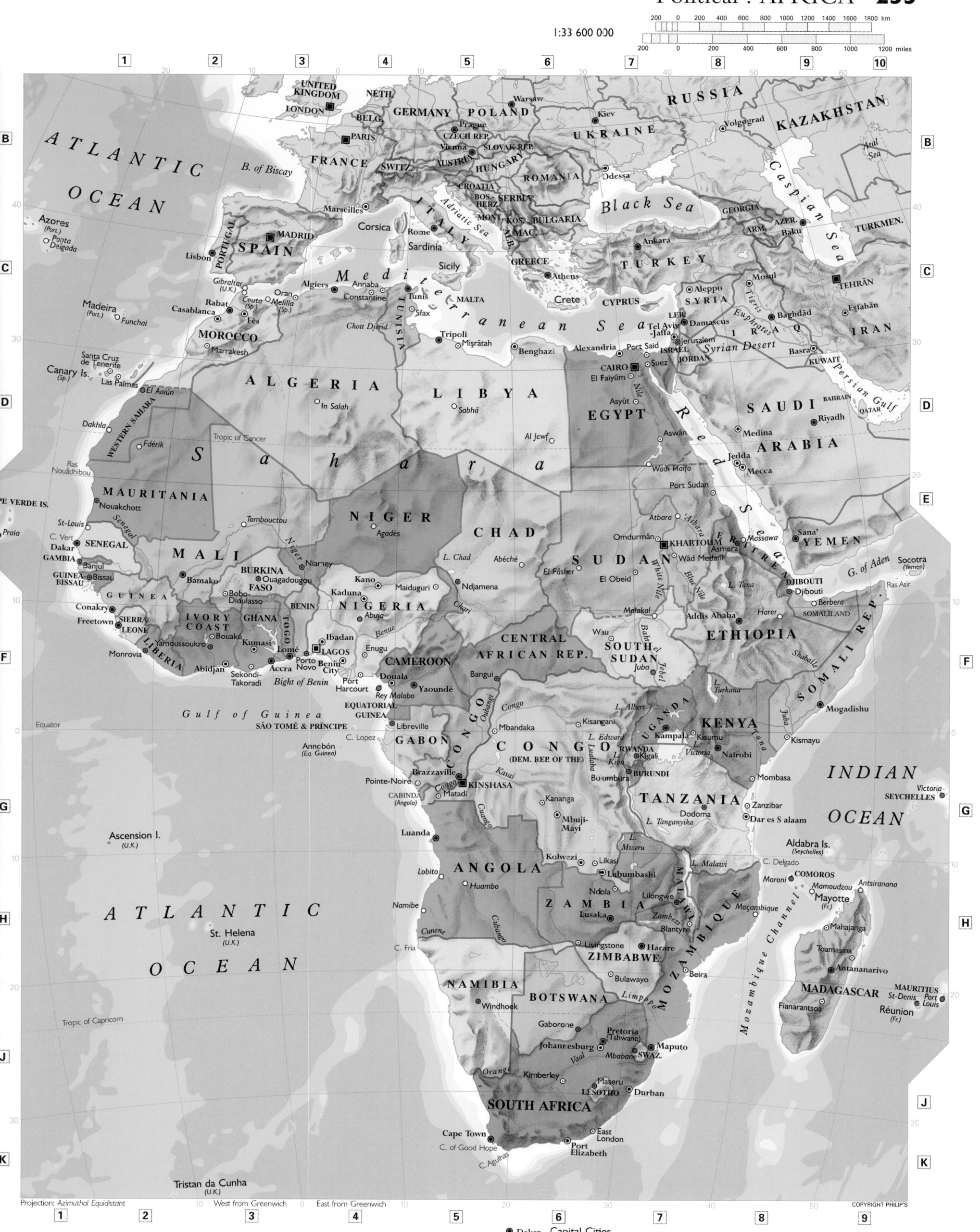

1:33 600 000

200 0 200 400 600 800 1000 1200 1400 1600 1800 km
200 0 200 400 600 800 1000 1200 miles

Projection: Azimuthal Equidistant

West from Greenwich East from Greenwich

● Dakar Capital Cities

COPYRIGHT PHILIP'S

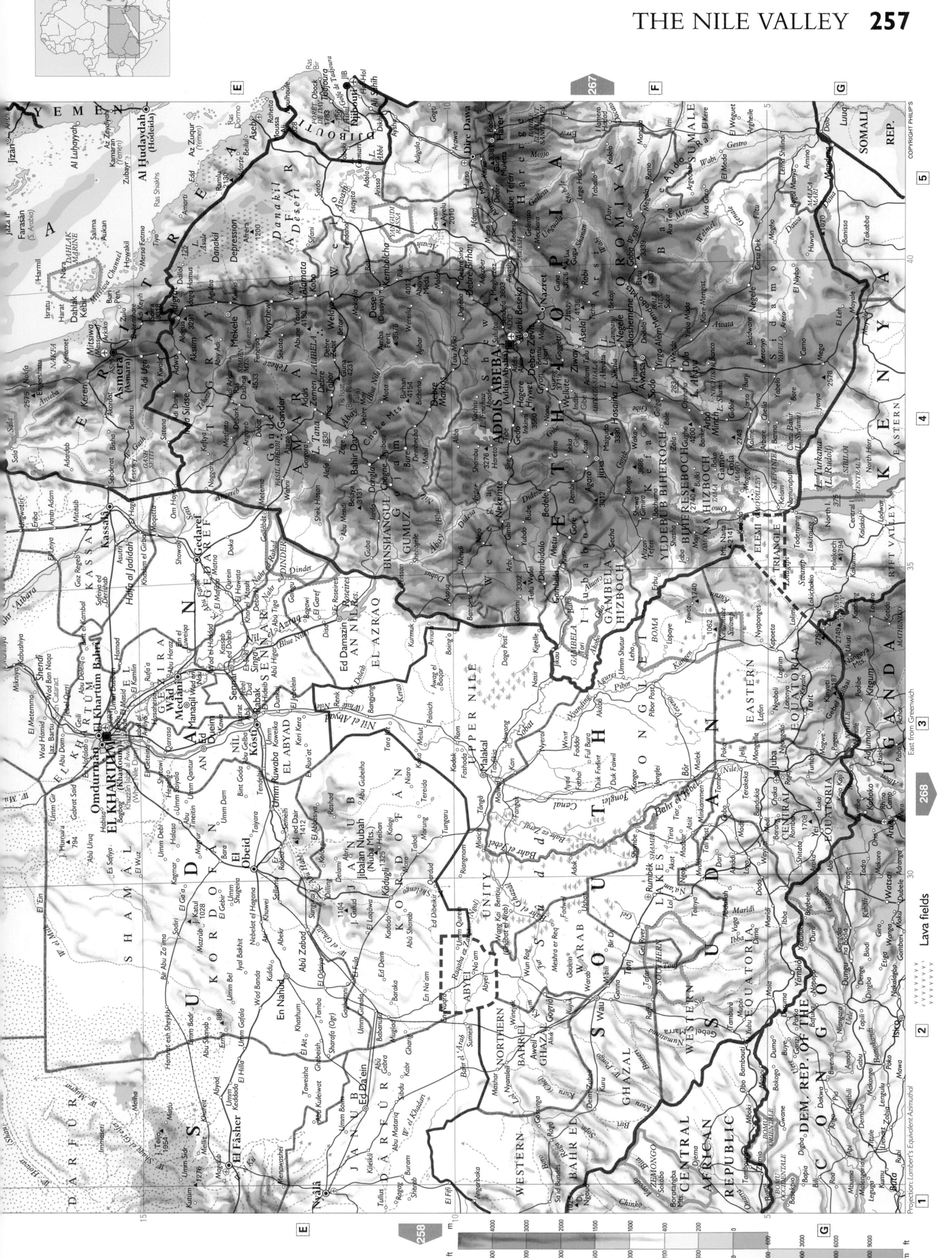

COPYRIGHT PHILIP'S

1:6 400 000

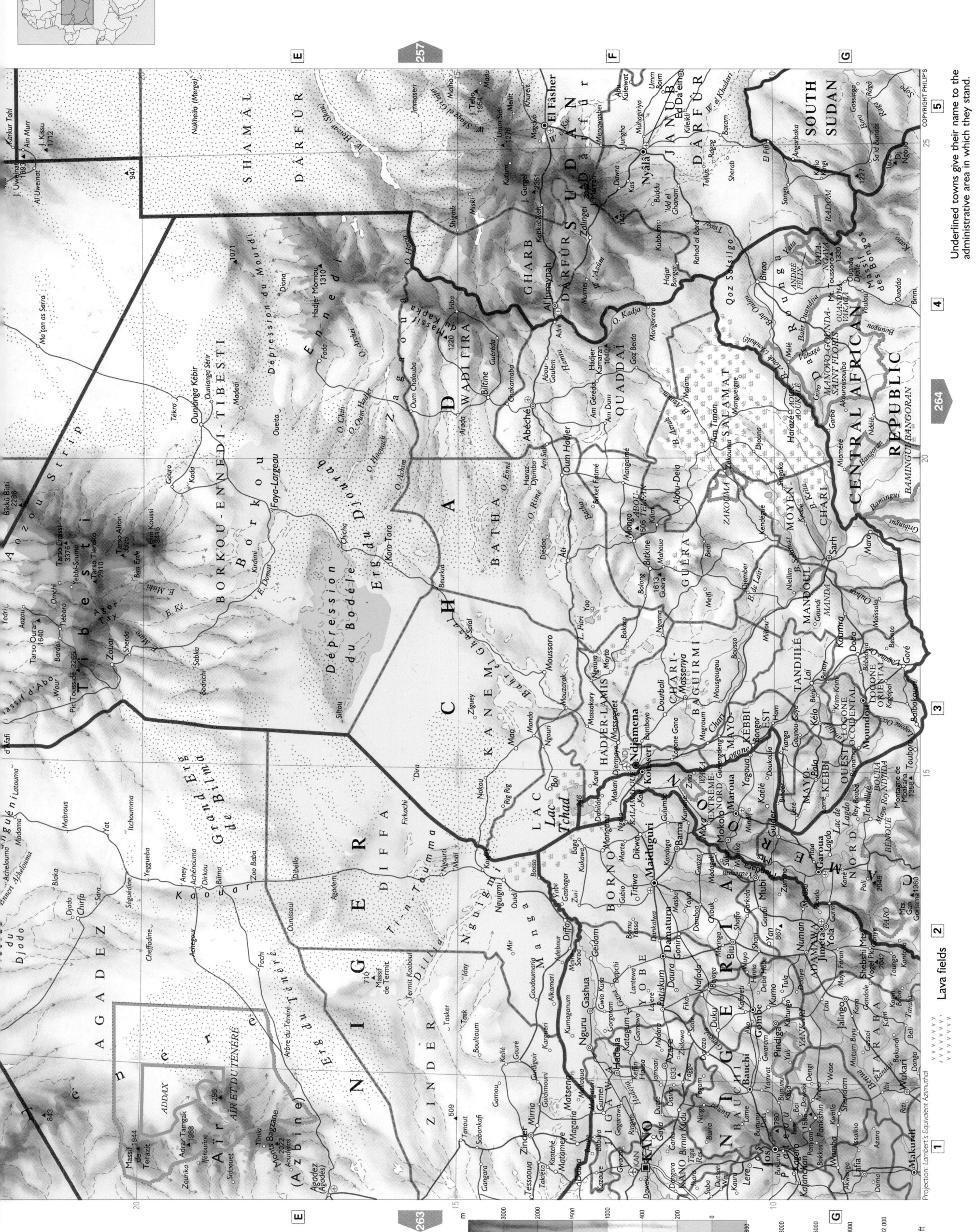

Underlined towns give their name to the administrative area in which they stand.

Lava fields

Projection: Lambert's Equivalent Azimuthal

COPYRIGHT PHILIP'S

263 264

1:6 400 000

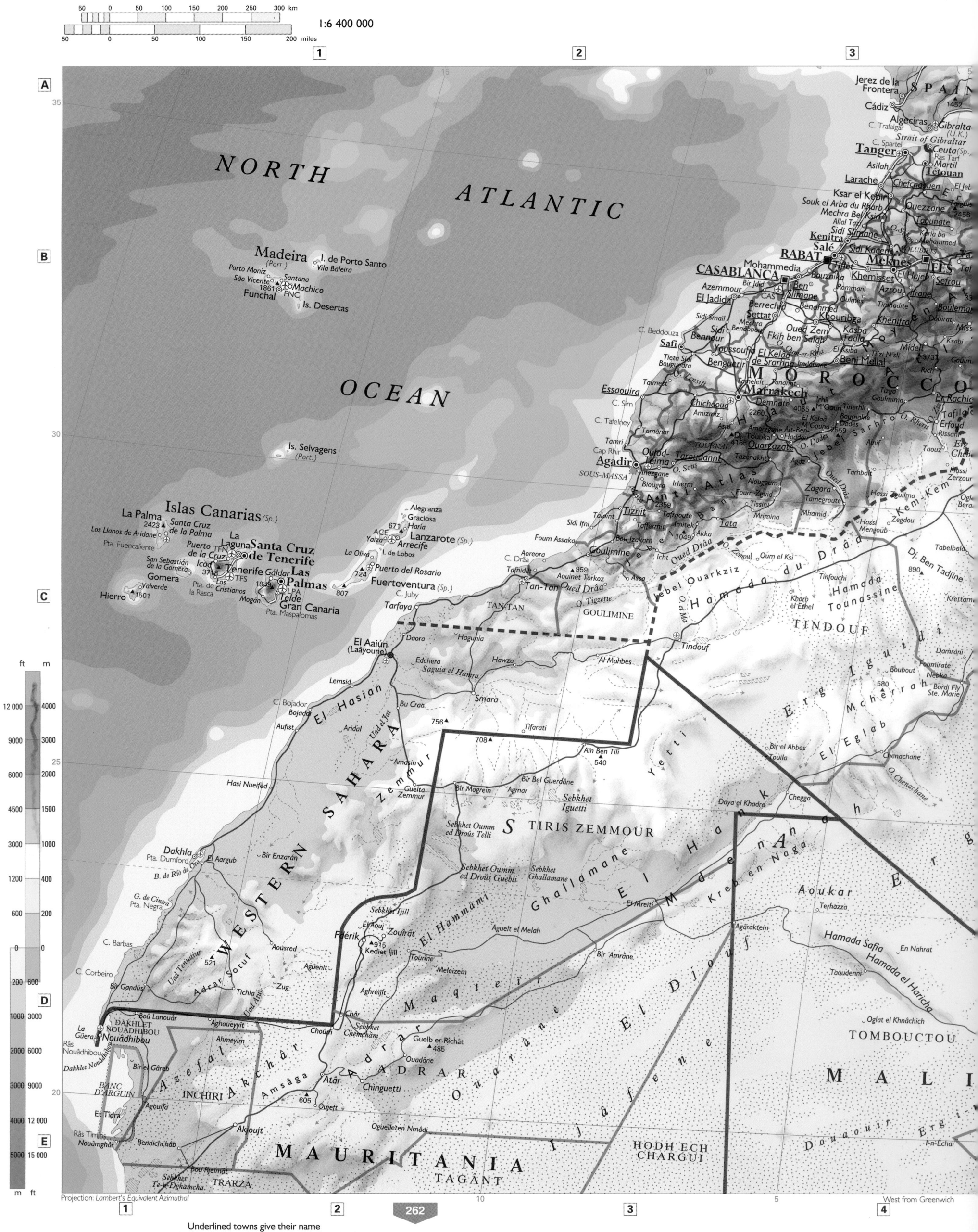

Projection: Lambert's Equivalent Azimuthal

West from Greenwich

Underlined towns give their name
to the administrative area in which they stand

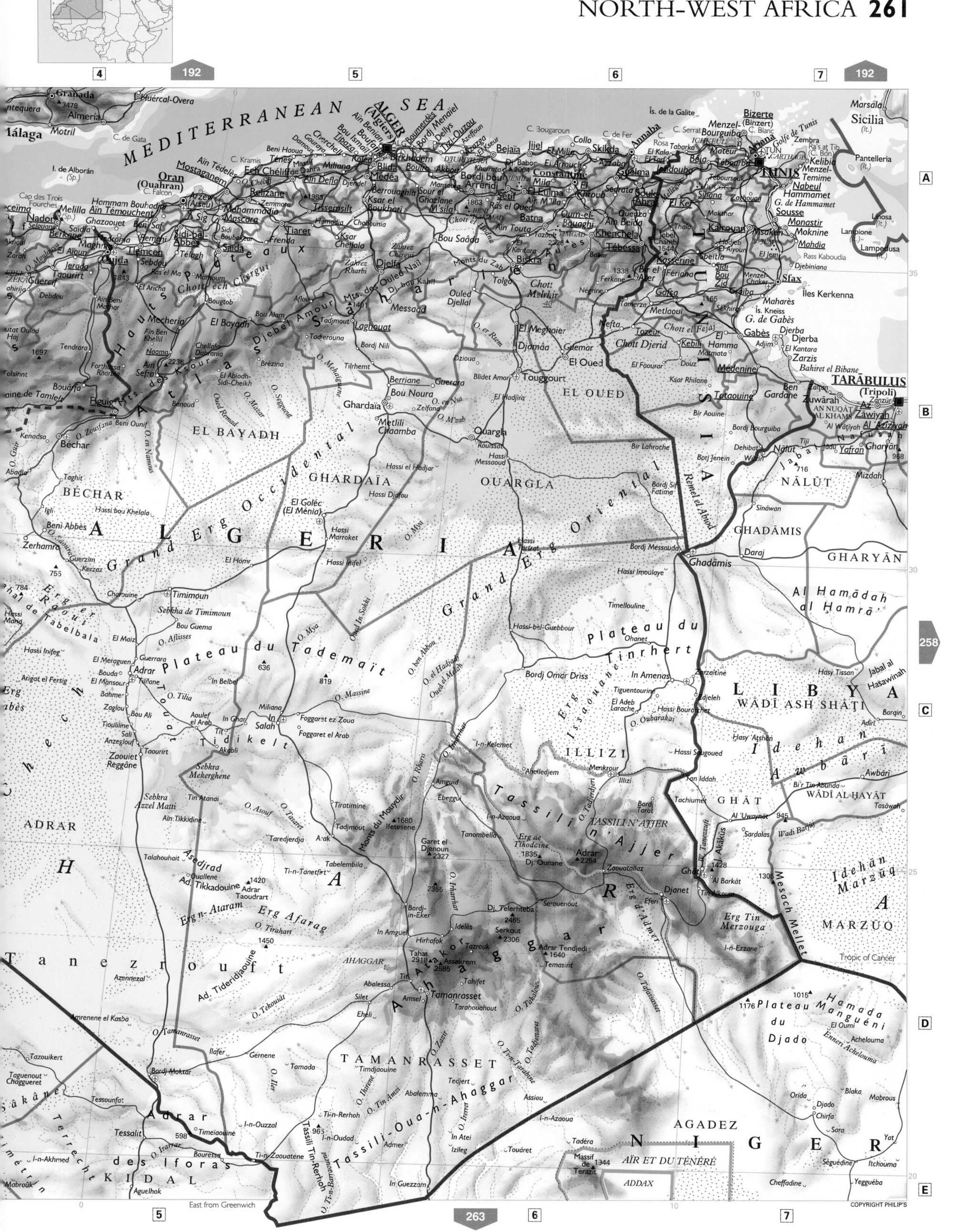

Projection : Lambert's Equivalent Azimuthal

Underlined towns give their name to the
administrative area in which they stand.

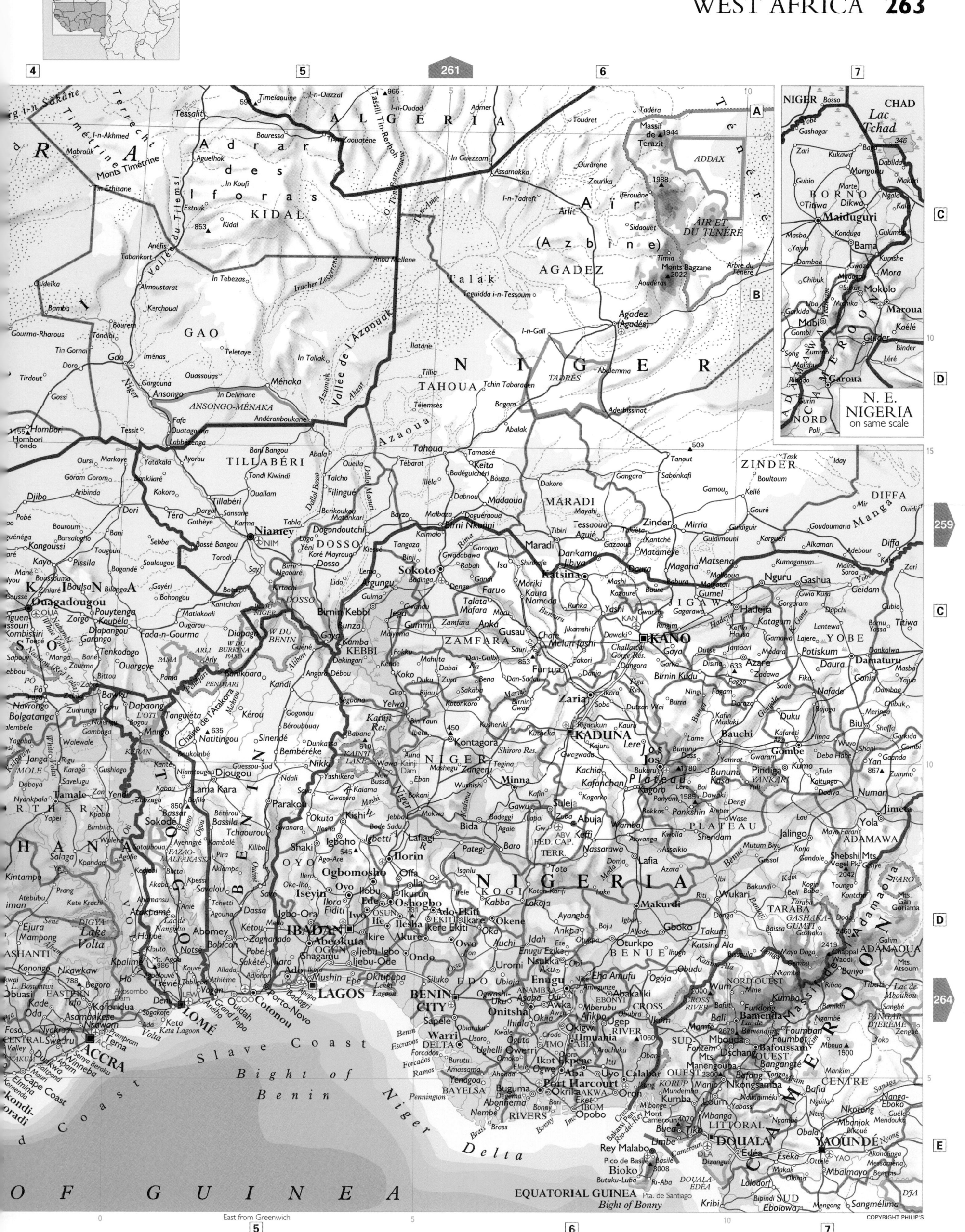

N. E.
NIGERIA
on same scale

East from Greenwich

COPYRIGHT PHILIP'S

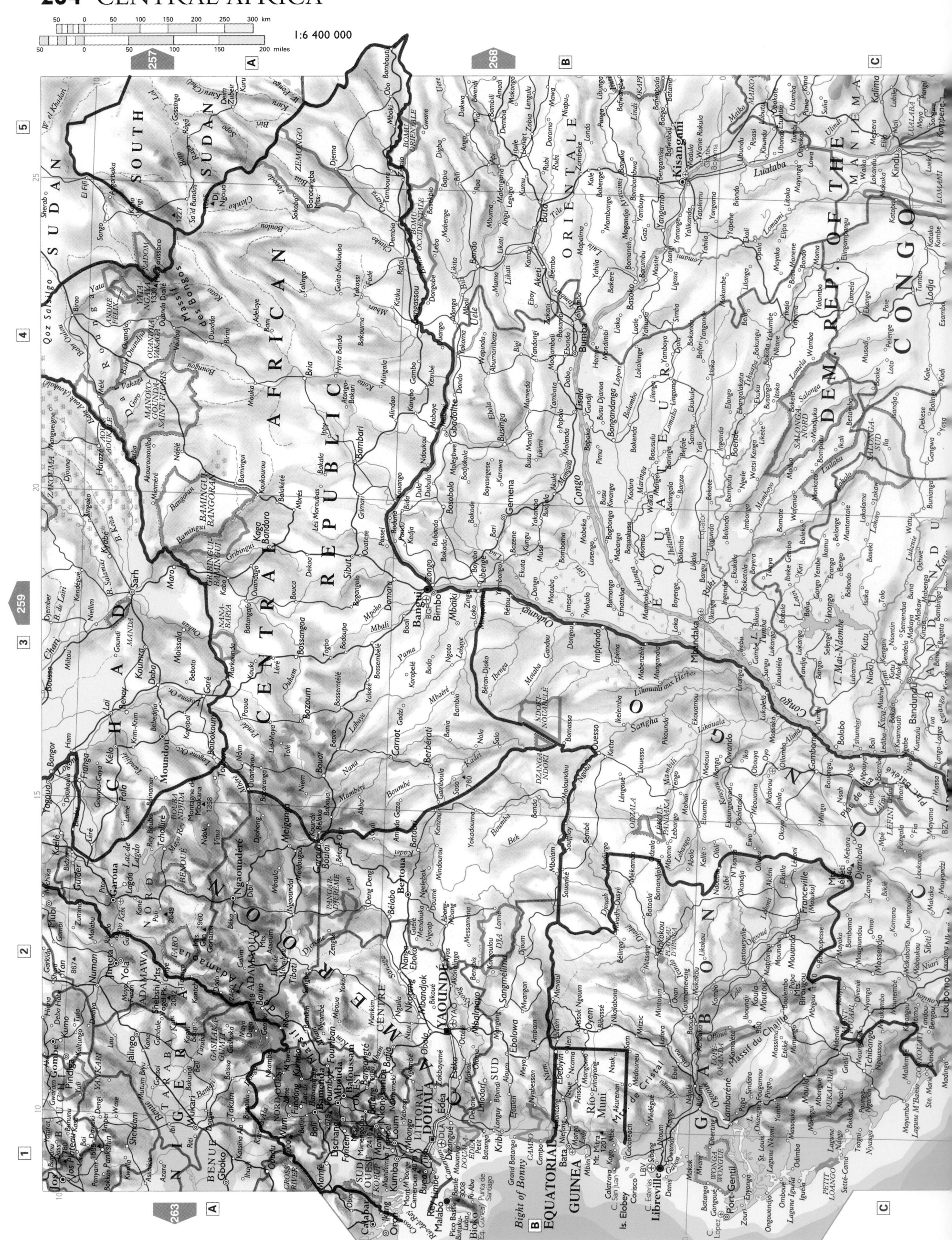

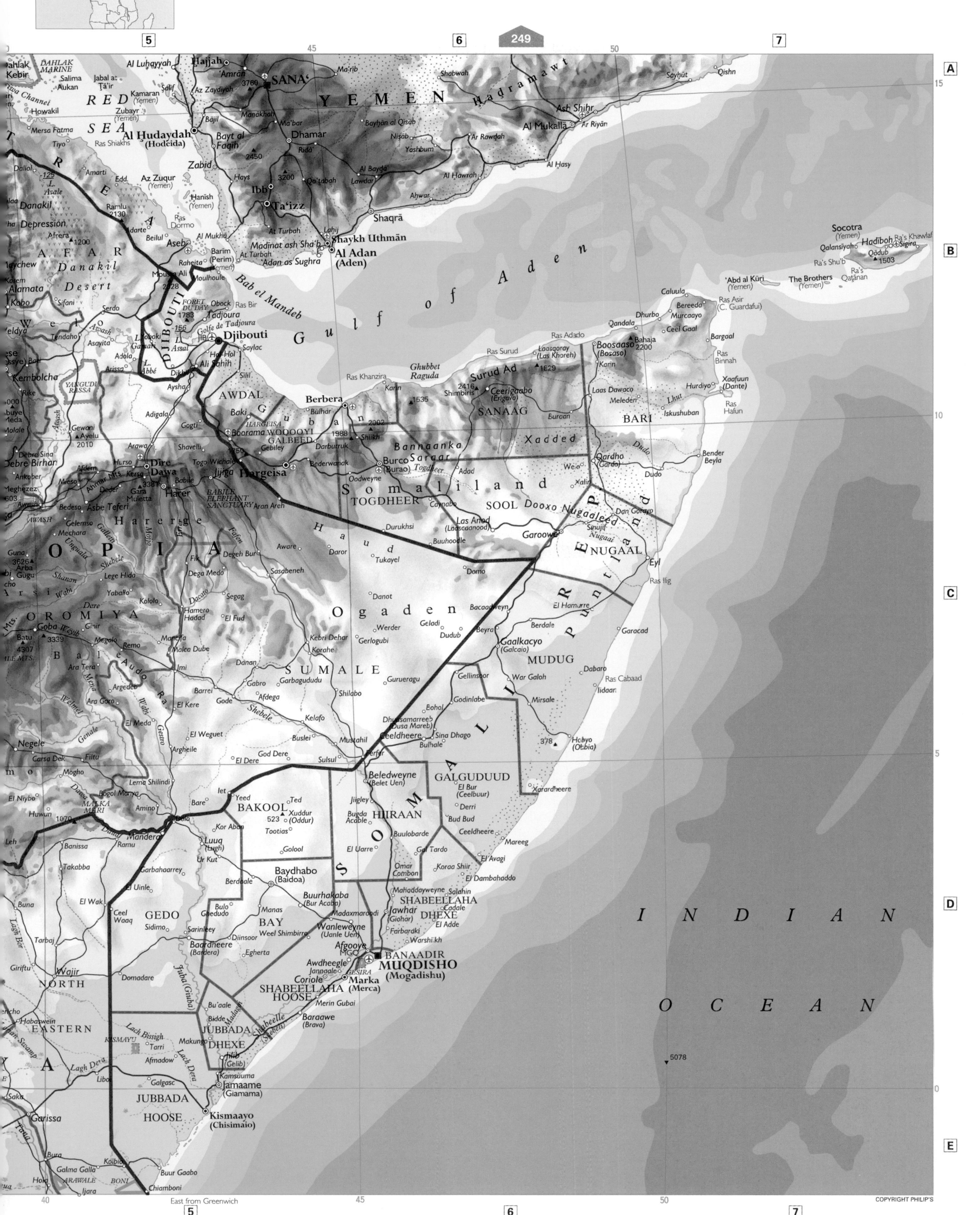

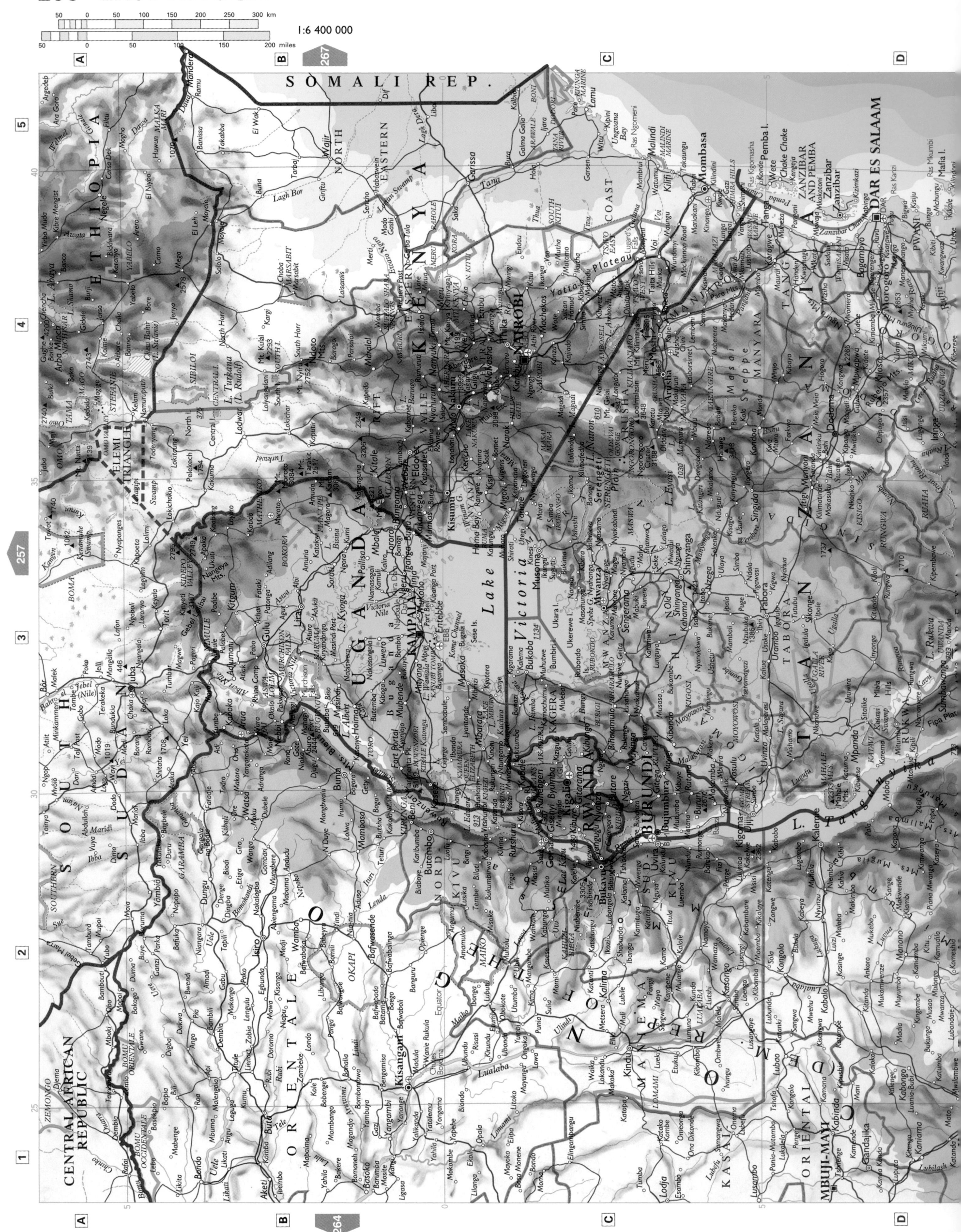

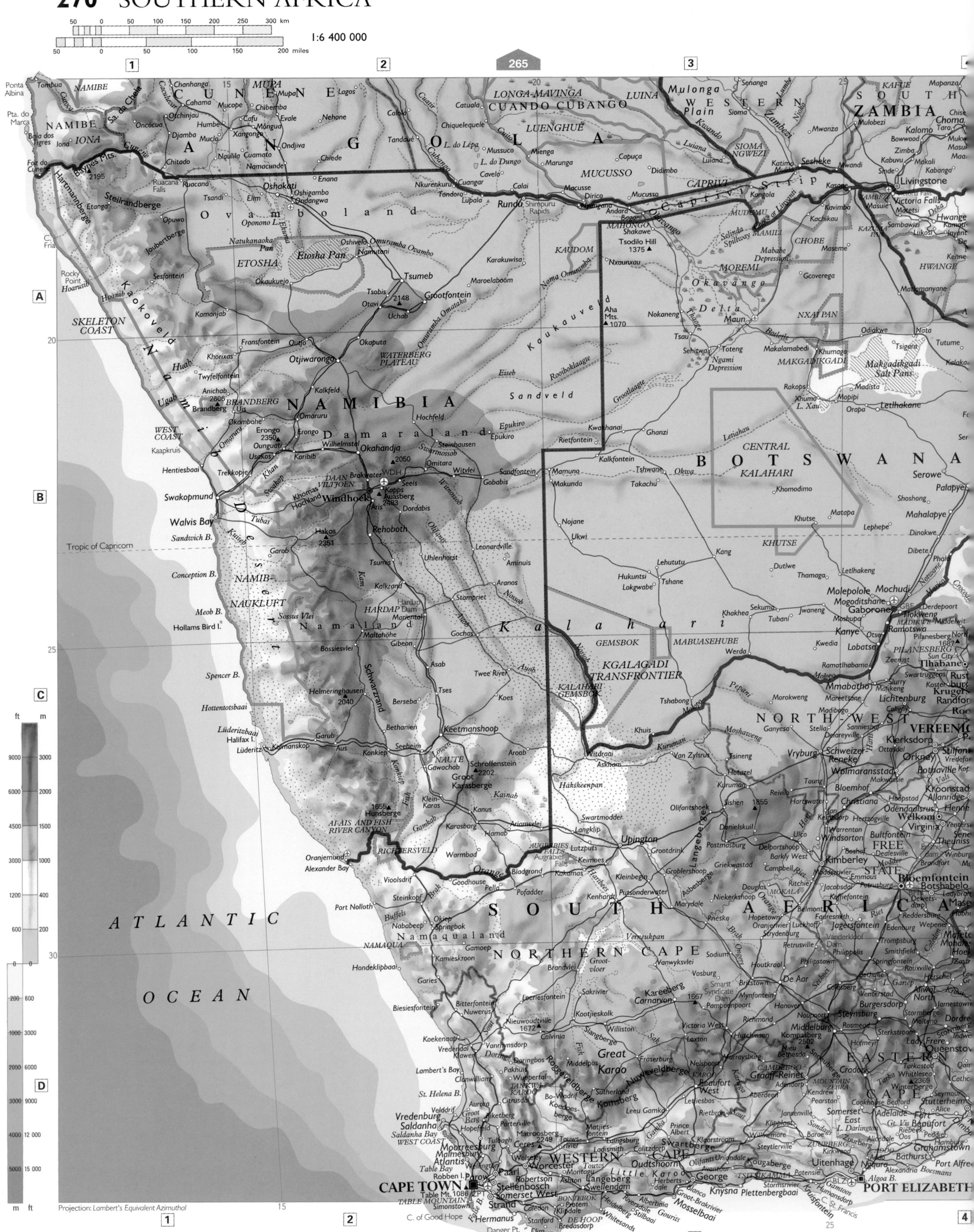

1:6 400 000

Projection: Lambert's Equivalent Azimuthal

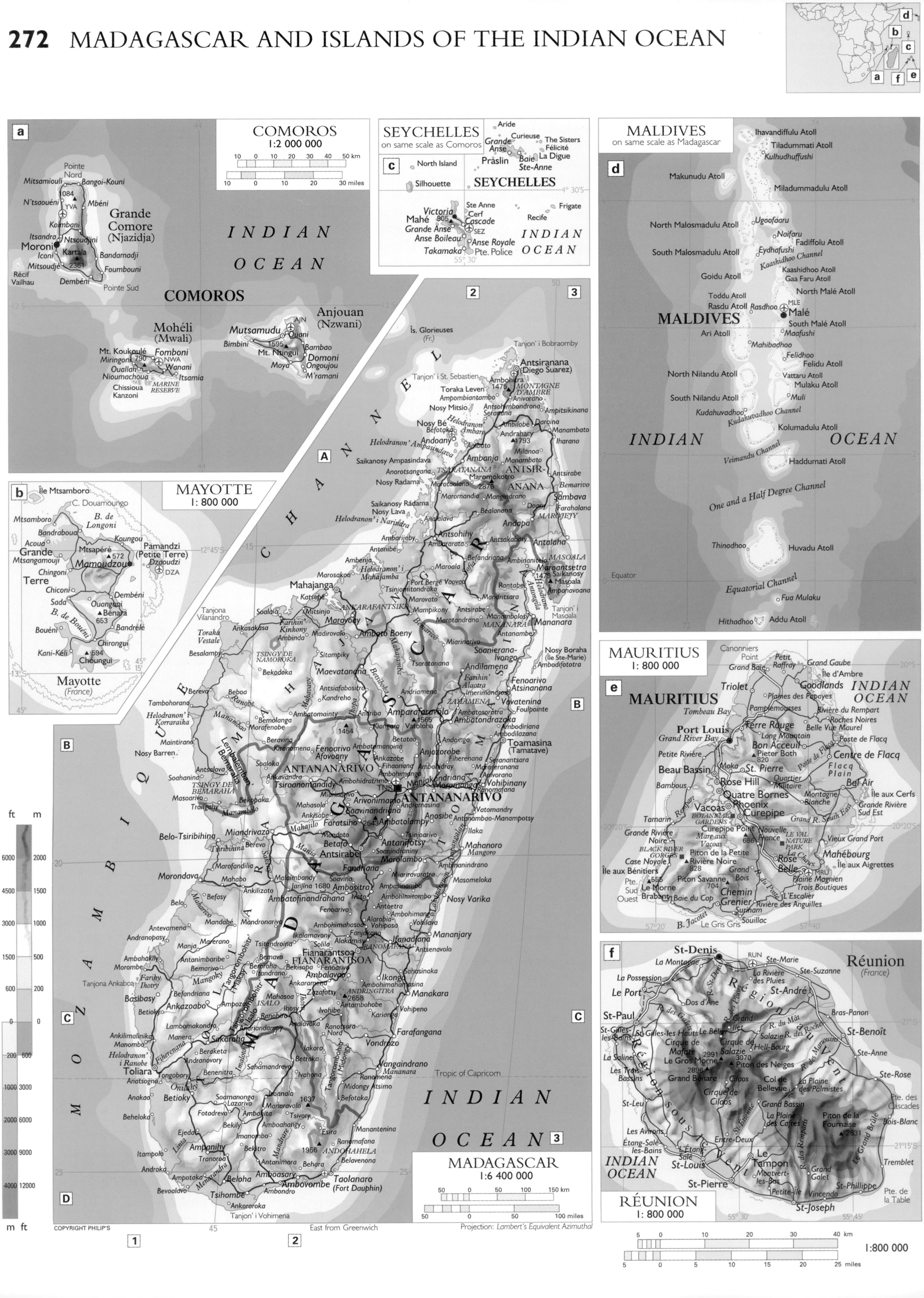

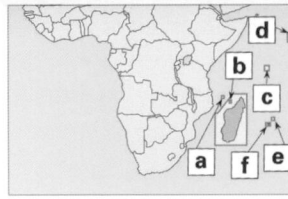

COMOROS
1:2 000 000

SEYCHELLES
on same scale as Comoros

SEYCHELLES

MALDIVES
on same scale as Madagascar

MAYOTTE
1: 800 000

MAURITIUS
1: 800 000

RÉUNION
1: 800 000

MADAGASCAR
1:6 400 000

COPYRIGHT PHILIP'S

East from Greenwich

Projection: Lambert's Equivalent Azimuthal

ft   m
6000   2000
4500   1500
3000   1000
1500   500
 600   200
   0   0
 200   600
 600   1000
1500   3000
3000   6000
4000   9000
        12000
m ft

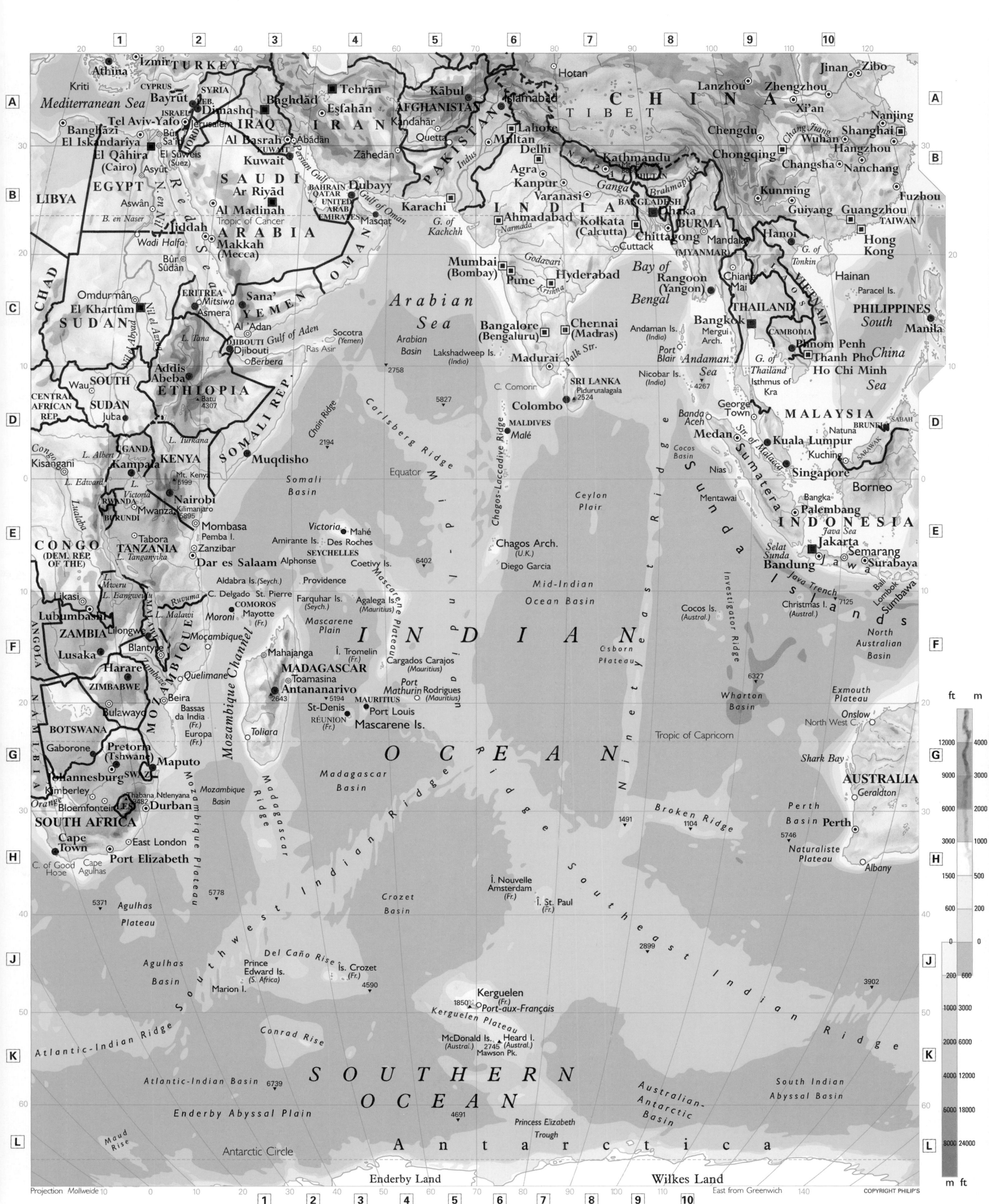

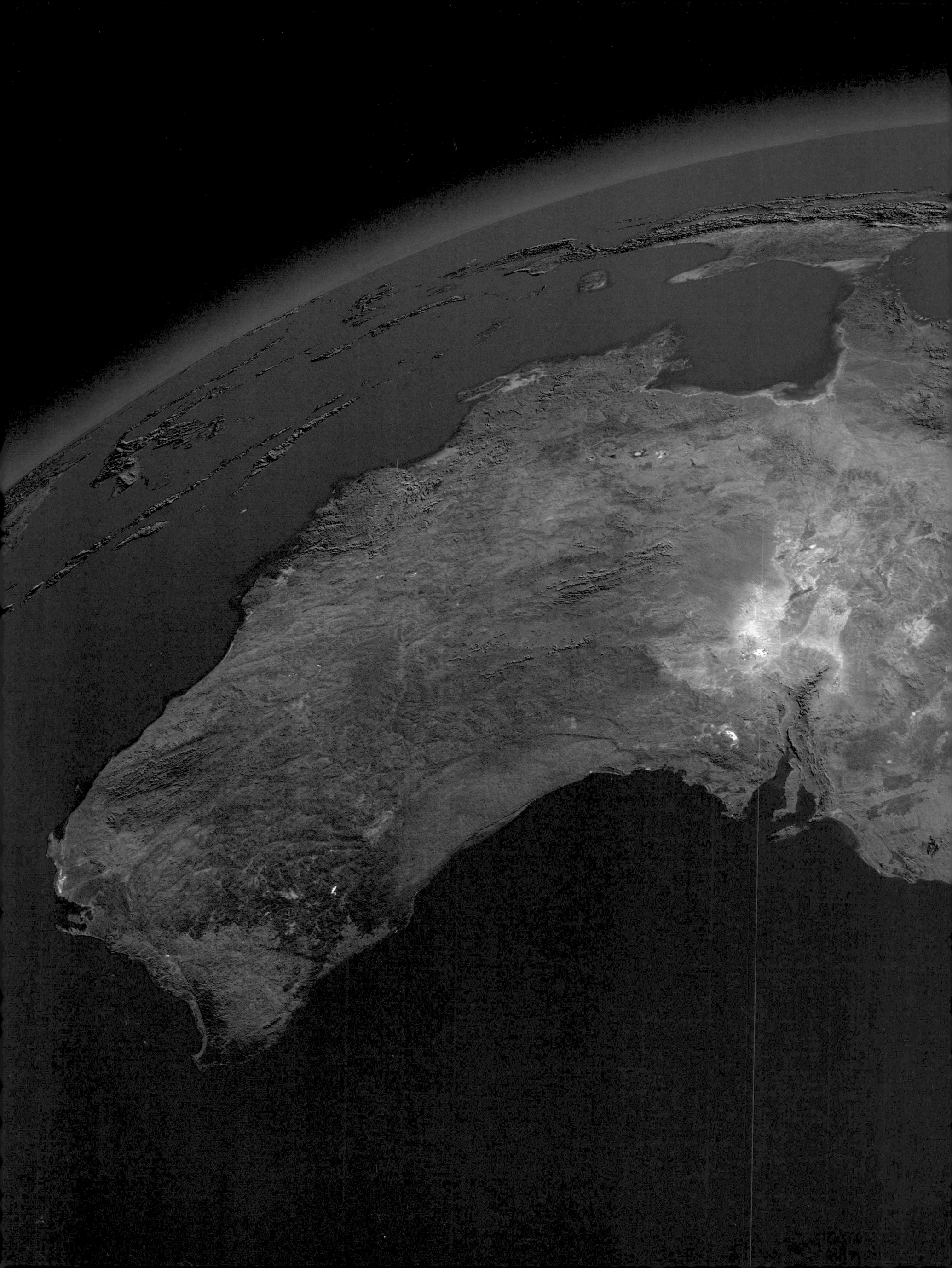

AUSTRALIA
AND
OCEANIA

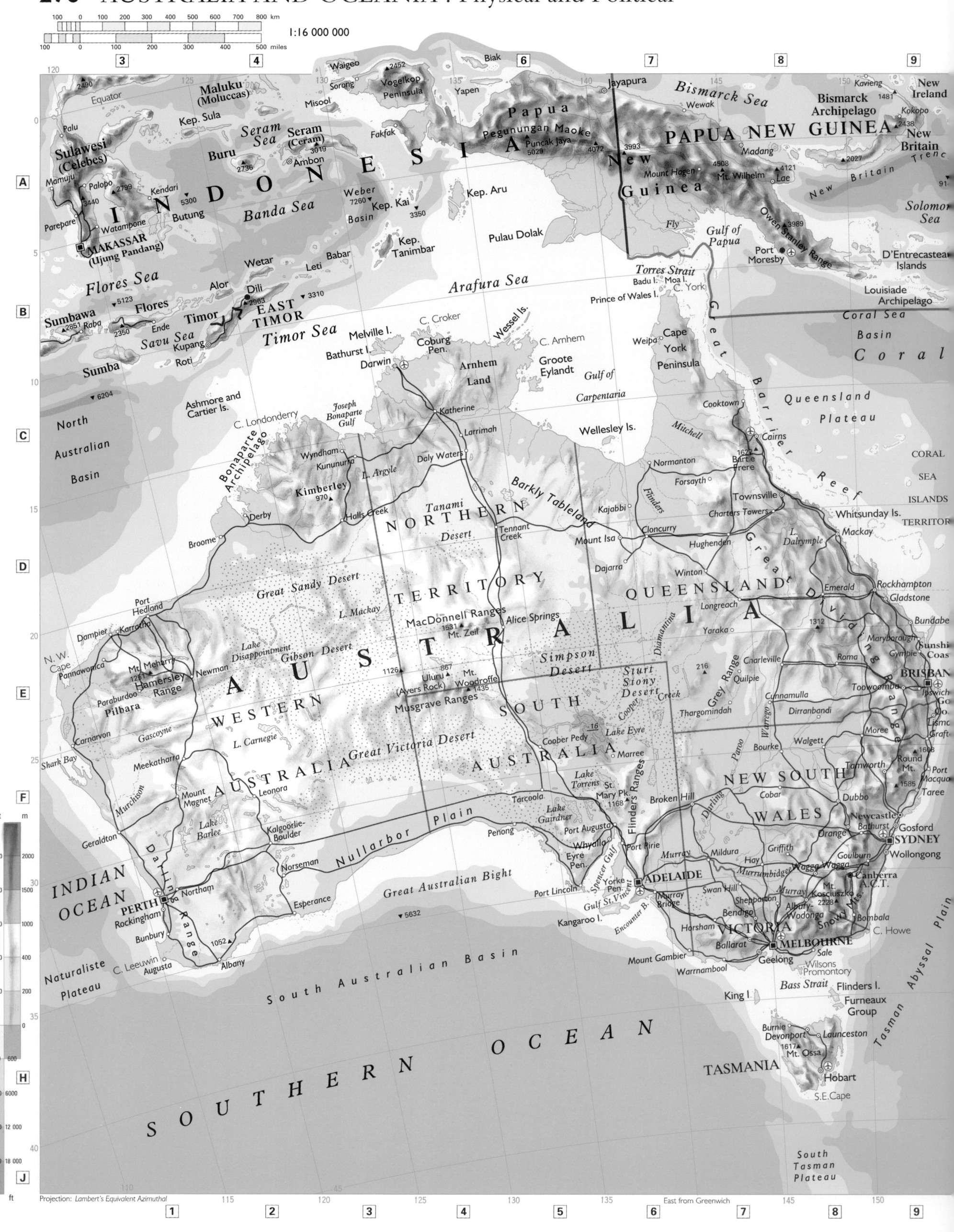

1:16 000 000

Projection: Lambert's Equivalent Azimuthal

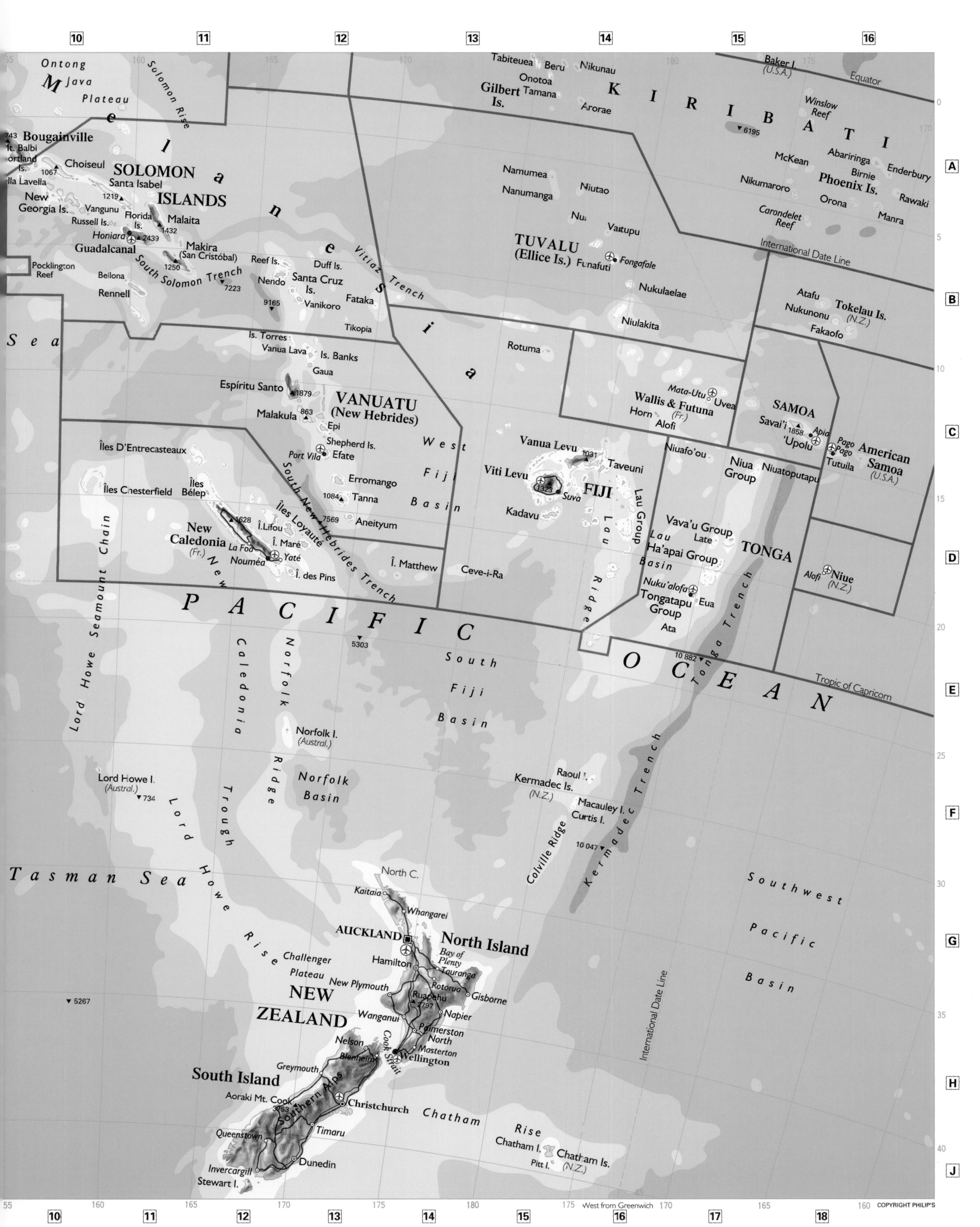

Ontong Java Plateau
Solomon Rise
Tabiteuea Beru Nikunau
Onotoa
Gilbert Tamana
Is.
Arorae
K I R I B A T I
Baker I.
(U.S.A.)
Equator

Bougainville
Mt. Balbi
2743
Choiseul
Portland
Is.
New Georgia Is.
1067
SOLOMON
Santa Isabel
Vangunu 1219
Russell Is. Florida Is.
Honiara 2439
Guadalcanal
1250
ISLANDS
Malaita
1432
Makira
(San Cristóbal)

Winslow Reef
McKean Abariringa Enderbury
Birnie
Nikumaroro Phoenix Is. Rawaki
Orona Manra
Carondelet Reef
International Date Line

Namumea
Nanumanga Niutao
Nui Vaitupu
TUVALU
(Ellice Is.) Funafuti Fongafale
Nukulaelae

Pocklington Reef
Bellona
Rennell
Sea
Reef Is.
Duff Is.
Nendo Santa Cruz
Is.
9165 Vanikoro
7223
Fataka
Tikopia
Vitiaz Trench

Niulakita
Rotuma

Atafu Tokelau Is.
Nukunonu (N.Z.)
Fakaofo

Is. Torres
Vanua Lava
Is. Banks
Gaua
Espíritu Santo 1879
Malakula 863
VANUATU
(New Hebrides)
Epi
Shepherd Is.
Port Vila Efate
Erromango
1084
Tanna
7569
Aneityum

M e l a n e s i a

West
Fiji
Basin

Vanua Levu 1031
Taveuni
Viti Levu
1323
Kadavu Suva
FIJI
Ceve-i-Ra

Mata-Utu Uvea
Wallis & Futuna
Horn (Fr.)
Alofi

Niuafo'ou
Niua Niuatoputapu
Group

SAMOA
Savai'i 1858
'Upolu Apia
Pago American
Pago Samoa
Tutuila (U.S.A.)

Îles D'Entrecasteaux
Îles Chesterfield
Îles
Bélep
New
Caledonia
(Fr.)
1628
La Foa
Nouméa
Îles Loyauté
Î. Lifou
Î. Maré
Yaté
Î. des Pins
Î. Matthew

Vava'u Group
Late
Lau Ha'apai Group
Group TONGA
Lau
Basin Nuku'alofa Eua
Tongatapu
Group
Ata

Alofi Niue
(N.Z.)

PACIFIC
5303
South
Fiji
Basin
10 882
Tonga Trench
OCEAN
Tropic of Capricorn

Lord Howe Seamount Chain
Caledonia
Norfolk Ridge
Caledonia Trough
Lord Howe Rise
Norfolk I.
(Austral.)
Norfolk Basin
Lord Howe I.
(Austral.)
734

South
Fiji
Basin

Raoul I.
Kermadec Is.
(N.Z.)
Macauley I.
Curtis I.
10 047
Kermadec Trench
Colville Ridge

Southwest

Pacific

Basin

Tasman Sea
5267

North C.
Kaitaia
Whangarei
AUCKLAND North Island
Hamilton Bay of
Challenger Tauranga Plenty
Plateau Rotorua
New Plymouth Gisborne
NEW Ruapehu
Wanganui 2797 Napier
ZEALAND Palmerston
North
Nelson Masterton
South Island Wellington
Greymouth Blenheim Cook Strait
Aoraki Mt. Cook Southern Alps
3753 Christchurch Chatham
Queenstown Timaru Rise
Chatham I. Chatham Is.
Pitt I. (N.Z.)
Invercargill Dunedin
Stewart I.

International Date Line

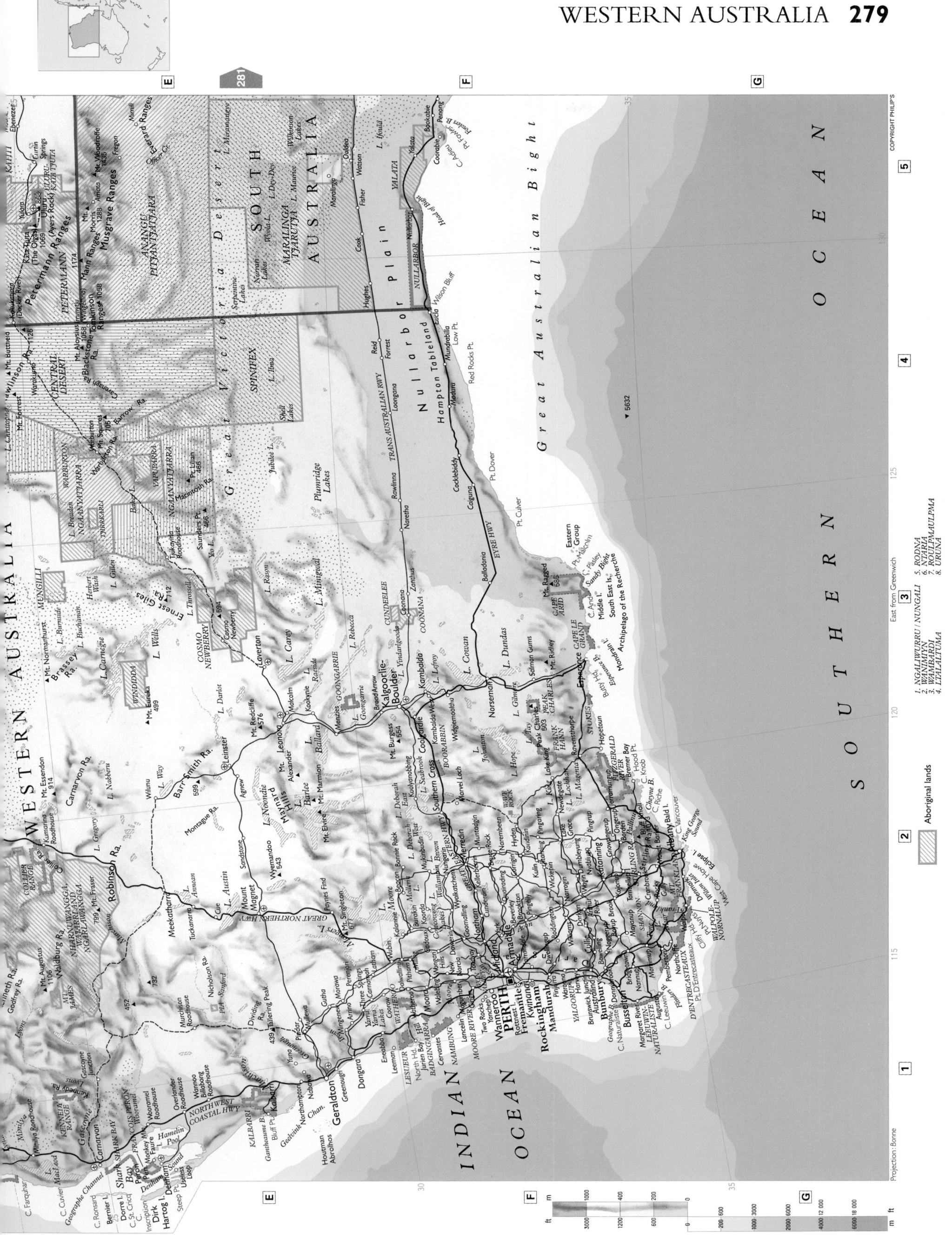

E   F   G

KATITI

ULURU (Ayers Rock) KATA TJUTA

Petermann Ranges

Musgrave Ranges

ANANGU PITJANTJATJARA

SOUTH

AUSTRALIA

Great Victoria Desert

SPINIFEX

WARBURTON NGAANYATJARRA

TJIRRKARLI

YAPU NGAANYATJARRA

WESTERN AUSTRALIA

MUNGILLI

COSMO NEWBERRY

Plumridge Lakes

Nullarbor Plain

Nullarbor

Hampton Tableland

TRANS-AUSTRALIAN RWY

EYRE HWY

Great Australian Bight

O C E A N

GOONGARRIE

Kalgoorlie-Boulder

CUNDEELEE

COOMANA

Archipelago of the Recherche

SOUTHERN

Mount Magnet

Meekatharra

GREAT NORTHERN HWY

GOLDEN PIPELINE

PERTH

Fremantle

Rockingham

Mandurah

Bunbury

Busselton

INDIAN

OCEAN

Geraldton

KALBARRI

NORTHWEST COASTAL HWY

Shark Bay

Carnarvon

KENNEDY RANGE

COLLIER RANGE

Robinson Ra.

COPYRIGHT PHILIP'S

East from Greenwich

Aboriginal lands

1. NGALIWURRU / NUNGALI   5. RODNA
2. WANMIYN   6. NTJARA
3. WARDARA   7. ROULPMAAULPMA
4. LTALALTUMA   8. URUNA

Projection: Bonne

m ft

1000 3000
400 1200
200 600
0 0
200 600
1000 3000
2000 6000
4000 12 000
6000 18 000

1   2   3   4   5

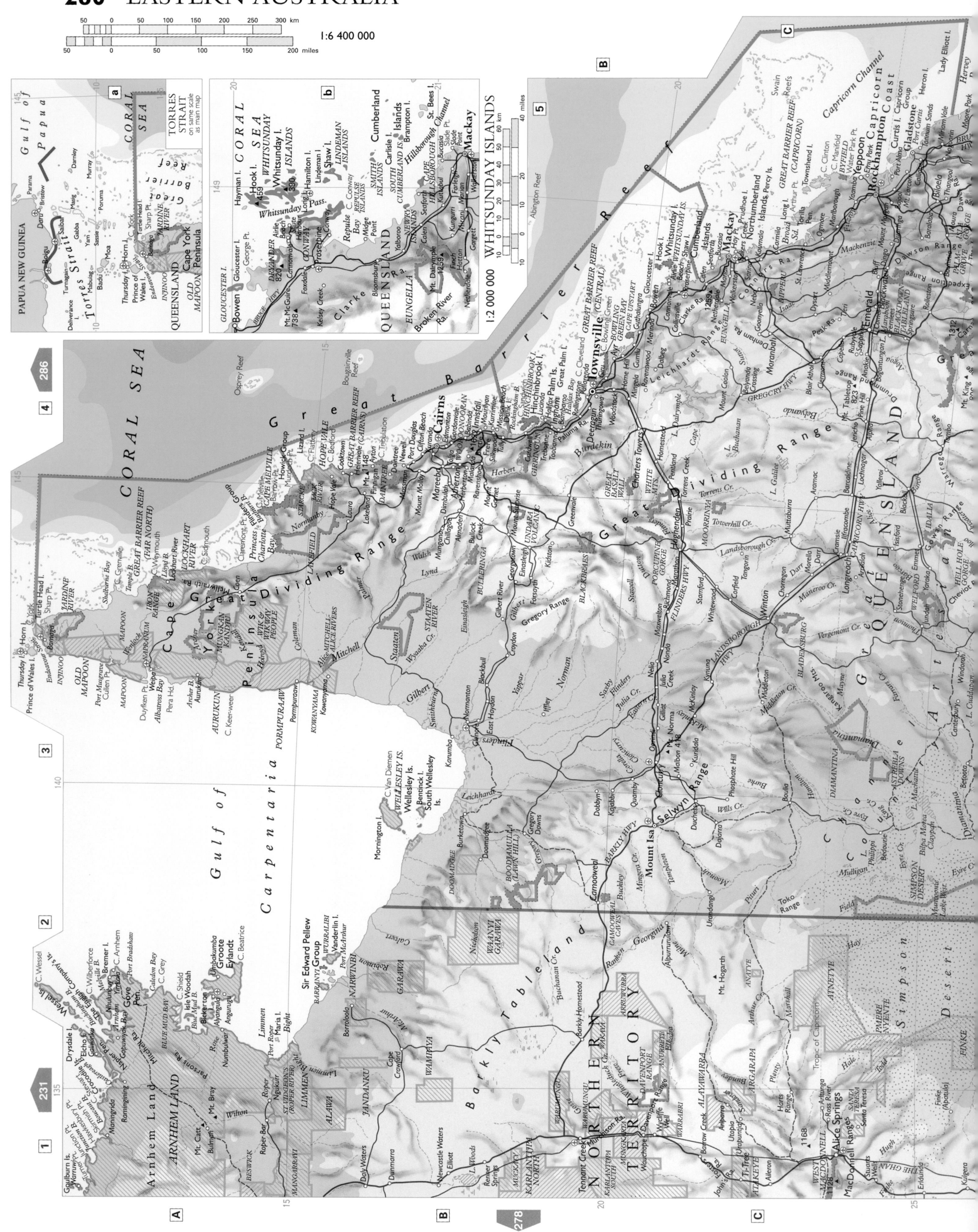

1:6 400 000

Scale bar: 50 0 50 100 150 200 250 300 km
50 0 50 100 150 200 miles

PAPUA NEW GUINEA

CORAL SEA

Gulf of Papua

Torres Strait

TORRES STRAIT on same scale as main map

QUEENSLAND

OLD MAPOON

Cape York Peninsula

GULF OF CARPENTARIA

CORAL SEA

WHITSUNDAY ISLANDS

1:2 000 000

QUEENSLAND

Mackay

Townsville

Cairns

Great Barrier Reef

Great Dividing Range

Cape York Peninsula

Gulf of Carpentaria

Barkly Tableland

NORTHERN TERRITORY

Arnhem Land

Alice Springs

Mount Isa

Rockhampton

Emerald

Gladstone

Tropic of Capricorn

Simpson Desert

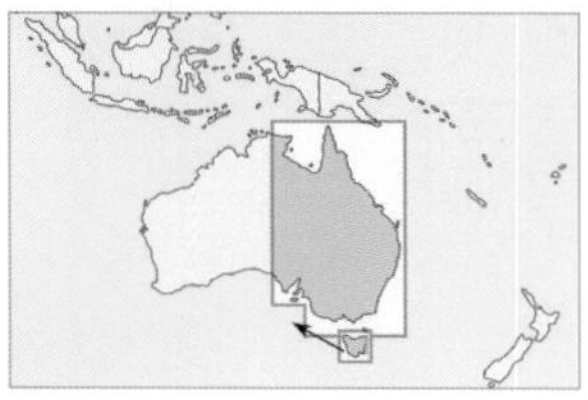

QUEENSLAND

NEW SOUTH WALES

SOUTH AUSTRALIA

VICTORIA

TASMANIA

BRISBANE
SYDNEY
MELBOURNE
ADELAIDE
Canberra (COMMONWEALTH TERRITORY)
Hobart
Newcastle
Wollongong
Geelong

TASMAN SEA

Bass Strait

Great Dividing Range

Darling Downs

Flinders Ranges

Lake Eyre

Murray
Darling

Furneaux Group
Flinders Island
Cape Barren I.
King Island

on same scale

Aboriginal lands

COPYRIGHT PHILIP'S

Projection: Bonne

East from Greenwich

279

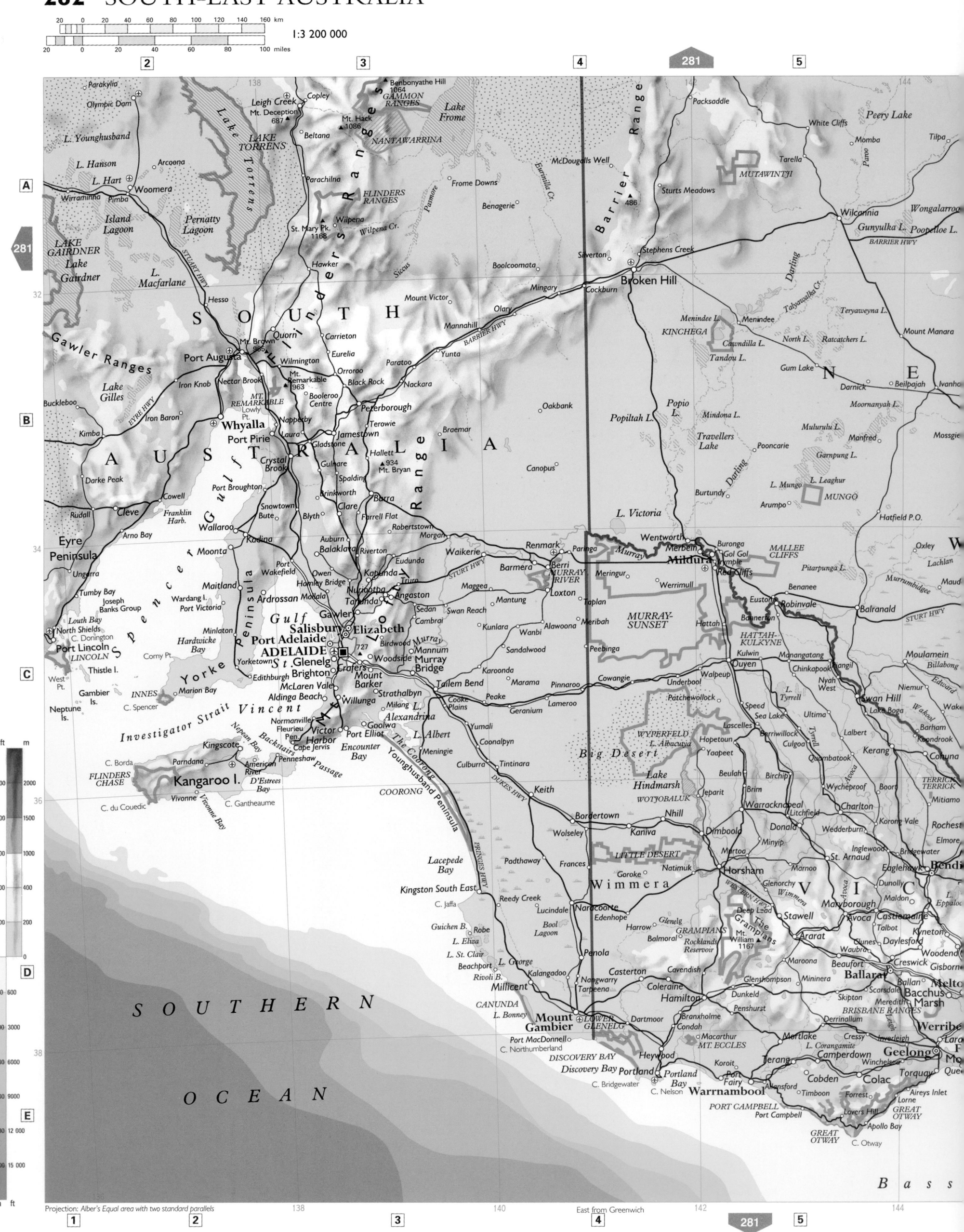

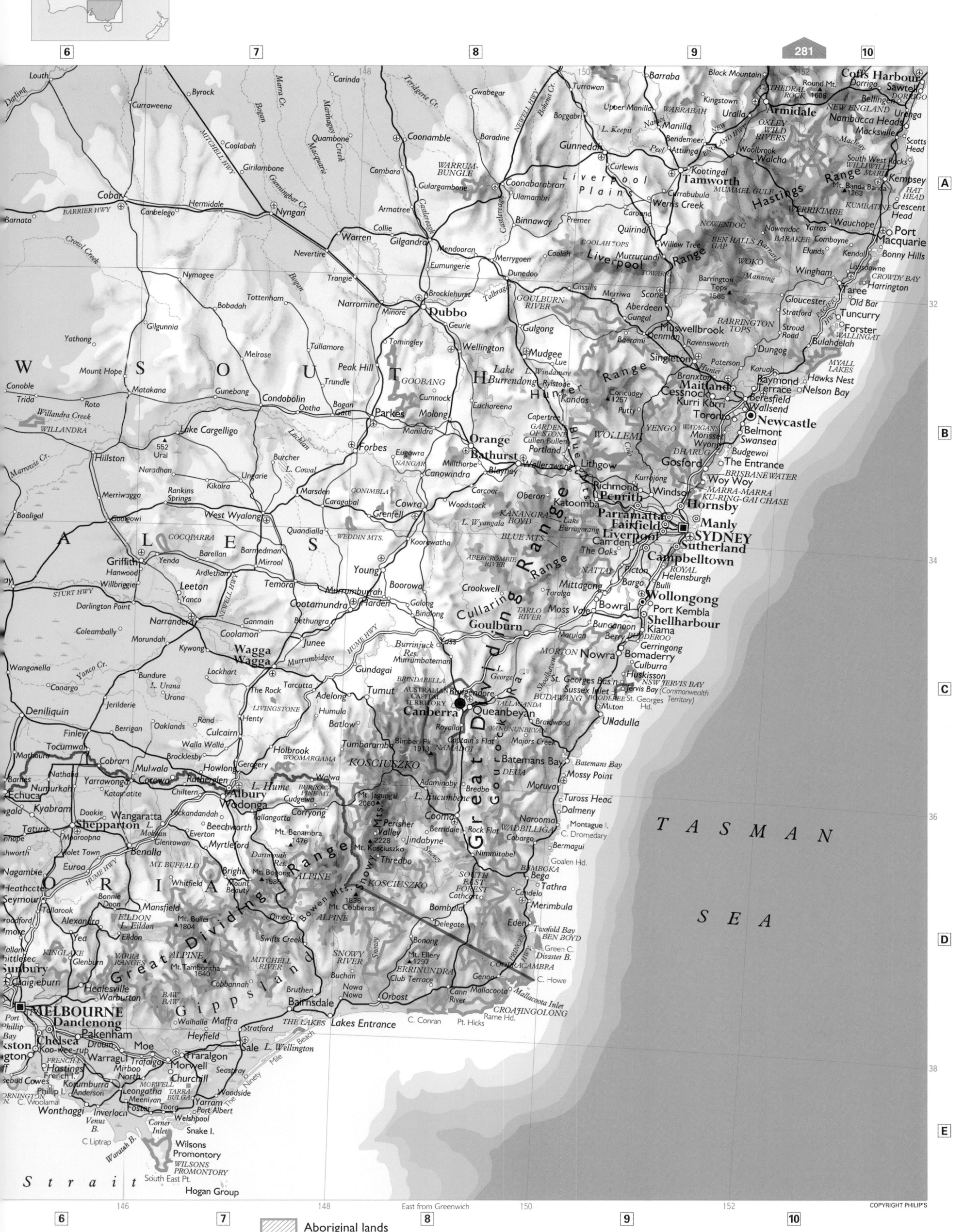

Aboriginal lands

East from Greenwich

10 0 20 40 60 80 100 120 140 km

1:2 800 000

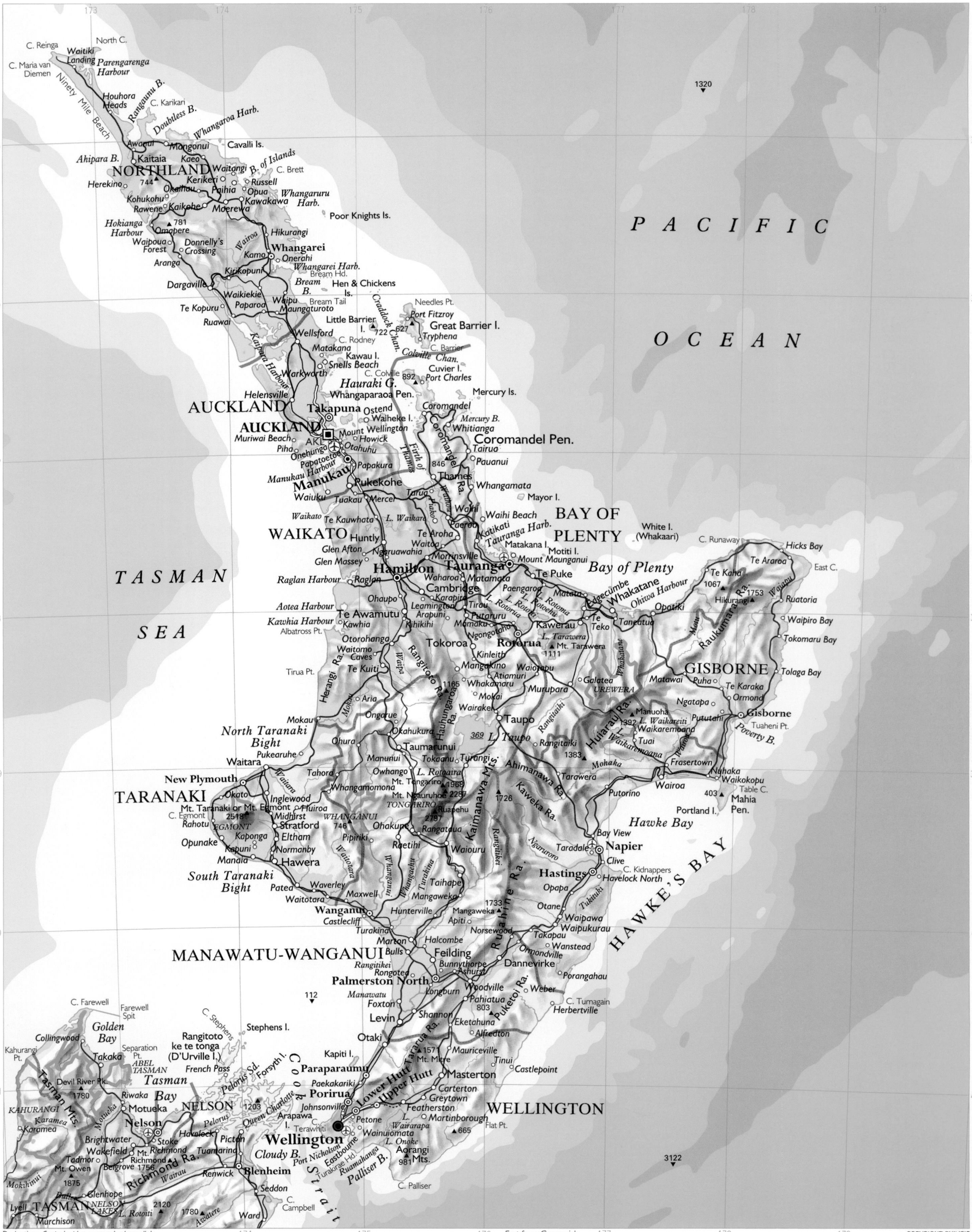

10 0 20 40 60 80 100 miles

1 2 3 4 5 6 7 8

P A C I F I C

O C E A N

NORTHLAND

C. Reinga
North C.
Waitiki Landing
C. Maria van Diemen
Parengarenga Harbour
Houhora Heads
Rangaunu B.
C. Karikari
Doubtless B.
Ninety Mile Beach
Awanui
Mongonui
Kaeo
Cavalli Is.
Ahipara B.
Kaitaia
Whangaroa Harb.
Herekino
Waitangi
B. of Islands
C. Brett
Okaihau
Kerikeri
Russell
Kohukohu
Paihia
Opua
Rawene
Kaikohe
Kawakawa
Whangaruru Harb.
Moerewa
Hokianga Harbour
Omapere
Hikurangi
Poor Knights Is.
Waipoua Forest
Donnelly's Crossing
Kamo
Aranga
Kirikopuni
Whangarei
Onerahi
Whangarei Harb.
Dargaville
Waikiekie
Bream Hd.
Te Kopuru
Paparoa
Waipu
Maungaturoto
Bream B.
Hen & Chickens
Ruawai
Bream Tail
Needles Pt.
Kaipara Harbour
Wellsford
Little Barrier I.
Port Fitzroy
Great Barrier I.
Matakana
Tryphena
Warkworth
C. Rodney
Kawau I.
Snells Beach
C. Barrier
Colville Chan.
AUCKLAND
Helensville
Whangaparaoa Pen.
Cuvier I.
Port Charles
Hauraki G.
C. Colville
Mercury Is.
Takapuna
Coromandel
Mercury B.
Whitianga
Ostend
Waiheke I.
AUCKLAND
AKL
Mount Wellington
Howick
Tairua
Muriwai Beach
Otahuhu
Pauanui
Piha
Onehunga
Papatoetoe
Firth of Thames
Manukau Harbour
Papakura
Thames
Whangamata
Manukau
Pukekohe
Tuakau
Mercer
Tairua Ra.
Mayor I.
Waiuku
Te Kauwhata
Waihi
BAY OF PLENTY
Waikato
L. Waikare
Paeroa
Waihi Beach
WAIKATO
Huntly
Te Aroha
Katikati
White I. (Whakaari)
Glen Afton
Ngaruawahia
Waitoa
Tauranga Harb.
C. Runaway
Hicks Bay
Glen Massey
Morrinsville
Tauranga
Matakana I.
Motiti I.
Te Araroa
Te Kaha
Hamilton
Waharoa
Mount Maunganui
Cambridge
Matamata
Te Puke
Bay of Plenty
Edgecumbe
Whakatane
Hikurangi
Ruatoria
Raglan
Raglan Harbour
Karapiro
Tirau
L. Rotorua
Matata
Ohiwa Harbour
Opotiki
Waipiro Bay
Aotea Harbour
Te Awamutu
Arapuni
Putaruru
L. Rotoiti
Te Teko
Taneatua
Tokomaru Bay
Kawhia
Kihikihi
Leamington
L. Rotoma
Kawhia Harbour
Memaku
Kawerau
GISBORNE
Albatross Pt.
Otorohanga
Mangakino
Ngongotaha
Rotorua
Galatea
Matawai
Tolaga Bay
Waitomo Caves
Waipa
Tokoroa
Kinleith
Mt. Tarawera
UREWERA
Puha
Te Karaka
Ormond
Tirua Pt.
Te Kuiti
Mangakino
Atiamuri
Waiotapu
Murupara
Ngatapa
Gisborne
Aria
Ongarue
Mokai
Wairakei
L. Waikareiti
Waikaremoana
Tuai
Pututahi
Tuaheni Pt.
Mokau
Okahukura
Taupo
Rangitaiki
Poverty B.
North Taranaki Bight
Ohura
Taumarunui
Tokaanu
Turangi
L. Rotoaira
369
L. Taupo
Ahimanawa Ra.
Mohaka
Frasertown
Waitara
Pukearuhe
Manunui
Owhango
Whangamomona
Mt. Tongariro
Kaweka Ra.
Wairoa
New Plymouth
Tahora
Mt. Ngauruhoe 2291
TONGARIRO
Putorino
Waikokopu
Okato
Inglewood
Ruapehu 2797
Mahia Pen.
TARANAKI
Mt. Taranaki or Mt. Egmont 2518
Huiroa
Ohakune
Rangataua
Hawke Bay
Rahotu
Midhirst
EGMONT
Stratford
Raetihi
Waiouru
Bay View
Kaponga
Eltham
Taradale
Napier
Opunake
Normanby
Ohura
Clive
Manaia
Hawera
Pipiriki
Taihape
C. Kidnappers
South Taranaki Bight
Patea
Waverley
Mangaweka
Hastings
Maxwell
Mangaweka
Havelock North
Waitotara
Hunterville
Mangaweka
Opapa
Otane
HAWKE'S BAY
Wanganui
Castlecliff
Apiti
Waipawa
Turakina
Norsewood
Waipukurau
MANAWATU-WANGANUI
Marton
Halcombe
Takapau
Wanstead
Bulls
Feilding
Ormondville
Rangitikei
Bunnythorpe
Dannevirke
Porangahau
Rongotea
Ashhurst
Palmerston North
Woodville
112
Foxton
Longburn
Pahiatua
Weber
Shannon
Mauriceville
Herbertville
Levin
Eketahuna
Otaki
Alfredton
Tinui
Kapiti I.
Castlepoint
Mt. Mere 1571
Paraparaumu
Masterton
Porirua
Paekakariki
Carterton
Lower Hutt
Greytown
Upper Hutt
Featherston
WELLINGTON
Johnsonville
Martinborough
Wellington
Petone
Wainuiomata
Flat Pt.
C. Palliser

T A S M A N

S E A

Golden Bay
Collingwood
C. Farewell
Farewell Spit
Takaka
C. Stephens
Stephens I.
Rangitoto ke te tonga (D'Urville I.)
Separation Pt.
ABEL TASMAN
French Pass
Devil River Pk.
Riwaka
Tasman Bay
Motueka
NELSON
Cook Strait
Terawhiti
Kahurangi Pt.
Karamea
KAHURANGI Mts.
Brightwater
Stoke
Nelson
Havelock
Pelorus Sd.
Picton
Wakefield
Mt. Richmond
Queen Charlotte
Arapawa I.
L. Onoke
Aorangi Mts. 981
Belgrove
Richmond Ra.
Tuamarina
Port Nicholson
Eastbourne
Turakirae Hd.
Ruamahanga
Palliser B.
Mokihinui
Murchison
Glenhope
L. Rotoiti
Renwick
Blenheim
NELSON LAKES
Seddon
TASMAN
Wairau
C. Campbell
Ward

3122

ft m

9000 3000
6000 2000
3000 1000
1200 400
600 200
0 0
200 600
1500 4500
3000 9000
m ft

Projection: Conical with two standard parallels

East from Greenwich

COPYRIGHT PHILIP'S

1:2 800 000

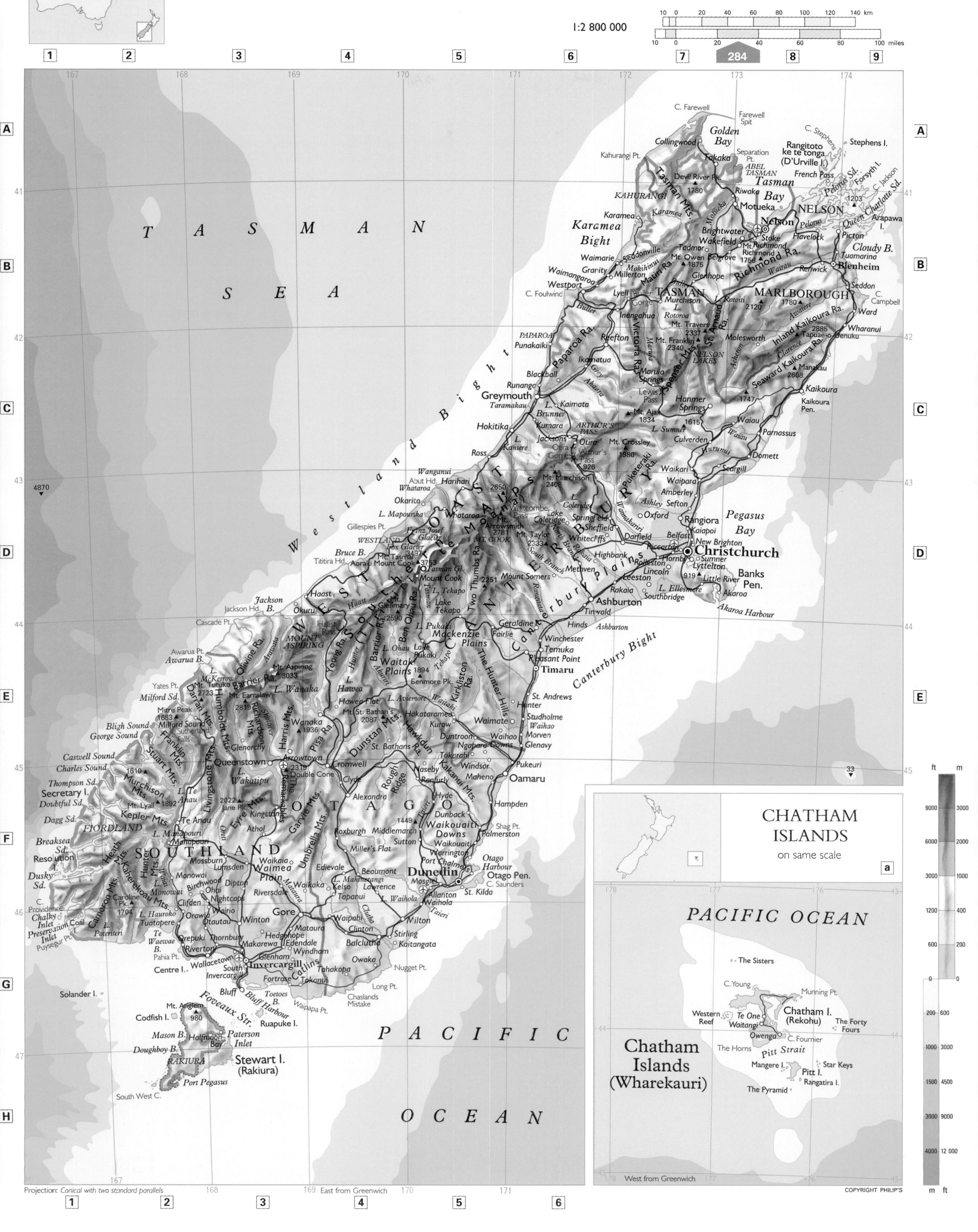

10 20 40 60 80 100 120 140 km
10 0 20 40 60 80 100 miles

284

T A S M A N   S E A

P A C I F I C   O C E A N

CHATHAM ISLANDS
on same scale

PACIFIC OCEAN

Chatham Islands (Wharekauri)

The Sisters

C. Young

Munning Pt.

Western Reef
Te One Waitangi
Chatham I. (Rekohu)
The Forty Fours

The Horns
Owenga
C. Fournier
Pitt Strait
Mangere I.
Pitt I.
Star Keys
Rangitira I.
The Pyramid

West from Greenwich

Projection: Conical with two standard parallels
East from Greenwich

COPYRIGHT PHILIP'S

NELSON
MARLBOROUGH
Blenheim
Picton
Golden Bay
Tasman Bay
C. Farewell
Farewell Spit
Collingwood
Takaka
Motueka
Westport
Greymouth
Hokitika
Ross
Harihari
Franz Josef Glacier
Fox Glacier
Mount Cook
Aoraki Mount Cook
Haast
Christchurch
Ashburton
Timaru
Oamaru
Dunedin
Invercargill
Bluff
Queenstown
Te Anau
Milford Sound
Gore
Stewart I. (Rakiura)
Port Pegasus
Codfish I.
Solander I.

WESTLAND
CANTERBURY
Canterbury Plains
OTAGO
SOUTHLAND
FIORDLAND
Mackenzie Plains
Waitaki Plains

SOUTHERN ALPS
Lake Tekapo
L. Pukaki
L. Wanaka
L. Hawea
L. Wakatipu
L. Te Anau
L. Manapouri

Westland Bight
Canterbury Bight
Foveaux Str.
Banks Pen.
Otago Pen.
Pegasus Bay

1:5 200 000

50 0 50 100 150 200 km
50 0 50 100 150 miles

COPYRIGHT PHILIP'S

Projection: Lambert Conformal Conic

East from Greenwich

PAPUA NEW GUINEA

Oceans and Seas: PACIFIC OCEAN, Bismarck Sea, Solomon Sea, New Britain, Coral Sea, Gulf of Papua, Huon Gulf, Milne Bay, Ward Hunt Sea

Islands and Groups: NORTH SOLOMONS, NEW IRELAND, NEW BRITAIN, WEST NEW BRITAIN, Admiralty Islands, MANUS, St. Matthias Group, New Hanover, Bismarck Archipelago, Lihir Group, Tanga Is., Feni Is., D'Entrecasteaux Islands, Trobriand Is., Woodlark I., Louisiade Archipelago, Bougainville I., Buka I.

Regions/Provinces: WEST SEPIK, EAST SEPIK, MADANG, WESTERN HIGHLANDS, SOUTHERN HIGHLANDS, ENGA, CHIMBU, EASTERN HIGHLANDS, MOROBE, NORTHERN, CENTRAL, WESTERN, GULF, PAPUA, New Guinea

Places: Port Moresby, Lae, Madang, Wewak, Wabag, Mendi, Goroka, Kundiawa, Mt. Hagen, Daru, Kerema, Popondetta, Rabaul, Kokopo, Kavieng, Lorengau, Samarai, Alotau, Buna, Gona, Wau, Bulolo, Finschhafen, Morobe

Mountains/Peaks: Owen Stanley Range, Bismarck Range, Central Range, Finisterre Ra., Adelbert Range, Torricelli Mts., Victor Emanuel Ra., Mt. Wilhelm 4508, Mt. Giluwe 4359, Mt. Michael 3647, Mt. Victoria 4035, Mt. Albert Edward 3990, Mt. Suckling 3676, Mt. Capella 3993, Mt. Balbi 2715

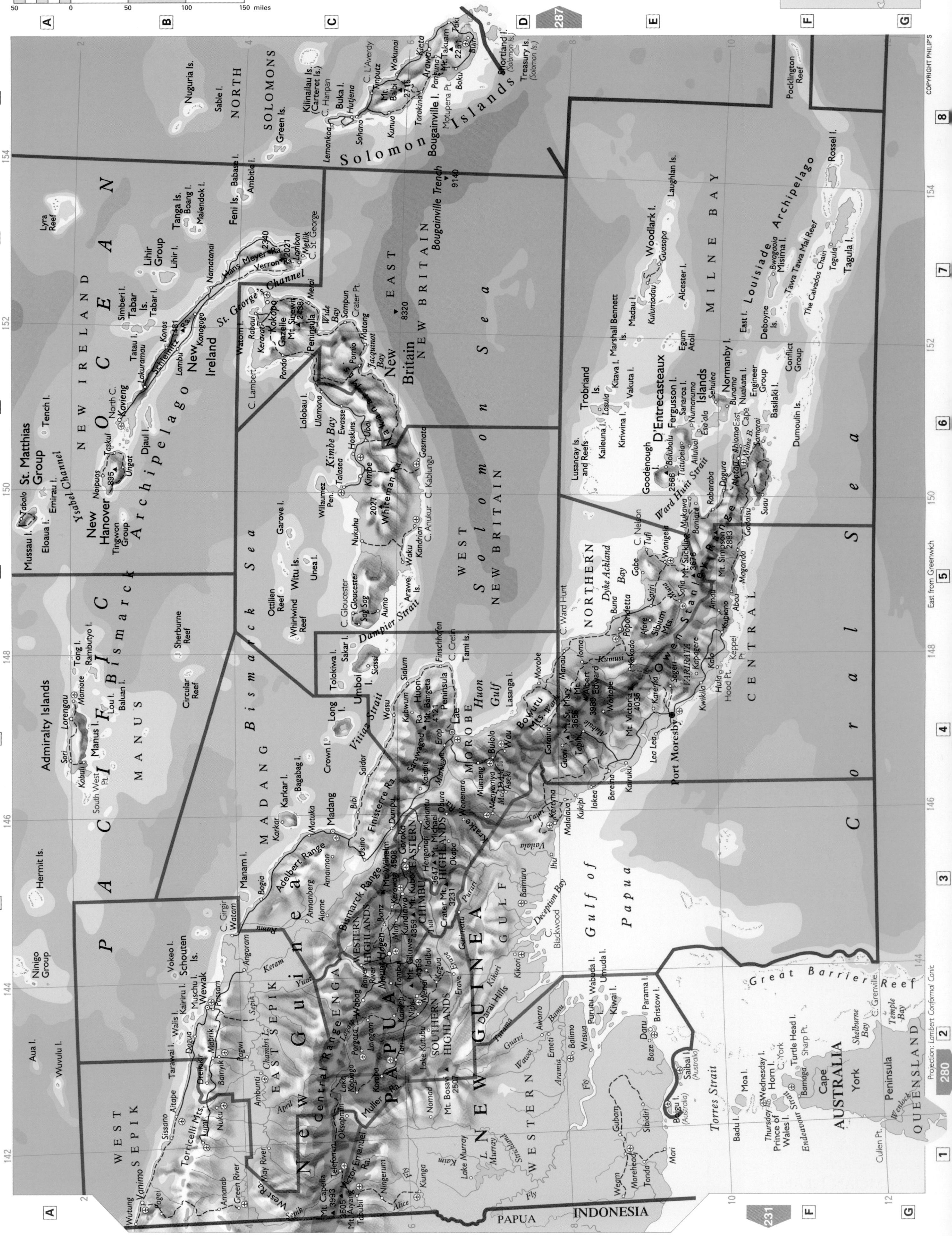

Straits: Torres Strait, Vitiaz Strait, Dampier Strait, Ward Hunt Strait, St. George's Channel

Australia: QUEENSLAND, Cape York Peninsula, Great Barrier Reef, Thursday I., Prince of Wales I., Saibai I.

Indonesia: PAPUA, INDONESIA

Sepik, Fly, Purari, Ramu, Markham, Lake Murray

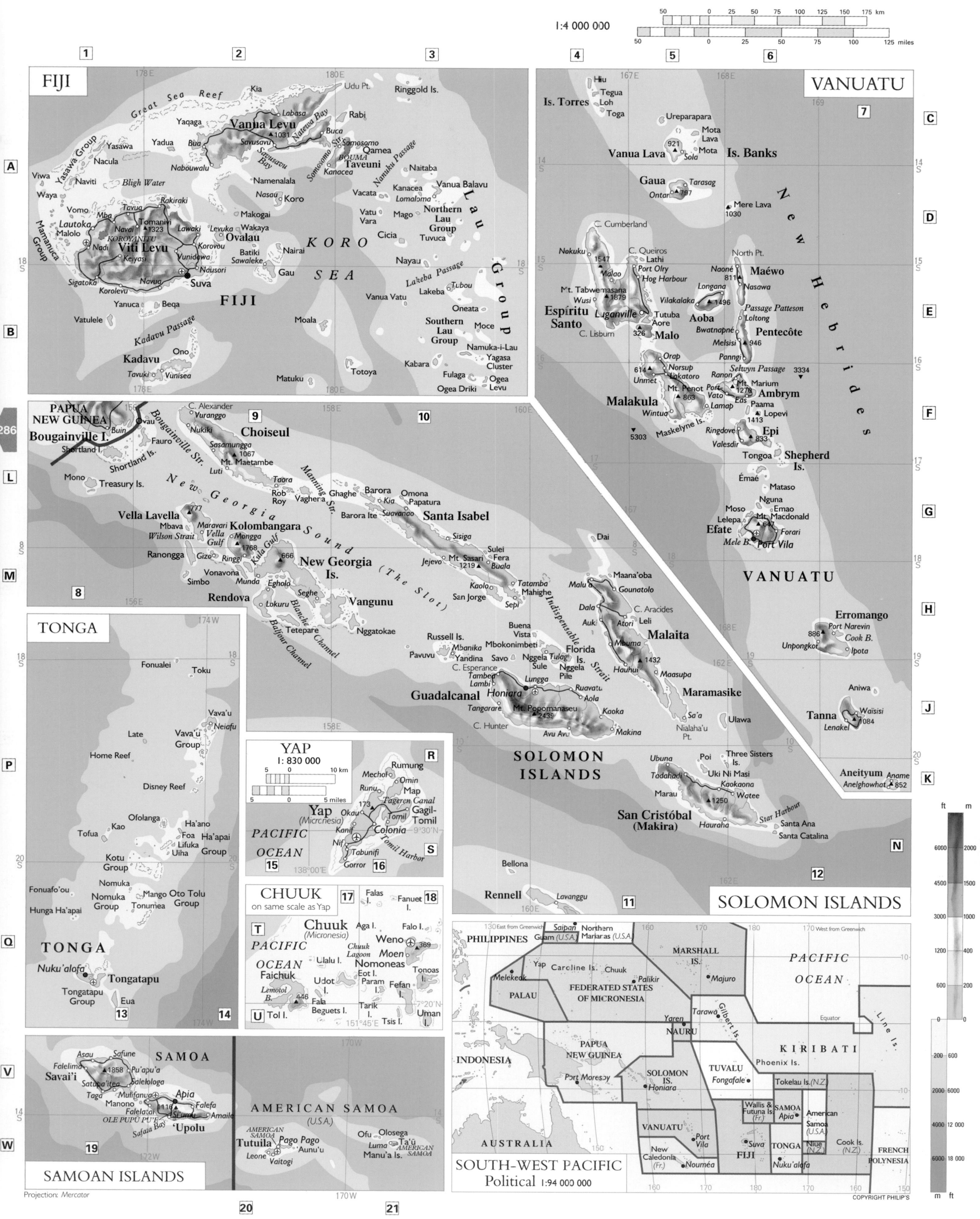

1:4 000 000

FIJI

VANUATU

TONGA

YAP
1: 830 000

CHUUK
on same scale as Yap

SOLOMON ISLANDS

SAMOAN ISLANDS

SOUTH-WEST PACIFIC
Political 1:94 000 000

Projection: Mercator

COPYRIGHT PHILIP'S

Equatorial Scale 1:43 200 000

OKINAWA
on same scale as Palau **a**

EAST CHINA SEA

Hedo-misaki · Hedo
Kunigami
Ie-shima · Kouri-shima · Yagaji-shima · 503 Yonaha-Dake
Seseko-shima · Nakijin
Minna-shima · Motobu · Nago
Onna · Arume-wan · Banno-saki
Okinawa (Japan) · Ishikawa · Kin-wan · Ikei-shima
Kadena · Gushikawa · Heanza-shima
Okinawa (Koza) · Henna · Tsuken-jima
Ginowan · Nakagusuku-wan · Kudaka-shima
Uraso · Naha · Shuri
Rukan-sho · Gushikami
Kyan-zaki · Itoman

PACIFIC OCEAN

128° E

Iwo-Jima
b
Kangoku Iwa · Kitano Hana · COAST GUARD STATION
Iwo-Jima (Japan) · 108
Kama Iwa · IWO-JIMA AIRFIELD
Suribachi Yama 167 · Fatatsu Ne
Tobiishi Hana · 141° 20' E
Hanare Iwa
PACIFIC OCEAN
26° 30' N
24° 45' N

IWO-JIMA **b**
1:200 000
0 1 2 3 km
1 0 1 2 mi

PALAU **c**
Ngeregur · Konrei
Ngardmau Bay · Ngardmau · 618
Babelthuap I. · Namai Bay
Melekeok
Komebail Lagoon · Garusuun
Koror · Garreru · Koror I.
Aulong · Urukthapel I.
Apurashokoru · Eil Malk I.
Ngobasangel · Ngeregong
Barnum Bay · Ngergoi
Ngesebus · Ngardololok · Kongauru I.
Peleliu I.
Angaur I.

PACIFIC OCEAN
134° 30' E

1:1 550 000
10 0 10 20 30 km
10 0 10 20 miles

RUSSIA
Lena · Irkutsk · Chita · Oz. Baykal
Ulaanbaatar · Blagoveshchensk · Amur · Khabarovsk
Sea of Okhotsk · Okhotsk
Poluostrov Kamchatka
Petropavlovsk-Kamchatskiy
Komandorskiye Ostrova (Russia)
Near Is. · Andreanof (U.S.A.)
Aleutian Basin · Bering Sea
7822
La Perouse Str. · Sakhalin
Kuril'skiye Ostrova (Russia)
Kuril-Kamchatka Trench
10,542
Aleutian Trench

MONGOLIA
Ürümqi
CHINA
Ulaanbaatar
Changchun · Harbin
Shenyang · Sapporo · Hokkaidō · Hakodate
Beijing · Vladivostok
Tianjin · NORTH KOREA · Sea of Japan
Taiyuan · Dalian · Seoul · Honshū
Lanzhou · SOUTH KOREA · Nagoya · Sendai
Xi'an · Qingdao · Kyōto · Tōkyō · Fuji-San 3776
Nanjing · Kitakyūshū · Osaka · Yokohama
Chengdu · Wuhan · Shikoku · JAPAN
Kunlun Shan · Lhasa · Chongqing · Shanghai · Kyūshū
XIZANG · Changsha · Hangzhou · East China Sea
Brahmaputra · Kunming · Fuzhou · Okinawa · Ryūkyū-rettō
Dhaka · Guangzhou · Taipei
Mandalay · Macau · Hong Kong · TAIWAN
Irrawaddy · Hainan
BURMA · Hanoi
LAOS · C. Engano
Salween · Luzon · Philippine Sea
Rangoon · Paracel Is. · Manila
THAILAND · Mekong · Philippine Basin
Bangkok · South China Sea · PHILIPPINES · Samar
CAMBODIA · Mindoro · 10,497
Phnom Penh · Palawan
VIETNAM · Thanh Pho Ho Chi Minh
G. of Thailand

Northwest Pacific Basin
Shatsky Rise
Midway Is. (U.S.A.)
Lisianski I. (U.S.A.)
Minami-Tori-Shima (Japan)
Wake I. (U.S.A.)
Emperor Seamount Chain
Hawaiian Ridge
Chinook Trough

Iwo-Jima (Japan) · Ogasawara Gunto (Japan)
Kazan-Rettō (Japan)
Kyushu-Palau Ridge
Ozima-Ridge

NORTHERN MARIANAS (U.S.A.)
West Mariana Basin · East Mariana Basin
Tinian · Saipan
GUAM (U.S.A.)
Challenger Deep 11,022
Mariana Trench
Yap · Caroline Is. · Chuuk · Micronesia
MARSHALL IS.
Bikini Atoll · Enewetak Atoll
Ralik Chain · Ratak Chain
Kwajalein · Majuro

FED. STATES OF MICRONESIA
PALAU · Melekeok · Palikir · Pohnpei
West Caroline Basin · East Caroline Basin
Eauripik Rise · Jaluit I.
Butaritari · Tarawa
Solomon Rise · Melanesian Basin · Gilbert Is.
Howland I. (U.S.A.) · Baker I. (U.S.A.)
Phoenix Is. · Abariringa · Enderbury

SRI LANKA
Colombo
Nicobar Is. (India)
MALAYSIA · Sulu Sea · Mindanao · Davao
Kuala Lumpur · PEN. MALAYSIA · BRUNEI · SABAH · 4101
Celebes Sea
Sumatera · Singapore · SARAWAK · Borneo
Maluku · Halmahera · Seram · Admiralty Is. · PAPUA NEW GUINEA · New Ireland
INDONESIA · Sulawesi · Buru · PAPUA Puncak Jaya 5029 · Bismarck Arch. · New Britain · Bougainville
Palembang · Java Sea · Makassar · Banda Sea · New Guinea · Lae · Kokopo
Jakarta · Flores Sea · 7440 · Kopo · SOLOMON IS.
Jawa · Surabaya · Bali · Flores · Port Moresby · Honiara · Guadalcanal
Sunda Island · Sumbawa · Dili · EAST TIMOR · Arafura Sea · Torres Strait · Louisiade Arch. · Santa Cruz Is. 9165

INDIAN OCEAN
Cocos Is. (Austral.)
Christmas I. (Austral.)
Sumba
North Australian Basin
C. York · C. Arnhem
Darwin
Gulf of Carpentaria
Broome
Exmouth Plateau
North West C.
Wharton Basin
Naturaliste Plateau
Geraldton
Perth Basin
Perth
Albany

AUSTRALIA
Alice Springs
L. Eyre
Mount Isa
Cairns
Townsville
Rockhampton
Great Barrier Reef
Great Dividing Ra.
Brisbane
Darling
Murray
Sydney · Canberra
Mt. Kosciuszko 2228
Adelaide
Great Australian Bight
Melbourne
Bass Str.
Tasmania · Hobart

Coral Sea Basin
Coral Sea
VANUATU · Espiritu Santo · Port Vila
Îs. Chesterfield · West Fiji Basin · Vanua Levu
NEW CALEDONIA (Fr.) · Nouméa · Viti Levu · FIJI · Suva
Rotuma · Is. Wallis & Futuna (Fr.) · SAMOA · Apia
Fongafale · TUVALU · Tokelau (N.Z.)
Norfolk I. (Austral.) · 7570
Lord Howe I. (Austral.)
Middleton Reef
South Fiji Basin
Lord Howe Rise
New Caledonia Ridge
Norfolk Ridge
Kermadec Is. (N.Z.) · 10,822
Kermadec Trench · 10,047

Fed. States of Micronesia
Yaren NAURU · Banaba
Nauru
Tarawa
KIRIBATI

Tonga Trench
Nuku'alofa · TONGA
Tasman Sea
Auckland
NEW ZEALAND
Aoraki Mt. Cook 3753
Christchurch
Dunedin
Invercargill
Wellington
Cook Strait
Chatham Rise
Chatham Is. (N.Z.)
Bounty Trough · Bounty Is. (N.Z.)
Antipodes Is. (N.Z.)
Auckland Is. (N.Z.)
Campbell Plateau
Macquarie Is. (Austral.)
Campbell I. (N.Z.)
East Tasman Plateau
South Tasman Rise
South Australian Basin

SOUTHERN OCEAN

NEW CALEDONIA **d**
1:5 750 000
50 0 50 100 km
50 0 50 miles

Îles Belep
Récif de Cook
Île Art
Île Balabio · Poum
Quégoa · Pouébo · Mt. Panié 1628
Koumac · Hienghène
Kaala-Gomen · Voh
Nouvelle-Calédonie (France)
Koné · Poindimié
3566 · Ponérihouen
Poya · Houaïlou
Bourail · Canala · Thio
La Foa · Bouloupari
Paita · Dumbéa · Yaté
Nouméa · Mont Dore
Grand Récif Sud
Îles Loyauté
Île Ouvéa · Fayaoué
Chépénéhé · Wé · Lifou
Ponérihouen · Île Tiga
La Roche · Mou · C. de Flotte
Tadine · C. Boyer · Île Maré
CORAL SEA
165° E · 166° E · 167° E

Projection: Mollweide's Homolographic
East from Greenwich

TAHITI

Pte. Aroa B. de Matavai Pte. Vénus
Papetoai Mahina
Papeete Arue Pirae Papenoo Tiarei
Mt. Tohiea Afareaitu Faaa Hitiaa
2207 Haapiti Pte. Nuupere Paea Mt. Orohena Lac Isthme de
Moorea Punaauia 2060 Mt. Tetufera Orohena 2241 Faaone Taravao Pte.
1789 Vairao Tautira
Maraa Papara Vaihiria Afaahiti Tatataa
Atimaono Mataiea Pueu Tautira
Vai'ao Mt. Rooniu
1332
PACIFIC Teahupoo Presqu'île de Taiarapu
OCEAN
149°30'W 149° 5'W

1:1 150 000
10   0 km
10   0   10 miles

FRENCH POLYNESIA
1:26 000 000
200 0 200 400 km
200 0 200 400 miles

Hatutu Eiao Îles
Marquises
Nuku Hiva Ua Huka
Ua Pu Hiva Oa
Tahuata Motané
4884

6513 Flint I. Î l e s T u a m o t u
(Kiribati)
Îles du Roi-Georges Manihi Îles du
Tikahau Ahé Takaroa Désappointement
Îles Sous- Matahiva Rangiroa Apataki Takume Puka Puka
le-Vent Bora Bora Îles du Kauehi Raroia Fangatau
Maupiti Huahine Vent Fakarava Makemo
Maupihaa Raiatea Tahiti Anaa Îles Raeuki Tatakoto
Moorea Papeete Méhétia Hao Marokau Amanu Puka Ruha
Îles de la Société Ravahere Vahitahi Réao
Héréhérétué Nengonengo Paraoa
Îles du Duc- Ahunui Vairaata
de-Gloucester Turéia Groupe
Îles Maria Vanavana Actéon
Rimatara Rurutu Tematagi Mururoa Fangataufa
Tropic of Capricorn Îles Gambier
Tubuaï Morané
Îles Tubuaï (Îles Australes) Raivavae Récif Récif
Président- Portland
Thiers
Rapa Récif
Neilson Îlots de Bass
PACIFIC
OCEAN

NIUE
1:830 000
5   0   10 km
3   0   5 miles

Hikutavake Mutalau
Namukulu Toi
Tuapa
Makefu Lakepa
Alofi Alofi Liku
Bay
Halangingie Fonuakula
Pt. Tamakautoga
Avatele Vaiea Hakupu
Tepa Pt.
PACIFIC OCEAN
170°W

RAROTONGA
1:415 000
5 km
5 miles

Rarotonga Avarua Harbour
(N.Z.) Avarua Pue
Nikao Avatiu Matavera
Arorangi 509 Avana Te Manga Ngatangiia
Maungaroa 588 653 Motu Tapu
222 Te Kou Avana Oneroa
Maungatangaiti 329 Muri Koromiri
Tarotume Taakoka
Titikaveka
PACIFIC OCEAN
159°45'W

Arctic Circle
ALASKA
(U.S.A.) **C A N A D A**
Anchorage 5959
Bristol Bay Juneau
Gulf of Alaska Edmonton
Prince of Wales I. Prince Rupert
Queen Charlotte Is. Calgary
(Canada)
Vancouver Victoria
Vancouver I. Seattle
Tufts **R**
Abyssal **O**
Plain Portland Boise **C**
Snake **K** **Y**
N o r t h e a s t **M**
Mendocino Fracture Zone C. Mendocino Salt Lake **t**
Sacramento City Denver **s**
San Francisco 4418
6741 **UNITED STATES**
Murray Fracture Zone Oklahoma City Memphis Atlanta
P a c i f i c Los Angeles Phoenix Dallas
San Diego **M** Houston Jacksonville
Guadalupe San Antonio New
(Mex.) Ciudad **E** Orleans
Molokai Fracture Zone Juárez **X** Mississippi
Baja California Gulf of Mexico Miami BAHAMAS
Tropic of Cancer **I** Monterrey 3504 Florida
B a s i n C. San Lucas Sigsbee La Habana CUBA Str.
Honolulu Gullo de California Deep Canal de Yucatan
O'ahu **HAWAI'I** Mexico Mérida 7680 JAMAICA HAITI
4205 (U.S.A.) Guadalajara Puebla BELIZE Kingston
Hawai'i Acapulco **O** GUATEMALA HONDURAS Caribbean
Clarion Fracture Zone Is. de Guatemala Sea
Revillagigedo Middle America Trench San Salvador NICARAGUA
(Mex.) EL SALVADOR Managua Barranquilla
Johnston I. Guatemala San José Cartagena **F**
(U.S.A.) Basin COSTA Colón Panamá
C I F I C Î. Clipperton RICA PANAMA
Palmyra Is. (Fr.) I. del Coco Panama
(U.S.A.) Clipperton Fracture Zone (Costa Rica) Basin Medellín
Teraina I. de Malpelo Cali
Tabuaeran (Colombia) **COLOMBIA**
Jarvis I. Kiritimati **G**
(U.S.A.) Galapagos Fracture Zone Quito
Equator **ECUADOR**
Malden I. Galápagos Guayaquil
E A N Starbuck I. (Ecuador) Carnegie Ridge C. Pariñas
Phoenix Is. Caroline I. Nuku
K I B A T I (Millennium I.) Hiva Trujillo
Manihiki Vostok I. Hiva Oa Marquesas Fracture Zone
Pukapuka Flint I. Îs. Marquises 6369 **PERU**
Manihiki Yupanqui Lima
Plateau Basin Cusco
Suwarrow Is. Îs. de la Mendaña L. Titicaca
Société Fracture Zone Arequipa 6550
Bora Bora Huahine 6866 La Paz
Cook Is. Raiatea Tahiti Peru- **BOLIVIA**
(N.Z.) Papeete Arica
Aitutaki Îs. Tuamotu Iquique Chile
Atiu Rangiroa P e r u B a s i n Basin PARAGUAY
Rarotonga **FRENCH POLYNESIA** Antofagasta 8064
Mangaia Îs. Gambier Trench San Miguel Asunción
Mururoa San Félix de Tucumán
Îs. Tubuaï (Chile) San Félix Córdoba
Oeno I. San Ambrosio Porto
Henderson I. Ducie I. (Chile) Alegre
Pitcairn I. Easter Fracture Zone Roggeveen Arch. de URUGUAY
(U.K.) Sala-y-Gómez Basin Juan Fernández Valparaíso Rosario Buenos
Rapa Sala y Gómez Ridge (Chile) Santiago Aires Montevideo
Easter Fracture Zone Aconcagua Río de la Plata
I. de Pascua 6962
(Chile) Concepción **ARGENTINA** Argentine
S o u t h w e s t Chile Rise Basin
P a c i f i c Menard Fracture Zone **A T L A N T I C**
B a s i n Nemo Point **O C E A N**
(furthest point 114 Falkland
from any land) Plateau 6212
Pacific-Antarctic Ridge Punta Arenas Falkland Is. Georgia Basin
S o u t h e a s t Est. de Magallanes (U.K.) South Georgia
P a c i f i c B a s i n C. de Hornos Tierra del Fuego South Georgia Ridge (U.K.)
Drake Passage 4402
West from Greenwich

ft m
10 12 000 4000
9000 3000
6000 2000
3000 1000
0 0
200 600
600
1000 3000
2000 6000
4000 12 000
6000 18 000
8000 24 000
m ft

NORTH
AMERICA

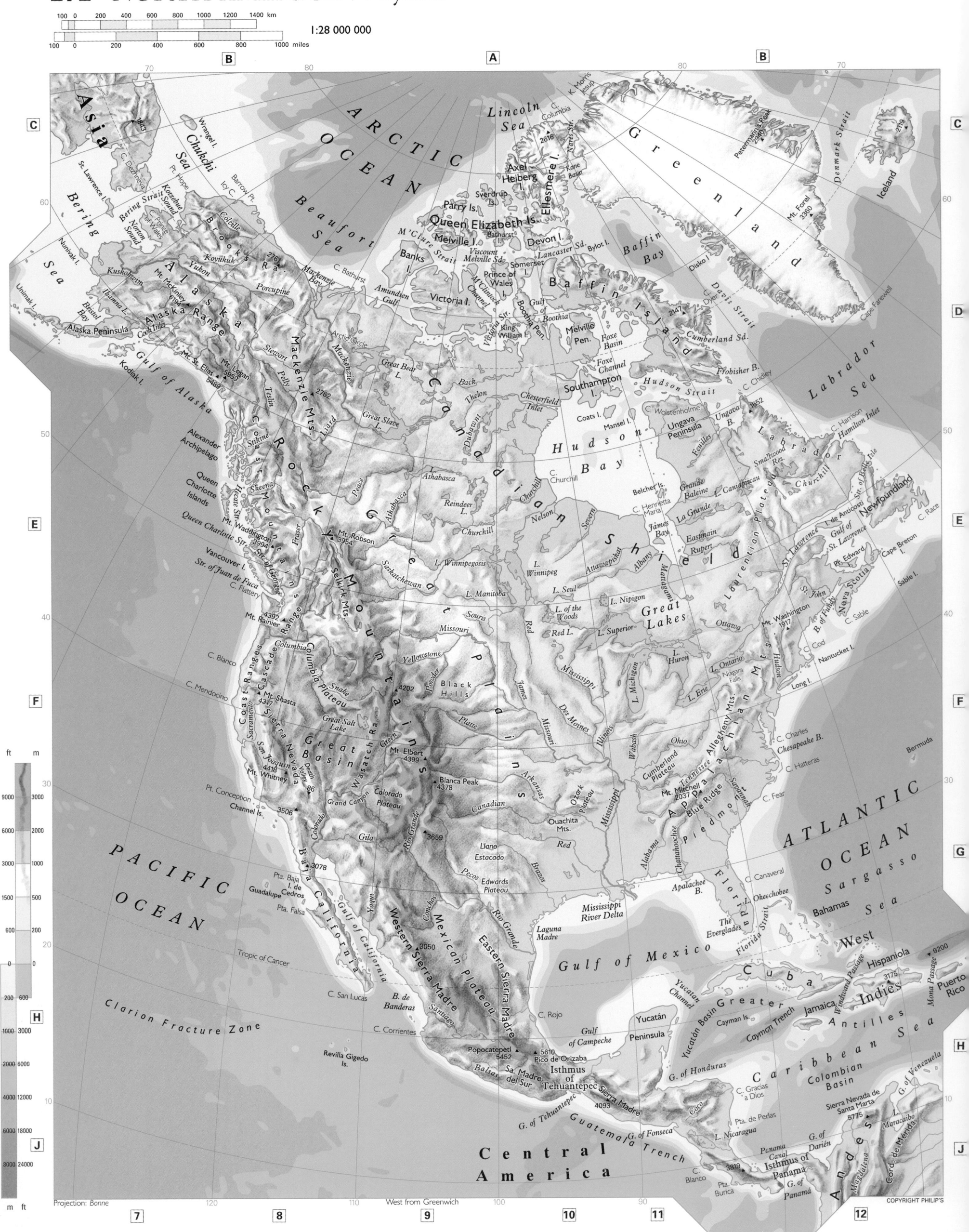

1:28 000 000

Projection: *Borne*

COPYRIGHT PHILIP'S

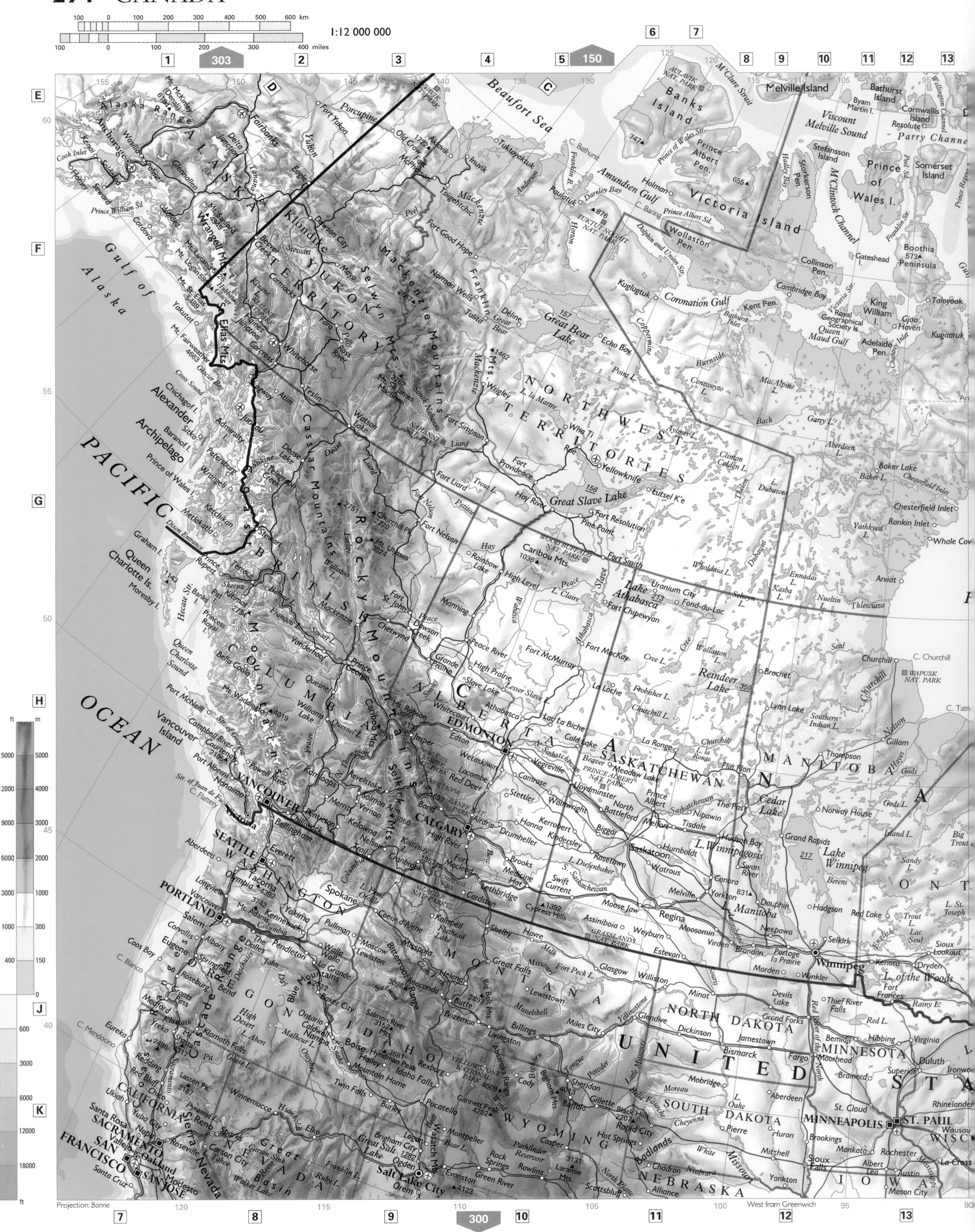

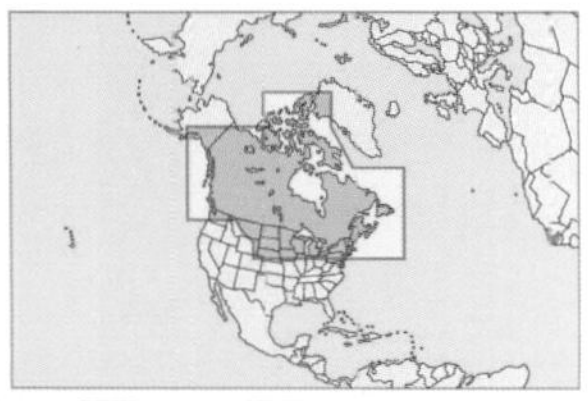

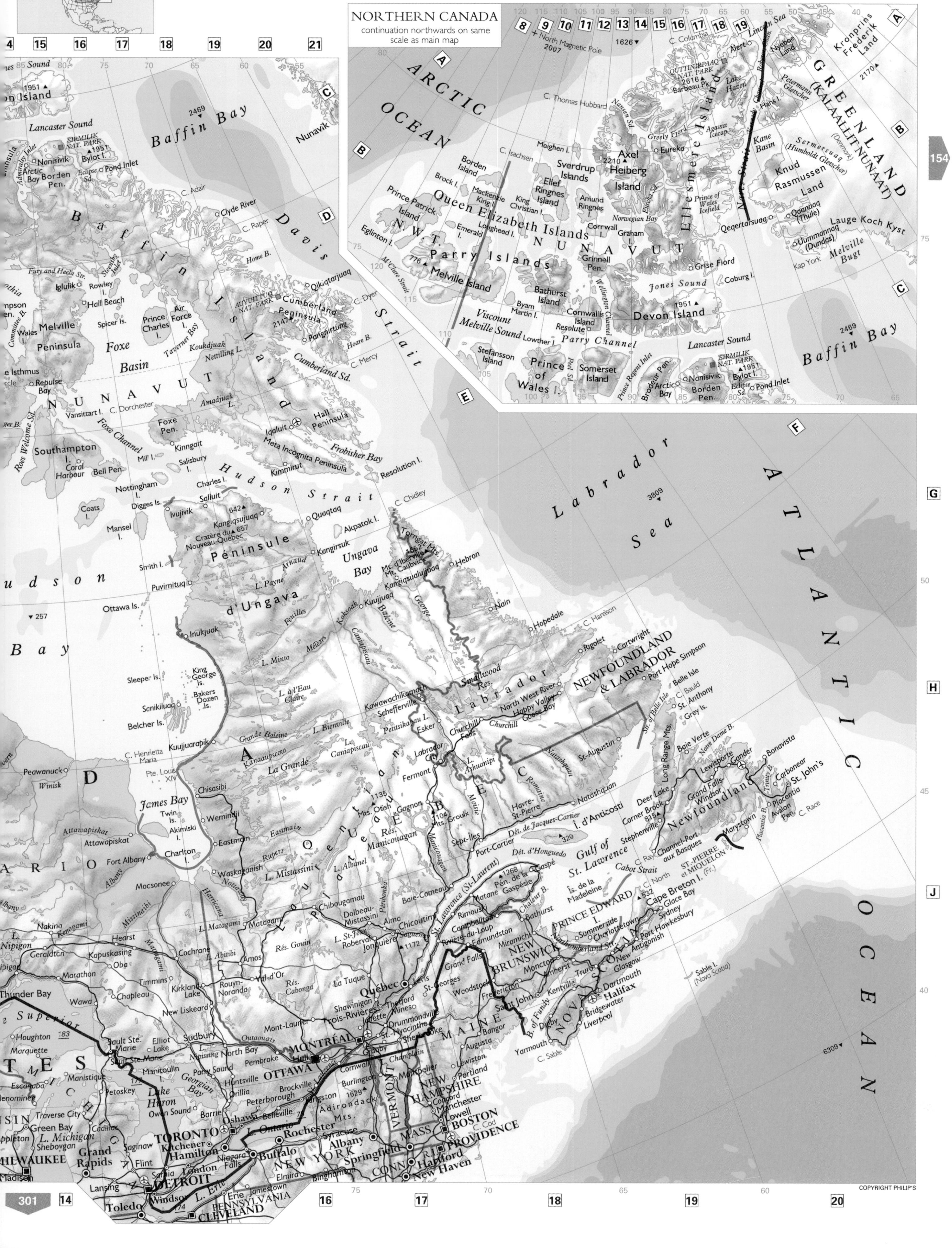

150

NORTHERN CANADA
continuation northwards on same scale as main map

ARCTIC OCEAN

North Magnetic Pole 2007

GREENLAND (KALAALLIT NUNAAT) (Denmark)

Kronprins Frederik Land

Ellesmere Island

Queen Elizabeth Islands

Sverdrup Islands

Axel Heiberg Island

Parry Islands

NUNAVUT

N.W.T.

Melville Island

Prince Patrick Island

Devon Island

Jones Sound

Parry Channel

Viscount Melville Sound

Prince of Wales I.

Somerset Island

Lancaster Sound

Baffin Bay

154

Baffin Bay

Lancaster Sound

SIRMILIK NAT. PARK

Nanisivik Arctic Bay Borden Pen. Bylot I. Pond Inlet

Baffin Island

Davis Strait

Cumberland Peninsula

AUYUITTUQ NAT. PARK

Pangnirtung

NUNAVUT

Foxe Basin

Melville Peninsula

Southampton I.

Foxe Channel

Hudson Strait

Frobisher Bay

Iqaluit

Meta Incognita Peninsula

Resolution I.

C. Chidley

Hudson Bay

Péninsule d'Ungava

Ungava Bay

Belcher Is.

James Bay

Labrador

LABRADOR Sea

ATLANTIC OCEAN

NEWFOUNDLAND & LABRADOR

Happy Valley-Goose Bay

Churchill Falls

Labrador City

Schefferville

Newfoundland

St. John's

Gulf of St. Lawrence

Cabot Strait

ST-PIERRE & MIQUELON (Fr.)

PRINCE EDWARD ISLAND

Charlottetown

NEW BRUNSWICK

NOVA SCOTIA

Halifax

Sydney

Cape Breton I.

QUÉBEC

Québec

MONTRÉAL

OTTAWA

TORONTO

Hamilton

L. Ontario

L. Erie

DETROIT

Lake Huron

L. Michigan

Thunder Bay

L. Superior

MAINE

VERMONT

NEW HAMPSHIRE

MASS.

BOSTON

PROVIDENCE

CONN.

NEW YORK

Hartford

New Haven

CLEVELAND

MILWAUKEE

COPYRIGHT PHILIP'S

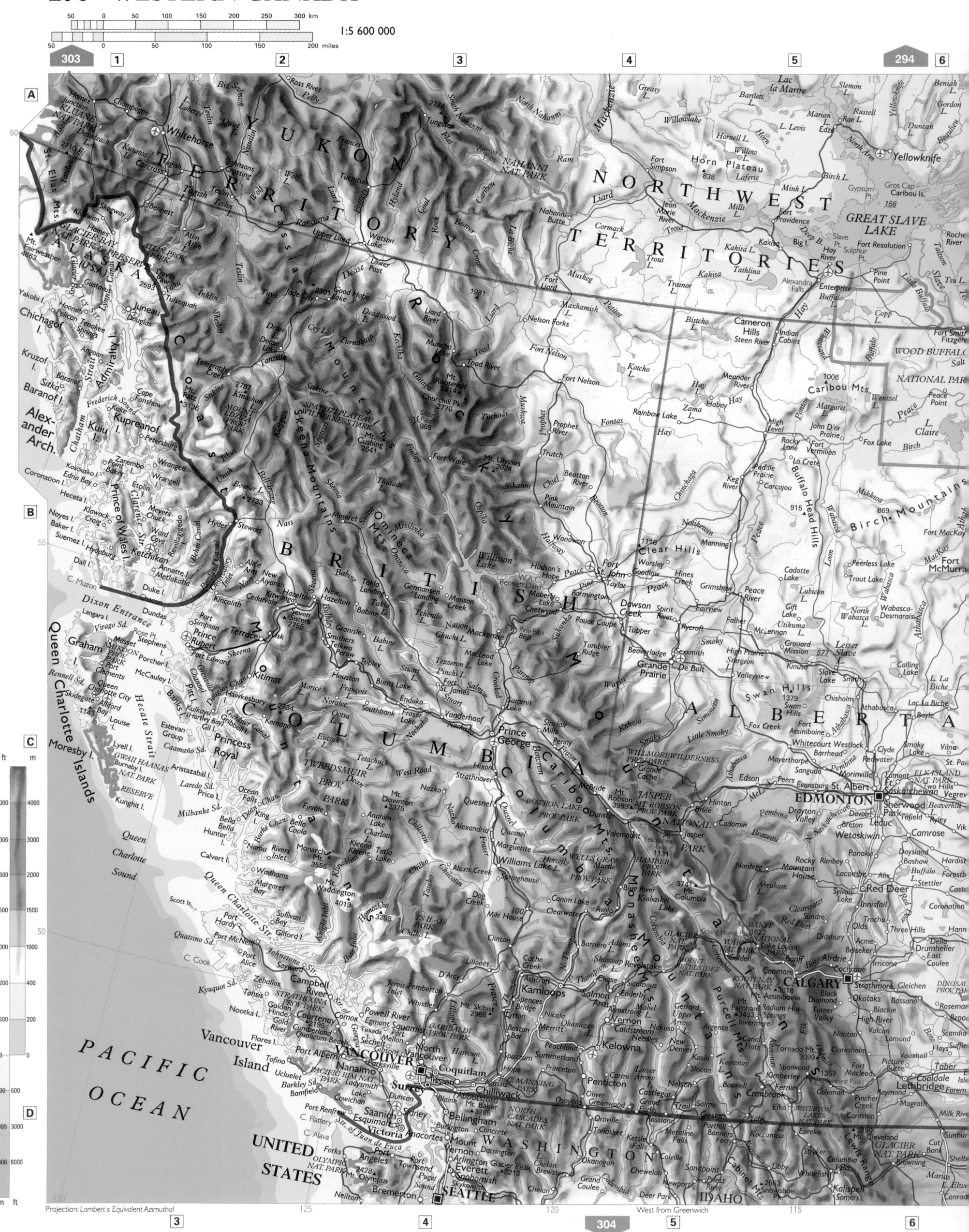

7
8
9
10
11
A
B
C
D
298
308
HUDSON
BAY
MANITOBA
SASKATCHEWAN
NORTH DAKOTA
MINNESOTA
MONTANA
LAKE WINNIPEG
Lake Athabasca
Reindeer Lake
Wollaston L.
Cedar Lake
Lake Winnipegosis
Lake Manitoba
Lake of the Woods
L. Sakakawea
Southern Indian L.
Walmsley L.
Artillery L.
Campbell L.
Tyrrell L.
Garde L.
Thelon
Mosquito L.
Nicholson L.
Dubawnt L.
Tulemalu L.
Yathkyed L.
Whale Cove (Tikirarjuaq)
Pistol B.
Kaminak L.
Bibby I.
Dawson Inlet
McLeod Bay
Reliance
Whitefish L.
Kamilukuak L.
Angikuni L.
Kazan
Lutsel K'e (Snowdrift)
Gagnon L.
Lynx L.
Carey L.
North Henik L.
South Henik L.
Maguse L.
Austin I.
Maguse Pt.
Arviat (Eskimo Point)
Nonacho L.
Taltson L.
Damant L.
Barlow L.
Porter L.
Rennie L.
Firedrake L.
Hicks L.
Tatinnai L.
Thaolintoa L.
Tha-anne
Thlewiaza
Hjalmar L.
Manchester L.
Doran L.
Smalltree L.
Snowbird L.
Ennadai L.
Edehon L.
Thekulthili L.
Thoa
Anaunethad L.
Wholdaia L.
Kasba L.
Nueltin L.
266
Hill Island L.
Dunvegan L.
Selwyn L.
Baralzon L.
CARIBOU RIVER PARK RESERVE
Caribou
Hubbart Pt.
Tazin L.
Scott L.
Putahow L.
Kasmere L.
Nejanilini L.
Charles L.
Camsell Portage
Uranium City
Fond-du-Lac
Dodge L.
Stony Rapids
Black L.
Porcupine
Phelps L.
Munroe L.
Stony L.
Seal
Button B.
C. Churchill
Churchill
Bylot
213
Black Lake
Fond-du-Lac
Riou L.
Misty L.
North Seal
Shethanei L.
North Knife
ATHABASCA SAND DUNES PROV. PARK
Davy L.
Hatchet L.
Lac Brochet
Whiskey Jack L.
Tadoule L.
South Knife
WAPUSK NATIONAL PARK
Fort Chipewyan
William
Pine
Pasfield L.
Cochrane
SAND LAKES PROV. PARK
South Seal
Etawney L.
NUMAYKOOS LAKE PROV. PARK
Owl
Deer
Herchmer
C. Tatnam
524
Rabbit Lake Mine
396
Wollaston Lake
Lac Brochet
Big Sand L.
Northern Indian L.
Waterbury L.
McFarlane
Cree
Richardson
Engemann L.
350
254
Little Churchill
Weir River
Weir
Nelson
Sundance
Machichi
Kaskattama
Kettle
Black Duck
Nishibi
Clearwater
Lloyd L.
Cree L.
478
Key Lake Mine
Geikie
Wathaman L.
Nokomis L.
Kinoosao
Goldsand L.
Barrington L.
Gauer L.
South Indian Lake
Waskaiowaka L.
Limestone
Stephens L.
Gillam
Bird
Hayes
Gods
Shamattawa
Beaver
Firebag
Careen L.
Black Birch L.
Upper Foster L.
Wathaman
Oliver L.
Lynn Lake
Leaf Rapids
AMISK PROV. PARK
Rat
Baldock L.
Split Lake
Split L.
Ilford
Fox
Beaverstone
CLEARWATER RIVER PROV. PARK
Clearwater
Wasekamio L.
Deception L.
Laurie L.
Granville L.
Rat L.
Odei
Gordon L.
Turnor L.
La Loche
Frobisher L.
Mudjatik
Daly L.
Macoun L.
Herriot
Southend
Kamuchawie L.
Thompson
Pikwitonei
Arnot
Stupart
Echoing
Sachigo
Garson L.
Porter L.
Haultain
Foster
Brabant L.
Reinder
Loon
Russell L.
Highrock L.
Nelson L.
Nelson House
Burntwood
Knee L.
Atik L.
Gods River
Severn
Christina
Peter Pond L.
Dillon
Churchill
Patuanak
Sandfly L.
McIntosh L.
Pukatawagan
Paint L.
Thicket Portage
Bear L.
Oxford L.
Edmund L.
Stull L.
Swan L.
Big Trout Lake
Conklin
Buffalo Narrows
Knee L.
Pine-house L.
Besnard L.
Stanley Mission
Sandy Bay
Sisipuk L.
Kipahigan L.
Setting L.
Sipiwesk L.
Cross L.
Walker L.
Gods L.
Sharpe L.
Bearskin Lake
Winefred L.
McCusker
Île-à-la-Crosse
Lac Île-à-la-Crosse
Canoe L.
Beauval
Nemeiben L.
LAC LA RONGE PROV. PARK
Lac la Ronge
Wood L.
Manawan L.
Pelican Narrows
Mirond L.
Sherridon
Snow Lake
Wabowden
Beaver Hill L.
Red Sucker L.
Ponask L.
Sachigo L.
Big Trout L.
Arsenault L.
Lac la Plonge
La Ronge
365
Kississing L.
Reed L.
Wekusko L.
Cross Lake
Primrose L.
Doré L.
Egg
Wapawekka L.
Creighton
Jan L.
Flin Flon
Minago
Molson L.
Stevenson L.
OPASQUIA PROV. PARK
Island L.
Keeley L.
Smoothstone L.
680
Deschambault L.
Amisk L.
Cranberry Portage
Namew L.
Wanless
Cormorant L.
GRASS RIVER PROV. PARK
Cormorant
N. Moose L.
Playgreen L.
Norway House
Bigstone L.
North Caribou L.
Cold Lake
Pierceland
MEADOW LAKE PROV. PARK
Delaronde L.
Cream L.
Montreal L.
NARROW HILLS PROV. PARK
Cumberland L.
CLEARWATER L. PROV. PARK
Clearwater
The Pas
Gunisao
Gunisao L.
Sandy Lake
Finger L.
Sandy L.
Meadow Lake
Green Lake
Waskesiu Lake
Montreal Lake
Candle L.
Tobin L.
Saskatchewan
Carrot
Moose Lake
S. Moose L.
Mukutawa
Horse I.
Pipestone
Elk Point
Loon Lake
Cowan L.
PRINCE ALBERT NAT. PARK
Big River
Westray
Grand Rapids
Deer L.
Deer Lake
MacDowell L.
St. Walburg
Turtle L.
Paradise Hill
Leoville
Debden
Smeaton
Nipawin
Carrot River
Easterville
Poplar
McInnes L.
Cat Lake
Cat L.
Lloydminster
Turtleford
Glaslyn
Spiritwood
Meath Park
Shellbrook
Prince Albert
Carruthers L.
Arborfield
Red Deer L.
Dawson B.
Hudson Bay
Berens River
Fishing L.
Berens
Stout L.
Pikangikum
Lashburn
Maidstone
Edam
North Battleford
Leask
Blaine Lake
Duck Lake
Kinistino
Birch Hills
Melfort
Tisdale
Star City
Mafeking
Swan L.
Birch River
217
253
Reindeer I.
Berens I.
Little Grand Rapids
Family L.
ATIKAKI PROV. WILDERNESS PARK
Cairns L.
Birch L.
Trout L.
Bamaji L.
St. Joseph L.
Wainwright
Battle
Manitou L.
Battleford
Denholm
Rosthern
Wakaw
Naicam
Lenore L.
Red Deer
GREENWATER LAKE PROV. PARK
Woody
Bowsman
Swan
Swan River
Pelican L.
Camperville
Birch
Waterhen L.
Sturgeon B.
Bloodvein
Chauvin
Provost
Macklin
Unity
Wilkie
Radisson
Aberdeen
Prud'homme
Humboldt
Lake Lenore
Rose Valley
Kelvington
Wadena
Sturgis
Pine River
Gypsumville
L. St. Martin
Fisher B.
Black L.
Manigotagan
Gammon
WOODLAND CARIBOU PROV. PARK
Red L.
Red Lake
Balmertown
Ear Falls
Lac Seul
Sioux Lookout
Salvador
Warman
Saskatoon
Asquith
Watson
Big Quill L.
Preeceville
Norquay
DUCK MT. PROV. PARK
Kamsack
Winnipegosis
Ethelbert
831
Sifton
Fairford
Steep Rock
Hodgson
Riverton
Hecla I.
Victoria Beach
Manigotagan
Sydney L.
Hudson
English
Luseland
Kerrobert
Biggar
Colonsay
Delisle
Allan
Lanigan
Wynyard
Foam Lake
Buchanan
Canora
Theodore
L. of the Prairies
Roblin
Dauphin L.
Ste. Rose du Lac
Ashern
Dog L.
Arborg
Eriksdale
Gimli
Pine Falls
NOPIMING PROV. PARK
Dodsland
Rosetown
Young
Watrous
Nokomis
Conquest
Outlook
Lestock
Yorkton
Grandview
Dauphin
RIDING MOUNTAIN NAT. PARK
Kindersley
Alsask
Milden
Imperial
Raymore
Last Mountain L.
Strasbourg
Ituna
McCreary
248
Manitoba
Winnipeg Beach
Minaki
Minnitaki L.
Oyen
Eatonia
Eston
Elrose
Davidson
Craik
Cupar
Melville
Langenburg
Russell
Rossburn
Amaranth
St. Laurent
Teulon
Pinawa
Whiteshell
Winnipeg
Wabigoon L.
Dinorwic
Dryden
Red Lake Road
Vermilion Bay
Keewatin
Kenora
S. Saskatchewan
Elbow
Riverhurst
Beechy
Central Butte
Regina Beach
Lumsden
Fort Qu'Appelle
Balcarres
Esterhazy
Binscarth
Shoal Lake
Wasagaming
Neepawa
Gladstone
Stonewall
Selkirk
Beausejour
WHITESHELL PROV. PARK
Falcon Lake
Eagle L.
Ignace
White Otter L.
Red Deer
Leader
Empress
Kyle
Diefenbaker L.
Mortlach
Regina
Indian Head
Grenfell
Whitewood
Moosomin
Birtle
Minnedosa
Rivers
Portage la Prairie
Winnipeg
Elma
Sioux Narrows
Lower Manitou L.
Burstall
Cabri
Pennant
Herbert
Chaplin
Moose Jaw
Pense
Rouleau
Sedley
Montmartre
Pipestone
Elkhorn
Carberry
Assiniboine
Niverville
Ste. Anne
Steinbach
Shoal L.
Rainy L.
Atikokan
Schuler
Fox Valley
Swift Current
Hodgeville
Old Wives L.
Moose Jaw
Milestone
Kipling
Maryfield
Virden
Brandon
St. Claude
Treherne
Carman
Morris
Woodridge
323
Lake of the Woods
Fort Frances
QUETICO PROV. PARK
Redcliff
Gull Lake
Irvine
Vanguard
Neville
Avonlea
Mossbank
MOOSE MT. PROV. PARK
Weyburn
Redvers
Reston
Souris
Wawanesa
Pilot Mound
Manitou
Morden
Altona
Emerson
Vassar
Warroad
Rainy River
Emo
Medicine Hat
1466
Cypress Hills
CYPRESS HILLS PROV. PARK
Piapot
Maple Creek
Shaunavon
Gravelbourg
Assiniboia
Pangman
Stoughton
Midale
Carlyle
Hartney
Boissevain
Killarney
Winkler
Pembina
Roseau
International Falls
VOYAGEURS NAT. PARK
Lac la Croix
Eastend
Pontiex
Frenchman
Mankota
Lafleche
Bengough
Radville
Lampman
Oxbow
Carnduff
Melita
Deloraine
Minto
Greenbush
Orion
Pakowki L.
Consul
Val Marie
GRASSLANDS NAT. PARK
Willow Bunch
Port of Coronach
Minton
Estevan
North Portal
Northgate
Bowbells
Mohall
766
Bottineau
Rolla
Langdon
Cando
Karlstad
Thief River Falls
Upper Red L.
Lower Red L.
Big Falls
Little Fork
Northome
Port of Climax
Rockglen
Westby
Plentywood
Scobey
Opheim
Turner
Kenmare
Souris
Rugby
Grafton
Grand Forks
East Grand Forks
Warren
Red Lake Falls
Virginia
Hibbing
Winnibigoshish
Fresno Res.
Chinook
Harlem
Malta
Saco
Havre
Milk
Chester
Big Sandy
Glasgow
Nashua
Poplar
Culbertson
Williston
Ray
Stanley
Minot
Granville
Velva
Towner
Devils Lake
Lakota
Larimore
Northwood
Crookston
Erskine
Bagley
Bemidji
Cass Lake
Deer River
Grand Rapids
Duluth
Cloquet
Superior
Fort Peck
Fort Peck Lake
Wolf Point
Missouri
Fairview
Alexander
Watford City
Garrison
Turtle Lake
Drake
Harvey
Carrington
New Rockford
Mayville
Cooperstown
Hillsboro
Ada
Mahnomen
Leech L.
Walker
Park Rapids
Pine River
Hill City
Floodwood
Mississippi
Red
110
105
100
95
90
60
55
50

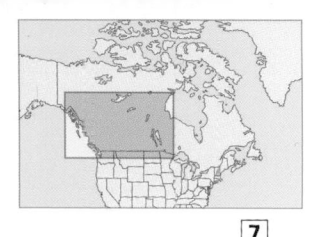

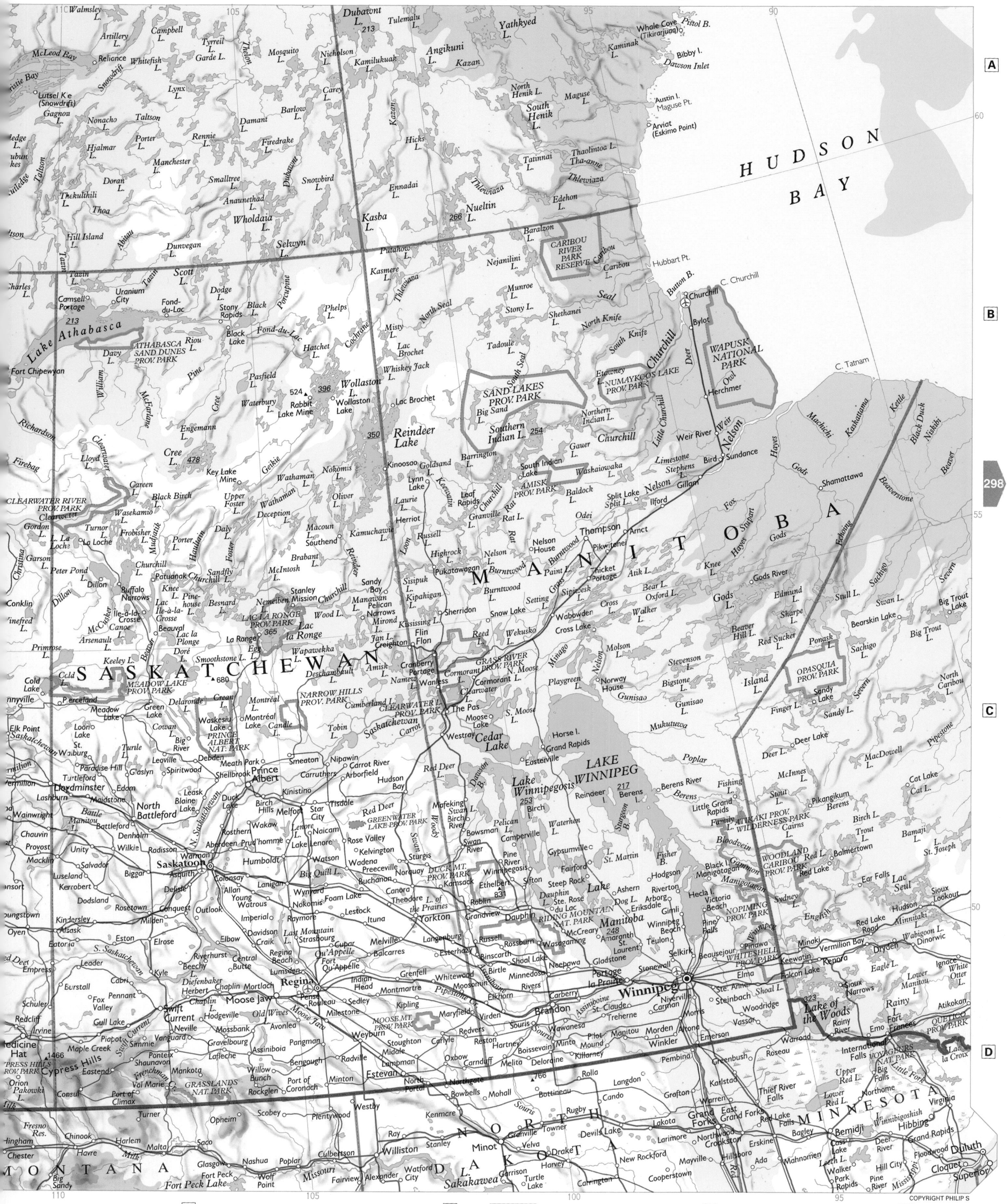

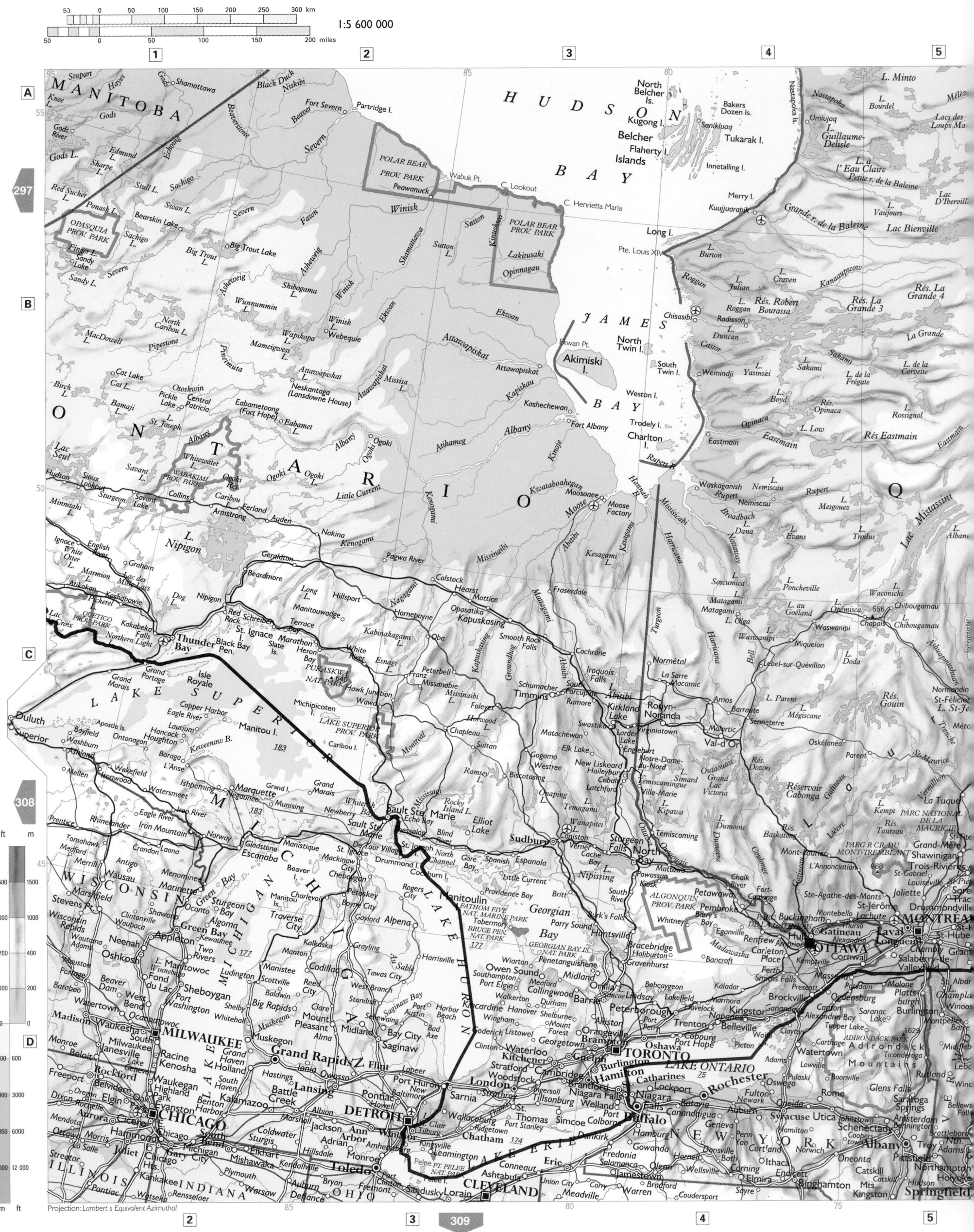

Projection: Lambert's Equivalent Azimuthal

A

B

C

D

LABRADOR SEA

NEWFOUNDLAND &

Labrador

LABRADOR

Newfoundland

QUÉBEC

Smallwood Reservoir

GULF OF ST. LAWRENCE

Île d'Anticosti

Pén. de la Gaspésie

St. Lawrence

NEW BRUNSWICK

PRINCE EDWARD ISLAND

NOVA SCOTIA

ST-PIERRE-ET-MIQUELON (France)

Cabot Strait

St. John's

MAINE

NEW HAMPSHIRE

ATLANTIC

OCEAN

Sable I. (Nova Scotia)

Halifax

UNITED STATES

BOSTON

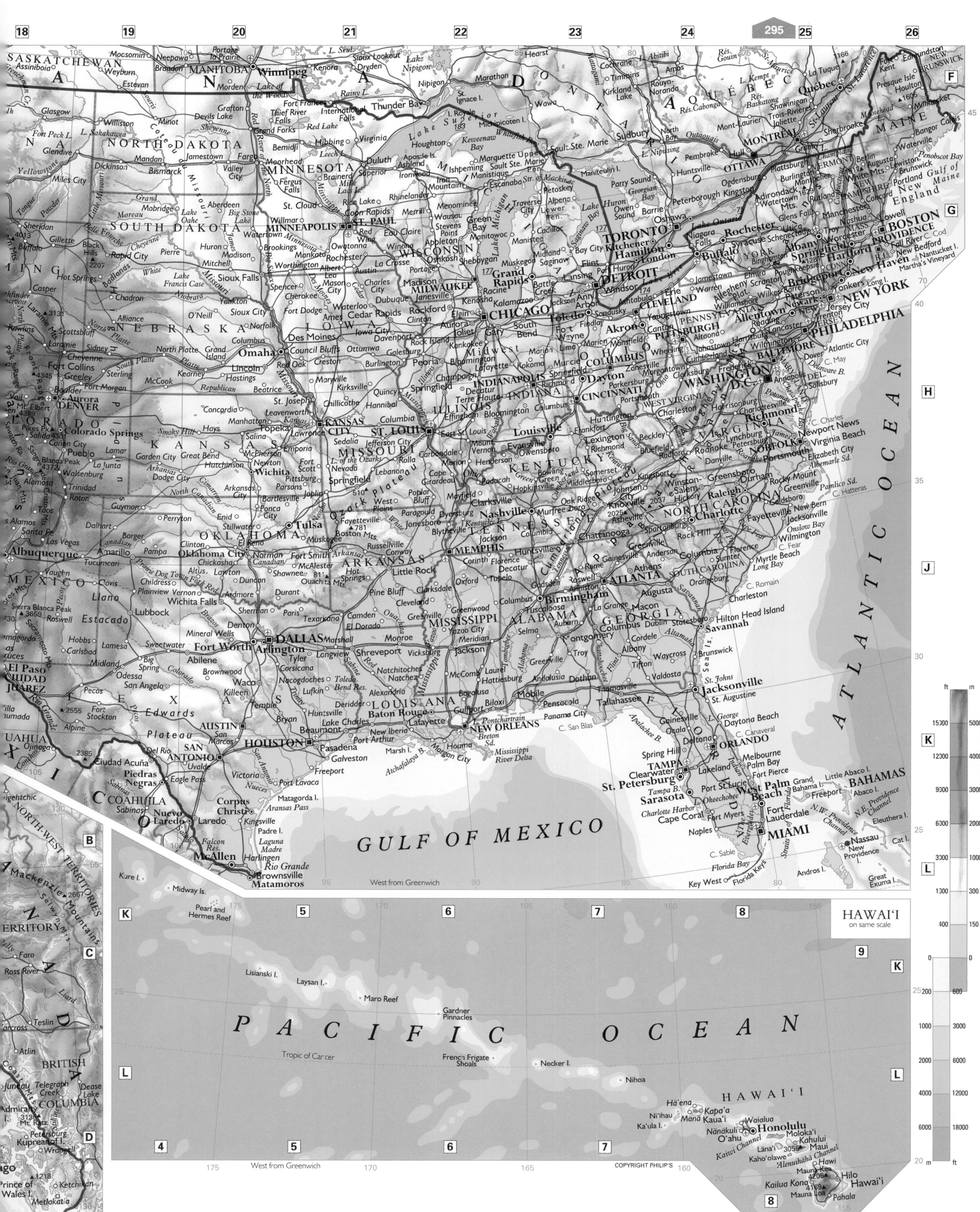

GULF OF MEXICO

PACIFIC OCEAN

ATLANTIC OCEAN

HAWAI'I
on same scale

HAWAI'I

COPYRIGHT PHILIP'S

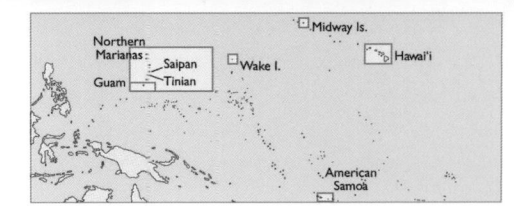

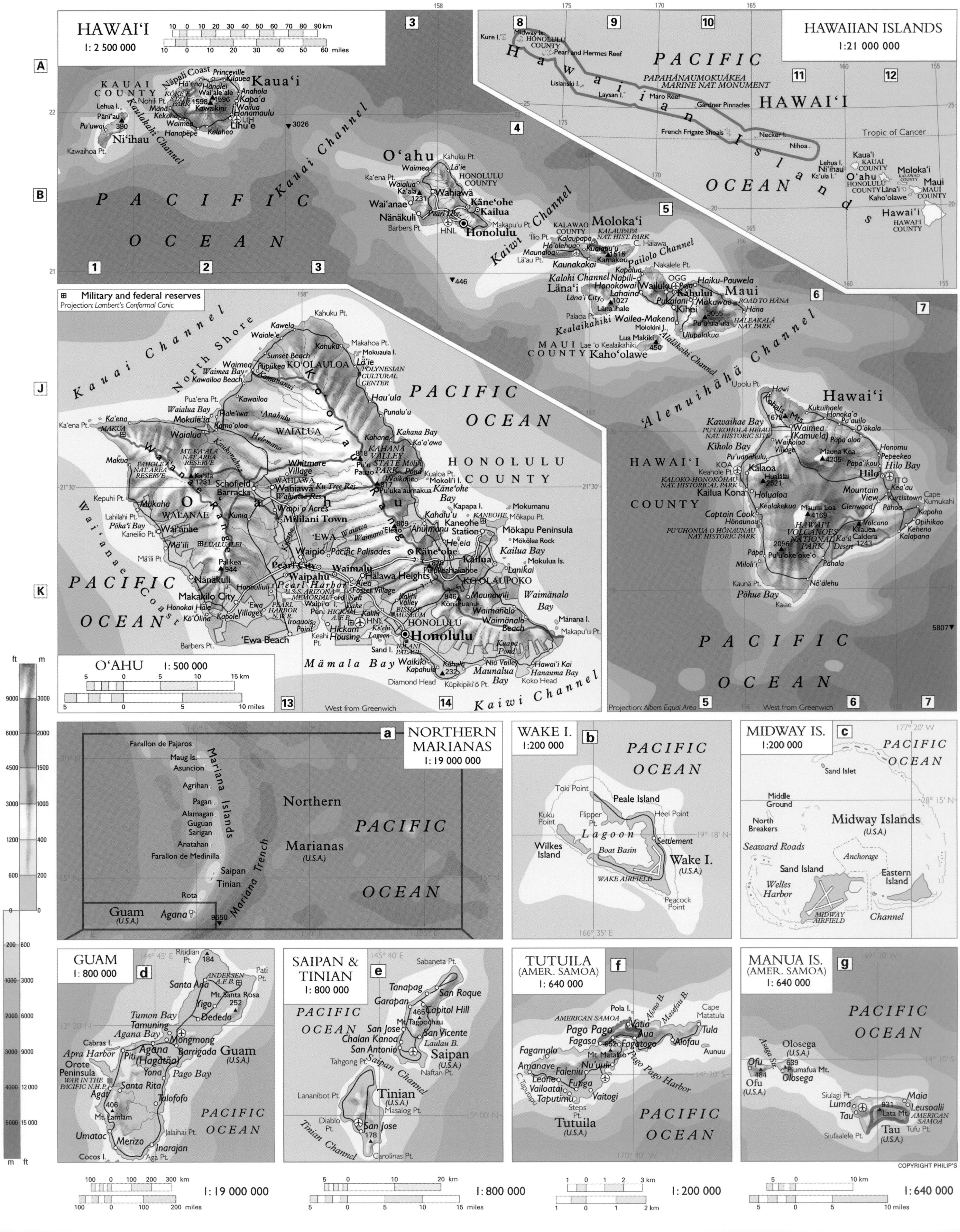

HAWAI'I
1: 2 500 000

HAWAIIAN ISLANDS
1: 21 000 000

Military and federal reserves
Projection: Lambert's Conformal Conic

O'AHU 1: 500 000

Projection: Albers Equal Area

NORTHERN MARIANAS
1: 19 000 000

WAKE I.
1: 200 000

MIDWAY IS.
1: 200 000

GUAM
1: 800 000

SAIPAN & TINIAN
1: 800 000

TUTUILA
(AMER. SAMOA)
1: 640 000

MANUA IS.
(AMER. SAMOA)
1: 640 000

COPYRIGHT PHILIP'S

1: 19 000 000

1: 800 000

1: 200 000

1: 640 000

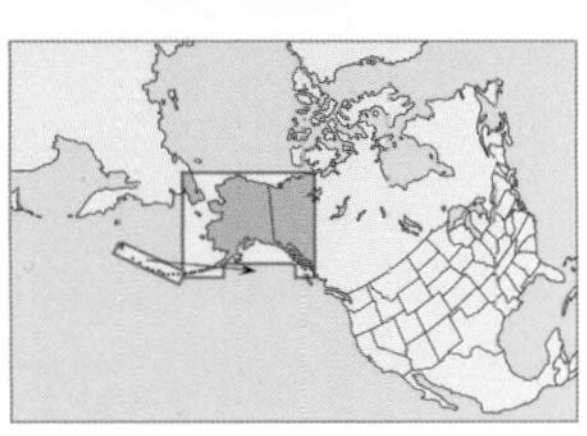

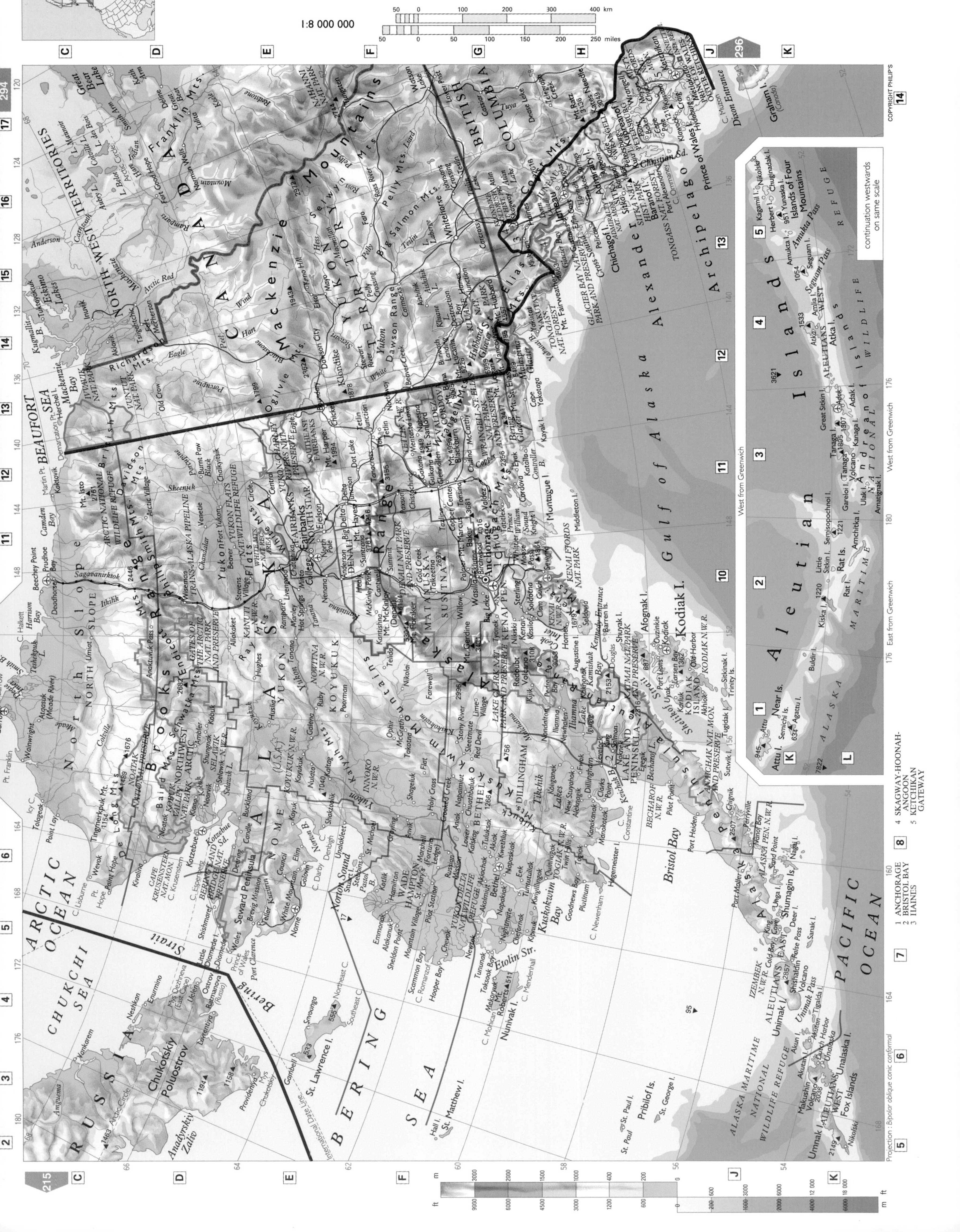

1:8 000 000

50 0 100 200 300 400 km
50 0 50 100 150 200 250 miles

COPYRIGHT PHILIP'S

continuation westwards
on same scale

ARCTIC OCEAN

BEAUFORT SEA

CHUKCHI SEA

BERING SEA

PACIFIC OCEAN

Gulf of Alaska

Aleutian Islands

Alexander Archipelago

RUSSIA

CANADA

NORTH-WEST TERRITORIES

YUKON TERRITORY

BRITISH COLUMBIA

ALASKA (U.S.A.)

Brooks Range

Alaska Range

North Slope

Seward Peninsula

Bristol Bay

Kodiak I.

1 ANCHORAGE
2 BRISTOL BAY
3 HAINES
4 SKAGWAY–HOONAH–
  ANGOON
5 KETCHIKAN
  GATEWAY

Projection: Bipolar oblique conic conformal

m ft

1:5 360 000

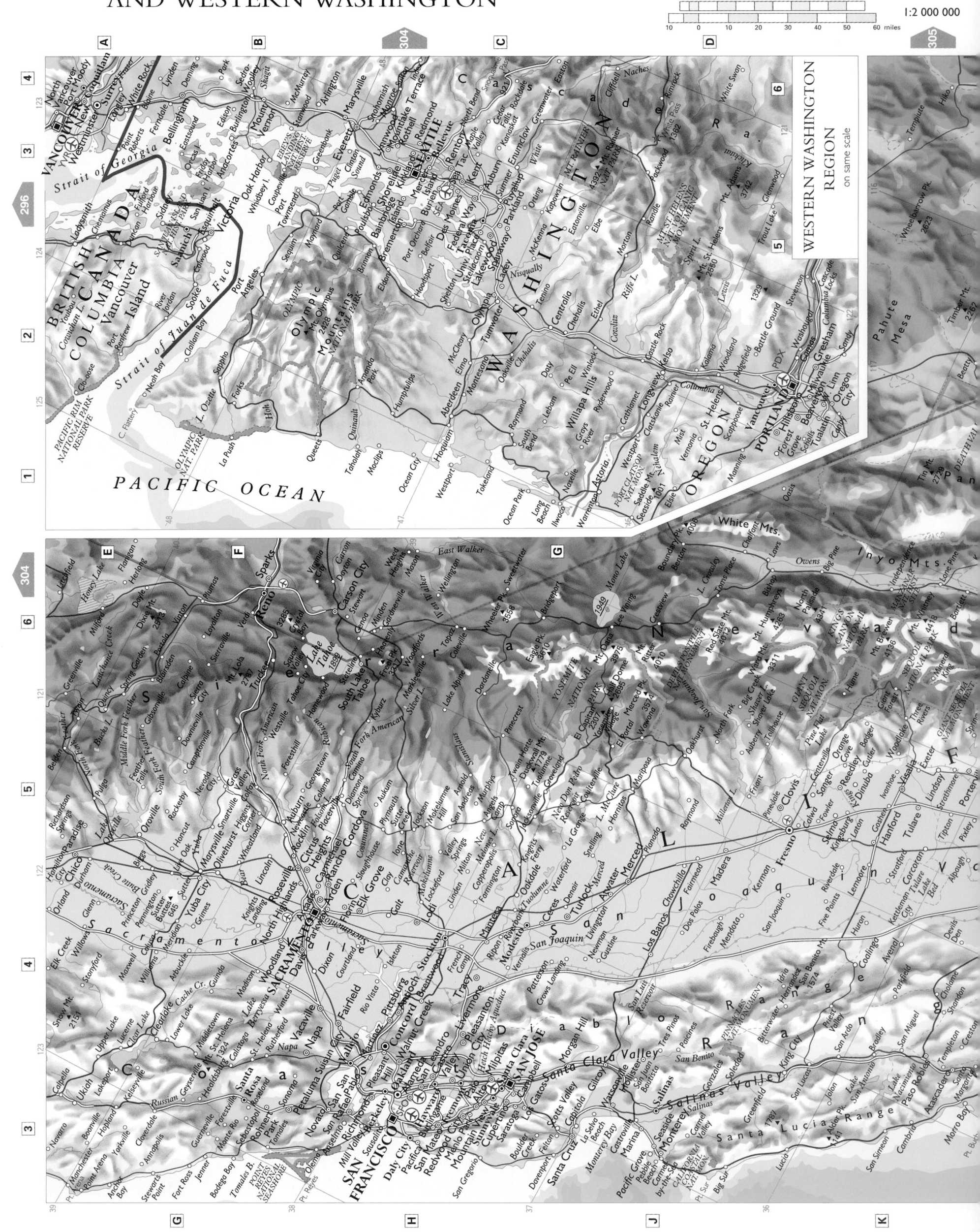

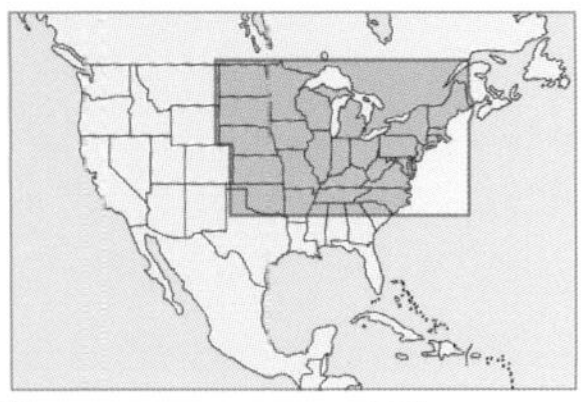

ONTARIO
QUÉBEC
MAINE
NEW HAMPSHIRE
VERMONT
NEW YORK
PENNSYLVANIA
OHIO
WEST VIRGINIA
VIRGINIA
MARYLAND
NEW JERSEY
NORTH CAROLINA
SOUTH CAROLINA
GEORGIA
NEW BRUNSWICK

LAKE HURON
LAKE ERIE
LAKE ONTARIO
LAKE SUPERIOR

Gulf of Maine

ATLANTIC OCEAN

Chesapeake Bay
Delaware Bay

MONTREAL
OTTAWA
Québec
Laval
Longueuil
TORONTO
Hamilton
Buffalo
Rochester
Syracuse
Albany
BOSTON
PROVIDENCE
Hartford
NEW YORK
Newark
PHILADELPHIA
Camden
BALTIMORE
WASHINGTON D.C.
Arlington
Alexandria
PITTSBURGH
CLEVELAND
Akron
COLUMBUS
CINCINNATI
Dayton
DETROIT
Windsor
Toledo
Grand Rapids
Lansing
Flint
Richmond
Norfolk
Virginia Beach
Chesapeake
Portsmouth
Newport News
Hampton
Charlotte
Raleigh
Greensboro
Winston-Salem
Durham
High Point
ATLANTA

COPYRIGHT PHILIP'S

1:2 000 000

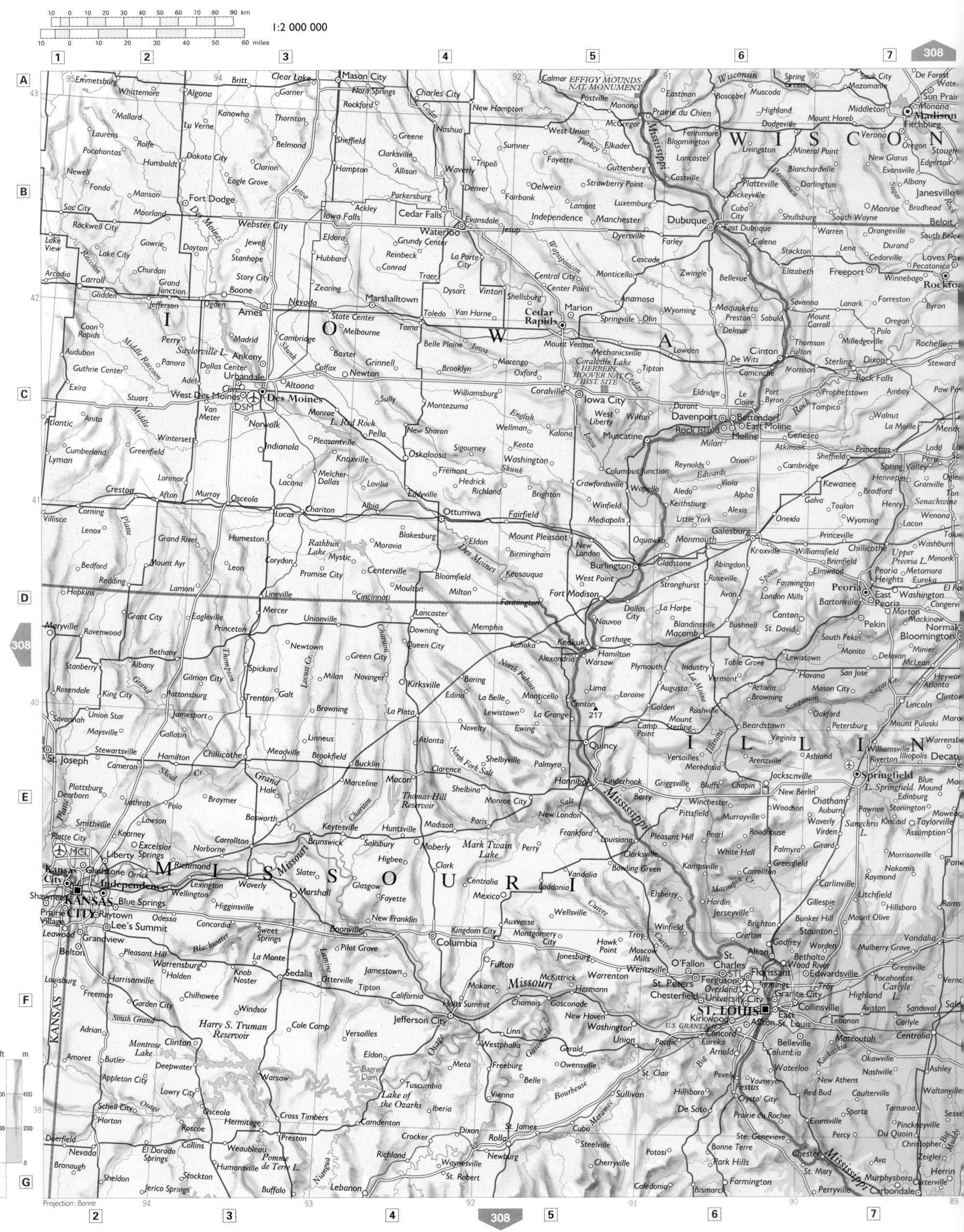

Projection: Bonne

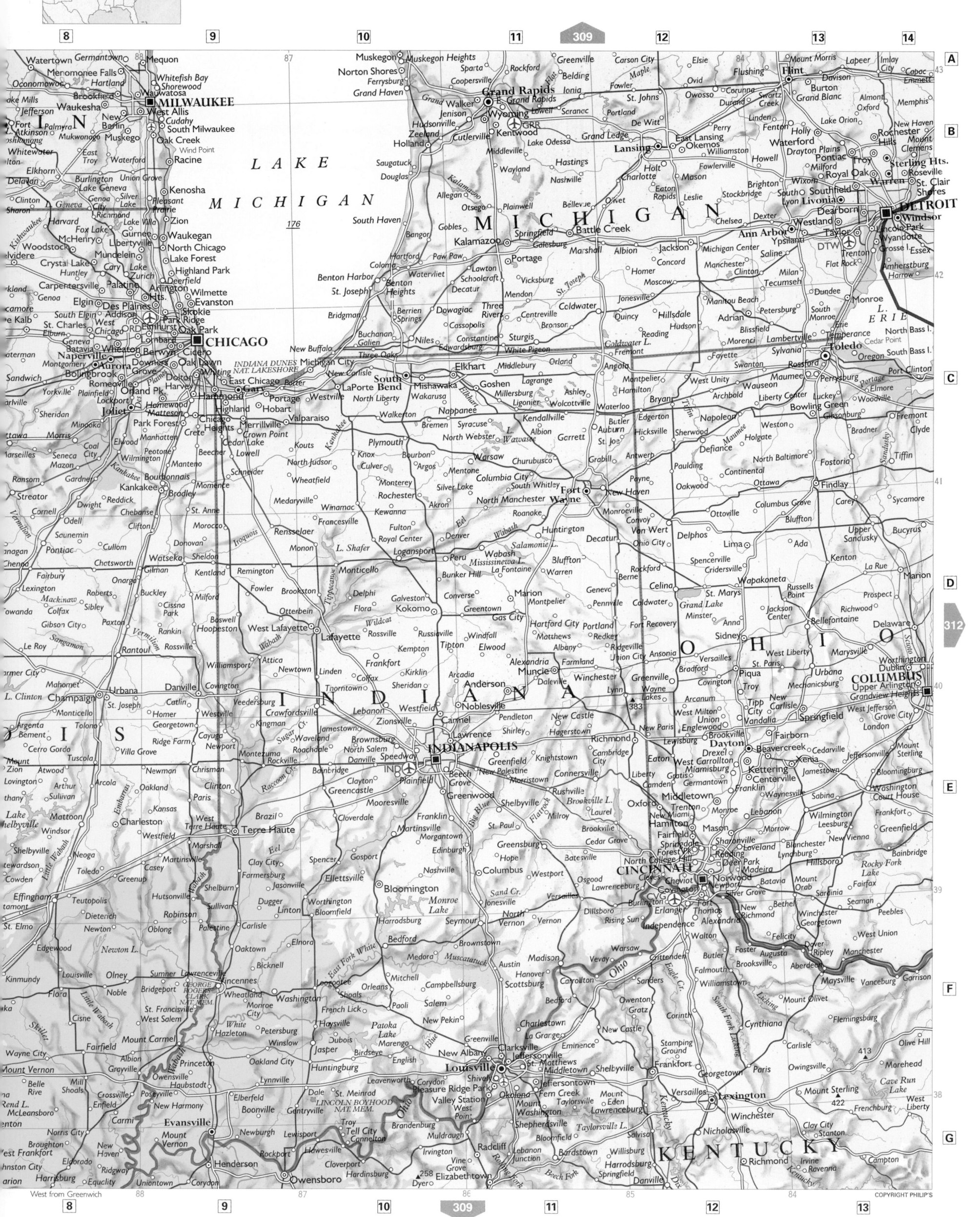

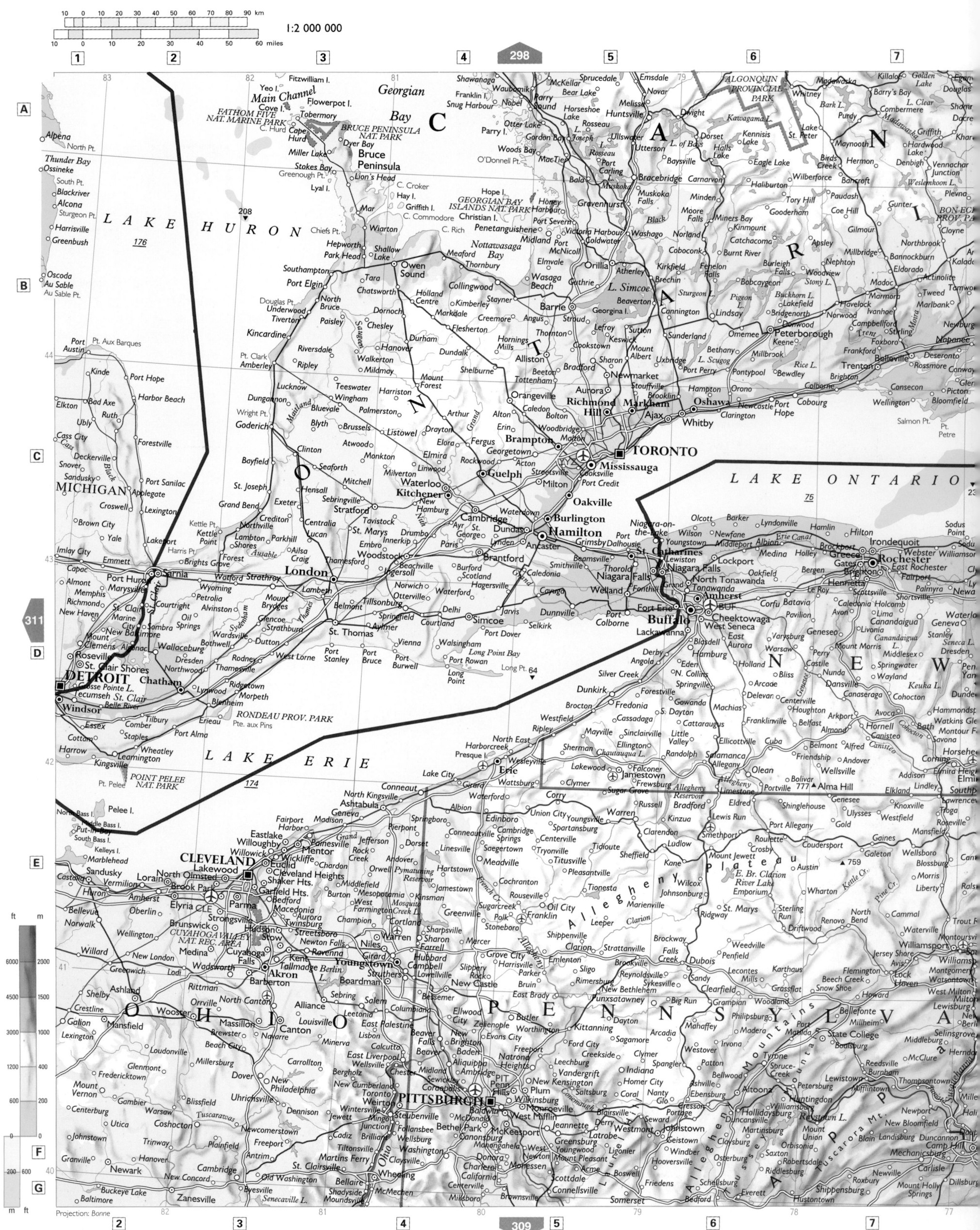

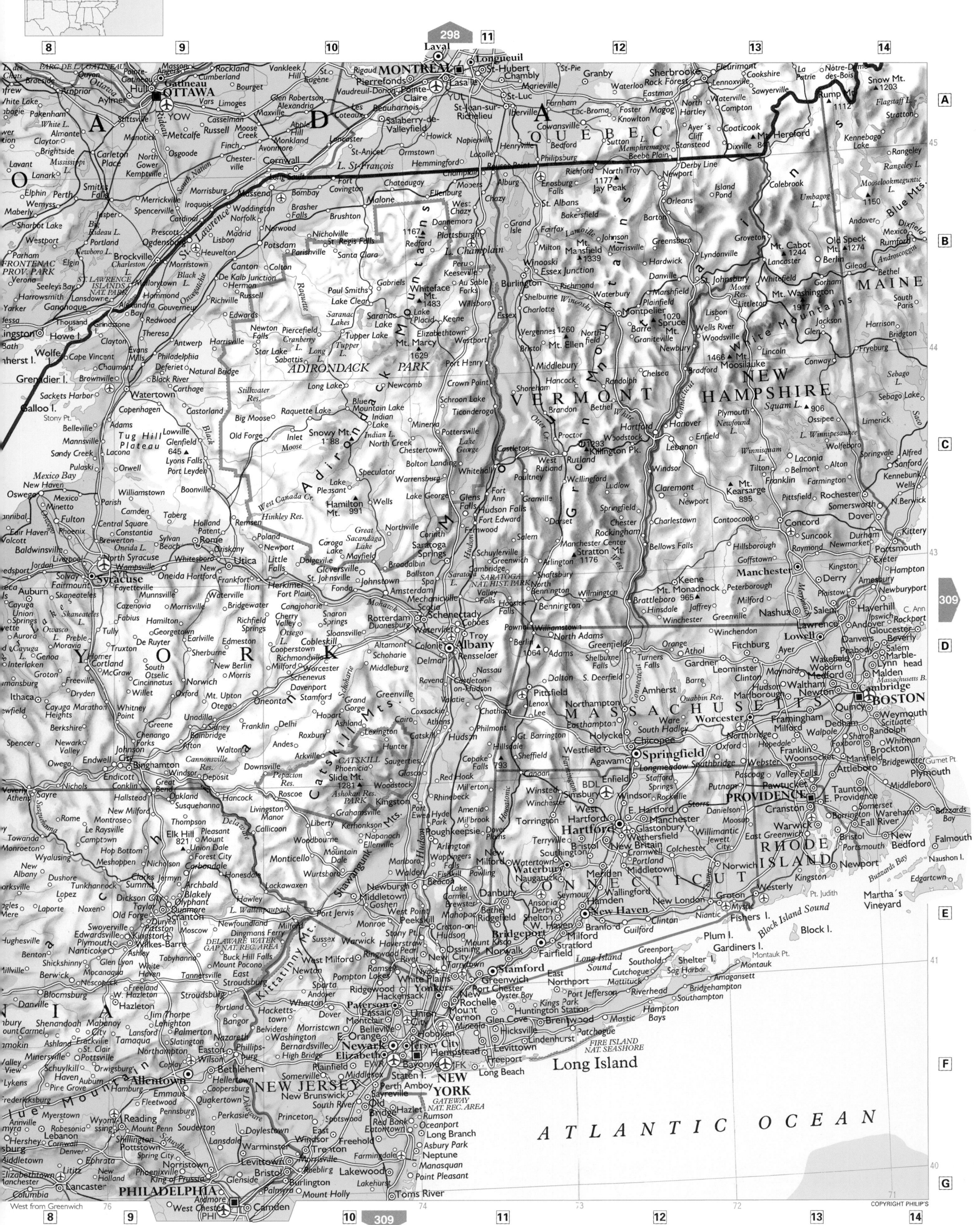

MONTREAL Longueuil

PARC DE LA GATINEAU
Pointe-Gatineau
Gatineau **Ottawa**

C A N A D A

Q U E B E C

A

B

ST. LAWRENCE ISLANDS NAT. PARK

A D I R O N D A C K   P A R K

Mt. Marcy
1629

V E R M O N T

N E W
H A M P S H I R E

M A I N E

C

Tug Hill Plateau

Syracuse

Utica

Albany

M A S S A C H U S E T T S

BOSTON

Massachusetts B.

D

N E W   Y O R K

Catskill Mts.

CATSKILL PARK
Slide Mt.
1281

Springfield

Hartford

PROVIDENCE

RHODE
ISLAND

309

Long Island Sound

Block Island Sound
Block I.

Martha's
Vineyard

E

DELAWARE WATER
GAP NAT. REC. AREA

C O N N E C T I C U T

New Haven

Bridgeport

Stamford

Yonkers

Long Island

FIRE ISLAND
NAT. SEASHORE

F

P E N N S Y L V A N I A

Allentown

Bethlehem

N E W   J E R S E Y

Newark
Jersey City

**NEW
YORK**

GATEWAY
NAT. REC. AREA

A T L A N T I C   O C E A N

G

PHILADELPHIA

Trenton

ILLINOIS
INDIANA
OHIO
PENNSYLVANIA
PITTSBURGH
PHILADELPHIA
INDIANAPOLIS
COLUMBUS
CINCINNATI
WEST VIRGINIA
MARYLAND
DELAWARE
BALTIMORE
WASHINGTON D.C.
ST. LOUIS
LOUISVILLE
VIRGINIA
KENTUCKY
Richmond
NORFOLK
Virginia Beach
Nashville
TENNESSEE
NORTH CAROLINA
Charlotte
MEMPHIS
Knoxville
Asheville
Greensboro
Durham
Raleigh
Wilmington
Chattanooga
Birmingham
ATLANTA
SOUTH CAROLINA
Columbia
Charleston
North Charleston
Mount Pleasant
MISSISSIPPI
ALABAMA
GEORGIA
Macon
Savannah
Hilton Head Island
Montgomery
Jackson
Columbus
Albany
Mobile
Pensacola
Tallahassee
NEW ORLEANS
Jacksonville
FLORIDA
St. Augustine
Gainesville
Ocala
Panama City
Daytona Beach
ORLANDO
Cape Canaveral
Melbourne
Spring Hill
TAMPA
St. Petersburg
Sarasota
Fort Pierce
Port St. Lucie
West Palm Beach
Fort Myers
Cape Coral
Boca Raton
Pompano Beach
Fort Lauderdale
Hollywood
MIAMI
Miami Beach
Hialeah
Coral Gables
Kendall
Homestead
Key West
Key Largo
Florida Keys
Str. of Florida
Florida Bay
EVERGLADES NAT. PARK
BIG CYPRESS NAT. PRESERVE
Lake Okeechobee

OF MEXICO

ATLANTIC OCEAN

BAHAMAS
Grand Bahama
Freeport
Abaco I.
Grand Cay
Little Abaco I.
New Providence
Nassau
Andros I.
Bimini Is.

Mississippi River Delta

APPALACHIAN MTS.
Cumberland Plateau
GREAT SMOKY MTS. NAT. PARK
SHENANDOAH NAT. PARK
Sea Islands

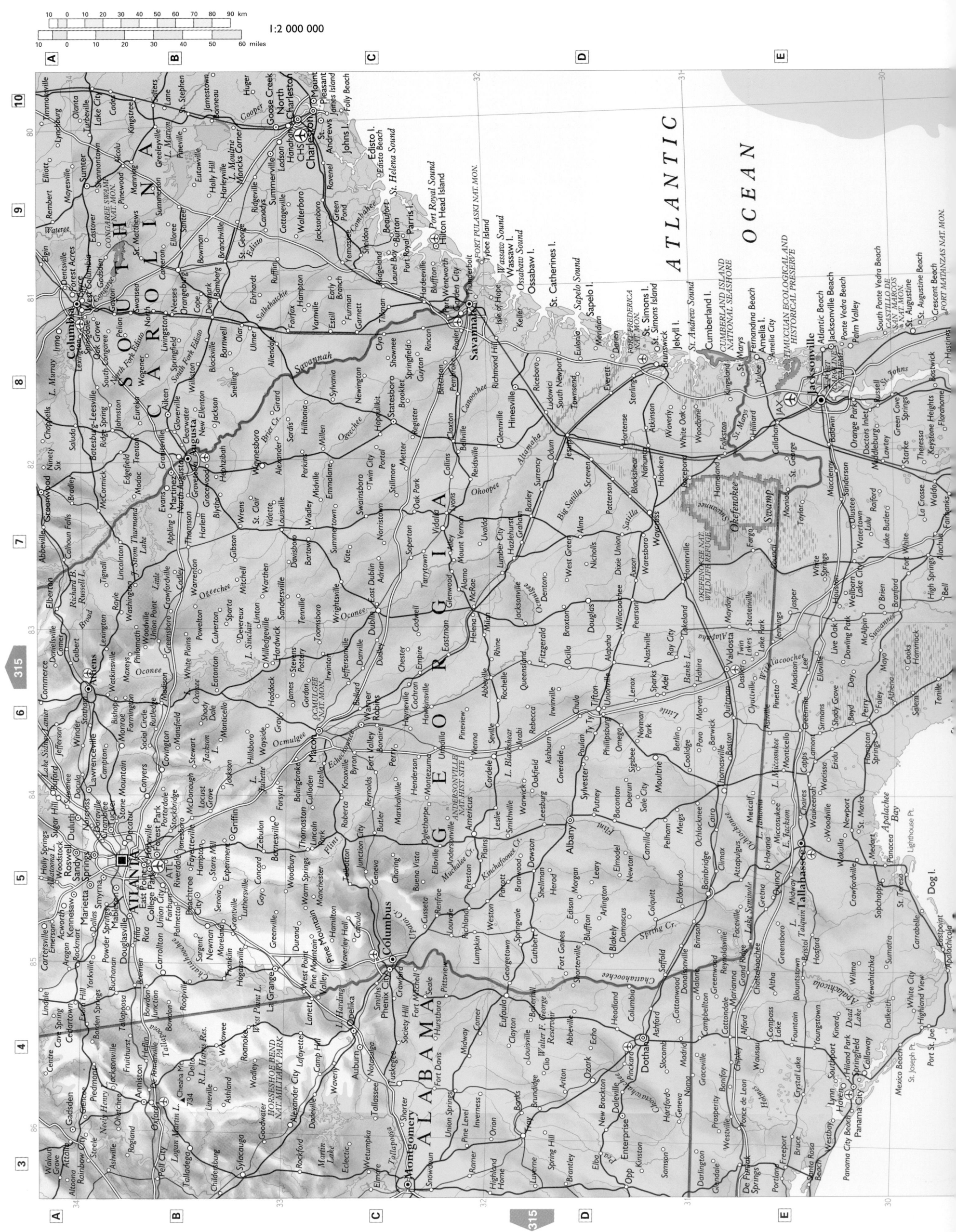

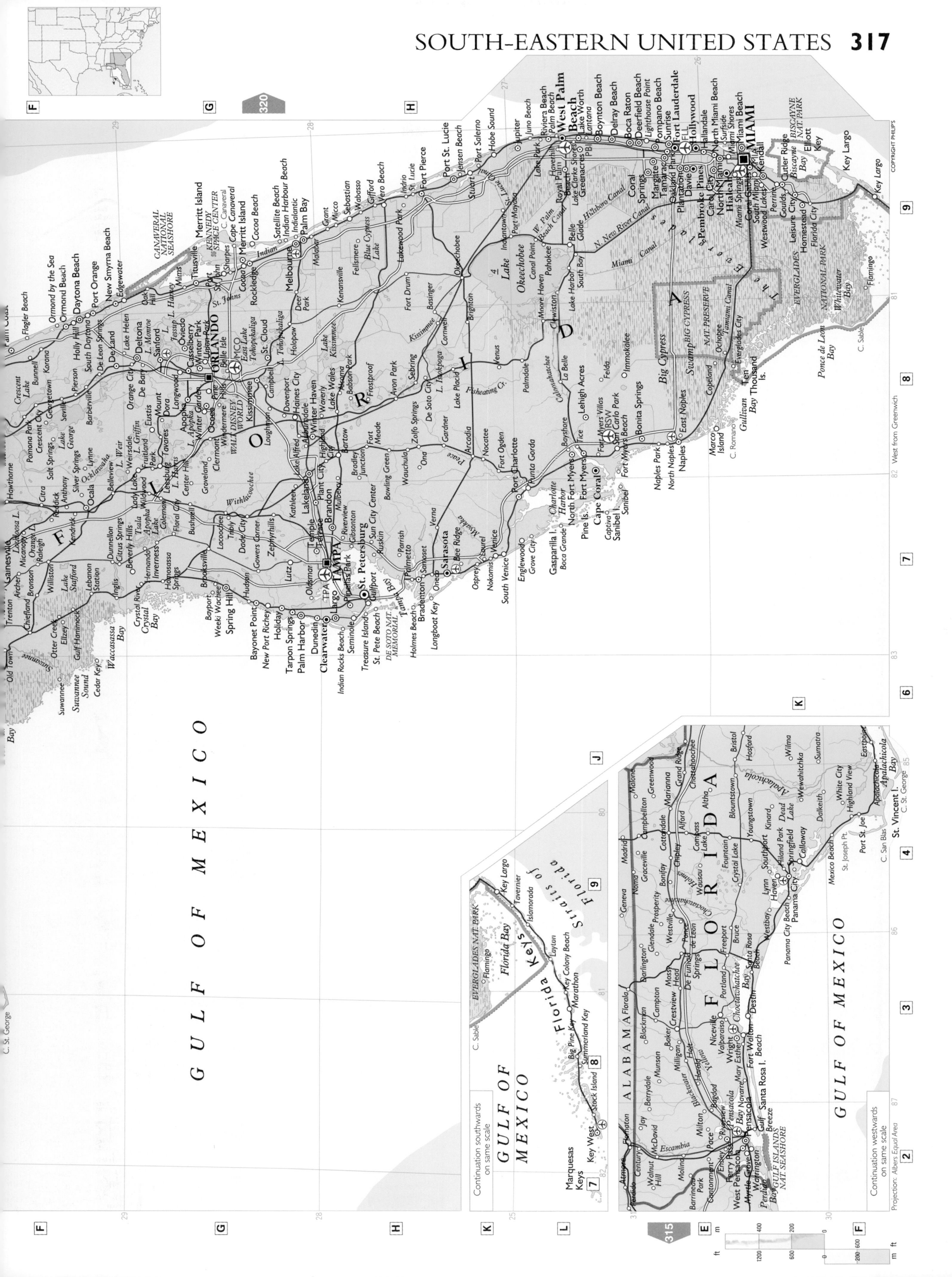

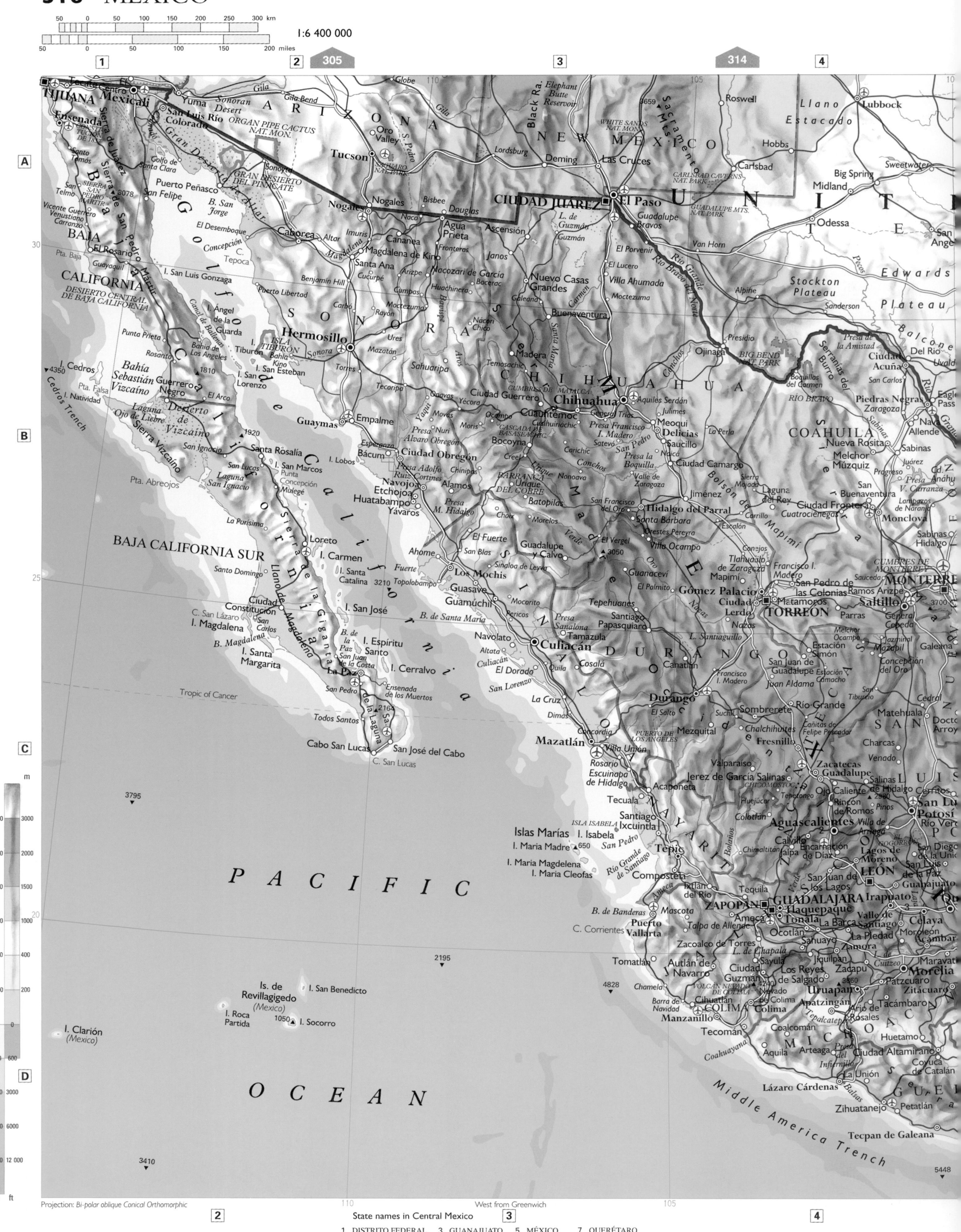

50 0   50   100 150 200 250 300 km

1:6 400 000

50 0   50   100   150 200 miles

Projection: Bi-polar oblique Conical Orthomorphic

West from Greenwich

State names in Central Mexico

1 DISTRITO FEDERAL 3 GUANAJUATO 5 MÉXICO 7 QUERÉTARO
2 AGUASCALIENTES   4 HIDALGO   6 MORELOS 8 TLAXCALA

JAMAICA
1:1 600 000

CARIBBEAN SEA

JAMAICA

Gulf of Mexico

MEXICO

GUATEMALA

BELIZE

HONDURAS

EL SALVADOR

NICARAGUA

COSTA RICA

PANAMA

CUBA

LA HABANA (Havana)

FLORIDA U.S.A.

MIAMI

Straits of Florida

Florida Keys

Cayman Islands (U.K.)

Yucatan Basin

Cayman Trench

Mosquitia

CARIBBEAN

PANAMA CANAL
1:800 000

CARIBBEAN SEA

PACIFIC OCEAN

1:6 400 000

Projection: Conical with two standard parallels

Isthmus of Panama

PUERTO RICO AND THE VIRGIN IS.
1:1 600 000

10 0 10 20 30 40 50 60 70 km
10 0 10 20 30 40 50 miles

ATLANTIC OCEAN

VIRGIN ISLANDS (U.K.)

Ruffling Pt. The Settlement Anegada East Pt.

Pta. Aguijereada Quebradillas Hatillo
Aguadilla Isabela Camuy Arecibo
Pta. Higuero Moca Barceloneta Vega Baja Levittown
Rincon Aguada PARQUE DE LAS CAVERNAS DEL RIO CAMUY OBSERVATORIO DE ARECIBO Manati Vega Alta **SAN JUAN** Carolina
San Sebastian Florida Ciales Río Grande Luquillo Fajardo
Añasco Lares **Bayamón** Guaynabo Sierra de El Yunque Ceiba
Mayagüez Maricao Utuado Cordillera Central Caguas Gurabo Luquillo Naguabo Pta. Puerca
Hormigueros Adjuntas 1338 Cerro de Punta Villalba Las Piedras Humacao
Cabo Rojo San German Sabana Grande Yauco **PUERTO RICO** (U.S.A.) Cayey Cidra Pta. Arenas
Parguera Sabana Grande Juana Diaz Coamo Salinas **Ponce** Guayama Patillas Maunabo
Guanica Santa Isabel I. Caja de Muertos

Dewey Culebra Isabel Segunda Esperanza Vieques

Jost Van Dyke I. Guana I. Great Camanoe Virgin Gorda
Hans Lollik I. Tortola 521 Road Town Spanish Town Beef I.
Charlotte Amalie Cruz Bay VIRGIN IS. NAT. PARK Peter I.
St. Thomas I. St. John I.
VIRGIN ISLANDS (U.S.A.)

CARIBBEAN SEA

Frederiksted 353 Mt. Eagle Christiansted East Pt.
Southwest Pt. **St. Croix I.** (U.S.A.)

West from Greenwich

ATLANTIC OCEAN

Puerto Rico Trench

BAHAMAS

Arthur's Town
New Bight Cat I.
San Salvador I.
Conception I.
Rum Cay
Long I. Tropic of Cancer
Clarence Town Samana Cay
Crooked I. Passage Crooked I.
Albert Town Plana Cays
Acklins I. Snug Corner
Mira por vos Cay
Cay Verde
Hogsty Reef
Santa Domingo
Little Inagua I.
Lake Rose Great Inagua I.
Mayari Matthew Town
Moa Baracoa
C. Lucrecia Pta. de Maisi
GUANTANAMO Maisi
BAY (U.S.A.) Paso de los Vientos (Windward Passage)

Turks & Caicos Is. (U.K.)
Caicos Is. Cockburn Town Turks Is.
Turks Island Passage
Silver Bank Passage

Mouchoir Bank
Silver Bank
Navidad Bank

Caicos Passage

Cap-Haïtien Monte Cristi LA ISABELA
Port-de-Paix Puerto Plata Santiago de los Caballeros San Francisco de Macorís
Cap-à-Foux Fort Liberté La Vega Nagua
Jean Rabel Gonaïves Hinche 3175 Pico Duarte Sánchez Samana
Î. de la Tortue St-Marc CORD. CENTRAL HAITISES Sabana de la Mar
Î. de la Gonâve **HAITI** **DOMINICAN REP.** Hato Mayor Aguadilla Arecibo Bayamón **SAN JUAN**
Jérémie **PORT-AU-PRINCE** San Juan San Pedro de Macorís Higüey C. Engaño Ponce **PUERTO RICO** (U.S.A.)
Dame Marie Massif de la Hotte 2680 SIERRA DE BAORUCO L. Enriquillo **SANTO DOMINGO** B. de Yuma Mayagüez Guayama
Les Cayes Petit Goâve Jacmel Azua de Compostela Barahona San Cristóbal I. Saona Isla Mona (U.S.A.)
Pointe-à-Gravois Aquin Pedernales C. Beata Freder ksted

Virgin Gorda Virgin Is. (U.K.) Sombrero (U.K.)
Anegada Road Town Anguilla (U.K.)
St. Thomas Tortola St.-Martin (Fr.)
Fajardo Virgin Is. (U.S.A.) Charlotte Amalie St. Maarten (Neth.) St.-Barthélemy (Fr.)
Culebra Vieques St. Croix (U.S.A.) Christiansted St. Eustatius (Neth.) Barbuda
1156 ST. KITTS Mt. Liamuiga 1156 **ANTIGUA & BARBUDA**
Basseterre Nevis St. John's Antigua
Redonda (U.K.) Brades 914 Soufrière Hills Guadeloupe Passage
Montserrat (U.K.) Ste.-Rose Le Moule La Désirade
GUADELOUPE (Fr.) 1467 Pointe-à-Pitre Marie-Galante (Fr.)
Basse-Terre I. des Saintes (Fr.) Grand-Bourg
Dominica Passage
Portsmouth 1419 **DOMINICA** Morne Diablotin MORNE TROIS PITONS
Roseau Martinique Passage
Mt. Pelée Ste.-Marie
1397 Le François
Fort-de-France Rivière-Pilote **MARTINIQUE**
St. Lucia Channel (Fr.)
Castries Soufrière **ST. LUCIA**
St. Vincent Passage
Soufrière 1234 St. Vincent Speightstown 340
Kingstown Bridgetown **BARBADOS**
Bequia **ST. VINCENT & THE GRENADINES**
Canouan
840 Carriacou
St. George's **GRENADA**

Hispaniola

Antilles

Beata Ridge

CARIBBEAN SEA

Venezuelan Basin

Colombian Basin

I. de Aves (Venezuela)

Aves Ridge

Leeward Islands

Windward Islands

Lesser Antilles

ABC Lesser Islands
Oranjestad Aruba (Neth.) Curaçao (Neth.) Bonaire (Neth.)
Pta. Gallinas MACUIRA Pen. de Willemstad
C. San Román Paraguaná
Pen. de la Guajira Pta. Espada Punto Fijo
ARC. LOS ROQUES
I. Las Aves (Ven.) Is. Los Roques (Ven.)
I. Blanquilla (Ven.)
Is. Los Hermanos (Ven.)

COLOMBIA
Santa Marta Ríohacha Uribia GUAJIRA
TAYRONA Golfo de Venezuela Punta Cardón Puerto Cumarebo
Ciénaga SIERRA NEVADA DE SANTA MARTA San Rafael MÉDANOS DE CORO La Vela
Soledad Valledupar CUEVA DE LA QUEBRADA EL TORO
Barranquilla CÉSAR FALCÓN Tucacas Puerto Cabello
Baranoa Mene de Mauroa Maracay
Subanalarga Maracaibo La Concepción Altagracia Baragua LARA CARABOBO **CARACAS**
Fundación Villa del Rosario Santa Rita Cabimas San Felipe VALENCIA MIRANDA
Calamar Ciudad Ojeda **BARQUISIMETO** **VALENCIA** Villa de Cura
Magangué ZULIA Lago de Maracaibo **MARACAIBO** Yaritagua San Juan de los Morros
Machiques TRUJILLO El Tocuyo GUÁRICO
Zambrano Betijoque Acarigua Calabozo
Mompós Trujillo Guanare Santa María de Ipire
El Banco Valera PORTUGUESA El Baúl
CUCUTA Mérida Barinas COJEDES Valle de la Pascua
Mérida SIERRA NEVADA Libertad San Carlos ANZOÁTEGUI
NORTE DE SANTANDER Ciudad Bolivia San Fernando de Apure
Ocaña TÁCHIRA BARINAS Bruzual
Cúcuta **VENEZUELA** Achaguas Orinoco Apure Calcara

I. de Margarita NUEVA ESPARTA
La Asunción Porlamar
Is. Los Testigos (Ven.)
Tobago Scarborough
I. La Tortuga (Ven.) CERRO EL COPEY Pampatar
Carúpano Pen. de Paria Port of Spain 949
Cumaná Cariaco SUCRE Güiria Arima Point
Puerto La Cruz MONAGAS Caripito **TRINIDAD & TOBAGO**
Barcelona Caicara Serpent's Mouth
Anaco Maturín MARIUSA
Cantaura DELTA
Valle de la Pascua El Tigre AMACURO Tucupita
San Mateo Pariaguán Santa María de Ipire Ciudad Guayana
Los Barrancos
BOLÍVAR El Pao Ciudad Bolívar Upata
Ciudad Bolívar Caroní Guasipati El Callao Tumeremo
Embalse de Guri

Sierra Imataca

West from Greenwich

COPYRIGHT PHILIP'S

4000 3000 2000 1500 1000 400 200 0
12 000 9000 6000 4500 3000 1200 600 0 ft
200 2000 4000 6000 8000 m
600 6000 12 000 18 000 24 000

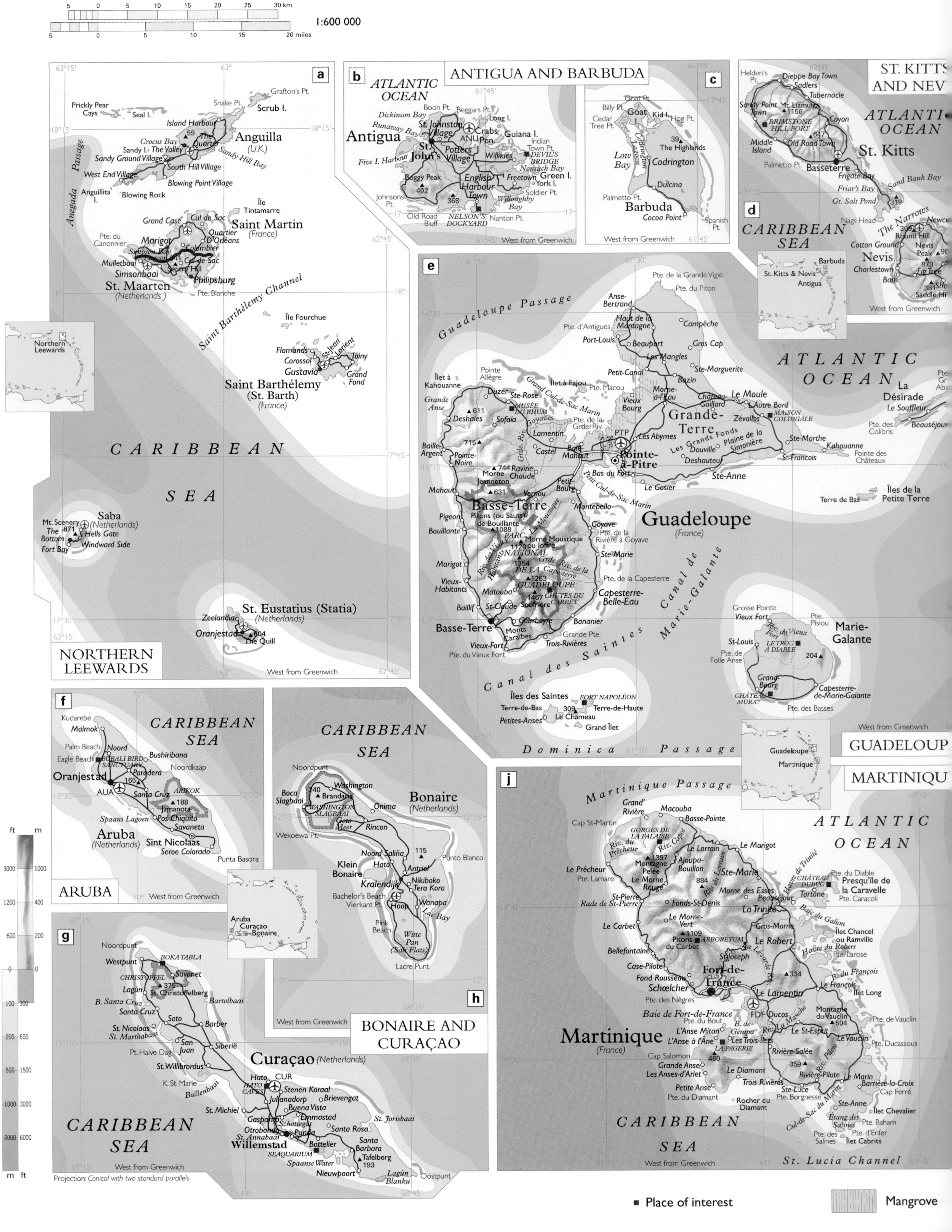

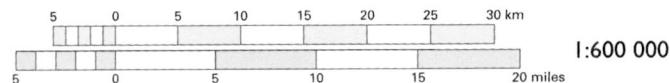

5 0 5 10 15 20 25 30 km
1:600 000
5 0 5 10 15 20 miles

a — Anguilla (U.K.); Saint Martin (France); St. Maarten (Netherlands); Saint Barthélemy (St. Barth) (France)

Prickly Pear Cays, Seal I., Snake Pt., Grafton's Pt., Island Harbour, Scrub I., Crocus Bay, The Valley, Sandy I., The Quarter, Anguilla, Sandy Ground Village, South Hill Village, Sandy Hill Bay, West End Village, Blowing Point Village, Anguillita I., Blowing Rock, Île Tintamarre, Grand Case, Cul de Sac, Quartier D'Orleans, Saint Martin (France), Marigot, Colombier, Pte. du Canonnier, Mulletbaai, Simsonbaai, St. Maarten (Netherlands), Philipsburg, Pte. Blanche, Saint Barthélemy Channel, Île Fourchue, Flamands, Corossol, Gustavia, St. Jean, Lorient, Toiny, Grand Fond, Saint Barthélemy (St. Barth) (France)

Angada Passage

Northern Leewards

CARIBBEAN SEA

Saba (Netherlands), Mt. Scenery 871, The Bottom, Hells Gate, Windward Side, Fort Bay

St. Eustatius (Statia) (Netherlands), Zeelandia, Oranjestad, 604 The Quill

NORTHERN LEEWARDS

West from Greenwich

b — ANTIGUA AND BARBUDA

ATLANTIC OCEAN, Dickinson Bay, Runaway Bay, Boon Pt., Beggars Pt., Long I., St. Johnston Village, Crabs Pen, Guiana I., Antigua, Five I. Harbour, St. John's, Potters Village, Willikies, Indian Town Pt., Boggy Peak 402, English Harbour Town, Freetown, Green I., York I., Soldier Pt., Johnsons Pt., 368, Willoughby Bay, NELSON'S DOCKYARD, Old Road Bluff, Nanton Pt., DEVIL'S BRIDGE, Nonsuch Bay

West from Greenwich

c — Billy Pt., Goat Pt., Cedar Tree Pt., Goat I., Kid I., Hog Pt., 39, The Highlands, Low Bay, Codrington, Dulcina, Palmetto Pt., Barbuda, Cocoa Point, Spanish Pt.

West from Greenwich

d — ST. KITTS AND NEVIS

Helden's Pt., Sandy Point Town, Dieppe Bay Town, Sadlers, Tabernacle, Mt. Liamuiga 1156, BRIMSTONE HILL FORT, Middle Island, Cayon, Old Road Town, St. Kitts, Palmetto Pt., Basseterre, Frigate Bay, Friar's Bay, Gt. Salt Pond, 319, Nags Head, Sand Bank Bay, The Narrows, Cotton Ground, Round Hill, Nevis Peak 985, Charlestown, Nevis, Bath, Saddle Hi, 873

ATLANTIC OCEAN, CARIBBEAN SEA

St. Kitts & Nevis, Barbuda, Antigua

West from Greenwich

e — GUADELOUPE (France)

Guadeloupe Passage, Pte. de la Grande Vigie, Pte. du Piton, Anse-Bertrand, Campêche, Haut de la Montagne, Pte. d'Antigues, Port-Louis, Beauport, Gros Cap, Les Mangles, Ste-Marguerite, Petit-Canal, Bazin, Morne-à-l'Eau, Vieux Bourg, Le Moule, Chateau-Gaillard, Autre Bord, Grande-Terre, Zévallos, MAISON COLONIALE, Îlet à Kahouanne, Pointe Allègre, Îlet à Fajou, Pte. Macou, Grand Cul-de-Sac Marin, Grande Anse, Duzer, Ste-Rose, Goyaves, Pte. de la Grde Riv., Les Abymes, Les Grands Fonds, Plaine de la Simonière, Deshaies, 611, MUSÉE DU RHUM, Sofaia, Lamentin, Castel, Douville, Deshauteur, PTP, Pointe-à-Pitre, Ste-Marthe, Pointe-Noire, 715, Baille-Argent, Pte. de la Grde Riv., Morne Jeanneton, 744, Ravine Chaude, Bas du Fort, Petit Bourg, Petit Cul-de-Sac Marin, Le Gosier, S-François, Pointe des Châteaux, Mahaut, 631, Vernou, Montebello, Goyave, Îles de la Petite Terre, Basse-Terre, Pigeon, Pitons (ou Sauts) de Bouillante 1088, Pte. de la Rivière à Goyave, Bouillante, PARC NATIONAL 1100, Morne Moustique, Matouba 1467, St-Claude, 1354, 1263, DE LA GUADELOUPE, Ste-Marie, Grde Riv. de la Capesterre, Pte. de la Capesterre, Marigot, Vieux-Habitants, CHUTES DU CARBET, Capesterre-Belle-Eau, Baillif, Soufrière, Bananier, Monts Caraïbes, Gourbeyre, Grande Pte., Trois-Rivières, Vieux-Fort, Pte. du Vieux Fort, Canal des Saintes, Canal de Marie-Galante, Grosse Pointe, Vieux Fort, Pte. Pisiou, St-Louis, Riv. du Vieux Fort, LE TROU À DIABLE, Marie-Galante, 204, Pte. de Folle Anse, Grand Bourg, Capesterre-de-Marie-Galante, CHÂTEAU MURAT, Pte. des Basses

Guadeloupe, Martinique

ATLANTIC OCEAN, La Désirade, Le Souffleur, Pte. des Colibris, Beauséjour

Dominica Passage, Îles des Saintes, FORT NAPOLÉON, Terre-de-Bas, 309, Terre-de-Haute, Petites-Anses, Le Chameau, Grand Îlet

GUADELOUPE
MARTINIQUE

f — ARUBA (Netherlands)

CARIBBEAN SEA, Kudarebe, Malmok, Bushiribana, Noord, Palm Beach, Eagle Beach, BUBALI BIRD SANCTUARY, Noordkaap, Oranjestad, Paradera, 165, AUA, Santa Cruz, ARIKOK, 188, Jamanota, Spaans Lagoen, Pos Chiquito, Savaneta, Aruba, Sint Nicolaas, Seroe Colorado, Punta Basora

West from Greenwich

g — Curaçao (Netherlands)

Noordpunt, Westpunt, BOKA TABLA, Savonet, CHRISTOFFEL, Lagun, 375, St. Christoffelberg, Bartolbaai, B. Santa Cruz, Santa Cruz, St. Nicolaas, St. Marthabai, Soto, Barber, San Juan, Siberië, Pt. Halve Dag, K. St. Marie, St. Willibrordus, Bullenbai, St. Michiel, HATO CAVES, CUR, Juliandorp, Stenen Koraal, Brievengat, Buena Vista, Santa Rosa, Gasparito, Enmastad, St. Annabaai, Schottegat, Punda, Santa Barbara, Willemstad, Otrobanda, Bottelier, SEAQUARIUM, Tafelberg 193, Spaanse Water, Nieuwpoort, Lagun Blanku, Oostpunt, St. Jorisbaai

CARIBBEAN SEA

BONAIRE AND CURAÇAO

Bonaire (Netherlands), Noordpunt, Boca Slagbaai, 240, Washington, Brandaris, WASHINGTON SLAGBAAI, Onima, Goto Meer, Rincon, Klein Bonaire, Noord Saliña, 115, Hato, Antriol, Nikiboko, Tera Kora, Kralendijk, Bachelor's Beach, Wanapa, Lac Bay, Vierkant Pt., Hoop, Witte Pan (Salt Flats), Pink Beach, Lacre Punt, Punta Basora, Punto Blanco, Wekoewa Pt.

Aruba, Curaçao, Bonaire

West from Greenwich

j — MARTINIQUE (France)

Martinique Passage, Grand' Rivière, Macouba, Cap St-Martin, Basse-Pointe, GORGES DE LA FALAISE, Riv. du Prêcheur, Le Lorrain, Le Marigot, Le Prêcheur, 1397, Montagne Pelée, Ajoupa-Bouillon, Ste-Marie, Pte. du Diable, Presqu'île de la Caravelle, Pte. Lamare, Le Morne Rouge, 884, Morne des Esses, Tartane, Pte. Caracoli, St-Pierre, Rade de St-Pierre, Fonds-St-Denis, La Trinité, Îlet Chancel ou Ramville, Le Carbet, 1109, Le Morne-Vert, Gros-Morne, ARBORÉTUM, Le Robert, Bellefontaine, Pitons du Carbet, St-Joseph, Îlet Larose, Case-Pilote, Fond Rousseau, 334, Du François, Fort-de-France, FDF, Schoelcher, Pte. des Nègres, Le Lamentin, Le François, Îlet Long, Baie de Fort-de-France, Ducos, Montagne du Vauclin 504, Pte. de Vauclin, B. de Génipa, Rivière Salée, 460, Le St-Esprit, Le Vauclin, L'Anse Mitan, L'Anse à l'Ane, Les Trois-Îlets, LA PAGERIE, Rivière-Salée, Cap Salomon, Grande Anse, 359, Rivière-Pilote, Le Marin, Les Anses-d'Arlet, Le Diamant, Trois Rivières, Ste-Luce, Barrière-la-Croix, Cap Ferré, Petite Anse, Rocher du Diamant, Pte. du Diamant, Ste-Anne, Cul-de-Sac du Marin, Étang des Salines, Pte. Baham, Pte. d'Enfer, Îlet Cabrits

ATLANTIC OCEAN, CARIBBEAN SEA, St. Lucia Channel

West from Greenwich

Projection: Conical with two standard parallels

ft / m elevation scale: 3000/1000, 1200/400, 600/200, 0, 200/600, 500/1500, 2000/6000

■ Place of interest   Mangrove

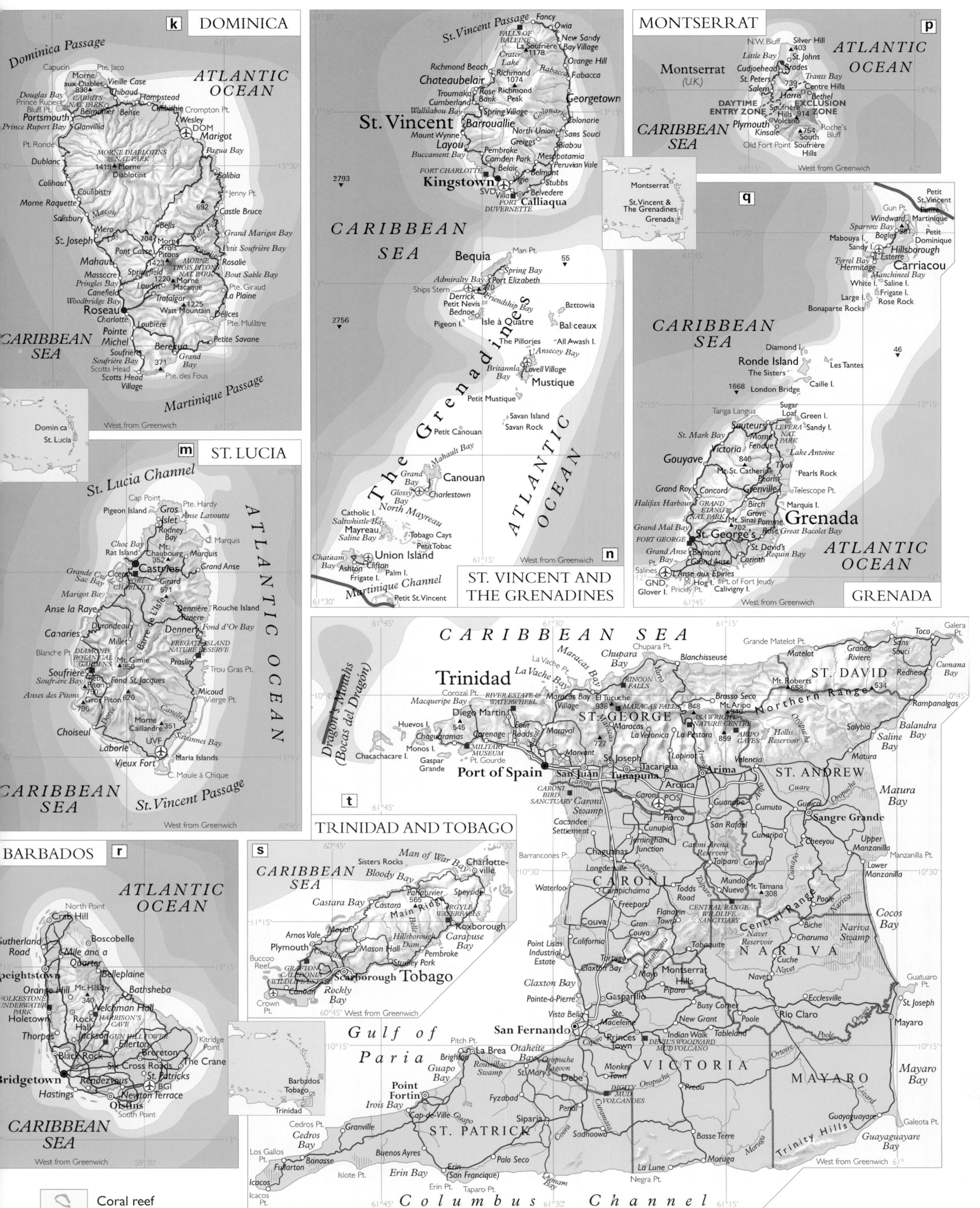

SOUTH AMERICA

100 0 200   400   600   800 1000 1200 1400 km
100 0   200   400   600   800   1000 miles
1:28 000 000

Projection: Lambert's Azimuthal Equal Area

COPYRIGHT PHILIP'S

1:28 000 000

Projection: Lambert's Azimuthal Equal Area

COPYRIGHT PHILIP'S

■ LIMA   Capital Cities

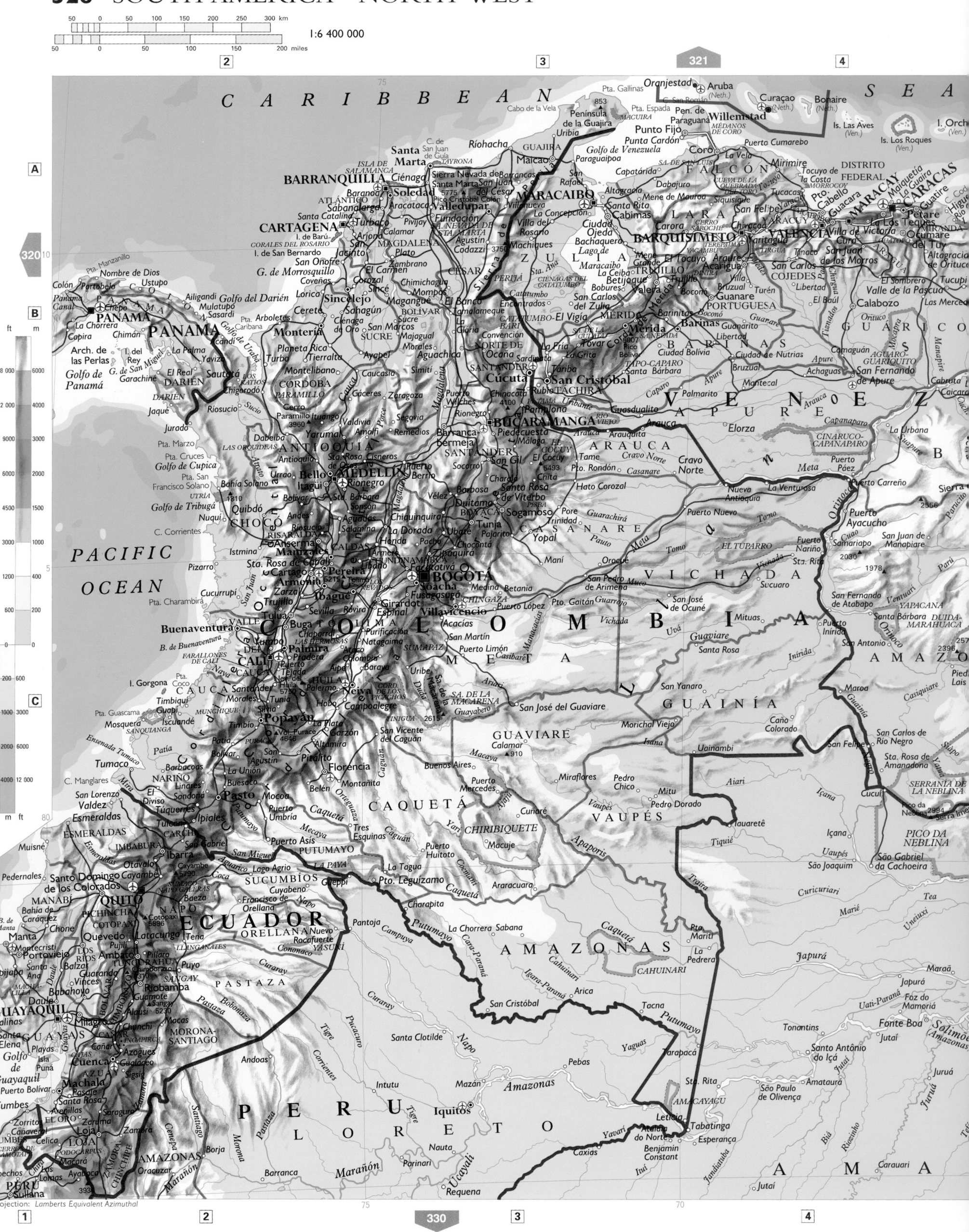

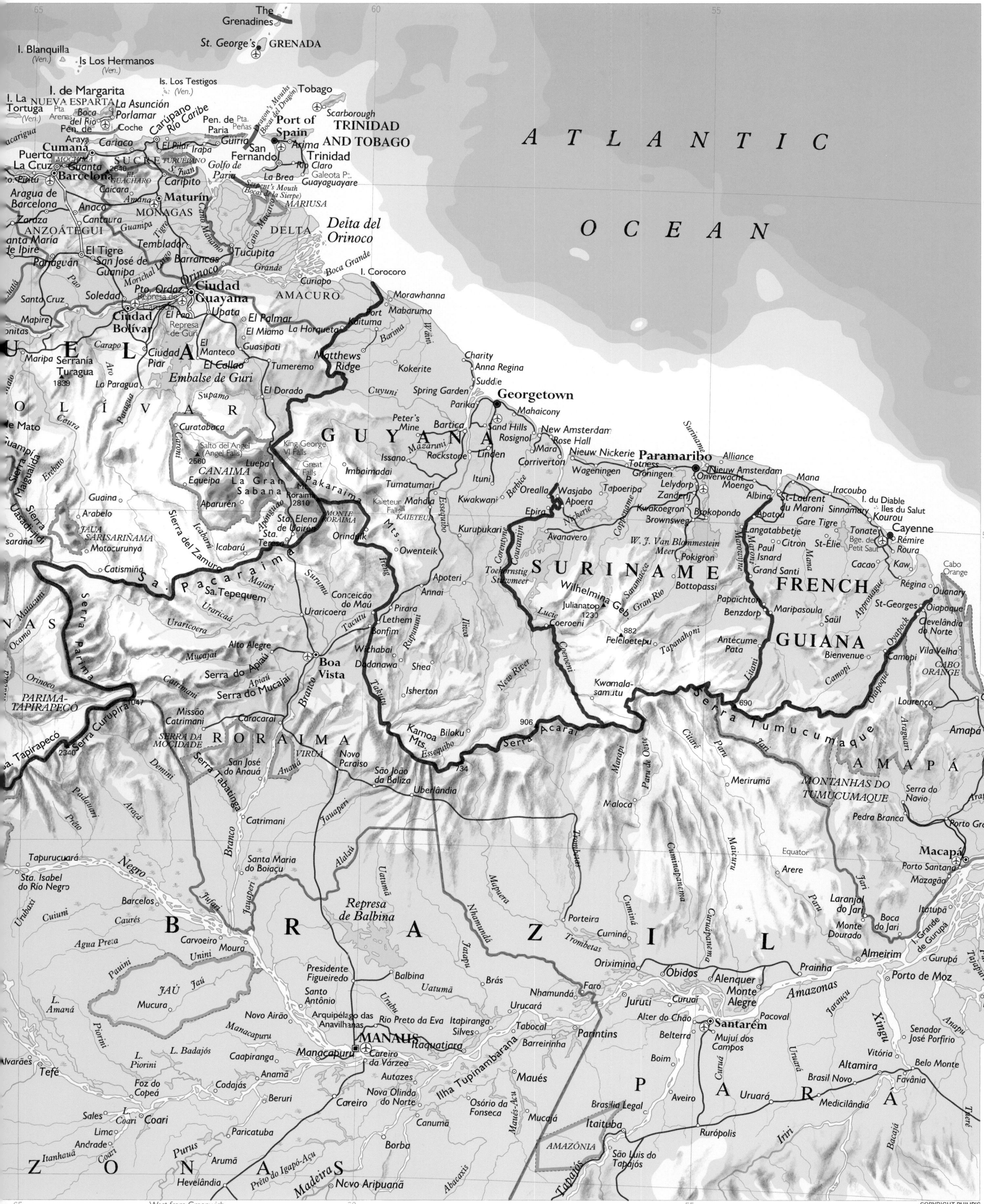

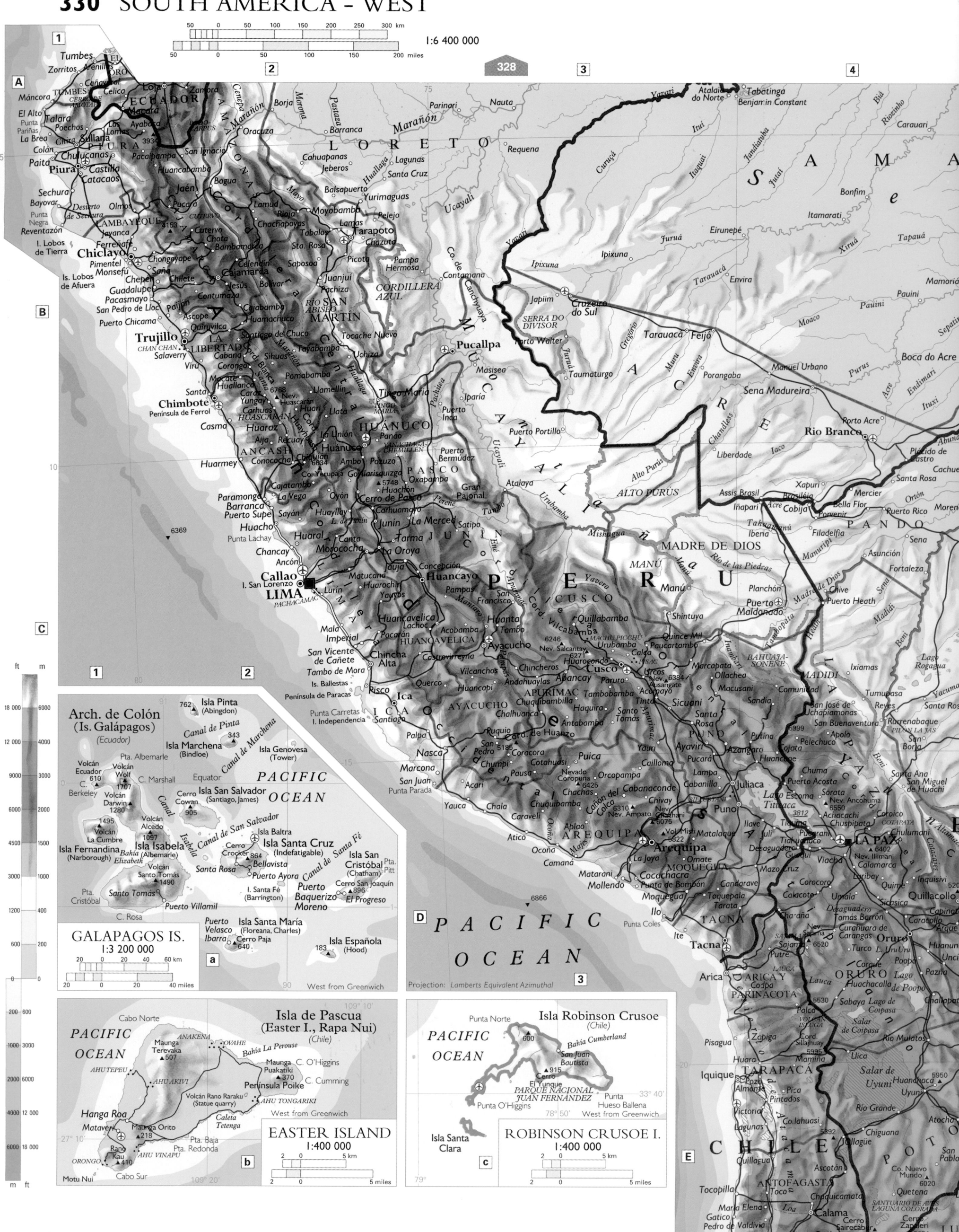

50 0 50 100 150 200 250 300 km
1:6 400 000
50 0 50 100 150 200 miles

328

GALAPAGOS IS.
1:3 200 000
20 0 20 40 60 km
20 0 20 40 miles

EASTER ISLAND
1:400 000
2 0 2 4 5 km
2 0 2 4 5 miles

ROBINSON CRUSOE I.
1:400 000
2 0 2 4 5 km
2 0 2 4 5 miles

Projection: Lamberts Equivalent Azimuthal

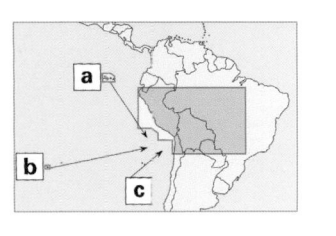

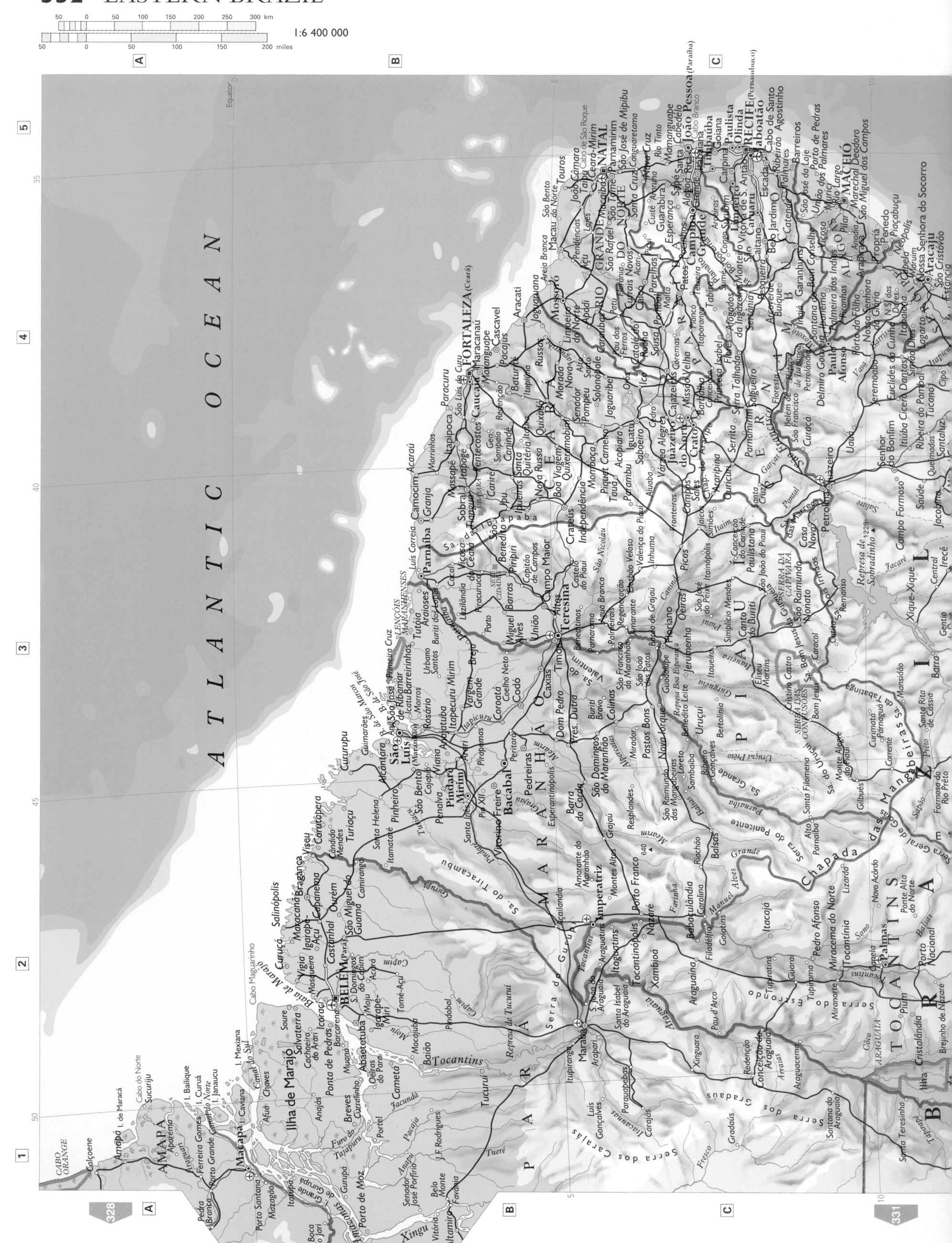

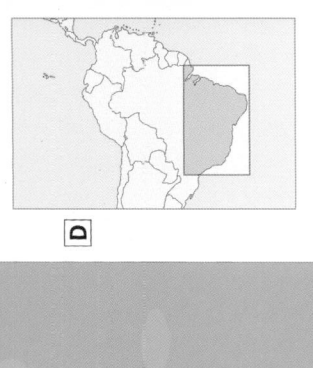

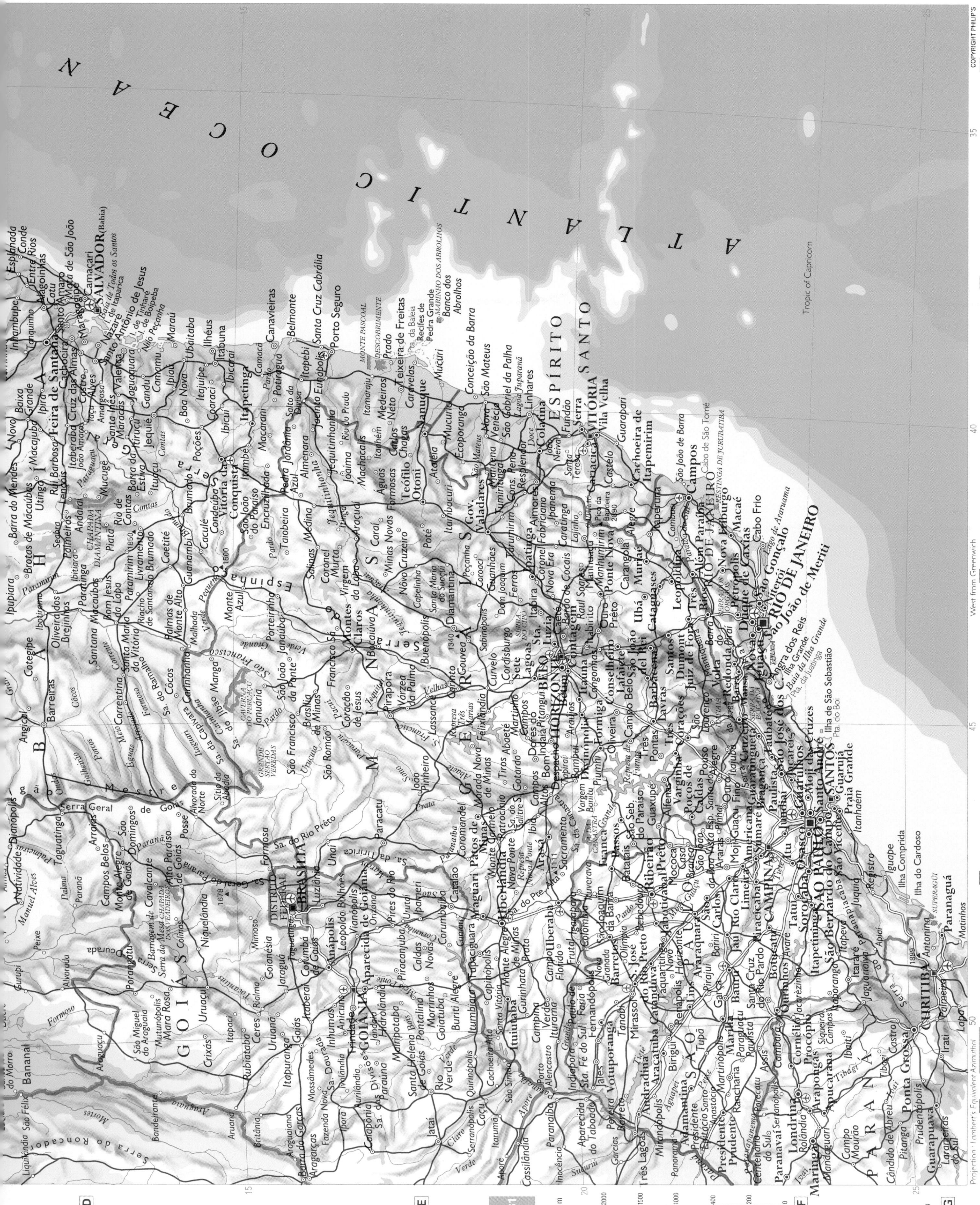

ATLANTIC OCEAN
BAHIA
GOIÁS
MINAS GERAIS
ESPÍRITO SANTO
RIO DE JANEIRO
SÃO PAULO
PARANÁ
DISTRITO FEDERAL
SALVADOR (Bahia)
Baía de Todos os Santos
BRASÍLIA
GOIÂNIA
BELO HORIZONTE
VITÓRIA
RIO DE JANEIRO
SÃO PAULO
CURITIBA
SANTOS
CAMPINAS
Banco dos Abrolhos
MARINHO DOS ABROLHOS
Serra Geral de Goiás
Serra do Espinhaço
CHAPADA DIAMANTINA
Serra da Mantiqueira
Tropic of Capricorn
West from Greenwich
Projection : Lambert's Equivalent Azimuthal
COPYRIGHT PHILIP'S
331
335

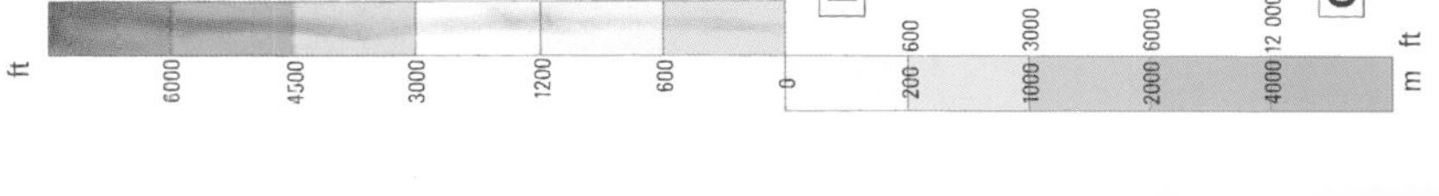

m
ft
2000
1500
1000
400
200
0
6000
4500
3000
1200
600
200
1000
2000
4000

1:6 400 000

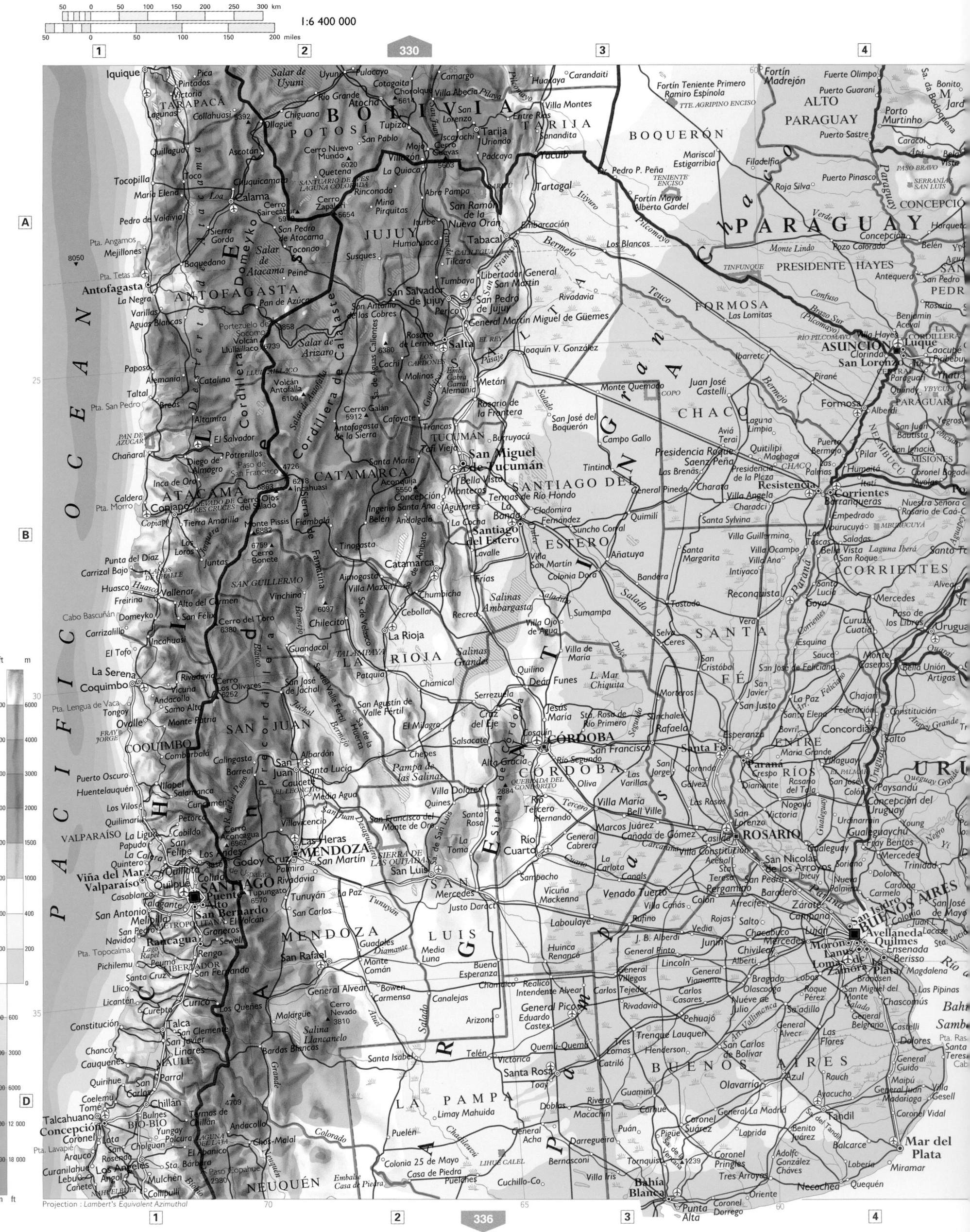

Projection : Lambert's Equivalent Azimuthal

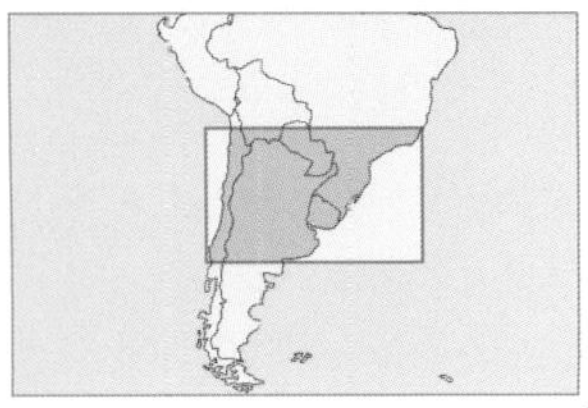

MATO GROSSO DO SUL

BRAZIL

PARANÁ

SANTA CATARINA

RIO GRANDE DO SUL

URUGUAY

SÃO PAULO

RIO DE JANEIRO

BELO HORIZONTE

CAMPINAS

CURITIBA

PORTO ALEGRE

MONTEVIDEO

VITÓRIA

Tropic of Capricorn

A T L A N T I C

O C E A N

Vila Velha
Guarapari
Cachoeiro de Itapemirim
Castelo
Alegre
Muriaé
Carangola
Ponte Nova
Ouro Prêto
Congonhas
Contagem
Betim
Itabirito
Lafaiete
Conselheiro
Oliveira
Campo Belo
São João del Rei
Barbacena
Ubá
Cataguases
Leopoldina
Além Paraíba
Nova Friburgo
Petrópolis
Macaé
Cabo Frio
L. de Araruama
Niterói
São Gonçalo
João de Meriti
Duque de Caxias
Angra dos Reis
Santos
Santos
São Vicente
Praia Grande
Guarujá
Pta. do Boi
Ilha de São Sebastião
Moji das Cruzes
Santo André
São Bernardo do Campo
Guarulhos
São José dos C.
Osasco
Jundiaí
Sorocaba
Itu
Tatuí
Itapetininga
Itapeva
Registro
Iguape
Ilha Comprida
Ilha do Cardoso
Antonina
Paranaguá
Guaratuba
Matinhos
Joinville
São Francisco do Sul
Itajaí
Brusque
Blumenau
Santa Cecília
Rio do Sul
Curitibanos
Campos Novos
São José
Ilha de Santa Catarina
Florianópolis
Lages
Laguna
Tubarão
Cabo Santa Marta Grande
Criciúma
Araranguá
Torres
Osório
Canoas
São Leopoldo
Novo Hamburgo
Caxias do Sul
Bento Gonçalves
Montenegro
Taquara
Viamão
Rio Pardo
Cachoeira do Sul
São Gabriel
Dom Pedrito
Bagé
Pelotas
Rio Grande
São José do Norte
Mostardas
LAGOA DO PEIXE
Lagoa dos Patos
Lagoa Mirim
Lagoa Mangueira
Santa Vitória do Palmar
Chuy
SANTA TERESA
Castillos
Rocha
Maldonado
PTA. DEL ESTE
La Plata

COPYRIGHT PHILIP'S

West from Greenwich

1:6 400 000

50 0 50 100 150 200 250 300 km
50 0 50 100 150 200 miles

Projection : Lambert's Equivalent Azimuthal

COPYRIGHT PHILIP'S

West from Greenwich

Provinces / Regions

LA PAMPA · BUENOS AIRES · RÍO NEGRO · NEUQUÉN · LA ARAUCANIA · LOS RÍOS · LOS LAGOS · CHUBUT · SANTA CRUZ · ARGENTINA · PATAGONIA

Oceans

ATLANTIC OCEAN
PACIFIC OCEAN

Selected place names

Temuco · Neuquén · Bahía Blanca · Valdivia · Osorno · Puerto Montt · San Carlos de Bariloche · Esquel · Viedma · Puerto Madryn · Trelew · Rawson · Comodoro Rivadavia · Caleta Olivia · Puerto Deseado · Gobernador Gregores · Puerto San Julián · Río Gallegos · Puerto Natales · Punta Arenas · Ushuaia · Río Grande · Porvenir

Islands & features

Isla de Chiloé · Archipiélago de los Chonos · Península de Taitao · Golfo de Penas · Golfo San Matías · Golfo San Jorge · Península Valdés · Isla Grande de Tierra del Fuego · Estrecho de Magallanes · Magellan's Strait · Cabo de Hornos (Cape Horn)

FALKLAND ISLANDS (U.K.)
(ISLAS MALVINAS)

West Falkland · East Falkland · Stanley · Port Darwin · Mt Usborne · Beauchêne I.

GEOGRAPHICAL GLOSSARY

This is a list of the geographical terms from various foreign languages that are found in the place names on the maps and in the index. Each is followed by the language and its English meaning.

Afr. Afrikaans
Alb. Albanian
Amh. Amharic
Ar. Arabic
Belo. Belorussian
Berb. Berber
Bulg. Bulgarian
Burm. Burmese
Cam. Cambodian
Cat. Catalan
Chin. Chinese
Czec. Czech
Dan. Danish
Dut. Dutch
Est. Estonian
Fin. Finnish
Fr. French
Gae. Gaelic
Ger. German
Gr. Greek
Heb. Hebrew
Hin. Hindi
Hung. Hungarian
I.-C. Indo-Chinese
Ice. Icelandic
It. Italian
Indo. Indonesian
Jap. Japanese
Kaz. Kazakh
Kor. Korean
Kyrg. Kyrgyz
Lapp. Lapp (Sami)
Lat. Latvian
Lith. Lithuanian
Malag. Malagasy
Mong. Mongolian
Nor. Norway
Pash. Pashto
Per. Persian
Pol. Polish
Port. Portuguese
Rom. Romanian
Russ. Russian
Sin. Sinhalese
Ser.-Cr. Serbo-Croat
Slov. Slovene
Som. Somali
Span. Spanish
Swe. Swedish
Tib. Tibetan
Turk. Turkish
Ukr. Ukrainian
Viet. Vietnamese

-á *Ice.* river
-å *Dan., Nor., Swe.* stream
-abad *Farsi, Russ.* town
Abyad *Ar.* white mountain
Ada, Adasi *Turk.* island
Addis *Amh.* new
Adrar *Ar., Berb.* mountains
Aiguille *Fr.* peak
Aïn, Aïn (A.) *Ar.* spring
Ákra *Gr.* cape, point
Akrotíri *Gr.* cape, point
Alb *Ger.* mountains
Albufera *Span.* lagoon
-ålen *Nor.* islands
Alpen *Ger.* mountain ranges
Alpes *Fr.* mountains
Alpi *It.* mountains
Alt *Ger.* old
Alta, Alto *Port.* high, upper
Altos *Span.* mountains
-älv, -älven *Swe.* stream, river
Amtskommune (Amt.) *Dan.* first-order administrative division
-ån *Swe.* river
Anse *Fr.* bay
Ao *Thai* bay
Appennino *It.* mountain range
Archipel *Fr.* archipelago
Archipiélago (Arch.) *Span.* archipelago
Arcipélago *It.* archipelago
Arquipélago (Arq.) *Port.* archipelago
Arrecife *Span.* reef
Arroyo (Arr.) *Span.* stream
-ås, -åsen *Nor., Swe.* hill
Ayios *Gr.* island
Ayn *Ar.* well, waterhole

Baai, -baai *Afr., Dut.* bay
Bāb *Ar.* gate, strait
Bäck, -bäcken *Swe.* stream
Back, -backen, *Swe.* hill
Bad, -baden *Ger.* spa
Badia *Cat.* bay
Bādiyah, Bādiyat *Ar.* desert
Bæk *Dan.* stream
Bælt *Dan.* strait
Baharu *Malay* new
Bahía (B.) *Span.* bay
Bahiret *Ar.* lagoon
Bahr *Ar.* sea, lake, river
Bahra Bahrat *Ar.* lake
Baía (B.) *Port.* bay
Baie (B.) *Fr.* bay
Baixa, Baixo *Port.* lower
Baja, Bajo *Span.* lower
Bakke *Nor.* hill
Bala *Farsi* upper
Ballon *Fr.* dome
Baltă *Rom.* marsh, lake
Ban *Lao, Thai* village
-Bana *Jap.* cape
Banc *Fr.* bank
Banco *Span.* bank
Bandao *Chin.* peninsula
Bandar *Ar., Malay* port, harbour
Bandar *Farsi* bay
Banja *Ser.-Cr.* spa, resort
Banjaran *Malay* mountain range
Baraji *Turk.* dam
Barat *Indo., Malay* western
Barrage (Barr.) *Fr.* dam
Barragem (Barr.) *Port.* dam, reservoir
Bas, basse *Fr.* lower
Bassin *Fr.* basin
-batang *Indo.* river
Baţlaq *Farsi* marsh
Batu *Malay* mountain
Bayt *Heb.* house, village
Bazar *Hin.* market, bazaar
-beek *Afr., Dut.* river
Be'er *Heb.* well
Bei *Chin.* north, northern
Beinn, Ben *Gae.* mountain
Beit *Heb.* village
Belaya, Belo, Beloye, Belyy *Russ.* white
Belogorye *Russ.* hills, mountain range
Bender *Som.* harbour
Berg(e), -berg(e) *Afr., Ger.* mountain(s)
-berg, -en, -et *Nor., Swe.* hill, mountain, rock
Besar *Indo., Malay* big
Bet *Heb.* house, village
Bir, Bîr, Bi'r *Ar.* well
Birkat, Birket *Ar.* lake, marsh, well
Bishti *Alb.* cape
-bjerg *Dan.* hill, point
Blaenau *Welsh* upland
-bo *Chin.* lake
Boca *Port., Span.* river mouth, inlet
Bodden *Ger.* bay, inlet
Bogaz, Boğazı *Turk.* channel, strait
Bogd *Mong.* mountain range
Bois *Fr.* woods
Boka *Ser.-Cr.* gulf, inlet
Bolshoi, Bolshaya, Bolshoye (Bol.) *Russ.* great, large
Bordj (Bj.) *Ar.* fort
-borg *Dan., Nor., Swe.* castle, fort
Bory *Pol.* woods
Bosque *Span.* woods
-botn *Nor.* valley floor
Bouche(s) *Fr.* mouth(s)
Braţul *Rom.* distributary stream, branch
-bre, -breen *Nor.* glacier
Bredning *Dan.* bay
Brücke *Ger.* bridge
-brug *Dut.* bridge
-brunn *Swe.* well, spring
Bucht *Ger.* bay
Bugt *Dan.* bay
-bugten *Dan.* bay
Buheirat *Ar.* lake, reservoir
Bukit *Malay* hill
-bukt, -a *Nor.* bay
-bukten *Swe.* bay
-bulag *Mong.* spring
Bulag *Chin.* lake
Bulu *Malay* mountain
Bum *Burm.* mountain
Bûr *Ar.* port
Burg. *Ar.* fort
Burg, -burg *Ger.* castle
Burnu, Burun *Turk.* cape
Butt *Gae.* promontory
Büyük *Turk.* big
-by *Dan., Nor., Swe.* town
-byen *Nor., Swe.* town

Cabeza *Span.* peak, hill
Cabo (C.) *Port., Span.* headland, cape
Cachoeira *Port.* waterfall
Cala Cat. *It.* bay
Camp Port. *Span.* land, field
Câmpia *Rom.* plain
Campo *It., Port., Span.* plain
Campos *Span.* upland
Canal (Can.) *Fr., Port., Span.* canal, channel
Canale (Can.) *It.* channel
Canalul (Can.) *Ser.-Cr.* canal
Cao Nguyen *Thai* plateau, tableland
Cap (C.) *Cat., Fr.* cape
Capo (C) *It.* cape
Carn *Gae.* hill
Carse *Gae.* valley
Catarata *Port., Span.* cataract
Cauce *Span.* intermittent stream
Causse *Fr.* limestone plateau
Cay, Cayi, -cay, -cayi *Turk.* river
Cayo(s) *Span.* rock(s), islet(s)
Cefn *Welsh* hill
Cerro *Span.* hill, peak
Česká, Český, České *Czec.* Czech
Chaco *Span.* jungle
Chaîne(s) *Fr.* mountain range(s)
Chang *Chin.* mountain
Chapa *Span.* hills, upland
Chapada *Port.* hills, upland
Chaung *Burm.* stream, river
Chi *Chin.* small lake
-ch'ŏn *Kor.* river
-chŏsuji *Kor.* reservoir
Chott *Ar.* salt lake, depression
Chu *Tib.* river
Chute *Fr.* waterfall
Città *It.* city
Ciudad *Span.* city
Co *Tib.* lake
Cochilla (Coch.) *Port.* hills
Col *Fr., It.* pass
Colina(s) *Span.* hill(s)
Colle *It.* pass
Colline(s) *Fr.* hill(s)
Conca *It.* plain, basin
Cordillera (Cord.) *Span.* mountain range
Costa *It., Port., Span.* coast
Côte *Fr.* coast, slope, hill
Coteaux *Fr.* hills
Cuchilla *Span.* hills
Cuenca *Span.* river basin
Cu-Lao *Viet.* island

Da *Chin.* big
Da *Viet.* river
Daban *Mong.* pass
Dağ(ı) *Turk.* mountain(s)
Dāgh *Farsi* mountain
Dağları *Turk.* mountain range
-dai, -daichi *Jap.* plateau
-Dake *Jap.* mountain
-dal, -e *Dan., Swe.* valley
-dal, -en *Swe., Nor.* valley, stream
Dalay Mong. large lake
-ðalir, -ðalur *Ice.* valley
-damm, -en *Swe.* lake
Danau *Malay* lake
Dao *Chin., Viet.* island
Dar *Ar.* region
Darya *Russ.* river
Daryācheh *Farsi* marshy lake, lake
Dasht *Farsi* desert, steppe
Daung *Burm.* mountain, hill
Dayr *Ar.* monastery
Debre *Amh.* hill
Deli *Ser.-Cr.* mountain
Deniz, -i *Turk.* sea
Département (Dépt.) *Fr.* first-order administrative division
Dere *Turk.* stream
Desierto (Des.) *Span.* desert
Détroit *Fr.* strait
Dhar *Ar.* region, mountain range
Diep *Dut.* channel
Dijk *Dut.* dyke
Ding *Chin.* mountain
Dingzi *Chin.* hill, mountain
Djebel (Dj.) *Ar.* mountain
-djúp *Ice.* fjord
-djupet *Swe.* channel, sound
-Do *Jap., Kor.* island
Dolina *Russ.* valley
Dolna, Dolni *Bulg.* lower
Dolna, Dolne, Dolny *Russ.* lower
Dolní *Czec.* lower
Dolok (D.) *Malay* mountain
-dong *Kor.* village, town
Dong *Chin.* east, eastern
Donja, Donji *Ser.-Cr.* lower
-dorf *Ger.* village
-dorp *Afr.* village
-drif *Afr.* ford
-dybet *Dan.* marine channel
Dzong *Tib.* town, settlement
Dzüün *Mong.* east, eastern

-egga *Nor.* peak
-eiland, -en (eil.) *Afr., Dut.* island(s)
Eilean *Gae.* island
-elv, -a *Nor.* river
Embalse *Span.* reservoir
'Emeq *Heb.* plain, valley
Ensenada *Span.* bay
Erg *Ar.* sand desert
Estero *Span.* estuary
Estrada *Span.* bay
Estrecho *Span.* strait
Estuaire *Fr.* estuary
Estuario *Span.* estuary
Étang *Fr.* lagoon, lake
-ey, -jar *Ice.* island(s)
-ežeras *Lith.* lake
-ezers *Lat.* lake

Falaise *Fr.* cliff
-fallet *Swe.* waterfall
Farihy *Malag.* lake
Faro *Span.* lighthouse
-feld *Ger.* field
-fell *Ice.* mountain, hill
Feng *Chin.* mountain range
Fiume (F.) *It.* river
-fjäll, -en, -et *Swe.* hill(s), mountain(s), ridge
-fjärden *Swe.* fjord
Fjeld *Dan.* mountain
-fjell, -et *Nor.* mountain range
-fjord, -en *Dan., Nor., Swe.* fjord
-fjorður *Ice.* fjord, bay, inlet
Fleuve (Fl.) *Fr.* river
-flói *Ice.* bay, marshy country
Fluss (F.) *Ger.* river
Foce, Foci *It.* mouth(s)
Folyó (F.) *Hung.* river
-fonn *Nor.* glacier
-fontein *Afr.* fountain, spring
Forêt *Fr.* forest
-fors, -en *Swe.* waterfall, rapids
-foss, -en *Ice., Nor.* waterfall
Forst *Ger.* forest
Foum *Ar.* pass
Fuente *Span.* source
-furt *Ger.* ford
Fylke *Nor.* first-order administrative division

-gang *Chin.* bay, harbour
-gang *Kor.* river
Ganga *Hin., Sin.* river
Gangri *Tib.* mountain
Gaoyuan *Chin.* plateau
-gat *Dan.* sound
-Gata *Jap.* lake
-gau *Ger.* district
-Gawa *Jap.* river
Gebel (G.) *Ar.* mountain
Gebirge (Geb.) *Ger.* hills, mountains
Gezirat, Geziret *Ar.* island
Ghat *Hin.* range of hills
Ghiol *Rom.* lake
Ghubbat *Ar.* bay, inlet
Gjiri *Alb.* bay
Gjol *Alb.* lagoon, lake
Glava (Gl.) *Ser.-Cr.* mountain, peak
Glen *Gae.* valley
Gletscher (Gl.) *Ger.* glacier
Gobi *Mong.* desert
Gol *Mong.* river
Göl *Azeri, Turk.* lake
Golfe (G.) *Fr.* gulf
Golfo (G.) *It., Span.* gulf
Gölü *Turk.* lake
Gomba *Tib.* settlement
Gora, Góra *Bulg., Russ., Ser.-Cr., Pol.* mountain
Gorje *Ser.-Cr.* hills, mountains
Gorno *Russ.* mountainous
-gorod *Russ.* small town
Gory, Góry *Pol., Russ.* mountain
-grad *Bulg. Russ., Ser.-Cr.* town, city
-grada *Russ.* ridge
Gran *It., Span.* big, great
Grand, -e *Fr.* big, great
Groot (Gt.) *Afr., Dut.* big, great
Gross, -e, -en, -er *Ger.* big, great(er)
Grupo *Span.* group
Gruppo *It.* group
Guan *Chin.* pass
Guba (G.) *Russ.* bay
-Guntō *Jap.* island group
Gunong, Gunung (G.) *Indo., Malay* mountain
Gură *Rom.* passage

Hadabat *Ar.* plateau
Hadjer *Ar.* mountain
-hafen *Ger.* harbour, port
Haff *Ger.* bay, lagoon
Hai *Chin.* lake, sea
Haixia *Chin.* channel, strait
Halbinsel *Ger.* peninsula
Halvø *Dan.* peninsula
Halvøya *Nor.* peninsula
Hāmad, Hamada, Hammādah, Hammādat *Ar.* stony desert, plateau
-hamn *Swe., Nor.* harbour, anchorage
Hāmūn *Farsi* marsh, lake
-Hantō *Jap.* peninsula
Har(e) *Heb.* hill(s), mountain(s)
Hassi (Hi.) *Ar.* well
-haug *Nor.* hill
Hav, Havet *Nor., Swe.* sea
-havn *Dan., Nor.* bay, harbour
Havre *Fr.* harbour
Hawd *Ar.* oasis
Hawr *Ar.* lake, marsh
He *Chin.* river
-hegység *Hung.* hills, forest
Heide *Ger.* heath, moor
Helodranon' *Malag.* bay
Higashi *Jap.* east, eastern
-ho *Kor.* lake
-hø *Nor.* peak
Hoch *Ger.* high
Hochland *Afr.* highland
Hoek, -hoek *Afr., Dut.* cape, point
-höfn *Ice.* harbour, port
-hög, -en, -högar, -högarna *Swe.* hill(s), peak, mountain
Höhe *Ger.* height
Hohen *Ger.* high, upper
-hoi *Chin.* bay
-høj, -e *Dan.* hills
-holm, -holme, -holmen *Dan., Nor., Swe.* island
Hon *Viet.* island
Hoog *Dut.* high
Hora *Czec., Ukr.* mountain
-horn *Ger.* peak
Hory *Czec.* mountains, hills
-hot *Mong.* town
-hoved *Dan.* point, headland, peninsula
-hrad *Czec.* town
Hráun *Ice.* lava
-hsi *Chin.* river
-hsia *Chin.* gorge, strait
-hsien *Chin.* district
Hu *Chin.* lake, reservoir
Huk *Dan., Ger.* cape
-huk *Swe.* cape
Huken *Nor.* cape

Idd *Ar.* well
Idehan *Ar., Berb.* sandy plain, dunes
-ike *Jap.* lake
Île(s) (I(s).) *Fr.* island(s)
Ilha(s) (I(s).) *Port.* island(s)
imeni *Russ.* 'in the name of'
Inish *Gae.* island
Insel(n) (I.) *Ger.* island(s)
Irmak *Turk.* river
'Irq *Ar.* dunes
Isla(s) (I(s).) *Span.* island(s)
Iso *Fin.* big, great
Isol, -a, -e (I.) *It.* island(s)
Isthme *Fr.* isthmus
Istmo *Span.* isthmus
-iwa *Jap.* island

Jabal *Ar.* mountain range
Järv *Est.* lake
järvi *Fin.* lake, bay, pond
-jaur, -javre *Lapp.* lake
Jazā'ir *Ar.* islands
Jazīra, jazīrat *Ar.* island
Jazireh *Farsi* island
Jebel *Ar.* mountain
Jezero *Ser.-Cr.* lake
Jezioro *Pol.* lake
Jiang *Chin.* river
Jiao *Chin.* cape
-Jima *Jap.* island
Jøkulen *Nor.* glacier, ice cap
-joki *Fin.* river
-jökull *Ice.* glacier, ice cap
Jūras Līcis *Lat.* bay, gulf

Kaap (K.) *Afr.* cape
-kai *Jap.* bay, channel, sea
-kaikyō *Jap.* strait
-kaise *Lapp.* mountain
kalnas *Lith.* hill
Kamennyy *Russ.* stony
Kampong *Cam.* village
Kampung *Malay* village
-kanaal *Dut.* canal
Kanal *Dan.* channel, gulf
Kanal *Ger., Swe.* canal
-kanal *Ser.-Cr.* channel, canal
Kanava *Fin.* canal
Kang *Kor.* river, bay
Kap (K.) *Dan., Ger.* cape, point
-kapp *Nor.* cape, point
-kaupstaður *Ice.* market town
-kaupunki *Fin.* town
Kavīr *Farsi* salt desert
Kébir *Ar.* great
Kecil *Malay* lesser, little
Kefar *Heb.* village, hamlet
-Ken *Jap.* first-order administrative division
Kep, -i (K.) *Alb.* cape
Kepulauan (Kep.) *Indo., Malay* archipelago
Keski- *Fin.* middle, central
Khalīg, Khalīj *Ar.* gulf
-khamba *Tib.* source, spring
Khawr *Ar.* bay, channel, wadi
Khlong *Thai* river
Kho Khot *Thai* isthmus
Khōr *Farsi* bay, estuary
Khrebet *Russ.* mountain range
Kita- *Jap.* north
Klein,-e, -er *Ger.* small
-klint *Dan.* cliff
Klintar *Swe.* hills
-kloof *Afr.* gorge, pass
Knude *Dan.* point
-Ko *Jap.* lake
Ko *Thai* island
-kōchi *Jap.* mountainous region
-kōgen *Jap.* plateau
Kohi *Pash.* mountains
Kol *Kaz., Kyrg.* lake
Kólpos *Gr., Turk.* gulf, bay
Kolymskoye *Russ.* mountain range
Kompong *Malay* landing place
-kop *Afr.* hill
-kopf *Ger.* hill
-köping *Swe.* market town
Körfäzi *Azeri* gulf
Körfezi *Turk.* gulf
Kosa *Russ., Ukr.* spit
-koski *Fin.* rapids
-kraal *Afr.* native village
-kraj *Czec., Pol., Ser.-Cr.* region
Krasnyy *Russ.* red
Kryazh *Russ.* ridge, hills
Kuala *Malay* bay
-kuan *Chin.* pass
Kūh(ha) *Farsi* mountain(s)
Kul *Russ.* lake
-kulle *Swe.* hill
Kum *Russ.* sandy desert
Kumpu *Fin.* hill
Kwe *Burm.* bay, gulf
-kylä *Fin.* village
Kyst, -en *Dan., Nor.* coast
Kyun(zu) *Burm.* island(s)

La *Tib.* pass
-laagte *Afr.* watercourse

Lääni *Fin.* first-order administrative division
Lac (L.) *Fr.* lake
Lacul (L.) *Rom.* lake, lagoon
Lago (L.) *It., Port., Span.* lake, lagoon
Lagoa (L.) *Port.* lagoon
Lagos *Port., Span.* lakes
Laguna (L.) *It., Span.* lagoon, lake
Lagune (L.) *Fr.* lake
-laht *Est.* bay
Lahti *Fin.* bay, gulf, cove
Lakhti *Russ.* bay, gulf
Lam *Thai* river
Lampi *Fin.* lake
Län *Swe.* first-order administrative division
Land *Ger.* first-order administrative division
-land *Dan.* region
-land *Afr., Nor.* land, province
Lande *Fr.* heath
Laut *Indo.* sea
Law *Gae.* hill, mountain
Līcis *Lat.* gulf
Lido *It.* beach, shore
Liedao *Chin.* islands
Lilla *Swe.* small
Lille *Dan., Nor.* small
Liman *Russ.* bay, gulf
Límni (L.) *Gr.* lake
Ling *Chin.* mountain range
-linna *Fin.* fort
Llano *Span.* prairie, plain
Llyn *Welsh* lake
Loch (L.) *Gae.* lake, inlet
Lough (L.) *Gae.* lake, inlet
Lum *Alb.* river
Lund *Dan.* forest
-lund, -en *Swe.* wood(s)
-luoto *Fin.* island

-maa *Est.* island
Madīnat *Ar.* town, city
Madiq *Ar.* strait
Maja *Alb.* mountains
-mäki *Fin.* hill, hillside
Mal *Alb.* mountain
Maloye, Malyy, Malyya *Russ.* little, small
Mala, Mali, Malo *Ser.-Cr.* little, small
Malaya *Belo.* small
Malé *Czec., Slovak* small
Mali *Alb.* mountain
-man *Kor.* bay
Mar *Span.* lagoon, sea
Marais *Fr.* marsh
Mare *It.* sea
Mare *Rom.* great
Marisma *Span.* marsh
-mark *Dan., Nor.* land
Marsâ *Ar.* anchorage, bay, inlet
Masabb *Ar.* river mouth, estuary
Massif *Fr.* upland, mountains
Mato *Port.* forest
Mazar *Farsi* shrine, tomb
Meer, -meer *Afr., Dut., Ger.* lake, sea
-men *Chin.* bay, gorge, channel
Mesto *Ser.-Cr., Czec.* town
Mezzo *It.* middle
Midbar *Heb.* wilderness
Mierzeja *Pol.* spit
Mifraz *Heb.* bay
Mina *Ar.* port
Minami *Jap.* south, southern
-misaki *Jap.* cape, point
Mittel *Ger.* central, middle
-mo *Nor., Swe.* heath, island
-mon *Swe.* heath
Mong *Burm.* town
Mont(s) (Mt(s).) *Fr.* hill(s), mountain(s)
Montagna (Mt.) *It.* mountain
Montagne(s) (Mt(s).) *Fr.* hill(s), mountain(s)
Montaña(s) (Mt(s).) *Span.* mountain(s)
Montanyes *Cat.* mountains
Monte(s) (Mte(s).) *It., Port., Span.* mountain(s)
Monti (Mti.) *It.* mountains
More *Russ.* sea
Mörön *Mong.* river
Moyen *Fr.* central, middle
Muang *Malay* town
Mui *Viet.* cape
Mull *Gae.* promontory
Mund, -mund *Afr.* mouth
Munkhafed *Ar.* depression
Munte (Mte.) *Rom.* mount
Munți(i) (Mti.) *Rom.* mountain(s)
Muong *Malay* village
Myit *Burm.* river
Myitwanya *Burm.* mouths of river
Mynydd *Welsh* mountain
-myr *Nor., Swe.* swamp
-mýri *Ice.* swamp
Mys (M.) *Russ.* cape

-Nada *Jap.* bay, gulf
-næs *Dan.* point, cape
Nafūd *Ar.* sandy desert
Nagorye *Russ.* hills, mountains
Nagy *Hung.* big
Nahal (N.) *Heb.* river
Nahr (N.) *Ar.* river, stream
Najd *Ar.* plateau, pass
Nakhon *Thai* town
Nam *Kor., Viet.* river
-nam *Kor.* south
Namakzār *Per.* salt flat
Nan *Chin.* south, southern
-nao *Chin.* lake
-näs *Swe.* cape
Neder *Dut.* lower
Nedre *Nor.* lower
Nei *Chin.* inner
Nek *Afr.* pass
-nes *Ice., Nor.* cape
Ness, -ness *Gae.* promontory, cape
Nevada, Nevado *Span.* snow-capped mountain
Nez *Fr.* cape
Nieder *Ger.* lower
-niemi *Fin.* cape, point, peninsula, island
Nieuw, -e *Dut.* new
Nishi *Jap.* west, western
Nisos, Nisoi *Gr.* island(s)
Nizhneye, Nizhniy *Russ.* lower
Nizina *Belo., Pol.* lowland
Nizmennost *Russ.* plain, lowland
Nízní *Czec.* lower
Noord *Dut.* north, northern
Nord *Fr.* north, northern
Norra *Swe.* north, northern
Nørre *Dan.* north, northern
Norte *Port., Span.* north, northern
Nos *Bulg., Russ.* cape, point
Nosy *Malag.* island
Nouveau, Nouvelle *Fr.* new
Nova, Novi *Bulg., Port., Serb.-Cr.* new
Novaya, Novo, Novoye, Novyy *Russ.* new
Nové, Novy *Czec., Slovak* new
Novo *Port.* new
Nowa, Nowe, Nowy *Pol.* new
Nudo *Span.* mountain
Nueva, Nuevo *Span.* new
Nur *Chin.* lake
Nur *Tib.* peak
Nuruu *Mong.* mountain range
Nusa *Indo.* island
Nuur *Mong.* lake
Ny *Dan., Nor., Swe.* new

-ø *Dan., Nor.* island
-ö *Swe.* island,
-öar, -na *Swe.* islands
Ober *Ger., Ukr.* upper
Oblast *Russ.* administrative division
Öbor *Mong.* inner
Occidental *Fr., Span.* western
-odde *Dan., Nor.* point, peninsula, cape
Oeste *Span.* west, western
Oglat *Ar.* well
Oji *Alb.* bay
Ojo *Span.* spring
-Oki *Jap.* bay
-ön *Swe.* island
Ondör *Mong.* upper
Oost(er) *Dut.* east(ern)
Oraşu *Rom.* city
Ord *Gae.* point
Óri *Gr.* mountains
Oriental, -e *Fr., Span.* east, eastern
Órmos *Gr.* bay
Óros *Gr.* mountain(s)
Ort *Ger.* point, cape
Ost *Ger.* east
Øst(er) *Den., Nor.* east(ern)
Öst(ra) *Swe.* east(ern)
Ostriv *Ukr.* island
Ostrov(a) *Russ.* island(s)
Otok(i) *Ser.-Cr.* island(s)
Ouabi, Ouadi (O.) *Ar.* dry watercourse, wadi
Oud, -e *Dut.* old
Oued, -i (O.) *Ar.* watercourse
Ouest *Fr.* west, western
Ouzan *Farsi* river
Ova, -si *Turk.* plains, lowlands
Over- *Dan., Dut.* upper
Över-, Övre *Nor., Swe.* upper
-øy, -a *Nor.* island(s)
Oya *Hin.* point
Oya *Sin.* river
Ozero, Ozera (Oz.) *Russ., Ukr.* lake(s)

-pää *Fin.* hill(s), mountain
Pahta *Lapp.* hill
Pampa(s) *Span.* plain(s)
Pantanal *Port.* marsh
Pantano *Span.* reservoir
Pantao *Chin.* peninsula
Parbat *Urdu* mountain
Pas *Fr.* strait
Paso (P.) *Span.* pass
Passage *Fr.* channel
Passe *Fr.* channel
Passo (P.) *It.* pass
Pasul (P.) *Rom.* pass
Patam *Hin.* small village
Patna, -patnam *Hin.* small village
Pegunungan *Indo., Malay* mountain range
Pei, -pei *Chin.* north
Pélagos *Gr.* sea
Pen *Welsh* hill
Peña *Span.* rock, peak
Pendi *Chin.* basin, depression
Péninsule *Fr.* peninsula
Penisola (Pen.) *It.* peninsula
Pereval (Per.) *Russ.* pass
Pervo-, Pervyy- *Russ.* first
Pertuis *Fr.* channel, strait
Peski *Russ.* sand desert
Petit, -e *Fr.* small
Phanom *Thai* mountain
Phnum *Cam.* mountain
Phou *Lao.* mountain
Phu *Thai, Viet.* mountain
Piano *It.* plain
Pic *Cat., Fr.* peak
Pico(s) *Span.* peak(s)
-piggen *Dan.* peak
Pik *Russ.* peak
Pingyuan *Chin.* plain
Pique *Fr.* peak
Piton *Fr.* peak
Pivostriv *Ukr.* peninsula
Piz, Pizzo *It.* peak
Plage *Fr.* beach
Plaine *Fr.* plain
Planalto *Port.* plateau
Planina (Pl.) *Bulg., Ser.-Cr.* mountain range
Plato *Russ., Bulg.* plateau
Playa *Span.* beach
-po *Chin.* lake, wetland
Pointe (Pte.) *Fr.* point, cape
Pojezierze *Pol.* lakes
Polder *Dut.* reclaimed farmland
-pólis *Gr.* city, town
Poluostrov (Pov.) *Russ.* peninsula
Półwysep *Pol.* peninsula
Pont *Fr.* bridge
Ponta (Pta.) *Port.* point, cape
Ponte *Port.* bridge
Poort *Afr.* passage, gate
-poort *Dut.* port
Porta *Port.* pass
Porțile *Rom.* gate
Portillo *Span.* pass
Porto *It., Port., Span.* port
Potámi, Potamós *Gr.* river
Pradesh *Hin.* state
Praia *Port.* beach, shore
Presa *Span.* reservoir
Presqu'île *Fr.* peninsula
Prokhod *Bulg.* pass
Proliv *Russ.* strait
Promontorio *Span.* promontory
Průsmyk (Pr.) *Czec.* pass
Pueblo *Span.* village
Puerto (Pto.) *Span.* port
Puig *Cat.* peak
Pulau (P.) *Indo., Malay* island
Puna *Span.* desert plateau
Puncak *Indo.* peak
Punta (Pta.) *It., Span.* point, peak
Puy *Fr.* peak

Qal'at *Ar.* fort
Qanat *Ar.* canal
Qasr *Ar.* fort
Qiryat *Heb.* town
Qiuling *Chin.* plateau
Qolleh *Farsi* mountain
-qundao *Chin.* islands

Rach *Viet.* river
Rags *Lat.* cape
Rambla *Cat.* river
Ramlat *Ar.* sandy desert
Rão (R.) *Port.* river
Rann *Hin.* swampy region
Rao *I.-C.* river
Ras *Amh., Ar., Farsi* cape, point
Récif(s) *Fr.* reef(s)
Recife(s) *Port.* reef(s)
Reka *Bulg.* river
Repede *Rom.* rapids
Represa *Port.* reservoir
Reshteh *Farsi* mountain range
-rettō *Jap.* group of islands, chain
Ria *Port., Span.* estuary, bay
Ribeirão (R.) *Port.* river
Ribera (R.) *Span.* river bank
Rijeka *Ser.-Cr.* river
Rio (R.) *Port., Span.* river
Rivier (R.) *Afr., Dut.* river
Riviera *It.* coastal plain, coast
Rivière (R.) *Fr.* river
Roca *Span.* rock
Rocca *It.* rock, peak
Roche *Fr.* rock
Rt *Ser.-Cr.* cape, point
Rubh', Rubha *Gae.* cape, point
-rück *Ger.* ridge
Rūd *Farsi* stream, river
Rudohorie *Slovak* mountains
Rzeka (R.) *Pol.* river

-saar *Est.* island
-saari *Fin.* island
Sabkhat, Sabkhet *Ar.* salt flats
Sadd *Ar.* dam
Sagar,-a *Hin., Urdu* lake
Sahrâ *Ar.* desert
-Saki *Jap.* cape, point
Salar *Span.* salt flat
Salina(s) *Span.* salt marsh(es)
-salmi *Fin.* strait, sound, lake, channel
Saltsjöbad *Swe.* resort
-Sammyaku *Jap.* mountain range
Samut *Thai* gulf
San (S.) *It., Port., Span.* saint
-San *Jap., Kor.* hill, mountain
-Sanchi *Jap.* mountain range
Sankt (St.) *Ger., Russ.* saint
-sanmaek *Kor.* mountain range
-sanmyaku *Jap.* mountain range
Santa (Sta.) *It., Port., Span.* saint
Santo (Sto.) *It. Port., Span.* saint
São (S.) *Port.* saint
Sarīr *Ar.* desert
Sasso *It.* mountain
Satu *Rom.* village
Saurums *Lat.* strait
Sebkha, Sebkhet *Ar.* salt flat
See, -see *Ger.* lake
-şehir *Turk.* town
Selat *Indo., Malay* strait
Selatan *Indo.* southern
-selkä *Fin.* bay, lake, ridge, hills
Selo *Ser.-Cr., Russ.* village
Selva *Port., Span.* forest, wood
Seno *Span.* bay, sound
Serir *Ar.* stony desert
Serra (Sa.) *Cat., Port.* range of hills
Serranía *Span.* mountain ridge
Severo, Severnaya, Severnoye, Severnyy (Sev.) *Russ.* north, northern
Sfântu *Rom.* saint
Shahr, -shahr *Farsi* city, town
Shamo *Chin.* desert
Shan *Chin.* hills, mountains
Shankou *Chin.* pass
Shanmo *Chin.* mountain range
Sharm *Ar.* bay
Shatt *Ar.* river mouth, estuary
-Shima *Jap.* island
Shimāli *Ar.* northern
-Shotō *Jap.* group of islands
-shui *Chin.* river
-shuiku *Chin.* reservoir
Sierra (Sa.) *Span.* mountain range
-sjö, -sjön, -sjø *Swe., Nor.* lake
-sjøen *Dan.* sea
-sjór *Ice.* lake
-sker *Ice.* island
-skär *Swe.* island, rock, cape
-skog, -skogen *Nor., Swe.* wood(s)
-skov *Dan.* forest
Slieve *Gae.* hill, mountain
Sø *Dan., Nor.* lake
Söder, Södra *Swe.* south, southern
Sør *Nor.* south, southern
Solonchak *Russ.* salt lake, marsh
Sønder, Søndra *Dan.* south, southern
Song *Viet.* river
Souk *Ar.* market
-spitze *Ger.* peak, mountain
-spruit *Afr.* stream
Sredna, Sredno *Bulg.* middle, central
Sredne, Sredneye *Russ.* middle, central
Srednja *Ser.-Cr.* middle, central
-stad *Afr., Nor., Swe.* town
-stadt *Ger.* town
-staður *Ice.* town
Stara, Stari *Ser.-Cr.* old
Stará, Staré, Stary *Czec.* old
Staraya, Staroye, Staryy *Russ.* old
Stare, Staro, Stary *Ukr.* old
Stausee *Ger.* reservoir
Stenón *Gr.* strait, pass
Step *Russ.* steppe
Stor, -a *Swe.* big
Store *Dan.* big
-strand *Dan., Ger., Nor., Swe.* beach
-strede *Nor.* straits
Strelka *Russ.* spit
-strete *Nor.* straits
Stretto (Str.) *It.* strait
Strædet (Str.) *Dan.* strait
-ström, -strömmen *Swe.* stream(s)
-stroom *Afr.* large river
Sud *Fr.* south, southern
Süd, -er *Ger.* south, southern
Suid *Afr.* south, southern
-Suidō *Jap.* strait, channel
Sul *Port.* south, southern
Sûn *Burm.* cape
-sund, -et *Swe., Nor.* sound, estuary, inlet
Sungai *Indo., Malay* river
Sur *Span.* south, southern
Sveti *Bulg.* saint
Syd *Dan., Swe.* south, southern
Sýsla *Ice.* first-order administrative division

-tag *Uighur* mountain
Tai -tai *Chin.* tower
-Take *Jap.* mountain
Tal *Mong.* plain, steppe
-tal *Ger.* valley
Tall *Ar.* hills
Tanjona *Malag.* cape, point
Tanjung, Tanjong (Tg.) *Indo., Malay.* cape, point
Tao *Chin.* island
Tasik *Malay* lake
Tassili *Ar.* rocky plateau
Tau *Russ.* mountain range
Taung *Burm.* mountain
Taungdan. *Burm.* mountain range
Taunggya *Burm.* pass
-tekojärvi *Fin.* reservoir
Teluk *Indo., Malay* bay, gulf
Ténéré *Berb.* desert
Tengah *Indo.* middle, central
-thal *Ger.* valley
Thok *Tib.* town
Tien *Chin.* lake, marsh
Tierra *Span.* land, country
Timur *Indo.* eastern
-tind *Nor.* peak
-ting *Chin.* mountain
Tjärn, -en, -et *Swe.* lake
-Tō *Jap.* island
Tong *Kor.* village, town
Tong *Burm., Thai, Kor.* mountain range
Tonlé *Cam.* lake
Top *Dut.* peak
-topp, -en *Nor.* peak
-träsk *Swe.* lake, swamp
Tsangpo *Tib.* large river
Tso *Tib.* lake
Tsu *Jap.* entrance, bay
Tsui *Chin.* cape, point
Tulur *Ar.* hill
-tunturi *Fin.* hill(s), mountain(s), ridge

Uad *Ar.* dry watercourse, wadi
Über *Ger.* upper
-udde, -udden *Swe.* point, cape
Uebi *Som.* river
Ujung *Indo., Malay* cape
Unter- *Ger.* lower
Us *Mong.* water
Ust, Ustye *Russ.* river mouth
Utara *Indo.* north, northern
Uttar *Hin.* north, northern
Uul *Mong., Russ.* mountain range

-vaara *Fin.* hill, mountain ridge, peak
Vaart *Dut.* canal
-våg *Nor.* bay
Val *Fr., Port., Span.* valley
Valea *Rom.* valley
-vall, -en *Swe.* mountain
Valle *It., Span.* valley
Vallée *Fr.* valley
Valli *It.* lake, lagoon
-város *Hung.* town
-varre *Nor.* mountain
Väst, Västra *Swe.* west, western
-vatn *Ice., Nor.* lake
-vatnet *Nor.* lake
-vatten, vattnet *Swe.* lake
-vecchio *It.* old
Vechi *Rom.* old
-ved, -veden *Swe.* hills
Veld, -veld *Afr.* field
Velha, Velho *Port.* old
Velika, Velike, Veliki, Veliko *Ser.-Cr., Slov.* big, large
Velikaya, Velikiy *Russ.* big, large
Velká, Velké, Velký *Czec.* big, large
Verkhne, Verkhniy *Russ.* upper
-vesi *Fin.* water, lake, bay, sound, strait
Vest, Vester, Vestre *Dan., Nor.* west, western
-vidda *Nor.* plateau
Vieille, Vieux *Fr.* old
Vieja, Vejo *Span.* old
Vig *Dan.* bay, inlet, cove, lagoon, lake
-vik *Ice.* bay
-vik, -a, -en *Nor., Swe.* bay, gulf, inlet, lake
Vila *Port.* small town
Villa *Span.* town
Ville *Fr.* town
Vinh *Viet.* bay
Vîrful (Vf.) *Rom.* peak, mountain
-viz *Hung.* river
-víztároló *Hung.* reservoir
-vlei *Afr.* lake, salt pan
-vliet *Dut.* canal
-vloer *Afr.* salt pan
Vodokhranilishche (Vdkhr.) *Russ.* reservoir
Vodoskovyshche (Vdskh.) *Ukr.* reservoir
Volcán (Vol.) *Span.* volcano, mountain
Vorota *Russ.* pass, channel, strait
Vostochno, Vostochnyy *Russ.* east, eastern
-vötn *Ice.* lakes
Vozvyshennost *Russ.* heights, uplands
Vozyera *Belo.* lake
Vrata *Bulg.* gate, pass
Vrchovina *Czec.* mountainous country
Vrch(y) *Czec.* mountain (range)
Vung *Viet.* bay, gulf
-vuori *Fin.* mountain, hill
Vychodné *Slovak* east, eastern
Vysochyna *Ukr.* upland

-waard *Dut.* polder
Wadi (W.) *Ar.* dry watercourse
Wâhât *Ar.* oasis
Wald *Ger.* forest, mountains
-Wan *Chin., Jap.* bay, harbour
Wāw *Ar.* well
Webi *Amh.* river
Wes *Afr.* west, western
Wielka, Wielki, Wielko *Pol.* big, large
Woestyn *Afr.* desert
Wysoka, Wysoki *Pol.* upper
Wyżyna *Pol.* plateau

Xi *Chin.* river
Xia *Chin.* gorge, strait
Xiao *Chin.* small

Yam *Heb.* sea
-Yama *Jap.* mountain
-yan *Chin.* gorge, island
Yang *Chin.* bay, sea, sound
Yangi *Russ.* new
Yazovir *Bulg.* reservoir
Yeni *Turk.* new
Yli *Fin.* upper
Ynys *Welsh* island
Yoma *Burm.* mountain range
Ytre-, Ytter- *Nor., Swe.* outer
-yuan *Chin.* stream
Yugo- *Ser.-Cr.* south, southern
Yunhe *Chin.* canal
Yuzhni, Yuzhno *Russ.* south, southern

-Zaki *Jap.* point
Zalew *Pol.* lagoon, swamp
Zaliv *Russ.* bay, gulf
-Zan *Jap.* mountain
Zangbo *Tib.* stream, river
Zapadnaya, Zapadno, Zapadnyi (Zap.) *Russ.* west, western
Zatoka *Pol., Ukr.* bay, gulf
-zee *Dut.* lake, sea
Zemlya *Russ.* land, island(s)
Zhang *Chin.* mountain
-zhou *Chin.* island
Zhong *Chin.* middle, central
Zhou *Chin.* island
Zizhiqu *Chin.* autonomous region
Zuid, Zuider *Dut.* south, southern

INDEX TO WORLD MAPS

340 A 'Âli an Nîl INDEX

A

A 'Âli an Nîl = Upper Nile □ South Sudan 9°30N 33°0E 257 F3
A Baña Spain 42°58N 8°46W 194 C2
A Cañiza Spain 42°13N 8°16W 194 C2
A Coruña Spain 43°20N 8°25W 194 B2
A Coruña □ Spain 43°10N 8°30W 194 B2
A Cruz do Incio Spain 42°39N 7°21W 194 C3
A Estrada Spain 42°43N 8°27W 194 C2
A Fonsagrada Spain 43°8N 7°4W 194 B3
A Guarda Spain 41°56N 8°52W 194 D2
A Gudiña Spain 42°4N 7°8W 194 C3
A Pobre Spain 42°58N 7°3W 194 C3
A Ramallosa Spain 42°45N 8°30W 194 C2
A Rúa Spain 42°24N 7°6W 194 C3
A Serra de Outes Spain 42°52N 8°55W 194 C2
A Shau Vietnam 16°6N 107°22E 236 D6
Aabenraa Denmark 55°3N 9°25E 163 J3
Aabybro Denmark 57°10N 9°44E 163 G3
Aachen Germany 50°45N 6°6E 178 E2
Aalām Iraq 33°19N 44°23E 113 B2
Aalborg Denmark 57°2N 9°54E 163 G3
Aalborg Bugt Denmark 56°50N 10°35E 163 H4
Aalen Germany 48°51N 10°6E 179 G6
Aalestrup Denmark 56°42N 9°29E 163 H3
Aalsmeer Neths. 52°16N 4°46E 112 B1
Aalst Belgium 50°56N 4°2E 170 D4
Aalten Neths. 51°56N 6°35E 170 C6
Aalter Belgium 51°5N 3°28E 170 C3
Äänekoski Finland 62°36N 25°44E 160 E21
Aarau Switz. 47°23N 8°4E 179 H4
Aarberg Switz. 47°2N 7°16E 179 H3
Aare → Switz. 47°33N 8°14E 179 H4
Aargau □ Switz. 47°26N 8°10E 179 H4
Aarhus = Århus Denmark 56°8N 10°11E 163 H4
Aarlen = Arlon Belgium 49°42N 5°49E 170 E5
Aars Denmark 56°48N 9°30E 163 H3
Aarschot Belgium 50°59N 4°49E 170 D4
Aasiaat Greenland 68°43N 52°56W 154 D5
Ab-i-Istada Afghan. 32°29N 67°55E 240 B3
Ab-i-Panja = Pyandzh → Asia 37°6N 68°20E 240 A2
Aba Sichuan, China 32°59N 101°42E 228 A3
Aba Dem. Rep. of the Congo 3°58N 30°17E 268 B3
Aba Nigeria 5°10N 7°19E 263 D6
Âbâ, Jazîrat Sudan 13°30N 32°31E 257 E3
Abacaxis → Brazil 3°54S 58°47W 329 D6
Abaco I. Bahamas 26°25N 77°10W 320 A4
Abadab, J. Sudan 18°54N 35°56E 256 D4
Ābādān Iran 30°22N 48°20E 247 D6
Abade Ethiopia 9°22N 38°3E 257 F4
Ābādeh Iran 31°8N 52°40E 247 D7
Abadín Spain 43°21N 7°29W 194 B3
Abadla Algeria 31°2N 2°45W 261 B4
Abaeté Brazil 19°9S 45°27W 333 E2
Abaeté → Brazil 18°2S 45°12W 333 E2
Abaetetuba Brazil 1°40S 48°50W 332 B2
Abagnar Qi = Xilinhot China 43°52N 116°2E 226 C9
Abah, Tanjung Indonesia 8°46S 115°38E 231 K18
Abai Paraguay 25°58S 55°54W 335 B4
Abakaliki Nigeria 6°22N 8°2E 263 D6
Abakan Russia 53°40N 91°10E 217 B12
Abala Congo 1°17S 15°35E 264 C3
Abala Niger 14°56N 3°22E 263 C5
Abalak Niger 15°22N 6°21E 263 B6
Abalemma Algeria 20°51N 5°59E 261 D6
Abalemma Niger 16°12N 7°50E 263 B6
Abalessa Algeria 22°58N 4°47E 261 D5
Abana Turkey 41°59N 34°1E 212 B6
Abancay Peru 13°35S 72°55W 330 C3
Abang, Gunung Indonesia 8°16S 115°25E 231 J18
Abanga → Gabon 0°20S 10°30E 264 C2
Abano Terme Italy 45°22N 11°46E 199 C8
Abapó Bolivia 18°48S 63°25W 331 D5
Abarán Spain 38°12N 1°23W 197 G3
Abariringa Kiribati 2°50S 171°40W 277 A16
Abarqū Iran 31°10N 53°20E 247 D7
Abasha Georgia 42°11N 42°13E 191 J6
Abashiri Japan 44°0N 144°15E 220 B12
Abashiri-Wan Japan 44°0N 144°30E 220 C12
Abau Papua N. G. 10°11S 148°46E 286 F5
Abaújszántó Hungary 48°16N 21°12E 182 B6
Abava → Latvia 57°6N 21°54E 184 A8
Ābay = Nîl el Azraq → Sudan 15°38N 32°31E 257 D3
Abay Kazakhstan 49°38N 72°53E 217 C8
Abaya, L. Ethiopia 6°30N 37°50E 257 F4
Abaza Russia 52°39N 90°6E 217 B12
Abba C.A.R. 5°20N 15°11E 264 A3
Abbadia di Fiastra ⌂ Italy 43°12N 13°24E 199 E10
Abbadia San Salvatore Italy 42°53N 11°41E 199 F8
'Abbāsābād Iran 33°34N 58°23E 247 C8
Abbay = Nîl el Azraq → Sudan 15°38N 32°31E 257 D3
Abbaye, Pt. U.S.A. 46°58N 88°8W 308 B9
Abbazia = Opatija Croatia 45°21N 14°17E 199 C11
Abbé, L. Ethiopia 11°8N 41°47E 257 E5
Abbeville Somme, France 50°6N 1°49E 173 B8
Abbeville Ala., U.S.A. 31°34N 85°15W 316 D4
Abbeville Ga., U.S.A. 31°59N 83°18W 316 D6
Abbeville La., U.S.A. 29°58N 92°8W 314 G8
Abbeville S.C., U.S.A. 34°11N 82°23W 316 A7
Abbey Wood U.K. 51°29N 0°7E 125 B4
Abbeyfeale Ireland 52°23N 9°18W 166 D2
Abbiategrasso Italy 45°24N 8°54E 198 C5
Abbot Ice Shelf Antarctica 73°0S 92°0W 151 D16
Abbotsford Canada 49°5N 122°20W 296 D4
Abbottabad Pakistan 34°10N 73°15E 242 B5
Abbou, O. ben → Algeria 28°32N 5°14E 261 C5
ABC Islands W. Indies 12°15N 69°0W 321 D6
Abcoude Neths. 52°17N 4°59E 112 B2
Abd al Kūrī Yemen 12°5N 52°20E 249 D6
Ābdānān Iran 32°56N 47°28E 213 F12
Ābdar Iran 30°16N 55°19E 247 D7
Âbdin Egypt 30°2N 31°14E 117 A2
'Abdolābād Iran 34°12N 56°30E 247 C8
Abdulino Russia 53°42N 53°40E 216 B4
Abdullah South Sudan 5°30N 29°55E 257 F3
Abdulpur Bangla. 24°15N 88°59E 241 C2
Abéché Chad 13°50N 20°35E 259 F4
Abejar Spain 41°48N 2°47W 196 D2
Abekr Sudan 12°45N 28°50E 257 E2
Abel Tasman △ N.Z. 40°59S 173°3E 285 A8
Abengourou Ivory C. 6°42N 3°27W 262 D4
Abeno Japan 34°38N 135°31E 133 B2
Abenójar Spain 38°53N 4°21W 195 G6
Åbenrå = Aabenraa Denmark 55°3N 9°25E 163 J3
Abensberg Germany 48°48N 11°51E 179 G7
Abeokuta Nigeria 7°3N 3°19E 263 D5
Aberaeron U.K. 52°15N 4°15W 169 E3
Aberayron = Aberaeron U.K. 52°15N 4°15W 169 E3
Aberchirder U.K. 57°34N 2°37W 167 D6
Abercorn = Mbala Zambia 8°46S 31°24E 269 D3
Abercorn Australia 25°12S 151°5E 281 D5
Abercrombie River △ Australia 34°5S 149°40E 283 C8
Aberdare U.K. 51°43N 3°27W 169 F4
Aberdare △ Kenya 0°22S 36°44E 268 C4
Aberdare Ra. Kenya 0°15S 36°50E 268 C4
Aberdeen N.S.W., Australia 32°9S 150°56E 283 B9
Aberdeen Sask., Canada 52°20N 106°8W 297 C7
Aberdeen Hong Kong, China 22°14N 114°8E 122 B1
Aberdeen Eastern Cape, S. Africa 32°28S 24°2E 270 D3
Aberdeen C. of Aberd., U.K. 57°9N 2°5W 167 D6
Aberdeen Idaho, U.S.A. 42°57N 112°50W 304 E7
Aberdeen Md., U.S.A. 39°31N 76°10W 309 F15
Aberdeen Miss., U.S.A. 33°49N 88°33W 315 E10
Aberdeen Ohio, U.S.A. 38°39N 83°46W 311 F13
Aberdeen S. Dak., U.S.A. 45°28N 98°29W 308 C4
Aberdeen Wash., U.S.A. 46°59N 123°50W 306 D3
Aberdeen, City of □ U.K. 57°10N 2°10W 167 D6
Aberdeen L. Canada 64°30N 99°0W 294 E12
Aberdeenshire □ U.K. 57°17N 2°36W 167 D6
Aberdour U.K. 56°3N 3°18W 121 A2
Aberdour Castle U.K. 56°3N 3°18W 121 A2
Aberdovey = Aberdyfi U.K. 52°33N 4°3W 169 E3
Aberdyfi U.K. 52°33N 4°3W 169 E3
Aberfeldy U.K. 56°37N 3°51W 167 E5
Aberfoyle U.K. 56°11N 4°23W 167 E4
Abergavenny U.K. 51°49N 3°1W 169 F4
Abergele U.K. 53°17N 3°35W 168 D4
Abernathy U.S.A. 33°50N 101°51W 314 E4
Abert, L. U.S.A. 42°38N 120°14W 304 E3
Aberystwyth U.K. 52°25N 4°5W 169 E3
Abfanggraben → Germany 48°10N 11°41E 131 A3
Abhā Si. Arabia 18°0N 42°34E 248 C3
Abhar Iran 36°9N 49°13E 213 D13
Abhayapuri India 26°24N 90°38E 241 B3
Abia □ Nigeria 5°30N 7°35E 263 D6
Abide Turkey 38°55N 29°20E 205 C11
Abidiya Sudan 18°18N 34°3E 256 D3
Abidjan Ivory C. 5°26N 3°58W 262 D4
Abilene Kans., U.S.A. 38°55N 97°13W 308 F5
Abilene Tex., U.S.A. 32°28N 99°43W 314 E5
Abingdon Oxon., U.K. 51°40N 1°17W 169 F6
Abingdon Ill., U.S.A. 40°48N 90°24W 310 D6
Abingdon Va., U.S.A. 36°43N 81°59W 309 G13
Abingdon, I. = Pinta, I. Ecuador 0°35N 90°44W 330 a
Abington Reef Australia 18°0S 149°35E 280 B4
Abiod, Remel el Tunisia 31°45N 9°35E 261 B6
Abitau → Canada 59°53N 109°3W 297 B7
Abitibi → Canada 51°3N 80°55W 298 B3
Abitibi, L. Canada 48°40N 79°40W 298 C4
Abiy Adi Ethiopia 13°39N 39°3E 257 E4
Abiyata, L. Ethiopia 7°37N 38°36E 266 C4
Abiyata-Shala △ Ethiopia 7°40N 38°37E 257 F4
Abkhaz Republic = Abkhazia □ Georgia 43°12N 41°5E 191 J5
Abkhazia □ Georgia 43°12N 41°5E 191 J5
Ablon-sur-Seine France 48°43N 2°25E 134 B3
Abminga Australia 26°8S 134°51E 281 D1
Abnûb Egypt 27°18N 31°4E 256 B3
Åbo = Turku Finland 60°30N 22°19E 188 B2
Abo, Massif d' Chad 21°41N 16°8E 259 D3
Abohar India 30°10N 74°10E 242 D6
Aboisso Ivory C. 5°30N 3°5W 262 D4
Abolo Congo 0°8N 14°16E 264 B2
Abomey Benin 7°10N 2°5E 263 D5
Abong-Mbang Cameroon 4°0N 13°8E 264 B2
Abongabong Indonesia 4°15N 96°48E 234 B1
Abonnema Nigeria 4°41N 6°49E 263 E6
Abony Hungary 47°12N 20°3E 182 C5
Abor Hills India 28°25N 94°46E 241 A5
Aborlan Phil. 9°26N 118°33E 233 G2
Aboso Ghana 5°23N 1°57W 262 D4
Abou-Deïa Chad 11°20N 19°20E 259 F3
Abou-Goulem Chad 13°37N 21°38E 259 F4
Abou-Telfan ⌂ Chad 12°2N 18°58E 259 F3
Abovian Armenia 40°16N 44°37E 191 K7
Aboyne U.K. 57°4N 2°47W 167 D6
Abra □ Phil. 17°35N 120°45E 232 C3
Abra de Ilog Phil. 13°27N 120°44E 232 E3
Abra Pampa Argentina 22°43S 65°42W 334 A2
Abraham L. Canada 52°15N 116°35W 296 C5
Abramtsevo Russia 55°49N 37°49E 129 B4
Abrantes Portugal 39°24N 8°7W 195 F2
Abreojos, Pta. Mexico 26°50N 113°40W 318 B2
Abri Esh Shamâliya, Sudan 20°50N 30°27E 256 C3
Abri Janub Kordofân, Sudan 11°40N 30°21E 257 E3
Abrolhos, Banco dos Brazil 18°0S 38°0W 333 E4
Abrud Romania 46°19N 23°5E 182 D8
Abruzzo □ Italy 42°15N 14°0E 199 F10
Absaroka Range U.S.A. 44°45N 109°50W 304 D9
Abtenau Austria 47°33N 13°21E 180 D6
Abu India 24°41N 72°50E 242 G5
Abū aḍ Ḍuhūr Syria 35°44N 37°2E 250 C8
Abū al Abyad U.A.E. 24°11N 53°50E 247 E7
Abū al Khaşīb Iraq 30°25N 48°0E 246 D5
Abū 'Alī Si. Arabia 27°20N 49°27E 247 E6
Abū 'Alī → Lebanon 34°25N 35°50E 250 D6
Abū 'Arīsh Si. Arabia 16°53N 42°48E 248 C3
Abu 'Aweigîla Egypt 30°50N 34°7E 251 H5
Abû Ballas Egypt 24°26N 27°36E 256 C2
Abu Deleiq Sudan 15°57N 33°48E 257 D3
Abu Dhabi = Abū Ẓāby U.A.E. 24°28N 54°22E 247 E7
Abû Dis Sudan 19°12N 33°38E 256 D3
Abu Dis West Bank 31°46N 35°16E 123 B2
Abu Dom Sudan 16°18N 32°25E 257 D3
Abū Du'ān Syria 36°25N 38°15E 213 D8
Abu el Gaîn, W. → Egypt 29°35N 33°30E 251 J4
Abû en Numrus Egypt 29°57N 31°12E 117 B2
Abu Fatma, Ras Sudan 22°25N 36°25E 256 C4
Abû Gabra Sudan 11°2N 26°50E 257 E2
Abu Ga'da, W. → Egypt 29°15N 32°53E 251 J3
Abu Gelba Sudan 13°11N 31°52E 257 E3
Abu Ghosh Israel 31°48N 35°6E 123 B1
Abu Gubeiha Sudan 11°30N 31°15E 257 E3
Abu Habl, Khawr → Sudan 12°37N 31°0E 257 E3
Abū Ḩadrīyah Si. Arabia 27°20N 48°58E 247 E6
Abu Hamed Sudan 19°32N 33°13E 256 D3
Abû Haraz An Nîl el Azraq, Sudan 18°1N 33°58E 256 D3
Abu Haraz El Gezira, Sudan 14°35N 33°30E 257 E3
Abû Haraz Esh Shamâliya, Sudan 19°8N 32°18E 256 D3
Abû Higar Sudan 12°50N 33°59E 257 E3
Abū Kamāl Syria 34°30N 41°0E 213 E9
Abu Kebîr Egypt 30°43N 31°40E 251 H2
Abu Kuleiwat Sudan 12°20N 26°0E 257 E2
Abū Madd, Ra's Si. Arabia 24°50N 37°7E 246 E3
Abu Matariq Sudan 10°59N 26°9E 257 E2
Abu Mendi Ethiopia 11°48N 35°42E 257 E4
Abū Mūsā U.A.E. 25°52N 55°3E 247 E7
Abū Qaşr Si. Arabia 30°21N 38°34E 246 D3
Abu Qireiya Egypt 24°5N 35°28E 256 C4
Abu Qurqâs Egypt 28°1N 30°44E 256 B3
Abū Raşāş, Ra's Oman 20°10N 58°38E 249 B7
Abu Rudeis Egypt 28°54N 33°11E 251 K4
Abu Shagara, Ras Sudan 21°4N 37°19E 256 C4
Abû Shanab Janub Kordofân, Sudan 10°47N 29°32E 266 B2
Abû Shanab Shamâl Kordofân, Sudan 13°58N 27°49E 257 E2
Abu Simbel Egypt 22°18N 31°40E 256 C3
Abū Şukhayr Iraq 31°54N 44°30E 213 G11
Abu Sultân Egypt 30°24N 32°21E 256 H8
Abu Tabari Sudan 17°32N 28°32E 256 D2
Abu Tig Egypt 27°4N 31°15E 256 B3
Abu Tiga Sudan 12°47N 34°12E 257 E3
Abu Tineitin Sudan 14°24N 31°1E 257 E3
Abû Uruq Sudan 15°52N 30°25E 257 D3
Abû Zabad Sudan 12°25N 29°10E 257 E2
Abū Ẓāby U.A.E. 24°28N 54°22E 247 E7
Abū Zeydābād Iran 33°54N 51°45E 247 C6
Abufari Brazil 5°25S 62°59W 331 B5
Abuja Nigeria 9°5N 7°32E 263 D6
Abukuma-Gawa → Japan 38°6N 140°52E 220 E10
Abukuma-Sammyaku Japan 37°30N 140°45E 220 F10
Abulug Phil. 18°27N 121°27E 232 B3
Abumombazi Dem. Rep. of the Congo 3°42N 22°10E 264 B4
Abunã Brazil 9°40S 65°20W 331 B4
Abunã → Brazil 9°41S 65°20W 331 B4
Abune Yosef Ethiopia 12°5N 39°12E 257 E4
Aburatsu Japan 31°34N 131°24E 222 F3
Aburo Dem. Rep. of the Congo 2°4N 30°53E 268 B3
Abut Hd. N.Z. 43°7S 170°15E 285 D5
Abuye Meda Ethiopia 10°30N 39°49E 257 E4
Abuyog Phil. 10°45N 125°0E 233 F5
Abwong South Sudan 9°2N 32°14E 257 F3
Åby Sweden 58°40N 16°10E 163 F10
Aby, Lagune Ivory C. 5°15N 3°14W 262 D4
Abyad Sudan 13°47N 26°24E 257 E2
Abyei Sudan 9°36N 28°26E 257 F2
Abyei □ Sudan 9°36N 28°26E 257 F2
Ābyek Iran 36°4N 50°33E 247 B6
Acacías Colombia 3°59N 73°46W 328 C3
Acacias Madrid, Spain 127 c2
Academy Gletscher Greenland 82°2N 34°0W 154 A7
Acadia △ U.S.A. 44°20N 68°13W 309 C19
Açailandia Brazil 5°0S 47°30W 332 C2
Acajutla El Salv. 13°36N 89°50W 320 D2
Acámbaro Mexico 20°2N 100°44W 318 D4
Acandí Colombia 8°32N 77°14W 328 B2
Acanthus Greece 40°27N 23°47E 202 F7
Acaponeta Mexico 22°30N 105°22W 318 C3
Acapulco Mexico 16°51N 99°55W 319 D5
Acapulco Trench Pac. Oc. 12°0N 88°0W 320 D2
Acará Brazil 1°57S 48°11W 332 B2
Acaraí, Serra Brazil 1°50N 57°50W 329 C6
Acaraú Brazil 2°53S 40°7W 332 B3
Acari Brazil 6°31S 36°38W 332 C4
Acarí Peru 15°25S 74°36W 330 D3
Acarigua Venezuela 9°33N 69°12W 328 B4
Acassuso Argentina 34°29S 58°30W 117 A2
Acatlán Mexico 18°12N 98°3W 319 D5
Acayucán Mexico 17°57N 94°55W 319 D6
Accéglio Italy 44°28N 7°0E 198 D4
Accomac U.S.A. 37°43N 75°40W 309 G16
Accotink, L. U.S.A. 38°47N 77°13W 143 C2
Accotink Cr. → U.S.A. 38°51N 77°15W 143 B2
Accous France 43°0N 0°36W 174 E3
Accra Ghana 5°35N 0°6W 263 D4
Accrington U.K. 53°45N 2°22W 168 D5
Acebal Argentina 33°20S 60°50W 334 C3
Aceh □ Indonesia 4°15N 97°30E 234 B1
Acerra Italy 40°57N 14°22E 201 B7
Aceuchal Spain 38°39N 6°30W 195 G4
Achacachi Bolivia 16°3S 68°43W 330 D4
Achaguas Venezuela 7°46N 68°14W 328 B4
Achaia □ Greece 38°5N 21°45E 204 C3
Achalpur India 21°22N 77°32E 244 D3
Achao Chile 42°28S 73°30W 336 B2
Acharnes Greece 38°5N 23°44E 204 C5
Achegour Niger 19°10N 11°54E 259 E2
Acheloos → Greece 38°19N 21°7E 204 C3
Achelouma Niger 22°12N 12°50E 259 D2
Achelouma, Enneri → Niger 21°55N 13°35E 259 D2
Acheng China 45°30N 126°58E 227 B14
Achenkirch Austria 47°32N 11°45E 180 D4
Achénouma Niger 19°7N 12°55E 259 E2
Achensee Austria 47°26N 11°45E 180 D4
Achentrias Greece 34°59N 25°13E 205 G7
Acher India 23°10N 72°32E 242 H5
Achères France 48°57N 2°3E 134 A1
Achern Germany 48°37N 8°4E 179 G4
Acheron → N.Z. 42°16S 173°4E 285 C8
Achill Hd. Ireland 53°58N 10°15W 166 C1
Achill I. Ireland 53°58N 10°1W 166 C1
Achim Germany 53°1N 9°3E 178 B5
Achinsk Russia 56°20N 90°20E 215 D10
Achladokambos Greece 37°31N 22°35E 204 D4
Achouka Gabon 0°52S 9°45E 264 C2
Acıgöl Turkey 37°50N 29°50E 205 D11
Acília Italy 41°47N 12°21E 136 C1
Acıpayam Turkey 37°26N 29°22E 205 D11
Acireale Italy 37°37N 15°10E 201 E8
Ackerman U.S.A. 33°19N 89°11W 315 E10
Ackley U.S.A. 42°33N 93°3W 310 B3
Acklins I. Bahamas 22°30N 74°0W 321 B5
Aclimação Brazil 23°34S 46°37W 137 B2
Acme Alta., Canada 51°33N 113°30W 296 C6
Acme Pa., U.S.A. 40°8N 79°26W 312 F5
Acobamba Peru 12°52S 74°35W 330 C3
Acomayo Peru 13°55S 71°38W 330 C3
Aconcagua, Cerro Argentina 32°39S 70°0W 334 C2
Aconquija, Mt. Argentina 27°0S 66°0W 334 B2
Acopiara Brazil 6°6S 39°27W 332 C4
Açores, Is. dos Atl. Oc. 38°0N 27°0W 153 d1
Acorizal Brazil 15°12S 56°22W 331 D6
Acornhoek S. Africa 24°37S 31°2E 271 B5
Acoua Mayotte 12°43S 45°4E 272 b
Acquapendente Italy 42°44N 11°52E 199 F8
Acquasanta Terme Italy 42°46N 13°24E 199 F10
Acquasparta Italy 42°41N 12°33E 199 F9
Acquaviva delle Fonti Italy 40°54N 16°50E 201 B9
Ácqui Terme Italy 44°41N 8°28E 198 D5
Acraman, L. Australia 32°2S 135°23E 281 E2
Acre = 'Akko Israel 32°55N 35°4E 250 F6
Acre □ Brazil 9°1S 71°0W 330 B3
Acre → Brazil 8°45S 67°22W 330 B4
Acri Italy 39°29N 16°23E 201 C9
Acropolis Athens, Greece 112 c2
Acs Hungary 47°42N 18°2E 182 C3
Actæon Mt. St. Helena 15°58S 5°42W 153 h
Actéon, Groupe French Polynesia 21°20S 136°30W 289 f
Actinolite Canada 44°32N 77°19W 312 B7
Actium Greece 38°57N 20°45E 207 B2
Acton Ont., Canada 43°38N 80°3W 312 C4
Acton London, U.K. 51°30N 0°16W 125 A2
Açu Brazil 5°34S 36°54W 332 C4
Açúcar, Pão de Brazil 22°56S 43°9W 135 B2
Acul = Vidin Bulgaria 43°59N 22°50E 202 C6
Acworth U.S.A. 34°4N 84°41W 316 A5
Ad Dafinah Si. Arabia 23°18N 41°58E 248 B3
Aḍ Ḍafrah U.A.E. 23°30N 54°30E 249 B6
Ad Daghghāran Iraq 32°8N 44°55E 213 G11
Ad Dahnā Si. Arabia 24°30N 48°10E 249 A5
Aḍ Ḍālī' Yemen 13°42N 44°44E 248 D4
Ad Dammām Si. Arabia 26°20N 50°5E 247 E6
Ad Dāmūr Lebanon 33°43N 35°27E 250 E6
Ad Darb Si. Arabia 18°2N 43°7E 248 C3
Ad Dawādimī Si. Arabia 24°35N 44°15E 246 E5
Ad Dawḩah Qatar 25°15N 51°35E 247 E6
Ad Dawr Iraq 34°27N 43°47E 213 E10
Aḍ Ḍiffah Libya 30°30N 24°30E 258 B4
Ad Dilam Si. Arabia 23°55N 47°10E 248 B4
Ad Dir'īyah Si. Arabia 24°44N 46°35E 246 E5
Ad Dīwānīyah Iraq 32°0N 45°0E 213 F11
Ad Dujayl Iraq 33°51N 44°14E 213 F11
Ad Duwayd Si. Arabia 30°15N 42°17E 246 D4
Ada Ghana 5°44N 0°40E 263 D5
Ada Serbia 45°49N 20°9E 182 E5
Ada Minn., U.S.A. 47°18N 96°31W 308 B5
Ada Ohio, U.S.A. 40°46N 83°49W 311 D13
Ada Okla., U.S.A. 34°46N 96°41W 314 D6
Ada Beja Portugal 38°47N 9°13W 126 A1
Adad Somali Rep. 9°27N 46°49E 267 C6
Adado, Ras Somali Rep. 11°19N 48°39E 267 B6
Adair, C. Canada 71°30N 71°34W 295 C17
Adaja → Spain 41°32N 4°52W 194 D6
Adak U.S.A. 51°45N 176°45W 303 L3
Adak I. U.S.A. 51°45N 176°45W 303 L3
Ådalsbruk Norway 60°43N 11°19E 164 D8
Adam Oman 22°15N 57°28E 249 B7
Adam, Mt. Falk. Is. 51°34S 60°4W 153 f
Adamantina Brazil 21°42S 51°4W 333 F1
Adamaoua □ Cameroon 6°30N 13°30E 263 D7
Adamaoua, Massif de l' Cameroon 7°20N 12°20E 263 D7
Adamawa □ Nigeria 9°20N 12°30E 263 D7
Adamawa Highlands = Adamaoua, Massif de l' Cameroon 7°20N 12°20E 263 D7
Adamello, Mte. Italy 46°9N 10°30E 198 B7
Adamello ⌂ Italy 46°4N 10°28E 198 B7
Adami Tulu Ethiopia 7°53N 38°41E 257 F4
Adaminaby Australia 36°0S 148°45E 283 D8
Adams Mass., U.S.A. 42°38N 73°7W 313 D11
Adams N.Y., U.S.A. 43°49N 76°1W 313 C8
Adams Wis., U.S.A. 43°57N 89°49W 308 D9
Adams, Mt. U.S.A. 46°12N 121°30W 306 D5
Adam's Bridge Sri Lanka 9°15N 79°40E 245 K4
Adams L. Canada 51°10N 119°40W 296 C5
Adams Park U.S.A. 33°43N 84°27W 113 B2
Adam's Peak Sri Lanka 6°48N 80°30E 245 L5
Adamuz Spain 38°2N 4°32W 195 G6
Adana Turkey 37°0N 35°16E 250 B6
Adana □ Turkey 37°0N 35°30E 250 B6
Adanero Spain 40°56N 4°36W 194 E6
Adang, Ko Thailand 6°33N 99°18E 237 J2
Adapazarı = Sakarya Turkey 40°48N 30°25E 212 B4
Adar Gwagwa, J. Sudan 22°15N 35°20E 256 C4
Adarama Sudan 17°10N 34°52E 257 D3
Adare, C. Antarctica 71°0S 171°0E 151 D11
Adarte Eritrea 13°18N 42°8E 257 E5
Adaut Indonesia 8°8S 131°7E 231 F8
Adavale Australia 25°52S 144°32E 281 D3
Adda → Italy 45°8N 9°53E 198 C6
Addatigala India 17°31N 82°3E 244 F6
Addax ⌂ Niger 19°17N 9°22E 259 E1
Addis Ababa = Addis Abeba Ethiopia 9°2N 38°42E 257 F4
Addis Abeba Ethiopia 9°2N 38°42E 257 F4
Addis Alem Ethiopia 9°0N 38°17E 257 F4
Addis Zemen Ethiopia 12°7N 37°47E 257 E4
Addiscombe U.K. 51°22N 0°4W 125 B3
Addison Ill., U.S.A. 41°55N 88°0W 311 C8
Addison N.Y., U.S.A. 42°1N 77°14W 312 D7
Addo S. Africa 33°32S 25°45E 270 D4
Addo △ S. Africa 33°30S 25°50E 270 D4
Addu Atoll Maldives 0°38S 73°10E 272 d
Adebour Niger 13°17N 11°50E 259 F2
Ādeh Iran 37°42N 45°11E 246 B5
Adel Ga., U.S.A. 31°8N 83°25W 316 D6
Adel Iowa, U.S.A. 41°37N 94°1W 310 C2
Adel Bagrou Mauritania 15°29N 6°57W 262 B3
Adelaide S. Austral., Australia 34°52S 138°30E 282 C3
Adelaide Eastern Cape, S. Africa 32°42S 26°20E 270 D4
Adelaide I. Antarctica 67°15S 68°30W 151 C17
Adelaide Pen. Canada 68°15N 97°30W 294 D12
Adelaide River Australia 13°15S 131°7E 278 B5
Adelaide Village Bahamas 25°0N 77°31W 153 b
Adelanto U.S.A. 34°35N 117°22W 307 L9
Adelaye C.A.R. 7°7N 22°49E 264 A4
Adele I. Australia 15°32S 123°9E 278 C3
Adélie, Terre Antarctica 68°0S 140°0E 151 C10
Adelie Land = Adélie, Terre Antarctica 68°0S 140°0E 151 C10
Adelong Australia 35°16S 148°4E 283 C8
Adelphi U.S.A. 39°0N 76°58W 143 A4
Adelsk Belarus 53°24N 23°47E 184 E10
Ademuz Spain 40°5N 1°13W 196 E3
Aden = Al 'Adan Yemen 12°45N 45°0E 248 D4
Aden, G. of Ind. Oc. 12°30N 47°30E 267 B6
Adendorp S. Africa 32°15S 24°30E 270 D3
Aderbissinat Niger 15°34N 7°54E 263 B6
Aderklaa Austria 48°17N 16°32E 142 A3
Adh Dhayd U.A.E. 25°17N 55°53E 247 E7
Adhoi India 23°26N 70°32E 242 H4
Adi Indonesia 4°15S 133°30E 231 E8
Adi Arkai Ethiopia 13°35N 37°57E 257 E4
Adi Daro Ethiopia 14°20N 38°14E 257 E4
Adi Keyih Eritrea 14°51N 39°22E 257 E4
Adi Kwala Eritrea 14°38N 38°48E 257 E4
Adi Ugri Eritrea 14°58N 38°48E 257 E4
Adieu, C. Australia 32°0S 132°10E 279 F5
Adieu Pt. Australia 15°14S 124°35E 278 C3
Adigala Ethiopia 10°24N 42°15E 257 E5
Adige → Italy 45°9N 12°20E 199 C9
Adigrat Ethiopia 14°20N 39°26E 257 E4
Adıgüzel Barajı Turkey 38°13N 29°14E 205 C11
Adilabad India 19°33N 78°20E 244 E4
Adilcevaz Turkey 38°47N 42°43E 213 C10
Adīrī Libya 27°32N 13°2E 258 C2
Adirondack ⌂ U.S.A. 44°0N 74°20W 313 C10
Adirondack Mts. U.S.A. 44°0N 74°0W 313 C10
Adis Abeba = Addis Abeba Ethiopia 9°2N 38°42E 257 F4
Adıyaman Turkey 37°45N 38°16E 213 D8
Adıyaman □ Turkey 37°30N 38°10E 213 D8
Adjim Tunisia 33°47N 10°50E 258 B2
Adjohon Benin 6°41N 2°32E 263 D5
Adjud Romania 46°7N 27°10E 183 D12
Adjumani Uganda 3°20N 31°50E 268 B3
Adjuntas Puerto Rico 18°10N 66°43W 321 b
Adlavik Is. Canada 55°0N 58°40W 299 B8
Adler Russia 43°28N 39°52E 191 J4
Adler Planetarium Chicago, U.S.A. 119 e3
Admer Algeria 20°21N 5°27E 261 D6
Admer, Erg d' Algeria 24°0N 9°5E 261 D6
Admiralteyskaya Storona Russia 59°56N 30°20E 137 B2
Admiralty G. Australia 14°20S 125°55E 278 B4
Admiralty Gulf ✪ Australia 14°16S 125°52E 278 B4
Admiralty I. U.S.A. 57°30N 134°30W 296 B2
Admiralty Inlet Canada 72°30N 86°0W 295 C14
Admiralty Is. Papua N. G. 2°0S 147°0E 286 B4
Admiralty Island ⌂ U.S.A. 57°40N 134°10W 303 H14
Adnan Menderes, İzmir ✈ (ADB) Turkey 38°23N 27°6E 205 C9
Ado Nigeria 6°36N 2°56E 263 D5
Ado-Ekiti Nigeria 7°38N 5°12E 263 D6
Adok South Sudan 8°10N 30°20E 257 F3
Adola Ethiopia 11°14N 41°44E 257 E5
Adolfo González Chaves Argentina 38°2S 60°5W 334 D3
Adolfo Ruiz Cortines, Presa Mexico 27°15N 109°6W 318 B3
Adonara Indonesia 8°15S 123°5E 231 F6
Adoni India 15°33N 77°18E 245 G3
Adony Hungary 47°6N 18°52E 182 C3
Adour → France 43°32N 1°32W 174 E2
Adra India 23°30N 86°42E 243 H12
Adra Spain 36°43N 3°3W 195 J7
Adrano Italy 37°40N 14°50E 201 E7
Adrar Algeria 27°51N 0°11E 261 C4
Adrar □ Algeria 25°45N 1°0E 261 C5
Adrar □ Mauritania 21°0N 10°0W 260 D3
Adrar des Iforas Africa 19°40N 1°40E 261 D5
Adré Chad 13°40N 22°20E 259 F4
Ádria Italy 45°3N 12°3E 199 C9
Adrian Ga., U.S.A. 32°33N 82°35W 316 C7
Adrian Mich., U.S.A. 41°54N 84°2W 311 C12
Adrian Mo., U.S.A. 38°24N 94°21W 310 F2
Adrian Tex., U.S.A. 35°16N 102°40W 314 D3
Adrianople = Edirne Turkey 41°40N 26°34E 203 E10
Adriatic Sea Medit. S. 43°0N 16°0E 193 C7
Adua Indonesia 1°45S 129°50E 231 E7
Adung Long Burma 28°7N 97°42E 241 A6
Adur India 9°8N 76°40E 245 K3
Adwa Ethiopia 14°15N 38°52E 257 E4
Adygea □ Russia 45°0N 40°0E 191 H5
Adzhar Republic = Ajaria □ Georgia 41°30N 42°0E 191 K6
Adzhibakul = Qazımämmäd Azerbaijan 40°3N 49°0E 191 K9
Adzopé Ivory C. 6°7N 3°49W 262 D4
Ægean Sea Medit. S. 38°30N 25°0E 205 C7
Aerhtai Shan Mongolia 46°40N 92°45E 217 C12
Ærø Denmark 54°52N 10°25E 163 K4
Ærøskøbing Denmark 54°53N 10°24E 163 K4
Aetos Greece 37°15N 21°50E 204 D3
Afaahiti Tahiti 17°45S 149°17W 289 e
Afafi, Massif d' Niger 22°11N 15°10E 259 D3
'Afak Iraq 32°4N 45°15E 213 F11
Afandou Greece 36°18N 28°12E 206 E12
Afar □ Ethiopia 12°0N 41°0E 257 E5
Afarag, Erg Algeria 23°50N 2°47E 261 D5
Afareaitu Moorea 17°33S 149°47W 289 e
Åfarnes Norway 62°40N 7°32E 164 B4
Afdega Ethiopia 6°4N 43°30E 267 C5
Afdem Ethiopia 9°28N 41°0E 267 C5
Áffori Italy 45°31N 9°10E 129 A2
Affton U.S.A. 38°33N 90°20W 310 F6
Afghanistan ■ Asia 33°0N 65°0E 240 B2
Afgooye Somali Rep. 2°7N 44°59E 267 D5
'Afīf Si. Arabia 23°53N 42°56E 248 B3
Afikpo Nigeria 5°53N 7°54E 263 D6
Aflandshage Denmark 55°33N 12°35E 118 B3
Aflisses, O. → Algeria 28°40N 0°50E 261 C5
Aflou Algeria 34°7N 2°3E 261 B5
Afmadow Somali Rep. 0°31N 42°4E 267 D5
Afogados da Ingàzeira Brazil 7°45S 37°39W 332 C4
Afognak I. U.S.A. 58°15N 152°30W 303 G9
Afono B. Amer. Samoa 14°15S 170°38W 302 f
Afore Papua N. G. 9°9S 148°23E 286 E5
Afragóla Italy 40°55N 14°18E 201 B7
Afram → Ghana 7°0N 0°52W 263 D4
Afrera Ethiopia 13°16N 41°5E 257 E5
Africa 10°0N 20°0E 254 E6
'Afrīn Syria 36°32N 36°50E 250 B7
'Afrīn → Syria 36°20N 36°35E 250 B7
Afşar → Turkey 37°2N 32°35E 250 A3
Afsarīyeh Iran 35°39N 51°30E 141 B2
Afşin Turkey 38°14N 36°55E 212 C7
Afton Iowa, U.S.A. 41°2N 94°12W 310 C2
Afton N.Y., U.S.A. 42°14N 75°32W 313 D9
Afton Wyo., U.S.A. 42°44N 110°56W 304 E8
Afuá Brazil 0°15S 50°20W 329 D7
'Afula Israel 32°37N 35°17E 250 F6
Afumba Zambia 15°38S 24°56E 265 F4
Afyon Turkey 38°45N 30°33E 205 C12
Afyon □ Turkey 38°25N 30°30E 205 C12
Afyonkarahisar = Afyon Turkey 38°45N 30°33E 205 C12
Aga Egypt 30°55N 31°10E 256 H7
Aga I. Micronesia 7°29N 151°43E 287 T18
Āgā Jarī Iran 30°42N 49°50E 247 D6
Agadem Niger 16°50N 13°11E 259 E2
Agadés = Agadez Niger 16°58N 7°59E 259 E1
Agadez Niger 16°58N 7°59E 259 E1
Agadir Morocco 30°28N 9°55W 260 B3
Agadir □ Morocco 30°42N 9°0W 260 B3
Agaete Canary Is. 28°6N 15°43W 153 e1
Agaie Nigeria 9°1N 6°18E 263 D6
Agalas Greece 37°43N 20°47E 207 D2
Agalega Is. Mauritius 11°0S 57°0E 273 F4
Agana Guam 13°28N 144°45E 302 d
Agana B. Guam 13°29N 144°45E 302 d
Ağapınar Turkey 39°48N 30°47E 205 B12
Agar India 23°40N 76°2E 242 H7
Agar → India 21°0N 82°57E 244 D6
Agâraktem Mali 23°8N 6°22W 260 D3
Agaro Ethiopia 7°50N 36°38E 257 F4
Agartala India 23°50N 91°23E 241 D3
Agăş Romania 46°28N 26°15E 183 D11
Agassiz Canada 49°14N 121°46W 296 D4
Agassiz Icecap Canada 80°15N 76°0W 295 A16
Agat Guam 13°25N 144°40E 302 d
Agats Indonesia 5°33S 138°0E 231 F9
Agatti I. India 10°50N 72°12E 245 J1
Agattu I. U.S.A. 52°25N 173°35E 303 K1
Agawam U.S.A. 42°5N 72°37W 313 D12
Agbélouvé Togo 6°35N 1°14E 263 D5
Agboville Ivory C. 5°55N 4°15W 262 D4
Agboyi Cr. → Nigeria 6°33N 3°24E 124 A2
Ağcabädi Azerbaijan 40°5N 47°27E 191 K8
Ağdam Azerbaijan 40°0N 46°58E 191 L8
Ağdaş Azerbaijan 40°44N 47°22E 191 K8
Agde France 43°19N 3°28E 174 E7
Agde, C. d' France 43°16N 3°28E 174 E7
Agdz Morocco 30°47N 6°30W 260 B3
Agdzhabedi = Ağcabädi Azerbaijan 40°5N 47°27E 191 K8
Agen France 44°12N 0°38E 174 D4
Ageo Japan 35°58N 139°36E 223 B11
Ager Tay Chad 20°0N 17°41E 259 E3
Agerbæk Denmark 55°36N 8°48E 163 J2
Agersø Denmark 55°13N 11°12E 163 J5
Ågerup Denmark 55°43N 12°19E 118 A1
Ågesta Sweden 59°12N 18°6E 139 B2
Ageyevo Russia 54°10N 36°27E 188 E9
Aggteleki △ Hungary 48°27N 20°36E 182 B5
Āgh Kand Iran 37°15N 48°4E 213 D13
Aghathonisi Greece 37°28N 27°0E 205 D8
Aghia Anna Greece 38°52N 23°24E 204 C5
Aghia Deka Greece 35°3N 24°58E 207 E5
Aghia Ekaterinis, Akra Greece 39°50N 19°50E 206 B9
Aghia Galini Greece 35°6N 24°41E 207 E5
Aghia Marina Athina, Greece 37°48N 23°51E 112 C3
Aghia Marina Kasos, Greece 35°27N 26°53E 205 F8
Aghia Marina Leros, Greece 37°11N 26°48E 205 D8
Aghia Paraskevi Athina, Greece 38°1N 23°49E 112 A2
Aghia Paraskevi Voreio Aigaio, Greece 39°14N 26°21E 205 B8
Aghia Roumeli Greece 35°14N 23°58E 207 E4
Aghia Varvara Greece 35°8N 25°1E 207 E6
Aghiasos Greece 39°5N 26°23E 205 B8
Aghio Theodori Greece 37°55N 23°9E 204 D5
Aghion Oros □ Greece 40°25N 24°6E 203 F8
Aghios Andreas Greece 37°21N 22°45E 204 D4
Aghios Dimitrios Greece 37°53N 23°44E 112 B2
Aghios Efimia Greece 38°18N 20°36E 207 C2
Aghios Efstratios Greece 39°34N 24°58E 204 B6
Aghios Georgios Greece 37°28N 23°57E 204 D5
Aghios Ioannis, Akra Greece 35°20N 25°40E 207 E6
Aghios Ioannis Rendis Greece 37°57N 23°39E 112 B1
Aghios Isidoros Greece 36°9N 27°51E 206 E11
Aghios Kirikos Greece 37°34N 26°17E 205 D8
Aghios Leon Greece 37°47N 20°43E 207 D2
Aghios Matheos Greece 39°30N 19°47E 206 C9
Aghios Mironas Greece 35°15N 25°1E 207 E6
Aghios Nikolaos Etoloakarnania, Greece 38°52N 20°48E 207 B2
Aghios Nikolaos Kriti, Greece 35°11N 25°41E 207 E6
Aghios Nikolaos Lefkada, Greece 38°36N 20°34E 207 B2
Aghios Oros = Athos Greece 40°9N 24°22E 203 F8
Aghios Petros Greece 38°40N 20°36E 207 B2
Aghios Stephanos Greece 39°46N 19°39E 206 B9
Aghios Thekli Greece 38°15N 20°23E 207 C1
Aghios Thomas Greece 38°58N 20°47E 207 B2
Aghiou Orous, Kolpos Greece 40°6N 24°0E 202 F7
Aghireşu Romania 46°53N 23°15E 183 D8
Aghoueyyît Mauritania 21°10N 15°6W 260 D1
Aghreïjît Mauritania 21°58N 12°11W 260 D2
Agia Greece 39°43N 22°45E 204 B4
Agincourt Canada 43°47N 79°16W 141 A3
Aginskoye Russia 51°6N 114°32E 215 D12
Agjert Mauritania 16°23N 9°17W 262 B3
Ağlasun Turkey 37°39N 30°31E 205 D12
Agly → France 42°46N 3°3E 174 F7
Agmar Mauritania 25°18N 10°50W 260 C2
Agnew Australia 28°1S 120°31E 279 E3
Agnibilékrou Ivory C. 7°10N 3°11W 262 D4
Agnita Romania 45°59N 24°40E 183 E9
Agnone Italy 41°48N 14°22E 199 G11
Ago Japan 34°20N 136°51E 223 C8
Ago-Are Nigeria 8°30N 3°25E 263 D5
Agofie Ghana 8°27N 0°15E 263 D5
Agogna → Italy 45°4N 8°54E 198 C5
Agoitz = Aoiz Spain 42°46N 1°22W 196 C3
Agön Sweden 61°34N 17°23E 162 C11
Agon Coutainville France 49°2N 1°34W 172 C5
Agoo Phil. 16°20N 120°22E 232 C3
Agora Athens, Greece 112 c1
Ágordo Italy 46°18N 12°2E 199 B9
Agori India 24°33N 82°57E 243 G10
Agouifa Mauritania 19°57N 16°10W 260 E1
Agouna Benin 7°39N 1°47E 263 D5
Agout → France 43°47N 1°41E 174 E5
Agra India 27°17N 77°58E 242 F7
Agra Canal India 28°33N 77°17E 120 B2
Agrakhanskiuy Poluostrov Russia 43°42N 47°36E 191 J8
Agram = Zagreb Croatia 45°50N 15°58E 199 C12
Agramunt Spain 41°48N 1°6E 196 D6
Ágreda Spain 41°51N 1°55W 196 D3
Ağri Turkey 39°44N 43°3E 213 C10
Ağri □ Turkey 39°45N 43°5E 213 C10
Agri → Italy 40°13N 16°44E 201 B9
Ağrı Dağı Turkey 39°50N 44°15E 213 C11
Ağri Karakose = Ağri Turkey 39°44N 43°3E 213 C10
Agria Greece 39°20N 23°1E 204 B5
Agricola Oriental Mexico 19°23N 99°4W 128 B2
Agrigento Italy 37°19N 13°34E 200 E6
Agrihan N. Marianas 18°46N 145°40E 302 a
Agrinio Greece 38°37N 21°27E 204 C3
Agrópoli Italy 40°21N 14°59E 201 B7
Ağstafa Azerbaijan 41°7N 45°27E 191 K7
Água Branca Brazil 5°50S 42°40W 332 C3
Agua Caliente Mexico 32°29N 116°59W 307 N10
Agua Caliente Springs U.S.A. 32°56N 116°19W 307 N10
Água Clara Brazil 20°25S 52°45W 331 E7
Água Espraiada → Brazil 23°36S 46°41W 137 B2
Agua Fria ⌂ U.S.A. 34°14N 112°0W 305 J8
Agua Hechicera Mexico 32°28N 116°15W 307 N10
Água Preta → Brazil 1°41S 63°48W 329 D5
Agua Prieta Mexico 31°18N 109°34W 318 A3
Aguachica Colombia 8°19N 73°38W 328 B3
Aguada Puerto Rico 18°23N 67°11W 321 b
Aguada Cecilio Argentina 40°51S 65°51W 336 B3
Aguadas Colombia 5°40N 75°38W 328 B2
Aguadilla Puerto Rico 18°26N 67°10W 321 C6
Aguadulce Panama 8°15N 80°32W 320 E3
Agualva-Cacem Portugal 38°46N 9°15W 126 A1
Aguanga U.S.A. 33°27N 116°51W 307 M10
Aguanish Canada 50°14N 62°2W 299 B7
Aguanish → Canada 50°13N 62°5W 299 B7
Aguapeí Brazil 16°12S 59°43W 331 D6
Aguapeí → Brazil 21°0S 51°0W 333 F1
Aguapey → Argentina 29°7S 56°36W 334 B4
Aguaray Guazú → Paraguay 24°47S 57°19W 334 A4
Aguarico → Ecuador 0°59S 75°11W 328 D2
Aguaro-Guariquito △ Venezuela 8°20N 66°35W 328 B4
Aguas → Spain 41°20N 0°30W 196 D4
Aguas Blancas Chile 24°15S 69°55W 334 A2
Aguas Calientes, Sierra de Argentina 25°26S 66°40W 334 B2
Águas Formosas Brazil 17°5S 40°57W 333 E3
Aguascalientes Mexico 21°53N 102°18W 318 C4
Aguascalientes □ Mexico 22°0N 102°20W 318 C4
Agudo Spain 38°59N 4°52W 195 G6
Águeda Portugal 40°34N 8°27W 194 E2
Agueda → Spain 41°2N 6°56W 194 D4
Aguelhok Mali 19°29N 0°52E 261 E5
Aguelt el Melah Mauritania 23°3N 10°40W 260 D2
Agüenit W. Sahara 22°11N 13°8W 260 D2
Aguié Niger 13°31N 7°46E 263 C6
Aguila, Punta Puerto Rico 17°57N 67°13W 321 b
Aguilafuente Spain 41°13N 4°7W 194 D6
Aguilar de Campóo Spain 42°47N 4°15W 194 C6
Aguilar de la Frontera Spain 37°31N 4°40W 195 H6
Aguilares Argentina 27°26S 65°35W 334 B2
Águilas Spain 37°23N 1°35W 197 H3
Agüimes Canary Is. 27°58N 15°27W 153 e1
Aguja, C. de la Colombia 11°18N 74°12W 328 A3
Agujereada, Pta. Puerto Rico 18°30N 67°8W 321 b
Agulaa Ethiopia 13°40N 39°40E 257 E4
Agulhas, C. S. Africa 34°52S 20°0E 270 D3
Agulhas Ridge Atl. Oc. 42°0S 15°0E 152 L13
Agulo Canary Is. 28°11N 17°12W 153 e1
Agung, Gunung Indonesia 8°20S 115°28E 231 J18

Aguni-Jima Japan 26°30N 127°10E 221 L3
Agur Uganda 2°28N 32°55E 268 B3
Agurei → South Sudan 7°45N 33°0E 257 F3
Agusan → Phil. 9°0N 125°30E 233 G5
Agusan del Norte □ Phil. 9°20N 125°10E 233 G5
Agusan del Sur □ Phil. 8°30N 125°30E 233 G5
Agustín Codazzi Colombia 10°2N 73°14W 328 A3
Agutaya I. Phil. 11°9N 120°58E 233 F3
Ağva Turkey 41°8N 29°51E 203 E13
Agvali Russia 42°36N 46°8E 191 J8
Aha Mts. Botswana 19°45S 21°0E 270 A3
Ahad Rifaydah Si. Arabia 17°50N 42°50E 248 C3
Ahaggar Algeria 23°0N 6°30E 261 D6
Ahaggar △ Algeria 23°0N 4°50E 261 D5
Ahal □ Turkmenistan 37°0N 57°0E 216 E5
Ahamansu Ghana 7°38N 0°35E 263 D5
Ahar Iran 38°35N 47°0E 213 C12
Ahat Turkey 38°39N 29°47E 205 C11
Ahaura → N.Z. 42°21S 171°34E 285 C6
Ahaus Germany 52°4N 7°0E 178 C2
Ahé French Polynesia 14°30S 146°18W 289 f
Åheim Norway 62°2N 5°13E 164 B2
Ahelledjem Algeria 26°37N 6°58E 261 C6
Ahimanawa Ra. N.Z. 39°3S 176°30E 284 F5
Ahioma Papua N. G. 10°20S 150°33E 286 F6
Ahipara B. N.Z. 35°5S 173°5E 284 B2
Ahir Dağı Turkey 38°45N 30°10E 205 C12
Ahiri India 19°30N 80°0E 244 E5
Ahlat Turkey 38°45N 42°29E 213 C10
Ahlen Germany 51°45N 7°53E 178 D3
Ahmad Wal Pakistan 29°18N 65°58E 242 E1
Ahmadabad India 23°0N 72°40E 242 H5
Aḩmadābād Khorāsān, Iran 35°3N 60°50E 247 C9
Aḩmadābād Khorāsān, Iran 35°49N 59°42E 247 C8
Aḩmadī Iran 27°56N 56°42E 247 E8
Ahmadnagar India 19°7N 74°46E 244 E2
Ahmadpur India 18°40N 76°57E 244 E3
Ahmadpur East Pakistan 29°12N 71°10E 242 E4
Ahmadpur Lamma Pakistan 28°19N 70°3E 242 E4
Ahmanson Theater Los Angeles, U.S.A. 127 b2
Ahmar, Mts. Ethiopia 9°20N 41°15E 257 F5
Ahmedabad = Ahmadabad India 23°0N 72°40E 242 H5
Ahmednagar = Ahmadnagar India 19°7N 74°46E 244 E2
Ahmetbey Turkey 41°26N 27°34E 203 E11
Ahmetler Turkey 38°28N 29°5E 205 C11
Ahmetli Turkey 38°32N 27°57E 205 C9
Ahmeyim Mauritania 20°51N 14°25W 260 D2
Ahoada Nigeria 5°8N 6°36E 263 D6
Ahome Mexico 25°55N 109°11W 318 B3
Ahon, Tarso Chad 20°23N 18°18E 259 D3
Ahoskie U.S.A. 36°17N 76°59W 315 C16
Ahr → Germany 50°32N 7°16E 178 E3
Ahram Iran 28°52N 51°16E 247 D6
Ahrax Pt. Malta 36°0N 14°22E 206 F7
Ahrensbök Germany 54°2N 10°35E 178 A6
Ahrensburg Germany 53°40N 10°13E 178 B6
Ahrensfelde Germany 52°34N 13°34E 115 A4
Ahu Akivi Chile 27°7S 109°24W 330 b
Ahu Tepeu Chile 27°6S 109°25W 330 b
Ahu Tongariki Chile 27°8S 109°17W 330 b
Ahu Vinapu Chile 27°10S 109°25W 330 b
Ahuachapán El Salv. 13°54N 89°52W 320 D2
'Āhuimanu U.S.A. 21°26N 157°50W 302 K14
Ahun France 46°4N 2°5E 173 F9
Ahuntsic Canada 45°32N 73°41W 130 A1
Ahunui French Polynesia 19°39S 140°25W 289 f
Ahuriri → N.Z. 44°31S 170°12E 285 E5
Åhus Sweden 55°56N 14°18E 163 J8
Ahvāz Iran 31°20N 48°40E 247 D6
Ahvenanmaa = Åland Finland 60°15N 20°0E 161 F19
Aḩwar Yemen 13°30N 46°40E 248 D4
Ahzar → Mali 15°30N 3°20E 263 B5
Ai → India 26°26N 90°44E 241 B3
Ai → Ōsaka, Japan 34°46N 135°35E 133 A2
Ai-Ais Namibia 27°54S 17°59E 270 C2
Ai-Ais and Fish River Canyon △ Namibia 24°45S 17°15E 270 B2
Aiari → Brazil 1°22N 68°36W 328 C4
Aichach Germany 48°27N 11°8E 179 G7
Aichi □ Japan 35°0N 137°15E 223 C9
'Aiea U.S.A. 21°23N 157°56W 302 K14
Aigle Switz. 46°18N 6°58E 179 J2
Aignay-le-Duc France 47°40N 4°43E 173 E11
Aigoual, Mt. France 44°8N 3°35E 174 D7
Aigre France 45°54N 0°1E 174 C4
Aigremont France 48°54N 2°1E 134 A1
Aigrettes, Île aux Mauritius 20°25S 57°43E 272 e
Aiguá Uruguay 34°13S 54°46W 335 C5
Aigueperse France 46°3N 3°13E 173 F10
Aigues → France 44°7N 4°43E 175 D8
Aigues-Mortes France 43°35N 4°12E 175 E8
Aigues-Mortes, G. d' France 43°31N 4°3E 175 E8
Aigües-Tortes i Estany de St. Maurici △ Spain 42°38N 0°31E 196 C4
Aiguilles France 44°47N 6°51E 175 D10
Aiguillon France 44°18N 0°21E 174 D4
Aigurande France 46°27N 1°49E 173 F8
Aihui = Heihe China 50°10N 127°30E 219 A14
Aija Peru 9°50S 77°45W 330 B2
Aikawa Japan 38°2N 138°15E 220 E9
Aiken U.S.A. 33°34N 81°43W 316 B8
Ailao Shan China 24°0N 101°20E 228 F3
Aileron Australia 22°39S 133°20E 280 C1
Ailey U.S.A. 32°11N 82°34W 316 C7
Ailigandi Panama 9°14N 78°1W 328 B2
Aillant-sur-Tholon France 47°52N 3°20E 173 E10
Aillik Canada 55°11N 59°18W 299 A8
Ailsa Craig Ont., Canada 43°8N 81°33W 312 C3
Ailsa Craig S. Ayrs., U.K. 55°15N 5°6W 167 F3
Ailulual Papua N. G. 9°38S 150°35E 286 E6
Aim Russia 59°0N 133°55E 215 D14
Aimere Indonesia 8°45S 121°3E 231 F6
Aimogasta Argentina 28°33S 66°50W 334 B2
Aimorés Brazil 19°30S 41°4W 333 E3
Ain □ France 46°5N 5°20E 173 F12
Ain → France 45°45N 5°11E 175 C9
Aïn Beïda Algeria 35°50N 7°29E 261 A6
Aïn Ben Khellil Algeria 33°15N 0°49W 261 B4
Aïn Ben Tili Mauritania 25°59N 9°27W 260 C3
Aïn Beni Mathar Morocco 34°1N 2°0W 261 B4
Aïn Benian Algeria 36°48N 2°55E 261 A5
Ain Dalla Egypt 27°20N 27°23E 256 B2
Ain Defla Algeria 36°16N 1°58E 261 A5
Ain Defla □ Algeria 36°10N 2°10E 261 A5
Ain el Akhḑar Egypt 28°50N 33°55E 251 K4
Ain el Mafki Egypt 27°30N 28°15E 256 B2
Ain Girba Egypt 29°20N 25°14E 256 B2
Aïn M'lila Algeria 36°2N 6°35E 261 A6
Ain Murr Sudan 21°50N 25°9E 256 C2
Ain Qeiqab Egypt 29°42N 24°55E 256 B1
Aïn Salah = In Salah Algeria 27°10N 2°32E 261 C5
Aïn-Sefra Algeria 32°47N 0°37W 261 B4
Ain Sheikh Murzûk Egypt 26°47N 27°45E 256 B2
Ain Sudr Egypt 29°50N 33°6E 251 J4
Ain Sukhna Egypt 29°32N 32°20E 256 J8
Aïn Tédelès Algeria 36°0N 0°21E 261 A5
Aïn Témouchent Algeria 35°16N 1°8W 261 A4
Aïn Témouchent □ Algeria 35°20N 1°5W 261 A4
Aïn Tikkidine Algeria 25°33N 1°24E 261 C5
Aïn Touta Algeria 35°26N 5°54E 261 A6
Ain Zeitûn Egypt 29°10N 25°48E 256 B2
Aïn Zorah Morocco 34°37N 3°32W 261 B4
Ainaži Latvia 57°50N 24°24E 188 D3
Ainos Oros Greece 38°9N 20°40E 207 C2
Ainsworth U.S.A. 42°33N 99°52W 308 D4
Aintab = Gaziantep Turkey 37°6N 37°23E 250 A8
Aioi Japan 34°48N 134°28E 222 C6
Aiome Papua N. G. 5°8S 144°44E 286 C3
Aipe Colombia 3°13N 75°15W 328 C2
Aiquile Bolivia 18°10S 65°10W 331 D4
Aïr Niger 18°30N 8°0E 259 E1
Air Canada Centre Toronto, Canada 141 c2
Aïr et Ténéré ⌓ Niger 18°12N 9°56E 263 B6
Air Force I. Canada 67°58N 74°5W 295 D17
Air Hitam Malaysia 1°55N 103°11E 237 M4
Air View Park Singapore 1°20N 103°46E 138 A2
Aira Japan 31°43N 130°43E 222 F2
Airaines France 49°58N 1°55E 173 C8
Airão Brazil 1°56S 61°22W 329 D5
Airbangis Indonesia 0°12N 99°22E 234 B1
Airdrie Alta., Canada 51°18N 114°2W 296 C6
Airdrie N. Lanarks., U.K. 55°52N 3°57W 167 F5
Aire → Meuse, France 49°18N 4°49E 173 C11
Aire → N. Yorks., U.K. 53°43N 0°55W 168 D7
Aire, I. de l' Spain 39°48N 4°16E 206 B5
Aire-sur-la-Lys France 50°37N 2°22E 173 B9
Aire-sur-l'Adour France 43°42N 0°15W 174 E3
Aireys Inlet Australia 38°29S 144°5E 282 E6
Airlie Beach Australia 20°16S 148°43E 280 b
Airport West Australia 37°42S 144°52E 128 A1
Airvault France 46°50N 0°8W 172 F6
Aisch → Germany 49°49N 10°58E 179 F6
Aisen □ Chile 46°30S 73°0W 336 C2
Aisne □ France 49°42N 3°40E 173 C10
Aisne → France 49°26N 2°50E 173 C9
Ait India 25°54N 79°14E 243 G8
Ait Ben Haddou Morocco 31°3N 7°7W 260 B3
Aitana, Sierra de Spain 38°35N 0°24W 197 G4
Aitape Papua N. G. 3°11S 142°22E 286 B2
Aitkin U.S.A. 46°32N 93°42W 308 B7
Aitutaki Cook Is. 18°52S 159°45W 289 J12
Aiuaba Brazil 6°38S 40°7W 332 C3
Aiud Romania 46°19N 23°44E 183 D8
Aix-en-Provence France 43°32N 5°27E 175 E9
Aix-la-Chapelle = Aachen Germany 50°45N 6°6E 178 E2
Aix-les-Bains France 45°41N 5°53E 175 C9
Aixe-sur-Vienne France 45°47N 1°9E 174 C5
Aiyang, Mt. Papua N. G. 5°10S 141°20E 286 C1
Aíyina = Egina Greece 37°45N 23°26E 204 D5
Aizawl India 23°40N 92°44E 241 D4
Aizenay France 46°44N 1°38W 172 F5
Aizkraukle Latvia 56°36N 25°11E 188 D3
Aizpute Latvia 56°43N 21°40E 184 B8
Aizuwakamatsu Japan 37°30N 139°56E 220 F9
Ajabshir Iran 37°28N 45°54E 213 D11
Ajaccio France 41°55N 8°40E 175 G12
Ajaccio, G. d' France 41°52N 8°40E 175 G12
Ajai ⌓ Uganda 2°52N 31°16E 268 B3
Ajaigarh India 24°52N 80°16E 243 G9
Ajajú → Colombia 0°59N 72°20W 328 C3
Ajalpan Mexico 18°22N 97°15W 319 D5
Ajanta India 20°30N 75°48E 244 D2
Ajanta Ra. India 20°28N 75°50E 244 D2
Ajari Rep. = Ajaria □ Georgia 41°30N 42°0E 191 K6
Ajaria □ Georgia 41°30N 42°0E 191 K6
Ajax Canada 43°50N 79°1W 312 C5
Ajax, Mt. N.Z. 42°35S 172°5E 285 C7
Ajdābiyā Libya 30°54N 20°4E 258 B4
Ajdābiyā □ Libya 29°0N 20°0E 258 C4
Ajdovščina Slovenia 45°54N 13°54E 199 C10
Ajegunle Nigeria 6°26N 3°20E 124 B2
Aji Japan 34°40N 135°27E 133 A1
Ajibar Ethiopia 10°35N 38°36E 257 E4
Ajka Hungary 47°4N 17°31E 182 C2
'Ajlūn Jordan 32°18N 35°47E 251 F6
'Ajmān U.A.E. 25°25N 55°30E 247 E7
Ajmer India 26°28N 74°37E 242 F6
Ajnala India 31°50N 74°48E 242 D6
Ajo U.S.A. 32°22N 112°52W 305 K7
Ajo, C. de Spain 43°31N 3°35W 194 B7
Ajoupa-Bouillon Martinique 14°49N 61°7W 322 j
Ajuda Portugal 38°42N 9°12W 126 A1
Ajuda, Pta. da Azores 37°52N 25°19W 153 c3
Ajuy Phil. 11°10N 123°1E 233 F4
Ak Dağ Turkey 36°30N 29°32E 205 E11
Ak Dağlar Turkey 39°32N 36°12E 212 C7
Ak Dağları Turkey 36°30N 29°30E 205 E11
Ak-Dovurak Russia 51°11N 90°36E 217 B12
Ak-Mechet = Qyzylorda Kazakhstan 44°48N 65°28E 217 C7
Ak-Mednet = Chornomorske Ukraine 45°31N 32°40E 189 K7
Ak-Sheikh = Razdolnoye Ukraine 45°46N 33°29E 189 K7
Akaba Togo 8°10N 1°2E 263 C5
Akabira Japan 43°33N 142°5E 220 C11
Akabli Algeria 26°49N 1°31E 261 C5
Akademika Obrucheva, Khrebet Russia 51°50N 96°0E 217 B13
Akagera △ Rwanda 1°31S 30°33E 268 C3
Akaishi-Dake Japan 35°27N 138°9E 223 B10
Akaishi-Sammyaku Japan 35°25N 138°10E 223 B10
Akaki Beseka Ethiopia 8°55N 38°45E 257 F4
Akākūs, J. Libya 25°20N 10°30E 258 C2
Akalkot India 17°32N 76°13E 244 F3
Akalla Sweden 59°24N 17°55E 139 A1
Akamas Cyprus 35°3N 32°18E 207 E8
Akan △ Japan 43°20N 144°20E 220 C12
Akanthou Cyprus 35°22N 33°45E 207 E9
Akarca Turkey 38°35N 29°35E 205 C11
Akaroa N.Z. 43°49S 172°59E 285 D7
Akaroa Harbour N.Z. 43°50S 172°55E 285 D7
Akasaka Tokyo, Japan 140 b3
Akasha Sudan 21°10N 30°32E 256 C3
Akashi Japan 34°45N 134°58E 222 C6
Akbarābād Iran 35°40N 51°20E 141 A2
Akbarpur Bihar, India 24°39N 83°58E 243 G10
Akbarpur Ut. P., India 26°25N 82°32E 243 F10
Akbou Algeria 36°31N 4°31E 261 A5
Akbulak Russia 51°1N 55°37E 216 B5
Akçaabat Turkey 41°1N 39°34E 213 B8
Akçadağ Turkey 38°27N 37°43E 212 C7
Akçakale Turkey 36°41N 38°56E 213 D8
Akçakoca Turkey 41°5N 31°8E 212 B4
Akçalı Dağları Turkey 36°18N 33°21E 250 B4
Akçaova Turkey 41°3N 29°57E 203 E13
Akçay Turkey 36°36N 29°45E 205 E11
Akçay → Turkey 37°50N 28°15E 205 D10
Akchâr Mauritania 20°20N 14°28W 260 D2
Akchi-Karasu = Toktogul Kyrgyzstan 41°50N 72°50E 217 D8
Akdağ Antalya, Turkey 37°0N 32°0E 250 B3
Akdağ İzmir, Turkey 38°33N 26°30E 205 C8
Akdağmadeni Turkey 39°39N 35°53E 212 C6
Akdere Turkey 36°14N 33°46E 250 B4
Akdoğan = Lysi Cyprus 35°6N 33°41E 207 E9
Akechi Japan 35°18N 137°23E 223 B9
Akelamo Indonesia 1°35N 129°40E 231 D7
Åkernes = Åknes Norway 58°45N 7°30E 164 F4
Åkers styckebruk Sweden 59°15N 17°5E 162 E11
Åkersberga Sweden 59°29N 18°18E 162 E12
Akershus □ Norway 60°0N 11°10E 164 D8
Akershus Slott Oslo, Norway 133 c1
Akeru → India 17°25N 80°5E 244 F5
Aketi Dem. Rep. of the Congo 2°38N 23°47E 264 B4
Akhalkalaki Georgia 41°27N 43°25E 191 K6
Akhaltsikhe Georgia 41°40N 43°0E 191 K6
Akhḑar, W. al → Si. Arabia 28°36N 36°36E 251 K7
Akhiok U.S.A. 56°57N 154°10W 303 H9
Akhisar Turkey 38°56N 27°48E 205 C9
Akhmîm Egypt 26°31N 31°47E 256 B3
Akhnur India 32°52N 74°45E 243 C6
Akhtarīn Syria 36°31N 37°20E 250 B8
Akhtopol Bulgaria 42°6N 27°56E 203 D11
Akhtuba → Russia 47°41N 46°55E 191 G8
Akhtubinsk Russia 48°13N 46°7E 191 F8
Akhty Russia 41°30N 47°45E 191 K8
Akhtyrka = Okhtyrka Ukraine 50°25N 35°0E 189 G8
Aki Japan 33°30N 133°54E 222 D5
Aki-Nada Japan 34°5N 132°40E 222 C4
Akiachak U.S.A. 60°55N 161°26W 303 F7
Akiak U.S.A. 60°55N 161°13W 303 F7
Akiéni Gabon 1°11S 13°53E 264 C2
Akihabara Tokyo, Japan 140 a5
Akimiski I. Canada 52°50N 81°30W 298 B3
Akıncı Burnu Turkey 36°19N 35°46E 250 B6
Akincilar = Louroujina Cyprus 35°0N 33°28E 207 F9
Åkirkeby Denmark 55°4N 14°55E 163 J8
Akita Japan 39°45N 140°7E 220 E10
Akita □ Japan 39°40N 140°30E 220 E10
Akjoujt Mauritania 19°45N 14°15W 262 B2
Akka Mali 15°24N 4°11W 262 B4
Akka Morocco 29°22N 8°9W 260 C3
Akkaraipattu Sri Lanka 7°13N 81°51E 245 L5
Akkaya Tepesi Turkey 37°25N 29°38E 205 D11
Akkerman = Bilhorod-Dnistrovskyy Ukraine 46°11N 30°23E 189 J6
Akkeshi Japan 43°2N 144°51E 220 C12
'Akko Israel 32°55N 35°4E 250 F6
Akköy Turkey 37°29N 27°15E 205 D9
Akkuş Turkey 40°47N 37°0E 212 B7
Aklampa Benin 8°15N 2°10E 263 D5
Aklan □ Phil. 11°50N 122°30E 233 F4
Aklavik Canada 68°12N 135°0W 294 D4
Aklera India 24°26N 76°32E 242 G7
Akmenė Lithuania 56°15N 22°45E 184 B9
Akmenrags Latvia 56°50N 21°4E 184 B8
Akmolinsk = Astana Kazakhstan 51°10N 71°30E 217 B8
Akmonte = Almonte Spain 37°13N 6°38W 195 H4
Åknes Norway 58°45N 7°30E 164 F4
Aknoul Morocco 34°40N 3°55W 261 B4
Akō Japan 34°45N 134°24E 222 C6
Ako Nigeria 10°19N 10°48E 263 C7
Akôbô South Sudan 7°47N 33°1E 257 F3
Akobo → Ethiopia 7°48N 33°3E 257 F3
Akola Maharashtra, India 20°42N 77°2E 244 D3
Akola Maharashtra, India 19°32N 74°3E 244 E2
Akolmiut U.S.A. 60°55N 162°20W 303 F7
Akonolinga Cameroon 3°50N 12°18E 263 E7
Akor Mali 14°59N 6°58W 262 C3
Akordat Eritrea 15°30N 37°40E 257 D4
Akosombo Dam Ghana 6°20N 0°5E 263 D5
Akot India 21°10N 77°10E 244 D3
Akot South Sudan 6°31N 30°9E 257 F3
Akoupé Ivory C. 6°23N 3°54W 262 D4
Akourousoulba C.A.R. 8°58N 20°46E 264 A4
Akpatok I. Canada 60°25N 68°8W 295 E18
Åkrahamn Norway 59°15N 5°10E 164 E2
'Akramah Libya 32°2N 23°41E 258 B4
Akranes Iceland 64°19N 22°5W 155 C4
Akreïjit Mauritania 18°19N 9°11W 262 B3
Akritas, Akra Greece 36°43N 21°54E 204 E3
Akron Colo., U.S.A. 40°10N 103°13W 304 F12
Akron Ind., U.S.A. 41°2N 86°1W 311 C10
Akron Ohio, U.S.A. 41°5N 81°31W 312 E3
Akrotiri Cyprus 34°36N 32°57E 207 F8
Akrotiri, Akra Greece 40°26N 25°27E 203 F9
Akrotiri Bay Cyprus 34°35N 33°10E 207 F9
Aksai Chin China 35°15N 79°55E 243 B8
Aksaray Turkey 38°25N 34°2E 212 C6
Aksaray □ Turkey 38°20N 33°45E 212 C5
Aksay = Aqsay Kazakhstan 51°11N 53°0E 187 D9
Akşehir Turkey 38°18N 31°30E 212 C4
Akşehir Gölü Turkey 38°30N 31°25E 212 C4
Akseki Turkey 37°2N 31°47E 250 A2
Akstafa = Ağstafa Azerbaijan 41°7N 45°27E 191 K7
Aksu Xinjiang Uygur, China 41°5N 80°10E 217 D10
Aksu Turkey 36°57N 30°50E 250 B1
Aksu → Turkey 36°52N 30°57E 250 B1
Aksu He → China 40°26N 80°59E 217 D10
Aksum Ethiopia 14°5N 38°40E 257 E4
Aktash Russia 55°2N 52°3E 190 C11
Aktepe Turkey 36°42N 36°27E 250 B7
Aktio Greece 38°57N 20°46E 207 B2
Akto China 39°5N 75°59E 217 E9
Aktsyabrski Belarus 52°38N 28°53E 177 B15
Aktyubinsk = Aqtöbe Kazakhstan 50°17N 57°10E 187 D10
Aku Nigeria 6°40N 7°18E 263 D6
Akula Dem. Rep. of the Congo 2°22N 20°12E 264 B4
Akun I. U.S.A. 54°11N 165°32W 303 J6
Akune Japan 32°1N 130°12E 222 E2
Akure Nigeria 7°15N 5°5E 263 D6
Akurenan Eq. Guin. 1°2N 10°40E 264 B2
Akuressa Sri Lanka 6°5N 80°29E 245 L5
Akureyri Iceland 65°40N 18°6W 155 B8
Akuseki-Shima Japan 29°27N 129°37E 221 K4
Akusha Russia 42°18N 47°30E 191 J8
Akutan U.S.A. 54°8N 165°46W 303 J6
Akutan I. U.S.A. 54°7N 165°55W 303 J6
Akwa-Ibom □ Nigeria 4°30N 7°30E 263 E6
Akwanga Nigeria 8°55N 8°23E 263 D6
Akyab = Sittwe Burma 20°18N 92°45E 241 E4
Akyazı Turkey 40°40N 30°38E 212 B4
Ål Norway 60°38N 8°33E 164 D5
Al Abyaḑ Libya 26°49N 14°1E 258 C2
Al Abyār Libya 32°9N 20°29E 258 B4
Al 'Adam Libya 31°51N 23°55E 258 B4
Al 'Adan Yemen 12°45N 45°0E 248 D4
Al Aḩsā = Hasa Si. Arabia 25°50N 49°0E 247 E6
Al Ajfar Si. Arabia 27°26N 43°0E 246 E4
Al Amādīyah Iraq 37°5N 43°30E 213 D10
Al 'Amārah Iraq 31°55N 47°15E 213 G12
Al Anbār □ Iraq 33°25N 42°0E 246 C4
Al 'Aqabah Jordan 29°31N 35°0E 251 J6
Al 'Aqabah □ Jordan 29°30N 35°0E 251 J6
Al 'Aqīq Si. Arabia 20°39N 41°25E 248 B3
Al Arak Syria 34°38N 38°35E 213 E8
Al 'Aramah Si. Arabia 25°30N 46°0E 246 E5
Al 'Ariḑah Si. Arabia 17°3N 43°5E 248 C3
Al 'Arţāwīyah Si. Arabia 26°31N 45°20E 246 E5
Al Ashkhara Oman 21°50N 59°30E 249 B7
Al 'Āşimah = 'Ammān □ Jordan 31°40N 36°30E 251 G7
Al 'Assāfīyah Si. Arabia 28°17N 38°59E 246 D3
Al Atārib Syria 36°9N 36°49E 250 B7
Al 'Awdah Si. Arabia 25°32N 45°41E 246 E5
Al 'Ayn Si. Arabia 25°4N 38°6E 246 E3
Al 'Ayn U.A.E. 24°15N 55°45E 247 E7
Al 'Azamīyah Iraq 33°22N 44°22E 113 A2
Al 'Azīzīyah Iraq 32°54N 45°4E 213 F11
Al 'Azīzīyah Libya 32°30N 13°1E 258 B2
Al 'Azīzīyah □ Libya 32°31N 13°1E 261 B7
Al Bāb Syria 36°23N 37°29E 250 B8
Al Bad' Si. Arabia 28°28N 35°1E 246 D2
Al Bādī Iraq 35°56N 41°32E 246 C4
Al Badī' Si. Arabia 22°0N 46°35E 248 B4
Al Bāḩah Si. Arabia 20°1N 41°28E 256 C5
Al Bāḩah □ Si. Arabia 20°30N 41°30E 248 B3
Al Baḩrah Kuwait 29°40N 47°52E 246 D5
Al Baḩral Mayyit = Dead Sea Asia 31°30N 35°30E 251 G6
Al Balqā' □ Jordan 32°5N 35°45E 251 F6
Al Barkāt Libya 24°56N 10°14E 258 D2
Al Bārūk, J. Lebanon 33°39N 35°40E 250 E6
Al Başrah Iraq 30°30N 47°50E 246 D5
Al Baţḩā Iraq 31°6N 45°53E 246 D5
Al Batinah Oman 24°10N 56°50E 249 A7
Al Batrūn Lebanon 34°15N 35°40E 250 D6
Al Bayāḑ Si. Arabia 22°0N 47°0E 248 B4
Al Bayḑā Libya 32°50N 21°44E 258 B4
Al Bayḑā' Yemen 14°5N 45°42E 248 D4
Al Bi'ār Si. Arabia 22°39N 39°40E 248 B2
Al Biqā Lebanon 34°10N 36°10E 250 D7
Al Biqā □ Lebanon 34°0N 36°5E 250 E7
Al Bi'r Si. Arabia 28°51N 36°16E 251 K7
Al Birk Si. Arabia 18°13N 41°33E 248 C3
Al Bu'ayrāt al Ḩasūn Libya 31°24N 15°44E 258 B3
Al Bukayrīyah Si. Arabia 26°9N 43°40E 246 E4
Al Bumbah Libya 32°24N 23°8E 258 B4
Al Burayj Syria 34°15N 36°46E 250 D7
Al Buţnām □ Libya 30°0N 24°0E 258 B4
Al Buţnān □ Libya 31°40N 24°30E 258 B4
Al Faḑilī Si. Arabia 26°58N 49°10E 247 E6
Al Fallūjah Iraq 33°20N 43°55E 213 F10
Al Fatḩah Iraq 35°3N 43°33E 213 E10
Al Fāw Iraq 30°0N 48°30E 247 D6
Al Faydamī Yemen 16°25N 52°26E 249 C6
Al Fujayrah U.A.E. 25°7N 56°18E 247 E8
Al Ghadaf, W. → Jordan 31°26N 36°43E 251 G7
Al Ghammās Iraq 31°45N 44°37E 246 D5
Al Gharīb Libya 32°35N 21°11E 258 B4
Al Ghayḑah Ḩaḑramaut Yemen 14°55N 50°0E 249 D5
Al Ghayḑah Qamar, Yemen 16°13N 52°11E 249 C6
Al Ghayl Yemen 15°30N 50°54E 249 D5
Al Ghazālah Si. Arabia 26°48N 41°19E 246 E4
Al Ḩadd Oman 22°32N 59°48E 249 B7
Al Ḩaddār Si. Arabia 21°58N 45°57E 248 B4
Al Ḩadīthah Iraq 34°0N 41°13E 213 E10
Al Ḩadīthah Si. Arabia 31°28N 37°8E 246 D3
Al Ḩaḑr Iraq 35°35N 42°44E 213 E10
Al Ḩaffah Syria 35°36N 36°1E 250 C7
Al Ḩājānah Syria 33°20N 36°33E 250 E7
Al Ḩajar al Gharbī Oman 24°10N 56°15E 247 E8
Al Hallānīyah Oman 17°30N 56°1E 249 C7
Al Hāmad Si. Arabia 31°30N 39°30E 246 D3
Al Ḩamādah al Ḩamrā' Libya 29°30N 12°0E 258 C2
Al Ḩamar Si. Arabia 22°26N 46°12E 248 B4
Al Ḩamdānīyah Syria 35°25N 36°50E 250 C7
Al Ḩamīdīyah Syria 34°42N 35°57E 250 D6
Al Ḩammār Iraq 30°57N 46°51E 246 D5
Al Ḩamrā' Si. Arabia 24°2N 38°55E 246 E3
Al Ḩamrā' Syria 35°19N 37°5E 250 C8
Al Ḩamzah Iraq 31°43N 44°58E 246 D5
Al Ḩanākīyah Si. Arabia 24°51N 40°31E 246 E4
Al Ḩarīq Si. Arabia 23°29N 46°27E 248 B4
Al Harūj al Aswad Libya 27°0N 17°10E 258 C3
Al Ḩasakah Syria 36°35N 40°45E 213 D9
Al Ḩasakah □ Syria 36°40N 40°50E 213 D9
Al Hāshimīyah Iraq 32°22N 44°39E 213 G11
Al Hāsikīyah Oman 17°28N 55°36E 249 C6
Al Ḩasy Yemen 14°3N 48°40E 249 D5
Al Hawīyah Ash Sharqīyah, Si. Arabia 24°45N 49°6E 249 A5
Al Hawīyah Makkah, Si. Arabia 21°26N 40°30E 248 B3
Al Ḩawrah Yemen 13°50N 47°35E 248 D4
Al Hawtah = Laḩij Yemen 13°4N 44°53E 248 D4
Al Ḩawţah Si. Arabia 23°30N 47°0E 248 B4
Al Ḩayy Iraq 32°5N 46°5E 213 F12
Al Ḩijarah Asia 30°0N 44°0E 246 D4
Al Ḩillah Iraq 32°30N 44°25E 213 F11
Al Ḩillah Si. Arabia 23°35N 46°50E 248 B4
Al Hindīyah Iraq 32°30N 44°10E 213 F11
Al Hirmil Lebanon 34°26N 36°24E 250 D7
Al Hoceïma Morocco 35°8N 3°58W 261 A4
Al Ḩudaydah Yemen 14°50N 43°0E 248 D3
Al Ḩudūd ash Shamālīyah □ Si. Arabia 29°10N 42°30E 246 D4
Al Ḩufrah Libya 25°32N 14°1E 258 C2
Al Hufūf Si. Arabia 25°25N 49°45E 247 E6
Al Ḩulwah Si. Arabia 23°24N 46°48E 248 B4
Al Ḩumayḑah Si. Arabia 29°14N 34°56E 251 J5
Al Ḩunayy Si. Arabia 25°58N 48°45E 247 E6
Al Husayyāt Libya 30°24N 20°37E 258 B4
Al 'Irqah Yemen 13°39N 47°22E 248 D4
Al Īsāwīyah Si. Arabia 30°43N 37°59E 246 D3
Al Ittihad = Madīnat ash Sha'b Yemen 12°50N 45°0E 248 D4
Al Jabal al Akhḑar Libya 32°30N 21°30E 258 B4
Al Jabal al Akhḑar □ Libya 32°30N 21°41E 258 B4
Al Jafr Jordan 30°18N 36°14E 251 H7
Al Jāfūrah Si. Arabia 25°0N 50°15E 247 E7
Al Jaghbūb Libya 29°42N 24°38E 258 C4
Al Jahrah Kuwait 29°25N 47°40E 246 D5
Al Jalāmīd Si. Arabia 31°20N 40°6E 246 D3
Al Jamalīyah Qatar 25°37N 51°5E 247 E6
Al Janūb □ Lebanon 33°20N 35°20E 250 E6
Al Jawf Libya 24°10N 23°24E 258 D4
Al Jawf Si. Arabia 29°55N 39°40E 246 D3
Al Jawf □ Si. Arabia 29°30N 39°30E 246 D3
Al Jazair = Algeria ■ Africa 28°30N 2°0E 261 C5
Al Jazirah Iraq 33°30N 44°0E 213 E10
Al Jithāmīyah Si. Arabia 27°41N 41°43E 246 E4
Al Jubayl Si. Arabia 27°0N 49°50E 247 E6
Al Jubaylah Si. Arabia 24°55N 46°25E 246 E5
Al Jubb Si. Arabia 27°11N 42°17E 246 E4
Al Jufrah Libya 29°10N 16°0E 258 C3
Al Jufrah □ Libya 27°30N 17°30E 258 C3
Al Jumūm Si. Arabia 21°37N 39°42E 248 B2
Al Junaynah Sudan 13°27N 22°45E 259 F4
Al Kabā'ish Iraq 30°58N 47°0E 246 D5
Al Kāmil Oman 22°13N 59°12E 249 B7
Al Karak Jordan 31°11N 35°42E 251 G6
Al Karak □ Jordan 31°0N 36°0E 251 H7
Al Kāẓimīyah Iraq 33°22N 44°18E 213 F11
Al Khābūrah Oman 23°57N 57°5E 247 F8
Al Khafji Si. Arabia 28°24N 48°29E 247 E6
Al Khalīl West Bank 31°32N 35°6E 251 G6
Al Khāliş Iraq 33°49N 44°32E 213 F11
Al Khamāsīn Si. Arabia 20°29N 44°46E 248 B4
Al Kharj Si. Arabia 24°0N 47°0E 248 B4
Al Kharsānīyah Si. Arabia 27°13N 49°18E 247 E6
Al Khaşab Oman 26°14N 56°15E 247 E8
Al Khāşirah Si. Arabia 23°30N 43°47E 248 B3
Al Khawr Qatar 25°41N 51°30E 247 E6
Al Khiḑr Iraq 31°12N 45°33E 246 D5
Al Khiyām Lebanon 33°20N 35°36E 250 E6
Al Khobar Si. Arabia 26°17N 50°12E 247 E6
Al Khums Libya 32°40N 14°17E 258 B2
Al Kifl Iraq 32°13N 44°22E 213 G11
Al Kiswah Syria 33°23N 36°14E 250 E7
Al Kūfah Iraq 32°2N 44°24E 213 F11
Al Kufrah Libya 24°17N 23°15E 258 D4
Al Kuhayfīyah Si. Arabia 27°12N 43°3E 246 E4
Al Kumayt Iraq 32°2N 46°52E 213 G12
Al Kūt Iraq 32°30N 46°0E 213 F11
Al Kuwayt Kuwait 29°30N 48°0E 246 D5
Al Labwah Lebanon 34°11N 36°20E 250 D7
Al Lādhiqīyah Syria 35°30N 35°45E 250 C6
Al Lādhiqīyah □ Syria 35°45N 36°0E 250 C7
Al Līth Si. Arabia 20°9N 40°15E 248 B3
Al Liwā' Oman 24°31N 56°36E 247 E8
Al Luḩayyah Yemen 15°45N 42°40E 248 D3
Al Madīnah Iraq 30°57N 47°16E 246 D5
Al Madīnah Si. Arabia 24°35N 39°52E 246 E3
Al Madīnah □ Si. Arabia 23°50N 40°30E 248 B3
Al Mafraq Jordan 32°17N 36°14E 251 F7
Al Mafraq □ Jordan 32°17N 36°15E 251 F7
Al Maghārīm Yemen 15°1N 47°49E 248 D4
Al Maghreb = Morocco ■ N. Afr. 32°0N 5°50W 260 B3
Al Mahbes W. Sahara 27°10N 9°50W 260 C3
Al Maḩmūdīyah Iraq 33°3N 44°21E 213 F11
Al Majma'ah Si. Arabia 25°57N 45°22E 246 E5
Al Makhruq, W. → Jordan 31°28N 37°0E 251 G8
Al Makḩūl Si. Arabia 26°37N 42°39E 246 E4
Al Mālikīyah Syria 37°10N 42°8E 213 D10
Al Manāmah Bahrain 26°10N 50°30E 247 E6
Al Maqwa' Kuwait 29°10N 47°59E 246 D5
Al Marāḩ Si. Arabia 25°35N 49°35E 247 E6
Al Marj Libya 32°25N 20°30E 258 B4
Al Marj □ Libya 32°0N 21°0E 258 B4
Al Marqab □ Libya 32°32N 14°35E 258 B2
Al Maţlā Kuwait 29°24N 47°40E 246 D5
Al Mawşil Iraq 36°15N 43°5E 213 D10
Al Mayādin Syria 35°1N 40°27E 213 E9
Al Mazār Jordan 31°4N 35°41E 251 G6
Al Midhnab Si. Arabia 25°50N 44°18E 246 E5
Al Minā' Lebanon 34°24N 35°49E 250 D6
Al Miqdādīyah Iraq 34°0N 45°0E 213 E11
Al Mubarraz Si. Arabia 25°30N 49°40E 247 E6
Al Mudawwarah Jordan 29°19N 36°0E 251 J7
Al Muḑaybī Oman 22°34N 58°7E 249 B7
Al Mughayrā' U.A.E. 24°5N 53°32E 247 E7
Al Muḩarraq Bahrain 26°15N 50°40E 247 E6
Al Mukallā Yemen 14°33N 49°2E 249 D5
Al Mukhā Yemen 13°18N 43°15E 248 D3
Al Mukhaylī Libya 32°10N 22°17E 258 B4
Al Musayjīd Si. Arabia 24°5N 39°5E 246 E3
Al Musayyib Iraq 32°49N 44°20E 213 F11
Al Muthanná □ Iraq 30°30N 45°15E 246 D5
Al Muwayh Si. Arabia 22°41N 41°37E 256 C5
Al Muwayliḩ Si. Arabia 27°40N 35°30E 246 E2
Al Muzāḩimīyah Si. Arabia 24°29N 46°18E 248 A4
Al Owuho = Otukpa Nigeria 7°9N 7°41E 263 D6
Al Qaddāḩīyah Libya 31°15N 15°9E 258 B3
Al Qaḑīmah Si. Arabia 22°20N 39°13E 248 B2
Al Qādisīyah □ Iraq 32°0N 45°0E 246 D5
Al Qadmūs Syria 35°5N 36°10E 250 C7
Al Qaḩmah Si. Arabia 18°0N 41°41E 248 C3
Al Qā'im Iraq 34°21N 41°7E 213 E9
Al Qā'iyah Si. Arabia 24°33N 43°15E 248 A3
Al Qalībah Si. Arabia 28°24N 37°42E 246 D3
Al Qāmishlī Syria 37°2N 41°14E 213 D9
Al Qardāḩah Syria 35°27N 36°3E 250 C7
Al Qaryah ash Sharqīyah Libya 30°28N 13°40E 258 B2
Al Qaryatayn Syria 34°12N 37°13E 250 D8
Al Qaşabāt Libya 32°39N 14°1E 258 B2
Al Qaşīm □ Si. Arabia 26°0N 43°0E 246 E4
Al Qaţ'ā Syria 34°40N 40°48E 213 E9
Al Qaţīf Si. Arabia 26°35N 50°0E 247 E6
Al Qaţn Yemen 15°51N 48°26E 249 D5
Al Qatrānah Jordan 31°12N 36°6E 251 G7
Al Qaţrūn Libya 24°56N 15°3E 258 D3
Al Qawz Si. Arabia 18°58N 41°26E 248 C3
Al Qayşūmah Si. Arabia 28°20N 46°7E 246 D5
Al Qiblīyah Oman 17°30N 56°20E 249 C7
Al Qubbah □ Libya 31°0N 23°40E 258 B4
Al Quds = Jerusalem Israel/West Bank 31°47N 35°10E 123 B2
Al Qunayţirah Syria 33°5N 35°45E 250 F6
Al Qunfudhah Si. Arabia 19°3N 41°4E 248 C3
Al Qurayyāt Oman 23°17N 58°53E 249 B7
Al Qurḩ Yemen 16°44N 51°29E 249 C5
Al Qurnah Iraq 31°1N 47°25E 246 D5
Al Quşayr Iraq 30°39N 45°50E 246 D5
Al Quşayr Syria 34°31N 36°34E 250 D7
Al Qutayfah Syria 33°44N 36°36E 250 E7
Al Quway'īyah Si. Arabia 24°3N 45°15E 248 A4
Al Quwayr Iraq 36°2N 43°29E 213 D10
Al 'Ubaylah Si. Arabia 21°59N 50°57E 249 B5
Al 'Uḑaylīyah Si. Arabia 25°8N 49°18E 247 E6
Al 'Ulā Si. Arabia 26°35N 38°0E 246 E3
Al 'Ulayyah Si. Arabia 19°39N 41°54E 248 C3
Al Uqaylah ash Sharqīgah Libya 30°12N 19°10E 258 B3
Al 'Uqayr Si. Arabia 25°40N 50°15E 247 E6
Al 'Urūq al Mutariḑah Si. Arabia 21°0N 53°30E 249 B6
Al 'Uwaynāt Libya 25°47N 10°33E 261 C7
Al 'Uwaynid Si. Arabia 24°50N 46°0E 246 E5
Al 'Uwayqīlah Si. Arabia 30°30N 42°10E 246 D4
Al Uweinat Libya 21°34N 24°50E 259 D4
Al 'Uyūn Ḩijāz, Si. Arabia 24°33N 39°35E 246 E3
Al 'Uyūn Najd, Si. Arabia 26°30N 43°50E 246 E4
Al 'Uzayr Iraq 31°19N 47°25E 246 D5
Al Wāhāt □ Libya 29°0N 22°0E 258 C4
Al Wajh Si. Arabia 26°10N 36°30E 246 E3
Al Wakrah Qatar 25°10N 51°40E 247 E6
Al-Walaja West Bank 31°44N 35°9E 123 B1
Al Waqbah Si. Arabia 28°48N 45°33E 246 D5
Al Wari'āh Si. Arabia 27°51N 47°25E 246 E5
Al Wāţīyah Libya 32°28N 11°57E 258 B2
Al Wīgh Libya 24°16N 14°58E 258 D2
Al Yaman = Yemen ■ Asia 15°0N 44°0E 248 D4
Ala Italy 45°45N 11°0E 198 C8
Ala Dağ Turkey 37°44N 35°9E 246 B2
Ala Dağları Turkey 39°15N 43°33E 213 C10
Ala Tau Asia 45°30N 80°40E 217 C10
Ala Tau Shankou = Dzungarian Gate Asia 45°10N 82°0E 217 C10
Alabama □ U.S.A. 33°0N 87°0W 315 E11
Alabama → U.S.A. 31°8N 87°57W 315 F11
Alabaster U.S.A. 33°15N 86°49W 315 E11
Alabat I. Phil. 14°7N 122°3E 232 D4
Alabel Phil. 6°4N 125°16E 233 H5
Alabule → Papua N. G. 8°31S 146°56E 286 E4
Alaca Turkey 40°10N 34°51E 212 B6
Alacaatlı Turkey 39°15N 28°3E 205 B10
Alaçam Turkey 41°36N 35°36E 212 B6
Alaçam Dağları Turkey 39°18N 28°49E 205 B10
Alacant = Alicante Spain 38°23N 0°30W 197 G4
Alaçatı Turkey 38°15N 26°22E 205 C8
Alachua U.S.A. 29°47N 82°30W 316 F7
Alaejos Spain 41°18N 5°13W 194 D5
Alagir Russia 43°3N 44°14E 191 J7
Alagna Valsésia Italy 45°51N 7°56E 198 C4
Alagoa de Baixo = Sertânia Brazil 8°5S 37°20W 332 C4
Alagoa Grande Brazil 7°3S 35°35W 332 C4
Alagoas = Marechal Deodoro Brazil 9°43S 35°54W 332 C4
Alagoas □ Brazil 9°0S 36°0W 332 C4
Alagoinhas Brazil 12°7S 38°20W 333 D4
Alagón Spain 41°46N 1°12W 196 D3
Alagón → Spain 39°44N 6°53W 194 F4
Alaguntan Nigeria 6°25N 3°29E 124 B2
Alagyoz = Aragats Armenia 40°30N 44°15E 191 K7
Alahan Turkey 36°46N 33°19E 250 B4
Alaheaieatnu = Altaelva → Norway 69°54N 23°17E 160 B20
Alai Range Asia 39°45N 72°0E 217 E8
Alaior Spain 39°57N 4°8E 206 B5
Alajero Canary Is. 28°3N 17°13W 153 e1
Alajuela Costa Rica 10°2N 84°8W 320 D3
Alajuela, L. Panama 9°14N 79°34W 320 c
Alakamisy Madag. 21°19S 47°14E 272 C2
Alakanuk U.S.A. 62°41N 164°37W 303 E6
Alaknanda → India 30°8N 78°36E 243 D8
Alaköl Kazakhstan 46°0N 81°5E 217 C10
Alakurtti Russia 66°58N 30°25E 160 C24
'Alaläkeiki Channel U.S.A. 20°30N 156°30W 302 C5
Alalapura Suriname 2°20N 56°25W 329 C6
Alalaú → Brazil 0°30S 61°9W 329 D5
Alamagan N. Marianas 17°36N 145°50E 302 a
Alamarvdasht Iran 27°37N 52°59E 247 E7
Alamata Ethiopia 12°25N 39°33E 257 E4
Alameda Calif., U.S.A. 37°46N 122°15W 136 B3
Alameda N. Mex., U.S.A. 35°11N 106°37W 305 J10
Alameda, Parque Mexico City, Mexico 128 b2
Alameda Memorial State Beach Park U.S.A. 37°45N 122°16W 136 B3
Alaminos Phil. 16°10N 119°59E 232 C2
Alamo Ga., U.S.A. 32°9N 82°47W 316 C7
Alamo Nev., U.S.A. 37°22N 115°10W 307 H11
Alamogordo U.S.A. 32°54N 105°57W 305 K11
Alamos Mexico 27°1N 108°56W 318 B3
Alamosa U.S.A. 37°28N 105°52W 305 H11
Alampur India 15°55N 78°6E 245 G4
Åland Finland 60°15N 20°0E 161 F19
Aland India 17°36N 76°35E 244 F3
Alandroal Portugal 38°41N 7°24W 195 G3
Ålands hav Europe 60°0N 19°30E 161 G18
Ålandsbro Sweden 62°40N 17°51E 162 B11
Alandur India 13°0N 80°15E 245 H5
Alang Indonesia 4°7N 117°0E 235 B5
Alange, Embalse d' Spain 38°45N 6°18W 195 G4
Alania = North Ossetia □ Russia 43°30N 44°30E 191 J7
Alanís Spain 38°3N 5°43W 195 G5
Alanya Turkey 36°38N 32°0E 250 B3
Alaotra, Farihin' Madag. 17°30S 48°30E 272 B2
Alapaha U.S.A. 31°23N 83°13W 316 D6
Alapayevsk Russia 57°52N 61°42E 214 D7
Alappuzha = Alleppey India 9°30N 76°28E 245 K3
'Alāqān Si. Arabia 29°10N 35°21E 251 J6
Alar del Rey Spain 42°38N 4°20W 194 C6
Alara → Turkey 36°38N 31°39E 250 B2
Alaraz Spain 40°45N 5°17W 194 E5
Alarcón, Embalse de Spain 39°36N 2°10W 196 F2
Alaró Spain 39°42N 2°47E 206 B3
Alarobia-Vohiposa Madag. 20°59S 47°9E 272 C2
Alas Indonesia 8°29S 117°0E 235 D5
Alas, Selat Indonesia 8°40S 116°40E 235 D5
Alaşehir Turkey 38°23N 28°30E 205 C10
Alashtar Iran 33°51N 48°15E 213 F13
Alaska □ U.S.A. 64°0N 154°0W 303 D9
Alaska, G. of Pac. Oc. 58°0N 145°0W 303 G11
Alaska Maritime Nat. Wildlife Refuge ⌓ U.S.A. 52°0N 174°0W 303 L4
Alaska Peninsula U.S.A. 56°0N 159°0W 303 H8
Alaska Peninsula Nat. Wildlife Refuge ⌓ U.S.A. 56°0N 159°0W 303 J8
Alaska Range U.S.A. 62°50N 151°0W 303 E10
Alássio Italy 44°0N 8°10E 198 E5
Älät Azerbaijan 39°58N 49°25E 191 L9
Alatau Shan = Ala Tau Asia 45°30N 80°40E 217 C10
Alatri Italy 41°43N 13°21E 199 G10
Alatyr Russia 54°55N 46°35E 190 C8
Alatyr → Russia 54°52N 46°36E 190 C8
Alaungdaw Kathapa △ Burma 22°30N 94°30E 241 D5
Alausi Ecuador 2°0S 78°50W 328 D2
Álava □ Spain 42°48N 2°28W 196 C2
Alava, C. U.S.A. 48°10N 124°44W 304 B1
Alaverdi Armenia 41°15N 44°37E 191 K7
Alavo = Alavus Finland 62°35N 23°36E 160 E20
Alavus Finland 62°35N 23°36E 160 E20
Alawa ☼ Australia 15°42S 134°39E 280 B1
Alawoona Australia 34°45S 140°30E 282 C4
Alayawarra ☼ Australia 22°0S 134°30E 280 C1
'Alayh Lebanon 33°46N 35°33E 250 E6
Alazani → Azerbaijan 41°5N 46°40E 191 K8
Alba Italy 44°42N 8°2E 198 D5
Alba □ Romania 46°10N 23°30E 183 D8
Alba Adriática Italy 42°50N 13°56E 199 F10
Alba de Tormes Spain 40°50N 5°30W 194 E5
Alba-Iulia Romania 46°8N 23°39E 183 D8
Albac Romania 46°28N 22°58E 182 D7
Albacete Spain 39°0N 1°50W 197 F3
Albacete □ Spain 38°50N 2°0W 197 G3
Albacutya, L. Australia 35°45S 141°58E 282 C4
Ålbæk Denmark 57°36N 10°25E 163 G4
Ålbæk Bugt Denmark 57°35N 10°40E 163 G4
Albaida Spain 38°51N 0°31W 197 G4
Albalate de las Nogueras Spain 40°22N 2°18W 196 E2
Albalate del Arzobispo Spain 41°6N 0°31W 196 D4
Alban France 43°53N 2°28E 174 E6
Albanel, L. Canada 50°55N 73°12W 298 B5
Albania ■ Europe 41°0N 20°0E 202 E4
Albano Laziale Italy 41°44N 12°39E 199 G9
Albany W. Austral., Australia 35°1S 117°58E 279 G2
Albany Ga., U.S.A. 31°35N 84°10W 316 D5
Albany Ind., U.S.A. 40°18N 85°14W 311 D11
Albany Mo., U.S.A. 40°15N 94°20W 310 D2
Albany N.Y., U.S.A. 42°39N 73°45W 313 D11
Albany Oreg., U.S.A. 44°38N 123°6W 304 D2
Albany Tex., U.S.A. 32°44N 99°18W 314 E5
Albany Wis., U.S.A. 42°42N 89°26W 310 B7
Albany → Canada 52°17N 81°31W 298 B3
Albarca, C. d' Spain 39°4N 1°22E 206 C1
Albardón Argentina 31°20S 68°30W 334 C2
Albarracín Spain 40°25N 1°26W 196 E3
Albarracín, Sierra de Spain 40°30N 1°30W 196 E3
Albatera Spain 38°11N 0°52W 197 G4
Albatross B. Australia 12°45S 141°30E 280 A3
Albatross Pt. N.Z. 38°7S 174°44E 284 E3
Albay □ Phil. 13°13N 123°33E 232 E4
Albegna → Italy 42°30N 11°11E 199 F8
Albemarle U.S.A. 35°21N 80°12W 315 D14
Albemarle, I. = Isabela, I. Ecuador 0°30S 91°4W 330 a
Albemarle, Pta. Ecuador 0°11N 91°21W 330 a
Albemarle Sd. U.S.A. 36°5N 76°0W 315 C16
Albenga Italy 44°3N 8°13E 198 D5
Alberche → Spain 39°58N 4°46W 194 F6
Alberdi Paraguay 26°14S 58°20W 334 B4
Albères, Mts. France 42°28N 2°56E 174 F6

Ålberga Sweden 58°44N 16°35E 163 F10
Alberga → Australia 27°6S 135°33E 281 D2
Albern Austria 48°9N 16°29E 142 B2
Albersdorf Germany 54°8N 9°17E 178 A5
Albert France 50°0N 2°38E 173 C9
Albert, L. Africa 1°30N 31°0E 268 B3
Albert, L. S. Austral., Australia 35°30S 139°10E 282 C3
Albert Edward, Mt. Papua N. G. 8°20S 147°24E 286 E4
Albert Edward Ra. Australia 18°17S 127°57E 278 C4
Albert Lea U.S.A. 43°39N 93°22W 308 D7
Albert Nat. Park = Virunga △ Dem. Rep. of the Congo 0°5N 29°38E 268 B2
Albert Nile → Uganda 3°36N 32°2E 268 B3
Albert Park Australia 37°51S 144°58E 128 B1
Albert Town Bahamas 22°37N 74°33W 321 B5
Albert Town Jamaica 18°17N 77°33W 320 a
Alberta □ Canada 54°40N 115°0W 296 C6
Alberti Argentina 35°1S 60°16W 334 D3
Albertinia S. Africa 34°11S 21°34E 270 D3
Albertirsa Hungary 47°14N 19°37E 182 C4
Alberto de Agostini △ Chile 54°38S 71°37W 336 D2
Alberton P.E.I., Canada 46°50N 64°0W 299 C7
Alberton Gauteng, S. Africa 26°15S 28°7E 123 B2
Albertslund Denmark 55°39N 12°21E 118 B2
Albertville = Kalemie Dem. Rep. of the Congo 5°55S 29°9E 268 D2
Albertville Savoie, France 45°40N 6°22E 175 C10
Albertville Ala., U.S.A. 34°16N 86°13W 315 D11
Albi France 43°56N 2°9E 174 E6
Albia U.S.A. 41°2N 92°48W 310 C4
Albina Suriname 5°37N 54°15W 329 B7
Albina, Ponta Angola 15°52S 11°44E 265 F2
Albino Italy 45°46N 9°47E 198 C6
Albion Ill., U.S.A. 38°23N 88°4W 311 F8
Albion Ind., U.S.A. 41°24N 85°25W 311 C11
Albion Mich., U.S.A. 42°15N 84°45W 311 B12
Albion Nebr., U.S.A. 41°42N 98°0W 308 E4
Albion Pa., U.S.A. 41°53N 80°22W 312 E4
Albocásser Spain 40°21N 0°1E 196 E5
Albolote Spain 37°14N 3°39W 195 H7
Alborán Medit. S. 35°57N 3°0W 195 K7
Alborea Spain 39°17N 1°24W 197 F3
Ålborg = Aalborg Denmark 57°2N 9°54E 163 G3
Ålborg Bugt = Aalborg Bugt Denmark 56°50N 10°35E 163 H4
Alborz, Reshteh-ye Kūhhā-ye Iran 36°0N 52°0E 247 C7
Albox Spain 37°23N 2°8W 197 H2
Albuera Phil. 10°55N 124°42E 233 F5
Albufeira Portugal 37°5N 8°15W 195 H2
Albula → Switz. 46°38N 9°28E 179 J5
Albuñol Spain 36°48N 3°11W 195 J7
Albuquerque Brazil 19°23S 57°26W 331 D6
Albuquerque N. Mex., U.S.A. 35°5N 106°39W 305 J10
Albuquerque, Cayos de Caribbean 12°10N 81°50W 320 D3
Alburg U.S.A. 44°59N 73°18W 313 B11
Alburno, Mte. Italy 40°33N 15°17E 201 B8
Alburquerque Spain 39°15N 6°59W 195 F4
Albury Australia 36°3S 146°56E 283 D7
Alby Sweden 62°30N 15°28E 162 B9
Alcácer do Sal Portugal 38°22N 8°33W 195 G2
Alcáçovas Portugal 38°23N 8°9W 195 G2
Alcala Phil. 17°54N 121°39E 232 C3
Alcalá de Guadaira Spain 37°20N 5°50W 195 H5
Alcalá de Henares Spain 40°28N 3°22W 194 E7
Alcalá de los Gazules Spain 36°29N 5°43W 195 J5
Alcalá de Xivert Spain 40°19N 0°13E 196 E5
Alcalá del Júcar Spain 39°12N 1°26W 197 F3
Alcalá del Río Spain 37°31N 5°59W 195 H5
Alcalá del Valle Spain 36°54N 5°10W 195 J5
Alcalá la Real Spain 37°27N 3°57W 195 H7
Álcamo Italy 37°59N 12°55E 200 E5
Alcanadre Spain 42°24N 2°7W 196 C2
Alcanadre → Spain 41°43N 0°12W 196 D4
Alcanar Spain 40°33N 0°28E 196 E5
Alcanede Portugal 39°25N 8°49W 195 F2
Alcanena Portugal 39°27N 8°40W 195 F2
Alcañices Spain 41°41N 6°21W 194 D4
Alcañiz Spain 41°2N 0°8W 196 D4
Alcântara Brazil 2°20S 44°30W 332 B3
Alcantara Lisboa, Portugal 38°43N 9°10W 126 A1
Alcántara Spain 39°41N 6°57W 194 F4
Alcántara, Embalse de Spain 39°44N 6°50W 194 F4
Alcantarilla Spain 37°59N 1°12W 197 H3
Alcaracejos Spain 38°24N 4°58W 195 G6
Alcaraz Spain 38°40N 2°29W 197 G2
Alcaraz, Sierra de Spain 38°40N 2°20W 197 G2
Alcatraz I. U.S.A. 37°49N 122°25W 136 B2
Alcaudete Spain 37°35N 4°5W 195 H6
Alcázar de San Juan Spain 39°24N 3°12W 195 F7
Alcazarquivir = Ksar el Kebir Morocco 35°0N 6°0W 260 B3
Alcedo, Volcán Ecuador 0°24S 91°6W 330 a
Alchevsk Ukraine 48°30N 38°45E 189 H10
Alcira = Alzira Spain 39°9N 0°30W 197 F4
Alcobaça = Tucuruí Brazil 3°42S 49°44W 332 B2
Alcobaça Portugal 39°32N 8°58W 195 F2
Alcobendas Spain 40°32N 3°38W 127 A2
Alcolea del Pinar Spain 41°2N 2°28W 196 D2
Alcoma U.S.A. 27°54N 81°29W 317 H8
Alcorcón Spain 40°20N 3°48W 127 B1
Alcoutim Portugal 37°25N 7°28W 195 H3
Alcova U.S.A. 42°34N 106°43W 304 E10
Alcoy Spain 38°43N 0°30W 197 G4
Alcubierre, Sierra de Spain 41°45N 0°22W 196 D4
Alcublas Spain 39°48N 0°43W 196 F4
Alcúdia Spain 39°51N 3°7E 206 B4
Alcúdia, B. d' Spain 39°47N 3°15E 206 B4
Alcúdia, Sierra de la Spain 38°34N 4°30W 195 G6
Aldabra Is. Seychelles 9°22S 46°28E 255 G8
Aldama Mexico 22°55N 98°4W 319 C5
Aldan Russia 58°40N 125°30E 215 D13
Aldan → Russia 63°28N 129°35E 215 C13
Aldea, Pta. de la Canary Is. 28°0N 15°50W 153 e1
Aldeburgh U.K. 52°10N 1°37E 169 E9
Alden Norway 61°19N 4°45E 164 C1
Alder Pk. U.S.A. 35°53N 121°22W 306 K5
Alderney U.K. 49°42N 2°11W 169 H5
Aldershof Germany 52°26N 13°33E 115 B4
Aldershot U.K. 51°15N 0°44W 169 F7
Aldinga Beach Australia 35°17S 138°27E 282 C3
Aldo Bonzi Argentina 34°42S 58°31W 117 C1
Åled Sweden 56°44N 12°57E 163 H6
Aledo U.S.A. 41°12N 90°45W 310 C6
Alefa Ethiopia 11°55N 36°55E 257 E4
Aleg Mauritania 17°3N 13°55W 262 B2
Alegranza Canary Is. 29°23N 13°32W 260 C2
Alegranza, I. Canary Is. 29°23N 13°32W 153 e2
Alegre Brazil 20°50S 41°30W 333 F3
Alegrete Brazil 29°40S 56°0W 335 B4
Aleknagik U.S.A. 59°17N 158°36W 303 G8
Aleksandriya = Oleksandriya Kirovohrad, Ukraine 48°42N 33°3E 189 H7
Aleksandriya = Oleksandriya Rivne, Ukraine 50°37N 26°19E 177 C14
Aleksandriyskaya Russia 43°58N 47°14E 191 J8
Aleksandropol = Gyumri Armenia 40°47N 43°50E 191 K6
Aleksandrov Russia 56°23N 38°44E 188 D10
Aleksandrov Gay Russia 50°9N 48°34E 190 E9
Aleksandrovac Serbia 43°28N 21°3E 202 C5
Aleksandrovac Serbia 44°28N 21°13E 202 B5
Aleksandrovka = Oleksandrivka Ukraine 48°55N 32°20E 189 H7
Aleksandrovka = Ordzhonikīdze Ukraine 47°39N 34°3E 189 J8
Aleksandrovo Bulgaria 43°14N 24°51E 203 C8
Aleksandrovsk = Belogorsk Russia 51°0N 128°20E 215 D13
Aleksandrovsk = Polyarny Russia 69°8N 33°20E 160 B25
Aleksandrovsk = Zaporizhzhya Ukraine 47°50N 35°10E 189 J8
Aleksandrovsk-Grushevsky = Shakhty Russia 47°40N 40°16E 191 G5
Aleksandrovsk-Sakhalinskiy Russia 50°50N 142°20E 219 A17
Aleksandrovskoye Russia 59°51N 30°20E 137 B2
Aleksandrów Kujawski Poland 52°53N 18°43E 185 F5
Aleksandrów Łódźki Poland 51°49N 19°17E 185 G6
Aleksandry, Zemlya Russia 80°25N 48°0E 214 A5
Alekseyevka Samara, Russia 52°35N 51°17E 190 D10
Alekseyevka Voronezh, Russia 50°43N 38°40E 189 G10
Alekseyevsk = Svobodnyy Russia 51°20N 128°0E 215 D13
Alekseyevskoye = Qazyghurt Kazakhstan 41°45N 69°23E 217 D7
Aleksin Russia 54°31N 37°9E 188 E9
Aleksinac Serbia 43°31N 21°42E 202 C5
Além Paraíba Brazil 21°52S 42°41W 333 F3
Alemania Argentina 25°40S 65°30W 334 B2
Alemania Chile 25°10S 69°55W 334 B2
Alen Eq. Guin. 1°58N 11°19E 264 B2
Alençon France 48°27N 0°4E 172 D7
'Alenuihähä Channel U.S.A. 20°30N 156°0W 302 C5
Alépé Ivory C. 5°29N 3°40W 262 D4
Aleppo = Ḩalab Syria 36°10N 37°15E 250 B8
Alerce Andino △ Chile 41°33S 72°29W 336 B2
Aléria France 42°5N 9°26E 175 F13
Alert Canada 83°2N 60°0W 295 A20
Aleru India 17°39N 79°3E 244 F4
Alès France 44°9N 4°5E 175 D8
Aleşd Romania 47°3N 22°22E 182 C7
Alessándria Italy 44°54N 8°37E 198 D5
Ålesund Norway 62°28N 6°12E 164 B3
Alet-les-Bains France 42°59N 2°14E 174 F6
Aletschhorn Switz. 46°28N 8°0E 179 J4
Aleutian Basin Pac. Oc. 57°0N 177°0E 288 B9
Aleutian Is. Pac. Oc. 52°0N 175°0W 303 K3
Aleutian Range U.S.A. 60°0N 154°0W 303 G9
Aleutian Trench Pac. Oc. 48°0N 180°0E 150 D17
Alexander Ga., U.S.A. 33°1N 81°53W 316 B8
Alexander N. Dak., U.S.A. 47°51N 103°39W 308 B2
Alexander, C. Solomon Is. 6°34S 156°32E 287 L9
Alexander, Mt. Australia 28°58S 120°16E 279 E3
Alexander Arch. U.S.A. 56°0N 136°0W 303 J14
Alexander Bay S. Africa 28°40S 16°30E 270 C2
Alexander City U.S.A. 32°56N 85°58W 316 C4
Alexander I. Antarctica 69°0S 70°0W 151 C17
Alexander Nevsky Abbey Russia 59°54N 30°23E 137 B2
Alexander Soutzos Museum Athens, Greece 112 b3
Alexandra Vic., Australia 37°8S 145°40E 283 D6
Alexandra N.Z. 45°14S 169°25E 285 F4
Alexandra Singapore, Singapore 1°17N 103°49E 138 B2
Alexandra Gauteng, S. Africa 26°6S 28°5E 123 A2
Alexandra Channel Burma 14°7N 93°13E 245 G11
Alexandra Falls Canada 60°29N 116°18W 296 A5
Alexandretta = İskenderun Turkey 36°32N 36°10E 250 B7
Alexandria = El Iskandarîya Egypt 31°13N 29°58E 256 H7
Alexandria B.C., Canada 52°35N 122°27W 296 C4
Alexandria Ont., Canada 45°19N 74°38W 313 A10
Alexandria Romania 43°57N 25°24E 183 G10
Alexandria Eastern Cape, S. Africa 33°38S 26°28E 270 D4
Alexandria W. Dunb., U.K. 55°59N 4°35W 167 F4
Alexandria Ind., U.S.A. 40°16N 85°41W 311 D11
Alexandria Ky., U.S.A. 38°58N 84°23W 311 F12
Alexandria La., U.S.A. 31°18N 92°27W 314 F8
Alexandria Minn., U.S.A. 45°53N 95°22W 308 C6
Alexandria Mo., U.S.A. 40°27N 91°28W 310 D5
Alexandria S. Dak., U.S.A. 43°39N 97°47W 308 D5
Alexandria Va., U.S.A. 38°49N 77°5W 143 C3
Alexandria Bay U.S.A. 44°20N 75°55W 313 B9
Alexandrina, L. Australia 35°25S 139°10E 282 C3
Alexandroupoli Greece 40°50N 25°54E 203 F9
Alexis U.S.A. 41°4N 90°33W 310 C6
Alexis → Canada 52°33N 56°8W 299 B8
Alexis Creek Canada 52°10N 123°20W 296 C4
Aley → Russia 52°51N 83°36E 217 B10
Aleysk Russia 52°40N 83°0E 217 B10
Alfabia Spain 39°44N 2°44E 206 B3
Alfama Lisbon, Portugal 126 c3
Alfambra Spain 40°33N 1°5W 196 E3
Alfândega da Fé Portugal 41°20N 6°59W 194 D4
Alfaro Spain 42°10N 1°50W 196 C3
Alfatar Bulgaria 43°59N 27°13E 203 C11
Alfeld Germany 51°59N 9°50E 178 D5
Alfenas Brazil 21°20S 46°10W 335 A6
Alföld Hungary 46°30N 20°0E 182 D5
Alfonsine Italy 44°30N 12°3E 199 D9
Alford Aberds., U.K. 57°14N 2°41W 167 D6
Alford Lincs., U.K. 53°15N 0°10E 168 D8
Alford Fla., U.S.A. 30°42N 85°24W 316 E4
Alfortville France 48°48N 2°24E 134 B3
Ålfotbreen Norway 61°45N 5°39E 164 C2
Ålfoten Norway 61°51N 5°41E 164 C2
Alfred Maine, U.S.A. 43°29N 70°43W 313 C14
Alfred N.Y., U.S.A. 42°16N 77°48W 312 D7
Alfredton N.Z. 40°41S 175°54E 284 G4
Alfreton U.K. 53°6N 1°24W 168 D6
Alfta Sweden 61°21N 16°4E 162 C10
Algaida Spain 39°33N 2°53E 206 B3
Algar Spain 36°40N 5°39W 195 J5
Ålgård Norway 58°46N 5°53E 164 F2
Algarinejo Spain 37°19N 4°9W 195 H6
Algarve Portugal 36°58N 8°20W 195 J2
Algeciras Spain 36°9N 5°28W 195 J5
Algemesí Spain 39°11N 0°27W 197 F4
Alger Algeria 36°42N 3°8E 261 A5
Alger □ Algeria 36°45N 3°10E 197 J8
Alger ✈ (ALG) Algeria 36°39N 3°13E 197 J8
Algeria ■ Africa 28°30N 2°0E 261 C5
Algés Portugal 38°42N 9°13W 126 A1
Algha Kazakhstan 49°53N 57°20E 187 E10
Alghero Italy 40°33N 8°19E 200 B1
Älghult Sweden 57°0N 15°35E 163 G9
Algiers = Alger Algeria 36°42N 3°8E 261 A5
Algiers U.S.A. 29°56N 90°2W 131 B2
Algoa B. S. Africa 33°50S 25°45E 270 D4
Algodonales Spain 36°54N 5°24W 195 J5
Algodor → Spain 39°55N 3°53W 194 F7
Algoma U.S.A. 44°36N 87°26W 308 C10
Algona U.S.A. 43°4N 94°14W 310 A2
Algonac U.S.A. 42°37N 82°32W 312 D2
Algonquin ⌓ Canada 45°50N 78°30W 298 C4
Alhama de Almería Spain 36°57N 2°34W 195 J8
Alhama de Aragón Spain 41°18N 1°54W 196 D3
Alhama de Granada Spain 37°0N 3°59W 195 H7
Alhama de Murcia Spain 37°51N 1°25W 197 H3
Alhambra U.S.A. 34°5N 118°7W 126 B4
Alhaurín el Grande Spain 36°39N 4°41W 195 J6
Alhucemas = Al Hoceïma Morocco 35°8N 3°58W 261 A4
'Alī al Gharbī Iraq 32°30N 46°45E 213 F12
'Alī ash Sharqī Iraq 32°7N 46°44E 213 F12
Äli Bayramlı Azerbaijan 39°59N 48°52E 191 L9
'Alī Khēl Afghan. 33°57N 69°43E 242 C3
Ali Sahîh Djibouti 11°10N 42°44E 257 E5
Alī Shāh Iran 38°9N 45°50E 246 B5
Ália Italy 37°47N 13°43E 200 E6
'Alīābād Golestān, Iran 36°40N 54°33E 247 B7
'Alīābād Khorāsān, Iran 32°30N 57°30E 247 C8
'Alīābād Kordestān, Iran 35°4N 46°58E 246 C5
'Alīābād Yazd, Iran 31°41N 53°49E 247 D7
Aliade Nigeria 7°18N 8°29E 263 D6
Aliaga Spain 40°40N 0°42W 196 E4
Aliağa Turkey 38°47N 26°59E 205 C8
Aliakmonas → Greece 40°30N 22°36E 202 F6
Alibag India 18°38N 72°56E 244 E1
Alibey → Turkey 41°3N 28°56E 122 B1
Alibey Barajı Turkey 41°8N 28°53E 122 B1
Alibeyköy Turkey 41°4N 28°56E 122 B1
Alibo Ethiopia 9°52N 37°5E 257 F4
Alibori → Benin 11°56N 3°17E 263 C5
Alibunar Serbia 45°5N 20°57E 182 E5
Alicante Spain 38°23N 0°30W 197 G4
Alicante □ Spain 38°30N 0°37W 197 G4
Alicante ✈ (ALC) Spain 38°14N 0°36W 197 G4
Alice Eastern Cape, S. Africa 32°48S 26°55E 270 D4
Alice Tex., U.S.A. 27°45N 98°5W 314 H5
Alice → Queens., Australia 24°2S 144°50E 280 C3
Alice → Queens., Australia 15°35S 142°20E 280 B3
Alice → Papua N. G. 6°10S 141°8E 286 D1
Alice, Punta Italy 39°24N 17°9E 201 C10
Alice Arm Canada 55°29N 129°31W 296 B3
Alice Springs Australia 23°40S 133°50E 280 C1
Alicedale S. Africa 33°15S 26°4E 270 D4
Aliceville U.S.A. 33°8N 88°9W 315 E10
Alicia Bohol, Phil. 9°54N 124°26E 233 G5
Alicia Isabela, Phil. 16°46N 121°42E 232 C3
Alicudi Italy 38°33N 14°20E 201 D7
Alien Taiwan 22°52N 120°19E 225 D2
Aliganj India 27°30N 79°10E 243 F8
Aligarh Raj., India 25°55N 76°15E 242 G7
Aligarh Ut. P., India 27°55N 78°10E 242 F8
Alīgūdarz Iran 33°25N 49°45E 247 C6
Alijó Portugal 41°16N 7°27W 194 D3
Alikanas Greece 37°51N 20°47E 207 D2
Alima → Congo 1°35S 16°37E 264 C3
Alimia Greece 36°16N 27°43E 206 E11
Alimodian Phil. 10°49N 122°26E 233 F4
Alimos Greece 37°52N 23°43E 112 B2
Alindao C.A.R. 5°2N 21°13E 264 A4
Alingsås Sweden 57°56N 12°31E 163 G6
Alipur W. Bengal, India 22°43N 88°12E 124 B1
Alipur Pakistan 29°25N 70°55E 242 E4
Alipur Duar India 26°30N 89°35E 241 B2
Aliquippa U.S.A. 40°37N 80°15W 312 F4
Alishan Taiwan 23°31N 120°48E 225 C2
Aliste → Spain 41°34N 5°58W 194 D5
Alitus = Alytus Lithuania 54°24N 24°3E 188 E3
Aliveri Greece 38°24N 24°2E 204 C6
Aliwal North S. Africa 30°45S 26°45E 270 D4
Alix Canada 52°24N 113°11W 296 C6
Aljezur Portugal 37°18N 8°49W 195 H2
Aljustrel Portugal 37°55N 8°10W 195 H2
Alkamari Niger 13°27N 11°10E 259 F2
Alkmaar Neths. 52°37N 4°45E 170 B4
All American Canal U.S.A. 32°45N 115°15W 305 K6
Allacapan Phil. 18°15N 121°35E 232 B3
Allach Germany 48°11N 11°27E 131 A1
Allada Benin 6°41N 2°9E 263 D5
Allagadda India 15°8N 78°30E 245 G4
Allagash → U.S.A. 47°5N 69°3W 309 B19
Allah Dad Pakistan 25°38N 67°34E 242 G2
Allahabad India 25°25N 81°58E 243 G9
Allakaket U.S.A. 66°34N 152°39W 303 C9
Allal Tazi Morocco 34°30N 6°20W 260 B3
Allambie Heights Australia 33°46S 151°15E 139 A2
Allan Canada 51°53N 106°4W 297 C7
Allanche France 45°14N 2°57E 174 C6
Allanmyo Burma 19°30N 95°17E 241 F5
Allanridge S. Africa 27°45S 26°40E 270 C4
Allansford Australia 38°26S 142°39E 282 E5
Allanton N.Z. 45°55S 170°15E 285 F5
Allaqi, Wadi → Egypt 23°7N 32°47E 256 C3
Allariz Spain 42°11N 7°50W 194 C3
Allassac France 45°15N 1°29E 174 C5
Allatoona L. U.S.A. 34°10N 84°44W 316 A5
Ålleberg Sweden 58°8N 13°36E 163 F7
Allegan U.S.A. 42°32N 85°51W 311 B11
Allegany U.S.A. 42°6N 78°30W 312 D6
Allegheny → U.S.A. 40°27N 80°1W 312 F5
Allegheny Mts. U.S.A. 38°15N 80°10W 309 F13
Allegheny Plateau U.S.A. 41°30N 78°30W 309 E14
Allegheny Res. U.S.A. 41°50N 79°0W 312 E6
Allègre France 45°12N 3°41E 174 C7
Allègre, Pte. Guadeloupe 16°22N 61°46W 322 e
Allen Argentina 38°58S 67°50W 336 A3
Allen Phil. 12°30N 124°17E 232 E5
Allen, Bog of Ireland 53°15N 7°0W 166 C5
Allen, L. Ireland 54°8N 8°4W 166 B3
Allendale U.S.A. 33°1N 81°18W 316 B8
Allende Mexico 28°20N 100°51W 318 B4
Allenstein = Olsztyn Poland 53°48N 20°29E 184 E7
Allentown U.S.A. 40°37N 75°29W 313 F9
Allentsteig Austria 48°41N 15°20E 180 C8
Alleppey India 9°30N 76°28E 245 K3
Allepuz Spain 40°29N 0°44W 196 E4
Aller → Germany 52°56N 9°12E 178 C5
Allermuir Hill U.K. 55°53N 3°14W 121 B2
Alley, The Jamaica 17°48N 77°17W 320 a
Alliance Suriname 5°50N 54°50W 329 B7
Alliance Nebr., U.S.A. 42°6N 102°52W 308 D2
Alliance Ohio, U.S.A. 40°55N 81°6W 312 F3
Allier □ France 46°25N 2°40E 173 F9
Allier → France 46°57N 3°4E 173 F10
Alliford Bay Canada 53°12N 131°58W 296 C2
Alligator Pond Jamaica 17°52N 77°34W 320 a
Allinagaram India 10°2N 77°30E 245 J3
Allinge Denmark 55°17N 14°50E 163 J8
Allison U.S.A. 42°45N 92°48W 310 B4
Alliston Canada 44°9N 79°52W 312 B5
Alloa U.K. 56°7N 3°47W 167 E5
Allones France 48°20N 1°40E 172 D8
Allora Australia 28°2S 152°0E 281 D5
Allos France 44°15N 6°38E 175 D10
Allstate Arena U.S.A. 42°2N 87°54W 119 A1
Allston U.S.A. 42°21N 71°7W 116 A2
Alluitsup Paa Greenland 60°30N 45°35W 154 E6
Allur India 14°40N 80°4E 245 G5
Alluru Kottapatnam India 15°24N 80°7E 245 G5
Alma Qué., Canada 48°35N 71°40W 299 C5
Alma Ga., U.S.A. 31°33N 82°28W 316 D7
Alma Kans., U.S.A. 39°1N 96°17W 308 F5
Alma Mich., U.S.A. 43°23N 84°39W 309 D11
Alma Nebr., U.S.A. 40°6N 99°22W 308 E4
Alma Wis., U.S.A. 44°20N 91°55W 308 C8
Alma Ata = Almaty Kazakhstan 43°15N 76°57E 217 D9
Alma Hill U.S.A. 42°2N 78°0W 312 D7
Almacelles Spain 41°43N 0°27E 196 D5
Almada Portugal 38°41N 9°8W 126 A2
Almaden Queens., Australia 17°22S 144°40E 280 B3
Almadén Spain 38°49N 4°52W 195 G6
Almagro Argentina 34°38S 58°24W 117 B2
Almagro I. Phil. 11°55N 124°18E 233 F5
Almalyk = Olmaliq Uzbekistan 40°50N 69°35E 217 D7
Almanor, L. U.S.A. 40°14N 121°9W 304 F3
Almansa Spain 38°51N 1°5W 197 G3
Almanza Spain 42°39N 5°3W 194 C5
Almanzor, Pico Spain 40°15N 5°18W 194 E5
Almanzora → Spain 37°14N 1°46W 197 H3
Almargem do Bispo Portugal 38°49N 9°17W 126 A1
Almas Brazil 11°33S 47°9W 333 D2
Almaş, Munţii Romania 44°49N 22°12E 182 F7
Almassora Spain 39°57N 0°3W 196 F4
Almaty Kazakhstan 43°15N 76°57E 217 D9
Almaty □ Kazakhstan 44°30N 78°0E 217 D9
Almazán Spain 41°30N 2°30W 196 D2
Almazovo Russia 55°50N 38°3E 129 A6
Almeirim Brazil 1°30S 52°34W 329 D7
Almeirim Portugal 39°12N 8°37W 195 F2
Almelo Neths. 52°22N 6°42E 170 B6
Almenar de Soria Spain 41°43N 2°12W 196 D2
Almenara Brazil 16°11S 40°42W 333 E3
Almenara Spain 39°46N 0°14W 196 F4
Almenara, Sierra de Spain 37°34N 1°32W 197 H3
Almendra, Embalse de Spain 41°10N 6°5W 194 D4
Almendralejo Spain 38°41N 6°26W 195 G4
Almere-Stad Neths. 52°20N 5°15E 170 B5
Almería Spain 36°52N 2°27W 195 J8
Almería □ Spain 37°20N 2°20W 197 H2
Almería, G. de Spain 36°41N 2°28W 197 J2
Almetyevsk Russia 54°53N 52°20E 190 C11
Älmhult Sweden 56°33N 14°8E 163 H8
Almirante Panama 9°10N 82°30W 320 E3
Almirante G. Brown, Parque Argentina 34°40S 58°28W 117 C2
Almirante Montt, G. Chile 51°52S 72°50W 336 D2
Almiropotamos Greece 38°16N 24°11E 204 C6
Almiros Greece 39°11N 22°45E 204 B4
Almodôvar Portugal 37°31N 8°2W 195 H2
Almodóvar del Campo Spain 38°43N 4°10W 195 G6
Almodóvar del Río Spain 37°48N 5°1W 195 H5
Almon West Bank 31°49N 35°17E 123 B2
Almond U.S.A. 42°19N 77°44W 312 D7
Almond → U.K. 55°58N 3°18W 121 B2
Almont U.S.A. 42°55N 83°3W 312 D1
Almonte Ont., Canada 45°14N 76°12W 313 A8
Almonte Spain 37°13N 6°38W 195 H4
Almora India 29°38N 79°40E 243 E8
Almoradí Spain 38°7N 0°46W 197 G4
Almorox Spain 40°14N 4°24W 194 E6
Almoustarat Mali 17°35N 0°8E 263 B5
Älmsta Sweden 59°58N 18°50E 162 E12
Almudévar Spain 42°3N 0°35W 196 C4
Almuñécar Spain 36°43N 3°41W 195 J7
Almunge Sweden 59°53N 18°3E 162 E12
Almuradiel Spain 38°32N 3°28W 195 G7
Almus Turkey 40°22N 36°54E 212 B7
Almvik Sweden 57°49N 16°30E 163 G10
Almyrou, Ormos Greece 35°23N 24°20E 207 E5
Alna Norway 59°55N 10°50E 133 A4
Alness U.K. 57°41N 4°16W 167 D4
Alnif Morocco 31°10N 5°8W 260 B3
Alnmouth U.K. 55°24N 1°37W 168 B6
Alnsjøen Norway 59°57N 10°51E 133 A4
Alnwick U.K. 55°24N 1°42W 168 B6
Alofau Amer. Samoa 14°16S 170°36W 302 f
Alofi Niue 19°1S 169°55W 289 g
Alofi, I. Wall. & F. Is. 14°27S 178°5W 277 C15
Alofi B. Niue 19°1S 169°56W 289 g
Aloi Uganda 2°16N 33°10E 268 B3
Alon Burma 22°12N 95°5E 241 D5
Along India 28°10N 94°46E 241 A5
Alonissos Greece 39°12N 23°50E 204 B5
Alonissos-Northern Sporades △ Greece 39°15N 24°5E 204 B6
Alor Indonesia 8°15S 124°30E 231 F6
Alor Setar Malaysia 6°7N 100°22E 237 J3
Álora Spain 36°49N 4°46W 195 J6
Alosno Spain 37°33N 7°7W 195 H3
Alost = Aalst Belgium 50°56N 4°2E 170 D4
Alot India 23°56N 75°40E 242 H6
Alotau Papua N. G. 10°16S 150°30E 286 F6
Alougoum Morocco 30°17N 6°56W 260 B3
Aloum Cameroon 2°16N 10°34E 264 B2
Aloysius, Mt. Australia 26°0S 128°38E 279 E4
Alpaugh U.S.A. 35°53N 119°29W 306 K7
Alpe Apuane ⌓ Italy 44°4N 10°15E 198 D7
Alpedrinha Portugal 40°6N 7°27W 194 E3
Alpena U.S.A. 45°4N 83°27W 309 C12
Alpercatas → Brazil 6°2S 44°19W 332 C3
Alperton U.K. 51°32N 0°17W 125 A2
Alpes-de-Haute-Provence □ France 44°8N 6°10E 175 D10
Alpes-Maritimes □ France 43°55N 7°10E 175 E11
Alpha Queens., Australia 23°39S 146°37E 280 C4
Alpha Ill., U.S.A. 41°12N 90°23W 310 C6
Alpha Ridge Arctic 84°0N 118°0W 150 A2
Alphen aan den Rijn Neths. 52°7N 4°40E 170 B4
Alphios → Greece 37°40N 21°33E 204 D3
Alphonse Seychelles 7°0S 52°45E 273 E4
Alpiarça Portugal 39°15N 8°35W 195 F2
Alpine Ariz., U.S.A. 33°51N 109°9W 305 K9
Alpine Calif., U.S.A. 32°50N 116°46W 307 N10
Alpine N.J., U.S.A. 40°57N 73°57W 132 A2
Alpine Tex., U.S.A. 30°22N 103°40W 314 F3
Alpine △ Australia 36°56S 148°10E 283 D7
Alps Europe 46°30N 9°30E 171 C8
Alpu Turkey 39°46N 30°58E 212 C4
Alpurrurulam Australia 20°59S 137°50E 280 C2
Alqueta, Barragem do Portugal 38°20N 7°25W 195 G3
Alrø Denmark 55°52N 10°5E 163 J4
Alrode S. Africa 26°17S 28°7E 123 B2
Als Denmark 54°59N 9°55E 163 K3
Alsace □ France 48°15N 7°25E 173 D14
Alsask Canada 51°21N 109°59W 297 C7
Alsasua Spain 42°54N 2°10W 196 C2
Alsek → U.S.A. 59°10N 138°12W 296 B1
Alsemberg Belgium 50°44N 4°20E 116 B2
Alsergrund Austria 48°13N 16°21E 142 A2
Alsfeld Germany 50°44N 9°16E 178 E5
Alsip U.S.A. 41°40N 87°44W 119 C2
Alsta Norway 65°58N 12°40E 160 D15
Ålsten Sweden 59°19N 17°57E 139 B1
Alsterbro Sweden 56°57N 15°55E 163 H9
Alstermo Sweden 56°58N 15°38E 163 H9
Alston U.K. 54°49N 2°25W 168 C5
Alta Finnmark, Norway 69°57N 23°10E 160 B20
Älta Sweden 59°15N 18°11E 139 B3
Alta, Sierra Spain 40°31N 1°30W 196 E3
Alta Floresta Brazil 9°57S 55°58W 331 B6
Alta Gracia Argentina 31°40S 64°30W 334 C3
Alta Sierra U.S.A. 35°42N 118°33W 307 K8
Altadena U.S.A. 34°11N 118°8W 126 A4
Altaelva → Norway 69°54N 23°17E 160 B20
Altafjorden Norway 70°5N 23°5E 160 A20
Altagracia Venezuela 10°45N 71°30W 328 A3
Altagracia de Orituco Venezuela 9°52N 66°23W 328 B4
Altai = Aerhtai Shan Mongolia 46°40N 92°45E 217 C12
Altai = Gorno-Altay □ Russia 51°0N 86°0E 217 B11
Altamachi → Bolivia 16°8S 66°50W 330 D4
Altamaha → U.S.A. 31°20N 81°20W 316 D8
Altamira Brazil 3°12S 52°10W 329 D7
Altamira Chile 25°47S 69°51W 334 B2
Altamira Colombia 2°3N 75°47W 328 C2
Altamira Tamaulipas, Mexico 22°24N 97°55W 319 C5
Altamira, Cuevas de Spain 43°20N 4°5W 194 B6
Altamont Ill., U.S.A. 39°4N 88°45W 311 E8
Altamont N.Y., U.S.A. 42°42N 74°2W 313 D10
Altamura Italy 40°49N 16°33E 201 B9
Altanbulag Mongolia 50°16N 106°30E 218 A10
Altar Mexico 30°43N 111°44W 318 A2
Altar, Gran Desierto de Mexico 31°50N 114°10W 318 B2
Altata Mexico 24°40N 107°55W 318 C3
Altavas Phil. 11°32N 122°29E 233 F4
Altavista U.S.A. 37°6N 79°17W 309 G14
Altay Xinjiang Uygur, China 47°48N 88°10E 217 C11
Altay Mongolia 46°22N 96°15E 218 B8
Altdorf Switz. 46°52N 8°36E 179 J4
Alte-Donau → Austria 48°14N 16°25E 142 A2
Alte Mellum Germany 53°43N 8°10E 178 B4
Altea Spain 38°38N 0°2W 197 G4
Altenberg Germany 50°45N 13°45E 178 E9
Altenbruch Germany 53°49N 8°46E 178 B4
Altenburg Germany 50°59N 12°25E 178 E8
Altenkirchen Mecklenburg-Vorpommern, Germany 54°38N 13°22E 178 A9
Altenkirchen Rhld-Pfz., Germany 50°41N 7°39E 178 E3
Altenmarkt Austria 47°43N 14°39E 180 D7
Alter do Chão Brazil 2°31S 54°57W 329 D6
Alter do Chão Portugal 39°12N 7°40W 195 F3
Alter Finkenkrug Germany 52°35N 13°3E 115 A1
Altes Rathaus Munich, Germany 131 b3
Altglienicke Germany 52°25N 13°32E 115 B4
Altha U.S.A. 30°34N 85°8W 316 E4
Altınkaya Barajı Turkey 41°18N 35°30E 212 B6
Altınoluk Turkey 39°34N 26°45E 205 B8
Altınova Turkey 39°12N 26°47E 205 B8
Altınözü Turkey 36°7N 36°14E 250 B7
Altıntaş Turkey 39°4N 30°7E 205 B12
Altınyaka Turkey 36°33N 30°20E 205 E12
Altınyayla Turkey 37°0N 29°33E 205 D11
Altiplano Bolivia 17°0S 68°0W 330 D4
Altkirch France 47°37N 7°15E 173 E14
Altlandsberg Germany 52°33N 13°43E 115 A5
Altlandsberg Nord Germany 52°34N 13°43E 115 A5
Altmannsdorf Austria 48°9N 16°18E 142 B1
Altmark Germany 52°45N 11°30E 178 C7
Altmühl → Germany 48°54N 11°52E 179 G7
Altmühltal ⌓ Germany 48°55N 11°15E 179 G7
Altmunster Austria 47°54N 13°45E 180 D6
Alto Adige = Trentino-Alto Adige □ Italy 46°30N 11°20E 199 B8
Alto Alegre Brazil 2°50N 61°20W 329 C5
Alto Araguaia Brazil 17°15S 53°20W 331 D7
Alto Chicapa Angola 10°52S 19°17E 265 E3
Alto Cuchumatanes = Cuchumatanes, Sierra de los Guatemala 15°35N 91°25W 320 C1
Alto Cuito = Tempué Angola 13°27S 18°49E 265 E3
Alto da Boa Vista Brazil 22°57S 43°16W 135 B1
Alto da Moóca Brazil 23°34S 46°33W 137 B2
Alto del Carmen Chile 28°46S 70°30W 334 B1
Alto do Pina Portugal 38°44N 9°7W 126 A2
Alto Garças Brazil 16°56S 53°32W 331 D7
Alto Garda Bresciano ⌓ Italy 45°42N 10°38E 198 C7
Alto Iriri → Brazil 8°50S 53°25W 331 B7
Alto Ligonha Mozam. 15°30S 38°11E 269 F4
Alto Molocue Mozam. 15°50S 37°35E 269 F4
Alto Paraguai Brazil 14°30S 56°31W 331 C6
Alto Paraguay □ Paraguay 21°0S 58°30W 334 A4
Alto Paraiso de Goiás Brazil 14°7S 47°31W 333 D2
Alto Paraná □ Paraguay 25°30S 54°50W 335 B5
Alto Parnaíba Brazil 9°6S 45°57W 332 C2
Alto Purús → Peru 9°12S 70°28W 330 B3
Alto Río Senguerr Argentina 45°2S 70°50W 336 C2
Alto Santo Brazil 5°31S 38°15W 332 C4
Alto Sucuriú Brazil 19°19S 52°47W 331 D7
Alton Ont., Canada 43°54N 80°5W 312 C4
Alton Hants., U.K. 51°9N 0°59W 169 F7
Alton Ill., U.S.A. 38°53N 90°11W 310 F6
Alton N.H., U.S.A. 43°27N 71°13W 313 C13
Altona Vic., Australia 37°51S 144°49E 128 B1
Altona Man., Canada 49°6N 97°33W 297 D9
Altoona Ala., U.S.A. 34°2N 86°20W 316 A3
Altoona Iowa, U.S.A. 41°39N 93°28W 310 C3
Altoona Pa., U.S.A. 40°31N 78°24W 312 F6
Altos Brazil 5°3S 42°28W 332 C3
Altötting Germany 48°12N 12°39E 179 G8
Altstätten Switz. 47°22N 9°33E 179 H5
Altun Kupri Iraq 35°45N 44°9E 213 E11
Altun Shan Xinjiang Uygur, China 38°30N 88°0E 217 E11
Altun Shan Xinjiang Uygur, China 39°18N 93°42E 218 D7
Alturas U.S.A. 41°29N 120°32W 304 F3
Altus U.S.A. 34°38N 99°20W 314 D5
Alubijid Phil. 8°35N 124°29E 233 G5
Alucra Turkey 40°22N 38°47E 213 B8
Aluk South Sudan 8°25N 27°30E 257 F2
Alūksne Latvia 57°24N 27°3E 188 D4
Alunda Sweden 60°4N 18°5E 162 D12
Alunite U.S.A. 35°59N 114°55W 307 K12
Aluoro → Ethiopia 8°26N 33°24E 257 F3
Alupka Ukraine 44°23N 34°2E 189 K8
Alur India 15°24N 77°15E 245 E3
Alur Gajah Malaysia 2°23N 102°13E 234 B2
Alushta Ukraine 44°40N 34°25E 189 K8
Alusi Indonesia 7°35S 131°40E 231 F8
Alustante Spain 40°36N 1°40W 196 E3
Alutgama Sri Lanka 6°26N 79°59E 245 L4
Alutnuwara Sri Lanka 7°19N 80°59E 245 L5
Aluva = Alwaye India 10°8N 76°24E 245 J3
Alva U.S.A. 36°48N 98°40W 314 C5
Alvaiázere Portugal 39°49N 8°23W 194 F2
Älvängen Sweden 57°58N 12°8E 163 G6
Alvão ⌓ Portugal 41°22N 7°48W 194 D3
Alvarado Veracruz, Mexico 18°46N 95°46W 319 D5
Alvarado Tex., U.S.A. 32°24N 97°13W 314 E6
Alvarães Brazil 3°12S 64°50W 329 D5
Alvaro Obregón, Presa Mexico 27°52N 109°52W 318 B3
Alvdal Norway 62°6N 10°37E 164 B7
Älvdalen Sweden 61°13N 14°4E 162 C8
Alvear Argentina 29°5S 56°30W 334 B4
Alverca Portugal 38°56N 9°1W 195 G1
Alvesta Sweden 56°54N 14°35E 163 H8
Alvik Sweden 59°19N 17°58E 139 B1
Alvin U.S.A. 29°26N 95°15W 314 G7
Alvin Callendar Naval Air Station U.S.A. 29°50N 90°1W 131 B2
Alvinston Canada 42°49N 81°52W 312 D3
Alvito Portugal 38°15N 7°58W 195 G3
Älvkarleby Sweden 60°34N 17°26E 162 D11
Alvorado Brazil 12°28S 49°6W 333 D2
Alvord Desert U.S.A. 42°30N 118°25W 304 E4
Älvros Sweden 62°3N 14°38E 162 B8
Älvsbyn Sweden 65°40N 21°0E 160 D19
Älvsjo Sweden 59°16N 18°0E 139 B2
Ålvundeid Norway 62°45N 8°33E 164 B5
Älvvik Sweden 59°21N 18°15E 139 A3
Alwar India 27°38N 76°34E 242 F7
Alwaye India 10°8N 76°24E 245 J3
Alxa Zuoqi China 38°50N 105°40E 226 E3
Alyangula Australia 13°55S 136°30E 280 A2
Alyata = Älät Azerbaijan 39°58N 49°25E 191 L9
Alyth U.K. 56°38N 3°13W 167 E5
Alytus Lithuania 54°24N 24°3E 188 E3
Alzada U.S.A. 45°2N 104°25W 304 D11
Alzamay Russia 55°33N 98°39E 215 D10
Alzey Germany 49°45N 8°7E 179 F4
Alzira Spain 39°9N 0°30W 197 F4
Am Dam Chad 12°40N 20°35E 259 F4
Am Géréda Chad 12°53N 21°14E 259 F4
Am Hasenbergl Germany 48°12N 11°33E 131 A2
Am Sak Chad 13°39N 20°8E 259 F4
Am Steinhof Austria 48°12N 16°17E 142 A1
Am Timan Chad 11°0N 20°10E 259 F4
Am Wald Germany 48°3N 11°36E 131 B2
Ama Keng Singapore 1°23N 103°41E 138 A2
Amacayacu △ Colombia 3°21S 70°8W 328 D3
Amada Gaza C.A.R. 4°46N 15°9E 264 B3
Amådalen Sweden 61°20N 14°44E 162 C8
Amadeus, L. Australia 24°54S 131°0E 279 D5
Amadi Dem. Rep. of the Congo 3°40N 26°40E 268 B2
Amâdi South Sudan 5°29N 30°25E 257 F3
Amadjuak L. Canada 65°0N 71°8W 295 E17
Amadora Portugal 38°45N 9°13W 126 A1
Amagansett U.S.A. 40°59N 72°9W 313 F12
Amagasaki Japan 34°42N 135°23E 133 A1
Amager Denmark 55°36N 12°35E 118 B3
Amagi Japan 33°25N 130°39E 222 D2
Amagunze Nigeria 6°20N 7°40E 263 D6
Amahai Indonesia 3°20S 128°55E 231 E7
Amaile Samoa 13°59S 171°22W 287 V20
Amaimon Papua N. G. 5°12S 145°30E 286 C3
Amaiun-Maia Spain 43°12N 1°29W 196 B3
Amakusa-Nada Japan 32°35N 130°5E 222 E2
Amakusa-Shotō Japan 32°15N 130°10E 222 E2
Amal Oman 18°21N 55°39E 249 C6
Åmål Sweden 59°3N 12°42E 162 E6
Amāl Qādisiya Iraq 33°16N 44°20E 113 B2
Amalapuram India 16°35N 81°55E 245 F5
Amalfi Colombia 6°55N 75°4W 328 B2
Amalfi Italy 40°38N 14°36E 201 B7
Amaliada Greece 37°47N 21°22E 204 D3
Amalienborg Slot Copenhagen, Denmark 118 b3
Amalner India 21°5N 75°5E 244 D2
Amamapare Indonesia 4°53S 136°38E 231 E9
Amambaí Brazil 23°5S 55°13W 335 A4
Amambaí → Brazil 23°22S 53°56W 335 A5
Amambay □ Paraguay 23°0S 56°0W 335 A4
Amambay, Cordillera de S. Amer. 23°0S 55°45W 335 A4
Amami-Guntō Japan 27°16N 129°21E 221 L4
Amami-Ō-Shima Japan 28°16N 129°21E 221 K4
Aman, Pulau Malaysia 5°16N 100°24E 237 c
Amana → Venezuela 9°45N 62°39W 329 B5
Amaná, L. Brazil 2°35S 64°40W 329 D5
Amanab Papua N. G. 3°40S 141°14E 286 B1
Amanat → India 24°7N 84°4E 243 G11
Amanave Amer. Samoa 14°20S 170°50W 302 f
Amanda Park U.S.A. 47°28N 123°55W 306 C3
Amankeldi Kazakhstan 50°10N 65°10E 217 B7
Amanohashidate Japan 35°40N 135°15E 223 B7
Amantea Italy 39°8N 16°4E 201 C9
Amanu French Polynesia 17°48S 140°46W 289 f
Amapá Brazil 2°5N 50°50W 329 C7
Amapá □ Brazil 1°40N 52°0W 329 C7
Amapari = Ferreira Gomes Brazil 0°48N 51°8W 332 A1
Amapari Brazil 0°37N 51°39W 329 C7
Amara Sudan 10°25N 34°10E 257 E3
Amara □ Ethiopia 12°30N 37°30E 257 E4
Amaração = Luís Correia Brazil 3°0S 41°35W 332 B3
Amarante Brazil 6°14S 42°50W 332 C3
Amarante Portugal 41°16N 8°5W 194 D2
Amarante do Maranhão Brazil 5°36S 46°45W 332 C2
Amaranth Canada 50°36N 98°43W 297 C9
Amarapura Burma 21°54N 96°3E 241 E6
Amaravati → India 11°0N 78°15E 245 J4
Amareleja Portugal 38°12N 7°13W 195 G3
Amargosa Brazil 13°2S 39°36W 333 D4
Amargosa → U.S.A. 36°14N 116°51W 307 J10
Amargosa Desert U.S.A. 36°40N 116°30W 307 J10
Amargosa Range U.S.A. 36°20N 116°45W 307 J10
Amari Greece 35°13N 24°40E 207 E5
Amarillo U.S.A. 35°13N 101°50W 314 D4
Amarkantak India 22°40N 81°45E 243 H9
Amârna, Tell el' Egypt 27°38N 30°52E 256 B3
Amarnath India 19°12N 73°22E 244 E1
Amaro, Mte. Italy 42°5N 14°5E 199 F11
Amarpur Bihar, India 25°5N 87°0E 243 G12
Amarpur Tripura, India 23°31N 91°39E 241 D3
Amarti Eritrea 14°17N 41°6E 257 E5
Amarwara India 22°18N 79°10E 243 H8
Amasin W. Sahara 25°45N 13°20W 260 C2
Amasra Turkey 41°45N 32°23E 212 B5
Amassama Nigeria 5°1N 6°2E 263 D6
Amasya Turkey 40°40N 35°50E 212 B6
Amasya □ Turkey 40°40N 35°50E 212 B6
Amata S. Austral., Australia 26°9S 131°9E 279 E5
Amata Piemonte, Italy 45°34N 9°8E 129 A1
Amataurá Brazil 3°29S 68°6W 328 D4
Amatignak I. U.S.A. 51°16N 179°6W 303 L3
Amatikulu S. Africa 29°3S 31°33E 271 C5
Amatitlán Guatemala 14°29N 90°38W 320 D1
Amatrice Italy 42°38N 13°17E 199 F10
Amau Papua N. G. 10°2S 148°34E 286 F5
Amay Belgium 50°33N 5°19E 170 D5
Amazon = Amazonas → S. Amer. 0°5S 50°0W 329 D8
Amazonas □ Brazil 5°0S 65°0W 331 B5
Amazonas □ Peru 5°0S 78°0W 330 B2
Amazonas □ Venezuela 3°30N 66°0W 328 C4
Amazonas → S. Amer. 0°5S 50°0W 329 D8
Amba Ferit Ethiopia 10°55N 38°50E 257 E4
Ambad India 19°38N 75°50E 244 E2

Ambagarh Chowki *India* 20°47N 80°43E 244 D5
Ambah *India* 26°43N 78°13E 242 F8
Ambahakily *Madag.* 21°36S 43°41E 272 C1
Ambahita *Madag.* 24°1S 45°16E 272 C2
Ambajogal *India* 18°44N 76°23E 244 E3
Ambala *India* 30°23N 76°56E 242 D7
Ambalangoda *Sri Lanka* 6°15N 80°5E 245 L5
Ambalapulai *India* 9°25N 76°25E 245 K3
Ambalavao *Madag.* 21°50S 46°56E 272 C2
Ambam *Cameroon* 2°20N 11°15E 264 B2
Ambanja *Madag.* 13°40S 48°27E 272 A2
Ambararata *Madag.* 15°3S 48°33E 272 B2
Ambarchik *Russia* 69°40N 162°20E 215 C17
Ambarijeby *Madag.* 14°56S 47°41E 272 A2
Ambaro, Helodranon' *Madag.* 13°23S 48°38E 272 A2
Ambasamudram *India* 8°43N 77°25E 245 K3
Ambato *Ecuador* 1°5S 78°42W 328 D2
Ambato *Madag.* 13°24S 48°29E 272 A2
Ambato, Sierra de *Argentina* 28°25S 66°10W 334 B2
Ambato Boeny *Madag.* 16°28S 46°43E 272 B2
Ambatofinandrahana *Madag.* 20°33S 46°48E 272 C2
Ambatolampy *Madag.* 19°20S 47°35E 272 B2
Ambatomainty *Madag.* 17°41S 45°40E 272 B2
Ambatomainana *Madag.* 18°18S 47°37E 272 B2
Ambatondrazaka *Madag.* 17°55S 48°28E 272 B2
Ambatosoratra *Madag.* 17°37S 48°31E 272 B2
Ambelokipi *Greece* 37°58N 23°47E 112 B2
Ambelonas *Greece* 39°45N 22°22E 204 B4
Ambenja *Madag.* 15°17S 46°58E 272 B2
Amberg *Germany* 49°26N 11°52E 179 F7
Ambergris Cay *Belize* 18°0N 87°55W 320 C2
Ambérieu-en-Bugey *France* 45°57N 5°20E 175 C9
Amberley *Ont., Canada* 44°2N 81°42W 312 B3
Amberley *N.Z.* 43°9S 172°44E 285 D7
Ambert *France* 45°33N 3°44E 174 C7
Ambidédi *Mali* 14°35N 11°47W 262 C2
Ambikapur *India* 23°15N 83°15E 243 H10
Ambikol *Sudan* 21°20N 30°50E 256 C3
Ambil I. *Phil.* 13°48N 120°18E 232 E3
Ambilobé *Madag.* 13°10S 49°3E 272 A2
Ambinanindrano *Madag.* 20°5S 48°23E 272 C2
Ambinanitelo *Madag.* 15°21S 49°35E 272 B2
Ambinda *Madag.* 16°25S 45°52E 272 B2
Ambitle I. *Papua N. G.* 4°5S 153°37E 286 C7
Amble *U.K.* 55°20N 1°36W 168 B6
Ambler *U.S.A.* 67°5N 157°52W 303 C8
Ambleside *U.K.* 54°26N 2°58W 168 C5
Ambo *Peru* 10°5S 76°10W 330 C2
Amboahangy *Madag.* 24°15S 46°22E 272 C2
Amboasary *Madag.* 25°1S 46°45E 272 D2
Ambodifototra *Madag.* 16°59S 49°52E 272 B2
Ambodilazana *Madag.* 18°6S 49°10E 272 B2
Ambodiriana *Madag.* 17°55S 49°18E 272 B2
Ambohidratrimo *Madag.* 18°50S 47°26E 272 B2
Ambohidray *Madag.* 18°36S 48°18E 272 B2
Ambohimahamasina *Madag.* 21°56S 47°11E 272 C2
Ambohimahasoa *Madag.* 21°7S 47°13E 272 C2
Ambohimanga *Madag.* 20°52S 47°36E 272 C2
Ambohimitombo *Madag.* 20°43S 47°26E 272 C2
Ambohitra *Madag.* 12°30S 49°10E 272 A2
Amboise *France* 47°24N 1°2E 172 E8
Amboiva *Angola* 11°33S 14°43E 265 E2
Ambon *Indonesia* 3°43S 128°12E 231 E7
Ambondro *Madag.* 25°13S 45°44E 272 D2
Amboró △ *Bolivia* 17°39S 64°3W 331 D5
Amboseli, L. *Kenya* 2°40S 37°10E 268 C4
Amboseli △ *Kenya* 2°37S 37°13E 268 C4
Ambositra *Madag.* 20°31S 47°25E 272 C2
Ambovombe *Madag.* 25°11S 46°5E 272 D2
Amboy *Calif., U.S.A.* 34°33N 115°45W 307 L11
Amboy *Ill., U.S.A.* 41°44N 89°20W 310 C7
Amboyna Cay *S. China Sea* 7°50N 112°50E 230 C4
Ambre, Île d' *Mauritius* 20°2S 57°41E 272 e
Ambridge *U.S.A.* 40°36N 80°14W 312 F4
Ambriz *Angola* 7°48S 13°8E 265 D2
Ambriz △ *Angola* 7°56S 10°27E 265 D2
Ambrolauri *Georgia* 42°31N 43°9E 213 A10
Ambrym *Vanuatu* 16°15S 168°10E 287 F6
Ambulong I. *Phil.* 12°13N 121°1E 232 E3
Ambunti *Papua N. G.* 4°13S 142°52E 286 C2
Ambur *India* 12°48N 78°43E 245 H4
Amchitka I. *U.S.A.* 51°32N 179°0E 303 L2
Amderma *Russia* 69°45N 61°30E 214 C7
Amdhi *India* 23°51N 81°27E 243 H9
Amdo *China* 32°20N 91°40E 218 E7
Ameca *Mexico* 20°33N 104°2W 318 C4
Ameca ➔ *Mexico* 20°41N 105°18W 318 C3
Amecameca de Juárez *Mexico* 19°8N 98°46W 319 D5
Amed *Indonesia* 8°19S 115°39E 231 J18
Ameixoeira *Portugal* 38°46N 9°8W 126 A2
Ameland *Neths.* 53°27N 5°45E 170 A5
Amélia *Italy* 42°33N 12°25E 199 F9
Amelia City *U.S.A.* 30°35N 81°28W 316 E8
Amelia I. *U.S.A.* 30°40N 81°25W 316 E8
Amendolara *Italy* 39°57N 16°35E 201 C9
Amenia *U.S.A.* 41°51N 73°33W 313 E11
América *Brazil* 23°35S 46°41W 137 B1
America-Antarctica Ridge *S. Ocean* 59°0S 16°0W 151 B2
American Falls *U.S.A.* 42°47N 112°51W 304 E7
American Falls Res. *U.S.A.* 42°47N 112°52W 304 E7
American Fork *U.S.A.* 40°23N 111°48W 304 F8
American Highland *Antarctica* 73°0S 75°0E 151 D6
American Indian Museum *Washington, D.C., U.S.A.* 143 b3
American Museum of Natural History *New York, U.S.A.* 132 b2
American Police Hall of Fame *U.S.A.* 25°49N 80°11W 128 B2
American River *Australia* 35°47S 137°46E 282 C2
American Samoa ☑ *Pac. Oc.* 14°20S 170°0W 302 f
American Samoa △ *Amer. Samoa* 14°15S 170°28W 302 g
American Univ. *U.S.A.* 38°56N 77°15W 143 B3
Americana *Brazil* 22°45S 47°20W 335 A6
Americus *U.S.A.* 32°4N 84°14W 316 C5
Amerigo Vespucci, Firenze ✕ (FLR) *Italy* 43°49N 11°13E 199 E8
Amerika = Nakhodka *Russia* 42°53N 132°54E 220 C6
Amersfoort *Neths.* 52°9N 5°23E 170 B5
Amersfoort *Mpumalanga, S. Africa* 26°59S 29°53E 271 C4
Amery Basin *S. Ocean* 68°15S 74°30E 151 C6
Amery Ice Shelf *Antarctica* 69°30S 72°0E 151 C6
Amerzgane *Morocco* 31°4N 7°14W 260 B3
Ames = Bertamirans *Spain* 42°54N 8°38W 194 C2
Ames *U.S.A.* 42°2N 93°37W 310 C3
Amesbury *U.S.A.* 42°51N 70°56W 313 D14
Amet *India* 25°18N 73°56E 242 G5
Amfiklia *Greece* 38°38N 22°35E 204 C4
Amfilochia *Greece* 38°52N 21°9E 204 C3
Amfipoli *Greece* 40°48N 23°52E 202 F7
Amfissa *Greece* 38°32N 22°22E 204 C4
Amga *Russia* 60°50N 132°0E 215 C14
Amga ➔ *Russia* 62°38N 134°32E 215 C14
Amgaon *India* 21°22N 80°22E 244 D5
Amgu *Russia* 45°45N 137°15E 220 B8
Amguid *Algeria* 26°26N 5°22E 261 C6
Amgun ➔ *Russia* 52°56N 139°38E 215 D14
Amherst = Kyaikkami *Burma* 16°4N 97°34E 241 G6
Amherst *N.S., Canada* 45°48N 64°8W 299 C7
Amherst *Mass., U.S.A.* 42°23N 72°31W 313 D12
Amherst *N.Y., U.S.A.* 42°59N 78°48W 312 D6
Amherst *Ohio, U.S.A.* 41°24N 82°14W 312 E2
Amherst I. *Canada* 44°8N 76°43W 313 B8
Amherstburg *Canada* 42°6N 83°6W 311 B13
Amiata, Mte. *Italy* 42°53N 11°37E 199 F8
Amidon *U.S.A.* 46°29N 103°19W 308 B2
Amiens *France* 49°54N 2°16E 173 C9
Amik Gölü *Turkey* 36°22N 36°17E 250 B7
Amili *India* 28°25N 95°52E 241 A5
Amin *Iraq* 33°19N 44°29E 113 B2
Aminadav *Israel* 31°45N 35°8E 123 B1
Amindeo *Greece* 40°42N 21°42E 202 F5
Amindivi Is. *India* 11°23N 72°23E 245 J1
Amingaon *India* 26°11N 91°40E 241 B3
Amini I. *India* 11°6N 72°45E 245 J1
Amino *Ethiopia* 4°25N 41°52E 257 G5
Aminuis *Namibia* 23°43S 19°21E 270 B2
Aminyevo *Russia* 55°41N 37°25E 129 B2
Āmir, Ra's *Libya* 32°57N 21°43E 258 B4
Amīrābād *Īlām, Iran* 33°20N 46°16E 246 C5
Amīrābād *Tehrān, Iran* 35°43N 51°24E 141 A2
Amirante Is. *Seychelles* 6°0S 53°0E 210 J7
Amisk △ *Canada* 56°43N 98°0W 297 B9
Amisk L. *Canada* 54°35N 102°15W 297 C8
Amistad, Presa de la *Mexico* 29°26N 101°3W 318 B4
Amistad △ *U.S.A.* 29°32N 101°12W 314 G4
Amite *U.S.A.* 30°44N 90°30W 315 F9
Amizmiz *Morocco* 31°12N 8°15W 260 B3
Amla *India* 21°56N 78°7E 242 J8
Amlapura *Indonesia* 8°27S 115°37E 231 J18
Åmli *Norway* 58°45N 8°32E 164 F5
Amlia I. *U.S.A.* 52°4N 173°30W 303 K4
Amlwch *U.K.* 53°24N 4°20W 168 D3
Amm Adam *Sudan* 16°20N 36°1E 257 D4
'Ammān *Jordan* 31°57N 35°52E 251 G6
'Ammān ☐ *Jordan* 31°40N 36°30E 251 G7
Ammanford *U.K.* 51°48N 3°59W 169 F4
Ammassalik = Tasiilaq *Greenland* 65°40N 37°20W 154 C7
Ammerån ➔ *Sweden* 63°9N 16°13E 162 A10
Ammersee *Germany* 48°0N 11°7E 179 G7
Ammochostos = Famagusta *Cyprus* 35°8N 33°55E 207 E9
Ammon *U.S.A.* 43°28N 111°58W 304 E8
Amnat Charoen *Thailand* 15°51N 104°38E 236 E5
Amnura *Bangla.* 24°37N 88°25E 243 G13
Amo Jiang ➔ *China* 23°0N 101°50E 228 F3
Āmol *Iran* 36°23N 52°20E 247 E7
Amora *Portugal* 38°37N 9°6W 126 E2
Amoreira *Portugal* 38°48N 9°11W 126 A1
Amoret *U.S.A.* 38°15N 94°35W 310 F2
Amorgos *Greece* 36°50N 25°57E 205 E7
Amory *U.S.A.* 33°59N 88°29W 315 E10
Amos *Canada* 48°35N 78°5W 298 C4
Åmot *Buskerud, Norway* 59°57N 9°54E 164 E6
Åmot *Oppland, Norway* 61°0N 10°2E 164 C7
Åmot *Telemark, Norway* 59°34N 8°0E 164 E5
Åmot *Sweden* 60°58N 16°27E 162 D10
Åmotfors *Sweden* 59°47N 12°22E 162 E6
Åmotsdal *Norway* 59°37N 8°26E 164 E5
Amour, Djebel *Algeria* 33°42N 1°37E 261 B5
Amoy = Xiamen *China* 24°25N 118°4E 229 E12
Ampah *Indonesia* 1°46S 115°7E 235 C5
Ampanavoana *Madag.* 15°41S 50°22E 272 B3
Ampang *Malaysia* 3°8N 101°45E 237 L3
Ampangalana, Lakandranon' *Madag.* 22°48S 47°50E 272 C2
Ampani *India* 19°35N 82°38E 244 E6
Ampanihy *Madag.* 24°40S 44°45E 272 C1
Amparafaravola *Madag.* 17°35S 48°13E 272 B2
Ampasimanbo *Madag.* 20°31S 48°0E 272 C2
Ampasindava, Helodranon' *Madag.* 13°40S 48°15E 272 A2
Ampasindava, Saikanosy *Madag.* 13°42S 47°55E 272 A2
Ampato, Nevado *Peru* 15°40S 71°56W 330 D3
Ampenan *Indonesia* 8°34S 116°4E 231 K18
Amper *Nigeria* 9°25N 9°40E 263 D6
Amper ➔ *Bayern, Germany* 48°29N 11°55E 179 G7
Amper ➔ *Oberbayern, Germany* 48°14N 11°25E 131 A1
Ampezzo *Italy* 46°25N 12°48E 199 B9
Amphoe Kathu *Thailand* 7°55N 98°21E 237 a
Amphoe Thalang *Thailand* 8°1N 98°20E 237 a
Ampitsikinana *Madag.* 12°57S 49°49E 272 A2
Ampombiantambo *Madag.* 12°42S 48°57E 272 A2
Amposta *Spain* 40°43N 0°34E 196 E5
Ampotaka *Madag.* 25°3S 44°41E 272 D1
Ampoza *Madag.* 22°20S 44°44E 272 C1
Amqui *Canada* 48°28N 67°27W 299 C6
Amrabad *India* 16°23N 78°50E 245 F4
'Amrān *Yemen* 15°41N 43°55E 248 D3
Amraoti = Amravati *India* 20°55N 77°45E 244 D3
Amravati *India* 20°55N 77°45E 244 D3
Amreli *India* 21°35N 71°17E 242 J4
Amrenene el Kasba *Algeria* 22°10N 0°30E 261 D5
Amritsar *India* 31°35N 74°57E 242 D6
Amroha *India* 28°53N 78°30E 243 E8
Amrum *Germany* 54°38N 8°22E 178 A4
Amsâga *Mauritania* 20°7N 14°10W 260 D2
Amsel *Algeria* 22°47N 5°29E 261 D6
Amstel *Amsterdam, Neths.* 112 b2
Amstel ➔ *Amsterdam, Neths.* 112 b3
Amstel-Drecht-Kanaal *Neths.* 52°18N 4°54E 112 B2
Amstelveen *Neths.* 52°18N 4°51E 112 B2
Amsterdam *Neths.* 52°23N 4°54E 112 A2
Amsterdam *N.Y., U.S.A.* 42°56N 74°11W 313 D10
Amsterdam ✕ (AMS) *Neths.* 52°18N 4°45E 112 B1
Amsterdam, I. = Nouvelle Amsterdam, Î. *Ind. Oc.* 38°30S 77°30E 273 H3
Amsterdam-Rijnkanaal *Neths.* 51°53N 5°28E 112 B3
Amsterdam Zuidoost *Neths.* 52°18N 4°58E 112 B2
Amsterdamse Bos *Neths.* 52°19N 4°50E 112 B2
Amstetten *Austria* 48°7N 14°51E 180 C7
'Amūdah *Syria* 37°6N 40°55E 213 D9
Amudarya *Turkmenistan* 37°53N 65°15E 216 E7
Amudarya ➔ *Uzbekistan* 43°58N 59°34E 216 D5
Amukta I. *U.S.A.* 52°30N 171°16W 303 K5
Amukta Pass *U.S.A.* 52°0N 171°0W 303 K5
Amulung *Phil.* 17°50N 121°43E 232 C3
Amund Ringnes I. *Canada* 78°20N 96°25W 295 B12
Amundsen Abyssal Plain *S. Ocean* 65°0S 125°0W 151 C14
Amundsen Basin *Arctic* 87°30N 80°0E 150 A
Amundsen Gulf *Canada* 71°0N 124°0W 294 C7
Amundsen Ridges *S. Ocean* 69°15S 123°0W 151 C14
Amundsen-Scott *Antarctica* 90°0S 166°0E 151 E
Amundsen Sea *Antarctica* 72°0S 115°0W 151 D15
Amungen *Sweden* 61°10N 15°40E 162 C9
Amuntai *Indonesia* 2°28S 115°25E 235 C5
Amur ➔ *Russia* 52°56N 141°10E 215 D15
Amur, W. ➔ *Sudan* 18°56N 33°34E 256 D3
Amurang *Indonesia* 1°5N 124°40E 231 D6
Amurrio *Spain* 43°3N 3°0W 196 B1
Amursk *Russia* 50°14N 136°54E 215 D14
Amusco *Spain* 42°10N 4°28W 194 C6
Amvrakikos Kolpos *Greece* 39°0N 20°55E 204 C2
Amvrosiyivka *Ukraine* 47°43N 38°30E 189 J10
Amyderya = Amudarya ➔ *Uzbekistan* 43°58N 59°34E 216 D5
An *Burma* 19°48N 94°0E 241 F5
An Bien *Vietnam* 9°45N 105°0E 237 H5
An Cabhán = Cavan *Ireland* 54°0N 7°22W 166 B4
An Cóbh = Cóbh *Ireland* 51°51N 8°17W 166 E3
An Daingean = Dingle *Ireland* 52°9N 10°17W 166 D1
An Hoa *Vietnam* 15°40N 108°5E 236 E7
An Khe *Vietnam* 13°57N 108°51E 236 F7
An Longfort = Longford *Ireland* 53°43N 7°49W 166 C4
An Muileann gCearr = Mullingar *Ireland* 53°31N 7°21W 166 C4
An Nabatīyah at Tahta *Lebanon* 33°23N 35°27E 250 E6
An Nabk *Si. Arabia* 31°20N 37°20E 246 D3
An Nabk *Syria* 34°2N 36°44E 250 D7
An Nafūd *Si. Arabia* 28°15N 41°0E 246 D4
An Nāḥiyah *Iraq* 34°26N 41°33E 213 E9
An Najaf *Iraq* 32°3N 44°15E 213 G11
An Namāş *Si. Arabia* 19°7N 42°8E 248 C3
An Nás = Naas *Ireland* 53°12N 6°40W 166 C5
An Nāşirīyah *Iraq* 31°0N 46°15E 246 D5
An Nawfalīyah *Libya* 30°54N 17°58E 258 B3
An Nhon = Binh Dinh *Vietnam* 13°55N 109°7E 236 F7
An Nîl ☐ *Sudan* 19°30N 33°0E 256 D3
An Nîl el Abyad ☐ *Sudan* 14°0N 32°15E 257 E3
An Nîl el Azraq ☐ *Sudan* 11°30N 34°30E 257 E3
An Nu'ayrīyah *Si. Arabia* 27°30N 48°30E 247 E6
An Nu'mānīyah *Iraq* 32°32N 45°25E 213 F11
An Nuqat Alkhams ☐ *Libya* 32°42N 11°57E 261 B7
An Ros = Rush *Ireland* 53°31N 6°6W 166 C5
An tAonach = Nenagh *Ireland* 52°52N 8°11W 166 D3
An Thoi, Quan Dao *Vietnam* 9°58N 104°0E 237 H5
An tInbhear Mór = Arklow *Ireland* 52°48N 6°10W 166 D5
An Uaimh *Ireland* 53°39N 6°41W 166 C5
Åna-Sira *Norway* 58°17N 6°25E 164 F3
Anaa *French Polynesia* 17°25S 145°30W 289 f
Anabar ➔ *Russia* 73°8N 113°36E 215 B12
Anaco *Venezuela* 9°27N 64°28W 329 B5
Anaconda *U.S.A.* 46°8N 112°57W 304 C7
Anacortes *U.S.A.* 48°30N 122°37W 306 B4
Anacosta ➔ *U.S.A.* 38°52N 77°1W 143 B4
Anacostia *U.S.A.* 38°51N 76°59W 143 B4
Anacuao, Mt. *Phil.* 16°16N 121°53E 232 C3
Anadarko *U.S.A.* 35°4N 98°15W 314 D5
Anadia *Brazil* 9°42S 36°18W 332 C4
Anadia *Portugal* 40°26N 8°27W 194 E2
Anadolu *Turkey* 39°0N 30°0E 212 C5
Anadoluhisarı *Turkey* 41°4N 29°3E 122 B2
Anadolukavağı *Turkey* 41°10N 29°7E 122 A2
Anadyr *Russia* 64°35N 177°20E 215 C18
Anadyr ➔ *Russia* 64°55N 176°5E 215 C18
Anadyrskiy Zaliv *Russia* 64°0N 180°0E 215 C19
Anafi *Greece* 36°22N 25°48E 205 E7
Anafonitria *Greece* 37°51N 20°39E 207 D2
Anaga, Pta. de *Canary Is.* 28°34N 16°9W 153 e1
Anagni *Italy* 41°44N 13°9E 199 G10
'Ānah *Iraq* 34°25N 42°0E 213 E10
Anaheim *U.S.A.* 33°50N 117°55W 307 M9
Anahim Lake *Canada* 52°28N 125°18W 296 C3
Anahola *U.S.A.* 22°9N 159°19W 302 A2
'Anahulu ➔ *U.S.A.* 21°37N 158°6W 302 J13
Anai Mudi *India* 10°12N 77°4E 245 J3
Anaichak △ *U.S.A.* 56°50N 158°15W 303 H8
Anaimalai Hills *India* 10°20N 76°40E 245 J3
Anajás *Brazil* 0°59S 49°57W 332 B2
Anajatuba *Brazil* 3°16S 44°37W 332 B3
Anakao *Madag.* 23°40S 43°39E 272 C1
Anakapalle *India* 17°42N 83°6E 244 F6
Anakena *Chile* 27°5S 109°20W 330 b
Anakie *Australia* 23°32S 147°45E 280 C4
Anaklia *Georgia* 42°22N 41°35E 191 J5
Anaktuvuk Pass *U.S.A.* 68°8N 151°45W 303 B10
Analalava *Madag.* 14°35S 48°0E 272 A2
Analavoka *Madag.* 22°23S 46°30E 272 C2
Analipsis *Greece* 39°36N 19°55E 206 B9
Anamã *Brazil* 3°35S 61°22W 329 D5
Anambar ➔ *Pakistan* 30°15N 68°50E 242 D3
Anambas, Kepulauan *Indonesia* 3°20N 106°30E 234 B3
Anambas Is. = Anambas, Kepulauan *Indonesia* 3°20N 106°30E 234 B3
Anambra ☐ *Nigeria* 6°20N 7°0E 263 D6
Aname *Vanuatu* 20°8S 169°47E 287 K7
Anamosa *U.S.A.* 42°7N 91°17W 310 B5
Anamur *Turkey* 36°8N 32°58E 250 B3
Anamur ➔ *Turkey* 36°5N 32°53E 250 B3
Anamur Burnu *Turkey* 36°2N 32°47E 250 B3
Anan *Japan* 33°54N 134°40E 222 D6
Anand *India* 22°32N 72°59E 242 H5
Anandapuram *India* 14°5N 75°12E 245 G2
Anandpur *India* 21°16N 86°13E 244 D8
Anantapur *India* 14°39N 77°42E 245 G3
Anantnag *India* 33°45N 75°10E 243 C6
Ananyiv *Ukraine* 47°44N 29°58E 183 C14
Anapa *Russia* 44°55N 37°25E 189 K9
Anapodiaris ➔ *Greece* 34°59N 25°20E 207 E6
Anápolis = Simão Dias *Brazil* 10°44S 37°49W 332 D4
Anápolis *Brazil* 16°15S 48°50W 333 E2
Anapu ➔ *Brazil* 1°53S 50°53W 329 D7
Anār *Iran* 30°55N 55°13E 247 D7
Anār Darreh *Afghan.* 32°46N 61°39E 240 B1
Anārak *Iran* 33°25N 53°40E 247 C7
Anarisfjällen *Sweden* 63°6N 13°10E 162 A7
Anas ➔ *India* 23°26N 74°0E 242 H5
Añasco *Puerto Rico* 18°17N 67°8W 321 b
Anata *West Bank* 31°49N 35°16E 123 B2
Anatahan *N. Marianas* 16°21N 145°40E 302 a
Anatolia = Anadolu *Turkey* 39°0N 30°0E 212 C5
Anatsogno *Madag.* 23°33S 43°46E 272 C1
Añatuya *Argentina* 28°20S 62°50W 334 B3
Anatye ✪ *Australia* 22°29S 137°3E 280 C2
Anauá ➔ *Brazil* 0°58N 61°21W 329 C5
Anaunethad L. *Canada* 60°55N 104°25W 297 A8
Anavilhanas, Arquipélago das *Brazil* 2°42S 60°45W 329 D5
Anbyŏn *N. Korea* 39°1N 127°35E 224 C3
Ancares, Sierra dos *Spain* 42°51N 6°52W 194 C4
Ancares △ *Spain* 42°50N 6°40W 194 C4
Ancash ☐ *Peru* 9°30S 77°45W 330 B2
Ancaster *Canada* 43°13N 79°59W 312 C5
Ancenis *France* 47°21N 1°10W 172 E5
Anchieta = Piatã *Brazil* 13°9S 41°48W 333 D3
Anch'ing = Anqing *China* 30°30N 117°3E 229 B11
Ancho, Canal *Chile* 50°0S 74°20W 336 D2
Anchor Bay *U.S.A.* 38°48N 123°34W 306 G3
Anchorage *U.S.A.* 61°13N 149°54W 303 F10
Anchorage ✕ (ANC) *U.S.A.* 61°10N 150°0W 303 F10
Anci *China* 39°20N 116°40E 226 E9
Ancohuma, Nevado *Bolivia* 16°0S 68°50W 330 D4
Ancol *Indonesia* 6°7S 106°49E 122 A1
Ancón *Peru* 11°50S 77°10W 330 C2
Ancona *Italy* 43°38N 13°30E 199 E10
Ancud *Chile* 42°0S 73°50W 336 B2
Ancud, G. de *Chile* 42°0S 73°0W 336 B2
Ancy-le-Franc *France* 47°46N 4°10E 173 E11
Anda *Heilongjiang, China* 46°24N 125°19E 219 B14
Anda *Phil.* 16°17N 119°57E 232 C2
Andacollo *Argentina* 37°10S 70°42W 334 D1
Andacollo *Chile* 30°14S 71°6W 334 C1
Andahuaylas *Peru* 13°40S 73°25W 330 C3
Andaingo *Madag.* 18°12S 48°17E 272 B2
Andalgalá *Argentina* 27°40S 66°30W 334 B2
Åndalsnes *Norway* 62°35N 7°43E 164 B4
Andalucía ☐ *Spain* 37°35N 5°0W 195 H6
'Andalus *Iraq* 33°19N 44°18E 113 B1
Andalusia = Andalucía ☐ *Spain* 37°35N 5°0W 195 H6
Andalusia *U.S.A.* 31°18N 86°29W 315 F11
Andaman & Nicobar Is. ☐ *India* 10°0N 93°0E 245 K11
Andaman Is. *Ind. Oc.* 12°30N 92°45E 245 H11
Andaman Sea *Ind. Oc.* 13°0N 96°0E 230 B1
Andamooka *Australia* 30°27S 137°9E 281 E2
Andapa *Madag.* 14°39S 49°39E 272 A2
Andara *Namibia* 18°2S 21°9E 270 A3
Andaraí *Bahia, Brazil* 12°48S 41°20W 333 D3
Andaraí *Rio de J., Brazil* 22°56S 43°14W 135 B1
Andelot-Blancheville *France* 48°15N 5°18E 173 D12
Andenes *Norway* 69°19N 16°18E 160 B17
Andenne *Belgium* 50°28N 5°5E 170 D5
Andéranboukane *Mali* 15°26N 3°2E 263 B5
Anderlecht *Belgium* 50°50N 4°19E 116 A1
Andermatt *Switz.* 46°38N 8°35E 179 J4
Andernach *Germany* 50°26N 7°24E 178 E3
Andernos-les-Bains *France* 44°44N 1°6W 174 D2
Andersen Air Force Base *Guam* 13°35N 144°55E 302 d
Anderslöv *Sweden* 55°26N 13°19E 163 J7
Anderson *Vic., Australia* 38°31S 145°26E 283 E6
Anderson *Alaska, U.S.A.* 64°25N 149°15W 303 D10
Anderson *Calif., U.S.A.* 40°27N 122°18W 304 F2
Anderson *Ind., U.S.A.* 40°10N 85°41W 311 D11
Anderson *Mo., U.S.A.* 36°39N 94°27W 308 G6
Anderson *S.C., U.S.A.* 34°31N 82°39W 315 D13
Anderson ➔ *Canada* 69°42N 129°0W 294 D6
Anderson I. *India* 12°46N 92°43E 245 H11
Anderson Park *U.S.A.* 33°45N 84°27W 113 B2
Andersonville *U.S.A.* 32°12N 84°9W 316 C5
Andersonville △ *U.S.A.* 32°12N 84°1W 316 C5
Anderstorp *Sweden* 57°19N 13°39E 163 G7
Andes *Colombia* 5°39N 75°54W 328 B2
Andes *N.Y., U.S.A.* 42°12N 74°47W 313 D10
Andes, Cord. de los *S. Amer.* 20°0S 68°0W 330 E4
Andfjorden *Norway* 69°10N 16°20E 160 B17
Andhra, L. *India* 18°54N 73°32E 244 E1
Andhra Pradesh ☐ *India* 18°0N 79°0E 244 F4
Andijon *Uzbekistan* 41°10N 72°15E 217 D8
Andijon ☐ *Uzbekistan* 40°45N 72°20E 217 D8
Andikithira = Antikythira *Greece* 35°52N 23°15E 204 F5
Andilamena *Madag.* 17°1S 48°35E 272 B2
Andīmeshk *Iran* 32°27N 48°21E 213 F13
Andimilos = Antimilos *Greece* 36°47N 24°12E 204 E6
Andingmen *China* 39°55N 116°23E 114 B2
Andiparos = Antiparos *Greece* 37°0N 25°3E 205 D7
Andipaxoi = Antipaxi *Greece* 39°9N 20°13E 204 B2
Andipsara *Greece* 38°30N 25°29E 205 C7
Andizhan = Andijon *Uzbekistan* 41°10N 72°15E 217 D8
Andkhvoy *Afghan.* 36°52N 65°8E 240 A2
Andoain *Spain* 43°13N 2°1W 196 B2
Andoany *Madag.* 13°25S 48°16E 272 A2
Andoas *Peru* 2°55S 76°25W 328 D2
Andohahela △ *Madag.* 24°4S 46°44E 272 C2
Andol *India* 17°51N 78°4E 244 F4
Andola *India* 16°57N 76°50E 244 F3
Andong *S. Korea* 36°40N 128°43E 224 D4
Andorra *Spain* 40°59N 0°28W 196 E4
Andorra ■ *Europe* 42°30N 1°30E 174 F5
Andorra La Vella *Andorra* 42°31N 1°32E 174 F5
Andover *Hants., U.K.* 51°12N 1°29W 169 F6
Andover *Maine, U.S.A.* 44°38N 70°45W 313 B14
Andover *Mass., U.S.A.* 42°40N 71°8W 313 D13
Andover *N.J., U.S.A.* 40°59N 74°45W 313 F10
Andover *N.Y., U.S.A.* 42°10N 77°48W 312 D7
Andover *Ohio, U.S.A.* 41°36N 80°34W 312 E4
Andøya *Norway* 69°10N 15°50E 160 B16
Andrade *Brazil* 4°40S 63°45W 329 D5
Andradina *Brazil* 20°54S 51°23W 333 F1
Andrahary *Madag.* 13°37S 49°17E 272 A2
Andramasina *Madag.* 19°11S 47°35E 272 B2
Andranopasy *Madag.* 21°17S 43°44E 272 C1
Andranovory *Madag.* 23°8S 44°10E 272 C1
Andratx *Spain* 39°39N 2°25E 206 B3
André Félix △ *C.A.R.* 9°29N 23°18E 264 A4
Andreanof Is. *U.S.A.* 51°30N 176°0W 303 L4
Andreapol *Russia* 56°40N 32°17E 188 D7
Andrée Land *Greenland* 73°40N 26°0W 154 C8
Andrews *S.C., U.S.A.* 33°27N 79°34W 315 E15
Andrews *Tex., U.S.A.* 32°19N 102°33W 314 E3
Andreyev = Jędrzejów *Poland* 50°35N 20°15E 185 H7
Andreyevka *Russia* 52°19N 51°55E 190 D10
Ándria *Italy* 41°13N 15°17E 201 A9
Andriamena *Madag.* 17°26S 47°30E 272 B2
Andriandampy *Madag.* 22°45S 45°41E 272 C2
Andriba *Madag.* 17°30S 45°58E 272 B2
Andrijevica *Montenegro* 42°45N 19°48E 202 D3
Andringitra △ *Madag.* 22°13S 46°5E 272 C2
Andritsena *Greece* 37°29N 21°52E 204 D3
Androka *Madag.* 24°58S 44°2E 272 C1
Andropov = Rybinsk *Russia* 58°5N 38°50E 188 C10
Andros *Greece* 37°50N 24°57E 204 D6
Andros I. *Bahamas* 24°30N 78°0W 320 B4
Andros Town *Bahamas* 24°43N 77°47W 320 B4
Androscoggin ➔ *U.S.A.* 43°58N 69°52W 313 C14
Androth I. *India* 10°50N 73°41E 245 J1
Andrychów *Poland* 49°51N 19°18E 185 J6
Andselv *Norway* 69°4N 18°34E 160 B18
Andújar *Spain* 38°3N 4°5W 195 G6
Andulo *Angola* 11°25S 16°45E 265 E3
Åneby *Akershus, Norway* 60°5N 10°51E 164 D7
Aneby *Sweden* 57°48N 14°49E 163 G8
Anéfis *Mali* 18°2N 0°36E 263 B5
Anegada *Br. Virgin Is.* 18°45N 64°20W 321 C7
Anegada, B. *Argentina* 40°20S 62°20W 336 B4
Anegada Passage *W. Indies* 18°15N 63°45W 321 C7
Anécho *Togo* 6°12N 1°34E 263 D5
Aneityum *Vanuatu* 20°12S 169°45E 287 K7
Anelghowhat *Vanuatu* 20°19S 169°43E 287 K7
Añelo *Argentina* 38°20S 68°45W 336 A3
Anenni-Noi *Moldova* 46°53N 29°15E 183 D14
Aneto, Pico de *Spain* 42°37N 0°40E 196 C5
Änew *Turkmenistan* 37°52N 58°31E 216 E5
Aney *Niger* 19°15N 12°50E 259 E2
Añez *Bolivia* 15°40S 63°10W 331 D5
Anfu *China* 27°21N 114°40E 229 D10
Ang Mo Kio *Singapore* 1°23N 103°50E 138 A3
Ang Thong *Thailand* 14°35N 100°31E 236 E3
Ang Thong, Ko *Thailand* 9°37N 99°41E 237 b
Ang Thong, Mu Ko △ *Thailand* 9°40N 99°43E 237 H2
Angadanan *Phil.* 16°45N 121°45E 232 C3
Angamos, Punta *Chile* 23°1S 70°32W 334 A1
Angara ➔ *Russia* 58°5N 94°20E 215 D10
Angara-Débou *Benin* 11°19N 3°3E 263 C5
Angarbaka *South Sudan* 9°44N 24°44E 257 F1
Angarsk *Russia* 52°30N 104°0E 218 A9
Angas Hills *Australia* 23°0S 127°50E 278 D4
Angaston *Australia* 34°30S 139°8E 282 C3
Angat *Phil.* 14°56N 121°2E 232 D3
Angaur I. *Palau* 6°54N 134°9E 288 c
Ångby *Sweden* 59°20N 17°53E 139 A1
Ånge *Sweden* 62°31N 15°35E 162 B9
Ángel, Salto = Angel Falls *Venezuela* 5°57N 62°30W 329 B5
Ángel de la Guarda, I. *Mexico* 29°20N 113°25W 318 B2
Angel Falls *Venezuela* 5°57N 62°30W 329 B5
Angel I. *U.S.A.* 37°52N 122°25W 136 A2
Angel Island State Park △ *U.S.A.* 37°52N 122°25W 136 A2
Angeles *Phil.* 15°9N 120°33E 232 D3
Ängelholm *Sweden* 56°15N 12°50E 163 H6
Angels Camp *U.S.A.* 38°4N 120°32W 306 G6
Ängelsberg *Sweden* 59°58N 16°0E 162 E10
Anger ➔ *Ethiopia* 9°37N 36°6E 257 F4
Angerburg = Węgorzewo *Poland* 54°13N 21°43E 184 D8
Angereb *Ethiopia* 13°11N 37°7E 257 E4
Angereb ➔ *Ethiopia* 13°45N 36°40E 257 E4
Ångermanälven ➔ *Sweden* 64°0N 17°20E 162 A11
Ångermanland *Sweden* 63°36N 17°45E 160 E17
Angermünde *Germany* 53°0N 14°0E 178 B9
Angers *Qué., Canada* 45°31N 75°29W 313 A9
Angers *Maine-et-Loire, France* 47°30N 0°35W 172 E6
Angerville *France* 48°19N 2°0E 173 D9
Ängesån ➔ *Sweden* 66°16N 22°47E 160 C20
Angical *Brazil* 12°0S 44°42W 333 D3
Angikuni L. *Canada* 62°12N 99°59W 297 A9
Angke, Kali ➔ *Indonesia* 6°6S 106°46E 122 A1
Angkor *Cambodia* 13°22N 103°50E 236 F4
Angledool *Australia* 29°5S 147°55E 281 D4
Anglem, Mt. *N.Z.* 46°45S 167°53E 285 G2
Anglès *Spain* 41°57N 2°38E 196 D7
Anglesey *U.K.* 53°17N 4°20W 168 D3
Anglesey, Isle of ☐ *U.K.* 53°16N 4°18W 168 D3
Anglet *France* 43°29N 1°31W 174 E2
Angleton *U.S.A.* 29°10N 95°26W 314 G7
Anglin ➔ *France* 46°42N 0°52E 174 B4
Anglisidhes *Cyprus* 34°51N 33°27E 207 F9
Anglure *France* 48°35N 3°50E 173 D10
Angmagssalik = Tasiilaq *Greenland* 65°40N 37°20W 154 D7
Ango *Dem. Rep. of the Congo* 4°10N 26°5E 268 B2
Angoche *Mozam.* 16°8S 39°55E 269 F4
Angoche, I. *Mozam.* 16°20S 39°50E 269 F4
Angol *Chile* 37°56S 72°45W 334 D1
Angola *Ind., U.S.A.* 41°38N 85°0W 311 C12
Angola *N.Y., U.S.A.* 42°38N 79°2W 312 D5
Angola ■ *Africa* 12°0S 18°0E 265 E3
Angola Abyssal Plain *Atl. Oc.* 15°0S 2°0E 152 H12
Angola Basin *Atl. Oc.* 15°0S 3°0E 152 H12
Angoon *U.S.A.* 57°30N 134°35W 303 H14
Angora = Ankara *Turkey* 39°57N 32°54E 212 C5
Angoram *Papua N. G.* 4°4S 144°4E 286 C3
Angoulême *France* 45°39N 0°10E 174 C4
Angoumois *France* 45°50N 0°25E 174 C4
Angra do Heroismo *Azores* 38°39N 27°13W 153 d1
Angra dos Reis *Brazil* 23°0S 44°10W 335 A7
Angrapa ➔ *Russia* 54°37N 21°54E 184 D8
Angren *Uzbekistan* 41°1N 70°12E 217 D8
Angtassom *Cambodia* 11°1N 104°41E 237 G5
Angu *Dem. Rep. of the Congo* 3°23N 24°30E 264 B4
Anguang *China* 45°15N 123°45E 227 B12
Anguilla ☑ *W. Indies* 18°14N 63°5W 322 a
Anguilla I. *Anguilla* 18°13N 63°11W 322 a
Angul *India* 20°51N 85°6E 244 D7
Anguo *China* 38°28N 115°15E 226 E8
Angurugu *Australia* 14°0S 136°25E 280 A2
Angus *Canada* 44°19N 79°53W 312 B5
Angus ☐ *U.K.* 56°46N 2°56W 167 E6
Angwa ➔ *Zimbabwe* 16°0S 30°23E 271 A5
Angyalföld *Hungary* 47°32N 19°5E 117 A2
Anhanduí ➔ *Brazil* 21°46S 52°9W 335 A5
Anholt *Denmark* 56°42N 11°33E 163 H5
Anhua *China* 28°23N 111°12E 229 C8
Anhui ☐ *China* 32°0N 117°0E 229 B11
Anhwei = Anhui ☐ *China* 32°0N 117°0E 229 B11
Aniak *U.S.A.* 61°35N 159°32W 303 F8
Anichab *Namibia* 21°0S 14°46E 270 B1
Anicuns *Brazil* 16°28S 49°58W 333 E2
Anidros *Greece* 36°38N 25°43E 205 E7
Anié *Togo* 7°42N 1°8E 263 D5
Anik *India* 19°1N 72°53E 130 A2
Anil *Brazil* 2°32S 44°14W 332 B3
Animas ➔ *U.S.A.* 36°43N 108°13W 305 H9
Anin *Burma* 15°36N 97°50E 236 E1
Anin *Warszawa, Poland* 52°13N 21°9E 142 B2
Anina *Romania* 45°6N 21°51E 182 E6
Anini-y *Phil.* 10°25N 121°55E 233 F3
Aninoasa *Romania* 44°47N 24°10E 183 F9
Añisoc *Eq. Guin.* 1°51N 10°46E 264 B2
Anita *U.S.A.* 41°27N 94°46W 310 C2
Anivorano *Antsiranana, Madag.* 12°44S 49°14E 272 A2
Anivorano *Toamasina, Madag.* 18°44S 48°58E 272 B2
Aniwa *Vanuatu* 19°17S 169°35E 287 J7
Anjalankoski *Finland* 60°45N 26°51E 188 A2
Anjangaon *India* 21°10N 77°20E 244 D3
Anjar *India* 23°6N 70°10E 242 H4
Anjengo *India* 8°40N 76°46E 245 K3
Anji *China* 30°46N 119°40E 229 B12
Anjidiv I. *India* 14°40N 74°10E 245 G2
Anjō *Japan* 34°57N 137°5E 223 C9
Anjou *Qué., Canada* 45°36N 73°33W 130 A2
Anjou *Maine-et-Loire, France* 47°20N 0°15W 172 E6
Anjouan *Comoros Is.* 12°15S 44°20E 272 a
Anjouan ✕ (AJN) *Comoros Is.* 12°9S 44°26E 272 a
Anjozorobe *Madag.* 18°22S 47°52E 272 B2
Anju *N. Korea* 39°36N 125°40E 224 C2
Anka *Nigeria* 12°13N 5°58E 263 C6
Ankaboa, Tanjona *Madag.* 21°58S 43°20E 272 C1
Ankang *China* 32°40N 109°1E 226 H5
Ankara *Turkey* 39°57N 32°54E 212 C5
Ankara ☐ *Turkey* 39°55N 32°50E 212 C5
Ankarafantsika △ *Madag.* 16°8S 47°5E 272 B2
Ankaramena *Madag.* 21°57S 46°39E 272 C2
Ankarsrum *Sweden* 57°41N 16°20E 163 G10
Ankasakasa *Madag.* 16°21S 44°52E 272 B1
Ankavandra *Madag.* 18°46S 45°18E 272 B2
Ankazoabo *Madag.* 22°18S 44°31E 272 C1
Ankazobe *Madag.* 18°20S 47°10E 272 B2
Ankeny *U.S.A.* 41°44N 93°36W 310 C3
Ankhialo = Pomorie *Bulgaria* 42°32N 27°41E 203 D11
Ankilimalinika *Madag.* 22°58S 43°45E 272 C1
Ankilizato *Madag.* 20°25S 45°1E 272 C2
Anking = Anqing *China* 30°30N 117°3E 229 B11
Ankisabe *Madag.* 19°17S 46°29E 272 B2
Anklam *Germany* 53°51N 13°41E 178 B9
Ankleshwar *India* 21°38N 73°3E 244 D1
Ankober *Ethiopia* 9°35N 39°40E 257 F4
Ankola *India* 14°40N 74°18E 245 G2
Ankoro *Dem. Rep. of the Congo* 6°45S 26°55E 268 D2
Ankororoka *Madag.* 25°30S 45°11E 272 D2
Ankpa *Nigeria* 7°22N 7°38E 263 D6
Anlong *China* 25°2N 105°27E 228 E5
Anlong Veng *Cambodia* 14°14N 104°5E 236 E5
Anlu *China* 31°15N 113°45E 229 B9
Anmyeondo *S. Korea* 36°25N 126°25E 224 D3
Ånn *Sweden* 63°19N 12°33E 162 A6
Ann, C. *U.S.A.* 42°38N 70°35W 313 D14
Ann Arbor *U.S.A.* 42°17N 83°45W 311 B13
Anna *Russia* 51°28N 40°23E 190 E5
Anna *Ill., U.S.A.* 37°28N 89°15W 308 G9
Anna *Ohio, U.S.A.* 40°24N 84°11W 311 D12
Anna Regina *Guyana* 7°10N 58°30W 329 B6
Annaba *Algeria* 36°50N 7°46E 261 A6
Annaba ☐ *Algeria* 36°12N 7°45E 261 A6
Annaberg-Buchholz *Germany* 50°34N 13°0E 178 E9
Annai *Guyana* 3°57N 59°8W 329 C6
Annaka *Japan* 36°19N 138°54E 223 A10
Annalee ➔ *Ireland* 54°2N 7°24W 166 B4
Annalee Heights *U.S.A.* 38°51N 77°10W 143 B2
Annam = Trung-Phan *Vietnam* 17°0N 109°0E 236 D6
Annamitique, Chaîne *Asia* 17°0N 106°40E 236 D6
Annan *U.K.* 54°59N 3°16W 167 G5
Annan ➔ *U.K.* 54°58N 3°16W 167 G5
Annanberg *Papua N. G.* 4°52S 144°42E 286 C3
Annandale *U.S.A.* 38°50N 77°11W 143 C2
Annapolis *U.S.A.* 38°59N 76°30W 309 F15
Annapolis Royal *Canada* 44°44N 65°32W 299 D6
Annapurna *Nepal* 28°34N 83°50E 243 E10
Anne Frankhuis *Amsterdam, Neths.* 112 a1
Annean, L. *Australia* 26°54S 118°14E 279 E2
Anneberg *Sweden* 57°44N 14°49E 163 G8
Annecy *France* 45°55N 6°8E 175 C10
Annecy, Lac d' *France* 45°52N 6°10E 175 C10
Annemasse *France* 46°12N 6°16E 173 F13
Annenfeld = Şämkir *Azerbaijan* 40°50N 46°0E 191 K8
Annenskiy Most *Russia* 60°45N 37°10E 188 B9
Annette I. *U.S.A.* 55°9N 131°28W 296 B2
Annette Island *U.S.A.* 55°9N 131°28W 303 J15
Annigeri *India* 15°26N 75°26E 245 G2
Anning *China* 24°55N 102°26E 228 E4
Anniston *U.S.A.* 33°39N 85°50W 316 B4
Annobón *Atl. Oc.* 1°25S 5°36E 255 G4
Annonay *France* 45°15N 4°40E 175 C8
Annot *France* 43°58N 6°38E 175 E10
Annotto B. *Jamaica* 18°17N 76°45W 320 a
Annotto Bay *Jamaica* 18°16N 76°47W 320 a
Ånnsjön *Sweden* 63°19N 12°34E 162 A6
Annville *U.S.A.* 40°20N 76°31W 313 F8
Annweiler *Germany* 49°12N 7°57E 179 F3
Ano Poroia *Greece* 41°17N 23°2E 202 E7
Ano Siros *Greece* 37°29N 24°56E 204 D6
Anogi *Greece* 38°25N 20°40E 207 C2
Anogia *Greece* 35°16N 24°52E 207 E5
Anorotsangana *Madag.* 13°56S 47°55E 272 A2
Anosibe *Madag.* 19°26S 48°13E 272 B2
Anou Mellene *Mali* 17°29N 0°33E 263 B5
Anoumaba *Ivory C.* 6°23N 4°38W 262 D4
Anping *Hebei, China* 38°15N 115°30E 226 E8
Anping *Liaoning, China* 41°5N 123°30E 224 B1
Anpu Gang *China* 21°25N 109°50E 228 G7
Anqing *China* 30°30N 117°3E 229 B11
Anqiu *China* 36°25N 119°10E 227 F10
Anren *China* 26°43N 113°18E 229 D9
Ansager *Denmark* 55°43N 8°45E 163 J2
Ansai *China* 36°50N 109°20E 226 F5
Ansan *S. Korea* 37°21N 126°52E 224 D3
Ansbach *Germany* 49°28N 10°34E 179 F6
Anse-Bertrand *Guadeloupe* 16°28N 61°32W 322 e
Anse Boileau *Seychelles* 4°43S 55°29E 272 c
Anse Royale *Seychelles* 4°44S 55°31E 272 c
Anseba ➔ *Eritrea* 16°0N 38°30E 257 D4
Anseong *S. Korea* 37°0N 127°16E 224 D3
Anserma *Colombia* 5°13N 75°48W 328 B2
Ansfelden *Austria* 48°12N 14°17E 180 C7
Anshan *China* 41°5N 122°58E 224 B1
Anshun *China* 26°18N 105°57E 228 D5
Ansião *Portugal* 39°56N 8°27W 194 F2
Ansley *U.S.A.* 41°18N 99°23W 308 E4
Ansó *Spain* 42°51N 0°48W 196 C4
Ansoáin *Spain* 42°50N 1°38W 196 C3
Anson *U.S.A.* 32°45N 99°54W 314 E5
Anson B. *Australia* 13°20S 130°6E 278 B5
Ansongo *Mali* 15°25N 0°35E 263 B5
Ansongo-Ménaka △ *Mali* 15°3N 1°37E 263 B5
Ansonia *Conn., U.S.A.* 41°21N 73°5W 313 E11
Ansonia *Ohio, U.S.A.* 40°13N 84°38W 311 D12
Anstruther *U.K.* 56°14N 2°41W 167 E6
Ansudu *Indonesia* 2°11S 139°22E 231 E9
Antabamba *Peru* 14°40S 73°0W 330 C3
Antagarh *India* 20°6N 81°9E 244 D5
Antakya = Hatay *Turkey* 36°14N 36°10E 250 B7
Antalaha *Madag.* 14°57S 50°20E 272 A3
Antalāt *Libya* 31°8N 20°42E 258 B4
Antalya *Turkey* 36°52N 30°45E 250 B1
Antalya ☐ *Turkey* 36°50N 30°45E 250 B1
Antalya Körfezi *Turkey* 36°15N 31°30E 250 B2
Antambohobe *Madag.* 22°20S 46°47E 272 C2
Antanambao-Manampotsy *Madag.* 19°29S 48°34E 272 B2
Antanambe *Madag.* 16°26S 49°52E 272 B2
Antananarivo *Madag.* 18°55S 47°31E 272 B2
Antananarivo ☐ *Madag.* 19°0S 47°0E 272 B2
Antanifotsy *Madag.* 19°39S 47°19E 272 B2
Antanimbaribe *Madag.* 21°30S 44°48E 272 C1
Antanimora *Madag.* 24°49S 45°40E 272 C2
Antarctic Pen. *Antarctica* 67°0S 60°0W 151 C18
Antarctica 90°0S 0°0 151 E3
Antécume Pata *Fr. Guiana* 3°17N 54°4W 329 C7
Antelope *Zimbabwe* 21°2S 28°31E 269 G2
Antequera *Paraguay* 24°8S 57°7W 334 A4
Antequera *Spain* 37°5N 4°33W 195 H6
Antero, Mt. *U.S.A.* 38°41N 106°15W 304 G10
Antevamena *Madag.* 21°2S 44°8E 272 C1
Anthony *Fla., U.S.A.* 29°18N 82°7W 317 G4
Anthony *Kans., U.S.A.* 37°9N 98°2W 308 G4
Anthony *N. Mex., U.S.A.* 32°0N 106°36W 305 K10
Anti Atlas *Morocco* 30°0N 8°30W 260 C3

Anti-Lebanon = Sharqi, Al Jabal ash *Lebanon* 33°40N 36°10E **250** E7
Antibes *France* 43°34N 7°6E **175** E11
Antibes, C. d' *France* 43°31N 7°7E **175** E11
Anticosti, Î. d' *Canada* 49°30N 63°0W **299** C7
Antifer, C. d' *France* 49°41N 0°10E **172** C7
Antigo *U.S.A.* 45°9N 89°9W **308** C9
Antigonish *Canada* 45°38N 61°58W **299** C7
Antigua *Canary Is.* 28°24N 14°1W **153** e2
Antigua *Guatemala* 14°34N 90°41W **320** D1
Antigua *W. Indies* 17°0N 61°50W **322** b
Antigua & Barbuda ■ *W. Indies* 17°20N 61°48W **322** b
Antigua Int. ✈ (ANU) *Antigua & B.* 17°8N 61°47W **322** b
Antigues, Pte. d' *Guadeloupe* 16°26N 61°32W **322** e
Antikythira *Greece* 35°52N 23°15E **204** F5
Antilla *Cuba* 20°40N 75°50W **320** B4
Antilles = West Indies *Cent. Amer.* 15°0N 65°0W **321** D7
Antimilos *Greece* 36°47N 24°12E **204** E6
Anting *Taiwan* 23°7N 120°14E **225** C2
Antioch = Hatay *Turkey* 36°14N 36°10E **250** B7
Antioch *U.S.A.* 38°1N 121°48W **306** G5
Antioche, Pertuis d' *France* 46°6N 1°20W **174** B2
Antioquia *Colombia* 6°40N 75°55W **328** B2
Antioquia □ *Colombia* 7°0N 75°30W **328** B2
Antiparos *Greece* 37°0N 25°3E **205** D7
Antipaxi *Greece* 39°9N 20°13E **204** B2
Antipodes Is. *Pac. Oc.* 49°45S 178°40E **288** M9
Antipolo *Phil.* 14°35N 121°10E **232** D3
Antique □ *Phil.* 11°10N 122°5E **233** F4
Antirio *Greece* 38°20N 21°46E **204** C3
Antlers *U.S.A.* 34°14N 95°37W **314** D7
Antoetra *Madag.* 20°46S 47°20E **272** C2
Antofagasta *Chile* 23°50S 70°30W **334** A1
Antofagasta □ *Chile* 24°0S 69°0W **334** A2
Antofagasta de la Sierra *Argentina* 26°5S 67°20W **334** B2
Antofalla *Argentina* 25°30S 68°5W **334** B2
Antofalla, Salar de *Argentina* 25°40S 67°45W **334** B2
Antoine, L. *Grenada* 12°11N 61°36W **323** q
Anton *U.S.A.* 33°49N 102°10W **314** E3
Antongila, Helodrano *Madag.* 15°30S 49°50E **272** B2
Antonibé *Madag.* 15°7S 47°24E **272** B2
Antonina *Brazil* 25°26S 48°42W **335** B6
Antonio B. Won Pat Int. ✈ (GUM) *Guam* 13°29N 144°48E **302** d
António Enes = Angoche *Mozam.* 16°8S 39°55E **269** F4
Antony *France* 48°44N 2°17E **134** B2
Antrain *France* 48°28N 1°30W **172** D5
Antrim *Antrim, U.K.* 54°43N 6°14W **166** B5
Antrim *Ohio, U.S.A.* 40°7N 81°21W **312** F3
Antrim □ *U.K.* 54°56N 6°25W **166** B5
Antrim, Mts. of *U.K.* 55°3N 6°14W **166** A5
Antrim Plateau *Australia* 18°8S 128°20E **278** C4
Antriol *Bonaire* 12°12N 68°16W **322** h
Antrodoco *Italy* 42°25N 13°5E **199** F10
Antropovo *Russia* 58°24N 43°6E **190** A6
Antsakabary *Madag.* 15°3S 48°56E **272** B2
Antsalova *Madag.* 18°40S 44°37E **272** B1
Antsenavolo *Madag.* 21°24S 48°3E **272** C2
Antsiafabositra *Madag.* 17°18S 46°57E **272** B2
Antsirabe *Antananarivo, Madag.* 19°55S 47°2E **272** B2
Antsirabe *Antsiranana, Madag.* 14°0S 49°59E **272** A2
Antsirabe *Mahajanga, Madag.* 15°57S 48°58E **272** B2
Antsiranana *Madag.* 12°25S 49°20E **272** A2
Antsiranana □ *Madag.* 12°16S 49°17E **272** A2
Antsohihy *Madag.* 14°50S 47°59E **272** A2
Antsohimbondrona Seranana *Madag.* 13°7S 48°48E **272** A2
Antu *China* 42°30N 128°20E **227** C15
Antufash *Yemen* 15°42N 42°25E **248** D3
Antung *Taiwan* 23°18N 121°20E **225** C3
Antwerp = Antwerpen *Belgium* 51°13N 4°25E **170** C4
Antwerp *N.Y., U.S.A.* 44°12N 75°37W **313** B9
Antwerp *Ohio, U.S.A.* 41°11N 84°45W **311** C12
Antwerpen *Belgium* 51°13N 4°25E **170** C4
Antwerpen □ *Belgium* 51°15N 4°40E **170** C4
Anukur, C. *Papua N. G.* 6°18S 149°37E **286** D5
Anupgarh *India* 29°10N 73°10E **242** E5
Anuppur *India* 23°6N 81°41E **243** H9
Anuradhapura *Sri Lanka* 8°22N 80°28E **245** K5
Anurrete ◎ *Australia* 20°50S 135°38E **280** C2
Anveh *Iran* 27°23N 54°11E **247** E7
Anvers = Antwerpen *Belgium* 51°13N 4°25E **170** C4
Anvers I. *Antarctica* 64°30S 63°40W **151** C17
Anvik *U.S.A.* 62°39N 160°13W **303** E7
Anwen *China* 29°4N 120°26E **229** C13
Anxi *Fujian, China* 25°2N 118°12E **229** E12
Anxi *Gansu, China* 40°30N 95°43E **218** C8
Anxian *China* 31°40N 104°25E **228** B5
Anxiang *China* 29°27N 112°11E **229** C9
Anxious B. *Australia* 33°24S 134°45E **281** E1
Anyama *Ivory C.* 5°30N 4°3W **262** D4
Anyang *Henan, China* 36°5N 114°21E **226** F8
Anyang *S. Korea* 37°23N 126°55E **224** D3
Anyer *Indonesia* 6°4S 105°53E **234** D3
Anyi *Jiangxi, China* 28°49N 115°25E **229** C10
Anyi *Shanxi, China* 35°2N 111°2E **226** G6
Anyuan *China* 25°9N 115°21E **229** E10
Anyue *China* 30°9N 105°50E **228** B5
Anza *U.S.A.* 33°35N 116°39W **307** M10
Anze *China* 36°10N 112°12E **226** F7
Anzegdouf *Algeria* 26°50N 0°1E **261** C5
Anzhero-Sudzhensk *Russia* 56°10N 86°0E **214** D9
Ánzio *Italy* 41°27N 12°37E **200** A5
Anzoátegui □ *Venezuela* 9°0N 64°30W **329** B5
Ao Makham *Thailand* 7°50N 98°24E **237** a
Ao Phangnga △ *Thailand* 8°10N 98°32E **237** a
Aoba *Vanuatu* 15°25S 167°50E **287** E5
Aoga-Shima *Japan* 32°28N 139°46E **223** E11
Aohan Qi *China* 43°18N 119°43E **227** C10
Aoiz *Spain* 42°46N 1°22W **196** C3
Aoji *N. Korea* 42°31N 130°23E **224** A5
Aola *Solomon Is.* 9°30S 160°30E **287** M11
Aomen = Macau *China* 22°12N 113°33E **229** F9
Aomori *Japan* 40°45N 140°45E **220** D10
Aomori □ *Japan* 40°45N 140°40E **220** D10
AON Center *Chicago, U.S.A.* **119** b2
Aonla *India* 28°16N 79°11E **243** E8
Aono-Yama *Japan* 34°28N 131°48E **222** C3
Aorai, Mt. *Tahiti* 17°34S 149°30W **289** e
Aoraki Mount Cook *N.Z.* 43°36S 170°9E **285** D5
Aoral, Phnum *Cambodia* 12°0N 104°15E **237** G5
Aorangi Ra. *N.Z.* 41°28S 175°22E **284** H4
Aore *Vanuatu* 15°35S 167°10E **287** E5
Aoreora *Morocco* 28°51N 10°53W **260** C2
Aosta *Italy* 45°45N 7°20E **198** C4
Aotea Harbour *N.Z.* 38°0S 174°50E **284** E3
Aotearoa = New Zealand ■ *Oceania* 40°0S 176°0E **284** G5
Aoudéras *Niger* 17°45N 8°20E **259** E1
Aouinet Torkoz *Morocco* 28°31N 9°46W **260** C3
Aouk, Bahr → *Africa* 8°51N 18°53E **259** G3
Aouk-Aoukalé ⌂ *C.A.R.* 9°52N 21°25E **264** A4
Aoukar *Mali* 23°50N 2°45W **260** D4
Aoukâr *Mauritania* 17°40N 10°0W **262** B3
Aoulef el Arab *Algeria* 26°55N 1°2E **261** C5
Aousred *W. Sahara* 22°32N 14°17W **260** D2
Aoyama *Tokyo, Japan* **140** b2
Aozou *Chad* 21°45N 17°28E **259** D3
Aozou, Couloir d' *Chad* 22°0N 19°0E **259** D3
Ap Lei Chau *China* 22°14N 114°9E **122** B1
Apá → *S. Amer.* 22°6S 58°2W **334** A4
Apache *U.S.A.* 34°54N 98°22W **314** D5
Apache Junction *U.S.A.* 33°25N 111°33W **305** K8
Apalachee B. *U.S.A.* 30°0N 84°0W **316** E5
Apalachicola *U.S.A.* 29°43N 84°59W **316** F5
Apalachicola → *U.S.A.* 29°43N 84°58W **316** F5
Apalachicola B. *U.S.A.* 29°40N 85°0W **316** F5
Apam *Ghana* 5°19N 0°42W **263** D4
Apamea *Syria* 35°31N 36°28E **250** C7
Apapa *Nigeria* 6°26N 3°21E **124** B2
Apapa Quays *Nigeria* 6°26N 3°23E **124** B2
Apaporis → *Colombia* 1°23S 69°25W **328** D4
Aparados da Serra △ *Brazil* 29°10S 50°8W **335** B5
Aparecida = Bertolínia *Brazil* 7°38S 43°57W **332** C3
Aparecida de Goiânia *Brazil* 16°45S 49°16W **333** E2
Aparecida do Taboado *Brazil* 20°5S 51°5W **333** F1
Aparri *Phil.* 18°22N 121°38E **232** B3
Aparurén *Venezuela* 5°6N 62°8W **329** B5
Apataki *French Polynesia* 15°26S 146°20W **289** f
Apateu *Romania* 46°36N 21°47E **182** D6
Apatin *Serbia* 45°40N 19°0E **182** E4
Apatity *Russia* 67°34N 33°22E **160** C25
Apatou *Fr. Guiana* 5°9N 54°20W **329** B7
Apatula = Finke *Australia* 25°34S 134°35E **280** D1
Apatzingán *Mexico* 19°5N 102°21W **318** D4
Apayao □ *Phil.* 18°10N 121°10E **232** B3
Apelacão *Portugal* 38°48N 9°7W **126** A2
Apeldoorn *Neths.* 52°13N 5°57E **170** B5
Apen *Germany* 53°13N 7°48E **178** B3
Apennines = Appennini *Italy* 44°30N 10°0E **198** D7
Apenrade = Aabenraa *Denmark* 55°3N 9°25E **163** J3
Apere → *Bolivia* 13°44S 65°18W **331** C4
Aphrodisias *Turkey* 37°42N 28°46E **205** D10
Api *Nepal* 30°0N 80°57E **218** F5
Apia *Samoa* 13°50S 171°50W **287** V20
Apiacás, Serra dos *Brazil* 9°50S 57°0W **331** B6
Apiaí *Brazil* 24°31S 48°50W **333** F2
Apiaú → *Brazil* 2°39N 61°12W **329** C5
Apiaú, Serra do *Brazil* 2°30N 62°0W **329** C5
Apidiá → *Brazil* 11°39S 61°11W **331** C5
Apies → *S. Africa* 25°15S 28°8E **271** C4
Apinajé *Brazil* 11°31S 48°18W **333** D2
Apiti *N.Z.* 39°58S 175°54E **284** F4
Apizaco *Mexico* 19°25N 98°8W **319** D5
Aplao *Peru* 16°0S 72°40W **330** D3
Apo, Mt. *Phil.* 6°53N 125°14E **233** H5
Apo East Pass. *Phil.* 12°40N 120°40E **232** E3
Apo Reef △ *Phil.* 12°50N 120°50E **232** E3
Apo West Pass. *Phil.* 12°31N 120°22E **232** E3
Apodi *Brazil* 5°39S 37°48W **332** C4
Apoera *Suriname* 5°12N 57°10W **329** B6
Apolakia *Greece* 36°5N 27°48E **206** E11
Apolakia, Ormos *Greece* 36°5N 27°45E **206** E11
Apolda *Germany* 51°2N 11°32E **178** D7
Apollo Bay *Australia* 38°45S 143°40E **282** E5
Apollonia = Marsá Sūsah *Libya* 32°52N 21°59E **258** B4
Apollonia *Greece* 36°15N 27°58E **206** E11
Apolo *Bolivia* 14°30S 68°30W **330** C4
Apolonia *Greece* 36°58N 24°43E **204** E6
Apónguao → *Venezuela* 4°48N 61°36W **329** C5
Apopa *El Salv.* 13°48N 89°10W **320** D2
Apopka *U.S.A.* 28°40N 81°31W **317** G8
Apopka, L. *U.S.A.* 28°37N 81°37W **133** A1
Apoquindo *Chile* 33°24S 70°32W **128** B2
Aporé *Brazil* 18°58S 52°1W **331** D7
Aporé → *Brazil* 19°27S 50°57W **333** E1
Aporema *Brazil* 1°14N 50°49W **332** A1
Apostle Is. *U.S.A.* 47°0N 90°40W **308** B8
Apostle Islands ⌂ *U.S.A.* 46°55N 91°0W **308** B8
Apóstoles *Argentina* 28°0S 56°0W **335** B4
Apostolos Andreas, C. *Cyprus* 35°42N 34°35E **207** E10
Apostolovo *Ukraine* 47°39N 33°39E **189** J7
Apoteri *Guyana* 4°2N 58°32W **329** C6
Appalachian Mts. *U.S.A.* 38°0N 80°0W **309** G14
Äppelbo *Sweden* 60°29N 14°1E **162** D8
Appennini *Italy* 44°30N 10°0E **198** D7
Appennino Ligure *Italy* 44°30N 9°0E **198** D6
Appenzell-Ausser Rhoden □ *Switz.* 47°23N 9°23E **179** H5
Appenzell-Inner Rhoden □ *Switz.* 47°20N 9°25E **179** H5
Appiano *Italy* 46°28N 11°15E **199** B8
Apple Hill *Canada* 45°13N 74°46W **313** A10
Apple Valley *U.S.A.* 34°32N 117°14W **307** L9
Appleby-in-Westmorland *U.K.* 54°35N 2°29W **168** C5
Appledore *U.K.* 51°3N 4°13W **169** F3
Appleton *U.S.A.* 44°16N 88°25W **308** C9
Appleton City *U.S.A.* 38°11N 94°2W **310** F2
Appleton Rum Distillery *Jamaica* 18°10N 77°44W **320** a
Appling *U.S.A.* 33°33N 82°19W **316** B7
Approuague *Fr. Guiana* 4°20N 52°0W **329** C7
Apra Harbor *Guam* 13°26N 144°40E **302** d
Apricena *Italy* 41°47N 15°27E **199** G12
April → *Papua N. G.* 4°18S 142°26E **286** C2
Aprília *Italy* 41°36N 12°39E **200** A5
Apsheronsk *Russia* 44°28N 39°42E **191** H4
Apsley *Canada* 44°45N 78°6W **312** B6
Apt *France* 43°53N 5°24E **175** E9
Apterkarskiy Ostrov *Russia* 59°57N 30°20E **137** B2
Apuane, Alpi *Italy* 44°7N 10°14E **198** D7
Apuaú *Brazil* 2°25S 60°53W **329** D5
Apucarana *Brazil* 23°55S 51°33W **335** A5
Apulia = Púglia □ *Italy* 41°15N 16°15E **201** A9
Apurashokoru *Palau* 7°16N 134°17E **288** c
Apurauan *Phil.* 9°35N 118°20E **233** G2
Apure □ *Venezuela* 7°10N 68°50W **328** B4
Apure → *Venezuela* 7°37N 66°25W **328** B4
Apurímac □ *Peru* 14°0S 73°0W **330** C3
Apurímac → *Peru* 12°17S 73°56W **330** C3
Apuseni, Munţii *Romania* 46°30N 22°45E **182** D7
Āq Qālā *Iran* 37°10N 54°30E **247** B7
Aqaba = Al 'Aqabah *Jordan* 29°31N 35°0E **251** J6
Aqaba, G. of *Red Sea* 29°0N 34°40E **251** K5
'Aqabah, Khalīj al = Aqaba, G. of *Red Sea* 29°0N 34°40E **251** K5
Aqadyr *Kazakhstan* 48°17N 74°50E **217** C8
Āqchah *Afghan.* 36°56N 66°11E **240** A2
'Aqdā *Iran* 32°26N 53°37E **247** C7
Aqiq *Sudan* 18°14N 38°12E **256** D4
Aqiq, Khalîg *Sudan* 18°20N 38°10E **256** D4
'Aqīq, W. al → *Si. Arabia* 20°16N 41°40E **248** C3
Aqköl *Kazakhstan* 51°59N 70°56E **217** B8
Aqmola = Astana *Kazakhstan* 51°10N 71°30E **217** B8
Aqmola □ *Kazakhstan* 51°30N 70°0E **217** B8
'Aqrah *Iraq* 36°46N 43°45E **213** D10
Aqsay *Kazakhstan* 51°11N 53°0E **187** D9
Aqshatau *Kazakhstan* 47°59N 74°3E **217** C8
Aqsū *Ongtüstik Qazaqstan, Kazakhstan* 42°25N 69°50E **217** D7
Aqsū *Pavlodar, Kazakhstan* 52°2N 76°55E **217** B9
Aqsūat *Kazakhstan* 44°37N 74°30E **217** D8
Aqtaū *Mangghystaū, Kazakhstan* 43°39N 51°12E **187** F9
Aqtaū *Qaraghandy, Kazakhstan* 50°14N 73°3E **217** B8
Aqtöbe *Kazakhstan* 50°17N 57°10E **187** D10
Aqtoghay *Kazakhstan* 46°57N 79°40E **217** C9
Aquarium of the Americas *New Orleans, U.S.A.* **131** b3
Aquidauana *Brazil* 20°30S 55°50W **331** E6
Aquidauana → *Brazil* 19°44S 56°50W **331** D6
Aquila *Mexico* 18°36N 103°30W **318** D4
Aquiles Serdán *Mexico* 28°36N 105°53W **318** B3
Aquin *Haiti* 18°16N 73°24W **321** C5
Aquitain, Bassin *France* 44°0N 0°30W **171** D3
Aquitaine □ *France* 44°25N 0°30W **174** D3
Ar Horqin Qi *China* 43°45N 120°0E **227** C11
Ar Kazimiyah *Iraq* 33°22N 44°20E **113** B1
Ar Rafid *Syria* 32°57N 35°52E **250** F6
Ar Raḥḥālīyah *Iraq* 32°44N 43°23E **213** F10
Ar Ram *West Bank* 31°51N 35°15E **123** A2
Ar Ramādī *Iraq* 33°25N 43°20E **213** F10
Ar Raml *Libya* 26°45N 19°40E **258** C3
Ar Ramthā *Jordan* 32°34N 36°0E **251** F7
Ar Raqqah *Syria* 35°59N 39°8E **213** E8
Ar Raqqah □ *Syria* 36°20N 39°10E **213** D8
Ar Rashidiya = Er Rachidia *Morocco* 31°58N 4°20W **260** B4
Ar Rass *Si. Arabia* 25°50N 43°40E **246** E4
Ar Rastan *Syria* 34°55N 36°43E **250** D7
Ar Rawḍah *Si. Arabia* 21°16N 42°50E **248** B3
Ar Rawḍah *Yemen* 14°28N 47°17E **248** D4
Ar Rayyan *Qatar* 25°17N 51°25E **247** E6
Ar Rifā'ī *Iraq* 31°50N 46°10E **246** D5
Ar Rijā' *Yemen* 13°1N 44°35E **248** D4
Ar Riyāḍ *Si. Arabia* 24°41N 46°42E **246** E5
Ar Riyāḍ □ *Si. Arabia* 23°0N 45°50E **248** B4
Ar Riyān *Yemen* 14°39N 49°19E **267** B6
Ar Rimās, W. → *Syria* 35°47N 36°50E **250** C7
Ar Ru'ays *Qatar* 26°8N 51°12E **247** E6
Ar Rukhaymīyah *Iraq* 29°22N 45°38E **246** D5
Ar Rumaythah *Iraq* 31°31N 45°12E **246** D5
Ar Ruṣāfah *Syria* 35°45N 38°49E **213** E8
Ar Rutbah *Iraq* 33°0N 40°15E **213** F9
Ar Ruwayḍah *Si. Arabia* 23°40N 44°40E **248** B4
Ara *India* 25°35N 84°32E **243** G11
Ara → *Japan* 35°41N 139°50E **140** A4
Ara Goro *Ethiopia* 5°48N 41°18E **257** F5
Ara Terra *Ethiopia* 6°38N 40°57E **257** F5
Arab *U.S.A.* 34°19N 86°30W **315** D11
'Arab, Bahr el → *South Sudan* 9°0N 29°30E **257** F2
Arab, Khalîg el *Egypt* 30°55N 29°0E **256** A2
Arab, Shatt al → *Asia* 29°57N 48°34E **247** D6
'Araba, W. → *Egypt* 28°19N 33°31E **256** J8
'Arabābād *Iran* 33°2N 57°41E **247** C8
'Arabah, W. → *Yemen* 18°5N 51°26E **249** C5
Araban *Turkey* 37°28N 37°44E **212** D7
Arabatskaya Strelka *Ukraine* 45°40N 35°0E **189** K8
Arabba *Italy* 46°30N 11°52E **199** B8
Arabelo *Venezuela* 4°55N 64°13W **329** C5
Arabi *U.S.A.* 31°50N 83°44W **316** D6
Arabia *Asia* 25°0N 45°0E **210** F6
Arabian Basin *Ind. Oc.* 11°30N 65°0E **273** C5
Arabian Desert = Es Sahrâ' Esh Sharqîya *Egypt* 27°30N 32°30E **256** B3
Arabian Gulf = Persian Gulf *Asia* 27°0N 50°0E **247** E6
Arabian Sea *Ind. Oc.* 16°0N 65°0E **238** F9
Arabistan = Khūzestān □ *Iran* 31°0N 49°0E **247** D6
Araç *Turkey* 41°15N 33°21E **212** B5
Aracaju *Brazil* 10°55S 37°4W **332** D4
Aracataca *Colombia* 10°38N 74°9W **328** A3
Aracati *Brazil* 4°30S 37°44W **332** B4
Araçatuba *Brazil* 21°10S 50°30W **335** A5
Araceli *Phil.* 10°33N 119°59E **233** F2
Aracena *Spain* 37°53N 6°38W **195** H4
Aracena, Sierra de *Spain* 37°50N 6°50W **195** H4
Arachova *Greece* 38°28N 22°35E **204** C4
Arachthos → *Greece* 39°20N 21°4E **204** B3
Aracides, C. *Solomon Is.* 8°21S 161°0E **287** M11
Aračinovo *Macedonia* 42°1N 21°34E **202** D5
Araçuaí *Brazil* 16°52S 42°4W **333** E3
Araçuaí → *Brazil* 16°46S 42°2W **333** E3
'Arad *Israel* 31°15N 35°12E **251** G6
Arad *Romania* 46°10N 21°20E **182** D6
Arad □ *Romania* 46°20N 22°0E **182** D6
Arada *Chad* 15°0N 20°20E **259** F4
Arādān *Iran* 35°21N 52°30E **247** C7
Aradhippou *Cyprus* 34°57N 33°36E **207** F9
Arafura Sea *E. Indies* 9°0S 135°0E **288** H5
Aragarças *Brazil* 15°55S 52°15W **331** D7
Aragats *Armenia* 40°30N 44°15E **191** K7
Aragon *U.S.A.* 34°2N 85°3W **316** A4
Aragón □ *Spain* 41°25N 0°40W **196** D4
Aragón → *Spain* 42°13N 1°44W **196** C3
Aragona *Italy* 37°24N 13°37E **200** E6
Aragua □ *Venezuela* 10°0N 67°10W **328** B4
Aragua de Barcelona *Venezuela* 9°28N 64°49W **329** B5
Araguacema *Brazil* 8°50S 49°20W **332** C2
Araguaçu = Paraguaçu Paulista *Brazil* 22°22S 50°35W **335** A5
Araguaia *Brazil* 12°49S 49°51W **333** D2
Araguaia → *Brazil* 5°21S 48°41W **332** C2
Araguaia △ *Brazil* 10°30S 50°0W **332** D2
Araguaína *Brazil* 7°12S 48°12W **332** C2
Araguari *Brazil* 18°38S 48°11W **333** E2
Araguari → *Brazil* 1°15N 49°55W **329** C8
Araguatins *Brazil* 5°38S 48°7W **332** C2
Arahal *Spain* 37°15N 5°33W **195** H5
Arain *India* 26°27N 75°2E **242** F6
Araioses *Brazil* 2°53S 41°55W **332** B3
Arak *Algeria* 25°20N 3°45E **261** C5
Arāk *Iran* 34°0N 49°40E **247** C6
Araka *South Sudan* 4°20N 30°23E **257** G3
Arakan □ *Burma* 19°0N 94°15E **241** F5
Arakan Coast *Burma* 19°0N 94°0E **241** F4
Arakan Yoma *Burma* 20°0N 94°40E **241** F5
Arakawa *Japan* 35°44N 139°48E **140** A3
Arakkonam *India* 13°7N 79°43E **245** H4
Araklı *Turkey* 41°6N 40°2E **213** B9
Araks = Aras, Rūd-e → *Asia* 40°5N 48°29E **213** B13
Araks → *Iran* 39°10N 47°10E **216** E3
Aral *Kazakhstan* 46°41N 61°45E **216** C6
Aral Mangy Qaraqumy *Kazakhstan* 46°50N 63°10E **216** C6
Aral Sea *Asia* 44°30N 60°0E **216** C5
Aral Tengizi = Aral Sea *Asia* 44°30N 60°0E **216** C5
Aralık *Turkey* 39°52N 44°31E **213** C11
Aralqum *Asia* 44°30N 60°35E **216** D6
Aralsk = Aral *Kazakhstan* 46°41N 61°45E **216** C6
Aralskoye More = Aral Sea *Asia* 44°30N 60°0E **216** C5
Aralsor, Ozero = Aralsor Köli *Kazakhstan* 49°5N 48°12E **191** F9
Aralsor Köli *Kazakhstan* 49°5N 48°12E **191** F9
Aramac *Australia* 22°58S 145°14E **280** C4
Aramia → *Papua N. G.* 7°55S 143°22E **286** D2
Aran → *India* 19°55N 78°12E **244** E4
Aran Areh *Ethiopia* 9°2N 43°54E **267** C5
Aran I. *Ireland* 55°0N 8°30W **166** A3
Aran Is. *Ireland* 53°6N 9°38W **166** C2
Aranda de Duero *Spain* 41°39N 3°42W **194** D7
Arandān *Iran* 35°23N 46°55E **246** C5
Aranđelovac *Serbia* 44°18N 20°34E **202** B4
Aranga *N.Z.* 35°44S 173°40E **284** B2
Arani *Bolivia* 17°34S 65°46W **331** D4
Arani *India* 12°43N 79°19E **245** H4
Aranjuez *Spain* 40°1N 3°40W **194** E7
Aranos *Namibia* 24°9S 19°7E **270** B2
Aransas Pass *U.S.A.* 27°55N 97°9W **314** H6
Arany-hegyi-patak → *Hungary* 47°34N 19°4E **117** A2
Aranyaprathet *Thailand* 13°41N 102°30E **236** F4
Arao *Japan* 32°59N 130°25E **222** E2
Araouane *Mali* 18°55N 3°30W **262** B4
Arapahoe *U.S.A.* 40°18N 99°54W **308** E4
Arapari *Brazil* 5°34S 49°15W **332** C2
Arapawa I. *N.Z.* 41°11S 174°17E **285** B9
Arapey Grande → *Uruguay* 30°55S 57°49W **334** C4
Arapgir *Turkey* 39°5N 38°30E **213** C8
Arapiraca *Brazil* 9°45S 36°39W **332** C4
Arapis, Akra *Greece* 40°27N 24°0E **203** F8
Arapongas *Brazil* 23°29S 51°28W **335** A5
Arapuni *N.Z.* 38°4S 175°39E **284** E4
Ar'ar *Si. Arabia* 30°59N 41°2E **246** D4
Araracuara *Colombia* 0°24S 72°17W **328** D3
Araranguá *Brazil* 29°0S 49°30W **335** B6
Araraquara *Brazil* 21°50S 48°0W **333** F2
Araras *Brazil* 22°22S 47°23W **333** F2
Ararás, Serra das *Brazil* 25°0S 53°10W **335** B5
Ararat *Armenia* 39°48N 44°50E **213** C11
Ararat *Vic., Australia* 37°16S 142°58E **282** D5
Ararat, Mt. = Ağrı Dağı *Turkey* 39°50N 44°15E **213** C11
Arari *Brazil* 3°28S 44°47W **332** B3
Araria *India* 26°9N 87°33E **243** F12
Araripe, Chapada do *Brazil* 7°20S 40°0W **332** C4
Araripina *Brazil* 7°33S 40°34W **332** C3
Araruama, L. de *Brazil* 22°53S 42°12W **333** F3
Araruna *Brazil* 6°52S 35°44W **332** C4
Aras, Rūd-e → *Asia* 40°5N 48°29E **213** B13
Aratāne *Mauritania* 18°24N 8°32W **262** B3
Araticu = Oeiras do Para *Brazil* 1°58S 49°51W **329** D8
Arauca *Colombia* 7°0N 70°40W **328** B3
Arauca □ *Colombia* 6°40N 71°0W **328** B3
Arauca → *Venezuela* 7°24N 66°35W **328** B4
Arauco *Chile* 37°16S 73°25W **334** D1
Araújos *Brazil* 19°56S 45°14W **333** E2
Arauquita *Colombia* 7°2N 71°25W **328** B3
Araure *Venezuela* 9°34N 69°13W **328** B4
Aravaca *Spain* 40°27N 3°47W **127** B1
Aravalli Range *India* 25°0N 73°30E **242** G5
Arawa *Ethiopia* 9°57N 41°58E **257** F5
Arawale ⌂ *Kenya* 1°24S 40°9E **266** C5
Arawe Is. *Papua N. G.* 6°6S 149°0E **286** D5
Arawhata → *N.Z.* 44°0S 168°40E **285** E3
Araxá *Brazil* 19°35S 46°55W **333** E2
Araya, Pen. de *Venezuela* 10°40N 64°0W **329** A5
Arayat *Phil.* 15°10N 120°46E **232** D3
Arba Gugu *Ethiopia* 8°40N 40°15E **257** F5
Arba Minch *Ethiopia* 6°0N 37°30E **257** F4
Arbat *Iraq* 35°25N 45°35E **213** E11
Arbataash *Iraq* 33°20N 44°19E **113** A1
Árbatax *Italy* 39°56N 9°42E **200** C2
Arbi *Ethiopia* 9°4N 35°7E **257** F4
Arbīl *Iraq* 36°15N 44°5E **213** D11
Arbīl □ *Iraq* 36°20N 44°20E **213** D11
Arboga *Sweden* 59°24N 15°52E **162** E9
Arbois *France* 46°55N 5°46E **173** F12
Arboletes *Colombia* 8°51N 76°26W **328** B2
Arbore *Ethiopia* 5°3N 36°50E **257** F4
Arboréa *Italy* 39°46N 8°35E **200** C1
Arborfield *Canada* 53°6N 103°39W **297** C8
Arborg *Canada* 50°54N 97°13W **297** C9
Arbre du Ténéré *Niger* 17°50N 10°4E **259** E2
Arbroath *U.K.* 56°34N 2°35W **167** E6
Arbuckle *U.S.A.* 39°1N 122°3W **306** F4
Arbus *Italy* 39°30N 8°33E **200** C1
Arc → *France* 45°34N 6°12E **175** C10
Arc de Triomphe *Paris, France* **134** a2
Arc-lès-Gray *France* 47°28N 5°34E **173** E12
Arcachon *France* 44°40N 1°10W **174** D2
Arcachon, Bassin d' *France* 44°42N 1°10W **174** D2
Arcade *U.S.A.* 42°32N 78°25W **312** D6
Arcadia *Calif., U.S.A.* 34°7N 118°1W **126** B4
Arcadia *Fla., U.S.A.* 27°13N 81°52W **317** H8
Arcadia *Ind., U.S.A.* 40°11N 86°1W **311** D10
Arcadia *Iowa, U.S.A.* 42°5N 95°3W **310** B1
Arcadia *La., U.S.A.* 32°33N 92°55W **314** E8
Arcadia *Pa., U.S.A.* 40°47N 78°51W **312** F6
Arcanum *U.S.A.* 39°59N 84°33W **311** E12
Arcata *U.S.A.* 40°52N 124°5W **304** F1
Arcévia *Italy* 43°30N 12°56E **199** E9
Archanes *Greece* 35°16N 25°11E **205** F7
Archangel = Arkhangelsk *Russia* 64°38N 40°36E **186** B7
Archangelos *Preveza, Greece* 39°6N 20°42E **207** A2
Archangelos *Rhodes, Greece* 36°13N 28°7E **206** E12
Archar *Bulgaria* 43°50N 22°54E **202** C6
Archbald *U.S.A.* 41°30N 75°32W **313** E9
Archbold *U.S.A.* 41°31N 84°18W **311** C12
Archena *Spain* 38°9N 1°16W **197** G3
Archenu, J. *Libya* 22°15N 24°45E **259** D4
Archer *U.S.A.* 29°32N 82°32W **317** F7
Archer → *Australia* 13°28S 141°41E **280** A3
Archer B. *Australia* 13°20S 141°30E **280** A3
Archer Bend = Mungkan Kandju △ *Australia* 13°35S 142°52E **280** A3
Archers Post *Kenya* 0°35N 37°35E **268** B4
Arches △ *U.S.A.* 38°45N 109°25W **304** G9
Archidona *Spain* 37°6N 4°22W **195** H6
Archipel-de-Mingan △ *Canada* 50°13N 63°10W **299** B7
Archipiélago Chinijo △ *Canary Is.* 29°20N 13°30W **153** e2
Archipiélago Los Roques △ *Venezuela* 11°50N 66°44W **321** D6
Archives Navy Memorial *Washington, D.C., U.S.A.* **143** b2
Arci, Mte. *Italy* 39°47N 8°45E **200** C1
Arcidosso *Italy* 42°52N 11°33E **199** F8
Arcila = Asilah *Morocco* 35°29N 6°0W **260** A3
Arcipelago de la Maddalena △ *Italy* 41°14N 9°24E **200** A2
Arcipelago Toscano △ *Italy* 42°45N 10°15E **198** F7
Arcis-sur-Aube *France* 48°32N 4°10E **173** D11
Arckaringa Cr. → *Australia* 28°10S 135°22E **281** D2
Arco *Italy* 45°55N 10°53E **198** C7
Arco *Idaho, U.S.A.* 43°38N 113°18W **304** E7
Arco Plaza *Los Angeles, U.S.A.* **127** b1
Arcola *U.S.A.* 39°41N 88°19W **311** E9
Arcoona *Australia* 31°2S 137°1E **282** A2
Arcos de Jalón *Spain* 41°12N 2°16W **196** D2
Arcos de la Frontera *Spain* 36°45N 5°49W **195** J5
Arcos de Valdevez *Portugal* 41°55N 8°22W **194** D2
Arcot *India* 12°53N 79°20E **245** H4
Arcoverde *Brazil* 8°25S 37°4W **332** C4
Arcozelo *Portugal* 40°32N 7°47W **194** E3
Arctic Bay *Canada* 73°1N 85°7W **295** C14
Arctic Mid-Ocean Ridge *Arctic* 87°0N 90°0E **150** A
Arctic Ocean *Arctic* 78°0N 160°0W **150** B18
Arctic Red River = Tsiigehtchic *Canada* 67°15N 134°0W **294** D5
Arctic Village *U.S.A.* 68°8N 145°32W **303** B11
Arctowski *Antarctica* 62°30S 58°0W **151** C18
Arcueil *France* 48°48N 2°19E **134** B2
Arda → *Bulgaria* 41°40N 26°30E **203** E10
Arda → *Italy* 45°2N 10°2E **198** C7
Ardabīl *Iran* 38°15N 48°18E **213** C13
Ardabīl □ *Iran* 38°15N 48°20E **247** B6
Ardahan *Turkey* 41°7N 42°41E **213** B10
Ardahan □ *Turkey* 41°10N 42°50E **213** B10
Ardakān = Sepīdān *Iran* 30°20N 52°5E **247** D7
Ardakān *Iran* 32°19N 53°59E **247** C7
Ardala *Sweden* 58°22N 13°19E **163** F7
Ardales *Spain* 36°53N 4°51W **195** J6
Årdalstangen *Norway* 61°14N 7°43E **164** C4
Ardara *Ireland* 54°46N 8°25W **166** B3
Ardas → *Greece* 41°40N 26°30E **203** E10
Ardèche □ *France* 44°42N 4°16E **175** D8
Ardèche → *France* 44°16N 4°39E **175** D8
Ardee *Ireland* 53°52N 6°33W **166** C5
Arden *Ont., Canada* 44°43N 76°56W **312** B8
Arden *Denmark* 56°46N 9°52E **163** H3
Arden *Calif., U.S.A.* 38°36N 121°33W **306** G5
Arden *Nev., U.S.A.* 36°1N 115°14W **307** J11
Ardenne *Belgium* 49°50N 5°5E **170** E5
Ardennes = Ardenne *Belgium* 49°50N 5°5E **170** E5
Ardennes □ *France* 49°35N 4°40E **173** C11
Ardentes *France* 46°45N 1°50E **173** F8
Arderin *Ireland* 53°2N 7°39W **166** C4
Ardeşen *Turkey* 41°12N 41°2E **213** B9
Ardestān *Iran* 33°20N 52°25E **247** C7
Ardfert *Ireland* 52°20N 9°47W **166** D2
Ardglass *U.K.* 54°17N 5°36W **166** B6
Ardhéa = Aridea *Greece* 40°58N 22°3E **202** F6
Ardila → *Portugal* 38°12N 7°28W **195** G3
Ardino *Bulgaria* 41°34N 25°9E **203** E9
Ardivachar Pt. *U.K.* 57°23N 7°26W **167** D1
Ardlethan *Australia* 34°22S 146°53E **283** C7
Ardmore *Okla., U.S.A.* 34°10N 97°8W **314** D6
Ardmore *Pa., U.S.A.* 40°2N 75°17W **313** F9
Ardnamurchan, Pt. of *U.K.* 56°43N 6°14W **167** E2
Ardnave Pt. *U.K.* 55°53N 6°20W **167** F2
Ardon *Russia* 43°10N 44°18E **191** J7
Ardore *Italy* 38°11N 16°10E **201** D9
Ardres *France* 50°50N 1°59E **173** B8
Ardrossan *S. Austral., Australia* 34°26S 137°53E **282** C2
Ardrossan *N. Ayrs., U.K.* 55°39N 4°49W **167** F4
Ards Pen. *U.K.* 54°33N 5°34W **166** B6
Arduan *Sudan* 19°54N 30°20E **256** D3
Ardud *Romania* 47°37N 22°52E **182** C7
Åre *Sweden* 63°22N 13°15E **162** A7
Arecibo *Puerto Rico* 18°29N 66°43W **321** C6
Areia Branca *Brazil* 5°0S 37°0W **332** C4
Arena, Pt. *U.S.A.* 38°57N 123°44W **306** G3
Arena I. *Phil.* 9°14N 120°45E **233** G3
Arenal *Honduras* 15°21N 86°50W **320** C2
Arenales, Cerro *Chile* 47°5S 73°40W **336** C2
Arenápolis *Brazil* 14°26S 56°49W **331** C6
Arenas = Las Arenas *Spain* 43°17N 4°50W **194** B6
Arenas, Pta. *Venezuela* 10°31N 64°14W **329** A5
Arenas de San Pedro *Spain* 40°12N 5°5W **194** E5
Arendal *Norway* 58°28N 8°46E **164** F5
Arendsee *Germany* 52°52N 11°27E **178** C7
Arenillas *Ecuador* 3°33S 80°10W **328** D1
Arensburg = Kuressaare *Estonia* 58°15N 22°30E **188** C2
Arenys de Mar *Spain* 41°35N 2°33E **196** D7
Arenzano *Italy* 44°24N 8°41E **198** D5
Arenzville *U.S.A.* 39°53N 90°22W **310** E6
Areopoli *Greece* 36°40N 22°22E **204** E4
Arequipa *Peru* 16°20S 71°30W **330** D3
Arequipa □ *Peru* 16°0S 72°50W **330** D3
Arere *Brazil* 0°16S 53°52W **329** D7
Arero *Ethiopia* 4°41N 38°50E **257** G4
Arès *France* 44°47N 1°8W **174** D2
Arese *Italy* 45°32N 9°4E **129** A1
Arévalo *Spain* 41°3N 4°43W **194** D6
Arezzo *Italy* 43°25N 11°53E **199** E8
Arga *Turkey* 38°21N 37°59E **246** B3
Arga → *Spain* 42°18N 1°47W **196** C3
Argalasti *Greece* 39°13N 23°13E **204** B5
Argamasilla de Alba *Spain* 39°8N 3°5W **195** F7
Argamasilla de Calatrava *Spain* 38°44N 4°4W **195** G6
Arganda del Rey *Spain* 40°19N 3°26W **194** E7
Arganil *Portugal* 40°13N 8°3W **194** E2
Arganzuela *Spain* 40°23N 3°42W **127** B1
Argao *Phil.* 9°52N 123°36E **233** G4
Argarapa ◎ *Australia* 22°20S 134°58E **280** C1
Argedeb *Ethiopia* 6°11N 41°13E **257** F5
Argelès-Gazost *France* 43°0N 0°6W **174** E3
Argelès-sur-Mer *France* 42°34N 3°1E **174** F7
Argens → *France* 43°24N 6°44E **175** E10
Argent-sur-Sauldre *France* 47°33N 2°25E **173** E9
Argenta = North Little Rock *U.S.A.* 34°45N 92°16W **314** D8
Argenta *B.C., Canada* 50°11N 116°56W **296** C5
Argenta *Italy* 44°37N 11°50E **199** D8
Argenta *Ill., U.S.A.* 39°59N 88°49W **311** E8
Argentan *France* 48°45N 0°1W **172** D6
Argentário, Mte. *Italy* 42°24N 11°9E **199** F8
Argentat *France* 45°6N 1°56E **174** C5
Argentera *Italy* 44°12N 7°5E **198** D4
Argenteuil *France* 48°56N 2°15E **134** A2
Argentia *Canada* 47°18N 53°58W **299** C9
Argentiera, C. dell' *Italy* 40°44N 8°8E **200** B1
Argentina ■ *S. Amer.* 35°0S 66°0W **327** G4
Argentine Abyssal Plain *Atl. Oc.* 46°0S 52°0W **152** L6
Argentine Basin *Atl. Oc.* 45°0S 45°0W **152** L7
Argentino, L. *Argentina* 50°10S 73°0W **336** D2
Argenton-Château *France* 46°59N 0°27W **172** F6
Argenton-sur-Creuse *France* 46°36N 1°30E **173** F8
Argeş □ *Romania* 45°0N 24°45E **183** F9
Argeş → *Romania* 44°5N 26°38E **183** F11
Arghandab → *Afghan.* 31°30N 64°15E **242** D1
Argheile *Ethiopia* 5°19N 42°4E **257** F5
Argirades *Greece* 39°27N 19°58E **206** C9
Argiroupoli *Athina, Greece* 37°55N 23°44E **112** B2
Argiroupoli *Kriti, Greece* 35°17N 24°20E **207** E5
Argo *Sudan* 19°28N 30°30E **256** D3
Argolida □ *Greece* 37°38N 22°50E **204** D4
Argolikos Kolpos *Greece* 37°20N 22°52E **204** D4
Argonne *France* 49°10N 5°0E **173** C12
Argonne Forest *U.S.A.* 41°42N 87°53W **119** C1
Argos *Greece* 37°40N 22°43E **204** D4
Argos *Ind., U.S.A.* 41°14N 86°15W **311** C10
Argos Orestiko *Greece* 40°27N 21°18E **202** F5
Argostoli *Greece* 38°11N 20°29E **207** C2
Argostoliou, Kolpos *Greece* 38°10N 20°27E **207** C1
Arguedas *Spain* 42°11N 1°36W **196** C3
Argüelles *Madrid, Spain* **127** a1
Arguello, Pt. *U.S.A.* 34°35N 120°39W **307** L6
Arguineguín *Canary Is.* 27°46N 15°41W **153** e1
Argun *Russia* 43°18N 45°52E **191** J7
Argun → *Russia* 53°20N 121°28E **219** A13
Argungu *Nigeria* 12°40N 4°31E **263** C5
Argus Pk. *U.S.A.* 35°52N 117°26W **307** K9
Argyle, L. *Australia* 16°20S 128°40E **278** C4
Argyle Waterfalls *Trin. & Tob.* 11°15N 60°35W **323** s
Argyll ⌂ *U.K.* 56°5N 5°0W **167** E4
Argyll & Bute □ *U.K.* 56°13N 5°28W **167** E3
Arhavi *Turkey* 41°21N 41°18E **213** B9
Århus *Denmark* 56°8N 10°11E **163** H4
Ari Atoll *Maldives* 3°53N 72°50E **272** d
Aria *N.Z.* 38°33S 175°0E **284** E4
Ariadnoye *Russia* 45°8N 134°25E **220** B7
Ariamsvlei *Namibia* 28°9S 19°51E **270** C2
Ariana *Tunisia* 36°52N 10°12E **258** A2
Ariana □ *Tunisia* 36°50N 9°52E **261** A6
Ariano Irpino *Italy* 41°9N 15°5E **201** A8
Ariari → *Colombia* 2°35N 72°47W **328** C3
Aribinda *Burkina Faso* 14°17N 0°52W **263** C4
Arica *Chile* 18°32S 70°20W **330** D3
Arica *Colombia* 2°0S 71°50W **328** D3
Arica y Parinacota □ *Chile* 17°40S 69°50W **330** D4
Arico *Canary Is.* 28°9N 16°29W **153** e1
Arid, C. *Australia* 34°1S 123°10E **279** F3
Arida *Japan* 34°5N 135°8E **223** C7
Aridal *W. Sahara* 25°59N 13°54W **260** C2
Aride *Seychelles* 4°13S 55°40E **272** c
Aridea *Greece* 40°58N 22°3E **202** F6
Ariège □ *France* 42°56N 1°30E **174** F5
Ariège → *France* 43°30N 1°25E **174** E5
Arieș → *Romania* 46°24N 23°20E **183** D8
Arigat el Fersig *Algeria* 27°35N 2°7W **261** C4
Arīhā *Israel* 31°51N 35°27E **256** A4
Arīḥā *Syria* 35°49N 36°35E **250** C7
Arikok ⌂ *Aruba* 12°31N 69°56W **322** f
Arila, Akra *Greece* 39°43N 19°39E **206** B9
Arilje *Serbia* 43°44N 20°7E **202** C4
Arima *Kanagawa, Japan* 35°33N 139°33E **140** B2
Arima *Trin. & Tob.* 10°38N 61°17W **323** t
Arima → *Trin. & Tob.* 10°35N 61°16W **323** t
Aringay *Phil.* 16°26N 120°21E **232** C3
Arinos → *Brazil* 10°25S 58°20W **331** C6
Ario de Rosales *Mexico* 19°12N 101°43W **318** D4
Ariogala *Lithuania* 55°16N 23°28E **184** C10
Arios Pagos *Athens, Greece* **112** c1
Aripo → *Trin. & Tob.* 10°35N 61°14W **323** t
Aripo, Mt. *Trin. & Tob.* 10°45N 61°15W **323** t
Aripo Caves *Trin. & Tob.* 10°43N 61°14W **323** t
Aripuanã *Brazil* 9°25S 60°30W **331** B5
Aripuanã → *Brazil* 5°7S 60°25W **331** B5
Ariquemes *Brazil* 9°55S 63°6W **331** B5
Arisaig *U.K.* 56°55N 5°51W **167** E3
Arish, W. el → *Egypt* 31°9N 33°49E **256** A3
Arissa *Ethiopia* 11°10N 41°35E **257** E5
Aristazabal I. *Canada* 52°40N 129°10W **296** C3
Arita *Japan* 33°11N 129°54E **222** D1
Aritao *Phil.* 16°18N 121°2E **232** C3
Ariton *U.S.A.* 31°36N 85°43W **316** D4
Arivonimamo *Madag.* 19°1S 47°11E **272** B2
Ariyalur *India* 11°8N 79°8E **245** J4
Ariza *Spain* 41°19N 2°3W **196** D2
Arizaro, Salar de *Argentina* 24°40S 67°50W **334** A2
Arizona *Argentina* 35°45S 65°25W **334** D2
Arizona □ *U.S.A.* 34°0N 112°0W **305** J8
Arizpe *Mexico* 30°20N 110°10W **318** A2
'Arjah *Si. Arabia* 24°43N 44°17E **246** E5
Årjäng *Sweden* 59°24N 12°8E **162** E6
Arjeplog *Sweden* 66°3N 17°54E **160** C17
Arjepluovve = Arjeplog *Sweden* 66°3N 17°54E **160** C17
Arjona *Colombia* 10°14N 75°22W **328** A2
Arjona *Spain* 37°56N 4°4W **195** H6
Arjuna *Indonesia* 7°49S 112°34E **235** D4
Arka *Russia* 60°15N 142°0E **215** C15
Arkadak *Russia* 51°58N 43°30E **190** E6
Arkadelphia *U.S.A.* 34°7N 93°4W **314** D8
Arkadia □ *Greece* 37°30N 22°20E **204** D4
Arkaig, L. *U.K.* 56°59N 5°10W **167** E3
Arkalgud *India* 12°46N 76°3E **245** H3
Arkalyk = Arqalyk *Kazakhstan* 50°13N 66°50E **217** B7
Arkansas □ *U.S.A.* 35°0N 92°30W **314** D8
Arkansas → *U.S.A.* 33°47N 91°4W **314** E9
Arkansas City *U.S.A.* 37°4N 97°2W **308** G5
Arkaroola *Australia* 30°20S 139°22E **281** E2
Arkavāz *Iran* 33°22N 46°35E **213** F12
Arkhangelsk *Russia* 64°38N 40°36E **186** B7
Arkhangelskoye *Russia* 51°32N 40°58E **190** E5
Arkhangelyskoye *Russia* 55°47N 37°17E **129** B1
Arki *Greece* 37°24N 26°44E **205** D8
Arki *India* 31°9N 76°58E **242** D7
Arkiko *Eritrea* 15°33N 39°30E **257** D4
Arklow *Ireland* 52°48N 6°10W **166** D5
Arkona *Germany* 54°42N 13°26E **178** A9
Arkösund *Sweden* 58°29N 16°56E **163** F10
Arkoudi *Greece* 38°33N 20°43E **204** C2
Arkport *U.S.A.* 42°24N 77°42W **312** D7
Arkticheskiy, Mys *Russia* 81°10N 95°0E **215** A10
Arkul *Russia* 57°17N 50°3E **190** B10
Arkville *U.S.A.* 42°9N 74°37W **313** D10
Årla *Sweden* 59°17N 16°40E **162** E10
Arlanda, Stockholm ✈ (ARN) *Sweden* 59°41N 17°56E **139** A1
Arlanza → *Spain* 42°6N 4°9W **194** C6
Arlanzón → *Spain* 42°3N 4°17W **194** C6
Arlbergpass *Austria* 47°9N 10°12E **180** D3
Arlbergtunnel *Austria* 47°9N 10°12E **180** D3
Arles *France* 43°41N 4°40E **175** E8
Arli *Burkina Faso* 11°35N 1°28E **263** C5
Arli △ *Burkina Faso* 11°35N 1°28E **263** C5
Arlington *Free State, S. Africa* 28°1S 27°53E **271** C4
Arlington *Ga., U.S.A.* 31°26N 84°44W **316** D5
Arlington *Mass., U.S.A.* 42°24N 71°10W **116** A1
Arlington *N.Y., U.S.A.* 41°42N 73°54W **313** E11
Arlington *Oreg., U.S.A.* 45°43N 120°12W **304** D3
Arlington *S. Dak., U.S.A.* 44°22N 97°8W **308** C5
Arlington *Tex., U.S.A.* 32°44N 97°6W **314** E6
Arlington *Va., U.S.A.* 38°53N 77°7W **143** B3
Arlington *Vt., U.S.A.* 43°5N 73°9W **313** C11
Arlington *Wash., U.S.A.* 48°12N 122°8W **306** B4
Arlington Heights *Ill., U.S.A.* 42°5N 87°59W **311** B9
Arlington Heights *Mass., U.S.A.* 42°25N 71°10W **116** A1
Arlington Nat. Cemetery *U.S.A.* 38°52N 77°4W **143** B3
Arlon *Belgium* 49°42N 5°49E **170** E5
Arlparra *Australia* 22°11S 134°30E **280** C1
Arltunga *Australia* 23°26S 134°41E **280** C1
Armação *Brazil* 22°52S 43°6W **135** B2
Armadale *Vic., Australia* 37°51S 145°0E **128** B2
Armadale *W. Austral., Australia* 32°9S 116°0E **279** F2

Armagh *U.K.* 54°21N 6°39W **166** B5
Armagh □ *U.K.* 54°18N 6°37W **166** B5
Armagnac *France* 43°50N 0°10E **174** E4
Armançon → *France* 47°59N 3°30E **173** E10
Armando Bermudez △ *Dom. Rep.* 19°3N 71°0W **321** C5
Armant *Egypt* 25°37N 32°32E **256** B3
Armatree *Australia* 31°26S 148°28E **283** A8
Armavir *Russia* 45°2N 41°7E **191** H5
Armenia *Colombia* 4°35N 75°45W **328** C2
Armenia ■ *Asia* 40°20N 45°0E **191** K7
Armenian Quarter *Jerusalem* **123** b3
Armeniş *Romania* 45°13N 22°17E **182** E7
Armenistis, Akra *Greece* 36°8N 27°42E **206** E11
Armentières *France* 50°40N 2°50E **173** B9
Armero *Colombia* 4°58N 74°54W **328** C3
Armidale *Australia* 30°30S 151°40E **283** A9
Armilla *Spain* 37°9N 3°37W **195** H7
ARMM = Muslim Mindanao □ *Phil.* 8°0N 123°0E **233** H3
Armori *India* 20°28N 79°59E **244** D4
Armorique ⌂ *France* 48°22N 3°50W **172** D3
Armour *U.S.A.* 43°19N 98°21W **308** D4
Armour Heights *Canada* 43°45N 79°25W **141** A2
Armstrong *B.C., Canada* 50°25N 119°10W **296** C5
Armstrong *Ont., Canada* 50°18N 89°4W **298** B2
Armur *India* 18°48N 78°16E **244** E4
Armutlu *Bursa, Turkey* 40°31N 28°50E **203** F12
Armutlu *İzmir, Turkey* 38°24N 27°34E **205** C9
Arnarfjörður *Iceland* 65°48N 23°40W **155** B3
Arnaud → *Canada* 59°59N 69°46W **295** F18
Arnauti, C. *Cyprus* 35°6N 32°17E **207** E8
Arnay-le-Duc *France* 47°10N 4°27E **173** E11
Arncliffe *Australia* 33°56S 151°8E **139** B1
Arnea *Greece* 40°30N 23°38E **202** F7
Arnedillo *Spain* 42°13N 2°14W **196** C2
Arnedo *Spain* 42°12N 2°5W **196** C2
Árnes *Iceland* 66°1N 21°31W **155** A5
Årnes *Akershus, Norway* 60°7N 11°28E **164** D8
Árnessýsla □ *Iceland* 64°15N 20°30W **155** C6
Arnett *U.S.A.* 36°8N 99°46W **314** C5
Arnhem *Neths.* 51°58N 5°55E **170** C5
Arnhem, C. *Australia* 12°20S 137°30E **280** A2
Arnhem B. *Australia* 12°20S 136°10E **280** A2
Arnhem Land *Australia* 13°10S 134°30E **280** A1
Arnhem Land ✪ *Australia* 12°50S 134°50E **280** A1
Arnissa *Greece* 40°47N 21°49E **202** F5
Arno → *Italy* 43°41N 10°17E **198** E7
Arno Bay *Australia* 33°54S 136°34E **282** B2
Arnold *Notts., U.K.* 53°1N 1°7W **168** D6
Arnold *Calif., U.S.A.* 38°15N 120°21W **306** G6
Arnold *Mo., U.S.A.* 38°26N 90°23W **310** F6
Arnold Arboretum *U.S.A.* 42°18N 71°8W **116** B2
Arnoldstein *Austria* 46°33N 13°43E **180** E6
Arnon → *France* 47°13N 2°1E **173** E9
Arnos Vale *Trin. & Tob.* 11°13N 60°45W **323** s
Arnot *Canada* 55°56N 96°41W **297** B9
Arnøya *Norway* 70°9N 20°40E **160** A19
Arnprior *Canada* 45°26N 76°21W **313** A8
Arnsberg *Germany* 51°24N 8°5E **178** D4
Arnsberger Wald ⌂ *Germany* 51°25N 8°20E **178** D4
Arnstadt *Germany* 50°50N 10°56E **178** E6
Arnswalde = Choszczno *Poland* 53°7N 15°25E **185** E2
Aro → *Venezuela* 8°1N 64°11W **329** B5
Aroa, Pte. *Moorea* 17°28S 149°46W **289** e
Aroab *Namibia* 26°41S 19°39E **270** C2
Aroania Oros *Greece* 37°56N 22°12E **204** D4
Aroche *Spain* 37°56N 6°57W **195** H4
Arochuku *Nigeria* 5°21N 7°54E **263** D6
Aroeiras *Brazil* 7°31S 35°41W **332** C4
Arolsen *Germany* 51°23N 9°2E **178** D5
Aron *India* 25°57N 77°56E **242** G6
Aron → *France* 46°50N 3°28E **173** F10
Arona *Canary Is.* 28°6N 16°40W **153** e1
Arona *Italy* 45°46N 8°34E **198** C5
Arorae *Kiribati* 2°38S 176°49E **277** A14
Arorangi *Cook Is.* 21°13S 159°49W **289** h
Aroroy *Phil.* 12°31N 123°24E **232** E4
Aros → *Mexico* 29°9N 107°57W **318** B3
Arouca *Trin. & Tob.* 10°38N 61°20W **323** t
Arousa, Ría de → *Spain* 42°28N 8°57W **194** C2
Årøysund *Norway* 59°10N 10°27E **164** E7
Arpa → *Asia* 39°28N 44°56E **213** C11
Arpaçay *Turkey* 40°50N 43°19E **213** B10
Árpádföld *Hungary* 47°32N 19°8E **117** A3
Arpajon *France* 48°36N 2°15E **173** D9
Arpajon-sur-Cère *France* 44°53N 2°28E **174** D6
Arpaşu de Jos *Romania* 45°47N 24°37E **183** E9
Arqalyk *Kazakhstan* 50°13N 66°50E **217** B7
Arque *Bolivia* 17°48S 66°23W **330** D4
Arrah = Ara *India* 25°35N 84°32E **243** G11
Arrah *Ivory C.* 6°40N 3°58W **262** D4
Arraias *Brazil* 12°56S 46°57W **333** D2
Arraias → *Mato Grosso, Brazil* 11°10S 53°35W **331** C7
Arraias → *Pará, Brazil* 7°30S 49°20W **332** C2
Arraijan *Panama* 8°56N 79°36W **320** c
Arraiolos *Portugal* 38°44N 7°59W **195** G3
Arran *U.K.* 55°34N 5°12W **167** F3
Arras *France* 50°17N 2°46E **173** B9
Arrasate *Spain* 43°4N 2°30W **196** B2
Arrats → *France* 44°6N 0°52E **174** D4
Arreau *France* 42°54N 0°22E **174** F4
Arrecife *Canary Is.* 28°57N 13°37W **153** e2
Arrecifes *Argentina* 34°6S 60°9W **334** C3
Arrée, Mts. d' *France* 48°26N 3°55W **172** D3
Arrentela *Portugal* 38°37N 9°6W **126** B2
Arresø *Denmark* 55°58N 12°6E **163** J6
Arriaga *Mexico* 16°14N 93°54W **319** D6
Arribes del Duero ⌂ *Spain* 41°11N 6°39W **194** D4
Arrilalah *Australia* 23°43S 143°54E **280** C3
Arrino *Australia* 29°30S 115°40E **279** E2
Arriondas *Spain* 43°23N 5°11W **194** B5
Arrojado → *Brazil* 13°24S 44°20W **333** D3
Arromanches-les-Bains *France* 49°20N 0°38W **172** C6
Arronches *Portugal* 39°8N 7°16W **195** F3
Arros → *France* 43°40N 0°2W **174** E3
Arrow, L. *Ireland* 54°3N 8°19W **166** B3
Arrowsmith, Mt. *N.Z.* 43°20S 170°55E **285** D5
Arrowtown *N.Z.* 44°57S 168°50E **285** E3
Arroyo de la Luz *Spain* 39°30N 6°38W **195** F4
Arroyo del Puerco = Arroyo de la Luz *Spain* 39°30N 6°38W **195** F4
Arroyo Grande *U.S.A.* 35°7N 120°35W **307** K6
Arroyo Seco Park *U.S.A.* 34°6N 118°11W **126** B3
Ars *Iran* 37°9N 47°46E **246** B5
Ars-sur-Moselle *France* 49°5N 6°4E **173** C13
Arsenault L. *Canada* 55°6N 108°32W **297** B7
Arsenev *Russia* 44°10N 133°15E **220** B6
Arsi *Ethiopia* 7°45N 39°0E **257** F4
Arsiero *Italy* 45°48N 11°21E **199** C8
Arsikere *India* 13°15N 76°15E **245** H3
Arsin *Turkey* 41°8N 39°55E **213** B8
Arsk *Russia* 56°10N 49°50E **190** B9
Arslanköy *Turkey* 37°0N 34°17E **250** B5
Årsta *Sweden* 59°17N 18°3E **139** B2
Årsunda *Sweden* 60°31N 16°45E **162** D10
Art, Î. *N. Cal.* 19°43S 163°38E **288** d
Arta *Greece* 39°8N 21°2E **204** B3
Artà *Spain* 39°41N 3°21E **206** B4
Arta □ *Greece* 39°15N 21°5E **204** B3
Artà, Coves d *Spain* 39°40N 3°24E **206** E4
Artane *Ireland* 53°22N 6°12W **120** A2
Artas *West Bank* 31°41N 35°11E **123** E2
Artashat *Armenia* 40°0N 44°35E **213** B11
Arteaga *Mexico* 18°28N 102°25W **318** D4
Arteche *Phil.* 12°17N 125°22E **232** E5
Arteijo = Arteixo *Spain* 43°19N 8°29W **194** E2
Arteixo *Spain* 43°19N 8°29W **194** E2
Artem = Artyom *Azerbaijan* 40°28N 50°20E **191** K10
Artem *Russia* 43°22N 132°13E **220** C6
Artemovsk *Sib., Russia* 54°45N 93°35E **215** D10
Artemovsk *Ukraine* 48°35N 38°0E **189** H9
Artemovskiy *Russia* 47°45N 40°16E **191** G5
Artenay *France* 48°5N 1°50E **173** D8
Artern *Germany* 51°22N 11°18E **178** D7
Artesa de Segre *Spain* 41°54N 1°3E **196** D6
Artesia = Mosomane *Botswana* 24°2S 26°19E **270** E4
Artesia *U.S.A.* 32°51N 104°24W **305** K11
Arthington *Liberia* 6°35N 10°45W **262** D2
Arthur *Ont., Canada* 43°50N 80°32W **312** C4
Arthur *Ill., U.S.A.* 39°43N 88°28W **311** E8
Arthur → *Australia* 41°2S 144°40E **281** G3
Arthur Cr. → *Australia* 22°30S 136°25E **280** C2
Arthur Pt. *Australia* 22°7S 150°3E **280** C5
Arthur River *Australia* 33°20S 117°2E **279** F2
Arthur's Pass *N.Z.* 42°54S 171°35E **285** C6
Arthur's Pass △ *N.Z.* 42°53S 171°42E **285** C6
Arthur's Seat *U.K.* 55°56N 3°9W **121** B3
Arthur's Town *Bahamas* 24°38N 75°42W **321** B4
Artigas = Río Branco *Uruguay* 32°40S 53°40W **335** C5
Artigas *Antarctica* 62°30S 58°0W **151** C18
Artigas *Uruguay* 30°20S 56°30W **334** C4
Artik *Armenia* 40°38N 43°58E **191** K6
Artillery L. *Canada* 63°9N 107°52W **297** A7
Artois *France* 50°20N 2°30E **173** B9
Artotina *Greece* 38°42N 22°2E **204** C4
Artova *Turkey* 40°5N 36°28E **212** B7
Artrutx, C. de *Spain* 39°55N 3°49E **206** B4
Arts, Place des *Montréal, Canada* **130** b2
Arts Bogd Uul *Mongolia* 44°40N 102°20E **226** B2
Artsyz *Ukraine* 46°4N 29°26E **183** D14
Artux *China* 39°40N 76°10E **217** E9
Artvin *Turkey* 41°14N 41°44E **213** B9
Artvin □ *Turkey* 41°10N 41°50E **213** B9
Artyk *Russia* 64°12N 145°6E **215** C15
Artyom *Azerbaijan* 40°28N 50°20E **191** K10
Aru, Kepulauan *Indonesia* 6°0S 134°30E **231** F8
Aru Is. = Aru, Kepulauan *Indonesia* 6°0S 134°30E **231** F8
Arua *Uganda* 3°1N 30°58E **268** B3
Aruanã *Brazil* 14°54S 51°10W **333** D1
Aruba ⊠ *W. Indies* 12°30N 70°0W **322** f
Arudy *France* 43°7N 0°28W **174** E3
Arué *Tahiti* 17°31S 149°30W **289** e
Arumã *Brazil* 4°44S 62°8W **329** D5
Arume-wan *Japan* 26°35N 128°8E **288** a
Arumpo *Australia* 33°48S 142°55E **282** B5
Arun *Bangkok, Thailand* **113** b1
Arun → *Nepal* 26°55N 87°10E **243** F12
Arun → *W. Susx., U.K.* 50°49N 0°33W **169** G7
Arunachal Pradesh □ *India* 28°0N 95°0E **241** B5
Aruppukkottai *India* 9°31N 78°8E **245** K4
Arusha *Tanzania* 3°20S 36°40E **268** C4
Arusha □ *Tanzania* 4°0S 36°30E **268** C4
Arusha △ *Tanzania* 3°16S 36°47E **268** C4
Arusha Chini *Tanzania* 3°32S 37°20E **268** C4
Arut → *Indonesia* 2°42S 111°34E **235** C4
Aruvi → *Sri Lanka* 8°48N 79°53E **245** K4
Aruwimi → *Dem. Rep. of the Congo* 1°13N 23°36E **264** B4
Arvada *Colo., U.S.A.* 39°48N 105°5W **304** G11
Arvada *Wyo., U.S.A.* 44°39N 106°8W **304** D10
Arvakalu *Sri Lanka* 8°20N 79°58E **245** K4
Arvayheer *Mongolia* 46°15N 102°48E **218** B9
Arve → *France* 46°11N 6°8E **173** F13
Arvi *Kriti, Greece* 34°59N 25°28E **207** F6
Arvi *India* 20°59N 78°16E **244** D4
Arviat *Canada* 61°6N 93°59W **297** A10
Arvidsjaur *Sweden* 65°35N 19°10E **160** D18
Arvika *Sweden* 59°40N 12°36E **162** E6
Arvin *U.S.A.* 35°12N 118°50W **307** K8
Arwad *Syria* 34°51N 35°51E **250** D6
Arwal *India* 25°15N 84°41E **243** G11
Arxan *China* 47°11N 119°57E **219** B12
Åryd *Sweden* 56°49N 14°59E **163** H8
Arys *Kazakhstan* 42°26N 68°48E **217** D7
Arzachena *Italy* 41°5N 9°23E **200** A2
Arzamas *Russia* 55°27N 43°55E **190** C6
Arzanah *U.A.E.* 24°47N 52°34E **247** E7
Arzew *Algeria* 35°50N 0°23W **261** A4
Arzgir *Russia* 45°18N 44°23E **191** H7
Arzignano *Italy* 45°31N 11°20E **199** C8
Arzúa *Spain* 42°56N 8°9W **194** C2
Aš *Czech Rep.* 50°13N 12°12E **180** A5
Ås *Akershus, Norway* 59°40N 10°48E **164** E7
Ås *Sweden* 63°15N 14°34E **162** A8
As Pontes de García Rodríguez *Spain* 43°27N 7°50W **194** B3
As Sa'an *Syria* 35°16N 37°22E **250** C8
Aş Şafā *Syria* 33°10N 37°0E **250** E8
As Saffānīyah *Si. Arabia* 27°55N 48°50E **247** E6
As Safīrah *Syria* 36°5N 37°21E **250** B8
Aş Şahm *Oman* 24°10N 56°53E **247** E8
As Sājir *Si. Arabia* 25°11N 44°36E **246** E5
As Salamīyah *Syria* 35°1N 37°2E **250** C8
As Salmān *Iraq* 30°30N 44°32E **246** D5
As Salţ *Jordan* 32°2N 35°43E **251** F6
As Sal'w'a *Qatar* 24°23N 50°50E **247** E6
As Samāwah *Iraq* 31°15N 45°15E **246** D5
As Sanamayn *Syria* 33°3N 36°10E **250** E7
As Sawāḑah *Si. Arabia* 22°24N 44°28E **248** B4
As Sayl al Kabīr *Si. Arabia* 21°38N 40°25E **248** B3
As Shawawra *West Bank* 31°41N 35°15E **123** B2
As Sohar = Şuḩār *Oman* 24°20N 56°40E **247** E8
As Sukhnah *Syria* 34°52N 38°52E **213** E8
As Sulaymānīyah *Iraq* 35°35N 45°29E **213** E11
As Sulaymānīyah *Si. Arabia* 24°9N 47°18E **248** A4
As Sulaymānīyah □ *Iraq* 35°50N 45°30E **213** E11
As Sulaymī *Si. Arabia* 26°17N 41°21E **246** E4
As Sulayyil *Si. Arabia* 20°27N 45°34E **248** B4
As Sulţān *Libya* 31°4N 17°8E **258** B3
As Summān *Si. Arabia* 25°0N 47°0E **246** E5
Aş Şurrah *Yemen* 13°57N 46°14E **248** D4
Aş Şuwar *Syria* 35°30N 40°38E **213** E9
As Suwaydā' *Syria* 32°40N 36°30E **250** F7
As Suwaydā' □ *Syria* 32°45N 36°45E **250** F7
As Suwayq *Oman* 23°51N 57°26E **247** F8
Aş Şuwayrah *Iraq* 32°55N 45°0E **213** F11
Åsa *Sweden* 57°21N 12°8E **163** G6
Asa Wright Nature Centre *Trin. & Tob.* 10°43N 61°17W **323** t
Asab *Namibia* 25°30S 18°0E **270** C2
Asaba *Nigeria* 6°12N 6°38E **263** D6
Asad, Buḩayrat al *Syria* 36°0N 38°15E **213** D8
Asadābād *Iran* 34°47N 48°7E **213** E13
Asafo *Ghana* 6°20N 2°40W **262** D4
Asaga Str. *Amer. Samoa* 14°10S 169°37W **302** g
Asagaya *Japan* 35°41N 139°38E **140** A2
Asahi *Chiba, Japan* 35°43N 140°39E **223** B12
Asahi *Ōsaka, Japan* 34°43N 135°31E **133** A2
Asahi-Gawa → *Japan* 34°36N 133°58E **222** C5
Asahigawa = Asahikawa *Japan* 43°46N 142°22E **220** C11
Asahikawa *Japan* 43°46N 142°22E **220** C11
Asakusa *Japan* 35°42N 139°47E **140** A3
Asakusabashi *Tokyo, Japan* **140** a5
Asale, L. *Ethiopia* 14°0N 40°20E **257** E5
Asaluyeh *Iran* 27°29N 52°37E **247** E7
Asama-Yama *Japan* 36°24N 138°31E **223** A10
Asamankese *Ghana* 5°50N 0°40W **263** D4
Asan *S. Korea* 36°48N 127°1E **224** D3
Asan → *India* 26°37N 78°24E **243** F8
Asansol *India* 23°40N 87°1E **243** H12
Åsarna *Sweden* 62°39N 14°22E **162** B8
Asati *India* 22°28N 88°15E **124** C1
Asau *Samoa* 13°27S 172°33W **287** V19
Asayita *Ethiopia* 11°35N 41°23E **257** E5
Asba Littoria = Asbe Teferi *Ethiopia* 9°4N 40°49E **257** F5
Asbe Teferi *Ethiopia* 9°4N 40°49E **257** F5
Asbesberge *S. Africa* 29°0S 23°0E **270** C3
Asbestos *Canada* 45°47N 71°58W **299** C5
Asbury Park *U.S.A.* 40°13N 74°1W **313** F10
Åsby *Sweden* 57°14N 12°18E **163** G6
Ascea *Italy* 40°8N 15°11E **201** B8
Ascensión *Mexico* 31°6N 107°59W **318** A3
Ascensión, B. de la *Mexico* 19°40N 87°30W **319** D7
Ascension I. *Atl. Oc.* 7°57S 14°23W **153** g
Aschach an der Donau *Austria* 48°22N 14°2E **180** C7
Aschaffenburg *Germany* 49°58N 9°6E **179** F5
Aschendorf *Germany* 53°3N 7°19E **178** B3
Aschersleben *Germany* 51°45N 11°29E **178** D7
Aschheim *Germany* 48°10N 11°42E **131** A3
Asciano *Italy* 43°14N 11°33E **199** E8
Áscoli Piceno *Italy* 42°51N 13°34E **199** F10
Áscoli Satriano *Italy* 41°11N 15°32E **201** A8
Ascope *Peru* 7°46S 79°8W **330** B2
Ascot Vale *Australia* 37°46S 144°53E **128** A1
Ascotán *Chile* 21°45S 68°17W **334** A2
Ascuncion *Phil.* 7°35N 125°45E **233** H5
Aseb *Eritrea* 13°0N 42°40E **257** E5
Åseda *Sweden* 57°10N 15°20E **163** G9
Asedjrad *Algeria* 24°51N 1°29E **261** D5
Aseki *Papua N. G.* 7°21S 146°12E **286** D4
Asela *Ethiopia* 8°0N 39°0E **257** F4
Åsen *Sweden* 61°17N 13°50E **162** C7
Asenovgrad *Bulgaria* 42°1N 24°51E **203** D8
Asfeld *France* 49°27N 4°5E **173** C11
Asfûn el Matâ'na *Egypt* 25°26N 32°30E **256** B3
Aşgabat = Ashgabat *Turkmenistan* 38°0N 57°50E **247** B8
Åsgårdstrand *Norway* 59°22N 10°27E **164** E7
Asgata *Cyprus* 34°46N 33°15E **207** F9
Ash Fork *U.S.A.* 35°13N 112°29W **305** J7
Ash Grove *U.S.A.* 37°19N 93°35W **308** G7
Ash Shabakah *Iraq* 30°49N 43°39E **246** D4
Ash Shafa *Si. Arabia* 21°27N 39°49E **248** B2
Ash Shamāl □ *Lebanon* 34°25N 36°0E **250** D7
Ash Shāmīyah *Iraq* 31°55N 44°35E **213** G11
Ash Sha'rā' *Si. Arabia* 24°16N 44°11E **248** A4
Ash Shāriqah *U.A.E.* 25°23N 55°26E **247** E7
Ash Sharmah *Si. Arabia* 28°1N 35°16E **251** K6
Ash Sharqāt *Iraq* 35°27N 43°16E **213** E10
Ash Sharqīyah □ *Si. Arabia* 23°0N 50°30E **249** B6
Ash Shāţi *Libya* 27°30N 12°30E **258** C2
Ash Shaţrah *Iraq* 31°30N 46°10E **246** D5
Ash Shawbak *Jordan* 30°32N 35°34E **246** D2
Ash Shaykh Ḩumayd *Si. Arabia* 28°6N 34°33E **251** K5
Ash Shifā' *Si. Arabia* 28°30N 35°30E **251** K6
Ash Shiḩr *Yemen* 14°45N 49°36E **249** D5
Ash Shināfīyah *Iraq* 31°35N 44°39E **246** D5
Ash Shu'bah *Si. Arabia* 28°54N 44°44E **246** D5
Ash Shumlūl *Si. Arabia* 26°31N 47°20E **246** E5
Ash Shuqayq *Si. Arabia* 17°44N 42°1E **248** C3
Ash Shūr'a *Iraq* 35°58N 43°13E **246** C4
Ash Shurayf *Si. Arabia* 25°43N 39°14E **246** E3
Ash Shuwayfāt *Lebanon* 33°45N 35°30E **250** E6
Ash Shuwayrif *Libya* 29°59N 14°16E **258** C2
Asha *Russia* 55°0N 57°16E **186** D10
Ashanti □ *Ghana* 7°30N 1°30W **263** D4
Ashbourne *U.K.* 53°2N 1°43W **168** D6
Ashbridge's Bay Park *Canada* 43°40N 79°18W **141** B3
Ashburn *Ga., U.S.A.* 31°43N 83°39W **316** D6
Ashburn *Ill., U.S.A.* 41°45N 87°43W **119** C2
Ashburton *Vic., Australia* 37°51S 145°4E **128** B2
Ashburton *N.Z.* 43°53S 171°48E **285** D6
Ashburton → *Australia* 21°40S 114°56E **278** D1
Ashburton, North Branch → *N.Z.* 43°54S 171°44E **285** D6
Ashburton, South Branch → *N.Z.* 43°54S 171°44E **285** D6
Ashcroft *Canada* 50°40N 121°20W **296** C4
Ashdod *Israel* 31°49N 34°35E **251** G5
Ashdown *U.S.A.* 33°40N 94°8W **314** E7
Asheboro *U.S.A.* 35°43N 79°49W **315** D15
Åsheim *Norway* 61°42N 11°11E **164** C8
Ashern *Canada* 51°11N 98°21W **297** C9
Asherton *U.S.A.* 28°27N 99°46W **314** G5
Asheville *U.S.A.* 35°36N 82°33W **315** D13
Ashewat *Pakistan* 31°22N 68°32E **242** D3
Asheweig → *Canada* 54°17N 87°12W **298** B2
Ashfield *Australia* 33°53S 151°7E **139** B1
Ashford *N.S.W., Australia* 29°15S 151°3E **281** D5
Ashford *Kent, U.K.* 51°8N 0°53E **169** F8
Ashford *Surrey, U.K.* 51°25N 0°26W **125** B1
Ashford *Ala., U.S.A.* 31°11N 85°14W **316** D4
Ashgabat *Turkmenistan* 38°0N 57°50E **247** B8
Ashhurst *N.Z.* 40°16S 175°45E **284** G4
Ashibetsu *Japan* 43°31N 142°11E **220** C11
Ashikaga *Japan* 36°28N 139°29E **223** A11
Ashington *U.K.* 55°11N 1°33W **168** B6
Ashio *Japan* 36°38N 139°27E **223** A11
Ashizuri-Uwakai △ *Japan* 32°56N 132°32E **222** E4
Ashizuri-Zaki *Japan* 32°44N 133°0E **222** E5
Ashkarkot *Afghan.* 33°3N 67°58E **242** C2
Ashkhabad = Ashgabat *Turkmenistan* 38°0N 57°50E **247** B8
Āshkhāneh *Iran* 37°26N 56°55E **247** B8
Ashland *Ala., U.S.A.* 33°16N 85°50W **316** B4
Ashland *Ill., U.S.A.* 39°53N 90°1W **310** E7
Ashland *Kans., U.S.A.* 37°11N 99°46W **308** G4
Ashland *Ky., U.S.A.* 38°28N 82°38W **309** F12
Ashland *Maine, U.S.A.* 46°38N 68°24W **309** B19
Ashland *Mont., U.S.A.* 45°36N 106°16W **304** D10
Ashland *Ohio, U.S.A.* 40°52N 82°19W **312** F2
Ashland *Oreg., U.S.A.* 42°12N 122°43W **304** E2
Ashland *Pa., U.S.A.* 40°45N 76°22W **313** F8
Ashland *Va., U.S.A.* 37°46N 77°29W **309** G15
Ashland *Wis., U.S.A.* 46°35N 90°53W **308** B8
Ashley *Ill., U.S.A.* 38°20N 89°11W **310** F7
Ashley *Ind., U.S.A.* 41°32N 85°4W **311** C11
Ashley *N. Dak., U.S.A.* 46°2N 99°22W **308** B4
Ashley *Pa., U.S.A.* 41°12N 75°55W **313** E9
Ashley → *N.Z.* 43°17S 172°44E **285** D7
Ashmore and Cartier Is. *Ind. Oc.* 12°15S 123°0E **278** B3
Ashmore Reef *Australia* 12°14S 123°5E **278** B3
Ashmûn *Egypt* 30°18N 30°58E **251** H1
Ashmyany *Belarus* 54°26N 25°52E **177** A13
Ashokan Res. *U.S.A.* 41°56N 74°13W **313** E10
Ashoknagar *India* 24°34N 77°43E **244** B3
Ashqelon *Israel* 31°42N 34°35E **251** G5
Ashraf = Behshahr *Iran* 36°45N 53°35E **247** B7
Ashta *India* 23°1N 76°43E **242** H7
Ashtabula *U.S.A.* 41°52N 80°47W **312** E4
Ashti *Maharashtra, India* 21°12N 78°11E **244** D4
Ashti *Maharashtra, India* 18°50N 75°15E **244** E2
Āshtiyān *Iran* 34°31N 50°0E **247** C6
Ashton *Western Cape, S. Africa* 33°50S 20°5E **270** D3
Ashton *Idaho, U.S.A.* 44°4N 111°27W **304** D8
Ashtown *Ireland* 53°22N 6°19W **120** A2
Ashuanipi, L. *Canada* 52°45N 66°15W **299** B6
Ashuapmushuan → *Canada* 48°37N 72°20W **298** C5
Ashville *Ala., U.S.A.* 33°50N 86°15W **316** B3
Ashville *Fla., U.S.A.* 30°37N 83°39W **316** E6
Ashville *Pa., U.S.A.* 40°34N 78°33W **312** F6
'Āşī → *Asia* 36°1N 35°59E **250** B6
Asia 45°0N 75°0E **210** E9
Asia, Kepulauan *Indonesia* 1°0N 131°13E **231** D8
Asiago *Italy* 45°52N 11°30E **199** C8
Asid G. *Phil.* 12°10N 123°29E **232** E4
Asidonhoppo *Suriname* 3°50N 55°30W **329** C6
Asifabad *India* 19°20N 79°24E **244** E4
Asilah *Morocco* 35°29N 6°0W **260** A3
Asinara *Italy* 41°4N 8°16E **200** A1
Asinara, G. dell' *Italy* 41°0N 8°30E **200** A1
Asino *Russia* 57°0N 86°0E **214** D9
Asipovichy *Belarus* 53°19N 28°33E **177** B15
'Asir *Si. Arabia* 18°40N 42°30E **248** C3
Asir, Ras *Somali Rep.* 11°55N 51°10E **267** B7
Aska *India* 19°2N 84°42E **244** E7
Aşkale *Turkey* 39°55N 40°41E **213** C9
Asker *Norway* 59°50N 10°29E **164** E7
Askersund *Sweden* 58°53N 14°55E **163** F8
Askham *S. Africa* 26°59S 20°47E **270** C3
Askī Mawşil *Iraq* 36°30N 42°44E **213** D10
Askim *Norway* 59°35N 11°10E **164** E8
Askio, Oros *Greece* 40°25N 21°35E **202** F5
Askisto *Finland* 60°16N 24°47E **121** B1
Askja *Iceland* 65°3N 16°48W **155** B10
Asklipio *Greece* 36°4N 27°56E **206** E11
Askøyna *Norway* 60°29N 5°10E **164** D2
Askrikefjärden *Sweden* 59°22N 18°13E **139** A3
Askvoll *Norway* 61°21N 5°4E **164** C2
Asl *Egypt* 29°33N 32°44E **256** B3
Aslan Burnu *Turkey* 38°44N 26°45E **205** C8
Aslanapa *Turkey* 39°13N 29°52E **205** B11
Aslānduz *Iran* 39°26N 47°24E **213** C12
Āsmār *Afghan.* 35°10N 71°27E **240** B3
Asmara = Asmera *Eritrea* 15°19N 38°55E **257** D4
Asmera *Eritrea* 15°19N 38°55E **257** D4
Asnæs *Denmark* 55°40N 11°0E **163** J4
Åsnen *Sweden* 56°37N 14°45E **163** H8
Asni *Morocco* 31°17N 7°58W **260** B3
Asnières *France* 48°54N 2°16E **134** A2
Aso *Japan* 32°55N 131°5E **222** E3
Aso Kujū △ *Japan* 32°53N 131°6E **222** E3
Aso-Zan *Japan* 32°53N 131°6E **222** E3
Ásola *Italy* 45°13N 10°24E **198** C7
Asos *Greece* 38°22N 20°33E **207** C2
Asosa *Ethiopia* 10°3N 34°32E **257** E3
Asoteriba, Jebel *Sudan* 21°51N 36°30E **256** C4
Asouf, O. → *Algeria* 25°40N 2°8E **261** C5
Aspatria *U.K.* 54°47N 3°19W **168** C4
Aspe *Spain* 38°20N 0°40W **197** G4
Aspen *U.S.A.* 39°11N 106°49W **304** G10
Aspendos *Turkey* 36°54N 31°7E **250** B2
Aspermont *U.S.A.* 33°8N 100°14W **314** E4
Aspern *Austria* 48°13N 16°29E **142** A2
Aspet *France* 43°1N 0°48E **174** E4
Aspiring, Mt. *N.Z.* 44°23S 168°46E **285** E3
Aspres-sur-Buëch *France* 44°32N 5°44E **175** D9
Asprokavos, Akra *Greece* 39°21N 20°6E **206** C10
Aspromonte △ *Italy* 38°9N 15°58E **201** D8
Aspur *India* 23°58N 74°7E **242** H6
Asquith *Canada* 52°8N 107°13W **297** C7
Assa *Morocco* 28°35N 9°6W **260** C3
Assab = Aseb *Eritrea* 13°0N 42°40E **257** E5
Assâba □ *Mauritania* 16°40N 11°40W **262** B2
Assâba, Massif de l' *Mauritania* 16°10N 11°45W **262** B2
Assagny △ *Ivory C.* 5°10N 4°48W **262** D4
Assago *Italy* 45°24N 9°7E **129** B1
Assaikio *Nigeria* 8°34N 8°55E **263** D6
Assal, L. *Djibouti* 11°40N 42°26E **257** E5
Assam □ *India* 26°0N 93°0E **241** C4
Assamakka *Niger* 19°21N 5°38E **263** B6
Assateague Island ⌂ *U.S.A.* 38°15N 75°10W **309** F16
Assaye *India* 20°15N 75°53E **244** D2
Asse *Belgium* 50°24N 4°10E **170** D4
Assekrem *Algeria* 23°16N 5°49E **261** D6
Assémini *Italy* 39°17N 9°0E **200** C1
Assen *Neths.* 53°0N 6°35E **170** A6
Assendelft *Neths.* 52°28N 4°45E **112** A1
Assens *Denmark* 55°16N 9°55E **163** J3
Assiano *Italy* 45°27N 9°3E **129** B1
Assini *Ivory C.* 5°9N 3°17W **262** D4
Assiniboia *Canada* 49°40N 105°59W **297** D7
Assiniboine → *Canada* 49°53N 97°8W **297** D9
Assiniboine, Mt. *Canada* 50°52N 115°39W **296** C5
Assiou *Algeria* 21°7N 7°36E **261** D6
Assis *Brazil* 22°40S 50°20W **335** A5
Assis Brasil *Brazil* 10°55S 69°32W **330** C4
Assisi *Italy* 43°4N 12°37E **199** E9
Åsskard *Norway* 63°1N 8°30E **164** A5
Assok Ngoum *Gabon* 1°45N 11°39E **264** B2
Assumption *U.S.A.* 39°31N 89°3W **310** E7
Assynt, L. *U.K.* 58°10N 5°3W **167** C3
Astaffort *France* 44°4N 0°40E **174** D4
Astakida *Greece* 35°53N 26°50E **205** F8
Astakos *Greece* 38°32N 21°5E **207** B3
Astana *Kazakhstan* 51°10N 71°30E **217** B8
Āstāneh *Iran* 37°17N 49°59E **247** B6
Astapovo = Lev Tolstoy *Russia* 53°13N 39°29E **188** F10
Astara *Azerbaijan* 38°30N 48°50E **213** C13
Āstārā *Iran* 38°20N 48°52E **213** C13
Astarabad = Gorgān *Iran* 36°55N 54°30E **247** B7
Asterousia *Greece* 34°59N 25°3E **207** F6
Asti *Italy* 44°54N 8°12E **198** D5
Astipalea *Greece* 36°32N 26°22E **205** E8
Astola I. *Pakistan* 25°7N 63°51E **240** D1
Astorga *Davao del S., Phil.* 6°54N 125°27E **233** H5
Astorga *Spain* 42°29N 6°8W **194** C4
Astoria *Ill., U.S.A.* 40°14N 90°21W **310** D6
Astoria *N.Y., U.S.A.* 40°46N 73°55W **132** B2
Astoria *Oreg., U.S.A.* 46°11N 123°50W **306** D3
Åstorp *Sweden* 56°6N 12°55E **163** H6
Astrakhan *Russia* 46°25N 48°5E **191** G9
Astrakhan □ *Russia* 47°45N 46°20E **191** G8
Astrebla Downs *Australia* 24°12S 140°34E **280** C3
Astrolabe, Récifs de l' *N. Cal.* 19°48S 165°37E **288** d
Astrolabe Park *Australia* 33°57S 151°12E **139** B2
Astudillo *Spain* 42°12N 4°22W **194** C6
Asturias □ *Spain* 43°15N 6°0W **194** B5
Asturias ✈ **(OVD)** *Spain* 43°33N 6°3W **194** B4
Asumman *S. Korea* 37°4N 126°40E **224** D3
Asunción *Bolivia* 11°46S 67°50W **330** C4
Asuncion *N. Marianas* 19°40N 145°24E **302** a
Asunción *Paraguay* 25°10S 57°30W **334** B4
Asunción Nochixtlán *Mexico* 17°28N 97°14W **319** D5
Åsunden *Sweden* 58°0N 15°51E **163** F9
Asutri *Sudan* 15°25N 35°45E **257** D4
Aswa → *Uganda* 3°43N 31°55E **268** B3
Aswa-Lolim ⌂ *Uganda* 2°43N 31°35E **268** B3
Aswad, Ra's al *Si. Arabia* 21°20N 39°0E **248** B2
Aswân *Egypt* 24°4N 32°57E **256** C3
Aswan High Dam = Sadd el Aali *Egypt* 23°54N 32°54E **256** C3
Asyût *Egypt* 27°11N 31°4E **256** B3
Asyûti, Wadi → *Egypt* 27°11N 31°16E **256** B3
Aszód *Hungary* 47°39N 19°28E **182** C4
At-Bashy *Kyrgyzstan* 41°10N 75°48E **217** D9
At Ţafīlah *Jordan* 30°45N 35°30E **251** H6
At Ţafīlah □ *Jordan* 30°45N 35°30E **251** H6
Aţ Ţā'if *Si. Arabia* 21°5N 40°27E **248** B3
At Tāj *Libya* 24°13N 23°18E **258** D4
At Ta'mīm □ *Iraq* 35°30N 44°20E **246** C5
At Tamīmī *Libya* 32°20N 23°4E **258** B4
Aţ Ţirāq *Si. Arabia* 27°19N 44°33E **246** E5
Aţ Tubayq *Si. Arabia* 29°30N 37°0E **251** J8
Aţ Ţunayb *Jordan* 31°48N 35°57E **251** G6
At Turbah *Laḩij, Yemen* 12°40N 43°30E **248** D3
At Turbah *Ta'izz, Yemen* 13°13N 44°7E **248** D4
Atabey *Turkey* 37°57N 30°39E **205** D12
Atacama □ *Chile* 27°30S 70°0W **334** B2
Atacama, Desierto de *Chile* 24°0S 69°20W **334** A2
Atacama, Salar de *Chile* 23°30S 68°20W **334** A2
Ataco *Colombia* 3°35N 75°23W **328** C2
Atafu *Pac. Oc.* 8°32S 172°31W **277** B16
Atakeye ✪ *Australia* 22°30S 133°45E **278** D5
Atakor *Algeria* 23°27N 5°31E **261** D6
Atakpamé *Togo* 7°31N 1°13E **263** D5
Atalaia do Norte *Brazil* 4°20S 70°12W **328** D3
Atalandi *Greece* 38°39N 22°58E **204** C4
Atalaya *Peru* 10°45S 73°50W **330** C3
Atalaya de Femes *Canary Is.* 28°56N 13°47W **153** e2
Ataléia *Brazil* 18°3S 41°6W **333** E3
Atami *Japan* 35°5N 139°4E **223** B11
Atamyrat *Turkmenistan* 37°50N 65°12E **217** E7
Atankawng *Burma* 25°50N 97°47E **241** C6
Atap *Indonesia* 3°51N 117°1E **235** B5
Atapupu *Indonesia* 9°0S 124°51E **231** F6
Atâr *Mauritania* 20°30N 13°5W **260** D2
Ataram, Erg n- *Algeria* 23°57N 2°0E **261** D5
Atarfe *Spain* 37°13N 3°40W **195** H7
Atari *Pakistan* 30°56N 74°2E **242** D6
Atarot *West Bank* 31°52N 35°13E **123** A2
Atarot ✈ **(JRS)** *West Bank* 31°52N 35°14E **123** A2
Atascadero *U.S.A.* 35°29N 120°40W **306** K6
Atasū *Kazakhstan* 48°30N 71°0E **217** C8
Atatürk, İstanbul ✈ **(IST)** *Turkey* 40°59N 28°49E **203** F12
Atatürk Barajı *Turkey* 37°28N 38°30E **213** D8
Atauro *E. Timor* 8°10S 125°30E **231** F7
Ataviros *Greece* 36°12N 27°50E **206** E11
Atbara *Sudan* 17°42N 33°59E **256** D3
'Atbara, Nahr → *Sudan* 17°40N 33°56E **256** D3
Atbasar *Kazakhstan* 51°48N 68°20E **217** B7
Atbashi = At-Bashy *Kyrgyzstan* 41°10N 75°48E **217** D9
Atça *Turkey* 37°53N 28°13E **205** D10
Atchafalaya B. *U.S.A.* 29°25N 91°25W **314** G9
Atchison *U.S.A.* 39°34N 95°7W **308** F6
Atebubu *Ghana* 7°47N 1°0W **263** D4
Ateca *Spain* 41°20N 1°49W **196** D3
Aterno → *Italy* 42°11N 13°51E **199** F10
Āteshān *Iran* 35°35N 52°37E **247** C7
Atesine, Alpi *Italy* 46°55N 11°30E **199** B8
Atessa *Italy* 42°4N 14°27E **199** F11
Atfîh *Egypt* 29°25N 31°15E **256** J7
Atghara *India* 22°37N 88°26E **124** B2
Ath *Belgium* 50°38N 3°47E **170** D3
Athabasca *Canada* 54°45N 113°20W **296** C6
Athabasca → *Canada* 58°40N 110°50W **297** B6
Athabasca, L. *Canada* 59°15N 109°15W **297** B7
Athabasca Sand Dunes ⌂ *Canada* 59°4N 108°43W **297** B7
Athagarh *India* 20°32N 85°37E **244** D7
Athamanon Oros *Greece* 39°30N 21°26E **204** B3
Athboy *Ireland* 53°37N 6°56W **166** C5
Athena *U.S.A.* 29°59N 83°30W **316** F6
Athenry *Ireland* 53°18N 8°44W **166** C3
Athens = Athina *Greece* 37°58N 23°43E **112** B2
Athens *Ala., U.S.A.* 34°48N 86°58W **315** D11
Athens *Ga., U.S.A.* 33°57N 83°23W **316** B6
Athens *N.Y., U.S.A.* 42°16N 73°49W **313** D11
Athens *Ohio, U.S.A.* 39°20N 82°6W **309** F12
Athens *Pa., U.S.A.* 41°57N 76°31W **313** E8
Athens *Tenn., U.S.A.* 35°27N 84°36W **315** D12
Athens *Tex., U.S.A.* 32°12N 95°51W **314** E7
Atheras *Greece* 38°19N 20°25E **207** C1
Atherley *Canada* 44°37N 79°20W **312** B5
Atherton *Australia* 17°17S 145°30E **280** B4
Athi River *Kenya* 1°28S 36°58E **268** C4
Athiéme *Benin* 6°37N 1°40E **263** D5
Athienou *Cyprus* 35°3N 33°32E **207** E9
Athina *Greece* 37°58N 23°43E **112** B2
Athina ✈ **(ATH)** *Greece* 37°56N 23°56E **112** A3
Athínai = Athina *Greece* 37°58N 23°43E **112** B2
Athis-Mons *France* 48°42N 2°23E **134** B3
Athlone *Westmeath, Ireland* 53°25N 7°56W **166** C4
Athlone *Western Cape, S. Africa* 33°57S 18°30E **118** A2
Athmalik *India* 20°43N 84°32E **244** D7
Athna *Cyprus* 35°3N 33°47E **207** E9
Athni *India* 16°44N 75°6E **244** F2
Athol *N.Z.* 45°30S 168°35E **285** F3
Athol *Mass., U.S.A.* 42°36N 72°14W **313** D12
Athol I. *Bahamas* 25°5N 77°16W **153** b
Atholl *S. Africa* 26°7S 28°3E **123** A2
Atholl, Forest of *U.K.* 56°51N 3°50W **167** E5
Atholl, Kap *Greenland* 76°25N 69°30W **154** B4
Atholville *Canada* 47°59N 66°43W **299** C6
Athos *Greece* 40°9N 24°22E **203** F8
Athy *Ireland* 53°0N 7°0W **166** C5
Ati *Chad* 13°13N 18°20E **259** F3
Ati *Sudan* 13°5N 29°2E **257** E2
Ati, J. *Libya* 23°24N 14°21E **258** D2
Atiak *Uganda* 3°12N 32°2E **268** B3
Atiamuri *N.Z.* 38°24S 176°5E **284** E5
Atico *Peru* 16°14S 73°40W **330** D3
Atienza *Spain* 41°12N 2°52W **196** D2
Atīfiya *Iraq* 33°21N 44°21E **113** A2
Atiit *South Sudan* 6°10N 30°35E **257** F3
Atik L. *Canada* 55°15N 96°0W **297** B9
Atikaki ⌂ *Canada* 51°30N 95°31W **297** C9
Atikameg → *Canada* 52°30N 82°46W **298** B3
Atikokan *Canada* 48°45N 91°37W **298** C1
Atikonak L. *Canada* 52°40N 64°32W **299** B7
Atimaono *Tahiti* 17°46S 149°28W **289** e
Atimonan *Phil.* 14°0N 121°55E **232** D3
'Ātinah, W. → *Oman* 18°23N 53°28E **249** C6
Atirampattinam *India* 10°28N 79°20E **245** J4
Atişalen *Turkey* 41°3N 28°52E **122** B1
Atitlán △ *Cent. Amer.* 14°38N 91°10W **320** D1
Atiu *Cook Is.* 20°0S 158°10W **289** J12
Atka *Russia* 60°50N 151°48E **215** C16
Atka *Alaska, U.S.A.* 52°12N 174°12W **303** K4
Atka I. *U.S.A.* 52°7N 174°30W **303** K4
Atkarsk *Russia* 51°55N 45°2E **190** E7
Atkinson *Ga., U.S.A.* 31°13N 81°47W **316** D8
Atkinson *Ill., U.S.A.* 41°25N 90°1W **310** C6
Atkinson *Nebr., U.S.A.* 42°32N 98°59W **308** D4
Atlanta *Ga., U.S.A.* 33°45N 84°23W **113** B2
Atlanta *Ill., U.S.A.* 40°16N 89°14W **310** D7
Atlanta *Mo., U.S.A.* 39°54N 92°29W **310** E4
Atlanta *Tex., U.S.A.* 33°7N 94°10W **314** E7
Atlanta Hartsfield Int. ✈ **(ATL)** *U.S.A.* 33°38N 84°26W **113** C2
Atlanta History Center *U.S.A.* 33°45N 84°22W **113** B2
Atlanta Zoo *U.S.A.* 33°44N 84°22W **113** B2
Atlantic *U.S.A.* 41°24N 95°1W **310** C2
Atlantic Beach *U.S.A.* 30°20N 81°24W **316** E8
Atlantic City *U.S.A.* 39°21N 74°27W **309** F16
Atlantic-Indian Basin *Antarctica* 60°0S 30°0E **151** B4
Atlantic Ocean 0°0 20°0W **152** F8
Atlántico □ *Colombia* 10°45N 75°0W **328** A3
Atlantis *S. Africa* 33°34S 18°29E **270** D2
Atlas Mts. = Haut Atlas *Morocco* 32°30N 5°0W **260** B4
Atlin *Canada* 59°31N 133°41W **296** B2
Atlin, L. *Canada* 59°26N 133°45W **296** B2
Atlin ⌂ *Canada* 59°10N 134°30W **296** B2
Atløyna *Norway* 61°21N 4°58E **164** C1
Atmakur *Andhra Pradesh, India* 18°45N 78°39E **244** E4
Atmakur *Andhra Pradesh, India* 14°37N 79°40E **245** G4
Atmakur *Andhra Pradesh, India* 15°53N 78°35E **245** G4
Atmore *U.S.A.* 31°2N 87°29W **315** F11
Atna *Norway* 61°44N 10°49E **164** C7
Atna → *Norway* 61°44N 10°49E **164** C7
Atō *Japan* 34°25N 131°40E **222** C3
Atocha *Bolivia* 20°56S 66°14W **330** E4
Atok *Phil.* 16°35N 120°41E **232** C3
Atoka *U.S.A.* 34°23N 96°8W **314** D6
Atokos *Greece* 38°28N 20°49E **207** C2
Atolia *U.S.A.* 35°19N 117°37W **307** K9
Atomium *Belgium* 50°54N 4°20E **116** A2
Atongo-Bakari *C.A.R.* 5°49N 21°35E **264** A4
Atori *Solomon Is.* 8°42S 160°59E **287** M11
Atqasuk *U.S.A.* 70°28N 157°24W **303** A8
Atqasuk → *U.S.A.* 70°52N 155°55W **303** A9
Atrå *Norway* 59°59N 8°45E **164** E5
Atrai → *Bangla.* 24°7N 89°22E **241** C2
Atrak = Atrek → *Turkmenistan* 37°35N 53°58E **247** B8
Ätran *Sweden* 57°7N 12°57E **163** G6
Ätran → *Sweden* 56°53N 12°30E **163** H6
Atrato → *Colombia* 8°17N 76°58W **328** B2
Atrauli *India* 28°2N 78°20E **242** E8
Atrek → *Turkmenistan* 37°35N 53°58E **247** B8
Atri *Italy* 42°35N 13°58E **199** F10
Atsiki *Greece* 39°56N 25°13E **205** B7
Atsoum, Mts. *Cameroon* 6°41N 12°57E **263** D7
Atsugi *Japan* 35°25N 139°21E **223** B11
Atsumi *Japan* 34°35N 137°4E **223** C9
Atsuta *Japan* 43°24N 141°26E **220** C10
Attalla *U.S.A.* 34°1N 86°6W **316** A3
Attapeu *Laos* 14°48N 106°50E **236** E6
Attapulgus *U.S.A.* 30°45N 84°29W **316** E5
Attawapiskat *Canada* 52°56N 82°24W **298** B3
Attawapiskat → *Canada* 52°57N 82°18W **298** B3
Attawapiskat L. *Canada* 52°18N 87°54W **298** B2
Attersee *Austria* 47°55N 13°32E **180** D6
Attica *Ind., U.S.A.* 40°18N 87°15W **311** D9
Attica *Ohio, U.S.A.* 41°4N 82°53W **312** E2
Attichy *France* 49°25N 3°3E **173** C10
Attigny *France* 49°28N 4°35E **173** C11
Attika = Attiki □ *Greece* 37°10N 23°40E **204** D5
Attikamagen L. *Canada* 55°0N 66°30W **299** B6
Attiki *Greece* 38°0N 23°43E **112** A2
Attiki □ *Greece* 37°10N 23°40E **204** D5
Attleboro *U.S.A.* 41°57N 71°17W **313** E13
Attock *Pakistan* 33°52N 72°20E **242** C5
Attopu = Attapeu *Laos* 14°48N 106°50E **236** E6
Attu *U.S.A.* 52°56N 173°15E **303** K1
Attu I. *U.S.A.* 52°55N 172°55E **303** K1
Attunga *Australia* 30°55S 150°50E **283** A9
Attur *India* 11°35N 78°30E **245** J4
'Atūd *Yemen* 14°53N 48°10E **249** D5
Atuel → *Argentina* 36°17S 66°50W **334** D2
Atura *Uganda* 2°7N 32°20E **268** B3
Åtvidaberg *Sweden* 58°12N 16°0E **163** F10
Atwater *U.S.A.* 37°21N 120°37W **306** H6
Atwood *Ont., Canada* 43°40N 81°1W **312** C3
Atwood *Ill., U.S.A.* 39°48N 88°28W **311** E8
Atwood *Kans., U.S.A.* 39°48N 101°3W **308** F3
Atyraū *Kazakhstan* 47°5N 52°0E **187** E9
Atzgersdorf *Austria* 48°8N 16°18E **142** B1
Au Sable *U.S.A.* 44°25N 83°20W **312** B1
Au Sable → *U.S.A.* 44°25N 83°20W **309** C12
Au Sable Forks *U.S.A.* 44°27N 73°41W **313** B11
Au Sable Pt. *U.S.A.* 44°20N 83°20W **312** B1
Au Vent, Région *Réunion* 21°0S 55°35E **272** f
Aua *Amer. Samoa* 14°17S 170°40W **302** f
Auas *Honduras* 15°29N 84°20W **320** C3
Auasberg *Namibia* 22°37S 17°13E **270** B2
Aubagne *France* 43°17N 5°37E **175** E9
Aube □ *France* 48°15N 4°10E **173** D11
Aube → *France* 48°34N 3°43E **173** D10
Aubenas *France* 44°37N 4°24E **175** D8
Aubenton *France* 49°50N 4°12E **173** C11
Auberry *U.S.A.* 37°7N 119°29W **306** H7
Aubervilliers *France* 48°54N 2°22E **134** A3
Aubigny-sur-Nère *France* 47°30N 2°24E **173** E9
Aubin *France* 44°33N 2°15E **174** D6
Aubing *Germany* 48°9N 11°25E **131** B1
Aubrac, Mts. d' *France* 44°40N 3°2E **174** D7
Auburn *S. Austral., Australia* 34°1S 138°42E **282** C3
Auburn *Ala., U.S.A.* 32°36N 85°29W **316** C4
Auburn *Calif., U.S.A.* 38°54N 121°4W **306** G5
Auburn *Ill., U.S.A.* 39°36N 89°45W **310** E7
Auburn *Ind., U.S.A.* 41°22N 85°4W **311** C11
Auburn *Maine, U.S.A.* 44°6N 70°14W **309** C18
Auburn *N.Y., U.S.A.* 42°56N 76°34W **313** D8
Auburn *Nebr., U.S.A.* 40°23N 95°51W **308** E6
Auburn *Pa., U.S.A.* 40°36N 76°6W **313** F8
Auburn *Wash., U.S.A.* 47°18N 122°14W **306** C4
Auburn Ra. *Australia* 25°15S 150°30E **281** D5
Auburndale *Fla., U.S.A.* 28°4N 81°48W **317** G8
Auburndale *Mass., U.S.A.* 42°20N 71°14W **116** A1
Aubusson *France* 45°57N 2°11E **174** C6
Auce *Latvia* 56°28N 22°53E **184** B9
Auch *France* 43°39N 0°36E **174** E4
Auchendinny *U.K.* 55°51N 3°11W **121** B2
Auchi *Nigeria* 7°6N 6°13E **263** D6
Auchterarder *U.K.* 56°18N 3°41W **167** E5
Auchtermuchty *U.K.* 56°18N 3°13W **167** E5
Auckland *N.Z.* 36°52S 174°46E **284** C3
Auckland □ *N.Z.* 36°50S 175°0E **284** C3
Auckland Is. *Pac. Oc.* 50°40S 166°5E **288** N8
Auckland Park *S. Africa* 26°11S 28°0E **123** B2
Aude □ *France* 43°8N 2°28E **174** E6
Aude → *France* 43°13N 3°14E **174** E7
Auden *Canada* 50°14N 87°53W **298** B2
Auderghem *Belgium* 50°49N 4°26E **116** B2
Auderville *France* 49°43N 1°57W **172** C5
Audierne *France* 48°1N 4°34W **172** D2
Audincourt *France* 47°30N 6°50E **173** E13
Audo Ra. *Ethiopia* 6°20N 41°50E **257** F5
Audubon *U.S.A.* 41°43N 94°56W **310** C2
Aue *Germany* 50°35N 12°41E **178** E8
Auerbach *Germany* 50°30N 12°24E **178** E8

Aufist W. Sahara 25°44N 14°39W 260 C2
Augathella Australia 25°48S 146°35E 281 D4
Aughnacloy U.K. 54°25N 6°59W 166 B5
Aughrim Ireland 53°18N 8°19W 166 C3
Augrabies Falls S. Africa 28°35S 20°20E 270 C3
Augrabies Falls △
  S. Africa 28°40S 20°22E 270 C3
Augsburg Germany 48°25N 10°52E 179 G6
Augsburg-Westliche Wälder △
  Germany 48°22N 10°40E 179 G6
August Town Jamaica 17°59N 76°44W 320 a
Augusta W. Austral.,
  Australia 34°19S 115°9E 279 F2
Augusta Italy 37°13N 15°13E 201 E8
Augusta Ga., U.S.A. 33°28N 81°58W 316 B8
Augusta Ark., U.S.A. 35°17N 91°22W 314 D9
Augusta Kans., U.S.A. 37°41N 96°59W 308 D5
Augusta Maine, U.S.A. 44°19N 69°47W 309 C19
Augusta Mont., U.S.A. 47°30N 112°24W 304 C7
Augusta, Mausoleo di Rome, Italy 136 b2
Augustenborg Denmark 54°57N 9°53E 163 K3
Augustine I. U.S.A. 59°22N 153°26W 303 G9
Augusto Cardosa = Metangula
  Mozam. 12°40S 34°50E 269 E3
Augustów Poland 53°51N 23°0E 184 E9
Augustówka Poland 52°11N 21°5E 142 B2
Augustus, Mt. Australia 24°20S 116°50E 279 D2
Augustus I. Australia 15°20S 124°30E 278 C3
Aujuittuq = Grise Fiord
  Canada 76°25N 82°57W 295 B15
Aukan Eritrea 15°29N 40°50E 257 D5
Auki Solomon Is. 8°45S 160°42E 287 M11
Aukra Norway 62°47N 6°55E 164 B3
Aukrug △ Germany 54°5N 9°45E 178 A5
Aukštaitija △ Lithuania 55°15N 26°0E 161 J22
Aukum U.S.A. 38°34N 120°43W 306 G6
Aul India 20°41N 86°39E 244 C8
Aulavik △ Canada 73°42N 119°55W 294 C8
Auld, L. Australia 22°25S 123°50E 278 D3
Âõliekõl Kazakhstan 52°32N 62°45E 216 B6
Aulifeltet Norway 60°30N 11°21E 162 D5
Auliye-Ata = Taraz
  Kazakhstan 42°54N 71°22E 217 D8
Aulla Italy 44°12N 9°58E 198 D6
Aulnay France 46°2N 0°22W 174 B3
Aulnay-sous-Bois France 48°56N 2°29E 134 A3
Aulne → France 47°48N 4°16W 172 D2
Aulnoye-Aymeries France 50°12N 3°50E 173 B10
Aulong Palau 7°16N 134°17E 288 c
Ault Somme, France 50°8N 1°26E 172 B8
Ault Colo., U.S.A. 40°35N 104°44W 304 F11
Aulus-les-Bains France 42°49N 1°19E 174 F5
Aumale = Sour el Ghozlane
  Algeria 36°10N 3°45E 261 A5
Aumale France 49°46N 1°46E 173 C8
Aumo Papua N. G. 5°44S 148°30E 286 C5
Aumont-Aubrac France 44°43N 3°17E 174 D7
Auna Nigeria 10°9N 4°42E 263 C5
Aundah India 19°32N 77°3E 244 E3
Aundh India 17°33N 74°23E 244 F2
Auning Denmark 56°26N 10°22E 163 H4
Aunis France 46°5N 0°50W 174 B3
Aunu'u Amer. Samoa 14°20S 170°31W 302 f
Auponhia Indonesia 1°58S 125°27E 231 E7
Aups France 43°37N 6°15E 175 E10
Aur, Pulau Malaysia 2°35N 104°10E 237 L5
Aura Burma 26°59N 97°57E 241 B6
Auraiya India 26°28N 79°33E 243 F8
Aurangabad Bihar, India 24°45N 84°18E 243 G11
Aurangabad Maharashtra,
  India 19°50N 75°23E 244 E2
Auray France 47°40N 2°59W 172 E4
Aurdal Norway 60°55N 9°26E 164 D6
Aure Norway 63°16N 8°33E 164 A5
Aurelio Italy 41°54N 12°26E 136 B1
Aurès Algeria 35°8N 6°30E 261 A6
Aurich Germany 53°28N 7°28E 178 B3
Aurilândia Brazil 16°44S 50°28W 333 E1
Aurillac France 44°55N 2°26E 176 D6
Aurlandsfjorden Norway 61°3N 7°1E 164 C4
Aurlandsvangen Norway 60°55N 7°12E 164 D4
Auronzo di Cadore Italy 46°33N 12°21E 199 B9
Aurora = Maéwo
  Vanuatu 15°10S 168°10E 287 E6
Aurora = San Francisco
  Phil. 13°21N 122°31E 232 E4
Aurora Ont., Canada 44°0N 79°28W 312 C5
Aurora Isabela, Phil. 16°59N 121°38E 232 D4
Aurora Zamboanga del S.,
  Phil. 7°57N 123°36E 233 H4
Aurora Western Cape,
  S. Africa 32°40S 18°29E 270 D2
Aurora Colo., U.S.A. 39°43N 104°49W 304 G11
Aurora Ill., U.S.A. 41°45N 88°19W 311 C8
Aurora Mo., U.S.A. 36°58N 93°43W 308 G7
Aurora N.Y., U.S.A. 42°45N 76°42W 313 D8
Aurora Nebr., U.S.A. 40°52N 98°0W 308 E5
Aurora Ohio, U.S.A. 41°21N 81°20W 312 E3
Aurora △ Phil. 15°30N 121°30E 232 D3
Aurora Memorial △
  Phil. 15°40N 121°20E 232 D3
Aursmoen Norway 59°55N 11°26E 164 D6
Aursunden Norway 62°40N 11°40E 164 B8
Aurukun Australia 13°20S 141°45E 280 A3
Aurukun ◇ Australia 13°36S 141°48E 280 A3
Aus Namibia 26°35S 16°12E 270 C2
Ausa India 18°15N 76°30E 244 E3
Ausable → Canada 43°19N 81°46W 312 C3
Auschwitz = Oświęcim
  Poland 50°2N 19°11E 185 H6
Ausim Egypt 30°7N 31°9E 117 A1
Auski Roadhouse
  Australia 22°22S 118°41E 278 D2
Auspitz = Hustopeče
  Czech Rep. 48°57N 16°43E 181 C9
Aussig = Ústí nad Labem
  Czech Rep. 50°41N 14°3E 180 A7
Aust-Agder □ Norway 58°45N 8°0E 164 F4
Austad Norway 58°58N 7°37E 164 F4
Austen Harbour Japan 12°55N 92°45E 245 H11
Austerlitz = Slavkov u Brna
  Czech Rep. 49°10N 16°52E 181 B9
Austerlitz, Gare d' France 48°50N 2°22E 134 A3
Austevoll Norway 60°5N 5°13E 164 D2
Austin Ind., U.S.A. 38°45N 85°49W 311 F11
Austin Minn., U.S.A. 43°40N 92°58W 308 D7
Austin Nev., U.S.A. 39°30N 117°4W 304 G5
Austin Pa., U.S.A. 41°38N 78°6W 312 E6
Austin Tex., U.S.A. 30°17N 97°45W 314 F6
Austin, L. Australia 27°40S 118°0E 278 E2
Austin I. Canada 61°10N 94°0W 297 A10
Austmarka Norway 60°6N 12°21E 164 D8
Austnes Norway 62°8N 6°16E 164 B3
Austral Is. = Tubuaï, Îs.
  French Polynesia 25°0S 150°0W 289 f
Austral Seamount Chain
  Pac. Oc. 24°0S 150°0W 289 K13
Australia ■ Oceania 23°0S 135°0E 276 E3
Australian-Antarctic Basin
  S. Ocean 60°0S 120°0E 151 C9
Australian Capital Territory □
  Australia 35°30S 149°0E 283 C8

Australind Australia 33°17S 115°42E 279 F2
Austria ■ Europe 47°0N 14°0E 180 E7
Austur-Skaftafellssýsla □
  Iceland 64°15N 16°0W 155 C10
Austvågøya Norway 68°20N 14°40E 160 B16
Autazes Brazil 3°35S 59°8W 329 D6
Auterive France 43°21N 1°29E 174 E5
Authie → France 50°22N 1°38E 173 B8
Authon-du-Perche France 48°12N 0°54E 172 D7
Autlán de Navarro
  Mexico 19°46N 104°22W 318 D4
Autun France 46°58N 4°17E 173 F11
Auvergne □ France 45°20N 3°15E 174 C7
Auvergne, Mts. d' France 45°20N 2°55E 174 C6
Auvézère → France 45°12N 0°50E 174 C4
Auxerre France 47°48N 3°32E 173 E10
Auxi-le-Château France 50°15N 2°8E 173 B9
Auxonne France 47°10N 5°20E 173 E12
Auxvasse U.S.A. 39°1N 91°54W 310 F5
Auyittuq □ Canada 67°30N 66°0W 295 D18
Auzances France 46°2N 2°30E 173 F9
Av-Dovurak Russia 51°17N 91°35E 215 D10
Ava Ill., U.S.A. 37°53N 89°30W 310 G7
Ava Mo., U.S.A. 36°57N 92°40W 308 G7
Avaldsnes Norway 59°21N 5°20E 164 E2
Avallon France 47°30N 3°53E 173 E10
Avalon Calif., U.S.A. 33°21N 118°20W 307 M8
Avalon Pen. Canada 47°30N 53°20W 299 C9
Avanavero Suriname 4°51N 57°22W 329 C6
Avanigadda India 16°0N 80°56E 245 G5
Avannaarsua □ Greenland 80°0N 55°0W 154 B5
Avanos Turkey 38°43N 34°51E 212 C6
Avantas Greece 40°57N 25°56E 203 F9
Avaré Brazil 23°4S 48°58W 335 A6
Avarua Cook Is. 21°12S 159°46W 289 b
Avarua Harb. Cook Is. 21°12S 159°46W 289 b
Avatele Cook Is. 19°6S 169°55W 289 g
Avatiu Cook Is. 21°12S 159°47W 289 b
Avawatz Mts. U.S.A. 35°40N 116°30W 307 K10
Avdan India 40°23N 29°46E 203 F13
Avedøre Denmark 55°37N 12°27E 118 B2
Aveiro Brazil 3°10S 55°5W 329 D6
Aveiro Portugal 40°37N 8°38W 194 E2
Aveiro □ Portugal 40°40N 8°35W 194 E2
Åvej Iran 35°40N 49°15E 247 C6
Avellaneda Argentina 34°40S 58°22W 337 D7
Avellino Italy 40°54N 14°47E 201 B7
Avenal U.S.A. 36°0N 120°8W 306 K6
Avenel U.S.A. 38°59N 76°59W 143 B4
Averøya Norway 63°0N 7°35E 164 A4
Aversa Italy 40°58N 14°12E 201 B7
Avery U.S.A. 47°15N 115°49W 304 C6
Aves, I. de W. Indies 15°45N 63°55W 321 C7
Aves, Is. las Venezuela 12°0N 67°30W 321 D6
Aves Laguna Colorada, Santuario
  de ◇ Bolivia 22°30S 67°30W 330 E4
Aves Ridge W. Indies 14°0N 63°30W 321 D7
Avesnes-sur-Helpe France 50°8N 3°57E 173 B10
Avesnois ◇ France 50°10N 3°45E 173 B10
Avesta Sweden 60°9N 16°10E 162 D10
Aveyron □ France 44°22N 2°45E 174 D6
Aveyron → France 44°5N 1°16E 174 D5
Avezzano Italy 42°2N 13°25E 199 F10
Avgo Greece 35°33N 25°37E 205 F7
Aviá Teraí Argentina 26°45S 60°50W 334 B3
Aviano Italy 46°4N 12°36E 199 B9
Aviatu → Cook Is. 21°12S 159°49W 289 b
Aviemore U.K. 57°12N 3°50W 167 D5
Aviemore, L. N.Z. 44°37S 170°18E 285 D5
Avigliana Italy 45°5N 7°23E 198 C4
Avigliano Italy 40°44N 15°43E 201 B8
Avignon France 43°57N 4°50E 175 E8
Ávila Spain 40°39N 4°43W 194 E6
Ávila □ Spain 40°30N 5°0W 194 E6
Ávila, Sierra de Spain 40°40N 5°15W 194 E5
Avila Beach U.S.A. 35°11N 120°44W 307 K6
Avilés Spain 43°35N 5°57W 194 B5
Avintes Portugal 41°7N 8°33W 194 D2
Avis Portugal 39°4N 7°53W 195 F3
Avis Pa., U.S.A. 41°11N 77°19W 312 E7
Avísio → Italy 46°7N 11°5E 199 B8
Avissawella Sri Lanka 6°56N 80°11E 245 L5
Aviston U.S.A. 38°36N 89°36W 310 F7
Avize France 48°59N 4°1E 173 C11
Avize = Avis Portugal 39°4N 7°53W 195 F3
Avlona = Vlorë Albania 40°32N 19°28E 202 F3
Avlonari Greece 38°31N 24°8E 204 C5
Avlum Denmark 56°16N 8°47E 163 H2
Avoca Vic., Australia 37°5S 143°26E 282 D5
Avoca N.Y., U.S.A. 42°25N 77°25W 312 D7
Avoca → Vic., Australia 35°40S 143°43E 282 D5
Avoca → Wicklow, Ireland 52°48N 6°10W 166 D5
Avola B.C., Canada 51°45N 119°19W 296 C5
Avola Italy 36°56N 15°7E 201 F8
Avon Ill., U.S.A. 40°40N 90°26W 310 D6
Avon N.Y., U.S.A. 42°55N 77°45W 312 D7
Avon → W. Austral.,
  Australia 31°40S 116°7E 279 F2
Avon → Bristol, U.K. 51°29N 2°41W 169 F5
Avon → Dorset, U.K. 50°44N 1°46W 169 G6
Avon → Warks., U.K. 52°0N 2°8W 169 E5
Avon Park U.S.A. 27°36N 81°31W 317 H8
Avondale Ill., U.S.A. 41°56N 87°41W 119 B2
Avondale U.S.A. 29°54N 90°12W 131 B1
Avondale Zimbabwe 17°43S 30°58E 269 F3
Avondale Heights
  Australia 37°45S 144°52E 128 A1
Avonlea Canada 50°0N 105°0W 297 D8
Avonmore Canada 45°10N 74°58W 313 A10
Avonmouth U.K. 51°30N 2°42W 169 F5
Avramov Bulgaria 42°45N 26°38E 203 D10
Avranches France 48°40N 1°20W 172 D5
Avre → France 48°47N 1°22E 172 D8
Avrig Romania 45°43N 24°21E 183 E9
Avrillé France 47°30N 0°35W 172 E6
Avtovac Bos.-H. 43°9N 18°35E 202 C2
Avtovo Russia 59°51N 30°16E 137 B1
Avu Avu Solomon Is. 9°50S 160°22E 287 M11
Awa-Shima Japan 38°27N 139°14E 220 E9
Awag el Baqar
  South Sudan 10°10N 33°10E 257 B3
A'waj → Syria 33°23N 36°20E 250 B5
Awaji Japan 34°32N 135°1E 223 C7
Awaji-Shima Japan 34°30N 134°50E 222 C6
'Awālī Bahrain 26°0N 50°30E 247 E6
Awantipur India 33°55N 75°3E 243 C6
Awanui N.Z. 35°4S 173°17E 284 B2
Aware Ethiopia 8°16N 44°9E 257 C5
Awarja → India 17°5N 76°15E 244 E2
Awaroa B. N.Z. 44°28S 168°4E 285 E3
Awasa Ethiopia 7°2N 38°28E 257 F4
Awasa, L. Ethiopia 7°20N 38°30E 257 F4
Awash Ethiopia 9°1N 40°10E 257 F5
Awash → Ethiopia 11°45N 41°5E 257 E5
Awash △ Ethiopia 8°40N 39°40E 257 F5
Awaso Ghana 6°15N 2°22W 262 D4
Awat China 40°35N 80°24E 217 D10
Awatere → N.Z. 41°37S 174°10E 285 D5
Awbārī Libya 26°46N 12°57E 258 C2
Awbārī, Idehan Libya 27°10N 11°30E 258 C2
Awjilah Somali Rep. 10°30N 43°30E 267 B5

Awdheegle Somali Rep. 1°59N 44°50E 267 D5
Awe, L. U.K. 56°17N 5°16W 167 E3
Awgu Nigeria 6°4N 7°24E 263 D6
Awjilah Libya 29°8N 21°7E 258 C4
Awka Nigeria 6°12N 7°5E 263 D6
Aworro Papua N. G. 7°43S 143°11E 286 D2
Awsard Mauritania 22°37N 14°22W 260 D2
Ax-les-Thermes France 42°44N 1°50E 174 F5
Axat France 42°48N 2°13E 174 F6
Axe → U.K. 50°42N 3°4W 169 F5
Axel Heiberg I. Canada 80°0N 90°0W 295 B14
Axim Ghana 4°51N 2°15W 262 E4
Axininm Brazil 4°2S 59°22W 329 D6
Axintele Romania 44°37N 26°47E 183 F11
Axioma Brazil 6°45S 64°31W 331 B5
Axios → Greece 40°57N 22°35E 202 F6
Axminster U.K. 50°46N 3°0W 169 G4
Axson U.S.A. 31°17N 82°44W 316 D7
Axvall Sweden 58°23N 13°34E 163 F6
Ay France 49°3N 4°1E 173 C11
Ayaantang Eq. Guin. 1°58N 10°24E 264 B2
Ayabaca Peru 4°40S 79°53W 330 A2
Ayabe Japan 35°20N 135°20E 223 B7
Ayacucho Argentina 37°5S 58°20W 334 D4
Ayacucho Peru 13°0S 74°0W 330 C3
Ayacucho □ Peru 14°0S 74°0W 330 C3
Ayaguz = Ayaköz
  Kazakhstan 48°10N 80°10E 217 C10
Ayakkum Hu China 37°30N 89°20E 217 E11
Ayaköz Kazakhstan 46°40N 79°14E 217 C9
Ayakudi India 10°28N 77°56E 245 G3
Ayala Phil. 6°57N 121°57E 233 H3
Ayamé Ivory C. 5°35N 3°9W 262 D4
Ayamonte Spain 37°12N 7°24W 195 H3
Ayan Russia 56°30N 138°16E 215 D14
Ayancik Turkey 41°57N 34°35E 212 B6
Ayangba Nigeria 7°31N 7°8E 263 D6
Ayapel Colombia 8°19N 75°9W 328 B2
Ayaş Turkey 40°10N 32°21E 212 B5
Ayaviri Peru 14°50S 70°35W 330 C3
Ayazağa Turkey 41°6N 28°59E 128 E1
Aybak Afghan. 36°15N 68°5E 240 A3
Aybastı Turkey 40°41N 37°23E 212 B7
Aydarköl Uzbekistan 40°50N 67°10E 217 D7
Aydın Turkey 37°51N 27°51E 205 D2
Aydın □ Turkey 37°50N 28°0E 205 D2
Aydın Dağları Turkey 38°0N 28°0E 205 D10
Aydıncık Turkey 36°9N 33°21E 250 B4
Aydingkol Hu China 42°40N 89°15E 217 D11
Ayelu Ethiopia 10°5N 40°42E 257 E5
Ayenngré Togo 8°40N 1°1E 263 D5
Ayer U.S.A. 42°34N 71°35W 313 D13
Ayer Chawan, Pulau
  Singapore 1°16N 103°41E 138 B2
Ayer Hitam Malaysia 5°24N 100°16E 237 c
Ayer Merbau, Pulau
  Singapore 1°16N 103°42E 138 B2
Ayerbe Spain 42°17N 0°41W 196 C4
Ayer's Cliff Canada 45°10N 72°3W 313 A12
Ayers Rock = Uluru
  Australia 25°23S 131°5E 279 E5
Ayeyarwady = Irrawaddy →
  Burma 15°50N 95°6E 241 L19
Áyia Napa Cyprus 34°59N 34°0E 207 E13
Áyia Phyla Cyprus 34°43N 33°1E 207 E12
Áyios Amvrósios Cyprus 35°20N 33°35E 207 E12
Áyios Seryios Cyprus 35°12N 33°53E 207 E12
Áyios Theodhoros Cyprus 35°22N 34°1E 207 E10
Áyios Yeóryios = Aghios Georgios
  Greece 37°28N 23°57E 204 D5
Aykhal Russia 66°0N 111°30E 215 C12
Aykino Russia 62°15N 49°56E 188 B9
Aykirikçi Turkey 39°8N 30°9E 205 B12
Aylesbury U.K. 51°49N 0°49W 169 F7
Aylmer Canada 42°46N 80°59W 312 D4
Aylmer, L. Canada 64°5N 108°30W 294 E10
'Ayn, Wādī al Oman 22°15N 55°28E 247 F7
'Ayn al Ghazālah Libya 32°10N 23°20E 258 B4
Ayn Dār S. Arabia 25°55N 49°10E 247 E7
Ayn Sifni Iraq 36°41N 43°20E 213 D10
Ayn Zālah Iraq 36°45N 42°35E 213 D10
Ayna Spain 38°34N 2°3W 197 G2
Aynāt Yemen 16°4N 49°9E 249 C5
'Aynūnah Si. Arabia 28°5N 35°8E 246 E4
Ayod South Sudan 8°7N 31°26E 257 F3
Ayolas Paraguay 27°10S 56°59W 334 B4
Ayon, Ostrov Russia 69°50N 169°0E 215 C17
Ayora Spain 39°3N 1°3W 197 G3
Ayorou Niger 14°53N 1°0E 263 C5
Ayos Cameroon 3°53N 12°31E 264 B2
'Ayoûn el 'Atroûs
  Mauritania 16°38N 9°37W 262 B3
Ayr Queens., Australia 19°35S 147°25E 280 B4
Ayr Ont., Canada 43°17N 80°27W 312 C4
Ayr S. Ayrs., U.K. 55°28N 4°38W 167 F4
Ayr → U.K. 55°28N 4°38W 167 F4
Ayrancı Turkey 37°21N 33°41E 250 B5
Ayrancılar Turkey 38°15N 27°18E 205 C9
Ayre, Pt. of I. of Man 54°25N 4°21W 168 C3
Ayribaba Turkmenistan 37°50N 66°34E 217 F7
Aysha Ethiopia 10°50N 42°23E 257 E5
Ayton Australia 15°56S 145°22E 280 B4
Aytos Bulgaria 42°42N 27°16E 203 D11
Aytoska Planina
  Bulgaria 42°45N 27°30E 203 D11
Ayu, Kepulauan Indonesia 0°35N 131°5E 231 D8
Ayutla Guatemala 14°40N 92°10W 320 D1
Ayutla de los Libres
  Mexico 16°54N 99°13W 319 D5
Ayvacık Turkey 39°36N 26°24E 212 C2
Ayvalık Turkey 39°20N 26°46E 212 C2
Az Zabadānī Syria 33°43N 36°5E 250 B5
Az Zāhirīyah West Bank 31°25N 34°58E 251 G5
Az Zahrān S. Arabia 26°10N 50°7E 247 E6
Az Zarqā Jordan 32°5N 36°4E 251 F7
Az Zarqā' U.A.E. 24°53N 53°4E 247 E7
Az Zāwiyah Libya 32°52N 12°56E 258 B2
Az Zaydīyah Yemen 15°20N 43°1E 248 D3
Az Zilfī Si. Arabia 26°12N 44°52E 246 E5
Az Zubayr Iraq 30°26N 47°40E 246 D5
Az Zuqur Yemen 14°0N 42°45E 248 E3
Az Zuwaytīnah Libya 30°58N 20°7E 258 B4
Azabu Tokyo, Japan 140 c3
Azad Kashmir □ Pakistan 33°50N 73°50E 243 C5
Azamabuja Portugal 39°4N 8°51W 195 F2
Azamgarh India 26°5N 83°13E 243 F10
Azangaro Peru 14°55S 70°13W 330 C3
Azaouad Mali 19°0N 3°18E 262 B5
Azaouak, V. de l' Mali 15°50N 3°20E 263 B5
Āzār Shahr Iran 37°45N 45°59E 246 B5
Azara Nigeria 8°22N 9°26E 263 D7
Azarān Iran 37°26N 47°16E 246 B5
Āzārbāyjān = Azerbaijan ■
  Asia 40°20N 48°0E 191 K9
Āzārbāyjān-e Gharbī □
  Iran 37°0N 44°30E 246 B5
Āzārbāyjān-e Sharqī □
  Iran 37°20N 47°0E 246 B5

Azare Nigeria 11°55N 10°10E 263 C7
Azay-le-Rideau France 47°16N 0°30E 172 E7
A'zāz Syria 36°36N 37°4E 250 B8
Azazga Algeria 36°48N 4°22E 261 A6
Azbine = Aïr Niger 18°30N 8°0E 259 E1
Azcapotzalco Mexico 19°28N 99°10W 128 B1
Azefal Mauritania 21°0N 14°45W 260 D2
Azeffoun Algeria 36°51N 4°26E 261 A6
Azemmour Morocco 33°20N 9°20W 260 B3
Azennezal Algeria 22°58N 0°43E 261 D5
Azerbaijan ■ Asia 40°20N 48°0E 191 K9
Azezo Ethiopia 12°28N 37°15E 257 E4
Azimganj India 24°14N 88°16E 243 G13
Azimganj India 24°14N 88°16E 243 G13
Azilal Morocco 31°55N 6°33W 260 B3
Azkoabá Chad 33°20N 9°20W 260 B3
Aznalcóllar Spain 37°32N 6°17W 195 H4
Azogues Ecuador 2°35S 78°0W 328 D2
Azores = Açores, Is. dos
  Atl. Oc. 38°0N 27°0W 153 d1
Azores-Biscay Rise Atl. Oc. 42°0N 20°0W 152 B9
Azov Russia 47°3N 39°25E 191 G4
Azov, Sea of Europe 46°0N 36°30E 189 J9
Azovskoye More = Azov, Sea of
  Europe 46°0N 36°30E 189 J9
Azrak, B. → Chad 10°52N 20°35E 259 G4
Azraq ash Shīshān Jordan 31°50N 36°49E 251 G7
Azrou Morocco 33°28N 5°19W 260 B3
Aztec U.S.A. 36°49N 107°59W 305 H10
Azteca, Estadia Mexico 19°18N 99°9W 128 C2
Azúa de Compostela
  Dom. Rep. 18°25N 70°44W 321 C5
Azuaga Spain 38°16N 5°39W 195 G5
Azuara Spain 41°15N 0°53W 196 D4
Azuay □ Ecuador 2°55S 79°0W 328 D2
Azúcar, Cerro Pan de
  Chile 23°19S 70°41W 137 A1
Azuer → Spain 39°8N 3°36W 195 F7
Azuero, Pen. de Panama 7°30N 80°30W 320 E3
Azuga Romania 45°27N 25°33E 183 E10
Azul Argentina 36°42S 59°43W 334 D4
Azul, Lagoa Azores 37°52N 25°47W 153 d3
Azul, Serra Brazil 14°50S 54°50W 331 C7
Azumino Japan 36°20N 137°50E 223 A9
Azurduy Bolivia 19°59S 64°29W 331 D5
Azusa U.S.A. 34°8N 117°52W 307 L9
Azzaba Algeria 36°48N 7°6E 261 A6
Azzano Décimo Italy 45°53N 12°42E 199 C9
Azzel Matti, Sebkra Algeria 26°10N 0°43E 261 C5

B

Ba Be △ Vietnam 22°25N 105°37E 236 A5
Ba Don Vietnam 17°45N 106°26E 236 D6
Ba Dong Vietnam 9°40N 106°33E 237 H6
Ba Ngoi Vietnam 11°54N 109°10E 237 G7
Ba Ria Vietnam 10°30N 107°10E 237 G6
Ba Tri Vietnam 10°2N 106°36E 237 H6
Ba Vi → Vietnam 21°1N 105°22E 236 B5
Ba Xian = Bazhou China 39°8N 116°22E 226 E9
Baa Indonesia 10°50S 123°0E 278 B3
Baambrugge Neths. 52°15N 4°59E 112 B2
Baamonde Spain 43°7N 7°44W 194 B3
Baao Phil. 13°27N 123°22E 232 E4
Baardheere Somali Rep. 2°20N 42°27E 267 D5
Baarle-Nassau Belgium 51°27N 4°56E 170 C4
Bab el Mandeb Red Sea 12°35N 43°25E 248 D3
Baba Bulgaria 42°44N 23°59E 202 D7
Baba, B. do Angola 14°50S 12°14E 265 C2
Bābā, Koh-i- Afghan. 34°30N 67°0E 240 B2
Baba Budan Hills India 13°30N 75°44E 245 H2
Baba Burnu Turkey 39°29N 26°2E 205 B8
Baba Channel Pakistan 24°48N 66°58E 242 G3
Baba dag Azerbaijan 41°0N 48°19E 191 K9
Babaçlândia Brazil 7°13S 47°46W 332 C2
Babada Turkey 37°49N 28°52E 205 D10
Babaeski Turkey 41°26N 27°6E 203 E11
Babahoyo Ecuador 1°40S 79°30W 328 D2
Babai = Sarju → India 27°21N 81°23E 243 F9
Babak Phil. 7°8N 125°41E 233 H5
Babana Nigeria 10°31N 3°46E 263 C5
Babanusa Sudan 11°20N 27°48E 256 F3
Babar Algeria 35°10N 7°6E 261 A6
Babar Indonesia 8°0S 129°30E 231 F7
Babar Pakistan 31°7N 69°32E 242 D3
Babarpur India 28°41N 77°16E 120 A2
Babase I. Papua N. G. 4°0S 153°42E 286 B7
Babayevo Russia 59°24N 35°55E 188 C6
Babb U.S.A. 48°51N 113°27W 304 A7
Babelthuap Palau 7°30N 134°30E 288 c
Babenhausen Germany 49°57N 8°57E 179 F4
Bābeni Romania 44°59N 24°11E 183 F9
Baberu India 25°33N 80°43E 243 G9
Babi Besar, Pulau
  Malaysia 2°25N 103°59E 237 L4
Babia Gora Europe 49°38N 19°38E 185 J6
Babian Jiang → China 22°35N 101°50E 234 F3
Bābil □ Iraq 32°30N 44°30E 246 C5
Babile Ethiopia 9°16N 42°11E 257 F5
Babile □ Ethiopia 8°45N 42°0E 257 F5
Babimost Poland 52°10N 15°49E 185 F2
Babina India 25°24N 78°28E 243 G8
Babinda Australia 17°20S 145°56E 280 B4
Babine Canada 55°22N 126°37W 296 B3
Babine → Canada 55°45N 127°44W 296 B3
Babine L. Canada 54°48N 126°0W 296 C3
Babiogórski △ Poland 49°38N 19°38E 185 J6
Babócsa Hungary 46°2N 17°21E 182 D2
Babol Iran 36°40N 52°50E 247 B7
Babol Sar Iran 36°45N 52°45E 247 B7
Babor, Dj. Algeria 36°31N 5°25E 261 A6
Baborów Poland 50°7N 18°1E 185 H5
Baboua C.A.R. 5°49N 14°58E 264 C2
Babruysk Belarus 53°10N 29°15E 177 B15
Babson Park U.S.A. 27°49N 81°32W 317 H8
Babuhri India 26°30N 71°0E 242 F4
Babuna Macedonia 41°30N 21°40E 202 F5
Babura Nigeria 12°51N 8°59E 263 C6
Babusar Pass Pakistan 35°12N 73°59E 243 B5
Babushkin Russia 55°41N 109°32E 215 D12
Babušnica Serbia 43°7N 22°27E 202 C6
Babuyan Chan. Phil. 18°50N 121°30E 232 A4
Babuyan I. Phil. 19°32N 121°57E 232 B3
Babuyan Is. Phil. 19°10N 121°40E 232 B3
Babylon Iraq 32°34N 44°22E 213 F11
Babylon U.S.A. 40°42N 73°19W 313 F11
Bac = Moldova 46°55N 29°36E 183 D14
Bắc → Vietnam 22°43N 103°59E 234 F3
Bac Serbia 45°29N 19°13E 182 B4
Bac Can Vietnam 22°8N 105°49E 236 A5
Bac Giang Vietnam 21°16N 106°11E 236 B6
Bac Lieu Vietnam 9°17N 105°43E 237 H5
Bac Ninh Vietnam 21°13N 106°4E 236 B6
Bac Phan Vietnam 22°0N 105°0E 236 B5
Bacaadweyn Somali Rep. 7°5N 47°40E 267 C6
Bacabal Brazil 4°15S 44°45W 332 B3
Bacacay Brazil 13°18N 123°47E 232 E4
Bacalar Mexico 18°43N 88°27W 319 D7
Bacan, Kepulauan
  Indonesia 0°35S 127°30E 231 E7

Bacarra Phil. 18°15N 120°37E 232 B3
Bacău Romania 46°35N 26°55E 183 D11
Bacău □ Romania 46°30N 26°44E 183 D11
Baccarat France 48°28N 6°42E 173 D13
Bacerac Mexico 30°18N 108°50W 318 A3
Bāceşti Romania 46°50N 27°11E 183 D12
Bach Long Vi. Dao
  Vietnam 20°10N 107°40E 236 B6
Bach Ma △ Vietnam 16°11N 107°49E 236 D6
Badlands U.S.A. 43°55N 102°30W 308 D2
Badlands △ U.S.A. 43°38N 102°56W 308 D2
Badli India 28°44N 77°8E 120 A1
Badnera India 20°48N 77°44E 244 D3
Badoc Phil. 17°56N 120°28E 232 B3
Badogo Mali 11°2N 8°13W 262 C3
Badoumbé Mali 13°42N 10°15W 262 C2
Badr Ḥunayn Si. Arabia 23°44N 38°46E 248 B2
Badrah Iraq 33°6N 45°58E 213 F11
Badrain Jaran Shamo
  China 40°40N 103°0E 226 D2
Badrinath India 30°45N 79°30E 243 D8
Badu Australia 10°7S 142°11E 280 a
Badulla Sri Lanka 7°1N 81°7E 245 L5
Badung, Bukit Indonesia 8°49S 115°10E 231 K18
Badung, Selat Indonesia 8°40S 115°22E 231 K18
Badupi Burma 21°36N 93°27E 241 E4
Badvel India 14°45N 79°3E 245 G4
Baena Spain 37°37N 4°20W 195 H6
Baengnyeongdo S. Korea 37°57N 124°40E 224 D2
Baerami Australia 32°27S 150°27E 283 B9
Bærum Norway 59°54N 10°36E 133 A2
Baetov Kyrgyzstan 41°13N 74°54E 217 D8
Baeza Ecuador 0°25S 77°53W 328 D2
Baeza Spain 37°57N 3°25W 195 H7
Bafang Cameroon 5°9N 10°11E 263 D7
Bafatá Guinea-Biss. 12°8N 14°40W 262 C2
Baffin B. N. Amer. 72°0N 64°0W 292 B13
Baffin I. Canada 68°0N 75°0W 295 D17
Bafia Cameroon 4°40N 11°10E 263 E7
Bafilo Togo 9°22N 1°22E 263 D5
Bafing → Mali 13°49N 10°50W 262 C2
Bafing ~ Mali 12°38N 10°18W 262 C2
Bafliyūn Syria 36°37N 36°59E 246 B3
Bafoulabé Mali 13°50N 10°55W 262 C2
Bafoussam Cameroon 5°28N 10°25E 263 D7
Bāfq Iran 31°40N 55°25E 247 D7
Bafra Turkey 41°34N 35°54E 212 B6
Bafra Burnu Turkey 41°45N 36°2E 212 B7
Bāft Iran 29°15N 56°38E 247 D8
Bafut Cameroon 6°6N 10°2E 263 D7
Bafwasende
  Dem. Rep. of the Congo 1°3N 27°5E 266 D2
Bagabag Phil. 16°30N 121°15E 232 C3
Bagabag I. Papua N. G. 4°48S 146°14E 286 C4
Bagac Phil. 14°36N 120°20E 232 D3
Bagaha India 27°6N 84°5E 244 A7
Bagalkot India 16°10N 75°40E 245 F2
Bagamanoc Phil. 13°57N 124°17E 232 E5
Bagamoyo Tanzania 6°28S 38°55E 268 D4
Bagan = Pagan Burma 21°10N 94°52E 241 H19
Bagan Datoh Malaysia 3°59N 100°47E 237 L3
Bagan Serai Malaysia 5°1N 100°32E 237 K3
Baganga Phil. 7°34N 126°33E 233 H6
Bagani Namibia 18°7S 21°41E 270 A3
Bagansiapiapi Indonesia 2°12N 100°50E 234 B2
Bagasra India 21°30N 71°0E 242 J4
Bagata
  Dem. Rep. of the Congo 3°44S 17°57E 266 E3
Bagaud India 22°19N 75°53E 242 H6
Bagawi Sudan 15°23N 31°30E 257 D3
Bağcılar Turkey 41°2N 28°49E 122 B1
Bagdad Calif., U.S.A. 34°35N 115°53W 307 L11
Bagdad Fla., U.S.A. 30°36N 87°2W 317 E2
Bagdarin Russia 54°26N 113°36E 215 D12
Bagé Brazil 31°20S 54°15W 335 C5
Bagenalstown = Muine Bheag
  Ireland 52°42N 6°58W 166 D5
Bagepalli India 13°47N 77°47E 245 H3
Bagevadi India 16°35N 75°58E 244 F2
Baggao Phil. 17°56N 121°46E 232 C3
Baggs U.S.A. 41°2N 107°39W 304 F10
Bagh Pakistan 33°59N 73°45E 243 C5
Baghain → India 25°32N 81°1E 243 G9
Baghdād Iraq 33°20N 44°23E 113 A2
Baghdād al Muthana ✈ (BGW)
  Iraq 33°17N 44°30E 113 B2
Baghdad Int. ✈ (SDA)
  Iraq 33°15N 44°14E 113 B1
Baghdati Georgia 42°5N 42°49E 213 A10
Baghelkhand India 24°20N 81°0E 243 G9
Bagheria Italy 38°5N 13°30E 200 D6
Baghlān Afghan. 32°12N 68°46E 240 A4
Baghlān □ Afghan. 36°0N 68°30E 240 A4
Bagley U.S.A. 47°32N 95°24W 308 B6
Bagmari India 22°34N 88°23E 148 A2
Bagn Norway 60°49N 9°34E 164 D6
Bagnara Cálabra Italy 38°17N 15°48E 201 D8
Bagnasco Italy 44°13N 8°3E 198 D5
Bagnell Dam U.S.A. 38°14N 92°36W 310 F4
Bagnères-de-Bigorre France 43°5N 0°9E 174 E4
Bagnères-de-Luchon
  France 42°47N 0°38E 174 F4
Bagneux France 42°47N 0°38E 134 B2
Bagni di Lucca Italy 44°1N 10°35E 198 D7
Bagno di Romagna Italy 43°50N 11°57E 199 E8
Bagnoles-de-l'Orne France 48°32N 0°25W 172 D6
Bagnolet France 48°52N 0°9E 134 A3
Bagnols-sur-Cèze France 44°10N 4°36E 175 D8
Bagnorégio Italy 42°37N 12°5E 199 F9
Bago = Pegu Burma 17°20N 96°29E 241 L20
Bago □ Burma 19°0N 96°0E 241 K20
Bago Phil. 10°32N 122°50E 233 F4
Bagodar India 24°5N 85°52E 243 G11
Bagrationovsk Russia 54°23N 20°39E 184 D7
Bagrdan Serbia 44°5N 21°11E 202 B5
Bagua Peru 5°35S 78°22W 330 B2
Baguiati India 22°37N 88°25E 148 A2
Baguio Phil. 16°26N 120°34E 232 C3
Bagzane, Monts Niger 17°43N 8°45E 263 E7
Bağyurdu Turkey 38°28N 27°41E 205 C9
Bahabón de Esgueva
  Spain 41°52N 3°43W 194 D7
Bahadurabad Ghat
  Bangla. 25°11N 89°44E 243 G13
Bahadurganj India 26°16N 87°49E 243 F12
Bahadurgarh India 28°41N 76°57E 242 E7
Baha'i Temple U.S.A. 42°4N 87°41W 119 A2
Bahamas ■ N. Amer. 24°0N 75°0W 321 B5
Bahara, Canal Viejo de
  W. Indies 22°10N 77°30W 320 B4
Bahār Iran 34°54N 48°26E 213 E13
Bahārak Afghan. 37°2N 88°27E 240 A5
Baharampur India 24°2N 88°27E 243 G13

Baharīya, El Wâhât al
Egypt 28°0N 28°50E **256** B2
Baharu Pandan = Pandan
Malaysia 1°32N 103°46E **237** d
Bahawalnagar *Pakistan* 30°0N 73°15E **242** E5
Bahawalpur *Pakistan* 29°24N 71°40E **242** E4
Bahçe *Turkey* 37°13N 36°34E **212** D7
Bahçecik *Turkey* 40°41N 29°44E **203** F13
Bahçeköy *Turkey* 41°10N 28°59E **122** A1
Bahçelievler *Turkey* 41°0N 28°50E **122** B1
Baheli *Phil.* 10°0N 118°47E **233** F2
Bäherden *Turkmenistan* 38°25N 57°26E **247** B8
Baheri *India* 28°45N 79°34E **243** E8
Bahgul → *India* 27°45N 79°36E **243** F8
Bahi *Tanzania* 5°58S 35°21E **268** D4
Bahi Swamp *Tanzania* 6°10S 35°0E **268** D4
Bahia = Salvador *Brazil* 13°0S 38°30W **333** D4
Bahia □ *Brazil* 12°0S 42°0W **333** D3
Bahía, Is. de la *Honduras* 16°45N 86°15W **320** C2
Bahía Blanca *Argentina* 38°35S 62°13W **334** D3
Bahía de Caráquez
Ecuador 0°40S 80°27W **328** D1
Bahía Kino *Mexico* 28°47N 111°58W **318** B2
Bahía Laura *Argentina* 48°10S 66°30W **336** C3
Bahía Mansa *Chile* 40°33S 73°46W **336** B2
Bahía Negra *Paraguay* 20°5S 58°5W **331** E6
Bahía Solano *Colombia* 6°14N 77°25W **328** B2
Bahir Dar *Ethiopia* 11°37N 37°10E **257** E4
Bahlah *Oman* 22°58N 57°18E **249** B7
Bahmanzād *Iran* 31°15N 51°47E **247** D6
Bahmer *Algeria* 27°32N 0°10W **261** C4
Bahr el Ahmar □ *Egypt* 28°40N 31°30E **251** K2
Bahr el Ahmar □ *Sudan* 20°0N 35°0E **256** D4
Bahr el Jebel = Central Equatoria □
South Sudan 4°0N 31°0E **257** G3
Bahraich *India* 27°38N 81°37E **243** F9
Bahrain ■ *Asia* 26°0N 50°35E **247** E6
Bahror *India* 27°51N 76°20E **242** F7
Bahtîm *Egypt* 30°8N 31°16E **117** A2
Bāhū Kalāt *Iran* 25°43N 61°25E **247** E9
Bai *Mali* 13°35N 3°28W **262** C4
Bai Bung, Mui = Ca Mau, Mui
Vietnam 8°38N 104°44E **237** H5
Bai Thuong *Vietnam* 19°54N 105°23E **236** C5
Baia de Aramā *Romania* 45°0N 22°50E **182** E7
Baía dos Tigres *Angola* 16°40S 11°47E **265** F2
Baía Farta *Angola* 12°40S 13°11E **265** E2
Baia Mare *Romania* 47°40N 23°35E **183** C8
Baia-Sprie *Romania* 47°41N 23°43E **183** C8
Baião *Brazil* 2°40S 49°40W **332** B2
Baïbokoum *Chad* 7°46N 15°43E **259** G3
Baicheng *Jilin, China* 45°38N 122°42E **227** B12
Baicheng *Xinjiang Uygur, China* 41°46N 81°52E **217** D10
Băicoi *Romania* 45°3N 25°52E **183** E10
Baidoa = Baydhabo
Somali Rep. 3°8N 43°30E **267** D5
Baie-Comeau *Canada* 49°12N 68°10W **299** C6
Baie du Cap *Mauritius* 20°29S 57°22E **272** e
Baie-Mahault *Guadeloupe* 16°16N 61°35W **322** e
Baie-St-Paul *Canada* 47°28N 70°32W **299** C5
Baie Ste-Anne *Seychelles* 4°18S 55°45E **272** c
Baie-Trinité *Canada* 49°25N 67°20W **299** C6
Baie Verte *Canada* 49°55N 56°12W **299** C8
Baignes-Ste-Radegonde
France 45°23N 0°25W **174** C3
Baigneux-les-Juifs *France* 47°31N 4°39E **173** E11
Baihar *India* 22°6N 80°33E **243** H9
Baihe *Hubei, China* 32°50N 110°5E **226** H6
Baihe *Jilin, China* 42°27N 128°9E **227** C15
Baihetan Dam *China* 27°11N 102°54E **228** D4
Ba'ījī *Iraq* 35°0N 43°30E **213** E10
Baijnath *India* 29°55N 79°37E **243** E8
Baikal, L. = Baykal, Oz.
Russia 53°0N 108°0E **215** D11
Baikonur = Bayqongyr
Kazakhstan 45°40N 63°20E **216** C6
Baikunthpur *India* 23°15N 82°33E **243** H10
Bailadila, Mt. *India* 18°43N 81°15E **244** E5
Baile Átha Cliath = Dublin
Ireland 53°21N 6°15W **120** A2
Baile Átha Fhirdhia = Ardee
Ireland 53°52N 6°33W **166** C5
Baile Átha I = Athy *Ireland* 53°0N 7°0W **166** C5
Baile Átha Luain = Athlone
Ireland 53°25N 7°56W **166** C4
Baile Átha Troim = Trim
Ireland 53°33N 6°48W **166** C5
Baile Brigín = Balbriggan
Ireland 53°37N 6°11W **166** C5
Băile Govora *Romania* 45°5N 24°11E **183** E9
Băile Herculane *Romania* 44°53N 22°26E **182** F7
Băile Olănești *Romania* 45°12N 24°14E **183** E9
Băile Tuşnad *Romania* 46°9N 25°51E **183** D10
Bailén *Spain* 38°8N 3°48W **195** G7
Băilești *Romania* 44°1N 23°20E **183** F8
Baileys Crossroads *U.S.A.* 38°50N 77°6W **143** B3
Bailhongal *India* 15°55N 74°53E **245** G2
Bailique, Ilha *Brazil* 1°2N 49°58W **332** A2
Baille-Argent *Guadeloupe* 16°15N 61°48W **322** e
Baillif *Guadeloupe* 16°1N 61°44W **322** e
Bailly *France* 48°50N 2°4E **134** A1
Bailugh *Afghan.* 32°40N 66°47E **240** B2
Bailundo = Luau *Angola* 10°40S 22°10E **265** E4
Bailundo *Angola* 12°10S 15°50E **265** E3
Baima *China* 33°0N 100°26E **228** A3
Baimuru *Papua N. G.* 7°35S 144°51E **286** D3
Bain-de-Bretagne *France* 47°50N 1°40W **172** E5
Bainbridge *Ga., U.S.A.* 30°55N 84°35W **316** E5
Bainbridge *Ind., U.S.A.* 39°46N 86°49W **311** E10
Bainbridge *N.Y., U.S.A.* 42°18N 75°29W **313** D9
Bainbridge *Ohio, U.S.A.* 39°14N 83°16W **311** E13
Bainbridge Island *U.S.A.* 47°38N 122°32W **306** C4
Baine *China* 42°0N 128°0E **219** C14
Baing *Indonesia* 10°14S 120°34E **231** F6
Bainiu *China* 32°50N 112°15E **226** H7
Bainyik *Papua N. G.* 3°40S 143°4E **286** B2
Baiona *Spain* 42°6N 8°52W **194** C2
Bā'ir *Jordan* 30°45N 36°55E **251** H7
Bā'ir, W. → *Jordan* 30°59N 37°24E **251** H8
Baird Mts. *U.S.A.* 67°0N 160°0W **303** C7
Bairiki = Tarawa *Kiribati* 1°30N 173°0E **288** G9
Bairin Youqi *China* 43°30N 118°35E **227** C10
Bairin Zuoqi *China* 43°58N 119°15E **227** C10
Bairnsdale *Australia* 37°48S 147°36E **283** D7
Bairro Alto *Lisbon, Portugal* **126** c1
Bairro Lopes *Lisbon, Portugal* **126** b3
Bais *Phil.* 9°35N 123°7E **233** G4
Baisha *Guangdong, China* 23°8N 113°11E **121** B2
Baisha *Henan, China* 34°20N 112°32E **226** G7
Baisha Li *China* 19°12N 109°20E **236** C7
Baishan *China* 42°43N 127°14E **227** C14
Baissa *Nigeria* 7°14N 10°38E **263** D7
Baitadi *Nepal* 29°35N 80°25E **243** E9
Baitarani → *India* 20°45N 86°48E **244** D8
Baixa *Lisbon, Portugal* **126** c2
Baixa Grande *Brazil* 11°57S 40°11W **333** D3
Baixa Limia-Sierra do Xurés △
Spain 41°59N 8°2W **194** D2
Baixo-Longa *Angola* 15°41S 18°45E **265** F3
Baiyer River *Papua N. G.* 5°32S 144°9E **286** C3
Baiyin *China* 36°45N 104°14E **226** F3
Baiyü *China* 31°16N 98°50E **228** B2
Baiyu Shan *China* 37°15N 107°30E **226** F4
Baiyuda *Sudan* 17°35N 32°7E **256** D3
Baiyun *China* 23°11N 113°16E **121** A2
Baiyun Hill *China* 23°8N 113°15E **121** B2
Baiyun Mountain Scenic Area
China 23°11N 113°17E **121** A2
Baj Baj *India* 22°30N 88°5E **243** H13
Baja *Hungary* 46°12N 18°59E **182** D3
Baja, Pta. *Easter I., Chile* 27°10S 109°22W **330** b
Baja, Pta. *Baja Calif., Mexico* 29°58N 115°49W **318** B1
Baja California *Mexico* 31°10N 115°12W **318** A1
Baja California □ *Mexico* 30°0N 115°0W **318** B2
Baja California Sur □
Mexico 25°50N 111°50W **318** B2
Bajag *India* 22°40N 81°21E **243** H9
Bajamar *Canary Is.* 28°33N 16°20W **153** a1
Bajana *India* 23°7N 71°49E **242** H4
Bajatrejo *Indonesia* 8°29S 114°19E **231** J17
Bajera *Indonesia* 8°31S 115°2E **231** J18
Bājgīrān *Iran* 37°36N 58°24E **247** B8
Bājil *Yemen* 15°4N 43°17E **248** D3
Bajimba, Mt. *Australia* 29°17S 152°6E **281** D5
Bajina Bašta *Serbia* 43°58N 19°35E **202** C3
Bajmok *Serbia* 45°57N 19°24E **182** E4
Bajo Boquete *Panama* 8°46N 82°27W **320** E3
Bajo Caracoles *Argentina* 47°27S 70°56W **336** C2
Bajo Nuevo *Caribbean* 15°40N 78°50W **320** C4
Bajoga *Nigeria* 10°57N 11°20E **263** C7
Bajool *Australia* 23°40S 150°35E **280** C5
Bak *Hungary* 46°43N 16°51E **182** D1
Bakala *C.A.R.* 6°15N 20°20E **264** A4
Bakar *Croatia* 45°18N 14°32E **199** C11
Bakassi Pen. *Cameroon* 4°42N 8°20E **263** E6
Bakel *Senegal* 14°56N 12°20W **262** C2
Baker *Calif., U.S.A.* 35°16N 116°4W **307** K10
Baker *Fla., U.S.A.* 30°48N 86°41W **317** E3
Baker *Mont., U.S.A.* 46°22N 104°17W **304** C11
Baker, Canal *Chile* 47°45S 74°45W **336** C2
Baker, L. *Canada* 64°0N 96°0W **294** E12
Baker, Mt. *U.S.A.* 48°50N 121°49W **304** B3
Baker City *U.S.A.* 44°47N 117°50W **304** D5
Baker I. *Pac. Oc.* 0°10N 176°35W **277** A15
Baker I. *Alaska, U.S.A.* 55°20N 133°40W **296** B2
Baker L. *Australia* 26°54S 126°5E **279** E4
Baker Lake *Canada* 64°20N 96°3W **294** E12
Bakere
Dem. Rep. of the Congo 1°36N 23°50E **264** B4
Bakerhill *U.S.A.* 31°47N 85°18W **316** D4
Bakers Creek *Australia* 21°13S 149°7E **280** C4
Bakers Dozen Is. *Canada* 56°45N 78°45W **298** A4
Bakersfield *Calif., U.S.A.* 35°23N 119°1W **307** K8
Bakersfield *Vt., U.S.A.* 44°45N 72°48W **313** B12
Bakharden = Bäherden
Turkmenistan 38°25N 57°26E **247** B8
Bakhchysaray *Ukraine* 44°40N 33°45E **189** K7
Bakhmach *Ukraine* 51°10N 32°45E **189** G7
Bakhmut = Artemovsk
Ukraine 48°35N 38°0E **189** H9
Bākhtarān = Kermānshāh
Iran 34°23N 47°0E **213** E12
Bākhtarān = Kermānshāh □
Iran 34°0N 46°30E **246** C5
Baki = Krasnyye Baki
Russia 57°8N 45°10E **190** B7
Bakı *Azerbaijan* 40°29N 49°56E **191** K9
Baki *Somali Rep.* 10°30N 43°48E **267** B5
Bakır → *Turkey* 38°55N 27°0E **205** C9
Bakırdağı *Turkey* 38°13N 35°46E **212** C6
Bakırköy *Turkey* 40°58N 28°52E **122** C1
Bakkafjörður *Iceland* 66°2N 14°48W **155** A12
Bakkaflói *Iceland* 66°10N 14°45W **155** A12
Bakkagerði *Iceland* 65°31N 13°49W **155** B13
Baklan *Turkey* 38°0N 29°36E **205** C11
Bako *Ethiopia* 5°51N 36°23E **257** F4
Bako *Ivory C.* 9°8N 7°40W **262** D3
Bako △ *Malaysia* 1°43N 110°28E **235** B4
Bakony *Hungary* 47°10N 17°30E **182** C2
Bakony Forest = Bakony
Hungary 47°10N 17°30E **182** C2
Bakool □ *Somali Rep.* 4°0N 44°0E **267** D5
Bakori *Nigeria* 11°34N 7°25E **263** C6
Bakouma *C.A.R.* 5°40N 22°56E **264** A4
Bakovka *Russia* 55°40N 37°19E **129** B2
Baksan *Russia* 43°42N 43°32E **191** J6
Bakswaho *India* 24°15N 79°18E **243** G8
Baku = Bakı *Azerbaijan* 40°29N 49°56E **191** K9
Bakun Dam *Malaysia* 2°50N 113°50E **235** B4
Bakundi *Nigeria* 8°2N 10°45E **263** D7
Bakung *Indonesia* 0°5N 104°26E **234** B2
Bakungan *Indonesia* 2°55N 97°28E **234** B1
Bakuriani *Georgia* 41°44N 43°31E **213** B10
Bakutis Coast *Antarctica* 74°0S 120°0W **151** D15
Bakwa-Kenge
Dem. Rep. of the Congo 4°51S 22°4E **265** C4
Bakwanga = Mbuji-Mayi
Dem. Rep. of the Congo 6°9S 23°40E **265** D4
Baky = Bakı *Azerbaijan* 40°29N 49°56E **191** K9
Bal Harbor *U.S.A.* 25°53N 80°7W **128** A2
Bala *Ont., Canada* 45°1N 79°37W **312** A5
Bala *Senegal* 14°1N 13°8W **262** C2
Balâ *Turkey* 39°32N 33°6E **212** C5
Bala *Gwynedd, U.K.* 52°54N 3°36W **168** E4
Bala, L. *U.K.* 52°53N 3°37W **168** E4
Bālā Morghāb *Afghan.* 35°35N 63°20E **240** B1
Balabac *Phil.* 7°59N 117°4E **233** H1
Balabac I. *Phil.* 8°0N 117°0E **233** H1
Balabac Str. *E. Indies* 7°53N 117°5E **230** C5
Balabagh *Afghan.* 34°25N 70°12E **242** B4
Ba'labakk *Lebanon* 34°0N 36°10E **250** E7
Balabalangan, Kepulauan
Indonesia 2°20S 117°30E **235** C5
Balabio, Î. *N. Cal.* 20°7S 164°11E **286** d
Bălăcița *Romania* 44°23N 23°8E **183** F8
Balad *Iraq* 34°0N 44°9E **213** F11
Balad Rūz *Iraq* 33°42N 45°5E **213** F11
Bālādeh *Fārs, Iran* 29°17N 51°56E **247** D6
Bālādeh *Māzandaran, Iran* 36°12N 51°48E **247** B6
Balaghat *India* 21°49N 80°12E **244** D5
Balaghat Ra. *India* 18°50N 76°30E **244** E3
Balaguer *Spain* 41°50N 0°50E **196** D5
Balaikarangan *Indonesia* 0°49N 110°25E **235** B4
Balaipungut *Indonesia* 1°3N 101°17E **234** B2
Balaisabut *Indonesia* 0°28N 110°49E **235** B4
Balaka
Dem. Rep. of the Congo 4°52S 19°57E **265** C3
Balakän *Azerbaijan* 41°43N 46°24E **191** K8
Balakété *C.A.R.* 6°56N 19°54E **264** A3
Balakhna *Russia* 56°25N 43°32E **190** B6
Balaklava *S. Austral., Australia* 34°7S 138°22E **282** C3
Balaklava *Ukraine* 44°30N 33°30E **189** K7
Balakliya *Ukraine* 49°28N 36°55E **189** H9
Balakovo *Russia* 52°4N 47°55E **190** D8
Balamau *India* 27°10N 80°21E **243** F9
Balamban *Phil.* 10°30N 123°43E **233** F4
Balambangan, Pulau
Malaysia 7°17N 116°55E **235** A5
Bălan *Romania* 46°39N 25°49E **183** D10
Balancán *Mexico* 17°48N 91°32W **319** D6
Balanda = Kalininsk
Russia 51°30N 44°40E **190** E7
Balandra B. *Trin. & Tob.* 10°42N 61°0W **323** t
Balanga *Phil.* 14°41N 120°32E **232** D3
Balangala
Dem. Rep. of the Congo 0°30N 19°56E **264** B3
Balangiga *Phil.* 11°7N 125°23E **233** F5
Balangir *India* 20°43N 83°35E **244** D6
Balaoan *Phil.* 16°49N 120°24E **232** C3
Balapur *India* 20°40N 76°45E **244** D3
Balara *Phil.* 14°39N 121°3E **127** B2
Balashikha *Russia* 55°48N 37°58E **129** B5
Balashov *Russia* 51°30N 43°10E **190** E6
Balasinor *India* 22°57N 73°23E **242** H5
Balasore = Baleshwar
India 21°35N 87°3E **244** D8
Balassagyarmat *Hungary* 48°4N 19°15E **182** B4
Balât *Egypt* 25°36N 29°19E **256** B2
Balaton *Hungary* 46°50N 17°40E **182** D2
Balaton-Felvidéki △
Hungary 46°52N 17°30E **182** D2
Balatonboglár *Hungary* 46°46N 17°40E **182** D2
Balatonfüred *Hungary* 46°58N 17°54E **182** D2
Balatonszentgyörgy
Hungary 46°41N 17°19E **182** D2
Balayan *Phil.* 13°57N 120°44E **232** E3
Balayan B. *Phil.* 13°51N 120°48E **232** E3
Balazote *Spain* 38°54N 2°9W **197** G2
Balbalan *Phil.* 17°27N 121°12E **232** C3
Balbalasang-Balbalan △
Phil. 17°23N 121°1E **232** C3
Balbi, Mt. *Papua N. G.* 5°55S 154°58E **286** C8
Balbieriškis *Lithuania* 54°32N 23°53E **184** D10
Balbigny *France* 45°49N 4°11E **175** C8
Balbina *Brazil* 1°58S 59°29W **329** D6
Balbina, Represa de *Brazil* 2°0S 59°30W **329** D6
Balboa *Panama* 8°57N 79°34W **320** c
Balbriggan *Ireland* 53°37N 6°11W **166** C5
Balcarce *Argentina* 38°0S 58°10W **334** D4
Balcarres *Canada* 50°50N 103°35W **297** C8
Bălcești *Romania* 44°37N 23°57E **183** F8
Balchik *Bulgaria* 43°28N 28°11E **203** C12
Balclutha *N.Z.* 46°15S 169°45E **285** G4
Balcones Escarpment
U.S.A. 29°30N 99°15W **314** G5
Balçova *Turkey* 38°22N 27°4E **205** C9
Bald I. *Australia* 34°57S 118°27E **279** F2
Bald Knob *U.S.A.* 35°19N 91°34W **314** D9
Baldenburg = Biały Bór
Poland 53°53N 16°51E **184** E3
Baldia *Pakistan* 24°54N 66°58E **123** A1
Baldock L. *Canada* 56°33N 97°57W **297** B9
Baldoyle *Ireland* 53°24N 6°8W **120** A3
Baldwin *Fla., U.S.A.* 30°18N 81°59W **316** E8
Baldwin *Mich., U.S.A.* 43°54N 85°51W **309** D11
Baldwin *Pa., U.S.A.* 40°21N 79°58W **312** F5
Baldwin, L. *U.S.A.* 28°34N 81°19W **133** A3
Baldwin Hills *U.S.A.* 34°0N 118°21W **126** B2
Baldwin Hills Res. *U.S.A.* 34°0N 118°21W **126** B2
Baldwinsville *U.S.A.* 43°10N 76°20W **313** C8
Baldy Peak *U.S.A.* 33°54N 109°34W **305** K9
Bale *Croatia* 45°4N 13°46E **199** C10
Bale *Oromiya, Ethiopia* 6°57N 40°8E **257** F5
Bale *Oromiya, Ethiopia* 6°20N 41°30E **257** F5
Bale Mts. △ *Ethiopia* 6°59N 39°52E **257** F4
Baleares, Is. *Spain* 39°30N 3°0E **206** B4
Balearic Is. = Baleares, Is.
Spain 39°30N 3°0E **206** B4
Baleh → *Malaysia* 2°1N 113°1E **235** B4
Baleia, Pta. da *Brazil* 17°40S 39°7W **333** E4
Baleine → *Canada* 58°15N 67°40W **299** A6
Baleine, Petite R. de la →
Canada 56°0N 76°45W **298** A4
Băleni *Romania* 45°48N 27°51E **183** E12
Baler *Phil.* 15°46N 121°34E **232** D3
Baler B. *Phil.* 15°50N 121°35E **232** D3
Baleshare *U.K.* 57°31N 7°22W **167** D1
Baleshwar *India* 21°35N 87°3E **244** D8
Balestrand *Norway* 61°11N 6°31E **164** C3
Baley *Russia* 51°36N 116°37E **215** D12
Balezino *Russia* 58°2N 53°6E **190** B11
Balfate *Honduras* 15°48N 86°25W **320** C2
Balfour Channel
Solomon Is. 8°43S 157°27E **287** M9
Balgo *Australia* 20°9S 127°58E **278** D4
Balgowlah *Australia* 33°47S 151°16E **139** A2
Balgowlah Heights
Australia 33°48S 151°16E **139** A2
Balham *U.K.* 51°26N 0°8W **125** B3
Balharshah *India* 19°50N 79°23E **244** E4
Bali *Cameroon* 5°54N 10°0E **263** D7
Bali *Dem. Rep. of the Congo* 2°50S 16°12E **264** C3
Bali *Kriti, Greece* 35°25N 24°47E **207** E5
Bali *Raj., India* 25°11N 73°17E **242** G5
Bali *W. Bengal, India* 22°39N 88°20E **124** B1
Bali *Indonesia* 8°20S 115°0E **231** J18
Bali □ *Indonesia* 8°20S 115°0E **231** J17
Bali, Selat *Indonesia* 8°18S 114°25E **231** J17
Bali Barat △ *Indonesia* 8°12S 114°35E **231** J17
Bali Sea *Indonesia* 8°0S 115°0E **231** J17
Balia *S. Leone* 9°22N 11°1W **262** D2
Baliapal *India* 21°40N 87°17E **243** J12
Baliceaux *St. Vincent* 12°57N 61°8W **323** n
Balicuatro Is. *Phil.* 12°39N 124°24E **232** E5
Baliganja *India* 22°31N 88°22E **124** B2
Balige *Indonesia* 2°14N 99°7E **234** B1
Baligród *Poland* 49°20N 22°17E **185** J9
Baliguda *India* 20°12N 83°55E **244** D6
Balik Pulau *Malaysia* 5°21N 100°14E **237** c
Balıkesir *Turkey* 39°39N 27°53E **205** B9
Balıkesir □ *Turkey* 39°45N 28°0E **205** B9
Balīkh → *Syria* 35°52N 39°12E **213** E8
Balıkçeşme *Turkey* 40°18N 27°5E **203** F11
Balikpapan *Indonesia* 1°10S 116°55E **235** C5
Balimbing *Phil.* 5°5N 119°58E **233** J2
Balimo *Papua N. G.* 8°6S 142°57E **286** E2
Baling *Malaysia* 5°41N 100°55E **237** K3
Balingasag *Phil.* 8°45N 124°47E **233** G5
Balinge *Sweden* 59°57N 17°33E **162** E11
Balingen *Germany* 48°16N 8°51E **179** G4
Balingsnäs *Sweden* 59°13N 18°0E **139** B2
Balingsta *Sweden* 59°12N 18°0E **139** B2
Balinsasayao Twin Lakes △
Phil. 9°21N 123°9E **233** G4
Balinț *Romania* 45°48N 21°54E **182** E6
Balintang Channel *Phil.* 19°49N 121°40E **232** B3
Balintang I. *Phil.* 19°58N 122°9E **232** B3
Balintawak *Phil.* 14°39N 120°59E **127** B1
Baliza *Brazil* 16°0S 52°20W **331** D7
Baljurashī *Si. Arabia* 19°51N 41°33E **248** C3
Balkan □ *Turkmenistan* 40°0N 54°30E **216** D5
Balkan Mts. = Stara Planina
Bulgaria 43°15N 23°0E **202** C7
Balkanabat *Turkmenistan* 39°30N 54°22E **247** B7
Balkh *Afghan.* 36°44N 66°47E **217** E7
Balkh □ *Afghan.* 36°50N 67°0E **240** A2
Balkhash = Balqash
Kazakhstan 46°50N 74°50E **214** E8
Balkhash, Ozero = Balqash Köli
Kazakhstan 46°0N 74°50E **217** C8
Balkonda *India* 18°52N 78°21E **244** E4
Ballachulish *U.K.* 56°41N 5°8W **167** E3
Balladonia *Australia* 32°27S 123°51E **279** F3
Ballaghaderreen *Ireland* 53°55N 8°34W **166** C3
Ballan *Australia* 37°35S 144°13E **282** D6
Ballarat *Australia* 37°33S 143°50E **282** D5
Ballard, L. *Australia* 29°20S 120°40E **279** E3
Ballater *U.K.* 57°3N 3°3W **167** D5
Ballé *Mali* 15°18N 8°33W **262** B3
Ballenas, Canal de
Mexico 29°10N 113°29W **318** B2
Balleny Is. *Antarctica* 66°30S 163°0E **151** C11
Balleroy *France* 49°11N 0°50W **172** C6
Ballerup *Denmark* 55°43N 12°21E **118** A2
Ballestas, Is. *Peru* 13°44S 76°25W **330** C2
Ballı *Turkey* 40°50N 27°3E **203** F11
Ballia *India* 25°46N 84°12E **243** G11
Ballina *N.S.W., Australia* 28°50S 153°31E **281** D5
Ballina *Mayo, Ireland* 54°7N 9°9W **166** B2
Ballinasloe *Ireland* 53°20N 8°13W **166** C3
Ballinger *U.S.A.* 31°45N 99°57W **314** F5
Ballinrobe *Ireland* 53°38N 9°13W **166** C2
Ballinskelligs B. *Ireland* 51°48N 10°13W **166** E1
Ballinteer *Ireland* 53°17N 6°15W **120** B2
Ballon *France* 48°10N 0°14E **172** D7
Ballons des Vosges △ *France* 48°0N 7°0E **173** E14
Ballsh *Albania* 40°36N 19°44E **202** F3
Ballston Spa *U.S.A.* 43°0N 73°51W **313** D11
Ballyboden *Ireland* 53°17N 6°18W **120** B2
Ballyboghil *Ireland* 53°32N 6°16W **166** C5
Ballybrack *Ireland* 53°15N 6°7W **120** B3
Ballybunion *Ireland* 52°31N 9°40W **166** D2
Ballycanew *Ireland* 52°37N 6°19W **166** D5
Ballycastle *U.K.* 55°12N 6°15W **166** A5
Ballyclare *U.K.* 54°46N 6°0W **166** B5
Ballydehob *Ireland* 51°34N 9°28W **166** E2
Ballyfermot *Ireland* 53°20N 6°21W **120** A1
Ballygawley *U.K.* 54°27N 7°2W **166** B4
Ballyhaunis *Ireland* 53°46N 8°46W **166** C3
Ballyheige *Ireland* 52°23N 9°49W **166** D2
Ballymena *U.K.* 54°52N 6°17W **166** B5
Ballymoney *U.K.* 55°5N 6°31W **166** A5
Ballymorefinn Hill *Ireland* 53°14N 6°22W **120** B1
Ballymote *Ireland* 54°5N 8°31W **166** B3
Ballymun *Ireland* 53°23N 6°16W **120** A2
Ballynahinch *U.K.* 54°24N 5°54W **166** B6
Ballyquintin Pt. *U.K.* 54°20N 5°30W **166** B6
Ballyshannon *Ireland* 54°30N 8°11W **166** B3
Balmaceda *Chile* 46°0S 71°50W **336** C2
Balmain *Australia* 33°51S 151°11E **139** B2
Balmaseda *Spain* 43°11N 3°12W **196** B1
Balmazújváros *Hungary* 47°37N 21°21E **182** C6
Balmertown *Canada* 51°4N 93°41W **297** C10
Balmoral *Australia* 37°15S 141°48E **282** D4
Balmorhea *U.S.A.* 30°59N 103°45W **314** F3
Balochistan = Baluchistan □
Pakistan 27°30N 65°0E **240** D2
Balod *India* 20°44N 81°13E **244** D5
Balombo *Angola* 12°21S 14°46E **265** E2
Balombo → *Angola* 11°57S 13°48E **265** E2
Balonne → *Australia* 28°47S 147°56E **281** D4
Balotra *India* 25°50N 72°14E **242** G5
Balpyq Bī *Kazakhstan* 44°52N 78°12E **217** D9
Balqash *Kazakhstan* 46°50N 74°50E **214** E8
Balqash Köli *Kazakhstan* 46°0N 74°50E **217** C8
Balrampur *India* 27°30N 82°20E **243** F10
Balranald *Australia* 34°38S 143°33E **282** C5
Balş *Romania* 44°22N 24°5E **183** F9
Balsapuerto *Peru* 5°48S 76°33W **330** B2
Balsas → *Maranhão, Brazil* 7°15S 44°35W **332** C3
Balsas → *Tocantins, Brazil* 9°58S 47°52W **332** C2
Balsas → *Michoacán,*
Mexico 17°55N 102°10W **318** D4
Balsas del Norte *Mexico* 18°0N 99°46W **319** D5
Bålsta *Sweden* 59°35N 17°30E **162** E11
Balta *Romania* 44°54N 22°38E **182** F7
Balta *Ukraine* 47°56N 29°45E **183** C14
Baltaköl *Kazakhstan* 43°7N 67°46E **217** D7
Baltanás *Spain* 41°56N 4°15W **194** D6
Bălți *Moldova* 47°48N 27°58E **183** C12
Baltic Sea *Europe* 57°0N 19°0E **161** H18
Baltîm *Egypt* 31°35N 31°10E **256** H7
Baltimore *Cork, Ireland* 51°29N 9°22W **166** E2
Baltimore *Md., U.S.A.* 39°17N 76°36W **309** F15
Baltimore *Ohio, U.S.A.* 39°51N 82°36W **312** G2
Baltinglass *Ireland* 52°56N 6°43W **166** D5
Baltit *Pakistan* 36°15N 74°40E **243** A6
Baltiysk *Russia* 54°41N 19°58E **184** D6
Baltiyskiy = Paldiski
Estonia 59°23N 24°9E **188** C3
Baltra, I. *Ecuador* 0°26S 90°16W **330** a
Baltrum *Germany* 53°43N 7°24E **178** B3
Baluan I. *Papua N. G.* 2°33S 147°17E **286** B4
Baluchistan □ *Pakistan* 27°30N 65°0E **240** D2
Balud *Phil.* 12°2N 123°12E **232** E4
Baluhati *India* 22°39N 88°15E **124** B1
Baluqtybulaq *Kazakhstan* 50°51N 51°8E **190** E10
Baluran △ *Indonesia* 7°50S 114°23E **235** D4
Balurghat *India* 25°15N 88°44E **241** C2
Balut I. *Phil.* 5°24N 125°23E **233** J5
Balvanera *Argentina* 34°37S 58°23W **117** B2
Balvi *Latvia* 57°8N 27°15E **188** D4
Balwyn *Australia* 37°48S 145°4E **128** A2
Balwyn North *Australia* 37°47S 145°4E **128** A2
Balya *Turkey* 39°44N 27°35E **205** B9
Balykchy *Kyrgyzstan* 42°26N 76°12E **217** D9
Balyqshy *Kazakhstan* 47°4N 51°52E **187** E9
Balzar *Ecuador* 2°2S 79°54W **328** D2
Bam *Iran* 29°7N 58°14E **247** D8
Bama *Guangxi Zhuangzu,*
China 24°8N 107°12E **228** E6
Bama *Nigeria* 11°33N 13°41E **263** C7
Bamaga *Australia* 10°50S 142°25E **280** A3
Bamaji L. *Canada* 51°9N 91°25W **298** B1
Bamako *Mali* 12°34N 7°55W **262** C3
Bamba
Dem. Rep. of the Congo 5°45S 18°23E **265** D3
Bamba *Mali* 17°5N 1°24W **263** B4
Bambama *Congo* 2°32S 13°32E **264** C2
Bambamarca *Peru* 6°36S 78°32W **330** B2
Bamban *Phil.* 16°23N 121°6E **232** C3
Bambannan I. *Phil.* 5°37N 120°17E **233** J3
Bambao *Comoros Is.* 12°11S 44°31E **272** a
Bambara Maoundé *Mali* 13°26N 4°3W **262** B4
Bambari *C.A.R.* 5°40N 20°35E **264** A4
Bambaroo *Australia* 18°50S 146°10E **280** B4
Bambaya *Guinea* 10°55N 13°38W **262** D2
Bamberg *Bayern, Germany* 49°54N 10°54E **179** F6
Bamberg *S.C., U.S.A.* 33°18N 81°2W **316** B8
Bambesi *Ethiopia* 9°45N 34°40E **257** F3
Bambey *Senegal* 14°42N 16°28W **262** C1
Bambili
Dem. Rep. of the Congo 3°40N 26°0E **268** B2
Bambinga
Dem. Rep. of the Congo 3°43S 18°53E **264** C3
Bambio *C.A.R.* 3°55N 16°57E **264** B3
Bamboi *Ghana* 8°13N 2°1W **262** D4
Bamboo Avenue *Jamaica* 18°6N 77°47W **320** a
Bambous *Mauritius* 20°15S 57°24E **272** e
Bambouti *C.A.R.* 5°24N 27°12E **264** A5
Bambuí *Brazil* 20°1S 45°58W **333** F2
Bamburgh *U.K.* 55°37N 1°43W **168** B6
Bamenda *Cameroon* 5°57N 10°11E **263** D7
Bamendjing, L. de
Cameroon 5°50N 10°30E **263** D7
Bamfield *Canada* 48°45N 125°10W **296** D3
Bāmīān *Afghan.* 34°49N 67°49E **217** F7
Bāmīān □ *Afghan.* 35°0N 67°0E **240** B2
Bamiancheng *China* 43°15N 124°2E **227** C13
Bamingui *C.A.R.* 7°34N 20°11E **264** A4
Bamingui → *C.A.R.* 8°33N 19°5E **264** A3
Bamingui-Bangoran △
C.A.R. 8°30N 19°46E **264** A3
Bamkin *Cameroon* 6°3N 11°27E **263** D7
Bampūr *Iran* 27°15N 60°21E **247** E9
Bampūr → *Iran* 27°24N 59°0E **247** E8
Bamu → *Papua N. G.* 8°1S 143°33E **286** E2
Ban *Burkina Faso* 14°5N 2°27W **262** C4
Ban Ao Tu Khun *Thailand* 8°9N 98°20E **237** a
Ban Ban *Laos* 19°31N 103°30E **236** C4
Ban Bang Hin *Thailand* 9°32N 98°35E **237** H2
Ban Bang Khu *Thailand* 7°57N 98°23E **237** a
Ban Bang Rong *Thailand* 8°3N 98°25E **237** a
Ban Bo Phut *Thailand* 9°33N 100°2E **237** b
Ban Chaweng *Thailand* 9°32N 100°3E **237** b
Ban Chiang *Thailand* 17°30N 103°10E **236** D4
Ban Chiang Klang
Thailand 19°25N 100°55E **236** C3
Ban Choho *Thailand* 15°2N 102°9E **236** E4
Ban Dan Lan Hoi *Thailand* 17°0N 99°35E **236** D2
Ban Don = Surat Thani
Thailand 9°6N 99°20E **237** H2
Ban Don *Vietnam* 12°53N 107°48E **236** F6
Ban Don, Ao → *Thailand* 9°20N 99°25E **237** H2
Ban Dong *Thailand* 19°30N 100°59E **236** C3
Ban Hong *Thailand* 18°18N 98°50E **236** C2
Ban Hua Thanon *Thailand* 9°26N 100°1E **237** b
Ban Kantang *Thailand* 7°25N 99°31E **237** J2
Ban Karon *Thailand* 7°51N 98°18E **237** a
Ban Kata *Thailand* 7°50N 98°18E **237** a
Ban Keun *Laos* 18°22N 102°35E **236** C4
Ban Khai *Thailand* 12°46N 101°18E **236** F3
Ban Kheun *Laos* 20°13N 101°7E **236** B3
Ban Khlong Khian *Thailand* 8°10N 98°26E **237** a
Ban Khlong Kua *Thailand* 6°57N 100°8E **237** J3
Ban Khuan *Thailand* 8°20N 98°25E **237** a
Ban Ko Yai Chim *Thailand* 11°17N 99°26E **237** G2
Ban Laem *Thailand* 13°13N 99°59E **236** F2
Ban Lamai *Thailand* 9°28N 100°3E **237** b
Ban Lao Ngam *Laos* 15°28N 106°10E **236** E6
Ban Le Kathe *Thailand* 15°49N 98°53E **236** E2
Ban Lo Po Noi *Thailand* 8°1N 98°34E **237** a
Ban Mae Chedi *Thailand* 19°11N 99°31E **236** C2
Ban Mae Nam *Thailand* 9°34N 100°0E **237** b
Ban Mae Sariang *Thailand* 18°10N 97°56E **236** C1
Ban Mê Thuột = Buon Ma Thuot
Vietnam 12°40N 108°3E **236** F7
Ban Mi *Thailand* 15°3N 100°32E **236** E3
Ban Muang Mo *Laos* 19°4N 103°58E **236** C4
Ban Na Bo *Thailand* 9°19N 99°41E **237** b
Ban Na San *Thailand* 8°53N 99°52E **237** H2
Ban Na Tong *Laos* 20°56N 101°47E **236** B3
Ban Nam Bac *Laos* 20°38N 102°20E **236** B4
Ban Nammi *Laos* 17°7N 105°40E **236** D5
Ban Nong Bok *Laos* 17°5N 104°48E **236** D5
Ban Nong Pling *Thailand* 15°40N 100°10E **236** E3
Ban Pak Chan *Thailand* 10°32N 98°51E **237** G2
Ban Patong *Thailand* 7°54N 98°18E **237** a
Ban Phai *Thailand* 16°4N 102°44E **236** D4
Ban Phak Chit *Thailand* 8°0N 98°24E **237** a
Ban Pong *Thailand* 13°50N 99°55E **236** F2
Ban Rawai *Thailand* 7°47N 98°20E **237** a
Ban Ron Phibun *Thailand* 8°9N 99°51E **237** H2
Ban Sakhu *Thailand* 8°4N 98°18E **237** a
Ban Sanam Chai *Thailand* 7°33N 100°25E **237** J3
Ban Tak *Thailand* 17°2N 99°4E **236** D2
Ban Tako *Thailand* 14°5N 102°40E **236** E4
Ban Tha Nun *Thailand* 8°12N 98°18E **237** a
Ban Tha Rua *Thailand* 7°59N 98°22E **237** a
Ban Tha Yu *Thailand* 8°17N 98°22E **237** a
Ban Thong Krut *Thailand* 9°25N 99°57E **237** b
Ban Xien Kok *Laos* 20°54N 100°39E **236** B3
Ban Yen Nhan *Vietnam* 20°57N 106°2E **236** B6
Banā, W. → *Yemen* 13°3N 45°24E **248** D4
Banaadir □ *Somali Rep.* 2°7N 45°24E **267** D6
Banaba *Kiribati* 0°45S 169°50E **288** H8
Banalia
Dem. Rep. of the Congo 1°32N 25°5E **268** B2
Banam *Cambodia* 11°20N 105°17E **237** G5
Banamba *Mali* 13°29N 7°22W **262** C3
Banana Is. *S. Leone* 8°7N 13°15W **262** D2
Bananal, I. do *Brazil* 11°30S 50°30W **333** D1
Bananga *India* 6°57N 93°54E **245** L11
Bananier *Guadeloupe* 16°0N 61°36W **322** e
Banaras = Varanasi *India* 25°22N 83°0E **243** G10
Banas → *Gujarat, India* 23°45N 71°25E **242** H4
Banas → *Mad. P., India* 24°15N 81°30E **243** G9
Bânâs, Ras *Egypt* 23°57N 35°59E **256** C4
Banática *Portugal* 38°40N 9°11W **126** A1
Banaue *Phil.* 16°55N 121°4E **232** C3
Banaz *Turkey* 38°46N 29°46E **205** C11
Banaz → *Turkey* 38°12N 29°14E **205** C11
Banbridge *U.K.* 54°22N 6°16W **166** B5
Banbury *U.K.* 52°4N 1°20W **169** E6
Banc d'Arguin △
Mauritania 20°10N 16°20W **260** D1
Banchory *U.K.* 57°3N 2°29W **167** D6
Banco *Ethiopia* 6°12N 38°13E **257** F4
Banco do Brasil, Centro Cultural
Rio de J., Brazil **135** a2
Bancoran *Phil.* 7°45N 118°30E **233** H2
Bancroft = Chililabombwe
Zambia 12°18S 27°43E **269** E2
Bancroft *Canada* 45°3N 77°51W **312** A7
Band *Romania* 46°30N 24°25E **183** D9
Band Bonī *Iran* 25°30N 59°33E **247** E8
Band-e Torkestan *Afghan.* 35°30N 64°0E **240** B2
Band Qīr *Iran* 31°39N 48°53E **247** D6
Banda *Cameroon* 3°58N 14°32E **264** B2
Banda *Mad. P., India* 24°3N 78°57E **243** G8
Banda *Maharashtra, India* 15°49N 73°52E **245** G1
Banda *Ut. P., India* 25°30N 80°26E **243** G9
Banda, Kepulauan
Indonesia 4°37S 129°50E **231** E7
Banda Aceh *Indonesia* 5°35N 95°20E **234** A1
Banda Banda, Mt.
Australia 31°10S 152°28E **283** A10
Banda Elat *Indonesia* 5°40S 133°5E **231** F8
Banda Is. = Banda, Kepulauan
Indonesia 4°37S 129°50E **231** E7
Banda Kani
Dem. Rep. of the Congo 4°48S 13°52E **265** C2
Banda Sea *Indonesia* 6°0S 130°0E **231** F8
Bandai-Asahi △ *Japan* 37°38N 140°5E **220** F10
Bandai-San *Japan* 37°36N 140°4E **220** F10
Bandak *Norway* 59°23N 8°29E **164** E5
Bandama → *Ivory C.* 6°32N 4°30W **262** D3
Bandama Blanc → *Ivory C.* 6°55N 5°30W **262** D4
Bandama Rouge →
Ivory C. 6°55N 5°30W **262** D4
Bandamadji *Comoros Is.* 11°47S 43°26E **272** a
Bandān *Iran* 31°23N 60°44E **247** D9
Bandanaira *Indonesia* 4°32S 129°54E **231** E7
Bandanwara *India* 26°9N 74°38E **242** F6
Bandar = Machilipatnam
India 16°12N 81°8E **245** F5
Bandar-e Abbās *Iran* 27°15N 56°15E **247** E8
Bandar-e Anzalī *Iran* 37°30N 49°30E **213** D13
Bandar-e Bushehr = Būshehr
Iran 28°55N 50°55E **247** D6
Bandar-e Chārak *Iran* 26°45N 54°20E **247** E7
Bandar-e Deylam *Iran* 30°5N 50°10E **247** D6
Bandar-e Emām Khomeynī
Iran 30°30N 49°5E **247** D6
Bandar-e Lengeh *Iran* 26°35N 54°58E **247** E7
Bandar-e Maqām *Iran* 26°56N 53°29E **247** E7
Bandar-e Ma'shur *Iran* 30°35N 49°10E **247** D6
Bandar-e Rīg *Iran* 29°29N 50°38E **247** D6
Bandar-e Torkeman *Iran* 37°0N 54°10E **247** B7
Bandar Labuan *Malaysia* 5°20N 115°14E **235** A5
Bandar Lampung
Indonesia 5°20S 105°10E **234** D3
Bandar Maharani = Muar
Malaysia 2°3N 102°34E **237** L4
Bandar Penggaram = Batu Pahat
Malaysia 1°50N 102°56E **237** M4
Bandar Seri Begawan
Brunei 4°52N 115°0E **235** B4
Bandar Sri Aman
Malaysia 1°15N 111°32E **235** B4
Bandawe *Malawi* 11°58S 34°5E **269** E3
Bande *Spain* 42°3N 7°58W **194** C3
Bandeira, Pico da *Brazil* 20°26S 41°47W **333** F3
Bandeirante *Brazil* 13°41S 50°48W **333** D1
Bandera *Argentina* 28°55S 62°20W **334** B3
Banderas, B. de *Mexico* 20°40N 105°25W **318** C3
Bandhavgarh *India* 23°40N 81°2E **243** H9
Bandhavgarh △ *India* 23°45N 81°10E **244** C5
Bandi → *India* 26°12N 75°47E **242** F6
Bandia → *India* 19°2N 80°28E **244** E5
Bandiagara *Mali* 14°12N 3°29W **262** C4
Bandikui *India* 27°3N 76°34E **242** F7
Bandipur △ *India* 11°45N 76°30E **245** J3
Bandırma *Turkey* 40°20N 28°0E **203** F11
Bandjarmasin = Banjarmasin
Indonesia 3°20S 114°35E **235** C4
Bandol *France* 43°8N 5°46E **175** E9
Bandon *Ireland* 51°44N 8°44W **166** E3
Bandon → *Ireland* 51°43N 8°37W **166** E3
Bandra *India* 19°3N 72°49E **130** A1
Bandra Pt. *India* 19°2N 72°49E **130** A1
Bandraboua *Mayotte* 12°42S 45°8E **272** b
Bandrélé *Mayotte* 12°54S 45°11E **272** b
Bandula *Mozam.* 19°0S 33°7E **269** F3
Bandundu
Dem. Rep. of the Congo 3°15S 17°22E **264** C3
Bandundu □
Dem. Rep. of the Congo 3°30S 17°30E **264** C3
Bandung *Indonesia* 6°54S 107°36E **235** D3
Bané *Burkina Faso* 11°42N 0°15W **263** C4
Băneasa *Romania* 45°56N 27°55E **183** E12
Bāneh *Iran* 35°59N 45°53E **213** E11
Banes *Cuba* 21°0N 75°42W **320** B4
Banff *Alta., Canada* 51°10N 115°34W **296** C5
Banff *Aberds., U.K.* 57°40N 2°33W **167** D6
Banff △ *Canada* 51°30N 116°15W **296** C5
Banfora *Burkina Faso* 10°40N 4°40W **262** C4
Bang Fai → *Laos* 16°57N 104°45E **236** D5
Bang Hieng → *Laos* 16°10N 105°10E **236** D5
Bang Kapi *Thailand* 13°45N 100°38E **113** B2
Bang Krathum *Thailand* 16°34N 100°18E **236** D3
Bang Lamung *Thailand* 13°3N 100°56E **236** F3
Bang Lang △ *Thailand* 5°58N 101°19E **237** K3
Bang Lang Res. *Thailand* 6°6N 101°17E **237** J3
Bang Mun Nak *Thailand* 16°2N 100°23E **236** D3
Bang Na *Thailand* 13°40N 100°36E **113** B2
Bang Pa In *Thailand* 14°14N 100°35E **236** E3
Bang Phlad *Bangkok, Thailand* **113** a1
Bang Rakam *Thailand* 16°45N 100°7E **236** D3
Bang Saphan *Thailand* 11°14N 99°28E **237** G2
Bang Thao *Thailand* 7°59N 98°18E **237** a
Banga *Angola* 8°43S 15°13E **265** D3
Banga *Dem. Rep. of the Congo* 5°25S 20°28E **265** D4
Banga *Aklan, Phil.* 11°38N 122°20E **233** F4
Banga *S. Cotabato, Phil.* 6°21N 124°47E **233** H5
Bangaduni I. *India* 21°34N 88°52E **241** E2
Bangala Dam *Zimbabwe* 21°7S 31°25E **269** G3
Bangalore *India* 12°59N 77°40E **245** H3
Banganapalle *India* 15°19N 78°14E **245** G4
Banganga → *India* 27°6N 77°25E **242** F6
Bangangté *Cameroon* 5°8N 10°32E **263** D7
Bangaon *India* 23°0N 88°47E **243** H13
Bangar *Brunei* 4°43N 115°4E **235** B4
Bangar *La Union, Phil.* 16°54N 120°25E **232** C3
Bangassou *C.A.R.* 4°55N 23°7E **264** B4
Bangbae *S. Korea* 37°29N 126°59E **137** C1
Bangeta, Mt. *Papua N. G.* 6°21S 147°3E **286** D4
Banggai *Indonesia* 1°34S 123°30E **231** E6
Banggai, Kepulauan
Indonesia 1°40S 123°30E **231** E6
Banggai Arch. = Banggai,
Kepulauan *Indonesia* 1°40S 123°30E **231** E6
Banggi, Pulau *Malaysia* 7°17N 117°12E **235** A5
Banghāzī *Libya* 32°11N 20°3E **258** B4
Banghāzī □ *Libya* 32°7N 20°4E **258** B4
Bangil *Indonesia* 7°36S 112°50E **235** D4
Bangjang *South Sudan* 11°23N 32°41E **257** E3
Bangka *Sulawesi, Indonesia* 1°50N 125°5E **231** D7
Bangka *Sumatera, Indonesia* 2°0S 105°50E **234** C3
Bangka, Selat *Indonesia* 2°30S 105°30E **234** C3
Bangka-Belitung □
Indonesia 2°30S 107°0E **234** C3
Bangkalan *Indonesia* 7°2S 112°46E **235** D4
Bangkaru *Indonesia* 2°4N 97°7E **234** B1
Bangkhen *Thailand* 13°52N 100°36E **113** A2
Bangkinang *Indonesia* 0°18N 101°5E **234** B2
Bangko *Indonesia* 2°5S 102°9E **234** C2
Bangkok *Thailand* 13°45N 100°35E **113** B2
Bangkok, Bight of
Thailand 12°55N 100°30E **236** F3
Bangkok Don Muang Int. ✈ (BKK)
Thailand 13°53N 100°36E **113** A2
Bangkok Noi *Thailand* 13°45N 100°29E **113** B1
Bangkok Yai *Thailand* 13°43N 100°29E **113** B1
Bangla = West Bengal □
India 23°0N 88°0E **243** H13
Bangladesh ■ *Asia* 24°0N 90°0E **241** D2
Bangli *Indonesia* 8°27S 115°21E **231** J18
Banglo *India* 22°31N 88°14E **124** B1
Bangoi-Kouni *Comoros Is.* 11°22S 43°21E **272** a
Bangolo *Ivory C.* 7°1N 7°29W **262** D3
Bangong Co *China* 33°45N 78°43E **243** C8
Bangor *Down, U.K.* 54°40N 5°40W **166** B6
Bangor *Gwynedd, U.K.* 53°14N 4°8W **168** D3
Bangor *Maine, U.S.A.* 44°48N 68°46W **309** C19
Bangor *Mich., U.S.A.* 42°18N 86°7W **311** B10
Bangor *Pa., U.S.A.* 40°52N 75°13W **313** F9
Bangoran → *C.A.R.* 8°42N 19°6E **264** A3
Bangrak *Thailand* 13°43N 100°31E **113** B2
Bangsu *Thailand* 13°49N 100°31E **113** B2
Bangu *Dem. Rep. of the Congo* 0°3S 19°12E **264** C3
Bangued *Phil.* 17°40N 120°37E **232** C3
Bangui *C.A.R.* 4°23N 18°35E **264** B3
Bangui *Phil.* 18°32N 120°46E **232** B3
Bangui B. *Phil.* 18°33N 120°43E **232** B3
Banguru
Dem. Rep. of the Congo 0°30N 27°10E **268** B2
Bangweulu, L. *Zambia* 11°0S 30°0E **269** E3
Bangweulu Swamp
Zambia 11°20S 30°15E **269** E3
Banhine △ *Mozam.* 22°49S 32°55E **271** B5
Bani *Burkina Faso* 13°43N 0°10W **263** C4
Bani *C.A.R.* 7°6N 22°50E **264** A4
Baní *Dom. Rep.* 18°16N 70°22W **321** C5
Bani *Phil.* 16°11N 119°52E **232** C2
Bani → *Mali* 14°30N 4°12W **262** C4
Bani, Jebel *Morocco* 29°16N 8°0W **260** C3
Bani Bangou *Niger* 15°3N 2°42E **263** B5
Banī Sa'd *Iraq* 33°34N 44°32E **213** F11
Banī Walīd *Libya* 31°36N 13°53E **258** B2
Banī Walīd □ *Libya* 31°46N 13°59E **258** B2
Bania *C.A.R.* 4°1N 15°7E **264** B3
Bania *Ivory C.* 9°4N 3°6W **262** D4
Baniara *Papua N. G.* 9°44S 149°54E **286** E5
Banihal Pass *India* 33°30N 75°12E **243** C6
Banikoara *Benin* 11°18N 2°26E **263** C5
Banīnah *Libya* 32°0N 20°12E **258** B4

Banissa *Kenya* 3°55N 40°19E **257 G5**
Bāniyās *Syria* 35°10N 36°0E **250 C7**
Banja Luka *Bos.-H.* 44°49N 17°11E **182 F2**
Banjar *India* 31°38N 77°21E **242 D7**
Banjar → *India* 22°36N 80°22E **243 H9**
Banjarbaru *Indonesia* 3°25S 114°49E **235 C4**
Banjarmasin *Indonesia* 3°20S 114°35E **235 C4**
Banjul *Gambia* 13°28N 16°40W **262 C1**
Bank *London, U.K.* **125 b5**
Bank of America *San Francisco, U.S.A.* **136 b2**
Bank of China Tower *Hong Kong, China* **122 c1**
Banka *India* 24°53N 86°55E **243 G12**
Bankas *Mali* 14°4N 3°31W **262 C4**
Bankeryd *Sweden* 57°53N 14°6E **163 G8**
Banket *Zimbabwe* 17°27S 30°19E **269 F3**
Bankilaré *Niger* 14°35N 0°44E **263 C5**
Bankot *India* 17°58N 73°2E **244 F1**
Banks *U.S.A.* 31°49N 85°51W **316 D4**
Banks, C. *Australia* 34°0S 151°16E **139 C2**
Banks I. = Moa *Australia* 10°11S 142°16E **280 a**
Banks I. *B.C., Canada* 53°20N 130°0W **296 C3**
Banks I. *N.W.T., Canada* 73°15N 121°30W **294 C7**
Banks Is. *Vanuatu* 13°50S 167°30E **287 C5**
Banks L. *U.S.A.* 31°2N 83°6W **316 D6**
Banks Pen. *N.Z.* 43°45S 173°15E **285 D8**
Banks Str. *Australia* 40°40S 148°10E **281 G4**
Banksmeadow *Australia* 33°57S 151°12E **139 B2**
Bankumuna
Dem. Rep. of the Congo 4°28S 19°57E **265 C3**
Bankura *India* 23°11N 87°18E **243 H12**
Bankya *Bulgaria* 42°43N 23°8E **202 D7**
Banmankhi *India* 25°53N 87°11E **243 G12**
Banmauk *Burma* 24°24N 95°51E **241 C5**
Bann → *Armagh, U.K.* 54°30N 6°31W **166 B5**
Bann → *L'derry., U.K.* 55°8N 6°41W **166 A5**
Bannaanka Saraar
Somali Rep. 9°20N 46°17E **267 C6**
Bannalec *France* 47°57N 3°42W **172 E3**
Bannang Sata *Thailand* 6°16N 101°16E **237 J3**
Bannerton *Australia* 34°42S 142°47E **282 C5**
Banning *U.S.A.* 33°56N 116°53W **307 M10**
Banningville = Bandundu
Dem. Rep. of the Congo 3°15S 17°22E **264 C3**
Banno *Ethiopia* 4°51N 37°24E **257 G4**
Bannō-saki *Japan* 26°33N 128°8E **288 a**
Bannockburn *Ont., Canada* 44°39N 77°33W **312 B7**
Bannockburn *Stirling, U.K.* 56°5N 3°55W **167 E5**
Bannockburn *Zimbabwe* 20°17S 29°48E **269 G2**
Bannu *Pakistan* 33°0N 70°18E **240 B3**
Bano *India* 22°40N 84°55E **243 H11**
Bañolas = Banyoles *Spain* 42°16N 2°44E **196 C7**
Banon *France* 44°2N 5°38E **175 D9**
Baños de la Encina *Spain* 38°10N 3°46W **195 G7**
Baños de Molgas *Spain* 42°15N 7°40W **194 C3**
Bánovce nad Bebravou
Slovak Rep. 48°44N 18°16E **181 C11**
Banovići *Bos.-H.* 44°25N 18°32E **182 F3**
Bansagar Dam *India* 24°11N 81°17E **244 B5**
Bansalan *Phil.* 6°55N 125°13E **233 H5**
Bansgaon *India* 26°33N 83°21E **243 F10**
Banská Bystrica
Slovak Rep. 48°46N 19°14E **181 C12**
Banská Štiavnica
Slovak Rep. 48°25N 18°55E **181 C11**
Bansko *Bulgaria* 41°52N 23°28E **202 E7**
Banskobystrický □
Slovak Rep. 48°20N 19°0E **181 C12**
Banstala *India* 22°31N 88°24E **124 B2**
Banswara *India* 23°32N 74°24E **242 H6**
Bantaeng *Indonesia* 5°32S 119°56E **235 D5**
Bantayan *Phil.* 11°10N 123°43E **233 F4**
Bantayan I. *Phil.* 11°13N 123°44E **233 F4**
Banteay Prei Nokor
Cambodia 11°56N 105°40E **237 G5**
Banten *Indonesia* 6°5S 106°8E **234 D3**
Banten □ *Indonesia* 6°30S 106°0E **234 D3**
Banton I. *Phil.* 12°56N 122°4E **232 E4**
Bantra *India* 22°35N 88°18E **124 B1**
Bantry *Ireland* 51°41N 9°27W **166 E2**
Bantry B. *Ireland* 51°37N 9°44W **166 E2**
Bantva *India* 21°29N 70°12E **242 J4**
Bantval *India* 12°55N 75°0E **245 H2**
Banya *Bulgaria* 42°33N 24°50E **203 D8**
Banyak, Kepulauan
Indonesia 2°10N 97°10E **234 B1**
Banyalbufar *Spain* 39°42N 2°31E **206 B3**
Banyeres de Mariola *Spain* 38°44N 0°38W **197 G4**
Banyo *Cameroon* 6°52N 11°45E **263 D7**
Banyoles *Spain* 42°16N 2°44E **196 C7**
Banyuls-sur-Mer *France* 42°28N 3°8E **174 F7**
Banyuwangi *Indonesia* 8°13S 114°21E **231 J17**
Banz *Papua N. G.* 5°45S 144°37E **286 C3**
Banza *Dem. Rep. of the Congo* 0°26N 20°10E **264 B4**
Banzare Coast *Antarctica* 68°0S 125°0E **151 C9**
Banzyville = Mobayi
Dem. Rep. of the Congo 4°15N 21°8E **264 B4**
Bao Ha *Vietnam* 22°11N 104°21E **228 F5**
Bao Lac *Vietnam* 22°57N 105°40E **236 A5**
Bao Loc *Vietnam* 11°32N 107°48E **237 G6**
Bao'an *China* 22°34N 113°52E **219 a**
Baocheng *China* 33°12N 106°56E **228 A6**
Baode *China* 39°1N 111°5E **226 E6**
Baodi *China* 39°38N 117°20E **227 E9**
Baoding *China* 38°50N 115°28E **226 E8**
Baoji *China* 34°20N 107°5E **226 G4**
Baojing *China* 28°45N 109°41E **228 C7**
Baokang *China* 31°54N 111°12E **229 B8**
Baoro *C.A.R.* 5°40N 15°58E **264 A3**
Baoshan *Shanghai, China* 31°24N 121°28E **138 A1**
Baoshan *Yunnan, China* 25°10N 99°5E **228 E2**
Baotou *China* 40°32N 110°2E **226 D6**
Baotow = Baotou *China* 40°32N 110°2E **226 D6**
Baoulé → *Mali* 12°36N 9°45W **262 C3**
Baoxing *China* 30°24N 102°50E **228 B4**
Baoying *China* 33°17N 119°20E **227 H10**
Baoyou = Ledong *China* 18°41N 109°5E **236 C7**
Bap *India* 27°23N 72°18E **242 F5**
Bapatla *India* 15°55N 80°30E **245 G5**
Bapaume *France* 50°7N 2°50E **173 B9**
Baqar, Bahr el → *Egypt* 31°7N 32°6E **251 G3**
Bāqerābād *Iran* 33°2N 51°58E **247 C6**
Ba'qūbah *Iraq* 33°45N 44°50E **213 F11**
Baquedano *Chile* 23°20S 69°52W **334 A2**
Bar *Montenegro* 42°8N 19°6E **202 D3**
Bar *Ukraine* 49°4N 27°40E **217 H4**
Bar Bigha *India* 25°21N 85°47E **243 G11**
Bar Giyora *Israel* 31°45N 35°5E **123 B1**
Bar Harbor *U.S.A.* 44°23N 68°13W **309 C19**
Bar-le-Duc *France* 48°47N 5°10E **173 D12**
Bar-sur-Aube *France* 48°14N 4°40E **173 D11**
Bar-sur-Seine *France* 48°7N 4°20E **173 D11**
Bara *India* 25°16N 81°43E **243 G9**
Bâra *Romania* 47°2N 27°3E **183 C12**
Bara *Sudan* 13°42N 30°22E **266 B3**
Bara Banki *India* 26°55N 81°12E **243 F9**
Baraawe *Somali Rep.* 1°20N 44°8E **267 D5**
Barabai *Indonesia* 2°32S 115°34E **235 C5**
Baraboo *U.S.A.* 43°28N 89°45W **308 D9**
Baracoa *Cuba* 20°20N 74°30W **321 B5**
Baradā → *Syria* 33°33N 36°34E **250 E7**
Baradero *Argentina* 33°52S 59°29W **334 C4**
Baradine *Australia* 30°56S 149°4E **283 A8**
Baraga *U.S.A.* 46°47N 88°30W **308 B9**
Bărăganul *Romania* 44°49N 27°31E **183 F12**
Baragoi *Kenya* 1°47N 36°47E **268 B4**
Barah → *India* 27°42N 77°5E **242 F6**
Barahanagar *India* 22°39N 88°22E **124 B2**
Barahona *Dom. Rep.* 18°13N 71°7W **321 C5**
Barail Range *India* 25°15N 93°20E **241 C4**
Barajas *Spain* 40°28N 3°34W **127 B2**
Barajas, Madrid ✕ (MAD)
Spain 40°26N 3°34W **127 B2**
Barak → *India* 24°52N 92°30E **241 C4**
Baraka *Sudan* 10°59N 27°59E **257 E2**
Baraka → *Sudan* 18°13N 37°35E **256 D4**
Barakaldo *Spain* 43°18N 2°59W **196 B2**
Barakar → *India* 24°7N 86°14E **243 G12**
Barakee △ *Australia* 31°37S 151°53E **283 A9**
Barakot *India* 21°33N 84°59E **243 J11**
Barakpur *India* 22°47N 88°21E **124 A2**
Baralaba *Australia* 24°13S 149°50E **280 C4**
Baralla *Spain* 42°53N 7°15W **194 C3**
Baralzon L. *Canada* 60°0N 98°3W **297 B9**
Baram → *Malaysia* 4°35N 113°58E **235 B4**
Baramati *India* 18°11N 74°33E **244 E2**
Baramba *India* 20°25N 85°23E **244 D7**
Barameiya *Sudan* 18°32N 36°38E **256 D4**
Baramula *India* 34°15N 74°20E **243 B6**
Baran *India* 25°9N 76°40E **242 G7**
Baran → *Pakistan* 25°13N 68°17E **242 G3**
Barañain *Spain* 42°48N 1°40W **196 C3**
Baranavichy *Belarus* 53°10N 26°0E **177 B14**
Barani *Burkina Faso* 13°9N 3°51W **262 C4**
Baranoa *Colombia* 10°48N 74°55W **328 A3**
Baranof *U.S.A.* 57°5N 134°50W **296 B2**
Baranof I. *U.S.A.* 57°0N 135°0W **303 H14**
Baranów Sandomierski
Poland 50°29N 21°30E **185 H8**
Baranowicze = Baranavichy
Belarus 53°10N 26°0E **177 B14**
Baranya □ *Hungary* 46°0N 18°15E **182 E3**
Barão de Cocais *Brazil* 19°56S 43°28W **333 E3**
Barão de Grajaú *Brazil* 6°45S 43°1W **332 C3**
Barão de Melgaço *Mato Grosso,*
Brazil 16°14S 55°52W **331 D6**
Barão de Melgaço *Rondônia,*
Brazil 11°50S 60°45W **331 C5**
Baraolt *Romania* 46°5N 25°34E **183 D10**
Baraona *Spain* 41°17N 2°39W **196 D2**
Barapasi *Indonesia* 2°15S 137°5E **231 E9**
Barapina = Panguna
Papua N. G. 6°21S 155°25E **286 D8**
Baras *Phil.* 13°40N 124°22E **232 E5**
Barasat *India* 22°46N 88°31E **243 H13**
Barat Daya, Kepulauan
Indonesia 7°30S 128°0E **231 F7**
Baratang I. *India* 12°13N 92°45E **245 H11**
Barataria B. *U.S.A.* 29°20N 89°55W **315 G10**
Barauda *India* 23°33N 75°15E **242 H6**
Baraut *India* 29°13N 77°7E **242 E7**
Baraya *Colombia* 3°10N 75°4W **328 C2**
Barbacan = Roxas *Phil.* 10°20N 119°21E **233 F2**
Barbacena *Brazil* 21°15S 43°56W **333 F3**
Barbacoas *Colombia* 1°45N 78°0W **328 C2**
Barbados ■ *W. Indies* 13°10N 59°30W **323 r**
Barbalha *Brazil* 7°19S 39°17W **332 C4**
Barban *Croatia* 45°5N 14°2E **199 C11**
Barbària, C. de *Spain* 38°39N 1°24E **206 D1**
Barbaros *Turkey* 40°54N 27°27E **203 F11**
Barbas, C. *W. Sahara* 22°20N 16°42W **260 D1**
Barbastro *Spain* 42°2N 0°5E **196 C5**
Barbate *Spain* 36°13N 5°56W **195 J5**
Barbaza *Phil.* 11°12N 122°2E **233 F4**
Barbeau Pk. *Canada* 81°54N 75°1W **295 A16**
Barber *Curaçao* 12°17N 69°4W **322 g**
Barberini, Palazzo *Rome, Italy* **136 b3**
Barberino di Mugello *Italy* 44°0N 11°15E **199 E8**
Barbers Pt. *U.S.A.* 21°18N 158°7W **302 K13**
Barberton *Mpumalanga,*
S. Africa 25°42S 31°2E **271 C5**
Barberton *Ohio, U.S.A.* 41°1N 81°39W **312 E3**
Barberville *U.S.A.* 29°11N 81°26W **317 F8**
Barbezieux-St-Hilaire
France 45°28N 0°9W **174 C3**
Barbican *London, U.K.* **125 a4**
Barbosa *Colombia* 5°57N 73°37W **328 B3**
Barbourville *U.S.A.* 36°52N 83°53W **309 G12**
Barbuda *W. Indies* 17°30N 61°40W **322 c**
Bârca *Romania* 43°59N 23°36E **183 G8**
Barcaldine *Australia* 23°43S 145°6E **280 C4**
Barcarena *Brazil* 1°30S 48°40W **332 B2**
Barcarena *Lisboa, Portugal* 38°43N 9°16W **126 A1**
Barcarena, Rib. de →
Portugal 38°41N 9°16W **126 A1**
Barcarrota *Spain* 38°31N 6°51W **195 G4**
Barce = Al Marj *Libya* 32°25N 20°30E **258 B4**
Barcellona Pozzo di Gotto
Italy 38°9N 15°13E **201 D8**
Barcelona *Spain* 41°22N 2°10E **114 A2**
Barcelona *Venezuela* 10°10N 64°40W **329 A5**
Barcelona □ *Spain* 41°30N 2°0E **196 D7**
Barcelona-Prat ✕ (BCN)
Spain 41°18N 2°5E **114 B1**
Barceloneta *Puerto Rico* 18°27N 66°32W **321 b**
Barcelonette *France* 44°23N 6°40E **175 D10**
Barcelos *Brazil* 1°0S 63°0W **329 D5**
Barcin *Poland* 52°52N 17°55E **185 F4**
Barclayville *Liberia* 4°48N 8°10W **262 E3**
Barcoo → *Australia* 25°30S 142°50E **280 D3**
Barcroft, L. *U.S.A.* 38°52N 77°9W **143 B3**
Barcs *Hungary* 45°58N 17°28E **182 E2**
Barczewo *Poland* 53°50N 20°42E **184 E7**
Bärdä *Azerbaijan* 40°25N 47°10E **191 K8**
Barda del Medio
Argentina 38°45S 68°11W **336 A3**
Bardaï *Chad* 21°25N 17°0E **259 D3**
Bardas Blancas *Argentina* 35°49S 69°45W **334 D2**
Bardawîl, Sabkhet el
Egypt 31°10N 33°15E **251 G4**
Barddhaman *India* 23°14N 87°39E **243 H12**
Bardejov *Slovak Rep.* 49°18N 21°15E **181 B14**
Bardera = Baardheere
Somali Rep. 2°20N 42°27E **267 D5**
Barð *Iceland* 66°3N 19°8W **155 A7**
Barðarbunga *Iceland* 64°38N 17°32W **155 C9**
Barðastrandarsýsla □
Iceland 65°40N 23°0W **155 B3**
Bardi *Italy* 44°38N 9°44E **198 D6**
Bardīyah *Libya* 31°45N 25°5E **258 B5**
Bardoli *India* 21°12N 73°5E **244 D1**
Bardolino *Italy* 45°33N 10°43E **198 C7**
Bardonècchia *Italy* 45°5N 6°42E **198 C3**
Bardsey I. *U.K.* 52°45N 4°47W **168 E3**
Bardstown *U.S.A.* 37°49N 85°28W **311 G11**
Bare *Ethiopia* 4°37N 42°43E **267 D5**
Bareilly *India* 28°22N 79°27E **243 E8**
Barela *India* 23°6N 80°3E **243 H9**
Barellan *Australia* 34°16S 146°24E **283 C7**
Barentin *France* 49°33N 0°58E **172 C7**
Barenton *France* 48°38N 0°50W **172 D6**
Barents Sea *Arctic* 73°0N 39°0E **150 B9**
Barentsøya *Svalbard* 78°25N 21°20E **154 B13**
Barentu *Eritrea* 15°2N 37°35E **257 D4**
Barfleur *France* 49°40N 1°17W **172 C5**
Barfleur, Pte. de *France* 49°42N 1°16W **172 C5**
Barfurush = Bābol *Iran* 36°40N 52°50E **247 B7**
Barga *Italy* 44°4N 10°29E **198 D7**
Bargaal *Somali Rep.* 11°25N 51°0E **267 B7**
Bargara *Australia* 24°50S 152°25E **280 C5**
Bargarh *India* 21°20N 83°37E **244 D6**
Bargas *Spain* 39°56N 4°3W **194 F6**
Bârgăului Bistriţa
Romania 47°13N 24°46E **183 C9**
Barge *Italy* 44°43N 7°20E **198 D4**
Bargi Dam *India* 22°59N 80°0E **244 C5**
Bargo *Australia* 34°18S 150°35E **283 C9**
Bargteheide *Germany* 53°44N 10°14E **178 B6**
Barguzin *Russia* 53°37N 109°37E **215 D11**
Barh *India* 25°29N 85°46E **243 G11**
Barhaj *India* 26°18N 83°44E **243 F10**
Barham *Australia* 35°36S 144°8E **282 C6**
Barharwa *India* 24°52N 87°47E **243 G12**
Barhi *India* 24°15N 85°25E **243 G11**
Bari *Dem. Rep. of the Congo* 3°20N 19°25E **264 B3**
Bari *India* 26°39N 77°39E **242 F7**
Bari *Italy* 41°8N 16°51E **201 A9**
Bari □ *Somali Rep.* 10°0N 50°0E **267 B6**
Bari Doab *Pakistan* 30°20N 73°0E **242 D5**
Bari Sadri *India* 24°28N 74°30E **242 G6**
Bari Sardo *Italy* 39°50N 9°38E **200 C2**
Barīdī, Ra's *Si. Arabia* 24°17N 37°31E **246 E3**
Barīm *Yemen* 12°39N 43°25E **248 D3**
Barima → *Guyana* 8°33N 60°25W **329 B5**
Barinas *Venezuela* 8°36N 70°15W **328 B3**
Barinas □ *Venezuela* 8°10N 69°50W **328 B4**
Baring *U.S.A.* 40°15N 92°12W **310 D4**
Baring, C. *Canada* 70°0N 117°30W **294 D8**
Baringa
Dem. Rep. of the Congo 0°45N 20°52E **264 B4**
Baringo *Kenya* 0°38N 36°16E **266 D4**
Baringo, L. *Kenya* 0°47N 36°16E **268 B4**
Barinitas *Venezuela* 8°45N 70°25W **328 B3**
Baripada *India* 21°57N 86°45E **244 D8**
Bariri *Brazil* 22°4S 48°44W **333 F2**
Bârîs *Egypt* 24°42N 30°31E **256 C3**
Barisal *Bangla.* 22°45N 90°20E **241 D3**
Barisal □ *Bangla.* 22°45N 90°20E **241 D3**
Barisan, Pegunungan
Indonesia 3°30S 102°15E **234 C2**
Barit I. *Phil.* 18°51N 121°15E **232 B3**
Barito → *Indonesia* 4°0S 114°50E **235 C4**
Baritú △ *Argentina* 23°43S 64°40W **334 A3**
Barjac *France* 44°20N 4°22E **175 D8**
Barjols *France* 43°34N 6°2E **175 E10**
Barjūj, Wadi → *Libya* 25°26N 12°12E **258 C2**
Bark L. *Canada* 45°27N 77°51W **312 A7**
Barka = Baraka → *Sudan* 18°13N 37°35E **256 D4**
Barkā' *Oman* 23°40N 58°0E **249 B7**
Barkakana *India* 23°37N 85°29E **243 H11**
Barkal, J. *Sudan* 18°32N 31°50E **256 D3**
Barkald *Norway* 61°59N 10°53E **164 C7**
Barkam *China* 31°51N 102°28E **228 B4**
Barker *U.S.A.* 43°20N 78°33W **312 C6**
Barking *U.K.* 51°32N 0°5E **125 A4**
Barkingside *U.K.* 51°35N 0°4E **125 A4**
Barkley, L. *U.S.A.* 37°1N 88°14W **315 C10**
Barkley Sound *Canada* 48°50N 125°10W **296 D3**
Barkly East *S. Africa* 30°58S 27°33E **270 D4**
Barkly Homestead
Australia 19°52S 135°50E **280 B2**
Barkly Tableland
Australia 17°50S 136°40E **280 B2**
Barkly West *S. Africa* 28°5S 24°31E **270 C3**
Barkol, Wadi → *Sudan* 17°40N 32°0E **256 D3**
Barkol Kazak Zizhixian
China 43°37N 93°2E **218 C7**
Barla Dağı *Turkey* 38°5N 30°40E **205 C12**
Bârlad *Romania* 46°15N 27°38E **183 D12**
Bârlad → *Romania* 45°38N 27°32E **183 E12**
Barlee, L. *Australia* 29°15S 119°30E **279 E2**
Barlee, Mt. *Australia* 24°38S 128°13E **279 D4**
Barletta *Italy* 41°19N 16°17E **201 A9**
Barlinek *Poland* 53°0N 15°15E **185 F2**
Barlovento *Canary Is.* 28°48N 17°48W **153 e1**
Barlovento *C. Verde Is.* 17°0N 25°0W **153 j**
Barlow L. *Canada* 62°0N 103°0W **297 A8**
Barmedman *Australia* 34°9S 147°21E **283 C7**
Barmer *India* 25°45N 71°20E **242 G4**
Barmera *Australia* 34°15S 140°28E **282 C4**
Barmouth *U.K.* 52°44N 4°4W **168 E3**
Barmstedt *Germany* 53°47N 9°46E **178 B5**
Barn, The *St. Helena* 15°55S 5°40W **153 h**
Barna → *India* 25°21N 83°3E **243 G10**
Barnagar *India* 23°7N 75°19E **242 H6**
Barnala *India* 30°23N 75°33E **242 D6**
Barnard → *Australia* 31°34S 151°25E **283 A9**
Barnard Castle *U.K.* 54°33N 1°55W **168 C6**
Barnato *Australia* 31°38S 145°0E **283 A6**
Barnaul *Russia* 53°20N 83°40E **217 B10**
Barnes *N.S.W., Australia* 36°2S 144°49E **282 D6**
Barnes *London, U.K.* 51°28N 0°14W **125 B2**
Barnes Ice Cap *Canada* 70°10N 73°15W **295 C17**
Barnesville *Ga., U.S.A.* 33°3N 84°9W **316 B5**
Barnesville *Minn., U.S.A.* 46°43N 96°28W **308 B5**
Barnet *U.K.* 51°39N 0°11W **125 A2**
Barnet □ *U.K.* 51°38N 0°9W **169 F7**
Barneveld *Neths.* 52°7N 5°36E **170 B5**
Barneville-Cartevert
France 49°23N 1°46W **172 C5**
Barnhart *U.S.A.* 31°8N 101°10W **314 F4**
Barnsley *U.K.* 53°34N 1°27W **168 D6**
Barnstable *U.S.A.* 41°42N 70°18W **309 E18**
Barnstaple *U.K.* 51°5N 4°4W **169 F3**
Barnstaple Bay = Bideford Bay
U.K. 51°5N 4°20W **169 F3**
Barnum B. *Palau* 7°6N 134°15E **288 c**
Barnwell *U.S.A.* 33°15N 81°23W **316 B8**
Baro *Nigeria* 8°35N 6°18E **263 D6**
Baro → *Ethiopia* 8°26N 33°13E **257 F3**
Barobo *Phil.* 8°33N 126°7E **233 G6**
Baroda = Vadodara *India* 22°20N 73°10E **242 H5**
Baroda *India* 25°29N 76°35E **242 G7**
Baroe *S. Africa* 33°13S 24°33E **270 D3**
Baron Ra. *Australia* 23°30S 127°45E **278 D4**
Barong *China* 31°3N 99°20E **228 B2**
Barora Solomon *Is.* 7°30S 158°20E **287 L10**
Barora Ite *Solomon Is.* 7°36S 158°24E **287 L10**
Barotse = Western □
Zambia 15°0S 24°4E **265 F4**
Barotseland *Zambia* 15°0S 24°0E **265 F4**
Barouéli *Mali* 13°4N 6°50W **262 C3**
Barpali *India* 21°11N 83°35E **244 D6**
Barpathar *India* 26°17N 93°53E **241 B4**
Barpeta *India* 26°20N 91°10E **241 B3**
Barqa *Libya* 27°0N 23°0E **258 B4**
Barqin *Libya* 27°33N 13°34E **258 C2**
Barques, Pt. Aux *U.S.A.* 44°4N 82°58W **312 B2**
Barquisimeto *Venezuela* 10°4N 69°19W **328 A4**
Barr, Ras el *Egypt* 31°32N 31°50E **256 H7**
Barr Smith Range
Australia 27°4S 120°20E **279 E3**
Barra *Brazil* 11°5S 43°10W **332 D3**
Barra *Gambia* 13°28N 16°32W **262 C1**
Barra *W. Isles, U.K.* 57°0N 7°29W **167 E1**
Barra, Sd. of *U.K.* 57°4N 7°25W **167 D1**
Barra Andai *Pakistan* 24°47N 66°59E **123 B2**
Barra Bonita = Ibaiti
Brazil 23°50S 50°10W **333 F1**
Barra da Estiva *Brazil* 13°38S 41°19W **333 D3**
Barra de Navidad
Mexico 19°12N 104°41W **318 D4**
Barra de São Manuel *Brazil* 7°19S 58°5W **331 B6**
Barra do Bugres *Brazil* 15°0S 57°11W **331 D6**
Barra do Corda *Brazil* 5°30S 45°10W **332 C2**
Barra do Dande *Angola* 8°28S 13°22E **265 D2**
Barra do Garças *Brazil* 15°54S 52°16W **331 D7**
Barra do Mendes *Brazil* 11°43S 42°4W **333 D3**
Barra do Piraí *Brazil* 22°30S 43°50W **333 F3**
Barra Falsa, Pta. da
Mozam. 22°58S 35°37E **271 B6**
Barra Funda *Brazil* 23°31S 46°39W **137 B2**
Barra Hd. *U.K.* 56°47N 7°40W **167 E1**
Barra Mansa *Brazil* 22°35S 44°12W **333 F3**
Barraba *Australia* 30°21S 150°35E **283 A9**
Barracão do Barreto *Brazil* 8°48S 58°24W **331 B6**
Barracas *Argentina* 34°39S 58°24W **117 B2**
Barracas al Sur = Avellaneda
Argentina 34°40S 58°22W **117 C2**
Barrackpur = Barakpur
India 22°47N 88°21E **124 A2**
Barrafranca *Italy* 37°22N 14°12E **201 E7**
Barraigh = Barra *U.K.* 57°0N 7°29W **167 E1**
Barrāmīya *Egypt* 25°4N 33°47E **256 B3**
Barranca *Lima, Peru* 10°45S 77°50W **330 C2**
Barranca *Loreto, Peru* 4°50S 76°50W **328 D2**
Barranca del Cobre △
Mexico 27°18N 107°40W **318 B3**
Barrancabermeja *Colombia* 7°0N 73°50W **328 B3**
Barrancas *Colombia* 10°57N 72°50W **328 A3**
Barrancas *Venezuela* 8°55N 62°5W **329 B5**
Barranco *Peru* 12°9S 77°2W **124 B2**
Barrancones Pt.
Trin. & Tob. 10°31N 61°28W **323 t**
Barrancos *Portugal* 38°10N 6°58W **195 G4**
Barranqueras *Argentina* 27°30S 59°0W **334 B4**
Barranquilla *Colombia* 11°0N 74°50W **328 A3**
Barranquitas *Puerto Rico* 18°11N 66°19W **321 b**
Barras *Brazil* 4°15S 42°18W **332 B3**
Barras *Colombia* 1°45S 73°13W **328 D3**
Barraute *Canada* 48°26N 77°38W **298 C4**
Barre *Mass., U.S.A.* 42°25N 72°6W **313 D12**
Barre *Vt., U.S.A.* 44°12N 72°30W **313 B12**
Barre de L'Isle Ridge
St. Lucia 13°55N 60°58W **323 m**
Barreal *Argentina* 31°33S 69°28W **334 C2**
Barrei *Ethiopia* 6°10N 42°49E **267 C5**
Barreiras *Brazil* 12°8S 45°0W **333 D2**
Barreirinha *Brazil* 2°47S 57°3W **329 D6**
Barreirinhas *Brazil* 2°30S 42°50W **332 B3**
Barreiro *Portugal* 38°39N 9°5W **126 B2**
Barreiros *Brazil* 8°49S 35°12W **332 C4**
Barrême *France* 43°57N 6°23E **175 E10**
Barren I. *India* 12°16N 93°51E **245 H11**
Barren Is. *U.S.A.* 58°55N 152°15W **303 G9**
Barreto *Brazil* 22°50S 43°5W **135 B2**
Barretos *Brazil* 20°30S 48°35W **333 F2**
Barrhead *Canada* 54°10N 114°24W **296 C6**
Barrie *Canada* 44°24N 79°40W **312 B5**
Barrier, C. *N.Z.* 36°25S 175°32E **284 C4**
Barrier Ra. *N.S.W.,*
Australia 31°0S 141°30E **282 A4**
Barrier Ra. *Otago, N.Z.* 44°15S 169°32E **285 E4**
Barrier Ra. *W. Coast, N.Z.* 44°30S 168°30E **285 E3**
Barrier Reef *Belize* 17°9N 88°3W **319 D7**
Barrière *Canada* 51°12N 120°7W **296 C4**
Barrière-la-Croix
Martinique 14°27N 60°51W **322 j**
Barrigada *Guam* 13°28N 144°48E **302 d**
Barrineau Park *U.S.A.* 30°42N 87°26W **317 E2**
Barrington *U.S.A.* 41°44N 71°18W **313 E13**
Barrington, I. = Santa Fé, I.
Ecuador 0°49S 90°5W **330 a**
Barrington L. *Canada* 56°55N 100°15W **297 B8**
Barrington Tops *Australia* 32°6S 151°28E **283 B9**
Barrington Tops △
Australia 32°4S 151°25E **283 B9**
Barringun *Australia* 29°1S 145°41E **281 D4**
Barrit-Luluno = Luba
Phil. 17°19N 120°42E **232 C3**
Barron *U.S.A.* 45°24N 91°51W **308 C8**
Barrouallie *St. Vincent* 13°14N 61°17W **323 n**
Barrow *U.S.A.* 71°18N 156°47W **303 A8**
Barrow → *Ireland* 52°25N 6°58W **166 D5**
Barrow, Pt. *U.S.A.* 71°23N 156°29W **303 A8**
Barrow Creek *Australia* 21°30S 133°55E **280 C1**
Barrow I. *Australia* 20°45S 115°20E **278 D2**
Barrow-in-Furness *U.K.* 54°7N 3°14W **168 C4**
Barrow Pt. *Australia* 14°20S 144°40E **280 A3**
Barrow Ra. *Australia* 26°0S 127°40E **279 E4**
Barrow Str. *Canada* 74°20N 95°0W **150 B3**
Barruecopardo *Spain* 41°4N 6°40W **194 D4**
Barruelo de Santullán
Spain 42°54N 4°17W **194 C6**
Barry *V. of Glam., U.K.* 51°24N 3°16W **169 F4**
Barry *Ill., U.S.A.* 39°42N 91°2W **310 E5**
Barry's Bay *Canada* 45°29N 77°41W **312 A7**
Barsalogho *Burkina Faso* 13°25N 1°3W **263 C4**
Barsat *Pakistan* 36°10N 72°45E **243 A5**
Barsham *Syria* 35°21N 40°33E **213 E9**
Barshatas *Kazakhstan* 48°10N 78°39E **217 C9**
Barsi *India* 18°10N 75°50E **244 E2**
Barsinghausen *Germany* 52°18N 9°28E **178 C5**
Barsoi *India* 25°48N 87°57E **241 C1**
Barstow *U.S.A.* 34°54N 117°1W **307 L9**
Bartala *India* 22°32N 88°15E **124 B1**
Bartenstein = Bartoszyce
Poland 54°15N 20°55E **184 D7**
Bartfeld = Bardejov
Slovak Rep. 49°18N 21°15E **181 B14**
Barth *Germany* 54°22N 12°42E **178 A8**
Bartica *Guyana* 6°25N 58°40W **329 B6**
Bartin *Turkey* 41°38N 32°21E **212 B5**
Bartle Frere *Australia* 17°27S 145°50E **280 B4**
Bartlesville *U.S.A.* 36°45N 95°59W **314 C7**
Bartlett *Calif., U.S.A.* 36°29N 118°2W **306 J8**
Bartlett *Tenn., U.S.A.* 35°12N 89°52W **315 D10**
Bartlett, L. *Canada* 63°5N 118°20W **296 A5**
Bartolo Solomon *Is.* 7°30S 158°20E **287 L10**
Bartolomeu Dias *Mozam.* 21°10S 35°8E **269 G4**
Barton *Phil.* 10°24N 119°8E **233 F2**
Barton *Vt., U.S.A.* 44°45N 72°11W **313 B12**
Barton Park *Australia* 33°56S 151°9E **139 B1**
Barton upon Humber
U.K. 53°41N 0°25W **168 D7**
Bartonville *U.S.A.* 40°39N 89°39W **310 D7**
Bartoszyce *Poland* 54°15N 20°55E **184 D7**
Bartow *Fla., U.S.A.* 27°54N 81°50W **317 H8**
Bartow *Ga., U.S.A.* 32°53N 82°29W **316 C7**
Bartyki *Poland* 52°10N 21°2E **126 C2**
Barú, I. de *Colombia* 10°15N 75°35W **328 A2**
Barú, Volcan *Panama* 8°55N 82°35W **320 E3**
Barumba
Dem. Rep. of the Congo 1°3N 23°37E **268 B1**
Barumbu
Dem. Rep. of the Congo 1°14N 23°31E **264 B4**
Barung, Nusa *Indonesia* 8°30S 113°30E **235 D4**
Barus *Indonesia* 2°0N 98°24E **234 B1**
Baruth *Germany* 52°4N 13°30E **178 C9**
Baruun Urt *Mongolia* 46°46N 113°15E **219 B11**
Baruunsuu *Mongolia* 43°43N 105°35E **226 C3**
Barvikha *Russia* 55°44N 37°16E **129 B1**
Barvinkove *Ukraine* 48°57N 37°0E **189 H9**
Bärwalde = Barwice
Poland 53°44N 16°21E **184 E3**
Barwani *India* 22°2N 74°57E **242 H6**
Barwice *Poland* 53°44N 16°21E **184 E3**
Barwick *U.S.A.* 30°54N 83°44W **316 E6**
Barycz → *Poland* 51°42N 16°15E **185 G3**
Barysaw *Belarus* 54°17N 28°28E **177 A15**
Barysh *Russia* 53°39N 47°8E **190 D8**
Barzān *Iraq* 36°55N 44°3E **246 B5**
Bârzava *Romania* 46°7N 21°59E **182 D6**
Bas-Congo □
Dem. Rep. of the Congo 5°0S 15°0E **265 D2**
Bas du Fort *Guadeloupe* 16°13N 61°30W **322 e**
Bas-Kouilou *Congo* 4°28S 11°42E **265 C2**
Bas-Rhin □ *France* 48°40N 7°30E **173 D14**
Bašaid *Serbia* 45°38N 20°25E **182 E5**
Bāsa'idū *Iran* 26°35N 55°20E **247 E7**
Basal *Pakistan* 33°33N 72°13E **242 C5**
Basankusa
Dem. Rep. of the Congo 1°5N 19°50E **264 B3**
Basarabeasca *Moldova* 46°21N 28°58E **183 D13**
Basarabi *Romania* 44°10N 28°26E **183 F13**
Basarabia = Bessarabiya
Moldova 47°0N 28°10E **177 E15**
Basauri *Spain* 43°13N 2°53W **196 B2**
Basawa *Afghan.* 34°15N 70°50E **242 B4**
Basco *Phil.* 20°27N 121°58E **232 A3**
Bascuñán, C. *Chile* 28°52S 71°35W **334 B1**
Basekpio
Dem. Rep. of the Congo 4°43N 24°36E **264 B4**
Basel *Switz.* 47°35N 7°35E **179 H3**
Basel, Euroairport ✕ (BSL)
Europe 47°36N 7°33E **173 E14**
Basel-Landschaft □ *Switz.* 47°26N 7°45E **179 H3**
Basento → *Italy* 40°20N 16°49E **201 B9**
Baserah *Indonesia* 0°25S 101°43E **234 C2**
Basey *Phil.* 11°17N 125°4E **233 F5**
Bashākerd, Kūhhā-ye
Iran 26°42N 58°35E **247 E8**
Bashanta = Gorodovikovsk
Russia 46°8N 41°58E **191 G5**
Bashaw *Canada* 52°35N 112°58W **296 C6**
Bāshī *Iran* 28°41N 51°4E **247 D6**
Bashi Channel *Asia* 21°25N 121°30E **225 E2**
Bashkir Republic =
Bashkortostan □ *Russia* 54°0N 57°0E **186 D10**
Bashkortostan □ *Russia* 54°0N 57°0E **186 D10**
Bashtanivka *Ukraine* 45°46N 29°29E **183 E14**
Basibasy *Madag.* 22°10S 43°40E **272 C1**
Basilaki I. *Papua N. G.* 10°35S 151°0E **286 F6**
Basilan □ *Phil.* 6°33N 122°4E **233 H4**
Basilan I. *Phil.* 6°35N 122°0E **233 H4**
Basilan Str. *Phil.* 6°50N 122°0E **233 H4**
Basildon *U.K.* 51°34N 0°28E **169 F8**
Basilé *Eq. Guin.* 3°42N 8°48E **263 E6**
Basilé, Pico de *Eq. Guin.* 3°36N 8°49E **263 E6**
Basilicata □ *Italy* 40°30N 16°30E **201 B9**
Basim = Washim *India* 20°3N 77°0E **244 D3**
Basin *U.S.A.* 44°23N 108°2W **304 D9**
Basinger *U.S.A.* 27°23N 81°2W **317 H8**
Basingstoke *U.K.* 51°15N 1°5W **169 F6**
Basirhat *Bangla.* 22°40N 88°54E **241 D2**
Basīt, Ra's al *Syria* 35°51N 35°48E **250 C6**
Baška *Croatia* 44°58N 14°45E **199 D11**
Başkale *Turkey* 38°2N 43°59E **213 C10**
Baskatong, Rés. *Canada* 46°46N 75°50W **298 C4**
Basle = Basel *Switz.* 47°35N 7°35E **179 H3**
Başmakçı *Turkey* 37°54N 30°1E **205 D12**
Basmat *India* 19°15N 77°12E **244 E3**
Basoda *India* 23°52N 77°54E **242 H7**
Basoko
Dem. Rep. of the Congo 1°16N 23°40E **264 B4**
Basongo
Dem. Rep. of the Congo 4°15S 20°20E **265 C4**
Basora, Pta. *Aruba* 12°25N 69°51W **322 f**
Basque, Pays *France* 43°15N 1°20W **174 E2**
Basque Provinces = País Vasco □
Spain 42°50N 2°45W **196 C2**
Basra = Al Başrah *Iraq* 30°30N 47°50E **246 D5**
Bass, Îs. de
French Polynesia 27°55S 143°26W **289 f**
Bass Str. *Australia* 39°15S 146°30E **281 F4**
Bassano *Canada* 50°48N 112°20W **296 C6**
Bassano del Grappa *Italy* 45°46N 11°44E **199 C8**
Bassar *Togo* 9°19N 0°57E **263 D5**
Bassas da India *Ind. Oc.* 22°0S 39°0E **269 G4**
Basse-Normandie □
France 48°45N 0°30W **172 D6**
Basse-Pointe *Martinique* 14°52N 61°8W **322 j**
Basse Santa-Su *Gambia* 13°13N 14°15W **262 C2**
Basse-Terre *Guadeloupe* 16°0N 61°44W **322 e**
Basse Terre *Trin. & Tob.* 10°7N 61°19W **323 t**
Bassein *Burma* 16°45N 94°30E **241 G5**
Bassein *India* 19°26N 72°48E **244 E1**
Basses, Pte. des *Guadeloupe* 15°52N 61°17W **322 e**
Basses-Alpes = Alpes-de-Haute-
Provence □ *France* 44°8N 6°10E **175 D10**
Basses-Pyrénées = Pyrénées-
Atlantiques □ *France* 43°10N 0°50W **174 E3**
Basseterre *St. Kitts & Nevis* 17°17N 62°43W **322 d**
Bassett *U.S.A.* 42°35N 99°32W **308 D4**
Bassi *India* 30°44N 76°21E **242 D7**
Bassigny *France* 48°0N 5°30E **173 E12**
Bassikounou *Mauritania* 15°55N 6°1W **262 B3**
Bassila *Benin* 9°1N 1°46E **263 D5**
Bassum *Germany* 52°50N 8°40E **178 C4**
Båstad *Sweden* 56°25N 12°51E **163 H6**
Bastak *Iran* 27°15N 54°25E **247 E7**
Baştām *Iran* 36°29N 55°4E **247 B7**
Bastar *India* 19°15N 81°40E **244 E5**
Bastelica *France* 42°1N 9°3E **175 F13**
Basti *India* 26°52N 82°55E **243 F10**
Bastia *France* 42°40N 9°30E **175 F13**
Bastille, Place de la *Paris, France* **134 c5**
Bastogne *Belgium* 50°1N 5°43E **170 D5**
Bastrop *La., U.S.A.* 32°47N 91°55W **314 E9**
Bastrop *Tex., U.S.A.* 30°7N 97°19W **314 F6**
Basuo = Dongfang *China* 18°50N 108°33E **236 C7**
Basus *Egypt* 30°7N 31°12E **117 A2**
Basutoland = Lesotho ■
Africa 29°40S 28°0E **271 C4**
Başyayla *Turkey* 36°45N 32°40E **250 B3**
Bat-ongan Caves *Phil.* 12°20N 123°15E **232 E4**
Bat Yam *Israel* 32°2N 34°44E **251 F5**
Bata *Eq. Guin.* 1°57N 9°50E **264 B1**
Bata *Romania* 46°1N 22°4E **182 D7**
Bataan □ *Phil.* 14°40N 120°25E **232 D3**
Bataan △ *Phil.* 14°45N 120°27E **232 D3**
Batabanó *Cuba* 22°41N 82°18W **320 B3**
Batabanó, G. de *Cuba* 22°30N 82°30W **320 B3**
Batac *Phil.* 18°3N 120°34E **232 B3**
Batagai *Russia* 67°38N 134°38E **215 C14**
Batajnica *Serbia* 44°54N 20°17E **202 B4**
Batak *Bulgaria* 41°57N 24°12E **203 E8**
Batakan *Indonesia* 4°5S 114°37E **235 C4**
Batala *India* 31°48N 75°12E **242 D6**
Batalha *Portugal* 39°40N 8°50W **194 F2**
Batalpashinsk = Cherkessk
Russia 44°15N 42°5E **191 H6**
Batam *Indonesia* 1°5N 104°3E **234 B2**
Batama
Dem. Rep. of the Congo 0°58N 26°33E **268 B2**
Batamay *Russia* 63°30N 129°15E **215 C13**
Batan I. *Albay, Phil.* 13°15N 124°0E **232 E4**
Batan I. *Batanes, Phil.* 20°26N 121°58E **232 A3**
Batan Is. *Phil.* 20°30N 122°0E **232 A3**
Batanagar *India* 22°31N 88°15E **124 B1**
Batanes □ *Phil.* 20°40N 121°55E **232 A3**
Batang *Sichuan, China* 30°1N 99°0E **228 B2**
Batang *Indonesia* 6°55S 109°45E **235 D3**
Batang Ai △ *Malaysia* 1°32N 112°2E **235 B4**
Batang Gadis △ *Indonesia* 0°28N 99°12E **234 B1**
Batanga *Gabon* 0°21S 9°18E **264 C1**
Batangafo *C.A.R.* 7°25N 18°20E **264 A3**
Batangas *Phil.* 13°35N 121°10E **232 E3**
Batangas □ *Phil.* 13°40N 121°5E **232 E3**
Batanta *Indonesia* 0°55S 130°40E **231 E8**
Batarasa *Phil.* 8°40N 117°37E **233 G1**
Batas I. *Phil.* 11°10N 119°36E **233 F2**
Batatais *Brazil* 20°54S 47°37W **335 A6**
Batavia = Jakarta *Indonesia* 6°9S 106°52E **122 A2**
Batavia *Ill., U.S.A.* 41°51N 88°19W **311 C8**
Batavia *N.Y., U.S.A.* 43°0N 78°11W **312 D6**
Batavia *Ohio, U.S.A.* 39°5N 84°11W **311 F12**
Bataysk *Russia* 47°3N 39°45E **189 J10**
Batbakara = Amankeldi
Kazakhstan 50°10N 65°10E **217 B7**
Batchelor *Australia* 13°4S 131°1E **278 B5**
Batdambang *Cambodia* 13°7N 103°12E **236 F4**
Batéké, Plateau *Congo* 3°30S 15°45E **264 C3**
Batemans B. *Australia* 35°40S 150°12E **283 C9**
Batemans Bay *Australia* 35°44S 150°11E **283 C9**
Batesburg-Leesville
U.S.A. 33°54N 81°33W **316 B8**
Batesville *Ark., U.S.A.* 35°46N 91°39W **314 D9**
Batesville *Ind., U.S.A.* 39°18N 85°13W **311 E11**
Batesville *Miss., U.S.A.* 34°19N 89°57W **315 D10**
Batesville *Tex., U.S.A.* 28°58N 99°37W **314 G5**
Bath *Ont., Canada* 44°11N 76°47W **313 B8**
Bath *St. Kitts & Nevis* 17°8N 62°37W **322 d**
Bath *Bath & N.E. Somerset,*
U.K. 51°23N 2°22W **169 F5**
Bath *Maine, U.S.A.* 43°55N 69°49W **309 D19**
Bath *N.Y., U.S.A.* 42°20N 77°19W **312 D7**
Bath & North East Somerset □
U.K. 51°21N 2°27W **169 F5**
Bath Beach *U.S.A.* 40°36N 74°0W **132 C1**
Bath I. *Pakistan* 24°49N 67°1E **123 B2**
Batha □ *Chad* 14°0N 19°0E **259 F3**
Batha → *Chad* 12°47N 17°34E **259 F3**
Batheay *Cambodia* 11°59N 104°57E **237 G5**
Bathsheba *Barbados* 13°13N 59°32W **323 r**
Bathurst = Banjul
Gambia 13°28N 16°40W **262 C1**
Bathurst *N.S.W.,*
Australia 33°25S 149°31E **283 B8**
Bathurst *N.B., Canada* 47°37N 65°43W **299 C6**
Bathurst *Eastern Cape,*
S. Africa 33°30S 26°50E **270 D4**
Bathurst, C. *Canada* 70°34N 128°0W **294 C6**
Bathurst B. *Australia* 14°16S 144°25E **280 A3**
Bathurst Harb. *Australia* 43°15S 146°10E **281 G4**
Bathurst I. *N. Terr.,*
Australia 11°30S 130°10E **278 B5**
Bathurst I. *Nunavut,*
Canada 76°0N 100°30W **295 B11**
Bathurst Inlet *Canada* 66°50N 108°1W **294 D10**
Bati *Ethiopia* 11°10N 40°0E **257 E5**
Batié *Burkina Faso* 9°53N 2°53W **262 D4**
Batiki *Fiji* 17°48S 179°10E **287 A2**
Batir *West Bank* 31°43N 35°8E **123 B1**
Batken *Kyrgyzstan* 40°3N 70°50E **217 D8**
Batken □ *Kyrgyzstan* 39°50N 71°0E **217 E8**
Batlow *Australia* 35°31S 148°9E **283 C8**
Batman *Turkey* 37°55N 41°5E **213 D9**
Baṭn al Ghūl *Jordan* 29°36N 35°56E **251 J6**
Batna *Algeria* 35°34N 6°15E **261 A6**
Batna □ *Algeria* 35°30N 5°55E **261 A6**
Batnfjordsøra *Norway* 62°53N 7°42E **164 B4**
Bato *Catanduanes, Phil.* 13°36N 124°18E **232 E5**
Bato *Leyte, Phil.* 10°13N 124°48E **233 F5**
Bato Bato *Phil.* 5°6N 119°49E **233 J2**
Batoala *Gabon* 0°48N 13°27E **264 B2**
Batobato = San Isidro *Phil.* 6°50N 126°5E **233 H6**
Batočina *Serbia* 44°7N 21°5E **202 B5**
Batok, Bukit *Singapore* 1°21N 103°46E **138 A2**
Batoka *Zambia* 16°45S 27°15E **269 F2**
Baton Rouge *U.S.A.* 30°27N 91°11W **314 F9**
Batong, Ko *Thailand* 6°32N 99°12E **237 J2**
Bátonyterenye *Hungary* 47°59N 19°50E **182 C4**
Batopilas *Mexico* 27°1N 107°44W **318 B3**
Batouri *Cameroon* 4°30N 14°25E **264 B2**
Batovany = Partizánske
Slovak Rep. 48°38N 18°23E **181 C11**
Båtsfjord *Norway* 70°38N 29°39E **160 A23**
Batsi *Greece* 37°52N 24°47E **204 D6**
Battambang = Batdambang
Cambodia 13°7N 103°12E **236 F4**
Battersea *U.K.* 51°28N 0°9W **125 B3**
Battery Park *New York, U.S.A.* **132 f1**
Batti Malv *India* 8°50N 92°51E **245 K11**
Batticaloa *Sri Lanka* 7°43N 81°45E **245 L5**
Battipáglia *Italy* 40°37N 14°58E **201 B7**
Battle *U.K.* 50°55N 0°30E **169 G8**
Battle → *Canada* 52°43N 108°15W **297 C7**
Battle Creek *U.S.A.* 42°19N 85°11W **311 B11**
Battle Ground *U.S.A.* 45°47N 122°32W **306 E4**
Battle Harbour *Canada* 52°16N 55°35W **299 B8**
Battle Lake *U.S.A.* 46°17N 95°43W **308 B6**
Battle Mountain *U.S.A.* 40°38N 116°56W **304 F5**
Battlefields *Zimbabwe* 18°37S 29°47E **269 F2**
Battleford *Canada* 52°45N 108°15W **297 C7**
Battonya *Hungary* 46°16N 21°3E **182 D6**
Batu *Ethiopia* 6°55N 39°45E **257 F4**
Batu *Malaysia* 3°15N 101°40E **237 L3**
Batu, Bukit *Malaysia* 2°16N 113°43E **235 B4**
Batu, Kepulauan *Indonesia* 0°30S 98°25E **234 C1**
Batu Bora, Bukit *Malaysia* 2°43N 114°43E **235 B4**
Batu Ferringhi *Malaysia* 5°28N 100°15E **237 c**
Batu Gajah *Malaysia* 4°28N 101°3E **237 K3**
Batu Is. = Batu, Kepulauan
Indonesia 0°30S 98°25E **234 C1**
Batu Pahat *Malaysia* 1°50N 102°56E **237 M4**
Batu Puteh *Malaysia* 5°25N 117°55E **235 A5**
Batu Puteh, Gunung
Malaysia 4°15N 101°31E **237 K3**
Batuan *Phil.* 12°25N 123°46E **232 E4**
Batuata *Indonesia* 6°12S 122°42E **231 F6**
Batugondang, Tanjung
Indonesia 8°6S 114°29E **231 J17**
Batukaru, Gunung
Indonesia 8°20S 115°5E **231 J18**
Batulaki *Phil.* 5°34N 125°19E **233 J5**
Batuli = San Isidro *Phil.* 6°50N 126°5E **233 H6**
Batumi *Georgia* 41°39N 41°44E **191 K5**
Batuputih *Indonesia* 1°24N 118°28E **235 B5**
Baturr, Gunung *Indonesia* 8°14S 115°23E **231 J18**
Batura Sar *Pakistan* 36°30N 74°31E **243 A6**
Baturaja *Indonesia* 4°11S 104°15E **234 C2**
Baturité *Brazil* 4°28S 38°45W **332 B4**
Baturiti *Indonesia* 8°19S 115°11E **231 J18**
Batusangkar *Indonesia* 0°27S 100°35E **234 C2**
Batys Qazaqstan □
Kazakhstan 50°0N 50°0E **216 C3**
Bau *Malaysia* 1°25N 110°9E **235 B4**
Bauang *Phil.* 16°31N 120°20E **232 C3**
Baubau *Indonesia* 5°25S 122°38E **231 F6**
Baucau *E. Timor* 8°27S 126°27E **231 F7**
Bauchi *Nigeria* 10°22N 9°48E **263 C6**
Bauchi □ *Nigeria* 10°30N 10°0E **263 C7**
Baud *France* 47°52N 3°1W **172 E3**
Baudette *U.S.A.* 48°43N 94°36W **308 A6**

Bauer, C. *Australia* 32°44S 134°4E 281 E1
Bauerwitz = Baborów
 Poland 50°7N 18°1E 185 H5
Bauguen = Salcedo *Phil.* 11°9N 125°40E 233 F5
Baukau = Baucau
 E. Timor 8°27S 126°27E 231 F7
Bauko *Phil.* 17°0N 120°52E 232 C3
Baulai → *Bangla.* 24°22N 91°1E 241 C3
Bauld, C. *Canada* 51°38N 55°26W 295 D20
Bauman *Russia* 55°45N 37°40E 129 B4
Baume-les-Dames *France* 47°27N 6°22E 173 E13
Baumgarten *Austria* 48°12N 16°17E 142 A1
Baunatal *Germany* 51°14N 9°24E 178 D5
Baunei *Italy* 40°2N 9°40E 200 B2
Baure *Nigeria* 12°52N 8°50E 263 C6
Baures *Bolivia* 13°35S 63°35W 331 C5
Bauru *Brazil* 22°10S 49°0W 335 A6
Baús *Brazil* 18°22S 52°47W 331 D7
Bausi *India* 24°48N 87°1E 243 G12
Bauska *Latvia* 56°24N 24°15E 184 B11
Bautino *Kazakhstan* 44°35N 50°14E 191 H10
Bautzen *Germany* 51°10N 14°26E 178 D10
Bauya *S. Leone* 8°12N 12°38W 262 D2
Bavānāt *Iran* 30°28N 53°27E 247 D7
Bavānište *Serbia* 44°49N 20°55E 182 F5
Bavaria = Bayern ☐
 Germany 48°50N 12°0E 179 G7
Båven *Sweden* 59°0N 16°56E 162 E10
Bavispe → *Mexico* 29°15N 109°11W 318 B3
Baw Baw △ *Australia* 37°50S 146°17E 283 D7
Bawal *Indonesia* 7°52S 111°13E 235 C4
Bawan *Indonesia* 1°42S 113°55E 235 C4
Bawdwin *Burma* 23°5N 97°20E 241 D6
Bawean *Indonesia* 5°46S 112°35E 235 D4
Bawku *Ghana* 11°3N 0°19W 263 C4
Bawlake *Burma* 19°11N 97°21E 241 F6
Bawolung *China* 28°50N 101°16E 228 C3
Bawomataluwo *Indonesia* 0°38N 97°44E 234 B1
 U.S.A. 31°47N 82°21W 316 D7
Baxter *Iowa, U.S.A.* 41°49N 93°9W 310 C3
Baxter *Minn., U.S.A.* 46°21N 94°17W 308 B6
Baxter Springs *U.S.A.* 37°2N 94°44W 308 G6
Baxter State ☐ *U.S.A.* 46°5N 68°57W 309 B19
Bay ☐ *Somali Rep.* 3°0N 43°30E 267 G3
Bay, L. *U.S.A.* 28°25N 81°34W 133 A2
Bay, Laguna de *Phil.* 14°22N 121°11E 232 D3
Bay City *Mich., U.S.A.* 43°36N 83°54W 309 D12
Bay City *Tex., U.S.A.* 28°59N 95°58W 314 G7
Bay Harbor Islands *U.S.A.* 25°53N 80°7W 128 A2
Bay Hill *U.S.A.* 28°28N 81°30N 133 A1
Bay Minette *U.S.A.* 30°53N 87°46W 315 F11
Bay of Plenty ☐ *N.Z.* 38°0S 177°0E 284 D5
Bay Ridge *Canada* 40°37N 74°1W 132 C1
Bay Roberts *Canada* 47°36N 53°16W 299 C9
Bay St. Louis *U.S.A.* 30°19N 89°20W 315 F10
Bay Springs *U.S.A.* 31°59N 89°17W 315 F10
Bay View *N.Z.* 39°25S 176°50E 284 F5
Baya *Dem. Rep. of the Congo* 11°53S 27°25E 269 G2
Bayambang *Phil.* 15°49N 120°27E 232 C3
Bayamo *Cuba* 20°20N 76°40W 320 B4
Bayamón *Puerto Rico* 18°24N 66°9W 321 C6
Bayan Har Shan *China* 34°0N 98°0E 218 E8
Bayan Hot = Alxa Zuoqi
 China 38°50N 105°40E 226 C4
Bayan Lepas *Malaysia* 5°17N 100°16E 237 c
Bayan Obo *China* 41°52N 109°59E 226 D5
Bayan-Ovoo = Erdenetsogt
 Mongolia 42°55N 106°5E 226 C4
Bayan-Turen = Choybalsan
 Mongolia 48°4N 114°30E 219 B11
Bayana *India* 26°55N 77°18E 242 F7
Bayanaūyl *Kazakhstan* 50°45N 75°45E 217 B9
Bayanhongor *Mongolia* 46°8N 102°43E 218 B9
Bayard *N. Mex., U.S.A.* 32°46N 108°8W 305 K9
Bayard *Nebr., U.S.A.* 41°45N 103°20W 308 E2
Baybay *Phil.* 10°40N 124°55E 233 F5
Bayburt *Turkey* 40°15N 40°20E 213 B9
Bayburt ☐ *Turkey* 40°35N 39°25E 213 B9
Baydaratskaya Guba
 Russia 69°0N 67°30E 214 C7
Baydhabo *Somali Rep.* 3°8N 43°30E 267 G3
Bayelsa ☐ *Nigeria* 4°30N 6°0E 263 D6
Bayerische Alpen
 Germany 47°35N 11°30E 179 H7
Bayerische Rhön ☐
 Germany 50°15N 10°5E 179 E6
Bayerischer Spessart ☐
 Germany 49°58N 10°15E 179 F6
Bayerischer Wald
 Germany 48°56N 12°50E 179 G8
Bayern ☐ *Germany* 48°50N 12°0E 179 G7
Bayeux *France* 49°17N 0°42W 172 C8
Bayfield *Ont., Canada* 43°34N 81°42W 312 C3
Bayfield *U.S.A.* 46°49N 90°49W 308 B8
Bayḩān al Qiṣāb *Yemen* 15°48N 45°44E 248 D4
Bayindir *Turkey* 31°46N 35°11E 123 B2
Bayit Va-Gan *Israel* 31°46N 35°11E 123 B2
Baykal, Oz. *Russia* 53°0N 108°0E 215 D11
Baykan *Turkey* 38°7N 41°44E 213 C9
Baymak *Russia* 52°36N 58°19E 186 D10
Baynes Mts. *Namibia* 17°15S 13°0E 270 A1
Bayombong *Phil.* 16°30N 121°10E 232 C3
Bayon *France* 48°30N 6°20E 173 D13
Bayona = Baiona *Spain* 42°6N 8°52W 194 C2
Bayonet Point *U.S.A.* 28°20N 82°41W 317 G7
Bayonne *Pyrénées-Atlantiques,*
 France 43°30N 1°28W 174 E2
Bayonne *N.J., U.S.A.* 40°40N 74°6W 132 B1
Bayou Boeuf *U.S.A.* 29°50N 90°10W 131 B1
Bayou Segnette State Park ☐
 U.S.A. 29°53N 90°10W 131 B2
Bayovar *Peru* 5°50S 81°0W 330 B1
Bayport *Kazakhstan* 28°32N 82°39W 317 G7
Bayqongyr *Kazakhstan* 45°40N 63°20E 216 C6
Bayram-Ali = Bayramaly
 Turkmenistan 37°37N 62°10E 247 B9
Bayramaly *Turkmenistan* 37°37N 62°10E 247 B9
Bayramiç *Turkey* 41°12N 26°56E 205 B8
Bayreuth *Germany* 49°56N 11°35E 179 F7
Bayrischzell *Germany* 47°41N 12°0E 179 H8
Bayrüt *Lebanon* 33°53N 35°31E 250 B4
Bays, L. of *Canada* 45°15N 79°4W 312 A5
Bayshore *Calif., U.S.A.* 37°42N 122°24W 137 H4
Bayshore *U.S.A.* 26°43N 81°50W 317 J8
Baysville *Canada* 45°9N 79°7W 312 A5
Bayswater *London, U.K.* 125 b2
Bayt al Faqīh *Yemen* 14°31N 43°19E 248 E3
Bayt Lahm *West Bank* 31°43N 35°12E 123 B2
Baytik Shan *China* 45°15N 90°50E 217 C12
Baytown *U.S.A.* 29°43N 94°59W 314 H7
Bayugan *Phil.* 8°43N 125°48E 233 G5
Bayview = Kirkwood
 S. Africa 33°22S 25°15E 270 D4
Bayview *London, U.K.* 125 b2
Bayt al Kabir, W. *Libya* 31°10N 15°53E 258 B3
Bāzār Dūzī = Bazardüzü
 Russia 41°12N 47°50E 191 K8

Ben Wyvis U.K. 57°43N 4°35W 167 D4
Bena Nigeria 11°20N 5°50E 263 C6
Bena-Dibele Dem. Rep. of the Congo 4°4S 22°50E 265 C4
Bena-Leka Dem. Rep. of the Congo 5°8S 22°10E 265 D4
Bena-Tshadi Dem. Rep. of the Congo 4°40S 22°49E 265 C4
Benagerie Australia 31°25S 140°22E 282 A4
Benahmed Morocco 33°4N 7°9W 260 B3
Benaki Museum Athens, Greece 112 b3
Benalla Australia 36°30S 146°0E 283 D7
Benalmádena Spain 36°36N 4°34W 195 J6
Benambra, Mt. Australia 36°31S 147°34E 283 D7
Benanee Australia 34°31S 142°52E 282 C5
Benangin Indonesia 0°58S 115°19E 235 C5
Bénara Mayotte 12°53S 45°9E 272 b
Benares = Varanasi India 25°22N 83°0E 243 G10
Bénat, C. France 43°5N 6°22E 175 E10
Benavente Portugal 38°59N 8°49W 195 G2
Benavente Spain 42°2N 5°43W 194 C5
Benavides U.S.A. 27°36N 98°25W 314 H5
Benavides de Órbigo Spain 42°30N 5°54W 194 C5
Benbecula U.K. 57°26N 7°21W 167 D1
Benbonyathe Hill Australia 30°25S 139°11E 282 A3
Bend U.S.A. 44°4N 121°19W 304 D3
Bendale Canada 43°45N 79°13W 141 A3
Bendela Dem. Rep. of the Congo 3°18S 17°36E 264 C3
Bendemeer Australia 30°53S 151°8E 283 A9
Bender Beyla Somali Rep. 9°30N 50°48E 267 C7
Bendery = Tighina Moldova 46°50N 29°30E 183 D14
Bendigo Australia 36°40S 144°15E 282 D6
Bendin = Będzin Poland 50°19N 19°7E 185 H6
Bendorf Germany 50°25N 7°35E 178 E3
Bendsburg = Będzin Poland 50°19N 19°7E 185 H6
Benē Beraq Israel 32°6N 34°51E 251 F5
Beneditinos Brazil 5°27S 42°22W 332 C3
Benedito Leite Brazil 7°13S 44°34W 332 C3
Benefica Brazil 22°52S 43°14W 135 B1
Bénéna Mali 13°9N 4°17W 262 C4
Benenitra Madag. 23°27S 45°5E 272 C2
Benešov Czech Rep. 49°46N 14°41E 180 B7
Benevento Italy 41°8N 14°45E 201 A7
Benfeld France 48°22N 7°34E 173 D14
Benfica Portugal 38°45N 9°11W 126 A1
Beng Mealea Cambodia 13°28N 104°14E 236 F5
Benga Mozam. 16°11S 33°40E 269 F3
Bengal = West Bengal □ India 23°0N 88°0E 243 H13
Bengal, Bay of Ind. Oc. 15°0N 90°0E 239 F14
Bengaluru = Bangalore India 12°59N 77°40E 245 H3
Bengbis Cameroon 3°27N 12°36E 263 E7
Bengbu China 32°58N 117°20E 227 H9
Benghazi = Banghāzī Libya 32°11N 20°3E 258 B4
Benghisa Point Malta 35°49N 14°33E 206 F8
Bengkalis Indonesia 1°30N 102°10E 237 M4
Bengkayang Indonesia 0°49N 109°28E 235 B3
Bengkulu Indonesia 3°50S 102°12E 234 C2
Bengkulu □ Indonesia 3°48S 102°16E 234 C2
Bengo Dem. Rep. of the Congo 2°11S 19°5E 264 C3
Bengo □ Angola 9°0S 13°10E 265 D2
Bengough Canada 49°25N 105°10W 297 D7
Bengtsfors Sweden 59°2N 12°14E 162 E6
Benguela Angola 12°37S 13°25E 265 E2
Benguela □ Angola 13°0S 13°30E 265 E2
Benguerir Morocco 32°16N 7°56W 260 B3
Benguérua, I. Mozam. 21°58S 35°28E 271 B6
Benguet □ Phil. 16°30N 120°40E 232 C3
Benha Egypt 30°26N 31°8E 256 H7
Benham Seamount Pac. Oc. 15°40N 124°30E 232 D5
Beni Dem. Rep. of the Congo 0°30N 29°27E 268 B2
Beni □ Bolivia 14°0S 65°0W 331 C5
Beni → Bolivia 10°23S 65°24W 331 C4
Beni Abbès Algeria 30°5N 2°5W 261 B4
Beni Hammad Algeria 35°49N 4°47E 261 A5
Beni Haoua Algeria 36°30N 1°30E 261 A5
Beni Mazâr Egypt 28°32N 30°44E 256 J7
Beni Mellal Morocco 32°21N 6°21W 260 B3
Beni Mellal □ Morocco 32°0N 6°30W 260 B3
Beni Ounif Algeria 32°0N 1°10W 261 B4
Beni Saf Algeria 35°17N 1°15W 261 A4
Beni Suef Egypt 29°5N 31°6E 256 J7
Beniah L. Canada 63°23N 112°17W 296 A6
Benicarló Spain 40°23N 0°23E 196 E5
Benicássim Spain 40°3N 0°4E 196 E5
Benidorm Spain 38°33N 0°9W 197 G4
Benin ■ Africa 10°0N 2°0E 263 D5
Benin → Nigeria 5°45N 5°4E 263 D6
Benin, Bight of W. Afr. 5°0N 3°0E 263 E5
Benin City Nigeria 6°20N 5°31E 263 D6
Benissa Spain 38°43N 0°3E 197 G5
Benitez Int. ✈ (SCL) Chile 33°23S 70°42W 137 B1
Bénitiers, Île aux Mauritius 20°24S 57°20E 272 e
Benito Juárez Argentina 37°4S 59°43W 334 D4
Benito Juárez, Int. ✈ (MEX) Mexico 19°25N 99°5W 128 B2
Benitses Greece 39°32N 19°55E 206 B9
Benjamin Aceval Paraguay 24°58S 57°34W 334 A4
Benjamin Constant Brazil 4°40S 70°15W 328 D3
Benjamín Hill Mexico 30°9N 111°7W 318 A2
Benkelman U.S.A. 40°3N 101°32W 308 E3
Benkovac Croatia 44°2N 15°37E 199 D12
Benmore Pk. N.Z. 44°25S 170°8E 285 E5
Bennett Canada 59°51N 135°0W 296 B2
Bennett, L. Australia 22°50S 131°2E 278 D5
Bennetta, Ostrov Russia 76°21N 148°56E 215 B15
Bennettsville U.S.A. 34°37N 79°41W 315 D15
Bennichchâb Mauritania 19°32N 15°12W 262 B1
Bennington N.H., U.S.A. 43°0N 71°55W 313 D11
Bennington Vt., U.S.A. 42°53N 73°12W 313 D11
Beno Dem. Rep. of the Congo 3°41S 17°49E 264 C3
Bénodet France 47°53N 4°7W 172 E2
Benom Malaysia 3°50N 102°6E 237 L4
Benoni S. Africa 26°11S 28°18E 271 C4
Benoud Algeria 32°20N 0°16E 261 B5
Benoué △ Cameroon 8°33N 13°55E 264 A2
Benoy Chad 8°59N 16°19E 259 G3
Benque Viejo Belize 17°5N 89°8W 320 C2
Bense Dominica 15°35N 61°22W 323 k
Bensheim Germany 49°40N 8°38E 179 F4
Benson Ariz., U.S.A. 31°58N 110°18W 305 L8
Benson Minn., U.S.A. 45°19N 95°36W 308 C6
Bensonhurst U.S.A. 40°35N 73°59W 132 C2
Bent Iran 26°20N 59°31E 247 E8
Benteng Indonesia 6°10S 120°30E 231 F6
Bentiaba Angola 14°15S 12°21E 265 E2
Bentinck I. Queens., Australia 17°3S 139°35E 280 B2
Bentinck I. Burma 11°45N 98°3E 237 G2
Bentiu South Sudan 9°10N 29°55E 257 F2
Bentley Subglacial Trench Antarctica 80°0S 115°0W 151 E15
Bento Gonçalves Brazil 29°10S 51°31W 335 B5
Benton Ark., U.S.A. 34°34N 92°35W 314 D8
Benton Calif., U.S.A. 37°48N 118°32W 306 H8
Benton Ill., U.S.A. 38°0N 88°55W 310 G8
Benton Pa., U.S.A. 41°12N 76°23W 313 E8
Benton Harbor U.S.A. 42°6N 86°27W 311 D10
Benton Heights U.S.A. 42°7N 86°24W 311 B10
Bentong Malaysia 3°31N 101°55E 237 L3
Bentonville U.S.A. 36°22N 94°13W 314 C7
Bentu Liben Ethiopia 8°32N 38°21E 257 F4
Benue □ Nigeria 7°20N 8°45E 263 D6
Benue → Nigeria 7°48N 6°46E 263 D6
Benxi China 41°20N 123°48E 224 B1
Benza Dem. Rep. of the Congo 4°49S 13°17E 265 D2
Benzdorp Suriname 3°44N 54°5W 329 C7
Beo Indonesia 4°25N 126°50E 231 D7
Beograd Serbia 44°50N 20°37E 202 B4
Beograd ✈ (BEG) Serbia 43°49N 20°17E 202 C4
Beolgyo S. Korea 34°51N 127°21E 224 E3
Beoumi Ivory C. 7°45N 5°23W 262 D3
Beppu Japan 33°15N 131°30E 222 D3
Beppu-Wan Japan 33°18N 131°34E 222 D3
Beqa Fiji 18°23S 178°8E 287 B2
Beqaa Valley = Al Biqā Lebanon 34°10N 36°10E 250 D7
Bequia St. Vincent 13°0N 61°15W 323 n
Ber Mota India 23°27N 68°34E 242 H3
Bera Bangla. 24°5N 89°37E 241 C2
Bera, Tasik Malaysia 3°5N 102°38E 237 L4
Berach → India 25°15N 75°2E 242 G6
Beraketa Madag. 23°7S 44°25E 272 C1
Béran-Djoko Congo 3°15N 17°0E 264 B3
Berane Montenegro 42°51N 19°52E 202 D3
Berastagi Indonesia 3°11N 98°31E 237 L2
Berat Albania 40°43N 19°59E 202 F3
Berau = Tanjungredeb Indonesia 2°9N 117°29E 235 B5
Berau → Indonesia 2°10N 117°42E 235 B5
Berau, Teluk Indonesia 2°30S 132°30E 231 E8
Beravina Madag. 18°10S 45°14E 272 B2
Berbak △ Indonesia 1°27S 104°19E 234 C2
Berber Sudan 18°0N 34°0E 256 D3
Berbera Somali Rep. 10°30N 45°2E 267 B6
Berbérati C.A.R. 4°15N 15°40E 264 B3
Berbice → Guyana 6°20N 57°32W 329 B6
Berceto Italy 44°31N 9°51E 198 D6
Berchem-Ste-Agathe Belgium 50°52N 4°17E 116 A1
Berchidda Italy 40°47N 9°10E 200 B2
Berchtesgaden Germany 47°38N 13°0E 179 H8
Berchtesgaden △ Germany 47°34N 12°55E 179 H8
Berck France 50°25N 1°36E 173 B8
Berdaale Somali Rep. 3°14N 43°11E 267 D5
Berdale Somali Rep. 7°4N 47°51E 267 C6
Berdichev = Berdychiv Ukraine 49°57N 28°30E 177 D15
Berdsk Russia 54°47N 83°2E 217 B10
Berdyansk Ukraine 46°45N 36°50E 189 J9
Berdychiv Ukraine 49°57N 28°30E 177 D15
Béré Chad 9°20N 16°9E 259 G3
Berea U.S.A. 37°34N 84°17W 309 G11
Berebere Indonesia 2°25N 128°45E 231 D7
Bereeda Somali Rep. 11°45N 51°0E 267 B7
Berehomet Ukraine 48°10N 25°19E 183 B10
Berehove Ukraine 48°15N 22°35E 182 B7
Bereina Papua N. G. 8°39S 146°30E 286 E4
Bereket Turkmenistan 39°16N 55°32E 247 B7
Berekua Dominica 15°14N 61°20W 323 k
Berekum Ghana 7°29N 2°34W 262 D4
Berenice Egypt 24°2N 35°25E 256 C4
Berens → Canada 52°25N 97°2W 297 C9
Berens I. Canada 52°18N 97°18W 297 C9
Berens River Canada 52°25N 97°0W 297 C9
Beresfield Australia 32°50S 151°40E 283 B9
Beresford U.S.A. 43°5N 96°47W 308 D5
Berestechko Ukraine 50°22N 25°5E 177 C13
Berești Romania 46°6N 27°50E 183 D12
Berettău → Romania 47°10N 21°50E 182 C6
Berettyó → Hungary 46°59N 21°7E 182 D6
Berettyóújfalu Hungary 47°13N 21°33E 182 C6
Berevo Mahajanga, Madag. 17°14S 44°17E 272 B1
Berevo Toliara, Madag. 19°44S 44°58E 272 B1
Bereza = Byaroza Belarus 52°31N 24°51E 177 B13
Berezhany Ukraine 49°26N 24°58E 177 D13
Berezina = Byarezina → Belarus 52°33N 30°14E 177 B16
Berezivka Ukraine 47°14N 30°55E 189 J6
Berezna Ukraine 51°35N 31°46E 189 G6
Bereznik Russia 62°51N 42°40E 186 B7
Berezniki Russia 59°24N 56°46E 186 C10
Berezovo Russia 64°0N 65°0E 214 C7
Berezyne Ukraine 46°14N 29°12E 183 D14
Berg am Laim Germany 48°7N 11°38E 131 B2
Berga Spain 42°6N 1°48E 196 C6
Berga Kalmar, Sweden 57°14N 16°3E 163 G10
Bergama Turkey 39°8N 27°11E 205 B9
Bérgamo Italy 45°41N 9°43E 198 C6
Bergaon India 20°41N 80°27E 244 D5
Bergara Spain 43°9N 2°28W 196 B2
Bergby Sweden 60°57N 17°2E 162 D11
Berge Norway 59°34N 8°10E 162 E2
Bergedorf Germany 53°28N 10°6E 178 B6
Bergeforsen Sweden 62°32N 17°23E 162 B11
Bergen Mecklenburg-Vorpommern, Germany 54°25N 13°25E 178 A9
Bergen Niedersachsen, Germany 52°49N 9°57E 178 C5
Bergen Neths. 52°40N 4°43E 170 B4
Bergen Hordaland, Norway 60°20N 5°20E 164 D2
Bergen N.Y., U.S.A. 43°5N 77°57W 312 C7
Bergen ✈ (BGO) Norway 60°17N 5°19E 162 D1
Bergen op Zoom Neths. 51°28N 4°18E 170 C4
Bergenfield U.S.A. 40°55N 73°59W 132 A2
Bergerac France 44°51N 0°30E 174 D4
Bergham Germany 48°2N 11°37E 131 B2
Bergheim Germany 50°57N 6°38E 178 E2
Bergholz U.S.A. 40°31N 80°53W 312 F4
Bergisch Gladbach Germany 50°59N 7°8E 170 D7
Bergisches Land ⌂ Germany 51°0N 7°30E 178 D3
Bergkamen Germany 51°37N 7°38E 178 D3
Bergkvara Sweden 56°23N 16°5E 163 H10
Bergshamra Sweden 59°38N 18°37E 162 E12
Bergsjö Sweden 61°59N 17°3E 162 C11
Bergstadt = Leśnica Poland 50°26N 18°11E 185 H5
Bergstrasse-Odenwald ⌂ Germany 49°45N 5°55E 179 F1
Bergues France 50°58N 2°24E 173 B9
Bergviken Sweden 61°15N 16°40E 162 C10
Bergville S. Africa 28°52S 29°18E 271 C4
Bergvliet S. Africa 34°2S 18°25E 118 B1
Berhala, Selat Indonesia 1°0S 104°15E 234 C2
Berhampore = Baharampur India 24°2N 88°27E 243 G13
Berhampur = Brahmapur India 19°15N 84°54E 244 E7
Berheci → Romania 45°58N 27°28E 183 E12
Beri Spain 41°20N 2°1E 114 A1
Berikat, Tanjung Indonesia 2°34S 106°52E 234 C3
Bering Glacier U.S.A. 60°20N 143°30W 303 F12
Bering Land Bridge ⌂ U.S.A. 66°20N 165°0W 303 C6
Bering Sea Pac. Oc. 58°0N 171°0W 292 D2
Bering Strait Pac. Oc. 65°30N 169°0W 303 D5
Beringovskiy Russia 63°3N 179°19E 215 C18
Berisso Argentina 34°56S 57°50W 334 C4
Berja Spain 36°50N 2°56W 195 J8
Berkåk Norway 62°50N 10°0E 164 B6
Berkane Morocco 34°52N 2°20W 261 B4
Berkeley U.S.A. 37°51N 122°16W 136 A3
Berkeley, C. Ecuador 0°1N 91°35W 330 a
Berkner I. Antarctica 79°30S 50°0W 151 D18
Berkovitsa Bulgaria 43°16N 23°8E 202 C7
Berkshire U.S.A. 42°19N 76°11W 313 D8
Berkshire Downs U.K. 51°33N 1°29W 169 F6
Berlanga Spain 38°17N 5°50W 195 G5
Berlenga, I. Portugal 39°25N 9°30W 195 F1
Berlengas = Valença do Piauí Brazil 6°20S 41°45W 332 C3
Berlin = Kitchener Canada 43°27N 80°29W 312 C4
Berlin Berlin, Germany 52°31N 13°23E 115 A3
Berlin Ga., U.S.A. 31°4N 83°37W 316 D6
Berlin Md., U.S.A. 38°20N 75°13W 309 F16
Berlin N.H., U.S.A. 44°28N 71°11W 313 B13
Berlin N.Y., U.S.A. 42°42N 73°23W 313 D11
Berlin Wis., U.S.A. 43°58N 88°57W 308 D9
Berlin □ Germany 52°30N 13°20E 178 C9
Berlin Dom Germany 32°31N 13°24E 115 A3
Berlin L. U.S.A. 41°3N 81°0W 312 E4
Berlin Tegel ✈ (TXL) Germany 52°35N 13°14E 115 A2
Berlinchen = Barlinek Poland 53°0N 15°15E 185 F2
Bermagui Australia 36°25S 150°4E 283 D9
Bermeja, Sierra Spain 36°30N 5°11W 195 J5
Bermejo → Formosa, Argentina 26°51S 58°23W 334 B4
Bermejo → San Juan, Argentina 32°30S 67°30W 334 C2
Bermejo, Paso = Uspallata, P. de Argentina 32°37S 69°22W 334 C2
Bermen, L. Canada 53°35N 68°55W 299 B6
Bermeo Spain 43°25N 2°47W 196 B2
Bermillo de Sayago Spain 41°22N 6°8W 194 D4
Bermondsey U.K. 51°29N 0°3W 125 B3
Bermuda ☑ Atl. Oc. 32°18N 64°45W 153 a
Bermuda Int. ✈ (BDA) Bermuda 32°22N 64°41W 153 a
Bermuda Rise Atl. Oc. 32°30N 65°0W 152 C5
Bern Switz. 46°57N 7°28E 179 J3
Bern □ Switz. 46°45N 7°40E 179 J3
Bernabeu, Estadio Spain 40°27N 3°41W 127 B1
Bernal Heights U.S.A. 37°44N 122°24W 136 B2
Bernalda Italy 40°24N 16°41E 201 B9
Bernalillo U.S.A. 35°18N 106°33W 305 J10
Bernam → Malaysia 3°45N 101°5E 234 B2
Bernardo de Irigoyen Argentina 26°15S 53°40W 335 B5
Bernardo O'Higgins △ Chile 48°50S 75°36W 336 C1
Bernardsville U.S.A. 40°43N 74°34W 313 F10
Bernasconi Argentina 37°55S 63°44W 334 D3
Bernau Bayern, Germany 47°47N 12°22E 179 H8
Bernau Brandenburg, Germany 52°40N 13°35E 178 C9
Bernay France 49°5N 0°35E 172 C7
Bernburg Germany 51°47N 11°44E 178 D7
Berndorf Austria 47°59N 16°1E 180 D9
Berne = Bern Switz. 46°57N 7°28E 179 J3
Berne = Bern □ Switz. 46°45N 7°40E 179 J3
Berne U.S.A. 40°39N 84°57W 311 D12
Berner Alpen Switz. 46°27N 7°35E 179 J3
Berneray U.K. 57°43N 7°11W 167 D1
Bernier I. Australia 24°50S 113°12E 279 D1
Bernina, Piz Switz. 46°20N 9°54E 179 J5
Bernkastel-Kues Germany 49°55N 7°3E 179 F3
Bernstadt = Bierutów Poland 51°7N 17°32E 185 G4
Bernstein = Pełczyce Poland 53°3N 15°16E 185 E2
Bero → Angola 15°10S 12°9E 265 F2
Beroroha Madag. 21°40S 45°10E 272 C2
Béroubouay Benin 10°34N 2°46E 263 C5
Beroun Czech Rep. 49°57N 14°5E 180 B7
Berounka → Czech Rep. 50°0N 14°22E 180 B7
Berovo Macedonia 41°38N 22°51E 202 E6
Berre, Étang de France 43°27N 5°5E 175 E9
Berre-l'Étang France 43°27N 5°10E 175 E9
Berrechid Morocco 33°18N 7°36W 260 B3
Berri Australia 34°14S 140°35E 282 C4
Berriane Algeria 32°50N 3°46E 261 B5
Berridale Australia 36°22S 148°48E 283 D8
Berrien Springs U.S.A. 41°57N 86°20W 311 C10
Berrigan Australia 35°38S 145°49E 283 C6
Berriwillock Australia 35°36S 142°59E 282 C5
Berrouaghia Algeria 36°10N 2°53E 261 A5
Berry N.S.W., Australia 34°46S 150°43E 283 C9
Berry Indre, France 46°50N 2°0E 173 F8
Berry Is. Bahamas 25°40N 77°50W 320 A4
Berrydale U.S.A. 30°53N 87°3W 317 E2
Berryessa, L. U.S.A. 38°31N 122°6W 306 G4
Berryville U.S.A. 36°22N 93°34W 314 C8
Berseba Namibia 26°0S 17°46E 270 C2
Bersenbrück Germany 52°34N 7°56E 178 C3
Bershad Ukraine 48°22N 29°31E 183 B14
Bertamirans Spain 42°54N 8°38W 194 C2
Berthold U.S.A. 48°19N 101°44W 308 A3
Berthoud U.S.A. 40°19N 105°5W 304 F11
Bertincourt France 50°5N 2°58E 173 B9
Bertolínia Brazil 7°38S 43°57W 332 C3
Bertoua Cameroon 4°30N 13°45E 264 B2
Bertraghboy B. Ireland 53°22N 9°54W 166 C2
Bertys = Balqash Kazakhstan 46°50N 74°50E 214 E8
Beru Kiribati 1°20S 176°0E 277 A14
Berufjörður Iceland 64°48N 14°29W 155 C12
Beruness Iceland 64°42N 14°16W 155 C12
Beruni Uzbekistan 41°41N 60°45E 216 D6
Beruri Brazil 3°54S 61°22W 329 D5
Berwick U.S.A. 41°3N 76°14W 313 E8
Berwick-upon-Tweed U.K. 55°46N 2°0W 168 B6
Berwyn U.S.A. 41°50N 87°47W 119 B2
Berwyn Heights U.S.A. 38°59N 76°55W 143 B4
Berwyn Mts. U.K. 52°54N 3°26W 168 E4
Beryslav Ukraine 46°50N 33°30E 189 J7
Berzasca Romania 44°39N 21°58E 182 F6
Berzence Hungary 46°12N 17°11E 182 D2
Besal Pakistan 35°4N 73°56E 243 B5
Besalampy Madag. 16°43S 44°29E 272 B1
Besançon France 47°15N 6°2E 173 E13
Besar Indonesia 2°40S 116°0E 235 C5
Besar, Gunung Malaysia 5°10N 101°18E 234 A2
Beshenkovichi Belarus 55°2N 29°29E 188 E5
Beşiktaş Turkey 41°2N 29°0E 122 B2
Beška Serbia 45°8N 20°6E 182 E5
Beslan Russia 43°15N 44°28E 191 J7
Besna Kobila Serbia 42°31N 22°10E 202 D6
Besnard L. Canada 55°25N 106°0W 297 B7
Besni Turkey 37°41N 37°52E 212 D7
Besor, N. → Egypt 31°28N 34°22E 251 G5
Besòs → Spain 41°24N 2°13E 114 A2
Bessa Monteiro Angola 7°7S 13°44E 265 D2
Bessarabiya Moldova 47°0N 28°10E 177 E15
Bessarabka = Basarabeasca Moldova 46°21N 28°58E 183 D13
Bessèges France 44°18N 4°8E 175 D8
Bessemer Ala., U.S.A. 33°24N 86°58W 315 E11
Bessemer Mich., U.S.A. 46°29N 90°3W 308 B8
Bessemer Pa., U.S.A. 40°59N 80°30W 312 F4
Bessie, L. U.S.A. 28°29N 81°31W 133 B1
Bessines-sur-Gartempe France 46°6N 1°22E 174 B5
Beswick Australia 14°34S 132°53E 278 B5
Beswick ⌂ Australia 14°31S 132°51E 278 B5
Bet Horon West Bank 31°52N 35°7E 123 A1
Bet She'an Israel 32°30N 35°30E 251 F6
Bet Shemesh Israel 31°44N 35°0E 251 G6
Betafo Madag. 19°50S 46°51E 272 B2
Betamba Dem. Rep. of the Congo 2°17S 21°24E 264 C4
Betancuria Canary Is. 28°25N 14°3W 153 e2
Betancuria, Mt. Canary Is. 28°25N 14°6W 153 e2
Betania Colombia 4°22N 72°54W 328 C3
Betanzos Bolivia 19°34S 65°27W 331 D4
Betanzos Spain 43°15N 8°12W 194 B2
Bétaré Oya Cameroon 5°40N 14°5E 264 A2
Betatao Madag. 18°11S 47°52E 272 B2
Bétera Spain 39°35N 0°28W 197 F4
Bétérou Benin 9°12N 2°16E 263 D5
Bethal S. Africa 26°27S 29°28E 271 C4
Bethalto U.S.A. 38°55N 90°2W 310 F6
Bethanien Namibia 26°31S 17°8E 270 C2
Bethany Ont., Canada 44°11N 78°34W 312 B6
Bethany Ill., U.S.A. 39°39N 88°45W 311 E8
Bethany Mo., U.S.A. 40°16N 94°2W 310 D2
Bethany Okla., U.S.A. 35°31N 97°38W 314 D6
Bethel Montserrat 16°44N 62°9W 323 p
Bethel Alaska, U.S.A. 60°48N 161°45W 303 F7
Bethel Conn., U.S.A. 41°22N 73°25W 313 E11
Bethel Maine, U.S.A. 44°25N 70°47W 313 B14
Bethel Ohio, U.S.A. 38°58N 84°5W 311 F12
Bethel Vt., U.S.A. 43°50N 72°38W 313 C12
Bethel Park U.S.A. 40°19N 80°2W 312 F4
Béthenville France 49°18N 4°23E 173 C11
Bethesda U.S.A. 38°59N 77°6W 143 B3
Bethlehem = Bayt Lahm West Bank 31°43N 35°12E 123 B2
Bethlehem Free State, S. Africa 28°14S 28°18E 271 C4
Bethlehem Pa., U.S.A. 40°37N 75°23W 313 F9
Bethnal Green U.K. 51°31N 0°2W 125 A3
Bethulie S. Africa 30°30S 25°59E 270 D4
Béthune France 50°30N 2°38E 173 B9
Béthune → France 49°53N 1°9E 172 C8
Bethungra Australia 34°45S 147°51E 283 C7
Betijoque Venezuela 9°23N 70°44W 328 B3
Betim Brazil 19°58S 44°13W 333 E3
Betioky Toliara, Madag. 23°48S 44°20E 272 C1
Betioky Toliara, Madag. 22°27S 43°43E 272 C1
Betong Malaysia 1°24N 111°31E 234 B4
Betong Thailand 5°45N 101°5E 237 K3
Betoota Australia 25°45S 140°42E 280 D3
Betor Ethiopia 11°37N 39°2E 257 E4
Betor W. Bengal, India 22°34N 88°17E 120 B1
Bétou Congo 3°2N 18°32E 264 B3
Betpaqdala Kazakhstan 45°45N 70°30E 217 C8
Betroka Madag. 23°16S 46°0E 272 C2
Betsiamites Canada 48°56N 68°40W 299 C6
Betsiamites → Canada 48°56N 68°38W 299 C6
Betsiboka → Madag. 16°3S 46°36E 272 B2
Bettendorf U.S.A. 41°32N 90°30W 310 C6
Bettiah India 26°48N 84°33E 243 F11
Bettna Sweden 58°55N 16°38E 163 F10
Béttola Italy 44°47N 9°36E 198 D6
Betul India 21°58N 77°59E 244 D3
Betung Indonesia 3°58S 104°34E 234 C2
Betung Kerihun △ Indonesia 1°11N 113°38E 235 B4
Betws-y-Coed U.K. 53°5N 3°48W 168 D4
Betxi Spain 39°56N 0°12W 196 F4
Betzdorf Germany 50°46N 7°52E 178 E3
Béu Angola 6°15S 15°32E 265 D3
Beuil France 44°6N 6°59E 175 D10
Beulah Vic., Australia 35°58S 142°29E 282 C5
Beulah Fla., U.S.A. 28°32N 81°34W 133 A1
Beulah Mich., U.S.A. 44°38N 86°6W 308 C10
Beulah N. Dak., U.S.A. 47°16N 101°47W 308 B3
Beulah, L. U.S.A. 28°32N 81°33W 133 A1
Beurkia Chad 15°20N 17°56E 259 E3
Beurs van Berlage Amsterdam, Neths. 112 a2
Beuthen = Bytom Poland 50°25N 18°54E 185 H5
Beuthen an der Oder = Bytom Odrzański Poland 51°44N 15°48E 185 G2
Beuvron → France 47°29N 1°15E 172 E8
Beveren Belgium 51°12N 4°16E 170 C4
Beverley W. Austral., Australia 32°9S 116°56E 279 F2
Beverley E. Riding, U.K. 53°51N 0°26W 168 D7
Beverley Hills Australia 33°56S 151°5E 139 B1
Beverley Park Australia 33°58S 151°8E 139 B1
Beverly Ill., U.S.A. 41°42N 87°39W 119 C3
Beverly Mass., U.S.A. 42°33N 70°53W 313 D14
Beverly Arts Center U.S.A. 41°41N 87°40W 119 C2
Beverly Glen U.S.A. 34°6N 118°26W 126 B2
Beverly Hills Calif., U.S.A. 34°5N 118°24W 126 B2
Beverly Hills Fla., U.S.A. 28°55N 82°28W 317 G7
Beverly Hills - Morgan Park Historic District U.S.A. 41°41N 87°40W 119 C2
Beverungen Germany 51°39N 9°22E 178 D5
Bevoalavo Madag. 25°13S 45°26E 272 D2
Bewas → India 23°59N 79°21E 243 H8
Bewdley Canada 44°5N 78°19W 312 B6
Bex Switz. 46°15N 7°1E 179 J3
Bexhill U.K. 50°51N 0°29E 169 G8
Bexley Australia 33°56S 151°7E 139 B1
Bexley □ U.K. 51°27N 0°9E 125 B4
Bexleyheath U.K. 51°27N 0°8E 125 B4
Bey Dağları Turkey 36°38N 30°29E 205 E12
Beyānlū Iran 36°0N 47°51E 246 C5
Beyazköy Turkey 41°21N 27°42E 203 E11
Beyçayırı Turkey 40°15N 26°55E 203 F10
Beydağ Turkey 38°5N 28°13E 205 C10
Beyeğaç Turkey 37°14N 28°53E 205 D10
Beyin Ghana 5°1N 2°41W 262 D4
Beykoz Turkey 41°7N 29°7E 122 B2
Beyla Guinea 8°30N 8°38W 262 D3
Beylerbeyi Turkey 41°2N 29°2E 122 B2
Beynat France 45°8N 1°44E 174 C5
Beyneu Kazakhstan 45°18N 55°9E 187 G10
Beyoba Turkey 38°48N 27°47E 205 C9
Beyoğlu Turkey 41°1N 28°58E 122 B1
Beyoneisu Retsugan Japan 31°55N 139°55E 223 F11
Beypazarı Turkey 40°10N 31°56E 212 B4
Beypore → India 11°10N 75°47E 245 J2
Beyra Somali Rep. 6°57N 47°19E 267 C6
Beyşehir Turkey 37°41N 31°43E 212 D4
Beyşehir Gölü Turkey 37°41N 31°33E 212 D4
Beytüşşebap Turkey 37°35N 43°10E 213 D10
Bezdan Serbia 45°50N 18°57E 182 E3
Bezhetsk Russia 57°47N 36°39E 188 D9
Béziers France 43°20N 3°12E 174 E7
Bezons France 48°56N 2°13E 134 A2
Bezuidenhout Park S. Africa 26°10S 28°5E 123 B2
Bezwada = Vijayawada India 16°31N 80°39E 244 F5
Bhabua India 25°3N 83°37E 243 G10
Bhachau India 23°20N 70°16E 242 H4
Bhadar → Gujarat, India 22°17N 72°20E 242 H5
Bhadar → Gujarat, India 21°27N 69°47E 242 J3
Bhadarwah India 32°58N 75°46E 243 C6
Bhadgaon = Bhaktapur Nepal 27°38N 85°24E 243 F11
Bhadohi India 25°25N 82°34E 243 G10
Bhadra India 29°8N 75°14E 242 E6
Bhadra → India 14°0N 75°20E 245 H2
Bhadrachalam India 17°40N 80°53E 244 F5
Bhadrakali India 22°40N 88°20E 124 A2
Bhadrakh India 21°10N 86°30E 244 D8
Bhadran India 22°19N 72°6E 242 H5
Bhadravati India 13°49N 75°40E 245 H2
Bhag Pakistan 29°2N 67°49E 242 E2
Bhagalpur India 25°10N 87°0E 243 G12
Bhagirathi → Uttarakhand, India 30°8N 78°35E 243 D8
Bhagirathi → W. Bengal, India 23°25N 88°23E 243 H13
Bhainsa India 19°10N 77°58E 244 E3
Bhairab → Bangla. 22°51N 89°34E 241 D2
Bhairab Bazar Bangla. 24°4N 90°58E 241 C3
Bhakkar Pakistan 31°40N 71°5E 242 D4
Bhakra Dam India 31°30N 76°45E 242 D7
Bhaktapur Nepal 27°38N 85°24E 243 F11
Bhalki India 18°2N 77°13E 244 E3
Bhalswa India 28°44N 77°10E 120 A2
Bhambo Khan Qarmati Pakistan 24°49N 67°7E 123 B2
Bhamo Burma 24°15N 97°15E 241 C6
Bhamragarh India 19°30N 80°40E 244 E5
Bhandara India 21°5N 79°42E 244 D4
Bhanpura India 24°31N 75°44E 242 G6
Bhanrer Ra. India 23°40N 79°45E 243 H8
Bhaptiahi India 26°19N 86°44E 243 F12
Bharat = India ■ Asia 20°0N 78°0E 239 F11
Bharatpur Chhattisgarh, India 23°44N 81°46E 243 H9
Bharatpur Raj., India 27°15N 77°30E 242 F7
Bharatpur Nepal 27°34N 84°10E 243 F11
Bharno India 23°14N 84°53E 243 H11
Bharuch India 21°47N 73°0E 244 D1
Bhatghar L. India 18°10N 73°48E 244 E1
Bhatiapara Ghat Bangla. 23°13N 89°42E 241 D2
Bhatinda India 30°15N 74°57E 242 D6
Bhatkal India 13°58N 74°35E 245 H2
Bhatpara India 22°50N 88°25E 243 H13
Bhatsala India 22°30N 88°16E 124 B1
Bhattu India 29°36N 75°19E 242 E6
Bhaun Pakistan 32°55N 72°40E 242 C5
Bhaunagar = Bhavnagar India 21°45N 72°10E 244 D1
Bhavani India 11°27N 77°43E 245 J3
Bhavnagar India 21°45N 72°10E 244 D1
Bhawanipatna India 19°55N 83°10E 244 E6
Bhawanipur India 22°32N 88°21E 124 B2
Bhawari India 25°42N 73°4E 242 G5
Bhayavadar India 21°51N 70°15E 242 J4
Bhendkhal India 18°52N 72°59E 130 B2
Bhera Pakistan 32°29N 72°57E 242 C5
Bhikangaon India 21°52N 75°57E 242 J6
Bhilai = Bhilainagar-Durg India 21°13N 81°26E 244 D5
Bhilainagar-Durg India 21°13N 81°26E 244 D5
Bhilsa = Vidisha India 23°28N 77°53E 242 H7
Bhilwara India 25°25N 74°38E 242 G6
Bhima → India 16°25N 77°17E 244 F3
Bhimavaram India 16°30N 81°30E 245 F5
Bhimbar Pakistan 32°59N 74°3E 243 C6
Bhind India 26°30N 78°46E 243 F8
Bhinga India 27°43N 81°56E 243 F9
Bhinmal India 25°0N 72°15E 242 G5
Bhisho S. Africa 32°50S 27°23E 270 D4
Bhiwandi India 19°20N 73°0E 244 E1
Bhiwani India 28°50N 76°9E 242 E7
Bhogava → India 22°26N 72°20E 242 H5
Bhokardan India 20°16N 75°46E 244 D2
Bhola Bangla. 22°45N 90°35E 241 D3
Bholari Pakistan 25°19N 68°13E 242 G3
Bhongir India 17°30N 78°56E 244 F4
Bhopal India 23°20N 77°30E 242 H7
Bhopalpatnam India 18°52N 80°23E 244 E5
Bhor India 18°12N 73°53E 244 E1
Bhuban India 20°53N 85°50E 244 D7
Bhubaneshwar India 20°15N 85°50E 244 D7
Bhuj India 23°15N 69°49E 242 H3
Bhuleshwar Mumbai, India 130 b2
Bhumiphol Res. Thailand 17°20N 98°40E 236 D2
Bhusawal India 21°3N 75°46E 244 D2
Bhutan ■ Asia 27°25N 90°30E 241 B3
Biá → Brazil 3°28S 67°23W 328 D4
Biafra, B. of = Bonny, Bight of Africa 3°30N 9°20E 263 E6
Biak Indonesia 1°10S 136°6E 231 E9
Biała Poland 50°24N 17°40E 185 H4
Biała → Poland 50°3N 20°55E 185 H7
Biała Piska Poland 53°37N 22°5E 184 E9
Biała Podlaska Poland 52°4N 23°6E 185 F10
Biała Rawska Poland 51°48N 20°29E 185 G7
Białobrzegi Poland 51°39N 20°57E 185 G7
Białogard Poland 54°2N 15°58E 184 D2
Białołeka Dworska Poland 52°19N 21°1E 142 B2
Białowieski △ Poland 52°43N 23°50E 185 F10
Białowieża Poland 52°41N 23°49E 185 F10
Biały Bór Poland 53°53N 16°51E 184 E3
Białystok Poland 53°10N 23°10E 185 E10
Biancavilla Italy 37°38N 14°52E 201 E7
Bianco Italy 38°5N 16°9E 201 D9
Biankouma Ivory C. 7°50N 7°40W 262 D3
Biaora India 23°56N 76°56E 242 H7
Bīārjmand Iran 36°6N 55°53E 247 B7
Biaro Indonesia 2°5N 125°26E 231 D7
Biarritz France 43°29N 1°33W 174 E2
Biasca Switz. 46°22N 8°58E 179 J4
Biavela Angola 14°43S 19°47E 265 E3
Biba Egypt 28°55N 31°0E 256 J7
Bibai Japan 43°19N 141°52E 220 C10
Bibala Angola 14°44S 13°24E 265 E2
Bibane, Bahiret el Tunisia 33°16N 11°13E 258 B2
Bibassé Gabon 1°27N 11°37E 264 B2
Bibbiena Italy 43°42N 11°49E 199 E8
Bibby I. Canada 61°55N 93°0W 297 A10
Bibei → Spain 42°24N 7°13W 194 C3
Biberach Germany 48°5N 9°47E 179 G5
Bibi Papua N. G. 5°30S 146°2E 286 C4
Bibiani Ghana 6°30N 2°8W 262 D4
Bibile Sri Lanka 7°10N 81°25E 245 L5
Bibungwa Dem. Rep. of the Congo 2°40S 28°15E 268 C2
Bicaj Albania 41°58N 20°25E 202 E4
Bicaz Romania 46°53N 26°5E 183 D11
Bicazu Ardelean Romania 46°51N 25°56E 183 D10
Biccari Italy 41°23N 15°12E 201 A8
Bicentennial Park N.S.W., Australia 33°51S 151°5E 139 B1
Bicentennial Park Calif., U.S.A. 34°1N 118°1W 126 B4
Bicester U.K. 51°54N 1°9W 169 F6
Biche Trin. & Tob. 10°26N 61°8W 323 t
Bichena Ethiopia 10°28N 38°10E 257 E4
Bicheno Australia 41°52S 148°18E 281 G4
Bichia India 22°27N 80°42E 243 H9
Bichvinta Georgia 43°9N 40°21E 191 J5
Bickerton I. Australia 13°45S 136°10E 280 A2
Bickley U.K. 51°23N 0°3E 125 B4
Bicknell U.S.A. 38°47N 87°19W 311 F9
Bicol △ Phil. 13°55N 122°58E 232 E4
Bicske Hungary 47°29N 18°38E 182 C3
Bicuari △ Angola 15°14S 14°45E 265 F2
Bicutan Phil. 14°30N 121°3E 127 C2
Bid = Bir India 19°4N 75°46E 244 E2
Bida Dem. Rep. of the Congo 4°55N 19°56E 264 B3
Bida Nigeria 9°3N 5°58E 263 D6
Bidar India 17°55N 77°35E 244 F3
Bidde Somali Rep. 0°58N 42°37E 267 D5
Biddeford U.S.A. 43°30N 70°28W 309 D18
Biddwara Ethiopia 5°11N 38°34E 257 F4
Bideford U.K. 51°1N 4°13W 169 F3
Bideford Bay U.K. 51°5N 4°20W 169 F3
Bidhan Nagar India 22°35N 88°25E 124 B2
Bidhuna India 26°49N 79°31E 243 F8
Bīdokht Iran 34°20N 58°46E 247 C8
Bidor Malaysia 4°6N 101°15E 237 K3
Bidu West Bank 31°50N 35°9E 123 B1
Bidyadanga Australia 18°45S 121°43E 278 C3
Bidzar Cameroon 9°54N 14°7E 264 A2
Bie Sweden 59°5N 16°12E 162 E10
Bié □ Angola 12°30S 17°0E 265 E3
Bié, Planalto de Angola 12°0S 16°0E 265 E3
Bieber U.S.A. 41°7N 121°8W 304 F3
Biebrza → Poland 53°13N 22°25E 185 E9
Biebrzański △ Poland 53°36N 22°45E 184 E9
Biecz Poland 49°44N 21°15E 185 J8
Biel Switz. 47°8N 7°14E 179 H3
Bielany Poland 52°17N 20°57E 142 B1
Bielawa Dolnośląskie, Poland 50°43N 16°37E 185 H3
Bielawa Warszawa, Poland 52°8N 21°9E 142 C2
Bielefeld Germany 52°1N 8°33E 178 C4
Bielersee Switz. 47°6N 7°5E 179 H3
Bielitz = Bielsko-Biała Poland 49°50N 19°2E 185 J6
Biella Italy 45°34N 8°3E 198 C5
Bielsk Podlaski Poland 52°47N 23°12E 185 F10
Bielsko-Biała Poland 49°50N 19°2E 185 J6
Bien Hoa Vietnam 10°57N 106°49E 237 G6
Bienne = Biel Switz. 47°8N 7°14E 179 H3
Bienvenida Spain 38°18N 6°12W 195 G4
Bienvenue Fr. Guiana 3°0N 52°30W 329 C7
Bienville, L. Canada 55°5N 72°40W 298 A5
Bierné France 47°48N 0°33W 172 E6
Bierun Poland 50°6N 19°6E 185 H6
Bierutów Poland 51°7N 17°32E 185 G4
Biescas Spain 42°37N 0°20W 196 C4
Biesdorf Germany 52°30N 13°33E 115 A4
Biese → Germany 52°53N 11°46E 178 C7
Biesiesfontein S. Africa 30°57S 17°58E 270 D2
Bieszczadzki △ Poland 49°5N 22°43E 185 J9
Bietigheim-Bissingen Germany 48°58N 9°8E 179 G5
Bièvre → France 48°44N 2°9E 134 B1
Bièvres France 48°45N 2°13E 134 B2
Bieżuń Poland 52°58N 19°55E 185 F6
Biferno → Italy 41°59N 15°2E 199 G12
Bifoum Gabon 0°20S 10°23E 264 C2
Big → Nfld. & L., Canada 54°50N 58°55W 299 B8
Big → Mo., U.S.A. 38°28N 90°37W 310 F6
Big B. = Awarua B. N.Z. 44°28S 168°4E 285 E3
Big B. Canada 55°43N 60°35W 299 A7
Big Bear City U.S.A. 34°16N 116°51W 307 L10
Big Bear Lake U.S.A. 34°15N 116°56W 307 L10
Big Belt Mts. U.S.A. 46°30N 111°25W 304 C8
Big Bend Swaziland 26°50S 31°58E 271 C5
Big Bend △ U.S.A. 29°20N 103°5W 314 G3
Big Black → U.S.A. 32°3N 91°4W 315 E9
Big Blue → Ind., U.S.A. 39°12N 85°56W 311 E11
Big Blue → Kans., U.S.A. 39°35N 96°34W 308 F5
Big Creek U.S.A. 37°11N 119°14W 306 H7
Big Cypress ⌂ U.S.A. 26°0N 81°10W 317 J8
Big Cypress Swamp U.S.A. 26°15N 81°30W 317 J8
Big Delta U.S.A. 64°10N 145°51W 303 D11
Big Desert Australia 35°45S 141°10E 281 F3
Big Falls U.S.A. 48°12N 93°48W 308 A7
Big Fork → U.S.A. 48°31N 93°43W 308 A7
Big Horn Mts. = Bighorn Mts. U.S.A. 44°25N 107°0W 304 D10
Big I. Canada 61°7N 116°45W 296 A5
Big Lake Alaska, U.S.A. 61°20N 150°20W 303 F10
Big Lake Tex., U.S.A. 31°12N 101°28W 314 F4
Big Moose U.S.A. 43°49N 74°58W 313 C10
Big Muddy → U.S.A. 37°33N 89°32W 310 G8
Big Muddy Cr. → U.S.A. 48°8N 104°36W 304 B11
Big Pine U.S.A. 37°10N 118°17W 306 H8
Big Pine Key U.S.A. 24°40N 81°21W 317 L8
Big Piney U.S.A. 42°32N 110°7W 304 E8
Big Quill L. Canada 51°55N 104°30W 297 C8
Big Rapids U.S.A. 43°42N 85°29W 309 D11
Big Rideau L. Canada 44°40N 76°15W 313 B8
Big River Canada 53°50N 107°0W 297 C7
Big Run U.S.A. 40°57N 78°55W 312 F6
Big Sable Pt. U.S.A. 44°3N 86°1W 308 C10
Big Salmon → Canada 61°52N 134°55W 296 A2
Big Sand L. Canada 57°45N 99°45W 297 B9
Big Sand Lake U.S.A. 28°25N 81°29W 133 B2
Big Sandy U.S.A. 48°11N 110°7W 304 B8
Big Sandy → U.S.A. 38°25N 82°36W 309 F12
Big Sandy Cr. = Sandy Cr. → U.S.A. 41°51N 109°47W 304 F9
Big Sandy Cr. → U.S.A. 38°7N 102°29W 304 G12
Big Satilla Cr. → U.S.A. 31°27N 82°3W 316 D7
Big Sioux → U.S.A. 42°29N 96°27W 308 D5
Big South Fork ⌂ U.S.A. 36°27N 84°47W 315 C12
Big Spring U.S.A. 32°15N 101°28W 314 E4
Big Stone City U.S.A. 45°18N 96°28W 308 C5
Big Stone Gap U.S.A. 36°52N 82°47W 309 G12
Big Stone L. U.S.A. 45°18N 96°27W 308 C5
Big Sur U.S.A. 36°15N 121°48W 306 J5
Big Timber U.S.A. 45°50N 109°57W 304 D9
Big Trout L. Canada 53°40N 90°0W 298 B2
Big Trout Lake Canada 53°45N 90°0W 298 B2
Biga Turkey 40°13N 27°14E 203 F11
Biga → Turkey 40°20N 27°14E 203 F11
Bigadiç Turkey 39°22N 28°7E 205 B10
Biganos France 44°39N 0°59W 174 D3
Bigeumdo S. Korea 34°45N 126°56E 224 E3
Biggar Sask., Canada 52°4N 108°0W 297 C7
Biggar S. Lanarks., U.K. 55°38N 3°32W 167 F5
Bigge I. Australia 14°35S 125°10E 278 B4
Biggenden Australia 25°31S 152°4E 281 D5
Biggleswade U.K. 52°5N 0°14W 169 E7
Biggs U.S.A. 39°25N 121°43W 306 F5
Bighorn U.S.A. 46°10N 107°27W 304 C10
Bighorn → U.S.A. 46°10N 107°28W 304 C10
Bighorn Canyon ⌂ U.S.A. 45°10N 108°0W 304 D10
Bighorn L. U.S.A. 44°55N 108°15W 304 D9
Bighorn Mts. U.S.A. 44°25N 107°0W 304 D10
Bigi Dem. Rep. of the Congo 3°2N 22°25E 264 B4
Bignona Senegal 12°52N 16°14W 262 C1
Bigorre France 43°10N 0°5E 174 E4
Bigstone L. Canada 53°42N 95°44W 297 C9
Biguglia, Étang de France 42°36N 9°29E 175 F13
Bigwa Tanzania 7°10S 39°10E 268 D4
Bihać Bos.-H. 44°49N 15°57E 199 D12
Bihar India 25°5N 85°40E 243 G11
Bihar □ India 25°0N 86°0E 243 G12
Biharamulo Tanzania 2°25S 31°25E 268 C3
Biharamulo ⌂ Tanzania 2°24S 31°26E 268 C3
Bihariganj India 25°44N 86°59E 243 G12
Biharkeresztes Hungary 47°8N 21°44E 182 C6
Bihor □ Romania 47°0N 22°10E 182 D7
Bihor, Munţii Romania 46°29N 22°47E 182 D7
Bijagós, Arquipélago dos Guinea-Biss. 11°15N 16°10W 262 C1
Bijaipur India 26°2N 77°20E 242 F7

Bijapur Chhattisgarh, India 18°50N 80°50E 244 E5
Bijapur Karnataka, India 16°50N 75°55E 244 F2
Bījār Iran 35°52N 47°35E 213 E12
Bijawar India 24°38N 79°30E 243 G8
Bijbels Museum Amsterdam, Neths. 112 b1
Bijela Montenegro 42°28N 18°39E 202 D2
Bijeljina Bos.-H. 44°46N 19°14E 182 F4
Bijelo Polje Montenegro 43°1N 19°45E 202 C3
Bijie China 27°20N 105°16E 228 D5
Bijnor India 29°27N 78°11E 242 E8
Bikaner India 28°2N 73°18E 242 E5
Bikapur India 26°30N 82°7E 243 F10
Bikeqi China 40°43N 111°20E 226 D6
Bikfayyā Lebanon 33°55N 35°41E 250 E6
Bikié Congo 3°7S 13°52E 264 C2
Bikin Russia 46°50N 134°20E 220 A7
Bikin → Russia 46°51N 134°2E 220 A7
Bikini Atoll Marshall Is. 12°0N 167°30E 288 F8
Bikita Zimbabwe 20°6S 31°41E 271 B5
Bīkkū Bīttī Libya 22°0N 19°12E 259 D3
Bikoro
Dem. Rep. of the Congo 0°48S 18°15E 264 C3
Bikoué Cameroon 3°55N 11°50E 263 E7
Bila Tserkva Ukraine 49°45N 30°10E 177 D16
Bilanga Burkina Faso 12°40N 0°1W 263 C4
Bilara India 26°14N 73°53E 242 F5
Bilasipara India 26°13N 90°14E 241 B3
Bilaspur Chhattisgarh, India 22°2N 82°15E 243 H10
Bilaspur Punjab, India 31°19N 76°50E 242 D7
Biläsuvar Azerbaijan 39°27N 48°32E 213 C13
Bilauk Taungdan Thailand 13°0N 99°0E 236 F2
Bilbao Spain 43°16N 2°56W 196 B2
Bilbao ✕ (BIO) Spain 43°18N 2°57W 196 B2
Bilbeis Egypt 30°25N 31°34E 256 H7
Bilbo = Bilbao Spain 43°16N 2°56W 196 B2
Bilbor Romania 47°6N 25°30E 183 C10
Bilche-Zolote Ukraine 48°47N 25°53E 183 B10
Bilciureşti Romania 44°44N 25°48E 183 F10
Bíldudalur Iceland 65°41N 23°36W 155 B3
Bílé Karpaty Europe 49°5N 18°0E 181 B11
Bileća Bos.-H. 42°53N 18°27E 202 D2
Bilecik Turkey 40°5N 30°5E 212 B4
Bilecik □ Turkey 40°0N 30°0E 212 B3
Bilećko Jezero Bos.-H. 42°48N 18°28E 202 D2
Bileh Savār Iran 39°21N 48°21E 213 C13
Bilgoraj Poland 50°33N 22°42E 185 H9
Bilgram India 27°11N 80°2E 243 F9
Bilhaur India 26°51N 80°5E 243 F9
Bilhorod-Dnistrovskyy
Ukraine 46°11N 30°23E 189 J6
Bili → Dem. Rep. of the Congo 4°9N 22°29E 264 B4
Bilibino Russia 68°3N 166°20E 215 C17
Bilibiza Mozam. 12°30S 40°20E 269 E5
Bilimora India 20°45N 72°57E 244 D1
Bilin Burma 17°14N 97°15E 241 G6
Biliran Phil. 11°28N 124°28E 233 F5
Biliran □ Phil. 11°35N 124°28E 233 F5
Bilisht Albania 40°37N 21°2E 202 F5
Billabong Cr. → Australia 35°5S 144°2E 282 C6
Billdal Sweden 57°35N 11°57E 163 G5
Billiluna Australia 19°37S 127°41E 278 C4
Billings U.S.A. 45°47N 108°30W 304 D9
Billiton Is. = Belitung
Indonesia 3°10S 107°50E 235 C3
Billsta Sweden 63°20N 18°28E 162 A12
Billund Denmark 55°44N 9°6E 163 J3
Billy Pt. Antigua & B. 17°44N 61°52W 322 c
Bilma Niger 18°50N 13°30E 259 E2
Bilo Gora Croatia 45°53N 17°15E 182 E2
Biloela Australia 24°24S 150°31E 280 C5
Bilohirsk Ukraine 45°3N 34°35E 189 K8
Biloku Guyana 1°50N 58°25W 329 C6
Biloli India 18°46N 77°44E 244 E3
Bilopillya Ukraine 51°14N 34°20E 189 G8
Bilovodsk Ukraine 49°13N 39°36E 189 H10
Biloxi U.S.A. 30°24N 88°53W 315 F10
Bilpa Morea Claypan
Australia 25°0S 140°0E 280 D3
Bilqās Qism Auwal Egypt 31°12N 31°21E 251 G2
Bilston U.K. 55°52N 3°10W 121 B2
Biltine Chad 14°40N 20°50E 259 F4
Bilugyun Burma 16°24N 97°32E 241 G6
Bilyarsk Russia 54°58N 50°22E 190 C10
Bim Son Vietnam 20°4N 105°51E 236 B5
Bima Indonesia 8°22S 118°49E 235 D5
Bimban Egypt 24°24N 32°54E 256 C3
Bimbe Angola 11°50S 15°50E 265 E3
Bimberi Pk. Australia 35°44S 148°51E 283 C8
Bimbila Ghana 8°54N 0°5E 263 D5
Bimbini Comoros Is. 12°11S 44°14E 272 a
Bimbo C.A.R. 4°15N 18°33E 264 B3
Bimini Is. Bahamas 25°42N 79°25W 320 A4
Bin Ghunaymah, Jabal
Libya 25°0N 15°30E 258 D3
Bin Jawwād Libya 30°47N 18°4E 258 B3
Bin Xian Heilongjiang,
China 45°42N 127°32E 227 B14
Bin Xian Shaanxi, China 35°2N 108°4E 226 G5
Bin Yauri Nigeria 10°46N 4°45E 263 C5
Bina-Etawah India 24°13N 78°14E 242 G8
Binacayan Phil. 14°27N 120°55E 127 C1
Binalbagan Phil. 10°12N 122°50E 233 F4
Binalong Australia 34°40S 148°39E 283 C8
Bīnālūd, Kūh-e Iran 36°30N 58°30E 247 B8
Binanga Indonesia 1°24N 99°46E 234 B1
Binangonan de Lampon = Infanta
Phil. 14°45N 121°39E 232 C5
Binatang = Bintangau
Malaysia 2°10N 111°40E 235 B4
Binche Belgium 50°26N 4°10E 170 D4
Binchuan China 25°42N 100°38E 228 E3
Binda Dem. Rep. of the Congo 5°52S 13°14E 265 D2
Binder Chad 9°56N 14°27E 259 G2
Bindki India 26°2N 80°36E 243 F9
Bindloe, I. = Marchena, I.
Ecuador 0°19N 90°29W 330 a
Bindoy Phil. 9°48N 123°5E 233 G4
Bindslev Denmark 57°33N 10°11E 163 G4
Bindura Zimbabwe 17°18S 31°18E 269 F3
Binéfar Spain 41°51N 0°18E 196 D5
Bingara Australia 29°52S 150°36E 281 D5
Bingaram I. India 10°56N 72°17E 245 J1
Bingen Germany 49°57N 7°55E 179 F3
Bingerau = Węgrów
Poland 52°24N 22°0E 185 F9
Bingerville Ivory C. 5°18N 3°49W 262 D4
Bingham U.S.A. 45°3N 69°53W 309 C19
Binghamton U.S.A. 42°6N 75°55W 313 D9
Bingo-Ochiai Japan 34°59N 133°8E 222 C4
Bingöl Turkey 38°53N 40°29E 213 C9
Bingöl □ Turkey 38°55N 40°30E 213 C9
Bingöl Dağları Turkey 39°16N 41°9E 213 C9
Bingsjö Sweden 61°1N 15°39E 162 C9
Binh Dinh Vietnam 13°55N 109°7E 236 F7
Binh Son Vietnam 15°20N 108°40E 236 E7
Binhai China 34°2N 119°49E 227 G10
Bini Erde Chad 20°6N 18°1E 259 D3
Binic France 48°46N 2°50W 172 D4
Binisatua Spain 39°50N 4°11E 206 B5
Binissalem Spain 39°41N 2°50E 206 B3
Binjai Kepulauan Riau,
Indonesia 3°48N 108°13E 235 B3
Binjai Sumatera Utara,
Indonesia 3°20N 98°30E 234 B1
Binji Nigeria 13°10N 4°55E 263 C5
Binka India 21°2N 83°48E 244 D6
Binnah, Ras Somali Rep. 11°9N 51°10E 267 B7
Binnaway Australia 31°28S 149°24E 283 A3
Binondo Phil. 14°36N 120°58E 127 B1
Binongko Indonesia 5°57S 124°2E 231 F6
Binscarth Canada 50°37N 101°17W 297 C3
Binshangul Gumuz □
Ethiopia 11°0N 35°30E 257 E4
Bint Goda Sudan 13°17N 31°33E 257 E3
Bintan Indonesia 1°0N 104°0E 234 B2
Bintangau Malaysia 2°10N 111°40E 235 B4
Bintaro Jaya Indonesia 6°16S 106°44E 122 B1
Bintuhan Indonesia 4°48S 103°22E 234 C2
Bintulu Malaysia 3°10N 113°0E 235 B4
Bintuni Indonesia 2°7S 133°32E 231 E3
Binyang China 23°12N 108°47E 228 F7
Binz Germany 54°24N 13°35E 178 A9
Binza Dem. Rep. of the Congo 4°21S 15°14E 265 C3
Binzert = Bizerte Tunisia 37°15N 9°50E 258 A1
Binzhou China 37°20N 118°2E 227 F10
Bío Bío □ Chile 37°35S 72°0W 334 D1
Biobío → Chile 36°49S 73°10W 334 D1
Biograd na Moru Croatia 43°56N 15°29E 199 E12
Biogradska Gora △
Montenegro 42°55N 19°40E 202 D3
Bioko Eq. Guin. 3°30N 8°40E 263 E3
Biokovo Croatia 43°23N 17°0E 199 E14
Biougra Morocco 30°15N 9°14W 260 B3
Bipindi Cameroon 3°6N 10°30E 263 E7
Bir India 19°4N 75°46E 244 E2
Bir, Ras Djibouti 12°0N 43°20E 257 E5
Bîr Abu Hashim Egypt 23°42N 34°6E 256 C3
Bîr Abu Minqar Egypt 26°33N 27°33E 256 B2
Bîr Abu Muḥammad
Egypt 29°44N 34°14E 251 J5
Bîr Abu Sandûq Egypt 29°24N 32°30E 251 J3
Bir Adal Deib Sudan 22°35N 36°10E 256 C4
Bi'r al Butayyihāt Jordan 29°47N 35°20E 251 J6
Bi'r al Ḥamdah Si. Arabia 28°30N 34°55E 251 K5
Bi'r al Mārī Jordan 30°4N 35°33E 251 H6
Bi'r al Musallam Si. Arabia 28°56N 35°38E 251 K6
Bi'r al Qattār Jordan 29°47N 35°32E 251 J6
Bir 'Ali Yemen 14°1N 48°20E 249 D5
Bîr 'Amrâne Mauritania 22°45N 8°39W 260 D3
Bir Aouine Tunisia 32°25N 9°18E 258 B1
Bîr 'Asal Egypt 25°55N 34°20E 256 B3
Bi'r ash Shakkūsīyah
Syria 35°23N 37°26E 250 C8
Bir Atrun Sudan 18°15N 26°40E 256 D2
Bîr Beiḍa Egypt 30°25N 34°29E 251 H5
Bîr Bel Guerdâne
Mauritania 25°24N 10°31W 260 C2
Bîr Bireida Egypt 29°8N 32°7E 251 J3
Bîr Buerât Egypt 28°59N 32°11E 251 K3
Bi'r Dhu'fān Libya 31°59N 14°32E 258 B2
Bîr Di South Sudan 7°34N 28°49E 257 F2
Bîr Diqnash Egypt 31°3N 25°23E 256 A2
Bîr el Abbes Algeria 26°7N 6°9W 260 C3
Bîr el 'Abd Egypt 31°2N 33°0E 251 G4
Bîr el 'Agramīya Egypt 29°38N 31°50E 251 J2
Bîr el Ater Algeria 34°46N 8°3E 261 B6
Bîr el Basur Egypt 29°51N 25°49E 256 B2
Bîr el Biarât Egypt 29°30N 34°43E 251 J5
Bîr el Dakhal Egypt 28°39N 32°23E 251 K3
Bîr el Duweidar Egypt 30°56N 32°32E 251 H3
Bîr el Garârât Egypt 31°3N 33°34E 251 G4
Bîr el Gâreb Mauritania 20°33N 16°12W 260 D1
Bîr el Gellaz Egypt 30°50N 26°40E 256 A2
Bîr el Ghamr Egypt 28°43N 31°20E 251 K2
Bîr el Heisi Egypt 29°22N 34°36E 251 J5
Bîr el Jafir Egypt 30°50N 32°41E 251 H3
Bîr el Mâlḥi Egypt 30°38N 33°19E 251 H4
Bîr el Manâyif Egypt 30°31N 32°12E 251 H3
Bîr el-Naṣb Egypt 29°3N 33°2E 251 J4
Bîr el Ṣafra Egypt 28°45N 34°21E 251 K5
Bîr el-Saura Egypt 29°9N 34°30E 251 J5
Bîr el Shaqqa Egypt 30°54N 25°1E 256 A2
Bîr el Thamâda Egypt 30°12N 33°27E 251 H4
Bîr Enzarān W. Sahara 23°53N 14°32W 260 D2
Bîr Fuad Egypt 30°35N 26°28E 256 A2
Bîr Gandús W. Sahara 21°36N 16°30W 260 D1
Bîr Gebeil Ḥiṣn Egypt 30°2N 33°18E 251 H4
Bi'r Ghadīr Syria 34°6N 37°3E 250 D8
Bîr Ghalla Egypt 28°23N 32°19E 251 K3
Bi'r Gharr Si. Arabia 28°7N 35°32E 251 K6
Bîr Gindali Egypt 29°55N 31°40E 251 J2
Bîr Haimur Egypt 22°45N 33°40E 256 C3
Bîr Ḥasana Egypt 30°29N 33°46E 251 H4
Bîr Hôôker Egypt 30°22N 30°21E 256 H7
Bi'r Īdimah Si. Arabia 18°31N 44°12E 248 C4
Bi'r Jadīd Si. Arabia 29°10N 35°6E 251 K6
Bîr Jdid Morocco 33°26N 8°0W 260 B3
Bîr Kanayis Egypt 24°59N 33°15E 256 C3
Bîr Kaseiba Egypt 31°0N 33°17E 251 H4
Bîr Kerawein Egypt 27°10N 28°25E 256 B2
Bîr Lahfân Egypt 31°0N 33°51E 251 H4
Bîr Lahrache Algeria 32°1N 8°12E 261 B6
Bîr Madkûr Egypt 30°44N 32°33E 251 H3
Bîr Maql Egypt 23°7N 33°40E 256 C3
Bîr Mineiga Sudan 22°47N 35°12E 256 C4
Bîr Misaha Egypt 22°13N 27°59E 256 C2
Bîr Mogreïn Mauritania 25°10N 11°25W 260 C2
Bîr Mureir Egypt 28°25N 31°15E 251 K2
Bîr Murr Egypt 23°28N 30°10E 256 C3
Bi'r Muṭribah Kuwait 29°54N 47°17E 246 D5
Bîr Nabala West Bank 31°51N 35°12E 123 A2
Bîr Nakheila Egypt 24°1N 30°50E 256 C3
Bîr Nakhul Egypt 29°5N 33°16E 251 J4
Bîr Qaṭia Egypt 30°58N 32°45E 251 H3
Bîr Qatrani Egypt 30°55N 26°10E 256 A2
Bîr Ranga Egypt 24°25N 35°15E 256 C4
Bîr Sahara Egypt 22°54N 28°40E 256 C2
Bîr Sa'id Egypt 29°38N 31°24E 251 J2
Bîr Seiyâla Egypt 26°10N 33°50E 256 B3
Bîr Shalatein Egypt 23°5N 35°25E 256 C4
Bîr Shebb Egypt 22°25N 29°40E 256 C2
Bîr Shût Egypt 23°50N 35°15E 256 C4
Bîr Sidri Egypt 28°53N 33°28E 251 K4
Bîr Tâba Egypt 29°29N 34°55E 251 J5
Bîr Terfawi Egypt 22°57N 28°55E 256 C2
Bi'r Tin Abunda Libya 26°28N 12°27E 261 C7
Bîr Umm Qubûr Egypt 24°35N 34°2E 256 C3
Bîr Ungât Egypt 22°8N 33°48E 256 C3
Bîr Wuseit Egypt 29°14N 33°21E 251 J4
Bîr Za'farâna Egypt 29°10N 32°40E 251 J3
Bîr Zeidûn Egypt 25°45N 33°40E 256 B3
Birāk Libya 27°31N 14°20E 258 C2
Birak el Kiyam Egypt 30°2N 31°9E 117 A1
Birambo Rwanda 2°0S 29°45E 268 C2
Biramféro Guinea 11°40N 9°10W 262 C3
Birao C.A.R. 10°20N 22°47E 264 A4
Biratnagar Nepal 26°27N 87°17E 243 F12
Birawa
Dem. Rep. of the Congo 2°20S 28°48E 268 C2
Birch → Canada 58°28N 112°17W 296 B6
Birch Cliff Canada 43°41N 79°16W 141 A3
Birch Grove Grenada 12°6N 61°40W 323 q
Birch Hills Canada 52°59N 105°25W 297 C7
Birch I. Canada 52°26N 99°54W 297 C9
Birch L. N.W.T., Canada 62°4N 116°33W 296 A5
Birch L. Ont., Canada 51°23N 92°18W 298 B1
Birch Mts. Canada 57°30N 113°10W 296 B6
Birch River Canada 52°24N 101°6W 297 C8
Birchip Australia 35°56S 142°55E 282 C5
Birchiş Romania 45°58N 22°9E 182 E7
Birchwood N.Z. 45°55S 167°53E 285 F2
Birchwood Alaska,
U.S.A. 61°24N 149°28W 303 F10
Bird Canada 56°30N 94°13W 297 B10
Bird I. = Aves, I. de
W. Indies 15°45N 63°55W 321 C7
Bird I. S. Georgia 54°0S 38°3W 151 B1
Birds Creek Canada 45°6N 77°52W 312 A7
Birdseye U.S.A. 38°19N 86°42W 311 F10
Birdsville Australia 25°51S 139°20E 280 D2
Birdum Cr. → Australia 15°14S 133°0E 278 C5
Birecik Turkey 37°2N 38°0E 213 D8
Birein Israel 30°50N 34°28E 251 H5
Bireuen Indonesia 5°14N 96°39E 234 A1
Birganj Nepal 27°1N 84°52E 243 F11
Birgu = Vittoriosa Malta 35°54N 14°31E 206 F8
Birhan Ethiopia 10°45N 38°4E 266 B4
Biri Norway 60°58N 10°35E 164 D7
Biri → South Sudan 7°56N 26°33E 257 F2
Birifo Gambia 13°30N 14°0W 262 C2
Birigüi Brazil 21°18S 50°16W 335 A5
Birini C.A.R. 7°51N 22°24E 264 A4
Bīrjand Iran 32°53N 59°13E 247 C8
Birkeland Norway 58°24N 7°12E 164 F5
Birkenfeld Germany 49°38N 7°9E 179 F3
Birkenhead U.K. 53°23N 3°2W 168 D4
Birkenstein Germany 52°31N 13°40E 115 A5
Birkerød Denmark 55°50N 12°25E 163 J6
Birket Fatmé Chad 12°55N 19°7E 259 F3
Birket Qârûn Egypt 29°30N 30°40E 256 J7
Birkfeld Austria 47°21N 15°45E 180 D8
Birkhadem Algeria 36°43N 3°3E 261 A5
Birkholz Germany 52°37N 13°34E 115 A4
Birkholzaue Germany 52°38N 13°36E 115 A4
Birkirkara Malta 35°54N 14°28E 206 F7
Bîrlad = Bârlad Romania 46°15N 27°38E 183 D12
Birmingham W. Mids.,
U.K. 52°29N 1°52W 169 E6
Birmingham Ala., U.S.A. 33°31N 86°48W 315 E11
Birmingham Iowa, U.S.A. 40°53N 91°57W 310 D5
Birmingham Int. ✕ (BHX)
U.K. 52°26N 1°45W 169 E6
Birmitrapur India 22°24N 84°46E 244 C7
Birni Ngaouré Niger 13°5N 2°51E 263 C5
Birni Nkonni Niger 13°55N 5°15E 263 C6
Birnie Kiribati 3°35S 171°31W 277 A16
Birnin Gwari Nigeria 11°0N 6°45E 263 C6
Birnin Kebbi Nigeria 12°32N 4°12E 263 C5
Birnin Kudu Nigeria 11°30N 9°29E 263 C6
Birobidzhan Russia 48°50N 132°50E 219 B15
Birougou, Mts. Gabon 1°51S 12°20E 264 C2
Birr Ireland 53°6N 7°54W 166 C4
Birrarung Park Australia 37°45S 145°4E 128 A2
Birrie → Australia 29°43S 146°37E 281 D4
Birsilpur India 28°11N 72°15E 242 E5
Birsk Russia 55°25N 55°30E 186 C10
Birtle Canada 50°30N 101°5W 297 C8
Biryuchiy Ukraine 46°10N 35°0E 189 J8
Biržai Lithuania 56°11N 24°45E 188 D3
Birzebbugga Malta 35°50N 14°32E 206 F8
Birzhi = Madona Latvia 56°53N 26°5E 188 D4
Birzula = Kotovsk
Ukraine 47°45N 29°35E 177 E15
Bisa Indonesia 1°15S 127°28E 231 E7
Bisáccia Italy 41°1N 15°22E 201 A8
Bisacquino Italy 37°42N 13°15E 200 E6
Bisai Japan 35°16N 136°44E 223 B8
Bisalpur India 28°14N 79°48E 243 E8
Bisbee U.S.A. 31°27N 109°55W 305 L9
Biscarrosse France 44°22N 1°20W 174 D2
Biscarrosse et de Parentis, Étang de
France 44°21N 1°10W 174 D2
Biscay, B. of Atl. Oc. 45°0N 2°0W 171 D1
Biscay Abyssal Plain
Atl. Oc. 45°0N 8°0W 152 B11
Biscayne ⌂ U.S.A. 25°25N 80°12W 317 K9
Biscayne B. U.S.A. 25°40N 80°12W 317 K9
Biscayne Park U.S.A. 25°52N 80°10W 128 A2
Biscéglie Italy 41°14N 16°30E 201 A9
Bischheim France 48°37N 7°46E 173 D14
Bischoflack = Škofja Loka
Slovenia 46°9N 14°19E 199 B11
Bischofsburg = Biskupiec
Poland 53°53N 20°58E 184 E7
Bischofshofen Austria 47°26N 13°14E 180 D6
Bischofstal = Ujazd Poland 50°23N 18°21E 185 H5
Bischofstein = Bisztynek
Poland 54°8N 20°53E 184 D7
Bischofswerda Germany 51°7N 14°10E 178 D10
Bischwiller France 48°46N 7°50E 173 D14
Biscoe Is. Antarctica 66°0S 67°0W 151 C17
Biscoitos Azores 38°47N 27°15W 153 d1
Biscotasing Canada 47°18N 82°9W 298 C3
Biševo Croatia 42°57N 16°3E 199 F13
Bisha Eritrea 15°30N 37°31E 257 D4
Bishah, W. → Si. Arabia 21°24N 43°26E 248 B3
Bishan China 29°33N 106°12E 228 C6
Bishanga
Dem. Rep. of the Congo 4°31S 21°2E 265 C4
Bishkek Kyrgyzstan 42°54N 74°46E 218 C3
Bishnath India 26°40N 93°10E 241 B4
Bishnupur India 23°8N 87°20E 243 H12
Bisho = Bhisho S. Africa 32°50S 27°23E 270 D4
Bishop Calif., U.S.A. 37°22N 118°24W 306 H8
Bishop Ga., U.S.A. 33°49N 83°26W 316 B6
Bishop Tex., U.S.A. 27°35N 97°48W 314 H6
Bishop Auckland U.K. 54°39N 1°40W 168 C6
Bishop Lavis S. Africa 33°56S 18°35E 118 A2
Bishop Museum U.S.A. 21°20N 157°52W 302 K14
Bishop's Falls Canada 49°2N 55°30W 299 C8
Bishop's Stortford U.K. 51°52N 0°10E 169 F8
Bishopscourt S. Africa 33°59S 18°27E 118 A1
Bisignano Italy 39°31N 16°17E 201 C9
Bisina, L. Uganda 1°38N 33°56E 268 B3
Biskra Algeria 34°50N 5°44E 261 B6
Biskra Malta 35°58N 14°21E 206 F7
Biskra □ Algeria 34°40N 5°25E 261 B6
Biskupiec Poland 53°53N 20°58E 184 E7
Bislig Phil. 8°12N 126°18E 233 G6
Bismarck Mo., U.S.A. 37°46N 90°38W 310 G6
Bismarck N. Dak., U.S.A. 46°48N 100°47W 308 B3
Bismarck Arch. Papua N. G. 2°30S 150°0E 286 B6
Bismarck Ra. Papua N. G. 5°35S 145°0E 286 C3
Bismarck Sea Papua N. G. 4°10S 146°50E 286 C4
Bismarckburg = Kasanga
Tanzania 8°30S 31°10E 269 D3
Bismark Germany 52°40N 11°33E 178 C7
Bismil Turkey 37°51N 40°40E 213 D9
Bismo Norway 61°54N 8°15E 164 C5
Biso Uganda 1°44N 31°26E 268 B3
Bison U.S.A. 45°31N 102°28W 308 C2
Bīsotūn Iran 34°23N 47°26E 213 E12
Bispebjerg Denmark 55°42N 12°31E 118 A3
Bispgården Sweden 63°2N 16°40E 162 A10
Bissagos = Bijagós, Arquipélago dos
Guinea-Biss. 11°15N 16°10W 262 C1
Bissam Cuttack India 19°31N 83°31E 244 E6
Bissau Guinea-Biss. 11°45N 15°45W 262 C1
Bissaula Nigeria 7°0N 10°27E 263 D7
Bissigh, Lach →
Somali Rep. 0°45N 41°33E 267 D5
Bissikrima Guinea 10°50N 10°58W 262 C2
Bissonet Plaza U.S.A. 30°1N 90°13W 131 A1
Bissorã Guinea-Biss. 12°16N 15°35W 262 C1
Bistcho L. Canada 59°45N 118°50W 296 B5
Bistreţ Romania 43°54N 23°23E 183 G8
Bistrica = Ilirska-Bistrica
Slovenia 45°34N 14°14E 199 C11
Bistriţa Romania 47°9N 24°35E 183 C9
Bistriţa → Romania 46°30N 26°57E 183 D11
Bistriţa Năsăud □
Romania 47°15N 24°30E 183 C9
Bistriţei, Munţii Romania 47°15N 25°40E 183 C10
Biswan India 27°29N 81°2E 243 F9
Bisztynek Poland 54°8N 20°53E 184 D7
Bita → C.A.R. 6°26N 24°43E 264 A4
Bitam Gabon 2°5N 11°25E 264 B2
Bitburg Germany 49°58N 6°31E 179 F2
Bitche France 49°2N 7°25E 173 C14
Bithynia Turkey 40°40N 31°0E 212 B4
Bitkine Chad 11°59N 18°13E 259 F3
Bitlis Turkey 38°20N 42°3E 213 C10
Bitlis □ Turkey 38°20N 42°5E 213 C10
Bitola Macedonia 41°1N 21°20E 202 E5
Bitolj = Bitola Macedonia 41°1N 21°20E 202 E5
Bitonto Italy 41°6N 16°41E 201 A9
Bitra I. India 11°33N 72°9E 245 J1
Bitter Creek U.S.A. 41°33N 108°33W 304 F9
Bitter L. = Buheirat-Murrat-el-
Kubra Egypt 30°18N 32°26E 256 H8
Bitterfeld Germany 51°37N 12°20E 178 D8
Bitterfontein S. Africa 31°1S 18°32E 270 D2
Bitterroot → U.S.A. 46°52N 114°7W 304 C6
Bitterroot Range U.S.A. 46°0N 114°20W 304 C6
Bitterwater U.S.A. 36°23N 121°0W 306 J6
Bitti Italy 40°29N 9°23E 200 B2
Bittou Burkina Faso 11°17N 0°18W 263 C4
Biu Nigeria 10°40N 12°3E 263 C7
Bivolari Romania 47°31N 27°27E 183 C12
Bivolu, Vf. Romania 47°16N 25°58E 183 C10
Biwa-Ko Japan 35°15N 136°10E 223 B8
Biwabik U.S.A. 47°32N 92°21W 308 B7
Bixad Romania 47°56N 23°28E 183 C8
Bixby U.S.A. 35°57N 95°53W 314 D7
Biya → Russia 52°25N 85°0E 217 B11
Biyala Egypt 31°10N 31°13E 251 G2
Biyang China 32°38N 113°21E 226 H7
Biysk Russia 52°40N 85°0E 217 B11
Bizana S. Africa 30°50S 29°52E 271 D4
Bizen Japan 34°43N 134°8E 222 C6
Bizerte Tunisia 37°15N 9°50E 258 A1
Bizerte □ Tunisia 37°5N 9°35E 261 A6
Bjåen fjellstove Norway 59°37N 7°26E 164 E4
Bjargtangar Iceland 65°30N 24°30W 155 B2
Bjarkalundur Iceland 65°33N 22°9W 155 B3
Bjärnum Sweden 56°17N 13°43E 163 H7
Bjästa Sweden 63°12N 18°29E 162 A12
Bjelasica Montenegro 42°50N 19°40E 202 D3
Bjelašnica Bos.-H. 43°43N 18°9E 182 G3
Bjelland Norway 58°23N 7°32E 164 F4
Bjelovar Croatia 45°56N 16°49E 199 C13
Bjerringbro Denmark 56°23N 9°39E 163 H3
Bjervamoen Norway 59°17N 9°5E 164 E6
Bjøberg Norway 60°56N 8°13E 164 D5
Björbo Sweden 60°27N 14°44E 162 D8
Björkelangen Norway 59°53N 11°34E 164 E8
Björklinge Sweden 60°2N 17°33E 162 D11
Björkö Sweden 59°19N 18°12E 139 B3
Björkö Sweden 59°52N 19°2E 162 E13
Bjørnafjorden Norway 60°7N 5°28E 164 D2
Björneborg = Pori Finland 61°29N 21°48E 188 B1
Björneborg Sweden 59°14N 14°16E 162 E8
Bjørnevatn Norway 69°40N 30°0E 160 B24
Bjørnøya Arctic 74°30N 19°0E 150 B8
Bjursås Sweden 60°44N 15°25E 162 D9
Bjuv Sweden 56°5N 12°55E 163 H6
Bla Mali 12°56N 5°47W 262 C3
Blå Jungfrun △ Sweden 57°16N 16°47E 163 G10
Blace Serbia 43°18N 21°17E 202 C5
Blachownia Poland 50°49N 18°56E 185 H5
Black = Da → Vietnam 21°15N 105°20E 228 G5
Black → Ont., Canada 44°42N 79°19W 312 B5
Black → Alaska, U.S.A. 66°42N 144°42W 303 C11
Black → Ariz., U.S.A. 33°44N 110°13W 305 K8
Black → Ark., U.S.A. 35°38N 91°20W 314 D9
Black → La., U.S.A. 31°16N 91°50W 314 F9
Black → Mich., U.S.A. 42°59N 82°27W 312 D2
Black → N.Y., U.S.A. 43°59N 76°4W 313 C8
Black → Wis., U.S.A. 43°57N 91°22W 308 D8
Black Bay Pen. Canada 48°38N 88°21W 298 C2
Black Birch L. Canada 56°53N 107°45W 297 B7
Black Canyon of the Gunnison ⌂
U.S.A. 38°40N 107°35W 304 G10
Black Cr. → Canada 43°40N 73°30W 141 A2
Black Creek Pioneer Village
Canada 43°46N 73°30W 141 A1
Black Diamond = Pittsburg
U.S.A. 38°2N 121°53W 306 G5
Black Diamond Canada 50°45N 114°14W 296 C6
Black Duck → Canada 56°51N 39°2W 298 A2
Black Forest = Schwarzwald
Germany 48°30N 8°20E 179 G4
Black Forest U.S.A. 39°0N 104°43W 304 G11
Black Hd. Ireland 53°9N 3°16W 166 C2
Black Hills U.S.A. 44°0N 103°45W 308 D2
Black I. Canada 51°12N 96°30W 297 C9
Black L. Canada 59°12N 105°15W 297 B7
Black L. Sask., Canada 59°12N 105°15W 297 B7
Black L. Mich., U.S.A. 45°28N 84°16W 309 C11
Black L. N.Y., U.S.A. 44°31N 75°36W 313 B9
Black Lake Canada 59°11N 105°20W 297 B7
Black Mesa U.S.A. 36°58N 102°58W 314 C3
Black Mountain
Australia 30°18S 151°39E 283 A9
Black Mt. = Mynydd Du
U.K. 51°52N 3°50W 169 F4
Black Mt. Bhutan 27°20N 90°25E 241 B3
Black Mts. U.K. 51°55N 3°7W 169 F4
Black Range U.S.A. 33°15N 107°50W 305 K10
Black River Jamaica 18°0N 77°50W 320 a
Black River N.Y., U.S.A. 44°0N 75°47W 313 C9
Black River B. Jamaica 18°0N 77°51W 320 a
Black River Falls U.S.A. 44°18N 90°51W 308 C8
Black River Gorges
Mauritius 20°24S 57°25E 272 e
Black Rock S. Austral.,
Australia 32°50S 138°44E 282 B3
Black Rock Barbados 13°7N 59°37W 323 r
Black Rock Desert
U.S.A. 41°10N 118°50W 304 F4
Black Sea Eurasia 43°30N 35°0E 187 F6
Black Tickle Canada 53°28N 55°45W 299 B8
Black Volta → Africa 8°41N 1°33W 262 D4
Black Warrior →
U.S.A. 32°32N 87°51W 315 E11
Blackall Australia 24°25S 145°45E 280 C4
Blackball N.Z. 42°22S 171°26E 285 C6
Blackbraes △ Australia 19°10S 144°10E 280 B3
Blackbull Australia 17°55S 141°45E 280 B3
Blackburn U.K. 53°45N 2°29W 168 D5
Blackburn, Mt. U.S.A. 61°44N 143°26W 303 F12
Blackburn with Darwen □
U.K. 53°45N 2°29W 168 D5
Blackdown Tableland △
Australia 23°52S 149°8E 280 C4
Blackfen U.K. 51°26N 0°6E 125 B4
Blackfoot U.S.A. 43°11N 112°21W 304 E7
Blackfoot → U.S.A. 46°52N 113°53W 304 C7
Blackfoot Res. U.S.A. 42°55N 111°39W 304 E8
Blackheath U.K. 51°28N 0°0 125 B4
Blackman U.S.A. 30°56N 86°38W 317 E3
Blackpool U.K. 53°49N 3°3W 168 D4
Blackpool □ U.K. 53°49N 3°3W 168 D4
Blackriver U.S.A. 44°46N 83°17W 312 B1
Blackrock Ireland 53°18N 6°11W 120 B2
Blacks Harbour Canada 45°3N 66°49W 299 C6
Blacksburg U.S.A. 37°14N 80°25W 309 G13
Blackshear U.S.A. 31°18N 82°14W 316 D7
Blackshear, L. U.S.A. 31°51N 83°56W 316 D6
Blacksod B. Ireland 54°6N 10°0W 166 B1
Blackstairs Mt. Ireland 52°33N 6°48W 166 D5
Blackstone U.S.A. 37°5N 78°0W 309 G14
Blackstone Ra. Australia 26°0S 128°30E 279 E4
Blackville U.S.A. 33°22N 81°16W 316 B8
Blackwater = West Road →
Canada 53°18N 122°53W 296 C4
Blackwater Australia 23°35S 148°53E 280 C4
Blackwater → Meath,
Ireland 53°39N 6°41W 166 C4
Blackwater → Waterford,
Ireland 52°4N 7°52W 166 D4
Blackwater → Armagh,
U.K. 54°31N 6°35W 166 B5
Blackwater → Fla., U.S.A. 30°36N 87°2W 317 E2
Blackwater → Mo.,
U.S.A. 38°56N 92°57W 310 F4
Blackwell U.S.A. 36°48N 97°17W 314 C6
Blackwells Corner
U.S.A. 35°37N 119°47W 307 K7
Blackwood, C. Papua N. G. 7°49S 144°31E 286 D3
Bladensburg U.S.A. 38°55N 76°55W 143 B4
Bladensburg △ Australia 22°30S 142°59E 280 C3
Blaenau Ffestiniog U.K. 53°0N 3°56W 168 E4
Blaenau Gwent □ U.K. 51°48N 3°12W 169 F4
Bláfell Iceland 64°30N 19°51W 155 C7
Bláfjall Iceland 65°26N 16°50W 155 B10
Blagaj Bos.-H. 43°16N 17°55E 202 C1
Blagnac France 43°37N 1°23E 174 E5
Blagnac, Toulouse ✕ (TLS)
France 43°37N 1°22E 174 E5
Blagodarnoye = Blagodarnyy
Russia 45°7N 43°37E 191 H6
Blagodarnyy Russia 45°7N 43°37E 191 H6
Blagoevgrad Bulgaria 42°2N 23°5E 202 D7
Blagoevgrad □ Bulgaria 42°2N 23°5E 202 D7
Blagoveshchensk
Russia 50°20N 127°30E 219 A14
Blahkiuh Indonesia 8°31S 115°12E 231 J18
Blain Loire-Atlantique,
France 47°29N 1°45W 172 E5
Blain Pa., U.S.A. 40°20N 77°31W 312 F7
Blaine Minn., U.S.A. 45°10N 93°13W 308 C7
Blaine Wash., U.S.A. 48°59N 122°45W 306 B4
Blaine Lake Canada 52°51N 106°52W 297 C7
Blair U.S.A. 41°33N 96°8W 308 E5
Blair Athol Australia 22°42S 147°31E 280 C4
Blair Atholl U.K. 56°46N 3°50W 167 E5
Blair Village U.S.A. 33°40N 84°23W 113 C2
Blairgowrie Gauteng, S. Africa 26°6S 28°0E 123 A2
Blairgowrie Perth & Kinr.,
U.K. 56°35N 3°21W 167 E5
Blairsden U.S.A. 39°47N 120°37W 306 F6
Blairsville U.S.A. 40°26N 79°16W 312 F5
Blaj Romania 46°10N 23°57E 183 D8
Blaka Niger 21°21N 12°47E 259 D2
Blakang Mati, Pulau
Singapore 1°15N 103°50E 237 d
Blake House U.S.A. 42°19N 71°3W 116 B2
Blake Pt. U.S.A. 48°11N 88°25W 308 A9
Blakehurst Australia 33°59S 151°6E 139 B1
Blakely Ga., U.S.A. 31°23N 84°56W 316 D5
Blakely Pa., U.S.A. 41°28N 75°37W 313 E9
Blakesburg U.S.A. 40°58N 92°38W 310 D4
Blakstad Akershus, Norway 59°49N 10°28E 133 B1
Blakstad Aust-Agder,
Norway 58°30N 8°39E 164 F5
Blambangan, Semenanjung
Indonesia 8°42S 114°29E 231 K17
Blâmont France 48°35N 6°50E 173 D13
Blanc, C. Spain 39°21N 2°51E 206 B3
Blanc, C. Tunisia 37°15N 9°56E 258 A1
Blanc, Mont Europe 45°48N 6°50E 175 C10
Blanca, B. Argentina 39°10S 61°30W 336 A4
Blanca Peak U.S.A. 37°35N 105°29W 305 H11
Blanchardville U.S.A. 42°49N 89°52W 310 B7
Blanche, C. Australia 33°1S 134°9E 281 E1
Blanche, L. S. Austral.,
Australia 29°15S 139°40E 281 D2
Blanche, L. W. Austral.,
Australia 22°25S 123°17E 278 D3
Blanche, L. Fla., U.S.A. 28°28N 81°30W 133 B1
Blanche, Pte. St. Lucia 13°53N 61°5W 323 m
Blanche, Pte. St.-Maarten 18°0N 63°2W 322 a
Blanche Channel
Solomon Is. 8°30S 157°30E 287 M9
Blanchester U.S.A. 39°17N 83°59W 311 E13
Blanchisseuse Trin. & Tob. 10°48N 61°18W 323 t
Blanco Western Cape,
S. Africa 33°55S 22°23E 270 D3
Blanco Tex., U.S.A. 30°6N 98°25W 314 F5
Blanco → Argentina 30°20S 68°42W 334 C2
Blanco → Bolivia 12°30S 64°18W 331 C5
Blanco, C. Costa Rica 9°34N 85°8W 320 E2
Blanco, C. Oreg., U.S.A. 42°51N 124°34W 304 E1
Blanco, Pta. Bonaire 12°13N 68°14W 322 h
Blanda → Iceland 65°37N 20°9W 155 B6
Blandford Forum U.K. 50°51N 2°9W 169 G5
Blanding U.S.A. 37°37N 109°29W 305 H9
Blandinsville U.S.A. 40°33N 90°52W 310 D6
Blanes Spain 41°40N 2°48E 196 D7
Blangkejeren Indonesia 3°59N 97°20E 234 B1
Blangpidie Indonesia 3°44N 96°49E 234 B1
Blangy-sur-Bresle France 49°55N 1°37E 173 C8
Blanice → Czech Rep. 49°10N 14°5E 180 B7
Blankaholm Sweden 57°36N 16°31E 163 G10
Blankenberge Belgium 51°20N 3°9E 170 C3
Blankenburg Berlin,
Germany 52°35N 13°27E 115 A3
Blankenburg Sachsen-Anhalt,
Germany 51°47N 10°57E 178 D6
Blankenfelde Germany 52°37N 13°23E 115 A3
Blanku, L. Curaçao 12°2N 68°47W 322 g
Blanquefort France 44°55N 0°38W 174 D3
Blanquilla Venezuela 11°51N 64°37W 321 D7
Blanquillo Uruguay 32°53S 55°37W 335 C4
Blansko Czech Rep. 49°22N 16°40E 181 B9
Blantyre Malawi 15°45S 35°0E 269 F4
Blarney Ireland 51°56N 8°33W 166 E3
Blasdell U.S.A. 42°48N 78°50W 312 D6
Błåsjø Norway 59°20N 6°50E 164 E4
Błaszki Poland 51°38N 18°30E 185 G5
Blatná Czech Rep. 49°25N 13°52E 180 B6
Blato Croatia 42°56N 16°48E 199 F13
Blaubeuren Germany 48°25N 9°47E 179 G5
Blaustein Germany 48°25N 9°53E 179 G5
Blåvands Huk Denmark 55°33N 8°4E 163 J2
Blaydon U.K. 54°58N 1°42W 168 C6
Blaye France 45°8N 0°40W 174 C3
Blaye-les-Mines France 44°1N 2°8E 174 D6
Blayney Australia 33°32S 149°14E 283 B8
Blaze, Pt. Australia 12°56S 130°11E 278 B5
Błażowa Poland 49°53N 22°7E 185 J9
Blechhammer = Blachownia
Poland 50°49N 18°56E 185 H5
Bleckede Germany 53°17N 10°43E 178 B6
Bled Slovenia 46°27N 14°7E 199 B11
Blefjell Norway 59°48N 9°10E 164 E6
Bleiburg Austria 46°35N 14°49E 180 E7
Blejeşti Romania 44°19N 25°27E 183 F10
Blekinge Sweden 56°25N 15°20E 161 H16
Blekinge län □ Sweden 56°20N 15°20E 163 H9
Blenheim Ont., Canada 42°20N 82°0W 312 D3
Blenheim N.Z. 41°38S 173°57E 285 B8
Bléone → France 44°5N 6°3E 175 D10
Blérancourt France 49°31N 3°9E 173 C10
Bletchley U.K. 51°59N 0°44W 169 F7
Bleus, Monts
Dem. Rep. of the Congo 1°30N 30°30E 268 B3
Blida Algeria 36°30N 2°49E 261 A5
Blida □ Algeria 36°30N 2°0E 261 A5
Blidet Amor Algeria 32°59N 5°58E 261 B6
Blidö Sweden 59°37N 18°53E 162 E12
Blidsberg Sweden 57°56N 13°30E 163 G7
Blieskastel Germany 49°14N 7°12E 179 F3
Bligh Sound N.Z. 44°47S 167°32E 285 E2
Bligh Water Fiji 17°0S 178°0E 287 A2
Blind River Canada 46°10N 82°58W 298 C3
Blinisht Albania 41°52N 19°59E 202 E3
Bliss Idaho, U.S.A. 42°56N 114°57W 304 E6
Bliss N.Y., U.S.A. 42°34N 78°15W 312 D6
Blissfield Mich., U.S.A. 41°50N 83°52W 311 C13
Blissfield Ohio, U.S.A. 40°24N 81°58W 312 F3
Blitar Indonesia 8°5S 112°11E 235 D4
Blitchton U.S.A. 32°12N 81°26W 316 C8
Blitta Togo 8°23N 1°6E 263 D5
Blizne Poland 52°14N 20°52E 142 B1
Block I. U.S.A. 41°11N 71°35W 313 E13
Block Island Sd. U.S.A. 41°15N 71°40W 313 E13
Bloemenmarkt Amsterdam, Neths. 112 b2
Bloemfontein S. Africa 29°6S 26°7E 270 C4
Bloemhof S. Africa 27°38S 25°32E 270 C4
Blois France 47°35N 1°20E 172 E8
Blomskog Sweden 59°16N 12°2E 162 E6
Blomstermåla Sweden 56°59N 16°21E 163 H10
Blomvåg Norway 60°32N 4°53E 164 D1
Blönduós Iceland 65°40N 20°12W 155 B6
Blongas Indonesia 8°53S 116°2E 231 K19
Blonie Poland 52°12N 20°37E 185 F7
Bloodvein → Canada 51°47N 96°43W 297 C9
Bloody B. Trin. & Tob. 11°18N 60°38W 323 s
Bloody Foreland Ireland 55°10N 8°17W 166 A3
Bloom = Chicago Heights
U.S.A. 41°30N 87°38W 311 C9
Bloomer U.S.A. 45°6N 91°29W 308 C8
Bloomfield Ont., Canada 43°59N 77°14W 312 C7
Bloomfield Ind., U.S.A. 39°1N 86°57W 311 E10
Bloomfield Iowa, U.S.A. 40°45N 92°25W 310 D4
Bloomfield Ky., U.S.A. 37°55N 85°19W 311 G11
Bloomfield N. Mex.,
U.S.A. 36°43N 107°59W 305 H10
Bloomfield Nebr., U.S.A. 42°36N 97°39W 308 D5
Bloomingburg U.S.A. 39°36N 83°24W 311 E13
Bloomington Ill., U.S.A. 40°28N 89°0W 310 D8
Bloomington Ind., U.S.A. 39°10N 86°32W 311 E10
Bloomington Minn.,
U.S.A. 44°50N 93°17W 308 C7
Bloomington Wis., U.S.A. 42°53N 90°55W 310 B6
Bloomsburg U.S.A. 41°0N 76°27W 313 F8
Bloomsbury Australia 20°48S 148°38E 280 b
Bloomsbury London, U.K. 125 a3
Blora Indonesia 6°57S 111°25E 235 D4
Blossburg U.S.A. 41°41N 77°4W 312 E7
Blosseville Kyst Greenland 68°50N 26°30W 154 D8
Błota Poland 52°9N 21°11E 142 C3
Blouberg S. Africa 23°8S 28°59E 271 B4
Blountstown U.S.A. 30°27N 85°3W 316 E4
Blowing Point Village
Anguilla 18°11N 63°6W 322 a
Blowing Rock Anguilla 18°9N 63°10W 322 a
Bludenz Austria 47°10N 9°50E 180 D2
Blue → U.S.A. 38°11N 86°13W 311 F10
Blue Cypress L. U.S.A. 27°44N 80°45W 317 H9
Blue Earth U.S.A. 43°38N 94°6W 308 D6
Blue Hole Jamaica 18°10N 76°24W 320 a
Blue Hole △ Belize 17°24N 88°30W 320 C2
Blue Island U.S.A. 41°40N 87°40W 119 D2
Blue Lagoon △ Zambia 15°28S 27°26E 269 F2
Blue Mesa Res. U.S.A. 38°28N 107°20W 304 G10
Blue Mosque = Sultanahme Camil
Turkey 41°0N 28°58E 122 B1
Blue Mound U.S.A. 39°42N 89°7W 310 E7
Blue Mountain Lake
U.S.A. 43°51N 74°27W 313 C10
Blue Mountain Pk. Jamaica 18°3N 76°36W 320 a
Blue Mountains and John Crow
Mountains Nat. Park △
Jamaica 18°5N 76°34W 320 a
Blue Mt. U.S.A. 40°30N 76°30W 313 F8
Blue Mts. N.S.W.,
Australia 33°40S 150°15E 283 B9
Blue Mts. Jamaica 18°3N 76°36W 320 a
Blue Mts. Maine, U.S.A. 44°50N 70°35W 313 B14
Blue Mts. Oreg., U.S.A. 45°0N 118°20W 304 D4
Blue Mts. △ Australia 34°2S 150°15E 283 C9
Blue Mud B. Australia 13°30S 136°0E 280 A2
Blue Mud Bay ✪ Australia 13°25S 136°2E 280 A2
Blue Nile = Nîl el Azraq →
Sudan 15°38N 32°31E 257 D3
Blue Nile Falls = Tis Issat
Ethiopia 11°25N 37°45E 257 E4
Blue Rapids U.S.A. 39°41N 96°39W 308 F5
Blue Ridge U.S.A. 36°40N 80°50W 309 G13
Blue River Canada 52°6N 119°18W 296 C5
Blue Springs U.S.A. 39°1N 94°17W 310 E2
Bluebell Ireland 53°19N 6°21W 120 B1
Bluefield U.S.A. 37°15N 81°17W 309 G13
Bluefields Nic. 12°20N 83°50W 320 D3
Bluevale Canada 43°51N 81°15W 312 C3
Bluff Queens., Australia 23°35S 149°4E 280 C4
Bluff N.Z. 46°37S 168°20E 285 G3
Bluff Utah, U.S.A. 37°17N 109°33W 305 H9
Bluff Harbour N.Z. 46°36S 168°21E 285 G3
Bluff Hd. China 22°11N 114°12E 122 B2
Bluff Knoll Australia 34°24S 118°15E 279 F2
Bluff Pt. Australia 27°50S 114°5E 279 E1
Bluffers Park Canada 43°43N 79°14W 141 A3
Bluffs U.S.A. 39°45N 90°32W 310 E6
Bluffton Ga., U.S.A. 31°31N 84°52W 316 D5
Bluffton Ind., U.S.A. 40°44N 85°11W 311 D11
Bluffton Ohio, U.S.A. 40°54N 83°54W 311 D13
Bluffton S.C., U.S.A. 32°14N 80°52W 316 C9
Blumberg Germany 52°36N 13°39E 115 A4
Blumenau = Stettler
Canada 52°19N 112°40W 296 C6
Blumenau Brazil 27°0S 49°0W 335 B6
Blunt U.S.A. 44°31N 99°59W 308 C4
Blunt Pt. U.S.A. 37°51N 122°25W 136 A2
Blutenberg Germany 48°9N 11°27E 131 B1
Bly U.S.A. 42°24N 121°3W 304 E3
Blyde River Canyon ⌂
S. Africa 24°37S 31°2E 271 B5
Blylaget Norway 59°56N 10°41E 133 B3
Blyth S. Austral., Australia 33°49S 138°28E 282 B3
Blyth Ont., Canada 43°44N 81°26W 312 C3
Blyth Northumberland, U.K. 55°8N 1°31W 168 B6
Blythe Calif., U.S.A. 33°37N 114°36W 307 M12
Blythe Ga., U.S.A. 33°17N 82°12W 316 B7
Blytheville U.S.A. 35°56N 89°55W 315 D10
Bø Telemark, Norway 59°25N 9°3E 164 E6
Bo S. Leone 7°55N 11°50W 262 D2
Bo Duc Vietnam 11°58N 106°50E 237 G6

Bo-eun S. Korea 36°29N 127°43E 224 D3
Bo Hai China 39°0N 119°0E 227 E10
Bo Hai Haixia Asia 38°25N 121°10E 227 E11
Bo-Kaap Museum Cape Town, S. Africa 118 c2
Bō-no-Misaki Japan 31°15N 130°13E 222 F2
Bo Xian = Bozhou China 33°55N 115°41E 226 H8
Boa Esperança Brazil 3°21N 61°23W 329 C5
Boa Esperança, Represa Brazil 6°50S 43°50W 332 C3
Boa Nova Brazil 14°22S 40°10W 333 D3
Boa Viagem Brazil 5°7S 39°44W 332 C4
Boa Vista = Tocantinópolis Brazil 6°20S 47°25W 332 C2
Boa Vista Brazil 2°48N 60°30W 329 C5
Boa Vista C. Verde Is. 16°0N 22°49W 153 j
Boa Vista, Alto do Brazil 22°58S 43°16W 135 B1
Boa Vista do Erechim = Erechim Brazil 27°35S 52°15W 335 B5
Boac Phil. 13°27N 121°50E 232 E3
Boaco Nic. 12°29N 85°35W 320 D2
Bo'ai China 35°10N 113°3E 226 G7
Boal Spain 43°25N 6°49W 194 B4
Boali C.A.R. 4°48N 18°7E 264 B3
Boalsburg U.S.A. 40°47N 77°49W 312 F7
Boane Mozam. 26°6S 32°19E 271 C5
Boang I. Papua N. G. 3°23S 153°18E 286 B7
Boao China 19°8N 110°34E 236 C8
Boardman U.S.A. 41°2N 80°40W 312 E4
Boardwalk U.S.A. 40°34N 73°49W 132 C3
Boath India 19°20N 78°20E 244 E4
Boatswain Bird I. Ascension I. 7°56S 14°18W 153 g
Boavista Portugal 38°48N 9°8W 126 A2
Boayan I. Phil. 10°34N 119°9E 233 F2
Boaz I. Bermuda 32°18N 64°51W 153 a
Bob Marley Mausoleum Jamaica 18°18N 77°18W 320 a
Bobadah Australia 32°19S 146°41E 283 B7
Bobai China 22°17N 109°59E 228 F7
Bobbili India 18°35N 83°30E 244 E6
Bóbbio Italy 44°46N 9°23E 198 D6
Bobcaygeon Canada 44°33N 78°33W 312 B6
Bobigny France 48°54N 2°26E 134 A3
Boblad India 17°13N 75°26E 244 F2
Böblingen Germany 48°40N 9°1E 179 G5
Bobo-Dioulasso Burkina Faso 11°8N 4°13W 262 C4
Bobolice Poland 53°58N 16°37E 184 E3
Bobon Phil. 12°32N 124°34E 232 E5
Bobonaza → Ecuador 2°36S 76°38W 328 D2
Bobonong Botswana 21°58S 28°20E 271 B4
Boboshevo Bulgaria 42°9N 23°0E 202 D7
Bobov Dol Bulgaria 42°20N 23°0E 202 D6
Bóbr → Poland 52°4N 15°4E 185 F2
Bobraomby, Tanjon' i Madag. 12°40S 49°10E 272 A2
Bobrov Russia 51°5N 40°2E 190 E5
Bobrovytsya Ukraine 50°45N 31°23E 189 G6
Bobruysk = Babruysk Belarus 53°10N 29°15E 177 B15
Bobrynets Ukraine 48°4N 32°5E 189 H7
Bobures Venezuela 9°15N 71°11W 328 B3
Boca del Río Mexico 19°5N 96°4W 319 D5
Boca do Acre Brazil 8°50S 67°27W 330 B4
Boca do Jari Brazil 1°7S 51°58W 329 D7
Boca Grande Fla., U.S.A. 26°45N 82°16W 317 J7
Boca Grande Venezuela 8°40N 60°40W 329 B5
Boca Raton U.S.A. 26°21N 80°5W 317 J9
Boca Slagbaai Bonaire 12°16N 68°24W 322 h
Bocaiúva Brazil 17°7S 43°49W 333 E3
Bocanda Ivory C. 7°5N 4°31W 262 D4
Bocanegra Peru 12°1S 77°7W 124 B2
Bocaranga C.A.R. 7°0N 15°35E 264 A3
Bocas del Dragón = Dragon's Mouths Venezuela 11°0N 61°50W 323 t
Bocas del Toro Panama 9°15N 82°20W 320 E3
Boceguillas Spain 41°20N 3°39W 194 D7
Bochkarevo = Belogorsk Russia 51°0N 128°20E 215 D13
Bochmanivka Ukraine 47°40N 29°34E 183 C14
Bochnia Poland 49°58N 20°27E 185 J7
Bocholt Germany 51°50N 6°36E 178 D2
Bochum = Senwabarana S. Africa 23°17S 29°7E 271 B4
Bochum Germany 51°28N 7°13E 178 D3
Bockenem Germany 52°1N 10°8E 178 C6
Boćki Poland 52°39N 23°3E 185 F10
Bocognano France 42°5N 9°4E 175 F13
Bocoio Angola 12°28S 14°10E 265 E2
Boconó Venezuela 9°15N 70°16W 328 B3
Boconó → Venezuela 8°43N 69°34W 328 B4
Bocoyna Mexico 27°52N 107°35W 318 B3
Bocşa Romania 45°21N 21°47E 182 E6
Boda C.A.R. 4°19N 17°26E 264 B3
Boda Dalarna, Sweden 61°1N 15°13E 162 C9
Böda Kalmar, Sweden 57°15N 17°3E 163 G11
Boda Västernorrland, Sweden 62°52N 16°39E 162 B10
Bodafors Sweden 57°48N 14°23E 163 G8
Bodaybo Russia 57°50N 114°0E 215 D12
Boddam U.K. 59°56N 1°17W 167 B7
Boddington Australia 32°50S 116°30E 279 F2
Bode Sadu Nigeria 9°0N 4°47E 263 D5
Bodega Bay U.S.A. 38°20N 123°3W 306 G3
Boden Sweden 65°50N 21°42E 160 D19
Bodensee Europe 47°35N 9°25E 179 H5
Bodenteich Germany 52°50N 10°42E 178 C6
Bodhan India 18°40N 77°44E 244 E3
Bodinayakkanur India 10°2N 77°10E 245 J3
Bodinga Nigeria 12°58N 5°10E 263 C6
Bodmin U.K. 50°28N 4°43W 169 G3
Bodmin Moor U.K. 50°33N 4°36W 169 G3
Bodø Norway 67°17N 14°24E 160 C16
Bodoquena, Serra da Brazil 21°0S 56°50W 331 E6
Bodoupa C.A.R. 5°43N 17°36E 264 A3
Bodrichi Chad 19°11N 15°54E 259 E3
Bodrog → Hungary 48°11N 21°22E 182 B6
Bodrum Turkey 37°3N 27°30E 205 D9
Boduna Dem. Rep. of the Congo 5°5N 19°44E 264 A3
Bódva → Hungary 48°19N 20°45E 182 B5
Boedo Argentina 34°38S 58°26W 117 B2
Boembé Congo 2°54S 15°39E 264 C3
Boën France 45°44N 4°1E 175 C8
Boende Dem. Rep. of the Congo 0°24S 21°12E 264 C4
Boerne U.S.A. 29°47N 98°44W 314 G5
Boesmans → S. Africa 33°42S 26°39E 270 D4
Boffa Guinea 10°16N 14°3W 262 C2
Bog Walk Jamaica 18°6N 77°1W 320 a
Bogal, Lagh → Kenya 0°41N 40°57E 267 D5
Bogale Burma 16°17N 95°24E 241 G5
Bogalusa U.S.A. 30°47N 89°52W 315 F10
Bogan → Australia 30°20S 146°55E 283 A7
Bogan Gate Australia 33°7S 147°49E 283 B7
Bogandé Burkina Faso 13°2N 0°8W 263 C4
Bogangolo C.A.R. 5°34N 18°15E 264 A3
Bogantungan Australia 23°41S 147°17E 280 C4
Bogata U.S.A. 33°28N 95°13W 314 E7
Bogatić Serbia 44°51N 19°30E 202 B3
Boğazkale Turkey 40°2N 34°37E 212 B6
Boğazlıyan Turkey 39°11N 35°14E 212 C6
Bogbonga Dem. Rep. of the Congo 1°36N 19°24E 264 B3
Bogda Shan China 43°35N 89°40E 217 D11
Bogen Sweden 60°4N 12°33E 162 D6
Bogenhausen Germany 48°8N 11°36E 131 B2
Bogense Denmark 55°34N 10°5E 163 J4
Bogetići Montenegro 42°41N 18°58E 202 D2
Boggabilla Australia 28°36S 150°24E 281 D5
Boggabri Australia 30°45S 150°5E 283 A9
Boggeragh Mts. Ireland 52°2N 8°55W 166 D3
Boggy Peak Antigua & B. 17°2N 61°52W 322 b
Boghari = Ksar el Boukhari Algeria 35°51N 2°52E 261 A5
Bogia Papua N. G. 4°9S 145°0E 286 C3
Bogildo S. Korea 34°9N 126°32E 224 E3
Boglan = Solhan Turkey 38°57N 41°3E 213 C9
Bogles Grenada 12°30N 61°26W 323 q
Bognor Regis U.K. 50°47N 0°40W 169 G7
Bogo Phil. 11°3N 124°0E 233 F4
Bogodukhov = Bohodukhiv Ukraine 50°9N 35°33E 189 G8
Bogol Manya Ethiopia 4°34N 41°29E 257 G5
Bogong, Mt. Australia 36°47S 147°17E 283 D7
Bogor Indonesia 6°36S 106°48E 234 D3
Bogoroditsk Russia 53°47N 38°8E 188 F10
Bogorodsk = Noginsk Russia 55°50N 38°25E 188 E10
Bogorodsk Russia 56°4N 43°30E 190 B6
Bogorodskoye = Kamskoye Ustye Russia 55°10N 49°20E 190 C9
Bogorodskoye = Leninskoye Russia 58°23N 47°3E 190 A8
Bogorodskoye Russia 55°48N 37°42E 129 B4
Bogoslovsky = Karpinsk Russia 59°45N 60°1E 186 C11
Bogoso Ghana 5°38N 2°3W 262 D4
Bogotá Colombia 4°34N 74°0W 328 C3
Bogota N.J., U.S.A. 40°52N 74°2W 132 A1
Bogotol Russia 56°15N 89°50E 214 D9
Bogou Togo 10°40N 0°12E 263 C5
Bogra Bangla. 24°51N 89°22E 241 C2
Bogstadvatnet Norway 59°58N 10°37E 133 A2
Boguchany Russia 58°40N 97°30E 215 D10
Boguchar Russia 49°55N 40°32E 190 F5
Bogué Mauritania 16°45N 14°10W 262 B2
Boguszów-Gorce Poland 50°45N 16°12E 185 H3
Bohain-en-Vermandois France 49°59N 3°28E 173 C10
Bohdan Ukraine 48°2N 24°22E 183 B9
Bohemian Forest = Böhmerwald Germany 49°8N 13°14E 179 F9
Bohena Cr. → Australia 30°17S 149°42E 283 A8
Bohinjska Bistrica Slovenia 46°17N 14°1E 199 B11
Böhmerwald Germany 49°8N 13°14E 179 F9
Böhmisch-Brod = Český Brod Czech Rep. 50°4N 14°52E 180 A7
Böhmisch-Leipa = Česká Lípa Czech Rep. 50°45N 14°30E 180 A7
Böhmisch-Trübau = Česká Třebová Czech Rep. 49°54N 16°27E 181 B9
Bohmte Germany 52°22N 8°19E 178 C4
Bohnsdorf Germany 52°23N 13°34E 115 B4
Bohodukhiv Ukraine 50°9N 35°33E 189 G8
Bohol Somali Rep. 5°45N 46°9E 267 C6
Bohol □ Phil. 9°50N 124°10E 233 G5
Bohol Sea Phil. 9°0N 124°0E 233 G5
Bohol Str. Phil. 9°45N 123°40E 233 G4
Bohongou Burkina Faso 12°30N 0°40E 263 C5
Böhönye Hungary 46°25N 17°28E 182 D2
Bohorodchany Ukraine 48°48N 24°32E 183 B9
Bohorok Indonesia 3°30N 98°12E 237 L2
Böhöt Mongolia 45°13N 108°16E 226 B5
Bohu China 41°58N 86°37E 217 D11
Bohuslän Sweden 58°25N 12°0E 163 F5
Bohuslav Ukraine 49°33N 30°56E 189 H6
Boi Nigeria 9°35N 9°27E 263 D6
Boi, Pta. do Brazil 23°55S 45°15W 335 A6
Boiaçu Brazil 0°27S 61°46W 329 D5
Boigu Australia 9°16S 142°13E 280 a
Boigu I. Australia 9°15S 142°14E 286 E2
Boileau, C. Australia 17°40S 122°7E 278 C3
Boim Brazil 2°49S 55°10W 329 D6
Boing'o South Sudan 9°58N 33°44E 257 F3
Boipariguda India 18°46N 82°26E 244 E6
Boipeba, I. de Brazil 13°39S 38°55W 333 D4
Boiro Spain 42°39N 8°54W 194 C2
Bois → Brazil 18°35S 50°2W 333 E1
Bois-Blanc Réunion 21°11S 55°49E 272 f
Bois-Colombes France 48°55N 2°16E 134 A2
Bois-d'Arcy France 48°48N 2°1E 134 B1
Boise U.S.A. 43°37N 116°13W 304 E5
Boise City U.S.A. 36°44N 102°31W 314 C3
Boissevain Canada 49°15N 100°5W 297 D8
Boissy-St-Léger France 48°44N 2°31E 134 B4
Bôite → Italy 46°5N 12°5E 199 B9
Boitzenburg Germany 53°16N 13°35E 178 B9
Boizenburg Germany 53°23N 10°43E 178 B6
Bojador W. Sahara 23°56N 15°49W 260 D1
Bojador, C. W. Sahara 26°0N 14°30W 260 C2
Bojana → Albania 41°52N 19°22E 202 E3
Bojano Italy 41°29N 14°29E 201 A7
Bojanowo Poland 51°43N 16°42E 185 G3
Bøjden Denmark 55°6N 10°7E 163 J4
Bojnūrd Iran 37°30N 57°20E 247 B8
Bojonegoro Indonesia 7°11S 111°54E 235 D4
Boju Nigeria 7°22N 7°55E 263 D6
Boka Serbia 45°22N 20°52E 182 E5
Boka Kotorska Montenegro 42°23N 18°32E 202 D2
Boka Tabla Curaçao 12°22N 69°8W 322 g
Bokada Dem. Rep. of the Congo 4°8N 19°23E 264 B3
Bokala Dem. Rep. of the Congo 3°8S 17°4E 264 C3
Bokala Ivory C. 8°31N 4°33W 262 D4
Bokani Nigeria 9°28N 5°10E 263 D6
Bokaro India 23°46N 85°55E 243 H11
Bokatola Dem. Rep. of the Congo 0°38S 18°46E 264 C3
Boké Guinea 10°56N 14°17W 262 C2
Bokela Dem. Rep. of the Congo 1°10S 21°59E 264 C4
Bokenda Dem. Rep. of the Congo 1°16N 21°22E 264 B4
Bokhara → Australia 29°55S 146°42E 281 D4
Bokkos Nigeria 9°17N 9°1E 263 D6
Boklar Dağları Turkey 37°5N 33°55E 250 A4
Boknafjorden Norway 59°14N 5°40E 164 E2
Boko Congo 4°46S 14°36E 265 C2
Bokode Dem. Rep. of the Congo 3°55N 19°36E 264 B3
Bokolo Gabon 2°40S 10°10E 264 C2
Bokondo Dem. Rep. of the Congo 0°15N 22°32E 264 B4
Bokor △ Cambodia 10°50N 104°1E 237 G5
Bokora △ Uganda 2°12N 31°32E 268 B3
Bokoro Chad 12°25N 17°14E 259 F3
Bokota Dem. Rep. of the Congo 0°56S 22°24E 264 C4
Bokote Dem. Rep. of the Congo 0°12S 21°8E 264 C4
Bokpyin Burma 11°18N 98°42E 237 G2
Boksitogorsk Russia 59°22N 33°50E 188 C7
Boku Papua N. G. 6°34S 155°21E 286 D8
Bokungu Dem. Rep. of the Congo 0°35S 22°50E 264 C4
Bol Chad 13°30N 14°40E 259 F2
Bol Croatia 43°18N 16°38E 199 E13
Bolama Guinea-Biss. 11°30N 15°30W 262 C1
Bolan → Pakistan 28°38N 67°42E 242 E2
Bolan Pass Pakistan 29°50N 67°20E 240 C2
Bolaños → Mexico 21°12N 104°5W 318 C4
Bolaños de Calatrava Spain 38°54N 3°40W 195 G7
Bolayır Turkey 40°31N 26°45E 203 F10
Bolbec France 49°30N 0°30E 172 C7
Boldājī Iran 31°56N 51°3E 247 D6
Boldeşti-Scăeni Romania 45°3N 26°2E 183 E11
Boldinasco Italy 45°29N 9°8E 129 B1
Bole Xinjiang Uygur, China 44°55N 81°37E 217 C10
Bole Ethiopia 6°36N 37°20E 257 F4
Bole Ghana 9°3N 2°23W 262 D4
Bolekhiv Ukraine 49°0N 23°57E 177 D12
Boleko Dem. Rep. of the Congo 1°35S 19°50E 264 C3
Bøler Norway 59°53N 10°50E 133 A4
Bolesławiec Poland 51°17N 15°37E 185 G2
Bolgatanga Ghana 10°44N 0°53W 263 C4
Bolgrad = Bolhrad Ukraine 45°40N 28°32E 183 E13
Bolhrad Ukraine 45°40N 28°32E 183 E13
Bolia Dem. Rep. of the Congo 1°36S 18°22E 264 C3
Bolinao Phil. 16°23N 119°54E 232 C2
Bolinao, C. Phil. 16°23N 119°55E 232 C2
Bolingbroke U.S.A. 32°57N 83°48W 316 C6
Bolingbrook U.S.A. 41°42N 88°4W 311 C8
Bolingo Dem. Rep. of the Congo 3°31S 21°43E 264 C4
Bolintin-Vale Romania 44°27N 25°46E 183 F10
Bolívar Antioquia, Colombia 5°50N 76°1W 328 B2
Bolívar Cauca, Colombia 2°0N 77°0W 328 C2
Bolívar Peru 7°18S 77°48W 330 B2
Bolivar Mo., U.S.A. 37°37N 93°25W 308 G7
Bolivar N.Y., U.S.A. 42°4N 78°10W 312 D6
Bolivar Tenn., U.S.A. 35°12N 89°0W 315 D10
Bolívar □ Colombia 9°0N 74°40W 328 B3
Bolívar □ Ecuador 1°15S 79°5W 328 D2
Bolívar □ Venezuela 6°20N 63°30W 329 B5
Bolivia ■ S. Amer. 17°6S 64°0W 331 D5
Bolivian Plateau = Altiplano Bolivia 17°0S 68°0W 330 D4
Boljevac Serbia 43°51N 21°58E 202 C5
Bolkhov Russia 53°25N 36°0E 188 F9
Bolków Poland 50°55N 16°6E 185 H3
Bollate Italy 45°32N 9°7E 129 A1
Bollebeek Belgium 50°55N 4°11E 116 A1
Bollebygd Sweden 57°40N 12°35E 163 G6
Bollène France 44°18N 4°45E 175 D8
Bollensdorf Germany 52°30N 13°42E 115 A5
Bollmora Sweden 59°14N 18°14E 139 B3
Bollnäs Sweden 61°21N 16°24E 162 C10
Bollon Australia 28°2S 147°29E 281 D4
Bollstabruk Sweden 62°59N 17°40E 162 B11
Bolmen Sweden 56°55N 13°40E 163 H7
Bolnisi Georgia 41°26N 44°32E 191 K7
Bolobo Dem. Rep. of the Congo 2°6S 16°20E 264 C3
Bologna Italy 44°29N 11°20E 199 D8
Bologna ✈ (BLQ) Italy 44°34N 11°16E 199 D8
Bologoye Russia 57°55N 34°5E 188 D8
Bolomba Dem. Rep. of the Congo 0°35N 19°0E 264 B3
Bolombo → Dem. Rep. of the Congo 1°32N 21°14E 264 B4
Bolonchén Mexico 20°1N 89°45W 319 D7
Bolondo Dem. Rep. of the Congo 2°12S 18°42E 264 C3
Bolong Chad 12°3N 17°45E 259 F3
Bolong Phil. 7°6N 122°14E 233 H4
Bolongongo Angola 8°28S 15°16E 265 D3
Bolótana Italy 40°20N 8°52E 200 B1
Boloven, Cao Nguyen Laos 15°10N 106°30E 236 E6
Bolpur India 23°40N 87°45E 243 H12
Bolsena Italy 42°39N 11°59E 199 F8
Bolsena, L. di Italy 42°36N 11°56E 199 F8
Bolshakovo Russia 54°53N 21°40E 184 D8
Bolshaya Chernigovka Russia 52°6N 50°52E 190 D10
Bolshaya Garmanda = Evensk Russia 62°12N 159°30E 215 C16
Bolshaya Glushitsa Russia 52°28N 50°30E 190 D10
Bolshaya Martynovka Russia 47°19N 41°37E 191 G5
Bolshaya Okhta Russia 59°56N 30°26E 137 B2
Bolshaya Tsaryovshchina = Volzhskiy Russia 48°56N 44°46E 191 F7
Bolshaya Vradiyevka Ukraine 47°50N 30°40E 189 J6
Bolshevik, Ostrov Russia 78°30N 102°0E 215 B11
Bolshoy Anyuy → Russia 68°30N 160°49E 215 C17
Bolshoy Begichev, Ostrov Russia 74°20N 112°30E 215 B12
Bolshoy Kamen Russia 43°7N 132°19E 220 C6
Bolshoy Kavkas = Caucasus Mountains Eurasia 42°50N 44°0E 191 J7
Bolshoy Lyakhovskiy, Ostrov Russia 73°35N 142°0E 215 B15
Bolshoy Theatre Moscow, Russia 129 b2
Bolshoy Tokmak = Tokmak Kyrgyzstan 42°49N 75°15E 217 D9
Bolshoy Tyuters, Ostrov Russia 59°51N 27°13E 188 C4
Bólstaðarhlíð Iceland 65°31N 19°49W 155 B7
Bolsward Neths. 53°3N 5°32E 170 A5
Bolt Head U.K. 50°12N 3°48W 169 G4
Boltaña Spain 42°28N 0°4E 196 C5
Boltigen Switz. 46°38N 7°24E 179 J3
Bolton Ont., Canada 43°54N 79°45W 312 C5
Bolton Gt. Man., U.K. 53°35N 2°26W 168 D5
Bolton Georgia, U.S.A. 33°48N 84°28W 113 B2
Bolton Landing U.S.A. 43°32N 73°35W 313 C11
Bolu Turkey 40°45N 31°35E 212 B4
Bolu □ Turkey 40°40N 31°30E 212 B4
Bolubolu Papua N. G. 9°21S 150°20E 286 E6
Bolungavík Iceland 66°9N 23°15W 155 A3
Boluo China 23°3N 114°21E 229 F10
Bolvadin Turkey 38°45N 31°4E 212 C4
Bolzano Italy 46°31N 11°22E 199 B8
Bom Comércio Brazil 9°45S 65°54W 331 B4
Bom Conselho Brazil 9°10S 36°41W 332 C4
Bom Despacho Brazil 19°43S 45°15W 333 E2
Bom Jesus Angola 9°11S 13°34E 265 D2
Bom Jesus Brazil 9°4S 44°22W 332 C3
Bom Jesus da Gurguéia, Serra Brazil 9°0S 43°0W 332 C3
Bom Jesus da Lapa Brazil 13°15S 43°25W 333 D3
Bom Retiro Brazil 23°31S 46°38W 137 B2
Boma Dem. Rep. of the Congo 5°50S 13°4E 265 D2
Boma △ South Sudan 7°0N 34°0E 257 F3
Bomaderry Australia 34°52S 150°37E 283 C9
Bomandjokou Congo 0°34N 14°23E 264 B2
Bomaneh Dem. Rep. of the Congo 1°18N 23°47E 264 B4
Bomassa Congo 2°12N 16°12E 264 B3
Bomate Dem. Rep. of the Congo 2°14N 25°15E 264 C3
Bombala Australia 36°56S 149°15E 283 D8
Bombarral Portugal 39°15N 9°9W 195 F1
Bombay = Mumbai India 18°56N 72°50E 130 B2
Bombay U.S.A. 44°56N 74°34W 313 B10
Bombedor, Pta. Venezuela 9°53N 61°37W 329 G9
Bomberai, Semenanjung Indonesia 3°0S 133°0E 231 E8
Bombo Kasani Dem. Rep. of the Congo 5°51S 21°54E 265 D4
Bomboma Dem. Rep. of the Congo 2°25N 18°55E 264 B3
Bombombwa Dem. Rep. of the Congo 1°40N 25°40E 268 B2
Bomboyo Chad 12°1N 15°28E 259 F3
Bomdila India 27°18N 92°22E 241 B4
Bomdo India 28°44N 94°54E 241 A5
Bomet Kenya 0°47S 35°21E 266 E4
Bomi China 29°50N 95°45E 218 F8
Bomi Hills Liberia 7°1N 10°38W 262 D2
Bomili Dem. Rep. of the Congo 1°45N 27°5E 268 B2
Bømlo Norway 59°37N 5°13E 164 E2
Bomokandi → Dem. Rep. of the Congo 3°39N 26°8E 268 B2
Bomongo Dem. Rep. of the Congo 1°27N 18°21E 264 B3
Bompoka India 8°15N 93°13E 245 K11
Bomputu Dem. Rep. of the Congo 0°23S 20°6E 264 C4
Bomst = Babimost Poland 52°10N 15°49E 185 F2
Bomu → C.A.R. 4°40N 22°30E 264 B4
Bomu Occidentale ⌂ Dem. Rep. of the Congo 4°48N 24°17E 264 B4
Bomu Orientale ⌂ Dem. Rep. of the Congo 5°0N 25°50E 264 B2
Bon, C. = Ra's aṭ Tib Tunisia 37°1N 11°2E 258 A2
Bon Acceuil Mauritius 20°10S 57°39E 272 e
Bon Echo ⌂ Canada 44°55N 77°16W 312 B7
Bon Sar Pa Vietnam 12°24N 107°35E 236 F6
Bona, Mt. U.S.A. 61°23N 141°45W 303 F12
Bonāb Āzarbājān-e Sharqī, Iran 37°20N 46°4E 213 D12
Bonāb Zanjān, Iran 36°35N 48°41E 213 D13
Bonaigarh India 21°50N 84°57E 243 J11
Bonaire Ga., U.S.A. 32°33N 83°36W 316 C6
Bonaire W. Indies 12°10N 68°15W 322 h
Bonampak Mexico 16°44N 91°5W 319 D6
Bonang Australia 37°11S 148°41E 283 D8
Bonanza Nic. 13°54N 84°35W 320 D3
Bonaparte Arch. Australia 14°0S 124°30E 278 B3
Bonaparte Rocks Grenada 12°24N 61°30W 323 q
Boñar Spain 42°52N 5°19W 194 C5
Bonar Bridge U.K. 57°54N 4°20W 167 D4
Bonasse Trin. & Tob. 10°5N 61°54W 323 t
Bonaventure Canada 48°5N 65°32W 299 C6
Bonaventure, Place Montréal, Canada 130 c2
Bonavista Canada 48°40N 53°5W 299 C9
Bonavista, C. Canada 48°42N 53°5W 299 C9
Bonavista B. Canada 48°45N 53°25W 299 C9
Bondeno Italy 44°53N 11°25E 199 D8
Bondi Australia 33°53S 151°16E 139 B2
Bondo Équateur, Dem. Rep. of the Congo 1°22S 23°54E 264 C4
Bondo Orientale, Dem. Rep. of the Congo 3°55N 23°53E 264 B4
Bondoc Pen. Phil. 13°26N 122°33E 232 E4
Bondoukou Ivory C. 8°2N 2°47W 262 D4
Bondowoso Indonesia 7°55S 113°49E 235 D4
Bondy France 48°54N 2°28E 134 A3
Bondy, Forêt de France 48°54N 2°33E 134 A4
Bône = Annaba Algeria 36°50N 7°46E 261 A6
Bone, Teluk Indonesia 4°10S 120°50E 231 E6
Bonefish Pond Bahamas 25°59N 77°23W 153 b
Bonerate Indonesia 7°25S 121°5E 231 F6
Bonerate, Kepulauan Indonesia 6°30S 121°10E 231 F6
Bo'ness U.K. 56°1N 3°37W 167 E5
Bonete, Cerro Argentina 27°55S 68°40W 334 B2
Bonfim = Senhor-do-Bonfim Brazil 10°30S 40°10W 332 D3
Bonfim Brazil 3°33N 59°25W 329 C6
Bong Son = Hoai Nhon Vietnam 14°28N 109°1E 236 E7
Bonga Ethiopia 7°15N 36°14E 257 F4
Bongabon Phil. 15°38N 121°8E 232 D3
Bongabong Phil. 12°45N 121°29E 232 E3
Bongaigaon India 26°28N 90°34E 241 B3
Bongandanga Dem. Rep. of the Congo 1°24N 21°3E 264 B4
Bongao Phil. 5°2N 119°46E 233 J2
Bongo Dem. Rep. of the Congo 1°47S 17°41E 264 C3
Bongo, Sa. de Angola 10°3S 15°15E 265 E3
Bongo I. Phil. 7°20N 124°3E 233 H5
Bongor Chad 10°35N 15°20E 259 F3
Bongos, Massif des C.A.R. 8°40N 22°25E 264 A4
Bongouanou Ivory C. 6°42N 4°15W 262 D4
Bonham U.S.A. 33°35N 96°11W 314 E6
Boni Mali 15°3N 2°10W 262 B4
Boni ⌂ Kenya 1°35S 41°18E 268 C5
Bonifacio France 41°24N 9°10E 175 G13
Bonifacio, Bouches de Medit. S. 41°12N 9°15E 200 A2
Bonifacio Monument Phil. 14°38N 120°58E 127 B1
Bonifay U.S.A. 30°47N 85°41W 316 E4
Bonin Is. = Ogasawara Gunto Pac. Oc. 27°0N 142°0E 211 F16
Bonita Springs U.S.A. 26°21N 81°47W 317 J8
Bonito Brazil 21°8S 56°28W 331 E6
Bonjol Indonesia 0°1S 100°13E 234 C2
Bonke Ethiopia 6°5N 37°16E 257 F4
Bonkoukou Niger 14°0N 3°15E 263 C5
Bonn Germany 50°46N 7°6E 178 E3
Bonnabel Place U.S.A. 30°0N 90°8W 131 A2
Bonnat France 46°20N 1°54E 173 F8
Bonne Terre U.S.A. 37°55N 90°33W 310 G6
Bonneau U.S.A. 33°16N 79°58W 316 B10
Bonners Ferry U.S.A. 48°42N 116°19W 304 B5
Bonnétable France 48°11N 0°25E 172 D7
Bonneuil-sur-Marne France 48°46N 2°30E 134 B4
Bonneval France 45°22N 7°3E 175 C11
Bonneval-sur-Arc France 48°11N 1°24E 172 D8
Bonneville France 46°4N 6°24E 173 F13
Bonney, L. Australia 37°50S 140°20E 282 D4
Bonnie Doon Australia 37°2S 145°53E 283 D6
Bonnie Rock Australia 30°29S 118°22E 279 F2
Bonnington U.K. 55°54N 3°25W 121 B1
Bonny Nigeria 4°25N 7°13E 263 E6
Bonny → Nigeria 4°20N 7°10E 263 E6
Bonny, Bight of Africa 3°30N 9°20E 263 E6
Bonny Hills Australia 31°36S 152°51E 283 A10
Bonny-sur-Loire France 47°33N 2°50E 173 E9
Bonnyrigg U.K. 55°53N 3°6W 167 F5
Bonnyrigg and Lasswade U.K. 55°52N 3°6W 121 B3
Bonnyville Canada 54°20N 110°45W 297 C6
Bono Italy 40°25N 9°2E 200 B2
Bonoi Indonesia 1°45S 137°41E 231 E9
Bonorva Italy 40°25N 8°46E 200 B1
Bonsall U.S.A. 33°16N 117°14W 307 M9
Bonsucesso Brazil 22°51S 43°15W 135 B1
Bontang Indonesia 0°10N 117°30E 235 B5
Bontebok △ S. Africa 34°5S 20°28E 270 D3
Bonteheuwel S. Africa 33°57S 18°33E 118 A2
Bonthe S. Leone 7°30N 12°33W 262 D2
Bontoc Phil. 17°7N 120°58E 232 C3
Bontosunggu Indonesia 5°41S 119°42E 235 D5
Bonyeri Ghana 5°1N 2°46W 262 D4
Bonyhád Hungary 46°18N 18°32E 182 D3
Bonython Ra. Australia 23°40S 128°45E 278 D4
Boo Sweden 59°20N 18°16E 139 A3
Booderee △ Australia 35°12S 150°42E 283 C9
Boodjamulla △ Australia 18°15S 138°6E 280 B2
Bookabie Australia 31°50S 132°41E 279 F5
Booke Dem. Rep. of the Congo 2°34S 22°3E 264 C4
Booker U.S.A. 36°27N 100°32W 314 C4
Bool Lagoon Australia 37°7S 140°40E 282 D4
Boola Guinea 8°22N 8°41W 262 D3
Boolcoomata Australia 31°57S 140°33E 282 A4
Booleroo Centre Australia 32°53S 138°21E 282 B3
Booligal Australia 33°58S 144°53E 283 B6
Boon Pt. Antigua & B. 17°10N 61°50W 322 b
Böön Tsagaan Nuur Mongolia 45°35N 99°9E 218 B8
Boonah Australia 27°58S 152°41E 281 D5
Boone Iowa, U.S.A. 42°4N 93°53W 310 B3
Boone N.C., U.S.A. 36°13N 81°41W 315 C14
Booneville Ark., U.S.A. 35°8N 93°55W 314 D8
Booneville Miss., U.S.A. 34°39N 88°34W 315 D10
Boonville Calif., U.S.A. 39°1N 123°22W 306 F3
Boonville Ind., U.S.A. 38°3N 87°16W 311 F9
Boonville Mo., U.S.A. 38°58N 92°44W 310 F4
Boonville N.Y., U.S.A. 43°29N 75°20W 313 C9
Boorabbin △ Australia 31°30S 120°10E 279 F3
Boorama Somali Rep. 9°55N 43°7E 267 C5
Boorindal Australia 30°22S 146°11E 281 E4
Boorowa Australia 34°28S 148°44E 283 C8
Boort Australia 36°7S 143°46E 282 D5
Boosaaso Somali Rep. 11°12N 49°18E 267 B6
Booterstown Ireland 53°19N 6°12W 120 B2
Boothia, Gulf of Canada 71°0N 90°0W 294 C14
Boothia Pen. Canada 71°0N 94°0W 294 C13
Bootle U.K. 53°28N 3°1W 168 D4
Booué Gabon 0°5S 11°55E 264 C2
Bopako Dem. Rep. of the Congo 1°53N 21°13E 264 B4
Boppard Germany 50°13N 7°35E 179 E3
Boquerón □ Paraguay 23°0S 60°0W 331 E6
Boquilla, Presa de la Mexico 27°31N 105°30W 318 B3
Boquillas del Carmen Mexico 29°11N 102°58W 318 B4
Bor Czech Rep. 49°41N 12°45E 180 B5
Bor Russia 56°28N 43°59E 190 B7
Bor Serbia 44°5N 22°7E 202 B6
Bôr South Sudan 6°10N 31°40E 257 F3
Bor Sweden 57°9N 14°10E 163 G8
Bor Turkey 37°54N 34°32E 212 D6
Bor, Lagh → Kenya 1°18N 40°40E 267 D5
Bor Mashash Israel 31°7N 34°50E 251 G5
Bor u Ceske Lipy = Nový Bor Czech Rep. 50°46N 14°35E 180 A7
Bora Bora French Polynesia 16°30S 151°45W 289 f
Borah Peak U.S.A. 44°8N 113°47W 304 D7
Borang South Sudan 4°50N 30°59E 257 G3
Borangapara India 25°14N 90°14E 241 C3
Borås Sweden 57°43N 12°56E 163 G6
Borāzjān Iran 29°22N 51°10E 247 D6
Borba Brazil 4°12S 59°34W 329 D6
Borba Portugal 38°50N 7°26W 195 G3
Borbon Phil. 10°50N 124°2E 233 F5
Borborema, Planalto da Brazil 7°0S 37°0W 332 C4
Borcea Romania 44°20N 27°45E 183 F12
Borchalo = Marneuli Georgia 41°30N 44°48E 191 K7
Borçka Turkey 41°25N 41°41E 213 B9
Bord Khūn-e Now Iran 28°3N 51°28E 247 D6
Borda, C. Australia 35°45S 136°34E 282 C2
Bordeaux France 44°50N 0°36W 174 D3
Bordeaux ✈ (BOD) France 44°50N 0°35W 174 D3
Borden Australia 34°3S 118°12E 279 F2
Borden-Carleton Canada 46°18N 63°47W 299 C7
Borden I. Canada 78°30N 111°30W 295 B9
Borden Pen. Canada 73°0N 83°0W 295 C15
Borden Springs U.S.A. 33°56N 85°28W 316 B4
Border Ranges △ Australia 28°24S 152°56E 281 D5
Borders = Scottish Borders □ U.K. 55°35N 2°50W 167 F6
Bordertown Australia 36°19S 140°45E 282 D4
Borðeyri Iceland 65°12N 21°6W 155 B5
Bordighera Italy 43°46N 7°39E 198 E4
Bordj bou Arreridj Algeria 36°4N 4°45E 261 A5
Bordj Bourguiba Tunisia 32°12N 10°2E 258 B2
Bordj Fly Ste. Marie Algeria 27°19N 2°32W 260 C4
Bordj-in-Eker Algeria 24°9N 5°3E 261 D6
Bordj Menaïel Algeria 36°46N 3°43E 261 A5
Bordj Messouda Algeria 30°12N 9°25E 261 B6
Bordj Mokhtar Algeria 21°20N 0°56E 261 D5
Bordj Nili Algeria 33°28N 3°2E 261 B5
Bordj Omar Driss Algeria 28°10N 6°40E 261 C6
Bordj Sif Fatima Algeria 31°6N 8°41E 261 B6
Bordj Tarat Algeria 25°55N 9°3E 261 C6
Borduttighat India 26°57N 93°58E 241 B4
Bore Ethiopia 4°39N 37°39E 257 G4
Borehamwood U.K. 51°40N 0°15W 169 F7
Borek Wielkopolski Poland 51°54N 17°11E 185 G4
Borensberg Sweden 58°34N 15°17E 163 F9
Borgå = Porvoo Finland 60°24N 25°40E 188 B3
Borgampad India 17°39N 80°52E 244 F5
Borgarfjarðarsýsla □ Iceland 64°30N 21°30W 155 C5
Borgarfjörður Borgarfjarðarsýsla, Iceland 64°30N 22°0W 155 C4
Borgarfjörður Norður-Múlasýsla, Iceland 65°33N 13°47W 155 B13
Borgarnes Iceland 64°32N 21°55W 155 C5
Børgefjellet Norway 65°20N 13°45E 160 D15
Borger Neths. 52°54N 6°44E 170 B6
Borger Tex., U.S.A. 35°39N 101°24W 314 D4
Borgholm Sweden 56°52N 16°39E 163 H10
Bórgia Italy 38°49N 16°30E 201 D9
Borgnesse, Pte. Martinique 14°26N 60°54W 322 j
Borgo San Dalmazzo Italy 44°20N 7°30E 198 D4
Borgo San Donnino = Fidenza Italy 44°52N 10°3E 198 D7
Borgo San Lorenzo Italy 43°57N 11°23E 199 E8
Borgo Val di Taro Italy 44°29N 9°46E 198 D6
Borgo Valsugana Italy 46°3N 11°27E 199 B8
Borgomanero Italy 45°42N 8°28E 198 C5
Borgorose Italy 42°11N 13°13E 199 F10
Borgosésia Italy 45°43N 8°16E 198 C5
Borgotaro = Borgo Val di Taro Italy 44°29N 9°46E 198 D6
Borgund Norway 61°3N 7°48E 164 C4
Borhoyn Tal Mongolia 43°50N 111°58E 226 C6
Bori Nigeria 4°42N 7°21E 263 E6
Borigumma India 19°3N 82°33E 244 E6
Borikhane Laos 18°33N 103°43E 236 C4
Borisoglebsk Russia 51°27N 42°5E 190 E6
Borisov = Barysaw Belarus 54°17N 28°28E 177 A15
Borisovgrad = Pŭrvomay Bulgaria 42°8N 25°17E 203 D9
Borisovka Russia 50°36N 36°1E 189 G9
Borisovo Russia 55°38N 37°44E 129 C4
Borj Jenein Tunisia 31°45N 10°9E 258 B2
Borja Peru 4°20S 77°40W 328 D2
Borja Spain 41°48N 1°34W 196 D3
Borjas Blancas = Les Borges Blanques Spain 41°31N 0°52E 196 D5
Borjomi Georgia 41°48N 43°28E 191 K6
Børkop Denmark 55°39N 9°39E 163 J3
Borkou Chad 18°15N 18°50E 259 E3
Borkou-Ennedi-Tibesti □ Chad 18°0N 19°0E 259 E3
Borkum Germany 53°34N 6°40E 178 B2
Borlänge Sweden 60°29N 15°26E 162 D9
Borle India 19°2N 72°54E 130 A2
Borley, C. Antarctica 66°15S 52°30E 151 C5
Borlu Turkey 38°44N 28°27E 205 C10
Bormida → Italy 44°23N 8°13E 198 D5
Bórmio Italy 46°28N 10°22E 198 B7
Borna Germany 51°7N 12°29E 178 D8
Borne Sulinowo Poland 53°32N 16°36E 184 E3
Borneo E. Indies 1°0N 115°0E 235 B4
Bornholm Denmark 55°10N 15°0E 163 J8
Bornholmsgattet Europe 55°15N 14°20E 163 J8
Borno □ Nigeria 11°30N 13°0E 263 C7
Bornos Spain 36°48N 5°42W 195 J5
Bornova Turkey 38°27N 27°14E 205 C9
Bornu Yassa Nigeria 12°14N 12°25E 263 C7
Boro → South Sudan 8°52N 26°11E 257 F2
Borobudur △ Indonesia 7°36S 110°12E 231 G14
Borobudur Indonesia 7°40S 110°11E 235 D4
Borocay I. Phil. 11°58N 121°55E 233 F3
Borodino Russia 55°31N 35°40E 188 E8
Borodino Ukraine 46°18N 29°15E 183 D14
Borogontsy Russia 62°42N 131°8E 215 C14
Borohoro Shan China 44°6N 83°10E 217 D10
Boromo Burkina Faso 11°45N 2°58W 262 C4
Boron U.S.A. 35°0N 117°39W 307 L9
Borongan Phil. 11°37N 125°26E 233 F5
Boronia Park Australia 33°49S 151°8E 139 A1
Borotangba Mts. C.A.R. 6°30N 25°0E 257 F2
Borotou Ivory C. 8°46N 7°30W 262 D3
Borovan Bulgaria 43°27N 23°45E 202 C7
Borovichi Russia 58°25N 33°55E 188 C7
Borovsk Russia 55°12N 36°24E 188 E9
Borovskoy Kazakhstan 53°48N 64°9E 216 B6
Borrby Sweden 55°27N 14°10E 163 J8
Borrego Springs U.S.A. 33°15N 116°23W 307 M10
Borriol Spain 40°4N 0°4W 196 E4
Borrisokane Ireland 53°0N 8°7W 166 D3
Borroloola Australia 16°4S 136°17E 280 B2
Borşa Cluj, Romania 46°56N 23°40E 183 D8
Borşa Maramureş, Romania 47°41N 24°50E 183 C9
Borsad India 22°25N 72°54E 242 H5
Borsec Romania 46°57N 25°34E 183 D10
Borshchiv Ukraine 48°48N 26°3E 183 B11
Borsod-Abaúj-Zemplén □ Hungary 48°20N 21°0E 182 B6
Bort-les-Orgues France 45°24N 2°29E 174 C6
Borth U.K. 52°29N 4°2W 169 E3
Börtnan Sweden 62°45N 13°50E 162 B7
Borūjerd Iran 33°55N 48°50E 213 F13
Boryeong S. Korea 36°21N 126°36E 224 D3
Borynya Ukraine 49°4N 23°0E 185 J10
Boryslav Ukraine 49°18N 23°28E 185 J10
Boryspil Ukraine 50°21N 30°59E 189 G6
Borzhomi = Borjomi Georgia 41°48N 43°28E 191 K6
Borzna Ukraine 51°18N 32°26E 189 G7
Borzya Russia 50°24N 116°31E 219 A12
Bosa Italy 40°18N 8°30E 200 B1
Bosa Monene Dem. Rep. of the Congo 1°16S 23°40E 264 C4
Bosaga Turkmenistan 37°33N 65°41E 240 A2
Bosambi Dem. Rep. of the Congo 2°24N 22°39E 264 B4
Bosanska Dubica Bos.-H. 45°10N 16°50E 199 C13
Bosanska Gradiška Bos.-H. 45°10N 17°15E 182 E2
Bosanska Kostajnica Bos.-H. 45°11N 16°33E 199 C13
Bosanska Krupa Bos.-H. 44°53N 16°10E 199 D13
Bosanski Brod Bos.-H. 45°10N 18°0E 182 E2
Bosanski Novi Bos.-H. 45°2N 16°22E 199 C13
Bosanski Petrovac Bos.-H. 44°35N 16°21E 199 D13
Bosanski Šamac Bos.-H. 45°3N 18°29E 182 E3
Bosansko Grahovo Bos.-H. 44°12N 16°26E 199 D13
Bosavi, Mt. Papua N. G. 6°30S 142°49E 286 D2
Boscastle U.K. 50°41N 4°42W 169 G3
Boscobel U.S.A. 43°8N 90°42W 310 A6
Boscobelle Barbados 13°17N 59°35W 323 r
Bose China 23°53N 106°35E 228 F6
Boseki Dem. Rep. of the Congo 2°34S 19°38E 264 C3
Boseong S. Korea 34°46N 127°5E 224 E3
Boshan China 36°28N 117°49E 227 F9
Boshof S. Africa 28°31S 25°13E 270 C4
Boshrūyeh Iran 33°50N 57°30E 247 C8
Bosilegrad Serbia 42°30N 22°27E 202 D6
Boskovice Czech Rep. 49°29N 16°40E 181 B9
Bosmont S. Africa 26°10S 27°57E 123 B1
Bosna → Bos.-H. 45°4N 18°29E 182 E3
Bosna i Hercegovina = Bosnia-Herzegovina ■ Europe 44°0N 18°0E 182 G2
Bosnia-Herzegovina ■ Europe 44°0N 18°0E 182 G2
Bosnik Indonesia 1°5S 136°10E 231 E9
Bōsō-Hantō Japan 35°20N 140°20E 223 B12
Bosobolo Dem. Rep. of the Congo 4°15N 19°50E 264 B3
Bosön Sweden 59°22N 18°11E 139 A3
Bosporus = İstanbul Boğazı Turkey 41°5N 29°3E 122 B2
Bosque Farms U.S.A. 35°51N 106°42W 305 J10
Bossangoa C.A.R. 6°35N 17°30E 264 A3
Bossé Bangou Niger 13°20N 1°18E 263 C5
Bossembélé C.A.R. 5°25N 17°40E 264 A3
Bossemtélé C.A.R. 5°41N 16°38E 264 A3
Bossier City U.S.A. 32°31N 93°44W 314 E8
Bossiesvlei Namibia 25°1S 16°44E 270 C2
Bosso Niger 13°43N 13°19E 259 F2
Bosso, Dallol → Niger 12°25N 2°50E 263 C5
Bostan Pakistan 30°26N 67°2E 242 D2
Bostānābād Iran 37°50N 46°50E 213 D12
Bostancı Turkey 40°57N 29°5E 122 C2
Bosten Hu China 41°55N 87°40E 217 D11
Boston Phil. 7°52N 126°22E 233 H6
Boston Lincs., U.K. 52°59N 0°2W 168 E7
Boston Ga., U.S.A. 30°47N 83°47W 316 E6
Boston Mass., U.S.A. 42°22N 71°3W 114 C2
Boston Bar Canada 49°52N 121°30W 296 D4
Boston Bay Jamaica 18°9N 76°22W 320 a
Boston Common Boston, U.S.A. 116 c1
Boston Logan Int. ✈ (BOS) U.S.A. 42°22N 71°1W 116 A2
Boston Mts. U.S.A. 35°42N 93°15W 314 D8
Boston Tea Party Ship & Museum Boston, U.S.A. 116 c3
Bostwick U.S.A. 29°46N 81°38W 316 F8
Bosumtwi, L. Ghana 6°30N 1°25W 263 D4
Bosusulu Dem. Rep. of the Congo 0°50N 20°45E 264 B4
Bosut → Croatia 45°20N 18°45E 182 E3
Boswell B.C., Canada 49°28N 116°45W 296 D5
Boswell Ind., U.S.A. 40°31N 87°23W 311 D9
Boswell Pa., U.S.A. 40°10N 79°2W 312 F5
Bosworth U.S.A. 39°28N 93°20W 310 E3
Botad India 22°15N 71°40E 242 H4
Botafogo Brazil 22°56S 43°10W 135 B1
Botan → Turkey 37°57N 42°2E 213 D10

Botanic Gardens *Washington, D.C., U.S.A.* 143 b3
Botanisk Have *Copenhagen, Denmark* 118 b2
Botany *Australia* 33°56S 151°12E 139 B2
Botany B. *Australia* 33°58S 151°11E 139 B2
Botany Bay △ *Australia* 34°0S 151°14E 139 B2
Botene *Laos* 17°35N 101°12E 236 D3
Botera *Angola* 11°37S 14°16E 265 E2
Botev *Bulgaria* 42°44N 24°52E 203 D8
Botevgrad *Bulgaria* 42°55N 23°47E 202 D7
Bothaville *S. Africa* 27°23S 26°34E 270 C4
Bothnia, G. of *Europe* 62°0N 20°0E 160 F19
Bothwell *Tas., Australia* 42°20S 147°1E 281 G4
Bothwell *Ont., Canada* 42°38N 81°52W 312 D3
Botič → *Czech Rep.* 50°4N 14°26E 135 B3
Botica Sete *Portugal* 38°49N 9°10W 126 A1
Boticas *Portugal* 41°41N 7°40W 194 D3
Botletle → *Botswana* 20°10S 23°15E 270 B3
Botlikh *Russia* 42°39N 46°11E 191 J8
Botna → *Moldova* 46°45N 29°34E 183 D14
Botola *Dem. Rep. of the Congo* 1°17S 18°13E 264 C3
Botolan *Phil.* 15°17N 120°1E 232 D3
Botoroaga *Romania* 44°8N 25°32E 183 F10
Botoşani *Romania* 47°42N 26°41E 183 C11
Botoşani □ *Romania* 47°50N 26°50E 183 C11
Botou *Burkina Faso* 12°42N 1°59E 263 C5
Botou *China* 38°4N 116°34E 226 E9
Botricello *Italy* 38°56N 16°51E 201 D9
Botro *Ivory C.* 7°51N 5°19W 262 D3
Botshabelo *S. Africa* 29°14S 26°44E 270 C4
Botswana ■ *Africa* 22°0S 24°0E 270 B3
Bottelier *Curaçao* 12°6N 68°54W 322 g
Bottineau *U.S.A.* 48°50N 100°27W 308 A3
Bottnaryd *Sweden* 57°47N 13°50E 163 G7
Bottom, The *Saba* 17°38N 63°15W 322 a
Bottopassi *Suriname* 4°14N 55°27W 329 C6
Bottrop *Germany* 51°31N 6°58E 170 C6
Botucatu *Brazil* 22°55S 48°30W 335 A6
Botum Sakor △ *Cambodia* 11°5N 103°15E 237 G4
Botwood *Canada* 49°6N 55°23W 299 C8
Bou Alam *Algeria* 33°50N 1°26E 261 B5
Bou Ali *Algeria* 27°11N 0°4W 261 C4
Bou Djébéha *Mali* 18°25N 2°45W 262 B4
Bou Guema *Algeria* 28°49N 0°19E 261 C5
Bou Ismaïl *Algeria* 36°38N 2°42E 261 A5
Bou Izakarn *Morocco* 29°12N 9°46W 260 C3
Boû Lanouâr *Mauritania* 21°12N 16°34W 260 D1
Bou Naga *Mauritania* 18°49N 13°20W 262 B2
Bou Noura *Algeria* 32°29N 3°43E 261 B5
Boû Rjeïmât *Mauritania* 19°4N 15°3W 262 B1
Bou Saâda *Algeria* 35°11N 4°9E 261 A5
Bou Salem *Tunisia* 36°45N 9°2E 258 A1
Bouaflé *Ivory C.* 7°1N 5°47W 262 D3
Bouaké *Ivory C.* 7°40N 5°2W 262 D3
Bouanga *Congo* 2°7S 16°8E 264 C3
Bouar *C.A.R.* 6°0N 15°40E 264 A3
Bouârfa *Morocco* 32°32N 1°58W 261 B4
Bouba Ndjida △ *Cameroon* 8°50N 14°45E 264 A2
Boubout *Algeria* 27°26N 4°30W 260 C4
Bouca *C.A.R.* 6°45N 18°25E 264 A3
Boucaut B. *Australia* 12°0S 134°25E 280 A1
Boucherville *Canada* 45°36N 73°28W 130 A3
Boucherville, Îs. de *Canada* 45°36N 73°28W 130 A3
Bouches-du-Rhône □ *France* 43°37N 5°2E 175 E9
Boucle de Baoulé △ *Mali* 13°53N 9°0W 262 C3
Boucles de la Seine Normande ⌓ *France* 49°32N 0°35E 172 C7
Bouctouche *Canada* 46°30N 64°45W 299 C7
Bouda *Algeria* 27°50N 0°27W 261 C4
Boudenib *Morocco* 31°59N 3°31W 260 B4
Bouéni *Mayotte* 12°54S 45°4E 272 b
Bouéni, B. de *Mayotte* 12°55S 45°7E 272 b
Boufarik *Algeria* 36°34N 2°58E 261 A5
Bougainville, C. *Australia* 13°57S 126°4E 278 B4
Bougainville I. *Papua N. G.* 6°0S 155°0E 287 L8
Bougainville Reef *Australia* 15°30S 147°5E 280 B4
Bougainville Str. *Solomon Is.* 6°40S 156°10E 287 L9
Bougaroun, C. *Algeria* 37°6N 6°30E 261 A6
Bougie = Bejaïa *Algeria* 36°42N 5°2E 261 A6
Bougival *France* 48°51N 2°8E 134 A1
Bougouni *Mali* 11°30N 7°20W 262 C3
Bougtob *Algeria* 34°2N 0°5E 261 B5
Bouillante *Guadeloupe* 16°8N 61°46W 322 e
Bouillante, Pitons de *Guadeloupe* 16°8N 61°43W 322 e
Bouillon *Belgium* 49°44N 5°3E 170 E5
Bouïra *Algeria* 36°20N 3°59E 261 A5
Bouïra □ *Algeria* 36°15N 3°55E 261 A5
Boukombé *Benin* 10°13N 1°9E 263 C5
Boulal *Mali* 15°8N 8°21W 262 B3
Boulazac *France* 45°10N 0°47E 174 C4
Boulder *Colo., U.S.A.* 40°1N 105°17W 304 F11
Boulder *Mont., U.S.A.* 46°14N 112°7W 304 C7
Boulder City *U.S.A.* 35°58N 114°49W 307 K12
Boulder Creek *U.S.A.* 37°7N 122°7W 306 H4
Boulder Dam = Hoover Dam *U.S.A.* 36°1N 114°44W 307 K12
Boulder Pt. *China* 22°14N 114°6E 122 B1
Boulemane □ *Morocco* 33°10N 4°0W 260 B4
Boulembo *Gabon* 1°26S 12°0E 264 C2
Bouli *Mauritania* 15°17N 12°18W 262 B2
Boulia *Australia* 22°52S 139°51E 280 C2
Bouligny *France* 49°17N 5°45E 173 C12
Boulogne → *France* 47°12N 1°47W 172 E5
Boulogne, Bois de *France* 48°51N 2°14E 134 A2
Boulogne-Billancourt *France* 48°50N 2°14E 134 A2
Boulogne-sur-Gesse *France* 43°18N 0°38E 174 E4
Boulogne-sur-Mer *France* 50°42N 1°36E 173 B8
Bouloire *France* 47°59N 0°45E 172 E7
Boulou → *C.A.R.* 6°45N 24°16E 264 A4
Boulouli *Mali* 15°30N 9°25W 262 B3
Bouloupari *N. Cal.* 21°52S 166°4E 288 d
Bouloupesse *Congo* 1°58S 12°40E 264 C2
Boulsa *Burkina Faso* 12°39N 0°34W 263 C4
Boultoum *Niger* 14°45N 10°25E 259 F2
Bouma △ *Fiji* 16°50S 179°52E 287 A2
Boumalne Dadès *Morocco* 31°25N 6°0W 260 B3
Boumba → *Cameroon* 2°2N 15°12E 264 B2
Boumbé → *C.A.R.* 4°4N 15°23E 264 B3
Boûmdeïd *Mauritania* 17°25N 11°50W 262 B2
Boumerdès *Algeria* 36°46N 3°28E 261 A5
Boumerdès □ *Algeria* 36°45N 3°40E 261 A5
Boun Neua *Laos* 21°38N 101°54E 236 B3
Boun Tai *Laos* 21°23N 101°58E 236 B3
Bouna *Ivory C.* 9°10N 3°0W 262 D4
Boundary *U.S.A.* 64°5N 141°1W 303 D12
Boundary Peak *U.S.A.* 37°51N 118°21W 306 H8
Boundiali *Ivory C.* 9°30N 6°20W 262 D3
Boungou → *C.A.R.* 8°21N 23°48E 264 A4
Bountiful *U.S.A.* 40°53N 111°52W 304 F8
Bounty Is. *Pac. Oc.* 48°0S 178°30E 288 M9
Bounty Trough *Pac. Oc.* 46°0S 178°0E 288 M9
Boura *Mali* 12°25N 4°33W 262 C4
Bourail *N. Cal.* 21°34S 165°30E 288 d
Bourbeuse → *U.S.A.* 38°24N 90°53W 310 F6
Bourbon *U.S.A.* 41°18N 86°7W 311 C10
Bourbon-Lancy *France* 46°37N 3°45E 173 F10
Bourbon-l'Archambault *France* 46°36N 3°4E 173 F10
Bourbon Street *New Orleans, U.S.A.* 131 b2
Bourbonnais *Allier, France* 46°28N 3°0E 173 F10
Bourbonnais *Ill., U.S.A.* 41°9N 87°52W 311 C9
Bourbonne-les-Bains *France* 47°54N 5°45E 173 E12
Bourbourg *France* 50°56N 2°12E 173 B9
Bourdel L. *Canada* 56°43N 74°10W 298 A5
Bourem *Mali* 17°0N 0°24W 263 B4
Bouressa *Mali* 20°0N 2°15E 261 E5
Bourg *France* 45°3N 0°34W 174 C3
Bourg-Argental *France* 45°18N 4°32E 175 C8
Bourg-de-Péage *France* 45°2N 5°3E 175 C9
Bourg-en-Bresse *France* 46°13N 5°12E 173 F12
Bourg-la-Reine *France* 48°46N 2°19E 134 B2
Bourg-Lastic *France* 45°39N 2°35E 174 C6
Bourg-Madame *France* 42°26N 1°55E 174 F5
Bourg-St-Andéol *France* 44°23N 4°39E 175 D8
Bourg-St-Maurice *France* 45°35N 6°46E 175 C10
Bourganeuf *France* 45°57N 1°45E 174 C5
Bourgas = Burgas *Bulgaria* 42°33N 27°29E 203 D11
Bourges *France* 47°9N 2°25E 173 E9
Bourget *Canada* 45°26N 75°9W 313 A9
Bourget, Lac du *France* 45°44N 5°52E 175 C9
Bourgneuf, B. de *France* 47°3N 2°10W 172 E4
Bourgneuf-en-Retz *France* 47°2N 1°58W 172 E5
Bourgogne □ *France* 47°0N 4°50E 173 F11
Bourgoin-Jallieu *France* 45°36N 5°17E 175 C9
Bourgueil *France* 47°17N 0°10E 172 E7
Bourke *Australia* 30°8S 145°55E 281 E4
Bourne *U.K.* 52°47N 0°22W 168 E7
Bournemouth *U.K.* 50°43N 1°52W 169 G6
Bournemouth □ *U.K.* 50°43N 1°52W 169 G6
Bouroum *Burkina Faso* 13°37N 0°39W 263 C4
Bouse *U.S.A.* 33°56N 114°0W 307 M13
Boussac *France* 46°22N 2°13E 173 F9
Boussé *Burkina Faso* 12°39N 1°53W 263 C4
Bousso *Chad* 10°34N 16°52E 259 F3
Boussouma *Burkina Faso* 12°52N 1°13W 263 C4
Bout, Pte. du *Martinique* 14°33N 61°3W 322 j
Bout Stable Bay *Dominica* 15°21N 61°15W 323 k
Boutilimit *Mauritania* 17°45N 14°40W 262 B2
Boutonne → *France* 45°54N 0°50W 174 C3
Bouvet I. = Bouvetøya *Antarctica* 54°26S 3°24E 152 M12
Bouvetøya *Antarctica* 54°26S 3°24E 152 M12
Bouviers *France* 48°46N 2°4E 134 B1
Bouxwiller *France* 48°49N 7°27E 173 D14
Bouza *Niger* 14°29N 6°2E 263 C6
Bouznika *Morocco* 33°46N 7°6W 260 B3
Bouzonville *France* 49°17N 6°32E 173 C13
Bova Marina *Italy* 37°56N 15°55E 201 E8
Bovalino Marina *Italy* 38°10N 16°10E 201 D9
Bovec *Slovenia* 46°20N 13°33E 199 B10
Boven Kapuas, Pegunungan *Malaysia* 1°25N 113°15E 235 B4
Bovenkerk *Neths.* 52°18N 4°51E 112 B2
Bovenkerker Polder *Neths.* 52°16N 4°52E 112 B2
Bøverdal *Norway* 61°44N 8°20E 164 C5
Bøverfjorden *Norway* 63°1N 8°32E 164 A5
Bovill *U.S.A.* 46°51N 116°24W 304 C5
Bovino *Italy* 41°15N 15°20E 201 A8
Bovisa *Italy* 45°30N 9°10E 129 A2
Bovril *Argentina* 31°21S 59°26W 334 C4
Bow *U.K.* 51°31N 0°1W 125 A3
Bow → *Canada* 49°57N 111°41W 296 C6
Bow Island *Canada* 49°50N 111°23W 304 B8
Bowbells *U.S.A.* 48°48N 102°15W 308 A2
Bowdle *U.S.A.* 45°27N 99°39W 308 C4
Bowdon *U.S.A.* 33°32N 85°15W 316 B4
Bowdon Junction *U.S.A.* 33°40N 85°9W 316 B4
Bowelling *Australia* 33°25S 116°30E 279 F2
Bowen *Argentina* 35°0S 67°31W 334 D2
Bowen *Queens., Australia* 20°0S 148°16E 280 J5
Bowen Mts. *Australia* 37°0S 147°50E 283 D7
Bowers Basin *Pac. Oc.* 53°45N 176°0E 150 D16
Bowers Ridge *Pac. Oc.* 54°0N 180°0E 150 D17
Bowery *New York, U.S.A.* 132 e2
Bowie *Ariz., U.S.A.* 32°19N 109°29W 305 K9
Bowie *Tex., U.S.A.* 33°34N 97°51W 314 E6
Bowkān *Iran* 36°31N 46°12E 213 D12
Bowland, Forest of *U.K.* 54°0N 2°30W 168 D5
Bowling Green *Fla., U.S.A.* 27°38N 81°50W 317 H8
Bowling Green *Ky., U.S.A.* 36°59N 86°27W 308 G10
Bowling Green *Mo., U.S.A.* 39°21N 91°12W 310 E5
Bowling Green *Ohio, U.S.A.* 41°23N 83°39W 311 C13
Bowling Green, C. *Australia* 19°19S 147°25E 280 B4
Bowling Green Bay △ *Australia* 19°26S 146°57E 280 B4
Bowman *N. Dak., U.S.A.* 46°11N 103°24W 308 B2
Bowman *S.C., U.S.A.* 33°21N 80°41W 316 B9
Bowman I. *Antarctica* 65°0S 104°0E 151 C8
Bowmanville = Clarington *Canada* 43°55N 78°41W 312 C6
Bowmore *U.K.* 55°45N 6°17W 167 F2
Bowral *Australia* 34°26S 150°27E 283 C9
Bowraville *Australia* 30°37S 152°52E 281 E5
Bowron → *Canada* 54°3N 121°50W 296 C4
Bowron Lake ⌓ *Canada* 53°10N 121°5W 296 C4
Bowser L. *Canada* 56°30N 129°30W 296 B3
Bowsman *Canada* 52°14N 101°12W 297 C8
Bowutu Mts. *Papua N. G.* 7°45S 147°10E 286 D4
Bowwood *Zambia* 17°5S 26°20E 269 F2
Box Cr. → *Australia* 34°10S 143°50E 281 E3
Boxholm *Sweden* 58°12N 15°3E 163 F9
Boxmeer *Neths.* 51°38N 5°56E 170 C5
Boxtel *Neths.* 51°36N 5°20E 170 C5
Boyabat *Turkey* 41°28N 34°47E 212 B6
Boyabo *Dem. Rep. of the Congo* 3°43N 18°46E 264 B3
Boyacá □ *Colombia* 5°30N 73°20W 328 B3
Boyacıköy *Turkey* 41°5N 29°2E 122 B2
Boyalıca *Turkey* 40°29N 29°33E 203 F13
Boyang *China* 29°0N 116°38E 229 C11
Boyany *Ukraine* 48°17N 26°8E 183 B11
Boyasegese *Dem. Rep. of the Congo* 3°29N 20°33E 264 B4
Boyce *U.S.A.* 31°23N 92°40W 314 F8
Boyd *U.S.A.* 30°11N 83°37W 316 E6
Boyd Conservation Area *Canada* 43°49N 79°35W 141 A1
Boyd L. *Canada* 52°46N 76°42W 298 B4
Boyenge *Dem. Rep. of the Congo* 0°14N 18°55E 264 B3
Boyer, C. *N. Cal.* 21°37S 168°6E 288 c
Boyera *Dem. Rep. of the Congo* 0°40S 19°23E 264 C3
Boyle *Alta., Canada* 54°35N 112°49W 296 C6
Boyle *Roscommon, Ireland* 53°59N 8°18W 166 C3
Boyle Heights *U.S.A.* 34°1N 118°12W 126 B3
Boyne → *Ireland* 53°43N 6°15W 166 C5
Boyne City *U.S.A.* 45°13N 85°1W 309 C11
Boyni Qara *Afghan.* 36°20N 67°0E 240 A2
Boynitsa *Bulgaria* 43°58N 22°32E 202 C6
Boynton Beach *U.S.A.* 26°32N 80°4W 317 J9
Boyoma, Chutes *Dem. Rep. of the Congo* 0°35N 25°23E 264 B5
Boysen Res. *U.S.A.* 43°25N 108°11W 304 E9
Boyup Brook *Australia* 33°50S 116°23E 279 F2
Boz Burun *Turkey* 40°32N 28°46E 203 F12
Boz Dağ *Turkey* 37°18N 29°11E 205 D11
Boz Dağları *Turkey* 38°20N 28°0E 205 C10
Bozai Gumbaz *Afghan.* 37°8N 74°0E 240 A4
Bozburun *Turkey* 36°43N 28°4E 205 E10
Bozcaada *Turkey* 39°49N 26°3E 212 C2
Bozdağ *Turkey* 36°50N 36°22E 250 B7
Bozdoğan *Turkey* 37°40N 28°17E 205 D10
Boze *Papua N. G.* 9°3S 143°3E 286 E2
Bozeman *U.S.A.* 45°41N 111°2W 304 D8
Bozen = Bolzano *Italy* 46°31N 11°22E 199 B8
Bozene *Dem. Rep. of the Congo* 2°56N 19°12E 264 B3
Boževac *Serbia* 44°32N 21°24E 202 B5
Bozhou *China* 33°55N 115°41E 226 H8
Bozkır *Turkey* 37°11N 32°14E 212 D5
Bozkurt *Turkey* 37°50N 29°37E 205 D11
Bozouls *France* 44°28N 2°43E 174 D6
Bozoum *C.A.R.* 6°25N 16°35E 264 A3
Bozova *Antalya, Turkey* 37°13N 30°18E 205 D12
Bozova *Sanliurfa, Turkey* 37°21N 38°32E 213 D8
Bozovici *Romania* 44°56N 22°0E 182 F7
Bozüyük *Turkey* 39°54N 30°3E 205 B12
Bozyazı *Turkey* 36°6N 33°0E 250 B4
Bra *Italy* 44°42N 7°51E 198 D4
Braås *Sweden* 57°4N 15°3E 163 G9
Brabant □ *Belgium* 50°46N 4°30E 170 D4
Brabant L. *Canada* 55°58N 103°43W 297 B8
Brabrand *Denmark* 56°9N 10°7E 163 H4
Brač *Croatia* 43°20N 16°40E 199 E13
Bracadale, L. *U.K.* 57°20N 6°30W 167 D2
Bracciano *Italy* 42°6N 12°10E 199 F9
Bracciano, L. di *Italy* 42°7N 12°14E 199 F9
Bracebridge *Canada* 45°2N 79°19W 312 A5
Bracieux *France* 47°30N 1°30E 172 E8
Bräcke *Sweden* 62°45N 15°26E 162 B9
Brackettville *U.S.A.* 29°19N 100°25W 314 G4
Brački Kanal *Croatia* 43°24N 16°40E 199 E13
Bracknell *U.K.* 51°25N 0°43W 169 F7
Bracknell Forest □ *U.K.* 51°25N 0°44W 169 F7
Brad *Romania* 46°10N 22°50E 182 D7
Brádano → *Italy* 40°23N 16°51E 201 B9
Bradbury Building *Los Angeles, U.S.A.* 127 b2
Bradenton *U.S.A.* 27°30N 82°34W 317 H7
Brades *Montserrat* 16°47N 62°13W 321 C7
Bradford *Ont., Canada* 44°7N 79°34W 312 B5
Bradford *W. Yorks., U.K.* 53°47N 1°45W 168 D6
Bradford *Ill., U.S.A.* 41°11N 89°39W 310 C7
Bradford *Ohio, U.S.A.* 40°8N 84°27W 311 D12
Bradford *Pa., U.S.A.* 41°58N 78°38W 312 E6
Bradford *Vt., U.S.A.* 43°59N 72°9W 313 C12
Bradley *Ark., U.S.A.* 33°6N 93°39W 314 E8
Bradley *Calif., U.S.A.* 35°52N 120°48W 306 K6
Bradley *Ill., U.S.A.* 41°9N 87°52W 311 C9
Bradley Institute *Zimbabwe* 17°7S 31°25E 269 F3
Bradley Junction *U.S.A.* 27°48N 81°59W 317 H8
Bradner *U.S.A.* 41°20N 83°26W 311 C13
Brady *U.S.A.* 31°9N 99°20W 314 F5
Brædstrup *Denmark* 55°58N 9°37E 163 J3
Braemar *Australia* 33°12S 139°35E 282 B3
Braepark *U.K.* 55°58N 3°18W 121 B2
Braeside *Canada* 45°28N 76°24W 313 A8
Braeton *Jamaica* 17°57N 76°53W 320 a
Braga *Portugal* 41°35N 8°25W 194 D2
Braga □ *Portugal* 41°30N 8°30W 194 D2
Bragadiru *Romania* 43°46N 25°31E 183 G10
Bragado *Argentina* 35°2S 60°27W 334 D3
Bragança *Brazil* 1°0S 47°2W 332 B2
Bragança *Portugal* 41°48N 6°50W 194 D4
Bragança □ *Portugal* 41°30N 6°45W 194 D4
Bragança Paulista *Brazil* 22°55S 46°32W 335 A6
Bragg's Spur = West Memphis *U.S.A.* 35°8N 90°10W 315 D9
Brahestad = Raahe *Finland* 64°40N 24°28E 160 D21
Brahmakund *India* 27°52N 96°22E 241 B6
Brahmanbaria *Bangla.* 23°58N 91°15E 241 D3
Brahmani → *India* 20°39N 86°46E 244 D8
Brahmapur *India* 19°15N 84°54E 244 E7
Brahmaputra → *Asia* 23°40N 90°35E 241 D3
Braich-y-pwll *U.K.* 52°47N 4°46W 168 E3
Braid *U.K.* 55°55N 3°11W 121 B2
Braidwood *Australia* 35°27S 149°49E 283 C8
Brăila *Romania* 45°19N 27°59E 183 E12
Brăila □ *Romania* 45°5N 27°30E 183 E12
Brainerd *U.S.A.* 46°22N 94°12W 308 B6
Braintree *Essex, U.K.* 51°53N 0°34E 169 F8
Braintree *Mass., U.S.A.* 42°13N 71°0W 313 D14
Brak → *S. Africa* 29°35S 22°55E 270 C3
Brake *Germany* 53°20N 8°28E 178 B4
Brakel *Germany* 51°42N 9°11E 178 D5
Brakna □ *Mauritania* 17°0N 13°20W 262 B2
Bräkne-Hoby *Sweden* 56°14N 15°6E 163 H9
Brakwater *Namibia* 22°28S 17°3E 270 B2
Brålanda *Sweden* 58°34N 12°21E 163 F6
Bramberg *Germany* 50°6N 10°40E 179 E6
Bramdrupdam *Denmark* 55°31N 9°28E 163 J3
Bramhapuri *India* 20°36N 79°52E 244 D4
Bramley *S. Africa* 26°7S 28°4E 123 A2
Bramming *Denmark* 55°28N 8°42E 163 J2
Brämön *Sweden* 62°14N 17°40E 162 B11
Brampton *Ont., Canada* 43°45N 79°45W 312 C5
Brampton *Cumb., U.K.* 54°57N 2°44W 168 C5
Brampton I. *Australia* 20°49S 149°16E 280 b
Bramsche *Germany* 52°24N 7°59E 178 C3
Branchville *U.S.A.* 33°15N 80°49W 316 B9
Branco → *Brazil* 1°20S 61°50W 329 D5
Branco, C. *Brazil* 7°9S 34°47W 332 C5
Brandaris *Bonaire* 12°16N 68°23W 322 h
Brandberg *Namibia* 21°10S 14°33E 270 B1
Brandberg ⌓ *Namibia* 21°10S 14°30E 270 B1
Brandbu *Norway* 60°26N 10°28E 164 D7
Brande *Denmark* 55°57N 9°8E 163 J3
Brandeis Univ. *U.S.A.* 42°21N 71°17W 116 A1
Brandenburg = Neubrandenburg *Germany* 53°33N 13°15E 178 B9
Brandenburg *Brandenburg, Germany* 52°25N 12°33E 178 C8
Brandenburg *Ky., U.S.A.* 38°0N 86°10W 311 G10
Brandenburg □ *Germany* 52°50N 13°0E 178 C9
Brandenburger Tor *Germany* 52°30N 13°21E 115 A3
Brandfort *S. Africa* 28°40S 26°30E 270 C4
Brando *France* 42°47N 9°27E 175 F13
Brandon *Man., Canada* 49°50N 99°57W 297 D9
Brandon *Fla., U.S.A.* 27°56N 82°17W 317 H7
Brandon *Vt., U.S.A.* 43°48N 73°6W 313 C11
Brandon B. *Ireland* 52°17N 10°8W 166 D1
Brandon Mt. *Ireland* 52°15N 10°15W 166 D1
Brandsen *Argentina* 35°10S 58°15W 334 D4
Brandvlei *S. Africa* 30°25S 20°30E 270 D3
Brandýs nad Labem *Czech Rep.* 50°10N 14°40E 180 A7
Brăneşti *Romania* 44°27N 26°20E 183 F11
Branford *Conn., U.S.A.* 41°17N 72°49W 313 E12
Branford *Fla., U.S.A.* 29°58N 82°56W 316 F7
Brani, Pulau *Singapore* 1°15N 103°50E 138 B3
Braniewo *Poland* 54°25N 19°50E 184 D6
Branik *Czech Rep.* 50°1N 14°25E 135 B2
Brännkyrka *Sweden* 59°17N 18°0E 139 B2
Bransfield Str. *Antarctica* 63°0S 59°0W 151 C18
Brańsk *Poland* 52°45N 22°50E 185 F9
Branson *U.S.A.* 36°39N 93°13W 308 G7
Brantford *Canada* 43°10N 80°15W 312 C4
Brantley *U.S.A.* 31°35N 86°16W 316 D3
Brantôme *France* 45°22N 0°39E 174 C4
Branxholme *Australia* 37°52S 141°49E 282 D4
Branxton *Australia* 32°38S 151°21E 283 B9
Branzi *Italy* 46°1N 9°46E 198 B6
Brás *Amazonas, Brazil* 2°5S 53°10W 329 D6
Brás *São Paulo, Brazil* 23°32S 46°36W 137 B2
Bras d'Or L. *Canada* 45°50N 60°50W 299 C7
Bras-Panon *Réunion* 20°59S 55°41E 272 f
Brasher Falls *U.S.A.* 44°49N 74°47W 313 B10
Brasil = Brazil ■ *S. Amer.* 12°0S 50°0W 327 E6
Brasil, Planalto *Brazil* 18°0S 46°30W 326 E6
Brasil Novo *Brazil* 3°19S 52°38W 329 D7
Brasilândia *Brazil* 23°28S 46°42W 137 A1
Brasiléia *Brazil* 11°0S 68°45W 330 C4
Brasília *Distrito Federal, Brazil* 15°47S 47°55W 333 E2
Brasília *Minas Gerais, Brazil* 16°12S 44°26W 333 E3
Brasília △ *Brazil* 15°41S 48°8W 333 E2
Brasília Legal *Brazil* 3°49S 55°36W 329 D6
Braskereidfoss *Norway* 60°44N 11°46E 164 D8
Braslaw *Belarus* 55°38N 27°0E 188 E4
Braslovče *Slovenia* 46°21N 15°3E 199 B12
Braşov *Romania* 45°38N 25°35E 183 E10
Braşov □ *Romania* 45°45N 25°15E 183 E10
Brass *Nigeria* 4°35N 6°14E 263 E6
Brass → *Nigeria* 4°15N 6°13E 263 E6
Brassac-les-Mines *France* 45°24N 3°20E 174 C7
Brasschaat *Belgium* 51°19N 4°27E 170 C4
Brassey, Banjaran *Malaysia* 5°0N 117°15E 235 B5
Brassey Ra. *Australia* 25°8S 122°15E 279 E3
Brasso Seco *Trin. & Tob.* 10°45N 61°16W 323 t
Brasstown Bald *U.S.A.* 34°53N 83°49W 315 D13
Brastad *Sweden* 58°23N 11°30E 163 F5
Brastavățu *Romania* 43°55N 24°24E 183 G9
Bratan = Morozov *Bulgaria* 42°30N 25°10E 203 D9
Brateş *Romania* 45°50N 26°4E 183 E11
Brateyevo *Russia* 55°39N 37°45E 129 C4
Bratislava *Slovak Rep.* 48°10N 17°7E 181 C10
Bratislava M.R. Štefánik ✈ (BTS) *Slovak Rep.* 48°11N 17°9E 181 C10
Bratislavský □ *Slovak Rep.* 48°15N 17°20E 181 C10
Bratsberg = Telemark □ *Norway* 59°25N 8°30E 164 E5
Bratsevo *Russia* 55°51N 37°24E 129 A2
Bratsigovo *Bulgaria* 42°1N 24°22E 203 D8
Bratsk *Russia* 56°10N 101°30E 215 D11
Brattleboro *U.S.A.* 42°51N 72°34W 313 D12
Brattvåg *Norway* 62°37N 6°25E 164 B3
Bratunac *Bos.-H.* 44°13N 19°21E 182 F4
Braunau *Austria* 48°15N 13°3E 180 C6
Braunsberg = Braniewo *Poland* 54°25N 19°50E 184 D6
Braunschweig *Germany* 52°15N 10°31E 178 C6
Braunton *U.K.* 51°7N 4°10W 169 F3
Brava = Baraawe *Somali Rep.* 1°20N 44°8E 267 D5
Brava *C. Verde Is.* 15°0N 24°40W 153 j
Bravicea *Moldova* 47°22N 28°27E 183 C13
Bråviken *Sweden* 58°38N 16°32E 163 F10
Bravo del Norte, Rio = Grande, Rio → *N. Amer.* 25°58N 97°9W 314 J6
Brawley *U.S.A.* 32°59N 115°31W 307 N11
Bray *Ireland* 53°13N 6°7W 166 C5
Bray, Mt. *Australia* 14°0S 134°30E 280 A1
Bray, Pays de *France* 49°46N 1°26E 171 B4
Bray-sur-Seine *France* 48°25N 3°14E 173 D10
Braybrook *Australia* 37°46S 144°51E 128 A1
Braymer *U.S.A.* 39°35N 93°48W 310 E3
Brázdim *Czech Rep.* 50°10N 14°35E 135 A3
Brazeau → *Canada* 52°55N 115°14W 296 C5
Brazil *U.S.A.* 39°32N 87°8W 311 E9
Brazil ■ *S. Amer.* 12°0S 50°0W 327 E6
Brazil Basin *Atl. Oc.* 15°0S 25°0W 152 H9
Brazilian Highlands = Brasil, Planalto *Brazil* 18°0S 46°30W 326 E6
Brazo Sur → *S. Amer.* 25°21S 57°42W 334 B4
Brazos → *U.S.A.* 28°53N 95°23W 314 G7
Brazzaville *Congo* 4°9S 15°12E 265 C3
Brčko *Bos.-H.* 44°54N 18°46E 182 F3
Brda → *Poland* 53°8N 18°8E 185 E5
Brdy *Czech Rep.* 49°43N 13°55E 180 B6
Bré = Bray *Ireland* 53°13N 6°7W 166 C5
Breach Candy *Mumbai, India* 130 a1
Breaden, L. *Australia* 25°51S 125°28E 279 E4
Breakheart Reservation *U.S.A.* 42°28N 71°1W 116 A2
Breaksea Sd. *N.Z.* 45°35S 166°35E 285 F1
Bream B. *N.Z.* 35°56S 174°28E 284 B3
Bream Hd. *N.Z.* 35°51S 174°36E 284 B3
Bream Tail *N.Z.* 36°3S 174°36E 284 C3
Breas *Chile* 25°29S 70°24W 334 B1
Breaza *Romania* 45°11N 25°40E 183 E10
Brebes *Indonesia* 6°52S 109°3E 235 D3
Brechin *Ont., Canada* 44°32N 79°10W 312 B5
Brechin *Angus, U.K.* 56°44N 2°39W 167 E6
Brecht *Belgium* 51°21N 4°38E 170 C4
Breckenridge *Colo., U.S.A.* 39°29N 106°3W 304 G10
Breckenridge *Minn., U.S.A.* 46°16N 96°35W 308 B5
Breckenridge *Tex., U.S.A.* 32°45N 98°54W 314 E5
Breckland *U.K.* 52°30N 0°40E 169 E8
Brecknock, Pen. *Chile* 54°35S 71°30W 336 D2
Břeclav *Czech Rep.* 48°46N 16°53E 181 C9
Brecon *U.K.* 51°57N 3°23W 169 F4
Brecon Beacons *U.K.* 51°53N 3°26W 169 F4
Brecon Beacons △ *U.K.* 51°50N 3°30W 169 F4
Breda *Neths.* 51°35N 4°45E 170 C4
Bredaryd *Sweden* 57°10N 13°45E 163 G7
Bredasdorp *S. Africa* 34°33S 20°2E 270 D3
Bredbo *Australia* 35°58S 149°10E 283 C8
Brede *Denmark* 55°47N 12°30E 118 A3
Bredebro *Denmark* 55°4N 8°50E 163 J2
Bredstedt *Germany* 54°37N 8°55E 178 A4
Bredy *Russia* 52°26N 60°21E 216 B6
Bree *Belgium* 51°8N 5°35E 170 C5
Breezy Point *U.S.A.* 40°33N 73°56W 132 C2
Bregalnica → *Macedonia* 41°43N 22°9E 202 E6
Bregenz *Austria* 47°30N 9°45E 180 D2
Bregovo *Bulgaria* 44°9N 22°39E 202 B6
Bréhal *France* 48°53N 1°30W 172 D5
Bréhat, Î. de *France* 48°51N 3°0W 172 D4
Breiðafjörður *Iceland* 65°15N 23°15W 155 B3
Breiðdalsvík *Iceland* 64°44N 14°0W 155 C13
Breil-sur-Roya *France* 43°56N 7°31E 175 E11
Breim *Norway* 61°44N 6°25E 164 C3
Breisach *Germany* 48°1N 7°36E 179 G3
Breitenlee *Austria* 48°15N 16°30E 142 A3
Brejinho de Nazaré *Brazil* 11°1S 48°34W 332 D2
Brejo *Brazil* 3°41S 42°47W 332 B3
Brekke *Norway* 61°1N 5°26E 164 C2
Brekken *Norway* 62°40N 11°51E 164 B8
Brekkestø *Norway* 58°11N 8°22E 164 F5
Bremanger *Norway* 61°51N 4°58E 164 C1
Bremangerlandet *Norway* 61°51N 5°0E 164 C1
Bremen *Bremen, Germany* 53°4N 8°47E 178 B4
Bremen *Ga., U.S.A.* 33°43N 85°9W 316 B4
Bremen *Ind., U.S.A.* 41°27N 86°9W 311 C10
Bremen □ *Germany* 53°4N 8°50E 178 B4
Bremer Bay *Australia* 34°21S 119°20E 279 F2
Bremer I. *Australia* 12°5S 136°45E 280 A2
Bremerhaven *Germany* 53°33N 8°36E 178 B4
Bremersdorp = Manzini *Swaziland* 26°30S 31°25E 271 C5
Bremerton *U.S.A.* 47°34N 122°37W 306 C4
Bremervörde *Germany* 53°29N 9°8E 178 B5
Bremnes *Norway* 59°47N 5°8E 164 E2
Bremsnes *Norway* 63°6N 7°40E 164 A4
Breña *Peru* 12°3S 77°3W 124 B2
Brenes *Spain* 37°32N 5°54W 195 H5
Brenham *U.S.A.* 30°10N 96°24W 314 F6
Brenne *France* 46°44N 1°14E 174 B5
Brenne ⌓ *France* 46°40N 1°15E 174 B5
Brennerpass *Austria* 47°2N 11°30E 180 D4
Brennhaug *Norway* 61°54N 9°21E 164 C6
Breno *Italy* 45°57N 10°18E 198 C7
Brent *U.S.A.* 32°56N 87°10W 315 E11
Brent □ *U.K.* 51°33N 0°16W 125 A2
Brent Res. *U.K.* 51°34N 0°14W 125 A2
Brenta → *Italy* 45°11N 12°18E 199 C9
Brentford *U.K.* 51°28N 0°18W 125 B2
Brentwood *Essex, U.K.* 51°37N 0°19E 169 F8
Brentwood *Calif., U.S.A.* 34°3N 118°28W 126 B2
Brentwood *Calif., U.S.A.* 37°56N 121°42W 306 H5
Brentwood *N.Y., U.S.A.* 40°47N 73°15W 313 F11
Brentwood Park *U.S.A.* 34°3N 118°29W 126 B2
Brera *Italy* 45°28N 9°11E 129 B2
Brereton *Barbados* 13°7N 59°30W 323 r
Bréscia *Italy* 45°33N 10°15E 198 C7
Breskens *Neths.* 51°23N 3°33E 170 C3
Breslau = Wrocław *Poland* 51°5N 17°5E 185 G4
Bresle → *France* 50°4N 1°22E 172 B8
Bressanone *Italy* 46°43N 11°39E 199 B8
Bressay *U.K.* 60°9N 1°6W 167 A7
Bresse *France* 46°50N 5°10E 173 F12
Bresso *Italy* 45°32N 9°11E 129 A2
Bressuire *France* 46°51N 0°30W 172 F6
Brest *Belarus* 52°10N 23°40E 177 B12
Brest *Finistère, France* 48°24N 4°31W 172 D2
Brest □ *Belarus* 52°30N 26°10E 177 B13
Brest-Litovsk = Brest *Belarus* 52°10N 23°40E 177 B12
Bretagne □ *France* 48°10N 3°0W 172 D3
Bretanha, Pta. da *Azores* 37°54N 25°47W 153 d3
Bretçu *Romania* 46°7N 26°18E 183 D11
Bretenoux *France* 44°54N 1°51E 174 D5
Breteuil *Eure, France* 48°50N 0°57E 172 D7
Breteuil *Oise, France* 49°38N 2°18E 173 C9
Breton *Canada* 53°7N 114°28W 296 C6
Breton, Pertuis *France* 46°17N 1°25W 174 B2
Breton Sd. *U.S.A.* 29°35N 89°15W 315 G10
Brett, C. *N.Z.* 35°10S 174°20E 284 B3
Bretten *Germany* 49°2N 8°42E 179 F4
Breueh *Indonesia* 5°44N 95°3E 234 A1
Breuil-Cervínia *Italy* 45°56N 7°38E 198 C4
Brevard *U.S.A.* 35°14N 82°44W 315 D13
Breves *Brazil* 1°40S 50°29W 332 B1
Brevig Mission *U.S.A.* 65°20N 166°29W 303 D6
Brevik *Telemark, Norway* 59°4N 9°42E 164 E6
Brevik *Stockholm, Sweden* 59°20N 18°12E 139 A3
Břevnov *Czech Rep.* 50°4N 14°22E 135 B2
Brewarrina *Australia* 30°0S 146°51E 281 E4
Brewer *U.S.A.* 44°48N 68°46W 309 C19
Brewer, Mt. *U.S.A.* 36°44N 118°28W 306 J8
Brewerville *Liberia* 6°26N 10°47W 262 D2
Brewster *N.Y., U.S.A.* 41°24N 73°36W 313 E11
Brewster *Ohio, U.S.A.* 40°43N 81°36W 312 F3
Brewster *Wash., U.S.A.* 48°6N 119°47W 304 B4
Brewster, Kap = Kangikajik *Greenland* 70°7N 22°0W 154 C8
Brewton *U.S.A.* 31°7N 87°4W 315 F11
Breyten *S. Africa* 26°16S 30°0E 271 C5
Breza *Bos.-H.* 44°2N 18°16E 182 F3
Brežice *Slovenia* 45°54N 15°35E 199 C12
Brézina *Algeria* 33°4N 1°14E 261 B5
Březnice *Czech Rep.* 49°32N 13°57E 180 B6
Breznik *Bulgaria* 42°44N 22°55E 202 D6
Brezno *Slovak Rep.* 48°50N 19°40E 181 C12
Brezoi *Romania* 45°21N 24°15E 183 E9
Brezovica *Kosovo* 42°15N 21°3E 202 D5
Brezovo *Bulgaria* 42°21N 25°5E 203 D9
Bria *C.A.R.* 6°30N 21°58E 264 A4
Briançon *France* 44°54N 6°39E 175 D10
Briare *France* 47°38N 2°45E 173 E9
Briars, The *St. Helena* 15°56S 5°43W 153 h
Briático *Italy* 38°43N 16°2E 201 D9
Bribie I. *Australia* 27°0S 153°10E 281 D5
Bribri *Costa Rica* 9°38N 82°50W 320 E3
Briceni *Moldova* 48°22N 27°6E 183 B12
Brickyard, The *U.S.A.* 41°55N 87°47W 119 B2
Bricquebec *France* 49°28N 1°38W 172 C5
Bridge City *U.S.A.* 29°55N 90°9W 131 B2
Bridgehampton *U.S.A.* 40°56N 72°19W 313 F12
Bridgend *U.K.* 51°30N 3°34W 169 F4
Bridgend □ *U.K.* 51°36N 3°36W 169 F4
Bridgenorth *Canada* 44°23N 78°23W 312 B6
Bridgeport *Calif., U.S.A.* 38°15N 119°14W 306 G7
Bridgeport *Conn., U.S.A.* 41°11N 73°12W 313 E11
Bridgeport *Ill., U.S.A.* 41°50N 87°38W 119 B3
Bridgeport *Ill., U.S.A.* 38°43N 87°46W 311 F9
Bridgeport *N.Y., U.S.A.* 43°9N 75°58W 313 C9
Bridgeport *Nebr., U.S.A.* 41°40N 103°6W 308 E2
Bridgeport *Tex., U.S.A.* 33°13N 97°45W 314 E6
Bridger *U.S.A.* 45°18N 108°55W 304 D9
Bridgeton *U.S.A.* 39°26N 75°14W 309 F16
Bridgetown *W. Austral., Australia* 33°58S 116°7E 279 F2
Bridgetown *Barbados* 13°6N 59°37W 323 r
Bridgetown *N.S., Canada* 44°55N 65°18W 299 D6
Bridgetown *Western Cape, S. Africa* 33°58S 18°33E 118 A2
Bridgeview *U.S.A.* 41°45N 87°48W 119 C2
Bridgewater *Tas., Australia* 42°44S 147°14E 281 G4
Bridgewater *Vic., Australia* 36°36S 143°59E 282 D5
Bridgewater *N.S., Canada* 44°25N 64°31W 299 D7
Bridgewater *Mass., U.S.A.* 41°59N 70°58W 313 E14
Bridgewater *N.Y., U.S.A.* 42°53N 75°15W 313 D9
Bridgewater, C. *Australia* 38°23S 141°23E 282 E4
Bridgman *U.S.A.* 41°57N 86°33W 311 C10
Bridgnorth *U.K.* 52°32N 2°25W 169 E5
Bridgton *U.S.A.* 44°3N 70°42W 313 B14
Bridgwater *U.K.* 51°8N 2°59W 169 F5
Bridgwater B. *U.K.* 51°15N 3°15W 169 F4
Bridlington *U.K.* 54°5N 0°12W 168 C7
Bridlington B. *U.K.* 54°4N 0°10W 168 C7
Bridport *Tas., Australia* 40°59S 147°23E 281 G4
Bridport *Dorset, U.K.* 50°44N 2°45W 169 G5
Briec *France* 48°6N 4°0W 172 D2
Brieg = Brzeg *Poland* 50°52N 17°30E 185 H4
Brienne-le-Château *France* 48°24N 4°30E 173 D11
Brienon-sur-Armançon *France* 47°59N 3°38E 173 E10
Brienz *Switz.* 46°46N 8°2E 179 J4
Brienzersee *Switz.* 46°44N 7°53E 179 J3
Brier Cr. → *U.S.A.* 32°44N 81°26W 316 C8
Brière ⌓ *France* 47°22N 2°13W 172 E4
Brievengat *Curaçao* 12°9N 68°54W 322 g
Brig *Switz.* 46°18N 7°59E 179 J3
Brigg *U.K.* 53°34N 0°28W 168 D7
Brigham City *U.S.A.* 41°31N 112°1W 304 F7
Bright *Australia* 36°42S 146°56E 283 D7
Brighton *S. Austral., Australia* 35°5S 138°30E 282 C3
Brighton *Vic., Australia* 37°55S 144°59E 128 B1
Brighton *Ont., Canada* 44°2N 77°44W 312 B7
Brighton *Trin. & Tob.* 10°13N 61°39W 323 t
Brighton *Brighton & Hove, U.K.* 50°49N 0°7W 169 G7
Brighton *Fla., U.S.A.* 27°14N 81°6W 317 H8
Brighton *Ill., U.S.A.* 39°2N 90°8W 310 E6
Brighton *Iowa, U.S.A.* 41°10N 91°49W 310 C5
Brighton *Mass., U.S.A.* 42°21N 71°9W 116 A2
Brighton *Mich., U.S.A.* 42°32N 83°47W 311 B13
Brighton *N.Y., U.S.A.* 43°8N 77°34W 312 C7
Brighton Beach *U.S.A.* 40°34N 73°57W 132 C2
Brighton-Le-Sands *Australia* 33°57S 151°9E 139 B1
Brighton Park *U.S.A.* 41°48N 87°41W 119 C2
Brightside *Canada* 45°7N 76°29W 313 A8
Brightwater *N.Z.* 41°22S 173°9E 285 B8
Brightwood *U.S.A.* 38°57N 77°1W 143 B3
Brigittenau *Austria* 48°14N 16°22E 142 A2
Brignogan-Plage *France* 48°40N 4°20W 172 D2
Brignoles *France* 43°25N 6°5E 175 E10
Brihuega *Spain* 40°45N 2°52W 196 E2
Brikama *Gambia* 13°15N 16°45W 262 C1
Brilliant *U.S.A.* 40°15N 80°39W 312 F4
Brilon *Germany* 51°23N 8°35E 178 D4
Brim *Australia* 36°3S 142°27E 282 D5
Brimbank Park *Australia* 37°43S 144°50E 128 A1
Brimfield *U.S.A.* 40°50N 89°53W 310 D7
Brimstone Hill Fort *St. Kitts & Nevis* 17°20N 62°50W 322 d
Brindabella △ *Australia* 35°14S 148°5E 283 C8
Bríndisi *Italy* 40°39N 17°55E 201 B10
Brinje *Croatia* 44°59N 15°9E 199 D12
Brinkley *U.S.A.* 34°53N 91°12W 314 D9
Brinkworth *Australia* 33°42S 138°26E 282 B3
Brinnon *U.S.A.* 47°41N 122°54W 306 C4
Brinson *U.S.A.* 30°59N 84°44W 316 E5
Brion, Î. *Canada* 47°46N 61°26W 299 C7
Brionne *France* 49°11N 0°43E 172 C7
Brionski *Croatia* 44°55N 13°45E 199 D10
Brioude *France* 45°18N 3°24E 174 C7
Briouze *France* 48°42N 0°23W 172 D6
Brisay *Canada* 54°26N 70°31W 299 B5
Brisbane *Queens., Australia* 27°25S 153°2E 281 D5
Brisbane *Calif., U.S.A.* 37°40N 122°23W 136 B2
Brisbane → *Australia* 27°24S 153°9E 281 D5
Brisbane Ranges △ *Australia* 37°47S 144°16E 282 D6
Brisbane Water △ *Australia* 33°26S 151°13E 283 B9
Brisighella *Italy* 44°13N 11°46E 199 D8
Bristol *Bristol, U.K.* 51°26N 2°35W 169 F5
Bristol *Conn., U.S.A.* 41°40N 72°57W 313 E12
Bristol *Fla., U.S.A.* 30°26N 84°59W 316 E5
Bristol *Pa., U.S.A.* 40°6N 74°51W 313 F10
Bristol *R.I., U.S.A.* 41°40N 71°16W 313 E13
Bristol *Tenn., U.S.A.* 36°36N 82°11W 315 C13
Bristol *Vt., U.S.A.* 44°8N 73°4W 313 B11
Bristol, City of □ *U.K.* 51°27N 2°36W 169 F5
Bristol B. *U.S.A.* 58°0N 160°0W 303 H8
Bristol Channel *U.K.* 51°18N 4°30W 169 F3
Bristol I. *Antarctica* 58°45S 28°0W 151 B1
Bristol L. *U.S.A.* 34°28N 115°41W 305 J6
Bristow *U.S.A.* 35°50N 96°23W 314 D6
Bristow I. *Papua N. G.* 9°8S 143°14E 286 E2
Britain = Great Britain *Europe* 54°0N 2°15W 158 E5
Britânia *Brazil* 15°14S 51°9W 331 D7
British Central Africa = Malawi ■ *Africa* 11°55S 34°0E 269 E3
British Columbia □ *Canada* 55°0N 125°15W 296 C3
British East Africa = Kenya ■ *Africa* 1°0N 38°0E 268 B4
British Guiana = Guyana ■ *S. Amer.* 5°0N 59°0W 329 C6
British Honduras = Belize ■ *Cent. Amer.* 17°0N 88°30W 320 C2
British Indian Ocean Terr. = Chagos Arch. ☑ *Ind. Oc.* 6°0S 72°0E 211 J9
British Isles *Europe* 54°0N 4°0W 165 D5
British Mts. *N. Amer.* 68°50N 140°0W 300 B12
British Museum *London, U.K.* 125 a3
British Virgin Is. ☑ *W. Indies* 18°30N 64°30W 321 C7
Brits *S. Africa* 25°37S 27°48E 271 C4
Britstown *S. Africa* 30°37S 23°30E 270 D3
Britt *Ont., Canada* 45°46N 80°34W 298 C3
Britt *Iowa, U.S.A.* 43°6N 93°48W 310 A3
Brittany = Bretagne □ *France* 48°10N 3°0W 172 D3
Britton *U.S.A.* 45°48N 97°45W 308 C5
Britz *Germany* 52°26N 13°27E 115 B3
Brive-la-Gaillarde *France* 45°10N 1°32E 174 C5
Briviesca *Spain* 42°32N 3°19W 194 C7
Brixen = Bressanone *Italy* 46°43N 11°39E 199 B8
Brixham *U.K.* 50°23N 3°31W 169 G4
Brixton *U.K.* 51°27N 0°8W 125 B3
Brnaze *Croatia* 43°41N 16°40E 199 E13
Brnenský □ *Czech Rep.* 49°10N 16°40E 181 B9
Brno *Czech Rep.* 49°10N 16°35E 181 B9
Broach = Bharuch *India* 21°47N 73°0E 244 D1
Broad → *Ga., U.S.A.* 33°59N 82°39W 316 B7
Broad → *S.C., U.S.A.* 34°1N 81°4W 315 D14
Broad Arrow *Australia* 30°23S 121°15E 279 F3
Broad B. *U.K.* 58°14N 6°18W 167 C2
Broad Haven *Ireland* 54°20N 9°55W 166 B2
Broad Law *U.K.* 55°30N 3°21W 167 F5
Broad Pk. = Faichan Kangri *India* 35°48N 76°34E 243 B7
Broad Sd. *Australia* 22°0S 149°45E 280 C4
Broadalbin *U.S.A.* 43°4N 74°12W 313 C10
Broadback → *Canada* 51°21N 78°52W 298 B4
Broadford *Australia* 37°14S 145°4E 283 D6
Broadhurst Ra. *Australia* 22°30S 122°30E 278 D3
Broadmeadows *Australia* 37°40S 144°55E 128 A1
Broadmoor *U.S.A.* 37°41N 122°29W 136 B2
Broads, The *U.K.* 52°45N 1°30E 168 E9
Broadus *U.S.A.* 45°27N 105°25W 304 D11
Broadview *U.S.A.* 41°51N 87°52W 119 B1
Broadway *New York, U.S.A.* 132 d2
Broager *Denmark* 54°53N 9°40E 163 K3
Broby *Sweden* 56°15N 14°4E 163 H8
Brocēni *Latvia* 56°42N 22°32E 184 B9
Brochet *Canada* 57°53N 101°40W 297 B8
Brochet, L. *Canada* 58°36N 101°35W 297 B8
Brock I. *Canada* 77°52N 114°19W 295 B9
Brocken *Germany* 51°47N 10°37E 178 D6
Brocklehurst *Australia* 32°9S 148°38E 283 B8
Brocklesby *Australia* 35°48S 146°40E 283 C7
Brockley *U.K.* 51°27N 0°2W 125 B3
Brockport *U.S.A.* 43°13N 77°56W 312 C7
Brockton *U.S.A.* 42°5N 71°1W 313 D13
Brockville *Canada* 44°35N 75°41W 313 B9
Brockway *Mont., U.S.A.* 47°18N 105°45W 304 C11
Brockway *Pa., U.S.A.* 41°15N 78°47W 312 E6
Brocton *U.S.A.* 42°23N 79°26W 312 D5
Brod *Macedonia* 41°32N 21°17E 202 E5
Brodarevo *Serbia* 43°14N 19°44E 202 C3
Brodeur Pen. *Canada* 72°30N 88°10W 295 C14
Brodhead *U.S.A.* 42°37N 89°22W 310 B7
Brodick *U.K.* 55°35N 5°9W 167 F3
Brodnica *Poland* 53°15N 19°25E 185 E6
Bródno *Poland* 52°17N 21°1E 142 B2
Bródnowski, Kanal *Poland* 52°17N 21°3E 142 B2
Brody *Ukraine* 50°5N 25°10E 177 C13

Broek Neths. 52°26N 5°0E 112 A2
Brogan U.S.A. 44°15N 117°31W 304 D5
Broglie France 49°2N 0°30E 172 C7
Brok Poland 52°43N 21°52E 185 F8
Broken Arrow U.S.A. 36°3N 95°48W 314 C7
Broken Bow Nebr., U.S.A. 41°24N 99°38W 308 E4
Broken Bow Okla., U.S.A. 34°2N 94°44W 314 D7
Broken Bow Lake U.S.A. 34°9N 94°40W 314 D7
Broken Hill = Kabwe Zambia 14°30S 28°29E 269 E2
Broken Hill Australia 31°58S 141°29E 282 A4
Broken River Ra. Australia 21°0S 148°22E 280 b
Brokind Sweden 58°13N 15°42E 163 F9
Brokopondo Suriname 5°3N 54°59W 329 B7
Bromberg = Bydgoszcz Poland 53°10N 18°0E 185 E5
Bromley □ U.K. 51°24N 0°2E 125 B4
Bromley Common U.K. 51°22N 0°2E 125 B4
Bromma Sweden 59°21N 17°55E 139 A1
Bromma ✈ (BMA) Sweden 59°21N 17°56E 139 A1
Bromo Tengger Semeru △ Indonesia 7°56S 112°57E 235 D4
Bromölla Sweden 56°5N 14°28E 163 H8
Brompton London, U.K. 125 c2
Bromsgrove U.K. 52°21N 2°2W 169 E5
Bronaugh U.S.A. 37°41N 94°28W 310 G2
Brøndby Strand Denmark 55°36N 12°25E 118 B2
Brøndbyøster Denmark 55°39N 12°26E 118 B2
Brøndbyvester Denmark 55°37N 12°23E 118 B2
Brønderslev Denmark 57°16N 9°57E 163 G3
Brondesbury U.K. 51°32N 0°12W 125 A2
Brong-Ahafo □ Ghana 7°50N 2°0W 262 D4
Broni Italy 45°4N 9°16E 198 C6
Bronkhorstspruit S. Africa 25°46S 28°45E 271 C4
Brønnøya Norway 59°51N 10°32E 133 A2
Brønnøysund Norway 65°28N 12°14E 160 D15
Brønshøj Denmark 55°41N 12°29E 118 A2
Bronson Fla., U.S.A. 29°27N 82°39W 317 F7
Bronson Mich., U.S.A. 41°52N 85°12W 311 C11
Bronte Italy 37°47N 14°50E 201 E7
Bronwood U.S.A. 31°50N 84°22W 316 D5
Bronxville U.S.A. 40°56N 73°49W 132 A3
Brook Park U.S.A. 41°23N 81°48W 312 E4
Brooke's Point Phil. 8°47N 117°50E 233 G1
Brookfield Ill., U.S.A. 41°48N 87°50W 119 C1
Brookfield Mo., U.S.A. 39°47N 93°4W 310 E3
Brookfield Wis., U.S.A. 43°4N 88°9W 311 A8
Brookhaven Georgia, U.S.A. 33°52N 84°19W 113 A2
Brookhaven Miss., U.S.A. 31°35N 90°26W 315 F9
Brookings Oreg., U.S.A. 42°3N 124°17W 304 E1
Brookings S. Dak., U.S.A. 44°19N 96°48W 308 C5
Brookland = West Columbia U.S.A. 33°59N 81°4W 316 B8
Brooklet U.S.A. 32°23N 81°40W 316 C8
Brooklin Canada 43°55N 78°55W 312 C6
Brookline U.S.A. 42°19N 71°8W 116 B2
Brooklyn N.Z. 41°18S 174°46E 143 B1
Brooklyn Western Cape, S. Africa 33°54S 18°29E 118 A1
Brooklyn Iowa, U.S.A. 41°44N 92°27W 310 C4
Brooklyn New York, U.S.A. 132 f3
Brooklyn-Battery Tunnel New York, U.S.A. 132 f1
Brooklyn Bridge New York, U.S.A. 132 f2
Brooklyn Heights New York, U.S.A. 132 f2
Brooklyn Park U.S.A. 45°6N 93°23W 308 C7
Brookmont U.S.A. 38°57N 77°7W 143 B3
Brooks Canada 50°35N 111°55W 296 C6
Brooks Range U.S.A. 68°0N 152°0W 303 C9
Brookston U.S.A. 40°36N 86°52W 311 D10
Brooksville Fla., U.S.A. 28°33N 82°23W 317 G7
Brooksville Ky., U.S.A. 38°41N 84°4W 311 F12
Brookton Australia 32°22S 117°0E 279 F2
Brookville Ind., U.S.A. 39°25N 85°1W 311 E12
Brookville Ohio, U.S.A. 39°50N 84°24W 311 E12
Brookville Pa., U.S.A. 41°10N 79°5W 312 E5
Brookville L. U.S.A. 39°28N 85°0W 311 E11
Broom, L. U.K. 57°55N 5°15W 167 D3
Broome Australia 18°0S 122°15E 278 C3
Broons France 48°20N 2°16W 172 D4
Brora U.K. 58°0N 3°52W 167 C5
Brora → U.K. 58°0N 3°51W 167 C5
Brørup Denmark 55°29N 9°1E 163 J2
Brösarp Sweden 55°43N 14°6E 163 J8
Brosna → Ireland 53°14N 7°58W 166 C4
Brossard Canada 45°27N 73°28W 130 B3
Broşteni Mehedinţi, Romania 44°45N 22°59E 182 F7
Broşteni Suceava, Romania 47°14N 25°43E 183 C10
Brøsterud Norway 60°18N 8°34E 164 D5
Brotas de Macaúbas Brazil 12°0S 42°38W 333 D2
Brothers U.S.A. 43°49N 120°36W 304 E3
Brothers, The Yemen 12°8N 53°10E 249 E6
Brøttum Norway 61°2N 10°34E 164 C7
Brou France 48°13N 1°11E 172 D8
Brou-sur-Chantereine France 48°53N 2°37E 134 A4
Brouage France 45°52N 1°4W 174 C2
Brough U.K. 54°32N 2°18W 168 C5
Brough Hd. U.K. 59°8N 3°20W 167 B5
Broughton U.S.A. 37°56N 88°27W 311 G8
Broughton Island = Qikiqtarjuaq Canada 67°33N 63°0W 295 D19
Broumov Czech Rep. 50°35N 16°20E 181 A9
Brovary Ukraine 50°34N 30°48E 189 G6
Brovst Denmark 57°6N 9°31E 163 G3
Brown Canada 43°48N 79°14W 141 A3
Brown, L. Australia 31°5S 118°15E 279 F2
Brown, Mt. Australia 32°30S 138°0E 282 B3
Brown, Pt. Australia 32°32S 133°50E 281 E1
Brown City U.S.A. 43°13N 82°59W 312 C2
Brown Willy U.K. 50°35N 4°37W 169 G3
Brownfield U.S.A. 33°11N 102°17W 314 E3
Browning Ill., U.S.A. 40°8N 90°22W 310 D6
Browning Mo., U.S.A. 40°3N 93°12W 310 D3
Browning Mont., U.S.A. 48°34N 113°1W 304 B7
Browns Town Jamaica 18°24N 77°22W 320 a
Brownsburg U.S.A. 39°51N 86°24W 311 E10
Brownstown U.S.A. 38°53N 86°3W 311 F10
Brownsville Oreg., U.S.A. 44°24N 122°59W 304 D2
Brownsville Pa., U.S.A. 40°1N 79°53W 312 F5
Brownsville Tenn., U.S.A. 35°36N 89°16W 315 D10
Brownsville Tex., U.S.A. 25°54N 97°30W 314 J6
Brownsweg Suriname 5°5N 55°15W 329 B6
Brownville U.S.A. 44°0N 75°59W 313 C9
Brownwood U.S.A. 31°43N 98°59W 314 F5
Browse I. Australia 14°7S 123°33E 278 B3
Broxton U.S.A. 31°38N 82°53W 316 D7
Broyhill Park U.S.A. 38°52N 77°12W 143 B2
Bru Norway 61°32N 5°11E 164 C2
Bruas Malaysia 4°30N 100°47E 237 K3
Bruay-la-Buissière France 50°29N 2°33E 173 B9
Bruce U.S.A. 30°28N 85°58W 316 E4
Bruce, Mt. Australia 22°37S 118°8E 278 D2
Bruce B. N.Z. 43°35S 169°42E 285 D4
Bruce Pen. Canada 45°0N 81°30W 312 B3
Bruce Peninsula △ Canada 45°14N 81°36W 312 A3
Bruce Rock Australia 31°52S 118°8E 279 F2
Bruche → France 48°34N 7°43E 173 D14
Bruchsal Germany 49°7N 8°35E 179 F4
Bruck an der Leitha Austria 48°1N 16°47E 181 C9
Bruck an der Mur Austria 47°24N 15°16E 180 D8
Brue → U.K. 51°13N 2°59W 169 F5
Bruflat Norway 60°53N 9°37E 164 D6
Bruges = Brugge Belgium 51°13N 3°13E 170 C3
Brugg Switz. 47°29N 8°11E 179 H4
Brugge Belgium 51°13N 3°13E 170 C3
Brughério Italy 45°33N 9°17E 129 A2
Bruin U.S.A. 41°3N 79°43W 312 E5
Bruini India 29°10N 96°11E 241 A6
Bruit, Pulau Malaysia 2°35N 111°20E 235 B4
Brûk, W. el → Egypt 30°15N 33°50E 251 H4
Bruksvallarna Sweden 62°38N 12°27E 162 B6
Brûlé Canada 53°15N 117°58W 296 C5
Brûlé, L. Canada 53°35N 64°4W 299 B7
Brûlon France 47°58N 0°15W 172 E6
Brumado Brazil 14°14S 41°40W 333 D3
Brumado → Brazil 14°13S 41°40W 333 D3
Brumath France 48°43N 7°40E 173 D14
Brumunddal Norway 60°53N 10°56E 164 D7
Brundidge U.S.A. 31°43N 85°49W 316 D4
Bruneau U.S.A. 42°53N 115°48W 304 E6
Bruneau → U.S.A. 42°56N 115°57W 304 E6
Bruneck = Brunico Italy 46°48N 11°56E 199 B8
Brunei = Bandar Seri Begawan Brunei 4°52N 115°0E 235 B4
Brunei ■ Asia 4°50N 115°0E 235 B4
Brunflo Sweden 63°5N 14°50E 162 A8
Brunico Italy 46°48N 11°56E 199 B8
Brünn = Brno Czech Rep. 49°10N 16°35E 181 B9
Brunnen Switz. 46°59N 8°37E 179 J4
Brunner, L. N.Z. 42°37S 171°27E 285 C6
Brunnhóll Iceland 64°17N 15°26W 155 C11
Brunnsberg Sweden 61°17N 13°56E 162 C8
Brunsbüttel Germany 53°53N 9°6E 178 B5
Brunssum Neths. 50°57N 5°59E 170 D5
Brunswick = Braunschweig Germany 52°15N 10°31E 178 C6
Brunswick Vic., Australia 37°45S 144°57E 128 A1
Brunswick Ga., U.S.A. 31°10N 81°30W 316 D8
Brunswick Maine, U.S.A. 43°55N 69°58W 309 D19
Brunswick Md., U.S.A. 39°19N 77°38W 309 F15
Brunswick Mo., U.S.A. 39°26N 93°8W 310 E3
Brunswick Ohio, U.S.A. 41°14N 81°51W 312 E3
Brunswick, Pen. de Chile 53°30S 71°30W 336 D2
Brunswick B. Australia 15°15S 124°50E 278 C3
Brunswick Junction Australia 33°15S 115°50E 279 F2
Brunt Ice Shelf Antarctica 75°30S 25°0W 151 D2
Bruntál Czech Rep. 49°59N 17°27E 181 B10
Brus Laguna Honduras 15°47N 84°35W 320 C3
Brusa = Bursa Turkey 40°15N 29°5E 203 F13
Brusartsi Bulgaria 43°40N 23°5E 202 C7
Brush U.S.A. 40°15N 103°37W 304 F12
Brushton U.S.A. 44°50N 74°31W 313 B10
Brusio Switz. 46°14N 10°8E 179 J6
Brusque Brazil 27°5S 49°0W 335 B6
Brussegem Belgium 50°56N 4°16E 116 A1
Brussel Belgium 50°51N 4°21E 116 A2
Brussel ✈ (BRU) Belgium 50°54N 4°29E 116 A2
Brussels = Brussel Belgium 50°51N 4°21E 116 A2
Brussels Canada 43°44N 81°15W 312 C3
Brusy Poland 53°53N 17°43E 184 E4
Bruthen Australia 37°42S 147°50E 283 D7
Bruvoll Norway 60°27N 11°29E 164 D8
Bruxelles = Brussel Belgium 50°51N 4°21E 116 A2
Bruyères France 48°10N 6°40E 173 D13
Bruz France 48°1N 1°46W 172 D5
Bruzzano Italy 45°31N 9°10E 129 A2
Brwinów Poland 52°9N 20°40E 185 F7
Bry-sur-Marne France 48°50N 2°32E 134 A4
Bryagovo Bulgaria 41°58N 25°8E 203 E9
Bryan Ohio, U.S.A. 41°28N 84°33W 311 C12
Bryan Tex., U.S.A. 30°40N 96°22W 314 F6
Bryan, L. U.S.A. 28°22N 81°29W 133 B2
Bryan, Mt. Australia 33°30S 139°5E 282 B3
Bryanka Ukraine 48°32N 38°45E 189 H10
Bryansk Bryansk, Russia 53°13N 34°25E 189 F8
Bryansk Dagestan, Russia 44°20N 47°10E 191 H8
Bryansk □ Russia 53°10N 33°10E 189 F7
Bryanskoye = Bryansk Russia 44°20N 47°10E 191 H8
Bryanston S. Africa 26°4S 28°0E 123 A1
Bryant Park New York, U.S.A. 132 c2
Bryce Canyon △ U.S.A. 37°30N 112°10W 305 H7
Bryn Norway 59°55N 10°27E 133 A1
Bryne Norway 58°44N 5°38E 164 F2
Bryson City U.S.A. 35°26N 83°27W 315 D13
Bryukhovetskaya Russia 45°48N 39°0E 189 K10
Brza Palanka Serbia 44°28N 22°27E 202 B6
Brzeg Poland 50°52N 17°30E 185 H4
Brzeg Dolny Poland 51°16N 16°41E 185 G3
Brześć Kujawski Poland 52°36N 18°55E 185 F5
Brzešć nad Bugiem = Brest Belarus 52°10N 23°40E 177 B12
Brzesko Poland 49°59N 20°34E 185 J7
Brzeziny Łódzkie, Poland 51°49N 19°42E 185 G6
Brzeziny Warszawa, Poland 52°19N 21°2E 142 B2
Brzozów Poland 49°41N 22°3E 185 J9
Bsharri Lebanon 34°15N 36°0E 250 D7
Bū al Ḩijān, W. → Libya 27°25N 19°22E 258 C3
Bū Athlah Libya 30°9N 15°39E 258 B3
Bū Baqarah U.A.E. 25°35N 56°25E 247 E8
Bu Craa W. Sahara 26°45N 12°50W 260 C2
Bū Ḩasā U.A.E. 23°30N 53°20E 247 F7
Bū Tummayyim, W. → Libya 26°56N 19°13E 258 C3
Bua Fiji 16°48S 178°37E 287 A2
Bua Sweden 57°14N 12°7E 163 G6
Bua → Malaysia 12°45S 34°16E 269 E3
Bua Yai Thailand 15°33N 102°26E 236 E4
Bu'aale Somali Rep. 1°5N 42°35E 267 D5
Buad I. Phil. 11°40N 124°51E 233 F5
Buala Solomon Is. 8°10S 159°35E 287 M10
Buan S. Korea 35°44N 126°44E 224 E3
Buapinang Indonesia 4°40S 121°30E 231 E6
Buatan Indonesia 0°44N 101°49E 234 B2
Buayan = General Santos Phil. 6°5N 125°14E 233 H5
Buba Guinea-Biss. 11°40N 14°59W 262 C2
Bubali Bird Sanctuary Aruba 12°33N 70°2W 322 f
Bubanda Dem. Rep. of the Congo 4°14N 19°38E 264 B3
Bubanza Burundi 3°6S 29°23E 268 C2
Bubaque Guinea-Biss. 11°16N 15°51W 262 C1
Bube Ethiopia 8°46N 35°48E 257 F4
Bubeneč Czech Rep. 50°6N 14°24E 135 B2
Bubi → Zimbabwe 22°20S 31°7E 271 B5
Būbiyān Kuwait 29°45N 48°15E 247 D6
Buc France 48°46N 2°7E 134 B1
Buca Fiji 16°38S 179°52E 287 A2
Buca Turkey 38°22N 27°11E 205 C9
Bucaco Angola 11°26S 20°10E 265 E4
Bucak Turkey 37°28N 30°36E 205 D12
Bucakkışla Turkey 36°57N 33°1E 205 D13
Bucaramanga Colombia 7°0N 73°0W 328 B3
Bucas Grande I. Phil. 9°40N 125°57E 233 G5
Bucasia Australia 21°2S 149°10E 280 b
Bucay Phil. 17°32N 120°43E 232 C3
Buccaneer Arch. Australia 16°7S 123°20E 278 C3
Buccino Italy 40°38N 15°22E 201 B8
Buccoo Reef Trin. & Tob. 11°10N 60°51W 323 s
Bucecea Romania 47°47N 26°28E 183 C11
Bucegi △ Romania 45°25N 25°25E 183 E10
Buchach Ukraine 49°5N 25°25E 177 D13
Buchan Vic., Australia 37°30S 148°12E 283 D8
Buchan Aberds., U.K. 57°32N 2°21W 167 D6
Buchan Ness U.K. 57°29N 1°46W 167 D7
Buchanan Sask., Canada 51°40N 102°45W 297 C8
Buchanan Liberia 5°57N 10°2W 262 D2
Buchanan Ga., U.S.A. 33°48N 85°11W 316 B4
Buchanan Mich., U.S.A. 41°50N 86°22W 311 C10
Buchanan, L. Queens., Australia 21°35S 145°52E 280 C4
Buchanan, L. W. Austral., Australia 25°33S 123°2E 279 E3
Buchanan, L. Tex., U.S.A. 30°45N 98°25W 314 F5
Buchanan Cr. → Australia 19°13S 136°33E 280 B2
Buchans Canada 48°50N 56°52W 299 C8
Bucharest = Bucureşti Romania 44°27N 26°10E 183 F11
Buchen Germany 49°32N 9°20E 179 F5
Buchenhain Germany 48°1N 11°29E 131 B1
Bucheon S. Korea 37°28N 126°45E 224 D3
Buchholz Berlin, Germany 52°36N 13°25E 115 A3
Buchholz Niedersachsen, Germany 53°19N 9°52E 178 B5
Buchloe Germany 48°1N 10°44E 179 G6
Buchon, Pt. U.S.A. 35°15N 120°54W 306 K6
Buciumi Romania 47°3N 23°1E 182 C8
Buck Hill Falls U.S.A. 41°11N 75°16W 313 E9
Bückeburg Germany 52°16N 9°2E 178 C5
Buckeye Lake U.S.A. 39°55N 82°29W 312 G2
Buckhannon U.S.A. 39°0N 80°8W 309 F13
Buckhaven U.K. 56°11N 3°3W 167 E5
Buckhead U.S.A. 33°51N 84°24W 113 A2
Buckhorn L. Canada 44°29N 78°23W 312 B6
Buckie U.K. 57°41N 2°58W 167 D6
Buckingham Qué., Canada 45°37N 75°24W 298 C4
Buckingham Bucks., U.K. 51°59N 0°57W 169 F7
Buckingham B. Australia 12°10S 135°40E 280 A2
Buckingham Canal India 14°0N 80°5E 245 H5
Buckingham Fountain Chicago, U.S.A. 119 d2
Buckingham Palace London, U.K. 125 b3
Buckinghamshire □ U.K. 51°53N 0°55W 169 F7
Buckland U.S.A. 65°59N 161°8W 303 D7
Buckle Hd. Australia 14°26S 127°52E 278 B4
Buckleboo Australia 32°54S 136°12E 282 B2
Buckley Flints., U.K. 53°10N 3°5W 168 D4
Buckley Ill., U.S.A. 40°36N 88°2W 311 D8
Buckley → Australia 20°10S 138°49E 280 C2
Bucklin Kans., U.S.A. 37°33N 99°38W 308 G4
Bucklin Mo., U.S.A. 39°47N 92°53W 310 E4
Buckow Germany 52°25N 13°26E 115 B3
Bucks L. U.S.A. 39°54N 121°12W 306 F5
Bucktown U.S.A. 30°1N 90°8W 131 A2
Buco Zau Angola 4°46S 12°33E 265 C2
Bucquoy France 50°9N 2°43E 173 B9
Bucureşti Romania 44°27N 26°10E 183 F11
Bucureşti Otopeni ✈ (OTP) Romania 44°30N 26°11E 183 F11
Bucyrus U.S.A. 40°48N 82°59W 311 D14
Bud Norway 62°55N 6°55E 164 B3
Bud Bud Somali Rep. 4°11N 46°28E 267 D6
Buda Hungary 47°30N 19°2E 117 A2
Buda Castle = Budaváripalota Budapest, Hungary 117 b2
Budacu, Vf. Romania 47°7N 25°41E 183 C10
Budafok Hungary 47°25N 19°2E 117 B2
Budalin Burma 22°20N 95°10E 241 D5
Budaörs Hungary 47°27N 18°57E 117 B1
Budapest Hungary 47°29N 19°3E 117 B2
Budapest □ Hungary 47°29N 19°5E 182 C4
Budapest ✈ (BUD) Hungary 47°26N 19°14E 117 B3
Budatétény Hungary 47°25N 19°2E 117 B2
Budaun India 28°5N 79°10E 243 E8
Budaváripalota Budapest, Hungary 117 b2
Budawang △ Australia 35°10S 150°12E 283 C9
Budd Coast Antarctica 68°0S 112°0E 151 C8
Buddenbrock = Brodnica Poland 53°15N 19°25E 185 E6
Budderoo △ Australia 35°40S 150°41E 283 C9
Buddinge Denmark 55°44N 12°30E 118 A3
Buddusò Italy 40°35N 9°15E 200 B2
Bude U.K. 50°49N 4°34W 169 G3
Budennovsk Russia 44°50N 44°10E 191 H7
Budeşti Romania 44°13N 26°30E 183 F11
Budeyi Ukraine 48°3N 29°16E 183 B14
Budge Budge = Baj Baj India 22°30N 88°5E 243 H13
Budgewoi Australia 33°13S 151°34E 283 B9
Búðardalur Iceland 65°7N 21°46W 155 B5
Budia Spain 40°38N 2°46W 192 E2
Büdingen Germany 50°16N 9°7E 179 E5
Budjala Dem. Rep. of the Congo 2°50N 19°40E 264 B3
Budo-Sungai Padi △ Thailand 6°19N 101°42E 237 J3
Budokan Tokyo, Japan 140 a4
Budoni Italy 40°40N 9°45E 200 B2
Búdrio Italy 44°32N 11°32E 199 D8
Budszentmihály = Tiszavasvári Hungary 47°58N 21°18E 182 C6
Budva Montenegro 42°17N 18°50E 202 D2
Budweis = České Budějovice Czech Rep. 48°55N 14°25E 180 C7
Budyonnovka = Novoazovsk Ukraine 47°15N 38°4E 189 J10
Budzyń Poland 52°54N 16°59E 185 F3
Bue Norway 58°40N 5°58E 164 F2
Buea Cameroon 4°10N 9°9E 263 E6
Buela Angola 5°54S 14°40E 265 D2
Buellton U.S.A. 34°37N 120°12W 307 L6
Buena Esperanza Argentina 34°45S 65°15W 334 C2
Buena Park U.S.A. 33°52N 117°59W 307 M9
Buena Vista Bolivia 17°27S 63°40W 331 D5
Buena Vista Curaçao 12°8N 68°57W 322 g
Buena Vista Solomon Is. 8°52S 160°3E 287 M11
Buena Vista Colo., U.S.A. 38°51N 106°8W 304 G10
Buena Vista Ga., U.S.A. 32°19N 84°31W 316 C5
Buena Vista Va., U.S.A. 37°44N 79°21W 309 G14
Buena Vista Lake Bed U.S.A. 35°12N 119°18W 307 K7
Buenaventura Colombia 3°53N 77°4W 328 C2
Buenaventura Chihuahua, Mexico 29°51N 107°29W 318 B3
Buenaventura, B. de Colombia 3°48N 77°17W 328 C2
Buenavista Agusan del N., Phil. 8°59N 125°24E 233 G5
Buenavista Quezon, Phil. 13°35N 122°34E 232 E4
Buendía, Embalse de Spain 40°25N 2°43W 196 E2
Buenópolis Brazil 17°54S 44°11W 333 E2
Buenos Aires Argentina 34°36S 58°22W 117 B2
Buenos Aires Colombia 1°36N 73°18W 328 C3
Buenos Aires Costa Rica 9°10N 83°20W 320 E3
Buenos Aires □ Argentina 36°30S 60°0W 334 D4
Buenos Aires, L. Argentina 46°35S 72°30W 336 C2
Buenos Aires Ezeiza ✈ (EZE) Argentina 34°49S 58°32W 117 C1
Buenos Ayres Trin. & Tob. 10°6N 61°41W 323 t
Buesaco Colombia 1°23N 77°9W 328 C2
Bufalotta Italy 41°59N 12°33E 136 B2
Buff Bay Jamaica 18°14N 76°40W 320 a
Buffalo Mo., U.S.A. 37°39N 93°6W 310 G3
Buffalo N.Y., U.S.A. 42°53N 78°53W 312 D6
Buffalo Okla., U.S.A. 36°50N 99°38W 314 C5
Buffalo S. Dak., U.S.A. 45°35N 103°33W 308 C2
Buffalo Wyo., U.S.A. 44°21N 106°42W 304 D10
Buffalo → Alta., Canada 60°5N 115°5W 296 A5
Buffalo → S. Africa 28°43S 30°37E 271 C5
Buffalo △ U.S.A. 36°14N 92°36W 314 C8
Buffalo Head Hills Canada 57°25N 115°55W 296 B5
Buffalo L. Alta., Canada 52°27N 112°54W 296 C6
Buffalo L. N.W.T., Canada 60°12N 115°25W 296 A5
Buffalo Narrows Canada 55°51N 108°29W 297 B7
Buffalo Springs △ Kenya 0°32N 37°35E 268 B4
Buffels → S. Africa 29°36S 17°3E 270 C2
Buford U.S.A. 34°10N 84°0W 315 D12
Bug = Buh → Ukraine 46°59N 31°58E 189 J6
Bug → Poland 52°31N 21°5E 185 F8
Buga Colombia 4°0N 76°15W 328 C2
Bugala I. Uganda 0°40S 32°20E 268 C3
Buganda Uganda 0°0 31°30E 268 C3
Buganga Uganda 0°3S 32°0E 268 C3
Bugasong Phil. 11°3N 122°4E 233 F4
Bugda Acable Somali Rep. 4°4N 45°15E 267 D6
Bugeat France 45°36N 1°55E 174 C5
Bugel, Tanjung Indonesia 6°26S 111°3E 235 D4
Búger Spain 39°45N 2°59E 206 B3
Bugibba Malta 35°57N 14°25E 206 F7
Bugio Portugal 38°39N 9°18W 126 B1
Bugojno Bos.-H. 44°2N 17°25E 182 F2
Bugsuk I. Phil. 8°12N 117°18E 233 G1
Buguey Phil. 18°17N 121°50E 232 B3
Buguias Phil. 16°43N 120°50E 232 C3
Bugulma Russia 54°33N 52°48E 186 D9
Buguma Nigeria 4°42N 6°55E 263 E6
Bugungu △ Uganda 2°17N 31°50E 268 B3
Buguruslan Russia 53°39N 52°26E 186 D9
Buh → Ukraine 46°59N 31°58E 189 J6
Buharkent Turkey 37°58N 28°44E 205 D10
Buheirat-Murrat-el-Kubra Egypt 30°18N 32°26E 256 H8
Buhera Zimbabwe 19°18S 31°29E 271 A5
Bühl Baden-W., Germany 48°40N 8°8E 179 G4
Buhl Idaho, U.S.A. 42°36N 114°46W 304 E6
Buhl Minn., U.S.A. 47°30N 92°46W 308 B7
Buhuşi Romania 46°41N 26°45E 183 D11
Bui △ Ghana 8°21N 2°21W 262 D4
Buiksloot Neths. 52°24N 4°55E 112 A2
Builth Wells U.K. 52°9N 3°25W 169 E4
Buin Papua N. G. 6°48S 155°42E 287 L8
Buinsk Russia 55°0N 48°18E 190 C9
Buique Brazil 8°37S 37°9W 332 C4
Buir Nur Mongolia 47°50N 117°42E 219 B12
Buis-les-Baronnies France 44°17N 5°16E 175 D9
Buitenveldert Neths. 52°20N 4°53E 112 B2
Buitenzorg = Bogor Indonesia 6°36S 106°48E 234 D3
Buitrago del Lozoya Spain 40°58N 3°38W 194 E7
Buizingen Belgium 50°44N 4°15E 116 B1
Bujalance Spain 37°54N 4°23W 195 H6
Bujanovac Serbia 42°28N 21°44E 202 D5
Bujaraloz Spain 41°29N 0°10W 196 D4
Buje Croatia 45°24N 13°39E 199 C10
Buji China 22°37N 114°5E 219 a
Bujumbura Burundi 3°16S 29°18E 268 C2
Bük Hungary 47°22N 16°45E 182 C1
Buk Poland 52°21N 16°30E 185 F3
Buka I. Papua N. G. 5°10S 154°35E 286 C8
Bukachacha Russia 52°55N 116°50E 215 D12
Bukama Dem. Rep. of the Congo 9°10S 25°50E 269 D2
Bukavu Dem. Rep. of the Congo 2°20S 28°52E 268 C2
Bukene Tanzania 4°15S 32°48E 268 C3
Bukhansan S. Korea 37°38N 126°58E 137 B1
Bukhara = Buxoro Uzbekistan 39°48N 64°25E 216 E6
Bukhoro = Buxoro Uzbekistan 39°48N 64°25E 216 E6
Bukhtarma Res. = Zaysan Köli Kazakhstan 48°0N 83°0E 217 C10
Bukidnon □ Phil. 8°0N 125°0E 233 G5
Bukima Tanzania 1°50S 33°25E 268 C3
Bukit Baka Bukit Raya △ Indonesia 0°43S 112°40E 235 C4
Bukit Barisan Selatan △ Indonesia 5°8S 104°4E 234 D2
Bukit Bendera Malaysia 5°25N 100°15E 237 c
Bukit Duabelas △ Indonesia 2°3S 102°48E 234 C2
Bukit Mertajam Malaysia 5°22N 100°28E 237 c
Bukit Nil Malaysia 1°22N 104°12E 237 d
Bukit Panjang Singapore 1°23N 103°46E 237 d
Bukit Panjang Nature Reserve Singapore 1°22N 103°45E 138 A2
Bukit Tengah Malaysia 5°22N 100°25E 237 c
Bukit Tigapuluh △ Indonesia 1°15S 102°25E 234 C2
Bukit Timah Nature Reserve Singapore 1°20N 103°47E 138 A2
Bukitkemuning Indonesia 4°51S 104°33E 234 C2
Bukittinggi Indonesia 0°20S 100°20E 234 C2
Bükk Hungary 48°0N 20°30E 182 B5
Bukkapatnam India 14°14N 77°46E 245 G3
Bükki △ Hungary 48°3N 20°30E 182 B5
Bukoba Tanzania 1°20S 31°49E 268 C3
Bukum, Pulau Singapore 1°14N 103°46E 138 C2
Bukuru Nigeria 9°42N 8°48E 263 D6
Bukuya Uganda 0°40N 31°52E 268 B3
Būl, Kuh-e Iran 30°48N 52°45E 247 D7
Bula Guinea-Biss. 12°7N 15°43W 262 C1
Bula Indonesia 3°6S 130°30E 231 E8
Bula Camarines S., Phil. 13°28N 123°16E 232 E4
Bula-Atumba Angola 8°41S 14°52E 265 D2
Bulabog-Putian △ Phil. 11°2N 122°4E 233 F4
Bulacan □ Phil. 15°0N 121°5E 232 D3
Bülach Switz. 47°31N 8°32E 179 H4
Bŭlaevo Kazakhstan 54°54N 70°26E 217 B8
Bulahdelah Australia 32°23S 152°13E 283 B10
Bulalacao Phil. 12°31N 121°26E 232 E3
Bulan Phil. 12°40N 123°52E 232 E4
Bulancak Turkey 40°56N 38°14E 213 B8
Búland Iceland 63°46N 18°30W 155 D8
Bulandshahr India 28°28N 77°51E 242 E7
Bulanık Turkey 39°4N 42°14E 213 C10
Bûlâq El Khârga, Egypt 25°10N 30°38E 256 B3
Bûlâq El Qâhira, Egypt 30°3N 31°14E 117 A2
Bulawayo Zimbabwe 20°7S 28°32E 269 G2
Buldan Turkey 38°2N 28°50E 205 C10
Buldana India 20°30N 76°18E 244 D3
Buldir I. U.S.A. 52°21N 175°56E 303 K1
Buldon Phil. 7°33N 124°25E 233 H5
Bule Phil. 14°26N 121°2E 127 C2
Bulenga Ghana 9°56N 2°12W 262 D4
Bulgan Mongolia 48°45N 103°34E 218 B9
Bulgar Russia 54°57N 49°4E 190 C9
Bulgaria ■ Europe 42°35N 25°30E 203 D9
Bulgheria, Monte Italy 40°4N 15°26E 201 B8
Bulgurca Turkey 38°9N 27°9E 205 C9
Bulhale Somali Rep. 5°20N 46°29E 267 C6
Bulhar Somali Rep. 10°25N 44°30E 267 B5
Buli, Teluk Indonesia 0°48N 128°25E 231 D7
Buliluyan, C. Phil. 8°20N 117°15E 233 G1
Bulim Singapore 1°22N 103°43E 138 A2
Bulki Ethiopia 6°11N 36°31E 257 F4
Bulkley → Canada 55°15N 127°40W 296 B3
Bull Head Jamaica 18°10N 77°16W 320 a
Bull Savanna Jamaica 17°53N 77°35W 320 a
Bull Shoals L. U.S.A. 36°22N 92°35W 314 C8
Bullaque → Spain 38°59N 4°17W 195 G6
Bullard U.S.A. 32°38N 83°30W 316 C6
Bullas Spain 38°2N 1°40W 197 G3
Bulle Switz. 46°37N 7°3E 179 J3
Bullen Park Australia 37°46S 145°4E 128 A2
Bullenbaai Curaçao 12°11N 69°2W 322 g
Buller → N.Z. 41°44S 171°36E 285 B6
Buller, Mt. Australia 37°10S 146°28E 283 D7
Buller Gorge N.Z. 41°40S 172°10E 285 B7
Bulleringa △ Australia 17°39S 143°56E 280 B3
Bullhead City U.S.A. 35°8N 114°32W 307 K12
Bulli Australia 34°15S 150°57E 283 C9
Büllingen Belgium 50°25N 6°16E 170 D6
Bullock Creek Australia 17°43S 144°31E 280 B3
Bulloo → Australia 28°43S 142°30E 281 D3
Bulloo L. Australia 28°43S 142°25E 281 D3
Bulls N.Z. 40°10S 175°24E 284 G4
Bully-les-Mines France 50°27N 2°44E 173 B9
Bulman Australia 13°39S 134°20E 280 A1
Bulnes Chile 36°42S 72°19W 334 D1
Bulo Ghedudo Somali Rep. 2°52N 43°1E 267 D5
Bulolo Papua N. G. 7°10S 146°40E 286 D4
Bulongo Dem. Rep. of the Congo 4°45S 21°30E 265 C4
Bulqizë Albania 41°30N 20°21E 202 E4
Bulsar = Valsad India 20°40N 72°58E 244 D1
Bultfontein S. Africa 28°18S 26°10E 270 C4
Buluan Phil. 6°44N 124°47E 233 H5
Buluan, L. Phil. 6°40N 124°49E 233 H5
Bulukumba Indonesia 5°33S 120°11E 231 F6
Bulun Russia 70°37N 127°30E 215 B13
Bulungkol China 38°36N 74°58E 217 E8
Bulungu Bandundu, Dem. Rep. of the Congo 4°33S 18°36E 265 C3
Bulungu Kasai-Occ., Dem. Rep. of the Congo 6°4S 21°54E 265 D4
Bulusan Phil. 12°45N 124°8E 232 E5
Bulusan Vol. Phil. 12°46N 124°3E 232 E5
Bumba Bandundu, Dem. Rep. of the Congo 6°58S 19°19E 265 D3
Bumba Equateur, Dem. Rep. of the Congo 2°13N 22°30E 264 B4
Bumbah, Khalīj Libya 32°20N 23°15E 258 B4
Bumbeşti-Jiu Romania 45°10N 23°24E 183 E8
Bumbiri I. Tanzania 1°40S 31°55E 268 C3
Bumbuna S. Leone 9°2N 11°49W 262 D2
Bumhkang Burma 26°51N 97°40E 241 B6
Bumhpa Bum Burma 26°51N 97°14E 241 B6
Bumi → Zimbabwe 17°0S 28°20E 269 F2
Bumtang → Bhutan 26°56N 90°53E 241 B3
Bumthang = Jakar Dzong Bhutan 27°33N 90°43E 241 B3
Buna Dem. Rep. of the Congo 3°14S 18°59E 264 C3
Buna North Eastern, Kenya 2°58N 39°30E 268 B4
Buna Papua N. G. 8°42S 148°27E 286 E5
Bunaken Indonesia 1°37N 124°46E 231 D6
Bunama Papua N. G. 10°9S 151°9E 286 F6
Bunawan Phil. 8°12N 125°57E 233 G5
Bunazi Tanzania 1°3S 31°23E 268 C3
Bunbury Australia 33°20S 115°35E 279 F2
Bunclody Ireland 52°39N 6°40W 166 D5
Buncrana Ireland 55°8N 7°27W 166 A4
Bund, The China 31°14N 121°30E 138 B1
Bunda Dem. Rep. of the Congo 4°58S 14°29E 265 C3
Bundaberg Australia 24°54S 152°22E 281 C5
Bundanoon Australia 34°40S 150°16E 283 C9
Bünde Germany 52°11N 8°35E 178 C4
Bundestag = Reichstag Berlin, Germany 115 a3
Bundey → Australia 21°46S 135°37E 280 C2
Bundi India 25°30N 75°35E 242 G6
Bundjalung △ Australia 29°16S 153°21E 281 D5
Bundoora North Australia 37°41S 145°2E 128 A2
Bundoora Park Australia 37°42S 145°2E 128 A2
Bundoran Ireland 54°28N 8°16W 166 B3
Bundukia South Sudan 5°14N 30°55E 257 F3
Bundure Australia 35°10S 146°1E 283 C7
Bung Kan Thailand 18°23N 103°37E 236 C4
Bunga → Nigeria 11°23N 9°56E 263 C6
Bungalaut, Selat Indonesia 2°0S 99°25E 234 C1
Bungay U.K. 52°27N 1°28E 169 E9
Bungendore Australia 35°14S 149°30E 283 C8
Bungil Cr. → Australia 27°5S 149°5E 281 D4
Bungle Bungle = Purnululu △ Australia 17°20S 128°20E 278 C4
Bungo Angola 7°26S 15°33E 265 D3
Bungo, Gunung Malaysia 1°16N 110°9E 235 B4
Bungo-Suidō Japan 33°0N 132°15E 222 E4
Bungoma Kenya 0°34N 34°34E 268 B3
Bungotakada Japan 33°35N 131°25E 222 D3
Bungu Tanzania 7°35S 39°0E 268 D4
Bunia Dem. Rep. of the Congo 1°35N 30°20E 268 B3
Bunianga Dem. Rep. of the Congo 3°28S 20°11E 264 C4
Bunji Pakistan 35°45N 74°40E 243 B6
Bunker Hill Ill., U.S.A. 39°3N 89°57W 310 E7
Bunker Hill Ind., U.S.A. 40°40N 86°6W 311 D10
Bunker Hill Memorial U.S.A. 42°22N 71°4W 116 A2
Bunker I. Pakistan 24°48N 66°57E 123 B1
Bunkie U.S.A. 30°57N 92°11W 314 F8
Bunkyō Japan 35°42N 139°45E 140 A3
Bunnefjorden Norway 59°50N 10°44E 133 A3
Bunnell U.S.A. 29°28N 81°16W 317 F8
Bunnythorpe N.Z. 40°16S 175°39E 284 G4
Buñol Spain 39°25N 0°47W 197 F4
Bunsuru → Nigeria 13°21N 6°23E 263 C6
Buntok Indonesia 1°40S 114°58E 235 C4
Bununu Dass Nigeria 10°5N 9°31E 263 C6
Bununu Kasa Nigeria 9°51N 9°32E 263 D6
Bunya Mts. △ Australia 26°51S 151°34E 281 D5
Bünyan Turkey 38°51N 35°51E 212 C6
Bunyola Spain 39°41N 2°42E 206 B3
Bunyu Indonesia 3°35N 117°50E 235 B5
Bunza Nigeria 12°8N 4°0E 263 C5
Bunzlau = Bolesławiec Poland 51°17N 15°37E 185 G2
Buol Indonesia 1°15N 121°32E 231 D6
Buon Brieng Vietnam 13°9N 108°12E 236 F7
Buon Ho Vietnam 12°57N 108°18E 236 F7
Buon Ma Thuot Vietnam 12°40N 108°3E 236 F7
Buona Vista Park Singapore 1°16N 103°47E 138 B2
Buong Long Cambodia 13°44N 106°59E 236 F6
Buorkhaya, Mys Russia 71°50N 132°40E 215 B14
Buqayq Si. Arabia 26°0N 49°45E 247 E6
Buqbuq Egypt 31°29N 25°29E 256 A2
Bur Acaba = Buurhakaba Somali Rep. 3°12N 44°20E 267 D5
Bûr Fuad Egypt 31°15N 32°20E 256 H8
Bûr Safâga Egypt 26°43N 33°57E 246 E2
Bûr Sa'îd Egypt 31°16N 32°18E 256 H8
Bûr Sûdân Sudan 19°32N 37°9E 256 D4
Bûr Taufiq Egypt 29°54N 32°32E 256 J8
Bura Kenya 1°4S 39°58E 268 C4
Buraan Somali Rep. 10°14N 48°44E 267 B6
Burakin Australia 30°31S 117°10E 279 F2
Buram Sudan 10°51N 25°9E 257 E2
Buran = Buraan Somali Rep. 10°14N 48°44E 267 B6
Burang China 30°15N 81°10E 218 E5
Burao = Burco Somali Rep. 9°32N 45°32E 267 C6
Burāq Syria 33°11N 36°29E 250 E7
Burauen Phil. 10°58N 124°53E 233 F5
Buraydah Si. Arabia 26°20N 43°59E 246 E4
Burbank Calif., U.S.A. 34°12N 118°18W 126 A3
Burbank Ill., U.S.A. 41°44N 87°46W 119 C2
Burç Turkey 36°59N 37°8E 250 B8
Burcher Australia 33°30S 147°16E 283 B7
Burco Somali Rep. 9°32N 45°32E 267 C6
Burda India 25°50N 77°35E 242 G7
Burdekin → Australia 19°38S 147°25E 280 B4
Burden, L. U.S.A. 28°27N 81°33W 133 B1
Burdeos Phil. 14°50N 121°58E 232 D3
Burdeos B. Phil. 14°44N 122°6E 232 D4
Burdur Turkey 37°45N 30°17E 205 D12
Burdur □ Turkey 37°45N 30°15E 205 D12
Burdur Gölü Turkey 37°44N 30°10E 205 D12
Burdwan = Barddhaman India 23°14N 87°39E 243 H12
Burdwood Bank Atl. Oc. 54°0S 59°0W 152 M6
Bure Gojam, Ethiopia 10°40N 37°4E 257 E4
Bure Ilubabor, Ethiopia 8°19N 35°8E 257 F4
Bure → U.K. 52°38N 1°43E 168 E9
Büren Germany 51°33N 8°35E 178 D4
Bureya → Russia 49°27N 129°30E 215 E13
Burford Canada 43°7N 80°27W 312 C4
Burg Germany 52°16N 11°51E 178 C7
Burg auf Fehmarn Germany 54°28N 11°9E 178 A7
Burg el Arab Egypt 30°54N 29°32E 256 H6
Burg et Tuyur Sudan 20°55N 27°56E 256 C2
Burg Stargard Germany 53°29N 13°18E 178 B9
Burgas Bulgaria 42°33N 27°29E 203 D11
Burgas □ Bulgaria 42°30N 27°20E 203 D11
Burgaski Zaliv Bulgaria 42°30N 27°39E 203 D11
Burgdorf Niedersachsen, Germany 52°27N 10°1E 178 C6
Burgdorf Switz. 47°3N 7°37E 179 H3
Burgenland □ Austria 47°20N 16°20E 181 D9
Burgeo Canada 47°37N 57°38W 299 C8
Burgersdorp S. Africa 31°0S 26°20E 270 D4
Burgess, Mt. Australia 30°50S 121°5E 279 F3
Burghausen Germany 48°9N 12°49E 179 G8
Burghead U.K. 57°43N 3°30W 167 D5
Búrgio Italy 37°36N 13°17E 200 E6
Burglengenfeld Germany 49°12N 12°2E 179 F8
Burgohondo Spain 40°26N 4°47W 194 E6
Burgos Ilocos N., Phil. 18°31N 120°39E 232 B3
Burgos Pangasinan, Phil. 16°4N 119°52E 232 C2
Burgos Spain 42°21N 3°41W 194 C7
Burgos □ Spain 42°21N 3°42W 194 C7
Burgstädt Germany 50°54N 12°49E 178 E8
Burgsvik Sweden 57°3N 18°19E 163 G12
Burguillos del Cerro Spain 38°23N 6°35W 195 G4
Burgundy = Bourgogne □ France 47°0N 4°50E 173 F11
Burhaniye Turkey 39°30N 26°58E 205 B8
Burhanpur India 21°18N 76°14E 244 D3
Burhi Gandak → India 25°20N 86°37E 243 G12
Burhner → India 22°43N 80°31E 243 H9
Buri Pen. Eritrea 15°25N 39°55E 257 D4
Burias I. Phil. 12°55N 123°5E 232 E4
Burias Pass. Phil. 13°0N 123°15E 232 E4
Burica, Pta. Costa Rica 8°3N 82°51W 320 E3
Burien U.S.A. 47°28N 122°20W 306 C4
Burigi, L. Tanzania 2°2S 31°22E 268 C3
Burigi △ Tanzania 2°20S 31°6E 268 C3
Burin Canada 47°1N 55°14W 299 C8
Buriram Thailand 15°0N 103°0E 236 E4
Buriti Alegre Brazil 18°9S 49°3W 333 E2
Buriti Bravo Brazil 5°50S 43°50W 332 C3
Buriti dos Lopes Brazil 3°10S 41°52W 332 B3
Burji Ethiopia 5°29N 37°51E 257 F4
Burkburnett U.S.A. 34°6N 98°34W 314 D5
Burke → Australia 23°12S 139°33E 280 C2
Burke Chan. Canada 52°10N 127°30W 296 C3
Burketown Australia 17°45S 139°33E 280 B2
Burkina Faso ■ Africa 12°0N 1°0W 262 C4
Burk's Falls Canada 45°37N 79°24W 298 C4
Burlada Spain 42°49N 1°36W 196 C3
Burleigh Falls Canada 44°33N 78°12W 312 B6
Burley U.S.A. 42°32N 113°48W 304 E7
Burlingame U.S.A. 37°35N 122°21W 306 H4
Burlington Ont., Canada 43°18N 79°45W 312 C5
Burlington Colo., U.S.A. 39°18N 102°16W 304 G12
Burlington Iowa, U.S.A. 40°49N 91°14W 310 D5
Burlington Kans., U.S.A. 38°12N 95°45W 308 F6
Burlington Ky., U.S.A. 39°2N 84°43W 311 E12
Burlington Mass., U.S.A. 42°30N 71°13W 116 A1
Burlington N.C., U.S.A. 36°6N 79°26W 315 C15
Burlington N.J., U.S.A. 40°4N 74°51W 313 F10
Burlington Vt., U.S.A. 44°29N 73°12W 313 B11
Burlington Wash., U.S.A. 48°28N 122°20W 306 B4
Burlington Wis., U.S.A. 42°41N 88°17W 311 B8
Burma ■ Asia 21°0N 96°30E 241 E6
Burnaby I. Canada 52°25N 131°19W 296 C2
Burnet U.S.A. 30°45N 98°14W 314 F5
Burney U.S.A. 40°53N 121°40W 304 F3
Burnham U.S.A. 40°38N 77°34W 312 F7
Burnham-on-Sea U.K. 51°14N 3°0W 169 F5
Burnham Park U.S.A. 41°49N 87°35W 119 C3
Burnham Park Harbor Chicago, U.S.A. 119 e3
Burnhamthorpe Canada 43°37N 79°35W 141 B1
Burnie Australia 41°4S 145°56E 281 G4
Burnley U.K. 53°47N 2°14W 168 D5
Burns U.S.A. 43°35N 119°3W 304 E4
Burns Junction U.S.A. 42°47N 117°51W 304 E5
Burns Lake Canada 54°14N 125°45W 296 C3
Burnside → Canada 66°51N 108°4W 294 D10
Burnside, L. Australia 25°22S 123°0E 279 E3
Burnsville U.S.A. 44°47N 93°17W 308 C7
Burnt Oak U.K. 51°36N 0°15W 125 A2
Burnt Paw U.S.A. 66°54N 143°44W 303 C12
Burnt River Canada 44°41N 78°42W 312 B6
Burntisland U.K. 56°4N 3°13W 121 A2
Burntwood → Canada 56°8N 96°34W 297 B9
Burntwood L. Canada 55°22N 100°26W 297 B8
Burnwynd U.K. 55°54N 3°23W 121 B1
Buronga Australia 34°18S 142°20E 282 C5
Burqa West Bank 31°54N 35°15E 123 A2
Burqān Kuwait 29°0N 47°57E 246 D5
Burqin China 47°43N 87°0E 217 C11
Burra S. Austral., Australia 33°40S 138°55E 282 B3
Burra Nigeria 11°0N 8°56E 263 C6
Burragorang, L. Australia 33°52S 150°37E 283 B9
Burray U.K. 58°51N 2°54W 167 C6
Burrel Albania 41°36N 20°1E 202 E4
Burren Ireland 53°9N 9°5W 166 C2
Burren △ Ireland 53°1N 8°58W 166 C2
Burren Junction Australia 30°7S 148°58E 281 E4
Burrendong, L. Australia 32°45S 149°10E 283 B8
Burriana Spain 39°50N 0°4W 196 F4
Burrinjuck, L. Australia 35°0S 148°36E 283 C8
Burro, Serranías del Mexico 28°56N 102°5W 318 B4
Burrow Hd. U.K. 54°41N 4°24W 167 G4
Burrowa-Pine Mountain △ Australia 36°6S 147°45E 283 D7
Burrum Coast △ Australia 25°13S 152°36E 281 D5
Burruyacú Argentina 26°30S 64°40W 334 B3
Burry Port U.K. 51°41N 4°15W 169 F3
Bursa Turkey 40°15N 29°5E 203 F13
Bursa □ Turkey 40°10N 29°5E 212 B3
Burseryd Sweden 57°12N 13°17E 163 G7
Burstall Canada 50°39N 109°54W 297 C7
Burton Mich., U.S.A. 43°0N 83°40W 311 B13
Burton Ohio, U.S.A. 41°28N 81°8W 312 E3

Burton S.C., U.S.A. 32°26N 80°43W 315 E14
Burton, L. Canada 54°45N 78°20W 298 B4
Burton upon Trent U.K. 52°48N 1°38W 168 E6
Burtundy Australia 33°45S 142°15E 282 B5
Burtus Egypt 30°8N 31°8E 117 A1
Buru Indonesia 3°30S 126°30E 231 E7
Buruanga Phil. 11°51N 121°53E 233 F3
Burudvatn Norway 59°58N 10°35E 133 A2
Burullus, Bahra el Egypt 31°25N 31°0E 256 H7
Burūm Yemen 14°22N 48°59E 249 D5
Burûn, Râs Egypt 31°14N 33°7E 251 G4
Burundi ■ Africa 3°15S 30°0E 268 C3
Burunny = Tsagan Aman
Russia 47°34N 46°43E 191 G8
Bururi Burundi 3°57S 29°37E 268 C2
Burutu Nigeria 5°20N 5°29E 263 D6
Burwell U.S.A. 41°47N 99°8W 308 E4
Burwick U.K. 58°45N 2°58W 167 C5
Burwood Australia 33°52S 151°5E 139 B1
Bury U.K. 53°35N 2°17W 168 D5
Bury St. Edmunds U.K. 52°15N 0°43E 169 E8
Buryatia □ Russia 53°0N 110°0E 215 D12
Bürylbaytal Kazakhstan 44°56N 74°0E 217 D8
Buryn Ukraine 51°13N 33°50E 189 G7
Burzenin Poland 51°28N 18°47E 185 G5
Busa, Mt. Phil. 6°8N 124°39E 233 H5
Busalla Italy 44°34N 8°57E 198 D5
Busan S. Korea 35°5N 129°0E 224 E4
Busanga
Dem. Rep. of the Congo 0°53S 22°7E 264 C4
Busango Swamp Zambia 14°15S 25°45E 269 E2
Busaso = Boosaaso
Somali Rep. 11°12N 49°18E 267 B6
Buşayrah Syria 35°9N 40°26E 213 E9
Busca Italy 44°31N 7°29E 198 D4
Bûsh Egypt 29°9N 31°8E 251 J2
Bushat Albania 41°58N 19°34E 202 E3
Büshehr Iran 28°55N 50°55E 247 D6
Büshehr □ Iran 28°20N 51°45E 247 D6
Bushenyi Uganda 0°35S 30°10E 268 C3
Bushimaie →
Dem. Rep. of the Congo 6°2S 23°45E 265 D4
Bushire = Büshehr Iran 28°55N 50°55E 247 D6
Bushiribana Aruba 12°33N 69°58W 322 f
Bushnell Fla., U.S.A. 28°40N 82°7W 317 G7
Bushnell Ill., U.S.A. 40°33N 90°31W 310 D6
Bushtyna Ukraine 48°3N 23°28E 183 B8
Bushwick U.S.A. 40°41N 73°54W 132 B2
Bushy Park U.K. 51°24N 0°20W 125 B1
Busie Ghana 10°29N 2°22W 262 C4
Businga
Dem. Rep. of the Congo 3°16N 20°59E 264 B4
Büsingen Germany 47°42N 8°41E 179 H4
Buskerud □ Norway 60°20N 9°0E 164 D5
Busko-Zdrój Poland 50°28N 20°42E 185 H7
Buslei Ethiopia 5°28N 44°25E 267 C5
Busovača Bos.-H. 44°6N 17°53E 182 F2
Buşra ash Shām Syria 32°30N 36°25E 251 F7
Busselton Australia 33°42S 115°15E 279 F2
Busseri → South Sudan 7°41N 28°3E 257 F2
Busseto Italy 44°59N 10°2E 198 D7
Bussière-Badil France 45°39N 0°36E 174 C4
Bussolengo Italy 45°28N 10°51E 198 C7
Bussum Neths. 52°16N 5°10E 170 B5
Bustamante, B. Argentina 45°5S 66°18W 336 C3
Buşteni Romania 45°24N 25°32E 183 E10
Busto, C. Spain 43°34N 6°28W 194 B4
Busto Arsizio Italy 45°37N 8°51E 198 C5
Busu Djanoa
Dem. Rep. of the Congo 1°43N 21°23E 264 B4
Busu Kwanga
Dem. Rep. of the Congo 1°48N 20°21E 264 B4
Busu Mandji
Dem. Rep. of the Congo 2°52N 21°14E 264 B4
Busuanga Phil. 12°14N 119°52E 232 E2
Busuanga I. Phil. 12°10N 120°0E 232 E2
Büsum Germany 54°7N 8°51E 178 A4
Busungbiu Indonesia 8°16S 114°58E 231 J17
Busy Corner Trin. & Tob. 10°18N 61°17W 323 t
Buta Dem. Rep. of the Congo 2°50N 24°53E 264 B4
Butantã Brazil 23°34S 46°42W 137 B1
Butare Rwanda 2°31S 29°52E 268 C2
Butaritari Kiribati 3°30N 174°0E 288 G9
Butcher I. India 18°57N 72°53E 130 B2
Bute S. Austral., Australia 33°51S 138°0E 282 B3
Bute Scotland, U.K. 55°48N 5°2W 167 F3
Bute Inlet Canada 50°40N 124°53W 296 C4
Butemba Uganda 1°9N 31°37E 268 B3
Butembo
Dem. Rep. of the Congo 0°9N 29°18E 268 B2
Buteni Romania 46°19N 22°7E 182 D7
Butera Italy 37°11N 14°11E 201 E7
Butere Kenya 0°13N 34°30E 268 B3
Butha-Buthe Lesotho 28°47S 28°14E 271 C4
Butha Qi China 48°0N 122°32E 219 B13
Buthidaung Burma 20°52N 92°32E 241 E4
Butiaba Uganda 1°50N 31°20E 268 B3
Butler Ga., U.S.A. 32°33N 84°14W 316 C5
Butler Ind., U.S.A. 41°26N 84°52W 311 C12
Butler Ky., U.S.A. 38°47N 84°22W 311 F12
Butler Mo., U.S.A. 38°16N 94°20W 310 F2
Butler Pa., U.S.A. 40°52N 79°54W 312 F5
Butler, L. U.S.A. 28°29N 81°33W 133 B1
Buton Indonesia 5°0S 122°45E 231 E6
Bütow = Bytów Poland 54°10N 17°30E 184 D4
Butrintit, L. e Albania 39°43N 20°5E 206 B10
Butte Mont., U.S.A. 46°0N 112°32W 304 C7
Butte Nebr., U.S.A. 42°58N 98°51W 308 D4
Butte Creek → U.S.A. 39°12N 121°56W 306 F5
Butterworth = Gcuwa
S. Africa 32°20S 28°11E 271 D4
Butterworth Malaysia 5°24N 100°23E 237 c
Buttevant Ireland 52°14N 8°40W 166 D3
Buttfield, Mt. Australia 24°45S 128°9E 279 D4
Button B. Canada 58°45N 94°23W 297 B10
Buttonwillow U.S.A. 35°24N 119°28W 307 K7
Butts Corner U.S.A. 38°46N 77°19W 143 C2
Butty Hd. Australia 33°54S 121°39E 279 F3
Butuan Phil. 8°57N 125°33E 233 G5
Butuan B. Phil. 9°4N 125°21E 233 G5
Butuku-Luba Eq. Guin. 3°29N 8°33E 263 E6
Butung = Buton Indonesia 5°0S 122°45E 231 E6
Buturlinovka Russia 50°50N 40°35E 190 E5
Butwal Nepal 27°33N 83°31E 243 F10
Butzbach Germany 50°25N 8°40E 179 E4
Bützow Germany 53°50N 11°58E 178 B7
Buuhoodle Somali Rep. 8°20N 46°25E 267 C6
Buulobarde Somali Rep. 3°50N 45°33E 267 D6
Buur Gaabo Somali Rep. 1°13S 41°51E 267 E5
Buurhakaba Somali Rep. 3°12N 44°20E 267 D5
Buvika Norway 63°18N 10°11E 164 A7
Buxa Duar India 27°45N 89°35E 243 F13
Buxar India 25°34N 83°58E 243 G10
Buxoro Uzbekistan 39°48N 64°25E 216 E6
Buxtehude Germany 53°28N 9°39E 178 B5
Buxton U.K. 53°16N 1°54W 168 D6
Buxy France 46°44N 4°40E 173 F11
Buy Russia 58°28N 41°28E 190 A5
Buyant-Uhaa Mongolia 44°55N 110°11E 226 B6
Buynaksk Russia 42°48N 47°7E 191 J8
Buyo Ivory C. 6°21N 7°5W 262 D3
Buyo, L. de Ivory C. 6°16N 7°10W 262 D3
Büyük Menderes →
Turkey 37°28N 27°11E 205 D9
Büyükçekmece Turkey 41°2N 28°35E 203 E12
Büyükdere Turkey 41°9N 29°2E 122 E2
Büyükeğri Dağı Turkey 36°45N 33°33E 250 E4
Büyükkariştiran Turkey 41°18N 27°33E 203 E11
Büyükkemikli Burnu
Turkey 40°18N 26°14E 203 F10
Büyükorhan Turkey 39°46N 28°56E 205 B10
Büyükyoncalı Turkey 41°20N 27°55E 203 E11
Buyun Shan China 40°4N 122°43E 227 D12
Buzançais France 46°54N 1°25E 172 F8
Buzău Romania 45°10N 26°50E 183 E11
Buzău □ Romania 45°20N 26°30E 183 E11
Buzău → Romania 45°26N 27°44E 183 E12
Buzău, Pasul Romania 45°35N 26°12E 183 E11
Buzaymah Libya 24°55N 22°2E 258 C4
Buzen Japan 33°35N 131°5E 222 C3
Buzet Croatia 45°24N 13°58E 199 C10
Buzi → Mozam. 19°50S 34°43E 269 F3
Buziaş Romania 45°38N 21°36E 182 E6
Büzmeýin Turkmenistan 38°3N 58°12E 247 E8
Buzuluk Russia 52°48N 52°12E 186 C9
Buzuluk → Russia 50°15N 42°7E 190 E6
Buzzards Bay U.S.A. 41°45N 70°37W 313 E14
Bwagaoia Papua N. G. 10°40S 152°52E 286 F7
Bwana Mkubwa Zambia 13°8S 28°38E 269 E2
Bwasa Dem. Rep. of the Congo 3°55S 18°24E 264 C3
Bwatnapné Vanuatu 15°41S 168°9E 287 E6
Bwindi △ Uganda 1°2S 29°42E 268 C2
Byakar Dzong = Jakar Dzong
Bhutan 27°33N 90°43E 241 E3
Byala Ruse, Bulgaria 43°28N 25°44E 203 C9
Byala Varna, Bulgaria 42°53N 27°55E 203 D11
Byala Slatina Bulgaria 43°26N 23°55E 202 C7
Byam Martin I. Canada 75°15N 104°15W 295 B11
Byarezina → Belarus 52°33N 30°14E 177 B16
Byaroza Belarus 52°31N 24°51E 177 B13
Bychawa Poland 51°1N 22°36E 185 G9
Byculla India 18°58N 72°50E 130 E2
Byczyna Poland 51°7N 18°12E 185 G5
Bydgoszcz Poland 53°10N 18°0E 185 E5
Byelorussia = Belarus ■
Europe 53°30N 27°0E 177 B14
Byeonsan △ S. Korea 35°40N 126°30E 224 E3
Byers U.S.A. 39°43N 104°14W 304 G11
Byesville U.S.A. 39°58N 81°32W 312 G3
Byfield △ Australia 22°52S 150°45E 280 C5
Bygdin Norway 61°21N 8°32E 164 C5
Bygdøy Norway 59°54N 10°40E 133 A3
Bygland Norway 58°50N 7°48E 164 F4
Byglandsfjorden Norway 58°44N 7°50E 164 F4
Bygstad Norway 61°23N 5°40E 164 C2
Bykhaw Belarus 53°31N 30°14E 177 B16
Bykhov = Bykhaw
Belarus 53°31N 30°14E 177 B16
Bykle Norway 59°20N 7°22E 164 E4
Bykovo Russia 49°50N 45°25E 190 F7
Bylas U.S.A. 33°8N 110°7W 305 K8
Bylot Canada 58°25N 94°8W 297 B10
Bylot I. Canada 73°13N 78°34W 295 C16
Byrd, C. Antarctica 69°38S 76°7W 151 C17
Byrock Australia 30°40S 146°27E 283 A7
Byron Ga., U.S.A. 32°39N 83°46W 316 C6
Byron Ill., U.S.A. 42°8N 89°15W 310 E7
Byron, C. Australia 28°43S 153°38E 281 D5
Byron Bay Australia 28°43S 153°37E 281 D5
Byrranga, Gory Russia 75°0N 100°0E 215 B11
Byrranga Mts. = Byrranga, Gory
Russia 75°0N 100°0E 215 B11
Byrum Denmark 57°16N 11°0E 163 G5
Byske Sweden 64°57N 21°11E 160 D19
Byskeälven → Sweden 64°57N 21°13E 160 D19
Bystrytsya Ukraine 48°27N 24°14E 183 B9
Bystrzyca → Dolnośląskie,
Poland 51°12N 16°55E 185 G3
Bystrzyca → Lubelskie,
Poland 51°21N 22°46E 185 G9
Bystrzyca Kłodzka Poland 50°19N 16°39E 185 H3
Bytča Slovak Rep. 49°13N 18°34E 181 B11
Bytkiv Ukraine 48°38N 24°28E 183 B9
Bytom Poland 50°25N 18°54E 185 H5
Bytom Odrzański Poland 51°44N 15°48E 185 G2
Bytów Poland 54°10N 17°30E 184 D4
Byumba Rwanda 1°35S 30°4E 268 C3
Bywater U.S.A. 29°58N 90°2W 131 B2
Bzenec Czech Rep. 48°58N 17°18E 181 C10
Bzura → Poland 52°25N 20°15E 185 F7

C

C.B.S. Fox Studios U.S.A. 34°9N 118°24W 126 B2
C.N.N. Center U.S.A. 33°45N 84°23W 113 B2
C.N. Tower Toronto, Canada 141 c1
C.W. McConaughy, L.
U.S.A. 41°14N 101°40W 308 E3
Ca → Vietnam 18°45N 105°45E 236 C5
Ca Mau Vietnam 9°7N 105°8E 237 H5
Ca Mau, Mui Vietnam 8°38N 104°44E 237 H5
Ca Na Vietnam 11°20N 108°54E 237 G7
Caacupé Paraguay 25°23S 57°5W 334 B4
Caaguazú △ Paraguay 26°5S 55°31W 335 B4
Caála Angola 12°46S 15°30E 265 E3
Caamaño Sd. Canada 52°55N 129°25W 296 C3
Caapiranga Brazil 3°18S 61°13W 329 D6
Caazapá Paraguay 26°8S 56°19W 334 B4
Caazapá □ Paraguay 26°10S 56°0W 335 B4
Cabaad, Ras Somali Rep. 6°18N 49°4E 267 C6
Cabadbaran Phil. 9°10N 125°38E 233 G5
Cabagan Phil. 17°26N 121°46E 232 C3
Cabalete I. Phil. 14°16N 121°49E 232 D3
Caballan = San Juan
Phil. 10°16N 125°10E 233 F5
Caballeria, C. de Spain 40°5N 4°5E 206 A5
Caballito Argentina 34°37S 58°25W 117 B2
Cabana Peru 8°25S 78°5W 330 B2
Cabana de Bergantiños
Spain 43°13N 8°54W 194 B2
Cabanaconde Peru 15°38S 71°58W 330 D3
Cabañaquinta Spain 43°10N 5°38W 194 B5
Cabanatuan Phil. 15°30N 120°58E 232 D3
Cabañeros ⌓ Spain 39°18N 4°35W 195 F6
Cabanes Spain 40°9N 0°2E 196 E5
Cabangon Phil. 15°10N 120°3E 232 D3
Cabanilla Peru 15°36S 70°28W 330 D3
Cabano Canada 47°40N 68°56W 299 C6
Čabar Croatia 45°36N 14°39E 199 C11
Cabarroguis Phil. 16°50N 121°30E 232 C3
Cabarruyan I. Phil. 16°18N 119°59E 232 C2
Cabazon U.S.A. 33°55N 116°47W 307 M10
Cabedelo Brazil 7°0S 34°50W 332 C5
Cabeza del Buey Spain 38°44N 5°13W 195 G5
Cabezón de la Sal Spain 43°18N 4°14W 194 B6
Cabildo Chile 32°30S 71°5W 334 C1
Cabimas Venezuela 10°23N 71°25W 328 A3
Cabin John U.S.A. 38°58N 77°10W 143 B2
Cabin John Regional Park ⌓
U.S.A. 39°0N 77°10W 143 A2
Cabinda Angola 5°33S 12°11E 265 D2
Cabinda □ Angola 5°0S 12°30E 265 D2
Cabinet Mts. U.S.A. 48°10N 115°50W 304 B6
Cabinteely Ireland 53°16N 6°9W 120 B3
Cabiri Angola 8°52S 13°39E 265 D2
Cable Beach Bahamas 25°4N 77°24W 153 b
Cabo Blanco Argentina 47°15S 65°47W 336 C3
Cabo de Gata-Níjar ⌓ Spain 36°5N 1°56W 197 J2
Cabo de Hornos △ Chile 55°42S 67°20W 336 E3
Cabo de Santo Agostinho
Brazil 8°20S 34°55W 332 C5
Cabo Frio Brazil 22°51S 42°3W 333 F3
Cabo Pantoja Peru 1°0S 75°10W 328 D2
Cabo Raso Argentina 44°20S 65°15W 336 B3
Cabo Rojo Puerto Rico 18°5N 67°9W 321 b
Cabo San Lucas Mexico 22°53N 109°54W 318 C3
Cabo Verde = Cape Verde Is. ■
Atl. Oc. 16°0N 24°0W 153 j
Cabo Yubi = Tarfaya
Morocco 27°55N 12°55W 260 C2
Cabonga, Réservoir
Canada 47°20N 76°40W 298 C4
Cabool U.S.A. 37°7N 92°6W 308 G7
Caboolture Australia 27°5S 152°58E 281 D5
Cabora Bassa Dam = Cahora Bassa,
Lago de Mozam. 15°20S 32°50E 269 F3
Caborca Mexico 30°37N 112°6W 318 A2
Cabot, Mt. U.S.A. 44°30N 71°25W 313 B13
Cabot Hd. Canada 45°14N 81°17W 312 A3
Cabot Str. Canada 47°15N 59°40W 299 C8
Cabra Dublin, Ireland 53°21N 6°18W 120 A2
Cabra Spain 37°30N 4°28W 195 H6
Cabra del Santo Cristo
Spain 37°42N 3°16W 195 H7
Cabra I. India 7°18N 93°50E 245 L11
Cabra I. Phil. 13°53N 120°2E 232 E3
Cábras Italy 39°56N 8°32E 200 C1
Cabras I. Guam 13°27N 144°44E 302 d
Cabrera Spain 39°8N 2°57E 206 B3
Cabrera, Sierra Spain 42°12N 6°40W 194 C4
Cabrera △ Spain 39°13N 2°53E 197 F7
Cabri Canada 50°35N 108°25W 297 C7
Cabriel → Spain 39°14N 1°3W 197 F3
Cabrits, Î. Martinique 14°23N 60°52W 322 j
Cabrits △ Dominica 15°35N 61°26W 323 k
Cabruta Venezuela 7°50N 66°10W 328 B4
Cabuçú de Baixo →
Brazil 23°30S 46°40W 137 A1
Cabuçú de Cima →
Brazil 23°30S 46°33W 137 A2
Cabugao Phil. 17°48N 120°27E 232 C3
Cabulauan Is. Phil. 11°25N 120°8E 233 F3
Cabulo Angola 10°18S 16°22E 265 E3
Caburan = Jose Abad Santos
Phil. 5°55N 125°39E 233 J5
Cabuta Angola 9°48S 14°58E 265 D2
Cabuyaro Colombia 4°18N 72°49W 328 C3
Cacabelos Spain 42°36N 6°44W 194 C4
Caçador Brazil 26°47S 51°0W 335 B5
Čačak Serbia 43°54N 20°20E 202 C4
Cacandee Settlement
Trin. & Tob. 10°33N 61°26W 323 t
Cacao Fr. Guiana 4°33N 52°26W 329 C7
Caçapava do Sul Brazil 30°30S 53°30W 335 C5
Cáccamo Italy 37°56N 13°40E 200 E6
Cacém Portugal 38°46N 9°18W 195 G1
Cáceres Brazil 15°5S 57°40W 331 D6
Cáceres Colombia 7°35N 75°20W 328 B2
Cáceres Spain 39°26N 6°23W 195 F4
Cáceres □ Spain 39°45N 6°0W 194 F5
Cachan France 48°47N 2°19E 134 B2
Cache Bay Canada 46°22N 80°0W 298 C4
Cache Cr. → U.S.A. 38°42N 121°42W 306 G5
Cache Creek Canada 50°48N 121°19W 296 C4
Cachenka → Russia 55°46N 37°17E 129 B1
Cacheu Guinea-Biss. 12°14N 16°8W 262 C1
Cachi Argentina 25°5S 66°10W 334 B2
Cachimbo Brazil 8°57S 54°54W 331 B7
Cachimbo, Serra do Brazil 9°30S 55°30W 331 B6
Cachimo Angola 8°21S 21°24E 265 D4
Cachinal de la Sierra
Chile 24°58S 69°32W 334 A2
Cachingues Angola 13°5S 16°43E 265 E3
Cachoeira = Solonópole
Brazil 5°44S 39°1W 332 C4
Cachoeira Brazil 12°30S 39°0W 333 D4
Cachoeira, Rib. da →
Brazil 23°38S 46°43W 137 B1
Cachoeira Alta Brazil 18°48S 50°58W 333 E1
Cachoeira do Sul Brazil 30°3S 52°53W 335 C5
Cachoeiro de Itapemirim
Brazil 20°51S 41°7W 333 F3
Cachoeiro do Arari Brazil 1°1S 48°58W 332 B2
Cachopo Portugal 37°20N 7°49W 195 H3
Cachuela Esperanza
Bolivia 10°32S 65°38W 331 C4
Cacilhas Portugal 38°41N 9°8W 126 A2
Cacine Guinea-Biss. 11°8N 14°57W 262 C1
Cacoal Brazil 11°32S 61°18W 331 C5
Cacólo Angola 10°9S 19°21E 265 E3
Caconda Angola 13°48S 15°8E 265 E3
Cacongo Angola 5°11S 12°5E 265 D2
Caçu Brazil 18°37S 51°4W 333 E1
Cacuaco Angola 6°47S 13°21E 265 D2
Cacuchi → Angola 14°26S 16°46E 265 E3
Cacula Angola 14°29S 14°10E 265 E2
Caculé Brazil 14°30S 42°13W 333 D3
Caculuvar → Angola 16°47S 14°56E 265 F2
Cacuso Angola 9°25S 15°45E 265 D3
Cadale Somali Rep. 2°45N 46°19E 267 D6
Čadca Slovak Rep. 49°26N 18°45E 181 B11
Caddo U.S.A. 34°7N 96°16W 314 D6
Cader Idris U.K. 52°42N 3°53W 169 E4
Cadereyta de Jiménez
Mexico 25°36N 100°0W 318 B5
Cades U.S.A. 33°47N 79°47W 316 B10
Cadi, Sierra del Spain 42°17N 1°42E 196 C6
Cadí-Moixeró ⌓ Spain 42°17N 1°44E 196 C6
Cadibarrawirracanna, L.
Australia 28°52S 135°27E 281 D2
Cadillac Gironde, France 44°38N 0°20W 174 D3
Cadillac Mich., U.S.A. 44°15N 85°24W 309 C11
Cadiz Phil. 10°57N 123°15E 233 F4
Cádiz Spain 36°30N 6°20W 195 J4
Cadiz Calif., U.S.A. 34°30N 115°28W 307 L11
Cadiz Ohio, U.S.A. 40°22N 81°0W 312 F4
Cádiz □ Spain 36°36N 5°45W 195 J5
Cádiz, G. de Spain 36°40N 7°0W 195 J3
Cadiz L. U.S.A. 34°18N 115°24W 305 J6
Cadley U.S.A. 33°32N 82°40W 316 B7
Cadney Park Australia 27°55S 134°3E 281 D1
Cadomin Canada 53°2N 117°20W 296 C5
Cadotte Lake Canada 56°26N 116°23W 296 B5
Cadours France 43°44N 1°2E 174 E5
Cadoux Australia 30°46S 117°7E 279 F2
Cadwell U.S.A. 32°20N 83°3W 316 C6
Caen France 49°10N 0°22W 172 C6
Caernarfon U.K. 53°8N 4°16W 168 D3
Caernarfon B. U.K. 53°4N 4°40W 168 D3
Caernarvon = Caernarfon
U.K. 53°8N 4°16W 168 D3
Caerphilly U.K. 51°35N 3°13W 169 F4
Caerphilly □ U.K. 51°37N 3°12W 169 F4
Caesarea Israel 32°30N 34°53E 251 F5
Caeté Brazil 19°55S 43°40W 333 E3
Caetité Brazil 13°50S 42°32W 333 D3
Cafayate Argentina 26°2S 66°0W 334 B2
Cafu Angola 16°30S 15°8E 265 F3
Cagayan □ Phil. 18°0N 121°50E 232 C3
Cagayan → Phil. 18°25N 121°42E 232 B3
Cagayan de Oro Phil. 8°30N 124°40E 233 G5
Cagayan Is. Phil. 9°40N 121°16E 233 G3
Cagayan Sulu I. Phil. 7°1N 118°30E 233 H2
Cagli Italy 43°33N 12°39E 199 E9
Cágliari Italy 39°13N 9°7E 200 C2
Cágliari, G. di Italy 39°8N 9°11E 200 C2
Cagnano Varano Italy 41°49N 15°47E 199 G12
Cagnes-sur-Mer France 43°40N 7°9E 175 E11
Caguán → Colombia 0°8S 74°18W 328 D3
Caguas Puerto Rico 18°14N 66°2W 321 C6
Caha Mts. Ireland 51°45N 9°40W 166 E2
Cahama Angola 16°17S 14°19E 265 F2
Caher Ireland 52°22N 7°56W 166 D4
Cahersiveen Ireland 51°56N 10°14W 166 E1
Cahora Bassa, Lago de
Mozam. 15°20S 32°50E 269 F3
Cahore Pt. Ireland 52°33N 6°12W 166 D5
Cahors France 44°27N 1°27E 174 D5
Cahuapanas Peru 5°15S 77°0W 330 B2
Cahuenga Park U.S.A. 34°8N 118°19W 126 B3
Cahuinari → Colombia 1°21S 73°44W 328 D3
Cahuinari △ Colombia 1°20S 71°10W 328 D3
Cahul Moldova 45°50N 28°15E 183 E13
Cai Bau, Dao Vietnam 21°10N 107°27E 228 G6
Cai Be Vietnam 10°20N 106°2E 237 G6
Cai Nuoc Vietnam 8°56N 105°1E 237 H5
Caia Mozam. 17°51S 35°24E 269 F4
Caiabis, Serra dos Brazil 11°30S 53°30W 331 C6
Caianda Angola 11°2S 23°31E 265 E4
Caiapó, Serra do Brazil 17°0S 52°0W 331 D7
Caiapônia Brazil 16°57S 51°49W 331 D7
Caibarién Cuba 22°30N 79°30W 320 B4
Caibiran Phil. 11°34N 124°35E 233 F5
Caiçara = Alvarães Brazil 3°12S 64°50W 329 D5
Caicara Bolívar, Venezuela 7°38N 66°10W 328 B4
Caicara Monagas, Venezuela 9°52N 63°38W 329 B5
Caicó Brazil 6°20S 37°0W 332 C4
Caicos Is. Turks & Caicos 21°40N 71°40W 321 B5
Caicos Passage W. Indies 22°45N 72°45W 321 B5
Caidian China 30°35N 114°2E 229 B10
Caiguna Australia 32°16S 125°29E 279 F4
Caillandre, Morne
St. Lucia 13°46N 60°57W 323 m
Caille I. Grenada 12°16N 61°34W 323 q
Cailloma Peru 15°9S 71°45W 330 D3
Cain, L. U.S.A. 28°28N 81°28W 133 B2
Căinari Moldova 46°41N 29°3E 183 D14
Cainde Angola 15°29S 13°24E 265 F2
Caine → Bolivia 18°23S 65°21W 331 D4
Caird Coast Antarctica 75°0S 25°0W 151 D1
Cairn Gorm U.K. 57°7N 3°39W 167 D5
Cairngorm Mts. U.K. 57°6N 3°42W 167 D5
Cairngorms △ U.K. 57°10N 3°50W 167 D5
Cairnryan U.K. 54°59N 5°1W 167 G3
Cairns Australia 16°57S 145°45E 280 B4
Cairns L. Canada 51°42N 94°30W 297 C10
Cairo = El Qâhira Egypt 30°2N 31°13E 117 A2
Cairo Ga., U.S.A. 30°52N 84°13W 316 E5
Cairo Ill., U.S.A. 37°0N 89°11W 308 G9
Cairo N.Y., U.S.A. 42°18N 74°0W 313 D10
Cairo Int. ✕ (CAI) Egypt 30°7N 31°24E 117 A3
Cairo Montenotte Italy 44°23N 8°16E 198 D5
Caírofa Angola 14°3S 13°54E 265 E2
Caiseal = Cashel Ireland 52°30N 7°53W 166 D4
Caisleán an Bharraigh = Castlebar
Ireland 53°52N 9°18W 166 C2
Caithness U.K. 58°25N 3°35W 167 C5
Caithness, Ord of U.K. 58°8N 3°36W 167 C5
Caitou Angola 14°28S 13°7E 265 E2
Caiuás = Rio Brilhante
Brazil 21°48S 54°33W 335 A5
Caiundo Angola 15°50S 17°28E 265 F3
Caiza Bolivia 20°2S 65°40W 331 E4
Caja de Muertos, I.
Puerto Rico 17°54N 66°32W 321 b
Cajabamba Peru 7°38S 78°4W 330 B2
Cajamarca Peru 7°5S 78°28W 330 B2
Cajamarca □ Peru 6°15S 78°50W 330 B2
Cajamarquilla = Bolívar
Peru 7°18S 77°48W 330 B2
Cajapió Brazil 2°58S 44°48W 332 B3
Cajarc France 44°29N 1°50E 174 D5
Cajas △ Ecuador 2°48S 79°15W 328 D2
Cajatambo Peru 10°30S 77°2W 330 C2
Cajazeiras Brazil 6°52S 38°30W 332 C4
Čajetina Serbia 43°47N 19°42E 202 C3
Cajidiocan Phil. 12°22N 122°41E 232 E4
Caju Brazil 22°52S 43°12W 135 B1
Çakırgöl Turkey 40°33N 39°40E 213 B8
Çakırlar Turkey 36°52N 30°33E 205 E12
Čakovec Croatia 46°23N 16°26E 199 B13
Čakovice Czech Rep. 50°9N 14°31E 135 B3
Çal Turkey 38°4N 29°23E 205 C11
Cala Spain 37°59N 6°21W 195 H4
Cala → Spain 37°38N 6°5W 195 H4
Cala Cadolar, Punta de = Rotja, Pta.
Spain 38°38N 1°35E 206 D2
Cala d'Or Spain 39°23N 3°14E 206 B4
Cala en Porter Spain 39°52N 4°8E 206 B5
Cala Figuera Spain 39°20N 3°10E 206 B4
Cala Figuera, C. de Spain 39°27N 2°31E 206 B3
Cala Forcat Spain 40°0N 3°47E 206 B4
Cala Major Spain 39°33N 2°37E 206 B3
Cala Mezquida = Sa Mesquida
Spain 39°55N 4°16E 206 B5
Cala Millor Spain 39°35N 3°22E 206 B4
Cala Murada Spain 39°27N 3°17E 206 B4
Cala Ratjada Spain 39°43N 3°27E 206 B4
Cala Santa Galdana Spain 39°56N 3°58E 206 B4
Calabanga Phil. 13°42N 123°17E 232 E4
Calabar Nigeria 4°57N 8°20E 263 E6
Calabogie Canada 45°18N 76°43W 313 A8
Calabozo Venezuela 9°0N 67°28W 328 B4
Calábria □ Italy 39°0N 16°30E 201 C9
Calábria △ Italy 39°6N 16°35E 201 C9
Calaburras, Pta. de Spain 36°30N 4°38W 195 J6
Calaceite Spain 41°1N 0°11E 196 D5
Calacoto Bolivia 17°16S 68°38W 330 D4
Calacuccia France 42°21N 9°1E 175 F13
Calafat Romania 43°58N 22°59E 182 G7
Calafell Spain 41°11N 1°34E 196 D6
Calagnaan I. Phil. 11°29N 123°12E 233 F4
Calagua Is. Phil. 14°30N 122°55E 232 D4
Calahorra Spain 42°18N 1°59W 196 C3
Calai Angola 17°47S 19°41E 265 F3
Calais Pas-de-Calais, France 50°57N 1°56E 173 B8
Calais Maine, U.S.A. 45°11N 67°17W 309 C20
Calakmul ⌓ Mexico 18°14N 89°48W 319 D7
Calalaste, Cord. de
Argentina 25°0S 67°0W 334 B2
Calama Brazil 8°0S 62°50W 331 B5
Calama Chile 22°30S 68°55W 334 A2
Calamar Bolívar, Colombia 10°15N 74°55W 328 A3
Calamar Vaupés, Colombia 1°58N 72°32W 328 C3
Calamba Cavite, Phil. 14°13N 121°10E 232 D3
Calamba Mis. Occ., Phil. 8°35N 123°39E 233 G4
Calamian Group Phil. 11°50N 119°55E 233 F2
Calamocha Spain 40°50N 1°17W 196 E3
Calamonte Spain 38°53N 6°23W 195 G4
Călan Romania 45°44N 22°59E 182 E7
Calañas Spain 37°40N 6°53W 195 H4
Calanda Spain 40°56N 0°15W 196 E4
Calandagan I. Phil. 10°39N 120°15E 233 F3
Calandula Angola 9°6S 15°57E 265 D3
Calang Indonesia 4°37N 95°37E 234 B1
Calangiánus Italy 40°56N 9°11E 200 B2
Calanscio, Sarîr Libya 27°30N 21°30E 258 C4
Calapan Phil. 13°25N 121°7E 232 E3
Călăraşi Moldova 47°16N 28°19E 183 C13
Călăraşi Romania 44°12N 27°20E 183 F12
Călăraşi □ Romania 44°10N 27°0E 183 F12
Calasparra Spain 38°14N 1°41W 197 G3
Calatafimi Italy 37°55N 12°52E 200 E5
Calatagan Phil. 13°50N 120°38E 232 E3
Calatayud Spain 41°20N 1°40W 196 D3
Călăţele Romania 46°46N 23°1E 182 D8
Calato = Kalathos Greece 36°9N 28°8E 206 E12
Calatrava Eq. Guin. 1°6N 9°25E 264 B1
Calatrava Phil. 10°35N 123°28E 233 F4
Calauag Phil. 13°55N 122°15E 232 E4
Calavà, C. Italy 38°11N 14°55E 201 D7
Calavite, C. Phil. 13°26N 120°20E 232 E3
Calavite Pass. Phil. 13°36N 120°25E 232 E3
Calayan Phil. 19°16N 121°28E 232 B3
Calayan I. Phil. 19°20N 121°27E 232 B3
Calbayog Phil. 12°4N 124°38E 232 E5
Calbiga Phil. 11°38N 125°0E 233 F5
Calca Peru 13°22S 72°0W 330 C3
Calcasieu L. U.S.A. 29°55N 93°18W 314 G8
Calcium U.S.A. 44°1N 75°50W 313 B9
Calcutta = Kolkata India 22°34N 88°21E 124 B2
Calcutta U.S.A. 40°40N 80°34W 312 F4
Caldaro Italy 46°25N 11°14E 199 B8
Caldas □ Colombia 5°15N 75°30W 328 B2
Caldas da Rainha Portugal 39°24N 9°8W 195 F1
Caldas de Reis Spain 42°36N 8°39W 194 C2
Caldas Novas Brazil 17°45S 48°38W 333 E2
Calder → U.K. 53°44N 1°22W 168 D6
Caldera Chile 27°5S 70°55W 334 B1
Caldera de Taburiente △
Canary Is. 28°43N 17°52W 153 e1
Caldwell Idaho, U.S.A. 43°40N 116°41W 304 E5
Caldwell Kans., U.S.A. 37°2N 97°37W 308 G5
Caldwell Tex., U.S.A. 30°32N 96°42W 314 F6
Caledon Ont., Canada 43°51N 79°51W 312 C5
Caledon Western Cape,
S. Africa 34°14S 19°26E 270 D2
Caledon → S. Africa 30°31S 26°5E 270 D4
Caledon B. Australia 12°45S 137°0E 280 A2
Caledonia Ont., Canada 43°7N 79°58W 312 C5
Caledonia N.Y., U.S.A. 42°58N 77°51W 312 D7
Calella Spain 41°37N 2°40E 196 D7
Calemba Angola 16°0S 15°44E 270 A2
Calen Australia 20°56S 148°48E 280 b
Calenzana France 42°31N 8°51E 175 F12
Caleta Olivia Argentina 46°25S 67°25W 336 C3
Caletones Chile 34°6S 70°27W 334 C1
Calexico U.S.A. 32°40N 115°30W 307 N11
Calf of Man I. of Man 54°3N 4°48W 168 C3
Calgary Canada 51°0N 114°10W 296 C6
Calheta Azores 38°36N 28°1W 153 d1
Calheta Madeira 32°44N 17°11W 153 c
Calheta de Nesquim
Azores 38°24N 28°5W 153 d1
Calhoun U.S.A. 34°30N 84°57W 315 D12
Calhoun Falls U.S.A. 34°6N 82°36W 316 A7
Cali Colombia 3°25N 76°35W 328 C2
Calibishie Dominica 15°35N 61°21W 323 k
Calicoan I. Phil. 10°59N 125°48E 233 F5
Calicut India 11°15N 75°43E 245 J2
Caliente U.S.A. 37°37N 114°31W 305 H6
California Trin. & Tob. 10°24N 61°28W 323 t
California Mo., U.S.A. 38°38N 92°34W 310 F4
California Pa., U.S.A. 40°4N 79°54W 312 F5
California □ U.S.A. 37°30N 119°30W 306 H7
California, Baja, T.N. = Baja
California □ Mexico 30°0N 115°0W 318 B2
California, Baja, T.S. = Baja
California Sur □
Mexico 25°50N 111°50W 318 B2
California, G. de Mexico 27°0N 111°0W 318 B2
California City U.S.A. 35°10N 117°55W 307 K9
California Hot Springs
U.S.A. 35°51N 118°41W 307 K8
California Inst. of Tech.
U.S.A. 34°8N 118°8W 126 B4
California Los Angeles, Univ. of
U.S.A. 34°4N 118°27W 126 B2
California Plaza Los Angeles, U.S.A. 127 b1
California State Univ.
U.S.A. 34°4N 118°10W 126 B3
Călilabad Azerbaijan 39°12N 48°29E 213 C13
Calilegua △ Argentina 25°36S 64°50W 334 B3
Călimăneşti Romania 45°14N 24°20E 183 E9
Călimani, Munţii Romania 47°12N 25°0E 183 C10
Calingasta Argentina 31°15S 69°30W 334 C2
Calinog Phil. 11°7N 122°32E 233 F4
Calintaan Phil. 12°35N 120°57E 232 E3
Calipatria U.S.A. 33°8N 115°31W 307 M11
Calistoga U.S.A. 38°35N 122°35W 306 G4
Calitri Italy 40°54N 15°26E 201 B8
Calitzdorp S. Africa 33°33S 21°42E 270 D3
Calivigny I. Grenada 12°0N 61°43W 323 q
Callabonna, L. Australia 29°40S 140°5E 281 D3
Callac France 48°25N 3°27W 172 D3
Callahan U.S.A. 30°34N 81°50W 316 E8
Callahan Tunnel Boston, U.S.A. 116 a3
Callan Ireland 52°32N 7°24W 166 D4
Callander U.K. 56°15N 4°13W 167 E4
Callang = San Manuel
Phil. 16°4N 120°40E 232 C3
Callao Peru 12°3S 77°8W 124 B2
Callaway U.S.A. 30°8N 85°36W 316 E4
Calliaqua St. Vincent 13°8N 61°12W 323 n
Callicoon U.S.A. 41°46N 75°3W 313 E9
Calling Lake Canada 55°15N 113°12W 296 B6
Calliope Australia 24°0S 151°16E 280 C5
Callosa de Segura Spain 38°7N 0°53W 197 G4
Callosa d'En Sarrià Spain 38°40N 0°8W 197 G4
Calma, Costa de la Spain 39°28N 2°26E 206 B3
Calmar U.S.A. 43°11N 91°52W 310 A5
Calne U.K. 51°26N 2°0W 169 F6
Calola Angola 16°25S 17°48E 265 F3
Calolbon = San Andres
Phil. 13°36N 124°6E 232 E5
Calonge Spain 41°52N 3°5E 196 D8
Caloocan Phil. 14°39N 120°58E 127 B1
Caloosahatchee → U.S.A. 26°31N 82°1W 317 H7
Calore → Italy 41°11N 14°28E 201 A7
Caloundra Australia 26°45S 153°10E 281 D5
Calpe Spain 38°39N 0°3E 197 G5
Calpella U.S.A. 39°14N 123°12W 306 F3
Calpine U.S.A. 39°40N 120°27W 306 F6
Calstock Canada 49°47N 84°9W 298 C3
Caltabellotta Italy 37°34N 13°13E 200 E6
Caltagirone Italy 37°14N 14°31E 201 E7
Caltanissetta Italy 37°29N 14°4E 201 E7
Çaltılıbük Turkey 39°57N 28°36E 203 G12
Caluango Angola 8°20S 19°39E 265 D3
Calubian Phil. 11°27N 124°26E 233 F5
Calucinga Angola 11°18S 16°12E 265 E3
Caluire-et-Cuire France 45°48N 4°52E 173 G11
Calulo Angola 10°1S 14°56E 265 E2
Calumet L. U.S.A. 41°41N 87°35W 119 C3
Calumet Park U.S.A. 41°40N 87°39W 119 C3
Calumet Sag Channel →
U.S.A. 41°40N 87°47W 119 C2
Calunda Angola 12°7S 23°36E 265 E4
Caluquembe Angola 13°47S 14°44E 265 E2
Caluso Italy 45°18N 7°53E 198 C4
Caluula Somali Rep. 11°50N 50°45E 267 B7
Caluya I. Phil. 11°55N 121°34E 233 F3
Calvados □ France 49°5N 0°15W 172 C6
Calvados Chain, The
Papua N. G. 11°10S 152°45E 286 F7
Calvairate Italy 45°27N 9°13E 129 B2
Calvert → Australia 16°17S 137°44E 280 B2
Calvert I. Canada 51°30N 128°0W 296 C3
Calvert Ra. Australia 24°0S 122°30E 278 D3
Calvi France 42°34N 8°45E 175 F12
Calvià Spain 39°34N 2°31E 206 B3
Calvillo Mexico 21°51N 102°43W 318 C4
Calvinia S. Africa 31°28S 19°45E 270 D2
Calvo, Mte. Italy 41°44N 15°46E 199 G12
Calwa U.S.A. 36°42N 119°46W 306 J7
Calzada Almuradiel = Almuradiel
Spain 38°32N 3°28W 195 G7
Calzada de Calatrava
Spain 38°42N 3°46W 195 G7
Cam → U.K. 52°21N 0°16E 169 E8
Cam Lam = Ba Ngoi
Vietnam 11°54N 109°10E 237 G7
Cam Pha Vietnam 21°7N 107°18E 228 G6
Cam Ranh Vietnam 11°54N 109°12E 237 G7
Cam Xuyen Vietnam 18°15N 106°0E 236 C6
Camabatela Angola 8°20S 15°26E 265 D3
Camacã Brazil 15°24S 39°30W 333 E4
Camaçari Brazil 12°41S 38°18W 333 D4
Camacha Madeira 32°41N 16°49W 153 c
Camacupa Angola 11°58S 17°22E 265 E3
Camaguán Venezuela 8°6N 67°36W 328 B4
Camagüey Cuba 21°20N 77°55W 320 B4
Camagüey, Arch. de Cuba 22°18N 78°0W 320 B4
Camaiore Italy 43°56N 10°18E 198 E7
Camamu Brazil 13°57S 39°7W 333 D4
Camaná Peru 16°30S 72°50W 330 D3
Camanche U.S.A. 41°47N 90°15W 310 C6
Camanche Res. U.S.A. 38°14N 121°1W 306 G6
Camapuã Brazil 19°30S 54°5W 331 D7
Camaquã Brazil 30°51S 51°49W 335 C5
Camaquã → Brazil 31°17S 51°47W 335 C5
Câmara de Lobos Madeira 32°39N 16°59W 153 c
Camararé → Brazil 12°15S 58°55W 331 C6
Camarat, C. France 43°12N 6°41E 175 E10
Camarate Portugal 38°48N 9°7W 126 A2
Çamardı Turkey 37°49N 34°58E 212 D6
Camarès France 43°49N 2°53E 174 E6
Camaret-sur-Mer France 48°16N 4°37W 172 D2
Camargo Bolivia 20°38S 65°15W 331 E4
Camargo Tamaulipas,
Mexico 26°19N 98°50W 319 B5
Camargue France 43°34N 4°34E 175 E8
Camargue ⌓ France 43°30N 4°40E 175 E8
Camarillo U.S.A. 34°13N 119°2W 307 L7
Camariñas Spain 43°8N 9°12W 194 B1
Camarines Norte □ Phil. 14°10N 122°45E 232 D4
Camarines Sur □ Phil. 13°40N 123°20E 232 E4
Camaroes Portugal 38°49N 9°14W 126 A1
Camarón, C. Honduras 16°0N 85°5W 320 C2
Camarones Argentina 44°50S 65°40W 336 B3
Camarones, B. Argentina 44°45S 65°35W 336 B3
Camas Spain 37°24N 6°2W 195 H4
Camas Wash., U.S.A. 45°35N 122°24W 306 E4
Camas Valley U.S.A. 43°2N 123°40W 304 E2
Camatambo Angola 6°31S 15°21E 265 D3
Camataquí = Villa Abecia
Bolivia 21°0S 68°18W 334 A2
Camaxilo Angola 8°21S 18°56E 265 D3
Camba Cassai Angola 9°47S 16°9E 265 D3
Camballin Australia 17°59S 124°12E 278 C3
Cambamba Angola 8°53S 14°44E 265 D2
Cambará Brazil 23°2S 50°5W 335 A5
Cambay = Khambhat
India 22°23N 72°33E 242 H5
Cambay, G. of = Khambhat, G. of
India 20°45N 72°30E 239 E10
Camberwell Vic., Australia 37°50S 145°5E 128 B2
Camberwell London, U.K. 51°28N 0°5W 125 B3
Cambil Spain 37°40N 3°33W 195 H7
Cambo Angola 10°55S 20°6E 265 D3
Cambo-les-Bains France 43°22N 1°23W 174 E2
Cambodia ■ Asia 12°15N 105°0E 236 F5
Camborne U.K. 50°12N 5°19W 169 G2
Cambrai S. Austral.,
Australia 34°40S 139°16E 282 C3
Cambrai Nord, France 50°11N 3°14E 173 B10
Cambre Spain 43°17N 8°20W 194 B2
Cambria U.S.A. 35°34N 121°5W 306 K5
Cambrian Mts. U.K. 52°3N 3°57W 169 E4
Cambridge Ont., Canada 43°23N 80°15W 312 C4
Cambridge Jamaica 18°18N 77°54W 320 a
Cambridge N.Z. 37°54S 175°29E 284 D4
Cambridge Cambs., U.K. 52°12N 0°8E 169 E8
Cambridge Ill., U.S.A. 41°18N 90°12W 310 C6
Cambridge Iowa, U.S.A. 41°54N 93°32W 310 C3
Cambridge Mass., U.S.A. 42°23N 71°7W 116 A2
Cambridge Minn., U.S.A. 45°34N 93°13W 308 C7
Cambridge N.Y., U.S.A. 43°2N 73°22W 313 C11
Cambridge Nebr., U.S.A. 40°17N 100°10W 308 E3
Cambridge Ohio, U.S.A. 40°2N 81°35W 312 F3
Cambridge B. Canada 69°10N 105°0W 294 D11
Cambridge City U.S.A. 39°49N 85°10W 311 E11
Cambridge G. Australia 14°55S 128°15E 278 B4
Cambridge Springs U.S.A. 41°48N 80°4W 312 E4
Cambridgeshire □ U.K. 52°25N 0°7W 169 E7
Cambrils Spain 41°8N 1°3E 196 D6
Cambuci Rio de J., Brazil 21°35S 41°55W 333 F3
Cambuci São Paulo, Brazil 23°33S 46°47W 137 B2
Cambulo Angola 7°49S 21°15E 265 D4
Cambundi-Catembo
Angola 10°10S 17°35E 265 E3
Camdeboo △ S. Africa 32°28S 24°25E 270 D3
Camden N.S.W., Australia 34°1S 150°43E 283 C9
Camden Ala., U.S.A. 31°59N 87°17W 315 F11
Camden Ark., U.S.A. 33°35N 92°50W 314 E8
Camden Maine, U.S.A. 44°13N 69°4W 309 C19
Camden N.J., U.S.A. 39°55N 75°7W 313 G9
Camden N.Y., U.S.A. 43°20N 75°45W 313 C9
Camden Ohio, U.S.A. 39°38N 84°39W 311 E12
Camden S.C., U.S.A. 34°16N 80°36W 315 D14
Camden □ U.K. 51°32N 0°8W 125 A3
Camden Bay U.S.A. 70°10N 145°15W 303 A11
Camden Sd. Australia 15°27S 124°25E 278 C3
Camdenton U.S.A. 38°1N 92°45W 310 F4
Cameia △ Angola 12°5S 21°40E 265 E4
Camelford U.K. 50°37N 4°42W 169 G3
Çameli Turkey 37°5N 29°24E 205 D11
Camenca Moldova 48°3N 28°42E 183 B13
Camerino Italy 43°8N 13°4E 199 E10
Camerón Chile 53°38S 69°39W 336 D3
Cameron Ariz., U.S.A. 35°53N 111°25W 305 J8
Cameron La., U.S.A. 29°48N 93°20W 314 G8
Cameron Mo., U.S.A. 39°44N 94°14W 310 E2
Cameron S.C., U.S.A. 33°34N 80°43W 316 B9
Cameron Tex., U.S.A. 30°51N 96°59W 314 F6
Cameron, Mt. N.Z. 41°20S 174°52E 143 B2
Cameron Highlands
Malaysia 4°27N 101°22E 237 K3
Cameron Hills Canada 59°48N 118°0W 296 B5
Cameron Mts. N.Z. 46°1S 167°0E 285 G2
Cameroon ■ Africa 6°0N 12°30E 264 A2
Camerota Italy 40°2N 15°22E 201 B8
Cameroun → Cameroon 4°0N 9°35E 263 E6
Cameroun, Mt. Cameroon 4°13N 9°10E 263 E6
Cametá Brazil 2°12S 49°30W 332 B2
Çamiçi Gölü Turkey 37°29N 27°28E 205 D9
Camiguin □ Phil. 9°11N 124°42E 233 G5

356 Camiguin I.
INDEX

Camiguin I. Phil. 18°56N 121°55E 232 B3
Camiling Phil. 15°42N 120°24E 232 D3
Camilla U.S.A. 31°14N 84°12W 316 D5
Caminha Portugal 41°50N 8°50W 194 D2
Camino U.S.A. 38°44N 120°41W 306 G6
Camiranga Brazil 1°48S 46°17W 332 B2
Camiri Bolivia 20°3S 63°31W 331 E5
Camissombo Angola 8°7S 20°38E 265 D4
Çamlıca Turkey 41°1N 29°3E 122 B2
Çamlıyayla Turkey 37°10N 34°36E 250 A5
Cammal U.S.A. 41°24N 77°28W 312 E7
Cammarata Italy 37°38N 13°38E 200 E6
Cammin = Kamień Pomorski Poland 53°57N 14°43E 184 E1
Camo Ethiopia 4°29N 38°24E 266 D4
Camocim Brazil 2°55S 40°50W 332 B3
Camooweal Australia 19°56S 138°7E 280 B2
Camooweal Caves △ Australia 20°1S 138°11E 280 C2
Camopi Fr. Guiana 3°12N 52°17W 329 C7
Camopi → Fr. Guiana 3°10N 52°20W 329 C7
Camorta India 8°8N 93°30E 245 K11
Camotes Is. Phil. 10°40N 124°24E 233 F5
Camotes Sea Phil. 10°30N 124°15E 233 F5
Camp Coulter = Powell U.S.A. 44°45N 108°46W 304 D9
Camp Hill Ala., U.S.A. 32°48N 85°39W 316 C4
Camp Hill Pa., U.S.A. 40°14N 76°55W 312 F8
Camp Nelson U.S.A. 36°8N 118°39W 307 J8
Camp Pendleton U.S.A. 33°13N 117°24W 307 M9
Camp Point U.S.A. 40°3N 91°4W 310 D5
Camp Springs U.S.A. 38°48N 76°55W 143 C4
Camp Verde U.S.A. 34°34N 111°51W 305 J8
Camp Wood U.S.A. 29°40N 100°1W 314 G4
Campagna Italy 40°40N 15°6E 201 B8
Campamento Spain 40°23N 3°46W 127 B1
Campana Argentina 34°10S 58°55W 334 C4
Campana, I. Chile 48°20S 75°20W 336 C1
Campanário Madeira 32°39N 17°2W 153 c
Campanario Spain 38°52N 5°36W 195 G5
Campanet Spain 39°46N 2°58E 206 B3
Campánia □ Italy 41°0N 14°30E 201 B7
Campbell Northern Cape, S. Africa 28°48S 23°44E 270 C3
Campbell Calif., U.S.A. 37°17N 121°57W 306 H5
Campbell Fla., U.S.A. 28°16N 81°27W 317 G8
Campbell Ohio, U.S.A. 41°5N 80°37W 312 E4
Campbell, C. N.Z. 41°47S 174°18E 285 B9
Campbell I. Pac. Oc. 52°30S 169°0E 288 N8
Campbell L. Canada 63°14N 106°55W 297 A7
Campbell Plateau S. Ocean 50°0S 170°0E 151 A11
Campbell River Canada 50°5N 125°20W 296 C3
Campbellfield Australia 37°41S 144°57E 128 A1
Campbellford Canada 44°18N 77°48W 312 B7
Campbellpur Pakistan 33°46N 72°26E 242 C5
Campbellsburg U.S.A. 38°39N 86°16W 311 F10
Campbellsville U.S.A. 37°21N 85°20W 309 G11
Campbellton N.B., Canada 47°57N 66°43W 299 C6
Campbellton Fla., U.S.A. 30°57N 85°24W 316 E4
Campbelltown = Bluff N.Z. 46°37S 168°20E 285 G3
Campbelltown Australia 34°4S 150°49E 283 C9
Campbeltown U.K. 55°25N 5°36W 167 F3
Campêche Guadeloupe 16°25N 61°26W 322 e
Campeche Campeche, Mexico 19°51N 90°32W 319 D6
Campeche □ Mexico 19°0N 90°30W 319 D6
Campeche, Banco Mexico 22°30N 88°0W 320 B2
Campeche, Golfo de Mexico 19°30N 93°0W 319 D6
Câmpeni Romania 46°22N 23°3E 182 D8
Camperdown N.S.W., Australia 33°53S 151°11E 139 B2
Camperdown Vic., Australia 38°14S 143°9E 282 E5
Camperville Canada 51°59N 100°9W 297 C8
Campi Salentina Italy 40°24N 18°1E 201 B11
Câmpia Turzii Romania 46°34N 23°53E 183 D8
Campidano Italy 39°30N 8°47E 200 C1
Campidoglio, Piazza de Rome, Italy 136 c3
Campíglia Maríttima Italy 43°4N 10°37E 198 E7
Campillo de Altobuey Spain 39°36N 1°49W 197 F3
Campillos Spain 37°4N 4°51W 195 H6
Câmpina Romania 45°10N 25°45E 183 E10
Campina Grande Brazil 7°20S 35°47W 332 C4
Campina Verde Brazil 19°31S 49°28W 333 E2
Campinas Brazil 22°50S 47°0W 335 A6
Campione Italy 45°58N 8°58E 175 C12
Campli Italy 42°43N 13°41E 199 F10
Campo = Ntem → Cameroon 2°21N 9°49E 264 B2
Campo Cameroon 2°22N 9°50E 264 B1
Campo Spain 42°25N 0°24E 196 C5
Campo, Casa de Spain 40°25N 3°45W 127 B1
Campo ⌓ Cameroon 2°23N 10°5E 264 B2
Campo Belo Brazil 20°52S 45°16W 333 F2
Campo de Criptana Spain 39°24N 3°7W 195 F7
Campo de Diauarum Brazil 11°12S 53°14W 331 C7
Campo de Gibraltar Spain 36°15N 5°25W 195 J5
Campo F.C. Barcelona Spain 41°22N 2°7E 114 A1
Campo Florido Brazil 19°47S 48°35W 333 E2
Campo Formoso = Campo Florido Brazil 19°47S 48°35W 333 E2
Campo Formoso Brazil 10°30S 40°20W 332 D3
Campo Grande Brazil 20°25S 54°40W 331 E7
Campo Grando Portugal 38°45N 9°9W 126 A2
Campo Maior Brazil 4°50S 42°12W 332 B3
Campo Maior Portugal 39°2N 7°7W 195 F3
Campo Mourão Brazil 24°3S 52°22W 335 A5
Campo Pequeño Portugal 38°44N 9°8W 126 A2
Campo Túres Italy 46°53N 11°55E 199 B8
Campoalegre Colombia 2°41N 75°20W 328 C2
Campobasso Italy 41°34N 14°39E 201 A7
Campobello di Licata Italy 37°15N 13°55E 200 E6
Campobello di Mazara Italy 37°38N 12°45E 200 E5
Campofelice di Roccella Italy 37°59N 13°53E 200 E6
Campolide Portugal 38°43N 9°9W 126 A2
Campomarino Italy 41°57N 15°2E 199 G12
Camporeale Italy 37°54N 13°6E 200 E6
Camporrobles Spain 39°39N 1°24W 196 F3
Campos Brazil 21°50S 41°20W 333 F3
Campos Spain 39°26N 3°1E 206 B4
Campos Altos Brazil 19°47S 46°10W 333 E2
Campos Belos Brazil 13°10S 47°3W 333 D2
Campos del Paraíso = Carrascosa del Campo Spain 40°2N 2°45W 196 E2
Campos Novos Brazil 27°21S 51°50W 335 B5
Campos Sales Brazil 7°4S 40°23W 332 C3
Camprodon Spain 42°19N 2°23E 196 C7
Camps Bay S. Africa 33°57S 18°23E 118 A1
Campton Fla., U.S.A. 30°53N 86°31W 317 E3
Campton Ga., U.S.A. 33°52N 83°43W 316 B6
Campton Ky., U.S.A. 37°44N 83°33W 311 G13
Camptonville U.S.A. 39°27N 121°3W 306 F5
Camptown U.S.A. 41°44N 76°14W 313 E8
Câmpulung Argeș, Romania 45°17N 25°3E 183 E10
Câmpulung Suceava, Romania 47°32N 25°30E 183 C10
Câmpuri Romania 46°0N 26°50E 183 D11
Campuya → Peru 1°40S 73°30W 328 D3
Campville U.S.A. 29°40N 82°7W 316 F7
Camrose Canada 53°0N 112°50W 296 C6
Camsell Portage Canada 59°37N 109°15W 297 B7
Camucuio Angola 14°7S 13°15E 265 E2
Camuy Puerto Rico 18°29N 66°51W 321 b
Çamyuva Turkey 36°30N 30°30E 205 E12
Çan Turkey 40°2N 27°3E 203 F11
Can Clavo Spain 38°57N 1°27E 206 D1
Can Creu Spain 38°58N 1°28E 206 D1
Can Gio Vietnam 10°25N 106°58E 237 G6
Can Pastilla Spain 39°32N 2°42E 206 B3
C'an San Joan Spain 41°28N 2°11E 114 A2
Can Tho Vietnam 10°2N 105°46E 237 G5
Canaan Trin. & Tob. 11°9N 60°49W 323 s
Canaan Conn., U.S.A. 42°2N 73°20W 313 D11
Canaan Hill Jamaica 18°23N 77°14W 320 a
Cañacao B. Phil. 14°29N 120°54E 127 C1
Canacona India 15°1N 74°4E 245 G2
Canada ■ N. Amer. 60°0N 100°0W 294 G11
Canada Abyssal Plain Arctic 80°0N 140°0W 150 B18
Canada Basin Arctic 80°0N 145°0W 150 B18
Cañada de Gómez Argentina 32°40S 61°30W 334 C3
Canadian U.S.A. 35°55N 100°23W 314 D4
Canadian → U.S.A. 35°28N 95°3W 314 D7
Canadian Shield Canada 53°0N 75°0W 292 D12
Canadys U.S.A. 33°3N 80°37W 316 B9
Canajoharie U.S.A. 42°54N 74°35W 313 D10
Çanakkale Turkey 40°8N 26°24E 203 F10
Çanakkale □ Turkey 40°10N 26°25E 203 F10
Çanakkale Boğazı Turkey 40°17N 26°32E 203 F10
Canal Flats Canada 50°10N 115°48W 296 C5
Canal Point U.S.A. 26°52N 80°38W 317 J9
Canal Street New Orleans, U.S.A. 131 b2
Canala N. Cal. 21°32S 165°57E 288 d
Canalejas Argentina 35°15S 66°34W 334 D2
Canals Argentina 33°35S 62°53W 334 C3
Canals Spain 38°58N 0°35W 197 G4
Canandaigua U.S.A. 42°54N 77°17W 312 D7
Canandaigua L. U.S.A. 42°47N 77°19W 312 D7
Cananea Mexico 31°0N 110°18W 318 A2
Cañar Ecuador 2°33S 78°56W 328 D2
Cañar □ Ecuador 2°30S 79°0W 328 D2
Canarias, Is. Atl. Oc. 28°30N 16°0W 153 e1
Canaries St. Lucia 13°55N 61°4W 323 m
Canarreos, Arch. de los Cuba 21°35N 81°40W 320 B3
Canarsie U.S.A. 40°38N 73°53W 132 C2
Canary Is. = Canarias, Is. Atl. Oc. 28°30N 16°0W 153 e1
Canaseraga U.S.A. 42°27N 77°45W 312 D7
Canastra, Serra da Brazil 20°0S 46°20W 333 F2
Canatlán Mexico 24°31N 104°47W 318 C4
Cañaveral Peru 3°56S 80°39W 328 D1
Canaveral, C. U.S.A. 28°27N 80°32W 317 G9
Canaveral ⌓ U.S.A. 28°28N 80°34W 317 G9
Cañaveruelas Spain 40°24N 2°38W 196 E2
Canavieiras Brazil 15°39S 39°0W 333 E4
Canbelego Australia 31°32S 146°18E 283 A7
Canberra Australia 35°15S 149°8E 283 C8
Canby Calif., U.S.A. 41°27N 120°52W 304 F3
Canby Minn., U.S.A. 44°43N 96°16W 308 C5
Canby Oreg., U.S.A. 45°16N 122°42W 306 E4
Cancale France 48°40N 1°50W 172 D5
Cancelleria, Palazzo dei Rome, Italy 136 c2
Canche → France 50°31N 1°39E 173 B8
Canchungo = Teixeira Pinto Guinea-Biss. 12°3N 16°0W 262 C1
Canchungo Guinea-Biss. 12°26N 16°5W 262 C1
Canchyuaya, Cordillera de Peru 7°30S 74°0W 330 B3
Cancún Mexico 21°8N 86°44W 319 C7
Candanchú Spain 42°47N 0°32W 196 C4
Candarave Peru 17°15S 70°13W 330 D3
Çandarlı Turkey 38°56N 26°56E 205 C8
Çandarlı Körfezi Turkey 38°52N 26°55E 205 C8
Candás Spain 43°35N 5°45W 194 B5
Candé France 47°34N 1°2W 172 E5
Candeias → Brazil 8°39S 63°31W 331 B5
Candela Italy 41°8N 15°31E 201 A8
Candelaria Argentina 27°29S 55°44W 335 B4
Candelaria Canary Is. 28°22N 16°22W 153 e1
Candelaria Phil. 13°56N 121°25E 232 E3
Candelario ⌓ Spain 40°20N 5°46W 194 E5
Candeleda Spain 40°10N 5°14W 194 E5
Candelo Australia 36°47S 149°43E 283 D8
Candi Dasa Indonesia 8°30S 115°34E 231 J18
Candia = Iraklio Greece 35°20N 25°12E 207 E6
Candia, Sea of = Crete, Sea of Greece 36°0N 25°0E 205 E7
Candiac Canada 45°23N 73°29W 130 B3
Cândido de Abreu Brazil 24°35S 51°20W 333 F1
Cândido Mendes Brazil 1°27S 45°43W 332 B2
Candle U.S.A. 65°55N 161°56W 303 D7
Candle L. Canada 53°50N 105°18W 297 C7
Candlemas I. Antarctica 57°3S 26°40W 151 B1
Cando U.S.A. 48°32N 99°12W 308 A4
Candon Phil. 17°12N 120°27E 232 C3
Canea = Chania Greece 35°30N 24°4E 207 E5
Caneças Portugal 38°48N 9°13W 126 A1
Canefield Dominica 15°20N 61°24W 323 k
Canela Brazil 10°15S 48°25W 332 D2
Canelles → St. Lucia 13°47N 60°55W 323 m
Canelli Italy 44°43N 8°17E 198 D5
Canelones Uruguay 34°32S 56°17W 335 C4
Canet-Plage France 42°41N 3°2E 174 F7
Cañete Chile 37°50S 73°30W 334 D1
Cañete Spain 40°3N 1°54W 196 E3
Cañete de las Torres Spain 37°53N 4°19W 195 H6
Cangamba Angola 13°40S 19°54E 265 E3
Cangandala Angola 9°45S 16°33E 265 D3
Cangandala △ Angola 9°53S 16°42E 265 D3
Cangas Spain 42°16N 8°47W 194 C2
Cangas de Onís Spain 43°21N 5°8W 194 B5
Cangas de Tineo = Cangas del Narcea Spain 43°10N 6°32W 194 B4
Cangas del Narcea Spain 43°10N 6°32W 194 B4
Cangnan China 27°30N 120°23E 229 D13
Cangoa Angola 13°8S 18°30E 265 E3
Cangola Angola 7°58S 15°53E 265 D3
Cangolo Angola 15°0S 13°52E 265 E2
Cangombe Angola 14°24S 19°59E 265 E3
Cangongo Angola 9°24S 17°30E 265 D3
Cangshan China 34°50N 118°2E 227 G10
Canguaretama Brazil 6°20S 35°5W 332 C4
Canguçu Brazil 31°22S 52°43W 335 C5
Canguçu, Serra do Brazil 31°20S 52°40W 335 C5
Cangumbe Angola 11°58S 19°12E 265 E3
Cangxi China 31°47N 105°59E 228 B5
Cangyuan China 23°12N 99°14E 228 F2
Cangzhou China 38°19N 116°52E 226 E9
Canhoca Angola 9°15S 14°41E 265 D2
Cani, I. Tunisia 36°21N 10°5E 258 A2
Caniapiscau → Canada 56°40N 69°30W 299 A6
Caniapiscau, L. Canada 54°10N 69°55W 299 B6
Canicattì Italy 37°21N 13°51E 200 E6
Canicattini Bagni Italy 37°2N 15°4E 201 E8
Canigao Channel Phil. 10°15N 124°42E 233 F5
Caniles Spain 37°26N 2°43W 195 H8
Canillas Spain 40°27N 3°38W 127 B2
Canillejas Spain 40°26N 3°36W 127 B2
Canim Lake Canada 51°47N 120°54W 296 C4
Canindé Brazil 4°22S 39°19W 332 B4
Canindé → Brazil 6°15S 42°52W 332 C3
Canindeyu □ Paraguay 24°10S 55°0W 335 A5
Canino Italy 42°28N 11°45E 199 F8
Canisteo U.S.A. 42°16N 77°36W 312 D7
Canisteo → U.S.A. 42°7N 77°8W 312 D7
Cañitas de Felipe Pescador Mexico 23°36N 102°43W 318 C4
Cañizal Spain 41°12N 5°22W 194 D5
Canjáyar Spain 37°1N 2°44W 195 H8
Canjinge Angola 10°12S 21°17E 265 E4
Çankırı Turkey 40°40N 33°37E 212 B5
Çankırı □ Turkey 40°40N 33°30E 212 B5
Cankuzo Burundi 3°10S 30°31E 268 C3
Canlaon Phil. 10°22N 123°12E 233 F4
Canlaon Volcano Phil. 10°25N 123°8E 233 F4
Canmore Canada 51°7N 115°18W 296 C5
Cann River Australia 37°35S 149°7E 283 D8
Canna U.K. 57°3N 6°33W 167 D2
Cannanore India 11°53N 75°27E 245 J2
Cannanore Is. India 10°30N 72°30E 245 J1
Cannelton U.S.A. 37°55N 86°45W 311 G10
Cannery, The San Francisco, U.S.A. 136 a1
Cannes France 43°32N 7°1E 175 E11
Canning Town = Port Canning India 22°23N 88°40E 243 H13
Canning Town U.K. 51°30N 0°1E 125 A4
Cannington Canada 44°20N 79°2W 312 B5
Cannóbio Italy 46°4N 8°42E 198 B5
Cannock U.K. 52°41N 2°1W 169 E5
Cannonball → U.S.A. 46°26N 100°35W 308 B3
Cannondale Mt. Australia 25°13S 148°57E 280 D4
Cannonsville Res. U.S.A. 42°4N 75°22W 313 D9
Cannonvale Australia 20°17S 148°43E 280 b
Caño Colorado Colombia 2°18N 68°22W 328 C4
Canoas Brazil 29°56S 51°11W 335 B5
Canoe L. Canada 55°10N 108°15W 297 B7
Cañon City U.S.A. 38°27N 105°14W 304 G11
Cañón de Río Blanco △ Mexico 18°43N 97°15W 319 D5
Cañón del Río Lobos ⌓ Spain 41°46N 3°28W 194 D7
Cañón del Sumidero △ Mexico 19°22N 96°24W 319 D5
Canonnier, Pte. du St.-Martin 18°4N 63°7W 322 a
Canonniers Pt. Mauritius 20°2S 57°32E 272 e
Canoochee → U.S.A. 31°59N 81°19W 316 D8
Canopus Australia 33°29S 140°42E 282 B4
Canora Canada 51°40N 102°30W 297 C8
Canosa di Púglia Italy 41°13N 16°4E 201 A9
Canouan St. Vincent 12°43N 61°20W 323 n
Canowindra Australia 33°35S 148°38E 283 B8
Canso Canada 45°20N 61°0W 299 C7
Canta Peru 11°29S 76°37W 330 C2
Cantabria □ Spain 43°10N 4°0W 194 B7
Cantabria, Sierra de Spain 42°40N 2°30W 196 C2
Cantabrian Mts. = Cantábrica, Cordillera Spain 43°0N 5°10W 194 C5
Cantábrica, Cordillera Spain 43°0N 5°10W 194 C5
Cantal □ France 45°5N 2°45E 174 C6
Cantal, Plomb du France 45°3N 2°45E 174 C6
Cantanhede Portugal 40°20N 8°36W 194 E2
Cantaura Venezuela 9°19N 64°21W 329 B5
Cantavieja Spain 40°31N 0°25W 196 E4
Čantavir Serbia 45°55N 19°46E 182 E4
Cantemir Moldova 46°17N 28°14E 183 D13
Canteras de Vallecas Spain 40°20N 3°37W 127 B2
Canterbury = Invermere Canada 50°30N 116°2W 296 C5
Canterbury N.S.W., Australia 33°55S 151°7E 139 B1
Canterbury Queens., Australia 25°23S 141°53E 280 D3
Canterbury Vic., Australia 37°49S 145°4E 128 A2
Canterbury Kent, U.K. 51°16N 1°6E 169 F9
Canterbury □ N.Z. 43°45S 171°19E 285 D6
Canterbury Bight N.Z. 44°16S 171°55E 285 E6
Canterbury Plains N.Z. 43°55S 171°22E 285 D6
Cantil U.S.A. 35°18N 117°58W 307 K9
Cantilan Phil. 9°20N 125°58E 233 G5
Cantillana Spain 37°36N 5°50W 195 H5
Canto do Buriti Brazil 8°7S 42°58W 332 C3
Canton = Guangzhou China 23°6N 113°13E 121 B2
Canton Ga., U.S.A. 34°14N 84°29W 315 D12
Canton Ill., U.S.A. 40°33N 90°2W 310 D6
Canton Miss., U.S.A. 32°37N 90°2W 315 E9
Canton Mo., U.S.A. 40°8N 91°32W 310 D5
Canton N.Y., U.S.A. 44°36N 75°10W 313 B9
Canton Ohio, U.S.A. 40°48N 81°23W 312 F3
Canton Pa., U.S.A. 41°39N 76°51W 312 E8
Canton S. Dak., U.S.A. 43°18N 96°35W 308 D5
Canton L. U.S.A. 36°6N 98°35W 314 C5
Cantonment U.S.A. 30°37N 87°20W 317 E2
Cantù Italy 45°44N 9°8E 198 C6
Cantwell U.S.A. 63°24N 148°57W 303 E10
Canudos Brazil 7°13S 58°5W 331 B6
Canumã Amazonas, Brazil 4°2S 59°4W 329 D6
Canumã Amazonas, Brazil 6°8S 60°10W 331 B5
Canumã → Brazil 3°55S 59°10W 331 A6
Canunda △ Australia 37°42S 140°16E 282 D4
Canutama Brazil 6°30S 64°20W 331 B5
Canutillo U.S.A. 31°55N 106°36W 314 F1
Canvey U.K. 51°31N 0°37E 169 F8
Canyon U.S.A. 34°59N 101°55W 314 D4
Canyon De Chelly ⌓ U.S.A. 36°10N 109°20W 305 H9
Canyonlands △ U.S.A. 38°15N 110°0W 305 G9
Canyons of the Ancients ⌓ U.S.A. 37°30N 108°55W 305 H9
Canyonville U.S.A. 42°56N 123°17W 304 E2
Canzar Angola 7°35S 21°34E 265 D4
Cao Bang Vietnam 22°40N 106°15E 228 F6
Cao He → China 40°10N 124°32E 227 D13
Cao Lanh Vietnam 10°27N 105°38E 237 G5
Cao Xian China 34°50N 115°35E 226 G8
Caoheijing China 31°10N 121°25E 138 B1
Caombo Angola 8°42S 16°33E 265 D3
Cáorle Italy 45°36N 12°53E 199 C9
Cap-aux-Meules Canada 47°23N 61°52W 299 C7
Cap-Chat Canada 49°6N 66°40W 299 C6
Cap-de-la-Madeleine Canada 46°22N 72°31W 298 C5
Cap de Ville Trin. & Tob. 10°9N 61°42W 323 t
Cap-Haïtien Haiti 19°40N 72°20W 321 C5
Cap I. Phil. 5°57N 120°6E 233 J3
Cap Pt. St. Lucia 14°7N 60°57W 323 m
Capac U.S.A. 43°1N 82°56W 312 C2
Capáccio Italy 40°25N 15°5E 201 B8
Capaci Italy 38°10N 13°14E 200 D6
Capaia Angola 8°27S 20°13E 265 D4
Capalonga Phil. 14°20N 122°30E 232 D4
Capanaparo → Venezuela 7°1N 67°7W 328 B4
Capanema Brazil 1°12S 47°11W 332 B2
Capangombe Angola 15°6S 13°8E 265 F2
Capánnori Italy 43°50N 10°34E 198 E7
Capão Redondo Brazil 23°39S 46°45W 137 B1
Caparaó △ Brazil 20°25S 41°46W 333 F3
Caparica Portugal 38°40N 9°9W 126 A2
Caparica, Costa da Portugal 38°38N 9°15W 126 B1
Caparo → Trin. & Tob. 10°31N 61°28W 323 t
Capas Phil. 15°38N 120°28E 232 D3
Capatárida Venezuela 11°11N 70°37W 328 A3
Capayas Phil. 10°28N 119°39E 233 F2
Capbreton France 43°39N 1°26W 174 E2
Capdenac France 44°34N 2°5E 174 D6
Capdepera Spain 39°42N 3°26E 206 B4
Cape → Australia 20°59S 146°51E 280 C4
Cape Arid △ Australia 33°58S 123°13E 279 F3
Cape Barren I. Australia 40°25S 148°15E 281 G4
Cape Basin Atl. Oc. 34°0S 7°0W 152 K12
Cape Breton Highlands △ Canada 46°50N 60°40W 299 C7
Cape Breton I. Canada 46°0N 60°30W 299 C7
Cape Canaveral U.S.A. 28°24N 80°36W 317 G9
Cape Charles U.S.A. 37°16N 76°1W 309 G15
Cape Coast Ghana 5°5N 1°15W 263 D4
Cape Cod ⌓ U.S.A. 41°56N 70°6W 309 E18
Cape Coral U.S.A. 26°33N 81°57W 317 J8
Cape Crawford Australia 16°41S 135°43E 280 B2
Cape Dorset = Kinngait Canada 64°14N 76°32W 295 E16
Cape Fear → U.S.A. 33°53N 78°1W 315 E15
Cape Flats S. Africa 34°3S 18°33E 118 B2
Cape Girardeau U.S.A. 37°19N 89°32W 308 G9
Cape Hatteras ⌓ U.S.A. 35°30N 75°28W 315 D17
Cape Hillsborough △ Australia 20°54S 149°2E 280 b
Cape Jervis Australia 35°40S 138°5E 282 C3
Cape Krusenstern ⌓ U.S.A. 67°30N 163°30W 303 C7
Cape Le Grand △ Australia 33°54S 122°26E 279 F3
Cape Lisburne = Wevok U.S.A. 68°53N 166°13W 303 B6
Cape Lookout ⌓ U.S.A. 35°45N 76°25W 315 D16
Cape May U.S.A. 38°56N 74°56W 309 F16
Cape May Point U.S.A. 38°56N 74°58W 309 F16
Cape Melville △ Australia 14°26S 144°28E 280 A3
Cape Mount △ Liberia 6°44N 11°24W 262 D2
Cape Pole U.S.A. 55°58N 133°48W 303 J14
Cape Range △ Australia 22°3S 114°0E 278 D1
Cape St. George Canada 48°28N 59°14W 299 C8
Cape Tormentine Canada 46°8N 63°47W 299 C7
Cape Town S. Africa 33°55S 18°22E 118 A1
Cape Town Int. ✕ (CPT) S. Africa 33°58S 18°35E 118 A2
Cape Upstart △ Australia 19°45S 147°48E 280 B4
Cape Verde Abyssal Plain Atl. Oc. 23°0N 26°0W 152 D9
Cape Verde Is. ■ Atl. Oc. 16°0N 24°0W 153 j
Cape Verde Plateau Atl. Oc. 18°0N 20°0W 152 E10
Cape Vincent U.S.A. 44°8N 76°20W 313 B8
Cape Yakataga U.S.A. 60°4N 142°26W 303 F12
Cape York Peninsula Australia 12°0S 142°30E 286 F2
Capela Brazil 10°30S 37°0W 332 D4
Capelas Azores 37°50N 25°41W 153 d3
Capele Angola 13°39S 14°53E 265 E2
Capelengue Angola 8°53S 19°42E 265 D3
Capelinha Brazil 17°42S 42°31W 333 E3
Capelinhos, Pta. dos Azores 38°36N 28°50W 153 d1
Capella Australia 23°2S 148°1E 280 C4
Capella, Mt. Papua N. G. 5°4S 141°8E 286 C1
Capelongo Angola 14°54S 15°8E 265 E3
Capenda Camulemba Angola 9°24S 18°27E 265 D3
Capendu France 43°11N 2°31E 174 E6
Capertree Australia 33°6S 149°58E 283 B8
Capestang France 43°20N 3°2E 174 E7
Capesterre, Grande Rivière de la → Guadeloupe 16°3N 61°33W 322 e
Capesterre, Pte. de la Guadeloupe 16°3N 61°33W 322 e
Capesterre-Belle-Eau Guadeloupe 16°4N 61°36W 322 e
Capesterre-de-Marie-Galante Guadeloupe 15°53N 61°14W 322 e
Capim → Brazil 1°40S 47°47W 332 B2
Capinópolis Brazil 18°41S 49°35W 333 E2
Capinota Bolivia 17°43S 66°14W 330 D4
Capira Panama 8°45N 79°53W 328 B2
Capistrello Italy 41°57N 13°23E 199 G10
Capitan U.S.A. 33°35N 105°35W 305 K11
Capitán Aracena, I. Chile 54°10S 71°20W 336 D2
Capitán Arturo Prat Antarctica 63°0S 61°0W 151 C17
Capitán Pastene Chile 38°13S 73°1W 336 A2
Capitão de Campos Brazil 4°40S 41°55W 332 B3
Capitol Heights U.S.A. 38°52N 76°55W 143 B4
Capitol Hill N. Marianas 15°13N 145°45E 302 e
Capitol Reef △ U.S.A. 38°15N 111°10W 305 G8
Capitola U.S.A. 36°59N 121°57W 306 J5
Capitolini, Musei Rome, Italy 136 c3
Capivara, Serra da Brazil 14°35S 45°0W 333 D3
Capiz □ Phil. 11°35N 122°30E 233 F4
Capizzi Italy 37°51N 14°29E 201 E7
Capoche → Mozam. 15°35S 33°0E 269 F3
Capodichino, Nápoli ✕ (NAP) Italy 40°53N 14°16E 201 B7
Capoeira Brazil 5°37S 59°33W 331 B6
Capolo Angola 10°22S 14°7E 265 E2
Caporetto = Kobarid Slovenia 46°15N 13°30E 199 B10
Caporolo → Angola 12°56S 12°58E 265 E2
Capot → Martinique 14°50N 61°5W 322 j
Capoterra Italy 39°11N 8°58E 200 C1
Cappadocia Turkey 39°0N 35°0E 212 C6
Capps U.S.A. 30°24N 83°54W 316 E6
Capraia Italy 43°2N 9°50E 198 E6
Caprara, Pta. Italy 41°7N 8°19E 200 A1
Caprarola Italy 42°19N 12°14E 199 F9
Caprera Italy 41°12N 9°28E 200 A2
Capri Italy 40°33N 14°14E 201 B7
Capricorn Coast Australia 23°16S 150°49E 280 C5
Capricorn Group Australia 23°30S 151°55E 280 C5
Capricorn Ra. Australia 23°20S 116°50E 278 D2
Caprino Veronese Italy 45°36N 10°47E 198 C7
Caprivi ⌓ Namibia 17°55S 22°37E 270 A3
Caprivi Strip Namibia 18°0S 23°0E 270 A3
Caps et Marais d'Opale ⌓ France 50°40N 2°0E 173 B9
Captain Cook U.S.A. 19°30N 155°55W 302 D6
Captain Cook Bridge Australia 34°0S 151°7E 139 C1
Captain Cook Landing Place Park Australia 34°1S 151°14E 139 C2
Captains Flat Australia 35°35S 149°27E 283 C8
Captieux France 44°18N 0°16W 174 D3
Captiva U.S.A. 26°31N 82°11W 317 J7
Capuça Angola 17°22S 21°18E 265 F4
Capuchos Portugal 38°38N 9°16W 126 B1
Capucin Dominica 15°38N 61°28W 323 k
Capul I. Phil. 12°26N 124°10E 232 E5
Capulin Volcano ⌓ U.S.A. 36°47N 103°58W 314 C3
Capunda Angola 10°41S 17°23E 265 E3
Caquetá □ Colombia 1°0N 74°0W 328 C3
Caquetá → Colombia 1°15S 69°15W 328 D4
Car Nicobar India 9°10N 92°47E 245 K11
Cara-Paraná → Colombia 1°45S 73°13W 328 D3
Carabanchel Alto Spain 40°22N 3°44W 127 B1
Carabanchel Bajo Spain 40°23N 3°44W 127 B1
Carabao I. Phil. 12°4N 121°56E 232 E3
Carabobo □ Venezuela 10°10N 68°5W 328 A4
Caracal Romania 44°8N 24°22E 183 F9
Caracaraí Brazil 1°50N 61°8W 329 C5
Caracas Venezuela 10°30N 66°55W 328 A4
Caracol Belize 16°45N 89°6W 320 C2
Caracol Mato Grosso do Sul, Brazil 22°18S 57°1W 334 A4
Caracol Piauí, Brazil 9°15S 43°22W 332 C3
Caracoli, Pte. Martinique 14°45N 60°52W 322 j
Caracollo Bolivia 17°39S 67°10W 330 D4
Caraga Phil. 7°20N 126°34E 233 H6
Caraga □ Phil. 9°40N 125°30E 233 G6
Caragabal Australia 33°49S 147°45E 283 B7
Caráglio Italy 44°25N 7°26E 198 D4
Carahue Chile 38°43S 73°12W 336 A2
Caraí Brazil 17°12S 41°42W 333 E3
Caraïbes, Mts. Guadeloupe 15°58N 61°41W 322 e
Carajás Brazil 2°57S 51°22W 332 C1
Carajás, Serra dos Brazil 6°0S 51°30W 332 C1
Caramoan Phil. 13°46N 123°52E 232 E4
Caramoan Pen. Phil. 13°47N 123°44E 232 E4
Caramoran Phil. 14°0N 124°8E 232 D5
Caranapatuba Brazil 6°38S 62°34W 331 B5
Carandaiti Bolivia 20°45S 63°4W 331 E5
Carangola Brazil 20°44S 42°5W 333 F3
Caransebeș Romania 45°28N 22°18E 182 E7
Carantec France 48°40N 3°55W 172 D3
Carapachay Argentina 34°31S 58°32W 117 B1
Carapichaima Trin. & Tob. 10°28N 61°27W 323 t
Carapo → Barinas, Venezuela 7°46N 70°23W 328 B3
Carapo → Bolívar, Venezuela 7°30N 64°0W 329 B5
Carapuse B. Trin. & Tob. 11°14N 60°35W 323 s
Caraquet Canada 47°48N 64°57W 299 C6
Caraș Severin □ Romania 45°10N 22°10E 182 E7
Carașova Romania 45°11N 21°51E 182 E6
Caratasca, L. de Honduras 15°20N 83°40W 320 C3
Caratinga Brazil 19°50S 42°10W 333 E3
Carauaí Brazil 4°52S 66°54W 328 D4
Caraúbas Brazil 5°43S 37°33W 332 C4
Caravaca de la Cruz Spain 38°8N 1°52W 197 G3
Caravággio Italy 45°30N 9°38E 198 C6
Caravela Guinea-Biss. 11°30N 16°30W 262 C1
Caravelas Brazil 17°45S 39°15W 333 E4
Caraveli Peru 15°45S 73°25W 330 D3
Caravelle, Presqu'île de la Martinique 14°46N 60°48W 322 j
Caraz Peru 9°3S 77°47W 330 B2
Caraza Argentina 34°41S 58°25W 117 C2
Carazinho Brazil 28°16S 52°46W 335 B5
Carballino = O Carballiño Spain 42°26N 8°5W 194 C2
Carballo Spain 43°13N 8°41W 194 B2
Carberry Canada 49°50N 99°25W 297 D9
Carbet, Chutes du Guadeloupe 16°2N 61°38W 322 e
Carbet, Pitons du Martinique 14°42N 61°7W 322 j
Carbó Mexico 29°42N 110°58W 318 B2
Carbón, L. del Argentina 49°35S 68°21W 336 C3
Carbonara, C. Italy 39°6N 9°31E 200 C2
Carbondale Colo., U.S.A. 39°24N 107°13W 304 G10
Carbondale Ill., U.S.A. 37°44N 89°13W 310 G7
Carbondale Pa., U.S.A. 41°35N 75°30W 313 E9
Carbonear Canada 47°42N 53°13W 299 C9
Carboneras Spain 36°59N 1°53W 197 J3
Carboneras de Guadazaón Spain 39°54N 1°50W 196 F3
Carbónia Italy 39°10N 8°30E 200 C1
Carcabuey Spain 37°27N 4°17W 195 H6
Carcagente = Carcaixent Spain 39°8N 0°28W 197 F4
Carcaixent Spain 39°8N 0°28W 197 F4
Carcajou Canada 57°47N 117°6W 296 B5
Carcar Phil. 10°6N 123°38E 233 F4
Carcarana → Argentina 32°27S 60°48W 334 C3
Carcasse, C. Haiti 18°30N 74°28W 321 C5
Carcassonne France 43°13N 2°20E 174 E6
Carchi □ Ecuador 0°45N 78°0W 328 C2
Carcoar Australia 33°36S 149°8E 283 B8
Carcross Canada 60°13N 134°45W 296 A2
Çardak Çanakkale, Turkey 40°22N 26°43E 203 F10
Çardak Denizli, Turkey 37°49N 29°39E 205 D11
Cardamon Hills India 9°30N 77°15E 245 K3
Cardamon Mts. = Kravanh, Chuor Phnum Cambodia 12°0N 103°32E 237 G4
Cardeña Spain 38°16N 4°20W 195 G6
Cárdenas Cuba 23°0N 81°30W 320 B3
Cárdenas San Luis Potosí, Mexico 22°0N 99°38W 319 C5
Cárdenas Tabasco, Mexico 17°59N 93°22W 319 D6
Cardener → Spain 41°41N 1°51E 196 D6
Cardenete Spain 39°46N 1°41W 196 F3
Cardiel, L. Argentina 48°55S 71°10W 336 C2
Cardiff U.K. 51°29N 3°10W 169 F4
Cardiff □ U.K. 51°31N 3°12W 169 F4
Cardiff-by-the-Sea U.S.A. 33°1N 117°17W 307 M9
Cardigan U.K. 52°5N 4°40W 169 E3
Cardigan B. U.K. 52°30N 4°30W 169 E3
Cardinal Canada 44°47N 75°23W 313 B9
Cardón, Punta Venezuela 11°37N 70°14W 328 A3
Cardona Spain 41°56N 1°40E 196 D6
Cardona Uruguay 33°53S 57°18W 334 C4
Cardoso, Ilha do Brazil 25°8S 47°58W 335 B5
Cardston Canada 49°15N 113°20W 296 D6
Cardwell Australia 18°14S 146°2E 280 B4
Careen L. Canada 57°0N 108°11W 297 B7
Carei Romania 47°40N 22°29E 182 C7
Careiro Brazil 3°12S 59°45W 329 D6
Carenage Trin. & Tob. 10°41N 61°36W 323 t
Carentan France 49°19N 1°15W 172 C5
Carey Idaho, U.S.A. 43°19N 113°57W 304 E7
Carey Ohio, U.S.A. 40°57N 83°23W 311 D13
Carey, L. Australia 29°0S 122°15E 279 E3
Carey L. Canada 62°12N 102°55W 297 A8
Careysburg Liberia 6°34N 10°30W 262 D2
Cargados Carajos Ind. Oc. 17°0S 59°0E 273 F4
Cargèse France 42°7N 8°35E 175 F12
Carhaix-Plouguer France 48°18N 3°36W 172 D3
Carhuamayo Peru 10°51S 76°4W 330 C2
Carhuas Peru 9°15S 77°39W 330 B2
Carhué Argentina 37°10S 62°50W 334 D3
Caria Turkey 37°20N 28°10E 205 D10
Cariacica Brazil 20°16S 40°25W 333 F3
Cariaco Venezuela 10°29N 63°33W 329 A5
Cariango Angola 10°37S 15°20E 265 E3
Cariati Italy 39°30N 16°57E 201 C9
Caribbean Sea W. Indies 15°0N 75°0W 320 C4
Cariboo Mts. Canada 53°0N 121°0W 296 C4
Caribou U.S.A. 46°52N 68°1W 309 B19
Caribou → Man., Canada 59°20N 94°44W 297 B10
Caribou → N.W.T., Canada 61°27N 125°45W 296 A3
Caribou I. Canada 47°22N 85°49W 298 C2
Caribou Is. Canada 61°55N 113°15W 296 A6
Caribou L. Man., Canada 59°21N 96°10W 297 B9
Caribou L. Ont., Canada 50°25N 89°5W 298 B2
Caribou Mts. Canada 59°12N 115°40W 296 B5
Caribou River ⌓ Canada 59°35N 96°35W 297 B9
Caribrod = Dimitrovgrad Serbia 43°2N 22°48E 202 C6
Carichíc Mexico 27°56N 107°3W 318 B3
Caridad Phil. 14°28N 120°53E 127 C1
Carigara Phil. 11°18N 124°41E 233 F5
Carigara B. Phil. 11°22N 124°37E 233 F5
Carignan France 49°38N 5°10E 173 C12
Carignano Italy 44°55N 7°40E 198 D4
Carinda Australia 30°28S 147°41E 283 A7
Cariñena Spain 41°20N 1°13W 196 D3
Carinhanha Brazil 14°15S 44°46W 333 D3
Carinhanha → Brazil 14°20S 43°47W 333 D3
Carini Italy 38°8N 13°11E 200 D6
Cariño Spain 43°45N 7°52W 194 B3
Carínola Italy 41°11N 13°58E 200 A6
Carinthia = Kärnten □ Austria 46°52N 13°30E 180 E6
Carioca, Sa. da Brazil 22°57S 43°13W 135 B1
Caripito Venezuela 10°8N 63°6W 329 A5
Cariré Brazil 3°57S 40°27W 332 B3
Caritianas Brazil 9°20S 63°6W 331 B5
Carles Phil. 11°34N 123°8E 233 F4
Carlet Spain 39°14N 0°31W 197 F4
Carleton, Mt. Canada 47°23N 66°53W 299 C6
Carleton Place Canada 45°8N 76°9W 313 A8
Carletonville S. Africa 26°23S 27°22E 270 C4
Cârlibaba Romania 47°35N 25°8E 183 C10
Carlin U.S.A. 40°43N 116°7W 304 F5
Carlingford L. U.K. 54°3N 6°9W 166 B5
Carlinville U.S.A. 39°17N 89°53W 310 E7
Carlisle Cumb., U.K. 54°54N 2°56W 168 C5
Carlisle Ind., U.S.A. 38°58N 87°24W 311 F9
Carlisle Ky., U.S.A. 38°19N 84°1W 311 F12
Carlisle Pa., U.S.A. 40°12N 77°12W 312 F7
Carlisle I. Australia 20°49S 149°18E 280 b
Carlit, Pic France 42°35N 1°55E 174 F5
Carloforte Italy 39°8N 8°18E 200 C1
Carlos Casares Argentina 35°32S 61°20W 334 D3
Carlos Chagas Brazil 17°43S 40°45W 333 E3
Carlos Tejedor Argentina 35°25S 62°25W 334 D3
Carlota I. Phil. 13°1N 121°53E 232 E3
Carlow Ireland 52°50N 6°56W 166 D5
Carlow □ Ireland 52°43N 6°50W 166 D5
Carlsbad = Karlovy Vary Czech Rep. 50°13N 12°51E 180 A5
Carlsbad Calif., U.S.A. 33°10N 117°21W 307 M9
Carlsbad N. Mex., U.S.A. 32°25N 104°14W 305 K11
Carlsbad Caverns △ U.S.A. 32°10N 104°35W 305 K11
Carlsberg Ridge Ind. Oc. 1°0N 66°0E 273 D5
Carlstadt U.S.A. 40°50N 74°6W 132 A1
Carlton Australia 37°47S 144°57E 128 A1
Carluke U.K. 55°45N 3°50W 167 F5
Carlyle Sask., Canada 49°40N 102°20W 297 D8
Carlyle Ill., U.S.A. 38°37N 89°22W 310 F7
Carlyle L. U.S.A. 38°37N 89°21W 310 F7
Carmacks Canada 62°5N 136°16W 294 E4
Carmagnola Italy 44°51N 7°43E 198 D4
Carman Canada 49°30N 98°0W 297 D9
Carmarthen U.K. 51°52N 4°19W 169 F3
Carmarthen B. U.K. 51°40N 4°30W 169 F3
Carmarthenshire □ U.K. 51°55N 4°13W 169 F3
Carmaux France 44°3N 2°10E 174 D6
Carmel Ind., U.S.A. 39°58N 86°7W 311 E10
Carmel N.Y., U.S.A. 41°26N 73°41W 313 E11
Carmel-by-the-Sea U.S.A. 36°33N 121°55W 306 J5
Carmel Valley U.S.A. 36°29N 121°43W 306 J5
Carmelo Uruguay 34°0S 58°20W 334 C4
Carmen Bolivia 11°40S 67°51W 330 C4
Carmen Paraguay 27°13S 56°12W 335 B4
Carmen Bohol, Phil. 9°50N 124°12E 233 G5
Carmen Cebu, Phil. 10°35N 124°1E 233 F5
Carmen N. Cotabato, Phil. 7°13N 124°45E 233 H5
Carmen Venezuela 1°16N 66°52W 328 C4
Carmen → Mexico 30°42N 106°29W 318 A3
Carmen, I. Mexico 25°57N 111°12W 318 B2
Carmen de Huechuraba Chile 33°20S 70°40W 137 B1
Carmen de la Legua Peru 12°3S 77°7W 124 B2
Carmen de Patagones Argentina 40°50S 63°0W 336 B4
Cármenes Spain 42°58N 5°34W 194 C5
Carmensa Argentina 35°15S 67°40W 334 D2
Carmi B.C., Canada 49°36N 119°8W 296 D5
Carmi Ill., U.S.A. 38°5N 88°10W 311 F8
Carmichael U.S.A. 38°38N 121°19W 306 G5
Carmichael Village Bahamas 25°0N 77°26W 153 b
Carmila Australia 21°55S 149°24E 280 C4
Carmona Costa Rica 10°0N 85°15W 320 E2
Carmona Spain 37°28N 5°42W 195 H5
Carn Ban U.K. 57°7N 4°15W 167 D4
Carn Eige U.K. 57°17N 5°8W 167 D3
Carnac France 47°35N 3°6W 172 E3
Carnamah Australia 29°41S 115°53E 279 E2
Carnarvon W. Austral., Australia 24°51S 113°42E 279 D1
Carnarvon Ont., Canada 45°3N 78°41W 312 A6
Carnarvon Northern Cape, S. Africa 30°56S 22°8E 270 D3
Carnarvon △ Australia 24°54S 148°2E 280 C4
Carnarvon Ra. Queens., Australia 25°15S 148°30E 280 D4
Carnarvon Ra. W. Austral., Australia 25°20S 120°45E 279 E3
Carnatic India 9°40N 77°50E 245 K3
Carnation U.S.A. 47°39N 121°55W 306 C5
Carnaxide Portugal 38°43N 9°14W 126 A1
Carncastle U.K. 54°54N 5°53W 166 B6
Carndonagh Ireland 55°16N 7°15W 166 A4
Carnduff Canada 49°10N 101°50W 297 D8
Carnegie Vic., Australia 37°53S 145°3E 128 B2
Carnegie Pa., U.S.A. 40°24N 80°5W 312 F4
Carnegie, L. Australia 26°5S 122°30E 279 E3
Carnegie Hall New York, U.S.A. 132 c2
Carnegie Ridge Pac. Oc. 1°0S 87°0W 289 H19
Carnic Alps = Karnische Alpen Europe 46°36N 13°0E 180 E6
Carniche Alpi = Karnische Alpen Europe 46°36N 13°0E 180 E6
Carnide Portugal 38°45N 9°10W 126 A1
Carnot C.A.R. 4°59N 15°56E 264 B3
Carnot, C. Australia 34°57S 135°38E 281 E2
Carnot B. Australia 17°20S 122°15E 278 C3
Carnoustie U.K. 56°30N 2°42W 167 E6
Carnsore Pt. Ireland 52°10N 6°22W 166 D5
Caro U.S.A. 43°29N 83°24W 309 D12
Caroço São Tomé & Príncipe 1°32N 7°27E 265 a
Caroga Lake U.S.A. 43°8N 74°28W 313 C10
Carol City U.S.A. 25°56N 80°14W 128 A1
Carolina Brazil 7°10S 47°30W 332 C2
Carolina Puerto Rico 18°23N 65°58W 321 C6
Carolina Mpumalanga, S. Africa 26°5S 30°6E 271 C5
Carolinas Pt. N. Marianas 14°55N 145°38E 302 e
Caroline I. Kiribati 9°58S 150°13W 289 H12
Caroline Is. Micronesia 8°0N 150°0E 288 G6
Caroline Pk. N.Z. 45°57S 167°15E 285 F2
Carondelet Reef Kiribati 5°33S 173°50E 277 B16
Caroni Trin. & Tob. 10°34N 61°23W 323 t
Caroni □ Trin. & Tob. 10°30N 61°22W 323 t
Caroni → Trin. & Tob. 10°37N 61°30W 323 t
Caroní → Venezuela 8°21N 62°43W 329 B5
Caroni Arena Res. Trin. & Tob. 10°33N 61°15W 323 t
Caroni Bird Sanctuary Trin. & Tob. 10°36N 61°28W 323 t
Caroni Swamp Trin. & Tob. 10°36N 61°27W 323 t
Caroníe = Nébrodi, Monti Italy 37°54N 14°35E 201 E7

Caroona Australia 31°24S 150°26E 283 A9
Carora Venezuela 10°11N 70°5W 328 A3
Carpathians Europe 49°30N 21°0E 177 D11
Carpaţii Meridionali Romania 45°30N 25°0E 183 E9
Carpentaria, G. of Australia 14°0S 139°0E 280 A2
Carpentersville U.S.A. 42°6N 88°17W 311 B8
Carpentras France 44°3N 5°2E 175 D9
Carpi Italy 44°47N 10°53E 198 D7
Carpina Brazil 7°51S 35°15W 332 C4
Cărpineni Moldova 46°46N 28°22E 183 D13
Carpinteria U.S.A. 34°24N 119°31W 307 L7
Carpio Spain 41°13N 5°7W 194 D5
Carr Boyd Ra. Australia 16°15S 128°35E 278 C4
Carra, L. Ireland 53°41N 9°14W 166 C2
Carrabelle U.S.A. 29°51N 84°40W 316 F5
Carraig Mhachdire Rois = Carrickmacross Ireland 53°59N 6°43W 166 C5
Carraig na Siúire = Carrick-on-Suir Ireland 52°21N 7°24W 166 D4
Carral Spain 43°14N 8°21W 194 B2
Carranglan Phil. 15°58N 121°4E 232 D3
Carranya ✪ Australia 19°13S 127°46E 278 C4
Carranza, Presa V. Mexico 27°20N 100°50W 318 B4
Carrara Italy 44°5N 10°6E 198 D7
Carrascal Santiago, Chile 33°25S 70°42W 137 B1
Carrascal Phil. 9°22N 125°56E 233 G5
Carrasco △ Bolivia 17°23S 64°59W 331 D5
Carrascosa del Campo Spain 40°2N 2°45W 196 E2
Carrauntoohill Ireland 52°0N 9°45W 166 D2
Carretas, Punta Peru 14°12S 76°17W 330 C2
Carriacou Grenada 12°29N 61°26W 323 q
Carrick-on-Shannon Ireland 53°57N 8°5W 166 C3
Carrick-on-Suir Ireland 52°21N 7°24W 166 D4
Carrickfergus U.K. 54°43N 5°49W 166 B6
Carrickmacross Ireland 53°59N 6°43W 166 C5
Carrickmines Ireland 53°15N 6°10W 120 B3
Carrières-sous-Bois France 48°55N 2°6E 134 A1
Carrières-sous-Poissy France 48°56N 2°2E 134 A1
Carrières-sur-Seine France 48°55N 2°11E 134 A2
Carrieton Australia 32°25S 138°31E 282 B3
Carrigeen B. Ireland 53°24N 6°5W 120 A3
Carrillo Mexico 26°54N 103°55W 318 B4
Carrington U.S.A. 47°27N 99°8W 308 B4
Carrión ➔ Spain 41°53N 4°32W 194 D6
Carrión de los Condes Spain 42°20N 4°37W 194 C6
Carrizal Bajo Chile 28°5S 71°20W 334 B1
Carrizalillo Chile 29°5S 71°30W 334 B1
Carrizo Cr. ➔ U.S.A. 36°55N 103°55W 305 H12
Carrizo Plain ⌂ U.S.A. 35°11N 119°47W 306 K7
Carrizo Springs U.S.A. 28°31N 99°52W 314 G5
Carrizozo U.S.A. 33°38N 105°53W 305 K11
Carroll U.S.A. 42°4N 94°52W 310 D2
Carrollton Ga., U.S.A. 33°35N 85°5W 316 B4
Carrollton Ill., U.S.A. 39°18N 90°24W 310 E6
Carrollton Ky., U.S.A. 38°41N 85°11W 311 F11
Carrollton Mo., U.S.A. 39°22N 93°30W 310 E3
Carrollton Ohio, U.S.A. 40°34N 81°5W 312 F3
Carron ➔ U.K. 57°53N 4°22W 167 D4
Carron, L. U.K. 57°22N 5°35W 167 D3
Carrot ➔ Canada 53°50N 101°17W 297 C8
Carrot River Canada 53°17N 103°35W 297 C8
Carrouges France 48°34N 0°10W 172 D6
Carrù Italy 44°29N 7°52E 198 D4
Carruthers Canada 52°52N 109°16W 297 C7
Carsa Dek Ethiopia 5°13N 39°50E 257 F4
Çarşamba Turkey 41°11N 36°44E 212 B7
Carsòli Italy 42°6N 13°5E 199 F10
Carson Calif., U.S.A. 33°49N 118°16W 307 M8
Carson N. Dak., U.S.A. 46°25N 101°34W 308 B3
Carson ➔ U.S.A. 39°45N 118°40W 306 F8
Carson City Mich., U.S.A. 43°11N 84°51W 311 A12
Carson City Nev., U.S.A. 39°10N 119°46W 306 F7
Carson Sink U.S.A. 39°50N 118°25W 304 G4
Carstensz Pyramid = Jaya, Puncak Indonesia 3°57S 137°17E 231 E9
Cartagena Colombia 10°25N 75°33W 328 A2
Cartagena Spain 37°38N 0°59W 197 H4
Cartago Colombia 4°45N 75°55W 328 C2
Cartago Costa Rica 9°50N 83°55W 320 E3
Cártama Spain 36°43N 4°39W 195 J6
Cartaxo Portugal 39°10N 8°47W 195 F2
Cartaya Spain 37°16N 7°9W 195 H3
Carteret Is. = Kilinailau Is. Papua N. G. 4°45S 155°20E 286 C8
Cartersville U.S.A. 34°10N 84°48W 316 A5
Carterton N.Z. 41°2S 175°31E 284 H4
Carterville U.S.A. 37°46N 89°5W 310 G7
Carthage Tunisia 36°52N 10°20E 200 F3
Carthage Ill., U.S.A. 40°25N 91°8W 310 D5
Carthage Mo., U.S.A. 37°11N 94°19W 308 G6
Carthage N.Y., U.S.A. 43°59N 75°37W 309 D16
Carthage Tex., U.S.A. 32°9N 94°20W 314 E7
Cartier I. Australia 12°31S 123°29E 278 B3
Cartierville Canada 45°31N 73°42W 130 A1
Cartwright Canada 53°41N 56°58W 299 B8
Caruachi, Represa de Venezuela 8°9N 62°50W 248 B5
Caruaru Brazil 8°15S 35°55W 332 C4
Carúpano Venezuela 10°39N 63°15W 329 A5
Caruray Phil. 10°20N 119°0E 233 F2
Carutapera Brazil 1°13S 46°1W 332 B2
Caruthersville U.S.A. 36°11N 89°39W 308 G9
Carvalho Brazil 2°16S 51°29W 329 D7
Carvin France 50°30N 2°57E 173 B9
Carvoeiro Brazil 1°30S 61°59W 329 D5
Carvoeiro, C. Portugal 39°21N 9°24W 195 F1
Cary Ill., U.S.A. 42°13N 88°14W 311 B8
Cary N.C., U.S.A. 35°47N 78°46W 315 D15
Casa, Pas de la = Envalira, Port d' Europe 42°33N 1°43E 196 C6
Casa Branca Brazil 21°46S 47°4W 333 F2
Casa Branca Portugal 38°29N 8°12W 195 G2
Casa de Piedra Argentina 38°5S 67°28W 334 D2
Casa de Piedra, Embalse Argentina 38°5S 67°32W 334 D2
Casa Grande U.S.A. 32°53N 111°45W 305 K8
Casa Loma Canada 43°41N 79°24W 141 A2
Casa Nova Brazil 9°25S 41°5W 332 C3
Casa Verde Brazil 23°29S 46°40W 137 A1
Casablanca Chile 33°20S 71°25W 334 C1
Casablanca Morocco 33°36N 7°36W 260 B3
Casablanca ☐ Morocco 33°38N 7°30W 260 B3
Casacalenda Italy 41°44N 14°51E 199 G11
Casal Morena Italy 41°49N 12°37E 136 C2
Casalbordino Italy 42°9N 14°35E 199 F11
Casale Monferrato Italy 45°8N 8°27E 198 C5
Casalmaggiore Italy 44°59N 10°26E 198 D7
Casalotti Italy 41°54N 12°22E 136 B1
Casalpusterlengo Italy 45°11N 9°39E 198 C6
Casamance ➔ Senegal 12°33N 16°46W 262 C1
Casanare ☐ Colombia 5°30N 72°0W 328 B3
Casanare ➔ Colombia 6°2N 69°51W 328 B4
Casarano Italy 40°0N 18°10E 201 B11
Casares Spain 36°27N 5°16W 195 J5
Casas Ibáñez Spain 39°17N 1°30W 197 F3
Casasimarro Spain 39°22N 2°3W 197 F2
Casatejada Spain 39°54N 5°40W 194 F5
Casavieja Spain 40°17N 4°46W 194 E6
Cascada de Basaseachic △ Mexico 28°9N 108°15W 318 B3
Cascade Seychelles 4°39S 55°29E 272 c
Cascade Idaho, U.S.A. 44°31N 116°2W 304 C5
Cascade Iowa, U.S.A. 42°18N 91°0W 310 B6
Cascade Mont., U.S.A. 47°16N 111°42W 304 C8
Cascade Heights U.S.A. 33°43N 84°26W 113 E2
Cascade Locks U.S.A. 45°40N 121°54W 306 E5
Cascade Pt. N.Z. 44°1S 168°20E 285 E3
Cascade Ra. U.S.A. 47°0N 121°30W 306 C5
Cascade Res. U.S.A. 44°32N 116°3W 304 D5
Cascades, Pte. des Réunion 21°9S 55°51E 272 f
Cascais Portugal 38°41N 9°25W 195 G1
Cascavel Ceará, Brazil 4°7S 38°14W 332 B4
Cascavel Paraná, Brazil 24°57S 53°28W 335 A5
Cáscina Italy 43°41N 10°33E 198 E7
Casco B. U.S.A. 43°45N 70°0W 309 D19
Case Noyale Mauritius 20°23S 57°22E 272 e
Case-Pilote Martinique 14°38N 61°9W 322 j
Caselle Torinese Italy 45°10N 7°39E 198 C4
Caserta Italy 41°4N 14°20E 201 A7
Casey Antarctica 66°0S 76°0E 151 C8
Casey Ill., U.S.A. 39°18N 87°59W 311 E9
Caseyr, Raas = Asir, Ras Somali Rep. 11°55N 51°10E 267 E7
Cashel Ireland 52°30N 7°53W 166 D4
Casibare ➔ Colombia 3°48N 72°18W 328 C3
Casiguran Phil. 16°22N 122°7E 232 C4
Casiguran Sound Phil. 16°6N 121°58E 232 C3
Casilda Argentina 33°10S 61°10W 334 C3
Casim = General Toshevo Bulgaria 43°42N 28°6E 203 C12
Casimcea Romania 44°45N 28°23E 183 F13
Casino N.S.W., Australia 28°52S 153°3E 281 D5
Casino New Orleans, U.S.A. 131 b2
Casiquiare ➔ Venezuela 2°1N 67°7W 328 C4
Casitas Peru 3°54S 80°39W 330 A1
Čáslav Czech Rep. 49°54N 15°22E 180 B8
Casma Peru 9°30S 78°20W 330 B2
Casmalia U.S.A. 34°50N 120°32W 307 L6
Cásola Valsénio Italy 44°12N 11°40E 199 D8
Cásoli Italy 42°7N 14°18E 199 F11
Caspe Spain 41°14N 0°1W 196 D4
Casper U.S.A. 42°51N 106°19W 304 E10
Caspian Depression Eurasia 47°0N 48°0E 191 G9
Caspian Sea Eurasia 43°0N 50°0E 187 F9
Cass City U.S.A. 43°36N 83°10W 312 C1
Cass Lake U.S.A. 47°23N 94°37W 308 B6
Cassà de la Selva Spain 41°53N 2°52E 196 D7
Cassadaga U.S.A. 42°20N 79°19W 312 D5
Cassai Angola 10°33S 21°59E 265 E4
Cassai ➔ Angola 3°2S 16°57E 265 E4
Cassamba Angola 13°6S 20°18E 265 E4
Cassano allo Iónio Italy 39°47N 16°20E 201 C9
Cassel France 50°48N 2°30E 173 B9
Casselberry U.S.A. 28°41N 81°20W 317 G8
Casselman Canada 45°19N 75°5W 313 A9
Casselton U.S.A. 46°54N 97°13W 308 B5
Cassiar Mts. Canada 59°30N 130°30W 296 B2
Cassilândia Brazil 19°9S 51°45W 331 D7
Cassilis Australia 32°3S 149°58E 283 B8
Cassinga Angola 15°5S 16°4E 265 F3
Cassino Italy 41°30N 13°49E 200 A6
Cassis France 43°14N 5°32E 175 E9
Cassoalala Angola 9°30S 14°22E 265 D2
Cassoango Angola 13°42S 20°56E 265 E4
Cassongue Angola 11°53S 15°2E 265 E3
Cassopolis U.S.A. 41°55N 86°1W 311 C10
Cassunda Angola 10°57S 21°3E 265 E4
Cassville Mo., U.S.A. 36°41N 93°52W 308 G7
Cassville Wis., U.S.A. 42°43N 90°59W 310 B6
Castagneto Carducci Italy 43°9N 10°36E 198 E7
Castaic U.S.A. 34°30N 118°38W 307 L8
Castalia U.S.A. 41°24N 82°49W 312 E2
Castanhal Brazil 1°18S 47°55W 332 B2
Castara Trin. & Tob. 11°17N 60°42W 323 s
Castara B. Trin. & Tob. 11°17N 60°42W 323 s
Castéggio Italy 45°0N 9°7E 198 C5
Castejón de Monegros Spain 41°37N 0°15W 196 D4
Castel Guadeloupe 16°15N 61°35W 322 b
Castèl di Leva Italy 41°46N 12°33E 136 C2
Castèl di Sangro Italy 41°47N 14°6E 199 G11
Castèl San Giovanni Italy 45°4N 9°26E 198 C6
Castèl San Pietro Terme Italy 44°24N 11°35E 199 D8
Castèl Sant'Angelo Rome, Italy 136 b1
Castelbuono Italy 37°56N 14°5E 201 E7
Castelfidardo Italy 43°28N 13°33E 199 E10
Castelfiorentino Italy 43°36N 10°58E 198 E7
Castelfranco Emília Italy 44°37N 11°3E 198 D8
Castelfranco Véneto Italy 45°40N 11°55E 199 C8
Casteljaloux France 44°19N 0°6E 174 D4
Castellabate Italy 40°17N 14°57E 201 B7
Castellammare, G. di Italy 38°8N 12°54E 200 D5
Castellammare del Golfo Italy 38°1N 12°53E 200 D5
Castellammare di Stábia Italy 40°42N 14°29E 201 B7
Castellamonte Italy 45°23N 7°42E 198 C4
Castellane France 43°50N 6°31E 175 E10
Castellaneta Italy 40°38N 16°56E 201 B9
Castelli Argentina 36°7S 57°47W 334 D4
Castelló de la Plana Spain 39°58N 0°3W 196 F4
Castellón de la Plana ☐ Spain 40°15N 0°5W 196 E4
Castellote Spain 40°48N 0°15W 196 E4
Castelmáuro Italy 41°50N 14°43E 199 G11
Castelnau-de-Médoc France 45°2N 0°48W 174 C3
Castelnau-Magnoac France 43°17N 0°31E 174 E4
Castelnaudary France 43°20N 1°58E 174 E5
Castelnovo ne' Monti Italy 44°26N 10°24E 198 D7
Castelnuovo di Val di Cécina Italy 43°12N 10°59E 198 E7
Castelo = Manuel Urbano Brazil 8°53S 69°18W 330 B4
Castelo Brazil 20°33S 41°14W 333 F3
Castelo, Pta. do Azores 36°56N 25°1W 153 d4
Castelo Branco Azores 38°31N 28°44W 153 d1
Castelo Branco Portugal 39°50N 7°31W 194 F3
Castelo Branco ☐ Portugal 39°52N 7°45W 194 F3
Castelo de Paiva Portugal 41°2N 8°16W 194 D2
Castelo de Vide Portugal 39°25N 7°27W 195 F3
Castelo do Piauí Brazil 5°20S 41°33W 332 C3
Castelrosso = Megisti Greece 36°8N 29°34E 205 E11
Castelsardo Italy 40°55N 8°43E 200 B1
Castelsarrasin France 44°2N 1°7E 174 D5
Casteltérmini Italy 37°32N 13°39E 200 E6
Castelvetrano Italy 37°41N 12°47E 200 E5
Castendo Angola 8°39S 14°10E 265 D2
Casterton Australia 37°30S 141°30E 282 D4
Castets France 43°52N 1°6W 174 E2
Castiglion Fiorentino Italy 43°20N 11°55E 199 E8
Castiglione = Bou Ismaïl Algeria 36°38N 2°42E 261 A5
Castiglione del Lago Italy 43°7N 12°3E 199 E9
Castiglione della Pescáia Italy 42°46N 10°53E 198 F7
Castiglione delle Stiviere Italy 45°23N 10°29E 198 C7
Castilblanco Spain 39°17N 5°5W 195 F5
Castile U.S.A. 42°38N 78°3W 312 D6
Castilla Peru 5°12S 80°38W 330 B1
Castilla, Playa de Spain 37°0N 6°33W 195 J4
Castilla-La Mancha ☐ Spain 39°30N 3°30W 195 F7
Castilla y Leon ☐ Spain 42°0N 5°0W 194 D6
Castillo de Locubín Spain 37°32N 3°56W 195 H7
Castillo de San Marcos ⌂ U.S.A. 29°54N 81°19W 316 F8
Castillon-en-Couserans France 42°56N 1°1E 174 F5
Castillonès France 44°39N 0°37E 174 D4
Castillos Uruguay 34°12S 53°52W 335 C5
Castle Bruce Dominica 15°26N 61°16W 323 k
Castle Dale U.S.A. 39°13N 111°1W 304 G8
Castle Douglas U.K. 54°56N 3°56W 167 G5
Castle Harbour Bermuda 32°21N 64°40W 153 a
Castle Mt. Jamaica 18°8N 76°22W 320 a
Castle of Good Hope Cape Town, S. Africa 118 c3
Castle Roads Bermuda 32°20N 64°40W 153 a
Castle Rock Colo., U.S.A. 39°22N 104°51W 304 G11
Castle Rock Wash., U.S.A. 46°17N 122°54W 306 D4
Castle Rock Pt. St. Helena 16°1S 5°45W 153 h
Castlebar Ireland 53°52N 9°18W 166 C2
Castlebay U.K. 56°57N 7°31W 167 E1
Castleblaney Ireland 54°7N 6°44W 166 B5
Castlecliff N.Z. 39°57S 175°5E 284 F4
Castlederg U.K. 54°42N 7°35W 166 B4
Castleford U.K. 53°43N 1°21W 168 D6
Castlegar Canada 49°20N 117°40W 296 D5
Castleknock Ireland 53°22N 6°21W 120 A1
Castlemaine Vic., Australia 37°2S 144°12E 282 D6
Castlemaine Kerry, Ireland 52°10N 9°42W 166 D2
Castlepoint N.Z. 40°54S 176°15E 284 G5
Castlepollard Ireland 53°41N 7°19W 166 C4
Castlerea Ireland 53°46N 8°29W 166 C3
Castlereagh ➔ Australia 30°12S 147°32E 283 A7
Castlereagh B. Australia 12°10S 135°10E 280 A2
Castleton U.S.A. 43°37N 73°11W 313 C11
Castleton Corners U.S.A. 40°36N 74°8W 132 C1
Castleton-on-Hudson U.S.A. 42°31N 73°45W 313 D11
Castletown I. of Man 54°5N 4°38W 168 C3
Castletown Bearhaven Ireland 51°39N 9°55W 166 E2
Castor Canada 52°15N 111°50W 296 C6
Castor ➔ Canada 53°24N 78°58W 298 B4
Castorland U.S.A. 43°53N 75°31W 313 C9
Castres France 43°37N 2°13E 174 E6
Castricum Neths. 52°33N 4°40E 170 B4
Castries St. Lucia 14°2N 60°58W 323 m
Castril Spain 37°48N 2°46W 195 H8
Castro Brazil 24°45S 50°0W 335 A6
Castro Chile 42°30S 73°50W 336 B2
Castro Alves Brazil 12°46S 39°33W 333 D4
Castro del Río Spain 37°41N 4°29W 195 H6
Castro-Urdiales Spain 43°23N 3°11W 194 B7
Castro Valley U.S.A. 37°41N 122°5W 306 H4
Castro Verde Portugal 37°41N 8°4W 195 H2
Castrogiovanni = Enna Italy 37°34N 14°16E 201 E7
Castrojeriz Spain 42°17N 4°9W 194 C6
Castropol Spain 43°32N 7°0W 194 B3
Castroreale Italy 38°6N 15°12E 201 D8
Castrovillari Italy 39°49N 16°12E 201 C9
Castroville U.S.A. 36°46N 121°45W 306 J5
Castrovirreyna Peru 13°20S 75°18W 330 C2
Castuera Spain 38°43N 5°37W 195 G5
Caswell Sound N.Z. 44°59S 167°8E 285 E2
Çat Turkey 39°40N 41°3E 213 C9
Cat Ba, Dao Vietnam 20°50N 107°0E 236 B6
Cat Ba △ Vietnam 20°47N 107°3E 236 B6
Cat I. Bahamas 24°30N 75°30W 321 B4
Cat L. Canada 51°40N 91°50W 298 B1
Cat Lake Canada 51°40N 91°50W 298 B1
Cat Tien △ Vietnam 11°25N 107°17E 237 G6
Čata Slovak Rep. 47°58N 18°38E 181 D11
Catabola Angola 12°9S 17°16E 265 E3
Catacamas Honduras 14°54N 85°56W 320 D2
Catacaos Peru 5°20S 80°45W 330 B1
Cataguases Brazil 21°23S 42°39W 333 F3
Catagupan Phil. 8°1N 116°58E 233 G1
Cataingan Phil. 12°0N 124°0E 232 E4
Çatak Turkey 38°1N 43°8E 213 C10
Çatalağzı Turkey 41°30N 31°59E 212 B4
Catalão Brazil 18°10S 47°57W 333 E2
Çatalca Turkey 41°8N 28°27E 203 E12
Catalina Nfld. & L., Canada 48°31N 53°4W 299 C9
Catalina Chile 25°13S 69°43W 334 B2
Catalina Ariz., U.S.A. 32°30N 110°50W 305 K8
Catalonia = Cataluña ☐ Spain 41°40N 1°15E 196 D6
Cataluña ☐ Spain 41°40N 1°15E 196 D6
Çatalzeytin Turkey 41°57N 34°12E 212 B6
Catamarca Argentina 28°30S 65°50W 334 B2
Catamarca ☐ Argentina 27°0S 65°50W 334 B2
Catanauan Phil. 13°36N 122°19E 232 E4
Catanduanes ☐ Phil. 13°50N 124°20E 232 E5
Catanduva Brazil 21°5S 48°58W 335 A6
Catánia Italy 37°30N 15°6E 201 E8
Catánia, G. di Italy 37°24N 15°8E 201 E8
Cataño Puerto Rico 18°27N 66°7W 321 b
Catanzaro Italy 38°54N 16°35E 201 D9
Cataouatche, L. U.S.A. 29°50N 90°14W 131 B1
Catarman Camiguin, Phil. 9°8N 124°40E 233 G5
Catarman N. Samar, Phil. 12°28N 124°35E 232 E5
Catatumbo ➔ Venezuela 9°21N 71°45W 328 B3
Cataula U.S.A. 32°39N 84°52W 316 C5
Catbalogan Phil. 11°46N 124°53E 233 F5
Catchacoma Canada 44°44N 78°19W 312 B6
Cateco Cangola Angola 8°28S 15°51E 265 D3
Cateel Phil. 7°47N 126°24E 233 H6
Cateel B. Phil. 7°54N 126°25E 233 H6
Catembe Mozam. 26°0S 32°33E 271 C5
Catende Angola 11°14S 21°30E 265 E4
Catende Brazil 8°40S 35°43W 332 C4
Caterham U.K. 51°15N 0°4W 169 F7
Catete Angola 9°6S 13°43E 265 D2
Catete Rio de J., Brazil 22°54S 43°10W 135 B1
Catford U.K. 51°26N 0°1W 125 B3
Cathair na Mart = Westport Ireland 53°48N 9°31W 166 C2
Cathair Saidhbhín = Cahersiveen Ireland 51°56N 10°14W 166 E1
Cathcart N.S.W., Australia 36°52S 149°24E 283 D8
Cathcart Eastern Cape, S. Africa 32°18S 27°10E 270 D4
Cathedral City U.S.A. 33°47N 116°28W 307 M10
Cathedral Rock △ Australia 30°24S 152°15E 283 A10
Catherine, L. U.S.A. 28°30N 81°24W 133 B2
Cathlamet U.S.A. 46°12N 123°23W 306 D3
Catió Guinea-Biss. 11°17N 15°15W 262 C1
Catisimiña Venezuela 4°5N 63°40W 329 C5
Catita Brazil 9°31S 43°1W 332 C3
Cativa Panama 9°21N 79°49W 320 c
Catlettsburg U.S.A. 38°25N 82°36W 309 F12
Catlin U.S.A. 40°4N 87°42W 311 D9
Catlins N.Z. 46°22S 169°17E 285 G4
Çatma Dağı Turkey 38°25N 29°50E 205 C11
Catmon Phil. 10°43N 124°1E 233 F5
Catoche, C. Mexico 21°35N 87°5W 319 C7
Catolé do Rocha Brazil 6°21S 37°45W 332 C4
Catota Angola 13°57S 17°30E 265 E3
Cátria, Mte. Italy 43°28N 12°42E 199 E9
Catriló Argentina 36°26S 63°24W 334 D3
Catrimani Brazil 0°27N 61°41W 329 C5
Catrimani ➔ Brazil 0°28N 61°44W 329 C5
Catskill U.S.A. 42°14N 73°52W 313 D11
Catskill ⌂ U.S.A. 42°8N 74°39W 313 D10
Catskill Mts. U.S.A. 42°10N 74°25W 313 D10
Catt, Mt. Australia 13°49S 134°23E 280 A1
Cattaraugus U.S.A. 42°20N 78°52W 312 D6
Cattaro = Kotor Montenegro 42°25N 18°47E 202 D2
Catterick U.K. 54°23N 1°37W 168 C6
Cattólica Italy 43°58N 12°44E 199 E9
Cattólica Eraclea Italy 37°26N 13°24E 200 E6
Catu Brazil 12°21S 38°23W 333 D4
Catuala Angola 16°25S 19°2E 265 F3
Catuane Mozam. 26°48S 32°18E 271 C5
Catubig Phil. 12°24N 125°3E 232 E5
Catumbela Angola 12°25S 13°34E 265 E2
Catumbela ➔ Angola 12°29S 13°28E 265 E2
Catur Mozam. 13°45S 35°30E 269 E4
Catwick Is. = Hon Hai Vietnam 10°0N 109°0E 237 H7
Cauayan Isabela, Phil. 16°56N 121°46E 232 C3
Cauayan Neg. Occ., Phil. 9°58N 122°37E 233 G4
Caubvick, Mt. = Iberville, Mt. d' Canada 58°50N 63°50W 295 F19
Cauca ☐ Colombia 2°30N 76°50W 328 C2
Cauca ➔ Colombia 8°54N 74°28W 328 B3
Caucaia Brazil 3°40S 38°35W 332 B4
Caucasia Colombia 8°0N 75°12W 328 B2
Caucasus Mountains Eurasia 42°50N 44°0E 191 J7
Caucete Argentina 31°38S 68°20W 334 C2
Caudete Spain 38°42N 1°2W 197 G3
Caudry France 50°7N 3°22E 173 B10
Cauese Mts. Mozam. 15°14S 30°33E 269 F3
Caulfield Australia 37°52S 145°1E 128 B2
Caulnes France 48°18N 2°10W 172 D4
Caulónia Italy 38°23N 16°24E 201 D9
Caungula Angola 8°26S 18°38E 265 D3
Cauquenes Chile 36°0S 72°22W 334 D1
Caura ➔ Venezuela 7°38N 64°53W 329 B5
Caurés ➔ Brazil 1°21S 62°20W 329 D5
Cauresi ➔ Mozam. 17°8S 33°0E 269 F3
Căuşani Moldova 46°38N 29°25E 183 D14
Causapscal Canada 48°19N 67°12W 299 C6
Causeway Bay Hong Kong, China 122 c3
Caussade France 44°10N 1°33E 174 D5
Causse-Méjean France 44°18N 3°42E 174 D7
Causses du Quercy ⌂ France 44°35N 1°35E 174 D5
Cauterets France 42°52N 0°8W 174 F3
Cauvery ➔ India 11°9N 78°52E 245 J4
Caux, Pays de France 49°38N 0°35E 172 C7
Cava de' Tirreni Italy 40°42N 14°42E 201 B7
Cávado ➔ Portugal 41°32N 8°48W 194 D2
Cavagrande del Cassibile ⌂ Italy 36°58N 15°6E 201 F8
Cavaillon France 43°50N 5°2E 175 E9
Cavalaire-sur-Mer France 43°10N 6°33E 175 E10
Cavalcante Brazil 13°48S 47°30W 333 D2
Cavalese Italy 46°17N 11°27E 199 B8
Cavalier U.S.A. 48°48N 97°37W 308 A5
Cavalla = Cavally ➔ Africa 4°22N 7°32W 262 E3
Cavalla △ Liberia 5°8N 7°20W 262 D3
Cavalli Is. N.Z. 35°0S 173°58E 284 B2
Cavallo, Î. de France 41°22N 9°16E 175 G13
Cavally ➔ Africa 4°22N 7°32W 262 E3
Cavan Ireland 54°0N 7°22W 166 B4
Cavan ☐ Ireland 54°1N 7°16W 166 C4
Cavárzere Italy 45°8N 12°5E 199 C9
Cavazuccherina = Iésolo Italy 45°32N 12°38E 199 C9
Çavdarhisar Turkey 39°12N 29°37E 205 B11
Çavdır Turkey 37°10N 29°42E 205 D11
Cave Creek U.S.A. 33°50N 111°57W 305 K8
Cave Run L. U.S.A. 38°5N 83°25W 311 F13
Cave Spring U.S.A. 34°6N 85°20W 316 A4
Cavenagh Ra. Australia 26°12S 127°55E 279 E4
Cavendish Australia 37°31S 142°2E 282 D5
Caverna do Peruaçu Brazil 15°0S 44°45W 333 E3
Caverna do Peruaçu △ Brazil 15°0S 44°35W 333 E3
Caviana, I. Brazil 0°10N 50°10W 329 C7
Cavili I. Phil. 9°16N 120°49E 233 G3
Cavite Phil. 14°29N 120°54E 127 C1
Cavite ☐ Phil. 14°15N 120°50E 232 D3
Caviúna = Rolândia Brazil 23°18S 51°23W 335 A5
Cavnic Romania 47°40N 23°52E 183 C8
Cavour Italy 44°47N 7°22E 198 D4
Cavtat Croatia 42°35N 18°13E 202 D2
Cawayan Phil. 11°56N 123°46E 233 F4
Cawayanon = Vintar Phil. 18°14N 120°39E 232 B3
Cawndilla L. Australia 32°30S 142°15E 282 B5
Cawnpore = Kanpur India 26°28N 80°20E 243 F9
Caxias Brazil 4°55S 43°20W 332 B3
Caxias Lisboa, Portugal 38°42N 9°16W 126 A1
Caxias do Sul Brazil 29°10S 51°10W 335 B5
Caxito Angola 8°30S 13°30E 265 D2
Caxopa Angola 11°52S 23°52E 265 E4
Çay Turkey 38°35N 31°1E 212 C4
Cay Pt. Bahamas 25°59N 77°25W 153 b
Cay Sal Bank Bahamas 23°45N 80°0W 320 B4
Cayambe Napo, Ecuador 0°2N 77°59W 328 C2
Cayambe Quito, Ecuador 0°3N 78°8W 328 C2
Cayce U.S.A. 33°58N 81°4W 316 B8
Çaycuma Turkey 41°25N 32°4E 212 B5
Çayeli Turkey 41°5N 40°45E 213 B9
Cayenne Fr. Guiana 5°5N 52°18W 329 B7
Cayenne ☐ Fr. Guiana 5°0N 53°0W 329 C7
Cayey Puerto Rico 18°7N 66°10W 321 b
Caygören Barajı Turkey 39°15N 28°12E 205 B10
Çayıralan Turkey 39°17N 35°38E 212 C6
Çaylı Azerbaijan 40°20N 46°49E 191 K8
Caylus France 44°15N 1°47E 174 D5
Cayman Brac Cayman Is. 19°43N 79°49W 320 C4
Cayman Is. ☑ W. Indies 19°40N 80°30W 320 C3
Cayman Trench Caribbean 17°0N 83°0W 320 C3
Caynabo Somali Rep. 9°20N 46°25E 267 C6
Cayon St. Kitts & Nevis 17°21N 62°52W 322 d
Cayres France 44°55N 3°48E 174 D7
Cayuga Ont., Canada 42°59N 79°50W 312 D5
Cayuga Ind., U.S.A. 39°57N 87°28W 311 E9
Cayuga N.Y., U.S.A. 42°54N 76°44W 313 D8
Cayuga Heights U.S.A. 42°27N 76°29W 313 D8
Cayuga L. U.S.A. 42°41N 76°41W 313 D8
Cazage Angola 11°2S 20°45E 265 E4
Cazalla de la Sierra Spain 37°56N 5°45W 195 H5
Căzăneşti Romania 44°36N 27°3E 183 F12
Cazaubon France 43°56N 0°3W 174 E3
Cazaux et de Sanguinet, Étang de France 44°29N 1°10W 174 D2
Cazenovia U.S.A. 42°56N 75°51W 313 D9
Cazères France 43°13N 1°5E 174 E5
Cazin Bos.-H. 44°57N 15°57E 199 D12
Čazma Croatia 45°45N 16°39E 199 C13
Cazombo Angola 11°54S 22°56E 265 E4
Cazorla Spain 37°55N 3°2W 195 H7
Cazorla, Sierra de Spain 38°5N 2°55W 195 G8
Cea ➔ Spain 42°0N 5°36W 194 C5
Ceamurlia de Jos Romania 44°43N 28°47E 183 F13
Ceanannus Mor Ireland 53°44N 6°53W 166 C5
Ceará = Fortaleza Brazil 3°45S 38°35W 332 B4
Ceará ☐ Brazil 5°0S 40°0W 332 C4
Ceara Abyssal Plain Atl. Oc. 0°0 36°0W 152 F7
Ceara Rise Atl. Oc. 4°30N 43°30W 152 F7
Ceará-Mirim Brazil 5°38S 35°25W 332 C4
Ceatharlach = Carlow Ireland 52°50N 6°56W 166 D5
Ceauru, L. Romania 44°58N 23°11E 183 F8
Cébaco, I. de Panama 7°33N 81°9W 320 E3
Cebeci Turkey 41°7N 28°52E 122 B1
Cebollar Argentina 29°10S 66°35W 334 B2
Cebollera, Sierra de Spain 42°0N 2°30W 196 D2
Cebreros Spain 40°27N 4°28W 194 E6
Cebu Phil. 10°18N 123°54E 233 F4
Cebu ☐ Phil. 10°20N 123°40E 233 F4
Čečava Bos.-H. 44°42N 17°44E 182 F2
Ceccano Italy 41°34N 13°20E 200 A6
Cecchignola Italy 41°48N 12°29E 136 C2
Cece Hungary 46°46N 18°39E 182 D3
Cecil Ivory C. 6°15N 4°25W 262 D4
Cecil Plains Australia 27°30S 151°11E 281 D5
Cecilienhof, Schloss Germany 52°35N 13°5E 115 B1
Cécina Italy 43°19N 10°31E 198 E7
Cécina ➔ Italy 43°18N 10°29E 198 E7
Ceclavín Spain 39°50N 6°45W 194 F4
Cedar ➔ U.S.A. 41°17N 91°21W 310 C5
Cedar City U.S.A. 37°41N 113°4W 305 H7
Cedar Creek Res. U.S.A. 32°11N 96°4W 314 E6
Cedar Falls Iowa, U.S.A. 42°32N 92°27W 310 B4
Cedar Falls Wash., U.S.A. 47°25N 121°45W 306 C5
Cedar Grove Georgia, U.S.A. 33°40N 84°16W 113 C3
Cedar Grove Ind., U.S.A. 39°22N 84°56W 311 E12
Cedar Key U.S.A. 29°8N 83°2W 317 F6
Cedar L. Canada 53°10N 100°0W 297 C9
Cedar Lake U.S.A. 41°22N 87°26W 311 C9
Cedar Park U.S.A. 30°30N 97°49W 314 F6
Cedar Point U.S.A. 41°44N 83°21W 311 C13
Cedar Rapids U.S.A. 41°59N 91°40W 310 C5
Cedar Tree Pt. Antigua & B. 17°42N 61°53W 322 c
Cedartown U.S.A. 34°1N 85°15W 316 A4
Cedarvale Canada 55°1N 128°22W 296 B3
Cedarvale Park Canada 43°42N 79°26W 141 A2
Cedarville KwaZulu Natal, S. Africa 30°23S 29°3E 271 D4
Cedarville Ill., U.S.A. 42°23N 89°38W 310 B7
Cedarville Ohio, U.S.A. 39°44N 83°49W 311 E13
Cedeira Spain 43°39N 8°2W 194 B2
Cedral Mexico 23°50N 100°45W 318 C4
Cedrino ➔ Italy 40°11N 9°24E 200 B2
Cedro Brazil 6°34S 39°3W 332 C4
Cedros Azores 38°38N 28°42W 153 d1
Cedros, I. Mexico 28°12N 115°15W 318 B1
Cedros B. Trin. & Tob. 10°16N 61°54W 323 t
Cedros Pt. Trin. & Tob. 10°7N 61°49W 323 t
Ceduna Australia 32°7S 133°46E 281 E1
Cedynia Poland 52°53N 14°12E 185 F1
Cée Spain 42°57N 9°10W 194 C1
Ceel Gaal Somali Rep. 10°58N 50°20E 267 B7
Ceel Waaq Kenya 2°49N 40°56E 267 D5
Ceelbuur = El Bur Somali Rep. 4°40N 46°37E 267 D6
Ceeldheere Galguduud, Somali Rep. 3°50N 47°8E 267 D6
Ceeldheere Galguduud, Somali Rep. 5°22N 46°11E 267 C6
Ceerigaabo Somali Rep. 10°35N 47°20E 267 B6
Cefalù Italy 38°2N 14°1E 201 D7
Cega ➔ Spain 41°33N 4°46W 194 D6
Cegléd Hungary 47°11N 19°47E 182 C4
Céglie Messápico Italy 40°39N 17°31E 201 B10
Cehegín Spain 38°6N 1°48W 197 G3
Ceheng China 24°58N 105°48E 228 E5
Cehu-Silvaniei Romania 47°24N 23°9E 183 C8
Ceiba Puerto Rico 18°16N 65°39W 321 b
Ceica Romania 46°53N 22°10E 182 D7
Ceira ➔ Portugal 40°13N 8°16W 194 E2
Çekerek Turkey 40°4N 35°29E 212 B6
Cekik Indonesia 8°12S 114°27E 231 J17
Cela Angola 11°25S 15°7E 265 E3
Čelákovice Czech Rep. 50°10N 14°46E 180 A7
Celano Italy 42°5N 13°33E 199 F10
Celanova Spain 42°9N 7°58W 194 C3
Celaque △ Honduras 14°30N 88°43W 320 D2
Celaya Mexico 20°31N 100°37W 318 C4
Celebes = Sulawesi Indonesia 2°0S 120°0E 235 C5
Celebes Sea Indonesia 3°0N 123°0E 231 D6
Celendín Peru 6°52S 78°10W 330 B2
Celestial Mts. = Tian Shan Asia 40°30N 76°0E 217 D9
Čelić Bos.-H. 44°43N 18°49E 182 F3
Celica Ecuador 4°7S 79°59W 328 D2
Celina U.S.A. 40°33N 84°35W 311 D12
Celinac Bos.-H. 44°44N 17°22E 182 F2
Celje Slovenia 46°16N 15°18E 199 B12
Celldömölk Hungary 47°16N 17°10E 182 C2
Celle Germany 52°37N 10°4E 178 C6
Celorico da Beira Portugal 40°38N 7°24W 194 E3
Celtic Sea Atl. Oc. 50°9N 9°34W 165 F2
Çeltikçi Turkey 37°32N 30°29E 205 D12
Çemişgezek Turkey 39°3N 38°56E 213 C8
Cempaka Putih Indonesia 6°10S 106°51E 122 B2
Cempi, Teluk Indonesia 8°44S 118°22E 235 D5
Cenderawasih, Teluk Indonesia 3°0S 135°20E 231 E9
Cenepa ➔ Peru 4°40S 78°10W 328 D2
Cengelköy Turkey 41°2N 29°3E 122 B2
Cengkareng Indonesia 6°9S 106°45E 122 A1
Cengong China 27°13N 108°44E 228 D7
Ceno ➔ Italy 44°43N 10°5E 198 D7
Centallo Italy 44°30N 7°35E 198 D4
Centelles Spain 41°50N 2°14E 196 D7
Centenário do Sul Brazil 22°48S 51°36W 333 F1
Centennial Olympic Park U.S.A. 33°46N 84°23W 113 B2
Centennial Park Australia 33°53S 151°14E 139 B2
Center N. Dak., U.S.A. 47°7N 101°18W 308 B3
Center Tex., U.S.A. 31°48N 94°11W 314 F7
Center Hill Fla., U.S.A. 28°38N 82°3W 317 G7
Center Hill Georgia, U.S.A. 33°46N 84°29W 113 B2
Center Point U.S.A. 42°12N 91°46W 310 B5
Centerburg U.S.A. 40°18N 82°42W 312 F2
Centerville Calif., U.S.A. 36°44N 119°30W 306 J7
Centerville Iowa, U.S.A. 40°44N 92°52W 310 D4
Centerville Ohio, U.S.A. 39°38N 84°8W 311 E12
Centerville Pa., U.S.A. 40°3N 79°59W 312 F5
Centerville Tenn., U.S.A. 35°47N 87°28W 315 D11
Centerville Tex., U.S.A. 31°16N 95°59W 314 F7
Cento Italy 44°43N 11°17E 199 D8
Centola Italy 40°3N 15°18E 201 B8
Centraal Station Amsterdam, Neths. 112 a3
Central = Tsentralnyy ☐ Russia 52°0N 40°0E 190 D3
Central Brazil 11°8S 42°8W 332 D3
Central Alaska, U.S.A. 65°35N 144°48W 303 D11
Central ☐ Ghana 5°30N 1°0W 263 D4
Central ☐ Kenya 0°30S 37°0E 268 C4
Central ☐ Malawi 13°30S 33°30E 269 E3
Central ☐ Papua N. G. 10°10S 148°0E 286 F5
Central ☐ Zambia 14°25S 28°50E 269 E2
Central, Cordillera Bolivia 18°30S 64°55W 331 D5
Central, Cordillera Colombia 5°0N 75°0W 328 C3
Central, Cordillera Costa Rica 10°10N 84°5W 320 D3
Central, Cordillera Dom. Rep. 19°15N 71°0W 321 C5
Central, Cordillera Peru 7°0S 77°30W 330 B2
Central, Cordillera Phil. 17°20N 120°57E 232 C3
Central, Cordillera Puerto Rico 18°8N 66°35W 321 b
Central, Gare Montréal, Canada 130 c2
Central African Empire = Central African Rep. ■ Africa 7°0N 20°0E 264 A4
Central African Rep. ■ Africa 7°0N 20°0E 264 A4
Central America America 12°0N 85°0W 292 H11
Central Australia ✪ Australia 22°30S 128°30E 278 D4
Central Bedfordshire ☐ U.K. 52°5N 0°20W 169 E7
Central Butte Canada 50°48N 106°31W 297 C7
Central City Colo., U.S.A. 39°48N 105°31W 304 G11
Central City Iowa, U.S.A. 42°12N 91°32W 310 B5
Central City Ky., U.S.A. 37°18N 87°7W 308 G10
Central City Nebr., U.S.A. 41°7N 98°0W 308 E4
Central Desert ✪ Australia 19°56S 130°46E 278 C5
Central Equatoria ☐ South Sudan 4°0N 31°0E 257 G3
Central I. Kenya 3°30N 36°0E 268 B4
Central Island △ Kenya 2°33N 36°1E 268 B4
Central Japan Int. ✕ (CJJ) Japan 34°53N 136°45E 223 C8
Central Kalahari ⌂ Botswana 22°36S 23°58E 270 B3
Central Makran Range Pakistan 26°30N 64°15E 240 D2
Central Pacific Basin Pac. Oc. 8°0N 175°0W 288 G10
Central Park New York, U.S.A. 132 a3
Central Park Zoo New York, U.S.A. 132 b2
Central Patricia Canada 51°30N 90°9W 298 B1
Central Point U.S.A. 42°23N 122°55W 304 E2
Central Provinces = Madhya Pradesh ☐ India 22°50N 78°0E 242 J8
Central Ra. Papua N. G. 5°0S 143°0E 286 C2
Central Ra. Trin. & Tob. 10°25N 61°15W 323 t
Central Range Wildlife Sanctuary Trin. & Tob. 10°27N 61°14W 323 t
Central Russian Uplands Europe 54°0N 36°0E 158 E13
Central Siberian Plateau Russia 65°0N 105°0E 210 B12
Central Square U.S.A. 43°17N 76°9W 313 C8
Central Village Jamaica 17°59N 76°55W 320 a
Centralia Ont., Canada 43°17N 81°28W 312 C3
Centralia Ill., U.S.A. 38°32N 89°8W 310 F7
Centralia Mo., U.S.A. 39°13N 92°8W 310 E4
Centralia Wash., U.S.A. 46°43N 122°58W 306 D4
Centre U.S.A. 34°9N 85°41W 316 A4
Centre ☐ Cameroon 4°45N 12°0E 263 E7
Centre de Flacq Mauritius 20°12S 57°43E 272 e
Centreville Mich., U.S.A. 41°55N 85°32W 311 C11
Centreville N.Y., U.S.A. 42°28N 78°14W 312 D6
Centreville Pa., U.S.A. 41°44N 79°45W 312 E5
Century U.S.A. 30°58N 87°16W 317 E2
Century City U.S.A. 34°3N 118°25W 126 B2
Cenxi China 22°57N 110°57E 229 F8
Čeotina ➔ Bos.-H. 43°36N 18°50E 202 C2
Cephalonia = Kefalonia Greece 38°15N 20°30E 207 C2
Čepin Croatia 45°32N 18°34E 182 E3
Ceprano Italy 41°33N 13°31E 200 A6
Ceptia Angola 12°56S 17°35E 265 E3
Ceptura Romania 45°1N 26°21E 183 E11
Cepu Indonesia 7°9S 111°35E 235 D4
Ceram = Seram Indonesia 3°10S 129°0E 231 E7
Ceram Sea = Seram Sea Indonesia 2°30S 128°30E 231 E7
Cerbère France 42°26N 3°10E 174 F7
Cerbicales, Îs. France 41°33N 9°22E 175 G13
Cercal Portugal 37°48N 8°40W 195 H2
Cerdaña Spain 42°22N 1°35E 196 C6
Cerdanyola del Vallès Spain 41°27N 2°8E 114 A1
Cère ➔ France 44°55N 1°49E 174 D5
Cerea Italy 45°12N 11°13E 199 C8
Ceredigion ☐ U.K. 52°16N 4°15W 169 E3
Ceres Argentina 29°55S 61°55W 334 B3
Ceres Brazil 15°17S 49°35W 333 E2
Ceres Western Cape, S. Africa 33°21S 19°18E 270 D2
Ceres Calif., U.S.A. 37°35N 120°57W 306 H6
Céret France 42°30N 2°42E 174 F6
Cereté Colombia 8°53N 75°48W 328 B2
Cerf Seychelles 4°38S 55°40E 272 c
Cerfs, Î. aux Mauritius 20°16S 57°47E 272 e
Cergy France 49°2N 2°4E 173 C9
Cerignola Italy 41°17N 15°53E 201 A8
Cerigo = Kythira Greece 36°8N 23°0E 204 E5
Cerillos Chile 33°29S 70°42W 137 B1
Cérilly France 46°37N 2°50E 173 F9
Cerisiers France 48°8N 3°30E 173 D10
Cerizay France 46°50N 0°40W 172 F6
Çerkeş Turkey 40°49N 32°52E 212 B5
Çerkezköy Turkey 41°17N 28°0E 203 E12
Cerknica Slovenia 45°48N 14°21E 199 C11
Cerkovica Bulgaria 43°41N 24°50E 203 C8
Cermerno Serbia 43°35N 20°25E 202 C4
Çermik Turkey 38°8N 39°26E 213 C8
Cerna Romania 45°4N 28°17E 183 E13
Cerna ➔ Romania 44°38N 23°58E 183 F8
Cernăuţi = Chernivtsi Ukraine 48°15N 25°52E 183 B10
Cernavodă Romania 44°22N 28°3E 183 F13
Cernay France 47°44N 7°10E 173 E14
Cernik Croatia 45°17N 17°22E 182 E2
Cerralvo, I. Mexico 24°15N 109°55W 318 C3
Cërrik Albania 41°2N 19°58E 202 E3
Cerritos Mexico 22°25N 100°15W 318 C4
Cerro Chato Uruguay 33°6S 55°8W 335 C4
Cerro Chovoreca △ Paraguay 19°19S 59°7W 331 D6
Cerro Cofre de Perote △ Mexico 19°29N 97°8W 319 D5
Cerro Corá △ Paraguay 22°35S 56°2W 335 A4
Cerro de la Estrella △ Mexico 19°23N 99°5W 128 B2
Cerro de los Angeles Spain 40°18N 3°41W 127 C1
Cerro de Pasco Peru 10°45S 76°10W 330 C2
Cerro Gordo U.S.A. 39°53N 88°44W 311 E8
Cerro Hoya △ Panama 7°17N 80°45W 320 E3
Cerro Navia Chile 33°25S 70°42W 137 B1
Cerro Saroche △ Venezuela 10°8N 69°33W 328 A4
Cerro Sombrero Chile 52°45S 69°15W 336 D3
Certaldo Italy 43°33N 11°2E 198 E8
Cervantes Phil. 17°0N 120°44E 232 C3
Cervaro ➔ Italy 41°30N 15°52E 201 A8
Cervati, Monte Italy 40°17N 15°29E 201 B8
Cerventes Australia 30°31S 115°3E 279 F2
Cervera Spain 41°40N 1°16E 196 D6
Cervera de Pisuerga Spain 42°51N 4°30W 194 C6
Cervera del Río Alhama Spain 42°2N 1°58W 196 C3
Cervéteri Italy 42°0N 12°6E 199 F9
Cérvia Italy 44°15N 12°22E 199 D9

Cervignano del Friuli
Italy 45°49N 13°20E **199** C10
Cervinara *Italy* 41°1N 14°37E **201** A7
Cervione *France* 42°20N 9°29E **175** F13
Cervo *Spain* 43°40N 7°24W **194** B3
Cesano Boscone *Italy* 45°26N 9°5E **129** B1
César □ *Colombia* 9°0N 73°30W **328** B3
Cesarò *Italy* 37°50N 14°38E **201** E7
Cesate *Italy* 45°35N 9°4E **129** A1
Cesena *Italy* 44°8N 12°15E **199** D9
Cesenático *Italy* 44°12N 12°24E **199** D9
Cēsis *Latvia* 57°18N 25°15E **188** D3
Česká Lípa *Czech Rep.* 50°45N 14°30E **180** A7
Česká Rep. = Czech Rep. ■
Europe 50°0N 15°0E **180** B8
Česká Třebová *Czech Rep.* 49°54N 16°27E **181** B9
České Budějovice
Czech Rep. 48°55N 14°25E **180** C7
České Velenice *Czech Rep.* 48°45N 14°57E **180** C7
Českobudějovický □
Czech Rep. 49°10N 14°30E **180** B7
Českomoravská Vrchovina
Czech Rep. 49°30N 15°40E **180** B8
Český Brod *Czech Rep.* 50°4N 14°52E **180** A7
Český Krumlov *Czech Rep.* 48°43N 14°21E **180** C7
Český Těšín *Czech Rep.* 49°45N 18°39E **181** B11
Česma ➔ *Croatia* 45°35N 16°29E **200** C7
Çeşme *Turkey* 38°20N 26°23E **205** C8
Cessnock *Australia* 32°50S 151°21E **283** B9
Cesson-Sévigné *France* 48°7N 1°36W **172** D5
Cestas *France* 44°44N 0°41W **174** D3
Cestos ➔ *Liberia* 5°40N 9°10W **262** D3
Cestos Sehnkwehn △
Liberia 5°40N 9°10W **262** D3
Cetaceo, Mt. *Phil.* 17°42N 122°3E **232** C4
Cetate *Romania* 44°7N 23°2E **182** F8
Cetatea-Albă = Bilhorod-
Dnistrovskyy *Ukraine* 46°11N 30°23E **189** J6
Cetin Grad *Croatia* 45°9N 15°45E **199** C12
Cetina ➔ *Croatia* 43°26N 16°42E **199** E13
Cetinje *Montenegro* 42°23N 18°59E **202** D2
Çetmi *Turkey* 36°52N 32°38E **250** B3
Cetraro *Italy* 39°31N 15°55E **201** C8
Ceuta *N. Afr.* 35°52N 5°18W **260** A3
Ceva *Italy* 44°23N 8°2E **198** D5
Ceve-i-Ra *Fiji* 21°46S 174°31E **277** E13
Cévennes *France* 44°10N 3°50E **174** D7
Cévennes △ *France* 44°15N 3°45E **174** D7
Ceyhan *Turkey* 37°4N 35°47E **250** A6
Ceyhan ➔ *Turkey* 36°38N 35°40E **250** B6
Ceylanpınar *Turkey* 36°50N 40°2E **213** D9
Ceylon = Sri Lanka ■ *Asia* 7°30N 80°50E **245** L5
Ceylon Plain *Ind. Oc.* 4°0S 82°0E **273** E7
Cèze ➔ *France* 44°6N 4°43E **175** D8
Cha-am *Thailand* 12°48N 99°58E **236** F2
Cha Kwo Ling *China* 22°18N 114°13E **122** B2
Chá Pungana *Angola* 13°44S 18°39E **265** E3
Chabanais *France* 45°52N 0°48E **174** C4
Chabeuil *France* 44°54N 5°3E **175** D9
Chablais *France* 46°20N 6°36E **173** F13
Chablis *France* 47°47N 3°48E **173** E10
Chabounia *Algeria* 35°30N 2°38E **261** A5
Chacabuco *Argentina* 34°40S 60°27W **334** C3
Chacachacare I.
Trin. & Tob. 10°41N 61°45W **323** t
Chacao, Canal *Chile* 41°47S 73°42W **336** B2
Chacarrita *Argentina* 34°35S 58°27W **117** B2
Chachani, Nevado *Peru* 16°11S 71°31W **330** D3
Chachapoyas *Peru* 6°15S 77°50W **330** B2
Chachasp *Peru* 15°30S 72°15W **330** D3
Chachoengsao *Thailand* 13°42N 101°5E **236** F3
Chachran *Pakistan* 28°55N 70°30E **242** E4
Chachro *Pakistan* 25°5N 70°15E **242** G4
Chaco □ *Argentina* 26°30S 61°0W **334** B3
Chaco □ *Paraguay* 26°0S 60°0W **334** B4
Chaco ➔ *U.S.A.* 36°46N 108°39W **305** H9
Chaco △ *Argentina* 27°0S 59°30W **334** B4
Chaco Culture △ *U.S.A.* 36°3N 107°58W **305** H10
Chacon, C. *U.S.A.* 54°42N 132°0W **296** C2
Chad ■ *Africa* 15°0N 17°15E **259** F3
Chad, L. = Tchad, L. *Chad* 13°30N 14°30E **259** F2
Chadileuvú ➔ *Argentina* 37°46S 66°0W **334** D2
Chadiza *Zambia* 14°45S 32°27E **269** E3
Chadron *U.S.A.* 42°50N 103°0W **308** D2
Chadwell Heath *U.K.* 51°34N 0°8E **125** A4
Chadyr-Lunga = Ciadâr-Lunga
Moldova 46°3N 28°51E **183** D13
Chae Hom *Thailand* 18°43N 99°35E **236** C2
Chae Son △ *Thailand* 18°42N 99°20E **236** C2
Chaem ➔ *Thailand* 18°11N 98°38E **236** C2
Chaeryŏng *N. Korea* 38°24N 125°36E **224** C2
Chafe *Nigeria* 11°59N 6°50E **263** C6
Chagai Hills = Chāh Gay Hills
Afghan. 29°30N 64°0E **240** C2
Chagang-do □ *N. Korea* 40°50N 126°30E **224** B3
Chagda *Russia* 58°45N 130°38E **215** D14
Chagdo Kangri *China* 34°15N 84°10E **217** F10
Chaghcharān *Afghan.* 34°31N 65°15E **240** B2
Chagne *Ethiopia* 10°57N 36°30E **266** B4
Chagny *France* 46°57N 4°45E **173** F11
Chagoda *Russia* 59°10N 35°15E **188** C8
Chagos Arch. ☑ *Ind. Oc.* 6°0S 72°0E **211** J9
Chagos-Laccadive Ridge
Ind. Oc. 3°0N 73°0E **273** D6
Chagres ➔ *Panama* 9°10N 79°40W **320** c
Chagres △ *Panama* 9°33N 79°37W **320** c
Chaguanas *Trin. & Tob.* 10°30N 61°26W **323** t
Chaguaramas *Trin. & Tob.* 10°41N 61°38W **323** t
Chāh Ākhvor *Iran* 32°41N 59°40E **247** C8
Chāh Bahar *Iran* 25°20N 60°40E **247** E9
Chāh-e Āb *Afghan.* 37°23N 69°48E **240** A3
Chāh-e Kavīr *Iran* 34°29N 56°52E **247** C8
Chāh Gay Hills *Afghan.* 29°30N 64°0E **240** C2
Chahār Borj *Iran* 37°6N 45°59E **213** D11
Chahār Borjak *Afghan.* 30°17N 62°3E **240** C1
Chahār Mahāll va Bakhtīarī □
Iran 32°0N 49°0E **247** C6
Chahtung *Burma* 26°41N 98°10E **241** B7
Chai Badan *Thailand* 15°12N 101°8E **236** E3
Chai Chee *Singapore* 1°19N 103°46E **138** B3
Chai Wan *China* 22°16N 114°14E **122** B2
Chai Wan Kok *China* 22°22N 114°6E **122** A1
Chaibasa *India* 22°42N 85°49E **243** H11
Chaidari *Greece* 38°2N 23°38E **112** A1
Chaillé-les-Marais *France* 46°25N 1°2W **174** B2
Chaillot, Palais de *Paris, France* **134** b2
Chaillu, Massif du *Gabon* 2°32S 11°10E **264** C2
Chain Ridge *Ind. Oc.* 6°0N 54°0E **273** D4
Chainat *Thailand* 15°11N 100°8E **236** E3
Chaires *U.S.A.* 30°26N 84°7W **316** F4
Chaitén *Chile* 42°55S 72°43W **336** B2
Chaiya *Thailand* 9°23N 99°14E **237** H2
Chaiyaphum *Thailand* 15°43N 102°2E **236** E4
Chaj Doab *Pakistan* 32°15N 73°0E **242** C5
Chajari *Argentina* 30°42S 58°0W **334** C4
Chak Amru *Pakistan* 32°22N 75°11E **242** C6
Chaka *South Sudan* 4°49N 31°14E **257** G3
Chakar ➔ *Pakistan* 29°29N 68°2E **242** E3
Chakari *Zimbabwe* 18°5S 29°51E **271** A4
Chakaria *Bangla.* 21°45N 92°5E **241** E4
Chakarnaba *Chad* 14°13N 20°51E **259** F4
Chakdaha *India* 22°23N 88°19E **124** C1
Chake Chake *Tanzania* 5°15S 39°45E **268** D4
Chakhānsūr *Afghan.* 31°10N 62°0E **240** C1
Chakonipau, L. *Canada* 56°18N 68°30W **299** A6
Chakradharpur *India* 22°45N 85°40E **243** H11
Chakrata *India* 30°42N 77°51E **242** D7
Chakwadam *Burma* 27°29N 98°31E **241** B7
Chakwal *Pakistan* 32°56N 72°53E **242** C5
Chala *Peru* 15°48S 74°20W **330** D3
Chalais *France* 45°16N 0°3E **174** C4
Chalakudi *India* 10°18N 76°20E **245** J3
Chalan Kanoa *N. Marianas* 15°9N 145°42E **302** e
Chalandri *Greece* 38°3N 23°48E **112** A2
Chalchihuites *Mexico* 23°29N 103°53W **318** C4
Chalcis = Chalkida *Greece* 38°27N 23°42E **204** C5
Châlette-sur-Loing *France* 48°1N 2°44E **173** D9
Chaleur B. *Canada* 47°55N 65°30W **299** C6
Chalfant *U.S.A.* 37°32N 118°21W **306** H8
Chalhuanca *Peru* 14°15S 73°15W **330** C3
Chaliki *Greece* 39°36N 22°30E **204** B4
Chalindrey *France* 47°43N 5°26E **173** E12
Chaling *China* 26°58N 113°30E **229** D9
Chalisgaon *India* 20°30N 75°10E **244** D2
Chalk River *Canada* 46°1N 77°27W **298** C4
Chalkar, Ozero = Shalkar Köli
Kazakhstan 50°35N 51°47E **190** E10
Chalki *Greece* 36°17N 27°35E **205** E9
Chalkida *Greece* 38°27N 23°42E **204** C5
Chalkidiki □ *Greece* 40°25N 23°20E **202** F7
Chalky Inlet *N.Z.* 46°3S 166°31E **285** G1
Chalkyitsik *U.S.A.* 66°39N 143°43W **303** C12
Challakere *India* 14°19N 76°39E **245** G3
Challans *France* 46°50N 1°52W **172** F5
Challapata *Bolivia* 18°53S 66°50W **330** D4
Challawa Gorge Res.
Nigeria 11°54N 8°25E **263** C6
Challenger Deep *Pac. Oc.* 11°30N 142°0E **288** F6
Challenger Fracture Zone
Pac. Oc. 35°0S 105°0W **289** L17
Challis *U.S.A.* 44°30N 114°14W **304** D6
Chalmette *U.S.A.* 29°56N 89°57W **315** G10
Chaloem Rattanakosin △
Thailand 14°40N 99°17E **236** E2
Chalon-sur-Saône *France* 46°48N 4°50E **173** F11
Chalong *Thailand* 7°50N 98°22E **237** a
Chalonnes-sur-Loire
France 47°20N 0°45W **172** E6
Châlons-en-Champagne
France 48°58N 4°20E **173** D11
Chálten, Cerro = Fitz Roy, Cerro
Argentina 49°17S 73°5W **336** C2
Châlus *Haute-Vienne, France* 45°39N 0°58E **174** C4
Chālūs *Iran* 36°38N 51°26E **247** B6
Cham *Germany* 49°13N 12°39E **179** F8
Cham, Cu Lao *Vietnam* 15°57N 108°30E **236** E7
Chama *U.S.A.* 36°54N 106°35W **305** H10
Chamah, Gunung
Malaysia 5°13N 101°35E **234** A2
Chamaicó *Argentina* 35°3S 64°58W **334** D3
Chaman *Pakistan* 30°58N 66°25E **240** C2
Chamartin *Spain* 40°27N 3°40W **127** B1
Chamba *India* 32°35N 76°10E **242** C7
Chamba *Tanzania* 11°37S 37°0E **269** E4
Chambal ➔ *India* 26°29N 79°15E **243** F8
Chamberi *Spain* 40°26N 3°42W **127** B1
Chamberlain *U.S.A.* 43°49N 99°20W **308** D4
Chamberlain ➔
Australia 15°30S 127°54E **278** C4
Chamberlain L. *U.S.A.* 46°14N 69°19W **309** B19
Chambers *U.S.A.* 35°11N 109°26W **305** J9
Chambersburg *U.S.A.* 39°56N 77°40W **309** F15
Chambéry *France* 45°34N 5°55E **175** C9
Chambi, Jebel *Tunisia* 35°11N 8°39E **261** A6
Chamblee *U.S.A.* 33°53N 84°18W **316** B5
Chambly *Canada* 45°27N 73°17W **313** A11
Chambord *Canada* 48°25N 72°6W **299** C5
Chamboulive *France* 45°26N 1°42E **174** C5
Chambourcy *France* 48°54N 2°2E **134** A1
Chambri L. *Papua N. G.* 4°15S 143°10E **286** C2
Chamchamal *Iraq* 35°32N 44°50E **213** E11
Chamela *Mexico* 19°32N 105°5W **318** D3
Chamical *Argentina* 30°22S 66°27W **334** C2
Chamili *Greece* 35°50N 26°15E **205** F8
Chamkar Luong *Cambodia* 11°0N 103°45E **237** G4
Chamois *U.S.A.* 38°41N 91°46W **310** F5
Chamoli *India* 30°24N 79°21E **243** D8
Chamonix-Mont Blanc
France 45°55N 6°51E **175** C10
Chamouchuane =
Ashuapmushuan ➔
Canada 48°37N 72°20W **298** C5
Champ de Mars, Parc du *Paris, France* **134** c2
Champa *India* 22°2N 82°43E **243** H10
Champagne *Canada* 60°49N 136°30W **296** A1
Champagne *France* 48°40N 4°20E **173** D11
Champagnole *France* 46°45N 5°55E **173** F12
Champaign *U.S.A.* 40°7N 88°15W **311** D8
Champássak *Laos* 14°53N 105°52E **236** E5
Champaubert *France* 48°50N 3°45E **173** D10
Champawat *India* 29°20N 80°6E **243** E9
Champdeniers-St-Denis
France 46°29N 0°25W **174** B3
Champdoré, L. *Canada* 55°55N 65°49W **299** A6
Champeix *France* 45°37N 3°8E **174** C7
Champigny-sur-Marne
France 48°49N 2°30E **134** B4
Champion *U.S.A.* 41°19N 80°51W **312** E4
Champlain *U.S.A.* 44°59N 73°27W **313** B11
Champlain, L. *U.S.A.* 44°40N 73°20W **313** B11
Champlain, Pont *Canada* 45°28N 73°31W **130** B2
Champlitte *France* 47°32N 5°31E **173** E12
Champotón *Mexico* 19°21N 90°43W **319** D6
Champs Elysées, Avenue des
Paris, France **134** b2
Champs-sur-Marne *France* 48°50N 2°34E **134** A4
Champua *India* 22°5N 85°40E **243** H11
Chamrail *India* 22°38N 88°17E **124** B1
Chamrajnagar *India* 11°52N 76°52E **245** J3
Chamusca *Portugal* 39°21N 8°29W **195** F2
Chan Chan *Peru* 8°7S 79°0W **330** B2
Chana *Thailand* 6°55N 100°44E **237** J3
Chanakyapuri *India* 28°35N 77°11E **120** B2
Chañaral *Chile* 26°23S 70°40W **334** B1
Chanārān *Iran* 36°39N 59°6E **247** B8
Chanasma *India* 23°44N 72°5E **242** H5
Chancay *Peru* 11°32S 77°25W **330** C2
Chancel, Î. *Martinique* 14°41N 60°53W **322** j
Chanchiang = Zhanjiang
China 21°15N 110°20E **229** G8
Chanco *Chile* 35°44S 72°32W **334** D1
Chand *India* 21°57N 79°7E **243** J8
Chandalar ➔ *U.S.A.* 66°37N 146°0W **303** C11
Chandan *India* 24°38N 86°40E **243** G12
Chandan Chauki *India* 28°33N 80°47E **243** E9
Chandannagar *India* 22°52N 88°24E **243** H13
Chandausi *India* 28°27N 78°49E **243** E8
Chandeleur Is. *U.S.A.* 29°55N 88°57W **315** G10
Chandeleur Sd. *U.S.A.* 29°55N 89°0W **315** G10
Chandigarh *India* 30°43N 76°47E **242** D7
Chandil *India* 22°58N 86°3E **243** H12
Chanditala *India* 22°41N 88°15E **124** A1
Chandler *S. Austral., Australia* 27°0S 133°19E **281** D1
Chandler *Qué., Canada* 48°18N 64°46W **299** C7
Chandler *Ariz., U.S.A.* 33°18N 111°50W **305** K8
Chandler *Okla., U.S.A.* 35°42N 96°53W **310** H6
Chandless ➔ *Brazil* 9°8S 69°51W **330** B4
Chandod *India* 21°59N 73°28E **242** J5
Chandpur *Bangla.* 23°8N 90°45E **241** D3
Chandra *Greece* 35°3N 26°8E **205** F8
Chandragiri *India* 13°35N 79°19E **245** H4
Chandrapur *India* 19°57N 79°25E **244** E4
Chandrupatla *India* 18°33N 80°24E **244** E5
Chānf *Iran* 26°38N 60°29E **247** E9
Chang *Pakistan* 26°59N 68°30E **242** F3
Chang, Ko *Thailand* 12°0N 102°23E **237** G4
Chang, Ko *Thailand* 9°50N 98°27E **237** H2
Ch'ang Chiang = Chang Jiang ➔
China 31°48N 121°10E **229** B13
Chang Jiang ➔ *China* 31°48N 121°10E **229** B13
Chang-won *S. Korea* 35°16N 128°37E **224** E4
Changan = Xi'an *China* 34°15N 109°0E **226** G5
Changane ➔ *Mozam.* 22°48N 113°48E **219** a
Changanacheri *India* 9°25N 76°31E **245** K3
Changanassery = Changanacheri
India 9°25N 76°31E **245** K3
Changane ➔ *Mozam.* 24°30S 33°30E **271** B5
Changbai *China* 41°25N 128°5E **224** B4
Changbai Shan *China* 42°20N 129°0E **224** A4
Changchiak'ou = Zhangjiakou
China 40°48N 114°55E **226** D8
Ch'angchih = Changzhi
China 36°10N 113°6E **226** F7
Changchih *Taiwan* 22°41N 120°32E **225** D2
Ch'angchou = Changzhou
China 31°47N 119°58E **229** B12
Changchow = Changzhou
China 31°47N 119°58E **229** B12
Changchun *China* 43°57N 125°17E **227** C13
Changchunling *China* 45°18N 125°27E **227** B13
Changde *China* 29°4N 111°35E **229** C8
Changdo-ri *N. Korea* 38°30N 127°40E **224** C3
Changfeng *China* 32°28N 117°10E **229** A11
Changfeng Park *China* 31°14N 121°24E **138** B1
Changge *China* 34°13N 113°46E **226** G7
Changhai = Shanghai
China 31°15N 121°26E **138** B2
Changhua *Zhejiang, China* 30°12N 119°12E **229** B12
Changhua *Taiwan* 24°2N 120°30E **225** B2
Changhua □ *Taiwan* 24°15N 120°55E **225** B2
Changhŭngni *N. Korea* 40°24N 128°19E **224** B4
Changi *Singapore* 1°23N 103°59E **138** A3
Changi, Singapore ✕ (SIN)
Singapore 1°23N 103°59E **138** A3
Changji *China* 44°1N 87°19E **217** D11
Changjiang *China* 19°20N 108°55E **236** C7
Changjiang Shuiku *China* 22°29N 113°27E **219** a
Changjin *N. Korea* 40°23N 127°15E **224** B3
Changjin-ho *N. Korea* 40°30N 127°15E **224** B3
Changle *China* 25°59N 119°27E **229** E12
Changli *China* 39°40N 119°13E **227** E10
Changling *China* 44°20N 123°58E **227** B12
Changlun *Malaysia* 6°25N 100°26E **237** J3
Changning *Hunan, China* 26°28N 112°22E **229** D9
Changning *Shanghai, China* 31°13N 121°24E **138** B1
Changning *Sichuan, China* 28°40N 104°56E **228** C5
Changning *Yunnan, China* 24°45N 99°30E **228** E2
Ch'angpin *Taiwan* 23°19N 121°27E **225** C3
Changping *China* 40°14N 116°12E **226** D9
Changsha *China* 28°12N 113°0E **229** C9
Changshan *China* 28°55N 118°27E **229** C12
Changshan Qundao
China 39°11N 122°32E **227** E12
Changshou *China* 29°50N 107°4E **228** C6
Changshu *China* 31°38N 120°43E **229** B13
Changshun *China* 26°3N 106°25E **228** D6
Changtai *China* 24°35N 117°42E **229** E11
Changt'e = Chongde
China 30°32N 120°26E **229** B13
Changting *China* 25°50N 116°22E **229** E11
Changtu *China* 42°46N 124°6E **227** C13
Changuinola *Panama* 9°26N 82°31W **320** E3
Changwu *Guangxi Zhuangzu, China* 23°25N 111°17E **229** F8
Changwu *Shaanxi, China* 35°10N 107°45E **226** G4
Changxing *China* 31°0N 119°55E **229** B12
Changyang *China* 30°30N 111°10E **229** B8
Changyi *China* 36°40N 119°30E **227** F10
Changyŏn *N. Korea* 38°15N 125°6E **224** C2
Changyuan *Henan, China* 35°15N 114°42E **226** G8
Changyuan *Taiwan* 23°25N 121°29E **225** C3
Changzhi *China* 36°10N 113°6E **226** F7
Changzhou *China* 31°47N 119°58E **229** B12
Chanhanga *Angola* 16°0S 14°8E **265** F2
Chania *Greece* 35°30N 24°4E **207** E5
Chania □ *Greece* 35°30N 24°0E **207** E5
Chania ✕ (CHQ) *Greece* 35°30N 24°6E **207** E5
Chanion, Kolpos *Greece* 35°33N 23°55E **207** E4
Chankar = Xanlar
Azerbaijan 40°37N 46°12E **191** K8
Channagiri *India* 14°2N 75°56E **245** G2
Channapatna *India* 12°40N 77°15E **245** H3
Channel Is. *U.K.* 49°19N 2°24W **169** H5
Channel Is. *Calif., U.S.A.* 33°40N 119°15W **307** M7
Channel Islands △ *U.S.A.* 34°0N 119°24W **307** L7
Channel-Port aux Basques
Canada 47°30N 59°9W **299** C8
Channel Tunnel *Europe* 51°0N 1°30E **169** F9
Channing *U.S.A.* 35°41N 102°20W **314** D3
Chantada *Spain* 42°36N 7°46W **194** C3
Chantereine *France* 48°53N 2°37E **134** A4
Chanthaburi *Thailand* 12°38N 102°12E **236** F4
Chantian *China* 23°12N 113°16E **121** A2
Chantilly *France* 49°12N 2°29E **173** C9
Chantonnay *France* 46°40N 1°3W **172** F5
Chantrey Inlet *Canada* 67°48N 96°20W **294** D12
Chanumla *India* 8°19N 93°5E **245** K11
Chanute *U.S.A.* 37°41N 95°27W **308** G6
Chany, Ozero *Russia* 54°49N 77°29E **217** B9
Chanza ➔ *Spain* 37°32N 7°30W **195** H3
Chao Hu *China* 31°30N 117°30E **229** B11
Chao Phraya ➔ *Thailand* 13°40N 100°31E **236** F3
Chao Phraya Lowlands
Thailand 15°30N 100°0E **236** E3
Chaocheng *China* 36°4N 115°37E **226** F8
Ch'aochou *Taiwan* 22°33N 120°32E **225** D2
Chaohu *China* 31°38N 117°50E **229** B11
Chaoyang *Beijing, China* 39°53N 116°26E **114** B2
Chaoyang *Guangdong, China* 23°17N 116°30E **229** F11
Chaoyang *Liaoning, China* 41°35N 120°22E **227** D11
Chaoyangmen *China* 39°54N 116°23E **114** B2
Chaozhou *China* 23°42N 116°32E **229** F11
Chapada Diamantina △
Brazil 12°52S 41°30W **333** D3
Chapada dos Guimarães
Brazil 15°26S 55°45W **331** D6
Chapada dos Guimarães △
Brazil 15°18S 55°54W **331** D6
Chapada dos Veadeiros △
Brazil 14°0S 47°30W **333** D2
Chapaev *Kazakhstan* 50°25N 51°10E **190** E10
Chapais *Canada* 49°47N 74°51W **298** C5
Chapala *Mozam.* 15°50S 37°35E **269** F4
Chapala, L. de *Mexico* 20°15N 103°0W **318** C4
Chaparé ➔ *Bolivia* 15°58S 64°42W **331** D5
Chaparmukh *India* 26°12N 92°31E **241** B4
Chaparral *Colombia* 3°43N 75°28W **328** C2
Chapayev = Chapaev
Kazakhstan 50°25N 51°10E **190** E10
Chapayevsk *Russia* 53°0N 49°40E **190** D9
Chapecó *Brazil* 27°14S 52°41W **335** B5
Chapel Hill *U.S.A.* 35°55N 79°4W **315** D15
Chapelizod *Ireland* 53°21N 6°20W **120** A1
Chapelton *Jamaica* 18°5N 77°16W **320** a
Chapin = Edinburg
U.S.A. 26°18N 98°10W **314** H5
Chapin *U.S.A.* 39°46N 90°24W **310** E6
Chapleau *Canada* 47°50N 83°24W **298** C3
Chaplin *Canada* 50°28N 106°40W **297** C7
Chaplin L. *Canada* 50°22N 106°36W **297** C7
Chaplino *Ukraine* 48°8N 36°15E **189** H9
Chaplygin *Russia* 53°15N 40°0E **188** F11
Chappell *U.S.A.* 41°6N 102°28W **308** E2
Chappells *U.S.A.* 34°11N 81°52W **316** A8
Chapra = Chhapra *India* 25°48N 84°44E **243** G11
Chapultepec, Bosque de
Mexico 19°25N 99°11W **128** B1
Chapultepec, Castillo de
Mexico 19°25N 99°10W **128** B1
Chaqābel *Iran* 33°16N 47°30E **213** F12
Châr *Mauritania* 21°32N 12°45W **260** D2
Chara *Russia* 56°54N 118°20E **215** D12
Charadai *Argentina* 27°35S 59°55W **334** B4
Charagua *Bolivia* 19°45S 63°10W **331** D5
Charakas *Greece* 35°1N 25°7E **207** E6
Charalá *Colombia* 6°17N 73°10W **328** B3
Charambirá, Punta
Colombia 4°16N 77°32W **328** C2
Charaña *Bolivia* 17°30S 69°25W **330** D4
Charantsavan *Armenia* 40°35N 44°41E **191** K7
Charanwala *India* 27°51N 72°10E **242** F5
Charapita *Colombia* 0°37S 74°21W **328** D3
Charata *Argentina* 27°13S 61°14W **334** B3
Charcas *Mexico* 23°8N 101°7W **318** C4
Charcot I. *Antarctica* 70°0S 70°0W **151** C17
Chard *U.K.* 50°52N 2°58W **169** G5
Chardon *U.S.A.* 41°35N 81°12W **312** E3
Charduar *India* 26°51N 92°46E **241** B4
Chardzhou = Türkmenabat
Turkmenistan 39°6N 63°34E **247** B9
Charente □ *France* 45°50N 0°16E **174** C4
Charente ➔ *France* 45°57N 1°5W **174** C2
Charente-Inférieure = Charente-
Maritime □ *France* 45°45N 0°45W **174** C3
Charente-Maritime □
France 45°45N 0°45W **174** C3
Charenton-du-Cher *France* 46°44N 2°39E **173** F9
Charenton-le-Pont *France* 48°49N 2°25E **134** B3
Chari ➔ *Chad* 12°58N 14°31E **259** F2
Chari-Baguirmi □ *Chad* 11°0N 17°0E **259** F3
Chārīkār *Afghan.* 35°0N 69°10E **240** B3
Charing *U.S.A.* 32°28N 84°22W **316** C5
Charing Cross *London, U.K.* **125** b4
Chariton *U.S.A.* 41°1N 93°19W **310** C3
Chariton ➔ *U.S.A.* 39°19N 92°58W **310** E4
Charity *Guyana* 7°24N 58°36W **329** B6
Chärjew = Türkmenabat
Turkmenistan 39°6N 63°34E **247** B9
Charkhari *India* 25°24N 79°45E **243** G8
Charkhi Dadri *India* 28°37N 76°17E **242** E7
Charleroi *Belgium* 50°24N 4°27E **170** D4
Charleroi *Pa., U.S.A.* 40°9N 79°57W **312** F5
Charleroi, Kanal de ➔
Belgium 50°51N 4°19E **116** B1
Charles, C. *U.S.A.* 37°7N 75°58W **309** G16
Charles, I. = Santa María, I.
Ecuador 1°17S 90°26W **330** a
Charles, Peak *Australia* 32°52S 121°11E **279** F3
Charles Bridge = Karlův most
Prague, Czech Rep. **135** b1
Charles City *U.S.A.* 43°4N 92°41W **310** A4
Charles de Gaulle, Paris ✕ (CDG)
France 49°0N 2°32E **173** D9
Charles Gates Dawes House
U.S.A. 42°2N 87°40W **119** A2
Charles I. *Canada* 62°39N 74°15W **295** E17
Charles L. *Canada* 59°50N 110°33W **297** B6
Charles Sound *N.Z.* 45°2S 167°4E **285** F2
Charles Square = Karlovo náměstí
Prague, Czech Rep. **135** c1
Charles Town *U.S.A.* 39°17N 77°52W **309** F15
Charlesbourg *Canada* 46°51N 71°16W **309** B18
Charleston *Ill., U.S.A.* 39°30N 88°10W **311** E8
Charleston *Miss., U.S.A.* 34°1N 90°4W **315** D9
Charleston *Mo., U.S.A.* 36°55N 89°21W **308** G9
Charleston *S.C., U.S.A.* 32°46N 79°56W **316** C10
Charleston *W. Va., U.S.A.* 38°21N 81°38W **309** F13
Charleston L. *Canada* 44°32N 76°0W **313** B9
Charleston Peak *U.S.A.* 36°16N 115°42W **307** J11
Charlestown *Mayo, Ireland* 53°58N 8°48W **166** C3
Charlestown
St. Kitts & Nevis 17°8N 62°37W **322** d
Charlestown *KwaZulu Natal, S. Africa* 27°26S 29°53E **271** C4
Charlestown *Ind., U.S.A.* 38°27N 85°40W **311** F11
Charlestown *Mass., U.S.A.* 42°22N 71°4W **116** A2
Charlestown *N.H., U.S.A.* 43°14N 72°25W **313** C12
Charlestown Bridge *Boston, U.S.A.* **116** a2
Charlestown of Aberlour
U.K. 57°28N 3°14W **167** D5
Charleville = Rath Luirc
Ireland 52°21N 8°40W **166** D3
Charleville *Australia* 26°24S 146°15E **281** D4
Charleville-Mézières
France 49°44N 4°40E **173** C11
Charlevoix *U.S.A.* 45°19N 85°16W **309** C11
Charlie Gibbs Fracture Zone
Atl. Oc. 52°45N 35°30W **152** B8
Charlieu *France* 46°10N 4°10E **173** F11
Charlotte *Dominica* 15°17N 61°24W **323** k
Charlotte *Mich., U.S.A.* 42°34N 84°50W **311** B12
Charlotte *N.C., U.S.A.* 35°13N 80°50W **315** D14
Charlotte *Vt., U.S.A.* 44°19N 73°16W **313** B11
Charlotte Amalie
U.S. Virgin Is. 18°21N 64°56W **321** C7
Charlotte Harbor *U.S.A.* 26°57N 82°4W **317** J7
Charlotte L. *Canada* 52°12N 125°19W **296** C3
Charlottenberg *Sweden* 59°54N 12°17E **162** E6
Charlottenburg *Germany* 52°31N 13°14E **115** A2
Charlottenburg, Schloss
Germany 52°31N 13°18E **115** A2
Charlottenlund *Denmark* 55°44N 12°35E **118** A3
Charlottesville *U.S.A.* 38°2N 78°30W **309** F14
Charlottetown *Nfld. & L., Canada* 52°46N 56°7W **299** B8
Charlottetown *P.E.I., Canada* 46°14N 63°8W **299** C7
Charlotteville *Trin. & Tob.* 11°20N 60°33W **323** s
Charlton *Vic., Australia* 36°16S 143°24E **282** D5
Charlton *London, U.K.* 51°29N 0°1E **125** B4
Charlton I. *Canada* 52°0N 79°20W **298** B4
Charmes *France* 48°22N 6°17E **173** D13
Charneca *Lisboa, Portugal* 38°47N 9°8W **126** A2
Charneca *Setúbal, Portugal* 38°37N 9°12W **126** B1
Charny *Canada* 46°43N 71°15W **299** C5
Charnyany *Belarus* 51°59N 24°12E **185** G11
Charolles *France* 46°27N 4°16E **173** F11
Chârost *France* 47°0N 2°7E **173** F9
Charouine *Algeria* 29°0N 0°15W **261** C4
Charre *Mozam.* 17°13S 35°10E **269** F4
Charroux *France* 46°9N 0°25E **174** B4
Charsadda *Pakistan* 34°7N 71°45E **242** B4
Charshanga = Köýtendag
Turkmenistan 37°30N 66°1E **240** A2
Charters Towers *Australia* 20°5S 146°13E **280** C4
Chartres *France* 48°29N 1°30E **172** D8
Chartreuse ⌂ *France* 45°22N 5°42E **175** C9
Charuma *Trin. & Tob.* 10°24N 61°9W **323** t
Charysh ➔ *Russia* 52°22N 83°45E **217** B10
Chascomús *Argentina* 35°30S 58°0W **334** D4
Chase *Canada* 50°50N 119°41W **296** C5
Chase, L. *U.S.A.* 28°28N 81°31W **133** B1
Chasefu *Zambia* 11°55S 33°8E **269** E3
Chashma Barrage
Pakistan 32°27N 71°20E **242** C4
Chaslands Mistake *N.Z.* 46°38S 169°22E **285** G4
Chasong *N. Korea* 41°27N 126°38E **224** B3
Chasseneuil-sur-Bonnieure
France 45°52N 0°29E **174** C4
Chāt *Iran* 37°59N 55°16E **247** B7
Chatal Balkan = Udvoy Balkan
Bulgaria 42°50N 26°50E **203** D10
Chatanika *U.S.A.* 65°7N 147°28W **303** D11
Château-Arnoux-St-Auban
France 44°6N 6°0E **175** D10
Château-Chinon *France* 47°4N 3°56E **173** E10
Château-d'Olonne *France* 46°30N 1°44W **174** B2
Château-du-Loir *France* 47°40N 0°25E **172** E7
Château Dubug *Martinique* 14°46N 60°55W **322** j
Château Gaillard
Guadeloupe 16°18N 61°23W **322** e
Château-Gontier *France* 47°50N 0°48W **172** E6
Château-la-Vallière *France* 47°30N 0°20E **172** E7
Château-Landon *France* 48°8N 2°40E **173** D9
Château Murat *Guadeloupe* 15°52N 61°17W **322** e
Château-Renard *France* 47°56N 2°55E **173** E9
Château-Renault *France* 47°36N 0°56E **172** E7
Château-Salins *France* 48°50N 6°30E **173** D13
Château-Thierry *France* 49°3N 3°20E **173** C10
Chateaubelair *St. Vincent* 13°17N 61°15W **323** n
Châteaubourg *France* 48°7N 1°25W **172** D5
Châteaubriant *France* 47°43N 1°23W **172** E5
Châteaudun *France* 48°3N 1°20E **172** D8
Châteaudufort *France* 48°44N 2°5E **134** B1
Chateaugay *U.S.A.* 44°56N 74°5W **313** B10
Châteaugiron *France* 48°3N 1°30W **172** D5
Châteauguay, L. *Canada* 56°26N 70°3W **299** A5
Châteaulin *France* 48°11N 4°8W **172** D2
Châteaumeillant *France* 46°35N 2°12E **173** F9
Châteauneuf-du-Faou
France 48°11N 3°50W **172** D3
Châteauneuf-sur-Charente
France 45°36N 0°3W **174** C3
Châteauneuf-sur-Cher
France 46°52N 2°18E **173** F9
Châteauneuf-sur-Loire
France 47°52N 2°13E **173** E9
Châteaurenard *France* 43°53N 4°51E **175** E8
Châteauroux *France* 46°50N 1°40E **173** F8
Châteauvillain *France* 48°2N 4°55E **173** D11
Châteaux, Pte. des
Guadeloupe 16°15N 61°10W **322** e
Châtelaillon-Plage *France* 46°5N 1°5W **174** B2
Châtelguyon *France* 45°55N 3°4E **174** C7
Châtellerault *France* 46°50N 0°30E **172** F7
Châtelus-Malvaleix *France* 46°18N 2°1E **173** F9
Châtenay-Malabry *France* 48°46N 2°16E **134** B2
Chatham = Miramichi
Canada 47°2N 65°28W **299** C6
Chatham *Ont., Canada* 42°24N 82°11W **312** D2
Chatham *Medway, U.K.* 51°22N 0°32E **169** F8
Chatham *Ill., U.S.A.* 41°45N 87°36W **119** C3
Chatham *Ill., U.S.A.* 39°40N 89°42W **310** E7
Chatham *N.Y., U.S.A.* 42°21N 73°36W **313** D11
Chatham, I. = San Cristóbal, I.
Ecuador 0°50S 89°26W **330** a
Chatham, I. *Chile* 50°40S 74°25W **336** D2
Chatham I. *N.Z.* 43°50S 176°20W **285** a
Chatham Is. *Pac. Oc.* 44°0S 176°40W **285** a
Chatham Rise *Pac. Oc.* 43°30S 180°0E **288** M10
Châtillon *Hauts-de-Seine, France* 48°48N 2°17E **134** B2
Châtillon *Italy* 45°45N 7°37E **198** C4
Châtillon-Coligny *France* 47°50N 2°51E **173** E9
Châtillon-en-Diois *France* 44°41N 5°29E **175** D9
Châtillon-sur-Indre *France* 46°59N 1°10E **172** F8
Châtillon-sur-Loire *France* 47°35N 2°44E **173** E9
Châtillon-sur-Seine
France 47°50N 4°33E **173** E11
Chatmohar *Bangla.* 24°15N 89°15E **243** G13
Chatou *France* 48°53N 2°9E **134** A1
Chatpur *India* 22°36N 88°22E **124** B2
Chatra *India* 24°12N 84°56E **243** G11
Chatrapur *India* 19°22N 85°2E **244** E7
Chats, L. des *Canada* 45°30N 76°20W **313** A8
Chatsu *India* 26°36N 75°57E **242** F6
Chatswood *Australia* 33°47S 151°11E **139** A2
Chatsworth *Ont., Canada* 44°27N 80°54W **312** B4
Chatsworth *Ill., U.S.A.* 40°45N 88°18W **311** D8
Chatsworth *Zimbabwe* 19°38S 31°13E **269** F3
Chatta-Hantō *Japan* 34°45N 136°55E **223** C8
Chāttagām = Chittagong
Bangla. 22°19N 91°48E **241** D3
Chattahoochee *U.S.A.* 30°42N 84°51W **316** E5
Chattahoochee ➔ *U.S.A.* 30°54N 84°57W **316** E5
Chattanooga *U.S.A.* 35°3N 85°19W **315** D12
Chatteris *U.K.* 52°28N 0°2E **169** E8
Chatturat *Thailand* 15°40N 101°51E **236** E3
Chatuchak *Thailand* 13°48N 100°33E **113** B2
Chatuchak Park
Thailand 13°48N 100°32E **113** B2
Chau Doc *Vietnam* 10°42N 105°7E **237** G5
Chaubourg, Mt. *St. Lucia* 14°2N 60°57W **323** m
Chaudes-Aigues *France* 44°51N 3°1E **174** D7
Chauffailles *France* 46°13N 4°20E **173** F11
Chauk *Burma* 20°53N 94°49E **241** E5
Chaukan Pass *Burma* 27°8N 97°10E **241** B6
Chauki *Pakistan* 24°55N 66°56E **123** A1
Chaumont *Haute-Marne, France* 48°7N 5°8E **173** D12
Chaumont *N.Y., U.S.A.* 44°4N 76°8W **313** B8
Chaumont-en-Vexin
France 49°16N 1°53E **173** C8
Chaumont-sur-Loire
France 47°29N 1°11E **172** E8
Chaunay *France* 46°13N 0°9E **174** B4
Chaunskaya G. *Russia* 69°0N 169°0E **215** C17
Chauny *France* 49°37N 3°12E **173** C10
Chaura *India* 8°27N 93°2E **245** K11
Chausey, Îs. *France* 48°52N 1°49W **172** D5
Chaussin *France* 46°59N 5°22E **173** F12
Chautauqua L. *U.S.A.* 42°10N 79°24W **312** D5
Chauvigny *France* 46°34N 0°39E **172** F7
Chauvin *Canada* 52°45N 110°10W **297** C6
Chavakachcheri *Sri Lanka* 9°39N 80°9E **245** K5
Chavanges *France* 48°30N 4°35E **173** D11
Chavantina *Brazil* 14°40S 52°21W **331** C7
Chavarria *Peru* 12°0S 77°7W **124** B1
Chavdata *Greece* 38°12N 20°23E **207** D1
Chaves *Brazil* 0°15S 49°55W **332** B2
Chaves *Portugal* 41°45N 7°32W **194** D3
Chaville *France* 48°48N 2°11E **134** B2
Chavuma *Zambia* 13°4S 22°40E **265** E4
Chawang *Thailand* 8°25N 99°30E **237** H2
Chayang *S. Korea* 37°32N 127°3E **137** B2
Chaykovskiy *Russia* 56°47N 54°9E **186** C9
Chazelles-sur-Lyon *France* 45°39N 4°22E **175** C8
Chazuta *Peru* 6°30S 76°0W **330** B2
Chazy *U.S.A.* 44°53N 73°26W **313** B11
Cheaha Mt. *U.S.A.* 33°29N 85°49W **316** B4
Cheb *Czech Rep.* 50°9N 12°28E **180** A5
Chebanse *U.S.A.* 41°0N 87°54W **311** D9
Chebbi, Erg *Africa* 31°12N 3°58W **260** B4
Cheboksarskoye Vdkhr.
Russia 56°13N 46°58E **190** B8
Cheboksary *Russia* 56°8N 47°12E **190** B8
Cheboygan *U.S.A.* 45°39N 84°29W **309** C11
Chebsara *Russia* 59°10N 38°59E **188** C10
Chech, Erg *Africa* 25°0N 2°15W **260** D4
Chechelnyk *Ukraine* 48°13N 29°22E **183** B14
Chechen, Ostrov *Russia* 43°59N 47°40E **191** H8
Ch'ech'eng *Taiwan* 22°5N 120°42E **225** D2
Chechenia □ *Russia* 43°30N 45°29E **191** J7
Checheno-Ingush Republic =
Chechenia □ *Russia* 43°30N 45°29E **191** J7
Chechnya = Chechenia □
Russia 43°30N 45°29E **191** J7
Chęciny *Poland* 50°46N 20°28E **185** H7
Checotah *U.S.A.* 35°28N 95°31W **314** D7
Chedabucto B. *Canada* 45°25N 61°8W **299** C7
Cheduba I. *Burma* 18°45N 93°40E **241** F4
Cheektowaga *U.S.A.* 42°54N 78°45W **312** D6
Cheepie *Australia* 26°33S 145°0E **281** D4
Cheeyou *Trin. & Tob.* 10°33N 61°8W **323** t
Chef-Boutonne *France* 46°7N 0°4W **174** B3
Chefchaouen *Morocco* 35°9N 5°15W **260** A3
Chefchaouen □ *Morocco* 35°10N 5°15W **260** A3
Cheffadine *Niger* 19°57N 12°11E **259** D2
Chefoo = Yantai *China* 37°34N 121°22E **227** F11
Chefornak *U.S.A.* 60°13N 164°12W **303** D6
Chegdomyn *Russia* 51°7N 133°1E **215** D14
Chegga *Mauritania* 25°27N 5°40W **260** C3
Chegutu *Zimbabwe* 18°10S 30°14E **269** F3
Chehalis *U.S.A.* 46°40N 122°58W **306** D4
Chehalis ➔ *U.S.A.* 46°57N 123°50W **306** D3
Cheile Nerei-Beusnita △
Romania 44°56N 21°52E **182** F6
Cheiron, Mt. *France* 43°49N 6°58E **175** E10
Cheju = Jeju *S. Korea* 33°31N 126°32E **224** a
Cheju-do = Jeju-do
S. Korea 33°29N 126°34E **224** a
Chek Lap Kok *China* 22°18N 113°56E **219** a
Chekalin *Russia* 54°10N 36°10E **188** E9
Chekhovo *Russia* 54°33N 20°43E **184** D7
Chekiang = Zhejiang □
China 29°0N 120°0E **229** C13
Chel = Kuru, Bahr el ➔
South Sudan 8°10N 26°50E **257** F2
Chela, Sa. da *Angola* 16°20S 13°20E **265** F2
Chelan *U.S.A.* 47°51N 120°1W **304** C3
Chelan, L. *U.S.A.* 48°11N 120°30W **304** B3
Cheleken = Hazar
Turkmenistan 39°34N 53°16E **187** G9
Cheleken Yarymadasy
Turkmenistan 39°30N 53°15E **247** B7
Chelforó *Argentina* 39°0S 66°33W **336** A3
Chéliff, O. ➔ *Algeria* 36°0N 0°8E **261** A5
Chelkar = Shalqar
Kazakhstan 47°48N 59°39E **216** C5
Chella *Ethiopia* 5°0N 37°26E **257** F4
Chellala Dahrania *Algeria* 33°2N 0°1E **261** B5
Chelles *France* 48°53N 2°35E **134** A4
Chelles, Canal de *France* 48°51N 2°35E **134** A4
Chells-le-Pin ✕ *France* 48°53N 2°36E **134** A4
Chełm *Poland* 51°8N 23°30E **185** G10
Chełmno *Poland* 53°20N 18°30E **185** E5
Chelmsford *U.K.* 51°44N 0°29E **169** F8
Chełmża *Poland* 53°10N 18°39E **185** E5
Chelny = Naberezhnyye Chelny
Russia 55°42N 52°19E **190** C11
Chelsea *Vic., Australia* 38°5S 145°8E **283** E6
Chelsea *London, U.K.* 51°29N 0°10W **125** B2
Chelsea *Mass., U.S.A.* 42°23N 71°1W **116** A2
Chelsea *Mich., U.S.A.* 42°19N 84°1W **311** B12
Chelsea *New York, U.S.A.* **132** c1
Chelsea *Vt., U.S.A.* 43°59N 72°27W **313** C12
Cheltenham *U.K.* 51°54N 2°4W **169** F5
Chelva *Spain* 39°45N 1°0W **196** F4
Chelyabinsk *Russia* 55°10N 61°24E **216** A6
Chelyakobi = Kopeysk
Russia 55°7N 61°37E **216** A6
Chelyuskin, C. = Chelyuskin, Mys
Russia 77°30N 103°0E **215** B11
Chelyuskin, Mys *Russia* 77°30N 103°0E **215** B11
Chemainus *Canada* 48°55N 123°42W **306** B3
Chembar = Belinskiy
Russia 53°0N 43°25E **190** D6
Chembur *India* 19°3N 72°53E **130** A2
Chemchâm, Sebkhet
Mauritania 21°2N 12°4W **260** D2
Chemillé *France* 47°14N 0°45W **172** E6
Chemin Grenier *Mauritius* 20°29S 57°28E **272** e
Chemnitz *Germany* 50°51N 12°54E **178** E8
Chemulpho = Incheon
S. Korea 37°27N 126°40E **224** D3
Chemult *U.S.A.* 43°14N 121°47W **304** E3
Chen, Gora *Russia* 65°16N 141°50E **215** C15
Chenab ➔ *Pakistan* 30°23N 71°2E **242** D4
Chenab Nagar *Pakistan* 31°45N 72°55E **242** D5
Chenachane *Algeria* 26°0N 4°15W **260** C4
Chenachane, O. ➔
Algeria 25°20N 3°20W **260** C4
Chenango Forks *U.S.A.* 42°15N 75°51W **313** D9
Chencha *Ethiopia* 6°15N 37°32E **257** F4
Chenchiang = Zhenjiang
China 32°11N 119°26E **229** A12
Cheney *U.S.A.* 47°30N 117°35W **304** C5
Cheng Xian *China* 33°43N 105°42E **226** H3
Chengalpattu *India* 12°42N 79°58E **245** H4
Chengbu *China* 26°18N 110°16E **229** D8
Chengcheng *China* 35°8N 109°56E **226** G5
Chengchou = Zhengzhou
China 34°45N 113°34E **226** G7
Chengde *China* 40°59N 117°58E **227** D9
Chengdong Hu *China* 32°15N 116°20E **229** A11
Chengdu *China* 30°38N 104°2E **228** B5
Chengele *India* 28°47N 96°16E **241** A6
Chenggong *China* 24°52N 102°56E **228** E4
Chenggu *China* 33°10N 107°21E **228** A6
Chenghai *China* 23°30N 116°42E **229** F11
Chengjiang *China* 24°39N 103°0E **228** E4
Chengkou *China* 31°54N 108°31E **228** B7
Ch'engkung *Taiwan* 23°6N 121°22E **225** C3
Chengmai *China* 19°50N 109°58E **236** C7
Chengnan *China* 23°25N 116°20E **219** a
Chengshan Jiao *China* 37°25N 122°44E **227** F12
Chengshousi *China* 39°49N 116°24E **114** C2
Chengteh = Chengde
China 40°59N 117°58E **227** D9
Ch'engtu = Chengdu
China 30°38N 104°2E **228** B5
Chengwu *China* 34°58N 115°50E **226** G8
Chengxi Hu *China* 32°15N 116°10E **229** A11
Chengyang *China* 36°18N 120°21E **227** F11
Chenjiagang *China* 34°23N 119°47E **227** G10
Chenkaladi *Sri Lanka* 7°47N 81°35E **245** L5
Chennai *India* 13°8N 80°19E **245** H5
Chennevières-sur-Marne
France 48°47N 2°31E **134** B4
Chenoa *U.S.A.* 40°45N 88°43W **311** D8
Chenôve *France* 47°16N 5°1E **173** E12
Chenxi *China* 28°2N 110°12E **229** C8

Chenzhou China 25°47N 113°1E 229 E9
Cheò, Eilean a' = Skye
  U.K. 57°15N 6°10W 167 D2
Cheom Ksan Cambodia 14°13N 104°56E 236 E1
Cheonan S. Korea 36°48N 127°9E 224 D3
Cheongdam S. Korea 37°31N 127°2E 137 B2
Cheongdo S. Korea 35°38N 128°42E 224 G4
Cheongju S. Korea 36°39N 127°27E 224 D3
Cheongsando S. Korea 34°11N 126°53E 224 G4
Cheongsong S. Korea 36°25N 129°3E 224 D4
Cheonho S. Korea 37°32N 127°6E 137 B2
Cheonsumman S. Korea 36°35N 126°25E 224 D3
Cheops Egypt 29°58N 31°8E 117 B1
Cheorwon S. Korea 38°15N 127°10E 224 C3
Chepelare Bulgaria 41°44N 24°40E 203 E8
Chepén Peru 7°15S 79°23W 330 B2
Chépénéhé N. Cal. 20°47S 167°9E 288 d
Chepes Argentina 31°20S 66°35W 334 C2
Chepo Panama 9°10N 79°6E 320 E4
Chepstow U.K. 51°38N 2°41W 169 F5
Chequamegon B. U.S.A. 46°39N 90°51W 308 B8
Cher □ France 47°10N 2°30E 173 E9
Cher → France 47°21N 0°29E 172 E7
Cherasco Italy 40°27N 17°10E 201 B10
Cheran India 25°45N 90°44E 241 C2
Cherasco Italy 44°39N 7°51E 198 D4
Cherating Malaysia 3°35S 103°5E 234 B2
Cheraw U.S.A. 34°42N 79°53W 315 D15
Cherbourg France 49°39N 1°40W 172 C5
Cherchell Algeria 36°35N 2°12E 261 A5
Cherdakly Russia 54°25N 48°50E 190 C9
Cherdyn Russia 60°24N 56°29E 186 B10
Cheremkhovo Russia 53°8N 103°1E 216 D11
Cherepanovo Russia 54°15N 83°30E 217 B10
Cherepkovo Russia 55°45N 37°21E 129 B2
Cherepovets Russia 59°5N 37°55E 188 C9
Chergui, Chott ech Algeria 34°21N 0°25E 261 B5
Chergui, Zahrez Algeria 35°11N 3°31E 261 B5
Cherial India 17°55N 78°59E 244 F4
Cheribon = Cirebon
  Indonesia 6°45S 108°32E 235 D3
Cherikov = Cherykaw
  Belarus 53°32N 31°20E 177 B16
Cheriyam I. India 10°9N 73°40E 245 J1
Cherkasy Ukraine 49°27N 32°4E 189 H7
Cherkasy □ Ukraine 48°55N 30°50E 189 H6
Cherkessk Russia 44°15N 42°5E 191 H6
Cherla India 18°5N 80°49E 245 D4
Cherlak Russia 54°15N 74°55E 217 B8
Chernaya Russia 70°30N 89°10E 215 B9
Cherial Taiwan 23°29N 120°25E 225 C2
Chiai Taiwan 23°30N 120°30E 225 C2
Chiaksan □ S. Korea 37°15N 128°0E 224 C4
Chiali Taiwan 23°9N 120°10E 225 C2
Chialulantsun Taiwan 22°49N 121°1E 225 C3
Chiamboni Somali Rep. 1°39S 41°35E 267 E5
Chiamussu = Jiamusi
  China 46°40N 130°26E 219 B15
Chiana Terme Italy 43°3N 11°49E 199 E8
Chianapu Taiwan 22°47N 120°36E 225 C2
Chiang Dao Thailand 19°22N 98°58E 236 C2
Chiang Dao, Doi Thailand 19°23N 98°54E 236 C2
Chiang Kham Thailand 19°32N 100°18E 236 C3
Chiang Khong Thailand 20°17N 100°24E 228 G3
Chiang Mai Thailand 18°47N 98°59E 236 C2
Chiang Rai Thailand 19°52N 99°50E 228 H2
Chiang Saen Thailand 20°16N 100°5E 228 G3
Chiangchun Taiwan 23°12N 120°9E 225 C2
Chiange Angola 15°35S 13°40E 265 F2
Chianti Italy 43°20N 11°20E 199 E8
Chiaohsi Taiwan 24°49N 121°46E 225 B3
Chiaotou Taiwan 22°45N 120°18E 225 C2
Chiapa → Mexico 16°42N 93°0W 319 D6
Chiapa de Corzo Mexico 16°42N 93°0W 319 D6
Chiapas □ Mexico 16°30N 92°30W 319 D6
Chiapas, Sa. Madre de
  Mexico 15°40N 93°0W 319 D6
Chiaramonti Italy 40°45N 8°41E 201 B1
Chiaravalle Italy 43°36N 13°19E 199 E10
Chiaravalle Centrale Italy 38°41N 16°25E 201 D9
Chiaravalle Milanese Italy 45°24N 9°16E 189 M7
Chiari Italy 45°32N 9°56E 198 C6
Chiatung Taiwan 22°25N 120°32E 225 C2
Chiautla de Tapia Mexico 18°18N 98°36W 319 D5
Chiàvari Italy 44°19N 9°19E 198 D6
Chiavenna Italy 46°19N 9°24E 198 B6
Chiba Japan 35°30N 140°7E 223 B12
Chiba □ Japan 35°30N 140°20E 223 B12
Chibabava Angola 13°38S 21°56E 265 E4
Chibemba, Cunene, Angola 15°48S 14°8E 265 F2
Chibemba Hulla, Angola 16°20S 15°20E 265 F3
Chibi Zimbabwe 20°18S 30°25E 271 B5
Chibia Angola 15°10S 13°42E 265 F2
Chibougamau Canada 49°56N 74°24W 298 C5
Chibougamau L. Canada 49°50N 74°20W 298 C5
Chibuk Nigeria 10°52N 12°50E 263 C7
Chibuto Mozam. 24°40S 33°33E 271 C5
Chibyu = Ukhta Russia 63°34N 53°41E 186 B9
Chic-Chocs, Mts. Canada 48°55N 66°0W 299 C6
Chicacole = Srikakulam
  India 18°14N 83°58E 244 E8
Chicago U.S.A. 41°52N 87°38W 119 B3
Chicago, Univ. of U.S.A. 41°47N 87°35W 119 c3
Chicago Harbor Chicago, U.S.A. 119 d3
Chicago Heights U.S.A. 41°30N 87°38W 311 C9
Chicago Lawn U.S.A. 41°47N 87°41W 119 C3
Chicago-Midway ✈ (MDW)
  U.S.A. 41°47N 87°45W 119 C2
Chicago O'Hare Int. ✈ (ORD)
  U.S.A. 41°57N 87°54W 119 B1
Chicago Ridge U.S.A. 41°41N 87°46W 119 C2
Chicago River → Chicago, U.S.A. 119 b2
Chicago River, North Branch →
  U.S.A. 41°53N 87°42W 119 C1
Chicago Sanitary and Ship Canal
  U.S.A. 41°49N 87°40W 119 C1
Chicago State Univ.
  U.S.A. 41°43N 87°36W 119 C3
Chicago Zoo U.S.A. 41°43N 87°36W 119 C3
Chicapa → Dem. Rep. of the Congo 6°25S 20°48E 265 D4
Chicha Chad 16°57N 18°34E 258 D4
Chichagof I. U.S.A. 57°30N 135°30W 303 H14
Chichaoua Morocco 31°32N 8°44W 260 B4
Chichawatni Pakistan 30°32N 72°42E 242 D5
Chichén-Itzá Mexico 20°37N 88°35W 322 b
Chicheng China 40°55N 115°55E 226 D7
Chichester U.K. 50°50N 0°47W 169 G7
Chichester Ra. Australia 22°12S 119°15E 278 D2
Chichibu Japan 35°59N 139°10E 223 A11
Chichibu-Tama-Kai △
  Japan 35°52N 138°42E 223 B10
Chichi'an China 47°26N 124°0E 219 B13
Chi'chi'ou Taiwan 22°11N 77°40E 242 H3
Chichola India 22°11N 79°33E 225 J9
Chiclana de la Frontera
  Spain 36°26N 6°9W 195 J4
Chiclayo Peru 6°42S 79°50W 330 B2
Chico → Chubut, Argentina 50°0S 68°30W 336 D3
Chico → Santa Cruz,
  Argentina 44°0S 67°0W 336 F3
Chico → Phil. 17°57N 121°36E 232 C3
Chicoa Mozam. 15°36S 32°20E 269 F3
Chicomba Angola 14°10S 14°52E 265 E2
Chicomo Mozam. 24°31S 34°6E 271 B5
Chicomostoc Mexico 22°28N 102°46W 318 C4
Chiconi Mayotte 12°50S 45°7E 272 b
Chicontepec Mexico 20°58N 98°10W 319 C5
Chicopee U.S.A. 42°9N 72°37W 313 D12
Chicualacuala Mozam. 22°6S 31°42E 271 B5
Chicuma Angola 13°26S 14°50E 265 E2
Chidambaram India 11°20N 79°45E 245 J4
Chidenguele Mozam. 24°55S 34°11E 271 B5
Chidley, C. Canada 60°23N 64°26W 295 E14
Chiducuane Mozam. 24°35S 34°25E 271 B5
Chiede Angola 17°15S 16°22E 265 F3
Chiefland U.S.A. 29°29N 82°52W 317 F7
Chiefs Pt. Canada 44°41N 81°18W 312 B3
Chiehting Taiwan 22°54N 120°11E 225 C2
Chiem Hoa Vietnam 22°12N 105°17E 236 A5
Chiemsee Germany 47°53N 12°28E 179 H8
Chienchen Taiwan 22°35N 120°18E 225 C2
Chiengi Zambia 8°45S 29°10E 269 D2
Chiengmai = Chiang Mai
  Thailand 18°47N 98°59E 236 C2
Chiengo Angola 13°20S 21°55E 265 E4
Chienti → Italy 43°18N 13°45E 199 E10
Chienzuci China 23°12N 113°22E 121 A3
Chieri Italy 45°1N 7°49E 198 D4
Chiers → France 49°39N 4°59E 173 C11
Chiesa in Valmalenco Italy 46°16N 9°51E 198 B6
Chiese → Italy 45°8N 10°25E 198 C7
Chieti Italy 42°21N 14°10E 199 F11
Chifeng China 42°18N 118°58E 227 C10
Chigasaki Japan 35°19N 139°24E 223 B11
Chigirin Ukraine 49°4N 32°38E 189 H7
Chignecto B. Canada 45°30N 64°40W 299 C7
Chignik U.S.A. 56°18N 158°24W 303 H8
Chigorodó Colombia 7°41N 76°42W 328 B2
Chiguana Bolivia 21°0S 67°58W 334 A2
Chigwell U.K. 51°37N 0°6E 169 F8
Chihli, G. of = Bo Hai
  China 39°0N 119°0E 227 C10
Ch'ihpen Taiwan 22°42N 121°2E 225 C3
Ch'ihshang Taiwan 23°7N 121°12E 225 C3
Chihu = Jixi China 45°20N 130°50E 227 B8
Chihu Taiwan 23°54N 120°24E 225 C2
Chihuahua Mexico 28°38N 106°5W 318 B3
Chihuahua □ Mexico 28°30N 106°0W 318 B3
Chiili = Shieli Kazakhstan 44°20N 66°15E 217 D7
Chik Bollapur India 13°25N 77°45E 245 H3
Chik Sha China 22°17N 114°16E 122 B2
Chikalda India 21°24N 77°19E 244 D3
Chikhli Ahmadnad, India 20°36N 73°4E 244 D1
Chikhli Maharashtra, India 20°20N 76°18E 244 D3
Chikmagalur India 13°15N 75°45E 245 H2
Chiknayakanhalli India 13°26N 76°37E 245 H3
Chikodi India 16°26N 74°38E 245 G2
Chila Taiwan 23°8N 120°7E 225 C2
Chikugo Japan 33°14N 130°28E 222 D2
Chikuma-Gawa →
  Japan 36°59N 138°35E 223 A10
Chikura Japan 34°55N 139°57E 223 C11
Chikushino Japan 33°30N 130°30E 222 D2
Chikwawa Malawi 16°2S 34°50E 269 F3
Chila Angola 14°35S 21°20E 265 E2
Chilapa Mexico 17°36N 99°10W 319 D5
Chilas Sri Lanka 35°25N 74°5E 243 B6
Chilaw Sri Lanka 7°30N 79°50E 245 L4
Chilcotin → Canada 51°44N 122°23W 305 D7
Childers Australia 25°15S 152°17E 281 D5
Childersburg U.S.A. 33°16N 86°21W 316 B3
Childress U.S.A. 34°25N 100°13W 314 D4
Child's Hill U.K. 51°33N 0°12W 125 A2
Chile ■ S. Amer. 35°0S 72°0W 327 G3
Chile, Univ. de Chile 33°26S 70°39W 137 B2
Chile Basin Pac. Oc. 33°0S 80°0W 289 L20
Chile Chico Chile 46°33S 71°44W 336 C2
Chile Rise Pac. Oc. 38°0S 92°0W 289 L18
Chilecito Argentina 29°10S 67°30W 334 B2
Chilengue, Serra de
  Angola 3°18S 15°22E 265 E2
Chilesso Angola 11°35S 16°40E 265 E2
Chilete Peru 7°10S 78°50W 330 B2
Chilhowee U.S.A. 38°36N 93°51W 311 F7
Chília, Braţul →
  Romania 45°14N 29°42E 183 E14
Chililbre Panama 9°9N 79°37W 320 c
Chilik Kazakhstan 43°33N 78°17E 217 D9
Chilin = Jilin China 43°44N 126°30E 227 C14
Chiliomodi Greece 37°48N 22°51E 204 D4
Chilka L. India 19°40N 85°25E 244 E7
Chilko → Canada 52°0N 123°40W 296 C4
Chilko L. Canada 51°20N 124°10W 296 C4
Chilla Saroda India 28°35N 77°18E 120 B2
Chillagoe Australia 17°7S 144°33E 280 B3
Chillán Chile 36°40S 72°10W 334 D1
Chillicothe Ill., U.S.A. 40°55N 89°29W 310 E7
Chillicothe Mo., U.S.A. 39°48N 93°33W 310 F7
Chillicothe Ohio, U.S.A. 39°20N 82°59W 309 F12
Chilliwack Canada 49°10N 121°54W 296 D4
Chillum U.S.A. 38°58N 76°58W 148 B4
Chilo India 27°25N 73°32E 242 F5
Chiloane, I. de Chile 42°30S 73°50W 336 B2
Chiloé □ Chile 42°11S 73°50W 336 B2
Chilonda Angola 11°59S 16°12E 265 E3
Chilongo Angola 13°55S 16°16E 265 E3
Chilpancingo Mexico 17°33N 99°30W 319 D5
Chiltern Australia 36°10S 146°36E 283 D7
Chiltern Hills U.K. 51°40N 0°53W 169 F7
Chilton U.S.A. 44°2N 88°10W 308 D9
Chiluage Angola 9°30S 21°50E 265 D4
Chilubi Zambia 11°5S 29°58E 269 E2
Chilubula Malawi 10°14S 31°51E 269 E3
Chilumba Malawi 10°28S 34°12E 269 E3
Chilung Taiwan 25°3N 121°45E 225 A3
Chilwa, L. Malawi 15°15S 35°40E 269 F3
Chimaltepec Mexico 17°35N 96°13W 319 D5
Chimán Panama 8°45N 78°40W 320 E4
Chimanimani Zimbabwe 19°48S 32°52E 271 A5
Chimanimani △ Zimbabwe 19°48S 33°0E 271 A5
Chimay Belgium 50°3N 4°20E 170 D4
Chimayo U.S.A. 36°0N 105°56W 305 J11
Chimba Zambia 9°54S 31°28E 269 D3
Chimbay Uzbekistan 42°57N 59°47E 216 D5
Chimborazo Ecuador 1°29S 78°55W 328 D2
Chimborazo □ Ecuador 1°0S 78°40W 328 D2
Chimbote Peru 9°0S 78°35W 330 B2
Chimboy Uzbekistan 42°57N 59°47E 216 D5
Chi'mei Taiwan 23°12N 119°26E 225 C1
Ch'imei Yü Taiwan 9°10N 82°0W 320 E3
Chimichagua Colombia 9°15N 73°49W 328 B3
Chimkent = Shymkent
  Kazakhstan 42°18N 69°36E 217 D7
Chimoio Mozam. 19°4S 33°30E 269 F3
Chimpembe Zambia 9°31S 29°33E 269 D2
Chimur India 20°30N 79°23E 244 D4
Chin □ Burma 22°0N 93°0E 241 E4
Chin Hills Burma 22°30N 93°30E 241 D4
Chin Ling Shan = Qinling Shandi
  China 33°50N 108°10E 226 H5
China Mexico 25°42N 99°14W 319 B5
China ■ Asia 30°0N 110°0E 219 E11
China, Great Plain of Asia 35°0N 115°0E 210 E13
China Basin San Francisco, U.S.A. 136 c3
China Lake U.S.A. 35°44N 117°37W 307 K9
China Town Toronto, Canada 141 b1
Chinacota Colombia 7°37N 72°36W 328 B3
Chinan = Jinan China 36°38N 117°1E 226 F9
Chinandega Nic. 12°35N 87°12W 320 D2
Chinati Peak U.S.A. 29°57N 104°29W 314 G2
Chinatown Singapore 138 c2
Chinatown Boston, U.S.A. 116 c2
Chinatown Chicago, U.S.A. 119 f1
Chinatown Los Angeles, U.S.A. 127 a3
Chinatown New York, U.S.A. 132 e2
Chincha Alta Peru 13°25S 76°7W 330 C2
Chinchaga → Canada 58°53N 118°20W 296 B5
Chincheros Peru 13°30S 73°44W 330 C3
Chinchilla Australia 26°45S 150°38E 281 D5
Chinchilla de Monte Aragón
  Spain 38°53N 1°40W 197 G3
Chinchorro, Banco
  Mexico 18°35N 87°22W 319 D7
Chinchou = Jinzhou
  China 41°5N 121°3E 227 D11
Chincoteague U.S.A. 37°56N 75°23W 309 G16
Chinde Mozam. 18°35S 36°30E 269 F4
Chindwin → Burma 21°26N 95°15E 241 E5
Chineni India 33°2N 75°15E 243 C6
Chinga Mozam. 15°13S 38°35E 269 F4
Chingaza △ Colombia 4°30N 73°40W 328 C3
Chingola Zambia 12°31S 27°53E 269 E2
Chingole Malawi 13°4S 34°17E 269 E3
Chingoni Mayotte 12°48S 45°8E 272 b
Chingu Taiwan 23°28N 121°29E 225 C3
Ch'ingshui Changhua,
  Taiwan 24°16N 120°34E 225 B2
Chingshui Hualien,
  Taiwan 24°1N 121°41E 225 B3
Chingshui Ilan, Taiwan 24°39N 121°55E 225 B3
Ch'ingtao = Qingdao
  China 36°5N 120°20E 227 F11
Chinguar Angola 12°25S 16°45E 265 E3
Chinguetti Mauritania 20°25N 12°24W 260 D2
Chingune Mozam. 20°33S 34°58E 271 B5
Chinguota India 22°29N 68°14E 124 C1
Chinhae S. Korea 35°9N 128°47E 224 D4
Chinhanguanine Mozam. 25°21S 32°30E 271 C5
Chinhoyi Zimbabwe 17°20S 30°8E 269 F3
Chinhsien = Jinxian
  China 32°1N 119°26E 229 A12
Chini India 31°32N 78°15E 242 D8
Chiniot Pakistan 31°45N 73°0E 242 D5
Chinipas Mexico 27°23N 108°32W 318 B3
Chinji Pakistan 32°42N 72°22E 242 C5
Chinju = Jinju S. Korea 35°12N 128°2E 224 D4
Chinkai Afghan. 31°57N 67°26E 242 D2
Chinkapook Australia 34°5S 142°57E 282 C5
Chinko → C.A.R. 4°50N 23°53E 264 B4
Chinle U.S.A. 36°9N 109°33W 305 H9
Ch'inlun Taiwan 22°32N 120°57E 225 C2
Chinmen Taiwan 24°26N 118°19E 225 a
Chinmen Tao Taiwan 24°26N 118°22E 225 a
Chinna Cr. → Pakistan 24°50N 67°0E 123 B2
Chinnamanur India 9°50N 77°24E 245 K3
Chinnampo = Namp'o
  N. Korea 38°52N 125°10E 224 E2
Chino Japan 35°59N 138°9E 223 B10
Chino Calif., U.S.A. 34°1N 117°41W 307 L9
Chino Valley U.S.A. 34°45N 112°27W 305 J7
Chinois, Quartier Montréal, Canada 130 b2
Chinon France 47°10N 0°15E 172 E7
Chinook U.S.A. 48°35N 109°14W 304 A9
Chinook Trough Pac. Oc. 44°0N 175°0W 288 C10
Chinoya Zambia 13°55S 23°16E 265 E4
Chinsali Zambia 10°30S 32°2E 269 E3
Chinshan Taiwan 23°13N 121°38E 225 C3
Chinshan = Chunchura
  India 22°53N 88°27E 243 H13
Chintalapudi India 17°4N 80°50W 245 F5
Chintamani India 13°26N 78°3E 245 H4
Chinwangtao = Qinhuangdao
  China 39°56N 119°30E 227 E10
Chióggia Italy 45°13N 12°17E 199 C9
Chíos Greece 38°27N 26°9E 205 C8
Chíos □ Greece 38°25N 26°5E 205 C8
Chipata Zambia 13°38S 32°28E 269 E3
Chipei Tao Taiwan 23°45N 119°37E 225 C1
Chipercani Moldova 47°31N 28°50E 183 C13
Chipindo Angola 13°49S 15°48E 265 E2
Chipinge Zimbabwe 20°13S 32°28E 269 G3
Chipinge △ Zimbabwe 20°10S 32°40E 271 B5
Chipiona Spain 36°44N 6°26W 195 J4
Chipley U.S.A. 30°47N 85°32W 316 F4
Chiplun India 17°31N 73°34E 244 F1
Chipman Canada 46°6N 65°53W 299 C6
Chipoka Malawi 13°57S 34°28E 269 E3
Chippenham U.K. 51°27N 2°6W 169 F6
Chippewa → U.S.A. 44°25N 92°5W 308 C7
Chippewa Falls U.S.A. 44°56N 91°24W 308 C8
Chipping Norton U.K. 51°56N 1°32W 169 F6
Chiprovtsi Bulgaria 43°24N 22°52E 202 C6
Chiquelequele Angola 16°44S 19°5E 265 F3
Chiquián Peru 10°10S 77°0W 330 B2
Chiquibul □ Belize 16°57N 88°50W 320 D2
Chiquinquirá Colombia 5°37N 73°50W 328 B3
Chiquita, Mar Argentina 30°42S 62°30W 334 C3
Chir → Russia 48°30N 43°0E 191 F7
Chirala India 15°50N 80°26E 245 G5
Chiramba Mozam. 16°55S 34°39E 269 F3
Chirawa India 28°14N 75°42E 242 E6
Chirayinkil India 8°41N 76°49E 245 K3
Chirchiq Uzbekistan 41°29N 69°35E 217 D7
Chiredzi Zimbabwe 21°0S 31°38E 271 B5
Chirfa Niger 20°55N 12°22E 269 B2
Chirgua → Venezuela 8°54N 67°56W 328 B4
Chiribiquete △ Colombia 0°31N 72°50W 328 C3
Chiricahua △ U.S.A. 32°0N 109°20W 305 K9
Chiricahua Peak U.S.A. 31°52N 109°20W 305 L9
Chirikof I. U.S.A. 55°50N 155°40W 300 D1
Chiriquí, G. de Panama 8°0N 82°10W 320 E3
Chiriquí, L. de Panama 9°10N 82°0W 320 E3
Chirisa △ Zimbabwe 17°53S 28°15E 269 F2
Chirivira Falls Zimbabwe 21°10S 32°12E 269 G3
Chirmiri India 23°15N 82°20E 243 H10
Chirnogi Romania 44°7N 26°32E 183 F11
Chirongui Mayotte 12°55S 45°9E 272 b
Chirpan Bulgaria 42°10N 25°19E 203 D9
Chirripó Grande, Cerro
  Costa Rica 9°29N 83°29W 320 E3
Chirundu Zimbabwe 16°3S 28°50E 271 A4
Chisamba Zambia 14°55S 28°20E 269 E2
Chisapani Nepal 28°37N 81°16E 243 E9
Chisasa Zambia 12°6S 25°30E 265 E5
Chisasibi Canada 53°50N 79°0W 298 B4
Ch'ishan Taiwan 22°51N 120°31E 225 C2
Chisholm Alta., Canada 54°55N 114°10W 296 C6
Chisholm Minn., U.S.A. 47°29N 92°53W 308 B7
Chishtian Mandi Pakistan 29°50N 72°55E 242 E5
Chishui He → China 28°30N 105°40E 228 C5
Chisimaio = Kismaayo
  Somali Rep. 0°22S 42°32E 267 E5
Chisimba Falls Zambia 10°12S 30°56E 269 E3
Chişinău Moldova 47°2N 28°50E 183 C13
Chişinău ✈ (KIV) Moldova 47°3N 28°46E 183 C13
Chişineu Criş Romania 46°32N 21°37E 182 D6
Chislehurst U.K. 51°24N 0°6E 125 B4
Chisone → Italy 44°49N 7°25E 198 D4
Chisos Mts. U.S.A. 29°5N 103°15W 314 G3
Chissengue Angola 9°13S 20°34E 265 D4
Chissilo Angola 13°30S 16°55E 265 E3
Chistochina U.S.A. 62°34N 144°40W 303 E11
Chistopol Russia 55°25N 50°38E 190 D10
Chiswick U.K. 51°29N 0°16W 125 B2
Chiswick House U.K. 51°28N 0°15W 125 B2
Chita Colombia 6°11N 72°28W 328 B3
Chita Russia 52°0N 113°35E 219 A11
Chitado Angola 17°10S 14°8E 265 F2
Chitagá Colombia 6°59S 21°12E 265 D4
Chitambo Zambia 12°59S 16°8E 265 E3
Chitipa Malawi 9°41S 33°19E 269 D3
Chitose Hokkaidō, Japan 42°49N 141°39E 220 C10
Chitose Kanagawa, Japan 35°33N 139°37E 140 B2
Chitradurga India 14°14N 76°24E 245 H3
Chitrakot India 19°10N 81°40E 244 E5
Chitral Pakistan 35°50N 71°56E 240 B7
Chitravati → India 14°45N 78°15E 245 G4
Chitré Panama 7°59N 80°27W 320 E3
Chittagong Bangla. 22°19N 91°48E 241 F8
Chittagong □ Bangla. 24°5N 91°0E 241 E8
Chittaurgarh India 24°52N 74°38E 242 G6
Chittoor India 13°15N 79°5E 245 H4
Chittur India 10°40N 76°45E 245 J3
Chitungwiza Zimbabwe 18°0S 31°6E 269 F3
Chiusa Italy 46°38N 11°34E 199 B8
Chiusi Italy 43°1N 11°57E 199 E8
Chiva Spain 39°27N 0°41W 197 F4
Chivacoa Venezuela 10°10N 68°54W 328 A4
Chivasso Italy 45°11N 7°53E 198 C4
Chivay Peru 15°40S 71°35W 330 D3
Chive Bolivia 12°23S 68°33W 330 C4
Chivhu Zimbabwe 19°2S 30°52E 269 F3
Chivilcoy Argentina 34°55S 60°0W 334 C3
Chiwanda Tanzania 11°23S 34°55E 269 E3
Chixi China 21°58N 110°58E 229 G9
Chiyoda Tokyo, Japan 140 b1
Chizarira △ Zimbabwe 17°36S 27°45E 269 F2
Chizarira △ Zimbabwe 17°44S 27°55E 269 F2
Chizela Zambia 13°8S 25°0E 265 E5
Chizu Japan 35°16N 134°14E 222 B6
Chkalov = Orenburg
  Russia 51°45N 55°6E 186 D10
Chkalovsk Russia 56°50N 43°10E 190 B6
Chloride U.S.A. 35°25N 114°12W 307 K12
Chlumec nad Cidlinou
  Czech Rep. 50°9N 15°29E 180 A8
Chmielnik Poland 50°37N 20°43E 185 H7
Cho-do N. Korea 38°30N 124°50E 224 C2
Cho Phuoc Hai Vietnam 10°26N 107°18E 237 G6
Choa Chu Kang Singapore 1°22N 103°41E 138 A2
Choba Kenya 2°30N 38°5E 266 D4
Chobe △ Botswana 18°37S 24°23E 270 A4
Choc B. St. Lucia 14°3N 60°59W 323 m
Chocianów Poland 51°27N 15°55E 185 G2
Chociwel Poland 53°29N 15°21E 184 E2
Chocó □ Colombia 6°0N 77°0W 328 B2
Chocolate Mts. U.S.A. 33°15N 115°15W 307 M11
Chocontá Colombia 5°9N 73°41W 328 B3
Chocowinity U.S.A. 35°31N 77°6W 315 D16
Choctawhatchee → U.S.A. 30°25N 86°8W 316 F3
Choctawhatchee B. U.S.A. 30°20N 86°20W 317 F2
Chodavaram Andhra Pradesh,
  India 17°50N 82°57E 244 F6
Chodavaram Andhra Pradesh,
  India 17°27N 81°54E 244 F5
Chodecz Poland 52°24N 19°2E 185 F6
Chodov u Prahy Czech Rep. 50°1N 14°30E 135 B2
Chodzież Poland 52°58N 16°58E 185 F4
Choele Choel Argentina 39°11S 65°40W 336 A3
Choiseul St. Lucia 13°47N 61°3W 323 m
Choiseul Solomon Is. 7°0S 156°40E 287 B7
Choisy-le-Roi France 48°46N 2°24E 134 B3
Choix Mexico 26°43N 108°17W 318 B3
Chojna Poland 52°58N 14°25E 185 F1
Chojnice Poland 53°42N 17°32E 185 E4
Chojnów Poland 51°18N 15°58E 185 G2
Chok Chai Thailand 14°44N 102°10E 236 E4
Chōkai-San Japan 39°6N 140°3E 220 E10
Choke Canyon Res.
  U.S.A. 28°30N 98°20W 314 G5
Choke Mts. Ethiopia 11°18N 37°15E 257 E4
Chokurdakh Russia 70°38N 147°55E 215 B15
Chokwé Mozam. 24°25S 32°50E 271 B5
Cholame U.S.A. 35°44N 120°18W 306 K6
Cholargos Greece 37°59N 23°48E 138 A2
Cholet France 47°4N 0°52W 172 E6
Cholguan Chile 37°10S 72°3W 334 D1
Choloma Honduras 15°37N 87°57W 320 C2
Cholpon-Ata Kyrgyzstan 42°40N 77°0E 217 D9
Choluteca Honduras 13°20N 87°14W 320 D2
Choluteca → Honduras 13°0N 87°20W 320 D2
Chom Bung Thailand 13°37N 99°36E 236 F2
Chom Thong Bangkok,
  Thailand 13°41N 100°29E 113 B1
Chom Thong Chiang Mai,
  Thailand 18°25N 98°41E 236 C2
Choma Zambia 16°48S 26°59E 269 F2
Chomolungma = Everest, Mt.
  Nepal 28°5N 86°58E 243 F12
Chomun India 27°15N 75°40E 242 F6
Chomutov Czech Rep. 50°28N 13°23E 180 A6
Chon Buri Thailand 13°21N 101°1E 236 F3
Chon Thanh Vietnam 11°24N 106°36E 237 G6
Chone Ecuador 0°40S 80°0W 328 D2
Chong Kai Cambodia 13°57N 103°35E 236 F4
Chong Mek Thailand 15°10N 105°27E 236 E5
Chong Pang Singapore 1°26N 103°49E 138 A2
Chong Phangan Thailand 9°39N 100°0E 237 b
Chong Samui Thailand 9°21N 99°50E 237 b
Chongde China 30°32N 120°26E 229 B12
Ch'ŏngjin N. Korea 41°47N 129°50E 224 B4
Chŏngju N. Korea 39°40N 125°5E 224 C2
Chongli China 40°58N 115°15E 226 D8
Chongming China 31°38N 121°23E 229 B13
Chongming Dao China 31°40N 121°30E 229 B13
Chongoroi Angola 13°37S 14°1E 265 E2
Chongoyape Peru 6°35S 79°25W 330 B2
Ch'ŏngp'yŏng N. Korea 39°47N 127°24E 224 C3
Chongqing Chongqing,
  China 29°35N 106°25E 228 C6
Chongqing Sichuan,
  China 30°38N 103°40E 228 B4
Chongqing Shi □ China 30°0N 108°0E 228 C6
Chongren China 27°46N 116°3E 229 D11
Chonguene Mozam. 25°3S 33°49E 271 C5
Chongwe Zambia 15°21S 28°42E 269 F2
Chongwen Beijing, China 114 c2
Chongyi China 25°42N 114°22E 229 E10
Chongzuo China 22°23N 107°20E 228 E6
Chonogol Mongolia 45°54N 115°22E 226 B8
Chonos, Arch. de los Chile 45°0S 75°0W 336 C2
Chop Ukraine 48°26N 22°12E 182 B7
Chopda India 21°20N 75°15E 244 D2
Chopim → Brazil 25°35S 53°5W 335 B5
Chopin Museum Warsaw, Poland 142 b2
Chor Pakistan 25°31N 69°46E 242 G3
Chora Greece 37°3N 21°42E 204 D3
Chora Sfakion Greece 35°15N 24°9E 207 E6
Chorbat La India 34°42N 76°37E 243 B7
Chorley U.K. 53°39N 2°38W 168 D5
Chorna Ukraine 47°36N 29°48E 183 C14
Chornaya → Russia 55°41N 38°0E 129 B6
Chornobyl Ukraine 51°20N 30°15E 177 C16
Chornomorske Ukraine 45°31N 32°46E 189 K7
Choroluque, Cerro Bolivia 20°59S 66°5W 334 A2
Choroszcz Poland 53°10N 22°59E 185 E9
Chorregon Australia 22°40S 143°32E 280 C3
Chorrillos Peru 12°10S 77°1W 124 C2
Chortkiv Ukraine 49°2N 25°46E 177 D3
Chorzele Poland 53°15N 20°55E 185 E7
Chorzów Poland 50°18N 18°57E 185 H5
Chos-Malal Argentina 37°20S 70°15W 334 D1
Ch'osan N. Korea 40°50N 125°47E 224 B2
Chosheta Shan Taiwan 23°27N 120°57E 225 C3
Chōshi Japan 35°45N 140°51E 223 B12
Choshui Hsi → Taiwan 23°50N 120°15E 225 C2
Choszczno Poland 53°7N 15°25E 185 E2
Chota Peru 6°33S 78°39W 330 B2
Choteau U.S.A. 47°49N 112°11W 304 C7
Chotěboř Czech Rep. 49°43N 15°40E 180 B8
Chotila India 22°23N 71°15E 242 H4
Chotta Udepur India 22°19N 74°1E 242 H6
Choûm Mauritania 21°11N 13°36W 260 D2
Chounguui Mayotte 12°57S 45°8E 272 b
Chowchilla U.S.A. 37°7N 120°16W 306 H6
Chowpatty Beach Mumbai, India 130 b1
Choybalsan Mongolia 48°4N 114°30E 219 B11
Choyr Mongolia 46°24N 108°30E 219 B10
Chrisman U.S.A. 39°48N 87°41W 311 E9
Chrisoupoli Greece 40°58N 24°42E 203 F8
Christ Church Cathedral
  Montréal, Canada 130 c2
Christburg = Dzierzgoń
  Poland 53°58N 19°20E 184 E6
Christchurch N.Z. 43°33S 172°47E 285 E7
Christchurch Dorset, U.K. 50°44N 1°47W 169 G6
Christian I. Canada 44°50N 80°12W 312 B4
Christian Quarter Jerusalem 123 b3
Christian Sd. U.S.A. 55°56N 134°40W 303 J14
Christiana Greece 36°14N 25°13E 205 D7
Christiana Jamaica 18°10N 77°29W 320 a
Christiana North West,
  S. Africa 27°52S 25°8E 270 C4
Christiansborg Slot
  Copenhagen, Denmark 118 c2
Christiansfeld Denmark 55°21N 9°29E 163 J3
Christianshåb = Qasigiannguit
  Greenland 68°50N 51°18E 154 C5
Christianshavn Denmark 55°40N 12°35E 118 A3
Christiansted
  U.S. Virgin Is. 17°45N 64°42W 321 C7
Christie B. Canada 62°32N 111°10W 296 A7
Christina → Canada 56°40N 111°3W 297 B6
Christmas Cr. →
  Australia 18°29S 125°23E 278 C4
Christmas I. = Kiritimati
  Kiribati 1°58N 157°27W 289 G12
Christmas I. Ind. Oc. 10°30S 105°40E 273 F9
Christofel △ Curaçao 12°13N 69°8W 322 g
Christopher, I. Australia 24°49S 127°42E 278 E4
Christyakovo = Thorez
  Ukraine 48°4N 38°34E 189 H10
Chrudim Czech Rep. 49°58N 15°43E 180 B8
Chrysler Building New York, U.S.A. 132 c2
Chrzanów Małopolskie,
  Poland 50°10N 19°21E 185 H6
Chrzanów Warszawa,
  Poland 52°13N 20°53E 142 B1
Chtapodia Greece 37°24N 25°34E 205 D7
Chtimba Malawi 10°35S 34°13E 269 E3
Chü = Shū China 43°36N 73°42E 217 D8
Chū → Kazakhstan 45°0N 67°44E 217 D7
Chü = Shū → Kazakhstan 45°0N 67°44E 217 D7
Chu Lai Vietnam 15°28N 108°45E 236 E7
Chu Mom Ray △
  Vietnam 14°29N 107°38E 236 E6
Chu Se Vietnam 13°40N 108°6E 236 E7
Chuadanga Bangla. 23°38N 88°51E 241 D7
Chuak, Ko Thailand 9°28N 99°41E 237 b
Ch'uanchou = Quanzhou
  China 24°55N 118°34E 229 E12
Chüanchow = Quanzhou
  China 24°55N 118°34E 229 E12
Chuangwei China 24°40N 121°49E 225 b
Chuankou China 34°20N 110°59E 226 G6
Chuathbaluk U.S.A. 61°42N 159°54W 300 C8
Chubarovka = Pology
  Ukraine 47°29N 36°15E 189 J9
Chubbuck U.S.A. 42°55N 112°28W 304 E7
Chūbu □ Japan 36°45N 137°30E 223 A9
Chūbu-Sangaku △ Japan 36°30N 137°40E 223 A9
Chubut □ Argentina 43°20S 65°5W 336 B3
Chubut → Argentina 43°20S 65°5W 336 B3

Chuch'i *Taiwan* 23°31N 120°33E **225** C2
Chuchi L. *Canada* 55°12N 124°30W **296** B4
Chuchow = Zhuzhou *China* 27°49N 113°12E **229** D9
Chuda *India* 22°29N 71°41E **242** H4
Chudovo *Russia* 59°10N 31°41E **188** C6
Chudskoye, Ozero *Russia* 58°13N 27°30E **188** C4
Chuen Lung *China* 22°23N 114°6E **122** A1
Chugach Mts. *U.S.A.* 60°45N 147°0W **303** F11
Chuginadak I. *U.S.A.* 52°50N 169°45W **303** K5
Chūgoku ☐ *Japan* 35°0N 133°0E **222** C5
Chūgoku-Sanchi *Japan* 35°0N 133°0E **222** B5
Chuguyev = Chuhuyiv *Ukraine* 49°55N 36°45E **189** H9
Chugwater *U.S.A.* 41°46N 104°50W **304** F11
Chuhuyiv *Ukraine* 49°55N 36°45E **189** H9
Chuk Kok *China* 22°20N 114°15E **122** A2
Chuka *Kenya* 0°20S 37°39E **268** C4
Chukchi Plateau *Arctic* 78°0N 165°0W **150** B17
Chukchi Sea *Russia* 68°0N 175°0W **215** C19
Chukotskiy Mys *Russia* 64°14N 173°8W **300** C5
Chukotskiy Poluostrov *Russia* 66°0N 174°0W **300** B5
Chukotskoye Nagorye *Russia* 68°0N 175°0E **215** C18
Chula *U.S.A.* 31°33N 83°32W **316** D6
Chula Vista *U.S.A.* 32°38N 117°5W **307** N9
Chulalongkorn Univ. *Thailand* 13°44N 100°31E **113** B2
Chulband → *India* 20°40N 79°54E **244** D4
Ch'ulin *Taiwan* 22°8N 120°42E **225** D2
Chulucanas *Peru* 5°8S 80°10W **330** B1
Chulumani *Bolivia* 16°24S 67°31W **330** D4
Chulym → *Russia* 57°43N 83°51E **214** D9
Chum Phae *Thailand* 16°40N 102°6E **236** D4
Chum Saeng *Thailand* 15°55N 100°15E **236** E3
Chuma *Bolivia* 15°24S 68°56W **330** D4
Chumar *India* 32°40N 78°35E **243** C8
Chumbicha *Argentina* 29°0S 66°10W **334** B2
Chumerna *Bulgaria* 42°45N 25°55E **203** D9
Chumikan *Russia* 54°40N 135°10E **215** D14
Chumphon *Thailand* 10°35N 99°14E **237** G2
Chumpi *Peru* 15°4S 73°46W **330** D3
Chumuare *Mozam.* 14°31S 31°50E **269** E3
Chuna → *Russia* 57°47N 94°37E **215** D10
Chun'an *Zhejiang, China* 29°35N 119°3E **229** C12
Chunan *Taiwan* 24°41N 120°52E **225** B2
Chuncheon *S. Korea* 37°58N 127°44E **224** D3
Chunchura *India* 22°53N 88°27E **243** H13
Chunga *Zambia* 15°0S 26°2E **269** F2
Chungcheongbuk-do ☐ *S. Korea* 36°45N 128°0E **224** D4
Chungcheongnam-do ☐ *S. Korea* 36°30N 127°0E **224** D3
Ch'ungch'ing = Chongqing *China* 29°35N 106°25E **228** C6
Chunggang-ŭp *N. Korea* 41°48N 126°48E **224** B3
Chungho *Taiwan* 25°0N 121°28E **225** A3
Chunghwa *N. Korea* 38°52N 125°47E **224** C2
Chungju *S. Korea* 36°58N 127°58E **224** D3
Chungking = Chongqing *China* 29°35N 106°25E **228** C6
Chungli *Taiwan* 24°57N 121°13E **225** B3
Chungpu *Taiwan* 23°26N 120°31E **225** C2
Chungt'iaoshan = Zhongtiao Shan *China* 35°0N 111°10E **226** G6
Chungtungwan *Taiwan* 24°31N 120°40E **225** B2
Chungyang Shanmo *Taiwan* 23°10N 121°0E **225** C3
Chunian *Pakistan* 30°57N 74°0E **242** D6
Chunya *Tanzania* 8°30S 33°27E **269** D3
Chunyang *China* 43°38N 129°23E **227** C15
Chuō *Tokyo, Japan* **140** b5
Chupara B. *Trin. & Tob.* 10°48N 61°22W **323** t
Chupara Pt. *Trin. & Tob.* 10°49N 61°22W **323** t
Chupei *Taiwan* 24°50N 121°0E **225** B3
Chuquibamba *Peru* 15°47S 72°44W **330** D3
Chuquibambilla *Peru* 14°7S 72°41W **330** C3
Chuquicamata *Chile* 22°15S 69°0W **334** A2
Chuquisaca ☐ *Bolivia* 20°30S 63°30W **331** E5
Chur *Switz.* 46°52N 9°32E **179** J5
Churachandpur *India* 24°20N 93°40E **241** C4
Church End *U.K.* 51°35N 0°11W **125** A2
Church of our Lady = Frauenkirche *Munich, Germany* **131** b2
Church Stretton *U.K.* 52°32N 2°48W **169** E5
Churchill *Vic., Australia* 38°19S 146°25E **283** E7
Churchill *Man., Canada* 58°47N 94°11W **297** B10
Churchill → *Man., Canada* 58°47N 94°12W **297** B10
Churchill → *Nfld. & L., Canada* 53°19N 60°10W **299** B7
Churchill, C. *Canada* 58°46N 93°12W **297** B10
Churchill Falls *Canada* 53°36N 64°19W **299** B7
Churchill L. *Canada* 55°55N 108°20W **297** B7
Churchill Pk. *Canada* 58°10N 125°10W **296** B3
Churchtown *Ireland* 53°18N 6°16W **120** B2
Churdan *U.S.A.* 42°9N 94°29W **310** B2
Churki *India* 23°50N 83°12E **243** H10
Churu *India* 28°20N 74°50E **242** E6
Churubusco *U.S.A.* 41°14N 85°19W **311** C11
Churún Merú = Angel Falls *Venezuela* 5°57N 62°30W **329** B5
Chushal *India* 33°40N 78°40E **243** C8
Chushan *Taiwan* 23°45N 120°40E **225** C2
Chuska Mts. *U.S.A.* 36°15N 108°50W **305** H9
Chusovoy *Russia* 58°22N 57°50E **186** C10
Chusovskoy Zavod = Chusovoy *Russia* 58°22N 57°50E **186** C10
Chuspipata *Bolivia* 16°18S 67°48W **330** D4
Chust = Khust *Ukraine* 48°10N 23°18E **183** B8
Chust *Uzbekistan* 41°0N 71°13E **217** D8
Chute-aux-Outardes *Canada* 49°7N 68°24W **299** C6
Chutung *Taiwan* 24°44N 121°5E **225** B3
Chuuk = Truk *Micronesia* 7°25N 151°46E **287** T17
Chuuk Lagoon *Micronesia* 7°24N 151°45E **287** T18
Chuvash Republic = Chuvashia ☐ *Russia* 55°30N 47°0E **190** C8
Chuvashia ☐ *Russia* 55°30N 47°0E **190** C8
Chuwārtah *Iraq* 35°43N 45°34E **213** E11
Chuwei *Taiwan* 25°6N 121°14E **225** A3
Chuxiong *China* 25°2N 101°28E **228** E3
Chüy *Kyrgyzstan* 42°55N 75°15E **217** C9
Chuy *Uruguay* 33°41S 53°27W **335** C5
Chüy ☐ *Kyrgyzstan* 42°25N 75°16E **217** D9
Chuzenji-Ko *Japan* 36°44N 139°27E **223** A11
Chuzhou *China* 32°19N 118°20E **229** A12
Chynadiyeve *Ukraine* 48°29N 22°50E **182** B7
Ci Xian *China* 36°20N 114°25E **226** F8
Ciacova *Romania* 45°35N 21°10E **182** E6
Ciadâr-Lunga *Moldova* 46°3N 28°51E **183** D13
Ciales *Puerto Rico* 18°20N 66°28W **321** b
Ciamis *Indonesia* 7°20S 108°21E **235** G13
Ciampino *Italy* 41°47N 12°36E **136** C2
Ciampino ✈ (CIA) *Italy* 41°47N 12°35E **136** C2
Cianjur *Indonesia* 6°49S 107°8E **234** D3
Cianorte *Brazil* 23°37S 52°37W **335** A5
Cibola *U.S.A.* 33°17N 114°42W **307** M12
Çiçekdağı *Turkey* 39°36N 34°24E **212** C6
Cicero *U.S.A.* 41°51N 87°44W **119** B2
Cicero Dantas *Brazil* 10°36S 38°23W **332** D4
Ciceron *St. Lucia* 13°59N 61°1W **323** m
Cicia *Fiji* 17°45S 179°18W **287** A3
Cidacos → *Spain* 42°21N 1°38W **197** C3
Cidade de Minas = Belo Horizonte *Brazil* 19°55S 43°56W **333** E3
Cide *Turkey* 41°53N 33°1E **212** B5
Cidra *Puerto Rico* 18°11N 66°10W **321** b
Ciechanów *Poland* 52°52N 20°38E **185** F7
Ciechanowiec *Poland* 52°40N 22°31E **185** F9
Ciechocinek *Poland* 52°53N 18°45E **185** F5
Ciego de Ávila *Cuba* 21°50N 78°50W **320** B4
Ciénaga *Colombia* 11°1N 74°15W **328** A3
Ciénaga de Oro *Colombia* 8°53N 75°37W **328** B2
Ciénagas del Catatumbo △ *Venezuela* 9°26N 72°8W **328** B3
Cienfuegos *Cuba* 22°10N 80°30W **320** B3
Cierp-Gaud *France* 42°55N 0°40E **174** F4
Cíes, Is. *Spain* 42°12N 8°55W **194** C2
Cieszanów *Poland* 50°14N 23°8E **185** H10
Cieszyn *Poland* 49°45N 18°35E **185** J5
Cieza *Spain* 38°17N 1°23W **197** G3
Çifteler *Turkey* 39°22N 31°2E **212** C4
Cifuentes *Spain* 40°47N 2°37W **196** E2
Cihanbeyli *Turkey* 38°40N 32°55E **212** C5
Cihuatlán *Mexico* 19°14N 104°35W **318** D4
Cijara, Embalse de *Spain* 39°18N 4°52W **195** F6
Cijara ⌓ *Spain* 39°18N 4°35W **195** F6
Cijulang *Indonesia* 7°42S 108°27E **235** D3
Cilacap *Indonesia* 7°43S 109°0E **235** D3
Cilandak *Indonesia* 6°17S 106°47E **122** B1
Cilao, Cirque de *Réunion* 21°7S 55°28E **272** f
Cilaos *Réunion* 21°8S 55°27E **272** f
Çıldır *Turkey* 41°7N 43°8E **213** B10
Çıldır Gölü *Turkey* 41°5N 43°15E **213** B10
Cilento e Vallo di Diano △ *Italy* 40°15N 15°20E **201** B8
Cili *China* 29°30N 111°8E **229** C8
Cilibia *Romania* 45°4N 27°4E **183** E12
Cilicia *Turkey* 36°30N 35°0E **250** B5
Cilincing *Indonesia* 6°6S 106°54E **122** A2
Ciliwung → *Indonesia* 6°6S 106°47E **122** B2
Cill Airne = Killarney *Ireland* 52°4N 9°30W **166** D2
Cill Chainnigh = Kilkenny *Ireland* 52°39N 7°15W **166** D4
Cill Dara = Kildare *Ireland* 53°9N 6°55W **166** C5
Cill Mhantáin = Wicklow *Ireland* 52°59N 6°3W **166** D5
Cilo Dağı *Turkey* 37°28N 43°55E **213** D10
Cima *U.S.A.* 35°14N 115°30W **307** K11
Cimarron *Kans., U.S.A.* 37°48N 100°21W **308** G3
Cimarron *N. Mex., U.S.A.* 36°31N 104°55W **305** H11
Cimarron → *U.S.A.* 36°10N 96°16W **314** C6
Čimice *Czech Rep.* 50°8N 14°25E **135** B2
Cimişlia *Moldova* 46°34N 28°44E **183** D13
Cimone, Mte. *Italy* 44°12N 10°42E **198** D7
Cina, Tanjung *Indonesia* 5°55S 104°45E **234** D2
Çınar *Turkey* 37°46N 40°19E **213** D9
Çınarcık *Turkey* 40°38N 29°5E **203** F13
Cinaruco-Capanaparo △ *Venezuela* 6°51N 67°32W **328** B4
Cinca → *Spain* 41°26N 0°21E **196** D5
Cincar *Bos.-H.* 43°55N 17°5E **182** G2
Cincinnati *Iowa, U.S.A.* 40°38N 92°56W **310** D4
Cincinnati *Ohio, U.S.A.* 39°9N 84°27W **311** E12
Cincinnati-Northern Kentucky Int. ✈ (CVG) *U.S.A.* 39°3N 84°40W **311** E12
Cincinnatus *U.S.A.* 42°33N 75°54W **313** D9
Çine *Turkey* 37°37N 28°2E **205** D10
Cinecittà *Italy* 41°51N 12°34E **136** B2
Ciney *Belgium* 50°18N 5°5E **170** D5
Cingoli *Italy* 43°23N 13°10E **199** E10
Cinigiano *Italy* 42°53N 11°24E **199** F8
Cinisello Bálsamo *Italy* 45°33N 9°13E **129** A2
Cinkota *Hungary* 47°31N 19°14E **117** A3
Cinque I. *India* 11°16N 92°42E **245** J11
Cinto, Mte. *France* 42°24N 8°54E **175** F12
Cintra, G. de *W. Sahara* 23°0N 16°15W **260** D1
Cintruénigo *Spain* 42°5N 1°49W **196** C3
Ciocile *Romania* 44°49N 27°14E **183** F12
Ciolănești din Deal *Romania* 44°19N 25°5E **183** F10
Ciorani *Romania* 44°45N 26°25E **183** F11
Čiovo *Croatia* 43°30N 16°17E **199** E13
Cipero → *Trin. & Tob.* 10°16N 61°28W **323** t
Cipete *Indonesia* 6°15S 106°47E **122** B1
Cipó *Brazil* 11°6S 38°31W **332** D4
Cipolletti *Argentina* 38°56S 67°59W **336** A3
Circeo, Mte. *Italy* 41°14N 13°3E **200** A6
Çirçir *Turkey* 40°3N 36°47E **212** C7
Circle *Alaska, U.S.A.* 65°50N 144°4W **303** D11
Circle *Mont., U.S.A.* 47°25N 105°35W **304** C11
Circleville *U.S.A.* 39°36N 82°57W **309** F12
Circular Reef *Papua N. G.* 3°25S 147°47E **286** B4
Cirebon *Indonesia* 6°45S 108°32E **235** D3
Cirencester *U.K.* 51°43N 1°57W **169** F6
Cireşu *Romania* 44°47N 22°31E **182** F7
Cirey-sur-Vezouze *France* 48°35N 6°57E **173** D13
Ciriè *Italy* 45°14N 7°36E **198** C4
Cirium *Cyprus* 34°40N 32°53E **207** F8
Cirò *Italy* 39°23N 17°4E **201** C10
Cirò Marina *Italy* 39°22N 17°8E **201** C10
Ciron → *France* 44°36N 0°18W **174** D3
Cisco *U.S.A.* 32°23N 98°59W **314** E5
Cislău *Romania* 45°14N 26°20E **183** E11
Cisna *Poland* 49°12N 22°20E **185** J9
Cisnădie *Romania* 45°42N 24°9E **183** E9
Cisne *U.S.A.* 38°31N 88°26W **311** F8
Cisneros *Colombia* 6°33N 75°4W **328** B2
Cissna Park *U.S.A.* 40°34N 87°54W **311** D9
Cisterna di Latina *Italy* 41°35N 12°49E **200** A5
Cisternino *Italy* 40°44N 17°25E **201** B10
Cistierna *Spain* 42°48N 5°7W **194** C5
Citadel = Kastellet *Copenhagen, Denmark* **118** a3
Citadel *Budapest, Hungary* **117** c2
Citaré → *Brazil* 1°11N 54°41W **329** C7
Citeli-Ckaro = Tsiteli-Tsqaro *Georgia* 41°33N 46°0E **191** K8
Citlaltépetl = Orizaba, Pico de *Mexico* 18°58N 97°15W **319** D5
Citra *U.S.A.* 29°25N 82°7W **317** F7
Citron *Fr. Guiana* 4°44N 53°57W **329** C7
Citrus Heights *U.S.A.* 38°42N 121°17W **306** G5
Citrus Springs *U.S.A.* 29°2N 82°27W **317** F7
Citrusdal *S. Africa* 32°35S 19°0E **270** D2
Città della Studi *Italy* 45°28N 9°12E **129** B2
Città del Vaticano = Vatican City ■ *Europe* 41°54N 12°27E **136** B1
Città della Pieve *Italy* 42°57N 12°1E **199** F9
Città di Castello *Italy* 43°27N 12°14E **199** E9
Città Sant' Angelo *Italy* 42°32N 14°5E **199** F11
Cittadella *Italy* 45°39N 11°47E **199** C8
Cittaducale *Italy* 42°23N 12°57E **199** F9
Cittanova *Italy* 38°21N 16°5E **201** D9
City, The *U.K.* 51°30N 0°6W **125** A3
City Hall = Rådhus *Oslo, Norway* **133** b1
City Hall = Stadshuset *Stockholm, Sweden* **139** b1
City of the Dead *Egypt* 30°0N 31°15E **117** A2
City Park *U.S.A.* 30°0N 90°5W **131** A2
City Terrace *U.S.A.* 34°3N 118°11W **126** B3
Ciuc, Munții *Romania* 46°25N 26°5E **183** D11
Ciucaş, Vf. *Romania* 45°31N 25°56E **183** E10
Ciucea *Romania* 46°57N 22°49E **182** D7
Ciuciulea *Moldova* 47°40N 27°29E **183** C12
Ciuciuleni *Moldova* 47°2N 28°25E **183** C13
Ciudad Acuña *Mexico* 29°18N 100°55W **318** B4
Ciudad Altamirano *Mexico* 18°20N 100°40W **318** D4
Ciudad Anáhuac *Mexico* 27°14N 100°7W **318** B4
Ciudad Bolívar *Venezuela* 8°5N 63°36W **329** B5
Ciudad Bolivia *Venezuela* 8°21N 70°34W **328** B3
Ciudad Camargo *Mexico* 27°40N 105°10W **318** B3
Ciudad Cortés *Costa Rica* 8°55N 84°0W **320** E3
Ciudad de México *Mexico* 19°24N 99°9W **128** B2
Ciudad de Nutrias *Venezuela* 8°5N 69°18W **328** B4
Ciudad de Valles *Mexico* 22°0N 99°0W **319** C5
Ciudad del Carmen *Mexico* 18°38N 91°50W **319** D6
Ciudad del Este *Paraguay* 25°30S 54°50W **335** B5
Ciudad Delicias = Delicias *Mexico* 28°13N 105°28W **318** B3
Ciudad Deportiva *Mexico* 19°24N 99°5W **128** B2
Ciudad Fin de Semana *Spain* 40°26N 3°34W **127** B2
Ciudad Frontera *Mexico* 26°56N 101°27W **318** B4
Ciudad General Belgrano *Argentina* 34°43S 58°33W **117** C1
Ciudad Guayana *Venezuela* 8°0N 62°30W **329** B5
Ciudad Guerrero *Mexico* 28°33N 107°30W **318** B3
Ciudad Guzmán *Mexico* 19°41N 103°29W **318** D4
Ciudad Juárez *Mexico* 31°44N 106°29W **318** A3
Ciudad Lerdo *Mexico* 25°32N 103°32W **318** B4
Ciudad Lineál *Spain* 40°26N 3°38W **127** B2
Ciudad Madero *Mexico* 22°19N 97°50W **319** C5
Ciudad Mante *Mexico* 22°44N 98°59W **319** C5
Ciudad Obregón *Mexico* 27°29N 109°56W **318** B3
Ciudad Ojeda *Venezuela* 10°12N 71°19W **328** A3
Ciudad Piar *Venezuela* 7°27N 63°19W **329** B5
Ciudad Porfirio Díaz = Piedras Negras *Mexico* 28°42N 100°31W **318** B4
Ciudad Real *Spain* 38°59N 3°55W **195** G7
Ciudad Real ☐ *Spain* 38°50N 4°0W **195** G7
Ciudad Rodrigo *Spain* 40°35N 6°32W **194** E4
Ciudad Satélite *Mexico* 19°30N 99°13W **128** A1
Ciudad Trujillo = Santo Domingo *Dom. Rep.* 18°30N 69°59W **321** C6
Ciudad Universitaria *B. Aires, Argentina* 34°33S 58°27W **117** B2
Ciudad Universitaria *México, Mexico* 19°20N 99°11W **128** C1
Ciudad Victoria *Mexico* 23°44N 99°8W **319** C5
Ciudadela *Spain* 40°0N 3°50E **206** B4
Ciulnița *Romania* 44°26N 27°22E **183** F12
Ciumeghiu *Romania* 46°44N 21°35E **182** D6
Ciuperceni *Romania* 44°54N 23°4E **182** F8
Ciutadella, Parc de la *Barcelona, Spain* **114** b3
Civa Burnu *Turkey* 41°21N 36°38E **212** B7
Civic Center *Los Angeles, U.S.A.* **127** b2
Cividale del Friuli *Italy* 46°6N 13°25E **199** B10
Cività Castellana *Italy* 42°18N 12°24E **199** F9
Civitanova Marche *Italy* 43°18N 13°44E **199** E10
Civitavécchia *Italy* 42°6N 11°48E **199** F8
Civray *France* 46°10N 0°17E **174** B4
Çivril *Turkey* 38°20N 29°43E **205** C11
Cixerri → *Italy* 39°17N 8°59E **200** C1
Cixi *China* 30°17N 121°9E **229** B13
Cizre *Turkey* 37°19N 42°10E **213** D10
Clackmannanshire ☐ *U.K.* 56°10N 3°43W **167** E5
Clacton-on-Sea *U.K.* 51°47N 1°11E **169** F9
Clain → *France* 46°47N 0°33E **172** F7
Claire, L. *Canada* 58°35N 112°5W **296** B6
Claireville Res. *Canada* 43°45N 79°39W **141** A1
Clairton *U.S.A.* 40°18N 79°53W **312** F5
Clairvaux-les-Lacs *France* 46°35N 5°45E **173** F12
Claise → *France* 46°56N 0°42E **174** B5
Clallam Bay *U.S.A.* 48°15N 124°16W **306** B2
Clam Gulch *U.S.A.* 60°15N 151°23W **303** F10
Clamart *France* 48°48N 2°15E **134** B2
Clamecy *France* 47°28N 3°30E **173** E10
Clanton *U.S.A.* 32°51N 86°38W **315** E11
Clanwilliam *S. Africa* 32°11S 18°52E **270** D2
Clapham *U.K.* 51°27N 0°8W **125** B3
Clapton *U.K.* 51°33N 0°3W **125** A3
Clara *Ireland* 53°21N 7°37W **166** C4
Claraville *U.S.A.* 35°24N 118°20W **307** K8
Clare *S. Austral., Australia* 33°50S 138°37E **282** B3
Clare *Mich., U.S.A.* 43°49N 84°46W **309** D11
Clare ☐ *Ireland* 52°45N 9°0W **166** D3
Clare → *Ireland* 53°20N 9°2W **166** C2
Clare I. *Ireland* 53°49N 10°0W **166** C1
Claremont *Jamaica* 18°19N 77°11W **320** a
Claremont *Western Cape, S. Africa* 34°8S 18°28E **118** A1
Claremont *Calif., U.S.A.* 34°6N 117°43W **307** L9
Claremont *N.H., U.S.A.* 43°23N 72°20W **313** C12
Claremont Pt. *Australia* 14°1S 143°41E **280** A3
Claremore *U.S.A.* 36°19N 95°36W **314** C7
Claremorris *Ireland* 53°45N 9°0W **166** C3
Clarence *U.S.A.* 39°45N 92°16W **310** E4
Clarence → *N.S.W., Australia* 29°25S 153°22E **281** D5
Clarence → *N.Z.* 42°10S 173°56E **285** C8
Clarence, I. *Chile* 54°0S 72°0W **336** D2
Clarence, Port *U.S.A.* 65°15N 166°40W **303** D6
Clarence B. *Ascension I.* 7°55S 14°25W **153** g
Clarence I. *Antarctica* 61°10S 54°0W **151** C18
Clarence Str. *Australia* 12°0S 131°0E **278** B5
Clarence Town *Bahamas* 23°6N 74°59W **321** B5
Clarendon *Pa., U.S.A.* 41°47N 79°6W **312** E5
Clarendon *Tex., U.S.A.* 34°56N 100°53W **314** D4
Clarenville *Canada* 48°10N 54°1W **299** C9
Claresholm *Canada* 50°2N 113°33W **296** D6
Clarie Coast *Antarctica* 68°0S 135°0E **151** C9
Clarinda *U.S.A.* 40°44N 95°2W **308** E6
Clarington *Canada* 43°55N 78°41W **312** C6
Clarion *Iowa, U.S.A.* 42°44N 93°44W **310** B3
Clarion *Pa., U.S.A.* 41°13N 79°23W **312** E5
Clarion → *U.S.A.* 41°7N 79°41W **312** E5
Clarion Fracture Zone *Pac. Oc.* 20°0N 120°0W **292** H7
Clark *Mo., U.S.A.* 39°17N 92°21W **310** E4
Clark *S. Dak., U.S.A.* 44°53N 97°44W **308** C5
Clark, Pt. *Canada* 44°4N 81°45W **312** B3
Clark Fork *U.S.A.* 48°9N 116°11W **304** B5
Clark Fork → *U.S.A.* 48°9N 116°15W **304** B5
Clarkdale *U.S.A.* 34°46N 112°3W **305** J7
Clarke City *Canada* 50°12N 66°38W **299** B6
Clarke I. *Australia* 40°32S 148°10E **281** G4
Clarke Ra. *Australia* 20°40S 148°30E **280** b
Clarks Fork Yellowstone → *U.S.A.* 45°32N 108°50W **304** D9
Clark's Harbour *Canada* 43°25N 65°38W **299** D6
Clarks Hill L. = J. Strom Thurmond L. *U.S.A.* 33°40N 82°12W **316** B7
Clarks Point *U.S.A.* 58°51N 158°33W **303** G8
Clarks Summit *U.S.A.* 41°30N 75°42W **313** E9
Clarks Town *Jamaica* 18°25N 77°33W **320** a
Clarksburg *U.S.A.* 39°17N 80°30W **309** F13
Clarksdale *U.S.A.* 34°12N 90°35W **315** D9
Clarkston *U.S.A.* 46°25N 117°3W **304** C5
Clarksville *Ark., U.S.A.* 35°28N 93°28W **314** D8
Clarksville *Ind., U.S.A.* 38°17N 85°45W **311** F11
Clarksville *Iowa, U.S.A.* 42°47N 92°40W **310** B4
Clarksville *Mo., U.S.A.* 39°22N 90°54W **310** E6
Clarksville *Tenn., U.S.A.* 36°32N 87°21W **315** C11
Clarksville *Tex., U.S.A.* 33°37N 95°3W **314** E7
Claro → *Brazil* 19°8S 50°40W **333** E1
Clatskanie *U.S.A.* 46°6N 123°12W **306** D3
Claude *U.S.A.* 35°7N 101°22W **314** D4
Claveria *Cagayan, Phil.* 18°37N 121°4E **232** B3
Claveria *Masbate, Phil.* 12°54N 123°15E **232** E4
Claveria *Mis. Or., Phil.* 8°38N 124°55E **233** G5
Clavering Ø *Greenland* 74°15N 21°0W **154** C8
Claxton *U.S.A.* 32°10N 81°55W **316** C8
Claxton B. *Trin. & Tob.* 10°21N 61°28W **323** t
Claxton Bay *Trin. & Tob.* 10°21N 61°28W **323** t
Clay *U.S.A.* 38°17N 121°10W **306** G5
Clay Center *U.S.A.* 39°23N 97°8W **308** F5
Clay City *Ind., U.S.A.* 39°17N 87°7W **311** E9
Clay City *Ky., U.S.A.* 37°52N 83°55W **311** G13
Clayhall *U.K.* 51°35N 0°3E **125** A4
Claypool *U.S.A.* 33°25N 110°51W **305** K8
Claysburg *U.S.A.* 40°17N 78°27W **312** F6
Claysville *U.S.A.* 40°7N 80°25W **312** F4
Clayton *Ont., Canada* 45°11N 76°19W **313** A8
Clayton *Ala., U.S.A.* 31°53N 85°27W **316** D4
Clayton *Ind., U.S.A.* 39°41N 86°31W **311** E10
Clayton *N. Mex., U.S.A.* 36°27N 103°11W **305** H12
Clayton *N.Y., U.S.A.* 44°14N 76°5W **313** B8
Clear, C. *Ireland* 51°25N 9°32W **166** E2
Clear, L. *Ont., Canada* 45°26N 77°12W **312** A7
Clear, L. *Fla., U.S.A.* 28°31N 81°24W **133** A2
Clear Hills *Canada* 56°40N 119°30W **296** B5
Clear I. *Ireland* 51°26N 9°30W **166** E2
Clear L. *U.S.A.* 39°2N 122°47W **306** F4
Clear Lake *Iowa, U.S.A.* 43°8N 93°23W **310** A3
Clear Lake *S. Dak., U.S.A.* 44°45N 96°41W **308** C5
Clear Lake Res. *U.S.A.* 41°56N 121°5W **304** F3
Clearfield *Pa., U.S.A.* 41°2N 78°27W **312** E6
Clearfield *Utah, U.S.A.* 41°7N 112°2W **304** F7
Clearlake *U.S.A.* 38°57N 122°38W **306** G4
Clearwater *B.C., Canada* 51°38N 120°2W **296** C4
Clearwater *Fla., U.S.A.* 27°59N 82°48W **317** H7
Clearwater → *Alta., Canada* 52°22N 114°57W **296** C6
Clearwater → *Alta., Canada* 56°44N 111°23W **297** B6
Clearwater L. *Canada* 53°34N 99°49W **297** C9
Clearwater Lake ⌓ *Canada* 54°0N 101°0W **297** C8
Clearwater Mts. *U.S.A.* 46°5N 115°20W **304** C6
Clearwater River ⌓ *Canada* 56°55N 109°10W **297** B7
Cleburne *U.S.A.* 32°21N 97°23W **314** E6
Clee Hills *U.K.* 52°26N 2°35W **169** E5
Cleethorpes *U.K.* 53°33N 0°3W **168** D7
Cleeve Cloud *U.K.* 51°56N 2°0W **169** F6
Clelles *France* 44°50N 5°38E **175** D9
Clemson *U.S.A.* 34°41N 82°50W **315** D13
Cleopatra Needle *Phil.* 10°7N 118°58E **233** F2
Clerke Reef *Australia* 17°22S 119°20E **278** C2
Clerkenwell *London, U.K.* **125** a4
Clermiston *U.K.* 55°57N 3°17W **121** B2
Clermont *Queens., Australia* 22°49S 147°39E **280** C4
Clermont *Oise, France* 49°23N 2°24E **173** C9
Clermont *Fla., U.S.A.* 28°33N 81°46W **317** G8
Clermont-en-Argonne *France* 49°5N 5°4E **173** C12
Clermont-Ferrand *France* 45°46N 3°4E **174** C7
Clermont-l'Hérault *France* 43°38N 3°26E **174** E7
Clerval *France* 47°25N 6°30E **173** E13
Clervaux *Lux.* 50°4N 6°2E **170** D6
Cles *Italy* 46°22N 11°2E **198** B8
Cleve *Australia* 33°43S 136°30E **282** B2
Clevedon *U.K.* 51°26N 2°52W **169** F5
Cleveland *Miss., U.S.A.* 33°45N 90°43W **315** E9
Cleveland *Ohio, U.S.A.* 41°29N 81°41W **312** E3
Cleveland *Okla., U.S.A.* 36°19N 96°28W **314** C6
Cleveland *Tenn., U.S.A.* 35°10N 84°53W **315** D12
Cleveland *Tex., U.S.A.* 30°21N 95°5W **314** F7
Cleveland, C. *Australia* 19°11S 147°1E **280** B4
Cleveland, Mt. *U.S.A.* 48°56N 113°51W **304** B7
Cleveland Heights *U.S.A.* 41°31N 81°33W **312** E3
Clevelândia *Brazil* 26°24S 52°23W **335** B5
Clevelândia do Norte *Brazil* 3°49N 51°52W **329** C7
Cleves *U.S.A.* 39°10N 84°45W **311** E12
Clew B. *Ireland* 53°50N 9°49W **166** C2
Clewiston *U.S.A.* 26°45N 80°56W **317** J9
Clichy *France* 48°54N 2°18E **134** A2
Clichy-sous-Bois *France* 48°54N 2°32E **134** A4
Clifden *Galway, Ireland* 53°29N 10°1W **166** C1
Clifden *N.Z.* 46°1S 167°42E **285** G2
Cliffdell *U.S.A.* 46°56N 121°5W **306** D5
Cliffside *Canada* 43°44N 79°14W **141** A3
Cliffside Park *U.S.A.* 40°49N 73°59W **132** B2
Cliffy Hd. *Australia* 35°1S 116°29E **279** G2
Clifton *Queens., Australia* 27°59S 151°53E **281** D5
Clifton *Sindh, Pakistan* 24°48N 67°1E **123** B2
Clifton *Western Cape, S. Africa* 33°56S 18°22E **118** A1
Clifton *Ariz., U.S.A.* 33°3N 109°18W **305** K9
Clifton *Colo., U.S.A.* 39°7N 108°25W **304** G9
Clifton *Ill., U.S.A.* 40°56N 87°56W **311** D9
Clifton *N.J., U.S.A.* 40°37N 74°4W **132** C1
Clifton *Tex., U.S.A.* 31°47N 97°35W **314** F6
Clifton Beach *Queens., Australia* 16°46S 145°39E **280** B4
Clifton Beach *Sindh, Pakistan* 24°48N 67°2E **123** B2
Clifton Pt. *Bahamas* 25°1N 77°34W **153** b
Cliftondale *U.S.A.* 42°26N 71°0W **116** A2
Climax *U.S.A.* 30°53N 84°26W **316** E5
Clinch → *U.S.A.* 35°53N 84°29W **315** D12
Clingmans Dome *U.S.A.* 35°34N 83°30W **315** D13
Clint *U.S.A.* 31°35N 106°14W **314** F1
Clinton *B.C., Canada* 51°6N 121°35W **296** C4
Clinton *Ont., Canada* 43°37N 81°32W **312** C3
Clinton *N.Z.* 46°12S 169°23E **285** G4
Clinton *Ark., U.S.A.* 35°36N 92°28W **314** D8
Clinton *Conn., U.S.A.* 41°17N 72°32W **313** E12
Clinton *Ill., U.S.A.* 40°9N 88°57W **310** D8
Clinton *Ind., U.S.A.* 39°40N 87°24W **311** E9
Clinton *Iowa, U.S.A.* 41°51N 90°12W **310** C6
Clinton *Mass., U.S.A.* 42°25N 71°41W **313** D13
Clinton *Mich., U.S.A.* 42°4N 83°58W **311** B13
Clinton *Mo., U.S.A.* 38°22N 93°46W **310** F3
Clinton *N.C., U.S.A.* 35°0N 78°22W **315** D15
Clinton *Okla., U.S.A.* 35°31N 98°58W **314** D5
Clinton *S.C., U.S.A.* 34°29N 81°53W **315** D14
Clinton *Tenn., U.S.A.* 36°6N 84°8W **315** C12
Clinton *Wash., U.S.A.* 47°59N 122°21W **306** C4
Clinton *Wis., U.S.A.* 42°34N 88°52W **311** B8
Clinton, C. *Australia* 22°30S 150°45E **280** C5
Clinton, L. *U.S.A.* 40°15N 88°45W **311** D8
Clinton Colden L. *Canada* 63°58N 107°27W **294** E10
Clintonville *U.S.A.* 44°37N 88°46W **308** C9
Clio *U.S.A.* 31°43N 85°37W **316** D4
Clipperton, I. *Pac. Oc.* 10°18N 109°13W **289** F17
Clipperton Fracture Zone *Pac. Oc.* 19°0N 122°0W **289** G16
Clisham *U.K.* 57°58N 6°49W **167** D2
Clisson *France* 47°5N 1°16W **172** E5
Clitheroe *U.K.* 53°53N 2°22W **168** D5
Clive *N.Z.* 39°36S 176°58E **284** F5
Clive L. *Canada* 63°13N 118°54W **296** A5
Cliza *Bolivia* 17°36S 65°56W **331** D4
Clo-oose *Canada* 48°39N 124°49W **306** B2
Cloates, Pt. *Australia* 22°43S 113°40E **278** D1
Clocolan *S. Africa* 28°55S 27°34E **271** C4
Clodomira *Argentina* 27°35S 64°14W **334** B3
Clogher Hd. *Ireland* 53°48N 6°14W **166** C5
Cloghran *Ireland* 53°27N 6°14W **120** A2
Clonakilty *Ireland* 51°37N 8°53W **166** E3
Clonakilty B. *Ireland* 51°35N 8°51W **166** E3
Cloncurry *Queens., Australia* 20°40S 140°28E **280** C3
Cloncurry *Kildare, Ireland* 53°25N 6°48W **166** C5
Cloncurry → *Australia* 18°37S 140°40E **280** B3
Clondalkin *Ireland* 53°19N 6°25W **166** C5
Clones *Ireland* 54°11N 7°15W **166** B4
Clonmel *Ireland* 52°21N 7°42W **166** D4
Clonskeagh *Ireland* 53°19N 6°14W **120** B2
Clontarf *N.S.W., Australia* 33°48S 151°16E **139** A2
Clontarf *Dublin, Ireland* 53°22N 6°11W **120** A2
Cloppenburg *Germany* 52°51N 8°1E **178** C4
Cloquet *U.S.A.* 46°43N 92°28W **308** B7
Clorinda *Argentina* 25°16S 57°45W **334** B4
Cloud Peak *U.S.A.* 44°23N 107°11W **304** D10
Cloudcroft *U.S.A.* 32°58N 105°45W **305** K11
Cloudy B. *N.Z.* 41°25S 174°10E **285** B9
Clovelly *Australia* 33°54S 151°15E **139** B2
Cloverdale *Calif., U.S.A.* 38°48N 123°1W **306** G4
Cloverdale *Ind., U.S.A.* 39°31N 86°48W **311** E10
Cloverport *U.S.A.* 37°50N 86°38W **311** G10
Clovis *Calif., U.S.A.* 36°49N 119°42W **306** J7
Clovis *N. Mex., U.S.A.* 34°24N 103°12W **305** J12
Cloyes-sur-le-Loir *France* 48°0N 1°14E **172** E8
Cloyne *Canada* 44°49N 77°11W **312** B7
Cluain Meala = Clonmel *Ireland* 52°21N 7°42W **166** D4
Club Terrace *Australia* 37°35S 148°58E **283** D8
Cluj ☐ *Romania* 46°45N 23°30E **183** D8
Cluj-Napoca *Romania* 46°47N 23°38E **183** D8
Clunes *Australia* 37°20S 143°45E **282** D5
Cluny *France* 46°26N 4°38E **173** F11
Cluses *France* 46°5N 6°35E **173** F13
Clusone *Italy* 45°53N 9°57E **198** C6
Clutha → *N.Z.* 46°20S 169°49E **285** G4
Clwyd → *U.K.* 53°19N 3°31W **168** D4
Clyattville *U.S.A.* 30°42N 83°19W **316** E6
Clyde *Alta., Canada* 54°9N 113°39W **296** C6
Clyde *N.Z.* 45°12S 169°20E **285** F4
Clyde *N.Y., U.S.A.* 43°5N 76°52W **312** C8
Clyde *Ohio, U.S.A.* 41°18N 82°59W **311** C14
Clyde → *U.K.* 55°55N 4°30W **167** F4
Clyde, Firth of *U.K.* 55°22N 5°1W **167** F3
Clyde Muirshiel ⌓ *U.K.* 55°50N 4°40W **167** F4
Clyde River *Canada* 70°30N 68°30W **295** C18
Clydebank *U.K.* 55°54N 4°23W **167** F4
Clymer *N.Y., U.S.A.* 42°1N 79°37W **312** D5
Clymer *Pa., U.S.A.* 40°40N 79°1W **312** F5
Clyo *U.S.A.* 32°29N 81°16W **316** C8
Ćmielów *Poland* 50°53N 21°31E **185** H8
Côa → *Portugal* 41°5N 7°6W **194** D3
Coachella *U.S.A.* 33°41N 116°10W **307** M10
Coachella Canal *U.S.A.* 32°43N 114°57W **307** N12
Coahoma *U.S.A.* 32°18N 101°18W **314** E4
Coahuayana → *Mexico* 18°41N 103°45W **318** D4
Coahuila ☐ *Mexico* 27°20N 102°0W **318** B4
Coal → *Canada* 59°39N 126°57W **296** B3
Coal City *U.S.A.* 41°17N 88°17W **311** C8
Coal I. *N.Z.* 46°8S 166°40E **285** G1
Coalane *Mozam.* 17°48S 37°2E **269** F4
Coalcomán *Mexico* 18°47N 103°9W **318** D4
Coaldale *Canada* 49°45N 112°35W **296** D6
Coalgate *U.S.A.* 34°32N 96°13W **314** D6
Coalinga *U.S.A.* 36°9N 120°21W **306** J6
Coalisland *U.K.* 54°33N 6°42W **166** B5
Coalville *Leics., U.K.* 52°44N 1°23W **168** E6
Coalville *Utah, U.S.A.* 40°55N 111°24W **304** F8
Coamo *Puerto Rico* 18°5N 66°22W **321** b
Coaraci *Brazil* 14°38S 39°32W **333** D4
Coari *Brazil* 4°8S 63°7W **329** D5
Coari → *Brazil* 4°30S 63°33W **329** D5
Coari, L. *Brazil* 4°15S 63°22W **329** D5
Coast ☐ *Kenya* 2°40S 39°45E **268** C4
Coast Mts. *Canada* 55°0N 129°20W **296** C3
Coast Ranges *U.S.A.* 39°0N 123°0W **306** G4
Coatbridge *U.K.* 55°52N 4°6W **167** F4
Coatepec *Mexico* 19°27N 96°58W **319** D5
Coatepeque *Guatemala* 14°46N 91°55W **320** D1
Coatesville *U.S.A.* 39°59N 75°50W **309** F16
Coaticook *Canada* 45°10N 71°46W **313** A13
Coats I. *Canada* 62°30N 83°0W **295** E15
Coats Land *Antarctica* 77°0S 25°0W **151** D1
Coatzacoalcos *Mexico* 18°7N 94°25W **319** D6
Cobá *Mexico* 20°31N 87°45W **319** C7
Cobadin *Romania* 44°5N 28°13E **183** F13
Cobalt *Canada* 47°25N 79°42W **298** C4
Cobán *Guatemala* 15°30N 90°21W **320** C1
Çobanlar *Turkey* 38°41N 30°47E **205** C12
Cobar *Australia* 31°27S 145°48E **283** A6
Cobargo *Australia* 36°20S 149°55E **283** D8
Cobbannah *Australia* 37°37S 147°13E **283** D7
Cobberas, Mt. *Australia* 36°53S 148°12E **283** D8
Cobden *Australia* 38°20S 143°3E **282** E5
Cóbh *Ireland* 51°51N 8°17W **166** E3
Cobija *Bolivia* 11°0S 68°50W **330** C4
Cobleskill *U.S.A.* 42°41N 74°29W **313** D10
Coboconk *Canada* 44°39N 78°48W **312** B6
Cobourg *Canada* 43°58N 78°10W **312** C6
Cobourg Pen. *Australia* 11°20S 132°15E **278** B5
Cobram *Australia* 35°54S 145°40E **283** C6
Cobras, I. das *Brazil* 22°53S 43°9W **135** B2
Cóbuè *Mozam.* 12°0S 34°58E **269** E3
Coburg *Vic., Australia* 37°44S 144°56E **128** A1
Coburg *Bayern, Germany* 50°15N 10°58E **179** E6
Coburg I. *Canada* 75°57N 79°26W **295** B16
Coca *Spain* 41°13N 4°32W **194** D6
Coca → *Ecuador* 0°29S 76°58W **328** D2
Cocachacra *Peru* 17°5S 71°45W **330** D3
Cocal *Brazil* 3°28S 41°34W **332** B3
Cocanada = Kakinada *India* 16°57N 82°11E **244** F6
Cocentaina *Spain* 38°45N 0°27W **197** G4
Cochabamba *Bolivia* 17°26S 66°10W **331** D4
Coche, I. *Venezuela* 10°47N 63°56W **329** A5
Cochem *Germany* 50°9N 7°9E **179** E3
Cochemane *Mozam.* 17°0S 32°54E **269** F3
Cochin *India* 9°58N 76°20E **245** K3
Cochin China = Nam-Phan *Vietnam* 10°30N 106°0E **237** G6
Cochran *U.S.A.* 32°23N 83°21W **316** C6
Cochrane *Alta., Canada* 51°11N 114°30W **296** C6
Cochrane *Ont., Canada* 49°0N 81°0W **298** C3
Cochrane *Chile* 47°15S 72°33W **336** C2
Cochrane → *Canada* 59°0N 103°40W **297** B8
Cochrane, L. *Chile* 47°10S 72°0W **336** C2
Cochranton *U.S.A.* 41°31N 80°3W **312** E4
Cockburn *Australia* 32°5S 141°0E **282** B4
Cockburn, Canal *Chile* 54°30S 72°0W **336** D2
Cockburn I. *Canada* 45°55N 83°22W **298** C3
Cockburn Ra. *Australia* 15°46S 128°0E **278** C4
Cockermouth *U.K.* 54°40N 3°22W **168** C4
Cocklebiddy *Australia* 32°0S 126°3E **279** F4
Cockpit *Jamaica* 18°16N 77°39W **320** a
Cockpit Country, The *Jamaica* 18°15N 77°45W **320** a
Côco → *Brazil* 9°27S 50°2W **332** C2
Coco → *Cent. Amer.* 15°0N 83°8W **320** D3
Coco, I. del *Pac. Oc.* 5°25N 87°55W **289** G19
Coco, Pta. *Colombia* 2°58N 77°43W **328** C2
Coco Channel *Asia* 13°45N 93°10E **245** H11
Cocoa *U.S.A.* 28°21N 80°44W **317** G9
Cocoa Beach *U.S.A.* 28°19N 80°37W **317** G9
Cocoa Point *Antigua & B.* 17°33N 61°46W **322** c
Cocobeach *Gabon* 0°59N 9°34E **264** B1
Coconarra △ *Australia* 34°10S 146°12E **283** C7
Cocora *Romania* 44°45N 27°3E **183** F12
Côcos *Brazil* 14°10S 44°33W **333** D3
Côcos → *Brazil* 12°44S 44°48W **333** D3
Cocos B. *Trin. & Tob.* 10°25N 61°2W **323** t
Cocos Basin *Ind. Oc.* 1°0N 94°0E **273** D8
Cocos I. *Guam* 13°14N 144°39E **302** d
Cocos Is. *Ind. Oc.* 12°10S 96°55E **273** F8
Cocos Ridge *Pac. Oc.* 4°0N 88°0W **289** G19
Cocotá *Brazil* 22°48S 43°11W **135** A1
Cod, C. *U.S.A.* 42°5N 70°10W **309** D18
Codajás *Brazil* 3°55S 62°0W **329** D5
Codera, C. *Venezuela* 10°35N 66°4W **328** A4
Codfish I. *N.Z.* 46°47S 167°38E **285** G2
Codigoro *Italy* 44°49N 12°8E **199** D9
Codlea *Romania* 45°42N 25°27E **183** E10
Codó *Brazil* 4°30S 43°55W **332** B3
Codogno *Italy* 45°9N 9°42E **198** C6
Codpa *Chile* 18°50S 69°44W **330** D4
Codrington *Antigua & B.* 17°38N 61°50W **322** c
Codrington Lagoon *Antigua & B.* 17°39N 61°50W **322** c
Codróipo *Italy* 45°58N 13°0E **199** C10
Codru, Munții *Romania* 46°30N 22°15E **182** D7
Cody *U.S.A.* 44°32N 109°3W **304** D9
Coe Hill *Canada* 44°52N 77°50W **312** B7
Coelemu *Chile* 36°30S 72°48W **334** D1
Coelho Neto *Brazil* 4°15S 43°0W **332** B3
Coen *Australia* 13°52S 143°12E **280** A3
Coeroeni *Suriname* 3°22N 57°21W **329** C6
Coeroeni → *Suriname* 3°21N 57°31W **329** C6
Coesfeld *Germany* 51°56N 7°10E **178** D3
Coetivy Is. *Seychelles* 7°8S 56°16E **273** E4
Cœuilly *France* 48°48N 2°32E **134** B4
Coeur d'Alene *U.S.A.* 47°41N 116°46W **304** C5
Coeur d'Alene L. *U.S.A.* 47°32N 116°49W **304** C5
Coevorden *Neths.* 52°40N 6°44E **170** B6
Cofete *Canary Is.* 28°6N 14°23W **153** e2
Coffeyville *U.S.A.* 37°2N 95°37W **308** G6
Coffin B. *Australia* 34°38S 135°28E **281** E2
Coffin Bay *Australia* 34°37S 135°29E **281** E2
Coffin Bay △ *Australia* 34°34S 135°19E **281** E2
Coffin Bay Peninsula *Australia* 34°32S 135°15E **281** E2
Coffs Harbour *Australia* 30°16S 153°5E **283** A10
Cofrentes *Spain* 39°13N 1°5W **197** F3
Cogalnic = Kohylnyk → *Ukraine* 45°49N 29°40E **183** E14
Cogealac *Romania* 44°36N 28°36E **183** F13
Coghinas → *Italy* 40°55N 8°48E **200** B1
Coghinas, L. del *Italy* 40°46N 9°3E **200** B2
Cognac *France* 45°41N 0°20W **174** C3
Cogne *Italy* 45°37N 7°21E **198** C4
Cogolin *France* 43°15N 6°32E **175** E10
Cogolludo *Spain* 40°59N 3°10W **196** E1
Cohocton *U.S.A.* 42°30N 77°30W **312** D7
Cohocton → *U.S.A.* 42°9N 77°6W **312** D7
Cohoes *U.S.A.* 42°46N 73°42W **313** D11
Cohuna *Australia* 35°45S 144°15E **282** C6
Coiba, I. de *Panama* 7°30N 81°40W **320** E3
Coig → *Argentina* 51°0S 69°10W **336** D3
Coigeach, Rubha *U.K.* 58°6N 5°26W **167** C3
Coihaique *Chile* 45°30S 71°45W **336** C2
Coimbatore *India* 11°2N 76°59E **245** J3
Coimbra *Mato Grosso, Brazil* 19°55S 57°48W **331** D6
Coimbra *Portugal* 40°15N 8°27W **194** E2
Coimbra ☐ *Portugal* 40°12N 8°25W **194** E2
Coín *Spain* 36°40N 4°48W **195** J6
Coina *Portugal* 38°39N 9°5W **126** B2
Coipasa, L. de *Bolivia* 19°12S 68°7W **330** D4
Coipasa, Salar de *Bolivia* 19°26S 68°9W **330** D4
Coit Tower *San Francisco, U.S.A.* **136** a2
Cojata *Peru* 15°2S 69°25W **330** D4
Cojedes ☐ *Venezuela* 9°20N 68°20W **328** B4
Cojedes → *Venezuela* 8°34N 68°5W **328** B4
Cojimies *Ecuador* 0°20N 80°0W **328** C1
Cojocna *Romania* 46°45N 23°50E **183** D8
Cojutepequé *El Salv.* 13°41N 88°54W **320** D2
Čoka *Serbia* 45°57N 20°12E **182** E5
Cokeville *U.S.A.* 42°5N 110°57W **304** E8
Colaba *India* 18°53N 72°48E **130** B1
Colaba Pt. *India* 18°53N 72°48E **130** B1
Colac *Australia* 38°21S 143°35E **282** E5
Colachel = Kolachel *India* 8°10N 77°15E **245** K3
Colán *Peru* 5°0S 81°0W **330** B1
Colatina *Brazil* 19°32S 40°37W **333** E3
Colbeck, C. *Antarctica* 77°6S 157°48W **151** D13
Colbert *U.S.A.* 34°2N 83°13W **316** A6
Colborne *Canada* 44°0N 77°53W **312** C7
Colby *U.S.A.* 39°24N 101°3W **308** F3
Colca, Cañón del *Peru* 15°50S 72°20W **330** D3
Colchester *Essex, U.K.* 51°54N 0°55E **169** F8
Colchester *Conn., U.S.A.* 41°35N 72°20W **313** E12
Cold Bay *U.S.A.* 55°12N 162°42W **303** J7
Cold L. *Canada* 54°33N 110°5W **297** C7
Cold Lake *Canada* 54°27N 110°10W **297** C6
Coldstream *B.C., Canada* 50°13N 119°11W **296** C5
Coldstream *Borders, U.K.* 55°39N 2°15W **167** F6
Coldwater *Ont., Canada* 44°42N 79°40W **312** B5
Coldwater *Kans., U.S.A.* 37°16N 99°20W **308** G4
Coldwater *Mich., U.S.A.* 41°57N 85°0W **311** C11
Coldwater *Ohio, U.S.A.* 40°29N 84°38W **311** D12
Colebrook *U.S.A.* 41°48N 84°59W **311** C11
Cole Camp *U.S.A.* 38°28N 93°12W **310** F3
Coleambally *Australia* 34°49S 145°52E **283** C6
Colebrook *U.S.A.* 44°54N 71°30W **313** B13
Colegiales *Argentina* 34°34S 58°27W **117** B2
Coleman *Alta., Canada* 49°40N 114°30W **296** D6
Coleman *Fla., U.S.A.* 28°48N 82°4W **317** G7
Coleman *Tex., U.S.A.* 31°50N 99°26W **314** F5
Coleman → *Australia* 15°6S 141°38E **280** B3
Colenso *S. Africa* 28°44S 29°50E **271** C4
Coleraine *Australia* 37°36S 141°40E **282** D4
Coleraine *L'derry., U.K.* 55°8N 6°41W **166** A5
Coleridge, L. *N.Z.* 43°17S 171°30E **285** D6
Coleroon → *India* 11°25N 79°50E **245** J4
Colesberg *S. Africa* 30°45S 25°5E **270** D4
Coleville *U.S.A.* 38°34N 119°30W **306** G7
Colfax *Calif., U.S.A.* 39°6N 120°57W **306** F6
Colfax *Ill., U.S.A.* 40°34N 88°37W **311** D8
Colfax *Ind., U.S.A.* 40°12N 86°40W **311** D10
Colfax *Iowa, U.S.A.* 41°41N 93°14W **310** C3
Colfax *La., U.S.A.* 31°31N 92°42W **314** F8
Colfax *Wash., U.S.A.* 46°53N 117°22W **304** C5
Colhué Huapi, L. *Argentina* 45°30S 69°0W **336** C3
Colibaşi *Moldova* 45°43N 28°11E **183** E13
Colibaşi *Romania* 44°56N 24°54E **183** F9
Colibris, Pte. des *Guadeloupe* 16°17N 61°5W **322** e
Cólico *Italy* 46°8N 9°22E **198** B6
Colider *Brazil* 10°45S 55°25W **331** C6
Coligny *Ain, France* 46°23N 5°21E **173** F12
Coligny *North West, S. Africa* 26°17S 26°15E **271** C4
Colihaut *Dominica* 15°29N 61°29W **323** k
Colima *Mexico* 19°14N 103°43W **318** D4
Colima ☐ *Mexico* 19°10N 104°0W **318** D4
Colima, Nevado de *Mexico* 19°33N 103°38W **318** D4
Colina *Chile* 33°13S 70°45W **334** C1
Colinas do Norte *Guinea-Biss.* 12°28N 15°0W **262** C2

Colinas *Goiás, Brazil* 14°15S 48°2W **333** D2
Colinas *Maranhão, Brazil* 6°0S 44°10W **332** C3
Colindale *U.K.* 51°35N 0°15W **125** A2
Colindres *Spain* 43°24N 3°27W **194** B7
Clinton *U.K.* 55°55N 3°14W **121** B2
Coll *U.K.* 56°39N 6°34W **167** E2
Collahuasi *Chile* 21°5S 68°45W **334** A2
Collarada, Peña *Spain* 42°43N 0°29W **196** C4
Collarenebri *Australia* 29°33S 148°34E **281** D4
Colle di Val d'Elsa *Italy* 43°25N 11°7E **198** E8
Collécchio *Italy* 44°45N 10°13E **198** D7
Colleen Bawn *Zimbabwe* 21°0S 29°12E **269** G2
College *U.S.A.* 64°52N 147°49W **303** D11
College Park *Ga., U.S.A.* 33°39N 84°27W **113** C2
College Park *Md., U.S.A.* 38°59N 76°55W **143** B4
College Point *U.S.A.* 40°47N 73°50W **132** B2
College Station *U.S.A.* 30°37N 96°21W **314** F6
Collégien *France* 48°50N 2°41E **134** A4
Collesalvetti *Italy* 43°34N 10°27E **198** E7
Colli Euganei △ *Italy* 45°18N 11°43E **199** C8
Collie *N.S.W., Australia* 31°41S 148°18E **283** A8
Collie *W. Austral., Australia* 33°22S 116°8E **279** F2
Collier B. *Australia* 16°10S 124°15E **278** C3
Collier Ra. *Australia* 24°45S 119°10E **279** D2
Collier Range △ *Australia* 24°39S 119°7E **279** D2
Collier Row *U.K.* 51°35N 0°9E **125** A4
Colliers Wood *U.K.* 51°24N 0°10W **125** B2
Collierville *U.S.A.* 35°3N 89°40W **315** D10
Collina, Passo di *Italy* 44°2N 10°56E **198** D7
Collingwood *Ont., Canada* 44°29N 80°13W **312** B4
Collingwood *N.Z.* 40°41S 172°40E **285** A7
Collins *Ont., Canada* 50°17N 89°27W **298** B2
Collins *Ga., U.S.A.* 32°11N 82°7W **316** C7
Collins *Mo., U.S.A.* 37°54N 93°37W **310** G3
Collins Bay *Canada* 44°14N 76°36W **313** B8
Collinson Pen. *Canada* 69°58N 101°24W **294** D11
Collinsville *Queens., Australia* 20°30S 147°56E **280** C4
Collinsville *Ill., U.S.A.* 38°40N 89°59W **310** F7
Collipulli *Chile* 37°55S 72°30W **334** D1
Collo *Algeria* 36°58N 6°37E **261** A6
Collooney *Ireland* 54°11N 8°29W **166** B3
Colma *U.S.A.* 37°40N 122°27W **136** B2
Colmar *France* 48°5N 7°20E **173** D14
Colmars *France* 44°11N 6°39E **175** D10
Colmenar *Spain* 36°54N 4°20W **195** J6
Colmenar de Oreja *Spain* 40°6N 3°25W **194** E7
Colmenar Viejo *Spain* 40°39N 3°47W **194** E7
Colney Hatch *U.K.* 51°36N 0°9W **125** A3
Colo → *Australia* 33°25S 150°52E **283** B9
Cologne = Köln *Germany* 50°56N 6°57E **178** E2
Cologno Monzese *Italy* 45°31N 9°16E **129** A2
Colom, I. d'en *Spain* 39°58N 4°16E **206** B5
Coloma *Calif., U.S.A.* 38°48N 120°53W **306** G6
Coloma *Mich., U.S.A.* 42°11N 86°19W **311** B10
Colomb-Béchar = Béchar *Algeria* 31°38N 2°18W **261** B4
Colombes *France* 48°55N 2°15E **134** A2
Colombey-les-Belles *France* 48°32N 5°54E **173** D12
Colombey-les-Deux-Églises *France* 48°13N 4°50E **173** D11
Colômbia *Brazil* 20°10S 48°40W **333** F2
Colombia ■ *S. Amer.* 3°45N 73°0W **328** C3
Colombian Basin *Caribbean* 14°0N 76°0W **321** D5
Colombier *St.-Martin* 18°5N 63°4W **322** a
Colombo *Sri Lanka* 6°56N 79°58E **245** L4
Colomiers *France* 43°36N 1°21E **174** E5
Colón *B. Aires, Argentina* 33°53S 61°7W **334** C3
Colón *Entre Ríos, Argentina* 32°12S 58°10W **334** C4
Colón *Cuba* 22°42N 80°54W **320** B3
Colón *Panama* 9°20N 79°54W **320** c
Colón, Arch. de *Ecuador* 0°0 91°0W **330** a
Colón, Monumento a *Barcelona, Spain* **114** c3
Colon, Plaza de *Madrid, Spain* **127** a3
Colón Ridge *Pac. Oc.* 2°0N 96°0W **289** G18
Colonarie *St. Vincent* 13°14N 61°8W **323** n
Colonia *Micronesia* 9°30N 138°10E **287** R16
Colonia 25 de Mayo *Argentina* 37°48S 67°41W **336** A3
Colònia de Sant Jordi *Spain* 39°19N 2°59E **206** B3
Colonia del Sacramento *Uruguay* 34°25S 57°50W **334** C4
Colonia Dora *Argentina* 28°34S 62°59W **334** B3
Colonia Güell *Spain* 41°21N 2°2E **114** A1
Colonial Beach *U.S.A.* 38°15N 76°58W **309** F15
Colonial Knob *N.Z.* 41°9S 174°48E **143** A1
Colonie *U.S.A.* 42°43N 73°50W **313** D11
Colonna, C. *Italy* 39°2N 17°12E **201** C10
Colonsay *Sask., Canada* 51°59N 105°52W **297** C7
Colonsay *Argyll & Bute, U.K.* 56°5N 6°12W **167** E2
Colorado □ *U.S.A.* 39°30N 105°30W **304** G11
Colorado → *Argentina* 39°50S 62°8W **336** A4
Colorado → *N. Amer.* 31°45N 114°40W **305** L6
Colorado → *Tex., U.S.A.* 28°36N 95°59W **314** G7
Colorado City *U.S.A.* 32°24N 100°52W **314** E4
Colorado Plateau *U.S.A.* 37°0N 111°0W **305** H8
Colorado River Aqueduct *U.S.A.* 33°50N 117°23W **307** L12
Colorado Springs *U.S.A.* 38°50N 104°49W **304** G11
Colorno *Italy* 44°56N 10°23E **198** D7
Colosseo *Rome, Italy* **136** c3
Colosseum = Colosseo *Rome, Italy* **136** c3
Cotlotlán *Mexico* 22°6N 103°16W **318** C4
Colquechaca *Bolivia* 18°40S 66°1W **331** D4
Colquitt *U.S.A.* 31°10N 84°44W **316** D5
Colstrip *U.S.A.* 45°53N 106°38W **304** D10
Colton *U.S.A.* 44°33N 74°56W **313** B10
Columbia *Ala., U.S.A.* 31°18N 85°7W **316** D4
Columbia *Ill., U.S.A.* 38°27N 90°12W **310** F6
Columbia *Ky., U.S.A.* 37°6N 85°18W **309** G11
Columbia *La., U.S.A.* 32°6N 92°5W **314** E8
Columbia *Miss., U.S.A.* 31°15N 89°50W **315** F10
Columbia *Mo., U.S.A.* 38°57N 92°20W **310** F4
Columbia *Pa., U.S.A.* 40°2N 76°30W **313** F8
Columbia *S.C., U.S.A.* 34°0N 81°2W **316** A8
Columbia *Tenn., U.S.A.* 35°37N 87°2W **315** D11
Columbia → *N. Amer.* 46°15N 124°5W **306** D2
Columbia, C. *Canada* 83°6N 69°57W **295** A18
Columbia, District of □ *U.S.A.* 38°55N 77°0W **309** F15
Columbia, Mt. *Canada* 52°8N 117°20W **296** C5
Columbia Basin *U.S.A.* 46°45N 119°5W **304** C4
Columbia City *U.S.A.* 41°10N 85°29W **311** C11
Columbia Falls *U.S.A.* 48°23N 114°11W **304** B6
Columbia Mts. *Canada* 52°0N 119°0W **296** C5
Columbia Plateau *U.S.A.* 44°0N 117°30W **304** E5
Columbiana *U.S.A.* 40°53N 80°42W **312** F4
Columbretes, Is. *Spain* 39°50N 0°50E **196** F5
Columbus *Ga., U.S.A.* 32°28N 84°59W **316** C5
Columbus *Ind., U.S.A.* 39°13N 85°55W **311** E11
Columbus *Kans., U.S.A.* 37°10N 94°50W **308** G6
Columbus *Miss., U.S.A.* 33°30N 88°25W **315** E10
Columbus *Mont., U.S.A.* 45°38N 109°15W **304** D9
Columbus *N. Mex., U.S.A.* 31°50N 107°38W **305** L10
Columbus *Nebr., U.S.A.* 41°26N 97°22W **308** E5
Columbus *Ohio, U.S.A.* 39°58N 83°0W **311** E13
Columbus *Tex., U.S.A.* 29°42N 96°33W **314** G6
Columbus Circle *Washington, D.C., U.S.A.* **143** b3
Columbus Circle *New York, U.S.A.* **132** b2
Columbus Grove *U.S.A.* 40°55N 84°4W **311** D12
Columbus Junction *U.S.A.* 41°17N 91°22W **310** C5
Columbus Monument = Colón, Monumento a *Barcelona, Spain* **114** c3
Columbus Park *Jamaica* 18°28N 77°25W **320** a
Columbus Park *Boston, U.S.A.* **116** b3
Colunga *Spain* 43°29N 5°16W **194** B5
Colusa *U.S.A.* 39°13N 122°1W **306** F4
Colville *U.S.A.* 48°33N 117°54W **304** B5
Colville → *U.S.A.* 70°25N 150°30W **303** A10
Colville, C. *N.Z.* 36°29S 175°21E **284** C4
Colville Channel *N.Z.* 36°25S 175°27E **284** C4
Colville Ridge *Pac. Oc.* 30°0S 180°0E **277** G15
Colwood *Canada* 48°26N 123°29W **306** B3
Colwyn Bay *U.K.* 53°18N 3°44W **168** D4
Coma *Ethiopia* 8°29N 36°53E **257** F4
Comácchio *Italy* 44°42N 12°11E **199** D9
Comalcalco *Mexico* 18°16N 93°13W **319** D6
Comallo *Argentina* 41°0S 70°5W **336** B2
Comana *Romania* 44°10N 26°10E **183** F11
Comanche *U.S.A.* 31°54N 98°36W **314** F5
Comandante Arbues = Mirandópolis *Brazil* 21°9S 51°6W **335** A5
Comandante Ferraz *Antarctica* 62°30S 58°0W **151** C18
Comandante Luis Piedrabuena *Argentina* 49°59S 68°54W **336** C3
Comăneşti *Romania* 46°25N 26°26E **183** D11
Comarapa *Bolivia* 17°54S 64°29W **331** D5
Comarnic *Romania* 45°15N 25°38E **183** E10
Comayagua *Honduras* 14°25N 87°37W **320** D2
Combahee → *U.S.A.* 32°31N 80°31W **315** E14
Combara *Australia* 31°10S 148°22E **283** A8
Combarbalá *Chile* 31°11S 71°2W **334** C1
Combault *France* 48°48N 2°37E **134** B4
Combe Martin *U.K.* 51°12N 4°3W **169** F3
Combeaufontaine *France* 47°38N 5°54E **173** E12
Comber *Ont., Canada* 42°14N 82°33W **312** D2
Comber *Down, U.K.* 54°33N 5°45W **166** B6
Combermere *Canada* 45°22N 77°37W **312** A7
Combermere Bay *Burma* 19°37N 93°34E **241** F4
Comblain-au-Pont *Belgium* 50°29N 5°35E **170** D5
Combourg *France* 48°25N 1°46W **172** D5
Comboyne *Australia* 31°34S 152°27E **283** A10
Combrailles *France* 46°8N 2°8E **173** F9
Combronde *France* 45°58N 3°5E **174** C7
Comer *Ala., U.S.A.* 32°2N 85°23W **316** C4
Comer *Ga., U.S.A.* 34°4N 83°8W **316** A6
Comeragh Mts. *Ireland* 52°18N 7°34W **166** D4
Comércio, Praça do *Portugal* 38°41N 9°9W **126** A2
Comerío *Puerto Rico* 18°12N 66°13W **321** b
Comet *Australia* 23°36S 148°38E **280** C4
Comilla *Bangla.* 23°28N 91°10E **241** D3
Comino *Malta* 36°1N 14°20E **206** E7
Comino, C. *Italy* 40°32N 9°49E **200** B2
Cómiso *Italy* 36°56N 14°36E **201** F7
Comitán de Domínguez *Mexico* 16°15N 92°8W **319** D6
Commentry *France* 46°20N 2°46E **173** F9
Commerce *Calif., U.S.A.* 34°0N 118°9W **126** B4
Commerce *Ga., U.S.A.* 34°12N 83°28W **315** D13
Commerce *Tex., U.S.A.* 33°15N 95°54W **314** E7
Commercy *France* 48°43N 5°34E **173** D12
Commissioner's Pt. *Bermuda* 32°19N 64°49W **153** a
Committee B. *Canada* 68°30N 86°30W **295** C14
Commodore, C. *Canada* 44°47N 80°54W **312** B4
Commonwealth B. *Antarctica* 67°0S 144°0E **151** C10
Commoron Cr. → *Australia* 28°22S 150°8E **281** D5
Communism Pk. = imeni Ismail Samani, Pik *Tajikistan* 39°0N 72°2E **217** E8
Como *Italy* 45°47N 9°5E **198** C6
Como, Lago di *Italy* 46°0N 9°11E **198** B6
Comodoro Rivadavia *Argentina* 45°50S 67°40W **336** C3
Comoé → *Ivory C.* 5°12N 3°44W **262** D4
Comoé △ *Ivory C.* 9°0N 3°35W **262** D4
Comoraşte *Romania* 45°10N 21°35E **182** E6
Comorin, C. = Kannyakumari *India* 8°3N 77°40E **245** K3
Comoros ■ *Ind. Oc.* 12°10S 44°15E **272** a
Comox *Canada* 49°42N 124°55W **296** D4
Company's Gardens *Cape Town, S. Africa* **118** c2
Compass Lake *U.S.A.* 30°36N 85°24W **316** E4
Compiègne *France* 49°24N 2°50E **173** C9
Comporta *Portugal* 38°22N 8°46W **195** G2
Compostela *Nayarit, Mexico* 21°14N 104°55W **318** C4
Compostela *Phil.* 7°40N 126°2E **233** H6
Comprida, I. *Brazil* 24°50S 47°42W **335** A6
Compton *Qué., Canada* 45°14N 71°49W **313** A13
Compton *Calif., U.S.A.* 33°53N 118°13W **307** M8
Comrat *Moldova* 46°18N 28°40E **183** D13
Comunidad *Peru* 13°59S 69°20W **330** C4
Con Cuong *Vietnam* 19°2N 104°54E **236** C5
Con Dao △ *Vietnam* 8°42N 106°35E **237** H6
Con Son, Dao *Vietnam* 8°41N 106°37E **237** H6
Cona Niyeu *Argentina* 41°58S 67°0W **336** B3
Conakry *Guinea* 9°29N 13°49W **262** D2
Conara *Australia* 41°50S 147°26E **281** G4
Conargo *Australia* 35°16S 145°10E **283** C6
Concarneau *France* 47°52N 3°56W **172** E3
Conceição *Paraíba, Brazil* 7°33S 38°31W **332** C4
Conceição *Mozam.* 18°47S 36°7E **269** F4
Conceição, I. da *Brazil* 22°52S 43°6W **135** B2
Conceição da Barra *Brazil* 18°35S 39°45W **333** E4
Conceição do Araguaia *Brazil* 8°0S 49°2W **332** C2
Conceição do Canindé *Brazil* 7°54S 41°34W **332** C3
Conceição do Maú *Brazil* 3°35N 59°53W **329** C6
Conceição do Paraíba = Capela *Brazil* 10°30S 37°0W **332** D4
Concepción *Argentina* 27°20S 65°35W **334** B2
Concepción *Bolivia* 16°15S 62°8W **331** D5
Concepción *Chile* 36°50S 73°0W **334** D1
Concepción *Mexico* 18°15N 90°5W **319** D6
Concepción *Paraguay* 23°22S 57°26W **334** A4
Concepción *Peru* 11°54S 75°19W **330** C2
Concepción *Tarlac, Phil.* 15°27N 120°47E **232** D3
Concepción □ *Chile* 37°0S 72°30W **334** D1
Concepción → *Mexico* 30°32N 113°2W **318** A2
Concepción, Est. de *Chile* 50°30S 74°55W **336** D2
Concepción, L. *Bolivia* 17°20S 61°20W **331** D5
Concepción, Pta. *Mexico* 26°53N 111°50W **318** B2
Concepción del Oro *Mexico* 24°38N 101°25W **318** C4
Concepción del Uruguay *Argentina* 32°35S 58°20W **334** C4
Conception, Pt. *U.S.A.* 34°27N 120°28W **307** L6
Conception B. *Nfld. & L., Canada* 47°45N 53°0W **299** C9
Conception B. *Namibia* 23°55S 14°22E **270** B1
Conception I. *Bahamas* 23°52N 75°9W **321** B4
Concession *Zimbabwe* 17°27S 30°56E **269** F3
Conchali *Chile* 33°22S 70°39W **137** B2
Conchas Dam *U.S.A.* 35°22N 104°11W **305** J11
Conches-en-Ouche *France* 48°58N 0°56E **172** D7
Concho *U.S.A.* 34°28N 109°36W **305** J9
Concho → *U.S.A.* 31°34N 99°43W **314** F5
Conchos → *Chihuahua, Mexico* 29°35N 104°25W **318** B4
Conchos → *Chihuahua, Mexico* 27°29N 106°45W **318** B3
Conchos → *Tamaulipas, Mexico* 24°55N 97°38W **319** B5
Concord *N.S.W., Australia* 33°52S 151°6E **139** B1
Concord *Ont., Canada* 43°48N 79°29W **141** A2
Concord *Grenada* 12°17N 61°44W **323** q
Concord *Calif., U.S.A.* 37°59N 122°2W **306** H4
Concord *Ga., U.S.A.* 33°5N 84°27W **316** B5
Concord *Mich., U.S.A.* 42°11N 84°38W **311** B12
Concord *Mo., U.S.A.* 38°32N 90°23W **310** F6
Concord *N.C., U.S.A.* 35°25N 80°35W **315** D14
Concord *N.H., U.S.A.* 43°12N 71°32W **313** C13
Concorde, Place de la *Paris, France* **134** b3
Concordia *Antarctica* 75°6S 123°23E **151** D9
Concordia *Argentina* 31°20S 58°2W **334** C4
Concórdia *Amazonas, Brazil* 4°36S 66°36W **328** D4
Concórdia *Sta. Catarina, Brazil* 27°14S 52°1W **335** B5
Concordia *Sinaloa, Mexico* 23°17N 106°4W **318** C3
Concordia *Kans., U.S.A.* 39°34N 97°40W **308** F5
Concordia *Mo., U.S.A.* 38°59N 93°34W **310** F3
Concordia Univ. *Montréal, Canada* **130** c1
Concorezzo *Italy* 45°35N 9°19E **129** A2
Concrete *U.S.A.* 48°32N 121°45W **304** B3
Conda *Angola* 11°9S 14°20E **265** E2
Condah *Australia* 37°57S 141°44E **282** D4
Condamine *Australia* 26°56S 150°9E **281** D5
Condat *France* 45°21N 2°46E **174** C6
Condé *Angola* 10°50S 14°37E **265** E2
Conde *Brazil* 11°49S 37°37W **333** D4
Conde *S. Dak., U.S.A.* 45°9N 98°6W **308** C4
Condé-sur-Noireau *France* 48°51N 0°33W **172** D6
Condet *Indonesia* 6°17S 106°51E **122** A2
Condeúba *Brazil* 14°52S 42°0W **333** D3
Condobolin *Australia* 33°4S 147°6E **283** B7
Condom *France* 43°57N 0°22E **174** E4
Condon *U.S.A.* 45°14N 120°11W **304** D3
Conegliano *Italy* 45°53N 12°18E **199** C9
Conejera, I. = Conills, I. des *Spain* 39°11N 2°58E **206** B3
Conejos *Mexico* 26°14N 103°53W **318** B4
Conemaugh → *U.S.A.* 40°28N 79°19W **312** F5
Conero △ *Italy* 43°32N 13°35E **199** E10
Coney Island *U.S.A.* 40°34N 74°0W **132** C2
Conflict Group *Papua N. G.* 10°47S 151°45E **286** F6
Confolens *France* 46°2N 0°40E **174** B4
Confuso → *Paraguay* 25°9S 57°34W **334** B4
Congaree → *U.S.A.* 33°44N 80°38W **316** B9
Congaree △ *U.S.A.* 33°47N 80°47W **316** B9
Congaz *Moldova* 46°7N 28°36E **183** D13
Congerville *U.S.A.* 40°38N 89°11W **310** D7
Conghua *China* 23°36N 113°31E **229** F9
Congjiang *China* 25°43N 108°52E **228** E7
Congleton *U.K.* 53°10N 2°13W **168** D5
Congo *Brazil* 7°48S 36°40W **332** C4
Congo (Brazzaville) = Congo ■ *Africa* 1°0S 16°0E **264** C3
Congo (Kinshasa) = Congo, Dem. Rep. of the ■ *Africa* 3°0S 23°0E **265** C4
Congo ■ *Africa* 1°0S 16°0E **264** C3
Congo → *Africa* 6°4S 12°24E **265** D2
Congo, Dem. Rep. of the ■ *Africa* 3°0S 23°0E **265** C4
Congo Basin *Africa* 0°10S 24°30E **254** G6
Congo Free State = Congo, Dem. Rep. of the ■ *Africa* 3°0S 23°0E **265** C4
Congonhas *Brazil* 20°30S 43°52W **333** F3
Congonhas São Paulo ✕ (CGH) *Brazil* 23°38S 46°39W **137** B2
Congress *U.S.A.* 34°9N 112°51W **305** J7
Conguillio △ *Chile* 38°40S 71°42W **336** A2
Conil de la Frontera *Spain* 36°17N 6°10W **195** J4
Conills, I. des *Spain* 39°11N 2°58E **206** B3
Conimbla △ *Australia* 33°45S 148°28E **283** B8
Coniston *Canada* 46°29N 80°51W **298** C3
Conjeeveram = Kanchipuram *India* 12°52N 79°45E **245** H4
Conklin *Alta., Canada* 55°38N 111°5W **297** B6
Conklin *N.Y., U.S.A.* 42°2N 75°49W **313** D9
Conkouati △ *Congo* 3°50S 11°28E **264** C2
Conlendas, Pta. das *Azores* 38°38N 27°14W **153** d1
Conley → *U.S.A.* 33°40N 84°17W **113** C3
Conn, L. *Ireland* 54°3N 9°15W **166** B2
Connacht □ *Ireland* 53°43N 9°12W **166** C2
Connaught Place *Delhi, India* **120** b2
Conneaut *U.S.A.* 41°57N 80°34W **312** E4
Conneautville *U.S.A.* 41°45N 80°22W **312** E4
Connecticut □ *U.S.A.* 41°30N 72°45W **313** E12
Connecticut → *U.S.A.* 41°16N 72°20W **313** E12
Connell *U.S.A.* 46°40N 118°52W **304** C4
Connellsville *U.S.A.* 40°1N 79°35W **312** F5
Connemara *Ireland* 53°29N 9°45W **166** C2
Connemara △ *Ireland* 53°32N 9°52W **166** C2
Conner *Phil.* 17°48N 121°19E **232** C3
Connerré *France* 48°3N 0°30E **172** D7
Connersville *U.S.A.* 39°39N 85°8W **311** E11
Connors Ra. *Australia* 21°40S 149°10E **280** C4
Conoble *Australia* 32°55S 144°33E **283** B6
Conococha *Peru* 10°7S 77°18W **330** C2
Conónaco → *Ecuador* 1°32S 75°35W **328** D2
Conques *France* 44°36N 2°23E **174** D6
Conquest *Canada* 51°32N 107°14W **297** C7
Conquista = Vitória da Conquista *Brazil* 14°51S 40°51W **333** D3
Conrad *Iowa, U.S.A.* 42°14N 92°52W **310** B4
Conrad *Mont., U.S.A.* 48°10N 111°57W **304** B8
Conrad Rise *S. Ocean* 53°0S 41°0E **151** B5
Conran, C. *Australia* 37°49S 148°44E **283** D8
Conroe *U.S.A.* 30°19N 95°27W **314** F7
Consecon *Canada* 44°0N 77°31W **312** C7
Conselheiro Lafaiete *Brazil* 20°40S 43°48W **333** F3
Conselheiro Pena *Brazil* 19°10S 41°30W **333** E3
Consell *Spain* 39°40N 2°49E **206** B3
Conselve *Italy* 45°14N 11°52E **199** C8
Conservatori, Palazzo dei *Rome, Italy* **136** c3
Consett *U.K.* 54°51N 1°50W **168** C6
Consolação *Brazil* 23°32S 46°38W **137** B2
Consort *Canada* 52°1N 110°46W **297** C6
Constance = Konstanz *Germany* 47°40N 9°10E **179** H5
Constance, L. = Bodensee *Europe* 47°35N 9°25E **179** H5
Constanţa *Romania* 44°14N 28°38E **183** F13
Constanţa □ *Romania* 44°15N 28°15E **183** F13
Constantia *S. Africa* 34°2S 18°26E **118** B1
Constantina *Spain* 37°51N 5°40W **195** H5
Constantine *Algeria* 36°25N 6°42E **261** A6
Constantine *Mich., U.S.A.* 41°50N 85°40W **311** C11
Constantine □ *Algeria* 36°30N 6°40E **261** A6
Constantine, Arch of = Costantino, Arco di *Rome, Italy* **136** c3
Constantine, C. *U.S.A.* 53°24N 158°54W **303** G8
Constantinople = İstanbul *Turkey* 41°0N 28°58E **122** C1
Constitución *B. Aires, Argentina* 34°38S 58°23W **117** B2
Constitución *Chile* 35°20S 72°30W **334** D1
Constitución *Uruguay* 31°0S 57°50W **334** C4
Constitución de 1857 △ *Mexico* 32°4N 115°55W **318** A1
Constitution *U.S.A.* 33°42N 84°20W **113** B2
Constitution Avenue *Washington, D.C., U.S.A.* **143** b2
Constitution Square = Syntagma Square *Athens, Greece* **112** b2
Consuegra *Spain* 39°23N 3°36W **195** F7
Consul *Canada* 49°20N 109°30W **297** D7
Contact *U.S.A.* 41°46N 114°45W **304** F6
Contagem *Brazil* 19°55S 44°6W **333** E3
Contai *India* 21°54N 87°46E **243** J12
Contamana *Peru* 7°19S 74°55W **330** B3
Contarina *Italy* 45°1N 12°13E **199** C9
Contas → *Brazil* 14°17S 39°1W **333** D4
Contes *France* 43°49N 7°19E **175** E11
Continental *U.S.A.* 41°6N 84°16W **311** C12
Contoocook *U.S.A.* 43°13N 71°45W **313** C13
Contra Costa *Mozam.* 25°9S 33°30E **271** C5
Contres *France* 47°24N 1°26E **172** E8
Contrexéville *France* 48°10N 5°53E **173** D12
Controller B. *U.S.A.* 60°7N 144°15W **303** F11
Contumaza *Peru* 7°23S 78°57W **330** B2
Contwoyto L. *Canada* 65°42N 110°50W **294** D9
Convención *Colombia* 8°28N 73°21W **328** B3
Convention Center *U.S.A.* 34°3N 118°16W **126** B3
Conversano *Italy* 40°56N 17°7E **201** B10
Converse *U.S.A.* 40°35N 85°52W **311** D11
Convoy *U.S.A.* 40°55N 84°43W **311** D12
Conway = Conwy *U.K.* 53°17N 3°50W **168** D4
Conway = Conwy → *U.K.* 53°17N 3°50W **168** D4
Conway *Australia* 20°24S 148°41E **280** b
Conway *Ont., Canada* 44°6N 76°54W **312** B8
Conway *Ark., U.S.A.* 35°5N 92°26W **314** D8
Conway *Fla., U.S.A.* 28°30N 81°19W **133** B2
Conway *N.H., U.S.A.* 43°59N 71°7W **313** C13
Conway *S.C., U.S.A.* 33°51N 79°3W **315** E15
Conway, C. *Australia* 20°34S 148°46E **280** b
Conway, L. *S. Austral., Australia* 28°17S 135°35E **281** D2
Conway, L. *Fla., U.S.A.* 28°28N 81°21W **133** B2
Conwy *U.K.* 53°17N 3°50W **168** D4
Conwy □ *U.K.* 53°10N 3°44W **168** D4
Conwy → *U.K.* 53°17N 3°50W **168** D4
Conyers *U.S.A.* 33°40N 84°1W **316** B5
Coober Pedy *Australia* 29°1S 134°43E **281** D1
Cooch Behar = Koch Bihar *India* 26°22N 89°29E **241** B2
Coogee *Australia* 33°55S 151°16E **139** B2
Cooinda *Australia* 13°15S 130°5E **278** B5
Cook *S. Austral., Australia* 30°37S 130°25E **279** F5
Cook *Minn., U.S.A.* 47°51N 92°41W **308** B7
Cook, B. *Chile* 55°10S 70°0W **336** E3
Cook, C. *Canada* 50°8N 127°55W **296** C3
Cook, Mt. = Aoraki Mount Cook *N.Z.* 43°36S 170°9E **285** D5
Cook, Récif de *N. Cal.* 19°25S 163°50E **288** d
Cook Bay *Vanuatu* 18°46S 169°15E **287** H7
Cook Inlet *U.S.A.* 60°0N 152°0W **303** G10
Cook Is. ∅ *Pac. Oc.* 17°0S 160°0W **289** J12
Cook Strait *N.Z.* 41°15S 174°29E **284** H3
Cooke Plains *Australia* 35°23S 139°34E **282** C3
Cookeville *U.S.A.* 36°10N 85°30W **315** C12
Cookhouse *S. Africa* 32°44S 25°47E **270** D4
Cooks Hammock *U.S.A.* 29°56N 83°17W **316** F6
Cooks Harbour *Canada* 51°36N 55°52W **299** B8
Cookshire *Canada* 45°25N 71°38W **313** A13
Cookstown *Ont., Canada* 44°11N 79°42W **312** B5
Cookstown *Tyrone, U.K.* 54°39N 6°45W **166** B5
Cooksville *Canada* 43°35N 79°38W **141** B1
Cooktown *Australia* 15°30S 145°16E **280** B4
Coolabah *Australia* 31°1S 146°43E **283** A7
Cooladdi *Australia* 26°37S 145°23E **281** D4
Coolah *Australia* 31°48S 149°41E **283** A8
Coolah Tops △ *Australia* 31°52S 150°0E **283** A9
Coolamon *Australia* 34°46S 147°8E **283** C7
Coolgardie *Australia* 30°55S 121°8E **279** F3
Coolidge *Ariz., U.S.A.* 32°59N 111°31W **305** K8
Coolidge *Ga., U.S.A.* 31°1N 83°52W **316** D6
Coolidge Dam *U.S.A.* 33°10N 110°32W **305** K8
Coolock *Ireland* 53°22N 6°12W **120** A2
Cooma *Australia* 36°12S 149°8E **283** D8
Coon Rapids *Iowa, U.S.A.* 41°53N 94°41W **310** C2
Coon Rapids *Minn., U.S.A.* 45°9N 93°19W **308** C7
Coonabarabran *Australia* 31°14S 149°18E **283** A8
Coonalpyn *Australia* 35°43S 139°52E **282** C3
Coonamble *Australia* 30°56S 148°27E **283** A8
Coonana *Australia* 31°0S 123°0E **279** F3
Coonana ✪ *Australia* 30°51S 122°53E **279** F3
Coondapoor *India* 13°42N 74°40E **245** H2
Cooninnie, L. *Australia* 26°4S 139°59E **281** D2
Coonoor *India* 11°21N 76°45E **245** J3
Cooper *U.S.A.* 33°23N 95°42W **314** E7
Cooper → *U.S.A.* 32°50N 79°56W **316** C10
Cooper Cr. → *Australia* 28°29S 137°46E **281** D2
Cooper Ridge *Pac. Oc.* 10°0N 150°30W **289** G12
Cooper's Hill *Jamaica* 18°4N 76°51W **320** a
Cooperstown *N. Dak., U.S.A.* 47°27N 98°8W **308** B4
Cooperstown *N.Y., U.S.A.* 42°42N 74°56W **313** D10
Coopersville *U.S.A.* 43°4N 85°57W **311** A11
Coopracambra △ *Australia* 37°20S 149°20E **283** D8
Coora → *Trin. & Tob.* 10°10N 61°28W **323** t
Coorabie *Australia* 31°54S 132°18E **279** F5
Coorong, The *Australia* 35°50S 139°20E **282** C3
Coorong △ *Australia* 36°0S 139°29E **282** D3
Coorow *Australia* 29°53S 116°2E **279** E2
Cooroy *Australia* 26°22S 152°54E **281** D5
Coos Bay *U.S.A.* 43°22N 124°13W **304** E1
Coosa → *U.S.A.* 32°30N 86°16W **315** E11
Cootamundra *Australia* 34°36S 148°1E **283** C8
Cootehill *Ireland* 54°4N 7°5W **166** B4
Copacabana *Brazil* 22°58S 43°11W **135** B1
Copahue Paso *Argentina* 37°49S 71°8W **334** D1
Copainalá *Mexico* 17°4N 93°18W **319** D6
Copake *U.S.A.* 42°7N 73°33W **313** D11
Copalnic Mănăştur *Romania* 47°30N 23°41E **183** C8
Copán *Honduras* 14°50N 89°9W **320** D2
Copatana *Brazil* 2°48S 67°4W **328** D4
Cope *Colo., U.S.A.* 39°40N 102°51W **304** G12
Cope *S.C., U.S.A.* 33°23N 81°0W **316** B8
Cope, C. *Spain* 37°26N 1°28W **197** H3
Copeland *U.S.A.* 25°57N 81°22W **317** K8
Copenhagen = København *Denmark* 55°40N 12°26E **118** A2
Copenhagen *U.S.A.* 43°54N 75°41W **313** C9
Copertino *Italy* 40°16N 18°3E **201** B11
Copiapó *Chile* 27°30S 70°20W **334** B1
Copiapó → *Chile* 27°19S 70°56W **334** B1
Coplay *U.S.A.* 40°44N 75°29W **313** F9
Copley *Australia* 30°36S 138°26E **282** A3
Copo △ *Argentina* 25°53S 61°41W **334** B3
Copp L. *Canada* 60°14N 114°40W **296** A6
Copparo *Italy* 44°54N 11°49E **199** D8
Coppename → *Suriname* 5°48N 55°55W **329** B6
Copper → *U.S.A.* 60°18N 145°3W **303** F11
Copper Canyon = Barranca del Cobre △ *Mexico* 27°18N 107°40W **318** B3
Copper Center *U.S.A.* 61°58N 145°18W **303** F11
Copper Cliff = Invermere *Canada* 50°30N 116°2W **296** C5
Copper Harbor *U.S.A.* 47°28N 87°53W **308** B10
Copper Queen *Zimbabwe* 17°29S 29°18E **269** F2
Copperas Cove *U.S.A.* 31°8N 97°54W **314** F6
Copperbelt □ *Zambia* 13°15S 27°30E **269** E2
Coppermine = Kugluktuk *Canada* 67°50N 115°5W **294** D8
Coppermine → *Canada* 67°49N 116°4W **294** D8
Copperopolis *U.S.A.* 37°58N 120°38W **306** H6
Copşa Mică *Romania* 46°7N 24°15E **183** D9
Coquet → *U.K.* 55°20N 1°32W **168** B6
Coquilhatville = Mbandaka *Dem. Rep. of the Congo* 0°1N 18°18E **264** B3
Coquille *U.S.A.* 43°11N 124°11W **304** E1
Coquimbo *Chile* 30°0S 71°20W **334** C1
Coquimbo □ *Chile* 31°0S 71°0W **334** C1
Coquitlam *Canada* 49°17N 122°45W **296** D4
Corabia *Romania* 43°48N 24°30E **183** G9
Coração de Jesus *Brazil* 16°43S 44°22W **333** E3
Coracora *Peru* 15°5S 73°45W **330** D3
Coraki *Australia* 28°59S 153°17E **281** D5
Coral *U.S.A.* 40°29N 79°10W **312** F5
Coral B. *Phil.* 8°25N 117°20E **233** G1
Coral Bay *Australia* 23°8S 113°46E **278** D1
Coral Gables *U.S.A.* 25°43N 80°16W **128** B2
Coral Harbour *Bahamas* 24°58N 77°28W **153** b
Coral Harbour *Nunavut, Canada* 64°8N 83°10W **295** E15
Coral Heights *Bahamas* 25°0N 77°27W **153** b
Coral Hills *U.S.A.* 38°51N 76°55W **143** B4
Coral Sea *Pac. Oc.* 15°0S 150°0E **286** F4
Coral Sea Basin *Pac. Oc.* 14°0S 152°0E **288** J7
Coral Sea Islands Terr. □ *Australia* 20°0S 155°0E **276** D9
Coral Springs *U.S.A.* 26°16N 80°16W **317** J9
Corales del Rosario △ *Colombia* 10°8N 75°46W **328** A2
Coralville *U.S.A.* 41°40N 91°35W **310** C5
Coralville L. *U.S.A.* 41°42N 91°33W **310** C5
Corangamite, L. *Australia* 38°5S 143°30E **282** E5
Corantijn → *Suriname* 5°50N 57°8W **329** B6
Coraopolis *U.S.A.* 40°31N 80°10W **312** F4
Corato *Italy* 41°9N 16°25E **201** A9
Corbeil-Essonnes *France* 48°36N 2°26E **173** D9
Corbeiro, C. *W. Sahara* 21°50N 17°0W **260** D1
Corbett △ *India* 29°20N 79°0E **243** E8
Corbie *France* 49°54N 2°30E **173** C9
Corbières *France* 42°55N 2°35E **174** F6
Corbigny *France* 47°16N 3°40E **173** E10
Corbin *U.S.A.* 36°57N 84°6W **309** G11
Corbones → *Spain* 37°36N 5°39W **195** H5
Corbu *Romania* 44°25N 28°39E **183** F13
Corby *U.K.* 52°30N 0°41W **169** E7
Corcaigh = Cork *Ireland* 51°54N 8°29W **166** E3
Corcoran *U.S.A.* 36°6N 119°33W **306** J7
Corcovado, Cristo Redentar *Brazil* 22°57S 43°12W **135** B1
Corcovado △ *Costa Rica* 8°33N 83°35W **320** E3
Cordele *U.S.A.* 31°58N 83°47W **316** D6
Cordell *U.S.A.* 35°17N 98°59W **314** D5
Cordenòns *Italy* 45°59N 12°42E **199** C9
Cordes-sur-Ciel *France* 44°5N 1°57E **174** D5
Cordillera Azul △ *Peru* 7°30S 76°30W **330** B2
Cordillera de los Picachos △ *Colombia* 2°39N 74°30W **328** C3
Cordisburgo *Brazil* 19°7S 44°21W **333** E3
Córdoba *Argentina* 31°20S 64°10W **334** C3
Córdoba *Veracruz, Mexico* 18°53N 96°56W **319** D5
Córdoba *Spain* 37°50N 4°50W **195** H6
Córdoba □ *Argentina* 31°22S 64°15W **334** C3
Córdoba □ *Colombia* 8°20N 75°40W **328** B2
Córdoba □ *Spain* 38°5N 5°0W **195** G6
Córdoba, Sierra de *Argentina* 31°10S 64°25W **334** C3
Cordon *Phil.* 16°42N 121°32E **232** C3
Cordova *U.S.A.* 60°33N 145°45W **303** F11
Corduff *Ireland* 53°23N 6°21W **120** A1
Corella *Spain* 42°7N 1°48W **196** C3
Corella → *Australia* 19°34S 140°47E **280** B3
Coremas *Brazil* 7°1S 37°58W **332** C4
Corentyne → *Guyana* 5°50N 57°8W **329** B6
Corfield *Australia* 21°40S 143°21E **280** C3
Corfu = Kerkyra *Greece* 39°38N 19°50E **206** B9
Corfu *U.S.A.* 42°57N 78°24W **312** D6
Corfu ✕ (CFU) *Greece* 39°35N 19°54E **206** B11
Corfu, Str. of = Kerkyras, Notio Steno *Greece* 39°34N 20°0E **206** B10
Corgo = O Corgo *Spain* 42°56N 7°25W **194** C3
Corguinho *Brazil* 19°53S 54°52W **331** D7
Cori *Italy* 41°39N 12°55E **200** A5
Coria *Spain* 39°58N 6°33W **194** F4
Coria del Río *Spain* 37°16N 6°3W **195** H4
Coricudgy *Australia* 32°51S 150°24E **283** B9
Corigliano Cálabro *Italy* 39°36N 16°31E **201** C9
Corimba, Barra de *Angola* 8°52S 13°9E **265** D2
Coringa Is. *Australia* 16°58S 149°58E **280** B4
Corinth = Korinthos *Greece* 37°56N 22°55E **204** D4
Corinth *Grenada* 12°2N 61°40W **323** q
Corinth *Ky., U.S.A.* 38°30N 84°34W **311** F12
Corinth *Miss., U.S.A.* 34°56N 88°31W **315** D10
Corinth *N.Y., U.S.A.* 43°15N 73°49W **313** C11
Corinth, G. of = Korinthiakos Kolpos *Greece* 38°16N 22°30E **204** C4
Corinth Canal *Greece* 37°58N 23°0E **204** D4
Corinto *Brazil* 18°20S 44°30W **333** E3
Corinto *Nic.* 12°30N 87°10W **320** D2
Coriole *Somali Rep.* 1°47N 44°32E **267** D5
Corisco *Eq. Guin.* 0°55N 9°18E **264** B1
Cork *Ireland* 51°54N 8°29W **166** E3
Cork □ *Ireland* 51°57N 8°40W **166** E3
Cork Harbour *Ireland* 51°47N 8°16W **166** E3
Corlay *France* 48°20N 3°5W **172** D3
Corleone *Italy* 37°49N 13°18E **200** E6
Corleto Perticara *Italy* 40°23N 16°2E **201** B9
Çorlu *Turkey* 41°11N 27°49E **203** E11
Cormack L. *Canada* 60°56N 121°37W **296** A4
Cormano *Italy* 45°32N 9°10E **129** A2
Cormòns *Italy* 45°58N 13°28E **199** C10
Cormorant *Canada* 54°14N 100°35W **297** C8
Cormorant L. *Canada* 54°15N 100°50W **297** C8
Corn Is. = Maíz, Is. del *Nic.* 12°15N 83°4W **320** D3
Cornalvo △ *Spain* 39°1N 6°13W **195** F4
Cornaredo *Italy* 45°30N 9°1E **129** A1
Cornélio Procópio *Brazil* 23°7S 50°40W **335** A5
Cornell *U.S.A.* 41°0N 88°44W **311** D8
Corner Brook *Canada* 48°57N 57°58W **299** C8
Corner Inlet *Australia* 38°45S 146°20E **283** E7
Corner Seamounts *Atl. Oc.* 35°0N 52°0W **152** C6
Corneşti *Moldova* 47°21N 28°1E **183** C13
Corneto = Tarquinia *Italy* 42°15N 11°45E **199** F8
Corníglio *Italy* 44°29N 10°5E **198** D7
Corning *Ark., U.S.A.* 36°25N 90°35W **315** C9
Corning *Calif., U.S.A.* 39°56N 122°11W **304** G2
Corning *Iowa, U.S.A.* 40°59N 94°44W **310** D2
Corning *N.Y., U.S.A.* 42°9N 77°3W **312** D7
Corno Grande *Italy* 42°28N 13°34E **199** F10
Cornwall *Ont., Canada* 45°2N 74°44W **313** A10
Cornwall *Pa., U.S.A.* 40°17N 76°25W **313** F8
Cornwall □ *Jamaica* 18°15N 77°54W **320** a
Cornwall □ *U.K.* 50°26N 4°40W **169** G3
Cornwall I. *Canada* 77°37N 94°38W **295** B13
Cornwallis I. *Canada* 75°8N 95°0W **295** B13
Cornwell *U.S.A.* 27°23N 81°6W **317** H8
Corny Pt. *Australia* 34°55S 137°0E **282** C2
Coro *Venezuela* 11°25N 69°41W **328** A4
Coroaci *Brazil* 18°35S 42°17W **333** E3
Coroatá *Brazil* 4°8S 44°0W **332** B3
Corocoro *Bolivia* 17°15S 68°28W **330** D4
Corocoro, I. *Venezuela* 8°30N 60°10W **329** B5
Coroico *Bolivia* 16°0S 67°50W **330** D4
Coromandel *Brazil* 18°28S 47°13W **333** E2
Coromandel *N.Z.* 36°45S 175°31E **284** C4
Coromandel Coast *India* 12°30N 81°0E **245** H5
Coromandel Pen. *N.Z.* 37°0S 175°45E **284** D4
Coromandel Ra. *N.Z.* 37°0S 175°40E **284** D4
Coron *Phil.* 12°1N 120°12E **232** E3
Coron B. *Phil.* 11°54N 120°8E **233** F3
Coron I. *Phil.* 11°55N 120°14E **233** F3
Corona *Calif., U.S.A.* 33°53N 117°34W **307** M9
Corona *N. Mex., U.S.A.* 34°15N 105°36W **305** J11
Coronado *U.S.A.* 32°41N 117°10W **307** N9
Coronado, B. de *Costa Rica* 9°0N 83°40W **320** E3
Coronados, G. de los *Chile* 41°40S 74°0W **336** B2
Coronados, Is. Los *Mexico* 32°26N 117°19W **307** N9
Coronation *Canada* 52°5N 111°27W **296** C6
Coronation Gulf *Canada* 68°25N 110°0W **294** D10
Coronation I. *Antarctica* 60°45S 46°0W **151** C18
Coronation Is. *Australia* 14°57S 124°55E **278** B3
Coronda *Argentina* 31°58S 60°56W **334** C3
Coronel *Chile* 37°0S 73°10W **334** D1
Coronel Bogado *Paraguay* 27°11S 56°18W **334** B4
Coronel Dorrego *Argentina* 38°40S 61°10W **334** D3
Coronel Fabriciano *Brazil* 19°31S 42°38W **333** E3
Coronel Murta *Brazil* 16°37S 42°11W **333** E3
Coronel Oviedo *Paraguay* 25°24S 56°30W **334** B4
Coronel Ponce *Brazil* 15°34S 55°1W **331** D6
Coronel Pringles *Argentina* 38°0S 61°30W **334** D3
Coronel Suárez *Argentina* 37°30S 61°52W **334** D3
Coronel Vidal *Argentina* 37°28S 57°45W **334** D4
Corongo *Peru* 8°30S 77°53W **330** B2
Coropuna, Nevado *Peru* 15°30S 72°41W **330** D3
Corossol *St.-Martin* 17°54N 62°51W **322** a
Çorovodë *Albania* 40°31N 20°14E **202** F4
Corowa *Australia* 35°58S 146°21E **283** C7
Corozal *Colombia* 9°19N 75°18W **328** B2
Corozal *Puerto Rico* 18°21N 66°19W **321** b
Corozal □ *Belize* 18°23N 88°23W **319** D7
Corozal Pt. *Trin. & Tob.* 10°45N 61°37W **323** t
Corps *France* 44°50N 5°56E **175** D9
Corpus *Argentina* 27°10S 55°30W **335** B4
Corpus Christi *U.S.A.* 27°47N 97°24W **314** H6
Corpus Christi, L. *U.S.A.* 28°2N 97°52W **314** G6
Corque *Bolivia* 18°20S 67°41W **330** D4
Corral *Chile* 39°52S 73°26W **336** A2
Corral de Almaguer *Spain* 39°45N 3°10W **194** F7
Corralejo *Canary Is.* 28°43N 13°53W **153** e2
Corraun Pen. *Ireland* 53°54N 9°54W **166** C2
Corréggio *Italy* 44°46N 10°47E **198** D7
Corregidor *Phil.* 14°23N 120°35E **232** D3
Corrente *Brazil* 10°27S 45°10W **332** D2
Corrente → *Brazil* 13°8S 43°28W **333** D3
Correntes → *Brazil* 17°38S 55°8W **331** D6
Correntes, C. das *Mozam.* 24°6S 35°34E **271** B6
Correntina *Brazil* 13°20S 44°39W **333** D3
Corrèze □ *France* 45°20N 1°45E **174** C5
Corrèze → *France* 45°10N 1°28E **174** C5
Corrib, L. *Ireland* 53°27N 9°16W **166** C2
Corridónia *Italy* 43°15N 13°30E **199** E10
Corrientes *Argentina* 27°30S 58°45W **334** B4
Corrientes □ *Argentina* 28°0S 57°0W **334** B4
Corrientes → *Argentina* 30°42S 59°38W **334** C4
Corrientes → *Peru* 3°43S 74°35W **328** D3
Corrientes, C. *Colombia* 5°30N 77°34W **328** B2
Corrientes, C. *Cuba* 21°43N 84°30W **320** B3
Corrientes, C. *Jalisco, Mexico* 20°25N 105°42W **318** C3
Corrigan *U.S.A.* 31°0N 94°52W **314** F7
Corrigin *Australia* 32°20S 117°53E **279** F2
Corriverton *Guyana* 5°55N 57°20W **329** B6
Corry *U.S.A.* 41°55N 79°39W **312** E5
Corryong *Australia* 36°12S 147°53E **283** D7
Corse □ *France* 42°0N 9°0E **175** G13
Corse, C. *France* 43°1N 9°25E **175** E13
Corse △ *France* 42°14N 9°10E **175** F13
Corse-du-Sud □ *France* 41°45N 9°0E **175** G13
Corsica = Corse □ *France* 42°0N 9°0E **175** G13
Corsicana *U.S.A.* 32°6N 96°28W **314** E6
Córsico *Italy* 45°25N 9°6E **129** B1
Corsini, Palazzo *Rome, Italy* **136** c1
Corstorphine *U.K.* 55°56N 3°17W **121** B2
Corte *France* 42°19N 9°11E **175** F13
Corte Pinto *Portugal* 37°42N 7°29W **195** H3
Cortegana *Spain* 37°52N 6°49W **195** H4
Cortes *Phil.* 9°17N 126°11E **233** G6
Cortés, Mar de = California, G. de *Mexico* 27°0N 111°0W **318** B2
Cortez *U.S.A.* 37°21N 108°35W **305** H9
Cortina d'Ampezzo *Italy* 46°32N 12°8E **199** B9
Cortland *N.Y., U.S.A.* 42°36N 76°11W **313** D8
Cortland *Ohio, U.S.A.* 41°20N 80°44W **312** E4
Cortona *Italy* 43°16N 11°59E **199** E8
Corubal → *Guinea-Biss.* 11°57N 15°5W **262** C2
Coruche *Portugal* 38°57N 8°30W **195** G2
Çoruh → *Turkey* 41°38N 41°38E **191** K5
Çorum *Turkey* 40°30N 34°57E **212** B6
Çorum □ *Turkey* 40°40N 35°0E **212** B6
Corumbá *Brazil* 19°0S 57°30W **331** D6
Corumbá → *Brazil* 18°19S 48°55W **333** E2
Corumbá de Goiás *Brazil* 16°0S 48°50W **333** E2
Corumbaíba *Brazil* 18°9S 48°34W **333** E2
Corund *Romania* 46°30N 25°13E **183** D10
Corunna = A Coruña *Spain* 43°20N 8°25W **194** B2
Corunna *U.S.A.* 42°59N 84°7W **311** B12
Corvallis *U.S.A.* 44°34N 123°16W **304** D2
Corvette, L. de la *Canada* 53°25N 74°3W **298** B5
Corviale *Italy* 41°51N 12°25E **136** B1
Corvo *Azores* 39°42N 31°6W **153** d2
Coryal *Trin. & Tob.* 10°30N 61°11W **323** t
Corydon *Ind., U.S.A.* 38°13N 86°7W **311** F10
Corydon *Iowa, U.S.A.* 40°46N 93°19W **310** D3
Corydon *Ky., U.S.A.* 37°44N 87°43W **311** G9
Cosalá *Mexico* 24°23N 106°41W **318** C3
Cosamaloapan de Carpio *Mexico* 18°22N 95°48W **319** D5
Cosenza *Italy* 39°18N 16°15E **201** C9
Coşereni *Romania* 44°38N 26°35E **183** F11
Coshocton *U.S.A.* 40°16N 81°51W **312** F3
Coslada *Spain* 40°25N 3°35W **127** B2
Cosmo Newberry *Australia* 28°0S 122°54E **279** E3
Cosmo Newberry ✪ *Australia* 27°59S 122°53E **279** E3
Cosmonaut Sea *S. Ocean* 66°30S 40°0E **151** C5
Cosne-Cours-sur-Loire *France* 47°24N 2°54E **173** E9
Coso Junction *U.S.A.* 36°3N 117°57W **307** J9
Coso Pk. *U.S.A.* 36°13N 117°44W **307** J9
Cospeito *Spain* 43°12N 7°34W **194** B3
Cosquín *Argentina* 31°15S 64°30W **334** C3
Cossato *Italy* 45°34N 8°10E **198** C5
Cossé-le-Vivien *France* 47°57N 0°54W **172** E6
Cossigny *France* 48°43N 2°40E **134** B4
Cosson → *France* 47°30N 1°15E **172** E8
Costa Blanca *Spain* 38°25N 0°10W **197** G4
Costa Brava *Spain* 41°30N 3°0E **196** D8
Costa Cálida *Spain* 37°30N 1°30W **197** H3
Costa Daurada *Spain* 41°12N 1°15E **196** D6
Costa del Sol *Spain* 36°30N 4°30W **195** J6
Costa dels Pins *Spain* 39°38N 3°26E **206** B4
Costa Mesa *U.S.A.* 33°38N 117°55W **307** M9
Costa Rica ■ *Cent. Amer.* 10°0N 84°0W **320** E3

Czech Rep. ■ *Europe* 50°0N 15°0E **180** B8
Czechowice-Dziedzice
Poland 49°54N 18°59E **185** J5
Czempiń *Poland* 52°9N 16°43E **185** F3
Czeremcha *Poland* 52°31N 23°21E **185** F10
Czerniejewo *Poland* 52°26N 17°30E **185** F4
Czernowitz = Chernivtsi
Ukraine 48°15N 25°52E **183** B10
Czerniaków *Poland* 52°11N 21°3E **142** B2
Czersk *Poland* 53°46N 17°58E **184** E4
Czerwieńsk *Poland* 52°1N 15°23E **185** F2
Czerwionka-Leszczyny
Poland 50°7N 18°37E **185** H5
Częstochowa *Poland* 50°49N 19°7E **185** H6
Człopa *Poland* 53°6N 16°6E **185** E3
Człuchów *Poland* 53°41N 17°22E **184** E4
Czortów = Chortkiv
Ukraine 49°2N 25°46E **177** D13
Czyste *Poland* 52°13N 20°57E **142** B1
Czyżew-Osada *Poland* 52°48N 22°19E **185** F9

D

D.C. War Memorial
Washington, D.C., U.S.A. **143** b1
Da → *Vietnam* 21°15N 105°20E **228** G5
Da Hinggan Ling *China* 48°0N 121°0E **219** B13
Da Lat *Vietnam* 11°56N 108°25E **237** G7
Da Moóca → *Brazil* 23°35S 46°35W **137** B2
Da Nang *Vietnam* 16°4N 108°13E **236** D7
Da Qaidam *China* 37°50N 95°15E **218** D8
Da Yunhe → *Hopei, China* 39°10N 117°10E **227** E9
Da Yunhe → *Jiangsu, China* 34°25N 120°5E **227** G11
Da'an *China* 45°30N 124°7E **227** B13
Daan Viljoen ⌂ *Namibia* 22°2S 16°45E **270** B2
Daanbantayan *Phil.* 11°17N 124°2E **233** F5
Dab'a, Ras el *Egypt* 31°3N 28°31E **256** H6
Daba Shan *China* 32°0N 109°0E **228** B7
Dabai *Nigeria* 11°25N 5°15E **263** C6
Dabajuro *Venezuela* 11°2N 70°40W **328** A3
Dabakala *Ivory C.* 8°15N 4°20W **262** D4
Dabaro *Somali Rep.* 6°21N 48°43E **267** C6
Dabas *Hungary* 47°11N 19°19E **182** C4
Dabat *Ethiopia* 12°58N 37°41E **257** E4
Dabbagh, Jabal *Si. Arabia* 27°52N 35°45E **246** E2
Dabeiba *Colombia* 7°1N 76°16W **328** B2
Daber = Dobra *Poland* 53°34N 15°20E **184** E2
Dabhoi *India* 22°10N 73°20E **242** H5
Dąbie *Poland* 52°5N 18°50E **185** F5
Dabie Shan *China* 31°20N 115°20E **229** B10
Dabilda *Cameroon* 12°45N 14°35E **259** F2
Dabl, W. → *Si. Arabia* 29°5N 36°16E **251** J7
Ďablice *Czech Rep.* 50°8N 14°29E **135** B2
Dabnou *Niger* 14°10N 5°22E **263** C6
Dabo *Indonesia* 0°30S 104°33E **234** C2
Dabola *Guinea* 10°50N 11°5W **262** C2
Dabou *Ivory C.* 5°20N 4°23W **262** D4
Daboya *Ghana* 9°30N 1°20W **263** D4
Dabravolya *Belarus* 52°55N 23°59E **185** F10
Dąbrowa *Poland* 52°19N 20°52E **142** B1
Dąbrowa Białostocka
Poland 53°40N 23°21E **184** E10
Dąbrowa Górnicza *Poland* 50°15N 19°10E **185** H6
Dąbrowa Tarnowska
Poland 50°10N 20°59E **185** H7
Dabu *China* 24°22N 116°41E **229** E11
Dabugam *India* 19°27N 82°26E **244** E6
Dabung *Malaysia* 5°23N 102°1E **237** K4
Dabus → *Ethiopia* 10°48N 35°10E **257** E4
Dacato → *Ethiopia* 7°25N 42°40E **257** F5
Dacca = Dhaka *Bangla.* 23°43N 90°26E **241** D3
Dacca = Dhaka □ *Bangla.* 24°25N 90°25E **241** C3
Dachang *Jiangsu, China* 32°13N 118°45E **229** A12
Dachang *Shanghai, China* 31°17N 121°24E **138** B1
Dachang ✈ *China* 31°18N 121°25E **138** B1
Dachau *Germany* 48°15N 11°26E **131** A1
Dachau-Ost *Germany* 48°15N 11°27E **131** A1
Dachauer Moos *Germany* 48°13N 11°27E **131** A1
Dachigam △ *India* 34°10N 75°0E **242** B6
Dachstein, Hoher *Austria* 47°28N 13°35E **180** D6
Dačice *Czech Rep.* 49°5N 15°26E **180** B8
Dacre *Canada* 45°22N 76°57W **312** A8
Dacula *U.S.A.* 33°59N 83°54W **316** B6
Dadanawa *Guyana* 2°50N 59°30W **329** C6
Dadar *India* 19°0N 72°49E **130** A1
Daday *Turkey* 41°28N 33°27E **212** B5
Dade City *U.S.A.* 28°22N 82°11W **317** G7
Dadès, Oued → *Morocco* 30°58N 6°44W **260** B3
Dadeville *U.S.A.* 32°50N 85°46W **316** C4
Dadhar *Pakistan* 29°28N 67°39E **242** E2
Dadiya *Nigeria* 9°35N 11°24E **263** D7
Dadnah *U.A.E.* 25°32N 56°22E **247** E8
Dadohae Maritime Nat. Park △
S. Korea 34°0N 126°0E **224** E3
Dadra = Achalpur *India* 21°22N 77°32E **244** D3
Dadra & Nagar Haveli □
India 20°5N 73°0E **244** D1
Dadri = Charkhi Dadri
India 28°37N 76°17E **242** E7
Dadu *Pakistan* 26°45N 67°45E **242** F2
Dadu He → *China* 29°31N 103°46E **228** C4
Daebang *S. Korea* 37°30N 126°55E **137** B1
Daebudo *S. Korea* 37°14N 126°35E **224** D3
Daecheongdo *S. Korea* 37°49N 124°42E **224** D2
Daechi *S. Korea* 37°30N 127°2E **137** B2
Daegu *S. Korea* 35°50N 128°37E **224** E4
Daejeon *S. Korea* 36°20N 127°28E **224** D3
Daejeon □ *S. Korea* 36°20N 127°25E **224** D3
Daejeong *S. Korea* 33°8N 126°17E **224** a
Daemodo *S. Korea* 34°11N 126°45E **224** E3
Daet *Phil.* 14°2N 122°55E **232** D4
Dafang *China* 27°9N 105°39E **228** D5
Dafdaf, J. *Si. Arabia* 28°16N 35°35E **251** K6
Dafeng *China* 33°3N 120°45E **227** H11
Dafnes *Greece* 35°13N 25°3E **207** E6
Dafni *Athína, Greece* 37°55N 23°44E **112** B2
Dafni *Pelopónnese, Greece* 37°48N 22°1E **204** D4
Dafnoudi, Akra *Greece* 38°28N 20°32E **207** C2
Dağ *Turkey* 37°12N 30°31E **205** D12
Daga Post *South Sudan* 9°13N 33°58E **266** C3
Dagali *Norway* 60°25N 8°28E **164** D5
Dagana *Senegal* 16°30N 15°35W **262** B1
Dagash *Sudan* 19°19N 33°25E **256** D3
Dagenham *U.K.* 51°32N 0°8E **125** A4
Dagestan □ *Russia* 42°30N 47°0E **191** J8
Dagestanskiye Ogni *Russia* 42°6N 48°12E **191** J9
Dagg Sd. *N.Z.* 45°23S 166°45E **285** F1
Daggett *U.S.A.* 34°52N 116°52W **307** L10
Daghestan Republic = Dagestan □
Russia 42°30N 47°0E **191** J8
Daghfeli *Sudan* 19°18N 32°40E **256** D3
Daglfing *Germany* 48°8N 11°39E **131** B2
Dağlıq Qarabağ =
Nagorno-Karabakh □
Azerbaijan 39°55N 46°45E **213** C12
Dagö = Hiiumaa *Estonia* 58°50N 22°45E **188** C2
Dagu *China* 38°59N 117°40E **227** E9
Dagua *Papua N. G.* 3°27S 143°20E **286** B2
Daguan *China* 27°43N 103°56E **228** D4
Dagupan *Phil.* 16°3N 120°20E **232** C3
Daguragu *Australia* 17°33S 130°30E **278** C5
Daguragu ✪ *Australia* 17°24S 130°48E **278** C5
Dahab *Egypt* 28°31N 34°31E **251** K5
Dahab, Gezîret el *Egypt* 29°59N 31°13E **117** B2
Dahanu *India* 19°58N 72°44E **244** E1
Daheisha *West Bank* 31°42N 35°11E **123** B2
Dahivadi *India* 17°43N 74°33E **244** F2
Dahlak Kebir *Eritrea* 15°50N 40°10E **257** D5
Dahlak Marine △ *Eritrea* 15°35N 40°1E **257** D5
Dahlem *Germany* 52°27N 13°16E **115** B2
Dahlenburg *Germany* 53°11N 10°44E **178** B6
Dahlonega *U.S.A.* 34°32N 83°59W **315** D13
Dahlwitz-Hoppegarten
Germany 52°30N 13°41E **115** A5
Dahme *Germany* 51°52N 13°25E **178** D9
Dahod *India* 22°50N 74°15E **242** H6
Dahomey = Benin ■ *Africa* 10°0N 2°0E **263** D5
Dahong Shan *China* 31°25N 113°0E **229** B9
Dahongliutan *China* 35°45N 79°20E **243** B8
Dahongmen *China* 39°48N 116°21E **114** C2
Dahra *Libya* 29°30N 17°50E **258** C3
Dahra *Senegal* 15°22N 15°30W **262** B1
Dahra, Massif de *Algeria* 36°7N 1°21E **261** A5
Dahshûr *Egypt* 29°45N 31°14E **256** J7
Dahūk *Iraq* 36°50N 43°1E **213** D10
Dahūk □ *Iraq* 36°50N 42°50E **213** D10
Dahuofan Shuiku *China* 41°52N 124°12E **224** B2
Dahy, Nafūd ad *Si. Arabia* 22°0N 45°25E **248** B4
Dai *Solomon Is.* 7°54S 160°40E **287** L11
Dai Hao *Vietnam* 18°1N 106°25E **236** C6
Dai-Sen *Japan* 35°22N 133°32E **222** B5
Dai Shan *China* 30°25N 122°10E **229** E14
Dai Xian *China* 39°4N 112°58E **226** E7
Daicheng *China* 38°42N 116°38E **226** E9
Daigo *Japan* 36°46N 140°21E **223** F12
Daik-u *Burma* 17°47N 96°40E **241** G6
Daikondi = Day Kundī □
Afghan. 34°0N 66°0E **240** B2
Daimanji-San *Japan* 36°14N 133°20E **222** A5
Daimiel *Spain* 39°5N 3°35W **195** F7
Daingean *Ireland* 53°18N 7°17W **166** C4
Dainkog *China* 32°30N 97°58E **228** A1
Daintree *Australia* 16°20S 145°20E **280** B4
Daintree △ *Australia* 16°8S 145°2E **280** B4
Daiō-Misaki *Japan* 34°15N 136°45E **223** C8
Dair, J. ed *Sudan* 12°27N 30°42E **257** E3
Dairen = Dalian *China* 38°50N 121°40E **227** E11
Dairût *Egypt* 27°34N 30°43E **256** B3
Daisen-Oki △ *Japan* 35°23N 133°34E **222** B5
Daisetsu-Zan *Japan* 43°30N 142°57E **220** C11
Daisetsu-Zan △ *Japan* 43°30N 142°55E **220** C11
Daitari *India* 21°10N 85°46E **244** D7
Daitō *Japan* 35°19N 132°58E **222** B4
Daiyun Shan *China* 25°50N 118°15E **229** E12
Dajarra *Australia* 21°42S 139°30E **280** C2
Dajiaoting *China* 39°51N 116°27E **114** B2
Dajiawa *China* 37°9N 119°0E **227** F10
Dajin Chuan → *China* 31°16N 101°59E **228** B3
Dak Dam *Cambodia* 12°20N 107°21E **236** F6
Dak Nhe *Vietnam* 15°28N 107°48E **236** E6
Dak Pek *Vietnam* 15°4N 107°44E **236** E6
Dak Song *Vietnam* 12°19N 107°35E **237** F6
Dak Sui *Vietnam* 14°55N 107°43E **236** E6
Dakar *Senegal* 14°34N 17°29W **262** C1
Dakar □ *Senegal* 14°45N 17°20W **262** C1
Dakhal, W. el → *Egypt* 28°48N 32°47E **251** K3
Dakhin *Bangla.* 22°30N 90°45E **241** D3
Dakhla *W. Sahara* 23°50N 15°53W **260** D1
Dakhla, El Wâhât el
Egypt 25°30N 28°50E **256** B2
Dakhnoye *Russia* 59°49N 30°15E **137** C1
Dakingari *Nigeria* 11°37N 4°1E **263** C5
Dakoank *India* 7°2N 93°43E **245** L11
Dakor *India* 22°45N 73°11E **242** H5
Dakoro *Niger* 14°31N 6°46E **263** C6
Dakota City *Iowa, U.S.A.* 42°43N 94°12W **310** B2
Dakota City *Nebr., U.S.A.* 42°25N 96°25W **308** D5
Đakovica *Kosovo* 42°22N 20°26E **202** D4
Đakovo *Croatia* 45°19N 18°24E **182** E3
Dal *Norway* 59°53N 8°40E **164** E5
Dala *Lunda Sul, Angola* 11°3S 20°17E **265** E4
Dala *Uíge, Angola* 8°5S 15°49E **265** D3
Dala *Solomon Is.* 8°30S 160°41E **287** M11
Dala-Cachibo *Angola* 10°30S 14°41E **265** E2
Dala-Järna *Sweden* 60°33N 14°26E **162** D8
Dalaba *Guinea* 10°47N 12°12W **262** C2
Dalachi *China* 36°48N 105°0E **226** F3
Dalagan = San Antonio
Phil. 14°57N 120°5E **232** D3
Dalaguete *Phil.* 9°46N 123°32E **233** G4
Dalai Nur *China* 43°20N 116°45E **226** C9
Dālakī *Iran* 29°26N 51°17E **247** D6
Dalälven → *Sweden* 60°12N 16°43E **162** D10
Dalaman *Turkey* 36°48N 28°47E **205** E10
Dalaman → *Turkey* 36°41N 28°43E **205** E10
Dalandzadgad *Mongolia* 43°27N 104°30E **226** C3
Dalanganem Is. *Phil.* 10°40N 120°17E **233** F3
Dalap-Uliga-Darrit = Majuro
Marshall Is. 7°9N 171°12E **288** G9
Dalarna *Sweden* 61°0N 14°0E **162** D8
Dalarnas län □ *Sweden* 61°0N 14°15E **162** C8
Dalasýsla □ *Iceland* 65°15N 22°0W **155** B4
Dalat *Malaysia* 2°44N 111°56E **235** B4
Dalay *Mongolia* 43°28N 103°30E **226** C2
Dālbandīn *Pakistan* 29°0N 64°23E **240** C2
Dalbeattie *U.K.* 54°56N 3°50W **167** G5
Dalbeg *Australia* 20°16S 147°18E **280** C4
Dalbosjön *Sweden* 58°40N 12°45E **163** F6
Dalby *Queens., Australia* 27°10S 151°17E **281** D5
Dalby *Skåne, Sweden* 55°40N 13°22E **163** J7
Dalby Söderskog △
Sweden 55°41N 13°21E **163** J7
Dale *Sogn og Fjordane, Norway* 61°22N 5°23E **164** C2
Dale *Ind., U.S.A.* 38°10N 86°59W **311** F10
Dale City *U.S.A.* 38°38N 77°19W **309** F15
Dale Hollow L. *U.S.A.* 36°32N 85°27W **315** C12
Dalejsky potok →
Czech Rep. 50°2N 14°24E **135** B2
Dalen *Norway* 59°26N 8°0E **164** E4
Dalet *Burma* 19°59N 93°51E **241** F4
Daletme *Burma* 21°36N 92°46E **241** E4
Daleville *Ala., U.S.A.* 31°19N 85°43W **316** D4
Daleville *Ind., U.S.A.* 40°7N 85°33W **311** D11
Dalga *Egypt* 27°39N 30°41E **256** B3
Dalgān *Iran* 27°31N 59°19E **247** E8
Dalgety Bay *U.K.* 56°2N 3°20W **121** A1
Dalhart *U.S.A.* 36°4N 102°31W **314** C3
Dalhousie *N.B., Canada* 48°5N 66°26W **299** C6
Dalhousie *India* 32°38N 75°58E **242** C6
Dali *Shaanxi, China* 34°48N 109°58E **226** G5
Dali *Yunnan, China* 25°40N 100°10E **228** E3
Dalian *China* 38°50N 121°40E **227** E11
Daliang Shan *China* 28°0N 102°45E **228** D4
Daling He → *China* 40°55N 121°40E **227** D11
Dāliyat el Karmel *Israel* 32°43N 35°2E **250** F6
Dalj *Croatia* 45°29N 18°59E **182** E3
Dalkeith *Midloth., U.K.* 55°54N 3°4W **121** B3
Dalkeith *Fla., U.S.A.* 30°0N 85°9W **316** E4
Dalkey *Ireland* 53°16N 6°6W **120** B3
Dalkey I. *Ireland* 53°17N 6°5W **120** B3
Dallas *Ga., U.S.A.* 33°55N 84°51W **316** B5
Dallas *Oreg., U.S.A.* 44°55N 123°19W **304** D2
Dallas *Tex., U.S.A.* 32°47N 96°48W **314** E6
Dallas Center *U.S.A.* 41°41N 93°58W **310** C3
Dallas City *U.S.A.* 40°38N 91°10W **310** D5
Dalle = Yirga Alem
Ethiopia 6°48N 38°22E **257** F4
Dalles, The *U.S.A.* 45°36N 121°10W **304** D3
Dallgow *Germany* 52°32N 13°5E **115** A1
Dallol *Ethiopia* 14°14N 40°17E **257** E5
Dalmā *U.A.E.* 24°30N 52°20E **247** E7
Dalmacija *Croatia* 43°20N 17°0E **199** E13
Dalmas, L. *Canada* 53°30N 71°50W **299** B5
Dalmatia = Dalmacija
Croatia 43°20N 17°0E **199** E13
Dalmau *India* 26°4N 81°2E **243** F9
Dalmellington *U.K.* 55°19N 4°23W **167** F4
Dalmeny *N.S.W., Australia* 36°10S 150°8E **283** D9
Dalmeny *Edinburgh, U.K.* 55°59N 3°22W **121** B1
Dalnegorsk *Russia* 44°32N 135°33E **220** B7
Dalnerechensk *Russia* 45°50N 133°40E **220** B6
Dalnevostochnyy □
Russia 67°0N 140°0E **215** C14
Dalny = Dalian *China* 38°50N 121°40E **227** E11
Daloa *Ivory C.* 7°0N 6°30W **262** D3
Dalou Shan *China* 28°15N 107°0E **228** C6
Dalry *U.K.* 55°42N 4°43W **167** F4
Dalrymple, L. *Australia* 20°40S 147°0E **280** C4
Dalrymple, Mt. *Australia* 21°1S 148°39E **280** b
Dals Långed *Sweden* 58°56N 12°18E **163** F6
Dalsætra *Norway* 61°28N 9°26E **164** C6
Dalsjöfors *Sweden* 57°46N 13°5E **163** G7
Dalsland *Sweden* 58°50N 12°15E **163** F6
Dalsmynni *Iceland* 64°48N 21°29W **155** C5
Dalston *U.K.* 51°32N 0°4W **125** A3
Daltenganj *India* 24°0N 84°4E **243** H11
Dalton *Ga., U.S.A.* 34°46N 84°58W **315** D12
Dalton *Mass., U.S.A.* 42°28N 73°11W **313** D11
Dalton *Nebr., U.S.A.* 41°25N 102°58W **308** E2
Dalton, Kap *Greenland* 69°25N 24°3W **154** D8
Dalton-in-Furness *U.K.* 54°10N 3°11W **168** C4
Daludalu *Indonesia* 1°4N 100°15E **234** B2
Dalupiri I. *Cagayan, Phil.* 19°5N 121°12E **232** B3
Dalupiri I. *N. Samar, Phil.* 12°25N 124°16E **232** E5
Dalvík *Iceland* 65°58N 18°32W **155** B8
Dálvvadis = Jokkmokk
Sweden 66°35N 19°50E **160** C18
Dalwallinu *Australia* 30°17S 116°40E **279** F2
Daly → *Australia* 13°35S 130°19E **278** B5
Daly City *U.S.A.* 37°42N 122°27W **136** B2
Daly L. *Canada* 56°32N 105°39W **297** B7
Daly River *Australia* 13°46S 130°42E **278** B5
Daly River-Port Keats ✪
Australia 14°13S 129°36E **278** B4
Daly Waters *Australia* 16°15S 133°24E **280** B1
Dalyan *Turkey* 36°50N 28°39E **205** E10
Dam *Amsterdam, Neths.* **112** a2
Dam Doi *Vietnam* 8°50N 105°12E **237** H5
Dam Ha *Vietnam* 21°21N 107°36E **236** B6
Damachova *Belarus* 51°45N 23°36E **185** G10
Damaia *Portugal* 38°44N 9°12W **126** A1
Daman *India* 20°25N 72°57E **244** D1
Daman & Diu □ *India* 20°25N 72°56E **244** D1
Dāmaneh *Iran* 33°1N 50°29E **247** C6
Damanganga → *India* 20°25N 72°56E **244** D1
Damanhûr *Egypt* 31°0N 30°30E **256** H7
Damant L. *Canada* 61°45N 105°5W **297** A7
Damaq *Iran* 35°25N 48°49E **213** E13
Damar *Indonesia* 7°7S 128°40E **237** F7
Damara *C.A.R.* 4°58N 18°42E **264** B3
Damarakia *Greece* 37°58N 23°39E **112** B1
Damaraland *Namibia* 20°0S 15°0E **270** B2
Damascus = Dimashq
Syria 33°30N 36°18E **250** E7
Damascus *U.S.A.* 31°18N 84°43W **316** D5
Damasi *Greece* 39°43N 22°11E **204** B4
Damatura *Nigeria* 11°45N 11°55E **263** C7
Damāvand *Iran* 35°47N 52°0E **247** C7
Damāvand, Qolleh-ye
Iran 35°56N 52°10E **247** C7
Damba *Angola* 6°44S 15°20E **265** D3
Damboa *Nigeria* 11°15N 12°55E **259** F2
Dâmboviţa □ *Romania* 45°0N 25°30E **183** F10
Dâmboviţa → *Romania* 44°12N 26°26E **183** F11
Dâmbovnic → *Romania* 44°28N 25°18E **183** F10
Dambrowica = Dubrovytsya
Ukraine 51°31N 26°35E **177** C14
Dambulla *Sri Lanka* 7°51N 80°39E **245** L5
Dame Marie *Haiti* 18°36N 74°26W **321** C5
Dämeritzsee *Germany* 52°34N 13°43E **115** B5
Dāmghān *Iran* 36°10N 54°17E **247** B7
Dămienesti *Romania* 46°44N 26°59E **183** D11
Damietta = Dumyât
Egypt 31°24N 31°48E **251** G2
Daming *China* 36°15N 115°6E **226** F8
Damīr Qābū *Syria* 36°58N 41°51E **246** B4
Dammai I. *Phil.* 5°47N 120°25E **233** J3
Dammam = Ad Dammām
Si. Arabia 26°20N 50°5E **247** E6
Dammarie-les-Lys *France* 48°31N 2°39E **173** D9
Dammartin-en-Goële
France 49°3N 2°41E **173** C9
Damme *Germany* 52°32N 8°11E **178** C4
Damodar → *India* 23°17N 87°35E **243** H12
Damoh *India* 23°50N 79°28E **243** H8
Damous *Algeria* 36°31N 1°42E **261** A5
Dampier *Australia* 20°41S 116°42E **278** D2
Dampier, Selat *Indonesia* 0°40S 131°0E **231** E8
Dampier Arch. *Australia* 20°38S 116°32E **278** D2
Dampier Str. *Papua N. G.* 5°50S 148°0E **286** C5
Damqawt *Yemen* 16°34N 52°50E **249** C6
Damrak *Amsterdam, Neths.* **112** a2
Damrani *Algeria* 27°45N 2°56W **260** C4
Damrei, Chuor Phnum
Cambodia 11°30N 103°0E **237** G4
Damroh *India* 28°26N 95°14E **241** A5
Damvillers *France* 49°20N 5°21E **173** C12
Damyang *S. Korea* 35°19N 126°59E **224** E3
Dan Gorayo *Somali Rep.* 8°43N 49°20E **267** C6
Dan-Gulbi *Nigeria* 11°40N 6°15E **263** C6
Dan Ryan Woods *U.S.A.* 41°44N 87°40W **119** C2
Dan-Sadau *Nigeria* 11°17N 6°29E **263** C6
Dana *Indonesia* 11°0S 121°15E **231** F6
Dana *Jordan* 30°41N 35°37E **251** H6
Dana, L. *Canada* 50°53N 77°20W **298** B4
Dana, Mt. *U.S.A.* 37°54N 119°12W **306** H7
Danakil Depression *Ethiopia* 13°0N 41°0E **267** B5
Danakil Desert *Ethiopia* 12°45N 41°0E **257** E5
Danan *Ethiopia* 6°31N 43°30E **267** C5
Danané *Ivory C.* 7°16N 8°9W **262** D3
Danao *Phil.* 10°31N 124°1E **233** F5
Danau Sentarum △
Indonesia 0°51N 112°6E **235** B4
Danba *China* 30°54N 101°48E **228** B3
Danbury *U.S.A.* 41°24N 73°28W **313** E11
Danby L. *U.S.A.* 34°13N 115°5W **305** J6
Dand *Afghan.* 31°28N 65°32E **242** D1
Dande → *Angola* 8°28S 13°21E **265** D2
Dande ⌂ *Zimbabwe* 15°56S 30°16E **269** F3
Dandeldhura *Nepal* 29°20N 80°35E **243** E9
Dandeli *India* 15°5N 74°30E **245** G2
Dandenong *Australia* 38°0S 145°15E **283** E6
Danderhall *U.K.* 55°55N 3°7W **121** B3
Danderyd *Sweden* 59°24N 18°1E **139** A2
Dandī *Iran* 36°32N 47°37E **213** D12
Dandîl *Egypt* 29°10N 31°2E **256** J7
Dandong *China* 40°10N 124°20E **224** B2
Daneborg *Greenland* 74°18N 20°14W **154** C8
Danfeng *China* 33°45N 110°25E **226** H6
Danforth *Canada* 43°43N 79°16W **141** A3
Dangan Liedao *China* 22°2N 114°8E **229** F10
Dangcagan *Phil.* 7°36N 125°0E **233** H5
Dange *Angola* 7°56S 15°3E **265** D3
Dangé-St-Romain *France* 46°56N 0°36E **174** B4
Dângeni *Romania* 47°51N 26°58E **183** C11
Danger Is. = Pukapuka
Cook Is. 10°53S 165°49W **289** J11
Danger Pt. *S. Africa* 34°40S 19°17E **270** D2
Dangjin *S. Korea* 36°53N 126°37E **224** D3
Dangla *Ethiopia* 11°18N 36°56E **257** E4
Dangla Shan = Tanggula Shan
China 32°40N 92°10E **218** E7
Dangora *Nigeria* 11°30N 8°7E **263** C6
Dangouadougou
Burkina Faso 10°9N 4°56W **262** D4
Dangrek, Mts. = Dangrek, Phnom
Thailand 14°20N 104°0E **236** E5
Dangrek, Phnom *Thailand* 14°20N 104°0E **236** E5
Dangriga *Belize* 17°0N 88°13W **320** C2
Dangshan *China* 34°27N 116°22E **226** G9
Dangtu *China* 31°32N 118°25E **229** B12
Dangyang *China* 30°52N 111°44E **229** B8
Daniel *U.S.A.* 42°52N 110°4W **304** E8
Daniel's Harbour *Canada* 50°13N 57°35W **299** B8
Danielskuil *S. Africa* 28°11S 23°33E **270** C3
Danielson *U.S.A.* 41°48N 71°53W **313** E13
Danielsville *U.S.A.* 34°8N 83°13W **316** A6
Danilov *Russia* 58°16N 40°13E **188** C11
Danilovgrad *Montenegro* 42°38N 19°4E **202** D3
Danilovka *Russia* 50°25N 44°12E **190** E7
Daning *China* 36°28N 110°45E **226** F6
Danish West Indies = Virgin Is.
(U.S.) ☑ *W. Indies* 18°20N 65°0W **321** C7
Danissa *Kenya* 3°17N 40°59E **267** D5
Danja *Nigeria* 11°21N 7°30E **263** C6
Danje-la-Menha *Angola* 9°32S 14°39E **265** D2
Danjiangkou *China* 32°31N 111°30E **229** A8
Danjiangkou Shuiku
China 32°37N 111°30E **229** A8
Dank *Oman* 23°33N 56°16E **247** F8
Dankalwa *Nigeria* 11°52N 12°12E **263** C7
Dankama *Nigeria* 13°20N 7°44E **263** C6
Dankhar Gompa *India* 32°10N 78°10E **242** C8
Dankov *Russia* 53°20N 39°5E **188** F10
Danleng *China* 30°1N 103°31E **228** B4
Danlí *Honduras* 14°4N 86°35W **320** D2
Danmark = Denmark ■
Europe 55°45N 10°0E **163** J3
Danmark Fjord *Greenland* 81°30N 22°0W **154** A8
Danmarkshavn
Greenland 76°45N 18°50W **154** B9
Dannemora *U.S.A.* 44°43N 73°44W **313** B11
Dannenberg *Germany* 53°6N 11°5E **178** B7
Dannevirke *N.Z.* 40°12S 176°8E **284** G5
Dannhauser *S. Africa* 28°0S 30°3E **271** C5
Danot *Ethiopia* 7°33N 45°17E **267** C6
Dansalan = Marawi City
Phil. 8°0N 124°21E **233** G5
Dansville *U.S.A.* 42°34N 77°42W **312** D7
Danta *India* 24°11N 72°46E **242** G5
Dantan *India* 21°57N 87°20E **243** J12
Dante = Xaafuun
Somali Rep. 10°25N 51°16E **267** B7
Dantewara *India* 18°54N 81°21E **244** E5
Danube = Dunărea →
Europe 45°20N 29°40E **183** E14
Danubyu *Burma* 17°15N 95°35E **241** G5
Danvers *U.S.A.* 42°34N 70°56W **313** D14
Danville *Ga., U.S.A.* 32°37N 83°15W **316** C6
Danville *Ill., U.S.A.* 40°8N 87°37W **311** D9
Danville *Ind., U.S.A.* 39°46N 86°32W **311** E10
Danville *Ky., U.S.A.* 37°39N 84°46W **311** G12
Danville *Pa., U.S.A.* 40°58N 76°37W **313** F8
Danville *Va., U.S.A.* 36°36N 79°23W **309** G14
Danville *Vt., U.S.A.* 44°25N 72°9W **313** B12
Danyang *China* 32°0N 119°31E **229** B12
Danzhai *China* 26°11N 107°48E **228** D6
Danzhou *China* 19°31N 109°33E **236** C7
Danzig = Gdańsk *Poland* 54°22N 18°40E **184** D5
Dao *Antique, Phil.* 10°30N 121°57E **233** F3
Dao *Capiz, Phil.* 11°24N 122°41E **233** F4
Dão → *Portugal* 40°20N 8°11W **194** E2
Dao Xian *China* 25°36N 111°31E **229** E8
Daocheng *China* 29°0N 100°10E **228** C3
Daora *W. Sahara* 27°5N 12°59W **260** C2
Daoud = Aïn Beïda *Algeria* 35°50N 7°29E **261** A6
Daoukro *Ivory C.* 7°10N 3°58W **262** D4
Dapa *Phil.* 9°46N 126°3E **233** G6
Dapaong *Togo* 10°55N 0°16E **263** C5
Dapchi *Nigeria* 12°32N 11°31E **263** C7
Dapiak, Mt. *Phil.* 8°15N 123°28E **233** G4
Dapitan *Phil.* 8°39N 123°25E **233** G4
Dapoli *India* 17°46N 73°11E **244** F1
Daqahlîya □ *Egypt* 30°55N 31°30E **251** H2
Daqing *China* 46°35N 125°0E **219** B13
Daqing Shan *China* 40°40N 111°0E **226** D6
Daqq-e Sorkh, Kavīr *Iran* 33°45N 52°50E **247** C7
Daqu Shan *China* 30°25N 122°20E **229** B14
Dar Banda *Africa* 8°0N 23°0E **254** F6
Dar el Beida = Casablanca
Morocco 33°36N 7°36W **260** B3
Dar es Salaam *Tanzania* 6°50S 39°12E **268** D4
Dar Mazār *Iran* 29°14N 57°20E **247** D8
Dar Rounga *C.A.R.* 0°45N 22°20E **264** A4
Dār Ta'izzah *Syria* 36°20N 36°52E **250** B7
Dar'ā *Syria* 32°36N 36°7E **250** F7
Dar'ā □ *Syria* 32°55N 36°10E **250** F7
Dara Dere = Zlatograd
Bulgaria 41°22N 25°7E **203** E9
Dārāb *Iran* 28°50N 54°30E **247** D7
Daraban *Pakistan* 31°44N 70°20E **242** D4
Darabani *Romania* 48°10N 26°39E **183** B11
Darai Hills *Papua N. G.* 7°8S 143°33E **286** D2
Daraina *Madag.* 13°12S 49°40E **272** A2
Daraj *Libya* 30°10N 10°28E **258** B2
Darakeh *Iran* 35°49N 51°22E **141** A2
Daram *Phil.* 11°38N 124°48E **233** F5
Dārān *Iran* 32°59N 50°24E **247** C6
Đaravica *Kosovo* 42°32N 20°8E **202** D4
Daraw *Egypt* 24°22N 32°51E **256** C3
Dārayyā *Syria* 33°28N 36°15E **250** E7
Darazo *Nigeria* 11°1N 10°24E **263** C7
Darband *Tehrān, Iran* 35°49N 51°27E **141** A2
Darband *Pakistan* 34°20N 72°50E **242** B5
Darband, Kūh-e *Iran* 31°34N 57°8E **247** D8
Darbhanga *India* 26°15N 85°55E **243** F11
Darburruk *Somali Rep.* 9°44N 44°31E **267** C5
Darby, C. *U.S.A.* 64°19N 162°47W **303** D7
D'Arcy *Canada* 50°33N 122°29W **296** C4
Dardanelle *Ark., U.S.A.* 35°13N 93°9W **314** D8
Dardanelle *Calif., U.S.A.* 38°20N 119°50W **306** G7
Dardanelles = Çanakkale Boğazı
Turkey 40°17N 26°32E **203** F10
Dare → *Ethiopia* 7°20N 42°11E **257** F5
Darende *Turkey* 38°31N 37°30E **212** C7
Dārestān *Iran* 29°9N 58°42E **247** D8
Darfield *N.Z.* 43°29S 172°7E **285** D7
Darfo *Italy* 45°53N 10°11E **198** C7
Dārfūr *Sudan* 13°40N 24°0E **259** F4
Dargai *Pakistan* 34°25N 71°55E **242** B4
Dargaville *N.Z.* 35°57S 173°52E **284** B2
Dargol *Niger* 13°54N 1°22E **263** C5
Darhan *Mongolia* 49°37N 106°21E **218** B10
Darhan Muminggan
China 41°40N 110°28E **226** D6
Dari *South Sudan* 5°48N 30°26E **257** F3
Darıca *Turkey* 40°45N 29°23E **212** B3
Darien *U.S.A.* 31°23N 81°26W **316** D8
Darién, G. del *Colombia* 9°0N 77°0W **320** E4
Darién, Serranía del
Colombia 8°30N 77°30W **320** E4
Darién △ *Panama* 7°36N 77°57W **320** E4
Dariganga = Ovoot
Mongolia 45°21N 113°45E **226** B7
Daringbadi *India* 19°54N 84°8E **244** E7
Darjeeling = Darjiling
India 27°3N 88°18E **241** B2
Darjiling *India* 27°3N 88°18E **241** B2
Darkan *Australia* 33°20S 116°43E **279** F2
Darke Peak *Australia* 33°27S 136°12E **282** B2
Darkhana *Pakistan* 30°39N 72°11E **242** D5
Darkhazīneh *Iran* 31°54N 48°39E **247** D6
Darkot Pass *Pakistan* 36°45N 73°26E **243** A5
Darling → *Australia* 34°4S 141°54E **282** C4
Darling Downs *Australia* 27°30S 150°30E **281** D5
Darling Harbour *Sydney, Australia* **139** b1
Darling Point *Australia* 33°52S 151°15E **139** B2
Darling Ra. *Australia* 32°30S 116°20E **279** F2
Darlington *Durham, U.K.* 54°32N 1°33W **168** C6
Darlington *Fla., U.S.A.* 30°57N 86°3W **316** E3
Darlington *S.C., U.S.A.* 34°18N 79°52W **315** D15
Darlington *Wis., U.S.A.* 42°41N 90°7W **310** B6
Darlington □ *U.K.* 54°32N 1°33W **168** C6
Darlington, L. *S. Africa* 33°10S 25°9E **270** D4
Darlington Point *Australia* 34°37S 146°1E **283** C7
Darlot, L. *Australia* 27°48S 121°35E **279** E3
Darłowo *Poland* 54°25N 16°25E **184** D3
Dărmăneşti *Bacău, Romania* 46°21N 26°33E **183** D11
Dărmăneşti *Suceava, Romania* 47°44N 26°9E **183** C11
Darmstadt *Germany* 49°51N 8°39E **179** F4
Darnah *Libya* 32°45N 22°45E **258** B4
Darnall *S. Africa* 29°23S 31°18E **271** C5
Darndale *Ireland* 53°23N 6°12W **120** A2
Darney *France* 48°5N 6°2E **173** D13
Darnick *Australia* 32°48S 143°38E **282** B5
Darnley *Australia* 9°35S 143°46E **280** a
Darnley, C. *Antarctica* 68°0S 69°0E **151** C6
Darnley B. *Canada* 69°30N 123°30W **294** D7
Daroca *Spain* 41°9N 1°25W **196** D3
Daror *Ethiopia* 8°14N 44°42E **267** C5
Darou-Mousti *Senegal* 15°3N 16°3W **262** B1
Darr → *Australia* 23°39S 143°50E **280** C3
Darra Pezu *Pakistan* 32°19N 70°44E **242** C4
Darran Mts. *N.Z.* 44°37S 167°59E **285** E2
Darreh Shahr *Iran* 33°7N 47°22E **213** F12
Darrequeira *Argentina* 37°42S 63°10W **334** D3
Darrington *U.S.A.* 48°15N 121°36W **304** B3
Darrūs *Iran* 35°46N 51°27E **141** A2
Darsana *Bangla.* 23°35N 88°48E **241** D2
Darsi *India* 15°46N 79°44E **245** G4
Darsser Ort *Germany* 54°28N 12°32E **178** A8
Dart → *U.K.* 50°24N 3°39W **169** G4
Dart, C. *Antarctica* 73°6S 126°20W **151** D14
Dartford *U.K.* 51°26N 0°13E **125** B5
Dartmoor *Vic., Australia* 37°56S 141°19E **282** D4
Dartmoor *Devon, U.K.* 50°38N 3°57W **169** G4
Dartmoor △ *U.K.* 50°37N 3°59W **169** G4
Dartmouth *N.S., Canada* 44°40N 63°30W **299** D7
Dartmouth *Devon, U.K.* 50°21N 3°36W **169** G4
Dartmouth, Res.
Australia 36°34S 147°32E **283** D7
Dartmouth Res. *Australia* 26°4S 145°18E **281** D4
Dartuch, C. = Artrutx, C. de
Spain 39°55N 3°49E **206** B4
Daru *Papua N. G.* 9°3S 143°13E **286** E2
Daruvar *Croatia* 45°35N 17°14E **182** E2
Darvaza = Içoguz
Turkmenistan 40°11N 58°24E **216** D5
Darvel, Teluk = Lahad Datu, Teluk
Malaysia 4°50N 118°20E **235** B5
Darvi *Mongolia* 46°27N 94°7E **217** C12
Darwen *U.K.* 53°42N 2°29W **168** D5
Darwendale *Zimbabwe* 17°41S 30°33E **271** A5
Darwha *India* 20°15N 77°45E **244** D3
Darwin *N. Terr., Australia* 12°25S 130°51E **278** B5
Darwin *Calif., U.S.A.* 36°15N 117°35W **307** J9
Darwin, Mt. *Chile* 54°47S 69°55W **336** D3
Darwin, Volcán *Ecuador* 0°10S 91°18W **330** a
Darya Ganj *Delhi, India* **120** a3
Darya Khan *Pakistan* 31°48N 71°6E **242** D4
Daryācheh-ye Bakhtegān
Iran 29°40N 53°50E **247** D7
Daryapur *India* 20°55N 77°20E **244** D3
Daryoi Amu = Amudarya →
Uzbekistan 43°58N 59°34E **216** D5
Dās *U.A.E.* 25°20N 53°30E **247** E7
Dashahe *China* 42°44N 128°12E **224** A4
Dashen, Ras *Ethiopia* 13°8N 38°26E **257** E4
Dasher *U.S.A.* 30°45N 83°13W **316** D6
Dashetai *China* 41°0N 109°5E **226** D5
Dashi *China* 23°11N 113°17E **121** B2
Dashiqiao *China* 40°38N 122°30E **227** D12
Dashkesan = Daşkäsän
Azerbaijan 40°25N 46°0E **191** K7
Dashköpri *Turkmenistan* 36°16N 62°8E **247** B9
Dashoguz *Turkmenistan* 41°49N 59°58E **216** D5
Dasht → *Pakistan* 25°10N 61°40E **240** D1
Dasht-i-Tahlab *Pakistan* 28°40N 62°25E **240** C1
Daska *Pakistan* 32°20N 74°20E **242** C6
Daşkäsän *Azerbaijan* 40°25N 46°0E **191** K7
Dasmariñas *Phil.* 14°20N 120°56E **232** D3
Dasol B. *Phil.* 15°52N 119°50E **232** D2
Dassa *Benin* 7°46N 2°14E **263** D5
Dasuya *India* 31°49N 75°38E **242** D6
Datadian *Indonesia* 2°1N 115°13E **235** B5
Datansha *China* 23°8N 113°12E **121** B2
Datça *Turkey* 36°46N 27°40E **205** E9
Datia *India* 25°39N 78°27E **243** G8
Datian *China* 25°40N 117°50E **229** E11
Datong *Anhui, China* 30°48N 117°44E **229** B11
Datong *Qinghai, China* 36°20N 102°50E **218** D9
Datong *Shanxi, China* 40°6N 113°18E **226** D7
Dattakhel *Pakistan* 32°54N 69°46E **242** C3
Dattapur = Dhamangaon
India 20°48N 78°9E **244** D4
Datteln *Germany* 51°39N 7°21E **178** D3
Datu, Tanjung *Indonesia* 2°5N 109°39E **235** B3
Datu Piang *Phil.* 7°2N 124°30E **233** H5
Datuk, Tanjong = Datu, Tanjung
Indonesia 2°5N 109°39E **235** B3
Datun *China* 40°0N 116°23E **114** B2
Daua = Dawa → *Africa* 4°11N 42°6E **257** G5
Daud Khel *Pakistan* 32°53N 71°34E **242** C4
Daudnagar *India* 25°2N 84°24E **243** G11
Daugava → *Latvia* 57°4N 24°3E **188** D3
Daugavpils *Latvia* 55°53N 26°32E **188** E4
Daulatabad *India* 19°57N 75°15E **244** E2
Daulatpur *India* 28°44N 77°6E **120** A1
Daule *Ecuador* 1°56S 79°56W **328** D2
Daule → *Ecuador* 2°10S 79°52W **328** D2
Daule-Peripa, Presa
Ecuador 1°0S 79°35W **328** D2
Daulpur *India* 26°45N 77°59E **242** F7
Daun *Germany* 50°11N 6°49E **179** E2
Daund *India* 18°26N 74°40E **244** E2
Daung Kyun *Burma* 12°13N 98°4E **237** F2
Dauphin *Man., Canada* 51°9N 100°5W **297** C8
Dauphin *Pa., U.S.A.* 40°22N 76°56W **312** F8
Dauphin L. *Canada* 51°20N 99°45W **297** C9
Dauphiné *France* 45°15N 5°25E **175** C9
Daura *Borno, Nigeria* 11°31N 11°24E **263** C7
Daura *Katsina, Nigeria* 13°2N 8°21E **263** C6
Dausa *India* 26°52N 76°20E **242** F7
Däväçi *Azerbaijan* 41°15N 48°57E **191** K9
Davangere *India* 14°25N 75°55E **245** G2
Davao *Phil.* 7°0N 125°40E **233** H5
Davao □ *Phil.* 7°0N 125°55E **233** H5
Davao del Sur □ *Phil.* 6°30N 125°25E **233** H5
Davao G. *Phil.* 6°30N 125°48E **233** H5
Davao Oriental □ *Phil.* 7°10N 126°30E **233** H6
Dāvar Panāh = Sarāvān
Iran 27°25N 62°15E **247** E9
Davenport *Calif., U.S.A.* 37°1N 122°12W **306** H4
Davenport *Fla., U.S.A.* 28°10N 81°36W **317** G8
Davenport *Iowa, U.S.A.* 41°32N 90°35W **310** C6
Davenport *Wash., U.S.A.* 47°39N 118°9W **304** C4
Davenport Ra. *Australia* 20°28S 134°0E **280** C1
Davenport Range △
Australia 20°36S 134°22E **280** C1
Daventry *U.K.* 52°16N 1°10W **169** E6
David *Panama* 8°30N 82°30W **320** E3
David City *U.S.A.* 41°15N 97°8W **308** E5
David Glacier *Antarctica* 75°20S 162°0E **151** D11
David Gorodok = Davyd Haradok
Belarus 52°4N 27°8E **177** B14
David's Citadel *Jerusalem* **123** b3
David's Tomb *Jerusalem* **123** b3
Davidson *Canada* 51°16N 105°59W **297** C7
Davidson, Mt. *U.S.A.* 37°44N 122°27W **136** B2
Davidson Mts. *U.S.A.* 68°41N 142°22W **303** B12
Davidson's Mains *U.K.* 55°58N 3°16W **121** B2
Davie *U.S.A.* 26°3N 80°14W **317** J9
Davis *Antarctica* 68°34S 77°55E **151** C6
Davis *Calif., U.S.A.* 38°33N 121°44W **306** G5
Davis Dam *U.S.A.* 35°12N 114°34W **307** K12
Davis Inlet *Canada* 55°50N 60°59W **299** A7
Davis Mts. *U.S.A.* 30°50N 103°55W **314** F3
Davis Sea *Antarctica* 66°0S 92°0E **151** C7
Davis Str. *N. Amer.* 65°0N 58°0W **295** D19
Davisboro *U.S.A.* 32°59N 82°36W **316** C7
Davison *U.S.A.* 43°2N 83°31W **311** A13
Davlos *Cyprus* 35°25N 33°54E **207** E9
Davo → *Ivory C.* 5°0N 6°10W **262** D3
Davos *Switz.* 46°48N 9°49E **179** J5
Dāvūdiyeh *Iran* 35°45N 51°25E **141** A2
Davutlar *Turkey* 37°43N 27°17E **205** D9
Davy L. *Canada* 58°53N 108°18W **297** B7
Davyd Haradok *Belarus* 52°4N 27°8E **177** B14
Davydkovo *Russia* 55°43N 37°29E **129** B2
Dawa → *Africa* 4°11N 42°6E **257** G5
Dawaki *Bauchi, Nigeria* 9°25N 9°33E **263** D6
Dawaki *Kano, Nigeria* 12°5N 8°23E **263** C6
Dawei = Tavoy *Burma* 14°2N 98°12E **236** E2
Dawes Ra. *Australia* 24°40S 150°40E **280** C5
Dawidy *Poland* 52°8N 20°58E **142** C1
Dawkah *Oman* 18°39N 54°5E **249** C6
Dawley = Telford *U.K.* 52°40N 2°27W **169** E5
Dawlish *U.K.* 50°35N 3°28W **169** G4
Dawna Ra. *Burma* 16°30N 98°30E **236** D2
Dawnyein *Burma* 15°54N 95°36E **241** G5
Dawqah *Si. Arabia* 19°36N 40°54E **248** C3
Dawros Hd. *Ireland* 54°50N 8°33W **166** B3
Dawson *U.S.A.* 31°46N 84°27W **316** D5
Dawson, I. *Chile* 53°50S 70°50W **336** D2
Dawson B. *Canada* 52°53N 100°49W **297** C8
Dawson City *Canada* 64°10N 139°30W **294** E4
Dawson Creek *Canada* 55°45N 120°15W **296** B4
Dawson Inlet *Canada* 61°50N 93°25W **297** A10
Dawson Ra. *Australia* 24°30S 149°48E **280** C4
Dawu *Hubei, China* 31°34N 114°7E **229** B9
Dawu *Sichuan, China* 30°55N 101°10E **228** B3
Dawwah *Oman* 20°33N 58°48E **249** B7
Dawwara, Ras id- *Malta* 35°52N 14°21E **206** F7
Dax *France* 43°44N 1°3W **174** E2
Daxian *China* 31°15N 107°23E **228** B6
Daxin *China* 22°50N 107°11E **228** F6
Daxindian *China* 37°30N 120°50E **227** F11
Daxing *China* 39°47N 116°24E **114** C2
Daxinggou *China* 43°25N 129°40E **227** C15
Daxue Shan *Sichuan, China* 30°30N 101°30E **228** B3
Daxue Shan *Yunnan, China* 23°42N 99°48E **228** F2
Day *U.S.A.* 30°12N 83°17W **316** E6
Day Kundī □ *Afghan.* 34°0N 66°0E **240** B2
Daya el Khadra *Mauritania* 25°14N 6°2W **260** C3
Dayang He → *China* 39°51N 123°36E **224** C1
Dayao *China* 25°43N 101°20E **228** E3
Daye *China* 30°6N 114°58E **229** B10
Dayet en Naharat *Mali* 17°39N 3°10W **262** B4
Dayi *China* 30°41N 103°29E **228** B4
Daylesford *Australia* 37°21S 144°9E **282** D6
Dayong *China* 29°11N 110°30E **229** C8
Dayr az Zawr *Syria* 35°20N 40°5E **213** E9
Dayr az Zawr □ *Syria* 34°50N 40°10E **213** E9
Days Bay *N.Z.* 41°17S 174°54E **143** B2
Daysland *Canada* 52°50N 112°20W **296** C6
Dayton *Iowa, U.S.A.* 42°16N 94°4W **310** B2
Dayton *Nev., U.S.A.* 39°14N 119°36W **306** F7
Dayton *Ohio, U.S.A.* 39°45N 84°12W **311** E12
Dayton *Pa., U.S.A.* 40°53N 79°15W **312** F5
Dayton *Tenn., U.S.A.* 35°30N 85°1W **315** D12
Dayton *Wash., U.S.A.* 46°19N 117°59W **304** C5
Dayton *Wyo., U.S.A.* 44°53N 107°16W **304** D10
Daytona Beach *U.S.A.* 29°13N 81°1W **317** F9
Dayu *China* 25°24N 114°22E **229** E10
Dayville *U.S.A.* 44°28N 119°32W **304** D4
Dazaifu *Japan* 33°32N 130°32E **222** D2
Dazhu *China* 30°41N 107°15E **228** B6
Dazkırı *Turkey* 37°57N 29°52E **205** D11
Dazu *China* 29°40N 105°42E **228** C5
De Aar *S. Africa* 30°39S 24°0E **270** D3
De Armanville *U.S.A.* 33°38N 85°45W **316** B4
De Bary *U.S.A.* 28°54N 81°18W **317** G8
De Biesbosch △ *Neths.* 51°45N 4°48E **170** C4
De Forest *U.S.A.* 43°15N 89°20W **310** A7
De Funiak Springs *U.S.A.* 30°43N 86°7W **316** E3
De Grey → *Australia* 20°12S 119°13E **278** D2
De Haan *Belgium* 51°16N 3°2E **170** C3
De Hoge Veluwe △ *Neths.* 52°5N 5°46E **170** B5
De Hoop △ *S. Africa* 34°30S 20°28E **270** D3
De Kalb Junction *U.S.A.* 44°30N 75°16W **313** B9
De Kennemerduinen △
Neths. 52°27N 4°33E **170** B4
De Land *U.S.A.* 29°2N 81°18W **317** F8
De Leon *U.S.A.* 32°7N 98°32W **314** E5
De Leon Springs *U.S.A.* 29°7N 81°21W **317** F8
De Long Mts. *U.S.A.* 68°10N 163°0W **303** B7
De Panne *Belgium* 51°6N 2°34E **170** C2
De Pere *U.S.A.* 44°27N 88°4W **308** C9
De Queen *U.S.A.* 34°2N 94°21W **314** D7
De Quincy *U.S.A.* 30°27N 93°26W **314** F8
De Ruyters *U.S.A.* 42°45N 75°53W **313** D9
De Smet *U.S.A.* 44°23N 97°33W **308** C5
De Soto *U.S.A.* 38°8N 90°34W **310** F6
De Soto City *U.S.A.* 27°27N 81°24W **317** H8
De Tour Village *U.S.A.* 46°0N 83°56W **309** B12
De Witt *Ark., U.S.A.* 34°18N 91°20W **314** D9
De Witt *Iowa, U.S.A.* 41°49N 90°33W **310** C6
De Witt *Mich., U.S.A.* 42°51N 84°34W **311** B12
Dead L. *U.S.A.* 30°10N 85°10W **316** E4
Dead Sea *Asia* 31°30N 35°30E **251** G6
Deadhorse *U.S.A.* 70°11N 148°27W **303** A10
Deadman B. *U.S.A.* 29°30N 83°30W **317** F6

Deadwood U.S.A. 44°23N 103°44W 308 C2
Deadwood L. Canada 59°10N 128°30W 296 B3
Deal U.K. 51°13N 1°25E 169 F9
Deal I. Australia 39°30S 147°20E 281 F4
Dealesville S. Africa 28°41S 25°44E 270 C4
De'an China 29°21N 115°46E 229 C10
Dean → Canada 52°49N 126°58W 296 C3
Dean, Forest of U.K. 51°45N 2°33W 169 F5
Dean Chan. Canada 52°30N 127°15W 296 C3
Deán Funes Argentina 30°20S 64°20W 334 C3
Dearborn Mich., U.S.A. 42°19N 83°10W 311 B13
Dearborn Mo., U.S.A. 39°32N 94°46W 310 E2
Dease → Canada 59°56N 128°32W 296 B3
Dease Inlet U.S.A. 71°2N 155°26W 303 A9
Dease L. Canada 58°40N 130°5W 296 B2
Dease Lake Canada 58°25N 130°6W 296 B2
Death Valley U.S.A. 36°15N 116°50W 307 J10
Death Valley △ U.S.A. 36°29N 117°6W 307 J9
Death Valley Junction U.S.A. 36°20N 116°25W 307 J10
Deatnu = Tana → Norway 70°30N 28°14E 160 A23
Deauville France 49°23N 0°2E 172 C7
Deba Spain 43°18N 2°21W 196 B2
Deba Habe Nigeria 10°14N 11°20E 263 C7
Debagram India 23°51N 90°33E 243 H14
Debak Malaysia 1°34N 111°25E 235 B4
Debaltsevo Ukraine 48°22N 38°26E 189 H10
Debao China 23°21N 106°46E 228 F6
Debar Macedonia 41°31N 20°30E 202 E4
Debark Ethiopia 13°1N 37°48E 257 E4
Debden Canada 53°30N 106°50W 297 C7
Debdou Morocco 33°59N 3°0W 261 B4
Debe Trin. & Tob. 10°22N 61°27W 323 t
Dębica Poland 50°2N 21°25E 185 H8
Dęblin Poland 51°34N 21°50E 185 G8
Dębno Poland 52°44N 14°41E 185 F1
Débo, L. Mali 15°14N 4°15W 262 B4
DeBolt Canada 55°12N 118°1W 296 B5
Deborah East, L. Australia 30°45S 119°0E 279 F2
Deborah West, L. Australia 30°45S 119°5E 279 F2
Deboyne Is. Papua N. G. 10°43S 152°22E 286 F7
Debrc Serbia 44°38N 19°53E 202 B3
Debre Birhan Ethiopia 9°41N 39°31E 257 F4
Debre Markos Ethiopia 10°20N 37°40E 257 E4
Debre May Ethiopia 11°20N 37°25E 257 E4
Debre Sina Ethiopia 9°51N 39°50E 257 F4
Debre Tabor Ethiopia 11°50N 38°26E 257 E4
Debre Zebit Ethiopia 11°48N 38°30E 257 E4
Debre Zevit Ethiopia 8°50N 39°0E 257 F4
Debrecen Hungary 47°33N 21°42E 182 C6
Debrzno Poland 53°31N 17°14E 184 E4
Dečani Kosovo 42°30N 20°18E 202 D4
Decatur Ala., U.S.A. 34°36N 86°59W 315 D11
Decatur Ga., U.S.A. 33°46N 84°16W 113 B3
Decatur Ill., U.S.A. 39°51N 88°57W 310 E8
Decatur Ind., U.S.A. 40°50N 84°56W 311 D12
Decatur Mich., U.S.A. 42°7N 85°58W 311 B11
Decatur Tex., U.S.A. 33°14N 97°35W 314 E6
Decazeville France 44°34N 2°15E 174 D6
Deccan India 18°0N 79°0E 244 F4
Deception, Mt. Australia 30°42S 138°16E 282 A3
Deception B. Papua N. G. 7°45S 144°40E 286 D3
Deception Bay Australia 27°10S 153°5E 281 D5
Deception I. Antarctica 63°0S 60°15W 151 C17
Deception L. Canada 56°33N 104°13W 297 B8
Dechang China 27°25N 102°11E 228 D4
Dechhu India 26°46N 72°20E 242 F5
Děčín Czech Rep. 50°47N 14°12E 180 A7
Decize France 46°50N 3°28E 173 F10
Deckerville U.S.A. 43°32N 82°44W 312 C2
Decollatura Italy 39°3N 16°21E 201 C9
Decorah U.S.A. 43°18N 91°48W 308 D8
Deda Romania 46°56N 24°50E 183 D9
Dedaye Burma 16°24N 95°53E 241 G5
Dedéagach = Alexandroupoli Greece 40°50N 25°54E 203 F9
Dededo Guam 13°31N 144°50E 302 d
Deder Ethiopia 9°19N 41°27E 257 F5
Dedham U.S.A. 42°15N 71°10W 116 B1
Dedoplis Tskaro = Tsiteli-Tsqaro Georgia 41°33N 46°0E 191 K8
Dédougou Burkina Faso 12°30N 3°25W 262 C4
Dedovichi Russia 57°32N 29°56E 188 D5
Dedza Malawi 14°20S 34°20E 269 E3
Dee → Aberds., U.K. 57°9N 2°5W 167 D6
Dee → Dumf. & Gall., U.K. 54°51N 4°3W 167 G4
Dee → Wales, U.K. 53°22N 3°17W 168 D4
Deep B. Canada 61°15N 116°35W 296 A5
Deep Bay = Chilumba Malawi 10°28S 34°12E 269 E3
Deep Bay = Shenzhen Wan China 22°27N 113°55E 219 a
Deep Lead Australia 37°0S 142°43E 282 D5
Deepwater N.S.W., Australia 29°25S 151°51E 281 D5
Deepwater Mo., U.S.A. 38°16N 93°47W 310 F7
Deer → Canada 58°23N 94°13W 297 B10
Deer I. U.S.A. 54°55N 162°18W 302 E7
Deer L. Canada 52°40N 94°20W 297 C10
Deer Lake Nfld. & L., Canada 49°11N 57°27W 299 C8
Deer Lake Ont., Canada 52°36N 94°20W 297 C10
Deer Lodge U.S.A. 46°24N 112°44W 304 C7
Deer Park Fla., U.S.A. 28°6N 80°54W 317 G9
Deer Park Ohio, U.S.A. 39°12N 84°23W 311 E12
Deer Park Wash., U.S.A. 47°57N 117°28W 304 C5
Deer River U.S.A. 47°20N 93°48W 308 B7
Deeragun Australia 19°16S 146°33E 280 B4
Deerfield Ill., U.S.A. 42°10N 87°51W 311 B9
Deerfield Mo., U.S.A. 37°50N 94°30W 310 G2
Deerfield Beach U.S.A. 26°19N 80°6W 317 J9
Deering U.S.A. 66°4N 162°42W 303 C7
Defensores del Chaco △ Paraguay 20°13S 60°27W 331 E5
Defiance U.S.A. 41°17N 84°22W 311 C12
Dega Medo Ethiopia 7°59N 43°1E 267 C5
Degana India 26°50N 74°20E 242 F6
Dêgê China 31°44N 98°39E 228 B2
Degebe → Portugal 38°13N 7°29W 195 G3
Degeberga Sweden 55°51N 14°5E 163 J8
Degeh Bur Ethiopia 8°11N 43°31E 267 C5
Dégelis Canada 47°30N 68°35W 299 C6
Degema Nigeria 4°50N 6°48E 263 E6
Degerfors Sweden 59°15N 14°27E 162 E8
Degerhamn Sweden 56°20N 16°24E 163 H10
Deggendorf Germany 48°50N 12°57E 179 G8
Degh → Pakistan 31°3N 73°21E 242 D5
Değirmendere Turkey 40°42N 29°47E 203 F13
Degirmenlik = Kythréa Cyprus 35°15N 33°29E 207 E9
Degunino Russia 55°52N 37°33E 129 A3
Deh Bīd Iran 30°39N 53°11E 247 D7
Deh Dasht Iran 30°47N 50°33E 247 D6
Deh-e Shīr Iran 31°29N 53°45E 247 D7
Deh Nugaleed = Nugaaleed, Dooxo Somali Rep. 8°35N 48°35E 267 C6
Dehaj Iran 30°42N 54°53E 247 D7
Dehak Iran 27°11N 62°37E 240 D1
Déhané Cameroon 3°30N 10°5E 264 B2
Dehdez Iran 31°43N 50°17E 247 D6
Dehej India 21°44N 72°40E 242 J5
Dehestān Iran 28°30N 55°35E 247 D7
Dehgolān Iran 35°17N 47°25E 213 E12
Dehibat Tunisia 32°0N 10°47E 258 B2
Dehiwala Sri Lanka 6°50N 79°51E 245 L4
Dehlorān Iran 32°41N 47°16E 213 F12
Dehnow-e Kūhestān Iran 27°58N 58°32E 247 E8
Dehra Dun India 30°20N 78°4E 242 D8
Dehri India 24°50N 84°15E 243 G11
Dehua China 25°26N 118°14E 229 E12
Dehui China 44°30N 125°40E 227 B13
Deim Zubeir South Sudan 7°49N 26°16E 257 F2
Deinze Belgium 50°59N 3°32E 170 D3
Deir Dibwan West Bank 31°55N 35°16E 123 A2
Deir Ibzi'e West Bank 31°55N 35°7E 123 A1
Dej Romania 47°10N 23°52E 183 C8
Deje Sweden 59°35N 13°29E 162 E7
Dejiang China 28°18N 108°7E 228 C7
Dejvice Czech Rep. 50°6N 14°23E 135 B2
Deka → Zimbabwe 18°4S 26°42E 270 A4
Dekabristov, Ostrov Russia 59°56N 30°15E 137 B1
DeKalb U.S.A. 41°56N 88°46W 311 C8
Dekemhare Eritrea 15°6N 39°0E 257 D4
Dekese Dem. Rep. of the Congo 3°24S 21°24E 264 C4
Dekoa C.A.R. 6°19N 19°4E 264 A3
Del Caño Rise Ind. Oc. 45°15S 44°15E 273 J3
Del Carmen Phil. 9°50N 126°0E 233 G6
Del Mar U.S.A. 32°58N 117°16W 307 N9
Del Norte U.S.A. 37°41N 106°21W 305 H10
Del Rey U.S.A. 33°59N 118°25W 126 C2
Del Rio U.S.A. 29°22N 100°54W 314 G4
Delai Sudan 17°21N 36°6E 256 D4
Delambre I. Australia 20°26S 117°5E 278 D2
Delami Sudan 11°38N 30°23E 257 E3
Delano U.S.A. 35°46N 119°15W 307 K7
Delano Peak U.S.A. 38°22N 112°22W 304 G7
Delārām Afghan. 32°9N 63°25E 240 B1
Delareyville S. Africa 26°41S 25°26E 270 C4
Delaronde L. Canada 54°3N 107°3W 297 C7
Delavan Ill., U.S.A. 40°22N 89°33W 310 D7
Delavan Wis., U.S.A. 42°38N 88°39W 311 B8
Delaware U.S.A. 40°18N 83°4W 311 D13
Delaware □ U.S.A. 39°0N 75°20W 309 F16
Delaware → U.S.A. 39°15N 75°20W 313 G9
Delaware B. U.S.A. 39°0N 75°10W 309 F16
Delaware Water Gap ⌓ U.S.A. 41°10N 74°55W 313 E10
Delay → Canada 56°56N 71°28W 299 A5
Delbrück Germany 51°46N 8°34E 178 D4
Delčevo Macedonia 41°58N 22°46E 202 E6
Delémont Switz. 47°22N 7°20E 179 H3
Delevan U.S.A. 42°29N 78°29W 312 D6
Delft Neths. 52°1N 4°22E 170 B4
Delft I. Sri Lanka 9°30N 79°40E 245 K4
Delfzijl Neths. 53°20N 6°55E 170 A6
Delgada, Punta Chile 52°28S 69°32W 336 D3
Delgado, C. Mozam. 10°45S 40°40E 269 E5
Delgerhet Mongolia 45°50N 110°30E 226 B6
Delgo Sudan 20°6N 30°40E 256 C3
Delhi Ont., Canada 42°51N 80°30W 312 D4
Delhi India 28°39N 77°13E 120 B2
Delhi La., U.S.A. 32°28N 91°30W 314 E9
Delhi N.Y., U.S.A. 42°17N 74°55W 313 D10
Delhi Gate Delhi, India 120 b3
Delhi Indira Gandhi Int. ✈ (DEL) India 28°34N 77°5E 120 B1
Deli Jovan Serbia 44°13N 22°9E 202 B6
Delia Canada 51°38N 112°23W 296 C6
Delice Turkey 39°54N 34°2E 212 C6
Délices Dominica 15°17N 61°17W 323 k
Delicias Mexico 28°13N 105°28W 318 B3
Delījān Iran 33°59N 50°40E 247 C6
Delimara Point Malta 35°49N 14°34E 206 F8
Déline Canada 65°11N 123°25W 294 D7
Delingha China 37°23N 97°23E 218 D8
Delisle Canada 51°55N 107°8W 297 C7
Delitzsch Germany 51°31N 12°20E 178 D8
Deliverance I. Australia 9°31S 141°34E 280 a
Dell City U.S.A. 31°56N 105°12W 314 F2
Dell Rapids U.S.A. 43°50N 96°43W 308 D5
Delle France 47°30N 7°2E 173 E14
Dellys Algeria 36°57N 3°57E 261 A5
Delmar Iowa, U.S.A. 42°0N 90°37W 310 C6
Delmar N.Y., U.S.A. 42°37N 73°47W 313 D11
Delmenhorst Germany 53°3N 8°37E 178 B4
Delmiro Gouveia Brazil 9°24S 38°6W 332 C4
Delnice Croatia 45°23N 14°50E 199 C11
Delonga, Ostrova Russia 76°40N 149°20E 215 B15
Deloraine Tas., Australia 41°30S 146°40E 281 G4
Deloraine Man., Canada 49°15N 100°29W 297 D8
Delphi Greece 38°28N 22°30E 204 C4
Delphi Ind., U.S.A. 40°36N 86°41W 311 D10
Delphos U.S.A. 40°51N 84°21W 311 D12
Delportshoop S. Africa 28°22S 24°20E 270 C3
Delray Beach U.S.A. 26°28N 80°4W 317 J9
Delsbo Sweden 61°48N 16°32E 162 C10
Delta Ala., U.S.A. 33°26N 85°42W 316 B4
Delta Colo., U.S.A. 38°44N 108°4W 304 G9
Delta Utah, U.S.A. 39°21N 112°35W 304 G7
Delta □ Nigeria 5°30N 6°0E 263 D6
Delta Amacuro □ Venezuela 8°30N 61°30W 329 B5
Delta del Ebre ⌓ Spain 40°43N 0°43E 196 E5
Delta del Po ⌓ Italy 44°50N 12°15E 199 D9
Delta du Saloum △ Senegal 13°42N 16°43W 262 C1
Delta Dunării ⌓ Romania 45°15N 29°25E 183 E14
Delta Junction U.S.A. 64°2N 145°44W 303 D11
Deltona U.S.A. 28°54N 81°16W 317 G8
Delungra Australia 29°39S 150°51E 281 D5
Delvada India 20°46N 71°2E 242 J4
Delvinaki Greece 39°57N 20°32E 204 B2
Delvinë Albania 39°59N 20°6E 202 G4
Delyatyn Ukraine 48°32N 24°38E 183 B9
Demagiri India 22°55N 92°28E 241 D4
Demak Indonesia 6°53S 110°38E 235 D4
Demanda, Sierra de la Spain 42°15N 3°0W 196 C2
Demarcation Pt. U.S.A. 69°41N 141°18W 303 B12
Demarest U.S.A. 40°57N 73°57W 132 A2
Demavend = Damāvand, Qolleh-ye Iran 35°56N 52°10E 247 C7
Demba Dem. Rep. of the Congo 5°28S 22°15E 265 D4
Demba Chio Angola 9°41S 13°41E 265 D2
Dembecha Ethiopia 10°32N 37°30E 257 E4
Dembéni Comoros Is. 11°52S 43°23E 272 a
Dembéni Mayotte 12°50S 45°11E 272 b
Dembi Ethiopia 8°5N 36°25E 257 F4
Dembia C.A.R. 4°56N 23°53E 264 B4
Dembia Dem. Rep. of the Congo 3°33N 25°48E 268 B2
Dembica = Dębica Poland 50°2N 21°25E 185 H8
Dembidolo Ethiopia 8°34N 34°50E 257 F3
Demchok India 32°42N 79°29E 243 C8
Demer → Belgium 50°57N 4°42E 170 D4
Demerara Abyssal Plain Atl. Oc. 10°0N 48°0W 152 F7
Demetrias Greece 39°22N 23°1E 204 B5
Demidov Russia 55°16N 31°30E 188 E6
Deming N. Mex., U.S.A. 32°16N 107°46W 305 K10
Deming Wash., U.S.A. 48°50N 122°13W 306 B4
Demini → Brazil 0°46S 62°56W 329 D5
Demirci Turkey 39°2N 28°38E 205 B10
Demirköprü Barajı Turkey 38°42N 28°25E 205 C10
Demirköy Turkey 41°49N 27°45E 203 E11
Demirtas Turkey 36°25N 32°11E 250 B3
Demmin Germany 53°54N 13°2E 178 B9
Demnate Morocco 31°44N 6°59W 260 B3
Democracia Brazil 5°48S 61°26W 331 B5
Demonte Italy 44°19N 7°17E 198 D4
Demopolis U.S.A. 32°31N 87°50W 315 E11
Dempo Indonesia 4°2S 103°15E 234 C2
Demyansk Russia 57°40N 32°27E 188 D7
Den Bosch = 's-Hertogenbosch Neths. 51°42N 5°17E 170 C5
Den Burg Neths. 53°3N 4°47E 170 A4
Den Chai Thailand 17°59N 100°4E 236 D3
Den Haag = 's-Gravenhage Neths. 52°7N 4°17E 170 B4
Den Helder Neths. 52°57N 4°45E 170 B4
Den Ilp Neths. 52°27N 4°55E 112 A2
Den Lille Havfrue Copenhagen, Denmark 118 a3
Den Oever Neths. 52°56N 5°2E 170 B5
Denain France 50°20N 3°22E 173 B10
Denair U.S.A. 37°32N 120°48W 306 H6
Denali = McKinley, Mt. U.S.A. 63°4N 151°0W 303 D10
Denali △ U.S.A. 63°30N 152°0W 303 E10
Denau Uzbekistan 38°16N 67°54E 217 E7
Denbigh Ont., Canada 45°8N 77°15W 312 A7
Denbigh Denbs., U.K. 53°12N 3°25W 168 D4
Denbigh, C. U.S.A. 64°23N 161°32W 303 D7
Denbighshire □ U.K. 53°8N 3°22W 168 D4
Dendang Indonesia 3°7S 107°56E 235 C3
Dendi = Ndindi Gabon 3°46S 11°9E 264 C2
Dendermonde Belgium 51°2N 4°5E 170 C4
Deneba Ethiopia 9°47N 39°10E 257 F4
Deng Deng Cameroon 5°12N 13°31E 264 A2
Dengchuan China 25°59N 100°3E 228 E3
Denge Nigeria 12°52N 5°21E 263 C6
Dengfeng China 34°25N 113°2E 226 G7
Dengi Nigeria 9°25N 9°55E 263 D6
Dengkou China 40°18N 106°55E 226 D4
Dengzhou China 32°34N 112°4E 229 A9
Denham Australia 25°56S 113°31E 279 E1
Denham, Mt. Jamaica 18°13N 77°32W 320 a
Denham Ra. Australia 21°55S 147°46E 280 C4
Denham Sd. Australia 25°45S 113°15E 279 E1
Denholm Canada 52°39N 108°1W 297 C7
Denia Spain 38°49N 0°8E 197 G5
Denial B. Australia 32°14S 133°32E 281 E1
Deniliquin Australia 35°30S 144°58E 283 C6
Denimoo = Fort Resolution Canada 61°10N 113°40W 296 A6
Denis Gabon 0°19N 9°22E 264 B1
Denison Iowa, U.S.A. 42°1N 95°21W 308 D6
Denison Tex., U.S.A. 33°45N 96°33W 314 E6
Denison Plains Australia 18°35S 128°0E 278 C4
Denisovka Kazakhstan 52°27N 61°39E 216 B6
Denistone Heights Australia 33°48S 151°8E 139 A1
Deniyaya Sri Lanka 6°21N 80°33E 245 L5
Denizli Turkey 37°42N 29°2E 205 D11
Denizli □ Turkey 37°45N 29°5E 205 D11
Denman Australia 32°24S 150°42E 283 B9
Denman Glacier Antarctica 66°45S 100°0E 151 C8
Denmark W. Austral., Australia 34°59S 117°25E 279 F2
Denmark S.C., U.S.A. 33°19N 81°9W 316 B8
Denmark ■ Europe 55°45N 10°0E 163 J3
Denmark Str. Atl. Oc. 66°0N 30°0W 154 D8
Dennery St. Lucia 13°55N 60°54W 323 m
Dennison U.S.A. 40°24N 81°19W 312 F3
Denny U.K. 56°1N 3°55W 167 E5
Denpasar Indonesia 8°39S 115°13E 231 K18
Denpasar ✈ (DPS) Indonesia 8°44S 115°10E 231 K18
Denton Ga., U.S.A. 31°44N 82°42W 316 D7
Denton Mont., U.S.A. 47°19N 109°57W 304 C9
Denton Tex., U.S.A. 33°13N 97°8W 314 E6
Dentonia Park Canada 43°42N 79°17W 141 A3
D'Entrecasteaux, Îs. N. Cal. 18°0S 163°0E 277 D11
D'Entrecasteaux, Pt. Australia 34°50S 115°57E 279 F2
D'Entrecasteaux △ Australia 34°20S 115°33E 279 F2
D'Entrecasteaux Is. Papua N. G. 9°0S 151°0E 286 E6
Dentsville U.S.A. 34°4N 80°58W 316 A9
Denu Ghana 6°4N 1°8E 263 D5
Denver Colo., U.S.A. 39°42N 104°59W 304 G11
Denver Ind., U.S.A. 40°52N 86°5W 311 D10
Denver Iowa, U.S.A. 42°40N 92°20W 310 B4
Denver Pa., U.S.A. 40°14N 76°8W 313 F8
Denver City U.S.A. 32°58N 102°50W 314 E3
Denwood = Wainwright Canada 52°50N 110°50W 297 C6
Deoband India 29°42N 77°43E 242 E7
Deobhog India 19°53N 82°44E 244 E6
Deodrug India 16°26N 76°55E 245 F3
Deogarh Orissa, India 21°32N 84°45E 244 D7
Deogarh Raj., India 25°32N 73°54E 242 G5
Deoghar India 24°30N 86°42E 243 G12
Deogyusan △ S. Korea 35°54N 127°40E 224 E3
Deokjeokdo S. Korea 37°13N 126°7E 224 D3
Deolali India 19°58N 73°50E 244 E1
Deoli = Devli India 25°50N 75°20E 242 G6
Déols France 46°50N 1°43E 173 F8
Deora India 26°22N 70°55E 242 F4
Deorha = Jubbal India 31°5N 77°40E 242 D7
Deori India 23°24N 79°1E 243 H8
Deoria India 26°31N 83°48E 243 F10
Deosai Mts. Pakistan 35°40N 75°0E 243 B6
Deosri India 26°46N 90°29E 241 B3
Depalpur India 22°51N 75°33E 242 H6
DePaul Univ. U.S.A. 41°55N 87°39W 119 B3
Deposit U.S.A. 42°4N 75°25W 313 D9
Deptford U.K. 51°28N 0°1W 125 B3
Depuch I. Australia 20°37S 117°44E 278 D2
Deputati, Camera dei Rome, Italy 136 b2
Deputatskiy Russia 69°18N 139°54E 215 C14
Dêqên China 28°34N 98°51E 228 C2
Deqing China 23°8N 111°42E 229 F8
Dera, Lach → Somali Rep. 0°15N 42°17E 267 D5
Dera Ghazi Khan Pakistan 30°5N 70°43E 242 D4
Dera Ismail Khan Pakistan 31°50N 70°50E 242 D4
Derabugti Pakistan 29°2N 69°9E 242 E3
Derawar Fort Pakistan 28°46N 71°20E 242 E4
Derbent Russia 42°5N 48°15E 191 J9
Derbent Turkey 38°11N 28°33E 205 C10
Derby W. Austral., Australia 17°18S 123°38E 278 C3
Derby Derby City, U.K. 52°56N 1°28W 168 E6
Derby Conn., U.S.A. 41°19N 73°5W 313 E11
Derby Kans., U.S.A. 37°33N 97°16W 308 G5
Derby N.Y., U.S.A. 42°41N 78°58W 312 D6
Derby City □ U.K. 52°56N 1°28W 168 E6
Derby Line U.S.A. 45°0N 72°6W 313 B12
Derbyshire □ U.K. 53°11N 1°38W 168 D6
Đerdap △ Serbia 44°40N 22°23E 202 B6
Derdepoort S. Africa 24°38S 26°24E 270 B4
Derecske Hungary 47°20N 21°33E 182 C6
Dereham U.K. 52°41N 0°57E 169 E8
Dereköy Turkey 41°55N 27°21E 203 E11
Dereli Turkey 40°44N 38°26E 213 B8
Derg → U.K. 54°44N 7°26W 166 B4
Derg, L. Ireland 53°0N 8°20W 166 D3
Dergachi = Derhaci Ukraine 50°9N 36°11E 189 G9
Derhaci Ukraine 50°9N 36°11E 189 G9
Deridder U.S.A. 30°51N 93°17W 314 F8
Derik Turkey 37°21N 40°18E 213 D9
Derinkuyu Turkey 38°22N 34°45E 212 C6
Dermantsi Bulgaria 43°8N 24°17E 203 C8
Dermott U.S.A. 33°32N 91°26W 314 E9
Dernière Rivière St. Lucia 13°57N 60°55W 323 m
Dêrong China 28°44N 99°9E 228 C2
Derri Somali Rep. 4°20N 46°37E 267 D6
Derrinallum Australia 37°57S 143°15E 282 D5
Derry = Londonderry U.K. 55°0N 7°20W 166 B4
Derry = Londonderry □ U.K. 55°0N 7°20W 166 B4
Derry N.H., U.S.A. 42°53N 71°19W 313 D13
Derry Pa., U.S.A. 40°20N 79°18W 312 F5
Derryveagh Mts. Ireland 54°56N 8°11W 166 B3
Derudub Sudan 17°31N 36°7E 256 D4
Derval France 47°40N 1°41W 172 E5
Derveni Greece 38°8N 22°25E 204 C4
Derventa Bos.-H. 44°59N 17°55E 182 F2
Derwent → Cumb., U.K. 54°39N 3°33W 168 C4
Derwent → Derby, U.K. 52°57N 1°28W 168 E6
Derwent → N. Yorks., U.K. 53°45N 0°58W 168 D7
Derwent Water U.K. 54°35N 3°9W 168 C4
Derzhavīnsk Kazakhstan 51°6N 66°19E 217 B7
Des Moines Iowa, U.S.A. 41°35N 93°37W 310 C3
Des Moines N. Mex., U.S.A. 36°46N 103°50W 305 H12
Des Moines Wash., U.S.A. 47°24N 122°19W 306 C4
Des Moines → U.S.A. 40°23N 91°25W 310 D5
Des Moines ✈ (DSM) U.S.A. 41°32N 93°40W 310 C3
Des Plaines U.S.A. 42°2N 87°54W 119 A1
Des Plaines → U.S.A. 41°23N 88°15W 311 C8
Desa Romania 43°52N 23°2E 182 G8
Desaguadero → Argentina 34°30S 66°46W 334 C2
Desaguadero → Bolivia 16°35S 69°5W 330 D4
Desantne Ukraine 45°34N 29°32E 183 E14
Désappointement, Is. du French Polynesia 14°10S 141°20W 289 f
Desaru Malaysia 1°31N 104°17E 237 d
Descanso, Pta. Mexico 32°21N 117°3W 307 N9
Descartes France 46°59N 0°42E 174 B4
Deschaillons-sur-St-Laurent Canada 46°32N 72°7W 299 C5
Deschambault L. Canada 54°50N 103°30W 297 C8
Deschutes → U.S.A. 45°38N 120°55W 304 D3
Descobrimento △ Brazil 16°53S 39°21W 333 E4
Dese Ethiopia 11°5N 39°40E 257 E4
Deseado, C. Chile 52°45S 74°42W 336 D2
Desenzano del Garda Italy 45°28N 10°32E 198 C7
Deseronto Canada 44°12N 77°3W 312 B7
Desert Center U.S.A. 33°43N 115°24W 307 M11
Desert Hot Springs U.S.A. 33°58N 116°30W 307 M10
Desert Wetlands Park U.S.A. 36°7N 115°2W 124 B2
Desertas, Ilhas Madeira 32°30N 16°30W 260 B1
Deset Norway 61°20N 11°26E 164 C8
Desfina Greece 38°25N 22°31E 204 C4
Deshaies Guadeloupe 16°18N 61°47W 322 e
Deshauteur Guadeloupe 16°15N 61°25W 322 e
Deshnok India 27°48N 73°21E 242 F5
Desierto Central de Baja California ⌓ Mexico 29°40N 114°50W 318 B2
Desjardins, Complexe Montréal, Canada 130 b2
Deskati Greece 39°55N 21°49E 202 G5
Desna → Ukraine 50°33N 30°32E 177 C16
Desnătui → Romania 43°53N 23°35E 183 G8
Desolación, I. Chile 53°0S 74°0W 336 D2
Despeñaperros, Paso Spain 38°24N 3°30W 195 G7
Despeñaperros ⌓ Spain 38°23N 3°32W 195 G7
Despotiko Greece 36°57N 24°58E 204 E6
Despotovac Serbia 44°6N 21°30E 202 B5
Dessau Germany 51°51N 12°14E 178 D8
Dessye = Dese Ethiopia 11°5N 39°40E 257 E4
Destin U.S.A. 30°24N 86°30W 317 E3
D'Estrees B. Australia 35°55S 137°45E 282 C2
Desuri India 25°18N 73°35E 242 G5
Desvres France 50°40N 1°48E 173 B8
Det Udom Thailand 14°54N 105°5E 236 E5
Deta Romania 45°24N 21°13E 182 E6
Dete Zimbabwe 18°38S 26°50E 270 A4
Detinja → Serbia 43°51N 20°5E 202 C4
Detmold Germany 51°56N 8°52E 178 D4
Detour, Pt. U.S.A. 45°40N 86°40W 308 C10
Detroit U.S.A. 42°19N 83°12W 312 D1
Detroit Lakes U.S.A. 46°49N 95°51W 308 B6
Detroit Metropolitan Wayne County ✈ (DTW) U.S.A. 42°13N 83°21W 311 B13
Detskoye Selo = Pushkin Russia 59°45N 30°25E 188 C6
Dettifoss Iceland 65°48N 16°24W 155 B10
Detva Slovak Rep. 48°34N 19°25E 181 C12
Deua △ Australia 35°32S 149°46E 283 C8
Deurne Neths. 51°27N 5°49E 170 C5
Deutsch = Przemyśl Poland 49°50N 22°45E 185 J9
Deutsch Brod = Havlíčkův Brod Czech Rep. 49°36N 15°33E 180 B8
Deutsch-Eylau = Iława Poland 53°36N 19°34E 184 E6
Deutsch Krone = Wałcz Poland 53°17N 16°27E 185 E3
Deutsch-Luxemburgischer ⌓ Germany 49°58N 6°12E 179 F2
Deutsche Bucht Germany 54°15N 8°0E 178 A4
Deutsche Oper Germany 52°30N 13°19E 115 A2
Deutsches Museum Germany 48°7N 11°35E 131 B2
Deutschland = Germany ■ Europe 51°0N 10°0E 178 E6
Deutschlandsberg Austria 46°49N 15°14E 180 E8
Deux-Sèvres □ France 46°35N 0°20W 172 F6
Deva Romania 45°53N 22°55E 182 E7
Devakottai India 9°55N 78°45E 245 K4
Devaprayag India 30°13N 78°35E 243 D8
Devarkonda India 16°42N 78°56E 244 F4
Dévaványa Hungary 47°2N 20°59E 182 C5
Deveci Dağları Turkey 40°6N 36°15E 212 B7
Devecikonağı Turkey 39°55N 28°34E 203 G12
Devecser Hungary 47°6N 17°26E 182 C2
Develi Turkey 38°23N 35°29E 212 C6
Deventer Neths. 52°15N 6°10E 170 B6
Devereux U.S.A. 33°13N 83°5W 316 B6
Deveron → U.K. 57°41N 2°32W 167 D6
Devesel Romania 44°28N 22°41E 182 F7
Devgad I. India 14°48N 74°5E 245 G2
Devgadh Bariya India 22°40N 73°55E 242 H5
Devgarh India 21°16N 73°23E 245 E1
Devi → India 19°59N 86°24E 244 E8
Devikot India 26°42N 71°12E 242 F4
Devil River Pk. N.Z. 40°56S 172°37E 285 A7
Devil's Bridge Antigua & B. 17°6N 61°41W 322 b
Devils Den U.S.A. 35°46N 119°58W 306 K7
Devils Hole = Death Valley △ U.S.A. 36°29N 117°6W 307 J9
Devils Island, I. = Diable, Île du Fr. Guiana 5°16N 52°34W 329 B7
Devils Lake U.S.A. 48°7N 98°52W 308 A4
Devils Paw Canada 58°47N 134°0W 296 B2
Devil's Peak S. Africa 33°57S 18°27E 118 A1
Devil's Pt. Sri Lanka 9°26N 80°6E 245 K5
Devils Postpile ⌓ U.S.A. 37°37N 119°5W 306 H7
Devils Tower U.S.A. 44°35N 104°42W 304 D11
Devils Tower △ U.S.A. 44°48N 104°55W 304 D11
Devil's Woodyard Mud Volcano Trin. & Tob. 10°16N 61°22W 323 t
Devin Bulgaria 41°44N 24°24E 203 E8
Devine U.S.A. 29°8N 98°54W 314 G5
Devipattinam India 9°29N 78°54E 245 K4
Devizes U.K. 51°22N 1°58W 169 F6
Devli India 25°50N 75°20E 242 G6
Devnya Bulgaria 43°13N 27°33E 203 C11
Devoll → Albania 40°57N 20°15E 202 F4
Devon Canada 53°24N 113°44W 296 C6
Devon □ U.K. 50°50N 3°40W 169 G4
Devon I. Canada 75°10N 85°0W 295 B15
Devonport Australia 41°10S 146°22E 281 G4
Devrek Turkey 41°13N 31°57E 212 B4
Devrekâni Turkey 41°36N 33°50E 212 B5
Devrez → Turkey 41°6N 34°25E 212 B6
Devrukh India 17°3N 73°37E 244 F1
Dewas India 22°59N 76°3E 242 H7
Dewetsdorp S. Africa 29°33S 26°39E 270 C4
Dewey Puerto Rico 18°18N 65°18W 321 b
Dexing China 28°46N 117°30E 229 C11
Dexter Maine, U.S.A. 45°1N 69°18W 309 C19
Dexter Mich., U.S.A. 42°20N 83°53W 311 B13
Dexter Mo., U.S.A. 36°48N 89°57W 308 G9
Dexter N. Mex., U.S.A. 33°12N 104°22W 305 K11
Dey-Dey, L. Australia 29°12S 131°4E 279 E5
Deyang China 31°3N 104°27E 228 B5
Deyhūk Iran 33°15N 57°30E 247 C8
Deyyer Iran 27°55N 51°55E 247 E6
Dez → Iran 31°39N 48°52E 213 F13
Dezadeash L. Canada 60°28N 136°58W 296 A1
Dezfūl Iran 32°20N 48°30E 213 F13
Dezhneva, Mys Russia 66°5N 169°40W 215 C19
Dezhou China 37°26N 116°18E 226 F9
Dhadhar → India 24°56N 85°24E 243 G11
Dhahabān Si. Arabia 21°58N 39°3E 248 B2
Dhahiriya = Aẓ Ẓāhirīyah West Bank 31°25N 34°58E 251 G5
Dhahran = Aẓ Ẓahrān Si. Arabia 26°10N 50°7E 247 E6
Dhak Pakistan 32°25N 72°33E 242 C5
Dhaka Bangla. 23°43N 90°26E 241 D3
Dhaka □ Bangla. 24°25N 90°25E 241 C3
Dhakuria India 22°30N 88°22E 124 B2
Dhali Cyprus 35°1N 33°25E 207 E9
Dhamangaon India 20°48N 78°9E 244 D4
Dhamār Yemen 14°30N 44°20E 248 D4
Dhampur India 29°19N 78°33E 243 E8
Dhamra → India 20°47N 86°58E 244 D8
Dhamtari India 20°42N 81°35E 244 D5
Dhanbad India 23°50N 86°30E 243 H12
Dhangarhi Nepal 28°55N 80°40E 243 E9
Dhankuta Nepal 26°55N 87°40E 243 F12
Dhanora India 20°20N 80°22E 244 D5
Dhanpuri India 23°13N 81°30E 244 C5
Dhanushkodi India 9°11N 79°24E 245 K4
Dhar India 22°35N 75°26E 242 H6
Dharampur Gujarat, India 20°32N 73°17E 244 D1
Dharampur Mad. P., India 22°13N 75°18E 242 H6
Dharamsala = Dharmsala India 32°16N 76°23E 242 C7
Dharan Nepal 26°49N 87°17E 243 F12
Dharangaon India 21°1N 75°16E 244 D2
Dharapuram India 10°45N 77°34E 245 J3
Dharavi India 19°1N 72°51E 130 A2
Dhariwal India 31°57N 75°19E 242 D6
Dharla → Bangla. 25°46N 89°42E 243 G13
Dharmapuri India 12°10N 78°10E 245 H4
Dharmavaram India 14°29N 77°44E 245 G3
Dharmjaygarh India 22°28N 83°13E 243 H10
Dharmsala India 32°16N 76°23E 242 C7
Dharni India 21°33N 76°53E 242 J7
Dharug △ Australia 33°20S 151°2E 283 B9
Dharur India 18°3N 76°8E 244 E3
Dharwad India 15°30N 75°4E 245 G2
Dhasan → India 25°48N 79°24E 243 G8
Dhaulagiri Nepal 28°39N 83°28E 243 E10
Dhebar, L. India 24°10N 74°0E 242 G6
Dheftera Cyprus 35°5N 33°16E 207 E9
Dhenkanal India 20°45N 85°35E 244 D7
Dherinia Cyprus 35°3N 33°57E 207 E9
Dheskáti = Deskati Greece 39°55N 21°49E 202 G5
Dhī Qār □ Iraq 31°0N 46°15E 246 D5
Dhiarrizos → Cyprus 34°41N 32°34E 207 F8
Dhībān Jordan 31°30N 35°46E 251 G6
Dhilwan India 31°31N 75°21E 242 D6
Dhimarkhera India 23°28N 80°22E 243 H9
Dhodhekánisos = Dodecanese Greece 36°35N 27°0E 205 E8
Dholka India 22°44N 72°29E 242 H5
Dhomokós = Domokos Greece 39°10N 22°18E 204 B4
Dhond = Daund India 18°26N 74°40E 244 E2
Dhone India 15°25N 77°53E 245 G3
Dhoraji India 21°45N 70°37E 242 J4
Dhragonísi = Tragonhsi Greece 37°27N 25°29E 205 D7
Dhrangadhra India 22°59N 71°31E 242 H4
Dhrol India 22°33N 70°25E 242 H4
Dhubāb Yemen 12°56N 43°25E 248 D3
Dhuburi India 26°2N 89°59E 241 B2
Dhulasar Bangla. 21°52N 90°14E 241 E3
Dhule India 20°58N 74°50E 244 D2
Dhupdhara India 26°10N 91°4E 241 B3
Dhurbo Somali Rep. 11°37N 50°20E 267 B7
Dhuusamarreeb Somali Rep. 5°30N 46°15E 267 C6
Di-ib, W. → Sudan 22°38N 36°6E 256 C4
Di Linh Vietnam 11°35N 108°4E 237 G7
Di Linh, Cao Nguyen Vietnam 11°30N 108°0E 237 G7
Dia Greece 35°28N 25°14E 207 D6
Diabakania Guinea 10°38N 10°58W 262 C2
Diable, Île du Fr. Guiana 5°16N 52°34W 329 B7
Diable, Pte. du Martinique 14°40N 60°53W 322 j
Diables, Morne aux Dominica 15°37N 61°27W 323 k
Diablo Pt. N. Marianas 15°0N 145°35E 302 e
Diablo Range U.S.A. 37°20N 121°25W 306 J5
Diablotins, Morne Dominica 15°30N 61°24W 323 k
Diadema Brazil 23°41S 46°37W 137 C2
Diafarabé Mali 14°9N 4°57W 262 C4
Diala Mali 14°10N 9°58W 262 C3
Dialakoro Mali 12°18N 7°54W 262 C3
Dialakoto Senegal 13°21N 13°19W 262 C2
Diallassagou Mali 13°47N 3°41W 262 C4
Diamant, Pte. du Martinique 14°27N 61°3W 322 j
Diamant, Rocher du Martinique 14°27N 61°2W 322 j
Diamante Argentina 32°5S 60°40W 334 C3
Diamante Italy 39°41N 15°49E 201 C8
Diamante → Argentina 34°30S 66°46W 334 C2
Diamantina Brazil 18°17S 43°40W 333 E3
Diamantina → Australia 26°45S 139°10E 281 D2
Diamantina △ Australia 23°33S 141°23E 280 C3
Diamantino Brazil 14°30S 56°30W 331 C6
Diamond Bar U.S.A. 34°1N 117°48W 307 L9
Diamond Harbour India 22°11N 88°14E 243 H13
Diamond Head U.S.A. 21°16N 157°49W 302 K14
Diamond I. Grenada 12°20N 61°35W 323 q
Diamond Is. Australia 17°25S 151°5E 280 B5
Diamond Mts. U.S.A. 39°40N 115°50W 304 G6
Diamond Springs U.S.A. 38°42N 120°49W 306 G6
Diamou Mali 14°5N 11°16W 262 C2
Dian Chi China 24°50N 102°43E 228 E4
Dianalund Denmark 55°32N 11°30E 163 J5
Dianbai China 21°33N 111°0E 229 G8
Diancheng China 21°30N 111°4E 229 G8
Dianjiang China 30°24N 107°20E 228 B6
Diano Marina Italy 43°54N 8°5E 198 E5
Dianópolis Brazil 11°38S 46°50W 333 D2
Dianra Ivory C. 8°45N 6°14W 262 D3
Diaoyu Dao = Senkaku-Shotō E. China Sea 25°45N 123°30E 221 M1
Diaoyu Tai = Senkaku-Shotō E. China Sea 25°45N 123°30E 221 M1
Diapaga Burkina Faso 12°5N 1°46E 263 C5
Diapangou Burkina Faso 12°5N 0°10E 263 C5
Diariguila Guinea 10°35N 10°2W 262 C2
Diavolo, Mt. India 12°40N 92°56E 245 H11
Dībā U.A.E. 25°45N 56°16E 247 E8
Dibagah Iraq 35°52N 43°48E 213 E10
Dibai India 28°13N 78°15E 242 E8
Dibaya Dem. Rep. of the Congo 6°30S 22°57E 265 D4
Dibaya-Lubue Dem. Rep. of the Congo 4°12S 19°54E 265 C3
Dibbeen △ Jordan 32°20N 35°45E 251 F6
Dibella Niger 17°32N 13°6E 259 E2
D'Iberville, Lac Canada 55°55N 73°15W 298 A5
Dibete Botswana 23°45S 26°32E 270 B4
Dibi Cameroon 7°8N 13°43E 264 A2
Dibru-Saikhowa △ India 27°40N 95°25E 241 B5
Dibrugarh India 27°29N 94°55E 241 B5
Diciosânmartin = Târnăveni Romania 46°19N 24°13E 183 D9
Dickens U.S.A. 33°37N 100°50W 314 E4
Dickeyville U.S.A. 42°38N 90°36W 310 B6
Dickinson U.S.A. 46°53N 102°47W 308 B2
Dickinson B. Antigua & B. 17°10N 61°51W 322 b
Dick's Pt. Bahamas 25°4N 77°18W 153 b
Dickson = Dikson Russia 73°40N 80°5E 214 B9
Dickson U.S.A. 36°5N 87°23W 315 C11
Dickson City U.S.A. 41°28N 75°36W 313 E9
Dicle Barajı Turkey 38°20N 40°11E 213 C9
Dicle Nehri → Turkey 37°44N 41°10E 213 D9
Dicomano Italy 43°53N 11°31E 199 E8
Didesa, W. → Ethiopia 10°2N 35°32E 257 E4
Didiéni Mali 13°53N 8°6W 262 C3
Didimbo Angola 17°30S 21°45E 265 F4
Didimoticho Greece 41°22N 26°29E 203 E10
Didsbury Canada 51°35N 114°10W 296 C6
Didwana India 27°23N 74°36E 242 F6
Die France 44°47N 5°22E 175 D9
Diébougou Burkina Faso 11°0N 3°15W 262 C4
Diecke Guinea 7°27N 8°54W 262 D3
Diedenhofen = Thionville France 49°20N 6°10E 173 C13
Diefenbaker, L. Canada 51°0N 106°55W 297 C7
Diegen Belgium 50°53N 4°26E 116 A2
Diego de Almagro Chile 26°22S 70°3W 334 B1
Diego Garcia Ind. Oc. 7°50S 72°50E 273 E6
Diego Martin Trin. & Tob. 10°43N 61°34W 323 t
Diego Ramírez, Islas Chile 56°30S 68°44W 336 E3
Diego Suarez = Antsiranana Madag. 12°25S 49°20E 272 A2
Diekirch Lux. 49°52N 6°10E 170 E6
Diéma Mali 14°32N 9°12W 262 C3
Diembéring Senegal 12°29N 16°47W 262 C1
Diemelsee ⌓ Germany 51°20N 8°40E 178 D4
Diemen Neths. 52°21N 4°58E 112 A2
Dien Ban Vietnam 15°53N 108°16E 236 E7
Dien Bien Phu Vietnam 21°20N 103°0E 228 G4
Dien Chau, Vinh Vietnam 19°0N 105°55E 236 C5
Dien Khanh Vietnam 12°15N 109°6E 237 F7
Diepholz Germany 52°37N 8°22E 178 C4
Diepkloof S. Africa 26°14S 27°57E 123 B1
Dieppe France 49°54N 1°4E 172 C8
Dieppe Bay Town St. Kitts & Nevis 17°25N 62°48W 322 d
Dieprivier S. Africa 34°2S 18°27E 118 B1
Dierks U.S.A. 34°7N 94°1W 314 D7
Diest Belgium 50°58N 5°4E 170 D5
Dieterich U.S.A. 39°4N 88°23W 311 E8
Dietikon Switz. 47°24N 8°24E 179 H4
Dieulefit France 44°32N 5°4E 175 D9
Dieuze France 48°49N 6°43E 173 D13
Dievenow = Dziwnów Poland 54°2N 14°45E 184 D1
Dif Somali Rep. 0°59N 40°58E 267 D5
Diffa Niger 13°18N 12°36E 263 C7
Diffa □ Niger 14°0N 12°30E 263 C7
Differdange Lux. 49°31N 5°54E 170 E5
Difficult Run → U.S.A. 38°55N 77°18W 143 B2
Diffun Phil. 16°36N 121°33E 232 C3
Dig India 27°28N 77°20E 242 F7
Digba Dem. Rep. of the Congo 4°25N 25°48E 268 B2
Digboi India 27°23N 95°38E 241 B5
Digby Canada 44°38N 65°50W 299 D6
Digges Is. Canada 62°40N 77°50W 295 E16
Diggi India 26°22N 75°26E 242 F6
Dighinala Bangla. 23°15N 92°5E 241 D4
Dighton U.S.A. 38°29N 100°28W 308 F3
Digity Mud Volcanoes Trin. & Tob. 10°12N 61°25W 323 t
Diglur India 18°34N 77°33E 244 E3
Digna Mali 14°48N 8°10W 262 C3
Digne-les-Bains France 44°5N 6°12E 175 D10
Digoin France 46°29N 4°1E 173 F11
Digor Turkey 40°22N 43°25E 213 B10
Digos Phil. 6°45N 125°20E 233 H5
Digranes Iceland 66°4N 14°44W 155 A12
Digras India 20°6N 77°45E 244 D3
Digul → Indonesia 7°7S 138°42E 231 F9
Digya △ Ghana 7°15N 0°5E 263 D5
Dihang = Brahmaputra → Asia 23°40N 90°35E 241 D3
Diinsoor Somali Rep. 2°24N 42°59E 267 D5
Dijlah, Nahr → Asia 31°0N 47°25E 246 D5
Dijon France 47°20N 5°3E 173 E12
Dikhil Djibouti 11°8N 42°20E 257 E5
Dikili Turkey 39°4N 26°53E 205 B8
Dikirnis Egypt 31°6N 31°35E 256 H7
Dikkil = Dikhil Djibouti 11°8N 42°20E 257 E5
Dikodougou Ivory C. 9°4N 5°45W 262 D3
Diksmuide Belgium 51°2N 2°52E 170 C2
Dikson Russia 73°40N 80°5E 214 B9
Dikti Oros Greece 35°8N 25°30E 207 D7
Dikwa Nigeria 12°4N 13°30E 263 C7
Dila Ethiopia 6°21N 38°22E 257 F4
Dilasag Phil. 16°25N 122°11E 232 C4
Dilbeek Belgium 50°51N 4°17E 116 A1
Dilek Yarimadisi △ Turkey 37°40N 27°10E 205 D9

Dili *E. Timor* 8°39S 125°34E **231** F7
Diligent Strait *India* 12°11N 92°57E **245** H11
Dilijan *Armenia* 40°46N 44°57E **191** K7
Dilijan *Armenia* 40°46N 44°57E **191** K7
Dilinata *Greece* 38°13N 20°31E **207** C2
Dilinata *Greece*
Dilj *Croatia* 45°29N 18°1E **182** E3
Dillenburg *Germany* 50°43N 8°17E **178** E4
Dilley *U.S.A.* 28°40N 99°10W **314** G5
Dilli = Delhi *India* 28°39N 7°13E **120** B2
Dilli *Mali* 15°1N 7°40W **262** G3
Dillia → *Niger* 14°9N 12°50E **259** F2
Dilling *Sudan* 12°3N 29°35E **257** E2
Dillingen *Bayern, Germany* 48°36N 10°30E **179** G6
Dillingen *Saarland, Germany* 49°22N 6°43E **179** F2
Dillingham *U.S.A.* 59°3N 158°28W **303** G8
Dillon *Sask., Canada* 55°56N 108°35W **297** B7
Dillon *Mont., U.S.A.* 45°13N 112°38W **304** D7
Dillon *S.C., U.S.A.* 34°25N 79°22W **315** D15
Dillon → *Canada* 55°56N 108°56W **297** B7
Dillsboro *U.S.A.* 39°1N 85°4W **311** E11
Dillsburg *U.S.A.* 40°7N 77°2W **312** F7
Dilolo
Dem. Rep. of the Congo 10°28S 22°18E **265** E4
Dilos *Greece* 37°23N 25°15E **205** D7
Dilove *Ukraine* 47°56N 24°11E **183** D9
Dimapur *India* 25°54N 93°45E **241** C4
Dimas *Mexico* 23°43N 106°47W **318** C3
Dimashq *Syria* 33°30N 36°18E **250** E7
Dimashq □ *Syria* 33°30N 36°30E **250** E7
Dimbaza *S. Africa* 32°50S 27°14E **271** D4
Dimbelenge
Dem. Rep. of the Congo 5°33S 23°7E **265** D4
Dimbokro *Ivory C.* 6°45N 4°46W **262** D4
Dimboola *Australia* 36°28S 142°7E **282** D5
Dîmbovița = Dâmbovița □
Romania 44°12N 26°26E **183** F11
Dimbulah *Australia* 17°8S 145°4E **280** B4
Dimitrovgrad *Bulgaria* 42°5N 25°35E **203** D9
Dimitrovgrad *Russia* 54°14N 49°39E **190** C9
Dimitrovgrad *Serbia* 43°2N 22°48E **202** C6
Dimitrovo = Pernik
Bulgaria 42°35N 23°2E **202** C6
Dimitsana *Greece* 37°36N 22°3E **204** D4
Dimmitt *U.S.A.* 34°33N 102°19W **314** D3
Dimo *South Sudan* 5°19N 29°10E **257** F2
Dimona *Israel* 31°2N 35°1E **251** D6
Dimonika → *Congo* 4°13S 12°21E **264** C2
Dimovo *Bulgaria* 43°43N 22°50E **202** C6
Dinagat → *Phil.* 10°0N 125°35E **233** C5
Dinagat I. *Phil.* 10°10N 125°40E **233** F5
Dinaig *Phil.* 7°11N 124°10E **233** H5
Dinajpur *Bangla.* 25°33N 88°43E **241** C2
Dinalupihan *Phil.* 14°52N 120°28E **233** D4
Dinan *France* 48°28N 2°2W **172** D4
Dīnān Āb *Iran* 32°4N 56°49E **247** C8
Dinant *Belgium* 50°16N 4°55E **170** D4
Dinapur *India* 25°38N 85°5E **243** G11
Dinar *Turkey* 38°5N 30°10E **205** C12
Dīnār, Kūh-e *Iran* 30°42N 51°46E **247** D6
Dinara Planina *Croatia* 44°0N 16°30E **199** D13
Dinard *France* 48°38N 2°6W **172** D4
Dinaric Alps = Dinara Planina
Croatia 44°0N 16°30E **199** D13
Dinas *Phil.* 7°38N 123°20E **233** H4
Dindanko *Mali* 14°8N 9°30W **262** C3
Dinde *Angola* 14°17S 13°42E **265** G2
Dinder, Nahr ed → *Sudan* 14°6N 33°40E **257** E3
Dinder → *Sudan* 12°30N 35°10E **257** E4
Dindi → *India* 16°24N 78°15E **245** A4
Dindigul *India* 10°25N 78°0E **245** J4
Dindori *India* 22°57N 81°5E **243** H9
Ding Xian = Dingzhou
China 38°30N 114°59E **226** D8
Dinga *Dem. Rep. of the Congo* 5°17S 16°42E **265** D3
Dinga *Pakistan* 25°26N 67°10E **242** G2
Dingalan *Phil.* 15°18N 121°25E **233** D3
Dingalan B. *Phil.* 15°18N 121°25E **233** D3
Ding'an *China* 19°42N 110°19E **236** D6
Dingbian *China* 37°35N 107°32E **226** F4
Dingelstädt *Germany* 51°18N 10°19E **178** D6
Dingle *Kerry, Ireland* 52°9N 10°17W **166** D1
Dingle *Sweden* 58°32N 11°55E **163** F5
Dingle B. *Ireland* 52°3N 10°20W **166** D1
Dingli *Malta* 35°51N 14°22E **205** D1
Dingmans Ferry *U.S.A.* 41°13N 74°55W **313** E10
Dingnan *China* 24°45N 115°0E **239** E10
Dingo *Australia* 23°38S 149°19E **280** C4
Dingolfing *Germany* 48°37N 12°30E **179** G8
Dingras *Phil.* 18°6N 120°42E **233** A3
Dingtao *China* 35°5N 115°35E **226** G8
Dinguiraye *Guinea* 11°18N 10°49W **262** C2
Dingwall *U.K.* 57°36N 4°26W **167** D4
Dingxi *China* 35°30N 104°33E **226** G3
Dingxiang *China* 38°30N 112°58E **226** E7
Dingyuan *China* 32°32N 117°41E **229** A11
Dingzhou *China* 38°30N 114°59E **226** D8
Dinh, Mui *Vietnam* 11°22N 109°1E **237** G7
Dinh Lap *Vietnam* 21°33N 107°6E **236** B6
Dinhata *India* 26°8N 89°27E **241** B2
Dinin → *Ireland* 52°43N 7°18W **166** D4
Dinira △ *Venezuela* 9°57N 70°6W **328** B3
Dinokwe *Botswana* 23°29S 26°37E **270** B4
Dinorwic *Canada* 49°41N 92°30W **297** D10
Dinosaur △ *Alta.,
Canada* 50°47N 111°30W **296** C6
Dinosaur △ *Colo., U.S.A.* 40°30N 108°45W **304** F9
Dinuba *U.S.A.* 36°32N 119°23W **306** J7
Diö *Sweden* 56°37N 14°15E **163** H8
Dioïla *Mali* 12°23N 6°50W **262** C3
Dioka *Mali* 14°5N 10°40W **262** C2
Diomede *U.S.A.* 65°47N 169°0W **303** D5
Diona *Chad* 17°51N 22°36E **259** E4
Diongoï *Mali* 14°38N 8°34W **262** C3
Dionísodes → *Cameroon* 35°20N 26°10E **207** D7
Dionysos, Theatro *Athens, Greece* 112 C2
Diósgyör *Hungary* 48°7N 20°43E **182** B5
Diosig *Romania* 47°18N 22°2E **182** D7
Diougani *Mali* 14°19N 2°44W **262** C4
Diouloulou *Senegal* 13°5N 16°38W **262** C1
Dioura *Mali* 14°59N 5°12W **262** C3
Diourbel *Senegal* 14°39N 16°12W **262** C1
Diourbel □ *Senegal* 14°45N 16°15W **262** C1
Dipalpur *Pakistan* 30°40N 73°39E **242** D5
Diphu *India* 25°51N 93°32E **241** C4
Dipkarpaz = Rizokarpaso
Cyprus 35°36N 34°23E **207** E10
Diplo *Pakistan* 24°35N 69°35E **242** G3
Dipolog *Phil.* 8°36N 123°20E **233** H4
Dipperu △ *Australia* 21°56S 148°42E **280** C4
Dir *Pakistan* 35°8N 71°59E **240** B3
Diré *Mali* 16°20N 3°25W **262** B4
Dire Dawa *Ethiopia* 9°35N 41°45E **257** F5
Dirfis Oros *Greece* 38°40N 23°54E **204** C5
Diriamba *Nic.* 11°51N 86°19W **320** D2
Dirico *Angola* 17°50S 20°42E **268** B3
Dirk Hartog I. *Australia* 25°50S 113°5E **279** E1
Dirkou *Niger* 18°35N 12°49E **259** D2
Dirnismaning *Germany* 48°13N 11°38E **131** A2
Dirranbandi *Australia* 28°33S 148°17E **281** D4
Dirs *Si. Arabia* 18°32N 42°25E **248** G3
Dirschau = Tczew *Poland* 54°8N 18°50E **184** D5

Disa *India* 24°18N 72°10E **242** G5
Disa *Sudan* 12°5N 34°15E **257** E3
Disappointment, C.
U.S.A. 46°18N 124°5W **304** C1
Disappointment, L.
Australia 23°20S 122°40E **278** D3
Disaster B. *Australia* 37°15S 149°58E **283** D8
Discovery B. *Vic.,
Australia* 38°10S 140°40E **282** E4
Discovery B. *China* 22°18N 114°1E **219** a
Discovery Bay *Australia* 38°9S 141°16E **282** E4
Discovery Seamount
Atl. Oc. 42°0S 0°10E **152** L12
Disentis Muster *Switz.* 46°42N 8°50E **179** J4
Dishna *Egypt* 26°9N 32°32E **256** B3
Disina *Nigeria* 11°35N 9°50E **263** C6
Disko = Qeqertarsuaq
Greenland 69°45N 53°30W **154** D5
Disko Bugt *Greenland* 69°10N 52°0W **154** D5
Disna = Dzisna →
Belarus 55°34N 28°12E **188** E5
Disney-M.G.M. Studios
U.S.A. 28°21N 81°33W **133** B1
Disney Reef *Tonga* 19°17S 174°7W **287** P13
Disney Studios *U.S.A.* 34°9N 118°19W **126** B3
Disneyland Hong Kong
China 22°18N 114°2E **219** a
Dispur *India* 26°3N 91°52E **241** B3
Diss *U.K.* 52°23N 1°7E **169** E9
Disteghil Sar *Pakistan* 36°20N 75°12E **243** A6
District Heights *U.S.A.* 38°51N 76°53W **143** B4
District of Columbia □
U.S.A. 38°55N 77°0W **309** F15
Distrito Federal □ *Brazil* 15°45S 47°45W **333** E2
Distrito Federal □ *Mexico* 19°15N 99°10W **319** D5
Distrito Federal □
Venezuela 10°30N 66°55W **328** A4
Disûq *Egypt* 31°8N 30°35E **256** H7
Ditan Park *Beijing, China* 114 A2
Diu *India* 20°45N 70°58E **242** J4
Diuata Mts. *Phil.* 9°0N 125°50E **233** G5
Dīvāndarreh *Iran* 35°55N 47°2E **213** E12
Divarata *Greece* 38°20N 20°33E **207** C2
Divenié *Congo* 2°43S 12°1E **264** C2
Dives → *France* 49°18N 0°7W **172** C5
Dives-sur-Mer *France* 49°18N 0°8W **172** C5
Divi Pt. *India* 15°59N 81°9E **245** G5
Divichi
Azerbaijan 41°15N 48°57E **191** K9
Divide *U.S.A.* 45°45N 112°45W **304** D7
Dividing Ra. *Australia* 27°45S 116°0E **279** E2
Divilican B. *Phil.* 17°21N 122°19E **232** C4
Divinópolis *Brazil* 20°10S 44°54W **333** F3
Divisões, Serra dos *Brazil* 15°0S 51°0W **333** E1
Divjakë *Albania* 41°0N 19°32E **202** F3
Divnoye *Russia* 45°55N 43°21E **191** H6
Divo *Ivory C.* 5°48N 5°15W **262** D3
Divriği *Turkey* 39°22N 38°7E **213** C8
Diwāl Kol *Afghan.* 34°23N 67°52E **242** B2
Dix → *U.S.A.* 37°49N 84°43W **311** G12
Dix Mt. *U.S.A.* 35°50N 120°16W **306** F5
Dixie Union *U.S.A.* 31°20N 82°28W **316** D7
Dixon *Calif., U.S.A.* 38°27N 121°49W **306** G5
Dixon *Ill., U.S.A.* 41°50N 89°29W **310** C7
Dixon *Mont., U.S.A.* 37°59N 92°6W **310** G4
Dixon Entrance *U.S.A.* 54°30N 132°0W **303** J14
Dixville *Canada* 45°4N 71°46W **313** A12
Diyadin *Turkey* 39°33N 43°40E **213** C10
Diyālā □ *Iraq* 33°45N 44°50E **248** C5
Diyālā → *Iraq* 33°13N 44°30E **213** F11
Diyarb Nigm *Egypt* 30°45N 31°26E **251** H2
Diyarbakır *Turkey* 37°55N 40°18E **213** D9
Diyarbakır □ *Turkey* 38°0N 40°0E **213** D9
Diyodar *India* 24°8N 71°50E **242** G4
Dizangué *Cameroon* 3°46N 9°59E **264** B1
Dja → *Cameroon* 3°10N 12°58E **264** B2
Djadié → *Cameroon* 0°46N 12°58E **264** B2
Djado *Niger* 21°4N 12°14E **259** D2
Djado, Plateau du *Niger* 21°29N 12°12E **259** D2
Djakarta = Jakarta
Indonesia 6°9S 106°52E **122** A2
Djalma Dutra = Miguel Calmon
Brazil 11°26S 40°36W **332** D3
Djalma Dutra = Poções
Brazil 14°31S 40°21W **333** D3
Djamâa *Algeria* 33°32N 5°59E **261** B6
Djambala *Angola* 16°45S 13°58E **265** F2
Djambala *Congo* 2°32S 14°30E **264** C2
Djanet *Algeria* 24°35N 9°32E **261** D6
Djaul I. *Papua N. G.* 2°58S 150°57E **286** B5
Djawa = Jawa *Indonesia* 7°0S 110°0E **235** D4
Djebel Tazzeka △ *Morocco* 34°6N 4°11W **260** B4
Djebiniana *Tunisia* 35°1N 11°0E **258** A2
Djédaa *Chad* 13°31N 18°34E **259** F3
Djelfa *Algeria* 34°40N 3°15E **261** B5
Djelfa □ *Algeria* 34°20N 3°40E **261** B5
Djema *C.A.R.* 6°3N 25°15E **264** A5
Djember *Chad* 10°25N 17°50E **259** F3
Djembo
Dem. Rep. of the Congo 9°54S 22°18E **265** D4
Djendel *Algeria* 36°15N 2°25E **261** A5
Djenné *Mali* 14°0N 4°30W **262** C4
Djenoun, Garet el *Algeria* 25°4N 5°31E **261** C6
Djerba *Tunisia* 33°48N 10°54E **258** B2
Djerba, Î. de *Tunisia* 33°50N 10°48E **258** B2
Djérem → *Cameroon* 5°20N 13°24E **264** A2
Djerid, Chott *Tunisia* 33°42N 8°30E **258** B1
Djermaya *Chad* 12°42N 15°3E **259** F3
Djibo *Burkina Faso* 14°9N 1°35W **263** C4
Djibouti *Djibouti* 11°30N 43°5E **257** E5
Djibouti ■ *Africa* 12°0N 43°0E **257** E5
Djohong *Cameroon* 6°47N 14°20E **264** A2
Djolu *Dem. Rep. of the Congo* 0°35N 22°5E **264** B4
Djouab → *Gabon* 1°13N 13°12E **264** B2
Djoudj △ *Senegal* 16°24N 16°14W **262** B2
Djougou *Benin* 9°40N 1°45E **263** D5
Djoum *Cameroon* 2°41N 12°35E **264** B2
Djouna *Chad* 10°27N 20°42E **259** F4
Djugu *Dem. Rep. of the Congo* 1°55N 30°35E **268** B3
Djukbini △ *Australia* 13°15N 131°2E **278** B5
Djúpavík *Iceland* 65°57N 21°34W **155** B5
Djúpivogur *Iceland* 64°39N 14°17W **155** C12
Djursland *Sweden* 60°34N 15°58E **162** D3
Djurås *Sweden* 60°34N 15°58E **162** D3
Djurdjura △ *Algeria* 35°20N 4°15E **261** A5
Djurö *Sweden* 58°52N 13°58E **139** A2
Djursholm *Sweden* 59°24N 18°6E **139** A2
Dmitriya Lapteva, Proliv
Russia 73°0N 140°0E **215** B13
Dmitriyev Lgovskiy *Russia* 52°10N 35°0E **189** F3
Dmitrievsk = Makiyivka
Ukraine 48°0N 38°0E **189** H3
Dmitriyevskoye = Talas
Kyrgyzstan 42°30N 72°13E **217** D3
Dmitrov *Russia* 56°25N 37°32E **188** D3
Dmitrovsk-Orlovskiy
Russia 52°29N 35°10E **189** F3
Dnepr = Dnipro →
Ukraine 46°30N 32°18E **189** J7
Dneprodzerzhinsk =
Dniprodzerzhynsk
Ukraine 48°32N 34°37E **189** H3
Dneprodzerzhinskoye Vdkhr. =
Dniprodzerzhynske Vdskh.
Ukraine 48°49N 34°48E **189** H3

Dnepropetrovsk = Dnipropetrovsk
Ukraine 48°30N 35°0E **189** H8
Dneprorudnoye = Dniprorudne
Ukraine 47°21N 34°58E **189** J8
Dnestr = Dnister →
Europe 46°18N 30°17E **177** E16
Dnestrovski = Belgorod
Russia 50°35N 36°35E **189** G9
Dnieper = Dnipro →
Ukraine 46°30N 32°18E **189** J7
Dniester = Dnister →
Europe 46°18N 30°17E **177** E16
Dnipro → *Ukraine* 46°30N 32°18E **189** J7
Dniprodzerzhynsk
Ukraine 48°32N 34°37E **189** H8
Dniprodzerzhynske Vdskh.
Ukraine 48°49N 34°48E **189** H8
Dnipropetrovsk *Ukraine* 48°30N 35°0E **189** H8
Dnipropetrovsk □
Ukraine 48°15N 34°50E **189** H8
Dniprorudne *Ukraine* 47°21N 34°58E **189** J8
Dnister → *Europe* 46°18N 30°17E **177** E16
Dnistrovskyy Lyman
Ukraine 46°15N 30°17E **189** J6
Dno *Russia* 57°50N 29°58E **188** D5
Dnyapro = Dnipro →
Ukraine 46°30N 32°18E **189** J7
Do Gonbadān = Gachsārān
Iran 30°15N 50°45E **247** D6
Doabi *Afghan.* 36°1N 69°32E **240** A3
Doaktown *Canada* 46°33N 66°8W **299** C6
Doan Hung *Vietnam* 21°30N 105°10E **236** B5
Doany *Madag.* 14°21S 49°30E **272** A2
Doba *Chad* 8°40N 16°50E **259** G3
Dobandi *Pakistan* 31°13N 66°50E **242** D2
Dobbiaco *Italy* 46°44N 12°14E **199** B7
Dobbyn *Australia* 19°44S 140°2E **280** B3
Dobczyce *Poland* 49°52N 20°25E **185** J7
Dobele *Latvia* 56°37N 23°16E **184** B10
Dobele □ *Latvia* 56°45N 23°10E **184** B9
Döbeln *Germany* 51°6N 13°7E **178** D9
Doberai, Jazirah *Indonesia* 1°25S 133°0E **231** E8
Döberitz *Germany* 52°32N 13°3E **115** A1
Dobiegniew *Poland* 52°59N 15°45E **185** F2
Doblas *Argentina* 37°5S 64°0W **334** D3
Döbling *Austria* 48°14N 16°20E **142** A2
Dobo *Dem. Rep. of the Congo* 2°20N 22°11E **264** B4
Dobo *Indonesia* 5°45S 134°15E **231** F8
Doboj *Bos.-H.* 44°46N 18°4E **182** F3
Dobong *S. Korea* 37°39N 127°2E **137** B2
Dobongsan *S. Korea* 37°40N 127°0E **137** B2
Dobra *Wielkopolskie, Poland* 51°55N 18°37E **185** G5
Dobra *Zachodnio-Pomorskie,
Poland* 53°34N 15°20E **184** E2
Dobra *Dâmbovița,
Romania* 44°52N 25°40E **183** F10
Dobra *Hunedoara, Romania* 45°54N 22°36E **182** E7
Dobre Miasto *Poland* 46°51N 21°58E **182** D7
Dobrich *Bulgaria* 43°37N 27°49E **203** D12
Dobrich □ *Bulgaria* 43°37N 27°49E **203** D11
Dobrinishta *Bulgaria* 41°49N 23°34E **202** E7
Dobříš *Czech Rep.* 49°46N 14°10E **180** B7
Dobrodzień *Poland* 50°45N 18°25E **185** H5
Dobromyl *Ukraine* 49°34N 22°46E **185** J9
Dobron *Ukraine* 48°25N 22°23E **182** B7
Dobropole *Ukraine* 48°25N 37°2E **189** H9
Dobrovolsk *Russia* 54°46N 22°31E **184** D9
Dobruja *Europe* 44°30N 28°15E **183** F13
Dobrush *Belarus* 52°25N 31°22E **177** B16
Dobrzany *Poland* 53°22N 15°25E **184** E2
Dobrzyń nad Wisłą *Poland* 52°39N 19°22E **185** F6
Doc, Mui *Vietnam* 17°58N 106°30E **236** D6
Doc Can I. *Phil.* 5°55N 119°56E **233** J2
Doce → *Brazil* 19°37S 39°49W **333** E4
Docker River = Kaltukatjara
Australia 24°52S 129°5E **279** D4
Docklands *U.K.* 51°30N 0°1W **125** A3
Docksta *Sweden* 63°3N 18°18E **162** A12
Doctor Arroyo *Mexico* 23°40N 100°11W **318** C4
Doctor Pedro P. Peña
Paraguay 22°27S 62°21W **331** E5
Doctor Phillips *U.S.A.* 28°26N 81°29W **133** B2
Doctors Inlet *U.S.A.* 30°6N 81°47W **316** E8
Doda *India* 33°10N 75°34E **243** C6
Doda, La *Canada* 49°25N 75°13W **298** C4
Doda Betta *India* 11°24N 76°44E **245** J3
Dodballapur *India* 13°18N 77°32E **245** H3
Dodder → *Ireland* 53°20N 6°13W **120** B1
Dodecanese = Dodecanese
Greece 36°35N 27°0E **205** E8
Dodekanisa = Dodecanese
Greece 36°35N 27°0E **205** E8
Dodge City *U.S.A.* 37°45N 100°1W **308** E4
Dodge L. *Canada* 59°50N 105°36W **297** B7
Dodger Stadium *U.S.A.* 34°4N 118°14W **126** B3
Dodgeville *U.S.A.* 42°58N 90°8W **310** B6
Dodo *Cameroon* 7°30N 12°3E **263** D7
Dodo *South Sudan* 5°10N 29°57E **257** F2
Dodola *Ethiopia* 6°59N 39°11E **257** F4
Dodoma *Tanzania* 6°8S 35°45E **268** D4
Dodoma □ *Tanzania* 6°0S 36°0E **268** D4
Dodoni *Greece* 39°40N 20°46E **204** B2
Dodori △ *Kenya* 1°55S 41°7E **268** C5
Dodsland *Canada* 51°50N 108°45W **297** C7
Dodson *U.S.A.* 48°24N 108°15W **304** B9
Dodurga *Turkey* 39°49N 29°57E **205** B11
Doerun *U.S.A.* 31°19N 83°55W **316** D6
Doesburg *Neths.* 52°1N 6°9E **170** B6
Doetinchem *Neths.* 51°59N 6°18E **170** C6
Dog Creek *Canada* 51°35N 122°14W **296** C4
Dog L. *Man., Canada* 51°2N 98°31W **297** C9
Dog L. *Ont., Canada* 48°48N 89°30W **298** C2
Dogankent *Turkey* 36°52N 35°18E **250** B2
Doğanşehir *Turkey* 38°5N 37°53E **212** D7
Dogliani *Italy* 44°32N 7°56E **198** D4
Dōgo *Japan* 36°15N 133°16E **222** A5
Dōgo-San *Japan* 36°15N 133°16E **222** A5
Dogondoutchi *Niger* 13°38N 4°2E **263** C5
Dogran *Pakistan* 31°48N 73°35E **242** D5
Dogs, Isle of *U.K.* 51°29N 0°1W **125** B3
Doğubayazıt *Turkey* 39°31N 44°5E **213** C11
Doguéraoua *Niger* 14°0N 5°31E **263** C6
Dogura *Papua N. G.* 10°6S 150°6E **286** C6
Doha = Ad Dawḥah
Qatar 25°15N 51°35E **247** E6
Dohazari *Bangla.* 22°10N 92°5E **241** D4
Dohinog = Manukan
Phil. 8°32N 123°12E **233** G4
Dohrighat *India* 26°16N 83°31E **243** F10
Doi *Indonesia* 2°14N 127°49E **231** D7
Doi Inthanon *Thailand* 18°35N 98°29E **236** C2
Doi Inthanon △ *Thailand* 18°33N 98°34E **236** C2
Doi Khuntan △ *Thailand* 18°30N 99°14E **236** C2
Doi Luang *Thailand* 18°30N 101°0E **236** C3
Doi Luang △ *Thailand* 19°8N 99°38E **236** C2
Doi Phukha △ *Thailand* 19°8N 101°9E **236** C3
Doi Saket *Thailand* 18°52N 99°2E **236** C2
Doi Suthep Pui △ *Thailand* 18°50N 98°55E **236** C2
Doi Toa *Thailand* 18°5N 98°12E **236** C2
Dois Irmãos, Sa. *Brazil* 9°0S 42°30W **332** D3
Dojransko Jezero
Macedonia 41°13N 22°44E **202** F6
Doka *Sudan* 13°31N 35°46E **257** E4

Dokka *Norway* 60°49N 10°7E **164** D7
Dokka → *Norway* 60°49N 10°7E **164** D7
Dokkum *Neths.* 53°20N 5°59E **170** A5
Dokos *Greece* 37°20N 23°20E **204** D5
Dokri *Pakistan* 27°25N 68°7E **242** F3
Dokshukino = Nartkala
Russia 43°33N 43°51E **191** J6
Dokuchayevsk *Ukraine* 47°44N 37°40E **189** J9
Dol-de-Bretagne *France* 48°34N 1°47W **172** D5
Dolac *Kosovo* 42°36N 20°36E **202** D4
Dolak, Pulau *Indonesia* 8°0S 138°30E **231** F9
Dolbeau-Mistassini
Canada 48°53N 72°14W **299** C5
Dole *France* 47°7N 5°31E **173** E12
Doleib, Wadi → *Sudan* 12°10N 53°15E **257** E3
Dolenji Logatec *Slovenia* 45°56N 14°15E **199** C11
Dolgellau *U.K.* 52°45N 3°53W **168** E4
Dolgelley = Dolgellau
U.K. 52°45N 3°53W **168** E4
Dolgoe Ozero *Russia* 60°0N 30°15E **137** A1
Dolhasca *Romania* 47°26N 26°36E **183** C11
Doliana *Greece* 39°54N 20°32E **204** B2
Dolianova *Italy* 39°22N 9°10E **200** C2
Dolinsk *Russia* 47°21N 142°48E **215** E15
Dolinskaya = Dolynska
Ukraine 48°6N 32°46E **189** H7
Dolj □ *Romania* 44°10N 23°30E **183** F8
Doll Museum *Delhi, India* 120 b3
Dollard *Neths.* 53°20N 7°10E **170** A7
Dollis Hill *U.K.* 51°33N 0°13W **125** A2
Dollymount *Ireland* 53°22N 6°11W **120** A2
Dolna Banya *Bulgaria* 42°18N 23°44E **202** D7
Dolni Chabry *Czech Rep.* 50°8N 14°26E **135** B2
Dolni Chiflik *Bulgaria* 42°59N 27°43E **203** D11
Dolni Dŭbnik *Bulgaria* 43°24N 24°26E **203** C8
Dolni Počernice *Czech Rep.* 50°5N 14°34E **135** B3
Dolnośląskie □ *Poland* 51°10N 16°30E **185** G3
Dolný Kubín *Slovak Rep.* 49°12N 19°18E **181** B12
Dolo *Ethiopia* 4°11N 42°3E **257** G5
Dolo *Italy* 45°25N 12°5E **199** C9
Dolomites = Dolomiti
Italy 46°23N 11°51E **199** B8
Dolomiti *Italy* 46°23N 11°51E **199** B8
Dolomiti Bellunesi △ *Italy* 46°10N 12°5E **199** B9
Dolores *Argentina* 36°20S 57°40W **334** D4
Dolores *Phil.* 12°2N 125°29E **232** E5
Dolores *Uruguay* 33°34S 58°15W **334** C4
Dolores *Colo., U.S.A.* 37°28N 108°30W **305** H9
Dolores → *U.S.A.* 38°49N 109°17W **304** G9
Dolovo *Serbia* 44°55N 20°52E **182** F5
Dolphin, C. *Falk. Is.* 51°10S 59°0W **153** f
Dolphin and Union Str.
Canada 69°5N 114°45W **294** D9
Dolphin Head *Jamaica* 18°22N 78°10W **320** a
Dolphin I. *Jamaica* 17°48N 77°10W **320** a
Dolphins Barn *Ireland* 53°20N 6°17W **120** B2
Dolsk *Poland* 51°59N 17°3E **185** G4
Dolton *U.S.A.* 41°38N 87°36W **311** C9
Dolungmukh *India* 27°30N 94°18E **241** B5
Dolyna *Ukraine* 48°58N 24°1E **183** D8
Dolynske *Ukraine* 48°6N 32°46E **189** H7
Dolynske *Ukraine* 47°32N 29°55E **183** C14
Dolzhanskaya *Russia* 46°37N 37°48E **189** J9
Dom Joaquim *Brazil* 18°57S 43°16W **333** E3
Dom Pedrito *Brazil* 31°0S 54°40W **335** C5
Dom Pedro *Brazil* 4°59S 44°27W **332** B3
Dom Pedro II, Parque
Brazil 23°33S 46°36W **137** B3
Doma = Gombe *Nigeria* 10°19N 11°2E **263** D7
Doma *Nigeria* 8°25N 8°18E **263** D6
Doma → *Zimbabwe* 16°28S 30°12E **269** B5
Domaçara *Somali Rep.* 1°52N 41°15E **267** D5
Domain, The *Sydney, Australia* 139 b2
Domaniç *Turkey* 39°48N 29°36E **205** B11
Domar, Enneri → *Chad* 18°11N 18°4E **259** D3
Domariaganj → *India* 26°17N 83°44E **243** F10
Domasi *Malawi* 15°15S 35°22E **269** F4
Domažlice *Czech Rep.* 49°28N 12°58E **180** B5
Dombarovka = Dombarovskiy
Russia 50°46N 59°32E **214** D6
Dombarovskiy *Russia* 50°46N 59°32E **214** D6
Dombås *Norway* 62°4N 9°8E **164** B6
Dombasle-sur-Meurthe
France 48°38N 6°21E **173** D13
Dombe Grande *Angola* 12°57S 13°6E **265** E2
Dombes *France* 45°58N 5°0E **175** C9
Dombóvár *Hungary* 46°21N 18°9E **182** E3
Dombrád *Hungary* 48°13N 21°54E **182** B6
Dombrova = Dąbrowa Górnicza
Poland 50°15N 19°10E **185** H6
Dombrowitsa = Dubrovytsya
Ukraine 51°31N 26°35E **177** C14
Dome Argus *Antarctica* 80°50S 76°30E **151** E6
Dome C. *Antarctica* 75°12S 123°37E **151** D9
Dome Fuji *Antarctica* 77°20S 39°45E **151** D5
Dome of the Rock *Jerusalem* 123 B3
Domel I. = Letsôk-aw Kyun
Burma 11°30N 98°25E **237** G2
Domérat *France* 46°21N 2°32E **173** F9
Domett *N.Z.* 42°53S 173°12E **285** D5
Domeyko *Chile* 29°0S 71°0W **334** B1
Domeyko, Cordillera *Chile* 24°30S 69°0W **334** A2
Domfront *France* 48°37N 0°40W **172** D6
Dominador *Chile* 24°21S 69°20W **334** A2
Dominica ■ *W. Indies* 15°20N 61°20W **323** k
Dominica Passage
W. Indies 15°10N 61°20W **321** C7
Dominican Rep. ■
W. Indies 19°0N 70°30W **321** C5
Dominion Centre *Toronto, Canada* 141 b2
Domingo
Dem. Rep. of the Congo 4°37S 21°15E **265** D4
Dömitz *Germany* 53°8N 11°15E **178** B7
Domme *France* 44°48N 1°12E **174** D5
Domnești *Romania* 45°13N 24°50E **183** E9
Domo *Ethiopia* 7°50N 47°10E **267** D5
Domodossola *Italy* 46°7N 8°17E **198** B5
Domokos *Greece* 39°10N 22°18E **204** B4
Domoni *Comoros Is.* 12°15S 44°32E **272** a
Dompaire *France* 48°14N 6°14E **173** D13
Dompierre-sur-Besbre
France 46°31N 3°41E **173** F10
Dompim *Ghana* 5°10N 2°5W **262** D4
Domsjö *Sweden* 63°32N 18°37E **162** A12
Domusnovas *Italy* 39°19N 8°39E **200** D1

Doña Mencía *Spain* 37°33N 4°21W **195** H6
Doña L. *Canada* 61°13N 108°36W **297** A7
Donaghadee *U.K.* 54°39N 5°33W **166** B6
Donaghmede *Ireland* 53°23N 6°9E **120** A2
Donaghmore *Ireland* 52°52N 7°36W **166** D4
Donald *Australia* 36°23S 143°0E **282** C5
Donaldsonville *U.S.A.* 30°6N 90°59W **314** F9
Donalsonville *U.S.A.* 31°3N 84°53W **316** D5
Doñana △ *Spain* 36°59N 6°23W **195** J4
Donau = Dunărea →
Europe 45°20N 29°40E **183** E14
Donau → *France* 45°5N 0°40E **174** C7
Donau Auen △ *Austria* 48°10N 16°40E **181** C9
Donau-Oder Kanal
Austria 48°12N 16°32E **142** A3
Donaueschingen *Germany* 47°56N 8°29E **179** H4
Donaufeld *Austria* 48°14N 16°24E **142** A2
Donaupark *Austria* 48°14N 16°24E **142** A2
Donaustadt *Austria* 48°12N 16°32E **142** A3
Donauwörth *Germany* 48°43N 10°47E **179** G6
Dondo *Angola* 9°45S 14°25E **265** D2
Dondo
Dem. Rep. of the Congo 4°11N 21°39E **264** B4
Dondo *Mozam.* 19°33S 34°46E **269** F3
Dondo, Teluk *Indonesia* 0°50N 120°30E **231** D6
Dondra Head *Sri Lanka* 5°55N 80°40E **245** M5
Doneşti *Romania* 48°14N 27°36E **183** B12
Donegal *Ireland* 54°39N 8°5W **166** B3
Donegal □ *Ireland* 54°53N 8°0W **166** B4
Donegal B. *Ireland* 54°31N 8°49W **166** B3
Donets → *Russia* 47°33N 40°55E **191** G5
Donets Basin *Ukraine* 49°0N 38°0E **158** F13
Donetsk *Ukraine* 48°0N 37°45E **189** J9
Donetsk □ *Ukraine* 47°30N 37°50E **189** H9
Dornes *France* 46°48N 3°18E **173** F10
Dorneşti *Romania* 47°52N 26°1E **183** C11
Dornie *U.K.* 57°17N 5°31W **167** D3
Dornoch *U.K.* 57°53N 4°2W **167** D4
Dornoch *Ont., Canada* 44°18N 80°51W **312** B4
Dornoch *Highl., U.K.* 57°53N 4°2W **167** D4
Dornoch Firth *U.K.* 57°51N 4°4W **167** D4
Dornogovi □ *Mongolia* 44°0N 110°0E **226** C6
Doro *Mali* 16°9N 0°51W **263** B4
Doro, Kavo *Greece* 38°9N 24°38E **204** C6
Dorog *Hungary* 47°42N 18°45E **182** C3
Dorogobuzh *Russia* 54°50N 33°18E **188** E7
Dorohoi *Romania* 47°56N 26°23E **183** C11
Döröö Nuur *Mongolia* 48°0N 93°0E **217** C12
Dorpat = Tartu *Estonia* 58°20N 26°44E **188** B4
Dorr *Iran* 33°17N 50°38E **247** C6
Dorre I. *Australia* 25°13S 113°12E **279** E1
Dorrigo *Australia* 30°20S 152°44E **283** A10
Dorrigo △ *Australia* 30°22S 152°47E **283** A10
Dorris *U.S.A.* 41°58N 121°55W **304** F3
Dorset *Ont., Canada* 45°14N 78°54W **312** A6
Dorset *Ohio, U.S.A.* 41°40N 80°40W **312** E4
Dorset *Vt., U.S.A.* 43°15N 73°6W **313** C11
Dorset □ *U.K.* 50°45N 2°26W **169** G5
Dorsten *Germany* 51°40N 6°58E **178** D2
Dortmund *Germany* 51°30N 7°28E **178** D3
Dortmund-Ems-Kanal →
Germany 51°50N 7°26E **178** D3
Dörtyol *Turkey* 36°50N 36°13E **250** B7
Doruk *Turkey* 36°53N 35°45E **250** B6
Dorum *Germany* 53°41N 8°34E **178** B4
Doruma
Dem. Rep. of the Congo 4°42N 27°33E **268** B2
Dorüneh *Iran* 35°10N 57°18E **247** C8
Dorval Int., Montréal ✈ (YUL)
Canada 45°27N 73°44W **130** B1
Dos Bahías, C. *Argentina* 44°58S 65°32W **334** B3
Dos d'Âne *Réunion* 20°58S 55°23E **272** f
Dos Hermanas *Spain* 37°16N 5°55W **195** H5
Dos Moninos → *Brazil* 23°40S 46°33W **137** C2
Dos Palos *U.S.A.* 36°59N 120°37W **306** J6
Döşemealtı *Turkey* 37°4N 30°33E **205** D12
Dosso *Niger* 13°0N 3°13E **263** C5
Dosso □ *Niger* 13°30N 3°30E **263** C5
Dosso → *Niger* 12°9N 3°36E **263** C5
Dostyq *Kazakhstan* 45°15N 82°29E **217** C10
Dot Lake *U.S.A.* 63°40N 144°4W **303** E11
Dothan *U.S.A.* 31°13N 85°24W **316** D6
Doty *U.S.A.* 46°38N 123°17W **306** D3
Douai *France* 50°21N 3°4E **173** B10
Douako *Guinea* 9°45N 10°6W **262** C2
Douala *Cameroon* 4°0N 9°45E **264** B1
Douala-Édéa △ *Cameroon* 3°20N 9°41E **264** B1
Douamoungo, L. *Mayotte* 12°38S 45°8E **272** b
Douaouir *Mali* 20°45N 3°0W **262** B4
Douarnenez *France* 48°6N 4°21W **172** D2
Double Cone *N.Z.* 44°41N 168°25E **285** F3
Double Island Pt.
Australia 25°56S 153°11E **281** D5
Double Mountain Fork →
U.S.A. 33°16N 100°0W **314** E4
Doubrava → *Czech Rep.* 50°0N 15°20E **188** a8
Doubs □ *France* 47°10N 6°20E **173** E13
Doubs → *France* 46°53N 5°1E **173** E12
Doubtful Sd. *N.Z.* 45°20S 166°49E **285** F1
Doubtless B. *N.Z.* 34°55S 173°26E **284** A4
Doudeville *France* 49°43N 0°47E **172** C7
Doué-la-Fontaine *France* 47°11N 0°16W **172** E6
Douentza *Mali* 15°0N 2°56W **262** C4
Douentza △ *Mali* 15°40N 2°25W **262** C4
Dougga *Tunisia* 36°25N 9°10E **261** A7
Doughboy B. *N.Z.* 47°2S 167°40E **285** H1
Douglas *S. Africa* 29°4S 23°46E **270** D3
Douglas *I. of Man* 54°10N 4°28W **168** C3
Douglas *Northern Cape,
S. Africa* 29°4S 23°46E **270** D3
Douglas *Alaska, U.S.A.* 58°17N 134°24W **303** G14
Douglas *Ariz., U.S.A.* 31°21N 109°33W **305** L9
Douglas *Ga., U.S.A.* 31°31N 82°51W **316** D7
Douglas *Mich., U.S.A.* 42°39N 86°14W **311** D10
Douglas *Wyo., U.S.A.* 42°45N 105°24W **304** E11
Douglas Apsley △
Australia 41°45S 148°11E **281** G4
Douglas B. *Dominica* 15°36N 61°29W **323** k
Douglas C. *Antarctica* 58°51N 153°15W **303** G9
Douglas Chan. *Canada* 53°40N 129°20W **296** C3
Douglas Park *Australia* 34°12N 150°42E **139** D1
Douglas Pt. *Canada* 44°19N 81°37W **312** B3
Douglastown *Canada* 48°46N 64°24W **299** C7
Douglasville *U.S.A.* 33°45N 84°45W **316** B5
Douirat *Morocco* 33°2N 4°11W **260** B4
Doukaton, Akra *Greece* 38°34N 20°33E **207** B2
Doulevant-le-Château
France 48°22N 4°53E **173** D11
Doullens *France* 50°10N 2°20E **173** B9
Doumé *Cameroon* 4°15N 13°25E **264** B2
Doumen *China* 22°10N 113°18E **229** F9
Douna *Mali* 14°58N 3°14W **262** C4
Dounreay *U.K.* 58°35N 3°44W **167** C5
Dourada, Serra *Brazil* 13°10S 48°45E **333** D2
Dourados *Brazil* 22°9S 54°50W **333** F1
Dourados → *Brazil* 21°58S 54°18W **333** F1
Dourados, Serra dos
Brazil 23°30S 53°30W **335** A5
Dourbali *Chad* 11°49N 15°32E **259** F3
Dourdan *France* 48°30N 2°1E **173** D9
Douro → *Europe* 41°8N 8°40W **194** D2
Douvaine *France* 46°19N 6°16E **173** F13
Douvres-la-Délivrande
France 49°17N 0°23W **172** C6
Douz *Tunisia* 33°25N 9°0E **258** B1

Douze → France 43°54N 0°30W 174 E3
Dove → U.K. 52°51N 1°36W 168 E6
Dove Creek U.S.A. 37°46N 108°54W 305 H9
Dover Tas., Australia 43°18S 147°2E 281 G4
Dover Kent, U.K. 51°7N 1°19E 169 F9
Dover Del., U.S.A. 39°10N 75°32W 309 F16
Dover Ky., U.S.A. 38°43N 83°52W 311 F13
Dover N.H., U.S.A. 43°12N 70°56W 313 C14
Dover N.J., U.S.A. 40°53N 74°34W 313 F10
Dover Ohio, U.S.A. 40°32N 81°29W 312 F3
Dover, Pt. Australia 32°32S 125°32E 279 F4
Dover, Str. of Europe 51°0N 1°30E 169 G9
Dover-Foxcroft U.S.A. 45°11N 69°13W 309 C19
Dover Heights Australia 33°52S 151°16E 139 B2
Dover Plains U.S.A. 41°43N 73°35W 313 E11
Dovey = Dyfi → U.K. 52°32N 4°3W 169 E3
Dovhe Ukraine 48°22N 23°17E 183 B8
Dovlen = Devin Bulgaria 41°44N 24°24E 203 E8
Dovre Norway 61°58N 9°15E 164 C6
Dovre △ Norway 62°10N 9°30E 164 B6
Dovrefjell Norway 62°15N 9°33E 164 B6
Dovrefjell △ Norway 62°20N 9°25E 164 B6
Dovrefjell-Sunndalsfjella △
Norway 62°23N 9°11E 164 B6
Dow Rūd Iran 33°28N 49°4E 247 C6
Dowa Malawi 13°38S 33°58E 269 E3
Dowagiac U.S.A. 41°59N 86°6W 311 C10
Dowerin Australia 31°12S 117°2E 279 F2
Dowgha'i Iran 36°54N 58°32E 247 B8
Dowlat Yār Afghan. 34°30N 65°45E 240 B2
Dowlatābād Farāh,
Afghan. 32°47N 62°40E 240 B1
Dowlatābād Fāryāb,
Afghan. 36°26N 64°55E 240 A2
Dowlatābād Kermān, Iran 28°20N 56°40E 247 D8
Dowlatābād Khorāsān,
Iran 35°16N 59°29E 247 C8
Dowlatābād Tehrān, Iran 35°38N 51°27E 141 B2
Dowling Park U.S.A. 30°15N 83°15W 316 E6
Down □ U.K. 54°23N 6°2W 166 B5
Down, L. U.S.A. 28°30N 81°31W 133 A1
Downers Grove U.S.A. 41°48N 88°1W 311 C8
Downey Calif., U.S.A. 33°56N 118°9W 126 C4
Downey Idaho, U.S.A. 42°26N 112°7W 304 E7
Downham Market U.K. 52°37N 0°23E 169 E8
Downieville U.S.A. 39°34N 120°50W 306 F6
Downing U.S.A. 40°29N 92°22W 310 D4
Downpatrick U.K. 54°20N 5°43W 166 B6
Downpatrick Hd. Ireland 54°20N 9°21W 166 B2
Downsview Canada 43°43N 79°30W 141 A1
Downsville U.S.A. 42°5N 75°0W 313 D10
Downton, Mt. Canada 52°42N 124°52W 296 C4
Dowsārī Iran 28°25N 57°59E 247 D8
Dowshī Afghan. 35°35N 68°43E 240 B3
Doxato Greece 41°9N 24°16E 203 E8
Doyle U.S.A. 40°2N 120°6W 306 E6
Doylestown U.S.A. 40°21N 75°10W 313 F9
Dozen Japan 36°5N 133°5E 222 A5
Dozois, Rés. Canada 47°30N 77°5W 298 C4
Dra Khel Pakistan 27°58N 66°45E 242 F2
Drâa, C. Morocco 28°47N 11°0W 260 C2
Drâa, Hamada du Algeria 28°0N 7°0W 260 C3
Drâa, Oued → Morocco 28°40N 11°10W 260 C2
Drac → France 45°12N 5°42E 175 C9
Drac, Coves del Spain 39°31N 3°19E 206 B4
Dračevo Macedonia 41°56N 21°31E 202 E5
Drachten Neths. 53°7N 6°5E 170 A6
Drăgănești Moldova 47°43N 28°15E 183 C13
Drăgănești-Olt Romania 44°9N 24°32E 183 F9
Drăgănești-Vlașca
Romania 44°5N 25°33E 183 F10
Dragaš Kosovo 42°5N 20°41E 202 D4
Drăgășani Romania 44°39N 24°17E 183 F9
Dragichyn Belarus 52°15N 25°8E 177 B13
Dragocvet Serbia 43°58N 21°15E 202 C5
Dragon's Mouths Venezuela 11°0N 61°50W 323 t
Dragør Denmark 55°35N 12°38E 118 B3
Dragovishtitsa Bulgaria 42°22N 22°39E 202 D6
Draguignan France 43°32N 6°27E 175 E10
Drahove Ukraine 48°14N 23°33E 183 B8
Drain U.S.A. 43°40N 123°19W 304 E2
Drake U.S.A. 47°55N 100°23W 308 B3
Drake Passage S. Ocean 58°0S 68°0W 151 B17
Drakensberg S. Africa 31°0S 28°0E 271 D4
Drama Greece 41°9N 24°10E 203 E8
Drama □ Greece 41°20N 24°0E 203 E8
Dramburg = Drawsko Pomorskie
Poland 53°35N 15°50E 184 E2
Drammen Norway 59°42N 10°12E 164 E7
Drancy France 48°55N 2°26E 134 A3
Dranesville U.S.A. 39°0N 77°20W 143 A1
Drangajökull Iceland 66°9N 22°15W 155 A4
Drangedal Norway 59°6N 9°3E 164 E6
Drangsnes Iceland 65°41N 21°27W 155 B5
Dranov, Ostrov Romania 44°55N 29°30E 183 F14
Drapetsona Greece 37°56N 23°37E 112 B1
Dras India 34°25N 75°48E 243 B6
Drastis, Akra Greece 39°48N 19°40E 206 B9
Drau = Drava → Croatia 45°33N 18°55E 182 E3
Drava → Croatia 45°33N 18°55E 182 E3
Dravograd Slovenia 46°36N 15°5E 199 B12
Drawa → Poland 52°52N 15°59E 185 F2
Drawieński △ Poland 53°6N 15°58E 185 E2
Drawno Poland 53°13N 15°46E 185 E2
Drawsko Pomorskie
Poland 53°35N 15°50E 184 E2
Drayton Canada 43°46N 80°40W 312 C4
Drayton Plains U.S.A. 42°41N 83°23W 311 B13
Drayton Valley Canada 53°12N 114°58W 296 C6
Dreieich Germany 50°1N 8°41E 179 E4
Dreikikir Papua N. G. 3°35S 142°46E 286 B2
Dreilinden Germany 52°24N 13°10E 115 B2
Dren Kosovo 43°8N 20°46E 202 C4
Drenthe □ Neths. 52°52N 6°40E 170 B6
Drepano, Akra Greece 35°28N 24°14E 207 E5
Drepanum, C. Cyprus 34°54N 32°19E 207 F8
Dresden Ont., Canada 42°35N 82°11W 312 D2
Dresden Sachsen, Germany 51°3N 13°44E 178 D9
Dresden N.Y., U.S.A. 42°41N 76°57W 312 D8
Dreux France 48°44N 1°23E 172 D8
Drevsjø Norway 61°53N 12°1E 164 C9
Drewnica Poland 52°18N 21°6E 142 B2
Drexel U.S.A. 39°45N 84°18W 311 E12
Drezdenko Poland 52°50N 15°49E 185 F2
Driesen = Drezdenko
Poland 52°50N 15°49E 185 F2
Driffield U.K. 54°0N 0°26W 167 C8
Driftwood U.S.A. 41°20N 78°8W 312 E6
Driggs U.S.A. 43°44N 111°6W 304 E8
Drigh Road Pakistan 24°52N 67°7E 123 A2
Drimnagh Ireland 53°19N 6°19W 120 B2
Drin → Albania 42°1N 19°38E 202 D3
Drin i Zi → Albania 41°37N 20°28E 202 E4
Drina → Bos.-H. 44°53N 19°21E 202 B3
Drincea → Romania 44°20N 22°55E 182 F7
Drinjača → Bos.-H. 44°15N 19°8E 182 F4
Driopida Greece 37°25N 24°26E 204 D6
Drissa = Vyerkhnyadzvinsk
Belarus 55°45N 27°58E 188 E4
Driva → Norway 62°41N 9°31E 164 B6
Drivstoggo Norway 62°26N 9°47E 164 B6
Drniš Croatia 43°51N 16°10E 199 E13
Drøbak Norway 59°39N 10°39E 164 E7
Drobeta-Turnu Severin
Romania 44°39N 22°41E 182 F7
Drobin Poland 52°42N 19°58E 185 F6
Drochia Moldova 48°2N 27°48E 183 B12
Drogenbos Belgium 50°47N 4°19E 116 B1
Drogheda Ireland 53°43N 6°22W 166 C5
Drogichin = Dragichyn
Belarus 52°15N 25°8E 177 B13
Drogobych = Drohobych
Ukraine 49°20N 23°30E 185 J10
Drohiczyn Poland 52°24N 22°39E 185 F9
Drohobych Ukraine 49°20N 23°30E 185 J10
Droichead Atha = Drogheda
Ireland 53°43N 6°22W 166 C5
Droichead na Bandan = Bandon
Ireland 51°44N 8°44W 166 E3
Droichead Nua Ireland 53°11N 6°48W 166 C5
Droitwich U.K. 52°16N 2°8W 169 E5
Drôme □ France 44°38N 5°15E 175 D9
Drôme → France 44°46N 4°46E 175 D8
Dromedary, C. Australia 36°17S 150°10E 283 D9
Drömling ⌂ Germany 52°29N 11°5E 178 C7
Dromore U.K. 54°31N 7°28W 166 B4
Dromore West Ireland 54°15N 8°52W 166 B3
Dronero Italy 44°28N 7°22E 198 D4
Dronfield U.K. 53°19N 1°27W 168 D6
Dronne → France 45°2N 0°9W 174 C3
Dronning Ingrid Land
Greenland 64°25N 52°5W 154 E5
Dronning Maud Land
Antarctica 72°30S 12°0E 151 D3
Dronninglund Denmark 57°10N 10°19E 163 G4
Dronten Neths. 52°32N 5°43E 170 B5
Dropt → France 44°35N 0°6W 174 D3
Drosendorf Austria 48°52N 15°37E 180 C8
Drosh Pakistan 35°33N 71°48E 240 B3
Droué France 48°3N 1°6E 172 D8
Drouin Australia 38°10S 145°53E 283 E6
Druid Hills U.S.A. 33°47N 84°21W 113 B2
Drujba Uzbekistan 41°13N 61°18E 216 D6
Druk Yul = Bhutan ■
Asia 27°25N 90°30E 241 B3
Drum Tower Beijing, China 114 a3
Drumbo Canada 43°16N 80°35W 312 C4
Drumcliff Ireland 54°20N 8°29W 166 B3
Drumcondra Ireland 53°21N 6°16W 120 A2
Drumheller Canada 51°25N 112°40W 296 C6
Drummond U.S.A. 46°40N 113°9W 304 C7
Drummond I. U.S.A. 46°1N 83°39W 309 B12
Drummond Pt. Australia 34°9S 135°16E 281 E2
Drummond Ra. Australia 23°45S 147°10E 280 C4
Drummondville Canada 45°55N 72°25W 298 C5
Drummoyne Australia 33°51S 151°9E 139 B1
Drumright U.S.A. 35°59N 96°36W 314 D6
Druskeniki = Druskininkai
Lithuania 54°3N 23°58E 188 E2
Druskininkai Lithuania 54°3N 23°58E 188 E2
Drut → Belarus 53°8N 30°5E 177 B16
Druya Belarus 55°45N 27°28E 188 E4
Druzhba Bulgaria 43°15N 28°1E 203 C12
Druzhina Russia 68°14N 145°18E 215 C15
Drvar Bos.-H. 44°21N 16°23E 199 D13
Drvenik Croatia 43°27N 16°3E 199 E13
Drwęca → Poland 53°0N 18°42E 185 E5
Dry Harbour Mts. Jamaica 18°19N 77°24W 320 a
Dry Tortugas U.S.A. 24°38N 82°55W 315 F13
Dryander △ Australia 20°13S 148°34E 280 b
Dryanovo Bulgaria 42°59N 25°28E 203 D9
Dryden Ont., Canada 49°47N 92°50W 297 D10
Dryden N.Y., U.S.A. 42°30N 76°18W 313 D8
Drygalski I. Antarctica 66°0S 92°0E 151 C7
Drygalski Ice Tongue
Antarctica 75°24S 163°30E 151 D11
Drylaw U.K. 55°58N 3°15W 121 B2
Drysdale → Australia 13°59S 126°51E 278 B4
Drysdale I. Australia 11°41S 136°0E 280 A2
Drysdale River △
Australia 14°56S 127°2E 278 B4
Drzewica Poland 51°27N 20°29E 185 G7
Drzewiczka → Poland 51°36N 20°36E 185 G7
Dschang Cameroon 5°32N 10°3E 263 D7
Du Gué → Canada 57°21N 70°45W 298 A5
Du He → China 32°48N 110°40E 229 A8
Du Quoin U.S.A. 38°1N 89°14W 310 G7
Du'an China 23°59N 108°3E 228 F7
Duanesburg U.S.A. 42°45N 74°11W 313 D10
Duaringa Australia 23°42S 149°42E 280 C4
Duarte, Pico Dom. Rep. 19°2N 70°59W 321 C5
Dubai = Dubayy U.A.E. 25°18N 55°20E 247 E7
Dubăsari Moldova 47°15N 29°10E 183 C14
Dubăsari Vdkhr. Moldova 47°30N 29°0E 183 C13
Dubawnt → Canada 64°33N 100°6W 297 A8
Dubawnt L. Canada 63°8N 101°28W 297 A8
Dubayy U.A.E. 25°18N 55°20E 247 E7
Dubbo Australia 32°11S 148°35E 283 B8
Dube → Liberia 5°16N 7°29W 262 D3
Dubeč Czech Rep. 50°3N 14°35E 135 B3
Dubele
Dem. Rep. of the Congo 2°56N 29°35E 268 B2
Dübendorf Switz. 47°24N 8°37E 179 H4
Dubica Croatia 45°11N 16°48E 199 C13
Dublanc Dominica 15°31N 61°28W 323 k
Dublin Dublin, Ireland 53°21N 6°15W 120 A2
Dublin Ga., U.S.A. 32°32N 82°54W 316 C7
Dublin Ohio, U.S.A. 40°5N 83°7W 311 D13
Dublin Tex., U.S.A. 32°5N 98°21W 314 E5
Dublin □ Ireland 53°24N 6°20W 166 C5
Dublin ✈ (DUB) Ireland 53°26N 6°15W 120 A2
Dublin B. Ireland 53°19N 6°7W 120 B3
Dublin Castle Dublin, Ireland 120 c2
Dublin Harbour Ireland 53°21N 6°11W 120 A2
Dubna Russia 56°44N 37°10E 188 D9
Dubnica nad Váhom
Slovak Rep. 48°58N 18°11E 181 C11
Dubno Ukraine 50°25N 25°45E 177 C13
Dubois Idaho, U.S.A. 44°10N 112°14W 304 D7
Dubois Ind., U.S.A. 38°27N 86°48W 311 F10
DuBois Pa., U.S.A. 41°7N 78°46W 312 E6
Dubossary = Dubăsari
Moldova 47°15N 29°10E 183 C14
Dubossary Vdkhr. = Dubăsari
Vdkhr. Moldova 47°30N 29°0E 183 C13
Dubove Ukraine 48°10N 23°53E 183 B8
Dubovka Russia 49°5N 44°50E 191 F7
Dubovskoye Russia 47°28N 42°46E 191 G6
Dubrajpur India 23°48N 87°25E 243 H12
Dubréka Guinea 9°46N 13°31W 262 D2
Dubrovitsa = Dubrovytsya
Ukraine 51°31N 26°35E 177 C14
Dubrovnik Croatia 42°39N 18°6E 202 D2
Dubrovytsya Ukraine 51°31N 26°35E 177 C14
Dubulu
Dem. Rep. of the Congo 4°18N 20°16E 264 B4
Dubuque U.S.A. 42°30N 90°41W 310 B6
Dubysa → Lithuania 55°5N 23°26E 184 C10
Duc de Gloucester, Îs.
French Polynesia 20°38S 143°20W 289 f
Duc Tho Vietnam 18°32N 105°35E 236 C5
Ducassous, Pte. Martinique 14°32N 60°50W 322 j
Duchang China 29°18N 116°12E 229 C11
Duchesne U.S.A. 40°10N 110°24W 304 F8
Duchess Australia 21°20S 139°50E 280 C2
Ducie I. Pac. Oc. 24°40S 124°48W 289 K15
Duck → U.S.A. 36°2N 87°52W 315 C11
Duck Cr. → Australia 22°37S 116°53E 278 D2
Duck Lake Canada 52°50N 106°16W 297 C7
Duck Mountain ⌂
Canada 51°45N 101°0W 297 C8
Duckwall, Mt. U.S.A. 37°58N 120°7W 306 H6
Ducos Martinique 14°33N 60°59W 322 j
Duda → Colombia 2°34N 74°3W 328 C3
Duddingston U.K. 55°56N 3°8W 121 B3
Duderstadt Germany 51°31N 10°15E 178 D6
Dudhi India 24°15N 83°10E 243 G10
Dudhnai India 25°59N 90°47E 241 C3
Dudinka Russia 69°30N 86°13E 215 C9
Dudley W. Mids., U.K. 52°31N 2°5W 169 E5
Dudley Ga., U.S.A. 32°32N 83°5W 316 C6
Dudna → India 19°17N 76°54E 244 E3
Dudo Somali Rep. 9°20N 50°12E 267 C7
Dudo, W. → Somali Rep. 9°14N 50°40E 267 C7
Dudub Ethiopia 6°55N 46°43E 267 C6
Dudwa India 28°30N 80°41E 243 E9
Dudwa △ India 28°30N 80°40E 243 E9
Duékoué Ivory C. 6°40N 7°15W 262 D3
Duenas Phil. 11°4N 122°37E 233 F4
Dueñas Spain 41°52N 4°33W 194 D6
Duerê Brazil 11°20S 49°17W 333 D2
Duero = Douro → Europe 41°8N 8°40W 194 D2
Duff Is. Pac. Oc. 9°50S 167°10E 277 B12
Dufftown U.K. 57°27N 3°8W 167 D5
Dufourspitz Switz. 45°56N 7°52E 179 K3
Dugger U.S.A. 39°4N 87°18W 311 E9
Dugi Otok Croatia 44°0N 15°3E 199 D11
Duguima Somali Rep. 1°15N 42°34E 267 D5
Dugnano Italy 45°33N 9°11E 129 A2
Dugo Selo Croatia 45°51N 16°18E 199 C13
Duida-Marahuaca △
Venezuela 3°33N 65°33W 328 C4
Duisburg Germany 51°26N 6°45E 178 D2
Duitama Colombia 5°50N 73°2W 328 B3
Duivendrecht Neths. 52°20N 4°55E 112 B2
Duiwelskloof = Modjadjiskloof
S. Africa 23°42S 30°10E 271 B5
Dujiangyan China 31°2N 103°38E 228 B4
Duk Fadiat South Sudan 7°45N 31°25E 257 F3
Duk Faiwil South Sudan 7°30N 31°29E 257 F3
Dukat Albania 40°16N 19°32E 202 F3
Dūkdamīn Iran 35°59N 57°43E 247 C8
Dukelský Průsmyk
Slovak Rep. 49°25N 21°42E 181 B14
Dukhān Qatar 25°25N 50°50E 247 E6
Dukhovshchina Russia 55°15N 32°27E 188 E7
Duki Pakistan 30°14N 68°25E 240 C3
Dukla Poland 49°30N 21°35E 185 J8
Duku Bauchi, Nigeria 10°43N 10°43E 263 C7
Duku Sokoto, Nigeria 11°11N 4°55E 263 C5
Dula Dem. Rep. of the Congo 4°40N 20°21E 264 B4
Dūlāb Iran 35°39N 51°27E 141 B2
Dulag Phil. 10°57N 125°2E 233 F5
Dulan China 36°0N 97°11E 218 D8
Dulawan = Datu Piang
Phil. 7°2N 124°30E 233 H5
Dulce U.S.A. 36°56N 107°0W 305 H10
Dulce → Argentina 30°32S 62°33W 334 C3
Dulce, G. Costa Rica 8°40N 83°20W 320 E3
Dulcina Antigua & B. 17°35N 61°49W 322 c
Dulf Iraq 35°7N 45°51E 246 C5
Dŭlgopol Bulgaria 43°3N 27°22E 203 C11
Duliu China 39°2N 116°55E 226 E9
Dullabchara India 24°30N 92°26E 241 C4
Dulles Int. ✈ (IAD)
U.S.A. 38°57N 77°27W 143 B1
Dullewala Pakistan 31°50N 71°25E 242 D4
Dullstroom S. Africa 25°27S 30°7E 271 C5
Dülmen Germany 51°49N 7°17E 178 D3
Dulovo Bulgaria 43°48N 27°9E 203 C11
Dulpetorpet Norway 60°34N 12°19E 164 D9
Dulq Maghār Syria 36°22N 38°39E 213 D8
Duluth Ga., U.S.A. 34°0N 84°9W 316 A5
Duluth Minn., U.S.A. 46°47N 92°6W 308 B7
Dulwich U.K. 51°27N 0°5W 125 B3
Dum Dum India 22°39N 88°26E 124 B2
Dum Dum Int. ✈ (CCU)
India 22°38N 88°26E 124 B2
Dum Duma India 27°40N 95°40E 241 B5
Dūmā Syria 33°34N 36°24E 250 E7
Dumaguete Phil. 9°17N 123°15E 233 G4
Dumai Indonesia 1°35N 101°28E 234 B2
Dumalinao Phil. 7°49N 123°23E 233 H4
Dumanjug Phil. 10°4N 123°26E 233 F4
Dumanquilas B. Phil. 7°34N 123°4E 233 H4
Dumaran Phil. 10°33N 119°50E 233 F2
Dumaran I. Phil. 10°33N 119°51E 233 F2
Dumarao Phil. 11°16N 122°41E 233 F4
Dumaresq → Australia 28°40S 150°28E 281 D5
Dumas Ark., U.S.A. 33°53N 91°29W 314 E9
Dumas Tex., U.S.A. 35°52N 101°58W 314 D4
Dumayr Syria 33°39N 36°42E 250 E7
Dumbarton U.K. 55°57N 4°33W 167 F4
Dumbéa N. Cal. 22°10S 166°27E 288 d
Ďumbier Slovak Rep. 48°56N 19°38E 181 C12
Dumbleyung Australia 33°17S 117°42E 279 F2
Dumbo Angola 14°6S 17°24E 265 E3
Dumbrăveni Romania 46°14N 24°34E 183 D9
Dumfries U.K. 55°4N 3°37W 167 F5
Dumfries & Galloway □
U.K. 55°9N 3°58W 167 F5
Dumingag Phil. 8°20N 123°20E 233 G4
Dumitrești Romania 45°33N 26°55E 183 E11
Dumka India 24°12N 87°15E 243 G12
Dumlupınar Turkey 38°53N 30°0E 205 C12
Dümmer Germany 52°31N 8°20E 178 C4
Dümmer ⌂ Germany 52°31N 8°21E 178 C4
Dumoine → Canada 46°13N 77°51W 298 C4
Dumoine, L. Canada 46°55N 77°55W 298 B4
Dumont U.S.A. 40°56N 73°59W 132 A2
Dumont d'Urville
Antarctica 66°40S 140°0E 151 C10
Dumont d'Urville Sea
S. Ocean 63°30S 138°0E 151 C9
Dumoulin Is. Papua N. G. 10°54S 150°46E 286 F6
Dumpu Papua N. G. 5°53S 145°44E 286 C3
Dumraon India 25°33N 84°8E 243 G11
Dumyât Egypt 31°24N 31°48E 251 G2
Dumyât, Far → Egypt 31°32N 31°51E 251 G2
Dumyât, Masabb Egypt 31°28N 31°51E 251 G2
Dún Dealgan = Dundalk
Ireland 54°1N 6°24W 166 B5
Dún Garbhán = Dungarvan
Ireland 52°5N 7°37W 166 D4
Dún Laoghaire Ireland 53°17N 6°8W 120 B3
Dun-le-Palestel France 46°18N 1°39E 173 F8
Dun-sur-Auron France 46°53N 2°33E 173 F9
Dun-sur-Meuse France 49°23N 5°11E 173 C12
Duna = Dunărea →
Europe 45°20N 29°40E 183 E14
Duna-Drava △ Hungary 46°15N 18°50E 182 D3
Duna-völgyi-főcsatorna
Hungary 46°40N 19°14E 182 D4
Dünaburg = Daugavpils
Latvia 55°53N 26°32E 188 E4
Dunaföldvár Hungary 46°50N 18°57E 182 D3
Dunagiri India 30°31N 79°52E 243 D8
Dunaj = Dunărea →
Europe 45°20N 29°40E 183 E14
Dunajec → Poland 50°15N 20°44E 185 H7
Dunajská Streda
Slovak Rep. 48°0N 17°37E 181 C10
Dunakeszi Hungary 47°37N 19°8E 182 C4
Dunapataj Hungary 46°39N 19°4E 182 D4
Dunărea → Europe 45°20N 29°40E 183 E14
Dunaszekcső Hungary 46°6N 18°45E 182 D3
Dunaújváros Hungary 46°58N 18°57E 182 D3
Dunav = Dunărea →
Europe 45°20N 29°40E 183 E14
Dunavațu de Jos
Romania 44°59N 29°13E 183 F14
Dunavtsi Bulgaria 43°57N 22°53E 202 C6
Dunay Russia 42°52N 132°22E 220 C6
Dunayivtsi Ukraine 48°54N 26°50E 183 B11
Dunback N.Z. 45°23S 170°36E 285 F5
Dunbar U.K. 56°0N 2°31W 167 E6
Dunblane U.K. 56°11N 3°58W 167 E5
Duncan B.C., Canada 48°45N 123°40W 306 B3
Duncan Ariz., U.S.A. 32°43N 109°6W 305 K9
Duncan Okla., U.S.A. 34°30N 97°57W 314 D6
Duncan, L. Canada 53°29N 77°58W 298 B4
Duncan Dock Cape Town, S. Africa 118 a3
Duncan L. Canada 62°51N 113°58W 296 A6
Duncan Passage India 11°0N 92°0E 245 J11
Duncan Town Bahamas 22°15N 75°45W 320 B4
Duncannon U.S.A. 40°23N 77°2W 312 F7
Duncans Jamaica 18°27N 77°32W 320 a
Duncansby Head U.K. 58°38N 3°1W 167 C5
Duncansville U.S.A. 40°25N 78°26W 312 F6
Dund-Us Mongolia 48°1N 91°38E 217 C12
Dundaga Latvia 57°31N 22°21E 184 A9
Dundalk Ont., Canada 44°10N 80°24W 312 B4
Dundalk Louth, Ireland 54°1N 6°24W 166 B5
Dundalk Md., U.S.A. 39°15N 76°31W 309 F15
Dundalk Bay Ireland 53°55N 6°15W 166 C5
Dundas = Uummannaq
Greenland 77°33N 68°52W 154 B4
Dundas Canada 43°17N 79°59W 312 C5
Dundas, L. Australia 32°35S 121°50E 279 F3
Dundas I. Canada 54°30N 130°50W 296 C2
Dundas Str. Australia 11°15S 131°35E 278 B5
Dundee KwaZulu Natal,
S. Africa 28°11S 30°15E 271 C5
Dundee Dundee C., U.K. 56°28N 2°59W 167 E6
Dundee Mich., U.S.A. 41°57N 83°40W 311 C13
Dundee N.Y., U.S.A. 42°32N 76°59W 312 D8
Dundee City □ U.K. 56°30N 2°58W 167 E6
Dundgovĭ □ Mongolia 45°10N 106°0E 226 B4
Dundrum Dublin, Ireland 53°18N 6°14W 120 B2
Dundrum Down, U.K. 54°16N 5°52W 166 B6
Dundrum B. U.K. 54°13N 5°47W 166 B6
Dunearn Singapore 1°19N 103°49E 138 B2
Dunedin N.Z. 45°50S 170°33E 285 F5
Dunedin Fla., U.S.A. 28°1N 82°46W 317 G7
Dunedoo Australia 32°0S 149°25E 283 A8
Dunfanaghy Ireland 55°11N 7°58W 166 A4
Dunfermline U.K. 56°5N 3°27W 167 E5
Dungannon Ont., Canada 43°51N 81°36W 312 C3
Dungannon Tyrone, U.K. 54°31N 6°46W 166 B5
Dungarpur India 23°52N 73°45E 242 H5
Dungarvan Ireland 52°5N 7°37W 166 D4
Dungarvan Harbour
Ireland 52°4N 7°35W 166 D4
Dungeness U.K. 50°54N 0°59E 169 G8
Dunglow Ireland 54°57N 8°21W 166 B3
Dungo, L. do Angola 17°15S 19°0E 265 F3
Dungog Australia 32°22S 151°46E 283 B9
Dungu
Dem. Rep. of the Congo 3°40N 28°32E 268 B2
Dungun Malaysia 4°45N 103°25E 237 K4
Dungunâb Sudan 21°10N 37°9E 256 C4
Dungunâb, Khalîg Sudan 21°5N 37°12E 256 C4
Dunhua China 43°20N 128°14E 227 C15
Dunhuang China 40°8N 94°36E 218 C7
Dunk I. Australia 17°59S 146°29E 280 B4
Dunkassa Benin 10°21N 3°10E 263 C5
Dunkeld Queens.,
Australia 33°25S 149°29E 281 E4
Dunkeld Vic., Australia 37°40S 142°22E 282 D5
Dunkeld Perth & Kinr.,
U.K. 56°34N 3°35W 167 E5
Dunkerque France 51°2N 2°20E 173 A9
Dunkery Beacon U.K. 51°9N 3°36W 169 F4
Dunkirk = Dunkerque
France 51°2N 2°20E 173 A9
Dunkirk U.S.A. 42°29N 79°20W 312 D5
Dunkuj Sudan 12°50N 32°49E 257 E3
Dunkwa Central, Ghana 6°0N 1°47W 262 D4
Dunkwa Central, Ghana 5°30N 1°0W 263 D4
Dúnleary = Dún Laoghaire
Ireland 53°17N 6°8W 120 B3
Dunleer Ireland 53°50N 6°24W 166 C5
Dunmanus B. Ireland 51°31N 9°50W 166 E2
Dunmanway Ireland 51°43N 9°6W 166 E2
Dunmarra Australia 16°42S 133°25E 280 B1
Dunmore U.S.A. 41°25N 75°38W 313 E9
Dunmore East Ireland 52°9N 7°0W 166 D5
Dunmore Hd. Ireland 52°10N 10°35W 166 D1
Dunmore Town Bahamas 25°30N 76°39W 320 A4
Dunn U.S.A. 35°19N 78°37W 315 D15
Dunn Loring U.S.A. 38°54N 77°13W 143 B2
Dunnellon U.S.A. 29°3N 82°28W 317 F7
Dunnet Hd. U.K. 58°40N 3°21W 167 C5
Dunning Ill., U.S.A. 41°56N 87°48W 119 B2
Dunning Nebr., U.S.A. 41°50N 100°6W 308 E3
Dunn's River Falls Jamaica 18°25N 77°8W 320 a
Dunnville Canada 42°54N 79°36W 312 D5
Dunolly Australia 36°51S 143°44E 282 D5
Dunoon U.K. 55°57N 4°56W 167 F4
Dunqul Egypt 23°26N 31°37E 256 C3
Duns U.K. 55°47N 2°20W 167 F6
Dunseith U.S.A. 48°50N 100°3W 308 A3
Dunsmuir U.S.A. 41°13N 122°16W 304 F2
Dunstable U.K. 51°53N 0°32W 169 F7
Dunstan Mts. N.Z. 44°53S 169°35E 285 E4
Dunster Canada 53°8N 119°50W 296 C5
Duntroon N.Z. 44°51S 170°40E 285 E5
Dunvegan Gauteng, S. Africa 26°9S 28°8E 123 A2
Dunvegan Highl., U.K. 57°27N 6°35W 167 D2
Dunvegan L. Canada 60°8N 107°10W 297 A7
Duolun China 42°12N 116°28E 226 C9
Duomo Italy 45°28N 9°11E 129 B2
Duomula China 34°8N 82°29E 217 F10
Duong Dong Vietnam 10°13N 103°58E 237 G4
Dupax del Norte Phil. 16°17N 121°5E 232 C3
Dupree U.S.A. 45°4N 101°35W 308 C3
Dupuyer U.S.A. 48°13N 112°30W 304 B7
Duqm Oman 19°39N 57°42E 249 C7
Duque de Caxias Brazil 22°46S 43°18W 135 A1
Duque de York, I. Chile 50°37S 75°25W 336 D1
Durack → Australia 15°33S 127°52E 278 C4
Durack Ra. Australia 16°50S 127°40E 278 C4
Durack River Australia 15°32S 127°39E 278 C4
Durağan Turkey 41°25N 35°3E 212 B6
Durak Turkey 39°42N 28°17E 205 B10
Đurakovac Kosovo 42°43N 20°29E 202 D4
Durance → France 43°55N 4°45E 175 E8
Durand Ga., U.S.A. 32°55N 84°46W 316 C5
Durand Ill., U.S.A. 42°26N 89°20W 310 B7
Durand Mich., U.S.A. 42°55N 83°59W 311 B13
Durand Wis., U.S.A. 44°38N 91°58W 308 C8
Durandeau St. Lucia 13°56N 60°59W 323 m
Durango Mexico 24°3N 104°39W 318 C4
Durango Colo., U.S.A. 37°16N 107°53W 305 H10
Durango □ Mexico 25°0N 105°20W 318 C4
Durankulak Bulgaria 43°41N 28°32E 203 C12
Durant Iowa, U.S.A. 41°36N 90°54W 310 C6
Durant Miss., U.S.A. 33°4N 89°51W 315 E10
Durant Okla., U.S.A. 33°59N 96°25W 314 E6
Duratón → Spain 41°37N 4°7W 194 D6
Durazno Uruguay 33°25S 56°31W 334 C4
Durazzo = Durrës Albania 41°19N 19°28E 202 E3
Durban Aude, France 42°59N 2°49E 174 F6
Durban KwaZulu Natal,
S. Africa 29°49S 31°1E 271 C5
Durbuy Belgium 50°21N 5°28E 170 D5
Dúrcal Spain 36°59N 3°34W 195 J7
Đurđevac Croatia 46°2N 17°3E 182 D2
Düren Germany 50°48N 6°29E 178 E2
Duren Sawit Indonesia 6°13S 106°54E 122 A2
Durg = Bhilainagar-Durg
India 21°13N 81°26E 244 D5
Durgapur India 23°30N 87°20E 243 H12
Durham Ont., Canada 44°10N 80°49W 312 B4
Durham Darlington, U.K. 54°47N 1°34W 168 C6
Durham Calif., U.S.A. 39°39N 121°48W 306 F5
Durham N.C., U.S.A. 35°59N 78°54W 315 D15
Durham N.H., U.S.A. 43°8N 70°56W 313 C14
Durham □ U.K. 54°42N 1°45W 168 C6
Duri Indonesia 1°27N 101°15E 234 B2
Durlas = Thurles Ireland 52°41N 7°49W 166 D4
Durlești Moldova 47°1N 28°46E 183 C13
Ḍurmā Si. Arabia 24°37N 46°8E 246 E5
Durmitor Montenegro 43°10N 19°0E 202 C2
Durmitor △ Montenegro 43°15N 19°5E 202 C3
Durness U.K. 58°34N 4°45W 167 C4
Durnford, Pta. W. Sahara 23°37N 16°0W 260 D1
Durrës Albania 41°19N 19°28E 202 E3
Durrow Ireland 52°51N 7°24W 166 D4
Dursey I. Ireland 51°36N 10°12W 166 E1
Dursley U.K. 51°40N 2°21W 169 F5
Dursunbey Turkey 39°35N 28°37E 205 B10
Durtal France 47°40N 0°18W 172 E6
Duru Dem. Rep. of the Congo 4°14N 28°50E 268 B2
Duru Gölü Turkey 41°20N 28°35E 203 E12
Durukhsi Ethiopia 8°31N 45°28E 267 C6
Durusu Turkey 41°17N 28°41E 203 E12
Durūz, Jabal ad Jordan 32°35N 36°40E 250 F7
D'Urville, Tanjung
Indonesia 1°28S 137°54E 231 E9
D'Urville I. N.Z. 40°50S 173°55E 285 A8
Duryea U.S.A. 41°20N 75°45W 313 E9
Dusa Mareb = Dhuusamarreeb
Somali Rep. 5°30N 46°15E 267 C6
Dûsh Egypt 24°35N 30°41E 256 C3
Dushak Turkmenistan 37°13N 60°1E 247 B9
Dushan China 25°48N 107°30E 228 E6
Dushanbe Tajikistan 38°33N 68°48E 217 E7
Dusheti Georgia 42°10N 44°42E 191 J7
Dushore U.S.A. 41°31N 76°24W 313 E8
Dusit Bangkok, Thailand 113 a2
Dusit Zoo Bangkok, Thailand 113 a2
Dusky Sd. N.Z. 45°47S 166°30E 285 F1
Dussejour, C. Australia 14°45S 128°13E 278 B4
Düsseldorf Germany 51°14N 6°47E 178 D2
Düsseldorf Rhein-Ruhr ✈ (DUS)
Germany 51°17N 6°46E 178 D2
Dusti Tajikistan 37°20N 68°40E 217 E7
Duszniki-Zdrój Poland 50°24N 16°24E 185 H3
Dutch East Indies = Indonesia ■
Asia 5°0S 115°0E 235 C4
Dutch Guiana = Suriname ■
S. Amer. 4°0N 56°0W 329 C6
Dutch Harbor U.S.A. 53°53N 166°32W 303 K6
Dutlwe Botswana 23°58S 23°46E 270 B3
Dutsan Wai Nigeria 10°50N 8°10E 263 C6
Dutse Nigeria 11°46N 9°20E 263 C6
Dutton Canada 42°39N 81°30W 312 D3
Dutton → Australia 20°44S 143°10E 280 C3
Dutywa S. Africa 32°8S 28°18E 271 D4
Duved Sweden 63°23N 12°55E 162 A6
Düvertepe Turkey 39°14N 28°27E 205 B10
Dúvida = Roosevelt →
Brazil 7°35S 60°20W 331 B5
Duwayhin, Khawr U.A.E. 24°20N 51°25E 247 E6
Duyfken Pt. Australia 12°33S 141°38E 280 A3
Duyun China 26°18N 107°29E 228 D6
Düzağaç Turkey 38°48N 30°10E 205 C12
Düzce Turkey 40°50N 31°10E 212 B4
Düzce □ Turkey 40°50N 31°10E 212 B4
Duzdab = Zāhedān Iran 29°30N 60°50E 247 D9
Duzer Guadeloupe 16°20N 61°44W 322 e
Dve Mogili Bulgaria 43°35N 25°55E 203 C9
Dvigatelstroy = Kaspiysk
Russia 42°52N 47°40E 191 J8
Dvina, Severnaya →
Russia 64°32N 40°30E 186 B7
Dvinsk = Daugavpils
Latvia 55°53N 26°32E 188 E4
Dvinskaya Guba Russia 65°0N 39°0E 186 B6
Dvor Croatia 45°4N 16°22E 199 C13
Dvůr Králové nad Labem
Czech Rep. 50°27N 15°50E 180 A8
Dwarka India 22°18N 69°8E 242 H3
Dwellingup Australia 32°43S 116°4E 279 F2
Dwight Ont., Canada 45°20N 79°1W 312 A5
Dwight Ill., U.S.A. 41°5N 88°26W 311 C8
Dworp Belgium 50°44N 4°18E 116 B1
Dyakove Ukraine 48°1N 23°0E 182 B7
Dyakovo Russia 55°40N 37°39E 129 B3
Dyatkovo Russia 53°40N 34°27E 188 F8
Dyatlovo = Dzyatlava
Belarus 53°28N 25°28E 177 B13
Dyce U.K. 57°13N 2°12W 167 D6
Dyer, C. Canada 66°37N 61°16W 295 D19
Dyer Bay Canada 45°10N 81°20W 312 A3
Dyer Plateau Antarctica 70°45S 65°30W 151 D17
Dyersburg U.S.A. 36°3N 89°23W 315 C10
Dyersville U.S.A. 42°29N 91°8W 310 B5
Dyfi → U.K. 52°32N 4°3W 169 E3
Dyhernfurth = Brzeg Dolny
Poland 51°16N 16°41E 185 G3
Dyje → Czech Rep. 48°37N 16°56E 181 C9
Dyke Ackland B.
Papua N. G. 9°0S 148°45E 286 E5
Dyker Beach Park U.S.A. 40°36N 74°1W 132 C1
Dymer Ukraine 50°47N 30°18E 177 C16
Dynów Poland 49°50N 22°11E 185 J9
Dyranut Norway 60°22N 7°31E 164 D4
Dyrhólaey Iceland 63°24N 19°8W 155 D7
Dyrnes Norway 63°25N 7°52E 164 A4
Dysart Queens., Australia 22°32S 148°23E 280 C4
Dysart Iowa, U.S.A. 42°10N 92°18W 310 B4
Dyushambe = Dushanbe
Tajikistan 38°33N 68°48E 217 E7
Dyviziya Ukraine 45°55N 29°59E 183 E14
Dzamin Üüd = Borhoyn Tal
Mongolia 43°50N 111°58E 226 C6
Dzaoudzi Mayotte 12°47S 45°16E 272 b
Dzaoudzi ✈ (DZA) Mayotte 12°48S 45°18E 272 b
Dzaudzhikau = Vladikavkaz
Russia 43°0N 44°35E 191 J7
Dzavhan □ Mongolia 48°0N 96°0E 217 C13
Dzavhan Gol → Mongolia 48°54N 93°23E 218 B7
Dzerzhinsk Russia 56°14N 43°30E 190 B6
Dzerzhinskiy Moskva,
Russia 55°38N 37°51E 129 C5
Dzerzhinskiy Moskva,
Russia 55°47N 37°37E 129 B3
Dzerzhinskiy Park Russia 55°50N 37°37E 129 B3
Dzhalal-Abad = Jalal-Abad
Kyrgyzstan 40°56N 73°0E 217 D8
Dzhalal-Ogly = Stepanavan
Armenia 41°1N 44°23E 191 K7
Dzhalinda Russia 53°26N 124°0E 215 D13
Dzhambeyty = Zhympīty
Kazakhstan 50°16N 52°35E 216 B4
Dzhambul = Taraz
Kazakhstan 42°54N 71°22E 217 D8
Dzhankoy Ukraine 45°40N 34°20E 189 K8
Dzhanybek = Zhānibek
Kazakhstan 49°25N 46°50E 190 F8
Dzhargalantu = Hovd □
Mongolia 48°2N 91°37E 217 C12
Dzharkent = Zharkent
Kazakhstan 44°10N 80°0E 217 D10
Dzharylhach, Ostriv
Ukraine 46°2N 32°55E 189 J7
Dzhezkazgan = Zhezqazghan
Kazakhstan 47°44N 67°40E 217 C7
Dzhibkhalantu = Uliastay
Mongolia 47°56N 97°28E 218 B8
Dzhizak = Jizzax Uzbekistan 40°6N 67°50E 217 D7
Dzhugdzur, Khrebet
Russia 57°30N 138°0E 215 D14
Dzhulynk Ukraine 48°26N 29°45E 183 B14
Dzhumgoltau, Khrebet
Kyrgyzstan 42°15N 74°30E 217 D8
Dzhungarskiye Vorota =
Dzungarian Gate Asia 45°10N 82°0E 217 C10
Dzhuryn Ukraine 48°41N 28°18E 183 B13
Dzhvari = Jvari Georgia 42°42N 42°4E 191 J6
Działdowo Poland 53°15N 20°15E 185 E7
Działoszyce Poland 50°22N 20°20E 185 H7
Działoszyn Poland 51°6N 18°50E 185 G5
Dzibilchaltún Mexico 21°10N 89°35W 319 C7
Dzierzgoń Poland 53°58N 19°20E 184 E6
Dzierżoniów Poland 50°45N 16°39E 185 H3
Dzilam de Bravo Mexico 21°24N 88°53W 319 C7
Dzioua Algeria 33°14N 5°14E 261 B6
Dzisna Belarus 55°34N 28°12E 188 E5
Dzisna → Belarus 55°34N 28°12E 188 E5
Dziwnów Poland 54°2N 14°45E 184 D1
Dzūkija △ Lithuania 54°10N 24°30E 161 J21
Dzungarian Basin = Junggar Pendi
China 44°30N 86°0E 217 D11
Dzungarian Gate Asia 45°10N 82°0E 217 C10
Dzur Mongolia 49°39N 95°46E 217 C13
Dzüünbayan Mongolia 44°29N 110°2E 226 B6
Dzüünharaa Mongolia 48°52N 106°28E 218 B10
Dzüünmod Mongolia 47°45N 106°58E 218 B10
Dzyarzhynsk Belarus 53°40N 27°1E 177 B14
Dzyatlava Belarus 53°28N 25°28E 177 B13

E

E.C. Manning ⌂ Canada 49°5N 120°45W 296 D4
E.T. Joshua ✈ (SVD)
St. Vincent 13°8N 61°13W 323 n
E.U.R. = Esposizione Universale di
Roma Italy 41°49N 12°28E 136 C1
Eabamet L. Canada 51°30N 87°46W 298 B2
Eabametoong Canada 51°30N 88°0W 298 B2
Éadan Doire = Edenderry
Ireland 53°21N 7°4W 166 C4
Eads U.S.A. 38°29N 102°47W 304 G12
Eagar U.S.A. 34°6N 109°17W 305 J9
Eagle Alaska, U.S.A. 64°47N 141°12W 303 D12
Eagle Colo., U.S.A. 39°39N 106°50W 304 G10
Eagle → Canada 53°36N 57°26W 299 B8
Eagle, Mt. U.S. Virgin Is. 17°46N 64°49W 321 b
Eagle Beach Aruba 12°32N 70°3W 322 f
Eagle Butte U.S.A. 45°0N 101°10W 308 C3
Eagle Cr. → U.S.A. 38°36N 85°4W 311 F11
Eagle Grove U.S.A. 42°40N 93°54W 310 B3
Eagle L. Ont., Canada 49°42N 93°13W 297 D10
Eagle L. Calif., U.S.A. 40°39N 120°45W 304 F3
Eagle L. Maine, U.S.A. 46°20N 69°22W 309 B19
Eagle Lake Ont., Canada 45°8N 78°29W 312 A6
Eagle Lake Maine, U.S.A. 47°3N 68°36W 309 B19
Eagle Lake Tex., U.S.A. 29°35N 96°20W 314 G6
Eagle Mountain U.S.A. 33°49N 115°27W 307 M11
Eagle Nest U.S.A. 36°33N 105°16W 305 H11
Eagle Pass U.S.A. 28°43N 100°30W 314 G4
Eagle Pk. U.S.A. 38°10N 119°25W 306 G7
Eagle Pt. Australia 16°11S 124°23E 278 C3
Eagle River Mich., U.S.A. 47°25N 88°18W 308 B9
Eagle River Wis., U.S.A. 45°55N 89°15W 308 C9
Eagle Rock U.S.A. 34°8N 118°12W 126 B3
Eaglehawk Australia 36°44S 144°15E 282 D6
Eagles Mere U.S.A. 41°25N 76°33W 313 E8
Eagleville U.S.A. 40°28N 93°59W 310 D3
Ealing □ U.K. 51°31N 0°20W 125 A2
Ear Falls Canada 50°38N 93°13W 297 C10
Earle U.S.A. 35°16N 90°28W 315 D9
Earlimart U.S.A. 35°53N 119°16W 307 K7
Earl's Court London, U.K. 125 c1
Earlsfield U.K. 51°26N 0°10W 125 B2
Earlville Ill., U.S.A. 41°35N 88°55W 311 C8
Earlville N.Y., U.S.A. 42°44N 75°32W 313 D9
Earlwood Australia 33°55S 151°8E 139 B1
Early Branch U.S.A. 32°45N 80°55W 316 C9
Earn → U.K. 56°21N 3°18W 167 E5
Earn, L. U.K. 56°23N 4°13W 167 E4
Earnslaw, Mt. N.Z. 44°32S 168°27E 285 E3
Earth U.S.A. 34°14N 102°24W 314 D3
Eas Vanuatu 16°20S 168°15E 287 F6
Easley U.S.A. 34°50N 82°36W 315 D13
East Anglia U.K. 52°30N 1°0E 168 E9
East Angus Canada 45°30N 71°40W 299 C5
East Antarctica Antarctica 80°0S 90°0E 151 D7
East Arlington Mass.,
U.S.A. 42°24N 71°8W 116 A2
East Arlington Va., U.S.A. 38°51N 77°4W 143 B3
East Aurora U.S.A. 42°46N 78°37W 312 D6
East Ayrshire □ U.K. 55°26N 4°11W 167 F4
East Bedfont U.K. 51°26N 0°28W 125 B1
East Beskids = Vychodné Beskydy
Europe 49°20N 22°0E 181 B15
East Boston U.S.A. 42°22N 71°1W 116 A2
East Brady U.S.A. 40°59N 79°37W 312 F5
East Branch Clarion River L.
U.S.A. 41°35N 78°35W 312 E6
East C. = Dezhneva, Mys
Russia 66°5N 169°40W 215 C19
East C. N.Z. 37°42S 178°35E 284 D7
East C. Papua N. G. 10°13S 150°53E 286 F6
East Caroline Basin
Pac. Oc. 4°0N 146°45E 288 G6
East Chicago U.S.A. 41°38N 87°27W 311 C9
East China Sea Asia 30°0N 126°0E 219 F14
East Coulee Canada 51°23N 112°27W 296 C6
East Dereham = Dereham
U.K. 52°41N 0°57E 169 E8
East Don → Canada 43°48N 79°25W 141 A2
East Don Parkland
Canada 43°47N 79°22W 141 A2
East Dublin U.S.A. 32°32N 82°52W 316 C7
East Dubuque U.S.A. 42°30N 90°39W 310 B6
East Dunbartonshire □
U.K. 55°57N 4°13W 167 F4
East Elmhurst U.S.A. 40°45N 73°52W 132 B2
East End Pt. Bahamas 25°33N 76°31W 153 b
East Falkland Falk. Is. 51°30S 58°30W 153 f
East Finchley U.K. 51°35N 0°10W 125 A2
East Flatbush U.S.A. 40°39N 73°55W 132 C2
East Fork White →
U.S.A. 38°33N 87°14W 311 F9
East Grand Forks U.S.A. 47°56N 97°1W 308 B5
East Grand Rapids
U.S.A. 42°58N 85°37W 311 B11

East Greenwich U.S.A. 41°40N 71°27W 313 E13
East Grinstead U.K. 51°7N 0°0 169 F8
East Ham U.K. 51°32N 0°3E 125 A4
East Hartford U.S.A. 41°46N 72°39W 313 E12
East Haydon Australia 18°0S 141°30E 280 B3
East Helena U.S.A. 46°35N 111°56W 304 C8
East Humber → Canada 43°47N 79°35W 141 A1
East Indies Asia 0°0 120°0E 210 J14
East Kilbride U.K. 55°47N 4°11W 167 F4
East Lamma Channel China 22°14N 114°9E 122 B1
East Lansing U.S.A. 42°44N 84°29W 311 B12
East Las Vegas = Whitney U.S.A. 36°4N 115°5W 124 B2
East Lexington U.S.A. 42°25N 71°12W 116 A1
East Livermore = Livermore Falls U.S.A. 44°29N 70°11W 309 C18
East Liverpool U.S.A. 40°37N 80°35W 312 F4
East London S. Africa 33°0S 27°55E 271 D4
East Los Angeles U.S.A. 34°1N 118°10W 126 B3
East Lothian □ U.K. 55°58N 2°44W 167 F6
East Main = Eastmain Canada 52°10N 78°30W 298 B4
East Mariana Basin Pac. Oc. 12°0N 153°0E 288 F7
East Milwaukee = Shorewood U.S.A. 43°5N 87°53W 311 A9
East Molesey U.K. 51°24N 0°21W 125 B1
East Moline U.S.A. 41°32N 90°26W 310 C6
East Naples U.S.A. 26°8N 81°46W 317 J8
East New Britain □ Papua N. G. 6°30S 152°30E 286 D7
East New York U.S.A. 40°40N 73°53W 132 B2
East Northport U.S.A. 40°53N 73°20W 313 F11
East Orange U.S.A. 40°46N 74°12W 313 F10
East Pacific Rise Pac. Oc. 15°0S 110°0W 289 J17
East Pakistan = Bangladesh ■ Asia 24°0N 90°0E 241 D3
East Palatka U.S.A. 29°39N 81°36W 316 F8
East Palestine U.S.A. 40°50N 80°33W 312 F4
East Peoria U.S.A. 40°40N 89°34W 310 D7
East Pine Canada 55°48N 120°12W 296 B4
East Pines U.S.A. 38°57N 76°54W 143 B4
East Point U.S.A. 33°41N 84°25W 113 B2
East Potomac Park Washington, D.C., U.S.A. 143 c1
East Providence U.S.A. 41°49N 71°23W 313 E13
East Pt. Br. Virgin Is. 18°40N 64°18W 321 b
East Pt. N.S., Canada 46°27N 61°58W 299 C7
East Pt. U.S. Virgin Is. 17°45N 64°34W 321 b
East Renfrewshire □ U.K. 55°46N 4°21W 167 F4
East Retford = Retford U.K. 53°19N 0°56W 168 D7
East Riding of Yorkshire □ U.K. 53°55N 0°30W 168 D7
East River → New York, U.S.A. 132 e3
East Rochester U.S.A. 43°7N 77°29W 312 C7
East Rutherford U.S.A. 40°50N 74°5W 132 A1
East St. Louis U.S.A. 38°37N 90°9W 310 F6
East Schelde = Oosterschelde → Neths. 51°33N 4°0E 170 C4
East Sea = Japan, Sea of Asia 40°0N 135°0E 220 E7
East Sepik □ Papua N. G. 4°0S 143°45E 286 C2
East Sheen U.K. 51°27N 0°16W 125 B2
East Siberian Sea Russia 73°0N 160°0E 215 B17
East Stroudsburg U.S.A. 41°1N 75°11W 313 E9
East Sussex □ U.K. 50°56N 0°19E 169 G8
East Talpiyot West Bank 31°45N 35°13E 123 B2
East Tasman Plateau Pac. Oc. 43°30S 152°0E 288 M7
East Tawas U.S.A. 44°17N 83°29W 309 C12
East Timor ■ Asia 8°50S 126°0E 231 F7
East Toorale Australia 30°27S 145°28E 281 E4
East Troy U.S.A. 42°47N 88°24W 311 B8
East Village New York, U.S.A. 132 e2
East Walker → U.S.A. 38°52N 119°10W 306 G7
East Wickham U.K. 51°28N 0°5E 125 B4
East Windsor U.S.A. 40°17N 74°34W 313 F10
East York Canada 43°40N 79°22W 141 A2
East Youngstown = Campbell U.S.A. 41°5N 80°37W 312 E4
Eastbourne N.Z. 41°19S 174°55E 143 B2
Eastbourne E. Sussex, U.K. 50°46N 0°18E 169 G8
Eastcote U.K. 51°34N 0°23W 125 A1
Eastend Canada 49°32N 108°50W 297 D7
Easter Fracture Zone Pac. Oc. 25°0S 115°0W 289 K16
Easter Howgate U.K. 55°52N 3°12W 121 B2
Easter I. = Pascua, I. de Chile 27°7S 109°23W 330 b
Eastern □ Ghana 6°30N 0°30W 263 D4
Eastern □ Kenya 0°0 38°30E 268 C4
Eastern □ S. Leone 8°15N 11°0W 262 D2
Eastern Cape □ S. Africa 32°0S 26°0E 270 D4
Eastern Cr. → Australia 20°40S 141°35E 280 C3
Eastern Desert = Es Sahrâ' Esh Sharqîya Egypt 27°30N 32°30E 256 B3
Eastern Equatoria □ South Sudan 5°0N 33°0E 257 G3
Eastern Ghats India 14°0N 78°50E 245 H4
Eastern Group = Lau Group Fiji 17°0S 178°30W 287 A3
Eastern Group Australia 33°30S 124°30E 279 F3
Eastern Guruma ✪ Australia 22°0S 117°30E 278 D2
Eastern Highlands □ Papua N. G. 6°30S 145°35E 286 D3
Eastern I. Midway Is. 28°12N 177°19W 302 c
Eastern Samar □ Phil. 11°40N 125°40E 233 F5
Eastern Transvaal = Mpumalanga □ S. Africa 26°0S 30°0E 271 C5
Easterville Canada 53°8N 99°49W 297 C9
Easthampton U.S.A. 42°16N 72°40W 313 D12
Eastlake U.S.A. 41°40N 81°26W 312 E3
Eastland U.S.A. 32°24N 98°49W 314 E5
Eastleigh U.K. 50°58N 1°21W 169 G6
Eastmain Canada 52°10N 78°30W 298 B4
Eastmain → Canada 52°27N 78°26W 298 B4
Eastman Qué., Canada 45°18N 72°19W 313 A12
Eastman Ga., U.S.A. 32°12N 83°11W 316 C6
Eastman Wis., U.S.A. 43°10N 91°1W 310 A5
Easton Md., U.S.A. 38°47N 76°5W 309 F15
Easton Pa., U.S.A. 40°41N 75°13W 313 F9
Easton Wash., U.S.A. 47°14N 121°11W 306 C5
Eastover U.S.A. 33°52N 80°41W 316 B9
Eastpoint U.S.A. 29°44N 84°53W 316 F5
Eastpoint Park Canada 43°46N 79°10W 141 A4
Eastport U.S.A. 44°56N 67°0W 309 C20
Eastsound U.S.A. 48°42N 122°55W 306 B4
Eastwood Australia 33°47S 151°4E 139 A1
Eaton Colo., U.S.A. 40°32N 104°42W 304 F11
Eaton Ohio, U.S.A. 39°45N 84°38W 311 E12
Eaton Canyon Park U.S.A. 34°10N 118°7W 126 A4
Eaton Centre Toronto, Canada 141 a2
Eaton Rapids U.S.A. 42°31N 84°39W 311 B12
Eatonia Canada 51°13N 109°25W 297 C7
Eatonton U.S.A. 33°20N 83°23W 316 B6
Eatontown U.S.A. 40°19N 74°4W 313 F10
Eatonville U.S.A. 46°52N 122°16W 306 D4
Eau Claire Fr. Guiana 3°30N 53°40W 329 C7
Eau Claire Wis., U.S.A. 44°49N 91°30W 308 C8
Eau Claire, L. à l' Canada 56°10N 74°25W 298 A5
Eauripik Rise Pac. Oc. 2°0N 142°0E 288 G6
Eauze France 43°53N 0°7E 174 E4
Eban Nigeria 9°40N 4°50E 263 D5
Ebanga Angola 12°45S 14°45E 265 E2
Ebangalakata Dem. Rep. of the Congo 0°29S 21°29E 264 C4
Ebano Mexico 22°13N 98°24W 319 C5
Ebara Japan 35°35N 139°42E 140 B3
Ebbegebirge ⌂ Germany 51°10N 7°55E 178 D3
Ebbw Vale U.K. 51°46N 3°12W 169 F4
Ebebiyín Eq. Guin. 2°9N 11°20E 264 B2
Ebel Gabon 0°7N 11°5E 264 B2
Ebeltoft Denmark 56°12N 10°41E 163 H4
Ebeltoft Vig Denmark 56°10N 10°35E 163 H4
Ebensburg U.S.A. 40°29N 78°44W 312 F6
Ebensee Austria 47°48N 13°46E 180 D6
Eber Gölü Turkey 38°38N 31°11E 212 C4
Eberbach Germany 49°28N 8°59E 179 F4
Eberswalde-Finow Germany 52°50N 13°49E 178 C9
Ebetsu Japan 43°7N 141°34E 220 C10
Ebey's Landing ⌂ U.S.A. 48°12N 122°41W 306 E4
Ebian China 29°11N 103°13E 228 C4
Ebingen Germany 48°13N 9°1E 179 G5
Ebino Japan 32°2N 130°48E 222 E2
Ebinur Hu China 44°55N 82°55E 217 D10
Ebisu Japan 35°38N 139°42E 140 E3
Ebla Syria 35°50N 36°48E 250 C7
Ebo Angola 11°40S 14°40E 265 E2
Ebola → Dem. Rep. of the Congo 3°20N 20°57E 264 E4
Éboli Italy 40°39N 15°2E 201 E8
Ebolowa Cameroon 2°55N 11°10E 263 E7
Ebonda Dem. Rep. of the Congo 2°12N 22°21E 264 E4
Ebonyi □ Nigeria 6°20N 8°0E 263 D6
Eboy Dem. Rep. of the Congo 2°50N 23°11E 264 E4
Ebrach Germany 49°51N 10°29E 179 F6
Ebre = Ebro → Spain 40°43N 0°54E 196 E5
Ébrié, Lagune Ivory C. 5°12N 4°26W 262 D4
Ebro → Spain 40°43N 0°54E 196 E5
Ebro, Embalse del Spain 43°0N 3°58W 194 C7
Ebstorf Germany 53°2N 10°24E 178 B6
Ebute-Ikorodu Nigeria 6°35N 3°29E 124 A2
Ebute-Metta Nigeria 6°28N 3°23E 124 B2
Ecatepec de Morelos Mexico 19°36N 99°3W 319 D5
Ecbatana = Hamadān Iran 34°52N 48°32E 213 E13
Ecclesville Trin. & Tob. 10°19N 61°8W 323 t
Eceabat Turkey 40°11N 26°21E 203 F10
Ech Chéliff Algeria 36°10N 1°20E 261 A5
Ech Chéliff □ Algeria 36°15N 1°30E 261 A5
Echague Phil. 16°42N 121°38E 232 C3
Echechonnee → U.S.A. 32°39N 83°36W 316 C6
Echigo-Sammyaku Japan 36°50N 139°50E 221 F9
Echinades Greece 38°25N 21°2E 207 C3
Echinos Greece 41°16N 25°1E 203 E9
Échirolles France 45°8N 5°44E 175 C9
Echizen-Misaki Japan 35°59N 135°57E 223 E7
Echmiadzin = Yejmiadzin Armenia 40°12N 44°19E 191 K7
Echo U.S.A. 31°29N 85°28W 316 D4
Echo Bay N.W.T., Canada 66°5N 117°55W 294 D8
Echo Bay Ont., Canada 46°29N 84°4W 298 C3
Echo Park Los Angeles, U.S.A. 127 a1
Echoing → Canada 55°51N 92°5W 298 B1
Echterdingen, Stuttgart ✈ (STR) Germany 48°42N 9°11E 179 G5
Echternach Lux. 49°49N 6°25E 170 E6
Echuca Australia 36°10S 144°45E 283 D6
Écija Spain 37°30N 5°10W 195 H5
Eckental Germany 49°35N 11°12E 179 F7
Eckernförde Germany 54°28N 9°50E 178 A5
Eclectic U.S.A. 32°38N 86°2W 316 C3
Eclipse I. Australia 35°5S 117°58E 279 G2
Eclipse Is. Australia 13°54S 126°19E 278 B4
Eclipse Sd. Canada 72°38N 79°0W 295 C16
Écommoy France 47°50N 0°17E 172 E7
Economy = Ambridge U.S.A. 40°36N 80°14W 312 F4
Ecoporanga Brazil 18°23S 40°50W 333 E3
Écouché France 48°42N 0°10W 172 D6
Ecrins △ France 44°54N 6°18E 175 D10
Ecuador ■ S. Amer. 2°0S 78°0W 328 D2
Ecuador, Volcán Ecuador 1°1S 91°32W 330 a
Écueillé France 47°5N 1°21E 172 E8
Ed Sweden 58°55N 11°55E 163 F5
Ed Dabbura Sudan 17°40N 34°15E 256 D3
Ed Da'ein Sudan 11°26N 26°9E 257 E2
Ed Damazin Sudan 11°46N 34°21E 266 E3
Ed Dâmer Sudan 17°27N 34°0E 256 D3
Ed Dar el Beida = Casablanca Morocco 33°36N 7°36W 260 B3
Ed Debba Sudan 18°0N 30°51E 256 D3
Ed Déffa Egypt 30°40N 26°30E 256 A2
Ed Deim Sudan 10°10N 28°20E 257 E2
Ed Dibeikir Sudan 10°23N 29°9E 266 E2
Ed Dueim Sudan 14°0N 32°10E 257 E3
Eda Japan 35°33N 139°33E 140 E2
Edam Sask., Canada 53°11N 108°46W 297 C7
Edam Neths. 52°31N 5°3E 170 B5
Edane Sweden 59°38N 12°49E 162 E6
Edapally India 11°19N 78°3E 245 J4
Eday U.K. 59°11N 2°47W 167 B6
Edchera W. Sahara 27°2N 13°4W 260 C2
Edd Eritrea 14°0N 41°38E 257 E5
Eddrachillis B. U.K. 58°17N 5°14W 167 C3
Eddystone U.K. 50°11N 4°16W 169 G3
Eddystone Pt. Australia 40°59S 148°20E 281 G4
Eddyville U.S.A. 41°9N 92°38W 310 C4
Ede Neths. 52°4N 5°40E 170 B5
Ede Nigeria 7°45N 4°29E 263 D5
Édéa Cameroon 3°51N 10°9E 263 E7
Edebäck Sweden 60°4N 13°32E 162 D7
Edehon L. Canada 60°25N 97°15W 297 A9
Edelény Hungary 48°18N 20°44E 182 B5
Eden = Bar Harbor U.S.A. 44°23N 68°13W 309 C19
Eden N.S.W., Australia 37°3S 149°55E 283 D8
Eden N.C., U.S.A. 36°29N 79°53W 315 C15
Eden N.Y., U.S.A. 42°39N 78°55W 312 D6
Eden Tex., U.S.A. 31°13N 99°51W 314 F5
Eden → U.K. 54°57N 3°1W 168 C4
Edenburg S. Africa 29°43S 25°58E 270 C4
Edendale Gauteng, S. Africa 26°8S 28°9E 123 A2
Edendale KwaZulu Natal, S. Africa 29°39S 30°18E 271 C5
Edenderry Ireland 53°21N 7°4W 166 C4
Edenhope Australia 37°4S 141°19E 282 D4
Edenmore Ireland 53°22N 6°11W 120 A2
Edenton U.S.A. 36°4N 76°39W 315 C16
Edenville S. Africa 27°37S 27°34E 271 C4
Eder → Germany 51°12N 9°28E 178 D5
Eder-Stausee Germany 51°10N 8°57E 178 D4
Edessa Greece 40°48N 22°5E 202 F6
Edewecht Germany 53°8N 7°58E 178 B3
Edfu = Idfû Egypt 24°55N 32°49E 256 C3
Edgar U.S.A. 40°22N 97°58W 308 E5
Edgars Cr. → Australia 37°43S 144°58E 128 A1
Edgartown U.S.A. 41°23N 70°31W 313 E14
Edge Hill U.K. 52°8N 1°26W 169 E6
Edgecumbe N.Z. 37°59S 176°47E 284 D5
Edgefield U.S.A. 33°47N 81°56W 316 B8
Edgeley Ont., Canada 43°47N 79°31W 141 A1
Edgeley N. Dak., U.S.A. 46°22N 98°43W 308 B4
Edgemar U.S.A. 37°39N 122°29W 136 C2
Edgemont U.S.A. 43°18N 103°50W 308 D2
Edgeøya Svalbard 77°45N 22°30E 150 B9
Edgerton Ohio, U.S.A. 41°27N 84°45W 311 C12
Edgerton Wis., U.S.A. 42°50N 89°4W 310 B7
Edgewater Fla., U.S.A. 28°59N 80°54W 317 G9
Edgewater N.J., U.S.A. 40°49N 73°58W 132 B2
Edgewood Fla., U.S.A. 28°29N 81°22W 133 B2
Edgewood Ill., U.S.A. 38°55N 88°40W 311 F8
Édhessa = Edessa Greece 40°48N 22°5E 202 F6
Edievale N.Z. 45°49S 169°22E 285 F4
Edina Liberia 6°0N 10°10W 262 D2
Edina Mo., U.S.A. 40°10N 92°11W 310 D4
Edinboro U.S.A. 41°52N 80°8W 312 E4
Edinburg Ill., U.S.A. 39°39N 89°23W 310 E7
Edinburg Tex., U.S.A. 26°18N 98°10W 314 H5
Edinburgh Edinburgh, U.K. 55°57N 3°13W 121 B2
Edinburgh Ind., U.S.A. 39°21N 85°58W 311 E11
Edinburgh ✈ (EDI) U.K. 55°54N 3°22W 121 B1
Edinburgh, City of □ U.K. 55°57N 3°17W 167 F5
Edinburgh Castle Edinburgh, U.K. 121 b2
Edineţ Moldova 48°9N 27°18E 183 B12
Edirne Turkey 41°40N 26°34E 203 E10
Edirne □ Turkey 41°12N 26°30E 203 E10
Edison Ga., U.S.A. 31°34N 84°44W 316 D5
Edison Wash., U.S.A. 48°33N 122°27W 306 B4
Edison Park U.S.A. 42°1N 87°48W 119 A2
Edisto → U.S.A. 32°29N 80°21W 316 C9
Edisto Beach U.S.A. 32°29N 80°20W 316 C9
Edisto I. U.S.A. 32°35N 80°20W 316 C9
Edithburgh Australia 35°5S 137°43E 282 C2
Edjeleh Algeria 28°38N 9°50E 261 C6
Edmeston U.S.A. 42°42N 75°15W 313 D9
Edmond U.S.A. 35°39N 97°29W 314 D6
Edmonds U.S.A. 47°48N 122°22W 306 C4
Edmondston U.S.A. 38°56N 76°54W 143 B4
Edmondstown Ireland 53°17N 6°18W 120 B2
Edmonton Queens., Australia 17°2S 145°46E 280 B4
Edmonton Alta., Canada 53°30N 113°30W 296 C6
Edmund L. Canada 54°45N 93°17W 298 B1
Edmundston Canada 47°23N 68°20W 299 C6
Edna U.S.A. 28°59N 96°39W 314 G6
Edo □ Nigeria 6°30N 6°0E 263 D6
Edo → Japan 35°38N 139°52E 140 B4
Edogawa Japan 35°43N 139°52E 140 A4
Edolo Italy 46°10N 10°21E 198 B7
Edøya Norway 63°18N 8°10E 164 A5
Edremit Turkey 39°34N 27°0E 205 B9
Edremit Körfezi Turkey 39°30N 26°45E 205 B8
Edsberg Sweden 59°26N 17°57E 139 A1
Edsbro Sweden 59°54N 18°29E 162 E12
Edsbruk Sweden 58°1N 16°29E 163 F10
Edsbyn Sweden 61°23N 15°49E 162 C9
Edson Canada 53°35N 116°28W 296 C5
Eduardo Castex Argentina 35°50S 64°18W 334 D3
Edward → Australia 35°5S 143°30E 282 C5
Edward, L. Africa 0°25S 29°40E 268 C2
Edward VII Land Antarctica 80°0S 150°0W 151 E13
Edwardesabad = Bannu Pakistan 33°0N 70°18E 240 B3
Edwards Calif., U.S.A. 34°50N 117°40W 307 L9
Edwards N.Y., U.S.A. 44°20N 75°15W 313 B9
Edwards → U.S.A. 41°9N 90°59W 310 C6
Edwards, L. Australia 37°42S 144°59E 128 A1
Edwards Plateau U.S.A. 30°45N 101°20W 314 F4
Edwardsburg U.S.A. 41°48N 86°6W 311 C10
Edwardsville Ill., U.S.A. 38°49N 89°58W 310 F7
Edwardsville Pa., U.S.A. 41°15N 75°56W 313 E9
Edzná Mexico 19°39N 90°19W 319 D6
Edzo Canada 62°49N 116°4W 296 A5
Eek U.S.A. 60°14N 162°2W 303 F7
Eeklo Belgium 51°11N 3°33E 170 C3
Eel → Ind., U.S.A. 39°7N 86°57W 311 E10
Eel → Ind., U.S.A. 40°45N 86°22W 311 D10
Eesti = Estonia ■ Europe 58°30N 25°30E 188 C3
Efate, I. Vanuatu 17°40S 168°25E 287 G6
Eferding Austria 48°18N 14°1E 180 C7
Effigy Mounds ⌂ U.S.A. 43°5N 91°11W 310 A5
Effingham U.S.A. 39°7N 88°33W 311 E8
Eforie Romania 44°1N 28°37E 183 F13
Efoulen Cameroon 2°46N 10°43E 264 B2
Eftelöt Norway 59°33N 9°49E 164 E6
Efxinoupoli Greece 39°12N 22°44E 204 B4
Efzonos Greece 37°55N 23°49E 112 B2
Ega → Spain 42°19N 1°55W 196 C3
Égadi, Ísole Italy 37°55N 12°16E 200 E5
Egaleo Greece 37°59N 23°40E 112 B2
Egaleo, Oros Greece 38°0N 23°36E 112 B1
Egan Range U.S.A. 39°35N 114°55W 304 G6
Eganville Canada 45°32N 77°5W 312 A7
Egedesminde = Aasiaat Greenland 68°43N 52°56W 154 D5
Egegik U.S.A. 58°13N 157°22W 303 G8
Eger = Cheb Czech Rep. 50°9N 12°28E 180 A5
Eger Hungary 47°53N 20°27E 182 C5
Eger → Hungary 47°38N 20°50E 182 C5
Egersund Norway 58°26N 6°1E 164 F3
Egg I. St. Helena 15°58S 5°47W 153 h
Egg L. Canada 55°5N 105°30W 297 B7
Eggedal Norway 60°14N 9°22E 164 D6
Eggegebirge Südlicher Teutoburger Wald ⌂ Germany 51°40N 8°59E 178 D4
Eggenburg Austria 48°38N 15°50E 180 C8
Eggenfelden Germany 48°23N 12°46E 179 G8
Egherta Somali Rep. 2°4N 43°11E 267 D5
Éghezée Belgium 50°35N 4°55E 170 D4
Egholo Solomon Is. 8°25S 157°25E 287 M9
Egilsstaðir Iceland 65°16N 14°25W 155 B12
Egina Greece 37°45N 23°26E 204 D5
Eginio Greece 40°28N 22°28E 202 F6
Egio Greece 38°15N 22°5E 204 C4
Egito Angola 12°4S 13°58E 265 E2
Égletons France 45°24N 2°3E 174 C6
Eglinton I. Canada 75°48N 118°30W 295 B8
Egmont Canada 49°45N 123°56W 296 D4
Egmont, C. N.Z. 39°16S 173°45E 284 F2
Egmont, Mt. = Taranaki, Mt. N.Z. 39°17S 174°5E 284 F3
Egmont △ N.Z. 39°17S 174°4E 284 F3
Egra India 21°54N 87°32E 243 J12
Eğridir Turkey 37°52N 30°51E 212 D4
Eğridir Gölü Turkey 37°53N 30°50E 212 D4
Egtved Denmark 55°38N 9°18E 163 J3
Éguas → Brazil 13°26S 44°14W 333 D3
Egum Atoll Papua N. G. 9°25S 152°0E 286 E7
Éguzon-Chantôme France 46°27N 1°33E 173 F8
Egvekinot Russia 66°19N 179°50W 215 C19
Egyek Hungary 47°39N 20°52E 182 C5
Egypt ■ Africa 28°0N 31°0E 256 B3
Eha Amufu Nigeria 6°30N 7°46E 263 D6
Eheli Algeria 22°26N 4°40E 261 D5
Ehime □ Japan 33°30N 132°40E 222 D4
Ehingen Germany 48°16N 9°43E 179 G5
Ehrenberg U.S.A. 33°36N 114°31W 307 M12
Ehrhardt U.S.A. 33°6N 81°1W 316 B8
Ehrwald Austria 47°24N 10°56E 180 D3
Eiao French Polynesia 8°0S 140°40W 289 f
Eibar Spain 43°11N 2°28W 196 B2
Eibenschitz = Ivančice Czech Rep. 49°6N 16°23E 181 B9
Eiche Germany 52°33N 13°35E 115 A4
Eiche Süd Germany 52°33N 13°35E 115 A4
Eichstätt Germany 48°54N 11°11E 179 G7
Eide Hordaland, Norway 60°31N 6°44E 164 D3
Eide Møre og Romsdal, Norway 62°55N 7°27E 164 B4
Eider → Germany 54°19N 8°57E 178 A4
Eidsbugarden Norway 61°23N 8°16E 164 C5
Eidsbygda Norway 62°36N 7°30E 164 B4
Eidsdalen Norway 62°16N 7°10E 164 B4
Eidsvåg Norway 62°46N 8°2E 164 B5
Eidsvold Australia 25°25S 151°12E 281 D5
Eidsvoll Norway 60°19N 11°14E 164 D8
Eielson U.S.A. 64°40N 147°4W 303 D11
Eifel Germany 50°15N 6°50E 179 E2
Eiffel, Tour Paris, France 134 c2
Eiffel Flats Zimbabwe 18°20S 30°0E 269 F3
Eiger Switz. 46°34N 8°1E 198 B5
Eigg U.K. 56°54N 6°10W 167 E2
Eighty Mile Beach Australia 19°30S 120°40E 278 C3
Eikefjord Norway 61°35N 5°27E 164 C2
Eikelandsosen Norway 60°15N 5°43E 164 D2
Eiken Norway 58°29N 7°14E 164 F4
Eikeren Norway 59°38N 9°58E 164 E6
Eikesdalen Norway 62°28N 8°12E 164 B5
Eil, L. U.K. 56°51N 5°16W 167 E3
Eil Malk Palau 7°0N 134°23E 288 c
Eildon Australia 37°14S 145°55E 283 D6
Eildon, L. Australia 37°10S 146°0E 283 D7
Eilean Sar = Western Isles □ U.K. 57°30N 7°10W 167 D1
Eilenburg Germany 51°27N 12°36E 178 D8
Ein Arik West Bank 31°54N 35°8E 123 A1
Ein el Luweiqa Sudan 14°5N 33°50E 257 E3
Ein Naquba Israel 31°47N 35°7E 123 B1
Ein Rafa Israel 31°47N 35°7E 123 B1
Eina Norway 60°38N 10°35E 164 D7
Einarsstaðir Iceland 65°44N 17°24W 155 B9
Einasleigh Australia 18°32S 144°5E 280 B3
Einasleigh → Australia 17°30S 142°17E 280 B3
Einbeck Germany 51°49N 9°53E 178 D5
Eindhoven Neths. 51°26N 5°28E 170 C5
Einsiedeln Switz. 47°7N 8°46E 179 H4
Eire = Ireland ■ Europe 53°50N 7°52W 166 C4
Eiríksjökull Iceland 64°46N 20°24W 155 C6
Eiríksstaðir Iceland 65°7N 15°25W 155 B11
Eirunepé Brazil 6°35S 69°53W 330 B4
Eiseb → Namibia 20°33S 20°59E 270 B2
Eisenach Germany 50°58N 10°19E 178 E6
Eisenberg Germany 50°58N 11°54E 178 E7
Eisenerz Austria 47°32N 14°54E 180 D7
Eisenhüttenstadt Germany 52°9N 14°38E 178 C10
Eisenkappel Austria 46°29N 14°36E 180 E7
Eisenstadt Austria 47°51N 16°31E 181 D9
Eisenstein = Železná Ruda Czech Rep. 49°8N 13°15E 180 B6
Eisfeld Germany 50°25N 10°54E 179 E6
Eisleben Germany 51°32N 11°32E 178 D7
Eislingen Germany 48°41N 9°42E 179 G5
Eivindvik Norway 60°59N 5°5E 164 D2
Eivissa Spain 38°54N 1°26E 206 D1
Eixe, Serra do Spain 42°24N 3°54W 194 C4
Eizariya West Bank 31°46N 35°16E 123 B2
Ejby Denmark 55°41N 12°24E 118 A2
Ejea de los Caballeros Spain 42°7N 1°9W 196 C3
Ejeda Madag. 24°20S 44°31E 272 C1
Ejigbo Nigeria 6°33N 3°18E 124 A1
Ejura Ghana 7°23N 1°15W 263 D4
Ejutla Mexico 16°34N 96°44W 319 D5
Ekalaka U.S.A. 45°53N 104°33W 304 D11
Ekalla Gabon 1°27S 14°0E 264 C2
Ekanga Dem. Rep. of the Congo 2°23S 23°14E 264 C4
Ekaterinburg = Yekaterinburg Russia 56°50N 60°30E 214 D7
Ekeberg Norway 59°53N 10°46E 133 A3
Ekenäs = Raasepori Finland 60°0N 23°26E 188 B2
Ekenässjön Sweden 57°28N 15°1E 163 G9
Ekerö Sweden 59°16N 17°45E 162 E11
Eket Nigeria 4°38N 7°56E 263 E6
Eketahuna N.Z. 40°38S 175°43E 284 G4
Ekibastuz Kazakhstan 51°50N 75°10E 217 B9
Ekiti □ Nigeria 7°25N 5°20E 263 D6
Eklutna U.S.A. 61°27N 149°22W 303 F10
Eknäs Sweden 59°8N 18°13E 139 B3
Ekoli Dem. Rep. of the Congo 0°23S 24°13E 264 C4
Ekoln Sweden 59°45N 17°37E 162 E11
Ekouamou Congo 0°8N 16°31E 264 B3
Ekoungounou Congo 1°10S 15°52E 264 C3
Ekshärad Sweden 60°10N 13°30E 162 D7
Eksjö Sweden 57°40N 14°58E 163 G8
Ekukola Dem. Rep. of the Congo 0°31S 18°56E 264 C3
Ekuku Dem. Rep. of the Congo 0°41S 21°42E 264 C4
Ekukula Dem. Rep. of the Congo 0°15N 21°30E 264 B4
Ekuma → Namibia 18°40S 16°2E 270 A2
Ekuta Dem. Rep. of the Congo 3°0N 18°50E 264 B3
Ekwan → Canada 53°12N 82°15W 298 B3
Ekwan Pt. Canada 53°16N 82°7W 298 B3
Ekwok U.S.A. 59°22N 157°30W 303 G8
El Aaiún W. Sahara 27°9N 13°12W 260 C2
El Aargub Mauritania 23°37N 15°52W 260 D1
El Abanico Chile 37°20S 71°31W 334 D1
El 'Abbasîya El Qâhira, Egypt 30°3N 31°16E 117 A2
El Abbasiya Sudan 12°10N 31°18E 257 E3
El Abiodh-Sidi-Cheikh Algeria 32°53N 0°31E 261 B5
El Adde Somali Rep. 2°35N 46°9E 267 D6
El Adeb Larache Algeria 27°22N 8°52E 261 C6
El 'Agrûd Egypt 30°14N 34°24E 251 H5
El Agustino Peru 12°2S 77°0W 124 B2
El Agustino, Cerro Peru 12°3S 76°59W 124 B3
El Aïoun Morocco 34°33N 2°30W 261 B4
El Ait Sudan 12°22N 27°27E 257 E2
El 'Aiyat Egypt 29°36N 31°15E 256 J7
El Alamein Egypt 30°48N 28°58E 256 A2
El Alto Peru 4°15S 81°14W 330 A1
El Aouj Mauritania 22°53N 12°49W 260 D2
El 'Aqaba, W. → Egypt 30°7N 33°54E 251 H4
El 'Arag Egypt 28°40N 26°20E 256 B2
El Aricha Algeria 34°13N 1°10W 261 B4
El Arîhâ West Bank 31°52N 35°27E 251 G6
El 'Arîsh Egypt 31°8N 33°50E 251 G3
El 'Arîsh, W. → Egypt 31°8N 33°47E 251 G3
El Arrouch Algeria 36°37N 6°53E 261 A6
El Asnam = Ech Chéliff Algeria 36°10N 1°20E 261 A5
El Astillero Spain 43°24N 3°49W 194 B7
El Avagi Somali Rep. 3°36N 46°57E 267 D6
El Badâri Egypt 27°4N 31°25E 256 B3
El Badrshein Egypt 29°51N 31°16E 251 J2
El Bagur Egypt 30°25N 31°2E 251 H2
El Bahrein Egypt 28°30N 26°25E 256 B2
El Ballâs Egypt 26°2N 32°43E 256 B3
El Balyana Egypt 26°10N 32°3E 256 B3
El Banco Colombia 9°0N 73°58W 328 B3
El Baqeir Sudan 18°40N 33°40E 256 D3
El Baragil Egypt 30°4N 31°9E 117 A1
El Barco de Ávila Spain 40°21N 5°31W 194 E5
El Barco de Valdeorras = O Barco Spain 42°23N 6°58W 194 C4
El Basâlîn Egypt 29°58N 31°16E 117 B2
El Bauga Sudan 18°18N 33°52E 256 D3
El Baúl Venezuela 8°57N 68°17W 328 B4
El Bawiti Egypt 28°25N 28°45E 256 B2
El Bayadh Algeria 33°40N 1°1E 261 B5
El Bayadh □ Algeria 32°30N 1°10E 261 B5
El Bierzo Spain 42°45N 6°30W 194 C4
El Bira West Bank 31°54N 35°12E 123 A2
El Bluff Nic. 11°59N 83°40W 320 D3
El Bolsón Argentina 41°55S 71°30W 336 B2
El Bonillo Spain 38°57N 2°35W 197 G2
El Bosque Chile 33°32S 70°40W 137 C2
El Buheirat = Lakes □ South Sudan 7°0N 30°0E 257 F3
El Bur Somali Rep. 4°40N 46°37E 267 D6
El Burgo de Osma Spain 41°35N 3°4W 196 D1
El Caín Argentina 41°38S 68°19W 336 B3
El Cajon U.S.A. 32°48N 116°58W 307 N10
El Calafate Argentina 50°19S 72°15W 336 D2
El Callao Venezuela 7°18N 61°50W 329 B5
El Campello Spain 38°26N 0°24W 197 G4
El Campo U.S.A. 29°12N 96°16W 314 G6
El Capitan U.S.A. 37°44N 119°38W 306 H7
El Carbón Honduras 15°25N 85°32W 320 C2
El Carmen Bolivia 13°40S 63°55W 331 C5
El Carmen Santiago, Chile 33°22S 70°43W 137 B1
El Carmen Colombia 9°43N 75°8W 328 B2
El Centro U.S.A. 32°48N 115°34W 307 N11
El Cerro Bolivia 17°30S 61°40W 331 D5
El Cerro de Andévalo Spain 37°45N 6°57W 195 H4
El Cocuy Colombia 6°25N 72°27W 328 B3
El Cocuy △ Colombia 6°33N 72°35W 328 B3
El Compadre Mexico 32°20N 116°14W 307 N10
El Corcovado Argentina 43°25S 71°35W 336 B2
El Coronil Spain 37°5N 5°38W 195 H5
El Cortijo Chile 33°22S 70°42W 137 B1
El Cristo, Vaso Regulador Mexico 19°30N 99°5W 128 B1
El Cuy Argentina 39°55S 68°25W 336 A3
El Cuyo Mexico 21°31N 87°41W 319 C7
El Dab'a Egypt 31°0N 28°27E 256 H6
El Daheir Egypt 31°13N 34°10E 251 G5
El Dambahaddo Somali Rep. 3°17N 46°40E 267 D6
El Deir Egypt 25°25N 32°20E 256 B3
El Dere = Ceeldheere Somali Rep. 5°22N 46°11E 267 C6
El Dere Ethiopia 5°6N 43°5E 267 C5
El Descanso Mexico 32°12N 116°58W 307 N10
El Desemboque Mexico 30°33N 113°1W 318 A2
El Dilingat Egypt 30°50N 30°31E 256 H7
El Diviso Colombia 1°22N 78°14W 328 C2
El Djouf Africa 21°25N 6°40W 260 D3
El Djouf Mauritania 20°0N 9°0W 260 C3
El Dorado Sinaloa, Mexico 24°17N 107°21W 318 C3
El Dorado Ark., U.S.A. 33°12N 92°40W 314 E8
El Dorado Kans., U.S.A. 37°49N 96°52W 308 G5
El Dorado Venezuela 6°55N 61°37W 329 B5
El Dorado Springs U.S.A. 37°52N 94°1W 310 G2
El Duqqi Egypt 30°1N 31°12E 117 A2
El Eglab Algeria 26°20N 4°30W 260 C4
El 'Ein Sudan 16°35N 29°22E 257 D2
El Ejido Spain 36°47N 2°49W 195 J8
El Encinar de los Reyes Spain 40°30N 3°39W 127 A2
El Escorial Spain 40°35N 4°7W 194 E6
El Espinar Spain 41°43N 4°15W 194 D6
El Eulma Algeria 36°9N 5°42E 261 A6
El Faiyûm Egypt 29°19N 30°50E 256 J7
El Faourar Tunisia 33°22N 8°45E 258 B1
El Fâsher Sudan 13°33N 25°26E 257 E2
El Fashn Egypt 28°50N 30°54E 256 J7
El Ferrol = Ferrol Spain 43°29N 8°15W 194 B2
El Fifi Sudan 10°4N 25°0E 257 E2
El Fud Ethiopia 7°15N 42°52E 267 C5
El Fuerte Mexico 26°25N 108°39W 318 B3
El Ga'a Sudan 14°16N 29°59E 257 E2
El Gamâliya Egypt 31°10N 31°52E 251 G2
El Garef Sudan 12°3N 34°19E 257 E3
El Gebir Sudan 13°40N 29°40E 257 E2
El Gedida Egypt 25°40N 28°30E 256 B2
El Geneina = Al Junaynah Sudan 13°27N 22°45E 259 F4
El Geteina Sudan 14°50N 32°27E 257 E3
El Gezira Egypt 30°2N 31°13E 117 A2
El Gezira □ Sudan 15°0N 33°0E 257 E3
El Gharbîya □ Egypt 30°50N 31°0E 251 H2
El Ghurîya Egypt 30°2N 31°15E 117 A2
El Gir Sudan 19°50N 28°18E 256 D2
El Gîza Egypt 30°0N 31°12E 117 A2
El Gîza □ Egypt 29°46N 31°18E 251 J2
El Gogorrón △ Mexico 21°49N 100°57W 318 C4
El Goléa Algeria 30°30N 2°50E 261 B5
El Golfo de Santa Clara Mexico 31°42N 114°30W 318 A2
El Gouna Egypt 27°5N 33°47E 256 B3
El Grau Spain 39°0N 0°7W 197 G4
El Hadjira Algeria 32°36N 5°30E 261 B6
El Hagiz Sudan 15°15N 35°50E 257 D4
El Hâi Egypt 29°39N 31°18E 256 J7
El Hajeb Morocco 33°43N 5°13W 260 B3
El Hamma Tunisia 33°54N 9°48E 258 B1
El Hammam Egypt 30°52N 29°25E 256 A2
El Hammâmi Mauritania 23°3N 11°30W 260 D2
El Hâmûl Egypt 31°18N 31°9E 251 G2
El Hamurre Somali Rep. 7°13N 48°54E 267 C6
El Hank Mauritania 24°30N 7°0W 260 D3
El Hasian W. Sahara 26°20N 14°0W 260 C2
El Hawata Sudan 13°25N 34°42E 257 E3
El Hideib Sudan 13°10N 32°0E 257 E3
El Hilla Sudan 13°24N 27°2E 257 E2
El Homr Algeria 29°43N 1°45E 261 C5
El 'Idisât Egypt 25°30N 32°35E 256 B3
El Iskandarîya Egypt 31°13N 29°58E 256 H7
El Jadida Morocco 33°11N 8°17W 260 B3
El Jadida □ Morocco 32°45N 8°30W 260 B3
El Jardal Honduras 14°54N 88°50W 320 D2
El Jebelein Sudan 12°40N 32°55E 257 E3
El Jebha Morocco 35°11N 4°43W 260 A4
El Jem Tunisia 35°19N 10°41E 258 A2
El Kab Sudan 19°27N 32°46E 256 D3
El Kafr el Sharqi Egypt 31°16N 31°10E 256 H7
El Kala Algeria 36°53N 8°26E 261 A6
El Kamlin Sudan 15°3N 33°11E 257 D3
El Kantara Algeria 35°14N 5°45E 261 A6
El Kantara Tunisia 33°45N 10°58E 258 B2
El Karaba Sudan 18°32N 33°41E 256 D3
El Kef Tunisia 36°12N 8°47E 258 A1
El Kef □ Tunisia 36°0N 9°0E 261 A6
El Keläa de Srahna Morocco 32°4N 7°27W 260 B3
El Keläa de Srahna □ Morocco 32°10N 7°45W 260 B3
El Keläa M'Gouna Morocco 31°14N 6°7W 260 B3
El Kere Ethiopia 5°50N 42°5E 257 F5
El Khadr West Bank 31°42N 35°10E 123 B1
El Khalîfa Egypt 30°0N 31°15E 117 A2
El Khandaq Sudan 18°30N 30°30E 256 D3
El Khanka Egypt 30°13N 31°21E 251 H2
El Khârga Egypt 25°30N 30°33E 256 B3
El Khartûm Sudan 15°31N 32°35E 257 D3
El Khartûm □ Sudan 15°30N 33°0E 257 D3
El Khartûm Bahri Sudan 15°40N 32°31E 257 D3
El Khroub Algeria 36°10N 6°55E 261 A6
El Kôm el Ahmar Egypt 30°6N 31°10E 117 A2
El Kseur Algeria 36°46N 4°49E 261 A5
El Ksiba Morocco 32°45N 6°1W 260 B3
El Kuntilla Egypt 30°1N 34°45E 251 H5
El Laqâwa Sudan 11°25N 29°1E 257 E2
El Leh Ethiopia 3°46N 39°13E 257 G4
El Leiya Sudan 16°15N 35°28E 257 D4
El Leoncito △ Argentina 31°58S 69°10W 334 C2
El Limón Panama 9°15N 79°49W 320 c
El Lucero Mexico 30°37N 106°31W 318 A3
El Ma'âdi Egypt 29°57N 31°15E 117 B2
El Maestrazgo Spain 40°30N 0°25W 196 E4
El Mafâza Sudan 13°38N 34°30E 257 E3
El Maghra Egypt 30°15N 28°55E 256 A2
El Mahalla el Kubra Egypt 31°0N 31°0E 256 H7
El Mahârîq Egypt 25°35N 30°35E 256 B3
El Maîmûn Egypt 29°14N 31°12E 256 J7
El Maitén Argentina 42°3S 71°10W 336 B2
El Maiz Algeria 28°19N 0°9W 261 C4
El Maks el Bahari Egypt 24°30N 30°40E 256 C3
El Malpais ⌂ U.S.A. 34°53N 108°3W 305 J10
El Manshâh Egypt 26°26N 31°50E 256 B3
El Mansour Algeria 27°47N 0°14W 261 C4
El Mansûra Egypt 31°0N 31°19E 256 H7
El Manteco Venezuela 7°38N 62°45W 329 B5
El Manzala Egypt 31°10N 31°50E 256 H7
El Marâgha Egypt 26°35N 31°10E 256 B3
El Masid Sudan 15°15N 33°0E 257 D3
El Masnou Spain 41°28N 2°20E 196 D7
El Matarîya El Mansûra, Egypt 31°15N 32°0E 256 H8
El Matarîya El Qâhira, Egypt 30°7N 31°18E 117 A2
El Meda Ethiopia 5°39N 41°47E 257 F5
El Medano Canary Is. 28°3N 16°32W 153 e1
El Meghaier Algeria 33°55N 5°58E 261 B6
El Ménia = El Goléa Algeria 30°30N 2°50E 261 B5
El Meraguen Algeria 28°0N 0°7W 261 C4
El Metemma Sudan 16°50N 33°10E 257 D3
El Miamo Venezuela 7°39N 61°46W 329 B5
El Milagro Argentina 30°59S 65°59W 334 C2
El Milia Algeria 36°51N 6°13E 261 A6
El Minufîya □ Egypt 30°30N 31°0E 251 H2
El Minyâ Egypt 28°7N 30°33E 256 B3
El Mohandessin Egypt 30°2N 31°11E 117 A2
El Monte U.S.A. 34°4N 118°1W 126 B4
El Montseny Spain 41°55N 2°25E 196 D7
El Mreiti Mauritania 23°29N 7°51W 260 D3
El Mreyye Mauritania 18°0N 6°0W 262 B3
El Muqattam Egypt 30°1N 31°17E 117 A2
El Mûski Egypt 30°3N 31°15E 117 A2
El Nido Phil. 11°10N 119°25E 233 F2
El Niybo Ethiopia 4°40N 39°55E 257 G4
El Obeid Sudan 13°8N 30°10E 257 E3
El Odaiya Sudan 12°8N 28°12E 257 E2
El Oro Mexico 19°51N 100°7W 319 D4
El Oro □ Ecuador 3°30S 79°50W 328 D2
El Oued Algeria 33°20N 6°58E 261 B6
El Oued □ Algeria 33°10N 7°15E 261 B6
El Palmar Bolivia 17°50S 63°9W 331 D5
El Palmar Venezuela 7°58N 61°53W 329 B5
El Palmar △ Argentina 32°10S 58°31W 334 C4
El Palmito, Presa Mexico 25°40N 105°30W 318 B3
El Pardo Spain 40°30N 3°46W 127 A1
El Paso = Derby U.S.A. 37°33N 97°16W 308 G5
El Paso Ill., U.S.A. 40°44N 89°1W 310 D7
El Paso Tex., U.S.A. 31°45N 106°29W 314 F1
El Pedernoso Spain 39°29N 2°45W 197 F2
El Pedroso Spain 37°51N 5°45W 195 H5
El Pilar Venezuela 10°32N 63°9W 329 A5
El Pinacate y Gran Desierto de Altar = Gran Desierto del Pinacate ⌂ Mexico 31°51N 113°32W 318 A2
El Pobo de Dueñas Spain 40°46N 1°39W 196 E3
El Portal Calif., U.S.A. 37°41N 119°47W 306 H7
El Portal Fla., U.S.A. 25°51N 80°11W 128 A2
El Porvenir Mexico 31°15N 105°51W 318 A3
El Prat de Llobregat Spain 41°19N 2°5E 114 B1
El Progreso Galápagos Is., Ecuador 0°54S 89°33W 330 a
El Progreso Honduras 15°26N 87°51W 320 C2
El Pueblito Mexico 29°6N 105°7W 318 B3
El Pueblo Canary Is. 28°36N 17°47W 153 e1
El Pueblo de Los Angeles Historic Park Los Angeles, U.S.A. 127 b2
El Puente del Arzobispo Spain 39°48N 5°10W 194 F5
El Puerto de Santa María Spain 36°36N 6°13W 195 J4
El Qâhira Egypt 30°2N 31°13E 117 A2
El Qâhira □ Egypt 30°2N 31°13E 251 H2
El Qanâyat Egypt 30°37N 31°27E 251 H2
El Qantara Egypt 30°51N 32°20E 251 H3
El Qasr Egypt 25°44N 28°42E 256 B2
El Qassâsîn Egypt 30°33N 31°55E 251 H2
El Qubâbât Egypt 29°28N 31°16E 256 J7
El Qubba Egypt 30°4N 31°16E 117 A2
El Quseima Egypt 30°40N 34°15E 251 H5
El Qusîya Egypt 27°29N 30°44E 256 B3
El Râshda Egypt 25°36N 28°57E 256 B2
El Reloj Mexico 19°19N 99°9W 128 C2
El Reno U.S.A. 35°32N 97°57W 301 H20
El Retiro Spain 40°25N 3°41W 127 B1
El Rey △ Argentina 24°40S 64°34W 334 A3
El Ridisiya Egypt 24°56N 32°51E 256 C3
El Rio U.S.A. 34°14N 119°10W 307 L7
El Ronquillo Spain 37°44N 6°10W 195 H4
El Roque, Pta. Canary Is. 28°10N 15°25W 153 e1
El Rosarito Mexico 28°38N 114°4W 318 B2
El Rubio Spain 37°22N 5°0W 195 H5
El Saff Egypt 29°34N 31°16E 256 J7
El Salto Santiago, Chile 33°22S 70°38W 137 B2
El Salto Durango, Mexico 23°47N 105°22W 318 C3
El Salvador ■ Cent. Amer. 13°50N 89°0W 320 D2
El Sauce Nic. 13°0N 86°40W 320 D2
El Saucejo Spain 37°4N 5°6W 195 H5
El Sereno U.S.A. 34°4N 118°10W 126 B3
El Shallal Egypt 24°0N 32°53E 256 C3
El Simbillawein Egypt 30°48N 31°13E 256 H7
El Sombrero Venezuela 9°23N 67°3W 328 B4
El Sueco Mexico 29°54N 106°24W 318 B3
El Suweis Egypt 29°58N 32°31E 256 J8
El Suweis □ Egypt 29°30N 32°15E 251 J3
El Tabbin Egypt 29°47N 31°18E 256 J7
El Talibîya Egypt 29°59N 31°10E 117 B2
El Tamá △ S. Amer. 7°25N 72°25W 328 B3
El Tamarâni, W. → Egypt 30°7N 34°43E 251 H5
El Tarf Algeria 36°46N 8°19E 261 A6
El Tarf □ Algeria 36°45N 8°10E 261 A6
El Thamad Egypt 29°40N 34°28E 251 J5
El Tigre Venezuela 8°44N 64°15W 329 B5
El Tîh, Gebel Egypt 29°40N 33°50E 251 J4
El Tîna Egypt 31°3N 32°22E 256 H8
El Tocuyo Venezuela 9°47N 69°48W 328 B4
El Tofo Chile 29°22S 71°18W 334 B1
El Tránsito Chile 28°52S 70°17W 334 B1
El Tucuche Trin. & Tob. 10°43N 61°25W 323 t
El Tuparro △ Colombia 5°19N 68°28W 328 B4
El Tûr Egypt 28°14N 33°36E 256 B3
El Turbio Argentina 51°45S 72°5W 336 D2
El Uarre Somali Rep. 3°4N 45°20E 267 D6
El Uqsur Egypt 25°41N 32°38E 256 B3
El Valle ⌂ Spain 37°56N 1°6W 197 H3
El Vendrell Spain 41°10N 1°30E 196 D6
El Vergel Chihuahua, Mexico 26°28N 106°22W 318 B3
El Vergel Distrito Federal, Mexico 19°18N 99°5W 128 C2

El Vigía Venezuela 8°38N 71°39W 328 B3
El Viso del Alcor Spain 37°23N 5°43W 195 H5
El Wabeira Egypt 29°34N 33°6E 251 J4
El Wâhli Egypt 30°3N 31°16E 117 A2
El Wak Somali Rep. 2°44N 41°1E 267 D5
El Weguet Ethiopia 5°28N 42°17E 257 F5
El Wuz Sudan 15°5N 30°7E 257 D3
El Yunque, Cerro Chile 33°39S 78°50W 330 c
El Yunque Puerto Rico 18°19N 65°48W 321 b
El Zamâlik Egypt 30°3N 31°12E 117 A2
El Zeitûn Egypt 30°6N 31°18E 117 A2
Elafonisos Greece 36°29N 22°56E 204 E4
Elamanchili India 17°33N 82°50E 244 F6
Élancourt France 48°47N 1°58E 173 D8
Elands Australia 31°37S 152°20E 283 A10
Elandsfontein Junc. = Germiston S. Africa 26°13S 28°10E 123 B2
Elasa Greece 35°18N 26°21E 205 F8
Elassona Greece 39°53N 22°12E 204 B4
Elat Israel 29°30N 34°56E 251 J5
Elati Oros Greece 38°43N 20°39E 207 B2
Elatia Greece 38°37N 22°46E 204 C4
Elâzığ Turkey 38°37N 39°14E 213 C8
Elâzığ □ Turkey 38°40N 39°15E 213 C8
Elba Italy 42°46N 10°17E 198 F7
Elba Ala., U.S.A. 31°25N 86°4W 316 D3
Elbasan Albania 41°9N 20°9E 202 E4
Elbe U.S.A. 46°45N 122°10W 306 D4
Elbe → Europe 53°50N 9°0E 178 B4
Elbe-Seitenkanal Germany 52°45N 10°32E 178 C6
Elberfeld U.S.A. 38°10N 87°27W 311 F9
Elbert, Mt. U.S.A. 39°7N 106°27W 304 G10
Elberton U.S.A. 34°7N 82°52W 316 A7
Elbeuf France 49°17N 1°2E 172 C8
Elbeyli Turkey 36°40N 37°27E 250 B8
Elbing = Elbląg Poland 54°10N 19°25E 184 D6
Elbistan Turkey 38°13N 37°15E 212 C7
Elbląg Poland 54°10N 19°25E 184 D6
Elbow Canada 51°7N 106°35W 297 C7
Elbrus Russia 43°21N 42°30E 191 J6
Elbufer-Drawehn ⌓ Germany 53°8N 10°58E 178 B6
Elburn U.S.A. 41°54N 88°28W 311 C8
Elburz Mts. = Alborz, Reshteh-ye Kūhhā-ye Iran 36°0N 52°0E 247 C7
Elche Spain 38°15N 0°42W 197 G4
Elche de la Sierra Spain 38°27N 2°3W 197 G2
Elcho I. Australia 11°55S 135°45E 280 A2
Elda Spain 38°29N 0°47W 197 G4
Eldama Ravine Kenya 0°3N 35°43E 268 B4
Elde → Germany 53°7N 11°15E 178 B7
Eldey Iceland 63°45N 22°55W 155 D4
Eldon Iowa, U.S.A. 40°55N 92°13W 310 D4
Eldon Mo., U.S.A. 38°21N 92°35W 310 F4
Eldon Wash., U.S.A. 47°33N 123°3W 306 C3
Eldora U.S.A. 42°22N 93°5W 310 B3
Eldorado = Echo Bay Canada 66°5N 117°55W 294 D8
Eldorado Argentina 26°28S 54°43W 335 B5
Eldorado Ont., Canada 44°35N 77°31W 312 B7
Eldorado Ill., U.S.A. 37°49N 88°26W 311 G8
Eldorado Tex., U.S.A. 30°52N 100°36W 314 F4
Eldorendo U.S.A. 31°3N 84°39W 316 D5
Eldoret Kenya 0°30N 35°17E 268 B4
Eldred U.S.A. 41°58N 78°23W 312 E6
Eldridge U.S.A. 41°39N 90°35W 310 C6
Elea, C. Cyprus 35°19N 34°4E 207 E10
Eleanora, Pk. Australia 32°57S 121°9E 279 F3
Eleao U.S.A. 21°27N 157°52W 302 K14
Elefantes → Africa 24°10S 32°40E 271 B5
Elefantes, B. das Angola 13°13S 12°44E 265 E2
Elefantes, G. Chile 46°28S 73°49W 336 C2
Elefsina Greece 38°4N 23°26E 204 C5
Eleftherios Venizelos ✈ (ATH) Greece 37°56N 23°56E 112 A3
Elektrogorsk Russia 55°56N 38°50E 188 E10
Elektroperedacha = Elektrogorsk Russia 55°56N 38°50E 188 E10
Elektrostal Russia 55°41N 38°32E 188 E10
Elektrovoz = Stupino Russia 54°57N 38°2E 188 E10
Elele Nigeria 5°5N 6°50E 263 D6
Elemi Triangle Africa 5°0N 35°20E 257 G4
Elena Bulgaria 42°55N 25°53E 203 D9
Elephant Butte Res. U.S.A. 33°9N 107°11W 305 K10
Elephant I. Antarctica 61°0S 55°0W 151 C18
Elephant Pass Sri Lanka 9°35N 80°25E 245 K5
Elephanta Caves India 18°57N 72°57E 130 B2
Elephanta I. India 18°57N 72°56E 130 B2
Elesbão Veloso Brazil 6°13S 42°8W 332 C3
Eleshnitsa Bulgaria 41°52N 23°36E 202 E7
Eleşkirt Turkey 39°50N 42°50E 213 C10
Eleuthera Bahamas 25°0N 76°20W 320 B4
Eleutheroupoli Greece 40°52N 24°20E 203 F8
Elfin Cove U.S.A. 58°12N 136°22W 303 G13
Elgå Norway 62°10N 11°56E 164 B8
Elgin Ont., Canada 44°36N 76°13W 313 B8
Elgin Moray, U.K. 57°39N 3°19W 167 D5
Elgin Ill., U.S.A. 42°2N 88°17W 311 B8
Elgin N. Dak., U.S.A. 46°24N 101°51W 308 B3
Elgin Oreg., U.S.A. 45°34N 117°55W 304 D5
Elgin S.C., U.S.A. 34°10N 80°48W 316 A9
Elgin Tex., U.S.A. 30°21N 97°22W 314 F6
Elgoibar Spain 43°13N 2°24W 196 B2
Elgon, Mt. Africa 1°10N 34°30E 268 B3
Elgspiggen Norway 62°10N 11°21E 164 B8
Eliase Indonesia 8°21S 130°48E 231 F8
Elikonos Oros Greece 38°18N 22°45E 204 C4
Elim Namibia 17°48S 15°31E 270 A2
Elim Western Cape, S. Africa 34°35S 19°45E 270 D2
Elim Alaska, U.S.A. 64°37N 162°15W 303 D7
Elin Pelin Bulgaria 42°40N 23°36E 202 D7
Elingampangu Dem. Rep. of the Congo 2°0S 24°4E 264 C4
Elipa Dem. Rep. of the Congo 1°3S 24°20E 264 C4
Eliseu Martins Brazil 8°13S 43°42W 332 C3
Elista Russia 46°16N 44°14E 191 G7
Eliza, L. Australia 37°15S 139°50E 282 D3
Elizabeth S. Austral., Australia 34°42S 138°41E 282 C3
Elizabeth Ill., U.S.A. 42°19N 90°13W 310 B6
Elizabeth N.J., U.S.A. 40°39N 74°12W 313 F10
Elizabeth, B. Ecuador 0°36S 91°12W 330 a
Elizabeth City U.S.A. 36°18N 76°14W 315 C16
Elizabethton U.S.A. 36°21N 82°13W 315 C13
Elizabethtown Ky., U.S.A. 37°42N 85°52W 311 G11
Elizabethtown N.Y., U.S.A. 44°13N 73°36W 313 B11
Elizabethtown Pa., U.S.A. 40°9N 76°36W 313 F8
Elizabethville = Lubumbashi Dem. Rep. of the Congo 11°40S 27°28E 269 E2
Elizondo Spain 43°12N 1°30W 196 B3
Ełk Poland 53°50N 22°21E 184 E9
Elk → B.C., Canada 49°11N 115°14W 296 C5
Ełk → Poland 53°41N 22°28E 184 E9
Elk → Ala., U.S.A. 34°46N 87°16W 315 D11
Elk City U.S.A. 35°25N 99°25W 314 D5
Elk Creek U.S.A. 39°36N 122°32W 306 F4
Elk Grove U.S.A. 38°25N 121°22W 306 G5
Elk Island △ Canada 53°35N 112°59W 296 C6
Elk Lake Canada 47°40N 80°25W 298 C3
Elk Point Canada 53°54N 110°55W 297 C6
Elk River Idaho, U.S.A. 46°47N 116°11W 304 C5
Elk River Minn., U.S.A. 45°18N 93°35W 308 C7
Elkader U.S.A. 42°51N 91°24W 310 B5
Elkedra → Australia 21°8S 136°22E 280 C2
Elkhart Ind., U.S.A. 41°41N 85°58W 311 C11
Elkhart Kans., U.S.A. 37°0N 101°54W 308 G3
Elkhart → U.S.A. 41°41N 85°58W 311 C11
Elkhorn Man., Canada 49°59N 101°14W 297 D8
Elkhorn Wis., U.S.A. 42°40N 88°33W 311 B8
Elkhorn → U.S.A. 41°8N 96°19W 308 E5
Elkhovo Bulgaria 42°10N 26°35E 203 D10
Elkin U.S.A. 36°15N 80°51W 315 C14
Elkins U.S.A. 38°55N 79°51W 309 F14
Elkland U.S.A. 41°59N 77°19W 312 E7
Elko B.C., Canada 49°20N 115°10W 296 D5
Elko Nev., U.S.A. 40°50N 115°46W 304 F6
Elkton U.S.A. 43°49N 83°11W 312 C1
Ellas = Greece ■ Europe 40°0N 23°0E 204 B3
Ellaville Fla., U.S.A. 30°23N 83°10W 316 E6
Ellaville Ga., U.S.A. 32°14N 84°19W 316 C5
Ellboda Sweden 59°24N 18°15E 139 A3
Ellef Ringnes I. Canada 78°30N 102°2W 295 B11
Ellen, Mt. U.S.A. 44°9N 72°56W 313 B12
Ellenburg U.S.A. 44°54N 73°48W 313 B11
Ellendale U.S.A. 46°0N 98°32W 308 B4
Ellenor, L. U.S.A. 28°28N 81°25W 133 B2
Ellensburg U.S.A. 46°59N 120°34W 304 C3
Ellenville U.S.A. 41°43N 74°24W 313 E10
Ellerton Barbados 13°7N 59°33W 323 r
Ellery, Mt. Australia 37°28S 148°47E 283 D8
Ellesmere = Scottsdale Australia 41°9S 147°31E 281 G4
Ellesmere, L. N.Z. 43°47S 172°28E 285 H7
Ellesmere I. Canada 79°30N 80°0W 295 B16
Ellesmere Island = Quttinirpaaq △ Canada 82°13N 72°13W 295 A17
Ellesmere Port U.K. 53°17N 2°54W 168 D5
Ellettsville U.S.A. 39°14N 86°38W 311 E10
Ellice Is. = Tuvalu ■ Pac. Oc. 8°0S 178°0E 277 B14
Ellicottville U.S.A. 42°17N 78°40W 312 D6
Ellington U.S.A. 42°13N 79°6W 312 D5
Elliniko Olympic Complex Greece 37°50N 23°45E 112 B2
Elliot N. Terr., Australia 17°33S 133°32E 280 B1
Elliot Eastern Cape, S. Africa 31°22S 27°48E 271 D4
Elliot Lake Canada 46°25N 82°35W 298 C3
Elliotdale = Xhora S. Africa 31°55S 28°38E 271 D4
Elliott U.S.A. 34°6N 80°10W 316 A9
Elliott Key U.S.A. 25°27N 80°12W 317 K9
Ellipse, The Washington, D.C., U.S.A. 143 b1
Ellis U.S.A. 38°56N 99°34W 308 F4
Ellis I. U.S.A. 40°41N 74°2W 132 B1
Elliston Australia 33°39S 134°53E 281 E1
Ellisville U.S.A. 31°36N 89°12W 315 F10
Ellon U.K. 57°22N 2°4W 167 D6
Ellora India 20°1N 75°10E 244 D2
Ellore = Eluru India 16°48N 81°8E 244 F5
Elloree U.S.A. 33°32N 80°34W 316 B9
Ellsworth Kans., U.S.A. 38°44N 98°14W 308 F4
Ellsworth Maine, U.S.A. 44°33N 68°25W 309 C19
Ellsworth Land Antarctica 76°0S 89°0W 151 D16
Ellsworth Mts. Antarctica 78°30S 85°0W 151 D16
Ellwangen Germany 48°57N 10°8E 179 G6
Ellwood City U.S.A. 40°52N 80°17W 312 F4
Ellzey U.S.A. 29°19N 82°48W 317 F7
Elm Switz. 46°54N 9°10E 179 J5
Elm-Lappwald ⌓ Germany 52°15N 10°50E 178 C6
Elma Man., Canada 49°52N 95°55W 297 D9
Elma Wash., U.S.A. 47°0N 123°25W 306 D3
Elmadağ Turkey 39°55N 33°14E 212 C5
Elmalı Turkey 36°44N 29°56E 205 E11
Elmers End U.K. 51°23N 0°2W 125 B3
Elmhurst Ill., U.S.A. 41°53N 87°56W 311 C9
Elmhurst N.Y., U.S.A. 40°44N 73°53W 132 B2
Elmina Ghana 5°5N 1°21W 263 D4
Elmira Ont., Canada 43°36N 80°33W 312 C4
Elmira N.Y., U.S.A. 42°6N 76°48W 312 D8
Elmira Heights U.S.A. 42°8N 76°50W 312 D8
Elmodel U.S.A. 31°21N 84°29W 316 D5
Elmore Vic., Australia 36°30S 144°37E 282 D6
Elmore Ala., U.S.A. 32°32N 86°19W 316 C3
Elmore Ohio, U.S.A. 41°29N 83°18W 311 C13
Elmshorn Germany 53°43N 9°40E 178 B5
Elmstead U.K. 51°24N 0°2E 125 B4
Elmvale Canada 44°35N 79°52W 312 B5
Elmwood Ill., U.S.A. 40°47N 89°58W 310 D7
Elmwood La., U.S.A. 29°57N 90°11W 131 B1
Elmwood Park Ill., U.S.A. 41°55N 87°48W 119 B2
Elmwood Park N.J., U.S.A. 40°54N 74°7W 132 A1
Elne France 42°36N 2°58E 174 F6
Elnesvågen Norway 62°52N 7°10E 164 B4
Elnora U.S.A. 38°53N 87°5W 311 F9
Eloaua I. Papua N. G. 1°38S 149°40E 286 A5
Elobey, Is. Eq. Guin. 1°1N 9°29E 264 B1
Elongo Dem. Rep. of the Congo 0°19S 21°39E 264 C4
Elora Canada 43°41N 80°26W 312 C4
Elorza Venezuela 7°3N 69°31W 328 B4
Elos Greece 36°46N 22°43E 204 E4
Elounda Greece 35°16N 25°42E 207 E6
Eloy U.S.A. 32°45N 111°33W 305 K8
Éloyes France 48°6N 6°36E 173 D13
Elphin Canada 44°55N 76°37W 313 B8
Elpitiya Sri Lanka 6°17N 80°10E 245 L5
Elrose Canada 51°12N 108°0W 297 C7
Elsberry U.S.A. 39°10N 90°47W 310 E6
Elsby △ Australia 14°55S 133°10E 278 B5
Elsdon N.Z. 41°8S 174°50E 143 A1
Elsdorf Germany 50°55N 6°34E 178 E2
Elsie Mich., U.S.A. 43°5N 84°23W 311 A12
Elsie Oreg., U.S.A. 45°52N 123°36W 306 E3
Elsiesrivier S. Africa 33°55S 18°35E 118 A2
Elsinore = Helsingør Denmark 56°2N 12°35E 163 H6
Elster → Germany 51°25N 11°57E 178 D7
Elsternwick Australia 37°52S 145°0E 128 B2
Elsterwerda Germany 51°27N 13°31E 178 D9
Eltanin Fracture Zone System S. Ocean 54°0S 130°0W 151 B14
Eltham N.Z. 39°26S 174°19E 284 F3
Eltham London, U.K. 51°27N 0°3E 125 B4
Elton Russia 49°5N 46°52E 191 F8
Elton, Ozero Russia 49°5N 46°42E 191 F8
Eltville Germany 50°2N 8°7E 179 E4
Eluru India 16°48N 81°8E 244 F5
Elvas Portugal 38°50N 7°10W 195 G3
Elven France 47°44N 2°36W 172 E4
Elverum Norway 60°53N 11°34E 164 D8
Elvire → Australia 17°51S 128°11E 278 C4
Elvire, Mt. Australia 29°22S 119°36E 279 E2
Elvo → Italy 45°23N 8°21E 198 C5
Elwell, L. = Tiber Res. U.S.A. 48°19N 111°6W 304 B8
Elwood Vic., Australia 37°53S 144°59E 128 B1
Elwood Ill., U.S.A. 41°24N 88°7W 311 C8
Elwood Ind., U.S.A. 40°17N 85°50W 311 D11
Elwood Nebr., U.S.A. 40°36N 99°52W 308 E4
Elx = Elche Spain 38°15N 0°42W 197 G4
Ely Cambs., U.K. 52°24N 0°16E 169 E8
Ely Minn., U.S.A. 47°55N 91°51W 308 B8
Ely Nev., U.S.A. 39°15N 114°54W 304 G6
Elyria U.S.A. 41°22N 82°7W 312 E2
Elyros Greece 35°15N 23°45E 204 F5
Élysée France 48°52N 2°19E 134 A2
Elysian Park Los Angeles, U.S.A. 127 a3
Elz → Germany 48°18N 7°44E 179 G3
Émaé Vanuatu 17°4S 168°24E 287 G6
eMalahleni S. Africa 25°51S 29°14E 271 C4
Emāmrūd Iran 36°30N 55°0E 247 B7
Emāmzādeh Sāleh Iran 35°48N 51°26E 141 A2
Emån → Sweden 57°8N 16°30E 163 G10
Emao Vanuatu 17°29S 168°30E 287 G6
Emas △ Brazil 18°2S 52°50W 331 D7
Emateloa Dem. Rep. of the Congo 1°16N 18°42E 264 B3
Embajadores Madrid, Spain 127 c2
Embalenhle S. Africa 26°32S 29°4E 271 C4
Embarcación Argentina 23°10S 64°0W 334 A3
Embarcadero, The San Francisco, U.S.A. 136 b3
Embarras → U.S.A. 38°39N 87°37W 311 F9
Embetsu Japan 44°44N 141°47E 220 B10
Embi Kazakhstan 48°50N 58°8E 216 C5
Embi → Kazakhstan 46°55N 53°28E 187 E9
Embonas Greece 36°13N 27°51E 206 E11
Embro Canada 43°9N 80°54W 312 C4
Embrun France 44°34N 6°30E 175 D10
Embu Kenya 0°32S 37°38E 268 C4
Emden Germany 53°21N 7°12E 178 B3
Emecik Turkey 36°46N 27°49E 205 E9
Emei Shan China 29°30N 103°18E 228 C4
Emeishan China 29°31N 103°23E 228 C4
Emek Refa'im Jerusalem 123 c2
Émerainville France 48°48N 2°37E 134 B4
Emerald Queens., Australia 23°32S 148°10E 280 C4
Emerald Vic., Australia 37°56S 145°29E 276 E8
Emerald Buddha = Phra Kaeo Bangkok, Thailand 113 b1
Emerald I. Canada 76°48N 114°10W 295 B9
Emerson Man., Canada 49°0N 97°10W 297 D9
Emerson Ga., U.S.A. 34°8N 84°45W 316 A5
Emeryville U.S.A. 37°49N 122°17W 136 A3
Emet Turkey 39°20N 29°15E 205 B11
Emeti Papua N. G. 7°53S 143°15E 286 D2
Emi Koussi Chad 19°45N 18°55E 259 E3
Emília-Romagna □ Italy 44°45N 11°0E 198 D8
Emilius, Mte. Italy 45°45N 7°20E 198 C4
Emin China 46°34N 83°36E 217 C10
Eminabad Pakistan 32°2N 74°8E 242 C6
Emine, Nos Bulgaria 42°40N 27°56E 203 D11
Eminence U.S.A. 38°22N 85°11W 311 F11
Eminönü Turkey 41°0N 28°57E 122 B1
Emirau I. Papua N. G. 1°40S 150°0E 286 A6
Emirdağ Turkey 39°2N 31°8E 212 C4
Emirgan Turkey 41°6N 29°2E 122 B2
Emissi, Tarso Chad 21°27N 18°36E 259 D3
Emlenton U.S.A. 41°11N 79°43W 312 E5
Emlichheim Germany 52°37N 6°51E 178 C2
Emmaboda Sweden 56°37N 15°32E 163 H9
Emmalane U.S.A. 32°46N 82°0W 316 C7
Emmarentia S. Africa 26°9S 28°0E 123 A2
Emmastad Curaçao 12°8N 68°55W 322 g
Emmaus S. Africa 29°2S 25°15E 270 C4
Emmaus Pa., U.S.A. 40°32N 75°30W 313 F9
Emme → Switz. 47°14N 7°32E 179 H3
Emmeloord Neths. 52°44N 5°46E 170 B5
Emmen Neths. 52°48N 6°57E 170 B6
Emmen Switz. 47°5N 8°18E 179 H4
Emmendingen Germany 48°6N 7°51E 179 G3
Emmental Switz. 46°55N 7°40E 179 J3
Emmerich Germany 51°50N 6°14E 178 D2
Emmet Australia 24°45S 144°30E 280 C3
Emmetsburg U.S.A. 43°7N 94°41W 310 A2
Emmett Idaho, U.S.A. 43°52N 116°30W 304 E5
Emmett Mich., U.S.A. 42°59N 82°46W 312 D2
Emmiganuru = Yemmiganur India 15°44N 77°29E 245 G3
Emmonak U.S.A. 62°47N 164°31W 303 E6
Emo Canada 48°38N 93°50W 297 D10
Emőd Hungary 47°57N 20°47E 182 C5
Emona Bulgaria 42°43N 27°53E 203 D11
Empalme Mexico 27°58N 110°51W 318 B2
Empangeni S. Africa 28°50S 31°52E 271 C5
Empedrado Argentina 28°0S 58°46W 334 B4
Emperor Seamount Chain Pac. Oc. 40°0N 170°0E 288 D9
Emperor Trough Pac. Oc. 43°0N 175°30E 288 C9
Empingham Res. = Rutland Water U.K. 52°39N 0°38W 169 E7
Empire U.S.A. 32°21N 83°18W 316 C6
Empire State Building New York, U.S.A. 132 c2
Empoli Italy 43°43N 10°57E 198 E7
Emporia Kans., U.S.A. 38°25N 96°11W 308 F5
Emporia Va., U.S.A. 36°42N 77°32W 309 G15
Emporium U.S.A. 41°31N 78°14W 312 E6
Empress Canada 50°57N 110°0W 297 C7
Empty Quarter = Rub' al Khālī Si. Arabia 19°0N 48°0E 249 C5
Ems → Germany 53°20N 7°12E 178 B3
Emsdale Canada 45°32N 79°19W 312 A5
Emsdetten Germany 52°10N 7°32E 178 C3
Emu China 43°40N 128°6E 227 C15
Emu Park Australia 23°13S 150°50E 280 C5
eMuziwezinto S. Africa 30°15S 30°45E 271 D5
'En 'Avrona Israel 29°43N 35°0E 251 J6
'En Boqeq Israel 31°12N 35°21E 251 G6
En Gannim = Ramat Gan Israel 32°4N 34°48E 251 F5
'En Gedi Israel 31°28N 35°25E 251 G6
En Na'am Sudan 10°21N 27°58E 266 B2
En Nahrat Mali 22°55N 3°36W 260 D4
En Nahud Sudan 12°45N 28°25E 257 E2
En Nofalab Sudan 15°52N 32°32E 257 D3
En Nuqra Sudan 10°4N 28°10E 266 B2
Ena Japan 35°25N 137°25E 223 B9
Ena-San Japan 35°26N 137°36E 223 B9
Enambú Colombia 1°1N 70°17W 328 C3
Enana Namibia 17°30S 16°23E 270 A2
Enånger Sweden 61°30N 17°9E 162 C11
Enard B. U.K. 58°5N 5°20W 167 C3
Enare träsk = Inarijärvi Finland 69°0N 28°0E 160 B23
Enarotali Indonesia 3°55S 136°21E 231 E9
Encampment U.S.A. 41°12N 106°47W 304 F10
Encantadas, Serra Brazil 30°40S 53°0W 335 C5
Encantado Brazil 22°53S 43°19W 135 B1
Encarnación Paraguay 27°15S 55°50W 335 B4
Encarnación de Díaz Mexico 21°31N 102°14W 318 C4
Enchi Ghana 5°53N 2°48W 262 D4
Encinitas U.S.A. 33°3N 117°17W 307 M9
Encino Calif., U.S.A. 34°9N 118°28W 126 B2
Encino N. Mex., U.S.A. 34°39N 105°28W 305 J11
Encino Res. U.S.A. 34°8N 118°30W 126 B1
Encontrados Venezuela 9°3N 72°14W 328 B3
Encounter B. Australia 35°45S 138°45E 282 C3
Encruzilhada Brazil 15°31S 40°54W 333 E3
Encs Hungary 48°20N 21°8E 182 B6
Endako Canada 54°6N 125°2W 296 C3
Endau Kenya 1°18S 38°31E 268 C4
Endau Rompin △ Malaysia 2°27N 103°45E 237 L4
Ende Indonesia 8°45S 121°40E 231 F6
Endeavour Str. Australia 10°45S 142°0E 286 F2
Endelave Denmark 55°46N 10°18E 163 J4
Enden Norway 61°47N 10°15E 164 C7
Enderbury Kiribati 3°8S 171°5W 277 A16
Enderby Canada 50°35N 119°10W 296 C5
Enderby Abyssal Plain S. Ocean 60°0S 40°0E 151 C5
Enderby I. Australia 20°35S 116°30E 278 D2
Enderby Land Antarctica 66°0S 53°0E 151 C5
Enderlin U.S.A. 46°38N 97°36W 308 B5
Enderrocat, C. Spain 39°28N 2°43E 206 B3
Endicott U.S.A. 42°6N 76°4W 313 D8
Endicott Mts. U.S.A. 68°0N 152°0W 303 C9
Endimari → Brazil 8°46S 66°7W 330 B4
Endwell U.S.A. 42°6N 76°2W 313 D8
Endyalgout I. Australia 11°40S 132°35E 278 B5
Ené → Peru 11°10S 74°18W 330 C3
Eneabba Australia 29°49S 115°16E 279 E2
Enebyberg Sweden 59°25N 17°59E 139 A1
Enewetak Atoll Marshall Is. 11°30N 162°15E 288 F8
Enez Turkey 40°45N 26°5E 203 F10
Enfer, Pte. d' Martinique 14°22N 60°54W 322 j
Enfield N.S.W., Australia 33°53S 151°6E 139 B1
Enfield N.S., Canada 44°56N 63°32W 299 D7
Enfield Conn., U.S.A. 41°58N 72°36W 313 E12
Enfield Ill., U.S.A. 38°6N 88°20W 311 F8
Enfield N.C., U.S.A. 36°11N 77°41W 315 C16
Enfield N.H., U.S.A. 43°39N 72°9W 313 C12
Enga □ Papua N. G. 5°30S 143°30E 286 C2
Engadin Switz. 46°45N 10°10E 179 J6
Engan Norway 63°8N 8°31E 164 A5
Engaño, C. Dom. Rep. 18°30N 68°20W 321 C6
Engaño, C. Phil. 18°35N 122°23E 232 B4
Engaru Japan 44°3N 143°31E 220 B11
Engcobo = Ngcobo S. Africa 31°37S 28°0E 271 D4
Engelberg Switz. 46°48N 8°26E 179 J4
Engels Russia 51°28N 46°6E 190 E8
Engemann L. Canada 58°0N 106°55W 297 B7
Engenho, I. do Brazil 22°50S 43°6W 135 B2
Engerdal Norway 61°45N 11°58E 164 C8
Engershatu Eritrea 16°7N 38°34E 257 D4
Enggano Indonesia 5°20S 102°40E 234 D2
Engineer Group Papua N. G. 10°35S 151°20E 286 F6
Engkilili Malaysia 1°3N 111°42E 235 B4
England U.S.A. 34°33N 91°58W 314 D9
England □ U.K. 53°0N 2°0W 169 E5
Englee Canada 50°45N 56°5W 299 B8
Englehart Canada 47°49N 79°52W 298 C4
Englewood Colo., U.S.A. 39°38N 104°59W 304 G11
Englewood Fla., U.S.A. 26°58N 82°21W 317 J7
Englewood Ill., U.S.A. 41°46N 87°38W 119 C3
Englewood N.J., U.S.A. 40°54N 73°58W 132 A2
Englewood Ohio, U.S.A. 39°53N 84°18W 311 E12
Englewood Cliffs U.S.A. 40°53N 73°59W 132 A2
English U.S.A. 38°20N 86°28W 311 F10
English → Ont., Canada 49°12N 91°5W 297 C10
English → Iowa, U.S.A. 41°29N 91°32W 310 C5
English B. Ascension I. 7°54S 14°23W 153 g
English Bazar = Ingraj Bazar India 24°58N 88°10E 243 G13
English Channel Europe 50°0N 2°0W 169 G6
English Company's Is., The Australia 11°50S 136°32E 280 A2
English Harbour Town Antigua & B. 17°1N 61°46W 322 b
English River Canada 49°14N 91°0W 298 C1
Engures ezers Latvia 57°16N 23°6E 184 A10
Enguri → Georgia 42°27N 41°38E 191 J5
Enid U.S.A. 36°24N 97°53W 314 C6
Enipeas → Greece 39°22N 22°17E 204 B4
Eniwa Japan 43°0N 141°30E 220 C10
Enkhuizen Neths. 52°42N 5°17E 170 B5
Enköping Sweden 59°37N 17°4E 162 E11
Enle China 24°0N 101°9E 228 F3
Enmore Australia 33°54S 151°10E 139 B2
Enna Italy 37°34N 14°16E 201 E7
Ennadai L. Canada 60°58N 101°20W 297 A8
Enné, O. → Chad 14°24N 18°45E 259 F4
Ennedi Chad 17°15N 22°0E 259 E4
Enneri Achelouma → Niger 21°55N 13°35E 261 D7
Enngonia Australia 29°21S 145°50E 281 D4
Ennigerloh Germany 51°50N 8°2E 178 D4
Ennis Clare, Ireland 52°51N 8°59W 166 D3
Ennis Mont., U.S.A. 45°21N 111°44W 304 D8
Ennis Tex., U.S.A. 32°20N 96°38W 314 E6
Enniscorthy Ireland 52°30N 6°34W 166 D5
Enniskillen U.K. 54°21N 7°39W 166 B4
Ennistimon Ireland 52°57N 9°17W 166 D2
Enns Austria 48°12N 14°28E 180 C7
Enns → Austria 48°14N 14°32E 180 C7
Eno Finland 62°47N 30°10E 160 E24
Enontekiö Finland 68°23N 23°37E 160 B20
Enosburg Falls U.S.A. 44°55N 72°48W 313 B12
Enping China 22°16N 112°21E 229 F9
Enrekang Indonesia 3°34S 119°47E 235 C5
Enrile Phil. 17°34N 121°42E 232 C3
Enriquillo, L. Dom. Rep. 18°20N 72°5W 321 C5
Enschede Neths. 52°13N 6°53E 170 B6
Ensenada Argentina 34°55S 57°55W 334 C4
Ensenada Chile 41°12S 72°33W 336 B2
Ensenada Baja Calif., Mexico 31°52N 116°37W 318 A1
Ensenada de los Muertos Mexico 23°59N 109°51W 318 C2
Enshi China 30°18N 109°29E 228 B7
Enshū-Nada Japan 34°27N 137°38E 223 C9
Ensiola, Pta. de n' Spain 39°7N 2°55E 206 B3
Ensisheim France 47°50N 7°20E 173 E14
Enskede Sweden 59°17N 18°4E 139 B2
Ensley U.S.A. 30°31N 87°16W 317 E2
Entebbe Uganda 0°4N 32°28E 268 B3
Enterprise N.W.T., Canada 60°47N 115°45W 296 A5
Enterprise Ala., U.S.A. 31°19N 85°51W 316 D4
Enterprise Nev., U.S.A. 36°13N 115°14W 124 B1
Enterprise Oreg., U.S.A. 45°25N 117°17W 304 D5
Entorno de Doñana ⌓ Spain 37°0N 6°26W 195 J4
Entrance, The Australia 33°21S 151°30E 283 B9
Entraygues-sur-Truyère France 44°38N 2°35E 174 D6
Entre-Deux Réunion 21°14S 55°28E 272 f
Entre Rios = Rio Brilhante Brazil 21°48S 54°33W 335 A5
Entre Rios = Três Rios Brazil 22°6S 43°15W 333 F3
Entre Ríos Bolivia 21°30S 64°25W 334 A3
Entre Rios Bahia, Brazil 11°56S 38°5W 333 D4
Entre Rios Pará, Brazil 5°24S 54°21W 331 B7
Entre Ríos □ Argentina 30°30S 58°30W 334 C4
Entrepeñas, Embalse de Spain 40°34N 2°42W 196 E2
Entrevias Spain 40°22N 3°40W 127 B1
Entroncamento Portugal 39°28N 8°28W 195 F2
Enugu Nigeria 6°30N 7°30E 263 D6
Enugu □ Nigeria 6°30N 7°45E 263 D6
Enugu Ezike Nigeria 7°0N 7°29E 263 D6
Enumclaw U.S.A. 47°12N 121°59W 306 C5
Envalira, Port d' Europe 42°33N 1°43E 196 C6
Envermeu France 49°53N 1°15E 172 C8
Envigado Colombia 6°10N 75°35W 328 B2
Enviken Sweden 60°49N 15°46E 162 D9
Envira Brazil 7°18S 70°13W 330 B3
Envira → Brazil 7°19S 70°15W 330 B3
Enying Hungary 46°56N 18°15E 182 D3
Enyonga Gabon 0°59S 9°22E 264 C1
Enza → Italy 44°54N 10°31E 198 D7
Enzan Japan 35°42N 138°44E 223 B10
Eochail = Youghal Ireland 51°56N 7°52W 166 E4
Eólie, Ís. Italy 38°30N 14°57E 201 D7
Eot I. Micronesia 7°23N 151°44E 287 T17
Epanomi Greece 40°25N 22°59E 202 F6
Epcot U.S.A. 28°21N 81°32W 133 B1
Epe Neths. 52°21N 5°59E 170 B5
Epe Nigeria 6°36N 3°59E 263 D5
Epéna Congo 1°22N 17°29E 264 B3
Épernay France 49°3N 3°56E 173 C10
Épernon France 48°35N 1°40E 173 D8
Ephesus Turkey 37°55N 27°22E 205 D9
Ephraim U.S.A. 39°22N 111°35W 304 G8
Ephrata Pa., U.S.A. 40°11N 76°11W 313 F8
Ephrata Wash., U.S.A. 47°19N 119°33W 304 C4
Epi Vanuatu 16°43S 168°15E 287 F6
Epidavros Limira Greece 36°46N 23°0E 204 E5
Épila Spain 41°36N 1°17W 196 D3
Épinac France 46°59N 4°31E 173 F11
Épinal France 48°10N 6°27E 173 D13
Epira Guyana 5°5N 57°20W 329 B6
Epiros □ Greece 39°30N 20°30E 204 B2
Episkopi Cyprus 34°40N 32°54E 207 F8
Episkopi Kriti, Greece 35°20N 24°20E 207 E5
Episkopi Bay Cyprus 34°35N 32°50E 207 F8
Epitalio Greece 37°37N 21°30E 204 D3
Eppalock, L. Australia 36°52S 144°34E 282 D6
Eppan = Appiano Italy 46°28N 11°15E 199 B8
Epping Australia 33°46S 151°5E 139 A1
Eppingen Germany 49°8N 8°53E 179 F4
Epsom U.K. 51°19N 0°16W 169 F7
Epukiro Namibia 21°40S 19°9E 270 B2
Equality U.S.A. 37°44N 88°20W 311 G8
Équateur □ Dem. Rep. of the Congo 2°0N 21°0E 264 B4
Equatorial Channel Maldives 0°0 73°10E 272 d
Equatorial Guinea ■ Africa 2°0N 8°0E 264 B1
Equeipa Venezuela 5°22N 62°43W 329 B5
Er Hai China 25°48N 100°11E 228 E3
Er Rachidia Morocco 31°58N 4°20W 260 B4
Er Rachidia □ Morocco 31°45N 4°30W 260 B4
Er Rahad Sudan 12°45N 30°32E 257 E3
Er Rif Morocco 35°1N 4°1W 261 A4
Er Rogel Sudan 18°10N 35°25E 256 D4
Er Roseires Sudan 11°55N 34°30E 257 E3
Er Rua'at Sudan 12°21N 32°17E 257 E3
Eraclea Italy 45°35N 12°40E 199 C9
Eran Phil. 9°4N 117°42E 233 G1
Eran B. Phil. 9°5N 117°43E 233 G1
Erandol India 20°56N 75°20E 244 D2
Eranga Dem. Rep. of the Congo 1°52S 18°56E 264 C3
Erap Papua N. G. 6°37S 146°51E 286 D4
Erasmus = Bronkhorstspruit S. Africa 25°46S 28°45E 271 C4
Erave Papua N. G. 6°39S 144°0E 286 D2
Erave → Papua N. G. 6°54S 144°47E 286 D3
Erāwadī Myit = Irrawaddy → Burma 15°50N 95°6E 241 G5
Erāwadī Myitwanya = Irrawaddy, Mouths of the Burma 15°30N 95°0E 241 H5
Erawan △ Thailand 14°25N 98°58E 236 E2
Erba Italy 45°48N 9°15E 198 C6
Erba Sudan 19°5N 36°51E 256 D4
Erba, J. Sudan 20°48N 36°47E 256 C4
Erbaa Turkey 40°42N 36°36E 212 B7
Erbeng Shan China 42°50N 84°59E 217 D10
Erbeskopf Germany 49°44N 7°2E 179 F3
Erbil = Arbīl Iraq 36°15N 44°5E 213 D11
Erbu Ethiopia 6°44N 34°53E 257 E3
Ercan, Nicosia ✈ (ECN) Cyprus 35°10N 33°30E 207 E9
Erçek Turkey 38°39N 43°36E 246 B4
Erçis Turkey 39°2N 43°21E 213 C10
Erciyaş Dağı Turkey 38°30N 35°30E 246 B2
Érd Hungary 47°22N 18°56E 182 C3
Erdao Jiang → China 42°37N 128°0E 224 A3
Erdek Turkey 40°23N 27°47E 203 F11
Erdély = Transilvania Romania 46°30N 24°0E 183 D9
Erdemli Turkey 36°36N 34°19E 250 B5
Erdene = Ulaan-Uul Mongolia 46°4N 100°49E 226 B6
Erdenet Mongolia 49°2N 104°5E 218 B9
Erdenetsogt Mongolia 42°55N 106°5E 226 C4
Erding Germany 48°18N 11°54E 179 G7
Erdre → France 47°13N 1°32W 172 E5
Erebato → Venezuela 5°54N 64°16W 329 B5
Erebus, Mt. Antarctica 77°35S 167°0E 151 D11
Erechim Brazil 27°35S 52°15W 335 B5
Ereğli Konya, Turkey 37°31N 34°4E 212 D6
Ereğli Zonguldak, Turkey 41°15N 31°24E 212 B4
Erei, Monti Italy 37°20N 14°20E 201 E7
Erenhot China 43°48N 112°2E 226 C7
Erenköy = Kokkina Cyprus 35°11N 32°36E 207 E8
Erenköy Turkey 40°58N 29°3E 122 C2
Eresfjord Norway 62°40N 8°8E 164 B5
Eresma → Spain 41°26N 4°45W 194 D6
Eresos Greece 39°11N 25°57E 205 B7
Ereymentaū Kazakhstan 51°37N 73°6E 217 B8
Erfelek Turkey 41°53N 34°55E 212 B6
Erfenisdam S. Africa 28°30S 26°50E 270 C4
Erfjord Norway 59°20N 6°14E 164 E3
Erfoud Morocco 31°30N 4°15W 260 B4
Erfstadt Germany 50°50N 6°50E 178 E2
Erft → Germany 51°11N 6°44E 178 D2
Erfurt Germany 50°58N 11°2E 178 E7
Ergani Turkey 38°17N 39°49E 213 C8
Ergel Mongolia 43°8N 109°5E 226 C5
Ergene → Turkey 41°1N 26°22E 203 E10
Ergeni Vozvyshennost Russia 47°0N 44°0E 191 G7
Ērgli Latvia 56°54N 25°38E 188 D3
Erhlin Taiwan 23°54N 120°22E 225 C2
Erhshui Taiwan 23°45N 120°37E 225 C2
Eria → Spain 42°3N 5°44W 194 C5
Eriba Sudan 16°40N 36°10E 257 D4
Eriboll, L. U.K. 58°30N 4°42W 167 C4
Érice Italy 38°2N 12°35E 200 D5
Eridu U.S.A. 30°18N 83°45W 316 E6
Erie Mich., U.S.A. 41°47N 83°31W 311 C13
Erie Pa., U.S.A. 42°8N 80°5W 312 D4
Erie, L. N. Amer. 42°15N 81°0W 312 D4
Erie Canal U.S.A. 43°5N 78°43W 312 C7
Erieau Canada 42°16N 81°57W 312 D3
Erigavo = Ceerigaabo Somali Rep. 10°35N 47°20E 267 B6
Erikoussa Greece 39°53N 19°34E 206 B9
Eriksdale Canada 50°52N 98°7W 297 C9
Erimanthos Greece 37°57N 21°50E 204 D3
Erimo-misaki Japan 41°50N 143°15E 220 D11
Erin Ont., Canada 43°45N 80°7W 312 C4
Erin Trin. & Tob. 10°5N 61°39W 323 t
Erin B. Trin. & Tob. 10°4N 61°43W 323 t
Erin Pt. Trin. & Tob. 10°3N 61°39W 323 t
Erinpura India 25°9N 73°3E 242 G5
Eriskay U.K. 57°4N 7°18W 167 D1
Erith U.K. 51°28N 0°11E 125 B5
Erithres Greece 38°13N 23°20E 204 C5
Eritrea ■ Africa 14°0N 38°30E 257 E4
Erivan = Yerevan Armenia 40°10N 44°31E 191 K7
Erjas → Portugal 39°40N 7°1W 194 F3
Erkech-Tam Pass Asia 39°46N 74°2E 217 E8
Erkelenz Germany 51°4N 6°19E 178 D2
Erkner Germany 52°25N 13°44E 178 C9
Erlaa Austria 48°9N 16°19E 142 B1
Erlangen Germany 49°36N 11°0E 179 F6
Erlanger U.S.A. 39°1N 84°36W 311 E12
Erldunda Australia 25°14S 133°12E 280 D1
Ermelo Neths. 52°18N 5°35E 170 B5
Ermelo Mpumalanga, S. Africa 26°31S 29°59E 271 C4
Ermenek Turkey 36°38N 33°0E 250 B4
Ermenek → Turkey 36°35N 33°23E 250 B4
Ermil Sudan 13°35N 27°40E 257 E2
Ermington Australia 33°48S 151°4E 139 A1
Ermioni Greece 37°23N 23°15E 204 D5
Ermita Phil. 14°35N 120°59E 127 B1
Ermones Greece 39°37N 19°46E 206 B9
Ermoupoli Greece 37°28N 24°57E 204 D6
Ernakulam India 9°59N 76°22E 245 K3
Erne → Ireland 54°30N 8°16W 166 B3
Erne, Lower L. U.K. 54°28N 7°47W 166 B4
Erne, Upper L. U.K. 54°14N 7°32W 166 B4
Ernée France 48°18N 0°56W 172 D6
Ernest Giles Ra. Australia 27°0S 123°45E 279 E3
Ernest N. Morial Convention Center New Orleans, U.S.A. 131 c3
Ernstberg Germany 50°13N 6°47E 179 E2
Erode India 11°24N 77°45E 245 J3
Eromanga Australia 26°40S 143°11E 281 D3
Erongo Namibia 21°39S 15°58E 270 B2
Erquy France 48°38N 2°29W 172 D4
Erramala Hills India 15°30N 78°15E 245 G4
Errentería Spain 43°19N 1°54W 196 B3
Errer → Ethiopia 7°32N 42°35E 257 F5
Errigal Ireland 55°2N 8°6W 166 A3
Errinundra △ Australia 37°20S 148°47E 283 D8
Erris Hd. Ireland 54°19N 10°0W 166 B1
Erromango Vanuatu 18°45S 169°5E 287 H7
Ersekë Albania 40°22N 20°40E 202 F4
Ersekújvár = Nové Zámky Slovak Rep. 48°2N 18°8E 181 C11
Ershatou China 23°6N 113°18E 121 B2
Erskine U.S.A. 47°40N 96°0W 308 B6
Erskineville Australia 33°54S 151°12E 139 B2
Erstein France 48°25N 7°38E 173 D14
Ertai China 46°3N 90°5E 217 C12
Ertan Shuiku China 27°5N 101°52E 228 D3
Ertholmene Denmark 55°19N 15°11E 163 J9
Ertil Russia 51°55N 40°50E 190 E5
Ertis = Irtysh → Russia 61°4N 68°52E 214 C7
Ertis Kazakhstan 53°20N 75°27E 217 B9
Ertis → Kazakhstan 47°52N 84°16E 217 C10
Ertvågøy Norway 63°13N 8°26E 164 A5
Eruh Turkey 37°46N 42°13E 213 D10
Erunkan Nigeria 6°36N 3°23E 124 A2
Ervy-le-Châtel France 48°2N 3°55E 173 D10
Erwin U.S.A. 36°9N 82°25W 315 C13
Eryuan China 26°7N 99°57E 228 D2
Erzgebirge Germany 50°27N 12°55E 178 E8
Erzin Russia 50°15N 95°10E 217 B13
Erzin Turkey 36°57N 36°11E 250 B7
Erzincan Turkey 39°46N 39°30E 213 C8
Erzincan □ Turkey 39°45N 39°30E 213 C8
Erzsébet-Telep Hungary 47°27N 19°10E 117 B3
Erzurum Turkey 39°57N 41°15E 213 C9
Erzurum □ Turkey 39°55N 41°15E 213 C9
Es Caló Spain 38°40N 1°30E 206 D2
Es Canar Spain 39°2N 1°36E 206 C2
Es Mercadal Spain 39°59N 4°5E 206 B5
Es Migjorn Gran Spain 39°57N 4°3E 206 B5
Es Safiya Sudan 15°31N 30°7E 257 D3
Es Sahrâ al Beida Egypt 27°50N 28°45E 256 B2
Es Sahrâ' Esh Sharqîya Egypt 27°30N 32°30E 256 B3
Es Sînâ' Egypt 29°0N 34°0E 246 D2
Es Sûkî Sudan 13°20N 33°58E 257 E3
Es Vedrà Spain 38°52N 1°12E 206 D1
Esa'ala Papua N. G. 9°45S 150°49E 286 E6
Esambo Dem. Rep. of the Congo 3°48S 23°30E 264 C4
Esan-Misaki Japan 41°40N 141°10E 220 D10
Esashi Hokkaidō, Japan 44°56N 142°35E 220 B11
Esashi Hokkaidō, Japan 41°52N 140°7E 220 D10
Esbjerg Denmark 55°29N 8°29E 163 J2
Esbo = Espoo Finland 60°12N 24°40E 188 B3
Escada Brazil 8°22S 35°8W 332 C4
Escalante Phil. 10°50N 123°33E 233 F4
Escalante Utah, U.S.A. 37°47N 111°36W 305 H8
Escalante → U.S.A. 37°24N 110°57W 305 H8
Escalón Mexico 26°45N 104°20W 318 B4
Escambia → U.S.A. 30°32N 87°11W 317 E2
Escanaba U.S.A. 45°45N 87°4W 308 C10
Escarparda Pt. Phil. 18°31N 122°13E 232 B4
Escarpé, C. N. Cal. 20°41S 167°13E 288 d
Escaut = Schelde → Belgium 51°15N 4°16E 170 C4
Esch-sur-Alzette Lux. 49°32N 6°0E 170 E6
Eschede Germany 52°44N 10°14E 178 C6
Eschenried Germany 48°13N 11°24E 131 A1
Eschwege Germany 51°11N 10°2E 178 D6
Eschweiler Germany 50°49N 6°15E 178 E2
Escobal Panama 9°6N 80°1W 320 c
Escoma Bolivia 15°40S 69°8W 330 D4
Escondido U.S.A. 33°7N 117°5W 307 M9
Escravos → Nigeria 5°35N 5°10E 263 D6
Escuinapa de Hidalgo Mexico 22°50N 105°50W 318 C3
Escuintla Guatemala 14°20N 90°48W 320 D1
Eséka Cameroon 3°41N 10°44E 263 E7
Eşen → Turkey 36°27N 29°16E 205 E11
Esenguly Turkmenistan 37°37N 53°59E 216 E4
Esenler Turkey 41°1N 28°52E 122 B1
Esens Germany 53°38N 7°36E 178 B3
Esenyurt Turkey 41°3N 28°48E 203 E12
Esera → Spain 42°6N 0°15E 196 C5
Eşfahān Iran 32°39N 51°43E 247 C6
Eşfahān □ Iran 32°50N 51°50E 247 C6
Esfarāyen Iran 37°4N 57°30E 247 B8
Esfideh Iran 33°39N 59°46E 247 C8
Esgueva → Spain 41°40N 4°43W 194 D6
Esh Sham = Dimashq Syria 33°30N 36°18E 250 E7
Esh Shamâlîya □ Sudan 19°0N 29°0E 256 D2
Esha Ness U.K. 60°29N 1°38W 167 A7
Eshan China 24°11N 102°24E 228 E4
Esher U.K. 51°21N 0°20W 125 B1
Eshkāshem = Ishkashim Tajikistan 36°44N 71°37E 217 E8
Eshkol △ Israel 31°20N 34°30E 251 G5
Eshowe S. Africa 28°50S 31°30E 271 C5
Esiama Ghana 4°56N 2°25W 262 E4
Esigodini Zimbabwe 20°18S 28°56E 271 B4
Esil = Ishim → Russia 57°45N 71°10E 214 D8
Esil Kazakhstan 51°57N 66°24E 217 B7
Esino → Italy 43°39N 13°22E 199 E10
Esira Madag. 24°20S 46°42E 272 C2
Esk → Dumf. & Gall., U.K. 54°58N 3°2W 167 G5
Esk → N. Yorks., U.K. 54°30N 0°37W 168 C7
Eskān Iran 26°48N 63°9E 240 D1
Eskbank U.K. 55°52N 3°4W 121 B3
Esker Siding Canada 53°53N 66°25W 299 B6
Eskifjörður Iceland 65°3N 13°55W 155 B13
Eskije = Xanthi Greece 41°10N 24°58E 203 E8
Eskilsäter Sweden 58°57N 13°10E 163 F7
Eskilstuna Sweden 59°22N 16°32E 162 E10
Eskimalatya Turkey 38°24N 38°22E 213 C8
Eskimo Point = Arviat Canada 61°6N 93°59W 297 A10

Eskişehir Turkey 39°50N 30°30E 205 B12
Eskişehir □ Turkey 39°40N 31°0E 205 B12
Esla → Spain 41°29N 6°3W 194 D4
Eslāmābād-e Gharb Iran 34°10N 46°30E 213 E12
Eslāmshahr Iran 35°40N 51°10E 247 C6
Eslöv Sweden 55°50N 13°20E 163 J7
Eşme Turkey 38°23N 28°58E 205 C10
Esmeralda, I. Chile 48°55S 75°25W 336 C1
Esmeraldas Ecuador 1°0N 79°40W 328 C2
Esmeraldas □ Ecuador 0°40N 79°30W 328 C2
Esmeraldas → Ecuador 0°58N 79°38W 328 C2
Esna = Isna Egypt 25°17N 32°30E 256 B3
Esnagi L. Canada 48°36N 84°33W 298 C3
Esom Hill U.S.A. 33°57N 85°23W 316 B4
Espa Norway 60°34N 11°16E 164 D8
Espada, Pta. Colombia 12°5N 71°7W 328 A3
Espalion France 44°32N 2°47E 174 D6
España = Spain ■ Europe 39°0N 4°0W 192 D3
Espanola Ont., Canada 46°15N 81°46W 298 C3
Espanola N. Mex., U.S.A. 35°59N 106°5W 305 J10
Española, I. Ecuador 1°23S 89°39W 330 a
Espanya, Plaça d' Barcelona, Spain 114 c1
Esparreguera Spain 41°33N 1°52E 196 D6
Esparza Costa Rica 9°59N 84°40W 320 E3
Espeland Norway 60°23N 5°28E 164 D2
Espelkamp Germany 52°24N 8°36E 178 C4
Espenberg, C. U.S.A. 66°33N 163°36W 303 C7
Esperança Amazonas, Brazil 4°24S 69°52W 328 D4
Esperança Paraíba, Brazil 7°1S 35°51W 332 C4
Esperance Australia 33°45S 121°55E 279 F3
Esperance, C. Solomon Is. 9°15S 159°43E 287 M10
Esperance B. Australia 33°48S 121°55E 279 F3
Esperantinópolis Brazil 4°53S 44°53W 332 B3
Esperanza Antarctica 65°0S 55°0W 151 C18
Esperanza Santa Cruz, Argentina 51°1S 70°49W 336 D2
Esperanza Santa Fe, Argentina 31°29S 61°3W 334 C3
Esperanza Mexico City, Mexico 128 c3
Esperanza Agusan del S., Phil. 8°43N 125°36E 233 G5
Esperanza Masbate, Phil. 11°45N 124°3E 233 F5
Esperanza Puerto Rico 18°6N 65°28W 321 b
Espéraza France 42°56N 2°14E 174 F6
Espevær Norway 59°35N 5°7E 164 E2
Espichel, C. Portugal 38°22N 9°16W 195 G1
Espiel Spain 38°11N 5°1W 195 G5
Espigão, Serra do Brazil 26°35S 50°30W 335 B5
Espinal Colombia 4°9N 74°53W 328 C3
Espinar Peru 14°51S 71°24W 330 C3
Espinazo, Sierra del = Espinhaço, Serra do Brazil 17°30S 43°30W 333 E3
Espinhaço, Serra do Brazil 17°30S 43°30W 333 E3
Espinho Portugal 41°1N 8°38W 194 D2
Espinilho, Serra do Brazil 28°30S 55°0W 335 B5
Espinosa de los Monteros Spain 43°5N 3°34W 194 B7
Espírito Santo □ Brazil 20°0S 40°45W 333 F3
Espírito Santo do Pinhal Brazil 22°10S 46°46W 335 A6
Espíritu Santo Vanuatu 15°15S 166°50E 287 E4
Espíritu Santo, B. del Mexico 19°20N 87°35W 319 D7
Espíritu Santo, I. Mexico 24°30N 110°22W 318 C2
Espita Mexico 21°1N 88°19W 319 C7
Espiye Turkey 40°56N 38°43E 213 B8
Esplanada Brazil 11°47S 37°57W 333 D4
Esplugas Spain 41°22N 2°5E 114 A1
Espoo Finland 60°12N 24°40E 188 B3
Esposizione Universale di Roma Italy 41°49N 12°28E 136 C1
Espuña, Sierra de Spain 37°51N 1°35W 197 H3
Espungabera Mozam. 20°29S 32°45E 271 B5
Esquel Argentina 42°55S 71°20W 336 B2
Esquimalt Canada 48°26N 123°25W 306 B3
Esquina Argentina 30°0S 59°30W 334 C4
Essandsjøen Norway 63°0N 12°0E 164 A8
Essaouira Morocco 31°32N 9°42W 260 B3
Essaouira □ Morocco 31°25N 9°30W 260 B3
Essen Belgium 51°28N 4°28E 170 C4
Essen Nordrhein-Westfalen, Germany 51°28N 7°2E 178 D3
Essendon Australia 37°44S 144°55E 128 A1
Essendon ✈ (MEB) Australia 37°43S 144°54E 128 A1
Essendon, Mt. Australia 25°0S 120°29E 279 E3
Essequibo → Guyana 6°50N 58°30W 329 B6
Essex Ont., Canada 42°10N 82°49W 312 D2
Essex Calif., U.S.A. 34°44N 115°15W 307 L11
Essex N.Y., U.S.A. 44°19N 73°21W 313 B11
Essex □ U.K. 51°54N 0°27E 169 F8
Essex Junction U.S.A. 44°29N 73°7W 313 B11
Essingen Sweden 59°19N 17°59E 139 B1
Essling Austria 48°12N 16°30E 142 A3
Esslingen Germany 48°44N 9°18E 179 G5
Essonne □ France 48°30N 2°20E 173 D9
Est, Gare de l' Paris, France 134 a5
Estaca de Bares, C. de Spain 43°46N 7°42W 194 B3
Estación Camacho Mexico 24°25N 102°18W 318 C4
Estación Simón Mexico 24°42N 102°35W 318 C4
Estadilla Spain 42°4N 0°16E 196 C5
Estado, Parque do Brazil 23°38S 46°38W 137 B2
Estados, I. de Los Argentina 54°40S 64°30W 336 D4
Estagel France 42°47N 2°40E 174 F6
Estagno Pt. Phil. 17°20N 122°24E 232 C4
Eşţahbānāt Iran 29°8N 54°4E 247 D7
Estância Brazil 11°16S 37°26W 332 D4
Estancia N. Mex., U.S.A. 34°46N 106°4W 305 J10
Estancia Monte León Argentina 50°14S 68°55W 336 D3
Estārm Iran 28°21N 58°21E 247 D8
Estarreja Portugal 40°45N 8°35W 194 E2
Estats, Pic d' Spain 42°40N 1°24E 196 C6
Estcourt S. Africa 29°0S 29°53E 271 C4
Este Italy 45°14N 11°39E 199 C8
Este △ Dom. Rep. 18°14N 68°42W 321 C6
Estefânia Lisbon, Portugal 126 a2
Estelí Nic. 13°9N 86°22W 320 D2
Estella Spain 42°40N 2°2W 196 C2
Estelle U.S.A. 29°50N 90°6W 131 B2
Estellencs Spain 39°39N 2°29E 206 B3
Estena → Spain 39°23N 4°44W 195 F6
Estepa Spain 37°17N 4°52W 195 H6
Estepona Spain 36°24N 5°7W 195 J5
Esterhazy Canada 50°37N 102°5W 297 C8
Esterias, C. Gabon 0°40N 9°20E 264 B1
Esternay France 48°44N 3°33E 173 D10
Esterri d'Aneu Spain 42°38N 1°5E 196 C6
Estevan Canada 49°10N 102°59W 297 D8
Estevan Group Canada 53°3N 129°38W 296 C3
Estherville U.S.A. 43°24N 94°50W 308 D6
Estill U.S.A. 32°45N 81°15W 316 C8
Estissac France 48°16N 3°48E 173 D10
Eston Canada 51°8N 108°40W 297 C7
Estonia ■ Europe 58°30N 25°30E 188 C3
Estoril Portugal 38°42N 9°23W 195 G1
Estouk Mali 18°14N 1°2E 263 B5
Estrela, Basilica da Portugal 38°42N 9°9W 126 A2
Estrela, Serra da Portugal 40°10N 7°45W 194 E3
Estrella Spain 38°25N 3°35W 195 G7
Estremoz Portugal 38°51N 7°39W 195 G3
Estrondo, Serra do Brazil 7°20S 48°0W 332 C2
Esutoru = Uglegorsk Russia 49°5N 142°2E 215 E15
Esztergom Hungary 47°47N 18°44E 182 C3
Et Tîdra Mauritania 19°45N 16°20W 262 B1
Etah India 27°35N 78°40E 243 F8
Étain France 49°13N 5°38E 173 C12
Étampes France 48°26N 2°10E 173 D9
Étang-Salé-les-Bains Réunion 21°15S 55°20E 272 f
Etanga Namibia 17°55S 13°0E 270 A1
Étaples France 50°30N 1°39E 173 B8
Etawah India 26°48N 79°6E 243 F8
Etawney L. Canada 57°50N 96°50W 297 B9
Etchojoa Mexico 26°55N 109°38W 318 B3
Ete Nigeria 7°2N 7°28E 263 D6
Etéké Gabon 1°29S 11°35E 264 C2
eThekwini = Durban S. Africa 29°49S 31°1E 271 C5
Ethel U.S.A. 46°32N 122°46W 306 D4
Ethelbert Canada 51°32N 100°25W 297 C8
Ethiopia ■ Africa 8°0N 40°0E 267 C4
Ethiopian Highlands Ethiopia 10°0N 37°0E 254 E7
Etili Turkey 39°59N 26°54E 203 G10
Etive, L. U.K. 56°29N 5°10W 167 E3
Etna Italy 37°50N 14°55E 201 E7
Etna → Norway 60°49N 10°7E 164 C6
Etne Norway 59°40N 5°58E 164 E2
Etobicoke Canada 43°39N 79°34W 141 B1
Etobicoke Cr. → Canada 43°35N 79°32W 141 B1
Etoile Dem. Rep. of the Congo 11°33S 27°30E 269 E2
Etoliko Greece 38°26N 21°21E 204 C3
Etolin Strait U.S.A. 60°20N 165°15W 303 F6
Etoloakarnania □ Greece 38°45N 21°18E 204 C3
Etosha △ Namibia 19°0S 16°0E 270 A2
Etosha Pan Namibia 18°40S 16°30E 270 A2
Etoumbi Congo 0°1S 14°57E 264 C2
Etowah U.S.A. 35°20N 84°32W 315 D12
Étréchy France 48°30N 2°12E 173 D9
Etrek Turkmenistan 37°36N 54°46E 247 B7
Étrépagny France 49°18N 1°36E 173 C8
Étretat France 49°42N 0°12E 172 C7
Etropole Bulgaria 42°50N 24°0E 203 D8
Ettelbruck Lux. 49°51N 6°5E 170 E6
Etterbeek Belgium 50°50N 4°23E 116 B2
Ettlingen Germany 48°56N 8°25E 179 G4
Ettrick Water → U.K. 55°31N 2°55W 167 F6
Etuku Dem. Rep. of the Congo 3°42S 25°45E 264 C5
Etulia Moldova 45°32N 28°27E 183 E13
Etzná-Tixmucuy = Edzná Mexico 19°39N 90°19W 319 D6
Eu France 50°3N 1°26E 172 E8
Eua Tonga 21°22S 174°56W 287 Q13
Euboea = Evia Greece 38°30N 24°0E 204 C6
Eucaliptus = Tomás Barrón Bolivia 17°35S 67°31W 330 D4
Euchareena Australia 32°57S 149°6E 283 E8
Eucla Australia 31°41S 128°52E 279 F4
Euclid U.S.A. 41°34N 81°32W 312 E3
Euclides da Cunha Brazil 10°31S 39°1W 332 D4
Eucumbene, L. Australia 36°2S 148°40E 283 D8
Eudora U.S.A. 33°7N 91°16W 314 E9
Eudunda Australia 34°12S 139°7E 282 C3
Eufaula Ala., U.S.A. 31°54N 85°9W 316 D4
Eufaula Okla., U.S.A. 35°17N 95°35W 314 D7
Eufaula L. U.S.A. 35°18N 95°21W 314 D7
Eugene U.S.A. 44°5N 123°4W 304 D2
Eugowra Australia 33°22S 148°24E 283 B8
Eulo Australia 28°10S 145°3E 281 D4
Eulonia U.S.A. 31°32N 81°26W 316 D8
Eumungerie Australia 31°56S 148°36E 283 A8
Eung-am S. Korea 37°34N 126°55E 137 B1
Eungella △ Australia 20°57S 148°40E 280 b
Eunice La., U.S.A. 30°30N 92°25W 314 F8
Eunice N. Mex., U.S.A. 32°26N 103°10W 305 K12
Eunpyeong S. Korea 37°36N 126°56E 137 B1
Eupen Belgium 50°37N 6°3E 170 D6
Euphrates = Furāt, Nahr al → Asia 31°0N 47°25E 246 D5
Eure □ France 49°10N 1°0E 172 C8
Eure → France 49°18N 1°12E 172 C8
Eure-et-Loir □ France 48°22N 1°30E 172 D8
Eureka Nunavut, Canada 80°0N 85°56W 295 B14
Eureka Calif., U.S.A. 40°47N 124°9W 304 F1
Eureka Ill., U.S.A. 40°43N 89°16W 310 D7
Eureka Kans., U.S.A. 37°49N 96°17W 308 G5
Eureka Mo., U.S.A. 38°30N 90°38W 310 F6
Eureka Mont., U.S.A. 48°53N 115°3W 304 B6
Eureka Nev., U.S.A. 39°31N 115°58W 304 G6
Eureka S.C., U.S.A. 33°42N 81°46W 316 B8
Eureka S. Dak., U.S.A. 45°46N 99°38W 308 C4
Eureka, Mt. Australia 26°35S 121°35E 279 E3
Eureka Sd. Canada 79°0N 85°0W 295 B15
Eurelia Australia 32°33S 138°35E 282 B3
Eurinilla Cr. → Australia 30°53S 140°11E 282 A4
Euroa Australia 36°44S 145°35E 283 D6
Europa, Île Ind. Oc. 22°20S 40°22E 271 B7
Europa, Picos de Spain 43°10N 4°49W 194 B6
Europa, Pt. Gib. 36°3N 5°21W 195 J5
Europe 50°0N 20°0E 158 E10
Europoort Neths. 51°57N 4°10E 170 C4
Euskirchen Germany 50°39N 6°48E 178 E2
Eustis U.S.A. 28°51N 81°41W 317 G8
Euston N.S.W., Australia 34°30S 142°46E 282 C5
Euston London, U.K. 125 a3
Eutawville U.S.A. 33°24N 80°21W 316 B9
Eutin Germany 54°8N 10°36E 178 A6
Eutsuk L. Canada 53°20N 126°45W 296 C3
Eva Perón = La Pampa □ Argentina 36°50S 66°0W 334 D2
Eva Perón = La Plata Argentina 35°0S 57°55W 334 C4
Evale Angola 16°33S 15°44E 265 F3
Evanger Norway 60°39N 6°7E 164 D3
Evanlı Turkey 36°46N 34°26E 250 B5
Evans U.S.A. 40°23N 104°41W 304 F11
Evans, L. Canada 50°50N 77°0W 298 B4
Evans City U.S.A. 40°46N 80°4W 312 F4
Evans Head Australia 29°7S 153°27E 281 D5
Evansburg Canada 53°36N 114°59W 296 C5
Evansdale U.S.A. 42°30N 92°17W 310 B4
Evanston Ill., U.S.A. 42°3N 87°40W 119 A2
Evanston Wyo., U.S.A. 41°16N 110°58W 304 F8
Evansville Ill., U.S.A. 38°5N 89°56W 310 F7
Evansville Ind., U.S.A. 37°58N 87°35W 311 G9
Evansville Wis., U.S.A. 42°47N 89°18W 310 B7
Évaux-les-Bains France 46°12N 2°29E 173 F9
Evaz Iran 27°46N 53°59E 247 E7
Evciler Afyon, Turkey 38°4N 29°54E 205 C11
Evciler Çanakkale, Turkey 39°47N 26°44E 205 B8
Eveleth U.S.A. 47°28N 92°32W 308 B7
Even Sapir Israel 31°46N 35°8E 123 B1
Evensk Russia 62°12N 159°30E 215 C16
Evenstad Norway 61°25N 11°7E 164 C8
Everard, L. Australia 31°30S 135°0E 281 E2
Everard Ranges Australia 27°5S 132°28E 279 E5
Evere Belgium 50°52N 4°25E 116 A2
Everest, Mt. Nepal 28°5N 86°58E 243 E12
Everett Ga., U.S.A. 31°24N 81°38W 316 D8
Everett Mass., U.S.A. 42°24N 71°3W 116 A2
Everett Pa., U.S.A. 40°1N 78°23W 312 F6
Everett Wash., U.S.A. 47°59N 122°12W 306 C4
Everglades, The U.S.A. 25°50N 81°0W 317 K9
Everglades △ U.S.A. 25°30N 81°0W 317 K9
Everglades City U.S.A. 25°52N 81°23W 317 K8
Evergreen Ala., U.S.A. 31°26N 86°57W 315 F11
Evergreen Mont., U.S.A. 48°14N 114°17W 304 B6
Evergreen Park U.S.A. 41°43N 87°42W 119 C2
Everöd Sweden 55°53N 14°5E 163 J8
Everton Australia 36°25S 146°33E 283 D7
Evertsberg Sweden 61°8N 13°58E 162 C7
Evesham U.K. 52°6N 1°56W 169 E6
Evia Greece 38°30N 24°0E 204 C6
Evia □ Greece 38°40N 23°40E 204 C5
Évian-les-Bains France 46°24N 6°35E 173 F13
Evīn Iran 35°47N 51°23E 141 A2
Evinayong Eq. Guin. 1°26N 10°35E 264 B2
Evinos → Greece 38°27N 21°40E 204 C3
Évisa France 42°15N 8°48E 175 F12
Evje Norway 58°36N 7°51E 164 F4
Évora Portugal 38°33N 7°57W 195 G3
Évora □ Portugal 38°33N 7°50W 195 G3
Evowghlī Iran 38°43N 45°13E 213 C11
Évreux France 49°3N 1°8E 172 C8
Evritania □ Greece 39°5N 21°30E 204 B3
Évron France 48°10N 0°24W 172 D6
Evros □ Greece 41°10N 26°0E 203 E10
Evros → Greece 41°40N 26°34E 203 F10
Evrotas → Greece 36°50N 22°40E 204 E4
Évry France 48°38N 2°27E 173 D9
Évvoia = Evia Greece 38°30N 24°0E 204 C6
'Ewa Beach U.S.A. 21°19N 158°1W 302 K13
'Ewa District U.S.A. 21°25N 158°0W 302 K14
'Ewa Villages U.S.A. 21°20N 158°3W 302 K13
Ewarton Jamaica 18°11N 77°6W 320 a
Ewasse Papua N. G. 5°19S 151°1E 286 C6
Ewe, L. U.K. 57°49N 5°38W 167 D3
Ewing Mo., U.S.A. 40°6N 91°43W 310 E5
Ewing Nebr., U.S.A. 42°16N 98°21W 308 D4
Ewo Congo 0°48S 14°45E 264 C2
Ewu Nigeria 6°33N 3°19E 124 A1
Exaltación Bolivia 13°10S 65°20W 331 C4
Excelsior Springs U.S.A. 39°20N 94°13W 310 E2
Exchange Square Hong Kong, China 122 c1
Excideuil France 45°20N 1°4E 174 C5
Exe → U.K. 50°41N 3°29W 169 G4
Exeter Ont., Canada 43°21N 81°29W 312 C3
Exeter Devon, U.K. 50°43N 3°31W 169 G4
Exeter Calif., U.S.A. 36°18N 119°9W 306 J7
Exeter N.H., U.S.A. 42°59N 70°57W 313 D14
Exhibition Place Canada 43°38N 79°25W 141 B2
Exira U.S.A. 41°35N 94°52W 310 C2
Exmoor U.K. 51°12N 3°45W 169 F4
Exmoor △ U.K. 51°8N 3°42W 169 F4
Exmouth W. Austral., Australia 21°54S 114°10E 278 D1
Exmouth Devon, U.K. 50°37N 3°25W 169 G4
Exmouth G. Australia 22°15S 114°15E 278 D1
Exmouth Plateau Ind. Oc. 19°0S 114°0E 288 J3
Expedition △ Australia 25°41S 149°7E 281 D4
Expedition Ra. Australia 24°30S 149°12E 280 C4
Experiment = Highland Mills U.S.A. 33°17N 84°17W 316 B5
Expo 2010 China 31°11N 121°29E 138 B1
Exposições, Palácio das Brazil 22°53S 43°13W 135 B1
Extremadura □ Spain 39°30N 6°5W 195 F4
Extrême-Nord □ Cameroon 11°0N 14°30E 259 F2
Exuma Sound Bahamas 24°30N 76°20W 320 B4
Eyak U.S.A. 60°32N 145°36W 303 F11
Eyasi, L. Tanzania 3°30S 35°0E 268 C4
Eydehavn Norway 58°30N 8°53E 164 F5
Eydhafushi Maldives 5°7N 73°2E 272 d
Eye Pen. U.K. 58°13N 6°10W 167 C2
Eyemouth U.K. 55°52N 2°5W 167 F6
Eygues = Aigues → France 44°7N 4°43E 175 D8
Eygurande France 45°40N 2°26E 173 G9
Eyjafjallajökull Iceland 63°38N 19°36W 155 D7
Eyjafjarðarsýsla □ Iceland 65°30N 18°30W 155 B8
Eyjafjörður Iceland 66°15N 18°30W 155 A8
Eyl Somali Rep. 8°0N 49°50E 267 C6
Eymet France 44°40N 0°25E 174 D4
Eymoutiers France 45°40N 1°45E 174 C5
Eynesil Turkey 41°4N 39°9E 213 B8
Eyrarbakki Iceland 63°52N 21°9W 155 D5
Eyre (North), L. Australia 28°30S 137°20E 281 D2
Eyre (South), L. Australia 29°18S 137°25E 281 D2
Eyre, L. Australia 29°30S 137°26E 276 F6
Eyre Mts. N.Z. 45°25S 168°25E 285 F3
Eyre Pen. Australia 33°30S 136°17E 282 C1
Eysturoy Færoe Is. 62°13N 6°54W 160 E9
Eyüp Turkey 41°2N 28°55E 122 B1
Eyvān = Jūy Zar Iran 33°50N 46°18E 213 F12
Eyvānkī Iran 35°24N 51°56E 247 C6
Ez Zeidab Sudan 17°25N 33°55E 256 D3
Ezcaray Spain 42°19N 3°0W 196 C1
Ezeiza ✈ (EZE) Argentina 34°49S 58°32W 117 C1
Ežerėlis Lithuania 54°53N 23°37E 184 D10
Ezhou China 30°23N 114°50E 229 B10
Ezine Turkey 39°48N 26°20E 205 B8
Ezouza → Cyprus 34°44N 32°27E 207 F8

F

F.Y.R.O.M. = Macedonia ■ Europe 41°53N 21°40E 202 E5
Faaa Tahiti 17°34S 149°35W 289 e
Faaborg Denmark 55°6N 10°15E 163 J4
Faaone Tahiti 17°40S 149°21W 289 e
Fabala Guinea 9°44N 9°5W 262 D3
Fabens U.S.A. 31°30N 106°10W 314 F1
Fåberg Norway 61°10N 10°25E 164 C7
Fabero Spain 42°46N 6°37W 194 C4
Fabius U.S.A. 42°50N 75°59W 313 D9
Fabour, Mt. Singapore 1°16N 103°49E 138 B2
Fabriano Italy 43°20N 12°54E 199 E9
Făcăeni Romania 44°32N 27°53E 183 F12
Facatativá Colombia 4°49N 74°22W 328 C3
Faceville U.S.A. 30°45N 84°38W 316 E5
Fachi Niger 18°6N 11°34E 259 E2
Facundo Argentina 45°18S 69°58W 336 C3
Fada Chad 17°13N 21°34E 259 E4
Fada-n-Gourma Burkina Faso 12°10N 0°30E 263 C5
Fadd Hungary 46°28N 18°49E 182 D3
Faddeyevskiy, Ostrov Russia 76°0N 144°0E 215 B15
Faddor South Sudan 8°7N 32°17E 257 F3
Fadghāmī Syria 35°53N 40°52E 213 E9
Fadiffolu Atoll Maldives 5°23N 73°29E 272 d
Fadlab Sudan 17°42N 34°2E 256 D3
Fadwel South Sudan 8°11N 29°20E 266 C2
Fælledparken Denmark 55°42N 12°34E 118 A3
Faenza Italy 44°17N 11°53E 199 D8
Færingehavn = Kangerluarsoruseq Greenland 63°45N 51°27W 154 E5
Færoe Is. = Føroyar ⊠ Atl. Oc. 62°0N 7°0W 160 F9
Fafa Mali 15°22N 0°48E 263 B5
Fafe Portugal 41°27N 8°11W 194 D2
Fafen → Ethiopia 5°59N 44°25E 267 C5
Fagam Nigeria 11°1N 10°1E 263 C7
Fagamalo Amer. Samoa 14°18S 170°48W 302 f
Făgăras Romania 45°48N 24°58E 183 E9
Făgăras, Munţii Romania 45°40N 24°40E 183 E9
Fagasa Amer. Samoa 14°17S 170°43W 302 f
Fagatogo Amer. Samoa 14°16S 170°41W 302 f
Fågelfors Sweden 57°12N 15°51E 163 H9
Fågelmara Sweden 56°16N 15°58E 163 H9
Fågelön Sweden 59°18N 17°55E 139 B1
Fagerheim Norway 60°23N 7°46E 164 D4
Fagerhult Sweden 57°8N 15°40E 163 G9
Fagernes Norway 60°59N 9°14E 164 D6
Fagersjö Sweden 59°14N 18°4E 139 B2
Fagersta Sweden 60°1N 15°46E 162 D9
Făget Romania 45°52N 22°10E 182 E7
Făget, Munţii Romania 47°40N 23°10E 183 C8
Faggo Nigeria 11°21N 9°57E 263 C6
Fagnano, L. Argentina 54°30S 68°0W 336 D3
Fagnières France 48°58N 4°20E 173 D11
Faguibine, L. Mali 16°45N 4°0W 262 B4
Fahlīān Iran 30°11N 51°28E 247 D6
Fahraj Kermān, Iran 29°0N 59°0E 247 D8
Fahraj Yazd, Iran 31°46N 54°36E 247 D7
Fai Tsi Long Vietnam 21°0N 107°30E 228 G6
Faial Azores 38°34N 28°42W 153 d1
Faial Madeira 32°47N 16°53W 153 c
Faial, Canal do Azores 38°33N 28°35W 153 d1
Faichan Kangri India 35°48N 76°34E 243 B7
Faichuk Micronesia 7°21N 151°38E 287 T17
Fair Haven N.Y., U.S.A. 43°18N 76°42W 313 C8
Fair Haven Vt., U.S.A. 43°36N 73°16W 309 D17
Fair Hd. U.K. 55°14N 6°9W 166 A5
Fair Isle U.K. 59°32N 1°38W 165 B6
Fair Oaks U.S.A. 38°39N 121°16W 306 G5
Fairbank U.S.A. 42°38N 92°3W 310 B4
Fairbanks Alaska, U.S.A. 64°51N 147°43W 303 D11
Fairbanks Fla., U.S.A. 29°44N 82°16W 316 F7
Fairborn U.S.A. 39°49N 84°2W 311 E12
Fairburn U.S.A. 33°34N 84°35W 316 B5
Fairbury Ill., U.S.A. 40°45N 83°31W 311 D8
Fairbury Nebr., U.S.A. 40°8N 97°11W 308 E5
Fairfax Ohio, U.S.A. 39°5N 83°37W 311 E13
Fairfax S.C., U.S.A. 32°59N 81°15W 316 C8
Fairfax Va., U.S.A. 38°50N 77°19W 143 B2
Fairfax Vt., U.S.A. 44°40N 73°1W 313 B11
Fairfax Station U.S.A. 38°48N 77°19W 143 C2
Fairfield N.S.W., Australia 33°53S 150°57E 283 B9
Fairfield Ala., U.S.A. 33°29N 86°55W 315 E11
Fairfield Calif., U.S.A. 38°15N 122°3W 306 G4
Fairfield Conn., U.S.A. 41°9N 73°16W 313 E11
Fairfield Idaho, U.S.A. 43°21N 114°44W 304 E6
Fairfield Ill., U.S.A. 38°23N 88°22W 311 F8
Fairfield Iowa, U.S.A. 40°56N 91°57W 310 D5
Fairfield Ohio, U.S.A. 39°20N 84°34W 311 E12
Fairfield Tex., U.S.A. 31°44N 96°10W 314 F6
Fairford Canada 51°37N 98°38W 297 C9
Fairhope U.S.A. 30°31N 87°54W 315 F11
Fairland S. Africa 26°8S 27°57E 123 A1
Fairlie N.Z. 44°5S 170°49E 285 E5
Fairmead U.S.A. 37°5N 120°10W 306 H6
Fairmilehead U.K. 55°54N 3°11W 121 B2
Fairmont Minn., U.S.A. 43°39N 94°28W 308 D6
Fairmont W. Va., U.S.A. 39°29N 80°9W 309 F13
Fairmount Calif., U.S.A. 34°45N 118°26W 307 L8
Fairmount N.Y., U.S.A. 43°5N 76°12W 313 C8
Fairmount Heights U.S.A. 38°54N 76°54W 143 B4
Fairplay U.S.A. 39°15N 106°2W 304 G10
Fairport Ont., Canada 43°49N 79°4W 141 A4
Fairport N.Y., U.S.A. 43°6N 77°27W 312 C7
Fairport Harbor U.S.A. 41°45N 81°17W 312 E3
Fairview Alta., Canada 56°5N 118°25W 296 B5
Fairview Mont., U.S.A. 47°51N 104°3W 304 C11
Fairview N.J., U.S.A. 40°48N 73°59W 132 B2
Fairview Okla., U.S.A. 36°16N 98°29W 314 C5
Fairview, L. U.S.A. 28°35N 81°24W 133 A2
Fairweather, Mt. U.S.A. 58°55N 137°32W 296 B1
Faisalabad Pakistan 31°30N 73°5E 242 D5
Faith U.S.A. 45°2N 102°2W 308 C2
Faizabad India 26°45N 82°10E 243 F10
Faizpur India 21°14N 75°49E 244 D2
Fajã Grande Azores 39°27N 31°16W 153 d2
Fajardo Puerto Rico 18°20N 65°39W 321 C6
Fajou, Îlet à Guadeloupe 16°21N 61°35W 322 e
Fajr, W. → Si. Arabia 29°10N 38°10E 246 D3
Fakaofo Pac. Oc. 9°23S 171°15W 277 B16
Fakarava French Polynesia 16°20S 145°37W 289 f
Fakenham U.K. 52°51N 0°51E 168 E8
Fåker Sweden 63°0N 14°34E 162 A8
Fakfak Indonesia 2°55S 132°18E 231 E8
Fakiya Bulgaria 42°10N 27°6E 203 D11
Fakobli Ivory C. 7°23N 7°23W 262 D3
Fakse Denmark 55°15N 12°8E 163 J6
Fakse Bugt Denmark 55°11N 12°15E 163 J6
Fakse Ladeplads Denmark 55°11N 12°9E 163 J6
Faku China 42°32N 123°21E 224 A1
Fala Beguets I. Micronesia 7°21N 151°41E 287 U17
Falaba S. Leone 9°54N 11°22W 262 D2
Falaise France 48°54N 0°12W 172 D6
Falakro Oros Greece 41°15N 23°58E 202 E7
Falam Burma 23°0N 93°45E 241 D4
Falas I. Micronesia 7°31N 151°44E 287 T18
Falces Spain 42°24N 1°48W 196 C3
Fălciu Romania 46°17N 28°7E 183 D13
Falcó, C. des Spain 38°50N 1°23E 206 D1
Falcón □ Venezuela 11°0N 69°50W 328 A4
Falcon, C. Algeria 35°50N 0°50W 261 A4
Falcón, Presa Mexico 26°35N 99°10W 319 B5
Falcon Lake Canada 49°42N 95°15W 297 D9
Falcon Res. U.S.A. 26°34N 99°10W 314 H5
Falconara Maríttima Italy 43°37N 13°24E 199 E10
Falcone, C. del Italy 40°58N 8°12E 200 B1
Falconer U.S.A. 42°7N 79°12W 312 D5
Faléa Mali 12°16N 11°17W 262 C2
Falefa Samoa 13°54S 171°31W 287 V20
Falelatai Samoa 13°55S 171°59W 287 V20
Falelima Samoa 13°32S 172°41W 287 V19
Falémé → Senegal 14°46N 12°14W 262 C2
Faleniu Amer. Samoa 14°19S 170°44W 302 f
Falenty Poland 52°8N 20°55E 142 C1
Falerum Sweden 58°8N 16°13E 163 F10
Faleshty = Făleşti Moldova 47°32N 27°44E 183 C12
Făleşti Moldova 47°32N 27°44E 183 C12
Falfurrias U.S.A. 27°14N 98°9W 314 H5
Falher Canada 55°44N 117°15W 296 B5
Faliraki Greece 36°22N 28°12E 206 E12
Faliro Greece 37°55N 23°39E 112 B1
Faliro, Ormos Greece 37°54N 23°40E 112 B2
Falkenberg Brandenburg, Germany 51°35N 13°14E 178 D9
Falkenberg Sweden 56°54N 12°30E 163 H6
Falkenburg = Niemodlin Poland 50°38N 17°38E 185 H4
Falkenburg Germany 52°34N 13°32E 115 A4
Falkenhagen Germany 52°34N 13°5E 115 A1
Falkensee Germany 52°34N 13°4E 115 A1
Falkirk U.K. 56°0N 3°47W 167 F5
Falkirk □ U.K. 55°58N 3°49W 167 F5
Falkland U.K. 56°16N 3°12W 167 E5
Falkland, East, I. Falk. Is. 51°40S 58°30W 336 D5
Falkland, West, I. Falk. Is. 51°40S 60°0W 336 D5
Falkland Is. ⊠ Atl. Oc. 51°30S 59°0W 153 f
Falkland Plateau Atl. Oc. 51°0S 50°0W 152 M7
Falkland Ridge Atl. Oc. 49°20S 40°0W 152 L8
Falkland Sd. Falk. Is. 52°0S 60°0W 153 f
Falknov nad Ohří = Sokolov Czech Rep. 50°12N 12°40E 180 A5
Falkonera Greece 36°50N 23°52E 204 E5
Falköping Sweden 58°12N 13°33E 163 F7
Fall River U.S.A. 41°43N 71°10W 313 E13
Fallbrook U.S.A. 33°23N 117°15W 307 M9
Fallon U.S.A. 39°28N 118°47W 304 G4
Falls Church U.S.A. 38°53N 77°12W 143 B2
Falls City U.S.A. 40°3N 95°36W 308 E6
Falls Creek U.S.A. 41°9N 78°48W 312 E6
Falmouth Jamaica 18°30N 77°40W 320 a
Falmouth Corn., U.K. 50°9N 5°5W 169 G2
Falmouth Ky., U.S.A. 38°41N 84°20W 311 F12
Falmouth Mass., U.S.A. 41°33N 70°37W 313 E14
Falo I. Micronesia 7°28N 151°52E 287 T18
Falomo Nigeria 6°26N 3°26E 124 B2
Falsa, Pta. Mexico 27°51N 115°3W 318 B1
False B. S. Africa 34°15S 18°40E 270 D2
False Bay S. Africa 34°6S 18°33E 118 B2
False Divi Pt. India 15°43N 80°50E 245 G5
False Pass U.S.A. 54°51N 163°25W 303 J7
False Pt. India 20°18N 86°48E 244 D8
Falso, C. Honduras 15°12N 83°21W 320 C3
Falster Denmark 54°45N 11°55E 163 K5
Fălticeni Romania 47°21N 26°20E 183 C11
Falun Sweden 60°37N 15°37E 162 D9
Famagusta Cyprus 35°8N 33°55E 207 E9
Famagusta Bay Cyprus 35°15N 34°0E 207 E10
Famatina, Sierra de Argentina 27°30S 68°0W 334 B2
Famenin Iran 35°5N 48°58E 213 E13
Family L. Canada 51°54N 95°27W 297 C9
Famoso U.S.A. 35°37N 119°12W 307 K7
Fan Xian China 35°55N 115°38E 226 G8
Fana Mali 13°0N 6°56W 262 C3
Fanad Hd. Ireland 55°17N 7°38W 166 A4
Fanahammaren Norway 60°16N 5°20E 164 D2
Fanari Greece 39°24N 21°47E 204 B3
Fandriana Madag. 20°14S 47°21E 272 C2
Faneuil Hall Marketplace Boston, U.S.A. 116 b3
Fánes-Sénnes e Braies ⌓ Italy 46°38N 12°4E 199 B9
Fang Thailand 19°55N 99°13E 236 C2
Fang Xian China 32°3N 110°40E 229 A8
Fangaga Sudan 17°40N 37°50E 256 D4
Fangak South Sudan 9°4N 30°53E 257 F3
Fangatau French Polynesia 15°22S 138°45W 289 f
Fangataufa French Polynesia 15°50S 140°52W 289 f
Fangchang China 31°5N 118°4E 229 B12
Fangcheng China 33°18N 112°59E 226 H7
Fangchenggang China 21°42N 108°21E 228 G7
Fangcun China 23°6N 113°13E 121 B2
Fangliao Taiwan 22°22N 120°38E 225 D2
Fangshan Beijing, China 39°41N 116°0E 226 E9
Fangshan Shanxi, China 38°3N 111°25E 226 E6
Fangshan Taiwan 22°15N 120°39E 225 D2
Fangyüan Taiwan 23°56N 120°19E 225 C2
Fangzi China 36°33N 119°10E 227 F10
Fani i Madh → Albania 41°56N 20°16E 202 E4
Fanjakana Madag. 21°10S 46°53E 272 C2
Fanjiatun China 43°40N 125°15E 227 C13
Fanling China 22°30N 114°8E 219 a
Fannich, L. U.K. 57°38N 4°59W 167 D4
Fannrem Norway 63°16N 9°50E 164 A6
Fannūj Iran 26°35N 59°38E 247 E8
Fanø Denmark 55°25N 8°25E 163 J2
Fano Italy 43°50N 13°1E 199 E10
Fanshi China 39°12N 113°20E 226 E7
Fantzuliao Hsi → Taiwan 22°42N 120°28E 225 D2
Fanuet I. Micronesia 7°32N 151°48E 287 T18
Fao = Al Fāw Iraq 30°0N 48°30E 247 D6
Faqirwali Pakistan 29°27N 73°0E 242 E5
Fâqûs Egypt 30°44N 31°47E 256 H7
Far East = Dalnevostochnyy □ Russia 67°0N 140°0E 215 C14
Far East Asia 40°0N 130°0E 210 E14
Fara in Sabina Italy 42°12N 12°43E 199 F9
Faradje Dem. Rep. of the Congo 3°50N 29°45E 268 B2
Farafangana Madag. 22°49S 47°50E 272 C2
Farafenni Gambia 13°34N 15°36W 262 C1
Farâfra, El Wâhât el Egypt 27°15N 28°20E 256 B2
Farāh Afghan. 32°20N 62°7E 240 B1
Farāh □ Afghan. 32°25N 62°10E 240 B1
Farāh → Afghan. 31°27N 61°28E 240 C1
Faraḩābād Iran 35°41N 51°30E 141 A2
Farahalana Madag. 14°26S 50°10E 272 A3
Faraid, Gebel Egypt 23°33N 35°19E 256 C4
Farako Ivory C. 10°45N 6°50W 262 D4
Farallon de Medinilla N. Marianas 16°1N 146°4E 302 a
Farallon de Pajaros N. Marianas 20°32N 144°54E 302 a
Farallones de Cali △ Colombia 3°13N 76°46W 328 C2
Faramana Burkina Faso 11°56N 4°45W 262 C4
Faranah Guinea 10°3N 10°45W 262 C2
Farap Turkmenistan 39°9N 63°36E 216 E6
Fararah Oman 17°55N 55°38E 249 C6
Farasān, Jazā'ir Si. Arabia 16°45N 41°55E 248 C3
Farasan Is. = Farasān, Jazā'ir Si. Arabia 16°45N 41°55E 248 C3
Faratsiho Madag. 19°24S 46°57E 272 B2
Farbaraki Somali Rep. 2°30N 45°30E 267 D6
Fardes → Spain 37°35N 3°0W 195 H7
Fareham U.K. 50°51N 1°11W 169 G6
Farewell U.S.A. 62°31N 153°54W 303 E9
Farewell, C. N.Z. 40°29S 172°43E 285 A7
Farewell C. = Nunap Isua Greenland 59°48N 43°55W 154 F6
Farewell Spit N.Z. 40°35S 173°0E 285 A8
Farforovskaya Russia 59°52N 30°27E 137 B2
Färgelanda Sweden 58°34N 12°0E 163 F5
Farghona Uzbekistan 40°23N 71°19E 217 D8
Farghona □ Uzbekistan 40°30N 71°15E 217 D8
Farghona Vodiysi Asia 40°46N 71°30E 217 D8
Fargo Ga., U.S.A. 30°41N 82°34W 316 E7
Fargo N. Dak., U.S.A. 46°53N 96°48W 308 B5
Fār'iah, W. al → West Bank 32°12N 35°27E 251 F6
Faribault U.S.A. 44°18N 93°16W 308 C7
Faridabad India 28°26N 77°19E 242 E6
Faridkot India 30°44N 74°45E 242 D6
Faridpur Bangla. 23°15N 89°55E 241 D2
Faridpur India 28°13N 79°33E 243 E8
Fārigh, W. al → Libya 30°28N 20°44E 258 B3
Färila Sweden 61°48N 15°50E 162 C9
Farim Guinea-Biss. 12°27N 15°9W 262 C1
Farīmān Iran 35°40N 59°49E 247 C8
Farinha → Brazil 6°51S 47°30W 332 C2
Fariones, Pta. Canary Is. 29°13N 13°28W 153 e2
Fâriskûr Egypt 31°20N 31°43E 256 H7
Färjestaden Sweden 56°39N 16°27E 163 H10
Farkadona Greece 39°36N 22°4E 204 B4
Farleigh Australia 21°4S 149°8E 280 b
Farley U.S.A. 42°27N 91°0W 310 B6
Farmakonisi Greece 37°17N 27°5E 205 D9
Farmer City U.S.A. 40°15N 88°39W 311 D8
Farmersburg U.S.A. 39°15N 87°23W 311 E9
Farmerville U.S.A. 32°47N 92°24W 314 E8
Farmingdale U.S.A. 40°12N 74°10W 313 F10
Farmington B.C., Canada 55°54N 120°30W 296 B4
Farmington Calif., U.S.A. 37°55N 120°59W 306 H6
Farmington Ga., U.S.A. 33°47N 83°26W 316 B6
Farmington Ill., U.S.A. 40°42N 90°0W 310 D7
Farmington Iowa, U.S.A. 40°38N 91°44W 310 D5
Farmington Maine, U.S.A. 44°40N 70°9W 309 C18
Farmington Mo., U.S.A. 37°47N 90°25W 310 G6
Farmington N.H., U.S.A. 43°24N 71°4W 313 C13
Farmington N. Mex., U.S.A. 36°44N 108°12W 305 H9
Farmington Utah, U.S.A. 40°59N 111°53W 304 F8
Farmington → U.S.A. 41°51N 72°38W 313 E12
Farmland U.S.A. 40°15N 85°5W 311 D11
Farmville U.S.A. 37°18N 78°24W 309 G14
Färnäs Sweden 61°0N 14°39E 162 D8
Farne Is. U.K. 55°38N 1°37W 168 B6
Färnebofjärden △ Sweden 60°10N 16°48E 162 D10
Farnham Canada 45°17N 72°59W 313 A12
Farnham, Mt. Canada 50°29N 116°30W 296 C5
Farningham U.K. 51°23N 0°12E 125 B5
Faro Brazil 2°10S 56°39W 329 D6
Faro Yukon, Canada 62°11N 133°22W 294 E5
Faro Portugal 37°2N 7°55W 195 H3
Fårö Gotland, Sweden 57°55N 19°5E 163 G13
Faro □ Portugal 37°12N 8°10W 195 H2
Faro ✈ (FAO) Portugal 37°2N 7°57W 195 H3
Faro ⌓ Cameroon 8°15N 12°37E 264 A2
Fårösund Sweden 57°52N 19°2E 163 G13
Farquhar, C. Australia 23°50S 113°36E 279 D1
Farquhar Is. Seychelles 11°0S 52°0E 273 F4
Farrars Cr. → Australia 25°35S 140°43E 280 D3
Farrāshband Iran 28°57N 52°5E 247 D7
Farrell U.S.A. 41°13N 80°30W 312 E4
Farrell Flat Australia 33°48S 138°48E 282 B3
Farrokhī Iran 33°50N 59°31E 247 C8
Farruch, C. = Ferrutx, C. de Spain 39°47N 3°21E 206 B4
Farrukhabad India 27°24N 79°34E 244 A4
Fārs □ Iran 29°30N 55°0E 247 D7
Farsala Greece 39°17N 22°23E 204 B4
Fārsī Afghan. 33°47N 63°15E 240 B1
Fārsī Iran 27°58N 50°11E 247 E6
Farsø Denmark 56°46N 9°19E 163 H3
Farson U.S.A. 42°7N 109°26W 304 E9
Farsta Sweden 59°14N 18°5E 139 B2
Farsund Norway 58°5N 6°55E 164 F3
Fartak, Râs Si. Arabia 28°5N 34°34E 246 D2
Fartak, Ra's Yemen 15°38N 52°15E 249 D6
Fârţăneşti Romania 45°49N 27°59E 183 E12
Fartura, Serra da Brazil 26°21S 52°52W 335 B5
Faru Nigeria 12°48N 6°12E 263 C6
Fārūj Iran 37°14N 58°14E 247 B8
Fårup Denmark 56°33N 9°51E 163 H3
Farvel, Kap = Nunap Isua Greenland 59°48N 43°55W 154 F6
Farwell U.S.A. 34°23N 103°2W 314 D3
Fāryāb □ Afghan. 36°0N 65°0E 240 B2
Fasā Iran 29°0N 53°39E 247 D7
Fasanerie-Nord Germany 48°11N 11°32E 131 A2
Fasangarten Germany 48°5N 11°36E 131 B2
Fasano Italy 40°50N 17°22E 201 B10
Fashoda South Sudan 9°50N 32°2E 257 F3
Fasil Ghebbi Ethiopia 12°36N 37°28E 266 B4
Fáskruðsfjörður Iceland 64°56N 14°1W 155 C12
Fassa Mali 13°26N 8°15W 262 C3
Fastiv Ukraine 50°7N 29°57E 177 C15
Fastnet Rock Ireland 51°22N 9°37W 166 E2
Fastov = Fastiv Ukraine 50°7N 29°57E 177 C15
Fatagar, Tanjung Indonesia 2°46S 131°57E 231 E8
Fataka Solomon Is. 11°55S 170°12E 277 C12
Fatatsu Ne Iwo Jima 24°45N 141°18E 288 b
Fatehabad Haryana, India 29°31N 75°27E 242 E6
Fatehabad Ut. P., India 27°1N 78°19E 242 F8
Fatehgarh India 27°25N 79°35E 243 F8
Fatehpur Bihar, India 24°38N 85°14E 243 G11
Fatehpur Raj., India 28°0N 74°40E 242 F6
Fatehpur Ut. P., India 25°56N 81°13E 243 G9
Fatehpur Ut. P., India 27°10N 81°13E 243 F9
Fatehpur Sikri India 27°6N 77°40E 242 F6
Fatesh Russia 52°8N 35°57E 189 F8
Fathai South Sudan 8°5N 31°48E 257 F3
Fathom Five ⌓ Canada 45°17N 81°40W 312 A3
Fatick Senegal 14°19N 16°27W 262 C1
Fatick □ Senegal 14°15N 16°30W 262 C1
Fatih Turkey 41°0N 28°56E 122 B1
Fatima Qué., Canada 47°24N 61°53W 299 C7
Fátima Portugal 39°37N 8°39W 195 F2
Fatoya Guinea 11°37N 9°10W 262 C3
Fatsa Turkey 41°2N 37°31E 212 B7
Fatshan = Foshan China 23°6N 113°9E 121 B2
Faucille, Col de la France 46°22N 6°2E 173 F13
Faulkton U.S.A. 45°2N 99°8W 308 C4
Faulquemont France 49°3N 6°36E 173 C13
Faure I. Australia 25°52S 113°50E 279 E1
Făurei Romania 45°6N 27°19E 183 E12
Fauresmith S. Africa 29°44S 25°17E 270 C4
Fauro Solomon Is. 6°55S 156°7E 287 L9
Fauske Norway 67°17N 15°25E 160 C16
Fåvang Norway 61°27N 10°11E 164 C7
Favânia Brazil 3°7S 51°48W 329 D7
Favara Italy 37°19N 13°39E 200 E6
Faváritx, C. de Spain 40°0N 4°15E 206 B5
Faverges France 45°45N 6°17E 175 C10
Favignana Italy 37°56N 12°20E 200 E5
Favignana, I. Italy 37°56N 12°19E 200 E5
Favoriten Austria 48°9N 16°23E 142 B2
Fawcett, Pt. Australia 11°46S 130°2E 278 B5
Fawkner Australia 37°42S 144°56E 128 A1
Fawkner Park Australia 37°50S 144°58E 128 B1
Fawn → Canada 55°20N 87°35W 298 A2
Fawnskin U.S.A. 34°16N 116°56W 307 L10
Faxaflói Iceland 64°29N 23°0W 155 C3
Faxälven → Sweden 63°13N 17°13E 162 A10
Faya-Largeau Chad 17°58N 19°6E 259 E3
Fayaoué N. Cal. 20°38S 166°33E 288 d
Fayd Si. Arabia 27°1N 42°52E 246 E4
Fayence France 43°38N 6°42E 175 E10
Fayette Ala., U.S.A. 33°41N 87°50W 315 E11
Fayette Iowa, U.S.A. 42°51N 91°48W 310 B5
Fayette Mo., U.S.A. 39°9N 92°41W 310 E4
Fayette N.Y., U.S.A. 42°48N 76°48W 313 D8
Fayette Ohio, U.S.A. 41°40N 84°20W 311 C12
Fayetteville Ark., U.S.A. 36°4N 94°10W 314 C7
Fayetteville Ga., U.S.A. 33°27N 84°27W 316 B5
Fayetteville N.C., U.S.A. 35°3N 78°53W 315 D15
Fayetteville N.Y., U.S.A. 43°1N 76°0W 313 C9
Fayetteville Tenn., U.S.A. 35°9N 86°34W 315 D11
Fayied Egypt 30°18N 32°16E 256 H8
Faylakah Kuwait 29°27N 48°20E 247 D6
Fayón Spain 41°15N 0°20E 196 D5
Fazao-Malfakassa △ Togo 8°45N 0°50E 263 D5
Fazenda Libongo Angola 8°24S 13°24E 265 D2
Fazenda Nova Brazil 16°11S 50°48W 333 E1
Fazilka India 30°27N 74°2E 242 D6
Fazilpur Pakistan 29°18N 70°29E 242 E4
Fdérik Mauritania 22°40N 12°45W 260 D2
Feakle Ireland 52°56N 8°40W 166 D3
Feale → Ireland 52°27N 9°37W 166 D2
Fear, C. U.S.A. 33°50N 77°58W 315 E16
Feather → U.S.A. 38°47N 121°36W 304 G3
Feather Falls U.S.A. 39°36N 121°16W 306 F5
Featherston N.Z. 41°6S 175°20E 284 H4
Featherstone Zimbabwe 18°42S 30°55E 269 F3
Fécamp France 49°45N 0°22E 172 C7
Feda Norway 58°17N 6°50E 164 F3

Fedala = Mohammedia
Morocco 33°44N 7°21W 260 B3
Federación Argentina 31°0S 57°55W 334 C4
Federal Capital Terr. ☐
Nigeria 9°0N 7°10E 263 D6
Federal Way U.S.A. 47°18N 122°19W 306 C4
Fedeshkūh Iran 28°49N 53°50E 247 D7
FedEx Stadium U.S.A. 38°54N 76°51W 143 B4
Fedje Norway 60°47N 4°43E 164 D1
Fedorovka Kazakhstan 53°37N 62°42E 216 B6
Fefan I. Pac. Oc. 7°21N 151°51E 287 T18
Fehérgyarmat Hungary 47°58N 22°30E 182 C7
Fehmarn Germany 54°27N 11°7E 178 A7
Fehmarn Bælt Europe 54°35N 11°20E 163 K5
Fehmarn Belt = Fehmarn Bælt
Europe 54°35N 11°20E 163 K5
Fei Xian China 35°18N 117°59E 227 G9
Feicheng China 36°14N 116°45E 226 F9
Feidong China 32°0N 117°35E 229 B11
Feijó Brazil 8°9S 70°21W 330 B3
Feilding N.Z. 40°13S 175°35E 284 G4
Feira de Santana Brazil 12°15S 38°57W 333 D4
Feirân, W. → Egypt 28°39N 33°12E 251 K4
Feirâni, G. Egypt 28°31N 34°19E 251 K5
Feiring Norway 60°30N 11°10E 164 D8
Feixi China 31°43N 117°59E 229 B11
Feixiang China 36°30N 114°45E 226 F8
Fejaj, Chott el Tunisia 33°52N 9°14E 258 B1
Fejér ☐ Hungary 47°9N 18°30E 182 C3
Fejø Denmark 54°55N 11°30E 163 K5
Feke Turkey 37°48N 35°56E 212 D6
Fekete → Hungary 45°47N 18°15E 182 E3
Felanitx Spain 39°28N 3°9E 206 B4
Felda U.S.A. 26°34N 81°26W 317 J8
Feldbach Austria 46°57N 15°52E 180 E8
Feldberg Baden-W., Germany 47°52N 8°0E 179 H3
Feldberg Mecklenburg-Vorpommern,
Germany 53°20N 13°25E 178 B9
Feldkirch Austria 47°15N 9°37E 180 D2
Feldkirchen Austria 46°44N 14°6E 180 E7
Feldkirchen Oberbayern,
Germany 48°8N 11°43E 131 B3
Feldmoching Germany 48°14N 11°32E 131 A2
Félicité Seychelles 4°19S 55°52E 272 c
Felicity U.S.A. 38°51N 84°6W 311 F12
Felidhoo Maldives 3°29N 73°32E 272 d
Felidu Atoll Maldives 3°29N 73°29E 272 d
Felipe Carrillo Puerto
Mexico 19°38N 88°3W 319 D7
Felixburg Zimbabwe 19°29S 30°51E 271 A5
Felixlândia Brazil 18°47S 44°55W 333 E3
Felixstowe U.K. 51°58N 1°23E 169 F9
Felletin France 45°53N 2°11E 174 C6
Fellingsbro Sweden 59°26N 15°37E 162 E9
Fellsmere U.S.A. 27°46N 80°36W 317 H9
Felshtin = Gvardeyskoye
Ukraine 45°7N 34°1E 189 K8
Felsogalla = Tatabánya
Hungary 47°32N 18°25E 182 C3
Feltham U.K. 51°26N 0°24W 125 B1
Felton U.S.A. 37°3N 122°4W 306 H4
Feltre Italy 46°1N 11°54E 199 B8
Femer Bælt = Fehmarn Bælt
Europe 54°35N 11°20E 163 K5
Femø Denmark 54°58N 11°35E 163 K5
Femunden Norway 62°10N 11°53E 164 B8
Femundsmarka △ Norway 62°18N 12°6E 164 B9
Fen He → China 35°36N 110°42E 226 G6
Fenchih Taiwan 23°30N 120°40E 225 C2
Fene Spain 43°27N 8°9W 194 B2
Fenelon Falls Canada 44°32N 78°45W 312 B6
Fener Turkey 41°1N 28°56E 122 B1
Fener Burnu Turkey 36°58N 27°18E 205 E9
Fenerbahçe Turkey 40°58N 29°2E 122 C2
Feneroa Ethiopia 13°5N 39°3E 257 E4
Feng Xian Jiangsu, China 34°43N 116°35E 226 G9
Feng Xian Shaanxi, China 33°54N 106°40E 226 H4
Fengari Greece 40°25N 25°32E 203 F9
Fengcheng Jiangxi,
China 28°12N 115°48E 229 C10
Fengcheng Liaoning, China 40°28N 124°5E 224 B2
Fengdu China 29°55N 107°48E 228 C6
Fengfeng China 36°28N 114°8E 226 F8
Fenggang China 27°57N 107°47E 228 D6
Fenghua China 29°40N 121°25E 229 C13
Fenghuang China 27°57N 109°29E 228 D7
Fengjie China 31°3N 109°31E 228 B7
Fengkai China 23°24N 111°30E 229 F8
Fengkang Taiwan 22°12N 120°41E 225 D2
Fengle China 31°29N 112°29E 229 B9
Fenglin Taiwan 23°45N 121°26E 225 C3
Fengning China 41°10N 116°33E 226 D9
Fengpin Taiwan 23°36N 121°31E 225 C3
Fengqing China 24°38N 99°55E 228 E2
Fengqiu China 35°2N 114°25E 226 G8
Fengrun China 39°48N 118°8E 227 E10
Fengshan Guangxi Zhuangzu,
China 24°39N 109°15E 228 E7
Fengshan Guangxi Zhuangzu,
China 24°31N 107°3E 228 E6
Fengshan Taiwan 22°38N 120°21E 225 D2
Fengshun China 23°46N 116°10E 229 F11
Fengtai Anhui, China 32°50N 116°40E 229 A11
Fengtai Beijing, China 39°49N 116°14E 114 C1
Fengtai Stadium China 39°51N 116°15E 114 B1
Fengtongzhai △ China 30°32N 102°54E 228 B4
Fengxiang China 34°29N 107°25E 226 G4
Fengxin China 28°41N 115°18E 229 C10
Fengyang China 32°51N 117°29E 227 H9
Fengyi China 25°37N 100°20E 228 E3
Fengyüan Taiwan 24°15N 120°35E 225 B2
Fengzhen China 40°25N 113°2E 226 D7
Feni Is. Papua N. G. 4°0S 153°40E 286 C7
Fenino Russia 55°43N 37°56E 129 B5
Fennimore U.S.A. 42°59N 90°39W 310 B6
Fenny Bangla. 22°55N 91°32E 241 D3
Feno, C. de France 41°58N 8°33E 175 G12
Fenoarivo Fianarantsoa,
Madag. 21°43S 46°24E 272 C2
Fenoarivo Fianarantsoa,
Madag. 20°52S 46°53E 272 C2
Fenoarivo Afovoany
Madag. 18°26S 46°34E 272 B2
Fenoarivo Atsinanana
Madag. 17°22S 49°25E 272 B2
Fens, The U.K. 52°38N 0°2W 168 E7
Fensmark Denmark 55°17N 11°48E 163 J5
Fenton U.S.A. 42°48N 83°42W 311 B13
Fenxi China 36°40N 111°31E 226 F6
Fenyang China 37°18N 111°48E 226 F6
Fenyi China 27°45N 114°47E 229 D10
Fenyuan Taiwan 24°1N 120°37E 225 B2
Feodosiya Ukraine 45°2N 35°16E 189 K8
Fer, C. de Algeria 37°3N 7°10E 261 A6
Fera Solomon Is. 8°6S 159°37E 287 M10
Ferbane Ireland 53°16N 7°50W 166 C4
Ferdows Iran 33°58N 58°2E 247 C8
Fère-Champenoise France 48°45N 3°59E 173 D10
Fère-en-Tardenois France 49°10N 3°30E 173 C10
Ferencváros Hungary 47°29N 19°5E 117 B2
Ferentino Italy 41°42N 13°15E 199 G10
Feres Greece 40°53N 26°10E 203 F10
Ferfer Somali Rep. 5°4N 45°9E 267 C6
Fergana = Farghona
Uzbekistan 40°23N 71°19E 217 D8
Fergana Range Asia 41°0N 73°50E 217 D8
Fergus Canada 43°43N 80°24W 312 C4
Fergus Falls U.S.A. 46°17N 96°4W 308 B5
Ferguson U.S.A. 38°44N 90°18W 310 F6
Fergusson I. Papua N. G. 9°30S 150°45E 286 E6
Fériana Tunisia 34°59N 8°33E 258 B1
Feričanci Croatia 45°32N 18°0E 182 E2
Ferihegy, Budapest ✈ (BUD)
Hungary 47°26N 19°14E 117 B3
Ferizaj = Uroševac Kosovo 42°23N 21°10E 202 D5
Ferkane Algeria 34°37N 7°26E 261 B6
Ferkéssédougou Ivory C. 9°35N 5°6W 262 D3
Ferlach Austria 46°32N 14°18E 180 E7
Ferland Canada 50°19N 88°27W 298 B2
Ferlo, Vallée du Senegal 15°15N 14°15W 262 B2
Ferlo-Nord ⌓ Senegal 15°43N 14°20W 262 B2
Ferlo-Sud ⌓ Senegal 15°43N 14°0W 262 B2
Fermanagh ☐ U.K. 54°21N 7°40W 166 B4
Fermo Italy 43°9N 13°43E 199 E10
Fermont Canada 52°47N 67°5W 299 B6
Fermoselle Spain 41°19N 6°27W 194 D4
Fermoy Ireland 52°9N 8°16W 166 D3
Fern Creek U.S.A. 38°9N 85°36W 311 G11
Fern Gully Jamaica 18°22N 77°9E 320 a
Fernán Núñez Spain 37°40N 4°44W 195 H6
Fernández Argentina 27°55S 63°50W 334 B3
Fernandina, I. Ecuador 0°25S 91°30W 330 a
Fernandina Beach U.S.A. 30°40N 81°27W 316 E8
Fernando de Noronha
Brazil 4°0S 33°10W 152 G8
Fernando Póo = Bioko
Eq. Guin. 3°30N 8°40E 263 E6
Fernandópolis Brazil 20°16S 50°14W 333 F1
Ferndale Ont., Canada 44°58N 81°17W 312 B3
Ferndale Gauteng, S. Africa 26°5S 28°0E 123 A2
Ferndale Wash., U.S.A. 48°51N 122°36W 306 B4
Fernie Canada 49°30N 115°5W 296 D5
Fernlees Australia 23°51S 148°7E 280 C4
Fernley U.S.A. 39°36N 119°15W 304 G4
Fernwood U.S.A. 43°16N 73°38W 313 C11
Feroke India 11°9N 75°46E 245 J2
Feroz Shah Kotla Cricket Stadium
Delhi, India 120 b3
Ferozepore = Firozpur
India 30°55N 74°40E 242 D6
Ferrandina Italy 40°29N 16°27E 201 B9
Ferrara Italy 44°50N 11°35E 199 D8
Ferrato, C. Italy 39°18N 9°38E 200 C2
Ferré, C. Martinique 14°27N 60°49W 322 j
Ferreira do Alentejo Portugal 38°4N 8°6W 195 G2
Ferreira Gomes Brazil 0°48N 51°8W 332 A1
Ferreñafe Peru 6°42S 79°50W 330 B2
Ferrerías Spain 39°59N 4°1E 206 B5
Ferret, C. France 44°38N 1°15W 174 D2
Ferrette France 47°30N 7°20E 173 E14
Ferriday U.S.A. 31°38N 91°33W 314 F9
Ferriere Italy 44°40N 9°30E 198 D6
Ferrières France 48°5N 2°48E 173 D9
Ferro, Capo Italy 41°9N 9°31E 200 A2
Ferrol Spain 43°29N 8°15W 194 B2
Ferrol, Pen. de Peru 9°10S 78°35W 330 B2
Ferron U.S.A. 39°5N 111°8W 304 G8
Ferros Brazil 19°14S 43°2W 333 E3
Ferrutx, C. de Spain 39°47N 3°21E 206 B4
Ferry Pass U.S.A. 30°31N 87°13W 317 E2
Ferryland Canada 47°2N 52°53W 299 C9
Ferrysburg U.S.A. 43°5N 86°13W 311 A10
Ferryville = Menzel-Bourguiba
Tunisia 37°9N 9°49E 258 A1
Fertile U.S.A. 47°32N 96°17W 308 B5
Fertő-Hanság △ Hungary 47°25N 16°50E 182 C1
Fertőszentmiklós Hungary 47°35N 16°53E 182 C1
Fès Morocco 34°0N 5°0W 260 B4
Fès ☐ Morocco 34°1N 5°0W 260 B4
Feshi Dem. Rep. of the Congo 6°8S 18°10E 265 D3
Fessenden U.S.A. 47°39N 99°38W 308 B4
Festenberg = Twardogóra
Poland 51°23N 17°28E 185 G4
Festøya Norway 62°22N 6°19E 164 B3
Festus U.S.A. 38°13N 90°24W 310 F6
Feté Bowé Senegal 14°56N 13°30W 262 C2
Fetești Romania 44°22N 27°51E 183 F12
Fethiye Turkey 36°36N 29°6E 205 E11
Fethiye Körfezi Turkey 36°40N 28°50E 205 E10
Fetlar U.K. 60°36N 0°52W 167 A8
Fetsund Norway 59°56N 11°10E 164 E8
Feuilles → Canada 58°47N 70°4W 295 F17
Feurs France 45°45N 4°13E 175 C8
Fevik Norway 58°22N 8°39E 164 F5
Fevzipaşa Turkey 37°6N 36°37E 250 A7
Feyzābād Badākhshān,
Afghan. 37°7N 70°33E 240 A3
Feyzābād Fāryāb, Afghan. 36°17N 64°52E 240 A2
Fez = Fès Morocco 34°0N 5°0W 260 B4
Fezzan Libya 27°0N 13°0E 258 C2
Fia Congo 3°25S 14°49E 264 C2
Fiambalá Argentina 27°45S 67°37W 334 B2
Fianarantsoa Madag. 21°26S 47°5E 272 C2
Fianarantsoa ☐ Madag. 22°30S 47°0E 272 B2
Fianga Cameroon 9°55N 15°9E 259 G3
Fiche Ethiopia 9°50N 38°46E 257 F4
Fichtelgebirge Germany 50°2N 11°55E 179 E7
Fichtelgebirge ⌓ Germany 50°8N 12°0E 179 E8
Fichtenau Germany 52°27N 13°42E 115 B4
Ficksburg S. Africa 28°51S 27°53E 271 C4
Fidenza Italy 44°52N 10°3E 198 D7
Fiditi Nigeria 7°45N 3°53E 263 D5
Fidjeland Norway 58°57N 6°56E 164 F3
Field → Australia 23°48S 138°0E 280 C2
Field I. Australia 12°5S 132°23E 278 B5
Field Museum of Natural History
Chicago, U.S.A. 119 e2
Fields Corner U.S.A. 42°18N 71°3W 116 B2
Fieni Romania 45°8N 25°25E 183 E10
Fier Albania 40°43N 19°33E 202 F3
Fiera Camp Italy 45°28N 9°9E 129 B1
Fierzë Albania 42°15N 20°1E 202 D4
Fife ☐ U.K. 56°16N 3°1W 167 E5
Fife ⌓ U.K. 56°13N 3°2W 167 E5
Fife Ness U.K. 56°17N 2°35W 167 E6
Fifth Cataract Sudan 18°22N 33°50E 256 D3
Fig Tree St. Kitts & Nevis 17°8N 62°35W 322 d
Figari France 41°29N 9°7E 175 G13
Figeac France 44°37N 2°2E 174 D6
Figeholm Sweden 57°22N 16°33E 163 G10
Figino Italy 45°29N 9°4E 129 B1
Figline Valdarno Italy 43°37N 11°28E 199 E8
Figtree Zimbabwe 20°22S 28°20E 269 G2
Figueira = Governador Valadares
Brazil 18°15S 41°57W 333 E3
Figueira Castelo Rodrigo
Portugal 40°57N 6°58W 194 E4
Figueira da Foz Portugal 40°7N 8°54W 194 E2
Figueiró dos Vinhos
Portugal 39°55N 8°16W 194 F2
Figueres Spain 42°18N 2°58E 196 C7
Figuig Morocco 32°5N 1°11W 261 B5
Figuig ☐ Morocco 32°50N 2°15W 261 B5
Fihaonana Madag. 18°36S 47°12E 272 B2
Fiherenana Madag. 18°29S 48°24E 272 B2
Fiherenana → Madag. 23°19S 43°37E 272 C1
Fiji ■ Pac. Oc. 17°20S 179°0E 287 A2
Fijir Iraq 33°21N 44°21E 113 A2
Fik Ethiopia 8°10N 42°19E 257 F5
Fika Nigeria 11°15N 11°13E 263 C7
Filabres, Sierra de los
Spain 37°13N 2°20W 195 H8
Filabusi Zimbabwe 20°34S 29°20E 271 B4
Filadelfia Bolivia 11°20S 68°46W 330 C4
Filadélfia Brazil 7°21S 47°30W 332 C2
Filadelfia Italy 38°47N 16°17E 201 D9
Filadelfia Paraguay 22°21S 60°2W 334 A3
Fil'akovo Slovak Rep. 48°17N 19°50E 181 C12
Filchner Ice Shelf Antarctica 79°0S 40°0W 151 D1
Filefjell Norway 61°8N 8°10E 164 C5
Filey U.K. 54°12N 0°18W 168 C7
Filey B. U.K. 54°12N 0°15W 168 C7
Filfla Malta 35°47N 14°24E 206 F7
Fili-Mazilovo Russia 55°44N 37°29E 129 B2
Filiaşi Romania 44°32N 23°31E 183 F8
Filiates Greece 39°38N 20°16E 206 B10
Filiatra Greece 37°9N 21°35E 204 D3
Filicudi Italy 38°35N 14°33E 201 D7
Filim Oman 20°37N 58°12E 249 B7
Filingué Niger 14°21N 3°22E 263 C5
Filiourí = Lissos → Greece 41°15N 25°40E 203 E9
Filipada Greece 39°12N 20°53E 204 B2
Filipstad Sweden 59°43N 14°9E 162 E8
Filisur Switz. 46°41N 9°40E 179 J5
Fillmore Calif., U.S.A. 34°24N 118°55W 307 L8
Fillmore Utah, U.S.A. 38°58N 112°20W 304 G7
Filothei Greece 38°2N 23°46E 112 A2
Filotio Greece 37°3N 25°30E 205 D7
Filottrano Italy 43°26N 13°21E 199 E10
Filtu Ethiopia 5°8N 40°35E 257 F5
Fimbul Ice Shelf S. Ocean 69°30S 1°0W 151 C2
Fimi →
Dem. Rep. of the Congo 3°1S 16°58E 264 C3
Fina ⌓ Mali 13°15N 8°46W 262 C3
Finale Emilia Italy 44°50N 11°18E 199 D8
Finale Ligure Italy 44°10N 8°20E 198 D5
Finalmarina = Finale Ligure
Italy 44°10N 8°20E 198 D5
Fiñana Spain 37°10N 2°50W 195 H8
Financial District San Francisco, U.S.A. 136 b3
Finch Canada 45°11N 75°7W 313 A9
Finch Hatton Australia 20°25S 148°39E 280 b
Finchaa, L. Ethiopia 9°35N 37°20E 266 C4
Finchley U.K. 51°36N 0°11W 125 A2
Findhorn → U.K. 57°38N 3°38W 167 D5
Findıklı Turkey 41°16N 41°9E 213 B9
Findlay U.S.A. 41°2N 83°39W 311 C13
Fine U.S.A. 44°14N 75°8W 313 B9
Fine Art, Museum of =
Kunsthistorischesmuseum
Vienna, Austria 142 b1
Fine Arts, Museum of
U.S.A. 42°20N 71°5W 116 A2
Finger L. Canada 53°33N 93°30W 298 B1
Finger Lakes U.S.A. 42°40N 76°30W 313 D8
Finglas Ireland 53°23N 6°19W 120 A2
Fingoè Mozam. 15°55S 31°50E 269 F3
Finike Turkey 36°21N 30°10E 205 E12
Finike Körfezi Turkey 36°17N 30°16E 205 E12
Finiq Albania 39°54N 20°3E 202 G4
Finistère ☐ France 48°20N 4°0W 172 D3
Finisterre = Fisterra Spain 42°54N 9°16W 194 C1
Finisterre, C. = Fisterra, C.
Spain 42°50N 9°19W 194 C1
Finisterre Ra. Papua N. G. 6°0S 146°30E 286 D4
Finke Australia 25°34S 134°35E 280 D1
Finke Gorge △ Australia 24°8S 132°49E 278 D5
Finland ■ Europe 63°0N 27°0E 160 E22
Finland, G. of Europe 60°0N 26°0E 188 C3
Finlay → Canada 57°0N 125°10W 296 B3
Finley N.S.W., Australia 35°38S 145°35E 283 C6
Finley N. Dak., U.S.A. 47°31N 97°50W 308 B5
Finn → Ireland 54°51N 7°28W 166 B4
Finnerödja Sweden 58°57N 14°24E 163 F8
Finnigan, Mt. Australia 15°49S 145°17E 280 B4
Finniss, C. Australia 33°8S 134°51E 281 E1
Finnmark Norway 69°37N 23°57E 160 B20
Finnsnes Norway 69°14N 18°0E 160 B18
Finsbury U.K. 51°31N 0°6W 125 A3
Finsbury Park U.K. 51°34N 0°6W 125 A3
Finschhafen Papua N. G. 6°33S 147°50E 286 D4
Finse Norway 60°36N 7°30E 164 D4
Finspång Sweden 58°43N 15°47E 163 F9
Finsteraarhorn Switz. 46°31N 8°10E 179 J4
Finsterwalde Germany 51°37N 13°42E 178 D9
Fiora → Italy 42°20N 11°34E 199 F8
Fiordland △ N.Z. 45°46S 167°0E 285 F2
Fiorenzuola d'Arda Italy 44°56N 9°55E 198 D6
Fiorito Argentina 34°42S 58°26W 117 C2
Fīq Syria 32°46N 35°41E 250 F6
Firat = Furāt, Nahr al →
Asia 31°0N 47°25E 246 D5
Fire Island ⌓ U.S.A. 40°38N 73°8W 313 F11
Firebag → Canada 57°45N 111°21W 297 B6
Firebaugh U.S.A. 36°52N 120°27W 306 J6
Firedrake L. Canada 61°25N 104°30W 297 A8
Firenze Italy 43°46N 11°15E 199 E8
Firenze Amerigo Vespucci ✈ (FLR)
Italy 43°49N 11°13E 199 E8
Firenze Pisa ✈ (PSA) Italy 43°40N 10°22E 198 E7
Firenzuola Italy 44°7N 11°23E 199 D8
Firhouse Ireland 53°17N 6°20W 120 B2
Firk, Sha'ib → Iraq 30°59N 44°34E 246 D5
Firkachi Niger 15°40N 14°20E 259 E2
Firmi France 44°33N 2°19E 174 D6
Firminy France 45°23N 4°18E 175 C8
Firozabad India 27°10N 78°25E 243 F8
Firozpur India 30°55N 74°40E 242 D6
Firozpur-Jhirka India 27°48N 76°57E 242 F7
Fīrūzābād Iran 28°52N 52°35E 247 D7
Fīrūzkūh Iran 35°50N 52°50E 247 C7
Firvale Canada 52°27N 126°13W 296 C3
Fischerhäuser Germany 48°14N 11°41E 131 A3
Fish → Namibia 28°7S 17°10E 270 C2
Fish → Northern Cape,
S. Africa 31°30S 20°16E 270 D3
Fish River Canyon
Namibia 27°40S 17°35E 270 C2
Fisheating Cr. → U.S.A. 26°57N 81°7W 317 J8
Fisher B. Canada 51°35N 97°13W 297 C9
Fisher Island U.S.A. 25°45N 80°8W 128 B2
Fishermans Bend
Australia 37°49S 144°55E 128 A1
Fisherman's Wharf
San Francisco, U.S.A. 136 a1
Fishers I. U.S.A. 41°15N 72°0W 313 E13
Fisherville Canada 43°46N 79°28W 141 A2
Fishguard U.K. 52°0N 4°58W 169 E3
Fishing L. Canada 52°10N 95°24W 297 C9
Fishkill U.S.A. 41°32N 73°54W 313 E11
Fiskardo Greece 38°28N 20°35E 207 C2
Fiskenæsset = Qeqertarsuatsiaat
Greenland 63°5N 50°45W 154 E5
Fiskstätra Sweden 59°17N 18°13E 139 B3
Fismes France 49°20N 3°40E 173 C10
Fisterra Spain 42°54N 9°16W 194 C1
Fisterra, C. Spain 42°50N 9°19W 194 C1
Fitchburg Mass., U.S.A. 42°35N 71°48W 313 D13
Fitchburg Wis., U.S.A. 42°58N 89°28W 310 B7
Fitjar Iceland 64°28N 21°18W 155 C5
Fitjar Hordaland, Norway 59°55N 5°17E 164 E2
Fitri, L. Chad 12°50N 17°28E 259 F3
Fitz Roy Argentina 47°0S 67°0W 336 F3
Fitz Roy, Cerro Argentina 49°17S 73°5W 336 C2
Fitzgerald Alta., Canada 59°51N 111°36W 296 B6
Fitzgerald Ga., U.S.A. 31°43N 83°15W 316 D6
Fitzgerald River △
Australia 33°53S 119°55E 279 F3
Fitzmaurice → Australia 14°45S 130°5E 278 B5
Fitzroy → Queens.,
Australia 23°32S 150°52E 280 C5
Fitzroy → W. Austral.,
Australia 17°31S 123°35E 278 C3
Fitzroy Crossing Australia 18°9S 125°38E 278 C4
Fitzroy Gardens Australia 37°48S 144°58E 128 A1
Fitzwilliam I. Canada 45°30N 81°45W 312 A3
Fiuggi Italy 41°48N 13°13E 199 G10
Fiume = Rijeka Croatia 45°20N 14°21E 199 C11
Fiumicino, Roma ✈ (FCO)
Italy 41°48N 12°15E 199 G9
Five Cowrie Cr. → Nigeria 6°26N 3°24E 124 B2
Five Dock Australia 33°52S 151°8E 139 B1
Five Island Harbour
Antigua & B. 17°6N 61°54W 322 b
Five Points U.S.A. 36°26N 120°6W 306 J6
Fivizzano Italy 44°14N 10°8E 198 D7
Fizi Dem. Rep. of the Congo 4°17S 28°55E 268 C2
Fjæra Norway 59°52N 6°22E 164 E3
Fjærland Norway 61°24N 6°43E 164 C3
Fjærlandsfjorden Norway 61°17N 6°40E 164 C3
Fjällbacka Sweden 58°36N 11°17E 163 F5
Fjällnäs Sweden 62°36N 12°11E 162 B6
Fjärdhundra Sweden 59°47N 16°56E 162 E10
Fjellerup Denmark 56°29N 10°34E 163 H4
Fjellstrand Norway 59°47N 10°36E 133 B2
Fjerritslev Denmark 57°5N 9°15E 163 G3
Fjugesta Sweden 59°11N 14°52E 162 E8
Fkih ben Salah Morocco 32°32N 6°45W 260 B3
Flå Norway 60°25N 9°28E 164 D6
Flacq Plain Mauritius 20°13S 57°43E 272 e
Flagler Beach U.S.A. 29°29N 81°8W 317 F8
Flagstaff U.S.A. 35°12N 111°39W 305 J8
Flagstaff B. St. Helena 15°54S 5°41W 153 h
Flagstaff L. U.S.A. 45°12N 70°18W 313 A14
Flaherty I. Canada 56°15N 79°15W 298 A4
Flåm Norway 60°50N 7°7E 164 D4
Flamands St.-Martin 17°55N 62°51W 322 a
Flambeau → U.S.A. 45°18N 91°14W 308 C8
Flamborough Hd. U.K. 54°7N 0°5W 168 C7
Flamengo Brazil 22°56S 43°11W 135 B1
Flamengos Azores 38°33N 28°39W 153 d1
Fläming Germany 52°6N 12°23E 178 C8
Flaming Gorge ⌓ U.S.A. 41°10N 109°25W 304 F9
Flaming Gorge Res.
U.S.A. 41°10N 109°25W 304 F9
Flamingo Fla., U.S.A. 28°22N 81°22W 133 B2
Flamingo Fla., U.S.A. 25°8N 80°57W 317 K9
Flamingo, Teluk Indonesia 5°30S 138°0E 231 F9
Flaminio Italy 41°55N 12°28E 136 C2
Flanagan U.S.A. 40°53N 88°52W 311 D8
Flanagin Town Trin. & Tob. 10°25N 61°19W 323 t
Flanders = Flandre Europe 50°50N 2°30E 173 B9
Flandre Europe 50°50N 2°30E 173 B9
Flandre-Occidentale = West-
Vlaanderen ☐ Belgium 51°0N 3°0E 170 D2
Flandre-Orientale = Oost-
Vlaanderen ☐ Belgium 51°5N 3°50E 170 C3
Flandreau U.S.A. 44°3N 96°36W 308 C5
Flanigan U.S.A. 40°10N 119°53W 304 F4
Flannan Is. U.K. 58°9N 7°52W 167 C1
Flåsjön Sweden 64°5N 15°40E 160 D16
Flaskebekk Norway 59°51N 10°39E 133 A2
Flat U.S.A. 62°28N 158°1W 303 E8
Flat → N.W.T., Canada 61°33N 125°18W 296 A3
Flat → Mich., U.S.A. 42°56N 85°20W 311 B11
Flat Pt. N.Z. 41°14S 175°57E 284 H4
Flat Rock U.S.A. 42°6N 83°17W 311 B13
Flatbush U.S.A. 40°39N 73°56W 132 C2
Flateby Norway 59°50N 11°10E 164 E8
Flaten Sweden 59°15N 18°9E 139 B2
Flatey Iceland 66°10N 17°52W 155 A9
Flateyri Iceland 66°3N 23°31W 155 A3
Flathead L. U.S.A. 47°51N 114°8W 304 C6
Flatiron Building New York, U.S.A. 132 d2
Flatlands U.S.A. 40°37N 73°56W 132 C2
Flatow = Złotów Poland 53°22N 17°2E 184 E4
Flatrock → U.S.A. 39°12N 85°56W 311 F10
Flattery, C. Queens.,
Australia 14°58S 145°21E 280 A4
Flattery, C. Wash.,
U.S.A. 48°23N 124°29W 306 B2
Flatts Village Bermuda 32°18N 64°43W 153 a
Flatwoods U.S.A. 38°31N 82°43W 309 F12
Flecha Pt. Phil. 7°22N 123°24E 233 H4
Flechas Pt. Phil. 10°22N 119°34E 233 F2
Fleet Center Boston, U.S.A. 116 a2
Fleetwood Lancs., U.K. 53°55N 3°1W 168 D4
Fleetwood Pa., U.S.A. 40°27N 75°49W 313 F9
Flekke Norway 61°19N 5°20E 164 C2
Flekkefjord Norway 58°18N 6°39E 164 F3
Flemingsburg U.S.A. 38°25N 83°45W 311 F13
Flemington U.S.A. 41°7N 77°28W 312 E7
Flemington Racecourse
Australia 37°47S 144°54E 128 A1
Flemish Cap Atl. Oc. 47°0N 45°0W 152 B7
Flen Sweden 59°4N 16°35E 162 E10
Flensburg Germany 54°47N 9°27E 178 A5
Flers France 48°47N 0°33W 172 D6
Flesberg Norway 59°51N 9°27E 164 E6
Flesherton Canada 44°16N 80°33W 312 B4
Flesko, Tanjung Indonesia 0°29N 124°30E 231 D6
Fletcher = Aurora
U.S.A. 39°43N 104°49W 304 G11
Fleurance France 43°52N 0°40E 174 E4
Fleurier Switz. 46°54N 6°35E 179 J2
Fleurieu Pen. Australia 35°40S 138°5E 282 C3
Flevoland ☐ Neths. 52°30N 5°30E 170 B5
Flin Flon Canada 54°46N 101°53W 297 C8
Flinders → Australia 17°36S 140°36E 280 B3
Flinders B. Australia 34°19S 115°19E 279 F2
Flinders Chase △
Australia 35°50S 136°42E 282 C2
Flinders Group Australia 14°11S 144°15E 280 A3
Flinders I. S. Austral.,
Australia 33°44S 134°41E 281 E1
Flinders I. Tas., Australia 40°0S 148°0E 281 G4
Flinders Ranges Australia 31°30S 138°30E 282 A3
Flinders Ranges △
Australia 31°30S 138°40E 282 A3
Flinders Reefs Australia 17°37S 148°31E 280 B4
Flint Flints., U.K. 53°15N 3°8W 168 D4
Flint Mich., U.S.A. 43°1N 83°41W 311 A13
Flint → U.S.A. 30°57N 84°34W 316 E5
Flint I. Kiribati 11°26S 151°48W 289 f
Flint Pk. U.S.A. 34°9N 118°11W 126 B3
Flintshire ☐ U.K. 53°17N 3°17W 168 D4
Flipper Pt. Wake I. 19°18N 166°37E 302 b
Flisa Norway 60°37N 12°0E 164 D9
Flisa → Norway 60°37N 12°0E 164 D9
Fliseryd Sweden 57°6N 16°15E 163 G10
Flix Spain 41°14N 0°32E 196 D5
Flixecourt France 50°1N 2°5E 173 B9
Floby Sweden 58°8N 13°20E 163 F7
Floda Sweden 57°49N 12°22E 163 G6
Flodden U.K. 55°37N 2°8W 168 B5
Flogny-la-Chapelle France 47°57N 3°57E 173 E10
Floodplains △ Sri Lanka 8°10N 81°10E 245 K5
Floodwood U.S.A. 46°56N 92°55W 308 B7
Flora Apayao, Phil. 18°14N 121°5E 232 B3
Flora Ill., U.S.A. 38°40N 88°29W 310 F8
Flora Ind., U.S.A. 40°33N 86°31W 311 D10
Florac France 44°20N 3°37E 174 D7
Florahome U.S.A. 29°44N 81°54W 316 F8
Floral City U.S.A. 28°45N 82°17W 317 G7
Florala U.S.A. 31°0N 86°20W 315 F11
Florânia Brazil 6°8S 36°49W 332 C4
Floreana, I. = Santa María, I.
Ecuador 1°17S 90°26W 330 a
Florence = Firenze Italy 43°46N 11°15E 199 E8
Florence Ala., U.S.A. 34°48N 87°41W 315 D11
Florence Ariz., U.S.A. 33°2N 111°23W 305 K8
Florence Calif., U.S.A. 33°57N 118°13W 126 C3
Florence Colo., U.S.A. 38°23N 105°8W 304 G11
Florence Oreg., U.S.A. 43°58N 124°7W 304 D1
Florence S.C., U.S.A. 34°12N 79°46W 315 D15
Florence, L. Australia 28°53S 138°9E 281 D2
Florence Bay = Chtimba
Malawi 10°35S 34°13E 269 E3
Florence Bloom Bird Sanctuary ⌓
S. Africa 26°7S 28°0E 123 A2
Florencia Colombia 1°36N 75°36W 328 C2
Florennes Belgium 50°15N 4°35E 170 D4
Florensac France 43°23N 3°28E 174 E7
Florentia S. Africa 26°16S 28°8E 123 B2
Florenville Belgium 49°40N 5°19E 170 E5
Flores = Florânia Brazil 6°8S 36°49W 332 C4
Flores = Timon Brazil 5°8S 42°52W 332 C3
Flores B. Aires, Argentina 34°38S 58°27W 117 B2
Flores Azores 39°26N 31°13W 153 d2
Flores Brazil 7°51S 37°59W 332 C4
Flores Guatemala 16°59N 89°50W 320 C2
Flores Indonesia 8°35S 121°0E 235 D5
Flores, Mercado de Mexico 19°19N 99°5W 128 C2
Flores I. Canada 49°20N 126°10W 296 D3
Flores Sea Indonesia 6°30S 120°0E 231 F6
Floresta B. Aires, Argentina 34°37S 58°27W 117 B2
Floresta Brazil 8°40S 37°26W 332 C4
Floreşti Moldova 47°53N 28°17E 183 C13
Floresville U.S.A. 29°8N 98°10W 314 G5
Floriano Brazil 6°50S 43°0W 332 C3
Florianópolis Brazil 27°30S 48°30W 335 B6
Florida B. Aires, Argentina 34°31S 58°28W 117 B2
Florida Cuba 21°32N 78°14W 320 B4
Florida Puerto Rico 18°22N 66°34W 321 b
Florida Gauteng, S. Africa 26°10S 27°55E 123 B1
Florida Uruguay 34°7S 56°10W 335 C4
Florida ☐ U.S.A. 28°0N 82°0W 315 G14
Florida, Straits of U.S.A. 25°0N 80°0W 320 B4
Florida B. U.S.A. 25°0N 80°45W 320 B3
Florida City U.S.A. 25°27N 80°29W 317 K9
Florida Is. Solomon Is. 8°55S 160°15E 287 M11
Florida Keys U.S.A. 24°40N 81°0W 317 L8
Floridablanca Phil. 14°59N 120°31E 232 D3
Floridia Italy 37°5N 15°9E 201 E8
Floridsdorf Austria 48°15N 16°26E 142 A2
Florin U.S.A. 38°30N 121°24W 306 G5
Florina Greece 40°48N 21°26E 202 F5
Florina ☐ Greece 40°45N 21°20E 202 F5
Florissant U.S.A. 38°47N 90°19W 310 F6
Florø Norway 61°35N 5°1E 164 C2
Flotte, C. de N. Cal. 21°10S 167°25E 288 d
Flower Station Canada 45°10N 76°41W 313 A8
Flowerpot I. Canada 45°18N 81°38W 312 A3
Floydada U.S.A. 33°59N 101°20W 314 E4
Fludir Iceland 64°7N 20°6W 155 C6
Flugumyri Iceland 65°34N 19°19W 155 B7
Fluk Indonesia 1°42S 127°44E 231 E7
Flúmen → Spain 41°43N 0°9W 196 D4
Flumendosa → Italy 39°26N 9°37E 200 C2
Fluminimaggiore Italy 39°26N 8°30E 200 C1
Flushing = Vlissingen
Neths. 51°26N 3°34E 170 C3
Flushing Mich., U.S.A. 43°4N 83°51W 311 A13
Flushing N.Y., U.S.A. 40°45N 73°49W 132 B3
Flushing Meadows Corona Park
U.S.A. 40°44N 73°50W 132 B2
Fluvià → Spain 42°12N 3°7E 196 C8
Fly → Papua N. G. 8°25S 143°0E 286 E2
Flying Fish, C. Antarctica 72°6S 102°29W 151 D15
Flysta Sweden 59°22N 17°54E 139 A1
Fo Tan China 22°23N 114°11E 122 A2
Foa Tonga 19°45S 174°18W 287 P13
Foam Lake Canada 51°40N 103°32W 297 C8
Foča Bos.-H. 43°31N 18°47E 202 C2
Foça Turkey 38°39N 26°46E 205 C8
Fochabers U.K. 57°37N 3°6W 167 D5
Focşani Romania 45°41N 27°15E 183 E12
Fodé C.A.R. 5°29N 23°18E 264 A4
Fodécontéa Guinea 10°50N 14°22W 262 C2
Fogang China 23°52N 113°30E 229 F9
Foggaret el Arab Algeria 27°13N 2°49E 261 C5
Foggaret ez Zoua Algeria 27°20N 2°53E 261 C5
Fóggia Italy 41°27N 15°34E 201 A8
Foggy Bottom U.S.A. 38°54N 77°3W 143 B3
Foglia → Italy 43°55N 12°54E 199 E9
Fogo Nfld. & L., Canada 49°43N 54°17W 299 C9
Fogo C. Verde Is. 15°5N 24°20W 153 j
Fogo I. Canada 49°40N 54°5W 299 C9
Fohnsdorf Austria 47°12N 14°40E 180 D7
Föhr Germany 54°43N 8°30E 178 A4
Föhrenhain Austria 48°19N 16°26E 142 A2
Foia Portugal 37°19N 8°37W 195 H2
Foix France 42°58N 1°38E 174 F5
Fojnica Bos.-H. 43°59N 17°51E 182 G2
Fokida ☐ Greece 38°30N 22°15E 204 C4
Fokino Russia 53°30N 34°22E 188 F8
Fokku Nigeria 11°36N 4°32E 263 C5
Fokstugu Norway 62°7N 9°17E 164 B6
Folda Nord-Trøndelag,
Norway 64°32N 10°30E 160 D14
Folda Nordland, Norway 67°38N 14°50E 160 C16
Földeák Hungary 46°19N 20°30E 182 D5
Folegandros Greece 36°40N 24°55E 204 E6
Foley Botswana 21°34S 27°21E 270 B4
Foley Ala., U.S.A. 30°24N 87°41W 315 F11
Foley Fla., U.S.A. 30°4N 83°32W 316 E6
Foleyet Canada 48°15N 82°25W 298 C3
Folgefonna Norway 60°3N 6°23E 164 D3
Folgefonna △ Norway 60°5N 6°15E 164 D3
Foligno Italy 42°57N 12°42E 199 F9
Folkestad Norway 62°7N 6°1E 164 B3
Folkestone U.K. 51°5N 1°12E 169 F9
Folkestone Underwater Park
Barbados 13°11N 59°38W 323 r
Folkston U.S.A. 30°50N 82°0W 316 E7
Folla → Norway 62°7N 10°37E 164 B7
Follansbee U.S.A. 40°19N 80°35W 312 F4
Folldal Norway 62°8N 10°0E 164 B6
Folle Anse, Pte. de
Guadeloupe 15°56N 61°19W 322 e
Follebu Norway 61°13N 10°16E 164 C7
Follónica Italy 42°55N 10°45E 198 F7
Follónica, G. di Italy 42°54N 10°43E 198 F7
Folsom L. U.S.A. 38°42N 121°9W 306 G5
Folteşti Romania 45°45N 28°3E 183 E13
Fomboni Comoros Is. 12°18S 43°46E 272 a
Fomm ir-Rih Bay Malta 35°54N 14°20E 206 F7
Fond-du-Lac Sask.,
Canada 59°19N 107°12W 297 B7
Fond du Lac Wis., U.S.A. 43°47N 88°27W 308 D9
Fond-du-Lac → Canada 59°17N 106°0W 297 B7
Fond Rousseau Martinique 14°38N 61°6W 322 j
Fond St. Jacques St. Lucia 13°50N 61°1W 323 m
Fonda Iowa, U.S.A. 42°35N 94°51W 310 B2
Fonda N.Y., U.S.A. 42°57N 74°22W 313 D10
Fondi Italy 41°21N 13°25E 200 A6
Fonds-St-Denis Martinique 14°43N 61°8W 322 j
Fonfría Spain 41°37N 6°9W 194 D4
Fongafale Tuvalu 8°31S 179°13E 277 B14
Fongen Norway 63°11N 11°38E 164 A8
Fonni Italy 40°7N 9°15E 200 B2
Fonsagrada = A Fonsagrada
Spain 43°8N 7°4W 194 B3
Fonseca, G. de
Cent. Amer. 13°10N 87°40W 320 D2
Font-Romeu-Odeillo-Via
France 42°31N 2°3E 174 F5
Fontaine-Française
France 47°32N 5°21E 173 E12
Fontainebleau Seine-et-Marne,
France 48°24N 2°40E 173 D9
Fontainebleau Gauteng,
S. Africa 26°6S 27°57E 123 A1
Fontana U.S.A. 34°6N 117°26W 307 L9
Fontana, L. Argentina 44°55S 71°30W 336 B2
Fontas → Canada 58°14N 121°48W 296 B4
Fonte Boa Brazil 2°33S 66°0W 328 D4
Fontem Cameroon 5°32N 9°52E 263 D6
Fontenay-aux-Roses
France 48°47N 2°17E 134 B2
Fontenay-le-Comte France 46°28N 0°48W 174 B3
Fontenay-le-Fleury France 48°48N 2°2E 134 B1
Fontenay-sous-Bois France 48°51N 2°28E 134 A3
Fontenelle Res. U.S.A. 42°1N 110°3W 304 E8
Fontur Iceland 66°23N 14°32W 155 A12
Fonuafo'ou Tonga 20°19S 175°25W 287 Q13
Fonuakula Cook Is. 19°2S 169°55W 289 g
Fonualei Tonga 18°1S 174°19W 287 P13
Fonyód Hungary 46°44N 17°33E 182 D2
Foochow = Fuzhou
China 26°5N 119°16E 229 D12
Foots Cray U.K. 51°24N 0°7E 125 B4
Footscray Australia 37°48S 144°56E 128 A1
Foping China 33°41N 108°0E 226 H5
Foraker, Mt. U.S.A. 62°58N 151°24W 303 E10
Forari Vanuatu 17°40S 168°31E 287 G6
Forbach France 49°10N 6°52E 173 C13
Forbes Australia 33°22S 148°5E 283 B8
Forbesganj India 26°17N 87°18E 243 F12
Forbidden City = Imperial Palace
Museum Beijing, China 114 b3
Forcados Nigeria 5°26N 5°26E 263 D6
Forcados → Nigeria 5°25N 5°19E 263 D6
Forcalquier France 43°58N 5°47E 175 E9
Forchheim Germany 49°43N 11°2E 179 F7
Ford City Calif., U.S.A. 35°9N 119°27W 307 K7
Ford City Pa., U.S.A. 40°46N 79°32W 312 F5
Fond d'Or B. St. Lucia 13°56N 60°54W 323 m
Ford I. U.S.A. 21°22N 157°58W 302 K14
Forda → Norway 62°57N 10°40E 164 B7
Førde Hordaland, Norway 59°36N 5°27E 164 E2
Førde Rogaland, Norway 59°26N 5°23E 164 E2
Førde Sogn og Fjordane,
Norway 61°27N 5°53E 164 C2
Førdefjorden Norway 61°29N 5°18E 164 C2
Fords Bridge Australia 29°41S 145°29E 281 D4
Ford's Theater Washington, D.C., U.S.A. 143 b2
Fordyce U.S.A. 33°49N 92°25W 314 E8
Forécariah Guinea 9°28N 13°10W 262 D2
Forel, Mt. Greenland 66°52N 36°55W 154 D7
Foremost Canada 49°26N 111°34W 296 D6
Foreshore Cape Town, S. Africa 118 a3
Forest Belgium 50°49N 4°20E 116 B1
Forest Ont., Canada 43°6N 82°0W 312 C3
Forest Miss., U.S.A. 32°22N 89°29W 315 E10
Forest Acres U.S.A. 34°1N 80°58W 316 A9
Forest City Iowa, U.S.A. 43°16N 93°39W 308 D7
Forest City N.C., U.S.A. 35°20N 81°52W 315 D14
Forest City Pa., U.S.A. 41°39N 75°28W 313 E9
Forest Gate U.K. 51°32N 0°1E 125 A4
Forest Grove U.S.A. 45°31N 123°7W 306 E3
Forest Heights U.S.A. 38°48N 77°0W 143 C3
Forest Hill Ont., Canada 43°41N 79°25W 141 A2
Forest Hill London, U.K. 51°26N 0°2W 125 B3
Forest Hills U.S.A. 40°42N 73°51W 132 B2
Forest Park Ga., U.S.A. 33°37N 84°22W 316 B5
Forest Park Ill., U.S.A. 41°51N 87°47W 119 B2
Forest Park N.Y., U.S.A. 40°42N 73°51W 132 B2
Forest Park Ohio, U.S.A. 39°17N 84°30W 311 E12
Forest View U.S.A. 41°48N 87°47W 119 C2
Forestburg Canada 52°35N 112°1W 296 C6
Foreste Casentinesi-Monte
Falterona-Campigna △
Italy 43°50N 11°48E 199 E8
Foresthill U.S.A. 39°1N 120°49W 306 F6
Forestier Pen. Australia 43°0S 148°0E 281 G4
Forestville Qué., Canada 48°48N 69°2W 299 C6
Forestville Calif., U.S.A. 38°28N 122°54W 306 G4
Forestville Md., U.S.A. 38°50N 76°52W 143 B4
Forestville N.Y., U.S.A. 42°28N 79°10W 312 D5
Forêt d'Orient ⌓ France 48°16N 4°25E 173 D11
Forêt du Day △ Djibouti 11°56N 42°40E 267 B5
Forez, Mts. du France 45°40N 3°50E 174 C7
Forfar U.K. 56°39N 2°53W 167 E6
Forillon △ Canada 48°46N 64°12W 299 C7
Forks U.S.A. 47°57N 124°23W 306 C2
Forks, The = Merritt
Canada 50°10N 120°45W 296 C4
Forksville U.S.A. 41°29N 76°35W 313 E8
Forli Italy 44°13N 12°3E 199 D9
Forman U.S.A. 46°7N 97°38W 308 B5
Formazza Italy 46°22N 8°26E 198 B5
Formby Pt. U.K. 53°33N 3°6W 168 D4
Formentera Spain 38°43N 1°27E 206 C1
Formentor, C. de Spain 39°58N 3°13E 206 B4
Formentor, Pen. de Spain 39°56N 3°11E 206 B4
Former Yugoslav Republic of
Macedonia = Macedonia ■
Europe 41°53N 21°40E 202 E5
Fórmia Italy 41°15N 13°37E 200 A6
Formiga Brazil 20°27S 45°25W 333 F2
Formigine Italy 44°37N 10°51E 198 D7
Formosa = Taiwan ■
Asia 23°30N 121°0E 225 C3
Formosa Argentina 26°15S 58°10W 334 B4
Formosa Brazil 15°32S 47°20W 333 E2
Formosa ☐ Argentina 25°0S 60°0W 334 B3
Formosa, Serra Brazil 12°0S 55°0W 331 C7
Formosa B. = Ungwana B.
Kenya 2°45S 40°20E 268 C5
Formosa do Rio Prêto
Brazil 11°2S 45°3W 332 D2
Formosa Strait = Taiwan Strait
Asia 24°40N 120°0E 229 E12
Formoso → Brazil 10°34S 49°56W 333 D2
Fornebu Norway 59°53N 10°36E 133 A2
Fornells Spain 40°3N 4°7E 206 A5
Fornos de Algodres
Portugal 40°38N 7°32W 194 E3
Fornovo di Taro Italy 44°42N 10°6E 198 D7
Foro Romano Rome, Italy 136 c3
Forollhogna △ Norway 62°39N 10°41E 164 B7
Føroyar ☑ Atl. Oc. 62°0N 7°0W 160 F9
Forres U.K. 57°37N 3°37W 167 D5
Forrest Vic., Australia 38°33S 143°47E 282 E5
Forrest W. Austral.,
Australia 30°51S 128°6E 279 F4
Forrest, Mt. Australia 24°48S 127°45E 279 D4
Forrest City U.S.A. 35°1N 90°47W 315 D9

Forreston U.S.A. 42°8N 89°35W 310 B7
Fors Sweden 60°14N 16°20E 162 D10
Forsand Norway 58°54N 6°5E 164 F3
Forsayth Australia 18°33S 143°34E 280 B3
Forserum Sweden 57°42N 14°30E 163 G8
Forshaga Sweden 59°33N 13°29E 162 E7
Förslöv Sweden 56°21N 12°48E 163 H6
Forsmo Sweden 63°16N 17°11E 162 A11
Forssa Finland 60°49N 23°38E 188 B2
Forst Germany 51°45N 14°37E 178 D10
Forstenried Germany 48°5N 11°29E 131 B1
Forstenrieder Park Germany 48°3N 11°27E 131 B1
Forster Australia 32°12S 152°31E 283 B10
Forsvik Sweden 58°35N 14°26E 163 F8
Forsyth Ga., U.S.A. 33°2N 83°56W 316 B6
Forsyth Mont., U.S.A. 46°16N 106°41W 304 C10
Forsyth I. N.Z. 40°58S 174°5E 285 A9
Fort Mumbai, India 130 c2
Fort Abbas Pakistan 29°12N 72°52E 242 E5
Fort Albany Canada 52°15N 81°35W 298 B3
Fort-Aleksandrovsky = Fort Shevchenko Kazakhstan 44°35N 50°23E 191 H10
Fort Archambault = Sarh Chad 9°5N 18°23E 259 G3
Fort Assiniboine Canada 54°20N 114°45W 296 C6
Fort Atkinson U.S.A. 42°56N 88°50W 311 B8
Fort Augustus U.K. 57°9N 4°42W 167 D4
Fort Bay Saba 17°37N 63°15W 322 a
Fort Bayard = Zhanjiang China 21°15N 110°20E 229 G8
Fort Beaufort S. Africa 32°46S 26°40E 270 D4
Fort Benton U.S.A. 47°49N 110°40W 304 C8
Fort Bragg U.S.A. 39°26N 123°48W 304 G2
Fort Bridger U.S.A. 41°19N 110°23W 304 F8
Fort Canning Park Singapore 138 b2
Fort Caroline △ U.S.A. 30°23N 81°30W 316 E8
Fort Charles Jamaica 17°55N 76°50W 320 a
Fort Charlotte St. Lucia 13°59N 61°0W 323 m
Fort Chipewyan Canada 58°42N 111°8W 297 B6
Fort Clatsop = Lewis and Clark △ U.S.A. 46°8N 123°53W 306 D3
Fort Collins U.S.A. 40°35N 105°5W 304 F11
Fort-Coulonge Canada 45°50N 76°45W 298 C4
Fort Covington U.S.A. 44°59N 74°29W 313 B10
Fort Dauphin = Taolanaro Madag. 25°2S 47°0E 272 D2
Fort Davis Ala., U.S.A. 32°15N 85°43W 316 C4
Fort Davis Tex., U.S.A. 30°35N 103°54W 314 F3
Fort-de-France Martinique 14°36N 61°2W 322 j
Fort-de-France, B. de Martinique 14°34N 61°4W 322 j
Fort de Kock = Bukittinggi Indonesia 0°20S 100°20E 234 C2
Fort de Polignac = Illizi Algeria 26°31N 8°32E 261 C6
Fort de Possel = Possel C.A.R. 5°5N 19°10E 264 A3
Fort Defiance U.S.A. 35°45N 109°5W 305 J9
Fort Dodge U.S.A. 42°30N 94°11W 310 B2
Fort Drum U.S.A. 27°32N 80°48W 317 H9
Fort Dupont Park U.S.A. 38°52N 76°56W 143 B4
Fort Edward U.S.A. 43°16N 73°35W 313 C11
Fort Erie Canada 42°54N 78°56W 312 D6
Fort Fairfield U.S.A. 46°46N 67°50W 309 B20
Fort Flatters = Bordj Omar Driss Algeria 28°10N 6°40E 261 C6
Fort Foote Village U.S.A. 38°46N 77°1W 143 C3
Fort-Foureau = Kousseri Cameroon 12°0N 14°55E 259 F2
Fort Frances Canada 48°36N 93°24W 297 D10
Fort Franklin = Déline Canada 65°11N 123°25W 294 D7
Fort Frederica △ U.S.A. 31°13N 81°23W 316 D8
Fort Gaines U.S.A. 31°36N 85°3W 316 D4
Fort Garland U.S.A. 37°26N 105°26W 305 H11
Fort George = Chisasibi Canada 53°50N 79°0W 298 B4
Fort George = Prince George Canada 53°55N 122°50W 296 C4
Fort George Grenada 12°3N 61°45W 323 q
Fort Good Hope Canada 66°14N 128°40W 294 D6
Fort Gouraud = Fdérik Mauritania 22°40N 12°45W 260 D2
Fort Hancock U.S.A. 31°18N 105°51W 314 F2
Fort Hertz = Putao Burma 27°28N 97°30E 241 B6
Fort Hill = Chitipa Malawi 9°41S 33°19E 269 D3
Fort Hope = Eabametoong Canada 51°30N 88°0W 298 B2
Fort Irwin U.S.A. 35°16N 116°41W 307 K10
Fort Jameson = Chipata Zambia 13°38S 32°28E 269 E3
Fort Jeudy, Pt. of Grenada 11°59N 61°42W 323 q
Fort Johnston = Mangoche Malawi 14°25S 35°16E 269 E4
Fort Kent U.S.A. 47°15N 68°36W 309 B19
Fort Klamath U.S.A. 42°42N 122°0W 304 D3
Fort Lamy = Ndjamena Chad 12°10N 15°0E 259 F3
Fort-Laperrine = Tamanrasset Algeria 22°50N 5°30E 261 D6
Fort Laramie U.S.A. 42°13N 104°31W 304 E11
Fort Lauderdale U.S.A. 26°7N 80°8W 317 J9
Fort Lee U.S.A. 40°50N 73°58W 132 A2
Fort Liard Canada 60°14N 123°30W 296 A4
Fort Liberté Haiti 19°42N 71°51W 321 C5
Fort Lupton U.S.A. 40°5N 104°49W 304 F11
Fort MacKay Canada 57°12N 111°41W 296 B6
Fort Macleod Canada 49°45N 113°30W 296 D6
Fort MacMahon = El Homr Algeria 29°43N 1°45E 261 C5
Fort McMurray Canada 56°44N 111°7W 296 B6
Fort McPherson Canada 67°30N 134°55W 294 D5
Fort Madison U.S.A. 40°38N 91°27W 310 D5
Fort Manning = Mchinji Malawi 13°47S 32°58E 269 E3
Fort Marlborough Indonesia 3°48S 102°15E 234 C2
Fort Mason Center San Francisco, U.S.A. 136 a1
Fort Matanzas △ U.S.A. 29°43N 81°14W 316 F8
Fort Meade U.S.A. 27°45N 81°48W 317 H8
Fort Mitchell U.S.A. 32°20N 85°1W 316 C4
Fort Morgan U.S.A. 40°15N 103°48W 304 F12
Fort Myers U.S.A. 26°39N 81°52W 317 J8
Fort Myers Beach U.S.A. 26°26N 81°52W 317 J8
Fort Myers Villas U.S.A. 26°33N 81°52W 317 J8
Fort Napoléon Guadeloupe 15°52N 61°35W 322 e
Fort Nelson Canada 58°50N 122°44W 296 B4
Fort Nelson → Canada 59°32N 124°0W 296 B4
Fort Norman = Tulita Canada 64°57N 125°30W 294 E6
Fort Ogden U.S.A. 27°5N 81°57W 317 H8
Fort Payne U.S.A. 34°26N 85°43W 315 D12
Fort Peck U.S.A. 48°1N 106°27W 304 B10
Fort Peck Dam U.S.A. 48°0N 106°26W 304 C10
Fort Peck L. U.S.A. 48°0N 106°26W 304 C10
Fort Pierce U.S.A. 27°27N 80°20W 317 H9
Fort Pierre U.S.A. 44°21N 100°22W 308 C3
Fort Pierre Bordes = Ti-n-Zaouatene Algeria 19°55N 2°55E 261 E5
Fort Plain U.S.A. 42°56N 74°37W 313 D10
Fort Portal Uganda 0°40N 30°20E 268 B3
Fort Providence Canada 61°3N 117°40W 296 A5
Fort Pulaski △ U.S.A. 32°2N 80°56W 316 C9
Fort Qu'Appelle Canada 50°45N 103°50W 297 C8
Fort Recovery U.S.A. 40°25N 84°47W 311 D12
Fort Resolution Canada 61°10N 113°40W 296 A6
Fort Rixon Zimbabwe 20°2S 29°17E 269 G2
Fort Rosebery = Mansa Zambia 11°13S 28°55E 269 E2
Fort Ross U.S.A. 38°32N 123°13W 306 G3
Fort-Rousset = Owando Congo 0°29S 15°55E 264 C3
Fort Rupert = Waskaganish Canada 51°30N 78°40W 298 B4
Fort St. James Canada 54°30N 124°10W 296 C4
Fort St. John Canada 56°15N 120°50W 296 B4
Fort Sandeman = Zhob Pakistan 31°20N 69°31E 242 D3
Fort Saskatchewan Canada 53°40N 113°15W 296 C6
Fort Scott U.S.A. 37°50N 94°42W 308 G6
Fort Severn Canada 56°0N 87°40W 298 A2
Fort Shevchenko Kazakhstan 44°35N 50°23E 191 H10
Fort Simpson Canada 61°45N 121°15W 296 A4
Fort Smith Alta., Canada 60°0N 111°51W 296 B6
Fort Smith Ark., U.S.A. 35°23N 94°25W 314 D7
Fort Stockton U.S.A. 30°53N 102°53W 314 F3
Fort Sumner U.S.A. 34°28N 104°15W 305 J11
Fort Thomas U.S.A. 39°4N 84°26W 311 E12
Fort Thompson U.S.A. 44°3N 99°26W 308 C4
Fort Trinquet = Bir Mogreïn Mauritania 25°10N 11°25W 260 C2
Fort Union △ U.S.A. 35°54N 105°1W 305 J11
Fort Uritskogo = Fort Shevchenko Kazakhstan 44°35N 50°23E 191 H10
Fort Valley U.S.A. 32°33N 83°53W 316 C6
Fort Vermilion Canada 58°24N 116°0W 296 B5
Fort Walton Beach U.S.A. 30°25N 86°36W 317 E3
Fort Ware Canada 57°26N 125°41W 296 B3
Fort Wayne U.S.A. 41°4N 85°9W 311 C11
Fort White U.S.A. 29°55N 82°43W 316 F7
Fort William U.K. 56°49N 5°7W 167 E3
Fort Worth U.S.A. 32°43N 97°19W 314 E6
Fort Yates U.S.A. 46°5N 100°38W 308 B3
Fort Yukon U.S.A. 66°34N 145°16W 303 C11
Fortaleza = Pedra Azul Brazil 16°2S 41°17W 333 E3
Fortaleza Bolivia 12°6S 66°49W 330 C4
Fortaleza Brazil 3°45S 38°35W 332 B4
Forteau Canada 51°28N 56°58W 299 B8
Fortescue → Australia 21°0S 116°4E 278 D2
Fortescue River Roadhouse Australia 21°17S 116°8E 278 D2
Forth → U.K. 56°9N 3°50W 167 E5
Forth, Firth of U.K. 56°5N 2°55W 121 A3
Forth Rail Bridge U.K. 56°0N 3°23W 121 A1
Forth Road Bridge U.K. 56°0N 3°24W 121 A1
Forthassa Rharbia Algeria 32°52N 1°18W 261 B4
Fortín General Pando Paraguay 19°45S 59°47W 331 D6
Fortín Madrejón Paraguay 20°45S 59°52W 331 E6
Fortín Teniente Primero Ramiro Espínola Paraguay 21°27S 61°30W 331 E5
Fortín Uno Argentina 38°50S 65°18W 336 A3
Fortore → Italy 41°55N 15°17E 199 G12
Fortrose N.Z. 46°38S 168°45E 285 G3
Fortrose Highl., U.K. 57°35N 4°9W 167 D4
Fortuna Spain 38°11N 1°7W 197 G3
Fortuna Calif., U.S.A. 40°36N 124°9W 304 F1
Fortuna N. Dak., U.S.A. 48°55N 103°47W 308 A2
Fortuna Ledge = Marshall U.S.A. 61°53N 162°5W 303 F7
Fortune Canada 47°4N 55°50W 299 C8
Fortune B. Canada 47°30N 55°22W 299 C8
Forūr Iran 26°17N 54°32E 247 E7
Fos-sur-Mer France 43°26N 4°56E 175 E8
Fosen Norway 63°50N 10°20E 160 E14
Foshan China 23°6N 113°9E 121 B2
Fosnavåg Norway 62°22N 5°38E 164 B2
Foso Ghana 5°43N 1°15W 263 D4
Foss Iceland 63°51N 17°52W 155 D9
Fossano Italy 44°33N 7°43E 198 D4
Fossil U.S.A. 45°0N 120°9W 304 D3
Fossil Butte △ U.S.A. 41°50N 110°27W 304 F8
Fossombrone Italy 43°41N 12°48E 199 E9
Fossvellir Iceland 65°27N 14°37W 155 B12
Foster Vic., Australia 38°40S 146°15E 283 E7
Foster Qué., Canada 45°17N 72°30W 313 A12
Foster Ky., U.S.A. 38°48N 84°13W 311 F12
Foster → Canada 55°47N 105°49W 297 B7
Foster Village U.S.A. 21°21N 157°55W 302 K14
Fosters Ra. Australia 21°35S 133°48E 280 C1
Fostoria U.S.A. 41°10N 83°25W 311 C13
Fót Hungary 47°35N 19°11E 117 A3
Fotadrevo Madag. 24°3S 45°1E 272 C2
Fouesnant France 47°53N 4°1W 172 E2
Fougamou Gabon 1°16S 10°30E 264 C2
Fougères France 48°21N 1°14W 172 D5
Foul Pt. Sri Lanka 8°35N 81°18E 245 K5
Foula U.K. 60°10N 2°5W 167 A6
Foulalaba Mali 10°40N 7°20W 262 C3
Foulness I. U.K. 51°36N 0°55E 169 F8
Foulpointe Madag. 17°41S 49°31E 272 B2
Foulwind, C. N.Z. 41°45S 171°28E 285 D6
Foum Assaka Morocco 29°8N 10°24W 260 C2
Foum Zguid Morocco 30°2N 6°59W 260 B3
Foumban Cameroon 5°45N 10°50E 263 D7
Foumbot Cameroon 5°31N 10°28E 263 D7
Foumbouni Comoros Is. 11°51S 43°29E 272 a
Foumirate Algeria 27°30N 3°12W 260 C4
Foundiougne Senegal 14°5N 16°32W 262 C1
Fountain Colo., U.S.A. 38°41N 104°42W 304 G11
Fountain Fla., U.S.A. 30°29N 85°25W 316 E4
Fountain Hills U.S.A. 33°37N 111°43W 305 K8
Fountain Springs U.S.A. 35°54N 118°51W 307 K8
Four Mountains, Is. of U.S.A. 53°0N 170°0W 303 K5
Four Roads Trin. & Tob. 10°41N 61°33W 323 t
Fourchambault France 47°2N 3°3E 173 E10
Fourchue, Île St.-Martin 17°58N 62°54W 322 a
Fouriesburg S. Africa 28°38S 28°14E 270 C4
Fourmies France 50°1N 4°2E 173 B11
Fourna Greece 39°3N 21°52E 204 B3
Fournaise, Piton de la Réunion 21°14S 55°43E 272 f
Fourni Greece 37°36N 26°32E 205 D8
Fourqueux France 48°53N 2°3E 134 A1
Fours France 46°50N 3°42E 173 F10
Fous, Pte. de Dominica 15°12N 61°20W 323 k
Fousinshin = Fuxin China 42°5N 121°48E 227 C11
Fouta Djallon Guinea 11°20N 12°10W 262 C2
Foux, Cap-à- Haiti 19°43N 73°27W 321 C5
Foveaux Str. N.Z. 46°42S 168°10E 285 G3
Fowey U.K. 50°20N 4°39W 169 G3
Fowler Calif., U.S.A. 36°38N 119°41W 306 J7
Fowler Colo., U.S.A. 38°8N 104°2W 304 G11
Fowler Ind., U.S.A. 40°37N 87°19W 311 D9
Fowler Mich., U.S.A. 43°0N 84°45W 311 B12
Fowlers Pt. Australia 32°2S 132°3E 279 F5
Fowlers B. Australia 31°59S 132°34E 279 F5
Fowlerville U.S.A. 42°40N 84°4W 311 C12
Fowman Iran 37°13N 49°19E 213 E13
Fox → Canada 56°3N 93°18W 297 B10
Fox Creek Canada 54°24N 116°48W 296 C5
Fox Is. U.S.A. 53°0N 168°0W 303 K6
Fox Lake Alta., Canada 58°28N 114°31W 296 B6
Fox Lake Ill., U.S.A. 42°24N 88°11W 311 B8
Fox Studios Australia 33°55S 151°13E 139 B2
Fox Valley Canada 50°30N 109°25W 297 C7
Foxboro Ont., Canada 44°14N 77°26W 312 B7
Foxboro Mass., U.S.A. 42°4N 71°16W 313 D13
Foxdale Australia 20°22S 148°35E 280 b
Foxe Basin Canada 66°0N 77°0W 295 D16
Foxe Chan. Canada 65°0N 80°0W 295 E16
Foxe Pen. Canada 65°0N 76°0W 295 E16
Foxen Sweden 59°25N 11°55E 162 E5
Foxford Ireland 53°59N 9°7W 166 C2
Foxrock Ireland 53°16N 6°11W 120 B2
Foxton N.Z. 40°29S 175°18E 284 G4
Foyle, Lough U.K. 55°7N 7°4W 166 A4
Foynes Ireland 52°37N 9°7W 166 D2
Foz Spain 43°33N 7°20W 194 B3
Foz do Copeá Brazil 3°52S 63°19W 329 D5
Foz do Cunene Angola 17°15S 11°48E 265 F2
Foz do Gregório Brazil 6°47S 70°44W 330 B3
Foz do Iguaçu Brazil 25°30S 54°30W 335 B5
Foz do Mamoriá Brazil 2°27S 66°32W 328 D4
Frackville U.S.A. 40°47N 76°14W 313 F8
Fraga Spain 41°32N 0°21E 196 D5
Fraile Muerto Uruguay 32°31S 54°32W 335 C5
Framingham U.S.A. 42°18N 71°24W 313 D13
Framnes Iceland 66°1N 20°26W 155 A6
Frampol Poland 50°41N 22°40E 185 H9
Franca Brazil 20°33S 47°30W 333 F2
Francavilla al Mare Italy 42°25N 14°17E 199 F11
Francavilla Fontana Italy 40°32N 17°35E 201 B10
France ■ Europe 47°0N 3°0E 171 C5
Frances Australia 36°41S 140°55E 282 D4
Frances → Canada 60°16N 129°10W 296 A3
Frances L. Canada 61°23N 129°30W 296 A3
Francesville U.S.A. 40°59N 86°53W 311 D10
Franceville Gabon 1°40S 13°32E 264 C2
Franche-Comté □ France 46°50N 5°55E 173 F12
Francis Case, L. U.S.A. 43°4N 98°34W 308 D4
Francisco Beltrão Brazil 26°5S 53°4W 335 B5
Francisco de Orellana Ecuador 0°28S 76°58W 328 D2
Francisco Ignacio Madero Coahuila, Mexico 25°48N 103°18W 318 B4
Francisco Ignacio Madero Durango, Mexico 24°26N 104°18W 318 C4
Francisco Ignacio Madero, Presa Mexico 28°10N 105°37W 318 B3
Francisco Sá Brazil 16°28S 43°30W 333 E3
Francistown Botswana 21°7S 27°33E 271 B4
Francofonte Italy 37°14N 14°53E 201 E7
François Canada 47°35N 56°45W 299 C8
François, B. du Martinique 14°38N 60°54W 322 j
François-Joseph, Chutes Dem. Rep. of the Congo 7°37S 17°17E 265 D3
François L. Canada 54°0N 125°30W 296 C3
Francois Peron △ Australia 25°42S 113°33E 279 E1
Franconia U.S.A. 38°47N 77°7W 143 C3
Francs Pk. U.S.A. 43°58N 109°20W 304 E9
Franeker Neths. 53°12N 5°33E 170 A5
Frank Hann △ Australia 32°52S 120°19E 279 F3
Frank Lloyd Wright Home U.S.A. 41°53N 87°47W 119 B2
Frankel Singapore 1°18N 103°55E 138 B3
Frankenberg Germany 51°3N 8°48E 178 D4
Frankenhöhe △ Germany 49°20N 10°25E 179 F6
Frankenstein = Ząbkowice Śląskie Poland 50°35N 16°50E 185 H3
Frankenwald Germany 50°20N 11°30E 179 E7
Frankenwald △ Germany 50°15N 11°30E 179 E7
Frankfield Jamaica 18°8N 77°22W 320 a
Frankford Ont., Canada 44°12N 77°36W 312 B7
Frankford U.S.A. 39°29N 91°19W 310 E5
Frankfort Free State, S. Africa 27°17S 28°30E 271 C4
Frankfort Ind., U.S.A. 40°17N 86°31W 311 D10
Frankfort Kans., U.S.A. 39°42N 96°25W 308 F5
Frankfort Ky., U.S.A. 38°12N 84°52W 311 F12
Frankfort N.Y., U.S.A. 43°2N 75°4W 313 C9
Frankfort Ohio, U.S.A. 39°24N 83°11W 311 E13
Frankfurt Brandenburg, Germany 52°20N 14°32E 178 C10
Frankfurt Hessen, Germany 50°7N 8°41E 179 E4
Frankfurt ✕ (FRA) Germany 50°1N 8°34E 179 E4
Fränkische Alb Germany 49°10N 11°23E 179 F7
Fränkische Rezat → Germany 49°11N 11°1E 179 F7
Fränkische Saale → Germany 50°3N 9°42E 179 E5
Fränkische Schweiz Germany 49°50N 11°10E 179 F7
Fränkische Schweiz-Veldensteiner Forst △ Germany 49°45N 11°22E 179 F7
Frankland → Australia 35°0S 116°48E 279 G2
Franklin Ga., U.S.A. 33°17N 85°6W 316 B4
Franklin Ind., U.S.A. 39°29N 86°3W 311 E10
Franklin Ky., U.S.A. 36°43N 86°35W 308 G10
Franklin La., U.S.A. 29°48N 91°30W 314 G9
Franklin Mass., U.S.A. 42°5N 71°24W 313 D13
Franklin N.H., U.S.A. 43°27N 71°39W 313 C13
Franklin N.Y., U.S.A. 42°20N 75°9W 313 D9
Franklin Nebr., U.S.A. 40°6N 98°57W 308 E4
Franklin Ohio, U.S.A. 39°34N 84°18W 311 E12
Franklin Pa., U.S.A. 41°24N 79°50W 312 E5
Franklin Va., U.S.A. 36°41N 76°56W 309 G15
Franklin W. Va., U.S.A. 38°39N 79°20W 309 F14
Franklin, Pt. U.S.A. 70°55N 158°48W 303 A8
Franklin B. Canada 69°45N 126°0W 294 D6
Franklin D. Roosevelt L. U.S.A. 48°18N 118°9W 304 B4
Franklin-Gordon Wild Rivers △ Australia 42°19S 145°51E 281 G4
Franklin Harb. Australia 33°43S 136°55E 282 B2
Franklin I. Antarctica 76°10S 168°30E 151 D11
Franklin I. Ont., Canada 45°24N 80°20W 312 A4
Franklin L. U.S.A. 40°25N 115°22W 304 F6
Franklin Mts. N.W.T., Canada 65°0N 125°0W 294 D6
Franklin Mts. N.Z. 44°55S 167°45E 285 F2
Franklin Park Ill., U.S.A. 41°55N 87°52W 119 B1
Franklin Park Mass., U.S.A. 42°18N 71°5W 116 B2
Franklin Park Va., U.S.A. 38°55N 77°9W 143 B3
Franklin Res. U.S.A. 34°5N 118°24W 126 B2
Franklin Str. Canada 72°0N 96°0W 294 C12
Franklinton U.S.A. 30°51N 90°9W 315 F9
Franklinville U.S.A. 42°20N 78°27W 312 D6
Franklyn Mt. N.Z. 42°4S 172°42E 285 C7
Frankston Australia 38°8S 145°8E 283 E6
Fränsö Sweden 62°55N 17°50E 162 B11
Fransfontein Namibia 20°12S 15°1E 270 B2
Fränsta Sweden 62°30N 16°11E 162 B10
Frantsa Iosifa, Zemlya Russia 82°0N 55°0E 214 A6
Franz Canada 48°25N 84°30W 298 C3
Franz Josef Land = Frantsa Iosifa, Zemlya Russia 82°0N 55°0E 214 A6
Franz Josef Strauss ✕ (MUC) Germany 48°21N 11°47E 131 A2
Franzburg Germany 54°11N 12°51E 178 A8
Frascati Italy 41°48N 12°41E 199 G9
Fraser U.S.A. 42°32N 82°57W 312 D2
Fraser → B.C., Canada 49°7N 123°11W 306 A3
Fraser → Nfld. & L., Canada 56°39N 62°10W 299 A7
Fraser, Mt. Australia 25°35S 118°20E 279 E2
Fraser I. Australia 25°15S 153°10E 281 D5
Fraser Lake Canada 54°0N 124°50W 296 C4
Fraserburg S. Africa 31°55S 21°30E 270 D3
Fraserburg Road = Leeu Gamka S. Africa 32°47S 21°59E 270 D3
Fraserburgh U.K. 57°42N 2°1W 167 D6
Fraserdale Canada 49°55N 81°37W 298 C3
Fraserpet = Kushalnagar India 12°14N 75°57E 245 H2
Frasertown N.Z. 38°58S 177°28E 284 E6
Fraserville = Rivière-du-Loup Canada 47°50N 69°30W 299 C6
Frashër Albania 40°23N 20°30E 202 F4
Frasne France 46°50N 6°10E 173 F13
Frătești Romania 43°58N 25°58E 183 G10
Frauenfeld Switz. 47°34N 8°54E 179 H4
Frauenkirche Munich, Germany 131 b2
Fraustadt = Wschowa Poland 51°48N 16°20E 185 G3
Fray Bentos Uruguay 33°10S 58°15W 334 C4
Fray Jorge △ Chile 30°42S 71°40W 334 C1
Frazier Downs ✪ Australia 18°48S 121°42E 278 C3
Frechilla Spain 42°8N 4°50W 194 C6
Fredericia Denmark 55°34N 9°45E 163 J3
Frederick Md., U.S.A. 39°25N 77°25W 309 F15
Frederick Okla., U.S.A. 34°23N 99°1W 314 D5
Frederick S. Dak., U.S.A. 45°50N 98°31W 308 C4
Frederick E. Hyde Fjord Greenland 83°25N 29°0W 154 A8
Fredericksburg Pa., U.S.A. 40°27N 76°26W 313 F8
Fredericksburg Tex., U.S.A. 30°16N 98°52W 314 F5
Fredericksburg Va., U.S.A. 38°18N 77°28W 309 F15
Fredericktown Mo., U.S.A. 37°34N 90°18W 308 G8
Fredericktown Ohio, U.S.A. 40°29N 82°33W 312 F2
Frederico Westphalen Brazil 27°22S 53°24W 335 B5
Fredericton Canada 45°57N 66°40W 299 C6
Fredericton Junction Canada 45°41N 66°40W 299 C6
Frederiksberg Denmark 55°40N 12°33E 118 A3
Frederiksdal Denmark 55°46N 12°25E 118 A2
Frederikshåb = Paamiut Greenland 62°0N 49°43W 154 E6
Frederikshald = Halden Norway 59°9N 11°23E 164 E8
Frederikshamn = Hamina Finland 60°34N 27°12E 188 B4
Frederikshavn Denmark 57°28N 10°31E 163 G4
Frederikssund Denmark 55°50N 12°3E 163 J6
Frederiksted U.S. Virgin Is. 17°43N 64°53W 321 C7
Frederiksværk Denmark 55°58N 12°4E 163 J6
Fredersdorf Germany 52°31N 13°45E 115 A5
Fredonia Ariz., U.S.A. 36°57N 112°32W 305 H7
Fredonia Kans., U.S.A. 37°32N 95°49W 308 G6
Fredonia N.Y., U.S.A. 42°26N 79°20W 312 D5
Fredriksberg Sweden 60°8N 14°23E 162 D8
Fredrikstad Norway 59°13N 10°57E 164 E7
Fredriksvern = Stavern Norway 59°0N 10°1E 164 F7
Free State □ S. Africa 28°30S 27°0E 270 C4
Freeburg U.S.A. 38°19N 91°56W 310 F5
Freehold U.S.A. 40°16N 74°17W 313 F10
Freeland U.S.A. 41°1N 75°54W 313 E9
Freels, C. Nfld. & L., Canada 49°15N 53°30W 299 C9
Freels, C. Nfld. & L., Canada 46°37N 53°32W 299 C9
Freeman Calif., U.S.A. 35°35N 117°53W 307 K9
Freeman Mo., U.S.A. 38°37N 94°30W 310 F2
Freeman S. Dak., U.S.A. 43°21N 97°26W 308 D5
Freeport Bahamas 26°30N 78°47W 320 A4
Freeport Trin. & Tob. 10°27N 61°25W 323 t
Freeport Fla., U.S.A. 30°30N 86°8W 316 E3
Freeport Ill., U.S.A. 42°17N 89°36W 310 B7
Freeport N.Y., U.S.A. 40°39N 73°35W 313 F11
Freeport Ohio, U.S.A. 40°12N 81°15W 312 F3
Freeport Pa., U.S.A. 40°41N 79°41W 312 F5
Freeport Tex., U.S.A. 28°57N 95°21W 314 G7
Freetown Antigua & B. 17°3N 61°42W 322 b
Freetown S. Leone 8°30N 13°17W 262 D2
Freeville U.S.A. 42°30N 76°20W 313 D8
Frégate, L. de la Canada 53°15N 74°45W 298 B5
Fregate Island Nature Reserve St. Lucia 13°52N 60°53W 323 m
Fregenal de la Sierra Spain 38°10N 6°39W 195 G4
Fregene Italy 41°51N 12°12E 199 G9
Fregon Australia 26°45S 132°1E 279 E5
Freguesia Brazil 22°48S 43°10W 135 A1
Fréhel, C. France 48°40N 2°20W 172 D4
Freiberg Germany 50°55N 13°20E 178 E9
Freibourg = Fribourg Switz. 46°49N 7°9E 179 J3
Freiburg Baden-W., Germany 47°59N 7°51E 179 H3
Freiburg Niedersachsen, Germany 53°49N 9°16E 178 B5
Freiburg in Schlesien = Świebodzice Poland 50°51N 16°20E 185 H3
Freidrichshain, Volkspark Germany 52°31N 13°25E 115 A3
Freienwalde = Chociwel Poland 53°29N 15°21E 184 E2
Freiham Germany 48°8N 11°25E 131 B1
Freilassing Germany 47°50N 12°58E 179 H8
Freimann Germany 48°11N 11°37E 131 A2
Freire Chile 38°54S 72°38W 336 A2
Freirina Chile 28°30S 71°10W 334 B1
Freising Germany 48°24N 11°45E 179 G7
Freistadt Austria 48°30N 14°30E 180 C7
Freital Germany 51°1N 13°39E 178 D9
Freiwaldau = Jeseník Czech Rep. 50°14N 17°8E 181 A10
Fréjus France 43°25N 6°44E 175 E10
Fremantle Australia 32°7S 115°47E 279 F2
Fremont Calif., U.S.A. 37°32N 121°57W 306 H4
Fremont Ind., U.S.A. 41°44N 84°56W 311 C12
Fremont Iowa, U.S.A. 41°13N 92°26W 310 C4
Fremont Mich., U.S.A. 43°28N 85°57W 309 D11
Fremont Nebr., U.S.A. 41°26N 96°30W 308 E5
Fremont Ohio, U.S.A. 41°21N 83°7W 311 C13
Fremont → U.S.A. 38°24N 110°42W 304 G8
French Camp U.S.A. 37°53N 121°16W 306 H5
French Cays = Plana Cays Bahamas 22°38N 73°30W 321 B5
French Creek → U.S.A. 41°24N 79°50W 312 E5
French Frigate Shoals U.S.A. 23°45N 166°10W 302 G10
French Guiana ☑ S. Amer. 4°0N 53°0W 329 C7
French Guinea = Guinea ■ W. Afr. 10°20N 11°30W 262 C2
French I. Australia 38°20S 145°22E 283 E6
French Island △ Australia 38°20S 145°22E 283 E6
French Lick U.S.A. 38°33N 86°37W 311 F10
French Market New Orleans, U.S.A. 131 a3
French Pass N.Z. 40°55S 173°55E 285 A8
French Polynesia ☑ Pac. Oc. 20°0S 145°0W 289 f
French Quarter New Orleans, U.S.A. 131 a2
French Sudan = Mali ■ Africa 17°0N 3°0W 262 B4
French Territory of the Afars and Issas = Djibouti ■ Africa 12°0N 43°0E 257 E5
French Togoland = Togo ■ W. Afr. 8°30N 1°35E 263 D5
Frenchburg U.S.A. 37°57N 83°38W 311 G13
Frenchman Cr. → N. Amer. 48°31N 107°10W 304 B10
Frenchman Cr. → Nebr., U.S.A. 40°14N 100°50W 308 E3
Frenda Algeria 35°2N 1°1E 261 A5
Frenštát pod Radhoštěm Czech Rep. 49°33N 18°13E 181 B11
Fresco Ivory C. 5°3N 5°31W 262 D3
Fresco → Brazil 7°15S 51°30W 331 B7
Fresh Pond U.S.A. 42°22N 71°8W 116 A2
Freshfield, C. Antarctica 68°25S 151°10E 151 C10
Fresnay-sur-Sarthe France 48°17N 0°1E 172 D7
Fresnes France 48°45N 2°18E 134 B2
Fresnillo Mexico 23°10N 102°53W 318 C4
Fresno U.S.A. 36°44N 119°47W 306 J7
Fresno Alhándiga Spain 40°42N 5°37W 194 E5
Fresno Res. U.S.A. 48°36N 109°57W 304 B9
Fresvik Norway 61°4N 6°55E 164 C3
Freudenau Austria 48°11N 16°25E 142 A2
Freudenstadt Germany 48°27N 8°24E 179 G4
Freudenthal = Bruntál Czech Rep. 49°59N 17°27E 181 B10
Frévent France 50°15N 2°17E 173 B9
Frew → Australia 20°0S 135°38E 280 C2
Frewsburg U.S.A. 42°3N 79°10W 312 D5
Freycinet △ Australia 42°11S 148°19E 281 G4
Freycinet Pen. Australia 42°10S 148°25E 281 G4
Freyming-Merlebach France 49°8N 6°48E 173 C13
Freystadt = Kisielice Poland 53°36N 19°16E 184 E6
Freystadt = Kożuchów Poland 51°45N 15°31E 185 G2
Freyung Germany 48°48N 13°31E 179 G9
Fria Guinea 10°27N 13°38W 262 C2
Fria, C. Namibia 18°0S 12°0E 270 A1
Friant U.S.A. 36°59N 119°43W 306 J7
Friar's B. St. Kitts & Nevis 17°16N 62°40W 322 d
Friarstown Ireland 53°15N 6°21W 120 B1
Frías Argentina 28°40S 65°5W 334 B2
Fribourg Switz. 46°49N 7°9E 179 J3
Fribourg □ Switz. 46°40N 7°0E 179 J3
Frick Collection New York, U.S.A. 132 b3
Fridafors Sweden 56°25N 14°39E 163 H8
Friday Harbor U.S.A. 48°32N 123°1W 306 B3
Friedberg Bayern, Germany 48°21N 10°59E 179 G6
Friedberg Hessen, Germany 50°19N 8°45E 179 E4
Friedeberg = Mirsk Poland 50°58N 15°23E 185 H2
Friedeberg in Neumark = Strzelce Krajeńskie Poland 52°52N 15°33E 185 F2
Friedenau Germany 52°28N 13°22E 115 B3
Friedens U.S.A. 40°3N 78°59W 312 F6
Friedland = Mieroszów Poland 50°40N 16°11E 185 H3
Friedland = Pravdinsk Russia 56°29N 43°28E 190 B6
Friedland Germany 53°40N 13°33E 178 B9
Friedrichsfelde Germany 52°29N 13°33E 115 B4
Friedrichshafen Germany 47°39N 9°30E 179 H5
Friedrichshagen Germany 52°27N 13°37E 115 B4
Friedrichshain Germany 52°31N 13°25E 115 A3
Friedrichskoog Germany 54°1N 8°53E 178 A4
Friedrichslust Germany 52°33N 13°43E 115 A5
Friedrichstadt Germany 54°23N 9°6E 178 A5
Friendly Is. = Tonga ■ Pac. Oc. 19°50S 174°30W 287 P13
Friendship U.S.A. 42°12N 78°8W 312 D6
Friesach Austria 46°57N 14°24E 180 E7
Friesack Germany 52°44N 12°34E 178 C8
Friesland □ Neths. 53°5N 5°50E 170 A5
Friesoythe Germany 53°1N 7°51E 178 B3
Frigate Seychelles 4°35S 55°56E 272 c
Frigate Bay St. Kitts & Nevis 17°16N 62°41W 322 d
Frigate I. Grenada 12°25N 61°29W 323 q
Friggesund Sweden 61°54N 16°33E 162 C10
Friherrs Finland 60°16N 24°49E 121 B1
Frillesås Sweden 57°20N 12°12E 163 G6
Frilufts Museum Finland 60°11N 24°52E 121 B2
Frinnaryd Sweden 57°55N 14°50E 163 G8
Frio → U.S.A. 28°26N 98°11W 314 G5
Frio, C. Brazil 22°50S 41°50W 326 F6
Friol Spain 43°2N 7°47W 194 B3
Friona U.S.A. 34°38N 102°43W 314 D3
Frisches Haff = Zalew Wiślany Poland 54°20N 19°50E 184 D6
Fristad Sweden 57°50N 13°0E 163 G6
Fritch U.S.A. 35°38N 101°36W 314 D4
Fritsla Sweden 57°33N 12°47E 163 G6
Fritzlar Germany 51°7N 9°16E 178 D5
Friuli-Venézia Giulia □ Italy 46°0N 13°0E 199 B9
Frobisher B. Canada 62°30N 66°0W 295 E18
Frobisher Bay = Iqaluit Canada 63°44N 68°31W 295 E18
Frobisher L. Canada 56°20N 108°15W 297 B7
Frohavet Norway 64°0N 9°30E 160 E13
Frohenbruck = Veselí nad Lužnicí Czech Rep. 49°12N 14°43E 180 B7
Frohnleiten Austria 47°16N 15°19E 180 D8
Frolovo Russia 49°45N 43°40E 190 F6
Frombork Poland 54°21N 19°41E 184 D6
Frome U.K. 51°14N 2°19W 169 F5
Frome → U.K. 50°41N 2°6W 169 G5
Frome, L. Australia 30°45S 139°45E 282 A3
Frome Downs Australia 31°13S 139°45E 282 A3
Frómista Spain 42°16N 4°25W 194 C6
Front Range U.S.A. 40°25N 105°45W 301 G18
Front Royal U.S.A. 38°55N 78°12W 309 F14
Fronteira Portugal 39°3N 7°39W 195 F3
Fronteiras Brazil 7°5S 40°37W 332 C3
Frontenac △ Canada 44°32N 76°30W 313 B8
Frontera Canary Is. 27°47N 17°59W 153 e1
Frontera Tabasco, Mexico 18°32N 92°38W 319 D6
Fronteras Mexico 30°56N 109°31W 318 A3
Frontignan France 43°27N 3°45E 174 E7
Frontón, I. Peru 12°7S 77°11W 124 B1
Frosinone Italy 41°38N 13°19E 200 A6
Frostburg U.S.A. 39°39N 78°56W 309 F14
Frostisen Norway 68°14N 17°10E 160 B17
Frostproof U.S.A. 27°45N 81°32W 317 H8
Frouard France 48°47N 6°8E 173 D13
Frövi Sweden 59°28N 15°24E 162 E9
Frøya Norway 63°43N 8°40E 160 E13
Fruitland Park U.S.A. 28°51N 81°54W 317 G8
Frumoasa Romania 46°28N 25°48E 183 D10
Frunze = Bishkek Kyrgyzstan 42°54N 74°46E 218 C3
Frunze Russia 55°47N 37°33E 129 B3
Frunzivka Ukraine 47°20N 29°45E 183 C14
Fruška Gora Serbia 45°7N 19°30E 182 E4
Fruška Gora △ Serbia 45°8N 19°40E 202 A3
Frutal Brazil 20°0S 49°0W 333 F2
Frutigen Switz. 46°35N 7°38E 179 J3
Frýdek-Místek Czech Rep. 49°40N 18°20E 181 B11
Frýdlant Czech Rep. 50°56N 15°9E 180 A8
Fryeburg U.S.A. 44°1N 70°59W 313 B14
Fryvaldov = Jeseník Czech Rep. 50°14N 17°8E 181 A10
Fthiotida □ Greece 38°50N 22°25E 204 C4
Fu Jiang → China 30°0N 106°16E 228 C6
Fu Xian = Wafangdian China 39°38N 121°58E 227 E11
Fu Xian China 36°0N 109°20E 226 G5
Fua Mulaku Maldives 0°17S 73°26E 272 d
Fu'an China 27°11N 119°36E 229 D12
Fubian China 31°17N 102°22E 228 B4
Fucécchio Italy 43°44N 10°48E 198 E7
Fucheng China 37°50N 116°10E 226 F9
Fuchou = Fuzhou China 26°5N 119°16E 229 D12
Fuchū Hiroshima, Japan 34°34N 133°14E 222 C5
Fuchū Tōkyō, Japan 35°40N 139°29E 140 A1
Fuchuan China 24°50N 111°5E 229 E8
Fuchun Jiang → China 30°5N 120°5E 229 B13
Fúcino, Piana del Italy 42°1N 13°31E 199 F10
Fuding China 27°20N 120°12E 229 D13
Fuencaliente Canary Is. 28°28N 17°50W 153 e1
Fuencaliente Spain 38°25N 4°18W 195 G6
Fuencaliente, Pta. Canary Is. 28°27N 17°51W 153 e1
Fuencarral Spain 40°29N 3°42W 127 B1
Fuengirola Spain 36°32N 4°41W 195 J6
Fuenlabrada Spain 40°17N 3°48W 127 C1
Fuensalida Spain 40°3N 4°12W 194 E6
Fuente-Álamo Spain 38°44N 1°24W 197 G3
Fuente Álamo de Murcia Spain 37°42N 1°6W 197 H3
Fuente de Cantos Spain 38°15N 6°18W 195 G4
Fuente del Maestre Spain 38°31N 6°28W 195 G4
Fuente el Fresno Spain 39°14N 3°46W 195 F7
Fuente Obejuna Spain 38°15N 5°25W 195 G5
Fuente Palmera Spain 37°42N 5°6W 195 H5
Fuentes de Andalucía Spain 37°28N 5°20W 195 H5
Fuentes de Ebro Spain 41°31N 0°38W 196 D4
Fuentes de León Spain 38°5N 6°32W 195 G4
Fuentes de Oñoro Spain 40°33N 6°52W 194 E4
Fuentesaúco Spain 41°15N 5°30W 194 D5
Fuerte → Mexico 25°54N 109°22W 318 B3
Fuerte Olimpo Paraguay 21°0S 57°51W 334 A4
Fuerteventura Canary Is. 28°30N 14°0W 153 e2
Fuerteventura ✕ (FUE) Canary Is. 28°24N 13°52W 153 e2
Fufeng China 34°22N 108°0E 226 G5
Fuga I. Phil. 18°52N 121°20E 232 B3
Fughmah Yemen 16°9N 49°26E 249 C5
Fugong China 27°5N 98°47E 228 D2
Fugou China 34°3N 114°25E 226 G8
Fugu China 39°2N 111°3E 226 E6
Fuhai China 47°2N 87°25E 217 C11
Fuḩaymī Iraq 34°16N 42°10E 213 E10
Fuhlsbüttel, Hamburg ✕ (HAM) Germany 53°35N 9°59E 178 B5
Fuhsien = Fu Xian China 36°0N 109°20E 226 G5
Fuhsing Changhua, Taiwan 24°3N 120°25E 225 B2
Fuhsing Kaohsiung, Taiwan 23°13N 120°48E 225 C2
Fuhsing Taoyüan, Taiwan 24°49N 121°21E 225 B3
Fuji Japan 35°9N 138°39E 223 B10
Fuji-Hakone-Izu △ Japan 35°15N 138°45E 223 B10
Fuji-San Japan 35°22N 138°44E 223 B10
Fuji-Yoshida Japan 35°30N 138°46E 223 B10
Fujian □ China 26°0N 118°0E 229 E12
Fujieda Japan 34°52N 138°16E 223 C10
Fujin China 47°16N 132°1E 219 B15
Fujinomiya Japan 35°10N 138°40E 223 B10
Fujioka Japan 36°15N 139°5E 223 A11
Fujisawa Japan 35°22N 139°29E 223 B11
Fujiyama, Mt. = Fuji-San Japan 35°22N 138°44E 223 B10
Fukagawa Hokkaidō, Japan 43°43N 142°2E 220 C11
Fukagawa Tōkyō, Japan 35°39N 139°48E 140 B3
Fukang China 44°10N 87°59E 217 D11
Fukaya Japan 36°12N 139°12E 223 A11
Fukiage Japan 31°27N 130°17E 222 F2
Fukiage Imperial Garden Tokyo, Japan 140 a4
Fukien = Fujian □ China 26°0N 118°0E 229 E12
Fukuchiyama Japan 35°19N 135°9E 223 B7
Fukue-Shima Japan 32°40N 128°45E 221 H4
Fukuei Chiao Taiwan 25°17N 121°32E 225 A3
Fukui Japan 36°5N 136°10E 223 A8
Fukui □ Japan 36°0N 136°12E 223 B8
Fukuma Japan 33°46N 130°28E 222 D2
Fukuoka Japan 33°39N 130°21E 222 D2
Fukuoka □ Japan 33°30N 131°0E 222 D2
Fukuoka Int. ✕ (FUK) Japan 33°34N 130°28E 222 D2
Fukuroi Japan 34°45N 137°55E 223 C9
Fukushima Fukushima, Japan 37°44N 140°28E 220 F10
Fukushima Ōsaka, Japan 34°41N 135°28E 133 A1
Fukushima □ Japan 37°30N 140°15E 220 F10
Fukuyama Japan 34°35N 133°20E 222 C5
Ful Bura South Sudan 7°50N 31°50E 257 F3
Fulacunda Guinea-Biss. 11°44N 15°3W 262 C1
Fulaga Fiji 19°8S 178°33W 287 B3
Fulan → Sweden 61°18N 13°4E 162 C7
Fulda Germany 50°32N 9°40E 178 E5
Fulda → Germany 51°25N 9°39E 178 D5
Fulford = North Miami Beach U.S.A. 25°55N 80°9W 128 A2
Fulford Harbour Canada 48°47N 123°27W 306 B3
Fulham U.K. 51°28N 0°12W 125 B2
Fuli Taiwan 23°11N 121°14E 225 C3
Fuliang China 29°23N 117°14E 229 C11
Fuling China 29°39N 107°17E 228 C6
Fullarton Trin. & Tob. 10°5N 61°54W 323 t
Fullerton Calif., U.S.A. 33°53N 117°56W 307 M9
Fullerton Nebr., U.S.A. 41°22N 97°58W 308 E5
Fulongquan China 44°20N 124°42E 227 B13
Fülöpszállás Hungary 46°49N 19°15E 182 D4
Fulton Ill., U.S.A. 41°52N 90°11W 310 C6
Fulton Ind., U.S.A. 40°57N 86°16W 311 D10
Fulton Mo., U.S.A. 38°52N 91°57W 310 F5
Fulton N.Y., U.S.A. 43°19N 76°25W 313 C8
Fulton Tenn., U.S.A. 36°31N 88°53W 315 C10
Fulufjället Sweden 61°32N 12°41E 162 C6
Fumay France 49°58N 4°40E 173 C11
Fumel France 44°30N 0°58E 174 D4
Fumin China 25°10N 102°20E 228 E4
Funabashi Japan 35°45N 140°0E 223 B12
Funabori Japan 35°41N 139°52E 140 A4
Funafuti = Fongafale Tuvalu 8°31S 179°13E 277 B14
Funafuti Pac. Oc. 8°31S 179°13E 277 B14
Funan China 32°39N 115°42E 229 A10
Funäsdalen Sweden 62°33N 12°32E 162 B6
Funchal Madeira 32°38N 16°54W 153 c
Funchal ✕ (FNC) Madeira 32°42N 16°45W 153 c
Fundación Colombia 10°31N 74°11W 328 A3
Fundão Brazil 19°55S 40°24W 333 E3
Fundão Portugal 40°8N 7°30W 194 E3
Fundão, I. do Brazil 22°51S 43°13W 135 B1
Fundong Cameroon 6°15N 10°16E 254 A2
Fundu Moldovei Romania 47°32N 25°24E 183 C10

Fundulea *Romania* 44°28N 26°31E **183** F11
Fundy, B. of *Canada* 45°0N 66°0W **299** D6
Fundy △ *Canada* 45°35N 65°10W **299** C6
Fünfhaus *Austria* 48°11N 16°20E **142** A2
Fünfkirchen = Pécs
Hungary 46°5N 18°15E **182** D3
Funhalouro *Mozam.* 23°3S 34°25E **271** B5
Funing *Hebei, China* 39°53N 119°12E **227** E10
Funing *Jiangsu, China* 33°45N 119°50E **227** H10
Funing *Yunnan, China* 23°35N 105°45E **228** F5
Funiu Shan *China* 33°30N 112°20E **226** H7
Funsi *Ghana* 10°21N 1°54W **262** C4
Funtua *Nigeria* 11°30N 7°18E **263** C6
Fuping *Hebei, China* 38°48N 114°12E **226** E8
Fuping *Shaanxi, China* 34°42N 109°10E **226** G5
Fuqing *China* 25°41N 119°21E **229** E12
Fuquan *China* 26°40N 107°27E **228** D6
Furano *Japan* 43°21N 142°23E **220** C11
Furāt, Nahr al → *Asia* 31°0N 47°25E **246** D5
Furesø *Denmark* 55°47N 12°25E **118** A2
Fūrg *Iran* 28°18N 55°13E **247** D7
Furkating *India* 26°28N 93°59E **241** B4
Furman *U.S.A.* 32°41N 81°11W **316** C8
Furmanov *Russia* 57°10N 41°9E **190** B5
Furnas *Azores* 37°46N 25°19W **153** d3
Furnás *Spain* 39°3N 1°32E **206** C2
Furnas, Represa de *Brazil* 20°50S 45°30W **333** F2
Furneaux Group
Australia 40°10S 147°50E **281** G4
Furqlus *Syria* 34°36N 37°8E **250** D8
Fürstenau *Germany* 52°31N 7°40E **178** C3
Fürstenberg = Eisenhüttenstadt
Germany 52°9N 14°38E **178** C10
Fürstenberg *Germany* 53°10N 13°8E **178** B9
Fürstenfeld *Austria* 47°3N 16°3E **180** D9
Fürstenfeldbruck
Germany 48°11N 11°15E **179** G7
Fürstenwalde *Germany* 52°22N 14°3E **178** C10
Fürth *Mittelfranken,*
Germany 49°28N 10°59E **179** F6
Fürth *Oberbayern, Germany* 48°2N 11°35E **131** B2
Fürth im Wald *Germany* 49°18N 12°50E **179** F8
Furtwangen *Germany* 48°2N 8°12E **179** G4
Furudal *Sweden* 61°10N 15°11E **162** C9
Furukawa *Gifu, Japan* 36°14N 137°11E **223** A9
Furukawa *Miyagi, Japan* 38°34N 140°58E **220** E10
Furulund *Sweden* 55°46N 13°6E **163** J7
Furuvik *Sweden* 61°38N 17°20E **162** D11
Fury and Hecla Str.
Canada 69°56N 84°0W **295** D15
Fusagasugá *Colombia* 4°21N 74°22W **328** C3
Fuscaldo *Italy* 39°25N 16°2E **201** C9
Fushan *Shandong, China* 37°30N 121°15E **227** F11
Fushan *Shanxi, China* 35°58N 111°51E **226** G6
Fushë Arrëz *Albania* 42°4N 20°2E **202** D4
Fushe Kosove = Kosovo Polje
Kosovo 42°40N 21°5E **202** D5
Fushë Krujë *Albania* 41°29N 19°43E **202** E3
Fushun *Liaoning, China* 41°50N 123°56E **224** B1
Fushun *Sichuan, China* 29°13N 104°52E **228** C5
Fusong *China* 42°20N 127°15E **224** A3
Füssen *Germany* 47°34N 10°42E **179** H6
Fusui *China* 22°40N 107°56E **228** F6
Futago-tamagawaen
Japan 35°36N 139°39E **140** B2
Futago-Yama *Japan* 33°35N 131°36E **222** D3
Futian *China* 22°32N 114°4E **219** a
Futiga *Amer. Samoa* 14°21S 170°45W **302** f
Futog *Serbia* 45°15N 19°42E **182** E4
Futrono *Chile* 40°8S 72°24W **336** B2
Futtsu *Japan* 35°13N 139°49E **223** B11
Fuwa *Egypt* 31°12N 30°33E **256** H7
Fuxian Hu *China* 24°30N 102°53E **228** E4
Fuxin *China* 42°5N 121°48E **227** C11
Fuxing Dao *China* 31°16N 121°33E **138** B2
Fuxing Park *China* 31°13N 121°27E **138** B1
Fuxinglu *China* 39°52N 116°16E **114** B1
Fuyang *Anhui, China* 33°0N 115°48E **226** H8
Fuyang *Zhejiang, China* 30°5N 119°57E **229** B12
Fuyang He → *China* 38°12N 117°0E **226** E9
Fuying Dao *China* 26°34N 120°9E **229** D13
Fuyong *China* 22°40N 113°49E **219** a
Fuyot Springs △ *Phil.* 17°1N 121°58E **232** C3
Fuyu *Heilongjiang, China* 47°49N 124°27E **219** B13
Fuyu *Jilin, China* 45°12N 124°43E **227** B13
Fuyuan *China* 25°40N 104°16E **228** E5
Fuyun *China* 47°0N 89°28E **217** C11
Füzesgyarmat *Hungary* 47°6N 21°14E **182** C6
Fuzhou = Linchuan
China 27°57N 116°15E **229** D11
Fuzhou *China* 26°5N 119°16E **229** D12
Füzuli *Azerbaijan* 39°36N 47°8E **213** C12
Fyn *Denmark* 55°20N 10°30E **163** J4
Fyne, L. *U.K.* 55°59N 5°23W **167** F3
Fynshav *Denmark* 54°59N 9°59E **163** K3
Fyresdal *Norway* 59°11N 8°5E **164** E5
Fyresvatn *Norway* 59°6N 8°10E **164** E5
Fyzabad = Faizabad *India* 26°45N 82°10E **243** F10
Fyzabad *Trin. & Tob.* 10°14N 61°33W **323** t

G

G. Ross Lord Park *Canada* 43°47N 79°28W **141** A2
Ga *Ghana* 9°47N 2°30W **262** D4
Ga-eun *S. Korea* 36°38N 128°5E **224** D4
Gaa Faru Atoll *Maldives* 4°45N 73°26E **272** d
Gaalkacyo *Somali Rep.* 6°30N 47°30E **267** C6
Gaanda *Nigeria* 10°10N 12°27E **263** C7
Gabaldon *Phil.* 15°37N 121°20E **232** D3
Gabas → *France* 43°46N 0°42W **174** E3
Gabba *Australia* 9°45S 142°38E **280** a
Gabela *Angola* 11°0S 14°24E **265** E2
Gaberones = Gaborone
Botswana 24°45S 25°57E **270** B4
Gabès *Tunisia* 33°53N 10°2E **258** B2
Gabès ☐ *Tunisia* 33°35N 9°30E **261** B6
Gabès, G. de *Tunisia* 34°0N 10°30E **258** B2
Gabgaba, W. → *Egypt* 22°10N 33°5E **256** C3
Gabia *Dem. Rep. of the Congo* 4°37S 17°14E **265** C3
Gabia la Grande *Spain* 37°8N 3°40W **195** H7
Gąbin *Poland* 52°23N 19°41E **185** F6
Gablonz = Jablonec nad Nisou
Czech Rep. 50°43N 15°10E **180** A8
Gabon ■ *Africa* 0°10S 10°0E **264** C2
Gabon → *Gabon* 0°25N 9°20E **264** B1
Gaborone *Botswana* 24°45S 25°57E **270** B4
Gabrat Sai'd *Sudan* 16°18N 31°50E **266** A3
Gabriels *U.S.A.* 44°26N 74°12W **313** B10
Gābrīk *Iran* 25°44N 58°28E **247** E8
Gabro *Ethiopia* 6°18N 43°16E **267** C5
Gabrovo *Bulgaria* 42°52N 25°19E **203** D9
Gabú = Nova Lamego
Guinea-Biss. 12°19N 14°11W **262** C2
Gacé *France* 48°49N 0°20E **172** D7
Gach Sār *Iran* 36°7N 51°19E **247** B6
Gachsārān *Iran* 30°15N 50°45E **247** D6
Gacko *Bos.-H.* 43°10N 18°33E **202** C2
Gad Hinglaj *India* 16°14N 74°21E **245** F2
Gadag *India* 15°30N 75°45E **245** G2
Gadaisu *Papua N. G.* 10°22S 149°46E **286** F5
Gadamai *Sudan* 17°11N 36°10E **257** D4
Gadap *Pakistan* 25°5N 67°28E **242** G2
Gadarwara *India* 22°50N 78°50E **243** H8
Gadebusch *Germany* 53°42N 11°7E **178** B7
Gadein *South Sudan* 8°10N 28°45E **257** F2
Gadhada *India* 22°0N 71°35E **242** J4
Gadis → *Indonesia* 1°2N 98°55E **234** B1
Gádor, Sierra de *Spain* 36°57N 2°45W **195** J8
Gadra *Pakistan* 25°40N 70°38E **242** G4
Gadsden *Ala., U.S.A.* 34°1N 86°1W **316** A3
Gadsden *S.C., U.S.A.* 33°51N 80°46W **316** B9
Gadwal *India* 16°10N 77°50E **245** F3
Gadyach = Hadyach
Ukraine 50°21N 34°0E **189** G8
Gadzi *C.A.R.* 4°47N 16°42E **264** B3
Gaebong *S. Korea* 37°29N 126°52E **137** C1
Găeşti *Romania* 44°48N 25°19E **183** F10
Gaeta *Italy* 41°12N 13°35E **200** A6
Gaeta, G. di *Italy* 41°6N 13°30E **200** A6
Gaffney *U.S.A.* 35°5N 81°39W **315** D14
Gafsa *Tunisia* 34°24N 8°43E **258** B1
Gafsa ☐ *Tunisia* 34°30N 8°48E **261** B6
Gagarawa *Nigeria* 12°25N 9°32E **263** C6
Gagaria *India* 25°43N 70°46E **242** G4
Gagarin *Russia* 55°38N 35°0E **188** E8
Găgăuzia ☐ *Moldova* 46°10N 28°40E **183** D13
Gage Park *U.S.A.* 41°47N 87°42W **119** C2
Gaggenau *Germany* 48°48N 8°18E **179** G4
Gaghamni *Sudan* 11°41N 28°19E **257** E2
Gagil-Tomil, I. *Pac. Oc.* 9°31N 138°12E **287** R16
Gagino *Russia* 55°15N 45°1E **190** C7
Gagliano del Capo *Italy* 39°50N 18°22E **201** C11
Gagnef *Sweden* 60°36N 15°5E **162** D9
Gagnoa *Ivory C.* 6°56N 5°16W **262** D3
Gagnon *Canada* 51°50N 68°5W **299** B6
Gagnon, L. *Canada* 62°3N 110°27W **297** A6
Gagny *France* 48°53N 2°32E **134** A4
Gago Coutinho
São Tomé & Principe 0°1S 6°32E **265** a
Gagra *Georgia* 43°20N 40°10E **191** J5
Gahini *Rwanda* 1°50S 30°30E **268** C3
Gahmar *India* 25°27N 83°49E **243** G10
Gai Xian = Gaizhou
China 40°22N 122°20E **224** B1
Gaibanda *Bangla.* 25°20N 89°36E **241** C2
Gaidouronisi *Greece* 34°53N 25°41E **207** E6
Gail *U.S.A.* 32°46N 101°27W **314** E4
Gail → *Austria* 46°36N 13°53E **180** E6
Gaillac *France* 43°54N 1°54E **174** E5
Gaillard Cut *Panama* 9°3N 79°40W **320** c
Gaillimh = Galway *Ireland* 53°17N 9°3W **166** C2
Gaillon *France* 49°10N 1°20E **172** C8
Gaimán *Argentina* 43°10S 65°25W **336** B3
Gaines *U.S.A.* 41°46N 77°35W **312** E7
Gainesville *Fla., U.S.A.* 29°40N 82°20W **317** F7
Gainesville *Ga., U.S.A.* 34°18N 83°50W **315** D13
Gainesville *Mo., U.S.A.* 36°36N 92°26W **308** G7
Gainesville *Tex., U.S.A.* 33°38N 97°8W **314** E6
Gainsborough *U.K.* 53°24N 0°46W **168** D7
Gairdner, L. *Australia* 31°30S 136°0E **282** A2
Gairloch *U.K.* 57°43N 5°41W **167** D3
Gairloch, L. *U.K.* 57°43N 5°45W **167** D3
Gaizhou *China* 40°22N 122°20E **224** B1
Gaj *Croatia* 45°28N 17°3E **182** E2
Gaj → *Pakistan* 26°26N 67°21E **242** F2
Gajendragarh *India* 15°44N 75°59E **245** G2
Gakona *U.S.A.* 62°18N 145°18W **303** E11
Gakuch *Pakistan* 36°7N 73°45E **243** A5
Gal Oya △ *Sri Lanka* 7°0N 81°20E **245** L5
Gal Oya Res. *Sri Lanka* 7°5N 81°30E **245** L5
Gal Tardo *Somali Rep.* 3°34N 45°58E **267** D6
Galachipa *Bangla.* 22°8N 90°26E **241** D3
Galâla, Gebel el *Egypt* 29°21N 32°22E **256** J8
Galâla el Baharîya, G. el
Egypt 29°22N 32°23E **251** J3
Galâla el Qiblîya, G. el
Egypt 28°42N 32°22E **251** K3
Galán, Cerro *Argentina* 25°55S 66°52W **334** B2
Galana → *Kenya* 3°9S 40°8E **268** C5
Galangue *Angola* 13°42S 16°9E **265** E3
Galangue, Serra *Angola* 14°18S 15°52E **265** E3
Galanta *Slovak Rep.* 48°11N 17°45E **181** C10
Galapagar *Spain* 40°36N 3°58W **194** E7
Galápagos = Colón, Arch. de
Ecuador 0°0 91°0W **330** a
Galapagos Fracture Zone
Pac. Oc. 3°0N 110°0W **289** G17
Galapagos Rise *Pac. Oc.* 15°0S 95°0W **289** J18
Galashiels *U.K.* 55°37N 2°49W **167** F6
Galata *Turkey* 41°1N 28°58E **122** B1
Galata Tower *Turkey* 41°1N 28°59E **122** B1
Galatas *Greece* 37°30N 23°26E **204** D5
Galatea *N.Z.* 38°24S 176°45E **284** E5
Galateia *Cyprus* 35°25N 34°4E **207** E10
Galaţi *Romania* 45°27N 28°2E **183** E13
Galaţi ☐ *Romania* 45°45N 27°30E **183** E12
Galatia *Turkey* 39°30N 33°0E **212** C5
Galatina *Italy* 40°10N 18°10E **201** B11
Galátone *Italy* 40°9N 18°4E **201** B11
Galatsi *Greece* 38°1N 23°45E **112** A2
Galax *U.S.A.* 36°40N 80°56W **309** G13
Galaxidi *Greece* 38°22N 22°23E **204** C4
Galbin Govĭ *Mongolia* 43°0N 107°0E **226** C4
Galcaio = Gaalkacyo
Somali Rep. 6°30N 47°30E **267** C6
Gáldar *Canary Is.* 28°9N 15°39W **153** e1
Galdhøpiggen *Norway* 61°38N 8°18E **164** C5
Galeana *Chihuahua,*
Mexico 30°7N 107°38W **318** A3
Galeana *Nuevo León,*
Mexico 24°50N 100°4W **318** A4
Galeão, Int. de ✕ **(GIG)**
Brazil 22°49S 43°15W **135** A1
Galegu *Sudan* 12°36N 35°2E **257** E4
Galela *Indonesia* 1°50N 127°49E **231** D7
Galena *Alaska, U.S.A.* 64°44N 156°56W **303** D8
Galena *Ill., U.S.A.* 42°25N 90°26W **310** B6
Galeota Pt. *Trin. & Tob.* 10°8N 60°59W **323** t
Galera *Spain* 37°45N 2°33W **197** H2
Galera, Pta. *Chile* 39°59S 73°43W **336** A2
Galera, Pta. da *Azores* 37°42N 25°30W **153** d3
Galera Pt. *Trin. & Tob.* 10°49N 60°54W **323** t
Galesburg *Ill., U.S.A.* 40°57N 90°22W **310** D6
Galesburg *Mich., U.S.A.* 42°17N 85°26W **311** B11
Galestan △ *Iran* 37°30N 56°0E **247** B8
Galeton *U.S.A.* 41°44N 77°39W **312** E7
Galets → *Réunion* 20°56S 55°17E **272** f
Galga *Ethiopia* 6°39N 37°47E **257** F4
Galgasc *Somali Rep.* 0°11N 41°38E **267** D5
Galguduud ☐ *Somali Rep.* 5°0N 47°0E **267** D6
Galheirão → *Brazil* 12°23S 45°5W **333** D2
Gali *Georgia* 42°37N 41°46E **191** J5
Galicea Mare *Romania* 44°4N 23°19E **183** F8
Galich *Russia* 58°22N 42°24E **190** A6
Galiche *Bulgaria* 43°34N 23°53E **202** C7
Galicia ☐ *Spain* 42°43N 7°45W **194** C3
Galičica △ *Macedonia* 41°2N 20°55E **202** E4
Galien *U.S.A.* 41°48N 86°30W **311** C10
Galilee = Hagalil *Israel* 32°53N 35°18E **250** F6
Galilee, L. *Australia* 22°20S 145°50E **280** C4
Galilee, Sea of = Yam Kinneret
Israel 32°45N 35°35E **250** F6
Galim *Cameroon* 7°6N 12°25E **263** D7
Galina Pt. *Jamaica* 18°24N 76°58W **320** a
Galinoporni *Cyprus* 35°31N 34°18E **207** E10
Galion *U.S.A.* 40°44N 82°47W **312** F2
Galion, B. du *Martinique* 14°44N 60°56W **322** j
Galite, Îs. de la *Tunisia* 37°30N 8°59E **261** A6
Galiuro Mts. *U.S.A.* 32°30N 110°20W **305** K8
Galiwinku *Australia* 12°2S 135°34E **280** A2
Gallâbât *Sudan* 12°58N 36°11E **257** E4
Gallan Hd. *U.K.* 58°15N 7°2W **167** C1
Gallarate *Italy* 45°40N 8°48E **198** C5
Gallatin *Mo., U.S.A.* 39°55N 93°58W **310** E3
Gallatin *Tenn., U.S.A.* 36°24N 86°27W **315** C11
Galle *Sri Lanka* 6°5N 80°10E **245** L5
Gállego → *Spain* 41°39N 0°51W **196** D4
Gallegos → *Argentina* 51°35S 69°0W **336** D3
Gallery of Infinit Art = Dominion
Centre *Toronto, Canada* **141** b2
Galletti → *Ethiopia* 8°46N 41°10E **257** F5
Galley Hd. *Ireland* 51°32N 8°55W **166** E3
Galliate *Italy* 45°29N 8°42E **198** C5
Gallinas, Pta. *Colombia* 12°28N 71°40W **328** A3
Gallipoli = Gelibolu
Turkey 40°28N 26°43E **203** F10
Gallípoli *Italy* 40°3N 17°58E **201** B10
Gallipolis *U.S.A.* 38°49N 82°12W **309** F12
Gällivare *Sweden* 67°9N 20°40E **160** C19
Gallneukirchen *Austria* 48°21N 14°25E **180** C7
Gällö *Sweden* 62°55N 15°13E **162** B9
Gallo, C. *Italy* 38°13N 13°19E **200** D6
Gallocanta, L. de *Spain* 40°58N 1°30W **196** E3
Galloo I. *U.S.A.* 43°55N 76°25W **313** C8
Galloway *U.K.* 55°1N 4°29W **167** F4
Galloway, Mull of *U.K.* 54°39N 4°52W **167** G4
Galloway △ *U.K.* 55°3N 4°20W **167** F4
Gallup *U.S.A.* 35°32N 108°45W **305** J9
Gallur *Spain* 41°52N 1°19W **196** D3
Galma Galla *Kenya* 1°11S 40°47E **267** E5
Galong *Australia* 34°37S 148°34E **283** C8
Galool *Somali Rep.* 3°38N 43°49E **267** D5
Galoya *Sri Lanka* 8°10N 80°55E **245** K5
Galt *Calif., U.S.A.* 38°15N 121°18W **306** G5
Galt *Mo., U.S.A.* 40°8N 93°23W **310** D3
Galten *Denmark* 56°9N 9°54E **163** H3
Galtür *Austria* 46°58N 10°11E **180** E3
Galty Mts. *Ireland* 52°22N 8°10W **166** D3
Galtymore *Ireland* 52°21N 8°11W **166** D3
Galugāh *Iran* 36°43N 53°48E **247** B7
Galva *U.S.A.* 41°10N 90°3W **310** C6
Galvarino *Chile* 38°24S 72°47W **336** A2
Galve de Sorbe *Spain* 41°13N 3°10W **196** D1
Galveston *Ind., U.S.A.* 40°35N 86°11W **311** D10
Galveston *Tex., U.S.A.* 29°18N 94°48W **314** G7
Galveston B. *U.S.A.* 29°36N 94°50W **314** G7
Gálvez *Argentina* 32°0S 61°14W **334** C3
Galway *Ireland* 53°17N 9°3W **166** C2
Galway ☐ *Ireland* 53°22N 9°1W **166** C2
Galway B. *Ireland* 53°13N 9°10W **166** C2
Galyanovo *Russia* 55°48N 37°47E **129** B4
Gam → *Vietnam* 21°55N 105°12E **236** B5
Gamagōri *Japan* 34°50N 137°14E **223** C9
Gamari, L. *Ethiopia* 11°32N 41°40E **257** E5
Gamawa *Nigeria* 12°10N 10°31E **263** C7
Gamay *Phil.* 12°23N 125°18E **232** E5
Gamay B. *Phil.* 12°21N 125°21E **232** E5
Gamba *Angola* 11°42S 17°14E **265** E3
Gambaga *Ghana* 10°30N 0°28W **263** C4
Gambat *Pakistan* 27°17N 68°26E **242** F3
Gambela *Ethiopia* 8°14N 34°38E **257** F3
Gambela △ *Ethiopia* 8°0N 34°0E **257** F3
Gambela Hizbech ☐ *Ethiopia* 8°0N 34°0E **257** F3
Gambell *U.S.A.* 63°47N 171°45W **303** E5
Gambhir → *India* 26°58N 77°27E **242** F6
Gambia ■ *W. Afr.* 13°25N 16°0W **262** C1
Gambia → *W. Afr.* 13°28N 16°34W **262** C1
Gambier *U.S.A.* 40°22N 82°23W **312** F2
Gambier, C. *Australia* 11°56S 130°57E **278** B5
Gambier, Îs.
French Polynesia 23°8S 134°58W **289** f
Gambier Is. *Australia* 35°3S 136°30E **282** C2
Gambier Village *Bahamas* 25°4N 77°30W **153** b
Gambir *Indonesia* 6°9S 106°48E **122** A1
Gambo *C.A.R.* 4°39N 22°16E **264** B4
Gambo *Canada* 48°47N 54°13W **299** C9
Gambo *Rio de J., Brazil* 22°53S 43°11W **135** B1
Gamboa *Panama* 9°7N 79°42W **320** c
Gamboli *Pakistan* 29°53N 68°24E **242** E3
Gambolòita *Italy* 45°26N 9°13E **129** B2
Gamboma *Congo* 1°55S 15°52E **264** C3
Gamboula *C.A.R.* 4°8N 15°9E **264** B3
Gamka → *S. Africa* 33°18S 21°39E **270** D3
Gamkab → *Namibia* 28°4S 17°54E **270** C2
Gamla Stan *Stockholm, Sweden* **139** c2
Gamla Uppsala *Sweden* 59°54N 17°40E **162** E11
Gamlakarleby = Kokkola
Finland 63°50N 23°8E **160** E20
Gamleby *Sweden* 57°54N 16°24E **163** G10
Gamlebyen *Norway* 59°54N 10°46E **133** A3
Gammon → *Canada* 51°24N 95°44W **297** C9
Gammon Ranges △
Australia 30°38S 139°8E **281** E2
Gamo-Gofa *Ethiopia* 5°40N 36°40E **257** F4
Gamoda-Saki *Japan* 33°50N 134°45E **222** D6
Gamou *Niger* 14°20N 9°55E **259** F1
Gampaha *Sri Lanka* 7°5N 79°59E **245** L4
Gampo *S. Korea* 35°48N 129°31E **224** E4
Gampola *Sri Lanka* 7°10N 80°34E **245** L5
Gamtoos → *S. Africa* 33°58S 25°1E **270** D4
Gan *France* 43°12N 0°27W **174** E3
Gan Gan *Argentina* 42°30S 68°10W **336** B3
Gan Goriama, Mts.
Cameroon 7°44N 12°45E **263** D7
Gan Jiang → *China* 29°15N 116°0E **229** C11
Ganado *U.S.A.* 35°43N 109°33W **305** J9
Gananita *Sudan* 18°22N 33°50E **256** D3
Gananoque *Canada* 44°20N 76°10W **313** B8
Ganassi *Phil.* 7°49N 124°6E **233** H5
Ganāveh *Iran* 29°35N 50°35E **247** D6
Gäncä *Azerbaijan* 40°45N 46°20E **191** K8
Gancheng *China* 18°51N 108°37E **236** C7
Gand = Gent *Belgium* 51°2N 3°42E **170** C3
Ganda *Angola* 13°3S 14°35E **265** E2
Gandajika
Dem. Rep. of the Congo 6°46S 23°58E **265** D4
Gandak → *India* 25°39N 85°13E **243** G11
Gandara *Phil.* 12°1N 124°49E **232** E5
Gandava *Pakistan* 28°32N 67°32E **242** E2
Gander *Canada* 48°58N 54°35W **299** C9
Gander L. *Canada* 48°58N 54°35W **299** C9
Ganderkesee *Germany* 53°2N 8°32E **178** B4
Ganderowe Falls *Zimbabwe* 17°20S 29°10E **269** F2
Gandesa *Spain* 41°3N 0°26E **196** D5
Gandhi Sagar *India* 24°40N 75°40E **242** G6
Gandhinagar *India* 23°15N 72°45E **242** H5
Gandi *Nigeria* 12°55N 5°49E **263** C6
Gandia *Spain* 38°58N 0°9W **197** G4
Gandino *Italy* 45°49N 9°54E **198** C6
Gando, Pta. *Canary Is.* 27°55N 15°22W **153** e1
Gandole *Nigeria* 8°28N 11°35E **263** D7
Gandou *Congo* 2°25N 17°25E **264** B3
Gandu *Brazil* 13°45S 39°30W **333** D4
Ganeb *Mauritania* 18°29N 10°8W **262** B2
Ganedidalem = Gani
Indonesia 0°48S 128°14E **231** E7
Ganga → *India* 23°20N 90°30E **241** D3
Ganga Sagar *India* 21°38N 88°5E **243** J13
Gangafani *Mali* 14°20N 2°20W **262** C4
Gangakher *India* 18°57N 76°45E **244** E3
Gangan → *India* 28°38N 78°58E **243** E8
Ganganagar *India* 29°56N 73°56E **242** E5
Gangapur *Maharashtra,*
India 19°41N 75°1E **244** E2
Gangapur *Raj., India* 26°32N 76°49E **242** F7
Gangara *Niger* 14°35N 8°29E **259** F1
Gangaw *Burma* 22°5N 94°5E **241** D5
Gangaw Taungdan
Burma 24°55N 96°35E **241** C6
Gangawati *India* 15°30N 76°36E **245** G3
Gangdisê Shan *China* 31°20N 81°0E **243** D9
Gangdong *S. Korea* 37°30N 127°5E **137** B2
Ganges = Ganga →
India 23°20N 90°30E **243** H14
Ganges *Canada* 48°51N 123°31W **296** D4
Ganges *Hérault, France* 43°56N 3°42E **174** E7
Ganges, Mouths of the
India 21°30N 90°0E **241** E3
Ganggyeong *S. Korea* 36°10N 127°0E **224** D3
Gånghester *Sweden* 57°42N 13°1E **163** G7
Ganghwa *S. Korea* 37°45N 126°30E **224** D3
Gangi *Italy* 37°48N 14°12E **201** E7
Gângiova *Romania* 43°54N 23°50E **183** G8
Gangnam *S. Korea* 37°30N 126°59E **137** B1
Gangneung *S. Korea* 37°45N 128°54E **224** D4
Gangoh *India* 29°46N 77°18E **242** E7
Gangotri *India* 30°50N 79°10E **243** D8
Gangotri △ *India* 30°50N 79°10E **243** D8
Gangseo *S. Korea* 37°32N 126°51E **137** B1
Gangseong *S. Korea* 38°24N 128°30E **224** C4
Gangtok *India* 27°20N 88°37E **241** B2
Gangtou *China* 23°12N 113°8E **121** A1
Gangu *China* 34°40N 105°15E **226** G3
Gangwa
Dem. Rep. of the Congo 3°30S 20°54E **264** C4
Gangwei *China* 23°4N 113°11E **121** B2
Gangwon-do ☐ *S. Korea* 37°45N 128°15E **224** D4
Gangyao *China* 44°12N 126°37E **227** B14
Gani *Indonesia* 0°48S 128°14E **231** E7
Ganj *India* 27°45N 78°57E **243** F8
Ganjam *India* 19°23N 85°4E **244** E7
Ganjiakou *China* 39°54N 116°16E **114** B1
Ganluo *China* 28°58N 102°59E **228** C4
Ganmain *Australia* 34°47S 147°1E **283** C7
Ganna *South Sudan* 7°30N 28°0E **266** C2
Gannat *France* 46°7N 3°11E **173** F10
Gannett Peak *U.S.A.* 43°11N 109°39W **304** E9
Ganquan *China* 36°20N 109°20E **226** F5
Gänserdorf *Austria* 48°20N 16°43E **181** C9
Ganshoren *Belgium* 50°52N 4°18E **116** A1
Ganshui *China* 28°40N 106°40E **228** C6
Gansu ☐ *China* 36°0N 104°0E **226** G3
Ganta *Liberia* 7°15N 8°59W **262** D3
Gantheaume, C. *Australia* 36°4S 137°32E **282** D2
Gantheaume B. *Australia* 27°40S 114°10E **279** E1
Gants Hill *U.K.* 51°34N 0°4E **125** A4
Gantsevichi = Hantsavichy
Belarus 52°49N 26°30E **177** B14
Gantung *Indonesia* 2°58S 108°9E **235** C3
Ganye *Nigeria* 8°25N 12°4E **263** D7
Ganyem = Genyem
Indonesia 2°46S 140°12E **231** E10
Ganyu *China* 34°50N 119°8E **227** G10
Ganyushkino *Kazakhstan* 46°35N 49°20E **191** G9
Ganzhou *China* 25°51N 114°56E **229** E10
Gao *Mali* 16°15N 0°5W **263** B4
Gao Xian *China* 28°21N 104°32E **228** C5
Gao'an *China* 28°26N 115°17E **229** C10
Gaobeidian *China* 39°19N 115°51E **226** E8
Gaocheng *China* 38°2N 114°49E **226** E8
Gaochun *China* 31°20N 118°49E **229** B12
Gaohebu *China* 30°43N 116°49E **229** B11
Gaokeng *China* 27°40N 113°58E **229** D9
Gaolan Dao *China* 21°55N 113°10E **229** G9
Gaoligong Shan *China* 24°45N 98°45E **228** E2
Gaomi *China* 36°20N 119°42E **227** F10
Gaoping *China* 35°45N 112°55E **226** G7
Gaoqiao *China* 31°21N 121°34E **138** A2
Gaotang *China* 36°50N 116°15E **226** F9
Gaoua *Burkina Faso* 10°20N 3°8W **262** C4
Gaoual *Guinea* 11°45N 13°25W **262** C2
Gaoxiong = Kaohsiung
Taiwan 22°35N 120°16E **225** D2
Gaoyang *China* 38°40N 115°45E **226** E8
Gaoyao *China* 23°3N 112°27E **229** F9
Gaoyou *China* 32°47N 119°26E **229** A12
Gaoyou Hu *China* 32°45N 119°20E **227** H10
Gaoyuan *China* 37°8N 117°58E **227** F9
Gaozhou *China* 21°58N 110°50E **229** G8
Gap *France* 44°33N 6°5E **175** D10
Gapan *Phil.* 15°19N 120°57E **232** D3
Gapat → *India* 24°30N 82°28E **243** G10
Gapuwiyak *Australia* 12°25S 135°43E **280** A2
Gar *China* 32°10N 79°58E **218** E4
Gara, L. *Ireland* 53°57N 8°26W **166** C3
Garāb *Iran* 33°27N 47°16E **213** F12
Garabogazköl Aylagy
Turkmenistan 41°0N 53°30E **187** F9
Garacad *Somali Rep.* 6°57N 49°24E **267** C6
Garachico *Canary Is.* 28°22N 16°46W **153** e1
Garachiné *Panama* 8°0N 78°12W **320** E4
Garafia *Canary Is.* 28°48N 17°57W **153** e1
Garagum *Turkmenistan* 39°30N 60°0E **247** B8
Garah *Australia* 29°5S 149°38E **281** D4
Garaina *Papua N. G.* 7°53S 147°8E **286** D4
Garajonay *Canary Is.* 28°7N 17°14W **153** e1
Garamba △
Dem. Rep. of the Congo 4°10N 29°40E **268** B2
Garango *Burkina Faso* 11°48N 0°34W **263** C4
Garanhuns *Brazil* 8°50S 36°30W **332** C4
Garapan *N. Marianas* 15°12N 145°43E **302** e
Garautha *India* 25°34N 79°18E **243** G8
Garawa ⊙ *Australia* 16°43S 136°51E **280** B2
Garawe *Liberia* 4°35N 8°0W **262** E3
Garba Harre = Garbahaarrey →
Somali Rep. 3°19N 42°13E **267** D5
Garba Tula *Kenya* 0°30N 38°32E **268** B4
Garbagnate Milanese *Italy* 45°34N 9°4E **129** A1
Garbagududu *Ethiopia* 6°12N 43°50E **267** C5
Garbahaarrey →
Somali Rep. 3°19N 42°13E **267** D5
Garbatella *Italy* 41°51N 12°30E **136** B2
Garberville *U.S.A.* 40°6N 123°48W **304** F2
Garbiyang *India* 30°8N 80°54E **243** D9
Garbsen *Germany* 52°26N 9°36E **178** C5
Garça *Brazil* 22°14S 49°37W **333** F2
Garças → *Mato Grosso,*
Brazil 15°54S 52°16W **331** D7
Garças → *Pernambuco,*
Brazil 8°43S 39°41W **332** C4
Garches *France* 48°50N 2°11E **134** A2
Garching *Germany* 48°14N 11°39E **131** A3
Garchitorena *Phil.* 13°52N 123°40E **232** E4
Garcia Hernandez *Phil.* 9°37N 124°18E **233** G5
Garcias *Brazil* 20°34S 52°13W **331** E7
Gard ☐ *France* 44°2N 4°10E **175** D8
Gard → *France* 43°51N 4°37E **175** E8
Garda, L. di *Italy* 45°40N 10°41E **198** C7
Gardabani *Georgia* 41°27N 45°5E **191** K7
Gardanne *France* 43°27N 5°27E **175** E9
Gårdby *Sweden* 56°36N 16°38E **163** H10
Garde L. *Canada* 62°50N 106°13W **297** A7
Gardelegen *Germany* 52°32N 11°24E **178** C7
Garden City *El Qâhira,*
Egypt 30°2N 31°14E **117** A2
Garden City *Ga., U.S.A.* 32°6N 81°9W **316** C8
Garden City *Kans.,*
U.S.A. 37°58N 100°53W **308** G3
Garden City *Mo., U.S.A.* 38°34N 94°12W **310** F2
Garden City *Tex., U.S.A.* 31°52N 101°29W **314** F4
Garden Grove *U.S.A.* 33°47N 117°55W **307** M9
Garden Reach *India* 22°33N 88°15E **124** B1
Gardens of Stone △
Australia 33°14S 150°11E **283** B9
Garder *Norway* 59°45N 10°38E **133** B2
Gardēz *Afghan.* 33°37N 69°9E **242** C3
Garðabær *Iceland* 64°5N 21°55W **155** C5
Garðskagi *Iceland* 64°5N 22°43W **155** C4
Garður *Iceland* 66°4N 16°46W **155** A10
Gardiki *Greece* 38°50N 21°55E **204** C3
Gardiner *Maine, U.S.A.* 44°14N 69°47W **309** C19
Gardiner *Mont., U.S.A.* 45°2N 110°22W **304** D8
Gardiners I. *U.S.A.* 41°6N 72°6W **313** E12
Gardner *Fla., U.S.A.* 27°21N 81°48W **317** H8
Gardner *Ill., U.S.A.* 41°12N 88°17W **311** C8
Gardner *Mass., U.S.A.* 42°34N 71°59W **313** D13
Gardner Canal *Canada* 53°27N 128°8W **296** C3
Gardner Pinnacles
U.S.A. 25°0N 167°55W **302** F10
Gardnerville *U.S.A.* 38°56N 119°45W **306** G7
Gardno, Jezioro *Poland* 54°40N 17°7E **184** D4
Gardo = Qardho *Somali Rep.* 9°30N 49°6E **267** C6
Gardone Val Trómpia
Italy 45°41N 10°11E **198** C7
Gárdony *Hungary* 47°12N 18°39E **182** C3
Gare Tigre *Fr. Guiana* 4°58N 53°9W **329** C7
Gareloi I. *U.S.A.* 51°48N 178°48W **303** L3
Gares = Puente la Reina
Spain 42°40N 1°49W **196** C3
Garešnica *Croatia* 45°36N 16°56E **199** C13
Garéssio *Italy* 44°12N 8°2E **198** D5
Garey *U.S.A.* 34°53N 120°19W **307** L6
Garfield *N.J., U.S.A.* 40°52N 74°7W **132** A1
Garfield *Wash., U.S.A.* 47°1N 117°9W **304** C5
Garfield Park *U.S.A.* 41°52N 87°42W **119** B2
Garforth *U.K.* 53°47N 1°24W **168** D6
Gargaliani *Greece* 37°4N 21°38E **204** D3
Gargan, Mt. *France* 45°37N 1°39E **174** C5
Gargano △ *Italy* 41°43N 15°52E **199** G12
Gargantua, C. *Canada* 47°36N 85°2W **309** B11
Gargareta *Greece* 37°57N 23°43E **112** B2
Gargett *Australia* 21°9S 148°46E **280** b
Gargouna *Mali* 15°56N 0°13E **263** B5
Gargždai *Lithuania* 55°43N 21°24E **184** C8
Garhchiroli *India* 20°10N 80°0E **244** D5
Garibaldi △ *Canada* 49°50N 122°40W **296** D4
Garibong *S. Korea* 37°29N 126°54E **137** C1
Gariep, L. *S. Africa* 30°40S 25°40E **270** D4
Garies *S. Africa* 30°32S 17°59E **270** D2
Garig Gunak Barlu △
Australia 11°26S 131°58E **278** B5
Garigliano → *Italy* 41°13N 13°45E **200** A6
Garissa *Kenya* 0°25S 39°40E **268** C4
Garkida *Nigeria* 10°27N 12°36E **263** C7
Garko *Nigeria* 11°45N 8°53E **263** C6
Garland *Tex., U.S.A.* 32°54N 96°38W **314** E6
Garland *Utah, U.S.A.* 41°45N 112°10W **304** F7
Garlasco *Italy* 45°12N 8°55E **198** C5
Garliava *Lithuania* 54°49N 23°52E **184** D10
Garlin *France* 43°33N 0°16W **174** E3
Garmāb *Semnān, Iran* 35°25N 56°45E **247** C8
Garmāb *Zanjān, Iran* 35°50N 48°11E **213** E13
Garmisch-Partenkirchen
Germany 47°30N 11°6E **179** H7
Garmo, Qullai = imeni Ismail
Samani, Pik *Tajikistan* 39°0N 72°2E **217** E8
Garmsār *Iran* 35°20N 52°25E **247** C7
Garner *U.S.A.* 43°6N 93°36W **310** A3
Garnett *U.S.A.* 38°17N 95°14W **308** F6
Garnpung L. *Australia* 33°25S 143°10E **282** B5
Garo Hills *India* 25°30N 90°30E **241** C3
Garoe = Garoowe
Somali Rep. 8°25N 48°33E **267** C6
Garonne → *France* 45°2N 0°36W **174** C3
Garonne, Canal Latéral à la
France 44°15N 0°18E **174** D4
Garoowe *Somali Rep.* 8°25N 48°33E **267** C6
Garorimman *S. Korea* 36°54N 126°21E **224** D3
Garot *India* 24°19N 75°41E **242** G6
Garou, L. *Mali* 16°2N 2°45W **262** B4
Garoua *Cameroon* 9°19N 13°21E **263** D7
Garoua Boulaï *Cameroon* 5°53N 14°33E **264** A2
Garove I. *Papua N. G.* 4°42S 149°30E **286** C5
Garpenberg *Sweden* 60°19N 16°12E **162** D10
Garphyttan *Sweden* 59°18N 14°56E **162** E8
Garrauli *India* 25°5N 79°22E **243** G8
Garrel *Germany* 52°57N 8°1E **178** C4
Garreru *Palau* 7°19N 134°32E **288** c
Garrett *U.S.A.* 41°21N 85°8W **311** C11
Garrigues *France* 43°40N 3°55E **174** E7
Garrison *Ky., U.S.A.* 38°36N 83°10W **311** F13
Garrison *Mont., U.S.A.* 46°31N 112°49W **304** C7
Garrison *N. Dak., U.S.A.* 47°40N 101°25W **308** B3
Garrison Res. = Sakakawea, L.
U.S.A. 47°30N 101°25W **308** B3
Garron Pt. *U.K.* 55°3N 5°59W **166** A6
Garrovillas de Alconétar
Spain 39°40N 6°33W **195** F4
Garrucha *Spain* 37°11N 1°49W **197** H3
Garry → *U.K.* 56°44N 3°47W **167** E5
Garry, L. *Canada* 65°58N 100°18W **294** D11
Garrygala *Turkmenistan* 38°31N 56°29E **247** B8
Garsen *Kenya* 2°20S 40°5E **268** C5
Gärsnäs *Sweden* 55°32N 14°10E **163** J8
Garson L. *Canada* 56°19N 110°2W **297** B6
Garstang *U.K.* 53°55N 2°46W **168** D5
Gartempe → *France* 46°47N 0°49E **174** B4
Gartz *Germany* 53°13N 14°22E **178** B10
Garu *Ghana* 10°55N 0°11W **263** C4
Garu *India* 23°40N 84°14E **243** H11
Garub *Namibia* 26°37S 16°0E **270** C2
Garusuun *Palau* 7°21N 134°31E **288** c
Garut *Indonesia* 7°14S 107°53E **235** D3
Garvanza *U.S.A.* 34°6N 118°11W **126** A3
Garvão *Portugal* 37°42N 8°21W **195** H2
Garvie Mts. *N.Z.* 45°30S 168°50E **285** F3
Garwa = Garoua *Cameroon* 9°19N 13°21E **263** D7
Garwa *India* 24°11N 83°47E **243** G10
Garwolin *Poland* 51°55N 21°38E **185** G8
Gary *U.S.A.* 41°36N 87°20W **311** C9
Garz *Germany* 54°19N 13°20E **178** A9
Garzê *China* 31°38N 100°1E **228** B3
Garzón *Colombia* 2°10N 75°40W **328** C2
Gas City *U.S.A.* 40°29N 85°37W **311** D11
Gas-San *Japan* 38°32N 140°1E **220** E10
Gasa *Bhutan* 27°55N 89°40E **241** B2
Gasan *Phil.* 13°19N 121°51E **232** E3
Gasan Kuli = Esenguly
Turkmenistan 37°37N 53°59E **216** E4
Gascogne *France* 43°45N 0°20E **174** E4
Gascogne, G. de *Europe* 44°0N 2°0W **174** E2
Gasconade *U.S.A.* 38°40N 91°34W **310** F5
Gasconade → *U.S.A.* 38°41N 91°33W **310** F5
Gascony = Gascogne
France 43°45N 0°20E **174** E4
Gascoyne → *Australia* 24°52S 113°37E **279** D1
Gascoyne Junction
Australia 25°2S 115°17E **279** E2
Gascueña *Spain* 40°18N 2°31W **196** E2
Gash, Wadi → *Africa* 16°48N 35°51E **257** D4
Gash Setit △ *Eritrea* 15°12N 36°58E **257** D4
Gåshaga *Sweden* 59°21N 18°13E **139** A3
Gashagar *Nigeria* 13°22N 12°47E **263** C7
Gashaka *Nigeria* 7°20N 11°29E **263** D7
Gashaka-Gumti △ *Nigeria* 7°23N 11°34E **263** D7
Gasherbrum *Pakistan* 35°40N 76°40E **243** B7
Gashua *Nigeria* 12°54N 11°0E **263** C7
Gasmata *Papua N. G.* 6°17S 150°20E **286** D6
Gasparilla I. *U.S.A.* 26°46N 82°16W **317** J7
Gasparillo *Trin. & Tob.* 10°18N 61°26W **323** t
Gasparito *Curaçao* 12°8N 68°56W **322** g
Gaspé *Canada* 48°52N 64°30W **299** C7
Gaspé, C. de *Canada* 48°48N 64°7W **299** C7
Gaspé Pen. = Gaspésie, Pén. de la
Canada 48°45N 65°40W **299** C6
Gasper Grande *Trin. & Tob.* 10°40N 61°39W **323** t
Gaspésie, Pén. de la
Canada 48°45N 65°40W **299** C6
Gaspésie ⌂ *Canada* 48°55N 66°10W **299** C6
Gassan *Burkina Faso* 12°49N 3°12W **262** C4
Gassen = Jasień *Poland* 51°46N 15°0E **185** G2
Gassol *Nigeria* 8°34N 10°25E **263** D7
Gasteiz = Vitoria-Gasteiz
Spain 42°50N 2°41W **196** C2
Gaston *U.S.A.* 33°49N 81°5W **316** B8
Gastonia *U.S.A.* 35°16N 81°11W **315** D14
Gastouni *Greece* 37°51N 21°15E **204** D3
Gastouri *Greece* 39°34N 19°54E **206** B9
Gastre *Argentina* 42°20S 69°15W **336** B3
Gästrikland *Sweden* 60°45N 16°40E **162** D10
Gata, C. *Cyprus* 34°34N 33°2E **207** F9
Gata, C. de *Spain* 36°41N 2°13W **197** J2
Gata, Sierra de *Spain* 40°20N 6°45W **194** E4
Gataga → *Canada* 58°35N 126°59W **296** B3
Gătaia *Romania* 45°26N 21°30E **182** E6
Gatchina *Russia* 59°35N 30°9E **188** C6
Gatehouse of Fleet *U.K.* 54°53N 4°12W **167** G4
Gates *U.S.A.* 43°9N 77°42W **312** C7
Gates of the Arctic ⌂
U.S.A. 67°45N 153°15W **303** C9
Gateshead *U.K.* 54°57N 1°35W **168** C6
Gateshead I. *Canada* 70°36N 100°26W **294** C11
Gatesville *U.S.A.* 31°26N 97°45W **314** F6
Gateway ⌂ *U.S.A.* 40°38N 73°51W **132** C2
Gateway of India *India* 18°55N 72°50E **130** B2
Gathsi *Zimbabwe* 20°2S 30°32E **269** G3
Gâtinais *France* 48°5N 2°40E **173** D9
Gâtine, Hauteurs de
France 46°35N 0°45W **174** B3
Gatineau *Canada* 45°29N 75°39W **313** A9
Gatineau → *Canada* 45°27N 75°42W **298** C4
Gatineau △ *Canada* 45°40N 76°0W **298** C4
Gatow *Germany* 52°29N 13°11E **115** B1
Gattaran *Phil.* 18°4N 121°38E **232** B3
Gattinara *Italy* 45°37N 8°22E **198** C5
Gatton *Australia* 27°32S 152°17E **281** D5
Gatún, L. *Panama* 9°7N 79°56W **320** c
Gatún Dam *Panama* 9°16N 79°55W **320** c
Gatún Locks *Panama* 9°16N 79°55W **320** c
Gatwick, London ✕ **(LGW)**
U.K. 51°10N 0°11W **169** F7
Gatyana *S. Africa* 32°16S 28°31E **271** D4
Gau *Fiji* 18°2S 179°18E **287** B2
Gaua *Vanuatu* 14°15S 167°30E **287** D5
Gaucín *Spain* 36°31N 5°19W **195** J5
Gauer L. *Canada* 57°0N 97°50W **297** B9
Gauhati = Guwahati
India 26°10N 91°45E **241** B3
Gauja → *Latvia* 57°10N 24°16E **188** D3
Gaujas △ *Latvia* 57°10N 24°50E **161** H21
Gaula → *Norway* 63°21N 10°14E **164** A7
Gaupne *Norway* 61°25N 7°18E **164** C4
Gaurdak = Gowurdak
Turkmenistan 37°50N 66°4E **217** E7
Gauri Phanta *India* 28°41N 80°36E **243** E9
Gauribidanur *India* 13°37N 77°32E **245** H3
Gaustatoppen *Norway* 59°48N 8°40E **164** E5
Gauteng ☐ *S. Africa* 26°0S 28°0E **271** C4
Gāv Koshī *Iran* 28°38N 57°12E **247** D8
Gavà *Spain* 41°18N 2°1W **114** B1
Gāvakān *Iran* 29°37N 53°10E **247** D7
Gavamar *Spain* 41°15N 2°1E **114** B1
Gavarnie *France* 42°44N 0°1W **174** F3
Gaväter *Iran* 25°10N 61°31E **247** E9
Gāvbandī *Iran* 27°12N 53°4E **247** E7
Gavdopoula *Greece* 34°56N 24°0E **207** E6
Gavdos *Greece* 34°50N 24°5E **207** F5
Gávea *Brazil* 22°58S 43°13W **135** B1
Gávea, Pedra da *Brazil* 22°59S 43°18W **135** B1
Gavi *Italy* 44°41N 8°49E **198** D5
Gavião *Portugal* 39°28N 7°56W **195** F3
Gaviota *U.S.A.* 34°29N 120°13W **307** L6
Gāvkhūnī, Bāţlāq-e *Iran* 32°6N 52°52E **247** C7
Gävle *Sweden* 60°40N 17°9E **162** D11
Gävleborgs län ☐ *Sweden* 61°30N 16°15E **162** C10
Gävlebukten *Sweden* 60°40N 17°20E **162** D11
Gavorrano *Italy* 42°55N 10°54E **198** F7
Gavray *France* 48°55N 1°20W **172** D5
Gavrilov Yam *Russia* 57°18N 39°49E **188** D10
Gavrio *Greece* 37°54N 24°44E **204** D6
Gawachab *Namibia* 27°4S 17°55E **270** C2
Gawai *Burma* 27°56N 97°30E **241** B6
Gawilgarh Hills *India* 21°15N 76°45E **244** D3
Gawler *Australia* 34°30S 138°42E **282** C3
Gawler Ranges *Australia* 32°30S 135°45E **282** B2
Gawu *Nigeria* 9°14N 6°52E **263** D6
Gaxun Nur *China* 42°22N 100°30E **218** C9
Gay *Russia* 51°27N 58°27E **186** D10
Gaya *Niger* 11°52N 3°28E **263** C5
Gaya *India* 24°47N 85°4E **243** G11
Gaya *Niger* 11°52N 3°28E **263** C5
Gaya *Nigeria* 11°57N 9°0E **263** C6
Gayasan △ *S. Korea* 35°45N 128°4E **225** C4
Gayéri *Burkina Faso* 12°39N 0°29E **263** C5
Gaylord *U.S.A.* 45°2N 84°41W **309** C11
Gayndah *Australia* 25°35S 151°32E **281** D5
Gaysin = Haysyn
Ukraine 48°57N 29°25E **183** B14
Gayvoron = Hayvoron
Ukraine 48°22N 29°52E **183** B14
Gaza *Gaza Strip* 31°30N 34°28E **251** G5
Gaza ☐ *Mozam.* 23°10S 32°45E **271** B5
Gaza Strip ■ *Asia* 31°29N 34°25E **251** G5
Gazanjyk = Bereket
Turkmenistan 39°16N 55°32E **247** B7
Gazaoua *Niger* 13°32N 7°55E **263** C6
Gāzbor *Iran* 28°5N 58°51E **247** D8
Gazdagrét *Hungary* 47°29N 19°0E **117** B1
Gazelle Pen. *Papua N. G.* 4°40S 152°0E **286** C7
Gazi *Dem. Rep. of the Congo* 1°3N 24°30E **264** B4
Gaziantep *Turkey* 37°6N 37°23E **250** A8
Gaziantep ☐ *Turkey* 37°0N 37°0E **250** B8
Gazimağusa = Famagusta
Cyprus 35°8N 33°55E **207** E9
Gaziosmanpaşa *Turkey* 41°5N 28°50E **122** B1
Gazipaşa *Turkey* 36°16N 32°18E **250** B3
Gazli *Uzbekistan* 40°8N 63°27E **216** D6
Gbadolite
Dem. Rep. of the Congo 4°17N 21°1E **264** B4
Gbarnga *Liberia* 7°19N 9°13W **262** D3
Gboko *Nigeria* 7°17N 9°4E **263** D6
Gcoverega *Botswana* 19°8S 24°18E **270** A3
Gcuwa *S. Africa* 32°20S 28°11E **271** D4
Gdańsk *Poland* 54°22N 18°40E **184** D5
Gdańsk ✕ **(GDN)** *Poland* 54°22N 18°30E **184** D5
Gdańska, Zatoka *Poland* 54°30N 19°20E **184** D6
Gdingen = Gdynia *Poland* 54°35N 18°33E **184** D5
Gdov *Russia* 58°48N 27°55E **188** C4
Gdynia *Poland* 54°35N 18°33E **184** D5

Geba → *Guinea-Biss.* 11°46N 15°36W **262** C1
Gebe *Indonesia* 0°5N 129°25E **231** D7
Gebeciler *Turkey* 38°46N 30°46E **205** C12
Gebeit Mine *Sudan* 21°3N 36°29E **256** C4
Gebel Abyad *Sudan* 19°0N 28°0E **256** D2
Gebel el Ahmar *Egypt* 30°2N 31°21E **117** A3
Gebel el Muqattam *Egypt* 30°1N 31°17E **117** A2
Gebel el Tura *Egypt* 29°56N 31°15E **117** B2
Gebel Iweibid *Egypt* 30°8N 32°13E **256** H8
Gebiley *Somali Rep.* 9°42N 43°37E **267** C5
Gebze *Turkey* 40°47N 29°25E **203** F13
Gecha *Ethiopia* 7°30N 35°18E **257** F4
Gedaref *Sudan* 14°2N 35°28E **257** E4
Gedaref □ *Sudan* 14°0N 35°0E **257** E4
Gede, Tanjung *Indonesia* 6°46S 105°12E **234** D3
Gediz *Turkey* 39°1N 29°24E **205** B11
Gediz → *Turkey* 38°35N 26°48E **205** C8
Gedo *Ethiopia* 9°2N 37°25E **257** F4
Gedo □ *Somali Rep.* 2°15N 42°10E **267** D5
Gèdre *France* 42°47N 0°2E **174** F4
Gedser *Denmark* 54°35N 11°55E **163** K5
Gedung, Pulau *Malaysia* 5°17N 100°23E **237** c
Geegully Cr. → *Australia* 18°32S 123°41E **278** C3
Geel *Belgium* 51°10N 4°59E **170** C4
Geelong *Australia* 38°10S 144°22E **282** E6
Geelvink B. = Cenderwasih, Teluk *Indonesia* 3°0S 135°20E **231** E9
Geelvink Chan. *Australia* 28°30S 114°0E **279** E1
Geesthacht *Germany* 53°26N 10°22E **178** B6
Geidam *Nigeria* 12°57N 11°57E **263** C7
Geikie → *Canada* 57°45N 103°52W **297** B8
Geikie Gorge △ *Australia* 18°3S 125°41E **278** C4
Geilenkirchen *Germany* 50°57N 6°8E **178** E2
Geili *Sudan* 16°1N 32°37E **257** D3
Geilo *Norway* 60°32N 8°14E **164** D5
Geiselgasteig *Germany* 48°3N 11°33E **131** B2
Geisingen *Germany* 47°54N 8°38E **179** H4
Geislingen *Germany* 48°37N 9°50E **179** G5
Geistown *U.S.A.* 40°18N 78°52W **312** F6
Geita *Tanzania* 2°48S 32°12E **268** C3
Geitastrand *Norway* 63°22N 9°56E **164** A6
Geithus *Norway* 59°57N 9°59E **164** E6
Gejiu *China* 23°20N 103°10E **228** F4
Gel → *South Sudan* 7°5N 29°10E **257** F2
Gel, Meydān-e *Iran* 29°4N 54°50E **247** D7
Gel River *South Sudan* 7°5N 29°10E **257** F2
Gela *Italy* 37°4N 14°15E **201** E7
Gela, G. di *Italy* 37°0N 14°20E **201** F7
Geladi *Ethiopia* 6°59N 46°30E **267** C6
Gelahun *Liberia* 7°55N 10°28W **262** D2
Gelam *Indonesia* 2°54S 110°11E **235** C4
Gelang Patah *Malaysia* 1°27N 103°35E **237** d
Gelderland □ *Neths.* 52°5N 6°10E **170** B6
Geldern *Germany* 51°31N 6°20E **178** D2
Geldrop *Neths.* 51°25N 5°32E **170** C5
Geleen *Neths.* 50°57N 5°49E **170** D5
Gelehun *S. Leone* 8°20N 11°40W **262** D2
Gelembe *Turkey* 39°10N 27°50E **205** B9
Gelemso *Ethiopia* 8°49N 40°31E **257** F5
Gelendost *Turkey* 38°7N 31°1E **212** C4
Gelendzhik *Russia* 44°33N 38°10E **189** K10
Gelib = Jilib *Somali Rep.* 0°29N 42°46E **267** D5
Gelibolu *Turkey* 40°28N 26°43E **203** F10
Gelibolu Yarımadası *Turkey* 40°20N 26°30E **203** F10
Gelidonya Burnu *Turkey* 36°12N 30°24E **212** D4
Gellinsoor *Somali Rep.* 6°28N 46°39E **267** C6
Gelnhausen *Germany* 50°11N 9°11E **179** E5
Gelnica *Slovak Rep.* 48°51N 20°55E **181** C13
Gelsenkirchen *Germany* 51°32N 7°6E **178** D3
Gelting *Germany* 54°45N 9°53E **178** A5
Gelugur *Malaysia* 5°22N 100°18E **237** c
Gemas *Malaysia* 2°37N 102°36E **237** L4
Gembloux *Belgium* 50°34N 4°43E **170** D4
Gembu *Nigeria* 6°42N 11°10E **263** D7
Gemena *Dem. Rep. of the Congo* 3°13N 19°48E **264** B3
Gemerek *Turkey* 39°15N 36°10E **212** C7
Gemla *Sweden* 56°52N 14°39E **163** H8
Gemlik *Turkey* 40°26N 29°9E **203** F13
Gemlik Körfezi *Turkey* 40°25N 28°55E **203** F12
Gemona del Friuli *Italy* 46°16N 13°9E **199** B10
Gemsa *Egypt* 27°39N 33°35E **256** B3
Gemsbok △ *Botswana* 25°5S 21°1E **270** C3
Gemünden *Germany* 50°3N 9°42E **179** E5
Genadi *Greece* 36°2N 27°56E **206** E11
Genale → *Ethiopia* 6°2N 39°1E **257** F4
Genç *Turkey* 38°44N 40°34E **213** C9
Gençay *France* 46°23N 0°23E **174** B4
General Acha *Argentina* 37°20S 64°38W **334** D3
General Alvear *B. Aires, Argentina* 36°0S 60°0W **334** D4
General Alvear *Mendoza, Argentina* 35°0S 67°40W **334** D2
General Artigas *Paraguay* 26°52S 56°16W **334** B4
General Belgrano *Argentina* 36°35S 58°47W **334** D4
General Bernardo O'Higgins *Antarctica* 63°0S 58°3W **151** C18
General Cabrera *Argentina* 32°53S 63°52W **334** C3
General Carrera, L. *Chile* 46°35S 72°0W **336** C2
General Cepeda *Mexico* 25°21N 101°22W **318** B4
General Conesa *Argentina* 40°6S 64°25W **336** B4
General Eugenio A. Garay *Paraguay* 20°31S 62°8W **331** E5
General Germán Busch = Villa Abecia *Bolivia* 21°0S 68°18W **334** A2
General Guido *Argentina* 36°40S 57°50W **334** D4
General Juan Madariaga *Argentina* 37°0S 57°0W **334** D4
General La Madrid *Argentina* 37°17S 61°20W **334** D3
General Lorenzo Vintter *Argentina* 40°45S 64°26W **336** B4
General Luna *Phil.* 13°41N 122°10E **232** E4
General MacArthur *Phil.* 11°18N 125°28E **233** F5
General Martin Miguel de Güemes *Argentina* 24°50S 65°0W **334** A3
General Pico *Argentina* 35°45S 63°50W **334** D3
General Pinedo *Argentina* 27°15S 61°20W **334** B3
General Pinto *Argentina* 34°45S 61°50W **334** C3
General Sampaio *Brazil* 4°2S 39°29W **332** B4
General San Martín *Argentina* 34°35S 58°32W **117** B1
General Santos *Phil.* 6°5N 125°14E **233** H5
General Tinio *Phil.* 15°39N 121°10E **232** D3
General Toshevo *Bulgaria* 43°42N 28°6E **203** C12
General Treviño *Mexico* 26°14N 99°29W **319** B5
General Trías *Mexico* 28°21N 106°22W **318** B3
General Uriburu = Zárate *Argentina* 34°7S 59°0W **334** C4
General Viamonte *Argentina* 35°1S 61°3W **334** D3
General Villegas *Argentina* 35°5S 63°0W **334** D3
General Vintter, L. *Argentina* 43°55S 71°40W **336** B2
Generoso Ponce = Jaci-Paraná *Brazil* 9°15S 64°23W **331** B5
Genesee *Idaho, U.S.A.* 46°33N 116°56W **304** C5
Genesee *Pa., U.S.A.* 41°59N 77°54W **312** E7
Genesee → *U.S.A.* 43°16N 77°36W **312** C7
Geneseo *Ill., U.S.A.* 41°27N 90°9W **310** C6
Geneseo *N.Y., U.S.A.* 42°48N 77°49W **312** D7
Geneva = Genève *Switz.* 46°12N 6°9E **179** J2
Geneva *Ala., U.S.A.* 31°2N 85°52W **316** D4
Geneva *Ga., U.S.A.* 32°35N 84°33W **316** C5
Geneva *Ill., U.S.A.* 41°53N 88°18W **311** C8
Geneva *Ind., U.S.A.* 40°36N 84°58W **311** D12
Geneva *N.Y., U.S.A.* 42°52N 76°59W **312** D8
Geneva *Nebr., U.S.A.* 40°32N 97°36W **308** E5
Geneva *Ohio, U.S.A.* 41°48N 80°57W **312** E4
Geneva, L. = Léman, L. *Europe* 46°26N 6°30E **173** F13
Geneva, L. *U.S.A.* 42°38N 88°30W **311** B8
Genève *Switz.* 46°12N 6°9E **179** J2
Geng *Afghan.* 31°22N 61°28E **240** C1
Gengenbach *Germany* 48°24N 8°1E **179** G4
Gengma *China* 23°32N 99°20E **228** F2
Genichesk = Henichesk *Ukraine* 46°12N 34°50E **189** J8
Genil → *Spain* 37°42N 5°19W **195** H5
Génipa, B. de *Martinique* 14°33N 61°0W **322** j
Genisea *Greece* 41°1N 24°57E **203** E8
Genk *Belgium* 50°58N 5°32E **170** D5
Genkai-Nada *Japan* 34°0N 130°0E **222** D2
Genlis *France* 47°11N 5°12E **173** E12
Gennargentu, Mti. del *Italy* 40°1N 9°19E **200** B2
Gennes *France* 47°20N 0°17W **172** E6
Gennevilliers *France* 48°56N 2°17E **134** A2
Genoa = Génova *Italy* 44°25N 8°57E **198** D5
Genoa *Vic., Australia* 37°29S 149°35E **283** D8
Genoa *Ill., U.S.A.* 42°6N 88°42W **311** B8
Genoa *N.Y., U.S.A.* 42°40N 76°32W **313** D8
Genoa *Nebr., U.S.A.* 41°27N 97°44W **308** E5
Genoa *Nev., U.S.A.* 39°2N 119°50W **306** F7
Genoa → *Argentina* 44°55S 70°5W **336** B2
Genoa City *U.S.A.* 42°30N 88°20W **311** B8
Génova *Italy* 44°25N 8°57E **198** D5
Génova ✕ (GOA) *Italy* 44°25N 8°56E **198** D5
Génova, G. di *Italy* 44°0N 9°0E **198** E6
Genovesa, I. *Ecuador* 0°20N 89°58W **330** a
Genriyetty, Ostrov *Russia* 77°6N 156°30E **215** B16
Gent *Belgium* 51°2N 3°42E **170** C3
Genteng *Jawa Barat, Indonesia* 7°22S 106°24E **234** D3
Genteng *Jawa Timur, Indonesia* 8°22S 114°9E **231** J17
Genthin *Germany* 52°25N 12°9E **178** C8
Gentilly *Val-de-Marne, France* 48°48N 2°21E **134** B3
Gentilly *La., U.S.A.* 30°0N 90°2W **131** A2
Gentio do Ouro *Brazil* 11°25S 42°30W **332** D3
Gentofte *Denmark* 55°44N 12°32E **118** A3
Gentryville *U.S.A.* 38°6N 87°2W **311** F9
Genval *Belgium* 50°43N 4°29E **116** B2
Genyem *Indonesia* 2°46S 140°12E **231** E10
Genzano di Lucánia *Italy* 40°51N 16°2E **201** B9
Genzano di Roma *Italy* 41°42N 12°41E **199** G9
Geoagiu *Romania* 45°55N 23°12E **183** E8
Geochang *S. Korea* 35°41N 127°55E **224** E3
Geogeumdo *S. Korea* 34°27N 127°10E **224** E3
Geographe B. *Australia* 33°30S 115°15E **279** F2
Geographe Chan. *Australia* 24°30S 113°0E **279** D1
Geographical Society Ø *Greenland* 72°57N 23°15W **154** C8
Geoje *S. Korea* 34°51N 128°35E **224** E4
Geojedo *S. Korea* 34°51N 128°38E **224** E4
Geokchay = Göyçay *Azerbaijan* 40°42N 47°43E **191** K8
Georga, Zemlya *Russia* 80°30N 49°0E **214** A5
George *S. Africa* 33°58S 22°29E **270** D3
George → *Canada* 58°49N 66°10W **299** A6
George, L. *N.S.W., Australia* 35°10S 149°25E **283** C8
George, L. *S. Austral., Australia* 37°25S 140°0E **282** D4
George, L. *W. Austral., Australia* 22°45S 123°40E **278** D3
George, L. *Uganda* 0°5N 30°10E **268** B3
George, L. *Fla., U.S.A.* 29°17N 81°36W **317** F8
George, L. *N.Y., U.S.A.* 43°37N 73°33W **313** C11
George Gill Ra. *Australia* 24°22S 131°45E **278** D5
George I. *Hong Kong, China* 22°13N 114°7E **122** B1
George I. *St. Helena* 15°58S 5°38W **153** h
George Pt. *Australia* 20°6S 148°36E **280** b
George River = Kangiqsualujjuaq *Canada* 58°30N 65°59W **295** F18
George Rogers Clark Nat. Memorial ⌂ *U.S.A.* 38°41N 87°32W **311** F9
George Sound *N.Z.* 44°52S 167°25E **285** E2
George Town *Tas., Australia* 41°6S 146°49E **281** G4
George Town *Bahamas* 23°33N 75°47W **320** B4
George Town *Cayman Is.* 19°20N 81°24W **320** C3
George Town *Malaysia* 5°25N 100°20E **237** c
George V Land *Antarctica* 69°0S 148°0E **151** C10
George VI Sound *Antarctica* 71°0S 68°0W **151** D17
George West *U.S.A.* 28°20N 98°7W **314** G5
Georges River Bridge *Australia* 34°0S 151°6E **139** C1
Georgetown = Janjanbureh *Gambia* 13°30N 14°47W **262** C2
Georgetown *Ascension I.* 7°56S 14°25W **153** g
Georgetown *Queens., Australia* 18°17S 143°33E **280** B3
Georgetown *Ont., Canada* 43°40N 79°56W **312** C5
Georgetown *P.E.I., Canada* 46°13N 62°24W **299** C7
Georgetown *Guyana* 6°50N 58°12W **329** B6
Georgetown *St. Vincent* 13°16N 61°7W **323** n
Georgetown *Calif., U.S.A.* 38°54N 120°50W **306** G6
Georgetown *Colo., U.S.A.* 39°42N 105°42W **304** G11
Georgetown *D.C., U.S.A.* 38°54N 77°3W **143** B3
Georgetown *Fla., U.S.A.* 29°23N 81°38W **317** F8
Georgetown *Ga., U.S.A.* 31°53N 85°6W **316** D4
Georgetown *Ill., U.S.A.* 39°59N 87°38W **311** E9
Georgetown *Ky., U.S.A.* 38°13N 84°33W **311** F12
Georgetown *N.Y., U.S.A.* 42°46N 75°44W **313** D9
Georgetown *Ohio, U.S.A.* 38°52N 83°54W **311** F13
Georgetown *S.C., U.S.A.* 33°23N 79°17W **315** E15
Georgetown *Tex., U.S.A.* 30°38N 97°41W **314** F6
Georgia □ *U.S.A.* 32°50N 83°15W **316** C6
Georgia ■ *Asia* 42°0N 43°0E **191** J6
Georgia, Str. of *N. Amer.* 49°25N 124°0W **306** A3
Georgia Basin *S. Ocean* 50°45S 35°30W **151** B1
Georgia Dome *U.S.A.* 33°45N 84°23W **113** B2
Georgian B. *Canada* 45°15N 81°0W **312** A4
Georgian Bay Islands △ *Canada* 44°53N 79°52W **312** B5
Georgīevka *Kazakhstan* 49°19N 84°34E **217** C10
Georgina → *Australia* 23°30S 139°47E **280** C2
Georgina I. *Canada* 44°22N 79°17W **312** B5
Georgioupoli *Greece* 35°20N 24°15E **207** E5
Georgiu-Dezh = Liski *Russia* 51°3N 39°30E **189** G10
Georgiyevsk *Russia* 44°12N 43°28E **191** H6
Georgsmarienhütte *Germany* 52°13N 8°3E **178** C4
Gera *Germany* 50°53N 12°4E **178** E8
Geraardsbergen *Belgium* 50°45N 3°53E **170** D3
Geraki *Greece* 37°0N 22°42E **204** D4
Geraki, Akra *Greece* 37°42N 20°59E **207** D2
Geral, Serra *Bahia, Brazil* 14°0S 41°0W **333** D3
Geral, Serra *Goiás, Brazil* 11°15S 46°30W **332** D2
Geral, Serra *Sta. Catarina, Brazil* 26°25S 50°0W **335** B6
Geral de Goiás, Serra *Brazil* 12°0S 46°0W **333** D2
Geral do Paranã, Serra *Brazil* 15°0S 47°30W **333** E2
Gerald *U.S.A.* 38°24N 91°20W **310** F5
Geraldine *N.Z.* 44°5S 171°15E **285** E6
Geraldine *Mont., U.S.A.* 47°36N 110°16W **304** C8
Geraldton = Innisfail *Australia* 17°33S 146°5E **280** B4
Geraldton *W. Austral., Australia* 28°48S 114°32E **279** E1
Geraldton *Ont., Canada* 49°44N 87°10W **298** C2
Geranium *Australia* 35°23S 140°11E **282** C4
Gérardmer *France* 48°3N 6°50E **173** D13
Gerasdorf bei Wien *Austria* 48°17N 16°28E **142** A2
Gerberau *Germany* 48°12N 11°27E **131** A1
Gercüş *Turkey* 37°34N 41°23E **213** D9
Gerdine, Mt. *U.S.A.* 61°35N 152°27W **303** F9
Gerede *Turkey* 40°45N 32°10E **212** B5
Gerês, Sierra do *Portugal* 41°48N 8°0W **194** D3
Gereshk *Afghan.* 31°47N 64°35E **240** C2
Geretsried *Germany* 47°51N 11°28E **179** H7
Gérgal *Spain* 37°7N 2°31W **197** H2
Gerik *Malaysia* 5°50N 101°15E **237** K3
Gering *U.S.A.* 41°50N 103°40W **308** E2
Geriş *Turkey* 36°57N 31°43E **250** B2
Gerlach *U.S.A.* 40°39N 119°21W **304** F4
Gerlachovský štít *Slovak Rep.* 49°11N 20°7E **181** B13
Gerli *Argentina* 34°41S 58°22W **117** C2
Gerlogubi *Ethiopia* 6°53N 45°3E **267** C6
German Bight = Deutsche Bucht *Germany* 54°15N 8°0E **178** A4
German East Africa = Tanzania ■ *Africa* 6°0S 34°0E **268** D3
German Planina *Macedonia* 42°20N 22°0E **202** D6
German South West Africa = Namibia ■ *Africa* 22°0S 18°9E **270** B2
Germania Land *Greenland* 77°5N 19°30W **154** B9
Germansen Landing *Canada* 55°43N 124°40W **296** B4
Germantown *Ohio, U.S.A.* 39°38N 84°22W **311** E12
Germantown *Tenn., U.S.A.* 35°5N 89°49W **315** D10
Germantown *Wis., U.S.A.* 43°14N 88°6W **311** A8
Germany ■ *Europe* 51°0N 10°0E **176** D3
Germencik *Turkey* 37°52N 27°37E **205** D9
Germering *Germany* 48°8N 11°22E **179** G7
Germersheim *Germany* 49°12N 8°22E **179** F4
Germī *Iran* 39°1N 48°3E **213** C13
Germiston *S. Africa* 26°13S 28°10E **123** B2
Gern *Germany* 48°10N 11°32E **131** B2
Gernene *Algeria* 21°40N 2°24E **261** D5
Gernika-Lumo *Spain* 43°19N 2°40W **196** B2
Gernsheim *Germany* 49°45N 8°30E **179** F4
Gero *Japan* 35°48N 137°14E **223** B9
Gerogery *Australia* 35°50S 147°1E **283** C7
Gerokgak *Indonesia* 8°11S 114°27E **231** J17
Gerolzhofen *Germany* 49°54N 10°21E **179** F6
Gerona = Girona *Spain* 41°58N 2°46E **196** D7
Gerona *Phil.* 15°36N 120°36E **232** D3
Geropotamos → *Greece* 35°3N 24°50E **207** E5
Gerrard *Canada* 50°30N 117°17W **296** C5
Gerringong *Australia* 34°46S 150°47E **283** C9
Gers □ *France* 43°35N 0°30E **174** E4
Gers → *France* 44°9N 0°39E **174** D4
Gersfeld *Germany* 50°27N 9°56E **178** E5
Gersoppa Falls *India* 14°12N 74°46E **245** G2
Gersthofen *Germany* 48°25N 10°53E **179** G6
Gertak Sanggul *Malaysia* 5°17N 100°12E **237** c
Gertak Sanggul, Tanjung *Malaysia* 5°16N 100°11E **237** c
Gerung *Indonesia* 8°43S 116°7E **231** K19
Géryville = El Bayadh *Algeria* 33°40N 1°1E **261** B5
Gerzat *France* 45°48N 3°8E **174** C7
Gerze *Turkey* 41°48N 35°12E **212** B6
Geseke *Germany* 51°38N 8°31E **178** D4
Geser *Indonesia* 3°50S 130°54E **231** E8
Gesira △ *Somali Rep.* 1°58N 44°59E **267** D5
Gesso → *Italy* 44°24N 7°33E **198** D4
Gestro, Wabi → *Ethiopia* 4°12N 42°2E **257** G5
Getafe *Spain* 40°18N 3°43W **127** C1
Getinge *Sweden* 56°49N 12°44E **163** H6
Getty Center, The *U.S.A.* 34°4N 118°29W **126** B2
Gettysburg *Pa., U.S.A.* 39°50N 77°14W **309** F15
Gettysburg *S. Dak., U.S.A.* 45°1N 99°57W **308** C4
Getxo *Spain* 43°21N 2°59W **196** B2
Getz Ice Shelf *Antarctica* 75°0S 130°0W **151** D14
Geumdo *S. Korea* 34°31N 127°45E **224** E3
Geumpang *Indonesia* 4°52N 96°6E **234** B1
Geunjeong *S. Korea* 37°28N 126°54E **137** C1
Geureudong, Gunung *Indonesia* 4°13N 96°42E **234** B1
Geurie *Australia* 32°22S 148°50E **283** B8
Geva Binyamin *West Bank* 31°51N 35°17E **123** A2
Gevaş *Turkey* 38°15N 43°6E **213** C10
Gévaudan *France* 44°40N 3°40E **174** D7
Gevgelija *Macedonia* 41°9N 22°30E **202** E6
Gévora → *Spain* 38°53N 6°57W **195** G4
Gevrai *India* 19°16N 75°45E **244** E2
Gewani *Ethiopia* 10°12N 40°42E **257** E5
Gex *France* 46°21N 6°3E **173** F13
Geyikli *Turkey* 39°48N 26°12E **205** B8
Geylang Serai *Singapore* 1°19N 103°53E **138** B3
Geyser *U.S.A.* 47°16N 110°30W **304** C8
Geyserville *U.S.A.* 38°42N 122°54W **306** G4
Geysir *Iceland* 64°19N 20°18W **155** C6
Geyve *Turkey* 40°30N 30°18E **212** B4
Ghâbat el Arab = Wang Kai *South Sudan* 9°3N 29°23E **257** F2
Ghabeish *Sudan* 12°9N 27°21E **257** E2
Ghadāf, W. al → *Iraq* 32°56N 43°30E **213** F10
Ghadāmis *Libya* 30°11N 9°29E **258** B1
Ghadāmis □ *Libya* 30°25N 10°25E **258** B2
Ghaddūwah *Libya* 26°26N 14°19E **258** C2
Ghaggar → *India* 29°30N 74°53E **242** E6
Ghaghara → *India* 25°45N 84°40E **243** G11
Ghaghat → *Bangla.* 25°19N 89°38E **241** C2
Ghaghe *Solomon Is.* 7°24S 158°15E **287** L10
Ghagra *India* 23°17N 84°33E **243** H11
Ghagra → *India* 27°29N 81°9E **243** F9
Ghajn Tuffieha Bay *Malta* 35°56N 14°21E **206** F7
Ghajnsielem *Malta* 36°2N 14°17E **206** E7
Ghalla, Wadi el → *Sudan* 10°25N 27°32E **257** E2
Ghallamane *Mauritania* 23°15N 10°0W **260** D3
Ghallamane, Sebkhet *Mauritania* 23°41N 9°50W **260** D3
Ghamid az Zenad *Si. Arabia* 19°35N 41°24E **248** C3
Ghana ■ *W. Afr.* 8°0N 1°0W **263** D4
Ghansor *India* 22°39N 80°1E **243** H9
Ghanzi *Botswana* 21°50S 21°34E **270** B3
Gharapuri *India* 18°57N 72°57E **130** B2
Gharb = Shahrak-e Qods *Iran* 35°47N 51°22E **141** A2
Gharb *Malta* 36°4N 14°13E **206** E6
Gharb Bahr el Ghazâl = Western Bahr el Ghazâl □ *South Sudan* 7°30N 25°30E **257** F2
Gharb Dârfûr □ *Sudan* 13°0N 23°0E **259** F4
Gharb el Istiwa'iya = Western Equatoria □ *South Sudan* 5°0N 30°0E **257** G3
Gharbîya, Es Sahrâ el *Egypt* 27°40N 26°30E **256** B2
Ghardaïa *Algeria* 32°20N 3°37E **261** B5
Ghardaïa □ *Algeria* 31°5N 3°10E **261** B5
Ghârib, G. *Egypt* 28°6N 32°54E **256** B3
Gharig *Sudan* 10°47N 27°33E **257** E2
Gharm *Tajikistan* 39°0N 70°20E **214** F8
Gharm, W. → *Oman* 19°57N 57°38E **249** C7
Gharyān *Libya* 32°10N 13°0E **258** B2
Gharyān □ *Libya* 30°35N 12°0E **258** B2
Ghāt *Libya* 24°59N 10°11E **258** D2
Ghāt □ *Libya* 25°35N 10°15E **258** C2
Ghatal *India* 22°40N 87°46E **243** H12
Ghatampur *India* 26°8N 80°13E **243** F9
Ghatgaon *India* 21°24N 85°53E **244** D7
Ghatkopar *India* 19°4N 72°54E **130** A2
Ghatprabha → *India* 16°15N 75°20E **245** F2
Ghats, Eastern *India* 14°0N 78°50E **245** H4
Ghats, Western *India* 14°0N 75°0E **245** H2
Ghatsila *India* 22°36N 86°29E **243** H12
Ghaṭṭī *Si. Arabia* 31°16N 37°31E **246** D3
Ghawdex = Gozo *Malta* 36°3N 14°15E **206** E7
Ghayl *Si. Arabia* 21°40N 46°20E **248** B4
Ghazal, Bahr el → *Chad* 13°0N 15°47E **259** F3
Ghazâl, Bahr el → *South Sudan* 9°31N 30°25E **257** F3
Ghazaouet *Algeria* 35°8N 1°50W **261** A4
Ghaziabad *India* 28°42N 77°26E **242** E7
Ghazipur *Delhi, India* 28°37N 77°19E **120** B2
Ghazipur *Ut. P., India* 25°38N 83°35E **243** G10
Ghaznī *Afghan.* 33°30N 68°28E **242** C3
Ghaznī □ *Afghan.* 32°10N 68°20E **240** B3
Ghedi *Italy* 45°24N 10°16E **198** C7
Ghelari *Romania* 45°38N 22°45E **182** E7
Ghent = Gent *Belgium* 51°2N 3°42E **170** C3
Gheorghe Gheorghiu-Dej = Onești *Romania* 46°17N 26°47E **183** D11
Gheorgheni *Romania* 46°43N 25°41E **183** D10
Gherla *Romania* 47°2N 23°57E **183** C8
Ghidigeni *Romania* 46°3N 27°30E **183** D12
Ghilarza *Italy* 40°7N 8°50E **200** B1
Ghimeș-Făget *Romania* 46°35N 26°2E **183** D11
Ghīnah, Wādī al → *Si. Arabia* 30°27N 38°14E **246** D3
Ghīrān, W. → *Si. Arabia* 20°52N 47°10E **248** B4
Ghirardelli Square *San Francisco, U.S.A.* **136** a1
Ghisonaccia *France* 42°1N 9°26E **175** F13
Ghisoni *France* 42°7N 9°12E **175** F13
Ghizar → *Pakistan* 36°15N 73°43E **243** A5
Ghizri *Pakistan* 24°49N 67°2E **123** B2
Ghizri Cr. → *Pakistan* 24°47N 67°5E **123** B2
Ghod → *India* 18°30N 74°35E **244** E2
Ghogha *India* 21°40N 72°20E **244** D1
Ghonda *India* 28°41N 77°16E **120** A2
Ghot Ogrein *Egypt* 31°10N 25°20E **256** A2
Ghotaru *India* 27°20N 70°1E **242** F4
Ghotki *Pakistan* 28°5N 69°21E **242** E3
Ghowr □ *Afghan.* 34°0N 64°20E **240** B2
Ghubbet el Bûs *Egypt* 29°35N 32°21E **251** J3
Ghughri *India* 22°39N 80°41E **243** H9
Ghugus *India* 19°58N 79°12E **244** E4
Ghulam Mohammad Barrage *Pakistan* 25°30N 68°20E **242** G3
Ghurayrah *Si. Arabia* 18°37N 42°41E **248** C3
Ghūrīān *Afghan.* 34°17N 61°25E **240** B1
Ghusuri *India* 22°37N 88°21E **124** B2
Ghuzzayil, Sabkhat *Libya* 29°30N 19°30E **258** C3
Gia Dinh *Vietnam* 10°49N 106°42E **237** G6
Gia Lai = Plei Ku *Vietnam* 13°57N 108°0E **236** F7
Gia Nghia *Vietnam* 11°58N 107°42E **237** G6
Gia Ngoc *Vietnam* 14°50N 108°58E **236** E7
Gia Vuc *Vietnam* 14°42N 108°34E **236** E7
Giali *Greece* 36°41N 27°11E **205** E9
Gialtra *Greece* 38°51N 22°59E **204** C4
Giamama = Jamaame *Somali Rep.* 0°4N 42°44E **267** D5
Gian *Phil.* 5°49N 125°12E **233** J5
Gianicolense *Italy* 41°53N 12°28E **136** B1
Gianicolo *Rome, Italy* **136** c1
Gianitsa *Greece* 40°46N 22°24E **202** F6
Giannutri *Italy* 42°15N 11°6E **198** F8
Giant Forest *U.S.A.* 36°36N 118°43W **306** J8
Giant Mts. = Krkonoše *Czech Rep.* 50°50N 15°35E **180** A8
Giant Sequoia ⌂ *U.S.A.* 36°10N 118°35W **306** K8
Giant Wheel = Riesenrad *Austria* 48°14N 16°23E **142** A2
Giants Causeway *U.K.* 55°16N 6°29W **166** A5
Giant's Tank *Sri Lanka* 8°51N 80°2E **245** K5
Gianyar *Indonesia* 8°32S 115°20E **231** K18
Giarabub = Al Jaghbūb *Libya* 29°42N 24°38E **258** C4
Giaros *Greece* 37°32N 24°40E **204** D6
Giarre *Italy* 37°43N 15°11E **201** E8
Giaveno *Italy* 45°2N 7°21E **198** C4
Gibara *Cuba* 21°9N 76°11W **320** B4
Gibbon *U.S.A.* 40°45N 98°51W **308** E4
Gibe → *Ethiopia* 7°20N 37°36E **257** F4
Gibe I *Ethiopia* 8°7N 37°0E **257** F4
Gibe II *Ethiopia* 8°0N 37°30E **257** F4
Gibe III *Ethiopia* 7°0N 37°30E **257** F4
Gibellina Nuova *Italy* 37°47N 12°58E **200** E5
Gibeon *Namibia* 25°9S 17°43E **270** C2
Gibraleón *Spain* 37°23N 6°58W **195** H4
Gibraltar ☑ *Europe* 36°7N 5°22W **195** J5
Gibraltar, Str. of *Medit. S.* 35°55N 5°40W **195** K5
Gibraltar Pt. *Canada* 43°36N 79°23W **141** B2
Gibraltar Range △ *Australia* 29°31S 152°19E **281** D5
Gibson *U.S.A.* 33°14N 82°36W **316** B7
Gibson City *U.S.A.* 40°28N 88°22W **311** D8
Gibson Desert *Australia* 24°0S 126°0E **278** D4
Gibsonburg *U.S.A.* 41°23N 83°19W **311** C13
Gibsons *Canada* 49°24N 123°32W **296** D4
Gibsonton *U.S.A.* 27°51N 82°23W **317** H7
Gibsonville *U.S.A.* 39°46N 120°54W **306** F6
Gidami *Ethiopia* 8°59N 34°37E **266** C3
Giddalur *India* 15°20N 78°57E **245** G4
Giddings *U.S.A.* 30°11N 96°56W **314** F6
Gidea Park *U.K.* 51°35N 0°11E **125** A5
Gidole *Ethiopia* 5°40N 37°25E **257** F4
Giebnegáisi = Kebnekaise *Sweden* 67°53N 13°33E **160** C18
Gien *France* 47°40N 2°36E **173** E9
Giengen *Germany* 48°37N 10°14E **179** G6
Giesing *Germany* 48°6N 11°35E **131** B2
Giessen *Germany* 50°34N 8°41E **178** E4
Gīfān *Iran* 37°54N 57°28E **247** B8
Gifatin, Geziret *Egypt* 27°10N 33°50E **256** B3
Gifford *U.S.A.* 27°40N 80°25W **317** H9
Gifhorn *Germany* 52°30N 10°33E **178** C6
Gift Lake *Canada* 55°53N 115°49W **296** B5
Gifu *Japan* 35°30N 136°45E **223** B8
Gifu □ *Japan* 35°40N 137°0E **223** B9
Gigant *Russia* 46°28N 41°20E **191** G5
Giganta, Sa. de la *Mexico* 26°0N 111°39W **318** B2
Gigen *Bulgaria* 43°40N 24°28E **203** C8
Gigha *U.K.* 55°42N 5°44W **167** F3
Giglio *Italy* 42°20N 10°52E **198** F7
Gignac *France* 43°39N 3°32E **174** E7
Gigüela → *Spain* 39°8N 3°44W **195** F7
Gijang *S. Korea* 35°14N 129°12E **224** E4
Gijón *Spain* 43°32N 5°42W **194** B5
Gikongoro *Rwanda* 2°28S 29°34E **268** C2
Gil I. *Canada* 53°12N 129°15W **296** C3
Gila → *U.S.A.* 32°43N 114°33W **305** K6
Gila Bend *U.S.A.* 32°57N 112°43W **305** K7
Gila Bend Mts. *U.S.A.* 33°10N 113°0W **305** K7
Gila Cliff Dwellings ⌂ *U.S.A.* 33°12N 108°16W **305** K9
Gīlān □ *Iran* 37°0N 50°0E **247** B6
Gīlān-e Gharb *Iran* 34°8N 45°55E **213** E11
Gilău *Romania* 46°45N 23°23E **183** D8
Gilbert → *Australia* 16°35S 141°15E **280** B3
Gilbert Is. *Kiribati* 1°0N 172°0E **277** A14
Gilbert River *Australia* 18°9S 142°52E **280** B3
Gilbert Seamounts *Pac. Oc.* 52°50N 150°10W **150** D18
Gilbués *Brazil* 9°50S 45°21W **332** C2
Gilead *U.S.A.* 44°24N 70°59W **313** B14
Gilf el Kebîr, Hadabat el *Egypt* 23°50N 25°50E **256** C2
Gilford I. *Canada* 50°40N 126°30W **296** C3
Gilgandra *Australia* 31°43S 148°39E **283** A8
Gilgil *Kenya* 0°30S 36°20E **268** C4
Gilgit *India* 35°50N 74°15E **243** B6
Gilgit → *Pakistan* 35°44N 74°37E **243** B6
Gilgunnia *Australia* 32°26S 146°2E **283** B7
Gili, Pulau 10°0S 115°0E **235** D5
Gili ⌂ *Mozam.* 16°39S 38°27E **269** F4
Gilimanuk *Indonesia* 8°10S 114°26E **231** J17
Giljeva Planina *Europe* 43°9N 20°0E **202** C3
Gill Pt. *St. Helena* 15°58S 5°38W **153** h
Gillam *Canada* 56°20N 94°40W **297** B10
Gilleleje *Denmark* 56°8N 12°19E **163** H6
Gillen, L. *Australia* 26°11S 124°38E **279** E3
Gilles, L. *Australia* 32°50S 136°45E **282** B2
Gillespie *U.S.A.* 39°8N 89°49W **310** E7
Gillespies Pt. *N.Z.* 43°24S 169°49E **285** D4
Gillette *U.S.A.* 44°18N 105°30W **304** D11
Gilliat *Australia* 20°40S 141°28E **280** C3
Gillingham *U.K.* 51°23N 0°33E **169** F8
Gilman *U.S.A.* 40°46N 88°0W **311** D9
Gilman City *U.S.A.* 40°8N 93°53W **310** D3
Gilmer *U.S.A.* 32°44N 94°57W **314** E7
Gilmerton *U.K.* 55°54N 3°7W **121** B3
Gilmore, L. *Australia* 32°29S 121°37E **279** F3
Gilmour *Canada* 44°48N 77°37W **312** B7
Gilo *West Bank* 31°44N 35°11E **123** B2
Gilo → *Ethiopia* 8°10N 33°15E **257** F3
Gilort → *Romania* 44°38N 23°32E **183** F8
Gilroy *U.S.A.* 37°1N 121°34W **306** H5
Giluwe, Mt. *Papua N. G.* 6°8S 143°52E **286** D2
Gimbi *Ethiopia* 9°3N 35°42E **257** F4
Gimcheon *S. Korea* 36°11N 128°4E **224** D4
Gimhae *S. Korea* 35°14N 128°53E **224** E4
Gimhwa *S. Korea* 38°17N 127°28E **224** C3
Gimie, Mt. *St. Lucia* 13°54N 61°0W **323** m
Gimje *S. Korea* 35°48N 126°45E **224** E3
Gimli *Canada* 50°40N 97°0W **297** C9
Gimmersta *Sweden* 59°14N 18°14E **139** B3
Gimo *Sweden* 60°11N 18°12E **162** D12
Gimone → *France* 44°0N 1°6E **174** E5
Gimont *France* 43°38N 0°52E **174** E4
Gin → *Sri Lanka* 6°5N 80°7E **245** L5
Gin Gin *Australia* 25°0S 151°58E **281** D5
Ginâh *Egypt* 25°21N 30°30E **256** B3
Ginatilan *Phil.* 9°34N 123°19E **233** G4
Gineifa *Egypt* 30°12N 32°25E **256** H8
Gingee *India* 12°15N 79°25E **245** H4
Gingin *Australia* 31°22S 115°54E **279** F2
Gingindlovu *S. Africa* 29°2S 31°30E **271** C5
Gingoog *Phil.* 8°50N 125°7E **233** G5
Gingoog B. *Phil.* 8°54N 125°7E **233** G5
Ginir *Ethiopia* 7°6N 40°40E **257** F5
Ginosa *Italy* 40°35N 16°45E **201** B9
Ginowan *Japan* 26°15N 127°45E **288** a
Ginza *Tokyo, Japan* **140** b5
Ginzo de Limia = Xinzo de Limia *Spain* 42°3N 7°47W **194** C3
Giofyros → *Greece* 35°20N 25°6E **207** E6
Giohar = Jawhar *Somali Rep.* 2°48N 45°30E **267** D6
Gióia, G. di *Italy* 38°30N 15°45E **201** D8
Gióia del Colle *Italy* 40°48N 16°55E **201** B9
Gióia Tàuro *Italy* 38°25N 15°54E **201** D8
Gioiosa Iónica *Italy* 38°20N 16°18E **201** D9
Gioiosa Marea *Italy* 38°10N 14°54E **201** D7
Giona, Oros *Greece* 38°38N 22°14E **204** C4
Giovi, Passo dei *Italy* 44°33N 8°57E **198** D5
Giovinazzo *Italy* 41°11N 16°40E **201** A9
Gippsland *Australia* 37°52S 147°0E **283** D7
Gir △ *India* 21°0N 71°0E **242** J4
Gir Hills *India* 21°0N 71°0E **242** J4
Girab *India* 26°2N 70°38E **242** F4
Girâfi, W. → *Egypt* 29°58N 34°39E **251** J5
Giraltovce *Slovak Rep.* 49°7N 21°32E **181** B14
Girapetra, Akra *Greece* 38°51N 20°41E **207** B2
Girard *St. Lucia* 13°59N 60°57W **323** m
Girard *Ga., U.S.A.* 33°3N 81°43W **316** B8
Girard *Ill., U.S.A.* 39°27N 89°47W **310** E7
Girard *Kans., U.S.A.* 37°31N 94°51W **308** G6
Girard *Ohio, U.S.A.* 41°9N 80°42W **312** E4
Girard *Pa., U.S.A.* 42°0N 80°19W **312** E4
Girardot *Colombia* 4°18N 74°48W **328** C3
Giraud, Pte. *Dominica* 15°20N 61°15W **323** k
Girdle Ness *U.K.* 57°9N 2°3W **167** D6
Giresun *Turkey* 40°55N 38°30E **213** B8
Giresun □ *Turkey* 40°30N 38°30E **213** B8
Girga *Egypt* 26°17N 31°55E **256** B3
Girgaum *Mumbai, India* **130** b2
Girgenti = Agrigento *Italy* 37°19N 13°34E **200** E6
Girgir, C. *Papua N. G.* 3°50S 144°35E **286** B3
Giri → *Dem. Rep. of the Congo* 0°28N 17°59E **264** B3
Giri → *India* 30°28N 77°41E **242** D7
Giridih *India* 24°10N 86°21E **243** G12
Girifalco *Italy* 38°49N 16°25E **201** D9
Giriftu *Kenya* 1°59N 39°46E **268** B4
Girilambone *Australia* 31°16S 146°57E **283** A7
Girne = Kyrenia *Cyprus* 35°20N 33°20E **207** E9
Giro *Nigeria* 11°7N 4°42E **263** C5
Giromagny *France* 47°45N 6°50E **173** E13
Giron = Kiruna *Sweden* 67°52N 20°15E **160** C19
Girona *Spain* 41°58N 2°46E **196** D7
Girona □ *Spain* 42°11N 2°30E **196** C7
Gironde □ *France* 44°45N 0°30W **174** D3
Gironde → *France* 45°32N 1°7W **174** C2
Gironella *Spain* 42°2N 1°53E **196** C6
Girraween △ *Australia* 28°46S 151°54E **281** D5
Girringun △ *Australia* 18°15S 145°32E **280** B4
Giru *Australia* 19°30S 147°5E **280** B4
Girvan *U.K.* 55°14N 4°51W **167** F4
Gisborne *Vic., Australia* 37°29S 144°36E **282** D6
Gisborne *N.Z.* 38°39S 178°5E **284** E7
Gisborne □ *N.Z.* 38°30S 178°0E **284** E7
Gisenyi *Rwanda* 1°41S 29°15E **268** C2
Gislaved *Sweden* 57°19N 13°32E **163** G7
Gisors *France* 49°15N 1°47E **173** C8
Gitarama *Rwanda* 2°4S 29°45E **268** C2
Gitega *Burundi* 3°26S 29°56E **268** C2
Githio *Greece* 36°46N 22°34E **204** E4
Gitschin = Jičín *Czech Rep.* 50°25N 15°28E **180** A8
Giuba = Juba → *Somali Rep.* 1°30N 42°35E **267** D5
Giugliano in Campania *Italy* 40°56N 14°12E **201** B7
Giulianova *Italy* 42°45N 13°57E **199** F10
Giura *Greece* 39°23N 24°10E **204** B6
Giurgeni *Romania* 44°45N 27°48E **183** F12
Giurgiu *Romania* 43°52N 25°57E **183** G10
Giurgiu □ *Romania* 44°20N 26°0E **183** F10
Giurgiulești *Moldova* 45°29N 28°12E **183** E13
Giv'at Ram *Israel* 31°47N 35°12E **123** B2
Giv'at Ye'arim *Israel* 31°47N 35°5E **123** B1
Giv'at Ze'ev *West Bank* 31°52N 35°10E **123** A2
Give *Denmark* 55°51N 9°13E **163** J3
Givet *France* 50°8N 4°49E **173** B11
Giv'on *West Bank* 31°51N 35°10E **123** A1
Givors *France* 45°35N 4°45E **175** C8
Givry *France* 46°41N 4°46E **173** F11
Giyani *S. Africa* 23°19S 30°43E **271** B5
Giyon *Ethiopia* 8°33N 38°1E **257** F4
Giza = El Gîza *Egypt* 30°0N 31°12E **117** A2
Giza Pyramids *Egypt* 29°58N 31°9E **117** B1
Gizab *Afghan.* 33°22N 66°17E **242** C1
Gizhiga *Russia* 62°3N 160°30E **215** C17
Gizhiginskaya Guba *Russia* 61°0N 158°0E **215** C16
Gizo *Solomon Is.* 8°7S 156°50E **287** M9
Giżycko *Poland* 54°2N 21°48E **184** D8
Gizzeria *Italy* 38°59N 16°12E **201** D9
Gjakovë = Dakovica *Kosovo* 42°22N 20°26E **202** D4
Gjalicë e Lumës, Mal. *Albania* 42°2N 20°25E **202** D4
Gjegjan *Albania* 41°58N 20°3E **202** E4
Gjendesheim *Norway* 61°30N 8°48E **164** C5
Gjermundshamn *Norway* 60°40N 5°55E **164** D2
Gjersjøen *Norway* 59°47N 10°47E **133** B3
Gjerstad *Norway* 58°54N 9°1E **164** F6
Gjevillvatnet *Norway* 62°43N 9°23E **164** B6
Gjilan = Gnjilane *Kosovo* 42°28N 21°29E **202** D5
Gjirokastër *Albania* 40°7N 20°10E **202** F4
Gjoa Haven *Canada* 68°38N 95°53W **294** D12
Gjøra *Norway* 62°33N 9°4E **164** B6
Gjøvik *Norway* 60°47N 10°43E **164** D7
Gjuhës, Kep i *Albania* 40°28N 19°15E **202** F3
Glace Bay *Canada* 46°11N 59°58W **299** C8
Glacier △ *B.C., Canada* 51°15N 117°30W **296** C5
Glacier △ *Mont., U.S.A.* 48°42N 113°48W **304** B7
Glacier Bay *U.S.A.* 58°40N 136°0W **303** G14
Glacier Bay ⌂ *U.S.A.* 58°45N 136°30W **296** B1
Glacier Peak *U.S.A.* 48°7N 121°7W **304** B3
Gladesville *Australia* 33°50S 151°8E **139** B1
Gladewater *U.S.A.* 32°33N 94°56W **314** E7
Gladsakse *Denmark* 55°45N 12°25E **118** A2
Gladstone *Queens., Australia* 23°52S 151°16E **280** C5
Gladstone *S. Austral., Australia* 33°15S 138°22E **282** B3
Gladstone *Man., Canada* 50°13N 98°57W **297** C9
Gladstone *Ill., U.S.A.* 40°52N 90°57W **310** D6
Gladstone *Mich., U.S.A.* 45°51N 87°1W **308** C10
Gladstone *Mo., U.S.A.* 39°13N 94°35W **310** E2
Gladwin *U.S.A.* 43°59N 84°29W **309** D11
Glafsfjorden *Sweden* 59°30N 12°37E **162** E6
Glagah *Indonesia* 8°13S 114°18E **231** J17
Głogów Małopolski *Poland* 50°10N 21°56E **185** H8
Glåma = Glomma → *Norway* 59°12N 10°57E **164** E7
Gláma *Iceland* 65°48N 23°0W **155** B4
Glamis *U.S.A.* 32°55N 115°5W **307** N11
Glamoč *Bos.-H.* 44°3N 16°51E **199** D13
Glamorgan, Vale of □ *U.K.* 51°28N 3°25W **169** F4
Glåmos *Norway* 62°41N 11°25E **164** B8
Glamsbjerg *Denmark* 55°17N 10°6E **163** J4
Glanvillia *Dominica* 15°34N 61°28W **323** k
Glarus *Switz.* 47°3N 9°4E **179** H5
Glarus □ *Switz.* 47°0N 9°5E **179** J5
Glasco *Kans., U.S.A.* 39°22N 97°50W **308** F5
Glasco *N.Y., U.S.A.* 42°3N 73°57W **313** D11
Glasgow *C. of Glasg., U.K.* 55°51N 4°15W **167** F4
Glasgow *Ky., U.S.A.* 37°0N 85°55W **309** G11
Glasgow *Mo., U.S.A.* 39°14N 92°51W **310** E4
Glasgow *Mont., U.S.A.* 48°12N 106°38W **304** B10
Glasgow, City of □ *U.K.* 55°51N 4°12W **167** F4
Glasgow Int. ✕ (GLA) *U.K.* 55°51N 4°21W **167** F4
Glaslyn *Canada* 53°22N 108°21W **297** C7
Glasnevin *Ireland* 53°22N 6°15W **120** A2
Glassmanor *U.S.A.* 38°49N 77°0W **143** C4
Glasthule *Ireland* 53°17N 6°7W **120** B3
Glastonbury *U.K.* 51°9N 2°43W **169** F5
Glastonbury *Conn., U.S.A.* 41°43N 72°37W **313** E12
Glatz = Kłodzko *Poland* 50°28N 16°38E **185** H3
Glauchau *Germany* 50°49N 12°31E **178** E8
Glava *Sweden* 59°33N 12°35E **162** E6
Glavice *Croatia* 43°43N 16°41E **199** E13
Glazov *Russia* 58°9N 52°40E **190** A11
Gleichen *Canada* 50°52N 113°3W **296** C6
Gleisdorf *Austria* 47°6N 15°44E **180** D8
Gleiwitz = Gliwice *Poland* 50°22N 18°41E **185** H5
Glen *U.S.A.* 44°7N 71°11W **313** B13
Glen Affric *U.K.* 57°17N 5°1W **167** D3
Glen Afton *N.Z.* 37°37S 175°4E **284** D4
Glen Canyon *U.S.A.* 37°30N 110°40W **305** H8
Glen Canyon ⌂ *U.S.A.* 37°15N 111°0W **305** H8
Glen Canyon Dam *U.S.A.* 36°57N 111°29W **305** H8
Glen Coe *U.K.* 56°40N 5°0W **167** E3
Glen Cove *U.S.A.* 40°51N 73°38W **313** F11
Glen Garry *U.K.* 57°3N 5°7W **167** D3
Glen Innes *Australia* 29°44S 151°44E **281** D5
Glen Iris *Australia* 37°51S 145°3E **128** B2
Glen Lyon *U.S.A.* 41°10N 76°5W **313** E8
Glen Mar Park *U.S.A.* 38°57N 77°7W **143** B3
Glen Massey *N.Z.* 37°38S 175°2E **284** D4
Glen Mor *U.K.* 57°9N 4°37W **167** D4
Glen More ⌂ *U.K.* 57°8N 3°40W **167** D5
Glen Moriston *U.K.* 57°11N 4°52W **167** D4
Glen Robertson *Canada* 45°22N 74°30W **313** A10
Glen Rouge Park *Canada* 43°49N 79°10W **141** A4
Glen Spean *U.K.* 56°53N 4°40W **167** E4
Glen Ullin *U.S.A.* 46°49N 101°50W **308** B3
Glénan, Îs. de *France* 47°42N 4°0W **172** E3
Glenarden *U.S.A.* 38°56N 76°51W **143** B4
Glenariff △ *Ireland* 55°2N 6°10W **166** A5
Glenasmole Reservoirs *Ireland* 53°15N 6°21W **120** B1
Glenavy *N.Z.* 44°54S 171°7E **285** E6
Glenbeigh *Ireland* 52°3N 9°58W **166** D2
Glenburn *Australia* 37°27S 145°26E **283** D6
Glencoe *Canada* 42°45N 81°43W **312** D3
Glencoe *KwaZulu Natal, S. Africa* 28°11S 30°11E **271** C5
Glencoe *Ala., U.S.A.* 33°57N 85°56W **316** B4
Glencoe *Minn., U.S.A.* 44°46N 94°9W **308** C6
Glencolumbkille *Ireland* 54°43N 8°42W **166** B3
Glencorse Res. *U.K.* 55°51N 3°15W **121** B2
Glencullen *Ireland* 53°14N 6°12W **120** B3
Glendale *Ariz., U.S.A.* 33°32N 112°11W **305** K7
Glendale *Calif., U.S.A.* 34°9N 118°15W **126** B3
Glendale *Fla., U.S.A.* 30°52N 86°7W **316** E3
Glendale *Zimbabwe* 17°22S 31°5E **269** F3
Glendive *U.S.A.* 47°7N 104°43W **304** C11
Glendo *U.S.A.* 42°30N 105°2W **304** E11
Glendoo Mt. *Ireland* 53°14N 6°16W **120** B2
Glenelg *Australia* 34°58S 138°31E **282** C3
Glenelg → *Australia* 38°4S 140°59E **282** E4
Glenfield *U.S.A.* 43°43N 75°24W **313** C9
Glengad Hd. *Ireland* 55°20N 7°10W **166** A4

Glengarriff Ireland 51°45N 9°34W 166 E2
Glengoffe Jamaica 18°10N 76°53W 320 a
Glenham U.S.A. 46°26S 168°52E 285 G3
Glenhope N.Z. 41°40S 172°39E 285 B7
Glenhuntly Australia 37°52S 145°1E 128 B2
Glenmary, Mt. N.Z. 43°55S 169°55E 285 D4
Glenmont U.S.A. 40°31N 82°6W 312 F2
Glenmorgan Australia 27°14S 149°42E 281 D4
Glenn U.S.A. 39°31N 122°1W 306 F4
Glennallen U.S.A. 62°7N 145°33W 303 E11
Glenns Ferry U.S.A. 42°57N 115°18W 304 E6
Glenora U.S.A. 31°56N 81°56W 316 D8
Glenora Canada 44°2N 77°3W 312 B7
Glenorchy Tas., Australia 42°49S 147°18E 281 G4
Glenorchy Vic., Australia 36°55S 142°41E 282 D5
Glenorchy N.Z. 44°51S 168°24E 285 E3
Glenore Australia 17°50S 141°12E 280 B3
Glenreagh Australia 30°2S 153°1E 281 E5
Glenrock U.S.A. 42°52N 105°52W 304 D11
Glenrothes U.K. 56°12N 3°10W 167 E5
Glenrowan Australia 36°28S 146°13E 283 D6
Glens Falls U.S.A. 43°19N 73°39W 313 C11
Glenside Wellington, N.Z. 41°12S 174°48E 143 B1
Glenside Pa., U.S.A. 40°6N 75°9W 313 F9
Glenthompson Australia 37°38S 142°32E 282 D5
Glenties Ireland 54°49N 8°16W 166 B3
Glenveagh △ Ireland 55°3N 8°1W 166 A3
Glenview U.S.A. 42°3N 87°48W 119 A2
Glenview Countryside U.S.A. 42°3N 87°49W 119 A2
Glenville U.S.A. 38°56N 80°50W 309 F13
Glenvista S. Africa 26°17S 28°3E 123 B2
Glenwood Nfld. & L., Canada 49°0N 54°58W 299 C9
Glenwood Ark., U.S.A. 34°20N 93°33W 314 D8
Glenwood Ga., U.S.A. 32°11N 82°40W 316 D7
Glenwood Hawai'i, U.S.A. 19°29N 155°9W 302 D6
Glenwood Iowa, U.S.A. 41°3N 95°45W 308 E6
Glenwood Minn., U.S.A. 45°39N 95°23W 308 C6
Glenwood Wash., U.S.A. 46°1N 121°17W 306 D5
Glenwood Springs U.S.A. 39°33N 107°19W 304 G10
Gletinganes Iceland 65°30N 13°37W 155 B13
Glidden U.S.A. 42°4N 94°44W 310 B2
Glifada Greece 37°52N 23°45E 112 B2
Glimåkra Sweden 56°19N 14°7E 163 H8
Glin Ireland 52°34N 9°17W 166 D2
Glina Croatia 45°20N 16°6E 199 C13
Glinojeck Poland 52°49N 20°21E 185 F7
Glittertind Norway 61°40N 8°32E 164 C5
Gliwice Poland 50°22N 18°41E 185 H5
Globe U.S.A. 33°24N 110°47W 305 K8
Glodeanu Siliştea Romania 44°50N 26°48E 183 F11
Glodeni Moldova 47°45N 27°31E 183 C12
Glödnitz Austria 46°53N 14°7E 180 E7
Glogau = Głogów Poland 51°37N 16°5E 185 D9
Gloggnitz Austria 47°41N 15°56E 180 D8
Głogów Poland 51°37N 16°5E 185 D9
Głogówek Poland 50°21N 17°53E 185 H4
Glomma → Norway 59°12N 10°57E 164 E7
Gloria Phil. 12°56N 121°30E 232 E3
Glorieuses, Îs. Ind. Oc. 11°30S 47°20E 272 A2
Glosa Greece 39°10N 23°45E 104 H7
Glossop U.K. 53°27N 1°56W 168 D6
Glostrup Denmark 55°39N 12°23E 118 B2
Gloucester N.S.W., Australia 32°0S 151°59E 283 B9
Gloucester Papua N. G. 5°31S 148°31E 286 C5
Gloucester Gloucs., U.K. 51°53N 2°15W 169 F5
Gloucester Mass., U.S.A. 42°37N 70°40W 313 D14
Gloucester, C. Papua N. G. 5°26S 148°21E 286 C5
Gloucester I. Australia 20°0S 148°30E 280 b
Gloucester Island △ Australia 20°2S 148°30E 280 b
Gloucester Point U.S.A. 37°15N 76°30W 309 G15
Gloucestershire □ U.K. 51°46N 2°15W 169 F5
Glover I. Grenada 11°59N 61°47W 323 q
Gloversville U.S.A. 43°3N 74°21W 313 C10
Glovertown Canada 48°40N 54°3W 299 C9
Gloverville = Warrenville U.S.A. 33°33N 81°48W 316 B8
Głowno Poland 51°59N 19°42E 185 G6
Głubczyce Poland 50°13N 17°52E 185 H4
Glubokiy Russia 48°35N 40°25E 191 F5
Glubokoe Kazakhstan 50°8N 82°18E 217 B10
Glubokoye = Hlybokaye Belarus 55°10N 27°45E 188 E4
Głucholazy Poland 50°19N 17°24E 185 H4
Glücksburg Germany 54°50N 9°33E 178 A5
Glückstadt Germany 53°45N 9°25E 178 B5
Glukhov = Hlukhiv Ukraine 51°42N 33°50E 189 J7
Glusk Belarus 52°53N 28°41E 177 B15
Głuszyca Poland 50°42N 16°22E 185 H3
Glyngøre Denmark 56°46N 8°52E 163 H2
Gmünd Kärnten, Austria 46°54N 13°31E 180 E6
Gmünd Niederösterreich, Austria 48°45N 15°0E 180 D8
Gmunden Austria 47°55N 13°48E 180 D6
Gnali Gabon 2°34S 11°18E 264 C2
Gnarp Sweden 62°3N 17°16E 162 B11
Gnesen = Gniezno Poland 52°30N 17°35E 185 F4
Gnesta Sweden 59°3N 17°17E 162 E11
Gniew Poland 53°50N 18°50E 184 E5
Gniewkowo Poland 52°54N 18°25E 185 F5
Gniezno Poland 52°30N 17°35E 185 F4
Gnjilane Kosovo 42°28N 21°29E 202 D5
Gnoien Germany 53°58N 12°41E 178 B8
Gnosjö Sweden 57°22N 13°43E 163 G7
Gnowangerup Australia 33°58S 117°59E 279 F2
Go Cong Vietnam 10°22N 106°40E 238 G6
Gō-Gawa → Japan 35°2N 132°13E 222 B4
Gō-no-ura Japan 33°44N 129°40E 222 D1
Goa India 15°33N 73°59E 245 G1
Goa Phil. 13°42N 123°29E 232 E4
Goa □ India 15°33N 73°59E 245 G1
Goalen Hd. Australia 36°33S 150°4E 283 D9
Goalpara India 26°10N 90°40E 241 B3
Goaltor India 22°43N 87°10E 243 H12
Goaso Ghana 6°48N 2°30W 262 C4
Goat Fell U.K. 55°38N 5°11W 167 F3
Goat I. Antigua & B. 17°4N 61°51W 322 c
Goat Pt. Antigua & B. 17°44N 61°51W 322 c
Goba Ethiopia 7°1N 39°59E 257 C5
Goba Mozam. 26°15S 32°13E 271 C5
Gobabis Namibia 22°30S 19°0E 270 B2
Gobe Papua N. G. 9°4S 149°0E 286 E5
Göbel Turkey 40°0N 28°9E 203 F12
Gobernador Gregores Argentina 48°46S 70°15W 336 C2
Gobichettipalayam India 11°31N 77°21E 245 J3
Gobles U.S.A. 42°22N 85°53W 311 B11
Gobō Japan 33°53N 135°10E 223 D7
Gobo South Sudan 5°40N 31°10E 257 F3
Göçbeyli Turkey 39°13N 27°26E 205 D9
Gochang S. Korea 35°26N 126°42E 224 G3
Gochas Namibia 24°59S 18°55E 270 B2
God Dere Ethiopia 5°12N 44°1E 267 C5
Godavari → India 16°25N 82°18E 244 F6

Godavari Pt. India 17°0N 82°20E 244 F6
Godbout Canada 49°20N 67°38W 299 C6
Godda India 24°50N 87°13E 243 G12
Gode Ethiopia 5°53N 43°35E 267 C5
Godech Bulgaria 43°1N 23°4E 202 D7
Goderich Canada 43°45N 81°41W 312 C3
Goderville France 49°38N 0°22E 172 C7
Godfrey U.S.A. 38°58N 90°11W 310 F6
Godfrey Ra. Australia 24°0S 117°0E 279 D2
Godhavn = Qeqertarsuaq Greenland 69°15N 53°38W 154 D5
Godhra India 22°49N 73°40E 242 H2
Godinlabe Somali Rep. 5°54N 46°38E 267 C6
Godöllő Hungary 47°38N 19°25E 182 D4
Godoy Cruz Argentina 32°56S 68°52W 334 C2
Gods → Canada 56°22N 92°51W 298 A1
Gods L. Canada 54°40N 94°15W 298 B1
Gods River Canada 54°50N 94°5W 297 C10
Godthåb = Nuuk Greenland 64°10N 51°35W 154 E5
Godwin Austen = K2 Pakistan 35°58N 76°32E 243 B7
Goeie Hoop, Kaap die = Good Hope, C. of S. Africa 34°24S 18°30E 270 D2
Goéland, L. au Canada 49°50N 76°48W 298 C4
Goélands, L. aux Canada 55°27N 64°17W 299 A7
Goeree Neths. 51°50N 4°0E 170 C3
Goes Neths. 51°30N 3°55E 170 C3
Gofca → Somali Rep. 1°10N 43°43E 267 D5
Goffstown U.S.A. 43°1N 71°36W 313 C13
Gogama Canada 47°35N 81°43W 298 C3
Gogar U.K. 55°56N 3°20W 121 B2
Gogebic, L. U.S.A. 46°30N 89°35W 308 B9
Goggetti Ethiopia 8°11N 38°35E 257 F4
Gogolin Poland 50°30N 18°0E 185 H5
Gogonou Benin 10°50N 2°50E 263 C5
Gogra = Ghaghara → India 25°45N 84°40E 243 G11
Gogrial South Sudan 8°30N 28°8E 257 F2
Gogti Ethiopia 10°7N 42°51E 257 E5
Gohana India 29°8N 76°42E 242 E7
Goharganj India 23°1N 77°41E 242 H7
Goheung S. Korea 34°36N 127°17E 224 E3
Goi → India 22°4N 74°46E 242 H6
Goiana Brazil 7°33S 34°59W 332 C5
Goianésia Brazil 15°18S 49°7W 333 E2
Goiânia Brazil 16°43S 49°20W 333 E2
Goiás Brazil 15°55S 50°10W 333 E1
Goiás □ Brazil 12°10S 48°0W 332 D2
Goiatins Brazil 7°42S 47°10W 332 C2
Goiatuba Brazil 18°1S 49°23W 333 E2
Goidu-Erē Brazil 24°12S 53°1W 335 A5
Goidu Atoll Maldives 4°53N 72°54E 272 d
Góis Portugal 40°10N 8°6W 194 E2
Gojam □ Ethiopia 10°55N 36°30E 257 E4
Gojeb, Wabi → Ethiopia 7°12N 36°40E 257 F4
Gojō Japan 34°21N 135°42E 223 D7
Gojra Pakistan 31°10N 72°40E 242 D5
Gokak India 16°11N 74°52E 245 F2
Gokarn India 14°33N 74°17E 245 G2
Gökçe → Sevana Lich Armenia 40°30N 45°20E 191 K7
Gökçeada Turkey 40°10N 25°50E 204 B3
Gökçedağ Turkey 39°33N 28°56E 205 B10
Gökçen Turkey 38°7N 27°53E 205 C9
Gökçeören Turkey 38°37N 28°35E 205 C10
Gökçeyazı Turkey 39°40N 27°40E 205 B9
Gökırmak → Turkey 41°25N 35°8E 212 B6
Gökova Turkey 37°1N 28°17E 205 D10
Gökova Körfezi Turkey 36°55N 27°50E 205 D9
Göksu → Turkey 36°30N 34°2E 212 D5
Göksun Turkey 38°2N 36°30E 212 C7
Gökteik Burma 22°26N 97°0E 241 D6
Göktepe Karaman, Turkey 36°37N 32°37E 205 D5
Göktepe Muğla, Turkey 37°25N 28°34E 205 D10
Göktürk Turkey 41°10N 28°53E 122 A1
Gokurt Pakistan 29°40N 67°26E 242 E2
Gokwe Zimbabwe 18°7S 28°58E 271 A4
Gol Gol Australia 34°12S 142°14E 282 C5
Gola India 28°3N 80°32E 243 E9
Golabari India 22°35N 88°20E 242 b
Golaghat India 26°8N 89°52E 241 B2
Golakganj India 26°8N 89°52E 241 B2
Golan Heights = Hagolan Syria 33°0N 35°45E 250 F6
Golanci Poland 52°57N 17°18E 185 F4
Gölashkerd Iran 27°59N 57°16E 247 E8
Golaya Pristen = Hola Prystan Ukraine 46°29N 32°32E 189 J7
Gölbaşı Adıyaman, Turkey 37°45N 37°35E 212 D7
Gölbaşı Ankara, Turkey 39°47N 32°49E 212 C5
Golconda Italy 17°24N 78°23E 244 F4
Golconda Nev., U.S.A. 40°58N 117°30W 304 F5
Gölcük Kocaeli, Turkey 40°42N 29°43E 203 F13
Gölcük Niğde, Turkey 38°14N 34°47E 212 C6
Gold U.S.A. 41°52N 77°50W 312 E7
Gold Beach U.S.A. 42°25N 124°25W 304 E1
Gold Coast = Ghana ■ W. Afr. 8°0N 1°0W 263 D4
Gold Coast Queens., Australia 28°0S 153°25E 276 b
Gold Coast Chicago, U.S.A. 119 a2
Gold Coast W. Afr. 4°0N 1°40W 263 E4
Gold Creek U.S.A. 46°26N 149°41W 303 E10
Gold Hill U.S.A. 42°26N 123°3W 304 E2
Gold River Canada 49°46N 126°3W 296 D3
Goldberg = Złotoryja Poland 51°8N 15°55E 185 G2
Goldberg Germany 53°35N 12°4E 178 B8
Golden B.C., Canada 51°20N 116°59W 296 C5
Golden Ill., U.S.A. 40°7N 91°1W 310 D5
Golden B. N.Z. 40°40S 172°50E 285 D7
Golden Buddha = Traimit Bangkok, Thailand 113 c2
Golden Gate U.S.A. 37°48N 122°29W 136 B2
Golden Gate □ U.S.A. 37°49N 122°31W 136 B2
Golden Gate Bridge U.S.A. 37°48N 122°29W 136 B2
Golden Gate Highlands △ S. Africa 28°40S 28°40E 271 C4
Golden Gate Park U.S.A. 37°46N 122°28W 136 B2
Golden Grove Middlesex, Jamaica 18°19N 77°9W 320 a
Golden Grove Surrey, Jamaica 17°55N 76°16W 320 a
Golden Hinde Canada 49°40N 125°44W 296 D3
Golden Horn = Haliç Turkey 41°1N 28°57E 122 B1
Golden Lake Canada 45°34N 77°21E 312 B7
Golden Rock India 10°45N 78°48E 245 J4
Golden Spike △ U.S.A. 41°37N 112°33W 304 F7
Golden Vale Ireland 52°33N 8°17W 166 D3
Goldendale U.S.A. 45°49N 120°50W 306 D5
Golders Green U.K. 51°34N 0°11W 125 A2
Goldfield U.S.A. 37°42N 117°14W 305 H5
Goldingen = Kuldīga Latvia 56°58N 21°59E 184 B8
Goldsand L. Canada 57°2N 101°8W 297 B8
Goldsboro U.S.A. 35°23N 77°59W 315 D16

Goldsmith U.S.A. 31°59N 102°37W 314 F3
Goldthwaite U.S.A. 31°27N 98°34W 314 F5
Golęga Portugal 39°24N 8°29W 195 F2
Goleniów Poland 53°35N 14°50E 184 E1
Golestān □ Iran 37°20N 55°25E 247 B7
Golestān Iran 30°36N 54°14E 247 D7
Goleta U.S.A. 34°27N 119°50W 307 L7
Golfito Costa Rica 8°41N 83°5W 320 E3
Golfo Aranci Italy 40°59N 9°38E 200 B2
Golfo di Orosei e del Gennargentu △ Italy 40°5N 9°15E 200 B2
Gölgeli Dağları Turkey 37°10N 28°55E 205 D10
Gölhisar Turkey 37°8N 29°31E 205 D11
Goliad U.S.A. 28°40N 97°23W 314 G6
Golija Montenegro 43°8N 19°25E 202 C2
Golija Serbia 43°22N 20°15E 202 C4
Golina Poland 52°15N 18°4E 185 F5
Goljam Bratan = Morozov Bulgaria 42°44N 24°8E 203 D9
Gölköy Turkey 40°41N 37°37E 212 B7
Gollans Stream → N.Z. 41°22S 174°52E 143 B2
Gollel = Lavumisa Swaziland 27°20S 31°55E 271 C5
Göllersdorf Austria 48°29N 16°7E 180 C9
Gollnow = Goleniów Poland 53°35N 14°50E 184 E1
Gölmarmara Turkey 38°42N 27°55E 205 C9
Golmud China 36°25N 94°53E 218 D7
Golo → France 42°31N 9°32E 175 F13
Golo I. Phil. 13°39N 120°22E 232 E3
Gölova Turkey 36°48N 30°5E 205 E12
Golovin U.S.A. 64°33N 163°2W 303 D7
Golpāyegān Iran 33°27N 50°18E 247 C6
Gölpazarı Turkey 40°16N 30°18E 203 F13
Golra Pakistan 33°37N 72°56E 242 C5
Golspie U.K. 57°58N 3°59W 167 D5
Golub-Dobrzyń Poland 53°7N 19°2E 185 E6
Golubac Serbia 44°38N 21°38E 202 B5
Golungo Alto Angola 9°8S 14°46E 265 D2
Golyam Perelik Bulgaria 41°36N 24°33E 203 E8
Golyama Kamchiya → Bulgaria 43°10N 27°55E 203 C11
Golyshi = Vetluzhskiy Russia 58°23N 45°26E 190 A7
Goma Dem. Rep. of the Congo 1°37S 29°10E 268 C5
Gomal Pass Pakistan 31°56N 69°20E 242 D3
Gomantong Caves Malaysia 5°40N 118°6E 235 A5
Gomati → India 25°32N 83°11E 243 G10
Gombari Dem. Rep. of the Congo 2°45N 29°3E 268 B2
Gombe → Tanzania 4°38S 31°40E 268 C3
Gombe Nigeria 10°19N 11°2E 263 C7
Gombe □ Nigeria 10°12N 11°20E 263 C7
Gombe Stream △ Tanzania 4°42S 29°37E 268 C2
Gombi Nigeria 10°12N 12°30E 263 C7
Gomel = Homyel Belarus 52°28N 31°0E 177 B16
Gomera Canary Is. 28°7N 17°14W 153 e1
Gómez Palacio Mexico 25°34N 103°30W 318 B4
Gomfi Greece 39°26N 21°36E 204 B3
Gomīshān Iran 37°4N 54°6E 247 B7
Gomogomo Indonesia 6°39S 134°43E 231 F8
Gomoh India 23°52N 86°10E 243 H12
Gompa = Ganta Liberia 7°15N 8°59W 262 D3
Gonābād Iran 34°15N 58°45E 247 C8
Gonaïves Haiti 19°20N 72°42W 321 C5
Gonarezhou △ Zimbabwe 21°32S 31°55E 269 G3
Gonâve, G. de la Haiti 19°29N 72°42W 321 C5
Gonâve, Île de la Haiti 18°51N 73°3W 321 C5
Gonbad-e Kāvūs Iran 37°20N 55°25E 247 B7
Gönc Hungary 48°28N 21°14E 182 B6
Gonda India 27°9N 81°58E 243 F9
Gondal India 21°58N 70°52E 242 J4
Gonder Ethiopia 12°39N 37°30E 257 E4
Gondia India 21°23N 80°10E 244 F4
Gondola Mozam. 19°10S 33°37E 269 F3
Gondomar Portugal 41°10N 8°35W 194 D2
Gondrecourt-le-Château France 48°31N 5°30E 173 D12
Gonen Israel 33°7N 35°39E 123 b
Gönen Balıkesir, Turkey 40°6N 27°39E 203 F11
Gönen Isparta, Turkey 37°57N 30°31E 205 D12
Gönen → Turkey 40°6N 27°39E 203 F11
Gong Xian China 28°23N 104°47E 228 C5
Gongchangling China 24°50N 110°49E 228 E7
Gongcheng China 24°50N 110°49E 228 E7
Gongga Shan China 29°40N 101°55E 228 C3
Gonggar China 29°23N 91°7E 218 F7
Gongguan China 21°48N 109°36E 228 F7
Gonghe China 36°18N 100°32E 218 D9
Gongju S. Korea 36°27N 127°2E 224 F3
Gongliu China 43°30N 82°28E 217 C10
Gongming China 22°47N 113°53E 219 a
Gongneung S. Korea 37°36N 127°3E 137 B2
Gongo Yembe Dem. Rep. of the Congo 1°58S 18°40E 264 C3
Gongola □ Nigeria 9°30N 12°0E 263 C7
Gongolgon Australia 30°21S 146°54E 281 E4
Gongshan China 27°43N 98°12E 228 C1
Gongtan China 28°55N 108°22E 228 C7
Gongtang China 34°45N 112°58E 226 D7
Gongzhuling China 43°30N 124°40E 227 C13
Goni India 33°3N 75°40E 243 C6
Goniadz Poland 53°30N 22°44E 184 E9
Goniri Nigeria 11°30N 12°15E 263 C7
Gonjo China 30°52N 98°17E 228 B2
Gonnesa Italy 39°16N 8°28E 200 C1
Gonnosfanádiga Italy 39°29N 8°39E 200 C1
Gonzaga Phil. 18°16N 122°2E 232 A4
Gonzales Calif., U.S.A. 36°30N 121°26W 306 J5
Gonzales Tex., U.S.A. 29°30N 97°27W 314 G6
González Mexico 22°48N 98°25W 319 C5
Goobang △ Australia 32°48S 148°24E 283 B8
Good Hope, C. of S. Africa 34°24S 18°30E 270 D2
Good Hope Lake Canada 59°16N 129°18W 296 B3
Good Hope Plantation Jamaica 18°25N 77°41W 320 a
Goodenough I. Papua N. G. 9°20S 150°15E 286 E6
Gooderham Canada 44°54N 78°21W 312 B6
Goodhouse S. Africa 28°57S 18°13E 270 C2
Gooding U.S.A. 42°56N 114°43W 304 E6
Goodland U.S.A. 39°21N 101°43W 308 F3
Goodlands Mauritius 20°2S 57°39E 272 e
Goodlow Canada 56°20N 120°8W 296 B4
Goodmayes U.K. 51°33N 0°6E 125 A4
Goodnews Bay U.S.A. 59°7N 161°35W 303 G7
Goodooga Australia 29°3S 147°28E 281 D4
Goodsprings U.S.A. 35°49N 115°27W 307 K11
Goodwater U.S.A. 33°4N 86°3W 316 C3
Goodwood S. Africa 33°55S 18°32E 118 A2
Goodwood A. U.K. 50°53N 0°43W 169 G7
Goole U.K. 53°42N 0°53W 168 D7
Goolgowi Australia 33°58S 145°41E 283 B6
Goolma Australia 32°30S 149°15E 283 B8
Goolwa Australia 35°30S 138°47E 282 C2
Goomalling Australia 31°15S 116°49E 279 F2
Goomeri Australia 26°12S 152°6E 281 D5

Goonda Mozam. 19°48S 33°57E 269 F3
Goondiwindi Australia 28°30S 150°21E 281 D5
Goongarrie △ Australia 30°7S 121°30E 279 F3
Goongarrie, L. Australia 30°3S 121°9E 279 F3
Goonyella Australia 21°47S 147°58E 280 C4
Goose → Canada 53°20N 60°35W 299 B7
Goose Creek U.S.A. 32°59N 80°2W 316 C9
Goose L. Calif., U.S.A. 41°56N 120°26W 304 F3
Goose L. Ill., U.S.A. 40°55N 89°27W 310 D7
Gooty India 15°7N 77°41E 245 G3
Gop India 22°5N 69°50E 242 H3
Gopalganj Bangla. 23°1N 89°50E 241 D2
Gopalganj India 26°28N 84°30E 243 F11
Gopalpur India 22°38N 88°26E 124 B2
Goppingen Germany 48°42N 9°39E 179 G5
Gospel Oak U.K. 51°32N 0°9W 125 A3
Gospić Croatia 44°35N 15°23E 199 D12
Gosport Hants., U.K. 50°48N 1°9W 169 G6
Gosport Ind., U.S.A. 39°21N 86°40W 311 C10
Gossa Norway 62°56N 6°50E 164 B3
Gossas Senegal 14°28N 16°7W 262 C1
Gosse → Australia 19°32S 134°37E 280 B1
Gossi Mali 15°48N 1°20E 263 B5
Gossinga South Sudan 8°36N 25°59E 257 F2
Gostivar Macedonia 41°48N 20°57E 202 E4
Gostyń Poland 51°50N 17°3E 185 G4
Gostynin Poland 52°26N 19°29E 185 F6
Göta älv → Sweden 57°42N 11°54E 163 G5
Göta kanal Sweden 58°30N 15°58E 163 F10
Götaland Sweden 57°30N 14°30E 163 G8
Gotanda Japan 35°37N 139°43E 140 B3
Göteborg Sweden 57°43N 11°59E 163 H5
Gotemba Japan 35°18N 138°56E 223 B10
Götene Sweden 58°32N 13°30E 163 F7
Gotha Germany 50°56N 10°42E 178 E6
Gothenburg = Göteborg Sweden 57°43N 11°59E 163 H5
Gothenburg U.S.A. 40°56N 100°10W 308 E3
Gothèye Niger 13°52N 1°34E 263 C5
Gotland Sweden 57°30N 18°33E 163 G12
Gotō-Rettō Japan 32°55N 129°5E 222 D1
Gotse Delchev Bulgaria 41°36N 23°46E 202 E7
Gotska Sandön Sweden 58°24N 19°15E 163 F13
Gōtsu Japan 35°0N 132°14E 222 C4
Göttero, Monte Italy 44°26N 9°42E 198 D6
Gottingen Germany 51°31N 9°55E 178 D5
Gottsche = Kočevje Slovenia 45°39N 14°50E 199 C11
Gottskär Sweden 57°25N 12°1E 163 G6
Gottwald = Zmiyev Ukraine 49°39N 36°27E 189 H9
Gottwaldov = Zlín Czech Rep. 49°14N 17°40E 181 B10
Gouarēro Guadeloupe 16°11N 61°38W 322 b
Gouda Neths. 52°1N 4°42E 170 C4
Goudiri Senegal 14°15N 12°45W 262 C2
Goudoumaria Niger 13°40N 11°10E 263 C7
Gouéké Guinea 8°2N 8°43W 262 D3
Gough I. Atl. Oc. 40°10S 9°45W 152 L11
Gouin, Rés. Canada 48°35N 74°40W 298 C5
Goulburn Australia 34°44S 149°44E 283 B9
Goulburn → Australia 36°6S 144°55E 283 C7
Goulburn Is. Australia 11°40S 133°20E 280 A1
Goulburn River △ Australia 32°19S 150°10E 283 B9
Goulds U.S.A. 25°33N 80°23W 317 K9
Goulia Ivory C. 10°1N 7°11W 262 C3
Goulimine Morocco 28°56N 10°0W 260 C3
Goulmima Morocco 31°41N 4°57W 260 B4
Goumbou Mali 15°2N 7°29E 262 B3
Goumenissa Greece 40°56N 22°37E 202 F6
Gounatolo Solomon Is. 8°25S 160°52E 287 M11
Goundam Mali 16°27N 3°40W 262 B4
Goundi Chad 9°21N 17°21E 259 G3
Goúnista Greece 38°50N 21°2E 202 G5
Gouménissa Greece 40°56N 22°37E 202 F6
Goura Greece 37°38N 22°18E 204 D4
Gourara Algeria 29°10N 0°50E 261 C5
Gouraya Algeria 36°31N 1°56E 261 A5
Gourbeyre Guadeloupe 16°0N 61°41W 322 b
Gourdon France 44°44N 1°23E 174 D5
Goúre Niger 14°0N 10°10E 263 C7
Gournyak Russia 50°59N 81°27E 217 D10
Gournyatskii Russia 67°32N 64°3E 186 A11
Gournyatskiy Russia 51°50N 48°30E 190 E9
Gournyy Saratov, Russia 41°50N 48°30E 190 E9
Gournyy Primorsk, Russia 44°57N 133°59E 222 A7
Goro → C.A.R. 9°14N 21°1E 264 A4
Gorodenka = Horodenka Ukraine 48°41N 25°29E 183 D10
Gorodishche = Horodyshche Ukraine 49°17N 31°27E 189 H6
Gorodishche Russia 53°13N 45°40E 190 D7
Gorodnya = Horodnya Ukraine 51°55N 31°33E 189 G6
Gorodok = Haradok Belarus 55°30N 30°3E 188 E6
Gorodok = Horodok Ukraine 49°46N 23°32E 177 D12
Gorodok = Zakamensk Russia 50°23N 103°17E 215 D11
Gorodovikovsk Russia 46°8N 41°58E 191 G5
Goroka Papua N. G. 6°7S 145°25E 286 E6
Goroke Australia 36°43S 141°29E 282 D4
Gorokhovets Russia 56°13N 42°39E 190 C6
Gorom Gorom Burkina Faso 14°26N 0°14W 263 C4
Goromonzi Zimbabwe 17°52S 31°22E 269 F3
Gorong, Kepulauan Indonesia 3°59S 131°25E 231 E4
Gorongose → Mozam. 20°30S 34°40E 269 F3
Gorongosa Mozam. 18°44S 34°2E 269 F3
Gorongoza, Sa. da Mozam. 18°50S 34°14E 269 F3
Gorontalo □ Indonesia 0°30S 121°0E 231 D6
Gorontalo □ Indonesia 0°50N 122°20E 231 D6
Goronyo Nigeria 13°29N 5°39E 263 C6
Gorshkovo Russia 51°50N 37°6E 189 G10
Gort Ireland 53°3N 8°49W 166 C3
Gortis Greece 35°4N 24°58E 207 E6
Gorumahisani India 22°20N 86°24E 243 H11
Góry Bystrzyckie Poland 50°20N 16°40E 185 H3
Góry Klyuch Russia 44°38N 39°58E 191 H4
Goryeong S. Korea 35°44N 128°15E 224 G2
Goryshkowe Poland 53°12N 19°35E 185 E6
Górzno Poland 53°12N 19°38E 185 E6

Gorzów Śląski Poland 51°3N 18°22E 185 G5
Gorzów Wielkopolski Poland 52°43N 15°15E 185 F2
Gose Japan 34°27N 135°44E 223 C7
Gosen Germany 52°23N 13°43E 115 B5
Goseong S. Korea 34°58N 128°19E 224 E4
Gosford U.S.A. 33°23S 151°18E 282 B5
Goshen Calif., U.S.A. 36°21N 119°25W 306 J7
Goshen Ind., U.S.A. 41°35N 85°50W 311 C11
Goshen N.Y., U.S.A. 41°24N 74°20W 313 E10
Goshogawara Japan 40°48N 140°27E 220 D10
Goslar Germany 51°54N 10°25E 178 D6
Gospel Oak U.K. 51°32N 0°9W 125 A3
Graaff-Reinet S. Africa 32°13S 24°32E 270 D3
Graben Vienna, Austria 142 b2
Grabill U.S.A. 41°13N 84°57W 311 C12
Grabo Ivory C. 4°57N 7°30W 262 D3
Grabow Mecklenburg-Vorpommern, Germany 53°17N 11°34E 178 B7
Grabów Warszawa, Poland 52°12N 16°5E 185 G3
Grabów nad Prosną Poland 51°31N 18°7E 185 G5
Graça Lisbon, Portugal 126 b3
Gračanica Croatia 44°18N 15°57E 199 D12
Gračanica Bos.-H. 44°43N 18°18E 182 F3
Graçay France 47°10N 1°50E 173 E8
Grace, Mt. U.K. 41°20S 174°55E 143 B2
Grace Cathedral San Francisco, U.S.A. 136 b2
Graceford U.S.A. 41°14S 174°55E 143 B2
Graceville U.S.A. 30°58N 85°31W 316 E4
Gracewood U.S.A. 33°22N 82°2W 316 B8
Grácia Spain 41°24N 2°10E 114 A2
Gracias a Dios, C. Honduras 15°0N 83°10W 320 D3
Graciosa Azores 39°4N 28°0W 153 e1
Graciosa, I. Canary Is. 29°15N 13°32W 153 e2
Grad Sofiya □ Bulgaria 42°35S 23°20E 202 D7
Gradac Montenegro 43°23N 19°9E 202 C3
Gradačac Bos.-H. 44°52N 18°26E 182 F3
Gradaús Brazil 7°43S 51°11W 332 C1
Gradaús, Serra dos Brazil 8°0S 50°45W 332 C1
Gradeška Planina Macedonia 41°30N 22°15E 202 E6
Gradets Bulgaria 42°46N 26°30E 203 D10
Gradište Slovenia 46°37N 15°50E 199 B12
Grădiştea de Munte Romania 45°37N 23°13E 183 E8
Grado Italy 45°40N 13°23E 199 C10
Grado Spain 43°23N 6°4W 194 B4
Graeca, Lacul Romania 44°5N 26°10E 183 F11
Grafarnes Iceland 64°55N 23°16W 155 C3
Gräfelfing Germany 48°7N 11°25E 131 B1
Grafenau Germany 48°51N 13°22E 179 G9
Gräfenberg Germany 49°39N 11°14E 179 F7
Grafham Water U.K. 52°19N 0°18W 169 E7
Grafton N.S.W., Australia 29°38S 152°58E 281 D5
Grafton Ill., U.S.A. 38°58N 90°26W 118 C3
Grafton N. Dak., U.S.A. 48°25N 97°25W 308 A5
Grafton W. Va., U.S.A. 39°21N 80°2W 309 F13
Grafton Caledonia Wildlife Estate U.S.A. 11°11N 60°47W 323 s
Grafton's Pt. Anguilla 18°20N 62°54W 322 a
Gragoatá Brazil 22°53S 43°8W 135 B2
Graham Ont., Canada 49°20N 90°30W 298 C1
Graham Tex., U.S.A. 33°6N 98°35W 314 E5
Graham Bell, Ostrov = Greem-Bell, Ostrov Russia 81°0N 62°0E 214 A7
Graham I. B.C., Canada 53°40N 132°30W 296 C2
Graham I. Nunavut, Canada 77°25N 90°30W 295 B13
Graham Land Antarctica 65°0S 64°0W 151 C17
Grahamstown S. Africa 33°19S 26°31E 270 D4
Grahamsville U.S.A. 41°51N 74°33W 313 E10
Grahovo Montenegro 42°40N 18°40E 202 D2
Graie, Alpi Europe 45°30N 7°10E 175 C11
Grain Coast W. Afr. 4°20N 10°0W 262 E3
Grajagan Indonesia 8°35S 114°13E 231 K17
Grajaú Brazil 5°50S 46°4W 332 C2
Grajaú → Brazil 3°41S 44°48W 332 B3
Grajewo Poland 53°39N 22°30E 184 E9
Gramada Bulgaria 43°49N 22°39E 202 C6
Gramat France 44°48N 1°43E 174 D5
Grammichele Italy 37°13N 14°38E 201 F7
Grámmos, Óros Greece 40°18N 20°47E 202 F4
Grampian □ U.K. 57°20N 3°0W 167 D6
Grampian Highlands = Grampian Mts. U.K. 56°50N 4°0W 167 E5
Grampian Mts. U.K. 56°50N 4°0W 167 E5
Grampians, The Australia 37°15S 142°20E 282 D5
Grampians △ Australia 37°0S 142°20E 282 D5
Gramsh Albania 40°52N 20°12E 202 F4
Gran Norway 60°24N 10°31E 164 D4
Gran → Suriname 4°1N 55°30W 329 C6
Gran Altiplanicie Central Argentina 49°0S 69°30W 336 C3
Gran Canaria Canary Is. 27°55N 15°35W 153 e1
Gran Chaco S. Amer. 25°0S 61°0W 334 B3
Gran Couva Trin. & Tob. 10°14N 61°22W 323 t
Gran Desierto del Pinacate △ Mexico 31°51N 113°32W 318 A2
Gran Laguna Salada Argentina 44°24S 67°23W 336 C3
Gran Pajonal Peru 10°45S 74°30W 330 C2
Gran Paradiso Italy 45°33N 7°17E 198 C4
Gran Sasso d'Itália Italy 42°27N 13°42E 199 F10
Gran Sasso e Monti Della Laga △ Italy 42°33N 13°22E 199 F10
Granada Nic. 11°58N 86°0W 320 D2
Granada Spain 37°10N 3°35W 195 H7
Granada Colo., U.S.A. 38°4N 102°19W 304 G12
Granada □ Spain 37°18N 3°0W 195 H7
Granadilla de Abona Canary Is. 28°7N 16°33W 153 e1
Granard Ireland 53°47N 7°30W 166 C4
Granbury U.S.A. 32°27N 97°47W 314 E6
Granby Qué., Canada 45°25N 72°45W 313 A12
Granby Colo., U.S.A. 40°5N 105°56W 304 F11
Granby Conn., U.S.A. 41°57N 72°47W 313 E12
Granby Mo., U.S.A. 36°55N 94°20W 310 G4
Granby L. U.S.A. 40°9N 105°54W 304 F11
Grand → Ont., Canada 42°51N 79°34W 312 D5
Grand → Mich., Canada 43°4N 86°15W 311 A10
Grand → Mo., U.S.A. 39°23N 93°7W 310 F4
Grand → S. Dak., U.S.A. 45°40N 100°45W 308 C3
Grand Abaque, Pte.du Guadeloupe 16°21N 61°0W 322 c
Grand Anse Grenada 12°1N 61°45W 323 j
Grand Anse B. Grenada 12°6N 61°45W 323 j
Grand B. Dominica 15°14N 61°18W 323 k
Grand Bahama I. Bahamas 26°40N 78°30W 320 A4
Grand Baie Mauritius 20°0S 57°35E 272 e
Grand Banks Atl. Oc. 47°6N 55°48W 299 C8
Grand Bassam Ivory C. 5°10N 3°49W 262 D4
Grand Batanga Cameroon 2°50N 9°56E 264 B1
Grand Bazar = Kapali Carsi Turkey 41°1N 28°58E 122 B1
Grand Béréré Réunion 21°6S 55°52E 272 f
Grand Bérébi Ivory C. 4°38N 6°55W 262 E3
Grand Blanc U.S.A. 42°56N 83°38W 311 B13
Grand Bois Mauritius 20°25S 57°32E 272 e
Grand-Bourg Guadeloupe 15°53N 61°19W 322 e
Grand Canal = Da Yunhe China 39°10N 117°10E 227 E9
Grand Canyon U.S.A. 36°3N 112°9W 305 H7
Grand Canyon Nat. Park U.S.A. 36°15N 112°30W 305 H7
Grand Canyon-Parashant U.S.A. 36°30N 113°45W 305 H6
Grand Case St.-Martin 18°6N 63°5W 322 c
Grand Cayman Cayman Is. 19°20N 81°20W 320 C3
Grand Central Station New York, U.S.A. 132 c2
Grand Cess Liberia 4°40N 8°12W 262 E3

Grand Coulee *U.S.A.* 47°57N 119°0W **304** C4
Grand Coulee Dam *U.S.A.* 47°57N 118°59W **304** C4
Grand Cul-de-Sac Marin *Guadeloupe* 16°20N 61°35W **322** e
Grand Erg de Bilma *Niger* 18°30N 14°0E **259** E2
Grand Étang △ *Grenada* 12°5N 61°42W **323** q
Grand Falls *Canada* 47°3N 67°44W **299** C6
Grand Falls-Windsor *Canada* 48°56N 55°40W **299** C8
Grand Fond *St.-Martin* 17°53N 62°48W **322** a
Grand Forks *B.C., Canada* 49°0N 118°30W **296** D5
Grand Forks *N. Dak., U.S.A.* 47°55N 97°3W **308** B5
Grand Galet *Réunion* 21°17S 55°38E **272** f
Grand Gaube *Mauritius* 20°0S 57°39E **272** e
Grand Gorge *U.S.A.* 42°21N 74°29W **313** D10
Grand Haven *U.S.A.* 43°4N 86°13W **311** A10
Grand I. *Mich., U.S.A.* 46°31N 86°40W **308** B10
Grand I. *N.Y., U.S.A.* 43°0N 78°58W **312** D6
Grand Îlet *Guadeloupe* 15°50N 61°35W **322** e
Grand Îlet *Réunion* 21°1S 55°29E **272** f
Grand Island *U.S.A.* 40°55N 98°21W **308** E4
Grand Isle *La., U.S.A.* 29°14N 90°0W **315** G9
Grand Isle *Vt., U.S.A.* 44°43N 73°18W **313** B11
Grand Junction *Colo., U.S.A.* 39°4N 108°33W **304** G9
Grand Junction *Iowa, U.S.A.* 42°2N 94°14W **310** B2
Grand L. *N.B., Canada* 45°57N 66°7W **299** C6
Grand L. *Nfld. & L., Canada* 49°0N 57°30W **299** C8
Grand L. *Nfld. & L., Canada* 53°40N 60°30W **299** B7
Grand L. *La., U.S.A.* 29°55N 92°47W **314** G8
Grand L. *Ohio, U.S.A.* 40°32N 84°25W **311** D12
Grand Lahou *Ivory C.* 5°10N 5°5W **262** D3
Grand Lake *U.S.A.* 40°15N 105°49W **304** F11
Grand Ledge *U.S.A.* 42°45N 84°45W **311** B12
Grand-Lieu, L. de *France* 47°6N 1°40W **172** E5
Grand Mal B. *Grenada* 12°4N 61°45W **323** q
Grand Manan I. *Canada* 44°45N 66°52W **299** D6
Grand Marais *Mich., U.S.A.* 46°40N 85°59W **309** B11
Grand Marais *Minn., U.S.A.* 47°45N 90°25W **298** C1
Grand Marigot B. *Dominica* 15°25N 61°16W **323** k
Grand-Mère *Canada* 46°36N 72°40W **298** C5
Grand Palace *Bangkok, Thailand* **113** b1
Grand Popo *Benin* 6°15N 1°57E **263** D5
Grand Portage *U.S.A.* 47°58N 89°41W **308** B9
Grand Prairie *U.S.A.* 32°44N 96°59W **314** E6
Grand Rapids = Wisconsin Rapids *U.S.A.* 44°23N 89°49W **308** C9
Grand Rapids *Man., Canada* 53°12N 99°19W **297** C9
Grand Rapids *Mich., U.S.A.* 42°58N 85°40W **311** B10
Grand Rapids *Minn., U.S.A.* 47°14N 93°31W **308** B7
Grand Rapids ✈ (GRR) *U.S.A.* 42°53N 85°31W **311** B11
Grand Récif Sud *N. Cal.* 22°47S 166°55E **288** d
Grand Ridge *U.S.A.* 30°43N 85°1W **316** E4
Grand River *U.S.A.* 40°49N 93°58W **310** D3
Grand River Bay *Mauritius* 20°9S 57°27E **272** e
Grand River South East → *Mauritius* 20°17S 57°46E **272** e
Grand' Rivière *Martinique* 14°52N 61°11W **322** j
Grand Roy *Grenada* 12°8N 61°45W **323** q
Grand St-Bernard, Col du *Europe* 45°50N 7°10E **179** K3
Grand Santi *Fr. Guiana* 4°20N 54°24W **329** C7
Grand Staircase-Escalante ⌓ *U.S.A.* 37°25N 111°33W **305** H8
Grand Teton *U.S.A.* 43°54N 110°50W **304** E8
Grand Teton △ *U.S.A.* 43°50N 110°50W **304** E8
Grand Union Canal *U.K.* 52°7N 0°53W **169** E7
Grandas de Salime *Spain* 43°13N 6°53W **194** B4
Grande → *Jujuy, Argentina* 24°20S 65°2W **334** A2
Grande → *Mendoza, Argentina* 36°52S 69°45W **334** D2
Grande → *Bolivia* 15°51S 64°39W **331** D5
Grande → *Bahia, Brazil* 11°30S 44°30W **332** D3
Grande → *Minas Gerais, Brazil* 20°6S 51°4W **333** F1
Grande → *Venezuela* 8°36N 61°39W **329** B5
Grande, B. *Argentina* 50°30S 68°20W **336** D3
Grande, I. *Brazil* 23°9S 44°14W **333** F3
Grande, Rio → *N. Amer.* 25°58N 97°9W **314** J6
Grande, Serra *Piauí, Brazil* 8°0S 45°10W **332** C2
Grande, Serra *Tocantins, Brazil* 11°15S 46°30W **332** D2
Grande Anse = Beauséjour *Guadeloupe* 16°18N 61°4W **322** e
Grande Anse *Guadeloupe* 16°19N 61°47W **322** e
Grande Anse *Martinique* 14°30N 61°5W **322** j
Grande Anse *St. Lucia* 14°1N 60°54W **323** m
Grande Anse *Seychelles* 4°18S 55°45E **272** c
Grande Baleine → *Canada* 55°16N 77°47W **298** A4
Grande Cache *Canada* 53°53N 119°8W **296** C5
Grande Casse, Pte. de la *France* 45°24N 6°49E **175** C10
Grande Comore *Comoros Is.* 11°35S 43°20E **272** a
Grande Cul de Sac B *St. Lucia* 13°59N 61°2W **323** m
Grande-Entrée *Canada* 47°30N 61°40W **299** C7
Grande Matelot Pt. *Trin. & Tob.* 10°49N 61°9W **323** t
Grande Place *Brussels, Belgium* **116** b2
Grande Prairie *Canada* 55°10N 118°50W **296** B5
Grande Pte. *Guadeloupe* 15°58N 61°37W **322** e
Grande-Rivière *Qué., Canada* 48°26N 64°30W **299** C7
Grande Riviere *Trin. & Tob.* 10°50N 61°3W **323** t
Grande Rivière, Pte. de la *Guadeloupe* 16°18N 61°36W **322** e
Grande Rivière Noire *Mauritius* 20°21S 57°21E **272** e
Grande Rivière Sud Est *Mauritius* 20°17S 57°46E **272** e
Grande Sertão Veredas △ *Brazil* 15°10S 45°40W **333** E2
Grande-Terre *Guadeloupe* 16°20N 61°25W **322** e
Grande Terre *Mayotte* 12°46S 45°7E **272** b
Grande-Vallée *Canada* 49°14N 65°8W **299** C6
Grande Vigie, Pte. de la *Guadeloupe* 16°32N 61°27W **322** e
Grandfalls *U.S.A.* 31°20N 102°51W **314** F3
Grândola *Portugal* 38°12N 8°35W **195** G2
Grandpré *France* 49°20N 4°50E **173** C11
Grands Causses ⌓ *France* 44°5N 2°58E **174** D6
Grands-Jardins ⌓ *Canada* 47°41N 70°51W **299** C5
Grandview *Man., Canada* 51°10N 100°42W **297** C8
Grandview *Mo., U.S.A.* 38°53N 94°32W **310** F2
Grandview *Wash., U.S.A.* 46°15N 119°54W **304** C4
Grandview Heights *U.S.A.* 39°58N 83°2W **311** E13
Grandvilliers *France* 49°40N 1°57E **173** C8
Graneros *Chile* 34°5S 70°45W **334** C1
Grange Hill *Jamaica* 18°18N 78°11W **320** a
Grangemouth *U.K.* 56°1N 3°42W **167** E5
Granger *U.S.A.* 41°35N 109°58W **304** F9
Grängesberg *Sweden* 60°6N 15°1E **162** D9
Grangeville *U.S.A.* 45°56N 116°7W **304** D5
Granisle *Canada* 54°53N 126°13W **296** C3
Granite City *U.S.A.* 38°42N 90°8W **310** F6
Granite Falls *U.S.A.* 44°49N 95°33W **308** C6
Granite L. *Canada* 48°8N 57°5W **299** C8
Granite Mt. *U.S.A.* 33°5N 116°28W **307** M10
Granite Pk. *U.S.A.* 45°10N 109°48W **304** D9
Graniteville *S.C., U.S.A.* 33°34N 81°49W **316** B8
Graniteville *Vt., U.S.A.* 44°8N 72°29W **313** B12
Granitola, C. *Italy* 37°34N 12°39E **200** E5
Granity *N.Z.* 41°39S 171°51E **285** B6
Granja *Brazil* 3°7S 40°50W **332** B3
Granja de Moreruela *Spain* 41°48N 5°44W **194** D5
Granja de Torrehermosa *Spain* 38°19N 5°35W **195** G5
Grankulla = Kauniainen *Finland* 60°13N 24°44E **121** B1
Gränna *Sweden* 58°1N 14°28E **163** F8
Granollers *Spain* 41°39N 2°18E **196** D7
Gransee *Germany* 53°1N 13°8E **178** B9
Grant *Fla., U.S.A.* 27°56N 80°32W **317** H9
Grant *Nebr., U.S.A.* 40°50N 101°43W **308** E3
Grant, Mt. *U.S.A.* 38°34N 118°48W **304** G4
Grant City *U.S.A.* 40°29N 94°25W **310** D2
Grant I. *Australia* 11°10S 132°52E **278** B5
Grant Park *Chicago, U.S.A.* **119** c2
Grant Range *U.S.A.* 38°30N 115°25W **304** G6
Grantham *U.K.* 52°55N 0°38W **168** E7
Grantley Adams Int. ✈ (BGI) *Barbados* 13°4N 59°29W **323** r
Granton *U.K.* 55°58N 3°14W **121** B2
Grantown-on-Spey *U.K.* 57°20N 3°36W **167** D5
Grants *U.S.A.* 35°9N 107°52W **305** J10
Grants Pass *U.S.A.* 42°26N 123°19W **304** E2
Grantsville *U.S.A.* 40°36N 112°28W **304** F7
Grantville *U.S.A.* 33°14N 84°50W **316** B5
Granville *Manche, France* 48°50N 1°35W **172** D5
Granville *Trin. & Tob.* 10°7N 61°48W **323** t
Granville *Ill., U.S.A.* 41°16N 89°14W **310** C7
Granville *N. Dak., U.S.A.* 48°16N 100°47W **308** A3
Granville *N.Y., U.S.A.* 43°24N 73°16W **313** C11
Granville *Ohio, U.S.A.* 40°4N 82°31W **312** F2
Granville L. *Canada* 56°18N 100°30W **297** B8
Granvin *Norway* 60°33N 6°45E **164** D3
Graskop *S. Africa* 24°56S 30°49E **271** B5
Gräsö *Sweden* 60°28N 18°35E **162** D12
Grass → *Canada* 56°3N 96°33W **297** B9
Grass Range *U.S.A.* 47°2N 108°48W **304** C9
Grass River ⌓ *Canada* 54°40N 100°50W **297** C8
Grass Valley *Calif., U.S.A.* 39°13N 121°4W **306** F6
Grass Valley *Oreg., U.S.A.* 45°22N 120°47W **304** D3
Grassano *Italy* 40°38N 16°17E **201** B9
Grasse *France* 43°38N 6°56E **175** E10
Grassflat *U.S.A.* 41°0N 78°6W **312** E6
Grasslands △ *Canada* 49°11N 107°38W **297** D7
Grassy *Australia* 40°3S 144°5E **281** G3
Grassy Park *S. Africa* 34°3S 18°30E **118** B2
Gråsten *Denmark* 54°55N 9°35E **163** K3
Grästorp *Sweden* 58°20N 12°40E **163** F6
Gratis *U.S.A.* 39°38N 84°32W **311** E12
Gratkorn *Austria* 47°8N 15°21E **180** D8
Gratosóglio *Italy* 45°24N 9°1E **129** B2
Gratz *U.S.A.* 38°28N 84°57W **311** F12
Gratzwalde *Germany* 52°28N 13°42E **115** B5
Graubünden ☐ *Switz.* 46°45N 9°30E **179** J5
Graudenz = Grudziądz *Poland* 53°30N 18°47E **184** E5
Graulhet *France* 43°45N 1°59E **174** E5
Graus *Spain* 42°11N 0°20E **196** C5
Gravberget *Norway* 60°53N 12°14E **164** D9
Grave, Pte. de *France* 45°34N 1°4W **174** C2
Gravelbourg *Canada* 49°50N 106°35W **297** D7
Gravelines *France* 51°1N 2°10E **173** A9
's-Gravenhage *Neths.* 52°7N 4°17E **170** B4
Gravenhurst *Canada* 44°52N 79°20W **312** B5
Gravesend *N.S.W., Australia* 29°35S 150°20E **281** D5
Gravesend *Kent, U.K.* 51°26N 0°22E **169** F8
Gravesend *N.Y., U.S.A.* 40°36N 73°56W **132** C2
Gravina in Púglia *Italy* 40°49N 16°25E **201** B9
Gravois, Pointe-à- *Haiti* 18°15N 73°56W **321** C5
Gravone → *France* 41°58N 8°45E **175** G12
Gray *Haute-Saône, France* 47°22N 5°35E **173** E12
Gray *Ga., U.S.A.* 33°1N 83°32W **316** B6
Grayling *Alaska, U.S.A.* 62°57N 160°3W **303** E7
Grayling *Mich., U.S.A.* 44°40N 84°43W **309** C11
Grays *U.K.* 51°28N 0°21E **169** F8
Grays Harbor *U.S.A.* 46°59N 124°1W **304** C1
Grays L. *U.S.A.* 43°4N 111°26W **304** E8
Grays River *U.S.A.* 46°21N 123°37W **306** D3
Grayville *U.S.A.* 38°16N 88°0W **311** F9
Grayvoron *Russia* 50°29N 35°41E **189** G8
Graz *Austria* 47°4N 15°27E **180** D8
Grazhdanka *Russia* 59°59N 30°24E **137** B2
Grdelica *Serbia* 42°55N 22°3E **202** D6
Greåker *Norway* 59°16N 11°12E **164** E8
Greasy L. *Canada* 62°55N 122°12W **296** A4
Great Abaco I. = Abaco I. *Bahamas* 26°25N 77°10W **320** A4
Great Artesian Basin *Australia* 23°0S 144°0E **280** C3
Great Australian Bight *Australia* 33°30S 130°0E **279** F5
Great Bacolet Bay *Grenada* 12°4N 61°37W **323** q
Great Bahama Bank *Bahamas* 23°15N 78°0W **320** B4
Great Barrier I. *N.Z.* 36°11S 175°25E **284** C4
Great Barrier Reef *Australia* 18°0S 146°50E **280** B4
Great Barrier Reef ⌓ *Australia* 20°0S 150°0E **280** B4
Great Barrington *U.S.A.* 42°12N 73°22W **313** D11
Great Basalt Wall △ *Australia* 19°52S 145°43E **280** B4
Great Basin *U.S.A.* 40°0N 117°0W **304** G5
Great Basin △ *U.S.A.* 38°56N 114°15W **304** G6
Great Basses *Sri Lanka* 6°11N 81°29E **245** L5
Great Bear → *Canada* 65°0N 126°0W **294** E7
Great Bear L. *Canada* 65°30N 120°0W **294** D8
Great Belt = Store Bælt *Denmark* 55°20N 11°0E **163** J4
Great Bend *Kans., U.S.A.* 38°22N 98°46W **308** F4
Great Bend *Pa., U.S.A.* 41°58N 75°45W **313** E9
Great Blasket I. *Ireland* 52°6N 10°32W **166** D1
Great Britain *Europe* 54°0N 2°15W **158** E5
Great Camanoe *Br. Virgin Is.* 18°30N 64°35W **321** b
Great Channel *Asia* 6°0N 94°0E **245** L11
Great Coco I. = Koko Kyunzu *Burma* 14°7N 93°22E **245** G11
Great Codroy *Canada* 47°51N 59°16W **299** C8
Great Divide, The = Great Dividing Ra. *Australia* 23°0S 146°0E **280** C4
Great Divide Basin *U.S.A.* 42°0N 108°0W **304** E9
Great Dividing Ra. *Australia* 23°0S 146°0E **280** C4
Great Driffield = Driffield *U.K.* 54°0N 0°26W **168** C7
Great Exuma I. *Bahamas* 23°30N 75°50W **320** B4
Great Falls *Guyana* 5°35N 61°0W **329** B5
Great Falls *Mont., U.S.A.* 47°30N 111°17W **304** C8
Great Falls *Va., U.S.A.* 38°59N 77°17W **143** B2
Great Falls Park *U.S.A.* 38°59N 77°14W **143** B2
Great Fish = Groot-Vis → *S. Africa* 33°28S 27°5E **270** D4
Great Goat I. *Jamaica* 17°52N 77°3W **320** a
Great Guana Cay *Bahamas* 24°0N 76°20W **320** B4
Great Hall of the People *Beijing, China* **114** c3
Great Himalayan △ *India* 31°30N 77°30E **242** D7
Great Inagua I. *Bahamas* 21°0N 73°20W **321** B5
Great Indian Desert = Thar Desert *India* 28°0N 72°0E **242** F5
Great Karoo *S. Africa* 31°55S 21°0E **270** D3
Great Khingan Mts. = Da Hinggan Ling *China* 48°0N 121°0E **219** B13
Great Lake *Australia* 41°50S 146°40E **281** G4
Great Lakes *N. Amer.* 46°0N 84°0W **292** E11
Great Limpopo Transfrontier △ *Africa* 23°0S 31°45E **271** B5
Great Malvern *U.K.* 52°7N 2°18W **169** E5
Great Miami → *U.S.A.* 39°7N 84°49W **309** F11
Great Nicobar *India* 7°0N 93°50E **245** L11
Great Ormes Head *U.K.* 53°20N 3°52W **168** D4
Great Otway △ *Australia* 38°50S 143°50E **282** E5
Great Ouse → *U.K.* 52°48N 0°21E **168** E8
Great Palm I. *Australia* 18°45S 146°40E **280** B4
Great Pedro Bluff *Jamaica* 17°51N 77°44W **320** a
Great Pee Dee → *U.S.A.* 33°21N 79°10W **315** E15
Great Plains *N. Amer.* 47°0N 105°0W **292** E9
Great Ruaha → *Tanzania* 7°56S 37°52E **268** D4
Great Sacandaga L. *U.S.A.* 43°6N 74°16W **313** C10
Great Saint Bernard Pass = Grand St-Bernard, Col du *Europe* 45°50N 7°10E **179** K3
Great Salt Desert = Kavīr, Dasht-e *Iran* 34°30N 55°0E **247** C7
Great Salt L. *U.S.A.* 41°15N 112°40W **304** F7
Great Salt Lake Desert *U.S.A.* 40°50N 113°30W **304** F7
Great Salt Plains L. *U.S.A.* 36°45N 98°8W **314** C5
Great Salt Pond *St. Kitts & Nevis* 17°14N 62°40W **322** d
Great Sand Dunes ⌓ *U.S.A.* 37°48N 105°45W **305** H11
Great Sand Sea *Libya* 29°0N 24°0E **258** C4
Great Sandy △ *Australia* 26°13S 153°2E **281** D5
Great Sandy Desert *Australia* 21°0S 124°0E **278** D3
Great Sangi = Sangihe, Pulau *Indonesia* 3°35N 125°30E **231** D7
Great Scarcies → *S. Leone* 9°0N 13°0W **262** D2
Great Sd. *Bermuda* 32°17N 64°51W **153** a
Great Sea Reef *Fiji* 16°15S 179°0E **287** A2
Great Sitkin I. *U.S.A.* 52°3N 176°6W **303** K3
Great Skellig *Ireland* 51°47N 10°33W **166** E1
Great Slave L. *Canada* 61°23N 115°38W **296** A5
Great Smoky Mts. △ *U.S.A.* 35°40N 83°40W **315** D13
Great Stour = Stour → *U.K.* 51°18N 1°22E **169** F9
Great Victoria Desert *Australia* 29°30S 126°30E **279** E4
Great Wall *Antarctica* 62°30S 58°0W **151** C18
Great Wall *China* 38°30N 109°30E **226** E5
Great Western Forum *U.S.A.* 33°57N 118°20W **126** C2
Great Whale River = Kuujjuarapik *Canada* 55°20N 77°35W **298** A4
Great Whernside *U.K.* 54°10N 1°58W **168** C6
Great Yarmouth *U.K.* 52°37N 1°44E **169** E9
Great Zab = Zāb al Kabīr → *Iraq* 36°1N 43°24E **213** D10
Great Zimbabwe *Zimbabwe* 20°16S 30°54E **269** G3
Greater Antilles *W. Indies* 17°40N 74°0W **321** C5
Greater London ☐ *U.K.* 51°31N 0°6W **169** F7
Greater Manchester ☐ *U.K.* 53°30N 2°15W **168** D5
Greater St. Lucia Wetlands ⌓ *S. Africa* 28°6S 32°27E **271** C5
Greater Sudbury = Sudbury *Canada* 46°30N 81°0W **298** C3
Greater Sunda Is. *Indonesia* 7°0S 112°0E **230** F4
Grebbestad *Sweden* 58°42N 11°15E **163** F5
Grebenka = Hrebenka *Ukraine* 50°9N 32°22E **189** G7
Greco *Italy* 45°30N 9°12E **129** A2
Greco, C. *Cyprus* 34°57N 34°5E **207** F10
Greco, Mte. *Italy* 41°48N 13°58E **199** G10
Gredos, Sierra de *Spain* 40°20N 5°0W **194** E6
Greece *U.S.A.* 43°13N 77°41W **312** C7
Greece ■ *Europe* 40°0N 23°0E **204** B3
Greeley *Colo., U.S.A.* 40°25N 104°42W **304** F11
Greeley *Nebr., U.S.A.* 41°33N 98°32W **308** E4
Greeleyville *U.S.A.* 33°40N 79°59W **316** B10
Greely Fd. *Canada* 80°30N 85°0W **295** A15
Greem-Bell, Ostrov *Russia* 81°0N 62°0E **214** A7
Green → *Ky., U.S.A.* 37°54N 87°30W **308** G10
Green → *Utah, U.S.A.* 38°11N 109°53W **304** G9
Green B. *U.S.A.* 45°0N 87°30W **308** C10
Green Bay *U.S.A.* 44°31N 88°0W **308** C9
Green C. *Australia* 37°13S 150°1E **283** D9
Green City *U.S.A.* 40°16N 92°57W **310** D4
Green Cove Springs *U.S.A.* 29°59N 81°42W **316** F8
Green I. = Lütao *Taiwan* 22°40N 121°30E **225** D3
Green I. *Antigua & B.* 17°2N 61°40W **322** b
Green I. *Hong Kong, China* 22°17N 114°6E **122** B1
Green I. *Grenada* 12°13N 61°35W **323** q
Green Is. *Papua N. G.* 4°35S 154°10E **286** C8
Green Island *Jamaica* 18°23N 78°17W **320** a
Green Island B. *Phil.* 10°12N 119°22E **233** F2
Green Lake *Canada* 54°17N 107°47W **297** C7
Green Mts. *U.S.A.* 43°45N 72°45W **313** C12
Green Point *S. Africa* 33°54S 18°25E **118** A1
Green Point Stadium *S. Africa* 33°54S 18°25E **118** A1
Green Pond *U.S.A.* 32°44N 80°37W **316** C9
Green River *Papua N. G.* 3°54S 141°11E **286** B1
Green River *Utah, U.S.A.* 38°59N 110°10W **304** G8
Green River *Wyo., U.S.A.* 41°32N 109°28W **304** F9
Green Valley *U.S.A.* 31°52N 110°56W **305** L8
Greenacres *U.S.A.* 26°38N 80°7W **317** J9
Greenbank *U.S.A.* 48°6N 122°34W **306** B4
Greenbelt *U.S.A.* 39°0N 76°53W **143** A4
Greenbelt Park *U.S.A.* 38°58N 76°53W **143** B4
Greenbush *Mich., U.S.A.* 44°35N 83°19W **312** B1
Greenbush *Minn., U.S.A.* 48°42N 96°11W **308** A5
Greencastle *U.S.A.* 39°38N 86°52W **311** E10
Greene *Iowa, U.S.A.* 42°54N 92°48W **310** B4
Greene *N.Y., U.S.A.* 42°20N 75°46W **313** D9
Greeneville *U.S.A.* 36°10N 82°50W **315** C13
Greenfield *Calif., U.S.A.* 36°19N 121°15W **306** J5
Greenfield *Calif., U.S.A.* 35°15N 119°0W **307** K8
Greenfield *Ill., U.S.A.* 39°21N 90°12W **310** E6
Greenfield *Ind., U.S.A.* 39°47N 85°46W **311** E11
Greenfield *Iowa, U.S.A.* 41°18N 94°28W **310** C2
Greenfield *Mass., U.S.A.* 42°35N 72°36W **313** D12
Greenfield *Mo., U.S.A.* 37°25N 93°51W **308** G7
Greenfield *Ohio, U.S.A.* 39°21N 83°23W **311** E13
Greenfield Park *Canada* 45°29N 73°28W **130** B3
Greenford *U.K.* 51°31N 0°21W **125** A1
Greenhill *U.K.* 51°34N 0°18W **125** A2
Greenhills *Ireland* 53°18N 6°20W **120** B1
Greenland ☒ *N. Amer.* 66°0N 45°0W **154** D6
Greenland Sea *Arctic* 73°0N 10°0W **154** B10
Greenmarket Square *Cape Town, S. Africa* **118** c2
Greenock *U.K.* 55°57N 4°46W **167** F4
Greenore *Ireland* 54°2N 6°8W **166** B5
Greenore Pt. *Ireland* 52°14N 6°19W **166** D5
Greenough *Australia* 28°58S 114°43E **279** E1
Greenough → *Australia* 28°51S 114°38E **279** E1
Greenough Pt. *Canada* 44°58N 81°26W **312** B3
Greenpoint *New York, U.S.A.* **132** e3
Greenport *U.S.A.* 41°6N 72°22W **313** E12
Greensboro *Fla., U.S.A.* 30°34N 84°45W **316** E5
Greensboro *Ga., U.S.A.* 33°35N 83°11W **316** B6
Greensboro *N.C., U.S.A.* 36°4N 79°48W **315** C15
Greensboro *Vt., U.S.A.* 44°36N 72°18W **313** B12
Greensburg *Ind., U.S.A.* 39°20N 85°29W **311** E11
Greensburg *Kans. U.S.A.* 37°36N 99°18W **308** G4
Greensburg *Pa., U.S.A.* 40°18N 79°33W **312** F5
Greenstone = Geraldton *Canada* 49°44N 87°10W **298** C2
Greenstone Pt. *U.K.* 57°55N 5°37W **167** D3
Greentown *U.S.A.* 40°29N 85°58W **311** D11
Greenup *U.S.A.* 39°15N 88°10W **311** E8
Greenvale *Australia* 18°59S 145°7E **280** B4
Greenville *Liberia* 5°1N 9°6W **262** D3
Greenville *Ala., U.S.A.* 31°50N 86°38W **315** F11
Greenville *Calif., U.S.A.* 40°8N 120°57W **306** E6
Greenville *Fla., U.S.A.* 30°28N 83°38W **316** E6
Greenville *Ga., U.S.A.* 33°2N 84°43W **316** B5
Greenville *Ill., U.S.A.* 38°53N 89°25W **310** F7
Greenville *Ind., U.S.A.* 38°22N 85°59W **311** F11
Greenville *Maine, U.S.A.* 45°28N 69°35W **309** C19
Greenville *Mich., U.S.A.* 43°11N 85°15W **311** A11
Greenville *Miss., U.S.A.* 33°24N 91°4W **315** E9
Greenville *Mo., U.S.A.* 37°8N 90°27W **308** G8
Greenville *N.C., U.S.A.* 35°37N 77°23W **315** D16
Greenville *N.H., U.S.A.* 42°46N 71°49W **313** D13
Greenville *N.Y., U.S.A.* 42°25N 74°1W **313** D10
Greenville *Ohio, U.S.A.* 40°6N 84°38W **311** D12
Greenville *Pa., U.S.A.* 41°24N 80°23W **312** E4
Greenville *S.C., U.S.A.* 34°51N 82°24W **315** D13
Greenville *Tex., U.S.A.* 33°8N 96°7W **314** E6
Greenwater Lake ⌓ *Canada* 52°32N 103°30W **297** C8
Greenwich *Conn., U.S.A.* 41°2N 73°38W **313** E11
Greenwich *N.Y., U.S.A.* 43°5N 73°30W **313** C11
Greenwich *Ohio, U.S.A.* 41°2N 82°31W **312** E2
Greenwich ☐ *U.K.* 51°29N 0°1E **125** B3
Greenwich Observatory *U.K.* 51°28N 0°0 **125** B3
Greenwich Village *New York, U.S.A.* **132** d1
Greenwood *B.C., Canada* 49°10N 118°40W **296** D5
Greenwood *Ark., U.S.A.* 35°13N 94°16W **314** D7
Greenwood *Fla., U.S.A.* 30°52N 85°10W **316** E4
Greenwood *Ind., U.S.A.* 39°37N 86°7W **311** E10
Greenwood *Mass., U.S.A.* 42°29N 71°2W **116** A2
Greenwood *Miss., U.S.A.* 33°31N 90°11W **315** E9
Greenwood *S.C., U.S.A.* 34°12N 82°10W **315** D13
Greenwood, Mt. *Australia* 13°48S 130°4E **278** B5
Greenwood Great House *Jamaica* 18°29N 77°44W **320** a
Grefsen *Norway* 59°56N 10°47E **133** A3
Gregbe *Ivory C.* 6°48N 6°43W **262** D3
Gregório → *Brazil* 6°50S 70°46W **330** B3
Gregory *U.S.A.* 43°14N 99°26W **308** D4
Gregory → *Australia* 17°53S 139°17E **280** B2
Gregory, L. *S. Austral., Australia* 28°55S 139°0E **281** D2
Gregory, L. *W. Austral., Australia* 20°0S 127°40E **278** D4
Gregory, L. *W. Austral., Australia* 25°38S 119°58E **279** E2
Gregory △ *Australia* 15°38S 131°15E **278** C5
Gregory Downs *Australia* 18°35S 138°45E **280** B2
Gregory Ra. *Queens., Australia* 19°30S 143°40E **280** B3
Gregory Ra. *W. Austral., Australia* 21°20S 121°12E **278** D3
Greifenberg = Gryfice *Poland* 53°55N 15°13E **184** E2
Greifenhagen = Gryfino *Poland* 53°16N 14°29E **185** E1
Greiffenberg = Gryfów Śląski *Poland* 51°2N 15°24E **185** G2
Greiffenberg *Germany* 53°5N 13°57E **178** B9
Greifswald *Germany* 54°5N 13°23E **178** A9
Greifswalder Bodden *Germany* 54°12N 13°35E **178** A9
Grein *Austria* 48°14N 14°51E **180** C7
Greiz *Germany* 50°39N 12°10E **178** E8
Gremikha *Russia* 67°59N 39°47E **186** A6
Grenaa *Denmark* 56°25N 10°53E **163** H4
Grenada *U.S.A.* 33°47N 89°49W **315** E10
Grenada ■ *W. Indies* 12°10N 61°40W **323** q
Grenade *France* 43°47N 1°17E **174** E5
Grenadier I. *U.S.A.* 44°3N 76°22W **313** B8
Grenadines, The *St. Vincent* 12°40N 61°20W **323** n
Grenchen *Switz.* 47°12N 7°24E **179** H3
Grenen *Denmark* 57°44N 10°40E **163** G4
Grenfell *N.S.W., Australia* 33°52S 148°8E **283** B8
Grenfell *Sask., Canada* 50°30N 102°56W **297** C8
Grenivík *Iceland* 65°57N 18°11W **155** B8
Grenjaðarstaður *Iceland* 65°49N 17°21W **155** B9
Grenoble *France* 45°12N 5°42E **175** C9
Grenville *Grenada* 12°7N 61°37W **323** q
Grenville, C. *Australia* 12°0S 143°13E **286** F2
Grenville Chan. *Canada* 53°40N 129°46W **296** C3
Gréoux-les-Bains *France* 43°45N 5°52E **175** E9
Gresham *U.S.A.* 45°30N 122°25W **306** E4
Gresham Park *U.S.A.* 33°43N 84°20W **113** B2
Gresik *Indonesia* 7°13S 112°38E **235** D4
Gretna *Dumf. & Gall., U.K.* 55°0N 3°3W **167** F5
Gretna *Fla., U.S.A.* 30°37N 84°40W **316** E5
Gretna *La., U.S.A.* 29°54N 90°3W **131** B2
Gretna City Park *U.S.A.* 29°54N 90°3W **131** B2
Greve Strand *Denmark* 55°34N 12°18E **118** B1
Greven *Germany* 52°6N 7°37E **178** C3
Grevena *Greece* 40°4N 21°25E **202** F5
Grevena ☐ *Greece* 40°2N 21°25E **202** F5
Grevenbroich *Germany* 51°5N 6°35E **178** D2
Grevenmacher *Lux.* 49°41N 6°26E **170** E6
Grevesmühlen *Germany* 53°52N 11°12E **178** B7
Grey → *Nfld. & L., Canada* 47°34N 57°6W **299** C8
Grey → *N.Z.* 42°27S 171°12E **285** C6
Grey, C. *Australia* 13°0S 136°35E **280** A2
Grey Is. *Canada* 50°50N 55°35W **295** G20
Grey Ra. *Australia* 27°0S 143°30E **281** D3
Greybull *U.S.A.* 44°30N 108°3W **304** D9
Greyfriars Kirk *Edinburgh, U.K.* **121** c3
Greymouth *N.Z.* 42°29S 171°13E **285** C6
Greystones *Ireland* 53°9N 6°5W **166** C5
Greytown *N.Z.* 41°5S 175°29E **284** H4
Greytown *KwaZulu Natal, S. Africa* 29°1S 30°36E **271** C5
Gribanovskiy *Russia* 51°28N 41°50E **190** E5
Gribbell I. *Canada* 53°23N 129°0W **296** C3
Gribës, Mal i *Albania* 40°17N 19°45E **202** F3
Gribingui → *C.A.R.* 8°33N 19°5E **264** A3
Gribingui-Bamingui ⌓ *C.A.R.* 7°45N 19°17E **264** A3
Gridley *U.S.A.* 39°22N 121°42W **306** F5
Griebeg, Ras il- *Malta* 35°58N 14°23E **206** F7
Griebnitzsee *Germany* 52°23N 13°8E **115** B1
Griekwastad *S. Africa* 28°49S 23°15E **270** C3
Griesheim *Germany* 49°51N 8°33E **179** F4
Grieskirchen *Austria* 48°16N 13°48E **180** C6
Griffin *U.S.A.* 33°15N 84°16W **316** B5
Griffin, L. *U.S.A.* 28°52N 81°51W **317** G8
Griffith *N.S.W., Australia* 34°18S 146°2E **283** C7
Griffith *Ont., Canada* 45°15N 77°10W **312** A7
Griffith I. *Canada* 44°50N 80°55W **312** B4
Griffith Park *U.S.A.* 34°8N 118°17W **126** B3
Griggsville *U.S.A.* 39°43N 90°43W **310** E6
Grignols *France* 44°23N 0°2W **174** D3
Grigoriopol *Moldova* 47°9N 29°18E **183** C14
Grimari *C.A.R.* 5°43N 20°6E **264** A4
Grimaylov = Hrymayliv *Ukraine* 49°20N 26°5E **177** D14
Grimbergen *Belgium* 50°56N 4°22E **116** A2
Grimes *U.S.A.* 39°4N 121°54W **306** F5
Grimm = Kamenskiy *Russia* 50°48N 45°25E **190** E7
Grimma *Germany* 51°14N 12°43E **178** D8
Grimmen *Germany* 54°7N 13°3E **178** A9
Grimsay *U.K.* 57°29N 7°14W **167** D1
Grimsby *Ont., Canada* 43°12N 79°34W **312** C5
Grimsby *N.E. Lincs., U.K.* 53°34N 0°5W **168** D7
Grímsey *Iceland* 66°33N 17°58W **155** A9
Grimshaw *Canada* 56°10N 117°40W **296** B5
Grimslöv *Sweden* 56°44N 14°34E **163** H8
Grímsstaðir *Iceland* 65°39N 16°7W **155** B10
Grimstad *Norway* 58°20N 8°35E **164** F5
Grímsvötn *Iceland* 64°26N 17°22W **155** C9
Grindavík *Iceland* 63°50N 22°26W **155** D4
Grindelwald *Switz.* 46°38N 8°2E **179** J4
Grindsted *Denmark* 55°46N 8°55E **163** J2
Grindstone I. *U.S.A.* 44°17N 76°27W **313** B8
Grindu *Romania* 44°44N 26°50E **183** F11
Grinnell *U.S.A.* 41°45N 92°43W **310** C4
Grinnell Pen. *Canada* 76°40N 95°0W **295** B13
Grintavec *Slovenia* 46°22N 14°32E **199** B11
Grinzing *Austria* 48°15N 16°20E **142** A2
Gris-Nez, C. *France* 50°52N 1°35E **173** B8
Grise Fiord *Canada* 76°25N 82°57W **295** B15
Grishino = Krasnoarmeisk *Ukraine* 48°18N 37°11E **189** H9
Grisolles *France* 43°49N 1°19E **174** E5
Grisons = Graubünden ☐ *Switz.* 46°45N 9°30E **179** J5
Grisslehamn *Sweden* 60°5N 18°49E **162** D12
Grmeč Planina *Bos.-H.* 44°43N 16°16E **199** D13
Groais I. *Canada* 50°55N 55°35W **299** B8
Gröbenried *Germany* 48°13N 11°25E **131** A1
Grobiņa *Latvia* 56°33N 21°10E **184** B8
Groblersdal *S. Africa* 25°15S 29°25E **271** C4
Grobming *Austria* 47°27N 13°54E **180** D6
Grochów *Poland* 52°15N 21°5E **142** B2
Grocka *Serbia* 44°40N 20°42E **202** B4
Gródek *Poland* 53°6N 23°40E **185** E10
Gródek Tagiellonski = Horodok *Ukraine* 49°46N 23°32E **177** D12
Grodekovo = Pogranichnyy *Russia* 44°25N 131°24E **220** B5
Grodków *Poland* 50°43N 17°21E **185** H4
Grodno = Hrodna *Belarus* 53°42N 23°52E **184** E10
Grodzisk *Poland* 52°19N 21°4E **142** B2
Grodzisk Mazowiecki *Poland* 52°7N 20°37E **185** F7
Grodzisk Wielkopolski *Poland* 52°15N 16°22E **185** F3
Grodzyanka = Hrodzyanka *Belarus* 53°31N 28°42E **177** B15
Groenendaal *Belgium* 50°46N 4°26E **116** B2
Groesbeck *U.S.A.* 31°31N 96°32W **314** F6
Grogol Petamburin *Indonesia* 6°9S 106°46E **122** A1
Groix *France* 47°38N 3°29W **172** E3
Groix, Î. de *France* 47°38N 3°28W **172** E3
Grójec *Poland* 51°50N 20°58E **185** G7
Gronau *Niedersachsen, Germany* 52°5N 9°47E **178** C5
Gronau *Nordrhein-Westfalen, Germany* 52°12N 7°2E **178** C3
Grong *Norway* 64°25N 12°8E **160** D15
Grönhögen *Sweden* 56°16N 16°24E **163** H10
Groningen *Neths.* 53°15N 6°35E **170** A6
Groningen *Suriname* 5°48N 55°28W **329** B6
Groningen ☐ *Neths.* 53°16N 6°40E **170** A6
Grønnedal = Kangilinnguit *Greenland* 61°20N 47°57W **154** E6
Gronsdorf *Germany* 48°7N 11°42E **131** B3
Groom *U.S.A.* 35°12N 101°6W **314** D4
Groot → *S. Africa* 33°45S 24°36E **270** D3
Groot-Berg → *S. Africa* 32°47S 18°8E **270** D2
Groot-Brakrivier *S. Africa* 34°2S 22°18E **270** D3
Groot Karasberge *Namibia* 27°20S 18°40E **270** C2
Groot Kei → *S. Africa* 32°41S 28°22E **271** D4
Groot-Vis → *S. Africa* 33°28S 27°5E **270** D4
Grootdrink *S. Africa* 28°33S 21°42E **270** C3
Groote Eylandt *Australia* 14°0S 136°40E **280** A2
Grootfontein *Namibia* 19°31S 18°6E **270** A2
Grootlaagte → *Africa* 20°55S 21°27E **270** B3
Grootvloer → *S. Africa* 30°0S 20°40E **270** D3
Grorud *Norway* 59°57N 10°52E **133** A4
Gros C. *Canada* 61°59N 113°32W **296** A6
Gros Cap *Guadeloupe* 16°24N 61°25W **322** e
Gros Islet *St. Lucia* 14°5N 60°58W **323** m
Gros-Morne *Martinique* 14°43N 61°2W **322** j
Gros Morne △ *Canada* 49°40N 57°50W **299** C8
Gros Piton *St. Lucia* 13°49N 61°5W **323** m
Grósio *Italy* 46°18N 10°16E **198** B7
Grosne → *France* 46°42N 4°56E **173** F11
Gross-Glienicke *Germany* 52°28N 13°6E **115** B1
Gross-Hadern *Germany* 48°6N 11°29E **131** B1
Gross-Lappen *Germany* 48°11N 11°35E **131** A2
Gross-Meseritsch = Velké Meziříčí *Czech Rep.* 49°21N 16°1E **180** B9
Gross-Strehlitz = Strzelce Opolskie *Poland* 50°31N 18°18E **185** H5
Gross Wartenberg = Syców *Poland* 51°19N 17°40E **185** G4
Grossa, Pta. *Spain* 39°6N 1°36E **206** C2
Grosse I. *U.S.A.* 42°8N 83°9W **311** B13
Grosse Krampe *Germany* 52°23N 13°40E **115** B5
Grosse Müggelsee *Germany* 52°26N 13°38E **115** B4
Grosse Point *U.S.A.* 42°23N 82°54W **312** D2
Grosse Point Lighthouse *U.S.A.* 42°2N 87°41W **119** A2
Grosse Pte. *Guadeloupe* 16°1N 61°17W **322** e
Grossenbrode *Germany* 54°21N 11°4E **178** A7
Grossenhain *Germany* 51°17N 13°32E **178** D9
Grossenzersdorf *Austria* 48°12N 16°33E **142** A3
Grossenzersdorfer Arm → *Austria* 48°12N 16°31E **142** A3
Grosser Arber *Germany* 49°6N 13°8E **179** F9
Grosser Biberhaufen *Austria* 48°12N 16°28E **142** A2
Grosser Plöner See *Germany* 54°10N 10°22E **178** A6
Grosser Wannsee *Germany* 52°25N 13°10E **115** B2
Grosseto *Italy* 42°46N 11°8E **199** F8
Grossfeld-Siedlung *Austria* 48°16N 16°26E **142** A2
Grossgerungs *Austria* 48°34N 14°57E **180** C7
Grossglockner *Austria* 47°5N 12°40E **180** D5
Grosshesselohe *Germany* 48°3N 11°32E **131** B2
Grossjedlersdorf *Austria* 48°16N 16°23E **142** A2
Grosswardein = Oradea *Romania* 47°2N 21°58E **182** C6
Grossziethen *Germany* 52°23N 13°26E **115** B3
Groswater B. *Canada* 54°20N 57°40W **299** B8
Grotli *Norway* 62°2N 7°42E **164** B4
Groton *Conn., U.S.A.* 41°21N 72°5W **313** E12
Groton *N.Y., U.S.A.* 42°36N 76°22W **313** D8
Groton *S. Dak., U.S.A.* 45°27N 98°6W **308** C4
Grottáglie *Italy* 40°32N 17°26E **201** B10
Grottaminarda *Italy* 41°4N 15°2E **201** A8
Grottammare *Italy* 42°59N 13°52E **199** F10
Grottkau = Grodków *Poland* 50°43N 17°21E **185** H4
Grouard Mission *Canada* 55°33N 116°9W **296** B5
Grouin, Pte. du *France* 48°43N 1°51W **172** D5
Ground Zero *New York, U.S.A.* **132** e1
Groundhog → *Canada* 48°45N 82°58W **298** C3
Grouw *Neths.* 53°5N 5°51E **170** A5
Grove, The *U.S.A.* 42°5N 87°52W **119** A1
Grove City *Fla., U.S.A.* 26°56N 82°19W **317** J7
Grove City *Ohio, U.S.A.* 39°53N 83°6W **311** E13
Grove City *Pa., U.S.A.* 41°10N 80°5W **312** E4
Grove Hall *U.S.A.* 42°18N 71°4W **116** B2
Grove Hill *U.S.A.* 31°42N 87°47W **315** F11
Grove Park *Hounslow, U.K.* 51°28N 0°15W **125** B2
Grove Park *Lewisham, U.K.* 51°25N 0°1E **125** B4
Grove Park *Georgia, U.S.A.* 33°46N 84°26W **113** B2
Groveland *Calif., U.S.A.* 37°50N 120°14W **306** H6
Groveland *Fla., U.S.A.* 28°34N 81°51W **317** G8
Grover = Tiltonsville *U.S.A.* 40°10N 80°41W **312** F4
Grover Beach *U.S.A.* 35°7N 120°37W **307** K6
Groves *U.S.A.* 29°57N 93°54W **314** G8
Groveton *N.H., U.S.A.* 44°36N 71°31W **313** B13
Groveton *Va., U.S.A.* 38°46N 77°6W **143** C3
Grovetown *U.S.A.* 33°27N 82°12W **316** B7
Grožnjan *Croatia* 45°22N 13°43E **199** C10
Groznyy *Russia* 43°20N 45°45E **191** J7
Grua *Norway* 60°16N 10°40E **164** D7
Grubišno Polje *Croatia* 45°44N 17°12E **182** E2
Grudovo *Bulgaria* 42°21N 27°10E **203** D11
Grudusk *Poland* 53°3N 20°38E **185** E7
Grudziądz *Poland* 53°30N 18°47E **184** E5
Gruinard B. *U.K.* 57°56N 5°35W **167** D3
Gruissan *France* 43°8N 3°7E **174** E7
Grumo Áppula *Italy* 41°1N 16°42E **201** A9
Grums *Sweden* 59°22N 13°5E **162** E7
Grünau *Germany* 52°25N 13°34E **115** B4
Grünberg *Germany* 50°35N 8°58E **178** E4
Grünberg in Schlesien = Zielona Góra *Poland* 51°57N 15°31E **185** G2
Grund *Iceland* 65°31N 13°9W **155** B8
Gründau *Germany* 50°10N 9°9E **179** E5
Grundy Center *U.S.A.* 42°22N 92°47W **310** B4
Grunewald *Germany* 52°28N 13°13E **115** B2
Grungedal *Norway* 59°44N 7°43E **164** E4
Grünstadt *Germany* 49°34N 8°9E **179** F4
Grünwald *Germany* 48°2N 11°31E **131** B2
Grünwalder Forst *Germany* 48°2N 11°33E **131** B2
Gruppo di Tessa ⌓ *Italy* 46°47N 11°0E **198** B8
Gruvberget *Sweden* 61°6N 16°10E **162** C10
Gruver *U.S.A.* 36°16N 101°24W **314** C4
Gruyères *Switz.* 46°35N 7°4E **179** J3
Gruža *Serbia* 43°54N 20°46E **202** C4
Gryazi *Russia* 52°30N 39°58E **189** F10
Gryazliv = Borovichi *Russia* 58°25N 33°55E **188** C7
Gryazovets *Russia* 58°50N 40°10E **188** C11
Grybów *Poland* 49°36N 20°55E **185** J7
Grycksbo *Sweden* 60°40N 15°29E **162** D9
Gryfice *Poland* 53°55N 15°13E **184** E2
Gryfino *Poland* 53°16N 14°29E **185** E1
Gryfów Śląski *Poland* 51°2N 15°24E **185** G2
Grymes Hill *U.S.A.* 40°36N 74°6W **132** C1
Gryt *Sweden* 58°12N 16°48E **163** F10
Grythyttan *Sweden* 59°41N 14°32E **162** E8
Grytviken *S. Georgia* 54°19S 36°33W **152** M8
Gstaad *Switz.* 46°28N 7°18E **179** J3
Gua *India* 22°18N 85°20E **243** H11
Gua Musang *Malaysia* 4°53N 101°58E **237** K3
Guabún, Pta. *Chile* 41°48S 74°2W **336** B2
Guacanayabo, G. de *Cuba* 20°40N 77°20W **320** B4
Guacara *Venezuela* 10°14N 67°53W **328** A4
Guachípas → *Argentina* 25°40S 65°30W **334** B2
Guadajoz → *Spain* 37°50N 4°51W **195** H6
Guadalajara *Jalisco, Mexico* 20°40N 103°20W **318** C4
Guadalajara *Spain* 40°37N 3°12W **196** E1
Guadalajara ☐ *Spain* 40°47N 2°30W **196** E2
Guadalcanal *Solomon Is.* 9°32S 160°12E **287** M11
Guadalcanal *Spain* 38°5N 5°52W **195** G5
Guadalén → *Spain* 38°5N 3°32W **195** G7
Guadales *Argentina* 34°30S 67°55W **334** C2
Guadalete → *Spain* 36°35N 6°13W **195** J4
Guadalimar → *Spain* 38°5N 3°28W **195** G7
Guadalmena → *Spain* 38°19N 2°56W **195** G8
Guadalmez → *Spain* 38°46N 5°4W **195** G5
Guadalope → *Spain* 41°15N 0°3W **196** D4
Guadalquivir → *Spain* 36°47N 6°22W **195** J4
Guadalupe = Guadeloupe ☒ *W. Indies* 16°20N 61°40W **322** e
Guadalupe *Brazil* 6°44S 43°47W **332** C3
Guadalupe *Zacatecas, Mexico* 22°45N 102°31W **318** C4
Guadalupe *Manila, Phil.* 14°34N 121°2E **127** B2
Guadalupe *Spain* 39°27N 5°17W **195** F5
Guadalupe *Calif., U.S.A.* 34°58N 120°34W **307** L6
Guadalupe → *U.S.A.* 28°27N 96°47W **314** G6
Guadalupe, Basilica de *Mexico* 19°29N 99°7W **128** B2
Guadalupe, Sierra de *Spain* 39°28N 5°30W **195** F5
Guadalupe Bravos *Mexico* 31°20N 106°10W **318** A3
Guadalupe I. *Pac. Oc.* 29°0N 118°50W **292** G8
Guadalupe Mts. △ *U.S.A.* 31°40N 104°30W **314** F2
Guadalupe Peak *U.S.A.* 31°50N 104°52W **314** F2
Guadalupe y Calvo *Mexico* 26°6N 106°58W **318** B3
Guadarrama, Sierra de *Spain* 41°0N 4°0W **194** E7
Guadeloupe ☒ *W. Indies* 16°20N 61°40W **322** e
Guadeloupe △ *Guadeloupe* 16°10N 61°40W **322** e
Guadeloupe Passage *W. Indies* 16°50N 62°15W **322** e
Guadelupe *Peru* 7°15S 79°29W **330** B2
Guadiamar → *Spain* 36°55N 6°24W **195** J4
Guadiana → *Portugal* 37°14N 7°22W **195** H3
Guadiana Menor → *Spain* 37°56N 3°15W **195** H7
Guadiaro → *Spain* 36°17N 5°17W **195** J5
Guadiato → *Spain* 37°48N 5°5W **195** H5
Guadiela → *Spain* 40°22N 2°49W **196** E2
Guadix *Spain* 37°18N 3°11W **195** H7
Guafo, Boca del *Chile* 43°35S 74°0W **336** B2
Guafo, I. *Chile* 43°35S 74°50W **336** B2
Guaico *Trin. & Tob.* 10°35N 61°9W **323** t
Guainía ☐ *Colombia* 2°30N 69°0W **328** C4
Guainía → *Colombia* 2°1N 67°7W **328** C4
Guaíra *Brazil* 24°5S 54°10W **335** A5
Guaíra ☐ *Paraguay* 25°45S 56°30W **334** B4
Guaire = Gorey *Ireland* 52°41N 6°18W **166** D5
Guaitecas, Is. *Chile* 44°0S 74°30W **336** B2
Guajará-Mirim *Brazil* 10°50S 65°20W **331** C4
Guajira ☐ *Colombia* 11°30N 72°30W **328** A3
Guajira, Pen. de la *Colombia* 12°0N 72°0W **328** A3
Gualaceo *Ecuador* 2°54S 78°47W **328** D2
Gualán *Guatemala* 15°8N 89°22W **320** C2

376 Gualdo Tadino INDEX

Gualdo Tadino Italy 43°14N 12°47E 199 E9
Gualeguay Argentina 33°10S 59°14W 334 C4
Gualeguaychú Argentina 33°3S 59°31W 334 C4
Gualequay → Argentina 33°19S 59°39W 334 C4
Gualicho, Salina Argentina 40°25S 65°20W 336 B3
Gualjaina Argentina 42°45S 70°30W 336 B2
Guam ⊠ Pac. Oc. 13°27N 144°45E 302 d
Guamá → Brazil 1°29S 48°30W 332 B2
Guamblin, I. Chile 44°50S 75°0W 336 B2
Guaminí Argentina 37°1S 62°28W 334 D3
Guamote Ecuador 1°56S 78°43W 328 D2
Guampí, Sierra de Venezuela 6°0N 65°35W 329 B4
Guamúchil Mexico 25°28N 108°6W 318 B3
Guana I. Br. Virgin Is. 18°30N 64°30W 321 b
Guanabacoa Cuba 23°8N 82°18W 320 B3
Guanabara, B. de Brazil 22°52S 43°10W 135 B1
Guanabara, Jardim Brazil 22°48S 43°11W 135 A1
Guanabara, Palácio da Brazil 22°56S 43°11W 135 B1
Guanacaste, Cordillera de Costa Rica 10°40N 85°4W 320 D2
Guanacaste △ Costa Rica 10°57N 85°30W 320 D2
Guanaceví Mexico 25°56N 105°57W 318 B3
Guanahani = San Salvador I. Bahamas 24°0N 74°40W 321 B5
Guanaja Honduras 16°30N 85°55W 320 C2
Guanajay Cuba 22°56N 82°42W 320 B3
Guanajuato Mexico 21°1N 101°15W 318 C4
Guanajuato □ Mexico 21°0N 101°0W 318 C4
Guanambi Brazil 14°13S 42°47W 333 D3
Guanapo Trin. & Tob. 10°36N 61°15W 323 t
Guanare Venezuela 8°42N 69°12W 328 B4
Guanare → Venezuela 8°13N 67°46W 328 B4
Guandacol Argentina 29°30S 68°40W 334 B2
Guandi Shan China 37°53N 111°29E 226 F6
Guane Cuba 22°10N 84°7W 320 B3
Guang'an China 30°28N 106°35E 228 B6
Guang'anmen China 39°51N 116°18E 114 B1
Guangchang China 26°50N 116°21E 229 D11
Guangde China 30°54N 119°25E 229 B12
Guangdong □ China 23°0N 113°0E 229 F9
Guangfeng China 28°20N 118°15E 229 C12
Guanghan China 30°58N 104°17E 228 B5
Guangling China 39°47N 114°22E 226 E8
Guangnan China 24°5N 105°4E 228 E5
Guangning China 23°40N 112°22E 229 F9
Guangqumen China 39°52N 116°25E 114 B2
Guangrao China 37°5N 118°25E 227 F10
Guangshui China 31°37N 114°0E 229 B9
Guangshun China 26°8N 106°21E 228 D6
Guangwu China 37°48N 105°57E 226 F3
Guangxi Zhuangzu Zizhiqu □ China 24°0N 109°0E 228 F7
Guangyuan China 32°26N 105°51E 226 H3
Guangze China 27°30N 117°12E 229 D11
Guangzhou China 23°6N 113°13E 121 B2
Guanhães Brazil 18°47S 42°57W 333 E3
Guanica Puerto Rico 17°58N 66°55W 321 b
Guanipa → Venezuela 9°56N 62°26W 329 B5
Guanling China 25°56N 105°35E 228 E5
Guannan China 34°8N 119°21E 227 G10
Guanshuo China 23°4N 113°22E 121 B3
Guanta Venezuela 10°14N 64°36W 329 A5
Guantánamo Cuba 20°10N 75°14W 321 B4
Guantánamo B. Cuba 19°59N 75°10W 321 C4
Guantao China 36°42N 115°25E 226 F8
Guanting Shuiku China 40°14N 115°35E 226 D8
Guanyang China 25°30N 111°8E 229 E8
Guanyun China 34°20N 119°18E 227 G10
Guapay = Grande → Bolivia 15°51S 64°39W 331 D5
Guapí Colombia 2°36N 77°54W 328 C2
Guapo → Trin. & Tob. 10°11N 61°40W 323 t
Guapo B. Trin. & Tob. 10°12N 61°41W 323 t
Guaporé = Rondônia Brazil 10°52S 61°57W 331 C5
Guaporé Brazil 28°51S 51°54W 335 B5
Guaporé → Brazil 11°55S 65°4W 331 C4
Guaqui Bolivia 16°41S 68°54W 330 D4
Guara, Sierra de Spain 42°19N 0°15W 196 C4
Guarabira Brazil 6°51S 35°29W 332 C4
Guaracara → Trin. & Tob. 10°18N 61°28W 323 t
Guarachirá → Colombia 5°27N 70°36W 328 B3
Guaranda Ecuador 1°36S 79°0W 328 D2
Guarani = Pacajus Brazil 4°10S 38°31W 332 B4
Guarapari Brazil 20°40S 40°30W 333 F3
Guarapuava Brazil 25°20S 51°30W 333 G1
Guaratinguetá Brazil 22°49S 45°9W 335 A6
Guaratuba Brazil 25°53S 48°38W 335 B6
Guarda Portugal 40°32N 7°20W 194 E3
Guarda □ Portugal 40°40N 7°20W 194 E3
Guardafui, C. = Asir, Ras Somali Rep. 11°55N 51°10E 267 B7
Guardamar del Segura Spain 38°5N 0°39W 197 G4
Guardavalle Italy 38°30N 16°30E 201 D9
Guárdia Sanframondi Italy 41°15N 14°36E 201 A7
Guardiagrele Italy 42°11N 14°13E 199 F11
Guardo Spain 42°47N 4°50W 194 C6
Guareña Spain 38°51N 6°6W 195 G4
Guareña → Spain 41°29N 5°23W 194 D5
Guari Papua N. G. 8°3S 146°52E 286 E4
Guárico □ Venezuela 8°40N 66°35W 328 B4
Guarrojo → Colombia 4°6N 70°42W 328 C3
Guarujá Brazil 24°2S 46°25W 335 A6
Guarulhos Brazil 23°29S 46°33W 335 A6
Guasave Mexico 25°34N 108°27W 318 B3
Guascama, Pta. Colombia 2°32N 78°24W 328 C2
Guasdualito Venezuela 7°15N 70°44W 328 B3
Guasipati Venezuela 7°28N 61°54W 329 B5
Guasopa Papua N. G. 9°12S 152°56E 286 E7
Guastalla Italy 44°55N 10°39E 198 D7
Guatemala Guatemala 14°40N 90°22W 320 D1
Guatemala ■ Cent. Amer. 15°40N 90°30W 320 C1
Guatemala Basin Pac. Oc. 11°0N 95°0W 289 F18
Guatemala Trench Pac. Oc. 14°0N 95°0W 292 H10
Guatire Venezuela 10°28N 66°32W 328 A4
Guatopo △ Venezuela 10°5N 66°30W 328 A4
Guatuaro Pt. Trin. & Tob. 10°19N 60°59W 323 t
Guavi → Papua N. G. 7°48S 143°16E 286 D2
Guaviare □ Colombia 2°0N 72°30W 328 C3
Guaviare → Colombia 4°3N 67°44W 328 C4
Guaxupé Brazil 21°10S 47°5W 335 A6
Guayabero → Colombia 2°36N 72°47W 328 C3
Guayaguayare Trin. & Tob. 10°8N 61°2W 323 t
Guayaguayare B. Trin. & Tob. 10°7N 61°2W 323 t
Guayama Puerto Rico 17°59N 66°7W 321 C6
Guayaneco, Arch. Chile 47°45S 75°10W 336 C1
Guayanilla Puerto Rico 18°1N 66°47W 321 b
Guayaquil Ecuador 2°15S 79°52W 328 D2
Guayaquil Baja Calif., Mexico 29°59N 115°4W 318 B1
Guayaquil, G. de Ecuador 3°10S 81°0W 328 D1
Guayaramerín Bolivia 10°48S 65°23W 331 C4
Guayas → Ecuador 2°36S 79°52W 328 D2
Guaymas Mexico 27°56N 110°54W 318 B2
Guaynabo Puerto Rico 18°22N 66°7W 321 b
Guba Dem. Rep. of the Congo 10°38S 26°27E 269 E2
Guba Ethiopia 11°17N 35°20E 257 E4
Gûbâl, Madîq Egypt 27°30N 34°0E 256 B3
Gubam Papua N. G. 8°39S 141°53E 286 E1
Guban Somali Rep. 10°30N 44°0E 267 B5
Gubat Phil. 12°55N 124°7E 232 E5
Gubbi India 13°19N 76°56E 245 H3
Gúbbio Italy 43°21N 12°35E 199 E9
Guben Germany 51°57N 14°42E 178 D10
Gubin Poland 51°57N 14°43E 185 G1
Gubio Nigeria 12°30N 12°42E 263 C7
Gubkin Russia 51°17N 37°32E 189 G9
Gubkinskiy Russia 64°27N 76°36E 214 C8
Guča Serbia 43°46N 20°15E 202 C4
Gucheng China 32°20N 111°30E 229 A8
Gudå Norway 63°27N 11°36E 164 A8
Gudalur India 11°30N 76°29E 245 J3
Gudauta Georgia 43°7N 40°32E 191 J5
Gudbrandsdalen Norway 61°33N 10°10E 164 C7
Guddu Barrage Pakistan 28°30N 69°50E 242 E3
Gudenå → Denmark 56°29N 10°13E 163 H4
Gudermes Russia 43°24N 46°5E 191 J8
Gudhjem Denmark 55°12N 14°58E 163 J8
Gudivada India 16°30N 81°3E 245 F5
Gudiyattam India 12°57N 78°55E 245 H4
Gudö Sweden 59°12N 18°12E 139 B3
Gudur India 14°12N 79°55E 245 G4
Gudvangen Norway 60°52N 6°49E 164 D3
Guebwiller France 47°55N 7°12E 173 E14
Guecho = Getxo Spain 43°21N 2°59W 196 B2
Guékédou Guinea 8°40N 10°5W 262 D2
Guelb er Rîchât Mauritania 21°7N 11°24W 260 D2
Guéle Mendouka Cameroon 4°23N 12°55E 263 E7
Guélengdeng Chad 10°55N 15°31E 259 F3
Güell, Parque de Spain 41°24N 2°10E 114 A2
Guelma Algeria 36°25N 7°29E 261 A6
Guelma □ Algeria 36°25N 7°25E 261 A6
Guelmine = Goulimine Morocco 28°56N 10°0W 260 C3
Guelph Canada 43°35N 80°20W 312 C4
Guelta Zemmur W. Sahara 25°8N 12°22W 260 C2
Guemar Algeria 33°30N 6°49E 261 B6
Guéméné-Penfao France 47°38N 1°50W 172 E5
Guéméné-sur-Scorff France 48°4N 3°13W 172 D3
Guéné Benin 11°44N 3°16E 263 C5
Güeppí Peru 0°7S 75°15W 328 D2
Guer France 47°54N 2°8W 172 E4
Güer Aike Argentina 51°39S 69°35W 336 D3
Guera Chad 11°55N 18°12E 259 F3
Guéra □ Chad 11°30N 18°30E 259 F3
Guérande France 47°20N 2°26W 172 E4
Guerara Algeria 32°51N 4°22E 261 B5
Guercif Morocco 34°14N 3°21W 261 B4
Guéréda Chad 14°31N 22°5E 259 F4
Guéret France 46°11N 1°51E 173 F8
Guérigny France 47°6N 3°10E 173 E10
Guerneville U.S.A. 38°30N 123°0W 306 G4
Guernica = Gernika-Lumo Spain 43°19N 2°40W 196 B2
Guernsey Chan. Is., U.K. 49°26N 2°35W 169 H5
Guernsey Wyo., U.S.A. 42°16N 104°45W 304 E11
Guerrara Algeria 28°5N 0°8W 261 C4
Guerrero Mexico City, Mexico 128 a1
Guerrero □ Mexico 17°40N 100°0W 319 D5
Guerzim Algeria 29°39N 1°40W 261 C4
Guessou-Sud Benin 10°3N 2°38E 263 C5
Gueugnon France 46°36N 4°4E 173 F11
Guéyo Ivory C. 5°25N 6°5W 262 D3
Gufuðalur Iceland 65°34N 22°25W 155 B4
Guggenheim Museum New York, U.S.A. 132 b3
Gughe Ethiopia 6°12N 37°30E 257 F4
Gūgher Iran 29°28N 56°27E 247 D8
Guglionesi Italy 41°55N 14°55E 199 G11
Guguan N. Marianas 17°18N 145°51E 302 a
Guhrau = Góra Poland 51°40N 16°31E 185 G3
Gui Jiang → China 23°30N 111°15E 229 F8
Guia Canary Is. 28°8N 15°38W 153 e1
Guia de Isora Canary Is. 28°12N 16°46W 153 e1
Guia Lopes da Laguna Brazil 21°26S 56°7W 335 A4
Guiana Venezuela 5°9N 63°36W 329 B5
Guiana Highlands S. Amer. 5°10N 60°40W 326 C4
Guiana I. Antigua & B. 17°6N 61°44W 322 b
Guibéroua Ivory C. 6°14N 6°10W 262 D3
Guichen B. Australia 37°10S 139°45E 282 D3
Guichi China 30°39N 117°27E 229 B11
Guider Cameroon 9°56N 13°57E 263 D7
Guidiguir Niger 13°40N 9°50E 259 F1
Guidimaka □ Mauritania 15°20N 12°0W 262 B2
Guidimouni Niger 13°42N 9°31E 259 F1
Guiding China 26°34N 107°11E 228 D6
Guidong China 26°7N 113°57E 229 D9
Guidónia-Montecélio Italy 42°1N 12°45E 199 F9
Guiers, L. de Senegal 16°10N 15°50W 262 B1
Guigang China 23°8N 109°35E 228 F7
Guiglo Ivory C. 6°45N 7°30W 262 D3
Guihulngan Phil. 10°7N 123°16E 233 F4
Guijá Mozam. 24°27S 33°0E 271 B5
Guijuelo Spain 40°33N 5°40W 194 E5
Guildford U.K. 51°14N 0°34W 169 F7
Guilford U.S.A. 41°17N 72°41W 313 E12
Guilin China 25°18N 110°15E 229 E8
Guillaume-Delisle, L. Canada 56°15N 76°17W 298 A4
Guillaumes France 44°5N 6°52E 175 D10
Guillestre France 44°39N 6°40E 175 D10
Guilvinec France 47°48N 4°17W 172 E2
Güimar Canary Is. 28°18N 16°24W 153 e1
Guimarães Brazil 2°9S 44°42W 332 B3
Guimarães Portugal 41°28N 8°24W 194 D2
Guimaras □ Phil. 10°35N 122°37E 233 F4
Guimaras Str. Phil. 10°38N 122°48E 233 F4
Guimba Phil. 15°40N 120°46E 232 D3
Guinardó Spain 41°24N 2°10E 114 A2
Guinayangan Phil. 13°54N 122°27E 232 E4
Guinda U.S.A. 38°50N 122°12W 306 G4
Guindulman Phil. 9°46N 124°29E 233 G5
Guinea Africa 8°0N 8°0E 254 F4
Guinea ■ W. Afr. 10°20N 11°30W 262 C2
Guinea, Gulf of Atl. Oc. 3°0N 2°30E 263 E5
Guinea Basin Atl. Oc. 0°0 5°0W 152 G11
Guinea-Bissau ■ Africa 12°0N 15°0W 262 C2
Güines Cuba 22°50N 82°0W 320 B3
Guingamp France 48°34N 3°10W 172 D3
Guinguinéo Senegal 14°20N 15°57W 262 C1
Guinobatan Phil. 13°11N 123°36E 232 E4
Guipavas France 48°26N 4°29W 172 D2
Guiping China 23°21N 110°2E 229 F8
Guipúzcoa □ Spain 43°12N 2°15W 196 B2
Guir Mali 18°52N 2°52W 262 B4
Guir, O. → Algeria 31°29N 2°17W 261 B4
Guiratinga Brazil 16°21S 53°45W 331 D7
Guirel Mauritania 15°30N 7°3W 262 B3
Güiria Venezuela 10°32N 62°18W 329 F8
Guiscard France 49°40N 3°1E 173 C10
Guise France 49°52N 3°35E 173 C10
Guita-Koulouba C.A.R. 5°58N 23°21E 264 A4
Guitiriz Spain 43°11N 7°50W 194 B3
Guitri Ivory C. 5°30N 5°14W 262 D3
Guiuan Phil. 11°5N 125°55E 233 F5
Guixi China 28°16N 117°15E 229 C11
Guiyang Guizhou, China 26°32N 106°40E 228 D6
Guiyang Hunan, China 25°46N 112°42E 229 E9
Guizhou □ China 27°0N 107°0E 228 D6
Gujan-Mestras France 44°38N 1°4W 174 D2
Gujar Khan Pakistan 33°16N 73°19E 242 C5
Gujarat □ India 23°20N 71°0E 242 H4
Gujiang China 27°11N 114°47E 229 D10
Gujiao China 37°54N 112°8E 226 F7
Gujranwala Pakistan 32°10N 74°12E 242 C6
Gujrat Pakistan 32°40N 74°2E 242 C6
Gukovo Russia 48°1N 39°58E 191 F5
Gulargambone Australia 31°20S 148°30E 283 A8
Gulbai Pakistan 24°52N 66°58E 123 A1
Gulbarga India 17°20N 76°50E 244 F3
Gulbene Latvia 57°8N 26°52E 188 D4
Gülchö Kyrgyzstan 40°19N 73°26E 217 D8
Guledagudda India 16°3N 75°48E 245 F2
Gülek Turkey 37°12N 34°48E 250 A5
Gulf □ Papua N. G. 8°0S 145°0E 286 D3
Gulf, The = Persian Gulf Asia 27°0N 50°0E 247 E6
Gulf Breeze U.S.A. 30°21N 87°9W 317 E2
Gulf Hammock U.S.A. 29°15N 82°43W 317 F7
Gulf Islands ⌓ U.S.A. 30°10N 87°10W 317 K2
Gulfport Fla., U.S.A. 27°44N 82°42W 317 H7
Gulfport Miss., U.S.A. 30°22N 89°6W 315 F10
Gulgong Australia 32°20S 149°49E 283 B8
Gulian China 52°56N 122°21E 219 A13
Gulin China 28°1N 105°50E 228 C5
Gulistan Pakistan 30°30N 66°35E 242 D2
Guliston Uzbekistan 40°29N 68°46E 217 D7
Gulja = Yining China 43°58N 81°10E 217 D10
Gulkana U.S.A. 62°16N 145°23W 303 E11
Gull Lake Canada 50°10N 108°29W 297 C7
Gullbrå Norway 60°50N 6°17E 164 D3
Gullbrandstorp Sweden 56°42N 12°43E 163 H6
Gullbringusýsla □ Iceland 64°0N 22°0W 155 D4
Gullfoss Iceland 64°20N 20°8W 155 C6
Gullhaug Norway 59°30N 10°15E 164 E7
Gullivan B. U.S.A. 25°45N 81°40W 317 K8
Gullspång Sweden 58°59N 14°6E 163 F8
Gullstein Norway 63°13N 8°9E 164 A5
Güllük Turkey 37°14N 27°35E 205 D9
Güllük Dağı △ Turkey 37°0N 30°30E 205 E12
Güllük Korfezi Turkey 37°12N 27°30E 205 D9
Gulma Nigeria 12°40N 4°23E 263 C5
Gulmarg India 34°3N 74°25E 243 B6
Gülnar Turkey 36°19N 33°24E 250 B4
Gulnare Australia 33°27S 138°27E 282 B3
Gülpınar Turkey 39°32N 26°7E 205 B8
Gülşehir Turkey 38°44N 34°37E 212 C6
Gülshat Kazakhstan 46°38N 74°21E 217 C8
Gulsvik Norway 60°24N 9°38E 164 D6
Gulu Uganda 2°48N 32°17E 268 B3
Gŭlŭbovo Bulgaria 42°8N 25°55E 203 D9
Gulud, J. Sudan 11°41N 29°31E 257 E2
Gulwe Tanzania 6°30S 36°25E 268 D4
Gulyaypole = Hulyaypole Ukraine 47°45N 36°21E 189 J9
Gum Lake Australia 32°42S 143°9E 282 B5
Gumaca Phil. 13°55N 122°6E 232 E4
Gumal → Pakistan 31°40N 71°50E 242 D4
Gumbaz Pakistan 30°2N 69°0E 242 D3
Gumbinnen = Gusev Russia 54°35N 22°10E 184 D9
Gumdag Turkmenistan 39°9N 54°56E 216 E4
Gumel Nigeria 12°39N 9°22E 263 C6
Gumi S. Korea 36°10N 128°12E 224 D4
Gumiel de Hizán Spain 41°46N 3°41W 194 D7
Gumla India 23°3N 84°33E 243 H11
Gumlu Australia 19°53S 147°41E 280 B4
Gumma □ Japan 36°30N 138°20E 223 A10
Gummersbach Germany 51°1N 7°34E 178 D3
Gummi Nigeria 12°4N 5°9E 263 C6
Gümüldür Turkey 38°6N 27°0E 205 C9
Gumuljina = Komotini Greece 41°9N 25°26E 203 E9
Gümüşçay Turkey 40°16N 27°17E 203 F11
Gümüşhacıköy Turkey 40°50N 35°18E 212 B6
Gümüşhane Turkey 40°30N 39°30E 213 B8
Gümüşsu Turkey 38°14N 29°1E 205 C11
Gumzai Indonesia 5°28S 134°42E 231 F8
Gun Hill Tower Barbados 13°8N 59°33W 323 r
Gun Pt. Grenada 12°32N 61°37W 323 q
Guna Amara, Ethiopia 11°43N 38°14E 266 B4
Guna Oromiya, Ethiopia 8°18N 39°52E 257 F4
Guna India 24°40N 77°19E 242 G7
Gunbalanya Australia 12°20S 133°4E 278 B5
Gundabooka △ Australia 30°30S 145°20E 281 E4
Gundagai Australia 35°3S 148°6E 283 C8
Gundarehi India 20°57N 81°17E 244 D5
Gundelfingen Germany 48°34N 10°22E 179 G6
Gundji Dem. Rep. of the Congo 2°5N 21°27E 264 B4
Gundlakamma → India 15°30N 80°15E 245 G5
Gundlupet India 11°48N 76°41E 245 J3
Gündoğmuş Turkey 36°48N 32°0E 250 B3
Gunebang Australia 33°1S 146°38E 283 B7
Güney Burdur, Turkey 37°29N 29°34E 205 D11
Güney Denizli, Turkey 38°9N 29°4E 205 C11
Güneydoğu Toroslar Turkey 38°20N 40°30E 213 C9
Gungal Australia 32°17S 150°32E 283 B9
Gungo Angola 10°58S 15°30E 265 E2
Güngören Turkey 41°1N 28°52E 122 B1
Gungu Dem. Rep. of the Congo 5°43S 19°20E 265 D3
Gunisao → Canada 53°56N 97°53W 297 C9
Gunisao L. Canada 53°33N 96°15W 297 C9
Gunjur Gambia 13°12N 16°44W 262 C1
Gunjyal Pakistan 32°20N 71°55E 242 C4
Günlüce Turkey 36°50N 28°20E 205 E10
Gunnarskog Sweden 59°49N 12°34E 162 E6
Gunnbjørn Fjeld Greenland 68°55N 29°47W 154 D8
Gunnebo Sweden 57°44N 16°32E 163 G10
Gunnedah Australia 30°59S 150°15E 283 A9
Gunnersbury U.K. 51°29N 0°17W 125 B2
Gunnewin Australia 25°59S 148°33E 281 D4
Gunningbar Cr. → Australia 31°14S 147°6E 283 A7
Gunnison Colo., U.S.A. 38°33N 106°56W 304 G10
Gunnison Utah, U.S.A. 39°9N 111°49W 304 G8
Gunnison → U.S.A. 39°4N 108°35W 304 G9
Gunsan S. Korea 35°59N 126°45E 224 E3
Guntakal India 15°11N 77°27E 245 G3
Gunter Canada 44°52N 77°32W 312 B7
Guntersville U.S.A. 34°21N 86°18W 315 D11
Guntong Malaysia 4°36N 101°3E 237 K3
Guntur India 16°23N 80°30E 245 F5
Gunung Buda △ Malaysia 4°12N 114°57E 235 B4
Gunung Ciremay △ Indonesia 6°53S 108°24E 235 D3
Gunung Gading △ Malaysia 2°2N 109°52E 235 B3
Gunung Leuser △ Indonesia 3°39N 97°32E 234 B1
Gunung Mulu △ Malaysia 4°6N 114°53E 235 B4
Gunung Palung △ Indonesia 1°9S 110°13E 235 C4
Gunungapi Indonesia 6°45S 126°30E 231 F7
Gunungsitoli Indonesia 1°15N 97°30E 234 B1
Gunungtua Indonesia 1°30N 99°37E 234 B1
Gunupur India 19°5N 83°50E 244 E6
Günz → Germany 48°27N 10°16E 179 G6
Gunza Angola 10°50S 13°50E 265 E2
Günzburg Germany 48°26N 10°17E 179 G6
Gunzenhausen Germany 49°7N 10°44E 179 F6
Guo He → China 32°59N 117°10E 227 H9
Guomao China 39°54N 116°26E 114 B2
Guoyang China 33°32N 116°12E 226 H9
Gupis Pakistan 36°15N 73°20E 243 A5
Gura Humorului Romania 47°35N 25°53E 183 C10
Gura-Teghii Romania 45°30N 26°25E 183 E11
Gurabo Puerto Rico 18°16N 65°58W 321 b
Gurag Ethiopia 8°20N 38°20E 257 F4
Gurahonţ Romania 46°16N 22°21E 182 D7
Gurbantünggüt Shamo China 45°8N 87°20E 217 C11
Gurdaspur India 32°5N 75°31E 242 C6
Gurdon U.S.A. 33°55N 93°9W 314 E8
Güre Balıkesir, Turkey 39°36N 26°54E 205 B8
Güre Uşak, Turkey 38°39N 29°10E 205 C11
Gurgaon India 28°27N 77°1E 242 E7
Gürgentepe Turkey 40°51N 37°50E 212 B7
Gurghiu, Munţii Romania 46°41N 25°15E 183 D10
Gurgueia → Brazil 6°50S 43°24W 332 C3
Gurha India 25°12N 71°39E 242 G4
Guri, Embalse de Venezuela 7°50N 62°52W 329 B5
Gurimatu Papua N. G. 6°45S 144°45E 286 D3
Gurin Nigeria 9°5N 12°54E 263 D7
Gurinhatã Brazil 19°14S 49°48W 333 E2
Gurjaani Georgia 41°43N 45°52E 191 K7
Gurk → Austria 46°35N 14°31E 180 E7
Gurkfeld = Krško Slovenia 45°57N 15°30E 199 C12
Gurkha Nepal 28°5N 84°40E 243 E11
Gurla Mandhata = Naimona'nyi Feng Nepal 30°26N 81°18E 243 D9
Gurley Australia 29°45S 149°48E 281 D4
Gurnee U.S.A. 42°22N 87°55W 311 B9
Gurnet Point U.S.A. 42°1N 70°34W 313 D14
Guro Mozam. 17°26S 32°30E 269 F3
Gürpınar İstanbul, Turkey 40°59N 28°37E 203 F12
Gürpınar Van, Turkey 38°18N 43°25E 213 C10
Gürsu Turkey 40°13N 29°11E 203 F13
Gurué Mozam. 15°25S 36°58E 269 F4
Gurueragu Ethiopia 6°23N 45°31E 267 C6
Gurun Malaysia 5°49N 100°27E 237 K3
Gürün Turkey 38°43N 37°15E 212 C7
Gurupá Brazil 1°25S 51°35W 329 D7
Gurupá, I. Grande de Brazil 1°25S 51°45W 329 D7
Gurupi Brazil 11°43S 49°4W 333 D2
Gurupi → Brazil 1°13S 46°6W 332 B2
Gurupi, Serra do Brazil 5°0S 47°50W 332 C2
Guruwe Zimbabwe 16°40S 30°42E 271 A5
Gurvan Sayhan Uul Mongolia 43°50N 104°0E 226 C3
Guryev = Atyraū Kazakhstan 47°5N 52°0E 187 E9
Guryevsk Russia 54°47N 20°38E 184 D7
Gus-Khrustalnyy Russia 55°42N 40°44E 190 C5
Gusau Nigeria 12°12N 6°40E 263 C6
Gusev Russia 54°35N 22°10E 184 D9
Gushan China 39°50N 123°35E 224 C1
Gushgy = Serhetabat Turkmenistan 35°20N 62°18E 247 C9
Gushi China 32°11N 115°41E 229 A10
Gushiago Ghana 9°55N 0°15W 263 D4
Gushikami Japan 26°7N 127°44E 288 a
Gushikawa Japan 26°21N 127°52E 288 a
Gusinje Montenegro 42°35N 19°50E 202 D3
Gusinoozersk Russia 51°16N 106°27E 215 D11
Gúspini Italy 39°32N 8°37E 200 C1
Güssing Austria 47°3N 16°20E 181 D9
Gustav Holm, Kap Greenland 66°36N 34°15W 154 D7
Gustavia St.-Martin 17°53N 62°51W 322 a
Gustavo A. Madero Mexico 19°29N 99°8W 128 B2
Gustavus U.S.A. 58°25N 135°44W 296 B1
Gustine U.S.A. 37°16N 121°0W 306 H6
Güstrow Germany 53°47N 12°10E 178 B8
Gusum Sweden 58°16N 16°30E 163 F10
Guta = Kolárovo Slovak Rep. 47°54N 18°0E 181 D10
Gütersloh Germany 51°54N 8°24E 178 D4
Gutha Australia 28°58S 115°55E 279 E2
Guthalungra Australia 19°52S 147°50E 280 B4
Guthrie Ont., Canada 44°28N 79°32W 312 B5
Guthrie Okla., U.S.A. 35°53N 97°25W 314 D6
Guthrie Tex., U.S.A. 33°37N 100°19W 314 E4
Guthrie Center U.S.A. 41°41N 94°30W 310 C2
Gutian China 26°32N 118°43E 229 D12
Gutiérrez Bolivia 19°25S 63°34W 331 D5
Guttenberg Iowa, U.S.A. 42°47N 91°6W 310 B5
Guttenberg New York, U.S.A. 132 a1
Guttentag = Dobrodzień Poland 50°45N 18°25E 185 H5
Guttstadt = Dobre Miasto Poland 53°58N 20°26E 184 E7
Gutu Zimbabwe 19°41S 31°9E 271 A5
Gutulia △ Norway 62°2N 12°11E 164 B9
Gutuyevskiy, Ostrov Russia 59°53N 30°15E 137 B1
Guwahati India 26°10N 91°45E 241 B3
Guy Fawkes River △ Australia 30°0S 152°20E 281 D5
Guy-Fayreau, Complexe Montréal, Canada 130 b2
Guyana ■ S. Amer. 5°0N 59°0W 329 C6
Guyancourt France 48°46N 2°4E 134 B1
Guyane française = French Guiana ⊠ S. Amer. 4°0N 53°0W 329 C7
Guyang China 41°0N 110°5E 226 D6
Guyenne France 44°30N 0°40E 174 D4
Guymon U.S.A. 36°41N 101°29W 314 C4
Guyotville = Aïn Benian Algeria 36°48N 2°55E 261 A5
Guyra Australia 30°15S 151°40E 281 E5
Guyton U.S.A. 32°20N 81°24W 316 C8
Guyuan Hebei, China 41°37N 115°40E 226 D8
Guyuan Ningxia Huizu, China 36°0N 106°20E 226 F4
Guzar Uzbekistan 38°36N 66°15E 217 E7
Güzelbağ Turkey 36°44N 31°53E 250 B2
Güzelbahçe Turkey 38°21N 26°54E 205 C8
Güzeloluk Turkey 36°47N 34°4E 250 B5
Güzelsu Turkey 36°53N 31°51E 250 B2
Güzelyurt = Morphou Cyprus 35°12N 32°59E 207 E8
Guzhang China 28°42N 109°58E 228 C7
Guzhen China 33°22N 117°18E 227 H9
Guzmán, L. de Mexico 31°20N 107°30W 318 A3
Gvardeysk Russia 54°39N 21°5E 184 D8
Gvardeyskoye Ukraine 45°7N 34°1E 189 K8
Gvarv Norway 59°23N 9°9E 164 E6
Gwa Burma 17°36N 94°34E 241 G5
Gwaai Zimbabwe 19°15S 27°45E 269 F2
Gwaai → Zimbabwe 17°59S 26°52E 269 F2
Gwabegar Australia 30°37S 148°59E 283 A8
Gwadabawa Nigeria 13°28N 5°15E 263 C6
Gwādar Pakistan 25°10N 62°18E 240 D1
Gwagwada Nigeria 10°15N 7°15E 263 C6
Gwaii Haanas △ Canada 52°21N 131°26W 296 C2
Gwalior India 26°12N 78°10E 242 F8
Gwanak S. Korea 37°29N 126°57E 137 C1
Gwanaksan S. Korea 37°27N 126°58E 137 C1
Gwanara Nigeria 8°55N 3°9E 263 D5
Gwanda Zimbabwe 20°55S 29°0E 269 G2
Gwandu Nigeria 12°30N 4°41E 263 C5
Gwane Dem. Rep. of the Congo 4°45N 25°48E 268 B2
Gwang-yang S. Korea 34°58N 127°35E 224 E3
Gwangju S. Korea 35°9N 126°54E 224 E3
Gwangju □ S. Korea 35°10N 126°45E 224 E3
Gwanju = Gwangju S. Korea 35°9N 126°54E 224 E3
Gwaram Nigeria 10°15N 10°25E 263 C7
Gwarzo Nigeria 12°20N 8°55E 263 C6
Gwasero Nigeria 9°29N 3°30E 263 D5
Gwda → Poland 53°3N 16°44E 185 E3
Gweebarra B. Ireland 54°51N 8°23W 166 B3
Gweedore Ireland 55°3N 8°13W 166 A3
Gweru Zimbabwe 19°28S 29°45E 269 F2
Gwi Nigeria 9°0N 7°10E 263 D6
Gwinn U.S.A. 46°19N 87°27W 308 B10
Gwio Kura Nigeria 12°40N 11°2E 263 C7
Gwoza Nigeria 11°5N 13°40E 263 C7
Gwydir → Australia 29°27S 149°48E 281 D4
Gwynedd □ U.K. 52°52N 4°10W 168 E3
Gyál Hungary 47°23N 19°13E 117 B3
Gyáli-patak → Hungary 47°23N 19°7E 117 B2
Gyandzha = Gäncä Azerbaijan 40°45N 46°20E 191 K8
Gyangzê China 29°5N 89°47E 218 F6
Gyaring Hu China 34°50N 97°40E 218 E8
Gydanskiy Poluostrov Russia 70°0N 78°0E 214 C8
Gyeonggi-do □ S. Korea 36°37N 127°15E 224 D3
Gyeongju S. Korea 35°51N 129°14E 224 E4
Gyeongsan S. Korea 35°49N 128°44E 224 E4
Gyeongsangbuk-do □ S. Korea 36°20N 128°45E 224 D4
Gyeongsangnam-do □ S. Korea 35°15N 128°15E 224 E4
Gyeryongsan △ S. Korea 36°20N 127°15E 224 D3
Gyl Norway 62°57N 8°7E 164 B5
Gyldenløve Fjord Greenland 64°15N 40°30W 154 E6
Gympie Australia 26°11S 152°38E 281 D5
Gyobingauk Burma 18°13N 95°39E 241 F5
Gyōda Japan 36°10N 139°30E 223 A11
Gyodongdo S. Korea 37°47N 126°15E 224 D3
Gyomaendrőd Hungary 46°56N 20°50E 182 D5
Gyöngyös Hungary 47°48N 19°56E 182 C4
Győr Hungary 47°41N 17°40E 182 C2
Győr-Moson-Sopron □ Hungary 47°40N 17°20E 182 C2
Gypsum Pt. Canada 61°53N 114°35W 296 A6
Gypsumville Canada 51°45N 98°40W 297 C9
Gyueshevo Bulgaria 42°14N 22°28E 202 D6
Gyula Hungary 46°38N 21°17E 182 D6
Gyumri Armenia 40°47N 43°50E 191 K6
Gyzylarbat = Serdar Turkmenistan 39°4N 56°23E 247 B8
Gyzyletrek = Etrek Turkmenistan 37°36N 54°46E 247 B7
Gzhatsk = Gagarin Russia 55°38N 35°0E 188 E8
Gzira Malta 35°54N 14°29E 206 F7

H

H. Neely Henry L. U.S.A. 33°55N 86°2W 316 B3
Ha 'Arava → Israel 30°50N 35°20E 251 H6
Ha Coi Vietnam 21°26N 107°46E 228 G6
Ha Dong Vietnam 20°58N 105°46E 228 G5
Ha Giang Vietnam 22°50N 104°59E 228 F5
Ha Karmel △ Israel 32°45N 35°5E 250 F6
Ha Long = Hong Gai Vietnam 20°57N 107°5E 228 G6
Ha Long, Vinh Vietnam 20°56N 107°3E 236 B6
Ha Tien Vietnam 10°23N 104°29E 237 G5
Ha Tinh Vietnam 18°20N 105°54E 236 C5
Ha Trung Vietnam 19°58N 105°50E 236 C5
Haaga Finland 60°13N 24°53E 121 B2
Haakon VII Topp Norway 71°0N 8°20W 154 C10
Haaksbergen Neths. 52°9N 6°45E 170 B6
Ha'ano Tonga 19°41S 174°18W 287 P13
Ha'apai Group Tonga 19°47S 174°27W 287 P13
Haapiti Moorea 17°34S 149°52W 289 e
Haapsalu Estonia 58°56N 23°30E 188 C2
Haar Germany 48°6N 11°43E 131 B3
Haarby Denmark 55°13N 10°7E 163 J4
Haarlem Neths. 52°23N 4°39E 170 B4
Haas-Lilienthal House San Francisco, U.S.A. 136 b1
Haast N.Z. 43°51S 169°1E 285 D4
Haast → N.Z. 43°50S 169°2E 285 D4
Haast Pass N.Z. 44°6S 169°21E 285 E4
Haasts Bluff Australia 23°22S 132°0E 278 D5
Haasts Bluff ⚙ Australia 23°39S 130°34E 278 D5
Hab → Pakistan 24°53N 66°41E 242 G3
Hab Nadi Chauki Pakistan 25°0N 66°50E 242 G2
Habahe China 48°3N 86°23E 217 C11
Ḩabarūt Yemen 17°18N 52°44E 249 C6
Habaswein Kenya 1°2N 39°30E 268 B4
Ḩabawnah, W. → Si. Arabia 17°57N 44°58E 248 C4
Habay Alta., Canada 58°50N 118°44W 296 B5
Habay Manila, Phil. 14°27N 120°56E 127 C1
Ḩabbān Yemen 14°21N 47°5E 248 D4
Ḩabbānīyah Iraq 33°17N 43°29E 213 F10
Ḩabbānīyah, Hawr al Iraq 33°17N 43°29E 213 F10
Habelschwerdt = Bystrzyca Kłodzka Poland 50°19N 16°39E 185 H3
Habibas, Îles Algeria 35°44N 1°8W 197 K3
Habichtswald ⌓ Germany 51°15N 9°15E 178 D5
Habiganj Bangla. 24°24N 91°30E 241 C3
Habirag China 42°17N 115°42E 226 C8
Habisa Sudan 15°38N 31°18E 266 A3
Habo Sweden 57°55N 14°6E 163 G8
Haboro Japan 44°22N 141°42E 220 B10
Ḩabshān U.A.E. 23°50N 53°37E 247 F7
Hachenburg Germany 50°40N 7°49E 178 E3
Hachi India 27°48N 94°2E 241 B5
Hachijō-Jima Japan 33°5N 139°45E 223 D11
Hachiman Japan 35°45N 136°57E 223 B8
Hachinohe Japan 40°30N 141°29E 220 D10
Hachiōji Japan 35°40N 139°20E 223 B11
Hacı Zeynalabdin Azerbaijan 40°37N 49°33E 191 K9
Hacıbektaş Turkey 38°56N 34°33E 212 C6
Hacılar Turkey 38°38N 35°26E 212 C6
Hack, Mt. Australia 30°45S 138°55E 282 A3
Hackås Sweden 62°56N 14°30E 162 B8
Hackbridge U.K. 51°23N 0°9W 125 B3
Hackensack U.S.A. 40°52N 74°4W 132 A1
Hackensack → U.S.A. 40°42N 74°7W 132 B1
Hackettstown U.S.A. 40°51N 74°50W 313 F10
Hackney □ U.K. 51°33N 0°3W 125 A3
Hackney Wick U.K. 51°32N 0°1W 125 A3
Håckrenmagasinet Sweden 63°15N 13°30E 162 C7
Haco Angola 10°15S 15°44E 265 E3
Hadali Pakistan 32°16N 72°11E 242 C5
Hadano Japan 35°22N 139°14E 223 B11
Hadarba, Ras Sudan 22°4N 36°51E 256 C4
Hadarom □ Israel 31°0N 35°0E 251 H6
Ḩadbaram Oman 17°27N 55°15E 249 C6
Ḩadd, Ra's al Oman 22°35N 59°50E 249 B7
Ḩaddā Si. Arabia 21°27N 39°34E 248 B2
Haddington U.K. 55°57N 2°47W 167 F6
Haddock U.S.A. 33°2N 83°26W 316 B6
Haddummati Atoll Maldives 2°0N 73°30E 272 d
Hadejia Nigeria 12°30N 10°5E 263 C7
Hadejia → Nigeria 12°50N 10°51E 263 C7
Hadera Israel 32°27N 34°55E 251 F5
Hadersleben = Haderslev Denmark 55°15N 9°30E 163 J3
Haderslev Denmark 55°15N 9°30E 163 J3
Hadgaon India 19°30N 77°40E 244 E3
Hadhramaut = Haḑramawt Yemen 15°30N 49°30E 249 D5
Hadībоh Yemen 12°39N 54°2E 249 D6
Hadilik China 37°56N 86°6E 217 E11
Hadım Turkey 36°58N 32°26E 250 B3
Hadithah Si. Arabia 31°27N 37°9E 251 G8
Hadjadj, O. el → Algeria 28°18N 5°20E 261 C6
Hadjeb el Aïoun Tunisia 35°21N 9°32E 258 A1
Hadjer Kamaran Chad 12°41N 21°46E 259 F4
Hadjer-Lamis □ Chad 12°55N 16°0E 259 F3
Hadjer Mornou Chad 17°12N 23°8E 259 E4
Hadlaskar Norway 60°15N 7°9E 164 D4
Hadley B. Canada 72°31N 108°12W 294 C10
Hadong S. Korea 35°5N 127°44E 224 E3
Hadr, Warrâq el Egypt 30°5N 31°12E 117 A2
Haḑramawt Yemen 15°30N 49°30E 249 D5
Ḩaḑramawt, W. → Yemen 15°10N 51°8E 249 D5
Ḩadrānīyah Iraq 35°38N 43°14E 246 C4
Hadrian's Wall U.K. 55°0N 2°30W 168 B5
Hadsten Denmark 56°19N 10°3E 163 H4
Hadsund Denmark 56°44N 10°8E 163 H4
Hadyach Ukraine 50°21N 34°0E 189 G8
Hae, Ko Thailand 7°44N 98°22E 237 a
Hægeland Norway 58°22N 7°45E 164 F4
Haeinsa S. Korea 35°45N 128°10E 224 E4
Haeju N. Korea 38°3N 125°45E 224 C2
Haeju-man N. Korea 37°54N 125°45E 224 D2
Hä'ena U.S.A. 22°14N 159°34W 302 A2
Haenam S. Korea 34°34N 126°35E 224 E3
Haenertsburg S. Africa 24°0S 29°50E 271 B4
Haerhpin = Harbin China 45°48N 126°40E 227 B14
Hafar al Bāţin Si. Arabia 28°32N 45°52E 246 D5
Hafik Turkey 39°51N 37°23E 212 C7
Ḩafīrat al 'Aydā Si. Arabia 26°26N 39°12E 246 E3
Ḩafit Oman 23°59N 55°49E 247 F7
Hafizabad Pakistan 32°5N 73°40E 242 C5
Haflong India 25°10N 93°5E 241 C4
Hafnarfjörður Iceland 64°4N 21°57W 155 C5
Hafnir Iceland 63°56N 22°41W 155 D4
Hafslo Norway 61°19N 7°10E 164 C4
Haft Gel Iran 31°30N 49°32E 247 D6
Haga Sweden 59°21N 18°1E 139 A2
Hagalil Israel 32°53N 35°18E 250 F6
Hagari → India 15°40N 77°0E 245 G3
Hagby Sweden 56°34N 16°11E 163 H10
Hagemeister I. U.S.A. 58°39N 160°54W 303 G7
Hagen Germany 51°21N 7°27E 178 D3
Hagenbrunn Austria 48°19N 16°27E 142 A2
Hagenow Germany 53°26N 11°12E 178 B7
Hagere Hiywet Ethiopia 8°59N 37°51E 266 C4
Hagerman U.S.A. 33°7N 104°20W 305 K11
Hagerman Fossil Beds ⌓ U.S.A. 42°48N 114°57W 304 E6
Hägersten Sweden 59°18N 17°59E 139 B1
Hagerstown Ind., U.S.A. 39°55N 85°10W 311 E11
Hagerstown Md., U.S.A. 39°39N 77°43W 309 F15
Hagersville Canada 42°58N 80°3W 312 D4
Hagetmau France 43°39N 0°37W 174 E3
Hagfors Sweden 60°3N 13°45E 162 D7
Häggvik Sweden 59°26N 17°56E 139 A1
Hagi Iceland 65°28N 23°25W 155 B3
Hagi Japan 34°30N 131°22E 222 C3
Hagolan Syria 33°0N 35°45E 250 F6
Hagondange France 49°16N 6°11E 173 C13
Hágöngulón Iceland 64°35N 18°8W 155 C8
Hagonoy Bulacan, Phil. 14°50N 120°44E 232 D3
Hagonoy Manila, Phil. 14°31N 121°3E 127 B2
Hags Hd. Ireland 52°57N 9°28W 166 D2
Hague, C. de la France 49°44N 1°56W 172 C5
Hague, The = 's-Gravenhage Neths. 52°7N 4°17E 170 B4
Hague Park Canada 43°45N 79°14W 141 A3
Haguenau France 48°49N 7°47E 173 D14
Hagunía W. Sahara 27°26N 12°24W 260 C2
Hahira U.S.A. 30°59N 83°22W 316 E6
Hai Duong Vietnam 20°56N 106°19E 228 G6
Hai'an Guangdong, China 20°18N 110°11E 229 G8
Hai'an Jiangsu, China 32°37N 120°27E 229 A13
Haian Shanmo Taiwan 23°25N 121°25E 225 C3
Haicheng China 40°50N 122°45E 224 B1
Haidar Khel Afghan. 33°58N 68°38E 242 C3
Haidarâbâd = Hyderabad India 17°22N 78°29E 244 F4
Haidargarh India 26°37N 81°22E 243 F9
Haidari = Chaidari Greece 38°2N 23°38E 112 A1
Haidarpur India 28°43N 77°8E 120 A1
Haidhausen Germany 48°7N 11°36E 131 B2
Haidian China 39°59N 116°16E 114 B1
Haifa = Hefa Israel 32°46N 35°0E 250 F6
Haifeng China 22°58N 115°10E 229 F10
Haiger Germany 50°43N 8°12E 178 E4
Haight-Ashbury U.S.A. 37°46N 122°26W 136 B2
Haikou China 20°1N 110°16E 236 B8
Haiku-Pauwela U.S.A. 20°56N 156°19W 302 C5
Ḩā'īl Si. Arabia 27°28N 41°45E 246 E4
Ḩā'īl □ Si. Arabia 26°40N 41°40E 246 E4
Hailakandi India 24°42N 92°34E 241 C4
Hailar China 49°10N 119°38E 219 B12
Hailey U.S.A. 43°31N 114°19W 304 E6
Haileybury Canada 47°30N 79°38W 298 C4
Hailin China 44°37N 129°30E 227 B15
Hailing Dao China 21°35N 111°47E 229 G8
Hailun China 47°28N 126°50E 219 B14
Hailuoto Finland 65°3N 24°45E 160 D21
Haimen Guangdong, China 23°15N 116°38E 229 F11
Haimen Jiangsu, China 31°52N 121°10E 229 B13
Hainan □ China 19°0N 109°30E 236 C7
Hainan Dao China 19°0N 109°30E 236 C7
Hainan Str. = Qiongzhou Haixia China 20°10N 110°15E 236 B8
Hainault U.K. 51°36N 0°6E 125 A4
Hainaut □ Belgium 50°30N 4°0E 170 D4
Hainburg Austria 48°9N 16°56E 181 C9
Haines Alaska, U.S.A. 59°14N 135°26W 296 B1
Haines Oreg., U.S.A. 44°55N 117°56W 304 D5
Haines City U.S.A. 28°7N 81°38W 317 G8
Haines Junction Canada 60°45N 137°30W 296 A1
Hainfeld Austria 48°3N 15°48E 180 C8
Haining China 30°28N 120°40E 229 B13
Haiphong Vietnam 20°47N 106°41E 228 G6
Haitan Dao China 25°30N 119°45E 229 E12
Haiti ■ W. Indies 19°0N 72°30W 321 C5
Haiya Sudan 18°20N 36°21E 256 D4
Haiyan Qinghai, China 36°53N 100°59E 218 D9
Haiyan Zhejiang, China 30°28N 120°58E 229 B13
Haiyang China 36°47N 121°9E 227 F11
Haiyang Dao China 39°2N 123°10E 224 C1
Haiyuan Guangxi Zhuangzu, China 22°8N 107°35E 228 F6
Haiyuan Ningxia Huizu, China 36°35N 105°52E 226 F3
Haizhou Guangdong, China 23°5N 113°18E 121 B2
Haizhou Jiangsu, China 34°37N 119°7E 227 G10
Haizhou Wan China 34°50N 119°20E 227 G10
Haizhu Guangchang China 23°6N 113°14E 121 B2
Haj Ali Qoli, Kavīr Iran 35°55N 54°50E 247 C7
Hajar Bangar Sudan 10°40N 22°45E 259 F4
Hajdú-Bihar □ Hungary 47°30N 21°30E 182 C6
Hajdúböszörmény Hungary 47°40N 21°30E 182 C6
Hajdúdorog Hungary 47°48N 21°30E 182 C6

Hajdúhadház Hungary 47°40N 21°40E 182 C6
Hajdúnánás Hungary 47°50N 21°26E 182 C6
Hajdúsámson Hungary 47°37N 21°42E 182 C6
Hajdúszoboszló Hungary 47°27N 21°22E 182 C6
Haji Ibrahim Iraq 36°40N 44°30E 213 D11
Ḩājjābād Iran 33°37N 60°0E 247 C9
Hajiganj Bangla. 23°15N 90°50E 241 D3
Hajipur India 25°45N 85°13E 243 G11
Ḩajjah Yemen 15°42N 43°36E 248 D3
Ḩājjīābād Iran 28°19N 55°55E 247 D7
Ḩājjīābād-e Zarrīn Iran 33°9N 54°51E 247 C7
Hajnówka Poland 52°47N 23°35E 185 F10
Hajodo S. Korea 34°17N 126°3E 224 E3
Ḩajrah Si. Arabia 20°14N 41°3E 248 B3
Haka Burma 22°39N 93°37E 241 D4
Hakansson, Mts. Dem. Rep. of the Congo 8°40S 25°45E 265 D5
Hakataramea N.Z. 44°43S 170°30E 285 E5
Hakkâri Turkey 37°34N 43°44E 213 D10
Hakkâri □ Turkey 37°30N 44°0E 213 D10
Hakkâri Dağları Turkey 38°2N 42°58E 213 C10
Hakken-Zan Japan 34°10N 135°54E 223 D7
Hakkōda San Japan 40°50N 141°0E 220 D10
Hakodate Japan 41°45N 140°44E 220 D10
Hakos Namibia 23°13S 16°21E 270 B2
Hakota Japan 36°5N 140°30E 223 A12
Håksberg Sweden 60°11N 15°12E 162 D9
Hakskeenpan S. Africa 26°48S 20°13E 270 C3
Haku-San Japan 36°9N 136°46E 223 A8
Haku-San △ Japan 36°15N 136°45E 223 A8
Hakuba Japan 36°42N 137°51E 223 A9
Hakui Japan 36°53N 136°47E 221 F8
Hakun Burma 26°46N 95°42E 241 B5
Hakunila Finland 60°16N 25°6E 121 B3
Hakupu Cook Is. 19°6S 169°50W 289 g
Hala Pakistan 25°43N 68°20E 240 D3
Ḩalab Syria 36°10N 37°15E 250 B8
Ḩalab □ Syria 36°10N 37°10E 250 B8
Ḩalaban Si. Arabia 23°29N 44°23E 248 B4
Halabjah Iraq 35°10N 45°58E 213 E11
Halaib Sudan 22°12N 36°30E 256 C4
Halaib Triangle Africa 22°30N 35°20E 256 C4
Halandri = Chalandri Greece 38°3N 23°48E 112 A2
Halangingie Pt. Cook Is. 19°2S 169°58W 289 g
Halasa Sudan 14°26N 30°39E 257 E3
Halásztelek Hungary 47°22N 19°0E 117 B1
Hālat 'Ammār Si. Arabia 29°10N 36°4E 246 D3
Hālawa, C. U.S.A. 21°10N 156°43W 302 B5
Hālawa Heights U.S.A. 21°23N 157°55W 302 K14
Ḩalbā Lebanon 34°34N 36°6E 250 D5
Halberstadt Germany 51°54N 11°3E 178 D7
Halcombe N.Z. 40°8S 175°30E 284 G4
Halcon, Mt. Phil. 13°16N 121°0E 232 E3
Halde Fjäll = Haltiatunturi Finland 69°17N 21°18E 160 B19
Halden Norway 59°9N 11°23E 164 E8
Haldensleben Germany 52°17N 11°24E 178 C7
Haldia Bangla. 22°1N 88°3E 243 H13
Haldwani India 29°31N 79°30E 243 E8
Hale U.S.A. 39°36N 93°20W 310 E3
Hale → Australia 24°56S 135°53E 280 C2
Haleakalā △ U.S.A. 20°40N 156°15W 302 C5
Hale'iwa U.S.A. 21°36N 158°6W 302 J13
Halesowen U.K. 52°27N 2°3W 169 E5
Halesworth U.K. 52°20N 1°31E 169 E9
Haleyville U.S.A. 34°14N 87°37W 315 D11
Half Assini Ghana 5°1N 2°50W 262 D4
Half Dome U.S.A. 37°44N 119°32W 306 H7
Halfa al Jadidah Sudan 15°20N 35°36E 266 A4
Halfeti Turkey 37°15N 37°52E 212 D7
Halfmoon Bay N.Z. 46°50S 168°5E 285 G3
Halfway → Canada 56°12N 121°32W 296 B4
Halfway Tree Jamaica 18°0N 76°48W 320 a
Halia India 24°50N 82°19E 243 G10
Haliburton Canada 45°3N 78°30W 312 A6
Haliç Turkey 41°1N 28°57E 122 B1
Halifax Queens., Australia 18°32S 146°22E 280 B4
Halifax N.S., Canada 44°38N 63°35W 299 D7
Halifax W. Yorks., U.K. 53°43N 1°52W 168 D6
Halifax Pa., U.S.A. 40°25N 76°55W 312 F8
Halifax B. Australia 18°50S 147°0E 280 B4
Halifax Harbour Grenada 12°6N 61°45W 323 q
Halifax I. Namibia 26°38S 15°4E 270 C2
Halik Shan China 42°20N 81°22E 217 D10
Halīl → Iran 27°40N 58°30E 247 E8
Halim Perdana Kusuma Int. ✕ (HLP) Indonesia 6°16S 106°53E 122 B2
Halimun △ Indonesia 6°42S 106°26E 234 D3
Halkett, C. U.S.A. 70°48N 152°11W 303 A9
Halki = Chalki Greece 36°17N 27°35E 205 E9
Halkida = Chalkida Greece 38°27N 23°42E 204 C5
Halkidiki = Chalkidiki □ Greece 40°25N 23°20E 202 F7
Halkirk U.K. 58°30N 3°29W 167 C5
Hall Beach Canada 68°46N 81°12W 295 D15
Hall I. U.S.A. 60°40N 173°6W 303 F4
Hall in Tirol Austria 47°17N 11°30E 180 D4
Hall Pen. Canada 63°30N 66°0W 295 E18
Hall Pt. Australia 15°40S 124°23E 278 C3
Hallabro Sweden 56°22N 15°5E 163 H9
Halland Sweden 57°8N 12°47E 161 H15
Hallandale Beach U.S.A. 25°58N 80°8W 317 K9
Hallands län □ Sweden 57°0N 12°40E 163 H6
Hallands Väderö Sweden 56°27N 12°34E 163 H6
Hallandsås Sweden 56°22N 13°0E 163 H7
Hallāniyat, Ghubbat al Oman 17°40N 55°45E 249 C6
Hallāniyat, Jazā'ir al Oman 17°30N 55°58E 249 C6
Hallasan S. Korea 33°22N 126°32E 224 a
Hallasan △ S. Korea 33°20N 126°30E 224 a
Hällbybrunn Sweden 59°24N 16°25E 162 E10
Halle Belgium 50°44N 4°13E 116 B1
Halle Nordrhein-Westfalen, Germany 52°3N 8°22E 178 C4
Halle Sachsen-Anhalt, Germany 51°30N 11°56E 178 D7
Hällefors Sweden 59°47N 14°31E 162 E8
Hälleforsnäs Sweden 59°10N 16°30E 162 E10
Hallein Austria 47°40N 13°5E 180 D6
Hällekis Sweden 58°38N 13°27E 163 F7
Hallen Sweden 63°11N 14°4E 162 A8
Hallett Australia 33°25S 138°55E 282 B3
Hallettsville U.S.A. 29°27N 96°57W 314 G6
Halley Antarctica 75°35S 26°39W 151 D1
Hallia → India 16°55N 79°20E 244 F4
Hallim S. Korea 33°24N 126°15E 224 a
Hallingby Norway 60°7N 10°10E 164 D7
Hallingdal Norway 60°40N 9°8E 164 D6
Hallingdalselva → Norway 60°23N 9°35E 164 D6
Hallingskarvet Norway 60°36N 7°47E 164 D4
Hallingskarvet △ Norway 60°37N 7°45E 164 D4
Hallingskeid Norway 60°40N 7°17E 164 D4
Hallock U.S.A. 48°47N 96°57W 308 A5
Hallormsstaður Iceland 65°6N 14°45W 155 B12
Halls Creek Australia 18°16S 127°38E 278 C4
Halls Gap Australia 37°8S 142°34E 281 F3
Halls Lake Canada 45°7N 78°45W 312 A6
Hallsberg Sweden 59°5N 15°7E 162 E9
Hallstahammar Sweden 59°38N 16°15E 162 E10
Hallstatt Austria 47°33N 13°38E 180 D6
Hallstavik Sweden 60°5N 18°37E 162 D12
Hallstead U.S.A. 41°58N 75°45W 313 E9
Hallyeo △ S. Korea 34°45N 128°25E 224 E4
Halmahera Indonesia 0°40N 128°0E 231 D7
Halmeu Romania 47°57N 23°2E 182 C8
Halmstad Sweden 56°41N 12°52E 163 H6
Halq el Oued Tunisia 36°53N 10°18E 258 A2
Hals Denmark 57°0N 10°18E 163 H4
Halsa Norway 63°3N 8°14E 164 A5
Halsafjorden Norway 63°5N 8°10E 164 A5
Hälsingborg = Helsingborg Sweden 56°3N 12°42E 163 H6
Hälsingland Sweden 61°40N 16°5E 162 C10
Halstead U.K. 51°57N 0°40E 169 F8
Haltdalen Norway 62°56N 11°8E 164 B8
Haltern Germany 51°44N 7°11E 178 D3
Haltiala Finland 60°16N 24°57E 121 B2
Haltiatunturi Finland 69°17N 21°18E 160 B19
Haltiavuori Finland 60°16N 24°56E 121 B2
Halton □ U.K. 53°22N 2°45W 168 D5
Haltwhistle U.K. 54°58N 2°26W 168 C5
Ḩālūl Qatar 25°40N 52°40E 247 E7
Halvad India 23°1N 71°11E 242 H4
Ḩalvān Iran 33°57N 56°15E 247 C8
Halve Dag, Pt. Curaçao 12°14N 69°7W 322 g
Ham Chad 10°1N 15°35E 259 F3
Ham Somme, France 49°45N 3°4E 173 C10
Ham London, U.K. 51°25N 0°18W 125 B2
Hamab Namibia 28°7S 19°16E 270 C2
Hamad Sudan 15°20N 33°32E 257 D3
Hamada Japan 34°56N 132°4E 222 C4
Hamadān Iran 34°52N 48°32E 213 E13
Hamadān □ Iran 35°0N 49°0E 247 C6
Hamadia Algeria 35°28N 1°57E 261 A5
Ḩamāh Syria 35°5N 36°40E 250 C7
Ḩamāh □ Syria 35°10N 37°0E 250 C8
Hamakita Japan 34°45N 137°47E 223 C9
Hamamatsu Japan 34°45N 137°45E 223 C9
Haman S. Korea 35°14N 128°28E 224 E4
Hamar Norway 60°48N 11°7E 164 D8
Hamâta, Gebel Egypt 24°17N 35°0E 246 E2
Hamatonbetsu Japan 45°10N 142°20E 220 B11
Hambantota Sri Lanka 6°10N 81°10E 245 L5
Hamber △ Canada 52°20N 118°0W 296 C5
Hamburg Hamburg, Germany 53°33N 9°59E 178 B5
Hamburg Ark., U.S.A. 33°14N 91°48W 314 E9
Hamburg N.Y., U.S.A. 42°43N 78°50W 312 D6
Hamburg Pa., U.S.A. 40°33N 75°59W 313 F9
Hamburg □ Germany 53°30N 10°0E 178 B5
Hamburg Fuhlsbüttel ✕ (HAM) Germany 53°35N 9°59E 178 B5
Ḩamḑ, W. al → Si. Arabia 24°55N 36°20E 246 E3
Ḩamdah Si. Arabia 19°2N 43°36E 248 C3
Ḩamdānah Si. Arabia 19°59N 40°34E 248 C3
Hamden U.S.A. 41°23N 72°54W 313 E12
Hamdibey Turkey 39°50N 27°15E 205 B9
Häme Finland 61°38N 25°10E 160 F21
Hämeenkylä Finland 60°16N 24°48E 121 B1
Hämeenlinna Finland 61°0N 24°28E 188 B3
Hamélé Ghana 10°56N 2°45W 262 C4
Hamelin Pool Australia 26°22S 114°20E 279 E1
Hameln Germany 52°6N 9°21E 178 C5
Hamerkaz □ Israel 32°15N 34°55E 251 F5
Hamero Hadad Ethiopia 7°27N 42°14E 267 C5
Hamersley Ra. Australia 22°0S 117°45E 278 D2
Hamgyŏng-sanmaek N. Korea 41°35N 129°15E 224 B4
Hamgyŏngbuk-do □ N. Korea 41°50N 129°25E 224 B4
Hamgyŏngnam-do □ N. Korea 40°0N 127°30E 224 C3
Hamhŭng N. Korea 39°54N 127°30E 224 C3
Hamhŭng-man N. Korea 39°48N 127°37E 224 C3
Hami China 42°55N 93°25E 218 C7
Hamilton = Churchill → Canada 53°19N 60°10W 299 B7
Hamilton Vic., Australia 37°45S 142°2E 282 D5
Hamilton Bermuda 32°17N 64°47W 153 a
Hamilton Ont., Canada 43°15N 79°50W 312 C5
Hamilton N.Z. 37°47S 175°19E 284 D4
Hamilton S. Lanarks., U.K. 55°46N 4°2W 167 F4
Hamilton Ala., U.S.A. 34°9N 87°59W 315 D11
Hamilton Alaska, U.S.A. 62°54N 163°53W 303 E7
Hamilton Ga., U.S.A. 32°45N 84°53W 316 C5
Hamilton Ill., U.S.A. 40°24N 91°21W 310 D5
Hamilton Ind., U.S.A. 41°33N 84°56W 311 C12
Hamilton Mo., U.S.A. 39°45N 94°0W 310 E2
Hamilton Mont., U.S.A. 46°15N 114°10W 304 C6
Hamilton N.Y., U.S.A. 42°50N 75°33W 313 D9
Hamilton Ohio, U.S.A. 39°24N 84°34W 311 E12
Hamilton Tex., U.S.A. 31°42N 98°7W 314 F5
Hamilton → Queens., Australia 23°30S 139°47E 280 C2
Hamilton → S. Austral., Australia 26°40S 135°19E 281 D2
Hamilton City U.S.A. 39°45N 122°1W 306 F4
Hamilton I. Australia 20°21S 148°56E 280 b
Hamilton Inlet Canada 54°0N 57°30W 299 B8
Hamilton Mt. U.S.A. 43°25N 74°22W 313 C10
Hamina Finland 60°34N 27°12E 188 B4
Hamirpur H.P., India 31°41N 76°31E 242 D7
Hamirpur Ut. P., India 25°57N 80°9E 243 G9
Hamitabat Turkey 41°30N 27°17E 203 E11
Hamju N. Korea 39°51N 127°26E 224 C3
Hamlet U.S.A. 34°53N 79°42W 315 D15
Hamley Bridge Australia 34°17S 138°35E 282 C3
Hamlin = Hameln Germany 52°6N 9°21E 178 C5
Hamlin N.Y., U.S.A. 43°17N 77°55W 312 C7
Hamlin Tex., U.S.A. 32°53N 100°8W 314 E4
Hamm Germany 51°40N 7°50E 178 D3
Ḩammām al ʻAlī Iraq 36°9N 43°15E 213 D10
Hammam Bouhadjar Algeria 35°23N 0°58W 261 A4
Hammamet Tunisia 36°24N 10°38E 258 A2
Hammamet, G. de Tunisia 36°10N 10°48E 258 A2
Ḩammār, Hawr al Iraq 30°50N 47°10E 246 D5
Hammarby Sweden 59°17N 18°5E 139 B2
Hammarstrand Sweden 63°7N 16°20E 162 A10
Hamme Belgium 50°55N 4°17E 116 A1
Hammelburg Germany 50°6N 9°53E 179 E5
Hammeren Denmark 55°18N 14°47E 163 J8
Hammerfest Norway 70°39N 23°41E 160 A20
Hammersmith U.K. 51°29N 0°14W 125 B2
Hammerstein = Czarne Poland 53°42N 16°58E 184 E3
Hammerum Denmark 56°8N 9°3E 163 H3
Hamminkeln Germany 51°43N 6°35E 178 D2
Hammond Ind., U.S.A. 41°38N 87°30W 311 C9
Hammond La., U.S.A. 30°30N 90°28W 315 F9
Hammond N.Y., U.S.A. 44°27N 75°42W 313 B9
Hammondsport U.S.A. 42°25N 77°13W 312 D7
Hammonton U.S.A. 39°39N 74°48W 309 F16
Hamoyet, Jebel Sudan 17°33N 38°2E 256 D4
Hampden N.Z. 45°18S 170°50E 285 F5
Hampshire □ U.K. 51°7N 1°23W 169 F6
Hampshire Downs U.K. 51°15N 1°10W 169 F6
Hampstead Qué., Canada 45°28N 73°37W 130 E2
Hampstead Dominica 15°36N 61°23W 323 k
Hampstead London, U.K. 51°33N 0°10W 125 A2
Hampstead Garden Suburb U.K. 51°34N 0°11W 125 A2
Hampstead Heath U.K. 51°33N 0°10W 125 A2
Hampton N.B., Canada 45°32N 65°51W 299 C6
Hampton Ont., Canada 43°58N 78°45W 312 C6
Hampton London, U.K. 51°24N 0°21W 125 B1
Hampton Ark., U.S.A. 33°32N 92°28W 314 E8
Hampton Ga., U.S.A. 33°23N 84°17W 316 B5
Hampton Iowa, U.S.A. 42°45N 93°13W 310 B3
Hampton N.H., U.S.A. 42°57N 70°50W 313 D14
Hampton S.C., U.S.A. 32°52N 81°7W 316 B8
Hampton Va., U.S.A. 37°2N 76°21W 309 G15
Hampton Bays U.S.A. 40°53N 72°30W 313 F12
Hampton Court Palace U.K. 51°24N 0°20W 125 B1
Hampton Springs U.S.A. 30°5N 83°40W 316 E6
Hampton Tableland Australia 32°0S 127°0E 279 F4
Hampton Wick U.K. 51°24N 0°18W 125 B2
Hampyeong S. Korea 35°3N 126°31E 224 E3
Hampyeonggum S. Korea 35°6N 126°23E 224 E3
Hamrā' Baghdād, Iraq 33°18N 44°18E 113 B1
Hamra Gävleborg, Sweden 61°39N 14°59E 162 C8
Hamrat → Chad 12°52N 21°15E 259 F4
Ḩamrā, Al Ḩamādah al Libya 29°30N 12°57E 258 C2
Hamrat esh Sheykh Sudan 14°38N 27°55E 257 E2
Ḩamrīn, Jabal Iraq 34°30N 44°30E 213 E11
Hamrun Malta 35°53N 14°29E 206 F8
Hamtik Phil. 10°42N 121°59E 233 F3
Hamur Turkey 39°37N 43°3E 213 C10
Hamyang S. Korea 35°32N 127°42E 224 E3
Hamzalar Turkey 37°7N 32°33E 250 A3
Han i Hotit Albania 42°19N 19°27E 202 D3
Han Jiang → China 23°25N 116°40E 229 F11
Han Shui → China 30°34N 114°17E 229 B10
Hāna U.S.A. 20°45N 155°59W 302 C6
Hanahan U.S.A. 32°55N 80°0W 316 C10
Hanak Si. Arabia 25°32N 37°0E 246 E3
Hanak Turkey 41°14N 42°50E 213 B10
Hanala Finland 60°20N 25°4E 121 A3
Hanalei U.S.A. 22°12N 159°30W 302 A2
Hanamaki Japan 39°23N 141°7E 220 E10
Hanamaulu U.S.A. 21°59N 159°22W 302 B2
Hanang Tanzania 4°30S 35°25E 268 C4
Hanapēpē U.S.A. 21°55N 159°35W 302 B2
Hanare Iwa Iwo Jima 24°48N 141°21E 288 b
Hanau Germany 50°7N 8°56E 179 E4
Hanauma B. U.S.A. 21°15N 157°40W 302 K14
Hanbogd = Ihbulag Mongolia 43°11N 107°10E 226 C4
Hançalar Turkey 38°8N 29°24E 205 C11
Hânceşti Moldova 46°50N 28°36E 183 D13
Hancheng China 35°31N 110°25E 226 G6
Hanchuan China 30°40N 113°50E 229 B9
Hanchung = Hanzhong China 33°10N 107°1E 228 A6
Hancock Mich., U.S.A. 47°8N 88°35W 308 B9
Hancock N.Y., U.S.A. 41°57N 75°17W 313 E9
Hancock Vt., U.S.A. 43°55N 72°50W 313 C12
Handa Japan 34°53N 136°55E 223 C8
Handa I. U.K. 58°23N 5°11W 167 C3
Handan China 36°35N 114°28E 226 F8
Handeni Tanzania 5°25S 38°2E 268 D4
Handlová Slovak Rep. 48°45N 18°35E 181 C11
Handub Sudan 19°15N 37°16E 256 D4
Handwara India 34°21N 74°20E 243 B6
Haneda Japan 35°32N 139°44E 140 B3
Haneda, Tōkyō ✕ (HND) Japan 35°33N 139°46E 140 B3
Hanegev Israel 30°50N 35°0E 251 H6
Hanford U.S.A. 36°20N 119°39W 306 J7
Hanford Reach △ U.S.A. 46°40N 119°30W 304 C4
Hang Chat Thailand 18°20N 99°21E 236 C2
Hang Hau China 22°19N 114°16E 122 B2
Hanga Roa Chile 27°8S 109°26W 330 b
Hangang → S. Korea 37°50N 126°30E 227 F14
Hangayn Nuruu Mongolia 47°30N 99°0E 218 B8
Hangchou = Hangzhou China 30°18N 120°11E 229 B13
Hanger Sweden 57°6N 13°58E 163 G7
Hanggin Houqi China 40°58N 107°4E 226 D4
Hanggin Qi China 39°52N 108°50E 226 E5
Hanging Gardens Mumbai, India 130 b1
Hangkow = Wuhan China 30°31N 114°18E 229 B10
Hangku = Hangu China 39°18N 117°53E 227 E9
Hangu China 39°18N 117°53E 227 E9
Hangzhou China 30°18N 120°11E 229 B13
Hangzhou Wan China 30°15N 120°45E 229 B13
Hanh Mongolia 51°32N 100°35E 218 A9
Hanhöhiy Uul Mongolia 49°30N 94°30E 217 C12
Hanhongor Mongolia 43°55N 104°28E 226 C3
Hani Turkey 38°24N 40°23E 213 C9
Hania = Chania Greece 35°30N 24°4E 207 E5
Ḩanīdh Si. Arabia 26°35N 48°38E 247 E6
Ḩanīsh Yemen 13°45N 42°46E 248 D3
Haniska Slovak Rep. 48°37N 21°15E 181 C14
Hanjiang China 25°26N 119°6E 229 E12
Hankinson U.S.A. 46°4N 96°54W 308 B5
Hanko Finland 59°50N 22°57E 188 C2
Hankou China 30°35N 114°30E 229 B10
Hanksville U.S.A. 38°22N 110°43W 304 G8
Hanle India 32°42N 79°4E 243 C8
Hanlon Canada 43°38N 79°39W 141 B1
Hanmer Springs N.Z. 42°32S 172°50E 285 C7
Hann → Australia 17°26S 126°17E 278 C4
Hann, Mt. Australia 15°45S 126°0E 278 C4
Hanna Alta., Canada 51°40N 111°54W 296 C6
Hanna Wyo., U.S.A. 41°52N 106°34W 304 F10
Hannah B. Canada 51°40N 80°0W 298 B4
Hannibal Mo., U.S.A. 39°42N 91°22W 310 E5
Hannibal N.Y., U.S.A. 43°19N 76°35W 313 C8
Hannik Sudan 18°12N 32°20E 256 D3
Hannover Germany 52°22N 9°46E 178 C5
Hanö Sweden 56°1N 14°50E 163 H8
Hanöbukten Sweden 55°35N 14°30E 163 J8
Hanoi Vietnam 21°5N 105°55E 228 G5
Hanover = Hannover Germany 52°22N 9°46E 178 C5
Hanover Ont., Canada 44°9N 81°2W 312 B3
Hanover Northern Cape, S. Africa 31°4S 24°29E 270 D3
Hanover Ind., U.S.A. 38°43N 85°28W 311 F11
Hanover N.H., U.S.A. 43°42N 72°17W 313 C12
Hanover Ohio, U.S.A. 40°4N 82°16W 312 F2
Hanover Pa., U.S.A. 39°48N 76°59W 309 F15
Hanover, I. Chile 51°0S 74°50W 336 D2
Hanpan, C. Papua N. G. 5°0S 154°35E 286 C8
Hans Lollik I. U.S. Virgin Is. 18°24N 64°53W 321 b
Hans Meyer Ra. Papua N. G. 4°20S 152°55E 286 C7
Hansdiha India 24°36N 87°5E 243 G12
Hanshou China 28°56N 111°50E 229 C8
Hansi H.P., India 32°27N 77°50E 242 C7
Hansi Haryana, India 29°10N 75°57E 242 E6
Hanson, L. Australia 31°0S 136°15E 282 A2
Hanstholm Denmark 57°7N 8°36E 163 G2
Hantan = Handan China 36°35N 114°28E 226 F8
Hanting China 36°46N 119°12E 227 F10
Hantsavichy Belarus 52°49N 26°30E 177 B14
Hanumangarh India 29°35N 74°19E 242 E6
Hanwell U.K. 51°30N 0°20W 125 A1
Hanworth U.K. 51°26N 0°23W 125 B1
Hanyin China 32°54N 108°28E 226 H5
Hanyū Japan 36°10N 139°32E 223 A11
Hanyuan China 29°21N 102°40E 228 C4
Hanzhong China 33°10N 107°1E 228 A6
Hanzhuang China 34°33N 117°23E 227 G9
Hao French Polynesia 18°15S 140°54W 289 f
Haora India 22°34N 88°18E 124 B1
Haouach, O. → Chad 16°45N 19°35E 259 E4
Haoxue China 30°3N 112°24E 229 B9
Haparanda Sweden 65°52N 24°8E 160 D21
Hapdeok S. Korea 36°48N 126°46E 224 D3
Hapeville U.S.A. 33°39N 84°24W 113 C2
Happy U.S.A. 34°45N 101°52W 314 D4
Happy Camp U.S.A. 41°48N 123°23W 304 F2
Happy Valley China 22°16N 114°10E 122 B2
Happy Valley-Goose Bay Canada 53°15N 60°20W 299 B7
Hapsu N. Korea 41°13N 128°51E 224 B4
Hapur India 28°45N 77°45E 242 E7
Ḩaql Si. Arabia 29°10N 34°58E 251 J5
Haquira Peru 14°14S 72°12W 330 C3
Har Indonesia 5°16S 133°14E 231 F8
Har Adar West Bank 31°49N 35°8E 123 B1
Har Gilo West Bank 31°43N 35°10E 123 B2
Har Homa West Bank 31°44N 35°12E 123 B2
Har Hu China 38°20N 97°38E 218 D8
Har Nof Israel 31°47N 35°11E 123 B2
Har Tsiyon Jerusalem 123 b3
Har Us Nuur Mongolia 48°0N 92°0E 217 C12
Har Yehuda Israel 31°35N 34°57E 251 G5
Ḩaraḑ Si. Arabia 24°22N 49°0E 249 A5
Ḩaraḑ Yemen 16°26N 43°5E 248 C3
Haradok Belarus 55°30N 30°3E 188 E6
Häradsbäck Sweden 56°32N 14°26E 163 H8
Harahan U.S.A. 29°56N 90°12W 131 B1
Haraiki French Polynesia 17°38S 143°27W 289 f
Haramosh Pakistan 35°50N 74°54E 243 B6
Haranomachi Japan 37°38N 140°58E 220 F10
Harare Zimbabwe 17°43S 31°2E 269 F3
Ḩarāsīs, Jiddat al Oman 19°30N 56°0E 249 C7
Harat Eritrea 16°5N 39°26E 257 D4
Harau Indonesia 0°7S 100°35E 234 C2
Haraz-Djombo Chad 14°20N 19°12E 259 F3
Harazé Chad 9°57N 20°48E 259 G4
Harbel Liberia 6°16N 10°20W 262 D2
Harbhanga India 20°38N 84°36E 244 D7
Harbin China 45°48N 126°40E 227 B14
Harbiye Turkey 36°10N 36°8E 250 B7
Harbo Sweden 60°7N 17°12E 162 D11
Harboøre Denmark 56°38N 8°10E 163 H2
Harbor Beach U.S.A. 43°51N 82°39W 312 C2
Harborcreek U.S.A. 42°9N 79°57W 312 D5
Harbour Breton Canada 47°29N 55°50W 299 C8
Harbour Deep Canada 50°25N 56°32W 299 B8
Harbour View Jamaica 17°59N 76°50W 320 a
Harburg Germany 53°27N 9°58E 178 B5
Harburger Berge △ Germany 53°26N 9°51E 178 B5
Harda India 22°27N 77°5E 242 H7
Hardangerfjorden Norway 60°5N 6°0E 164 D3
Hardangerjøkulen Norway 60°30N 7°27E 164 D4
Hardangervidda Norway 60°7N 7°20E 164 D4
Hardangervidda △ Norway 60°10N 7°25E 164 D4
Hardap △ Namibia 24°29S 17°45E 270 B2
Hardap Dam Namibia 24°32S 17°50E 270 B2
Hardeeville U.S.A. 32°17N 81°5W 316 C8
Harden Australia 34°32S 148°24E 283 C8
Hardenberg Neths. 52°34N 6°37E 170 B6
Harderwijk Neths. 52°21N 5°38E 170 B5
Hardey → Australia 22°45S 116°8E 278 D2
Hardin Ill., U.S.A. 39°10N 90°37W 310 E6
Hardin Mont., U.S.A. 45°44N 107°37W 304 D10
Harding S. Africa 30°35S 29°55E 271 D4
Harding, L. U.S.A. 32°40N 85°5W 316 C4
Harding Ra. Australia 16°17S 124°55E 278 C3
Hardinsburg U.S.A. 37°47N 86°28W 311 G10
Hardisty Canada 52°40N 111°18W 296 C6
Hardoi India 27°26N 80°6E 243 F9
Hardwar = Haridwar India 29°58N 78°9E 242 E8
Hardwick Ga., U.S.A. 33°4N 83°14W 316 B6
Hardwick Vt., U.S.A. 44°30N 72°22W 313 B12
Hardwicke B. Australia 34°55S 137°20E 282 C2
Hardwood Lake Canada 45°12N 77°26W 312 A7
Hardy, Pen. Chile 55°30S 68°20W 336 E3
Hardy, Pte. St. Lucia 14°6N 60°56W 323 m
Hare B. Canada 51°15N 55°45W 299 B8
Hareid Norway 62°22N 6°1E 164 B3
Haren Brussels, Belgium 50°53N 4°25E 116 A2
Haren Niedersachsen, Germany 52°47N 7°13E 178 C3
Harer Ethiopia 9°20N 42°8E 257 F5
Harerge Ethiopia 7°12N 42°0E 257 F5
Hareskovby Denmark 55°45N 12°23E 118 A2
Harestua Norway 60°11N 10°44E 164 D7
Hareto Ethiopia 9°23N 37°6E 257 F4
Harfleur France 49°30N 0°10E 172 C7
Hargeisa Somali Rep. 9°30N 44°2E 267 C5
Hargeisa △ Somali Rep. 10°2N 44°2E 267 B5
Harghita □ Romania 46°30N 25°30E 183 D10
Harghita, Munţii Romania 46°25N 25°35E 183 D10
Hargshamn Sweden 60°12N 18°30E 162 D12
Hari → Indonesia 1°16S 104°5E 234 C2
Haria Canary Is. 29°8N 13°32W 153 e2
Ḩarīb Yemen 14°56N 45°30E 248 D4
Haricha, Hamada el Mali 22°40N 3°15W 260 D4
Harihar India 14°32N 75°44E 245 G2
Harihari N.Z. 43°9S 170°33E 285 D5
Ḩārim Syria 36°14N 36°29E 250 B7
Harim, Jabal al Oman 25°58N 56°14E 247 E8
Harima-Nada Japan 34°30N 134°35E 222 C6
Haringey □ U.K. 51°34N 0°5W 125 A3
Haringhata → Bangla. 22°0N 89°58E 241 E2
Haripad India 9°14N 76°28E 245 K3
Harīr, W. al → Syria 32°44N 35°59E 250 F6
Harīrūd → Asia 37°24N 60°38E 240 A1
Härjedalen Sweden 62°22N 13°5E 162 B7
Harjusuo Finland 60°19N 25°0E 121 B3
Harlaching Germany 48°5N 11°33E 121 B2
Harlan Iowa, U.S.A. 41°39N 95°19W 308 E6
Harlan Ky., U.S.A. 36°51N 83°19W 309 G12
Hârlău Romania 47°23N 26°55E 183 C11
Harlaw Res. U.K. 55°52N 3°18W 121 B2
Harlech U.K. 52°52N 4°6W 168 E3
Harlem Ga., U.S.A. 33°25N 82°19W 316 B7
Harlem Mont., U.S.A. 48°32N 108°47W 304 B9
Harlem New York, U.S.A. 132 a3
Harlesden U.K. 51°32N 0°14W 125 A2
Hårlev Denmark 55°21N 12°14E 163 J6
Harleyville U.S.A. 33°13N 80°27W 316 B9
Harlingen Neths. 53°11N 5°25E 170 A5
Harlingen Tex., U.S.A. 26°12N 97°42W 314 H6
Harlington U.K. 51°29N 0°25W 125 B1
Harlow U.K. 51°46N 0°8E 169 F8
Harlowton U.S.A. 46°26N 109°50W 304 C9
Harmaja Finland 60°6N 24°58E 121 C2
Harmancık Turkey 39°41N 29°9E 205 B11
Harmånger Sweden 61°55N 17°20E 162 C11
Harmashatar hegy Hungary 47°33N 19°0E 117 A2
Harmil Eritrea 16°30N 40°10E 257 D5
Harnai India 17°48N 73°6E 244 F1
Harnai Pakistan 30°6N 67°56E 242 D2
Harney, L. U.S.A. 28°45N 81°3W 317 G8
Harney Basin U.S.A. 43°0N 119°30W 304 E4
Harney L. U.S.A. 43°14N 119°8W 304 E4
Harney Peak U.S.A. 43°52N 103°32W 308 D2
Härnön Sweden 62°36N 18°0E 162 B12
Härnösand Sweden 62°38N 17°55E 162 B11
Haro Spain 42°35N 2°55W 196 C2
Harold U.S.A. 30°40N 86°53W 317 E3
Harold Pond Bahamas 25°2N 77°22W 153 b
Harolds Cross Ireland 53°19N 6°16W 120 B2
Haroldswick U.K. 60°48N 0°50W 167 A8
Háros Hungary 47°23N 19°2E 117 B2
Harp L. Canada 55°5N 61°50W 299 A7
Harpanahalli India 14°47N 76°2E 245 G3
Harper = Costa Mesa U.S.A. 33°38N 117°55W 307 M9
Harper Liberia 4°25N 7°43W 262 E3
Harper, Mt. U.S.A. 64°14N 143°51W 303 D12
Harperrig Res. U.K. 55°50N 3°26W 121 B1
Harplinge Sweden 56°45N 12°45E 163 H6
Harrai India 22°37N 79°13E 243 H8
Harrand Pakistan 29°28N 70°3E 242 E4
Harricana → Canada 50°56N 79°32W 298 B4
Harriman U.S.A. 35°56N 84°33W 315 D12
Harrington Australia 31°52S 152°42E 283 A10
Harrington Harbour Canada 50°31N 59°30W 299 B8
Harrington Sd. Bermuda 32°20N 64°44W 153 a
Harris Montserrat 16°44N 62°11W 323 p
Harris W. Isles, U.K. 57°50N 6°55W 167 D2
Harris, L. S. Austral., Australia 31°10S 135°10E 281 E2
Harris, L. Fla., U.S.A. 28°47N 81°49W 317 G8
Harris, Sd. of U.K. 57°44N 7°6W 167 D1
Harris Mts. N.Z. 44°49S 168°49E 285 E3
Harris Pt. Canada 43°6N 82°9W 312 C2
Harrisburg Ill., U.S.A. 37°44N 88°32W 311 G8
Harrisburg Nebr., U.S.A. 41°33N 103°44W 308 E2
Harrisburg Pa., U.S.A. 40°16N 76°53W 312 F8
Harrismith S. Africa 28°15S 29°8E 271 C4
Harrison Ark., U.S.A. 36°14N 93°7W 314 C8
Harrison Maine, U.S.A. 44°7N 70°39W 313 B14
Harrison Nebr., U.S.A. 42°41N 103°53W 308 D2
Harrison, C. Canada 54°55N 57°55W 299 B8
Harrison Bay U.S.A. 70°40N 151°0W 303 A10
Harrison L. Canada 49°33N 121°50W 296 D4
Harrisonburg U.S.A. 38°27N 78°52W 309 F14
Harrison's Cave Barbados 13°11N 59°34W 323 r
Harrisonville U.S.A. 38°39N 94°21W 310 F2
Harriston Canada 43°57N 80°53W 312 C4
Harrisville Mich., U.S.A. 44°39N 83°17W 312 B1
Harrisville N.Y., U.S.A. 44°9N 75°19W 313 B9
Harrisville Pa., U.S.A. 41°8N 80°0W 312 E5
Harrodsburg Ind., U.S.A. 39°1N 86°33W 311 E10
Harrodsburg Ky., U.S.A. 37°46N 84°51W 311 G12
Harrogate U.K. 54°0N 1°33W 168 C6
Harrow Vic., Australia 37°9S 141°35E 282 D4
Harrow Ont., Canada 42°2N 82°55W 312 D2
Harrow □ U.K. 51°35N 0°21W 125 A1
Harrow on the Hill U.K. 51°34N 0°21W 125 A1
Harrow School U.K. 51°34N 0°20W 125 A1
Harrow Weald U.K. 51°36N 0°20W 125 A1
Harrowsmith Canada 44°24N 76°40W 313 B8
Harry S. Truman Res. U.S.A. 38°16N 93°24W 310 F3
Harsefeld Germany 53°27N 9°30E 178 B5
Harsewinkel Germany 51°56N 8°14E 178 D4
Harsīn Iran 34°18N 47°33E 213 E12
Hârşova Romania 44°40N 27°59E 183 F12
Harstad Norway 68°48N 16°30E 160 B17
Harsud India 22°6N 76°44E 242 H7
Hart U.S.A. 43°42N 86°22W 308 D10
Hart, L. Australia 31°10S 136°25E 282 A2
Hartbees → S. Africa 28°45S 20°32E 270 C3
Hartberg Austria 47°17N 15°58E 181 D8
Hårteigen Norway 60°11N 7°3E 164 D4
Hartford Ala., U.S.A. 31°6N 85°42W 316 D4
Hartford Conn., U.S.A. 41°46N 72°41W 313 E12
Hartford Ky., U.S.A. 37°27N 86°55W 308 G10
Hartford Mich., U.S.A. 42°13N 86°10W 311 B10
Hartford S. Dak., U.S.A. 43°38N 96°57W 308 D5
Hartford Vt., U.S.A. 43°40N 72°20W 313 C12
Hartford Wis., U.S.A. 43°19N 88°22W 308 D9
Hartford City U.S.A. 40°27N 85°22W 311 D11
Hartingsburg = Bela Bela S. Africa 24°51S 28°19E 271 B4
Hartland N.B., Canada 46°20N 67°32W 299 C6
Hartland Wis., U.S.A. 43°6N 88°21W 311 A8
Hartland Pt. U.K. 51°1N 4°32W 169 F3
Hartlepool U.K. 54°42N 1°13W 168 C6
Hartlepool □ U.K. 54°42N 1°17W 168 C6
Hartley Bay Canada 53°25N 129°15W 296 C3
Hartmannberge Namibia 17°0S 13°0E 270 A1
Hartney Canada 49°30N 100°35W 297 D8
Hârtop Moldova 46°39N 28°40E 183 D13
Harts → S. Africa 28°24S 24°17E 270 C3
Harts Range Australia 23°6S 134°55E 280 C1
Hartselle U.S.A. 34°27N 86°56W 315 D11
Hartsfield-Atlanta Int. ✕ (ATL) U.S.A. 33°38N 84°26W 113 C2
Hartshorne U.S.A. 34°51N 95°34W 314 D7
Hartstown U.S.A. 41°33N 80°23W 312 E4
Hartsville U.S.A. 34°23N 80°4W 315 D14
Hartswater S. Africa 27°34S 24°43E 270 C3
Hartwell U.S.A. 34°21N 82°56W 315 D13
Harumi Tokyo, Japan 140 c5
Harunabad Pakistan 29°35N 73°8E 242 E5
Harur India 12°3N 78°29E 245 H4
Hārūt → Afghan. 31°29N 61°24E 240 C1
Harvand Iran 28°25N 55°43E 247 D7
Harvard U.S.A. 42°25N 88°37W 311 B8
Harvard Univ. U.S.A. 42°22N 71°7W 116 A2
Harvey W. Austral., Australia 33°5S 115°54E 279 F2
Harvey Ill., U.S.A. 41°36N 87°50W 311 C9
Harvey La., U.S.A. 29°54N 90°4W 131 B2
Harvey N. Dak., U.S.A. 47°47N 99°56W 308 B4
Harwich U.K. 51°56N 1°17E 169 F9
Harwood Heights U.S.A. 41°57N 87°46W 119 B2
Haryana □ India 29°0N 76°10E 242 E7
Haryn → Belarus 52°7N 27°17E 177 B14
Harz Germany 51°38N 10°44E 178 D6
Harz △ Germany 51°40N 10°18E 178 D6
Harzgerode Germany 51°38N 11°8E 178 D7
Hasa Si. Arabia 25°50N 49°0E 247 E6
Ḩasā, W. al → Jordan 31°4N 35°29E 251 D4
Hasaheisa Sudan 14°44N 33°20E 257 E3
Ḩasanābād Eşfahan, Iran 32°8N 52°44E 247 C7
Ḩasanābād Tehrān, Iran 35°44N 51°16E 141 A1
Hasankeyf Turkey 37°42N 41°24E 213 D9
Hasanparti India 18°4N 79°32E 244 E4
Hasawinah, Jabal al Libya 28°15N 14°0E 261 C7
Ḩasb, W. → Iraq 31°45N 44°17E 246 D5
Hasbrouck Heights U.S.A. 40°51N 74°4W 132 A1
Hasdo → India 21°44N 82°44E 243 J10
Haselhorst Germany 52°33N 13°14E 115 A2
Haselünne Germany 52°40N 7°29E 178 C3
Hashima Japan 35°20N 136°40E 223 B8
Hashimoto Japan 34°19N 135°37E 223 C7
Hashtjerd Iran 35°52N 50°40E 247 C6
Hashtpur = Tālesh Iran 37°58N 48°58E 213 D13
Hashtrud Iran 37°28N 47°4E 213 D12
Hasi Nueifed W. Sahara 24°54N 14°49W 260 D2
Ḩāsik Oman 17°22N 55°17E 249 C6
Haskell U.S.A. 33°10N 99°44W 314 E5
Haskovo = Khaskovo Bulgaria 41°56N 25°30E 203 E9
Hasköy Edirne, Turkey 41°38N 26°52E 203 E10
Hasköy İstanbul, Turkey 41°2N 28°57E 122 B1
Haslach Germany 48°16N 8°5E 179 G4
Hasle Denmark 55°11N 14°44E 163 J8
Hasle Oslo, Norway 59°46N 10°38E 133 B2
Haslemere U.K. 51°5N 0°43W 169 F7
Haslev Denmark 55°18N 11°57E 163 J5
Haslum Norway 59°55N 10°34E 133 A2
Hasparren France 43°24N 1°18W 174 E2
Hassa Turkey 36°48N 36°29E 250 B7
Hassan India 13°0N 76°5E 245 H3
Hassberge △ Germany 50°8N 10°45E 179 E6
Hassela Sweden 62°7N 16°42E 162 B10
Hasselt Belgium 50°56N 5°21E 170 D5
Hassfurt Germany 50°2N 10°30E 179 E6
Hassi bel Guebbour Algeria 28°30N 6°41E 261 C6
Hassi bou Khelala Algeria 30°17N 0°18W 261 B4
Hassi Bourarchet Algeria 27°26N 9°19E 261 C6
Hassi Djafou Algeria 30°55N 3°35E 261 B5
Hassi el Hadjar Algeria 31°28N 4°45E 261 B5
Hassi Imoulaye Algeria 29°54N 9°10E 261 C6
Hassi Inifeg Algeria 28°15N 1°30W 261 C4
Hassi Inifel Algeria 29°50N 3°41E 261 C5
Hassi Mana Algeria 28°48N 2°37W 261 C4
Hassi Marroket Algeria 30°10N 3°0E 261 B5
Hassi Mengoub Algeria 29°49N 5°26W 260 C3
Hassi Messaoud Algeria 31°51N 5°1E 261 B6
Hassi Sougoued Algeria 26°50N 9°28E 261 C6
Hassi Tartrat Algeria 30°5N 6°28E 261 B6
Hassi Zerzour Morocco 30°51N 3°56W 260 B4
Hassi Zguilma Algeria 30°19N 6°10W 260 B4
Hässleholm Sweden 56°10N 13°46E 163 H7
Hasslö Sweden 56°7N 15°28E 163 H9
Hassloch Germany 49°22N 8°16E 179 F4
Hästhagen Sweden 59°18N 13°9E 139 B2
Hästholmen Sweden 58°17N 14°38E 163 F8
Hastings Vic., Australia 38°18S 145°12E 283 E6
Hastings Barbados 13°4N 59°36W 323 r
Hastings N.Z. 39°39S 176°52E 284 F5
Hastings E. Sussex, U.K. 50°51N 0°35E 169 G8
Hastings Fla., U.S.A. 29°43N 81°31W 316 F8
Hastings Mich., U.S.A. 42°39N 85°17W 311 B11
Hastings Minn., U.S.A. 44°44N 92°51W 308 C7
Hastings Nebr., U.S.A. 40°35N 98°23W 308 E4
Hastings Ra. Australia 31°15S 152°14E 283 A10
Hästveda Sweden 56°17N 13°55E 163 H7
Hat Ukraine 48°19N 22°38E 182 B7
Hat Head △ Australia 31°3S 153°1E 283 A10
Hat Lot Vietnam 21°15N 104°7E 236 B5
Hat Yai Thailand 7°1N 100°27E 237 J3
Hataitai N.Z. 41°18S 174°48E 143 B1
Hatanbulag = Ergel Mongolia 43°8N 109°5E 226 C5
Hatay Turkey 36°14N 36°10E 250 B7
Hatay □ Turkey 36°25N 36°15E 250 B7
Hatch U.S.A. 32°40N 107°9W 305 K10
Hatch End U.K. 51°36N 0°22W 125 A1
Hatchet L. Canada 58°36N 103°40W 297 B8
Haţeg Romania 45°36N 22°55E 182 E7
Hateruma-Shima Japan 24°3N 123°47E 221 M1
Hatfield Australia 33°54S 143°49E 282 B5
Hatgal Mongolia 50°26N 100°9E 218 A9
Hathras India 27°36N 78°6E 242 F8
Hatia Bangla. 22°30N 91°5E 241 D3
Hatia Is. Bangla. 22°30N 91°0E 241 D3
Hatiara India 22°36N 88°26E 124 B2
Ḩāţibah, Ra's Si. Arabia 21°55N 38°57E 256 C4
Hatid India 17°17N 75°3E 244 F2
Hatillo Puerto Rico 18°29N 66°50W 321 b
Hato Bonaire 12°11N 68°17W 322 h
Hato Curaçao 12°11N 68°57W 322 g
Hato Caves Curaçao 12°11N 68°57W 322 g
Hato Corozal Colombia 6°11N 71°45W 328 B3
Hato Mayor Dom. Rep. 18°46N 69°15W 321 C6
Hatsukaichi Japan 34°22N 132°22E 222 C4
Hatta India 24°7N 79°36E 243 G8
Hatta U.A.E. 24°45N 56°4E 247 E8
Hattah Australia 34°48S 142°17E 282 C5
Hattah Kulkyne △ Australia 34°16S 142°33E 282 C5
Hatteras, C. U.S.A. 35°14N 75°32W 315 D17
Hatteras Abyssal Plain Atl. Oc. 28°0N 72°0W 152 D4
Hattiesburg U.S.A. 31°20N 89°17W 315 F10
Hatutu French Polynesia 7°56S 140°38W 289 f
Hatvan Hungary 47°40N 19°45E 182 C4
Hau → Vietnam 9°30N 106°13E 237 H6
Haubstadt U.S.A. 38°12N 87°34W 311 F9
Haud Ethiopia 8°0N 45°0E 267 C6
Hauganes Iceland 65°56N 18°27W 155 B8
Haugastøl Norway 60°30N 7°50E 164 D4
Hauge Norway 58°20N 6°15E 164 F3
Haugesund Norway 59°23N 5°13E 164 E2
Hauhui Solomon Is. 9°10S 160°59E 287 M11
Hauhungaroa Ra. N.Z. 38°42S 175°40E 284 E4
Haukeligrend Norway 59°44N 7°33E 164 E4
Hauketo Norway 59°50N 10°48E 133 A3
Haukipudas Finland 65°12N 25°20E 160 D21
Haultain → Canada 55°51N 106°46W 297 B7
Haungpa Burma 25°29N 96°7E 241 C6
Hauraha Solomon Is. 10°46S 161°59E 287 N11
Hauraki G. N.Z. 36°35S 175°5E 284 C4
Hauroko L. N.Z. 45°59S 167°21E 285 F2
Hausruck Austria 48°6N 13°30E 180 C6
Haut Atlas Morocco 32°30N 5°0W 260 B4
Haut de la Montagne Guadeloupe 16°26N 61°28W 322 e
Haut-Jura △ France 46°23N 2°23E 173 F9
Haut-Languedoc △ France 43°30N 2°43E 174 E6
Haut-Niger △ Guinea 10°20N 10°20W 262 C2
Haut-Rhin □ France 48°0N 7°15E 173 E14
Haut-Zaïre = Orientale □ Dem. Rep. of the Congo 2°20N 26°0E 268 B2
Haute-Corse □ France 42°30N 9°30E 175 F13
Haute-Garonne □ France 43°30N 1°30E 174 E5
Haute-Loire □ France 45°5N 3°50E 174 C7
Haute-Marne □ France 48°10N 5°20E 173 D12
Haute-Normandie □ France 49°20N 1°0E 172 C7
Haute-Saône □ France 47°45N 6°10E 173 E13
Haute-Savoie □ France 46°0N 6°20E 175 C10
Haute-Vienne □ France 45°50N 1°10E 174 C5
Hautes-Alpes □ France 44°42N 6°20E 175 D10
Hautes Fagnes = Hohes Venn Belgium 50°30N 6°5E 170 D6
Hautes-Pyrénées □ France 43°0N 0°10E 174 F4
Hauteville-Lompnès France 45°58N 5°36E 175 C9
Hautmont France 50°15N 3°55E 173 B10
Hauts-de-Seine □ France 48°52N 2°15E 173 D9
Hauts Plateaux Algeria 35°0N 1°0E 261 B5
Hau'ula U.S.A. 21°37N 157°55W 302 J14
Hauz Khas India 28°33N 77°11E 120 B2
Hauzenberg Germany 48°40N 13°37E 179 G9
Havana = La Habana Cuba 23°8N 82°22W 320 B3
Havana Fla., U.S.A. 30°37N 84°25W 316 E5
Havana Ill., U.S.A. 40°18N 90°4W 310 D6
Havant U.K. 50°51N 0°58W 169 G7
Havârna Romania 48°4N 26°43E 183 B11
Havasor = Kığzı Turkey 38°18N 43°25E 246 B4
Havasu, L. U.S.A. 34°18N 114°28W 307 L12
Havdhem Sweden 57°10N 18°20E 163 G12
Havel → Germany 52°50N 12°3E 115 A2
Havelian Pakistan 34°2N 73°10E 242 B5
Havelkanal Germany 52°36N 13°10E 115 A2
Havelock Ont., Canada 44°26N 77°53W 312 B7
Havelock N.Z. 41°17S 173°48E 285 B8
Havelock N.C., U.S.A. 34°53N 76°54W 315 D16
Havelock I. India 11°58N 93°0E 245 J11

Havelock North N.Z. 39°40S 176°53E 284 F5
Haverfordwest U.K. 51°48N 4°58W 169 F3
Haverhill Suffolk, U.K. 52°5N 0°28E 169 E8
Haverhill Fla., U.S.A. 26°42N 80°7W 317 J9
Haverhill Mass., U.S.A. 42°47N 71°5W 313 D13
Haveri India 14°53N 75°24E 245 G2
Havering-atte-Bower U.K. 51°37N 0°13E 125 A5
Havern Sweden 62°18N 15°7E 162 B9
Haverstraw U.S.A. 41°12N 73°58W 313 E11
Håverud Sweden 58°50N 12°28E 163 F6
Havirga Mongolia 45°41N 113°5E 226 B7
Havířov Czech Rep. 49°46N 18°20E 181 B11
Havlíčkův Brod Czech Rep. 49°36N 15°33E 180 B8
Havneby Denmark 55°5N 8°34E 163 J2
Havran Turkey 39°33N 27°6E 206 F5
Havre U.S.A. 48°33N 109°41W 304 B9
Havre-Aubert Canada 47°12N 61°56W 299 C7
Havre-St.-Pierre Canada 50°18N 63°33W 299 B7
Havsa Turkey 41°13N 26°48E 205 A11
Havza Turkey 41°0N 35°35E 212 B6
Haw → U.S.A. 35°36N 79°3W 315 D15
Hawai'i □ U.S.A. 19°30N 155°30W 302 D6
Hawai'i □ U.S.A. 19°30N 156°30W 302 D5
Hawai'i County U.S.A. 19°30N 155°30W 302 D6
Hawai'i Kai U.S.A. 21°16N 157°42W 302 K14
Hawai'i Volcanoes △ U.S.A. 19°30N 155°18W 302 D6
Hawaiian Is. Pac. Oc. 20°30N 156°0W 302 G12
Hawaiian Ridge Pac. Oc. 24°0N 165°0W 289 E11
Hawarden U.K. 43°0N 96°29W 308 D5
Hawashiyah, W. Egypt 28°31N 32°58E 251 K3
Hawea, L. N.Z. 44°28N 169°19E 285 E4
Hawea Flat N.Z. 44°40N 169°19E 285 E4
Hawera N.Z. 39°35S 174°19E 284 F3
Hawesville U.S.A. 37°54N 86°45W 311 G10
Hawi U.S.A. 20°14N 155°50W 302 C6
Hawick U.K. 55°26N 2°47W 167 F6
Hawk Junction Canada 48°5N 84°38W 298 C3
Hawk Point U.S.A. 38°58N 91°8W 310 F5
Hawkdun Ra. N.Z. 44°53S 170°5E 285 E5
Hawke B. N.Z. 39°25S 177°20E 284 F6
Hawker Australia 31°59S 138°22E 282 A3
Hawke's Bay Canada 50°36N 57°10W 299 B8
Hawke's Bay □ N.Z. 39°45S 176°35E 284 F5
Hawkesbury Canada 45°37N 74°37W 298 C5
Hawkesbury I. Canada 53°37N 129°3W 296 C3
Hawkesbury Pt. Australia 11°55S 134°5E 280 A1
Hawkinsville U.S.A. 32°17N 83°28W 316 H5
Hawks Nest Australia 32°41S 152°11E 283 B10
Hawley Minn., U.S.A. 46°53N 96°19W 308 B5
Hawley Pa., U.S.A. 41°28N 75°11W 313 E9
Haworth U.K. 53°50N 73°59W 132 A2
Hawrān, W. → Iraq 33°58N 42°34E 213 F10
Hawsh Mūssá Lebanon 33°45N 35°55E 250 B4
Hawthorne Nev., U.S.A. 29°36N 82°5W 317 F7
Hawthorne Nev., U.S.A. 38°32N 118°38W 304 G4
Hawthorne Racecourse U.S.A. 41°49N 87°44W 119 C2
Hay Australia 34°30S 144°51E 283 C6
Hay → N. Terr., Australia 24°50S 138°0E 280 C2
Hay → Alta., Canada 60°50N 116°26W 296 A5
Hay, C. Australia 14°5S 129°29E 278 B4
Hay I. Canada 44°53N 80°58W 312 B4
Hay L. Canada 58°50N 118°50W 296 B5
Hay-on-Wye U.K. 52°5N 3°8W 169 E4
Hay Point Australia 21°18S 149°17E 280 C4
Hay River Canada 60°51N 115°44W 296 A5
Hay Springs U.S.A. 42°41N 102°41W 308 D2
Haya = Tehoru Indonesia 3°20S 129°30E 231 E7
Hayange France 49°20N 6°2E 173 C13
Hayastan = Armenia ■ Asia 40°20N 45°0E 191 K7
Hayato Japan 31°40N 130°43E 222 F2
Haydān, W. al → Jordan 31°29N 35°34E 251 G6
Haydarlı Turkey 38°16N 30°23E 205 C12
Hayden U.S.A. 40°30N 107°16W 304 F10
Hayes Jamaica 17°52N 77°14W 320 a
Hayes Kent, U.K. 51°22N 0°0 125 B4
Hayes Middlesex, U.K. 51°30N 0°25W 125 A1
Hayes S. Dak., U.S.A. 44°23N 101°1W 308 C3
Hayes → Canada 57°3N 92°12W 298 A1
Hayes, Mt. U.S.A. 63°37N 146°43W 303 E11
Hayes Creek Australia 13°43S 131°22E 278 B5
Hayes End U.K. 51°31N 0°25W 125 A1
Hayford U.K. 41°45N 87°42W 119 C2
Hayle U.K. 50°11N 5°26W 169 G2
Hayling I. U.K. 50°48N 0°59W 169 G7
Haymā' Oman 19°56N 56°19E 249 C7
Hayman I. Australia 20°4S 148°53E 280 b
Haymana Turkey 39°26N 32°31E 212 C5
Haynan Yemen 15°50N 48°18E 249 E5
Haynau = Chojnów Poland 51°18N 15°58E 185 G2
Hayneville U.S.A. 32°11N 86°35W 316 C6
Hayrabolu Turkey 41°12N 27°5E 203 E11
Hays Alta., Canada 50°6N 111°48W 296 C6
Hays Kans., U.S.A. 38°53N 99°20W 308 F4
Haysville U.S.A. 38°28N 86°55W 311 F10
Haysyn Ukraine 48°57N 29°25E 183 B14
Hayvoron Ukraine 48°22N 29°52E 183 B14
Hayward Calif., U.S.A. 37°40N 122°4W 306 H4
Hayward Wis., U.S.A. 46°1N 91°29W 308 B8
Haywards N.Z. 41°9S 174°59E 143 A2
Haywards Heath U.K. 51°0N 0°5W 169 G7
Hazafon □ Israel 32°40N 35°0E 250 F6
Hazar Turkmenistan 39°34N 53°16E 187 G9
Hazārān, Kūh-e Iran 29°35N 57°20E 247 D8
Hazard U.S.A. 37°15N 83°12W 309 G12
Hazaribag India 23°58N 85°26E 243 H11
Hazaribag Road India 24°12N 85°57E 243 H11
Hazebrouck France 50°42N 2°31E 173 B9
Hazelton B.C., Canada 55°20N 127°42W 296 B3
Hazelton N. Dak., U.S.A. 46°29N 100°17W 308 B3
Hazen U.S.A. 47°18N 101°38W 308 B3
Hazen, L. Canada 81°47N 71°1W 154 A3
Hazlehurst Ga., U.S.A. 31°52N 82°36W 316 D5
Hazlehurst Miss., U.S.A. 31°52N 90°24W 315 F9
Hazleton Ind., U.S.A. 38°29N 87°33W 311 F9
Hazleton Pa., U.S.A. 40°57N 75°59W 313 E9
Hazlett, L. Australia 21°30S 128°48E 278 D4
Hazro Turkey 38°15N 40°47E 213 D9
He Xian Anhui, China 31°45N 118°20E 229 B12
He Xian Guangxi Zhuangzu, China 24°27N 111°30E 228 E8
Head of Bight Australia 31°30S 131°25E 280 D5
Headland U.S.A. 31°21N 85°21W 316 D4
Headlands Zimbabwe 18°15S 32°2E 269 F8
Healdsburg U.S.A. 38°37N 122°52W 306 G4
Healdton U.S.A. 34°14N 97°29W 314 D6
Healesville Australia 37°35S 145°30E 283 D6
Healy U.S.A. 63°52N 148°58W 303 E10
Heany Junction Zimbabwe 20°6S 28°54E 268 F5
Heanza-shima Japan 26°26N 127°57E 288 a
Heard I. Ind. Oc. 53°6S 72°36E 73 K11
Hearne U.S.A. 30°53N 96°36W 314 F6
Hearst Canada 49°40N 83°41W 298 C3
Heart → U.S.A. 46°46N 100°50W 308 B3
Heart's Content Canada 47°54N 53°27W 299 C9
Heath → Bolivia 12°31S 68°38W 330 C4
Heath, Pte. Canada 49°8N 61°40W 299 C7
Heath Mts. N.Z. 45°39S 167°9E 285 F2

Heathcote Australia 36°56S 144°45E 283 D6
Heatherwood = Edson Canada 53°35N 116°28W 296 C5
Heathfield S. Africa 34°3S 18°27E 118 B1
Heathrow, London ✈ (LHR) U.K. 51°28N 0°27W 125 B1
Heavener U.S.A. 34°53N 94°36W 314 D7
Hebbronville U.S.A. 27°18N 98°41W 314 H5
Hebe Haven China 22°21N 114°15E 122 A2
Hebei □ China 39°0N 116°0E 226 D6
Hebel Australia 28°58S 147°47E 281 D4
Heber U.S.A. 32°44N 115°32W 307 N11
Heber Springs U.S.A. 35°30N 92°2W 314 D8
Hebgen L. U.S.A. 44°52N 111°20W 304 D8
Hebi China 35°57N 114°7E 226 G8
Hebrides U.K. 57°30N 7°0W 158 D4
Hebrides, Sea of the U.K. 57°5N 7°0W 167 D2
Hebron = Al Khalīl West Bank 31°32N 35°6E 251 G6
Hebron Nfld. & L., Canada 58°5N 62°30W 295 F19
Hebron N. Dak., U.S.A. 46°54N 102°3W 308 B2
Hebron Nebr., U.S.A. 40°10N 97°35W 308 E5
Heby Sweden 59°56N 16°53E 162 E10
Hecate Str. Canada 53°10N 130°30W 296 C2
Heceta I. Canada 55°46N 133°40W 296 B2
Hechi China 24°40N 108°2E 228 E7
Hechingen Germany 48°21N 8°57E 179 G4
Hechuan China 30°2N 106°12E 228 B6
Hecla U.S.A. 45°53N 98°9W 308 C4
Hecla I. Canada 51°10N 96°43W 297 C9
Hedal Norway 60°37N 9°41E 162 D3
Heddal Norway 59°36N 9°9E 164 E6
Hédé Ille-et-Vilaine, France 48°18N 1°49W 172 D5
Hede Jämtland, Sweden 62°23N 13°30E 162 B7
Hedemora Sweden 60°18N 15°58E 162 D9
Hedensted Denmark 55°46N 9°42E 163 J3
Hedesunda Sweden 60°24N 17°0E 162 D10
Hedgehope N.Z. 46°12S 168°34E 285 G3
Hedmark □ Norway 61°17N 11°40E 164 F8
Hedo Japan 26°52N 128°15E 288 a
Hedo-misaki Japan 26°52N 128°15E 288 a
Hedong China 23°5N 113°14E 121 B2
Hedrick U.S.A. 41°11N 92°19W 310 C4
He'eia U.S.A. 21°25N 157°48W 302 K14
Heel Pt. Wake I. 19°18N 166°38E 302 b
Heerde Neths. 52°24N 6°2E 170 B6
Heerenveen Neths. 52°57N 5°55E 170 B5
Heerhugowaard Neths. 52°40N 4°51E 170 B4
Heerlen Neths. 50°55N 5°58E 170 D5
Heerwegen = Polkowice Poland 51°29N 16°3E 185 G3
Hefa Israel 32°46N 35°0E 250 F6
Hefa □ Israel 32°40N 35°0E 250 F6
Hefei China 31°52N 117°18E 229 B11
Hefeng China 29°55N 109°52E 228 C7
Heflin U.S.A. 33°39N 85°35W 316 B4
Hegang China 47°20N 130°19E 219 B15
Heggenes Norway 61°9N 9°4E 164 C6
Hegra Norway 63°27N 11°8E 164 A8
Hei Ling Chau China 22°15N 114°2E 219 a
Heiban Sudan 11°13N 30°31E 257 E5
Heichengzhen China 36°24N 106°3E 226 F4
Heidal Norway 61°45N 9°19E 164 C6
Heide Germany 54°11N 9°6E 178 A5
Heidelberg Baden-W., Germany 49°24N 8°42E 179 F4
Heidelberg Western Cape, S. Africa 34°6S 20°59E 270 D3
Heidelberg Heights Australia 37°45S 145°4E 128 A2
Heidelberg West Australia 37°45S 145°4E 128 A2
Heidelberg S. Africa 26°30S 28°21E 271 C4
Heidemühle Germany 52°29N 13°4E 178 B9
Heidenau Germany 50°57N 13°52E 178 E9
Heidenheim Germany 48°41N 10°9E 179 G6
Heideveld S. Africa 33°58S 18°32E 118 A2
Heigun-Tō Japan 33°47N 132°14E 222 D4
Heihe China 50°10N 127°30E 219 A14
Heijing China 25°22N 101°44E 228 E3
Heijō = P'yŏngyang N. Korea 39°0N 125°30E 224 C2
Heilbad Heiligenstadt Germany 51°22N 10°8E 178 D6
Heilbron S. Africa 27°16S 27°59E 271 C4
Heilbronn Germany 49°9N 9°13E 179 F5
Heiligenblut Austria 47°2N 12°51E 180 D5
Heiligenhafen Germany 54°22N 10°59E 178 A6
Heiligensee Germany 52°37N 13°13E 115 A2
Heiligenstadt Austria 48°14N 16°21E 142 A1
Heilongjiang □ China 48°0N 126°0E 219 B14
Heilprin Land Greenland 82°5N 33°0W 154 A7
Heilsberg = Lidzbark Warmiński Poland 54°7N 20°34E 184 D7
Heilunkiang = Heilongjiang □ China 48°0N 126°0E 219 B14
Heim Norway 63°26N 9°5E 164 A6
Heimaey Iceland 63°26N 20°17W 155 E3
Heimdal Norway 63°21N 10°22E 164 A7
Heinola Finland 61°13N 26°2E 164 F19
Heinsberg Germany 51°3N 6°5E 178 D2
Heinsun Burma 25°52N 95°35E 241 G3
Heinze Chaung Burma 14°42N 97°52E 236 E1
Heinze Kyun Burma 14°25N 97°45E 236 E1
Heirnkut Burma 25°14N 94°44E 241 G3
Heishan China 41°40N 122°5E 227 D12
Heishui Liaoning, China 42°8N 119°30E 227 C11
Heishui Sichuan, China 32°4N 103°2E 228 A4
Hejaz = Ḥijāz Si. Arabia 24°0N 40°0E 246 E3
Hejian China 38°25N 116°5E 226 E8
Hejiang China 28°43N 105°46E 228 C5
Hejin China 35°35N 110°42E 226 G6
Hejing China 42°18N 86°22E 217 F11
Hekimhan Turkey 38°50N 37°55E 212 C7
Hekinan Japan 34°52N 137°0E 223 B9
Hekla Iceland 63°56N 19°35W 155 D7
Hekou Gansu, China 36°10N 103°26E 226 F2
Hekou Guangdong, China 23°10N 112°45E 229 F9
Hekou Yunnan, China 22°30N 103°59E 228 F4
Hel Poland 54°37N 18°47E 184 D5
Helagsfjället Sweden 62°54N 12°25E 162 B6
Helan Shan China 38°30N 105°55E 226 E3
Helden's Pt. St. Kitts & Nevis 17°25N 62°51W 322 d
Helechosa de los Montes Spain 39°19N 4°52W 195 C5
Helemano → U.S.A. 21°35N 158°7W 302 J13
Helen Atoll Palau 2°40N 132°0E 230 D8
Helena U.S.A. 34°32N 90°36W 315 D9
Helena Ga., U.S.A. 32°5N 82°55W 316 C7
Helena Mont., U.S.A. 46°36N 112°2W 304 C7
Helendale U.S.A. 34°44N 117°19W 307 L9
Helensburgh Canada 45°31N 73°32W 130 A2
Helenelund Sweden 59°27N 17°58E 139 A1
Helensburgh N.S.W., Australia 34°11S 151°1E 283 C9
Helensburgh Argyll & Bute, U.K. 56°1N 4°43W 167 E4
Helensville N.Z. 36°41S 174°29E 284 C3
Helenvale U.S.A. 15°43S 145°14E 280 B4
Helgasjön Sweden 56°55N 14°50E 163 H6

Helgeland Norway 66°7N 13°29E 160 C15
Helgoland Germany 54°10N 7°53E 178 A3
Helheim Gletscher Greenland 66°24N 38°12W 154 D7
Heligoland = Helgoland Germany 54°10N 7°53E 178 A3
Heligoland B. = Deutsche Bucht Germany 54°15N 8°0E 178 A4
Heliopolis = Masr el Gedida Egypt 30°5N 31°21E 117 A2
Hell Norway 63°26N 10°54E 164 A7
Hell-Bourg Réunion 21°3S 55°32E 272 f
Hell Hole Gorge △ Australia 25°31S 144°12E 280 D3
Hella Iceland 63°50N 20°24W 155 D6
Hellas = Greece ■ Europe 40°0N 23°0E 204 B3
Helleland Norway 58°33N 6°7E 164 F3
Hellendoorn Neths. 52°32N 6°27E 170 B6
Hellersdorf Germany 52°33N 13°35E 115 A4
Hellerup Denmark 55°44N 12°34E 163 J6
Hellesylt Norway 62°6N 6°51E 164 B3
Hellevoetsluis Neths. 51°50N 4°8E 170 C4
Hellín Spain 38°31N 1°40W 197 G3
Hellissandur Iceland 64°55N 23°54W 155 C3
Hells Canyon → U.S.A. 45°30N 117°45W 304 D5
Hells Gate Saba 17°39N 63°14W 322 a
Hell's Gate △ Kenya 0°54S 36°19E 268 C4
Hellvik Norway 58°29N 5°52E 164 F2
Helm U.S.A. 36°33N 120°6W 306 J6
Helmand □ Afghan. 31°20N 64°0E 240 C2
Helmand → Afghan. 31°12N 61°34E 240 C1
Helme → Germany 51°20N 11°12E 178 D7
Helmeringhausen Namibia 25°54S 16°57E 270 C2
Helmond Neths. 51°29N 5°41E 170 C5
Helmsdale U.K. 58°7N 3°39W 167 C5
Helmsdale → U.K. 58°8N 3°43W 167 C5
Helmstedt Germany 52°12N 11°0E 178 C7
Helong China 42°40N 129°0E 224 A4
Helper U.S.A. 39°41N 110°51W 304 G8
Helsingborg Sweden 56°3N 12°42E 163 H6
Helsinge Denmark 56°2N 12°13E 163 H6
Helsingfors = Helsinki Finland 60°10N 24°55E 121 B2
Helsingør Denmark 56°2N 12°35E 163 H6
Helsinki Finland 60°10N 24°55E 121 B2
Helsinki-Vantaa ✈ (HEL) Finland 60°18N 24°58E 121 B2
Helska, Mierzeja Poland 54°45N 18°40E 184 D5
Helston U.K. 50°6N 5°17W 169 G2
Helvellyn U.K. 54°32N 3°1W 168 C4
Helwân Egypt 29°50N 31°20E 256 J7
Hemavati → India 12°30N 76°20E 245 H3
Hemel Hempstead U.K. 51°44N 0°28W 169 F7
Hemet U.S.A. 33°45N 116°58W 307 M10
Hemingford U.S.A. 42°19N 103°4W 308 D2
Hemis △ India 34°10N 77°11E 242 B7
Hemmingford Canada 45°3N 73°35W 313 A11
Hemphill U.S.A. 31°20N 93°51W 315 F7
Hempstead N.Y., U.S.A. 40°42N 73°37W 313 F11
Hempstead Tex., U.S.A. 30°6N 96°5W 314 F6
Hemse Sweden 57°15N 18°22E 163 G12
Hemsedal Norway 60°53N 8°30E 164 C5
Hemsö Sweden 62°42N 18°5E 162 B12
Hen Norway 60°13N 10°11E 164 D7
Hen and Chicken B. Australia 33°50S 151°7E 139 B1
Hen and Chickens Is. N.Z. 35°58S 174°45E 284 B3
Henån Sweden 58°14N 11°40E 163 F5
Henan □ China 34°0N 114°0E 226 H8
Henares → Spain 40°24N 3°30W 194 E7
Henashi-Misaki Japan 40°37N 139°51E 220 D9
Hendaye France 43°23N 1°47W 174 E2
Hendek Turkey 40°48N 30°44E 212 B4
Henderson Argentina 36°18S 61°43W 334 D3
Henderson Ga., U.S.A. 32°21N 83°47W 316 C6
Henderson Ky., U.S.A. 37°50N 87°35W 311 G9
Henderson N.C., U.S.A. 36°20N 78°25W 315 C15
Henderson Nev., U.S.A. 36°2N 114°58W 304 J6
Henderson Tenn., U.S.A. 35°26N 88°38W 315 D10
Henderson Tex., U.S.A. 32°9N 94°48W 314 E7
Henderson I. Pac. Oc. 24°22S 128°19W 289 K15
Hendersonville N.C., U.S.A. 35°19N 82°28W 315 D13
Hendersonville Tenn., U.S.A. 36°18N 86°37W 315 C11
Hendijān Iran 30°14N 49°43E 247 D6
Hendon U.K. 51°35N 0°14W 125 A2
Hendorābī Iran 26°40N 53°37E 247 E7
Heng Jiang → China 28°40N 104°25E 228 C5
Heng Xian China 22°40N 109°17E 228 F7
Hengâm Iran 26°38N 55°53E 249 H6
Henganofi Papua N. G. 6°15S 145°38E 286 D3
Hengcheng China 38°18N 106°28E 226 E4
Hengdaohezi China 44°52N 129°0E 227 B15
Hengduan Shan China 28°30N 98°50E 228 C2
Hengelo Neths. 52°16N 6°48E 170 B6
Henggang China 22°39N 114°12E 219 a
Hengmen China 22°33N 113°35E 219 a
Hengshan Hunan, China 27°16N 112°45E 229 D9
Hengshan Shaanxi, China 37°58N 109°5E 226 F5
Hengshui China 37°41N 115°40E 226 F8
Hengyang China 26°59N 112°22E 229 D9
Henichesk Ukraine 46°12N 34°56E 189 J8
Henima Australia 12°25N 93°36E 241 C4
Hénin-Beaumont France 50°25N 2°58E 173 B9
Hénin-Liétard = Hénin-Beaumont France 50°25N 2°58E 173 B9
Henley-on-Thames U.K. 51°32N 0°54W 169 F7
Henlopen, C. U.S.A. 38°48N 75°6W 309 F16
Henna Japan 26°19N 127°53E 288 a
Hennan Sweden 62°2N 15°54E 162 B9
Hennebont France 47°49N 3°19W 172 E3
Hennenman S. Africa 27°59S 27°1E 270 C4
Hennessey U.S.A. 36°6N 97°54W 314 C6
Hennigsdorf Germany 52°38N 13°12E 115 A2
Henrietta N.Y., U.S.A. 43°4N 77°37W 312 D7
Henrietta Tex., U.S.A. 33°49N 98°12W 314 E5
Henrietta, Ostrov = Genriyetty, Ostrov Russia 77°6N 156°30E 215 B16
Henrietta Maria, C. Canada 55°9N 82°20W 298 A3
Henry U.S.A. 41°7N 89°22W 310 D7
Henry Lawrence I. India 12°55N 93°7E 245 H11
Henryetta U.S.A. 35°27N 95°59W 314 D7
Henryków Poland 50°39N 16°58E 185 H3
Henryville Canada 45°8N 73°11W 130 A5
Hensall Canada 43°26N 81°30W 312 C3
Henson Cr. → U.S.A. 38°47N 76°58W 143 C4
Hentiesbaai Namibia 22°8S 14°18E 270 B1
Hentiyn Nuruu Mongolia 48°30N 108°30E 219 B9
Henttaa Finland 60°11N 24°41E 121 B1
Henty Australia 35°30S 147°0E 283 C7
Henzada Burma 17°38N 95°26E 241 G5
Hephaestia Greece 39°55N 25°14E 205 B7
Hephzibah U.S.A. 33°19N 82°6W 316 C6

Heping China 24°29N 115°0E 229 E10
Heping Park China 31°16N 121°30E 138 B2
Hepingli China 39°57N 116°23E 114 B2
Heppner U.S.A. 45°21N 119°33W 304 D4
Hepu China 21°40N 109°12E 228 G7
Hepworth Canada 44°37N 81°9W 312 B3
Heqing China 26°37N 100°11E 228 D3
Heqing China 26°37N 100°11E 228 D3
Hequ China 39°20N 111°15E 226 D6
Héraðsflói Iceland 65°42N 14°12W 155 B12
Héraðsvötn → Iceland 65°45N 19°25W 155 B5
Heradsbygd Norway 60°49N 11°39E 164 D8
Heraklion = Iraklio Greece 35°20N 25°12E 207 E6
Herald Cays Australia 16°58S 149°9E 280 B4
Herand Norway 60°20N 6°2E 164 D3
Herangi N.Z. 38°33S 174°48E 284 E3
Herāt Afghan. 34°20N 62°7E 240 B1
Herāt □ Afghan. 35°0N 62°0E 240 B1
Hérault □ France 43°34N 3°15E 174 E7
Hérault → France 43°17N 3°26E 174 E7
Herbault France 47°36N 1°8E 172 E8
Herbert → Australia 18°31S 146°17E 280 B4
Herbert Canada 50°30N 107°10W 297 C7
Herbert Hoover Nat. Historic Site U.S.A. 41°40N 91°21W 310 C5
Herbert I. U.S.A. 52°45N 170°7W 303 K5
Herbertabad India 11°43N 92°37E 245 J11
Herberton Australia 17°20S 145°25E 280 B4
Herbertsdale S. Africa 34°1S 21°46E 270 D3
Herbertville N.Z. 40°30S 176°33E 284 F6
Herbignac France 47°27N 2°18W 172 E4
Herborn Germany 50°40N 8°18E 178 E4
Herby Poland 50°45N 18°50E 185 H5
Herceg-Novi Montenegro 42°30N 18°33E 202 D2
Hercegfalva = Mezőfalva Hungary 46°55N 18°49E 182 D3
Herchmer Canada 57°22N 94°10W 297 B10
Herculaneum U.S.A. 38°16N 90°23W 310 F6
Herculândia Brazil 21°57S 50°40W 333 H8
Heréhérétué French Polynesia 19°45S 144°58W 289 f
Herefoss Norway 58°32N 8°23E 164 F5
Hereford Hereford, U.K. 52°4N 2°43W 169 E5
Hereford Tex., U.S.A. 34°49N 102°24W 314 E3
Herefordshire □ U.K. 52°8N 2°40W 169 E5
Herefoss Norway 58°32N 8°23E 164 F5
Herentals Belgium 51°12N 4°51E 170 C4
Herford Germany 52°7N 8°39E 178 C4
Héricourt France 47°32N 6°45E 173 E13
Herington U.S.A. 38°40N 96°57W 308 F5
Heris Iran 38°14N 47°6E 213 C12
Herisau Switz. 47°22N 9°17E 179 H5
Hérisson France 46°32N 2°42E 173 F9
Herkimer U.S.A. 43°2N 74°59W 313 D10
Herlen → Asia 48°48N 117°0E 219 B9
Herlong U.S.A. 40°8N 120°8W 306 E6
Herm U.K. 49°30N 2°28W 169 H9
Hermakivka Ukraine 48°42N 26°11E 183 B11
Herman U.S.A. 45°49N 96°9W 308 C5
Hermann U.S.A. 38°42N 91°27W 310 F5
Hermannsburg N. Terr., Australia 23°57S 132°45E 278 D5
Hermannsburg Germany 52°50N 10°5E 178 C6
Hermannsbad = Ciechocinek Poland 52°53N 18°45E 185 F5
Hermanus S. Africa 34°27S 19°12E 270 E2
Hermanus Mayor I. Phil. 15°47N 119°47E 232 D2
Hermel Lebanon 34°23N 36°24E 250 A5
Hermidale Australia 31°30S 146°42E 281 E4
Hermiston U.S.A. 45°51N 119°17W 304 D4
Hermit Is. Papua N. G. 1°32S 145°0E 286 A3
Hermitage Grenada 12°27N 61°28W 323 q
Hermitage and Winter Palace Russia 59°55N 30°19E 137 B2
Hermon, N.Y., U.S.A. 44°28N 75°14W 313 B10
Hermon, Mt. = Shaykh, J. ash Lebanon 33°25N 35°50E 250 E6
Hermosillo Mexico 29°10N 111°0W 318 B3
Hermsdorf Germany 52°37N 13°18E 115 A2
Hernád → Hungary 47°56N 21°8E 182 C6
Hernals Austria 48°13N 16°18E 142 A2
Hernandarias Paraguay 25°20S 54°40W 335 B5
Hernandez U.S.A. 36°24N 120°46W 306 J6
Hernando Argentina 32°28S 63°40W 334 C3
Hernando Fla., U.S.A. 28°54N 82°23W 317 G6
Hernando Miss., U.S.A. 34°50N 90°0W 315 D10
Hernando de Magallanes Chile 54°0S 72°40W 336 D2
Herndon U.S.A. 40°43N 76°51W 312 E8
Herne Germany 51°32N 7°14E 170 C7
Herne Bay U.K. 51°21N 1°8E 169 F9
Herne Hill U.K. 51°27N 0°6W 125 B3
Herning Denmark 56°8N 8°58E 163 H2
Heroica Caborca = Caborca Mexico 30°37N 112°6W 318 A2
Heroica Nogales = Nogales Mexico 31°19N 110°56W 318 A2
Heron Bay Canada 48°40N 86°25W 298 C2
Heron I. Australia 23°27S 151°55E 280 C5
Herón, Î. aux Canada 45°25N 73°34W 130 B2
Herradura, Pta. de la Canary Is. 28°26N 14°8W 153 f2
Herreid U.S.A. 45°50N 100°4W 308 C3
Herrenberg Germany 48°36N 8°52E 179 G4
Herrera Spain 37°26N 4°55W 195 H6
Herrera de Alcántara Spain 39°39N 7°25W 195 C2
Herrera del Duque Spain 39°10N 5°3W 195 C5
Herrin U.S.A. 37°48N 89°2W 310 G7
Herriot Canada 56°22N 101°16W 297 B8
Herrljunga Sweden 58°5N 13°1E 163 F6
Hersbruck Germany 49°30N 11°25E 179 F7
Herschel I. Canada 69°35N 139°5W 292 B5
Herschel S. Africa 30°39S 27°1E 271 E4
Hershey U.S.A. 40°17N 76°39W 313 F8
Herso = Cherso Greece 40°7N 22°48E 204 A4
Herstal Belgium 50°40N 5°38E 170 D5
Herstedøster Denmark 55°41N 12°21E 139 C2
Hertford U.K. 51°48N 0°4W 169 F7
's-Hertogenbosch Neths. 51°42N 5°17E 170 C5
Hertford, N.C., U.S.A. 36°11N 76°28W 315 C16
Hertfordshire □ U.K. 51°51N 0°5W 169 F7
Hertsa Ukraine 48°9N 26°6E 183 B10
Hertzogville S. Africa 28°9S 25°30E 270 C4
Hervás Spain 40°16N 5°52W 194 E5

Hervey B. Australia 25°0S 152°52E 280 C5
Herzberg Brandenburg, Germany 51°41N 13°14E 178 D9
Herzberg Niedersachsen, Germany 51°38N 10°20E 178 D6
Herzliyya Israel 32°10N 34°50E 250 C3
Herzogenburg Austria 48°17N 15°41E 180 C8
Heşār Fārs, Iran 29°52N 50°16E 247 D6
Heşār Markazī, Iran 35°50N 49°12E 247 C6
Hesdin France 50°21N 2°3E 173 B9
Heshan China 23°50N 108°53E 228 F7
Heshui China 35°48N 108°0E 226 G5
Heshun China 37°22N 113°32E 226 F7
Heskestad Norway 58°28N 6°22E 164 F3
Hesperia U.S.A. 34°25N 117°18W 307 L9
Hesse = Hessen □ Germany 50°30N 9°0E 178 E4
Hessen □ Germany 50°30N 9°0E 178 E4
Hestra Sweden 57°26N 13°35E 163 G7
Hetauda Nepal 27°25N 85°2E 243 F11
Hetch Hetchy Aqueduct U.S.A. 37°29N 122°19W 306 H5
Hettinger U.S.A. 46°0N 102°42W 308 B2
Hettstedt Germany 51°39N 11°31E 178 D7
Hetzendorf Austria 48°10N 16°16E 142 B2
Heuksando S. Korea 34°40N 125°30E 224 G2
Heunghae S. Korea 36°4N 129°21E 224 D4
Heuvelton U.S.A. 44°37N 75°25W 313 B9
Hevelândia Brazil 5°12S 61°50W 329 E5
Heves Hungary 47°36N 20°17E 182 C5
Heves □ Hungary 47°50N 20°0E 182 C5
Hewitt U.S.A. 31°28N 97°12W 314 F6
Hexham U.K. 54°58N 2°4W 168 C5
Hexi Yunnan, China 24°9N 102°38E 228 E4
Hexi Zhejiang, China 27°58N 119°38E 229 D12
Hexigten Qi China 43°18N 117°30E 227 C9
Hextable U.K. 51°24N 0°10E 125 B5
Heyang China 35°2N 110°22E 226 G6
Heydarābād Iran 30°33N 55°38E 247 D7
Heyfield Australia 37°59S 146°47E 283 D7
Heysham U.K. 54°3N 2°53W 168 C5
Heyuan China 23°39N 114°40E 229 F10
Heywood Australia 38°8S 141°37E 282 D4
Heyworth U.S.A. 40°19N 88°59W 310 D8
Heze China 35°14N 115°20E 226 G8
Hezhang China 27°8N 104°41E 228 D5
Hezheng China 35°14N 103°18E 226 G2
Hi-no-Misaki Japan 35°26N 132°38E 222 B4
Hi Vista U.S.A. 34°45N 117°46W 307 L9
Hialeah U.S.A. 25°51N 80°16W 317 N5
Hiawassa, L. U.S.A. 28°33N 81°28W 143 A2
Hiawatha U.S.A. 39°51N 95°32W 308 F6
Hibbing U.S.A. 47°25N 92°56W 308 B7
Hibernia Reef Australia 12°0S 123°23E 278 B3
Hibiki-Nada Japan 34°0N 130°0E 222 D2
Hickman U.S.A. 36°34N 89°11W 311 H8
Hickory U.S.A. 35°44N 81°21W 315 D14
Hickory Hills U.S.A. 41°43N 87°49W 119 C2
Hicks, Pt. Australia 37°49S 149°17E 283 D8
Hicks Bay N.Z. 37°34S 178°21E 284 E7
Hicks L. Canada 61°25N 100°0W 297 A9
Hicksville Ohio, U.S.A. 41°18N 84°46W 311 C12
Hida Romania 47°10N 23°19E 183 C8
Hida-Gawa → Japan 35°26N 137°3E 223 B9
Hida-Sammyaku Japan 36°30N 137°40E 223 A9
Hida-Sanchi Japan 36°10N 137°0E 223 A9
Hidaka Japan 35°30N 134°44E 222 B7
Hidaka-Sammyaku Japan 42°45N 142°45E 220 C11
Hidalgo □ Mexico 20°30N 99°0W 319 C5
Hidalgo, Presa M. Mexico 26°30N 108°35W 318 B3
Hidalgo del Parral Mexico 26°56N 105°40W 318 B3

Highlands, The Antigua & B. 17°38N 61°47W 322 c
Highlands North S. Africa 26°8S 28°5E 123 A2
Highmore U.S.A. 44°31N 99°26W 308 C4
Higüero, Pta. Puerto Rico 18°22N 67°16W 321 b
Higüey Dom. Rep. 18°37N 68°42W 321 C6
Hihya Egypt 30°40N 31°36E 256 H7
Hiiraan □ Somali Rep. 4°0N 45°30E 267 G4
Hiiumaa Estonia 58°50N 22°45E 188 C2
Hijar Spain 41°10N 0°27W 196 D4
Ḥijāz Si. Arabia 24°0N 40°0E 246 E3
Hijo = Tagum Phil. 7°33N 125°53E 233 H5
Hikari Japan 33°58N 131°58E 222 D3
Hiketa Japan 34°13N 134°24E 222 C6
Hikkaduwa Sri Lanka 6°19N 80°6E 245 L5
Hikmak, Ras el Egypt 31°15N 27°15E 256 A2
Hikone Japan 35°15N 136°10E 223 B8
Hikurangi Gisborne, N.Z. 37°55S 178°4E 284 E5
Hikurangi Northland, N.Z. 35°36S 174°17E 284 B5
Hikutavake Cook Is. 18°56S 169°53W 289 g
Hiland Park U.S.A. 30°12N 85°33W 316 H4
Hilawng Burma 21°23N 93°48E 241 E4
Hildburghausen Germany 50°26N 10°44E 178 E6
Hildesheim Germany 52°9N 9°56E 178 C5
Hliðarendi Iceland 63°44N 19°57W 155 D7
Hill → Australia 30°23S 115°3W 277 F2
Hill City Idaho, U.S.A. 43°18N 115°3W 304 E6
Hill City Kans., U.S.A. 39°22N 99°51W 308 F4
Hill City Minn., U.S.A. 46°59N 93°36W 308 B7
Hill City S. Dak., U.S.A. 43°56N 103°35W 308 D2
Hill Island L. Canada 60°30N 109°50W 297 A7
Hillaby, Mt. Barbados 13°12N 59°35W 323 g
Hillared Sweden 57°37N 13°10E 163 G7
Hillcrest Center U.S.A. 35°23N 118°57W 307 K8
Hillcrest Heights U.S.A. 38°49N 76°57W 143 C4
Hillegom Neths. 52°18N 4°35E 170 B4
Hillend U.K. 56°2N 3°22W 121 A1
Hillerød Denmark 55°56N 12°19E 163 J6
Hillerstorp Sweden 57°20N 13°52E 163 G7
Hilli Bangla. 25°17N 89°1E 243 G13
Hillman U.S.A. 45°4N 83°54W 312 B6
Hillsboro = Deerfield Beach U.S.A. 26°19N 80°6W 317 J9
Hillsboro Ga., U.S.A. 33°11N 83°38W 316 B6
Hillsboro Ill., U.S.A. 39°9N 89°29W 310 F7
Hillsboro Kans., U.S.A. 38°21N 97°12W 308 F5
Hillsboro N. Dak., U.S.A. 47°26N 97°3W 308 B5
Hillsboro Ohio, U.S.A. 39°12N 83°37W 311 F13
Hillsboro Oreg., U.S.A. 45°31N 122°59W 306 E4
Hillsboro Tex., U.S.A. 32°1N 97°8W 314 E6
Hillsboro Canal U.S.A. 26°30N 80°15W 317 J9
Hillsborough Grenada 12°28N 61°28W 323 q
Hillsborough N.H., U.S.A. 43°7N 71°54W 313 C13
Hillsborough Channel Australia 20°56S 149°15E 280 b
Hillsborough Dam Trin. & Tob. 11°13N 60°40W 323 s
Hillsborough Land = Belle Glade U.S.A. 26°41N 80°40W 317 J9
Hillsdale Mich., U.S.A. 41°56N 84°38W 311 C12
Hillsdale N.Y., U.S.A. 42°11N 73°32W 313 D11
Hillsport Canada 49°27N 85°34W 298 C2
Hilltonia U.S.A. 32°53N 81°40W 316 C8
Hillston Australia 33°30S 145°31E 283 B6
Hilo ✈ (ITO) U.S.A. 19°43N 155°4W 302 D6
Hilo B. U.S.A. 19°45N 155°5W 302 D6
Hilongos Phil. 10°22N 124°44E 233 F5
Hilton Canada 43°17N 77°48W 312 C7
Hilton Head Island U.S.A. 32°13N 80°45W 316 D7
Hilvan Turkey 37°34N 38°58E 213 D8
Hilversum Neths. 52°14N 5°10E 170 B5
Himachal Pradesh □ India 31°30N 77°0E 242 D7
Himalaya Asia 29°0N 84°0E 243 E11
Himalchuli Nepal 28°27N 84°38E 243 E11
Himarë Albania 40°8N 19°43E 202 F3
Himatnagar India 23°37N 72°57E 242 H5
Hime-Jima Japan 33°43N 131°40E 222 D3
Himeji Japan 34°50N 134°40E 222 C7
Himi Japan 36°50N 136°55E 223 A8
Himmerland Denmark 56°50N 9°50E 163 H3
Hims Syria 34°40N 36°45E 250 C5
Hims □ Syria 34°30N 37°0E 250 C6
Hin Keng China 22°22N 114°10E 219 a
Hinatuan Phil. 8°22N 126°20E 233 G6
Hinatuan Passage Phil. 9°45N 125°47E 233 G6
Hinche Haiti 19°9N 72°1W 321 C5
Hinchinbrook I. Australia 18°20S 146°15E 280 B4
Hinckley Leics., U.K. 52°33N 1°22W 169 E6
Hinckley Minn., U.S.A. 46°1N 92°56W 308 B7
Hindaun India 26°44N 77°5E 242 F7
Hindenburg = Zabrze Poland 50°18N 18°50E 185 H5
Hindmarsh, L. Australia 36°5S 141°55E 282 D4
Hindsholm Denmark 55°30N 10°40E 163 J4
Hindu Bagh Pakistan 30°56N 67°50E 240 D5
Hindu Kush Asia 36°0N 71°0E 240 B6
Hindupur India 13°49N 77°32E 245 H3
Hines Creek Canada 56°20N 118°40W 296 B5
Hinesville U.S.A. 31°51N 81°36W 316 D8
Hinganghat India 20°30N 78°52E 244 D4
Hingham U.S.A. 48°33N 110°25W 304 B8
Hingir India 21°57N 83°41E 243 J10
Hingol → Pakistan 25°23N 65°28E 240 G4
Hingoli India 19°41N 77°15E 244 E3
Hinis Turkey 39°20N 41°44E 213 C9
Hinna = Imi Ethiopia 6°28N 42°10E 267 F3
Hinnøya Norway 68°35N 15°50E 160 B10
Hino Japan 35°0N 136°15E 223 C8
Hinoba-an Phil. 9°52N 122°28E 233 H4
Hinojosa del Duque Spain 38°30N 5°9W 195 C5
Hinokage Japan 32°39N 131°24E 222 E3
Hinton Alta., Canada 53°26N 117°34W 296 C5
Hinton W. Va., U.S.A. 37°40N 80°54W 309 G14
Hirado Japan 33°22N 129°33E 222 E1
Hirado-Shima Japan 33°20N 129°27E 222 E1
Hirakata Japan 34°48N 135°40E 223 C7
Hirakud Dam India 21°32N 83°45E 244 D6

Hiran → India 23°6N 79°21E 243 H8
Hirapur India 24°22N 79°13E 243 G8
Hirara Japan 24°48N 125°17E 221 M2
Hirata Japan 35°24N 132°49E 222 B4
Hiratsuka Japan 35°19N 139°21E 223 B11
Hirekerur India 14°28N 75°23E 245 G2
Hirfanlı Barajı Turkey 39°18N 33°31E 212 C5
Hirhafok Algeria 23°49N 5°45E 261 D6
Hiromi Japan 33°13N 132°36E 222 D4
Hiroo Japan 42°17N 143°19E 220 C11
Hirosaki Japan 40°34N 140°28E 220 D10
Hiroshima Japan 34°24N 132°30E 222 C4
Hiroshima □ Japan 34°50N 133°0E 222 C5
Hiroshima-Wan Japan 34°5N 132°20E 222 C4
Hirota Japan 34°45N 135°20E 133 A1
Hirschberg = Jelenia Góra Poland 50°50N 15°45E 185 H2
Hirschstetten Austria 48°14N 16°27E 142 A2
Hirson France 49°55N 4°4E 173 C11
Hirtshals Denmark 57°36N 9°57E 163 G3
Hisai Japan 34°40N 136°28E 223 C8
Hisar India 29°12N 75°45E 242 E6
Hisarcık Turkey 39°15N 29°14E 205 B11
Hisaria Bulgaria 42°30N 24°44E 203 D8
Hisb, Sha ib = Ḩasb, W. → Iraq 31°45N 44°17E 246 D5
Ḩismá Si. Arabia 28°30N 36°0E 251 K7
Ḩişn al 'Abr Yemen 16°8N 47°14E 248 C4
Hispaniola W. Indies 19°0N 71°0W 321 C5
Hīt Iraq 33°38N 42°49E 213 F10
Hita Japan 33°20N 130°58E 222 D2
Hitachi Japan 36°36N 140°39E 223 A12
Hitachi-Ōta Japan 36°30N 140°30E 223 A12
Hitchin U.K. 51°58N 0°16W 169 F7
Hithadhoo Maldives 0°36S 73°5E 272 d
Hither Green U.K. 51°26N 0°0 125 B3
Hitiaa Tahiti 17°36S 149°18W 289 e
Hitoyoshi Japan 32°13N 130°45E 222 E2
Hitra Norway 63°30N 8°45E 164 A5
Hitzacker Germany 53°9N 11°2E 178 B7
Hiu Vanuatu 13°10S 166°35E 287 C4
Hiuchi-Nada Japan 34°5N 133°20E 222 C5
Hiva Oa French Polynesia 9°45S 139°0W 289 f
Hixon Canada 53°25N 122°35W 296 C4
Hiyoshi Japan 35°32N 139°38E 140 B2
Ḩiyyon, N. → Israel 30°25N 35°10E 251 H6
Hizma West Bank 31°50N 35°16E 123 B2
Hjalmar L. Canada 61°33N 109°25W 297 A7
Hjälmaren Sweden 59°18N 15°40E 162 E9
Hjältevad Sweden 57°38N 15°20E 163 G9
Hjalteyri Iceland 65°55N 18°18W 155 B8
Hjartdal Norway 59°37N 8°41E 164 E5
Hjelmelandsvågen Norway 59°14N 6°10E 164 E3
Hjelset Norway 62°48N 7°30E 164 B4
Hjerkinn Norway 62°13N 9°33E 164 B6
Hjo Sweden 58°22N 14°17E 163 F8
Hjørring Denmark 57°29N 9°59E 163 G3
Hjörsey Iceland 64°32N 22°21W 155 C4
Hjort Trench S. Ocean 58°0S 157°30E 151 B10
Hjortekær Denmark 55°47N 12°32E 118 A3
Hjortespring Denmark 55°44N 12°25E 118 A2
Hjortkvarn Sweden 58°54N 15°26E 163 F9
Hjukse Norway 59°31N 9°19E 164 E6
Hkakabo Razi Burma 28°25N 97°23E 228 C1
Hkakabo Razi △ Burma 28°0N 97°55E 241 A6
Hkamti = Singkaling Hkamti Burma 26°0N 95°39E 241 C5
Hko-lam Burma 21°7N 98°5E 241 E7
Hko-ut Burma 20°58N 98°2E 241 E7
Hkyenhpa Burma 27°43N 97°25E 241 B6
Hlaingbwe Burma 17°8N 97°50E 241 G6
Hlinsko Czech Rep. 49°45N 15°54E 180 B8
Hlobane S. Africa 27°42S 31°0E 271 C5
Hlohovec Slovak Rep. 48°26N 17°49E 181 C10
Hlubočepy Czech Rep. 50°2N 14°23E 135 B2
Hlučín Czech Rep. 49°54N 18°11E 181 B11
Hluhluwe S. Africa 28°1S 32°15E 271 C5
Hluhluwe ⌂ S. Africa 22°10S 32°5E 271 B5
Hlukhiv Ukraine 51°40N 33°58E 189 G7
Hlwaze Burma 18°54N 96°37E 241 F6
Hlyboka Ukraine 48°5N 25°56E 183 B10
Hlybokaye Belarus 55°10N 27°45E 188 E4
Hnappadalssýsla □ Iceland 64°50N 22°30W 155 C4
Hnífsdalur Iceland 66°7N 23°8W 155 A3
Hnúšt'a Slovak Rep. 48°35N 19°58E 181 C12
Ho Ghana 6°37N 0°27E 263 D5
Ho Chi Minh City = Thanh Pho Ho Chi Minh Vietnam 10°58N 106°40E 237 G6
Ho Chung China 22°21N 114°14E 122 A2
Ho Hoa Binh Vietnam 20°50N 105°0E 228 G5
Ho Thac Ba Vietnam 21°42N 105°1E 236 A5
Ho Thuong Vietnam 19°32N 105°48E 236 C5
Hoa Binh Vietnam 20°50N 105°20E 228 G5
Hoa Hiep Vietnam 11°34N 105°51E 237 G5
Hoai Nhon Vietnam 14°28N 109°1E 236 E7
Hoang Lien △ Vietnam 21°30N 105°32E 236 B5
Hoang Lien Son Vietnam 22°0N 104°0E 228 F4
Hoanib → Namibia 19°27S 12°46E 270 A2
Hoare B. Canada 65°17N 62°30W 295 D19
Hoarusib → Namibia 19°3S 12°36E 270 A2
Hobart Tas., Australia 42°50S 147°21E 281 G4
Hobart Ind., U.S.A. 41°32N 87°15W 311 C9
Hobart Okla., U.S.A. 35°1N 99°6W 314 D5
Hobbs U.S.A. 32°42N 103°8W 305 K12
Hobbs Coast Antarctica 74°50S 131°0W 151 D14
Hobe Sound U.S.A. 27°4N 80°8W 317 H9
Hobo Colombia 2°35N 75°30W 328 C2
Hoboken Ga., U.S.A. 31°11N 82°8W 316 D7
Hoboken New York, U.S.A. 132 d1
Hobro Denmark 56°39N 9°46E 163 H3
Hobsons B. Australia 37°51S 144°55E 128 B1
Hoburgen Sweden 56°55N 18°7E 163 H12
Hobyo Somali Rep. 5°25N 48°30E 267 C6
Hocalar Turkey 38°36N 30°0E 205 C11
Hochbrück Germany 48°14N 11°37E 131 A2
Hochelaga Canada 45°32N 73°33W 130 A2
Hochfeld Namibia 21°28S 17°58E 270 B2
Hochharz △ Germany 51°48N 10°38E 178 D6
Hochschwab Austria 47°35N 15°0E 180 D8
Höchstadt Germany 49°42N 10°47E 179 F6
Hochtaunus ⌂ Germany 50°20N 8°30E 179 E4
Hoch'uan = Hechuan China 30°2N 106°12E 228 B6
Hochwan = Hechuan China 30°2N 106°12E 228 B6
Hockenheim Germany 49°19N 8°32E 179 F4
Hockley = Levelland U.S.A. 33°35N 102°23W 314 E3
Hodaka-Dake Japan 36°17N 137°39E 223 A9
Hodeida = Al Ḩudaydah Yemen 14°50N 43°0E 248 D3
Hodgeville Canada 50°7N 106°58W 297 C7
Hodgkins U.S.A. 41°46N 87°53W 119 C1
Hodgson Canada 51°13N 97°36W 297 C9
Hodh El Gharbi □ Mauritania 16°30N 10°0W 262 B3
Hódmezővásárhely Hungary 46°28N 20°22E 182 D5
Hodna, Chott el Algeria 35°26N 4°43E 261 A6
Hodo-dan N. Korea 39°23N 127°32E 224 C3
Hodonín Czech Rep. 48°50N 17°10E 181 C10
Hœdic, Î. de France 47°20N 2°53W 172 E4
Hoegi S. Korea 37°35N 127°3E 137 B2
Hoeilaart Belgium 50°46N 4°28E 116 B2
Hoek van Holland Neths. 52°0N 4°7E 170 C4
Hoengseong S. Korea 37°29N 127°59E 224 D3
Hoeryong N. Korea 42°30N 129°45E 224 A4
Hoeyang N. Korea 38°43N 127°36E 224 C3
Hof Bayern, Germany 50°19N 11°55E 179 E7
Hof Norður-Múlasýsla, Iceland 65°39N 15°0W 155 B11
Hof Suður-Múlasýsla, Iceland 64°33N 14°40W 155 C12
Hof Vestfold, Norway 59°32N 10°5E 164 E7
Hofburg Vienna, Austria 142 b1
Hofei = Hefei China 31°52N 117°18E 229 B11
Hoffell Iceland 64°23N 15°20W 155 C11
Hoffman I. U.S.A. 40°34N 74°3W 132 C1
Hofgarten Munich, Germany 131 a3
Hofgeismar Germany 51°29N 9°23E 178 D5
Hofheim Germany 50°5N 8°26E 179 E4
Hofmeyr S. Africa 31°39S 25°50E 270 D4
Höfn Iceland 64°15N 15°13W 155 C11
Hofors Sweden 60°31N 16°15E 162 D10
Hofsjökull Iceland 64°49N 18°48W 155 C8
Hofsós Iceland 65°53N 19°26W 155 B7
Hōfu Japan 34°3N 131°34E 222 C3
Hog Harbour Vanuatu 15°8S 167°6E 287 E5
Hog I. = Paradise I. Bahamas 25°6N 77°19W 153 b
Hog I. Grenada 12°0N 61°44W 323 q
Hog Pt. Antigua & B. 17°41N 61°47W 322 c
Hogan Group Australia 39°13S 147°1E 281 F4
Höganäs Sweden 56°12N 12°33E 163 H6
Hogansville U.S.A. 33°10N 84°55W 316 B5
Hogarth, Mt. Australia 21°48S 136°58E 280 C2
Hoge Kempen △ Belgium 51°6N 5°35E 170 C5
Høgeloft Norway 61°3N 8°12E 164 C5
Hogenakai Falls India 12°6N 77°50E 245 H3
Hoggar = Ahaggar Algeria 23°0N 6°30E 261 D6
Högsäter Sweden 58°38N 12°5E 163 F6
Högsby Sweden 57°10N 16°1E 163 G10
Högsjö Sweden 59°4N 15°44E 162 E9
Hogsty Reef Bahamas 21°41N 73°48W 321 B5
Hoh → U.S.A. 47°45N 124°29W 306 C2
Hoh Xil Shan China 36°30N 89°0E 218 D6
Hohd ech Chargui □ Mauritania 19°0N 7°15W 260 E3
Hohe Acht Germany 50°22N 7°0E 179 E3
Hohe Tauern Austria 47°11N 12°40E 180 D5
Hohe Tauern △ Austria 47°5N 12°20E 180 D5
Hohenau Austria 48°36N 16°55E 181 C9
Hohenbrunn Germany 48°2N 11°42E 131 B3
Hohenelbe = Vrchlabí Czech Rep. 50°38N 15°37E 180 A8
Hohenems Austria 47°22N 9°42E 180 D2
Hohenloher Ebene Germany 49°14N 9°36E 179 F5
Hohenmauth = Vysoké Mýto Czech Rep. 49°58N 16°10E 181 B9
Hohensalza = Inowrocław Poland 52°50N 18°12E 185 F5
Hohensalzburg = Lunino Russia 53°38N 45°18E 190 D7
Hohenschönhausen Germany 52°33N 13°30E 115 A4
Hohenstadt = Zábřeh Czech Rep. 49°53N 16°52E 181 B9
Hohenstein = Olsztynek Poland 53°34N 20°19E 184 E7
Hohenwald U.S.A. 35°33N 87°33W 315 D11
Hohenwestedt Germany 54°5N 9°40E 178 A5
Hoher Rhön = Rhön Germany 50°24N 9°58E 178 E5
Hoher Vogelsberg ⌂ Germany 51°45N 9°35E 178 D5
Hohes Venn Belgium 50°30N 6°5E 170 D6
Hohes Venn-Eifel ⌂ Europe 50°30N 6°10E 178 E2
Hohhot China 40°52N 111°40E 226 D6
Hohoe Ghana 7°8N 0°32E 263 D5
Hoi An Vietnam 15°30N 108°19E 236 E7
Hoi Xuan Vietnam 20°25N 105°9E 228 G5
Hoihow = Haikou China 20°1N 110°16E 236 B8
Hoisington U.S.A. 38°31N 98°47W 308 F4
Hojai India 26°2N 92°54E 241 B4
Hojambaz Turkmenistan 38°7N 65°0E 216 E6
Højer Denmark 54°58N 8°42E 163 K2
Hōjō Japan 33°58N 132°46E 222 D4
Hok Sweden 57°31N 14°16E 163 G8
Hokang = Hegang China 47°20N 130°19E 219 B15
Hökensås Sweden 58°0N 14°5E 163 G8
Hökerum Sweden 57°51N 13°16E 163 G7
Hokianga Harbour N.Z. 35°31S 173°22E 284 B2
Hokitika N.Z. 42°42S 171°0E 285 C6
Hokkaidō □ Japan 43°30N 143°0E 220 C11
Hokksund Norway 59°48N 9°54E 164 E6
Hol-Hol Djibouti 11°20N 42°50E 257 E5
Hola Kenya 1°29S 40°2E 268 B4
Hola Prystan Ukraine 46°29N 32°32E 189 J7
Holakas Greece 35°57N 27°53E 206 F11
Holalkere India 14°2N 76°11E 245 G3
Hólar Iceland 65°44N 19°8W 155 B7
Holargos = Cholargos Greece 37°59N 23°48E 112 B2
Holbæk Denmark 55°43N 11°43E 163 J5
Holborn London, U.K. 125 a4
Holbrook N.S.W., Australia 35°42S 147°18E 283 C7
Holbrook Ariz., U.S.A. 34°54N 110°10W 305 J8
Holcomb U.S.A. 42°54N 77°25W 312 D7
Holden Mo., U.S.A. 38°43N 94°0W 310 F3
Holden Utah, U.S.A. 39°6N 112°16W 304 G7
Holden, L. U.S.A. 28°30N 81°23W 133 B2
Holdenville U.S.A. 35°5N 96°24W 314 D6
Holdich Argentina 45°57S 68°13W 336 C3
Holdrege U.S.A. 40°26N 99°23W 308 E4
Hole-Narsipur India 12°48N 76°16E 245 H3
Holešov Czech Rep. 49°20N 17°35E 181 B10
Holešovice Czech Rep. 50°6N 14°28E 135 B2
Holetown Barbados 13°11N 59°38W 323 r
Holgate U.S.A. 41°15N 84°8W 311 C12
Holguín Cuba 20°50N 76°20W 320 B4
Holíč Slovak Rep. 48°49N 17°10E 181 C10
Holice Czech Rep. 50°5N 16°0E 180 A8
Holiday U.S.A. 28°11N 82°44W 317 G7
Höljes Sweden 60°50N 12°35E 162 D6
Hollabrunn Austria 48°34N 16°5E 180 C9
Hollams Bird I. Namibia 24°40S 14°30E 270 B1
Holland = Netherlands ■ Europe 52°0N 5°30E 170 C5
Holland Mich., U.S.A. 42°47N 86°7W 311 B10
Holland N.Y., U.S.A. 42°38N 78°32W 312 D6
Holland B. Jamaica 17°57N 76°13W 320 a
Holland Centre Canada 44°23N 80°47W 312 B4
Holland Patent U.S.A. 43°14N 75°15W 313 C9
Holland Tunnel New York, U.S.A. 132 d1
Holland Village Singapore 1°18N 103°47E 138 B2
Hollandale U.S.A. 33°10N 90°51W 315 E9
Hollandia = Jayapura Indonesia 2°28S 140°38E 231 E10
Holley U.S.A. 43°14N 78°2W 312 C6
Hollfeld Germany 49°56N 11°18E 179 F7
Hollidaysburg U.S.A. 40°26N 78°24W 312 F6
Hollis U.S.A. 34°41N 99°55W 314 D5
Hollis Reservoir Trin. & Tob. 10°40N 61°10W 323 t
Hollister Calif., U.S.A. 36°51N 121°24W 306 J5
Hollister Idaho, U.S.A. 42°21N 114°35W 304 E6
Höllriegelskreuth Germany 48°2N 11°30E 131 B1
Höllviken Sweden 55°26N 12°58E 163 J6
Höllviksnäs = Höllviken Sweden 55°26N 12°58E 163 J6
Holly U.S.A. 42°48N 83°38W 311 B13
Holly Hill Fla., U.S.A. 29°16N 81°3W 317 F8
Holly Hill S.C., U.S.A. 33°19N 80°25W 316 B9
Holly Springs Ga., U.S.A. 34°10N 84°30W 316 A5
Holly Springs Miss., U.S.A. 34°46N 89°27W 315 D10
Hollywood Calif., U.S.A. 34°5N 118°19W 126 B3
Hollywood Fla., U.S.A. 26°0N 80°8W 317 J9
Hollywood Bowl U.S.A. 34°7N 118°20W 126 B2
Holman Canada 70°44N 117°44W 294 C8
Hólmavík Iceland 65°42N 21°40W 155 B5
Holmen Oppland, Norway 60°40N 10°22E 164 D7
Holmen Wis., U.S.A. 43°58N 91°15W 308 D8
Holmenkollen Norway 59°57N 10°41E 133 A3
Holmes Beach U.S.A. 27°31N 82°43W 317 H7
Holmes Cr. → U.S.A. 30°30N 85°50W 316 E4
Holmes Reefs Australia 16°27S 148°0E 280 B4
Holmes Run Acres U.S.A. 38°51N 77°13W 143 B2
Holmestrand Norway 59°31N 10°14E 164 E7
Holmgård Sweden 59°14N 18°0E 139 B1
Holmlia Norway 59°49N 10°46E 133 B3
Holmsjö Sweden 56°25N 15°32E 163 H9
Holmsjön Västernorrland, Sweden 62°41N 16°33E 162 B10
Holmsjön Västernorrland, Sweden 62°26N 15°20E 162 B9
Holmsland Klit Denmark 56°0N 8°5E 163 J2
Holmsund Sweden 63°41N 20°20E 160 E19
Holocaust Memorial Israel 31°47N 35°11E 123 B2
Holocaust Memorial Park Boston, U.S.A. 116 b2
Holod Romania 46°49N 22°8E 182 D7
Holon Israel 32°0N 34°46E 251 G5
Holopaw U.S.A. 28°8N 81°5W 317 G8
Holovne Ukraine 51°20N 24°5E 185 G11
Holøydal Norway 62°12N 11°27E 164 B8
Holozubyntsi Ukraine 48°50N 26°55E 183 B11
Holroyd → Australia 14°10S 141°36E 280 A3
Holstebro Denmark 56°22N 8°37E 163 H2
Holsteinische Schweiz ⌂ Germany 54°8N 10°30E 178 A6
Holsteinsborg = Sisimiut Greenland 66°40N 53°30W 154 D5
Holsworthy U.K. 50°48N 4°22W 169 G3
Holt Iceland 63°33N 19°48W 155 D7
Holt Fla., U.S.A. 30°43N 86°45W 317 E3
Holt Mich., U.S.A. 42°39N 84°31W 311 B12
Holton Nfld. & L., Canada 54°31N 57°12W 299 B8
Holton Kans., U.S.A. 39°28N 95°44W 308 F6
Holts Summit U.S.A. 38°38N 92°7W 310 F4
Holtville U.S.A. 32°49N 115°23W 307 N11
Holualoa U.S.A. 19°37N 155°57W 302 D6
Holum Norway 58°6N 7°32E 164 F4
Holwerd Neths. 53°22N 5°54E 170 A5
Holy Cross U.S.A. 62°12N 159°46W 303 E8
Holy I. Anglesey, U.K. 53°17N 4°37W 168 D3
Holy I. Northumberland, U.K. 55°40N 1°47W 168 B6
Holyhead U.K. 53°18N 4°38W 168 D3
Holyoke Colo., U.S.A. 40°35N 102°18W 304 F12
Holyoke Mass., U.S.A. 42°12N 72°37W 313 D12
Holyrood Canada 47°27N 53°8W 299 C9
Holyrood House, Palace of U.K. 55°57N 3°10W 121 B3
Holysloot Neths. 52°25N 5°2E 112 A3
Holzkirchen Germany 47°52N 11°42E 179 H7
Holzminden Germany 51°50N 9°28E 178 D5
Homa Bay Kenya 0°36S 34°30E 268 C3
Homalin Burma 24°55N 95°0E 241 C5
Homand Iran 32°28N 59°37E 247 C8
Homathko → Canada 51°0N 124°56W 296 C4
Homberg Germany 51°2N 9°25E 178 D5
Hombori Mali 15°20N 1°38W 263 B4
Hombori Tondo Mali 15°16N 1°40W 263 B4
Homburg Germany 49°28N 7°18E 179 F3
Home B. Canada 68°40N 67°10W 295 D18
Home Hill Australia 19°43S 147°25E 280 B4
Home Reef Tonga 18°59S 174°47W 287 P13
Homedale U.S.A. 43°37N 116°56W 304 E5
Homei Taiwan 24°7N 120°29E 225 B2
Homeland U.S.A. 30°51N 82°1W 316 E7
Homer Alaska, U.S.A. 59°39N 151°33W 303 G10
Homer Ill., U.S.A. 40°4N 87°57W 311 D9
Homer La., U.S.A. 32°48N 93°4W 314 E8
Homer Mich., U.S.A. 42°9N 84°49W 311 B12
Homer N.Y., U.S.A. 42°38N 76°10W 313 D8
Homer City U.S.A. 40°32N 79°10W 312 F5
Homert ⌂ Germany 51°15N 8°0E 178 D4
Homerton U.K. 51°32N 0°2W 125 A3
Homerville U.S.A. 31°2N 82°45W 316 D7
Homestead Queens., Australia 20°20S 145°40E 280 C4
Homestead Fla., U.S.A. 25°28N 80°29W 317 K9
Homestead ⌂ U.S.A. 40°17N 96°50W 308 E5
Hometown U.S.A. 41°44N 87°42W 119 C2
Homewood U.S.A. 41°34N 87°40W 311 C9
Hommelvik Norway 63°25N 10°48E 164 A7
Hommersåk Norway 58°56N 5°50E 164 F2
Homnabad India 17°45N 77°11E 244 F3
Homoine Mozam. 23°55S 35°8E 271 B6
Homoljske Planina Serbia 44°10N 21°45E 202 B5
Homonhon I. Phil. 10°44N 125°43E 233 F5
Homorod Romania 46°5N 25°15E 183 D10
Homosassa Springs U.S.A. 28°48N 82°35W 317 G7
Homs = Al Khums Libya 32°40N 14°17E 258 B2
Homs = Ḩimş Syria 34°40N 36°45E 250 D7
Homyel Belarus 52°28N 31°0E 177 B16
Homyel □ Belarus 52°40N 30°10E 189 F6
Hon Chong Vietnam 10°25N 104°30E 237 G5
Hon Hai Vietnam 10°0N 109°0E 237 H7
Hon Me Vietnam 19°23N 105°56E 236 C5
Honan = Henan □ China 34°0N 114°0E 226 H8
Hōnanchō Japan 35°40N 139°39E 140 A2
Hōnaunau U.S.A. 19°26N 155°55W 302 D6
Honavar India 14°17N 74°27E 245 G2
Honaz Turkey 37°46N 29°18E 205 D11
Honbetsu Japan 43°7N 143°37E 220 C11
Honcho Japan 35°40N 139°41E 140 A3
Honcut U.S.A. 39°20N 121°32W 306 F5
Honda Colombia 5°12N 74°45W 328 B3
Honda, Bahía Cuba 22°54N 83°10W 320 B3
Honda B. Phil. 9°53N 118°49E 233 G2
Hondarribia Spain 43°22N 1°47W 196 B3
Hondeklipbaai S. Africa 30°19S 17°17E 270 D2
Honden Japan 35°43N 139°50E 140 A4
Hondo Japan 32°27N 130°12E 222 E2
Hondo Tex., U.S.A. 29°21N 99°9W 314 G5
Hondo, Río → Belize 18°25N 88°21W 319 D7
Hondo, Rio → Calif., U.S.A. 34°2N 118°15W 126 B4
Honduras ■ Cent. Amer. 14°40N 86°30W 320 D2
Honduras, G. de Caribbean 16°50N 87°0W 320 C2
Hønefoss Norway 60°10N 10°18E 164 D7
Honesdale U.S.A. 41°34N 75°16W 313 E9
Honey Harbour Canada 44°52N 79°49W 312 B5
Honey L. U.S.A. 40°15N 120°19W 306 E6
Honfleur France 49°25N 0°13E 172 C7
Høng Denmark 55°31N 11°18E 163 J5
Hong → Vietnam 20°16N 106°34E 236 B5
Hong Gai Vietnam 20°57N 107°5E 228 G6
Hong He → China 32°25N 115°35E 226 H8
Hong Hu China 29°54N 113°24E 229 C9
Hong Kong China 22°17N 114°11E 122 B1
Hong Kong □ China 22°11N 114°14E 229 F10
Hong Kong, Univ. of China 22°16N 114°8E 122 B1
Hong Kong I. China 22°16N 114°12E 122 B2
Hong Kong Int. ✕ (HKG) China 22°19N 113°57E 219 a
Hong Kong Park Hong Kong, China 122 c1
Honga Angola 15°9S 15°12E 265 F3
Hong'an China 31°20N 114°40E 229 B10
Hongcheon S. Korea 37°44N 127°53E 224 D3
Hongdo S. Korea 34°41N 125°12E 224 E2
Honghai Wan China 22°40N 115°0E 229 F10
Honghe China 23°25N 102°25E 228 F4
Honghu China 29°50N 113°30E 229 C9
Hongje S. Korea 37°35N 126°56E 137 B1
Hongjiang China 27°7N 109°59E 228 D7
Hongjimun Tunnel S. Korea 37°37N 126°58E 137 B1
Hongkou China 31°16N 121°29E 138 B1
Hongliu He → China 38°0N 109°50E 226 F5
Hongor Mongolia 45°45N 112°50E 226 B7
Hongqiao China 31°11N 121°22E 138 B1
Hongseong S. Korea 36°37N 126°38E 224 D3
Hongshan China 36°38N 117°58E 227 F9
Hongshui He → China 23°48N 109°30E 228 F7
Hongtong China 36°16N 111°40E 226 F6
Honguedo, Détroit d' Canada 49°15N 64°0W 299 C7
Hongwon N. Korea 40°0N 127°56E 224 C3
Hongya China 29°57N 103°22E 228 C4
Hongyuan China 32°51N 102°40E 228 A4
Hongze Hu China 33°15N 118°35E 227 H10
Honiara Solomon Is. 9°27S 159°57E 287 M10
Honiton U.K. 50°47N 3°11W 169 G4
Honjō Akita, Japan 39°23N 140°3E 220 E10
Honjō Gumma, Japan 36°14N 139°11E 223 A11
Honjyo Japan 35°41N 139°48E 140 A3
Honkawane Japan 35°5N 138°5E 223 B10
Honkorâb, Ras Egypt 24°35N 35°10E 256 C4
Honnali India 14°15N 75°40E 245 G2
Honningsvåg Norway 70°59N 25°59E 160 A21
Hönö Sweden 57°41N 11°39E 163 G5
Honoka'a U.S.A. 20°5N 155°28W 302 C6
Honokai Hale U.S.A. 21°20N 158°6W 302 K13
Honolulu U.S.A. 21°19N 157°52W 302 K14
Honolulu District U.S.A. 21°19N 157°46W 302 K14
Honolulu Int. ✕ (HNL) U.S.A. 21°19N 157°55W 302 K14
Honomu U.S.A. 19°52N 155°7W 302 D6
Honoré Mercier, Pont Canada 45°24N 73°39W 130 B1
Honouliuli U.S.A. 21°22N 158°2W 302 K13
Hönow Germany 52°32N 13°38E 115 A4
Honshū Japan 36°0N 138°0E 223 A8
Hontoria del Pinar Spain 41°50N 3°10W 196 D1
Honu'apo B. U.S.A. 19°5N 155°33W 302 D6
Hood, I. = Española, I. Ecuador 1°23S 89°39W 330 a
Hood, Mt. U.S.A. 45°23N 121°42W 304 D3
Hood, Pt. Australia 34°23S 119°34E 279 F2
Hood Pt. Papua N. G. 10°4S 147°45E 286 F4
Hood River U.S.A. 45°43N 121°31W 304 D3
Hoodsport U.S.A. 47°24N 123°9W 306 C3
Hooge Germany 54°34N 8°33E 178 A4
Hoogeveen Neths. 52°44N 6°28E 170 B6
Hoogezand-Sappemeer Neths. 53°9N 6°45E 170 A6
Hooghly = Hugli → India 21°56N 88°4E 243 J13
Hooghly-Chinsura = Chunchura India 22°53N 88°27E 243 H13
Hook U.K. 51°22N 0°17W 125 B2
Hook Hd. Ireland 52°7N 6°56W 166 D5
Hook I. Australia 20°4S 149°0E 280 b
Hook of Holland = Hoek van Holland Neths. 52°0N 4°7E 170 C4
Hooker U.S.A. 36°52N 101°13W 314 C4
Hooker Creek = Lajamanu Australia 18°23S 130°38E 278 C5
Hooker Creek ✪ Australia 18°6S 130°23E 278 C5
Ho'olehua U.S.A. 21°10N 157°5W 302 B4
Hoonah U.S.A. 58°7N 135°27W 296 B1
Hoop Bonaire 12°7N 68°17W 322 h
Hooper Bay U.S.A. 61°32N 166°6W 303 F6
Hoopeston U.S.A. 40°28N 87°40W 311 D9
Hoopstad S. Africa 27°50S 25°55E 270 C4
Höör Sweden 55°56N 13°33E 163 J7
Hoorn Neths. 52°38N 5°4E 170 B5
Hoover U.S.A. 33°24N 86°49W 315 E11
Hoover Dam U.S.A. 36°1N 114°44W 307 K12
Hooversville U.S.A. 40°9N 78°55W 312 F6
Hop Bottom U.S.A. 41°42N 75°46W 313 E9
Hopa Turkey 41°28N 41°30E 213 B9
Hope B.C., Canada 49°25N 121°25W 296 D4
Hope Ariz., U.S.A. 33°43N 113°42W 307 M13
Hope Ark., U.S.A. 33°40N 93°36W 314 E8
Hope Ind., U.S.A. 39°18N 85°46W 311 E11
Hope, L. S. Austral., Australia 28°24S 139°18E 281 D2
Hope, L. W. Austral., Australia 32°35S 120°15E 279 F3
Hope, Pt. U.S.A. 68°21N 166°47W 303 B6
Hope Bay Jamaica 18°12N 76°34W 320 a
Hope I. Canada 44°55N 80°11W 312 B4
Hope Town Bahamas 26°35N 76°57W 320 A4
Hope Vale Australia 15°16S 145°20E 280 B4
Hope Vale ✪ Australia 15°8S 145°15E 280 B4
Hopedale Nfld. & L., Canada 55°28N 60°13W 299 A7
Hopedale Mass., U.S.A. 42°8N 71°33W 313 D13
Hopefield S. Africa 33°3S 18°22E 270 D2
Hopei = Hebei □ China 39°0N 116°0E 226 E9
Hopelchén Mexico 19°46N 89°51W 319 D7
Hopetoun Vic., Australia 35°42S 142°22E 282 C5
Hopetoun W. Austral., Australia 33°57S 120°7E 279 F3
Hopetown S. Africa 29°34S 24°3E 270 C3
Hopewell U.S.A. 37°18N 77°17W 309 G15
Hopfgarten Austria 47°27N 12°10E 180 D5
Hopin Burma 24°58N 96°30E 241 C6
Hoping Changhua, Taiwan 24°10N 120°56E 225 B2
Hoping T'aitung, Taiwan 23°4N 121°20E 225 C3
Hopkins U.S.A. 40°33N 94°49W 310 D2
Hopkins, L. Australia 24°15S 128°35E 278 D4
Hopkinsville U.S.A. 36°52N 87°29W 308 G10
Hopland U.S.A. 38°58N 123°7W 306 G3
Hopong Burma 20°47N 97°11E 241 E6
Hopwood's Ferry = Echuca Australia 36°10S 144°45E 283 D6
Hoque Angola 14°40S 13°55E 265 E2
Hoquiam U.S.A. 46°59N 123°53W 306 D3
Hora Hoverla Ukraine 48°7N 24°41E 183 B9
Hora Sfakion = Chora Sfakion Greece 35°15N 24°9E 207 E5
Hōrai Japan 34°58N 137°32E 223 C9
Horana Sri Lanka 6°43N 80°4E 245 L5
Horasan Turkey 40°3N 42°11E 213 B10
Horaždóvice Czech Rep. 49°19N 13°42E 180 B6
Horb Germany 48°26N 8°47E 179 G4
Hörby Sweden 55°51N 13°40E 163 J7
Horcajo de Santiago Spain 39°50N 3°1W 196 F1
Hordabø Norway 60°42N 4°54E 164 D1
Hordaland □ Norway 60°25N 6°15E 164 D3
Hordern Hills Australia 20°15S 130°0E 278 D5
Horezu Romania 45°6N 24°0E 183 E8
Horgen Switz. 47°15N 8°35E 179 H4
Horgoš Serbia 46°10N 20°0E 182 D4
Hořice Czech Rep. 50°21N 15°39E 180 A8
Horikiri Japan 35°44N 139°50E 140 A4
Horinchove Ukraine 48°16N 23°26E 183 B8
Horinger China 40°28N 111°48E 226 D6
Horizontina Brazil 27°37S 54°19W 335 B5
Horki Belarus 54°17N 30°59E 188 E6
Horlick Mts. Antarctica 84°0S 102°0W 151 E15
Horlivka Ukraine 48°19N 38°5E 189 H10
Hormak Iran 29°58N 60°51E 247 D9
Hormigueros Puerto Rico 18°8N 67°8W 321 b
Hormoz Iran 27°35N 55°0E 247 E7
Hormoz, Jaz.-ye Iran 27°8N 56°28E 247 E8
Hormozgān □ Iran 27°30N 56°0E 247 E8
Hormuz, Kūh-e Iran 27°27N 55°10E 247 E7
Hormuz, Str. of The Gulf 26°30N 56°30E 247 E8
Horn Austria 48°39N 15°40E 180 C8
Horn Iceland 66°28N 22°25W 155 A4
Horn Sweden 57°54N 15°51E 163 G9
Horn → Canada 61°30N 118°1W 296 A5
Horn, Cape = Hornos, C. de Chile 55°50S 67°30W 336 E3
Horn, Is. Wall. & F. Is. 14°16S 178°6W 277 C15
Horn Head Ireland 55°14N 8°0W 166 A3
Horn I. Australia 10°37S 142°17E 286 F2
Horn Plateau Canada 62°15N 119°15W 296 A5
Horn Pond U.S.A. 42°28N 71°9W 116 A1
Hornachuelos Spain 37°50N 5°14W 195 H5
Hornavan Sweden 66°15N 17°30E 160 C17
Hornbeck U.S.A. 31°20N 93°24W 314 F8
Hornbrook U.S.A. 41°55N 122°33W 304 F2
Hornburg Germany 52°2N 10°37E 178 C6
Hornby N.Z. 43°33S 172°33E 285 D7
Horncastle U.K. 53°13N 0°7W 168 D7
Hornchurch U.K. 51°33N 0°14E 125 A5
Horndal Sweden 60°18N 16°23E 162 D10
Hornell U.S.A. 42°20N 77°40W 312 D7
Hornell L. Canada 62°20N 119°25W 296 A5
Hornepayne Canada 49°14N 84°48W 298 C3
Horni Czech Rep. 50°2N 14°33E 135 B3
Horní Planá Czech Rep. 48°46N 14°2E 180 C7
Horni Počernice Czech Rep. 50°6N 14°36E 135 B3
Hornindal Norway 61°58N 6°30E 164 C3
Hornings Mills Canada 44°9N 80°12W 312 B4
Hornitos U.S.A. 37°30N 120°14W 306 H6
Hornopirén △ Chile 41°58S 72°17W 336 B2
Hornos, C. de Chile 55°50S 67°30W 336 E3
Hornos Is. Papua N. G. 2°12S 147°45E 286 B4
Hornoy-le-Bourg France 49°50N 1°54E 173 C8
Hornsby Australia 33°42S 151°2E 283 B9
Hornsea U.K. 53°55N 0°11W 168 D7
Hornsey U.K. 51°35N 0°7W 125 A3
Hornsjø Norway 61°19N 10°38E 164 C7
Hornslandet Sweden 61°35N 17°37E 162 C11
Hörnum Germany 54°45N 8°17E 178 A4
Horobetsu = Noboribetsu Japan 42°24N 141°6E 220 C10
Horodenka Ukraine 48°41N 25°29E 183 B10
Horodnya Ukraine 51°55N 31°33E 189 G6
Horodok Khmelnytskyy, Ukraine 49°10N 26°34E 177 D14
Horodok Lviv, Ukraine 49°46N 23°32E 177 D12
Horodyshche Ukraine 49°17N 31°27E 189 H6
Horokhiv Ukraine 50°30N 24°45E 177 C13
Horoměřice Czech Rep. 50°8N 14°20E 135 B1
Horovice Czech Rep. 49°48N 13°53E 180 B6
Horqin Youyi Qianqi China 46°5N 122°3E 227 A12
Horqin Zuoyi Zhongqi China 44°8N 123°18E 227 B12
Horqueta Paraguay 23°15S 56°55W 334 A4
Horred Sweden 57°22N 12°28E 163 G6
Horse Cr. → U.S.A. 41°57N 103°58W 304 F12
Horse I. Canada 53°20N 99°6W 297 C9
Horse Is. Canada 50°15N 55°50W 299 B8
Horsefly L. Canada 52°25N 121°0W 296 C4
Horseheads U.S.A. 42°10N 76°49W 312 D8
Horsens Denmark 55°52N 9°51E 163 J3
Horseshoe Bend ⌂ U.S.A. 32°59N 85°44W 316 C4
Horseshoe Lake Canada 45°17N 79°51W 312 A5
Horsham Vic., Australia 36°44S 142°13E 282 D5
Horsham W. Susx., U.K. 51°4N 0°20W 169 F7
Horšovský Týn Czech Rep. 49°31N 12°58E 180 B5
Horta Azores 38°32N 28°38W 153 d1
Hortaleza Spain 40°28N 3°38W 127 B2
Horten Norway 59°25N 10°32E 164 E7
Hortense U.S.A. 31°20N 81°57W 316 D8
Horti India 17°7N 75°47E 244 F2
Hortobágy → Hungary 47°30N 21°6E 182 C6
Hortobágyi △ Hungary 47°36N 21°10E 182 C6
Horton Kans., U.S.A. 39°40N 95°32W 308 F6
Horton Mo., U.S.A. 37°58N 94°22W 310 G2
Horton → Canada 69°56N 126°52W 294 D6
Hortus Botanicus Amsterdam, Neths. 112 b3
Horwood L. Canada 48°5N 82°20W 298 C3
Hosaina Ethiopia 7°30N 37°47E 257 F4
Hosapete = Hospet India 15°15N 76°20E 245 G3
Hosdrug = Kanhangad India 12°21N 74°58E 245 H2
Hosdurga India 13°49N 76°17E 245 H3
Hosenofu Libya 23°41N 21°4E 258 D4
Ḩoseynābād Khuzestān, Iran 32°45N 48°20E 247 C6
Ḩoseynābād Kordestān, Iran 35°33N 47°8E 213 E12
Hosford U.S.A. 30°23N 84°48W 316 E5
Hôsh 'Īsa Egypt 30°55N 30°17E 256 H7
Hoshangabad India 22°45N 77°45E 242 H7
Hoshiarpur India 31°30N 75°58E 242 D6
Hoskins Papua N. G. 5°29S 150°27E 286 C6
Hoskote India 13°4N 77°48E 245 H3
Hosoyama Japan 35°36N 139°31E 140 B2
Hospet India 15°15N 76°20E 245 G3
Hostafranchs Spain 41°21N 2°8E 114 A1
Hoste, I. Chile 55°0S 69°0W 336 E3
Hostens France 44°30N 0°40W 174 D3
Hostivař Czech Rep. 50°3N 14°31E 135 B3
Hosur India 12°43N 77°49E 245 H3
Hot Thailand 18°8N 98°29E 236 C2
Hot Creek Range U.S.A. 38°40N 116°20W 304 G5
Hot Springs = Truth or Consequences U.S.A. 33°8N 107°15W 305 K10
Hot Springs Ark., U.S.A. 34°31N 93°3W 314 D8
Hot Springs S. Dak., U.S.A. 43°26N 103°29W 308 D2
Hot Springs △ U.S.A. 34°31N 93°3W 314 D8
Hotagen Sweden 63°59N 14°12E 160 E16
Hotan China 37°25N 79°55E 217 E9
Hotan He → China 40°22N 80°56E 217 D10
Hotazel S. Africa 27°17S 22°58E 270 C3
Hotchkiss U.S.A. 38°48N 107°43W 304 G10
Hôtel des Invalides Paris, France 134 c2
Hotham, C. Australia 12°2S 131°18E 278 B5
Hoting Sweden 64°8N 16°15E 160 D17
Hotolisht Albania 41°10N 20°25E 202 E4
Hotspur Seamount Atl. Oc. 17°55S 35°55W 152 H8
Hotte, Massif de la Haiti 18°30N 73°45W 321 C5
Hottentotsbaai Namibia 26°8S 14°59E 270 C1
Hou Hai China 22°32N 113°56E 219 a
Houailou N. Cal. 21°17S 165°38E 288 d
Houat, Î. de France 47°24N 2°58W 172 E4
Houbětin Czech Rep. 50°6N 14°33E 135 B3
Houdan France 48°48N 1°35E 173 D8
Houei Sai Laos 20°18N 100°26E 228 G3
Houeillès France 44°12N 0°2E 174 D4
Houffalize Belgium 50°8N 5°48E 170 D5
Houghton Gauteng, S. Africa 26°10S 28°3E 123 B2
Houghton Mich., U.S.A. 47°7N 88°34W 308 B9
Houghton N.Y., U.S.A. 42°25N 78°10W 312 D6
Houghton L. U.S.A. 44°21N 84°44W 309 C11
Houghton-le-Spring U.K. 54°51N 1°28W 168 C6
Houhora Heads N.Z. 34°49S 173°9E 284 A2
Houilles France 48°56N 2°11E 134 A2
Houli Taiwan 24°19N 120°44E 225 B2
Houlton U.S.A. 46°8N 67°51W 309 B20
Houlung Taiwan 24°37N 120°47E 225 B2
Houma China 35°36N 111°20E 226 G6
Houma La., U.S.A. 29°36N 90°43W 315 G9
Houmt Souk = Djerba Tunisia 33°48N 10°54E 258 B2
Houndé Burkina Faso 11°34N 3°31W 262 C4
Hounslow □ U.K. 51°28N 0°21W 125 B1
Houpi Taiwan 23°22N 120°21E 225 C2
Hourtin France 45°11N 1°4W 174 C2
Hourtin-Carcans, Étang d' France 45°10N 1°6W 174 C2
Housatonic → U.S.A. 41°10N 73°7W 313 E11
House of Nobility = Riddarhuset Stockholm, Sweden 139 c2
House of Parliament = Riksdagshuset Stockholm, Sweden 139 b2
Houses of Parliament London, U.K. 125 c3
Houston B.C., Canada 54°25N 126°39W 296 C3
Houston Fla., U.S.A. 30°15N 82°54W 316 E7
Houston Mo., U.S.A. 37°22N 91°58W 308 G8
Houston Tex., U.S.A. 29°45N 95°21W 314 G7
Hout = Mogwadi → S. Africa 23°4S 29°36E 271 B4
Hout Bay S. Africa 34°2S 18°23E 118 B1
Houtkraal S. Africa 30°23S 24°5E 270 D3
Houtman Abrolhos Australia 28°43S 113°48E 279 E1
Hov Norway 60°42N 10°20E 164 D7
Hovd = Dund-Us Mongolia 48°1N 91°38E 217 C12
Hovd □ Mongolia 48°2N 91°37E 217 C12
Hovda Norway 60°53N 9°11E 164 D6
Hovden Aust-Agder, Norway 59°33N 7°22E 164 E4
Hovden Sogn og Fjordane, Norway 61°41N 4°52E 164 C1
Hove U.K. 50°50N 0°10W 169 G7
Hove Å → Denmark 55°43N 12°7E 118 B2
Hovedøya Norway 59°53N 10°43E 133 A3
Hovedstaden □ Denmark 56°0N 10°0E 163 J6
Hovenweep ⌂ U.S.A. 37°20N 109°0W 305 H9
Hovet Norway 60°38N 8°8E 164 D5
Hoveyzeh Iran 31°27N 48°4E 247 D6
Hovgaard Ø Greenland 79°55N 18°50W 154 B9
Høvik Norway 59°54N 10°34E 133 A2
Hovin Norway 59°51N 9°0E 164 E6
Hovmantorp Sweden 56°47N 15°7E 163 H9
Hovorčovice Czech Rep. 50°10N 14°31E 135 A3
Hövsgöl Mongolia 43°37N 109°39E 226 C5
Hövsgöl Nuur Mongolia 51°0N 100°30E 218 A9
Hovsta Sweden 59°22N 15°15E 162 E9
Howakil Eritrea 15°10N 40°16E 257 D5
Howar, Wadi → Sudan 17°30N 27°8E 257 D2
Howard Queens., Australia 25°16S 152°32E 281 D5
Howard Pa., U.S.A. 41°1N 77°40W 312 F7
Howard S. Dak., U.S.A. 44°1N 97°32W 308 C5
Howard Beach U.S.A. 40°39N 73°50W 132 C2
Howe U.S.A. 43°48N 113°0W 304 E7
Howe, C. Australia 37°30S 150°0E 283 D9
Howe, West Cape Australia 35°8S 117°36E 279 G2
Howe I. Canada 44°16N 76°17W 313 B8
Howell U.S.A. 42°36N 83°56W 311 B13
Howick Qué., Canada 45°11N 73°51W 313 A11
Howick N.Z. 36°54S 174°56E 284 C3
Howick KwaZulu Natal, S. Africa 29°28S 30°14E 271 C5
Howick Group Australia 14°20S 145°30E 280 A4
Howitt, L. Australia 27°40S 138°40E 281 D2
Howland I. Pac. Oc. 0°48N 176°38W 288 G10
Howlong Australia 35°59S 146°38E 283 C7
Howrah = Haora India 22°34N 88°18E 124 B1
Howth Ireland 53°23N 6°6W 120 A3
Howth Hd. Ireland 53°22N 6°4W 120 A3
Höxter Germany 51°46N 9°22E 178 D5
Hoxtolgay China 46°35N 85°59E 217 C11
Hoxton London, U.K. 125 a5
Hoxud China 42°15N 86°51E 217 D11
Hoy U.K. 58°50N 3°15W 167 C5
Hoya Niedersachsen, Germany 52°49N 9°8E 178 C5
Hōya Tōkyō, Japan 35°44N 139°34E 140 A2
Høyanger Norway 61°13N 6°4E 164 C3
Hoyerswerda Germany 51°26N 14°14E 178 D10
Hoylake U.K. 53°24N 3°10W 168 D4
Hōyo-Kaikyō Japan 33°20N 131°58E 222 D3
Hoyos Spain 40°9N 6°45W 194 E4
Hpa-an = Pa-an Burma 16°51N 97°40E 241 G6
Hpawlum Burma 27°12N 98°12E 241 B7
Hpettintha Burma 24°14N 95°23E 241 C5
Hpizow Burma 26°57N 98°24E 241 B7
Hpunan Pass Burma 27°30N 96°55E 241 A6
Hradčany Czech Rep. 50°5N 14°24E 135 B2
Hradec Králové Czech Rep. 50°15N 15°50E 180 A8
Hrádek Czech Rep. 48°46N 16°16E 181 C9
Hrafnseyri Iceland 65°46N 23°28W 155 B3
Hranice Czech Rep. 49°34N 17°45E 181 B10
Hrazdan Armenia 40°30N 44°46E 191 K7
Hrebenka Ukraine 50°9N 32°22E 189 G7
Hrífunes Iceland 63°38N 18°30W 155 D8
Hrísey Iceland 66°0N 18°23W 155 B8
Hrisoupoli = Chrisoupoli Greece 40°58N 24°42E 203 F8
Hrodna Belarus 53°42N 23°52E 184 E10
Hrodna □ Belarus 53°20N 24°45E 188 F3
Hrodzyanka Belarus 53°31N 28°42E 177 B15
Hron → Slovak Rep. 47°49N 18°45E 181 D11
Hrubieszów Poland 50°49N 23°51E 185 H10
Hrubý Jeseník Czech Rep. 50°5N 17°10E 181 A10
Hrvatska = Croatia ■ Europe 45°20N 16°0E 199 C13
Hrymayliv Ukraine 49°20N 26°5E 177 D14
Hrynyava Ukraine 47°59N 24°53E 183 C9
Hsa-paw Burma 19°1N 97°30E 241 F6
Hsenwi Burma 23°22N 97°55E 241 D6
Hsi-hkip Burma 20°25N 96°42E 241 E6
Hsiafu Taiwan 25°7N 121°17E 225 A3
Hsiamen = Xiamen China 24°25N 118°4E 229 E12
Hsian = Xi'an China 34°15N 109°0E 226 G5
Hsiangshan Taiwan 24°48N 120°54E 225 B2
Hsiaochinmen Tao Taiwan 24°26N 118°14E 225 a
Hsiaohungt'ou Hsü Taiwan 21°57N 121°36E 225 E3
Hsiaokang Taiwan 22°34N 120°20E 225 D2
Hsiatahsi Taiwan 22°28N 120°56E 225 D2
Hsiaying Taiwan 23°14N 120°15E 225 C2
Hsichih Taiwan 25°4N 121°39E 225 A3
Hsikang Taiwan 23°7N 120°12E 225 C2
Hsilo Taiwan 23°48N 120°27E 225 C2

Hsinche Taiwan 24°10N 120°50E 225 B2
Hsinch'eng Taiwan 24°8N 121°39E 225 B3
Hsinchu Taiwan 24°48N 120°58E 225 B2
Hsinchu □ Taiwan 24°45N 121°10E 225 B3
Hsinchuang Kaohsung, Taiwan 22°34N 120°29E 225 D2
Hsinchuang T'aipei, Taiwan 25°2N 121°27E 225 A3
Hsinfa Taiwan 23°1N 120°39E 225 C2
Hsinfeng Taiwan 24°54N 120°59E 225 B2
Hsinhailien = Lianyungang China 34°40N 119°11E 227 G10
Hsinhua Taiwan 23°2N 120°18E 225 C2
Hsini Taiwan 23°41N 120°51E 225 C2
Hsinking = Changchun China 43°57N 125°17E 227 C13
Hsinpi Taiwan 22°28N 120°33E 225 D2
Hsinshih Taiwan 23°4N 120°17E 225 C2
Hsintien Taiwan 24°57N 121°32E 225 B3
Hsinwu Taiwan 24°59N 121°6E 225 B3
Hsinying Taiwan 23°21N 120°17E 225 C2
Hsinyuan Taiwan 22°32N 120°27E 225 D2
Hsipaw Burma 22°37N 97°18E 241 D6
Hsiukuluan Hsi → Taiwan 23°28N 121°30E 225 C3
Hsiushui Taiwan 24°3N 120°30E 225 B2
Hsiyu Taiwan 23°36N 119°30E 225 C1
Hsopket Burma 23°11N 98°26E 228 F2
Hsüchou = Xuzhou China 34°18N 117°10E 227 G9
Hsüeh Shan China 24°24N 121°12E 225 B3
Hsüehchia Taiwan 23°14N 120°10E 225 C2
Hsühaitsun Taiwan 22°12N 120°52E 225 D2
Htawgaw Burma 25°57N 98°23E 241 C7
Hu Xian China 34°8N 108°42E 226 G5
Hua Hin Thailand 12°34N 99°58E 236 F2
Hua Lamphong Railway Station Bangkok, Thailand 113 c2
Hua Muang Laos 20°13N 103°52E 236 B4
Hua Shan China 34°28N 110°4E 226 G6
Hua Xian Henan, China 35°30N 114°30E 226 G8
Hua Xian Shaanxi, China 34°30N 109°48E 226 G5
Hua Yü Taiwan 23°24N 119°19E 225 C1
Hua'an China 25°1N 117°32E 229 E11
Huab → Namibia 20°52S 13°25E 270 A2
Huacaya Bolivia 20°45S 63°43W 331 E5
Huachacalla Bolivia 18°45S 68°17W 330 D4
Huacheng China 24°4N 115°37E 229 E10
Huachinera Mexico 30°9N 108°55W 318 A3
Huacho Peru 11°10S 77°35W 330 C2
Huachón Peru 10°35S 76°0W 330 C2
Huade China 41°55N 113°59E 226 D7
Huadian China 43°0N 126°40E 227 C14
Huadu China 23°22N 113°12E 229 F9
Huahine, Î. French Polynesia 16°46S 150°58W 289 f
Huai Hat △ Thailand 16°52N 104°17E 236 D5
Huai He → China 33°0N 118°30E 229 A12
Huai Kha Khaeng △ Thailand 15°48N 99°7E 236 E2
Huai Nam Dang △ Thailand 19°30N 98°30E 236 C2
Huai Yot Thailand 7°45N 99°37E 237 J2
Huai'an Hebei, China 40°30N 114°20E 226 D8
Huai'an Jiangsu, China 33°30N 119°10E 227 H10
Huaibei China 34°0N 116°48E 226 G9
Huaibin China 32°32N 115°27E 229 A10
Huaicho = Puerto Acosta Bolivia 15°32S 69°15W 330 D4
Huaide = Gongzhuling China 43°30N 124°40E 227 C13
Huaidezhen China 43°48N 124°50E 227 C13
Huaihua China 27°32N 109°57E 228 D7
Huaiji China 23°55N 112°12E 229 F9
Huainan China 32°38N 116°58E 229 A11
Huaining China 30°24N 116°40E 229 B11
Huairen China 39°48N 113°20E 226 E7
Huairou China 40°20N 116°35E 226 D9
Huaiyang China 33°40N 114°52E 226 H8
Huaiyin China 33°30N 119°2E 227 H10
Huaiyuan Anhui, China 32°55N 117°10E 227 H9
Huaiyuan Guangxi Zhuangzu, China 24°31N 108°22E 228 E7
Huajuapán de León Mexico 17°48N 97°46W 319 D5
Hualälai U.S.A. 19°42N 155°52W 302 D6
Hualapai Peak U.S.A. 35°5N 113°54W 305 J7
Hualien Taiwan 23°59N 121°36E 225 C3
Hualien □ Taiwan 23°45N 121°25E 225 C3
Huallaga → Peru 5°15S 75°30W 330 B2
Huallanca Peru 8°50S 77°56W 330 B2
Huamachuco Peru 7°50S 78°5W 330 B2
Huambo Angola 12°42S 15°54E 265 E3
Huambo □ Angola 13°0S 16°0E 265 E3
Huan Jiang → China 34°28N 109°0E 226 G5
Huan Xian China 36°33N 107°7E 226 F4
Huancabamba Peru 5°10S 79°15W 330 B2
Huancane Peru 15°10S 69°44W 330 D4
Huancapi Peru 13°40S 74°0W 330 C3
Huancavelica Peru 12°50S 75°5W 330 C2
Huancavelica □ Peru 13°0S 75°0W 330 C3
Huancayo Peru 12°5S 75°12W 330 C2
Huanchaca Bolivia 20°15S 66°40W 330 E4
Huanchaca, Serranía de Bolivia 14°30S 60°39W 331 C5
Huang Hai = Yellow Sea China 35°0N 123°0E 227 G12
Huang He → China 37°55N 118°50E 227 F10
Huang Xian China 37°38N 120°30E 227 F11
Huangchuan China 32°15N 115°10E 229 A10
Huangdao China 36°0N 120°7E 227 G11
Huanggang China 30°29N 114°52E 229 B10
Huangguoshu China 26°0N 105°40E 228 E5
Huanghua China 38°22N 117°20E 227 E9
Huanghuagang China 38°20N 117°54E 227 E9
Huanghuagang Mausoleum China 23°9N 113°17E 121 B2
Huangling China 35°34N 109°15E 226 G5
Huanglong China 35°30N 109°59E 226 G5
Huanglong △ China 32°44N 103°50E 228 A4
Huanglongtan China 32°40N 110°33E 229 A8
Huangmei China 30°5N 115°56E 229 B10
Huangpi China 30°50N 114°22E 229 B10
Huangping China 26°52N 107°54E 228 D6
Huangpu China 31°14N 121°30E 138 B2
Huangpu Jiang → China 31°11N 121°29E 138 B1
Huangpu Park China 31°14N 121°29E 138 B1
Huangshan Anhui, China 30°8N 118°9E 229 B12
Huangshan Anhui, China 29°42N 118°25E 229 C12
Huangshi China 30°10N 115°3E 229 B10
Huangsongdian China 43°45N 127°25E 227 C14
Huangtugang China 39°49N 116°15E 114 C1
Huangyan China 28°38N 121°19E 229 C13
Huangyangsi China 26°33N 111°39E 229 D8
Huaning China 24°17N 102°56E 228 E4
Huanjiang China 24°50N 108°18E 228 E7
Huanren China 41°23N 125°20E 224 B2
Huanren Shuiku China 41°17N 125°34E 224 B2
Huanta Peru 12°55S 74°20W 330 C3
Huantai China 36°58N 117°56E 227 F9
Huánuco Peru 9°55S 76°15W 330 B2
Huánuco □ Peru 9°55S 76°14W 330 B2
Huanuni Bolivia 18°16S 66°51W 330 D4
Huanzo, Cordillera de Peru 14°35S 73°20W 330 C3
Huaping China 26°46N 101°25E 228 D3
Huara Chile 19°59S 69°47W 330 D4
Huaral Peru 11°32S 77°13W 330 C2
Huaraz Peru 9°30S 77°32W 330 B2
Huari Peru 9°14S 77°14W 330 B2
Huarmey Peru 10°5S 78°5W 330 C2
Huarochiri Peru 12°9S 76°15W 330 C2
Huarocondo Peru 13°26S 72°14W 330 C3
Huarong China 29°29N 112°30E 229 C9
Huascar Peru 11°59S 77°1W 124 A2
Huascarán, Nevado Peru 9°7S 77°37W 330 B2
Huasco Chile 28°30S 71°15W 334 B1
Huasco → Chile 28°27S 71°13W 334 B1
Huasna U.S.A. 35°6N 120°24W 307 K6
Huatabampo Mexico 26°50N 109°38W 318 B3
Huauchinango Mexico 20°12N 98°3W 319 C5
Huautla de Jiménez Mexico 18°8N 96°51W 319 D5
Huaxi China 26°25N 106°40E 228 D6
Huay Khwang Thailand 13°47N 100°33E 113 B2
Huayhuash, Cordillera Peru 10°30S 76°45W 330 B2
Huayin China 34°35N 110°5E 226 G6
Huaying China 30°8N 106°44E 228 B6
Huayllay Peru 11°3S 76°21W 330 C2
Huayuan China 28°37N 109°29E 228 C7
Huazhou China 21°33N 110°33E 229 G8
Hubballi = Hubli India 15°22N 75°15E 245 G2
Hubbard Iowa, U.S.A. 42°18N 93°18W 310 B3
Hubbard Ohio, U.S.A. 41°9N 80°34W 312 E4
Hubbard Tex., U.S.A. 31°51N 96°48W 314 F6
Hubbard, Mt. N. Amer. 60°19N 139°4W 303 F13
Hubbard Glacier Canada 60°18N 139°22W 294 E4
Hubbart Pt. Canada 59°21N 94°41W 297 B10
Hubei □ China 31°0N 112°0E 229 B9
Hubli India 15°22N 75°15E 245 G2
Huch'ang N. Korea 41°25N 127°2E 224 B3
Huchow = Huzhou China 30°51N 120°8E 229 B13
Hucknall U.K. 53°3N 1°13W 168 D6
Huddersfield U.K. 53°39N 1°47W 168 D6
Huddinge Sweden 59°14N 18°0E 139 B2
Hude Germany 53°7N 8°26E 178 B4
Hudi Sudan 17°43N 34°18E 256 D3
Hudiksvall Sweden 61°43N 17°10E 162 C11
Hudson Ont., Canada 50°6N 92°9W 298 B1
Hudson Fla., U.S.A. 28°22N 82°42W 317 G7
Hudson Mass., U.S.A. 42°23N 71°34W 313 D13
Hudson Mich., U.S.A. 41°51N 84°21W 311 C12
Hudson N.Y., U.S.A. 42°15N 73°46W 313 D11
Hudson Wis., U.S.A. 44°58N 92°45W 308 C7
Hudson Wyo., U.S.A. 42°54N 108°35W 304 E9
Hudson → U.S.A. 40°42N 74°2W 313 F10
Hudson, C. Antarctica 68°21S 153°45E 151 C10
Hudson, Vol. Chile 46°4S 72°55W 336 C2
Hudson Bay Nunavut, Canada 60°0N 86°0W 295 F14
Hudson Bay Sask., Canada 52°51N 102°23W 297 C8
Hudson Falls U.S.A. 43°18N 73°35W 313 C11
Hudson Mts. Antarctica 74°32S 99°20W 151 D16
Hudson Str. Canada 62°0N 70°0W 295 E18
Hudson's Hope Canada 56°0N 121°54W 296 B4
Hudsonville U.S.A. 42°52N 85°52W 311 B11
Hue Vietnam 16°30N 107°35E 236 D6
Huebra → Spain 41°2N 6°48W 194 D4
Huechuraba Chile 33°22S 70°39W 137 B1
Huedin Romania 46°52N 23°2E 182 D8
Huehuetenango Guatemala 15°20N 91°28W 320 C1
Huejúcar Mexico 22°21N 103°13W 318 C4
Huélamo Spain 40°17N 1°48W 196 E3
Huelgoat France 48°22N 3°46W 172 D3
Huelma Spain 37°39N 3°28W 195 H7
Huelva Spain 37°18N 6°57W 195 H4
Huelva □ Spain 37°40N 7°0W 195 H4
Huelva → Spain 37°27N 6°0W 195 H5
Hueneme = Port Hueneme U.S.A. 34°7N 119°12W 307 L7
Huentelauquén Chile 31°38S 71°33W 334 C1
Huércal-Overa Spain 37°23N 1°57W 197 H3
Huerquehue △ Chile 39°6S 71°42W 336 A2
Huerta, Sa. de la Argentina 31°10S 67°30W 334 C2
Huertas, C. de las Spain 38°21N 0°24W 197 G4
Huerva → Spain 41°39N 0°52W 196 D4
Huesca Spain 42°8N 0°25W 196 C4
Huesca □ Spain 42°20N 0°1E 196 C5
Huéscar Spain 37°44N 2°35W 197 H2
Hueso Ballena, Pta. Chile 33°40S 78°46W 330 c
Huetamo Mexico 18°35N 100°53W 318 D4
Huete Spain 40°10N 2°43W 196 E2
Huevos I. Trin. & Tob. 10°42N 61°43W 323 t
Huger U.S.A. 33°6N 79°48W 316 B10
Hugh → Australia 25°1S 134°1E 280 D1
Hughenden Australia 20°52S 144°10E 280 C3
Hughes U.S.A. 66°3N 154°15W 303 C9
Hughesville U.S.A. 41°14N 76°44W 313 E8
Hugli → India 21°56N 88°4E 243 J13
Hugo Colo., U.S.A. 39°8N 103°28W 304 G12
Hugo Okla., U.S.A. 34°1N 95°31W 314 D7
Hugoton U.S.A. 37°11N 101°21W 308 G3
Huguang Opera Museum Beijing, China 114 c2
Huhehaote = Hohhot China 40°52N 111°40E 226 D6
Huhsi Taiwan 23°35N 119°39E 225 C1
Hui Xian = Huixian China 35°27N 113°12E 226 G7
Hui Xian China 33°50N 106°4E 226 H4
Hui'an China 25°1N 118°43E 229 E12
Hui'anbu China 37°28N 106°38E 226 F4
Huiarau Ra. N.Z. 38°45S 176°55E 284 E5
Huichang China 25°32N 115°45E 229 E10
Huichapan Mexico 20°23N 99°39W 319 C5
Huichon N. Korea 40°10N 126°16E 224 B3
Huidong Guangdong, China 22°58N 114°43E 229 F10
Huidong Sichuan, China 26°34N 102°35E 228 D4
Huifa He → China 43°0N 127°50E 227 C14
Huíla Angola 15°4S 13°32E 265 F2
Huíla □ Angola 14°0S 15°0E 265 E2
Huila □ Colombia 2°30N 75°45W 328 C2
Huila, Nevado del Colombia 3°0N 76°0W 328 C2
Huilai China 23°0N 116°18E 229 F11
Huili China 26°35N 102°17E 228 D4
Huimin China 37°27N 117°28E 227 F9
Huinan China 42°40N 126°2E 224 A3
Huinca Renancó Argentina 34°51S 64°22W 334 C3
Huining China 35°38N 105°0E 226 G3
Huinong China 39°5N 106°35E 226 E4
Huiroa N.Z. 39°15S 174°30E 284 F3
Huishui China 26°7N 106°38E 228 D6
Huisne → France 47°59N 0°11E 172 E7
Huiting China 34°5N 116°5E 226 G9
Huitong China 26°51N 109°45E 228 D7
Huixian China 35°27N 113°12E 226 G7
Huixtla Mexico 15°9N 92°28W 319 D6
Huize China 26°24N 103°15E 228 D4
Huizhou China 23°0N 114°23E 229 F10
Huizingen Belgium 50°45N 4°17E 116 B1
Hukawng Valley Burma 26°30N 96°30E 241 B6
Hukeri India 16°14N 74°36E 245 F2
Hukou Jiangxi, China 29°45N 116°21E 229 C11
Huk'ou Taiwan 24°54N 121°2E 225 B3
Hukuntsi Botswana 23°58S 21°45E 270 B3
Hula Papua N. G. 10°5S 147°43E 286 F4
Ḩulayfā' Si. Arabia 25°58N 40°45E 246 E4
Huld = Ulaanjirem Mongolia 45°5N 105°30E 226 B3
Hulin China 45°48N 132°59E 219 B15
Hulin He → China 45°0N 122°10E 227 B12
Hull = Kingston upon Hull U.K. 53°45N 0°21W 168 D7
Hull Canada 45°26N 75°43W 313 A9
Hull → U.K. 53°44N 0°20W 168 D7
Hulst Neths. 51°17N 4°2E 170 C4
Hultschin = Hlučín Czech Rep. 49°54N 18°11E 181 B11
Hultsfred Sweden 57°30N 15°52E 163 G9
Huludao China 40°45N 120°50E 227 D11
Hulun = Hailar China 49°10N 119°38E 219 B12
Hulun Nur China 49°0N 117°30E 219 B12
Hulyaypole Ukraine 47°45N 36°21E 189 J9
Huma, Tanjung Malaysia 5°29N 100°16E 237 c
Humacao Puerto Rico 18°9N 65°50W 321 b
Humahuaca Argentina 23°10S 65°25W 334 A2
Humaitá = Porto Walter Brazil 8°15S 72°40W 330 B3
Humaitá Brazil 7°35S 63°1W 331 B5
Humaitá Paraguay 27°2S 58°31W 334 B4
Humansdorp S. Africa 34°2S 24°46E 270 D3
Humansville U.S.A. 37°48N 93°35W 310 G3
Humara, J. Sudan 16°16N 30°59E 257 D3
Humayun's Tomb India 28°35N 77°15E 120 B2
Humbe Angola 16°40S 14°55E 265 F2
Humbe, Serra do Angola 12°10S 15°25E 265 E2
Humber → Ont., Canada 43°47N 79°38W 141 A1
Humber → England, U.K. 53°42N 0°27W 168 D7
Humber B. Canada 43°37N 79°27W 141 B2
Humber Bay Canada 43°38N 79°29W 141 B2
Humber Bay Park Canada 43°37N 79°28W 141 B2
Humber College Canada 43°35N 79°30W 141 B1
Humber Summit Canada 43°45N 79°32W 141 A1
Humber Valley Village Canada 43°40N 79°31W 141 A1
Humberlea Canada 43°43N 79°31W 141 A1
Humberwood Park Canada 43°44N 79°37W 141 A1
Humboldt Sask., Canada 52°15N 105°9W 297 C7
Humboldt Iowa, U.S.A. 42°44N 94°13W 310 B2
Humboldt Tenn., U.S.A. 35°50N 88°55W 315 D10
Humboldt → U.S.A. 39°59N 118°36W 304 G4
Humboldt Gletscher = Sermersuaq Greenland 79°30N 62°0W 154 B4
Humboldt Mts. N.Z. 44°30S 168°15E 285 E3
Humboldt Park U.S.A. 41°54N 87°42W 119 B2
Humbolt, Mt. N. Cal. 21°53S 166°25E 288 d
Hume U.S.A. 36°48N 118°54W 306 J8
Hume, L. Australia 36°0S 147°5E 283 D7
Humen China 22°50N 113°40E 219 a
Humenné Slovak Rep. 48°55N 21°50E 181 C14
Humera Spain 40°25N 3°46W 127 B1
Humeston U.S.A. 40°52N 93°30W 310 D3
Hummelsta Sweden 59°34N 16°58E 162 E10
Hummelvika Norway 63°29N 8°19E 164 A5
Hummingbird Centre Toronto, Canada 141 b3
Hummock Hill = Whyalla Australia 33°2S 137°30E 282 B2
Humpata Angola 15°2S 13°24E 265 F2
Humphreys, Mt. U.S.A. 37°17N 118°40W 306 H8
Humphreys Peak U.S.A. 35°21N 111°41W 305 J8
Humpolec Czech Rep. 49°31N 15°20E 180 B8
Humptulips U.S.A. 47°14N 123°57W 306 C3
Humula Australia 35°30S 147°46E 283 C7
Hūn Libya 29°2N 16°0E 258 C3
Hun He → China 40°41N 122°8E 224 B1
Hun Jiang → China 40°50N 125°38E 227 D13
Húnaflói Iceland 65°50N 20°50W 155 B6
Hunan □ China 27°30N 112°0E 229 D9
Húnavatnssýsla □ Iceland 65°30N 20°25W 155 B6
Hunaydī Iraq 33°18N 44°29E 113 B2
Hunchun China 42°52N 130°28E 227 C16
Hundested Denmark 55°58N 11°52E 163 J5
Hundewali Pakistan 31°55N 72°38E 242 D5
Hundige Denmark 55°35N 12°18E 118 B1
Hundige Strand Denmark 55°35N 12°20E 118 B2
Hundorp Norway 61°33N 9°59E 164 C7
Hundred Islands △ Phil. 16°10N 120°2E 232 C3
Hundred Mile House Canada 51°38N 121°18W 296 C4
Hundvåg Norway 59°0N 5°43E 164 E2
Hunedoara Romania 45°40N 22°50E 182 E7
Hunedoara □ Romania 45°50N 22°54E 182 E7
Hunei Taiwan 22°53N 120°14E 225 D2
Hünfeld Germany 50°39N 9°46E 178 E5
Hung Hom China 22°18N 114°11E 122 B2
Hung Yen Vietnam 20°39N 106°4E 228 G6
Hunga Ha'apai Tonga 20°41S 175°7W 287 Q13
Hungary ■ Europe 47°20N 19°20E 181 D12
Hungary, Plain of Europe 47°0N 20°0E 158 F10
Hungerford Australia 28°58S 144°24E 281 D3
Hŭngnam N. Korea 39°49N 127°45E 224 C3
Hungt'ou Hsü = Lan Yü Taiwan 22°4N 121°25E 225 D3
Hungund India 16°4N 76°3E 245 F3
Huni Valley Ghana 5°33N 1°56W 262 D4
Hunjiang China 41°54N 126°26E 224 B3
Hunneberg Sweden 58°18N 12°30E 163 F6
Hunnebostrand Sweden 58°27N 11°18E 163 F5
Hunsberge Namibia 27°45S 17°12E 270 C2
Hunsrück Germany 49°56N 7°27E 179 F3
Hunstanton U.K. 52°56N 0°29E 168 E8
Hunsur India 12°16N 76°16E 245 H3
Hunte → Germany 53°14N 8°28E 178 B4
Hunter N.Z. 44°36S 171°2E 285 E6
Hunter N.Y., U.S.A. 42°13N 74°13W 313 D10
Hunter → N.S.W., Australia 32°52S 151°46E 283 B9
Hunter → N.Z. 44°21S 169°27E 285 E4
Hunter, C. Solomon Is. 9°48S 159°50E 287 M10
Hunter Hills, The N.Z. 44°26S 170°46E 285 E5
Hunter I. Tas., Australia 40°30S 144°45E 281 G3
Hunter I. B.C., Canada 51°55N 128°0W 296 C3
Hunter Mts. N.Z. 45°43S 167°25E 285 F2
Hunter Ra. Australia 32°45S 150°15E 283 B9
Hunters Hill Australia 33°50S 151°9E 139 B1
Hunters Pt. U.S.A. 37°43N 122°21W 136 B2
Hunters Road Zimbabwe 19°9S 29°49E 269 F2
Hunters Valley U.S.A. 38°54N 77°17W 143 B2
Hunterville N.Z. 39°56S 175°35E 284 F4
Huntingburg U.S.A. 38°18N 86°57W 311 F10
Huntingdon Cambs., U.K. 52°20N 0°11W 169 E7
Huntingdon Pa., U.S.A. 40°30N 78°1W 312 F6
Huntington = Shelton U.S.A. 41°19N 73°5W 313 E11
Huntington Ind., U.S.A. 40°53N 85°30W 311 D11
Huntington N.Y., U.S.A. 40°52N 73°26W 313 F11
Huntington Oreg., U.S.A. 44°21N 117°16W 304 D5
Huntington Utah, U.S.A. 39°20N 110°58W 304 G8
Huntington Va., U.S.A. 38°47N 77°4W 143 C3
Huntington W. Va., U.S.A. 38°25N 82°27W 309 F12
Huntington Beach U.S.A. 33°40N 118°5W 307 M9
Huntington Park U.S.A. 33°58N 118°13W 126 C3
Huntley Jamaica 18°4N 77°35W 320 a
Huntley Ill., U.S.A. 42°10N 88°26W 311 B8
Huntly N.Z. 37°34S 175°11E 284 D4
Huntly Aberds., U.K. 57°27N 2°47W 167 D6
Huntsville Ont., Canada 45°20N 79°14W 312 A5
Huntsville Ala., U.S.A. 34°44N 86°35W 315 D11
Huntsville Mo., U.S.A. 39°26N 92°33W 310 E4
Huntsville Tex., U.S.A. 30°43N 95°33W 314 F7
Hunyani → Zimbabwe 15°57S 30°39E 269 F3
Hunyuan China 39°42N 113°42E 226 E7
Hunza → India 35°54N 74°20E 243 B6
Huo Shan China 36°26N 111°52E 226 F6
Huo Xian = Huozhou China 36°36N 111°42E 226 F6
Huocheng China 44°0N 80°48E 217 D10
Huolin Gol China 45°32N 119°38E 227 B10
Huon G. Papua N. G. 7°0S 147°30E 286 D4
Huon Pen. Papua N. G. 6°20S 147°30E 286 D4
Huong Khe Vietnam 18°13N 105°41E 236 C5
Huonville Australia 43°0S 147°5E 281 G4
Huoqiu China 32°20N 116°12E 229 A11
Huoshan China 31°25N 116°20E 229 B11
Huoshao Dao = Lütao Taiwan 22°40N 121°30E 225 D3
Huozhou China 36°36N 111°42E 226 F6
Hupeh = Hubei □ China 31°0N 112°0E 229 B9
Ḩūr Iran 30°50N 57°7E 247 D8
Hurānd Iran 38°51N 47°22E 213 C12
Ḩuraymīla Si. Arabia 25°8N 46°8E 246 E5
Hurbanovo Slovak Rep. 47°51N 18°11E 181 D11
Hurd, C. Canada 45°13N 81°44W 312 A3
Hurdiyo Somali Rep. 10°33N 51°6E 267 B7
Hure Qi China 42°45N 121°45E 227 C11
Hurezani Romania 44°49N 23°40E 183 F8
Hurghada Egypt 27°15N 33°50E 256 B3
Hurīya Iraq 33°21N 44°19E 113 A1
Hurley N. Mex., U.S.A. 32°42N 108°8W 305 K9
Hurley Wis., U.S.A. 46°27N 90°11W 308 B8
Huron Calif., U.S.A. 36°12N 120°6W 306 J6
Huron Ohio, U.S.A. 41°24N 82°33W 312 E2
Huron S. Dak., U.S.A. 44°22N 98°13W 308 C4
Huron, L. U.S.A. 44°30N 82°40W 312 B2
Huron East Canada 43°37N 81°18W 312 C3
Hurricane U.S.A. 37°11N 113°17W 305 H7
Hurso Ethiopia 9°35N 41°33E 257 F5
Hurstville Australia 33°57S 151°6E 139 B1
Hurtsboro U.S.A. 32°15N 85°25W 316 C4
Hurungwe ⌂ Zimbabwe 16°7S 29°5E 269 F2
Hurunui → N.Z. 42°54S 173°18E 285 C8
Hurup Denmark 56°46N 8°25E 163 H2
Húsafell Iceland 64°42N 20°53W 155 C6
Husan West Bank 31°42N 35°8E 123 B1
Húsavík Iceland 66°3N 17°21W 155 A9
Husby Sweden 59°24N 17°56E 139 A1
Huşi Romania 46°41N 28°7E 183 D13
Huskisson Australia 35°2S 150°41E 283 C9
Huskvarna Sweden 57°47N 14°15E 163 G8
Huslia U.S.A. 65°41N 156°24W 303 D8
Husnes Norway 59°52N 5°45E 164 E2
Hustad Norway 62°57N 7°6E 164 B4
Hustadvika Norway 63°0N 7°0E 164 A3
Hustontown U.S.A. 40°3N 78°2W 312 F6
Hustopeče Czech Rep. 48°57N 16°43E 181 C9
Husum København, Denmark 55°42N 12°27E 118 A2
Husum Schleswig-Holstein, Germany 54°28N 9°4E 178 A5
Husum Sweden 63°21N 19°12E 162 A13
Huszt = Khust Ukraine 48°10N 23°18E 183 B8
Hutanopan Indonesia 0°40N 99°42E 234 B1
Hutchinson Kans., U.S.A. 38°5N 97°56W 308 F5
Hutchinson Minn., U.S.A. 44°54N 94°22W 308 C6
Ḩūth Yemen 16°14N 43°58E 248 C3
Hutiao Xia China 27°13N 100°9E 228 D3
Hutjena Papua N. G. 5°23S 154°42E 286 C8
Hutsonville U.S.A. 39°7N 87°40W 311 E9
Hutt → N.Z. 41°14S 174°54E 143 B2
Hutte Sauvage, L. de la Canada 56°15N 64°45W 299 A7
Hütteldorf Austria 48°12N 16°15E 142 A1
Hüttenberg Austria 46°56N 14°33E 180 E7
Hüttener Berge ⌂ Germany 54°24N 9°40E 178 A5
Hutton, Mt. Australia 25°51S 148°20E 281 D4
Huvadu Atoll Maldives 0°30N 73°15E 272 d
Hüvösvölgy Hungary 47°32N 19°0E 117 A2
Huwei Taiwan 23°42N 120°26E 225 C2
Huwei Hsi → Taiwan 23°37N 120°22E 225 C2
Huwon Secret Garden S. Korea 37°34N 126°59E 137 B1
Huwun Ethiopia 4°23N 40°6E 257 G5
Huy Belgium 50°31N 5°15E 170 D5
Huzhou China 30°51N 120°8E 229 B13
Huzurabad India 18°12N 79°25E 244 E4
Huzurnagar India 16°54N 79°53E 244 F4
Hvalpsund Denmark 56°42N 9°11E 163 H3
Hvalstad Norway 59°51N 10°27E 133 A1
Hvalstrand Norway 59°50N 10°30E 133 A2
Hvammsfjörður Iceland 65°4N 22°5W 155 B4
Hvammstangi Iceland 65°24N 20°57W 155 B6
Hvammur Mýrasýsla, Iceland 64°50N 21°21W 155 C5
Hvammur Skagafjarðarsýsla, Iceland 65°53N 19°51W 155 B7
Hvannadalshnúkur Iceland 64°1N 16°41W 155 C10
Hvanneyri Iceland 64°34N 21°36W 155 C5
Hvar Croatia 43°11N 16°28E 199 E13
Hvarski Kanal Croatia 43°15N 16°35E 199 E13
Hveragerði Iceland 64°0N 21°12W 155 C5
Hvidovre Denmark 55°38N 12°27E 118 B2
Hvítá → Iceland 64°30N 21°58W 155 C5
Hvítárvatn Iceland 64°37N 19°50W 155 C7
Hvittingfoss Norway 59°29N 10°0E 164 E7
Hvizdets Ukraine 48°35N 25°17E 183 B10
Hvolsvöllur Iceland 63°45N 20°14W 155 D6
Hwacheon-Cheosuji S. Korea 38°5N 127°50E 224 C3
Hwagok S. Korea 37°32N 126°51E 137 B1
Hwainan = Huainan China 32°38N 116°58E 229 A11
Hwaiyin = Huaiyin China 33°30N 119°2E 227 H10
Hwang Ho = Huang He → China 37°55N 118°50E 227 F10
Hwange Zimbabwe 18°18S 26°30E 269 F2
Hwange △ Zimbabwe 19°0S 26°30E 270 A4
Hwanghaebuk-do □ N. Korea 38°30N 126°25E 224 C3
Hwanghaenam-do □ N. Korea 38°15N 125°30E 224 C2
Hwangju N. Korea 38°40N 125°46E 224 C2
Hwangshih = Huangshi China 30°10N 115°3E 229 B10
Hwaseong S. Korea 37°12N 126°48E 224 D3
Hwasun S. Korea 35°3N 126°59E 224 E3
Hwekum Burma 26°7N 95°22E 241 B5
Hyaing Burma 22°39N 94°44E 241 D5
Hyannis Mass., U.S.A. 41°39N 70°17W 309 E18
Hyannis Nebr., U.S.A. 42°0N 101°46W 308 E3
Hyargas Nuur Mongolia 49°0N 93°0E 217 C12
Hyattsville U.S.A. 38°57N 76°57W 143 B4
Hybo Sweden 61°49N 16°15E 162 C10
Hydaburg U.S.A. 55°15N 132°50W 296 B2
Hyde N.Z. 45°18S 170°16E 285 F5
Hyde Park Sydney, Australia 139 b2
Hyde Park Guyana 6°30N 58°16W 329 B6
Hyde Park Gauteng, S. Africa 26°6S 28°2E 123 A2
Hyde Park London, U.K. 51°30N 0°10W 125 A2
Hyde Park Calif., U.S.A. 33°58N 118°19W 126 C3
Hyde Park Ill., U.S.A. 41°47N 87°35W 119 C3
Hyde Park Mass., U.S.A. 42°15N 71°7W 116 B2
Hyde Park N.Y., U.S.A. 41°47N 73°56W 313 E11
Hyden Australia 32°24S 118°53E 279 F2
Hyder U.S.A. 55°55N 130°5W 296 B2
Hyderabad India 17°22N 78°29E 244 F4
Hyderabad Pakistan 25°23N 68°24E 242 G3
Hydra Greece 37°20N 23°28E 204 D5
Hyen Norway 61°44N 5°56E 164 C2
Hyères France 43°8N 6°9E 175 E10
Hyères, Îs. d' France 43°0N 6°20E 175 F10
Hyesan N. Korea 41°20N 128°10E 224 B4
Hyland → Canada 59°52N 128°12W 296 B3
Hylestad Norway 59°6N 7°29E 164 E4
Hyllestad Norway 61°10N 5°17E 164 C2
Hyltebruk Sweden 56°59N 13°15E 163 H7
Hyndman Peak U.S.A. 43°45N 114°8W 304 E6
Hynnekleiv Norway 58°36N 8°25E 164 F5
Hyōgo □ Japan 35°15N 134°50E 222 B6
Hyrra Banda C.A.R. 5°58N 22°1E 264 A4
Hyrum U.S.A. 41°38N 111°51W 304 F8
Hysham U.S.A. 46°18N 107°14W 304 C10
Hythe U.K. 51°4N 1°5E 169 F9
Hyūga Japan 32°25N 131°35E 222 E3
Hyvinge = Hyvinkää Finland 60°38N 24°50E 188 B3
Hyvinkää Finland 60°38N 24°50E 188 B3

I

I-n-Akhmed Mali 19°49N 0°56W 261 E4
I-n-Azaoua Illizi, Algeria 25°42N 6°54E 261 C6
I-n-Azaoua Tamanrasset, Algeria 20°46N 7°32E 261 D6
I-n-Échaï Mali 20°10N 2°5W 260 D4
I-n-Ezzane Algeria 23°29N 11°15E 261 D7
I-n-Gall Niger 16°51N 7°1E 263 B6
I-n-Kelemet Algeria 26°57N 5°47E 261 C6
I-n-Oudad Algeria 20°17N 4°38E 261 D5
I-n-Ouzzal Algeria 20°41N 2°34E 261 D5
I-n-Tadreft Niger 19°5N 6°38E 263 B6
Iabès, Erg Algeria 27°30N 2°2W 261 C4
Iablaniţa Romania 44°57N 22°19E 182 F7
Iaco → Brazil 9°3S 68°34W 330 B4
Iacobeni Romania 47°25N 25°20E 183 C10
Iaçu Brazil 12°45S 40°13W 333 D3
Iakora Madag. 23°6S 46°40E 272 C2
Ialibu Papua N. G. 6°17S 143°59E 286 D2
Ialissos Greece 36°24N 28°10E 206 E12
Ialomiţa □ Romania 44°30N 27°30E 183 F12
Ialomiţa → Romania 44°42N 27°51E 183 F12
Ialoveni Moldova 46°56N 28°47E 183 D13
Ialpug → Moldova 45°41N 28°35E 183 E13
Iamonia L. U.S.A. 30°38N 84°14W 316 E5
Ianca Romania 45°6N 27°29E 183 E12
Iara Romania 46°31N 23°35E 183 D8
Iarda Ethiopia 11°9N 35°53E 257 E4
Iargara Moldova 46°24N 28°23E 183 D13
Iaşi Romania 47°10N 27°40E 183 C12
Iaşi □ Romania 47°20N 27°0E 183 C12
Iasmos Greece 41°8N 25°11E 203 E9
Iauaretê Colombia 0°36N 69°12W 328 C4
Ib → India 21°34N 83°48E 243 J10
Iba Phil. 15°22N 120°0E 232 D2
Ibadan Nigeria 7°22N 3°58E 263 D5
Ibagué Colombia 4°20N 75°20W 328 C2
Ibaiti Brazil 23°50S 50°10W 333 F1
Ibajay Phil. 11°49N 122°10E 233 F4
Iballë Albania 42°12N 20°2E 202 D4
Ibăneşti Botoşani, Romania 48°4N 26°22E 183 B11
Ibăneşti Mureş, Romania 46°45N 24°57E 183 D9
Ibanshe Dem. Rep. of the Congo 4°58S 21°30E 265 C4
Ibar → Serbia 43°43N 20°45E 202 C4
Ibara Japan 34°36N 133°28E 222 C5
Ibaraki Japan 36°20N 140°30E 223 A12
Ibaraki Japan 34°49N 135°34E 223 C7
Ibaraki □ Japan 36°10N 140°10E 223 A12
Ibarra Ecuador 0°21N 78°7W 328 C2
Ibb Yemen 14°2N 44°10E 248 D4
Ibba South Sudan 4°49N 29°2E 257 G2
Ibba, Bahr el → South Sudan 5°30N 28°55E 257 F2
Ibbenbüren Germany 52°16N 7°43E 178 C3
Ibeke Gembo Dem. Rep. of the Congo 1°24S 18°51E 264 C3
Ibembo Dem. Rep. of the Congo 2°35N 23°35E 264 B4
Ibenga → Congo 2°19N 18°9E 264 B3
Ibera, L. Argentina 28°30S 57°9W 334 B4
Iberia Peru 11°21S 69°35W 330 C4
Iberia Mo., U.S.A. 38°5N 92°18W 310 F4
Iberian Peninsula Europe 40°0N 5°0W 158 H5
Iberville Canada 45°19N 73°17W 313 A11
Iberville, Mt. d' Canada 58°50N 63°50W 295 F19
Ibese Nigeria 6°33N 3°28E 124 A2
Ibeto Nigeria 10°29N 5°8E 263 C6
Ibi Nigeria 8°15N 9°44E 263 D6
Ibi Spain 38°38N 0°34W 197 G4
Ibiá Brazil 19°30S 46°30W 333 E2
Ibiapaba, Sa. da Brazil 4°0S 41°30W 332 B3
Ibicaraí Brazil 14°51S 39°36W 333 D4
Ibicuí Brazil 14°51S 39°59W 333 D4
Ibicuí → Brazil 29°25S 56°47W 335 B4
Ibicuy Argentina 33°55S 59°10W 334 C4
Ibirapuera Brazil 23°36S 46°40W 137 B1
Ibirapuera, Parque do Brazil 23°35S 46°38W 137 B2
Ibitiara Brazil 12°39S 42°13W 333 D3
Ibiza = Eivissa Spain 38°54N 1°26E 206 D1
Ibiza ✈ (IBZ) Spain 38°53N 1°22E 197 G6
Íblei, Monti Italy 37°15N 14°45E 201 E7
Ibn Hānī', Ra's Syria 35°35N 35°43E 250 C6
Ibo Mozam. 12°22S 40°40E 269 E5
Ibonma Indonesia 3°29S 133°31E 231 E8
Ibotirama Brazil 12°13S 43°12W 333 D3
Iboundji Gabon 1°0S 11°51E 264 C2
İbradı Turkey 37°4N 31°35E 250 A2
Ibrāhīm → Lebanon 34°4N 35°38E 250 D6
'Ibrī Oman 23°14N 56°30E 247 F8
İbriktepe Turkey 41°0N 26°30E 203 E10
Ibshawâi Egypt 29°21N 30°40E 256 J7
Ibu Indonesia 1°35N 127°33E 231 D7
Ibuki-Sanchi Japan 35°25N 136°18E 223 B8
Ibusuki Japan 31°12N 130°40E 222 F2
Ica Peru 14°0S 75°48W 330 C2
Ica □ Peru 14°20S 75°30W 330 C2
Iça → Brazil 2°55S 67°58W 330 A4
Icabarú Venezuela 4°20N 61°45W 329 C5
Icabarú → Venezuela 4°45N 62°15W 329 C5
Icacos Trin. & Tob. 10°3N 61°54W 323 t
Icacos Pt. Trin. & Tob. 10°3N 61°57W 323 t
Içana Brazil 0°21N 67°19W 328 C4
Içana → Brazil 0°26N 67°19W 328 C4
Icarai Brazil 22°54S 43°6W 135 B2
Icatu Brazil 2°46S 44°4W 332 B3
Icaturama = Santa Rosa de Viterbo Colombia 5°53N 72°59W 328 B3
İçel Turkey 36°51N 34°36E 250 B5
İcel □ Turkey 36°45N 34°0E 250 B5
Iceland ■ Europe 64°45N 19°0W 155 C8
Iceland Basin Atl. Oc. 61°0N 19°0W 150 C7
Icelandic Plateau Arctic 64°0N 10°0W 150 C7
Içerenköy Turkey 40°58N 29°6E 122 C2
İçeriçumra Turkey 37°34N 32°39E 212 D5
Ichalkaranji India 16°40N 74°33E 244 F2
Ich'ang = Yichang China 30°40N 111°20E 229 B8
Ichchapuram India 19°10N 84°40E 244 E7
Icheon S. Korea 37°17N 127°27E 224 D3
Ichgao Japan 35°32N 139°32E 140 B2
Ichhawar India 23°1N 77°1E 242 H7
Ichigaya Tokyo, Japan 140 a3
Ichihara Japan 35°28N 140°5E 223 B12
Ichikawa Japan 35°43N 139°54E 140 A4
Ichilo → Bolivia 15°57S 64°50W 331 D5
Ichinohe Japan 40°13N 141°17E 220 D10
Ichinomiya Gifu, Japan 35°18N 136°48E 223 B8
Ichinomiya Kumamoto, Japan 32°58N 131°5E 222 E3
Ichinoseki Japan 38°55N 141°8E 220 E10
Ichkeul △ Tunisia 37°5N 9°37E 258 A1
Ichnya Ukraine 50°52N 32°24E 189 G7
Icht Morocco 29°6N 8°54W 260 C3
Ichu Taiwan 23°20N 120°14E 225 C2
Ichun = Yichun China 47°44N 128°52E 219 B14
Ickenham U.K. 51°33N 0°26W 125 A1
Icó Brazil 6°24S 38°51W 332 C4
Icoca Angola 6°12S 16°20E 265 D3
Icod Canary Is. 28°22N 16°43W 153 e1
Içoguz Turkmenistan 40°11N 58°24E 216 D5
Iconi Comoros Is. 12°21S 43°51E 272 a
Icoraci Brazil 1°18S 48°28W 332 B2
Icy C. U.S.A. 70°20N 161°52W 303 A7
Ida Grove U.S.A. 42°21N 95°28W 308 D6
Idaan Somali Rep. 6°10N 48°55E 267 C6
Idabel U.S.A. 33°54N 94°50W 314 E7
Idaga Hamus Ethiopia 14°13N 39°48E 257 E4
Idah Nigeria 7°5N 6°40E 263 D6
Idaho □ U.S.A. 45°0N 115°0W 304 D6
Idaho City U.S.A. 43°50N 115°50W 304 E6
Idaho Falls U.S.A. 43°30N 112°2W 304 E7
Idalia △ Australia 24°49S 144°36E 280 C3
Idanha-a-Nova Portugal 39°50N 7°15W 194 F3
Idar-Oberstein Germany 49°43N 7°16E 179 F3
Iday Niger 14°54N 11°33E 259 F2
'Idd el Ghanam Sudan 11°30N 24°19E 259 F4
Iddo Nigeria 6°28N 3°22E 124 B2
Idelès Algeria 23°50N 5°53E 261 D6
Idensalmi = Iisalmi Finland 63°32N 27°10E 160 E22
Idfû Egypt 24°55N 32°49E 256 C3
Ídhra = Hydra Greece 37°20N 23°28E 204 D5
Idi Indonesia 5°2N 97°37E 234 A1
Idi, Oros = Psiloritis, Oros Greece 35°15N 24°45E 207 E5
Idi Amin Dada, L. = Edward, L. Africa 0°25S 29°40E 268 C2
Idi-Oro Nigeria 6°31N 3°21E 124 A2
İdil Turkey 37°20N 41°53E 213 D9
Idiofa Dem. Rep. of the Congo 4°55S 19°42E 265 C3
Idjil = Fdérik Mauritania 22°40N 12°45W 260 D2
Idkerberget Sweden 60°22N 15°15E 162 D9
Idku Egypt 31°18N 30°17E 256 H7
Idku, Bahra el Egypt 31°18N 30°18E 256 H7
Idlib Syria 35°55N 36°36E 250 C7
Idlib □ Syria 35°45N 36°45E 250 C7
Idre Sweden 61°52N 12°42E 162 C6
Idria U.S.A. 36°25N 120°41W 306 J6
Idrija Slovenia 46°0N 14°5E 199 C11
Idritsa Russia 56°17N 28°53E 188 D5
Idutywa = Dutywa S. Africa 32°8S 28°18E 271 D4
Ie Shima Japan 26°43N 127°48E 288 a
Ie Suido Japan 26°42N 127°51E 288 a
Ieper Belgium 50°51N 2°53E 170 D2
Ierapetra Greece 35°1N 25°44E 207 F6
Ierissos Greece 40°22N 23°52E 202 F7
Ierissos Kolpos Greece 40°27N 23°57E 202 F7
Iernut Romania 46°27N 24°15E 183 D9
Ieshima-Shotō Japan 34°40N 134°32E 222 C6
Iesi Italy 43°31N 13°14E 199 E10
Iésolo Italy 45°32N 12°38E 199 C9
Iet Ethiopia 4°33N 43°1E 267 D5
Ifac, Penyal d' Spain 38°38N 0°5E 197 G5
'Ifāl, W. al → Si. Arabia 28°7N 35°3E 251 K6
Ifanadiana Madag. 21°19S 47°39E 272 C2
Ife Nigeria 7°30N 4°31E 263 D5
Iférouâne Niger 19°5N 8°24E 259 E1
Ifetesene Algeria 25°30N 4°33E 261 C5
Iffley Australia 18°53S 141°12E 280 B3
Ifon Nigeria 6°58N 5°40E 263 D6
Iforas, Adrar des Africa 19°40N 1°40E 261 D5
Ifould, L. Australia 30°52S 132°6E 279 F5
Ifrane Morocco 33°33N 5°7W 260 B3
Ifrane □ Morocco 33°20N 5°15W 260 B3
Ifugao □ Phil. 16°40N 121°10E 232 C3
Iga Japan 34°45N 136°10E 223 C8
Igalo Montenegro 42°28N 18°30E 202 D2
Iganga Uganda 0°37N 33°28E 268 B3
Iganmu Nigeria 6°28N 3°22E 124 B2
Igara-Paraná → Colombia 2°9S 71°47W 328 D3
Igarapava Brazil 20°3S 47°47W 333 F2
Igarapé-Açu Brazil 1°4S 47°33W 332 B2
Igarapé-Miri Brazil 1°59S 48°58W 332 B2
Igarka Russia 67°30N 86°33E 214 C9
Igatpuri India 19°40N 73°35E 244 E1
Igbetti Nigeria 8°44N 4°8E 263 D5
Igbo-Ora Nigeria 7°29N 3°15E 263 D5
Igbobi Nigeria 6°31N 3°22E 124 A2
Igboho Nigeria 8°53N 3°50E 263 D5
Igbologun Nigeria 6°24N 3°19E 124 B1
Igbor Nigeria 7°27N 8°34E 263 D6
Iğdır Turkey 39°55N 44°2E 213 C11
Igelfors Sweden 58°52N 15°41E 163 F9
Iggesund Sweden 61°39N 17°10E 162 C11
Ighil Izane = Relizane Algeria 35°44N 0°31E 261 A5
Igiugig U.S.A. 59°20N 155°55W 303 G9
Iglau = Jihlava Czech Rep. 49°28N 15°35E 180 B8
Iglésias Italy 39°19N 8°32E 200 C1
Igli Algeria 30°25N 2°19W 261 B4
Igloolik = Iglulik Canada 69°20N 81°49W 295 D15
Igluligaarjuk = Chesterfield Inlet Canada 63°30N 90°45W 294 E13
Iglulik Canada 69°20N 81°49W 295 D15
'Igma, G. el Egypt 29°10N 34°0E 251 J5
'Igma, Gebel el Egypt 28°55N 34°0E 256 B3
Ignace Canada 49°30N 91°40W 298 C1
İğneada Turkey 41°52N 27°59E 203 E11
İğneada Burnu Turkey 41°53N 28°2E 203 E12
Igny France 48°44N 2°13E 134 B2
Igoumenitsa Greece 39°32N 20°18E 206 B10
Igrim Russia 63°12N 64°30E 214 C7
Iguaçu → Brazil 25°36S 54°36W 335 B5
Iguaçu, Cat. del Brazil 25°41S 54°26W 335 B5
Iguaçu △ Brazil 25°30S 54°0W 335 B5
Iguaçu Falls = Iguaçu, Cat. del Brazil 25°41S 54°26W 335 B5
Iguala Mexico 18°21N 99°32W 319 D5
Igualada Spain 41°37N 1°37E 196 D6
Iguape Brazil 24°43S 47°33W 333 F2
Iguaratinga = São Francisco do Maranhão Brazil 6°15S 42°52W 332 C3
Iguassu = Iguaçu → Brazil 25°36S 54°36W 335 B5
Iguatu Brazil 6°20S 39°18W 332 C4
Iguazú △ Argentina 25°42S 54°22W 335 B5

Iguéla Gabon 2°0S 9°16E 264 C1
Iguéla, Lagune Gabon 1°48S 9°16E 264 C2
Iguidi, Erg Africa 27°0N 6°0W 260 C3
Iguig Phil. 17°45N 121°44E 232 C3
Igumen = Cherven
Belarus 53°45N 28°28E 177 B15
Iharana Madag. 13°25S 50°0E 272 A3
Ihavandiffulu Atoll Maldives 7°0N 72°50E 272 d
Ihbulag Mongolia 43°11N 107°10E 226 C4
Iheya-Shima Japan 27°4N 127°58E 221 L3
Ihiala Nigeria 5°51N 6°55E 263 D6
Ihirene → Algeria 20°28N 4°37E 261 D5
Ihosy Madag. 22°24S 46°8E 272 C2
Ihotry, Farihy Madag. 21°56S 43°41E 272 C1
Ihu Papua N. G. 7°55S 145°24E 286 D3
Ihugh Nigeria 7°2N 9°0E 263 D6
Ii Finland 65°19N 25°22E 160 D21
Ii-Shima Japan 26°43N 127°47E 221 L3
Iida Japan 35°35N 137°50E 223 B9
Iijoki → Finland 65°20N 25°20E 160 D21
Iisalmi Finland 63°32N 27°10E 160 E22
Iiyama Japan 36°51N 138°22E 221 F9
Iizuka Japan 33°38N 130°42E 222 D2
IJ, Het → Neths. 52°23N 4°54E 112 A2
IJ-meer Neths. 52°23N 4°54E 112 A3
Ijâfene Mauritania 20°40N 8°0W 260 D3
Ijebu-Igbo Nigeria 6°56N 4°1E 263 D5
Ijebu-Ode Nigeria 6°47N 3°58E 263 D5
Ijesa-Tedo Nigeria 6°29N 3°19E 124 B1
Ijevan Armenia 40°52N 45°8E 191 K7
Ijill, Sebkhet Mauritania 22°47N 12°53W 260 D2
IJmuiden Neths. 52°28N 4°35E 170 B4
Ijo älv = Iijoki →
Finland 65°20N 25°20E 160 D21
Ijora Nigeria 6°27N 3°22E 124 B2
IJssel → Neths. 52°35N 5°50E 170 B5
IJsselmeer Neths. 52°45N 5°20E 170 B5
Ijuí Brazil 28°23S 53°55W 335 B5
Ijuí → Brazil 27°58S 55°20W 335 B4
Ijûin Japan 31°37N 130°24E 222 F2
Ikalamavony Madag. 21°9S 46°35E 272 C2
Ikali Dem. Rep. of the Congo 2°2S 21°4E 264 C4
Ikamatua N.Z. 42°16S 171°41E 285 E6
Ikang Nigeria 4°49N 8°30E 263 E6
Ikanga Kenya 1°42S 38°4E 268 C4
Ikara Nigeria 11°12N 8°15E 263 C6
Ikare Nigeria 7°32N 5°40E 263 D6
Ikaria Greece 37°35N 26°10E 205 D8
Ikast Denmark 56°8N 9°10E 163 H3
Ikebe Japan 35°31N 139°34E 140 B2
Ikebukuro Japan 35°43N 139°42E 140 A3
Ikeda Japan 34°1N 133°48E 222 C5
Ikegami Japan 35°33N 139°42E 140 B3
Ikei-shima Japan 26°23N 127°59E 288 a
Ikeja Nigeria 6°35N 3°20E 124 A2
Ikela Dem. Rep. of the Congo 1°6S 23°6E 264 C4
Ikélemba Congo 1°12N 16°38E 264 B3
Ikélemba →
Dem. Rep. of the Congo 0°7N 18°17E 264 B3
Ikengo Dem. Rep. of the Congo 0°8S 18°8E 264 C3
Ikere Nigeria 7°25N 5°19E 263 D6
Ikeuchi Japan 34°35N 135°32E 133 B2
Ikhtiman Bulgaria 42°27N 23°48E 202 D7
Iki Japan 33°45N 129°42E 222 D1
Iki-Kaikyō Japan 33°40N 129°45E 222 D1
Ikimba L. Tanzania 1°30S 31°20E 268 C3
Ikire Nigeria 7°23N 4°15E 263 D5
Ikitsuki-Shima Japan 33°23N 129°26E 222 D1
İkizdere Turkey 40°46N 40°32E 213 B9
Iko Congo 0°35S 16°0E 264 C3
Ikom Nigeria 6°0N 8°42E 263 D6
Ikoma Japan 34°30N 135°40E 223 C7
Ikomu
Dem. Rep. of the Congo 1°54S 19°40E 264 C3
Ikongo Madag. 21°52S 47°27E 272 C2
Ikopa → Madag. 16°45S 46°40E 272 B2
Ikorongo △ Tanzania 1°50S 34°53E 268 C3
Ikot Ekpene Nigeria 5°12N 7°40E 263 D6
Ikoyi Nigeria 6°27N 3°26E 124 B2
Ikparjuk = Arctic Bay
Canada 73°1N 85°7W 295 C14
Iksan S. Korea 35°59N 127°0E 224 E3
Ikuata Nigeria 6°24N 3°21E 124 B2
Ikungu Tanzania 1°33S 33°42E 268 C3
Ikuno Hyōgo, Japan 35°10N 134°48E 222 B6
Ikuno Ōsaka, Japan 34°40N 135°30E 133 A2
Ikuntji = Haasts Bluff
Australia 23°22S 132°0E 278 D5
Ikurun Nigeria 7°54N 4°40E 263 D5
Ikuta Japan 35°36N 139°32E 140 B2
Il-Kullana Malta 35°50N 14°24E 206 F7
Il-Munxar Malta 35°51N 14°34E 206 F8
Ila Dem. Rep. of the Congo 2°53S 21°7E 264 C4
Ila Nigeria 8°0N 4°39E 263 D5
Ila Oslo, Norway 59°57N 10°35E 133 A2
Ilafer Algeria 21°40N 1°58E 261 D5
Ilagan Phil. 17°7N 121°53E 232 C3
Ilaka Madag. 19°33S 48°52E 272 B2
Īlām Iran 33°36N 46°36E 213 F12
Ilam Nepal 26°58N 87°58E 243 F12
Īlām □ Iran 33°0N 47°0E 246 C5
Ilan Taiwan 24°45N 121°44E 225 B3
Ilan □ Taiwan 24°30N 121°35E 225 B3
Ilan, Mt. Phil. 10°26N 119°33E 233 F2
Ilanskiy Russia 56°14N 96°3E 215 D10
Ilaro Nigeria 6°53N 3°3E 263 D5
Ilatane Niger 16°30N 4°45E 263 B5
Ilave Peru 16°5S 69°40W 330 D4
Iława Poland 53°36N 19°34E 184 E6
Ilayangudi India 9°34N 78°37E 245 K4
Ile → Kazakhstan 45°53N 77°10E 217 C9
Île-à-la-Crosse Canada 55°27N 107°53W 297 B7
Île-à-la-Crosse, Lac
Canada 55°40N 107°45W 297 B7
Île-de-France □ France 49°0N 2°20E 173 D9
Ileanda Romania 47°20N 23°38E 183 C8
Ilebo Dem. Rep. of the Congo 4°17S 20°55E 265 C4
Ilek Russia 51°32N 53°21E 216 B4
Ilek → Russia 51°30N 53°22E 186 D9
Iler, O. → Algeria 20°59N 3°14E 261 D5
Ilero Nigeria 8°0N 3°20E 263 D5
Ilesha Kwara, Nigeria 8°57N 3°28E 263 D5
Ilesha Oyo, Nigeria 7°37N 4°40E 263 D5
Ilet = Krasnogorskiy
Russia 56°10N 48°28E 190 B9
Iletskaya = Sol Iletsk
Russia 51°10N 55°0E 186 D10
Iletsky Gorodok = Ilek
Russia 51°32N 53°21E 216 B4
Ilford Man., Canada 56°4N 95°35W 297 B9
Ilford London, U.K. 51°33N 0°4E 125 A4
Ilfracombe Queens.,
Australia 23°30S 144°30E 280 C3
Ilfracombe Devon, U.K. 51°12N 4°8W 169 F3
Ilgaz Turkey 40°55N 33°37E 212 B5
Ilgaz Dağları Turkey 41°10N 33°50E 212 B5
Ilgın Turkey 38°16N 31°55E 212 C4
Ilha, Pta. da Azores 38°25N 28°3W 153 d1
Ilha Grande Brazil 0°27S 65°2W 329 D4
Ilha Grande, B. da Brazil 23°9S 44°30W 333 F3
Ilha Grande, Represa
Brazil 23°10S 53°5W 335 A5
Ilha Grande △ Brazil 23°10S 53°20W 335 A5
Ílhavo Portugal 40°33N 8°43W 194 E2
Ilhéus Brazil 14°49S 39°2W 333 D4
Ili = Ile → Kazakhstan 45°53N 77°10E 217 C9
Ilia Romania 45°57N 22°40E 182 E7
Ilia □ Greece 37°45N 21°35E 204 D3
Iliamna U.S.A. 59°45N 154°55W 303 G9
Iliamna L. U.S.A. 59°30N 155°0W 303 G9
Ilias, Profitis Greece 36°17N 27°56E 206 E11
Iliç Turkey 39°27N 38°33E 213 C8
Ilica Turkey 39°52N 27°46E 205 B9
Ilig, Ras Somali Rep. 7°47N 49°50E 267 C6
Iligan Phil. 8°12N 124°13E 233 G5
Iligan B. Phil. 8°25N 124°5E 233 G5
Iligan Pt. Phil. 18°25N 122°25E 232 B4
Ilin I. Phil. 12°14N 121°5E 232 E3
'Ilio Pt. U.S.A. 21°13N 157°16W 302 B4
Ilion U.S.A. 43°1N 75°2W 313 D9
Ilioupoli Greece 37°54N 23°45E 112 B2
Ilirska-Bistrica Slovenia 45°34N 14°14E 199 C11
Iliwa = Rewa → Guyana 3°19N 58°42W 329 C6
Iliysk = Qapshaghay
Kazakhstan 43°51N 77°14E 217 D9
Ilkal India 15°57N 76°8E 245 G3
Ilkenau = Olkusz Poland 50°18N 19°33E 185 H6
Ilkeston U.K. 52°58N 1°19W 168 E6
Ilkley U.K. 53°56N 1°48W 168 D6
Illampu = Ancohuma, Nevado
Bolivia 16°0S 68°50W 330 D4
Illana B. Phil. 7°35N 123°45E 233 H4
Illapel Chile 32°0S 71°10W 334 C1
Ille-et-Vilaine □ France 48°10N 1°30W 172 D5
Ille-sur-Têt France 42°40N 2°38E 174 F6
Illéla Niger 14°32N 5°20E 263 C6
Iller → Germany 48°23N 9°58E 179 G5
Illertissen Germany 48°12N 10°7E 179 G6
Illescas Spain 40°8N 3°51W 194 E7
Illetas Spain 39°32N 2°35E 206 B3
Illichivsk Ukraine 46°20N 30°35E 189 J6
Illiers-Combray France 48°18N 1°15E 172 D8
Illimani, Nevado Bolivia 16°30S 67°50W 330 D4
Illinois □ U.S.A. 40°15N 89°30W 310 D7
Illinois → U.S.A. 38°58N 90°28W 310 F6
Illinois at Chicago, Univ. of
U.S.A. 41°52N 87°38W 119 B3
Illinois Institute of Technology
U.S.A. 41°50N 87°37W 119 B3
Illiopolis U.S.A. 39°51N 89°15W 310 E7
Illium = Troy Turkey 39°57N 26°12E 205 B8
Illizi Algeria 26°31N 8°32E 261 C6
Illizi □ Algeria 26°50N 8°10E 261 C6
Illkirch-Graffenstaden
France 48°34N 7°42E 173 D14
Íllora Spain 37°17N 3°53W 195 H7
Ilm → Germany 51°6N 11°40E 178 D7
Ilma, L. Australia 29°13S 127°46E 279 E4
Ilmajoki Finland 62°44N 22°34E 160 E20
Ilmen, Ozero Russia 58°15N 31°10E 188 C6
Ilmenau = Jordanów
Poland 49°41N 19°49E 185 J6
Ilmenau = Limanowa
Poland 49°42N 20°22E 185 J7
Ilmenau Germany 50°41N 10°54E 178 E6
Ilnytsya Ukraine 48°21N 23°5E 182 B8
Ilo Peru 17°40S 71°20W 330 D3
Ilobu Nigeria 7°45N 4°25E 263 D5
Iloc I. Phil. 11°17N 119°40E 233 F2
Ilocos Norte □ Phil. 18°10N 120°45E 232 B3
Ilocos Sur □ Phil. 17°20N 120°35E 232 C3
Iloilo Phil. 10°45N 122°33E 233 F4
Iloilo □ Phil. 11°0N 122°40E 233 F4
Ilomantsi Finland 62°38N 30°57E 160 E24
Ilora Nigeria 7°45N 3°50E 263 D5
Ilorin Nigeria 8°30N 4°35E 263 D5
Ilotkaya Russia 50°30N 45°50E 190 E7
Ilovlya Russia 49°15N 44°2E 191 F7
Ilovlya → Russia 49°14N 44°0E 191 F7
Iłowa Poland 51°30N 15°10E 185 G2
Ilpendam Neths. 52°28N 4°57E 112 A2
Ilsos → Greece 37°55N 23°41E 112 E2
Ilubabor Ethiopia 7°25N 35°0E 257 F4
Ilulissat Greenland 69°12N 51°10W 154 C5
Ilva Mică Romania 47°17N 24°40E 183 C9
Ilwaco U.S.A. 46°19N 124°3W 306 C2
Ilwaki Indonesia 7°55S 126°30E 231 F7
Ilyichevsk = Illichivsk
Ukraine 46°20N 30°35E 189 J6
Iłża Poland 51°10N 21°15E 185 G8
Ilzanka → Poland 51°14N 21°48E 185 G8
Imabari Japan 34°4N 133°0E 222 C5
Imagem e do Som, Museu da
Rio de J., Brazil 135 b3
Imaichi Japan 36°43N 139°46E 223 A11
Imaloto → Madag. 23°27S 45°13E 272 C2
İmamoğlu Turkey 37°15N 35°38E 212 D6
Iman = Dalnerechensk
Russia 45°50N 133°40E 220 B6
Imandra, Ozero Russia 67°30N 33°0E 160 C25
Imanombo Madag. 24°26S 45°49E 272 C2
Imari Japan 33°15N 129°52E 222 D1
Imasa Sudan 18°0N 36°12E 256 D4
Imathia □ Greece 40°30N 22°15E 202 F6
Imatra Finland 61°12N 28°48E 188 B5
Imbâbah Egypt 30°3N 31°12E 117 A2
Imbabura □ Ecuador 0°30N 78°45W 328 C2
Imbaimadai Guyana 5°44N 60°17W 329 B5
Imbonga
Dem. Rep. of the Congo 0°43S 19°44E 264 C3
Imdahane Morocco 32°8N 7°0W 260 B3
Iménas Mali 16°20N 0°40E 263 B5
imeni 26 Bakinskikh Komissarov =
Neftçala Azerbaijan 39°19N 49°12E 213 C13
imeni 26 Bakinskikh Komissarov
Turkmenistan 39°22N 54°10E 247 B7
imeni Dvadtsati Shesti Bakinskikh
Komissarov = Neftçala
Azerbaijan 39°19N 49°12E 213 C13
imeni Dzerzhinskogo =
Naryan-Mar Russia 67°42N 53°12E 186 A9
imeni Ismail Samani, Pik
Tajikistan 39°0N 72°2E 217 E8
imeni Mikoyana = Kara-Balta
Kyrgyzstan 42°50N 73°49E 217 D8
imeni Petrovskogo G.I. =
Horodyshche Ukraine 49°17N 31°27E 189 H6
imeni Sverdlova = Sverdlovsk
Ukraine 48°5N 39°47E 189 H10
imeni Tovarishcha Khateyevicha =
Synelnykove Ukraine 48°25N 35°30E 189 H8
imeni Tretyego Internatsionala =
Novoshakhtinsk
Russia 47°46N 39°58E 189 J10
Imeri, Serra Brazil 0°50N 65°25W 328 C4
Imerimandroso Madag. 17°26S 48°35E 272 B2
Imese Dem. Rep. of the Congo 2°8N 18°9E 264 B3
Imfolozi △ S. Africa 28°18S 31°50E 271 C5
Imi Ethiopia 6°28N 42°10E 257 F5
Imielin Poland 52°9N 21°0E 142 C2
Imirim Brazil 23°29S 46°39W 137 A2
Imishly = İmişli Azerbaijan 39°55N 48°4E 191 L9
İmişli Azerbaijan 39°55N 48°4E 191 L9
Imitek Morocco 29°43N 8°10W 260 C3
Imitos Greece 37°55N 23°45E 112 B2
Imitos, Oros Greece 37°53N 23°48E 112 B2
Imjado S. Korea 35°5N 126°5E 224 E3
Imjin-gang → N. Korea 37°47N 126°39E 224 D3
Imlay U.S.A. 40°40N 118°9W 304 F4
Imlay City U.S.A. 43°2N 83°5W 312 D1
Immaseri Sudan 15°40N 25°31E 257 D2
Immenstadt Germany 47°33N 10°13E 179 H6
Immingham U.K. 53°37N 0°13W 168 D7
Immokalee U.S.A. 26°25N 81°25W 317 J8
Imo □ Nigeria 5°30N 7°10E 263 D6
Imo → Nigeria 4°36N 7°35E 263 E6
Ímola Italy 44°20N 11°42E 199 D8
Imotski Croatia 43°27N 17°12E 199 E14
Impé Congo 2°45S 15°16E 264 C3
Imperatorskaya Gavan = Vanino
Russia 48°50N 140°5E 215 E15
Imperatriz Amazonas, Brazil 5°18S 67°11W 330 B4
Imperatriz Maranhão,
Brazil 5°30S 47°29W 332 C2
Impéria Italy 43°53N 8°3E 198 E5
Imperial Sask., Canada 51°21N 105°28W 297 C7
Imperial Peru 13°4S 76°21W 330 C2
Imperial Calif., U.S.A. 32°51N 115°34W 307 N11
Imperial Nebr., U.S.A. 40°31N 101°39W 308 E3
Imperial Beach U.S.A. 32°35N 117°6W 307 N9
Imperial Dam U.S.A. 32°55N 114°25W 307 N12
Imperial Palace = Paço Imperial
Rio de J., Brazil 135 a2
Imperial Palace Museum Beijing, China 114 b3
Imperial Res. U.S.A. 32°53N 114°28W 307 N12
Imperial Valley U.S.A. 33°0N 115°30W 307 N11
Imperieuse Reef Australia 17°36S 118°50E 278 C2
Impfondo Congo 1°40N 18°0E 264 B3
Imphal India 24°48N 93°56E 241 C4
Imphy France 46°55N 3°16E 173 F10
Impulo Angola 13°51S 13°39E 265 E2
İmranlı Turkey 39°54N 38°7E 213 C8
İmroz = Gökçeada Turkey 40°10N 25°50E 203 F9
İmroz Turkey 40°10N 25°55E 203 F9
Imst Austria 47°15N 10°44E 180 D3
Imuris Mexico 30°47N 110°52W 318 A2
Imuruan B. Phil. 10°40N 119°10E 233 F2
Imus Phil. 14°26N 120°56E 232 D3
In Aleï Mali 17°42N 2°30W 262 B4
In Amenas Algeria 28°5N 9°33E 261 C6
In Amguel Algeria 23°41N 5°9E 261 D6
In Atei Algeria 20°33N 6°4E 261 D6
In Belbel Algeria 27°55N 1°12E 261 C5
In Delimane Mali 15°52N 1°31E 263 B5
In Ghar Algeria 27°10N 1°59E 261 C5
In Guezzam Algeria 19°37N 5°52E 261 E6
In Koufi Mali 19°11N 1°25E 263 B5
In Salah Algeria 27°10N 2°32E 261 C5
In Tallak Mali 16°19N 3°15E 263 B5
In Tebezas Mali 17°49N 1°53E 263 B5
Ina Japan 35°50N 137°55E 223 B8
Ina Ill., U.S.A. 38°9N 88°54W 311 F8
Ina-Bonchi Japan 35°45N 137°58E 223 B8
Inabanga Phil. 10°2N 124°4E 233 F5
Inaccessible I. Atl. Oc. 37°18S 12°40W 152 K10
Inaguauan Phil. 9°33N 118°39E 233 G2
Inagi Japan 35°38N 139°31E 140 B2
Inajá Brazil 8°54S 37°49W 332 C4
Inambari → Peru 12°41S 69°44W 330 C4
Inangahua N.Z. 41°52S 171°59E 285 B6
Inanwatan Indonesia 2°8S 132°10E 231 E8
Iñapari Peru 11°0S 69°40W 330 C4
Inarajan Guam 13°16N 144°45E 302 d
Inari Finland 68°54N 27°1E 160 B22
Inarijärvi Finland 69°0N 28°0E 160 B23
Inawashiro-Ko Japan 37°29N 140°6E 220 F10
Inazawa Japan 35°15N 136°47E 223 B8
Inbin Burma 18°6N 95°16E 241 F5
Inca Spain 39°43N 2°54E 206 B3
Inca de Oro Chile 26°45S 69°54W 334 B2
Incahuasi Argentina 27°2S 68°18W 334 B2
Incahuasi Chile 29°12S 71°5W 334 B1
İnce Burun Turkey 42°7N 34°56E 212 A6
İncekum Burnu Turkey 36°13N 33°57E 250 B4
İncesu Turkey 38°38N 35°11E 212 C6
Inchcolm U.K. 56°2N 3°18W 121 A2
Incheon S. Korea 37°27N 126°40E 224 D3
Inchicore Ireland 53°20N 6°20W 120 A1
Inchiri □ Mauritania 20°0N 15°0W 260 E2
Inchkeith U.K. 56°2N 3°8W 121 A2
Inchmickery U.K. 56°0N 3°16W 121 A2
Incio = A Cruz do Incio
Spain 42°39N 7°21W 194 C3
Incirano Italy 45°34N 9°9E 129 A1
İncirliova Turkey 37°50N 27°41E 205 D9
Incline Village U.S.A. 39°10N 119°58W 304 G4
Incomáti → Mozam. 25°46S 32°43E 271 C5
Incudine, Mte. France 41°50N 9°12E 175 G13
Inda Silase Ethiopia 14°10N 38°15E 257 E4
Indal Sweden 62°36N 17°5E 162 B11
Indalsälven → Sweden 62°36N 17°30E 162 B11
Indaw Burma 24°15N 96°5E 241 C6
Indawgyi In Burma 25°8N 96°20E 241 C6
Indbir Ethiopia 8°7N 37°52E 257 F4
Indefatigable, I. = Santa Cruz, I.
Ecuador 0°38S 90°23W 330 a
Independence Calif.,
U.S.A. 36°48N 118°12W 306 J8
Independence Iowa,
U.S.A. 42°28N 91°54W 310 B5
Independence Kans.,
U.S.A. 37°14N 95°42W 308 G6
Independence Ky.,
U.S.A. 38°57N 84°33W 311 F12
Independence Mo., U.S.A. 39°6N 94°25W 310 E2
Independence Avenue
Washington, D.C., U.S.A. 143 c2
Independence Fjord
Greenland 82°10N 29°0W 154 A8
Independence Mts.
U.S.A. 41°20N 116°0W 304 F5
Independência Brazil 5°23S 40°19W 332 C3
Independencia Santiago,
Chile 33°25S 70°39W 137 B2
Independencia Lima, Peru 11°59S 77°3W 124 A2
Independencia, I. Peru 14°16S 76°12W 330 C2
Independenţa Romania 45°25N 27°42E 183 E12
Înderbor Kazakhstan 48°33N 51°47E 216 C4
Index U.S.A. 47°50N 121°33W 306 C5
India ■ Asia 20°0N 78°0E 239 F11
India Gate Delhi, India 120 c2
Indialantic U.S.A. 28°6N 80°34W 317 G9
Indian → U.S.A. 27°59N 80°34W 317 G9
Indian Cabins Canada 59°52N 117°40W 296 B5
Indian Creek Village
U.S.A. 25°52N 80°8W 128 A2
Indian Harbour Canada 54°27N 57°13W 299 B8
Indian Harbour Beach
U.S.A. 28°10N 80°35W 317 G9
Indian Head Canada 50°30N 103°41W 297 C8
Indian L. U.S.A. 43°45N 74°16W 313 C10
Indian Lake U.S.A. 43°47N 74°16W 313 C10
Indian Ocean 5°0S 75°0E 273 E6
Indian Rocks Beach
U.S.A. 27°52N 82°51W 317 H7
Indian Springs U.S.A. 36°35N 115°40W 307 J11
Indian Town Pt.
Antigua & B. 17°6N 61°40W 322 b
Indian Walk Trin. & Tob. 10°16N 61°20W 323 t
Indiana U.S.A. 40°37N 79°9W 312 F5
Indiana □ U.S.A. 40°0N 86°0W 311 E11
Indiana Dunes △ U.S.A. 41°40N 87°0W 311 C9
Indianapolis U.S.A. 39°46N 86°9W 311 E10
Indianapolis Int. ✈ (IND)
U.S.A. 39°43N 86°17W 311 E10
Indianola Iowa, U.S.A. 41°22N 93°34W 310 C3
Indianola Miss., U.S.A. 33°27N 90°39W 315 E9
Indianópolis Brazil 23°35S 46°38W 137 B2
Indiantown U.S.A. 27°1N 80°28W 317 H9
Indiapora Brazil 19°57S 50°17W 333 E1
Indiga Russia 67°38N 49°9E 186 A8
Indigirka → Russia 70°48N 148°54E 215 B15
Inđija Serbia 45°6N 20°7E 182 E5
Indio U.S.A. 33°43N 116°13W 307 M10
Indira Gandhi Canal India 28°0N 72°0E 242 F5
Indira Gandhi Int. ✈ (DEL)
India 28°34N 77°5E 120 B1
Indira Pt. India 6°44N 93°49E 245 L11
Indira Sagar India 22°15N 76°40E 242 H7
Indispensable Str.
Solomon Is. 9°0S 160°30E 287 M11
Indo-China Asia 15°0N 102°0E 210 G12
Indonesia ■ Asia 5°0S 115°0E 235 C4
Indore India 22°42N 75°53E 242 H6
Indramayu Indonesia 6°20S 108°19E 235 D3
Indrapura = Kerinci
Indonesia 1°40S 101°15E 234 C2
Indravati → India 19°20N 80°20E 244 E5
Indre □ France 46°50N 1°39E 173 F8
Indre → France 47°16N 0°11E 172 E7
Indre Ålvik Norway 60°26N 6°26E 164 D3
Indre Arna Norway 60°26N 5°30E 164 D2
Indre-et-Loire □ France 47°20N 0°40E 172 E7
Indrio U.S.A. 27°31N 80°21W 317 H9
Indulkana Australia 26°58S 133°5E 281 D1
Indungo Angola 14°48S 16°17E 265 E3
Indura Belarus 53°26N 23°53E 184 E10
Indus → Pakistan 24°20N 67°47E 242 G2
Indus, Mouths of the
Pakistan 24°0N 68°0E 242 H3
Industria S. Africa 26°11S 27°58E 123 B1
Industrial Canal U.S.A. 30°4N 90°4W 131 A2
Industry U.S.A. 40°20N 90°36W 310 D6
İnebolu Turkey 41°55N 33°40E 212 B5
İnecik Turkey 40°56N 27°16E 203 F11
İnegöl Turkey 40°5N 29°31E 203 F13
Inés, Mt. Argentina 48°30S 69°40W 336 C3
Ineu Romania 46°26N 21°51E 182 D6
Inezgane Morocco 30°25N 9°29W 260 B3
Infanta Phil. 14°45N 121°39E 232 D3
Infantes = Villanueva de los
Infantes Spain 38°43N 3°1W 195 G7
Infiernillo, Presa del
Mexico 18°35N 101°50W 318 D4
Infiesto Spain 43°21N 5°21W 194 B5
Inga, Barrage d'
Dem. Rep. of the Congo 5°39S 13°39E 265 D2
Ingabu Burma 17°37N 95°20E 241 G5
Inganda
Dem. Rep. of the Congo 0°5S 20°57E 264 C4
Ingapirca Ecuador 2°38S 78°56W 328 D2
Ingaro Sweden 59°12N 18°45E 162 E12
Ingelstad Sweden 56°45N 14°56E 163 H8
Ingende
Dem. Rep. of the Congo 0°12S 18°57E 264 C3
Ingeniero Jacobacci
Argentina 41°20S 69°36W 336 B3
Ingenio Canary Is. 27°55N 15°26W 153 e1
Ingenio Santa Ana
Argentina 27°25S 65°40W 334 B2
Ingersoll Canada 43°4N 80°55W 312 C4
Ingham Australia 18°43S 146°10E 280 B4
Ingierstrand Norway 59°49N 10°46E 133 B3
Ingleborough U.K. 54°10N 2°22W 168 C5
Inglefield Land Greenland 78°30N 70°0W 154 B4
Inglewood Queens.,
Australia 28°25S 151°2E 281 D5
Inglewood Vic., Australia 36°29S 143°53E 282 D5
Inglewood N.Z. 39°9S 174°14E 284 F3
Inglewood Calif., U.S.A. 33°58N 118°21W 126 C3
Inglis U.S.A. 29°2N 82°40W 317 F7
Ingliston U.K. 55°56N 3°23W 121 B1
Ingolf Fjord Greenland 80°35N 17°30W 154 A9
Ingólfshöfði Iceland 63°48N 16°39W 155 D10
Ingolstadt Germany 48°46N 11°26E 179 G7
Ingomar U.S.A. 46°35N 107°23W 304 C10
Ingonish Canada 46°42N 60°18W 299 C7
Ingore Guinea-Biss. 12°24N 15°48W 262 C1
Ingraj Bazar India 24°58N 88°10E 243 G13
Ingrid Christensen Coast
Antarctica 69°30S 76°0E 151 C6
Ingul = Inhul → Ukraine 46°50N 32°0E 189 J7
Ingulec = Inhulec Ukraine 47°42N 33°14E 189 J7
Ingulets = Inhulets →
Ukraine 46°46N 32°47E 189 J7
Inguri = Enguri →
Georgia 42°27N 41°38E 191 J5
Ingushetia □ Russia 43°20N 44°50E 191 J7
Ingwavuma S. Africa 27°9S 31°59E 271 C5
Inhaca Mozam. 26°1S 32°57E 271 C5
Inhaca, Pen. Mozam. 26°13S 32°55E 271 C5
Inhafenga Mozam. 20°36S 33°53E 271 B5
Inhambane Mozam. 23°54S 35°30E 271 B6
Inhambane □ Mozam. 22°30S 34°20E 271 B5
Inhambupe Brazil 11°47S 38°21W 333 D4
Inhaminga Mozam. 18°26S 35°0E 269 F4
Inharrime Mozam. 24°30S 35°0E 271 B6
Inharrime → Mozam. 24°30S 35°0E 271 B6
Inhaúma Brazil 22°51S 43°17W 135 B1
Inhisar Turkey 40°3N 30°23E 205 A12
Inhul → Ukraine 46°50N 32°0E 189 J7
Inhulec Ukraine 47°42N 33°14E 189 J7
Inhulets → Ukraine 46°46N 32°47E 189 J7
Inhuma Brazil 6°40S 41°42W 332 C3
Inhumas Brazil 16°22S 49°30W 333 E2
Iniesta Spain 39°27N 1°45W 197 F3
Ining = Yining China 43°58N 81°10E 217 D10
Inini □ Fr. Guiana 4°0N 53°0W 329 C7
Inírida → Colombia 3°55N 67°52W 328 C4
Inis = Ennis Ireland 52°51N 8°59W 166 D3
Inis Córthaidh = Enniscorthy
Ireland 52°30N 6°34W 166 D5
Inishbofin Ireland 53°37N 10°13W 166 C1
Inisheer Ireland 53°3N 9°32W 166 C2
Inishfree B. Ireland 55°4N 8°23W 166 A3
Inishkea North Ireland 54°9N 10°11W 166 B1
Inishkea South Ireland 54°7N 10°12W 166 B1
Inishmaan Ireland 53°5N 9°35W 166 C2
Inishmore Ireland 53°8N 9°45W 166 C2
Inishmurray I. Ireland 54°26N 8°39W 166 B3
Inishowen Pen. Ireland 55°14N 7°15W 166 A4
Inishshark Ireland 53°37N 10°16W 166 C1
Inishturk Ireland 53°42N 10°7W 166 C1
Inishvickillane Ireland 52°3N 10°37W 166 D1
Initao Phil. 8°56N 124°20E 233 G5
Injāna Iraq 34°29N 44°38E 213 E11
Injibara Ethiopia 10°59N 37°0E 257 E4
Injinoo ✪ Australia 10°56S 142°15E 280 A3
Injune Australia 25°53S 148°32E 281 D4
Inkisi →
Dem. Rep. of the Congo 4°46S 14°52E 265 D3
Inklin → N. Amer. 58°50N 133°10W 296 B2
Inland Kaikoura Ra.
N.Z. 41°59S 173°41E 285 B8
Inland Sea = Setonaikai
Japan 34°20N 133°30E 222 C5
Inle L. Burma 20°30N 96°58E 241 E6
Inlet U.S.A. 43°45N 74°48W 313 C10
Inn → Austria 48°35N 13°28E 180 C6
Innamincka Australia 27°44S 140°46E 281 D3
Innbygda Norway 61°19N 12°17E 164 C9
Inner Hebrides U.K. 57°0N 6°30W 167 E2
Inner Mongolia = Nei Mongol
Zizhiqu □ China 42°0N 112°0E 226 D7
Inner Port Shelter China 22°22N 114°17E 122 A2
Inner Sound U.K. 57°30N 5°55W 167 D3
Innerkip Canada 43°13N 80°42W 312 C4
Innes △ Australia 35°52S 136°53E 282 C2
Innetalling I. Canada 56°0N 79°0W 298 A4
Innisfail Queens., Australia 17°33S 146°5E 280 B4
Innisfail Alta., Canada 52°2N 113°57W 296 C6
Innoko Natl. Wildlife Refuge △
U.S.A. 63°20N 158°25W 303 E8
In'noshima Japan 34°19N 133°10E 222 C5
Innsbruck Austria 47°16N 11°23E 180 D4
Innviertel Austria 48°15N 13°15E 180 C6
Innvik Norway 61°51N 6°37E 164 C3
Inny → Ireland 53°30N 7°50W 166 C4
Ino Japan 33°33N 133°26E 222 D5
Inocência Brazil 19°47S 51°48W 333 E1
Inongo
Dem. Rep. of the Congo 1°55S 18°30E 264 C3
Inoni Congo 3°4S 15°39E 264 C3
İnönü Turkey 39°48N 30°9E 205 B12
Inoucdjouac = Inukjuak
Canada 58°25N 78°15W 295 F16
Inousses Greece 38°33N 26°14E 205 C8
Inowrocław Poland 52°50N 18°12E 185 F5
Inquisivi Bolivia 16°50S 67°10W 330 D4
Inscription, C. Australia 25°29S 112°59E 279 E1
Insein Burma 16°50N 96°5E 241 G6
Insjön Sweden 60°41N 15°6E 162 D9
Ińsko Poland 53°25N 15°32E 184 E2
Insterberg = Chernyakhovsk
Russia 54°36N 21°48E 184 D8
Însurăţei Romania 44°50N 27°40E 183 F12
Inta Russia 66°5N 60°8E 186 A11
Intendente Alvear
Argentina 35°12S 63°32W 334 D3
İntepe Turkey 40°1N 26°20E 205 A8
Interlachen U.S.A. 29°37N 81°53W 317 F8
Interlagos Brazil 23°41S 46°42W 137 C1
Interlaken Switz. 46°41N 7°50E 179 J3
Interlaken N.Y., U.S.A. 42°37N 76°44W 313 D8
International Falls U.S.A. 48°36N 93°25W 308 A7
Interview I. India 12°55N 92°43E 245 H11
Intiyaco Argentina 28°43S 60°5W 334 B3
Întorsura Buzăului
Romania 45°41N 26°2E 183 E11
Intramuros Phil. 14°35N 120°57E 127 B1
Intrepid Air and Space Museum
New York, U.S.A. 132 b1
Intutu Peru 3°32S 74°48W 328 D3
Inubō-Zaki Japan 35°42N 140°52E 223 B12
Inukjuak Canada 58°25N 78°15W 295 F16
Inútil, B. Chile 53°30S 70°15W 336 D2
Inuvik Canada 68°16N 133°40W 294 D5
Inuyama Japan 35°23N 136°56E 223 B8
Invalides France 48°51N 2°18E 134 A2
Inveraray U.K. 56°14N 5°5W 167 E3
Inverbervie U.K. 56°51N 2°17W 167 E6
Invercargill N.Z. 46°24S 168°24E 285 G3
Inverclyde □ U.K. 55°55N 4°49W 167 F4
Inverell Australia 29°45S 151°8E 281 D5
Invergordon U.K. 57°41N 4°10W 167 D4
Inverkeithing U.K. 56°2N 3°24W 121 A1
Inverleigh Australia 38°6S 144°3E 282 E6
Inverloch Australia 38°38S 145°45E 281 F4
Invermere Canada 50°30N 116°2W 296 C5
Inverness N.S., Canada 46°15N 61°19W 299 C7
Inverness Highl., U.K. 57°29N 4°13W 167 D4
Inverness Ala., U.S.A. 32°1N 85°45W 316 C4
Inverness Fla., U.S.A. 28°50N 82°20W 317 G7
Inverurie U.K. 57°17N 2°23W 167 D6
Investigator Group
Australia 34°45S 134°20E 281 E1
Investigator Ridge Ind. Oc. 11°30S 98°10E 273 F8
Investigator Str. Australia 35°30S 137°0E 282 C2
Inya Russia 50°28N 86°37E 217 B11
Inyanga Zimbabwe 18°12S 32°40E 269 F3
Inyangani Zimbabwe 18°5S 32°50E 269 F3
Inyantue Zimbabwe 18°33S 26°39E 270 A4
Inyo Mts. U.S.A. 36°40N 118°0W 306 J9
Inyokern U.S.A. 35°39N 117°49W 307 K9
Inyonga Tanzania 6°45S 32°5E 268 D3
Inywa Burma 23°56N 96°17E 241 D6
Inza Russia 53°55N 46°25E 190 D8
Inzersdorf Austria 48°8N 16°21E 142 B2
Inzhavino Russia 52°22N 42°30E 190 D6
Inzia →
Dem. Rep. of the Congo 3°45S 17°57E 265 C3
Iō-Jima Japan 30°48N 130°18E 221 J5
Ioannina Greece 39°42N 20°47E 204 B2
Ioannina □ Greece 39°39N 20°57E 204 B2
Iokea Papua N. G. 8°25S 146°16E 286 E4
Iola U.S.A. 37°55N 95°24W 308 G6
Iolani Palace U.S.A. 21°18N 157°51W 302 K14
Ioma Papua N. G. 8°19S 147°52E 286 E4
Ion Corvin Romania 44°7N 27°50E 183 F12
Iona Angola 16°54S 12°34E 265 F2
Iona Argyll & Bute, U.K. 56°20N 6°25W 167 E2
Iona △ Angola 16°47S 12°20E 265 F2
Ione U.S.A. 38°21N 120°56W 306 G6
Iongo Angola 9°11S 17°45E 265 D3
Ionia U.S.A. 42°59N 85°4W 311 B11
Ionian Is. = Ionioi Nisoi
Greece 38°40N 20°0E 204 C2
Ionian Sea Medit. S. 37°30N 17°30E 193 D7
Ionioi Nisoi Greece 38°40N 20°0E 204 C2
Ionioi Nisoi □ Greece 38°40N 20°0E 207 B2
Ios Greece 36°41N 25°20E 205 E7
Iowa □ U.S.A. 42°18N 93°30W 310 C3
Iowa → U.S.A. 41°10N 91°1W 310 C5
Iowa City U.S.A. 41°40N 91°32W 310 C5
Iowa Falls U.S.A. 42°31N 93°16W 310 B3
Iowa Park U.S.A. 33°57N 98°40W 314 E5
Ipala Tanzania 4°30S 32°52E 268 C3
Ipameri Brazil 17°44S 48°9W 333 E2
Ipanema Minas Gerais,
Brazil 19°47S 41°44W 333 E3
Ipanema Rio de J., Brazil 22°59S 43°12W 135 B1
Iparía Peru 9°17S 74°29W 330 B3
Ipati Greece 38°52N 22°14E 204 C4
Ipatinga Brazil 19°32S 42°30W 333 E3
Ipatovo Russia 45°45N 42°50E 191 H6
Ipek = Peć Kosovo 42°40N 20°17E 202 D4
Ipel' → Europe 47°48N 18°53E 181 D11
Ipiales Colombia 0°50N 77°37W 328 C2
Ipiaú Brazil 14°8S 39°44W 333 D4
Ipil Phil. 7°47N 122°35E 233 H4
Ipin = Yibin China 28°45N 104°32E 228 C5
Ipirá Brazil 12°10S 39°44W 333 D4
Ipiranga Brazil 23°35S 46°36W 137 B2
Ipiranga → Brazil 23°37S 46°37W 137 B2
Ipixuna Brazil 7°0S 71°40W 330 B3
Ipixuna → Amazonas,
Brazil 7°11S 71°51W 330 B3
Ipixuna → Amazonas, Brazil 5°45S 63°2W 331 B5
Ipoh Malaysia 4°35N 101°5E 237 K3
Ipomi Nigeria 6°28N 3°22E 124 B2
Iporá Brazil 16°28S 51°7W 331 D7
Ipota Vanuatu 18°52S 169°20E 287 H7
Ippy C.A.R. 6°5N 21°7E 264 A4
İpsala Turkey 40°55N 26°23E 203 F10
Ipsario, Oros Greece 40°40N 24°40E 203 F8
Ipsos Greece 39°43N 19°48E 206 B9
Ipswich Queens., Australia 27°35S 152°40E 281 D5
Ipswich Suffolk, U.K. 52°4N 1°10E 169 E9
Ipswich Mass., U.S.A. 42°41N 70°50W 313 D14
Ipswich S. Dak., U.S.A. 45°27N 99°2W 308 C4
Ipu Brazil 4°23S 40°44W 332 B3
Ipueiras Brazil 4°33S 40°43W 332 B3
Ipuh Indonesia 3°0S 101°30E 234 C2
Ipupiara Brazil 11°49S 42°37W 333 D3
Iqaluit Canada 63°44N 68°31W 295 E18
Iqaluktuutiaq = Cambridge Bay
Canada 69°10N 105°0W 294 D11
Iquique Chile 20°19S 70°5W 330 E3
Iquitos Peru 3°45S 73°10W 328 D3
Ir Gannim = Bat Yam
Israel 32°2N 34°44E 251 F3
Irabu-Jima Japan 24°50N 125°10E 221 M2
Iracoubo Fr. Guiana 5°30N 53°10W 329 B7
Īrafshān Iran 26°42N 61°56E 247 E9
Irago-Suidō Japan 34°25N 137°0E 223 C8
Irahuan Phil. 9°48N 118°41E 233 G2
Iraklia Cyclades, Greece 36°50N 25°28E 205 E7
Iraklia Serres, Greece 41°10N 23°16E 202 E7
Iraklio Greece 35°20N 25°12E 207 E6
Iraklio □ Greece 35°10N 25°10E 207 E6
Iraklio ✈ (HER) Greece 35°20N 25°15E 207 E6
Iraklion = Iraklio Greece 35°20N 25°12E 207 E6
Irakliou, Kolpos Greece 35°23N 25°8E 207 E6
Irako-Zaki Japan 34°35N 137°1E 223 C9
Irala Paraguay 25°55S 54°35W 335 B5
Iran ■ Asia 33°0N 53°0E 247 C7
Iran, Pegunungan
Malaysia 2°20N 114°50E 235 B4
Iran Ra. = Iran, Pegunungan
Malaysia 2°20N 114°50E 235 B4
Iranamadu Tank Sri Lanka 9°23N 80°29E 245 K5
Īrānshahr Iran 27°15N 60°40E 247 E9
Irapa Venezuela 10°34N 62°35W 329 A5
Irapuato Mexico 20°41N 101°28W 318 C4
Iraq ■ Asia 33°0N 44°0E 213 F10
Irarrar, O. → Mali 20°0N 1°30E 261 E5
Irati Brazil 25°25S 50°38W 335 B5
Irbes saurums Latvia 57°45N 22°5E 184 A9
Irbid Jordan 32°35N 35°48E 251 F6
Irbid □ Jordan 32°30N 35°50E 250 F6
Irebu Dem. Rep. of the Congo 0°40S 17°46E 264 C3
Irecê Brazil 11°18S 41°52W 332 D3
Iregua → Spain 42°27N 2°24E 196 C7
Ireland ■ Europe 53°50N 7°52W 166 C4
Ireland I. Bermuda 32°19N 64°50W 153 a
Ireland Island Bermuda 32°19N 64°50W 153 a
Ireland's Eye Ireland 53°24N 6°4W 120 A3
Irele Nigeria 7°40N 5°40E 263 D6
Ireng → Brazil 3°33N 59°51W 329 C6
Irerrer, O. → Algeria 19°25N 5°47E 261 E6
Irgiz = Yrghyz Kazakhstan 48°37N 61°16E 216 C6
Irgiz = Yrghyz →
Kazakhstan 48°6N 62°30E 216 C6
Irgiz, Bolshaya → Russia 52°10N 49°10E 190 D9
Irharrhar, O. → Algeria 28°3N 6°15E 261 C6
Irherm Morocco 30°7N 8°18W 260 B3
Irhil M'Goun Morocco 31°30N 6°28W 260 B3
Iri = Iksan S. Korea 35°59N 127°0E 224 E3
Irian Barat = Papua □
Indonesia 4°0S 137°0E 231 E9
Irian Jaya = Papua □
Indonesia 4°0S 137°0E 231 E9
Irian Jaya Barat □
Indonesia 2°5S 132°50E 231 E8
Iriba Chad 15°7N 22°15E 259 E4
Irié Guinea 8°15N 9°10W 262 D3
Iriga Phil. 13°25N 123°25E 232 E4
Iriklinskoye Vdkhr. Russia 52°0N 59°0E 218 B5
Iringa Tanzania 7°48S 35°43E 263 D4
Iringa □ Tanzania 7°48S 35°43E 263 D4
Irinjalakuda India 10°21N 76°14E 245 J3
Iriomote △ Japan 24°29N 123°53E 221 M1
Iriomote-Jima Japan 24°19N 123°48E 221 M1
Iriona Honduras 15°57N 85°11W 320 C2
Iriri → Brazil 3°52S 52°37W 329 D7
Iriri Novo → Brazil 8°46S 53°22W 331 B7
Irish Republic ■ Europe 53°50N 7°52W 166 C4
Irish Sea Europe 53°38N 4°48W 168 D3
Irkeshtam Pass = Erkech-Tam Pass
Asia 39°46N 74°2E 217 E8
Irkutsk Russia 52°18N 104°20E 218 A9
Irlığanlı Turkey 37°53N 29°12E 205 D11
Irma Canada 52°55N 111°14W 297 C6
Irō-Zaki Japan 34°36N 138°51E 223 C10
Irois B. Trin. & Tob. 10°9N 61°45W 323 t
Iroise, Mer d' France 48°15N 4°45W 172 D2
Iron Baron Australia 32°58S 137°11E 282 B2
Iron Gate = Portile de Fier
Europe 44°44N 22°30E 182 F7
Iron Knob Australia 32°46S 137°8E 282 B2
Iron Mountain U.S.A. 45°49N 88°4W 308 C9
Iron Range △ Australia 12°34S 143°18E 280 A3
Iron River U.S.A. 46°6N 88°39W 308 B9
Irondequoit U.S.A. 43°13N 77°35W 312 C7
Ironton Mo., U.S.A. 37°36N 90°38W 308 G8
Ironton Ohio, U.S.A. 38°32N 82°41W 309 F12
Ironwood U.S.A. 46°27N 90°9W 308 B8
Ironwood Forest △
U.S.A. 32°32N 111°28W 305 K8
Iroquois Canada 44°51N 75°19W 313 B9
Iroquois → U.S.A. 41°5N 87°49W 311 C9
Iroquois Falls Canada 48°46N 80°41W 298 C3
Iroquois Point U.S.A. 21°19N 157°58W 302 K14
Irosin Phil. 12°42N 124°2E 232 E5
Irpin Ukraine 50°30N 30°15E 177 C16
Irqieqa, Ras I- Malta 35°56N 14°29E 206 F7
Irrara Cr. → Australia 29°35S 145°31E 281 D4
Irrawaddy □ Burma 17°0N 95°0E 241 G5
Irrawaddy → Burma 15°50N 95°6E 241 G5
Irrawaddy, Mouths of the
Burma 15°30N 95°0E 241 H5
Irricana Canada 51°19N 113°37W 296 C6
Irrunytju Australia 26°3S 128°56E 279 E4
Irshava Ukraine 48°19N 23°3E 182 B8
Irsina Italy 40°45N 16°14E 201 B9
Irtysh → Russia 61°4N 68°52E 214 C7
Irumu Dem. Rep. of the Congo 1°32N 29°53E 268 B2
Irún Spain 43°20N 1°52W 196 B3
Irunea = Pamplona-Iruña
Spain 42°48N 1°38W 196 C3
Irurzun Spain 42°55N 1°50W 196 C3
Irvine Alta., Canada 49°57N 110°16W 297 D6
Irvine N. Ayrs., U.K. 55°37N 4°41W 167 F4
Irvine Calif., U.S.A. 33°41N 117°46W 307 M9
Irvine Ky., U.S.A. 37°42N 83°58W 311 G13
Irvinestown U.K. 54°28N 7°39W 166 B4
Irving U.S.A. 32°48N 96°55W 314 E6
Irving Park U.S.A. 41°57N 87°42W 119 B2
Irvington U.S.A. 37°53N 86°17W 311 G10
Irvona U.S.A. 40°46N 78°33W 312 F6
Irwin → Australia 29°15S 114°54E 279 E1
Irwinton U.S.A. 32°49N 83°10W 316 C6
Irwinville U.S.A. 31°39N 83°23W 316 D6
Irymple Australia 34°14S 142°8E 282 C5
Is, Jebel Sudan 22°3N 35°28E 256 C4
Is-sur-Tille France 47°30N 5°6E 173 E12
Isa Nigeria 13°14N 6°24E 263 C6
Isa Khel Pakistan 32°41N 71°17E 242 C4
Isaac → Australia 22°55S 149°20E 280 C4
Isabel Rio de J., Brazil 22°55S 43°14W 135 B1

Isabel *S. Dak., U.S.A.* 45°24N 101°26W **308** C3
Isabel, I. *Mexico* 21°51N 105°55W **318** C3
Isabel Segunda *Puerto Rico* 18°9N 65°27W **321** b
Isabela *Basilan, Phil.* 6°40N 121°59E **233** H3
Isabela *Negros, Phil.* 10°12N 122°59E **233** F4
Isabela *Puerto Rico* 18°30N 67°2W **321** b
Isabela □ *Phil.* 17°0N 122°0E **232** C4
Isabela, Canal *Ecuador* 0°20S 90°55W **330** a
Isabela, I. *Ecuador* 0°30S 91°4W **330** a
Isabella, Cord. *Nic.* 13°30N 85°25W **320** D2
Isabella Ra. *Australia* 21°0S 121°4E **278** D3
Isaccea *Romania* 45°16N 28°28E **183** E13
Isachsen, C. *Canada* 79°20N 105°28W **295** B10
Ísafjarðardjúp *Iceland* 66°10N 23°0W **155** A3
Ísafjarðarsýsla □ *Iceland* 66°0N 23°0W **155** B3
Ísafjörður *Iceland* 66°5N 23°9W **155** A3
Isagarh *India* 24°48N 77°51E **242** G7
Isagatedo *Nigeria* 6°31N 3°19E **124** A1
Isahaya *Japan* 32°52N 130°2E **222** E2
Isaka *Dem. Rep. of the Congo* 2°33S 18°54E **264** C3
Isaka *Tanzania* 3°56S 32°59E **268** C3
Işalniţa *Romania* 44°24N 23°44E **183** F8
Isalo, Tangorombohitr' *Madag.* 22°45S 45°15E **272** C2
Isalo △ *Madag.* 22°23S 45°16E **272** C2
Isan → *India* 26°51N 80°7E **243** F9
Isana = Içana → *Brazil* 0°26N 67°19W **328** C4
Isandja *Dem. Rep. of the Congo* 2°59S 21°59E **264** C4
Isangano △ *Zambia* 11°8S 30°35E **269** E3
Isangi *Dem. Rep. of the Congo* 0°52N 24°10E **264** B4
Isanlu Makutu *Nigeria* 8°20N 5°50E **263** D6
Isar → *Bayern, Germany* 48°48N 12°57E **179** G8
Isar → *Oberbayern, Germany* 48°15N 11°41E **131** A3
Isarco → *Italy* 46°27N 11°18E **199** B8
Isaris *Greece* 37°22N 22°0E **204** D3
Isarog, Mt. *Phil.* 13°39N 123°23E **232** E4
Isawa *Japan* 35°40N 138°35E **223** B10
Íscar *Spain* 41°22N 4°32W **194** D6
Iscayachi *Bolivia* 21°31S 65°3W **331** E4
İscehisar *Turkey* 38°51N 30°45E **205** C12
Íschia *Italy* 40°44N 13°57E **200** B6
Iscuandé *Colombia* 2°28N 77°59W **328** C2
Isdell → *Australia* 16°27S 124°51E **278** C3
Ise *Japan* 34°25N 136°45E **223** C8
Ise-Shima △ *Japan* 34°25N 136°48E **223** C8
Ise-Wan *Japan* 34°43N 136°43E **223** C8
Isefjord *Denmark* 55°53N 11°50E **163** J5
Isel → *Austria* 46°50N 12°47E **180** E5
Iseo *Italy* 45°39N 10°3E **198** C7
Iseo, L. d' *Italy* 45°43N 10°4E **198** C7
Iseramagazi *Tanzania* 4°37S 32°10E **268** C3
Isère □ *France* 45°15N 5°40E **175** C9
Isère → *France* 44°59N 4°51E **175** D8
Iserlohn *Germany* 51°22N 7°41E **178** D3
Isérnia *Italy* 41°36N 14°14E **201** A7
Isesaki *Japan* 36°19N 139°12E **223** A11
Iseyin *Nigeria* 8°0N 3°36E **263** D5
Isfahan = Eşfahān *Iran* 32°39N 51°43E **247** C6
Isfjorden *Norway* 62°35N 7°49E **164** B4
Ishbīlīya *Iraq* 33°21N 44°26E **113** A2
Ishëm *Albania* 41°33N 19°34E **202** E3
Ishenga Oshwe *Dem. Rep. of the Congo* 3°57S 22°33E **264** C4
Isherton *Guyana* 2°20N 59°25W **329** C6
Ishigaki *Japan* 24°26N 124°10E **221** M2
Ishigaki-Shima *Japan* 24°20N 124°10E **221** M2
Ishikari *Japan* 43°20N 141°15E **220** C10
Ishikari-Gawa → *Japan* 43°15N 141°23E **220** C10
Ishikari-Sammyaku *Japan* 43°30N 143°0E **220** C11
Ishikari-Wan *Japan* 43°25N 141°1E **220** C10
Ishikawa *Japan* 26°25N 127°49E **288** a
Ishikawa □ *Japan* 36°30N 136°30E **223** A8
Ishim *Russia* 56°10N 69°30E **214** D7
Ishim → *Russia* 57°45N 71°10E **214** D8
Ishimbay *Russia* 53°28N 56°2E **216** B5
Ishinomaki *Japan* 38°32N 141°20E **220** E10
Ishioka *Japan* 36°11N 140°16E **223** A12
Ishizuchi-Yama *Japan* 33°45N 133°6E **222** D5
Ishkashim *Tajikistan* 36°44N 71°37E **217** E8
Ishkoman *Pakistan* 36°30N 73°50E **243** A5
Ishøj Strand *Denmark* 55°36N 12°20E **118** B2
Ishpeming *U.S.A.* 46°29N 87°40W **308** B10
Ishurdi *Bangla.* 24°9N 89°3E **241** C2
Isiboro Sécure △ *Bolivia* 16°15S 65°50W **331** D4
Isigny-sur-Mer *France* 49°19N 1°6W **172** C5
Isıklar Dağı *Turkey* 40°45N 27°15E **203** F11
Işıklı *Turkey* 38°19N 29°51E **205** C11
Isil Kul *Russia* 54°55N 71°16E **217** B8
Ísili *Italy* 39°44N 9°6E **200** C2
Isiolo *Kenya* 0°24N 37°33E **268** B4
Isiro *Dem. Rep. of the Congo* 2°53N 27°40E **268** B2
Isisford *Australia* 24°15S 144°21E **280** C3
İskenderun *Turkey* 36°32N 36°10E **250** B7
İskenderun Körfezi *Turkey* 36°40N 35°50E **250** B6
İskilip *Turkey* 40°45N 34°29E **212** B6
Iskitim *Russia* 54°38N 83°18E **217** B10
Iskŭr → *Bulgaria* 43°45N 24°25E **203** C8
Iskŭr, Yazovir *Bulgaria* 42°23N 23°30E **202** D7
Iskushuban *Somali Rep.* 10°18N 50°12E **267** B7
Iskut → *Canada* 56°45N 131°49W **296** B2
Isla → *U.K.* 56°32N 3°20W **167** E5
Isla Coiba △ *Panama* 7°33N 81°36W **320** E4
Isla Cristina *Spain* 37°13N 7°17W **195** H3
Isla de Salamanca △ *Colombia* 10°59N 74°40W **328** A3
Isla Gorge △ *Australia* 25°10S 149°57E **280** D4
Isla Gorgona △ *Colombia* 2°59N 78°10W **328** C2
Isla Guamblin △ *Chile* 44°50S 75°4W **336** B1
Isla Isabel △ *Mexico* 21°54N 105°58W **318** C3
Isla Magdalena △ *Chile* 44°20S 73°13W **336** B2
Isla Tiburón y San Estebán ⌓ *Mexico* 29°0N 112°27W **318** B2
Isla Vista *U.S.A.* 34°25N 119°53W **307** L7
İslâhiye *Turkey* 37°0N 36°35E **250** B7
Islam Headworks *Pakistan* 29°49N 72°33E **242** E5
Islamabad *Pakistan* 33°40N 73°10E **242** C5
Islamgarh *Pakistan* 27°51N 70°48E **242** F4
Islamkot *Pakistan* 24°42N 70°13E **242** G4
Islamorada *U.S.A.* 24°56N 80°37W **317** L9
Islampur *Bihar, India* 25°9N 85°12E **243** G11
Islampur *Maharashtra, India* 17°2N 74°20E **244** F2
Islampur *W. Bengal, India* 26°16N 88°12E **243** F13
Island = Iceland ■ *Europe* 64°45N 19°0W **155** C8
Island B. *Phil.* 9°6N 118°10E **233** G2
Island Bay *N.Z.* 41°20S 174°46E **143** B1
Island Harbour *Anguilla* 18°12N 63°0W **322** a
Island L. *Canada* 53°47N 94°25W **297** C10
Island Lagoon *Australia* 31°30S 136°40E **282** A2
Island Park *Canada* 43°37N 79°22W **141** B2
Island Pond *U.S.A.* 44°49N 71°53W **313** B13
Islands, B. of *Nfld. & L., Canada* 49°11N 58°15W **299** C8
Islands, B. of *N.Z.* 35°15S 174°6E **284** B3
Islay *U.K.* 55°46N 6°10W **167** F2
Isle → *France* 44°55N 0°15W **174** D3
Isle aux Morts *Canada* 47°35N 59°0W **299** C8
Isle of Hope *U.S.A.* 31°58N 81°5W **316** D8
Isle of Wight □ *U.K.* 50°41N 1°17W **169** G6
Isle Royale △ *U.S.A.* 48°0N 88°55W **308** B9
Isleton *U.S.A.* 38°10N 121°37W **306** G5
Islev *Denmark* 55°41N 12°27E **118** A2
Isleworth *U.K.* 51°28N 0°19W **125** B2
Islington *Canada* 43°38N 79°30W **141** B1
Islington □ *U.K.* 51°33N 0°5W **125** A3
Islote Pt. *Trin. & Tob.* 10°4N 61°47W **323** t
Ismail = Izmayil *Ukraine* 45°22N 28°46E **183** E13
Ismâ'ilîya *Egypt* 30°37N 32°18E **251** H3
Ismâ'ilîya □ *Egypt* 30°35N 32°16E **251** H3
Ismâ'ilîya, Tir'at el → *Egypt* 30°4N 31°16E **251** H2
Ismaning *Germany* 48°13N 11°40E **131** A3
Ismayloskiy Park *Russia* 55°46N 37°46E **129** B4
Isna *Egypt* 25°17N 32°30E **256** B3
Isoanala *Madag.* 23°50S 45°44E **272** C2
Ísola del Liri *Italy* 41°41N 13°34E **199** G10
Ísola della Scala *Italy* 45°16N 11°0E **198** C7
Ísola di Capo Rizzuto *Italy* 38°58N 17°6E **201** D10
Isolo *Nigeria* 6°31N 3°19E **124** A1
İsparta *Turkey* 37°47N 30°30E **205** D12
İsparta □ *Turkey* 38°0N 31°0E **212** D4
Isperikh *Bulgaria* 43°43N 26°50E **203** C10
Íspica *Italy* 36°47N 14°55E **201** F7
İspir *Turkey* 40°28N 40°59E **213** B9
Israel ■ *Asia* 32°0N 34°50E **251** G5
Isratu *Eritrea* 16°20N 39°53E **257** D4
Issakly *Russia* 54°8N 51°32E **190** C10
Issano *Guyana* 5°49N 59°26W **329** B6
Issaouane, Erg *Algeria* 26°58N 8°42E **258** C1
Issia *Ivory C.* 6°33N 6°33W **262** D3
Issoire *France* 45°32N 3°15E **174** C7
Issoudun *France* 46°57N 1°59E **173** F8
Issy-les-Moulineaux *France* 48°49N 2°15E **134** B2
Issyk-Kul = Balykchy *Kyrgyzstan* 42°26N 76°12E **217** D9
Issyk-Kul, Ozero = Ysyk-Köl *Kyrgyzstan* 42°25N 77°15E **217** D9
Ist *Croatia* 44°17N 14°47E **199** D11
Istaihah *U.A.E.* 23°19N 54°4E **249** B6
Istállós-kő *Hungary* 48°4N 20°26E **182** B5
İstanbul *Turkey* 41°0N 28°58E **122** C1
İstanbul □ *Turkey* 41°0N 29°0E **203** E12
İstanbul ✈ **(IST)** *Turkey* 40°59N 28°49E **203** F12
İstanbul Boğazı *Turkey* 41°5N 29°3E **122** B2
Istaravshan = Ŭroteppa *Tajikistan* 39°55N 69°1E **217** E7
Isteren *Norway* 61°58N 11°47E **164** B8
Istiea *Greece* 38°57N 23°9E **204** C5
İstinye *Turkey* 41°6N 29°3E **122** B2
Istmina *Colombia* 5°10N 76°39W **328** B2
Isto, Mt. *U.S.A.* 69°12N 143°48W **303** B12
Istok *Kosovo* 42°45N 20°24E **202** D4
Istokpoga, L. *U.S.A.* 27°23N 81°17W **317** H8
Istra *Croatia* 45°10N 14°0E **199** C10
Istres *France* 43°31N 4°59E **175** E8
Istria = Istra *Croatia* 45°10N 14°0E **199** C10
Isugod *Phil.* 9°19N 118°5E **233** G2
Isulan *Phil.* 6°30N 124°29E **233** H5
Itá *Paraguay* 25°29S 57°21W **334** B4
Itä Hakkila *Finland* 60°17N 25°7E **121** B3
Itabaiana *Paraíba, Brazil* 7°18S 35°19W **332** C4
Itabaiana *Sergipe, Brazil* 10°41S 37°37W **332** D4
Itabaianinha *Brazil* 11°16S 37°47W **332** D4
Itaberaba *Brazil* 12°32S 40°18W **333** D3
Itaberaí *Brazil* 16°2S 49°48W **333** E2
Itabira *Brazil* 19°37S 43°13W **333** E3
Itabirito *Brazil* 20°15S 43°48W **333** F3
Itaboca *Brazil* 4°50S 62°40W **329** D5
Itabuna *Brazil* 14°48S 39°16W **333** D4
Itacajá *Brazil* 8°19S 47°46W **332** C2
Itacaunas → *Brazil* 5°21S 49°8W **332** C2
Itaewon *S. Korea* 37°32N 126°58E **137** B1
Itaguari → *Brazil* 14°11S 44°40W **333** D3
Itaguatins *Brazil* 5°47S 47°29W **332** C2
Itaim → *Brazil* 7°2S 42°2W **332** C3
Itainópolis *Brazil* 7°24S 41°31W **332** C3
Itaipú, Represa de *Brazil* 25°30S 54°30W **335** B5
Itaituba *Brazil* 4°10S 55°50W **329** D6
Itajaí *Brazil* 27°50S 48°39W **335** B6
Itajany do Sul = Rio do Sul *Brazil* 27°13S 49°37W **335** B6
Itajubá *Brazil* 22°24S 45°30W **333** F2
Itajuípe *Brazil* 14°41S 39°22W **333** D4
Itaka *Tanzania* 8°50S 32°49E **269** D3
Itako *Japan* 35°56N 140°33E **223** B12
Itala ⌓ *S. Africa* 27°30S 31°7E **271** C5
Italy ■ *Europe* 42°0N 13°0E **192** C6
Itamaraju *Brazil* 17°4S 39°32W **333** E4
Itamarati *Brazil* 6°24S 68°15W **330** B4
Itamataré *Brazil* 2°16S 46°24W **332** B2
Itambacuri *Brazil* 18°1S 41°42W **333** E3
Itambé *Brazil* 15°15S 40°37W **333** E3
Itami *Japan* 34°46N 135°24E **133** A1
Itampolo *Madag.* 24°41S 43°57E **272** C1
Itanagar *India* 27°6N 93°37E **241** B4
Itandrano *Madag.* 21°47S 45°17E **272** C2
Itanhaém *Brazil* 24°11S 46°47W **333** F2
Itanhanga *Brazil* 22°59S 43°19W **135** B1
Itanhauã → *Brazil* 4°45S 63°48W **329** D5
Itanhém *Brazil* 17°9S 40°20W **333** E3
Itano *Japan* 34°7N 134°28E **222** C6
Itapaci *Brazil* 14°57S 49°34W **333** D2
Itapagé *Brazil* 3°41S 39°34W **332** B4
Itaparica = Petrolândia *Brazil* 9°5S 38°20W **332** C4
Itaparica, I. de *Brazil* 12°54S 38°42W **333** D4
Itaparica, Represa de *Brazil* 11°3S 42°47W **332** D3
Itapebi *Brazil* 15°56S 39°32W **333** E4
Itapecuru Mirim *Brazil* 3°24S 44°20W **332** B3
Itaperuna *Brazil* 21°10S 41°54W **333** F3
Itapetinga *Brazil* 15°15S 40°15W **333** E3
Itapetininga *Brazil* 23°36S 48°7W **335** A6
Itapeva *Brazil* 23°59S 48°59W **335** A6
Itapicuru → *Bahia, Brazil* 11°47S 37°32W **332** D4
Itapicuru → *Maranhão, Brazil* 2°52S 44°12W **332** B3
Itapipoca *Brazil* 3°30S 39°35W **332** B4
Itapira = Ubaitaba *Brazil* 14°18S 39°20W **333** D4
Itapiranga *Brazil* 2°45S 58°1W **329** D6
Itapiúna *Brazil* 4°33S 38°57W **332** B4
Itaporanga *Paraíba, Brazil* 7°18S 38°0W **332** C4
Itaporanga *São Paulo, Brazil* 23°42S 49°29W **333** F2
Itapuá □ *Paraguay* 26°40S 55°40W **335** B4
Itapuranga *Brazil* 15°40S 49°59W **333** E2
Itaquai → *Brazil* 4°20S 70°12W **330** A3
Itaquatiara *Brazil* 2°58S 58°30W **329** D6
Itaquí *Brazil* 29°8S 56°30W **334** B4
Itararé *Brazil* 24°6S 49°23W **335** A6
Itarsi *India* 22°36N 77°51E **242** H7
Itarumã *Brazil* 18°42S 51°25W **333** E1
Itatí *Argentina* 27°16S 58°15W **334** B4
Itatiaia △ *Brazil* 22°22S 44°38W **335** A7
Itatira *Brazil* 4°30S 39°37W **332** B4
Itatuba *Brazil* 5°46S 63°20W **331** B5
Itatupã *Brazil* 0°37S 51°12W **329** D7
Itaueira *Brazil* 7°36S 43°2W **332** C3
Itaueira → *Brazil* 6°41S 42°55W **332** C3
Itaúna *Brazil* 20°4S 44°34W **333** F3
Itbayat *Phil.* 20°47N 121°51E **232** A3
Itbayat I. *Phil.* 20°45N 121°50E **232** A3
Itchen → *U.K.* 50°55N 1°22W **169** G6
Itchouma *Niger* 20°14N 13°32E **261** D7
Ite *Peru* 17°55S 70°57W **330** D3
Itea *Greece* 38°25N 22°25E **204** C4
Itezhi Tezhi, L. *Zambia* 15°30S 25°30E **269** F2
Ithaca = Ithaki *Greece* 38°25N 20°40E **207** C2
Ithaca *U.S.A.* 42°27N 76°30W **313** D8
Ithaki *Greece* 38°25N 20°40E **207** C2
Ithakis, Stenon *Greece* 38°22N 20°39E **207** C2
Iti △ *Greece* 38°50N 22°15E **204** C4
Itimbiri → *Dem. Rep. of the Congo* 2°2N 22°44E **264** B4
Itinga *Brazil* 16°36S 41°47W **333** E3
Itiquira *Brazil* 17°12S 54°7W **331** D7
Itiquira → *Brazil* 17°18S 56°44W **331** D6
Itiruçu *Brazil* 13°31S 40°9W **333** D3
Itiúba *Brazil* 10°43S 39°51W **332** D4
Itiyuro → *Argentina* 22°40S 63°50W **334** A3
Itkilik → *U.S.A.* 70°9N 150°56W **303** A10
Itō *Japan* 34°58N 139°5E **223** C11
Itogon *Phil.* 16°22N 120°41E **232** C3
Itoigawa *Japan* 37°2N 137°51E **221** F8
Itoko *Dem. Rep. of the Congo* 1°0S 21°48E **264** C4
Itoman *Japan* 26°7N 127°40E **288** a
Iton → *France* 49°9N 1°12E **172** C8
Itonamas → *Bolivia* 12°28S 64°24W **331** C5
Itri *Italy* 41°17N 13°32E **200** A6
Itsa *Egypt* 29°15N 30°47E **256** J7
Itsamia *Comoros Is.* 12°21S 43°52E **272** a
Itsandra *Comoros Is.* 11°40S 43°15E **272** a
Itsuki *Japan* 32°24N 130°50E **222** E2
Itsukushima Shrine *Japan* 34°15N 132°15E **222** C4
Íttiri *Italy* 40°36N 8°34E **200** B1
Ittoqqortoormiit *Greenland* 70°20N 23°0W **154** C8
Itu *Brazil* 23°17S 47°15W **335** A6
Itu *Nigeria* 5°10N 7°58E **263** D6
Itu Aba I. *S. China Sea* 10°23N 114°21E **230** B4
Ituaçu *Brazil* 13°50S 41°18W **333** D3
Ituango *Colombia* 7°4N 75°45W **328** B2
Ituí → *Brazil* 4°38S 70°19W **328** D3
Ituiutaba *Brazil* 19°0S 49°25W **333** E2
Itumbiara *Brazil* 18°20S 49°10W **333** E2
Ituna *Canada* 51°10N 103°24W **297** C8
Itunge Port *Tanzania* 9°40S 33°55E **269** D3
Ituni *Guyana* 5°28N 58°15W **329** B6
Itupiranga *Brazil* 5°9S 49°20W **332** C2
Iturama *Brazil* 19°44S 50°11W **333** E1
Iturbe *Argentina* 23°0S 65°25W **334** A2
Ituri → *Dem. Rep. of the Congo* 1°40N 27°1E **268** B2
Iturup, Ostrov *Russia* 45°0N 148°0E **215** E15
Ituverava *Brazil* 20°20S 47°47W **333** F2
Ituxi → *Brazil* 7°18S 64°51W **331** B5
Itzehoe *Germany* 53°55N 9°31E **178** B5
Iuka *U.S.A.* 38°37N 88°47W **311** F8
Iungsdalshytta *Norway* 60°49N 7°55E **164** D4
Ivahona *Madag.* 23°27S 46°10E **272** C2
Ivaí → *Brazil* 23°18S 53°42W **335** A5
Ivalo *Finland* 68°38N 27°35E **160** B22
Ivalojoki → *Finland* 68°40N 27°40E **160** B22
Ivanava *Belarus* 52°7N 25°29E **177** B13
Ivančice *Czech Rep.* 49°6N 16°23E **181** B9
Ivane-Puste *Ukraine* 48°39N 26°10E **183** B11
Ivăneşti *Romania* 46°39N 27°27E **183** D12
Ivangorod = Dęblin *Poland* 51°34N 21°50E **185** G8
Ivangorod *Russia* 59°27N 28°13E **188** C5
Ivanhoe *N.S.W., Australia* 32°56S 144°20E **282** B6
Ivanhoe *Vic., Australia* 37°45S 145°3E **128** A2
Ivanhoe *Ont., Canada* 44°23N 77°28W **312** B7
Ivanhoe *Calif., U.S.A.* 36°23N 119°13W **306** J7
Ivanhoe *Minn., U.S.A.* 44°28N 96°15W **308** C5
Ivanhorod *Ukraine* 48°48N 29°50E **183** B14
Ivanić Grad *Croatia* 45°41N 16°25E **199** C13
Ivanjica *Serbia* 43°35N 20°12E **202** C4
Ivanjska *Bos.-H.* 44°55N 17°4E **182** F2
Ivankoyskoye Vdkhr. *Russia* 56°37N 36°32E **188** D9
Ivano-Frankivsk *Ukraine* 48°40N 24°40E **183** B9
Ivano-Frankivsk □ *Ukraine* 48°45N 24°30E **183** B9
Ivanof Bay *U.S.A.* 55°54N 159°29W **303** J8
Ivanovo = Ivanava *Belarus* 52°7N 25°29E **177** B13
Ivanovo *Russia* 57°5N 41°0E **188** D11
Ivanovo □ *Russia* 57°10N 41°50E **190** B5
Ivanšćica *Croatia* 46°12N 16°13E **199** B13
Ivashchenkovo = Chapayevsk *Russia* 53°0N 49°40E **190** D9
Ivato *Madag.* 20°37S 47°10E **272** C2
Ivatsevichy *Belarus* 52°43N 25°21E **177** B13
Ivaylovgrad *Bulgaria* 41°32N 26°8E **203** E10
Ivdel *Russia* 60°42N 60°24E **186** B11
Ivgres = Komsomolsk *Russia* 57°2N 40°20E **188** D11
Ivindo → *Gabon* 0°9S 12°9E **264** C2
Ivinheima → *Brazil* 23°14S 53°42W **335** A5
Ivinhema *Brazil* 22°10S 53°37W **335** A5
Ivittuut *Greenland* 61°14N 48°12W **154** E6
Iviza = Eivissa *Spain* 38°54N 1°26E **206** D1
Ivohibe *Madag.* 22°31S 46°57E **272** C2
Ivolândia *Brazil* 16°34S 50°51W **333** E1
Ivory Coast *W. Afr.* 4°20N 5°0W **262** E4
Ivory Coast ■ *Africa* 7°30N 5°0W **262** D4
Ivösjön *Sweden* 56°8N 14°25E **163** H8
Ivrea *Italy* 45°28N 7°52E **198** C4
İvrindi *Turkey* 39°34N 27°30E **205** B9
Ivry-sur-Seine *France* 48°49N 2°22E **134** B3
Ivujivik *Canada* 62°24N 77°55W **295** E16
Ivvavik △ *Canada* 69°6N 139°30W **294** D4
Ivybridge *U.K.* 50°23N 3°56W **169** G4
Iwa *Japan* 36°5N 139°52E **223** A11
Iwai-Jima *Japan* 33°47N 131°58E **222** D3
Iwaizumi *Japan* 39°50N 141°45E **220** E10
Iwaki *Japan* 37°3N 140°55E **221** F10
Iwakuni *Japan* 34°15N 132°8E **222** C4
Iwami *Japan* 35°32N 134°15E **222** B6
Iwami Ginzan *Japan* 35°10N 132°30E **222** B4
Iwamizawa *Japan* 43°12N 141°46E **220** C10
Iwanai *Japan* 42°58N 140°30E **220** C10
Iwase *Japan* 36°21N 140°6E **223** A12
Iwata *Japan* 34°42N 137°51E **223** C9
Iwate □ *Japan* 39°30N 141°30E **220** E10
Iwate-San *Japan* 39°51N 141°0E **220** E10
Iwo *Nigeria* 7°39N 4°9E **263** D5
Iwo Jima *Pac. Oc.* 24°47N 141°20E **288** b
Iwŏn *N. Korea* 40°19N 128°39E **224** B4
Iwonicz-Zdrój *Poland* 49°37N 21°47E **185** J8
Iwungu *Dem. Rep. of the Congo* 5°16S 19°17E **265** D3
Ixelles *Belgium* 50°50N 4°22E **116** B2
Ixiamas *Bolivia* 13°50S 68°5W **330** C4
Ixopo *S. Africa* 30°11S 30°5E **271** D5
Ixtepec *Mexico* 16°34N 95°6W **319** D5
Ixtlán del Río *Mexico* 21°2N 104°22W **318** C4
'Iyādh *Yemen* 14°59N 46°51E **248** D4
Iyal Bakhit *Sudan* 13°20N 28°39E **257** E2
Iyo *Japan* 33°45N 132°45E **222** D4
Iyo-Mishima *Japan* 33°58N 133°30E **222** D5
Iyo-Nada *Japan* 33°40N 132°20E **222** D4
Izabal, L. de *Guatemala* 15°30N 89°10W **320** C2
Izamal *Mexico* 20°56N 89°1W **319** C7
Izberbash *Russia* 42°35N 47°52E **191** J8
Izbica *Poland* 50°53N 23°10E **185** H10
Izbica Kujawska *Poland* 52°25N 18°40E **185** F5
Izbiceni *Romania* 43°45N 24°40E **183** G9
Izembek Nat. Wildlife Refuge ⌓ *U.S.A.* 55°15N 162°45W **303** J7
Izena-Shima *Japan* 26°56N 127°56E **221** L3
Izgrev *Bulgaria* 43°36N 26°58E **203** C10
Izhevsk *Russia* 56°51N 53°14E **186** C9
Izhma = Sosnogorsk *Russia* 63°37N 53°51E **186** B9
Izhma → *Russia* 65°19N 52°54E **186** A9
Izileg *Algeria* 20°20N 6°4E **261** D6
Izkī *Oman* 22°56N 57°46E **249** B7
Izmayil *Ukraine* 45°22N 28°46E **183** E13
Izmaylovo *Russia* 55°47N 37°47E **129** B4
İzmir *Turkey* 38°25N 27°8E **205** C9
İzmir □ *Turkey* 38°15N 27°40E **205** C9
İzmir Adnan Menderes ✈ **(ADB)** *Turkey* 38°23N 27°6E **205** C9
İzmir Körfezi *Turkey* 38°30N 26°50E **205** C8
İzmit = Kocaeli *Turkey* 40°45N 29°50E **203** F13
Iznájar *Spain* 37°15N 4°19W **195** H6
Iznalloz *Spain* 37°24N 3°30W **195** H7
İznik *Turkey* 40°23N 29°46E **212** B3
İznik Gölü *Turkey* 40°27N 29°30E **203** F13
Izobilno-Tishchenskoye = Izobil'nyy *Russia* 45°25N 41°44E **191** H5
Izobil'nyy *Russia* 45°25N 41°44E **191** H5
Izola *Slovenia* 45°32N 13°39E **199** C10
Izozog, Bañados de *Bolivia* 18°48S 62°10W **331** D5
Izra *Syria* 32°51N 36°15E **250** F7
Iztacalco *Mexico* 19°23N 99°5W **128** B2
Iztapalapa *Mexico* 19°21N 99°6W **128** B2
Iztochni Rodopi *Bulgaria* 41°45N 25°30E **203** E9
Izu-Hantō *Japan* 34°45N 139°0E **223** C11
Izu-Shotō *Japan* 34°30N 140°0E **221** G10
Izúcar de Matamoros *Mexico* 18°36N 98°28W **319** D5
Izuhara *Japan* 34°12N 129°17E **222** C1
Izumi *Kagoshima, Japan* 32°5N 130°22E **222** E2
Izumi *Ōsaka, Japan* 34°28N 135°24E **223** C7
Izumi-Sano *Japan* 34°23N 135°18E **223** C7
Izumo *Japan* 35°20N 132°46E **222** B4
Izyaslav *Ukraine* 50°5N 26°50E **177** C14
Izyum *Ukraine* 49°12N 37°19E **189** H9

J

J.F.K. Int. ✈ **(JFK)** *U.S.A.* 40°38N 73°47W **313** F11
J.F. Rodrigues *Brazil* 2°55S 50°20W **332** B1
J.P. Koch Fjord *Greenland* 82°45N 44°0W **154** A6
J. Strom Thurmond L. *U.S.A.* 33°40N 82°12W **316** B7
Ja-ela *Sri Lanka* 7°5N 79°53E **245** L4
Ja-eundo *S. Korea* 34°53N 126°2E **224** E3
Jaba *Ethiopia* 6°20N 35°7E **257** F4
Jaba *West Bank* 31°51N 35°16E **123** A2
Jabal al Awliya' *Sudan* 15°14N 32°29E **266** A3
Jabalón → *Spain* 38°53N 4°5W **195** G6
Jabalpur *India* 23°9N 79°58E **243** H8
Jabbūl *Syria* 36°4N 37°30E **246** B3
Jabiru *Australia* 12°40S 132°53E **278** B5
Jablah *Syria* 35°20N 36°0E **250** C7
Jablanac *Croatia* 44°42N 14°56E **199** D11
Jablanica *Bos.-H.* 43°40N 17°45E **182** G2
Jablonec nad Nisou *Czech Rep.* 50°43N 15°10E **180** A8
Jablonica *Slovak Rep.* 48°37N 17°26E **181** C10
Jabłonowo Pomorskie *Poland* 53°23N 19°10E **184** E6
Jablunkov *Czech Rep.* 49°35N 18°46E **181** B11
Jaboatão *Brazil* 8°7S 35°1W **332** C4
Jabonga *Phil.* 9°20N 125°32E **233** G5
Jaboticabal *Brazil* 21°15S 48°17W **335** A6
Jabukovac *Serbia* 44°22N 22°21E **202** B6
Jaburu *Brazil* 5°30S 64°0W **331** B5
Jaca *Spain* 42°35N 0°33W **196** C4
Jacaré *Brazil* 22°53S 43°14W **135** B1
Jacaré → *Brazil* 10°3S 42°13W **332** D3
Jacareí *Brazil* 23°20S 46°0W **335** A6
Jacarèzinho *Brazil* 23°5S 49°58W **335** A6
Jaci-Paraná *Brazil* 9°15S 64°23W **331** B5
Jaciara *Brazil* 15°59S 54°57W **331** D7
Jacinto *Brazil* 16°10S 40°17W **333** E3
Jack River △ *Australia* 14°58S 144°19E **280** A3
Jackman *U.S.A.* 45°37N 70°15W **309** C18
Jacksboro *U.S.A.* 33°13N 98°10W **314** E5
Jackson *Barbados* 13°7N 59°36W **323** r
Jackson *Ala., U.S.A.* 31°31N 87°53W **315** F11
Jackson *Calif., U.S.A.* 38°21N 120°46W **306** G6
Jackson *Ga., U.S.A.* 33°20N 83°57W **316** B6
Jackson *Ky., U.S.A.* 37°33N 83°23W **309** G12
Jackson *Mich., U.S.A.* 42°15N 84°24W **311** B12
Jackson *Minn., U.S.A.* 43°37N 95°1W **308** D6
Jackson *Miss., U.S.A.* 32°18N 90°12W **315** E9
Jackson *Mo., U.S.A.* 37°23N 89°40W **308** G9
Jackson *N.H., U.S.A.* 44°10N 71°11W **313** B13
Jackson *Ohio, U.S.A.* 39°3N 82°39W **309** F12
Jackson *S.C., U.S.A.* 33°20N 81°47W **316** B8
Jackson *Tenn., U.S.A.* 35°37N 88°49W **315** D10
Jackson *Wyo., U.S.A.* 43°29N 110°46W **304** E8
Jackson, C. *N.Z.* 40°59S 174°20E **285** A9
Jackson B. *N.Z.* 43°58S 168°42E **285** D3
Jackson Center *U.S.A.* 40°27N 84°4W **311** D12
Jackson Hd. *N.Z.* 43°58S 168°37E **285** D3
Jackson Heights *U.S.A.* 40°44N 73°53W **132** B2
Jackson L. *Fla., U.S.A.* 30°30N 84°17W **316** E5
Jackson L. *Ga., U.S.A.* 33°19N 83°50W **316** B6
Jackson L. *Wyo., U.S.A.* 43°52N 110°36W **304** E8
Jackson Park *U.S.A.* 41°46N 87°34W **119** C3
Jacksons *N.Z.* 42°46S 171°32E **285** C6
Jackson's Arm *Canada* 49°52N 56°47W **299** C8
Jacksonville *Ala., U.S.A.* 33°49N 85°46W **316** B4
Jacksonville *Ark., U.S.A.* 34°52N 92°7W **314** D8
Jacksonville *Calif., U.S.A.* 37°52N 120°24W **306** H6
Jacksonville *Fla., U.S.A.* 30°20N 81°39W **316** E8
Jacksonville *Ga., U.S.A.* 31°49N 82°59W **316** D7
Jacksonville *Ill., U.S.A.* 39°44N 90°14W **310** E6
Jacksonville *N.C., U.S.A.* 34°45N 77°26W **315** D16
Jacksonville *Tex., U.S.A.* 31°58N 95°17W **314** F7
Jacksonville Beach *U.S.A.* 30°17N 81°24W **316** E8
Jacksonville Int. ✈ **(JAX)** *U.S.A.* 30°30N 81°41W **316** E8
Jacmel *Haiti* 18°14N 72°32W **321** C5
Jaco, Pte. *Dominica* 15°39N 61°24W **323** k
Jacob Lake *U.S.A.* 36°43N 112°13W **305** H7
Jacobabad *Pakistan* 28°20N 68°29E **242** E3
Jacobina *Brazil* 11°11S 40°30W **332** D3
Jacobshagen = Dobrzany *Poland* 53°22N 15°25E **184** E2
Jacon Javits Convention Center *New York, U.S.A.* **132** c1
Jacotet, B. *Mauritius* 20°30S 57°26E **272** e
Jacqueline Kennedy Onassis Res. *New York, U.S.A.* **132** a3
Jacques-Cartier *Canada* 45°31N 73°27W **130** A3
Jacques-Cartier, Dét. de *Canada* 50°0N 63°30W **299** C7
Jacques-Cartier, Mt. *Canada* 48°57N 66°0W **299** C6
Jacques-Cartier, Pont *Canada* 45°31N 73°32W **130** A2
Jacques-Cartier ⌓ *Canada* 47°15N 71°33W **299** C5
Jacqueville *Ivory C.* 5°12N 4°25W **262** D4
Jacuí → *Brazil* 30°2S 51°15W **335** C5
Jacumba *U.S.A.* 32°37N 116°11W **307** N10
Jacundá → *Brazil* 1°57S 50°26W **332** B1
Jadavpur *India* 22°28N 88°22E **124** C2
Jadcherla *India* 16°46N 78°9E **244** F4
Jade *Germany* 53°20N 8°14E **178** B4
Jade Buddha Temple *China* 31°15N 121°25E **138** B1
Jade City *Canada* 59°15N 129°37W **296** B3
Jade Dragon Snow Mt. = Yulong Xueshan *China* 27°6N 100°10E **228** D3
Jade Island *Beijing, China* **114** b2
Jade Mt. = Yü Shan *Taiwan* 23°25N 120°52E **225** C2
Jadebusen *Germany* 53°29N 8°12E **178** B4
Jadotville = Likasi *Dem. Rep. of the Congo* 10°55S 26°48E **269** E2
Jadovnik *Serbia* 43°20N 19°45E **202** C3
Jadraque *Spain* 40°55N 2°55W **196** E2
Jādū *Libya* 32°0N 12°0E **258** B2
Jægersborg *Denmark* 55°45N 12°31E **118** A3
Jægersborg Dyrehave *Denmark* 55°46N 12°33E **118** A3
Jaén *Peru* 5°25S 78°40W **330** B2
Jaén *Spain* 37°44N 3°43W **195** H7
Jaén □ *Spain* 37°50N 3°30W **195** H7
Jæren *Norway* 58°42N 5°47E **164** F2
Jærens Rev *Norway* 58°45N 5°45E **164** F2
Jafarabad *India* 20°52N 71°22E **242** J4
Jaffa = Tel Aviv-Yafo *Israel* 32°4N 34°48E **251** F5
Jaffa, C. *Australia* 36°58S 139°40E **282** D3
Jaffna *Sri Lanka* 9°45N 80°2E **245** K5
Jaffrey *U.S.A.* 42°49N 72°2W **313** D12
Jagadhri *India* 30°10N 77°20E **242** D7
Jagadishpur *Bihar, India* 25°30N 84°21E **243** G11
Jagadishpur *W. Bengal, India* 22°39N 88°17E **124** B1
Jagatpur *India* 28°44N 77°13E **120** A2
Jagdalpur *India* 19°3N 82°0E **244** E6
Jagdaqi *China* 50°25N 124°7E **219** A13
Jagersfontein *S. Africa* 29°44S 25°27E **270** C4
Jaghīn → *Iran* 27°17N 57°13E **247** E8
Jagna *Phil.* 9°39N 124°22E **233** G5
Jagodina *Serbia* 44°5N 21°15E **202** B5
Jagraon *India* 30°50N 75°25E **242** D6
Jagst → *Germany* 49°14N 9°10E **179** F5
Jagtial *India* 18°50N 79°0E **244** E4
Jaguaquara *Brazil* 13°32S 39°58W **333** D4
Jaguaré, Rib. do → *Brazil* 23°32S 46°45W **137** B1
Jaguariaíva *Brazil* 24°10S 49°50W **335** A6
Jaguaribe *Brazil* 5°53S 38°37W **332** C4
Jaguaribe → *Brazil* 4°25S 37°45W **332** B4
Jaguaruana *Brazil* 4°50S 37°47W **332** B4
Jagüey Grande *Cuba* 22°35N 81°7W **320** B3
Jagungal, Mt. *Australia* 36°8S 148°22E **283** D8
Jahanabad *India* 25°13N 84°59E **243** G11
Jahangirpur *India* 28°43N 77°12E **120** A2
Jahazpur *India* 25°37N 75°17E **242** G6
Jahrom *Iran* 28°30N 53°31E **247** D7
Jaicós *Brazil* 7°21S 41°8W **332** C3
Jaigarh *India* 17°17N 73°13E **244** F1
Jaijon *India* 31°21N 76°9E **242** D7
Jailolo *Indonesia* 1°5N 127°30E **231** D7
Jailolo, Selat *Indonesia* 0°5N 129°5E **231** D7
Jaintiapur *Bangla.* 25°8N 92°7E **241** C4
Jaipur *Assam, India* 27°16N 95°24E **241** B5
Jaipur *Raj., India* 27°0N 75°50E **242** F6
Jais *India* 26°15N 81°32E **243** F9
Jaisalmer *India* 26°55N 70°54E **242** F4
Jaisinghnagar *India* 23°38N 78°34E **243** H8
Jaitaran *India* 26°12N 73°56E **242** F5
Jaithari *India* 23°14N 78°37E **243** H8
Jājarm *Iran* 36°58N 56°27E **247** B8
Jajce *Bos.-H.* 44°19N 17°17E **182** F2
Jajpur *India* 20°53N 86°22E **244** D8
Jakam → *India* 23°54N 74°13E **242** H6
Jakar Dzong *Bhutan* 27°33N 90°43E **241** B3
Jakarta *Indonesia* 6°9S 106°52E **122** A2
Jakarta, Teluk *Indonesia* 6°5S 106°50E **122** A1
Jakarta Halim Perdana Kusuma Int. ✈ **(HLP)** *Indonesia* 6°16S 106°53E **122** B2
Jakhal *India* 29°48N 75°50E **242** E6
Jakharrah *Libya* 29°13N 21°34E **258** C4
Jakhau *India* 23°13N 68°43E **242** H3
Jakobshavn = Ilulissat *Greenland* 69°12N 51°10W **154** D5
Jakobstad = Pietarsaari *Finland* 63°40N 22°43E **160** E20
Jakupica *Macedonia* 41°45N 21°22E **202** E5
Jal *U.S.A.* 32°7N 103°12W **305** K12
Jalaihai Pt. *Guam* 13°18N 144°46E **302** d
Jalājil *Si. Arabia* 25°40N 45°27E **246** E5
Jalal-Abad *Kyrgyzstan* 40°56N 73°0E **217** D8
Jalal-Abad □ *Kyrgyzstan* 41°30N 72°30E **217** D8
Jalālābād *Afghan.* 34°30N 70°29E **242** B4
Jalalabad *India* 27°41N 79°42E **243** F8
Jalalpur Jattan *Pakistan* 32°38N 74°11E **242** C6
Jalama *U.S.A.* 34°29N 120°29W **307** L6
Jalan Kayu *Singapore* 1°24N 103°52E **138** A3
Jalandhar = Jullundur *India* 31°20N 75°40E **242** D6
Jalapa *Guatemala* 14°39N 89°59W **320** D2
Jalapa Enríquez = Xalapa *Mexico* 19°32N 96°55W **319** D5
Jalasjärvi *Finland* 62°29N 22°47E **160** E20
Jalaun *India* 26°8N 79°25E **243** F8
Jalāzin *Afghan.* 37°2N 64°49E **240** A2
Jaldak *Afghan.* 31°58N 66°43E **240** C2
Jaldhaka → *Bangla.* 26°16N 89°16E **241** B2
Jales *Brazil* 20°10S 50°33W **333** F1
Jalesar *India* 27°29N 78°19E **242** F8
Jaleswar *Nepal* 26°38N 85°48E **243** F11
Jalgaon *India* 21°0N 75°42E **244** D2
Jalībah *Iraq* 30°35N 46°32E **246** D5
Jalingo *Nigeria* 8°55N 11°25E **263** D7
Jalisco □ *Mexico* 20°20N 103°40W **318** D4
Jalkot *Pakistan* 35°14N 73°24E **243** B5
Jalna *India* 19°48N 75°38E **244** E2
Jalón → *Spain* 41°47N 1°4W **196** D3
Jalor *India* 25°21N 72°37E **242** G5
Jalpa *Mexico* 21°38N 102°58W **318** C4
Jalpaiguri *India* 26°32N 88°46E **241** B2
Jalpan *Mexico* 21°14N 99°29W **319** C5
Jālq *Iran* 27°35N 62°46E **240** D1
Jālū *Libya* 29°2N 21°33E **258** C4
Jaluit I. *Marshall Is.* 6°0N 169°30E **288** G8
Jalūlā *Iraq* 34°16N 45°10E **213** E11
Jamaame *Somali Rep.* 0°4N 42°44E **267** D5
Jamaari *Nigeria* 11°44N 9°53E **263** C6
Jamaica ■ *W. Indies* 18°10N 77°30W **320** a
Jamaica B. *U.S.A.* 40°36N 73°50W **132** C3
Jamaica Channel *Jamaica* 17°0N 76°0W **321** C4
Jamaica Plain *U.S.A.* 42°18N 71°6W **116** B2
Jamakpuri *India* 28°37N 77°5E **120** B1
Jamalpur *Bangla.* 24°52N 89°56E **241** C2
Jamalpur *India* 25°18N 86°28E **243** G12
Jamalpurganj *India* 23°2N 87°59E **243** H13
Jamanota *Aruba* 12°29N 69°57W **322** f
Jamanxim → *Brazil* 4°43S 56°18W **331** A6
Jamari *Brazil* 8°45S 63°27W **331** B5
Jamari → *Brazil* 8°27S 63°30W **331** B5
Jamba *Angola* 14°40S 16°2E **265** E3
Jambewangi *Indonesia* 8°17S 114°7E **231** J17
Jambi *Indonesia* 1°38S 103°30E **234** C2
Jambi □ *Indonesia* 1°30S 102°30E **234** C2
Jambongan, Pulau *Malaysia* 6°45N 117°20E **235** A5
Jambusar *India* 22°3N 72°51E **242** H5
James *U.S.A.* 32°58N 83°29W **316** C6
James → *S. Dak., U.S.A.* 42°52N 97°18W **308** D5
James → *Va., U.S.A.* 36°56N 76°27W **309** G15
James, I. = San Salvador, I. *Ecuador* 0°16S 90°42W **330** a
James B. *Canada* 54°0N 80°0W **298** B3
James I. *Gambia* 13°19N 16°21W **262** C1
James Island *U.S.A.* 32°45N 79°55W **316** C10
James Ranges *Australia* 24°10S 132°30E **278** D5
James Ross I. *Antarctica* 63°58S 57°50W **151** C18
Jamesabad *Pakistan* 25°17N 69°15E **242** G3
Jameson Land *Greenland* 71°0N 23°30W **154** C8
Jamesport *U.S.A.* 39°58N 93°48W **310** E3
Jamestown = Wawa *Canada* 47°59N 84°47W **298** C3
Jamestown *S. Austral., Australia* 33°10S 138°32E **282** B3
Jamestown *St. Helena* 15°55S 5°43W **153** h
Jamestown *Eastern Cape, S. Africa* 31°6S 26°45E **270** D4
Jamestown *Ind., U.S.A.* 39°56N 86°38W **311** E10
Jamestown *Mo., U.S.A.* 38°48N 92°30W **310** F4
Jamestown *N. Dak., U.S.A.* 46°54N 98°42W **308** B4
Jamestown *N.Y., U.S.A.* 42°6N 79°14W **312** D5
Jamestown *Ohio, U.S.A.* 39°39N 83°33W **311** E13
Jamestown *Pa., U.S.A.* 41°29N 80°27W **312** E4
Jamestown *S.C., U.S.A.* 33°17N 79°42W **316** B10
Jamīlābād *Iran* 34°24N 48°28E **247** C6
Jamira → *India* 21°35N 88°28E **243** J13
Jämjö *Sweden* 56°12N 15°49E **163** H9
Jamkhandi *India* 16°30N 75°15E **244** F2
Jamkhed *India* 18°43N 75°19E **244** E2
Jammalamadugu *India* 14°51N 78°25E **245** G4
Jammerbugten *Denmark* 57°15N 9°20E **163** G3
Jammu *India* 32°43N 74°54E **242** C6
Jammu & Kashmir □ *India* 34°25N 77°0E **243** B7
Jamnagar *India* 22°30N 70°6E **242** H4
Jamner *India* 20°45N 75°52E **244** D2
Jamni → *India* 25°13N 78°35E **243** G8
Jampur *Pakistan* 29°39N 70°40E **242** E4
Jamrud *Pakistan* 33°59N 71°24E **242** C4
Jämsä *Finland* 61°53N 25°10E **188** B3
Jamshedpur *India* 22°44N 86°12E **243** H12
Jamshīdīyeh *Iran* 35°42N 51°22E **141** A2
Jamsil *S. Korea* 37°30N 127°4E **137** B2
Jamtara *India* 23°59N 86°49E **243** H12
Jämtland *Sweden* 63°31N 14°0E **160** E16
Jämtlands län □ *Sweden* 63°0N 14°40E **162** B7
Jamuna → *Bangla.* 23°51N 89°45E **241** D2
Jamunamukh *India* 26°6N 92°44E **241** B4
Jamurki *Bangla.* 24°9N 90°2E **241** C3
Jamwon *S. Korea* 37°30N 127°0E **137** B2
Jan L. *Canada* 54°56N 102°55W **297** C8
Jan Mayen *Arctic* 71°0N 9°0W **150** B7
Janakkala *Finland* 60°54N 24°36E **188** B3
Janakpur *Nepal* 26°42N 85°55E **244** A7
Janaúba *Brazil* 15°48S 43°19W **333** E3
Janaucu, I. *Brazil* 0°30N 50°10W **332** A1
Jand *Pakistan* 33°30N 72°6E **242** C5
Jandaia *Brazil* 17°6S 50°7W **333** E1
Jandanku ✪ *Australia* 16°20S 135°45E **280** B2
Jandaq *Iran* 34°3N 54°22E **247** C7
Jandía *Canary Is.* 28°6N 14°21W **153** e2
Jandía, Pta. de *Canary Is.* 28°3N 14°31W **153** e2
Jandía △ *Canary Is.* 28°4N 14°19W **153** e2
Jandiatuba → *Brazil* 3°28S 68°42W **328** D4
Jandola *Pakistan* 32°20N 70°9E **242** C4
Jandowae *Australia* 26°45S 151°7E **281** D5
Jándula → *Spain* 38°3N 4°6W **195** G6
Jane Pk. *N.Z.* 45°15S 168°20E **285** F3
Janesville *U.S.A.* 42°41N 89°1W **310** B7
Janga *Ghana* 10°5N 1°0W **263** C4
Jangamo *Mozam.* 24°6S 35°21E **271** B6
Janghai *India* 25°33N 82°19E **243** G10
Jangheung *S. Korea* 34°41N 126°52E **224** E3
Janghowon *S. Korea* 37°7N 127°37E **224** D3
Jangoon *India* 17°44N 79°5E **244** F4
Jangsu *S. Korea* 35°38N 127°31E **224** E3
Janhtang Ga *Burma* 26°32N 96°38E **241** B6
Jani Khel *Afghan.* 32°46N 68°24E **240** B3
Janikowo *Poland* 52°45N 18°7E **185** F5
Janinà = Ioannina □ *Greece* 39°39N 20°57E **204** B2
Janiuay *Phil.* 10°58N 122°30E **233** F4
Janja *Bos.-H.* 44°40N 19°14E **182** F4
Janjanbureh *Gambia* 13°30N 14°47W **262** C2
Janjevo *Kosovo* 42°35N 21°19E **202** D5
Janjgir *India* 22°1N 82°34E **243** J10
Janjina *Croatia* 42°58N 17°25E **199** F14
Janjina *Madag.* 20°30S 45°50E **272** C2
Jankau = Janikowo *Poland* 52°45N 18°7E **185** F5
Janki *Poland* 52°8N 20°52E **142** C1
Jannaale *Somali Rep.* 1°48N 44°42E **267** D5
Janos *Mexico* 30°54N 108°10W **318** A3
Jánoshalma *Hungary* 46°18N 19°21E **182** D4
Jánosháza *Hungary* 47°8N 17°12E **182** C2
Jánossomorja *Hungary* 47°47N 17°11E **182** C2
Janów *Poland* 50°44N 19°27E **185** H6
Janów Lubelski *Poland* 50°48N 22°23E **185** H9
Janów Podlaski *Poland* 52°11N 23°11E **185** F10
Janowiec Wielkopolski *Poland* 52°45N 17°30E **185** F4
Jantho *Indonesia* 5°17N 95°38E **234** A1
Januária *Brazil* 15°25S 44°25W **333** E3
Janub = Southern △ *South Sudan* 6°50N 28°45E **257** F2
Janub Dârfûr □ *Sudan* 11°0N 25°0E **257** E2
Janub Kordofân □ *Sudan* 12°0N 30°0E **257** E3
Janûb Sînî □ *Egypt* 29°30N 33°50E **251** J4
Janubio *Canary Is.* 28°56N 13°50W **153** e2
Janville *France* 48°10N 1°50E **173** D8
Janwada *India* 18°0N 77°29E **244** E3
Janzé *France* 47°55N 1°28W **172** E5
Jaora *India* 23°40N 75°10E **242** H6
Japan ■ *Asia* 36°0N 136°0E **221** G8
Japan, Sea of *Asia* 40°0N 135°0E **220** E7
Japan Center *San Francisco, U.S.A.* **136** c1
Japan Trench *Pac. Oc.* 32°0N 142°0E **288** D6
Japen = Yapen *Indonesia* 1°50S 136°0E **231** E9
Japiim *Brazil* 7°37S 72°54W **330** B3
Japla *India* 24°33N 84°1E **243** G11
Japurá *Brazil* 1°48S 66°34W **328** D4
Japura *Indonesia* 0°19S 102°21E **234** C2
Japurá → *Brazil* 3°8S 65°46W **328** D4
Jaquarão *Brazil* 32°34S 53°23W **335** C5
Jaqué *Panama* 7°27N 78°8W **320** E4
Jarābulus *Syria* 36°49N 38°1E **213** D8
Jaraguá *Goiás, Brazil* 15°45S 49°20W **333** E2
Jaraguá *São Paulo, Brazil* 23°27S 46°44W **137** A1
Jaraguá, Pico de *Brazil* 23°27S 46°46W **137** A1
Jaraguari *Brazil* 20°9S 54°35W **331** E7
Jaraicejo *Spain* 39°40N 5°49W **195** F5
Jaraíz de la Vera *Spain* 40°4N 5°45W **194** E5
Jarama → *Spain* 40°24N 3°32W **194** E7
Jaramānah *Syria* 33°29N 36°21E **250** E7
Jaramillo *Argentina* 47°10S 67°7W **336** C3
Jarandilla de la Vera *Spain* 40°8N 5°39W **194** E5
Jaranwala *Pakistan* 31°15N 73°26E **242** D5
Jarash *Jordan* 32°17N 35°54E **251** F6
Jarash □ *Jordan* 32°17N 35°54E **251** F6
Jarauçu → *Brazil* 1°48S 52°22W **329** D7

Järbo Sweden 60°43N 16°36E 162 D10
Jarboesville = Lexington Park U.S.A. 38°16N 76°27W 309 F15
Jardas al 'Abīd Libya 32°18N 20°59E 258 B4
Jardim Brazil 21°28S 56°2W 334 A4
Jardim Paulista Brazil 23°34S 46°41W 137 B1
Jardín → Spain 38°50N 2°10W 197 G2
Jardín América Argentina 27°3S 55°14W 335 B4
Jardin Botanique Brussels, Belgium 116 a3
Jardine River △ Australia 11°9S 142°21E 280 A3
Jardines de la Reina, Arch. de los Cuba 20°50N 78°50W 320 B4
Jargalang China 43°5N 122°55E 227 C12
Jargalant = Hovd □ Mongolia 48°2N 91°37E 217 C12
Jari → Brazil 1°9S 51°54W 329 D7
Jaria Janjail Bangla. 25°0N 90°40E 241 C3
Jarīr, W. al → Si. Arabia 25°38N 42°30E 246 E4
Järlåsa Sweden 59°53N 17°12E 162 E11
Jarlsberg og Larvik = Vestfold □ Norway 59°15N 10°0E 164 E7
Jarmen Germany 53°54N 13°20E 178 B9
Järna Sweden 59°6N 17°34E 162 E11
Jarnac France 45°40N 0°11W 174 C3
Jarny France 49°9N 5°53E 173 C12
Jaro Phil. 11°11N 124°47E 233 F5
Jarocin Poland 51°59N 17°29E 185 G4
Jaroměř Czech Rep. 50°22N 15°52E 180 A8
Jarosław Poland 50°2N 22°42E 185 H9
Järpås Sweden 58°23N 12°57E 163 F6
Järpen Sweden 63°21N 13°26E 162 A7
Jarrahdale Australia 32°24S 116°5E 279 F2
Jarrahi → Iran 30°49N 48°48E 247 D6
Jarso Ethiopia 5°15N 37°30E 257 F4
Jartai China 39°45N 105°48E 226 E3
Jaru Brazil 10°26S 62°27W 331 C5
Jaru → Brazil 10°5S 61°59W 331 C5
Jarud Qi China 44°28N 120°50E 227 B11
Järvatältet Sweden 59°25N 17°54E 139 A1
Järvenpää Finland 60°29N 25°5E 188 B3
Jarvis Canada 42°53N 80°6W 312 D4
Jarvis I. Pac. Oc. 0°15S 160°5W 289 H12
Jarvorník Czech Rep. 50°23N 17°2E 181 A10
Järvsö Sweden 61°43N 16°10E 162 C10
Jarwa India 27°38N 82°30E 243 F10
Jaša Tomić Serbia 45°26N 20°50E 182 E5
Jasaan Phil. 8°39N 124°45E 233 G5
Jasdan India 22°2N 71°12E 242 H4
Jashpurnagar India 22°54N 84°9E 243 H11
Jasidih India 24°31N 86°39E 243 G12
Jasień Poland 51°46N 15°0E 185 G2
Jāsimīyah Iraq 33°45N 44°41E 213 F11
Jasin Malaysia 2°20N 102°26E 237 L4
Jāsk Iran 25°38N 57°45E 247 E8
Jaskhar India 18°54N 72°58E 130 B2
Jasło Poland 49°45N 21°30E 185 J8
Jasmund Germany 54°32N 13°35E 178 A9
Jasmund △ Germany 54°31N 13°38E 178 A9
Jaso India 24°30N 80°29E 243 G9
Jason Is. Falk. Is. 51°0S 61°0W 153 f
Jasonville U.S.A. 39°10N 87°12W 311 E9
Jasper Alta., Canada 52°55N 118°5W 296 C5
Jasper Ont., Canada 44°52N 75°57W 313 B9
Jasper Ala., U.S.A. 33°50N 87°17W 315 E11
Jasper Fla., U.S.A. 30°31N 82°57W 316 E7
Jasper Ind., U.S.A. 38°24N 86°56W 311 F10
Jasper Tex., U.S.A. 30°56N 94°1W 314 F7
Jasper △ Canada 52°50N 118°8W 296 C5
Jasrasar India 27°43N 73°49E 242 F5
Jassān Iraq 32°58N 45°52E 213 G11
Jassey = Iaşi Romania 47°10N 27°40E 183 C12
Jastarnia Poland 54°42N 18°40E 184 D5
Jastrebarsko Croatia 45°41N 15°39E 199 C12
Jastrow = Jastrowie Poland 53°26N 16°49E 184 E3
Jastrowie Poland 53°26N 16°49E 184 E3
Jastrzębie Zdrój Poland 49°57N 18°35E 185 J5
Jász-Nagykun-Szolnok □ Hungary 47°15N 20°30E 182 C5
Jászapáti Hungary 47°32N 20°10E 182 C5
Jászárokszállás Hungary 47°39N 19°58E 182 C4
Jászberény Hungary 47°30N 19°55E 182 C4
Jászkisér Hungary 47°27N 20°20E 182 C5
Jászladány Hungary 47°23N 20°10E 182 C5
Jataí Brazil 17°58S 51°48W 333 E1
Jatapu → Brazil 2°13S 58°17W 329 D6
Jath India 17°3N 75°13E 244 F2
Jati Pakistan 24°20N 68°19E 242 G3
Jatibarang Indonesia 6°28S 108°18E 235 D3
Jatiluwih Indonesia 8°23S 115°8E 231 J18
Jatinegara Indonesia 6°13S 106°52E 122 B2
Játiva = Xàtiva Spain 38°59N 0°32W 197 G4
Jatobá = Petrolândia Brazil 9°5S 38°20W 332 C4
Jättendal Sweden 61°58N 17°15E 162 C11
Jaú Angola 15°12S 13°31E 265 F2
Jaú Brazil 22°10S 48°30W 335 A6
Jaú → Brazil 1°54S 61°26W 329 D5
Jauaperi → Brazil 1°26S 61°35W 329 D5
Jauer = Jawor Poland 51°4N 16°11E 185 G3
Jauja Peru 11°45S 75°15W 330 C2
Jaunpur India 25°46N 82°44E 243 G10
Jauru → Brazil 16°22S 57°46W 331 D6
Java = Jawa Indonesia 7°0S 110°0E 235 D4
Java Sea Indonesia 4°35S 107°15E 235 C3
Java Trench Ind. Oc. 9°0S 105°0E 234 D2
Javadi Hills India 12°40N 78°40E 245 H4
Javādīyeh Iran 35°39N 51°22E 141 B2
Javalambre, Sa. de Spain 40°6N 1°0W 196 E4
Javānrud Iran 34°47N 46°31E 213 E12
Jávea Spain 38°48N 0°10E 197 G5
Javhlant = Uliastay Mongolia 47°56N 97°28E 218 B8
Javier, I. Chile 47°5S 74°25W 336 C2
Javla India 17°18N 75°9E 244 F2
Jawa Indonesia 7°0S 110°0E 235 D4
Jawa Barat □ Indonesia 7°0S 107°0E 231 G12
Jawa Tengah □ Indonesia 7°0S 110°0E 235 D3
Jawa Timur □ Indonesia 8°0S 113°0E 235 D4
Jawad India 24°36N 74°51E 242 G6
Jawf, W. al → Yemen 15°50N 45°30E 248 D4
Jawhar India 19°55N 73°14E 244 E1
Jawhar Somali Rep. 2°48N 45°30E 267 D6
Jawor Poland 51°4N 16°11E 185 G3
Jaworowa Poland 52°9N 20°56E 142 C1
Jaworzno Poland 50°13N 19°11E 185 H6
Jaworzyna Śląska Poland 50°55N 16°28E 185 H3
Jawoyn ✪ Australia 14°16S 132°28E 278 B5
Jay U.S.A. 30°57N 87°9W 317 E2
Jay Peak U.S.A. 44°55N 72°32W 313 B12
Jaya, Puncak Indonesia 3°57S 137°17E 231 E9
Jayanca Peru 6°24S 79°50W 330 B2
Jayanti India 26°45N 89°40E 241 B2
Jayapura Indonesia 2°28S 140°38E 231 E10
Jayawijaya, Pegunungan Indonesia 5°0S 139°0E 231 F9
Jaynagar India 26°43N 86°9E 243 F12
Jaypur = Jeypore India 18°50N 82°38E 244 E6
Jayrūd Syria 33°49N 36°44E 250 E7
Jayton U.S.A. 33°15N 100°34W 314 E4
Jāz Mūrīān, Hāmūn-e Iran 27°20N 58°55E 247 E8
Jazīreh-ye Shīf Iran 29°4N 50°54E 247 D6
Jazminal Mexico 24°52N 101°24W 318 C4
Jazz Museum New Orleans, U.S.A. 131 a3
Jazzīn Lebanon 33°31N 35°35E 250 E6
Jean U.S.A. 35°47N 115°20W 307 K11
Jean Lafitte Nat. Historical Park ⌂ U.S.A. 29°51N 90°9W 131 B1
Jean Marie River Canada 61°32N 120°38W 296 A4
Jean-Rabel Haiti 19°50N 73°5W 321 C5
Jeanerette U.S.A. 29°55N 91°40W 314 G9
Jeanette, Ostrov = Zhannetty, Ostrov Russia 76°43N 158°0E 215 B16
Jeanne-Mance, Parc Montréal, Canada 130 b1
Jeanneton, Morne Guadeloupe 16°14N 61°43W 322 e
Jeannette U.S.A. 40°20N 79°36W 312 F5
Jebāl Bārez, Kūh-e Iran 28°30N 58°20E 247 D8
Jebba Nigeria 9°9N 4°48E 263 D5
Jebel, Bahr el → South Sudan 9°30N 30°25E 257 F3
Jebel Ali = Minā' Jabal 'Alī U.A.E. 25°2N 55°8E 247 E7
Jebel Dud Sudan 13°25N 33°9E 257 E3
Jebel Qerri Sudan 16°16N 32°50E 257 D3
Jeberos Peru 5°15S 76°10W 330 B2
Jebus Indonesia 1°43S 105°28E 234 C3
Jecheon S. Korea 37°8N 128°12E 224 D4
Jedburgh U.K. 55°29N 2°33W 167 F6
Jedda = Jiddah Si. Arabia 21°29N 39°10E 248 B2
Jeddore L. Canada 48°3N 55°55W 299 C8
Jedlesee Austria 48°15N 16°23E 142 A2
Jedlicze Poland 49°43N 21°40E 185 J8
Jędrzejów Poland 50°35N 20°15E 185 H7
Jedwabne Poland 53°17N 22°18E 185 E9
Jeetzel → Germany 53°9N 11°3E 178 B7
Jefferson Ga., U.S.A. 34°7N 83°35W 316 A6
Jefferson Iowa, U.S.A. 42°1N 94°23W 310 B2
Jefferson La., U.S.A. 29°57N 90°9W 131 B2
Jefferson Ohio, U.S.A. 41°44N 80°46W 312 E4
Jefferson Tex., U.S.A. 32°46N 94°21W 314 E7
Jefferson Wis., U.S.A. 43°0N 88°48W 311 B8
Jefferson, Mt. Nev., U.S.A. 38°47N 116°56W 304 G5
Jefferson, Mt. Oreg., U.S.A. 44°41N 121°48W 304 D3
Jefferson City Mo., U.S.A. 38°34N 92°10W 310 F4
Jefferson City Tenn., U.S.A. 36°7N 83°30W 315 C13
Jefferson Memorial Washington, D.C., U.S.A. 143 c1
Jefferson Park Calif., U.S.A. 34°2N 118°19W 126 B3
Jefferson Park Ill., U.S.A. 41°58N 87°46W 119 B2
Jeffersontown U.S.A. 38°12N 85°35W 311 F11
Jeffersonville Ga., U.S.A. 32°41N 83°20W 316 C6
Jeffersonville Ind., U.S.A. 38°17N 85°44W 311 F11
Jeffersonville Ohio, U.S.A. 39°39N 83°34W 311 E13
Jeffrey City U.S.A. 42°30N 107°49W 304 E10
Jega Nigeria 12°15N 4°23E 263 C5
Jegi S. Korea 37°34N 127°1E 137 B2
Jejevo Solomon Is. 8°6S 159°8E 287 M10
Jeju S. Korea 33°31N 126°32E 224 a
Jeju-do S. Korea 33°29N 126°34E 224 a
Jeju-do □ S. Korea 33°25N 126°30E 224 a
Jēkabpils Latvia 56°29N 25°57E 188 D3
Jekyll I. U.S.A. 31°4N 81°25W 316 D8
Jelambar Indonesia 6°9S 106°47E 122 A1
Jelcz-Laskowice Poland 51°2N 17°19E 185 G4
Jelenia Góra Poland 50°50N 15°45E 185 H2
Jelgava Latvia 56°41N 23°49E 184 B10
Jelgava □ Latvia 56°35N 23°45E 184 B10
Jelica Serbia 43°50N 20°17E 202 C4
Jelli South Sudan 5°25N 31°45E 257 F3
Jelonki Poland 52°14N 20°54E 142 E1
Jelšava Slovak Rep. 48°37N 20°15E 181 C13
Jema'a Mallam = Kafanchan Nigeria 9°40N 8°20E 263 D6
Jemaja Indonesia 3°5N 105°45E 234 B3
Jemaluang Malaysia 2°16N 103°52E 237 L4
Jember Indonesia 8°11S 113°41E 235 D4
Jempang, Danau Indonesia 0°25S 116°12E 235 C5
Jena Thüringen, Germany 50°54N 11°35E 178 E7
Jena La., U.S.A. 31°41N 92°8W 314 F8
Jenai Taiwan 24°2N 121°8E 225 B3
Jenbach Austria 47°24N 11°47E 180 D4
Jendouba Tunisia 36°29N 8°47E 258 A1
Jendouba □ Tunisia 36°34N 8°52E 261 A6
Jeneponto Indonesia 5°40S 119°44E 235 D5
Jengish Chokoso = Pobedy, Pik Kyrgyzstan 42°0N 79°58E 217 D9
Jenho Taiwan 23°54N 121°36E 225 C3
Jenīn West Bank 32°28N 35°18E 251 F6
Jenison U.S.A. 42°54N 85°47W 311 B11
Jenkins U.S.A. 37°10N 82°38W 309 G12
Jenner U.S.A. 38°27N 123°7W 306 G3
Jennings Fla., U.S.A. 30°36N 83°6W 316 E6
Jennings La., U.S.A. 30°13N 92°40W 314 F8
Jennings Mo., U.S.A. 38°43N 90°15W 310 F6
Jenny Pt. Dominica 15°28N 61°15W 323 k
Jensen Beach U.S.A. 27°15N 80°14W 317 H9
Jente Taiwan 22°58N 120°16E 225 D2
Jenwu Taiwan 22°42N 120°20E 225 D2
Jeollabuk-do □ S. Korea 35°45N 127°15E 224 E3
Jeollanam-do □ S. Korea 34°45N 127°0E 224 E3
Jeong-eup S. Korea 35°35N 126°50E 224 E3
Jeongseon S. Korea 37°20N 128°45E 227 F15
Jeonju S. Korea 35°50N 127°4E 224 E3
Jepara Indonesia 7°40S 109°14E 235 D3
Jeparit Australia 36°8S 142°1E 282 D5
Jequié Brazil 13°51S 40°5W 333 D3
Jequitaí → Brazil 17°4S 44°50W 333 E3
Jequitinhonha Brazil 16°30S 41°0W 333 E3
Jequitinhonha → Brazil 15°51S 38°53W 333 E4
Jerada Morocco 34°17N 2°10W 261 B4
Jerantut Malaysia 3°56N 102°22E 237 L4
Jerejak, Pulau Malaysia 5°19N 100°19E 237 c
Jérémie Haiti 18°40N 74°10W 321 C5
Jeremoabo Brazil 10°4S 38°21W 332 D4
Jerez, Pta. Mexico 22°58N 97°40W 319 C5
Jerez de García Salinas Mexico 22°39N 103°0W 318 C4
Jerez de la Frontera Spain 36°41N 6°7W 195 J4
Jerez de los Caballeros Spain 38°20N 6°45W 195 G4
Jericho = El Arīḥā West Bank 31°52N 35°27E 251 G6
Jericho Australia 23°38S 146°6E 280 C4
Jerichow Germany 52°30N 12°1E 178 C8
Jerico Springs U.S.A. 37°37N 94°1W 310 G2
Jerid, Chott el = Djerid, Chott Tunisia 33°42N 8°30E 258 B1
Jerilderie Australia 35°20S 145°41E 283 C6
Jermyn U.S.A. 41°32N 75°33W 313 E9
Jerningham Junction Trin. & Tob. 10°33N 61°23W 323 t
Jerome U.S.A. 42°44N 114°31W 304 E6
Jerónimos, Mosteiro dos Portugal 38°41N 9°11W 126 A1
Jerramungup Australia 33°55S 118°55E 279 F2
Jersey U.K. 49°11N 2°7W 169 H5
Jersey City U.S.A. 40°42N 74°4W 132 B1
Jersey Shore U.S.A. 41°12N 77°15W 312 E7
Jerseyville U.S.A. 39°7N 90°20W 310 E6
Jerumenha Brazil 7°5S 43°30W 332 C3
Jerusalem Israel/West Bank 31°47N 35°10E 123 B2
Jervis B. Australia 35°8S 150°46E 283 C9
Jervis Bay △ Australia 35°9S 150°42E 283 C9
Jervis Inlet Canada 50°0N 123°57W 296 C4
Jerzu Italy 39°47N 9°31E 200 C2
Jesenice Slovenia 46°28N 14°3E 199 B11
Jeseník Czech Rep. 50°14N 17°8E 181 A10
Jesenké Slovak Rep. 48°20N 20°10E 181 C13
Jesi = Iesi Italy 43°31N 13°14E 199 E10
Jessamine, L. U.S.A. 28°28N 81°23W 133 B2
Jessel = Jasło Poland 49°45N 21°30E 185 J8
Jesselton = Kota Kinabalu Malaysia 6°0N 116°4E 235 A5
Jessheim Norway 60°9N 11°10E 164 D8
Jessnitz Germany 51°40N 12°18E 178 D8
Jessore Bangla. 23°10N 89°10E 241 D2
Jesup Ga., U.S.A. 31°36N 81°53W 316 D8
Jesup Iowa, U.S.A. 42°29N 92°4W 310 B4
Jesup, L. U.S.A. 28°43N 81°14W 317 G8
Jesús Peru 7°15S 78°25W 330 B2
Jésus, Î. Canada 45°36N 73°44W 130 A1
Jesús Carranza Mexico 17°26N 95°2W 319 D5
Jesús María Argentina 30°59S 64°5W 334 C3
Jesús María Lima, Peru 12°4S 77°3W 124 B2
Jetmore U.S.A. 38°4N 99°54W 308 F4
Jetpur India 21°45N 70°10E 242 J4
Jette Belgium 50°53N 4°20E 116 A1
Jeumont France 50°18N 4°6E 173 B11
Jeungdo S. Korea 34°56N 126°9E 224 E3
Jeungpyeong S. Korea 36°47N 127°34E 224 D3
Jevnaker Norway 60°15N 10°26E 164 D7
Jewell U.S.A. 42°20N 93°39W 308 D7
Jewett U.S.A. 40°22N 81°2W 312 F3
Jewett City U.S.A. 41°36N 71°59W 313 E13
Jewish Quarter Jerusalem 123 b3
Jey Iran 35°41N 51°20E 141 B2
Jeyḥūnābād Iran 34°58N 48°59E 247 C6
Jeypore India 18°50N 82°38E 244 E6
Jeziorak, Jezioro Poland 53°40N 19°35E 184 E6
Jeziorany Poland 53°58N 20°46E 184 E7
Jeziorka → Poland 52°8N 21°9E 185 F8
Jha Jha India 24°46N 86°22E 243 G12
Jhaarkand = Jharkhand □ India 24°0N 85°50E 243 H11
Jhabua India 22°46N 74°36E 242 H6
Jhajjar India 28°37N 76°42E 242 E7
Jhal Pakistan 28°17N 67°27E 242 E2
Jhal Jhao Pakistan 26°20N 65°35E 240 D2
Jhalakati Bangla. 22°39N 90°12E 241 D3
Jhalawar India 24°40N 76°10E 242 G7
Jhalida India 23°22N 85°58E 243 H11
Jhalrapatan India 24°33N 76°10E 242 G7
Jhang Maghiana Pakistan 31°15N 72°22E 242 D5
Jhansi India 25°30N 78°36E 243 G8
Jhargram India 22°27N 86°59E 243 H12
Jharia India 23°45N 86°26E 243 H12
Jharkhand □ India 24°0N 85°50E 243 H11
Jharsuguda India 21°56N 84°5E 244 D7
Jhelum Pakistan 33°0N 73°45E 242 C5
Jhelum → Pakistan 31°20N 72°10E 242 D5
Jhenaidah Bangla. 23°33N 89°10E 241 D2
Jhilmilli India 23°24N 82°51E 243 H10
Jhudo Pakistan 24°58N 69°18E 242 G3
Jhunjhunu India 28°10N 75°30E 242 E6
Ji-Paraná Brazil 10°50S 61°58W 331 C5
Ji Xian China 36°7N 110°40E 226 F6
Jia Xian Henan, China 33°59N 113°12E 226 H7
Jia Xian Shaanxi, China 38°12N 110°28E 226 E6
Jiading China 31°22N 121°15E 229 B13
Jiahe China 25°38N 112°19E 229 E9
Jiaji = Qionghai China 19°15N 110°26E 236 C8
Jialing Jiang → China 29°30N 106°20E 228 C6
Jiamusi China 46°40N 130°26E 219 B15
Ji'an Jiangxi, China 27°6N 114°59E 229 D10
Ji'an Jilin, China 41°5N 126°10E 227 D14
Jianchang China 40°55N 120°35E 227 D11
Jianchuan China 26°38N 99°55E 228 D2
Jiande China 29°23N 119°15E 229 C12
Jiang'an China 28°40N 105°3E 228 C5
Jiangbei China 29°40N 106°34E 228 C6
Jiangcheng China 22°36N 101°52E 228 F3
Jiangchuan China 24°8N 102°39E 228 E4
Jiangdi China 26°57N 103°37E 228 D4
Jiangdu China 32°27N 119°36E 229 A12
Jiange China 32°4N 105°32E 228 A5
Jianggao China 23°15N 113°13E 121 A2
Jianghua China 25°0N 111°47E 229 E8
Jiangjin China 29°14N 106°14E 228 C6
Jiangkou China 27°40N 108°49E 228 D7
Jiangle China 26°42N 117°23E 229 D11
Jiangmen China 22°32N 113°0E 229 F9
Jiangning China 31°55N 118°50E 229 B12
Jiangshan China 28°40N 118°37E 229 C12
Jiangsu □ China 33°0N 120°0E 227 H11
Jiangwan China 31°18N 121°28E 138 B1
Jiangxi □ China 27°30N 116°0E 229 D11
Jiangyan China 32°30N 120°7E 229 A13
Jiangyin China 31°54N 120°17E 229 B13
Jiangyong China 25°20N 111°22E 229 E8
Jiangyou China 31°44N 104°43E 228 B5
Jiangyuan China 42°2N 126°34E 227 C14
Jianhe China 26°37N 108°31E 228 D7
Jianli China 29°46N 112°56E 229 C9
Jianning China 26°50N 116°50E 229 D11
Jian'ou China 27°3N 118°17E 229 D12
Jianping China 41°53N 119°42E 227 D10
Jianshi China 30°37N 109°38E 228 B7
Jianshui China 23°36N 102°43E 228 F4
Jianyang Fujian, China 27°20N 118°5E 229 D12
Jianyang Sichuan, China 30°24N 104°33E 228 B5
Jiao Xian = Jiaozhou China 36°18N 120°1E 227 F11
Jiaohe Hebei, China 38°2N 116°20E 226 E9
Jiaohe Jilin, China 43°40N 127°22E 227 C14
Jiaoling China 24°41N 116°12E 229 E11
Jiaonan China 35°52N 119°58E 227 G10
Jiaozhou China 36°18N 120°1E 227 F11
Jiaozhou Wan China 36°5N 120°10E 227 F11
Jiaozuo China 35°16N 113°12E 226 G7
Jiashan China 30°55N 120°55E 229 B13
Jiawang China 34°28N 117°26E 227 G9
Jiaxiang China 35°25N 116°20E 226 G9
Jiaxing China 30°49N 120°45E 229 B13
Jiayi = Chiai Taiwan 23°29N 120°25E 225 C2
Jiayu China 29°55N 113°55E 229 C9
Jiayuguan China 39°49N 98°18E 218 D8
Jib West Bank 31°51N 35°11E 123 A2
Jibão, Serra do Brazil 14°48S 45°0W 333 D3
Jibiya Nigeria 13°5N 7°12E 263 C6
Jibou Romania 47°15N 23°17E 183 C8
Jibuti = Djibouti ■ Africa 12°0N 43°0E 257 E5
Jicarón, I. Panama 7°10N 81°50W 320 E3
Jičín Czech Rep. 50°25N 15°28E 180 A8
Jiddah Si. Arabia 21°29N 39°10E 248 B2
Jido India 29°2N 94°58E 241 A5
Jido S. Korea 35°4N 126°14E 224 E3
Jieshou China 33°18N 115°22E 226 H8
Jiexiu China 37°2N 111°55E 226 F6
Jieyang China 23°35N 116°21E 229 F11
Jigalong Australia 23°21S 120°47E 278 D3
Jigalong ✪ Australia 23°21S 120°46E 278 D3
Jigawa □ Nigeria 12°0N 9°45E 263 C6
Jigme Dorje △ Bhutan 28°0N 89°40E 241 B2
Jigme Singye Wangchuck Bhutan 27°20N 90°25E 241 B3
Jigni India 25°45N 79°25E 243 G8
Jihād Iraq 33°17N 44°19E 113 B1
Jihlava Czech Rep. 49°28N 15°35E 180 B8
Jihlava → Czech Rep. 48°55N 16°36E 181 C9
Jihlavský □ Czech Rep. 49°30N 15°30E 180 B8
Jihnan Taiwan 24°22N 120°39E 225 B2
Jihočeský □ Czech Rep. 49°8N 14°35E 180 B7
Jihomoravský □ Czech Rep. 49°5N 16°30E 181 B9
Jiiqley Somali Rep. 5°25N 45°20E 267 C6
Jijel Algeria 36°52N 5°50E 261 A6
Jijel □ Algeria 36°45N 6°0E 261 A6
Jijiga Ethiopia 9°20N 42°50E 267 C5
Jikamshi Nigeria 12°12N 7°45E 263 C6
Jikau South Sudan 8°28N 33°47E 257 F3
Jilib Somali Rep. 0°29N 42°46E 267 D5
Jilin China 43°44N 126°30E 227 C14
Jilin □ China 44°0N 127°0E 224 A3
Jiloca → Spain 41°21N 1°39W 196 D3
Jilong = Chilung Taiwan 25°3N 121°45E 225 A3
Jim Thompson's House Bangkok, Thailand 113 b3
Jim Thorpe U.S.A. 40°52N 75°44W 313 F9
Jima Ethiopia 7°40N 36°47E 257 F4
Jimbaran, Teluk Indonesia 8°46S 115°9E 231 K18
Jimbōchō Tokyo, Japan 140 a4
Jimbolia Romania 45°47N 20°43E 182 E5
Jimena de la Frontera Spain 36°27N 5°24W 195 J5
Jiménez Chihuahua, Mexico 27°8N 104°54W 318 B4
Jimenez Phil. 8°20N 123°50E 233 G4
Jimeta Nigeria 9°17N 12°28E 263 D7
Jimo China 36°23N 120°30E 227 F11
Jimsar China 43°59N 89°4E 217 D11
Jin Jiang → China 28°24N 115°48E 229 C10
Jin Xian = Jinzhou China 38°55N 121°42E 227 E11
Jinan China 36°38N 117°1E 226 F9
Jinchang China 38°30N 102°10E 218 D9
Jincheng China 35°29N 112°50E 226 G7
Jinchuan China 31°30N 102°3E 228 B4
Jind India 29°19N 76°22E 242 E7
Jindabyne Australia 36°25S 148°35E 283 D8
Jinding China 22°22N 113°33E 219 a
Jindo S. Korea 34°28N 126°15E 224 E3
Jindřichův Hradec Czech Rep. 49°10N 15°2E 180 B8
Jing He → China 34°27N 109°4E 226 G5
Jing Shan China 31°20N 111°35E 229 B8
Jing Xian China 30°38N 118°25E 229 B12
Jing'an Jiangxi, China 28°50N 115°17E 229 C10
Jingan Shanghai, China 31°14N 121°25E 138 B1
Jingbian China 37°20N 108°30E 226 F5
Jingchuan China 35°20N 107°20E 226 G4
Jingde China 30°15N 118°27E 229 B12
Jingdezhen China 29°20N 117°11E 229 C11
Jingdong China 24°23N 100°47E 228 E3
Jinggangshan China 26°58N 114°15E 229 D10
Jinggu China 23°35N 100°41E 228 F3
Jinghai Guangdong, China 22°59N 116°31E 229 F11
Jinghai Tianjin, China 38°55N 116°55E 226 E9
Jinghong China 22°0N 100°45E 228 G3
Jingjiang China 32°2N 120°16E 229 A13
Jingle China 38°20N 111°55E 226 E6
Jingmen China 31°0N 112°10E 229 B9
Jingning China 35°30N 105°43E 226 G3
Jingpo Hu China 43°55N 128°55E 227 C15
Jingshan China 31°1N 113°7E 229 B9
Jingtai China 37°10N 104°6E 226 F3
Jingtanggang China 39°10N 119°5E 227 E10
Jingu Outer Garden Tokyo, Japan 140 b2
Jingxi China 23°8N 106°27E 228 F6
Jingyang China 34°30N 108°50E 226 G5
Jingyu China 42°25N 126°45E 224 A3
Jingyuan China 36°30N 104°40E 226 F3
Jingzhou Hubei, China 30°21N 112°11E 229 B9
Jingzhou Hunan, China 26°33N 109°40E 228 D7
Jingziguan China 33°15N 111°0E 226 H6
Jinhua China 29°8N 119°38E 229 C12
Jining Nei Monggol Zizhiqu, China 41°5N 113°0E 226 D7
Jining Shandong, China 35°22N 116°34E 226 G9
Jinja Uganda 0°25N 33°12E 268 B3
Jinjang Malaysia 3°13N 101°39E 237 L3
Jinji China 37°58N 106°8E 226 F4
Jinjiang Fujian, China 24°43N 118°33E 229 E12
Jinjiang Yunnan, China 26°14N 100°34E 228 D3
Jinjini Ghana 7°26N 2°42W 262 D4
Jinju S. Korea 35°12N 128°2E 224 E4
Jinkou China 30°20N 114°8E 229 B10
Jinkouhe China 29°18N 103°4E 228 C4
Jinmu Jiao China 18°9N 109°34E 236 C7
Jinnah Barrage Pakistan 32°58N 71°33E 242 C4
Jinning China 24°38N 102°38E 228 E4
Jinočany Czech Rep. 50°2N 14°16E 135 B1
Jinonice Czech Rep. 50°3N 14°22E 135 B2
Jinotega Nic. 13°6N 85°59W 320 D2
Jinotepe Nic. 11°50N 86°10W 320 D2
Jinping Guizhou, China 26°41N 109°10E 228 D7
Jinping Yunnan, China 22°45N 103°18E 228 F4
Jinsha China 27°29N 106°12E 228 D6
Jinsha Jiang → China 28°50N 104°36E 228 C5
Jinshan China 30°54N 121°10E 229 B13
Jinshi China 29°40N 111°50E 229 C8
Jintan China 31°42N 119°36E 229 B12
Jintotolo Channel Phil. 11°48N 123°5E 233 F4
Jintotolo I. Phil. 11°51N 123°7E 233 F4
Jintur India 19°37N 76°42E 244 E3
Jinxi Jiangxi, China 27°56N 116°45E 229 D11
Jinxi Liaoning, China 40°52N 120°50E 227 D11
Jinxian China 28°26N 116°17E 229 C11
Jinxiang China 35°5N 116°22E 226 G9
Jinyang China 27°28N 103°5E 228 D4
Jinyun China 28°35N 120°5E 229 C13
Jinzhai China 31°40N 115°53E 229 B10
Jinzhong China 37°42N 112°46E 226 F7
Jinzhou Liaoning, China 38°55N 121°42E 227 E11
Jinzhou Liaoning, China 41°5N 121°3E 227 D11
Jiparaná → Brazil 8°3S 62°52W 331 B5
Jipijapa Ecuador 1°0S 80°40W 328 D1
Jiquilpan Mexico 19°59N 102°43W 318 D4
Jirisan S. Korea 35°20N 127°44E 224 E3
Jirisan △ S. Korea 35°15N 127°30E 224 E3
Jiroft Iran 28°45N 57°50E 247 D8
Jishan China 35°34N 110°58E 226 G6
Jishou China 28°21N 109°43E 228 C7
Jishui China 27°12N 115°8E 229 D10
Jisr ash Shughūr Syria 35°49N 36°18E 250 C7
Jitarning Australia 32°48S 117°57E 279 F2
Jitra Malaysia 6°16N 100°25E 237 J3
Jiu → Romania 43°47N 23°48E 183 G8
Jiudengkou China 39°56N 106°40E 226 E4
Jiujiang Guangdong, China 22°50N 113°0E 229 F9
Jiujiang Jiangxi, China 29°42N 115°58E 229 C10
Jiuling Shan China 28°40N 114°40E 229 C10
Jiulong = Kowloon China 22°19N 114°11E 122 B1
Jiulong China 28°57N 101°31E 228 C3
Jiuquan China 39°50N 98°20E 218 D8
Jiutai China 44°10N 125°50E 227 B13
Jiuxincheng China 39°17N 115°59E 226 E8
Jiuzhaigou △ China 33°8N 103°52E 228 A4
Jiwa U.A.E. 23°0N 54°10E 249 B6
Jiwani Pakistan 25°1N 61°44E 240 D1
Jiwani, Ras Pakistan 25°1N 61°44E 240 D1
Jixi Anhui, China 30°5N 118°34E 229 B12
Jixi Heilongjiang, China 45°20N 130°50E 227 B16
Jiyang China 37°0N 117°12E 227 F9
Jiyuan China 35°7N 112°57E 226 G7
Jiyūgaoka Japan 35°35N 139°40E 140 B3
Jiz', W. → Yemen 16°12N 52°14E 249 C6
Jizā'ir Iraq 33°15N 44°23E 113 B2
Jīzān Si. Arabia 17°0N 42°20E 248 C3
Jize China 36°54N 114°56E 226 F8
Jizera → Czech Rep. 50°10N 14°43E 180 A7
Jizhou China 37°35N 115°30E 226 F8
Jizīra Iraq 33°15N 44°25E 113 B2
Jizl, Wādī al → Si. Arabia 25°39N 38°25E 246 E3
Jizō-Zaki Japan 35°34N 133°20E 222 B5
Jizzax Uzbekistan 40°6N 67°50E 217 D7
Jizzax □ Uzbekistan 40°20N 67°40E 217 D7
Joaçaba Brazil 27°5S 51°31W 335 B5
Joaíma Brazil 16°39S 41°2W 333 E3
Joal Fadiout Senegal 14°9N 16°50W 262 C1
João Amaro Brazil 12°46S 40°22W 333 D3
João Belo = Xai-Xai Mozam. 25°6S 33°31E 271 C5
João Câmara Brazil 5°32S 35°48W 332 C4
João Neiva Brazil 19°45S 40°24W 333 E3
João Pessoa = Eirunepé Brazil 6°35S 69°53W 330 B4
João Pessoa = Porto Brazil 3°54S 42°42W 332 B3
João Pessoa Brazil 7°10S 34°52W 332 C5
João Pinheiro Brazil 17°45S 46°10W 333 E2
Joaquín V. González Argentina 25°10S 64°0W 334 B3
Jobat India 22°25N 74°34E 242 H6
Jobourg, Nez de France 49°41N 1°57W 172 C5
Jódar Spain 37°50N 3°21W 195 H7
Jodhpur India 26°23N 73°8E 242 F5
Jodiya India 22°42N 70°18E 242 H4
Joensuu Finland 62°37N 29°49E 160 E23
Jōetsu Japan 37°12N 138°10E 221 F9
Jœuf France 49°12N 6°0E 173 C12
Jofane Mozam. 21°15S 34°18E 271 B5
Joffre, Morne = Moustique, Morne Guadeloupe 16°7N 61°44W 322 e
Jog Falls = Gersoppa Falls India 14°12N 74°46E 245 G2
Jogbani India 26°25N 87°15E 243 F12
Jõgeva Estonia 58°45N 26°24E 188 C4
Jogjakarta = Yogyakarta Indonesia 7°49S 110°22E 235 D4
Joglo Indonesia 6°13S 106°45E 122 B1
Jōhana Japan 36°30N 136°57E 223 A8
Johannesburg Gauteng, S. Africa 26°11S 28°2E 123 B2
Johannesburg Calif., U.S.A. 35°22N 117°38W 307 K9
Johannesburg, Univ. of S. Africa 26°11S 28°0E 123 B2
Johanneskirchen Germany 48°10N 11°38E 131 A2
Johannesstift Germany 52°34N 13°12E 115 A2
Johannisburg = Pisz Poland 53°38N 21°49E 184 E8
Johannisthal Germany 52°26N 13°30E 115 B4
Johansfors Sweden 56°42N 15°32E 163 H9
Johilla → India 23°37N 81°14E 243 H9
John Crow Mts. Jamaica 18°5N 76°25W 320 a
John Day U.S.A. 44°25N 118°57W 304 D4
John Day → U.S.A. 45°44N 120°39W 304 D3
John Day Fossil Beds ⌂ U.S.A. 44°33N 119°38W 304 D4
John D'or Prairie Canada 58°30N 115°8W 296 B5
John F. Kennedy Nat. Historic Site ⌂ U.S.A. 42°20N 71°7W 116 A2
John F. Kennedy Space Center U.S.A. 28°40N 80°42W 317 G9
John H. Kerr Res. U.S.A. 36°36N 78°18W 315 C15
John Hancock Center Chicago, U.S.A. 119 a2
John McLaren Park U.S.A. 37°43N 122°24W 136 B2
John o' Groats U.K. 58°38N 3°4W 167 C5
Johnnie U.S.A. 36°25N 116°5W 307 J10
Johns I. U.S.A. 32°47N 80°7W 316 C9
John's Ra. Australia 21°55S 133°23E 280 C1
Johnson U.S.A. 44°38N 72°41W 313 B12
Johnson City Kans., U.S.A. 37°34N 101°45W 308 G3
Johnson City N.Y., U.S.A. 42°7N 75°58W 313 D9
Johnson City Tenn., U.S.A. 36°19N 82°21W 315 C13
Johnson City Tex., U.S.A. 30°17N 98°25W 314 F5
Johnsonburg U.S.A. 41°29N 78°41W 312 E6
Johnsondale U.S.A. 35°58N 118°32W 307 K8
Johnsons Crossing Canada 60°29N 133°18W 296 A2
Johnsons Pt. Antigua & B. 17°2N 61°53W 322 b
Johnsonville N.Z. 41°13S 174°48E 143 B1
Johnston U.S.A. 33°50N 81°48W 316 B8
Johnston, L. Australia 32°25S 120°30E 279 F3
Johnston City U.S.A. 37°49N 88°56W 310 G8
Johnston Falls = Mambilima Falls Zambia 10°31S 28°45E 269 E2
Johnston I. Pac. Oc. 17°10N 169°8W 289 F11
Johnstone Str. Canada 50°28N 126°0W 296 C3
Johnstown Kilkenny, Ireland 52°45N 7°33W 166 D4
Johnstown N.Y., U.S.A. 43°0N 74°22W 313 C10
Johnstown Ohio, U.S.A. 40°9N 82°41W 312 F2
Johnstown Pa., U.S.A. 40°20N 78°55W 312 F6
Johor □ Malaysia 2°5N 103°20E 237 M4
Johor, Selat Asia 1°28N 103°47E 237 d
Johor Bahru Malaysia 1°28N 103°46E 237 d
Jõhvi Estonia 59°22N 27°27E 188 C4
Joigny France 47°58N 3°20E 173 E10
Joinville Brazil 26°15S 48°55W 335 B6
Joinville Haute-Marne, France 48°27N 5°10E 173 D12
Joinville I. Antarctica 65°0S 55°30W 151 C18
Joinville-le-Pont France 48°49N 2°27E 134 B3
Jojutla Mexico 18°37N 99°11W 319 D5
Jøkelbugten Greenland 78°25N 20°20W 154 B9
Jokkmokk Sweden 66°35N 19°50E 160 C18
Jökulsá á Bru → Iceland 65°40N 14°16W 155 B12
Jökulsá á Fjöllum → Iceland 66°10N 16°30W 155 A10
Jökulsárgljúfur △ Iceland 65°56N 16°31W 155 B10
Jolfā Āzarbājān-e Sharqī, Iran 38°57N 45°38E 213 C11
Jolfā Eşfahan, Iran 32°58N 51°37E 247 C6
Joli-Bois Belgium 50°42N 4°24E 116 B2
Joliet U.S.A. 41°32N 88°5W 311 C8
Joliette Canada 46°3N 73°24W 298 C5
Jollas Finland 60°10N 25°5E 121 B3
Jolo Phil. 6°0N 121°0E 233 H3
Jolo Group Phil. 6°0N 121°9E 233 J3
Jolon U.S.A. 35°58N 121°9W 306 K5
Jølstravatnet Norway 61°32N 6°23E 164 C3
Jomalig I. Phil. 14°42N 122°22E 232 D4
Jombang Indonesia 7°33S 112°14E 235 D4
Jomda China 31°28N 98°12E 228 B2
Jonåker Sweden 58°45N 16°45E 163 F10
Jonava Lithuania 55°8N 24°12E 188 E3
Jondal Norway 60°16N 6°15E 164 D3
Jones Phil. 16°33N 121°42E 232 C3
Jones Sound Canada 76°0N 85°0W 295 B15
Jonesboro Ark., U.S.A. 35°50N 90°42W 315 D9
Jonesboro Ga., U.S.A. 33°31N 84°22W 316 B5
Jonesboro La., U.S.A. 32°15N 92°43W 314 E8
Jonesburg U.S.A. 38°51N 91°18W 310 F5
Jonesville Ind., U.S.A. 39°5N 85°54W 311 E11
Jonesville Mich., U.S.A. 41°59N 84°40W 311 C12
Jong → S. Leone 7°32N 12°23W 262 D2
Jonglei South Sudan 6°25N 31°30E 257 F3
Jonglei □ South Sudan 7°30N 32°30E 257 F3
Jonglei Canal South Sudan 9°20N 31°39E 266 C3
Jongmyo Royal Shrine S. Korea 37°34N 126°59E 137 B1
Jongno S. Korea 37°35N 126°59E 137 B1
Joniškis Lithuania 56°13N 23°35E 184 B10
Jönköping Sweden 57°45N 14°8E 163 G8
Jönköpings län □ Sweden 57°30N 14°30E 163 G8
Jonquière Canada 48°27N 71°14W 299 C5
Jonsered Sweden 57°45N 12°10E 163 G6
Jonstrup Denmark 55°45N 12°20E 118 A2
Jonzac France 45°27N 0°28W 174 C3
Joplin U.S.A. 37°6N 94°31W 308 G6
Joppa U.K. 55°57N 3°6W 121 B3
Jora India 26°20N 77°49E 242 F6
Jordan Guimaras, Phil. 10°40N 122°35E 233 F4
Jordan Mont., U.S.A. 47°19N 106°55W 304 C10
Jordan N.Y., U.S.A. 43°4N 76°29W 313 C8
Jordan ■ Asia 31°0N 36°0E 251 H7
Jordan → Asia 31°48N 35°32E 251 G6
Jordan Valley U.S.A. 42°59N 117°3W 304 E5
Jordânia Brazil 15°55S 40°11W 333 E3
Jordanów Poland 49°41N 19°49E 185 J6
Jordet Norway 61°25N 12°8E 164 C9
Jorge, C. Chile 51°40S 75°35W 336 D1
Jorge Chavez, Int. ✈ (LIM) Peru 12°2S 77°8W 124 B2
Jorge Newbery ✈ (AEP) Argentina 34°34S 58°25W 117 B2
Jorgen Brønlund Fjord Greenland 82°30N 31°0W 154 A7
Jorhat India 26°45N 94°12E 241 B5
Jori → Norway 62°4N 9°5E 162 B3
Jorm Afghan. 36°50N 70°52E 240 A3
Jörn Sweden 65°4N 20°1E 160 D19
Jorong Indonesia 3°58S 114°56E 235 C4
Jørpeland Norway 59°3N 6°1E 164 E3
Jorquera → Chile 28°3S 69°58W 334 B2
Joru S. Leone 7°41N 11°3W 262 D2
Jos Nigeria 9°53N 8°51E 263 D6
Jos Plateau Niger 9°30N 9°0E 259 G1
Jos Plateau Nigeria 9°55N 9°0E 263 D6
Jošanička Banja Serbia 43°24N 20°47E 202 C4
Jose Abad Santos Phil. 5°55N 125°39E 233 J5
José Batlle y Ordóñez Uruguay 33°20S 55°10W 335 C4
José Bonifácio = Erechim Brazil 27°35S 52°15W 335 B5
José de San Martín Argentina 44°4S 70°26W 336 B2
Jose Panganiban Phil. 14°17N 122°41E 232 D4
Jósefa Piłsudskiego Park Poland 52°15N 21°2E 142 B1
Joseni Romania 46°42N 25°29E 183 D10
Joseph, L. Canada 45°10N 79°44W 312 A5
Joseph Banks Group Australia 34°36S 136°16E 282 C2
Joseph Bonaparte G. Australia 14°35S 128°50E 278 B4
Joseph L. Canada 52°45N 65°18W 299 B6
Joshinath India 30°34N 79°34E 243 D8
Joshinetsu-Kōgen △ Japan 36°42N 138°32E 223 A10
Joshua Tree U.S.A. 34°8N 116°19W 307 L10
Joshua Tree △ U.S.A. 33°55N 116°0W 307 M10
Josselin France 47°57N 2°33W 172 E4
Jost Van Dyke I. Br. Virgin Is. 18°29N 64°47W 321 b
Jostedal Norway 61°35N 7°15E 164 C4
Jostedalsbreen Norway 61°40N 6°59E 164 C3
Jōtō Japan 34°42N 135°33E 133 A2
Jotunheimen Norway 61°35N 8°25E 164 C5
Jotunheimen △ Norway 61°32N 8°25E 164 C5
Joubertberge Namibia 18°30S 14°0E 270 A1
Joué-lès-Tours France 47°21N 0°40E 172 E7
Jourdanton U.S.A. 28°55N 98°33W 314 G5
Joutseno Finland 61°7N 28°31E 188 B5
Jouy-en-Josas France 48°46N 2°10E 134 B2
Jovellanos Cuba 22°40N 81°10W 320 B3
Jovellar Phil. 13°4N 123°36E 232 E4
Jowai India 25°26N 92°12E 241 C4
Jowkār Iran 34°25N 48°40E 213 E13
Jowzjān □ Afghan. 36°10N 66°0E 240 A2
Joyeuse France 44°29N 4°16E 175 D8
Jōyō Japan 34°50N 135°47E 223 C7
Józefów Lubelskie, Poland 50°28N 23°2E 185 H10
Józefów Mazowieckie, Poland 52°10N 21°11E 185 F8
Ju Xian China 36°35N 118°20E 227 F10
Juan Aldama Mexico 24°19N 103°21W 318 C4
Juan Anchorena Argentina 34°30S 58°29W 117 A2
Juan Bautista Alberdi Argentina 34°26S 61°43W 334 C3
Juan de Bolas Jamaica 18°5N 77°9W 320 a
Juan de Fuca, Str of. N. Amer. 48°15N 124°0W 306 B3
Juán de Nova Ind. Oc. 17°3S 43°45E 271 A7
Juan Fernández, Arch. de Pac. Oc. 33°50S 80°0W 326 G2
Juan Fernández △ Chile 33°38S 78°52W 330 c
Juan González Romero Mexico 19°30N 99°3W 128 A2
Juan José Castelli Argentina 25°27S 60°57W 334 B3
Juan L. Lacaze Uruguay 34°26S 57°25W 334 C4
Juana Díaz Puerto Rico 18°3N 66°31W 321 b
Juanjuí Peru 7°10S 76°45W 330 B2
Juankoski Finland 63°3N 28°19E 160 E23
Juara Brazil 11°20S 57°25W 331 C6
Juárez Mexico 27°37N 100°44W 318 B4
Juárez, Sierra de Mexico 32°0N 116°0W 318 A1
Juárez Int. ✈ (MEX) Mexico 19°25N 99°5W 128 B2
Juatinga, Pta. da Brazil 23°17S 44°30W 333 F3
Juàzeiro Brazil 9°30S 40°30W 332 C3
Juàzeiro do Norte Brazil 7°10S 39°18W 332 C4
Juazohn Liberia 5°22N 8°50W 262 D3
Juba South Sudan 4°50N 31°35E 257 G3
Juba → Somali Rep. 1°30N 42°35E 267 D5
Jubany Antarctica 62°30S 58°0W 151 C18
Jubayl Lebanon 34°5N 35°39E 250 D6
Jubbada Dhexe □ Somali Rep. 2°0N 41°30E 267 D5
Jubbada Hoose □ Somali Rep. 0°0 42°0E 267 E5
Jubbah Si. Arabia 28°2N 40°56E 246 D4
Jubbal India 31°5N 77°40E 242 D7
Jubbulpore = Jabalpur India 23°9N 79°58E 243 H8
Jübek Germany 54°33N 9°22E 178 A5
Jubga Russia 44°19N 38°48E 191 H4
Jubilee L. Australia 29°0S 126°50E 279 E4
Juby, C. Morocco 28°0N 12°59W 260 C2
Júcar = Xúquer → Spain 39°5N 0°10W 197 F4
Júcaro Cuba 21°37N 78°51W 320 B4
Juchitán de Zaragoza Mexico 16°26N 95°1W 319 D5
Judaberg Norway 59°10N 5°51E 164 E2
Judea = Har Yehuda Israel 31°35N 34°57E 251 G5
Judeira West Bank 31°52N 35°12E 123 A2
Judenburg Austria 47°12N 14°38E 180 D7
Judith → U.S.A. 47°44N 109°39W 304 C9
Judith, Pt. U.S.A. 41°22N 71°29W 313 E13
Judith Gap U.S.A. 46°41N 109°45W 304 C9
Juelsminde Denmark 55°43N 10°1E 163 J4
Jufari → Brazil 1°13S 62°0W 329 D5

Juhdum West Bank 31°42N 35°15E 123 B2
Juhu India 19°5N 73°0E 130 A2
Juifang Taiwan 25°7N 121°48E 225 A3
Juigalpa Nic. 12°6N 85°26W 320 D2
Juillac France 45°20N 1°19E 174 C5
Juist Germany 53°40N 6°59E 178 B2
Juisui Taiwan 23°30N 121°22E 225 C3
Juiz de Fora Brazil 21°43S 43°19W 333 F3
Jūjā Iran 35°45N 139°43E 140 A3
Jujuy □ Argentina 23°20S 65°40W 332 A2
Jukao = Rugao China 32°23N 120°31E 229 A13
Jukskeirivier → S. Africa 26°55 28°6E 123 A2
Julesburg U.S.A. 40°59N 102°16W 304 F12
Juli Peru 16°10S 69°25W 330 D3
Julia Cr. → Australia 20°0S 141°11E 280 C3
Julia Creek Australia 20°39S 141°44E 280 C3
Juliaca Peru 15°25S 70°10W 330 D3
Julian U.S.A. 33°4N 116°38W 307 M10
Julian, L. Canada 54°25N 77°57W 298 B4
Julian Alps = Julijske Alpe
   Slovenia 46°15N 14°1E 199 B11
Juliana Top = Mandala, Puncak
   Indonesia 4°44S 140°20E 231 E10
Julianadorp Curaçao 12°9N 68°57W 322 g
Julianatop Suriname 3°40N 56°30W 329 C6
Julianehåb = Qaqortoq
   Greenland 60°43N 46°0W 154 E6
Julianów Poland 52°10N 21°9E 142 B2
Jülich Germany 50°55N 6°22E 178 E2
Juliette, L. U.S.A. 33°2N 83°50W 316 B6
Julijske Alpe Slovenia 46°15N 14°1E 199 B11
Julimes Mexico 28°25N 105°27W 318 B3
Jullundur India 31°20N 75°40E 242 D6
Julu Zimbabwe 37°15S 115°2E 226 F8
Jumbo Zimbabwe 16°45S 30°48E 269 C5
Jumbo Pk. U.S.A. 36°12N 114°11W 307 J12
Jumentos Cays Bahamas 23°0N 75°40W 320 B4
Jumilla Spain 38°28N 1°19W 197 G3
Jumla Nepal 29°15N 82°13E 243 E10
Jumna = Yamuna →
   India 25°30N 81°53E 243 G9
Jumunjin S. Korea 37°55N 128°54E 224 C4
Junagadh India 21°30N 70°30E 242 J4
Junan China 35°12N 118°53E 227 G10
Juncos Puerto Rico 18°14N 65°55W 321 b
Junction Tex., U.S.A. 30°29N 99°46W 314 F5
Junction Utah, U.S.A. 38°14N 112°13W 305 G7
Junction B. Australia 11°52S 133°55E 280 A1
Junction City Ga., U.S.A. 32°36N 84°28W 316 C5
Junction City Kans., U.S.A. 39°2N 96°50W 308 F5
Junction City Oreg., U.S.A.
   44°13N 123°12W 304 D2
Junction Pt. Australia 11°45S 133°50E 280 A1
Jundah Australia 24°46S 143°2E 280 C3
Jundiaí Brazil 24°30S 47°0W 335 A6
Juneau U.S.A. 58°18N 134°25W 296 B2
Junee Australia 34°53S 147°35E 283 C7
Jung S. Korea 37°33N 126°59E 137 B1
Jungar Qi China 39°49N 110°57E 226 E6
Jungbunzlau = Mladá Boleslav
   Czech Rep. 50°27N 14°53E 180 A7
Jungfernheide, Volkspark
   Germany 52°32N 13°18E 115 A2
Jungfernsee Germany 52°25N 13°6E 115 B1
Jungfrau Switz. 46°32N 7°58E 179 J3
Junggar Pendi China 44°30N 86°0E 217 D11
Junghwa N. Korea 37°35N 127°3E 137 B2
Jungkat Indonesia 0°4N 109°13E 235 B3
Jungnang S. Korea 37°36N 127°7E 137 B2
Jungnangcheon →
   S. Korea 37°32N 126°55E 137 B1
Jungdalshytta = Iungdalshytta
   Norway 60°49N 7°55E 164 D4
Jungshahi Pakistan 24°52N 67°44E 242 G2
Juniata → U.S.A. 40°24N 77°1W 312 F7
Junín Argentina 34°33S 60°57W 334 C3
Junín Peru 11°12S 76°0W 330 C2
Junín □ Peru 11°30S 75°0W 330 C2
Junín, L. de Peru 11°25S 76°0W 330 C2
Junín de los Andes
   Argentina 39°45S 71°0W 336 A2
Juniper Green U.K. 55°54N 3°16W 121 B2
Jūniyah Lebanon 33°59N 35°38E 250 E6
Junk B. China 22°17N 114°15E 122 B2
Junlian China 28°8N 104°29E 228 C5
Junnar India 19°12N 73°58E 244 E1
Juno Beach U.S.A. 26°52N 80°3W 317 J9
Juntas Chile 28°24S 69°58W 334 B2
Juntura U.S.A. 43°45N 118°5W 304 E4
Juparanã, L. Brazil 19°16S 40°8W 333 E3
Jupiter U.S.A. 26°57N 80°6W 317 J9
Juquiá Brazil 24°19S 47°38W 335 B6
Jur, Nahr el → South Sudan 8°45N 29°15E 257 F2
Jura = Jura, Mts. du Europe 46°40N 6°5E 173 F13
Jura = Schwäbische Alb
   Germany 48°20N 9°30E 179 G5
Jura U.K. 56°0N 5°50W 167 F3
Jura □ France 46°47N 5°45E 173 F12
Jura □ Switz. 47°20N 7°20E 179 H3
Jura, Mts. du Europe 46°40N 6°5E 173 F13
Jura, Sd. of U.K. 55°57N 5°45W 167 F3
Jūra → Lithuania 55°3N 22°9E 184 C9
Jurado Colombia 7°7N 77°46W 328 B2
Jurbarkas Lithuania 55°4N 22°46E 184 C9
Jurien Bay Australia 30°18S 115°2E 279 F2
Jūrmala Latvia 56°58N 23°34E 184 B10
Jurong Jiangsu, China 31°57N 119°9E 229 B12
Jurong Singapore 1°19N 103°42E 138 B2
Jurong, Selat Singapore 1°17N 103°41E 138 B2
Jurong Industrial Estate
   Singapore 1°19N 103°40E 138 B1
Juruá Brazil 3°27S 66°3W 328 D4
Juruá → Brazil 2°37S 65°44W 328 D4
Juruena Brazil 13°0S 58°10W 331 C6
Juruena → Brazil 7°20S 58°3W 331 B6
Jurujuba, Enseada de
   Brazil 22°54S 43°6W 135 B2
Juruti Brazil 2°9S 56°4W 329 D6
Jūsō Japan 34°42N 135°27E 133 A1
Jussey France 47°50N 5°55E 173 E12
Justice U.S.A. 41°44N 87°49W 119 C2
Justicia Brazil 127 a3
Justo Daract Argentina 33°52S 65°12W 334 C2
Jutaí Amazonas, Brazil 2°43S 66°57W 328 D4
Jutaí Amazonas, Brazil 5°11S 68°54W 328 D4
Jutaí → Brazil 2°43S 66°57W 328 D4
Jüterbog Germany 51°59N 13°5E 178 D9
Juticalpa Honduras 14°40N 86°12W 320 D2
Jutland = Jylland Denmark 56°25N 9°30E 163 H3
Juuka Finland 63°13N 29°17E 160 E23
Juventud, I. de la Cuba 21°40N 82°40W 320 B3
Juvigny-sous-Andaine
   France 48°32N 0°30W 172 D6
Juwangsan △ S. Korea 36°20N 129°15E 224 D4
Jūy Zar Iran 33°50N 46°18E 213 F12
Juye China 35°22N 116°5E 226 G9
Juzennecourt France 48°10N 4°58E 173 D11
Jvari Georgia 42°42N 42°4E 191 J8
Jwalahri India 28°40N 77°6E 120 B1
Jyderup Denmark 55°40N 11°26E 163 J5
Jylland Denmark 56°25N 9°30E 163 H3
Jyväskylä Finland 62°14N 25°50E 160 E21

K

K2 Pakistan 35°58N 76°32E 243 B7
Ka → Nigeria 11°40N 4°0E 263 C5
Kaa-Iya □ Bolivia 18°35S 61°40W 331 D5
Ka'a'awa U.S.A. 21°33N 157°51W 302 J14
Kaakha = Kaka
   Turkmenistan 37°21N 59°36E 247 B8
Ka'ala U.S.A. 21°31N 158°9W 302 J13
Kaala-Gomén N. Cal. 20°40S 164°25E 288 d
Ka'alu'alu B. U.S.A. 18°58N 155°37W 302 E6
Kaap Plateau S. Africa 28°30S 24°0E 270 C3
Kaapkruis Namibia 21°55S 13°57E 270 B1
Kaapstad = Cape Town
   S. Africa 33°55S 18°22E 118 A1
Kaashidhoo Atoll Maldives 4°58N 73°28E 272 d
Kaashidhoo Channel
   Maldives 5°1N 73°28E 272 d
Kaataon, Mt. Phil. 8°10N 124°52E 233 G5
Kaba Guinea 10°9N 11°40W 262 C2
Kabacan Phil. 7°8N 124°49E 233 H5
Kabachishche = Zelenodolsk
   Russia 55°55N 48°30E 190 C9
Kabaena Indonesia 5°15S 122°0E 233 F6
Kabala S. Leone 9°38N 11°37W 262 D2
Kabale Uganda 1°15S 30°0E 268 C3
Kabalo Dem. Rep. of the Congo 6°0S 27°0E 265 D5
Kabambare
   Dem. Rep. of the Congo 4°41S 27°39E 268 C2
Kabango
   Dem. Rep. of the Congo 8°35S 28°30E 269 D2
Kabanjahe Indonesia 3°6N 98°30E 234 B1
Kabara Fiji 18°59S 178°56W 287 B3
Kabara Mali 16°40N 2°50W 262 B4
Kabardinka Russia 44°40N 37°57E 189 K10
Kabardino-Balkaria □
   Russia 43°30N 43°30E 191 J6
Kabarega Falls = Murchison Falls
   Uganda 2°15N 31°30E 268 B3
Kabarnet Kenya 0°30N 35°45E 264 D4
Kabasalan Phil. 7°47N 122°44E 233 H4
Kabat Indonesia 8°16S 114°19E 231 J17
Kabaty Poland 52°8N 21°4E 142 C2
Kabba Nigeria 7°50N 6°3E 263 D6
Kabbani → India 12°13N 76°54E 245 H3
Kabi Niger 13°30N 12°35E 263 C7
Kabin Buri Thailand 13°57N 101°43E 236 F3
Kabinakagami L. Canada 48°54N 84°25W 298 C3
Kabinda
   Dem. Rep. of the Congo 6°10S 24°29E 265 D4
Kabkabīyah Sudan 13°50N 24°0E 259 F4
Kablungu, C. Papua N. G. 6°20S 150°1E 286 D6
Kabna Sudan 19°6N 32°40E 258 D3
Kabo C.A.R. 7°35N 18°38E 264 A3
Kabompo Zambia 13°36S 24°14E 265 E4
Kabompo → Zambia 14°11S 23°11E 265 E4
Kabondo
   Dem. Rep. of the Congo 8°58S 25°40E 265 D5
Kabongo
   Dem. Rep. of the Congo 7°22S 25°33E 265 D5
Kabou Guinea 10°48N 14°57W 262 C2
Kabou Togo 9°28N 0°55E 263 D5
Kaboudia, Rass Tunisia 35°13N 11°10E 261 A8
Kabr Sudan 10°54N 26°50E 257 E2
Kabrît, G. el Egypt 29°42N 33°16E 251 F2
Kabrousse Senegal 12°25N 16°45W 262 C1
Kabubu
   Dem. Rep. of the Congo 9°42S 24°40E 265 D4
Kabūd Gonbad Iran 37°5N 59°45E 247 B8
Kabudar Ahang Iran 35°11N 48°43E 213 E13
Kabugao Phil. 18°2N 121°11E 232 B3
Kābul Afghan. 34°28N 69°11E 242 B3
Kābul □ Afghan. 34°28N 69°11E 242 B3
Kābul → Pakistan 33°55N 72°14E 242 C5
Kabuli Papua N. G. 2°7S 146°40E 286 B6
Kabunga
   Dem. Rep. of the Congo 1°38S 28°3E 268 C2
Kaburuang Indonesia 3°50N 126°30E 231 D7
Kabushiya Sudan 16°54N 33°41E 257 D3
Kabwanga
   Dem. Rep. of the Congo 7°2S 22°56E 268 C4
Kabwe Zambia 14°30S 28°29E 269 E2
Kačanik Kosovo 42°13N 21°12E 202 D5
Kačerginė Lithuania 54°56N 23°42E 184 D10
Kachar Kazakhstan 52°23N 62°55E 216 B6
Kachchh, Gulf of India 22°50N 69°15E 242 H3
Kachchh, Rann of India 24°0N 70°0E 242 H4
Kachchhidhana India 21°44N 78°46E 243 J8
Kachebera Zambia 13°50S 32°50E 269 E3
Kachia Nigeria 9°50N 7°55E 263 C6
Kachikau Botswana 18°8S 24°26E 270 A3
Kachira, L. Uganda 0°40S 31°7E 268 C3
Kachīry Kazakhstan 53°10N 75°50E 217 B9
Kachisi Ethiopia 9°40N 37°50E 257 F4
Kaçkar Turkey 40°45N 41°10E 213 B9
Kada Chad 19°20N 19°39E 259 F3
Kadaingti Burma 17°37N 97°32E 241 G6
Kadaiyanallur India 9°3N 77°22E 245 K3
Kadan Czech Rep. 50°23N 13°1E 180 A6
Kadan Kyun Burma 12°30N 98°20E 236 F2
Kadanai → Afghan. 31°22N 65°45E 242 D1
Kadarkút Hungary 46°13N 17°39E 182 D2
Kadavu Fiji 19°0S 178°17E 287 B2
Kadavu Passage Fiji 18°45S 178°0E 287 B2
Kade Ghana 6°7N 0°56W 263 D4
Kadei → C.A.R. 3°31N 16°3E 264 B3
Kademlija = Triglav
   Slovenia 46°21N 13°50E 199 B10
Kadena Japan 26°21N 127°45E 288 a
Kadhimain = Al Kāzimīyah
   Iraq 33°22N 44°18E 213 F11
Kadi India 23°18N 72°23E 242 H5
Kadiak I. = Kodiak I.
   U.S.A. 57°30N 152°45W 303 H9
Kadiana Mali 10°45N 6°23W 262 C3
Kadıköy Turkey 40°59N 29°1E 122 C2
Kadina Australia 33°55S 137°43E 282 B2
Kadınhanı Turkey 38°14N 32°13E 212 C5
Kadiolo Mali 10°35N 7°41W 262 C3
Kadipur India 26°10N 82°23E 243 F10
Kadiri India 14°12N 78°13E 245 G4
Kadirli Turkey 37°23N 36°5E 212 D7
Kadiyevka = Stakhanov
   Ukraine 48°35N 38°40E 189 H10
Kadmat I. India 11°14N 72°47E 245 H1
Kadodo Sudan 11°14N 29°31E 257 F2
Kadoka U.S.A. 43°50N 101°31W 308 D3
Kadoma Zimbabwe 18°20S 29°52E 269 C5
Kādūgli Sudan 11°0N 29°45E 257 F2
Kaduna Nigeria 10°30N 7°21E 263 C6
Kaduna □ Nigeria 11°0N 7°30E 263 C6
Kaduna → Nigeria 8°45N 5°48E 263 D6
Kadur India 13°34N 76°1E 245 H3

Kaduy Russia 59°12N 37°9E 188 C9
Kaédi Mauritania 16°9N 13°28W 262 B2
Kaélé Cameroon 10°7N 14°27E 259 F2
Ka'ena U.S.A. 21°34N 158°14W 302 J12
Ka'ena Pt. U.S.A. 21°35N 158°17W 302 J12
Kaeng Khoi Thailand 14°35N 101°0E 236 E3
Kaeng Krachan △
   Thailand 12°57N 99°23E 236 F2
Kaeng Krung △ Thailand 9°30N 98°50E 237 H2
Kaeng Tana △ Thailand 15°25N 105°32E 236 E5
Kaeo N.Z. 35°6S 173°49E 284 B2
Kaesŏng N. Korea 37°58N 126°35E 224 D3
Kaesŏng □ N. Korea 38°0N 126°37E 224 D3
Kāf Si. Arabia 31°25N 37°29E 246 D3
Kafakumba
   Dem. Rep. of the Congo 9°38S 23°46E 265 D4
Kafan = Kapan Armenia 39°18N 46°27E 213 C12
Kafanchan Nigeria 9°40N 8°20E 263 D6
Kafareti Nigeria 10°25N 11°12E 263 C7
Kaffrine Senegal 14°8N 15°36W 262 C1
Kafia Kingi Sudan 9°20N 24°25E 264 A4
Kafin Nigeria 9°30N 7°4E 263 D6
Kafin Madaki Nigeria 10°41N 9°46E 263 C6
Kafinda Zambia 12°32S 30°20E 269 E3
Kafr 'Aqab West Bank 31°52N 35°13E 123 A2
Kafr el Battikh Egypt 31°25N 31°44E 256 H7
Kafr el Dauwâr Egypt 31°8N 30°8E 256 H7
Kafr el Sheikh Egypt 31°15N 30°50E 251 G1
Kafr el Sheikh □ Egypt 31°15N 30°55E 251 G1
Kafr el Zaiyât Egypt 30°49N 30°48E 256 H7
Kafue Zambia 15°46S 28°9E 269 F2
Kafue → Zambia 15°12S 25°38E 269 F2
Kafue Flats Zambia 15°40S 27°25E 269 F2
Kafulwe Zambia 9°0S 29°1E 269 D2
Kafumba
   Dem. Rep. of the Congo 5°23S 18°55E 265 D3
Kaga Japan 36°16N 136°15E 223 A8
Kaga Bandoro C.A.R. 7°0N 19°10E 264 B3
Kagan Uzbekistan 39°43N 64°33E 216 F7
Kagawong Canada 45°54N 82°15E 312 A3
Kagera □ Tanzania 2°0S 31°30E 268 C3
Kagera → Uganda 0°57S 31°47E 268 C3
Kaganovich = Tovarkovsky
   Russia 53°40N 38°14E 188 F10
Kagarko Nigeria 9°28N 7°36E 263 D6
Kagawa □ Japan 34°15N 134°0E 222 C6
Kağıthane Turkey 41°4N 28°58E 122 B1
Kağıthane → Turkey 41°9N 28°56E 122 B1
Kağızman Turkey 40°5N 43°10E 213 B10
Kagologolo Indonesia 1°9S 98°37E 234 C1
Kagopal Chad 8°16N 16°23E 259 G3
Kagoro Nigeria 9°36N 8°23E 263 D6
Kagoshima Japan 31°35N 130°33E 222 F2
Kagoshima □ Japan 31°30N 130°30E 222 F2
Kagoshima-Wan Japan 31°25N 130°40E 222 F2
Kagran Austria 48°14N 16°26E 142 A2
Kagua Papua N. G. 6°26S 143°48E 286 D2
Kagul = Cahul Moldova 45°50N 28°15E 183 E13
Kahak Iran 36°6N 49°46E 247 B6
Kahala U.S.A. 21°16N 157°47W 302 K14
Kahalu'u U.S.A. 21°28N 157°50W 302 K14
Kahama Tanzania 4°8S 32°30E 268 C3
Kahan Pakistan 29°18N 68°54E 242 E3
Kahang Malaysia 2°12N 103°32E 237 L4
Kahayan → Indonesia 3°40S 114°0E 235 E4
Kahe Tanzania 3°30S 37°25E 268 C4
Kahemba
   Dem. Rep. of the Congo 7°18S 18°55E 265 D3
Kaherekoau Mts. N.Z. 45°45S 167°15E 285 F2
Kahil, Djebel bou Algeria 34°26N 4°0E 261 B5
Kahnawake Canada 45°24N 73°40W 130 B1
Kahnūj Iran 27°55N 57°40E 247 E8
Kahoka U.S.A. 40°25N 91°44W 312 C5
Kaho'olawe U.S.A. 20°33N 156°37W 302 C5
Kahouanne Guadeloupe 16°15N 61°12W 322 e
Kahouanne, Îlet à
   Guadeloupe 16°15N 61°12W 322 e
Kahramanmaraş Turkey 37°37N 36°53E 212 D7
Kahramanmaraş □
   Turkey 37°35N 36°33E 212 D7
Kâhta Turkey 37°46N 38°36E 213 D8
Kahuku U.S.A. 21°41N 157°57W 302 J14
Kahuku Pt. U.S.A. 21°43N 157°59W 302 J14
Kahul, Ozero Ukraine 45°24N 28°24E 183 E13
Kahului U.S.A. 20°54N 156°28W 302 C5
Kahurangi △ N.Z. 41°10S 172°32E 285 B7
Kahurangi Pt. N.Z. 40°50S 172°10E 285 A7
Kahuta Pakistan 33°35N 73°24E 242 C5
Kahuzi-Biega △
   Dem. Rep. of the Congo 1°50S 27°55E 268 C2
Kai, Kepulauan Indonesia 5°55S 132°45E 231 F8
Kai Besar Indonesia 5°35S 133°0E 231 F8
Kai Is. = Kai, Kepulauan
   Indonesia 5°55S 132°45E 231 F8
Kai Kecil Indonesia 5°45S 132°40E 231 F8
Kai Xian China 31°11N 108°21E 228 B7
Kaiama Nigeria 9°36N 4°1E 263 D5
Kaiapit Papua N. G. 6°18S 146°18E 286 D4
Kaiapoi N.Z. 43°24S 172°40E 285 D7
Kaidu → China 41°46N 86°31E 216 E9
Kaieteur Falls Guyana 5°1N 59°10W 329 B6
Kaifeng China 34°48N 114°21E 228 B8
Kaihua China 29°12N 118°20E 229 C12
Kaijiang China 31°7N 107°58E 228 B6
Kaikohe N.Z. 35°25S 173°49E 284 B2
Kaikoura N.Z. 42°25S 173°43E 285 C8
Kaikoura Pen. N.Z. 42°25S 173°43E 285 C8
Kailahun S. Leone 8°18N 10°39W 262 D2

Kaira India 22°45N 72°50E 242 H5
Kairana India 29°24N 77°15E 242 E7
Kairiru I. Papua N. G. 3°21S 143°34E 286 B2
Kairouan Tunisia 35°45N 10°5E 258 A2
Kairouan □ Tunisia 35°30N 9°46E 261 A8
Kairuku Papua N. G. 8°51S 146°35E 286 E4
Kaiser Wilhelm Kanal = Nord-
   Ostsee-Kanal Germany 54°12N 9°32E 178 A5
Kaiser Wilhelm Kirche Berlin, Germany 115 b2
Kaiser-Wilhelmsland = Papua □
   Indonesia 4°0S 137°0E 231 E9
Kaiserebersdorf Austria 48°9N 16°26E 142 B2
Kaiserslautern Germany 49°26N 7°45E 179 F3
Kaiserstuhl Germany 48°4N 7°40E 179 G3
Kaita Japan 34°22N 132°32E 222 C4
Kaitaia N.Z. 35°8S 173°17E 284 B2
Kaitangata N.Z. 46°17S 169°51E 285 G4
Kaithal India 29°48N 76°26E 242 E7
Kaitu → Pakistan 33°10N 70°30E 242 C4
Kaivoksela Finland 60°15N 24°53E 121 B2
Kaiwi Channel U.S.A. 21°15N 157°30W 302 K14
Kaiyang China 27°4N 106°59E 228 D6
Kaiyuan Liaoning, China 42°28N 124°1E 224 A2
Kaiyuan Yunnan, China 23°40N 103°12E 228 F4
Kaiyuh Mts. U.S.A. 64°30N 158°0W 303 D8
Kajaani Finland 64°17N 27°46E 160 D22
Kajabbi Australia 20°0S 140°1E 280 B3
Kajakī Afghan. 32°18N 65°5E 240 B2
Kajana = Kajaani
   Finland 64°17N 27°46E 160 D22
Kajang Malaysia 2°59N 101°48E 237 L3
Kajaran Armenia 39°10N 46°7E 213 C12
Kajiado Kenya 1°53S 36°48E 268 C4
Kajo Kaji South Sudan 3°58N 31°40E 257 G3
Kajok South Sudan 8°19N 28°0E 257 F2
Kajuru Nigeria 10°15N 7°34E 263 C6
Kaka South Sudan 10°38N 32°10E 257 E3
Kaka Turkmenistan 37°21N 59°36E 247 B8
Kakabeka Falls Canada 48°24N 89°37W 298 C2
Kakadu △ Australia 12°0S 132°3E 278 B5
Kakamas S. Africa 28°45S 20°33E 270 C3
Kakamega Kenya 0°20N 34°46E 268 B3
Kakamigahara Japan 35°28N 136°48E 223 A8
Kakana India 9°7N 92°48E 245 K11
Kakanj Bos.-H. 44°4N 18°4E 182 F3
Kakanui Mts. N.Z. 45°10S 170°30E 285 F5
Kakata Liberia 6°35N 10°20W 262 D2
Kakdwip India 21°53N 88°11E 243 J13
Kake Japan 34°36N 132°19E 222 C4
Kake U.S.A. 56°59N 133°57W 296 B2
Kakegawa Japan 34°45N 138°1E 223 C10
Kakeroma-Jima Japan 28°8N 129°14E 221 K4
Kakhib Russia 42°28N 46°34E 191 J8
Kakhk Iran 34°9N 58°38E 247 C8
Kakhonak U.S.A. 59°26N 154°51W 303 G9
Kakhovka Ukraine 46°45N 33°30E 189 J7
Kakhovske Vdskh. Ukraine 47°5N 34°0E 189 J7
Kakinada India 16°57N 82°11E 244 F6
Kakisa Canada 60°56N 117°25W 296 A5
Kakisa → Canada 61°3N 118°10W 296 A5
Kakisa L. Canada 60°56N 117°43W 296 A5
Kakogawa Japan 34°46N 134°51E 222 C6
Kaktovik U.S.A. 70°8N 143°38W 303 A12
Kakum △ Ghana 5°24N 1°20W 263 D4
Kakuma Kenya 3°43N 34°52E 268 B3
Kakwa → Canada 54°37N 118°28W 296 C5
Kala Nigeria 12°2N 14°40E 263 C7
Kala Oya → Sri Lanka 8°20N 79°45E 245 K4
Kala-Kebira Tunisia 35°59N 10°38E 261 A8
Kalaallit Nunaat = Greenland ☒
   N. Amer. 66°0N 45°0W 154 D6
Kalabagh Pakistan 33°0N 71°28E 242 C4
Kalabahi Indonesia 8°13S 124°31E 231 F6
Kalabak → Radomir
   Bulgaria 42°37N 22°59E 202 D6
Kalabakan Malaysia 4°25N 117°29E 235 B5
Kalabana Mali 14°10N 8°35W 262 C3
Kalabo Zambia 14°58S 22°40E 265 E4
Kalach Russia 50°22N 41°0E 190 E5
Kalach na Donu Russia 48°43N 43°32E 191 F6
Kalachinsk Russia 55°3N 74°20E 216 C7
Kaladan → Burma 20°20N 93°5E 241 E4
Kaladar Canada 44°37N 77°5W 312 B7
Kalae U.S.A. 18°55N 155°41W 302 E6
Kalahari Africa 24°0S 21°30E 270 B3
Kalahari Gemsbok △
   S. Africa 25°30S 20°30E 270 C3
Kalahoo U.S.A. 20°54N 156°32W 302 C5
Kalaikhum Tajikistan 38°28N 70°46E 218 F8
Kalaikunda India 22°21N 87°14E 243 H12
Kalajoki Finland 64°12N 24°10E 160 D21
Kalakamati Botswana 20°40S 27°25E 271 B4
Kalakan Russia 55°15N 116°45E 215 D12
Kalakol Kenya 3°33N 35°54E 266 D4
Kal'ak'unlun Shank'ou =
   Karakoram Pass Asia 35°33N 77°50E 243 B7
Kalam India 35°34N 72°30E 243 B5
Kalama
   Dem. Rep. of the Congo 2°52S 28°35E 268 C2
Kalama Wash., U.S.A. 46°1N 122°51W 306 E4
Kalámai = Kalamata Greece 37°3N 22°10E 205 D9
Kalamaloué △ Cameroon 12°11N 14°55E 263 C7
Kalamansig Phil. 6°33N 124°3E 233 H5
Kalamaria Greece 40°35N 22°55E 205 C10
Kalamata Greece 37°3N 22°10E 205 D9
Kalamazoo U.S.A. 42°17N 85°35W 311 B11
Kalamazoo → U.S.A. 42°40N 86°10W 311 B10
Kalamb India 18°3N 74°48E 244 E2
Kalambaka Greece 39°42N 21°39E 205 B9
Kalambo Falls Tanzania 8°37S 31°35E 269 D3
Kalamnuri India 19°40N 77°20E 244 E3
Kalamos Attiki, Greece 38°17N 23°52E 204 C5
Kalamos Lefkada, Greece 38°37N 20°55E 204 C3
Kalan Turkey 39°7N 39°32E 213 C8
Kalangadoo Australia 37°34S 140°41E 282 D4
Kalankalan Guinea 10°7N 9°54W 262 C3
Kalannie Australia 30°22S 117°5E 279 F2
Kalāntarī Iran 32°10N 54°8E 247 C7
Kalao Indonesia 7°21S 121°0E 231 F6
Kalaotoa Indonesia 7°20S 121°50E 231 F6
Kálarne Sweden 62°59N 16°8E 162 B10
Kalpitiya Sri Lanka 8°14N 79°47E 245 K4
Kalpi India 26°8N 79°47E 243 F8
Kalputhi I. India 10°49N 72°11E 245 J1
Kalrayan Hills India 11°45N 78°40E 245 J4
Kalsubai India 19°35N 73°45E 244 E1
Kaltag U.S.A. 64°20N 158°43W 303 D8
Kaltern = Caldaro Italy 46°25N 11°13E 198 E7
Kaltungo Nigeria 9°48N 11°19E 263 D7
Kalu → Pakistan 25°5N 67°39E 242 G2
Kaluga Russia 54°35N 36°10E 188 E9
Kalulushi Zambia 12°50S 28°3E 269 E2
Kalum → Slovenia 46°14N 14°37E 199 B11
Kalundborg Denmark 55°41N 11°5E 163 J5
Kalush Ukraine 49°3N 24°23E 177 D13

Kaluszyn Poland 52°13N 21°52E 185 F8
Kalutara Sri Lanka 6°35N 80°0E 245 L4
Kalvåg Norway 61°46N 4°51E 164 C1
Kalvarija Lithuania 54°24N 23°14E 184 D10
Kalvboda Fælled Denmark 55°35N 12°33E 118 B3
Kalveboderne Denmark 55°37N 12°31E 118 B3
Kalwakurti India 16°41N 78°30E 244 F4
Kalya Russia 60°15N 59°59E 186 B10
Kalyan Maharashtra, India 20°30N 74°3E 244 D2
Kalyan Maharashtra, India 19°15N 73°9E 244 E1
Kalyandrug India 14°33N 77°36E 245 G3
Kalyani India 17°52N 76°57E 244 F3
Kalyansingapuram India 19°7N 83°9E 244 E6
Kalyazin Russia 57°15N 37°55E 188 D9
Kam Albania 42°17N 20°18E 202 D4
Kam Burma 19°1N 95°4E 241 F5
Kama Dem. Rep. of the Congo 3°30S 27°6E 268 C2
Kama → Russia 55°45N 52°0E 186 D9
Kama Iwa Japan 24°47N 141°17E 288 b
Kamachumo Tanzania 3°1S 31°37E 268 C3
Kamae Japan 32°48N 131°56E 222 D3
Kamaing Burma 25°26N 96°35E 241 C6
Kamaishi Japan 39°16N 141°53E 222 E7
Kamakou U.S.A. 21°7N 156°52W 302 B5
Kamakura Japan 35°19N 139°33E 223 B11
Kamalapuram India 14°35N 78°39E 245 G4
Kamalété Gabon 0°43S 11°49E 264 C2
Kamalia Pakistan 30°44N 72°42E 242 D5
Kaman Turkey 39°22N 33°44E 212 C5
Kamana
   Dem. Rep. of the Congo 5°59S 24°58E 265 D4
Kamananui → U.S.A. 21°38N 158°4W 302 J13
Kamanjab Namibia 19°35S 14°51E 270 A2
Kamapanda Zambia 12°5S 24°0E 269 E1
Kamara Mali 14°38N 9°23W 262 C3
Kamarān Yemen 15°21N 42°35E 248 D3
Kamareddi India 18°19N 78°21E 244 E4
Kamarhati India 22°40N 88°23E 124 A2
Kamativi Zimbabwe 18°20S 27°6E 270 A4
Kamba Nigeria 11°50N 3°45E 263 C5
Kambalda West Australia 31°10S 121°37E 279 F3
Kambam India 9°45N 77°16E 245 K3
Kambangan, Nusa
   Indonesia 7°40S 108°10E 235 D3
Kambar Pakistan 27°37N 68°1E 242 F3
Kambarka Russia 56°15N 54°11E 186 C9
Kambia S. Leone 9°3N 12°53W 262 D2
Kambolé Togo 8°43N 1°9E 263 D5
Kambolé Zambia 8°47S 30°48E 269 D3
Kambos Cyprus 35°2N 32°44E 207 E8
Kambove
   Dem. Rep. of the Congo 10°51S 26°33E 269 E2
Kamchatka, Poluostrov
   Russia 57°0N 160°0E 215 D17
Kamchatka Pen. = Kamchatka,
   Poluostrov Russia 57°0N 160°0E 215 D17
Kamchiya → Bulgaria 43°4N 27°44E 203 C11
Kame Ruins Zimbabwe 20°7S 28°25E 270 B4
Kameari Japan 35°45N 139°50E 140 A4
Kameda-Hantō Japan 41°50N 141°0E 222 D10
Kameido Japan 35°42N 139°50E 140 A4
Kamen Russia 53°50N 81°30E 217 B10
Kamen-Rybolov Russia 44°46N 132°2E 220 B5
Kamende
   Dem. Rep. of the Congo 6°26S 24°35E 265 D4
Kamenica Serbia 43°27N 22°27E 202 C6
Kamenice nad Lipou
   Czech Rep. 49°18N 15°2E 180 B8
Kamenjak, Rt Croatia 44°47N 13°55E 199 D10
Kamenka = Kamyanka
   Ukraine 49°3N 32°6E 189 H7
Kamenka Arkhangelsk,
   Russia 65°58N 44°0E 186 A7
Kamenka Penza, Russia 53°10N 44°5E 190 D6
Kamenka Voronezh,
   Russia 50°47N 39°20E 189 G10
Kamenka Bugskaya = Kamyanka-
   Buzka Ukraine 50°8N 24°16E 177 C13
Kamenka Dneprovskaya =
   Kamyanka-Dniprovska
   Ukraine 47°29N 34°28E 189 J8
Kamenka-Shevchenkovskaya =
   Kamyanka-Buzka
   Ukraine 50°8N 24°16E 177 C13
Kamennomostskiy Russia 44°18N 40°13E 191 H5
Kameno Bulgaria 42°34N 27°18E 203 D11
Kamenolomni Russia 47°40N 40°14E 191 G5
Kamensk-Shakhtinskiy
   Russia 48°23N 40°20E 191 F5
Kamensk Uralskiy Russia 56°25N 62°2E 214 D7
Kamenskaya = Kamensk-
   Shakhtinskiy Russia 48°23N 40°20E 191 F5
Kamenskiy Russia 50°48N 45°25E 190 E7
Kamenskoye = Dniprodzerzhynsk
   Ukraine 48°30N 34°37E 189 H8
Kamenyak Bulgaria 43°24N 26°57E 203 C10
Kamenz Germany 51°15N 14°5E 178 D10
Kameoka Japan 35°0N 135°35E 223 C7
Kameyama Japan 34°51N 136°27E 223 C8
Kami-Itabashi Japan 35°46N 139°42E 140 A3
Kami-Jima Japan 34°25N 133°20E 222 C5
Kami-Koshiki-Jima
   Japan 31°50N 129°52E 222 F1
Kamiagata Japan 34°35N 129°29E 222 C1
Kamiah U.S.A. 46°14N 116°2W 304 C5
Kamień Krajeński Poland 53°32N 17°32E 185 E4
Kamień Pomorski Poland 53°57N 14°43E 184 E1
Kamienna → Poland 51°6N 21°47E 185 G8
Kamienna Góra Poland 50°47N 16°2E 185 H3
Kamieńsk Poland 51°12N 19°29E 185 G6
Kamilukuak L. Canada 62°22N 101°40W 297 A8
Kamin-Kashyrskyy
   Ukraine 51°39N 24°56E 177 C13
Kamina
   Dem. Rep. of the Congo 8°45S 25°0E 265 D5
Kaminoyama Japan 38°9N 140°17E 222 E9
Kamiros Greece 36°20N 27°56E 205 D12
Kamishak Bay U.S.A. 59°35N 153°45W 303 G9
Kamisu Japan 35°53N 140°45E 223 B12
Kamitsushima Japan 34°41N 129°26E 222 C1
Kamituga
   Dem. Rep. of the Congo 3°2S 28°10E 268 C2
Kamla → India 25°35N 86°36E 243 G12
Kamloops Canada 50°40N 120°20W 296 C4
Kamloops Slovenia 46°14N 14°37E 199 B11
Kamo Armenia 40°21N 45°7E 191 K7
Kamo N.Z. 35°42S 174°20E 284 B3
Kamoa Mts. Guyana 1°30N 59°0W 329 C6

Kamogawa *Japan* 35°5N 140°5E 223 B12
Kamojima *Japan* 34°4N 134°21E 222 C6
Kamoke *Pakistan* 32°4N 74°4E 242 C6
Kamo'oloa *U.S.A.* 21°34N 158°7W 302 J13
Kamoshida *Japan* 35°33N 139°31E 140 B2
Kamp → *Austria* 48°1N 15°42E 180 C8
Kampala *Uganda* 0°20N 32°30E 268 B3
Kampar *Malaysia* 4°18N 101°9E 237 K3
Kampar → *Indonesia* 0°30N 103°8E 234 B2
Kampen *Neths.* 52°33N 5°53E 170 B5
Kamphaeng Phet
 Thailand 16°28N 99°30E 236 D2
Kampinoski △ *Poland* 52°21N 20°4ΟE 185 F7
Kampolombo, L. *Zambia* 11°37S 29°42E 269 E2
Kampong Cham *Cambodia* 12°0N 105°30E 237 G5
Kampong Chhnang
 Cambodia 12°20N 104°35E 237 F5
Kampong Landing
 Singapore 1°20N 103°55E 138 A3
Kampong Pengerang
 Malaysia 1°22N 104°7E 237 d
Kampong Punggai
 Malaysia 1°27N 104°18E 237 d
Kampong Saom
 Cambodia 10°38N 103°30E 237 G4
Kampong Saom, Chaak
 Cambodia 10°50N 103°32E 237 G4
Kampong Tanjong Langsat
 Malaysia 1°28N 104°1E 237 d
Kampong Tanjong Penjuru
 Singapore 1°18N 103°45E 138 B2
Kampong Telok Ramunia
 Malaysia 1°22N 104°15E 237 d
Kampot *Cambodia* 10°36N 104°11E 237 G4
Kampsville *U.S.A.* 39°18N 90°37W 310 E6
Kampti *Burkina Faso* 10°7N 3°25W 262 C4
Kampuchea = Cambodia ■
 Asia 12°15N 105°0E 236 F5
Kampung Air Putih
 Malaysia 4°15N 103°10E 237 K4
Kampung Bali *Indonesia* 6°11S 106°48E 122 B1
Kampung Jerangau
 Malaysia 4°50N 103°10E 237 K4
Kampung Raja *Malaysia* 5°45N 102°35E 237 K4
Kampungbaru = Tolitoli
 Indonesia 1°5N 120°50E 231 D6
Kamrau, Teluk *Indonesia* 3°30S 133°36E 231 E8
Kamsack *Canada* 51°34N 101°54W 297 C8
Kamsar *Guinea* 10°40N 14°36W 262 C2
Kamskoye Ustye *Russia* 55°10N 49°20E 190 C9
Kamskoye Vdkhr. *Russia* 58°41N 56°7E 186 C10
Kamsuuma *Somali Rep.* 0°15N 42°46E 267 D5
Kamthi *India* 21°9N 79°19E 244 D4
Kamuchawie L. *Canada* 56°18N 101°59W 297 B8
Kamuela *U.S.A.* 20°1N 155°41W 302 C6
Kamui-Misaki *Japan* 43°20N 140°21E 220 C10
Kamyanets-Podilskyy
 Ukraine 48°45N 26°40E 183 B11
Kamyanka *Ukraine* 49°3N 32°8E 189 B7
Kamyanka-Buzka
 Ukraine 50°8N 24°16E 177 C13
Kamyanka-Dniprovska
 Ukraine 47°29N 34°28E 189 J8
Kamyanets *Belarus* 52°23N 23°49E 185 F10
Kamyanyezi *Belarus* 52°23N 23°49E 185 F10
Kāmyārān *Iran* 34°47N 46°56E 213 E12
Kamyshin *Russia* 50°10N 45°24E 190 E7
Kamyzyak *Russia* 46°4N 48°10E 191 G9
Kan → = Gan Jiang →
 China 29°15N 116°0E 229 C11
Kan *Burma* 22°25N 94°5E 241 D5
Kan *South Sudan* 9°1N 31°47E 257 F3
Kanaaupscow → *Canada* 54°2N 76°30W 298 B4
Kanab *U.S.A.* 37°3N 112°32W 305 H7
Kanab Cr. → *U.S.A.* 36°24N 112°38W 305 H7
Kanacea *Lau Group, Fiji* 17°15S 179°6W 287 A3
Kanacea *Taveuni, Fiji* 16°59S 179°56E 287 C3
Kanaga I. *U.S.A.* 51°45N 177°22W 303 L3
Kanagawa □ *Japan* 35°20N 139°20E 223 B11
Kanagi *Japan* 40°54N 140°27E 220 D10
Kanairiktok → *Canada* 55°2N 60°18N 299 A7
Kanakanak *U.S.A.* 59°0N 158°32W 303 G8
Kanalia *Greece* 39°30N 22°53E 204 B4
Kanamori *Japan* 35°31N 139°27E 140 B1
Kananga
 Dem. Rep. of the Congo 5°55S 22°18E 265 D4
Kanangra-Boyd △
 Australia 33°57S 150°15E 283 B9
Kanash *Russia* 55°30N 47°32E 190 C8
Kanaskat *U.S.A.* 47°19N 121°54W 306 C5
Kanastraíon, Ákra = Paliouri, Ákra
 Greece 39°57N 23°45E 202 G7
Kanawha → *U.S.A.* 38°50N 82°9W 309 F12
Kanazawa *Japan* 36°30N 136°38E 223 A8
Kanbalu *Burma* 23°12N 95°31E 241 D5
Kanchanaburi *Thailand* 14°2N 99°31E 236 E2
Kanchenjunga *Nepal* 27°50N 88°10E 243 F13
Kanchipuram *India* 12°52N 79°45E 245 H4
Kanchow = Ganzhou
 China 25°51N 114°56E 229 E10
Kańczuga *Poland* 49°59N 22°25E 185 J9
Kanda *Tokyo, Japan* 140 a3
Kanda Kanda
 Dem. Rep. of the Congo 6°52S 23°48E 265 D4
Kandagach = Qandyaghash
 Kazakhstan 49°28N 57°25E 187 E10
Kandaghat *India* 30°59N 77°7E 242 D7
Kandahār *Kandahār,*
 Afghan. 31°32N 65°43E 240 C2
Kandahar *India* 18°52N 77°12E 244 E3
Kandahār □ *Afghan.* 31°0N 65°0E 240 C2
Kandala
 Dem. Rep. of the Congo 6°20S 19°40E 265 D3
Kandalaksha *Russia* 67°9N 32°30E 160 C25
Kandalakshskiy Zaliv
 Russia 66°0N 35°0E 186 A6
Kandang *Indonesia* 3°3N 97°19E 234 B1
Kandangan *Indonesia* 2°50S 115°20E 235 C5
Kandanos *Greece* 35°19N 23°44E 204 E6
Kandava *Latvia* 57°2N 22°46E 184 A9
Kandavu = Kadavu *Fiji* 19°0S 178°15E 287 B2
Kandavu Passage = Kadavu
 Passage *Fiji* 18°45S 178°0E 287 B2
Kandep *Papua N. G.* 5°54S 143°32E 286 C2
Kandhla *India* 29°18N 77°19E 242 E7
Kandi *Benin* 11°7N 2°55E 263 C5
Kandi *India* 23°58N 88°5E 243 H13
Kandiaro *Pakistan* 27°4N 68°13E 242 F3
Kandila *Arkadia, Greece* 37°46N 22°22E 204 D4
Kandila *Etoloakarnania,*
 Greece 38°42N 20°56E 207 B2
Kandıra *Turkey* 41°4N 29°13E 202 C12
Kandra *Turkey* 41°4N 30°9E 212 B4
Kandla *India* 23°0N 70°10E 242 H3
Kandor, O. → *Chad* 17°13N 20°52E 259 F4
Kandos *Australia* 32°45S 149°58E 283 B8
Kandreho *Madag.* 17°29S 46°6E 272 B2
Kandrian *Papua N. G.* 6°14S 149°37E 286 D5
Kandy *Sri Lanka* 7°18N 80°43E 245 L5
Kane *U.S.A.* 41°40N 78°49W 312 E6
Kane Basin *Greenland* 79°1N 70°0W 154 B4
Kaneilio Pt. *U.S.A.* 21°27N 158°12W 302 K13
Kanel *Senegal* 15°30N 13°18W 262 B2

Kanem □ *Chad* 15°0N 16°0E 259 F3
Kāne'ohe *U.S.A.* 21°25N 157°48W 302 K14
Kāne'ohe B. *U.S.A.* 21°30N 157°50W 302 K14
Kaneohe Marine Corps Air Station
 U.S.A. 21°27N 157°46W 302 K14
Kanevskaya *Russia* 46°3N 38°57E 191 G4
Kanfanar *Croatia* 45°7N 13°50E 199 C10
Kang *Botswana* 23°41S 22°50E 270 B3
Kangaamiut *Greenland* 65°50N 53°20W 154 D5
Kangaatsiaq *Greenland* 68°18N 53°28W 154 D5
Kangaba *Mali* 11°56N 8°25W 262 C3
Kangal *Turkey* 39°14N 37°23E 212 C7
Kangān *Fārs, Iran* 27°50N 52°3E 247 E7
Kangān *Hormozgan, Iran* 25°48N 57°28E 247 E8
Kangar *Malaysia* 6°27N 100°12E 237 J3
Kangāvar *Iran* 11°36N 8°4W 262 C3
Kangaroo I. *Australia* 35°45S 137°0E 282 C2
Kangaroo Mts. *Australia* 23°29S 141°51E 280 C3
Kangasala *Finland* 61°28N 24°4E 186 B3
Kangāvar *Iran* 34°40N 48°0E 213 E12
Kangding *China* 30°2N 101°57E 228 B3
Kangdong *N. Korea* 39°9N 126°5E 224 C3
Kangean, Kepulauan
 Indonesia 6°55S 115°23E 235 D5
Kangean Is. = Kangean, Kepulauan
 Indonesia 6°55S 115°23E 235 D5
Kangen → *South Sudan* 6°47N 33°9E 257 F3
Kangerdlugssuak
 Greenland 68°10N 32°20W 154 D7
Kangerluarsoruseq
 Greenland 63°45N 51°27W 154 E5
Kangerluarsoruset =
 Kangerluarsoruseq
 Greenland 63°45N 51°27W 154 E5
Kangerlussuaq *Greenland* 66°59N 50°40W 154 D5
Kangertittivaq = Scoresby Sund
 Greenland 70°28N 21°46W 154 C8
Kangŏ *N. Korea* 41°0N 126°35E 224 B3
Kanghsi *Taiwan* 23°34N 120°8E 225 C2
Kangikajik *Greenland* 70°7N 22°0W 154 C8
Kangilinnguit *Greenland* 61°20N 47°57W 154 E6
Kangiqliniq = Rankin Inlet
 Canada 62°30N 93°0W 294 E13
Kangiqsualujjuaq
 Canada 58°30N 65°59W 295 F18
Kangiqtugaapik = Clyde River
 Canada 70°30N 68°30W 295 C18
Kangirsuk *Canada* 60°0N 70°0W 295 F18
Kangkar Chemaran
 Malaysia 1°34N 104°12E 237 d
Kangkar Sungai Tiram
 Malaysia 1°35N 103°55E 237 d
Kangkar Teberau *Malaysia* 1°32N 103°51E 237 d
Kango *Gabon* 0°11N 10°5E 264 B2
Kangoku Iwa *Iwo Jima* 24°48N 141°17E 288 b
Kangoya
 Dem. Rep. of the Congo 9°55S 22°48E 265 D4
Kangping *China* 42°43N 123°18E 227 C12
Kangpokpi *India* 25°8N 93°58E 241 C4
Kangra *India* 32°6N 76°16E 242 C7
Kangrinboqe Feng *China* 31°0N 81°25E 243 D9
Kangshan *Taiwan* 22°48N 120°17E 225 D2
Kangto *China* 27°50N 92°35E 241 C4
Kangtog *Taiwan* 22°50N 120°22E 225 D2
Kangwon-do □ *N. Korea* 38°47N 127°35E 224 C3
Kangyidaung *Burma* 16°56N 94°54E 241 H5
Kanha △ *India* 22°15N 80°40E 243 H9
Kanhan → *India* 21°4N 79°34E 244 D4
Kanhangad *India* 12°21N 74°58E 245 H2
Kanheri *India* 19°13N 72°52E 244 E1
Kani *Sagaing, Burma* 23°52N 95°22E 241 D5
Kani *Sagaing, Burma* 22°26N 94°51E 241 D5
Kani *Ivory C.* 8°29N 6°36W 262 D3
Kani *Japan* 35°25N 137°7E 223 B9
Kani-Keli *Mayotte* 12°57S 45°6E 272 b
Kaniama
 Dem. Rep. of the Congo 7°30S 24°12E 265 D4
Kaniapiskau = Caniapiscau →
 Canada 56°40N 69°30W 299 A6
Kaniapiskau, L. = Caniapiscau, L.
 Canada 54°10N 69°55W 299 B6
Kaniere, L. *N.Z.* 42°50S 171°10E 285 D6
Kanif *Micronesia* 9°31N 138°5E 287 R16
Kanigiri *India* 15°24N 79°31E 245 G4
Kanin, Poluostrov *Russia* 68°0N 45°0E 186 A8
Kanin Nos, Mys *Russia* 68°39N 43°32E 186 A7
Kanin Pen. = Kanin, Poluostrov
 Russia 68°0N 45°0E 186 A8
Kaniné *Albania* 40°23N 19°30E 202 F3
Kaniva *Australia* 36°22S 141°18E 282 C4
Kanjiža *Serbia* 46°3N 20°4E 182 C5
Kanjut Sar *Pakistan* 36°7N 75°25E 243 A6
Kankaanpää *Finland* 61°44N 22°50E 188 E2
Kankakee → *U.S.A.* 41°7N 87°52W 311 C9
Kankakee *U.S.A.* 41°23N 88°15W 311 C8
Kankan *Guinea* 10°23N 9°15W 262 C3
Kankendy = Xankändi
 Azerbaijan 39°52N 46°49E 213 C12
Kankesanturai *Sri Lanka* 9°49N 80°2E 245 K5
Kankossa *Mauritania* 15°54N 11°31W 262 B2
Kankroli *India* 25°4N 73°53E 242 G5
Kankurgachi *India* 22°34N 88°23E 124 B2
Kanlica *Turkey* 41°5N 29°3E 132 B2
Kanmaw Kyun *Burma* 11°40N 98°28E 237 G2
Kanmuri-Yama *Japan* 34°30N 132°4E 222 C4
Kannabe *Japan* 34°33N 133°22E 222 C4
Kannapolis *U.S.A.* 35°30N 80°37W 315 D14
Kannauj *India* 27°3N 79°56E 243 F13
Kanniyakumari *India* 8°3N 77°40E 245 K3
Kannur = Cannanore
 India 11°53N 75°27E 245 J2
Kannyakumari *India* 8°3N 77°40E 245 K3
Kano *Nigeria* 12°2N 8°30E 263 C6
Kano □ *Nigeria* 11°30N 8°30E 263 C6
Kanonerskiy, Ostrov
 Russia 59°53N 30°13E 137 B1
Kan'onji *Japan* 34°7N 133°39E 222 C5
Kanoroba *Ivory C.* 9°7N 6°8W 262 D3
Kanowha *U.S.A.* 42°57N 93°47W 310 B3
Kanowit *Malaysia* 2°14N 112°20E 235 B4
Kanoya *Japan* 31°25N 130°50E 222 F2
Kanpetlet *Burma* 21°10N 93°59E 241 E4
Kanpur *India* 26°28N 80°20E 243 F9
Kansai Int. ✈ (KIX)
 Japan 34°27N 135°12E 133 B2
Kansanshi *Zambia* 39°33N 87°56W 311 E9
Kansas □ *U.S.A.* 38°30N 99°0W 308 F7
Kansas → *U.S.A.* 39°7N 94°37W 310 F7
Kansas City *Kans., U.S.A.* 39°7N 94°38W 310 F7
Kansas City *Mo., U.S.A.* 39°6N 94°35W 310 F7
Kansas City Int. ✈ (MCI)
 U.S.A. 39°18N 94°43W 310 E7
Kansenia
 Dem. Rep. of the Congo 10°20S 26°0E 268 E5
Kansk *Russia* 56°20N 95°37E 215 D1C
Kansu = Gansu □ *China* 36°0N 104°0E 226 G3
Kantaban *India* 22°43N 88°30E 124 B1
Kantang *Thailand* 7°25N 99°31E 237 J2
Kantemirovka *Russia* 49°43N 39°55E 189 H10
Kanth *India* 29°10N 78°40E 242 E8
Kanthanpudi *India*
 Poland 51°32N 16°45E 185 G3

Kantharalak *Thailand* 14°39N 104°39E 236 E5
Kanthi = Contai *India* 21°54N 87°46E 243 J12
Kantishna *U.S.A.* 63°31N 150°57W 303 E10
Kantishna → *U.S.A.* 64°45N 149°58W 303 D10
Kantli → *India* 28°20N 75°30E 242 E6
Kantō □ *Japan* 36°15N 139°30E 223 A11
Kantō-Sanchi *Japan* 35°59N 138°50E 223 B10
Kantu-long *Burma* 19°57N 97°36E 241 F6
Kanturk *Ireland* 52°11N 8°54W 166 D3
Kanuma *Japan* 36°34N 139°42E 223 A11
Kanus *Namibia* 27°50S 18°39E 270 C2
Kanuti Nat. Wildlife Refuge △
 U.S.A. 66°25N 151°50W 303 C10
Kanye *Botswana* 24°55S 25°28E 270 B4
Kanzaki → *Japan* 34°41N 135°24E 133 A1
Kanzenze
 Dem. Rep. of the Congo 10°30S 25°12E 265 E5
Kanzi, Ras *Tanzania* 7°1S 39°33E 268 D4
Kanzonzi, Chissioua
 Comoros Is. 12°23S 43°40E 272 a
Kao *Tonga* 19°40S 175°1W 287 P13
Kao Phara *Thailand* 8°3N 98°22E 237 a
Kaohsiung *Taiwan* 22°35N 120°16E 225 D2
Kaohsiung □ *Taiwan* 23°0N 120°35E 225 D2
Kaoka *Solomon Is.* 9°42S 160°43E 287 M11
Kaokaona = Kirakira
 Solomon Is. 10°27S 161°56E 287 N11
Kaokoveld *Namibia* 19°15S 14°30E 270 A1
Kaolack *Senegal* 14°5N 16°8W 262 C1
Kaolack □ *Senegal* 14°0N 15°15W 262 C1
Kaolan = Lanzhou *China* 36°1N 103°52E 226 F2
Kaolo *Solomon Is.* 8°24S 159°38E 287 M10
Kaoshan *China* 44°38N 124°50E 227 B13
Kaoshu *Taiwan* 22°49N 120°36E 225 D2
Kaouar *Niger* 19°5N 12°52E 259 E2
Kaoyao = Zhaoqing *China* 23°0N 112°20E 229 F9
Kapa'a *U.S.A.* 22°5N 159°19W 302 H15
Kapadvanj *India* 23°5N 73°0E 242 H5
Kapagere *Papua N. G.* 9°46S 147°42E 286 E4
Kapahulu *U.S.A.* 21°16N 157°49W 302 K14
Kapaklı *Turkey* 41°19N 27°59E 203 E11
Kapaklı Carsi *Turkey* 41°1N 28°58E 132 B1
Kapan *Armenia* 39°18N 46°27E 213 C12
Kapanga
 Dem. Rep. of the Congo 8°30S 22°40E 265 D3
Kapanga *Katanga,*
 Dem. Rep. of the Congo 8°30S 22°40E 265 D3
Kapar *U.S.A.* 21°29N 157°48W 302 K14
Kapatagan *Phil.* 7°52N 123°44E 233 H4
Kapchagai = Qapshaghay
Kapchagaiskoye Vdkhr. =
 Qapshaghay Bögeni
 Kazakhstan 43°45N 77°50E 217 D9
Kapedo *Kenya* 1°10N 36°6E 268 B4
Kapela = Velika Kapela
 Croatia 45°10N 15°5E 199 C12
Kapellerfeld *Austria* 48°18N 16°26E 142 A2
Kapellskär *Sweden* 59°44N 19°2E 163 E12
Kapelo, Akra *Greece* 36°9N 23°3E 204 E5
Kapema
 Dem. Rep. of the Congo 10°45S 28°22E 269 E2
Kapenguria *Kenya* 1°14N 35°7E 268 B4
Kapfenberg *Austria* 47°26N 15°18E 180 D8
Kapit *Dagi Turkey* 27°50N 36°12E 203 F11
Kapiri Mposhi *Zambia* 13°59S 28°43E 269 E2
Kāpīsā □ *Afghan.* 35°0N 69°20E 240 B3
Kapiskau → *Canada* 52°47N 81°55W 298 B3
Kapit *Malaysia* 2°0N 112°55E 235 B4
Kapiti I. *N.Z.* 40°50S 174°56E 284 E3
Kaplan, Massif du *Chad* 15°7N 21°45E 259 E4
Kaplan *U.S.A.* 30°0N 92°17W 314 F8
Kaplice *Czech Rep.* 48°42N 14°30E 180 C7
Kapoe *Thailand* 9°34N 98°32E 237 H2
Kapoeta *South Sudan* 4°50N 33°35E 257 G3
Kapoli *U.S.A.* 19°30N 154°50W 302 D7
Kápolnásnyék *Hungary* 47°16N 18°41E 182 C3
Kapombo
 Dem. Rep. of the Congo 10°40S 23°30E 265 E4
Kaponga *N.Z.* 39°29S 174°9E 284 F3
Kápos → *Hungary* 46°44N 18°30E 182 D3
Kaposvár *Hungary* 46°25N 17°47E 182 D2
Kapotnya *Russia* 55°39N 37°48E 129 C4
Kapowsin *U.S.A.* 46°59N 122°13W 306 D4
Kapp *Norway* 60°43N 10°52E 163 D7
Kappala *Sweden* 59°21N 18°13E 139 A3
Kappeln *Germany* 54°40N 9°55E 178 A5
Kappelshamn *Sweden* 57°52N 18°47E 163 G12
Kapps *Namibia* 22°32S 17°18E 270 B2
Kaprije *Croatia* 43°42N 15°43E 199 E12
Kapsabet *Kenya* 0°12N 35°6E 268 B4
Kapsan *N. Korea* 41°4N 128°19E 224 B4
Kapsukas = Marijampolè
 Lithuania 54°33N 23°19E 184 D10
Kaptai *Bangla.* 22°21N 92°17E 241 D4
Kaptai L. *Bangla.* 22°40N 92°20E 241 D4
Kapuas = Kalimantan Barat,
 Indonesia 0°25S 109°20E 235 C3
Kapuas = Kalimantan Tengah,
 Indonesia 2°0S 113°30E 235 C4
Kapuas Hulu, Pegunungan
 Malaysia 1°30N 113°30E 235 B4
Kapuas Hulu Ra. = Kapuas Hulu,
 Pegunungan *Malaysia* 1°30N 113°30E 235 B4
Kapulo *Dem. Rep. of the Congo* 8°18S 29°15E 269 D2
Kapunda *Australia* 34°20S 138°56E 282 B2
Kapuni *N.Z.* 39°29S 174°8E 284 F3
Kapurthala *India* 31°23N 75°25E 242 D6
Kapuskasing → *Canada* 49°49N 82°0W 298 C3
Kapuskasing *Canada* 49°25N 82°30W 298 C3
Kaputar, Mt. *Australia* 30°15S 150°10E 281 E5
Kaputir *Kenya* 2°5N 35°28E 268 B4
Kapuvár *Hungary* 47°36N 17°1E 182 C2
Kapyla *Finland* 60°13N 24°57E 137 A2
Kara *U.S.A.* 19°51N 155°56E 302 L7
Kara, W. → *Si. Arabia* 21°0N 40°24E 254 C2
Kara Ada *Turkey* 36°58N 27°28E 205 D9
Kara Bogaz Gol, Zaliv =
 Garabogazköl Aylagy
 Turkmenistan 41°0N 53°30E 187 F9
Kara Burun *Turkey* 38°32N 27°58E 205 C8
Kara-Kala = Garrygala
 Turkmenistan 38°31N 56°29E 247 B8
Kara Kalpak Republic =
 Qoraqalpoghistan □
 Uzbekistan 43°0N 58°0E 216 D5
Kara-Köl *Kyrgyzstan* 41°40N 72°40E 217 C7
Kara Kum = Garagum
 Turkmenistan 39°30N 60°0E 247 B8
Kara-Saki *Japan* 34°41N 129°30E 222 C1
Kara Sea *Russia* 75°0N 70°0E 214 B8
Karaadilli *Turkey* 38°18N 30°33E 205 C12
Karabiğa *Turkey* 40°23N 27°17E 203 D11
Karabük *Turkey* 41°10N 32°37E 212 B5
Karabük □ *Turkey* 41°0N 32°30E 212 B5
Karaburun *Albania* 40°25N 19°20E 202 F3

Karaburun *Turkey* 38°41N 26°28E 205 C8
Karabutak = Qarabutaq
 Kazakhstan 50°0N 60°14E 216 C6
Karacabey *Turkey* 40°12N 28°21E 203 F12
Karacakılavuz *Turkey* 41°8N 27°21E 203 E11
Karaçal Tepesi *Turkey* 36°21N 32°38E 250 B3
Karacasu *Turkey* 37°43N 28°35E 205 D10
Karachala = Qaraçala
 Azerbaijan 39°45N 48°53E 191 L9
Karachayevsk *Russia* 43°50N 41°55E 191 J5
Karachev *Russia* 53°10N 35°5E 189 F8
Karachey-Cherkessia □
 Russia 43°40N 41°30E 191 J5
Karachi *Pakistan* 24°50N 67°0E 123 A2
Karachi Int. ✈ (KHI)
 Pakistan 24°53N 67°9E 123 A2
Karad *India* 17°15N 74°10E 244 F2
Karadirek *Turkey* 38°34N 30°11E 205 C12
Karaga *Ghana* 9°58N 0°28W 263 D4
Karaganda = Qaraghandy
 Kazakhstan 49°50N 73°10E 217 C8
Karagayly = Qaraghayly
 Kazakhstan 49°26N 76°0E 214 E8
Karaginskiy, Ostrov
 Russia 58°45N 164°0E 215 D17
Karagiye, Vpadina
 Kazakhstan 43°27N 51°45E 187 F9
Karagiye Depression = Karagiye,
 Vpadina *Kazakhstan* 43°27N 51°45E 187 F9
Karagola Road *India* 25°29N 87°23E 243 G12
Karagüney Dağları
 Turkey 40°30N 34°40E 212 B6
Karahalli *Turkey* 38°23N 29°33E 205 C11
Kārahnjúkar *Iceland* 64°57N 15°46W 155 C11
Karaikal *India* 10°59N 79°50E 245 J4
Karaikkudi *India* 10°5N 78°45E 245 J4
Karaisali *Turkey* 37°16N 35°2E 212 D6
Karaiskakis *Greece* 38°35N 21°4E 207 B3
Karaitivu I. *Sri Lanka* 9°45N 79°52E 245 K4
Karaj *Iran* 35°48N 51°0E 247 C6
Karajarri ◎ *Australia* 19°0S 22°30E 278 C3
Karak *Malaysia* 3°25N 102°2E 237 L4
Karakalpakstan =
 Qoraqalpoghistan □
 Uzbekistan 43°0N 58°0E 216 D5
Karakaya Baraji *Turkey* 38°31N 38°23E 213 C8
Karakelong *Indonesia* 4°35N 126°50E 231 D7
Karakitang *Indonesia* 3°14N 125°28E 231 D7
Karaklis = Vanadzor
 Armenia 40°48N 44°30E 191 K7
Karakoçan *Turkey* 38°57N 40°2E 213 C9
Karakol *Kyrgyzstan* 42°30N 78°20E 217 D9
Karakoram Pass *Asia* 35°33N 77°50E 243 B7
Karakoram Ra. *Pakistan* 35°30N 77°0E 243 B7
Karakul = Qarakol
 Uzbekistan 39°32N 63°50E 216 F6
Karakul, Ozero *Tajikistan* 39°1N 73°25E 217 F8
Karakurt *Turkey* 40°10N 42°37E 213 B10
Karakuwisa *Nam.bia* 18°56S 19°40E 270 A2
Karal *Chad* 12°50N 14°46E 259 F2
Karalon *Russia* 57°5N 115°50E 215 D12
Karaman *Balıkesir, Turkey* 39°39N 28°0E 205 B9
Karaman *Konya, Turkey* 37°14N 33°13E 212 D5
Karaman □ *Turkey* 37°5N 33°15E 212 D5
Karamanlı *Turkey* 37°23N 29°47E 205 D11
Karamay *China* 45°30N 84°58E 226 B3
Karambu *Indonesia* 3°53S 116°6E 235 C5
Karamea *N.Z.* 41°14S 172°6E 285 B7
Karamea → *N.Z.* 41°13S 172°26E 285 B7
Karamea Bight *N.Z.* 41°22S 171°40E 285 B6
Karamian *Indonesia* 5°5S 114°40E 235 D4
Karamnasa → *India* 25°31N 83°52E 243 G10
Karamürsel *Turkey* 40°41N 29°36E 203 F13
Kārān *Si. Arabia* 27°43N 49°49E 247 E6
Karand *Iran* 34°16N 46°15E 213 E12
Karanganyar *Indonesia* 7°38S 109°37E 235 D3
Karangasem = Amlapura
 Indonesia 8°27S 115°37E 231 J18
Karanja *Maharashtra,*
 India 21°1N 78°24E 244 D4
Karanja *Maharashtra,*
 India 20°29N 77°31E 244 D3
Karanjia *India* 21°47N 85°58E 243 J11
Karankasso *Burkina Faso* 10°50N 3°53W 262 C4
Karaova *Turkey* 37°5N 27°40E 205 D9
Karapınar *Turkey* 37°41N 33°30E 212 D5
Karapıro *N.Z.* 37°53S 175°32E 284 B5
Karasburg *Namibia* 28°0S 18°44E 270 C2
Karasino *Russia* 66°50N 66°50E 214 C9
Karasjok *Norway* 69°27N 25°30E 160 B21
Karasu *Sakarya, Turkey* 41°4N 30°46E 212 B4
Karasu *Antalya,*
 Turkey 36°18N 30°10E 205 D12
Karasu → *Hatay, Turkey* 36°10N 36°30E 250 B7
Karasubazar = Bilohirsk
 Ukraine 45°3N 34°35E 189 K8
Karasuk *Russia* 53°44N 78°2E 217 B9
Karasuyama *Japan* 36°39N 140°9E 223 A12
Karatas *Adana, Turkey* 36°36N 35°21E 250 B6
Karatas *Manisa, Turkey* 38°35N 28°0E 205 C9
Karatas Burnu *Turkey* 36°31N 35°24E 250 B6
Karatau, Khrebet = Qarataü
 Kazakhstan 43°30N 69°30E 217 D7
Karatax Shan *China* 35°57N 81°0E 217 F10
Karateki Shan *China* 37°54N 79°0E 217 F10
Karativu *Sri Lanka* 8°22N 79°47E 245 K4
Karatoprak *Turkey* 37°1N 27°18E 205 D9
Karatoya → *India* 24°7N 89°25E 243 G12
Karatsu *Japan* 33°26N 129°58E 222 D1
Karaul *Russia* 70°6N 83°15E 214 B9
Karauli *India* 26°30N 77°4E 242 F7
Karavastasë, L. e *Albania* 40°55N 19°30E 202 F3
Karavia *Greece* 36°20N 27°10E 205 D10
Karavostasi *Cyprus* 35°8N 32°50E 207 D11
Karawa
 Dem. Rep. of the Congo 3°18N 20°17E 264 B4
Karawang *Indonesia* 6°30S 107°15E 235 D3
Karawanken *Europe* 46°30N 14°40E 180 C7
Karayazı *Turkey* 39°41N 42°9E 213 C10
Karazhal = Qarazhal
 Kazakhstan 48°2N 70°49E 214 E8
Karbalā' *Iraq* 32°36N 44°3E 213 F11
Karbalā □ *Iraq* 32°30N 43°50E 213 F10
Kårböle *Sweden* 61°59N 15°22E 163 E9
Karcag *Hungary* 47°19N 20°57E 182 C5
Karcha → *India* 25°17N 81°56E 243 G9
Karczew *Poland* 52°1N 21°15E 185 F8
Kardak → *India* 19°35N 75°40E 244 E2
Kardamaina *Greece* 36°47N 27°9E 205 D9
Kardamili *Greece* 36°59N 22°13E 204 E4
Kardeljevo = Ploče
 Croatia 43°4N 17°26E 199 E14
Karditsa *Greece* 39°23N 21°54E 204 B3
Karditsa □ *Greece* 39°15N 21°50E 204 B3
Kärdla *Estonia* 58°59N 22°40E 184 A8
Kardzhali = Kŭrdzhali
 Bulgaria 41°38N 25°21E 203 D10
Kareeberge *S. Africa* 30°59S 21°50E 270 D3
Kareha → *India* 25°44N 86°21E 243 G12

Kareima *Sudan* 18°30N 31°49E 256 D3
Karelia □ *Russia* 65°30N 32°30E 186 A5
Karelian Republic = Karelia □
 Russia 65°30N 32°30E 186 A5
Karelo-Finnish S.S.R. = Karelia □
 Russia 65°30N 32°30E 186 A5
Karema *Papua N. G.* 9°12S 147°18E 286 E4
Karen = Kayin □ *Burma* 18°0N 97°30E 241 G6
Karenni = Kayah □
 Burma 19°15N 97°15E 241 F6
Karera *India* 25°32N 78°9E 242 G8
Kārevāndar *Iran* 27°53N 60°44E 247 E9
Kargasok *Russia* 59°3N 80°53E 214 D9
Kargat *Russia* 55°10N 80°15E 214 D9
Kargi *Eastern, Kenya* 2°31N 37°34E 268 B4
Kargil *India* 34°32N 76°12E 243 B7
Kargopol *Russia* 61°30N 38°58E 186 B6
Kargowa *Poland* 52°5N 15°51E 185 F2
Karguéri *Niger* 13°27N 10°30E 259 F2
Karhal *India* 27°1N 78°57E 243 F8
Kari *India* 41°11N 34°30E 212 B6
Karia ba Mohammed
 Morocco 34°22N 5°12W 260 B3
Kariab *Madag.* 22°25S 47°22E 272 C2
Kariba *Zimbabwe* 16°28S 28°50E 269 F2
Kariba, L. *Zimbabwe* 16°40S 28°25E 269 F2
Kariba Dam *Zimbabwe* 16°30S 28°35E 269 F2
Kariba Gorge *Zambia* 16°30S 28°50E 269 F2
Karibib *Namibia* 22°0S 15°56E 270 B2
Karies *Greece* 40°14N 24°19E 203 F8
Karijini △ *Australia* 23°8S 118°15E 278 D2
Karikari, C. N.Z. 34°46S 173°24E 284 A2
Karimata, Kepulauan
 Indonesia 1°25S 109°0E 235 C3
Karimata, Selat *Indonesia* 2°0S 108°40E 235 C3
Karimata Is. = Karimata,
 Kepulauan *Indonesia* 1°25S 109°0E 235 C3
Karimganj *India* 24°52N 92°20E 241 C4
Karimnagar *India* 18°26N 79°10E 244 E4
Karimun, Pulau *Indonesia* 1°3N 103°22E 237 d
Karimun Kecil, Pulau
 Indonesia 1°8N 103°22E 237 d
Karimunjawa, Kepulauan
 Indonesia 5°50S 110°30E 235 D4
Karin *Bari, Somali Rep.* 10°59N 49°13E 267 B6
Karin *Woqooyi Galbeed,*
 Somali Rep. 10°50N 45°52E 267 B6
Karistos *Greece* 38°1N 24°29E 204 C6
Karīt *Iran* 33°29N 56°55E 247 C8
Kariya *Japan* 34°58N 137°1E 223 C9
Kariyangwe *Zimbabwe* 18°0S 27°38E 269 F2
Karjala *Finland* 62°0N 30°25E 188 A5
Karjat *India* 18°33N 75°0E 244 E2
Karkal *India* 13°15N 74°56E 245 H2
Karkar *Papua N. G.* 4°32S 145°57E 286 C3
Karkar I. *Papua N. G.* 4°40S 146°0E 286 C4
Karkaralinsk = Qarqaraly
 Kazakhstan 49°26N 75°30E 217 C9
Karkh *Pakistan* 33°20N 44°22E 213 A2
Karkheh → *Iran* 31°2N 47°29E 246 D5
Karkinitska Zatoka
 Ukraine 45°56N 33°0E 189 K7
Karkinitskiy Zaliv = Karkinitska
 Zatoka *Ukraine* 45°56N 33°0E 189 K7
Karkuk = Kirkük *Iraq* 35°30N 44°21E 213 E11
Karkur Tohl *Egypt* 22°5N 25°5E 256 C2
Karl Liebknecht *Russia* 51°40N 35°35E 189 G8
Karl-Marx-Stadt = Chemnitz
 Germany 50°51N 12°54E 178 E8
Karla, L. = Volvi, L. *Greece* 40°40N 23°34E 202 F7
Karlantijpa North ◎
 Australia 19°27S 133°33E 278 C5
Karlantijpa South ◎
 Australia 20°31S 133°9E 278 C5
Karlby = Kokkola
 Finland 63°50N 23°8E 160 E20
Karlholmsbruk *Sweden* 60°31N 17°37E 162 D11
Karlin *Czech Rep.* 50°5N 14°26E 135 B2
Karlino *Poland* 54°3N 15°53E 184 D2
Karlivka *Ukraine* 49°29N 35°8E 189 H8
Karlobag *Croatia* 44°32N 15°5E 198 D12
Karlovac *Croatia* 45°31N 15°36E 199 C12
Karlovarský *Czech Rep.* 50°10N 12°51E 180 A5
Karlovasi *Greece* 37°45N 26°42E 205 D8
Karlovka = Karlivka
 Ukraine 49°29N 35°8E 189 H8
Karlovo *Bulgaria* 42°38N 24°47E 203 D8
Karlovo námésti *Prague, Czech Rep.* 135 c1
Karlovy Vary *Czech Rep.* 50°13N 12°51E 180 A5
Karlowitz = Sremski Karlovci
 Serbia 45°12N 19°57E 182 B4
Karlowitz = Velké Karlovice
 Czech Rep. 49°20N 18°17E 181 B11
Karlsbad = Karlovy Vary
 Czech Rep. 50°13N 12°51E 180 A5
Karlsborg *Sweden* 58°33N 14°33E 163 F8
Karlsburg = Alba-Iulia
 Romania 46°8N 23°39E 183 D8
Karlsena, Mys *Russia* 77°0N 67°24E 214 B7
Karlsfeld *Germany* 48°13N 11°28E 131 A1
Karlshamn *Sweden* 56°10N 14°51E 163 H8
Karlshorst *Germany* 52°29N 13°31E 115 B4
Karlskoga *Sweden* 59°28N 14°33E 162 E7
Karlskrona *Sweden* 56°10N 15°35E 163 H9
Karlsplatz *Munich, Germany* 131 b1
Karlsruhe *Germany* 49°0N 8°23E 179 F4
Karlstad = Karlovac
 Croatia 45°31N 15°36E 199 C12
Karlstad *Sweden* 59°23N 13°30E 162 E6
Karlstad *Minn., U.S.A.* 48°35N 96°31W 308 A3
Karlstad *Germany* 49°57N 9°47E 178 F5
Karluk *U.S.A.* 57°34N 154°28W 303 H9
Karlův most *Prague, Czech Rep.* 135 b1
Karma *Niger* 13°38N 1°52E 263 C5
Karmala *India* 18°25N 75°12E 244 E2
Karmiʼel *Israel* 32°55N 35°18E 248 F4
Karmøy *Norway* 59°15N 5°15E 163 E4
Karnak *Egypt* 25°43N 32°39E 256 C3
Karnal *India* 29°42N 77°2E 242 E7
Karnali → *Nepal* 28°45N 81°16E 243 E9
Karnaphuli Res. = Kaptai L.
 Bangla. 22°40N 92°20E 243 H18
Karnaprayag *India* 30°16N 79°15E 243 D8
Karnataka □ *India* 13°15N 77°0E 245 H3
Karnes City *U.S.A.* 28°53N 97°54W 314 G6
Karnische Alpen *Europe* 46°36N 13°0E 180 C6
Kärnten □ *Austria* 46°52N 13°30E 180 C6
Karnner Strasse *Vienna, Austria* 142 e2
Karo *Mali* 12°16N 3°18W 262 C4
Karoi *Zimbabwe* 16°48S 29°45E 269 F2
Karol Bagh *India* 28°39N 77°11E 128 D2
Kärdejoyo = Ploče
 Croatia 43°4N 17°26E 199 E14
Karon, Ao *Thailand* 7°51N 98°17E 237 a
Karonga *Malawi* 9°57S 33°55E 268 D3
Karoo △ *S. Africa* 32°18S 22°27E 270 D3
Karoonda *Australia* 35°1S 139°59E 282 B3
Karor *Pakistan* 31°15N 70°59E 242 D4
Karora *Sudan* 17°44N 38°15E 256 D4
Karori *N.Z.* 41°17S 174°44E 143 A5
Kasongo
 Dem. Rep. of the Congo 4°30S 26°33E 268 C2

Kasongo Lunda Dem. Rep. of the Congo 6°35S 16°49E 265 D3
Kasos Greece 35°20N 26°55E 205 F8
Kasos, Stenon Greece 35°30N 26°30E 205 F8
Kaspi Georgia 41°59N 44°26E 191 K7
Kaspichan Bulgaria 43°18N 27°11E 203 C11
Kaspiysk Russia 42°52N 47°40E 191 J8
Kaspiyskiy Russia 45°22N 47°23E 191 H8
Kassab Syria 35°55N 35°59E 250 C6
Kassab ed Doleib Sudan 13°30N 33°35E 257 E3
Kassaba Egypt 22°40N 29°55E 256 C2
Kassalâ Sudan 15°30N 36°0E 257 D4
Kassalâ □ Sudan 15°20N 36°26E 257 D4
Kassandrino Greece 40°1N 23°27E 202 F7
Kassel Germany 51°18N 9°26E 178 D5
Kasserine Tunisia 35°10N 8°50E 258 A1
Kasserine □ Tunisia 35°15N 9°0E 258 A1
Kassinger Sudan 18°46N 31°51E 256 D3
Kassiopi Greece 39°48N 19°53E 206 B9
Kasson U.S.A. 44°2N 92°45W 308 C7
Kastamonu Turkey 41°25N 33°43E 212 B5
Kastamonu □ Turkey 41°20N 34°0E 212 B5
Kastav Croatia 45°22N 14°20E 199 C11
Kasteli Greece 35°29N 23°38E 207 E4
Kastellet Copenhagen, Denmark 118 a3
Kastelli Greece 35°12N 25°20E 207 E6
Kastellorizo = Megisti Greece 36°8N 29°34E 205 E11
Kastelo, Akra Greece 35°30N 27°15E 205 F9
Kasterlee Belgium 51°15N 4°59E 170 C4
Kastlösa Sweden 56°26N 16°25E 163 H10
Kastoria Greece 40°30N 21°19E 202 F5
Kastoria □ Greece 40°30N 21°15E 202 F5
Kastorias, L. Greece 40°30N 21°20E 202 F5
Kastorio Greece 37°10N 22°17E 204 D4
Kastornoye Russia 51°55N 38°2E 189 G10
Kastos Greece 38°35N 20°55E 207 B2
Kastrosikia Greece 39°6N 20°38E 207 A2
Kastrup Denmark 55°38N 12°39E 118 B3
Kastrup, København ✈ (CPH) Denmark 55°37N 12°39E 118 B3
Kastsyukovichy Belarus 53°20N 32°4E 189 F7
Kasuga Fukuoka, Japan 33°32N 130°26E 222 D2
Kasuga Tōkyō, Japan 35°45N 139°38E 140 A2
Kasugai Japan 35°12N 136°59E 223 B8
Kasuge Japan 35°45N 139°49E 140 A3
Kasukabe Japan 35°58N 139°49E 223 B11
Kasulu Tanzania 4°37S 30°5E 268 C3
Kasumi Japan 35°38N 134°38E 222 B6
Kasumiga-Ura Japan 36°0N 140°25E 223 B12
Kasumigaseki Tokyo, Japan 140 b4
Kasumkent Russia 41°47N 48°15E 191 K9
Kasungu Malawi 13°0S 33°29E 269 E3
Kasungu △ Malawi 12°53S 33°9E 269 E3
Kasur Pakistan 31°5N 74°25E 242 D6
Kata, Ao Thailand 7°48N 98°18E 237 J2
Kata Archanes Greece 35°15N 25°10E 207 E6
Kata Tjuta Australia 25°20S 130°50E 279 E5
Kataba Zambia 16°5S 25°10E 269 F2
Katagum Nigeria 12°18N 10°21E 263 C7
Katahdin, Mt. U.S.A. 45°54N 68°56W 309 C19
Kataka = Cuttack India 20°25N 85°57E 244 D7
Katako Kombe Dem. Rep. of the Congo 3°25S 24°20E 264 C4
Katakolo Greece 37°38N 21°19E 204 D3
Katale Tanzania 4°52S 31°7E 268 C3
Katalla U.S.A. 60°12N 144°31W 303 F11
Katamatite Australia 36°6S 145°41E 283 D6
Katanda Katanga, Dem. Rep. of the Congo 7°52S 24°13E 265 D4
Katanda Nord-Kivu, Dem. Rep. of the Congo 0°55S 29°21E 268 C2
Katanga □ Dem. Rep. of the Congo 8°0S 25°0E 268 D2
Katangi India 21°56N 79°50E 244 D4
Katanning Australia 33°40S 117°33E 279 F2
Katapakishi Dem. Rep. of the Congo 8°15S 22°49E 265 D4
Katastari Greece 37°50N 20°45E 207 D2
Katavi △ Tanzania 6°51S 31°3E 268 D3
Katavi Swamp Tanzania 6°50S 31°10E 268 D3
Katchall India 7°57N 93°22E 245 L11
Katchiungo Angola 12°35S 16°13E 265 E3
Katerini Greece 40°18N 22°37E 202 F6
Katghora India 22°30N 82°33E 243 H10
Katha Burma 24°10N 96°30E 241 C6
Kathapa △ Burma 22°20N 94°30E 241 D5
Katherîna, Gebel Egypt 28°30N 33°57E 251 K4
Katherine Australia 14°27S 132°20E 278 B5
Katherine Gorge = Nitmiluk △ Australia 14°6S 132°15E 278 B5
Kathi India 21°47N 74°3E 242 J6
Kathiawar India 22°20N 71°0E 242 H4
Kathikas Cyprus 34°55N 32°25E 207 F8
Kathleen U.S.A. 28°7N 82°2W 317 G7
Kathmandu Nepal 27°45N 85°20E 243 F11
Kathua India 32°23N 75°34E 242 C6
Kati Mali 12°41N 8°4W 262 C3
Katihar India 25°34N 87°36E 243 G12
Katikati N.Z. 37°32S 175°57E 284 D4
Katima Mulilo Namibia 17°28S 24°13E 270 A3
Katimbira Malawi 12°40S 34°0E 269 E3
Katingan = Mendawai → Indonesia 3°30S 113°0E 235 C4
Katiola Ivory C. 8°10N 5°10W 262 D3
Katipunan Phil. 8°31N 123°17E 233 G4
Katiti ❂ Australia 25°1S 131°11E 279 E5
Katla Iceland 63°36N 19°7W 155 D7
Katlabukh, Ozero Ukraine 45°28N 29°0E 183 E14
Katlanovo Macedonia 41°52N 21°40E 202 E5
Katmai △ U.S.A. 58°20N 155°0W 303 G9
Katmandu = Kathmandu Nepal 27°45N 85°20E 243 F11
Katni = Murwara India 23°46N 80°28E 243 H9
Katni India 23°51N 80°24E 243 H9
Kato Achaia Greece 38°8N 21°33E 204 C3
Kato Chorio Greece 35°3N 25°47E 207 E6
Kato Korakiana Greece 39°42N 19°45E 206 B9
Káto Pyrgos Cyprus 35°11N 32°41E 207 E8
Katochi Greece 38°26N 21°15E 204 C3
Katol India 21°17N 78°38E 244 D4
Katompe Dem. Rep. of the Congo 6°2S 26°23E 265 D5
Katong Singapore 1°18N 103°53E 138 B3
Katonga → Uganda 0°34N 31°50E 268 B3
Katoomba Australia 33°41S 150°19E 283 B9
Katouna Greece 38°47N 21°7E 204 C3
Katowice Poland 50°17N 19°5E 185 H6
Katrancı Dağı Turkey 37°27N 30°25E 205 D12
Katrine, L. U.K. 56°15N 4°30W 167 E4
Katrineholm Sweden 59°0N 16°12E 162 E10
Katsepe Madag. 15°45S 46°15E 272 B2
Katsina Nigeria 13°0N 7°32E 263 C6
Katsina □ Nigeria 12°30N 7°30E 263 C6
Katsina Ala Nigeria 7°10N 9°30E 263 D6
Katsina Ala → Nigeria 7°10N 9°20E 263 D6
Katsumoto Japan 33°51N 129°42E 222 D1
Katsushika Japan 35°44N 139°51E 140 A4
Katsuta Japan 36°25N 140°31E 223 A12
Katsuura Japan 35°10N 140°20E 223 B12
Katsuyama Fukui, Japan 36°3N 136°30E 223 A8
Katsuyama Okayama, Japan 35°5N 133°41E 222 B5
Kattaqŭrghon Uzbekistan 39°55N 66°15E 217 E7
Kattavia Greece 35°57N 27°46E 206 F11
Kattegat Denmark 56°40N 11°20E 163 H5
Katthammarsvik Sweden 57°26N 18°51E 163 G12
Kattowitz = Katowice Poland 50°17N 19°5E 185 H6
Katul, J. Sudan 14°12N 29°25E 257 E2
Katumba Dem. Rep. of the Congo 7°40S 25°17E 265 D5
Katun → Russia 52°25N 85°1E 217 B11
Katwa India 23°30N 88°5E 243 H13
Katwijk Neths. 52°12N 4°24E 170 B4
Kąty Wrocławskie Poland 51°2N 16°45E 185 G3
Ka'ū Desert U.S.A. 19°21N 155°19W 302 D6
Kau Pai Chau China 22°12N 114°15E 122 B2
Kau-Ye Kyun Burma 11°1N 98°32E 237 G2
Kau Yi Chau China 22°17N 114°4E 122 B1
Kaua'i U.S.A. 22°3N 159°30W 302 A2
Kauai Channel U.S.A. 21°45N 158°50W 302 B3
Kauai Island Lihue Municipal ✈ (LIH) U.S.A. 21°58N 159°20W 302 B2
Kaub Germany 50°5N 7°46E 179 E3
Kaudom ⌂ Namibia 18°45S 20°51E 270 A3
Kauehi French Polynesia 15°49S 145°10W 289 f
Kaufbeuren Germany 47°53N 10°37E 179 H6
Kaufman U.S.A. 32°35N 96°19W 314 E6
Kauhajoki Finland 62°25N 22°10E 160 E20
Kaukauna U.S.A. 44°17N 88°17W 308 C9
Kaukauveld Namibia 20°0S 20°15E 270 B3
Kaukonahua → U.S.A. 21°35N 158°7W 302 J13
Ka'ula I. U.S.A. 21°40N 160°33W 302 B1
Kaulakahi Channel U.S.A. 22°0N 159°55W 302 B2
Kaulsdorf Germany 52°29N 13°34E 115 B4
Kaunā Pt. U.S.A. 19°2N 155°53W 302 D6
Kaunakakai U.S.A. 21°6N 157°1W 302 B4
Kaunas Lithuania 54°54N 23°54E 184 D10
Kaunas ✈ (KUN) Lithuania 54°57N 24°3E 184 D11
Kaunchi = Yangiyul Uzbekistan 41°0N 69°3E 217 D7
Kaunghein Burma 25°41N 95°26E 241 C5
Kaunia Bangla. 25°46N 89°26E 241 C2
Kauniainen Finland 60°13N 24°44E 121 B1
Kaunos Turkey 36°49N 28°39E 205 E10
Kaupangur Iceland 65°38N 18°2W 155 B8
Kaura Namoda Nigeria 12°37N 6°33E 263 C6
Kauru Nigeria 10°33N 8°12E 263 C6
Kautokeino Norway 69°0N 23°4E 160 B20
Kauwapur India 27°31N 82°18E 243 F10
Kavacha Russia 60°16N 169°51E 215 C17
Kavadarci Macedonia 41°26N 22°3E 202 E6
Kavajë Albania 41°11N 19°33E 202 E3
Kavak Turkey 41°4N 36°3E 212 B7
Kavak Dağı Turkey 37°10N 28°2E 205 D10
Kavaklı Turkey 41°39N 27°10E 203 E11
Kavaklıdere Turkey 37°27N 28°21E 205 D10
Kavaklii = Topolovgrad Bulgaria 42°5N 26°20E 203 D10
Kavala Greece 40°57N 24°28E 203 F8
Kavala □ Greece 41°5N 24°30E 203 E8
Kavala Kolpos Greece 40°50N 24°25E 203 F8
Kavalerovo Russia 44°15N 135°4E 220 B7
Kavali India 14°55N 80°1E 245 G5
Kavār Iran 29°11N 52°44E 247 D7
Kavaratti India 10°34N 72°37E 245 J1
Kavaratti I. India 10°33N 72°38E 245 J1
Kavarna Bulgaria 43°26N 28°22E 203 C12
Kavava Dem. Rep. of the Congo 8°52S 22°19E 265 D4
Kavi India 22°12N 72°38E 242 H5
Kavieng Papua N. G. 2°36S 150°51E 286 B6
Kavimba Botswana 18°2S 24°38E 270 A3
Kavīr, Dasht-e Iran 34°30N 55°0E 247 C7
Kavīr △ Iran 34°40N 52°0E 247 C7
Kavirondo G. = Winam G. Kenya 0°20S 34°15E 268 C3
Kavkaz Russia 45°20N 36°40E 189 K9
Kävlinge Sweden 55°47N 13°9E 163 J7
Kavos Greece 39°23N 20°3E 206 C10
Kavousi Greece 35°7N 25°51E 207 E6
Kavungo Angola 11°31S 23°3E 265 E4
Kaw Fr. Guiana 4°30N 52°15W 329 C7
Kawa Sudan 13°42N 32°34E 257 E3
Kawachi-Nagano Japan 34°28N 135°31E 223 C7
Kawagama L. Canada 45°18N 78°45W 312 A6
Kawagoe Japan 35°55N 139°29E 223 B11
Kawaguchi Japan 35°52N 139°45E 223 B11
Kawah Ijen △ Indonesia 8°3S 114°14E 235 D4
Kawaihae B. U.S.A. 20°0N 155°50W 302 C6
Kawaihoa Pt. U.S.A. 21°47N 160°12W 302 B1
Kawaikini U.S.A. 22°5N 159°29W 302 A2
Kawailoa U.S.A. 21°36N 158°3W 302 J13
Kawailoa Beach U.S.A. 21°37N 158°5W 302 J13
Kawakawa N.Z. 35°23S 174°6E 284 B3
Kawambwa Zambia 9°48S 29°3E 269 D2
Kawana Zambia 13°5S 25°58E 265 E5
Kawanabe Japan 31°23N 130°24E 222 F2
Kawanoe Japan 34°1N 133°34E 222 C5
Kawardha India 22°0N 81°17E 243 J9
Kawasaki Japan 35°31N 139°43E 140 B3
Kawasi Indonesia 1°38S 127°28E 231 E7
Kawau I. N.Z. 36°25S 174°52E 284 C3
Kawawa Japan 35°31N 139°33E 140 B2
Kawawachikamach Canada 54°48N 66°50W 299 B6
Kawęczyn Poland 52°16N 21°5E 142 B2
Kaweka Ra. N.Z. 39°17S 176°19E 284 F5
Kawela U.S.A. 21°42N 158°1W 302 J13
Kawerau N.Z. 38°7S 176°42E 284 E5
Kawhia N.Z. 38°4S 174°49E 284 E3
Kawhia Harbour N.Z. 38°5S 174°51E 284 E3
Kawio, Kepulauan Indonesia 4°30N 125°30E 231 D7
Kawkareik Burma 16°33N 98°14E 241 G7
Kawlin Burma 23°47N 95°41E 241 D5
Kawthaung Burma 10°5N 98°36E 237 H2
Kawthoolei = Kayin □ Burma 18°0N 97°30E 241 G6
Kawthule = Kayin □ Burma 18°0N 97°30E 241 G6
Kawya Burma 24°50N 94°58E 241 C5
Kaxgar He → China 39°45N 78°24E 217 E9
Kaxholmen Sweden 57°51N 14°19E 163 G8
Kaya Burkina Faso 13°4N 1°10W 263 C4
Kayah □ Burma 19°15N 97°15E 241 F6
Kayak I. U.S.A. 59°56N 144°23W 303 G11
Kayalıköy Barajı Turkey 41°50N 27°5E 203 E11
Kayan Burma 16°54N 96°34E 241 G6
Kayan → Indonesia 2°55N 117°35E 235 B5
Kayan Mentarang △ Indonesia 2°25N 115°30E 235 B5
Kayankulam India 9°10N 76°33E 245 K3
Kaycee U.S.A. 43°43N 106°38W 304 E10
Kayeli Indonesia 3°20S 127°10E 231 E7
Kayenda Dem. Rep. of the Congo 10°48S 23°6E 265 E4
Kayenta U.S.A. 36°44N 110°15W 305 H8
Kayes Congo 4°25S 11°41E 265 C2
Kayes Mali 14°25N 11°30W 262 C2
Kayes □ Mali 14°0N 11°0W 262 C2
Kayı Turkey 39°12N 30°46E 205 B12
Kayima S. Leone 8°54N 11°15W 262 D2
Kayin □ Burma 18°0N 97°30E 241 G6
Kaymakçı Turkey 38°10N 28°8E 205 C10
Kayoa Indonesia 0°1N 127°28E 231 D7
Kayomba Zambia 13°11S 24°2E 269 E1
Kayombo Zambia 13°3S 23°51E 265 E4
Kaysatskoye Russia 49°47N 46°49E 190 F8
Kayseri Turkey 38°45N 35°30E 212 C6
Kayseri □ Turkey 38°40N 36°0E 212 C7
Kaysville U.S.A. 41°2N 111°56W 304 F8
Kayts Sri Lanka 9°42N 79°51E 245 K4
Kayu Putih Indonesia 6°10S 106°53E 122 B2
Kayuagung Indonesia 3°24S 104°50E 234 C2
Kaz Dağı Turkey 39°42N 26°50E 205 B8
Kazachye Russia 70°52N 135°58E 215 B14
Kazakhstan ■ Asia 50°0N 70°0E 217 C8
Kazan Russia 55°50N 49°10E 190 C9
Kazan → Canada 64°2N 95°29W 297 A9
Kazan-Rettō Pac. Oc. 25°0N 141°0E 288 E6
Kazancı Turkey 36°29N 32°51E 250 B3
Kazanlı Turkey 36°49N 34°43E 250 B5
Kazanlŭk Bulgaria 42°38N 25°20E 203 D9
Kazanskaya Russia 49°50N 41°10E 190 F5
Kazatin = Kozyatyn Ukraine 49°45N 28°50E 177 D15
Kazaure Nigeria 12°42N 8°28E 263 C6
Kazbek Russia 42°42N 44°30E 191 J7
Kāzerūn Iran 29°38N 51°40E 247 D6
Kazi Magomed = Qazımämmäd Azerbaijan 40°3N 49°0E 191 K9
Kazimierz Dolny Poland 51°19N 21°57E 185 G8
Kazimierza Wielka Poland 50°15N 20°30E 185 H7
Kazincbarcika Hungary 48°17N 20°36E 182 B5
Kazipet India 17°58N 79°30E 244 F4
Kaziranga △ India 26°40N 93°30E 241 B4
Kaziza Dem. Rep. of the Congo 10°42S 23°52E 265 E4
Kazlų Rūda Lithuania 54°46N 23°30E 184 D10
Kazo Japan 36°7N 139°36E 223 A11
Kaztalovka Kazakhstan 49°47N 48°43E 190 F9
Kazu Burma 25°27N 97°46E 241 C6
Kazuma Pan △ Zimbabwe 18°20S 25°48E 269 F2
Kazumba Dem. Rep. of the Congo 6°25S 22°5E 265 D4
Kazungula Zambia 17°35S 25°15E 265 F5
Kazuno Japan 40°10N 140°45E 220 D10
Kazym → Russia 63°54N 65°50E 214 C7
Kbely Czech Rep. 50°8N 14°32E 135 B3
Kcynia Poland 53°0N 17°30E 185 F4
Ke-hsi Mansam Burma 21°56N 97°50E 241 E6
Ké-Macina Mali 13°58N 5°22W 262 C3
Kea Greece 37°35N 24°22E 204 D6
Kea'au U.S.A. 19°37N 155°2W 302 D6
Keady U.K. 54°15N 6°42W 166 B5
Keahi Pt. U.S.A. 21°19N 157°59W 302 K14
Keahole Pt. U.S.A. 19°44N 156°4W 302 D5
Kealaikahiki Channel U.S.A. 20°35N 156°50W 302 C5
Kealakekua U.S.A. 19°31N 155°55W 302 D6
Kearney Mo., U.S.A. 39°22N 94°22W 310 E2
Kearney Nebr., U.S.A. 40°42N 99°5W 308 E4
Kearney ❂ Australia 20°10S 128°4E 278 D4
Kearny U.S.A. 33°3N 110°55W 305 K8
Kearsarge, Mt. U.S.A. 43°22N 71°50W 313 C13
Keban Turkey 38°50N 38°50E 213 C8
Keban Barajı Turkey 38°41N 38°33E 213 C8
Kebara Congo 2°27S 14°25E 264 C2
Kebayoran Baru Indonesia 6°14S 106°47E 122 B1
Kebayoran Lama Indonesia 6°13S 106°46E 122 B1
Kebbi □ Nigeria 11°35N 4°0E 263 C5
Kébémèr Senegal 15°23N 16°34W 262 B1
Kébi Ivory C. 9°18N 6°37W 262 D3
Kebi, Mayo → Cameroon 9°18N 13°33E 264 A2
Kebili Tunisia 33°47N 9°0E 258 B1
Kebili □ Tunisia 33°30N 8°50E 261 B6
Kebnekaise Sweden 67°53N 18°33E 160 C18
Kebon Jeruk Indonesia 6°11S 106°46E 122 B1
Kebri Dehar Ethiopia 6°45N 44°17E 267 C5
Kebumen Indonesia 7°42S 109°40E 235 D3
Kecel Hungary 46°31N 19°16E 182 D4
Kechika → Canada 59°41N 127°12W 296 B3
Keçiborlu Turkey 37°57N 30°18E 205 D12
Kecskemét Hungary 46°57N 19°42E 182 D4
Kedada Ethiopia 5°25N 35°58E 257 F4
Kedah □ Malaysia 5°50N 100°40E 237 K3
Kėdainiai Lithuania 55°15N 24°2E 184 C11
Kedar West Bank 31°44N 35°18E 123 B2
Kedarnath India 30°44N 79°4E 243 D8
Kedgwick Canada 47°40N 67°20W 299 C6
Kediet Ijill Mauritania 22°38N 12°33W 260 D2
Kediri Indonesia 7°51S 112°1E 235 D4
Kedja Dem. Rep. of the Congo 4°50N 19°16E 264 B3
Kedjebi Ghana 8°12N 0°25E 263 D5
Kédougou Senegal 12°35N 12°10W 262 C2
Kedoya Indonesia 6°10S 106°45E 122 B1
Kedros Oros Greece 35°11N 24°37E 207 E5
Kędzierzyn-Koźle Poland 50°20N 18°12E 185 H5
Ke'ehi Lagoon U.S.A. 21°20N 157°54W 302 K14
Keeler U.S.A. 36°29N 117°52W 306 J9
Keeley L. Canada 54°54N 108°8W 297 C7
Keeling Is. = Cocos Is. Ind. Oc. 12°10S 96°55E 273 F8
Keelung = Chilung Taiwan 25°3N 121°45E 225 A3
Keenapusan Phil. 6°50N 118°50E 233 H2
Keene Ont., Canada 44°15N 78°10W 312 B6
Keene Calif., U.S.A. 35°13N 118°33W 307 K8
Keene N.H., U.S.A. 42°56N 72°17W 313 D12
Keene N.Y., U.S.A. 44°16N 73°46W 313 B11
Keep River △ Australia 15°49S 129°8E 278 C4
Keeper Hill Ireland 52°45N 8°16W 166 D3
Keepit, L. Australia 30°50S 150°30E 283 A9
Keerweer, C. Australia 14°0S 141°32E 280 A3
Keeseville U.S.A. 44°29N 73°30W 313 B11
Keetmanshoop Namibia 26°35S 18°8E 270 C2
Keewatin Canada 49°46N 94°34W 297 D10
Keewatin → Canada 56°29N 100°46W 297 B8
Kefa Ethiopia 6°55N 36°30E 257 F4
Kefalonia Greece 38°15N 20°30E 207 C2
Kefalonia □ Greece 38°15N 20°30E 207 C2
Kefalonia ✈ (EFL) Greece 38°10N 20°30E 207 C1
Kefalos Greece 36°45N 26°59E 205 E8
Kefamenanu Indonesia 9°28S 124°29E 231 F6
Kefar Sava Israel 32°11N 34°54E 251 F5
Keffi Nigeria 8°55N 7°43E 263 D6
Keffin Hausa Nigeria 12°13N 9°59E 263 C6
Keflavík Iceland 64°2N 22°35W 155 C4
Keflavík ✈ (KEF) Iceland 64°0N 22°45W 155 C4
Keftya Ethiopia 13°54N 37°7E 257 E4
Keg River Canada 57°54N 117°55W 296 B5
Kegalla Sri Lanka 7°15N 80°21E 245 L5
Kegaska Canada 50°9N 61°18W 299 B7
Kehancha Kenya 1°11S 34°37E 268 C3
Keheili Sudan 19°25N 32°50E 256 D3
Kehena U.S.A. 19°23N 154°55W 302 D7
Kehl Germany 48°34N 7°50E 179 G3
Keibul Lamjao △ India 24°30N 93°55E 241 C4
Keighley U.K. 53°52N 1°54W 168 D6
Keijo = Seoul S. Korea 37°31N 126°58E 137 B2
Keila Estonia 59°18N 24°25E 188 C3
Keilor Australia 37°42S 144°50E 128 A1
Keilor North Australia 37°44S 144°51E 128 A1
Keimoes S. Africa 28°41S 20°59E 270 C3
Keimola Finland 60°20N 24°49E 121 A1
Keita Niger 14°46N 5°56E 263 C6
Keïta, B. → Chad 9°14N 18°21E 259 G3
Keitele Finland 63°10N 26°20E 160 E22
Keith S. Austral., Australia 36°6S 140°20E 282 D4
Keith Moray, U.K. 57°32N 2°57W 167 D6
Keithsburg U.S.A. 41°6N 90°56W 310 C6
Keiyasi Fiji 17°53S 177°46E 287 A1
Keizer U.S.A. 44°57N 123°1W 304 D2
Kejimkujik △ Canada 44°25N 65°25W 299 D6
Kejserr Franz Joseph Fd. Greenland 73°30N 24°30W 154 C8
Kekaha U.S.A. 21°58N 159°43W 302 B2
Kekri India 26°0N 75°10E 242 G6
Keksgolm = Priozersk Russia 61°2N 30°7E 188 B6
Kelafo Ethiopia 5°37N 44°8E 267 C5
Kelam Ethiopia 4°48N 35°58E 257 G4
Kelamet Eritrea 16°0N 38°30E 257 D4
Kelan China 38°43N 111°31E 226 E6
Kelang = Klang Malaysia 3°2N 101°26E 237 L3
Kelani Ganga → Sri Lanka 6°58N 79°50E 245 L4
Kelantan □ Malaysia 5°10N 102°0E 237 K3
Kelantan → Malaysia 6°13N 102°14E 237 J4
Kelapa Gading Indonesia 6°9S 106°52E 122 A2
Këlcyrë Albania 40°20N 20°12E 202 F4
Kelekçi Turkey 37°15N 29°20E 205 D11
Kelenföld Hungary 47°27N 19°2E 117 B2
Keles Turkey 39°54N 29°14E 203 G13
Keleti-főcsatorna Hungary 47°45N 21°20E 182 C6
Kelheim Germany 48°54N 11°52E 179 G7
Kelibia Tunisia 36°50N 11°3E 258 A2
Kelkit Turkey 40°7N 39°16E 213 B8
Kelkit → Turkey 40°45N 36°32E 212 B7
Kellé Congo 0°8S 14°38E 264 C2
Kellé Niger 14°16N 10°7E 263 C7
Keller U.S.A. 31°50N 81°15W 316 D8
Kellerberrin Australia 31°36S 117°38E 279 F2
Kellett, C. Canada 72°0N 126°0W 150 B1
Kelleys I. U.S.A. 41°36N 82°42W 312 E2
Kellogg U.S.A. 47°32N 116°7W 304 C5
Kells = Ceanannus Mor Ireland 53°44N 6°53W 166 C5
Kelmė Lithuania 55°38N 22°56E 184 C9
Kelmentsi Ukraine 48°28N 26°50E 183 B11
Kélo Chad 9°10N 15°45E 259 G3
Kelokedhara Cyprus 34°48N 32°39E 207 F8
Kelowna Canada 49°50N 119°25W 296 D5
Kelsey Creek Australia 20°26S 148°31E 280 b
Kelseyville U.S.A. 38°59N 122°50W 306 G4
Kelso N.Z. 45°54S 169°15E 285 F4
Kelso Borders, U.K. 55°36N 2°26W 167 F6
Kelso Wash., U.S.A. 46°9N 122°54W 306 D4
Keluang = Kluang Malaysia 2°3N 103°18E 237 L4
Kelvin S. Africa 26°4S 28°5E 123 A2
Kelvington Canada 52°10N 103°30W 297 C8
Kem Russia 65°0N 34°38E 186 B5
Kem → Russia 64°57N 34°41E 186 B5
Kem-Kem Morocco 30°40N 4°30W 260 B4
Kema Indonesia 1°22N 125°8E 231 D7
Kemah Turkey 39°32N 39°5E 213 C8
Kemaliye Erzincan, Turkey 39°16N 38°29E 213 C8
Kemaliye Manisa, Turkey 38°27N 28°25E 205 C10
Kemalpaşa Turkey 38°25N 27°27E 205 C9
Kemaman Malaysia 4°12N 103°18E 237 K4
Kemang Indonesia 6°15S 106°48E 122 B1
Kemano Canada 53°35N 128°0W 296 C3
Kemapyu Burma 18°49N 97°19E 241 F6
Kemasik Malaysia 4°25N 103°27E 237 K4
Kemayoran Indonesia 6°10S 106°51E 122 B2
Kembé C.A.R. 4°36N 21°54E 264 B4
Kembolcha Ethiopia 11°2N 39°42E 257 E4
Kemer Antalya, Turkey 36°36N 30°34E 205 E12
Kemer Burdur, Turkey 37°21N 30°4E 205 D12
Kemer Muğla, Turkey 36°40N 29°22E 205 E11
Kemer Barajı Turkey 37°30N 28°37E 205 D10
Kemerburgaz Turkey 41°9N 28°54E 122 B1
Kemerovo Russia 55°20N 86°5E 214 D9
Kemerovo □ Russia 55°0N 86°0E 217 B11
Ķemeru △ Latvia 56°58N 23°25E 184 B10
Kemi Finland 65°44N 24°34E 160 D21
Kemi älv = Kemijoki → Finland 65°47N 24°32E 160 D21
Kemi träsk = Kemijärvi Finland 66°43N 27°22E 160 C22
Kemijärvi Finland 66°43N 27°22E 160 C22
Kemijoki → Finland 65°47N 24°32E 160 D21
Kemmerer U.S.A. 41°48N 110°32W 304 F8
Kemmuna = Comino Malta 36°1N 14°20E 206 E7
Kemp, L. U.S.A. 33°46N 99°9W 314 E5
Kemp Land Antarctica 69°0S 55°0E 151 C5
Kempas Malaysia 1°33N 103°42E 237 d
Kempen = Kępno Poland 51°18N 17°58E 185 G4
Kempsey Australia 31°1S 152°50E 283 A10
Kempt, L. Canada 47°25N 74°22W 298 C5
Kempten Germany 47°45N 10°17E 179 H6
Kempton Tas., Australia 42°31S 147°12E 281 G4
Kempton Ind., U.S.A. 40°17N 86°14W 311 D10
Kempton Park Races U.K. 51°24N 0°23W 125 B1
Kemptville Canada 45°0N 75°38W 313 B9
Ken → India 25°13N 80°27E 243 G9
Kenadsa Algeria 31°48N 2°26W 261 B4
Kenai U.S.A. 60°33N 151°16W 303 F10
Kenai Fjords △ U.S.A. 59°40N 149°50W 303 G10
Kenai Mts. U.S.A. 60°0N 150°0W 303 G10
Kenai Nat. Wildlife Refuge ⌂ U.S.A. 60°20N 150°30W 303 F10
Kenamuke Swamp South Sudan 5°55N 33°48E 257 F3
Kenansville U.S.A. 27°53N 80°59W 317 H9
Kendai India 22°45N 82°37E 243 H10
Kendal Indonesia 6°56S 110°14E 235 D4
Kendal Cumb., U.K. 54°20N 2°44W 168 C5
Kendall N.S.W., Australia 31°35S 152°44E 283 A10
Kendall Fla., U.S.A. 25°40N 80°19W 317 K9
Kendall → Australia 14°4S 141°35E 280 A3
Kendallville U.S.A. 41°27N 85°16W 311 C11
Kendari Indonesia 3°50S 122°30E 231 E6
Kendawangan Indonesia 2°32S 110°17E 235 C4
Kende Nigeria 11°30N 4°12E 263 C5
Kendégué Chad 10°0N 18°36E 259 F3
Kendi, Pulau Malaysia 5°13N 100°11E 237 c
Kendrapara India 20°35N 86°30E 244 D8
Këndrevicës, Maja e Albania 40°15N 19°52E 202 F3
Kendrew S. Africa 32°32S 24°30E 270 D3
Kendrick U.S.A. 29°15N 82°10W 317 F7
Kene Thao Laos 17°44N 101°10E 236 D3
Kenedy U.S.A. 28°49N 97°51W 314 G6
Kenema S. Leone 7°50N 11°14W 262 D2
Keng Kok Laos 16°26N 105°12E 236 D5
Keng Tawng Burma 20°45N 98°18E 241 E7
Keng Tung Burma 21°18N 99°39E 236 B2
Kengani Dem. Rep. of the Congo 2°59S 17°36E 264 C3
Kenge Dem. Rep. of the Congo 4°50S 17°4E 265 C3
Kengeja Tanzania 5°26S 39°45E 268 D4
Kenhardt S. Africa 29°19S 21°12E 270 C3
Kéniéba Mali 12°54N 11°17W 262 C2
Kenilworth S. Africa 33°59S 18°27E 118 A1
Keningau Malaysia 5°20N 116°10E 235 A5
Kenitra Morocco 34°15N 6°40W 260 B3
Kenitra □ Morocco 34°18N 6°25W 260 B3
Kenli China 37°30N 118°20E 227 F10
Kenmare Kerry, Ireland 51°53N 9°36W 166 E2
Kenmare N. Dak., U.S.A. 48°41N 102°5W 308 A2
Kenmare River Ireland 51°48N 9°51W 166 E2
Kennebago Lake U.S.A. 45°4N 70°40W 313 A14
Kennebec U.S.A. 43°54N 99°52W 308 D4
Kennebec → U.S.A. 43°45N 69°46W 309 D19
Kennebunk U.S.A. 43°23N 70°33W 313 C14
Kennedy Zimbabwe 18°52S 27°10E 270 A4
Kennedy, C. = Canaveral, C. U.S.A. 28°27N 80°32W 317 G9
Kennedy Channel Arctic 80°50N 66°0W 154 A4
Kennedy Entrance U.S.A. 59°1N 152°0W 303 G10
Kennedy Ra. Australia 24°45S 115°10E 279 D2
Kennedy Range △ Australia 24°34S 115°2E 279 D2
Kennedy Space Center U.S.A. 28°40N 80°42W 317 G9
Kennedy Town China 22°16N 114°6E 122 B1
Kenner U.S.A. 29°59N 90°14W 131 A1
Kennesaw U.S.A. 34°1N 84°37W 316 A5
Kennet → U.K. 51°27N 0°57W 169 F7
Kenneth Ra. Australia 23°50S 117°8E 279 D2
Kennett U.S.A. 36°14N 90°3W 308 G8
Kennewick U.S.A. 46°12N 119°7W 304 C4
Kennington London, U.K. 125 c4
Kennisis Lake Canada 45°13N 78°36W 312 A6
Kenogami → Canada 51°6N 84°28W 298 B3
Kenora Canada 49°47N 94°29W 297 D10
Kenosha U.S.A. 42°35N 87°49W 311 B9
Kensal Green U.K. 51°32N 0°13W 125 A2
Kensal Rise London, U.K. 125 a1
Kensington N.S.W., Australia 33°54S 151°13E 139 B2
Kensington P.E.I., Canada 46°28N 63°34W 299 C7
Kensington Gauteng, S. Africa 26°11S 28°6E 123 B2
Kensington London, U.K. 51°29N 0°10W 125 B2
Kensington N.Y., U.S.A. 40°38N 73°57W 132 C2
Kensington Palace U.K. 51°30N 0°11W 125 A2
Kent Ohio, U.S.A. 41°9N 81°22W 312 E3
Kent Tex., U.S.A. 31°4N 104°13W 314 F2
Kent Wash., U.S.A. 47°22N 122°14W 306 C4
Kent □ U.K. 51°12N 0°40E 169 F8
Kent Group Australia 39°30S 147°20E 281 F4
Kent Pen. Canada 68°30N 107°0W 294 D10
Kent Village U.S.A. 38°55N 76°53W 143 B4
Kentaū Kazakhstan 43°32N 68°36E 217 D7
K'enting △ Taiwan 21°57N 120°48E 225 E2
Kentish Town U.K. 51°32N 0°8W 125 A3
Kentland U.S.A. 40°46N 87°27W 311 D9
Kenton London, U.K. 51°34N 0°17W 125 A2
Kenton Ohio, U.S.A. 40°39N 83°37W 311 D13
Kentucky □ U.S.A. 37°0N 84°0W 309 G11
Kentucky → U.S.A. 38°41N 85°11W 311 F11
Kentucky L. U.S.A. 37°1N 88°16W 308 G9
Kentville Canada 45°6N 64°29W 299 C7
Kentwood La., U.S.A. 30°56N 90°31W 315 F9
Kentwood Mich., U.S.A. 42°52N 85°39W 311 B11
Kenwood House U.K. 51°34N 0°9W 125 A3
Kenya ■ Africa 1°0N 38°0E 268 B4
Kenya, Mt. Kenya 0°10S 37°18E 268 C4
Kenyir, Tasik Malaysia 5°1N 102°54E 237 K4
Kenzou Cameroon 4°10N 15°2E 264 B3
Keo Neua, Deo Vietnam 18°23N 105°10E 236 C5
Keokuk U.S.A. 40°24N 91°24W 310 D5
Keoladeo △ India 27°0N 77°20E 242 F7
Keonjhargarh India 21°28N 85°35E 243 J11
Keosauqua U.S.A. 40°44N 91°58W 310 D5
Keota U.S.A. 41°22N 91°57W 310 C5
Kep Cambodia 10°29N 104°19E 237 G5
Kep Vietnam 21°24N 106°16E 236 B6
Kep △ Cambodia 10°30N 104°18E 237 G5
Kepa Poland 52°13N 21°3E 142 B2
Kepala Batas Malaysia 5°31N 100°26E 237 c
Kepez Turkey 40°5N 26°24E 203 F10
Kepi Indonesia 6°32S 139°19E 231 F9
Kępice Poland 54°16N 16°51E 184 D3
Kepler Mts. N.Z. 45°25S 167°20E 285 F2
Kępno Poland 51°18N 17°58E 185 G4
Keppel Harbour Singapore 1°15N 103°49E 138 B2
Keppel Pt. Papua N. G. 10°10S 147°58E 286 F4
Kepsut Turkey 39°40N 28°9E 205 B10
Kepuhi Pt. U.S.A. 21°29N 158°14W 302 K13
Kepulauan Karimunjawa △ Indonesia 5°50S 110°25E 235 D4
Kerala □ India 11°0N 76°15E 245 J3
Keram → Papua N. G. 4°7S 144°5E 286 C3
Kerama-Rettō Japan 26°5N 127°15E 221 L3
Keramikos Athens, Greece 112 b1
Keran Pakistan 34°35N 73°59E 243 B5
Keran △ Togo 10°9N 0°41E 263 C5
Kerang Vic., Australia 35°40S 143°55E 282 C5
Kerang Indonesia 2°15S 116°3E 235 C5
Keranyo Ethiopia 5°3N 38°18E 257 F4
Kerao → South Sudan 11°0N 32°41E 257 E3
Keratea Greece 37°48N 23°58E 204 D5
Keraudren, C. Australia 19°58S 119°45E 278 C2
Kerava Finland 60°25N 25°5E 188 B3
Keravat Papua N. G. 4°17S 152°2E 286 C7
Kerch Ukraine 45°20N 36°20E 189 K9
Kerchenskiy Proliv Black Sea 45°10N 36°30E 189 K9
Kerchoual Mali 17°12N 0°20E 263 B5
Kerema Papua N. G. 7°58S 145°50E 286 D3
Kerempe Burnu Turkey 42°2N 33°20E 212 A5
Keren Eritrea 15°45N 38°28E 257 D4
Kerewan Gambia 13°29N 16°10W 262 C1
Kerguelen Ind. Oc. 49°15S 69°10E 273 J5
Kerguelen Plateau S. Ocean 55°0S 75°0E 273 K6
Keri Greece 37°40N 20°49E 207 D2
Keri Kera Sudan 12°21N 32°42E 257 E3
Kerian, Kuala Malaysia 5°10N 100°25E 237 c
Kericho Kenya 0°22S 35°15E 268 C4
Kerikeri N.Z. 35°12S 173°59E 284 B2
Kerinci Indonesia 1°40S 101°15E 234 C2
Kerinci Seblat △ Indonesia 2°30S 101°30E 234 C1
Kerintji = Kerinci Indonesia 1°40S 101°15E 234 C2
Keriya He → China 38°30N 82°10E 217 E10
Kerkenna, Îs. Tunisia 34°48N 11°11E 258 B2
Kerki = Atamyrat Turkmenistan 37°50N 65°12E 217 E7
Kerkini, L. Greece 41°12N 23°10E 202 E7
Kerkouane Tunisia 36°58N 11°2E 200 F4
Kerkrade Neths. 50°53N 6°4E 170 D6
Kerkyra Greece 39°38N 19°50E 206 B9
Kerkyra □ Greece 39°37N 19°50E 206 B9
Kerkyra ✈ (CFU) Greece 39°35N 19°54E 204 B1
Kerkyras, Notio Steno Greece 39°34N 20°0E 206 B10
Kerma Sudan 19°33N 30°32E 256 D3
Kermadec Is. Pac. Oc. 30°0S 178°15W 277 G15
Kermadec Trench Pac. Oc. 30°30S 176°0W 277 G15
Kermān Iran 30°15N 57°1E 247 D8
Kerman Calif., U.S.A. 36°43N 120°4W 306 J6
Kermān □ Iran 30°0N 57°0E 247 D8
Kermān, Bīābān-e Iran 28°45N 59°45E 247 D8
Kermānshāh Iran 34°23N 47°0E 213 E12
Kermānshāh □ Iran 34°0N 46°30E 246 C5
Kermen Bulgaria 42°30N 26°16E 203 D10
Kermine = Navoi Uzbekistan 40°9N 65°22E 217 D7
Kermit U.S.A. 31°52N 103°6W 314 F3
Kern → U.S.A. 35°16N 119°18W 307 K7
Kernhof Austria 47°49N 15°32E 180 D8
Kernow = Cornwall □ U.K. 50°26N 4°40W 169 G3
Kernville U.S.A. 35°45N 118°26W 307 K8
Keroh Malaysia 5°43N 101°1E 237 K3
Keros Greece 36°54N 25°40E 205 E7
Kérou Benin 10°50N 2°5E 263 C5
Kérouane Guinea 9°15N 9°0W 262 D3
Kerowagi Papua N. G. 5°51S 144°51E 286 C3
Kerpen Germany 50°51N 6°41E 178 E2
Kerrera U.K. 56°24N 5°33W 167 E3
Kerrobert Canada 51°56N 109°8W 297 C7
Kerrville U.S.A. 30°3N 99°8W 314 F5
Kerry □ Ireland 52°7N 9°35W 166 D2
Kerry Hd. Ireland 52°25N 9°56W 166 D2
Kersa Ethiopia 9°28N 41°48E 257 F5
Kertosono Indonesia 7°38S 112°9E 235 D4
Kerulen = Herlen → Asia 48°48N 117°0E 219 B12
Kervo = Kerava Finland 60°25N 25°5E 188 B3
Kerzaz Algeria 29°29N 1°37W 261 C4
Kesagami → Canada 51°40N 79°45W 298 B4
Kesagami L. Canada 50°23N 80°15W 298 B3
Keşan Turkey 40°49N 26°38E 203 F10
Kesariani Greece 37°57N 23°46E 112 B2
Kesennuma Japan 38°54N 141°35E 220 E10
Keshāvar Iran 36°50N 46°22E 213 D12
Keshit Iran 29°43N 58°17E 247 D8
Kesigi = Kosgi India 15°51N 77°16E 245 G3
Keşiş Dağ Turkey 39°47N 39°46E 213 C8
Keskal India 20°5N 81°35E 244 D5
Keskin Turkey 39°40N 33°36E 212 C5
Kestenga Russia 65°50N 31°45E 160 D24
Keswick U.K. 54°36N 3°8W 168 C4
Keszthely Hungary 46°50N 17°15E 182 D2
Ket → Russia 58°55N 81°32E 214 D9
Keta Ghana 5°49N 1°0E 263 D5
Keta Lagoon Ghana 5°55N 1°0E 263 D5
Ketapang Jawa Timur, Indonesia 8°9S 114°23E 231 J17
Ketapang Kalimantan Barat, Indonesia 1°55S 110°0E 235 C4
Ketchenery Russia 47°18N 44°32E 191 G7
Ketchikan U.S.A. 55°21N 131°39W 296 B2
Ketchum U.S.A. 43°41N 114°22W 304 E6
Kete Krachi Ghana 7°46N 0°1W 263 D4
Ketef, Khalîg Umm el Egypt 23°40N 35°35E 246 F2
Keti Bandar Pakistan 24°8N 67°27E 242 G2
Kétou Benin 7°25N 2°45E 263 D5
Ketri India 28°1N 75°50E 242 E6
Kętrzyn Poland 54°7N 21°22E 184 D8
Ketta Congo 1°28N 15°54E 264 B3
Kettering Northants., U.K. 52°24N 0°43W 169 E7
Kettering Md., U.S.A. 38°53N 76°49W 143 B5
Kettering Ohio, U.S.A. 39°41N 84°10W 311 E12
Kettle → Canada 56°40N 89°34W 297 B11
Kettle Falls U.S.A. 48°37N 118°3W 304 B4
Kettle Point Canada 43°10N 82°1W 312 C2
Kettle Pt. Canada 43°13N 82°1W 312 C2
Kettleman City U.S.A. 36°1N 119°58W 306 J7
Kęty Poland 49°51N 19°16E 185 J6
Keuka L. U.S.A. 42°30N 77°9W 312 D7
Keuruu Finland 62°16N 24°41E 188 A3
Kevelaer Germany 51°36N 6°15E 178 D2
Kew Vic., Australia 37°48S 145°2E 128 A2
Kew London, U.K. 51°28N 0°17W 125 B2
Kew Gardens Ont., Canada 43°39N 79°18W 141 A3
Kew Gardens London, U.K. 51°28N 0°17W 125 B2
Kewanee U.S.A. 41°14N 89°56W 310 C7
Kewanna U.S.A. 41°1N 86°25W 311 C10
Kewaunee U.S.A. 44°27N 87°31W 308 C10
Keweenaw B. U.S.A. 47°0N 88°15W 308 B9
Keweenaw Pen. U.S.A. 47°15N 88°15W 308 B9
Keweenaw Pt. U.S.A. 47°25N 87°43W 308 B10
Kexholm = Priozersk Russia 61°2N 30°7E 188 B6
Key, L. Ireland 54°0N 8°15W 166 C3
Key Biscayne U.S.A. 25°41N 80°9W 128 B2
Key Colony Beach U.S.A. 24°45N 80°57W 317 L9
Key Lake Mine Canada 57°5N 105°32W 297 B7
Key Largo U.S.A. 25°5N 80°27W 317 K9
Key West U.S.A. 24°33N 81°48W 317 L8
Keyala South Sudan 4°27N 32°52E 257 G3
Keynsham U.K. 51°24N 2°29W 169 F5
Keyser U.S.A. 39°26N 78°59W 309 F14
Keystone Heights U.S.A. 29°47N 82°2W 316 F7
Keytesville U.S.A. 39°26N 92°56W 310 E4
Kezhma Russia 58°59N 101°9E 215 D11
Kezi Zimbabwe 20°58S 28°32E 271 B4
Kežmarok Slovak Rep. 49°10N 20°28E 181 B13
Kgalagadi Transfrontier ⌂ Africa 25°10S 21°0E 270 C3
Khabarovsk Russia 48°30N 135°5E 219 B16
Khabr Iran 28°51N 56°22E 247 D8
Khābūr → Syria 35°17N 40°35E 213 E9
Khachmas = Xaçmaz Azerbaijan 41°31N 48°42E 191 K9
Khachrod India 23°25N 75°20E 242 H6
Khadari, W. el → Sudan 10°29N 27°15E 257 E2
Khadro Pakistan 26°11N 68°50E 242 F3
Khadyzhensk Russia 44°26N 39°32E 191 H4
Khadzhilyangar = Dahongliutan China 35°45N 79°20E 243 B8
Khaga India 25°47N 81°7E 243 G9
Khagaria India 25°30N 86°32E 243 G12
Khaipur Pakistan 29°34N 72°17E 242 E5
Khair India 27°57N 77°46E 242 F7
Khairabad India 27°33N 80°47E 243 F9
Khairagarh India 21°27N 81°2E 243 J9
Khairpur Pakistan 27°32N 68°49E 242 F3
Khairpur Nathan Shah Pakistan 27°6N 67°44E 242 F2
Khairwara India 23°58N 73°38E 242 H5
Khaisor → Pakistan 31°17N 68°59E 242 D3
Khajuri Kach Pakistan 32°4N 69°51E 242 C3
Khāk Dow Afghan. 34°57N 67°16E 240 B2
Khakassia □ Russia 53°0N 90°0E 217 B12
Khakhea Botswana 24°48S 23°22E 270 B3
Khalafābād Iran 30°54N 49°24E 247 D6
Khalfūt Yemen 15°52N 52°10E 249 D6
Khalīj Iraq 33°18N 44°28E 113 B2
Khalilabad India 26°48N 83°5E 243 F10
Khalīlī Iran 27°38N 53°17E 247 E7
Khalkhāl Iran 37°37N 48°32E 213 D13
Khalkís = Chalkida Greece 38°27N 23°42E 204 C5
Khalmer-Sede = Tazovskiy Russia 67°30N 78°44E 214 C8
Khalmer Yu Russia 67°58N 65°1E 214 C7
Khalturin Russia 58°40N 48°50E 186 C8
Kham Keut Laos 18°15N 104°43E 236 C5
Khamaria India 23°5N 80°48E 243 H9
Khambhaliya India 22°14N 69°41E 242 H3
Khambhat India 22°23N 72°33E 242 H5
Khambhat, G. of India 20°45N 72°30E 239 E10
Khamgaon India 20°42N 76°37E 244 D3
Khamīr Iran 26°57N 55°36E 247 E7
Khamir Yemen 16°2N 44°0E 248 C4
Khamīs Mushayţ Si. Arabia 18°18N 42°44E 248 C3
Khammam India 17°11N 80°6E 244 F5
Khamsa Egypt 30°27N 32°23E 251 H3
Khan → Namibia 22°37S 14°56E 270 B2
Khān Abū Shāmat Syria 33°39N 36°53E 250 E7
Khān al Baghdādī Iraq 33°51N 42°32E 213 G10
Khān al Ḩammād Iraq 32°19N 44°16E 213 G11
Khān Azād Iraq 33°7N 44°22E 246 C5

Khān Mujiddah *Iraq* 32°21N 43°48E **246** C4
Khān Shaykhūn *Syria* 35°26N 36°38E **212** E7
Khan Tengri, Pik *Asia* 42°12N 80°10E **217** D10
Khān Yūnis *Gaza Strip* 31°21N 34°18E **251** G5
Khānābād *Afghan.* 36°45N 69°5E **240** A3
Khanai *Pakistan* 30°30N 67°8E **242** D2
Khānaqīn *Iraq* 34°23N 45°25E **213** E11
Khanāşir *Syria* 35°45N 37°30E **250** C8
Khānbāghī *Iran* 36°10N 55°25E **247** B7
Khandallah *N.Z.* 41°15S 174°47E **143** B1
Khandwa *India* 21°49N 76°22E **244** D3
Khandyga *Russia* 62°42N 135°35E **215** C14
Khanewal *Pakistan* 30°20N 71°55E **242** D4
Khangah Dogran
Pakistan 31°50N 73°37E **242** D5
Khanh Duong *Vietnam* 12°44N 108°44E **236** F7
Khaniá = Chania *Greece* 35°30N 24°4E **207** E5
Khaniadhana *India* 25°1N 78°8E **242** G8
Khanka, L. *Asia* 45°0N 132°24E **220** B6
Khankendy = Xankändi
Azerbaijan 39°52N 46°49E **213** C12
Khanna *India* 30°42N 76°16E **242** D7
Khanozai *Pakistan* 30°37N 67°19E **242** D2
Khanpur *Pakistan* 28°42N 70°35E **242** E4
Khansā' *Iraq* 33°21N 44°28E **113** A2
Khanty-Mansiysk *Russia* 61°0N 69°0E **214** C7
Khanzire, Ras *Somali Rep.* 10°52N 45°48E **267** B6
Khao Khitchakut △
Thailand 12°50N 102°10E **236** F4
Khao Laem △ *Thailand* 14°56N 98°31E **236** E2
Khao Laem Res. *Thailand* 14°50N 98°30E **236** E2
Khao Lak △ *Malaysia* 8°38N 98°18E **237** H2
Khao Luang △ *Thailand* 8°34N 99°42E **237** H2
Khao Nam Khang △
Thailand 6°32N 100°35E **237** J3
Khao Phlu *Thailand* 9°29N 99°59E **237** b
Khao Pu-Khao Ya △
Thailand 7°26N 99°57E **237** J2
Khao Sam Roi Yot △
Thailand 12°13N 99°57E **237** F2
Khao Sok △ *Thailand* 8°55N 98°38E **237** H2
Khao Yai △ *Thailand* 14°21N 101°29E **236** E3
Khaoen Si Nakarin △
Thailand 14°47N 99°0E **236** E2
Khapalu *Pakistan* 35°10N 76°20E **243** B7
Khapcheranga *Russia* 49°42N 112°24E **215** E12
Khaptao △ *Nepal* 29°20N 81°10E **243** E9
Kharabali *Russia* 47°25N 47°15E **191** G8
Kharagauli *Georgia* 42°1N 43°12E **191** J6
Kharaghoda *India* 23°11N 71°46E **242** H4
Kharagpur *India* 22°20N 87°25E **243** H12
Kharan Kalat *Pakistan* 28°34N 65°21E **240** C2
Kharānaq *Iran* 32°20N 54°45E **247** C7
Kharavli *India* 18°54N 72°55E **130** B2
Kharda *India* 18°40N 75°34E **244** E2
Khardung La *India* 34°20N 77°43E **243** B7
Kharg = Khārk, Jazīreh-ye
Iran 29°15N 50°28E **247** D6
Khârga, El Wâhât el
Egypt 25°10N 30°35E **256** B3
Khargon *India* 21°45N 75°40E **244** D2
Khari → *India* 25°54N 74°31E **242** G6
Kharian *Pakistan* 32°49N 73°52E **242** C5
Khariar *India* 20°17N 82°46E **244** D6
Kharit, Wadi el → *Egypt* 24°26N 33°3E **256** C3
Khārk, Jazīreh-ye *Iran* 29°15N 50°28E **247** D6
Kharkiv *Ukraine* 49°58N 36°20E **189** H9
Kharkiv □ *Ukraine* 48°20N 36°20E **189** H9
Kharkov = Kharkiv
Ukraine 49°58N 36°20E **189** H9
Kharmanli *Bulgaria* 41°55N 25°55E **203** E9
Kharovsk *Russia* 59°56N 40°13E **188** C11
Kharsawangarh *India* 22°48N 85°50E **243** H11
Kharta *Turkey* 40°55N 29°7E **212** B3
Khartoum = El Khartûm
Sudan 15°31N 32°35E **257** D3
Khartum *Canada* 45°15N 77°5W **312** A7
Khasan *Russia* 42°25N 130°40E **220** C5
Khasavyurt *Russia* 43°16N 46°40E **191** J8
Khāsh *Iran* 28°15N 61°15E **240** C1
Khāsh, Dasht-e *Afghan.* 31°50N 62°30E **240** C1
Khashm el Girba *Sudan* 14°59N 35°58E **257** E4
Khashum *Sudan* 12°27N 28°12E **257** E2
Khashuri *Georgia* 42°3N 43°35E **191** J6
Khasi Hills *India* 25°30N 91°30E **241** C3
Khaskovo *Bulgaria* 41°56N 25°30E **203** E9
Khaskovo □ *Bulgaria* 42°0N 25°40E **203** E9
Khatanga *Russia* 72°0N 102°20E **215** B11
Khatanga → *Russia* 72°55N 106°0E **215** B11
Khatauli *India* 29°17N 77°43E **242** E7
Khatlon □ *Tajikistan* 37°50N 69°0E **217** E7
Khatra *India* 22°59N 86°51E **243** H12
Khātūnābād *Iran* 30°1N 55°25E **247** D7
Khatyrka *Russia* 62°3N 175°15E **215** C18
Khavda *India* 23°51N 69°43E **242** H3
Khawlaf, Ra's *Yemen* 12°40N 54°7E **249** E6
Khawr Fakkān *U.A.E.* 25°21N 56°22E **247** E8
Khay' *Si. Arabia* 18°45N 41°24E **248** C3
Khaybar, Harrat
Si. Arabia 25°30N 39°45E **246** E4
Khāzimiyah *Iraq* 34°46N 43°37E **246** C4
Khazzān Jabal al Awliyā
Sudan 15°24N 32°20E **257** D3
Khe Bo *Vietnam* 19°8N 104°41E **236** C5
Khe Long *Vietnam* 21°29N 104°46E **236** B5
Khe Sanh *Vietnam* 16°37N 106°45E **236** D6
Khed *Maharashtra, India* 17°43N 73°27E **244** F1
Khed *Maharashtra, India* 18°51N 73°56E **244** E1
Khed Brahma *India* 24°7N 73°5E **242** G5
Khefren *Egypt* 29°58N 31°8E **117** B1
Khekra *India* 28°52N 77°20E **242** E7
Khem-Beldyr = Kyzyl
Russia 51°50N 94°30E **217** B12
Khemarak Phouminville = Krong
Kaoh Kong *Cambodia* 11°37N 102°59E **237** G4
Khemisset *Morocco* 33°50N 6°1W **260** B3
Khemisset □ *Morocco* 33°40N 6°15W **260** B3
Khemmarat *Thailand* 16°10N 105°15E **236** D5
Khenāmān *Iran* 30°27N 56°29E **247** D8
Khenchela *Algeria* 35°28N 7°11E **261** A6
Khenchela □ *Algeria* 35°0N 7°0E **261** B6
Khenifra *Morocco* 32°58N 5°46W **260** B3
Kherrata *Algeria* 36°27N 5°13E **261** A6
Khersān → *Iran* 31°33N 50°22E **247** D6
Kherson *Ukraine* 46°35N 32°35E **189** J7
Kherson □ *Ukraine* 46°15N 33°10E **189** J7
Kheta → *Russia* 71°54N 102°6E **215** B11
Khewari *Pakistan* 26°36N 68°52E **242** F3
Khibinogorsk = Kirovsk
Russia 67°32N 33°41E **186** A5
Khichripur *India* 28°37N 77°18E **120** B2
Khidirpur *India* 22°32N 88°19E **124** B1
Khilchipur *India* 24°2N 76°34E **242** G7
Khilok *Russia* 51°30N 110°45E **215** D12
Khimki *Russia* 55°53N 37°26E **188** E9
Khimki-Khovrino *Russia* 55°51N 37°31E **129** A3
Khios = Chios *Greece* 38°27N 26°9E **205** C8
Khirbet Batin Abu Lihyah
West Bank 31°50N 35°16E **123** A1
Khirbet el-Misbah
West Bank 31°53N 35°4E **123** A1
Khirbet Jub e-Rum
West Bank 31°44N 35°16E **123** B2
Khirsadoh *India* 22°11N 78°47E **243** H8
Khiuma = Hiiumaa
Estonia 58°50N 22°45E **188** C2
Khiva *Uzbekistan* 41°30N 60°18E **216** D6
Khlebarovo *Bulgaria* 43°37N 26°15E **203** C10
Khlong Khlung *Thailand* 16°12N 99°43E **236** D2
Khlong Lan △ *Thailand* 16°12N 99°13E **236** D2
Khlong Phanom △
Thailand 8°45N 98°38E **237** H2
Khlong San *Thailand* 13°43N 100°29E **113** B2
Khlong Toey *Thailand* 13°43N 100°36E **113** B2
Khmelnik *Ukraine* 49°33N 27°58E **177** D14
Khmelnytskyy *Ukraine* 49°23N 27°0E **177** D14
Khmelnytskyy □
Ukraine 49°50N 26°40E **177** D14
Khmer Rep. = Cambodia ■
Asia 12°15N 105°0E **236** F5
Khoai, Hon *Vietnam* 8°26N 104°50E **237** H5
Khodoriv *Ukraine* 49°24N 24°19E **177** D13
Khodzent = Khŭjand
Tajikistan 40°17N 69°37E **217** D7
Khojak Pass *Afghan.* 30°51N 66°34E **242** D2
Khojayli *Uzbekistan* 42°29N 59°31E **216** D5
Khok Kloi *Thailand* 8°17N 98°19E **237** a
Khok Pho *Thailand* 6°43N 101°6E **237** J3
Khok Samrong *Thailand* 15°3N 100°43E **236** E3
Khokhropār *Pakistan* 25°42N 70°12E **240** D3
Kholm *Afghan.* 36°45N 67°40E **240** A2
Kholm *Russia* 57°10N 31°15E **188** D6
Kholmsk *Russia* 47°40N 142°5E **215** E15
Khomārlu *Iran* 39°6N 47°3E **213** C12
Khomas Hochland *Namibia* 22°40S 16°0E **270** B2
Khombole *Senegal* 14°43N 16°42W **262** C1
Khomeyn *Iran* 33°40N 50°7E **247** C6
Khomeynī Shahr *Iran* 32°41N 51°31E **247** C6
Khomodino *Botswana* 22°46S 23°52E **270** B3
Khon Kaen *Thailand* 16°30N 102°47E **236** D4
Khong → *Cambodia* 13°32N 105°58E **236** F5
Khong Sedone *Laos* 15°34N 105°49E **236** E5
Khonuu *Russia* 66°30N 143°12E **215** C15
Khoper → *Russia* 49°30N 42°20E **190** F6
Khor el 'Atash *Sudan* 13°20N 34°15E **257** E3
Khorāsān-e Janūb □ *Iran* 32°0N 59°0E **247** C8
Khorāsān-e Razavī □ *Iran* 35°0N 59°0E **247** C8
Khorāsān-e Shemālī □ *Iran* 37°0N 57°0E **247** B8
Khorat = Nakhon Ratchasima
Thailand 14°59N 102°12E **236** E4
Khorat, Cao Nguyen
Thailand 15°30N 102°50E **236** E4
Khorazm = Xorazm □
Uzbekistan 43°0N 60°0E **216** D6
Khorb el Ethel *Algeria* 28°30N 6°17W **260** C3
Khorel *India* 22°41N 88°18E **124** A1
Khorixas *Namibia* 20°16S 14°59E **270** B1
Khorol *Ukraine* 49°48N 33°15E **189** H7
Khorosovo *Russia* 55°46N 37°27E **129** B2
Khorramābād *Khorāsān,*
Iran 35°6N 57°57E **247** C8
Khorramābād *Lorestān,*
Iran 33°30N 48°25E **213** F13
Khorramdarreh *Iran* 36°11N 49°11E **213** D13
Khorrāmshahr *Iran* 30°29N 48°15E **247** D6
Khorugh *Tajikistan* 37°30N 71°36E **240** A3
Khosravī *Iran* 30°48N 51°28E **247** D6
Khosrowābād *Khuzestān,*
Iran 30°10N 48°25E **247** D6
Khosrowābād *Kordestān,*
Iran 35°31N 47°38E **213** E12
Khost *Pakistan* 30°13N 67°35E **242** D2
Khosūyeh *Iran* 28°32N 54°26E **247** D7
Khotan = Hotan *China* 37°25N 79°55E **217** E9
Khotyn *Ukraine* 48°31N 26°27E **183** B11
Khouribga *Morocco* 32°58N 6°57W **260** B3
Khouribga □ *Morocco* 32°56N 6°36W **260** B3
Khowai *Bangla.* 24°5N 91°40E **241** C3
Khowst *Afghan.* 33°22N 69°58E **242** C3
Khowst □ *Afghan.* 33°20N 70°0E **240** B3
Khoyniki *Belarus* 51°54N 29°55E **177** C15
Khram, Ko *Thailand* 12°42N 100°47E **236** F3
Khrami → *Georgia* 41°25N 45°0E **191** K7
Khrenovoye *Russia* 51°4N 40°16E **190** E5
Khromtaū *Kazakhstan* 50°17N 58°27E **216** B5
Khrysokhou B. *Cyprus* 35°6N 32°25E **207** E8
Khuan Wa *Thailand* 7°53N 98°17E **237** a
Khudrah, W. → *Yemen* 18°10N 50°20E **249** C5
Khudzhand = Khŭjand
Tajikistan 40°17N 69°37E **217** D7
Khuff *Si. Arabia* 24°55N 44°53E **246** E5
Khūgīānī *Afghan.* 31°34N 66°32E **242** D2
Khuis *Botswana* 26°40S 21°49E **270** C3
Khuiyala *India* 27°9N 70°25E **242** F4
Khŭjand *Tajikistan* 40°17N 69°37E **217** D7
Khŭjayli = Khojayli
Uzbekistan 42°29N 59°31E **216** D5
Khujner *India* 23°47N 76°36E **242** H7
Khukhan *Thailand* 14°42N 104°12E **236** E5
Khulayş *Si. Arabia* 22°9N 39°19E **248** B2
Khulna *Bangla.* 22°45N 89°34E **241** D2
Khulna □ *Bangla.* 22°25N 89°35E **241** D2
Khulo *Georgia* 41°33N 42°19E **191** K5
Khumago *Botswana* 20°26S 24°32E **270** B3
Khumrah *Si. Arabia* 21°22N 39°13E **248** B2
Khunjerab △ *Pakistan* 36°40N 75°30E **243** A3
Khunjerab Pass = Kinjirap Daban
Asia 36°40N 75°25E **240** A4
Khūnsorkh *Iran* 27°9N 56°7E **247** E8
Khunti *India* 23°5N 85°17E **243** H11
Khūr *Iran* 32°55N 58°18E **247** C8
Khurai *India* 24°3N 78°23E **242** G8
Khurayḑah *Yemen* 15°33N 48°18E **249** D5
Khurayş *Si. Arabia* 25°6N 48°2E **247** E6
Khurda *India* 20°11N 85°37E **244** D7
Khureit *Sudan* 13°59N 26°3E **257** E2
Khurja *India* 28°15N 77°58E **242** E7
Khūrmāl *Iraq* 35°18N 46°2E **213** E12
Khurr, Wādī al *Iraq* 32°3N 43°52E **246** C4
Khūsf *Iran* 32°46N 58°53E **247** C8
Khushab *Pakistan* 32°20N 72°20E **242** C5
Khust *Ukraine* 48°10N 23°18E **183** B8
Khutse △ *Botswana* 23°31S 24°12E **270** B3
Khuwei *Sudan* 13°5N 29°17E **257** E2
Khuzdar *Pakistan* 27°52N 66°30E **242** F2
Khūzestān □ *Iran* 31°0N 49°0E **247** D6
Khvāf *Iran* 34°33N 60°8E **247** C9
Khvājeh *Iran* 38°9N 46°35E **246** B5
Khvājeh Moḩammad, Kūh-e
Afghan. 36°22N 70°17E **240** A3
Khvalynsk *Russia* 52°30N 48°2E **190** D9
Khvānsār *Iran* 29°56N 54°8E **247** D7
Khvatovka *Russia* 52°24N 46°32E **190** D8
Khvor *Iran* 33°45N 55°0E **247** C7
Khvorgū *Iran* 27°34N 56°27E **247** E8
Khvormūj *Iran* 28°40N 51°30E **247** D6
Khvoy *Iran* 38°35N 45°0E **213** C11
Khvoynaya *Russia* 58°58N 34°28E **188** C8
Khwae Noi → *Thailand* 14°1N 99°32E **236** E2
Khyber Pass *Afghan.* 34°10N 71°8E **242** B4
Khyriv *Ukraine* 49°32N 22°50E **185** J9
Kia *Fiji* 16°16S 179°8E **287** a
Kia *Solomon Is.* 7°32S 158°26E **287** L10
Kiabukwa
Dem. Rep. of the Congo 8°40S 24°48E **265** D4
Kiadho → *India* 19°37N 77°40E **244** E3
Kiama *N.S.W., Australia* 34°40S 150°50E **283** C9
Kiamba
Dem. Rep. of the Congo 7°19S 17°49E **265** D3
Kiamari *Pakistan* 24°49N 66°58E **125** B1
Kiamba *Phil.* 6°2N 124°46E **233** H5
Kiambi *Dem. Rep. of the Congo* 7°15S 28°0E **268** D2
Kiambu *Kenya* 1°8S 36°50E **268** C4
Kiamusze = Jiamusi
China 46°40N 130°26E **219** B15
Kian = Ji'an *China* 41°5N 126°10E **227** D14
Kiana *U.S.A.* 66°58N 160°26W **303** C7
Kiang West △ *Gambia* 13°25N 15°50W **262** C1
Kiangara *Madag.* 17°58S 47°2E **272** B8
Kiangsi = Jiangxi □
China 27°30N 116°0E **229** D11
Kiangsu = Jiangsu □
China 33°0N 120°0E **227** H11
Kiato *Greece* 38°1N 22°45E **204** C4
Kibæk *Denmark* 56°2N 8°51E **163** H2
Kibale △ *Uganda* 0°16N 30°18E **268** B3
Kibanga Port *Uganda* 0°10N 32°58E **268** B3
Kibangou *Congo* 3°26S 12°22E **264** C2
Kibara *Tanzania* 2°8S 33°30E **268** C3
Kibare, Mts.
Dem. Rep. of the Congo 8°25S 27°10E **268** D2
Kibawe *Phil.* 7°34N 125°0E **233** H5
Kibenga
Dem. Rep. of the Congo 7°56S 17°30E **265** D3
Kibira △ *Burundi* 3°6S 30°24E **268** C3
Kiboga *Uganda* 0°58N 31°45E **268** B3
Kibombo
Dem. Rep. of the Congo 3°57S 25°53E **265** C5
Kibondo *Tanzania* 3°35S 30°45E **268** C3
Kibre Mengist *Ethiopia* 5°54N 38°59E **257** F4
Kıbrıs = Cyprus ■ *Asia* 35°0N 33°0E **207** F9
Kibumbu *Burundi* 3°32S 29°45E **268** C2
Kibungo *Rwanda* 2°10S 30°32E **268** C3
Kibuye *Burundi* 3°39S 29°59E **268** C2
Kibuye *Rwanda* 2°3S 29°21E **268** C2
Kibwesa *Tanzania* 6°30S 29°58E **268** D2
Kibwezi *Kenya* 2°27S 37°57E **268** C4
Kicasalih *Turkey* 41°23N 26°48E **203** E10
Kičevo *Macedonia* 41°34N 20°59E **202** E4
Kichha *India* 28°53N 79°30E **243** E8
Kichha → *India* 28°41N 79°18E **243** E8
Kichmengskiy Gorodok
Russia 59°59N 45°48E **186** B8
Kicking Horse Pass
Canada 51°28N 116°16W **296** C5
Kîd, W. → *Egypt* 28°9N 34°27E **251** K5
Kid I. *Antigua & B.* 17°42N 61°49W **322** c
Kidal *Mali* 18°26N 1°22E **263** B5
Kidal □ *Mali* 19°55N 1°5E **263** B5
Kidapawan *Phil.* 7°1N 125°3E **233** H5
Kidderminster *U.K.* 52°24N 2°15W **169** E5
Kidepo Valley △ *Uganda* 3°52N 33°50E **268** B3
Kidete *Tanzania* 6°25S 37°17E **268** D4
Kidira *Senegal* 14°28N 12°13W **262** C2
Kidnappers, C. *N.Z.* 39°38S 177°5E **284** F6
Kidsgrove *U.K.* 53°5N 2°14W **168** D5
Kidston *Australia* 18°52S 144°8E **280** B3
Kidugallo *Tanzania* 6°49S 38°15E **268** D4
Kidurong, Tanjong
Malaysia 3°16N 113°3E **235** B4
Kiel *Germany* 54°19N 10°8E **178** A6
Kiel Canal = Nord-Ostsee-Kanal
Germany 54°12N 9°32E **178** A5
Kiel-Kanal = Nord-Ostsee-Kanal
Germany 54°12N 9°32E **178** A5
Kielce *Poland* 50°52N 20°42E **185** H7
Kielder Water *U.K.* 55°11N 2°31W **168** B5
Kieler Bucht *Germany* 54°35N 10°25E **178** A6
Kiembara *Burkina Faso* 13°15N 2°44W **262** C4
Kienge
Dem. Rep. of the Congo 10°30S 27°30E **269** E2
Kierling *Austria* 48°18N 16°16E **142** A1
Kierlingbach → *Austria* 48°18N 16°19E **142** A1
Kiessé *Niger* 13°29N 4°1E **263** C5
Kieta *Papua N. G.* 6°12S 155°36E **286** D8
Kiev = Kyyiv *Ukraine* 50°30N 30°28E **177** C16
Kifaya *Guinea* 12°10N 13°4W **262** C2
Kiffa *Mauritania* 16°37N 11°24W **262** B2
Kifisos → *Athina, Greece* 37°58N 23°42E **112** B2
Kifisos → *Voiotia, Greece* 38°35N 23°20E **204** C5
Kifissia *Greece* 38°4N 23°49E **204** C5
Kifrī *Iraq* 34°45N 45°0E **213** E11
Kigali *Rwanda* 1°59S 30°4E **268** C3
Kigarama *Tanzania* 1°1S 31°50E **268** C3
Kigelle *South Sudan* 8°40N 34°2E **257** F3
Kigezi △ *Uganda* 0°34S 29°55E **268** C2
Kiği *Turkey* 39°18N 40°21E **213** C9
Kigoma □ *Tanzania* 5°0S 30°0E **268** D3
Kigoma-Ujiji *Tanzania* 4°55S 29°36E **268** C2
Kigomasha, Ras *Tanzania* 4°58S 38°58E **268** C4
Kigosi △ *Tanzania* 4°10S 31°45E **268** C3
Kığzı *Turkey* 38°18N 43°25E **246** B4
Kihei *U.S.A.* 20°47N 156°28W **302** C5
Kihikihi *N.Z.* 38°2S 175°22E **284** E4
Kihnu *Estonia* 58°9N 24°1E **188** C3
Kiholo B. *U.S.A.* 19°50N 155°56W **302** D6
Kii-Hantō *Japan* 34°0N 135°45E **223** D7
Kii-Nagashima *Japan* 34°12N 136°20E **223** D8
Kii-Sanchi *Japan* 34°20N 136°0E **223** C8
Kii-Suidō *Japan* 33°40N 134°45E **222** C5
Kiira Dam *Uganda* 0°25N 33°0E **268** B3
Kiire *Japan* 31°22N 130°33E **222** F2
Kijik *U.S.A.* 60°20N 154°20W **303** F9
Kikaiga-Shima *Japan* 28°19N 129°59E **221** K4
Kikiak = Rigolet *Canada* 54°10N 58°23W **299** B8
Kikinda *Serbia* 45°50N 20°30E **182** E5
Kikládhes = Cyclades
Greece 37°0N 24°30E **204** E6
Kikoira *Australia* 33°39S 146°40E **283** B7
Kikombo *Bandundu,*
Dem. Rep. of the Congo 5°37S 18°50E **265** D3
Kikombo *Bandundu,*
Dem. Rep. of the Congo 5°49S 17°45E **265** D3
Kikongo
Dem. Rep. of the Congo 4°16S 17°17E **265** C3
Kikori *Papua N. G.* 7°25S 144°15E **286** D3
Kikori → *Papua N. G.* 7°38S 144°20E **286** D3
Kikuchi *Japan* 32°59N 130°47E **222** D2
Kikuna *Japan* 35°30N 139°37E **140** B2
Kikwit *Dem. Rep. of the Congo* 5°0S 18°45E **265** D3
Kil *Sweden* 59°30N 13°20E **162** E7
Kilafors *Sweden* 61°14N 16°36E **162** D10
Kilakkarai *India* 9°12N 78°47E **245** K4
Kilar *India* 33°6N 76°25E **242** C7
Kilauea *U.S.A.* 22°13N 159°25W **302** A2
Kilauea Caldera *U.S.A.* 19°25N 155°17W **302** D6
Kilbarrack *Ireland* 53°23N 6°10W **120** A2
Kilbeggan *Ireland* 53°22N 7°30W **166** C4
Kilbirnie *N.Z.* 41°19S 174°48E **143** B1
Kilbrannan Sd. *U.K.* 55°37N 5°26W **167** F3
Kilbuck Mts. *U.S.A.* 60°36N 159°53W **303** F8
Kilburn *U.K.* 51°32N 0°11W **125** A2
Kilchu *N. Korea* 40°57N 129°25E **224** D4
Kilcoy *Australia* 26°59S 152°30E **281** D5
Kildare *Ireland* 53°9N 6°55W **166** C5
Kildare □ *Ireland* 53°10N 6°50W **166** C5
Kildinstroy *Russia* 68°48N 33°6E **186** B25
Kileikli *Sudan* 11°25N 25°31E **257** E2
Kilembe
Dem. Rep. of the Congo 5°42S 19°55E **265** D3
Kilen *Norway* 59°20N 8°49E **163** E6
Kilfinnane *Ireland* 52°21N 8°28W **166** D3
Kilgarvan *Ireland* 51°54N 9°27W **166** E2
Kilgore *U.S.A.* 32°23N 94°53W **314** E7
Kilgoris *Kenya* 1°0S 34°53E **268** C3
Kilibo *Benin* 8°32N 2°38E **263** D5
Kilifi *Kenya* 3°40S 39°48E **268** C4
Kilimanjaro *Tanzania* 3°7S 37°20E **268** C4
Kilimanjaro □ *Tanzania* 4°0S 38°0E **268** C4
Kilimanjaro △ *Tanzania* 3°2S 37°19E **268** C4
Kilimli *Turkey* 41°28N 31°50E **212** B4
Kilinailau Is. *Papua N. G.* 4°45S 155°20E **286** C8
Kilindini *Kenya* 4°4S 39°40E **268** C4
Kilis *Turkey* 36°42N 37°6E **250** B8
Kilis □ *Turkey* 36°50N 37°10E **212** D7
Kiliya *Ukraine* 45°28N 29°16E **183** E14
Kilkee *Ireland* 52°41N 9°39W **166** D2
Kilkeel *U.K.* 54°4N 6°0W **166** B5
Kilkenny *Ireland* 52°39N 7°15W **166** D4
Kilkenny □ *Ireland* 52°35N 7°15W **166** D4
Kilkieran B. *Ireland* 53°20N 9°41W **166** C2
Kilkis *Greece* 40°58N 22°57E **202** F6
Kilkis □ *Greece* 41°5N 22°50E **202** E6
Killakee *Ireland* 53°15N 6°19W **120** B2
Killala *Ireland* 54°13N 9°12W **166** B2
Killala B. *Ireland* 54°16N 9°8W **166** B2
Killaloe *Ont., Canada* 45°33N 77°25W **312** A7
Killaloe *Clare, Ireland* 52°48N 8°28W **166** D3
Killarney *Queens.,*
Australia 28°20S 152°18E **281** D5
Killarney *Man., Canada* 49°10N 99°40W **297** D9
Killarney *Kerry, Ireland* 52°4N 9°30W **166** D2
Killarney, L. *Bahamas* 25°3N 77°27W **153** b
Killarney △ *Ireland* 52°0N 9°33W **166** D2
Killary Harbour *Ireland* 53°38N 9°52W **166** C2
Killdeer *U.S.A.* 47°22N 102°45W **308** B2
Killeberg *Sweden* 56°29N 14°5E **163** H8
Killeen *U.S.A.* 31°7N 97°44W **314** F6
Killester *Ireland* 53°22N 6°11W **120** A2
Killin *U.K.* 56°28N 4°19W **167** E4
Killiney *Ireland* 53°16N 6°7W **120** B3
Killiney B. *Ireland* 53°15N 6°5W **120** B3
Killington Pk. *U.S.A.* 43°36N 72°49W **313** C12
Killini = Kyllini *Greece* 37°55N 21°8E **207** D3
Killini *Greece* 37°54N 22°25E **204** D4
Killorglin *Ireland* 52°6N 9°47W **166** D2
Killybegs *Ireland* 54°38N 8°26W **166** B3
Kilmacud *Ireland* 53°17N 6°13W **120** B2
Kilmainham *Ireland* 53°20N 6°17W **120** A2
Kilmainham Gaol *Ireland* 53°21N 6°19W **120** A2
Kilmarnock *U.K.* 55°37N 4°29W **167** F4
Kilmashogue Mt. *Ireland* 53°15N 6°15W **120** B2
Kilmez *Russia* 56°58N 50°55E **190** B10
Kilmez → *Russia* 56°58N 50°28E **190** B10
Kilmore *Vic., Australia* 37°25S 144°53E **283** D6
Kilmore *Dublin, Ireland* 53°23N 6°13W **120** A2
Kilmore Quay *Ireland* 52°10N 6°36W **166** D5
Kilnamanagh *Ireland* 53°18N 6°22W **120** B1
Kilo *Finland* 60°13N 24°47E **121** B1
Kilokri *India* 28°34N 77°15E **120** B2
Kilómetro 1082 = Joaquín V.
González *Argentina* 25°10S 64°0W **334** B3
Kilondo *Tanzania* 9°45S 34°20E **269** D3
Kilosa *Tanzania* 6°48S 37°0E **268** D4
Kilrush *Ireland* 52°38N 9°29W **166** D2
Kiltan I. *India* 11°29N 73°0E **245** J1
Kiltiernan *Ireland* 53°15N 6°11W **120** B2
Kilwa Kisiwani *Tanzania* 8°58S 39°32E **269** D4
Kilwa Kivinje *Tanzania* 8°45S 39°25E **269** D4
Kilwa Masoko *Tanzania* 8°55S 39°30E **269** D4
Kilwinning *U.K.* 55°39N 4°43W **167** F4
Kim *U.S.A.* 37°15N 103°21W **305** H12
Kim → *Cameroon* 5°28N 11°7E **263** D7
Kimaam *Indonesia* 7°58S 138°53E **231** F9
Kimamba *Tanzania* 6°45S 37°10E **268** D4
Kimba *Australia* 33°8S 136°23E **282** B2
Kimball *Nebr., U.S.A.* 41°14N 103°40W **308** E2
Kimball *S. Dak., U.S.A.* 43°45N 98°57W **308** D4
Kimbanda
Dem. Rep. of the Congo 4°16S 18°30E **265** C3
Kimbe *Papua N. G.* 5°33S 150°11E **286** C6
Kimbe B. *Papua N. G.* 5°15S 150°30E **286** C6
Kimberley *W. Austral.,*
Australia 16°20S 127°0E **278** C4
Kimberley *B.C., Canada* 49°40N 115°59W **296** D5
Kimberley *Ont., Canada* 44°23N 80°32W **312** B4
Kimberley *Northern Cape,*
S. Africa 28°43S 24°46E **270** C3
Kimberly *U.S.A.* 42°32N 114°22W **304** E6
Kimbongo
Dem. Rep. of the Congo 6°8S 18°1E **265** D3
Kimch'aek *N. Korea* 40°40N 129°10E **224** B4
Kimhae = Gimhae
S. Korea 35°14N 128°53E **224** E4
Kimhwa *N. Korea* 38°25N 127°36E **224** C3
Kimi *Greece* 38°38N 24°6E **204** C6
Kimitsu *Japan* 35°19N 139°54E **223** B11
Kimjŏngsugŭp *N. Korea* 41°24N 127°45E **224** B3
Kimmage *Ireland* 53°18N 6°17W **120** B2
Kimmirut *Canada* 62°50N 69°50W **295** E18
Kimolos *Greece* 36°48N 24°37E **204** E6
Kimongo *Congo* 4°27S 12°53E **265** C2
Kimovsk *Moskva, Russia* 55°21N 37°28E **188** E9
Kimovsk *Tula, Russia* 54°0N 38°29E **188** E10
Kimpangu
Dem. Rep. of the Congo 5°52S 15°3E **265** D3
Kimparana *Mali* 12°48N 5°0W **262** C4
Kimpese *Congo* 5°33S 14°26E **265** D2
Kimpese
Dem. Rep. of the Congo 5°35S 14°26E **265** D2
Kimry *Russia* 56°55N 37°15E **188** D9
Kimstad *Sweden* 58°35N 15°58E **163** F9
Kimvula
Dem. Rep. of the Congo 5°44S 15°58E **265** D3
Kin *Burma* 22°46N 94°22E **241** D5
Kin-u *Burma* 22°46N 95°37E **241** D5
Kin-wan *Japan* 26°23N 127°55E **288** a
Kinabalian, Mt. *Phil.* 8°12N 125°26E **233** G5
Kinabalu, Gunung
Malaysia 6°3N 116°14E **235** A5
Kinabalu △ *Malaysia* 6°0N 116°30E **235** A5
Kinango *Kenya* 4°8S 39°19E **268** C4
Kinard *U.S.A.* 30°16N 85°15W **316** E4
Kinaros *Greece* 36°59N 26°15E **205** E8
Kinaskan L. *Canada* 57°38N 130°8W **296** B2
Kinbasket L. *Canada* 52°0N 118°10W **296** C5
Kincaid *Canada* 49°40N 107°0W **297** D7
Kincaid *U.S.A.* 39°35N 89°25W **310** F9
Kincardine *Canada* 44°10N 81°40W **312** B3
Kinchafoonee Cr. →
U.S.A. 31°38N 84°10W **316** D5
Kinchega △ *Australia* 32°27S 142°15E **282** B5
Kincolith *Canada* 55°0N 129°57W **296** C3
Kinda *Kasai-Or.,*
Dem. Rep. of the Congo 9°18S 25°4E **265** D5
Kinda *Katanga,*
Dem. Rep. of the Congo 4°47S 21°48E **265** D4
Kindambi
Dem. Rep. of the Congo 5°6S 18°14E **265** D4
Kindberg *Austria* 47°30N 15°27E **180** D8
Kinde *U.S.A.* 43°56N 83°0W **312** C2
Kindele
Dem. Rep. of the Congo 8°39S 24°10E **265** D4
Kinder Scout *U.K.* 53°24N 1°52W **168** D6
Kinderhook *U.S.A.* 42°33N 73°42W **313** D10
Kindersley *Canada* 51°30N 109°10W **297** C7
Kindi *Iraq* 33°18N 44°22E **113** B2
Kindia *Guinea* 10°0N 12°52W **262** D2
Kindongo
Dem. Rep. of the Congo 3°58S 17°30E **264** C3
Kindu *Dem. Rep. of the Congo* 2°55S 25°50E **265** C5
Kinel *Russia* 53°15N 50°40E **190** D10
Kineshma *Russia* 57°30N 42°5E **190** B6
Kinesi *Tanzania* 1°25S 33°50E **268** C3
King, L. *Australia* 33°10S 119°35E **279** F2
King, Mt. *Australia* 25°10S 147°30E **280** D4
King Christian I.
Canada 77°48N 101°40W **295** B11
King City *Calif., U.S.A.* 36°13N 121°8W **306** J5
King City *Mo., U.S.A.* 40°3N 94°31W **310** D2
King Cove *U.S.A.* 55°3N 162°19W **303** J7
King Cr. → *Australia* 24°35S 139°30E **280** C2
King Edward →
Australia 14°14S 126°35E **278** B4
King Edward Point
S. Georgia 54°17S 36°30W **151** B1
King Frederick VI Land = Kong
Frederik VI.s Kyst
Greenland 63°0N 43°0W **154** E6
King George B. *Falk. Is.* 51°30S 60°30W **153** f
King George I. *Antarctica* 60°0S 60°0W **151** C18
King George Is. *Canada* 57°20N 80°30W **295** F15
King George Sd. *Australia* 35°5S 118°0E **279** G2
King George VI Falls
Guyana 5°42N 61°5W **329** B5
King I. = Kadan Kyun
Burma 12°30N 98°20E **236** F2
King I. *Tas., Australia* 39°50S 144°0E **281** F3
King I. *B.C., Canada* 52°10N 127°40W **296** C3
King Khalid Military City =
Madinat al Malik Khālid al
Askarīyah *Si. Arabia* 27°54N 45°31E **246** E5
King Leopold Ranges
Australia 17°30S 125°45E **278** C4
King of Prussia *U.S.A.* 40°5N 75°23W **313** F9
King Salmon *U.S.A.* 58°42N 156°40W **303** G8
King Sd. *Australia* 16°50S 123°20E **278** C3
King Sejong *Antarctica* 62°30S 58°0W **151** C18
King William I. *Canada* 69°10N 97°25W **294** D12
King William's Town
S. Africa 32°51S 27°22E **270** D4
Kingaok = Bathurst Inlet
Canada 66°50N 108°1W **294** D10
Kingaroy *Australia* 26°32S 151°51E **281** D5
Kingdom City *U.S.A.* 38°56N 91°56W **310** F5
Kingfisher *U.S.A.* 35°52N 97°56W **314** D6
Kinghorn *U.K.* 56°5N 3°10W **121** A2
Kingirbān *Iraq* 34°40N 44°54E **246** C5
Kingisepp = Kuressaare
Estonia 58°15N 22°30E **188** C2
Kingisepp *Russia* 59°25N 28°40E **188** C5
Kingking = Pantukan
Phil. 7°9N 125°54E **233** H5
Kinglake △ *Australia* 37°30S 145°22E **283** D6
Kingman *Ariz., U.S.A.* 35°12N 114°4W **307** K12
Kingman *Ind., U.S.A.* 39°58N 87°18W **311** E9
Kingman *Kans., U.S.A.* 37°39N 98°7W **308** G4
Kingoonya *Australia* 30°55S 135°19E **281** E2
Kingri *Pakistan* 30°27N 69°49E **242** D3
Kings → *U.S.A.* 36°3N 119°50W **306** J7
Kings Canyon *Australia* 24°15S 131°34E **278** D5
Kings Canyon △ *U.S.A.* 36°50N 118°40W **306** J8
Kings County = Offaly □
Ireland 53°15N 7°30W **166** C4
Kings Cross *Sydney, Australia* **139** c3
King's Cross *London, U.K.* **125** a4
Kings Domain *Australia* 37°49S 144°58E **126** B1
Kings Forest = Kongelunden
Denmark 55°34N 12°34E **118** B3
King's Lynn *U.K.* 52°45N 0°24E **168** E8
Kings Park *N.Y., U.S.A.* 40°53N 73°16W **313** F11
Kings Park *Va., U.S.A.* 38°48N 77°17W **143** C2
Kings Park West *U.S.A.* 38°48N 77°18W **143** C2
Kings Peak *U.S.A.* 40°46N 110°23W **304** F8
King's Trough *Atl. Oc.* 43°48N 22°0W **152** B9
Kingsbridge *U.K.* 50°17N 3°47W **169** G4
Kingsburg *U.S.A.* 36°31N 119°33W **306** J7
Kingsbury *Vic., Australia* 37°43S 145°2E **128** A2
Kingsbury *London, U.K.* 51°34N 0°15W **125** A2
Kingscote *Australia* 35°40S 137°38E **282** C2
Kingscourt *Ireland* 53°55N 6°48W **166** C5
Kingsford *N.S.W.,*
Australia 33°56S 151°14E **139** B2
Kingsford *Mich., U.S.A.* 45°48N 88°4W **308** C9
Kingsford Smith, Sydney ✕ (SYD)
Australia 33°57S 151°11E **139** B2
Kingsland *U.S.A.* 30°48N 81°41W **316** E8
Kingsport *U.S.A.* 36°33N 82°33W **315** C13
Kingston *Ont., Canada* 44°14N 76°30W **313** B8
Kingston *Jamaica* 18°0N 76°50W **320** a
Kingston *N.Z.* 45°20S 168°43E **285** F3
Kingston *N.H., U.S.A.* 42°56N 71°3W **313** D13
Kingston *N.Y., U.S.A.* 41°56N 73°59W **313** E11
Kingston *Pa., U.S.A.* 41°16N 75°54W **313** E9
Kingston *R.I., U.S.A.* 41°29N 71°30W **313** E13
Kingston Pk. *U.S.A.* 35°44N 115°55W **307** K11
Kingston South East
Australia 36°51S 139°55E **282** D3
Kingston upon Hull *U.K.* 53°45N 0°21W **168** D7
Kingston upon Hull □
U.K. 53°45N 0°21W **168** D7
Kingston-upon-Thames □
U.K. 51°24N 0°17W **125** B2
Kingston Vale *U.K.* 51°25N 0°25W **125** B2
Kingstown = Dún Laoghaire
Ireland 53°17N 6°8W **120** B3
Kingstown *N.S.W.,*
Australia 30°29S 151°6E **283** A9
Kingstown *St. Vincent* 13°10N 61°10W **323** n
Kingstree *U.S.A.* 33°40N 79°50W **316** B10
Kingsville *Ont., Canada* 42°2N 82°45W **312** D2
Kingsville *Tex., U.S.A.* 27°31N 97°52W **314** H6
Kingsway *Canada* 43°38N 79°32W **141** B1
Kingtechen = Jingdezhen
China 29°20N 117°11E **229** C11
Kingunda
Dem. Rep. of the Congo 6°36S 16°58E **265** D3
Kingussie *U.K.* 57°6N 4°2W **167** D4
Kingwood *U.S.A.* 30°2N 95°16W **314** F7
Kınık *Antalya, Turkey* 36°20N 29°20E **205** E11
Kınık *İzmir, Turkey* 39°6N 27°24E **205** B9
Kinistino *Canada* 52°57N 105°2W **297** C7
Kinjirap Daban *Asia* 36°40N 75°25E **240** A4
Kinkala *Congo* 4°18S 14°49E **265** C2
Kinki □ *Japan* 33°45N 136°0E **223** D8
Kinkony, Farihin' *Madag.* 16°8S 45°50E **272** B2
Kinleith *N.Z.* 38°20S 175°56E **284** E4
Kinlochleven *U.K.* 56°43N 5°0W **167** E4
Kinmount *Canada* 44°48N 78°45W **312** B6
Kinmundy *U.S.A.* 38°46N 88°51W **311** F8
Kinn *Norway* 61°34N 4°45E **164** C1
Kinna *Sweden* 57°32N 12°42E **163** G6
Kinnairds Hd. *U.K.* 57°43N 2°1W **167** D6
Kinnared *Sweden* 57°2N 13°7E **163** G7
Kinnarp *Sweden* 58°5N 13°32E **163** F7
Kinneviken *Sweden* 58°35N 13°15E **163** F7
Kinngait *Canada* 64°14N 76°32W **295** E16
Kino Nuevo *Mexico* 28°52N 112°3W **318** B2
Kinogitan *Phil.* 9°0N 124°48E **233** G5
Kinoje → *Canada* 52°8N 81°25W **298** B3
Kinokawa *Japan* 34°15N 135°20E **223** C7
Kinomoto *Japan* 35°30N 136°13E **223** B8
Kinoni *Uganda* 0°41S 30°28E **268** C3
Kinoosao *Canada* 57°5N 102°1W **297** B8
Kinross *U.K.* 56°13N 3°25W **167** E5
Kinsale *Cork, Ireland* 51°42N 8°31W **166** E3
Kinsale *Montserrat* 16°42N 62°13W **323** p
Kinsale, Old Hd. of *Ireland* 51°37N 8°33W **166** E3
Kinsaley *Ireland* 53°24N 6°10W **120** A2
Kinsarvik *Norway* 60°22N 6°43E **164** D3
Kinsha = Chang Jiang →
China 31°48N 121°10E **229** B13
Kinshasa
Dem. Rep. of the Congo 4°20S 15°15E **265** C3
Kinsley *U.S.A.* 37°55N 99°25W **308** G4
Kinsman *U.S.A.* 41°26N 80°35W **312** E4
Kinston *Ala., U.S.A.* 31°13N 86°10W **316** D3
Kinston *N.C., U.S.A.* 35°16N 77°35W **315** D16
Kintamani *Indonesia* 8°14S 115°19E **231** J18
Kintampo *Ghana* 8°5N 1°41W **263** D4
Kintap *Indonesia* 3°51S 115°13E **235** C5
Kintore *U.K.* 57°14N 2°20W **167** D6
Kintore Ra. *Australia* 23°15S 128°47E **278** D4
Kintshua
Dem. Rep. of the Congo 4°27S 19°38E **265** C3
Kintyre *U.K.* 55°30N 5°35W **167** F3
Kintyre, Mull of *U.K.* 55°17N 5°47W **167** F3
Kinu-Gawa → *Japan* 35°36N 139°57E **223** B11
Kinushseo → *Canada* 55°15N 83°45W **298** A3
Kinuso *Canada* 55°20N 115°25W **296** B5
Kinvarra *Ireland* 53°8N 8°56W **166** C3
Kinwat *India* 19°38N 78°12E **244** E4
Kinyangiri *Tanzania* 4°25S 34°37E **268** C3
Kinyeti *South Sudan* 3°57N 32°54E **257** G3
Kinzia *Dem. Rep. of the Congo* 3°36S 18°26E **264** C3
Kinzig → *Germany* 48°36N 7°49E **179** G3
Kinzua *U.S.A.* 41°52N 78°58W **312** E6
Kioni *Greece* 38°27N 20°41E **207** C2
Kiosk *Canada* 46°6N 78°53W **298** C4
Kiowa *Kans., U.S.A.* 37°1N 98°29W **308** G4
Kiowa *Okla., U.S.A.* 34°43N 95°54W **314** D7
Kipahigan L. *Canada* 55°20N 101°55W **297** B8
Kipanga *Tanzania* 6°15S 35°20E **268** D4
Kipapa → *U.S.A.* 21°24N 158°1W **302** K13
Kiparissia *Greece* 37°15N 21°40E **204** D3
Kiparissiakos Kolpos
Greece 37°25N 21°25E **204** D3
Kipawa, L. *Canada* 46°50N 79°0W **298** C4
Kipembawe *Tanzania* 7°38S 33°27E **268** D3
Kipengere Ra. *Tanzania* 9°12S 34°15E **269** D3
Kipili *Tanzania* 7°28S 30°32E **268** D3
Kipini *Kenya* 2°30S 40°32E **268** C5
Kipling *Canada* 50°6N 102°38W **297** C8
Kipling Heights *Canada* 43°43N 79°34W **141** A1
Kipnuk *U.S.A.* 59°56N 164°3W **303** G6
Kippure *Ireland* 53°11N 6°21W **166** C5
Kipseli *Athens, Greece* **112** a3
Kipushi
Dem. Rep. of the Congo 11°48S 27°12E **269** E2
Kira Panagia *Greece* 39°17N 24°4E **204** B6
Kirakira *Solomon Is.* 10°27S 161°56E **287** N11
Kirandul *India* 18°33N 81°10E **244** E5
Kirane *Mali* 15°20N 10°20W **262** B2
Kiranomena *Madag.* 18°17S 46°2E **272** B2
Kiraz *Turkey* 38°14N 28°13E **205** C10
Kirazlı *Turkey* 40°2N 26°41E **203** F10
Kirchhain *Germany* 50°47N 8°56E **178** E4
Kirchheim *Germany* 48°39N 9°27E **179** G5
Kirchheimbolanden
Germany 49°40N 8°0E **179** F3
Kirchschlag *Austria* 47°30N 16°19E **181** D9
Kirchstockbach *Germany* 48°1N 11°40E **131** B3
Kirchtrudering *Germany* 48°7N 11°40E **131** B3
Kirdâsa *Egypt* 30°2N 31°6E **251** H2
Kirdimi *Chad* 18°11N 18°31E **259** E3
Kireç *Turkey* 39°33N 28°22E **205** B10
Kirensk *Russia* 57°50N 107°55E **215** D11
Kirghiz Range *Asia* 42°40N 73°40E **217** D8
Kirghizia = Kyrgyzstan ■
Asia 42°0N 75°0E **217** D9
Kirgiz-Kulak = Chirchiq
Uzbekistan 41°29N 69°35E **217** D7
Kirgiziya Steppe *Eurasia* 50°0N 55°0E **187** E10
Kiri *Dem. Rep. of the Congo* 1°29S 19°0E **264** C3
Kiri Buru *India* 22°0N 85°0E **244** D7
Kiribati ■ *Pac. Oc.* 3°0S 180°0E **277** A15
Kırıkhan *Turkey* 36°31N 36°21E **250** B7
Kirikiri *Nigeria* 6°26N 3°18E **124** B1
Kırıkkale *Turkey* 39°51N 33°32E **212** C5
Kirikopuni *N.Z.* 35°50S 174°1E **284** B3
Kirillov *Russia* 59°49N 38°24E **188** C10
Kirin = Jilin *China* 43°44N 126°30E **227** C14
Kirindi Oya → *Sri Lanka* 6°15N 81°20E **245** L5
Kirinyaga = Kenya, Mt.
Kenya 0°10S 37°18E **268** C4
Kirirom △ *Cambodia* 11°18N 104°5E **237** G5
Kirishi *Russia* 59°28N 32°0E **188** C7
Kirishima Yaku △ *Japan* 31°24N 130°50E **221** J5
Kirishima-Yama *Japan* 31°58N 130°55E **222** F2
Kiritimati *Kiribati* 1°58N 157°27W **289** G12
Kiriwina I. *Papua N. G.* 8°40S 151°5E **286** D7
Kırka *Turkey* 39°17N 30°33E **205** B12
Kırkağaç *Turkey* 39°8N 27°40E **205** B9
Kirkby *U.K.* 53°30N 2°54W **168** D5
Kirkby-in-Ashfield *U.K.* 53°6N 1°14W **168** D6
Kirkby Lonsdale *U.K.* 54°12N 2°36W **168** C5
Kirkby Stephen *U.K.* 54°29N 2°21W **168** C5
Kirkcaldy *U.K.* 56°7N 3°9W **167** E5
Kirkcudbright *U.K.* 54°50N 4°2W **167** G4
Kirke Værløse *Denmark* 55°47N 12°19E **118** A1
Kirkehamn *Norway* 58°14N 6°31E **164** F3
Kirkenær *Norway* 60°27N 12°3E **164** D9
Kirkenes *Norway* 69°40N 30°5E **160** B24
Kirkfield *Canada* 44°34N 78°59W **312** B6
Kirkhill *U.K.* 55°50N 3°13W **121** B2
Kirkintilloch *U.K.* 55°56N 4°8W **167** F4
Kirkjubæjarklaustur
Iceland 63°47N 18°4W **155** D8
Kirkkonummi *Finland* 60°8N 24°26E **189** B4
Kirkland *Ill., U.S.A.* 42°6N 88°51W **311** B8
Kirkland *Wash., U.S.A.* 47°40N 122°12W **306** C4
Kirkland Lake *Canada* 48°9N 80°2W **298** C3
Kırklareli *Turkey* 41°44N 27°15E **203** E11
Kırklareli □ *Turkey* 41°45N 27°15E **203** E11
Kirklin *U.S.A.* 40°12N 86°22W **311** D10
Kirkliston *U.K.* 55°57N 3°24W **121** B1
Kirkliston Ra. *N.Z.* 44°25S 170°34E **285** E5
Kirknewton *U.K.* 55°53N 3°25W **121** B1
Kirknitz = Cerknica
Slovenia 45°48N 14°21E **199** C11
Kirksville *U.S.A.* 40°12N 92°35W **310** D4
Kirkūk *Iraq* 35°30N 44°21E **213** E11
Kirkwall *U.K.* 58°59N 2°58W **167** C6
Kirkwood *Eastern Cape,*
S. Africa 33°22S 25°15E **270** D4
Kirkwood *Mo., U.S.A.* 38°35N 90°24W **310** F6
Kirlampudi *India* 17°12N 82°12E **244** F6
Kirmasti = Mustafakemalpaşa
Turkey 40°2N 28°24E **203** F12
Kirn *Germany* 49°47N 7°27E **179** F3
Kirobasi *Turkey* 36°43N 33°52E **250** B4
Kirov *Kaluga, Russia* 54°3N 34°20E **188** E8
Kirov *Kirov, Russia* 58°35N 49°40E **186** C8
Kirov Palace of Culture
Russia 59°55N 30°15E **137** B1
Kirovabad = Gäncä
Azerbaijan 40°45N 46°20E **191** K8
Kirovakan = Vanadzor
Armenia 40°48N 44°30E **191** K7
Kirovo = Kirovohrad
Ukraine 48°35N 32°20E **189** H7

Kirovograd = Kirovohrad *Ukraine* 48°35N 32°20E **189** H7
Kirovohrad *Ukraine* 48°35N 32°20E **189** H7
Kirovohrad □ *Ukraine* 48°30N 31°30E **189** H6
Kirovsk *Russia* 67°32N 33°41E **186** A5
Kirovskiy = Balpyq Bī *Kazakhstan* 44°52N 78°12E **217** D9
Kirovskiy *Astrakhan, Russia* 45°51N 48°11E **191** H9
Kirovskiy *Kamchatka, Russia* 54°27N 155°42E **215** D16
Kirovskiy *Primorsk, Russia* 45°7N 133°30E **220** B6
Kirriemuir *U.K.* 56°41N 3°1W **167** E5
Kirsanov *Russia* 52°35N 42°40E **190** D6
Kırşehir *Turkey* 39°14N 34°5E **212** C6
Kirtachi *Niger* 12°52N 2°30E **263** C5
Kīrteh *Afghan.* 32°15N 63°0E **240** B1
Kirthar △ *Pakistan* 25°45N 67°30E **242** F2
Kirthar Range *Pakistan* 27°0N 67°0E **242** F2
Kirtland *U.S.A.* 36°44N 108°21W **305** H9
Kiruna *Sweden* 67°52N 20°15E **160** C19
Kirundu *Dem. Rep. of the Congo* 0°50S 25°35E **264** C5
Kirya *Russia* 55°8N 46°55E **190** C8
Kiryat Anavim *Israel* 31°49N 35°6E **123** B1
Kiryat Ha Yovel *Israel* 31°46N 35°10E **123** B1
Kiryū *Japan* 36°24N 139°20E **223** A11
Kisa *Sweden* 58°0N 15°39E **163** G9
Kisaga *Tanzania* 4°30S 34°23E **268** C3
Kisalföld *Hungary* 47°30N 17°0E **182** C2
Kisambo *Dem. Rep. of the Congo* 6°25S 18°14E **265** D3
Kisandji *Dem. Rep. of the Congo* 6°18S 19°16E **265** D3
Kisanga *Dem. Rep. of the Congo* 2°30N 26°35E **268** B2
Kisangani *Dem. Rep. of the Congo* 0°35N 25°15E **268** B2
Kisantu *Dem. Rep. of the Congo* 5°7S 15°5E **265** D3
Kisar *Indonesia* 8°5S 127°10E **231** F7
Kisaran *Indonesia* 3°0N 99°37E **234** B1
Kisarawe *Tanzania* 6°53S 39°0E **268** D4
Kisarazu *Japan* 35°23N 139°55E **223** B11
Kisbér *Hungary* 47°30N 18°2E **182** C3
Kiselevsk *Russia* 54°5N 86°39E **217** B11
Kish = Qeys *Iran* 26°32N 53°58E **249** A6
Kishanganga → *Pakistan* 34°18N 73°28E **243** B5
Kishanganj *India* 26°3N 88°14E **241** B2
Kishangarh *Raj., India* 26°34N 74°52E **242** F6
Kishangarh *Raj., India* 27°50N 70°30E **242** F4
Kishb, Ḩarrat al *Si. Arabia* 22°30N 40°15E **248** B3
Kishi *Nigeria* 9°1N 3°52E **263** D5
Kishinev = Chişinău *Moldova* 47°2N 28°50E **183** C13
Kishiwada *Japan* 34°28N 135°22E **223** C7
Kishkareny = Lazo *Moldova* 47°33N 28°2E **183** C13
Kishkeneköl *Kazakhstan* 53°38N 72°20E **217** B8
Kishorganj *Bangla.* 24°26N 90°40E **241** C3
Kishtwar *India* 33°20N 75°48E **242** C6
Kishwaukee → *U.S.A.* 42°12N 89°8W **310** B7
Kisielice *Poland* 53°36N 19°16E **184** E6
Kisigo ⌓ *Tanzania* 6°27S 34°17E **268** D3
Kisii *Kenya* 0°40S 34°45E **268** C3
Kisiju *Tanzania* 7°23S 39°19E **268** D4
Kısıklı *Turkey* 41°1N 29°2E **122** B2
Kisir *Turkey* 41°0N 43°5E **213** B10
Kisizi *Uganda* 1°0S 29°58E **268** C2
Kiska I. *U.S.A.* 51°59N 177°30E **303** L2
Kiskomárom = Zalakomár *Hungary* 46°33N 17°10E **182** D2
Kiskörei-víztároló *Hungary* 47°31N 20°36E **182** C5
Kiskőrös *Hungary* 46°37N 19°20E **182** D4
Kiskundorozsma *Hungary* 46°16N 20°5E **182** D5
Kiskunfélegyháza *Hungary* 46°42N 19°53E **182** D4
Kiskunhalas *Hungary* 46°28N 19°37E **182** D4
Kiskunmajsa *Hungary* 46°30N 19°48E **182** D4
Kiskunsági △ *Hungary* 46°39N 19°30E **182** D4
Kislovodsk *Russia* 43°50N 42°45E **191** J6
Kismaayo *Somali Rep.* 0°22S 42°32E **267** E5
Kismayu △ *Somali Rep.* 1°25N 41°30E **267** D5
Kiso-Gawa → *Japan* 35°20N 136°45E **223** B8
Kiso-Sammyaku *Japan* 35°45N 137°45E **223** B9
Kisofukushima *Japan* 35°52N 137°43E **223** B9
Kisoro *Uganda* 1°17S 29°48E **268** C2
Kispest *Hungary* 47°27N 19°8E **117** B2
Kissamos = Kasteli *Greece* 35°29N 23°38E **207** E4
Kissamos, Kolpos *Greece* 35°30N 23°38E **207** E4
Kissidougou *Guinea* 9°5N 10°5W **262** D2
Kissimmee *U.S.A.* 28°18N 81°24W **317** G8
Kissimmee → *U.S.A.* 27°9N 80°52W **317** H8
Kissimmee, L. *U.S.A.* 27°55N 81°17W **317** H8
Kississing L. *Canada* 55°10N 101°20W **297** B8
Kissónerga *Cyprus* 34°49N 32°24E **207** F8
Kissu, J. *Sudan* 21°37N 25°10E **256** C2
Kista *Sweden* 59°24N 17°57E **139** A1
Kistanje *Croatia* 43°58N 15°55E **199** E12
Kistna = Krishna → *India* 15°57N 80°59E **245** G5
Kisújszállás *Hungary* 47°12N 20°50E **182** C5
Kisuki *Japan* 35°17N 132°54E **222** B4
Kisumu *Kenya* 0°3S 34°45E **268** C3
Kisvárda *Hungary* 48°14N 22°4E **182** B7
Kiswani *Tanzania* 4°5S 37°57E **268** C4
Kiswere *Tanzania* 9°27S 39°30E **269** D4
Kit Carson *U.S.A.* 38°46N 102°48W **304** G12
Kita *Ōsaka, Japan* 34°41N 135°30E **133** A2
Kita *Tōkyō, Japan* 35°44N 139°44E **140** A3
Kita *Mali* 13°5N 9°25W **262** C3
Kita-Ura *Japan* 36°0N 140°34E **223** B12
Kitaa □ *Greenland* 70°0N 47°0W **154** C6
Kitaibaraki *Japan* 36°50N 140°45E **221** F10
Kitakami *Japan* 39°20N 141°10E **220** E10
Kitakami-Gawa → *Japan* 38°25N 141°19E **220** E10
Kitakami-Sammyaku *Japan* 39°30N 141°30E **220** E10
Kitakata *Japan* 37°39N 139°52E **220** F9
Kitakyūshū *Japan* 33°50N 130°50E **222** D2
Kitale *Kenya* 1°0N 35°0E **268** B4
Kitami *Japan* 43°48N 143°54E **220** C11
Kitami-Sammyaku *Japan* 44°22N 142°43E **220** B11
Kitangiri, L. *Tanzania* 4°5S 34°20E **268** C3
Kitanglad △ *Phil.* 8°57N 124°21E **233** G5
Kitano Hana *Iwo Jima* 24°49N 141°20E **288** b
Kitano-Kaikyō *Japan* 34°17N 134°58E **222** C6
Kitaotao *Phil.* 7°40N 125°1E **233** H5
Kitava I. *Papua N. G.* 8°40S 151°20E **286** E6
Kitaya *Tanzania* 10°38S 40°8E **269** E5
Kitazawa *Japan* 35°39N 139°40E **140** B3
Kitcharao *Phil.* 9°27N 125°36E **233** G5
Kitchener *Canada* 43°27N 80°29W **312** C4
Kitee *Finland* 62°5N 30°8E **188** A6
Kitega = Gitega *Burundi* 3°26S 29°56E **268** C2
Kitengo *Dem. Rep. of the Congo* 7°26S 24°8E **265** D4
Kitgum *Uganda* 3°17N 32°52E **268** B3
Kíthira = Kythira *Greece* 36°8N 23°0E **204** E5
Kíthnos *Greece* 37°26N 24°27E **204** D6
Kiti *Cyprus* 34°50N 33°34E **207** F9
Kiti, C. *Cyprus* 34°48N 33°36E **207** F9
Kitimat *Canada* 54°3N 128°38W **296** C3
Kitinen → *Finland* 67°14N 27°27E **160** C22
Kitiyab *Sudan* 17°13N 33°35E **257** D3
Kitombe *Dem. Rep. of the Congo* 5°22S 18°59E **265** D3
Kitridge Pt. *Barbados* 13°9N 59°25W **323** r
Kitros *Greece* 40°22N 22°34E **202** F6
Kitsman *Ukraine* 48°26N 25°46E **183** B10
Kitsuki *Japan* 33°25N 131°37E **222** D3
Kittakittaooloo, L. *Australia* 28°3S 138°14E **281** D2
Kittanning *U.S.A.* 40°49N 79°31W **312** F5
Kittatinny Mt. *U.S.A.* 41°19N 74°39W **313** F10
Kittery *U.S.A.* 43°5N 70°45W **313** C14
Kittilä *Finland* 67°40N 24°51E **160** C21
Kitui *Kenya* 1°17S 38°0E **268** C4
Kitwanga *Canada* 55°6N 128°4W **296** B3
Kitwe *Zambia* 12°54S 28°13E **269** E2
Kityang = Jieyang *China* 23°35N 116°21E **229** F11
Kitzbühel *Austria* 47°27N 12°24E **180** D5
Kitzbühler Alpen *Austria* 47°20N 12°20E **180** D5
Kitzingen *Germany* 49°44N 10°9E **179** F6
Kiu Tsiu *China* 22°22N 114°17E **122** A2
Kiukiang = Jiujiang *China* 29°42N 115°58E **229** C10
Kiunga *Papua N. G.* 6°7S 141°18E **286** D1
Kiunga Marine ⌓ *Kenya* 2°1S 41°14E **268** C5
Kivalina *U.S.A.* 67°44N 164°33W **303** C6
Kivarli *India* 24°33N 72°46E **242** G5
Kivertsi *Ukraine* 50°50N 25°28E **177** C13
Kividhes *Cyprus* 34°46N 32°51E **207** F8
Kivik *Sweden* 55°41N 14°13E **163** J8
Kivistö *Finland* 60°18N 24°50E **121** B2
Kivotos *Greece* 40°13N 21°26E **202** F5
Kivu, L. *Dem. Rep. of the Congo* 1°48S 29°0E **268** C2
Kiwai I. *Papua N. G.* 8°35S 143°30E **286** E2
Kiwirrkurra *Australia* 22°49S 127°45E **278** D4
Kiwirrkurra ✪ *Australia* 22°49S 127°45E **278** D4
Kiyev = Kyyiv *Ukraine* 50°30N 30°28E **177** C16
Kiyevskoye Vdkhr. = Kyyivske Vdskh. *Ukraine* 51°0N 30°25E **177** C16
Kıyıköy *Turkey* 41°38N 28°5E **203** E12
Kizel *Russia* 59°3N 57°40E **186** C10
Kizhi, Ostrov *Russia* 65°12N 35°28E **188** B8
Kiziba-Baluba ⌓ *Congo* 11°50S 28°0E **269** E2
Kiziguru *Rwanda* 1°46S 30°23E **268** C3
Kızıl Adalar *Turkey* 40°52N 29°5E **203** F13
Kızıl Dağ *Turkey* 36°19N 35°57E **250** B6
Kızıl Irmak → *Turkey* 41°44N 35°58E **212** B6
Kizil Jilga *China* 35°26N 78°50E **243** B8
Kizil Yurt *Russia* 43°13N 46°54E **191** J8
Kızılcabölük *Turkey* 37°37N 29°1E **205** D11
Kızılcadağ *Turkey* 37°1N 29°58E **205** D11
Kızılcahamam *Turkey* 40°30N 32°30E **212** B5
Kızıldağ △ *Turkey* 38°5N 31°20E **246** B1
Kızılhisar *Turkey* 37°32N 29°17E **212** D3
Kızılırmak *Turkey* 40°21N 33°59E **212** B5
Kızılkaya *Turkey* 37°18N 30°27E **205** D12
Kızılören *Turkey* 38°15N 30°10E **205** C12
Kızıltepe *Turkey* 37°12N 40°35E **213** D9
Kızıltoprak *Turkey* 40°58N 29°3E **122** C2
Kizimkazi *Tanzania* 6°28S 39°30E **268** D4
Kizlyar *Russia* 43°51N 46°40E **191** J8
Kizuri *Japan* 34°38N 135°34E **133** B2
Kizyl-Arvat = Serdar *Turkmenistan* 39°4N 56°23E **247** B8
Kjellerup *Denmark* 56°17N 9°25E **163** H3
Kjellmyra *Norway* 60°39N 12°1E **164** D9
Kjelsås *Norway* 59°57N 10°47E **133** A3
Kjølen *Norway* 62°3N 8°45E **164** C5
Kjölur *Iceland* 64°50N 19°25W **155** C7
Kjósarsýsla □ *Iceland* 64°15N 21°30W **155** C5
Kladanj *Bos.-H.* 44°14N 18°42E **182** F3
Kladnica *Serbia* 43°23N 20°2E **202** C4
Kladno *Czech Rep.* 50°10N 14°7E **180** A7
Kladovo *Serbia* 44°36N 22°33E **202** B6
Kladow *Germany* 52°27N 13°9E **115** B1
Klæbu *Norway* 63°18N 10°29E **164** A7
Klaeng *Thailand* 12°47N 101°39E **236** F3
Klagan *Malaysia* 5°58N 117°27E **235** A5
Klagenfurt *Austria* 46°38N 14°20E **180** E7
Klaipėda *Lithuania* 55°43N 21°10E **184** C8
Klaipėda □ *Lithuania* 55°43N 21°7E **184** C8
Klaksvík *Færoe Is.* 62°14N 6°35W **160** E9
Klamath → *U.S.A.* 41°33N 124°5W **304** F1
Klamath Falls *U.S.A.* 42°13N 121°46W **304** E3
Klamath Mts. *U.S.A.* 41°50N 123°20W **304** F2
Klamono *Indonesia* 1°8S 131°30E **231** E8
Klampenborg *Denmark* 55°46N 12°35E **118** A3
Klampo *Indonesia* 0°7N 116°58E **235** B5
Klang *Malaysia* 3°2N 101°26E **237** L3
Klangklang *Burma* 22°41N 93°26E **241** D4
Klanjec *Croatia* 46°3N 15°45E **199** B12
Klappan → *Canada* 58°0N 129°43W **296** B3
Klara = Trysilelva → *Norway* 61°2N 12°35E **164** C9
Klarälven → *Sweden* 59°23N 13°32E **162** E7
Klässbol *Sweden* 59°33N 12°45E **162** E6
Klaten *Indonesia* 7°43S 110°36E **235** D4
Klatovy *Czech Rep.* 49°23N 13°18E **180** B6
Klausenburg = Cluj-Napoca *Romania* 46°47N 23°38E **183** D8
Klawer *S. Africa* 31°44S 18°36E **270** D2
Klawock *U.S.A.* 55°33N 133°6W **303** J14
Klazienaveen *Neths.* 52°44N 7°0E **170** B6
Klé *Mali* 12°0N 6°28W **262** C3
Klečany *Czech Rep.* 50°10N 14°24E **135** A2
Kłecko *Poland* 52°38N 17°25E **185** F4
Kleczew *Poland* 52°22N 18°9E **185** F5
Kledering *Austria* 48°8N 16°26E **142** B2
Kleena Kleene *Canada* 52°0N 124°59W **296** C4
Klein Bonaire *Bonaire* 12°9N 68°18W **322** h
Klein Jukskei → *S. Africa* 26°6S 27°57E **123** A1
Klein-Karas *Namibia* 27°33S 18°7E **270** C2
Klein-Schlatten = Zlatna *Romania* 46°8N 23°11E **183** D8
Kleinbegin *S. Africa* 28°54S 21°40E **270** C3
Kleinmachnow *Germany* 52°24N 13°14E **115** B2
Kleinschönebeck *Germany* 52°29N 13°42E **115** B5
Klekovača *Bos.-H.* 44°25N 16°32E **199** D13
Klembivka *Ukraine* 48°23N 28°25E **183** B13
Klemetsrud *Norway* 59°50N 10°51E **133** A4
Klender *Indonesia* 6°12S 106°54E **122** A2
Klenoec *Macedonia* 41°32N 20°49E **202** E4
Klenovec *Slovak Rep.* 48°36N 19°54E **181** C12
Klerksdorp *S. Africa* 26°53S 26°38E **270** C4
Kleszczele *Poland* 52°35N 23°19E **185** F10
Kletnya *Russia* 53°23N 33°12E **188** F7
Kletsk = Klyetsk *Belarus* 53°5N 26°45E **177** B14
Kletskiy *Russia* 49°16N 43°11E **191** F6
Kleve *Germany* 51°47N 6°7E **178** D2
Kličany *Czech Rep.* 50°11N 14°25E **135** A2
Klickitat *U.S.A.* 45°49N 121°9W **304** D3
Klickitat → *U.S.A.* 45°42N 121°17W **306** E5
Klidhes *Cyprus* 35°42N 34°36E **207** E10
Klimovichi *Belarus* 53°36N 32°0E **188** F6
Klin *Russia* 56°20N 36°48E **188** D9
Klina *Kosovo* 42°37N 20°35E **202** D4
Klinaklini → *Canada* 51°21N 125°40W **296** C3
Klintehamn *Sweden* 57°24N 18°12E **163** G12
Klintsy *Russia* 52°50N 32°10E **189** F7
Klip → *S. Africa* 27°3S 29°3E **271** C4
Klipdale *S. Africa* 34°19S 19°57E **270** D2
Klippan *Sweden* 56°8N 13°10E **163** H7
Klipplaat *S. Africa* 33°1S 24°22E **270** D3
Klipriviersberg Nature Reserve *S. Africa* 26°16S 28°2E **123** B2
Klishkivtsi *Ukraine* 48°26N 26°16E **183** B11
Klisura *Bulgaria* 42°40N 24°28E **203** D8
Kljajićevo *Serbia* 45°45N 19°17E **182** E4
Ključ *Bos.-H.* 44°32N 16°48E **199** D13
Kłobuck *Poland* 50°55N 18°55E **185** H5
Klockestrand *Sweden* 62°53N 17°55E **162** B11
Kłodawa *Poland* 52°15N 18°55E **185** F5
Kłodzko *Poland* 50°28N 16°38E **185** H3
Kløfta *Norway* 60°4N 11°10E **164** D8
Klondike *Canada* 64°0N 139°26W **294** E4
Klondike Goldrush ⌓ *U.S.A.* 59°27N 135°19W **303** G14
Klong Wang Chao △ *Thailand* 16°20N 99°9E **236** D2
Klos *Albania* 41°28N 20°10E **202** E4
Klosterneuburg *Austria* 48°18N 16°19E **142** A1
Klosters *Switz.* 46°52N 9°52E **179** J5
Klötze *Germany* 52°37N 11°10E **178** C7
Klouto *Togo* 6°57N 0°44E **263** D5
Klövsjö *Sweden* 62°32N 14°11E **162** B8
Kluane △ *Canada* 60°45N 139°30W **296** A1
Kluane L. *Canada* 61°15N 138°40W **294** E4
Kluang *Malaysia* 2°3N 103°18E **237** L4
Kluczbork *Poland* 50°58N 18°12E **185** H5
Klukhori = Karachayevsk *Russia* 43°50N 41°55E **191** J5
Klukwan *U.S.A.* 59°24N 135°54W **296** B1
Klungkung *Indonesia* 8°32S 115°24E **231** K18
Klyetsk *Belarus* 53°5N 26°45E **177** B14
Klyuchevskaya, Gora *Russia* 55°50N 160°30E **215** D17
Klyuchi *Russia* 56°18N 160°51E **215** D17
Knaben *Norway* 58°40N 7°4E **164** F4
Knappavellir *Iceland* 63°54N 16°36W **155** D10
Knäred *Sweden* 56°31N 13°19E **163** H7
Knaresborough *U.K.* 54°1N 1°28W **168** C6
Knarvik *Norway* 60°32N 5°19E **164** D2
Knee L. *Man., Canada* 55°3N 94°45W **298** A1
Knee L. *Sask., Canada* 55°51N 107°0W **297** B7
Kneïss, Îs. *Tunisia* 34°22N 10°18E **258** B2
Knesset *Jerusalem* **123** b1
Knezha *Bulgaria* 43°30N 24°5E **203** C8
Knight I. *U.S.A.* 60°21N 147°45W **303** F11
Knight Inlet *Canada* 50°45N 125°40W **296** C3
Knighton *U.K.* 52°21N 3°3W **169** E4
Knights Ferry *U.S.A.* 37°50N 120°40W **306** H6
Knights Landing *U.S.A.* 38°48N 121°43W **306** G5
Knightsbridge *London, U.K.* **125** c2
Knightstown *U.S.A.* 39°48N 85°32W **311** E11
Knin *Croatia* 44°3N 16°17E **199** D13
Knislinge *Sweden* 56°12N 14°5E **163** H8
Knittelfeld *Austria* 47°13N 14°51E **180** D7
Knivsta *Sweden* 59°43N 17°48E **162** E11
Knjaževac *Serbia* 43°35N 22°18E **202** C6
Knob, C. *Australia* 34°32S 119°16E **279** F2
Knob Lake = Kawawachikamach *Canada* 54°48N 66°50W **299** B6
Knob Noster *U.S.A.* 38°46N 93°33W **310** F3
Knock *Ireland* 53°48N 8°55W **166** C3
Knockmealdown Mts. *Ireland* 52°14N 7°56W **166** D4
Knokke-Heist *Belgium* 51°21N 3°17E **170** C3
Knossos *Greece* 35°16N 25°10E **207** E6
Knowlton *Canada* 45°13N 72°31W **313** A12
Knox *U.S.A.* 41°18N 86°37W **311** C10
Knox Coast *Antarctica* 66°30S 108°0E **151** C8
Knoxville *Ga., U.S.A.* 32°47N 83°59W **316** C6
Knoxville *Ill., U.S.A.* 40°55N 90°17W **310** D6
Knoxville *Iowa, U.S.A.* 41°19N 93°6W **310** C4
Knoxville *Pa., U.S.A.* 41°57N 77°27W **312** E7
Knoxville *Tenn., U.S.A.* 35°58N 83°55W **315** D13
Knud Rasmussen Land *Greenland* 78°0N 60°0W **154** B4
Knysna *S. Africa* 34°2S 23°2E **270** D3
Knyszyn *Poland* 53°20N 22°56E **184** E9
Ko Kha *Thailand* 18°11N 99°24E **236** C2
Kō-Saki *Japan* 34°5N 129°13E **222** C1
Ko Tarutao △ *Thailand* 6°31N 99°26E **237** J2
Ko Yao *Thailand* 8°7N 98°35E **237** a
Koartac = Quaqtaq *Canada* 60°55N 69°40W **295** E18
Koba *Aru, Indonesia* 6°37S 134°37E **231** F8
Koba *Bangka, Indonesia* 2°26S 106°14E **234** C3
Kőbánya *Hungary* 47°28N 19°9E **117** B2
Kobarid *Slovenia* 46°15N 13°30E **199** B10
Kobayashi *Japan* 31°56N 130°59E **222** F2
Kobbegem *Belgium* 50°55N 4°15E **116** A1
Kobdo = Hovd □ *Mongolia* 48°2N 91°37E **217** C12
Kōbe *Japan* 34°41N 135°13E **223** C7
Kobelyaky *Ukraine* 49°11N 34°9E **189** H8
København *Denmark* 55°40N 12°26E **118** A2
København ✈ (CPH) *Denmark* 55°37N 12°39E **118** B3
Kobenni *Mauritania* 15°58N 9°24W **262** B3
Kōbi-Sho *Japan* 25°56N 123°41E **221** M1
Koblenz *Germany* 50°21N 7°36E **179** E3
Kobo *Dem. Rep. of the Congo* 4°54S 17°9E **265** C3
Kobo *Ethiopia* 12°2N 39°56E **257** E4
Kobryn *Belarus* 52°15N 24°22E **177** B13
Kobuchizawa *Japan* 35°52N 138°19E **223** B10
Kobuk *U.S.A.* 66°55N 156°52W **303** C8
Kobuk → *U.S.A.* 66°54N 160°38W **303** C7
Kobuk Valley △ *U.S.A.* 67°0N 160°0W **303** C7
Kobuleti *Georgia* 41°55N 41°45E **191** K5
Kobyletska Polyana *Ukraine* 48°3N 24°4E **183** B9
Kobylin *Poland* 51°43N 17°12E **185** G4
Kobylisy *Czech Rep.* 50°7N 14°26E **135** B2
Kobyłka *Poland* 52°20N 21°10E **142** A3
Kobylkino *Russia* 54°8N 43°56E **190** C6
Koca → *Turkey* 40°8N 27°57E **203** F11
Kocabaş *Turkey* 37°49N 29°20E **205** D11
Kocaeli *Turkey* 40°45N 29°50E **203** F13
Kocaeli □ *Turkey* 40°45N 29°55E **203** F13
Kočane *Serbia* 43°12N 21°52E **202** C5
Kočani *Macedonia* 41°55N 22°25E **202** E6
Koçarlı *Turkey* 37°45N 27°43E **205** D9
Koceljevo *Serbia* 44°28N 19°50E **202** B3
Kočevje *Slovenia* 45°39N 14°50E **199** C11
Kocgiri = Zara *Turkey* 39°58N 37°43E **212** C7
Koch Bihar *India* 26°22N 89°29E **241** B2
Kochas *India* 25°15N 83°56E **243** G10
Kocher → *Germany* 49°13N 9°12E **179** F5
Kochi = Cochin *India* 9°58N 76°20E **245** K3
Kōchi *Japan* 33°30N 133°35E **222** D5
Kōchi □ *Japan* 33°40N 133°30E **222** D5
Kochiu = Gejiu *China* 23°20N 103°10E **228** F4
Kochkor *Kyrgyzstan* 42°13N 75°46E **217** D9
Kochubey *Russia* 44°23N 46°32E **191** H8
Kock *Poland* 51°38N 22°27E **185** G9
Kodaira *Japan* 35°43N 139°28E **140** A1
Kodala *India* 19°38N 84°57E **244** E7
Kodanaka *Japan* 35°34N 139°37E **140** B2
Kodarma *India* 24°28N 85°36E **243** G11
Koddiyar B. *Sri Lanka* 8°33N 81°15E **245** K5
Kode *Sweden* 57°57N 11°51E **163** G5
Kodenmacho *Tokyo, Japan* **140** a5
Kodi *Dem. Rep. of the Congo* 3°34S 22°12E **264** C4
Kodi *Indonesia* 9°33S 119°0E **278** A2
Kodiak *U.S.A.* 57°47N 152°24W **303** H9
Kodiak I. *U.S.A.* 57°30N 152°45W **303** H9
Kodikkarai = Point Calimere *India* 10°17N 79°49E **245** J4
Kodinar *India* 20°46N 70°46E **242** J4
Kodinsk *Russia* 58°40N 99°10E **215** D10
Kodlipet *India* 12°48N 75°53E **245** H2
Kodok *South Sudan* 9°53N 32°7E **257** F3
Kodori → *Georgia* 42°47N 41°10E **191** J5
Kodoro *Dem. Rep. of the Congo* 1°16N 20°6E **264** B4
Kodungallur = Cranganore *India* 10°13N 76°13E **245** J3
Kodyma *Ukraine* 48°6N 29°7E **183** B14
Koedoesberge *S. Africa* 32°40S 20°11E **270** D3
Koekelberg *Belgium* 50°52N 4°20E **116** A1
Koes *Namibia* 26°0S 19°15E **270** C2
Kofarnihon *Tajikistan* 38°33N 69°1E **217** E7
Kofçaz *Turkey* 41°58N 27°12E **203** E11
Koffiefontein *S. Africa* 29°30S 25°0E **270** C4
Kofiau *Indonesia* 1°11S 129°50E **231** E7
Köflach *Austria* 47°4N 15°5E **180** D8
Koforidua *Ghana* 6°3N 0°17W **263** D4
Kōfu *Japan* 35°40N 138°30E **223** B10
Koga *Japan* 33°45N 130°25E **222** D2
Koga *Japan* 36°11N 139°43E **223** A11
Kogaluc → *Canada* 56°12N 61°44W **299** A7
Koganei *Japan* 35°42N 139°31E **140** A2
Kogarah *Australia* 33°57S 151°8E **139** B1
Køge *Denmark* 55°27N 12°11E **163** J6
Køge Bugt *Denmark* 55°34N 12°24E **163** J6
Kogi □ *Nigeria* 7°45N 6°45E **263** D6
Kogin Baba *Nigeria* 7°55N 11°35E **263** D7
Kogo *Eq. Guin.* 1°5N 9°42E **264** B1
Kogon *Uzbekistan* 39°43N 64°33E **216** E6
Koh-i-Khurd *Afghan.* 33°30N 65°59E **242** C1
Koh-i-Maran *Pakistan* 29°18N 66°50E **242** E2
Koh Ker *Cambodia* 13°47N 104°32E **236** F5
Koh Wai *Thailand* 11°54N 102°25E **237** H4
Kohala Mts. *U.S.A.* 20°5N 155°45W **302** C6
Kohat *Pakistan* 33°40N 71°29E **242** C4
Kohima *India* 25°35N 94°10E **241** C5
Kohkīlūyeh va Būyer Aḩmadi □ *Iran* 31°30N 50°30E **247** D6
Kohler Ra. *Antarctica* 77°0S 110°0W **151** D15
Kohlfurt = Węgliniec *Poland* 51°18N 15°10E **185** G2
Kohlu *Pakistan* 29°54N 69°15E **242** E3
Kohtla-Järve *Estonia* 59°20N 27°20E **188** C4
Kohukohu *N.Z.* 35°22S 173°38E **284** B2
Kohylnyk → *Ukraine* 45°49N 29°40E **183** E14
Koi Sanjaq *Iraq* 36°5N 44°38E **213** D11
Koidu *S. Leone* 8°38N 10°59W **262** D2
Koihoa *India* 8°12N 93°29E **245** K11
Koilkuntla *India* 15°14N 78°19E **245** G4
Koillismaa *Finland* 65°44N 28°36E **160** D23
Koimbani *Comoros Is.* 11°37S 43°21E **272** a
Koin *N. Korea* 40°28N 126°18E **224** B3
Koinare *Bulgaria* 43°21N 24°8E **203** C8
Koindu *S. Leone* 8°26N 10°19W **262** D2
Koivisto = Primorsk *Russia* 60°22N 28°37E **188** B5
Koivupää *Finland* 60°18N 24°53E **121** B2
Koja *Indonesia* 6°8S 106°52E **122** A2
Koja Utara *Indonesia* 6°5S 106°53E **122** A2
Kojetín *Czech Rep.* 49°21N 17°20E **181** B10
Kojŏ *N. Korea* 38°58N 127°58E **224** C3
Kojonup *Australia* 33°48S 117°10E **279** F2
Kojūr *Iran* 36°23N 51°43E **247** B6
Kokand = Qŭqon *Uzbekistan* 40°31N 70°56E **217** D8
Kokas *Indonesia* 2°42S 132°26E **231** E8
Kokava *Slovak Rep.* 48°35N 19°50E **181** C12
Kokcha → *Afghan.* 37°9N 69°24E **240** A3
Kokchetav = Kökshetaū *Kazakhstan* 53°20N 69°25E **217** B7
Köke'e State Park ⌓ *U.S.A.* 22°6N 159°40W **302** A2
Kokemäenjoki → *Finland* 61°32N 21°44E **188** B1
Kokerite *Guyana* 7°12N 59°35W **329** B6
Kokhav Ya'akov *West Bank* 31°53N 35°14E **123** A2
Kokhma *Russia* 56°57N 41°8E **190** B5
Koki *Senegal* 15°30N 15°59W **262** B1
Kokiu = Gejiu *China* 23°20N 103°10E **228** F4
Kokkilai *Sri Lanka* 9°0N 80°57E **245** K5
Kokkina *Cyprus* 35°11N 32°36E **207** E8
Kokkola *Finland* 63°50N 23°8E **160** E20
Koko *Nigeria* 11°28N 4°29E **263** C5
Koko Head *U.S.A.* 21°16N 157°43W **302** K14
Koko Kyunzu *Burma* 14°7N 93°22E **245** G11
Kokobunji *Japan* 35°42N 139°27E **140** A1
Kokobunji-Temple *Japan* 35°44N 139°55E **140** A4
Kokoda *Papua N. G.* 8°54S 147°47E **286** E4
Kokologo *Burkina Faso* 12°11N 1°53W **262** C4
Kokolopozo *Ivory C.* 5°8N 6°5W **262** D3
Kokomo *U.S.A.* 40°29N 86°8W **311** D10
Kokopo *Papua N. G.* 4°22S 152°19E **286** C7
Kokoro *Niger* 14°12N 0°55E **263** C5
Koksan *N. Korea* 38°46N 126°40E **224** C3
Kökshetaū *Kazakhstan* 53°20N 69°25E **217** B7
Koksoak → *Canada* 58°30N 68°10W **295** F18
Kokstad *S. Africa* 30°32S 29°29E **271** D4
Köktal *Kazakhstan* 44°8N 79°48E **217** D9
Kokubu *Japan* 31°44N 130°46E **222** F2
Kokyar *China* 37°23N 77°10E **217** E9
Kola *Indonesia* 5°35S 134°30E **231** F8
Kola *Russia* 68°45N 33°8E **160** B25
Kola Pen. = Kolskiy Poluostrov *Russia* 67°30N 38°0E **186** A6
Kolachel *India* 8°10N 77°15E **245** K3
Kolachi → *Pakistan* 27°8N 67°2E **242** F2
Kolahoi *India* 34°12N 75°22E **243** B6
Kolahun *Liberia* 8°15N 10°4W **262** D2
Kolaka *Indonesia* 4°3S 121°46E **231** E6
Kolar *India* 13°12N 78°15E **245** H4
Kolar Gold Fields *India* 12°58N 78°16E **245** H4
Kolarängen *Sweden* 59°16N 18°10E **139** B3
Kolaras *India* 25°14N 77°36E **242** G6
Kolari *Finland* 67°20N 23°48E **160** C20
Kolarovgrad = Shumen *Bulgaria* 43°18N 26°55E **203** C10
Kolárovo *Slovak Rep.* 47°54N 18°0E **181** D10
Kolašin *Montenegro* 42°50N 19°31E **202** D3
Kolayat *India* 27°50N 72°50E **242** F5
Kolbäck *Sweden* 59°34N 16°15E **162** E10
Kolbäcksån → *Sweden* 59°36N 16°16E **162** E10
Kolbeinsstaðir *Iceland* 64°59N 22°16W **155** C4
Kolberg = Kołobrzeg *Poland* 54°10N 15°35E **184** D2
Kolbermoor *Germany* 47°51N 12°4E **179** H8
Kolbio *Kenya* 1°8S 41°12E **267** E5
Kolbotn *Norway* 59°48N 10°48E **133** B3
Kolbu *Norway* 60°39N 10°45E **164** D7
Kolbuszowa *Poland* 50°15N 21°46E **185** H8
Kolchugino = Leninsk-Kuznetskiy *Russia* 54°44N 86°10E **217** B11
Kolchugino *Russia* 56°17N 39°22E **188** D10
Kolda *Senegal* 12°55N 14°57W **262** C2
Kolda □ *Senegal* 13°5N 14°50W **262** C2
Koldegi *Sudan* 12°3N 30°16E **257** E3
Kolding *Denmark* 55°30N 9°29E **163** J3
Kole *Dem. Rep. of the Congo* 3°16S 22°42E **264** C4
Koléa *Algeria* 36°38N 2°46E **261** A5
Kolepom = Dolak, Pulau *Indonesia* 8°0S 138°30E **231** F9
Kolguyev, Ostrov *Russia* 69°20N 48°30E **186** A8
Kolhapur *India* 16°43N 74°15E **244** F2
Kolia *Ivory C.* 9°46N 6°28W **262** D3
Koliganek *U.S.A.* 59°48N 157°25W **303** G8
Kolimbia *Greece* 36°15N 28°10E **206** E12
Kolín *Czech Rep.* 50°2N 15°9E **180** A8
Kolind *Denmark* 56°21N 10°34E **163** H4
Kolkas rags *Latvia* 57°46N 22°37E **184** A9
Kolkata *India* 22°34N 88°21E **124** B2
Kolkata Dum Dum Int. ✈ (CCU) *India* 22°38N 88°26E **124** B2
Kolkata Maidan *India* 22°33N 88°21E **124** B1
Kollam = Quilon *India* 8°50N 76°38E **245** K3
Kölleda *Germany* 51°11N 11°15E **178** D7
Kollegal *India* 12°9N 77°9E **245** H3
Kolleru L. *India* 16°40N 81°10E **244** F5
Kollum *Neths.* 53°17N 6°10E **170** A6
Kolmanskop *Namibia* 26°45S 15°14E **270** C2
Köln *Germany* 50°56N 6°57E **178** E2
Kolno *Poland* 53°25N 21°56E **184** E8
Koło *Warszawa, Poland* 52°14N 20°56E **142** B1
Koło *Wielkopolskie, Poland* 52°14N 18°40E **185** F5
Kołobrzeg *Poland* 54°10N 15°35E **184** D2
Kolochava *Ukraine* 48°26N 23°41E **183** B8
Kologi *Sudan* 10°51N 30°58E **257** E3
Kolokani *Mali* 13°35N 7°45W **262** C3
Kolokinthou *Greece* 38°0N 23°42E **112** B2
Koloko *Burkina Faso* 11°5N 5°19W **262** C3
Kololo *Ethiopia* 7°29N 41°58E **257** F5
Kolombangara *Solomon Is.* 8°0S 157°5E **287** M9
Kolomna *Russia* 55°8N 38°45E **188** E10
Kolomyagi *Russia* 60°0N 30°19E **137** A1
Kolomyya *Ukraine* 48°31N 25°2E **183** B10
Kolondiéba *Mali* 11°5N 6°54W **262** C3
Kolonodale *Indonesia* 2°0S 121°19E **231** E6
Kolonos *Greece* 37°59N 23°43E **112** B2
Kolonowskie *Poland* 50°39N 18°22E **185** H5
Kolosib *India* 24°15N 92°45E **241** C4
Kolpashevo *Russia* 58°20N 83°5E **214** D9
Kolpino *Russia* 59°44N 30°39E **188** C6
Kolpny *Russia* 52°17N 37°1E **189** F9
Kolsås *Norway* 59°55N 10°30E **133** A2
Kolskiy Poluostrov *Russia* 67°30N 38°0E **186** A6
Kolskiy Zaliv *Russia* 69°23N 34°0E **160** B26
Kolsva *Sweden* 59°36N 15°51E **162** E9
Kolubara → *Serbia* 44°35N 20°15E **202** B4
Kolumadulu Atoll *Maldives* 2°22N 73°7E **272** d
Koluszki *Poland* 51°45N 19°46E **185** G6
Kolwezi *Dem. Rep. of the Congo* 10°40S 25°25E **269** E2
Kolyma → *Russia* 69°30N 161°0E **215** C17
Kolymskoye Nagorye *Russia* 63°0N 157°0E **215** C16
Kôm Hamâda *Egypt* 30°46N 30°41E **256** H7
Kôm Ombo *Egypt* 24°25N 32°52E **256** C3
Komadugu Gana → *Nigeria* 13°5N 12°24E **263** C7
Komae *Japan* 35°37N 139°34E **140** B2
Komagane *Japan* 35°44N 137°58E **223** B9
Komagome *Japan* 35°43N 139°45E **140** A3
Komaki *Japan* 35°17N 136°55E **223** B8
Komandorskiye Is. = Komandorskiye Ostrova *Russia* 55°0N 167°0E **215** D17
Komandorskiye Ostrova *Russia* 55°0N 167°0E **215** D17
Komárno *Slovak Rep.* 47°49N 18°5E **181** D11
Komarnyky *Ukraine* 48°59N 23°3E **182** B8
Komárom *Hungary* 47°43N 18°7E **182** C3
Komárom-Esztergom □ *Hungary* 47°35N 18°20E **182** C3
Komáromújváros = Komárom *Hungary* 47°43N 18°7E **182** C3
Komatipoort *S. Africa* 25°25S 31°55E **271** C5
Komatou Yialou *Cyprus* 35°25N 34°8E **207** E10
Komatsu *Japan* 36°25N 136°30E **223** A8
Komatsushima *Japan* 34°0N 134°35E **222** D6
Komavangard = Sobinka *Russia* 56°0N 40°0E **188** E11
Komazawa *Japan* 35°37N 139°40E **140** B3
Komba *Dem. Rep. of the Congo* 2°52N 24°3E **264** B4
Kombissiri *Burkina Faso* 12°4N 1°20W **263** C4
Kombo *Gabon* 0°20S 12°22E **264** C2
Kombong *India* 28°7N 94°51E **241** A5
Kombori *Burkina Faso* 13°26N 3°56W **262** C4
Komboti *Greece* 39°6N 21°5E **204** B3
Kome Channel *Uganda* 0°10S 32°35E **268** C3
Komebail Lagoon *Palau* 7°25N 134°25E **288** c
Komen *Slovenia* 45°49N 13°45E **199** C10
Komenda *Ghana* 5°4N 1°28W **263** D4
Komi *Cyprus* 35°24N 34°0E **207** E10
Komi □ *Russia* 64°0N 55°0E **186** B10
Kominter = Novoshakhtinsk *Russia* 47°46N 39°58E **189** J10
Komintern = Marhanets *Ukraine* 47°40N 34°40E **189** J8
Komiža *Croatia* 43°3N 16°11E **199** E13
Komló *Hungary* 46°15N 18°16E **182** D3
Kommamur Canal *India* 16°0N 80°25E **245** G5
Kommunarsk = Alchevsk *Ukraine* 48°30N 38°45E **189** H10
Kommunizma, Pik = imeni Ismail Samani, Pik *Tajikistan* 39°0N 72°2E **217** E8
Komodo *Indonesia* 8°37S 119°20E **235** D5
Komodo △ *Indonesia* 8°36S 119°34E **235** D5
Komono *Congo* 3°10S 13°20E **264** C2
Komoran, Pulau *Indonesia* 8°18S 138°45E **231** F9
Komoro *Japan* 36°19N 138°26E **223** A10
Komotau = Chomutov *Czech Rep.* 50°28N 13°23E **180** A6
Komotini *Greece* 41°9N 25°26E **203** E9
Komovi *Montenegro* 42°41N 19°39E **202** D3
Kompasberg *S. Africa* 31°45S 24°32E **270** D3
Kompong Chhnang = Kampong Chhnang *Cambodia* 12°20N 104°35E **237** F5
Kompong Chikreng *Cambodia* 13°5N 104°18E **236** F5
Kompong Kleang *Cambodia* 13°6N 104°8E **236** F5
Kompong Luong *Cambodia* 11°49N 104°48E **237** G5
Kompong Pranak *Cambodia* 13°35N 104°55E **236** F5
Kompong Som = Kampong Saom *Cambodia* 10°38N 103°30E **237** G4
Kompong Som, Chhung = Kampong Saom, Chaak *Cambodia* 10°50N 103°32E **237** G4
Kompong Speu *Cambodia* 11°26N 104°32E **237** G5
Kompong Sralau *Cambodia* 14°5N 105°46E **236** E5
Kompong Thom *Cambodia* 12°35N 104°51E **236** F5
Kompong Trabeck *Cambodia* 13°6N 105°14E **236** F5
Kompong Trach *Cambodia* 11°25N 105°48E **237** G5
Kompong Tralach *Cambodia* 11°54N 104°47E **237** G5
Komrat = Comrat *Moldova* 46°18N 28°40E **183** D13
Komsberg *S. Africa* 32°40S 20°45E **270** D3
Komsomolets = Qarabalyq *Kazakhstan* 53°45N 62°2E **216** B6
Komsomolets, Ostrov *Russia* 80°30N 95°0E **215** A10
Komsomolsk *Russia* 57°2N 40°20E **188** D11
Komsomolsk-na-Amur *Russia* 50°30N 137°0E **219** A16
Komsomolskiy *Russia* 54°27N 45°33E **190** C7
Komsomolskoe *Kazakhstan* 50°25N 60°5E **216** B6
Komsomolsky = Chirchiq *Uzbekistan* 41°29N 69°35E **217** D7
Kömür Burnu *Turkey* 38°39N 26°12E **205** C8
Kon Ka Kinh △ *Vietnam* 14°19N 107°23E **236** E6
Kon Tum *Vietnam* 14°24N 108°0E **236** E7
Kon Tum, Plateau du *Vietnam* 14°30N 108°30E **236** E7
Kona *W. Bengal, India* 22°37N 88°18E **124** B1
Kona *Mali* 14°57N 3°53W **262** C4
Kona *Nigeria* 8°57N 11°21E **263** D7
Kona ✈ (KOA) *U.S.A.* 19°44N 156°3W **302** D5
Könähuanui *U.S.A.* 21°21N 157°47W **302** K14
Konakovo *Russia* 56°40N 36°51E **188** D9
Konala *Finland* 60°14N 24°52E **121** B2
Konar □ *Afghan.* 34°30N 71°3E **240** B3
Konarak *India* 19°54N 86°7E **244** E8
Konārak *Iran* 25°21N 60°23E **249** A8
Konārī *Iran* 28°13N 51°36E **247** D6
Konch *India* 26°0N 79°10E **243** G8
Kondagaon *India* 19°35N 81°35E **244** E5
Konde *Tanzania* 4°57S 39°45E **268** C4
Kondias *Greece* 39°49N 25°10E **205** B7
Kondinin *Australia* 32°34S 118°8E **279** F2
Kondli *India* 28°36N 77°19E **120** B2
Kondo *Dem. Rep. of the Congo* 5°35S 13°0E **265** D2
Kondoa *Tanzania* 4°55S 35°50E **268** C4
Kondopoga *Russia* 62°12N 34°17E **188** A8
Kondratyevo *Russia* 57°22N 98°15E **215** D10
Kondrovo *Russia* 54°48N 35°56E **188** E8
Konduga *Nigeria* 11°35N 13°26E **263** C7
Kondukur *India* 15°12N 79°57E **245** G4
Kondūz *Afghan.* 36°50N 68°50E **240** A3
Kondūz □ *Afghan.* 36°50N 68°50E **240** A3
Koné *Cameroon* 8°50N 13°17E **259** G2
Koné *N. Cal.* 21°4S 164°52E **288** d
Köneürgench *Turkmenistan* 42°19N 59°10E **216** D5
Konevo *Russia* 62°8N 39°20E **188** A10
Kong = Khong → *Cambodia* 13°32N 105°58E **236** F5
Kong *Ivory C.* 8°54N 4°36W **262** D4
Kong, Koh *Cambodia* 11°20N 103°0E **237** G4
Kong Christian IX.s Land *Greenland* 68°0N 36°0W **154** D7
Kong Christian X.s Land *Greenland* 74°0N 29°0W **154** C8
Kong Frederik IX.s Land *Greenland* 67°0N 52°0W **154** D5
Kong Frederik VI.s Kyst *Greenland* 63°0N 43°0W **154** E6
Kong Frederik VIII.s Land *Greenland* 78°30N 26°0W **154** B8
Kong Karls Land *Svalbard* 79°0N 28°0E **154** B13
Kong Oscar Fjord *Greenland* 72°20N 24°0W **154** C8
Kongauru I. *Palau* 7°3N 134°16E **288** c
Kongbo *C.A.R.* 4°44N 21°23E **264** B4
Kongeå → *Denmark* 55°23N 8°39E **163** J2
Kongelunden *Denmark* 55°34N 12°34E **118** B3
Kongens Lyngby *Denmark* 55°46N 12°30E **118** A3
Kongerslev *Denmark* 56°54N 10°6E **163** H4
Kongkemul *Indonesia* 1°52N 116°10E **235** B5
Konglu *Burma* 27°13N 97°57E **241** B6
Kongmoon = Jiangmen *China* 22°32N 113°0E **229** F9
Kongo *Finland* 60°20N 24°47E **121** A1
Kongola *Namibia* 17°45S 23°20E **270** A3
Kongolo *Kasai-Or., Dem. Rep. of the Congo* 5°26S 24°49E **265** D4
Kongolo *Katanga, Dem. Rep. of the Congo* 5°22S 27°0E **268** D2
Kongor *South Sudan* 7°1N 31°27E **257** F3
Kongossambougou ⌓ *Mali* 14°0N 8°30W **262** C3
Kongoulou *Cameroon* 2°59N 11°7E **264** B2
Kongoussi *Burkina Faso* 13°19N 1°32W **263** C4
Kongsberg *Norway* 59°39N 9°39E **164** E6
Kongsvinger *Norway* 60°12N 12°2E **164** D9
Kongur Shan *China* 38°34N 75°18E **217** E9
Kongwa *Tanzania* 6°11S 36°26E **268** D4
Koni *Dem. Rep. of the Congo* 10°40S 27°11E **269** E2
Koniakari *Mali* 14°35N 10°50W **262** C2
Koniecpol *Poland* 50°46N 19°40E **185** H6
Königgrätz = Hradec Králové *Czech Rep.* 50°15N 15°50E **180** A8
Königs Wusterhausen *Germany* 52°19N 13°38E **178** C9
Königsberg = Chojna *Poland* 52°58N 14°25E **185** F1
Königsberg = Kaliningrad *Russia* 54°42N 20°32E **184** D7
Königsbrunn *Germany* 48°16N 10°54E **179** G6
Königshütte = Chorzów *Poland* 50°18N 18°57E **185** H5
Königslutter *Germany* 52°15N 10°49E **178** C6
Konin *Poland* 52°12N 18°15E **185** F5
Köninginhof an der Elbe = Dvůr Králové nad Labem *Czech Rep.* 50°27N 15°50E **180** A8
Koninklijk Paleis *Amsterdam, Neths.* **112** a2
Konispol *Albania* 39°42N 20°10E **206** B10
Konitsa *Greece* 40°5N 20°48E **204** A2
Konjic *Bos.-H.* 43°42N 17°58E **182** G2
Konkiep *Namibia* 26°49S 17°15E **270** C2
Konkō *Japan* 34°33N 133°36E **222** C4
Konkouré → *Guinea* 9°50N 13°42W **262** D2
Konnagar *India* 22°42N 88°21E **124** A2
Könnern *Germany* 51°41N 11°47E **178** D7
Konnur *India* 16°14N 74°49E **245** F2
Kono *S. Leone* 8°30N 11°5W **262** D2
Konogogo *Papua N. G.* 3°29S 152°10E **286** B7
Konohana *Japan* 34°40N 135°26E **133** A1
Konongo *Ghana* 6°40N 1°15W **263** D4
Konos *Papua N. G.* 3°10S 151°44E **286** B6
Konosha *Russia* 61°0N 40°5E **188** B11
Kōnosu *Japan* 36°3N 139°31E **223** A11
Konotop *Ukraine* 51°12N 33°7E **189** G7
Konqi He → *China* 41°0N 86°0E **217** D11
Konradshof = Skawina *Poland* 49°59N 19°50E **185** J6
Konradshöhe *Germany* 52°35N 13°13E **115** A2
Konrei *Palau* 7°43N 134°36E **288** c
Konsankoro *Guinea* 9°2N 9°0W **262** D3
Końskie *Poland* 51°15N 20°23E **185** G7
Konsmo *Norway* 58°16N 7°23E **164** F4
Konstadt = Wołczyn *Poland* 51°1N 18°3E **185** G5
Konstancin-Jeziorna *Poland* 52°5N 21°7E **185** F8
Konstantinograd = Krasnohrad *Ukraine* 49°27N 35°27E **189** H8
Konstantinovka = Kostyantynivka *Ukraine* 48°32N 37°39E **189** H9
Konstantinovsk *Russia* 47°33N 41°10E **191** G5
Konstantynów Łódźki *Poland* 51°45N 19°20E **185** G6
Konstanz *Germany* 47°40N 9°10E **179** H5
Kont *Iran* 26°55N 61°50E **247** E9
Konta *India* 17°48N 81°23E **244** F5
Kontagora *Nigeria* 10°23N 5°27E **263** C6
Kontcha *Cameroon* 7°59N 12°15E **263** D7
Kontiolahti *Finland* 62°46N 29°50E **160** E23
Kontokali *Greece* 39°38N 19°51E **206** B9
Konya *Turkey* 37°52N 32°35E **212** D5
Konya □ *Turkey* 37°46N 32°20E **250** A3
Konya Ovası *Turkey* 38°9N 33°5E **212** C5

Konyin Burma 22°58N 94°42E 241 D5
Konz Germany 49°42N 6°34E 179 F2
Konza Kenya 1°45S 37°7E 268 C4
Koo-wee-rup Australia 38°13S 145°28E 283 E6
Koocanusa, L. Canada 49°20N 115°15W 304 B6
Kookynie Australia 29°17S 121°22E 279 E3
Ko'olau Range U.S.A. 21°35N 157°50W 302 J14
Ko'olauloa District U.S.A. 21°35N 157°55W 302 J14
Ko'olaupoko District U.S.A. 21°25N 157°50W 302 K14
Kö'Ōlina U.S.A. 21°19N 158°7W 302 K13
Koolyanobbing Australia 30°48S 119°36E 279 F2
Koondrook Australia 35°33S 144°8E 282 C6
Koonibba Australia 31°54S 133°25E 281 E1
Koorawatha Australia 34°2S 148°33E 283 C8
Koorda Australia 30°48S 117°35E 279 F2
Kooskia U.S.A. 46°9N 115°59W 304 C6
Kootenay → U.S.A. 49°19N 117°39W 296 D5
Kootenay △ Canada 51°0N 116°0W 296 C5
Kootenay L. Canada 49°45N 116°50W 304 B5
Kootingal Australia 31°3S 151°4E 283 A9
Kootjieskolk S. Africa 31°15S 20°21E 270 D3
Kopanina Czech Rep. 50°3N 14°17E 135 B1
Kopanovka Russia 47°28N 46°50E 191 G8
Kopaonik Serbia 43°10N 20°50E 202 C4
Kopaonik △ Serbia 43°20N 20°50E 202 C4
Kopargaon India 19°51N 74°28E 244 E2
Koparkhairna India 19°6N 72°59E 130 A2
Kópasker Iceland 66°18N 16°27W 155 A10
Kópavogur Iceland 64°6N 21°55W 155 C5
Kopayhorod Ukraine 48°52N 27°53E 183 B12
Köpenick Germany 52°26N 13°35E 115 B4
Koper Slovenia 45°31N 13°44E 199 C10
Kopervik Norway 59°17N 5°17E 164 E2
Kopet Dagh Asia 38°0N 58°0E 247 B8
Kopeysk Russia 55°7N 61°37E 216 A6
Kopi Australia 33°24S 135°40E 281 E2
Köping Sweden 59°31N 16°3E 162 E10
Köpingsvik Sweden 56°53N 16°43E 163 H10
Kopište Croatia 42°48N 16°42E 199 F13
Koplik Albania 42°15N 19°25E 202 D3
Köpmanholmen Sweden 63°10N 18°35E 162 A12
Koppa India 13°33N 75°21E 245 H2
Koppal India 15°23N 76°5E 245 G3
Koppang Norway 61°34N 11°3E 164 C8
Kopparberg Sweden 59°52N 15°0E 162 E9
Koppeh Dāgh = Kopet Dagh Asia 38°0N 58°0E 247 B8
Kopperå Norway 63°24N 11°50E 164 A8
Koppies S. Africa 27°20S 27°30E 271 C4
Koppom Sweden 59°43N 12°10E 162 E6
Koprivlen Bulgaria 41°31N 23°53E 202 E7
Koprivnica Croatia 46°12N 16°45E 199 B13
Kopřivnice Czech Rep. 49°36N 18°9E 181 B11
Koprivshtitsa Bulgaria 42°40N 24°19E 203 D8
Köprü → Turkey 36°48N 31°11E 250 B2
Köprübaşı Turkey 38°43N 28°23E 205 C10
Köprülü Turkey 36°43N 32°10E 250 B3
Köprülü △ Turkey 37°20N 31°5E 246 B1
Kopychyntsi Ukraine 49°7N 25°58E 177 D13
Kor Aban Somali Rep. 3°58N 42°44E 267 D5
Kora △ Kenya 0°14S 38°44E 268 C4
Koraa Shiir Somali Rep. 3°16N 46°16E 267 D6
Korab Macedonia 41°44N 20°40E 202 E4
Korahe Ethiopia 6°39N 44°5E 267 C5
Koral India 21°50N 73°12E 242 J5
Korangal India 17°6N 77°38E 244 E3
Korangi Pakistan 24°47N 67°8E 123 B2
Koraput India 18°50N 82°40E 244 E6
Korarou, L. Mali 15°15N 3°15W 262 B4
Korba India 22°20N 82°45E 243 H10
Korbach Germany 51°16N 8°52E 178 D4
Korbu, Gunung Malaysia 4°41N 101°18E 237 K3
Korçë Albania 40°37N 20°50E 202 F4
Korčula Croatia 42°56N 16°57E 199 F13
Korčulanski Kanal Croatia 43°3N 16°40E 199 E13
Kord Kūy Iran 36°48N 54°7E 247 B7
Kord Sheykh Iran 28°31N 52°53E 247 D7
Kordestan = Kurdistan Asia 37°20N 43°30E 213 D10
Kordestān □ Iran 36°0N 47°0E 246 C5
Kordié Burkina Faso 12°36N 2°22W 262 C4
Koré Mayroua Niger 13°18N 3°55E 263 C5
Korea, North ■ Asia 40°0N 127°0E 227 E14
Korea, South ■ Asia 36°0N 128°0E 227 G15
Korea Bay Korea 39°0N 124°0E 224 C2
Korea Strait Asia 34°0N 129°30E 227 H15
Koregaon India 17°40N 74°10E 244 F2
Korem Ethiopia 12°30N 39°32E 257 E4
Koremasa Japan 35°39N 139°29E 140 B1
Korenevo Kursk, Russia 51°27N 34°55E 189 G8
Korenevo Moskva, Russia 55°40N 38°0E 129 B6
Korenica = Titova Korenica Croatia 44°45N 15°41E 199 D12
Korenovsk Russia 45°30N 39°22E 191 H4
Korets Ukraine 50°40N 27°5E 177 C14
Korfantów Poland 50°29N 17°36E 185 H4
Korgan Turkey 40°44N 37°13E 212 B7
Korgus Sudan 19°16N 33°29E 256 D3
Korhogo Ivory C. 9°29N 5°28W 262 D3
Koribundu S. Leone 7°41N 11°46W 262 D2
Koridalos Greece 37°59N 23°39E 112 B1
Korienzé Mali 15°22N 3°50W 262 B4
Korinthia □ Greece 37°50N 22°35E 204 D4
Korinthiakos Kolpos Greece 38°16N 22°30E 204 C4
Korinthos Greece 37°56N 22°55E 204 D4
Korioumé Mali 16°35N 3°0W 262 B4
Korissia, L. Greece 39°27N 19°53E 206 C9
Korithi Greece 37°55N 20°42E 207 D2
Kōriyama Japan 37°24N 140°23E 220 F10
Korkino Russia 54°54N 61°23E 216 B6
Korkuteli Turkey 37°4N 30°13E 205 D12
Korla China 41°45N 86°4E 217 D11
Kormakiti, C. Cyprus 35°23N 32°56E 207 E8
Körmend Hungary 47°5N 16°35E 182 C1
Kormor Iraq 35°8N 44°50E 213 E11
Kornat Croatia 43°50N 15°20E 199 E12
Kornat △ Croatia 43°50N 15°12E 199 E12
Korneshty = Corneşti Moldova 47°21N 28°1E 183 C13
Korneuburg Austria 48°20N 16°20E 181 C9
Kórnik Poland 52°15N 17°6E 185 F4
Kornsjø Norway 58°57N 11°39E 164 F8
Koro Fiji 17°19S 179°23E 287 A2
Koro Ivory C. 8°32N 7°30W 262 D3
Koro Mali 14°1N 2°58W 262 C4
Koro Sea Fiji 17°30S 179°45W 287 A3
Koro Toro Chad 16°5N 18°30E 259 E3
Koroba Papua N. G. 5°44S 142°47E 286 C2
Korobkovo = Gubkin Russia 51°17N 37°32E 189 G9
Korocha Russia 50°54N 37°19E 189 G9
Köroğlu Dağları Turkey 40°38N 33°0E 212 B5
Korogwe Tanzania 5°5S 38°25E 268 D4
Koroit Australia 38°18S 142°24E 282 E5
Korokoro N.Z. 41°13S 174°52E 143 B2
Korokoro Stream → N.Z. 41°14S 174°52E 143 B2
Koroleve Ukraine 48°9N 23°8E 183 B8
Korolevu Fiji 18°12S 177°46E 287 B1
Koromiri Cook Is. 21°15S 159°43W 289 h
Korona U.S.A. 29°25N 81°12W 317 F8
Koronadal Phil. 6°12N 124°51E 233 H5
Korong Vale Australia 36°22S 143°45E 282 D5
Koroni Greece 36°48N 21°57E 204 E3
Koronia, L. Greece 40°47N 23°10E 202 F7
Koronos Greece 37°12N 25°35E 205 D7
Koronowo Poland 53°19N 17°55E 185 E4
Koropelé C.A.R. 4°44N 17°11E 264 B3
Koropets Ukraine 48°56N 25°10E 183 B10
Koror Palau 7°20N 134°28E 288 c
Körös → Hungary 46°43N 20°12E 182 D5
Körös Maros △ Hungary 47°8N 20°52E 182 C5
Köröstarcsa Hungary 46°53N 21°3E 182 D6
Korosten Ukraine 50°54N 28°36E 177 C15
Korostyshev Ukraine 50°19N 29°4E 177 C15
Korotoyak Russia 51°1N 39°2E 189 G10
Korovou Fiji 17°47S 178°32E 287 A2
Koroyanitu △ Fiji 17°40S 177°35E 287 A1
Korraraika, Helodranon' i Madag. 17°45S 43°57E 272 B1
Korror I. Palau 7°20N 134°29E 288 c
Korsakov Russia 46°36N 142°42E 215 E15
Korsberga Sweden 57°19N 15°7E 163 G9
Korshiv Ukraine 48°39N 25°1E 183 B10
Korshunovo Russia 58°37N 110°10E 215 D12
Korsør Denmark 55°20N 11°9E 163 J5
Korsun Shevchenkovskiy Ukraine 49°26N 31°16E 189 H6
Korsze Poland 54°11N 21°9E 184 D8
Korti Sudan 18°6N 31°33E 256 D3
Kortrijk Belgium 50°50N 3°17E 170 D3
Korucu Turkey 39°28N 27°22E 205 B9
Korumburra Australia 38°26S 145°50E 283 E6
Korup △ Cameroon 5°15N 9°2E 264 A1
Korwai India 24°7N 78°5E 242 G8
Koryakskoye Nagorye Russia 61°0N 171°0E 215 C18
Koryukovka Ukraine 51°46N 32°16E 189 G7
Kos Greece 36°50N 27°15E 205 E9
Kosa Ethiopia 7°50N 36°50E 257 F4
Kosai Japan 34°42N 137°32E 223 C9
Kosan N. Korea 38°52N 127°25E 224 C3
Kosaya Gora Russia 54°10N 37°30E 188 E9
Kościan Poland 52°5N 16°40E 185 F3
Kościerzyna Poland 54°8N 17°59E 184 D4
Kosciusko U.S.A. 33°4N 89°35W 315 E10
Kosciuszko, Mt. Australia 36°27S 148°16E 283 D8
Kosciuszko △ Australia 36°30S 148°20E 283 D8
Kösély → Hungary 47°25N 21°5E 182 C6
Kosgi Andhra Pradesh, India 16°58N 77°43E 244 F3
Kosgi Andhra Pradesh, India 15°51N 77°16E 245 G3
Kosha Sudan 20°50N 30°30E 256 C3
Koshava Bulgaria 44°4N 23°2E 202 B7
Kōshi Japan 32°53N 130°48E 222 E2
Koshigaya Japan 35°54N 139°48E 223 B11
K'oshih = Kashi China 39°30N 76°2E 217 E9
Koshiki-Kaikyo Japan 31°30N 130°0E 222 F1
Koshiki-Rettō Japan 31°45N 129°49E 222 F1
Koshim → Kazakhstan 49°20N 50°30E 190 F10
Koshkonong L. U.S.A. 42°52N 88°58W 311 B8
Kōshoku Japan 36°38N 138°6E 223 A10
Koshu-Kavak = Krumovgrad Bulgaria 41°29N 25°38E 203 E9
Kosi India 27°48N 77°29E 242 F7
Kosi → India 28°41N 78°57E 243 E8
Košice Slovak Rep. 48°42N 21°15E 181 C14
Košický □ Slovak Rep. 48°45N 21°0E 181 C14
Kosino Russia 55°43N 37°50E 129 B5
Kosiv Ukraine 48°19N 25°6E 183 B10
Kosjerić Serbia 44°0N 19°55E 202 B3
Köşk Turkey 37°50N 28°3E 205 D10
Koskinou Greece 36°23N 28°13E 206 E12
Koslan Russia 63°34N 49°14E 186 B8
Köslin = Koszalin Poland 54°11N 16°8E 184 D3
Kosmach Ukraine 48°20N 24°50E 183 B9
Kosŏng N. Korea 38°40N 128°22E 224 C4
Kosovo ■ Europe 42°30N 21°0E 202 D4
Kosovo Polje Kosovo 42°40N 21°5E 202 D5
Kosovska Kamenica Kosovo 42°35N 21°35E 202 D5
Kosovska Mitrovica Kosovo 42°54N 20°52E 202 D4
Kossou, L. de Ivory C. 6°59N 5°31W 262 D3
Kosta Sweden 56°50N 15°24E 163 H9
Kostajnica Croatia 45°17N 16°30E 199 C13
Kostanjevica Slovenia 45°51N 15°27E 199 C12
Kostenets = Pernik Bulgaria 42°35N 23°2E 202 D7
Kostenets Bulgaria 42°15N 23°52E 202 D7
Koster S. Africa 25°52S 26°54E 270 C4
Kôstî Sudan 13°8N 32°43E 257 E3
Kostinbrod Bulgaria 42°49N 23°13E 202 D7
Kostolac Serbia 44°37N 21°15E 202 B5
Kostopil Ukraine 50°51N 26°22E 177 C14
Kostroma Russia 57°50N 40°58E 188 D11
Kostromo □ Russia 58°10N 42°50E 190 A6
Kostromskoye Vdkhr. Russia 57°52N 40°49E 188 D11
Kostryzhivka Ukraine 48°39N 25°43E 183 B10
Kostrzyn Lubuskie, Poland 52°35N 14°39E 185 F1
Kostrzyn Wielkopolskie, Poland 52°24N 17°14E 185 F4
Kostyantynivka Ukraine 48°32N 37°39E 189 H9
Kostyukovichi = Kastsyukovichy Belarus 53°20N 32°4E 189 F7
Kosugi Japan 35°34N 139°39E 140 B2
Koszalin Poland 54°11N 16°8E 184 D3
Kőszeg Hungary 47°23N 16°33E 182 C1
Kot Addu Pakistan 30°30N 71°0E 242 D4
Kot Kapura India 30°35N 74°50E 242 D6
Kot Moman Pakistan 32°13N 73°0E 242 C5
Kot Sultan Pakistan 30°46N 70°56E 242 D4
Kota India 25°14N 75°49E 242 G6
Kota Jakarta, Indonesia 6°7S 106°48E 122 A1
Kota Barrage India 25°6N 75°51E 242 G6
Kota Belud Malaysia 6°21N 116°26E 235 A5
Kota Bharu Malaysia 6°7N 102°14E 237 J4
Kota Kinabalu Malaysia 6°0N 116°4E 235 A5
Kota Tinggi Malaysia 1°44N 103°53E 237 M4
Kotaagung Indonesia 5°38S 104°29E 234 D2
Kotabaru Kalimantan Barat, Indonesia 0°49S 111°31E 235 C4
Kotabaru Kalimantan Selatan, Indonesia 3°20S 116°20E 235 C5
Kotabaru Sumatera Barat, Indonesia 1°7S 101°43E 234 C2
Kotabesi Indonesia 2°24S 112°58E 235 C4
Kotabumi Indonesia 4°49S 104°54E 234 C2
Kotajawa Indonesia 5°37S 104°19E 234 D2
Kotamobagu Indonesia 0°57N 124°31E 231 D6
Kotapad India 19°9N 82°21E 244 E6
Kotapinang Indonesia 1°53N 100°5E 237 M3
Kotawaringin Indonesia 2°28S 111°27E 235 C4
Kotchandpur Bangla. 23°24N 89°1E 241 D2
Kotcho L. Canada 59°7N 121°12W 296 B4
Kotdwara India 29°45N 78°32E 243 E8
Kotel Bulgaria 42°52N 26°26E 203 D10
Kotelnich Russia 58°22N 48°24E 190 A9
Kotelnikovo Russia 47°38N 43°8E 191 G6
Kotelnyy, Ostrov Russia 75°10N 139°0E 215 B14
Kotelyniki Russia 55°39N 37°52E 129 C5
Kothagudem India 17°30N 80°40E 244 F5
Kothapet India 19°21N 79°28E 244 E4
Kothari → India 25°20N 75°4E 242 G6
Köthen Germany 51°45N 11°59E 178 D7
Kothi Chhattisgarh, India 23°21N 82°3E 243 H10
Kothi Mad. P., India 24°45N 80°40E 243 G9
Kotiro Pakistan 26°17N 67°13E 242 F2
Kotka Finland 60°28N 26°58E 188 B4
Kotlas Russia 61°17N 46°43E 186 B8
Kotlenska Planina Bulgaria 42°56N 26°30E 203 D10
Kotli Pakistan 33°30N 73°55E 242 C5
Kotlik U.S.A. 63°2N 163°33W 303 E7
Kotma India 23°12N 81°58E 243 H9
Kōtō Japan 35°40N 139°48E 140 A3
Kotohira Japan 34°11N 133°49E 222 C5
Koton-Karifi Nigeria 8°0N 6°48E 263 D6
Kotonkoro Nigeria 11°3N 5°58E 263 C6
Kotor Montenegro 42°25N 18°47E 202 D2
Kotor Varoš Bos.-H. 44°38N 17°22E 182 F2
Kotoriba Croatia 46°23N 16°48E 199 B13
Kotovo Russia 50°22N 44°45E 190 E7
Kotovsk Russia 52°36N 41°32E 190 D5
Kotovsk Ukraine 47°45N 29°35E 177 E15
Kotputli India 27°43N 76°12E 242 F7
Kotri Pakistan 25°22N 68°22E 242 G3
Kotri → India 19°15N 80°35E 244 E5
Kotronas Greece 36°38N 22°29E 204 E4
Kotrung India 22°41N 88°20E 124 A2
Kötschach-Mauthen Austria 46°41N 13°1E 180 E6
Kottayam India 9°35N 76°33E 245 K3
Kotto C.A.R. 4°14N 22°2E 264 B4
Kotto → C.A.R. 4°14N 22°2E 264 B4
Kottur India 10°34N 76°56E 245 J3
Kotturu India 14°45N 76°10E 245 G3
Kotu Group Tonga 20°0S 174°45W 287 Q13
Kotuy → Russia 71°54N 102°6E 215 B11
Kotyuzhany Ukraine 48°48N 27°42E 183 B12
Kotzebue U.S.A. 66°53N 162°39W 303 C7
Kotzebue Sound U.S.A. 66°20N 163°0W 303 C7
Kotzenau = Chocianów Poland 51°27N 15°55E 185 G2
Kouango C.A.R. 5°0N 20°10E 264 B4
Kouchibouguac △ Canada 46°50N 65°0W 299 C6
Koudougou Burkina Faso 12°10N 2°20W 262 C4
Koufey Niger 13°57N 7°56E 259 F1
Koufonisi Iraklio, Greece 34°56N 26°8E 207 F7
Koufonisi Notio Aigaio, Greece 36°57N 25°35E 205 E7
Kougaberge S. Africa 33°48S 23°50E 270 D3
K'ouhu Taiwan 23°35N 120°11E 225 C2
Kouibli Ivory C. 7°15N 7°14W 262 D3
Kouilou → Congo 4°10S 12°5E 265 C2
Koukdjuak → Canada 66°43N 73°0W 295 D17
Kouki C.A.R. 7°22N 17°3E 264 A3
Koukoulé, Mt. Comoros Is. 12°18S 43°41E 272 a
Koukourou C.A.R. 7°12N 20°2E 264 A4
Koula Greece 41°23N 24°44E 203 E8
Koula Moutou Gabon 1°15S 12°25E 264 C2
Koulen = Kulen Cambodia 13°50N 104°40E 236 F5
Koulikoro Mali 12°40N 7°50W 262 C3
Koulikoro □ Mali 14°0N 7°45W 262 C3
Kouloura Greece 39°42N 19°54E 206 B9
Koumac N. Cal. 20°33S 164°17E 288 d
Koumala Australia 21°38S 149°15E 280 C4
Koumameveng Gabon 0°11N 11°51E 264 B2
Koumankou Mali 11°58N 6°6W 262 C3
Koumbia Burkina Faso 11°10N 3°50W 262 C4
Koumbia Guinea 11°48N 13°29W 262 C2
Koumboum Guinea 10°25N 13°0W 262 C2
Koumpenntoum Senegal 13°59N 14°34W 262 C2
Koumra Chad 8°50N 17°35E 259 G3
Koun-Fao Ivory C. 7°30N 3°15W 262 D4
Koundara Guinea 12°29N 13°18W 262 C2
Koundé C.A.R. 6°7N 14°38E 264 A2
Koungheul Senegal 14°0N 14°50W 262 C2
Koungou Mayotte 12°43S 45°12E 272 b
Koungoulou Congo 3°31S 13°20E 264 C2
Kountze U.S.A. 30°22N 94°19W 314 F7
Koupéla Burkina Faso 12°11N 0°21W 263 C4
Kouponia Greece 37°57N 23°47E 112 B2
Kourémalé Mali 11°59N 8°42W 262 C3
Kouri-shima Japan 26°42N 128°1E 288 a
Kouris → Cyprus 34°38N 32°54E 207 F8
Kourizo, P. de Chad 22°28N 15°27E 258 D3
Kourou Fr. Guiana 5°9N 52°39W 329 B7
Kourouba Mali 13°22N 10°57W 262 C2
Koûroudjél Mauritania 16°12N 11°30W 262 B2
Kouroukoto Mali 12°35N 10°5W 262 C2
Kourouma Burkina Faso 11°35N 4°50W 262 C4
Kourouninkoto Mali 13°52N 9°35W 262 C3
Kouroussa Guinea 10°45N 9°45W 262 C3
Koussanar Senegal 13°52N 14°5W 262 C2
Koussané Mali 14°53N 11°14W 262 C2
Koussane Senegal 14°10N 12°22W 262 C2
Kousseri Cameroon 12°0N 14°55E 259 F2
Koutiala Mali 12°25N 5°23W 262 C3
Kouto Ivory C. 9°53N 6°25W 262 D3
Kouts U.S.A. 41°19N 87°2W 311 C9
Kouvé Togo 6°25N 1°25E 263 D5
Kouvola Finland 60°52N 26°43E 188 B4
Kouyi Congo 2°29S 12°25E 264 C2
Kouyou → Congo 0°44S 16°38E 264 C3
Kovačica Serbia 45°5N 20°38E 182 E5
Kovdor Russia 67°34N 30°24E 160 C24
Kovel Ukraine 51°11N 24°38E 177 C13
Kovilpatti India 9°10N 77°50E 245 K3
Kovin Serbia 44°44N 20°59E 182 F5
Kovno = Kaunas Lithuania 54°54N 23°54E 184 D10
Kovrov Russia 56°25N 41°25E 190 B5
Kovur Andhra Pradesh, India 17°3N 81°39E 244 F5
Kovur Andhra Pradesh, India 14°30N 80°1E 245 G5
Kowal Poland 52°32N 19°7E 185 F6
Kowalewo Pomorskie Poland 53°10N 18°52E 185 E5
Kowanyama Australia 15°29S 141°44E 280 B3
Kowanyama ✪ Australia 15°20S 141°47E 280 B3
Kowlīnī Afghan. 37°39N 65°58E 240 A2
Kowloon China 22°19N 114°11E 122 B1
Kowloon Park Hong Kong, China 122 a2
Kowloon Peak China 22°20N 114°13E 122 A2
Kowloon Res. China 22°21N 114°9E 122 A1
Kowloon Tong China 22°20N 114°10E 122 A2
Kowŏn N. Korea 39°26N 127°14E 224 C3
Kōyama Japan 31°20N 130°56E 222 F2
Koyampattur = Coimbatore India 11°2N 76°59E 245 J3
Köyceğiz Turkey 36°57N 28°40E 205 E10
Köyceğiz Gölü Turkey 36°56N 28°42E 205 E10
Köýtendag Turkmenistan 37°30N 66°1E 240 A2
Koyuk U.S.A. 64°56N 161°9W 303 D7
Koyukuk U.S.A. 64°53N 157°42W 303 D8
Koyukuk → U.S.A. 64°55N 157°32W 303 D8
Koyukuk Nat. Wildlife Refuge ⌂ U.S.A. 65°35N 156°30W 303 D8
Koyulhisar Turkey 40°20N 37°52E 212 B7
Koyunyeri Turkey 40°50N 26°26E 203 F10
Koza = Okinawa Japan 26°19N 127°46E 288 a
Kozak Turkey 39°15N 27°6E 205 B9
Kozaklı Turkey 39°13N 34°49E 212 C6
Kozan Turkey 37°26N 35°50E 212 D6
Kozani Greece 40°19N 21°47E 202 F5
Kozani □ Greece 40°18N 21°45E 202 F5
Kozara Bos.-H. 45°0N 17°0E 199 D14
Kozara △ Bos.-H. 45°0N 17°0E 182 F2
Kozarac Bos.-H. 44°58N 16°48E 199 D13
Kozelets Ukraine 50°55N 31°7E 189 G6
Kozelsk Russia 54°2N 35°48E 188 E8
Kozhikode = Calicut India 11°15N 75°43E 245 J2
Kozhukhovo Russia 55°43N 37°53E 129 B5
Kozhva Russia 65°10N 57°0E 186 A10
Koziegłowy Poland 50°37N 19°8E 185 H6
Kozienice Poland 51°35N 21°34E 185 G8
Kozje Slovenia 46°5N 15°35E 199 B12
Kozloduy Bulgaria 43°45N 23°42E 202 C7
Kozlov = Michurinsk Russia 52°58N 40°27E 190 D5
Kozlovets Bulgaria 43°30N 25°20E 203 C9
Kozlovka Russia 55°52N 48°14E 190 C9
Kozlu Turkey 41°26N 31°45E 212 B4
Kozluk Turkey 38°11N 41°31E 213 C9
Koźmin Poland 51°48N 17°27E 185 G4
Kozmodemyansk Russia 56°20N 46°36E 190 B8
Kōzu-Shima Japan 34°13N 139°10E 223 C11
Kożuchów Poland 51°45N 15°31E 185 G2
Kozyatyn Ukraine 49°45N 28°50E 177 D15
Kozyrevsk Russia 56°3N 159°51E 215 D16
Kpabia Ghana 9°10N 0°20W 263 D4
Kpalimé Togo 6°57N 0°44E 263 D5
Kpandae Ghana 8°30N 0°2W 263 D4
Kpessi Togo 8°4N 1°16E 263 D5
Kra, Isthmus of = Kra, Kho Khot Thailand 10°15N 99°30E 237 G2
Kra, Kho Khot Thailand 10°15N 99°30E 237 G2
Kra Buri Thailand 10°22N 98°46E 237 G2
Kraai → S. Africa 30°40S 26°45E 270 D4
Kraainem Belgium 50°52N 4°28E 116 A2
Krabi Thailand 8°4N 98°55E 237 H2
Kracheh = Kratie Cambodia 12°32N 106°10E 236 F6
Kragan Indonesia 6°43S 111°38E 235 D4
Kragerø Norway 58°52N 9°25E 164 F6
Kragujevac Serbia 44°2N 20°56E 202 B4
Krailling Germany 48°5N 11°25E 131 B1
Krainburg = Kranj Slovenia 46°16N 14°22E 199 B11
Krajenka Poland 53°18N 16°59E 185 E3
Krakatau = Rakata, Pulau Indonesia 6°10S 105°20E 234 D3
Krakatoa = Rakata, Pulau Indonesia 6°10S 105°20E 234 D3
Krakau = Kraków Poland 50°4N 19°57E 185 H6
Krakor Cambodia 12°32N 104°12E 236 F5
Kraków Poland 50°4N 19°57E 185 H6
Kraków ✈ (KRK) Poland 50°5N 19°52E 185 H6
Kraksaan Indonesia 7°43S 113°23E 235 D4
Kralanh Cambodia 13°35N 103°25E 236 F4
Kralendijk Bonaire 12°9N 68°16W 322 h
Králíky Czech Rep. 50°6N 16°45E 181 A9
Kraljevo Serbia 43°44N 20°41E 202 C4
Kralovéhradecký □ Czech Rep. 50°25N 15°50E 180 A8
Královský Chlmec Slovak Rep. 48°27N 22°0E 181 C14
Kralupy nad Vltavou Czech Rep. 50°13N 14°20E 180 A7
Kramatorsk Ukraine 48°50N 37°30E 189 H9
Kramfors Sweden 62°55N 17°48E 162 B11
Kramis, C. Algeria 36°26N 0°45E 261 A5
Krampnitz Germany 52°27N 13°3E 115 B1
Krampnitzsee Germany 52°27N 13°3E 115 B1
Krania Greece 39°53N 21°18E 202 G5
Krania Elasonas Greece 39°57N 22°2E 204 B4
Kranidi Greece 37°20N 23°10E 204 D5
Kranj Slovenia 46°16N 14°22E 199 B11
Kranji, Sungei → Singapore 1°26N 103°44E 138 A2
Kranji Industrial Estate Singapore 1°26N 103°45E 138 A2
Kranjska Gora Slovenia 46°29N 13°48E 199 B10
Krankskop S. Africa 28°0S 30°47E 271 C5
Kranz = Zelenogradsk Russia 54°53N 20°29E 184 D7
Krapina Croatia 46°10N 15°52E 199 B12
Krapina → Croatia 45°50N 15°50E 199 C12
Krapkowice Poland 50°29N 17°56E 185 H4
Krappitz = Krapkowice Poland 50°29N 17°56E 185 H4
Kras Croatia 45°35N 14°0E 199 C10
Krasavino Russia 60°58N 46°29E 186 B8
Krasieo Res. Thailand 14°49N 99°30E 236 E2
Kraskino Russia 42°44N 130°48E 220 C5
Kraskovo Russia 55°39N 37°58E 129 C5
Krāslava Latvia 55°54N 27°10E 188 E4
Kraslice Czech Rep. 50°19N 12°31E 180 A5
Krasnaya Gorbatka Russia 55°52N 41°45E 190 C5
Krasnaya Polyana Russia 43°40N 40°13E 191 J5
Krasnaya Sloboda = Krasnoslobodsk Russia 48°42N 44°33E 191 F7
Krasne Ukraine 46°7N 29°15E 183 D14
Krasni Okny Ukraine 47°32N 29°27E 183 C14
Kraśnik Poland 50°55N 22°15E 185 H9
Krasno-Presnenskaya Russia 55°45N 37°32E 129 B3
Krasnoarmeisk Ukraine 48°18N 37°11E 189 H9
Krasnoarmeysk = Tayynsha Kazakhstan 53°50N 69°45E 217 B7
Krasnoarmeysk Russia 51°0N 45°42E 190 E7
Krasnoarmeyskiy Russia 47°0N 42°12E 191 G6
Krasnoarmeysky Rudnik = Dobropole Ukraine 48°25N 37°2E 189 H9
Krasnobrod Poland 50°33N 23°12E 185 H10
Krasnodar Russia 45°5N 39°0E 191 H4
Krasnodar □ Russia 46°30N 39°30E 191 G4
Krasnodarskoye Vdkhr. Russia 45°1N 39°23E 191 H4
Krasnodon Ukraine 48°17N 39°44E 189 H10
Krasnogorsk Russia 55°49N 37°18E 129 B1
Krasnogorskiy Russia 56°10N 48°28E 190 B9
Krasnograd = Krasnohrad Ukraine 49°27N 35°27E 189 H8
Krasnogvardeysk = Gatchina Russia 59°35N 30°9E 188 C6
Krasnogvardeysk Ukraine 45°32N 34°16E 189 K8
Krasnogvardeyskoye Russia 45°52N 41°33E 191 H5
Krasnohrad Ukraine 49°27N 35°27E 189 H8
Krasnokamensk Russia 50°3N 118°0E 215 D12
Krasnokamsk Russia 58°4N 55°48E 186 C10
Krasnokokshaysk = Yoshkar Ola Russia 56°38N 47°55E 190 B8
Krasnokutsk Ukraine 50°10N 34°50E 189 G8
Krasnolesnyy Russia 51°53N 39°35E 189 G10
Krasnoperekopsk Ukraine 46°0N 33°54E 189 J7
Krasnorechenskiy Russia 44°41N 135°14E 220 B7
Krasnoselkup Russia 65°20N 82°10E 214 C9
Krasnoslobodsk Mordvinia, Russia 54°25N 43°45E 190 C6
Krasnoslobodsk Volgograd, Russia 48°42N 44°33E 191 F7
Krasnoturinsk Russia 59°46N 60°12E 186 C11
Krasnoufimsk Russia 56°36N 57°38E 186 C10
Krasnouralsk Russia 58°21N 60°3E 186 C11
Krasnovishersk Russia 60°23N 57°3E 186 B10
Krasnovodsk = Türkmenbashi Turkmenistan 40°5N 53°5E 247 A7
Krasnoyarsk Russia 56°8N 93°0E 215 D10
Krasnoyarskoye Russia 54°31N 21°56E 184 D8
Krasnoye = Krasnyy Russia 54°25N 31°30E 188 E6
Krasnoye = Ulan Erge Russia 46°19N 44°53E 191 G7
Krasnoyilsk Ukraine 47°59N 25°38E 183 C10
Krasnozavodsk Russia 56°27N 38°25E 188 D10
Krasnoznamensk Russia 54°57N 22°30E 184 D9
Krasny = Kyzyl Russia 51°50N 94°30E 217 B12
Krasny = Mozhga Russia 56°26N 52°15E 190 B11
Krasny Boyevik = Kotovsk Russia 52°36N 41°32E 190 D5
Krasny Sulin Russia 47°52N 40°8E 191 G5
Krasnystaw Poland 50°57N 23°5E 185 H10
Krasnyy Russia 54°25N 31°30E 188 E6
Krasnyy Kholm Russia 58°10N 37°10E 188 C9
Krasnyy Kut Russia 50°50N 47°0E 190 E8
Krasnyy Liman Ukraine 48°58N 37°50E 189 H9
Krasnyy Luch Ukraine 48°13N 39°0E 189 H10
Krasnyy Profintern Russia 57°45N 40°27E 188 D11
Krasnyy Yar Astrakhan, Russia 46°43N 48°23E 191 G9
Krasnyy Yar Samara, Russia 53°30N 50°22E 190 D10
Krasnyy Yar Volgograd, Russia 50°42N 44°45E 190 E7
Krasnyye Baki Russia 57°8N 45°10E 190 B7
Krasnyyoskolske Vdskh. Ukraine 49°27N 37°40E 189 H9
Kraszna → Hungary 48°4N 22°20E 182 B7
Kratie Cambodia 12°32N 106°10E 236 F6
Kratke Ra. Papua N. G. 6°45S 146°0E 286 D4
Kratovo Macedonia 42°6N 22°10E 202 D6
Krau Indonesia 3°19S 140°5E 231 E10
Kraulshavn = Nuussauq Greenland 74°8N 57°3W 154 C5
Kravanh, Chuor Phnum Cambodia 12°0N 103°32E 237 G4
Krč Czech Rep. 50°2N 14°26E 135 B2
Krefeld Germany 51°20N 6°33E 178 D2
Kremaston, L. Greece 38°52N 21°30E 204 C3
Kremen Croatia 44°28N 15°53E 199 D12
Kremenchuk Ukraine 49°5N 33°25E 189 H7
Kremenchuksk Vdskh. Ukraine 49°20N 32°30E 189 H7
Kremenets Ukraine 50°8N 25°43E 177 C13
Kremennaya Ukraine 49°1N 38°10E 189 H10
Kremges = Svitlovodsk Ukraine 49°2N 33°13E 189 H7
Kremlin Moscow, Russia 129 c2
Kremmen Germany 52°45N 13°1E 178 C9
Kremmling U.S.A. 40°4N 106°24W 304 F10
Kremnica Slovak Rep. 48°45N 18°50E 181 C11
Krems Austria 48°25N 15°36E 180 C8
Kremsmünster Austria 48°3N 14°8E 180 C7
Krenau = Chrzanów Poland 50°10N 19°21E 185 H6
Krestena Greece 37°35N 21°37E 204 D3
Krestovskiye, Ostrov Russia 59°57N 30°14E 137 B1
Kretinga Lithuania 55°53N 21°15E 184 C8
Krettamia Algeria 28°47N 3°27W 260 C4
Krettsy Russia 58°15N 32°30E 188 C7
Kreuzberg Bayern, Germany 50°22N 9°58E 179 E5
Kreuzberg Berlin, Germany 52°30N 13°24E 115 A3
Kreuzburg = Kluczbork Poland 50°58N 18°12E 185 H5
Kreuztal Germany 50°57N 8°0E 178 E4
Kria Vrisi Greece 40°41N 22°18E 202 F6
Kribi Cameroon 2°57N 9°56E 263 E6
Krichem Bulgaria 42°8N 24°28E 203 D8
Krichev = Krychaw Belarus 53°40N 31°41E 177 B16
Kril'on, Mys Russia 45°53N 142°5E 220 B11
Krim Slovenia 45°53N 14°30E 199 C11
Krim-Krim Chad 9°0N 15°24E 259 G3
Krindachyovka = Krasnyy Luch Ukraine 48°13N 39°0E 189 H10
Krios, Akra Greece 35°13N 23°34E 207 E4
Krishna → India 15°57N 80°59E 245 G5
Krishnagiri India 12°32N 78°16E 245 H4
Krishnanagar India 23°24N 88°33E 243 H13
Krishnaraja Sagar India 12°20N 76°30E 245 H3
Kristdala Sweden 57°24N 16°13E 163 G10
Kristians = Oppland □ Norway 61°15N 9°40E 164 C6
Kristiansand Norway 58°8N 8°1E 164 F5
Kristianstad Sweden 56°2N 14°9E 163 H8
Kristiansund Norway 63°7N 7°45E 164 A4
Kristiinankaupunki Finland 62°16N 21°21E 160 E19
Kristinehamn Sweden 59°18N 14°7E 162 E8
Kristinestad = Kristiinankaupunki Finland 62°16N 21°21E 160 E19
Kristinopol = Chervonohrad Ukraine 50°25N 24°10E 177 C13
Krithoti, Akra Greece 38°30N 21°2E 207 B3
Kriti Greece 35°15N 25°0E 207 E6
Kritsa Greece 35°10N 25°41E 207 E6
Kritzendorf Austria 48°19N 16°18E 142 A1
Kriva → Macedonia 42°5N 21°47E 202 D5
Kriva Palanka Macedonia 42°11N 22°19E 202 D6
Krivaja → Bos.-H. 44°27N 18°9E 182 F3
Krivelj Serbia 44°10N 22°5E 202 B6
Křivoklátsko ⌂ Czech Rep. 50°1N 13°51E 180 A6
Krivoy Rog = Kryvyy Rih Ukraine 47°51N 33°20E 189 J7
Križevci Croatia 46°3N 16°32E 199 B13
Krk Croatia 45°8N 14°40E 199 C11
Krka → Slovenia 45°50N 15°30E 199 C12
Krka △ Croatia 43°53N 15°56E 199 E12
Krkonoše Czech Rep. 50°50N 15°35E 180 A8
Krkonoše △ Czech Rep. 50°43N 15°39E 180 A8
Krnjaja = Kljajićevo Serbia 45°45N 19°17E 182 E4
Krnov Czech Rep. 50°5N 17°40E 181 A10
Krobia Poland 51°47N 16°59E 185 G3
Krøderen Norway 60°9N 9°49E 164 D6
Krokees Greece 36°53N 22°32E 204 E4
Krokek Sweden 58°40N 16°24E 163 F10
Krokodil = Umgwenya → Mozam. 25°14S 32°18E 271 C5
Krokom Sweden 63°20N 14°30E 162 A8
Krokowa Poland 54°47N 18°9E 184 D5
Króksfjarðarnes Iceland 65°27N 21°56W 155 B5
Krokstadelva Norway 59°56N 10°1E 164 E7
Krolevets Ukraine 51°35N 33°20E 189 G7
Królewska Huta = Chorzów Poland 50°18N 18°57E 185 H5
Kroměříž Czech Rep. 49°18N 17°21E 181 B10
Krompachy Slovak Rep. 48°54N 20°52E 181 C13
Kromy Russia 52°48N 35°48E 189 F8
Kronach Germany 50°14N 11°19E 179 E7
Kronau = Kranjska Gora Slovenia 46°29N 13°48E 199 B10
Krong Kaoh Kong Cambodia 11°37N 102°59E 237 G4
Kronobergs län □ Sweden 56°45N 14°30E 163 H8
Kronprins Christian Land Greenland 80°30N 22°0W 154 A8
Kronprins Frederik Land Greenland 81°0N 45°0W 154 A6
Kronprins Olav Kyst Antarctica 69°0S 42°0E 151 C5
Kronprinsesse Märtha Kyst Antarctica 73°30S 10°0W 151 D2
Kronshtadt Russia 59°57N 29°51E 188 C5
Kronstadt = Braşov Romania 45°38N 25°35E 183 E10
Kroonstad S. Africa 27°43S 27°19E 270 C4
Kröpelin Germany 54°4N 11°47E 178 A7
Kropotkin Russia 45°28N 40°28E 191 H5
Kropp Germany 54°24N 9°31E 178 A5
Krosna Lithuania 54°23N 23°33E 184 D10
Krośniewice Poland 52°15N 19°11E 185 F6
Krosno Poland 49°42N 21°46E 185 J8
Krosno Odrzańskie Poland 52°3N 15°7E 185 F2
Krotoszyn Poland 51°42N 17°23E 185 G4
Krotovka Russia 53°18N 51°10E 190 D10
Krousonas Greece 35°13N 24°59E 207 E5
Krrabë Albania 41°13N 20°0E 202 E3
Krško Slovenia 45°57N 15°30E 199 C12
Krstača Serbia 42°57N 20°8E 202 D4
Kruger △ S. Africa 24°50S 26°10E 271 B4
Krugersdorp S. Africa 26°5S 27°46E 271 C4
Krui Indonesia 5°10S 103°55E 234 D2
Kruisfontein S. Africa 33°59S 24°43E 270 D3
Krujë Albania 41°32N 19°46E 202 E3
Krulevshchina = Krulyewshchyna Belarus 55°5N 27°45E 188 E4
Krulyewshchyna Belarus 55°5N 27°45E 188 E4
Krumbach Germany 48°13N 10°22E 179 G6
Krumë Albania 42°14N 20°28E 202 D4
Krummau = Český Krumlov Czech Rep. 48°43N 14°21E 180 C7
Krumme Lanke Germany 52°27N 13°14E 115 B2
Krummensee Germany 52°35N 13°41E 115 A5
Krummhübel = Karpacz Poland 50°46N 15°46E 185 H2
Krumovgrad Bulgaria 41°29N 25°38E 203 E9
Krung Thep = Bangkok Thailand 13°45N 100°35E 113 B2
Krupanj Serbia 44°25N 19°22E 202 B3
Krupina Slovak Rep. 48°22N 19°5E 181 C12
Krupinica → Slovak Rep. 48°4N 18°55E 181 C11
Krupki Belarus 54°19N 29°8E 177 A15
Krusboda Sweden 59°13N 18°14E 139 B3
Krusenstern, C. U.S.A. 67°8N 163°45W 303 C7
Kruševac Serbia 43°35N 21°28E 202 C5
Kruševo Macedonia 41°23N 21°19E 202 E5
Krushchyov = Svitlovodsk Ukraine 49°2N 33°13E 189 H7
Krushelnyksya Ukraine 49°7N 23°29E 185 J10
Kruszwica Poland 52°40N 18°20E 185 F5
Krychaw Belarus 53°40N 31°41E 177 B16
Krylatskoye Russia 55°44N 37°23E 129 B2
Krymsk Russia 44°50N 38°0E 189 K10
Krymskiy Poluostrov = Krymskyy Pivostriv Ukraine 45°0N 34°0E 189 K8
Krymskyy Pivostriv Ukraine 45°0N 34°0E 189 K8
Krynica Poland 49°25N 20°57E 185 J7
Krynica Morska Poland 54°23N 19°28E 184 D6
Krynki Poland 53°17N 23°43E 185 E10
Krynychne Ukraine 45°32N 28°40E 183 E13
Kryvyy Rih Ukraine 47°51N 33°20E 189 J7
Kryzhopil Ukraine 48°23N 28°53E 183 B13
Krzemieniec = Kremenets Ukraine 50°8N 25°43E 177 C13
Krzepice Poland 50°58N 18°50E 185 H5
Krzeszów Poland 50°24N 22°21E 185 H9
Krzna → Poland 52°8N 23°32E 185 F10
Krzywiń Poland 51°58N 16°50E 185 G3
Krzyż Wielkopolski Poland 52°52N 16°0E 185 F2
Ksabi Morocco 32°51N 4°13W 260 B4
Ksar Chellala Algeria 35°13N 2°19E 261 A5
Ksar el Boukhari Algeria 35°51N 2°52E 261 A5
Ksar el Kebir Morocco 35°0N 6°0W 260 B3
Ksar es Souk = Er Rachidia Morocco 31°58N 4°20W 260 B4
Ksar Rhilane Tunisia 33°0N 9°39E 258 B1
Książ Wielkopolski Poland 52°4N 17°14E 185 F4
Ksour, Mts. des Algeria 32°45N 0°30W 261 B4
Kstovo Russia 56°12N 44°13E 190 B7
Ku, W. el → Sudan 13°37N 25°15E 257 E2
Ku-Ring-Gai Chase △ Australia 33°39S 151°14E 283 B9
Ku Tree Res. U.S.A. 21°30N 157°59W 302 J14
Kuah Malaysia 6°19N 99°51E 237 J2
Kuala Indonesia 2°55N 105°47E 234 B3
Kuala Belait Malaysia 4°35N 114°11E 235 B4
Kuala Berang Malaysia 5°5N 103°1E 237 K4
Kuala Dungun = Dungun Malaysia 4°45N 103°25E 237 K4
Kuala Kangsar Malaysia 4°46N 100°56E 237 K3
Kuala Kelawang Malaysia 2°56N 102°5E 237 L4
Kuala Kerai Malaysia 5°30N 102°12E 237 K4
Kuala Kubu Bharu Malaysia 3°34N 101°39E 237 L3
Kuala Lipis Malaysia 4°10N 102°3E 237 K4
Kuala Lumpur Malaysia 3°9N 101°41E 237 L3
Kuala Nerang Malaysia 6°16N 100°37E 237 J3
Kuala Pilah Malaysia 2°45N 102°15E 237 L4
Kuala Rompin Malaysia 2°49N 103°29E 237 L4
Kuala Selangor Malaysia 3°20N 101°15E 237 L3
Kuala Sepetang Malaysia 4°49N 100°28E 237 K3
Kuala Terengganu Malaysia 5°20N 103°8E 237 K4
Kualajelai Indonesia 2°58S 110°46E 235 C4
Kualakapuas Indonesia 2°55S 114°20E 235 C4
Kualakurun Indonesia 1°10S 113°50E 235 C4
Kualapembuang Indonesia 3°14S 112°38E 235 C4
Kualapesaguan Indonesia 2°1S 110°7E 235 C4
Kualapu'u U.S.A. 21°9N 157°2W 302 B4
Kualasimpang Indonesia 4°17N 98°3E 234 B1
Kualatungkal Indonesia 0°49S 103°28E 234 C2
Kualoa Pt. U.S.A. 21°31N 157°50W 302 J14
Kuamat Malaysia 5°13N 117°30E 235 A5
Kuan Shan Taiwan 23°14N 120°54E 225 C2
Kuanao Taiwan 24°31N 118°24E 225 a
Kuancheng China 40°37N 118°30E 227 D10
Kuandang Indonesia 0°56N 123°1E 231 D6
Kuandian China 40°45N 124°45E 224 B2
Kuangchou = Guangzhou China 23°6N 113°13E 121 B2
Kuangfu Taiwan 23°40N 121°25E 225 C3
Kuanhsi Taiwan 24°48N 121°10E 225 B3
Kuanmiao Taiwan 22°58N 120°19E 225 D2
Kuanshan Taiwan 23°3N 121°9E 225 C3
Kuantan Malaysia 3°49N 103°20E 237 L4
Kuanyin Ilan, Taiwan 24°23N 121°46E 225 B3
Kuanyin Taoyüan, Taiwan 25°2N 121°4E 225 A3
Kuapā Pond U.S.A. 21°17N 157°43W 302 K14
Kuapnit Balinsasayao △ Phil. 10°53N 124°55E 233 F5
Kuba = Quba Azerbaijan 41°21N 48°32E 191 K9
Kubah △ Malaysia 1°35N 110°9E 235 B4
Kuban → Russia 45°20N 37°30E 189 K9
Kuban Depression = Prikubanskaya Nizmennost Russia 45°39N 38°33E 191 H4
Kubaysah Iraq 33°35N 42°37E 213 G10
Kubenskoye, Ozero Russia 59°40N 39°25E 188 C10
Kuberle = Krasnoarmeyskiy Russia 47°0N 42°12E 191 G6
Kubokawa Japan 33°12N 133°8E 222 D5
Kubor, Mt. Papua N. G. 6°10S 144°44E 286 D3
Kubrat Bulgaria 43°49N 26°31E 203 C10
Kubu Indonesia 8°16S 115°35E 231 J18
Kubumesaai Indonesia 1°31N 115°6E 235 B5
Kubutambahan Indonesia 8°5S 115°10E 231 J18
Kucar, Tanjung Indonesia 8°39S 114°34E 231 K18

Kučevo Serbia 44°30N 21°40E 202 B5
Kuchaman India 27°13N 74°47E 242 F6
Kuchchaveli Sri Lanka 8°49N 81°6E 245 K5
Kuchenspitze Austria 47°7N 10°12E 180 D3
Kuchinda India 21°44N 84°21E 243 J11
Kuching Malaysia 1°33N 110°25E 235 B4
Kuchino-eruba-Jima Japan 30°28N 130°12E 221 J5
Kuchino-Shima Japan 29°57N 129°55E 221 K4
Kuchinotsu Japan 32°36N 130°11E 222 E2
Kuchl Austria 47°37N 13°9E 180 D6
Kūchnay Darvīshān Afghan. 30°59N 64°10E 240 C2
Kuchurhan → Ukraine 46°33N 29°57E 183 D14
Kucing = Kuching Malaysia 1°33N 110°25E 235 B4
Kuçovë Albania 40°47N 19°57E 202 F3
Küçükbahçe Turkey 38°33N 26°24E 205 C8
Küçükköy Balıkesir, Turkey 39°16N 26°42E 205 B8
Küçükköy İstanbul, Turkey 41°3N 28°52E 122 B1
Küçükkuyu Turkey 39°32N 26°36E 205 B8
Küçükmenderes → Turkey 37°57N 27°16E 205 D9
Küçüksu Turkey 41°5N 29°5E 122 B2
Kud → Pakistan 26°5N 66°20E 242 F2
Kuda India 23°10N 71°15E 242 H4
Kuda Indonesia 1°1N 112°58E 235 B4
Kudahuvadhoo Maldives 2°40N 72°54E 272 d
Kudahuvadhoo Channel Maldives 2°40N 73°0E 272 d
Kudaka-shima Japan 26°9N 127°53E 288 a
Kudal India 16°2N 73°41E 245 F1
Kudalier → India 18°35N 79°48E 244 E4
Kudamatsu Japan 34°0N 131°52E 222 D3
Kudankita Tokyo, Japan 140 a3
Kudarebe Aruba 12°37N 70°4W 322 f
Kudat Malaysia 6°55N 116°55E 235 A5
Kudirkos Naumiestis Lithuania 54°46N 22°53E 184 D9
Kudowa-Zdrój Poland 50°27N 16°15E 185 H3
Kudremukh India 13°15N 75°20E 245 H2
Kudrovo Russia 59°54N 30°30E 137 B3
Kudus Indonesia 6°48S 110°51E 235 D4
Kudymkar Russia 59°1N 54°39E 186 C9
Kueishan Tao Taiwan 24°51N 121°57E 225 B3
Kueiyang = Guiyang China 26°32N 106°40E 228 D6
Kufra Oasis = Al Kufrah Libya 24°17N 23°15E 258 D4
Kufstein Austria 47°35N 12°11E 180 D5
Kugaaruk = Pelly Bay Canada 68°38N 89°50W 295 D14
Kugluktuk Canada 67°50N 115°5W 294 D8
Kugong I. Canada 56°18N 79°50W 298 A4
Kūh Dasht Iran 33°32N 47°36E 213 F12
Kūh-e-Jebāl Bārez Iran 29°0N 58°0E 247 D8
Kūh-e Sorkh Iran 35°30N 58°45E 216 E5
Kūhak Iran 27°12N 63°10E 240 D1
Kuhan Pakistan 28°19N 67°14E 242 E2
Kūhbonān Iran 31°23N 56°19E 247 D8
Kūhestak Iran 26°47N 57°2E 247 E8
Kuhestān Afghan. 34°39N 61°12E 240 B1
Kuhin Iran 36°22N 49°40E 247 B6
Kūhīrī Iran 26°55N 61°2E 247 E9
Kūhiston-Badakhshon □ Tajikistan 38°30N 73°0E 217 E8
Kuhmo Finland 64°7N 29°31E 160 D23
Kuhn Chae △ Thailand 19°8N 99°24E 236 C2
Kuhnsdorf Austria 46°37N 14°38E 180 E7
Kūhpāyeh Eşfahan, Iran 32°44N 52°20E 247 C7
Kūhpāyeh Kermān, Iran 30°35N 57°15E 247 D8
Kūhrān, Kūh-e Iran 26°46N 58°12E 247 E8
Kui Buri Thailand 12°3N 99°52E 237 F2
Kuiburi △ Thailand 12°10N 99°37E 237 F2
Kuichong China 22°38N 114°25E 219 a
Kuiseb → Namibia 22°59S 14°31E 270 B1
Kuito Angola 12°22S 16°55E 265 E3
Kuiu I. U.S.A. 57°45N 134°10W 296 B2
Kujang N. Korea 39°57N 126°1E 224 C3
Kujawsko-Pomorskie □ Poland 53°20N 18°30E 184 E5
Kuji Japan 40°11N 141°46E 220 D10
Kujū-San Japan 33°5N 131°15E 222 D3
Kukarka = Sovetsk Russia 57°38N 48°53E 190 B9
Kukava Ukraine 48°37N 27°43E 183 B12
Kukavica Serbia 42°48N 21°57E 202 D5
Kukawa Nigeria 12°58N 13°27E 263 C7
Kuk'eng Taiwan 23°38N 120°33E 225 C2
Kukës Albania 42°5N 20°27E 202 D4
Kuki Japan 36°4N 139°40E 223 A11
Kukipi Papua N. G. 8°10S 146°6E 286 E4
Kukmor Russia 56°11N 50°54E 190 B10
Kukong = Shaoguan China 24°48N 113°35E 229 E9
Kuku Pt. Wake I. 19°18N 166°34E 302 b
Kukuan Taiwan 24°17N 121°2E 225 B3
Kukuihaele U.S.A. 20°5N 155°35W 302 C6
Kukup Malaysia 1°20N 103°27E 237 d
Kukup, Pulau Malaysia 1°18N 103°25E 237 d
Kukvidze Russia 50°40N 43°0E 190 E6
Kula Bulgaria 43°52N 22°36E 202 C6
Kula Serbia 45°37N 19°32E 182 E4
Kula Turkey 38°32N 28°40E 205 C10
Kula Gulf Solomon Is. 8°5S 157°18E 287 M9
K'ula Kangri Asia 28°14N 90°36E 241 A3
K'ula Shan Bhutan 28°14N 90°36E 218 F7
Kulachi Pakistan 31°56N 70°27E 242 D4
Kulai Malaysia 1°44N 103°35E 237 M4
Kulal, Mt. Kenya 2°43N 36°56E 266 D4
Kulaly, Ostrov = Kulaly Aral Kazakhstan 45°0N 50°5E 191 H10
Kulaly Aral Kazakhstan 45°0N 50°5E 191 H10
Kulasekarappattinam India 8°20N 78°5E 245 K4
Kulassein I. Phil. 6°25N 120°41E 233 H3
Kulaura Bangla. 24°32N 92°3E 241 C4
Kulautuva Lithuania 54°56N 23°36E 184 D10
Kuldīga Latvia 56°58N 21°59E 184 B8
Kuldīga □ Latvia 56°55N 22°0E 184 B8
Kuldja = Yining China 43°58N 81°10E 217 D10
Kuldu Sudan 12°50N 28°30E 257 E2
Kulebaki Russia 55°22N 42°25E 190 C6
Kulen Cambodia 13°50N 104°40E 236 F5
Kulen Vakuf Bos.-H. 44°35N 16°2E 199 D13
Kulgam India 33°36N 75°2E 243 C6
Kulgera Australia 25°50S 133°18E 280 D1
Kulhudhuffushi Maldives 6°37N 73°3E 272 d
Kulim Malaysia 5°22N 100°34E 237 K3
Kulin Australia 32°40S 118°2E 279 F2
Kulittalai India 10°55N 78°25E 245 J4
Kulkayu = Hartley Bay Canada 53°25N 129°15W 296 C3
Kullen Sweden 56°18N 12°26E 163 H6
Kullu India 31°58N 77°6E 242 D7
Kulmbach Germany 50°6N 11°26E 179 E7
Kŭlob Tajikistan 37°55N 69°50E 217 E7
Kulosaari Finland 60°11N 25°0E 121 B3
Kulp Turkey 38°29N 41°2E 213 C9
Kulpawn → Ghana 10°20N 1°5W 263 D4
Kulsary = Qulsary Kazakhstan 46°59N 54°1E 187 E9
Kulti India 23°43N 86°50E 243 H12
Kulu Turkey 39°5N 33°4E 212 C5
Kulumadau Papua N. G. 9°3S 152°43E 286 E7
Kulunda Russia 52°35N 78°57E 217 B9
Kulundinskoye, Ozero Russia 53°0N 79°36E 217 B9
Kulungar Afghan. 34°0N 69°2E 242 C3
Kūlvand Iran 31°21N 54°35E 247 D7
Kulwin Australia 35°2S 142°42E 282 C5
Kulyab = Kŭlob Tajikistan 37°55N 69°50E 217 E7
Kuma Japan 33°39N 132°54E 222 D4
Kuma → Russia 44°55N 47°0E 191 H8
Kumafşarı Turkey 37°19N 29°32E 205 D11
Kumaganum Nigeria 13°8N 10°38E 263 C7
Kumagaya Japan 36°9N 139°22E 223 A11
Kumai Indonesia 2°44S 111°43E 235 C4
Kumai, Teluk Indonesia 3°0S 111°43E 235 C4
Kumalar Dağı Turkey 38°15N 30°20E 205 C12
Kumamba, Kepulauan Indonesia 1°36S 138°45E 231 E9
Kumamoto Japan 32°45N 130°45E 222 E2
Kumamoto □ Japan 32°55N 130°55E 222 E2
Kumano Japan 33°54N 136°5E 223 D8
Kumano-Nada Japan 33°47N 136°20E 223 D8
Kumanovo Macedonia 42°9N 21°42E 202 D5
Kumar → Afghan. 34°30N 70°28E 240 B3
Kumara N.Z. 42°37S 171°12E 285 C6
Kumarina Roadhouse Australia 24°41S 119°32E 279 D2
Kumarkhali Bangla. 23°51N 89°15E 241 D2
Kumasi Ghana 6°41N 1°38W 262 D4
Kumba Cameroon 4°36N 9°24E 263 E6
Kumbağ Turkey 40°51N 27°27E 203 F11
Kumbakonam India 10°58N 79°25E 245 J4
Kumbarilla Australia 27°15S 150°55E 281 D5
Kumbatine △ Australia 31°8S 152°35E 283 A10
Kumbhraj India 24°22N 77°3E 242 G7
Kumbia Australia 26°41S 151°39E 281 D5
Kumbo Cameroon 6°15N 10°36E 263 D7
Kumbukkan Oya → Sri Lanka 6°35N 81°40E 245 L5
Kŭmch'on N. Korea 38°10N 126°29E 224 C3
Kumdah Si. Arabia 20°23N 45°5E 248 B4
Kume-Shima Japan 26°20N 126°47E 221 L3
Kumeny Russia 58°10N 49°47E 190 A9
Kumertau Russia 52°45N 55°57E 186 D10
Kumharsain India 31°19N 77°27E 242 D7
Kumi Uganda 1°30N 33°58E 268 B3
Kumkale Turkey 39°59N 26°11E 203 G10
Kumla Örebro, Sweden 59°8N 15°10E 162 E9
Kumla Stockholm, Sweden 59°13N 18°11E 139 B3
Kumlu Turkey 36°21N 36°27E 250 B7
Kumluca Turkey 36°22N 30°20E 205 E12
Kummerower See Germany 53°49N 12°51E 178 B8
Kumo Nigeria 10°1N 11°12E 263 C7
Kumo älv = Kokemäenjoki → Finland 61°32N 21°44E 188 B1
Kumon Bum Burma 26°30N 97°15E 241 B6
Kumotori-Yama Japan 35°51N 138°57E 223 B10
Kumta India 14°29N 74°25E 245 G2
Kumtag Shamo China 39°40N 92°0E 218 D7
Kumukahi, C. U.S.A. 19°31N 154°49W 302 D7
Kumusi → Papua N. G. 8°16S 148°13E 286 E5
Kumylzhenskaya Russia 49°51N 42°38E 190 F6
Kunágota Hungary 46°26N 21°3E 182 D6
Kunak Malaysia 4°41N 118°15E 235 B5
Kunashir, Ostrov Russia 44°0N 146°0E 215 E15
Kunchaung Burma 23°50N 96°35E 241 D6
Kunda Estonia 59°30N 26°34E 188 C4
Kunda India 25°43N 81°31E 243 G9
Kundar → Pakistan 31°56N 69°19E 242 D3
Kundelungu △ Dem. Rep. of the Congo 10°30S 27°40E 269 E2
Kundelungu Ouest △ Dem. Rep. of the Congo 9°55S 27°17E 269 D2
Kundian Pakistan 32°27N 71°28E 242 C4
Kundiawa Papua N. G. 6°2S 145°1E 286 D3
Kundla India 21°21N 71°25E 242 J4
Kundur Indonesia 0°45N 103°25E 234 B2
Kung, Ao Thailand 8°5N 98°24E 237 a
Kunga → Bangla. 21°46N 89°30E 241 E2
Kungälv Sweden 57°53N 11°59E 163 G5
Kungens kurva Sweden 59°15N 17°53E 139 B1
Kunghit I. Canada 52°6N 131°3W 296 C2
Kungkuan Taiwan 24°35N 120°44E 225 B2
Kungliao Taiwan 25°1N 121°54E 225 A3
Kungliga Slottet Stockholm, Sweden 139 b2
Kungrad = Qŭnghirot Uzbekistan 43°2N 58°50E 216 D5
Kungsängen Sweden 59°29N 17°45E 162 E11
Kungsbacka Sweden 57°30N 12°5E 163 G6
Kungsgården Sweden 60°37N 16°35E 162 D10
Kungshamn Sweden 58°22N 11°15E 163 F5
Kungshatt Sweden 59°17N 17°53E 139 B1
Kungsholmen Sweden 59°20N 18°2E 139 A2
Kungsör Sweden 59°25N 16°5E 162 E10
Kungsuliao Taiwan 24°37N 120°45E 225 B2
Kungu Dem. Rep. of the Congo 2°47N 19°12E 264 B3
Kungur Russia 57°25N 56°57E 186 C10
Kungurri Australia 21°4S 148°45E 280 b
Kungyangon Burma 16°27N 96°2E 241 G6
Kunhar → Pakistan 34°20N 73°30E 243 B5
Kunhegyes Hungary 47°22N 20°36E 182 C5
Kunia U.S.A. 21°28N 158°4W 302 K13
Kunigami Japan 26°46N 128°12E 288 a
Kunimi-Dake Japan 32°33N 131°1E 222 E3
Kuningan Jakarta, Indonesia 6°13S 106°49E 122 B1
Kuningan Jawa Barat, Indonesia 6°59S 108°29E 235 D3
Kunisaki Japan 33°33N 131°45E 222 D3
Kunitachi Japan 35°41N 139°27E 140 A1
Kunjirap Daban Pakistan 36°52N 75°27E 240 A4
Kunlara Australia 34°54S 139°55E 282 C3
Kunlong Burma 23°20N 98°50E 228 F2
Kunlun Shan Asia 36°0N 86°30E 217 E11
Kunlun Shankou China 35°38N 94°4E 218 D7
Kunmadaras Hungary 47°28N 20°45E 182 C5
Kunming China 25°1N 102°41E 228 E4
Kunming Hu China 39°59N 116°13E 114 B1
Kunmunya ✪ Australia 15°26S 124°42E 278 C3
Kunnamkulam India 10°38N 76°7E 245 J3
Kunów Poland 50°57N 21°17E 185 H8
Kunratice Czech Rep. 50°0N 14°28E 135 B2
Kunshan China 31°22N 120°58E 229 B13
Kunsthistorisches museum Vienna, Austria 142 b1
Kunszentmárton Hungary 46°50N 20°20E 182 D5
Kunszentmiklós Hungary 47°2N 19°8E 182 C4
Kuntaur Senegal 13°40N 14°48W 262 C2
Kuntsevo Russia 55°43N 37°23E 129 B2
Kunua Papua N. G. 5°46S 154°44E 286 C8
Kununurra Australia 15°40S 128°50E 278 C4
Kunwari → India 26°26N 79°11E 243 F8
Kunya-Urgench = Köneürgench Turkmenistan 42°19N 59°10E 216 D5
Künzelsau Germany 49°17N 9°42E 179 F5
Kunzulu Dem. Rep. of the Congo 3°28S 16°12E 264 C3
Kuohsing Taiwan 24°2N 120°51E 225 B2
Kuopio Finland 62°53N 27°35E 160 E22
Kupa → Croatia 45°28N 16°24E 199 C13
Kupang Indonesia 10°19S 123°39E 231 F6
Kupchino Russia 59°50N 30°23E 137 B2
Kupiano Papua N. G. 10°4S 148°14E 286 F5
Kūpikipiki'ō Pt. U.S.A. 21°15N 157°47W 302 K14
Kupino Russia 54°21N 77°16E 217 B9
Kupreanof I. U.S.A. 56°50N 133°30W 296 B2
Kupres Bos.-H. 43°56N 17°15E 182 G2
Kupyansk Ukraine 49°52N 37°35E 189 H9
Kupyansk-Uzlovoi Ukraine 49°40N 37°43E 189 H9
Kuqa China 41°35N 82°30E 217 D10
Kür → Azerbaijan 39°29N 49°15E 213 C13
Kur → Bhutan 26°50N 91°0E 241 B3
Kür Dili Azerbaijan 39°3N 49°13E 213 C13
Kura = Kür → Azerbaijan 39°29N 49°15E 213 C13
Kurahashi-Jima Japan 34°8N 132°31E 222 C4
Kuramo Waters Nigeria 6°25N 3°26E 124 B2
Kuranda Australia 16°48S 145°35E 280 B4
Kuranga India 22°4N 69°10E 242 H3
Kurashiki Japan 34°40N 133°50E 222 C5
Kurayn Si. Arabia 27°39N 49°50E 247 E6
Kurayoshi Japan 35°26N 133°50E 222 B5
Kurbağalı → Turkey 40°58N 29°1E 122 C2
Kürchatov Kazakhstan 50°45N 78°32E 217 B9
Kürdämir Azerbaijan 40°25N 48°3E 191 K9
Kurdistan Asia 37°20N 43°30E 213 D10
Kurduvadi India 18°8N 75°29E 244 E2
Kŭrdzhali Bulgaria 41°38N 25°21E 203 E9
Kŭrdzhali □ Bulgaria 41°38N 25°21E 203 E9
Kure Japan 34°14N 132°32E 222 C4
Küre Turkey 41°48N 33°43E 212 B5
Küre Dağları Turkey 41°50N 34°10E 212 B6
Kure I. U.S.A. 28°25N 178°25W 302 F8
Kuressaare Estonia 58°15N 22°30E 188 C2
Kurgan Russia 55°26N 65°18E 216 A7
Kurgan-Tyube = Qŭrghonteppa Tajikistan 37°50N 68°47E 217 F7
Kurganinsk Russia 44°54N 40°34E 191 H5
Kurgannaya = Kurganinsk Russia 44°54N 40°34E 191 H5
Kuri India 26°37N 70°43E 242 F4
Kuria Maria Is. = Hallāniyat, Jazā'ir al Oman 17°30N 55°58E 249 C6
Kurichchi India 11°36N 77°35E 245 J3
Kuridala Australia 21°16S 140°29E 280 C3
Kurigram Bangla. 25°49N 89°39E 241 C2
Kurihara Japan 35°45N 139°34E 140 A2
Kurikka Finland 62°36N 22°24E 160 E20
Kuril Basin Pac. Oc. 47°0N 150°0E 150 E15
Kuril Is. = Kurilskiye Ostrova Russia 45°0N 150°0E 215 E16
Kuril-Kamchatka Trench Pac. Oc. 44°0N 153°0E 288 C7
Kurilsk Russia 45°14N 147°53E 215 E15
Kurilskiye Ostrova Russia 45°0N 150°0E 215 E16
Kurino Japan 31°57N 130°43E 222 F2
Kurinskaya Kosa = Kür Dili Azerbaijan 39°3N 49°13E 213 C13
Kurisches Haff = Kurshskiy Zaliv Russia 55°9N 21°6E 184 C8
Kürkçü Turkey 36°34N 33°39E 250 B4
Kurkheda India 20°37N 80°12E 244 D5
Kurkur Egypt 23°50N 32°0E 256 C3
Kurla India 19°4N 72°52E 130 A2
Kurlkuta ✪ Australia 24°0S 127°5E 278 D4
Kurlovskiy Russia 55°25N 40°40E 190 C5
Kurmuk Sudan 10°33N 34°21E 257 E3
Kurmuri India 19°4N 72°53E 130 A2
Kurnool India 15°45N 78°0E 245 G4
Kuro-Shima Kagoshima, Japan 30°50N 129°57E 221 J4
Kuro-Shima Okinawa, Japan 24°14N 124°1E 221 M2
Kurobe-Gawe → Japan 36°55N 137°25E 223 A9
Kurogi Japan 33°12N 130°40E 222 D2
Kuror, J. Sudan 20°27N 31°30E 256 C3
Kurow N.Z. 44°44S 170°29E 285 E5
Kurów Poland 51°23N 22°12E 185 G9
Kurrajong Australia 33°33S 150°42E 283 B9
Kurram → Pakistan 32°36N 71°20E 242 C4
Kurri Kurri Australia 32°50S 151°28E 283 B9
Kurrimine Australia 17°47S 146°6E 280 B4
Kursavka Russia 44°29N 42°32E 191 H6
Kurse Korhi India 20°14N 80°46E 244 D5
Kurseong = Karsiyang India 26°56N 88°18E 241 B2
Kürshim Kazakhstan 48°34N 83°39E 217 C10
Kurshskaya Kosa ⌂ Russia 55°7N 20°45E 184 C7
Kurshskiy Zaliv Russia 55°9N 21°6E 184 C8
Kuršių Nerijos △ Lithuania 55°30N 21°6E 184 C8
Kursk Russia 51°42N 36°11E 189 G9
Kursk □ Russia 51°50N 36°10E 189 G9
Kursu = Salla Finland 66°50N 28°49E 160 C23
Kuršumlija Serbia 43°9N 21°19E 202 C5
Kuršumlijska Banja Serbia 43°3N 21°11E 202 C5
Kurşunlu Bursa, Turkey 40°3N 29°40E 203 F13
Kurşunlu Çankırı, Turkey 40°51N 33°15E 212 B5
Kurtalan Turkey 37°56N 41°44E 213 D9
Kurtbey Turkey 41°9N 26°35E 203 E10
Kurtistown U.S.A. 19°36N 155°4W 302 D6
Kuru South Sudan 7°43N 26°31E 257 F2
Kuru, Bahr el → South Sudan 8°10N 26°50E 257 F2
Kuruçaşile Turkey 41°49N 32°42E 212 B5
Kuruçay Turkey 39°39N 38°29E 246 B3
Kurukshetra = Thanesar India 30°1N 76°52E 242 D7
Kuruktag China 41°0N 89°0E 217 D11
Kuruman S. Africa 27°28S 23°28E 270 C3
Kuruman → S. Africa 26°56S 20°39E 270 C3
Kurume Fukuoka, Japan 33°15N 130°30E 222 D2
Kurume Tōkyō, Japan 35°45N 139°31E 140 A2
Kurun → South Sudan 5°30N 34°17E 257 F3
Kurunegala Sri Lanka 7°30N 80°23E 245 L5
Kurupukari Guyana 4°43N 58°37W 329 C6
Kuryanovo Russia 55°39N 37°42E 129 C4
Kus Gölü Turkey 40°10N 27°55E 203 F11
Kuşadası Turkey 37°52N 27°15E 212 D2
Kuşadası Körfezi Turkey 37°56N 27°0E 205 D8
Kusamba Indonesia 8°34S 115°27E 231 K18
Kusatsu Gumma, Japan 36°37N 138°36E 223 A10
Kusatsu Shiga, Japan 34°58N 135°57E 223 C7
Kusawa L. Canada 60°20N 136°13W 296 A1
Kusel Germany 49°32N 7°24E 179 F3
Kushaka Nigeria 10°32N 6°48E 263 C6
Kushalgarh India 23°10N 74°27E 242 H6
Kushalnagar India 12°14N 75°57E 245 H2
Kushchevskaya Russia 46°33N 39°35E 191 G4
Kusheriki Nigeria 10°33N 6°28E 263 C6
Kushikino Japan 31°44N 130°16E 222 F2
Kushima Japan 31°29N 131°14E 222 F3
Kushimoto Japan 33°28N 135°47E 223 D7
Kushiro Japan 43°0N 144°25E 220 C12
Kushiro-Gawa → Japan 42°59N 144°23E 220 C12
Kushiro Shitsugen △ Japan 43°9N 144°26E 220 C12
Kūshk Iran 28°46N 56°51E 247 D8
Kushka = Serhetabat Turkmenistan 35°20N 62°18E 247 C9
Kushmurun = Qusmuryn Kazakhstan 52°27N 64°36E 216 B6
Kushnytsya Ukraine 48°27N 23°15E 183 B8
Kushol India 33°40N 76°36E 243 C7
Kushtia Bangla. 23°55N 89°5E 241 D2
Kushva Russia 58°18N 59°45E 186 C10
Kuskan Turkey 36°29N 33°17E 250 B4
Kuskokwim → U.S.A. 60°5N 162°25W 303 F7
Kuskokwim B. U.S.A. 59°45N 162°25W 303 G7
Kuskokwim Mts. U.S.A. 62°30N 156°0W 303 E9
Kuskovo Russia 55°44N 37°48E 129 B4
Kusmi India 23°17N 83°55E 243 H10
Kusŏng N. Korea 39°59N 125°15E 224 C2
Kussharo-Ko Japan 43°38N 144°21E 220 C12
Kustanay = Qostanay Kazakhstan 53°10N 63°35E 216 B6
Küstenje = Constanţa Romania 44°14N 28°38E 183 F13
Kustia India 22°31N 88°23E 124 B2
Kustrin = Kostrzyn Poland 52°35N 14°39E 185 F1
Kusu Japan 33°16N 131°9E 222 D3
Kut, Ko Thailand 11°40N 102°35E 237 G4
Kuta Indonesia 8°43S 115°11E 231 K18
Kutacane Indonesia 3°50N 97°50E 234 B1
Kütahya Turkey 39°30N 30°2E 205 B12
Kütahya □ Turkey 39°10N 29°30E 205 B11
Kutai △ Indonesia 0°23N 117°16E 235 B5
Kutaisi Georgia 42°19N 42°40E 191 J6
Kutaraja = Banda Aceh Indonesia 5°35N 95°20E 234 A1
Kutch, Gulf of = Kachchh, Gulf of India 22°50N 69°15E 242 H3
Kutch, Rann of = Kachchh, Rann of India 24°0N 70°0E 242 H4
Kutina Croatia 45°29N 16°48E 199 C13
Kutiyana India 21°36N 70°2E 242 J4
Kutjevo Croatia 45°23N 17°55E 182 E2
Kutkai Burma 23°27N 97°56E 241 D6
Kutkashen Azerbaijan 40°58N 47°47E 191 K8
Kutná Hora Czech Rep. 49°57N 15°16E 180 B8
Kutno Poland 52°15N 19°23E 185 F6
Kutru India 19°5N 80°46E 244 E5
Kutse Botswana 21°7S 22°16E 270 B3
Kutsino Russia 55°44N 37°55E 129 B5
Kuttabul Australia 21°1S 148°54E 280 b
Kutu Dem. Rep. of the Congo 2°40S 18°11E 264 C3
Kutu Moke Dem. Rep. of the Congo 3°12S 17°21E 264 C3
Kutum Sudan 14°10N 24°40E 257 E1
Kúty Slovak Rep. 48°40N 17°3E 181 C10
Kuty Ukraine 48°16N 25°11E 183 B10
Kuujjuaq Canada 58°6N 68°15W 295 F18
Kuujjuarapik Canada 55°20N 77°35W 298 A4
Kuusamo Finland 65°57N 29°8E 160 D23
Kuusankoski Finland 60°55N 26°38E 188 B4
Kuvango Angola 14°28S 16°20E 265 E3
Kuvshinovo Russia 57°2N 34°11E 188 D8
Kuwait = Al Kuwayt Kuwait 29°30N 48°0E 246 D5
Kuwait ■ Asia 29°30N 47°30E 246 D5
Kuwana Japan 35°5N 136°43E 223 B8
Kuwana → India 26°25N 83°15E 243 F10
Kuwol-san N. Korea 38°30N 125°15E 224 C2
Kuybyshev = Samara Russia 53°8N 50°6E 190 D10
Kuybyshev Russia 55°27N 78°19E 214 D8
Kuybyshevka-Vostochnaya = Belogorsk Russia 51°0N 128°20E 215 D13
Kuybyshevo Ukraine 47°25N 36°40E 189 J9
Kuybyshevskoye Vdkhr. Russia 55°2N 49°30E 190 C9
Kuye He → China 38°23N 110°46E 226 E6
Kūyeh Iran 38°45N 47°57E 246 B5
Kuyto, Ozero Russia 65°6N 31°20E 160 D24
Kuytun China 44°25N 85°0E 217 D11
Kuyucak Turkey 37°55N 28°28E 205 D10
Kuyumba Russia 60°58N 96°59E 215 C10
Kuzey Anadolu Dağları Turkey 41°0N 36°45E 212 B7
Kuzguncuk Turkey 41°2N 29°2E 122 B2
Kuzhithurai India 8°18N 77°11E 245 K3
Kuzitrin → U.S.A. 65°10N 165°25W 303 D6
Kuzmin Serbia 45°2N 19°25E 182 E4
Kuznetsk Russia 53°12N 46°40E 190 D8
Kuznetsovo = Konakovo Russia 56°40N 36°51E 188 D9
Kuzomen Russia 66°22N 36°50E 186 A4
Kuzucubelen Turkey 36°51N 34°27E 250 B5
Kuzyminki Russia 55°42N 37°44E 129 B4
Kvænangen Norway 70°5N 21°15E 160 A19
Kværndrup Denmark 55°10N 10°31E 163 J4
Kvaløya Norway 69°40N 18°30E 160 B18
Kvam Norway 61°40N 9°42E 164 C6
Kvänum Sweden 58°18N 13°11E 163 F7
Kvareli = Qvareli Georgia 41°57N 45°47E 191 K7
Kvarner Croatia 44°50N 14°10E 199 D11
Kvarnerič Croatia 44°43N 14°37E 199 D11
Kvås Norway 58°16N 7°14E 164 F4
Kvernaland Norway 58°47N 5°45E 164 F2
Kvichak B. U.S.A. 58°48N 157°30W 303 G8
Kvicksund Sweden 59°27N 16°19E 162 E10
Kvikne Norway 62°35N 10°16E 164 B7
Kvillsfors Sweden 57°24N 15°29E 163 G9
Kvina → Norway 58°19N 6°55E 164 F3
Kvinlog Norway 58°31N 6°55E 164 F3
Kvirily = Zestaponi Georgia 42°6N 43°0E 191 J6
Kvismare kanal Sweden 59°11N 15°35E 162 E9
Kvissleby Sweden 62°18N 17°22E 162 B11
Kviteseid Norway 59°24N 8°29E 164 E5
Kvitøya Svalbard 80°8N 32°35E 154 A14
Kwabhaca S. Africa 30°51S 29°0E 271 D4
Kwai = Khwae Noi → Thailand 14°1N 99°32E 236 E2
Kwai Chung China 22°22N 114°7E 122 A1
Kwajalein Marshall Is. 9°5N 167°20E 288 G8
Kwakhanai Botswana 21°39S 21°16E 270 B3
Kwakoegron Suriname 5°12N 55°25W 329 B6
Kwale Coast, Kenya 4°15S 39°31E 268 C4
Kwale Nigeria 5°46N 6°26E 263 D6
Kwamalasamutu Suriname 2°20N 56°47W 329 C6
KwaMashu S. Africa 29°45S 30°58E 271 C5
Kwamouth Dem. Rep. of the Congo 3°9S 16°12E 264 C3
Kwando → Africa 18°27S 23°32E 265 F4
Kwangchow = Guangzhou China 23°6N 113°13E 121 B2
Kwangdaeri N. Korea 40°34N 127°33E 227 D14
Kwango → Dem. Rep. of the Congo 3°14S 17°22E 264 C3
Kwangsi-Chuang = Guangxi Zhuangzu Zizhiqu □ China 24°0N 109°0E 228 F7
Kwangtung = Guangdong □ China 23°0N 113°0E 229 F9
Kwara □ Nigeria 8°45N 4°30E 263 D6
Kwataboahegan → Canada 51°9N 80°50W 298 B3
Kwatisore Indonesia 3°18S 134°50E 231 E8
KwaZulu Natal □ S. Africa 29°0S 30°0E 271 C5
Kweichow = Guizhou □ China 27°0N 107°0E 228 D6
Kweilin = Guilin China 25°18N 110°15E 229 E8
Kweisui = Hohhot China 40°52N 111°40E 226 D6
Kweiyang = Guiyang China 26°32N 106°40E 228 D6
Kwekwe Zimbabwe 18°58S 29°48E 269 F2
Kwenge → Dem. Rep. of the Congo 4°50S 18°44E 265 C3
Kwethluk U.S.A. 60°49N 161°26W 303 F7
Kwidzyn Poland 53°44N 18°55E 184 E5
Kwigillingok U.S.A. 59°51N 163°8W 303 G7
Kwiha Ethiopia 13°29N 39°32E 257 E4
Kwikila Papua N. G. 9°49S 147°38E 286 E4
Kwilu → Dem. Rep. of the Congo 3°22S 17°22E 265 C3
Kwinana Australia 32°15S 115°47E 279 F2
Kwinbet Burma 16°20N 94°14E 241 G5
Kwisa → Poland 51°34N 15°24E 185 G2
Kwoka Indonesia 0°31S 132°27E 231 E8
Kwolla Nigeria 9°0N 9°15E 263 D6
Kwun Tong China 22°19N 114°13E 122 B2
Kya-in-Seikkyi Burma 16°2N 98°8E 241 G7
Kyabé Chad 9°30N 19°0E 259 G3
Kyabra Cr. → Australia 25°36S 142°55E 281 D3
Kyabram Australia 36°19S 145°4E 283 D6
Kyaikkami Burma 16°4N 97°34E 241 G6
Kyaiklat Burma 16°25N 95°40E 241 G5
Kyaikmaraw Burma 16°23N 97°44E 241 G6
Kyaikthin Burma 23°32N 95°40E 241 D5
Kyaikto Burma 17°20N 97°3E 236 D1
Kyaing Tong = Keng Tung Burma 21°18N 99°39E 236 B2
Kyakhta Russia 50°30N 106°25E 215 D11
Kyambura ⌂ Uganda 0°7S 30°9E 268 C3
Kyan-zaki Japan 26°5N 127°39E 288 a
Kyancutta Australia 33°8S 135°33E 281 E2
Kyangin Burma 18°20N 95°20E 241 F5
Kyaukhnyat Burma 18°15N 97°31E 241 F6
Kyaukki Burma 18°27N 96°56E 241 F6
Kyaukkyi Burma 18°15N 94°29E 241 F5
Kyaukme Burma 22°32N 97°2E 241 D6
Kyaukpadaung Burma 20°52N 95°8E 241 E5
Kyaukpyu Burma 19°28N 93°30E 241 E4
Kyaukse Burma 21°36N 96°10E 241 E6
Kyauktaga Burma 18°10N 96°37E 241 F6
Kyauktan Burma 16°38N 96°19E 241 G6
Kyauktaw Burma 20°51N 92°59E 241 E4
Kyaunggon Burma 17°6N 95°11E 241 G5
Kyawkku Burma 21°48N 96°56E 241 E6
Kybartai Lithuania 54°39N 22°45E 184 D9
Kyburz U.S.A. 38°47N 120°18W 306 G6
Kyeintali Burma 18°0N 94°29E 241 G5
Kyelang India 32°35N 77°2E 242 C7
Kyenjojo Uganda 0°40N 30°37E 268 B3
Kyidaunggan Burma 19°53N 96°12E 241 F6
Kyje Czech Rep. 50°6N 14°33E 135 B3
Kyjov Czech Rep. 49°1N 17°7E 181 B10
Kyle Canada 50°50N 108°2W 297 C7
Kyle Dam Zimbabwe 20°15S 31°0E 269 G3
Kyle of Lochalsh U.K. 57°17N 5°44W 167 D3
Kyll → Germany 49°48N 6°41E 179 F2
Kyllburg Germany 50°2N 6°34E 179 E2
Kyllini Greece 37°55N 21°8E 207 D3
Kyllini, Akra Greece 37°57N 21°8E 207 D3
Kymijoki → Finland 60°30N 26°55E 188 B4
Kymmene älv = Kymijoki → Finland 60°30N 26°55E 188 B4
Kyneton Australia 37°10S 144°29E 282 D6
Kynuna Australia 21°37S 141°55E 280 C3
Kyō-ga-Saki Japan 35°45N 135°15E 223 B7
Kyoga, L. Uganda 1°35N 33°0E 268 B3
Kyogle Australia 28°40S 153°0E 281 D5
Kyom → South Sudan 8°58N 28°13E 257 F2
Kyŏngju = Gyeongju S. Korea 35°51N 129°14E 224 E4
Kyŏngsŏng N. Korea 41°35N 129°36E 224 B4
Kyōto Japan 35°0N 135°45E 223 C7
Kyōto □ Japan 35°15N 135°45E 223 B7
Kyparissovouno Cyprus 35°19N 33°10E 207 E9
Kyperounda Cyprus 34°56N 32°58E 207 F8
Kypros = Cyprus ■ Asia 35°0N 33°0E 207 F9
Kyrenia Cyprus 35°20N 33°20E 207 E9
Kyrgyzstan ■ Asia 42°0N 75°0E 217 D9
Kyritz Germany 52°56N 12°24E 178 C8
Kyrkhult Sweden 56°22N 14°34E 163 H8
Kyrksæterøra Norway 63°18N 9°5E 164 A6
Kyrnasivka Ukraine 48°35N 28°58E 183 B13
Kyrnychky Ukraine 45°42N 29°4E 183 E14
Kyro älv = Kyrönjoki → Finland 63°14N 21°45E 160 E19
Kyrönjoki → Finland 63°14N 21°45E 160 E19
Kystatyam Russia 67°20N 123°10E 215 C13
Kysucké Nové Mesto Slovak Rep. 49°18N 18°47E 181 B11
Kytay, Ozero Ukraine 45°40N 29°13E 183 E14
Kythira Greece 36°8N 23°0E 204 E5
Kythréa Cyprus 35°15N 33°29E 207 E9
Kyu-hkok Burma 24°4N 98°4E 241 C7
Kyūhōji Japan 34°38N 135°33E 133 B2
Kyunhla Burma 23°25N 95°15E 241 D5
Kyuquot Sound Canada 50°2N 127°22W 296 D3
Kyurdamir = Kürdämir Azerbaijan 40°25N 48°3E 191 K9
Kyūshū Japan 33°0N 131°0E 222 E3
Kyūshū □ Japan 33°0N 131°0E 222 E3
Kyushu-Palau Ridge Pac. Oc. 20°0N 136°0E 288 E5
Kyūshū-Sanchi Japan 32°35N 131°17E 222 E3
Kyūshū Trench Japan 31°35N 134°0E 222 F6
Kyustendil Bulgaria 42°16N 22°41E 202 D6
Kyustendil □ Bulgaria 42°16N 22°41E 202 D6
Kyusyur Russia 70°19N 127°30E 215 B13
Kywong Australia 34°58S 146°44E 283 C7
Kyyiv Ukraine 50°30N 30°28E 177 C16
Kyyiv □ Ukraine 50°5N 30°45E 189 G6
Kyyivske Vdskh. Ukraine 51°0N 30°25E 177 C16
Kyzyl Russia 51°50N 94°30E 217 B12
Kyzyl-Adyr Kyrgyzstan 42°39N 71°35E 217 D8
Kyzyl-Burun = Siyăzăn Azerbaijan 41°3N 49°10E 191 K9
Kyzyl-Khoto = Kyzyl Russia 51°50N 94°30E 217 B12
Kyzyl Kum Asia 42°0N 65°0E 238 A9
Kyzyl Kum Uzbekistan 42°30N 65°0E 217 D7
Kyzyl Kyya Kyrgyzstan 40°16N 72°8E 217 D8
Kyzyl Orda = Qyzylorda Kazakhstan 44°48N 65°28E 217 D7
Kyzyl-Suu Kyrgyzstan 42°20N 78°0E 217 D9

L

La Albuera Spain 38°45N 6°49W 195 G4
La Alcarria Spain 40°31N 2°45W 196 E2
La Almarcha Spain 39°41N 2°24W 196 F2
La Almunia de Doña Godina Spain 41°29N 1°23W 196 D3
La Amistad △ Cent. Amer. 9°28N 83°18W 320 E3
La Asunción Venezuela 11°2N 63°53W 329 A5
La Baie Canada 48°19N 70°53W 299 C5
La Banda Argentina 27°45S 64°10W 334 B3
La Bañeza Spain 42°17N 5°54W 194 C5
La Barca Mexico 20°17N 102°34W 318 C4
La Barceloneta Spain 41°22N 2°11E 114 A2
La Barge U.S.A. 42°16N 110°12W 304 E8
La Barra Nic. 12°54N 83°33W 320 D3
La Bastide-Puylaurent France 44°35N 3°55E 174 D7
La Baule France 47°17N 2°24W 172 E4
La Belle Fla., U.S.A. 26°46N 81°26W 317 J8
La Belle Mo., U.S.A. 40°7N 91°55W 310 D5
La Biche → Canada 59°57N 123°50W 296 B4
La Biche, L. Canada 54°50N 112°3W 296 C6
La Bisbal d'Empordà Spain 41°58N 3°2E 196 D8
La Blanca Chile 33°30S 70°40W 137 C2
La Boca Argentina 34°38S 58°22W 117 B2
La Brea Peru 4°40S 81°7W 330 A1
La Brea Trin. & Tob. 10°15N 61°37W 323 t
La Brède France 44°41N 0°32W 174 D3
La Bresse France 48°2N 6°53E 173 D13
La Bretèche France 48°51N 2°1E 134 A1
La Bureba Spain 42°36N 3°24W 194 C7
La Cal → Bolivia 17°27S 58°15W 331 D6
La Calera Chile 32°50S 71°10W 334 C1
La Calle = El Kala Algeria 36°53N 8°26E 261 A6
La Campana △ Chile 32°58S 71°14W 334 C1
La Campiña Lima, Peru 12°11S 77°0W 124 C2
La Campiña Spain 37°45N 4°45W 195 H6
La Canal = Sa Canal Spain 38°51N 1°23E 206 D1
La Cañiza = A Cañiza Spain 42°13N 8°16W 194 C2
La Canourgue France 44°26N 3°13E 174 D7
La Capelle France 49°59N 3°50E 173 C10
La Carlota Argentina 33°30S 63°20W 334 C3
La Carlota Phil. 10°25N 122°55E 233 F4
La Carlota Spain 37°40N 4°56W 195 H6
La Carolina Spain 38°17N 3°38W 195 G7
La Castellana Phil. 10°20N 123°3E 233 F4
La Cavalerie France 44°1N 3°10E 174 D7
La Ceiba Honduras 15°40N 86°50W 320 C2
La Ceiba Venezuela 9°28N 71°4W 328 C3
La Celle-St-Cloud France 48°50N 2°9E 134 A1
La Chaise-Dieu France 45°18N 3°42E 174 C7
La Chapelle d'Angillon France 47°21N 2°25E 173 E9
La Chapelle-St-Luc France 48°20N 4°3E 173 D11
La Chapelle-sur-Erdre France 47°18N 1°34W 172 E5
La Charité-sur-Loire France 47°10N 3°1E 173 E10
La Chartre-sur-le-Loir France 47°44N 0°34E 172 E7
La Châtaigneraie France 46°39N 0°44W 174 B3
La Châtre France 46°35N 2°0E 173 F9
La Chaux → Mauritius 20°23S 57°41E 272 e
La Chaux-de-Fonds Switz. 47°7N 6°50E 179 H2
La Chorrera Colombia 0°44S 73°1W 328 D3
La Chorrera Panama 8°53N 79°47W 320 c
La Ciotat France 43°10N 5°37E 175 E9
La Cisterna Chile 33°32S 70°39W 137 C2
La Ciudadela Mexico City, Mexico 128 c2
La Clayette France 46°17N 4°19E 173 F11
La Cocha Argentina 27°50S 65°40W 334 B2
La Concepción = Ri-Aba Eq. Guin. 3°28N 8°40E 263 E6
La Concepción Panama 8°31N 82°37W 320 E3
La Concepción Venezuela 10°30N 71°50W 328 A3
La Concordia Mexico 16°5N 92°38W 319 D6
La Constitución, Plaza de = Zócalo Mexico City, Mexico 128 b3
La Coruña = A Coruña Spain 43°20N 8°25W 194 B2
La Côte-St-André France 45°24N 5°15E 175 C9
La Courneuve France 48°55N 2°22E 134 A3
La Courtine France 45°41N 2°15E 174 C6
La Crau Bouches-du-Rhône, France 43°32N 4°40E 175 E8
La Crau Var, France 43°9N 6°4E 175 E10
La Crescent U.S.A. 43°50N 91°18W 308 D8
La Crete Canada 58°11N 116°24W 296 B5
La Crosse Fla., U.S.A. 29°51N 82°24W 316 F7
La Crosse Kans., U.S.A. 38°32N 99°18W 308 F4
La Crosse Wis., U.S.A. 43°48N 91°15W 308 D8
La Cruz Costa Rica 11°4N 85°39W 320 D2
La Cruz Sinaloa, Mexico 23°55N 106°54W 318 C3
La Cumbre, Volcán Ecuador 0°21S 91°32W 330 a
La Dehesa Chile 33°21S 70°33W 137 B2
La Désirade Guadeloupe 16°18N 61°3W 322 e
La Digue Seychelles 4°20S 55°51E 272 c
La Dorada Colombia 5°30N 74°40W 328 B3
La Encantada Peru 12°13S 77°1W 124 C2
La Esperanza Argentina 40°26S 68°32W 336 B3
La Esperanza Cuba 22°46N 83°44W 320 B3
La Esperanza Honduras 14°15N 88°10W 320 D2
La Estación Spain 40°27N 3°48W 127 B1
La Estrada = A Estrada Spain 42°43N 8°27W 194 C2
La Falaise, Gorges de Martinique 14°49N 61°10W 322 j
La Faouët France 48°2N 3°30W 172 D3
La Fayette U.S.A. 34°42N 85°17W 315 D12
La Fé Cuba 22°2N 84°15W 320 B3
La Fère France 49°39N 3°21E 173 C10
La Ferté-Bernard France 48°10N 0°40E 172 D7
La Ferté-Gaucher France 48°47N 3°19E 173 D10
La Ferté-Macé France 48°35N 0°22W 172 D6
La Ferté-St-Aubin France 47°42N 1°57E 173 E8
La Ferté-sous-Jouarre France 48°56N 3°8E 173 D10
La Ferté-Vidame France 48°37N 0°53E 172 D7
La Flèche France 47°42N 0°4W 172 E6
La Floresta Spain 41°26N 2°3E 114 A1
La Florida Chile 33°33S 70°34W 137 C2
La Foa N. Cal. 21°43S 165°50E 288 d
La Follette U.S.A. 36°23N 84°7W 315 C12
La Fontaine U.S.A. 40°40N 85°43W 311 D11
La Fortuna Spain 40°21N 3°46W 127 B1
La França Spain 41°22N 2°9E 114 A1
La Fregeneda Spain 40°58N 6°54W 194 E4
La Fría Venezuela 8°13N 72°15W 328 B3
La Fuente de San Esteban Spain 40°49N 6°15W 194 E4
La Gacilly France 47°45N 2°8W 172 E4
La Garenne-Colombes France 48°54N 2°15E 134 A2
La Gi Vietnam 10°40N 107°45E 237 G6
La Gineta Spain 39°8N 2°1W 197 F2
La Giustiniana Italy 41°59N 12°24E 136 B1
La Glória Colombia 8°37N 73°48W 328 B3
La Goulette = Halq el Oued Tunisia 36°53N 10°18E 258 A2
La Gran Sabana Venezuela 5°30N 61°30W 329 B5
La Grand'Combe France 44°13N 4°2E 175 D8
La Grande U.S.A. 45°20N 118°5W 304 D4
La Grande → Canada 53°50N 79°0W 298 B5
La Grande 3, Rés. Canada 53°40N 75°10W 298 B4
La Grande 4, Rés. Canada 54°0N 73°15W 298 B5
La Grande-Motte France 43°23N 4°5E 175 E8
La Grange Calif., U.S.A. 37°42N 120°27W 306 H6
La Grange Ga., U.S.A. 33°2N 85°2W 316 B4
La Grange Ill., U.S.A. 41°48N 87°53W 119 C1
La Grange Ky., U.S.A. 38°24N 85°22W 311 F11
La Grange Mo., U.S.A. 40°3N 91°35W 310 D5
La Grange Tex., U.S.A. 29°54N 96°52W 314 G6
La Grange Park U.S.A. 41°49N 87°51W 119 C1
La Granja Chile 33°31S 70°38W 137 C2
La Grave France 45°3N 6°18E 175 C10
La Grita Venezuela 8°8N 71°59W 328 B3
La Guaira Venezuela 10°36N 66°56W 328 A4
La Guardia = A Guarda Spain 41°56N 8°52W 194 D2
La Guardia, New York ✈ (LGA) U.S.A. 40°46N 73°52W 132 B2
La Gudiña = A Gudiña Spain 42°4N 7°8W 194 C3
La Güera Mauritania 20°51N 17°0W 260 D1
La Guerche-de-Bretagne France 47°57N 1°16W 172 E5
La Guerche-sur-l'Aubois France 46°58N 2°56E 173 F9
La Habana Cuba 23°8N 82°22W 320 B3
La Harpe U.S.A. 40°35N 90°58W 310 D6

La Haute Vallée de Chevreuse ⌓ *France* 48°35N 1°58E **173** D8
La Haye-du-Puits *France* 49°17N 1°33W **172** C5
La Horqueta *Venezuela* 7°55N 60°20W **329** B5
La Horra *Spain* 41°44N 3°53W **194** D7
La Hulpe *Belgium* 50°43N 4°30E **116** B2
La Independencia *Mexico* 16°15N 92°1W **319** D6
La Isabela *Dom. Rep* 19°58N 71°2W **321** C5
La Jonquera *Spain* 42°25N 2°53E **196** C7
La Joya *Peru* 16°43S 71°52W **330** D3
La Junta *U.S.A.* 37°59N 103°33W **304** H12
La Laguna *Canary Is.* 28°28N 16°18W **153** e1
La Lézarde ➜ *Martinique* 14°35N 61°1W **322** j
La Libertad = Puerto Libertad *Mexico* 29°55N 112°43W **318** B2
La Libertad *Guatemala* 16°47N 90°7W **320** C1
La Libertad □ *Peru* 8°0S 78°30W **330** B2
La Ligua *Chile* 32°30S 71°16W **334** C1
La Línea de la Concepción *Spain* 36°15N 5°23W **195** J5
La Llacuna *Spain* 41°24N 2°12E **114** A2
La Loche *Canada* 56°29N 109°26W **297** B7
La Loma *Mexico* 19°31N 99°11W **128** A1
La Londe-les-Maures *France* 43°8N 6°14E **175** E10
La Lora *Spain* 42°45N 4°0W **194** C7
La Loupe *France* 48°29N 1°0E **172** D8
La Louvière *Belgium* 50°27N 4°10E **170** D4
La Lucila *Argentina* 34°30S 58°29W **117** B2
La Lune *Trin. & Tob.* 10°3N 61°22W **323** t
La Machine *France* 46°54N 3°27E **173** F10
La Maddalena *Italy* 41°13N 9°24E **200** A2
La Maladrerie *France* 48°54N 2°1E **134** A1
La Malbaie *Canada* 47°40N 70°10W **299** C5
La Malinche △ *Mexico* 19°15N 98°3W **319** D5
La Mancha *Spain* 39°10N 2°54W **197** F2
La Manche ➜ *Martinique* 14°33N 61°0W **322** j
La Mariña *Spain* 43°30N 7°40W **194** B3
La Martre, L. *Canada* 63°15N 117°55W **296** A5
La Merced *Peru* 11°3S 75°19W **330** C2
La Mesa *Baja Calif., Mexico* 32°30N 116°57W **307** N10
La Mesa *Calif., U.S.A.* 32°46N 117°1W **307** N9
La Mesilla *U.S.A.* 32°16N 106°48W **305** K10
La Milla, Cerro *Peru* 12°2S 77°5W **124** B2
La Misión *Mexico* 32°6N 116°53W **318** A1
La Moille *U.S.A.* 41°32N 89°17W **310** C7
La Moine ➜ *U.S.A.* 39°59N 90°31W **310** E6
La Monachina *Italy* 41°53N 12°21E **136** B1
La Montagne *Réunion* 20°53S 55°26E **272** f
La Monte *U.S.A.* 38°46N 93°26W **310** F3
La Moraleja *Spain* 40°30N 3°38W **127** A2
La Mothe-Achard *France* 46°37N 1°40W **172** F5
La Motte-Chalançon *France* 44°30N 5°21E **175** D9
La Motte-du-Caire *France* 44°20N 6°3E **175** D10
La Motte-Servolex *France* 45°35N 5°53E **175** C9
La Moure *U.S.A.* 46°21N 98°18W **308** B4
La Moustique ➜ *Guadeloupe* 16°10N 61°34W **322** e
La Muela *Spain* 41°36N 1°7W **196** D3
La Mure *France* 44°55N 5°48E **175** D9
La Negra *Chile* 23°46S 70°18W **334** A1
La Nopalera *Mexico* 19°18N 99°5W **128** C2
La Oliva *Canary Is.* 28°36N 13°57W **153** e2
La Oraya *Peru* 11°32S 75°54W **330** C2
La Orotava *Canary Is.* 28°22N 16°31W **153** e1
La Oroya *Peru* 11°32S 75°54W **330** C2
La Pacaudière *France* 46°11N 3°52E **173** F10
La Pagerie *Martinique* 14°32N 61°3W **322** j
La Palma *Canary Is.* 28°40N 17°50W **153** e1
La Palma *Panama* 8°15N 78°0W **320** E4
La Palma del Condado *Spain* 37°21N 6°38W **195** H4
La Paloma *Chile* 30°35S 71°0W **334** C1
La Pampa □ *Argentina* 36°50S 66°0W **334** D2
La Paragua *Venezuela* 6°50N 63°20W **329** B5
La Pastora *Trin. & Tob.* 10°42N 61°21W **323** t
La Paternal *Argentina* 34°35S 58°26W **117** B2
La Paya ⌓ *Colombia* 0°0 75°5W **328** C2
La Paz *Entre Ríos, Argentina* 30°50S 59°45W **334** C4
La Paz *San Luis, Argentina* 33°30S 67°20W **334** C2
La Paz *Bolivia* 16°20S 68°10W **330** D4
La Paz *Honduras* 14°20N 87°47W **320** D2
La Paz *Baja Calif. S., Mexico* 24°10N 110°18W **318** C2
La Paz *Abra, Phil.* 17°40N 120°41E **232** C3
La Paz *Tarlac, Phil.* 15°26N 120°45E **232** D3
La Paz □ *Bolivia* 15°30S 68°0W **330** D4
La Paz Centro *Nic.* 12°20N 86°41W **320** D2
La Pedrera *Colombia* 1°18S 69°43W **328** D4
La Pérade *Canada* 46°35N 72°12W **299** C5
La Perla *Chihuahua, Mexico* 28°18N 104°32W **318** B4
La Perla *Lima, Peru* 12°4S 77°7W **124** B2
La Perouse *Australia* 33°59S 151°14E **139** B2
La Perouse, Bahia *Chile* 27°5S 109°18W **330** b
La Perouse Str. *Asia* 45°40N 142°0E **220** B11
La Pesca *Mexico* 23°46N 97°47W **319** C5
La Piedad *Mexico* 20°21N 102°0W **318** C4
La Pine *U.S.A.* 43°40N 121°30W **304** E3
La Pisana *Italy* 41°51N 12°23E **136** B1
La Plaine *Dominica* 15°20N 61°15W **323** k
La Plaine des Cafres *Réunion* 21°13S 55°33E **272** f
La Plaine des Palmistes *Réunion* 21°7S 55°38E **272** f
La Plata *Argentina* 35°0S 57°55W **334** C4
La Plata *Colombia* 2°23N 75°53W **328** C2
La Plata *Mo., U.S.A.* 40°2N 92°29W **310** D4
La Plata, L. *Argentina* 44°55S 71°50W **336** B2
La Pobla de Lillet *Spain* 42°16N 1°59E **196** C6
La Pobla de Segur *Spain* 42°15N 0°58E **196** C5
La Pocatière *Canada* 47°22N 70°2W **299** C5
La Pola de Gordón *Spain* 42°51N 5°41W **194** C5
La Porta *France* 42°25N 9°21E **175** F13
La Porte *U.S.A.* 29°40N 95°1W **314** G7
La Porte City *U.S.A.* 42°19N 92°12W **310** B4
La Possession *Réunion* 20°55S 55°21E **272** f
La Prairie *Canada* 45°25N 73°29W **130** B3
La Presanella *Italy* 46°13N 10°40E **198** B7
La Puebla = Sa Pobla *Spain* 39°46N 3°1E **206** B4
La Puebla de Cazalla *Spain* 37°10N 5°20W **195** H5
La Puebla de los Infantes *Spain* 37°47N 5°24W **195** H5
La Puebla de Montalbán *Spain* 39°52N 4°22W **194** F6
La Puebla del Río *Spain* 37°16N 6°3W **195** H4
La Puerta de Segura *Spain* 38°22N 2°45W **195** G8
La Punta *Peru* 12°4S 77°10W **124** B1
La Puntigala *Spain* 41°27N 2°13E **114** A2
La Purísima *Mexico* 26°10N 112°4W **318** B2
La Push *U.S.A.* 47°55N 124°38W **306** C2
La Queue-en-Brie *France* 48°47N 2°34E **134** B4
La Quiaca *Argentina* 22°5S 65°35W **334** A2
La Reina *Chile* 33°26S 70°33W **137** B2
La Réole *France* 44°35N 0°1W **174** D3
La Republica, Plaza de *Mexico City, Mexico* **128** b1
La Restinga *Canary Is.* 27°38N 17°59W **153** e1
La Ribera *Spain* 41°21N 2°4E **114** A1
La Rioja *Argentina* 29°20S 67°0W **334** B2
La Rioja □ *Argentina* 29°30S 67°0W **334** B2
La Rioja □ *Spain* 42°20N 2°20W **196** C2
La Rivière des Pluies *Réunion* 20°54S 55°31E **272** f
La Robla *Spain* 42°50N 5°41W **194** C5
La Roche *N. Cal.* 21°26S 168°2E **288** d
La Roche-Bernard *France* 47°31N 2°19W **172** E4
La Roche-Canillac *France* 45°12N 1°57E **174** C5
La Roche-en-Ardenne *Belgium* 50°11N 5°35E **170** D5
La Roche-sur-Foron *France* 46°4N 6°19E **173** F13
La Roche-sur-Yon *France* 46°40N 1°25W **172** F5
La Rochefoucauld *France* 45°44N 0°24E **174** C4
La Rochelle *France* 46°10N 1°9W **174** B2
La Roda *Spain* 39°13N 2°15W **197** F2
La Roda de Andalucía *Spain* 37°12N 4°46W **195** H6
La Romaine *Canada* 50°13N 60°40W **299** B7
La Romana *Dom. Rep.* 18°27N 68°57W **321** C6
La Ronge *Canada* 55°5N 105°20W **297** B7
La Rue *U.S.A.* 40°35N 83°23W **311** D13
La Rumorosa *Mexico* 32°34N 116°6W **307** N10
La Sabina = Sa Savina *Spain* 38°44N 1°25E **206** D1
La Sagra *Spain* 37°57N 2°35W **197** H2
La Sagrera *Spain* 41°25N 2°11E **114** A2
La Salada *Argentina* 34°43S 58°28W **117** C2
La Saline *Réunion* 21°4S 55°16E **272** f
La Salle *U.S.A.* 41°20N 89°6W **310** C7
La Sanabria *Spain* 42°0N 6°30W **194** C4
La Santa *Canary Is.* 29°5N 13°40W **153** e2
La Sarre *Canada* 48°45N 79°15W **298** C4
La Scala *Italy* 45°28N 9°11E **129** B2
La Scie *Canada* 49°57N 55°36W **299** C8
La Selva *Spain* 42°0N 2°45E **196** C7
La Selva Beach *U.S.A.* 36°56N 121°51W **306** J5
La Selva del Camp *Spain* 41°13N 1°8E **196** D6
La Serena *Chile* 29°55S 71°10W **334** B1
La Serena *Spain* 38°45N 5°40W **195** G5
La Seu d'Urgell *Spain* 42°22N 1°23E **196** C6
La Seyne-sur-Mer *France* 43°7N 5°52E **175** E9
La Sila *Italy* 39°15N 16°35E **201** C9
La Solana *Spain* 38°59N 3°14W **195** G7
La Soufrière *St. Vincent* 13°20N 61°11W **323** n
La Souterraine *France* 46°15N 1°30E **173** F8
La Spézia *Italy* 44°7N 9°50E **198** D6
La Storta *Italy* 41°59N 12°20E **136** A1
La Suze-sur-Sarthe *France* 47°53N 0°2E **172** E7
La Tagua *Colombia* 0°3N 74°40W **328** C3
La Taxonera *Spain* 41°25N 2°10E **114** A2
La Teste-de-Buch *France* 44°37N 1°8W **174** D2
La Tortuga *Venezuela* 11°0N 65°22W **321** D6
La Tour-du-Pin *France* 45°33N 5°27E **175** C9
La Tranche-sur-Mer *France* 46°20N 1°27W **172** F5
La Tremblade *France* 45°46N 1°8W **174** C2
La Trinidad *Phil.* 16°28N 120°35E **232** C3
La Trinité *Martinique* 14°45N 60°58W **322** j
La Tuque *Canada* 47°30N 72°50W **298** C5
La Unión *Chile* 40°10S 73°0W **336** B2
La Unión *Colombia* 1°35N 77°5W **329** C2
La Unión *El Salv.* 13°20N 87°50W **320** D2
La Unión *Guerrero, Mexico* 17°58N 101°49W **318** D4
La Unión *Peru* 9°43S 76°45W **330** B2
La Unión *Spain* 37°38N 0°53W **197** H4
La Union □ *Phil.* 16°30N 120°25E **232** C3
La Urbana *Venezuela* 7°8N 66°56W **328** B4
La Vache B. *Trin. & Tob.* 10°45N 61°29W **323** t
La Vache Pt. *Trin. & Tob.* 10°47N 61°28W **323** t
La Vall d'Uixó *Spain* 39°49N 0°15W **196** F4
La Vega *Dom. Rep.* 19°20N 70°30W **321** C5
La Vega *Peru* 10°41S 77°44W **330** C2
La Vela de Coro *Venezuela* 11°27N 69°34W **328** A4
La Venta *Mexico* 18°5N 94°3W **319** D6
La Ventura *Colombia* 6°8N 68°48W **328** B4
La Vergne *U.S.A.* 36°1N 86°35W **315** C11
La Veronica *Trin. & Tob.* 10°42N 61°21W **323** t
La Victoria *Lima, Peru* 12°3S 77°2W **124** B2
La Victoria *Venezuela* 10°14N 67°20W **328** A4
La Villa Joiosa = Villajoyosa *Spain* 38°30N 0°12W **197** G4
La Voulte-sur-Rhône *France* 44°48N 4°46E **175** D8
Laa an der Thaya *Austria* 48°43N 16°23E **181** C9
Laaber, Grosse ➜ *Germany* 48°55N 12°30E **179** G8
Laage *Germany* 53°55N 12°21E **178** B8
Laajalahti *Finland* 60°11N 24°48E **121** B1
Laajasalo *Finland* 60°10N 25°1E **121** B3
Laaksolahti *Finland* 60°14N 24°45E **121** B1
Laas Dawaco *Somali Rep.* 10°28N 49°0E **267** B6
Laascaanood = Las Anod *Somali Rep.* 8°26N 47°19E **267** C6
Laasqoray *Somali Rep.* 11°10N 48°20E **267** B6
Laatzen *Germany* 52°19N 9°48E **178** C5
Lā'au Pt. *U.S.A.* 21°6N 157°19W **302** B4
Laba ➜ *Russia* 45°11N 39°42E **191** H4
Labagou National Forest Park *China* 40°1N 116°22E **114** A2
Laban *Burma* 25°52N 96°40E **241** C6
Labasa *Fiji* 16°30S 179°27E **287** A2
Labason *Phil.* 8°4N 122°31E **233** G4
Labastide-Murat *France* 44°39N 1°33E **174** D5
Labastide-Rouairoux *France* 43°28N 2°39E **174** E6
Labbézenga *Mali* 15°2N 0°48E **263** B5
Labdah = Leptis Magna *Libya* 32°40N 14°12E **258** B2
Labe = Elbe ➜ *Europe* 53°50N 9°0E **178** B4
Labé *Guinea* 11°24N 12°16W **262** C2
Laberge, L. *Canada* 61°11N 135°12W **296** A1
Labes = Łobez *Poland* 53°38N 15°39E **184** E2
Labian, Tanjong *Malaysia* 5°9N 119°13E **235** A5
Labiau = Polessk *Russia* 54°50N 21°8E **184** D8
Labig Pt. = Iligan Pt. *Phil.* 18°25N 122°25E **232** B4
Labin *Croatia* 45°5N 14°8E **199** C11
Labinsk *Russia* 44°40N 40°48E **191** H5
Labis *Malaysia* 2°22N 103°2E **237** L4
Labiszyn *Poland* 52°57N 17°54E **185** F4
Lablâba, W. el ➜ *Egypt* 30°1N 31°19E **117** A2
Labo *Phil.* 14°9N 122°51E **232** D4
Laboe *Germany* 54°24N 10°13E **178** A6
Laborec ➜ *Slovak Rep.* 48°37N 21°58E **181** C14
Laborie *St. Lucia* 13°45N 61°2W **323** m
Labouheyre *France* 44°13N 0°55W **174** D3
Laboulaye *Argentina* 34°10S 63°30W **334** C3
Labrador *Canada* 53°20N 61°0W **299** B7
Labrador City *Canada* 52°57N 66°55W **299** B6
Labrador Sea *Atl. Oc.* 57°0N 54°0W **295** F21
Lábrea *Brazil* 7°15S 64°51W **331** B5
Labruguière *France* 43°31N 2°16E **174** E6
Labuan □ *Malaysia* 5°20N 115°12E **235** A5
Labuan, Pulau *Malaysia* 5°21N 115°13E **235** A5
Labuha *Indonesia* 0°30S 127°30E **231** E7
Labuhan *Indonesia* 6°22S 105°50E **234** D3
Labuhanbajo *Indonesia* 8°28S 119°54E **235** D5
Labuhanbilik *Indonesia* 2°31N 100°10E **237** L3
Labuk, Telok *Malaysia* 6°10N 117°50E **235** A5
Labutta *Burma* 16°9N 94°46E **241** G5
Labyrinth, L. *Australia* 30°40S 135°11E **281** E2
Labytnangi *Russia* 66°39N 66°21E **186** A12
Laç *Albania* 41°38N 19°43E **202** E3
Lac □ *Chad* 13°30N 14°30E **259** F2
Lac Bay *Bonaire* 12°6N 68°13W **322** h
Lac-Bouchette *Canada* 48°16N 72°11W **299** C5
Lac Édouard *Canada* 47°40N 72°16W **298** C5
Lac La Biche *Canada* 54°45N 111°58W **296** C6
Lac la Martre = Wha Ti *Canada* 63°8N 117°16W **294** E8
Lac La Ronge ⌓ *Canada* 55°9N 104°41W **297** B7
Lac-Mégantic *Canada* 45°35N 70°53W **299** C5
Lac Thien *Vietnam* 12°25N 108°11E **236** F7
Lacanau *France* 44°58N 1°5W **174** D2
Lacanau, Étang de *France* 44°58N 1°7W **174** D2
Lacantún ➜ *Mexico* 16°36N 90°39W **319** D6
Lácara ➜ *Spain* 38°55N 6°25W **195** G4
Lacaune *France* 43°43N 2°40E **174** E6
Lacaune, Mts. de *France* 43°43N 2°50E **174** E6
Laccadive Is. = Lakshadweep Is. *India* 10°0N 72°30E **245** J1
Lacepede B. *Australia* 36°40S 139°40E **282** D3
Lacepede Is. *Australia* 16°55S 122°0E **278** C3
Lacerdónia *Mozam.* 18°3S 35°35E **269** F4
Lacey *U.S.A.* 47°7N 122°49W **306** C4
Lachania *Greece* 35°58N 27°54E **206** F11
Lachay, Pta. *Peru* 11°17S 77°44W **330** C2
Lachen *India* 27°46N 88°36E **241** B2
Lachhmangarh *India* 27°50N 75°4E **242** F6
Lachi *Pakistan* 33°25N 71°20E **242** C4
Lachia *Taiwan* 22°43N 120°53E **225** D2
Lachine *Canada* 45°26N 73°42W **130** B1
Lachine, Canal de *Canada* 45°26N 73°38W **130** B2
Lachlan ➜ *Australia* 34°22S 143°55E **282** C5
Lachoc *Peru* 12°50S 75°6W **330** C2
Lachute *Canada* 45°39N 74°21W **298** C5
Lackagh Hills *Ireland* 54°16N 8°10W **166** B3
Lackawanna *U.S.A.* 42°50N 78°50W **312** D6
Lackawaxen *U.S.A.* 41°29N 74°59W **313** E10
Lacolle *Canada* 45°5N 73°22W **313** A11
Lacombe *Canada* 52°30N 113°44W **296** C6
Lacon *U.S.A.* 41°2N 89°24W **310** C7
Lacona *Iowa, U.S.A.* 41°12N 93°23W **310** C3
Lacona *N.Y., U.S.A.* 43°39N 76°10W **313** C8
Láconi *Italy* 39°54N 9°4E **200** C2
Laconia *U.S.A.* 43°32N 71°28W **313** C13
Lacoochee *U.S.A.* 28°28N 82°11W **317** G7
Lacq *France* 43°25N 0°35W **174** E3
Lacre Punt *Bonaire* 12°1N 68°14W **322** h
Lad Phrao *Thailand* 13°47N 100°35E **113** B2
Ladakh Ra. *India* 34°0N 78°0E **243** C8
Ladário *Brazil* 19°1S 57°35W **331** D6
Ladd *U.S.A.* 41°23N 89°13W **310** C7
Laddonia *U.S.A.* 39°15N 91°39W **310** E5
Lądek-Zdrój *Poland* 50°21N 16°53E **185** H3
Ladera Heights *U.S.A.* 33°59N 118°22W **126** C2
Lâdik *Turkey* 40°57N 35°58E **212** B6
Ladismith *S. Africa* 33°28S 21°15E **270** D3
Ladispoli *Italy* 41°56N 12°5E **199** G9
Lādīz *Iran* 28°55N 61°15E **247** D9
Ladnun *India* 27°38N 74°25E **242** F6
Ladoga, L. = Ladozhskoye Ozero *Russia* 61°15N 30°30E **188** B6
Ladonas ➜ *Greece* 37°40N 21°50E **204** D3
Ladozhskoye Ozero *Russia* 61°15N 30°30E **188** B6
Ladrillero, G. *Chile* 49°20S 75°35W **336** C1
Ladson *U.S.A.* 32°59N 80°5W **316** C9
Ladushkin *Russia* 54°34N 20°10E **184** D7
Ládví *Czech Rep.* 50°8N 14°27E **135** B2
Lady *Poland* 52°8N 20°57E **142** C1
Lady Elliott I. *Australia* 24°7S 152°42E **280** C5
Lady Frere *S. Africa* 31°42S 27°14E **270** D4
Lady Grey *S. Africa* 30°43S 27°13E **270** D4
Lady Lake *U.S.A.* 28°55N 81°55W **317** G8
Ladybrand *S. Africa* 29°9S 27°29E **270** C4
Ladysmith *B.C., Canada* 49°0N 123°49W **306** B3
Ladysmith *KwaZulu Natal, S. Africa* 28°32S 29°46E **271** C4
Ladysmith *Wis., U.S.A.* 45°28N 91°12W **308** C8
Ladyzhyn *Ukraine* 48°40N 29°15E **183** B14
Lae *Papua N. G.* 6°40S 147°2E **286** C4
Lae 'o Kealaikahiki *U.S.A.* 20°32N 156°42W **302** C5
Laem Hin Khom *Thailand* 9°25N 99°56E **237** b
Laem Khat *Thailand* 8°6N 98°26E **237** a
Laem Nga *Thailand* 7°55N 98°27E **237** a
Laem Ngop *Thailand* 12°10N 102°26E **237** F4
Laem Phan Wa *Thailand* 7°47N 98°25E **237** a
Laem Pho *Thailand* 6°55N 101°19E **237** J3
Laem Phrom Thep *Thailand* 7°45N 98°19E **237** a
Laem Riang *Thailand* 8°7N 98°27E **237** a
Laem Sam Rong *Thailand* 9°35N 100°4E **237** b
Laem Son *Thailand* 7°59N 98°16E **237** a
Laem Son △ *Thailand* 9°29N 98°24E **237** H2
Laem Yamu *Thailand* 7°59N 98°26E **237** a
Lærdalsøyri *Norway* 61°6N 7°28E **164** C4
Laerma *Greece* 36°9N 27°57E **206** E11
Læsø *Denmark* 57°15N 11°5E **163** G5
Læsø Rende *Denmark* 57°20N 10°45E **163** G4
Lafayette *Ala., U.S.A.* 32°54N 85°24W **316** C4
Lafayette *Ind., U.S.A.* 40°25N 86°54W **311** D10
Lafayette *La., U.S.A.* 30°14N 92°1W **314** F8
Lafayette *Tenn., U.S.A.* 36°31N 86°2W **315** C11
Lafayette Park *San Francisco, U.S.A.* **136** b1
Lafayette Square *New Orleans, U.S.A.* **131** b2
Laferte ➜ *Canada* 61°53N 117°44W **296** A5
Lafia *Nigeria* 8°30N 8°34E **263** D6
Lafiagi *Nigeria* 8°52N 5°20E **263** D6
Lafkos *Greece* 39°9N 23°14E **204** B5
Lafleche *Canada* 49°45N 106°40W **297** D7
Lafon *South Sudan* 5°5N 32°29E **257** F3
Lafontaine *Montréal, Canada* **130** a1
Lafontaine, Parc *Canada* 45°33N 73°34W **130** A2
Laful *India* 7°10N 93°52E **245** L11
Lagaip ➜ *Papua N. G.* 5°4S 142°52E **286** C2
Lagan = Kaspiyskiy *Russia* 45°22N 47°23E **191** H8
Lagan *Sweden* 56°56N 13°58E **163** H7
Lagan ➜ *Sweden* 56°30N 12°58E **163** H6
Lagan ➜ *Antrim, U.K.* 54°36N 5°55W **166** B6
Lagana, Kolpos *Greece* 37°42N 20°53E **207** D2
Laganas *Greece* 37°44N 20°52E **207** D2
Lagangilang *Phil.* 17°37N 120°44E **232** C3
Lagarfljót ➜ *Iceland* 65°40N 14°18W **155** B12
Lagarto *Brazil* 10°54S 37°41W **332** D4
Lagawe *Phil.* 16°49N 121°6E **232** C3
Lagdo *Cameroon* 9°3N 13°44E **259** G2
Lagdo, L. de *Cameroon* 8°40N 14°0E **264** A2
Lage *Germany* 51°59N 8°48E **178** D4
Lågen ➜ *Oppland, Norway* 61°8N 10°25E **164** C7
Lågen ➜ *Vestfold, Norway* 59°3N 10°3E **164** E7
Lägerdorf *Germany* 53°53N 9°34E **178** B5
Lages *Brazil* 27°48S 50°20W **335** B5
Laggan = Lake Louise *Canada* 51°30N 116°10W **296** C5
Lagh Badana △ *Somali Rep.* 1°36N 41°49E **267** E4
Laghman □ *Afghan.* 34°20N 70°0E **240** B3
Laghouat *Algeria* 33°50N 2°59E **261** B5
Laghouat □ *Algeria* 33°50N 2°59E **261** B5
Lagnieu *France* 45°55N 5°20E **175** C9
Lagny-sur-Marne *France* 48°52N 2°44E **173** D9
Lago = Niassa □ *Mozam.* 13°30S 36°0E **269** E4
Lago *Italy* 39°10N 16°9E **201** C9
Lago Agrio *Ecuador* 0°5N 76°52W **328** C2
Lago de Sanabria y Entorno ⌓ *Spain* 42°9N 6°45W **194** C4
Lago Posadas *Argentina* 47°30S 71°40W **336** C2
Lago Puelo △ *Argentina* 42°30S 71°55W **336** B2
Lago Ranco *Chile* 40°19S 72°30W **336** B2
Lagoa *Azores* 37°45N 25°20W **153** d3
Lagoa *Rio de J., Brazil* 22°58S 43°11W **135** B1
Lagôa *Portugal* 37°8N 8°27W **195** H2
Lagoa do Peixe △ *Brazil* 31°12S 50°55W **335** C5
Lagoa Vermelha *Brazil* 28°13S 51°32W **335** B5
Lagoaça *Portugal* 41°11N 6°44W **194** D4
Lagodekhi *Georgia* 41°50N 46°22E **191** K8
Lagona = Laguna Beach *U.S.A.* 33°33N 117°47W **307** M9
Lagónegro *Italy* 40°8N 15°45E **201** B8
Lagonoy G. *Phil.* 13°35N 123°50E **232** E4
Lagos *Angola* 13°3S 16°35E **265** F3
Lagos *Greece* 41°1N 25°6E **203** E9
Lagos *Nigeria* 6°25N 3°27E **124** B2
Lagos *Portugal* 37°5N 8°41W **195** H2
Lagos □ *Nigeria* 6°28N 3°25E **263** D5
Lagos de Moreno *Mexico* 21°21N 101°55W **318** C4
Lagos Harbour *Nigeria* 6°26N 3°23E **124** B2
Lagos-Ikeja ✈ (LOS) *Nigeria* 6°34N 3°19E **124** A1
Lagos Island *Nigeria* 6°26N 3°23E **124** B2
Lagos Lagoon *Nigeria* 6°30N 3°28E **124** B2
Lagrange = Bidyadanga *Australia* 18°45S 121°43E **278** C3
Lagrange *U.S.A.* 41°39N 85°25W **311** C11
Lagrange B. *Australia* 18°38S 121°42E **278** C3
Laguardia *Spain* 42°33N 2°35W **196** C2
Laguépie *France* 44°8N 1°57E **174** D5
Lagún *Curaçao* 12°19N 69°10W **322** g
Laguna = Padilla *Bolivia* 19°19S 64°20W **331** D5
Laguna *Brazil* 28°30S 48°50W **335** B6
Laguna *N. Mex., U.S.A.* 35°2N 107°25W **305** J10
Laguna □ *Phil* 14°10N 121°20E **232** D3
Laguna, Sa. de la *Mexico* 23°35N 109°55W **318** C3
Laguna Beach *U.S.A.* 33°33N 117°47W **307** M9
Laguna Blanca △ *Argentina* 39°0S 70°5W **336** A2
Laguna de B. *Phil.* 14°29N 121°6E **127** C2
Laguna de Duera *Spain* 41°35N 4°43W **194** D6
Laguna de Lachuá △ *Guatemala* 15°55N 90°40W **320** C1
Laguna de Tacarigua △ *Venezuela* 10°59N 64°7W **328** A4
Laguna del Laja △ *Chile* 37°27S 71°20W **334** D1
Laguna del Tigre △ *Guatemala* 17°32N 90°56W **320** C1
Laguna Limpia *Argentina* 26°32S 59°45W **334** B4
Laguna San Rafael △ *Chile* 46°54S 73°31W **336** C2
Lagunas *Chile* 21°0S 69°45W **334** A2
Lagunas *Peru* 5°10S 75°35W **330** B2
Lagunas de Chacahua △ *Mexico* 16°0N 97°43W **319** D5
Lagunas de Montebello △ *Mexico* 16°4N 91°42W **319** D6
Lagunas de Ruidera ⌓ *Spain* 38°57N 2°52W **197** G2
Lagunillas *Bolivia* 19°38S 63°43W **331** D5
Lahad Datu *Malaysia* 5°0N 118°20E **235** A5
Lahad Datu, Telok *Malaysia* 4°50N 118°20E **235** B5
Lahaina *U.S.A.* 20°53N 156°41W **302** C5
Lahan Sai *Thailand* 14°25N 102°52E **236** E4
Lahanam *Laos* 16°16N 105°16E **236** D5
Lahar *India* 26°12N 78°57E **243** F8
Laharpur *India* 27°43N 80°56E **243** F9
Lahat *Indonesia* 3°45S 103°30E **234** C2
Lahe *Burma* 26°20N 95°26E **241** F5
Lahewa *Indonesia* 1°22N 97°12E **234** B1
Lahij *Yemen* 13°4N 44°53E **248** D4
Lāhījān *Iran* 37°10N 50°6E **247** B6
Lahilahi Pt. *U.S.A.* 21°28N 158°13W **302** K13
Lähn = Wleń *Poland* 51°2N 15°39E **185** G2
Lahn ➜ *Germany* 50°19N 7°37E **179** E3
Lahnstein *Germany* 50°15N 7°37E **179** E3
Laholm *Sweden* 56°30N 13°2E **163** H7
Laholmsbukten *Sweden* 56°30N 12°45E **163** H6
Lahore *Pakistan* 31°32N 74°22E **242** D6
Lahpongsel *Burma* 27°7N 98°25E **241** B7
Lahr *Germany* 48°20N 7°53E **179** G3
Lahri *Pakistan* 29°11N 68°13E **242** E3
Lāhrūd *Iran* 38°30N 47°52E **213** C12
Lahti *Finland* 60°58N 25°40E **188** B3
Lahtis = Lahti *Finland* 60°58N 25°40E **188** B3
Lahugala Kitulana △ *Sri Lanka* 6°50N 81°40E **245** L5
Laï *Chad* 9°25N 16°18E **259** G3
Lai Chau *Vietnam* 22°5N 103°3E **228** F4
Lai-hka *Burma* 21°16N 97°40E **241** E6
Laiagam *Papua N. G.* 5°33S 143°30E **286** C2
Lai'an *China* 32°28N 118°30E **229** A12
Laibach = Ljubljana *Slovenia* 46°4N 14°33E **199** B11
Laibin *China* 23°42N 109°14E **228** F7
Lā'ie *U.S.A.* 21°39N 157°56W **302** J14
Laifeng *China* 29°27N 109°20E **228** C7
L'Aigle *France* 48°46N 0°38E **172** D7
Laignes *France* 47°50N 4°20E **173** E11
L'Aiguillon-sur-Mer *France* 46°20N 1°18W **174** B2
Laila = Layla *Si. Arabia* 22°10N 46°40E **248** B4
Laim *Germany* 48°7N 11°30E **131** B2
Lainate *Italy* 45°34N 9°1E **129** A1
Laingsburg *S. Africa* 33°9S 20°52E **270** D3
Lainioälven ➜ *Sweden* 67°35N 22°40E **160** C20
Lainz *Austria* 48°10N 16°16E **142** B1
Lairg *U.K.* 58°2N 4°24W **167** C4
Laïri, B. de *Chad* 12°28N 16°45E **259** F3
Lais *Indonesia* 3°31S 102°3E **234** C2
Lais *Phil.* 6°20N 125°39E **233** H5
Laisamis *Kenya* 1°36N 37°48E **268** B4
Laissac *France* 44°23N 2°50E **174** D6
Láives *Italy* 46°26N 11°20E **199** B8
Laiwu *China* 36°15N 117°40E **227** F9
Laixi *China* 36°50N 120°31E **227** F11
Laiyang *China* 36°59N 120°45E **227** F11
Laiyuan *China* 39°20N 114°40E **226** E8
Laizhou *China* 37°8N 119°57E **227** F10
Laizhou Wan *China* 37°30N 119°30E **227** F10
Laja ➜ *Mexico* 20°55N 100°46W **318** C4
Lajamanu *Australia* 18°23S 130°38E **278** C5
Lajeado = Guiratinga *Brazil* 16°21S 53°45W **331** D7
Lajedo *Azores* 39°23N 31°15W **153** d2
Lajere *Nigeria* 12°10N 11°25E **263** C7
Lajes *Azores* 38°46N 27°6W **153** b1
Lajes *Rio Grande do N., Brazil* 5°41S 36°14W **332** C4
Lajes das Flores *Azores* 39°23N 31°10W **153** d2
Lajes do Pico *Azores* 38°23N 28°16W **153** d1
Lajinha *Brazil* 20°9S 41°37W **333** F3
Lajkovac *Serbia* 44°27N 20°14E **202** B4
Lajosmizse *Hungary* 47°3N 19°32E **182** C4
Lak Sao *Laos* 18°11N 104°59E **236** C5
Lakaband *Pakistan* 31°2N 69°15E **242** D3
Lakamané *Mali* 14°30N 9°55W **262** C3
Lakatoro *Vanuatu* 16°6S 167°25E **287** F5
Lake *U.S.A.* 44°33N 110°24W **304** D8
Lake Alfred *U.S.A.* 28°6N 81°44W **317** G8
Lake Alpine *U.S.A.* 38°29N 120°0W **306** G7
Lake Andes *U.S.A.* 43°9N 98°32W **308** D4
Lake Arthur *U.S.A.* 30°5N 92°41W **314** F8
Lake Bindegolly △ *Australia* 28°0S 144°12E **281** D3
Lake Boga *Australia* 35°26S 143°38E **282** C5
Lake Buena Vista *U.S.A.* 28°23N 81°32W **133** B1
Lake Butig △ *Phil.* 7°45N 124°16E **233** H5
Lake Butler *U.S.A.* 30°1N 82°21W **316** E7
Lake Cain Hills *U.S.A.* 28°29N 81°28W **133** B2
Lake Cargelligo *Australia* 33°15S 146°22E **283** B7
Lake Charles *U.S.A.* 30°14N 93°13W **314** F8
Lake City *Colo., U.S.A.* 38°2N 107°19W **304** G10
Lake City *Fla., U.S.A.* 30°11N 82°38W **316** E7
Lake City *Iowa, U.S.A.* 42°16N 94°44W **310** B2
Lake City *Mich., U.S.A.* 44°20N 85°13W **309** C11
Lake City *Minn., U.S.A.* 44°27N 92°16W **308** C7
Lake City *Pa., U.S.A.* 42°1N 80°21W **312** D4
Lake City *S.C., U.S.A.* 33°52N 79°45W **316** B10
Lake Clark △ *U.S.A.* 61°0N 154°0W **303** F9
Lake Clarke Shores *U.S.A.* 26°39N 80°5W **317** J9
Lake Coleridge *N.Z.* 43°17S 171°30E **285** D6
Lake Cowichan *Canada* 48°49N 124°3W **296** D4
Lake District △ *U.K.* 54°30N 3°21W **168** C4
Lake Eildon △ *Australia* 37°10S 145°56E **283** D6
Lake Elsinore *U.S.A.* 33°38N 117°20W **307** M9
Lake Eyre △ *Australia* 28°40S 137°31E **281** D2
Lake Fairfax Park *U.S.A.* 38°57N 77°19W **143** B2
Lake Forest *U.S.A.* 42°15N 87°50W **311** B9
Lake Gairdner △ *Australia* 31°41S 135°51E **281** E2
Lake Geneva *U.S.A.* 42°36N 88°26W **311** B8
Lake George *U.S.A.* 43°26N 73°43W **313** C11
Lake Grace *Australia* 33°7S 118°28E **279** F2
Lake Gregory ◎ *Australia* 20°12S 127°27E **278** D4
Lake Harbor *U.S.A.* 26°42N 80°48W **317** J9
Lake Harbour = Kimmirut *Canada* 62°50N 69°50W **295** E18
Lake Havasu City *U.S.A.* 34°27N 114°22W **307** L12
Lake Helen *U.S.A.* 28°59N 81°14W **317** G8
Lake Hughes *U.S.A.* 34°41N 118°26W **307** L8
Lake Isabella *U.S.A.* 35°38N 118°28W **307** K8
Lake Jackson *U.S.A.* 29°3N 95°27W **314** G7
Lake King *Australia* 33°5S 119°45E **279** F2
Lake Kopiago *Papua N. G.* 5°23S 142°31E **286** C2
Lake Kutubu *Papua N. G.* 6°20S 143°18E **286** D2
Lake Lenore *Canada* 52°24N 104°59W **297** C8
Lake Louise *Canada* 51°30N 116°10W **296** C5
Lake Mackay ◎ *Australia* 21°48S 129°46E **278** D4
Lake Mburo △ *Uganda* 0°33S 30°56E **268** C3
Lake Mead ⌓ *U.S.A.* 36°30N 114°22W **307** K12
Lake Meredith ⌓ *U.S.A.* 35°50N 101°50W **314** D4
Lake Mills *Iowa, U.S.A.* 43°25N 93°32W **308** D7
Lake Mills *Wis., U.S.A.* 43°5N 88°55W **311** A8
Lake Murray *Papua N. G.* 6°48S 141°29E **286** D1
Lake Nakura △ *Kenya* 0°21S 36°8E **268** C4
Lake Odessa *U.S.A.* 42°47N 85°8W **311** B11
Lake Orion *U.S.A.* 42°47N 83°14W **311** B13
Lake Park *Fla., U.S.A.* 26°48N 80°3W **317** J9
Lake Park *Ga., U.S.A.* 30°41N 83°11W **316** E6
Lake Placid *Fla., U.S.A.* 27°18N 81°22W **317** H8
Lake Placid *N.Y., U.S.A.* 44°17N 73°59W **313** B11
Lake Pleasant *U.S.A.* 43°28N 74°25W **313** C10
Lake Point Tower *Chicago, U.S.A.* **119** b3
Lake Providence *U.S.A.* 32°48N 91°10W **314** E9
Lake Pukaki *N.Z.* 44°11S 170°8E **285** E5
Lake Roosevelt ⌓ *U.S.A.* 48°5N 118°14W **304** B4
Lake St. Peter *Canada* 45°18N 78°2W **312** A6
Lake Shore Drive *Chicago, U.S.A.* **119** a2
Lake Shore Park *Chicago, U.S.A.* **119** a2
Lake Superior ⌓ *Canada* 47°45N 84°45W **298** C3
Lake Tekapo *N.Z.* 44°0S 170°30E **285** E5
Lake Torrens △ *Australia* 30°55S 137°40E **281** E2
Lake View *U.S.A.* 42°18N 95°3W **310** B1
Lake Villa *U.S.A.* 42°25N 88°5W **311** B8
Lake Village *U.S.A.* 33°20N 91°17W **314** E9
Lake Wales *U.S.A.* 27°54N 81°35W **317** H8
Lake Worth *U.S.A.* 26°37N 80°3W **317** J9
Lake Zurich *U.S.A.* 42°12N 88°5W **311** B8
Lakeba *Fiji* 18°13S 178°47W **287** B3
Lakeba Passage *Fiji* 18°0S 178°45W **287** B3
Lakefield *Canada* 44°25N 78°16W **312** B6
Lakefield △ *Australia* 15°24S 144°26E **280** B3
Lakehurst *U.S.A.* 40°1N 74°19W **313** F10
Lakeland *Queens., Australia* 15°49S 144°57E **280** B3
Lakeland *Fla., U.S.A.* 28°3N 81°57W **317** G8
Lakeland *Ga., U.S.A.* 31°2N 83°4W **316** D6
Lakemba = Lakeba *Fiji* 18°13S 178°47W **287** B3
Lakemba *Australia* 33°55S 151°5E **139** B1
Lakepa *Cook Is.* 18°59S 169°48W **289** g
Lakeport *Calif., U.S.A.* 39°3N 122°55W **306** F4
Lakeport *Mich., U.S.A.* 43°7N 82°30W **312** C2
Lakes □ *South Sudan* 7°0N 30°0E **257** F3
Lakes Entrance *Australia* 37°50S 148°0E **283** D8
Lakeside *Gauteng, S. Africa* 26°5S 28°8E **123** A2
Lakeside *Western Cape, S. Africa* 34°5S 18°27E **118** B1
Lakeside *Calif., U.S.A.* 32°52N 116°55W **307** N10
Lakeside *Nebr., U.S.A.* 42°3N 102°26W **308** D2
Lakeside Center *Chicago, U.S.A.* **119** f3
Lakeview *Ill., U.S.A.* 41°56N 87°38W **119** B3
Lakeview *La., U.S.A.* 30°0N 90°6W **131** A2
Lakeview *Oreg., U.S.A.* 42°11N 120°21W **304** E3
Lakeville *U.S.A.* 44°39N 93°14W **308** C7
Lakewood *Colo., U.S.A.* 39°42N 105°4W **304** G11
Lakewood *N.J., U.S.A.* 40°6N 74°13W **313** F10
Lakewood *N.Y., U.S.A.* 42°6N 79°19W **312** D5
Lakewood *Ohio, U.S.A.* 41°28N 81°47W **312** E3
Lakewood *Wash., U.S.A.* 47°11N 122°32W **306** C4
Lakewood Park *Fla., U.S.A.* 27°33N 80°24W **317** H9
Lakewood Park *Georgia, U.S.A.* 33°43N 84°24W **113** B2
Lakha *India* 26°9N 70°54E **242** F4
Lakhimpur *India* 27°57N 80°46E **243** F9
Lakhipur *Assam, India* 24°48N 93°0E **241** C4
Lakhipur *Assam, India* 26°2N 90°18E **243** F14
Lakhisarai *India* 25°11N 86°5E **243** G12
Lakhnadon *India* 22°36N 79°36E **243** H8
Lakhnau = Lucknow *India* 26°50N 81°0E **243** F9
Lakhonpheng *Laos* 15°54N 105°34E **236** E5
Lakhpat *India* 23°48N 68°47E **242** H3
Lakhtinskiy *Russia* 59°59N 30°9E **137** B1
Lakhtinskiy Razliv, Oz. *Russia* 59°59N 30°10E **137** B1
Lāki *Azerbaijan* 40°34N 47°22E **191** K8
Laki *Iceland* 64°4N 18°14W **155** C8
Lakin *U.S.A.* 37°57N 101°15W **308** G3
Lakitusaki ➜ *Canada* 54°21N 82°25W **298** B3
Lakka *Greece* 39°17N 20°9E **206** C10
Lakki *Greece* 35°24N 23°57E **207** E4
Lakki *Pakistan* 32°36N 70°55E **242** C4
Lakonia □ *Greece* 36°55N 22°30E **204** E4
Lakonikos Kolpos *Greece* 36°40N 22°40E **204** E4
Lakor *Indonesia* 8°15S 128°17E **231** F7
Lakota *Ivory C.* 5°50N 5°30W **262** D3
Lakota *N. Dak., U.S.A.* 48°2N 98°21W **308** A4
Laksar *India* 29°46N 78°3E **242** E8
Laksefjorden *Norway* 70°45N 26°50E **160** A22
Lakselv *Norway* 70°2N 25°0E **160** A21
Laksettipet *India* 18°52N 79°13E **244** E4
Lakshadweep □ *India* 10°0N 72°30E **245** J1
Lakshadweep Is. *India* 10°0N 72°30E **245** J1
Laksham *Bangla.* 23°14N 91°8E **241** D3
Lakshimpur *Bangla.* 22°58N 90°50E **241** D3
Lakshmanpur *Chhattisgarh, India* 22°58N 83°3E **243** H10
Lakshmanpur *W. Bengal, India* 22°38N 88°16E **124** B1
Lakshmeshwar *India* 15°9N 75°28E **245** G2
Lakshmikantapur *India* 22°5N 88°20E **243** H13
Laksi *Thailand* 13°53N 100°35E **113** A2
Lakuramau *Papua N. G.* 2°54S 151°15E **286** B6
Lal-lo *Phil.* 18°12N 121°40E **232** B3
Lal Qila *Delhi, India* **120** a3
Lala *Dem. Rep. of the Congo* 4°13S 20°30E **265** C4
Lala *Phil.* 7°59N 123°43E **233** H4
Lala Musa *Pakistan* 32°40N 73°57E **242** C5
Lalaghat *India* 24°30N 92°40E **241** C4
Lalago *Tanzania* 3°28S 33°58E **268** C3
Lalang ➜ *Indonesia* 2°24S 104°39E **234** C2
Lalapanzi *Zimbabwe* 19°20S 30°15E **269** F3
Lalapaşa *Turkey* 41°49N 26°44E **203** E10
Lalara *Gabon* 0°19N 11°32E **264** B2
Lalbenque *France* 44°19N 1°34E **174** D5
Lalbert *Australia* 35°38S 143°20E **282** C5
L'Albufera *Spain* 39°20N 0°27W **197** F4
L'Alcora *Spain* 40°5N 0°14W **196** E4
L'Alfàs del Pi *Spain* 38°35N 0°5W **197** G4
Lalganj *India* 25°52N 85°13E **243** G11
Lalgola *India* 24°25N 88°15E **243** G13
Lālī *Iran* 32°21N 49°6E **247** C6
Lalibela *Ethiopia* 12°3N 39°0E **257** E4
Lalin *Heilongjiang, China* 45°12N 127°0E **227** B14
Lalín *Spain* 42°40N 8°5W **194** C2
Lalin He ➜ *China* 45°32N 125°40E **227** B13
Lalinde *France* 44°50N 0°44E **174** D4
Lalitapur *Nepal* 27°40N 85°20E **243** F11
Lalitpur *India* 24°42N 78°28E **243** G8
Lalkua *India* 29°5N 79°31E **243** E8
Lalm *Norway* 61°50N 9°17E **164** C6
Lalsot *India* 26°34N 76°20E **242** F7
Lam Nam Nan △ *Thailand* 17°55N 100°28E **236** D3
Lam Pao Res. *Thailand* 16°50N 103°15E **236** D4
Lam Tin *China* 22°18N 114°14E **122** B2
Lama Kara *Togo* 9°30N 1°15E **263** D5
Lamae *Thailand* 9°51N 99°5E **237** H2
Lamag *Malaysia* 5°29N 117°49E **235** A5
Lamaing *Burma* 15°25N 97°53E **236** E1
Lamaipum *Burma* 25°40N 97°57E **241** C6
Lamap *Vanuatu* 16°26S 167°43E **287** F5
Lamar *Colo., U.S.A.* 38°5N 102°37W **304** G12
Lamar *Mo., U.S.A.* 37°30N 94°16W **308** G6
Lamarque *Argentina* 39°24S 65°40W **336** A3
Lamas *Peru* 6°28S 76°31W **330** B2
Lamastre *France* 44°59N 4°35E **175** D8
Lamayuru *India* 34°25N 76°56E **243** B7
Lambach *Austria* 48°6N 13°51E **180** C6
Lamballe *France* 48°29N 2°31W **172** D4
Lambaréné *Gabon* 0°41S 10°12E **264** C2
Lambasa = Labasa *Fiji* 16°30S 179°27E **287** A2
Lambay I. *Ireland* 53°29N 6°1W **166** C5
Lambayeque □ *Peru* 6°45S 80°0W **330** B2
Lambert *Norway* 59°52N 10°48E **133** A3
Lambert, C. *Papua N. G.* 4°11S 151°31E **286** C6
Lambert-St. Louis Int. ✈ (STL) *U.S.A.* 38°45N 90°22W **310** F6
Lambert's Bay *S. Africa* 32°5S 18°17E **270** D2
Lambertville *U.S.A.* 41°46N 83°35W **311** C13
Lambesc *France* 43°39N 5°16E **175** E9
Lambèse = Tazoult *Algeria* 35°29N 6°11E **261** A6
Lambeth *Canada* 42°54N 81°18W **312** D3
Lambeth □ *U.K.* 51°28N 0°6W **125** B3
Lambi *Solomon Is.* 9°22S 159°39E **287** M10
Lambia *Greece* 37°52N 21°53E **204** D3
Lambir Hills △ *Malaysia* 4°12N 114°1E **235** B4
Lambomakondro *Madag.* 22°41S 44°44E **272** C1
Lambon *Papua N. G.* 4°45S 152°48E **286** C7
Lambrate *Italy* 45°28N 9°16E **129** B2
Lambro ➜ *Italy* 45°8N 9°32E **198** C6
Lambro, Parco *Italy* 45°29N 9°14E **129** B2
Lambton Mills *Canada* 43°39N 79°30W **141** B1
Lambu *Papua N. G.* 3°18S 151°43E **286** B6
Lambunao *Phil.* 11°3N 122°29E **233** F4
Lamé *Chad* 9°15N 14°32E **259** G2
Lame *Nigeria* 10°30N 9°20E **263** C6
Lame Deer *U.S.A.* 45°37N 106°40W **304** D10
Lamego *Portugal* 41°5N 7°52W **194** D3
Lamentin *Guadeloupe* 16°16N 61°38W **322** e
Lamèque *Canada* 47°45N 64°38W **299** C7
Lameroo *Australia* 35°19S 140°33E **282** C4
Lamesa *U.S.A.* 32°44N 101°58W **314** E4
Lamia *Greece* 38°55N 22°26E **204** C4
Lamigan Pt. *Phil.* 6°48N 126°21E **233** H6
Lamine ➜ *U.S.A.* 38°59N 92°51W **310** F4
Lamington △ *Australia* 28°13S 153°12E **281** D5
Lamitan *Phil.* 6°39N 122°8E **233** H4
Lamlam, Mt. *Guam* 13°22N 144°41E **302** d
Lamma I. *China* 22°12N 114°7E **122** B1
Lammermuir Hills *U.K.* 55°50N 2°40W **167** F6
Lammeulo *Indonesia* 5°14N 95°56E **234** A1
Lammhult *Sweden* 57°10N 14°35E **163** G8
Lamoille ➜ *U.S.A.* 44°38N 73°13W **313** B11
Lamon B. *Phil.* 14°30N 122°20E **232** D4
Lamongan *Indonesia* 7°7S 112°25E **235** D4
Lamoni *U.S.A.* 40°37N 93°56W **310** D3
Lamont *Alta., Canada* 53°46N 112°50W **296** C6
Lamont *Calif., U.S.A.* 35°15N 118°55W **307** K8
Lamont *Fla., U.S.A.* 30°23N 83°49W **316** E6
Lamont *Iowa, U.S.A.* 42°36N 91°39W **310** B5
Lamont *Wyo., U.S.A.* 42°13N 107°29W **304** E10
Lamotte-Beuvron *France* 47°36N 2°2E **173** E9
Lampa *Peru* 15°22S 70°22W **330** D3
Lampang *Thailand* 18°16N 99°32E **236** C2
Lampasas *U.S.A.* 31°4N 98°11W **314** F5
Lampazos de Naranjo *Mexico* 27°1N 100°31W **318** B4
Lampedusa *Medit. S.* 35°36N 12°40E **261** A7
Lampertheim *Germany* 49°35N 8°27E **179** F4
Lampeter *U.K.* 52°7N 4°4W **169** E3
Lamphun *Thailand* 18°40N 99°2E **236** C2
Lampione *Medit. S.* 35°33N 12°20E **256** A2
Lampman *Canada* 49°25N 102°50W **297** D8
Lamprechtshausen *Austria* 48°0N 12°58E **180** D5
Lampung □ *Indonesia* 5°30S 104°30E **234** D2
Lampung, Teluk *Indonesia* 5°40S 105°20E **234** D3
Lamta *India* 22°8N 80°7E **243** H9
Lamu *Burma* 19°14N 94°10E **241** F5
Lamu *Coast, Kenya* 2°16S 40°55E **268** C5
Lamud *Peru* 6°10S 77°57W **330** B2
Lamy *U.S.A.* 35°29N 105°53W **305** J11
Lan Xian *China* 38°15N 111°35E **226** E6
Lan Yü *Taiwan* 22°4N 121°25E **225** D3
Lāna'i *U.S.A.* 20°50N 156°55W **302** C5
Lāna'i City *U.S.A.* 20°50N 156°55W **302** C5
Lāna'ihale *U.S.A.* 20°49N 156°52W **302** C5
Lanak La *China* 34°27N 79°32E **243** B8
Lanak'o Shank'ou = Lanak La *China* 34°27N 79°32E **243** B8
Lanao, L. *Phil.* 7°52N 124°15E **233** H5
Lanao del Norte □ *Phil.* 8°0N 124°10E **233** H5
Lanao del Sur □ *Phil.* 7°40N 124°10E **233** H5
Lanark *Ont., Canada* 45°1N 76°22W **313** A8
Lanark *S. Lanarks., U.K.* 55°40N 3°47W **167** F5
Lanark *Ill., U.S.A.* 42°6N 89°50W **310** B7
Lanbi Kyun *Burma* 10°50N 98°20E **237** G2
Lancang *China* 22°36N 99°58E **228** F2
Lancang Jiang ➜ *China* 21°40N 101°10E **228** G3
Lancashire □ *U.K.* 53°50N 2°48W **168** D5
Lancaster *Ont., Canada* 45°10N 74°30W **313** A10
Lancaster *Lancs., U.K.* 54°3N 2°48W **168** C5

Lancaster Calif., U.S.A. 34°42N 118°8W 307 L8
Lancaster Ky., U.S.A. 37°37N 84°35W 309 G11
Lancaster Mo., U.S.A. 40°31N 92°32W 310 D4
Lancaster N.H., U.S.A. 44°29N 71°34W 313 B13
Lancaster Ohio, U.S.A. 39°43N 82°36W 309 F12
Lancaster Pa., U.S.A. 40°2N 76°19W 313 F8
Lancaster S.C., U.S.A. 34°43N 80°46W 315 D14
Lancaster Wis., U.S.A. 42°51N 90°43W 310 B6
Lancaster, Récif = Neilson, Récif Pac. Oc. 27°1S 146°2W 289 f
Lancaster Sd. Canada 74°13N 84°0W 295 C15
Lancelin Australia 31°0S 115°18E 279 F2
Lanchow = Lanzhou China 36°1N 103°52E 226 F2
Lanchyn Ukraine 48°33N 24°45E 183 B9
Lanciano Italy 42°14N 14°23E 199 F11
Lanco Chile 39°24S 72°46W 336 A2
Lancones Peru 4°30S 80°30W 330 A1
Lancun China 36°25N 120°10E 227 F11
Łańcut Poland 50°10N 22°13E 185 H9
Land Between the Lakes △ U.S.A. 36°25N 88°0W 315 C11
Landau Bayern, Germany 48°40N 12°41E 179 G8
Landau Rhld-Pfz., Germany 49°12N 8°6E 179 F4
Landay Afghan. 30°31N 63°47E 240 C1
Landeck Austria 47°9N 10°34E 180 D3
Lander U.S.A. 42°50N 108°44W 304 E9
Lander → Australia 22°0S 132°0E 278 D5
Landerneau France 48°28N 4°17W 172 D2
Landeryd Sweden 57°7N 13°15E 163 G7
Landes France 44°0N 1°0W 174 D2
Landes □ France 43°57N 0°48W 174 E3
Landes de Gascogne △ France 44°23N 0°50W 174 D3
Landeshut = Kamienna Góra Poland 50°47N 16°2E 185 H3
Landete Spain 39°56N 1°25W 196 F3
Landfall I. India 13°40N 93°2E 245 H11
Landi Kotal Pakistan 34°7N 71°6E 242 B4
Landianchang China 39°56N 116°17E 114 B1
Landisburg U.S.A. 40°21N 77°19W 312 F7
Landivisiau France 48°31N 4°6W 172 D2
Landmannalaugar Iceland 63°59N 19°4W 155 D7
Landover Hills U.S.A. 38°56N 76°54W 143 B4
Landquart Switz. 46°58N 9°32E 179 J5
Landrecies France 50°7N 3°40E 173 B10
Land's End U.K. 50°4N 5°44W 169 G2
Landsberg = Górowo Iławeckie Poland 54°17N 20°30E 184 D7
Landsberg Germany 48°2N 10°53E 179 G6
Landsberg an der Warthe = Gorzów Wielkopolski Poland 52°43N 15°15E 185 F2
Landsberg in Oberschlesien = Gorzów Śląski Poland 51°3N 18°22E 185 G5
Landsborough Cr. → Australia 22°28S 144°35E 280 C3
Landsbro Sweden 57°24N 14°56E 163 G8
Landshut Germany 48°34N 12°8E 179 G8
Landskrona Sweden 55°53N 12°50E 163 J6
Landsmeer Neths. 52°26N 4°55E 112 A2
Landstrasse Austria 48°12N 16°23E 142 A2
Landstuhl Germany 49°24N 7°33E 179 F3
Landvetter Sweden 57°41N 12°17E 163 G6
Landwehr kanal Germany 52°29N 13°24E 115 B3
Lane U.S.A. 33°32N 79°53W 316 B10
Lane Cove Australia 33°48S 151°9E 139 A1
Lane Cove Nat. Park △ Australia 33°47S 151°8E 139 A1
Lanesboro U.S.A. 41°57N 75°34W 313 E9
Lanester France 47°46N 3°22W 172 E3
Lanett U.S.A. 32°52N 85°12W 316 C4
Lang Shan China 41°0N 106°30E 226 D4
Lang Son Vietnam 21°52N 106°42E 228 G6
Lang Suan Thailand 9°57N 99°4E 237 H2
Langå Midtjylland, Denmark 56°23N 9°54E 163 H3
Langa Western Cape, S. Africa 33°57S 18°31E 118 A2
La'nga Co China 30°45N 81°15E 243 D9
Langa-Langa Dem. Rep. of the Congo 3°50S 15°59E 264 C3
Langadas Greece 40°46N 23°6E 202 F7
Langadia Greece 37°43N 22°1E 204 D4
Långan → Sweden 63°19N 14°44E 162 A8
Langanes Iceland 66°20N 14°53W 155 A12
Langano, L. Ethiopia 7°36N 38°43E 257 F4
Langar Afghan. 37°2N 73°47E 240 A4
Langar Iran 35°23N 60°25E 247 C9
Langara I. Canada 54°14N 133°1W 296 C2
Langarūd Iran 37°11N 50°8E 247 B6
Langås Sweden 56°58N 12°26E 163 H6
Langatabbetje Suriname 4°59N 54°28W 329 C7
Langdai China 26°6N 105°21E 228 D5
Langdon U.S.A. 48°45N 98°22W 308 A4
Långe Jan = Ölands södra udde Sweden 56°12N 16°23E 163 H10
Langeac France 45°7N 3°29E 174 C7
Langeais France 47°20N 0°24E 172 E7
Langeb Baraka → Sudan 17°28N 36°50E 256 D4
Langeberg S. Africa 33°55S 21°0E 270 D3
Langeberge S. Africa 28°15S 22°33E 270 C3
Langeland Denmark 54°56N 10°48E 163 K4
Langelands Bælt Denmark 54°50N 10°55E 163 K4
Langen Hessen, Germany 49°59N 8°40E 179 F4
Langen Niedersachsen, Germany 53°36N 8°36E 178 B4
Langenbielau = Bielawa Poland 50°43N 16°37E 185 H3
Langenburg Canada 50°51N 101°43W 297 C8
Langeneß Germany 54°38N 8°36E 178 A4
Langenlois Austria 48°29N 15°40E 180 C8
Langenzersdorf Austria 48°18N 16°21E 142 A2
Langeoog Germany 53°45N 7°32E 178 B3
Langer See Germany 52°24N 13°37E 115 B4
Langeskov Denmark 55°22N 10°35E 163 J4
Langesund Norway 59°0N 9°45E 164 F6
Langevåg Norway 62°26N 6°13E 164 B3
Langfang China 39°30N 116°41E 226 E9
Langgapayung Indonesia 1°43N 99°58E 234 B1
Långhem Sweden 57°36N 13°14E 163 G7
Langhirano Italy 44°37N 10°16E 198 D7
Langholm U.K. 55°9N 3°0W 167 F5
Langisjór Iceland 64°11N 18°15W 155 C8
Langjökull Iceland 64°39N 20°12W 155 C6
Langkawi, Pulau Malaysia 6°25N 99°45E 237 J2
Langklip S. Africa 28°12S 20°20E 270 C3
Langkon Malaysia 6°30N 116°40E 235 A5
Langley B.C., Canada 49°7N 122°39W 306 A4
Langley Va., U.S.A. 38°57N 77°11W 143 B2
Langley Park U.S.A. 38°59N 76°58W 143 B4
Langnau Switz. 46°56N 7°47E 179 J3
Langogne France 44°43N 3°50E 174 D7
Langon France 44°33N 0°16W 174 D3
Langøya Norway 68°45N 14°50E 160 B16
Langreo Spain 43°18N 5°40W 194 B5
Langres France 47°52N 5°20E 173 E12
Langres, Plateau de France 47°45N 5°3E 173 E12
Langsa Indonesia 4°30N 97°57E 234 B1
Långsele Sweden 63°12N 17°4E 162 A11
Långshyttan Sweden 60°27N 16°2E 162 D10
Langtang △ Nepal 28°10N 85°30E 243 E11
Langtao Burma 27°15N 97°34E 241 B6
Langting India 25°31N 93°7E 241 C4
Langtou China 40°1N 124°19E 227 D13
Langtry U.S.A. 29°49N 101°34W 314 G4
Langu Thailand 6°53N 99°47E 237 J2
Langue de Barbarie △ Senegal 14°54N 16°30W 262 C1
Languedoc France 43°58N 3°55E 174 E7
Languedoc-Roussillon □ France 43°25N 3°0E 174 E6
Langwald Germany 48°10N 11°25E 131 A1
Langwang China 22°38N 113°27E 219 a
Langxi China 31°10N 119°12E 229 B12
Langzhong China 31°38N 105°58E 228 B5
Lanham U.S.A. 38°59N 76°51W 143 B4
Lanigan Canada 51°51N 105°2W 297 C7
Lanikai U.S.A. 21°23N 157°42W 302 K14
Lanín △ Argentina 40°0S 71°58W 336 A2
Lanjigarh India 19°43N 83°23E 244 E6
Lankao China 34°48N 114°50E 226 G8
Länkäran Azerbaijan 38°48N 48°52E 213 C13
Lankwitz Germany 52°25N 13°21E 115 B3
Lanmeur France 48°39N 3°43W 172 D3
Lannemezan France 43°8N 0°23E 174 E4
Lannilis France 48°35N 4°32W 172 D2
Lannion France 48°46N 3°29W 172 D3
L'Annonciation Canada 46°25N 74°55W 298 C5
L'Annunziatella Italy 41°49N 12°33E 136 C2
Lanouaille France 45°24N 1°9E 174 C5
Lanping China 26°28N 99°15E 228 D2
Lansang △ Thailand 16°45N 99°0E 236 D2
Lansdale U.S.A. 40°14N 75°17W 313 F9
Lansdowne N.S.W., Australia 31°48S 152°30E 283 A10
Lansdowne Ont., Canada 44°24N 76°1W 313 B8
Lansdowne India 29°50N 78°41E 243 E8
Lansdowne Western Cape, S. Africa 33°59S 18°30E 118 A2
Lansdowne House = Neskantaga Canada 52°14N 87°53W 298 B2
L'Anse U.S.A. 46°45N 88°27W 308 B9
L'Anse à l'Âne Martinique 14°32N 61°4W 322 j
L'Anse au Loup Canada 51°32N 56°50W 299 B8
L'Anse aux Epines Grenada 11°59N 61°45W 323 q
L'Anse aux Meadows Canada 51°36N 55°32W 299 B8
L'Anse la Raye St. Lucia 13°55N 61°3W 323 m
L'Anse Mitan Martinique 14°32N 61°3W 322 j
Lansford U.S.A. 40°50N 75°53W 313 F9
Lanshan China 25°24N 112°10E 229 E9
Lanshantou China 35°5N 119°20E 227 G10
Länsi-Turunmaa Finland 60°18N 22°18E 188 B2
Lansing Ont., Canada 43°45N 79°24W 141 A2
Lansing Mich., U.S.A. 42°44N 84°33W 311 B12
Lanslebourg-Mont-Cenis France 45°17N 6°52E 175 C10
Lanta, Ko Thailand 7°35N 99°3E 237 J2
Lantana U.S.A. 26°35N 80°3W 317 J9
Lantau I. China 22°15N 113°56E 219 a
Lantewa Nigeria 12°16N 11°44E 263 C7
Lantian China 34°11N 109°20E 226 G5
Lanus Argentina 34°42S 58°23W 117 C2
Lanusei Italy 39°52N 9°34E 200 C2
Lanuza Phil. 9°14N 126°4E 233 G6
Lanxi China 29°13N 119°28E 229 C12
Lanyang Hsi → Taiwan 24°43N 121°49E 225 B3
Lanyü Taiwan 22°2N 121°32E 225 D3
Lanzarote Canary Is. 29°0N 13°40W 153 e2
Lanzarote ✕ (ACE) Canary Is. 28°57N 13°40W 153 e2
Lanzhou China 36°1N 103°52E 226 F2
Lanzo Torinese Italy 45°16N 7°28E 198 C4
Lao → Italy 39°47N 15°48E 201 C8
Lao Bao Laos 16°35N 106°30E 239 F17
Lao Cai Vietnam 22°30N 103°57E 228 F4
Laoag Phil. 18°7N 120°34E 232 B3
Laoang Phil. 12°32N 125°8E 232 E5
Laoha He → China 43°25N 120°35E 227 C11
Laohekou China 32°22N 111°38E 229 A8
Laois □ Ireland 52°57N 7°36W 166 D4
Laon France 49°33N 3°35E 173 C10
Laona U.S.A. 45°34N 88°40W 308 C9
Laonung Hsi → Taiwan 22°47N 120°27E 225 D2
Laos ■ Asia 17°45N 105°0E 236 D5
Lapa Paraná, Brazil 25°46S 49°44W 335 B6
Lapa Rio de J., Brazil 22°54S 43°10W 135 B1
Lapac I. Phil. 5°32N 120°47E 233 J3
Lapai Nigeria 9°5N 6°32E 263 D6
Lapalisse France 46°15N 3°38E 173 F10
Laparan I. Phil. 5°57N 120°0E 233 J2
Lapeer U.S.A. 43°3N 83°19W 311 A13
Lapeyrade France 44°4N 0°3W 174 D3
Lapithos Cyprus 35°21N 33°11E 207 E9
Lapland = Lappland Europe 68°7N 24°0E 160 B21
LaPorte Ind., U.S.A. 41°36N 86°43W 311 C10
Laporte Pa., U.S.A. 41°25N 76°30W 313 E8
Lapovo Serbia 44°10N 21°2E 202 B5
Lappeenranta Finland 61°3N 28°12E 188 B5
Lappland Europe 68°7N 24°0E 160 B21
Lappo = Lapua Finland 62°58N 23°0E 160 E20
Laprida Argentina 37°34S 60°45W 334 D3
Lâpseki Turkey 40°20N 26°41E 203 F10
Laptev Sea Russia 76°0N 125°0E 215 B13
Lapu-Lapu Phil. 10°20N 123°55E 233 F4
Lapua Finland 62°58N 23°0E 160 E20
Lăpuş → Romania 47°25N 23°40E 183 C8
Lăpuş, Munţii Romania 47°20N 23°50E 183 C8
Lăpuşna Moldova 46°53N 28°25E 183 D13
Lapy Poland 52°59N 22°52E 185 F9
Laqiya Arba'in Sudan 20°1N 28°1E 256 C2
Laqiya Umran Sudan 19°55N 28°18E 256 D2
L'Àquila Italy 42°22N 13°22E 199 F10
Lār Iran 27°40N 54°14E 247 E7
Lara Australia 38°2S 144°26E 282 E6
Lara □ Venezuela 10°10N 69°50W 328 A4
Larabanga Ghana 9°16N 1°56W 262 D4
Larache Morocco 35°10N 6°5W 260 A3
Larache □ Morocco 35°10N 5°50W 260 A3
Laragaran = Plaridel Phil. 8°37N 123°43E 233 G4
Laragne-Montéglin France 44°18N 5°49E 175 D9
Lārak Iran 26°51N 56°21E 249 A7
Laramie U.S.A. 41°19N 105°35W 304 F11
Laramie Mts. U.S.A. 42°0N 105°30W 304 F11
Laranjal do Jari Brazil 0°51S 52°30W 329 D7
Laranjeiras Brazil 22°55S 43°10W 135 B1
Laranjeiras do Sul Brazil 25°23S 52°23W 335 B5
Larantuka Indonesia 8°21S 122°55E 231 F6
Larat Indonesia 7°0S 132°0E 231 F8
L'Arbresle France 45°50N 4°36E 175 C8
Lärbro Sweden 57°47N 18°50E 163 G12
Lärdal Norway 59°25N 8°10E 164 E5
Larde Mozam. 16°28S 39°43E 269 F4
Larder Lake Canada 48°5N 79°40W 298 C4
Lardos Greece 36°6N 28°1E 206 E12
Lardos, Akra = Lindos, Akra Greece 36°4N 28°10E 206 E12
Lardos, Ormos Greece 36°4N 28°2E 206 E12
Lare Kenya 0°20N 37°56E 268 C4
Laredo Spain 43°26N 3°28W 194 B7
Laredo Tex., U.S.A. 27°30N 99°30W 314 H5
Laredo Sd. Canada 52°30N 128°53W 296 C3
Larena Phil. 9°15N 123°35E 233 G4
Lares Puerto Rico 18°18N 66°53W 321 b
Large I. Grenada 12°24N 61°30W 323 q
Largentière France 44°34N 4°18E 175 D8
L'Argentière-la-Bessée France 44°47N 6°33E 175 D10
Largo U.S.A. 27°54N 82°47W 317 H7
Largo, Key U.S.A. 25°15N 80°15W 317 K9
Largs U.K. 55°47N 4°52W 167 F4
Lari Italy 43°34N 10°35E 198 E7
Lariang Indonesia 1°26S 119°17E 235 C5
Larimore U.S.A. 47°54N 97°38W 308 B5
Larino Italy 41°48N 14°54E 199 G11
Larisa Greece 39°36N 22°27E 204 B4
Larisis Station Athens, Greece 112 a1
Larissa = Larisa Greece 39°36N 22°27E 204 B4
Larissa □ Greece 39°39N 22°24E 204 B4
Larkana Pakistan 27°32N 68°18E 242 F3
Larkins = South Miami U.S.A. 25°42N 80°17W 128 B1
Larnaca Cyprus 34°55N 33°38E 207 F9
Larnaca ✕ (LCA) Cyprus 34°50N 33°34E 207 F9
Larnaca Bay Cyprus 34°53N 33°45E 207 F9
Larnare, Pte. Martinique 14°47N 61°13W 322 j
Larne U.K. 54°51N 5°51W 166 B6
Larned U.S.A. 38°11N 99°6W 308 F4
Laroquebrou France 44°58N 2°12E 174 D6
Larose U.S.A. 29°34N 90°23W 315 G9
Larose, Pte. Martinique 14°39N 60°53W 322 j
Larrimah Australia 15°35S 133°12E 278 C5
Larsen Bay U.S.A. 57°32N 153°59W 303 H9
Larsen Ice Shelf Antarctica 67°0S 62°0W 151 C17
Laruns France 43°0N 0°26W 174 F3
Larvik Norway 59°4N 10°2E 164 E7
Larzac, Causse du France 43°50N 3°17E 174 E7
Las Poland 52°13N 21°6E 142 B2
Las Alpujarras Spain 36°55N 3°20W 197 J7
Las Animas U.S.A. 38°4N 103°13W 304 G12
Las Anod Somali Rep. 8°26N 47°19E 267 C6
Las Arenas Spain 43°17N 4°50W 194 B6
Las Batuecas △ Spain 40°32N 6°5W 194 E4
Las Bonitas Venezuela 7°52N 65°40W 328 B4
Las Brenãs Argentina 27°5S 61°7W 334 B3
Las Cabezas de San Juan Spain 36°57N 5°58W 195 J5
Las Cañadas del Teide △ Canary Is. 28°15N 16°37W 153 e1
Las Chimeneas Mexico 32°8N 116°5W 307 N10
Las Coloradas Argentina 39°34S 70°36W 336 A2
Las Corts Spain 41°23N 2°7E 114 A1
Las Cruces U.S.A. 32°19N 106°47W 305 K10
Las Flores Argentina 36°10S 59°7W 334 D4
Las Gabias = Gabia la Grande Spain 37°8N 3°40W 195 H7
Las Heras Mendoza, Argentina 32°51S 68°49W 334 C2
Las Heras Santa Cruz, Argentina 46°33S 68°57W 336 C3
Las Hermosas △ Colombia 3°48N 75°51W 328 C2
Las Horquetas Argentina 48°14S 71°11W 336 C2
Las Kabacki Poland 52°7N 21°2E 142 C2
Las Khoreh = Laasqoray Somali Rep. 11°10N 48°20E 267 B6
Las Lajas Argentina 38°30S 70°25W 336 A2
Las Lomas Peru 4°40S 80°10W 330 A1
Las Lomitas Argentina 24°43S 60°35W 334 A3
Las Marismas Spain 37°5N 6°20W 195 H4
Las Mercedes Venezuela 9°7N 66°24W 328 B4
Las Minas Spain 38°20N 1°41W 197 G3
Las Navas de la Concepción Spain 37°56N 5°30W 195 H5
Las Navas del Marqués Spain 40°36N 4°20W 194 E6
Las Nieves Phil. 8°46N 125°34E 233 G5
Las Orquideas △ Colombia 6°36N 76°16W 328 B2
Las Palmas Argentina 27°8S 58°45W 334 B4
Las Palmas Canary Is. 28°7N 15°26W 153 e1
Las Palmas → Mexico 32°31N 116°58W 307 N10
Las Palmas ✕ (LPA) Canary Is. 27°55N 15°25W 153 e1
Las Pedroñas Spain 39°26N 2°40W 197 F2
Las Piedras Puerto Rico 18°11N 65°52W 321 b
Las Piedras Uruguay 34°44S 56°14W 335 C4
Las Pinas Phil. 14°29N 120°58E 127 C1
Las Pipinas Argentina 35°30S 57°19W 334 D4
Las Plumas Argentina 43°40S 67°15W 336 B3
Las Rejas Chile 33°27S 70°42W 137 B1
Las Rosas Argentina 32°30S 61°35W 334 C3
Las Rozas Spain 40°29N 3°52W 194 E7
Las Tablas Panama 7°49N 80°14W 320 E3
Las Toscas Argentina 28°21S 59°18W 334 B4
Las Truchas Mexico 17°57N 102°13W 318 D4
Las Tunas Cuba 20°58N 76°59W 320 B4
Las Varillas Argentina 31°50S 62°50W 334 C3
Las Vegas N. Mex., U.S.A. 35°36N 105°13W 305 J11
Las Vegas Nev., U.S.A. 36°10N 115°8W 124 A2
Las Vegas McCarran Int. ✕ (LAS) U.S.A. 36°5N 115°9W 124 B2
Lasa = Lhasa China 29°25N 90°58E 218 F7
LaSalle Canada 45°26N 73°38W 130 B2
LaSalle Street Chicago, U.S.A. 119 a1
LaSalle Street Station Chicago, U.S.A. 119 d1
Lasanga I. Papua N. G. 7°25S 147°15E 286 D4
Lasarte-Oria Spain 43°16N 2°1W 196 B2
Lascano Uruguay 33°35S 54°12W 335 C5
Lascelles Australia 35°34S 142°34E 282 C5
Lasek Bielański Poland 52°17N 20°57E 142 B1
Lasek Na Kole Poland 52°15N 20°56E 142 B1
Lash-e Joveyn Afghan. 31°45N 61°30E 240 C1
Lashburn Canada 53°10N 109°40W 297 C7
Lashio Burma 22°56N 97°45E 241 D6
Lashkar India 26°10N 78°10E 242 F8
Lashkar Gāh Afghan. 31°35N 64°21E 240 C2
Lasin Poland 53°30N 19°2E 184 E6
Lasithi Greece 35°11N 25°31E 207 E6
Lasithi □ Greece 35°5N 25°50E 207 E6
Lāsjerd Iran 35°24N 53°4E 247 C7
Lask Poland 51°34N 19°8E 185 G6
Łaskarzew Poland 51°48N 21°36E 185 G8
Laško Slovenia 46°10N 15°16E 199 B12
Lassance Brazil 17°54S 44°34W 333 E3
Lassay-les-Châteaux France 48°27N 0°30W 172 D6
Lassen Pk. U.S.A. 40°29N 121°30W 304 F3
Lassen Volcanic △ U.S.A. 40°30N 121°20W 304 F3
Lassongo Angola 12°5S 22°46E 265 E4
Last Mountain L. Canada 51°5N 105°14W 297 C7
Lastchance Cr. → U.S.A. 40°2N 121°15W 306 E5
Lastoursville Gabon 0°55S 12°38E 264 C2
Lastovo Croatia 42°46N 16°55E 199 F13
Lastovski Kanal Croatia 42°50N 17°0E 199 F14
Lat Yao Thailand 15°45N 99°48E 236 E2
Lata Mt. Amer. Samoa 14°14S 169°27W 302 f
Latacunga Ecuador 0°50S 78°35W 328 D2
Latakia = Al Lādhiqīyah Syria 35°30N 35°45E 250 C6
Latchford Canada 47°20N 79°50W 298 C4
Late Tonga 18°48S 174°39W 287 P13
Latehar India 23°45N 84°30E 243 H11
Laterza Italy 40°37N 16°48E 201 B9
Latham Australia 29°44S 116°20E 279 E2
Lathen Germany 52°52N 7°19E 178 C3
Lathi India 27°43N 71°23E 242 F4
Lathi Vanuatu 14°57S 167°8E 287 D5
Lathrop U.S.A. 39°33N 94°20W 310 E2
Lathrop Wells U.S.A. 36°39N 116°24W 307 J10
Latiano Italy 40°33N 17°43E 201 B10
Latin, Quartier Montréal, Canada 130 b2
Latina Italy 41°28N 12°52E 200 A5
Latina Madrid, Spain 40°24N 3°44W 127 B1
Latisana Italy 45°47N 13°0E 199 C10
Latium = Lazio □ Italy 42°10N 12°30E 199 F9
Laton U.S.A. 36°26N 119°41W 306 J7
Latorytsya → Slovak Rep. 48°28N 21°50E 181 C14
Latouche Treville, C. Australia 18°27S 121°49E 278 C3
Latouma Niger 22°10N 14°50E 259 D2
Látrar Iceland 66°24N 23°2W 155 A3
Latrobe Tas., Australia 41°14S 146°30E 281 G4
Latrobe Pa., U.S.A. 40°19N 79°23W 312 F5
Latrónico Italy 40°5N 16°1E 201 B9
Latur India 18°25N 76°40E 244 E3
Latvia ■ Europe 56°50N 24°0E 188 D2
Lau Nigeria 9°11N 11°19E 263 D7
Lau Basin Pac. Oc. 20°0S 177°0W 277 E15
Lau Fau Shan China 22°28N 113°59E 219 a
Lau Group Fiji 17°0S 178°30W 287 A3
Lau Ridge Pac. Oc. 21°0S 178°30W 277 E15
Lauban = Lubań Poland 51°5N 15°15E 185 G2
Lauca → Bolivia 19°9S 68°10W 330 D4
Lauchhammer Germany 51°29N 13°47E 178 D9
Lauda-Königshofen Germany 49°33N 9°42E 179 F5
Laudal Norway 58°15N 7°30E 164 F4
Laudat Dominica 15°20N 61°21W 323 k
Lauenburg = Lębork Poland 54°33N 17°46E 184 D4
Lauenburg Germany 53°22N 10°32E 178 B6
Lauenburgische Seen △ Germany 53°38N 10°45E 178 B6
Lauf Germany 49°30N 11°16E 179 F7
Laufás Iceland 65°53N 18°4W 155 B8
Laugar Iceland 65°15N 21°48W 155 B5
Laugarás Iceland 64°7N 20°30W 155 C6
Laugarbakki Iceland 65°20N 20°55W 155 B6
Laugarvatn Iceland 64°13N 20°44W 155 C6
Lauge Koch Kyst Greenland 75°45N 57°45W 295 B20
Laughlin U.S.A. 35°10N 114°34W 305 J6
Laujar de Andarax Spain 37°0N 2°54W 197 H2
Laukaa Finland 62°24N 25°56E 160 E21
Laulau, Bahia N. Marianas 15°8N 145°45E 302 e
Launceston Tas., Australia 41°24S 147°8E 281 G4
Launceston Corn., U.K. 50°38N 4°22W 169 G3
Laune → Ireland 52°7N 9°47W 166 D2
Launglon Bok Burma 13°50N 97°54E 236 F1
Laupheim Germany 48°14N 9°52E 179 G5
Laura Queens., Australia 15°32S 144°32E 280 B3
Laura S. Austral., Australia 33°10S 138°18E 282 B3
Laureana di Borrello Italy 38°30N 16°5E 201 D9
Laurel Fla., U.S.A. 27°8N 82°27W 317 H7
Laurel Ind., U.S.A. 39°30N 85°11W 311 E11
Laurel Miss., U.S.A. 31°41N 89°8W 315 F10
Laurel Mont., U.S.A. 45°40N 108°46W 304 D9
Laurel Bay U.S.A. 32°27N 80°47W 316 C9
Laurel Hill U.S.A. 40°14N 79°6W 312 F5
Laurencekirk U.K. 56°50N 2°28W 167 E6
Laurens Iowa, U.S.A. 42°51N 94°52W 310 B2
Laurens S.C., U.S.A. 34°30N 82°1W 315 D13
Laurentian Plateau Canada 52°0N 70°0W 299 B6
Lauria Italy 40°2N 15°50E 201 B8
Laurie L. Canada 56°35N 101°57W 297 B8
Laurinburg U.S.A. 34°47N 79°28W 315 D15
Laurium U.S.A. 47°14N 88°27W 308 B9
Lausanne Switz. 46°32N 6°38E 179 J2
Laut Indonesia 4°45N 108°0E 235 B3
Laut, Pulau Indonesia 3°40S 116°10E 235 C5
Laut Kecil, Kepulauan Indonesia 4°45S 115°40E 235 C5
Lautaro Chile 38°31S 72°27W 336 A2
Lauterbach Germany 50°37N 9°24E 178 E5
Lauterecken Germany 49°38N 7°35E 179 F3
Lautoka Fiji 17°37S 177°27E 287 A1
L'Autre Bord Guadeloupe 16°20N 61°20W 322 e
Lauttasaari Finland 60°9N 24°53E 121 C2
Lauzès France 44°34N 1°35E 174 D5
Lava → Russia 54°37N 21°14E 184 D8
Lava Beds △ U.S.A. 41°40N 121°30W 304 F3
Lavagh More Ireland 54°46N 8°6W 166 B3
Lavagna Italy 44°18N 9°20E 198 D6
Laval France 48°4N 0°48W 172 D6
Laval-des-Rapides Canada 45°33N 73°42W 130 A1
Lavalle Argentina 28°15S 65°15W 334 B2
Lāvān Iran 26°48N 53°22E 247 E7
Lavanggu Solomon Is. 11°36S 160°16E 287 N11
Lavant Canada 45°3N 76°42W 313 A8
Lāvar Meydān Iran 30°20N 54°30E 247 D7
Lavara Greece 41°19N 26°22E 203 E10
Lavardac France 44°12N 0°20E 174 D4
Lavaur France 43°40N 1°49E 174 E5
Lavelanet France 42°57N 1°51E 174 F5
Lavello Italy 41°3N 15°48E 201 A8
L'Averdy, C. Papua N. G. 5°33S 155°4E 286 C8
Lavers Hill Australia 38°40S 143°25E 282 E5
Laverton Australia 28°44S 122°29E 279 E3
Lavik Norway 61°6N 5°25E 164 C2
Lavis Italy 46°8N 11°7E 198 B8
Lavīzān Iran 35°47N 51°30E 132 A2
Lavos Portugal 40°6N 8°49W 194 E2
Lavoutte, Anse St. Lucia 14°5N 60°55W 323 m
Lavradio Portugal 38°40N 9°2W 126 A2
Lavras Brazil 21°20S 45°0W 333 F3
Lavre Portugal 38°46N 8°22W 195 G2
Lavrio Greece 37°40N 24°4E 204 D6
Lavris Greece 35°25N 24°40E 207 E5
Lavumisa Swaziland 27°20S 31°55E 271 C5
Lavushi Manda △ Zambia 12°46S 31°0E 269 E3
Lawa Phil. 6°12N 125°41E 233 H5
Lawa-an Phil. 11°51N 125°5E 233 F5
Lawaki Fiji 17°40S 178°35E 287 A2
Lawas Malaysia 4°55N 115°25E 235 B5
Lawdar Yemen 13°53N 45°52E 248 D4
Lawele Indonesia 5°13S 122°57E 231 F6
Lawit Indonesia 1°23N 112°55E 235 B4
Lawksawk Burma 21°15N 96°52E 241 E6
Lawn Hill = Boodjamulla △ Australia 18°15S 138°6E 280 B2
Lawndale U.S.A. 41°50N 87°42W 119 B2
Lawne L. U.S.A. 28°33N 81°26W 133 A2
Lawqah Si. Arabia 29°49N 42°45E 246 D4
Lawra Ghana 10°39N 2°51W 262 C4
Lawrence N.Z. 45°55S 169°41E 285 F4
Lawrence Ind., U.S.A. 39°50N 86°2W 311 E10
Lawrence Kans., U.S.A. 38°58N 95°14W 308 F6
Lawrence Mass., U.S.A. 42°43N 71°10W 313 D13
Lawrence Heights Canada 43°43N 79°25W 141 A2
Lawrenceburg Ind., U.S.A. 39°6N 84°52W 311 E12
Lawrenceburg Ky., U.S.A. 38°2N 84°54W 311 F12
Lawrenceburg Tenn., U.S.A. 35°14N 87°20W 315 D11
Lawrenceville Ga., U.S.A. 33°57N 83°59W 316 B6
Lawrenceville Ill., U.S.A. 38°44N 87°41W 311 F9
Lawrenceville Pa., U.S.A. 41°59N 77°8W 312 E7
Laws U.S.A. 37°24N 118°20W 306 H8
Lawson U.S.A. 39°26N 94°12W 310 E2
Lawtey U.S.A. 30°3N 82°5W 316 E7
Lawton Mich., U.S.A. 42°10N 85°50W 311 B11
Lawton Okla., U.S.A. 34°37N 98°25W 314 D5
Lawu Indonesia 7°40S 111°13E 235 D4
Lawz, J. al Si. Arabia 28°40N 35°20E 246 D2
Laxå Sweden 58°59N 14°37E 163 F8
Laxamýri Iceland 65°58N 17°29W 155 B9
Laxford, L. U.K. 58°24N 5°6W 167 C3
Laxou France 48°41N 6°8E 173 D13
Lay → France 46°18N 1°17W 174 B2
Layari Pakistan 24°52N 67°0E 123 A2
Layari → Pakistan 24°52N 66°58E 123 A1
Layla Si. Arabia 22°10N 46°40E 248 B4
Laylān Iraq 35°18N 44°31E 246 C5
Layon → France 47°20N 0°45W 172 E6
Layou St. Vincent 13°12N 61°17W 323 n
Layou → Dominica 15°23N 61°21W 323 k
Laysan I. U.S.A. 25°50N 171°50W 302 F9
Layton Fla., U.S.A. 24°50N 80°47W 317 L9
Layton Utah, U.S.A. 41°4N 111°58W 304 F8
Laytonville U.S.A. 39°41N 123°29W 304 G2
Laza Burma 26°30N 97°38E 241 B6
Lazarata Greece 38°47N 20°40E 207 B2
Lazarev Russia 52°13N 141°30E 215 D15
Lazarev Sea S. Ocean 67°30S 3°0W 151 C2
Lazarevac Serbia 44°23N 20°17E 202 B4
Lazarevskoye Russia 43°55N 39°21E 191 J4
Lazarivo Madag. 23°54S 44°59E 272 C1
Lázaro Cárdenas Mexico 17°55N 102°11W 318 D4
Lazdijai Lithuania 54°14N 23°31E 184 D10
Lazhuglung China 34°52N 81°24E 217 F10
Lazi Phil. 9°8N 123°38E 233 G4
Łazienki Palace Warsaw, Poland 142 c3
Łazienkowski Park Poland 52°13N 21°1E 142 B2
Lazio □ Italy 42°10N 12°30E 199 F9
Lazo Moldova 47°33N 28°2E 183 C13
Lazo Russia 43°25N 133°55E 220 C6
Lbishchensk = Chapaev Kazakhstan 50°25N 51°10E 190 E10
Le Beausset France 43°12N 5°48E 175 E9
Le Bélier Réunion 21°2S 55°28E 272 f
Le Bic Canada 48°20N 68°41W 299 C6
Le Blanc France 46°37N 1°3E 174 B5
Le Blanc-Mesnil France 48°56N 2°27E 134 A3
Le Bleymard France 44°30N 3°42E 174 D7
Le Bourget France 48°56N 2°25E 134 A3
Le Bourgneuf-la-Fôret France 48°10N 0°59W 172 D6
Le Bugue France 44°55N 0°56E 174 D4
Le Carbet Martinique 14°42N 61°11W 322 j
Le Cateau Cambrésis France 50°7N 3°32E 173 B10
Le Caylar France 43°51N 3°19E 174 E7
Le Chambon-Feugerolles France 45°24N 4°19E 175 C8
Le Chameau Guadeloupe 15°51N 61°35W 322 e
Le Châtelet France 46°38N 2°16E 173 F9
Le Chenoi Belgium 50°41N 4°18E 116 B2
Le Chesnay France 48°49N 2°8E 134 B1
Le Chesne France 49°30N 4°45E 173 C11
Le Cheylard France 44°55N 4°25E 175 D8
Le Christ de Saclay France 48°43N 1°59E 134 B2
Le Claire U.S.A. 41°36N 90°21W 310 C6
Le Conquet France 48°21N 4°46W 172 D2
Le Creusot France 46°48N 4°24E 173 F11
Le Croisic France 47°18N 2°30W 172 E4
Le Diamant Martinique 14°28N 61°2W 322 j
Le Donjon France 46°22N 3°48E 173 F10
Le Dorat France 46°14N 1°5E 174 B5
Le François Martinique 14°38N 60°57W 322 j
Le Gosier Guadeloupe 16°14N 61°29W 322 e
Le Grand Brûlé Réunion 21°14S 55°47E 272 f
Le Grand-Lucé France 47°52N 0°28E 172 E7
Le Grand-Pressigny France 46°55N 0°48E 172 F7
Le Grand-Quevilly France 49°24N 1°3E 172 C8
Le Gris Gris Mauritius 20°31S 57°32E 272 e
Le Gros Morne Réunion 21°5S 55°28E 272 f
Le Havre France 49°30N 0°5E 172 C7
Le Kremlin-Bicêtre France 48°48N 2°21E 134 B3
Le Lamentin Martinique 14°35N 61°2W 322 j
Le Lavandou France 43°8N 6°22E 175 E10
Le Lion-d'Angers France 47°37N 0°43W 172 E6
Le Lorrain Martinique 14°48N 61°3W 322 j
Le Louroux-Béconnais France 47°30N 0°55W 172 E6
Le Luc France 43°23N 6°21E 175 E10
Le Lude France 47°39N 0°9E 172 E7
Le Maire, Estr. de Argentina 54°50S 65°0W 336 D4
Le Mans France 48°0N 0°10E 172 E7
Le Marigot Martinique 14°50N 61°4W 322 j
Le Marin Martinique 14°27N 60°55W 322 j
Le Mars U.S.A. 42°47N 96°10W 308 D5
Le Mayet-de-Montagne France 46°4N 3°40E 173 F10
Le Mêle-sur-Sarthe France 48°31N 0°22E 172 D7
Le Mesnil-le-Roi France 48°56N 2°7E 134 A1
Le Monastier-sur-Gazeille France 44°57N 3°59E 174 D7
Le Monêtier-les-Bains France 44°58N 6°30E 175 D10
Le Mont-Dore France 45°35N 2°49E 174 C6
Le Mont-St-Michel France 48°40N 1°30W 172 D5
Le Morne Brabant Mauritius 20°27S 57°19E 272 e
Le Morne Rouge Martinique 14°47N 61°8W 322 j
Le Morne-Vert Martinique 14°42N 61°8W 322 j
Le Moule Guadeloupe 16°20N 61°22W 322 e
Le Moyne, L. Canada 56°45N 68°47W 299 A6
Le Muy France 43°28N 6°34E 175 E10
Le Palais France 47°20N 3°10W 172 E3
Le Pecq France 48°53N 2°6E 134 A1
Le Perreux France 48°50N 2°29E 134 A3
Le Perthus France 42°30N 2°53E 174 F6
Le Pin France 48°55N 2°37E 134 A4
Le Plessis-Robinson France 48°47N 2°15E 134 B2
Le Plessis-Trévise France 48°48N 2°34E 134 B4
Le Port Réunion 20°56S 55°18E 272 f
Le Port-Marly France 48°52N 2°6E 134 A1
Le Pré-St-Gervais France 48°53N 2°23E 134 A3
Le Prêcheur Martinique 14°48N 61°14W 322 j
Le Puy-en-Velay France 45°3N 3°52E 174 C7
Le Raincy France 48°53N 2°31E 134 A4
Le Raysville U.S.A. 41°50N 76°10W 313 E8
Le Robert Martinique 14°40N 60°56W 322 j
Le Roy Ill., U.S.A. 40°21N 88°46W 311 D8
Le Roy N.Y., U.S.A. 42°58N 77°59W 312 D7
Le St-Esprit Martinique 14°34N 60°56W 322 j
Le Souffleur Guadeloupe 16°19N 61°2W 322 e
Le Sueur U.S.A. 44°28N 93°55W 308 C7
Le Tampon Réunion 21°16S 55°32E 272 f
Le Teil France 44°33N 4°40E 175 D8
Le Teilleul France 48°32N 0°53W 172 D6
Le Theil France 48°16N 0°42E 172 D7
Le Thillot France 47°53N 6°46E 173 E13
Le Thuy Vietnam 17°14N 106°49E 236 D6
Le Touquet-Paris-Plage France 50°30N 1°36E 173 B8
Le Tréport France 50°3N 1°20E 172 B8
Le Trou à Diable Guadeloupe 15°57N 61°14W 322 e
Le Val-d'Ajol France 47°55N 6°30E 173 E13
Le Val Nature Park Mauritius 20°22S 57°37E 272 e
Le Vauclin Martinique 14°33N 60°52W 322 j
Le Verdon-sur-Mer France 45°33N 1°4W 174 C2
Le Vésinet France 48°54N 2°8E 134 A1
Le Vigan France 43°59N 3°36E 174 E7
Lea → U.K. 51°31N 0°1E 169 F8
Lea Bridge U.K. 51°33N 0°2W 115 A3
Lea Lea Papua N. G. 9°17S 146°59E 286 E4
Leach Cambodia 12°21N 103°46E 237 F4
Lead U.S.A. 44°21N 103°46W 308 C2
Leader Canada 50°50N 109°30W 297 C7
Leadville U.S.A. 39°15N 106°18W 304 G10
Leaf → U.S.A. 30°59N 88°44W 315 F10
Leaf Rapids Canada 56°30N 99°59W 297 B9
Leaghur, L. Australia 33°35S 143°3E 282 B5
Leaksville = Eden U.S.A. 36°29N 79°53W 315 C15
Lealui Zambia 15°10S 23°2E 265 F4
Leamington Canada 42°3N 82°36W 312 D2
Leamington N.Z. 37°55S 175°30E 284 D4
Leamington Utah, U.S.A. 39°32N 112°17W 304 G7
Leamington Spa = Royal Leamington Spa U.K. 52°18N 1°31W 169 E6
Le'an China 27°22N 115°48E 229 D10
Leandro Norte Alem Argentina 27°34S 55°15W 335 B4
Leane, L. Ireland 52°2N 9°32W 166 D2
Learmonth Australia 22°13S 114°10E 278 D1
Leary U.S.A. 31°29N 84°31W 316 D5
Leaside Canada 43°42N 79°22W 141 A2
Leask Canada 53°5N 106°45W 297 C7
Leatherhead U.K. 51°18N 0°20W 169 F7
Leavdnja = Lakselv Norway 70°2N 25°0E 160 A21
Leavenworth Ind., U.S.A. 38°12N 86°21W 311 F10
Leavenworth Kans., U.S.A. 39°19N 94°55W 308 F6
Leavenworth Wash., U.S.A. 47°36N 120°40W 304 C3
Leawood U.S.A. 38°58N 94°37W 310 F2
Łeba Poland 54°45N 17°32E 184 D4
Łeba → Poland 54°46N 17°33E 184 D4
Lebach Germany 49°25N 6°54E 179 F2
Lebak Phil. 6°32N 124°5E 233 H5
Lebam U.S.A. 46°34N 123°33W 306 D3
Lebane Serbia 42°56N 21°44E 202 D5
Lebango Congo 0°39N 14°21E 264 B2
Lebango → Congo 0°2N 14°52E 264 B2
Lebanon Fla., U.S.A. 29°10N 82°37W 317 F7
Lebanon Ill., U.S.A. 38°38N 89°49W 310 F7
Lebanon Ind., U.S.A. 40°3N 86°28W 311 D10
Lebanon Kans., U.S.A. 39°49N 98°33W 308 F4
Lebanon Ky., U.S.A. 37°34N 85°15W 309 G11
Lebanon Mo., U.S.A. 37°41N 92°40W 310 G4
Lebanon N.H., U.S.A. 43°39N 72°15W 313 C12
Lebanon Ohio, U.S.A. 39°26N 84°13W 311 E12
Lebanon Oreg., U.S.A. 44°32N 122°55W 304 D2
Lebanon Pa., U.S.A. 40°20N 76°26W 313 F8
Lebanon Tenn., U.S.A. 36°12N 86°18W 315 C11
Lebanon ■ Asia 34°0N 36°0E 250 E7
Lebanon Junction U.S.A. 37°50N 85°44W 311 G11
Lebap □ Turkmenistan 40°0N 63°0E 216 D6
Lebec U.S.A. 34°51N 118°52W 307 L8
Lebedyan Russia 53°0N 39°10E 189 F10
Lebedyn Ukraine 50°35N 34°30E 189 G8
Lebel-sur-Quévillon Canada 49°3N 76°59W 298 C4
Leblon Brazil 22°59S 43°14W 135 B1
Lebo Dem. Rep. of the Congo 4°30N 23°58E 264 B4
Lebomboberge S. Africa 24°30S 32°0E 271 B5
Lębork Poland 54°33N 17°46E 184 D4
Lebowakgomo S. Africa 24°12S 29°30E 271 B4
Lebrija Spain 36°53N 6°5W 195 J4
Łebsko, Jezioro Poland 54°40N 17°25E 184 D4
Lebu Chile 37°40S 73°47W 334 D1
Leca da Palmeira Portugal 41°12N 8°42W 194 D2
Lecce Italy 40°23N 18°11E 201 B11
Lecco Italy 45°51N 9°23E 198 C6
Lecco, L. di Italy 45°55N 9°19E 198 C6
Lécera Spain 41°13N 0°43W 196 D4
Lech Austria 47°13N 10°9E 180 D3
Lech → Germany 48°43N 10°56E 179 G6
Lechang China 25°10N 113°20E 229 E9
Lechena Greece 37°57N 21°16E 204 D3
Lechtaler Alpen Austria 47°15N 10°30E 180 D3
Lecontes Mills U.S.A. 41°5N 78°17W 312 E6
Lectoure France 43°56N 0°38E 174 E4
Łęczna Poland 51°18N 22°53E 185 G9
Łęczyca Poland 52°5N 19°15E 185 F6
Ledang, Gunung Malaysia 2°22N 102°37E 237 L4
Ledesma Spain 41°6N 5°59W 194 D5
Lediba Dem. Rep. of the Congo 3°1S 16°34E 264 C3
Lédo, Cabo Angola 9°43S 13°12E 265 D2
Ledong China 18°41N 109°5E 236 C7
Leduc Canada 53°15N 113°30W 296 C6
Lee London, U.K. 51°27N 0°0 125 B4
Lee Fla., U.S.A. 30°25N 83°18W 316 E6
Lee Mass., U.S.A. 42°19N 73°15W 313 D11
Lee → Ireland 51°53N 8°56W 166 E3
Lee Vining U.S.A. 37°58N 119°7W 306 H7
Leech L. U.S.A. 47°10N 94°24W 308 B6
Leechburg U.S.A. 40°37N 79°36W 312 F5
Leeds W. Yorks., U.K. 53°48N 1°33W 168 D6
Leeds Ala., U.S.A. 33°33N 86°33W 315 E11
Leek Neths. 53°10N 6°24E 170 A6
Leek Staffs., U.K. 53°7N 2°1W 168 D5
Leeman Australia 29°57S 114°58E 279 E1
Leeper U.S.A. 41°22N 79°18W 312 E5
Leer Germany 53°13N 7°26E 178 B3
Lee's Summit U.S.A. 38°55N 94°23W 310 F2
Leesburg Fla., U.S.A. 28°49N 81°53W 317 G8
Leesburg Ga., U.S.A. 31°44N 84°10W 316 D5
Leesburg Ohio, U.S.A. 39°21N 83°33W 311 E13
Leeston N.Z. 43°45S 172°19E 285 D7
Leesville U.S.A. 31°8N 93°16W 314 F8
Leeton Australia 34°33S 146°23E 283 C7
Leetonia U.S.A. 40°53N 80°45W 312 F4
Leeu Gamka S. Africa 32°47S 21°59E 270 D3
Leeuwarden Neths. 53°15N 5°48E 170 A5
Leeuwin, C. Australia 34°20S 115°9E 279 F2
Leeuwin Naturaliste △ Australia 34°6S 115°3E 279 F2
Leeward Is. Atl. Oc. 16°30N 63°30W 321 C7
Léfini Congo 2°55S 15°39E 264 C3
Léfini → Congo 2°56S 16°9E 264 C3
Léfini △ Congo 2°55S 15°20E 264 C3
Lefka Cyprus 35°6N 32°51E 207 E8
Lefkada Greece 38°40N 20°43E 207 B2
Lefkimi Greece 39°25N 20°3E 206 C10
Lefkimis, Akra Greece 39°29N 20°4E 206 C10
Lefkoniko Cyprus 35°18N 33°44E 207 E9
Lefroy Canada 44°16N 79°34W 312 B5
Lefroy, L. Australia 31°21S 121°40E 279 F3
Leg → Poland 50°42N 21°50E 185 H8
Leganés Spain 40°19N 3°45W 127 B1
Legazpi Phil. 13°10N 123°45E 232 E4
Legazpi Madrid, Spain 40°23N 3°41W 127 B1
Lège-Cap-Ferret France 44°48N 1°9W 174 D2
Lege Hida Ethiopia 7°56N 41°4E 257 F5
Legendre I. Australia 20°22S 116°55E 278 D2
Leghorn = Livorno Italy 43°33N 10°19E 198 E7
Legian Indonesia 8°42S 115°10E 231 K18
Legionowo Poland 52°25N 20°50E 185 F7
Legnago Italy 45°11N 11°18E 199 C8
Legnano Italy 45°36N 8°54E 198 C5
Legnica Poland 51°12N 16°10E 185 G3
Legrad Croatia 46°17N 16°51E 199 B13
Leh India 34°9N 77°35E 243 B7
Lehigh Acres U.S.A. 26°36N 81°39W 317 J8
Lehighton U.S.A. 40°50N 75°43W 313 F9
Lehliu Romania 44°29N 26°50E 183 F11
Leho South Sudan 7°7N 33°52E 257 F3
Lehrte Germany 52°22N 9°58E 178 C5
Lehtisaari Finland 60°10N 24°51E 121 B2

Lehua I. *U.S.A.* 22°1N 160°6W **302 A1**
Lehututu *Botswana* 23°54S 21°55E **270 B3**
Lei Shui *China* 26°55N 112°35E **229 D9**
Lei Yue Mun *China* 22°17N 114°14E **122 B2**
Leiah *Pakistan* 30°58N 70°58E **242 D4**
Leião *Portugal* 38°43N 9°17W **126 A1**
Leibnitz *Austria* 46°47N 15°34E **180 E8**
Leibo *China* 28°11N 103°34E **228 C4**
Leicester *U.K.* 52°38N 1°8W **169 E6**
Leicester City □ *U.K.* 52°38N 1°8W **169 E6**
Leicester Square *London, U.K.* **125 b3**
Leicestershire □ *U.K.* 52°41N 1°17W **169 E6**
Leichhardt *Australia* 33°53S 151°9E **139 B1**
Leichhardt → *Australia* 17°35S 139°48E **280 B2**
Leichhardt Ra. *Australia* 20°46S 147°40E **280 C4**
Leiden *Neths.* 52°9N 4°30E **170 B4**
Leie → *Belgium* 51°2N 3°45E **170 C3**
Leifers = Láives *Italy* 46°26N 11°20E **199 B8**
Leigh → *Australia* 38°18S 144°30E **282 E6**
Leigh Creek *Australia* 30°38S 138°26E **280 D2**
Leikang *Norway* 62°15N 5°47E **164 B2**
Leikanger *Sogn & Fjordane, Norway* 62°8N 5°18E **164 B2**
Leikanger *Sogn & Fjordane, Norway* 61°10N 6°51E **164 C3**
Leiktho *Burma* 19°13N 96°35E **241 F6**
Leimen *Germany* 49°21N 8°41E **179 F4**
Leimus *Nic.* 14°40N 84°3W **320 D3**
Leine → *Germany* 52°43N 9°36E **178 C5**
Leinefelde *Germany* 51°23N 10°19E **178 D6**
Leinster *Australia* 27°51S 120°36E **279 E3**
Leinster □ *Ireland* 53°3N 7°8W **166 C4**
Leinster, Mt. *Ireland* 52°37N 6°46W **166 D5**
Leipalingis *Lithuania* 54°5N 23°51E **184 D10**
Leipe = Lipno *Poland* 52°49N 19°15E **185 F6**
Leipzig *Germany* 51°18N 12°22E **178 D8**
Leira *Norway* 60°58N 9°17E **164 D6**
Leiria *Portugal* 39°46N 8°53W **194 F2**
Leiria □ *Portugal* 39°46N 8°53W **194 F2**
Leirvassbu *Norway* 61°33N 8°13E **164 C5**
Leirvik *Norway* 59°47N 5°28E **164 E2**
Leishan *China* 26°15N 108°20E **228 D7**
Leisler, Mt. *Australia* 23°23S 129°20E **278 D4**
Leisure City *U.S.A.* 25°30N 80°26W **317 K9**
Leith *U.K.* 55°59N 3°11W **121 B3**
Leith Hill *U.K.* 51°11N 0°22W **169 F7**
Leitha → *Europe* 47°54N 16°13E **181 D10**
Leitir Ceanainn = Letterkenny *Ireland* 54°57N 7°45W **166 B4**
Leitrim *Ireland* 54°0N 8°5W **166 B3**
Leitrim □ *Ireland* 54°8N 8°0W **166 B4**
Leitza *Spain* 43°5N 1°55W **196 B3**
Leiyang *China* 26°27N 112°45E **229 D9**
Leizhou *China* 20°52N 110°8E **229 G8**
Leizhou Bandao *China* 21°0N 110°0E **228 G7**
Leizhou Wan *China* 20°50N 110°20E **229 G8**
Lek → *Neths.* 51°54N 4°35E **170 C4**
Leka *Norway* 65°5N 11°35E **160 D14**
Lekani *Greece* 41°10N 24°35E **203 B3**
Lekbibaj *Albania* 42°17N 19°56E **202 D3**
Lekki *Nigeria* 43°20N 2°32W **196 B2**
Lékéti, Mt. *Congo* 2°34S 14°17E **264 C2**
Lekki *Nigeria* 6°26N 3°28E **264 B2**
Lekki Lagoon *Nigeria* 6°30N 4°7E **263 D5**
Léko *Mali* 13°37N 9°2W **262 C3**
Lékoli-Pandaka △ *Congo* 0°41N 14°56E **264 C2**
Lékoni *Gabon* 1°35S 14°14E **264 C2**
Lékoni → *Gabon* 1°35S 14°14E **264 C2**
Lekoui *Burkina Faso* 12°37N 3°40W **262 C4**
Leksand *Sweden* 60°44N 15°1E **162 D9**
Leksura = Lentekhi *Georgia* 42°47N 42°45E **191 J6**
Leland *Mich., U.S.A.* 45°1N 85°45W **309 C11**
Leland *Miss., U.S.A.* 33°24N 90°54W **313 H9**
Lelâng *Sweden* 59°10N 12°5E **162 E6**
Lelepa *Vanuatu* 17°35S 168°11E **287 M11**
Leleque *Argentina* 42°28S 71°0W **336 B2**
Leli *Solomon Is.* 8°42S 161°4E **287 M11**
Leling *China* 37°44N 117°13E **227 F9**
Léloumo *Guinea* 11°11N 12°56W **262 C2**
Lelu *Burma* 19°4N 95°30E **241 F5**
Lelydorp *Suriname* 5°42N 55°14W **329 B6**
Lelystad *Neths.* 52°30N 5°25E **170 B5**
Lem *Denmark* 56°1N 8°24E **163 H2**
Lema *Nigeria* 12°58N 4°13E **263 C5**
Lema Shilindi *Ethiopia* 4°50N 42°6E **257 G5**
Léman, L. *Europe* 46°26N 6°30E **173 F13**
Lemankoa *Papua N. G.* 5°3S 154°34E **288 G8**
Lembar *Indonesia* 8°45S 116°4E **231 K19**
Lemberg = Lviv *Ukraine* 49°50N 24°0E **177 D13**
Lembongan, Nusa *Indonesia* 8°40S 115°27E **231 K18**
Lembuak *Indonesia* 8°36S 116°11E **231 K19**
Leme *Brazil* 22°58S 43°10W **335 B5**
Lemera *Dem. Rep. of the Congo* 3°0S 28°55E **268 C2**
Lemery *Phil.* 13°51N 120°56E **232 E3**
Lemfu *Dem. Rep. of the Congo* 5°18S 15°13E **265 D3**
Lemhi Ra. *U.S.A.* 44°0N 113°0W **304 D7**
Lemmer *Neths.* 52°51N 5°43E **170 B5**
Lemmon *U.S.A.* 45°57N 102°10W **308 C2**
Lemon Grove *U.S.A.* 32°44N 117°1W **307 N9**
Lemoore *U.S.A.* 36°18N 119°46W **306 J7**
Lemotol B. *Micronesia* 7°21N 151°35E **287 T17**
Lemoyne *Canada* 45°29N 73°29W **130 B3**
Lempdes *France* 45°22N 3°17E **174 C7**
Lemsid *W. Sahara* 26°33N 13°51W **260 C2**
Lemukutan *Indonesia* 0°45N 108°43E **235 B3**
Lemvig *Denmark* 56°33N 8°20E **163 H2**
Lemyethna *Burma* 17°36N 95°9E **241 G5**
Lena *U.S.A.* 42°23N 89°49W **310 B7**
Lena → *Russia* 72°52N 126°40E **215 B13**
Lenadoon Pt. *Ireland* 54°18N 9°3W **166 B2**
Lenakel *Vanuatu* 19°38S 169°16E **287 N7**
Lenart *Slovenia* 46°36N 15°48E **199 B12**
Lenartovce *Slovak Rep.* 48°18N 20°20E **181 C13**
Lencloître *France* 46°50N 0°20E **172 F7**
Lençóis *Brazil* 12°35S 41°24W **333 D3**
Lençóis Maranhenses △ *Brazil* 2°30S 43°0W **332 B3**
Lendava *Slovenia* 46°34N 16°33E **199 B13**
Lendinara *Italy* 45°5N 11°36E **199 B8**
Lenger *Kazakhstan* 42°12N 69°54E **217 D7**
Lengerich *Germany* 52°11N 7°52E **178 C3**
Lenggong *Malaysia* 5°6N 100°58E **237 K3**
Lenggries *Germany* 47°41N 11°55E **179 H7**
Léngoué → *Congo* 1°15N 15°38E **264 B3**
Lengshuijiang *China* 27°40N 111°33E **229 D8**
Lengshuitan *China* 26°27N 111°35E **229 D8**
Lengua de Vaca, Pta. *Chile* 30°14S 71°38W **334 C1**
Lengwe △ *Malawi* 16°14S 34°45E **269 F3**
Lengwethen = Lunino *Russia* 54°44N 22°34E
Lengyeltóti *Hungary* 46°40N 17°40E **182 D2**
Lengyeltóthács = Lengyeltóti *Hungary* 46°40N 17°40E **182 D2**
Lenhovda *Sweden* 57°0N 15°16E **163 G9**
Lenin *Russia* 54°53N 37°36E **188 D9**
Lenin Mausoleum *Moscow, Russia* **129 B2**
Lenina, Kanal → *Russia* 43°44N 51°7E **217 D17**
Leninabad = Khüjand *Tajikistan* 40°17N 69°37E **217 D7**
Leninakan = Gyumri *Armenia* 40°47N 43°50E **191 K6**
Lenine *Ukraine* 45°17N 35°46E **189 K8**

Leningrad = Sankt-Peterburg *Russia* 59°55N 30°20E **137 B1**
Leningrad □ *Russia* 59°40N 32°0E **188 C7**
Leninogorsk *Kazakhstan* 50°20N 83°30E **217 B10**
Lenino *Russia* 54°44N 86°10E **217 B11**
Lenino = Leninsk-Kuznetskiy
Lenino *Russia* 55°38N 37°39E **129 C3**
Leninogorsk *Russia* 54°36N 52°30E **216 B4**
Leninsk = Petrodvorets *Russia* 59°52N 29°54E **188 C5**
Leninsk *Russia* 48°40N 45°15E **91 F7**
Leninsk-Kuznetskiy *Russia* 54°44N 86°10E **217 B11**
Lenin-Turkmensky = Türkmenabat *Turkmenistan* 39°6N 63°34E **247 B9**
L'Escala *Spain* 42°7N 3°8E **196 C8**
L'Escalier *Mauritius* 20°28S 57°36E **272 e**
Leschnitz = Leśnica *Poland* 50°26N 18°11E **185 H5**
L'Escoumins *Canada* 48°25N 69°24W **299 C6**
Lenin *Russia* 54°53N 37°36E **188 D9**
Leshukonskoye *Russia* 64°54N 45°46E **186 B8**
Leshwe → *Dem. Rep. of the Congo* 12°45S 29°30E **269 E2**
L'Ésigny *France* 48°44N 2°37E **134 B4**
Lésina *Italy* 41°52N 15°21E **199 G12**
Lésina, L. di *Italy* 41°53N 15°26E **199 G12**
Lesjaskog *Norway* 62°14N 8°22E **164 B5**
Lesjaverk *Norway* 62°12N 8°34E **164 B5**
Lesjöfors *Sweden* 59°58N 14°11E **162 E8**
Leskhimstroy = Syeverodonetsk *Ukraine* 48°53N 38°35E **189 H10**
Lesko *Poland* 49°30N 22°23E **185 J9**
Lesko I. *Antarctica* 56°0S 28°0W **151 B1**
Leskovac *Serbia* 43°0N 21°58E **202 C5**
Leskovik *Albania* 40°10N 20°34E **202 F4**
Leslau = Włocławek *Poland* 52°40N 19°3E **185 F6**
Leslie *Ga., U.S.A.* 31°57N 84°5W **316 D5**
Leslie *Mich., U.S.A.* 42°27N 84°26W **311 B12**
Leśna *Poland* 51°1N 15°15E **185 G2**
Lesneven *France* 48°35N 4°20W **172 D2**
Leśnica *Poland* 50°26N 18°11E **185 H5**
Leśnica *Serbia* 44°39N 19°20E **202 B3**
Lesnoi = Umba *Russia* 66°42N 34°11E **186 A5**
Lesnoye *Russia* 58°15N 35°18E **188 C8**
Lesnozavodskaya *Russia* 59°51N 30°29E **137 B2**
Lesopilnoye *Russia* 46°44N 134°20E **207 A7**
Lesotho ■ *Africa* 29°40S 28°0E **271 C4**
Lesozavodsk *Russia* 45°30N 133°29E **220 B6**
Lesparre-Médoc *France* 45°18N 0°57W **174 C3**
L'Espluga de Francolí *Spain* 41°24N 1°7E **196 D6**
Lessay *France* 49°14N 1°30W **172 C5**
Lesse → *Belgium* 50°15N 4°54E **170 D4**
Lesse et Lomme △ *Belgium* 50°8N 5°9E **170 D5**
Lessebo *Sweden* 56°45N 15°16E **163 H9**
Lesser Antilles *W. Indies* 15°0N 61°0W **321 D7**
Lesser Slave L. *Canada* 55°30N 115°25W **296 B5**
Lesser Sunda Is. *Indonesia* 8°0S 120°0E **235 D5**
Lessines *Belgium* 50°42N 3°50E **170 D3**
Lester B. Pearson Int., Toronto ✈ (YYZ) *Canada* 43°46N 79°35W **141 A1**
L'Esterre *Grenada* 12°28N 61°29W **323 q**
Lestershire = Johnson City *U.S.A.* 42°7N 75°58W **313 D9**
Lestock *Canada* 51°19N 103°59W **297 C8**
Lesuer *L. Australia* 13°50S 127°17E **278 B4**
Lesueur △ *Australia* 30°11S 115°10E **279 F2**
L'Étang-la-Ville *France* 48°52N 2°4E **134 A1**
L'Étang-Salé *Réunion* 21°15S 55°23E **272 f**
Letaváltés *Hungary* 47°23N 21°54E **182 C6**
Letchworth *U.K.* 51°59N 0°13W **169 F7**
Letea, Ostrov *Romania* 45°18N 29°20E **183 E14**
Lethbridge *Canada* 49°45N 112°45W **296 D6**
Lethem *Guyana* 3°20N 59°50W **329 C6**
Leti, Kepulauan *Indonesia* 8°10S 128°0E **237 F7**
Leti Is. = Leti, Kepulauan *Indonesia* 8°10S 128°0E **237 F7**
Letiahau → *Botswana* 21°16S 24°0E **270 B3**
Leticia *Colombia* 4°9S 70°0W **328 D4**
Leting *China* 39°23N 118°55E **227 E10**
Letjiesbos *S. Africa* 32°34S 22°16E **270 D3**
Letlhakane *Botswana* 21°27S 25°30E **270 B4**
Letlhakeng *Botswana* 24°0S 24°59E **270 B3**
Letná *Prague, Czech Rep.* **135 a2**
Letñany *Czech Rep.* 50°8N 14°30E **135 B**
Letopolis = Ausîm *Egypt* 30°7N 31°8E **117 A1**
Letpadan *Burma* 17°45N 95°45E **241 G5**
Letpan *Burma* 19°28N 94°10E **241 F5**
Letsôk-aw Kyun *Burma* 11°30N 98°25E **237 G2**
Letterkenny *Ireland* 54°57N 7°45W **166 B4**
Leu *Romania* 44°10N 24°0E **183 E8**
Leuca *Angola* 11°34S 20°32E **265 G4**
Leucadia *U.S.A.* 33°4N 117°18W **307 M9**
Leucate *France* 42°50N 3°0E **174 F7**
Leucate, Étang de *France* 42°50N 3°3E **174 F7**
Leuk *Switz.* 46°19N 7°37E **179 J3**
Leuşeni *Moldova* 46°49N 28°12E **183 D13**
Leuser, Gunung *Indonesia* 3°46N 97°12E **234 B1**
Leusoali Amer. Samoa 14°15S 169°25W **302 f**
Leutkirch *Germany* 47°49N 10°1E **179 H6**
Leutschau = Levoča *Slovak Rep.* 49°2N 20°35E **181 B13**
Leuven *Belgium* 50°52N 4°42E **170 D4**
Leuze-en-Hainaut *Belgium* 50°36N 3°37E **170 D3**
Lev Tolstoy *Russia* 53°13N 39°29E **188 F10**
Levan *Albania* 40°40N 19°28E **202 F3**
Levanger *Norway* 63°45N 11°19E **160 E14**
Levant, Î. du *France* 43°3N 6°28E **175 E10**
Lévanto *Italy* 44°10N 9°38E **198 D6**
Lévanzo *Italy* 38°0N 12°20E **200 D5**
Leveld *Norway* 60°44N 8°33E **164 D5**
Levelland *U.S.A.* 33°35N 102°23W **314 E3**
Levelock *U.S.A.* 59°7N 156°51W **303 G8**
Leven *U.K.* 56°12N 3°0W **121 B5**
Leven, L. *U.K.* 56°12N 3°22W **121 B5**
Leven, Toraka *Madag.* 12°30S 47°45E **272 A2**
Levêque C. *Australia* 16°20S 123°0E **278 C3**
Levera C. *Grenada* 12°13N 61°38W **323 q**
Leverano *Italy* 40°17N 18°0E **201 B10**
Leverburgh *U.K.* 57°46N 7°0W **170 D3**
Leverett Glacier *Antarctica* 85°30S 140°0W **151 E14**
Leverkusen *Germany* 51°1N 7°1E **178 D3**
Levice *Slovak Rep.* 48°13N 18°35E **181 C11**
Lévico Terme *Italy* 46°0N 11°18E **199 C8**
Levie *France* 41°42N 9°7E **175 G13**
Levier *France* 46°58N 6°8E **173 F13**
Levin *N.Z.* 40°37S 175°18E **284 G4**
Lévis *Canada* 46°48N 71°9W **299 C5**
Levis, L. *Canada* 62°37N 117°58W **296 A5**
Levítha *Greece* 37°0N 26°28E **205 D8**
Levittown *N.Y., U.S.A.* 40°44N 73°31W **313 F11**
Levittown *Pa., U.S.A.* 40°9N 74°51W **313 E10**
Levka *Bulgaria* 41°52N 26°15E **203 E10**
Levka Oros *Greece* 35°18N 24°3E **207 E5**
Levkás = Lefkada *Greece* 38°40N 20°43E **207 E3**
Levkôsia = Nicosia *Cyprus* 35°10N 33°25E **207 D11**

Les Minquiers, Plateau des *Chan. Is.* 48°58N 2°8W **172 D4**
Les Moroubas *C.A.R.* 6°11N 20°13E **264 A4**
Les Pavillons-sous-Bois *France* 48°54N 2°30E **134 A4**
Les Pieux *France* 49°30N 1°48W **172 C5**
Les Ponts-de-Cé *France* 47°25N 0°30W **172 E6**
Les Riceys *France* 47°59N 4°22E **173 E11**
Les Sables-d'Olonne *France* 46°30N 1°45W **174 B2**
Les Tantes *Grenada* 12°19N 61°33W **323 q**
Les Trois-Bassins *Réunion* 21°5S 55°18E **272 f**
Les Trois-Îlets *Martinique* 14°32N 61°2W **322 j**
Les Vans *France* 44°25N 4°7E **175 D8**
Lesbos = Lesvos *Greece* 39°10N 26°20E **205 B8**
Leshan *China* 29°33N 103°41E **228 C4**
L'Escala *Spain* 42°7N 3°8E **196 C8**

Levoča *Slovak Rep.* 49°2N 20°35E **181 B13**
Levroux *France* 46°59N 1°38E **173 F8**
Levski *Bulgaria* 43°21N 25°10E **203 C9**
Levskigrad = Karlovo *Bulgaria* 42°38N 24°47E **203 D8**
Levuka *Fiji* 17°34S 179°0E **287 A2**
Lewe *Burma* 19°38N 96°7E **241 F6**
Lewes *E. Sussex, U.K.* 50°52N 0°1E **169 G8**
Lewes *Del., U.S.A.* 38°46N 75°9W **309 F16**
Lewin Brzeski *Poland* 5C°45N 17°37E **185 H4**
Lewis *U.K.* 58°9N 6°40W **167 C2**
Lewis → *U.S.A.* 45°51N 122°48W **308 E4**
Lewis, Butt of *U.K.* 58°31N 6°16W **167 C2**
Lewis and Clark △ *U.S.A.* 46°8N 123°53W **306 D3**
Lewis Pass *N.Z.* 42°3′S 172°11E **285 C7**
Lewis Ra. *Australia* 2C°3S 128°50E **278 D4**
Lewis Range *U.S.A.* 48°5N 113°5W **304 B7**
Lewis Run *U.S.A.* 41°52N 78°40W **312 E6**
Lewisburg *Ohio, U.S.A.* 39°51N 84°33E **311 E12**
Lewisburg *Pa., U.S.A.* 40°58N 76°54W **312 F8**
Lewisburg *Tenn., U.S.A.* 35°27N 86°48W **315 D11**
Lewisburg *W. Va., U.S.A.* 37°48N 80°27W **309 G13**
Lewisham □ *U.K.* 51°27N 0°1W **125 B3**
Lewisport *U.S.A.* 37°56N 86°54W **311 G10**
Lewiston *Idaho, U.S.A.* 46°25N 117°1W **304 C5**
Lewiston *Maine, U.S.A.* 44°6N 70°13W **309 D18**
Lewiston *N.Y., U.S.A.* 43°11N 79°3W **312 C5**
Lewiston *Ill., U.S.A.* 40°24N 90°9W **310 D5**
Lewistown *Mont., U.S.A.* 47°4N 109°26W **304 C9**
Lewistown *Pa., U.S.A.* 40°36N 77°34W **312 F7**
Lexington *Ga., U.S.A.* 33°52N 83°7W **316 B6**
Lexington *Ky., U.S.A.* 38°3N 84°30W **311 F12**
Lexington *Mass., U.S.A.* 42°27N 71°14W **314 f10**
Lexington *Mich., U.S.A.* 43°16N 82°32W **312 C2**
Lexington *Miss., U.S.A.* 33°7N 90°3W **313 J9**
Lexington *N.C., U.S.A.* 35°49N 80°15W **315 D14**
Lexington *N.Y., U.S.A.* 42°15N 74°22W **313 D10**
Lexington *Nebr., U.S.A.* 40°47N 99°45W **308 E4**
Lexington *Ohio, U.S.A.* 40°41N 82°35W **312 F2**
Lexington *S.C., U.S.A.* 33°59N 81°11W **316 B5**
Lexington *Tenn., U.S.A.* 35°39N 88°24W **315 D10**
Lexington *Va., U.S.A.* 37°47N 79°27W **309 G14**
Leyburn *U.K.* 54°19N 1°48W **168 C6**
Leye *China* 24°4N 106°29E **228 C6**
Leyeh *Taiwan* 23°28N 120°42E **225 C2**
Leyland *U.K.* 53°42N 2°43W **168 D5**
Leyre → *France* 44°39N 1°1W **174 D2**
Leyte *Phil.* 10°30N 125°0E **233 F5**
Leyte □ *Phil.* 11°0N 125°0E **233 F5**
Leyte Gulf *Phil.* 10°50N 125°25E **233 F5**
Leyton *U.K.* 51°33N 0°1W **125 A3**
Leytonstone *U.K.* 51°34N 0°0 **125 A4**
Lezajsk *Poland* 50°1N 22°25E **185 H9**
Lezay *France* 46°15N 0°1W **174 B3**
Lezhë *Albania* 41°47N 19°39E **202 E3**
Lezhi *China* 30°16N 105°0E **228 B5**
Lézignan-Corbières *France* 43°13N 2°43E **174 E6**
Lezoux *France* 45°49N 3°21E **174 C7**
Lgov *Russia* 51°42N 35°16E **189 G8**
Lhasa *China* 29°25N 90°58E **218 F7**
L'Haÿ-les-Roses *France* 48°46N 2°20E **134 B3**
Lhazê *China* 29°5N 87°38E **218 F6**
L'Hermite, I. *Chile* 55°50S 68°0W **336 G3**
Lhokkruet *Indonesia* 4°55N 95°24E **234 B1**
Lhokseumawe *Indonesia* 5°10N 97°10E **234 A1**
Lhoksukon *Indonesia* 5°2N 97°19E **234 A1**
L'Hospitalet de Llobregat *Spain* 41°21N 2°6E **196 D7**
Lhotka □ *Czech Rep.* 50°1N 14°22E **135 B**
Lhuntsi Dzong *Bhutan* 27°39N 91°10E **241 B3**
Lhut, W. → *Somali Rep.* 10°1′7N 50°9E **267 B7**
Li *Thailand* 17°48N 98°57E **236 D2**
Li Jiang → *China* 24°45N 110°33E **229 E8**
Li Jiang □ *China* 24°45N 110°38E **229 E8**
Li Shan *China* 35°34N 111°16E **226 G6**
Li Shui → *China* 29°24N 111°37E **229 C9**
Li Xian *Gansu, China* 34°10N 105°5E **226 G3**
Li Xian *Hebei, China* 38°30N 115°35E **226 E8**
Li Xian *Hunan, China* 29°36N 111°42E **229 C9**
Li Yuba *South Sudan* 5°23N 27°25E **266 C2**
Lia-Moya *C.A.R.* 24°0S 24°59E **270 B3**
Liadi *Greece* 36°50N 26°11E **205 E8**
Lian Xian = Liancheng *China* 40°0N 112°25E **226 D7**
Lianga *Phil.* 8°38N 126°6E **233 G6**
Lianga B. *Phil.* 8°38N 126°12E **233 G6**
Liangcheng *Nei Monggol Zizhiqu, China* 40°28N 112°25E **226 D7**
Liangcheng *Shandong, China* 35°32N 119°37E **227 G10**
Liangdang *China* 33°56N 106°18E **226 H4**
Lianghekou *China* 29°11N 108°44E **228 C7**
Liangping *China* 30°38N 107°47E **228 B6**
Liangpran *Indonesia* 1°4N 114°23E **236 D4**
Lianhua *China* 27°3N 113°54E **229 D9**
Lianhua Shan *China* 23°40N 116°48E **229 F10**
Lianjiang *Fujian, China* 26°12N 119°27E **229 D12**
Lianjiang *Guangdong, China* 21°40N 110°20E **229 G8**
Lianping *China* 24°26N 114°30E **229 E10**
Lianshanguan *China* 40°53N 123°43E **227 D13**
Lianshui *China* 33°42N 119°20E **227 H10**
Lianyuan *China* 27°40N 111°38E **229 D8**
Lianyungang *China* 34°40N 119°11E **227 G10**
Lianzhou *China* 24°51N 112°22E **229 E9**
Liao He → *China* 41°0N 121°50E **227 D11**
Liaocheng *China* 36°28N 115°58E **226 F8**
Liaodong Bandao *China* 40°0N 122°22E **227 E12**
Liaodong Wan *China* 40°20N 121°10E **227 D11**
Liaoning □ *China* 41°40N 122°30E **227 D12**
Liaoyang *China* 41°15N 122°58E **227 D12**
Liaoyuan *China* 42°58N 125°2E **227 C13**
Liaozhong *China* 41°23N 122°50E **227 D12**
Liapádes *Greece* 39°42N 19°40E **203 F2**
Liard → *Canada* 61°51N 121°18W **296 A4**
Liard River *Canada* 59°25N 126°5W **296 B3**
Liari *Pakistan* 25°37N 66°30E **242 G2**
Liat *Indonesia* 2°53S 107°0E **235 E4**
Líbano *Colombia* 4°55N 75°4W **328 C3**
Libau = Liepāja *Latvia* 56°30N 21°0E **184 B8**
Libby *U.S.A.* 48°23N 115°33W **304 B6**
Libenge *Dem. Rep. of the Congo* 3°40N 18°55E **264 D3**

Leval *→ Laos* 18°31N 102°30E **236 C4**
Likala *Dem. Rep. of the Congo* 0°9N 19°12E **264 B3**
Likang *Taiwan* 22°47N 120°29E **225 D2**
Likasi *Dem. Rep. of the Congo* 10°55S 26°48E **269 E2**
Likati *Dem. Rep. of the Congo* 3°20N 24°0E **264 B4**
Likati → *Dem. Rep. of the Congo* 2°53N 24°3E **264 B4**
Likenäs *Sweden* 60°33N 13°3E **162 D7**
Likete *Dem. Rep. of the Congo* 0°48S 21°31E **264 C4**
Likhaya = Likhovskoy *Russia* 48°10N 40°10E **191 F5**
Likhoborka → *Russia* 55°50N 37°37E **129 A3**
Likhoslavl *Russia* 57°12N 35°30E **188 D8**
Likhovskoy *Russia* 48°10N 40°10E **191 F5**
Likhvin = Chekalin *Russia* 54°10N 36°10E **188 D8**
Likimi *Dem. Rep. of the Congo* 2°44N 20°47E **264 B4**
Likasi *Dem. Rep. of the Congo* 11°5N 23°36E **264 B4**
Liknes *Norway* 58°19N 6°59E **164 F3**
Likokoo *Gabon* 0°12S 12°48E **264 C2**
Likoma I. *Malawi* 12°3S 34°45E **269 E3**
Likouala → *Congo* 0°12S 14°53E **264 C3**
Likouala aux Herbes → *Congo* 0°52S 17°8E **264 C3**
Liku *Cook Is.* 19°2S 168°47W **289 g**
Likumburu *Tanzania* 9°43S 35°8E **269 D4**
Lilanga *Dem. Rep. of the Congo* 0°34S 23°56E **264 C4**
L'Île-Bouchard *France* 47°7N 0°26E **172 E7**
L'Île-Rousse *France* 42°38N 8°57E **175 F12**
Lilenga *Dem. Rep. of the Congo* 1°4N 22°2E **264 B4**
Liling *China* 27°42N 113°29E **229 D9**
Lilla Edet *Sweden* 58°9N 12°8E **163 F6**
Lilla Värtan *Sweden* 59°20N 18°11E **139 A3**
Lille *France* 50°38N 3°3E **173 B10**
Lille Bælt *Denmark* 55°20N 9°45E **163 J3**
Lille Værløse *Denmark* 55°47N 12°22E **118 A2**
Lillebonne *France* 49°3′C N 0°32E **172 C7**
Lillehammer *Norway* 61°8N 10°30E **164 C7**
Lillesand *Norway* 58°15N 8°23E **164 F5**
Lillestrøm *Norway* 59°57N 11°5E **164 E8**
Lillhärdal *Sweden* 61°51N 14°4E **162 C8**
Lillian Pt. *Australia* 27°40S 126°6E **279 E4**
Lillo *Spain* 39°45N 3°20W **194 F7**
Lillooet *Canada* 50°44N 121°57W **296 C4**
Lillooet → *Canada* 49°15N 121°57W **296 D4**
Lilongwe *Malawi* 14°0S 33°48E **269 E3**
Liloy *Phil.* 8°4N 122°39E **233 G5**
Liluah *India* 22°37N 88°19E **124 B1**
Lim → *Europe* 43°45S 19°15E **202 C3**
Lim Chu Kang *Singapore* 1°26N 103°43E **138 A2**
Lima *Brazil* 4°36S 63°40W **329 D5**
Lima *Indonesia* 3°39S 127°58E **231 E7**
Lima *Peru* 12°3S 77°2W **334 B2**
Lima *Ill., U.S.A.* 40°11N 91°23W **310 D5**
Lima *Mont., U.S.A.* 44°38N 112°36W **304 D7**
Lima *N.Y., U.S.A.* 42°54N 77°36W **312 D7**
Lima *Ohio, U.S.A.* 40°44N 84°6W **311 D12**
Lima □ *Peru* 12°3S 77°3W **334 B2**
Lima → *Portugal* 41°41N 8°50W **194 D2**
Lima Jorge Chavez, Int. ✈ (LIM) *Peru* 12°2S 77°8W **124 B2**
Liman = Krasnyy Liman *Ukraine* 48°58N 37°50E **189 H9**
Liman *Russia* 45°45N 47°12E **191 H8**
Limanowa *Poland* 49°42N 20°22E **185 J7**
Limassol = Cyprus *Cyprus* 34°42N 33°1E **207 F9**
Limavady *U.K.* 55°3N 6°56W **166 A5**
Limay → *Argentina* 39°0S 68°0W **336 A3**
Limay Mahuida *Argentina* 37°10S 66°45W **334 D2**
Limbach-Oberfrohna *Germany* 50°52N 12°43E **178 E8**
Limbang *Malaysia* 4°42N 115°6E **235 D3**
Limbara, Mte. *Italy* 40°51N 9°10E **200 B2**
Limbaži *Latvia* 57°31N 24°42E **188 D3**
Limbdi *India* 22°34N 71°51E **242 H4**
Limbe *Cameroon* 4°1N 9°10E **263 E6**
Limbiate *Italy* 45°35N 9°7E **124 A1**
Limbueta *Angola* 12°30S 18°42E **265 E3**
Limbuhan = Pio V. Corpuz *Phil.* 11°55N 124°2E **233 F5**
Limburg *Belgium* 50°22N 8°4E **179 E4**
Limburg □ *Belgium* 51°2N 5°25E **170 C5**
Limburg □ *Neths.* 51°20N 5°55E **170 C5**
Lime Village *U.S.A.* 61°21N 155°28W **303 F9**
Limedsforsen *Sweden* 60°52N 13°25E **162 D7**
Limehouse □ *U.K.* 51°30N 0°1W **125 A3**
Limeil-Brévannes *France* 48°44N 2°29E **134 B3**
Limeira = Joaçaba *Brazil* 27°5S 51°31W **335 B5**
Limeira *Brazil* 22°35S 47°28E **335 A6**
Limenária *Greece* 40°38N 24°32E **203 F8**
Limerick = Luimneach *Ireland* 52°40N 8°37W **166 D3**
Limerick *Maine, U.S.A.* 43°41N 70°48W **313 C14**
Limerick □ *Ireland* 52°30N 8°50W **166 D3**
Limestone *U.S.A.* 42°2N 78°38W **312 D6**
Limestone → *Canada* 56°31N 94°7W **297 B10**
Limestone Hill = Lackawanna *U.S.A.* 42°49N 78°49W **312 D5**
Limfjorden *Denmark* 56°55N 9°0E **163 H3**
Limía = Lima → *Portugal* 41°41N 8°50W **194 D2**
Limingen *Norway* 64°48N 13°35E **160 D15**
Limmared *Sweden* 57°34N 13°20E **163 G7**
Limmen △ *Australia* 15°15S 135°36E **280 B2**
Limmen Bight *Australia* 14°40S 135°35E **280 A2**
Limmen Bight → *Australia* 15°7S 135°44E **280 B2**
Límni *Greece* 38°45N 23°18E **205 B6**
Límnos *Greece* 39°50N 25°5E **205 B7**
Limoeiro *Brazil* 7°52S 35°27W **332 C4**
Limoeiro do Norte *Brazil* 5°5S 38°0W **332 C4**
Limoges *France* 45°50N 1°15E **174 C5**
Limoges *Canada* 45°20N 75°16W **131 A9**
Limón *Costa Rica* 10°0N 83°2W **320 E3**
Limon, Colo., U.S.A. 39°16N 103°41W **304 G12**
Limone Piemonte *Italy* 44°12N 7°34E **198 D4**
Limonu *Turkey* 36°34N 34°15E **250 B3**
Limousin □ *France* 45°30N 1°30E **174 C5**
Limousin, Plateau du *France* 45°45N 1°15E **174 C5**
Limoux *France* 43°4N 2°12E **174 E6**
Limpopo □ *S. Africa* 24°5S 29°38E **271 A4**
Limpopo → *Africa* 25°5S 33°30E **271 C5**
Limuru *Kenya* 1°2S 36°35E **268 C4**
Lin Xian *China* 37°57N 110°58E **226 F6**
Lin'an *China* 30°15N 119°42E **229 B12**
Linao Pt. *Phil.* 11°30N 119°52E **233 F2**
Linapacan I. *Phil.* 11°30N 119°52E **233 F2**
Linapacan Str. *Phil.* 11°37N 119°49E **259 F2**
Linares *Chile* 35°50S 71°40W **334 D1**
Linares *Colombia* 1°23N 77°31W **328 C3**
Linares *Mexico* 24°52N 99°34W **319 C5**
Linares *Spain* 38°10N 3°40W **196 C2**
Linares □ *Chile* 35°50S 71°0W **334 D1**
Linaria *Greece* 38°52N 24°31E **204 D1**
Linaro, Capo *Italy* 42°2N 11°55E **198 A4**
Linas, Mte. *Italy* 39°25N 8°38E **200 C1**

Lincang *China* 23°58N 100°1E **228** F3
Lincheng *China* 37°25N 114°30E **226** F8
Linchuan *China* 27°57N 116°15E **229** D11
Lincoln = Beamsville *Canada* 43°12N 79°28W **312** C5
Lincoln *Argentina* 34°55S 61°30W **334** C3
Lincoln *N.Z.* 43°38S 172°30E **285** D7
Lincoln *Lincs., U.K.* 53°14N 0°32W **168** D7
Lincoln *Calif., U.S.A.* 38°54N 121°17W **306** G5
Lincoln *Ill., U.S.A.* 40°9N 89°22W **310** D7
Lincoln *Kans., U.S.A.* 39°3N 98°9W **308** F4
Lincoln *Maine, U.S.A.* 45°22N 68°30W **309** C19
Lincoln *N.H., U.S.A.* 44°3N 71°40W **313** B13
Lincoln *N. Mex., U.S.A.* 33°30N 105°23W **305** K11
Lincoln *Nebr., U.S.A.* 40°49N 96°41W **308** E5
Lincoln Boyhood △ *U.S.A.* 38°7N 86°59W **311** F10
Lincoln Center for Performing Arts *New York, U.S.A.* **132** b2
Lincoln City *U.S.A.* 44°57N 124°1W **304** D1
Lincoln Hav = Lincoln Sea *Arctic* 84°0N 55°0W **154** A5
Lincoln Heights *U.S.A.* 34°4N 118°12W **126** B3
Lincoln Memorial *U.S.A.* 38°52N 77°4W **143** B3
Lincoln Park *Calif., U.S.A.* 37°47N 122°30W **136** B1
Lincoln Park *Ga., U.S.A.* 32°52N 84°20W **316** C5
Lincoln Park *Ill., U.S.A.* 41°57N 87°38W **119** B3
Lincoln Park *Mich., U.S.A.* 42°15N 83°11W **311** B13
Lincoln Park *N.J., U.S.A.* 40°55N 74°18W **132** B1
Lincoln Park Zoo *U.S.A.* 41°55N 87°38W **119** B3
Lincoln Sea *Arctic* 84°0N 55°0W **154** A5
Lincoln Tunnel *New York, U.S.A.* **132** c1
Lincolnshire □ *U.K.* 53°14N 0°32W **168** D7
Lincolnshire Wolds *U.K.* 53°26N 0°13W **168** D7
Lincolnton *Ga., U.S.A.* 33°48N 82°29W **316** B7
Lincolnton *N.C., U.S.A.* 35°29N 81°16W **315** D14
Lincolnwood *U.S.A.* 42°1N 87°43W **119** A2
Lind *U.S.A.* 46°58N 118°37W **304** C4
Linda *U.S.A.* 39°8N 121°34W **306** F5
Linda-a-Pastora *Portugal* 38°42N 9°15W **126** A1
Lindale *U.S.A.* 34°11N 85°11W **316** A4
Lindås *Norway* 60°44N 5°9E **164** D2
Lindau *Germany* 47°33N 9°42E **179** H5
Lindeman I. *Australia* 20°27S 149°3E **280** b
Lindeman Islands △ *Australia* 20°28S 149°5E **280** b
Linden = Gladstone *U.S.A.* 39°13N 94°35W **310** E2
Linden *Guyana* 6°0N 58°10W **329** B6
Linden *Wellington, N.Z.* 41°10S 174°50E **143** A1
Linden *Gauteng, S. Africa* 26°8S 28°0E **123** A2
Linden *Ala., U.S.A.* 32°18N 87°48W **315** E11
Linden *Calif., U.S.A.* 38°1N 121°5W **306** G5
Linden *Ind., U.S.A.* 40°11N 86°54W **311** D10
Linden *Mich., U.S.A.* 42°49N 83°47W **311** B13
Linden *Tex., U.S.A.* 33°1N 94°22W **314** E7
Lindenberg *Germany* 52°36N 13°31E **115** A4
Lindenhurst *U.S.A.* 40°41N 73°23W **313** F11
Lindenow Fjord *Greenland* 60°30N 43°25W **154** E6
Lindesberg *Sweden* 59°36N 15°15E **162** E9
Lindesnes *Norway* 57°58N 7°3E **164** G4
Lindi *Tanzania* 9°58S 39°38E **269** D4
Lindi □ *Tanzania* 9°40S 38°30E **269** D4
Lindi → *Dem. Rep. of the Congo* 0°33N 25°5E **268** B2
Lindley *U.S.A.* 42°1N 77°8W **312** D7
Lindö *Sweden* 58°37N 16°15E **163** F10
Lindome *Sweden* 57°35N 12°5E **163** G6
Lindos *Greece* 36°6N 28°4E **206** E12
Lindos, Akra *Greece* 36°4N 28°10E **206** E12
Lindoso *Portugal* 41°52N 8°11W **194** D2
Lindow *Germany* 52°58N 12°59E **178** C8
Lindøya *Norway* 59°53N 10°42E **133** A3
Lindsay *Ont., Canada* 44°22N 78°43W **312** B6
Lindsay *Calif., U.S.A.* 36°12N 119°5W **306** J7
Lindsay *Okla., U.S.A.* 34°50N 97°38W **314** D6
Lindsborg *U.S.A.* 38°35N 97°40W **308** F5
Lindsdal *Sweden* 56°44N 16°18E **163** H10
Line Islands *Pac. Oc.* 7°0N 160°0W **289** H12
Linesville *U.S.A.* 41°39N 80°26W **312** E4
Lineville *Ala., U.S.A.* 33°19N 85°45W **316** B4
Lineville *Iowa, U.S.A.* 40°35N 93°32W **310** D3
Linfen *China* 36°3N 111°30E **226** F6
Ling Xian *Hunan, China* 26°29N 113°48E **229** D9
Ling Xian *Shandong, China* 37°22N 116°30E **226** F9
Lingal *India* 16°17N 78°31E **245** F4
Linganamakki Res. *India* 14°6N 74°52E **245** G2
Lingao *China* 19°56N 109°42E **236** C7
Lingayen *Phil.* 16°1N 120°14E **232** C3
Lingayen G. *Phil.* 16°10N 120°15E **232** C3
Lingbao *China* 34°31N 110°51E **226** G6
Lingbi *China* 33°33N 117°33E **227** H9
Lingbo *Sweden* 61°3N 16°41E **162** C10
Lingchuan *Guangxi Zhuangzu, China* 25°26N 110°21E **229** E8
Lingchuan *Shanxi, China* 35°45N 113°12E **226** G7
Lingding Yang *China* 22°25N 113°44E **219** a
Lingen *Germany* 52°31N 7°19E **178** C3
Lingga *Indonesia* 0°12S 104°37E **234** C2
Lingga, Kepulauan *Indonesia* 0°10S 104°30E **234** C2
Lingga Arch. = Lingga, Kepulauan *Indonesia* 0°10S 104°30E **234** C2
Linghed *Sweden* 60°48N 15°55E **162** D9
Linghem *Sweden* 58°26N 15°47E **163** F9
Lingig *Phil.* 8°2N 126°24E **233** G6
Lingle *U.S.A.* 42°8N 104°21W **304** E11
Lingomo *Dem. Rep. of the Congo* 0°38N 22°3E **264** B4
Lingqiu *China* 39°28N 114°22E **226** E8
Lingshan *China* 22°25N 109°18E **228** F7
Lingshi *China* 36°48N 111°48E **226** F6
Lingshou *China* 38°20N 114°20E **226** E8
Lingshui *China* 18°27N 110°0E **236** C8
Lingsugur *India* 16°10N 76°31E **245** F3
Lingtai *China* 35°0N 107°40E **226** G4
Linguère *Senegal* 15°25N 15°5W **262** B1
Lingui *China* 25°12N 110°2E **229** E8
Lingunda *Dem. Rep. of the Congo* 0°49N 21°8E **264** C3
Lingwu *China* 38°6N 106°20E **226** E4
Lingyuan *China* 41°10N 119°15E **227** D10
Lingyun *China* 25°2N 106°35E **228** E6
Linhai *China* 28°50N 121°8E **229** C13
Linhares *Brazil* 19°25S 40°4W **333** E3
Linhe *China* 40°48N 107°20E **226** D4
Liniers *Argentina* 34°39S 58°30W **117** B1
Linjiang *China* 41°50N 127°0E **224** B3
Linkebeek *Belgium* 50°46N 4°20E **116** B2
Linköping *Sweden* 58°28N 15°36E **163** F9
Linkou *China* 45°15N 130°18E **227** B16
Linksfield *S. Africa* 26°9S 28°6E **123** A2
Linli *China* 29°27N 111°30E **229** C8
Linlithgow = West Lothian □ *U.K.* 55°54N 3°36W **167** F5
Linmeyer *S. Africa* 26°15S 28°4E **123** B2
Linn *U.S.A.* 38°29N 91°51W **310** F5
Linna *Finland* 60°20N 24°50E **121** A2
Linnei *Taiwan* 23°45N 120°36E **225** C2
Linneus *U.S.A.* 39°53N 93°11W **310** E3
Linnhe, L. *U.K.* 56°36N 5°25W **167** E3
Linosa *Medit. S.* 35°51N 12°50E **258** A2
Linpien *Taiwan* 22°26N 120°30E **225** D2
Linqi *China* 35°45N 113°52E **226** G7
Linqing *China* 36°50N 115°42E **226** F8
Linqu *China* 36°25N 118°30E **227** F10
Linquan *China* 33°5N 115°17E **229** A10
Lins *Brazil* 21°40S 49°44W **335** A6
Linshu *China* 34°53N 118°38E **227** G10
Linshui *China* 30°21N 106°57E **228** B6
Linsia = Linxia *China* 35°36N 103°10E **218** D9
Linstead *Jamaica* 18°8N 77°2W **320** a
Linta → *Madag.* 25°2S 44°5E **272** D1
Lintao *China* 35°26N 103°58E **226** G2
Linth → *Switz.* 47°7N 9°7E **179** H5
Linthal *Switz.* 46°54N 9°0E **179** J5
Linton *Ind., U.S.A.* 39°2N 87°10W **311** F9
Linton *N. Dak., U.S.A.* 46°16N 100°14W **308** B3
Lintong *China* 34°20N 109°10E **226** G5
Lintuvaara *Finland* 60°14N 24°49E **121** B1
Linwood *Canada* 43°35N 80°43W **312** C4
Linwu *China* 25°19N 112°31E **229** E9
Linxi *Hebei, China* 39°42N 118°26E **227** E10
Linxi *Liaoning, China* 43°36N 118°2E **227** C10
Linxia *China* 35°36N 103°10E **218** D9
Linxiang *China* 29°28N 113°23E **229** C9
Linyanti → *Africa* 17°50S 25°5E **270** A4
Linyi *Shandong, China* 37°13N 116°54E **226** F9
Linyi *Shandong, China* 35°5N 118°21E **227** G10
Linying *China* 33°48N 113°56E **226** H7
Linyuan *Taiwan* 22°30N 120°23E **225** D2
Linz *Austria* 48°18N 14°18E **180** C7
Linz *Rhld-Pfz., Germany* 50°34N 7°17E **178** E3
Linzhenzhen *China* 36°30N 109°59E **226** F5
Linzhou *China* 36°4N 113°49E **226** F7
Linzi *China* 36°50N 118°20E **227** F10
Lioko *Équateur, Dem. Rep. of the Congo* 0°2N 22°4E **264** B4
Lioko *Orientale, Dem. Rep. of the Congo* 1°25N 23°7E **264** B4
Liomseter *Norway* 61°15N 9°35E **164** C6
Lion, G. du *France* 43°10N 4°0E **174** E7
Lion Rock Country Park △ *China* 22°21N 114°11E **122** A2
Lionárisso *Cyprus* 35°28N 34°8E **207** E10
Lionel Town *Jamaica* 17°50N 77°15W **320** a
Lioni *Italy* 40°52N 15°11E **201** B8
Lions, G. of = Lion, G. du *France* 43°10N 4°0E **174** E7
Lion's Den *Zimbabwe* 17°15S 30°5E **269** F3
Lion's Head *Ont., Canada* 44°58N 81°15W **312** B3
Lion's Head *Western Cape, S. Africa* 33°56S 18°23E **118** A1
Liouesso *Congo* 1°2N 15°43E **264** B3
Lioumi *Greece* 38°0N 23°40E **112** B2
Liozno = Lyozna *Belarus* 55°0N 30°50E **188** E6
Lipa *Phil.* 13°57N 121°10E **232** E3
Lipali *Mozam.* 15°50S 35°50E **269** F4
Lipany *Slovak Rep.* 49°9N 20°58E **181** B13
Lipari *Italy* 38°26N 14°58E **201** D7
Lipari, I. *Italy* 38°29N 14°56E **201** D7
Lipari, Is. = Eólie, Is. *Italy* 38°30N 14°57E **201** D7
Lipatkain *Indonesia* 0°1N 101°12E **234** B2
Lipcani *Moldova* 48°14N 26°48E **183** B11
Liperi *Finland* 62°31N 29°24E **160** E23
Lipetsk *Russia* 52°37N 39°35E **189** F10
Lipetsk □ *Russia* 52°50N 38°50E **190** D4
Lipiany *Poland* 53°2N 14°58E **185** E1
Liping *China* 26°15N 109°7E **228** D7
Lipisi *Greece* 37°19N 26°50E **205** D8
Lipjan = Lipljan *Kosovo* 42°31N 21°7E **202** D5
Lipkany = Lipcani *Moldova* 48°14N 26°48E **183** B11
Lipljan *Kosovo* 42°31N 21°7E **202** D5
Lipník nad Bečvou *Czech Rep.* 49°32N 17°36E **181** B10
Lipno *Poland* 52°49N 19°15E **185** F6
Lipova *Romania* 46°8N 21°42E **182** D6
Lipovets *Ukraine* 49°12N 29°1E **177** D15
Lippe → *Germany* 51°39N 6°36E **178** D2
Lippehne = Lipiany *Poland* 53°2N 14°58E **185** E1
Lippstadt *Germany* 51°41N 8°22E **178** D4
Lipscomb *U.S.A.* 36°14N 100°16W **314** C4
Lipsk *Poland* 53°44N 23°24E **184** E10
Lipsko *Poland* 51°9N 21°40E **185** G8
Liptovský Hrádok *Slovak Rep.* 49°2N 19°44E **181** B12
Liptovský Mikuláš *Slovak Rep.* 49°6N 19°35E **181** B12
Liptrap, C. *Australia* 38°50S 145°55E **283** E6
Lipu *China* 24°30N 110°22E **229** E8
Lira *Uganda* 2°17N 32°57E **268** B3
Liranga *Congo* 0°43S 17°32E **264** C3
Liri → *Italy* 41°25N 13°52E **200** A6
Liria = Llíria *Spain* 39°37N 0°35W **197** F4
Lisakovsk *Kazakhstan* 52°33N 62°37E **216** B6
Lisala *Dem. Rep. of the Congo* 2°12N 21°38E **264** B4
Lisboa *Portugal* 38°42N 9°8W **126** A2
Lisboa □ *Portugal* 39°0N 9°12W **195** F1
Lisboa ✕ (LIS) *Portugal* 38°46N 9°8W **126** A2
Lisbon = Lisboa *Portugal* 38°42N 9°8W **126** A2
Lisbon *N. Dak., U.S.A.* 46°27N 97°41W **308** B5
Lisbon *N.H., U.S.A.* 44°13N 71°55W **313** B13
Lisbon *N.Y., U.S.A.* 44°43N 75°19W **313** B9
Lisbon *Ohio, U.S.A.* 40°46N 80°46W **312** F4
Lisbon Falls *U.S.A.* 44°0N 70°4W **309** D18
Lisburn *U.K.* 54°31N 6°3W **166** B5
Lisburn, C. *Vanuatu* 15°39S 166°46E **287** E4
Lisburne, C. *U.S.A.* 68°53N 166°13W **303** B6
Liscannor B. *Ireland* 52°55N 9°24W **166** D2
Liscia → *Italy* 41°11N 9°9E **200** A2
Lisdoonvarna *Ireland* 53°2N 9°18W **166** C2
Lishan *Taiwan* 24°16N 121°14E **225** B3
Lishe Jiang → *China* 24°15N 101°35E **228** E3
Lishi *China* 37°31N 111°8E **226** F6
Lishu *China* 43°20N 124°18E **227** C13
Lishui *Guangdong, China* 23°12N 113°9E **121** A1
Lishui *Jiangsu, China* 31°38N 119°2E **229** B12
Lishui *Zhejiang, China* 28°28N 119°54E **229** C12
Lisianski I. *U.S.A.* 26°2N 174°0W **302** F9
Lisichansk = Lysychansk *Ukraine* 48°55N 38°30E **189** H10
Lisieux *France* 49°10N 0°12E **172** C7
Liski *Russia* 51°3N 39°30E **189** G10
L'Isle-Jourdain *Gers, France* 43°36N 1°5E **174** E5
L'Isle-Jourdain *Vienne, France* 46°13N 0°31E **174** B4
L'Isle-sur-la-Sorgue *France* 43°54N 5°2E **175** E9
Lisle-sur-Tarn *France* 43°52N 1°49E **174** E5
Lismore *N.S.W., Australia* 28°44S 153°21E **281** D5
Lismore *Waterford, Ireland* 52°8N 7°55W **166** D4
Lissa = Leszno *Poland* 51°50N 16°30E **185** G3
Lissos → *Greece* 41°15N 25°40E **203** E9
Lista *Norway* 58°7N 6°39E **164** F3
Lister, Mt. *Antarctica* 78°0S 162°0E **151** D11
Lister og Mandals = Vest-Agder □ *Norway* 58°30N 7°15E **164** F4
Liston *Australia* 28°39S 152°6E **281** D5
Listowel *Ont., Canada* 43°44N 80°58W **312** C4
Listowel *Kerry, Ireland* 52°27N 9°29W **166** D2
Lit *Sweden* 63°19N 14°51E **162** A8
Lit-et-Mixe *France* 44°2N 1°15W **174** D2
Litang *Guangxi Zhuangzu, China* 23°12N 109°8E **228** F7
Litang *Sichuan, China* 30°1N 100°17E **228** B3
Litang *Malaysia* 5°27N 118°31E **235** A5
Litang Qu → *China* 28°4N 101°32E **228** C3
Litani → *Lebanon* 33°20N 35°15E **250** E6
Litchfield *Vic., Australia* 36°18S 142°52E **282** D5
Litchfield *Calif., U.S.A.* 40°24N 120°23W **306** E6
Litchfield *Conn., U.S.A.* 41°45N 73°11W **313** E11
Litchfield *Ill., U.S.A.* 39°11N 89°39W **310** E7
Litchfield *Minn., U.S.A.* 45°8N 94°32W **308** C6
Litchfield △ *Australia* 13°14S 131°1E **278** B5
Liteni *Romania* 47°32N 26°32E **183** C11
Lithakia *Greece* 37°43N 20°50E **207** D2
Lithgow *Australia* 33°25S 150°8E **283** B9
Lithino, Akra *Greece* 34°55N 24°44E **207** F5
Lithuania ■ *Europe* 55°30N 24°0E **188** E2
Litija *Slovenia* 46°3N 14°50E **199** B11
Lititz *U.S.A.* 40°9N 76°18W **313** F8
Litochoro *Greece* 40°8N 22°34E **202** F6
Litoko *Dem. Rep. of the Congo* 1°13S 24°47E **264** C4
Litoměřice *Czech Rep.* 50°33N 14°10E **180** A7
Litomyšl *Czech Rep.* 49°52N 16°20E **181** B9
Litschau *Austria* 48°58N 15°4E **180** C8
Little Abaco *Bahamas* 26°50N 77°30W **320** A4
Little Andaman I. *India* 10°45N 92°30E **245** J11
Little Aral Sea = Northern Aral Sea *Kazakhstan* 46°20N 60°30E **216** C6
Little B. *N.S.W., Australia* 33°58S 151°15E **139** B2
Little B. *Montserrat* 16°43N 62°11W **323** p
Little Barrier I. *N.Z.* 36°12S 175°8E **284** C4
Little Basses *Sri Lanka* 6°24N 81°43E **245** L5
Little Belt Mts. *U.S.A.* 46°40N 110°45W **304** C8
Little Bighorn Battlefield △ *U.S.A.* 45°34N 107°25W **304** D10
Little Blue → *U.S.A.* 39°42N 96°41W **308** F5
Little Buffalo → *Canada* 61°0N 113°46W **296** A6
Little Calumet → *U.S.A.* 41°39N 87°34W **119** D3
Little Cayman *Cayman Is.* 19°41N 80°3W **320** C3
Little Churchill → *Canada* 57°30N 95°22W **297** B9
Little Coco I. *Burma* 14°0N 93°13E **245** H11
Little Colorado → *U.S.A.* 36°12N 111°48W **305** H8
Little Current *Canada* 45°55N 82°0W **298** C3
Little Current → *Canada* 50°57N 84°36W **298** B3
Little Desert △ *Australia* 37°25S 141°30E **282** D4
Little Diomede I. *U.S.A.* 65°45N 168°56W **303** D5
Little Falls *Minn., U.S.A.* 45°59N 94°22W **308** C6
Little Falls *N.Y., U.S.A.* 43°3N 74°51W **313** C10
Little Ferry *U.S.A.* 40°50N 74°2W **132** A1
Little Fork → *U.S.A.* 48°31N 93°35W **308** A7
Little Grand Rapids *Canada* 52°0N 95°29W **297** C9
Little Humboldt → *U.S.A.* 41°1N 117°43W **304** F5
Little Inagua I. *Bahamas* 21°40N 73°50W **321** B5
Little Italy *New York, U.S.A.* **132** b2
Little Karoo *S. Africa* 33°45S 21°0E **270** D3
Little Khingan Mts. = Xiao Hinggan Ling *China* 49°0N 127°0E **219** B14
Little Lake *U.S.A.* 35°56N 117°55W **307** K9
Little Lake Conway *U.S.A.* 28°29N 81°21W **133** B2
Little Laut Is. = Laut Kecil, Kepulauan *Indonesia* 4°45S 115°40E **235** C5
Little London *Jamaica* 18°15N 78°13W **320** a
Little Mecatina = Petit-Mécatina → *Canada* 50°40N 59°30W **299** B8
Little Mermaid = Den Lille Havfrue *Copenhagen, Denmark* **118** a3
Little Minch *U.K.* 57°35N 6°45W **167** D2
Little Missouri → *U.S.A.* 47°36N 102°25W **308** B2
Little Nicobar *India* 7°20N 93°40E **245** L11
Little Ouse → *U.K.* 52°22N 1°12E **169** E9
Little Rann *India* 23°25N 71°25E **242** H4
Little Red → *U.S.A.* 35°11N 91°27W **314** D9
Little Red School House Nature Center *U.S.A.* 41°42N 87°51W **119** C1
Little River *N.Z.* 43°45S 172°49E **285** D7
Little Rock *U.S.A.* 34°45N 92°17W **314** D8
Little Rouge → *Canada* 43°45N 79°11W **141** A4
Little Ruaha → *Tanzania* 7°57S 37°53E **268** D4
Little Sable Pt. *U.S.A.* 43°38N 86°33W **308** D10
Little Scarcies → *S. Leone* 8°50N 13°10W **262** D2
Little Sioux → *U.S.A.* 41°48N 96°4W **308** E5
Little Sitkin I. *U.S.A.* 51°57N 178°31E **303** L2
Little Smoky → *Canada* 54°44N 117°11W **296** C5
Little Snake → *U.S.A.* 40°27N 108°26W **304** F9
Little Sound *Bermuda* 32°15N 64°50W **153** a
Little Tokyo *Los Angeles, U.S.A.* **127** c2
Little Valley *U.S.A.* 42°15N 78°48W **312** D6
Little Wabash → *U.S.A.* 37°55N 88°5W **311** G8
Little White → *U.S.A.* 43°40N 100°40W **308** D3
Little York *U.S.A.* 41°1N 90°45W **310** C6
Little Zab = Zāb aş Şaghīr → *Iraq* 35°17N 43°29E **213** E10
Littlefield *U.S.A.* 33°55N 102°20W **314** E3
Littlehampton *U.K.* 50°49N 0°32W **169** G7
Littleton *U.S.A.* 44°18N 71°46W **313** B13
Littoral □ *Cameroon* 4°0N 10°0E **263** E7
Littoria = Latina *Italy* 41°28N 12°52E **200** A5
Litunga *Angola* 13°19S 16°48E **265** E3
Litvinov *Czech Rep.* 50°36N 13°37E **180** A6
Liu He → *Jilin, China* 42°46N 126°13E **224** A3
Liu He → *Liaoning, China* 40°55N 121°35E **227** D11
Liu Jiang → *China* 23°55N 109°30E **228** F7
Liuba *China* 33°38N 106°55E **228** A6
Liucheng *China* 24°38N 109°14E **228** E7
Liuchia *Taiwan* 23°13N 120°21E **225** C2
Liuch'iu *Taiwan* 22°21N 120°23E **225** D2
Liuch'iu Yü *Taiwan* 22°20N 120°22E **225** D2
Liugou *China* 40°57N 118°15E **227** D10
Liuhang *China* 31°21N 121°21E **138** A1
Liuhe *China* 42°17N 125°43E **227** C13
Liuheng Dao *China* 29°40N 122°5E **229** C14
Liujiang *China* 24°26N 109°11E **228** E7
Liukang Tenggaja = Sabalana, Kepulauan *Indonesia* 6°45S 118°50E **231** F5
Liuli *Tanzania* 11°3S 34°38E **269** E3
Liupan Shan *China* 35°39N 106°12E **226** G4
Liupanshui *China* 26°38N 104°48E **228** D5
Liurong Temple *China* 23°8N 113°15E **121** B2
Liuwa Plain *Zambia* 14°20S 22°30E **265** E4
Liuwa Plain △ *Zambia* 14°45S 22°35E **265** E4
Liuyang *China* 28°10N 113°37E **229** C9
Liuying *Taiwan* 23°17N 120°18E **225** C2
Liuzhou *China* 24°22N 109°22E **228** E7
Liuzhuang *China* 33°12N 120°18E **227** H11
Livada *Romania* 47°52N 23°5E **182** C8
Livadero *Greece* 40°2N 21°57E **202** F5
Livadhia *Cyprus* 34°57N 33°38E **207** F9
Livadhje *Albania* 39°47N 20°7E **206** B10
Livadi *Greece* 40°8N 22°9E **204** A4
Livadia *Greece* 38°27N 22°54E **204** C4
Livarot *France* 48°58N 0°9E **172** D7
Live Oak *Calif., U.S.A.* 39°17N 121°40W **306** F5
Live Oak *Fla., U.S.A.* 30°18N 82°59W **316** E7
Live Oak Manor *U.S.A.* 29°57N 90°14W **131** B1
Lively *Canada* 46°26N 81°9W **309** B13
Livengood *U.S.A.* 65°32N 148°33W **303** D10
Liveras *Cyprus* 35°23N 32°57E **207** E8
Livermore *U.S.A.* 37°41N 121°47W **306** H5
Livermore, Mt. *U.S.A.* 30°38N 104°11W **314** F2
Livermore Falls *U.S.A.* 44°29N 70°11W **309** C18
Liverpool *N.S.W., Australia* 33°54S 150°58E **283** B9
Liverpool *N.S., Canada* 44°5N 64°41W **299** D7
Liverpool *Mersey., U.K.* 53°25N 3°0W **168** D4
Liverpool *N.Y., U.S.A.* 43°6N 76°13W **313** C8
Liverpool Bay *U.K.* 53°30N 3°20W **168** D4
Liverpool Plains *Australia* 31°15S 150°15E **283** A9
Liverpool Ra. *Australia* 31°50S 150°30E **283** A9
Liverpool Street *London, U.K.* **125** a5
Livigno *Italy* 46°35N 10°10E **198** B7
Livingston *Guatemala* 15°50N 88°50W **320** C2
Livingston *W. Lothian, U.K.* 55°54N 3°30W **167** F5
Livingston *Ala., U.S.A.* 32°35N 88°11W **315** E10
Livingston *Calif., U.S.A.* 37°23N 120°43W **306** H6
Livingston *Mont., U.S.A.* 45°40N 110°34W **304** D8
Livingston *S.C., U.S.A.* 33°38N 81°7W **315** E14
Livingston *Tenn., U.S.A.* 36°23N 85°19W **315** C12
Livingston *Tex., U.S.A.* 30°43N 94°56W **314** F7
Livingston *Wis., U.S.A.* 42°54N 90°26W **310** B6
Livingston, L. *U.S.A.* 30°50N 95°10W **314** F7
Livingston Manor *U.S.A.* 41°54N 74°50W **313** E10
Livingstone *Zambia* 17°46S 25°52E **269** F2
Livingstone △ *Australia* 35°22S 147°22E **283** C7
Livingstone Mts. *N.Z.* 45°15S 168°9E **285** F3
Livingstone Mts. *Tanzania* 9°40S 34°20E **269** D3
Livingstonia *Malawi* 10°38S 34°5E **269** E3
Livno *Bos.-H.* 43°50N 17°1E **182** G2
Livny *Russia* 52°30N 37°30E **189** F9
Livonia *Mich., U.S.A.* 42°23N 83°23W **311** B13
Livonia *N.Y., U.S.A.* 42°49N 77°40W **312** D7
Livorno *Italy* 43°33N 10°19E **198** E7
Livradois-Forez △ *France* 44°0N 3°0E **174** E7
Livramento = Nossa Senhora do Livramento *Brazil* 15°48S 56°22W **331** D6
Livramento *Brazil* 30°55S 55°30W **335** C4
Livramento do Brumado *Brazil* 13°39S 41°50W **333** D3
Livron-sur-Drôme *France* 44°46N 4°51E **175** D8
Livry-Gargan *France* 48°55N 2°31E **134** A4
Livyntsi *Ukraine* 48°25N 26°37E **183** B11
Liwale *Tanzania* 9°48S 37°58E **269** D4
Liwan *China* 23°3N 113°13E **121** B2
Liwiec → *Poland* 52°36N 21°34E **185** F8
Liwonde *Malaysia* 15°4S 35°13E **269** F4
Liwonde △ *Malawi* 14°48S 35°20E **269** E4
Lixi *China* 26°23N 101°59E **228** D3
Lixian *China* 31°23N 103°13E **228** B4
Lixin *China* 33°8N 116°13E **229** A11
Lixouri *Greece* 38°12N 20°26E **207** C2
Liyang *China* 31°26N 119°28E **229** B12
Lizard → *Trin. & Tob.* 10°9N 61°1W **323** t
Lizard I. *Australia* 14°42S 145°30E **280** A4
Lizard Pt. *U.K.* 49°57N 5°13W **169** H2
Lizarda *Brazil* 9°36S 46°41W **332** C2
Lizarra = Estella *Spain* 42°40N 2°2W **196** C2
Lizella *U.S.A.* 32°48N 83°49W **316** C6
Lizzano *Italy* 40°23N 17°27E **201** B10
Ljan *Norway* 59°50N 10°46E **133** A3
Ljig *Serbia* 44°13N 20°18E **202** B4
Ljøra → *Norway* 61°24N 12°35E **164** C9
Ljørdalen *Norway* 61°23N 12°41E **164** C9
Ljosland *Norway* 58°47N 7°22E **164** F4
Ljubija *Bos.-H.* 44°55N 16°35E **199** D13
Ljubinje *Bos.-H.* 42°58N 18°5E **202** D2
Ljubišnja *Europe* 43°18N 19°6E **202** C3
Ljubljana *Slovenia* 46°4N 14°33E **199** B11
Ljubljana ✕ (LJU) *Slovenia* 46°14N 14°33E **199** B11
Ljubno *Slovenia* 46°25N 14°46E **199** B11
Ljubovija *Serbia* 44°11N 19°22E **202** B3
Ljugarn *Sweden* 57°20N 18°43E **163** G12
Ljung *Sweden* 57°59N 13°3E **163** G7
Ljungan → *Sweden* 62°18N 17°23E **162** B11
Ljungaverk *Sweden* 62°30N 16°5E **162** B10
Ljungby *Sweden* 56°49N 13°55E **163** H7
Ljungbyholm *Sweden* 56°39N 16°5E **163** H10
Ljungdalen *Sweden* 62°51N 12°47E **162** B6
Ljungsbro *Sweden* 58°31N 15°30E **163** F9
Ljungskile *Sweden* 58°14N 11°55E **163** F5
Ljusdal *Sweden* 61°46N 16°3E **162** C10
Ljusfallshammar *Sweden* 58°48N 15°30E **163** F9
Ljusnan → *Sweden* 61°12N 17°8E **162** C11
Ljusne *Sweden* 61°13N 17°7E **162** C11
Ljusterö *Sweden* 59°31N 18°37E **162** E12
Ljustorp *Sweden* 62°38N 17°21E **162** B11
Ljutomer *Slovenia* 46°31N 16°11E **199** B13
Llagostera *Spain* 41°50N 2°54E **196** D7
Llamellín *Peru* 9°0S 76°54W **330** B2
Llancanelo, Salina *Argentina* 35°40S 69°8W **334** D2
Llandeilo *U.K.* 51°53N 3°59W **169** F4
Llandovery *U.K.* 51°59N 3°48W **169** F4
Llandrindod Wells *U.K.* 52°14N 3°22W **169** E4
Llandudno *U.K.* 53°19N 3°50W **168** D4
Llanelli *U.K.* 51°41N 4°10W **169** F3
Llanes *Spain* 43°25N 4°50W **194** B6
Llanganates △ *Ecuador* 0°51S 72°20W **328** D3
Llangollen *U.K.* 52°58N 3°11W **168** E4
Llanidloes *U.K.* 52°27N 3°31W **169** E4
Llano *U.S.A.* 30°45N 98°41W **314** F5
Llano → *U.S.A.* 30°39N 98°26W **314** F5
Llano de Can Gineu *Spain* 41°27N 2°10E **114** A2
Llano Estacado *U.S.A.* 33°30N 103°0W **314** E3
Llanos *S. Amer.* 5°0N 71°35W **326** C3
Llanos de Challe △ *Chile* 28°8S 71°1W **334** B1
Llanquihue, L. *Chile* 41°10S 72°50W **336** B1
Llanwrtyd Wells *U.K.* 52°7N 3°38W **169** E4
Llata *Peru* 9°25S 76°47W **330** B2
Llebeig, C. des *Spain* 39°33N 2°18E **206** B3
Lleida *Spain* 41°37N 0°39E **196** D5
Lleida □ *Spain* 42°6N 1°0E **196** C6
Llentrisca, C. *Spain* 38°52N 1°15E **206** D1
Llera de Canales *Mexico* 23°19N 99°1W **319** C5
Llerena *Spain* 38°17N 6°0W **195** G5
Llevant, Sa. de *Spain* 39°35N 3°17E **206** B4
Lleyn Peninsula *U.K.* 52°51N 4°36W **168** E3
Llica *Bolivia* 19°52S 68°16W **330** D4
Llico *Chile* 34°46S 72°5W **334** C1
Llíria *Spain* 39°37N 0°35W **197** F4
Llívia *Spain* 42°28N 1°59E **174** F5
Llobregat → *Spain* 41°19N 2°5E **196** D7
Llodio *Spain* 43°9N 2°58W **196** B2
Llorente *Phil.* 11°25N 125°33E **233** F5
Lloret de Mar *Spain* 41°41N 2°53E **196** D7
Lloseta *Spain* 39°43N 2°52E **206** B3
Lloyd B. *Australia* 12°45S 143°27E **280** A3
Lloyd L. *Canada* 57°22N 108°57W **297** B7
Lloydminster *Canada* 53°17N 110°0W **297** C7
Llubí *Spain* 39°42N 3°0E **206** B4
Llucena del Cid *Spain* 40°16N 0°17W **196** E4
Llucmajor *Spain* 39°29N 2°53E **206** B3
Lluidas Vale *Jamaica* 18°6N 77°5W **320** a
Llullaillaco, Volcán *S. Amer.* 24°43S 68°30W **334** A2
Llullaillaco △ *Chile* 24°50S 68°51W **334** A2
Lo → *Vietnam* 21°18N 105°25E **236** B5
Lo Aranguiz *Chile* 33°23S 70°43W **137** B2
Lo Boza *Chile* 33°23S 70°43W **137** B1
Lo Chau *China* 22°11N 114°15E **122** B2
Lo Chau Pak Mai *China* 22°11N 114°14E **122** B2
Lo Espejo *Chile* 33°31S 70°42W **137** C1
Lo Hermida *Chile* 33°28S 70°33W **137** B2
Lo Prado *Chile* 33°26S 70°42W **137** B1
Lo So Shing *China* 22°12N 114°7E **122** B1
Lo Wai *China* 22°22N 114°8E **122** A1
Loa *U.S.A.* 38°24N 111°39W **304** G8
Loa → *Chile* 21°26S 70°41W **334** A1
Loagan Bunut △ *Malaysia* 3°32N 114°40E **235** B4
Loaita I. *S. China Sea* 10°41N 114°25E **230** B4
Loakulu *Indonesia* 0°31S 117°1E **235** C5
Loange → *Dem. Rep. of the Congo* 4°17S 20°2E **265** C4
Loango *Congo* 4°38S 11°50E **265** C2
Loanhead *U.K.* 55°53N 3°9W **121** B3
Loano *Italy* 44°8N 8°15E **198** D5
Loay *Phil.* 9°36N 124°1E **233** G5
Lobamba *Swaziland* 26°28S 31°12E **271** C5
Lobatse *Botswana* 25°12S 25°40E **270** C4
Lobau *Wien, Austria* 48°10N 16°31E **142** A3
Löbau *Sachsen, Germany* 51°5N 14°40E **178** D10
Lobaye → *C.A.R.* 3°41N 18°35E **264** B3
Loben = Lubliniec *Poland* 50°43N 18°45E **185** H5
Lobenstein *Germany* 50°25N 11°39E **178** E7
Lobería *Argentina* 38°10S 58°40W **334** D4
Löberöd *Sweden* 55°47N 13°31E **163** J7
Łobez *Poland* 53°38N 15°39E **184** E2
Lobito *Angola* 12°18S 13°35E **265** E2
Lobo *Phil.* 13°39N 121°13E **232** E3
Lobo → *Ivory C.* 6°2N 6°45W **262** D3
Lobos *Argentina* 35°10S 59°0W **334** D4
Lobos, I. *Mexico* 27°20N 110°36W **318** B2
Lobos, I. de *Canary Is.* 28°45N 13°50W **153** e2
Lobos, Pt. *U.S.A.* 37°46N 122°30W **136** B1
Lobos de Afuera, Islas *Peru* 6°57S 80°42W **330** B1
Lobos de Tierra, I. *Peru* 6°27S 80°52W **330** B1
Łobżenica *Poland* 53°18N 17°15E **185** E4
Loc Binh *Vietnam* 21°46N 106°54E **236** B6
Loc Ninh *Vietnam* 11°50N 106°34E **237** G6
Locarno *Switz.* 46°10N 8°47E **179** J4
Loch Baghasdail = Lochboisdale *U.K.* 57°9N 7°20W **167** D1
Loch Garman = Wexford *Ireland* 52°20N 6°28W **166** D5
Loch Lomond and the Trossachs △ *U.K.* 56°10N 4°40W **167** E4
Loch Nam Madadh = Lochmaddy *U.K.* 57°36N 7°10W **167** D1
Lochaber *U.K.* 56°59N 5°1W **167** E3
Locham *Germany* 48°7N 11°26E **131** B1
Locharbriggs *U.K.* 55°7N 3°35W **167** F5
Lochboisdale *U.K.* 57°9N 7°20W **167** D1
Loche, L. La *Canada* 56°30N 109°30W **297** B7
Lochem *Neths.* 52°9N 6°26E **170** B6
Loches *France* 47°7N 1°0E **172** E7
Lochgilphead *U.K.* 56°2N 5°26W **167** E3
Lochino *Russia* 55°41N 37°17E **129** B1
Lochinvar △ *Zambia* 15°55S 27°15E **269** F2
Lochinver *U.K.* 58°9N 5°14W **167** C3
Lochkov *Czech Rep.* 50°0N 14°21E **135** B2
Lochloosa L. *U.S.A.* 29°30N 82°7W **317** F7
Lochmaddy *U.K.* 57°36N 7°10W **167** D1
Lochnagar *Queens., Australia* 23°33S 145°38E **280** C4
Lochnagar *Aberds., U.K.* 56°57N 3°15W **167** E5
Łochów *Poland* 52°33N 21°42E **185** F8
Lochy, L. *U.K.* 57°0N 4°53W **167** E4
Lock *Australia* 33°34S 135°46E **281** E2
Lock Haven *U.S.A.* 41°8N 77°28W **312** E7
Lockeford *U.S.A.* 38°10N 121°9W **306** G5
Lockeport *Canada* 43°47N 65°4W **299** D6
Lockerbie *U.K.* 55°7N 3°21W **167** F5
Lockhart *N.S.W., Australia* 35°14S 146°40E **283** C7
Lockhart *Tex., U.S.A.* 29°53N 97°40W **314** G6
Lockhart, L. *Australia* 33°15S 119°3E **279** F2
Lockhart River *Australia* 12°58S 143°30E **280** A3
Lockhart River ✪ *Australia* 12°47S 143°20E **280** A3
Lockhausen *Germany* 48°10N 11°24E **131** A1
Lockney *U.S.A.* 34°7N 101°27W **314** D4
Lockport *Ill., U.S.A.* 41°35N 88°3W **311** C8
Lockport *N.Y., U.S.A.* 43°10N 78°42W **312** C6
Locminé *France* 47°54N 2°51W **172** E3
Locri *Italy* 38°14N 16°16E **201** D9
Locronan *France* 48°7N 4°15W **172** D2
Locust Cr. → *U.S.A.* 39°40N 93°17W **310** E3
Locust Grove *U.S.A.* 33°21N 84°7W **316** B5
Lod *Israel* 31°57N 34°54E **251** G5
Lodalskåpa *Norway* 61°47N 7°13E **164** C4
Lodeinoye Pole *Russia* 60°44N 33°33E **188** B7
Lodève *France* 43°44N 3°19E **174** E7
Lodge Bay *Canada* 52°14N 55°51W **299** B8
Lodge Grass *U.S.A.* 45°19N 107°22W **304** D10
Lodhran *Pakistan* 29°32N 71°30E **242** E4
Lodi *Italy* 45°19N 9°30E **198** C6
Lodi *Calif., U.S.A.* 38°8N 121°16W **306** G5
Lodi *N.J., U.S.A.* 40°52N 74°5W **132** A1
Lodi *Ohio, U.S.A.* 41°2N 82°1W **312** E3
Lodi Estate *India* 28°36N 77°15E **120** B2
Lodja *Dem. Rep. of the Congo* 3°30S 23°23E **264** C4
Lodosa *Spain* 42°25N 2°4W **196** C2
Lödöse *Sweden* 58°2N 12°9E **163** F6
Lodwar *Kenya* 3°7N 35°36E **268** B4
Łódź *Poland* 51°45N 19°27E **185** G6
Łódzkie □ *Poland* 51°30N 19°30E **185** G6
Loei *Thailand* 17°29N 101°35E **236** D3
Loenga *Dem. Rep. of the Congo* 4°48S 26°30E **265** C5
Loeriesfontein *S. Africa* 31°0S 19°26E **270** D2
Lofa → *Liberia* 6°35N 11°8W **263** D2
Lofa Mano △ *Liberia* 7°55N 10°25W **262** D2
Lofer *Austria* 47°35N 12°41E **180** D5
Lofoten *Norway* 68°30N 13°59E **160** B16
Lofsdalen *Sweden* 62°10N 13°20E **162** B7
Lofsen → *Sweden* 62°7N 13°57E **162** B7
Loftahammar *Sweden* 57°54N 16°41E **163** G10
Loga *Niger* 13°40N 3°15E **263** C5
Logan *Iowa, U.S.A.* 41°39N 95°47W **308** E6
Logan *Ohio, U.S.A.* 39°32N 82°25W **309** F12
Logan *Utah, U.S.A.* 41°44N 111°50W **304** F8
Logan *W. Va., U.S.A.* 37°51N 81°59W **309** G13
Logan, Mt. *Canada* 60°34N 140°23W **294** E3
Logan Int., Boston ✕ (BOS) *U.S.A.* 42°22N 71°1W **116** A2
Logan Martin L. *U.S.A.* 33°26N 86°20W **316** B3
Logan Square *U.S.A.* 41°55N 87°42W **119** B2
Logandale *U.S.A.* 36°36N 114°29W **307** J12
Logansport *Ind., U.S.A.* 40°45N 86°22W **311** D10
Logansport *La., U.S.A.* 31°58N 94°0W **314** F8
Logirim *South Sudan* 4°43N 33°14E **257** G3
Lognes-Émerainville ✕ (XLG) *France* 48°49N 2°37E **134** B4
Logo *South Sudan* 5°20N 30°18E **257** F3
Logone → *Chad* 12°6N 15°2E **259** F3
Logone Gana *Chad* 11°36N 15°4E **259** F3
Logone Occidental □ *Chad* 8°30N 16°0E **259** G3
Logone Occidental → *Chad* 8°50N 16°0E **259** G3
Logone Oriental □ *Chad* 8°30N 16°30E **259** G3
Logone Oriental → *Chad* 9°7N 16°26E **259** G3
Logroño *Spain* 42°28N 2°27W **196** C2
Logrosán *Spain* 39°20N 5°32W **195** F5
Løgstør *Denmark* 56°58N 9°14E **163** H3
Logtak L. *India* 24°33N 93°50E **241** C4
Løgumkloster *Denmark* 55°4N 8°57E **163** J2
Loh *Vanuatu* 13°21S 166°38E **287** C4
Lohals *Denmark* 55°8N 10°55E **163** J4
Lohardaga *India* 23°27N 84°45E **243** H11
Loharia *India* 23°45N 74°14E **242** H6
Loharu *India* 28°27N 75°49E **242** E6
Lohja *Finland* 60°12N 24°5E **188** B3
Löhme *Germany* 52°37N 13°40E **115** A5
Löhne *Germany* 52°11N 8°40E **178** C4
Loho = Luohe *China* 33°32N 114°2E **226** H8
Lohr *Germany* 49°59N 9°35E **179** F5
Lohri Wah → *Pakistan* 27°27N 67°37E **242** F2
Loi-kaw *Burma* 19°40N 97°17E **241** F6
Loi-lem *Burma* 20°52N 97°28E **241** E6
Loimaa *Finland* 60°50N 23°5E **188** B2
Loir → *France* 47°33N 0°32W **172** E6
Loir-et-Cher □ *France* 47°40N 1°20E **172** E8
Loire □ *France* 45°40N 4°5E **175** C8
Loire → *France* 47°16N 2°10W **172** E4
Loire Anjou Touraine △ *France* 47°14N 0°5W **172** E6
Loire-Atlantique □ *France* 47°25N 1°40W **172** E5
Loire Inférieure = Loire-Atlantique □ *France* 47°25N 1°40W **172** E5
Loiret □ *France* 47°55N 2°30E **173** E9
Loitz *Germany* 53°58N 13°8E **178** B9
Loja *Ecuador* 3°59S 79°16W **330** A2
Loja *Spain* 37°10N 4°10W **195** H6
Loja □ *Ecuador* 4°0S 79°13W **328** D2
Loje → *Angola* 7°49S 13°6E **265** D2
Loji = Kawasi *Indonesia* 1°38S 127°28E **231** E7
Lojo = Lohja *Finland* 60°12N 24°5E **188** B3
Løjt Kirkeby *Denmark* 55°7N 9°26E **163** J3
Lojung *China* 24°27N 109°36E **228** E7
Loka *Dem. Rep. of the Congo* 0°22N 18°2E **264** B3
Loka *South Sudan* 4°13N 31°0E **257** G3
Lokako *Dem. Rep. of the Congo* 0°57S 18°55E **264** C4
Lokandu *Dem. Rep. of the Congo* 2°30S 25°45E **264** C5
Lokaw *Dem. Rep. of the Congo* 2°40S 20°12E **264** C4
Løken *Norway* 59°48N 11°29E **164** E8
Lokeren *Belgium* 51°6N 3°59E **170** C3
Lokgwabe *Botswana* 24°10S 21°50E **270** B3
Lokhvytsya *Ukraine* 50°25N 33°18E **189** G7
Lokichar *Kenya* 2°23N 35°39E **268** B4
Lokichokio *Kenya* 4°19N 34°13E **268** B3
Lokitaung *Kenya* 4°12N 35°48E **268** B4
Lokkan tekojärvi *Finland* 67°55N 27°35E **160** C22
Løkken *Denmark* 57°22N 9°41E **163** G3
Løkken *Sør-Trøndelag, Norway* 63°9N 9°41E **164** A6
Loknya *Russia* 56°49N 30°4E **188** D6
Loko *C.A.R.* 3°38N 18°2E **264** B3
Loko *Nigeria* 8°1N 7°53E **263** D6
Lokoja *Nigeria* 7°47N 6°45E **263** D6
Lokolama *Dem. Rep. of the Congo* 2°35S 19°50E **264** C3
Lokolenge *Dem. Rep. of the Congo* 1°12N 22°38E **264** B4
Lokolo → *Dem. Rep. of the Congo* 1°43S 18°23E **264** C3
Lokot *Russia* 52°34N 34°36E **189** F8
Loktak L. = Logtak L. *India* 24°33N 93°50E **241** C4
Lokuru *Solomon Is.* 8°20S 157°0E **287** M9
Lol *South Sudan* 6°26N 29°37E **257** F2
Lol → *South Sudan* 9°13N 26°30E **257** F2
Lola *Angola* 14°19S 13°37E **265** E2
Lola *Guinea* 7°52N 8°29W **262** D3
Lola, Mt. *U.S.A.* 39°26N 120°22W **306** F6
Lolgorien *Kenya* 1°14S 34°48E **268** C3
Lolibai, Gebel *South Sudan* 3°50N 33°0E **257** G3
Lolimi *South Sudan* 4°35N 34°0E **257** G3
Loliondo *Tanzania* 2°2S 35°39E **268** C4
Lolland *Denmark* 54°45N 11°30E **163** K5
Lollar *Germany* 50°37N 8°43E **178** E4
Lolo *U.S.A.* 46°45N 114°5W **304** C6
Lolo → *Eq. Guin.* 1°36N 9°37E **264** B1
Lolo → *Gabon* 0°18S 12°18E **264** C2
Lolobau I. *Papua N. G.* 4°55S 151°10E **286** C6
Lolodorf *Cameroon* 3°16N 10°49E **263** E7
Lolokhet *Pakistan* 24°54N 67°12E **123** A2
Loloma *Zambia* 13°24S 24°21E **265** E4
Loltong *Vanuatu* 15°32S 168°10E **287** E5
Lom *Bulgaria* 43°48N 23°12E **202** C7
Lom *Oppland, Norway* 61°50N 8°34E **164** C5
Lom → *Bulgaria* 43°45N 23°15E **202** C7
Lom → *Cameroon* 5°20N 13°24E **264** A2
Lom Kao *Thailand* 16°53N 101°14E **236** D3
Lom Sak *Thailand* 16°47N 101°15E **236** D3
Loma *U.S.A.* 47°56N 110°30W **304** C8
Loma Linda *U.S.A.* 34°3N 117°16W **307** L9
Loma Mansa *S. Leone* 9°13N 11°7W **262** D2
Loma Mts. *S. Leone* 9°10N 11°7W **262** D2
Lomako → *Dem. Rep. of the Congo* 0°50N 20°50E **264** B4
Lomaloma *Fiji* 17°17S 178°59W **287** A3
Lomami → *Dem. Rep. of the Congo* 0°46N 24°16E **264** B4
Lomas Chapultepec *Mexico* 19°25N 99°12W **128** B1
Lomas de San Angel Inn *Mexico* 19°20N 99°13W **128** B1
Lomas de Zamora *Argentina* 34°45S 58°24W **334** C4
Lombadina *Australia* 16°31S 122°54E **278** C3
Lombard *U.S.A.* 41°53N 88°1W **311** C8
Lombárdia □ *Italy* 45°40N 9°30E **198** C6
Lombardy = Lombárdia □ *Italy* 45°40N 9°30E **198** C6
Lombardy East *S. Africa* 26°6S 28°7E **123** A2
Lombe *Angola* 9°27S 16°13E **265** D3
Lombez *France* 43°29N 0°55E **174** E4
Lomblen *Indonesia* 8°30S 123°32E **231** F6
Lombok *Indonesia* 8°45S 116°30E **235** D5
Lombok, Selat *Indonesia* 8°30S 115°50E **231** K18
Lomé *Togo* 6°9N 1°20E **263** D5
Lomela *Dem. Rep. of the Congo* 2°19S 23°15E **264** C4
Lomela → *Dem. Rep. of the Congo* 0°15S 20°40E **264** C4
Lomianki *Poland* 52°21N 20°54E **142** A1
Lomié *Cameroon* 3°13N 13°38E **264** B2
Lomma *Sweden* 55°43N 13°6E **163** J7
Lommel *Belgium* 51°14N 5°19E **170** C5
Lomond *Canada* 50°24N 112°36W **296** C6
Lomond, L. *U.K.* 56°8N 4°38W **167** E4
Lomonosov Ridge *Arctic* 88°0N 140°0E **150** A
Lomphat *Cambodia* 13°30N 106°59E **236** F6
Lompobatang *Indonesia* 5°24S 119°56E **231** F5
Lompoc *U.S.A.* 34°38N 120°28W **307** L6
Lomsegga *Norway* 61°49N 8°21E **164** C5
Lomus Reforma *Mexico* 19°24N 99°14W **128** B1
Łomża *Poland* 53°10N 22°2E **185** E9
Lon, Ko *Thailand* 7°47N 98°23E **237** a
Lonavale *India* 18°46N 73°29E **244** E1
Loncoche *Chile* 39°20S 72°50W **336** A2
Loncopué *Argentina* 38°4S 70°37W **336** A2
Londa *India* 15°30N 74°30E **245** G2
Londiani *Kenya* 0°10S 35°33E **268** C4
Londinières *France* 49°50N 1°25E **172** C8
London *Ont., Canada* 42°59N 81°15W **312** D3
London *London, U.K.* 51°30N 0°3W **125** B3
London *Ky., U.S.A.* 37°8N 84°5W **309** G11
London *Ohio, U.S.A.* 39°53N 83°27W **311** E13
London, Greater □ *U.K.* 51°36N 0°5W **169** F7
London Avenue Canal *U.S.A.* 30°3N 90°6W **131** A2
London Bridge *Grenada* 12°15N 61°35W **323** q
London Bridge *London, U.K.* **125** b5

London City ✕ (LCY) U.K. 51°30N 0°3E 125 A4
London Gatwick ✕ (LGW) U.K. 51°10N 0°11W 169 F7
London Heathrow ✕ (LHR) U.K. 51°28N 0°27W 125 B1
London Mills U.S.A. 40°43N 90°11W 310 D6
London Stansted ✕ (STN) U.K. 51°54N 0°14E 169 F8
London Zoo U.K. 51°31N 0°9W 125 A3
Londonderry U.K. 55°0N 7°20W 166 B4
Londonderry □ U.K. 55°0N 7°20W 166 B4
Londonderry, C. Australia 13°45S 126°55E 278 B4
Londonderry, I. Chile 55°0S 71°0W 336 E2
Londrina Brazil 23°18S 51°10W 335 A5
Londuimbale Angola 12°15S 15°19E 265 E3
Lone Pine U.S.A. 36°36N 118°4W 306 J8
Lonely Mine Zimbabwe 19°30S 28°49E 271 A4
Long, Î. Martinique 14°36N 60°51W 322 j
Long Akah Malaysia 3°19N 114°47E 235 B4
Long B. N.S.W., Australia 33°59S 151°15E 139 B2
Long B. Cornwall, Jamaica 18°20N 78°20W 320 a
Long B. S.C., U.S.A. 33°35N 78°45W 315 E15
Long Beach Calif., U.S.A. 33°46N 118°11W 307 M8
Long Beach N.Y., U.S.A. 40°35N 73°39W 313 F11
Long Beach Wash., U.S.A. 46°21N 124°3W 306 D2
Long Branch Ont., Canada 43°35N 79°31W 141 B1
Long Branch N.J., U.S.A. 40°18N 74°0W 313 F11
Long Brook → U.S.A. 38°49N 77°15W 143 C2
Long Cay Bahamas 25°6N 77°22W 153 b
Long Creek U.S.A. 44°43N 119°6W 304 D4
Long Ditton U.K. 51°22N 0°19W 125 B2
Long Eaton U.K. 52°53N 1°15W 168 E6
Long I. Antigua & B. 17°8N 61°45W 322 b
Long I. Queens., Australia 20°22S 148°51E 280 b
Long I. Bahamas 23°20N 75°10W 321 B4
Long I. Nunavut, Canada 54°50N 79°20W 298 B4
Long I. Cork, Ireland 51°30N 9°34W 166 E2
Long I. Papua N. G. 5°20S 147°5E 286 C4
Long I. N.Y., U.S.A. 40°45N 73°30W 313 F11
Long Island City U.S.A. 40°45N 73°56W 132 B2
Long Island Sd. U.S.A. 41°10N 73°0W 313 E12
Long L. Ont., Canada 49°30N 86°50W 298 C2
Long L. N.Y., U.S.A. 44°0N 74°23W 313 C10
Long Lake U.S.A. 43°58N 74°25W 313 C10
Long Mountain Mauritius 20°8S 57°33E 272 e
Long Point Canada 42°34N 80°25W 312 D4
Long Point B. Canada 42°40N 80°10W 312 D4
Long Prairie U.S.A. 45°59N 94°52W 308 C6
Long Prairie → U.S.A. 46°20N 94°36W 308 B6
Long Pt. Bahamas 25°1N 77°20W 153 b
Long Pt. Ont., Canada 42°35N 80°2W 312 D4
Long Pt. Ont., Canada 43°56N 76°53W 313 C8
Long Pt. Otago, N.Z. 46°34S 169°36E 285 G4
Long Range Mts. Canada 49°30N 57°30W 299 C8
Long Reef Australia 14°1S 125°48E 278 B4
Long Sault Canada 45°2N 74°53W 313 A10
Long Str. = Longa, Proliv Russia 70°0N 175°0E 215 C18
Long Street Cape Town, S. Africa 118 c2
Long Thanh Vietnam 10°47N 106°57E 237 G6
Long Xian China 34°55N 106°55E 226 G4
Long Xuyen Vietnam 10°19N 105°28E 237 G5
Longa Angola 14°42S 18°32E 265 E3
Longa Greece 36°53N 21°55E 204 E3
Longa → Angola 10°14S 13°29E 265 E2
Longa, Proliv Russia 70°0N 175°0E 215 C18
Longa Mavinga ⌂ Angola 16°20S 20°15E 265 F4
Longagung Indonesia 2°16N 115°16E 235 B5
Long'an China 23°10N 107°40E 228 F6
Longana Vanuatu 15°18S 168°0E 287 E5
Longarone Italy 46°16N 12°18E 199 B9
Longbenton U.K. 55°1N 1°31W 168 B6
Longberang Indonesia 3°43N 116°7E 235 B5
Longbia Indonesia 2°37N 116°42E 235 B5
Longboat Key U.S.A. 27°23N 82°39W 317 H7
Longboh Indonesia 0°52N 115°1E 235 B5
Longburn N.Z. 40°23S 175°35E 284 G4
Longchamp, Hippodrome de France 48°51N 2°13E 134 A2
Longchang China 29°18N 105°15E 228 C5
Longchuan Guangdong, China 24°5N 115°17E 229 E10
Longchuan Yunnan, China 24°23N 97°58E 228 E1
Longde China 35°30N 106°20E 226 G4
Longdenville Trin. & Tob. 10°31N 61°23W 323 t
Longeau France 47°47N 5°20E 173 E12
Longford Tas., Australia 41°32S 147°3E 281 G4
Longford Longf., Ireland 53°43N 7°49W 166 C4
Longford □ Ireland 53°42N 7°45W 166 C4
Longgan Shan China 42°19N 126°30E 224 A3
Longhai China 24°25N 117°46E 229 E11
Longhua Guangdong, China 22°39N 114°0E 219 a
Longhua Hebei, China 41°18N 117°45E 227 D9
Longhua Pagoda China 31°10N 121°26E 138 B1
Longhua Park China 31°10N 121°26E 138 B1
Longhui China 27°7N 111°2E 229 D8
Longido Tanzania 2°43S 36°42E 268 C4
Longiram Indonesia 0°5S 115°45E 235 C5
Longjela Indonesia 2°28N 115°28E 235 B5
Longjing China 42°46N 129°25E 227 C15
Longjohn Slough U.S.A. 41°42N 87°52W 119 C1
Longkou Jiangxi, China 26°8N 115°10E 229 D10
Longkou Shandong, China 37°40N 120°18E 227 F11
Longli China 26°25N 106°58E 228 D6
Longlin China 24°47N 105°20E 228 E5
Longling China 24°37N 98°39E 228 E2
Longmeadow U.S.A. 42°3N 72°34W 313 D12
Longmen China 23°40N 114°18E 229 F10
Longmen Shiku China 34°34N 112°10E 226 G7
Longming China 22°59N 107°7E 228 F6
Longmont U.S.A. 40°10N 105°6W 304 F11
Longnan China 24°55N 114°47E 229 E10
Longnawan Indonesia 1°51N 114°55E 235 B4
Longobucco Italy 39°27N 16°37E 201 C9
Longoni, B. de Mayotte 12°41S 45°8E 272 b
Longonot △ Kenya 0°55S 36°28E 266 E4
Longos Greece 39°16N 20°7E 206 C10
Longquan China 28°7N 119°10E 229 C12
Longreach Australia 23°28S 144°14E 280 C3
Longshan China 29°29N 109°25E 228 C7
Longsheng China 25°48N 110°0E 229 E8
Longtan Dam China 25°5N 107°0E 228 E6
Longtan Hu → China 39°51N 116°24E 114 B2
Longué-Jumelles France 47°22N 0°8W 172 E6
Longue-Pointe Canada 45°35N 73°31W 130 A2
Longueau France 49°52N 2°21E 173 C9
Longueuil Canada 45°31N 73°29W 130 A3
Longuy Cameroon 3°5N 9°58E 264 B1
Longuyon France 49°27N 5°35E 173 C12
Longvic France 47°17N 5°4E 173 E12
Longview Tex., U.S.A. 32°30N 94°44W 314 E7
Longview Wash., U.S.A. 46°8N 122°57W 306 D4
Longwood St. Helena 15°57S 5°41W 153 h
Longwood Fla., U.S.A. 28°42N 81°21W 317 G8
Longwy France 49°30N 5°46E 173 C12
Longxi China 34°53N 104°40E 226 G3
Longxue Dao China 22°41N 113°38E 219 a
Longyan China 25°10N 117°0E 229 E11
Longyearbyen Svalbard 78°13N 15°40E 150 B8
Longyou China 29°1N 119°8E 229 C12
Longzhou China 22°22N 106°50E 228 F6
Loni India 28°45N 77°17E 120 A2
Lonigo Italy 45°23N 11°23E 199 C8
Löningen Germany 52°44N 7°46E 178 C3
Lonja → Croatia 45°22N 16°40E 199 C13
Lonkala Dem. Rep. of the Congo 4°37S 23°14E 265 C4
Lonkin Burma 25°39N 96°22E 241 C6
Lonoke U.S.A. 34°47N 91°54W 314 D9
Lonquimay Chile 38°26S 71°14W 336 A2
Lons-le-Saunier France 46°40N 5°31E 173 F12
Lönsboda Sweden 56°24N 14°20E 163 H8
Lønset Norway 62°46N 7°24E 164 B4
Lonton Burma 25°6N 96°17E 241 C6
Looc Phil. 12°15N 121°59E 232 E3
Looe U.K. 50°22N 4°28W 169 G3
Loogootee U.S.A. 38°41N 86°55W 311 F10
Lookout, C. Canada 55°18N 83°56W 298 A3
Lookout, C. N.C., U.S.A. 34°35N 76°32W 315 D16
Loolmalasin Tanzania 3°0S 35°53E 268 C4
Loon → Alta., Canada 57°8N 115°3W 296 B5
Loon → Man., Canada 55°53N 101°59W 297 B8
Loon Lake Canada 54°2N 109°10W 297 C7
Loongana Australia 30°52S 127°5E 279 F4
Loop, The Chicago, U.S.A. 119 c1
Loop Hd. Ireland 52°34N 9°56W 166 D2
Lop China 37°3N 80°11E 217 E10
Lop Nor = Lop Nur China 40°20N 90°10E 217 D12
Lop Nur China 40°20N 90°10E 217 D12
Lopare Bos.-H. 44°39N 18°46E 182 F3
Lopatin Russia 43°50N 47°35E 191 J8
Lopatina, Gora Russia 50°47N 143°10E 215 D15
Lopatino = Volzhsk Russia 55°57N 48°23E 190 C9
Lopatka, Mys Russia 50°52N 156°40E 215 D16
Lopaye South Sudan 6°37N 33°40E 257 F3
Lopburi Thailand 14°48N 100°37E 236 E3
Lopé-Okanda ⌂ Gabon 0°45S 11°34E 264 C2
Lopevi Vanuatu 16°30S 168°21E 287 E6
Lopez Phil. 13°53N 122°15E 232 E4
Lopez Pa., U.S.A. 41°27N 76°20W 313 E8
Lopez, C. Gabon 0°47S 8°40E 264 C1
López de Filippis = Mariscal Estigarribia Paraguay 22°3S 60°40W 334 A3
Lopinot Trin. & Tob. 10°41N 61°19W 323 t
Lopori → Dem. Rep. of the Congo 1°14N 19°49E 254 B3
Lopphavet Norway 70°27N 21°15E 160 A19
Lora Norway 62°8N 8°45E 164 B5
Lora → Afghan. 31°35N 66°32E 240 C2
Lora → Oppland, Norway 62°8N 8°42E 164 B5
Lora, Hāmūn-i- Pakistan 29°38N 64°58E 240 C2
Lora Cr. → Australia 28°10S 135°22E 281 D2
Lora del Río Spain 37°39N 5°33W 195 H5
Lorain U.S.A. 41°28N 82°11W 312 E2
Loraine U.S.A. 40°9N 91°13W 310 D5
Loralai Pakistan 30°20N 68°41E 242 D3
Lorca Spain 37°41N 1°42W 197 H3
Lord Howe I. Pac. Oc. 31°33S 159°6E 277 G11
Lord Howe Rise Pac. Oc. 30°0S 162°30E 277 H12
Lord Howe Seamount Chain Pac. Oc. 28°0S 159°0E 277 F10
Lord Loughborough I. Burma 10°25N 97°54E 237 G1
Lord's Cricket Ground U.K. 51°31N 0°10W 125 A2
Lordsburg U.S.A. 32°21N 108°43W 305 K9
Lorengau Papua N. G. 2°1S 147°15E 286 B4
Lorestān □ Iran 33°30N 48°40E 247 C6
Loreto Bolivia 15°13S 64°40W 331 D5
Loreto Brazil 7°5S 45°10W 332 C2
Loreto Marche, Italy 43°26N 13°36E 199 E10
Loreto Piemonte, Italy 45°29N 9°12E 129 B2
Loreto Baja Calif. S., Mexico 26°0N 111°21W 318 B2
Loreto Surigao N., Phil. 10°21N 125°34E 232 F5
Loreto □ Peru 5°0S 75°0W 328 E3
Lorgues France 43°28N 6°22E 175 E10
Lorhosso Burkina Faso 10°17N 3°38W 262 C4
Lorian Swamp Kenya 0°40N 39°35E 267 D4
Lorica Colombia 9°14N 75°49W 328 B2
Lorient Morbihan, France 47°45N 3°23W 172 E3
Lorient St.-Martin 17°54N 62°49W 322 a
Lorimor U.S.A. 41°8N 94°3W 310 C2
Lőrinci Hungary 47°44N 19°41E 182 C4
Lormi India 22°17N 81°41E 243 H9
Lorn U.K. 56°26N 5°10W 167 E3
Lorn, Firth of U.K. 56°20N 5°40W 167 E3
Lorne Australia 38°33S 143°59E 282 E5
Loronyo South Sudan 4°38N 32°38E 257 G3
Lorovouno Cyprus 35°8N 32°36E 207 E8
Lörrach Germany 47°36N 7°40E 179 H3
Lorrain → Martinique 14°50N 61°3W 322 j
Lorraine = Baker U.S.A. 46°22N 104°17W 304 C11
Lorraine □ France 48°53N 6°0E 173 D13
Lorraine ⌂ France 48°55N 5°50E 173 D12
Los Sweden 61°45N 15°10E 162 C9
Los, Îles de Guinea 9°30N 13°50W 262 D2
Los Alamos Calif., U.S.A. 34°44N 120°17W 307 L6
Los Alamos N. Mex., U.S.A. 35°53N 106°19W 305 J10
Los Alcornocales ⌂ Spain 36°21N 5°32W 195 J5
Los Alerces △ Argentina 42°55S 71°55W 336 B2
Los Altos U.S.A. 37°23N 122°7W 306 H4
Los Andes Chile 32°50S 70°40W 334 C1
Los Angeles Chile 37°28S 72°23W 334 D1
Los Angeles Calif., U.S.A. 34°4N 118°15W 125 B3
Los Angeles, Bahía de Mexico 28°56N 113°34W 318 B2
Los Angeles Aqueduct U.S.A. 35°22N 118°5W 307 K9
Los Angeles Int. ✕ (LAX) U.S.A. 33°57N 118°25W 123 C2
Los Antiguos Argentina 46°35S 71°40W 336 C2
Los Banos U.S.A. 37°4N 120°51W 306 H6
Los Barrios Spain 36°11N 5°30W 195 J5
Los Blancos Argentina 23°40S 62°30W 334 A3
Los Cardones △ Argentina 25°8S 65°55W 334 B2
Los Cerrillos ✕ (ULC) Chile 33°29S 70°42W 137 B1
Los Chiles Costa Rica 11°2N 84°43W 320 D3
Los Corrales de Buelna Spain 43°16N 4°4W 194 B6
Los Cristianos Canary Is. 28°3N 16°42W 153 e1
Los Gallardos Spain 37°10N 1°57W 197 H3
Los Gallos Pt. Trin. & Tob. 10°5N 61°55W 323 t
Los Gatos U.S.A. 37°14N 121°59W 306 H5
Los Glaciares △ Argentina 50°0S 73°55W 336 C2
Los Haïtises △ Dom. Rep. 19°4N 69°36W 321 C6
Los Hermanos Is. Venezuela 11°45N 64°25W 321 D7
Los Huemules △ Chile 46°10S 73°23W 336 C2
Los Islotes Canary Is. 29°4N 13°44W 153 e2
Los Katios △ Colombia 7°50N 77°10W 328 B2
Los Lagos Chile 39°51S 72°50W 336 A2
Los Llanos de Aridane Canary Is. 28°38N 17°54W 153 e1
Los Loros Chile 27°50S 70°6W 334 B1
Los Lunas U.S.A. 34°48N 106°44W 305 J10
Los Menucos Argentina 40°50S 68°10W 336 B3
Los Mochis Mexico 25°45N 108°57W 318 B3
Los Monegros Spain 41°29N 0°13W 196 D4
Los Monos Argentina 46°1S 69°36W 336 C3
Los Muermos Chile 41°24S 73°29W 336 B2
Los Nevados △ Colombia 4°41N 75°21W 328 C2
Los Nietos Spain 37°39N 0°47W 197 H4
Los Nietos Calif., U.S.A. 33°57N 118°4W 126 C4
Los Olivos Lima, Peru 11°59S 77°5W 124 A2
Los Olivos Calif., U.S.A. 34°40N 120°7W 307 L6
Los Palacios Cuba 22°35N 83°15W 320 B3
Los Palacios y Villafranca Spain 37°10N 5°55W 195 H5
Los Queñes Chile 35°1S 70°48W 334 D1
Los Remedios △ Mexico 19°28N 99°17W 128 B1
Los Reyes Mexico 19°21N 99°6W 128 B2
Los Reyes de Salgado Mexico 19°35N 102°29W 318 D4
Los Ríos □ Ecuador 1°30S 79°25W 328 D2
Los Roques Is. Venezuela 11°50N 66°45W 321 D6
Los Santos de Maimona Spain 38°27N 6°22W 195 G4
Los Teques Venezuela 10°21N 67°2W 328 A4
Los Testigos, Is. Venezuela 11°23N 63°6W 329 A5
Los Vilos Chile 32°10S 71°30W 334 C1
Los Yébenes Spain 39°36N 3°55W 195 F7
Loshan = Leshan China 29°33N 103°41E 228 C4
Łosice Poland 52°13N 22°43E 185 F9
Lošinj Croatia 44°30N 14°30E 199 D11
Loskop Dam S. Africa 25°23S 29°20E 271 C4
Løsning Denmark 55°48N 9°42E 163 J3
Losombo Dem. Rep. of the Congo 1°2N 19°44E 264 B3
Lossiemouth U.K. 57°42N 3°17W 167 D5
Lossnen Sweden 62°26N 12°45E 162 B6
Lostwithiel U.K. 50°24N 4°41W 169 G3
Losuia Papua N. G. 8°30S 151°4E 286 E6
Lot Belgium 50°46N 4°16E 116 B1
Lot □ France 44°39N 1°40E 174 D5
Lot → France 44°18N 0°20E 174 D4
Lot-et-Garonne □ France 44°22N 0°30E 174 D4
Lota Chile 37°5S 73°10W 334 D1
Lotagipi Swamp Sudan 4°36N 34°55E 257 G3
Løten Norway 60°51N 11°21E 164 D8
Lotfābād Iran 37°32N 59°20E 247 B8
Lothair S. Africa 26°22S 30°27E 271 C5
Loto Dem. Rep. of the Congo 2°48S 22°30E 264 C4
Lotoi → Dem. Rep. of the Congo 1°35S 18°30E 264 C3
Lotorp Sweden 58°44N 15°50E 163 F9
Lötschbergtunnel Switz. 46°26N 7°43E 179 J3
Lotta → Europe 68°42N 31°6E 160 B24
Lottefors Sweden 61°25N 16°24E 162 C10
Löttorp Sweden 57°10N 17°0E 163 G11
Lotung Taiwan 24°41N 121°46E 225 B3
Lotus River S. Africa 34°4S 18°31E 118 B2
Lotus Temple India 28°33N 77°15E 120 B2
Lötzen = Giżycko Poland 54°2N 21°48E 184 D8
Lou I. Papua N. G. 2°25S 147°22E 286 B4
Loubière Dominica 15°16N 61°23W 323 k
Loubomo Congo 4°9S 12°47E 264 C2
Loudéac France 48°11N 2°47W 172 D4
Loudi China 27°42N 111°59E 229 D8
Loudima Congo 4°6S 13°5E 264 C2
Loudonville U.S.A. 40°38N 82°14W 312 F2
Loudun France 47°3N 0°5E 172 E7
Loue → France 47°1N 5°28E 173 E12
Louga Senegal 15°45N 16°5W 262 B1
Louga □ Senegal 15°20N 15°35W 262 B1
Loughborough U.K. 52°47N 1°11W 168 E6
Lougheed I. Canada 77°26N 105°6W 295 B10
Loughlinstown Ireland 53°15N 6°7W 120 B3
Loughman U.S.A. 28°14N 81°34W 317 G8
Loughrea Ireland 53°12N 8°33W 166 C3
Loughros More B. Ireland 54°48N 8°32W 166 B3
Louhans France 46°38N 5°12E 173 F12
Louis Armstrong New Orleans Int. ✕ (MSY) U.S.A. 30°0N 90°15W 131 A1
Louis Armstrong Park New Orleans, U.S.A. 131 a2
Louis-Gentil = Youssoufia Morocco 32°16N 8°31W 260 B3
Louis Trichardt S. Africa 23°1S 29°43E 271 B4
Louis XIV, Pte. Canada 54°37N 79°45W 298 B4
Louisa U.S.A. 38°7N 82°36W 309 F12
Louisbourg Canada 45°55N 60°0W 299 C8
Louisburg U.S.A. 38°37N 94°41W 310 F2
Louisburgh Ireland 53°46N 9°49W 166 C2
Louise, L. U.S.A. 28°28N 81°32W 133 B1
Louise I. Canada 52°55N 131°50W 296 C2
Louiseville Canada 46°20N 72°56W 298 C5
Louisiade Arch. Papua N. G. 11°10S 153°0E 286 F7
Louisiana U.S.A. 39°27N 91°3W 310 E6
Louisiana □ U.S.A. 30°50N 92°0W 314 F9
Louisiana Superdome New Orleans, U.S.A. 131 b1
Louisville Ala., U.S.A. 31°47N 85°33W 316 D4
Louisville Ga., U.S.A. 33°0N 82°25W 316 B7
Louisville Ill., U.S.A. 38°46N 88°30W 311 F8
Louisville Ky., U.S.A. 38°15N 85°46W 311 F11
Louisville Miss., U.S.A. 33°7N 89°3W 315 E10
Louisville Ohio, U.S.A. 40°50N 81°16W 312 F3
Louisville Ridge Pac. Oc. 31°0S 172°30W 288 L10
Loukoléla Congo 1°4S 17°10E 264 C3
Loukouo Congo 3°38S 14°39E 264 C2
Loulay France 46°3N 0°30W 174 B3
Loulé Portugal 37°9N 8°0W 195 H3
Louloni Mali 10°54N 5°36W 262 C3
Loum Cameroon 4°42N 9°44E 264 B1
Louny Czech Rep. 50°20N 13°48E 180 A6
Loup City U.S.A. 41°17N 98°58W 308 E4
Loups Marins, Lacs des Canada 56°30N 73°45W 298 A5
Lourdes France 43°6N 0°3W 174 E3
Lourdes-de-Blanc-Sablon Canada 51°24N 57°12W 299 B8
Lourenço Brazil 2°30N 51°40W 329 C7
Lourenço Marques = Maputo Mozam. 25°58S 32°32E 271 C5
Loures Portugal 38°49N 9°10W 126 A1
Lourinhã Portugal 39°14N 9°17W 195 F1
Louros Greece 39°3N 20°47E 207 A2
Louroujina Cyprus 35°0N 33°28E 207 F9
Lousã Portugal 40°7N 8°14W 194 E2
Louta Burkina Faso 13°30N 3°13W 262 C4
Louth N.S.W., Australia 30°30S 145°8E 283 A6
Louth Ireland 53°58N 6°32W 166 C5
Louth Lincs., U.K. 53°22N 0°1W 168 D7
Louth □ Ireland 53°56N 6°34W 166 C5
Louth B. Australia 34°33S 135°56E 282 C1
Loutra Edipsou Greece 38°54N 23°2E 204 C5
Loutra Kyllinis Greece 37°52N 21°7E 207 D3
Loutraki Greece 37°58N 22°57E 204 D4
Loutropoli Thermis Greece 39°11N 26°29E 205 B8
Louvain = Leuven Belgium 50°52N 4°42E 170 D4
Louvale U.S.A. 32°10N 84°50W 316 C5
Louveciennes France 48°51N 2°8E 134 A1
Louviers France 49°12N 1°10E 172 C8
Louvre, Musée du Paris, France 134 b4
Louvre, Palais du Paris, France 134 b4
Louwsburg S. Africa 27°37S 31°7E 271 C5
Lovat → Russia 58°14N 31°28E 188 C6
Lovćen Montenegro 42°23N 18°51E 202 D2
Lovćen △ Montenegro 42°20N 18°50E 202 D2
Lovech Bulgaria 43°8N 24°42E 203 C8
Lovech □ Bulgaria 43°0N 24°45E 203 D8
Loveland Colo., U.S.A. 40°24N 105°5W 304 F11
Loveland Ohio, U.S.A. 39°16N 84°16W 311 E12
Lovell U.S.A. 44°50N 108°24W 304 D9
Lovelock U.S.A. 40°11N 118°28W 304 F4
Lóvere Italy 45°49N 10°4E 198 C7
Lovers Leap Jamaica 17°52N 77°39W 320 a
Loves Park U.S.A. 42°19N 89°3W 310 B7
Lövestad Sweden 55°40N 13°54E 163 J7
Loviisa Finland 60°28N 26°12E 188 B4
Lovilia U.S.A. 41°8N 92°55W 310 C4
Lovina Indonesia 8°9S 115°1E 231 J18
Loving U.S.A. 32°17N 104°6W 305 K11
Lovington Ill., U.S.A. 39°43N 88°38W 311 E8
Lovington N. Mex., U.S.A. 32°57N 103°21W 305 K12
Lovisa = Loviisa Finland 60°28N 26°12E 188 B4
Lovosice Czech Rep. 50°30N 14°2E 180 A7
Lovran Croatia 45°18N 14°15E 199 C11
Lovrin Romania 45°58N 20°48E 182 E5
Lövstabruk Sweden 60°25N 17°53E 162 D11
Lövstabukten Sweden 60°35N 17°45E 162 D11
Lóvua Lunda Norte, Angola 7°19S 20°12E 265 D4
Lóvua Moxico, Angola 11°33S 23°33E 265 E4
Lóvua → Dem. Rep. of the Congo 6°6S 20°37E 265 D4
Low, L. Canada 52°29N 76°17W 298 B4
Low B. Antigua & B. 17°39N 61°51W 322 b
Low Pt. Australia 32°25S 127°25E 279 F4
Low Tatra = Nízké Tatry Slovak Rep. 48°55N 19°30E 181 C12
Lowa Dem. Rep. of the Congo 1°25S 25°47E 268 C2
Lowa → Dem. Rep. of the Congo 1°24S 25°51E 268 C2
Lowden U.S.A. 41°52N 90°56W 310 C6
Lowell Ind., U.S.A. 41°18N 87°25W 311 C9
Lowell Mass., U.S.A. 42°38N 71°19W 313 D13
Lowell Mich., U.S.A. 42°56N 85°20W 311 B11
Lowellville U.S.A. 41°2N 80°32W 312 E4
Löwen = Lewin Brzeski Poland 50°45N 17°37E 185 H4
Löwen → Namibia 26°51S 18°17E 270 C2
Löwenberg = Lwówek Śląski Poland 51°7N 15°38E 185 G2
Löwenstadt = Brzeziny Poland 51°49N 19°42E 185 G6
Lower Alkali L. U.S.A. 41°16N 120°2W 304 F3
Lower Arrow L. Canada 49°40N 118°5W 296 D5
Lower Austria = Niederösterreich □ Austria 48°25N 15°40E 180 C8
Lower B. U.S.A. 40°32N 74°5W 132 C1
Lower California = Baja California Mexico 31°10N 115°12W 318 A1
Lower East Side New York, U.S.A. 132 e2
Lower Glenelg △ Australia 38°4S 141°41E 282 E4
Lower Hutt N.Z. 41°10S 174°55E 143 B2
Lower Kalskag U.S.A. 61°31N 160°22W 303 F7
Lower Lake U.S.A. 38°55N 122°37W 306 G4
Lower Manhattan New York, U.S.A. 132 e1
Lower Manitou L. Canada 49°15N 93°0W 297 D10
Lower Manzanilla Trin. & Tob. 10°31N 61°3W 323 t
Lower New York B. = Lower B. U.S.A. 40°22N 74°5W 132 C1
Lower Paia U.S.A. 20°55N 156°23W 302 C5
Lower Post Canada 59°58N 128°30W 296 B3
Lower Red L. U.S.A. 47°58N 95°0W 308 B6
Lower Saxony = Niedersachsen □ Germany 52°50N 9°0E 178 C4
Lower Shing Mun Res. China 22°22N 114°9E 122 A1
Lower Tunguska = Tunguska, Nizhnyaya → Russia 65°48N 88°4E 215 C9
Lower Zambezi △ Zambia 15°25S 29°40E 269 F2
Lowestoft U.K. 52°29N 1°45E 169 E9
Lowgar □ Afghan. 34°0N 69°0E 240 B3
Łowicz Poland 52°6N 19°55E 185 F6
Lowly, Pt. Australia 33°0S 137°46E 282 B2
Lowry B. N.Z. 41°15S 174°55E 143 B2
Lowry City U.S.A. 38°8N 93°44W 310 F3
Lowther I. Canada 74°33N 97°30W 295 C12
Lowville U.S.A. 43°47N 75°29W 313 C9
Loxton S. Austral., Australia 34°28S 140°31E 282 C4
Loxton Northern Cape, S. Africa 31°30S 22°22E 270 D3
Loyalton U.S.A. 39°41N 120°14W 306 F6
Loyalty Is. = Loyauté, Îs. N. Cal. 20°50S 166°30E 288 d
Loyang = Luoyang China 34°40N 112°26E 226 G7
Loyauté, Îs. N. Cal. 20°50S 166°30E 288 d
Loyev = Loyew Belarus 51°55N 30°46E 177 C16
Loyew Belarus 51°55N 30°46E 177 C16
Loyola Univ. U.S.A. 42°0N 87°39W 119 B3
Loyoro Uganda 3°22N 34°14E 268 B3
Lož Slovenia 45°43N 14°30E 199 C11
Lozère □ France 44°35N 3°30E 174 D7
Loznica Serbia 44°32N 19°14E 202 B3
Lozova Ukraine 49°0N 36°20E 189 H9
Ltalaltuma ✪ Australia 23°57S 132°25E 278 D5
Lu India 26°58N 95°14E 241 B5
Lü Shan China 29°30N 115°55E 229 C11
Lu Verne U.S.A. 42°55N 94°5W 310 B2
Lu Wo China 22°33N 114°6E 219 a
Lu Xun, Tomb of China 31°17N 121°29E 138 B1
Lu Xun Museum Beijing, China 114 b1
Lu Xun Park China 31°17N 121°28E 138 B1
Lua → Dem. Rep. of the Congo 2°46N 18°26E 264 B3
Lua Makiki U.S.A. 20°33N 156°37W 302 C5
Luachimo Angola 7°23S 20°48E 265 D4
Luacono Angola 11°15S 21°37E 265 E4
Luajan → India 24°44N 85°1E 243 G11
Lualaba → Dem. Rep. of the Congo 0°26N 25°20E 264 B5
Luale Dem. Rep. of the Congo 1°9N 23°5E 264 B4
Lualualei Naval Reserve U.S.A. 21°27N 158°6W 302 K13
Luambe △ Zambia 12°30S 32°15E 269 E3
Luampa Zambia 15°4S 24°20E 265 F4
Lu'an China 31°45N 116°29E 229 B11
Luan Chau Vietnam 21°38N 103°24E 228 G4
Luan He → China 39°20N 119°5E 227 E10
Luan Xian China 39°40N 118°40E 227 E10
Luancheng Guangxi Zhuangzu, China 22°48N 108°55E 228 F7
Luancheng Hebei, China 37°53N 114°40E 226 F8
Luanco Spain 43°37N 5°48W 194 B5
Luanda Angola 8°50S 13°15E 265 D2
Luando → Angola 10°21S 16°27E 265 E3
Luando ⌂ Angola 11°0S 17°32E 265 E3
Luang, Doi Thailand 18°30N 101°15E 236 C3
Luang, Thale Thailand 7°30N 100°15E 237 J3
Luang Nam Tha Laos 20°58N 101°30E 228 G3
Luang Prabang Laos 19°52N 102°10E 228 H4
Luanginga → Zambia 15°11S 22°55E 265 F4
Luangwa Zambia 15°35S 30°16E 269 F3
Luangwa → Zambia 14°25S 30°25E 269 E3
Luangwa Valley Zambia 13°30S 31°30E 269 E3
Luangwe = Loange → Dem. Rep. of the Congo 4°17S 20°2E 265 C4
Luania-Bubi Dem. Rep. of the Congo 7°28S 24°49E 265 D4
Luanne China 40°55N 117°40E 227 D9
Luanping China 40°53N 117°23E 227 D9
Luanshya Zambia 13°3S 28°28E 269 E2
Luapula □ Zambia 11°0S 29°0E 269 E2
Luapula → Africa 9°26S 28°33E 269 D2
Luar, Danau Indonesia 0°55N 112°15E 235 B4
Luarca Spain 43°32N 6°32W 194 B4
Luashi Dem. Rep. of the Congo 10°50S 23°36E 265 E4
Luatamba Angola 12°6S 20°19E 265 E4
Luatira Angola 12°52S 17°14E 265 E3
Luau Angola 10°40S 22°10E 265 E4
Luba Phil. 17°19N 120°42E 232 C3
Lubaczów Poland 50°10N 23°8E 185 H10
Lubalo Angola 9°10S 19°15E 265 D3
Lubamiti Dem. Rep. of the Congo 2°28S 17°47E 264 C3
Lubań Poland 51°5N 15°15E 185 G2
Lubana, Ozero = Lubānas Ezers Latvia 56°45N 27°0E 188 D4
Lubānas Ezers Latvia 56°45N 27°0E 188 D4
Lubang Phil. 13°52N 120°7E 232 E3
Lubang Is. Phil. 13°50N 120°12E 232 E3
Lubango Angola 14°55S 13°30E 265 E2
Lubao Dem. Rep. of the Congo 5°17S 25°42E 265 D5
Lubao Phil. 14°56N 120°36E 232 D3
Lübars Germany 52°37N 13°21E 115 A3
Lubartów Poland 51°28N 22°42E 185 G9
Lubawa Poland 53°30N 19°48E 184 E6
Lübbecke Germany 52°18N 8°37E 178 C4
Lübben Germany 51°56N 13°54E 178 D9
Lübbenau Germany 51°52N 13°57E 178 D9
Lubbock U.S.A. 33°35N 101°51W 314 E4
Lübeck Germany 53°52N 10°40E 178 B6
Lübecker Bucht Germany 54°3N 10°54E 178 A6
Lubefu Dem. Rep. of the Congo 4°47S 24°27E 265 C4
Lubefu → Dem. Rep. of the Congo 4°10S 23°0E 265 C4
Lubelskie □ Poland 51°20N 22°50E 185 G9
Lüben = Lubin Poland 51°24N 16°11E 185 G3
Lubero = Luofu Dem. Rep. of the Congo 0°10S 29°15E 268 C2
Luberon ⌂ France 43°52N 5°25E 175 E9
Lubersac France 45°26N 1°23E 174 C5
Lubicon L. Canada 56°23N 115°56W 296 B5
Lubień Kujawski Poland 52°23N 19°9E 185 F6
Lubilash → Dem. Rep. of the Congo 6°2S 23°45E 265 D4
Lubin Poland 51°24N 16°11E 185 G3
Lublin Poland 51°12N 22°38E 185 G9
Lubliniec Poland 50°43N 18°45E 185 H5
Lubnān = Lebanon ■ Asia 34°0N 36°0E 250 E7
Lubnān, Jabal Lebanon 33°45N 35°40E 250 E6
Lubniewice Poland 52°31N 15°15E 185 F2
Lubny Ukraine 50°3N 32°58E 189 G7
Lubomierz Poland 51°1N 15°31E 185 G2
Luboń Poland 52°21N 16°51E 185 F3
Lubondaie Dem. Rep. of the Congo 8°1S 26°32E 265 D4
Lubongola Dem. Rep. of the Congo 2°35S 27°50E 268 C2
L'ubotín Slovak Rep. 49°17N 20°53E 181 B13
Lubraniec Poland 52°33N 18°50E 185 F5
Lubsko Poland 51°45N 14°57E 185 G1
Lübtheen Germany 53°18N 11°5E 178 B7
Lubuagan Phil. 17°21N 121°10E 232 C3
Lubudi Dem. Rep. of the Congo 6°51S 21°18E 265 D4
Lubudi → Kasai-Occ., Dem. Rep. of the Congo 4°19S 20°23E 265 C4
Lubudi → Katanga, Dem. Rep. of the Congo 9°0S 25°35E 265 D5
Lubuklinggau Indonesia 3°15S 102°55E 234 C2
Lubukpakam Indonesia 3°33N 98°52E 234 B1
Lubuksikaping Indonesia 0°10N 100°15E 234 B2
Lubumbashi Dem. Rep. of the Congo 11°40S 27°28E 269 E2
Lubunda Dem. Rep. of the Congo 5°12S 26°41E 265 D5
Lubungu Zambia 14°35S 26°24E 269 E2
Lubuskie □ Poland 52°10N 15°20E 185 F2
Lubutu Dem. Rep. of the Congo 0°45S 26°30E 268 C2
Luc-en-Diois France 44°36N 5°28E 175 D9
Lucala Angola 9°7S 15°58E 265 D3
Lucala → Angola 9°38S 14°14E 265 D2
Lucan Canada 43°11N 81°24W 312 C3
Lucania, Mt. Canada 61°1N 140°27W 294 E3
Lucapa Angola 8°25S 20°45E 265 D4
Lucas U.S.A. 41°2N 93°29W 310 C3
Lucas Channel = Main Channel Canada 45°21N 81°45W 312 A3
Lucban Phil. 14°6N 121°33E 232 D3
Lucca Italy 43°50N 10°29E 198 E7
Lucé France 48°26N 1°27E 172 D8
Luce Bay U.K. 54°45N 4°48W 167 G4
Lucea Jamaica 18°27N 78°10W 320 a
Lucedale U.S.A. 30°56N 88°35W 315 F10
Lucena Phil. 13°56N 121°37E 232 E3
Lucena Spain 37°27N 4°31W 195 H6
Lučenec Slovak Rep. 48°18N 19°42E 181 C12
Lucera Italy 41°30N 15°20E 201 A8
Lucerne = Lake Worth U.S.A. 26°37N 80°3W 317 J9
Lucerne = Luzern Switz. 47°3N 8°18E 179 H4
Lucerne U.S.A. 39°6N 122°48W 306 F4
Lucerne Valley U.S.A. 34°27N 116°57W 307 L10
Lucero Mexico 30°49N 106°30W 318 A3
Luchena → Spain 37°44N 1°50W 197 H3
Lucheng China 36°20N 113°11E 226 F7
Lucheringo → Mozam. 11°43S 36°17E 269 E4
Luchow = Luzhou China 28°52N 105°20E 228 C5
Lüchow Germany 52°58N 11°8E 178 C7
Luchu Taiwan 22°52N 120°15E 225 D2
Luchuan China 22°21N 110°12E 229 F8
Lucia U.S.A. 36°2N 121°33W 306 J5
Luciara Brazil 10°45S 50°34W 333 D1
Lucie → Suriname 3°35N 57°38W 329 C6
Lucinda Australia 18°32S 146°20E 280 B4
Lucindale Australia 36°58S 140°26E 282 D4
Lucira Angola 14°0S 12°35E 265 E2
Luciras, B. das Angola 13°52S 12°31E 265 E2
Luckau Germany 51°50N 13°42E 178 D9
Luckenwalde Germany 52°5N 13°10E 178 C9
Luckey U.S.A. 41°27N 83°29W 311 C13
Luckhoff S. Africa 29°44S 24°43E 270 C3
Lucknow Ont., Canada 43°57N 81°31W 312 C3
Lucknow India 26°50N 81°0E 243 F9
Luçon France 46°28N 1°10W 174 B2
Lucusse Angola 12°32S 20°48E 265 E4
Lucy, L. U.S.A. 28°34N 81°29W 133 A2
Lüda = Dalian China 38°50N 121°40E 227 E11
Luda Kamchiya → Bulgaria 43°3N 27°29E 203 C11
Ludbreg Croatia 46°15N 16°38E 199 B13
Lüdenscheid Germany 51°13N 7°37E 178 D3
Lüderitz Namibia 26°41S 15°8E 270 C2
Lüderitzbaai Namibia 26°36S 15°8E 270 C2
Ludhiana India 30°57N 75°56E 242 D6
Ludian China 27°10N 103°33E 228 D4
Luding Qiao China 29°53N 102°12E 228 C4
Lüdinghausen Germany 51°46N 7°27E 178 D3
Ludington U.S.A. 43°57N 86°27W 308 D10
Ludlow Shrops., U.K. 52°22N 2°42W 169 E5
Ludlow Calif., U.S.A. 34°43N 116°10W 307 L10
Ludlow Pa., U.S.A. 41°43N 78°56W 312 E6
Ludlow Vt., U.S.A. 43°24N 72°42W 313 C12
Ludowici U.S.A. 31°43N 81°45W 316 D8
Luduş Romania 46°29N 24°5E 183 D9
Ludvika Sweden 60°8N 15°14E 162 D9
Ludwigsburg Germany 48°53N 9°11E 179 G5
Ludwigsfeld Germany 48°12N 11°27E 131 A1
Ludwigsfelde Germany 52°17N 13°17E 178 C9
Ludwigshafen Germany 49°29N 8°26E 179 F4
Ludwigslust Germany 53°19N 11°30E 178 B7
Ludza Latvia 56°32N 27°43E 188 D4
Lue Australia 32°38S 149°50E 283 B8
Luebo Dem. Rep. of the Congo 5°21S 21°23E 265 D4
Lueki Dem. Rep. of the Congo 3°20S 25°48E 264 C5
Luena Angola 12°13S 19°51E 265 E3
Luena Dem. Rep. of the Congo 9°28S 25°43E 269 D2
Luena Zambia 10°40S 30°25E 269 E3
Luena → Angola 12°30S 22°34E 265 E4
Luena → Zambia 14°46S 23°30E 265 E4
Luena Flats Zambia 14°47S 23°17E 265 E4
Luengué ⌂ Angola 16°55S 19°55E 265 F3
Luenha = Ruenya → Africa 16°24S 33°48E 269 F3
Luepa Venezuela 5°43N 61°31W 329 B5
Lueta → Dem. Rep. of the Congo 7°4S 21°40E 265 D4
Luete → Zambia 15°46S 23°10E 265 F4
Lüeyang China 33°22N 106°10E 226 H4
Lufeng Guangdong, China 22°57N 115°38E 229 F10
Lufeng Yunnan, China 25°0N 102°5E 228 E4
Lufico Angola 6°24S 13°23E 265 D2
Lufira → Dem. Rep. of the Congo 9°30S 27°0E 269 D2
Lufkin U.S.A. 31°21N 94°44W 314 F7
Lufupa Dem. Rep. of the Congo 10°37S 24°56E 265 E4
Luga Russia 58°40N 29°55E 188 C5
Luga → Russia 59°40N 28°18E 188 C5
Lugano Switz. 46°1N 8°57E 179 J4
Lugano, L. di Switz. 46°0N 9°0E 198 C6
Lugansk = Luhansk Ukraine 48°38N 39°15E 189 H10
Luganville Vanuatu 15°27S 167°10E 287 E5
Lugard's Falls Kenya 3°6S 38°41E 268 C4
Lugela Mozam. 16°25S 36°43E 269 F4
Lugenda → Mozam. 11°25S 38°33E 269 E4
Lugh = Luuq Somali Rep. 3°48N 42°34E 267 D5
Lugnaquillia Ireland 52°58N 6°28W 166 D5
Lugnvik Sweden 62°56N 17°55E 162 B11
Lugo Italy 44°25N 11°54E 199 D8
Lugo Spain 43°2N 7°35W 194 B3
Lugo □ Spain 43°0N 7°30W 194 C3
Lugoj Romania 45°42N 21°57E 182 E6
Lugovoy = Qulan Kazakhstan 42°55N 72°43E 214 E8
Lugus I. Phil. 5°41N 120°50E 233 J3
Luhansk Ukraine 48°38N 39°15E 189 H10
Luhansk □ Ukraine 49°10N 38°40E 189 H10
Luhe China 32°19N 118°50E 229 A12
Luhe → Germany 53°23N 10°13E 178 B6
Luhit → India 27°48N 95°28E 241 B5
Luhu China 23°9N 113°16E 121 B2
Luhuo China 31°21N 100°48E 228 B3
Lui → Angola 8°21S 17°33E 265 D3
Lui → Zambia 16°18S 23°17E 265 F4
Luia Angola 8°10S 21°32E 265 D4
Luia → Angola 8°32S 21°47E 265 D4
Luiana Angola 17°25S 22°59E 265 F4
Luiana → Angola 17°24S 23°3E 265 F4
Luiana ⌂ Angola 16°55S 22°20E 265 F4
Luichow = Liuzhou China 24°22N 109°22E 228 E7
Luichow Pen. = Leizhou Bandao China 21°0N 110°0E 228 G7
Luikuei Taiwan 23°0N 120°38E 225 D2
Luilaka → Dem. Rep. of the Congo 0°52S 20°12E 264 C4
Luimneach = Limerick Ireland 52°40N 8°37W 166 D3
Luing U.K. 56°14N 5°39W 167 E3
Luino Italy 45°59N 8°44E 198 C5
Luio → Angola 13°17S 21°37E 265 E4
Luís Correia Brazil 3°0S 41°35W 332 B3
Luís Gonçalves Brazil 5°37S 50°25W 332 C1
Luitpold Coast Antarctica 78°30S 32°0W 151 D1
Luiza Dem. Rep. of the Congo 7°40S 22°30E 265 D4
Luizi Dem. Rep. of the Congo 6°0S 27°25E 268 D2
Luján Argentina 34°45S 59°5W 334 C4
Lujiang China 31°20N 117°15E 229 B11
Lukala Dem. Rep. of the Congo 5°31S 14°32E 265 D2
Lukang Taiwan 24°1N 120°22E 225 B2
Lukanga Bandundu, Dem. Rep. of the Congo 1°41S 18°9E 264 C3
Lukanga Équateur, Dem. Rep. of the Congo 1°0S 18°8E 264 C3
Lukanga Swamp Zambia 14°30S 27°40E 269 E2
Lukavac Bos.-H. 44°33N 18°32E 182 F3
Lukenie → Dem. Rep. of the Congo 3°0S 18°50E 264 C3
Lŭki Bulgaria 41°50N 24°43E 203 E8
Lukk Libya 32°1N 24°46E 258 B4
Lukolela Équateur, Dem. Rep. of the Congo 1°10S 17°12E 264 C3
Lukolela Kasai-Or., Dem. Rep. of the Congo 5°23S 24°32E 265 D4
Lukosi Zimbabwe 18°30S 26°30E 269 F2
Lukovë Albania 39°59N 19°54E 202 G3
Lukovit Bulgaria 43°13N 24°11E 203 C8
Łuków Poland 51°55N 22°23E 185 G9
Lukoyanov Russia 55°2N 44°29E 190 C7
Luksefjell Norway 59°23N 9°34E 164 E6
Luku Taiwan 23°44N 120°45E 225 C2
Lukulu Zambia 14°23S 23°15E 265 E4
Lukuni Dem. Rep. of the Congo 5°50S 17°16E 265 D3
Lukusuzi △ Zambia 12°43S 32°36E 269 E3
Lula Dem. Rep. of the Congo 5°22S 16°2E 265 D3
Lülang Shan China 38°0N 111°15E 226 F6
Luleå Sweden 65°35N 22°10E 160 D20
Luleälven → Sweden 65°35N 22°10E 160 D20
Lüleburgaz Turkey 41°23N 27°22E 203 E11
Luliang China 25°0N 103°40E 228 E4
Lulima Dem. Rep. of the Congo 4°12S 25°36E 268 C2
Luling U.S.A. 29°41N 97°39W 314 G6
Lulong China 39°53N 118°51E 227 E10
Lulonga → Dem. Rep. of the Congo 1°0N 18°10E 264 B3
Lulu U.S.A. 30°7N 82°29W 316 E7
Lulu → Dem. Rep. of the Congo 1°18N 23°42E 264 B4
Lulua → Dem. Rep. of the Congo 4°30S 20°30E 265 C4
Luluabourg = Kananga Dem. Rep. of the Congo 5°55S 22°18E 265 D4
Luma Amer. Samoa 14°16S 169°33W 302 f
Lumai Angola 13°13S 21°25E 265 E4
Lumajang Indonesia 8°8S 113°13E 235 D4
Lumaku, Gunong Malaysia 4°52N 115°38E 235 B5
Lumār Iran 33°33N 46°49E 213 F12
Lumbala → Angola 12°39S 22°35E 265 E4
Lumbala Kaquengue Angola 12°39S 22°34E 265 E4
Lumbala N'guimbo Angola 14°18S 21°18E 265 E4
Lumbe → Zambia 16°44S 23°41E 265 F4
Lumber City U.S.A. 31°56N 82°41W 316 D7
Lumberton U.S.A. 34°37N 79°0W 315 D15
Lumbis Indonesia 4°18N 116°15E 235 B5

Lumding *India* 25°46N 93°10E 241 C4
Lumi *Papua N. G.* 3°30S 142°2E 286 B2
Lumiar *Portugal* 38°46N 9°10W 126 A2
Lumpkin *U.S.A.* 32°3N 84°48W 316 C5
Lumsden *Sask., Canada* 50°39N 104°52W 297 C8
Lumsden *N.Z.* 45°44S 168°27E 285 F3
Lumut *Malaysia* 4°13N 100°37E 237 K3
Lumut, Tanjung *Indonesia* 3°50S 105°58E 234 C3
Luna *India* 23°43N 69°16E 242 H3
Luna *Apayao, Phil.* 18°18N 121°21E 232 B3
Lunan *China* 24°40N 103°18E 228 E4
Lunavada *India* 23°8N 73°37E 242 H5
Lunca *Romania* 47°22N 25°1E 183 C10
Lunca Corbului *Romania* 44°42N 24°45E 183 F9
Lund *Sweden* 55°44N 13°12E 163 J7
Lunda Norte □ *Angola* 8°0S 20°0E 265 D4
Lunda Sul □ *Angola* 10°0S 20°0E 265 E4
Lundamo *Norway* 63°9N 10°19E 164 A7
Lundazi *Zambia* 12°20S 33°7E 269 E3
Lunde *Sweden* 62°53N 17°51E 162 B11
Lundenburg = Břeclav *Czech Rep.* 48°46N 16°53E 181 C9
Lunderskov *Denmark* 55°29N 9°19E 163 J3
Lundi → *Zimbabwe* 21°43S 32°34E 269 G3
Lundtofte *Denmark* 55°47N 12°32E 118 A3
Lundu *Malaysia* 1°40N 109°50E 235 B3
Lundy *U.K.* 51°10N 4°41W 169 F3
Lune → *U.K.* 54°0N 2°51W 168 C5
Lüneburg *Germany* 53°15N 10°24E 178 B6
Lüneburg Heath = Lüneburger Heide *Germany* 53°10N 10°12E 178 B6
Lüneburger Heide *Germany* 53°10N 10°12E 178 B6
Lunel *France* 43°39N 4°9E 175 E8
Lünen *Germany* 51°37N 7°32E 178 D3
Lunenburg *Canada* 44°22N 64°18W 299 D7
Lunéville *France* 48°36N 6°30E 173 D13
Lung Mei *China* 22°23N 114°15E 122 A2
Lunga *Dem. Rep. of the Congo* 5°46S 12°14E 265 C4
Lunga → *Zambia* 14°34S 26°25E 269 E2
Lunga Lunga *Kenya* 4°33S 39°7E 268 C4
Lungchin *Taiwan* 24°12N 120°31E 225 B2
Lunge *Angola* 12°13S 16°7E 265 E3
Lungga *Solomon Is.* 9°25S 160°3E 287 M11
Lungi *S. Leone* 8°40N 13°17W 262 D2
Lunglei *India* 22°55N 92°45E 241 D4
Lungngo *Burma* 21°57N 93°36E 241 E4
Lung'tan *Taiwan* 24°52N 121°12E 225 B3
Lungwebungu → *Zambia* 14°19S 23°14E 265 E4
Luni *India* 26°0N 73°6E 242 G5
Luni → *India* 24°41N 71°14E 242 G4
Luninets = Luninyets *Belarus* 52°15N 26°50E 177 B14
Luning *U.S.A.* 38°30N 118°11W 304 G4
Lunino *Russia* 53°38N 45°18E 190 D7
Luninyets *Belarus* 52°15N 26°50E 177 B14
Lunkaransar *India* 28°29N 73°44E 242 E5
Lunner *Norway* 60°19N 10°35E 164 D7
Lunpei *Taiwan* 24°45N 120°21E 225 C2
Lunsar *S. Leone* 8°41N 12°32W 262 D2
Lunsemfwa → *Zambia* 14°54S 30°12E 269 E3
Lunsemfwa Falls *Zambia* 14°30S 29°6E 269 E2
Luntai *China* 41°46N 84°14E 217 D10
Luo He → *China* 34°35N 110°20E 226 G6
Luocheng *China* 24°48N 108°53E 228 E7
Luochuan *China* 35°45N 109°26E 226 G5
Luoci *China* 25°19N 102°18E 228 E4
Luodian *China* 25°24N 106°43E 228 E6
Luoding *China* 22°45N 111°40E 229 F8
Luofu *Dem. Rep. of the Congo* 0°10S 29°15E 268 C2
Luohe *China* 33°32N 114°2E 226 H8
Luojiang *Guangdong, China* 23°5N 113°17E 121 B2
Luojiang *Sichuan, China* 31°18N 104°33E 228 B5
Luonan *China* 34°5N 110°10E 226 G6
Luoning *China* 34°35N 111°40E 226 G6
Luoshan *China* 32°13N 114°30E 229 A10
Luotian *China* 30°46N 115°22E 229 B10
Luoxiao Shan *China* 26°30N 114°1E 229 D10
Luoyang *China* 34°40N 112°26E 226 G7
Luoyuan *China* 26°28N 119°30E 229 D12
Luozi *Dem. Rep. of the Congo* 4°54S 14°0E 265 C2
Luozigou *China* 43°42N 130°18E 227 C16
Lupeni *Romania* 45°21N 23°13E 183 E8
Lupilichi *Mozam.* 11°47S 35°13E 269 E4
Lupire *Angola* 14°36S 19°29E 265 E3
Łupków *Poland* 49°15N 22°4E 185 J9
Lupoing *China* 24°53N 104°21E 228 E5
Lupon *Phil.* 6°54N 126°0E 233 H6
Luputa *Dem. Rep. of the Congo* 7°7S 23°43E 265 D4
Luqa *Malta* 35°52N 14°29E 206 F7
Luquan *Hebei, China* 38°4N 114°17E 226 E8
Luquan *Yunnan, China* 25°35N 102°25E 228 E4
Luque *Paraguay* 25°19S 57°25W 334 B4
Luquembo *Angola* 10°44S 17°43E 265 E3
Luquillo *Puerto Rico* 18°23N 65°43W 321 b
Luquillo, Sierra de *Puerto Rico* 18°20N 65°47W 321 b
Lúras *Italy* 40°56N 9°10E 200 B2
Luray *U.S.A.* 38°40N 78°28W 309 F14
Lure *France* 47°40N 6°30E 173 E13
Luremo *Angola* 8°30S 17°50E 265 D3
Lurgan *U.K.* 54°28N 6°19W 166 B5
Luribay *Bolivia* 17°6S 67°39W 330 D4
Lurín *Peru* 12°17S 76°52W 330 C2
Lúrio *Mozam.* 13°32S 40°30E 269 E5
Lusaka *Zambia* 15°28S 28°16E 269 F2
Lusaka □ *Zambia* 15°30S 29°0E 269 F2
Lusambo *Dem. Rep. of the Congo* 4°58S 23°28E 265 C4
Lusancay Is. and Reefs *Papua N. G.* 8°30S 150°30E 286 E6
Lusangaye *Dem. Rep. of the Congo* 4°54S 26°0E 265 C5
Luseland *Canada* 52°5N 109°24W 297 C7
Lusenga Plain △ *Zambia* 9°22S 29°14E 269 D2
Lusengo *Dem. Rep. of the Congo* 1°47N 19°31E 264 B3
Lushan *Henan, China* 33°45N 112°55E 226 H7
Lushan *Sichuan, China* 30°12N 102°52E 228 B4
Lushan △ *China* 29°33N 115°58E 229 C10
Lushi *China* 34°3N 111°3E 226 G6
Lushnjë *Albania* 40°55N 19°41E 202 F3
Lushoto *Tanzania* 4°47S 38°20E 268 C4
Lushui *China* 25°58N 98°44E 228 E2
Lushuihe *China* 42°31N 127°47E 224 A3
Lüshun *China* 38°45N 121°15E 227 E11
Lusignan *France* 46°26N 0°8E 174 B4
Lusigny-sur-Barse *France* 48°16N 4°15E 173 D11
Lusiye *Zambia* 15°30S 23°57E 265 F4
Lusk *U.S.A.* 42°46N 104°27W 304 E11
Lussac-les-Châteaux *France* 46°24N 0°43E 174 B4
Lustenau *Austria* 47°26N 9°39E 180 D2
Lustheim *Germany* 48°14N 11°34E 131 A2
Lustrafjorden *Norway* 61°23N 7°25E 164 C4
Lūt, Dasht-e *Iran* 31°30N 58°0E 247 D8
Luta = Dalian *China* 38°50N 121°40E 227 E11
Lütao *Taiwan* 22°40N 121°30E 225 D3
Lutembo *Angola* 13°26S 21°16E 265 E4
Lutherstadt Wittenberg *Germany* 51°53N 12°39E 178 D8
Luthersville *U.S.A.* 33°13N 84°45W 316 B5
Luti *Solomon Is.* 7°14S 157°0E 287 L9
Luton *U.K.* 51°53N 0°24W 169 F7
Luton □ *U.K.* 51°53N 0°24W 169 F7
Lutong *Malaysia* 4°28N 114°0E 235 B4
Łutsel K'e *Canada* 62°24N 110°44W 297 A6
Lutshima → *Dem. Rep. of the Congo* 5°22S 18°59E 265 D3
Lutsk *Ukraine* 50°50N 25°15E 177 C13
Luttenberg = Ljutomer *Slovenia* 46°31N 16°11E 199 B13
Lutto = Lotta → *Europe* 68°42N 31°6E 160 B24
Lutuai *Angola* 12°41S 20°7E 265 E4
Lutz *U.S.A.* 28°9N 82°28W 317 G7
Lützow Holmbukta *Antarctica* 69°10S 37°30E 151 C4
Lutzputs *S. Africa* 28°3S 20°40E 270 C3
Luuk *Phil.* 5°58N 121°18E 233 J3
Luuq *Somali Rep.* 3°48N 42°34E 267 D5
Luverne *Ala., U.S.A.* 31°43N 86°16W 316 D3
Luverne *Minn., U.S.A.* 43°39N 96°13W 308 D5
Luvo *Angola* 5°51S 14°5E 265 D2
Luvua *Dem. Rep. of the Congo* 8°48S 25°17E 265 D5
Luvua → *Dem. Rep. of the Congo* 6°50S 27°30E 268 D2
Luvuvhu → *S. Africa* 22°25S 31°18E 271 B5
Luwan *China* 31°12N 121°27E 138 B1
Luwegu → *Tanzania* 8°31S 37°23E 269 D4
Luwero *Uganda* 0°50N 32°28E 268 B3
Luwuk *Indonesia* 0°56S 122°47E 231 E6
Luxembourg *Lux.* 49°37N 6°9E 170 E6
Luxembourg □ *Belgium* 49°58N 5°30E 170 E5
Luxembourg ■ *Europe* 49°45N 6°0E 170 E5
Luxembourg ✈ (LUX) *Lux.* 49°37N 6°10E 170 E6
Luxembourg, Palais du *Paris, France* 134 c4
Luxemburg *U.S.A.* 42°36N 91°5W 310 B5
Luxeuil-les-Bains *France* 47°49N 6°24E 173 E13
Luxi *Hunan, China* 28°20N 110°7E 229 C8
Luxi *Yunnan, China* 24°40N 103°55E 228 E4
Luxi *Yunnan, China* 24°27N 98°36E 228 E2
Luxian *China* 29°9N 105°24E 228 C5
Luxor = El Uqsur *Egypt* 25°41N 32°38E 256 B3
Luy-de-Béarn → *France* 43°39N 0°48W 174 E3
Luy-de-France → *France* 43°39N 0°48W 174 E3
Luyeh *Hualien, Taiwan* 23°35N 121°32E 225 C3
Luyeh *T'aitung, Taiwan* 22°55N 121°8E 225 D3
Luyi *China* 33°50N 115°35E 226 H8
Luz *Azores* 39°1N 28°0W 153 d1
Luz-St-Sauveur *France* 42°53N 0°0 174 F4
Luza *Russia* 60°39N 47°10E 186 B8
Luzern *Switz.* 47°3N 8°18E 179 H4
Luzern □ *Switz.* 47°2N 7°55E 179 H3
Luzhai *China* 24°29N 109°42E 228 E7
Luzhany *Ukraine* 48°22N 25°47E 183 B10
Luzhi *China* 26°21N 105°16E 228 D5
Luzhniki Sports Centre *Russia* 55°43N 37°31E 129 B3
Luzhou *China* 28°52N 105°20E 228 C5
Luziânia *Brazil* 16°20S 48°0W 333 E2
Luzilândia *Brazil* 3°28S 42°22W 332 B3
Lužnice → *Czech Rep.* 49°14N 14°23E 180 B7
Luzon *Phil.* 16°0N 121°0E 232 C3
Luzon Strait *Asia* 21°0N 120°40E 229 G13
Luzy *France* 46°47N 3°58E 173 F10
Luzzi *Italy* 39°27N 16°17E 201 C9
Lviv *Ukraine* 49°50N 24°0E 177 D13
Lviv □ *Ukraine* 49°30N 23°45E 177 D12
Lvov = Lviv *Ukraine* 49°50N 24°0E 177 D13
Lwówek *Poland* 52°28N 16°10E 185 F3
Lwówek Śląski *Poland* 51°7N 15°38E 185 G2
Lyakhavichy *Belarus* 53°2N 26°32E 177 B14
Lyakhovskiye, Ostrova *Russia* 73°40N 141°0E 215 B15
Lyaki = Läki *Azerbaijan* 40°34N 47°22E 191 K8
Lyal I. *Canada* 44°57N 81°24W 312 B3
Lyall Mt. *N.Z.* 45°16S 167°32E 285 F2
Lyallpur = Faisalabad *Pakistan* 31°30N 73°5E 242 D5
Lyaskovets *Bulgaria* 43°6N 25°44E 203 C9
Lyasnaya → *Belarus* 52°9N 23°31E 185 F10
Lybster *U.K.* 58°18N 3°15W 167 C5
Lycabettus *Athens, Greece* 112 b3
Lycaonia *Turkey* 38°0N 33°0E 212 D5
Lychen *Germany* 53°12N 13°18E 178 B9
Lychkova *Russia* 57°55N 32°24E 188 D7
Lycia *Turkey* 36°30N 29°30E 205 E11
Lyck = Ełk *Poland* 53°50N 22°21E 184 E9
Lyckebyån → *Sweden* 56°12N 15°39E 163 H9
Lycksele *Sweden* 64°38N 18°40E 160 D18
Lycosura *Greece* 37°20N 22°3E 204 D4
Lydda = Lod *Israel* 31°57N 34°54E 251 G5
Lyddan I. *Antarctica* 74°0S 21°0W 151 D2
Lydenburg *S. Africa* 25°10S 30°29E 271 C5
Lydia *Turkey* 38°48N 28°19E 205 C10
Łydynia → *Poland* 52°43N 20°26E 185 F7
Lyell *N.Z.* 41°48S 172°4E 285 B7
Lyell I. *Canada* 52°40N 131°35W 296 C2
Lyepyel *Belarus* 54°50N 28°40E 188 E5
Lyford Cay *Bahamas* 25°2N 77°33W 153 b
Lygnern *Sweden* 57°30N 12°15E 163 G6
Lykavittos Hill = Lycabettus *Athens, Greece* 112 b3
Lykens *U.S.A.* 40°34N 76°42W 313 F8
Lyman *Ukraine* 45°41N 29°45E 183 E14
Lyman *Wyo., U.S.A.* 41°20N 110°18W 304 F8
Lymanske *Ukraine* 46°40N 29°58E 183 D14
Lyme B. *U.K.* 50°42N 2°53W 169 G4
Lyme Regis *U.K.* 50°43N 2°57W 169 G5
Lymington *U.K.* 50°45N 1°32W 169 G6
Łyna → *Poland* 54°37N 21°14E 184 D8
Lynchburg *Ohio, U.S.A.* 39°15N 83°48W 311 E13
Lynchburg *S.C., U.S.A.* 34°3N 80°4W 316 A9
Lynchburg *Va., U.S.A.* 37°25N 79°9W 309 G14
Lynd → *Australia* 16°28S 143°18E 280 B3
Lynd Ra. *Australia* 25°30S 149°20E 281 D4
Lynden *Ont., Canada* 43°14N 80°9W 312 C4
Lynden *Wash., U.S.A.* 48°57N 122°27W 306 B4
Lyndhurst *S. Austral., Australia* 30°15S 138°18E 281 E2
Lyndhurst *N.J., U.S.A.* 40°49N 74°7W 132 B1
Lyndon → *Australia* 23°29S 114°6E 279 D1
Lyndonville *N.Y., U.S.A.* 43°20N 78°23W 312 C6
Lyndonville *Vt., U.S.A.* 44°31N 72°1W 313 B12
Lyngdal *Buskerud, Norway* 59°54N 9°32E 164 E6
Lyngdal *Vest-Agder, Norway* 58°8N 7°7E 164 F4
Lyngen *Norway* 69°45N 20°30E 160 B19
Lyngør *Norway* 58°38N 9°8E 164 F6
Lynher Reef *Australia* 15°27S 121°55E 278 C3
Lynn *Ind., U.S.A.* 40°3N 84°56W 311 D12
Lynn *Mass., U.S.A.* 42°28N 70°57W 313 D14
Lynn Canal *U.S.A.* 58°50N 135°15W 303 G14
Lynn Haven *U.S.A.* 30°15N 85°39W 316 E4
Lynn Lake *Canada* 56°51N 101°3W 297 B8
Lynn Woods Res. *U.S.A.* 42°29N 71°0W 116 A2
Lynne *U.S.A.* 29°12N 81°55W 317 F8
Lynnville *U.S.A.* 38°12N 87°18W 311 F9
Lynnwood *U.S.A.* 47°49N 122°18W 306 C4
Lynton *U.K.* 51°13N 3°50W 169 F4
Lyntupy *Belarus* 55°4N 26°23E 188 E4
Lynx L. *Canada* 62°25N 106°15W 297 A7
Lyon *France* 45°46N 4°50E 175 C8
Lyon, Gare de *Paris, France* 134 c5
Lyon St-Exupery ✈ (LYS) *France* 45°44N 5°2E 175 C9
Lyonnais *France* 45°45N 4°15E 175 C8
Lyons = Lyon *France* 45°46N 4°50E 175 C8
Lyons *Ga., U.S.A.* 32°12N 82°19W 316 C7
Lyons *Ill., U.S.A.* 41°48N 87°49W 119 C2
Lyons *Kans., U.S.A.* 38°21N 98°12W 308 F4
Lyons *N.Y., U.S.A.* 43°5N 77°0W 312 C8
Lyons → *Australia* 25°2S 115°9E 279 E2
Lyons Falls *U.S.A.* 43°37N 75°22W 313 C9
Lyozna *Belarus* 55°0N 30°50E 188 E6
Lyra Reef *Papua N. G.* 1°50S 153°35E 286 A7
Lys = Leie → *Belgium* 51°2N 3°45E 170 C3
Lysá nad Labem *Czech Rep.* 50°11N 14°51E 180 A7
Lysaker *Norway* 59°54N 10°38E 133 A2
Lysakerselva → *Norway* 59°54N 10°38E 133 A2
Lysebotn *Norway* 59°3N 6°37E 164 E3
Lysefjorden *Norway* 59°0N 6°23E 164 E3
Lysekil *Sweden* 58°17N 11°26E 163 F5
Lysi *Cyprus* 35°6N 33°41E 207 E9
Lyskovo *Russia* 56°0N 45°3E 190 B7
Lysolaje *Czech Rep.* 50°8N 14°22E 135 B2
Lystrup *Denmark* 56°14N 10°14E 163 H4
Lysva *Russia* 58°7N 57°49E 186 C10
Lysvik *Sweden* 60°1N 13°9E 162 D7
Lysychansk *Ukraine* 48°55N 38°30E 189 H10
Lytham St. Anne's *U.K.* 53°45N 3°0W 168 D4
Lyttelton *N.Z.* 43°35S 172°44E 285 D7
Lytton *Canada* 50°13N 121°31W 296 C4
Lyuban *Russia* 59°16N 31°18E 188 C6
Lyubertsy *Russia* 55°40N 37°51E 129 B5
Lyubim *Russia* 58°20N 40°39E 188 C11
Lyubimets *Bulgaria* 41°50N 26°5E 203 E10
Lyublino *Russia* 55°41N 37°44E 129 B4
Lyuboml *Ukraine* 51°11N 24°4E 185 G11
Lyubotyn *Ukraine* 50°0N 36°0E 189 H8
Lyubytino *Russia* 58°50N 33°16E 188 C7
Lyudinovo *Russia* 53°52N 34°28E 188 F8

M

M.R. Stefanik, Bratislava ✈ (BTS) *Slovak Rep.* 48°11N 17°9E 181 C10
Ma → *Vietnam* 19°47N 105°56E 228 H5
Ma, O. el → *Algeria* 27°45N 7°52W 260 C3
Ma Nam Wat *China* 22°21N 114°16E 122 A2
Ma On Shan Country Park ⌓ *China* 22°22N 114°14E 122 A2
Ma'adaba *Jordan* 31°43N 35°47E 251 H6
Maafushi *Maldives* 3°59N 73°27E 272 d
Ma'ale Adumim *West Bank* 31°49N 35°17E 123 B2
Ma'ale Ha Khamisha *Israel* 31°49N 35°7E 123 B1
Ma'ale Mikhmas *West Bank* 31°52N 35°18E 123 A2
Maamba *Zambia* 17°17S 26°28E 270 A4
Ma'ān *Jordan* 30°12N 35°44E 251 H6
Ma'ān □ *Jordan* 30°0N 36°0E 251 J7
Maana'oba *Solomon Is.* 8°17S 160°50E 287 M11
Maanselkä *Finland* 63°52N 28°32E 160 E23
Ma'anshan *China* 31°44N 118°29E 229 B12
Maantiekylä *Finland* 60°20N 25°0E 121 A3
Maarianhamina = Mariehamn *Finland* 60°5N 19°55E 161 F18
Maarifa *Iraq* 33°15N 44°21E 113 B2
Maarmorilik *Greenland* 71°3N 51°0W 154 C5
Ma'arrat an Nu'mān *Syria* 35°43N 36°43E 250 C7
Maas → *Neths.* 51°45N 4°32E 170 C4
Maaseik *Belgium* 51°6N 5°45E 170 C5
Maasim *Phil.* 5°52N 125°0E 233 J5
Maasin *Phil.* 10°8N 124°50E 233 F5
Maastricht *Neths.* 50°50N 5°40E 170 D5
Maasupa *Solomon Is.* 9°16S 161°17E 287 M11
Maave *Mozam.* 21°4S 34°47E 271 B5
Mababe Depression *Botswana* 18°50S 24°15E 270 A3
Mabaia *Angola* 7°12S 14°2E 265 D2
Mabalane *Mozam.* 23°37S 32°31E 271 B5
Mabanga *Dem. Rep. of the Congo* 1°30N 19°6E 264 B3
Ma'bar *Yemen* 14°48N 44°17E 248 D4
Mabaruma *Guyana* 8°10N 59°50W 329 B6
Mabato Pt. *Phil.* 14°29N 121°3E 127 C2
Mabein *Burma* 23°29N 96°37E 241 D6
Mabel, L. *U.S.A.* 28°25N 81°32W 133 B1
Mabel L. *Canada* 50°35N 118°43W 296 C5
Mabenga *Dem. Rep. of the Congo* 3°39S 18°40E 264 C3
Mabenge *Dem. Rep. of the Congo* 4°15N 24°12E 264 B4
Maberly *Canada* 44°50N 76°32W 313 B8
Mabesi, L. *S. Leone* 7°10N 11°42W 262 D2
Mabian *China* 28°47N 103°37E 228 C4
Mabil *Ethiopia* 10°26N 36°52E 257 E4
Mabinay *Phil.* 9°48N 122°54E 233 G4
Mabirou *Congo* 1°3S 15°42E 264 C3
Mablethorpe *U.K.* 53°20N 0°15E 168 D8
Mableton *U.S.A.* 33°49N 84°35W 316 B5
Mably *France* 46°5N 4°4E 173 F11
Maboma *Dem. Rep. of the Congo* 2°30N 28°10E 268 B2
Mabonto *S. Leone* 8°53N 11°50W 262 D2
Maboukou *Congo* 3°39S 12°31E 264 C2
Mabouya I. *Grenada* 12°29N 61°30W 323 q
Mabroûk *Mali* 19°29N 1°15W 261 E4
Mabrous *Niger* 21°14N 13°35E 259 D2
Mabuasehube ⌓ *Botswana* 25°5S 21°10E 270 C3
Mabudis *Phil.* 20°55N 121°55E 232 A3
Mabuiag *Australia* 9°57S 142°11E 280 a
Mac Bac *Vietnam* 9°46N 106°7E 237 H6
Macachín *Argentina* 37°10S 63°43W 334 D3
Macaco, Morro do *Brazil* 22°56S 43°6W 135 B2
Macaé *Brazil* 22°20S 41°43W 333 F3
Macael *Spain* 37°20N 2°18W 197 H2
Macaíba *Brazil* 5°51S 35°21W 332 C4
Macajalar B. *Phil.* 8°55N 124°39E 233 G5
Macajuba *Brazil* 12°9S 40°22W 333 D3
McAlester *U.S.A.* 34°56N 95°46W 314 D7
McAllen *U.S.A.* 26°12N 98°14W 314 H5
McAlpin *U.S.A.* 30°8N 82°57W 316 E7
MacAlpine L. *Canada* 66°32N 102°45W 294 D11
Macamic *Canada* 48°45N 79°0W 298 C4
Macao = Macau *China* 22°12N 113°33E 229 F9
Macão *Portugal* 39°35N 7°59W 195 F3
Macapá *Brazil* 0°5N 51°4W 329 C7
Macaque, Morne *Dominica* 15°20N 61°20W 323 k
Macará *Ecuador* 4°23S 79°57W 328 D2
Macarani *Brazil* 15°33S 40°24W 333 E3
Macarena, Serranía de la *Colombia* 2°45N 73°55W 328 C3
Macareo, Caño → *Venezuela* 9°47N 61°36W 329 B5
Macarthur *Australia* 38°5S 142°0E 282 E5
McArthur → *Australia* 15°54S 136°40E 280 B2
McArthur, Port *Australia* 16°4S 136°23E 280 B2
Macas *Ecuador* 2°19S 78°7W 328 D2
Macate *Peru* 8°48S 78°7W 330 B2
Macau *Brazil* 5°15S 36°40W 332 C4
Macau *China* 22°12N 113°33E 229 F9
Macaúbas *Brazil* 13°2S 42°42W 333 D3
Macauley I. *Pac. Oc.* 30°12S 178°28W 277 G15
Macaya → *Colombia* 0°59N 72°20W 328 C3
McBride *Canada* 53°20N 120°19W 296 C4
McCall *U.S.A.* 44°55N 116°6W 304 D5
McCamey *U.S.A.* 31°8N 102°14W 314 F3
McCammon *U.S.A.* 42°39N 112°12W 304 E7
McCarran Int., Las Vegas ✈ (LAS) *U.S.A.* 36°5N 115°9W 124 B2
McCarthy *U.S.A.* 61°26N 142°56W 303 F12
McCauley I. *Canada* 53°40N 130°15W 296 C2
McCleary *U.S.A.* 47°3N 123°16W 306 C3
Macclenny *U.S.A.* 30°17N 82°7W 316 E7
Macclesfield *U.K.* 53°15N 2°8W 168 D5
M'Clintock Chan. *Canada* 72°0N 102°0W 294 C11
McClintock Ra. *Australia* 18°44S 127°38E 278 C4
McCloud *U.S.A.* 41°15N 122°8W 304 F2
McCluer I. *Australia* 11°5S 133°0E 278 B5
McClure *U.S.A.* 40°42N 77°19W 312 F7
McClure, L. *U.S.A.* 37°35N 120°16W 306 H6
M'Clure Str. *Canada* 75°0N 119°0W 295 C8
McClusky *U.S.A.* 47°29N 100°27W 308 B3
McComb *U.S.A.* 31°15N 90°27W 315 F9
McCook *Ill., U.S.A.* 41°47N 87°49W 119 C2
McCook *Nebr., U.S.A.* 40°12N 100°38W 308 E3
McCormick *U.S.A.* 33°55N 82°17W 316 B7
McCreary *Canada* 50°47N 99°29W 297 C9
McCullough Mt. *U.S.A.* 35°35N 115°13W 307 K11
McCusker → *Canada* 55°32N 108°39W 297 B7
McDavid *U.S.A.* 30°52N 87°19W 317 E2
McDermitt *U.S.A.* 41°59N 117°43W 304 F5
McDonald *U.S.A.* 40°22N 80°14W 312 F4
Macdonald, L. *Australia* 23°30S 129°0E 278 D4
Macdonald, Mt. *Vanuatu* 17°36S 168°23E 287 G6
McDonald Is. *Ind. Oc.* 53°0S 73°0E 273 K6
MacDonnell Ranges *Australia* 23°40S 133°0E 278 D5
McDonough *U.S.A.* 33°27N 84°9W 316 B5
McDougalls Well *Australia* 31°8S 141°15E 282 A4
MacDowell L. *Canada* 52°15N 92°45W 298 B1
Macduff *U.K.* 57°40N 2°31W 167 D6
Maceda *Spain* 42°16N 7°39W 194 C3
Macedonia *U.S.A.* 41°19N 81°31W 312 E3
Macedonia ■ *Europe* 41°53N 21°40E 202 E5
Maceió *Brazil* 9°40S 35°41W 332 C4
Maceira *Portugal* 39°41N 8°55W 194 F2
Macenta *Guinea* 8°35N 9°32W 262 D3
Macerata *Italy* 43°18N 13°27E 199 E10
McFarland *U.S.A.* 35°41N 119°14W 307 K7
McFarlane → *Canada* 59°12N 107°58W 297 B7
Macfarlane, L. *Australia* 32°0S 136°40E 282 B2
McGehee *U.S.A.* 33°38N 91°24W 314 E9
McGill *U.S.A.* 39°23N 114°47W 304 G6
McGill Univ. *Montréal, Canada* 130 b1
Macgillycuddy's Reeks *Ireland* 51°58N 9°45W 166 E2
McGrath *U.S.A.* 62°58N 155°36W 303 E9
McGraw *U.S.A.* 42°36N 76°8W 313 D8
McGregor *U.S.A.* 43°1N 91°11W 310 A5
McGregor Ra. *Australia* 27°0S 142°45E 281 D3
McGuire, Mt. *Australia* 20°18S 148°23E 280 b
Mach *Pakistan* 29°50N 67°20E 242 E2
Māch Kowr *Iran* 25°48N 61°28E 247 E9
Machacalis *Brazil* 17°5S 40°45W 333 E3
Machado = Jiparaná → *Brazil* 8°3S 62°52W 331 B5
Machagai *Argentina* 26°56S 60°2W 334 B3
Machakos *Kenya* 1°30S 37°15E 268 C4
Machala *Ecuador* 3°20S 79°57W 328 D2
Machalilla △ *Ecuador* 1°24S 80°42W 328 D1
Machanga *Mozam.* 20°59S 35°0E 271 B6
Machattie, L. *Australia* 24°50S 139°48E 280 C2
Machault *France* 49°21N 4°29E 173 C11
Machava *Mozam.* 25°54S 32°28E 271 C5
Machecoul *France* 47°0N 1°49W 172 F5
Macheke *Zimbabwe* 18°5S 31°51E 271 A5
Machelen *Belgium* 50°55N 4°26E 116 A2
Macheng *China* 31°12N 115°2E 229 B10
McHenry *U.S.A.* 42°21N 88°16W 311 B8
Macherado *Greece* 37°46N 20°49E 207 D2
Macherla *India* 16°29N 79°26E 244 F4
Machero *Spain* 39°21N 4°20W 195 F6
Machgaon *India* 20°5N 86°17E 244 D8
Machhu → *India* 23°6N 70°46E 242 H4
Machiara △ *Pakistan* 34°40N 73°30E 242 B5
Machias *Maine, U.S.A.* 44°43N 67°28W 309 C20
Machias *N.Y., U.S.A.* 42°25N 78°29W 312 D6
Machichi → *Canada* 57°3N 92°6W 297 B10
Machico *Madeira* 32°43N 16°44W 153 c
Machida *Japan* 35°32N 139°26E 140 B1
Machilipatnam *India* 16°12N 81°8E 245 F5
Machiques *Venezuela* 10°4N 72°34W 328 A3
Machu Picchu *Peru* 13°8S 72°30W 330 C3
Machynlleth *U.K.* 52°35N 3°50W 169 E4
Macia *Mozam.* 25°2S 33°8E 271 C5
Macias Nguema Biyoga = Bioko *Eq. Guin.* 3°30N 8°40E 263 E6
Maciejowice *Poland* 51°36N 21°26E 185 G8
McIlwraith Ra. *Australia* 13°50S 143°20E 280 A3
Măcin *Romania* 45°16N 28°8E 183 E13
Macina *Mali* 14°50N 5°0W 262 C4
McInnes L. *Canada* 52°13N 93°45W 297 C10
McIntosh *U.S.A.* 45°55N 101°21W 308 C3
McIntosh L. *Canada* 55°45N 105°0W 297 B8
Macintosh Ra. *Australia* 27°39S 125°32E 279 E4
Macintyre → *Australia* 28°37S 150°47E 281 D5
Maciołki *Poland* 52°19N 21°9E 142 B2
Macizo Galaico *Spain* 42°30N 7°30W 194 C3
Maçka *Turkey* 40°49N 39°36E 213 B8
Mackay *Queens., Australia* 21°8S 149°11E 280 K7
Mackay *Idaho, U.S.A.* 43°55N 113°37W 304 E7
MacKay → *Canada* 57°10N 111°38W 296 B6
Mackay, L. *Australia* 22°30S 129°0E 278 D4
McKay Ra. *Australia* 23°0S 122°30E 278 D3
McKean *Kiribati* 3°36S 174°8W 277 A16
McKeesport *U.S.A.* 40°20N 79°51W 312 F5
McKellar *Canada* 45°30N 79°55W 312 A5
McKenna *U.S.A.* 46°56N 122°33W 306 D4
Mackenzie *Canada* 55°20N 123°5W 296 B4
McKenzie *U.S.A.* 36°8N 88°31W 315 C10
Mackenzie → *Queens., Australia* 23°38S 149°46E 280 C4
Mackenzie → *N.W.T., Canada* 69°10N 134°20W 294 D5
McKenzie → *U.S.A.* 44°7N 123°6W 304 D2
Mackenzie Bay *Canada* 69°0N 137°30W 292 C6
Mackenzie City = Linden *Guyana* 6°0N 58°10W 329 B6
Mackenzie King I. *Canada* 77°45N 111°0W 295 B9
Mackenzie Mts. *Canada* 64°0N 130°0W 292 C6
Mackenzie Plains *N.Z.* 44°10S 170°25E 285 E5
McKerrow, L. *N.Z.* 44°25S 168°5E 285 E3
McKerrow, Mt. *N.Z.* 41°19S 174°58E 143 B2
Mackheim = Maków Mazowiecki *Poland* 52°52N 21°6E 185 F8
Mackinac, Straits of *U.S.A.* 45°50N 84°40W 301 F23
Mackinaw *U.S.A.* 40°32N 89°21W 310 D7
Mackinaw → *U.S.A.* 40°33N 89°44W 310 D7
Mackinaw City *U.S.A.* 45°47N 84°44W 309 C11
McKinlay *Australia* 21°16S 141°18E 280 C3
McKinlay → *Australia* 20°50S 141°28E 280 C3
McKinley, Mt. *U.S.A.* 63°4N 151°0W 303 E10
McKinley Park *Alaska, U.S.A.* 63°44N 148°55W 303 E10
McKinley Park *Ill., U.S.A.* 41°49N 87°40W 119 C2
McKinley Sea *Arctic* 82°0N 0°0 154 A11
McKinney *U.S.A.* 33°12N 96°37W 314 E6
Mackinnon Road *Kenya* 3°40S 39°1E 268 C4
McKittrick *Calif., U.S.A.* 35°18N 119°37W 307 K7
McKittrick *Mo., U.S.A.* 38°44N 91°27W 310 F5
Macklin *Canada* 52°20N 109°56W 297 C7
Macksville *Australia* 30°40S 152°56E 283 A10
McLaren Vale *Australia* 35°13S 138°31E 282 C3
McLaughlin *U.S.A.* 45°49N 100°49W 308 C3
Maclean *Australia* 29°26S 153°16E 281 D5
McLean *Ill., U.S.A.* 40°19N 89°10W 310 D7
McLean *Tex., U.S.A.* 35°14N 100°36W 314 D4
McLean *Va., U.S.A.* 38°56N 77°10W 143 B2
McLeansboro *U.S.A.* 38°6N 88°32W 311 F8
Maclear *S. Africa* 31°2S 28°23E 271 D4
Maclear, C. *Malawi* 13°58S 34°49E 269 E3
Macleay → *Australia* 30°56S 153°0E 283 A10
McLennan *Canada* 55°42N 116°50W 296 B5
MacLeod = Fort Macleod *Canada* 49°45N 113°30W 296 D6
McLeod → *Canada* 54°9N 115°44W 296 C5
MacLeod, L. *Australia* 24°9S 113°47E 279 D1
MacLeod B. *Canada* 62°53N 110°0W 297 A7
MacLeod Lake *Canada* 54°58N 123°0W 296 C4
McLoughlin, Mt. *U.S.A.* 42°27N 122°19W 304 E2
MacMahon = Aïn Touta *Algeria* 35°26N 5°54E 261 A6
McMechen *U.S.A.* 39°57N 80°44W 312 G4
McMinnville *Oreg., U.S.A.* 45°13N 123°12W 304 D2
McMinnville *Tenn., U.S.A.* 35°41N 85°46W 315 D12
McMurdo *Antarctica* 77°51S 166°37E 151 D11
McMurdo Sd. *Antarctica* 77°0S 170°0E 151 D11
McMurray = Fort McMurray *Canada* 56°44N 111°7W 296 B6
McMurray *U.S.A.* 48°19N 122°14W 306 B4
Maco *Phil.* 7°20N 125°50E 233 H5
Maçobere *Mozam.* 21°13S 32°47E 269 G3
Macocolo *Angola* 6°47S 16°8E 265 D3
Macodoene *Mozam.* 23°32S 35°5E 271 B6
Macolo *Angola* 7°5S 16°42E 265 D3
Macomb *U.S.A.* 40°27N 90°40W 310 D6
Macomer *Italy* 40°16N 8°47E 200 B1
Mâcon *Saône-et-Loire, France* 46°19N 4°50E 173 F11
Macon *Ga., U.S.A.* 32°51N 83°38W 316 C6
Macon *Ill., U.S.A.* 39°43N 89°0W 310 E8
Macon *Miss., U.S.A.* 33°7N 88°34W 315 E10
Macon *Mo., U.S.A.* 39°44N 92°28W 310 E4
Macondo *Angola* 12°37S 23°46E 265 E4
Macopocho → *Chile* 33°24S 70°40W 137 B1
Macossa *Mozam.* 17°55S 33°56E 269 F3
Macou, Pte. *Guadeloupe* 16°21N 61°31W 322 e
Macouba *Martinique* 14°52N 61°9W 322 j
Macoucherie → *Dominica* 15°25N 61°27W 323 k
Macoun L. *Canada* 56°32N 103°40W 297 B8
Macoupin Cr. → *U.S.A.* 39°11N 90°38W 310 E6
Macovane *Mozam.* 21°30S 35°2E 271 B6
MacPherson = Kapuskasing *Canada* 49°25N 82°30W 298 C3
McPherson *U.S.A.* 38°22N 97°40W 308 F5
McPherson Pk. *U.S.A.* 34°53N 119°53W 307 L7
McPherson Ra. *Australia* 28°15S 153°15E 281 D5
Macquarie → *Australia* 30°7S 147°24E 283 A7
Macquarie Harbour *Australia* 42°15S 145°23E 281 G4
Macquarie I. *Pac. Oc.* 54°36S 158°55E 288 N7
Macquarie Ridge *S. Ocean* 57°0S 159°0E 151 B10
Macqueripe B. *Trin. & Tob.* 10°44N 61°37W 323 t
McRae *U.S.A.* 32°4N 82°54W 316 C7
MacRitchie Res. *Singapore* 1°20N 103°49E 138 A2
MacRobertson Land *Antarctica* 71°0S 64°0E 151 D6
Macrohon *Phil.* 10°4N 124°56E 233 F5
Macroom *Ireland* 51°54N 8°57W 166 E3
MacTier *Canada* 45°8N 79°47W 312 A5
Macubela *Mozam.* 16°53S 37°49E 269 F4
Macugnaga *Italy* 45°58N 7°58E 198 C4
Macuira △ *Colombia* 12°9N 71°21W 328 A3
Macuje *Colombia* 0°24N 73°10W 328 C3
Macul *Chile* 33°30S 70°35W 137 C2
Macumba → *Australia* 27°52S 137°12E 281 D2
Macuro *Venezuela* 10°42N 61°55W 329 F9
Macusani *Peru* 14°4S 70°29W 330 C3
Macuse *Mozam.* 17°45S 37°10E 269 F4
Macuspana *Mexico* 17°46N 92°36W 319 D6
Macusse *Angola* 17°48S 20°23E 265 F4
Mada → *Nigeria* 7°59N 7°55E 263 D6
Ma'dabā □ *Jordan* 31°43N 35°47E 251 G6
Madadeni *S. Africa* 27°43S 30°3E 271 C5
Madadi *Chad* 18°28N 20°45E 259 E4
Madagali *Nigeria* 10°56N 13°33E 263 C7
Madagascar ■ *Africa* 20°0S 47°0E 272 B2
Madagoi → *Somali Rep.* 0°49N 42°58E 267 D5
Madā'in Sālih *Si. Arabia* 26°46N 37°57E 246 E3
Madakasira *India* 13°56N 77°16E 245 H3
Madalena *Azores* 38°32N 28°32W 153 d1
Madama *Niger* 22°0N 13°40E 259 D2
Madame, I. *Canada* 45°30N 60°58W 299 C7
Madame Tussaud's *London, U.K.* 125 a3
Madan *Bulgaria* 41°30N 24°57E 203 E8
Madanapalle *India* 13°33N 78°28E 245 H4
Madang *Papua N. G.* 5°12S 145°49E 286 C3
Madang □ *Papua N. G.* 5°0S 145°30E 286 C3
Madaoua *Niger* 14°5N 6°27E 263 C6
Madara *Nigeria* 11°45N 10°35E 263 C7
Madaripur *Bangla.* 23°19N 90°15E 241 D3
Madau I. *Papua N. G.* 8°58S 152°28E 286 E7
Madauk *Burma* 17°56N 96°52E 241 G6
Madawaska *Canada* 45°30N 78°0W 312 A7
Madawaska → *Canada* 45°27N 76°21W 312 A7
Madaxmaroodi *Somali Rep.* 2°39N 44°36E 267 D5
Madaya *Burma* 22°12N 96°10E 241 D6
Madbar *South Sudan* 6°17N 30°45E 257 F3
Maddalena *Italy* 41°16N 9°23E 200 A2
Maddaloni *Italy* 41°2N 14°23E 201 A7
Maddela *Phil.* 16°21N 121°41E 232 C3
Maddur *India* 12°36N 77°4E 245 H3
Madeira *Atl. Oc.* 32°50N 17°0W 153 c
Madeira *Ohio, U.S.A.* 39°11N 84°21W 311 E12
Madeira → *Brazil* 3°22S 58°45W 329 D6
Madeleine, Îs. de la *Canada* 47°30N 61°40W 299 C7
Maden *Turkey* 38°23N 39°40E 213 C8
Madera *Chihuahua, Mexico* 29°12N 108°7W 318 B3
Madera *Calif., U.S.A.* 36°57N 120°3W 306 J6
Madera *Pa., U.S.A.* 40°49N 78°26W 312 F6
Madgaon *India* 15°12N 73°58E 245 G1
Madha *India* 18°0N 75°30E 244 F2
Madhavpur *India* 21°15N 69°58E 242 J3
Madhepura *India* 26°11N 86°23E 243 F12
Madhira *India* 16°55N 80°22E 244 F5
Madhubani *India* 26°21N 86°7E 243 F12
Madhudaha *India* 22°30N 88°24E 124 B2
Madhugiri *India* 13°40N 77°12E 245 H3
Madhumati → *Bangla.* 22°53N 89°52E 241 D2
Madhupur *Bangla.* 24°37N 90°2E 241 C3
Madhupur *India* 24°16N 86°39E 243 G12
Madhya Pradesh □ *India* 22°50N 78°0E 242 J8
Madhyamgram *India* 22°41N 88°26E 124 A2
Madidi → *Bolivia* 12°32S 66°52W 330 C4
Madikeri *India* 12°30N 75°45E 245 H2
Madikwe ⌓ *S. Africa* 27°38S 32°15E 271 C5
Madill *U.S.A.* 34°6N 96°46W 314 D6
Madimba *Angola* 6°36S 14°23E 265 D2
Madimba *Dem. Rep. of the Congo* 4°58S 15°5E 265 C3
Madín *México, Mexico* 19°32N 99°16W 128 A1
Ma'din *Syria* 35°45N 39°36E 213 E8
Madín, L. *Mexico* 19°31N 99°16W 128 A1
Madina *Mali* 13°25N 8°50W 262 C3
Madīnah Al Mansūr *Iraq* 33°18N 44°20E 113 B2
Madinani *Ivory C.* 9°37N 6°57W 262 D3
Madinat al Malik Khālid al Askarīyah *Si. Arabia* 27°54N 45°31E 246 E5
Madīnat ash Sha'b *Yemen* 12°50N 45°0E 248 D4
Madīnat ath Thawrah *Syria* 35°50N 38°32E 213 E8
Mâdinet Nasr *Egypt* 30°4N 31°18E 117 A2
Madingo *Congo* 4°5S 11°24E 264 C2
Madingou *Congo* 4°10S 13°33E 264 C2
Madîq Gûbâl *Egypt* 27°47N 33°55E 251 L4
Madîq Tirân *Egypt* 27°55N 34°30E 251 L5
Madirovalo *Madag.* 16°26S 46°32E 272 B2
Madison *Calif., U.S.A.* 38°41N 121°59W 306 G5
Madison *Fla., U.S.A.* 30°28N 83°25W 316 E6
Madison *Ga., U.S.A.* 33°36N 83°28W 316 B6
Madison *Ind., U.S.A.* 38°44N 85°23W 311 F11
Madison *Mo., U.S.A.* 39°28N 92°13W 310 E4
Madison *Nebr., U.S.A.* 41°50N 97°27W 308 E5
Madison *Ohio, U.S.A.* 41°46N 81°3W 312 E3
Madison *S. Dak., U.S.A.* 44°0N 97°7W 308 C5
Madison *Wis., U.S.A.* 43°4N 89°24W 310 A7
Madison → *U.S.A.* 45°56N 111°31W 304 D8
Madison Avenue *New York, U.S.A.* 132 c2
Madison Heights *U.S.A.* 37°25N 79°8W 309 G14
Madison Square *New York, U.S.A.* 132 d2
Madison Square Garden *New York, U.S.A.* 132 c2
Madisonville *Ky., U.S.A.* 37°20N 87°30W 308 G10
Madisonville *Tex., U.S.A.* 30°57N 95°55W 314 F7
Madista *Botswana* 21°15S 25°6E 270 B4
Madiun *Indonesia* 7°38S 111°32E 235 D4
Madjingo *Gabon* 1°20N 14°4E 264 B2
Mado Gashi *Kenya* 0°44N 39°10E 268 B4
Madoc *Canada* 44°30N 77°28W 312 B7
Madoi *China* 34°46N 98°18E 218 E8
Madon → *France* 48°36N 6°6E 173 D13
Madona *Latvia* 56°53N 26°5E 188 D4
Madonie *Italy* 37°50N 13°50E 200 E6
Madonna di Campiglio *Italy* 46°14N 10°49E 198 B7
Madra Dağı *Turkey* 39°23N 27°12E 205 B9
Madrakah, Ra's al *Oman* 19°0N 57°50E 249 C7
Madras = Chennai *India* 13°8N 80°19E 245 H5
Madras = Tamil Nadu □ *India* 11°0N 77°0E 245 J3
Madras *U.S.A.* 44°38N 121°8W 304 D3
Madre, L. *U.S.A.* 25°15N 97°30W 314 J6
Madre, Sierra *Phil.* 17°0N 122°0E 232 C4
Madre de Dios □ *Peru* 12°0S 70°15W 330 C3
Madre de Dios → *Bolivia* 10°59S 66°8W 330 C4
Madre de Dios, I. *Chile* 50°20S 75°10W 336 D1
Madre del Sur, Sierra *Mexico* 17°30N 100°0W 319 D5
Madre Occidental, Sierra *Mexico* 27°0N 107°0W 318 B3
Madre Oriental, Sierra *Mexico* 25°0N 100°0W 318 C5
Madri *India* 24°16N 73°32E 242 G5
Madrid *Spain* 40°24N 3°42W 127 B1
Madrid *Ala., U.S.A.* 31°2N 85°24W 316 D4
Madrid *Iowa, U.S.A.* 41°53N 93°49W 310 C3
Madrid *N.Y., U.S.A.* 44°45N 75°8W 313 B9
Madrid □ *Spain* 40°30N 3°45W 194 E7
Madrid Barajas ✈ (MAD) *Spain* 40°26N 3°34W 127 B2
Madridejos *Spain* 39°28N 3°33W 195 F7
Madrigal de las Altas Torres *Spain* 41°5N 5°0W 194 D6
Madrona *Spain* 41°27N 2°1E 114 A1
Madrona, Sierra *Spain* 38°27N 4°16W 195 G6
Madroñera *Spain* 39°26N 5°42W 195 F5
Madrusah *Libya* 24°48N 14°32E 258 D2
Madu *Sudan* 14°37N 26°4E 257 E2
Madula *Dem. Rep. of the Congo* 0°27N 25°22E 264 B5
Maduo *Dem. Rep. of the Congo* 1°24S 20°44E 264 C4
Madura *W. Austral., Australia* 31°55S 127°0E 279 F4
Madura *Indonesia* 7°30S 114°0E 231 G15
Madura, Selat *Indonesia* 7°30S 113°20E 235 D4
Madura Oya △ *Sri Lanka* 7°20N 81°10E 245 L5
Madurai *India* 9°55N 78°10E 245 K4
Madurantakam *India* 12°30N 79°50E 245 H4
Madzhalis *Russia* 42°9N 47°47E 191 J8
Mae Chan *Thailand* 20°9N 99°52E 236 B2
Mae Charim △ *Thailand* 18°17N 100°59E 236 C3
Mae Hong Son *Thailand* 19°16N 97°56E 236 C2
Mae Khlong → *Thailand* 13°24N 100°0E 236 F3
Mae Moei △ *Thailand* 17°26N 98°7E 236 D2
Mae Phang △ *Thailand* 19°7N 99°13E 236 C2
Mae Phrik *Thailand* 17°27N 99°7E 236 D2
Mae Ping △ *Thailand* 17°37N 98°51E 236 D2
Mae Ramat *Thailand* 16°58N 98°31E 236 D2
Mae Rim *Thailand* 18°54N 98°57E 236 C2
Mae Sai *Thailand* 20°20N 99°55E 236 B2
Mae Sot *Thailand* 16°43N 98°34E 236 D2
Mae Suai *Thailand* 19°39N 99°33E 228 H2
Mae Tha *Thailand* 18°28N 99°8E 236 C2
Mae Tup Res. *Thailand* 17°52N 98°45E 236 D2
Mae Wa △ *Thailand* 17°23N 99°16E 236 D2
Mae Wong △ *Thailand* 15°54N 99°12E 236 E2
Mae Yom △ *Thailand* 18°43N 100°15E 236 C3
Maebaru *Japan* 33°33N 130°12E 222 D2
Maebashi *Japan* 36°24N 139°4E 223 A11
Maella *Spain* 41°8N 0°7E 196 D5
Maelpaeg L. *Canada* 48°20N 56°30W 299 C8
Maesawa *Japan* 35°44N 139°31E 140 A2
Maesteg *U.K.* 51°36N 3°40W 169 F4
Maestra, Sierra *Cuba* 20°15N 77°0W 320 B4
Maestre de Campo I. *Phil.* 12°56N 121°42E 232 E3
Maetambe, Mt. *Solomon Is.* 7°3S 157°1E 287 L9
Maevatanana *Madag.* 16°56S 46°49E 272 B2
Maéwo *Vanuatu* 15°10S 168°10E 287 E6
Mafadi *S. Africa* 29°12S 29°21E 271 C4
Mafate, Cirque de *Réunion* 21°3S 55°25E 272 f
Mafeking = Mafikeng *S. Africa* 25°50S 25°38E 270 C4
Mafeking *Canada* 52°40N 101°10W 297 C8
Maféré *Ivory C.* 5°30N 3°2W 262 D4
Mafeteng *Lesotho* 29°51S 27°15E 270 C4
Maffra *Australia* 37°53S 146°58E 283 D7
Mafia I. *Tanzania* 7°45S 39°50E 268 D4
Mafikeng *S. Africa* 25°50S 25°38E 270 C4
Mafra *Brazil* 26°10S 49°55W 335 B6
Mafra *Portugal* 38°55N 9°20W 195 G1
Mafungabusi Plateau *Zimbabwe* 18°30S 29°8E 269 F2
Magadan *Russia* 59°38N 150°50E 215 D16
Magadi *India* 12°58N 77°14E 245 H3
Magadi *Rift Valley, Kenya* 1°54S 36°19E 268 C4
Magadi, L. *Kenya* 1°54S 36°19E 268 C4
Magaliesburg *S. Africa* 26°0S 27°32E 271 C4
Magallanes = Punta Arenas *Chile* 53°10S 71°0W 336 D2
Magallanes *Phil.* 12°50N 123°50E 232 E4
Magallanes □ *Chile* 52°0S 72°0W 336 D2
Magallanes, Estrecho de *Chile* 52°30S 75°0W 336 D2
Magaluf *Spain* 39°29N 2°32E 206 B3

Magangué Colombia 9°14N 74°45W 328 B3
Maganoy Phil. 6°51N 124°31E 233 H5
Magaria Niger 13°4N 9°5E 259 F1
Magarida Papua N. G. 10°18S 149°20E 286 F5
Magburaka S. Leone 8°47N 12°0W 262 D2
Magdagachi Russia 53°27N 125°48E 215 D13
Magdalen Is. = Madeleine, Îs. de la Canada 47°30N 61°40W 299 C7
Magdalena Argentina 35°5S 57°30W 334 D4
Magdalena Bolivia 13°13S 63°57W 331 C5
Magdalena Lima, Peru 12°5S 77°5W 124 B2
Magdalena N. Mex., U.S.A. 34°7N 107°15W 305 J10
Magdalena □ Colombia 10°0N 74°0W 328 B3
Magdalena → Colombia 11°6N 74°51W 328 A3
Magdalena → Mexico 30°40N 112°25W 318 A2
Magdalena, B. Mexico 24°35N 112°0W 318 C2
Magdalena, I. Chile 44°40S 73°0W 336 B2
Magdalena, I. Mexico 24°40N 112°15W 318 C2
Magdalena, Llano de Mexico 25°0N 111°25W 318 C2
Magdalena Contreras Mexico 19°20N 99°13W 128 C1
Magdalena de Kino Mexico 30°38N 110°57W 318 A2
Magdeburg Germany 52°7N 11°38E 178 C7
Magdelaine Cays Australia 16°33S 150°18E 280 B5
Magdub Sudan 13°42N 25°5E 257 E2
Magee U.S.A. 31°52N 89°44W 315 F10
Magelang Indonesia 7°29S 110°13E 235 D4
Magellan's Str. = Magallanes, Estrecho de Chile 52°30S 75°0W 336 D2
Magenta Italy 45°28N 8°53E 198 C5
Magenta, L. Australia 33°30S 119°2E 279 F2
Magerøya Norway 71°3N 25°40E 160 A21
Maggea Australia 34°28S 140°2E 282 C4
Maggia → Switz. 46°18N 8°36E 179 J4
Maggiorasca, Mte. Italy 44°33N 9°29E 198 D6
Maggiore, Lago Italy 45°57N 8°39E 198 B5
Maggotty Jamaica 18°9N 77°46W 320 a
Maghâgha Egypt 28°38N 30°50E 256 B3
Maghama Mauritania 15°32N 12°57W 262 B2
Magherafelt U.K. 54°45N 6°37W 166 B5
Maghnia Algeria 34°50N 1°43W 261 B4
Maghreb Baghdād, Iraq 33°23N 44°22E 113 A2
Maghreb N. Afr. 32°0N 4°0W 254 C3
Maginu Japan 35°34N 139°34E 140 B2
Magione Italy 43°8N 12°12E 199 E9
Magistralnyy Russia 56°16N 107°36E 215 D11
Maglaj Bos.-H. 44°33N 18°7E 182 F3
Magliana Italy 41°50N 12°26E 136 B1
Magliano in Toscana Italy 42°36N 11°17E 199 F8
Máglie Italy 40°7N 18°18E 201 B11
Magnac-Laval France 46°13N 1°11E 174 B5
Magnetic Pole (North) Arctic 82°42N 114°24W 150 A1
Magnetic Pole (South) Antarctica 64°8S 138°8E 151 C9
Magnisia □ Greece 39°15N 23°0E 204 B5
Magnitogorsk Russia 53°27N 59°4E 186 D10
Magnolia Ark., U.S.A. 33°16N 93°14W 314 E8
Magnolia Miss., U.S.A. 31°9N 90°28W 315 F9
Magnor Norway 59°56N 12°15E 164 E9
Magny-en-Vexin France 49°9N 1°47E 173 C8
Magny-les-Hameaux France 48°44N 2°3E 134 B1
Mago Fiji 17°26S 179°8W 287 A3
Mago △ Ethiopia 5°40N 36°18E 257 F4
Magog Canada 45°18N 72°9W 313 A12
Magoro Uganda 1°45N 34°12E 268 B3
Mağosa = Famagusta Cyprus 35°8N 33°55E 207 E9
Magoye Zambia 16°1S 27°30E 269 F2
Magpet Phil. 7°6N 125°6E 233 H5
Magpie, L. Canada 51°0N 64°41W 299 B7
Magrath Canada 49°25N 112°50W 296 D6
Magre → Spain 39°11N 0°25W 197 F4
Magrur Sudan 14°1N 30°27E 257 E3
Magrur, Wadi → Sudan 16°5N 26°30E 257 D2
Magsingal Phil. 17°41N 120°25E 232 C3
Magta Lahjar Mauritania 17°28N 13°17W 262 B2
Magu Tanzania 2°30S 33°30E 268 C3
Maguan China 23°0N 104°21E 228 F5
Maguarinho, C. Brazil 0°15S 48°30W 332 B2
Magude Mozam. 25°2S 32°40E 271 C5
Maguindanao □ Phil. 7°5N 124°40E 233 H5
Magurski △ Poland 49°30N 21°30E 185 J8
Mağusa = Famagusta Cyprus 35°8N 33°55E 207 E9
Maguse L. Canada 61°37N 95°10W 297 A9
Maguse Pt. Canada 61°20N 93°50W 297 A10
Magvana India 23°13N 69°22E 242 H3
Magwe Burma 20°10N 95°0E 241 E5
Magwe South Sudan 4°8N 32°17E 257 G3
Magwe □ Burma 20°0N 95°0E 241 F5
Magyarorszag = Hungary ■ Europe 47°20N 19°20E 181 D12
Maha Oya Sri Lanka 7°31N 81°22E 245 L5
Maha Sarakham Thailand 16°12N 103°16E 236 D4
Mahābād Iran 36°50N 45°45E 213 D11
Mahabaleshwar India 17°58N 73°43E 244 F1
Mahabharat Lekh Nepal 28°30N 82°0E 243 E10
Mahabo Madag. 20°23S 44°40E 272 C1
Mahad India 18°6N 73°29E 244 E1
Mahaddayweyne Somali Rep. 2°58N 45°32E 267 D6
Mahadeo Hills India 22°20N 78°30E 243 H8
Mahadeopur India 18°48N 80°0E 244 E5
Mahaffey U.S.A. 40°53N 78°44W 312 F6
Mahagi Dem. Rep. of the Congo 2°20N 31°0E 268 B3
Mahagnao Volcano △ Phil. 10°52N 124°51E 233 F5
Mahaicony Guyana 6°36N 57°48W 329 B6
Mahajamba → Madag. 15°33S 47°8E 272 B2
Mahajamba, Helodranon' i Madag. 15°24S 47°5E 272 B2
Mahajan India 28°48N 73°56E 242 E5
Mahajanga Madag. 15°40S 46°25E 272 B2
Mahajanga □ Madag. 17°0S 47°0E 272 B2
Mahajilo → Madag. 19°42S 45°22E 272 B2
Mahakam → Indonesia 0°35S 117°17E 235 C5
Mahalapye Botswana 23°1S 26°51E 270 B4
Mahalaxmi Mumbai, India 130 a1
Mahalchhar Bangla. 22°55N 92°2E 241 D4
Mahale Mts. Tanzania 6°20S 30°0E 268 D3
Mahale Mts. △ Tanzania 6°10S 29°50E 268 D2
Maḩallāt Iran 33°55N 50°30E 247 C6
Māhān Iran 30°5N 57°18E 247 D8
Mahan → India 23°30N 82°50E 243 H10
Mahanadi → India 20°20N 86°25E 244 D8
Mahananda → India 25°12N 87°52E 243 G12
Mahanoro Madag. 19°54S 48°48E 272 B2
Mahanoy City U.S.A. 40°49N 76°9W 313 F8
Mahaplag Phil. 10°35N 124°57E 233 F5
Maharashtra □ India 20°30N 75°30E 244 D2
Maharès Tunisia 34°32N 10°29E 258 B2
Maharivo Madag. 20°26S 44°10E 272 C1
Mahasamund India 21°6N 82°6E 244 D6
Mahasham, W. → Egypt 30°15N 34°10E 251 H5
Mahasoa Madag. 23°23S 45°41E 272 C2
Mahasolo Madag. 19°7S 46°22E 272 B2
Mahattat ash Shīdīyah Jordan 29°55N 35°55E 251 J6
Mahattat 'Unayzah Jordan 30°30N 35°47E 251 H6
Mahaut Dominica 15°21N 61°24W 323 k
Mahaut Guadeloupe 16°11N 61°46W 322 e
Mahavavy → Madag. 15°57S 45°54E 272 B2
Mahaweli Ganga → Sri Lanka 8°27N 81°13E 245 K5
Mahaxay Laos 17°22N 105°12E 236 D5
Mahbubabad India 17°42N 80°2E 244 F5
Mahbubnagar India 16°45N 77°59E 244 F3
Mahd adh Dhahab Si. Arabia 23°30N 40°52E 248 B3
Mahda U.A.E. 25°20N 56°15E 247 E8
Maḩḑah Oman 24°24N 55°59E 247 E7
Mahdia Guyana 5°13N 59°8W 329 B6
Mahdia Tunisia 35°28N 11°0E 258 A2
Mahdia □ Tunisia 35°20N 10°35E 251 A7
Mahe Jammu & Kashmir, India 33°10N 78°32E 243 C8
Mahé Pondicherry, India 11°42N 75°34E 245 J2
Mahé Seychelles 5°0S 55°30E 272 c
Mahé ✈ (SEZ) Seychelles 4°40S 55°31E 272 c
Mahébourg Mauritius 20°24S 57°42E 272 e
Mahendra Giri India 8°20N 77°30E 245 K3
Mahendraganj India 25°20N 89°45E 241 C2
Mahendragarh India 28°17N 76°14E 242 E7
Mahendranagar Nepal 28°55N 80°20E 243 E9
Mahenge Tanzania 8°45S 36°41E 269 D4
Maheno N.Z. 45°10S 170°50E 235 F5
Mahesana India 23°39N 72°26E 242 H5
Maheshtala India 22°29N 88°15E 124 C1
Maheshwar India 22°11N 75°35E 242 H6
Mahgawan India 26°29N 78°37E 243 F8
Mahi → India 22°15N 72°55E 242 H5
Mahia Pen. N.Z. 39°9S 177°55E 284 F6
Mahibadhoo Maldives 3°47N 72°58E 272 d
Mahighe Solomon Is. 8°30S 159°58E 287 M10
Mahilyow Belarus 53°55N 30°18E 177 B16
Mahilyow □ Belarus 54°10N 30°50E 188 E6
Mahim Maharashtra, India 19°2N 72°50E 130 A2
Mahim Maharashtra, India 19°39N 72°44E 244 E1
Mahim B. India 19°2N 72°49E 130 A1
Mahina Tahiti 17°30S 149°27W 289 e
Mahirija Morocco 34°0N 3°16W 261 B4
Mahlaing Burma 21°6N 95°39E 241 E5
Mahlsdorf Germany 52°30N 13°37E 115 A4
Mahmiya Sudan 17°12N 33°43E 257 D3
Mahmoodabad Pakistan 24°51N 67°4E 123 A2
Mahmud Kot Pakistan 30°16N 71°0E 242 D4
Mahmudia Romania 45°5N 29°5E 183 E14
Mahmudiye Turkey 39°48N 30°15E 205 B12
Mahmutbey Turkey 41°3N 28°49E 203 E12
Mahmutlar Turkey 36°29N 32°5E 250 B3
Māhneshān Iran 36°44N 47°39E 213 D12
Mahnomen U.S.A. 47°19N 95°58W 308 B6
Maho Sri Lanka 7°49N 80°16E 245 L5
Mahoba India 25°15N 79°55E 243 G8
Mahomet U.S.A. 40°12N 88°24W 311 D8
Mahón = Maó Spain 39°53N 4°16E 206 B5
Mahon, Menorca ✈ (MAH) Spain 39°50N 4°16E 196 F9
Mahone Bay Canada 44°27N 64°23W 299 D7
Mahongo ⌓ Namibia 18°0S 23°15E 270 B3
Mahopac U.S.A. 41°22N 73°45W 313 E11
Mahoua Chad 11°49N 18°26E 259 F3
Mahrauli India 28°31N 77°10E 120 B2
Mährisch-Budwitz = Moravské Budějovice Czech Rep. 49°4N 15°49E 180 B8
Mährisch-Schönberg = Šumperk Czech Rep. 49°59N 16°59E 181 B9
Mährisch-Trubau = Moravská Třebová Czech Rep. 49°45N 16°40E 181 B9
Mahul India 19°0N 72°53E 130 A2
Mahuta Nigeria 11°32N 4°58E 263 C5
Mahuva India 21°5N 71°48E 242 J4
Mahya Daği Turkey 41°47N 27°36E 203 E11
Mai-Ndombe, L. Dem. Rep. of the Congo 2°0S 18°20E 264 C3
Mai Thon, Ko Thailand 7°40N 98°28E 237 a
Maia Amer. Samoa 14°13S 169°25W 302 g
Maia Azores 36°56N 25°1W 153 d4
Maia Portugal 41°14N 8°37W 194 D2
Maials Spain 41°22N 0°30E 196 D5
Maibong India 25°18N 93°10E 241 C4
Maicao Colombia 11°23N 72°13W 328 A3
Maîche France 47°16N 6°48E 173 E13
Maici → Brazil 6°30S 61°43W 331 B5
Maicuru → Brazil 2°14S 54°17W 329 D7
Máida Italy 38°51N 16°22E 201 D9
Maida Vale London, U.K. 125 a1
Maidan Khula Afghan. 33°36N 69°50E 242 C3
Maidenhead U.K. 51°31N 0°42W 169 F7
Maidstone Vic., Australia 37°47S 144°52E 128 A1
Maidstone Sask., Canada 53°5N 109°20W 297 C7
Maidstone Kent, U.K. 51°16N 0°32E 169 F8
Maiduguri Nigeria 12°0N 13°20E 263 C7
Maiella △ Italy 42°5N 14°5E 199 F11
Măieruş Romania 45°53N 25°31E 183 E10
Maigatari Nigeria 12°46N 9°27E 263 C6
Maigh Nuad = Maynooth Ireland 53°23N 6°34W 166 C5
Maignelay Montigny France 49°32N 2°30E 173 C9
Maigo Phil. 8°10N 123°57E 233 G4
Maigualida, Sierra Venezuela 5°30N 65°10W 329 B4
Maigudo Ethiopia 7°30N 37°8E 257 F4
Maihar India 24°16N 80°45E 243 G9
Maihara Japan 35°19N 136°17E 223 B8
Maikala Ra. India 22°0N 81°0E 244 D5
Maiko △ Dem. Rep. of the Congo 0°30S 27°50E 268 C2
Mailani India 28°17N 80°21E 243 E9
Mā'ili U.S.A. 21°25N 158°11W 302 K13
Mā'ili Pt. U.S.A. 21°24N 158°11W 302 K13
Maillezais France 46°22N 0°45W 174 B3
Mailsi Pakistan 29°48N 72°15E 242 E5
Maimbung Phil. 5°56N 121°2E 233 J3
Main → Bayern, Germany 50°0N 8°18E 179 F4
Main → Antrim, U.K. 54°48N 6°18W 166 B5
Main Channel Canada 45°21N 81°45W 312 A3
Main Range △ Australia 28°11S 152°27E 281 D5
Main Ridge Trin. & Tob. 11°16N 60°40W 323 s
Mainburg Germany 48°38N 11°47E 179 G7
Maindargi India 17°28N 76°18E 244 F3
Maine France 48°20N 0°15W 172 D6
Maine □ U.S.A. 45°20N 69°0W 309 C19
Maine → Ireland 52°9N 9°45W 166 D2
Maine, G. of U.S.A. 43°0N 68°30W 309 D19
Maine-et-Loire □ France 47°31N 0°30W 172 E6
Maïne-Soroa Niger 13°13N 12°2E 263 C7
Maingkaing Burma 24°48N 95°16E 241 C5
Maingkwan Burma 26°15N 96°37E 241 B6
Mainistir an Corann = Midleton Ireland 51°55N 8°10W 166 E3
Mainit Phil. 9°32N 125°32E 233 G5
Mainit, L. Phil. 9°31N 125°30E 233 G5
Mainland Orkney, U.K. 58°59N 3°8W 167 C5
Mainland Shet., U.K. 60°15N 1°22W 167 A7
Mainpuri India 27°18N 79°4E 243 F8
Maintal Germany 50°7N 8°52E 179 E4
Maintenon France 48°35N 1°35E 173 D8
Maintirano Madag. 18°3S 44°1E 272 B1
Mainz Germany 50°1N 8°14E 179 E4
Maio C. Verde Is. 15°10N 23°10W 153 j
Maipú Argentina 36°52S 57°50W 334 D4
Maipú Santiago, Chile 33°30S 70°45W 137 C1
Maiquetía Venezuela 10°36N 66°57W 328 A4
Máira → Italy 44°49N 7°38E 198 D4
Mairabari India 26°30N 92°22E 241 B4
Mairipotaba Brazil 17°18S 49°28W 333 E2
Maisi Cuba 20°17N 74°9W 321 B5
Maisi, Pta. de Cuba 20°10N 74°10W 321 B5
Maiskhal I. Bangla. 21°36N 91°56E 241 E3
Maison Coloniale Guadeloupe 16°18N 61°16W 322 e
Maisonneuve, Parc Canada 45°32N 73°33W 130 A2
Maisons-Alfort France 48°48N 2°26E 134 B3
Maisons-Laffitte France 48°57N 2°8E 134 A1
Maissoneuve Canada 45°32N 73°33W 130 A2
Maitland N.S.W., Australia 32°33S 151°36E 283 B9
Maitland S. Austral., Australia 34°23S 137°40E 282 C2
Maitland Western Cape, S. Africa 33°53S 18°29E 118 A1
Maitland → Canada 43°45N 81°43W 312 C3
Maitland, Banjaran Malaysia 4°55N 116°37E 235 B5
Maitri Antarctica 70°0S 3°0W 151 D3
Maitum Phil. 6°2N 124°30E 233 H5
Maiyema Nigeria 12°5N 4°25E 263 C5
Maiyuan China 25°34N 117°28E 229 E11
Maíz, Is. del Nic. 12°15N 83°4W 320 D3
Maizuru Japan 35°25N 135°22E 223 B7
Majagual Colombia 8°33N 74°38W 328 B3
Majalengka Indonesia 6°50S 108°13E 235 D3
Majanji Uganda 0°16N 34°0E 268 B3
Majari → Brazil 3°29N 60°58W 329 C5
Majdūl Libya 25°51N 15°7E 258 C3
Majene Indonesia 3°38S 118°57E 235 C5
Majes → Peru 16°40S 72°44W 330 D3
Majete ⌓ Malawi 15°54S 34°34E 269 F3
Majevica Bos.-H. 44°45N 18°50E 182 F3
Maji Ethiopia 6°12N 35°30E 257 F4
Majiang China 26°28N 107°32E 228 D6
Majorca = Mallorca Spain 39°30N 3°0E 206 B4
Majors Creek Australia 35°33S 149°45E 283 C8
Majuriã Brazil 7°30S 64°55W 331 B5
Majuro Marshall Is 7°9N 171°12E 288 G9
Mak, Ko Thailand 11°49N 102°29E 237 G4
Maka Senegal 13°40N 14°10W 262 C2
Mākaha Hawai'i, U.S.A. 21°29N 158°13W 302 K13
Makaha Zimbabwe 17°20S 32°39E 271 A5
Makahoa Pt. U.S.A. 21°41N 157°56W 302 J14
Makak Cameroon 3°36N 11°0E 263 E7
Makaka Congo 3°45S 13°39E 264 C2
Makakilo City U.S.A. 21°22N 158°5W 302 K13
Makakou Gabon 0°11S 12°12E 264 C2
Makalamabedi Botswana 20°19S 23°51E 270 B3
Makale Indonesia 3°6S 119°51E 235 C5
Makalu Asia 27°55N 87°8E 243 F12
Makalu-Barun △ Nepal 27°45N 87°10E 243 F12
Makamba Burundi 4°8S 29°49E 268 C2
Makapu'u Pt. U.S.A. 21°19N 157°39W 302 K14
Makarewa Junction N.Z. 46°20S 168°21E 285 G3
Makari Cameroon 12°35N 10°27E 259 F2
Makarikari = Makgadikgadi Salt Pans Botswana 20°40S 25°45E 270 B4
Makarov Basin Arctic 87°0N 150°0W 150 A
Makarovo Russia 57°40N 107°45E 215 D11
Makarska Croatia 43°20N 17°2E 199 E14
Makaryev Russia 57°52N 43°50E 190 B6
Makasar Indonesia 6°17S 106°52E 122 A2
Makassar Indonesia 5°10S 119°20E 235 D5
Makassar, Selat Indonesia 1°0S 118°20E 235 C5
Makassar, Str. of = Makassar, Selat Indonesia 1°0S 118°20E 235 C5
Makat = Maqat Kazakhstan 47°39N 53°19E 187 E9
Makati Phil. 14°33N 121°7E 127 B2
Makaw Dem. Rep. of the Congo 3°29S 18°20E 264 C3
Makawao U.S.A. 20°52N 156°17W 302 C5
Makaya Dem. Rep. of the Congo 3°21S 18°1E 264 C3
Makedonija = Macedonia ■ Europe 41°53N 21°40E 202 E5
Makefu Cook Is. 18°59S 169°55W 289 g
Makemo French Polynesia 16°35S 143°40W 289 f
Makeni S. Leone 8°55N 12°5W 262 D2
Makeyevka = Makiyivka Ukraine 48°0N 38°0E 189 H9
Makgadikgadi △ Botswana 20°27S 24°47E 270 B3
Makgadikgadi Salt Pans Botswana 20°40S 25°45E 270 B4
Makhachkala Russia 43°0N 47°30E 191 J8
Makhado = Louis Trichardt S. Africa 23°1S 29°43E 271 B4
Makham, Ao Thailand 7°51N 98°25E 237 a
Makharadze = Ozurgeti Georgia 41°55N 42°0E 191 K5
Makhfar al Buşayyah Iraq 30°0N 46°10E 246 D5
Makhmūr Iraq 35°46N 43°35E 213 E10
Makhtal India 16°30N 77°31E 245 E3
Makhyah, W. → Yemen 17°40N 49°1E 249 C5
Makian Indonesia 0°20N 127°20E 231 D7
Makina Solomon Is. 9°50S 160°50E 287 M11
Makindu Kenya 2°18S 37°50E 268 C4
Mäkiniitty Finland 60°20N 24°58E 121 A2
Makinka = Makīnsk Kazakhstan 52°37N 70°26E 217 B8
Makīnsk Kazakhstan 52°37N 70°26E 217 B8
Makira = San Cristóbal Solomon Is. 10°30S 161°0E 287 N11
Makiyivka Ukraine 48°0N 38°0E 189 H9
Makkah Si. Arabia 21°30N 39°54E 248 B2
Makkah □ Si. Arabia 21°30N 42°30E 248 B3
Makkovik Canada 55°10N 59°10W 299 A8
Makó Hungary 46°14N 20°33E 182 D5
Mako Senegal 12°52N 12°20W 262 C2
Makogai Fiji 17°28S 179°0E 287 A2
Makok Gabon 0°1S 9°35E 264 C1
Makokou Gabon 0°40N 12°50E 264 B2
Makongo Dem. Rep. of the Congo 3°25N 26°17E 268 B2
Makoro Dem. Rep. of the Congo 3°10N 29°59E 268 B2
Makoua Congo 0°5S 15°50E 264 C3
Maków Mazowiecki Poland 52°52N 21°6E 185 F8
Maków Podhalański Poland 49°43N 19°45E 185 J6
Makra Greece 36°15N 25°54E 205 E7
Makrai India 22°2N 77°0E 242 H7
Makran Asia 26°13N 61°30E 240 D1
Makran Coast Range Pakistan 25°40N 64°0E 240 D2
Makrana India 27°2N 74°46E 242 F6
Makrany Belarus 51°48N 24°17E 185 G11
Makri Greece 40°52N 25°40E 203 F9
Makri India 19°46N 81°55E 244 E5
Makrigialos Greece 35°2N 25°59E 207 E6
Makthar Tunisia 35°48N 9°12E 258 A1
Mākū Iran 39°15N 44°31E 213 C11
Mäkua U.S.A. 21°32N 158°13W 302 J13
Makua Military Reservation U.S.A. 21°32N 158°14W 302 J13
Makum India 27°30N 95°23E 241 B5
Makumbi Dem. Rep. of the Congo 5°50S 20°43E 265 D4
Makunda Botswana 22°30S 20°7E 270 B3
Makung Taiwan 23°34N 119°34E 225 C1
Makungo Somali Rep. 0°49N 42°35E 267 D5
Makunudu Atoll Maldives 6°20N 72°35E 272 d
Makunza Dem. Rep. of the Congo 8°52S 24°19E 265 D4
Makurazaki Japan 31°15N 130°20E 222 F2
Makurdi Nigeria 7°43N 8°35E 263 D6
Makushin Volcano U.S.A. 53°53N 166°55W 303 K6
Makūyeh Iran 28°7N 53°9E 247 D7
Makwassie S. Africa 27°17S 26°0E 270 C4
Makwiro Zimbabwe 17°58S 30°25E 271 A5
Mal India 26°51N 88°45E 241 B2
Mâl Mauritania 16°58N 13°23W 262 B2
Mal B. Ireland 52°50N 9°30W 166 D2
Mala = Mallow Ireland 52°8N 8°39W 166 D3
Mala Peru 12°40S 76°38W 330 C2
Mala ✪ Australia 21°39S 130°45E 278 D5
Mala, Pta. Panama 7°28N 80°2W 320 E3
Mala Belozërka Ukraine 47°12N 34°56E 189 J8
Malá Fatra △ Slovak Rep. 49°10N 19°0E 181 B12
Mala Kapela Croatia 44°45N 15°30E 199 D12
Mała Panew → Poland 50°43N 17°54E 185 H4
Malá Strana Czech Rep. 50°4N 14°24E 135 B2
Mala Vyska Ukraine 48°39N 31°36E 189 H6
Malabang Phil. 7°36N 124°3E 233 H5
Malabar N.S.W., Australia 33°58S 151°14E 139 B2
Malabar Fla., U.S.A. 28°0N 80°34W 317 H9
Malabar Coast India 11°0N 75°0E 245 J2
Malabar Hill India 18°57N 72°48E 130 B1
Malabar Pt. India 18°56N 72°48E 130 B1
Malabo = Rey Malabo Eq. Guin. 3°45N 8°50E 263 E6
Malabon Phil. 14°39N 120°56E 127 B1
Malabrigo = Puerto Chicama Peru 7°45S 79°20W 330 B2
Malabrigo Pt. Phil. 13°36N 121°15E 232 E3
Malabu Nigeria 9°32N 12°48E 263 D7
Malabuñgan Phil. 9°3N 117°38E 233 G1
Malacañang Palace Phil. 14°35N 120°59E 127 B1
Malacca, Straits of Indonesia 3°0N 101°0E 237 L3
Malacky Slovak Rep. 48°27N 17°0E 181 C10
Malad City U.S.A. 42°12N 112°15W 304 E7
Maladeta Spain 42°39N 0°39E 196 C5
Maladzyechna Belarus 54°20N 26°50E 177 A14
Málaga Colombia 6°42N 72°44W 328 B3
Málaga Spain 36°43N 4°23W 195 J6
Málaga □ Spain 36°38N 4°58W 195 J6
Malagarasi Tanzania 5°5S 30°50E 268 D3
Malagarasi → Tanzania 5°12S 29°47E 268 D2
Malagasy Rep. = Madagascar ■ Africa 20°0S 47°0E 272 B2
Malagón Spain 39°11N 3°52W 195 F7
Malagón → Spain 37°35N 7°29W 195 H3
Malah Syria 32°33N 36°54E 251 F7
Malahide Ireland 53°26N 6°9W 120 A3
Malaimbandy Madag. 20°20S 45°36E 272 C2
Malaita Solomon Is. 9°0S 161°0E 287 M11
Malakal South Sudan 9°33N 31°40E 257 F3
Malakal Harb. Palau 7°19N 134°27E 288 c
Malakanagiri India 18°21N 81°54E 244 E5
Malakand Pakistan 34°40N 71°55E 242 B4
Malakhovka Russia 55°39N 38°0E 129 C6
Malakoff France 48°49N 2°18E 134 B2
Malakula Vanuatu 16°15S 167°30E 287 F5
Malakwal Pakistan 32°34N 73°13E 242 C5
Malalag Phil. 6°36N 125°24E 233 H5
Malalaua Papua N. G. 8°4S 146°10E 286 E4
Malam Chad 11°27N 20°59E 259 F4
Malamala Indonesia 3°21S 120°55E 231 E6
Malanda Australia 17°22S 145°35E 280 B4
Malang Indonesia 7°59S 112°45E 235 D4
Malanga Mozam. 13°28S 36°7E 269 E4
Malangas Phil. 7°37N 123°1E 233 H4
Malange □ Angola 9°30S 16°0E 265 D3
Malangen Norway 69°24N 18°37E 160 B18
Malanje Angola 9°36S 16°17E 265 D3
Malanut B. Phil. 9°15N 117°59E 233 G1
Malapatan Phil. 5°59N 125°18E 233 J5
Mälaren Sweden 59°30N 17°10E 162 E11
Malargüe Argentina 35°32S 69°30W 334 D2
Mälarhöjaen Sweden 59°18N 17°58E 139 B1
Malartic Canada 48°9N 78°9W 298 C4
Malaryta Belarus 51°50N 24°3E 185 G11
Malasiqui Phil. 15°55N 120°24E 232 D3
Malaspina Glacier U.S.A. 59°50N 140°30W 303 G12
Malate Phil. 14°34N 120°59E 127 B1
Malatya Turkey 38°25N 38°20E 213 C8
Malatya □ Turkey 38°15N 38°0E 212 C7
Malawali, Pulau Malaysia 7°3N 117°18E 235 A5
Malawi ■ Africa 11°55S 34°0E 269 E3
Malawi, L. Africa 12°30S 34°30E 269 E3
Malay Phil. 11°54N 121°55E 233 F3
Malay Pen. Asia 7°25N 100°0E 237 J3
Malay Quarter Cape Town, S. Africa 118 c2
Malaya Belozërka = Mala Belozërka Ukraine 47°12N 34°56E 189 J8
Malaya Neva Russia 59°56N 30°16E 137 B1
Malaya Okhta Russia 59°55N 30°25E 137 B2
Malaya Vishera Russia 58°55N 32°25E 188 C7
Malaya Viska = Mala Vyska Ukraine 48°39N 31°36E 189 H6
Malaybalay Phil. 8°5N 125°7E 233 G5
Malāyer Iran 34°19N 48°51E 213 E13
Malaysia ■ Asia 5°0N 110°0E 237 K4
Malazgirt Turkey 39°10N 42°33E 213 C10
Malbaza Niger 13°59N 5°38E 263 C6
Malbon Australia 21°5S 140°17E 280 C3
Malbooma Australia 30°41S 134°11E 281 E1
Malbork Poland 54°3N 19°1E 184 D6
Malca Dube Ethiopia 6°47N 42°4E 267 C5
Malcésine Italy 45°46N 10°48E 198 C7
Malchin Germany 53°44N 12°44E 178 B8
Malchow Berlin, Germany 52°34N 13°29E 115 A3
Malchow Mecklenburg-Vorpommern, Germany 53°28N 12°25E 178 B8
Malcolm Australia 28°51S 121°25E 279 E3
Malcolm, Pt. Australia 33°48S 123°45E 279 F3
Malczyce Poland 51°14N 16°29E 185 G3
Maldah India 25°2N 88°9E 243 G13
Maldegem Belgium 51°14N 3°26E 170 C3
Malden London, U.K. 51°23N 0°15W 125 B2
Malden Mass., U.S.A. 42°26N 71°3W 116 A2
Malden Mo., U.S.A. 36°34N 89°57W 308 G9
Malden I. Kiribati 4°3S 155°1W 289 H12
Maldives ■ Ind. Oc. 5°0N 73°0E 272 d
Maldon Vic., Australia 37°0S 144°6E 282 D6
Maldon Essex, U.K. 51°44N 0°42E 169 F8
Maldonado Uruguay 34°59S 55°0W 335 C5
Maldonado, Pta. Mexico 16°20N 98°33W 319 D5
Malè Italy 46°21N 10°55E 198 B7
Malé Maldives 4°10N 73°28E 272 d
Malé ✈ (MLE) Maldives 4°11N 73°28E 272 d
Malé Atoll Maldives 4°45N 73°15E 272 d
Malé Karpaty Slovak Rep. 48°30N 17°20E 181 C10
Maleas, Akra Greece 36°28N 23°7E 204 E5
Malebo, Pool Africa 4°17S 15°20E 265 C3
Malegaon India 20°30N 74°38E 244 D2
Malei Mozam. 17°12S 36°58E 269 F4
Maleizen Belgium 50°45N 4°31E 116 B3
Malek South Sudan 6°4N 31°36E 257 F3
Malek Kandī Iran 37°9N 46°6E 213 D12
Malela Bas-Congo, Dem. Rep. of the Congo 5°59S 12°37E 265 D2
Malela Maniema, Dem. Rep. of the Congo 4°22S 26°8E 265 C5
Malema Mozam. 14°57S 37°20E 269 E4
Maleme Greece 35°31N 23°49E 207 E4
Malendok I. Papua N. G. 3°28S 153°13E 286 B7
Målerås Sweden 56°54N 15°34E 163 H9
Malerkotla India 30°32N 75°58E 242 D6
Males Greece 35°6N 25°35E 207 E6
Malesherbes France 48°15N 2°24E 173 D9
Maleshevska Planina Europe 41°38N 23°7E 202 E7
Malešice Czech Rep. 50°5N 14°30E 135 B3
Malesina Greece 38°37N 23°14E 204 C5
Malestroit France 47°49N 2°25W 172 E4
Malfa Italy 38°35N 14°50E 201 D7
Malgobek Russia 43°30N 44°34E 191 J7
Malgomaj Sweden 64°40N 16°30E 160 D17
Malgrat de Mar Spain 41°39N 2°46E 196 D7
Malha Sudan 15°8N 25°10E 257 D2
Malhada Brazil 14°21S 43°47W 333 D3
Malhargarh India 24°17N 74°59E 242 G6
Malheur → U.S.A. 44°4N 116°59W 304 D5
Malheur L. U.S.A. 43°20N 118°48W 304 E4
Mali Guinea 12°10N 12°20W 262 C2
Mali ■ Africa 17°0N 3°0W 262 B4
Mali → Burma 25°42N 97°30E 241 C6
Mali Kanal Serbia 45°36N 19°24E 182 E4
Mali Kyun Burma 13°0N 98°20E 236 F2
Malia Greece 35°17N 25°32E 207 E6
Malia, Kolpos Greece 35°19N 25°27E 207 E6
Maliao Taiwan 23°48N 120°13E 225 C2
Malibu U.S.A. 34°2N 118°41W 307 L8
Maligaya = Gloria Phil. 12°59N 121°30E 232 E3
Maliku = Minicoy I. India 8°17N 73°2E 245 K1
Maliku Indonesia 0°39S 123°16E 231 E6
Malili Indonesia 2°42S 121°6E 231 E6
Målilla Sweden 57°23N 15°48E 163 G9
Malimba, Mts. Dem. Rep. of the Congo 7°30S 29°30E 268 D2
Malin Hd. Ireland 55°23N 7°23W 166 A4
Malin Pen. Ireland 55°20N 7°17W 166 A4
Malindang, Mt. Phil. 8°13N 123°38E 233 G4
Malindi Kenya 3°12S 40°5E 268 C5
Malindi Marine ⌓ Kenya 3°15S 40°7E 268 C5
Malines = Mechelen Belgium 51°2N 4°29E 170 C4
Malino Indonesia 1°0N 121°0E 231 D6
Malinyi Tanzania 8°56S 36°0E 269 D4
Malipo China 23°7N 104°42E 228 F5
Maliq Albania 40°45N 20°48E 202 F4
Malir → Pakistan 24°49N 67°4E 123 B2
Malita Phil. 6°19N 125°39E 233 H5
Maliwun Burma 10°17N 98°40E 237 G2
Maliya India 23°5N 70°46E 242 H4
Maljenik Serbia 43°54N 21°43E 202 C5
Malka Mari △ Kenya 4°11N 40°46E 268 B5
Malkapur India 20°53N 76°12E 244 D3
Malkara Turkey 40°53N 26°53E 203 F10
Malkhangiri = Malakanagiri India 18°21N 81°54E 244 E5
Małkinia Górna Poland 52°42N 22°5E 185 F9
Malko Tŭrnovo Bulgaria 41°59N 27°31E 203 E11
Mall, The Washington, D.C., U.S.A. 143 b2
Mallacoota Australia 37°40S 149°40E 283 D8
Mallacoota Inlet Australia 37°34S 149°40E 283 D8
Mallaig U.K. 57°0N 5°50W 167 D3
Mallala Australia 34°26S 138°30E 282 C3
Mallaoua Niger 13°2N 9°36E 263 C6
Mallard U.S.A. 42°56N 94°41W 310 B2
Mallawan India 27°4N 80°12E 243 F9
Mallawi Egypt 27°44N 30°44E 256 B3
Mallee Cliffs △ Australia 34°16S 142°32E 282 C5
Mallembe Gabon 3°34S 10°53E 264 C2
Mallemort France 43°43N 5°11E 175 E9
Malleny Mills U.K. 55°52N 3°20W 121 B2
Málles Venosta Italy 46°41N 10°32E 198 B7
Mallicolo = Malakula Vanuatu 16°15S 167°30E 287 F5
Mallorca Spain 39°30N 3°0E 206 B4
Mallorytown Canada 44°29N 75°53W 313 B9
Mallow Ireland 52°8N 8°39W 166 D3
Malmbäck Sweden 57°34N 14°28E 163 G8
Malmberget Sweden 67°11N 20°40E 160 C19
Malmédy Belgium 50°25N 6°2E 170 D6
Malmesbury S. Africa 33°28S 18°41E 270 D2
Malmi Finland 60°15N 24°59E 121 B2
Malmivaara = Malmberget Sweden 67°11N 20°40E 160 C19
Malmköping Sweden 59°8N 16°44E 162 E10
Malmö Sweden 55°36N 12°59E 163 J7
Malmok Aruba 12°36N 70°4W 322 f
Malmøya Norway 59°52N 10°45E 133 A3
Malmslätt Sweden 58°27N 15°33E 163 F9
Malmyzh Russia 56°31N 50°41E 190 B10
Malnaş Romania 46°2N 25°49E 183 D10
Malo Vanuatu 15°40S 167°11E 287 E5
Malo Konare Bulgaria 42°12N 24°24E 203 D8
Maloarkhangelsk Russia 52°28N 36°30E 189 F9
Maloca Brazil 0°43N 55°57W 329 C6
Malolo Fiji 17°45S 177°11E 287 A1
Malolos Phil. 14°50N 120°49E 232 D3
Malolotja ⌓ Swaziland 26°4S 31°6E 271 C5
Malombe L. Malawi 14°40S 35°15E 269 E4
Małomice Poland 51°34N 15°29E 185 G2
Malomir Bulgaria 42°16N 26°32E 203 D10
Malone Fla., U.S.A. 30°57N 85°10W 316 E4
Malone N.Y., U.S.A. 44°51N 74°18W 313 B10
Malong China 25°24N 103°34E 228 E4
Malonga Dem. Rep. of the Congo 10°24S 23°10E 265 E4
Małopolskie □ Poland 49°50N 20°20E 185 J7
Malorad Bulgaria 43°28N 23°41E 202 C7
Måløv Denmark 55°44N 12°20E 118 A1
Måløy Norway 61°57N 5°6E 164 C2
Maloyaroslovets Russia 55°2N 36°20E 188 E9
Malpartida de Cáceres Spain 39°26N 6°30W 195 F4
Malpaso Canary Is. 27°43N 18°3W 153 e1
Malpaso, Presa = Netzahualcóyotl, Presa Mexico 17°8N 93°35W 319 D6
Malpelo, I. de Colombia 4°3N 81°35W 289 G19
Malpica de Bergantiños Spain 43°19N 8°50W 194 B2
Malprabha → India 16°20N 76°5E 245 F3
Malpur India 23°21N 73°27E 242 H5
Malpura India 26°17N 75°23E 242 F6
Mals = Málles Venosta Italy 46°41N 10°32E 198 B7
Malsiras India 17°52N 74°55E 244 F2
Malta Brazil 6°54S 37°31W 332 C4
Malta Idaho, U.S.A. 42°18N 113°22W 304 E7
Malta Mont., U.S.A. 48°21N 107°52W 304 B10
Malta ■ Europe 35°55N 14°26E 206 F7
Malta ✈ (MLA) Malta 35°52N 14°29E 206 F7
Maltahöhe Namibia 24°55S 17°0E 270 B2
Maltepe Turkey 40°55N 29°8E 203 F13
Malton Ont., Canada 43°42N 79°38W 141 A1
Malton N. Yorks., U.K. 54°8N 0°49W 168 C7
Malu'a Solomon Is. 8°20S 160°38E 287 M11
Maludam △ Malaysia 1°39N 111°2E 235 B4
Maluko = Manolo Fortich Phil. 8°28N 124°50E 233 G5
Maluku Indonesia 1°0S 127°0E 231 E7
Maluku □ Indonesia 3°0S 128°0E 231 E7
Maluku Sea = Molucca Sea Indonesia 0°0 125°0E 231 E6
Malumfashi Nigeria 11°48N 7°39E 263 C6
Malunda Indonesia 3°0S 118°50E 235 C5
Malundo Angola 14°51S 22°0E 265 E4
Malung Sweden 60°42N 13°44E 162 D7
Malungon Phil. 6°16N 125°14E 233 H5
Malungsfors Sweden 60°44N 13°33E 162 D7
Malur India 13°0N 77°55E 245 H3
Maluso Phil. 6°33N 121°53E 233 H3
Maluwe Ghana 8°40N 2°17W 262 D4
Malvalli India 12°28N 77°8E 245 H3
Malvan India 16°2N 73°30E 245 F1
Malvern Vic., Australia 37°50S 145°2E 128 B2
Malvern Ont., Canada 43°47N 79°13W 141 A3
Malvern Gauteng, S. Africa 26°11S 28°5E 123 B2
Malvern Ark., U.S.A. 34°22N 92°49W 314 D8
Malvern Hills U.K. 52°0N 2°19W 169 E5
Malvik Norway 63°25N 10°40E 164 A7
Malvinas, Is. = Falkland Is. ☑ Atl. Oc. 51°30S 59°0W 153 f
Malwal South Sudan 9°19N 31°35E 257 F3
Malý Dunaj → Slovak Rep. 47°45N 18°9E 181 D11
Malya Tanzania 3°5S 33°38E 268 C3
Malye Derbety Russia 47°57N 44°42E 191 G7
Malyn Ukraine 50°46N 29°3E 177 C15
Malyy Lyakhovskiy, Ostrov Russia 74°7N 140°36E 215 B15
Malyy Taymyr, Ostrov Russia 78°6N 107°15E 215 B11
Mama Russia 58°18N 112°54E 215 D12
Mamadysh Russia 55°44N 51°23E 190 C10
Mamaku N.Z. 38°5S 176°8E 284 E5
Mämala B. U.S.A. 21°15N 157°55W 302 K14
Mamanguape Brazil 6°50S 35°4W 332 C4
Mamanuca Group Fiji 17°35S 177°5E 287 A1
Mamarr Mitlā Egypt 30°2N 32°54E 251 H3
Mamasa Indonesia 2°55S 119°20E 235 C5
Mambajao Phil. 9°15N 124°43E 233 G5
Mambasa Dem. Rep. of the Congo 1°22N 29°3E 268 B2
Mamberamo → Indonesia 2°0S 137°50E 231 E9
Mambéré → C.A.R. 3°31N 16°3E 264 B3
Mambili → Congo 0°6N 16°5E 264 B3
Mambilima Falls Zambia 10°31S 28°45E 269 E2
Mambirima Dem. Rep. of the Congo 11°25S 27°33E 269 E2
Mambo Tanzania 4°52S 38°22E 268 C4
Mambrui Kenya 3°5S 40°5E 268 C5
Mamburao Phil. 13°13N 120°39E 232 E3
Mamedkala Russia 42°10N 48°7E 191 J9
Mameigwess L. Canada 52°35N 87°50W 298 B2
Mamers France 48°21N 0°22E 172 D7
Mamfé Cameroon 5°50N 9°15E 263 D6
Māmī, Ra's Yemen 12°32N 54°30E 249 D6
Mamili △ Namibia 18°2S 24°1E 270 A3
Mamiña Chile 20°5S 69°14W 330 E4
Mamlyutka Kazakhstan 54°56N 68°32E 217 B7
Mammoth U.S.A. 32°43N 110°39W 305 K8
Mammoth Cave △ U.S.A. 37°8N 86°13W 308 G10
Mamonovo Kaliningrad, Russia 54°28N 19°55E 184 D6
Mamonovo Moskva, Russia 55°41N 37°18E 129 B2
Mamoré → Bolivia 10°23S 65°53W 331 C4
Mamou Guinea 10°15N 12°0W 262 C2
Mamoudzou Mayotte 12°48S 45°14E 272 b
Mampang Prapatan Indonesia 6°15S 106°49E 122 B1
Mampikony Madag. 16°6S 47°38E 272 B2
Mampoko Dem. Rep. of the Congo 0°51N 18°42E 264 B3
Mampong Ghana 7°6N 1°26W 263 D4
Mampukuji Japan 35°36N 139°31E 140 B2
Mamry, Jezioro Poland 54°5N 21°50E 184 D8
Mamuil Malal, Paso S. Amer. 39°35S 71°28W 336 A2
Mamuju Indonesia 2°41S 118°50E 235 C5
Ma'mūl Oman 18°8N 55°16E 249 C6
Mamuno Botswana 22°16S 20°1E 270 B3
Mamuras Albania 41°34N 19°41E 202 E3
Man Ivory C. 7°30N 7°40W 262 D3
Man → India 17°31N 75°32E 244 F2
Man, I. of India 8°28N 93°36E 245 K11
Man, I. of U.K. 54°15N 4°30W 168 C3
Man-Bazar India 23°4N 86°39E 243 H12
Man Budrukh India 19°2N 72°55E 130 A2
Mān Kat Burma 22°5N 98°1E 241 D7
Man Khurd India 19°3N 72°55E 130 A2
Man Na Burma 23°27N 97°19E 241 D6
Man-of-War B. Trin. & Tob. 11°19N 60°34W 323 s
Man Tun Burma 23°52N 98°38E 241 D7
Mana Fr. Guiana 5°45N 53°55W 329 B7
Mänä Hawai'i, U.S.A. 22°2N 159°47W 302 A2
Mana → Fr. Guiana 5°45N 53°55W 329 B7
Mana Pools △ Zimbabwe 15°56S 29°25E 269 F2
Manaar, G. of = Mannar, G. of Asia 8°30N 79°0E 245 K4
Manabí □ Ecuador 0°40S 80°5W 328 D1
Manacacías → Colombia 4°23N 72°4W 328 C3
Manacapuru Brazil 3°16S 60°37W 329 D5
Manacapuru → Brazil 3°18S 60°37W 329 D5
Manacor Spain 39°34N 3°13E 206 B4
Manadas Azores 38°38N 28°6W 153 d1
Manado Indonesia 1°29N 124°51E 231 D6
Managua Nic. 12°6N 86°20W 320 D2
Managua, L. de Nic. 12°20N 86°30W 320 D2
Manaia N.Z. 39°33S 174°8E 284 F3
Manakara Madag. 22°8S 48°1E 272 C2
Manakau N.Z. 42°15S 173°42E 285 C8
Manākhah Yemen 15°5N 43°44E 248 D3
Manakhat Israel 31°45N 35°11E 123 B2
Manali India 32°16N 77°10E 242 C7
Manam I. Papua N. G. 4°5S 145°0E 286 C3
Manama = Al Manāmah Bahrain 26°10N 50°30E 247 E6
Manambao → Madag. 17°35S 44°0E 272 B1
Manambato Madag. 13°43S 49°7E 272 A2
Manambolo → Madag. 19°18S 44°22E 272 B1
Manambolosy Madag. 16°2S 49°40E 272 B2
Mánamo, Caño → Venezuela 9°55N 62°16W 329 B5
Mänana I. U.S.A. 21°20N 157°40W 302 K14
Mananara Madag. 16°10S 49°46E 272 B2
Mananara → Madag. 23°21S 47°42E 272 C2
Mananara ⌓ Madag. 16°14S 49°45E 272 B2
Manangatang Australia 35°5S 142°54E 282 C5
Mananjary Madag. 21°13S 48°20E 272 C2
Manankoro Mali 10°28N 7°25W 262 C3
Manantali, L. de Mali 13°12N 10°28W 262 C2
Manantavadi India 11°49N 76°1E 245 J3
Manantenina Madag. 24°17S 47°19E 272 C2
Manaos = Manaus Brazil 3°0S 60°0W 329 D6
Manapire → Venezuela 7°42N 66°7W 328 B4
Manapla Phil. 10°58N 123°5E 233 F4
Manapouri N.Z. 45°34S 167°39E 285 F2
Manapouri, L. N.Z. 45°32S 167°32E 285 F2
Manapparai India 10°36N 78°25E 245 J4
Manaqil Sudan 14°15N 32°59E 257 E3

Manar → India 18°50N 77°20E 244 E3
Manār, Jabal Yemen 14°2N 44°17E 248 D4
Manaravolo Madag. 23°59S 45°39E 272 C2
Manas Xinjiang Uygur, China 44°17N 86°10E 217 D11
Manas Somali Rep. 2°57N 43°28E 267 D5
Manas → India 26°12N 90°40E 241 B3
Manas △ India 26°40N 91°0E 241 B3
Manas He → China 45°38N 85°12E 218 B6
Manas Hu China 45°45N 85°55E 217 C11
Manaslu Nepal 28°33N 84°33E 243 E11
Manasquan U.S.A. 40°8N 74°3W 313 F10
Manassa U.S.A. 37°11N 105°56W 305 H11
Manatí Puerto Rico 18°26N 66°29W 321 b
Manati B. St. Helena 16°0S 5°46W 153 h
Manau Papua N. G. 8°4S 148°0E 286 E4
Manaung Burma 18°45N 93°40E 241 F4
Manaus Brazil 3°0S 60°0W 329 D6
Manavgat Turkey 36°47N 31°26E 250 B2
Manavgat → Turkey 36°43N 31°27E 250 B2
Manawan = Rizal Phil. 17°51N 121°21E 232 C3
Manawan L. Canada 55°24N 103°14W 297 B8
Manawatu → N.Z. 40°28S 175°12E 284 G4
Manawatu-Wanganui □ N.Z. 39°50S 175°30E 284 F4
Manay Phil. 7°17N 126°33E 233 H6
Manbij Syria 36°31N 37°57E 212 D7
Mancha Real Spain 37°48N 3°39W 195 H7
Manche □ France 49°10N 1°20W 172 C5
Manchegorsk Russia 67°54N 32°58E 214 C4
Manchester Gt. Man., U.K. 53°29N 2°12W 168 D5
Manchester Calif., U.S.A. 38°58N 123°41W 306 G3
Manchester Conn., U.S.A. 41°47N 72°31W 313 E12
Manchester Ga., U.S.A. 32°51N 84°37W 316 C5
Manchester Iowa, U.S.A. 42°29N 91°27W 310 B5
Manchester Ky., U.S.A. 37°9N 83°46W 309 G12
Manchester Mich., U.S.A. 42°9N 84°2W 311 B12
Manchester N.H., U.S.A. 42°59N 71°28W 313 D13
Manchester N.Y., U.S.A. 42°56N 77°16W 312 D7
Manchester Ohio, U.S.A. 38°41N 83°36W 311 F13
Manchester Pa., U.S.A. 40°4N 76°43W 313 F8
Manchester Tenn., U.S.A. 35°29N 86°5W 315 D11
Manchester Vt., U.S.A. 43°10N 73°5W 313 C11
Manchester Int. ✕ (MAN) U.K. 53°21N 2°17W 168 D5
Manchester L. Canada 61°28N 107°29W 297 A7
Manchhar L. Pakistan 26°25N 67°39E 242 F2
Manchineel Bay Grenada 12°26N 61°29W 323 q
Manchou Taiwan 22°1N 120°50E 225 D2
Manchuria = Dongbei China 45°0N 125°0E 227 D13
Manchurian Plain China 47°0N 124°0E 210 D14
Manciano Italy 42°35N 11°31E 199 F8
Mancifa Ethiopia 6°53N 41°50E 257 F5
Máncora Peru 4°9S 81°1W 330 A1
Mand → India 21°42N 83°15E 243 J10
Mand → Iran 28°20N 52°30E 247 D7
Manda Ludewe, Tanzania 10°30S 34°40E 269 E3
Manda Mbeya, Tanzania 7°58S 32°29E 268 D3
Manda Mbeya, Tanzania 8°30S 32°49E 269 D3
Manda △ Chad 9°45N 17°52E 259 G3
Mandabé Madag. 21°0S 44°55E 272 C1
Mandaguari Brazil 23°32S 51°42W 335 A5
Mandah = Töhöm Mongolia 44°27N 108°2E 226 B5
Mandal Norway 58°2N 7°25E 164 F4
Mandala, Puncak Indonesia 4°44S 140°20E 231 E10
Mandalay Burma 22°0N 96°4E 241 E6
Mandalay □ Burma 22°0N 96°5E 241 E5
Mandale = Mandalay Burma 22°0N 96°4E 241 E6
Mandalgarh India 25°12N 75°6E 242 G6
Mandalgovĭ Mongolia 45°45N 106°10E 226 B4
Mandalī Iraq 33°43N 45°28E 213 F11
Mandalselva → Norway 58°2N 7°28E 164 F4
Mandaluyong Phil. 14°35N 121°1E 127 B2
Mandan U.S.A. 46°50N 100°54W 308 B3
Mandaoli India 28°37N 77°17E 120 B2
Mandaon Phil. 12°13N 123°17E 232 E4
Mandaqui → Brazil 23°30S 46°40W 137 A2
Mandar, Teluk Indonesia 3°32S 119°21E 235 C5
Mandara Mts. Nigeria 10°40N 13°40E 259 F2
Mándas Italy 39°40N 9°8E 200 C2
Mandasor = Mandsaur India 24°3N 75°8E 242 G6
Mandaue Phil. 10°20N 123°56E 233 F4
Mandelieu-la-Napoule France 43°34N 6°57E 175 E10
Mandera Kenya 3°55N 41°53E 268 B5
Mandeville Jamaica 18°2N 77°31W 320 a
Mandi India 31°39N 76°58E 242 D7
Mandi Burewala Pakistan 30°9N 72°41E 242 D5
Mandi Dabwali India 29°58N 74°42E 242 E6
Mandiana Guinea 10°37N 8°39W 262 C3
Mandigos = Manica Mozam. 18°58S 32°59E 271 A5
Mandimba Mozam. 14°20S 35°40E 269 E4
Mandioli Indonesia 0°40S 127°20E 231 E7
Mandioré, L. S. Amer. 18°8S 57°33W 331 D6
Mandla India 22°39N 80°30E 243 H9
Mandø Denmark 55°18N 8°33E 163 J2
Mandoli India 28°41N 77°18E 120 A2
Mandorah Australia 12°32S 130°42E 278 B5
Mandoto Madag. 19°34S 46°17E 272 B2
Mandoudi Greece 38°48N 23°29E 204 C5
Mandoul Chad 9°40N 15°30E 259 G3
Mandra Greece 38°4N 23°30E 204 C5
Mandra Pakistan 33°23N 73°12E 242 C5
Mandraki Greece 36°36N 27°11E 205 E9
Mandrare → Madag. 25°10S 46°30E 272 D2
Mandritsara Madag. 15°50S 48°49E 272 B2
Mandronarivo Madag. 21°7S 45°38E 272 C2
Mandsaur India 24°3N 75°8E 242 G6
Mandurah Australia 32°36S 115°48E 279 F2
Mandúria Italy 40°24N 17°38E 201 B10
Mandvi Gujarat, India 22°51N 69°22E 242 H3
Mandvi Maharashtra, India 18°56N 72°50E 130 B2
Mandya India 12°30N 77°0E 245 H3
Mandzai Pakistan 30°55N 67°6E 242 D2
Mané Burkina Faso 12°59N 1°21W 263 C4
Maneh Iran 37°39N 57°7E 247 B8
Manenberg S. Africa 33°58S 18°33E 118 A2
Manengouba, Mts. Cameroon 5°0N 9°50E 263 E6
Maner → India 18°30N 79°40E 244 E4
Manera Madag. 22°55S 44°20E 272 C1
Manérbio Italy 45°21N 10°8E 198 C7
Maneroo Cr. → Australia 23°21S 143°53E 280 C3
Manfalût Egypt 27°20N 30°52E 256 B3
Manfred Australia 33°19S 143°45E 282 B5
Manfredónia Italy 41°38N 15°55E 199 G12
Manfredónia, G. di Italy 41°35N 16°5E 199 G13
Mang Kung Uk China 22°18N 114°16E 122 B2
Mang-won S. Korea 37°33N 126°55E 137 B1
Manga Brazil 14°46S 43°56W 333 C3
Manga Burkina Faso 11°40N 1°4W 263 C4
Manga Congo 0°13S 16°56E 264 C3
Manga Niger 15°0N 14°0E 259 F2
Mangabeiras, Chapada das Brazil 10°0S 46°30W 332 D2
Mangai Dem. Rep. of the Congo 4°2S 19°33E 265 C3
Mangaia Cook Is. 21°55S 157°55W 289 K12
Mangakino N.Z. 38°22S 175°47E 284 E4
Mangal Phil. 6°25N 121°58E 233 H3
Mangalagiri India 16°26N 80°36E 245 F5
Mangaldai India 26°26N 92°2E 241 B4
Mangaldan Phil. 16°4N 120°24E 232 C3
Mangalia Romania 43°50N 28°35E 183 G13
Mangalmé Chad 12°26N 19°37E 259 F3
Mangalore India 12°55N 74°47E 245 H2
Mangaluru = Mangalore India 12°55N 74°47E 245 H2
Mangalvedha India 17°31N 75°28E 244 F2
Mangan India 27°31N 88°32E 241 B2
Mangaon India 18°15N 73°20E 244 E1
Mangawan India 24°41N 81°33E 243 G9
Mangaweka N.Z. 39°48S 175°47E 284 F4
Mangaweka, Mt. N.Z. 39°49S 176°5E 284 F5
Mange Dem. Rep. of the Congo 0°54N 20°30E 264 B4
Manger Norway 60°38N 5°3E 164 D2
Manggar Indonesia 2°50S 108°10E 235 C3
Manggawitu Indonesia 4°8S 133°32E 231 E8
Mangghystaū Kazakhstan 43°40N 51°15E 216 D4
Mangghystaū □ Kazakhstan 45°0N 53°0E 216 D4
Mangghystaū Tübegi Kazakhstan 44°30N 52°30E 216 D4
Manggis Indonesia 8°29S 115°31E 231 J18
Mangin Taungdan Burma 24°15N 95°45E 241 C5
Mangindrano Madag. 14°17S 48°58E 272 A2
Mangkalihat, Tanjung Indonesia 1°2N 118°59E 235 B5
Mangkururrpa ⊙ Australia 20°35S 129°43E 278 D4
Mangla Pakistan 33°7N 73°39E 242 C5
Mangla Dam Pakistan 33°9N 73°44E 243 C5
Manglares, C. Colombia 1°36N 79°2W 328 C2
Manglaur India 29°44N 77°49E 242 E7
Manglisi Georgia 41°41N 44°22E 191 K7
Mangnai China 37°52N 91°43E 218 D7
Mangnai Zhen China 38°24N 90°14E 217 E12
Mango Togo 10°20N 0°30E 263 C5
Mango Tonga 20°17S 174°29W 287 Q13
Mangoche Malawi 14°25S 35°16E 269 E4
Mangoky → Madag. 21°29S 43°41E 272 C1
Mangole Indonesia 1°50S 125°55E 231 E6
Mangolpuri India 28°41N 77°6E 120 A1
Mangombe Dem. Rep. of the Congo 1°20S 26°48E 268 C2
Mangonui N.Z. 35°1S 173°32E 284 B2
Mangoro → Madag. 20°0S 48°45E 272 C2
Mangrol Mad. P., India 21°7N 70°7E 242 J4
Mangrol Raj., India 25°20N 76°31E 242 G6
Mangrul Pir India 20°19N 77°21E 244 D3
Manguaba = Pilar Brazil 9°36S 35°56W 332 C4
Mangualde Portugal 40°38N 7°48W 194 E3
Mangueigne Chad 10°30N 21°15E 259 F4
Mangueira, L. da Brazil 33°0S 52°50W 335 C5
Manguéni, Hamada Niger 22°35N 12°40E 258 D2
Manguinhos ✕ Brazil 22°52S 43°14W 135 B1
Mangum U.S.A. 34°53N 99°30W 314 D5
Mangungu Dem. Rep. of the Congo 5°16S 19°36E 265 D3
Manguri Australia 28°58S 134°22E 281 A1
Mangyshlak, Poluostrov = Mangghystaū Tübegi Kazakhstan 44°30N 52°30E 216 D4
Manhattan Kans., U.S.A. 39°11N 96°35W 308 F5
Manhattan New York, U.S.A. 132 d2
Manhattan Beach U.S.A. 40°34N 73°56W 132 C2
Manhattan Bridge New York, U.S.A. 132 f2
Manhatten U.S.A. 41°26N 87°59W 311 C9
Manhiça Mozam. 25°23S 32°49E 271 C5
Manhuaçu Brazil 20°15S 42°2W 333 F3
Manhumirim Brazil 20°22S 41°57W 333 F3
Maní Colombia 4°49N 72°17W 328 C3
Mania → Madag. 19°42S 45°22E 272 B2
Maniago Italy 46°10N 12°43E 199 B9
Manica Mozam. 18°58S 32°59E 271 A5
Manica □ Mozam. 19°10S 33°45E 271 A5
Manicahan Phil. 7°1N 122°12E 233 H4
Manicaland □ Zimbabwe 19°0S 32°30E 269 F3
Manicoré Brazil 5°48S 61°16W 331 B5
Manicoré → Brazil 5°51S 61°19W 331 B5
Manicouagan → Canada 49°30N 68°30W 299 C6
Manicouagan, Rés. Canada 51°5N 68°40W 299 B6
Maniema □ Dem. Rep. of the Congo 3°0S 26°0E 268 C2
Manīfah Si. Arabia 27°44N 49°0E 247 E6
Manifold, C. Australia 22°41S 150°50E 280 C5
Maniganggo China 31°56N 99°10E 228 B2
Manigotagan Canada 51°6N 96°18W 297 C9
Manigotagan → Canada 51°7N 96°20W 297 C9
Manihari India 25°21N 87°38E 243 G12
Manihi French Polynesia 14°24S 145°56W 289 f
Manihiki Cook Is. 10°24S 161°1W 289 J11
Manihiki Plateau Pac. Oc. 11°0S 164°0W 289 J11
Maniitsoq Greenland 65°26N 52°55W 154 D5
Manika, Plateau de la Dem. Rep. of the Congo 10°0S 25°5E 269 E2
Manikchhari Bangla. 22°51N 91°50E 241 D3
Manikganj Bangla. 23°52N 90°0E 241 D3
Manikpur India 25°4N 81°7E 243 G9
Manila Phil. 14°35N 120°58E 127 B1
Manila Utah, U.S.A. 40°59N 109°43W 304 F9
Manila B. Phil. 14°40N 120°35E 232 D3
Manila Ninoy Aquino Int. ✕ (MNL) Phil. 14°31N 121°0E 127 B2
Manildra Australia 33°11S 148°41E 283 B8
Manilla Australia 30°45S 150°43E 283 A9
Manimpé Mali 14°11N 5°28W 262 C3
Maningrida Australia 12°3S 134°13E 280 A1
Maninian Ivory C. 10°3N 7°52W 262 C3
Maninjau, Danau Indonesia 0°19S 100°11E 234 C2
Manipur □ India 25°0N 94°0E 241 C5
Manipur → Burma 23°45N 94°20E 241 D5
Manisa Turkey 38°38N 27°30E 205 C9
Manisa □ Turkey 38°40N 28°0E 205 C9
Manistee U.S.A. 44°15N 86°19W 308 C10
Manistee → U.S.A. 44°15N 86°21W 308 C10
Manistique U.S.A. 45°57N 86°15W 308 C10
Manito U.S.A. 40°26N 89°47W 310 D7
Manitoba □ Canada 53°30N 97°0W 297 B9
Manitoba, L. Canada 51°0N 98°45W 297 C9
Manitou Canada 49°15N 98°32W 297 D9
Manitou, L. Canada 50°55N 65°17W 299 B6
Manitou Beach U.S.A. 41°58N 84°19W 311 C12
Manitou Is. U.S.A. 45°8N 86°0W 308 C10
Manitou L. Canada 52°43N 109°43W 297 C7
Manitou Springs U.S.A. 38°52N 104°55W 304 G11
Manitoulin I. Canada 45°40N 82°30W 298 C3
Manitouwadge Canada 49°8N 85°48W 298 C2
Manitowoc U.S.A. 44°5N 87°40W 308 C10
Manitsauá-Missu → Brazil 10°58S 53°20W 331 C7
Maniyachi India 8°51N 77°55E 245 K3
Manizales Colombia 5°5N 75°32W 328 B2
Manja Madag. 21°26S 44°20E 272 C1
Manjacaze Mozam. 24°45S 34°0E 271 B5
Manjakandriana Madag. 18°55S 47°47E 272 B2
Manjeri India 11°7N 76°11E 245 J3
Manjhand Pakistan 25°50N 68°10E 242 G3
Manjiang China 41°56N 127°35E 224 B3
Manjimup Australia 34°15S 116°6E 279 F2
Manjlegaon India 19°9N 76°14E 244 E3
Manjo Cameroon 4°50N 9°49E 264 B1
Manjra → India 18°49N 77°52E 244 E3
Mankato Kans., U.S.A. 39°47N 98°13W 308 F4
Mankato Minn., U.S.A. 44°10N 94°0W 308 C6
Mankayan Phil. 16°52N 120°47E 232 C3
Mankayane Swaziland 26°40S 31°4E 271 C5
Mankera Pakistan 31°23N 71°26E 242 D4
Mankim Cameroon 5°6N 12°3E 263 D7
Mankkaa Finland 60°11N 24°47E 121 B1
Mankono Ivory C. 8°1N 6°10W 262 D3
Mankota Canada 49°25N 107°5W 297 D7
Mankulam Sri Lanka 9°8N 80°26E 245 K5
Manlay = Üydzin Mongolia 44°9N 107°0E 226 B4
Manleluag △ Phil. 15°4N 120°17E 232 D3
Manley Hot Springs U.S.A. 65°0N 150°38W 303 D10
Manlleu Spain 42°2N 2°17E 196 C7
Manly Australia 33°47S 151°17E 139 A2
Manmad India 20°18N 74°28E 244 D2
Mann, L. U.S.A. 28°32N 81°35W 133 A2
Mann Ranges Australia 26°6S 130°5E 279 E5
Manna Indonesia 4°25S 102°55E 234 C2
Mannahill Australia 32°25S 140°0E 282 B4
Mannar Sri Lanka 9°1N 79°54E 245 K4
Mannar, G. of Asia 8°30N 79°0E 245 K4
Mannar I. Sri Lanka 9°5N 79°45E 245 K4
Mannargudi India 10°45N 79°51E 245 J4
Mannheim Germany 49°29N 8°29E 179 F4
Manning Alta., Canada 56°53N 117°39W 296 B5
Manning Oreg., U.S.A. 45°45N 123°13W 306 E3
Manning S.C., U.S.A. 33°42N 80°13W 316 B9
Manning → Australia 31°52S 152°43E 283 A10
Manning Str. Solomon Is. 7°30S 158°0E 287 L10
Mann's Chinese Theatre U.S.A. 34°6N 118°20W 126 B2
Mannswörth Austria 48°8N 16°30E 142 B3
Mannu → Italy 39°16N 9°0E 200 C2
Mannu, C. Italy 40°3N 8°21E 200 B1
Mannum Australia 34°50S 139°20E 282 C3
Mano S. Leone 8°3N 12°2W 262 D2
Mano → Liberia 6°56N 11°30W 262 D2
Mano River Liberia 7°20N 11°6W 262 D2
Manoa Bolivia 9°40S 65°27W 331 B4
Manoharpur India 22°23N 85°12E 243 H11
Manokotak U.S.A. 58°58N 159°3W 303 G8
Manokwari Indonesia 0°54S 134°0E 231 E8
Manolada Greece 38°4N 21°21E 204 C3
Manolo Fortich Phil. 8°28N 124°50E 233 G5
Manombo Madag. 22°57S 43°28E 272 C1
Manono Dem. Rep. of the Congo 7°15S 27°25E 268 D2
Manono Samoa 13°50S 172°5W 287 V19
Manoppello Italy 42°15N 14°3E 199 F11
Manor Park Wellington, N.Z. 41°10S 174°59E 143 A2
Manor Park London, U.K. 51°32N 0°1E 125 A4
Manora Pakistan 24°47N 66°58E 123 B1
Manora Pt. Pakistan 24°47N 66°58E 123 B1
Manorhamilton Ireland 54°18N 8°9W 166 B3
Manosque France 43°49N 5°47E 175 E9
Manotick Canada 45°13N 75°41W 313 A9
Manouane → Canada 49°30N 71°10W 299 C5
Manouane, L. Canada 50°45N 70°45W 299 B5
Manovo-Gounda Saint Floris △ C.A.R. 9°30N 21°25E 264 A4
Manp'o N. Korea 41°6N 126°24E 224 B3
Manpojin = Manp'o N. Korea 41°6N 126°24E 224 B3
Manpur Chhattisgarh, India 23°17N 83°35E 243 H10
Manpur Chhattisgarh, India 20°22N 80°43E 244 D5
Manpur Mad. P., India 22°26N 75°37E 242 H6
Manquehue, Cerro Chile 33°21S 70°35W 137 B2
Manra Kiribati 4°27S 171°15W 277 A16
Manresa Spain 41°48N 1°50E 196 D6
Mansa Gujarat, India 23°27N 72°45E 242 H5
Mansa Punjab, India 30°0N 75°27E 242 E6
Mansa Zambia 11°13S 28°55E 269 E2
Mansa Konko Gambia 13°28N 15°33W 262 C1
Mansalay Phil. 12°31N 121°26E 232 E3
Månsåsen Sweden 63°5N 14°18E 162 A8
Mansehra Pakistan 34°20N 73°15E 242 B5
Mansel I. Canada 62°0N 80°0W 295 E15
Mansfield Vic., Australia 37°4S 146°6E 283 D7
Mansfield Notts., U.K. 53°9N 1°11W 168 D6
Mansfield Ga., U.S.A. 33°31N 83°44W 316 B6
Mansfield La., U.S.A. 32°2N 93°43W 314 E8
Mansfield Mass., U.S.A. 42°2N 71°13W 313 D13
Mansfield Ohio, U.S.A. 40°45N 82°31W 312 F2
Mansfield Pa., U.S.A. 41°48N 77°5W 312 E7
Mansfield Tex., U.S.A. 32°33N 97°8W 314 E6
Mansfield, Mt. U.S.A. 44°33N 72°49W 313 B12
Mansi Burma 24°48N 95°52E 241 C5
Mansidão Brazil 10°43S 44°2W 332 D3
Mansilla de las Mulas Spain 42°30N 5°25W 194 C5
Mansle France 45°52N 0°12E 174 C4
Manso → Brazil 13°50S 47°0W 333 D2
Mansôa Guinea-Biss. 12°0N 15°20W 262 C1
Manson U.S.A. 42°32N 94°32W 310 B2
Manson Creek Canada 55°37N 124°32W 296 B4
Mansoura Algeria 36°1N 4°31E 261 A5
Manta Ecuador 1°0S 80°40W 328 D1
Manta, B. de Ecuador 0°54S 80°44W 328 D1
Mantadia △ Madag. 18°54S 48°21E 272 B2
Mantalingajan, Mt. Phil. 8°55N 117°45E 233 G1
Mantantale Dem. Rep. of the Congo 2°10S 20°11E 264 C4
Mantare Tanzania 2°42S 33°13E 268 C3
Mantaro → Peru 12°16S 73°57W 330 C3
Manteca U.S.A. 37°48N 121°13W 306 H5
Mantecal Venezuela 7°34N 69°17W 328 B4
Mantena Brazil 18°47S 40°59W 333 E3
Manteo U.S.A. 35°55N 75°40W 315 D17
Mantes-la-Jolie France 48°58N 1°41E 173 D8
Mantha India 19°40N 76°23E 244 E3
Manthani India 18°40N 79°35E 244 E4
Manti U.S.A. 39°16N 111°38W 304 G8
Mantiqueira, Serra da Brazil 22°0S 44°0W 333 F3
Manton U.S.A. 44°25N 85°24W 309 C11
Mantorp Sweden 58°21N 15°20E 163 F9
Mántova Italy 45°9N 10°48E 198 C7
Mänttä Vilppula Finland 62°3N 24°40E 164 B21
Mantua = Mántova Italy 45°9N 10°48E 198 C7
Mantung Australia 34°35S 140°3E 282 C4
Manturovo Russia 58°23N 44°45E 190 A7
Manú Peru 12°10S 70°51W 330 C3
Manú → Peru 12°16S 70°55W 330 C3
Manu'a Is. Amer. Samoa 14°13S 169°35W 287 W21
Manuel Alves → Brazil 11°19S 48°28W 333 D2
Manuel Alves Grande → Brazil 7°27S 47°35W 332 C2
Manuel Urbano Brazil 8°53S 69°18W 330 B4
Manui Indonesia 3°35S 123°5E 231 E6
Manukan Phil. 8°32N 123°12E 233 G4
Manukau N.Z. 37°0S 174°52E 284 D3
Manukau Harbour N.Z. 37°3S 174°45E 284 D3
Manunui N.Z. 38°54S 175°21E 284 E4
Manurewa N.Z. 38°39S 177°7E 284 D3
Manuripi → Bolivia 11°6S 67°36W 330 C4
Manus □ Papua N. G. 2°0S 147°0E 286 B4
Manus I. Papua N. G. 2°0S 147°0E 286 B4
Manvi India 15°57N 76°59E 245 G3
Manwath India 19°19N 76°32E 244 E3
Many U.S.A. 31°34N 93°29W 314 F8
Manyallaluk ⊙ Australia 14°16S 132°49E 278 B5
Manyani Kenya 3°5S 38°30E 268 C4
Manyara, L. Tanzania 3°40S 35°50E 268 C4
Manyara △ Tanzania 3°35S 35°50E 268 C4
Manyas Turkey 40°2N 27°59E 203 F11
Manyas Gölü = Kus Gölü Turkey 40°10N 27°55E 203 F11
Manyava Ukraine 48°39N 24°21E 183 B9
Manych → Russia 47°13N 40°40E 191 G5
Manych-Gudilo, Ozero Russia 46°24N 42°38E 191 G6
Manyonga → Tanzania 4°10S 34°15E 268 C3
Manyoni Tanzania 5°45S 34°55E 268 D3
Manzai Pakistan 32°12N 70°15E 242 C4
Manzala, Bahra el Egypt 31°10N 31°56E 256 H7
Manzanar ⌓ U.S.A. 36°44N 118°9W 306 J7
Manzanares Spain 39°2N 3°22W 195 F7
Manzanares, Canal de Spain 40°19N 3°38W 127 C2
Manzaneda Spain 42°12N 7°15W 194 C3
Manzanillo Pt. Trin. & Tob. 10°31N 61°1W 323 t
Manzanillo Cuba 20°20N 77°31W 320 B4
Manzanillo Colima, Mexico 19°3N 104°20W 318 D4
Manzanillo, Pta. Panama 9°30N 79°40W 320 E4
Manzano Mts. U.S.A. 34°40N 106°20W 305 J10
Manzarīyeh Iran 34°53N 50°50E 247 C6
Manzhouli China 49°35N 117°25E 219 B12
Manzini Swaziland 26°30S 31°25E 271 C5
Manzur Vadisi △ Turkey 39°10N 39°30E 246 B3
Mao Chad 14°4N 15°19E 259 F3
Maó Spain 39°53N 4°16E 206 B5
Mao Mausoleum Beijing, China 114 c3
Maoka = Kholmsk Russia 47°40N 142°5E 215 E15
Maoke, Pegunungan Indonesia 3°40S 137°30E 231 E9
Maolin China 43°58N 123°30E 227 C12
Maoming China 21°50N 110°54E 229 G8
Maopi T'ou China 21°56N 120°43E 225 E2
Maouri, Dallol → Niger 12°5N 3°30E 263 C5
Maoxian China 31°41N 103°49E 228 B4
Maoxing China 45°28N 124°40E 227 B13
Map Micronesia 9°35N 138°10E 287 R16
Mapalma Dem. Rep. of the Congo 2°3N 24°30E 264 B4
Mapam Yumco China 30°45N 81°28E 243 D9
Mapastepec Mexico 15°26N 92°54W 319 D6
Mapfongui Gabon 1°15S 12°59E 264 C2
Maphrao, Ko Thailand 7°56N 98°26E 237 a
Mapia, Kepulauan Indonesia 0°50N 134°20E 231 D8
Mapimí Mexico 25°49N 103°51W 318 B4
Mapimí, Bolsón de Mexico 27°0N 104°15W 318 B4
Maping China 31°34N 113°32E 229 B9
Mapinga Tanzania 6°40S 39°12E 268 D4
Mapinhane Mozam. 22°20S 35°0E 271 B6
Mapire Venezuela 7°45N 64°42W 329 B5
Maple → U.S.A. 42°59N 84°57W 311 B12
Maple Creek Canada 49°55N 109°29W 297 D7
Maple Valley U.S.A. 47°25N 122°3W 306 C4
Mapleton U.S.A. 44°2N 123°52W 304 D2
Mapo S. Korea 37°32N 126°56E 137 B1
Mapoon ⊙ Australia 11°44S 142°8E 280 A3
Mapourika, L. N.Z. 43°16S 170°12E 285 D5
Maprik Papua N. G. 3°44S 143°3E 286 B2
Mapuca India 15°36N 73°46E 245 G1
Mapuera → Brazil 1°5S 57°2W 329 D6
Mapulanguene Mozam. 24°29S 32°6E 271 B5
Mapungubwe △ S. Africa 22°12S 29°22E 271 B4
Maputo Mozam. 25°58S 32°32E 271 C5
Maputo □ Mozam. 26°0S 32°25E 271 C5
Maputo, B. de Mozam. 25°50S 32°45E 271 C5
Maputo ⌓ Mozam. 26°23S 32°48E 271 C5
Maqanshy Kazakhstan 46°47N 82°1E 217 C10
Maqat Kazakhstan 47°39N 53°19E 187 E9
Maqên China 34°24N 100°6E 218 E9
Maqên Gangri China 34°55N 99°18E 218 E8
Maqiaohe China 44°40N 130°30E 227 B16
Maqnā Si. Arabia 28°25N 34°50E 251 K5
Maqran, W. → Si. Arabia 20°55N 47°12E 248 B4
Maqteïr Mauritania 21°50N 11°40W 260 D2
Maqu China 33°52N 101°42E 218 E9
Maquan He = Brahmaputra → Asia 23°40N 90°35E 241 D3
Maqueda Spain 40°4N 4°22W 194 E6
Maqueda Channel Phil. 13°42N 124°1E 232 E5
Maquela do Zombo Angola 6°0S 15°15E 265 D3
Maquinchao Argentina 41°15S 68°50W 336 B3
Maquoketa U.S.A. 42°4N 90°40W 310 B6
Mar Canada 44°49N 81°12W 312 B3
Mar, Serra do Brazil 25°30S 49°0W 335 B6
Mar Chiquita, L. Argentina 30°40S 62°50W 334 C3
Mar del Plata Argentina 38°0S 57°30W 334 D4
Mar Menor Spain 37°40N 0°45W 197 H4
Mar Vista U.S.A. 34°0N 118°25W 126 B2
Mara Guyana 6°0N 57°36W 329 B6
Mara India 28°11N 94°14E 241 A5
Mara Tanzania 1°30S 34°32E 268 C3
Mara □ Tanzania 1°45S 34°20E 268 C3
Maraã Brazil 1°52S 65°25W 328 D4
Maraa Tahiti 17°46S 149°34W 289 e
Marabá Brazil 5°20S 49°5W 332 C2
Marabahan Indonesia 3°0S 114°45E 235 C4
Maraboon, L. Australia 23°41S 148°0E 280 C4
Maracá, I. de Brazil 2°10N 50°30W 329 C7
Maracaibo Venezuela 10°40N 71°37W 328 A3
Maracaibo, L. de Venezuela 9°40N 71°30W 328 B3
Maracaju Brazil 21°38S 55°9W 335 A4
Maracajú, Serra de Brazil 20°57S 55°1W 331 E6
Maracanã Pará, Brazil 0°46S 47°27W 332 B2
Maracanã Rio de J., Brazil 22°54S 43°13W 135 B1
Maracanaú Brazil 3°52S 38°38W 332 B4
Maracás Brazil 13°26S 40°18W 333 D3
Maracas Trin. & Tob. 10°41N 61°24W 323 t
Maracas → Trin. & Tob. 10°34N 61°25W 323 t
Maracas B. Trin. & Tob. 10°45N 61°26W 323 t
Maracas Bay Village Trin. & Tob. 10°46N 61°28W 323 t
Maracas Falls Trin. & Tob. 10°44N 61°24W 323 t
Maracay Venezuela 10°15N 67°28W 328 A4
Maracena Spain 37°12N 3°38W 195 H7
Marādah Libya 29°15N 19°15E 258 C3
Maradi Niger 13°29N 7°20E 263 C6
Maradi □ Niger 14°15N 7°15E 263 C6
Marāgheh Iran 37°30N 46°12E 213 D12
Maragogipe Brazil 12°46S 38°55W 333 D4
Marāh Si. Arabia 25°0N 45°35E 246 E5
Marahoue △ Ivory C. 8°0N 7°8W 262 D3
Marais du Cotentin et du Bessin ⌓ France 49°10N 1°30W 172 C5
Marais Poitevin, Val de Sèvre et Vendée ⌓ France 46°18N 0°35W 174 B3
Maraisburg = Hofmeyr S. Africa 31°39S 25°50E 270 D4
Marajó, B. de Brazil 1°0S 48°30W 332 B2
Marajo, I. de Brazil 1°0S 49°30W 332 B1
Marākand Iran 38°51N 45°16E 246 B5
Marakele △ S. Africa 24°30S 25°30E 271 D4
Maralal Kenya 1°0N 36°38E 268 B4
Maralinga Australia 30°13S 131°32E 279 F5
Maralinga Tjarutja ⊙ Australia 29°30S 131°0E 279 E5
Maram India 25°25N 94°6E 241 C5
Marama Australia 35°10S 140°10E 282 C4
Maramag Phil. 7°46N 125°0E 233 H5
Maramaraereğlisi Turkey 40°57N 27°57E 203 F11
Maramasike Solomon Is. 9°30S 161°25E 287 M11
Marambio Antarctica 64°0S 56°0W 151 C18
Maramureş □ Romania 47°45N 24°0E 183 C9
Maran Malaysia 3°35N 102°45E 237 L4
Marana U.S.A. 32°27N 111°13W 305 K8
Maranboy Australia 14°40S 132°39E 278 B5
Maranchón Spain 41°6N 2°15W 196 D2
Marand Iran 38°30N 45°45E 213 C11
Marandochori Greece 38°38N 20°39E 207 B2
Marang Malaysia 5°12N 103°13E 237 K4
Maranguape Brazil 3°55S 38°50W 332 B4
Maranhão = São Luís Brazil 2°39S 44°15W 332 B3
Maranhão □ Brazil 5°0S 46°0W 332 C2
Marano, L. di Italy 45°44N 13°10E 199 C10
Maranoa → Australia 27°50S 148°37E 281 D4
Marañón → Peru 4°30S 73°35W 330 A3
Marão Mozam. 24°18S 34°2E 271 B5
Maraoli India 19°2N 72°53E 130 A2
Marapi → Brazil 0°37N 55°58W 329 C6
Marari Brazil 5°43S 67°47W 330 B4
Maraş = Kahramanmaraş Turkey 37°37N 36°53E 212 D7
Mărăşeşti Romania 45°52N 27°14E 183 E12
Maratea Italy 39°59N 15°43E 201 C8
Marateca Portugal 38°34N 8°40W 195 G2
Marathasa Cyprus 34°59N 32°51E 207 F8
Marathia, Akra Greece 37°39N 20°50E 207 D2
Marathokambos Greece 37°43N 26°42E 205 D8
Marathon Queens., Australia 20°51S 143°32E 280 C3
Marathon Ont., Canada 48°44N 86°23W 298 C2
Marathon Fla., U.S.A. 24°43N 81°5W 317 L8
Marathon N.Y., U.S.A. 42°27N 76°2W 313 D8
Marathon Tex., U.S.A. 30°12N 103°15W 314 F3
Marathonas Greece 38°11N 23°58E 204 C5
Marathóvouno Cyprus 35°13N 33°37E 207 E9
Maratua Indonesia 2°10N 118°35E 235 B5
Maraú Brazil 14°6S 39°0W 333 D4
Marau Indonesia 2°9S 110°42E 235 C4
Marau Solomon Is. 10°31S 161°31E 287 N11
Maraval Trin. & Tob. 10°42N 61°31W 323 t
Maraval → Trin. & Tob. 10°39N 61°32W 323 t
Maravari Solomon Is. 7°50S 156°42E 287 L9
Maravatío Mexico 19°54N 100°27W 318 D4
Marawi City Phil. 8°0N 124°21E 233 G5
Marāwih U.A.E. 24°18N 53°18E 247 E7
Marazliyivka Ukraine 46°8N 30°3E 183 D15
Marbella Spain 36°30N 4°57W 195 J6
Marble Bar Australia 21°9S 119°44E 278 D2
Marble Falls U.S.A. 30°35N 98°16W 314 F5
Marblehead Mass., U.S.A. 42°29N 70°51W 313 D14
Marblehead Ohio, U.S.A. 41°32N 82°44W 312 E2
Mårbu Norway 60°11N 8°9E 164 D5
Marburg = Maribor Slovenia 46°36N 15°40E 199 B12
Marburg Germany 50°47N 8°46E 178 E4
Marca, Pta. do Angola 16°31S 11°43E 265 F2
Marcal → Hungary 47°41N 17°40E 182 C2
Marcali Hungary 46°35N 17°25E 182 D2
Marcapata Peru 13°31S 70°52W 330 C3
Marcaria Italy 45°7N 10°32E 198 C7
Mărcăuţi Moldova 48°20N 27°14E 183 B12
Marcelin Poland 52°19N 20°59E 142 B1
Marceline U.S.A. 39°43N 92°57W 310 E4
Marcelino Brazil 1°0S 68°45W 328 D4
March U.K. 52°33N 0°5E 169 E8
Marchal Dem. Rep. of the Congo 5°16S 14°58E 265 D2
Marchand = Rommani Morocco 33°31N 6°40W 260 B3
Marche France 46°5N 1°20E 174 B5
Marche □ Italy 43°30N 13°15E 199 E10
Marché Bonsecours Montréal, Canada 130 b3
Marche-en-Famenne Belgium 50°14N 5°19E 170 D5
Marchena Spain 37°18N 5°23W 195 H5
Marchena, Canal de Ecuador 0°19N 90°12W 330 a
Marchena, I. Ecuador 0°19N 90°29W 330 a
Marches = Marche □ Italy 43°30N 13°15E 199 E10
Marchesale ⌓ Italy 38°32N 16°13E 201 D9
Marciana Marina Italy 42°48N 10°12E 198 F7
Marcianise Italy 41°2N 14°17E 201 A7
Marcigny France 46°17N 4°2E 173 F11
Marcillat-en-Combraille France 46°12N 2°38E 173 F9
Marck France 50°57N 1°57E 173 B8
Marckolsheim France 48°10N 7°30E 173 D14
Marco Island U.S.A. 25°58N 81°44W 317 K8
Marco Rondon Brazil 12°0S 60°56W 331 C5
Marcona Peru 15°10S 75°10W 330 D3
Marcos Juárez Argentina 32°42S 62°5W 334 C3
Mărculeşti Moldova 47°52N 28°14E 183 C13
Marcus Baker, Mt. U.S.A. 61°26N 147°45W 303 F11
Marcus I. = Minami-Tori-Shima Pac. Oc. 24°20N 153°58E 288 E7
Marcy, Mt. U.S.A. 44°7N 73°56W 313 B11
Mardan Pakistan 34°20N 72°0E 242 B5
Mardarivka Ukraine 47°32N 29°44E 183 C14
Mardie Australia 21°12S 115°59E 278 D2
Mardin Turkey 37°20N 40°43E 213 D9
Mårdsjö Sweden 63°18N 15°35E 162 A9
Maré, Î. N. Cal. 21°30S 168°0E 277 E12
Marécchia → Italy 44°4N 12°34E 199 D9
Marechal Deodoro Brazil 9°43S 35°54W 332 C4
Marechal Floriano = Piranhas Brazil 9°27S 37°46W 332 C4
Maree, L. U.K. 57°40N 5°26W 167 D3
Mareeba Australia 16°59S 145°28E 280 B4
Mareeg Somali Rep. 3°46N 47°18E 267 D6
Mareetsane S. Africa 26°9S 25°25E 270 C4
Mareil-Marly France 48°52N 2°4E 134 A1
Maremma Italy 42°30N 11°30E 199 F8
Maremma ⌓ Italy 42°35N 11°8E 198 F8
Maréna Kayes, Mali 14°36N 10°45W 262 C2
Maréna Koulikoro, Mali 13°55N 7°20W 262 C3
Marengo Ind., U.S.A. 38°22N 86°21W 311 F10
Marengo Iowa, U.S.A. 41°48N 92°4W 310 C4
Marennes France 45°49N 1°7W 174 C2
Marerano Madag. 21°23S 44°52E 272 C1
Marettimo Italy 37°58N 12°4E 200 E5
Mareuil France 45°26N 0°29E 174 C4
Marfa U.S.A. 30°19N 104°1W 314 F2
Marganets = Marhanets Ukraine 47°40N 34°40E 189 J8
Margao = Madgaon India 15°12N 73°58E 245 G1
Margaret → Australia 18°9S 125°41E 278 C4
Margaret Bay Canada 51°20N 127°35W 296 C3
Margaret L. Canada 58°56N 115°25W 296 B5
Margaret River Australia 33°57S 115°4E 279 F2
Margareten Austria 48°11N 16°20E 142 A2
Margarita, I. de Venezuela 11°0N 64°0W 329 A5
Margariti Greece 39°22N 20°26E 204 B2
Margaritovo Russia 43°25N 134°45E 220 C7
Margate KwaZulu Natal, S. Africa 30°50S 30°20E 271 D5
Margate Kent, U.K. 51°23N 1°23E 169 F9
Margate Fla., U.S.A. 26°15N 80°12W 317 J9
Margeride, Mts. de la France 44°43N 3°38E 174 D7
Margrabowa = Olecko Poland 54°2N 22°31E 184 D9
Margherita India 27°16N 95°40E 241 B5
Margherita di Savóia Italy 41°22N 16°9E 201 A9
Margherita Pk. Uganda 0°22N 29°51E 268 B3
Marghilon Uzbekistan 40°27N 71°42E 217 D8
Marghita Romania 47°22N 22°22E 182 C7
Margonin Poland 52°58N 17°5E 185 F4
Margosatubig Phil. 7°34N 123°10E 233 H4
Mārgow, Dasht-e Afghan. 30°40N 62°30E 240 C1
Marguerite Canada 52°30N 122°25W 296 C4
Marhanets Ukraine 47°40N 34°40E 189 J8
Marhoum Algeria 34°27N 0°11W 261 B4
Mari Papua N. G. 9°11S 141°42E 286 E1
Mārī Syria 36°29N 37°10E 250 B8
Mari El □ Russia 56°30N 48°0E 190 B8
Mari Indus Pakistan 32°57N 71°34E 242 C4
Mari Republic = Mari El □ Russia 56°30N 48°0E 190 B8
Maria Austria 48°11N 16°21E 142 A2
Maria, Îs. French Polynesia 21°48S 154°41W 289 f
María, Sa. de Spain 37°39N 2°14W 197 H2
Maria Aurora Phil. 15°48N 121°28E 232 D3
María de la Salut Spain 39°40N 3°5E 206 B4
María Elena Chile 22°18S 69°40W 334 A2
María Grande Argentina 31°45S 59°55W 334 C4
Maria I. N. Terr., Australia 14°52S 135°45E 280 A2
Maria I. Tas., Australia 42°35S 148°0E 281 G4
Maria Is. St. Lucia 13°44N 60°56W 323 m
Maria Island △ Australia 42°38S 148°5E 281 G4
Maria Pereira = Mombaça Brazil 5°43S 39°45W 332 C4
Maria Theresiopel = Subotica Serbia 46°6N 19°39E 182 D4
Maria van Diemen, C. N.Z. 34°29S 172°40E 284 A1
Mariager Denmark 56°40N 9°59E 163 H3
Mariager Fjord Denmark 56°42N 10°19E 163 H4
Mariahilferstrasse Vienna, Austria 142 b1
Mariakani Kenya 3°50S 39°27E 268 C4
Mariala △ Australia 25°57S 145°2E 281 D4
Marian Australia 21°9S 148°57E 280 b
Marian L. Canada 63°0N 116°15W 296 A5
Mariana Islands Pac. Oc. 15°15N 145°48E 302 a
Mariana Trench Pac. Oc. 13°0N 145°0E 302 a
Mariani India 26°39N 94°19E 241 B5
Marianica, Cord. = Morena, Sierra Spain 38°20N 4°0W 195 G7
Marianna Ark., U.S.A. 34°46N 90°46W 315 D9
Marianna Fla., U.S.A. 30°46N 85°14W 316 E4
Mariannelund Sweden 57°37N 15°35E 163 G9
Mariánské Lázně Czech Rep. 49°58N 12°41E 180 B5
Marias → U.S.A. 47°56N 110°30W 304 C8
Marías, Is. Mexico 21°25N 106°28W 318 C3
Mariato, Punta Panama 7°12N 80°52W 320 E3
Mariazell Austria 47°47N 15°19E 180 D8
Ma'rib Yemen 15°25N 45°21E 248 D4
Maribo Denmark 54°48N 11°30E 163 K5
Maribor Slovenia 46°36N 15°40E 199 B12
Maricaban I. Phil. 13°39N 120°53E 232 E3
Maricao Puerto Rico 18°11N 66°59W 321 b
Marico → Africa 23°35S 26°57E 270 B4
Maricopa Ariz., U.S.A. 33°4N 112°3W 305 K7
Maricopa Calif., U.S.A. 35°4N 119°24W 307 K7
Maridalen Norway 59°59N 10°45E 133 A3
Maridalsvatnet Norway 59°59N 10°46E 133 A3
Marīdī South Sudan 4°55N 29°25E 257 G2
Marīdī, Wadi → South Sudan 6°15N 29°21E 257 F2
Marié → Brazil 0°27S 66°26W 328 D4
Marie Byrd Land Antarctica 79°30S 125°0W 151 D14
Marie-Galante Guadeloupe 15°56N 61°16W 322 e
Marie-Galante, Canal de Guadeloupe 16°0N 61°25W 322 e
Mariecourt = Kangiqsujuaq Canada 61°30N 72°0W 295 E17
Mariefred Sweden 59°15N 17°12E 162 E11
Mariehamn Finland 60°5N 19°55E 161 F18
Marieholm Sweden 55°53N 13°10E 163 J7
Mariembourg Belgium 50°6N 4°31E 170 D4
Marienbad = Mariánské Lázně Czech Rep. 49°58N 12°41E 180 B5
Marienberg Germany 50°39N 13°9E 178 E9
Marienburg = Malbork Poland 54°3N 19°1E 184 D6
Mariendorf Germany 52°26N 13°23E 115 B3
Marienfelde Germany 52°24N 13°23E 115 B3
Marienplatz Munich, Germany 131 b2
Mariental Namibia 24°36S 18°0E 270 B2
Marienville U.S.A. 41°28N 79°8W 312 E5
Mariestad Sweden 58°43N 13°50E 163 F7
Marietta Ga., U.S.A. 33°57N 84°33W 316 B5
Marietta Ohio, U.S.A. 39°25N 81°27W 309 F13
Marieville Canada 45°26N 73°10W 313 A11
Mariga → Nigeria 9°40N 5°55E 263 C6
Marignane France 43°25N 5°13E 175 E9
Marigot Dominica 15°33N 61°18W 323 k
Marigot Guadeloupe 16°5N 61°46W 322 e
Marigot St.-Martin 18°4N 63°5W 322 a
Marigot Bay St. Lucia 13°58N 61°1W 323 m
Marihatag Phil. 8°48N 126°18E 233 G6
Mariinsk Russia 56°10N 87°20E 214 D9
Mariinsk Water = Volgo-Baltiyskiy Kanal Russia 60°0N 38°0E 188 B9
Mariinskiy Posad Russia 56°10N 47°45E 190 B8
Marijampolė Lithuania 54°33N 23°19E 184 D10
Marijampolė □ Lithuania 54°34N 23°21E 184 D10
Marikina Phil. 14°37N 121°5E 127 B2
Marikina → Phil. 14°33N 121°5E 127 B2
Marília Brazil 22°13S 50°0W 335 A6
Marimba Angola 8°28S 17°8E 265 D3
Marín Spain 42°23N 8°42W 194 C2
Marin, Cul-de-Sac du Martinique 14°27N 60°53W 322 j
Marin City U.S.A. 37°52N 122°30W 136 A1
Marin Pen. U.S.A. 37°50N 122°30W 136 A1
Marina U.S.A. 36°41N 121°48W 306 J5
Marina del Rey U.S.A. 33°58N 118°27W 126 C2
Marinduque Phil. 13°25N 122°0E 231 B6
Marinduque □ Phil. 13°18N 122°0E 232 E4
Marine City U.S.A. 42°43N 82°30W 312 D2
Marine Drive Mumbai, India 130 b1
Marineland U.S.A. 29°40N 81°13W 316 F8
Marineo Italy 37°57N 13°25E 200 E6
Marinette U.S.A. 45°6N 87°38W 308 C10
Maringá Brazil 23°26S 52°2W 335 A5
Maringa → Dem. Rep. of the Congo 1°14N 19°48E 264 B3
Marinha Grande Portugal 39°45N 8°56W 194 F2
Marinho dos Abrolhos △ Brazil 17°50S 39°0W 333 E4
Marino Dublin, Ireland 53°22N 6°14W 120 A2
Marino Italy 41°46N 12°39E 199 G9
Marion Ala., U.S.A. 32°38N 87°19W 315 E11
Marion Ill., U.S.A. 37°44N 88°56W 310 G8

Marion Ind., U.S.A. 40°32N 85°40W 311 D11
Marion Iowa, U.S.A. 42°2N 91°36W 310 B5
Marion Kans., U.S.A. 38°21N 97°1W 308 F5
Marion N.C., U.S.A. 35°41N 82°1W 315 D13
Marion Ohio, U.S.A. 40°35N 83°8W 311 D13
Marion S.C., U.S.A. 34°11N 79°24W 315 D15
Marion Va., U.S.A. 36°50N 81°31W 309 G13
Marion, L. U.S.A. 33°28N 80°10W 316 B9
Marion Bay Australia 35°12S 136°59E 282 C2
Marion I. Ind. Oc. 47°0S 38°0E 273 J2
Maripa Venezuela 7°26N 65°9W 329 B4
Maripasoula Fr. Guiana 3°40N 54°4W 329 C7
Maripipi I. Phil. 11°47N 124°19E 233 F5
Mariposa U.S.A. 37°29N 119°58W 306 H7
Mariscal Estigarribia
Paraguay 22°3S 60°40W 334 A3
Marisco, Ponta do Brazil 23°1S 43°18W 135 C1
Maritime Alps = Maritimes, Alpes
Europe 44°10N 7°10E 175 D11
Maritimes, Alpes Europe 44°10N 7°10E 175 D11
Maritsa = Evros ➝
Greece 41°40N 26°34E 203 F10
Maritsa Greece 36°22N 28°8E 206 E12
Mariupol Ukraine 47°5N 37°31E 189 J9
Marīvān Iran 35°30N 46°25E 213 E12
Mariveles Phil. 14°26N 120°29E 232 D3
Marj 'Uyūn Lebanon 33°21N 35°34E 250 E6
Marjan = Wazikhwah
Afghan. 32°11N 68°21E 240 B3
Mark Twain L. U.S.A. 39°28N 91°55W 310 E5
Marka Si. Arabia 18°14N 41°19E 256 D5
Marka Somali Rep. 1°48N 44°50E 267 D5
Markam China 29°42N 98°38E 228 C2
Markapur India 15°44N 79°19E 245 G4
Markaryd Sweden 56°28N 13°35E 163 H7
Markat Albania 39°44N 20°12E 206 B10
Markazī ☐ Iran 35°0N 49°30E 216 F3
Markdale Canada 44°19N 80°39W 312 B4
Marked Tree U.S.A. 35°32N 90°25W 315 D9
Markelsdorfer Huk
Germany 54°33N 11°4E 178 A7
Market Drayton U.K. 52°54N 2°29W 168 E5
Market Harborough U.K. 52°29N 0°55W 169 E7
Market Rasen U.K. 53°24N 0°20W 168 D7
Markham Canada 43°52N 79°16W 141 A2
Markham ➝ Papua N. G. 6°41S 147°2E 286 D4
Markham, Mt. Antarctica 83°0S 164°0E 151 E11
Marki Poland 52°19N 21°6E 142 B2
Märkisch Friedland = Mirosławiec
Poland 53°20N 16°5E 184 E3
Märkische Schweiz △
Germany 52°34N 14°2E 178 C10
Markit China 38°54N 77°40E 217 E9
Markkleeberg Germany 51°16N 12°23E 178 D8
Markland Wood Canada 43°38N 79°34W 141 B1
Markleeville U.S.A. 38°42N 119°47W 306 G7
Markopoulo Greece 37°53N 23°57E 204 D5
Markounda C.A.R. 7°39N 16°55E 264 A3
Markovac Serbia 44°14N 21°7E 202 B5
Markovo Russia 64°40N 170°24E 215 C17
Markoye Burkina Faso 14°39N 0°2E 263 C5
Marks Russia 51°45N 46°50E 190 E8
Marksshtadt = Marks
Russia 51°45N 46°50E 190 E8
Marksville U.S.A. 31°8N 92°4W 314 F8
Markt Schwaben
Germany 48°11N 11°52E 179 G7
Marktoberdorf Germany 47°45N 10°37E 179 H6
Marktredwitz Germany 50°1N 12°6E 179 E8
Marl Germany 51°39N 7°4E 178 D3
Marla Australia 27°19S 133°33E 281 D1
Marlbank Canada 44°26N 77°6W 312 B7
Marlboro U.S.A. 41°36N 73°59W 313 E11
Marlborough Queens.,
Australia 22°46S 149°52E 280 C4
Marlborough Wilts., U.K. 51°25N 1°43W 169 F6
Marlborough Mass.,
U.S.A. 42°21N 71°33W 313 D13
Marlborough ☐ N.Z. 41°40S 173°50E 285 B8
Marlborough Downs U.K. 51°27N 1°53W 169 F6
Marle France 49°43N 3°47E 173 C10
Marlin U.S.A. 31°18N 96°54W 314 F6
Marlow Mecklenburg-Vorpommern,
Germany 54°9N 12°33E 178 A8
Marlow Bucks., U.K. 51°34N 0°46W 169 F7
Marlow Okla., U.S.A. 34°39N 97°58W 314 D6
Marly, Forêt de France 48°52N 2°2E 134 A1
Marly-le-Roi France 48°52N 2°5E 134 A1
Marmagao India 15°25N 73°56E 245 G1
Marmande France 44°30N 0°10E 174 D4
Marmara Turkey 40°35N 27°34E 203 F11
Marmara, Sea of = Marmara Denizi
Turkey 40°45N 28°15E 203 F12
Marmara Denizi Turkey 40°45N 28°15E 203 F12
Marmara Gölü Turkey 38°37N 28°2E 205 C10
Marmaris Turkey 36°50N 28°14E 205 E10
Marmaris Limanı Turkey 36°50N 28°19E 205 E10
Marmelos ➝ Brazil 6°6S 61°46W 331 B5
Marmion, Mt. Australia 29°16S 119°50E 279 E2
Marmion L. Canada 48°55N 91°20W 298 C1
Marmolada, Mte. Italy 46°26N 11°51E 199 B8
Marmolejo Spain 38°3N 4°13W 195 G6
Marmora Canada 44°28N 77°41W 312 B7
Mármora, La Italy 39°59N 9°20E 200 C2
Marmugao = Marmagao
India 15°25N 73°56E 245 G1
Marnay France 47°16N 5°48E 173 E12
Marne Germany 53°56N 9°2E 178 B5
Marne ☐ France 48°50N 4°10E 173 D11
Marne ➝ France 48°47N 2°29E 173 D9
Marne-la-Vallée France 48°50N 2°37E 134 A4
Marneuli Georgia 41°30N 44°48E 191 K7
Marnia = Maghnia
Algeria 34°50N 1°43W 261 B4
Marnoo Australia 36°40S 142°52E 282 D5
Maro Chad 8°30N 19°0E 259 G3
Maro Reef U.S.A. 25°25N 170°35W 302 F9
Maro Rosa Brazil 13°58S 49°9W 333 D2
Maroa Ill., U.S.A. 40°2N 88°57W 310 D8
Maroa Venezuela 2°43N 67°33W 328 C4
Maroala Madag. 15°23S 47°59E 272 B2
Maroantsetra Madag. 15°26S 49°44E 272 B2
Maroelaboom Namibia 19°15S 18°53E 270 A2
Marofandilia Madag. 20°7S 44°34E 272 C1
Marojejy △ Madag. 14°26S 49°21E 272 A2
Marokau French Polynesia 18°2S 142°17W 289 f
Marolambo Madag. 20°2S 48°7E 272 C2
Marolles-en-Brie France 48°44N 2°33E 134 B4
Maromandia Madag. 14°13S 48°5E 272 A2
Maromokotro Madag. 14°0S 49°0E 272 A2
Marondera Zimbabwe 18°5S 31°42E 269 F3
Maroni ➝ Fr. Guiana 5°30N 54°0W 329 B7
Maronia Greece 40°53N 25°30E 203 F9
Maronne ➝ France 45°5N 1°56E 174 C5
Maroochydore Australia 26°29S 153°5E 281 D5
Maroon Town Jamaica 18°22N 77°48W 320 a
Maroona Australia 37°27S 142°54E 282 D5
Maros Indonesia 5°0S 119°34E 235 C5
Maros ➝ Hungary 46°15N 20°13E 182 D5
Marosakoa Madag. 15°26S 46°38E 272 B2
Maroseranana Madag. 18°32S 48°51E 272 B2
Maróstica Italy 45°44N 11°40E 199 C8
Marotandrano Madag. 16°10S 48°50E 272 B2
Marotaolano Madag. 12°47S 49°15E 272 A2
Marotiri, Îs. = Bass, Îs. de
French Polynesia 27°55S 143°26W 289 f
Maroua Cameroon 10°40N 14°20E 259 F2
Maroubra Australia 33°56S 151°16E 139 B2
Marovato Madag. 15°48S 48°5E 272 B2
Marovoay Madag. 16°6S 46°39E 272 B2
Marowijne ☐ Suriname 4°0N 55°0W 329 C7
Marowijne ➝ Suriname 5°45N 53°58W 329 B7
Marqakōl Kazakhstan 48°45N 85°45E 217 C11
Marquard S. Africa 28°40S 27°28E 270 C4
Marquesas Fracture Zone
Pac. Oc. 9°0S 125°0W 289 H15
Marquesas Is. = Marquises, Îs.
French Polynesia 9°30S 140°0W 289 f
Marquesas Keys U.S.A. 24°35N 82°10W 317 L7
Marquette U.S.A. 46°33N 87°24W 308 B10
Marquette Park U.S.A. 41°46N 87°42W 119 C2
Marquis St. Lucia 14°2N 60°54W 323 m
Marquis, C. St. Lucia 14°3N 60°54W 323 m
Marquis I. Grenada 12°5N 61°37W 323 q
Marquise France 50°50N 1°40E 173 B8
Marquises, Îs.
French Polynesia 9°30S 140°0W 289 f
Marra, Gebel South Sudan 7°20N 27°35E 257 F2
Marra, Pta. da Angola 16°31S 11°43E 265 F2
Marra Cr. ➝ Australia 30°8S 147°15E 283 A7
Marra-Marra △ Australia 33°30S 151°4E 283 B9
Marracuene Mozam. 25°45S 32°35E 271 C5
Marradi Italy 44°4N 11°37E 199 D8
Marrakech Morocco 31°9N 8°0W 250 B3
Marrakech ☐ Morocco 31°30N 7°30W 250 B3
Marratxi Spain 39°39N 2°48E 236 B3
Marrawah Australia 40°55S 144°42E 231 G3
Marrecas, Serra das Brazil 9°0S 41°0W 332 C3
Marree Australia 29°39S 138°1E 281 D2
Marrero U.S.A. 29°53N 90°6W 131 B2
Marrickville Australia 33°54S 151°9E 139 B1
Marrimane Mozam. 22°58S 33°34E 271 B5
Marromeu Mozam. 18°15S 36°25E 271 A6
Marromeu △ Mozam. 19°0S 36°0E 271 A6
Marroquí, Punta Spain 36°0N 5°37W 195 K5
Marrowie Cr. ➝
Australia 33°23S 145°40E 283 B6
Marruás = Porto Brazil 3°54S 42°42W 332 B3
Marrubane Mozam. 18°0S 37°0E 269 F4
Marrúbiu Italy 39°40N 8°35E 200 C1
Marrupa Mozam. 13°8S 37°30E 269 E4
Mars B. Ascension I. 7°59S 14°24W 153 g
Mars Hill U.S.A. 46°31N 67°52W 309 B20
Marsá al Burayqah Libya 30°24N 19°37E 258 B3
Marsá 'Alam Egypt 25°5N 34°54E 256 B3
Marsá Matrûḥ Egypt 31°19N 27°9E 256 A2
Marsá Sha'b Sudan 22°52N 35°47E 256 C4
Marsá Sūsah Libya 32°52N 21°59E 258 B4
Marsabit Kenya 2°18N 38°0E 268 B4
Marsabit △ Kenya 2°23N 37°56E 268 B4
Marsala Italy 37°48N 12°26E 200 E5
Marsalforn Malta 36°4N 14°16E 206 E7
Mârşani Romania 44°1N 24°1E 183 F9
Marsaskala Malta 35°52N 14°34E 206 F8
Marsaxlokk Malta 35°51N 14°33E 206 F8
Marsaxlokk Bay Malta 35°49N 14°33E 206 F8
Marsberg Germany 51°28N 8°52E 178 D4
Marsciano Italy 42°54N 12°20E 199 F9
Marsden Australia 33°47S 147°32E 283 B7
Marseillan France 43°23N 3°31E 174 E7
Marseille France 43°18N 5°23E 175 E9
Marseille-Marignane ✕ (MRS)
France 43°26N 5°14E 175 E9
Marseilles = Marseille
France 43°18N 5°23E 175 E9
Marseilles U.S.A. 41°20N 88°43W 311 C8
Marsfield Australia 33°46S 151°7E 139 A1
Marsh I. U.S.A. 29°34N 91°53W 314 G9
Marsha, L. U.S.A. 28°29N 81°29W 133 B2
Marshall Liberia 6°8N 10°22W 262 D2
Marshall Alaska, U.S.A. 61°53N 162°5W 303 F7
Marshall Ark., U.S.A. 35°55N 92°38W 314 D8
Marshall Ill., U.S.A. 39°23N 87°42W 311 E9
Marshall Mich., U.S.A. 42°16N 84°58W 311 B12
Marshall Minn., U.S.A. 44°27N 95°47W 303 C6
Marshall Mo., U.S.A. 39°7N 93°12W 313 E3
Marshall Tex., U.S.A. 32°33N 94°23W 314 E7
Marshall ➝ Australia 22°59S 136°59E 280 C2
Marshall, C. Ecuador 0°1S 91°12W 330 a
Marshall Bennett Is.
Papua N. G. 8°50S 151°55E 286 E6
Marshall Field's Chicago, U.S.A. 119 c2
Marshall Is. ■ Pac. Oc. 9°0N 171°0E 288 G9
Marshalltown U.S.A. 42°3N 92°55W 310 B4
Marshallville = Lewisporte
Canada 49°15N 55°3W 299 C8
Marshallville U.S.A. 32°27N 83°56W 316 C6
Marshbrook Zimbabwe 18°33S 31°9E 271 A5
Marshfield = Coos Bay
U.S.A. 43°22N 124°13W 304 E1
Marshfield Mo., U.S.A. 37°15N 92°54W 308 G7
Marshfield Vt., U.S.A. 44°20N 72°20W 313 312
Marshfield Wis., U.S.A. 44°40N 90°10W 308 C8
Marshūn Iran 36°19N 49°23E 247 B6
Mársico Nuovo Italy 40°25N 15°44E 201 B8
Marsouins, R. des ➝
Réunion 21°1S 55°44E 272 f
Märsta Sweden 59°37N 17°52E 162 E11
Marstal Denmark 54°51N 10°30E 163 K4
Marstrand Sweden 57°53N 11°35E 163 G5
Mart U.S.A. 31°33N 96°50W 314 F6
Marta ➝ Italy 42°14N 11°42E 199 F8
Martaban Burma 16°30N 97°35E 241 G6
Martaban, G. of Burma 16°5N 96°30E 241 G6
Martano Italy 40°12N 18°18E 201 B11
Martapura Kalimantan Selatan,
Indonesia 3°22S 114°47E 235 C4
Martapura Sumatera Selatan,
Indonesia 4°19S 104°22E 234 C2
Marte Nigeria 12°23N 13°46E 263 C7
Marte, Campo de Brazil 23°30S 46°38W 137 B2
Marte R. Gómez, Presa
Mexico 26°10N 99°0W 319 B5
Martel France 44°57N 1°37E 174 D5
Martelange Belgium 49°49N 5°43E 170 E5
Martellago Italy 45°33N 12°9E 199 C9
Martés, Sierra Spain 39°20N 1°0W 197 F4
Martesana, Naviglio della
Italy 45°31N 9°17E 129 A2
Martfű Hungary 47°1N 20°17E 182 C5
Marthaguy Cr. ➝
Australia 30°16S 147°35E 283 A7
Marthapal India 19°24N 81°37E 244 E5
Martha's Vineyard
U.S.A. 41°25N 70°38W 313 E14
Martigné-Ferchaud France 47°50N 1°20W 172 E5
Martigny Switz. 46°6N 7°3E 179 J3
Martigues France 43°24N 5°4E 175 E9
Martil Morocco 35°36N 5°15W 260 A3
Martin Slovak Rep. 49°6N 18°58E 181 B11
Martin S. Dak., U.S.A. 43°11N 101°44W 308 D3
Martin Tenn., U.S.A. 36°21N 88°51W 315 C10
Martin ➝ Spain 41°18N 0°19W 196 D4
Martin L. U.S.A. 32°41N 85°55W 316 C4
Martin Luther King Nat. Historic
Site △ U.S.A. 33°45N 84°22W 113 32
Martin Pt. U.S.A. 70°8N 143°16W 303 A12
Martin Vaz Atl. Oc. 20°30S 28°51W 152 J9
Martina Franca Italy 40°42N 17°20E 201 B10
Martinborough N.Z. 41°14S 175°29E 284 H4
Martinez B. Aires,
Argentina 34°29S 58°31W 117 A1
Martinez Calif., U.S.A. 38°1N 122°8W 306 G4
Martinez Ga., U.S.A. 33°31N 82°5W 315 E13
Martinho Campos Brazil 19°20S 45°13W 333 E2
Martinique ☑ W. Indies 14°40N 61°0W 322 j
Martinique Channel
St. Vincent 12°34N 61°25W 323 n
Martinique Passage
W. Indies 15°15N 61°0W 321 C7
Martinkylä Finland 60°17N 24°51E 121 B2
Martino Greece 38°35N 23°12E 204 C5
Martinópolis Brazil 22°11S 51°12W 335 A5
Martins Ferry U.S.A. 40°6N 80°44W 312 F4
Martinsberg Austria 48°22N 15°9E 180 C8
Martinsburg Pa., U.S.A. 40°19N 78°20W 312 F6
Martinsburg W. Va.,
U.S.A. 39°27N 77°58W 309 F15
Martinsicuro Italy 42°54N 13°54E 199 F10
Martinsried Germany 48°6N 11°27E 131 B1
Martinsville Ill., U.S.A. 39°20N 87°53W 311 E9
Martinsville Ind., U.S.A. 39°26N 86°25W 311 E10
Martinsville Va., U.S.A. 36°41N 79°52W 309 G14
Marton N.Z. 40°4S 175°23E 284 G4
Martorell Spain 41°28N 1°56E 196 D6
Martos Spain 37°44N 3°58W 195 H7
Martu ✪ Australia 22°30S 122°30E 278 D3
Martūbah Libya 32°35N 22°46E 258 B4
Martuni Armenia 40°8N 45°20E 191 K7
Maru Nigeria 12°22N 6°22E 263 C6
Marudi Malaysia 4°11N 114°19E 235 B4
Maruf Afghan. 31°30N 67°6E 240 C2
Marugame Japan 34°15N 133°40E 222 C5
Marui = Pagwi Papua N. G. 4°4S 143°2E 286 C2
Maruia ➝ N.Z. 41°47S 172°13E 285 B7
Maruim Brazil 10°45S 37°5W 332 D4
Maruko Japan 35°33N 139°40E 140 B3
Marulan Australia 34°43S 150°3E 283 C9
Marum, Mt. Vanuatu 16°15S 168°7E 287 F6
Marunga Angola 17°28S 23°2E 265 F4
Marungu, Mts.
Dem. Rep. of the Congo 7°30S 30°0E 268 D3
Marunouchi Tokyo, Japan 140 b4
Maruoka Japan 36°9N 136°16E 223 A8
Marusino Russia 55°41N 37°58E 129 B5
Maruwa ✪ Australia 22°30S 127°30E 278 D4
Marv Dasht Iran 29°50N 52°40E 247 D7
Marvão = Castelo do Piauí
Brazil 5°20S 41°33W 332 C3
Marvast Iran 30°30N 54°15E 247 D7
Marvejols France 44°33N 3°19E 174 D7
Marvel Loch Australia 31°28S 119°29E 279 F2
Marwar India 25°43N 73°45E 242 G5
Mary Turkmenistan 37°40N 61°50E 247 B9
Mary Esther U.S.A. 30°25N 86°40W 317 E3
Maryborough = Port Laoise
Ireland 53°2N 7°18W 166 C4
Maryborough Queens.,
Australia 25°31S 152°37E 281 D5
Maryborough Vic.,
Australia 37°3S 143°44E 282 D5
Maryfield Canada 49°50N 101°35W 297 D8
Maryino = Pristen Russia 51°15N 36°44E 189 G9
Maryino Russia 55°40N 37°45E 129 B4
Marymount Singapore 1°19N 103°47E 138 B2
Maryland ☐ U.S.A. 39°0N 76°30W 309 F15
Maryland Junction
Zimbabwe 17°45S 30°31E 269 F3
Marylebone London, U.K. 125 a2
Marymont Poland 52°16N 20°58E 142 B1
Maryport U.K. 54°44N 3°28W 168 C4
Mary's Harbour Canada 52°18N 55°51W 299 B8
Marysin Wawerski Poland 52°14N 21°9E 142 B2
Marystown Canada 47°10N 55°10W 299 C8
Marysville Calif., U.S.A. 39°9N 121°35W 306 F5
Marysville Kans., U.S.A. 39°51N 96°39W 308 F5
Marysville Mich., U.S.A. 42°54N 82°29W 312 D2
Marysville Ohio, U.S.A. 40°14N 83°22W 311 D13
Marysville Wash., U.S.A. 48°3N 122°11W 306 B4
Maryville Mo., U.S.A. 40°21N 94°52W 310 D2
Maryville Tenn., U.S.A. 35°46N 83°58W 315 D13
Marzahn Germany 52°32N 13°34E 115 A4
Marzo, Punta Colombia 6°50N 77°42W 328 B2
Marzūq Libya 25°53N 13°57E 258 C2
Marzūq ☐ Libya 25°0N 16°0E 258 D3
Marzūq, Idehān Libya 24°50N 13°51E 258 D2
Masada = Mesada Israel 31°20N 35°19E 251 G6
Masāʼdah Syria 33°13N 35°45E 250 E6
Masahunga Tanzania 2°6S 33°18E 268 C3
Masai Steppe Tanzania 4°30S 36°30E 268 C4
Masai Mara △ Kenya 1°25S 35°5E 268 C4
Masaka Uganda 0°21S 31°45E 268 C3
Masāl Iran 37°23N 49°8E 213 D12
Masalembo, Kepulauan
Indonesia 5°35S 114°30E 235 D4
Masalima, Kepulauan
Indonesia 5°4S 117°5E 235 D5
Masallı Azerbaijan 39°3N 48°40E 213 C13
Masalog Pt. N. Marianas 15°1N 145°40E 302 e
Masamba Indonesia 2°30S 120°15E 231 E6
Masan S. Korea 35°11N 128°32E 224 E4
Masandam, Ra's Oman 26°30N 56°30E 247 E8
Masasi Tanzania 10°45S 38°52E 269 E4
Masaya Nic. 12°0N 86°7W 320 D2
Masba Nigeria 11°35N 13°1E 263 C7
Masbate Phil. 12°21N 123°36E 232 E4
Masbate ☐ Phil. 12°20N 123°30E 232 E4
Masbate Pass. Phil. 12°30N 123°35E 232 E4
Máscali Italy 37°45N 15°12E 201 E8
Mascara Algeria 35°26N 0°6E 261 A5
Mascara ☐ Algeria 35°25N 0°10E 261 A5
Mascarene Is. Ind. Oc. 22°0S 55°0E 254 J9
Mascot Australia 33°55S 151°12E 139 B2
Mascota Mexico 20°32N 104°49W 318 C4
Mascoutah U.S.A. 38°29N 89°48W 310 F7
Masefau B. Amer. Samoa 14°15S 170°37W 302 f
Masein Burma 23°22N 94°21E 241 D5
Masela Indonesia 8°9S 129°51E 231 F7
Maseru Lesotho 29°18S 27°30E 270 C4
Masfjorden Norway 60°48N 5°18E 164 D2
Mashaba Zimbabwe 20°2S 30°29E 269 G3
Mashābih Si. Arabia 25°35N 36°30E 246 E3
Mashan China 23°40N 108°11E 228 F7
Mashang China 36°48N 117°57E 227 F9
Mashar South Sudan 9°16N 26°51E 257 F2
Mashatu △ Botswana 22°45S 29°5E 271 B4
Mashegu Nigeria 10°0N 5°35E 263 D6
Mashebrum Pakistan 35°38N 76°18E 243 B7
Mashhad Iran 36°20N 59°35E 247 B8
Mashi Nigeria 13°0N 7°54E 263 C6
Mashiki Japan 32°51N 130°53E 222 E2
Mashīz Iran 29°56N 56°37E 247 D8
Mashkel ➝ Pakistan 26°2N 65°19E 240 D2
Māshkel, Hāmūn-i-
Pakistan 28°20N 62°56E 240 C1
Mashki Chāh Pakistan 29°5N 62°30E 240 C1
Mashonaland Central ☐
Zimbabwe 17°30S 31°0E 271 A5
Mashonaland East ☐
Zimbabwe 18°0S 32°0E 271 A5
Mashonaland West ☐
Zimbabwe 17°30S 29°30E 271 A4
Mashrakh India 26°7N 84°48E 243 F11
Mashtaga = Maştağa
Azerbaijan 40°35N 50°1E 191 K10
Masi Manimba
Dem. Rep. of the Congo 4°40S 17°54E 265 C3
Masibi Angola 11°6S 22°41E 265 E4
Masig Australia 9°45S 143°24E 280 a
Masindi Uganda 1°40N 31°43E 268 B3
Masindi Port Uganda 1°43N 32°2E 268 B3
Masinga Res. Kenya 0°58S 37°38E 268 C4
Masinloc Phil. 15°32N 119°57E 232 D2
Maşīrah, Jazīrat Oman 21°0N 58°50E 249 B7
Maşīrah, Khalīj Oman 20°10N 58°10E 249 B7
Maşīrah, Tur'at Oman 20°30N 58°40E 249 B7
Masisea Peru 8°35S 74°22W 330 B3
Masisi Dem. Rep. of the Congo 1°23S 28°49E 268 C2
Masjed Soleyman Iran 31°55N 49°18E 247 D6
Mask, L. Ireland 53°36N 9°22W 166 C2
Maskelyne Is. Vanuatu 16°32S 167°49E 287 F5
Maski India 15°56N 76°46E 245 G3
Maskin Oman 23°44N 56°52E 247 F8
Maslen Nos Bulgaria 42°18N 27°48E 203 D11
Maslinica Croatia 43°24N 16°13E 199 E13
Masmo Sweden 59°15N 17°53E 139 B1
Maşna'ah Yemen 14°27N 48°17E 249 D5
Masnou = El Masnou
Spain 41°28N 2°20E 196 D7
Masoala, Tanjon' i
Madag. 15°59S 50°13E 272 B3
Masoala △ Madag. 15°30S 50°12E 272 B3
Masoarivo Madag. 19°3S 44°19E 272 B1
Masohi = Amahai
Indonesia 3°20S 128°55E 231 E7
Masomeloka Madag. 20°17S 48°37E 272 C2
Mason Mich., U.S.A. 42°35N 84°27W 311 B12
Mason Nev., U.S.A. 38°56N 119°8W 306 G7
Mason Ohio, U.S.A. 39°22N 84°19W 311 E12
Mason Tex., U.S.A. 30°45N 99°14W 314 F5
Mason B. N.Z. 46°55S 167°45E 285 G2
Mason City Ill., U.S.A. 40°12N 89°42W 310 D7
Mason City Iowa, U.S.A. 43°9N 93°12W 310 A3
Mason Hall Trin. & Tob. 11°3N 60°43W 323 s
Maspalomas Canary Is. 27°46N 15°35W 153 e1
Maspalomas, Pta.
Canary Is. 27°43N 15°36W 153 e1
Maspeth U.S.A. 40°43N 73°55W 132 B2
Masqat Oman 23°37N 58°36E 249 B7
Masr el Gedida Egypt 30°5N 31°21E 117 A2
Masr el Qadima Egypt 30°0N 31°14E 117 A2
Massa Congo 3°45S 15°29E 264 C3
Massa Italy 44°1N 10°9E 198 D7
Massa, O. ➝ Morocco 30°2N 9°40W 260 B3
Massa Maríttima Italy 43°3N 10°52E 198 E7
Massachusetts ☐ U.S.A. 42°30N 72°0W 313 D13
Massachusetts Avenue
Washington, D.C., U.S.A. 143 a2
Massachusetts B. U.S.A. 42°25N 70°50W 313 D14
Massachusetts Inst. of Tech.
U.S.A. 42°21N 71°5W 116 A2
Massacre Dominica 15°20N 61°25W 323 k
Massafra Italy 40°35N 17°7E 201 B10
Massaguet Chad 12°28N 15°26E 259 F3
Massakory Chad 13°0N 15°49E 259 F3
Massamá Portugal 38°45N 9°16W 126 A1
Massamba Mozam. 15°58S 33°31E 269 F3
Massanella Spain 39°48N 2°51E 206 B3
Massangano Angola 9°40S 14°13E 265 D2
Massangena Mozam. 21°34S 33°0E 271 B5
Massango Angola 8°2S 16°21E 265 D3
Massapê Brazil 3°31S 40°19W 332 B3
Massat France 42°53N 1°21E 174 F5
Massawa = Mitsiwa
Eritrea 15°35N 39°25E 257 D4
Massena U.S.A. 44°56N 74°54W 313 B10
Massenya Chad 11°21N 16°9E 259 F3
Masset Canada 54°2N 132°10W 296 C2
Masseube France 43°25N 0°34E 174 E4
Massey ➝ Canada 43°42N 79°19W 141 A3
Massey Hall Toronto, Canada 141 a3
Massiac France 45°15N 3°11E 174 C7
Massif Central France 44°55N 3°0E 174 D7
Massif des Bauges △
France 45°40N 6°10E 173 G13
Massigui Mali 11°46N 6°50W 262 C3
Massillon U.S.A. 40°48N 81°32W 312 F3
Massima Gabon 1°27S 11°33E 264 C2
Massinge, O. ➝ Algeria 36°13N 2°12E 261 A5
Massinga Mozam. 23°15S 35°22E 271 B6
Massingir Mozam. 23°51S 32°4E 271 B5
Masson-Angers Canada 45°32N 75°25W 313 A9
Masson I. Antarctica 66°10S 93°20E 151 C7
Massouka Gabon 1°37S 9°56E 264 C1
Massow = Maszewo Poland 53°23N 15°3E 184 E2
Massy France 48°43N 2°16E 134 B2
Mastābah Si. Arabia 20°49N 39°26E 248 B2
Maştağa Azerbaijan 40°35N 50°1E 191 K10
Mastanli = Momchilgrad
Bulgaria 41°33N 25°23E 203 E9
Masterton N.Z. 40°56S 175°39E 284 G4
Mastic U.S.A. 40°47N 72°54W 313 F12
Mastuj Pakistan 36°20N 72°36E 243 A5
Mastung Pakistan 29°50N 66°56E 240 C2
Mastūrah Si. Arabia 23°7N 38°52E 248 B2
Masty Belarus 53°27N 24°38E 177 B13
Masuda Japan 34°40N 131°51E 222 C3
Masuika
Dem. Rep. of the Congo 7°37S 22°32E 265 D4
Masuku = Franceville
Gabon 1°40S 13°32E 264 C2
Masurai Indonesia 2°30S 101°51E 234 C2
Masurian Lakes = Mazurski,
Pojezierze Poland 53°50N 21°0E 184 E7
Masvingo Zimbabwe 20°8S 30°49E 269 G3
Masvingo ☐ Zimbabwe 21°0S 31°30E 269 G3
Maswa △ Tanzania 2°53S 34°19E 268 C3
Maşyāf Syria 35°4N 36°20E 250 C7
Maszewo Poland 53°29N 15°3E 184 E2
Mat ➝ Albania 41°40N 19°35E 202 E3
Mât ➝ Réunion 20°57S 55°42E 272 f
Mata Israel 31°43N 35°4E 123 B1
Mata-au = Clutha ➝
N.Z. 46°20S 169°49E 285 G4
Mata de São João Brazil 12°31S 38°17W 333 D4
Mata-Utu Wall. & F. Is. 13°17S 176°8W 277 C15
Matabele Plain Zambia 16°20S 23°10E 265 F4
Matabeleland North ☐
Zimbabwe 19°0S 28°0E 269 F2
Matabeleland South ☐
Zimbabwe 21°0S 29°0E 269 G2
Matachel ➝ Spain 38°50N 6°17W 195 G4
Matachewan Canada 47°56N 80°39W 298 C3
Matacuni ➝ Venezuela 3°2N 65°16W 329 C4
Matadi
Dem. Rep. of the Congo 5°52S 13°31E 265 D2
Matafao, Mt. Amer. Samoa 14°17S 170°42W 302 f
Matagalpa Nic. 13°0N 85°58W 320 D2
Matagami Canada 49°45N 77°34W 298 C4
Matagami, L. Canada 49°50N 77°40W 298 C4
Matagorda B. U.S.A. 28°40N 96°12W 314 G6
Matagorda I. U.S.A. 28°15N 96°30W 314 G6
Matahiva French Polynesia 17°32S 149°20W 289 f
Mataiea Tahiti 17°46S 149°25W 289 e
Matak Indonesia 3°18N 106°16E 234 B3
Matakana N.S.W.,
Australia 32°59S 145°54E 283 B6
Matakana N.Z. 36°21S 174°43E 284 C3
Matala Angola 14°46S 15°4E 265 E3
Matala Kriti, Greece 34°59N 24°45E 207 F5
Matalam Phil. 7°5N 124°54E 233 H5
Matalaque Peru 16°26S 70°49W 330 D3
Matale Sri Lanka 7°30N 80°37E 245 L5
Matam Senegal 15°34N 13°17W 262 B2
Matam ☐ Senegal 15°37N 13°19W 262 B2
Matamata N.Z. 37°48S 175°47E 284 D4
Matameye Niger 13°26N 8°28E 259 F1
Matamoros Campeche,
Mexico 18°50N 90°50W 319 D6
Matamoros Coahuila,
Mexico 25°32N 103°15W 318 B4
Matamoros Tamaulipas,
Mexico 25°53N 97°30W 319 B5
Ma'ṭan as Sarra Libya 21°45N 22°0E 259 D4
Ma'ṭan Bishārah Libya 23°0N 22°32E 258 D4
Matandu ➝ Tanzania 8°45S 34°19E 269 D3
Matane Canada 48°50N 67°33W 299 C6
Matang China 23°30N 104°7E 228 F5
Matankari Niger 13°46N 4°1E 263 C5
Matanomadh India 23°33N 68°57E 242 H3
Matanzas Cuba 23°0N 81°40W 320 B3
Matapa Botswana 23°11S 24°39E 270 B3
Matapan, C. = Tenaro, Akra
Greece 36°22N 22°27E 204 E4
Matapédia Canada 48°0N 66°59W 299 C6
Matapo △ Zimbabwe 20°30S 29°40E 269 G2
Matara Sri Lanka 5°58N 80°30E 245 M5
Mataram Indonesia 8°35S 116°7E 231 K19
Matarani Peru 17°0S 72°10W 330 D3
Mataranka Australia 14°55S 133°4E 278 B5
Matarinao B. Phil. 11°12N 125°33E 233 F5
Matarma, Râs Egypt 30°27N 32°44E 251 H3
Mataró Spain 41°32N 2°29E 196 D7
Matarraña ➝ Spain 41°14N 0°22E 196 D5
Mataruška Banja Serbia 43°40N 20°40E 202 C4
Mataso Vanuatu 17°14S 168°26E 287 G6
Matata N.Z. 37°54S 176°48E 284 D5
Matatiele S. Africa 30°20S 28°49E 271 D4
Matatila Dam India 25°0N 78°22E 244 B4
Matatula, C. Amer. Samoa 14°15S 170°33W 302 f
Mataura N.Z. 46°11S 168°51E 285 G3
Mataura ➝ N.Z. 46°34S 168°44E 285 G3
Matavai, B. de Tahiti 17°30S 149°23W 289 e
Matavera Cook Is. 21°13S 159°44W 289 h
Mataveri Chile 27°9S 109°27W 330 b
Mategua Bolivia 13°1S 62°48W 331 C5
Matehuala Mexico 23°39N 100°39W 318 C4
Mateke
Dem. Rep. of the Congo 4°52S 24°25E 264 C3
Mateke Hills Zimbabwe 21°48S 31°0E 269 G3
Matelot Trin. & Tob. 10°50N 61°7W 323 t
Matera Italy 40°40N 16°36E 201 B9
Matese, Monti del Italy 41°27N 14°22E 201 A7
Matese △ Italy 41°24N 14°23E 201 A7
Mátészalka Hungary 47°58N 22°20E 182 C7
Matetsi Zimbabwe 18°12S 26°0E 269 F2
Mateur Tunisia 37°0N 9°40E 258 A1
Matfors Sweden 62°21N 17°2E 162 B11
Matha France 45°52N 0°20W 174 C3
Matheniko △ Uganda 2°49N 34°27E 268 B3
Mathis U.S.A. 28°6N 97°50W 314 G6
Mathoura Australia 35°50S 144°55E 283 C6
Mathraki Greece 39°48N 19°31E 206 B9
Mathura India 27°30N 77°40E 242 F7
Mati Phil. 6°55N 126°15E 233 H6
Matiakoali Burkina Faso 12°28N 1°2E 263 C5
Matiali India 26°56N 88°49E 243 F13
Matías Romero Mexico 16°53N 95°2W 319 D5
Matibane Mozam. 14°49S 40°45E 269 E5
Matinha Portugal 38°45N 9°5W 126 A2
Matinhos Brazil 25°49S 48°32W 333 G2
Matiri Ra. N.Z. 41°38S 172°20E 285 B7
Matjiesfontein S. Africa 33°14S 20°35E 270 D3
Matla ➝ India 21°40N 88°40E 243 J13
Matlamanyane Botswana 19°33S 25°57E 270 A4
Matli Pakistan 25°2N 68°39E 242 G3
Matlock U.K. 53°9N 1°33W 168 D6
Matmata Tunisia 33°37N 9°59E 258 B1
Matna Sudan 13°49N 35°10E 257 E4
Matnog Phil. 12°35N 124°5E 232 E5
Mato Dem. Rep. of the Congo 8°1S 24°24E 265 D4
Mato ➝ Venezuela 7°9N 65°7W 329 B4
Mato, Serranía de
Venezuela 6°25N 65°25W 328 B4
Mato Grosso ☐ Brazil 14°0S 55°0W 331 C7
Mato Grosso, Planalto do
Brazil 15°0S 55°0W 331 D7
Mato Grosso do Sul ☐
Brazil 18°0S 55°0W 331 D7
Matobo = Matapo △
Zimbabwe 20°30S 29°40E 269 G2
Matochkin Shar, Proliv
Russia 73°23N 55°12E 214 B6
Matola Mozam. 25°57S 32°27E 271 C5
Matong Papua N. G. 5°36S 151°50E 286 D6
Matopo Hills Zimbabwe 20°36S 28°20E 269 G2
Matopos Zimbabwe 20°20S 28°29E 269 G2
Matosinhos Portugal 41°11N 8°42W 194 D2
Matou Taiwan 23°11N 120°15E 225 C2
Matouba Guadeloupe 16°2N 61°41W 322 e
Matour France 46°19N 4°29E 173 F11
Matramam Indonesia 6°12S 106°51E 122 B2
Matroosberg S. Africa 33°23S 19°40E 270 D2
Maṭruḥ Oman 23°37N 58°30E 249 B7
Matsena Nigeria 13°5N 10°5E 263 C7
Matsesta Russia 43°34N 39°51E 191 J4
Matsu Tao Taiwan 26°8N 119°56E 225 b
Matsubara = Takahagi
Japan 36°43N 140°45E 221 F10
Matsubara Japan 34°34N 135°33E 133 B2
Matsubase Japan 32°40N 130°40E 222 E2
Matsudo Japan 35°47N 139°54E 223 B11
Matsue Japan 35°25N 133°10E 222 B5
Matsum, Ko Thailand 9°22N 99°59E 237 b
Matsumae Japan 41°26N 140°7E 220 D10
Matsumae-Hantō Japan 41°30N 140°15E 220 D10
Matsumoto Japan 36°15N 138°0E 223 A10
Matsusaka Japan 34°34N 136°32E 223 C8
Matsushima Japan 38°20N 141°10E 220 E10
Matsushima Kumamoto,
Japan 32°30N 130°25E 222 E2
Matsuura Japan 33°20N 129°49E 222 D1
Matsuyama Japan 33°45N 132°45E 222 D4
Matsuzaki Japan 34°43N 138°50E 223 C10
Mattagami ➝ Canada 50°43N 81°29W 298 B3
Mattancheri India 9°50N 76°15E 245 K3
Mattapan U.S.A. 42°16N 71°6W 116 B2
Mattawa Canada 46°20N 78°45W 298 C4
Matterhorn Switz. 45°58N 7°39E 179 K3
Mattersburg Austria 47°44N 16°24E 181 D9
Matteson U.S.A. 41°30N 87°42W 311 C9
Matthew, Î. N. Cal. 22°29S 171°15E 277 E13
Matthew Town Bahamas 20°57N 73°40W 321 B5
Matthews U.S.A. 40°23N 85°30W 311 D11
Matthews Ridge Guyana 7°37N 60°10W 329 B5
Mattias Church Budapest, Hungary 117 b1
Mattice Canada 49°40N 83°20W 298 C3
Mattili India 18°33N 82°12E 244 E6
Mattituck U.S.A. 40°59N 72°32W 313 F12
Mattō Japan 36°31N 136°34E 223 A8
Mattoon U.S.A. 39°29N 88°23W 311 E8
Matuba Mozam. 24°28S 32°49E 271 B5
Matucana Peru 11°55S 76°25W 330 C2
Matugama Sri Lanka 6°31N 80°7E 245 L5
Matuguinao Phil. 12°5N 124°55E 232 E5
Matuku Papua N. G. 4°54S 145°47E 286 C3
Matuku Fiji 19°10S 179°44E 287 B2
Matūn = Khowst Afghan. 33°22N 69°58E 242 C3
Matura Trin. & Tob. 10°40N 61°4W 323 t
Matura B. Trin. & Tob. 10°39N 61°1W 323 t
Maturín Venezuela 9°45N 63°11W 329 B5
Matusadona △ Zimbabwe 16°58S 28°42E 269 F2
Matutum, Mt. Phil. 6°22N 125°5E 233 H5
Matveyev Kurgan Russia 47°35N 38°57E 189 J10
Matxitxako, C. Spain 43°28N 2°47W 196 B2
Mátyásföld Hungary 47°30N 19°12E 117 A3
Mau Mad. P., India 26°17N 78°41E 243 F8
Mau Ut. P., India 25°56N 83°33E 243 G10
Mau Ut. P., India 25°17N 81°23E 243 G9
Mau Escarpment Kenya 0°40S 36°0E 268 C4
Mau Ranipur India 25°16N 79°8E 243 G8
Mau Tso Ngam China 22°22N 114°13E 122 A2
Maua Eastern, Kenya 0°14N 37°56E 268 C4
Maua Mozam. 13°53S 37°10E 269 E4
Mauban Phil. 14°12N 121°44E 232 D3
Maubeuge France 50°17N 3°57E 173 B10
Maubin Burma 16°44N 95°39E 241 G5
Mauborguet France 43°29N 0°1E 174 E4
Maud, Pt. Australia 23°6S 113°45E 278 D1
Maud Rise S. Ocean 66°0S 3°0E 151 C3
Maude Australia 34°29S 144°18E 282 C6
Maudin Sun Burma 16°0N 94°30E 241 G5
Mauer Austria 48°9N 16°16E 142 B1
Maués Brazil 3°20S 57°45W 329 D6
Maués-Acu ➝ Brazil 3°22S 57°44W 329 D6
Maug Is. N. Marianas 20°1N 145°13E 302 a
Mauganj India 24°50N 81°55E 243 G9
Maughold Hd. I. of Man 54°18N 4°18W 168 C3
Mauguio France 43°37N 4°1E 174 E7
Maui U.S.A. 20°48N 156°20W 300 C5
Maulamyaing = Moulmein
Burma 16°30N 97°40E 241 G6
Maule ☐ Chile 36°5S 72°30W 334 D1
Mauléon-Licharre France 43°14N 0°54W 174 E3
Maullín Chile 41°38S 73°37W 336 B2
Maulvibazar Bangla. 24°29N 91°42E 241 C3
Maumee U.S.A. 41°34N 83°39W 311 C13
Maumee ➝ U.S.A. 41°42N 83°28W 311 C13
Maumere Indonesia 8°38S 122°13E 231 F6
Maumusson, Pertuis de
France 45°48N 1°14W 174 C2
Maun Botswana 20°0S 23°26E 270 B3
Mauna Kea U.S.A. 19°50N 155°28W 302 D6
Mauna Loa U.S.A. 19°30N 155°35W 302 D6
Mauna Loa Forest Reserve
U.S.A. 19°35N 155°33W 302 D6
Maunabo Puerto Rico 18°1N 65°54W 321 b
Maunaloa U.S.A. 21°8N 157°13W 302 B4
Maunalua B. U.S.A. 21°15N 157°45W 302 K14
Maunath Bhanjan = Mau
India 25°56N 83°33E 243 G10
Maunawili U.S.A. 21°23N 157°46W 302 K14
Maunga Orito Chile 27°10S 109°25W 330 b
Maunga Puakatiki Chile 27°6S 109°15W 330 b
Maunga Terevaka Chile 27°5S 109°23W 330 b
Maungarooa Cook Is. 21°13S 159°48W 289 h
Maungatongaiti Cook Is. 21°14S 159°48W 289 h
Maungaturoto N.Z. 36°6S 174°23E 284 C3
Maungdow Burma 20°50N 92°21E 241 E4
Maungmagan Kyunzu
Burma 14°0N 97°48E 236 E1
Maungu Kenya 3°33S 38°45E 268 C4
Maupihaa
French Polynesia 16°50S 153°55W 289 f
Maupin U.S.A. 45°11N 121°5W 304 D3
Maupiti French Polynesia 16°27S 152°15W 289 f
Maure-de-Bretagne France 47°59N 1°58W 172 E5
Maurepas, L. U.S.A. 30°15N 90°30W 315 F9
Maures France 43°15N 5°15E 175 E10
Mauriac France 45°13N 2°19E 174 C6
Maurice, L. Australia 29°30S 131°0E 279 E5
Mauriceville N.Z. 40°45S 175°42E 284 G4
Mauricie △ Canada 46°45N 73°0W 298 C5
Maurienne France 45°13N 6°30E 175 C10
Mauripur Pakistan 24°52N 66°55E 123 A1
Mauritania ■ Africa 20°50N 10°0W 260 D3
Mauritius ■ Ind. Oc. 20°0S 57°0E 272 e
Mauritius ✕ (MRU)
Mauritius 20°25S 57°40E 272 e
Mauron France 48°9N 2°18W 172 D4
Maurs France 44°43N 2°12E 174 D6
Mauston U.S.A. 43°48N 90°5W 308 D8
Mauterndorf Austria 47°9N 13°40E 180 D6
Mauthen Austria 46°40N 13°0E 180 E6
Mauvezin France 43°44N 0°53E 174 E4
Mauzé-sur-le-Mignon
France 46°12N 0°41W 174 B3
Mavaca ➝ Venezuela 2°31N 65°11W 329 C4
Mavinga Angola 15°50S 20°21E 265 F4
Mavli India 24°45N 73°55E 242 G5
Mavrata Greece 38°4N 20°44E 207 C2
Mavrovë Albania 40°26N 19°32E 202 F3
Mavrovo △ Macedonia 41°36N 20°45E 202 E4
Mavuradonha Mts.
Zimbabwe 16°30S 31°30E 269 F3
Mawa Dem. Rep. of the Congo 2°45N 26°40E 268 B2
Mawai India 22°30N 81°4E 243 H9
Mawana India 29°6N 77°58E 242 E7
Mawand Pakistan 29°33N 68°38E 242 E3
Mawjib, W. al ➝ Jordan 31°28N 35°36E 251 G6
Mawk Mai Burma 20°14N 97°37E 241 E6
Mawlaik Burma 23°40N 94°26E 241 D5
Mawlamyine = Moulmein
Burma 16°30N 97°40E 241 G6
Mawlawkho Burma 17°50N 97°38E 241 G6
Mawqaq Si. Arabia 27°25N 41°8E 246 E4
Mawshij Yemen 13°43N 43°17E 248 D3
Mawson Antarctica 67°30S 62°53E 151 C6
Mawson Coast Antarctica 68°30S 63°0E 151 C6
Mawson Pk. Heard I. 53°6S 73°31E 273 K6
Mawsynram India 25°15N 91°30E 241 C3
Max U.S.A. 47°49N 101°18W 308 B3
Maxambamba = Nova Iguaçu
Brazil 22°45S 43°28W 333 F3
Maxcanú Mexico 20°35N 90°0W 319 C6
Maxesibeni S. Africa 30°49S 29°23E 271 D4
Maxeys U.S.A. 33°45N 83°11W 316 B6
Maxhamish L. Canada 59°50N 123°17W 296 B4
Maxhof Germany 48°4N 11°29E 131 B1
Maxixe Mozam. 23°54S 35°17E 271 B6
Maxville Canada 45°17N 74°51W 313 A10
Maxwell N.Z. 39°51S 174°49E 284 F3
Maxwell Calif., U.S.A. 39°17N 122°11W 306 F4
Maxwellton Australia 20°43S 142°41E 280 C3
May, C. U.S.A. 38°56N 74°58W 309 F16
May Downs Australia 22°38S 148°55E 280 C4
May Jirgui Niger 13°44N 8°8E 259 F1
May Pen Jamaica 17°58N 77°15W 320 a
May River Papua N. G. 4°19S 141°58E 286 C1
Maya Indonesia 1°10S 109°35E 235 C3
Maya ➝ Russia 60°28N 134°28E 215 D14
Maya Mts. Belize 16°30N 89°0W 320 C2
Mayabandar India 12°56N 92°56E 245 H11
Mayaguana Bahamas 22°30N 72°44W 321 B5
Mayagüez Puerto Rico 18°12N 67°9W 321 C6
Mayahi Niger 13°58N 7°40E 263 C6
Mayaky Ukraine 47°26N 29°33E 183 C14
Mayals = Maials Spain 41°22N 0°30E 196 D5
Mayama Congo 3°51S 14°54E 264 C2
Mayāmey Iran 36°24N 55°42E 247 B7
Mayang China 27°53N 109°49E 228 D7
Mayanup Australia 33°57S 116°27E 279 F2

Mayapán Mexico 20°29N 89°11W 319 C7
Mayarí Cuba 20°40N 75°41W 321 B4
Mayaro Trin. & Tob. 10°12N 61°1W 323 t
Mayaro □ Trin. & Tob. 10°10N 61°5W 323 t
Mayaro B. Trin. & Tob. 10°14N 60°59W 323 t
Mayavaram = Mayiladuthurai India 11°3N 79°42E 245 J4
Maybell U.S.A. 40°31N 108°5W 304 F9
Maybio Phil. 5°50N 125°35E 233 J5
Maybole U.K. 55°21N 4°42W 167 F4
Maychew Ethiopia 12°50N 39°31E 257 E4
Maydān Iraq 34°55N 45°37E 213 E11
Maydan Ukraine 48°36N 23°29E 183 B8
Maydī Yemen 16°19N 42°48E 248 C3
Mayen Germany 50°19N 7°13E 179 E3
Mayenne France 48°20N 0°38W 172 D6
Mayenne □ France 48°10N 0°40W 172 D6
Mayenne → France 47°30N 0°32W 172 E6
Mayer U.S.A. 34°24N 112°14W 305 J7
Mayerthorpe Canada 53°57N 115°8W 296 C5
Mayesville U.S.A. 34°0N 80°12W 316 A9
Mayfair Gauteng, S. Africa 26°11S 28°0E 123 B2
Mayfair London, U.K. 125 b3
Mayfield Ky., U.S.A. 36°44N 88°38W 308 G9
Mayfield N.Y., U.S.A. 43°6N 74°16W 313 C10
Mayhill U.S.A. 32°53N 105°29W 305 K11
Mayiladuthurai India 11°3N 79°42E 245 J4
Maykop Russia 44°35N 40°10E 191 H5
Mayma Russia 52°3N 85°55E 217 B11
Maymyo Burma 22°2N 96°28E 236 A1
Maynard Mass., U.S.A. 42°26N 71°27W 313 D13
Maynard Wash., U.S.A. 47°59N 122°55W 306 C4
Maynard Hills Australia 28°28S 119°49E 279 E2
Mayne → Australia 23°40S 141°55E 280 C3
Maynooth Ont., Canada 45°13N 77°56W 312 A7
Maynooth Kildare, Ireland 53°23N 6°34W 166 C5
Mayo Yukon, Canada 63°38N 135°57W 294 E4
Mayo Trin. & Tob. 10°21N 61°23W 323 t
Mayo Fla., U.S.A. 30°3N 83°10W 316 E6
Mayo □ Ireland 53°53N 9°3W 166 C2
Mayo → Argentina 45°45S 69°45W 336 C3
Mayo → Peru 6°38S 76°15W 330 B2
Mayo B. Phil. 6°56N 126°22E 233 H6
Mayo Daga Nigeria 6°59N 11°25E 263 D7
Mayo Faran Nigeria 8°57N 12°4E 263 D7
Mayo-Kébbi Est □ Chad 10°20N 15°30E 259 F3
Mayo-Kébbi Ouest □ Chad 9°40N 17°50E 259 G3
Mayoko Congo 2°18S 12°49E 264 C2
Mayoko Dem. Rep. of the Congo 1°6S 23°50E 264 C4
Mayon Volcano Phil. 13°15N 123°41E 232 E4
Mayor Buratovich Argentina 39°15S 62°37W 336 A4
Mayor I. N.Z. 37°16S 176°17E 284 D5
Mayor Pablo Lagerenza Paraguay 19°55S 60°47W 331 D5
Mayorga Spain 42°10N 5°16W 194 C5
Mayotte ☑ Ind. Oc. 12°50S 45°10E 272 b
Mayoyao Phil. 16°59N 121°14E 232 C3
Mayqayyng Kazakhstan 51°27N 75°47E 217 B9
Mayraira Pt. Phil. 18°39N 120°51E 232 B3
Mayreau St. Vincent 12°39N 61°23W 323 n
Maysān □ Iraq 31°55N 47°15E 246 D5
Mayskiy Russia 43°47N 44°2E 191 J7
Maysville Ky., U.S.A. 38°39N 83°46W 311 F13
Maysville Mo., U.S.A. 39°53N 94°22W 310 E2
Maytiguid I. Phil. 11°3N 119°36E 233 F2
Mayu Indonesia 1°30N 126°30E 231 D7
Mayumba Gabon 3°25S 10°39E 264 C2
Mayuram = Mayiladuthurai India 11°3N 79°42E 245 J4
Mayville N. Dak., U.S.A. 47°30N 97°20W 308 B5
Mayville N.Y., U.S.A. 42°15N 79°30W 312 D5
Maywood Calif., U.S.A. 33°59N 118°12W 126 C3
Maywood Ill., U.S.A. 41°52N 87°51W 119 B1
Maywood N.J., U.S.A. 40°53N 74°3W 132 A1
Maywood Park Race Track U.S.A. 41°54N 87°50W 119 B1
Mazabuka Zambia 15°52S 27°44E 269 F2
Mazagán = El Jadida Morocco 33°11N 8°17W 260 B3
Mazagão Brazil 0°7S 51°16W 329 D7
Mazagaon Mumbai, India 130 a2
Mazamet France 43°30N 2°20E 174 E6
Mazán Peru 3°30S 73°0W 328 D3
Māzandarān □ Iran 36°30N 52°0E 247 B7
Mazapil Mexico 24°39N 101°34W 318 C4
Mazar China 36°32N 77°1E 217 E9
Mazar, O. → Algeria 31°50N 1°36E 261 B5
Mazār-e Sharīf Afghan. 36°41N 67°0E 240 A2
Mazara del Vallo Italy 37°39N 12°35E 200 E5
Mazarredo Argentina 47°10S 66°50W 336 C3
Mazarrón Spain 37°38N 1°19W 197 H3
Mazarrón, G. de Spain 37°27N 1°19W 197 H3
Mazaruni → Guyana 6°25N 58°35W 329 B6
Mazatán Mexico 29°0N 110°8W 318 B2
Mazatenango Guatemala 14°35N 91°30W 320 D1
Mazatlán Mexico 23°13N 106°25W 318 C3
Mažeikiai Lithuania 56°20N 22°20E 184 B9
Mazhafa, J. Si. Arabia 28°52N 35°55E 251 K6
Māzhān Iran 32°30N 59°0E 247 C8
Mazıdağı Turkey 37°28N 40°29E 213 D9
Mazīnān Iran 36°19N 56°56E 247 B8
Mazo Cruz Peru 16°45S 69°44W 330 D4
Mazoe Mozam. 16°42S 33°7E 269 F3
Mazoe → Mozam. 16°20S 33°30E 269 F3
Mazomanie U.S.A. 43°11N 89°48W 310 A7
Mazon U.S.A. 41°14N 88°25W 311 C8
Mazowe Zimbabwe 17°28S 30°58E 269 F3
Mazowieckie □ Poland 52°40N 21°0E 185 F8
Mazrûb Sudan 14°0N 29°20E 257 E2
Mazurski, Pojezierze Poland 53°50N 21°0E 184 E7
Mazyr Belarus 51°59N 29°15E 177 B15
Mba Fiji 17°33S 177°41E 287 A1
Mbaba Senegal 14°59N 16°44W 262 C1
Mbabane Swaziland 26°18S 31°6E 271 C5
Mbaéré → C.A.R. 3°47N 17°31E 264 B3
Mbagne Mauritania 16°6N 14°47W 262 B2
M'bahiakro Ivory C. 7°33N 4°19W 262 D4
Mbaïki C.A.R. 3°53N 18°1E 264 B3
Mbakana, Mt. de Cameroon 7°57N 15°6E 264 A3
Mbala Zambia 8°46S 31°24E 269 D3
Mbalabala Zimbabwe 20°27S 29°3E 271 B4
Mbalam Cameroon 2°13N 13°49E 264 B2
Mbale Uganda 1°8N 34°12E 268 B3
Mbali → C.A.R. 4°27N 18°20E 264 B3
Mbalmayo Cameroon 3°33N 11°33E 263 E7
Mbam → Cameroon 4°24N 11°17E 263 E7
Mbamba Bay Tanzania 11°13S 34°49E 269 E3
Mbandaka Dem. Rep. of the Congo 0°1N 18°18E 264 B3
Mbandjok Cameroon 4°27N 11°54E 264 B2
Mbanga Cameroon 4°30N 9°33E 263 E6
Mbanika Solomon Is. 9°3S 159°13E 287 M10
M'Banio, Lagune Gabon 3°35S 11°0E 264 C2
Mbanza Congo Angola 6°18S 14°16E 265 D2
Mbanza Ngungu Dem. Rep. of the Congo 5°12S 14°53E 265 D2
Mbarangandu Tanzania 10°11S 36°48E 269 D4
Mbarara Uganda 0°35S 30°40E 268 C3
Mbari → C.A.R. 4°34N 22°43E 264 B4
Mbatto Ivory C. 6°28N 4°22W 262 D4
Mbava Solomon Is. 7°47S 156°33E 287 L9
Mbé Congo 3°14S 15°50E 264 C3
Mbe Eq. Guin. 1°47N 9°56E 264 B1
Mbengga = Beqa Fiji 18°23S 178°8E 287 B2
Mbengué Gabon 2°2S 11°7E 264 C2
Mbengui Gabon 2°3S 10°4E 264 C2
Mbéni Comoros Is. 11°30S 43°22E 272 a
Mbenkuru → Tanzania 9°25S 39°50E 269 D4
Mbéré → Cameroon 7°45N 15°36E 264 A3
Mberengwa Zimbabwe 20°29S 29°57E 269 G2
Mberengwa, Mt. Zimbabwe 20°37S 29°55E 269 G2
Mberubu Nigeria 6°10N 7°38E 263 D6
Mbesuma Zambia 10°0S 32°2E 269 E3
Mbeya Tanzania 8°54S 33°29E 269 D3
Mbeya □ Tanzania 8°15S 33°30E 268 D3
Mbhashe → S. Africa 32°15S 28°54E 271 D4
Mbigou Gabon 1°53S 11°56E 264 C2
M'bili South Sudan 7°35N 28°15E 257 F2
Mbinga Tanzania 10°50S 35°0E 269 E4
Mbini = Río Muni □ Eq. Guin. 1°30N 10°0E 264 B2
Mbini Eq. Guin. 1°35N 9°37E 264 B1
Mbizi Zimbabwe 21°23S 31°1E 269 G3
Mboi Dem. Rep. of the Congo 6°57S 21°54E 265 D4
Mboki C.A.R. 5°19N 25°58E 257 F2
Mbokonimbeti Solomon Is. 8°57S 160°7E 287 M11
Mboli Dem. Rep. of the Congo 4°8N 23°9E 264 B4
Mbomo Congo 0°25N 14°42E 264 B2
M'bonge Cameroon 4°33N 9°5E 263 E6
Mboro Senegal 15°9N 16°54W 262 B1
Mboua Cameroon 4°25N 14°16E 264 A2
Mbouda Cameroon 5°38N 10°15E 264 A2
M'boukou, L. de Cameroon 6°23N 12°50E 263 D7
Mboune Senegal 14°42N 13°34W 262 C2
Mbouoma Congo 0°52S 15°4E 264 C3
Mbour Senegal 14°22N 16°54W 262 C1
Mbout Mauritania 16°1N 12°38W 262 B2
Mbrés C.A.R. 6°40N 19°48E 264 A3
M'Bridge → Angola 7°12S 12°51E 265 D2
Mbuji-Mayi Dem. Rep. of the Congo 6°9S 23°40E 265 D4
Mbulu Tanzania 3°45S 35°30E 268 C4
Mbuma Dem. Rep. of the Congo 3°32N 24°50E 264 B4
Mbuma Solomon Is. 8°59S 160°46E 287 M11
Mburucuyá Argentina 28°1S 58°14W 334 B4
Mburucuyá △ Argentina 28°1S 58°12W 334 B4
M'bwat Cameroon 6°29N 10°45E 264 A2
Mcherrah Algeria 27°0N 4°30W 260 C4
Mchinga Tanzania 9°44S 39°45E 269 D4
Mchinji Malawi 13°47S 32°58E 269 E3
Mdantsane S. Africa 32°56S 27°46E 271 D4
Mdennah Mauritania 24°37N 6°0W 260 D3
Me'a She' Arim Jerusalem 123 a2
Mead, L. U.S.A. 36°0N 114°44W 307 J12
Meade = Atqasuk → U.S.A. 70°52N 155°55W 303 A9
Meade U.S.A. 37°17N 100°20W 308 G3
Meade River = Atqasuk U.S.A. 70°28N 157°24W 303 A8
Meadow Lake Canada 54°10N 108°26W 297 C7
Meadow Lake △ Canada 54°27N 109°0W 297 C7
Meadow Valley Wash → U.S.A. 36°40N 114°34W 307 J12
Meadowbank Park Australia 33°49S 151°6E 139 A1
Meadville Mo., U.S.A. 39°47N 93°18W 310 E3
Meadville Pa., U.S.A. 41°39N 80°9W 312 E4
Meaford Canada 44°36N 80°35W 312 B4
Meakan Dake Japan 43°15N 144°0E 220 C11
Mealhada Portugal 40°22N 8°27W 194 E2
Mealy Mts. Canada 53°10N 58°0W 299 B8
Meander River Canada 59°2N 117°42W 296 B5
Meares, C. U.S.A. 45°37N 124°0W 304 D1
Mearim → Brazil 3°4S 44°35W 332 B3
Meath □ Ireland 53°40N 6°57W 166 C5
Meath Park Canada 53°27N 105°22W 297 C7
Meaulne France 46°36N 2°36E 173 F9
Meaux France 48°58N 2°50E 173 D9
Mebechi-Gawa → Japan 40°31N 141°31E 220 D10
Mebonden Norway 63°13N 11°2E 164 A8
Mebulu, Tanjung Indonesia 8°50S 115°5E 231 K18
Mecanhelas Mozam. 15°12S 35°54E 269 F4
Mecaya → Colombia 0°29N 75°11W 328 C2
Mecca = Makkah Si. Arabia 21°30N 39°54E 248 C2
Mecca U.S.A. 33°34N 116°5W 307 M10
Mechanicsburg Ohio, U.S.A. 40°4N 83°33W 311 D13
Mechanicsburg Pa., U.S.A. 40°13N 77°1W 312 F8
Mechanicsville U.S.A. 41°54N 91°16W 310 C5
Mechanicville U.S.A. 42°54N 73°41W 313 D11
Mechara Ethiopia 8°36N 40°20E 257 F5
Mechelen Belgium 51°2N 4°29E 170 C4
Mecheria Algeria 33°35N 0°18W 261 B4
Mechernich Germany 50°35N 6°39E 178 E2
Mechetinskaya Russia 46°45N 40°32E 191 G5
Mechol Micronesia 9°37N 138°9E 287 R16
Méchouly Czech Rep. 50°3N 14°32E 135 B3
Mechra Bel Ksiri Morocco 34°34N 5°57W 260 B3
Mechra Benâbbou Morocco 32°39N 7°48W 260 B3
Měčice Czech Rep. 50°11N 14°31E 135 A3
Mecidiye Turkey 40°38N 26°32E 203 F10
Mecidiyeköy Turkey 41°4N 29°0E 122 B2
Mecitözü Turkey 40°32N 35°17E 212 B6
Mecklenburg Germany 53°33N 11°40E 176 B7
Mecklenburg-Vorpommern □ Germany 53°45N 12°15E 178 B8
Mecklenburger Bucht Germany 54°20N 11°40E 178 A7
Meconta Mozam. 14°59S 39°50E 269 E4
Mecsek Hungary 46°10N 18°18E 182 D3
Mecubúri Mozam. 14°39S 38°54E 269 E4
Mecubúri → Mozam. 14°10S 40°30E 269 E5
Mecúfi Mozam. 13°20S 40°32E 269 E5
Meda Portugal 40°57N 7°18W 194 E3
Medak India 18°1N 78°15E 244 E4
Medan Indonesia 3°40N 98°38E 234 B1
Medang Indonesia 8°9S 117°22E 235 D5
Médanos Argentina 38°50S 62°42W 336 A4
Médanos de Coro △ Venezuela 11°35N 69°44W 328 A4
Medanosa, Pta. Argentina 48°8S 66°0W 336 C3
Medart U.S.A. 30°5N 84°23W 316 E5
Medaryville U.S.A. 41°5N 86°55W 311 C10
Medawachchiya Sri Lanka 8°30N 80°30E 245 K5
Medchal India 17°37N 78°29E 244 F4
Mede Italy 45°6N 8°44E 198 C5
Médéa Algeria 36°12N 2°50E 261 A5
Médéa □ Algeria 35°0N 3°0E 261 B5
Mededa Bos.-H. 43°44N 19°10E 182 G4
Médégué Gabon 0°37N 10°8E 264 B2
Medeiros Neto Brazil 17°20S 40°14W 333 E3
Medellín Colombia 6°15N 75°35W 328 B2
Medelpad Sweden 62°33N 16°30E 162 B10
Medemblik Neths. 52°46N 5°8E 170 B5
Médenine Tunisia 33°21N 10°30E 258 B2
Médenine □ Tunisia 32°20N 10°0E 261 B7
Mederdra Mauritania 17°0N 15°38W 262 B1
Medford Mass., U.S.A. 42°25N 71°7W 116 A2
Medford Oreg., U.S.A. 42°19N 122°52W 304 E2
Medford Wis., U.S.A. 45°9N 90°20W 308 C8
Medgidia Romania 44°15N 28°19E 183 F13
Media South Sudan 5°4N 30°42E 257 F3
Media Agua Argentina 31°58S 68°25W 334 C2
Media Luna Argentina 34°45S 66°44W 334 C2
Medianeira Brazil 25°17S 54°5W 335 B5
Mediapolis U.S.A. 41°0N 91°10W 310 D5
Mediaş Romania 46°9N 24°22E 183 D9
Medicilândia Brazil 3°33S 53°8W 329 D7
Medicina Italy 44°28N 11°38E 199 D8
Medicine Bow U.S.A. 41°54N 106°12W 304 F10
Medicine Bow Mts. U.S.A. 40°40N 106°0W 304 F10
Medicine Bow Pk. U.S.A. 41°21N 106°19W 304 F10
Medicine Hat Canada 50°0N 110°45W 297 D6
Medicine Lake U.S.A. 48°30N 104°30W 304 B11
Medicine Lodge U.S.A. 37°17N 98°35W 308 G4
Medina = Al Madīnah Si. Arabia 24°35N 39°52E 246 E3
Medina Brazil 16°15S 41°29W 333 E3
Medina Colombia 4°30N 73°21W 328 C3
Medina Mis. Or., Phil. 8°55N 125°0E 233 G5
Medina N. Dak., U.S.A. 46°54N 99°18W 308 B4
Medina N.Y., U.S.A. 43°13N 78°23W 312 C6
Medina Ohio, U.S.A. 41°8N 81°52W 312 E3
Medina → U.S.A. 29°16N 98°29W 314 G5
Medina de Pomar Spain 42°56N 3°29W 194 C7
Medina de Rioseco Spain 41°53N 5°3W 194 D5
Medina del Campo Spain 41°18N 4°55W 194 D6
Médina Gounas Senegal 13°8N 13°45W 262 C2
Medina L. U.S.A. 29°32N 98°56W 314 G5
Medina Sidonia Spain 36°28N 5°57W 195 J5
Medinaceli Spain 41°12N 2°30W 196 D2
Medinipur India 22°25N 87°21E 243 H12
Mediodia Spain 40°22N 3°39W 127 B2
Mediterranean Sea Europe 35°0N 15°0E 193 D7
Medjerda, O. → Tunisia 37°7N 10°13E 258 A2
Mednogorsk Russia 51°24N 57°37E 216 B5
Medny = Mednogorsk Russia 51°24N 57°37E 216 B5
Médoc France 45°10N 0°50W 174 C3
Medora U.S.A. 38°49N 86°10W 311 F10
Médouneu Gabon 0°57N 10°47E 264 B2
Medulin Croatia 44°49N 13°55E 199 D10
Medveđa Serbia 42°50N 21°32E 202 D5
Medvedevo Russia 56°37N 47°47E 190 B8
Medveditsa → Tver, Russia 57°5N 37°30E 188 D9
Medveditsa → Volgograd, Russia 49°35N 42°41E 190 F6
Medvedok Russia 57°20N 50°1E 190 B10
Medvezhi, Ostrava Russia 71°0N 161°0E 215 B17
Medvezhiy Ozyora Russia 55°52N 37°59E 129 A5
Medvezhye = Krasnogvardeyskoye Russia 45°52N 41°33E 191 H5
Medvezhyegorsk Russia 63°0N 34°25E 186 B5
Medway □ U.K. 51°25N 0°32E 169 F8
Medway → U.K. 51°27N 0°46E 169 F8
Medzev Slovak Rep. 48°43N 20°55E 181 C13
Medzilaborce Slovak Rep. 49°17N 21°52E 181 B14
Medžitlija Macedonia 40°56N 21°26E 202 F5
Meekatharra Australia 26°32S 118°29E 279 E2
Meeker U.S.A. 40°2N 107°55W 304 F10
Meeniyan Australia 38°35S 146°3E 283 E7
Meersburg Germany 47°41N 9°16E 179 H5
Meerut India 29°1N 77°42E 242 E7
Meeteetse U.S.A. 44°9N 108°52W 304 D9
Mega Ethiopia 3°57N 38°19E 257 G4
Mega Indonesia 4°0S 101°2E 234 C2
Megalo Ethiopia 6°51N 40°47E 267 C5
Megalo Chorio Greece 36°27N 27°24E 205 E9
Megalonisos Greece 38°0N 24°15E 204 D6
Megalopoli Greece 37°25N 22°7E 204 D4
Meganisi Greece 38°38N 20°46E 207 B2
Megara Greece 37°58N 23°22E 204 D5
Megasini India 21°38N 86°21E 243 J12
Megdovas = Tavropos → Greece 39°10N 21°45E 204 B3
Megève France 45°51N 6°37E 175 C10
Meghalaya □ India 25°50N 91°0E 243 G17
Meghezez Ethiopia 9°18N 39°26E 257 F4
Meghna → Bangla. 22°50N 90°50E 241 D3
Megion Russia 61°3N 76°6E 214 C8
Mégiscane, L. Canada 48°35N 75°55W 298 C4
Megisti Greece 36°8N 29°34E 205 E11
Megisti Greece 36°8N 29°34E 205 E11
Megra Russia 60°11N 37°14E 188 B9
Meguro Japan 35°37N 139°42E 140 B3
Meguro → Japan 35°37N 139°45E 140 B3
Mehadia Romania 44°56N 22°23E 182 F7
Mehaïguene, O. → Algeria 32°15N 2°59E 261 B5
Meharry, Mt. Australia 22°59S 118°35E 278 D2
Mehedeby Sweden 60°27N 17°25E 162 D11
Mehedinţi □ Romania 44°40N 22°45E 182 F7
Meheisa Sudan 19°38N 32°57E 256 D3
Mehekar India 20°9N 76°34E 244 D3
Méhétia French Polynesia 17°52S 148°3W 289 f
Mehlville U.S.A. 38°31N 90°19W 308 F8
Mehndawal India 26°58N 83°5E 243 F10
Mehpalpur India 28°32N 77°7E 120 B1
Mehr Jān Iran 33°50N 55°6E 247 C7
Mehrābād Iran 36°53N 47°55E 213 D12
Mehrābād ✕ (THR) Iran 35°41N 51°18E 141 A1
Mehrabān Iran 38°4N 47°7E 213 C12
Mehram Nagar India 28°34N 77°8E 120 B1
Mehrān Iran 33°7N 46°10E 213 F12
Mehrān → Iran 26°45N 55°26E 247 E7
Mehrgarh Pakistan 29°30N 67°30E 242 E2
Mehrīz Iran 31°35N 54°28E 247 D7
Mehrow Germany 52°34N 13°37E 115 A4
Mehun-sur-Yèvre France 47°10N 2°13E 173 E9
Mei Jiang → China 24°25N 116°35E 229 E11
Mei Lanfang, Pantheon of Beijing, China 114 a2
Mei Xian China 34°18N 107°55E 226 G4
Meia Ponte → Brazil 18°32S 49°36W 333 E2
Meicheng China 29°29N 119°16E 229 C12
Meichengzhen China 28°9N 111°40E 229 C8
Meichuan China 30°8N 115°31E 229 B10
Meidling Austria 48°10N 16°20E 142 A2
Meidougou Cameroon 6°25N 14°13E 264 A2
Méier Brazil 22°52S 43°15W 135 B1
Meiganga Cameroon 6°30N 14°25E 264 A2
Meighen I. Canada 80°0N 99°30W 295 B12
Meigs U.S.A. 31°4N 84°6W 316 D5
Meigu China 28°16N 103°20E 228 C4
Meihekou China 42°32N 125°40E 224 A2
Meiji Shrine Tokyo, Japan 140 b1
Meiktila Burma 20°53N 95°54E 241 E5
Meili Xue Shan China 28°30N 98°39E 228 C2
Meinerzhagen Germany 51°6N 7°38E 178 D3
Meiningen Germany 50°34N 10°25E 178 E6
Meinung Taiwan 22°54N 120°32E 225 D2
Meio → Brazil 13°36S 44°7W 333 D3
Meira, Serra de Spain 43°15N 7°15W 194 B3
Meiringen Switz. 46°43N 8°12E 179 J4
Meise Belgium 50°56N 4°20E 116 A1
Meishan Sichuan, China 30°3N 103°23E 228 B4
Meishan Taiwan 23°35N 120°33E 225 C2
Meissen Germany 51°9N 13°29E 178 D9
Meissner Germany 51°13N 9°51E 178 D5
Meissner-Kaufunger Wald △ Germany 51°16N 9°45E 178 D5
Meitan China 27°45N 107°29E 228 D6
Meizhou China 24°16N 116°6E 229 E11
Meja India 25°9N 82°7E 243 G10
Mejillones Chile 23°10S 70°30W 334 A1
Mejiro Japan 35°43N 139°43E 140 A3
Mékambo Gabon 1°2N 13°50E 264 B2
Mekdela Ethiopia 11°24N 39°10E 257 E4
Mekele Ethiopia 13°33N 39°30E 257 E4
Mekerghene, Sebkra Algeria 26°21N 1°30E 261 C5
Mékhé Senegal 15°7N 16°38W 262 B1
Mekhomiya = Razlog Bulgaria 41°53N 23°28E 202 E7
Mekhtar Pakistan 30°30N 69°15E 240 C3
Meknès Morocco 33°57N 5°33W 260 B3
Meknès □ Morocco 33°3N 5°35W 260 B3
Meko Nigeria 7°27N 2°52E 263 D5
Mekong → Asia 9°30N 106°15E 237 H6
Mekongga Indonesia 3°39S 121°15E 231 E6
Mekoryuk U.S.A. 60°23N 166°11W 303 F6
Mekrou → Benin 12°25N 2°50E 263 C5
Mekvari = Kür → Azerbaijan 39°29N 49°15E 213 C13
Mel Italy 46°4N 12°5E 199 B9
Melagiri Hills India 12°20N 77°30E 245 H3
Melah, Oued el → Algeria 32°20N 2°28E 261 B5
Melaka Malaysia 2°15N 102°15E 237 L4
Melaka □ Malaysia 2°15N 102°15E 237 L4
Melambes Greece 35°8N 24°40E 207 E5
Melanesia Pac. Oc. 4°0S 155°0E 277 A10
Melanesian Basin Pac. Oc. 0°5N 160°35E 288 G8
Melapalaiyam India 8°39N 77°44E 245 K3
Melawi → Indonesia 0°5N 111°29E 235 B4
Melaya Indonesia 8°17S 114°30E 231 J17
Melbourne Vic., Australia 37°48S 144°58E 128 A1
Melbourne Fla., U.S.A. 28°5N 80°37W 317 G9
Melbourne Iowa, U.S.A. 41°57N 93°6W 310 C3
Melbourne ✕ (MEL) Australia 37°40S 144°50E 128 A1
Melcher-Dallas U.S.A. 41°14N 93°15W 310 C3
Melchor Múzquiz Mexico 27°53N 101°31W 318 B4
Melchor Ocampo Mexico 24°51N 101°39W 318 C4
Meldal Norway 63°3N 9°44E 164 A6
Méldola Italy 44°7N 12°5E 199 D9
Meldorf Germany 54°5N 9°5E 178 A5
Mélé C.A.R. 9°46N 21°33E 264 A4
Mele B. Vanuatu 17°44S 168°14E 287 G6
Meleden Somali Rep. 10°25N 49°51E 267 B6
Melegnano Italy 45°21N 9°19E 198 C6
Meleizem Mauritania 22°19N 11°24W 260 D2
Melekeok Palau 7°27N 134°38E 288 c
Melekess = Dimitrovgrad Russia 54°14N 49°39E 190 C9
Melenci Serbia 45°32N 20°20E 182 E5
Melenki Russia 55°20N 41°37E 190 C5
Meleuz Russia 52°58N 55°55E 216 B5
Mélèzes → Canada 57°40N 69°29W 298 A5
Melfi Chad 11°0N 17°59E 259 F3
Melfi Italy 41°0N 15°39E 201 B8
Melfort Sask., Canada 52°50N 104°37W 297 C8
Melfort Zimbabwe 18°0S 31°25E 269 F3
Melgaço Portugal 42°7N 8°15W 194 C2
Melgar de Fernamental Spain 42°27N 4°17W 194 C6
Melgraseyri Iceland 66°1N 22°27W 155 A4
Melhus Norway 63°17N 10°18E 164 A7
Melide Spain 42°55N 8°1W 194 C2
Meligales Greece 37°15N 21°59E 204 D3
Melilla N. Afr. 35°21N 2°57W 261 A4
Melilli Italy 37°11N 15°7E 201 E8
Melintang, Danau Indonesia 0°18S 116°20E 235 C5
Melipilla Chile 33°42S 71°15W 334 C1
Melissa Canada 45°24N 79°14W 312 A5
Melissa, Akra Greece 35°6N 24°33E 207 E5
Melissa Oros Greece 37°32N 26°4E 205 D8
Melissani Cave Greece 38°15N 20°38E 207 C2
Melita Canada 49°15N 101°0W 297 D8
Mélito di Porto Salvo Italy 37°55N 15°47E 201 E8
Melitopol Ukraine 46°50N 35°22E 189 J8
Melk Austria 48°13N 15°20E 180 C8
Melkki Finland 60°8N 24°53E 121 C2
Mellan Fryken Sweden 59°45N 13°10E 162 E7
Mellansel Sweden 63°26N 18°19E 160 E18
Mellbystrand Sweden 56°30N 12°56E 163 H6
Melle Deux-Sèvres, France 46°14N 0°10W 174 B3
Melle Niedersachsen, Germany 52°12N 8°20E 178 C4
Mellègue, O. → Tunisia 36°36N 9°14E 258 A1
Mellen U.S.A. 46°20N 90°40W 308 B8
Mellerud Sweden 58°41N 12°28E 163 F6
Mellette U.S.A. 45°9N 98°30W 308 C4
Mellid = Melide Spain 42°55N 8°1W 194 C2
Mellieħa Malta 35°57N 14°22E 206 F7
Mellieħa Bay Malta 35°59N 14°22E 206 F7
Mellit Sudan 14°7N 25°34E 257 E2
Mellizo Sur, Cerro Chile 48°33S 73°10W 336 C2
Mellrichstadt Germany 50°25N 10°17E 178 E6
Mellunkylä Finland 60°14N 25°5E 121 B3
Mellunmäki Finland 60°14N 25°6E 121 B3
Melnik Bulgaria 41°30N 23°25E 202 E7
Mělník Czech Rep. 50°22N 14°23E 180 A7
Melnytsya Podilska Ukraine 48°37N 26°10E 183 B11
Melo Uruguay 32°20S 54°10W 335 C5
Melolo Indonesia 9°53S 120°40E 231 F6
Melouprey Cambodia 13°48N 105°16E 236 F5
Melrhir, Chott Algeria 34°13N 6°30E 261 B6
Melrose N.S.W., Australia 32°42S 146°57E 283 B7
Melrose Borders, U.K. 55°36N 2°43W 167 F6
Melrose Mass., U.S.A. 42°27N 71°2W 116 A2
Melrose Minn., U.S.A. 45°40N 94°49W 308 C6
Melrose N. Mex., U.S.A. 34°26N 103°38W 305 J12
Melrose N.Y., U.S.A. 40°49N 73°55W 132 B2
Melrose Park U.S.A. 41°53N 87°50W 119 B1
Melsbroek Belgium 50°55N 4°29E 116 A2
Melsisi Vanuatu 15°46S 168°10E 287 E6
Melstone U.S.A. 46°36N 107°52W 304 C10
Melsungen Germany 51°7N 9°32E 178 D5
Melton Australia 37°41S 144°35E 282 D6
Melton Mowbray U.K. 52°47N 0°54W 168 E7
Melun France 48°32N 2°39E 173 D9
Melur India 10°2N 78°23E 245 J4
Melut South Sudan 10°30N 32°13E 257 E3
Melville Sask., Canada 50°55N 102°50W 297 C8
Melville Gauteng, S. Africa 26°11S 28°1E 123 B2
Melville, C. Queens., Australia 14°11S 144°30E 280 A3
Melville, C. Phil. 7°49N 117°0E 233 H1
Melville, L. Canada 53°30N 60°0W 299 B8
Melville B. N. Terr., Australia 12°0S 136°45E 280 A2
Melville B. Greenland 75°30N 63°0W 154 B4
Melville I. N. Terr., Australia 11°30S 131°0E 278 B5
Melville I. Canada 75°30N 112°0W 295 B9
Melville Pen. Canada 68°0N 84°0W 295 D15
Melvin, Lough Ireland 54°26N 8°10W 166 B3
Mélykút Hungary 46°11N 19°25E 182 D4
Memaliaj Albania 40°25N 19°56E 202 F3
Memba Mozam. 14°11S 40°30E 269 E5
Membalong Indonesia 3°9S 107°37E 235 C3
Memboro Indonesia 9°30S 119°30E 231 F5
Membrilla Spain 38°59N 3°21W 195 G7
Memel = Klaipėda Lithuania 55°43N 21°10E 184 C8
Memel S. Africa 27°38S 29°36E 271 C4
Memmingen Germany 47°58N 10°10E 179 H6
Mempawah Indonesia 0°30N 109°5E 235 B3
Memphis Egypt 29°52N 31°12E 256 J7
Memphis Mich., U.S.A. 42°54N 82°46W 312 D2
Memphis Mo., U.S.A. 40°28N 92°10W 310 D4
Memphis Tenn., U.S.A. 35°8N 90°2W 315 D9
Memphis Tex., U.S.A. 34°44N 100°33W 314 D4
Memphrémagog, L. N. Amer. 45°8N 72°17W 313 B12
Mena Ukraine 51°31N 32°13E 189 G7
Mena Ark., U.S.A. 34°35N 94°15W 314 D7
Mena → Ethiopia 5°40N 40°50E 257 F5
Menado = Manado Indonesia 1°29N 124°51E 231 D6
Menai Strait U.K. 53°11N 4°13W 168 D3
Ménaka Mali 15°59N 2°18E 263 B5
Menan = Chao Phraya → Thailand 13°40N 100°31E 236 F3
Menarandra → Madag. 25°17S 44°30E 272 D1
Menard U.S.A. 30°55N 99°47W 314 F5
Menard Fracture Zone Pac. Oc. 43°0S 97°0W 289 M18
Menate Indonesia 0°12S 113°3E 235 C4
Menawashei Sudan 12°41N 24°59E 257 E1
Mendaña Fracture Zone Pac. Oc. 16°0S 91°0W 289 J18
Mendawai → Indonesia 3°30S 113°0E 235 C4
Mende France 44°31N 3°30E 174 D7
Mendebo Mts. Ethiopia 7°0N 39°22E 257 F4
Mendeleyev Ridge Arctic 80°0N 178°0W 150 B17
Menden Germany 51°26N 7°47E 178 D3
Mendenhall, C. U.S.A. 59°45N 166°10W 303 G6
Menderes Turkey 38°14N 27°8E 205 C9
Mendhar India 33°35N 74°10E 243 C6
Mendi Ethiopia 9°47N 35°4E 257 F4
Mendi Papua N. G. 6°11S 143°39E 286 D2
Mendip Hills U.K. 51°17N 2°40W 169 F5
Mendocino U.S.A. 39°19N 123°48W 304 G2
Mendocino, C. U.S.A. 40°26N 124°25W 304 F1
Mendocino Fracture Zone Pac. Oc. 40°0N 142°0W 289 D13
Mendol Indonesia 0°36N 103°13E 234 B2
Mendon U.S.A. 42°0N 85°27W 311 B11
Mendooran Australia 31°50S 149°6E 283 A8
Mendota Calif., U.S.A. 36°45N 120°23W 306 J6
Mendota Ill., U.S.A. 41°33N 89°7W 310 C7
Mendoyo Indonesia 8°23S 114°42E 231 J17
Mendoza Argentina 32°50S 68°52W 334 C2
Mendoza □ Argentina 33°0S 69°0W 334 C2
Mene Grande Venezuela 9°49N 70°56W 328 B3
Menemen Turkey 38°34N 27°3E 205 C9
Menen Belgium 50°47N 3°7E 170 D3
Menéndez, L. Argentina 42°40S 71°51W 336 B2
Menfi Italy 37°36N 12°58E 200 E5
Mengcheng China 33°12N 116°36E 226 H9
Mengdingjie China 23°31N 98°58E 228 F2
Mengeš Slovenia 46°10N 14°35E 199 B11
Menggala Indonesia 4°30S 105°15E 234 C3
Menghai China 21°49N 100°55E 228 G3
Mengibar Spain 37°58N 3°48W 195 H7
Mengjin China 34°55N 112°45E 226 G7
Mengla China 21°20N 101°25E 228 G3
Menglian China 22°21N 99°27E 228 F2
Mengong Cameroon 2°56N 11°25E 264 B2
Mengshan China 24°14N 110°55E 229 E8
Mengyin China 35°40N 117°58E 227 G9
Mengzhe China 22°2N 100°15E 228 F3
Mengzi China 23°20N 103°22E 228 F4
Menihek Canada 54°28N 56°36W 299 B6
Menihek L. Canada 54°0N 67°0W 299 B6
Menin = Menen Belgium 50°47N 3°7E 170 D3
Menindee Australia 32°20S 142°25E 282 B5
Menindee L. Australia 32°20S 142°25E 282 B5
Meningie Australia 35°50S 139°18E 282 C3
Menjangan, Pulau Indonesia 8°7S 114°31E 231 J17
Menkrour Algeria 26°27N 8°9E 261 C6
Menlo Park U.S.A. 37°27N 122°12W 306 H4
Menngen © Australia 15°21S 131°16E 278 C5
Menominee U.S.A. 45°6N 87°37W 308 C10
Menominee → U.S.A. 45°6N 87°35W 308 C10
Menomonee Falls U.S.A. 43°10N 88°7W 311 A8
Menomonie U.S.A. 44°53N 91°55W 308 C8
Menongue Angola 14°48S 17°52E 265 E3
Menorca Spain 40°0N 4°0E 206 B5
Menorca ✕ (MAH) Spain 39°50N 4°16E 196 F9
Mentakab Malaysia 3°29N 102°21E 237 L4
Mentasta Lake U.S.A. 62°55N 143°45W 303 E12
Mentawai, Kepulauan Indonesia 2°0S 99°0E 234 C1
Mentawai, Selat Indonesia 1°45S 100°0E 234 C2
Menteng Indonesia 6°11S 106°49E 122 B1
Menton France 43°50N 7°29E 175 E11
Mentone U.S.A. 41°10N 86°2W 311 C10
Mentor U.S.A. 41°40N 81°21W 312 E3
Menyamya Papua N. G. 7°10S 145°59E 286 D3
Menyapa Indonesia 1°4N 116°4E 235 B5
Menzel-Bourguiba Tunisia 37°9N 9°49E 258 A1
Menzel-Chaker Tunisia 35°0N 10°26E 258 B2
Menzel-Temime Tunisia 36°46N 11°0E 258 A2
Menzelinsk Russia 55°47N 53°11E 186 C9
Menzies Australia 29°40S 121°2E 279 E3
Meob B. Namibia 24°25S 14°34E 270 B1
Me'ona Israel 33°1N 35°15E 250 E6
Mequi Mexico 28°17N 105°29W 318 B3
Mepaco Mozam. 15°57S 30°48E 269 F3
Meppel Neths. 52°42N 6°12E 170 B6
Meppen Germany 52°42N 7°17E 178 C3
Mequinenza Spain 41°22N 0°17E 196 D5
Mequinenza, Embalse de Spain 41°25N 0°15E 196 D5
Mequon U.S.A. 43°14N 87°59W 311 A9
Mer France 47°42N 1°30E 172 E8
Merai Papua N. G. 4°52S 152°19E 286 C7
Merak Indonesia 6°10N 106°26E 231 F12
Meråker Norway 63°25N 11°46E 164 A8
Meramangye, L. Australia 28°25S 132°13E 279 E5
Meramec → U.S.A. 38°24N 90°21W 310 F6
Meran = Merano Italy 46°40N 11°9E 199 B8
Merano Italy 46°40N 11°9E 199 B8
Mérantaise → France 48°42N 2°8E 134 B1
Merapi Indonesia 7°32S 110°26E 235 D4
Merate Italy 45°42N 9°25E 198 C6
Meratus, Pegunungan Indonesia 2°45S 115°40E 235 C5
Merauke Indonesia 8°29S 140°24E 231 F10
Merbein Australia 34°10S 142°2E 282 C5
Merca = Marka Somali Rep. 1°48N 44°50E 267 D5
Mercamadrid Spain 40°21N 3°39W 127 B2
Mercantour △ France 44°16N 6°43E 175 D10
Mercato Saraceno Italy 43°57N 12°12E 199 E9
Merced U.S.A. 37°18N 120°29W 306 H6
Merced → U.S.A. 37°21N 120°59W 306 H6
Merced, L. U.S.A. 37°43N 122°29W 136 B2
Merced Pk. U.S.A. 37°36N 119°24W 306 H7
Mercedes B. Aires, Argentina 34°40S 59°30W 334 C4
Mercedes Corrientes, Argentina 29°10S 58°5W 334 B4
Mercedes San Luis, Argentina 33°40S 65°21W 334 C2
Mercedes Camarines N., Phil. 14°7N 123°1E 232 D4
Mercedes Uruguay 33°12S 58°0W 334 C4
Merceditas Chile 28°20S 70°35W 334 B1
Mercer N.Z. 37°16S 175°5E 284 D4
Mercer Mo., U.S.A. 40°31N 93°32W 310 D3
Mercer Pa., U.S.A. 41°14N 80°15W 312 E4
Mercer Island U.S.A. 47°34N 122°13W 306 C4
Merchandise Mart Chicago, U.S.A. 119 b1
Mercier Bolivia 10°42S 68°5W 330 C4
Mercury U.S.A. 36°40N 115°59W 307 J11
Mercury B. N.Z. 36°48S 175°45E 284 C4
Mercury Is. N.Z. 36°37S 175°52E 284 C4
Mercy, C. Canada 65°0N 63°30W 295 E19
Merdrignac France 48°11N 2°27W 172 D4
Mere U.K. 51°6N 2°16W 169 F5
Mere Lava Vanuatu 14°25S 168°3E 287 D6
Merebuk, Gunung Indonesia 8°13S 114°39E 231 J17
Meredale S. Africa 26°16S 27°58E 123 B1
Meredith Australia 37°49S 144°5E 282 D6
Meredith, C. Falk. Is. 52°15S 60°40W 153 f
Meredith, L. U.S.A. 35°43N 101°33W 314 D4
Meredosia U.S.A. 39°50N 90°34W 310 E6
Merefa Ukraine 49°48N 36°3E 189 H9
Merei Romania 45°7N 26°43E 183 E11
Merga = Nukheila Sudan 19°1N 26°21E 256 D2
Mergui Burma 12°26N 98°34E 236 F2
Mergui Arch. = Myeik Kyunzu Burma 11°30N 97°30E 237 G1
Meribah Australia 34°43S 140°51E 282 C4
Méribel-les-Allues France 45°25N 6°34E 175 C10
Meriç Turkey 41°11N 26°25E 203 E10
Meriç → Turkey 40°52N 26°12E 203 F10
Mérida Yucatán, Mexico 20°58N 89°37W 319 C7
Mérida Phil. 10°55N 124°32E 233 F5
Mérida Spain 38°55N 6°25W 195 G4
Mérida Venezuela 8°24N 71°8W 328 B3
Mérida □ Venezuela 8°30N 71°10W 328 B3
Mérida, Cord. de Venezuela 9°0N 71°0W 328 B3
Meriden U.K. 52°26N 1°38W 169 E6
Meriden Conn., U.S.A. 41°32N 72°48W 313 E12
Meridian Calif., U.S.A. 39°9N 121°55W 306 F5
Meridian Ga., U.S.A. 31°27N 81°23W 316 D8
Meridian Idaho, U.S.A. 43°37N 116°24W 304 E5
Meridian Miss., U.S.A. 32°22N 88°42W 315 E10
Mérignac France 44°51N 0°39W 174 D3
Merimbula Australia 36°53S 149°54E 283 D8
Merin Gubai Somali Rep. 1°26N 44°20E 267 D5
Merinda Australia 20°2S 148°11E 280 C4
Mering Germany 48°16N 10°59E 179 G6
Meringa Nigeria 10°44N 12°9E 263 C7
Meringur Australia 34°20S 141°19E 282 C4
Merir Palau 4°10N 132°30E 231 D8
Merirumã Brazil 1°15N 54°50W 329 C7
Merizo Guam 13°16N 144°40E 302 d
Merkel U.S.A. 32°28N 100°1W 314 E4
Merlimau, Pulau Singapore 1°17N 103°42E 138 B2
Mermaid Reef Australia 17°6S 119°36E 278 C2
Mero Dominica 15°25N 61°26W 323 k
Meroe India 7°33N 93°33E 245 L11
Merowe Sudan 18°29N 31°46E 256 D3
Merowe Dam Sudan 18°35N 31°56E 256 D3
Merredin Australia 31°28S 118°18E 279 F2
Merri Cr. → Australia 37°47S 144°59E 128 A1
Merrick U.K. 55°8N 4°28W 167 F4
Merrickville Canada 44°55N 75°50W 313 B9
Merrill Oreg., U.S.A. 42°1N 121°36W 304 E3
Merrill Wis., U.S.A. 45°11N 89°41W 308 C9
Merrillville U.S.A. 41°29N 87°20W 311 C9
Merrimack → U.S.A. 42°49N 70°49W 313 D14
Merriman U.S.A. 42°55N 101°42W 308 D3
Merrion Ireland 53°19N 6°12W 120 B2
Merrionette Park U.S.A. 41°41N 87°40W 119 C2
Merritt Canada 50°10N 120°45W 296 C4
Merritt Island U.S.A. 28°21N 80°42W 317 G9
Merriwa Australia 32°6S 150°22E 283 B9
Merriwagga Australia 33°47S 145°43E 283 B6
Merry I. Canada 55°29N 77°31W 298 A4
Merrygoen Australia 31°51S 149°12E 283 A8
Merryville U.S.A. 30°45N 93°33W 315 F8
Mersa Fatma Eritrea 14°57N 40°17E 257 E5
Mersch Lux. 49°44N 6°7E 170 E6
Merse → Italy 43°5N 11°22E 199 E8
Mersea I. U.K. 51°47N 0°58E 169 F8
Merseburg Germany 51°22N 11°59E 178 D7
Mersey → U.K. 53°25N 3°1W 168 D4
Merseyside □ U.K. 53°31N 3°2W 168 D4
Mersin = İçel Turkey 36°51N 34°36E 250 B5
Mersing Malaysia 2°25N 103°50E 237 L4
Merta India 26°39N 74°4E 242 F6
Merta Road India 26°43N 73°55E 242 F5
Merthyr Tydfil U.K. 51°45N 3°22W 169 F4
Merthyr Tydfil □ U.K. 51°46N 3°21W 169 F4
Merti Kenya 1°4N 38°40E 268 B4
Mértola Portugal 37°40N 7°40W 195 H3
Merton □ U.K. 51°25N 0°11W 125 B2
Mertzon U.S.A. 31°16N 100°49W 314 F4
Méru Oise, France 49°13N 2°8E 173 C9
Meru Eastern, Kenya 0°3N 37°40E 268 B4
Meru Tanzania 3°15S 36°46E 268 C4
Meru △ Kenya 0°5N 38°10E 268 B4
Meru Betiri △ Indonesia 8°27S 113°51E 235 D4
Merv = Mary Turkmenistan 37°40N 61°50E 247 B9
Merville France 50°38N 2°38E 173 B9
Méry-sur-Seine France 48°31N 3°54E 173 D10
Merzifon Turkey 40°53N 35°32E 212 B6
Merzig Germany 49°26N 6°38E 179 F2
Merzouga, Erg Tin Algeria 24°0N 11°4E 261 D7
Mesa U.S.A. 33°25N 111°50W 305 K8
Mesa Verde △ U.S.A. 37°11N 108°29W 305 H9
Mesach Mellet Libya 24°30N 11°30E 258 D2
Mesada Israel 31°20N 35°19E 251 G6
Mesagne Italy 40°34N 17°48E 201 B10
Mesanagros Greece 36°1N 27°49E 206 E11
Mesaoría Cyprus 35°12N 33°14E 207 E9
Meschede Germany 51°20N 8°18E 178 D4
Mescit Turkey 40°21N 41°11E 213 B9
Mesemvriya = Nesebŭr Bulgaria 42°41N 27°46E 203 D11
Mesfinto Ethiopia 13°20N 37°22E 257 E4
Mesgarābād Iran 35°27N 51°30E 141 B3
Mesgouez, L. Canada 51°20N 75°0W 298 B5
Meshcherskiy Russia 55°40N 37°23E 129 B2
Meshchovsk Russia 54°22N 35°17E 188 E8
Meshed = Mashhad Iran 36°20N 59°35E 247 B8
Meshgīn Shahr Iran 38°30N 47°45E 213 C12
Meshkede-Ser = Bābol Sar Iran 36°45N 52°45E 247 B7
Meshoppen U.S.A. 41°36N 76°3W 313 E8
Meshra er Req South Sudan 8°25N 29°18E 257 F2
Mesilinka → Canada 56°6N 124°30W 296 B4
Meslay-du-Maine France 47°58N 0°33W 172 E6
Mesocco Switz. 46°23N 9°12E 179 J5
Mesologi Greece 38°21N 21°28E 204 C3
Mesongi Greece 39°29N 19°56E 206 C9
Mesopotamia = Al Jazirah Iraq 33°30N 44°0E 213 E10
Mesopotamia U.S.A. 41°27N 80°57W 312 E4
Mesopotamo Greece 39°14N 20°34E 204 B2
Mesoraca Italy 39°5N 16°48E 201 C9
Mésou Volímais = Volimes Greece 37°52N 20°39E 207 D2
Mesquite U.S.A. 36°48N 114°4W 305 H6
Messaad Algeria 34°8N 3°30E 261 B5

Messac France 47°49N 1°50W 172 E5
Messalo → Mozam. 12°25S 39°15E 269 E4
Messaména Cameroon 3°48N 12°49E 264 B2
Messara, Kolpos Greece 35°6N 24°47E 207 E5
Messe Austria 48°13N 16°24E 142 A2
Messier, Canal Chile 48°20S 74°33W 336 C2
Messina = Musina S. Africa 22°20S 30°5E 271 B5
Messina Italy 38°11N 15°34E 201 D8
Messina, Str. di Italy 38°15N 15°35E 201 D8
Messini Greece 37°4N 22°1E 204 D4
Messinia □ Greece 37°10N 22°0E 204 D3
Messiniakos Kolpos Greece 36°45N 22°5E 204 E4
Messkirch Germany 47°59N 9°7E 179 H5
Messlingen Sweden 62°40N 12°50E 162 B6
Mesta = Nestos → Europe 40°54N 24°49E 203 E8
Mesta, Akra Greece 38°16N 25°53E 205 C7
Mestanza Spain 38°35N 4°4W 195 G6
Mestersvig Greenland 72°10N 23°40W 154 C8
Mestre Italy 45°29N 12°15E 199 C9
Mestre, Espigão Brazil 12°30S 46°10W 333 D2
Mesudiye Turkey 40°28N 37°46E 212 B7
Meta U.S.A. 38°19N 92°10W 310 F4
Meta □ Colombia 3°30N 73°0W 328 C3
Meta → S. Amer. 6°12N 67°28W 328 B4
Meta Incognita Pen. Canada 62°45N 68°30W 295 E18
Metabetchouan Canada 48°26N 71°52W 299 C5
Metairie U.S.A. 29°59N 90°9W 131 A2
Metalici, Munţii Romania 46°15N 22°50E 182 D7
Metaline Falls U.S.A. 48°52N 117°22W 304 B5
Metallifere, Colline Italy 43°10N 11°0E 198 E8
Metamora U.S.A. 40°47N 89°22W 310 D7
Metán Argentina 25°30S 65°0W 334 B3
Metangula Mozam. 12°40S 34°50E 269 E3
Metanópoli Italy 45°24N 9°15E 129 B2
Metauro → Italy 43°50N 13°3E 199 E10
Metcalf U.S.A. 30°43N 83°59W 316 E6
Metcalfe Canada 45°14N 75°28W 313 A9
Metema Ethiopia 12°58N 36°12E 257 E4
Metengobalame Mozam. 14°49S 34°30E 269 E3
Methana Greece 37°35N 23°23E 204 D5
Methoni Greece 36°49N 21°42E 204 E3
Methven N.Z. 43°38S 171°40E 285 D6
Metil Mozam. 16°24S 39°0E 269 F4
Metkovets Bulgaria 43°37N 23°10E 202 C7
Metković Croatia 43°6N 17°39E 199 E14
Metlakatla U.S.A. 55°8N 131°35W 303 J15
Metlaoui Tunisia 34°24N 8°24E 258 B1
Metlik Papua N. G. 4°46S 152°55E 286 C7
Metlika Slovenia 45°40N 15°20E 199 C12
Metlili Chaamba Algeria 32°16N 3°38E 261 B5
Metro Indonesia 5°5S 105°20E 234 D3
Metro-Dade Cultural Centre U.S.A. 25°46N 80°12W 128 B2
Metro Toronto Zoo Canada 43°48N 79°10W 141 A3
Metropolis U.S.A. 37°9N 88°44W 308 G9
Metropolitan Museum of Art New York, U.S.A. 132 b3
Metropolitana □ Chile 33°30S 70°50W 334 C1
Metsovo Greece 39°48N 21°12E 204 B3
Metter U.S.A. 32°24N 82°3W 316 C7
Mettuppalaiyam India 11°18N 76°59E 245 J3
Mettur India 11°48N 77°47E 245 J3
Metu Ethiopia 8°18N 35°35E 257 F4
Metz France 49°8N 6°10E 173 C13
Metzingen Germany 48°31N 9°17E 179 G5
Meudon France 48°48N 2°14E 134 B2
Meulaboh Indonesia 4°11N 96°3E 234 B1
Meung-sur-Loire France 47°50N 1°40E 173 E8
Meureudu Indonesia 5°19N 96°10E 234 A1
Meurthe → France 48°47N 6°9E 173 D13
Meurthe-et-Moselle □ France 48°52N 6°0E 173 D13
Meuse □ France 49°8N 5°25E 173 C12
Meuse → Europe 50°45N 5°41E 170 D5
Meuselwitz Germany 51°2N 12°17E 178 D8
Meutapok, Mt. Malaysia 5°40N 117°0E 235 A5
Mevaseret Tsiyon Israel 31°48N 35°9E 123 B1
Mevo Beitar Israel 31°43N 35°6E 123 B1
Mexia U.S.A. 31°41N 96°29W 314 F6
Mexiana, I. Brazil 0°0 49°30W 332 B2
Mexicali Mexico 32°40N 115°30W 307 N11
Mexican Plateau Mexico 25°0N 104°0W 292 G9
Mexican Water U.S.A. 36°57N 109°32W 305 H9
México Distrito Federal, Mexico 19°24N 99°9W 128 B2
Mexico Maine, U.S.A. 44°34N 70°33W 313 B14
Mexico Mo., U.S.A. 39°10N 91°53W 310 E5
Mexico N.Y., U.S.A. 43°28N 76°14W 313 C8
México □ Mexico 19°20N 99°30W 319 D5
Mexico ■ Cent. Amer. 25°0N 105°0W 318 C4
México, Ciudad de Mexico 19°24N 99°9W 128 B2
Mexico, G. of Cent. Amer. 25°0N 90°0W 319 C7
Mexico B. U.S.A. 43°35N 76°20W 313 C8
Mexico Beach U.S.A. 29°57N 85°25W 316 F4
Mexico City Int. ✈ (MEX) Mexico 19°25N 99°5W 128 B2
Meydān-e Naftūn Iran 31°56N 49°18E 247 D6
Meydani, Ra's-e Iran 25°24N 59°6E 247 E8
Meyenburg Germany 53°18N 12°14E 178 B8
Meyers Chuck U.S.A. 55°45N 132°15W 296 B2
Meyersdal S. Africa 26°17S 28°5E 123 B2
Meymac France 45°32N 2°10E 174 C6
Meymaneh Afghan. 35°53N 64°38E 240 B2
Meyo Cameroon 2°50N 11°1E 264 B2
Meyrueis France 44°12N 3°27E 174 D7
Meyssac France 45°3N 1°40E 174 C5
Meyzieu France 45°46N 4°59E 175 C8
Mezdra Bulgaria 43°12N 23°42E 202 C7
Mèze France 43°27N 3°36E 174 E7
Mezen Russia 65°50N 44°20E 186 A7
Mezen → Russia 65°44N 44°22E 186 A7
Mézenc, Mt. France 44°54N 4°11E 175 D8
Mezeş, Munţii Romania 47°5N 23°5E 182 C8
Mezha → Russia 55°44N 31°33E 188 E6
Mezhdurechensk Russia 53°41N 88°3E 217 B11
Mezhdurechenskiy Russia 59°36N 65°56E 214 D7
Mezhdurechye = Shali Russia 43°9N 45°55E 191 J7
Mezhevaya Utka = Sinegorskiy Russia 47°55N 40°52E 191 G5
Mézidon-Canon France 49°5N 0°1W 172 C6
Mézières-en-Brenne France 46°49N 1°13E 174 B5
Mézilhac France 44°49N 4°21E 175 D8
Mézin France 44°4N 0°16E 174 D4
Mezitli Turkey 36°45N 34°29E 250 B5
Mezőberény Hungary 46°49N 21°3E 182 D6
Mezőfalva Hungary 46°55N 18°49E 182 D3
Mezőhegyes Hungary 46°19N 20°49E 182 D5
Mezőkövácsháza Hungary 46°25N 20°57E 182 D5
Mezőkövesd Hungary 47°49N 20°35E 182 C5
Mézos France 44°5N 1°10W 174 D2
Mezőtúr Hungary 47°1N 20°41E 182 C5
Mezquital Mexico 23°29N 104°23W 318 C4
Mezzate Italy 45°26N 9°17E 129 B2
Mezzolombardo Italy 46°13N 11°5E 198 B8
Mfolozi → S. Africa 28°25S 32°26E 271 C5
Mgarr Malta 35°55N 14°22E 206 F7
Mgarr Gozo, Malta 36°2N 14°18E 206 E7
Mgeta Tanzania 8°22S 36°6E 269 D4
Mglin Russia 53°2N 32°50E 189 F7
Mhamid Morocco 29°49N 5°43W 260 C3
Mhlaba Hills Zimbabwe 18°30S 30°30E 269 F3
Mhow India 22°33N 75°50E 242 H6
Mi-Shima Japan 34°46N 131°9E 222 C3
Miadong S. Korea 37°36N 127°0E 137 B2
Miagao Phil. 10°39N 122°14E 233 F4
Miahuatlán Mexico 16°20N 96°36W 319 D5
Miaich South Sudan 9°30N 30°30E 257 F3
Miajadas Spain 39°9N 5°54W 195 F5
Miami Fla., U.S.A. 25°46N 80°11W 128 B2
Miami Okla., U.S.A. 36°53N 94°53W 314 C7
Miami Tex., U.S.A. 35°42N 100°38W 314 D4
Miami Beach U.S.A. 25°47N 80°7W 128 B2
Miami Canal U.S.A. 25°45N 80°12W 128 A1
Miami Int. ✈ (MIA) U.S.A. 25°48N 80°17W 128 B1
Miami Shores U.S.A. 25°51N 80°11W 128 A2
Miami Springs U.S.A. 25°49N 80°17W 128 B1
Miamisburg U.S.A. 39°38N 84°17W 311 E12
Mian Xian China 33°10N 106°32E 228 A6
Mianchi China 34°48N 111°48E 226 G6
Mīāndarreh Iran 35°37N 53°39E 247 C7
Mīāndowāb Iran 37°0N 46°5E 213 D12
Miandrivazo Madag. 19°31S 45°29E 272 B2
Mīāneh Iran 37°30N 47°40E 213 D12
Mianning China 28°32N 102°9E 228 C4
Mianwali Pakistan 32°38N 71°28E 242 C4
Mianyang China 31°22N 104°47E 228 B5
Mianzhu China 31°22N 104°7E 228 B5
Miao Ling China 26°5N 107°30E 228 D6
Miaodao Qundao China 38°10N 120°45E 227 E11
Miaoli Taiwan 24°37N 120°49E 225 B2
Miaoli □ Taiwan 24°30N 120°55E 225 B2
Miarinarivo Antananarivo, Madag. 18°57S 46°55E 272 B2
Miarinarivo Toamasina, Madag. 16°38S 48°15E 272 B2
Miariravaratra Madag. 20°13S 47°31E 272 C2
Miass Russia 54°59N 60°6E 186 D11
Miasteczko Krajeńskie Poland 53°7N 17°1E 185 E4
Miastko Poland 54°0N 16°58E 184 E3
Miasto Poland 52°15N 21°0E 142 B2
Mica S. Africa 24°10S 30°48E 271 B5
Micanopy U.S.A. 29°30N 82°17W 317 F7
Micăsasa Romania 46°7N 24°7E 183 D9
Micco U.S.A. 27°53N 80°30W 317 H9
Miccosukee U.S.A. 30°36N 84°3W 316 E5
Miccosukee, L. U.S.A. 30°33N 83°53W 316 E6
Michael, Mt. Papua N. G. 6°27S 145°22E 286 D3
Michalovce Slovak Rep. 48°47N 21°58E 181 C14
Michałowice Poland 52°10N 20°52E 142 B1
Michigan □ U.S.A. 44°0N 85°0W 309 C11
Michigan, L. U.S.A. 44°0N 87°0W 311 B9
Michigan Avenue Chicago, U.S.A. 119 b2
Michigan Center U.S.A. 42°14N 84°20W 311 B12
Michigan City U.S.A. 41°43N 86°54W 311 C10
Michika Nigeria 10°36N 13°23E 263 C7
Michipicoten I. Canada 47°40N 85°40W 298 C2
Michle Czech Rep. 50°3N 14°28E 135 B2
Michoacán □ Mexico 19°10N 101°50W 318 D4
Michurin Bulgaria 42°9N 27°51E 203 D11
Michurinsk Russia 52°58N 40°27E 190 D5
Micoud St. Lucia 13°49N 60°54W 323 m
Micronesia Pac. Oc. 11°0N 160°0E 288 G7
Micronesia, Federated States of ■ Pac. Oc. 9°0N 150°0E 288 G7
Mid-Atlantic Ridge Atl. Oc. 0°0 20°0W 152 J10
Mid-City Calif., U.S.A. 34°4N 118°20W 126 B2
Mid City La., U.S.A. 29°58N 90°6W 131 B2
Mid-Indian Ocean Basin Ind. Oc. 10°0S 80°0E 273 F7
Mid-Indian Ridge Ind. Oc. 30°0S 75°0E 273 H6
Mid-Pacific Seamounts Pac. Oc. 18°0N 177°0W 288 F10
Midai Indonesia 3°0N 107°47E 235 B3
Midale Canada 49°25N 103°20W 297 D8
Middelburg Neths. 51°30N 3°36E 170 C3
Middelburg Eastern Cape, S. Africa 31°30S 25°0E 270 D4
Middelburg Mpumalanga, S. Africa 25°49S 29°28E 271 C4
Middelfart Denmark 55°30N 9°43E 163 J3
Middelpos S. Africa 31°55S 20°13E 270 D3
Middelwit S. Africa 24°51S 27°3E 270 B4
Middle → U.S.A. 41°26N 93°30W 310 C3
Middle Alkali L. U.S.A. 41°27N 120°5W 304 F3
Middle America Trench = Guatemala Trench Pac. Oc. 14°0N 95°0W 292 H10
Middle Andaman I. India 12°30N 92°50E 245 H11
Middle Bass I. U.S.A. 41°41N 82°48W 312 E2
Middle East Asia 35°0N 40°0E 210 E5
Middle Fork Feather → U.S.A. 38°33N 121°30W 306 F5
Middle Ground Midway Is. 28°14N 177°24W 302 c
Middle Harbour Australia 33°47S 151°14E 139 A2
Middle Hd. Australia 33°49S 151°16E 139 A2
Middle I. Australia 34°6S 123°11E 279 F3
Middle Island St. Kitts & Nevis 17°20N 62°48W 322 d
Middle Loup → U.S.A. 41°17N 98°24W 308 E4
Middle Park Australia 37°50S 144°57E 128 B1
Middle Raccoon → U.S.A. 41°35N 93°35W 310 C3
Middle Village U.S.A. 40°43N 73°52W 132 B2
Middleboro U.S.A. 41°54N 70°55W 313 E14
Middleburg Fla., U.S.A. 30°4N 81°52W 316 E8
Middleburg Pa., U.S.A. 40°47N 77°3W 312 F7
Middleburgh U.S.A. 42°36N 74°20W 313 D10
Middlebury Ind., U.S.A. 41°41N 85°42W 311 C11
Middlebury Vt., U.S.A. 44°1N 73°10W 313 B11
Middlefield U.S.A. 41°27N 81°4W 312 E3
Middlemarch N.Z. 45°30S 170°9E 285 F5
Middlemount Australia 22°50S 148°40E 280 C4
Middleport N.Y., U.S.A. 43°13N 78°29W 312 C6
Middleport Ohio, U.S.A. 39°0N 82°3W 309 F12
Middlesboro U.S.A. 36°36N 83°43W 309 G12
Middlesbrough U.K. 54°35N 1°13W 168 C6
Middlesbrough □ U.K. 54°28N 1°13W 168 C6
Middlesex Belize 17°2N 88°31W 320 C2
Middlesex N.J., U.S.A. 40°36N 74°30W 313 F10
Middlesex N.Y., U.S.A. 42°42N 77°16W 312 D7
Middlesex □ Jamaica 18°10N 77°5W 320 a
Middlesex Fells Reservation U.S.A. 42°27N 71°6W 116 A2
Middleton Queens., Australia 22°22S 141°32E 280 C3
Middleton N.S., Canada 44°57N 65°4W 300 D6
Middleton Wis., U.S.A. 43°6N 89°30W 310 A7
Middleton Cr. → Australia 22°35S 141°51E 280 C3
Middleton I. U.S.A. 59°26N 146°20W 303 G11
Middletown Armagh, U.K. 54°17N 6°51W 166 B5
Middletown Calif., U.S.A. 38°45N 122°37W 306 G4
Middletown Conn., U.S.A. 41°34N 72°39W 313 E12
Middletown Ky., U.S.A. 38°14N 85°32W 311 F11
Middletown N.Y., U.S.A. 41°27N 74°25W 313 E10
Middletown Ohio, U.S.A. 39°31N 84°24W 311 E12
Middletown Pa., U.S.A. 40°12N 76°44W 313 F8
Middleville U.S.A. 42°43N 85°28W 311 B11
Midelt Morocco 32°46N 4°44W 260 B4
Midge Point Australia 20°39S 148°43E 280 b
Midhirst N.Z. 39°17S 174°18E 284 F3
Miðsandur Iceland 64°24N 21°28W 155 C5
Midhurst Ont., Canada 44°26N 79°43W 312 B5
Midhurst W. Susx., U.K. 50°59N 0°44W 169 G7
Midi, Canal du → France 43°45N 1°21E 174 E5
Midi, Gare du Brussels, Belgium 116 c1
Midi d'Ossau, Pic du France 42°50N 0°26W 174 F3
Midi-Pyrénées □ France 43°55N 1°45E 174 E5
Midland W. Austral., Australia 31°54S 116°1E 279 F2
Midland Ont., Canada 44°45N 79°50W 312 B5
Midland Calif., U.S.A. 33°52N 114°48W 307 M12
Midland Mich., U.S.A. 43°37N 84°14W 309 D11
Midland Pa., U.S.A. 40°39N 80°27W 312 F4
Midland Tex., U.S.A. 32°0N 102°3W 314 F3
Midland Beach U.S.A. 40°34N 74°6W 132 C1
Midlands □ Zimbabwe 19°40S 29°0E 269 F2
Midleton Ireland 51°55N 8°10W 166 E3
Midlothian □ U.K. 55°51N 3°5W 167 F5
Midnapore = Medinipur India 22°25N 87°21E 243 H12
Midongy, Tangorombohitr' i Madag. 23°30S 47°0E 272 C2
Midongy Atsimo Madag. 23°35S 47°1E 272 C2
Midori Japan 36°30N 139°15E 223 A11
Midou → France 43°54N 0°30W 174 E3
Midouze → France 43°48N 0°51W 174 E3
Midsayap Phil. 7°12N 124°32E 233 H5
Midsund Norway 62°41N 6°40E 164 B3
Midtgulen Norway 61°44N 5°11E 164 C2
Midtjylland □ Denmark 56°30N 9°0E 163 H2
Midu China 25°18N 100°30E 228 E3
Midville U.S.A. 32°49N 82°14W 316 C7
Midway Ala., U.S.A. 32°5N 85°31W 316 C4
Midway Fla., U.S.A. 30°30N 84°27W 316 E5
Midway Is. Pac. Oc. 28°13N 177°22W 302 c
Midway Wells U.S.A. 32°41N 115°7W 307 N11
Midwest U.S.A. 42°0N 90°0W 301 G22
Midwest Wyo., U.S.A. 43°25N 106°16W 304 E10
Midwest City U.S.A. 35°27N 97°24W 314 D6
Midwood U.S.A. 40°37N 73°57W 132 C2
Midyat Turkey 37°25N 41°23E 213 D9
Midžor Bulgaria 43°24N 22°40E 202 C6
Mie Japan 32°58N 131°35E 222 E3
Mie □ Japan 34°30N 136°10E 223 C8
Miechów Poland 50°21N 20°5E 185 H7
Miedwie, Jezioro Poland 53°17N 14°54E 185 E1
Miedzeszyn Poland 52°10N 21°11E 142 B2
Międzybórz Poland 51°25N 17°34E 185 G4
Międzychód Poland 52°35N 15°53E 185 F2
Międzylesie Dolnośląskie, Poland 50°8N 16°40E 185 H3
Międzylesie Warszawa, Poland 52°12N 21°10E 142 B3
Międzyrzec Podlaski Poland 51°58N 22°45E 185 G9
Międzyrzecz Poland 52°26N 15°35E 185 F2
Międzyzdroje Poland 53°56N 14°26E 184 E1
Miejska Górka Poland 51°39N 16°58E 185 G3
Miélan France 43°27N 0°19E 174 E4
Mielau = Mława Poland 53°9N 20°25E 185 E7
Mielec Poland 50°15N 21°25E 185 H8
Mienga Angola 17°12S 19°43E 265 F3
Miercurea-Ciuc Romania 46°21N 25°48E 183 D10
Miercurea Sibiului Romania 45°53N 23°48E 183 E8
Mieres Spain 43°18N 5°48W 194 B5
Mieroszów Poland 50°40N 16°11E 185 H3
Mies = Stříbro Czech Rep. 49°44N 13°0E 180 A6
Mieso Ethiopia 9°15N 40°43E 257 F5
Miessaari Finland 60°8N 24°47E 121 C1
Mieszkowice Poland 52°47N 14°30E 185 F1
Mifflintown U.S.A. 40°34N 77°24W 312 F7
Mifraz Hefa Israel 32°52N 35°0E 250 F6
Migang Shan China 35°32N 106°13E 226 G4
Migennes France 47°58N 3°31E 173 E10
Migliarino Italy 44°46N 11°56E 199 D8
Migliarino-San Rossore-Massaciuccoli △ Italy 43°44N 10°20E 198 E7
Migori Kenya 1°4S 34°28E 268 C3
Miguasha △ Canada 48°5N 66°19W 299 C6
Miguel Alemán, Presa Mexico 18°15N 96°32W 319 D5
Miguel Alves Brazil 4°11S 42°55W 332 B3
Miguel Calmon Brazil 11°26S 40°36W 333 D3
Miguel Hidalgo Mexico 19°25N 99°12W 128 B1
Migueturra Spain 38°58N 3°53W 195 G7
Mihăileni Romania 47°58N 26°9E 183 C11
Mihăileşti Romania 44°20N 25°54E 183 F10
Mihailovca Moldova 46°33N 28°56E 183 D13
Mihalgazi Turkey 40°2N 30°34E 205 A12
Mihalıççık Turkey 39°53N 31°30E 212 C4
Mihara Japan 34°24N 133°5E 222 C5
Mihara-Yama Japan 34°43N 139°23E 223 C11
Mihesu de Cîmpie Romania 46°41N 24°25E 183 D9
Mijas Spain 36°36N 4°40W 195 J6
Mikawa-Wan Japan 34°44N 137°13E 223 C9
Mikese Tanzania 6°48S 37°55E 268 D4
Mikha-Tskhakaya = Senaki Georgia 42°15N 42°1E 191 J6
Mikhailovka = Mykhaylivka Ukraine 47°12N 35°15E 189 J8
Mikhaylov Russia 54°14N 39°0E 188 E10
Mikhaylovgrad = Montana Bulgaria 43°27N 23°16E 202 C7
Mikhaylovka = Kimovsk Russia 54°0N 38°29E 188 E10
Mikhaylovka Russia 50°3N 43°5E 190 E6
Mikhelysona Russia 55°42N 37°52E 129 B5
Mikhnevo Russia 55°4N 37°56E 188 E9
Miki Hyōgo, Japan 34°48N 134°59E 222 C6
Miki Kagawa, Japan 34°12N 134°7E 222 C6
Mikines Greece 37°43N 22°46E 204 D4
Mikir Hills India 26°10N 93°30E 241 D4
Mikkeli Finland 61°43N 27°15E 188 B4
Mikkwa → Canada 58°25N 114°46W 296 B6
Mikniya Sudan 17°0N 33°45E 257 D3
Mikołajki Poland 53°49N 21°37E 184 E8
Míkonos = Mykonos Greece 37°30N 25°25E 205 D7
Mikope Dem. Rep. of the Congo 4°58S 20°43E 265 C4
Mikoyan-Shakhar = Karachayevsk Russia 43°50N 41°55E 191 J5
Mikri Prespa, L. Greece 40°47N 21°3E 202 F5
Mikro Derio Greece 41°19N 26°6E 203 E10
Mikstat Poland 51°32N 17°59E 185 G4
Mikulov Czech Rep. 48°48N 16°39E 181 C9
Mikumi Tanzania 7°26S 37°0E 268 D4
Mikumi △ Tanzania 7°35S 37°15E 268 D4
Mikun Russia 62°20N 50°0E 186 B9
Mikuni Japan 36°13N 136°9E 223 A8
Mikuni-Tōge Japan 36°50N 138°50E 223 A10
Mikura-Jima Japan 33°52N 139°36E 223 D11
Mila Algeria 36°27N 6°16E 261 A6
Mila □ Algeria 36°25N 6°10E 261 A6
Milaca U.S.A. 45°45N 93°39W 308 C7
Miladummadulu Atoll Maldives 5°50N 73°30E 272 d
Milagro Ecuador 2°11S 79°36W 328 D2
Milagros Phil. 12°13N 123°30E 232 E4
Milan = Milano Italy 45°28N 9°10E 129 B1
Milan Ga., U.S.A. 32°1N 83°4W 316 C6
Milan Ill., U.S.A. 41°27N 90°34W 310 C6
Milan Mich., U.S.A. 42°5N 83°41W 311 B13
Milan Mo., U.S.A. 40°12N 93°7W 310 D3
Milan Tenn., U.S.A. 35°55N 88°46W 315 D10
Miland Norway 59°54N 8°45E 164 E5
Milando Angola 8°45S 17°36E 265 D3
Milando △ Angola 8°45S 17°10E 265 D3
Milanese, Parco Regionale △ Italy 45°35N 9°5E 129 A1
Milang Australia 35°24S 138°58E 282 C3
Milange Mozam. 16°3S 35°45E 269 F4
Milano Italy 45°28N 9°10E 129 B1
Milano Due Italy 45°29N 9°16E 129 B2
Milano Linate ✈ (LIN) Italy 45°27N 9°16E 129 B2
Milano San Felice Italy 45°28N 9°18E 129 B2
Milanoa Madag. 13°35S 49°47E 272 A2
Milâs Turkey 37°20N 27°50E 205 D9
Milatos Greece 35°18N 25°34E 207 E6
Milazzo Italy 38°13N 15°15E 201 D8
Milbank U.S.A. 45°13N 96°38W 308 C5
Milbanke Sd. Canada 52°19N 128°33W 296 C3
Milbertshofen Germany 48°10N 11°34E 131 A2
Milden Canada 51°29N 107°32W 297 C7
Mildenhall U.K. 52°21N 0°32E 169 E8
Mildmay Canada 44°3N 81°7W 312 B3
Mildura Australia 34°13S 142°9E 282 C5
Mile China 24°28N 103°20E 228 E4
Mile and a Quarter Barbados 13°16N 59°37W 323 r
Miles Australia 26°40S 150°9E 281 D5
Miles City U.S.A. 46°25N 105°51W 304 C11
Mileşti Moldova 47°13N 28°3E 183 C13
Milestone Canada 49°59N 104°31W 297 D8
Mileto Italy 38°36N 16°4E 201 D9
Miletto, Mte. Italy 41°27N 14°22E 201 A7
Miletus Turkey 37°30N 27°18E 205 D9
Milevsko Czech Rep. 49°27N 14°21E 180 B7
Milford Calif., U.S.A. 40°10N 120°22W 306 E6
Milford Conn., U.S.A. 41°14N 73°3W 313 E11
Milford Del., U.S.A. 38°55N 75°26W 309 F16
Milford Ill., U.S.A. 40°38N 87°42W 311 D9
Milford Mass., U.S.A. 42°8N 71°31W 313 D13
Milford Mich., U.S.A. 42°35N 83°36W 311 B13
Milford N.H., U.S.A. 42°50N 71°39W 313 D13
Milford N.Y., U.S.A. 42°35N 74°56W 313 D10
Milford Pa., U.S.A. 41°19N 74°48W 313 E10
Milford Utah, U.S.A. 38°24N 113°1W 304 G7
Milford Haven U.K. 51°42N 5°7W 169 F2
Milford Sd. N.Z. 44°41S 167°47E 285 E2
Milḩ, Baḩr al = Razāzah, Buḩayrat ar Iraq 32°40N 43°35E 213 F10
Miliana Aïn Salah, Algeria 27°20N 2°32E 261 C5
Miliana Médéa, Algeria 36°20N 2°15E 261 A5
Milicz Poland 51°31N 17°19E 185 G4
Milies Greece 39°20N 23°9E 204 B5
Milikapiti Australia 11°26S 130°40E 278 B5
Mililani Town U.S.A. 21°28N 158°1W 302 K13
Miling Australia 30°30S 116°17E 279 F2
Militello in Val di Catánia Italy 37°16N 14°48E 201 E7
Militsch = Milicz Poland 51°31N 17°19E 185 G4
Milk, Wadi el → Sudan 17°55N 30°20E 256 D3
Milk River Canada 49°10N 112°5W 296 D6
Milk River Spa Jamaica 17°50N 77°22W 320 a
Mill → U.S.A. 42°57N 83°23W 312 D1
Mill Hill U.K. 51°37N 0°14W 125 A2
Mill I. Antarctica 66°0S 101°30E 151 C8
Mill I. Nunavut, Canada 63°58N 77°47W 295 E16
Mill Shoals U.S.A. 38°15N 88°21W 311 F8
Mill Valley U.S.A. 37°54N 122°32W 306 H4
Millárs → Spain 39°55N 0°1W 196 F4
Millau France 44°8N 3°4E 174 D7
Millbridge Canada 44°41N 77°36W 312 B7
Millbrook Ont., Canada 44°10N 78°29W 312 B6
Millbrook Ala., U.S.A. 32°29N 83°22W 315 E11
Millbrook N.Y., U.S.A. 41°47N 73°42W 313 E11
Mille Lacs, L. des Canada 48°45N 90°35W 298 C1
Mille Lacs L. U.S.A. 46°15N 93°39W 308 B7
Milledgeville Ga., U.S.A. 33°5N 83°14W 316 B6
Milledgeville Ill., U.S.A. 41°58N 89°46W 310 C7
Millen U.S.A. 32°48N 81°57W 316 C8
Millennium Dome U.K. 51°30N 0°0 125 B4
Millennium I. = Caroline I. Kiribati 9°58S 150°13W 289 H12
Millennium Park Chicago, U.S.A. 119 c2
Miller U.S.A. 44°31N 98°59W 308 C4
Miller Lake Canada 45°6N 81°26W 312 A3
Miller Meadow U.S.A. 41°51N 87°49W 119 B2
Millerhill U.K. 55°55N 3°5W 121 B3
Millerovo Russia 48°57N 40°28E 191 F5
Miller's Flat N.Z. 45°39S 169°23E 285 F4
Millers Point Sydney, Australia 139 a1
Millersburg Ind., U.S.A. 41°32N 85°42W 311 C11
Millersburg Ohio, U.S.A. 40°33N 81°55W 312 F3
Millersburg Pa., U.S.A. 40°32N 76°58W 312 F8
Millerton N.Z. 41°39S 171°54E 285 B6
Millerton N.Y., U.S.A. 41°57N 73°31W 313 E11
Millerton L. U.S.A. 37°1N 119°41W 306 J7
Millet St. Lucia 13°55N 60°59W 323 m
Millevaches, Plateau de France 45°45N 2°0E 174 C6
Millheim U.S.A. 40°54N 77°29W 312 F7
Millicent Australia 37°34S 140°21E 282 D4
Milligan U.S.A. 30°45N 86°38W 317 E3
Millington U.S.A. 35°20N 89°53W 315 D10
Millinocket U.S.A. 45°39N 68°43W 309 C19
Millmerran Australia 27°53S 151°16E 281 D5
Millom U.K. 54°13N 3°16W 168 C4
Mills L. Canada 61°30N 118°20W 296 A5
Millsboro U.S.A. 40°0N 80°0W 312 G5
Millstream Chichester △ Australia 21°35S 117°6E 278 D2
Millstreet Ireland 52°4N 9°4W 166 D2
Millthorpe Australia 33°26S 149°12E 283 B8
Milltown Ireland 53°19N 6°14W 120 B2
Milltown Malbay Ireland 52°52N 9°24W 166 D2
Millville N.J., U.S.A. 39°24N 75°2W 309 F16
Millville Pa., U.S.A. 41°7N 76°32W 313 E8
Millwood U.S.A. 38°52N 76°52W 134 B3
Millwood L. U.S.A. 33°42N 93°58W 314 E8
Milna Croatia 43°20N 16°28E 199 E13
Milne → Australia 21°10S 137°33E 280 C2
Milne Bay □ Papua N. G. 10°0S 152°30E 286 E7
Milne Land Greenland 70°40N 26°30W 154 C8
Milnerton S. Africa 33°53S 18°29E 118 A1
Milo U.S.A. 45°15N 68°59W 309 C19
Milo → Guinea 8°52N 9°0W 262 D3
Miloli'i U.S.A. 19°11N 155°55W 302 D6
Milon, Akra Greece 36°15N 28°11E 206 E12
Milon-la-Chapelle France 48°43N 2°3E 134 B1
Milos Greece 36°44N 24°25E 204 E6
Miłosław Poland 52°12N 17°32E 185 F4
Milot Albania 41°41N 19°43E 202 E3
Milparinka Australia 29°46S 141°57E 281 D3
Milpitas U.S.A. 37°26N 121°55W 306 H5
Milroy U.S.A. 39°30N 85°28W 311 E11
Miltenberg Germany 49°41N 9°16E 179 F5
Milton N.S.W., Australia 35°20S 150°27E 283 C9
Milton N.S., Canada 44°4N 64°45W 299 D7
Milton Ont., Canada 43°31N 79°53W 312 C5
Milton N.Z. 46°7S 169°59E 285 G4
Milton Calif., U.S.A. 38°3N 120°51W 306 G6
Milton Fla., U.S.A. 30°38N 87°3W 317 E2
Milton Iowa, U.S.A. 40°41N 92°10W 310 D4
Milton Mass., U.S.A. 42°14N 71°2W 116 B2
Milton Pa., U.S.A. 41°1N 76°51W 312 F8
Milton Vt., U.S.A. 44°38N 73°7W 313 B11
Milton Wis., U.S.A. 42°47N 88°56W 311 B8
Milton Bridge U.K. 55°51N 3°11W 121 B2
Milton-Freewater U.S.A. 45°56N 118°23W 304 D4
Milton Keynes U.K. 52°1N 0°44W 169 E7
Milton Keynes □ U.K. 52°1N 0°44W 169 E7
Milton Park Montréal, Canada 130 b1
Miltou Chad 10°14N 17°26E 259 C8
Miluo China 29°0N 112°59E 229 C9
Milverton Canada 43°34N 80°55W 312 C4
Milwaukee U.S.A. 43°2N 87°54W 311 A9
Milwaukee Deep Atl. Oc. 19°50N 68°0W 321 C6
Milwaukie U.S.A. 45°26N 122°38W 306 E4
Mim Ghana 6°57N 2°33W 262 D4
Mimico Canada 43°36N 79°29W 141 B2
Mimico Creek → Canada 43°37N 79°28W 141 B1
Mimili Australia 27°0S 132°42E 279 E5
Mimizan France 44°12N 1°13W 174 D2
Mimoň Czech Rep. 50°38N 14°43E 180 A7
Mimongo Gabon 1°11S 11°36E 264 C2
Mimoso Brazil 15°10S 48°5W 333 E2
Mims U.S.A. 28°40N 80°51W 317 G9
Min Jiang → Fujian, China 26°0N 119°35E 229 E12
Min Jiang → Sichuan, China 28°45N 104°40E 228 C5
Min Xian China 34°25N 104°5E 226 G3
Minā' Jabal 'Alī U.A.E. 25°2N 55°8E 247 E7
Mina Pirquitas Argentina 22°40S 66°30W 334 A2
Mīnā Su'ud Si. Arabia 28°45N 48°28E 247 D6
Mīnā' al Aḩmadī Kuwait 29°5N 48°10E 247 D6
Minago → Canada 54°33N 98°59W 297 C9
Minakami Japan 36°49N 138°59E 223 A10
Minaki Canada 49°59N 94°40W 297 D10
Minakuchi Japan 34°58N 136°10E 223 C8
Minalungao △ Phil. 15°2N 121°8E 232 D3
Minamata Japan 32°10N 130°30E 222 E2
Minami Japan 34°40N 135°30E 133 A2
Minami-Arapusa △ Japan 35°30N 138°9E 223 B10
Minami-Tori-Shima Pac. Oc. 24°20N 153°58E 288 E7
Minamitsunashima Japan 35°32N 139°37E 140 B2
Minas Indonesia 0°50N 101°26E 234 B2
Minas Uruguay 34°20S 55°10W 335 C4
Minas, Sierra de las Guatemala 15°9N 89°31W 320 C2
Minas Basin Canada 45°20N 64°12W 299 C7
Minas de Riotinto Spain 37°42N 6°35W 195 H4
Minas Gerais □ Brazil 18°50S 46°0W 333 E2
Minas Novas Brazil 17°15S 42°36W 333 E3
Minatitlán Mexico 17°59N 94°31W 319 D6
Minato Ōsaka, Japan 34°39N 135°25E 133 B1
Minato Tokyo, Japan 140 c3
Minbu Burma 20°10N 94°52E 241 E5
Minbya Burma 20°22N 93°16E 241 E4
Minchinabad Pakistan 30°10N 73°34E 242 D5
Mincio → Italy 45°4N 10°59E 198 C7
Minčol Slovak Rep. 49°15N 20°58E 181 B13
Mindanao Phil. 8°0N 125°0E 233 H5
Mindanao Sea = Bohol Sea Phil. 9°0N 124°0E 233 G5
Mindanao Trench Pac. Oc. 12°0N 126°6E 232 E5
Mindel → Germany 48°31N 10°23E 179 G6
Mindelheim Germany 48°2N 10°29E 179 G6
Mindelo C. Verde Is. 16°24N 25°0W 153 j
Minden Ont., Canada 44°55N 78°43W 312 B6
Minden Nordrhein-Westfalen, Germany 52°17N 8°55E 178 C4
Minden La., U.S.A. 32°37N 93°17W 314 E8
Minden Nev., U.S.A. 38°57N 119°46W 306 G7
Mindibungu = Billiluna Australia 19°37S 127°41E 278 C4
Mindiptana Indonesia 5°55S 140°22E 231 F10
Mindon Burma 19°21N 94°44E 241 F5
Mindona L. Australia 33°6S 142°6E 282 B5
Mindoro Phil. 13°0N 121°0E 232 E3
Mindoro Occidental □ Phil. 13°0N 120°55E 232 E3
Mindoro Oriental □ Phil. 13°0N 121°25E 232 E3
Mindoro Str. Phil. 12°30N 120°30E 232 E3
Mindouli Congo 4°12S 14°28E 265 C2
Mindourou Cameroon 3°29N 13°26E 264 B2
Mine Japan 34°12N 131°7E 222 C3
Minehead U.K. 51°12N 3°29W 169 F4
Mineiros Brazil 17°34S 52°34W 331 D7
Mineola N.Y., U.S.A. 40°44N 73°38W 313 F11
Mineola Tex., U.S.A. 32°40N 95°29W 314 E7
Mineral Bath Jamaica 17°58N 76°22W 320 a
Mineral King U.S.A. 36°27N 118°36W 306 J8
Mineral Point U.S.A. 42°52N 90°11W 310 B6
Mineral Wells U.S.A. 32°48N 98°7W 314 E5
Mineralnyye Vody Russia 44°15N 43°8E 191 H6
Miners Bay Canada 44°49N 78°46W 312 B6
Minersville U.S.A. 40°41N 76°16W 313 F8
Minerva N.Y., U.S.A. 43°47N 73°59W 313 C11
Minerva Ohio, U.S.A. 40°44N 81°6W 312 F3
Minervino Murge Italy 41°5N 16°5E 201 A9
Minetto U.S.A. 43°24N 76°28W 313 C8
Minfeng China 37°4N 82°46E 217 E10
Ming-Kush Kyrgyzstan 41°40N 74°28E 217 D8
Mingäçevir Azerbaijan 40°45N 47°0E 191 K8
Mingäçevir Su Anbarı Azerbaijan 40°57N 46°50E 191 K8
Mingala C.A.R. 5°6N 21°49E 264 A4
Mingan Canada 50°20N 64°0W 299 B7
Mingary Australia 32°8S 140°45E 282 B4
Mingchien Taiwan 23°50N 120°42E 225 C2
Mingechaur = Mingäçevir Azerbaijan 40°45N 47°0E 191 K8
Mingechaurskoye Vdkhr. = Mingäçevir Su Anbarı Azerbaijan 40°57N 46°50E 191 K8
Mingela Australia 19°52S 146°38E 280 B4
Mingenew Australia 29°12S 115°21E 279 E2
Mingera Cr. → Australia 20°38S 137°45E 280 C2
Mingguang China 32°24N 117°3E 229 A11
Mingin Burma 22°50N 94°30E 241 D5
Mingir Moldova 46°40N 28°20E 183 D13
Minglanilla Spain 39°34N 1°38W 197 F3
Minglun China 25°10N 108°21E 228 E7
Mingo Congo 1°55S 15°1E 264 C3
Mingo Junction U.S.A. 40°19N 80°37W 312 F4
Mingora Pakistan 34°48N 72°22E 243 B5
Mingorria Spain 40°45N 4°40W 194 E6
Mingshan China 30°6N 103°10E 228 B4
Mingteke Daban = Mintaka Pass Pakistan 37°0N 74°58E 243 A6
Mingxi China 26°18N 117°12E 229 D11
Mingyuegue China 43°2N 128°50E 227 C15
Minhe China 36°9N 102°45E 218 D9
Minhla Magwe, Burma 19°58N 95°3E 241 F5
Minhla Pegu, Burma 17°59N 95°43E 241 G5
Minho = Miño → Spain 41°52N 8°40W 194 D2
Minhou China 26°0N 119°15E 229 E12
Minhsiung Taiwan 23°30N 120°35E 225 C2
Miničevo Serbia 43°42N 22°18E 182 G7
Minicoy I. India 8°17N 73°2E 245 K1
Minidoka U.S.A. 42°45N 113°29W 304 E7
Minier U.S.A. 40°26N 89°19W 310 D7
Minigwal, L. Australia 29°31S 123°14E 279 E3
Minilya → Australia 23°45S 114°0E 279 D1
Minilya Roadhouse Australia 23°55S 114°0E 279 D1
Mininera Australia 37°37S 142°58E 282 D5
Minipi L. Canada 52°25N 60°45W 299 B7
Minj Papua N. G. 5°54S 144°37E 286 C3
Minjilang Australia 11°8S 132°33E 278 B5
Mink L. Canada 61°54N 117°40W 296 A5
Minkammen South Sudan 6°3N 31°32E 257 F3
Minkebé Gabon 1°45N 12°45E 264 B2
Minlaton Australia 34°45S 137°35E 282 C2
Minna Nigeria 9°37N 6°30E 263 D6
Minna-shima Japan 26°39N 127°49E 288 a
Minneapolis Kans., U.S.A. 39°8N 97°42W 308 F5
Minneapolis Minn., U.S.A. 44°57N 93°16W 308 C7
Minnedosa Canada 50°14N 99°50W 297 C9
Minnesota □ U.S.A. 46°0N 94°15W 308 B6
Minnesota → U.S.A. 44°54N 93°9W 308 C7
Minnesund Norway 60°23N 11°14E 164 D8
Minnewaukan U.S.A. 48°4N 99°15W 308 A4
Minnipa Australia 32°51S 135°9E 281 E2
Minnitaki L. Canada 49°57N 92°10W 298 C1
Mino Japan 35°32N 136°55E 223 B8
Miño Spain 43°21N 8°12W 194 B2
Miño → Spain 41°52N 8°40W 194 D2
Mino-Kamo Japan 35°23N 137°2E 223 B9
Mino-Mikawa-Kōgen Japan 35°10N 137°23E 223 B9
Minoa Greece 35°6N 25°45E 205 F7
Minobu Japan 35°22N 138°26E 223 B10
Minobu-Sanchi Japan 35°14N 138°20E 223 B10
Minonk U.S.A. 40°54N 89°2W 310 D7
Minooka U.S.A. 41°27N 88°16W 311 C8
Minorca = Menorca Spain 40°0N 4°0E 206 B5
Minore Australia 32°14S 148°27E 283 B8
Minot U.S.A. 48°14N 101°18W 308 A3
Minqin China 38°38N 103°20E 226 E2
Minqing China 26°15N 118°50E 229 D12
Minsen Germany 53°41N 7°58E 178 B3
Minshât el Bekkari Egypt 30°0N 31°8E 117 A1
Minsk Belarus 53°52N 27°30E 177 B14
Minsk □ Belarus 53°15N 27°30E 188 F4
Mińsk Mazowiecki Poland 52°10N 21°33E 185 F8
Minster U.S.A. 40°24N 84°23W 311 D11
Mintabie Australia 27°15S 133°7E 281 D1
Mintaka Pass Pakistan 37°0N 74°58E 243 A6
Minthami Burma 23°55N 94°16E 241 D5
Minto N.B., Canada 46°5N 66°5W 299 C6
Minto Alaska, U.S.A. 64°53N 149°10W 303 D10
Minto, L. Canada 57°13N 75°0W 298 A5
Minton Canada 49°10N 104°35W 297 D8
Mintoum Gabon 0°27N 12°16E 264 B2
Minturn U.S.A. 39°35N 106°26W 304 G10
Minturno Italy 41°15N 13°45E 200 A6
Minudasht Iran 37°17N 56°7E 247 B8
Minûf Egypt 30°26N 30°52E 256 H7
Minusinsk Russia 53°43N 91°20E 217 B12
Minutang India 28°15N 96°30E 241 A6
Minvoul Gabon 2°9N 12°8E 264 B2
Minwakh Yemen 16°48N 48°6E 249 C5
Minya el Qamh Egypt 30°31N 31°21E 256 H7
Minya Konka = Gongga Shan China 29°40N 101°55E 228 C3
Minyip Australia 36°29S 142°36E 282 D5
Minzhong China 22°37N 113°30E 219 a
Mionica Bos.-H. 44°51N 18°29E 182 F3
Mionica Serbia 44°14N 20°6E 202 B4
Miquan China 43°58N 87°42E 217 D11
Miquelon Qué., Canada 49°25N 76°27W 298 C4
Miquelon St-P. & M. 47°8N 56°22W 299 C8
Mīr Niger 14°5N 11°59E 259 F2
Mīr Kūh Iran 26°22N 58°55E 247 E8
Mīr Shahdād Iran 26°15N 58°29E 247 E8
Mira Italy 45°26N 12°8E 199 C9
Mira Portugal 40°26N 8°44W 194 E2
Mira → Colombia 1°36N 79°1W 328 C2
Mira → Portugal 37°43N 8°47W 195 H2
Mira por vos Cay Bahamas 22°9N 74°30W 321 B5
Mīrābād Afghan. 30°25N 61°50E 240 D2
Mirabella Eclano Italy 41°2N 14°59E 201 A7
Mirabello, Kolpos Greece 35°10N 25°50E 207 E6
Miracema do Norte Brazil 9°33S 48°24W 332 C2
Mirador Brazil 6°22S 44°22W 332 C3
Mirador-Río Azul △ Guatemala 17°45N 89°50W 320 C1
Miraflores = Rovira Colombia 4°15N 75°20W 328 C2
Miraflores Colombia 1°25N 72°13W 328 C3
Miraflores Lima, Peru 12°7S 77°2W 124 B2
Miraflores, L. Panama 9°1N 79°36W 320 c
Miraflores Locks Panama 9°0N 79°36W 320 c
Miraj India 16°50N 74°45E 244 F2
Miram Shah Pakistan 33°0N 70°2E 242 C4
Miramar Argentina 38°15S 57°50W 334 D4
Miramar Mozam. 23°50S 35°35E 271 B6
Miramar N.Z. 41°18S 174°49E 143 B1
Miramas France 43°33N 4°59E 175 E8
Mirambeau France 45°23N 0°35W 174 C3
Miramichi Canada 47°2N 65°28W 299 C6
Miramichi B. Canada 47°15N 65°0W 299 C7
Miramont-de-Guyenne France 44°37N 0°21E 174 D4
Miranda Brazil 20°10S 56°15W 331 E6
Miranda □ Venezuela 10°15N 66°25W 328 A4
Miranda → Brazil 19°25S 57°20W 331 D6
Miranda de Ebro Spain 42°41N 2°57W 196 C2
Miranda do Corvo Portugal 40°6N 8°20W 194 E2
Miranda do Douro Portugal 41°30N 6°16W 194 D4
Mirande France 43°31N 0°25E 174 E4
Mirandela Portugal 41°32N 7°10W 194 D3
Mirándola Italy 44°53N 11°4E 198 D8
Mirandópolis Brazil 21°9S 51°6W 335 A5
Mirango Malawi 13°32S 34°58E 269 E3
Mirani Australia 21°8S 148°53E 280 b
Mirano Italy 45°30N 12°7E 199 C9
Miras Albania 40°30N 20°56E 202 F4
Mirassol Brazil 20°46S 49°28W 335 A6
Mirbāţ Oman 17°0N 54°45E 249 C6
Mirboo North Australia 38°24S 146°10E 283 E7
Mirear Egypt 23°15N 35°41E 256 C4
Mirebeau France 46°49N 0°10E 172 F7
Mirebeau-sur-Bèze France 47°25N 5°20E 173 E12
Mirecourt France 48°20N 6°10E 173 D13
Mires Greece 35°4N 24°56E 207 E5
Mirgorod = Myrhorod Ukraine 49°58N 33°37E 189 H7
Miri Malaysia 4°23N 113°59E 235 B4
Mirialguda India 16°52N 79°35E 244 F4
Miriam Vale Australia 24°20S 151°33E 280 C5
Miribel France 45°50N 4°57E 173 G11
Mirigama Sri Lanka 7°15N 80°8E 245 L5
Mirim, L. S. Amer. 32°45S 52°50W 335 C5
Mirimire Venezuela 11°10N 68°43W 328 A4
Miringi Comoros Is. 12°15S 43°38E 272 a
Miriti Brazil 6°15S 59°0W 331 B6
Miriuwung Gajerrong ✪ Australia 15°0S 128°45E 278 C4
Mirjāveh Iran 29°1N 61°30E 247 D9
Mirny Antarctica 66°50S 92°30E 151 C14
Mirnyy Russia 62°33N 113°53E 215 C12
Miroč Serbia 44°32N 22°16E 202 B6
Mirokhan Pakistan 27°46N 68°6E 242 F3
Mirond L. Canada 55°6N 102°47W 297 B8

Mirosławiec Poland 53°20N 16°5E 184 E3
Mirpur Pakistan 33°32N 73°56E 243 C5
Mirpur Batoro Pakistan 24°44N 68°16E 242 G3
Mirpur Bibiwari Pakistan 28°33N 67°44E 242 E2
Mirpur Khas Pakistan 25°30N 69°0E 242 G3
Mirpur Sakro Pakistan 24°33N 67°41E 242 G2
Mirria Niger 13°43N 9°7E 259 F1
Mirrool Australia 34°19S 147°10E 283 C7
Mirs Bay = Tai Pang Wan China 22°33N 114°24E 219 a
Mirsale Somali Rep. 5°57N 47°59E 267 C6
Mirsk Poland 50°58N 15°23E 185 H2
Mirtağ Turkey 38°23N 41°56E 246 B4
Mirtoo Sea Greece 37°0N 23°20E 204 D5
Mirtou, Kolpos Greece 38°20N 20°27E 207 C1
Miryang S. Korea 35°31N 128°44E 224 E4
Mirzaani Georgia 41°24N 46°5E 191 K8
Mirzachul = Guliston Uzbekistan 40°29N 68°46E 217 D7
Mirzapur India 25°10N 82°34E 243 G10
Mirzapur-cum-Vindhyachal = Mirzapur India 25°10N 82°34E 243 G10
Mirzoyan = Taraz Kazakhstan 42°54N 71°22E 217 D8
Misaki Japan 34°18N 135°9E 223 C7
Misamis = Ozamiz Phil. 8°15N 123°50E 233 G4
Misamis Occidental □ Phil. 8°20N 123°42E 233 G4
Misamis Oriental □ Phil. 8°45N 125°0E 233 G5
Misantla Mexico 19°56N 96°50W 319 D5
Misawa Japan 40°41N 141°24E 220 D10
Miscou I. Canada 47°57N 64°31W 299 C7
Misdroy = Międzyzdroje Poland 53°56N 14°26E 184 E1
Misericordia = Itaporanga Brazil 7°18S 38°0W 332 C4
Misericordia, Sa. da Brazil 22°51S 43°17W 135 B1
Misha India 7°59N 93°20E 245 L10
Mish'āb, Ra's al Si. Arabia 28°15N 48°43E 247 D6
Mishagua → Peru 11°12S 72°58W 330 C3
Mishamo Tanzania 5°41S 30°41E 268 D3
Mishan China 45°37N 131°48E 220 B5
Mishawaka U.S.A. 41°40N 86°11W 311 C10
Mishbih, Gebel Egypt 22°38N 34°44E 256 C3
Mishima Japan 35°10N 138°52E 223 B10
Mishmi Hills India 29°0N 96°0E 241 A6
Mishō Japan 32°57N 132°35E 222 E4
Misima I. Papua N. G. 10°40S 152°45E 286 F7
Misión Mexico 32°6N 116°53W 307 N10
Misión Fagnano Argentina 54°32S 67°17W 336 D3
Misiones □ Argentina 27°0S 55°0W 335 B5
Misiones □ Paraguay 27°0S 56°0W 334 B4
Miskah Si. Arabia 24°49N 42°56E 246 E4
Miski, E. → Chad 20°0N 17°55E 259 E3
Miskitos, Cayos Nic. 14°26N 82°50W 320 D3
Miskolc Hungary 48°7N 20°50E 182 B5
Misoke Dem. Rep. of the Congo 0°42S 28°2E 268 C2
Misool Indonesia 1°52S 130°10E 231 E8
Miṣr = Egypt ■ Africa 28°0N 31°0E 256 B3
Mişrātah Libya 32°24N 15°3E 258 B3
Mişrātah □ Libya 33°30N 15°0E 258 B3
Missanabie Canada 48°20N 84°6W 298 C3
Missão Catrimani Brazil 2°48N 62°18W 329 C5
Missão Velha Brazil 7°15S 39°10W 332 C4
Missinaibi → Canada 50°43N 81°29W 298 B3
Missinaibi L. Canada 48°23N 83°40W 298 C3
Mission B.C., Canada 49°10N 122°15W 296 D4
Mission Calif., U.S.A. 37°44N 122°25W 136 B2
Mission S. Dak., U.S.A. 43°18N 100°39W 308 D3
Mission Tex., U.S.A. 26°13N 98°20W 314 H5
Mission Beach Australia 17°53S 146°6E 280 B4
Mission Viejo U.S.A. 33°36N 117°40W 307 M9
Missirah Senegal 13°40N 16°30W 262 C1
Missisa L. Canada 52°20N 85°7W 298 B2
Missisicabi → Canada 51°14N 79°31W 298 B4
Mississagi → Canada 46°15N 83°9W 298 C3
Mississauga Canada 43°32N 79°35W 141 B1
Mississinewa L. U.S.A. 40°42N 85°52W 311 D10
Mississippi □ U.S.A. 33°0N 90°0W 315 E10
Mississippi → U.S.A. 29°9N 89°15W 310 E5
Mississippi L. Canada 45°5N 76°10W 313 A8
Mississippi River Delta U.S.A. 29°10N 89°15W 315 G10
Mississippi Sd. U.S.A. 30°20N 89°0W 315 F10
Missoula U.S.A. 46°52N 114°1W 304 C6
Missour Morocco 33°3N 4°0W 260 B4
Missouri □ U.S.A. 38°25N 92°30W 310 E3
Missouri → U.S.A. 38°49N 90°7W 310 F6
Missouri City U.S.A. 29°37N 95°32W 314 G7
Missouri Valley U.S.A. 41°34N 95°53W 308 E6
Mist U.S.A. 45°59N 123°15W 306 E3
Mistassibi → Canada 48°53N 72°13W 299 B5
Mistassini Canada 48°53N 72°12W 299 C5
Mistassini → Canada 48°42N 72°20W 299 C5
Mistassini, L. Canada 51°0N 73°30W 298 B5
Mistastin L. Canada 55°57N 63°20W 299 A7
Mistelbach Austria 48°34N 16°34E 181 C9
Misterbianco Italy 37°31N 15°1E 201 E8
Misteriosa Bank W. Indies 18°50N 83°50W 320 C3
Misti, Volcán Peru 16°18S 71°24W 330 D3
Mistinibi, L. Canada 55°56N 64°17W 299 A7
Mistissini Canada 48°53N 72°12W 299 C5
Mistretta Italy 37°56N 14°22E 201 E7
Misty Fjords Nat. Monument △ U.S.A. 55°40N 130°40W 303 J15
Misty L. Canada 58°53N 101°40W 297 B8
Misugi Japan 34°31N 136°16E 223 C8
Misumi Japan 32°37N 130°27E 222 E2
Misurata = Mişrātah Libya 32°24N 15°3E 258 B3
Mit Ghamr Egypt 30°42N 31°12E 256 H7
Mitaka Japan 35°41N 139°34E 142 A2
Mitande Mozam. 14°6S 35°58E 269 E4
Mitatib Sudan 15°59N 36°12E 257 D4
Mitau = Jelgava Latvia 56°41N 23°49E 184 B10
Mitava = Jelgava Latvia 56°41N 23°49E 184 B10
Mitcham U.K. 51°23N 0°10W 125 B2
Mitcham Common U.K. 51°23N 0°8W 125 B3
Mitchell Queens., Australia 26°29S 147°58E 281 D4
Mitchell Ont., Canada 43°28N 81°12W 312 C3
Mitchell Ga., U.S.A. 33°13N 82°42W 316 B7
Mitchell Ind., U.S.A. 38°44N 86°28W 311 F10
Mitchell Nebr., U.S.A. 41°57N 103°49W 308 E2
Mitchell Oreg., U.S.A. 44°34N 120°9W 304 D3
Mitchell S. Dak., U.S.A. 43°43N 98°2W 308 D4
Mitchell → Australia 15°12S 141°35E 280 B3
Mitchell, Mt. U.S.A. 35°46N 82°16W 315 D13
Mitchell-Alice Rivers △ Australia 15°28S 142°5E 280 B3
Mitchell Museum of the American Indian U.S.A. 42°4N 87°43W 119 A2
Mitchell Ra. Australia 12°49S 135°36E 280 A2
Mitchell River △ Australia 37°37S 147°22E 283 D7
Mitchell's Plain S. Africa 34°4S 18°35E 118 B2
Mitchelstown Ireland 52°15N 8°16W 168 D3
Mitha Tiwana Pakistan 32°13N 72°6E 242 C5
Mithi Pakistan 24°44N 69°48E 242 G3
Mithimna Greece 39°20N 26°12E 205 B8
Mithrao Pakistan 27°28N 69°40E 242 F3
Mitiamo Australia 36°12S 144°15E 282 D6
Mitikas Etoloakarnania, Greece 38°40N 20°56E 207 B2
Mitikas Preveza, Greece 39°0N 20°42E 207 B2
Mitilini Greece 39°6N 26°35E 205 B8
Mitilinii Greece 37°42N 26°56E 205 D8
Mitino Russia 55°51N 37°20E 129 A2
Mitla Pass = Mamarr Mitlā Egypt 30°2N 32°54E 251 H3
Mito Japan 36°20N 140°30E 223 A12
Mitra, Mt. Eq. Guin. 1°23N 9°19E 264 B1
Mitre, Mt. N.Z. 40°50S 175°30E 284 G4
Mitrofanovka Russia 49°58N 39°42E 189 H10
Mitrovica = Kosovska Mitrovica Kosovo 42°54N 20°52E 202 D4
Mitrowitz = Sremska Mitrovica Serbia 44°59N 19°38E 182 F4
Mitsamiouli Comoros Is. 11°20S 43°16E 272 a
Mitsang Gabon 0°42N 12°33E 264 B2
Mitsinjo Madag. 16°1S 45°52E 272 B2
Mitsiwa Eritrea 15°35N 39°25E 257 D4
Mitsiwa Channel Eritrea 15°30N 40°0E 257 D5
Mitsoudjé Comoros Is. 11°48S 43°16E 272 a
Mitsukaidō Japan 36°1N 139°59E 223 A11
Mitsushima Japan 34°15N 129°20E 222 C1
Mittagong Australia 34°28S 150°29E 283 C9
Mitte Germany 52°32N 13°24E 115 A3
Mittel Isarkanal → Germany 48°12N 11°40E 131 A3
Mittel Schreiberhau = Szklarska Poreba Poland 50°50N 15°33E 185 H2
Mittelberg Austria 47°20N 10°10E 180 D3
Mittelfranken □ Germany 49°25N 10°40E 179 F6
Mittellandkanal → Germany 52°20N 8°28E 178 C4
Mittelwalde = Międzylesie Poland 50°8N 16°40E 185 H3
Mittenwalde Germany 52°15N 13°31E 178 C9
Mittersill Austria 47°16N 12°29E 180 D5
Mitterteich Germany 49°57N 12°14E 179 F8
Mittimatalik = Pond Inlet Canada 72°40N 77°0W 295 C16
Mittweida Germany 50°59N 12°59E 178 E8
Mitú Colombia 1°15N 70°13W 328 C3
Mituas Colombia 3°52N 68°49W 328 C4
Mitumba Tanzania 7°8S 31°2E 268 D3
Mitumba, Mts. Dem. Rep. of the Congo 7°0S 27°30E 268 D2
Mitwaba Dem. Rep. of the Congo 8°2S 27°17E 269 D2
Mityana Uganda 0°23N 32°2E 268 B3
Mitzic Gabon 0°45N 11°40E 264 B2
Miura Japan 35°12N 139°40E 223 B11
Mixcoac Mexico 19°23N 99°11W 128 B1
Mixteco → Mexico 18°11N 98°30W 319 D5
Miyagi □ Japan 38°15N 140°45E 220 E10
Miyāh, W. el → Egypt 25°0N 33°23E 256 C3
Miyāh, W. el → Syria 34°44N 39°57E 246 C3
Miyake-Jima Japan 34°5N 139°30E 223 C11
Miyako Japan 39°40N 141°59E 220 E10
Miyako-Jima Japan 24°45N 125°20E 221 M2
Miyako-Rettō Japan 24°24N 125°0E 221 M2
Miyakojima Japan 34°42N 135°31E 133 A2
Miyakonojō Japan 31°40N 131°5E 222 F3
Miyān Rahan Iran 34°34N 47°26E 213 E12
Miyani India 21°50N 69°26E 242 J3
Miyanojō Japan 31°54N 130°27E 222 F2
Miyanoura-Dake Japan 30°20N 130°31E 221 J5
Miyata Japan 33°49N 130°42E 222 D2
Miyazaki Japan 31°56N 131°30E 222 F3
Miyazaki □ Japan 32°30N 131°30E 222 E3
Miyazu Japan 35°35N 135°10E 223 B7
Miyet, Bahr el = Dead Sea Asia 31°30N 35°30E 251 G6
Miyi China 26°47N 102°9E 228 D4
Miyoshi Japan 34°48N 132°51E 222 C4
Miyun China 40°28N 116°50E 226 D9
Miyun Shuiku China 40°30N 117°0E 227 D9
Mizan Teferi Ethiopia 6°57N 35°35E 257 F4
Mizdah Libya 31°30N 13°0E 258 B2
Mizdah □ Libya 31°26N 12°59E 258 B2
Mizen Hd. Cork, Ireland 51°27N 9°50W 166 E2
Mizen Hd. Wicklow, Ireland 52°51N 6°4W 166 D5
Mizhhirya Ukraine 48°32N 23°30E 183 B8
Mizhi China 37°47N 110°12E 226 F6
Mizil Romania 44°59N 26°29E 183 F11
Mizo Hills = Mizoram □ India 23°30N 92°40E 241 D4
Mizonokuchi Japan 35°35N 139°34E 140 B2
Mizoram □ India 23°30N 92°40E 241 D4
Mizpe Ramon Israel 30°34N 34°49E 251 H5
Mizue Japan 35°41N 139°54E 140 A4
Mizuho Antarctica 70°30S 41°0E 151 D5
Mizuho Japan 35°6N 135°17E 223 B7
Mizunami Japan 35°22N 137°15E 223 B9
Mizusawa Japan 39°8N 141°8E 220 E10
Mjällby Sweden 56°3N 14°40E 163 H8
Mjöbäck Sweden 57°28N 12°53E 163 G6
Mjölby Sweden 58°20N 15°10E 163 F9
Mjølfjell Norway 60°41N 6°55E 164 D3
Mjømna Norway 60°55N 4°55E 164 D1
Mjörn Sweden 57°55N 12°25E 163 G6
Mjøsa Norway 60°40N 11°0E 164 D8
Mkata Tanzania 5°45S 38°20E 268 D4
Mkhaya △ Swaziland 26°34S 31°45E 271 C5
Mkhuze △ S. Africa 29°27S 29°30E 271 C4
Mkokotoni Tanzania 5°55S 39°15E 268 D4
Mkomazi Tanzania 4°40S 38°7E 268 C4
Mkomazi → S. Africa 30°12S 30°50E 271 D5
Mkomazi △ Tanzania 4°4S 30°2E 268 C3
Mkulwe Tanzania 8°37S 32°20E 269 D3
Mkumbi, Ras Tanzania 7°38S 39°55E 268 D4
Mkushi Zambia 14°25S 29°15E 269 E2
Mkushi River Zambia 13°32S 29°45E 269 E2
Mkuze S. Africa 27°10S 32°0E 271 C5
Mladá Boleslav Czech Rep. 50°27N 14°53E 180 A7
Mladenovac Serbia 44°28N 20°44E 202 B4
Mlala Hills Tanzania 6°50S 31°40E 268 D3
M'lang Phil. 6°56N 124°52E 233 H5
Mlange = Mulanje, Mt. Malawi 16°2S 35°33E 269 F4
Mlava → Serbia 44°45N 21°13E 202 B5
Mława Poland 53°9N 20°25E 185 E7
Mlawula △ Swaziland 26°12S 32°2E 271 C5
Mliniště Bos.-H. 44°15N 16°50E 199 D13
Mljet Croatia 42°43N 17°30E 199 F14
Mljet △ Croatia 42°45N 17°25E 199 F14
Mljetski Kanal Croatia 42°48N 17°35E 199 F14
Mlocinski Park Poland 52°19N 20°57E 142 B1
Młociny Poland 52°18N 20°55E 142 B1
Młynary Poland 54°12N 19°46E 184 D6
Mmabatho S. Africa 25°49S 25°30E 270 C4
Mme Cameroon 6°18N 10°14E 263 D7
Mnevniki Russia 55°45N 37°28E 129 B2
Mnichovo Hradiště Czech Rep. 50°32N 14°59E 180 A7
Mo Hordaland, Norway 60°49N 5°48E 164 D2
Mo Møre og Romsdal, Norway 63°0N 8°59E 164 A5
Mo Telemark, Norway 59°28N 7°50E 164 E4
Mo i Rana Norway 66°20N 14°7E 160 C16
Moa Queens., Australia 10°11S 142°16E 280 a
Moa Cuba 20°40N 74°56W 321 B4
Moa Indonesia 8°0S 128°0E 231 F7
Moa → S. Leone 6°59N 11°36W 262 D2
Moab U.S.A. 38°35N 109°33W 304 G9
Moabi Gabon 2°24S 10°59E 264 C2
Moaco → Brazil 7°41S 68°18W 330 B4
Moala Fiji 18°36S 179°53E 287 B2
Moama Australia 36°7S 144°46E 281 F3
Moamba Mozam. 25°36S 32°15E 271 C5
Moapa U.S.A. 36°40N 114°37W 307 J12
Moate Ireland 53°24N 7°44W 166 C4
Moba Dem. Rep. of the Congo 7°0S 29°48E 268 D2
Moba Lagos, Nigeria 6°26N 3°28E 124 B2
Mobara Japan 35°25N 140°18E 223 B12
Mobārakābād Iran 28°24N 53°20E 247 D7
Mobaye C.A.R. 4°25N 21°5E 264 B4
Mobayi Dem. Rep. of the Congo 4°15N 21°8E 264 B4
Mobeka Dem. Rep. of the Congo 1°52N 19°49E 264 B3
Mobenzélé Congo 0°56N 17°50E 264 B3
Moberly U.S.A. 39°25N 92°26W 310 E4
Moberly Lake Canada 55°50N 121°44W 296 B4
Mobile U.S.A. 30°41N 88°3W 315 F10
Mobile B. U.S.A. 30°30N 88°0W 315 F11
Mobridge U.S.A. 45°32N 100°26W 308 C3
Mobutu Sese Seko, L. = Albert, L. Africa 1°30N 31°0E 268 B3
Moc Chau Vietnam 20°50N 104°38E 236 B5
Moc Hoa Vietnam 10°46N 105°56E 237 G5
Moca Puerto Rico 18°24N 67°10W 321 b
Mocabe Kasari Dem. Rep. of the Congo 9°58S 26°12E 269 D2
Mocajuba Brazil 2°35S 49°30W 332 B2
Moçambique = Mozambique ■ Africa 19°0S 35°0E 269 F4
Moçambique Mozam. 15°3S 40°42E 269 F5
Moçâmedes = Namibe Angola 15°7S 12°11E 265 F2
Mocanaqua U.S.A. 41°9N 76°8W 313 E8
Mocapra → Venezuela 7°56N 66°46W 328 B4
Mocco, Morro de Angola 12°28S 15°11E 265 E3
Moce Fiji 18°40S 178°29W 287 B3
Mocha = Al Mukhā Yemen 13°18N 43°15E 248 D3
Mocha, I. Chile 38°22S 73°56W 336 A2
Mochos Greece 35°16N 25°27E 207 E6
Mochudi Botswana 24°27S 26°7E 270 B4
Mocimboa da Praia Mozam. 11°25S 40°20E 269 E5
Mociu Romania 46°46N 24°3E 183 D9
Möckeln Sweden 56°40N 14°15E 163 H8
Mockfjärd Sweden 60°30N 14°57E 162 D8
Moclips U.S.A. 47°14N 124°13W 306 C2
Mocoa Colombia 1°7N 76°35W 328 C2
Mococa Brazil 21°28S 47°0W 335 A6
Mocorito Mexico 25°29N 107°55W 318 B3
Moctezuma Mexico 29°48N 109°42W 318 B3
Moctezuma → Mexico 21°59N 98°34W 319 C5
Mocuba Mozam. 16°54S 36°57E 269 F4
Moczydło Poland 52°8N 21°12E 142 C2
Moda Burma 24°22N 96°29E 241 C6
Modane France 45°12N 6°40E 175 C10
Modasa India 23°30N 73°21E 242 H5
Modder → S. Africa 29°2S 24°37E 270 C3
Modderfontein = Niekerkshoop S. Africa 29°19S 22°51E 270 C3
Modderfontein S. Africa 26°5S 28°10E 123 A2
Modderrivier S. Africa 29°2S 24°38E 270 C3
Módena Italy 44°40N 10°55E 198 D7
Modena Utah, U.S.A. 37°48N 113°56W 305 H7
Modernamuseet Stockholm, Sweden 139 b3
Modesto U.S.A. 37°39N 121°0W 306 H6
Möðrudalur Iceland 65°22N 15°53W 155 B11
Möðruvellir Iceland 65°46N 18°15W 155 B8
Módica Italy 36°52N 14°46E 201 F7
Modimolle S. Africa 24°42S 28°22E 271 B4
Modjadjiskloof S. Africa 23°42S 30°10E 271 B5
Modjamboli Dem. Rep. of the Congo 2°28N 22°6E 264 B4
Mödling Austria 48°5N 16°17E 181 C9
Modo South Sudan 5°31N 30°33E 257 F3
Modoc U.S.A. 33°44N 82°13W 316 B7
Modra Slovak Rep. 48°19N 17°20E 181 C10
Modřany Czech Rep. 50°0N 14°24E 125 B2
Modriča Bos.-H. 44°57N 18°17E 182 F3
Moe Australia 38°12S 146°19E 283 E7
Moebase Mozam. 17°3S 38°41E 269 F4
Moëlan-sur-Mer France 47°49N 3°38W 172 E3
Moelv Norway 60°56N 10°43E 164 D7
Moen I. = Weno Pac. Oc. 7°27N 151°52E 287 T18
Moengo Suriname 5°45N 54°20W 329 B7
Moerewa N.Z. 35°8S 174°1E 284 B3
Moffat U.K. 55°21N 3°27W 167 F5
Moga India 30°48N 75°8E 242 D6
Mogadishu = Muqdisho Somali Rep. 2°2N 45°25E 267 D6
Mogador = Essaouira Morocco 31°32N 9°42W 260 B3
Mogadouro Portugal 41°22N 6°47W 194 D4
Mogalakwena → S. Africa 22°38S 28°40E 271 B4
Mogami-Gawa → Japan 38°45N 140°0E 220 E10
Mogán Canary Is. 27°53N 15°43W 153 e1
Mogandjo Dem. Rep. of the Congo 1°23N 24°15E 264 B4
Mogaung Burma 25°20N 97°0E 241 C6
Mogen Norway 60°2N 7°52E 164 D4
Mogente = Moixent Spain 38°52N 0°45W 197 G4
Mogho Ethiopia 4°54N 40°16E 257 G5
Mogielnica Poland 51°42N 20°41E 185 G7
Mogila Ethiopia 5°24N 36°14E 257 F4
Mogilev = Mahilyow Belarus 53°55N 30°18E 177 B16
Mogilev-Podolskiy = Mohyliv-Podilskyy Ukraine 48°26N 27°48E 183 B12
Mogilno Poland 52°39N 17°55E 185 F4
Mogincual Mozam. 15°35S 40°25E 269 F5
Mogliano Véneto Italy 45°33N 12°14E 199 C9
Mogocha Russia 53°40N 119°50E 215 D12
Mogoditshane Botswana 24°37S 25°51E 270 B4
Mogok Burma 23°0N 96°40E 241 D6
Mogollon Rim U.S.A. 34°10N 110°50W 305 J8
Mógoro Italy 39°41N 8°47E 200 C1
Mograt Sudan 19°28N 33°16E 256 D3
Mogroum Chad 11°6N 15°25E 259 F3
Moguer Spain 37°15N 6°52W 195 H4
Mogumber Australia 31°2S 116°3E 279 F2
Mogwadi → S. Africa 23°4S 29°36E 271 B4
Mogyoród Hungary 47°35N 19°14E 117 A3
Mohács Hungary 45°58N 18°41E 182 E3
Mohaka → N.Z. 39°7S 177°12E 284 F6
Mohala India 20°35N 80°44E 244 D5
Mohales Hoek Lesotho 30°7S 27°26E 270 D4
Mohali Congo 0°15N 15°29E 264 B3
Mohall U.S.A. 48°46N 101°31W 308 A3
Moḩammadābād Iran 37°52N 59°5E 247 B8
Mohammadia Algeria 35°33N 0°3E 261 A5
Mohammedia Morocco 33°44N 7°21W 260 B3
Mohammerah = Khorrāmshahr Iran 30°29N 48°15E 247 D6
Mohana India 19°27N 84°16E 244 E7
Mohana → India 24°43N 85°0E 243 G11
Mohanganj Bangla. 24°54N 90°59E 241 C3
Mohanlalganj India 26°41N 80°58E 243 F9
Mohave, L. U.S.A. 35°12N 114°34W 307 K12
Mohawk → U.S.A. 42°47N 73°41W 313 D11
Moheda Sweden 57°1N 14°35E 163 G8
Mohéli Comoros Is. 12°20S 43°40E 272 a
Mohéli ✗ (NWA) Comoros Is. 12°19S 43°47E 272 a
Mohenjodaro Pakistan 27°19N 68°7E 242 F3
Moher, Cliffs of Ireland 52°58N 9°27W 166 D2
Mohican, C. U.S.A. 60°12N 167°25W 303 F6
Mohicanville Res. U.S.A. 40°45N 82°9W 312 F2
Möhne → Germany 51°29N 7°57E 178 D3
Mohns Ridge Arctic 72°30N 5°0W 150 B7
Mohnyin Burma 24°47N 96°22E 241 C6
Mohoro Tanzania 8°6S 39°8E 268 D4
Mohrin = Moryń Poland 52°51N 14°22E 185 F1
Mohsenābād Iran 36°40N 59°35E 247 B8
Mohyliv-Podilskyy Ukraine 48°26N 27°48E 183 B12
Moi Norway 58°27N 6°32E 164 F3
Moia South Sudan 5°3N 28°2E 257 F2
Moidart, L. U.K. 56°47N 5°52W 167 E3
Moinabad India 17°44N 77°16E 244 F3
Moinești Romania 46°28N 26°31E 183 D11
Moinho Velho, Cor. → Brazil 23°35S 46°35W 137 B2
Moira → Canada 44°21N 77°24W 312 B7
Moirang India 24°30N 93°46E 241 C4
Moirans France 45°20N 5°33E 175 C9
Moirans-en-Montagne France 46°26N 5°43E 173 F12
Moisaküla Estonia 58°3N 25°12E 188 C3
Moisie Canada 50°12N 66°1W 299 B6
Moisie → Canada 50°14N 66°5W 299 B6
Moissac France 44°7N 1°5E 174 D5
Moïssala Chad 8°21N 17°46E 259 G3
Moita Portugal 38°38N 8°58W 195 G2
Moixent Spain 38°52N 0°45W 197 G4
Möja Sweden 59°26N 18°55E 162 E12
Mojácar Spain 37°6N 1°55W 197 H3
Mojados Spain 41°26N 4°40W 194 D6
Mojave U.S.A. 35°3N 118°10W 307 K8
Mojave △ U.S.A. 35°7N 115°32W 307 K11
Mojave Desert U.S.A. 35°0N 116°30W 307 L10
Moji das Cruzes Brazil 23°31S 46°11W 335 A6
Moji-Guaçu Brazil 22°22S 46°57W 333 F2
Moji-Guaçu → Brazil 20°53S 48°10W 335 A6
Mojiang China 23°37N 101°35E 228 F3
Mojjo → Ethiopia 7°55N 42°0E 257 F5
Mojkovac Montenegro 42°58N 19°35E 202 D3
Mojo Bolivia 21°48S 65°33W 334 A2
Mojo Ethiopia 8°35N 39°5E 257 F4
Mojokerto Indonesia 7°28S 112°26E 235 D4
Mojos, Llanos de Bolivia 15°10S 65°0W 331 D5
Moju Brazil 1°53S 48°46W 332 B2
Moju → Brazil 1°40S 48°25W 332 B2
Mok S. Korea 37°32N 126°52E 137 B1
Moka Mauritius 20°13S 57°29E 272 e
Mokai N.Z. 38°32S 175°56E 284 E4
Mokala △ S. Africa 29°10S 24°10E 270 C3
Mokambo Dem. Rep. of the Congo 12°25S 28°20E 269 E2
Mokameh India 25°24N 85°55E 243 G11
Mokane U.S.A. 38°41N 91°53W 310 F5
Mōkapu Peninsula U.S.A. 21°25N 157°45W 302 K14
Mokau N.Z. 38°42S 174°39E 284 E3
Mokau → N.Z. 38°35S 174°35E 284 E3
Mokelumne → U.S.A. 38°13N 121°28W 306 G5
Mokelumne Hill U.S.A. 38°18N 120°43W 306 G6
Mokhotlong Lesotho 29°22S 29°2E 271 C4
Mokihinui → N.Z. 41°33S 171°58E 285 B6
Möklinta Sweden 60°4N 16°33E 162 D10
Moknine Tunisia 35°35N 10°58E 258 A2
Mokoan, L. Australia 36°27S 146°5E 283 D7
Mokokchung India 26°15N 94°30E 241 B5
Mōkōlea Rock U.S.A. 21°27N 157°44W 302 K14
Mokolo Cameroon 10°49N 13°54E 259 F2
Mokolo Dem. Rep. of the Congo 1°55N 18°6E 264 B3
Mokolo → S. Africa 23°14S 27°43E 271 B4
Mokombe Dem. Rep. of the Congo 0°14S 23°48E 264 C4
Mokopane S. Africa 24°10S 28°55E 271 B4
Mokotów Poland 52°12N 21°0E 142 B2
Mokpalin Burma 17°26N 96°53E 241 G6
Mokpo S. Korea 34°50N 126°25E 224 E3
Mokra Gora Europe 42°50N 20°30E 202 D4
Mokronog Slovenia 45°57N 15°9E 199 C12
Moksha → Russia 54°45N 41°53E 190 C6
Mokshan Russia 53°25N 44°35E 190 D7
Mokuauia I. U.S.A. 21°40N 157°56W 302 J14
Mokulē'ia U.S.A. 21°35N 158°9W 302 J13
Mokulua Is. U.S.A. 21°24N 157°42W 302 K14
Mokumanu U.S.A. 21°28N 157°43W 302 K14
Mokwa Nigeria 9°19N 5°0E 263 D6
Mol Belgium 51°11N 5°5E 170 C5
Mola di Bari Italy 41°4N 17°5E 201 A10
Molai Greece 36°49N 22°56E 204 E4
Molakalmuru India 14°55N 76°50E 245 G3
Molale Ethiopia 10°10N 39°41E 257 E4
Molaly Kazakhstan 45°27N 78°18E 217 C9
Molanda Dem. Rep. of the Congo 2°28N 20°48E 264 B4
Molara Italy 40°52N 9°43E 200 B2
Molat Croatia 44°15N 14°50E 199 D11
Molave Phil. 8°5N 123°30E 233 G4
Molchanovo Russia 57°40N 83°50E 214 D9
Mold U.K. 53°9N 3°8W 168 D4
Moldava nad Bodvou Slovak Rep. 48°38N 21°0E 181 C14
Moldavia = Moldova ■ Europe 47°0N 28°0E 183 C13
Moldavia Romania 46°30N 27°0E 183 D12
Molde Norway 62°45N 7°9E 164 B4
Moldova ■ Europe 47°0N 28°0E 183 C13
Moldova Nouă Romania 44°45N 21°41E 182 F6
Moldoveanu, Vf. Romania 45°36N 24°45E 183 E9
Moldovița Romania 47°41N 25°32E 183 C10
Mole → U.K. 51°24N 0°21W 169 F7
Mole △ Ghana 9°43N 1°44W 263 D4
Molegbwe Dem. Rep. of the Congo 4°12N 20°53E 264 B4
Molenbeek-St-Jean Belgium 50°51N 4°19E 116 A1
Molepolole Botswana 24°28S 25°28E 270 B4
Molesworth N.Z. 42°5S 173°16E 285 C8
Molfetta Italy 41°12N 16°36E 201 A9
Mōli'i Pond U.S.A. 21°31N 157°51W 302 J14
Molina de Aragón Spain 40°46N 1°52W 196 E3
Molina de Segura Spain 38°3N 1°12W 197 G3
Moline U.S.A. 41°30N 90°31W 310 C6
Molinella Italy 44°37N 11°40E 199 D8
Molino U.S.A. 30°43N 87°20W 317 E2
Molino de Rosas Mexico 19°21N 99°14W 128 B1
Molinos Argentina 25°28S 66°15W 334 B2
Moliro Dem. Rep. of the Congo 8°12S 30°30E 268 D3
Moliterno Italy 40°14N 15°52E 201 B8
Molkom Sweden 59°37N 13°44E 162 E7
Mölle Sweden 56°17N 12°31E 163 H6
Molledo Spain 43°8N 4°6W 194 B6
Mollem Belgium 50°56N 4°13E 116 A1
Mollendo Peru 17°0S 72°0W 330 D3
Mollerin, L. Australia 30°30S 117°35E 279 F2
Mollerussa Spain 41°37N 0°54E 196 D5
Mollina Spain 37°8N 4°38W 195 H6
Mollins de Rey Spain 41°24N 2°1E 114 A1
Mölln Germany 53°39N 10°42E 178 B6
Mölltorp Sweden 58°30N 14°26E 163 F8
Mölndal Sweden 57°40N 12°3E 163 G5
Mölnlycke Sweden 57°40N 12°8E 163 G6
Molo Burma 23°22N 96°53E 241 D6
Molo Rift Valley, Kenya 0°15S 35°44E 268 C4
Molochansk Ukraine 47°15N 35°35E 189 J8
Molochnoye, Ozero Ukraine 46°30N 35°20E 189 J8
Molodechno = Maladzyechna Belarus 54°20N 26°50E 177 A14
Molodezhnaya Antarctica 67°40S 45°51E 151 C9
Molodove Ukraine 46°13N 29°39E 183 D14
Moloka'i U.S.A. 21°8N 157°0W 302 B4
Molokai Fracture Zone Pac. Oc. 28°0N 125°0W 289 E15
Molokini I. U.S.A. 20°38N 156°30W 302 C5
Molong Australia 33°5S 148°54E 283 B8
Molopo → Africa 28°30S 20°12E 270 C3
Molos Greece 38°47N 22°37E 204 C4
Molotov = Perm Russia 58°0N 56°10E 186 C10
Molotov, Mys = Arkticheskiy, Mys Russia 81°10N 95°0E 215 A10
Molotovsk = Nolinsk Russia 57°28N 49°57E 190 B9
Molotovsk = Severodvinsk Russia 64°27N 39°58E 186 B6
Molotovskoye = Krasnogvardeyskoye Russia 45°52N 41°33E 191 H5
Moloundou Cameroon 2°8N 15°15E 264 B3
Molowaie Dem. Rep. of the Congo 5°47S 23°18E 265 D4
Molsheim France 48°33N 7°29E 173 D14
Molson L. Canada 54°22N 96°40W 297 C9
Molteno S. Africa 31°22S 26°22E 270 D4
Molu Indonesia 6°45S 131°40E 231 F8
Molucca Sea Indonesia 0°0 125°0E 231 E6
Moluccas = Maluku Indonesia 1°0S 127°0E 231 E7
Molundo Phil. 7°57N 124°23E 233 H5
Moma Dem. Rep. of the Congo 1°35S 23°52E 264 C4
Moma Mozam. 16°47S 39°4E 269 F4
Momba Australia 30°58S 143°30E 282 A5
Mombaça Brazil 5°43S 39°45W 332 C4
Mombango Dem. Rep. of the Congo 1°45N 24°26E 264 B4
Mombasa Kenya 4°3S 39°40E 268 C4
Mombetsu Japan 44°21N 143°22E 220 B11
Mombil Burma 27°46N 98°6E 241 B7
Momboyo → Dem. Rep. of the Congo 0°16S 19°0E 264 C3
Mombuey Spain 42°3N 6°20W 194 C4
Momchilgrad Bulgaria 41°33N 25°23E 203 E9
Momence U.S.A. 41°10N 87°40W 311 C9
Momi Dem. Rep. of the Congo 1°42S 27°0E 268 C2
Momote Papua N. G. 2°4S 147°27E 286 B4
Mompog Pass. Phil. 13°34N 122°13E 232 E4
Mompós Colombia 9°14N 74°26W 328 B3
Møn Denmark 54°57N 12°20E 163 K6
Møn Hordaland, Norway 60°37N 6°31E 164 D3
Mon □ Burma 16°0N 97°30E 241 G6
Mona, Canal de la = Mona Passage W. Indies 18°30N 67°45W 321 C6
Mona, Isla Puerto Rico 18°5N 67°54W 321 C6
Mona, Pta. Costa Rica 9°37N 82°36W 320 E3
Mona Passage W. Indies 18°30N 67°45W 321 C6
Mona Quimbundo Angola 9°55S 19°58E 265 D3
Monaca U.S.A. 40°41N 80°17W 312 F4
Monaco ■ Europe 43°46N 7°23E 175 E11
Monadhliath Mts. U.K. 57°10N 4°4W 167 D4
Monadnock, Mt. U.S.A. 42°52N 72°7W 313 D12
Monagas □ Venezuela 9°20N 63°0W 329 B5
Monaghan Ireland 54°15N 6°57W 166 B5
Monaghan □ Ireland 54°11N 6°56W 166 B5
Monahans U.S.A. 31°36N 102°54W 314 F3
Monapo Mozam. 14°56S 40°19E 269 E5
Monar, L. U.K. 57°26N 5°8W 167 D3
Monaragala Sri Lanka 6°52N 81°22E 245 L5
Monarch Mt. Canada 51°55N 125°57W 296 C3
Monashee Mts. Canada 51°0N 118°43W 296 C5
Monasterevin Ireland 53°8N 7°4W 166 C4
Monastir = Bitola Macedonia 41°1N 21°20E 202 E5
Monastir Tunisia 35°50N 10°49E 258 A2
Monastir □ Tunisia 35°37N 10°45E 261 A7
Monbetsu Japan 42°30N 142°10E 220 C11
Moncalieri Italy 45°0N 7°41E 198 D4
Moncalvo Italy 45°3N 8°16E 198 C5
Moncão Portugal 42°4N 8°27W 194 C2
Moncarapacho Portugal 37°5N 7°46W 195 H3
Moncayo, Sierra del Spain 41°48N 1°50W 196 D3
Moncha-Guba = Monchegorsk Russia 67°54N 32°58E 160 C25
Monchegorsk Russia 67°54N 32°58E 160 C25
Mönchengladbach Germany 51°11N 6°27E 178 D2
Monchique Portugal 37°19N 8°38W 195 H2
Moncks Corner U.S.A. 33°12N 80°1W 316 B9
Monclova Mexico 26°54N 101°25W 318 B4
Moncontour France 48°22N 2°38W 172 D4
Moncton Canada 46°7N 64°51W 299 C7
Mondariz Spain 42°14N 8°27W 194 C2
Mondego → Portugal 40°9N 8°52W 194 E2
Mondego, C. Portugal 40°11N 8°54W 194 E2
Mondeodo Indonesia 3°34S 122°9E 231 E6
Mondeor S. Africa 26°16S 28°0E 123 B2
Mondeville France 49°10N 0°18W 172 C6
Mondimbi Dem. Rep. of the Congo 1°48N 22°46E 264 B4
Mondjuku Dem. Rep. of the Congo 1°41S 21°12E 264 C4
Mondlo S. Africa 27°59S 30°43E 271 C5
Mondo Chad 13°47N 15°32E 259 F3
Mondolfo Italy 43°45N 13°6E 199 E10
Mondoñedo Spain 43°25N 7°23W 194 B3
Mondovì Italy 44°23N 7°49E 198 D4
Mondragó Spain 39°21N 3°12E 206 B10
Mondragon = Arrasate Spain 43°4N 2°30W 196 B2
Mondragon Phil. 12°31N 124°45E 232 E5
Mondragone Italy 41°7N 13°53E 200 A6
Mondrain I. Australia 34°9S 122°14E 279 F3
Moneague Jamaica 18°16N 77°7W 320 a
Moneda, Palacio de la Chile 33°26S 70°39W 137 B2
Monemvasia Greece 36°41N 23°3E 204 E5
Moneró Brazil 22°48S 43°11W 135 A1
Moneron, Ostrov Russia 46°15N 141°16E 220 A10
Monessen U.S.A. 40°9N 79°54W 312 F5
Monesterio Spain 38°6N 6°15W 195 G4
Monestier-de-Clermont France 44°55N 5°38E 175 D9
Monett U.S.A. 36°55N 93°55W 308 G7
Moneymore U.K. 54°41N 6°40W 166 B5
Monfalcone Italy 45°49N 13°32E 199 C10
Monflanquin France 44°32N 0°47E 174 D4
Monforte Portugal 39°6N 7°25W 195 F3
Monforte de Lemos Spain 42°31N 7°33W 194 C3
Mong Hpayak Burma 20°52N 99°55E 236 B2
Mong Hsat Burma 20°31N 99°15E 236 B2
Mong Hsu Burma 21°54N 98°30E 228 G2
Mong Hta Burma 19°50N 98°35E 241 F7
Mong Ket Burma 23°8N 98°22E 241 D7
Mong Kok China 22°19N 114°10E 122 B2
Mong Kung Burma 21°35N 97°35E 241 E6
Mong Kyawt Burma 19°56N 98°45E 241 F7
Mong Long Burma 22°47N 96°37E 241 D6
Mong Mit Burma 23°7N 96°41E 241 D6
Mong Nai Burma 20°32N 97°46E 241 E6
Mong Pan Burma 20°19N 98°22E 241 E7
Mong Ping Burma 21°22N 99°2E 228 G2
Mong Pu Burma 20°55N 98°44E 241 E7
Mong Ton Burma 20°17N 98°45E 241 E7
Mong Tung Burma 22°2N 97°41E 241 D6
Mong Yai Burma 22°21N 98°3E 241 D7
Mong Yang Burma 21°50N 99°41E 236 B2
Mong Yu Burma 23°30N 97°47E 241 D6
Monga Dem. Rep. of the Congo 4°12N 22°49E 264 B4
Mongala → Dem. Rep. of the Congo 1°53N 19°46E 264 B3
Mongalla South Sudan 5°8N 31°42E 257 F3
Mongandia Congo 0°45N 17°11E 264 B3
Mongers, L. Australia 29°25S 117°5E 279 E2
Mongga Solomon Is. 7°52S 157°0E 287 L9
Monghyr = Munger India 25°23N 86°30E 243 G12
Mongibello = Etna Italy 37°50N 14°55E 201 E7
Mongla Bangla. 22°8N 89°35E 241 D2
Mongmong Guam 13°28N 144°45E 302 d
Mongngaw Burma 22°47N 96°59E 241 D6
Mongo Chad 12°14N 18°43E 259 F3
Mongó Eq. Guin. 1°52N 10°10E 264 B2
Mongo → S. Leone 9°35N 12°10W 262 D2
Mongolia ■ Asia 47°0N 103°0E 218 B9
Mongolia, Plateau of Asia 45°0N 105°0E 210 D12
Mongomo Eq. Guin. 1°38N 11°19E 264 B2
Mongonu Nigeria 12°40N 13°32E 263 C7
Mongororo Chad 12°3N 22°26E 259 F4
Mongstad Norway 60°49N 5°2E 164 D2
Mongu Zambia 15°16S 23°12E 265 F4
Mônguá Angola 16°43S 15°20E 265 F3
Moniac U.S.A. 30°31N 82°14W 316 E7
Monifieth U.K. 56°30N 2°48W 167 E6
Monistrol-sur-Loire France 45°17N 4°11E 175 C8
Monkayo Phil. 7°50N 126°5E 233 H6
Monkey Bay Malawi 14°7S 35°1E 269 E4
Monkey Mia Australia 25°48S 113°43E 279 E1
Monkey River Belize 16°22N 88°29W 320 C2
Monkey Town Trin. & Tob. 10°12N 61°25W 323 t
Mońki Poland 53°23N 22°48E 184 E9
Monkland Canada 45°11N 74°52W 313 A10
Monkoto Dem. Rep. of the Congo 1°38S 20°35E 264 C4
Monkstown Ireland 53°18N 6°10W 120 B3
Monkton Canada 43°35N 81°5W 312 C3
Monmouth Monmouths., U.K. 51°48N 2°42W 169 F5
Monmouth Ill., U.S.A. 40°55N 90°39W 310 D6
Monmouth Oreg., U.S.A. 44°51N 123°14W 304 D2
Monmouthshire □ U.K. 51°48N 2°54W 169 F5
Monnickendam Neths. 52°28N 5°2E 112 A3
Mono Solomon Is. 7°20S 155°35E 287 L8
Mono → Togo 6°17N 1°51E 263 D5
Mono, Pta. Nic. 12°0N 83°30W 320 D3
Mono L. U.S.A. 38°1N 119°1W 306 H7
Monolith U.S.A. 35°7N 118°22W 307 K8
Monolithos Greece 36°7N 27°45E 206 E11
Monon U.S.A. 40°52N 86°53W 311 D10
Monona Iowa, U.S.A. 43°3N 91°23W 310 A5
Monona Wis., U.S.A. 43°4N 89°20W 310 A7
Monongahela U.S.A. 40°12N 79°56W 312 F5
Monópoli Italy 40°57N 17°18E 201 B10
Monor Hungary 47°21N 19°27E 182 C4
Monos I. Trin. & Tob. 10°42N 61°44W 323 t
Monóvar Spain 38°28N 0°53W 197 G4
Monowai N.Z. 45°53S 167°31E 285 F2
Monowai, L. N.Z. 45°53S 167°25E 285 F2
Monqoumba C.A.R. 3°33N 18°40E 264 B3
Monreal del Campo Spain 40°47N 1°20W 196 E3
Monreale Italy 38°5N 13°17E 200 D6
Monroe Ga., U.S.A. 33°47N 83°43W 316 B6
Monroe Iowa, U.S.A. 41°31N 93°6W 310 C3
Monroe La., U.S.A. 32°30N 92°7W 314 E8
Monroe Mich., U.S.A. 41°55N 83°24W 311 C13
Monroe N.C., U.S.A. 34°59N 80°33W 315 D14
Monroe N.Y., U.S.A. 41°20N 74°11W 313 E10
Monroe Ohio, U.S.A. 39°27N 84°22W 311 E12
Monroe Utah, U.S.A. 38°38N 112°7W 304 G7
Monroe Wash., U.S.A. 47°51N 121°58W 306 C5
Monroe Wis., U.S.A. 42°36N 89°38W 310 B7
Monroe, L. U.S.A. 28°50N 81°19W 317 G8
Monroe City Ind., U.S.A. 38°37N 87°20W 311 F9
Monroe City Mo., U.S.A. 39°39N 91°44W 310 E5
Monroe L. U.S.A. 39°1N 86°31W 311 E10
Monroeton U.S.A. 41°43N 76°29W 313 E8
Monroeville Ala., U.S.A. 31°31N 87°20W 315 F11
Monroeville Ind., U.S.A. 40°59N 84°52W 311 D12
Monroeville Pa., U.S.A. 40°26N 79°45W 312 F5
Monrovia Liberia 6°18N 10°47W 262 D2
Monrovia Calif., U.S.A. 34°9N 118°1W 126 B4
Mons Belgium 50°27N 3°58E 170 D3
Møns Klint Denmark 54°57N 12°33E 163 K6
Monsanto Portugal 38°44N 9°12W 126 A1
Monsanto, Parque Florestal de Portugal 38°43N 9°11W 126 A1
Monsaraz Portugal 38°28N 7°22W 195 G3
Monse Indonesia 4°7S 123°15E 231 E6
Monsefú Peru 6°52S 79°52W 330 B2
Monségur France 44°38N 0°4E 174 D4
Monsélice Italy 45°14N 11°45E 199 C8
Mönsterås Sweden 57°3N 16°26E 163 G10
Mont Cenis, Col du France 45°15N 6°55E 175 C10
Mont-de-Marsan France 43°54N 0°31W 174 E3
Mont-Dore N. Cal. 22°16S 166°34E 288 d
Mont Fouari △ Congo 2°52S 11°32E 264 C2
Mont-Joli Canada 48°37N 68°10W 299 C6
Mont-Laurier Canada 46°35N 75°30W 298 C4
Mont-Louis Canada 49°15N 65°44W 299 C6
Mont Peko △ Ivory C. 9°5N 7°15W 262 D3
Mont-roig del Camp Spain 41°5N 0°58E 196 D5
Mont-Royal Canada 45°30N 73°38W 130 A2
Mont-Royal, Parc Canada 45°30N 73°36W 130 A2
Mont-St-Michel, Le France 48°40N 1°30W 172 D5
Mont Sangbé △ Ivory C. 8°0N 7°10W 262 D3
Mont-Tremblant △ Canada 46°30N 74°30W 298 C5
Montabaur Germany 50°25N 7°50E 178 E3
Montagnac = Remchi Algeria 35°2N 1°26W 261 A4
Montagnac France 43°29N 3°28E 174 E7
Montagnana Italy 45°14N 11°28E 199 C8
Montagne Blanche Mauritius 20°16S 57°39E 272 e
Montagne d'Ambre △ Madag. 12°37S 49°8E 272 A2
Montagne de Reims △ France 49°8N 4°0E 173 C11
Montagu S. Africa 33°45S 20°8E 270 D3
Montagu I. Antarctica 58°25S 26°20W 151 B1
Montague Canada 46°10N 62°39W 299 C7
Montague, I. Mexico 31°45N 114°48W 318 A2
Montague I. N.S.W., Australia 36°16S 150°13E 283 D9
Montague I. Alaska, U.S.A. 60°0N 147°30W 303 G11
Montague Ra. Australia 27°15S 119°30E 279 E2
Montague Sd. Australia 14°28S 125°20E 278 B4
Montaigu France 46°59N 1°18W 172 F5
Montalbán Spain 40°50N 0°45W 196 E4
Montalbano Iónico Italy 40°17N 16°34E 201 B9
Montalbo Spain 39°53N 2°42W 196 F2
Montalcino Italy 43°3N 11°29E 199 E8

INDEX
Mount Buffalo 403

Montalegre *Angola* 8°45S 17°4E **265** D3
Montalegre *Portugal* 41°49N 7°47W **194** D3
Montalto *Italy* 38°10N 15°55E **201** D8
Montalto di Castro *Italy* 42°21N 11°37E **199** F8
Montalto Uffugo *Italy* 39°24N 16°9E **201** C9
Montalvo *U.S.A.* 34°15N 119°12W **307** L7
Montamarta *Spain* 41°39N 5°49W **194** D5
Montana *Bulgaria* 43°27N 23°16E **202** C7
Montaña *Peru* 6°0S 73°0W **330** B3
Montana □ *Bulgaria* 43°30N 23°10E **202** C7
Montana □ *U.S.A.* 47°0N 110°0W **304** C9
Montaña Clara, I. *Canary Is.* 29°17N 13°33W **153** e2
Montana de Montjuich *Spain* 41°21N 2°9E **114** A1
Montañas de Malaga ⌓ *Spain* 36°48N 4°32W **195** J6
Montánchez *Spain* 39°15N 6°8W **195** F4
Montanhas do Tumucumaque *Brazil* 2°5N 53°0W **329** C7
Montañita *Colombia* 1°22N 75°28W **328** C2
Montargil *Portugal* 39°5N 8°10W **195** F2
Montargis *France* 47°59N 2°43E **173** E9
Montauban *France* 44°2N 1°21E **174** D5
Montauk *U.S.A.* 41°3N 71°57W **313** E13
Montauk Pt. *U.S.A.* 41°4N 71°51W **313** E13
Montbard *France* 47°38N 4°20E **173** E11
Montbarrey *France* 47°1N 5°39E **173** E12
Montbéliard *France* 47°31N 6°48E **173** E13
Montblanc *Spain* 41°23N 1°4E **196** D6
Montbrison *France* 45°36N 4°3E **175** C8
Montcada i Reixac *Spain* 41°29N 2°12W **114** A2
Montcalm, Pic de *France* 42°40N 1°25E **174** F5
Montceau-les-Mines *France* 46°40N 4°23E **173** F11
Montcenis *France* 46°47N 4°23E **175** B8
Montclair *U.S.A.* 40°49N 74°12W **313** F10
Montcornet *France* 49°40N 4°1E **173** C11
Montcuq *France* 44°21N 1°13E **174** D5
Montdidier *France* 49°38N 2°35E **173** C9
Monte Albán *Mexico* 17°2N 96°46W **319** D5
Monte Alegre *Brazil* 2°0S 54°0W **329** D7
Monte Alegre de Goiás *Brazil* 13°14S 47°10W **333** D2
Monte Alegre de Minas *Brazil* 18°52S 48°52W **333** E2
Monte Alegre do Piauí *Brazil* 9°46S 45°18W **332** C2
Monte Azul *Brazil* 15°9S 42°53W **333** E3
Monte-Carlo *Monaco* 43°44N 7°25E **175** E11
Monte Carmelo *Brazil* 18°43S 47°29W **333** E2
Monte Caseros *Argentina* 30°10S 57°50W **334** C4
Monte Chingolo *Argentina* 34°43S 58°22W **117** C2
Monte Comán *Argentina* 34°40S 67°53W **334** C2
Monte Cristi *Dom. Rep.* 19°52N 71°39W **321** C5
Monte Cucco ⌓ *Italy* 43°22N 12°43E **199** E9
Monte Dinero *Argentina* 52°18S 68°33W **336** D3
Monte Dourado *Brazil* 0°52S 52°31W **329** D7
Monte Lindo → *Paraguay* 23°56S 57°12W **334** A4
Monte Palatino *Rome, Italy* **136** c3
Monte Pascoal △ *Brazil* 16°51S 39°21W **333** E4
Monte Patria *Chile* 30°42S 70°58W **334** C1
Monte Quemado *Argentina* 25°53S 62°41W **334** B3
Monte Redondo *Portugal* 39°53N 8°50W **194** F2
Monte Rio *U.S.A.* 38°28N 123°0W **306** G4
Monte San Giovanni Campano *Italy* 41°38N 13°31E **200** A6
Monte San Giuliano = Érice *Italy* 38°2N 12°35E **200** D5
Monte San Savino *Italy* 43°20N 11°43E **199** E8
Monte Sant' Ángelo *Italy* 41°42N 15°59E **199** G12
Monte Santu, C. di *Italy* 40°5N 9°44E **200** B2
Monte Sibillini △ *Italy* 42°55N 13°15E **199** F10
Monte Subasio ⌓ *Italy* 43°5N 12°40E **199** E9
Monte Vista *U.S.A.* 37°35N 106°9W **305** H10
Monteagudo *Argentina* 27°14S 54°8W **335** B5
Monteagudo *Bolivia* 19°49S 63°59W **331** D5
Montealegre del Castillo *Spain* 38°48N 1°17W **197** G3
Montebello *Qué., Canada* 45°40N 74°55W **298** C5
Montebello *Guadeloupe* 16°10N 61°36W **322** e
Montebello *Calif., U.S.A.* 34°1N 118°8W **126** B4
Montebello Iónico *Italy* 37°59N 15°45E **201** E8
Montebello Is. *Australia* 20°30S 115°45E **278** D2
Montebelluna *Italy* 45°47N 12°3E **199** C9
Montebourg *France* 49°30N 1°20W **172** C5
Montecarlo *Argentina* 26°34S 54°47W **335** B5
Montecastrilli *Italy* 42°39N 12°29E **199** F9
Montecatini Terme *Italy* 43°53N 10°46E **198** E7
Montecito *U.S.A.* 34°26N 119°40W **307** L7
Montecristi *Ecuador* 1°0S 80°40W **328** D1
Montecristo *Italy* 42°20N 10°19E **198** F7
Montefalco *Italy* 42°54N 12°39E **199** F9
Montefiascone *Italy* 42°32N 12°2E **199** F9
Montefrío *Spain* 37°20N 4°0W **195** H7
Montegiórgio *Italy* 43°6N 13°33E **199** E10
Montego B. *Jamaica* 18°28N 77°56W **320** a
Montego Bay *Jamaica* 18°28N 77°55W **320** a
Montehermoso *Spain* 40°5N 6°21W **194** E4
Monteiro *Brazil* 7°48S 37°2W **332** C4
Montejícar *Spain* 37°33N 3°30W **195** H7
Montelbaanstoren *Amsterdam, Neths.* **112** b3
Monteleone di Calabria = Vibo Valéntia *Italy* 38°40N 16°6E **201** D9
Montelíbano *Colombia* 8°5N 75°29W **328** B2
Montélimar *France* 44°33N 4°45E **175** D8
Montella *Italy* 40°51N 15°1E **201** B8
Montellano *Spain* 36°59N 5°29W **195** J5
Montello *U.S.A.* 43°48N 89°20W **308** D9
Montemayor, Meseta de *Argentina* 44°20S 66°10W **336** B3
Montemor *Portugal* 38°49N 9°12W **126** A1
Montemor-o-Novo *Portugal* 38°40N 8°12W **195** G2
Montemor-o-Velho *Portugal* 40°11N 8°40W **194** E2
Montemorelos *Mexico* 25°12N 99°49W **319** B5
Montendre *France* 45°16N 0°26W **174** C3
Montenegro *Brazil* 29°39S 51°29W **335** B5
Montenegro ■ *Europe* 42°40N 19°20E **202** D3
Montenero di Bisáccia *Italy* 41°57N 14°47E **199** G11
Montepuez *Mozam.* 13°8S 38°59E **269** E4
Montepuez → *Mozam.* 12°32S 40°27E **269** E5
Montepulciano *Italy* 43°5N 11°47E **199** E8
Montereale *Italy* 42°31N 13°15E **199** F10
Montereau-Faut-Yonne *France* 48°22N 2°57E **173** D9
Monterey *Calif., U.S.A.* 36°37N 121°55W **306** J5
Monterey *Ind., U.S.A.* 41°11N 86°30W **311** C10
Monterey B. *U.S.A.* 36°45N 122°0W **306** J5
Monterey Hills *U.S.A.* 34°6N 118°10W **126** B3
Monterey Park *U.S.A.* 34°3N 118°7W **126** B4
Montería *Colombia* 8°46N 75°53W **328** B2
Montero *Bolivia* 17°20S 63°15W **331** D5
Monteros *Argentina* 27°11S 65°30W **334** B2
Monterotondo *Italy* 42°3N 12°37E **199** F9
Monterrey *Mexico* 25°40N 100°19W **318** B4
Montes Altos *Brazil* 5°50S 47°4W **332** C2
Montes Azules ⌓ *Mexico* 16°21N 91°3W **319** D6
Montes Claros *Brazil* 16°30S 43°50W **333** E3
Montesano *U.S.A.* 46°59N 123°36W **306** D3
Montesano sulla Marcellana *Italy* 40°16N 15°42E **201** B8
Montesárchio *Italy* 41°4N 14°38E **201** A7
Montescaglioso *Italy* 40°33N 16°40E **201** B9
Montesilvano *Italy* 42°29N 14°8E **199** F11
Montesinho ⌓ *Portugal* 41°54N 6°52W **194** D4
Montespaccato *Italy* 41°54N 12°23E **136** B1
Montesson *France* 48°54N 2°8E **134** A1
Montevarchi *Italy* 43°31N 11°34E **199** E8
Monteverde Nuovo *Italy* 41°52N 12°26E **136** B1
Montevideo *Uruguay* 34°50S 56°11W **335** C4
Montevideo *Minn., U.S.A.* 44°57N 95°43W **308** C6
Montezuma *Ga., U.S.A.* 32°18N 84°2W **316** C5
Montezuma *Ind., U.S.A.* 39°48N 87°22W **311** E9
Montezuma *Iowa, U.S.A.* 41°35N 92°32W **310** C4
Montezuma Castle ⌓ *U.S.A.* 34°39N 111°45W **305** J8
Montfaucon *France* 47°6N 1°7W **172** E5
Montfaucon-d'Argonne *France* 49°16N 5°8E **173** C12
Montfaucon-en-Velay *France* 45°11N 4°20E **175** C8
Montfermeil *France* 48°54N 2°33E **134** A4
Montfort-le-Gesnois *France* 48°3N 0°25E **172** D7
Montfort-sur-Meu *France* 48°9N 1°58W **172** D5
Montfragüe ⌓ *Spain* 39°48N 5°52W **194** F5
Montgenèvre *France* 44°56N 6°43E **175** D10
Montgomery = Sahiwal *Pakistan* 30°45N 73°8E **242** D5
Montgomery *Powys, U.K.* 52°34N 3°8W **169** E4
Montgomery *Ala., U.S.A.* 32°23N 86°19W **316** C3
Montgomery *Ill., U.S.A.* 41°44N 88°21W **311** C8
Montgomery *Pa., U.S.A.* 41°10N 76°53W **312** E8
Montgomery *W. Va., U.S.A.* 38°11N 81°19W **309** F13
Montgomery City *U.S.A.* 38°59N 91°30W **310** F5
Montguyon *France* 45°12N 0°12W **174** C3
Monthermé *France* 49°52N 4°42E **173** C11
Monthey *Switz.* 46°15N 6°56E **179** J2
Monthois *France* 49°19N 4°43E **173** C11
Monti *Italy* 40°49N 9°19E **200** B2
Monti Lucrétili ⌓ *Italy* 42°5N 12°50E **199** F9
Monti Picentini ⌓ *Italy* 40°45N 15°2E **201** B8
Monti Simbruini ⌓ *Italy* 41°55N 13°13E **199** G10
Monticelli d'Ongina *Italy* 45°5N 9°56E **198** C6
Monticello *Ark., U.S.A.* 33°38N 91°47W **314** E9
Monticello *Fla., U.S.A.* 30°33N 83°52W **316** E6
Monticello *Ga., U.S.A.* 33°18N 83°40W **316** B6
Monticello *Ill., U.S.A.* 40°1N 88°34W **311** D8
Monticello *Ind., U.S.A.* 40°45N 86°46W **311** D10
Monticello *Iowa, U.S.A.* 42°15N 91°12W **310** B5
Monticello *Ky., U.S.A.* 36°50N 84°51W **309** G11
Monticello *Minn., U.S.A.* 45°18N 93°48W **308** C7
Monticello *Miss., U.S.A.* 31°33N 90°7W **315** F9
Monticello *Mo., U.S.A.* 40°7N 91°43W **310** D5
Monticello *N.Y., U.S.A.* 41°39N 74°42W **313** E10
Monticello *Utah, U.S.A.* 37°52N 109°21W **305** H9
Montichiari *Italy* 45°25N 10°23E **198** C7
Montier-en-Der *France* 48°30N 4°45E **173** D11
Montignac *France* 45°4N 1°10E **174** C5
Montigny-le-Bretonneux *France* 48°46N 2°1E **134** B1
Montigny-les-Metz *France* 49°7N 6°10E **173** C13
Montigny-sur-Aube *France* 47°57N 4°45E **173** E11
Montijo *Portugal* 38°41N 8°54W **195** G2
Montijo *Spain* 38°52N 6°39W **195** G4
Montilla *Spain* 37°36N 4°40W **195** H6
Montivilliers *France* 49°33N 0°12E **172** C7
Montjay-la-Tour *France* 48°54N 2°40E **134** A4
Montjuïc *Spain* 41°22N 2°10E **114** A2
Montjuïc, Parc de *Barcelona, Spain* **114** c1
Montluçon *France* 46°22N 2°36E **173** F9
Montmagny *Canada* 46°58N 70°34W **299** C5
Montmarault *France* 46°19N 2°57E **173** F9
Montmartre *Canada* 50°14N 103°27W **297** C8
Montmédy *France* 49°30N 5°20E **173** C12
Montmélian *France* 45°30N 6°4E **175** C10
Montmirail *France* 48°51N 3°30E **173** D10
Montmoreau-St-Cybard *France* 45°23N 0°8E **174** C4
Montmorillon *France* 46°26N 0°50E **174** B4
Montmort-Lucy *France* 48°55N 3°49E **173** D10
Monto *Australia* 24°52S 151°6E **280** C5
Montoire-sur-le-Loir *France* 47°45N 0°52E **172** E7
Montongbuwoh *Indonesia* 8°33S 116°4E **231** K19
Montório al Vomano *Italy* 42°35N 13°38E **199** F10
Montoro *Spain* 38°1N 4°27W **195** G6
Montour Falls *U.S.A.* 42°21N 76°51W **312** D8
Montoursville *U.S.A.* 41°15N 76°55W **312** E8
Montparnasse, Gare *France* 48°50N 2°19E **134** A2
Montpelier *Idaho, U.S.A.* 42°19N 111°18W **304** E8
Montpelier *Ind., U.S.A.* 40°33N 85°17W **311** D11
Montpelier *Ohio, U.S.A.* 41°35N 84°37W **311** C12
Montpelier *Vt., U.S.A.* 44°16N 72°35W **313** B12
Montpellier *France* 43°37N 3°52E **174** E7
Montpezat-de-Quercy *France* 44°15N 1°30E **174** D5
Montpon-Ménestérol *France* 45°0N 0°11E **174** D4
Montréal *Qué., Canada* 45°30N 73°33W **130** A2
Montréal *Aude, France* 43°13N 2°8E **174** E6
Montréal *Gers, France* 43°56N 0°11E **174** E4
Montreal → *Canada* 47°14N 84°39W **298** C3
Montréal, Î. de *Canada* 45°30N 73°40W **130** A2
Montréal, Univ. de *Canada* 45°29N 73°37W **130** B2
Montréal Est *Canada* 45°37N 73°31W **130** A2
Montréal L. *Canada* 54°20N 105°45W **297** C7
Montreal Lake *Canada* 54°3N 105°46W **297** C7
Montréal-Nord *Canada* 45°36N 73°36W **130** A2
Montréal-Ouest *Canada* 45°27N 73°39W **130** B1
Montréal Trudeau Int. ✕ (YUL) *Canada* 45°28N 73°44W **130** B1
Montredon-Labessonnié *France* 43°45N 2°18E **174** E6
Montrésor *France* 47°10N 1°10E **172** E8
Montret *France* 46°40N 5°7E **173** F12
Montreuil *Pas-de-Calais, France* 50°27N 1°45E **173** B8
Montreuil *Seine-St-Denis, France* 48°51N 2°27E **134** A3
Montreuil-Bellay *France* 47°8N 0°9W **172** E6
Montreux *Switz.* 46°26N 6°55E **179** J2
Montrevel-en-Bresse *France* 46°21N 5°8E **173** F12
Montrichard *France* 47°20N 1°10E **172** E8
Montrose *Angus, U.K.* 56°44N 2°27W **167** E6
Montrose *Colo., U.S.A.* 38°29N 107°53W **304** G10
Montrose *Pa., U.S.A.* 41°50N 75°53W **313** E9
Montrose, L. *U.S.A.* 38°18N 93°50W **310** F3
Montrouge *France* 48°48N 2°18E **134** B2
Monts, Pte. des *Canada* 49°20N 67°12W **299** C6
Montsalvy *France* 44°41N 2°30E **174** D6
Montsant, Serra de *Spain* 41°17N 1°0E **196** D6
Montsauche-les-Settons *France* 47°13N 4°2E **173** E11
Montsec, Serra del *Spain* 42°5N 0°45E **196** C5
Montseny ⌓ *Spain* 41°43N 2°22W **196** D2
Montserrat *B. Aires, Argentina* 34°37S 58°24W **117** B2
Montserrat *Spain* 41°36N 1°49E **196** D6
Montserrat ☒ *W. Indies* 16°40N 62°10W **323** p
Montserrat Hills *Trin. & Tob.* 10°23N 61°21W **323** t
Montuenga *Spain* 41°3N 4°38W **194** D6
Montuiri *Spain* 39°34N 2°59E **206** B3
Montvert-les-Bas *Réunion* 21°19S 55°32E **272** f
Monveda *Dem. Rep. of the Congo* 2°52N 21°30E **264** B4
Monyo *Burma* 17°59N 95°30E **241** G5
Monywa *Burma* 22°7N 95°11E **241** D5
Monza *Italy* 45°35N 9°16E **129** A2
Monze *Zambia* 16°17S 27°29E **269** F2
Monze, C. *Pakistan* 24°47N 66°37E **242** G2
Monzón *Spain* 41°52N 0°10E **196** D5
Monzoro *Italy* 45°27N 9°2E **129** B1
Moóca *Brazil* 23°33S 46°35W **137** B2
Moodyville = North Vancouver *Canada* 49°19N 123°4W **306** A3
Mooers *U.S.A.* 44°58N 73°35W **313** B11
Mooi → *S. Africa* 28°45S 30°34E **271** C5
Mooi River *S. Africa* 29°13S 29°50E **271** C4
Mo'oka *Japan* 36°26N 140°1E **223** A12
Mookgophong = Mookgopong *S. Africa* 24°31S 28°44E **271** B4
Mookgopong *S. Africa* 24°31S 28°44E **271** B4
Moomba *Australia* 28°6S 140°12E **281** A3
Moonachie *U.S.A.* 40°50N 74°2W **132** B1
Moonah → *Australia* 22°3S 138°33E **280** C2
Moonda, L. *Australia* 25°52S 140°25E **280** D3
Moonee Ponds *Australia* 37°45S 144°53E **128** A1
Moonee Valley Racecourse *Australia* 37°45S 144°55E **128** A1
Moonie *Australia* 27°46S 150°20E **281** D5
Moonie → *Australia* 29°19S 148°43E **281** D4
Moonta *Australia* 34°6S 137°32E **282** C2
Moora *Australia* 30°37S 115°58E **279** F2
Moorcroft *U.S.A.* 44°16N 104°57W **304** D11
Moore → *Australia* 31°22S 115°30E **279** F2
Moore, L. *Australia* 29°50S 117°35E **279** E2
Moore Falls *Canada* 44°48N 78°48W **312** B6
Moore Haven *U.S.A.* 26°50N 81°6W **317** J8
Moore Park *Australia* 24°43S 152°17E **280** C5
Moore Res. *U.S.A.* 44°20N 71°53W **313** B13
Moore River △ *Australia* 31°7S 115°39E **279** F2
Moorea *French Polynesia* 17°30S 149°50W **289** e
Moorefield *U.S.A.* 39°4N 78°58W **309** F14
Mooresville *U.S.A.* 39°37N 86°22W **311** E10
Moorfoot Hills *U.K.* 55°44N 3°8W **167** F5
Moorhead *U.S.A.* 46°53N 96°45W **308** B5
Moorland *U.S.A.* 42°26N 94°18W **310** B2
Moormerland *Germany* 53°20N 7°20E **178** B3
Moornanyah L. *Australia* 33°15S 143°42E **282** B5
Mooroopna *Australia* 36°25S 145°22E **283** D6
Moorpark *U.S.A.* 34°17N 118°53W **307** L8
Moorreesburg *S. Africa* 33°6S 18°38E **270** D2
Moorrinya △ *Australia* 21°42S 144°58E **280** C3
Moosach *Germany* 48°10N 11°30E **131** A2
Moosburg *Germany* 48°27N 11°56E **179** G7
Moose → *Ont., Canada* 51°20N 80°25W **298** B3
Moose → *N.Y., U.S.A.* 43°38N 75°24W **313** C9
Moose Creek *Canada* 45°15N 74°58W **313** A10
Moose Factory *Canada* 51°16N 80°32W **298** B3
Moose Jaw *Canada* 50°24N 105°30W **297** C7
Moose Jaw → *Canada* 50°34N 105°18W **297** C7
Moose Lake *Man., Canada* 53°46N 100°8W **297** C8
Moose Lake *Minn., U.S.A.* 46°27N 92°46W **308** B7
Moose Mountain ⌓ *Canada* 49°48N 102°25W **297** D8
Moose Pass *U.S.A.* 60°29N 149°22W **303** F10
Moosehead L. *U.S.A.* 45°38N 69°40W **309** C19
Mooselookmeguntic L. *U.S.A.* 44°55N 70°49W **313** B14
Moosilauke, Mt. *U.S.A.* 44°3N 71°40W **313** B13
Moosomin *Canada* 50°9N 101°40W **297** C8
Moosonee *Canada* 51°17N 80°39W **298** B3
Moosup *U.S.A.* 41°43N 71°53W **313** E13
Mootwingee △ *Australia* 31°10S 142°30E **282** A5
Mopane *S. Africa* 22°37S 29°52E **271** B4
Mopeia Velha *Mozam.* 17°30S 35°40E **269** F4
Mopipi *Botswana* 21°6S 24°55E **270** B3
Mopoi *C.A.R.* 5°6N 26°54E **268** A2
Mopti *Mali* 14°30N 4°0W **262** C4
Mopti □ *Mali* 14°40N 4°0W **262** C4
Moqatta *Sudan* 14°38N 35°50E **257** E4
Moqor *Afghan.* 32°50N 67°42E **242** C2
Moquegua *Peru* 17°15S 70°46W **330** D3
Moquegua □ *Peru* 16°50S 70°55W **330** D3
Mór *Hungary* 47°25N 18°12E **182** C3
Mora *Cameroon* 11°2N 14°7E **259** F2
Mora *Maharashtra, India* 18°54N 72°55E **130** B2
Móra *Portugal* 38°55N 8°10W **195** G2
Mora *Spain* 39°41N 3°46W **195** F7
Mora *Sweden* 61°2N 14°38E **162** C8
Mora *Minn., U.S.A.* 45°53N 93°18W **308** C7
Mora *N. Mex., U.S.A.* 35°58N 105°20W **305** J11
Mora de Rubielos *Spain* 40°15N 0°45W **196** E4
Móra d'Ebre *Spain* 41°6N 0°38E **196** D5
Móra la Nova *Spain* 41°7N 0°39E **196** D5
Morača → *Montenegro* 42°20N 19°9E **202** D3
Morada Nova *Brazil* 5°7S 38°23W **332** C4
Morada Nova de Minas *Brazil* 18°37S 45°22W **333** E2
Moradabad *India* 28°50N 78°50E **243** E8
Morafenobe *Madag.* 17°50S 44°53E **272** B1
Morąg *Poland* 53°55N 19°56E **184** E6
Moral de Calatrava *Spain* 38°51N 3°33W **195** G7
Moraleda, Canal *Chile* 44°30S 73°30W **336** B2
Moraleja *Spain* 40°6N 6°43W **194** E4
Morales *Bolívar, Colombia* 8°16N 73°51W **328** B3
Morales *Cauca, Colombia* 2°45N 76°38W **328** C2
Moramanga *Madag.* 18°56S 48°12E **272** B2
Moran *Kans., U.S.A.* 37°55N 95°10W **308** G6
Moran *Wyo., U.S.A.* 43°50N 110°31W **304** E8
Moranbah *Australia* 22°1S 148°6E **280** C4
Morané *French Polynesia* 23°10S 137°7W **289** f
Morang = Biratnagar *Nepal* 26°27N 87°17E **243** F12
Moranhat *India* 27°10N 94°50E **241** B5
Morano Cálabro *Italy* 39°50N 16°8E **201** C9
Morant Bay *Jamaica* 17°53N 76°25W **320** a
Morant Cays *Jamaica* 17°22N 76°0W **320** C4
Morant Pt. *Jamaica* 17°55N 76°12W **320** a
Morar *India* 26°14N 78°14E **242** F8
Morar, L. *U.K.* 56°57N 5°40W **167** E3
Moratalaz *Spain* 40°24N 3°39W **127** B2
Moratalla *Spain* 38°14N 1°49W **197** G3
Moratuwa *Sri Lanka* 6°45N 79°55E **245** L4
Morava → *Slovak Rep.* 48°10N 16°59E **181** C9
Moravia *Iowa, U.S.A.* 40°53N 92°49W **310** D4
Moravia *N.Y., U.S.A.* 42°43N 76°25W **313** D8
Moravian Hts. = Českomoravská Vrchovina *Czech Rep.* 49°30N 15°40E **180** B8
Moravica → *Serbia* 43°52N 20°8E **202** C4
Moravița *Romania* 45°17N 21°14E **182** E6
Moravská Třebová *Czech Rep.* 49°45N 16°40E **181** B9
Moravské Budějovice *Czech Rep.* 49°4N 15°49E **180** B8
Morawa *Australia* 29°13S 116°0E **279** E2
Morawhanna *Guyana* 8°30N 59°40W **329** B6
Moray □ *U.K.* 57°31N 3°18W **167** D5
Moray Firth *U.K.* 57°40N 3°52W **167** D5
Morbach *Germany* 49°48N 7°6E **179** F3
Morbegno *Italy* 46°8N 9°34E **198** B6
Morbi *India* 22°50N 70°42E **242** H4
Morbihan □ *France* 47°55N 2°50W **172** E4
Mörby *Sweden* 59°23N 18°3E **139** A2
Mörbylånga *Sweden* 56°32N 16°22E **163** H10
Morcenx *France* 44°3N 0°55W **174** D3
Morcone *Italy* 41°20N 14°40E **201** A7
Mordelles *France* 48°5N 1°52W **172** D5
Morden *Man., Canada* 49°15N 98°10W **297** D9
Morden *London, U.K.* 51°24N 0°13W **125** B2
Mordoğan *Turkey* 38°30N 26°37E **205** C8
Mordovian Republic = Mordvinia □ *Russia* 54°20N 44°30E **190** C7
Mordovo *Russia* 52°6N 40°50E **190** D5
Mordvinia □ *Russia* 54°20N 44°30E **190** C7
Mordy *Poland* 52°13N 22°31E **185** F9
Møre og Romsdal □ *Norway* 62°30N 8°0E **164** B4
Moreau → *U.S.A.* 45°18N 100°43W **308** C3
Morebeng *S. Africa* 23°30S 29°55E **271** B4
Morecambe *U.K.* 54°5N 2°52W **168** C5
Morecambe B. *U.K.* 54°7N 3°0W **168** C5
Moree *Australia* 29°28S 149°54E **281** D4
Morée → *France* 48°57N 2°25E **134** A3
Morehead *Papua N. G.* 8°41S 141°41E **286** E1
Morehead *Ky., U.S.A.* 38°11N 83°26W **311** F13
Morehead City *U.S.A.* 34°43N 76°43W **315** D16
Morel → *India* 26°13N 76°36E **242** F7
Moreland *U.S.A.* 33°17N 84°46W **316** B5
Morelia *Mexico* 19°42N 101°7W **318** D4
Morella *Queens., Australia* 23°0S 143°52E **280** C3
Morella *Spain* 40°35N 0°5W **196** E4
Morelos *Mexico* 26°42N 107°40W **318** B3
Morelos □ *Mexico* 18°45N 99°0W **319** D5
Moremi ⌓ *Botswana* 19°18S 23°10E **270** A3
Morena *India* 26°30N 78°4E **242** F8
Morena, Sierra *Spain* 38°20N 4°0W **195** G7
Morenci *U.S.A.* 41°43N 84°13W **311** C12
Moreni *Romania* 44°59N 25°36E **183** F10
Moreno *Bolivia* 11°9S 66°15W **330** C4
Moreno Valley *U.S.A.* 33°56N 117°14W **307** M10
Moreru → *Brazil* 10°10S 59°15W **331** C6
Moresby I. *Canada* 52°30N 131°40W **296** C2
Morestel *France* 45°40N 5°28E **175** C9
Moreton I. *Australia* 27°10S 153°25E **281** D5
Moreton Island △ *Australia* 27°2S 153°24E **281** D5
Moreuil *France* 49°46N 2°30E **173** C9
Morez *France* 46°31N 6°2E **173** F13
Morgan *S. Austral., Australia* 34°2S 139°35E **282** C3
Morgan *Ga., U.S.A.* 31°32N 84°36W **316** D5
Morgan *Utah, U.S.A.* 41°2N 111°41W **304** F8
Morgan City *U.S.A.* 29°42N 91°12W **314** G9
Morgan Hill *U.S.A.* 37°8N 121°39W **306** H5
Morgan Park *U.S.A.* 41°41N 87°38W **119** C3
Morganfield *U.S.A.* 37°41N 87°55W **308** G10
Morganton *U.S.A.* 35°45N 81°41W **315** D14
Morgantown *Ind., U.S.A.* 39°22N 86°16W **311** E10
Morgantown *W. Va., U.S.A.* 39°38N 79°57W **309** F14
Morgenzon *S. Africa* 26°45S 29°36E **271** C4
Morges *Switz.* 46°31N 6°29E **179** J2
Morghak *Iran* 29°7N 57°54E **247** D8
Morgongåva *Sweden* 59°57N 16°58E **162** E10
Morhange *France* 48°55N 6°38E **173** D13
Morhar → *India* 25°29N 85°11E **243** G11
Mori *China* 43°49N 90°11E **217** D12
Mori *Italy* 45°51N 10°59E **198** C7
Mori *Japan* 42°6N 140°35E **220** C10
Moriah *Trin. & Tob.* 11°15N 60°43W **323** s
Moriarty *U.S.A.* 34°59N 106°3W **305** J10
Moribaya *Guinea* 9°53N 9°32W **262** D3
Morice L. *Canada* 53°50N 127°40W **296** C3
Morichal Largo → *Venezuela* 9°27N 62°25W **329** B5
Morichal Viejo *Colombia* 2°13N 70°2W **328** C3
Moriguchi *Japan* 34°43N 135°34E **133** A2
Moriki *Nigeria* 12°52N 6°30E **263** C6
Morinville *Canada* 53°49N 113°41W **296** C6
Morioka *Japan* 39°45N 141°8E **220** E10
Moris *Mexico* 28°10N 108°32W **318** B3
Morisset *Australia* 33°6S 151°30E **283** B9
Morivione *Italy* 45°26N 9°12E **129** B2
Moriyama *Japan* 35°4N 135°59E **223** B7
Morlaàs *France* 43°21N 0°18W **174** E3
Morlaix *France* 48°36N 3°52W **172** D3
Mörlunda *Sweden* 57°19N 15°52E **163** G9
Mormanno *Italy* 39°53N 15°59E **201** C8
Mormant *France* 48°37N 2°52E **173** D9
Morne-à-l'Eau *Guadeloupe* 16°20N 61°27W **322** e
Morne des Esses *Martinique* 14°44N 61°1W **322** j
Morne Diablotins *Dominica* 15°30N 61°24W **323** k
Morne Fendue *Grenada* 12°12N 61°38W **323** q
Morne Raquette *Dominica* 15°27N 61°27W **323** k
Morne Trois Pitons △ *Dominica* 15°22N 61°20W **323** k
Morningside *Gauteng, S. Africa* 26°4S 28°3E **123** A2
Morningside *Edinburgh, U.K.* 55°56N 3°12W **121** B2
Morningside *Md., U.S.A.* 38°49N 76°53W **143** C4
Morningside Park *Ont., Canada* 43°47N 79°12W **141** A3
Morningside Park *Fla., U.S.A.* 28°26N 81°24W **133** B2
Mornington *Australia* 38°15S 145°5E **283** E6
Mornington, I. *Chile* 49°50S 75°30W **336** C1
Mornington I. *Australia* 16°30S 139°30E **280** B2
Mornington Peninsula △ *Australia* 38°28S 144°53E **283** E6
Mornos → *Greece* 38°25N 21°50E **204** C3
Moro *Pakistan* 26°40N 68°0E **242** F2
Moro *Sudan* 10°50N 30°9E **257** E3
Moro → *Pakistan* 29°42N 67°22E **242** E2
Moro G. *Phil.* 6°30N 123°0E **233** H4
Morobe *Papua N. G.* 7°49S 147°38E **286** D4
Morobe □ *Papua N. G.* 7°0S 147°0E **286** D4
Morocco *U.S.A.* 40°57N 87°27W **311** D9
Morocco ■ *N. Afr.* 32°0N 5°50W **260** B3
Morococha *Peru* 11°40S 76°5W **330** C2
Morogoro *Tanzania* 6°50S 37°40E **268** D4
Morogoro □ *Tanzania* 8°0S 37°0E **268** D4
Moroleón *Mexico* 20°8N 101°12W **318** C4
Morombe *Madag.* 21°45S 43°22E **272** C1
Moron = Morong *Phil.* 14°41N 120°16E **232** D3
Moron *Argentina* 34°39S 58°37W **334** C4
Morón *Cuba* 22°8N 78°39W **320** B4
Mörön *Mongolia* 49°38N 100°9E **218** B9
Morón de Almazán *Spain* 41°29N 2°27W **196** D2
Morón de la Frontera *Spain* 37°6N 5°28W **195** H5
Morona → *Peru* 4°40S 77°10W **328** D2
Morona-Santiago □ *Ecuador* 2°30S 78°0W **328** D2
Morondava *Madag.* 20°17S 44°17E **272** C1
Morondo *Ivory C.* 8°57N 6°47W **262** D3
Morong *Phil.* 14°41N 120°16E **232** D3
Morongo Valley *U.S.A.* 34°3N 116°37W **307** L10
Moroni *Comoros Is.* 11°40S 43°16E **272** a
Moroni *Utah, U.S.A.* 39°32N 111°35W **304** G8
Moroni Iconi ✕ (YVA) *Comoros Is.* 11°32S 43°15E **272** a
Moronou *Ivory C.* 6°16N 4°59W **262** D4
Morotai *Indonesia* 2°10N 128°30E **231** D7
Moroto *Uganda* 2°28N 34°42E **268** B3
Moroto, Mt. *Uganda* 2°30N 34°43E **268** B3
Morozov *Bulgaria* 42°30N 25°10E **203** D9
Morozovsk *Russia* 48°25N 41°50E **191** F5
Morpeth *Ont., Canada* 42°23N 81°50W **312** D3
Morpeth *Northumberland, U.K.* 55°10N 1°41W **168** B6
Morphou *Cyprus* 35°12N 32°59E **207** E8
Morphou Bay *Cyprus* 35°15N 32°50E **207** E8
Morrelganj *Bangla.* 22°28N 89°51E **241** D2
Morrilton *U.S.A.* 35°9N 92°44W **314** D8
Morrinhos *Ceará, Brazil* 3°14S 40°7W **332** B3
Morrinhos *Minas Gerais, Brazil* 17°45S 49°10W **333** E2
Morrinsville *N.Z.* 37°40S 175°32E **284** D4
Morris *Man., Canada* 49°25N 97°22W **297** D9
Morris *Ill., U.S.A.* 41°22N 88°26W **311** C8
Morris *Minn., U.S.A.* 45°35N 95°55W **308** C6
Morris *N.Y., U.S.A.* 42°33N 75°15W **313** D9
Morris *Pa., U.S.A.* 41°35N 77°17W **312** E7
Morris, Mt. *Australia* 26°9S 131°4E **279** E5
Morris Jesup, Kap *Greenland* 83°40N 34°0W **154** A7
Morrisburg *Canada* 44°55N 75°7W **313** B9
Morrison *U.S.A.* 41°49N 89°58W **310** C7
Morrisonville *U.S.A.* 39°25N 89°27W **310** E7
Morristown *Ariz., U.S.A.* 33°51N 112°37W **305** K7
Morristown *Ind., U.S.A.* 39°40N 85°42W **311** E11
Morristown *N.J., U.S.A.* 40°48N 74°29W **313** F10
Morristown *N.Y., U.S.A.* 44°35N 75°39W **313** B9
Morristown *Tenn., U.S.A.* 36°13N 83°18W **315** C13
Morrisville *N.Y., U.S.A.* 42°53N 75°35W **313** D9
Morrisville *Pa., U.S.A.* 40°13N 74°47W **313** F10
Morrisville *Vt., U.S.A.* 44°34N 72°36W **313** B12
Morro, Pta. *Chile* 27°6S 71°0W **334** B1
Morro Bay *U.S.A.* 35°22N 120°51W **306** K6
Morro Chico *Chile* 52°2S 71°26W **336** D2
Morro del Jable *Canary Is.* 28°3N 14°23W **153** e2
Morro do Chapéu *Brazil* 11°33S 41°9W **333** D3
Morro Grande = Barão de Cocais *Brazil* 19°56S 43°28W **333** E3
Morro Jable, Pta. de *Canary Is.* 28°2N 14°20W **153** e2
Morro Solar, Cerro *Peru* 12°11S 77°1W **124** C2
Morrocoy △ *Venezuela* 10°48N 68°13W **328** A4
Morros *Brazil* 2°52S 44°3W **332** B3
Morrosquillo, G. de *Colombia* 9°35N 75°40W **320** E4
Morrow *U.S.A.* 39°21N 84°8W **311** E12
Mörrum *Sweden* 56°12N 14°45E **163** H8
Morrumbene *Mozam.* 23°31S 35°16E **271** B6
Mörrumsån → *Sweden* 56°10N 14°45E **163** H8
Mors *Denmark* 56°50N 8°45E **163** H2
Morshansk *Russia* 53°28N 41°50E **190** D5
Morsi *India* 21°21N 78°0E **244** D4
Mörsil *Sweden* 63°19N 13°40E **162** A7
Mortagne → *France* 48°33N 6°27E **173** D13
Mortagne-au-Perche *France* 48°31N 0°33E **172** D7
Mortagne-sur-Gironde *France* 45°28N 0°47W **174** C3
Mortagne-sur-Sèvre *France* 47°0N 0°59W **172** F6
Mortain *France* 48°40N 0°57W **172** D6
Mortara *Italy* 45°15N 8°44E **198** C5
Morteau *France* 47°3N 6°35E **173** E13
Morteros *Argentina* 30°50S 62°0W **334** C3
Mortes, R. das → *Brazil* 11°45S 50°44W **333** D1
Mortlach *Canada* 50°27N 106°4W **297** C7
Mortlake *N.S.W., Australia* 33°50S 151°6E **139** B1
Mortlake *Vic., Australia* 38°5S 142°50E **282** E5
Mortlake *London, U.K.* 51°27N 0°15W **125** B2
Morton *Ill., U.S.A.* 40°37N 89°28W **310** D7
Morton *Tex., U.S.A.* 33°44N 102°46W **314** E3
Morton *Wash., U.S.A.* 46°34N 122°17W **306** D4
Morton △ *Australia* 35°0S 150°12E **283** C9
Morton Grove *U.S.A.* 42°2N 87°46W **119** A2
Moruga *Trin. & Tob.* 10°4N 61°16W **323** t
Moruga → *Trin. & Tob.* 10°5N 61°16W **323** t
Morumbi *Brazil* 23°35S 46°42W **137** B1
Morundah *Australia* 34°57S 146°19E **283** C7
Morung *Sudan* 10°32N 31°3E **266** B3
Moruya *Australia* 35°58S 150°3E **283** C9
Morvan *France* 47°5N 4°3E **173** E11
Morvan ⌓ *France* 47°12N 4°3E **173** E11
Morvant *Trin. & Tob.* 10°40N 61°29W **323** t
Morven *Queens., Australia* 26°22S 147°5E **281** D4
Morven *N.Z.* 44°50S 171°6E **285** E6
Morven *Ga., U.S.A.* 30°57N 83°30W **316** E6
Morvern *U.K.* 56°38N 5°44W **167** E3
Morwell *Australia* 38°10S 146°22E **283** E7
Morwell △ *Australia* 38°14S 146°23E **283** E7
Moryń *Poland* 52°51N 14°22E **185** F1
Morzhovets, Ostrov *Russia* 66°44N 42°35E **186** A7
Morzine *France* 46°11N 6°42E **173** F13
Mosakahiken = Moose Lake *Canada* 53°46N 100°8W **297** C8
Mosalsk *Russia* 54°30N 34°55E **188** E8
Mosbach *Germany* 49°21N 9°9E **179** F5
Mosby *Norway* 58°12N 7°55E **164** F4
Moscavide *Portugal* 38°47N 9°6W **126** A2
Mošćenice *Croatia* 45°17N 14°16E **199** C11
Moschato *Greece* 37°55N 23°40E **112** B2
Mosciano Sant' Ángelo *Italy* 42°42N 13°52E **199** F10
Moscone Convention Center *San Francisco, U.S.A.* **136** c2
Moscos Is. *Burma* 14°0N 97°30E **236** F1
Moscow = Moskva *Russia* 55°45N 37°37E **129** B3
Moscow *Idaho, U.S.A.* 46°44N 117°0W **304** C5
Moscow *Mich., U.S.A.* 42°3N 84°30W **311** B12
Moscow *Pa., U.S.A.* 41°20N 75°31W **313** E9
Moscow Mills *U.S.A.* 38°57N 90°55W **310** F6
Mosel → *Europe* 50°22N 7°36E **173** B14
Moselle = Mosel → *Europe* 50°22N 7°36E **173** B14
Moselle □ *France* 48°59N 6°33E **173** D13
Moses Lake *U.S.A.* 47°8N 119°17W **304** C4
Mosgiel *N.Z.* 45°53S 170°21E **285** F5
Moshaweng → *S. Africa* 26°35S 22°50E **270** C3
Moshchnyy, Ostrav *Russia* 60°1N 27°50E **188** B4
Moshi *Tanzania* 3°22S 37°18E **268** C4
Moshi → *Nigeria* 9°18N 4°38E **263** D5
Moshupa *Botswana* 24°46S 25°29E **270** B4
Mosina *Poland* 52°15N 16°50E **185** F3
Mosite *Dem. Rep. of the Congo* 0°53N 23°40E **264** B4
Mosjøen *Norway* 65°51N 13°12E **160** D15
Moskenesøya *Norway* 67°58N 13°0E **160** C15
Moskenstraumen *Norway* 67°47N 12°45E **160** C15
Moskog *Norway* 61°26N 6°0E **164** C2
Moskva *Russia* 55°45N 37°37E **129** B3
Moskva □ *Russia* 56°20N 37°20E **188** D9
Moskva → *Russia* 55°5N 38°51E **188** E10
Moskvoretskiy *Russia* 55°42N 37°37E **129** B3
Moslavačka Gora *Croatia* 45°40N 16°37E **199** C13
Mosman *Australia* 33°49S 151°15E **139** B2
Moso *Vanuatu* 17°30S 168°15E **287** G6
Mosomane *Botswana* 24°2S 26°19E **270** B4
Mosonmagyaróvár *Hungary* 47°52N 17°18E **182** C2
Mošorin *Serbia* 45°19N 20°4E **182** E5
Mospyne *Ukraine* 47°52N 38°0E **189** J9
Mosqueiro *Brazil* 1°10S 48°28W **332** B2
Mosquera *Colombia* 2°35N 78°24W **328** C2
Mosquero *U.S.A.* 35°47N 103°58W **305** J12
Mosqueruela *Spain* 40°21N 0°27W **196** E4
Mosquitia *Honduras* 15°20N 84°10W **320** C3
Mosquito Coast = Mosquitia *Honduras* 15°20N 84°10W **320** C3
Mosquito Creek L. *U.S.A.* 41°18N 80°46W **312** E4
Mosquito L. *Canada* 62°35N 103°20W **297** A8
Mosquitos, G. de los *Panama* 9°15N 81°10W **320** E3
Moss *Norway* 59°27N 10°40E **164** E7
Moss Vale *Australia* 34°32S 150°25E **283** C9
Mossaka *Congo* 1°15S 16°45E **264** C3
Mossâmedes *Brazil* 16°7S 50°11W **333** E1
Mossbank *Canada* 49°56N 105°56W **297** D7
Mossburn *N.Z.* 45°41S 168°15E **285** F3
Mosselbaai *S. Africa* 34°11S 22°8E **270** D3
Mossendjo *Congo* 2°55S 12°42E **264** C2
Mossfellsbær *Iceland* 64°11N 21°45W **155** C5
Mossgiel *Australia* 33°15S 144°5E **282** B6
Mossingen *Germany* 48°24N 9°4E **179** G5
Mossman *Australia* 16°21S 145°15E **280** B4
Mossoró *Brazil* 5°10S 37°15W **332** C4
Mossuril *Mozam.* 14°58S 40°42E **269** E5
Mossy Head *U.S.A.* 30°45N 86°19W **317** E3
Mossy Point *Australia* 35°50S 150°11E **283** C9
Most *Czech Rep.* 50°31N 13°38E **180** A6
Mosta *Malta* 35°55N 14°26E **206** F7
Mostaganem *Algeria* 35°54N 0°5E **261** A5
Mostaganem □ *Algeria* 35°40N 0°15E **261** A5
Mostar *Bos.-H.* 43°22N 17°50E **182** G2
Mostardas *Brazil* 31°2S 50°51W **335** C5
Mostefa, Rass *Tunisia* 36°55N 11°3E **258** A2
Mosteiros *Azores* 37°53N 25°49W **153** d3
Mosterhamn *Norway* 59°42N 5°21E **164** E2
Mostiska = Mostyska *Ukraine* 49°48N 23°4E **185** J10
Móstoles *Spain* 40°19N 3°53W **194** E7
Mosty = Masty *Belarus* 53°27N 24°38E **177** B13
Mostyska *Ukraine* 49°48N 23°4E **185** J10
Mosul = Al Mawşil *Iraq* 36°15N 43°5E **213** D10
Møsvatnet *Norway* 59°52N 8°5E **164** E5
Mota *Ethiopia* 11°5N 37°52E **257** E4
Mota *Vanuatu* 13°49S 167°42E **287** C5
Mota del Cuervo *Spain* 39°30N 2°52W **197** F2
Mota del Marqués *Spain* 41°38N 5°11W **194** D5
Mota Lava *Vanuatu* 13°40S 167°40E **287** C5
Motaba *Congo* 2°6N 18°2E **264** B3
Motagua → *Guatemala* 15°44N 88°14W **320** C2
Motala *Sweden* 58°32N 15°1E **163** F9
Motaze *Mozam.* 24°48S 32°52E **271** B5
Moțca *Romania* 47°15N 26°37E **183** C11
Motegi *Japan* 36°32N 140°11E **223** A12
Moth *India* 25°43N 78°57E **243** G8
Motherwell *U.K.* 55°47N 3°58W **167** F5
Moti Bagh *India* 28°33N 77°10E **120** B2
Motihari *India* 26°30N 84°55E **243** F11
Motilla del Palancar *Spain* 39°34N 1°55W **197** F3
Motiti I. *N.Z.* 37°38S 176°25E **284** D5
Motnik *Slovenia* 46°14N 14°54E **199** B11
Motobu *Japan* 26°39N 127°53E **288** a
Motocurunya *Venezuela* 4°24N 64°5W **329** C5
Motol *Czech Rep.* 50°3N 14°21E **135** B2
Motovun *Croatia* 45°20N 13°50E **199** C10
Motozintla de Mendoza *Mexico* 15°22N 92°14W **319** D6
Motril *Spain* 36°31N 3°37W **195** J7
Motru *Romania* 44°48N 22°59E **182** F7
Motru → *Romania* 44°32N 23°31E **183** F8
Motsa *Israel* 31°47N 35°9E **123** B2
Motsa Ilit *Israel* 31°48N 35°9E **123** B1
Motspur Park *U.K.* 51°23N 0°14W **125** B2
Mott *U.S.A.* 46°23N 102°20W **308** B2
Mottingham *U.K.* 51°26N 0°1E **125** B4
Möttling = Metlika *Slovenia* 45°40N 15°20E **199** C12
Móttola *Italy* 40°38N 17°2E **201** B10
Motu → *N.Z.* 37°52S 177°36E **284** D6
Motu Nui *Chile* 27°12S 109°28W **330** b
Motu Tapu *Cook Is.* 21°14S 159°43W **289** h
Motuba *Dem. Rep. of the Congo* 2°20N 13°34E **264** B3
Motueka *N.Z.* 41°7S 173°1E **285** B8
Motueka → *N.Z.* 41°5S 173°1E **285** B8
Motul *Mexico* 21°6N 89°17W **319** C7
Motupena Pt. *Papua N. G.* 6°30S 155°10E **286** D8
Mou *N. Cal.* 21°5S 167°26E **288** d
Mouanda *Gabon* 1°28S 13°7E **264** C2
Mouchalagane → *Canada* 50°56N 68°41W **299** B6
Mouchoir Bank *W. Indies* 20°57N 70°47W **321** B5
Mouding *China* 25°20N 101°28E **228** E3
Moudjeria *Mauritania* 17°50N 12°28W **262** B2
Moudon *Switz.* 46°40N 6°49E **179** J2
Moudros *Greece* 39°50N 25°18E **205** B7
Mougoundou *Congo* 2°40S 12°41E **264** C2
Mouhoun = Black Volta → *Africa* 8°41N 1°33W **262** D4
Mouila *Gabon* 1°50S 11°0E **264** C2
Mouka *C.A.R.* 7°16N 21°52E **264** A4
Moukalaba ⌓ *Gabon* 2°50S 10°35E **264** C2
Moukambo *Gabon* 3°5S 11°38E **264** C2
Moul *Niger* 15°5N 13°11E **259** F2
Moulamein *Australia* 35°3S 144°1E **282** C6
Moule à Chique, C. *St. Lucia* 13°43N 60°57W **323** m
Moulhoulé *Djibouti* 11°58N 42°58E **267** B5
Mouliana *Greece* 35°10N 25°59E **207** E6
Moulin Rouge *Paris, France* **134** a3
Moulins *France* 46°35N 3°19E **173** F10
Moulmein *Burma* 16°30N 97°40E **241** G6
Moulmeingyun *Burma* 16°23N 95°16E **241** G5
Moulouya, O. → *Morocco* 35°5N 2°25W **261** A4
Moulton *U.S.A.* 40°41N 92°41W **310** D4
Moultrie *U.S.A.* 31°11N 83°47W **316** D6
Moultrie, L. *U.S.A.* 33°20N 80°5W **316** B9
Mounana *Gabon* 1°18S 13°13E **264** C2
Mound City *Mo., U.S.A.* 40°7N 95°14W **308** E6
Mound City *S. Dak., U.S.A.* 45°44N 100°4W **308** C3
Moundou *Chad* 8°40N 16°10E **259** G3
Moundsville *U.S.A.* 39°55N 80°44W **312** G4
Mounembé *Congo* 3°20S 12°32E **264** C2
Moung *Cambodia* 12°46N 103°27E **236** F4
Moungoudi *Congo* 2°45S 11°46E **264** C2
Mount Airy *U.S.A.* 36°31N 80°37W **315** C14
Mount Albert *Canada* 44°8N 79°19W **312** B5
Mount Apo △ *Phil.* 7°0N 125°10E **233** H5
Mount Arayat △ *Phil.* 15°39N 120°44E **232** D3
Mount Aspiring △ *N.Z.* 44°19S 168°47E **285** E3
Mount Ayliff = Maxesibeni *S. Africa* 30°49S 29°23E **271** D4
Mount Ayr *U.S.A.* 40°43N 94°14W **310** D2
Mount Barker *S. Austral., Australia* 35°5S 138°52E **282** C3
Mount Barker *W. Austral., Australia* 34°38S 117°40E **279** F2
Mount Barnett Roadhouse *Australia* 16°39S 125°57E **278** C4
Mount Beauty *Australia* 36°47S 147°10E **283** D7
Mount Bellew Bridge *Ireland* 53°28N 8°31W **166** C3
Mount Brydges *Canada* 42°54N 81°29W **312** D3
Mount Buffalo △ *Australia* 36°43S 146°46E **283** D7

Mount Burr *Australia* 37°34S 140°26E 281 F3
Mount Carmel = Ha Karmel △
  Israel 32°45N 35°5E 250 F6
Mount Carmel *Ill., U.S.A.* 38°25N 87°46W 311 F9
Mount Carmel *Pa., U.S.A.* 40°47N 76°26W 313 F8
Mount Carroll *U.S.A.* 42°6N 89°59W 310 B7
Mount Clemens *U.S.A.* 42°35N 82°53W 312 D2
Mount Cook *N.Z.* 43°44S 170°5E 285 C5
Mount Cook △ *N.Z.* 43°35S 170°15E 285 D5
Mount Coolon *Australia* 21°25S 147°25E 280 C4
Mount Darwin *Zimbabwe* 16°47S 31°38E 269 F3
Mount Dennis *Canada* 43°40N 79°28W 141 A2
Mount Desert I. *U.S.A.* 44°21N 68°20W 309 C19
Mount Dora *U.S.A.* 28°48N 81°38W 317 G8
Mount Ebenezer *Australia* 25°6S 132°34E 279 E5
Mount Eccles △ *Australia* 38°5S 141°54E 282 E4
Mount Eden *U.S.A.* 37°33N 121°36W 311 F11
Mount Edziza △ *Canada* 57°30N 130°45W 296 B2
Mount Elgon △ *E. Afr.* 1°4N 34°42E 268 B3
Mount Field △ *S. Africa* 30°40S 28°30E 271 D4
Mount Forest *Canada* 43°59N 80°43W 312 C4
Mount Frankland △
  Australia 31°47S 116°37E 279 F2
Mount Frederick ○
  Australia 19°39S 129°18E 278 C4
Mount Frere = Kwabhaca
  S. Africa 30°51S 29°0E 271 D4
Mount Gambier
  Australia 37°50S 140°46E 282 E4
Mount Garnet *Australia* 17°37S 145°6E 280 B4
Mount Greenwood
  U.S.A. 41°42N 87°42W 119 C2
Mount Hagen *Papua N. G.* 5°52S 144°16E 286 C3
Mount Hamiguitan △
  Phil. 6°44N 126°10E 233 H6
Mount Holly *U.S.A.* 39°59N 74°47W 313 G10
Mount Holly Springs
  U.S.A. 40°7N 77°12W 312 F7
Mount Hood Memorial Park △
  U.S.A. 42°26N 71°1W 116 A2
Mount Hope *N.S.W.,*
  Australia 32°51S 145°51E 283 B6
Mount Hope *S. Austral.,*
  Australia 34°7S 135°23E 281 E2
Mount Horeb *U.S.A.* 43°1N 89°44W 310 B7
Mount Iglit-Mount Baco △
  Phil. 12°45N 121°8E 232 E3
Mount Isa *Australia* 20°42S 139°26E 280 C2
Mount Isarog △ *Phil.* 13°38N 123°24E 232 E4
Mount James ○ *Australia* 24°45S 122°8E 278 D2
Mount Jewett *U.S.A.* 41°44N 78°39W 312 E6
Mount Ka'ala Nat. Area Reserve △
  U.S.A. 21°31N 158°7W 302 J13
Mount Kaputar △
  Australia 30°16S 150°10E 281 E5
Mount Kenya △ *Kenya* 0°7S 37°21E 268 C4
Mount Kisco *U.S.A.* 41°12N 73°44W 313 E11
Mount Laguna *U.S.A.* 32°52N 116°25W 307 N10
Mount Larcom *Australia* 23°48S 150°59E 280 C5
Mount Lofty Ranges
  Australia 34°35S 139°5E 282 C3
Mount McKinley = Denali △
  U.S.A. 63°30N 152°0W 303 E10
Mount Magnet *Australia* 28°2S 117°47E 279 E2
Mount Malindang △
  Phil. 8°17N 123°32E 233 G4
Mount Manara *Australia* 32°45S 143°55E 282 B5
Mount Maunganui *N.Z.* 37°40S 176°14E 284 D5
Mount Merrion *Ireland* 53°18N 6°12W 120 B2
Mount Molloy *Australia* 16°42S 145°20E 280 B4
Mount Morgan *Australia* 23°40S 150°25E 280 C5
Mount Morris *Mich.,*
  U.S.A. 43°7N 83°42W 311 A13
Mount Morris *N.Y.,*
  U.S.A. 42°44N 77°52W 312 D7
Mount Olive *U.S.A.* 39°4N 89°44W 310 E7
Mount Olivet *U.S.A.* 38°32N 84°2W 311 F12
Mount Olympus *U.S.A.* 34°7N 118°21W 126 B2
Mount Orab *U.S.A.* 39°2N 83°55W 311 C13
Mount Pearl *Canada* 47°31N 52°47W 299 C9
Mount Penn *U.S.A.* 40°20N 75°54W 313 F9
Mount Perry *Australia* 25°13S 151°42E 281 D5
Mount Pleasant *Iowa,*
  U.S.A. 40°58N 91°33W 310 D5
Mount Pleasant *Mich.,*
  U.S.A. 43°36N 84°46W 309 D11
Mount Pleasant *Pa.,*
  U.S.A. 40°9N 79°33W 312 F5
Mount Pleasant *S.C.,*
  U.S.A. 32°47N 79°52W 316 C10
Mount Pleasant *Tenn.,*
  U.S.A. 35°32N 87°12W 315 D11
Mount Pleasant *Tex.,*
  U.S.A. 33°9N 94°58W 314 E7
Mount Pleasant *Utah,*
  U.S.A. 39°33N 111°27W 304 G8
Mount Pocono *U.S.A.* 41°7N 75°22W 313 E9
Mount Pulaski *U.S.A.* 40°1N 89°17W 310 E7
Mount Pulog △ *Phil.* 16°35N 120°57E 232 C3
Mount Rainier *U.S.A.* 38°56N 76°57W 143 B4
Mount Rainier △ *U.S.A.* 46°55N 121°50W 306 D5
Mount Remarkable △
  Australia 32°47S 138°3E 282 B2
Mount Revelstoke △
  Canada 51°5N 118°30W 296 C5
Mount Robson △ *Canada* 53°0N 119°0W 296 C5
Mount St. Helens △
  U.S.A. 46°14N 122°11W 306 D4
Mount Selinda *Zimbabwe* 20°24S 32°43E 271 B5
Mount Shasta *U.S.A.* 41°19N 122°19W 306 F2
Mount Signal *U.S.A.* 32°39N 115°37W 307 N11
Mount Somers *N.Z.* 43°45S 171°27E 285 D6
Mount Sterling *Ill.,*
  U.S.A. 39°59N 90°45W 310 E6
Mount Sterling *Ky.,*
  U.S.A. 38°4N 83°56W 311 F13
Mount Sterling *Ohio,*
  U.S.A. 39°43N 83°16W 311 E13
Mount Surprise *Australia* 18°10S 144°17E 280 B3
Mount Union *U.S.A.* 40°23N 77°53W 312 F7
Mount Upton *U.S.A.* 42°26N 75°23W 313 D9
Mount Vernon *Ga.,*
  U.S.A. 32°11N 82°36W 316 C12
Mount Vernon *Ill.,*
  U.S.A. 38°19N 88°55W 311 G8
Mount Vernon *Ind.,*
  U.S.A. 37°56N 87°54W 308 G10
Mount Vernon *Iowa,*
  U.S.A. 41°55N 91°23W 310 C5
Mount Vernon *N.Y.,*
  U.S.A. 40°54N 73°49W 132 A3
Mount Vernon *Ohio,*
  U.S.A. 40°23N 82°29W 312 F2
Mount Vernon *Wash.,*
  U.S.A. 48°25N 122°20W 306 B4
Mount Vernon Square
  Washington, D.C., U.S.A. 143 a2
Mount Victor *Australia* 32°11S 139°44E 282 B3
Mount Washington
  U.S.A. 39°5N 84°24W 311 F11
Mount Wellington *N.Z.* 36°55S 174°52E 284 C4
Mount William △
  Australia 40°56S 148°14E 281 E4
Mount Wynne *St. Vincent* 13°14N 61°16W 322 a1
Mount Zion = Har Tsiyon
  Jerusalem 123 b3

Mount Zion *U.S.A.* 39°46N 88°53W 311 E8
Mounta, Akra *Greece* 38°3N 20°47E 207 C2
Mountain □ *Phil.* 17°20N 121°10E 232 C3
Mountain Ash *U.K.* 51°40N 3°23W 169 F4
Mountain Center
  U.S.A. 33°42N 116°44W 307 M10
Mountain City *Nev.,*
  U.S.A. 41°50N 115°58W 304 F6
Mountain City *Tenn.,*
  U.S.A. 36°29N 81°48W 315 C14
Mountain Dale *U.S.A.* 41°41N 74°32W 313 E10
Mountain Grove *U.S.A.* 37°8N 92°16W 310 G8
Mountain Home *Ark.,*
  U.S.A. 36°20N 92°23W 314 C8
Mountain Home *Idaho,*
  U.S.A. 43°8N 115°41W 304 E6
Mountain Iron *U.S.A.* 47°32N 92°37W 308 B7
Mountain Pass *U.S.A.* 35°29N 115°35W 307 K11
Mountain View *Ark.,*
  U.S.A. 35°52N 92°7W 314 D8
Mountain View *Calif.,*
  U.S.A. 37°23N 122°5W 306 H4
Mountain View *Hawai'i,*
  U.S.A. 19°33N 155°7W 302 D6
Mountain Village *U.S.A.* 62°5N 163°43W 303 E7
Mountain Zebra △
  S. Africa 32°14S 25°27E 270 D4
Mountainair *U.S.A.* 34°31N 106°15W 305 J10
Mountlake Terrace
  U.S.A. 47°47N 122°18W 306 C4
Mountmellick *Ireland* 53°7N 7°20W 166 C4
Mountrath *Ireland* 53°0N 7°28W 166 C4
Moura *Queens., Australia* 24°35S 149°58E 280 C4
Moura *Brazil* 1°32S 61°38W 329 D5
Moura *Portugal* 38°7N 7°30W 195 G3
Mourão *Portugal* 38°22N 7°22W 195 G3
Mourdi, Dépression du
  Chad 18°10N 23°0E 259 E4
Mourdiah *Mali* 14°35N 7°25W 262 C3
Mourenx *France* 43°22N 0°38W 174 E3
Mouri *Ghana* 5°6N 1°14W 263 D4
Mourilyan *Australia* 17°35S 146°3E 280 B4
Mourmelon-le-Grand
  France 49°8N 4°22E 173 C11
Mourne → *U.K.* 54°52N 7°26W 166 B4
Mourne Mts. *U.K.* 54°10N 6°0W 166 B5
Mournies *Greece* 35°29N 24°1E 207 D6
Mouscron *Belgium* 50°45N 3°12E 170 D3
Mousgougou *Chad* 10°47N 16°9E 259 F3
Moussa 'Ali *Djibouti* 12°27N 42°24E 267 B5
Moussoro *Chad* 13°41N 16°35E 259 F3
Moustique, Morne
  Guadeloupe 16°7N 61°44W 322 e
Mouthe *France* 46°44N 6°12E 173 F13
Moutier *Switz.* 47°16N 7°21E 179 H3
Moûtiers *France* 45°29N 6°32E 175 C10
Moutong *Indonesia* 0°28N 121°13E 231 D6
Mouy *France* 49°18N 2°20E 173 C9
Mouydir, Monts du *Algeria* 25°30N 4°16E 261 C5
Mouzaki *Greece* 39°25N 21°37E 208 E3
Mouzarak *Chad* 13°17N 15°58E 259 F3
Mouzon *France* 49°36N 5°3E 173 C12
Movas *Mexico* 28°10N 109°25W 318 B3
Moville *Ireland* 55°11N 7°3W 166 A4
Mowandjum *Australia* 17°22S 123°40E 278 C3
Moweaqua *U.S.A.* 39°38N 89°1W 310 E7
Moxico □ *Angola* 12°0S 20°0E 265 H5
Moxotó → *Brazil* 9°19S 38°14W 332 C4
Moy → *Ireland* 54°8N 9°8W 166 B2
Moya *Comoros Is.* 12°18S 44°18E 272 a
Moyale *Ethiopia* 3°34N 39°5E 266 G4
Moyale *Kenya* 3°30N 39°4E 257 C4
Moyamba *S. Leone* 8°4N 12°30W 262 D2
Moyen Atlas *Morocco* 33°0N 5°0W 260 B4
Moyen-Chari □ *Chad* 9°40N 18°15E 259 G3
Moyo *Indonesia* 8°10S 117°40E 235 D5
Moyobamba *Peru* 6°0S 77°0W 330 B2
Moyowosi → *Tanzania* 3°50S 31°0E 268 C3
Moyto *Chad* 12°35N 16°33E 259 F3
Moyu *China* 37°15N 79°44E 217 E9
Moyyero → *Russia* 68°44N 103°42E 215 C11
Moyynqum *Zhambyl,*
  Kazakhstan 44°17N 72°57E 217 D8
Moyynqum *Zhambyl,*
  Kazakhstan 44°12N 71°0E 217 D8
Moyynty *Kazakhstan* 47°10N 73°18E 217 C8
Mozambique = Moçambique
  Mozam. 15°3S 40°42E 269 F5
Mozambique ■ *Africa* 19°0S 35°0E 269 F4
Mozambique Basin *Ind. Oc.* 30°0S 40°0E 273 G2
Mozambique Chan. *Africa* 17°30S 42°30E 271 A7
Mozarthaus *Vienna, Austria* 142 b2
Mozdok *Russia* 43°45N 44°48E 191 J7
Mozdūrān *Iran* 36°9N 60°35E 247 B9
Mozhaysk *Russia* 55°30N 36°2E 188 E9
Mozhga *Russia* 56°26N 52°15E 190 B11
Mozhnābād *Iran* 34°7N 60°6E 247 C9
Mozirje *Slovenia* 46°22N 14°58E 199 B11
Mozyr = Mazyr *Belarus* 51°59N 29°15E 177 B15
Mpanda *Tanzania* 6°23S 31°1E 268 D3
Mpé *Congo* 2°58S 14°38E 264 C2
Mpesoba *Mali* 12°31N 5°39W 262 C3
Mphoeng *Zimbabwe* 21°10S 27°51E 269 G2
Mpika *Zambia* 11°51S 31°25E 269 G3
Mpoko → *C.A.R.* 4°19N 18°33E 264 B3
Mpouya *Congo* 2°38S 16°13E 264 C3
Mpulungu *Zambia* 8°51S 31°5E 269 D3
Mpumalanga *S. Africa* 29°50S 30°33E 271 C5
Mpumalanga □ *S. Africa* 26°30S 30°0E 271 C5
Mpwapwa *Tanzania* 6°23S 36°30E 268 D4
Mqabba *Malta* 35°51N 14°28E 207 D1
Mqanduli *S. Africa* 31°49S 28°45E 271 D4
Mqinvartsveri = Kazbek
  Russia 42°42N 44°30E 191 J7
Mragowo *Poland* 53°52N 21°18E 185 B8
M'ramani *Comoros Is.* 12°20S 44°31E 272 a
Mramor *Serbia* 43°20N 21°45E 202 C5
Mrauk-u = Myohaung
  Burma 20°35N 93°11E 241 K18
Mrimina *Morocco* 29°50N 7°9W 260 C3
Mrkonjić Grad *Bos.-H.* 44°26N 17°4E 182 F2
Mrkopalj *Croatia* 45°21N 14°52E 199 C11
Mrocza *Poland* 53°16N 17°35E 185 B4
Msaken *Tunisia* 35°49N 10°33E 258 A2
Msambansovu *Zimbabwe* 15°50S 30°3E 269 F3
Msida *Malta* 35°54N 14°29E 207 F2
M'sila *Algeria* 35°46N 4°30E 261 A5
M'sila □ *Algeria* 35°20N 4°20E 261 A5
Msoro *Zambia* 13°35S 31°50E 269 G3
Msta → *Russia* 58°25N 31°20E 188 C6
Mstislavl = Mstsislaw
  Belarus 54°0N 31°50E 177 A16
Mstsislaw *Belarus* 54°0N 31°50E 177 A16
Mszana Dolna *Poland* 49°41N 20°5E 185 J7
Mszczonów *Poland* 51°58N 20°33E 185 G7
Mtama *Tanzania* 10°17S 39°21E 269 E4
Mtamvuna = Mthamvuna →
  S. Africa 31°6S 30°12E 271 D5
Mthatha *S. Africa* 31°36S 28°49E 271 D4
Mtilikwe → *Zimbabwe* 21°9S 31°30E 269 G3

Mtito Andei *Kenya* 2°41S 38°10E 268 C4
Mtsamboro *Mayotte* 12°42S 45°4E 272 a
Mtsamboro, Î. *Mayotte* 12°38S 45°2E 272 b
Mtsangamouji *Mayotte* 12°45S 45°11E 272 b
Mtsensk *Russia* 53°17N 36°36E 188 F9
Mtubatuba *S. Africa* 28°30S 32°8E 271 C5
Mtwalume *S. Africa* 30°30S 30°38E 271 D5
Mtwara-Mikindani
  Tanzania 10°20S 40°20E 269 E5
Mu → *Burma* 21°55N 95°19E 241 H19
Mu Gia, Deo *Vietnam* 17°40N 105°47E 236 D5
Mu Ko Chang △
  Thailand 11°59N 102°22E 237 G4
Mu Ko Surin *Thailand* 9°30N 97°55E 237 H1
Mu Us Shamo *China* 39°0N 109°0E 226 E5
Muacadala *Angola* 4°6S 24°0E 265 E4
Muan *S. Korea* 34°59N 126°28E 224 E3
Muaná *Brazil* 1°25S 49°15W 332 B2
Muanda
  Dem. Rep. of the Congo 6°0S 12°20E 265 D2
Muang Beng *Laos* 20°23N 101°46E 228 G3
Muang Chiang Rai = Chiang Rai
  Thailand 19°52N 99°50E 228 H2
Muang Et *Laos* 20°49N 104°1E 236 B5
Muang Hiam *Laos* 20°5N 103°22E 236 B4
Muang Hongsa *Laos* 19°43N 101°20E 236 C3
Muang Houn *Laos* 20°8N 101°23E 236 B3
Muang Kau *Laos* 15°6N 105°47E 236 E5
Muang Khao *Laos* 19°38N 103°32E 236 C4
Muang Khong *Laos* 14°7N 105°51E 236 E5
Muang Khoua *Laos* 21°5N 102°31E 236 B3
Muang Liap *Laos* 18°29N 101°40E 236 C3
Muang Mai *Thailand* 8°5N 98°21E 237 a
Muang May *Laos* 14°49N 106°56E 236 E6
Muang Na Mo *Laos* 21°3N 101°49E 228 G3
Muang Ngeun *Laos* 20°36N 101°3E 228 G3
Muang Ngoi *Laos* 20°43N 102°41E 228 G4
Muang Nong *Laos* 16°22N 106°30E 236 D6
Muang Ou Neua *Laos* 22°18N 101°48E 228 F3
Muang Ou Tay *Laos* 22°7N 101°48E 228 F3
Muang Pak Beng *Laos* 19°54N 101°8E 236 C3
Muang Phalane *Laos* 16°39N 105°34E 236 D5
Muang Phiang *Laos* 19°6N 101°32E 236 C3
Muang Phine *Laos* 16°32N 106°2E 236 D6
Muang Saiapoun *Laos* 18°24N 101°31E 236 C3
Muang Sing *Laos* 21°11N 101°9E 228 G3
Muang Son *Laos* 20°27N 103°19E 236 B4
Muang Soui *Laos* 19°33N 102°52E 236 C4
Muang Va *Laos* 21°53N 102°19E 228 F4
Muang Va *Laos* 21°18N 101°20E 236 B3
Muang Xai *Laos* 20°42N 101°59E 228 G3
Muang Xamteu *Laos* 19°59N 104°38E 236 C5
Muanghongsa *Laos* 12°32S 19°55E 265 E3
Muar *Malaysia* 2°3N 102°34E 237 L4
Muara Takus *Indonesia* 0°20N 100°33E 234 B2
Muaraaman *Indonesia* 3°7S 102°12E 234 C2
Muarabadak *Indonesia* 0°20S 117°26E 235 C5
Muarabeliti *Indonesia* 3°15S 103°11E 234 C2
Muarabungo *Indonesia* 1°28S 102°52E 234 C2
Muaradua *Indonesia* 4°31S 104°4E 234 C2
Muaraenim *Indonesia* 3°40S 103°50E 234 C2
Muarajuloi *Indonesia* 0°12S 114°3E 235 C4
Muarakaman *Indonesia* 0°2S 116°45E 235 C5
Muarasabak *Indonesia* 1°7S 103°51E 234 C2
Muarasiberut *Indonesia* 1°35S 99°12E 234 C1
Muaratebo *Indonesia* 1°30S 102°26E 234 C2
Muaratembesi *Indonesia* 1°42S 103°8E 234 C2
Muarateweh *Indonesia* 0°58S 114°52E 235 C4
Muarawahau *Indonesia* 1°1N 116°52E 235 B5
Mubarakpur *India* 26°6N 83°18E 243 F10
Mubarraz = Al Mubarraz
  Si. Arabia 25°30N 49°40E 247 E6
Mubende *Uganda* 0°33N 31°22E 268 B3
Mubi *Nigeria* 10°18N 13°16E 263 C7
Mucaba, Sa. de *Angola* 7°12S 15°0E 265 D3
Mucajá *Brazil* 3°57S 57°32W 329 D6
Mucajaí *Brazil* 2°25N 60°52W 329 C5
Mucajaí, Serra do *Brazil* 2°23N 61°10W 329 C5
Mucari *Angola* 9°30S 16°54E 265 D3
Muchachos, Roque de los
  Canary Is. 28°44N 17°52W 153 e1
Müchen *Germany* 51°17N 11°47E 178 D7
Muchinga Mts. *Zambia* 11°30S 31°30E 269 E3
Muchkapskiy *Russia* 51°52N 42°28E 190 E6
Muchuan *China* 28°57N 103°55E 228 C5
Muck *U.K.* 56°50N 6°15W 167 E2
Muckadilla *Australia* 26°35S 148°23E 281 D4
Muckalee Cr. → *U.S.A.* 31°38N 84°9W 316 B5
Muckaty ○ *Australia* 18°37S 133°52E 280 B1
Muckle Flugga *U.K.* 60°51N 0°54W 167 A8
Muco → *Colombia* 4°15N 70°21W 328 C3
Muconda *Angola* 10°31S 21°15E 265 E4
Mucope *Angola* 16°24S 14°52E 265 F2
Mucubela *Brazil* 13°0S 41°23W 333 D3
Mucuim → *Brazil* 6°33S 64°18W 331 B5
Mucur *Turkey* 39°3N 34°22E 212 C6
Mucura *Brazil* 2°31S 62°43W 329 D5
Mucuri *Brazil* 18°0S 39°36W 333 E4
Mucurici *Brazil* 18°6S 40°31W 333 E3
Mucusso *Angola* 18°1S 21°25E 265 F4
Mucussueje *Angola* 11°1S 21°56E 265 E4
Muda *Canary Is.* 28°34N 13°57W 153 e2
Mudanjiang *China* 44°38N 129°30E 227 B15
Mudanya *Turkey* 40°25N 28°50E 203 F12
Muddebihal *India* 16°20N 76°8E 245 F3
Muddy Cr. → *U.S.A.* 38°24N 110°42W 304 G8
Mudgee *Australia* 32°32S 149°31E 283 B8
Mudhol *Andhra Pradesh,*
  India 18°58N 77°55E 244 E3
Mudhol *Karnataka, India* 16°21N 75°17E 245 F2
Mudiata
  Dem. Rep. of the Congo 7°15S 22°1E 265 D4
Mudigere → *Canada* 56°1N 107°36W 297 B7
Mudon *Burma* 16°15N 97°44E 241 G6
Mudug → *Somali Rep.* 7°0N 48°0E 267 C6
Mudukulattur *India* 9°21N 78°31E 245 K4
Mudumu △ *Namibia* 18°5S 23°29E 270 B3
Mudurnu *Turkey* 40°28N 31°12E 212 B4

Mugi *Japan* 33°40N 134°25E 222 D6
Mugia = Muxía *Spain* 43°3N 9°10W 194 B1
Mugila, Mts.
  Dem. Rep. of the Congo 7°0S 28°50E 268 D2
Mugla *Turkey* 37°15N 28°22E 205 D10
Muğla □ *Turkey* 37°15N 28°0E 205 D10
Muglad *Sudan* 11°1N 27°50E 259 F6
Muglizh *Bulgaria* 42°37N 25°32E 203 D9
Mugodzhary = Mughalzhar Taūy
  Kazakhstan 49°0N 58°40E 216 C5
Mugu *Nepal* 29°45N 82°30E 243 E10
Muhagiriya *Sudan* 12°0N 25°38E 259 F5
Muhala *Congo* 5°40S 28°42E 268 D2
Muhammad, Râs *Egypt* 27°44N 34°16E 251 C5
Muhammad Qol *Sudan* 20°53N 37°9E 256 C4
Muhammadabad *India* 26°4N 83°25E 243 F10
Muḩayriqah *Si. Arabia* 23°59N 45°4E 248 B4
Muhesi → *Tanzania* 7°0S 35°20E 268 D4
Mühldorf *Germany* 48°14N 12°32E 179 G8
Mühlenfliess → *Germany* 52°32N 13°4E 115 A5
Mühlhausen = Milevsko
  Czech Rep. 49°27N 14°21E 180 H8
Mühlhausen *Germany* 51°12N 10°27E 178 D6
Mühlig Hofmann fjell
  Antarctica 72°30S 5°0E 151 D3
Mühlviertel *Austria* 48°30N 14°10E 180 C7
Muhos *Finland* 64°47N 25°59E 160 D21
Muḩradah *Syria* 35°15N 36°35E 250 C7
Muhu *Estonia* 58°36N 23°11E 188 C2
Muhutwe *Tanzania* 1°35S 31°45E 268 C3
Mui Wo *China* 22°16N 113°59E 219 a
Muiden *Neths.* 52°20N 5°4E 170 B6
Muie *Angola* 14°23S 20°25E 265 E4
Muika *Japan* 37°5N 138°50E 221 F9
Muine Bheag *Ireland* 52°42N 6°58E 166 D5
Muineachán = Monaghan
  Ireland 54°15N 6°57W 166 B5
Muir, L. *Australia* 34°30S 116°40E 279 F2
Muir of Ord *U.K.* 57°32N 4°28W 167 D8
Muisné *Ecuador* 0°36N 80°2W 328 C1
Muizenberg *S. Africa* 34°5S 18°27E 118 E1
Mujahidpur *India* 28°33N 77°14E 120 B2
Mujeres, I. *Mexico* 21°15N 86°43W 320 B2
Mujnak = Muynak
  Uzbekistan 43°44N 59°10E 216 D5
Mujui dos Campos *Brazil* 2°35S 54°41W 329 D7
Muka, Tanjung *Malaysia* 5°28N 100°11E 237 a
Mukacheve *Ukraine* 48°27N 22°45E 182 B7
Mukacheve = Mukacheve
  Ukraine 48°27N 22°45E 182 B7
Mukah *Malaysia* 2°55N 112°5E 235 B4
Mukandpur *India* 28°44N 77°11E 120 A2
Mukandwara *India* 24°49N 75°59E 242 G6
Mukawa *Papua N. G.* 9°38S 149°59E 286 E5
Mukawwa, Geziret *Egypt* 23°55N 35°53E 246 F2
Mukawwar *Sudan* 20°50N 37°17E 256 C4
Mukaylah *Si. Arabia* 19°16N 41°48E 248 C3
Mukdahan *Thailand* 16°32N 104°43E 236 D5
Mukden = Shenyang
  China 41°48N 123°27E 224 B1
Mukerian *India* 31°57N 75°37E 242 D6
Mukhavets → *Belarus* 52°5N 23°39E 185 F10
Mukher *India* 18°42N 77°22E 244 E3
Mukhmas *West Bank* 31°52N 35°17E 123 A2
Mukhtolovo *Russia* 55°29N 43°15E 190 C6
Mukhtuya = Lensk
  Russia 60°48N 114°55E 215 C12
Mukinbudin *Australia* 30°55S 118°5E 279 F2
Mukishi *Kasai-Occ.,*
  Dem. Rep. of the Congo 5°39S 21°3E 265 D4
Mukishi *Katanga,*
  Dem. Rep. of the Congo 8°30S 24°44E 265 D4
Muko *Japan* 34°55N 135°42E 223 C7
Muko → *Japan* 34°48N 135°22E 223 A1
Muko Phetra △ *Thailand* 6°57N 99°33E 237 J2
Mukojima *Japan* 34°53N 139°49E 140 A3
Mukomuko *Indonesia* 2°30S 101°10E 234 C2
Mukomwenze
  Dem. Rep. of the Congo 6°49S 27°15E 268 D2
Mukono *Uganda* 0°21N 32°45E 268 B3
Muktsar *India* 30°30N 74°30E 242 D6
Mukur = Moqor *Afghan.* 32°50N 67°42E 242 C2
Mukutuwa → *Canada* 53°10N 97°24W 297 C9
Mukwela *Zambia* 17°0S 26°40E 269 F2
Mukwonago *U.S.A.* 42°52N 88°20W 311 A8
Mul *India* 20°4N 79°4E 244 D4
Mula → *India* 38°3N 1°33W 197 G3
Mula → *Pakistan* 27°57N 67°36E 242 F2
Mulako Atoll *Maldives* 3°0N 73°30E 272 d
Mulamba
  Dem. Rep. of the Congo 6°21S 21°13E 265 D4
Mulanay *Phil.* 13°31N 122°24E 232 E4
Mulange
  Dem. Rep. of the Congo 4°30S 27°10E 268 C2
Mulanje, Mt. *Malawi* 16°2S 35°33E 269 F4
Mulatre, Pte. *Dominica* 15°17N 61°15W 323 k
Mulatupo Sasardi *Panama* 8°57N 77°45W 320 E4
Mulbagal *India* 13°10N 78°24E 245 H4
Mulben *S. Africa* 26°17S 28°32E 123 B2
Mulberry *U.S.A.* 27°54N 81°59W 317 H6
Mulberry Grove *U.S.A.* 38°56N 89°16W 310 F7
Mulchatna → *U.S.A.* 59°40N 157°7W 303 G8
Mulchén *Chile* 37°45S 72°20W 338 D1
Mulde → *Germany* 51°53N 12°15E 178 D8
Muldraugh *U.S.A.* 37°56N 85°59W 311 G11
Mule Creek Junction
  U.S.A. 43°23N 104°13W 304 E11
Mulegé *Mexico* 26°53N 111°59W 318 B2
Muleshoe *U.S.A.* 34°13N 102°43W 314 D3
Muletta, Gara *Ethiopia* 9°13N 41°27E 257 F5
Mulgrave *Canada* 45°38N 61°31W 299 C7
Mulgrave I. = Badu
  Australia 10°7S 142°11E 280 a
Mulhacén *Spain* 37°4N 3°20W 195 H7
Mülheim *Germany* 51°25N 6°54E 178 D2
Mulhouse *France* 47°40N 7°20E 173 E14
Muli *Sichuan, China* 27°52N 101°8E 228 D3
Muli *India* 22°40N 71°30E 244 B1
Mulifanua *Samoa* 13°50S 171°59W 287 V20
Muling *China* 44°35N 130°10E 227 B16
Mulki *India* 13°6N 74°48E 245 H2
Mull *U.K.* 56°25N 5°56W 167 E3
Mull, Sound of *U.K.* 56°30N 5°50W 167 E3
Mullach Íde = Malahide
  Ireland 53°26N 6°9W 120 A3
Mullaittivu *Sri Lanka* 9°15N 80°49E 245 K5
Mullen *U.S.A.* 42°3N 101°1W 308 D3
Mullengudgery *Australia* 31°43S 147°23E 283 B8
Mullens *U.S.A.* 37°35N 81°23W 309 G11
Muller, Pegunungan
  Indonesia 0°30N 113°30E 235 B4
Muller Ra. *Papua N. G.* 5°30S 142°52E 286 C3
Mullet Pen. *Ireland* 54°13N 10°2W 166 B1
Mullewa *Australia* 28°29S 115°30E 279 E2
Mulligan → *Australia* 25°0S 138°6E 280 D2
Mullingar *Ireland* 53°31N 7°21W 166 C4

Mullins *U.S.A.* 34°12N 79°15W 315 D15
Mullsjö *Sweden* 57°56N 13°55E 163 G7
Mullumbimby *Australia* 28°30S 153°30E 281 D5
Mulobezi *Zambia* 16°45S 25°7E 269 F2
Mulondo *Angola* 15°41S 15°12E 265 F3
Mulonga Plain *Zambia* 16°20S 22°40E 265 F4
Mulroy B. *Ireland* 55°15N 7°46W 166 A4
Mulshi I. *India* 18°30N 73°48E 244 E1
Multai *India* 21°50N 78°21E 244 D4
Multan *Pakistan* 30°15N 71°36E 242 D4
Mulu, Gunung *Malaysia* 4°3N 114°56E 235 B4
Mulug *India* 18°11N 79°57E 244 E4
Mulumbe, Mts.
  Dem. Rep. of the Congo 8°40S 27°30E 269 D2
Mulundu
  Dem. Rep. of the Congo 6°40S 20°33E 265 D4
Mulungushi Dam *Zambia* 14°48S 28°48E 269 F2
Mulvane *U.S.A.* 37°29N 97°15W 308 G5
Mulwad *Sudan* 18°45N 30°39E 256 D3
Mulwala *Australia* 35°59S 146°0E 283 C7
Mulwala, L. *Australia* 35°59S 146°0E 283 C7
Muma
  Dem. Rep. of the Congo 3°25N 23°21E 264 B4
Mumbai *India* 18°56N 72°50E 130 B2
Mumbai Chhatrapati Shivaji Int. ✈
  (BOM) *India* 19°5N 72°52E 130 A2
Mumbeji *Zambia* 13°51S 23°39E 265 E4
Mumbondo *Angola* 10°9S 14°15E 265 D2
Mumbwa *Zambia* 15°0S 27°0E 269 F2
Mumeng *Papua N. G.* 7°1S 146°37E 286 C4
Mumias *Kenya* 0°20N 34°29E 268 C4
Mumra *Russia* 45°45N 47°41E 191 H8
Mun → *Thailand* 15°19N 105°30E 236 E5
Mun-gyeong *S. Korea* 36°35N 128°12E 224 D4
Muna *Indonesia* 5°0S 122°30E 231 F6
Munabao *India* 25°45N 70°17E 242 G4
Munamagi *Estonia* 57°43N 27°4E 188 D4
Muncan *Indonesia* 8°34S 115°11E 231 K18
Muncar *Indonesia* 8°26S 114°20E 231 J17
Munch-museum *Norway* 59°55N 10°46E 133 A4
München *Germany* 48°8N 11°34E 179 G7
Müncheberg *Germany* 52°30N 14°9E 178 C9
Münchehofe *Germany* 52°29N 13°40E 115 B5
München Franz Josef Strauss Int. ✈
  (MUC) *Germany* 48°21N 11°47E 131 A2
Munchen-Gladbach =
  Mönchengladbach
  Germany 51°11N 6°27E 178 D2
Munchique *Colombia* 2°44N 77°1W 328 C2
Muncho Lake *Canada* 59°0N 125°50W 296 B3
Munch'ŏn *N. Korea* 39°14N 127°19E 224 E3
Muncie *U.S.A.* 40°12N 85°23W 311 D11
Muncoonie L. West
  Australia 25°12S 138°40E 280 D2
Munda *Solomon Is.* 8°20S 157°16E 287 M9
Mundabbera *Australia* 25°36S 151°18E 281 D5
Mundakayam *India* 9°30N 76°50E 245 K3
Mundal *Sri Lanka* 7°48N 79°48E 245 L4
Mundelein *U.S.A.* 42°16N 88°0W 311 B8
Mundemba *Cameroon* 4°57N 8°52E 264 B1
Munderfing *Austria* 48°2N 13°4E 180 C6
Münden *Germany* 51°25N 9°38E 178 D5
Mundiwindi *Australia* 23°47S 120°9E 278 D3
Mundo → *Spain* 38°30N 2°15W 197 G2
Mundo Novo *Brazil* 11°50S 40°29W 333 D3
Mundo Nuevo *Trin. & Tob.* 10°28N 61°15W 323 l
Mundra *India* 22°54N 69°48E 242 H3
Mundrabilla *Australia* 31°52S 127°51E 279 F4
Munduk *Indonesia* 8°17S 115°4E 231 J18
Munenga *Angola* 10°2S 14°41E 265 D2
Munera *Spain* 39°2N 2°29W 197 F2
Mungallala *Australia* 26°28S 147°34E 281 D4
Mungallala Cr. →
  Australia 28°53S 147°5E 281 D4
Mungana *Australia* 17°8S 144°27E 280 B3
Mungaoli *India* 24°24N 78°7E 243 G8
Mungari *Mozam.* 17°12S 33°30E 269 F3
Mungbere
  Dem. Rep. of the Congo 2°36N 28°28E 268 B2
Mungeli *India* 22°4N 81°41E 243 H9
Munger *India* 25°23N 86°30E 243 G12
Mungilli ○ *Australia* 24°31S 128°45E 279 C4

Muping *China* 37°22N 121°36E 227 F11
Muqaddam, Wadi → *Sudan* 18°4N 31°30E 256 D3
Muqdisho *Somali Rep.* 2°2N 45°25E 267 D6
Muqshin, W. → *Oman* 19°44N 55°14E 249 C6
Muquequete *Angola* 14°50S 14°16E 265 E2
Mur → *Austria* 46°18N 16°52E 181 E9
Mûr-de-Bretagne *France* 48°12N 3°0W 172 D4
Muradiye *Manisa, Turkey* 38°39N 27°21E 205 C9
Muradiye *Van, Turkey* 39°0N 43°44E 213 C10
Murai Res. *Singapore* 1°23N 103°43E 138 A2
Murakami *Japan* 38°14N 139°29E 220 E9
Muralla = Prince of Wales I.
  Australia 10°40S 142°10E 280 a
Murallón, Cerro *Chile* 49°48S 73°30W 338 C2
Muranda *Rwanda* 1°52S 29°20E 268 C2
Murang'a *Kenya* 0°45S 37°9E 268 C4
Muranów *Poland* 52°14N 20°58E 142 B1
Murashi *Russia* 59°30N 49°0E 186 C8
Murat *France* 45°7N 2°53E 174 C6
Murat → *Turkey* 38°46N 40°0E 213 C9
Murat Bay = Ceduna
  Australia 32°7S 133°46E 281 E1
Murat Daği *Turkey* 38°55N 29°43E 205 C11
Muratlı *Turkey* 41°10N 27°29E 203 E11
Murau *Austria* 47°6N 14°10E 180 C7
Murava *Belarus* 52°39N 24°15E 185 F11
Muravera *Italy* 39°25N 9°34E 200 C2
Muravyevo = Mažeikiai
  Lithuania 56°20N 22°20E 184 B9
Murayama *Japan* 38°30N 140°25E 220 E10
Murça *Portugal* 41°24N 7°28W 194 D3
Murcaayo *Somali Rep.* 11°41N 50°34E 267 B7
Murchison *N.Z.* 41°49S 172°21E 285 B7
Murchison → *Australia* 27°45S 114°0E 279 E1
Murchison, Mt.
  Antarctica 73°25S 166°22E 151 D11
Murchison, Mt. *N.Z.* 43°0S 171°22E 285 D6
Murchison Falls *Uganda* 2°15N 31°30E 268 B3
Murchison Falls = *Uganda* 2°15N 31°48E 268 B3
Murchison Mts. *N.Z.* 45°13S 167°23E 285 D2
Murchison Ra. *Australia* 20°0S 134°10E 280 C1
Murchison Rapids *Malawi* 15°55S 34°35E 269 F3
Murchison Roadhouse
  Australia 27°39S 116°14E 279 E2
Murcia *Spain* 38°5N 1°10W 197 G3
Murcia □ *Spain* 37°50N 1°30W 197 H3
Murdo *U.S.A.* 43°53N 100°43W 308 D3
Murdoch Pt. *Australia* 14°37S 144°55E 280 A4
Mürefte *Turkey* 40°40N 27°14E 203 F11
Mureş □ *Romania* 46°45N 24°40E 183 D9
Mureş → *Romania* 46°15N 20°13E 182 D5
Mureşul = Mureş →
  Romania 46°15N 20°13E 182 D5
Muret *France* 43°30N 1°20E 174 E5
Murewa *Zimbabwe* 17°39S 31°47E 271 A5
Murfreesboro *N.C.,*
  U.S.A. 36°27N 77°6W 315 C16
Murfreesboro *Tenn.,*
  U.S.A. 35°51N 86°24W 315 D11
Murgab *Tajikistan* 38°10N 74°2E 217 F8
Murgap = *Turkmenistan* 38°18N 61°12E 247 B9
Murgenella *Australia* 11°34S 132°56E 278 B5
Murgeni *Romania* 46°12N 28°1E 183 D13
Murgha Kibzai *Pakistan* 30°44N 69°25E 242 D3
Murghob = Murgap
  Tajikistan 38°10N 74°2E 217 F8
Muri *Cook Is.* 21°15S 159°43W 289 H5
Muri *India* 23°22N 85°52E 243 H11
Muria *Indonesia* 6°36S 110°53E 235 D4
Muriaé *Brazil* 21°8S 42°23W 333 F3
Murias de Paredes *Spain* 42°52N 6°11W 194 C4
Murici *Brazil* 9°19S 35°56W 332 C4
Muriége *Angola* 9°58S 21°11E 265 D4
Muriel Mine *Zimbabwe* 17°14S 30°40E 269 F3
Murilo *Angola* 10°44S 20°20E 265 E4
Murillo *Russia* 59°59N 30°29E 137 B2
Müritz *Germany* 53°25N 12°42E 178 B8
Müritz □ *Germany* 53°25N 12°40E 178 B8
Muriwai Beach *N.Z.* 36°50S 174°26E 284 C3
Murkong Selek *India* 27°44N 95°18E 241 K6
Murliganj *India* 25°54N 86°59E 243 G12
Murmansk *Russia* 68°57N 33°10E 186 A5
Murmashi *Russia* 68°47N 32°42E 160 B25
Muro *Haute-Corse, France* 42°34N 8°54E 175 F12
Muro *Spain* 39°44N 3°3E 199 A10
Muro, C. de *France* 41°44N 8°37E 175 G12
Muro de Alcoy *Spain* 38°46N 0°26W 197 G4
Muro Lucano *Italy* 40°45N 15°29E 201 B8
Muros *Spain* 42°45N 9°5W 194 C1
Muros e Noya, Ría de →
  Spain 42°45N 9°0W 194 C1
Muroto *Japan* 33°18N 134°9E 222 D6
Muroto-Misaki *Japan* 33°15N 134°10E 222 D6
Murovani Kurylivtsi
  Ukraine 48°44N 27°31E 183 D12
Murowana Goślina *Poland* 52°35N 17°0E 185 F3
Murphy *U.S.A.* 43°13N 116°33W 304 E5
Murphys *U.S.A.* 38°8N 120°28W 306 G6
Murphys Station = Sunnyvale
  U.S.A. 37°23N 122°2W 306 H4
Murphysboro *U.S.A.* 37°46N 89°20W 310 G7
Murrat Sudan 18°51N 29°33E 256 D2
Murrat Wells *Sudan* 18°9S ... E 256 D2
Murray *Iowa, U.S.A.* 41°3N 93°57W 310 C3
Murray *Ky., U.S.A.* 36°37N 88°19W 309 G9
Murray *Utah, U.S.A.* 40°40N 111°53W 304 F8
Murray → *Australia* 35°20S 139°22E 282 C3
Murray, L. *Papua N. G.* 7°0S 141°35E 286 D1
Murray, L. *U.S.A.* 34°3N 81°13W 316 B6
Murray Bridge *Australia* 35°6S 139°14E 282 C3
Murray Fracture Zone
  Pac. Oc. 35°0N 130°0W 289 D14
Murray Harbour *Canada* 46°0N 62°28W 299 C7
Murray River △ *Australia* 34°23S 140°32E 281 E3
Murray-Sunset △
  Australia 34°45S 141°30E 282 C4
Murrayfield *S. Africa* 31°58S 23°47E 121 B2
Murraysburg *S. Africa* 31°58S 23°47E 270 D3
Murree *Pakistan* 33°56N 73°28E 242 C5
Murrieta *U.S.A.* 33°33N 117°13W 307 M9
Murro di Porco, Capo *Italy* 37°0N 15°20E 201 F8
Murrumbateman *Australia* 34°58S 149°0E 283 C8
Murrumbidgee → *Australia* 34°43S 143°12E 282 B5
Murrumburrah *Australia* 34°32S 148°22E 283 C8
Murrurundi *Australia* 31°42S 150°51E 283 B9
Murshid *Sudan* 21°40N ... E 256 C3
Murshidabad *India* 24°11N 88°19E 243 G13
Murska Sobota *Slovenia* 46°39N 16°12E 199 B13
Murtajapur *India* 20°40N 77°25E 244 D3

Murtle L. Canada 52°8N 119°38W 296 C5
Murtoa Australia 36°35S 142°28E 282 D5
Murtosa Portugal 40°44N 8°40W 194 E2
Muru → Brazil 8°9S 70°45W 330 B3
Murud India 18°19N 72°58E 244 E1
Murung → Indonesia 0°12N 114°3E 235 B4
Murungu Tanzania 4°12S 31°10E 268 C3
Murupara N.Z. 38°28S 176°42E 284 E5
Mururoa French Polynesia 21°52S 138°55W 289 f
Murwara India 23°46N 80°28E 243 H9
Murwillumbah Australia 28°18S 153°27E 281 D5
Mürz → Austria 47°30N 15°25E 180 D8
Mürzzuschlag Austria 47°36N 15°41E 180 D8
Mus India 9°14N 92°47E 245 K11
Muş Turkey 38°45N 41°30E 213 C9
Muş □ Turkey 38°45N 41°30E 213 C9
Musa Dem. Rep. of the Congo 2°40N 19°18E 264 B3
Musa → Papua N. G. 9°3S 148°55E 286 E5
Mûsa, Gebel Egypt 28°33N 33°59E 251 K4
Musa Khel Pakistan 30°59N 69°52E 242 D3
Mūsa Qal'eh Afghan. 32°20N 64°50E 240 B2
Musabeyli Turkey 36°53N 36°55E 250 B7
Musadi Dem. Rep. of the Congo 2°31S 22°50E 264 C4
Musafirkhana India 26°22N 81°48E 243 F9
Musala Bulgaria 42°13N 23°37E 202 D7
Musala Indonesia 1°41N 98°28E 234 B1
Musan N. Korea 42°12N 129°12E 224 A4
Musandam, Ra's Oman 26°20N 56°20E 249 A7
Musangu Dem. Rep. of the Congo 10°28S 23°55E 265 E4
Musasa Tanzania 3°25S 31°30E 268 C3
Musashino Japan 35°42N 139°33E 140 A2
Musay'īd Qatar 25°0N 51°33E 247 E6
Musaymīr Yemen 13°27N 44°37E 248 D4
Muscat = Masqat Oman 23°37N 58°36E 249 B7
Muscat & Oman = Oman ■ Asia 23°0N 58°0E 249 B7
Muscatatuck → U.S.A. 38°46N 86°10W 311 F10
Muscatine U.S.A. 41°25N 91°3W 310 C5
Muschu I. Papua N. G. 3°25S 143°35E 286 B2
Muscle Shoals U.S.A. 34°45N 87°40W 315 D11
Muscoda U.S.A. 43°11N 90°27W 310 A6
Musengezi = Unsengedsi → Zimbabwe 15°43S 31°14E 269 F3
Museu Nacional Brazil 22°59S 43°13W 135 B1
Museumquartier Vienna, Austria 142 c1
Musgrave Harbour Canada 49°27N 53°58W 299 C9
Musgrave Ranges Australia 26°0S 132°0E 279 E5
Mushie Dem. Rep. of the Congo 2°56S 16°55E 264 C3
Mushima Zambia 14°10S 24°56E 265 E4
Mushin Nigeria 6°31N 3°21E 124 A2
Musi → India 16°41N 79°40E 244 F4
Musi → Indonesia 2°20S 104°56E 234 C2
Musiektheater Amsterdam, Neths. 112 b3
Musina S. Africa 22°20S 30°5E 271 B5
Musiri India 10°56N 78°27E 245 J4
Muskeg → Canada 60°20N 123°20W 296 A4
Muskego U.S.A. 42°55N 88°8W 311 B8
Muskegon U.S.A. 43°14N 86°16W 311 A10
Muskegon → U.S.A. 43°14N 86°21W 308 D10
Muskegon Heights U.S.A. 43°12N 86°16W 311 A10
Muskogee U.S.A. 35°45N 95°22W 314 D7
Muskoka, L. Canada 45°0N 79°25W 312 B5
Muskoka Falls Canada 44°59N 79°17W 312 B5
Muskwa → Canada 58°47N 122°48W 296 B4
Muslim Mindanao □ Phil. 8°0N 123°0E 233 H3
Muslim Quarter Jerusalem 123 a3
Muslīmiyah Syria 36°19N 37°12E 246 B3
Musmar Sudan 18°13N 35°40E 256 D4
Musocco Italy 45°29N 9°8E 129 B1
Musofu Zambia 13°30S 29°0E 269 E2
Musoma Tanzania 1°30S 33°48E 268 C3
Musquaro, L. Canada 50°38N 61°5W 299 B7
Musquodoboit Harbour Canada 44°50N 63°9W 299 D7
Mussau I. Papua N. G. 1°30S 149°40E 286 A5
Musselburgh U.K. 55°57N 3°2W 167 F5
Musselshell → U.S.A. 47°21N 107°57W 304 C10
Mussende Angola 10°32S 16°5E 265 E3
Musserra Angola 7°37S 13°2E 265 D2
Mussidan France 45°2N 0°22E 174 C4
Mussolinea di Sardegna = Arboréa Italy 39°46N 8°35E 200 C1
Mussolo Angola 9°59S 17°19E 265 D3
Mussomeli Italy 37°35N 13°45E 200 E6
Mussoorie India 30°27N 78°6E 242 D8
Mussuco Angola 17°2S 19°3E 265 F3
Mustafakemalpaşa Turkey 40°2N 28°24E 203 F12
Mustahil Ethiopia 5°16N 44°45E 267 C5
Mustang Nepal 29°10N 83°55E 243 E10
Mustansiriya Iraq 33°22N 44°24E 113 A2
Musters, L. Argentina 45°20S 69°25W 336 C3
Mustique I. St. Vincent 12°52N 61°11W 323 n
Musturud Egypt 30°8N 31°17E 117 A2
Musudan N. Korea 40°50N 129°43E 224 B4
Muswell Hill U.K. 51°35N 0°8W 125 A3
Muswellbrook Australia 32°16S 150°56E 283 B9
Muszyna Poland 49°22N 20°55E 185 J7
Mût Egypt 25°28N 28°58E 256 B2
Mut Turkey 36°40N 33°28E 250 B4
Mutalau Cook Is. 18°56S 169°50W 289 g
Mutanabi Iraq 33°19N 44°21E 113 B2
Mutanda Dem. Rep. of the Congo 5°17S 16°34E 265 D3
Mutanda Mozam. 21°0S 33°34E 271 B5
Mutanda Zambia 12°24S 26°13E 269 E2
Mutankiang = Mudanjiang China 44°38N 129°30E 227 B15
Mutanshe Taiwan 22°9N 120°48E 225 D2
Mutare Zimbabwe 18°58S 32°38E 269 F3
Mutawintji △ Australia 31°10S 142°30E 281 E3
Mutha Kenya 1°48S 38°26E 268 C4
Muthana Iraq 33°19N 44°27E 113 B2
Muting Indonesia 7°23S 140°20E 231 F10
Mutki = Mirtağ Turkey 38°23N 41°56E 246 B4
Mutoko Zimbabwe 17°24S 32°13E 271 A5
Mutomo Kenya 1°51S 38°12E 268 C4
Mutoray Russia 60°56N 101°0E 215 C11
Mutoto Dem. Rep. of the Congo 5°42S 22°42E 265 D4
Mutoxo Angola 12°17S 21°40E 265 E4
Mutsamudu Comoros Is. 12°10S 44°25E 272 a
Mutshatsha Dem. Rep. of the Congo 10°35S 24°20E 265 E4
Mutsu Japan 41°5N 140°55E 220 D10
Mutsu-Wan Japan 41°5N 140°55E 220 D10
Muttaburra Australia 22°38S 144°29E 280 C3
Muttalip Turkey 39°50N 30°32E 205 B12
Mutton I. Ireland 52°49N 9°32W 166 D2
Muttra = Mathura India 27°30N 77°40E 242 F7
Muttukuru India 14°16N 80°6E 245 G5
Mutuáli Mozam. 14°55S 37°0E 269 E4
Mutum Biyu Nigeria 8°40N 10°50E 263 D7
Mutumba Burundi 3°25S 29°21E 268 C2
Mutunópolis Brazil 13°40S 49°15W 333 D2
Mutur Sri Lanka 8°27N 81°16E 245 K5
Muweilih Egypt 30°42N 34°19E 251 H5
Muxaluando Angola 8°8S 14°18E 265 D2
Muxía Spain 43°3N 9°10W 194 B1
Muxima Angola 9°33S 13°58E 265 D2
Muy Muy Nic. 12°39N 85°36W 320 D2
Muyinga Burundi 3°14S 30°33E 268 C3
Muynak Uzbekistan 43°44N 59°10E 216 D5
Muyunkum, Peski = Moyynqum Kazakhstan 44°12N 71°0E 217 D8
Muz Tag China 36°25N 87°25E 217 E11
Muzaffarabad Pakistan 34°25N 73°30E 243 B5
Muzaffargarh Pakistan 30°5N 71°14E 242 D4
Muzaffarnagar India 29°26N 77°40E 242 E7
Muzaffarpur India 26°7N 85°23E 243 F11
Muzafirpur Pakistan 30°58N 69°9E 242 D3
Muzeze Angola 15°3S 17°43E 265 F3
Muzhi Russia 65°25N 64°40E 186 A11
Muzillac France 47°35N 2°30W 172 E4
Muzon, C. U.S.A. 54°40N 132°42W 303 J14
Muztagh-Ata China 38°17N 75°7E 217 E9
Muztor = Toktogul Kyrgyzstan 41°50N 72°50E 217 D8
Muzūra Egypt 28°53N 30°48E 256 J7
Mvadhi-Ousyé Gabon 1°13N 13°12E 264 B2
Mvam Gabon 0°13S 9°39E 264 C1
Mvangan Cameroon 2°17N 11°43E 264 B2
Mvôlô South Sudan 6°2N 29°53E 257 F2
Mvuma Zimbabwe 19°16S 30°30E 269 F3
Mvurwi Zimbabwe 17°0S 30°57E 269 F3
Mwabvi ⌓ Malawi 16°42S 35°0E 269 F3
Mwadi-Kalumbu Dem. Rep. of the Congo 7°53S 18°43E 265 D3
Mwadui Tanzania 3°26S 33°32E 268 C3
Mwali = Mohéli Comoros Is. 12°20S 43°40E 272 a
Mwambo Tanzania 10°30S 40°22E 269 E5
Mwandi Zambia 17°30S 24°51E 269 F1
Mwanza Katanga, Dem. Rep. of the Congo 7°55S 26°43E 265 D5
Mwanza Tanzania 2°30S 32°58E 268 C3
Mwanza Zambia 16°58S 24°28E 265 F4
Mwanza □ Tanzania 2°0S 33°0E 268 C3
Mwaya Tanzania 9°32S 33°55E 269 D3
Mweelrea Ireland 53°39N 9°49W 166 C2
Mweka Dem. Rep. of the Congo 4°50S 21°34E 265 C4
Mwendjila Dem. Rep. of the Congo 7°12S 18°51E 265 D3
Mwene-Ditu Dem. Rep. of the Congo 6°35S 22°27E 265 D4
Mwenezi Zimbabwe 21°15S 30°48E 269 G3
Mwenezi → Mozam. 22°40S 31°50E 269 G3
Mwenga Dem. Rep. of the Congo 3°1S 28°28E 268 C2
Mweru, L. Zambia 9°0S 28°40E 269 D2
Mweru Wantipa △ Zambia 8°39S 29°25E 269 D2
Mwetshi Dem. Rep. of the Congo 4°50S 22°38E 265 C4
Mweza Range Zimbabwe 21°0S 30°0E 269 G3
Mwilambwe Dem. Rep. of the Congo 8°7S 25°5E 265 D5
Mwimbi Tanzania 8°38S 31°39E 269 D3
Mwingi Kenya 0°56S 38°4E 268 C4
Mwinilunga Zambia 11°43S 24°25E 265 E4
My Son Vietnam 15°48N 108°7E 236 E7
My Tho Vietnam 10°29N 106°23E 237 G6
Mya, O. → Algeria 30°46N 4°54E 261 B5
Myajlar India 26°15N 70°20E 242 F4
Myakinino Russia 55°48N 37°22E 129 B2
Myakka → U.S.A. 26°56N 82°11W 317 J7
Myall Lakes △ Australia 32°25S 152°30E 283 B10
Myanaung Burma 18°18N 95°22E 241 F5
Myanmar = Burma ■ Asia 21°0N 96°30E 241 E6
Myaung Burma 21°50N 95°25E 241 E5
Myaungmya Burma 16°30N 94°40E 241 G5
Mycenæ = Mikines Greece 37°43N 22°46E 204 D4
Myebon Burma 20°3N 93°22E 241 E4
Myedna Belarus 51°52N 23°42E 185 G10
Myeik = Mergui Burma 12°26N 98°34E 236 F2
Myeik Kyunzu Burma 11°30N 97°30E 237 G1
Myerstown U.S.A. 40°22N 76°19W 313 F8
Myingyan Burma 21°30N 95°20E 241 E5
Myitkyina Burma 25°24N 97°26E 241 C6
Myitson Burma 23°16N 96°34E 241 D6
Myittha Burma 21°25N 96°8E 241 E6
Myittha → Burma 23°12N 94°17E 241 D5
Myjava Slovak Rep. 48°41N 17°37E 181 C10
Mykerinos Egypt 29°58N 31°8E 117 B1
Mykhaylivka Ukraine 47°12N 35°15E 189 J8
Mykines Færoe Is. 62°7N 7°35W 160 E9
Myking Norway 60°41N 5°19E 164 D2
Mykolayiv Ukraine 46°58N 32°0E 189 J7
Mykolayiv □ Ukraine 47°20N 31°50E 189 J6
Mykonos Greece 37°30N 25°25E 205 D7
Mylius Erichsen Land Greenland 81°30N 27°0W 154 A8
Myllypuro Finland 60°13N 25°3E 121 B3
Mymensingh Bangla. 24°45N 90°24E 241 C3
Mynydd Du U.K. 51°52N 3°50W 169 F4
Myo-gyi Burma 21°27N 96°22E 241 E6
Myohaung Burma 20°35N 93°11E 241 E4
Myohla Burma 19°16N 95°25E 241 F5
Myotha Burma 21°41N 95°43E 241 E5
Myothit Kachin, Burma 24°24N 97°24E 241 C6
Myothit Magwe, Burma 20°12N 95°27E 241 E5
Myrasýsla □ Iceland 64°45N 21°30W 155 C5
Mýrdalsjökull Iceland 63°40N 19°6W 155 D7
Myrhorod Ukraine 49°58N 33°37E 189 H7
Mýri Iceland 65°23N 17°23W 155 B9
Myrtle Beach U.S.A. 33°42N 78°53W 315 E15
Myrtle Creek U.S.A. 43°1N 123°17W 304 E2
Myrtle Grove U.S.A. 30°23N 87°17W 317 E2
Myrtle Point U.S.A. 43°4N 124°8W 304 E1
Myrtleford Australia 36°34S 146°44E 283 D7
Myrtou Cyprus 35°18N 33°4E 207 E9
Myrviken Sweden 62°58N 14°20E 162 B8
Mysen Norway 59°33N 11°20E 164 E8
Mysia Turkey 39°50N 27°0E 203 G11
Myślenice Poland 49°51N 19°57E 185 J6
Myślibórz Poland 52°55N 14°50E 185 F1
Mysłowice Poland 50°15N 19°12E 185 H6
Myslowitz = Mysłowice Poland 50°15N 19°12E 185 H6
Mysore = Karnataka □ India 13°15N 77°0E 245 H3
Mysore India 12°17N 76°41E 245 H3
Mystic Conn., U.S.A. 41°21N 71°58W 313 E13
Mystic Iowa, U.S.A. 40°47N 92°57W 310 D4
Mystic → U.S.A. 42°22N 71°3W 116 A2
Mysuru = Mysore India 12°17N 76°41E 245 H3
Myszków Poland 50°45N 19°22E 185 H6
Myszyniec Poland 53°23N 21°21E 184 E8
Mytishchi Russia 55°50N 37°50E 188 E9
Mývatn Iceland 65°36N 17°0W 155 B10
M'zab, Oued → Algeria 32°15N 5°0E 261 B6
Mže → Czech Rep. 49°46N 13°24E 180 B6
Mzimba Malawi 11°55S 33°39E 269 E3
Mzimkulu → S. Africa 30°44S 30°28E 271 D5
Mzimvubu → S. Africa 31°38S 29°33E 271 D4
Mzuzu Malawi 11°30S 33°55E 269 E3

N

Na Clocha Liatha = Greystones Ireland 53°9N 6°5W 166 C5
Na Haeo △ Thailand 17°31N 100°58E 236 D3
Na Hearadh = Harris U.K. 57°50N 6°55W 167 D2
Na-lang Burma 22°42N 97°33E 241 D6
Na Noi Thailand 18°19N 100°43E 236 C3
Na Phao Laos 17°35N 105°44E 236 D5
Na Sam Vietnam 22°3N 106°37E 228 F6
Na Thon Thailand 9°32N 99°56E 237 b
Naab → Germany 49°1N 12°2E 179 F8
Nä'älehu U.S.A. 19°4N 155°35W 302 D6
Na'am Sudan 9°42N 28°27E 257 F2
Na'am → South Sudan 6°48N 29°57E 257 F2
Naama Algeria 33°16N 0°19E 261 B5
Naama □ Algeria 33°15N 0°45E 261 B5
Naantali Finland 60°29N 22°2E 188 B1
Naas Ireland 53°12N 6°40W 166 C5
Nababeep S. Africa 29°36S 17°46E 270 C2
Nabadwip = Navadwip India 23°34N 88°20E 243 H13
Nabari Japan 34°37N 136°5E 223 C8
Nabawa Australia 28°30S 114°48E 279 E1
Nabberu, L. Australia 25°50S 120°30E 279 E3
Nabburg Germany 49°27N 12°11E 179 F8
Naberezhnyye Chelny Russia 55°42N 52°19E 190 C11
Nabesna U.S.A. 62°22N 143°0W 303 E12
Nabeul Tunisia 36°30N 10°44E 258 A2
Nabeul □ Tunisia 36°30N 10°40E 261 A7
Nabha India 30°26N 76°14E 242 D7
Nabi Sâlih Egypt 28°37N 33°59E 251 K4
Nabīd Iran 29°40N 57°38E 247 D8
Nabire Indonesia 3°15S 135°26E 231 E9
Nabisar Pakistan 25°8N 69°40E 242 G3
Nabisipi → Canada 50°14N 62°13W 299 B7
Nabiswera Uganda 1°27N 32°15E 268 B3
Nāblus = Nābulus West Bank 32°14N 35°15E 251 F6
Naboomspruit S. Africa 24°32S 28°40E 271 B4
Nabou Burkina Faso 11°25N 2°50W 262 C4
Nabouwalu Fiji 17°0S 178°45E 287 A2
Nabq Egypt 28°6N 34°25E 251 K5
Nabua Phil. 13°24N 123°22E 232 E4
Nābulus West Bank 32°14N 35°15E 251 F6
Nabunturan Phil. 7°35N 125°58E 233 H5
Nacala Mozam. 14°32S 40°34E 269 E5
Nacaome Honduras 13°31N 87°30W 320 D2
Nacaroa Mozam. 14°22S 39°56E 269 E4
Naches U.S.A. 46°44N 120°42W 304 C3
Naches → U.S.A. 46°38N 120°31W 306 D6
Nachicapau, L. Canada 56°40N 68°5W 299 A6
Nachikatsuura Japan 33°33N 135°58E 223 D7
Nachingwea Tanzania 10°23S 38°49E 269 E4
Nachna India 27°34N 71°41E 242 F4
Náchod Czech Rep. 50°25N 16°8E 180 A9
Nachuge India 10°47N 92°21E 245 J11
Nacimiento, L. U.S.A. 35°46N 120°53W 306 K6
Nacka Sweden 59°19N 18°10E 139 B3
Nackara Australia 32°48S 139°12E 282 B3
Naco Mexico 31°19N 109°56W 318 A3
Nacogdoches U.S.A. 31°36N 94°39W 314 F7
Nácori Chico Mexico 29°40N 108°57W 318 B3
Nacozari de García Mexico 30°25N 109°38W 318 A3
Nacula Fiji 16°54S 177°27E 287 A1
Nada = Danzhou China 19°31N 109°33E 236 C7
Nådendal = Naantali Finland 60°29N 22°2E 188 B1
Nadezhdinsky = Serov Russia 59°29N 60°35E 186 C11
Nadi Fiji 17°42S 177°20E 287 A1
Nadi Sudan 18°40N 33°41E 256 D3
Nadiad India 22°41N 72°56E 242 H5
Nădlac Romania 46°10N 20°50E 182 D5
Nador Morocco 35°14N 2°58W 261 A4
Nadur Malta 35°54N 14°22E 206 F7
Nadur Gozo, Malta 36°2N 14°18E 206 E7
Nadūshan Iran 32°2N 53°35E 247 C7
Nadvirna Ukraine 48°37N 24°30E 183 B9
Nadvoitsy Russia 63°52N 34°14E 186 B5
Nadvornaya = Nadvirna Ukraine 48°37N 24°30E 183 B9
Nadym Russia 65°35N 72°42E 214 C8
Nadym → Russia 66°12N 72°0E 214 C8
Naenae N.Z. 41°12S 174°57E 143 B2
Nærbø Norway 58°40N 5°39E 164 F2
Nærsnes Norway 59°45N 10°27E 133 B1
Næstved Denmark 55°13N 11°44E 163 J5
Nafada Nigeria 11°8N 11°20E 263 C7
Nafpaktos Greece 38°24N 21°50E 204 C3
Nafplio Greece 37°33N 22°50E 204 D4
Naft-e Safīd Iran 31°40N 49°17E 247 D6
Naftan Pt. N. Marianas 15°5N 145°45E 302 e
Naftshahr Iran 34°0N 45°30E 213 E11
Nafud Desert = An Nafūd Si. Arabia 28°15N 41°0E 246 D4
Nafūsah, Jabal Libya 32°12N 12°30E 258 B2
Nag Hammâdi Egypt 26°2N 32°18E 256 B3
Naga Japan 26°34N 127°43E 288 a
Naga Camarines S., Phil. 13°38N 123°15E 232 E4
Naga Cebu, Phil. 10°13N 123°45E 233 F4
Naga Zamboanga del S., Phil. 7°46N 122°45E 233 H4
Naga, Kreb en Africa 24°12N 6°0W 260 D3
Naga Hills = Nagaland □ India 26°0N 94°30E 241 C5
Naga-Shima Kagoshima, Japan 32°10N 130°9E 222 E2
Naga-Shima Yamaguchi, Japan 33°49N 132°5E 222 D4
Nagagami Canada 50°23N 84°20W 298 B3
Nagahama Ehime, Japan 33°36N 132°29E 222 D4
Nagahama Shiga, Japan 35°23N 136°16E 223 B8
Nagai Japan 38°6N 140°2E 220 E10
Nagai I. U.S.A. 55°5N 160°0W 303 J8
Nagaland □ India 26°0N 94°30E 241 C5
Nagambie Australia 36°47S 145°10E 283 D6
Nagano Japan 36°40N 138°10E 223 A10
Nagano □ Japan 36°15N 138°0E 223 A10
Nagaoka Japan 37°27N 138°51E 221 F9
Nagaon = Nowgong India 26°20N 92°50E 241 B4
Nagappattinam India 10°46N 79°51E 245 J4
Nagar → Bangla. 24°27N 89°12E 241 C2
Nagar Karnul India 16°29N 78°20E 245 F4
Nagar Parkar Pakistan 24°28N 70°46E 242 G4
Nagara-Gawa → Japan 35°40N 136°43E 223 B8
Nagaram India 18°21N 80°26E 244 E5
Nagarhole △ India 12°0N 76°10E 245 J3
Nagari Hills India 13°3N 79°45E 245 H4
Nagarjuna Sagar India 16°30N 79°13E 245 F4
Nagasaki Japan 32°47N 129°50E 222 E1
Nagasaki □ Japan 32°50N 129°40E 222 E1
Nagato Japan 34°19N 131°5E 222 C3
Nagatsuta Japan 35°32N 139°31E 140 B2
Nagaur India 27°15N 73°45E 242 F5
Nagayo Japan 32°48N 129°50E 222 E1
Nagbhir India 20°34N 79°55E 244 D4
Nagda India 23°27N 75°25E 242 H6
Nagercoil India 8°12N 77°26E 245 K3
Nagina India 29°30N 78°30E 243 E8
Nagīneh Iran 34°20N 57°15E 247 C8
Naginimara India 26°49N 94°50E 241 B5
Nagir Pakistan 36°12N 74°42E 243 A6
Naglarby Sweden 60°25N 15°34E 162 D9
Nagles Mts. Ireland 52°8N 8°30W 166 D3
Nago-wan Japan 26°34N 127°57E 288 a
Nagod India 24°34N 80°36E 243 G9
Nagold Germany 48°32N 8°43E 179 G4
Nagold → Germany 48°52N 8°42E 179 G4
Nagoorin Australia 24°17S 151°15E 280 C5
Nagorno-Karabakh □ Azerbaijan 39°55N 46°45E 213 C12
Nagornyy Russia 55°58N 124°57E 215 D13
Nagoya Indonesia 1°15N 104°5E 234 B2
Nagoya Japan 35°10N 136°50E 223 B8
Nagoya ✈ (NGO) Japan 35°14N 136°57E 223 B8
Nagpartian = Burgos Phil. 18°31N 120°39E 232 B3
Nagpur India 21°8N 79°10E 244 D4
Nagqu China 31°29N 92°3E 218 E7
Nags Head St. Kitts & Nevis 17°13N 62°38W 322 d
Nagua Dom. Rep. 19°23N 69°50W 321 C6
Naguabo Puerto Rico 18°13N 65°44W 321 b
Nagurunguru ✪ Australia 16°45S 129°45E 278 C4
Nagyatád Hungary 46°14N 17°22E 182 D2
Nagyecsed Hungary 47°53N 22°24E 182 C7
Nagykálló Hungary 47°53N 21°51E 182 C6
Nagykanizsa Hungary 46°28N 17°0E 182 D2
Nagykáta Hungary 47°25N 19°45E 182 C4
Nagykőrös Hungary 47°5N 19°48E 182 C4
Nagyszombat = Trnava Slovak Rep 48°23N 17°35E 181 C10
Nagytétény Hungary 47°23N 18°59E 117 B1
Nagyvárad = Oradea Romania 47°2N 21°58E 182 C6
Naha Japan 26°13N 127°42E 288 a
Nahabuan Indonesia 0°49N 114°4E 235 B4
Nahalin West Bank 31°41N 35°7E 123 B1
Nahan India 30°33N 77°18E 242 D7
Nahanni △ Canada 61°36N 125°41W 296 A4
Nahanni Butte Canada 61°2N 123°31W 296 A4
Nahargarh Mad. P., India 24°10N 75°14E 242 G6
Nahargarh Raj., India 24°55N 76°50E 242 G7
Nahariyya Israel 33°1N 35°5E 250 F6
Nahāvand Iran 34°10N 48°22E 213 E13
Nahe → Germany 49°58N 7°54E 179 F3
Nahirne Ukraine 45°26N 28°27E 183 E13
Nahîya, W. → Egypt 28°55N 31°0E 256 B3
Nahuel Huapi, L. Argentina 41°0S 71°32W 336 B2
Nahuel Huapi △ Argentina 41°3S 71°59W 336 B2
Nahuelbuta △ Chile 37°44S 72°57W 334 D1
Nahunta U.S.A. 31°12N 81°59W 316 D8
Nai Yong Thailand 8°14N 98°22E 237 a
Naic Phil. 14°19N 120°46E 232 D3
Naicá Mexico 27°53N 105°31W 318 B3
Naicam Canada 52°30N 104°30W 297 C8
Naifaru Maldives 5°25N 73°20E 272 d
Naikoon ⌓ Canada 53°55N 131°55W 296 C2
Naikul India 21°20N 84°58E 244 D7
Naila Germany 50°19N 11°42E 179 E7
Naimisharanya India 27°21N 80°30E 243 F9
Naimona'nyi Feng Nepal 30°26N 81°18E 243 D9
Nain Nfld. & L., Canada 56°34N 61°40W 299 A7
Nā'īn Iran 32°54N 53°0E 247 C7
Nain Jamaica 17°57N 77°38W 320 a
Naini Tal India 29°30N 79°30E 243 E8
Nainpur India 22°30N 80°10E 243 H9
Naintré France 46°46N 0°29E 172 F7
Nainwa India 25°46N 75°51E 242 G6
Naipu Romania 44°12N 25°47E 183 F10
Nairai Fiji 17°49S 179°15E 287 A2
Nairn U.K. 57°35N 3°53W 167 D5
Nairobi Kenya 1°17S 36°48E 268 C4
Nairobi △ Kenya 1°22S 36°50E 268 C4
Naissaar Estonia 59°34N 24°29E 188 C3
Naita, Mt. Ethiopia 5°30N 35°18E 257 F4
Naitaba Fiji 17°0S 179°16W 287 A3
Naivasha Kenya 0°40S 36°30E 268 C4
Naivasha, L. Kenya 0°48S 36°20E 268 C4
Najac France 44°14N 1°58E 174 D5
Najaf = An Najaf Iraq 32°3N 44°15E 213 G11
Najafābād Iran 32°40N 51°15E 247 C6
Najafgarh Drain → India 28°39N 77°4E 120 B1
Najd Si. Arabia 26°30N 42°0E 248 A3
Nájera Spain 42°26N 2°48W 196 C2
Najerilla → Spain 42°32N 2°48W 196 C2
Najibabad India 29°40N 78°20E 242 E8
Najin N. Korea 42°12N 130°15E 224 A5
Najmah Si. Arabia 26°42N 50°6E 247 E6
Najrān Si. Arabia 17°34N 44°18E 248 C4
Najrān □ Si. Arabia 18°30N 45°50E 248 C4
Naju S. Korea 35°3N 126°43E 224 E3
Naka Japan 36°30N 140°35E 223 A12
Naka-Gawa → Japan 36°20N 140°36E 223 A12
Nakadōri-Shima Japan 32°57N 129°4E 221 H4
Nakagusuku-wan Japan 26°14N 127°53E 288 a
Nakahara Japan 35°33N 139°37E 140 B2
Nakal = Nakło nad Notecią Poland 53°9N 17°38E 185 E4
Nakalagba Dem. Rep. of the Congo 2°50N 27°58E 268 B2
Nakalele Pt. U.S.A. 21°2N 156°35W 302 B5
Nakama Japan 33°56N 130°43E 222 D2
Nakambé = White Volta → Ghana 9°10N 1°15W 263 D4
Nakaminato Japan 36°21N 140°36E 223 A12
Nakamura Japan 32°59N 132°56E 222 E4
Nakanai Mts. Papua N. G. 5°40S 151°0E 286 C6
Nakano Nagano, Japan 36°45N 138°22E 223 A10
Nakano Tōkyō, Japan 35°42N 139°39E 140 A2
Nakano-Shima Japan 29°51N 129°52E 221 K4
Nakanojō Japan 36°35N 138°51E 223 A10
Nakashibetsu Japan 43°33N 144°59E 220 C12
Nakatsu Japan 33°34N 131°15E 222 D3
Nakatsugawa Japan 35°29N 137°30E 223 B9
Nakfa Eritrea 16°40N 38°32E 257 D4
Nakfa ⌓ Eritrea 17°28N 38°55E 257 D4
Nakha Yai, Ko Thailand 8°3N 98°28E 237 a
Nakhichevan = Naxçıvan Azerbaijan 39°12N 45°15E 213 C11
Nakhichevan Rep. = Naxçıvan □ Azerbaijan 39°25N 45°26E 213 C11
Nakhl Egypt 29°55N 33°43E 251 J4
Nakhl-e Taqī Iran 27°28N 52°36E 247 E7
Nakhodka Russia 42°53N 132°54E 220 C6
Nakhon Nayok Thailand 14°12N 101°13E 236 E3
Nakhon Pathom Thailand 13°49N 100°3E 236 F3
Nakhon Phanom Thailand 17°23N 104°43E 236 D5
Nakhon Ratchasima Thailand 14°59N 102°12E 236 E4
Nakhon Sawan Thailand 15°35N 100°10E 236 E3
Nakhon Si Thammarat Thailand 8°29N 100°0E 237 H3
Nakhon Thai Thailand 17°5N 100°44E 236 D3
Nakhtarana India 23°20N 69°15E 242 H3
Nakijin Japan 26°40N 127°58E 288 a
Nakina Canada 50°10N 86°40W 298 B2
Nakło nad Notecią Poland 53°9N 17°38E 185 E4
Naknek U.S.A. 58°44N 157°1W 303 G8
Nako Burkina Faso 10°40N 3°4W 262 C4
Nakodar India 31°8N 75°31E 242 D6
Nakskov Denmark 54°50N 11°8E 163 K5
Naktong → S. Korea 35°7N 128°57E 227 G15
Nakuru Kenya 0°15S 36°4E 268 C4
Nakuru, L. Kenya 0°23S 36°5E 268 C4
Nakusp Canada 50°20N 117°45W 296 C5
Nal Pakistan 27°40N 66°12E 242 F2
Nal → Pakistan 25°20N 65°30E 242 G1
Nalázi Mozam. 24°3S 33°20E 271 B5
Nalchik Russia 43°30N 43°33E 191 J6
Nałęczów Poland 51°17N 22°9E 185 G9
Nalerigu Ghana 10°35N 0°25W 263 C4
Nalgonda India 17°6N 79°15E 244 F4
Nalhati India 24°17N 87°52E 243 G12
Naliya India 23°16N 68°50E 242 H3
Nallamalai Hills India 15°30N 78°50E 245 G4
Nallıhan Turkey 40°11N 31°20E 212 B4
Nalolo Zambia 15°33S 23°7E 265 F4
Nalón → Spain 43°32N 6°4W 194 B4
Nalong Burma 24°44N 97°28E 241 C6
Nalubaale Dam Uganda 0°30N 33°5E 268 B3
Nalumasortoq Greenland 60°23N 44°28W 154 E6
Nālūt Libya 31°54N 11°0E 258 B2
Nālūt □ Libya 31°52N 10°58E 258 B2
Nam Can Vietnam 8°46N 104°59E 237 H5
Nam-ch'on N. Korea 38°15N 126°26E 224 C3
Nam Co China 30°30N 90°45E 218 E7
Nam Dinh Vietnam 20°25N 106°5E 228 G6
Nam Du, Quan Dao Vietnam 9°41N 104°21E 237 H5
Nam Hke → Burma 25°34N 95°41E 228 G2
Nam Loi → Burma 21°3N 98°27E 228 G3
Nam Nao △ Thailand 16°44N 101°32E 236 D3
Nam Ngum Res. Laos 18°35N 102°34E 236 C4
Nam-Phan Vietnam 10°30N 106°0E 237 G6
Nam Phong Thailand 16°42N 102°52E 236 D4
Nam Theun Res. Laos 17°51N 105°3E 236 D5
Nam Tok Thailand 14°21N 99°4E 236 E2
Nam Un Res. Thailand 17°13N 103°44E 236 D4
Namachire Angola 11°26S 22°43E 265 E4
Namacunde Angola 17°18S 15°50E 265 F3
Namacurra Mozam. 17°30S 36°50E 271 A6
Namadgi △ Australia 35°42S 149°0E 283 C8
Namai B. Palau 7°31N 134°38E 288 c
Namak, Daryācheh-ye Iran 34°30N 52°0E 247 C7
Namak, Kavir-e Iran 34°30N 57°30E 247 C8
Namakkal India 11°13N 78°13E 245 J4
Namakzār, Daryācheh-ye Iran 34°0N 60°30E 240 B1
Namaland Namibia 26°0S 17°0E 270 B2
Namanga Kenya 2°33S 36°47E 268 C4
Namangan Uzbekistan 41°0N 71°40E 217 D8
Namangan □ Uzbekistan 41°0N 71°15E 217 D8
Namapa Mozam. 13°43S 39°50E 269 E4
Namaqua △ S. Africa 30°0S 17°30E 270 D2
Namaqualand S. Africa 30°0S 17°25E 270 D2
Namasagali Uganda 1°2N 33°0E 268 B3
Namatanai Papua N. G. 3°40S 152°29E 286 B7
Namber Indonesia 1°2S 134°49E 231 E8
Nambour Australia 26°32S 152°58E 281 D5
Nambouwalu = Nabouwalu Fiji 17°0S 178°45E 287 A2
Nambuangongo Angola 8°1S 14°12E 265 D2
Nambucca Heads Australia 30°37S 153°0E 283 A10
Nambung △ Australia 30°30S 115°5E 279 F2
Namcha Barwa China 29°40N 95°10E 218 F8
Namche Bazar Nepal 27°51N 86°47E 243 F12
Namchonjŏm = Nam-ch'on N. Korea 38°15N 126°26E 224 C3
Namdapha △ India 27°30N 96°50E 241 B6
Namecunda Mozam. 14°54S 37°37E 269 E4
Nameh Indonesia 2°34N 116°21E 235 B5
Namen = Namur Belgium 50°27N 4°52E 170 D4
Namenalala Fiji 17°8S 179°9E 287 A2
Nameponda Mozam. 15°50S 39°50E 269 F4
Nameri △ India 26°55N 92°55E 241 B4
Namerikawa Japan 36°46N 137°20E 223 A9
Náměšť nad Oslavou Czech Rep. 49°12N 16°10E 181 B9
Námestovo Slovak Rep. 49°24N 19°25E 181 B12
Nametil Mozam. 15°40S 39°21E 269 F4
Namew L. Canada 54°14N 101°56W 297 C8
Namgia India 31°48N 78°40E 243 D8
Namhkam Burma 23°50N 97°41E 228 E1
Namho Burma 22°4N 99°1E 228 F2
Namhsan Burma 22°48N 97°2E 241 D6
Namialo Mozam. 14°55S 39°59E 269 E4
Namib Desert Namibia 22°30S 15°0E 270 B2
Namib-Naukluft ⌓ Namibia 24°40S 15°16E 270 B2
Namibe Angola 15°7S 12°11E 265 F2
Namibe □ Angola 16°35S 12°30E 265 F2
Namibe ⌓ Angola 16°35S 12°20E 265 F2
Namibia ■ Africa 22°0S 18°9E 270 B2
Namibia Abyssal Plain Atl. Oc. 30°0S 5°30E 152 J12
Namibwoestyn = Namib Desert Namibia 22°30S 15°0E 270 B2
Namīn Iran 38°25N 48°30E 213 C13
Namjeju S. Korea 33°14N 126°33E 224 a
Namlan Burma 22°15N 97°24E 241 D6
Namlea Indonesia 3°18S 127°5E 231 E7
Namoi → Australia 30°12S 149°30E 283 A9
Namous, O. en → Algeria 31°0N 0°15W 261 B4
Nampa U.S.A. 43°34N 116°34W 304 E5
Nampala Mali 15°20N 5°30W 262 B3
Namp'o N. Korea 38°52N 125°10E 224 C2
Namp'o □ N. Korea 38°52N 125°25E 224 C2
Nampō-Shotō Japan 32°0N 140°0E 221 J10
Nampula Mozam. 15°6S 39°15E 269 F4
Namrole Indonesia 3°46S 126°46E 231 E7
Namsan Park S. Korea 37°32N 126°59E 137 B1
Namsang Burma 20°53N 97°43E 241 E6
Namse Shankou China 30°0N 82°25E 243 E10
Namsen → Norway 64°28N 11°37E 160 D14
Namslau = Namysłów Poland 51°6N 17°42E 185 G4
Namsos Norway 64°29N 11°30E 160 D14
Namtok Chat Trakan △ Thailand 17°17N 100°40E 236 D3
Namtok Huay Yang △ Thailand 11°35N 99°30E 237 G2
Namtok Mae Surin △ Thailand 18°55N 98°2E 236 C2
Namtok Ngao △ Thailand 9°58N 98°46E 237 H2
Namtok Phlew △ Thailand 12°32N 102°13E 236 F4
Namtok Yong △ Thailand 8°15N 98°45E 237 H2
Namtsy Russia 62°43N 129°37E 215 C13
Namtu Burma 23°5N 97°28E 241 D6
Namtumbo Tanzania 10°30S 36°4E 269 E4
Namu Canada 51°52N 127°50W 296 C3
Namuka-i-Lau Fiji 18°53S 178°37W 287 B3
Namukulu Cook Is. 18°57S 169°54W 289 g
Namumea Tuvalu 5°41S 176°9E 277 B14
Namur Belgium 50°27N 4°52E 170 D4
Namur □ Belgium 50°17N 5°0E 170 D4
Namuruputh Kenya 4°34N 35°57E 268 B4
Namutoni Namibia 18°49S 16°55E 270 A2
Namwala Zambia 15°44S 26°30E 269 F2
Namwon Jeju-do, S. Korea 33°16N 126°43E 224 a
Namwon Jeollabuk-do, S. Korea 35°23N 127°23E 224 E3
Namyang N. Korea 42°57N 129°52E 224 A4
Namyangju S. Korea 37°38N 127°12E 224 D3
Namyeong S. Korea 37°32N 126°57E 137 B1
Namysłów Poland 51°6N 17°42E 185 G4
Nan Thailand 18°48N 100°46E 236 C3
Nan → Thailand 15°42N 100°9E 236 E3
Nan-ch'ang = Nanchang China 28°42N 115°55E 229 C10
Nan Ling China 25°0N 112°30E 229 E8
Nan Xian China 29°20N 112°22E 229 C9
Nana C.A.R. 5°0N 15°50E 264 A3
Nana Romania 44°17N 26°34E 183 F11
Nana-Barya ⌓ C.A.R. 7°40N 17°29E 264 A3
Nana Kru Liberia 4°55N 8°45W 262 E3
Nanaimo Canada 49°10N 124°0W 296 D4
Nänäkuli U.S.A. 21°24N 158°9W 302 K13
Nanam N. Korea 41°44N 129°40E 224 B4
Nan'an China 24°59N 118°21E 229 E12
Nanango Australia 26°40S 152°0E 281 D5
Nan'ao Guangdong, China 23°28N 117°5E 229 F11
Nanao Japan 37°0N 137°0E 221 F8
Nanao Taiwan 24°28N 121°48E 225 B3
Nanbiancun China 23°4N 113°10E 121 B1
Nanbu China 31°18N 106°3E 228 B6
Nanchang China 28°42N 115°55E 229 C10
Nanchang He → China 39°58N 116°14E 114 B1
Nancheng China 27°33N 116°35E 229 D11
Nanching = Nanjing China 32°2N 118°47E 229 A12
Nanchong China 30°43N 106°2E 228 B6
Nanchuan China 29°9N 107°6E 228 C6
Nanchung = Nanchong China 30°43N 106°2E 228 B6
Nancowry India 7°59N 93°32E 245 L11
Nancy France 48°42N 6°12E 173 D13
Nanda Devi India 30°23N 79°59E 243 D8
Nanda Devi △ India 30°30N 79°50E 243 D8
Nanda Kot India 30°17N 80°5E 243 D9
Nandan Guangxi Zhuangzu, China 24°58N 107°29E 228 E6
Nandan Japan 34°10N 134°42E 222 C6
Nandang China 23°6N 113°12E 121 B2
Nanded India 19°10N 77°20E 244 E3
Nandewar Ra. Australia 30°15S 150°35E 281 E5
Nandgaon India 20°19N 74°39E 244 D2
Nandi = Nadi Fiji 17°42S 177°20E 287 A1
Nandi Zimbabwe 20°58S 31°44E 269 G3
Nandigama India 16°47N 80°18E 244 F5
Nandigram India 22°1N 87°58E 243 H12
Nandikotkur India 15°52N 78°18E 245 G4
Nandura India 20°52N 76°25E 244 D3
Nandurbar India 21°20N 74°15E 244 D2
Nandyal India 15°30N 78°30E 245 G4
Nanfeng Guangdong, China 23°45N 111°47E 229 F8
Nanfeng Jiangxi, China 27°12N 116°28E 229 D11
Nang Rong Thailand 14°38N 102°48E 236 E4
Nanga-Eboko Cameroon 4°41N 12°22E 263 E7
Nanga Parbat Pakistan 35°10N 74°35E 243 B6
Nangade Mozam. 11°5S 39°36E 269 E4
Nangal Dewat India 28°33N 77°5E 120 B1
Nangalao I. Phil. 11°26N 120°10E 233 F3
Nangamau Indonesia 0°6S 111°55E 235 C4
Nangamentebah Indonesia 0°33N 112°46E 235 B4
Nangapinoh Indonesia 0°20S 111°44E 235 C4
Nangar △ Australia 33°23S 148°3E 283 B8
Nangarhār □ Afghan. 34°20N 70°0E 240 B3
Nangatayap Indonesia 1°32S 110°34E 235 C4
Nangbéto, L. de Togo 7°26N 1°25E 262 D5
Nangeya Mts. Uganda 3°30N 33°30E 268 B3
Nangis France 48°33N 3°1E 173 D10
Nangnim-sanmaek N. Korea 40°13N 126°51E 224 B3
Nangong China 37°23N 115°22E 226 F8
Nangtud, Mt. Phil. 11°17N 122°11E 233 F4
Nanguneri India 8°29N 77°40E 245 K3
Nangwarry Australia 37°33S 140°48E 282 D4
Nanhua Yunnan, China 25°13N 101°21E 228 E3
Nanhua Taiwan 23°2N 120°28E 225 C2
Nanhuang China 36°58N 121°48E 227 F11
Nanhui China 31°5N 121°44E 229 B13
Nanhunan Shan Taiwan 24°21N 121°26E 225 B3
Nanisivik Canada 73°2N 84°33W 295 C15
Naniwa Japan 34°39N 135°29E 133 B1
Nanjangud India 12°6N 76°43E 245 H3
Nanji Shan China 27°27N 121°4E 229 D13
Nanjian China 25°2N 100°25E 228 E3
Nanjiang China 32°28N 106°51E 228 A6
Nanjing Fujian, China 24°25N 117°20E 229 E11
Nanjing Jiangsu, China 32°2N 118°47E 229 A12
Nanjirinji Tanzania 9°41S 39°5E 269 D4
Nankana Sahib Pakistan 31°27N 73°38E 242 D5
Nankang Jiangxi, China 25°40N 114°45E 229 E10
Nankang Taiwan 25°3N 121°35E 225 A3
Nanking = Nanjing China 32°2N 118°47E 229 A12
Nankoku Japan 33°39N 133°44E 222 D5
Nanlang China 22°30N 113°32E 219 a
Nanliao Taiwan 24°50N 120°55E 225 B2
Nanling China 30°55N 118°20E 229 B12
Nannial India 19°4N 79°38E 244 E4
Nanning China 22°48N 108°20E 228 F7
Nannup Australia 33°59S 115°48E 279 F2
Nanole India 19°0N 72°55E 130 A2
Nanortalik Greenland 60°10N 45°17W 154 E6
Nanpan Jiang → China 25°10N 106°5E 228 E6
Nanpara India 27°52N 81°33E 243 F9
Nanping Fujian, China 26°38N 118°10E 229 D12
Nanping Henan, China 29°55N 112°3E 229 C9
Nanpu Bridge China 31°12N 121°30E 138 B2
Nanri Dao China 25°15N 119°25E 229 E12
Nansei-Shotō = Ryūkyū-Rettō Japan 26°0N 126°0E 221 M3
Nansen Basin Arctic 84°0N 50°0E 150 A10
Nansen Land Greenland 83°0N 43°0W 154 A6
Nansen Sd. Canada 81°0N 91°0W 295 A13
Nansha China 22°45N 113°34E 219 a
Nanshan China 18°19N 109°10E 236 C7
Nanshan I. S. China Sea 10°45N 115°49E 230 B5
Nanshi China 31°12N 121°29E 138 B1
Nansio Tanzania 2°3S 33°4E 268 C3
Nant France 44°1N 3°18E 174 D7
Nantawarrinna ✪ Australia 30°49S 138°58E 281 B2
Nanterre France 48°53N 2°12E 134 A2
Nantes France 47°12N 1°33W 172 E5
Nantiat France 46°1N 1°11E 174 B5
Nanticoke U.S.A. 41°12N 76°0W 313 E8
Nanton Canada 50°21N 113°46W 296 C6
Nanton Pt. Antigua & B. 17°0N 61°45W 322 b
Nantong China 32°1N 120°52E 229 A13
Nantou China 22°32N 113°55E 219 a
Nant'ou Taiwan 23°55N 120°41E 225 C2
Nant'ou □ Taiwan 23°50N 121°0E 225 C3
Nantua France 46°10N 5°35E 173 F12
Nantucket U.S.A. 41°17N 70°6W 309 E18
Nantucket I. U.S.A. 41°16N 70°5W 309 E18
Nantulo Mozam. 12°32S 38°45E 269 E4
Nantung = Nantong China 32°1N 120°52E 229 A13
Nantwich U.K. 53°4N 2°31W 168 D5
Nanty Glo U.S.A. 40°28N 78°50W 312 F6
Nantzu Taiwan 22°44N 120°19E 225 D2
Nanuku Passage Fiji 16°45S 179°15W 287 A3
Nanumanga Pac. Oc. 6°18S 176°20E 277 B14
Nanuque Brazil 17°50S 40°21W 333 E3
Nanusa, Kepulauan Indonesia 4°45N 127°1E 231 D7
Nanutarra Roadhouse Australia 22°32S 115°30E 278 D2
Nanwan Taiwan 21°57N 120°46E 225 E2
Nanxi China 28°54N 104°59E 228 C5
Nanxiong China 25°6N 114°15E 229 E10
Nanyang China 33°11N 112°30E 226 H7
Nanyi Hu China 31°5N 119°0E 229 B12
Nanyuan China 39°47N 116°24E 226 E9
Nanyuki Kenya 0°2N 37°4E 268 B4
Nanzhang China 31°45N 111°50E 229 B8
Nanzhao China 33°30N 112°20E 226 H7
Nao, C. de la Spain 38°44N 0°14E 197 G5

Naococane, L. Canada 52°50N 70°45W 299 B5
Naogaon Bangla. 24°52N 88°52E 241 G2
Naoné Vanuatu 15°0S 168°8E 287 E6
Naoussa Cyclades, Greece 37°7N 25°14E 205 D7
Naoussa Imathia, Greece 40°42N 22°9E 202 F6
Naozhou Dao China 20°55N 110°20E 229 G8
Napa U.S.A. 38°18N 122°17W 306 G4
Napa → U.S.A. 38°10N 122°19W 306 G4
Napaimiut U.S.A. 61°33N 158°42W 303 D3
Napakiak U.S.A. 60°42N 161°57W 303 F7
Nāpali Coast U.S.A. 22°11N 159°39W 302 A2
Napanee Canada 44°15N 77°0W 312 B8
Napanoch U.S.A. 41°44N 74°22W 313 E10
Napaskiak U.S.A. 60°43N 161°55W 303 F7
Nape Laos 18°18N 105°6E 236 C5
Nape Pass = Keo Neua, Deo
  Vietnam 18°23N 105°10E 236 C5
Naperville U.S.A. 41°46N 88°9W 311 C8
Napier N.Z. 39°30S 176°56E 284 F5
Napier Broome B.
  Australia 14°2S 126°37E 278 B4
Napier Mole Pakistan 24°49N 66°58E 123 B1
Napier Pen. Australia 12°4S 135°43E 280 A2
Napierville Canada 45°11N 73°25W 313 A11
Napili-Honokowai
  U.S.A. 20°58N 156°39W 302 C5
Naples = Nápoli Italy 40°50N 14°15E 201 B7
Naples U.S.A. 26°8N 81°48W 317 J8
Naples Park U.S.A. 26°17N 81°46W 317 J8
Napo China 23°22N 105°50E 228 F5
Napo □ Ecuador 0°30S 77°0W 328 D2
Napo → Peru 3°20S 72°40W 328 D3
Napoleon N. Dak., U.S.A. 46°30N 99°46W 308 B4
Napoleon Ohio, U.S.A. 41°23N 84°8W 311 C12
Napoleon's Tomb St. Helena 15°56S 5°42W 153 h
Nápoli Italy 40°50N 14°15E 201 B7
Nápoli, G. di Italy 40°43N 14°10E 201 B7
Nápoli Capodichino ✈ (NAP)
  Italy 40°53N 14°16E 201 B7
Napopo
  Dem. Rep. of the Congo 4°15N 28°0E 268 B2
Nappanee U.S.A. 41°27N 86°0W 311 C11
Napperby Australia 33°9S 138°7E 282 B3
Naqadeh Iran 36°57N 45°23E 213 D11
Naqb, Ra's an Jordan 29°48N 35°44E 251 A6
Naqqâsh Iran 35°40N 49°6E 247 C6
Nár Sweden 57°15N 18°35E 163 G10
Nara Japan 34°40N 135°49E 223 C7
Nara Mali 15°10N 7°20W 262 B3
Nara Canal Pakistan 24°30N 69°20E 242 G3
Nara Visa U.S.A. 35°37N 103°6W 305 J12
Naracoorte Australia 36°58S 140°45E 282 D4
Naradhan Australia 33°34S 146°17E 283 B7
Naraina India 28°36N 77°8E 120 B1
Naraini India 25°11N 80°29E 243 G9
Naranjos Mexico 21°21N 97°41W 319 C5
Narasannapeta India 18°25N 84°3E 244 E7
Narasapur India 16°26N 81°40E 245 F5
Narasaropet India 16°14N 80°4E 245 F5
Narathiwat Thailand 6°30N 101°48E 237 J3
Narayanapatnam India 18°53N 83°10E 244 E6
Narayangadh = Bharatpur
  Nepal 27°34N 84°10E 243 F11
Narayanganj Bangla. 23°40N 90°33E 241 D3
Narayanpet India 16°45N 77°30E 244 F3
Narbada = Narmada →
  India 21°38N 72°36E 242 J5
Narberth U.S.A. 51°47N 4°44W 169 F3
Narbonne France 43°11N 3°0E 174 E7
Narborough, I. = Fernandina, I.
  Ecuador 0°25S 91°30W 330 a
Narbuvoll Norway 62°21N 11°27E 164 B8
Narcea → Spain 43°33N 6°44W 194 B4
Narcondam I. India 13°20N 94°16E 245 H12
Nardīn Iran 37°3N 55°59E 247 B7
Nardò Italy 40°11N 18°2E 201 B11
Narembeen Australia 32°7S 118°24E 279 F2
Narendranagar India 30°10N 78°18E 242 D8
Nares Abyssal Plain
  Atl. Oc. 22°0N 67°0W 152 D5
Nares Str. Arctic 80°0N 70°0W 154 B3
Naretha Australia 31°0S 124°45E 279 F3
Narew → Poland 52°26N 20°41E 185 F7
Nari → Pakistan 28°0N 67°40E 242 F2
Nariman Point Mumbai, India 130 c1
Nariman Pt. India 18°55N 72°49E 130 B1
Narin Afghan. 36°5N 69°0E 246 B8
Narindra, Helodranon' i
  Madag. 14°55S 47°30E 272 A2
Narino □ Colombia 1°30N 78°0W 328 C2
Narita Japan 35°47N 140°19E 223 B12
Narita, Tōkyō ✈ (NRT)
  Japan 35°45N 140°25E 223 B12
Nariva □ Trin. & Tob. 10°22N 61°10W 323 L
Nariva → Trin. & Tob. 10°24N 61°14W 323 L
Nariva Swamp Trin. & Tob. 10°26N 61°14W 323 L
Närke Sweden 59°10N 15°0E 162 E8
Narmada → India 21°38N 72°36E 242 J5
Narmada Canal India 22°0N 73°45E 244 C1
Nārmak Iran 35°42N 51°33E 141 A2
Narman Turkey 40°26N 41°57E 213 B9
Narnaul India 28°5N 76°11E 242 E7
Narni Italy 42°30N 12°30E 199 F9
Naro Ghana 10°22N 2°27W 262 C4
Naro Fominsk Russia 55°23N 36°43E 188 C6
Narok Kenya 65°55N 59°58E 186 A10
Narón Spain 43°32N 8°9W 194 B2
Narooma Australia 36°14S 150°4E 283 D9
Narowal Pakistan 32°6N 74°52E 242 C6
Narrabri Australia 30°19S 149°46E 281 E4
Narrandera Australia 34°42S 146°31E 283 C7
Narrogin Australia 32°58S 117°14E 279 F2
Narromine Australia 32°12S 148°12E 283 B8
Narrow Hills △ Canada 54°0N 104°37W 297 C8
Narrows, The
  St. Kitts & Nevis 17°12N 62°40W 322 d
Narsampet India 17°57N 79°58E 244 F4
Narsaq Greenland 60°57N 46°4W 154 E6
Narsimhapur India 22°54N 79°14E 243 H8
Narsinghgarh India 23°45N 76°40E 242 H7
Narsinghpur India 20°28N 85°5E 244 D7
Narsipatnam India 17°40N 82°37E 244 E6
Nartes, L. e Albania 40°33N 19°20E 202 F3
Nartkala Russia 43°33N 43°51E 191 J6
Naruto Japan 34°43N 135°22E 133 A1
Naruto Kantō, Japan 34°11N 134°37E 222 C6
Naruto Shikoku, Japan 35°36N 140°25E 223 B12
Naruto-Kaikyō Japan 34°14N 134°39E 222 C6
Narva Estonia 59°23N 28°12E 188 C5
Narva → Russia 59°27N 28°2E 188 C4
Narva Bay = Narva Laht
  Estonia 59°35N 27°35E 161 G22
Narva Laht Estonia 59°35N 27°35E 161 G22
Narvacan Phil. 17°25N 120°28E 233 A3
Narvik Norway 68°28N 17°26E 160 B17
Narvskoye Vdkhr. Russia 59°18N 28°2E 188 C4
Narwana India 29°39N 76°6E 242 E7
Narwiański △ Poland 52°5N 22°53E 185 B9
Narwinbi △ Australia 16°1S 136°17E 280 B2
Naryan-Mar Russia 67°42N 53°12E 186 A9
Narym Russia 59°0N 81°30E 214 D9
Naryn Kyrgyzstan 41°26N 75°58E 217 D9

Naryn □ Kyrgyzstan 41°26N 75°58E 217 D9
Naryn → Uzbekistan 40°52N 71°36E 217 D8
Naryn Qum Kazakhstan 47°30N 49°0E 191 G9
Nasa Norway 66°29N 15°23E 160 C16
Nasau Fiji 17°19S 179°27E 287 A2
Năsăud Romania 47°19N 24°29E 183 D10
Nasawa Vanuatu 15°12S 168°9E 287 B2
Nasb, W. → Egypt 28°29N 34°31E 251 K5
Nasby Sweden 59°25N 18°5E 139 A2
Nasbypark Sweden 59°25N 18°5E 139 A2
Nasca Peru 14°50S 74°57W 330 G4
Nasca Ridge Pac. Oc. 20°0S 80°0W 289 K19
Naseby N.Z. 45°1S 170°10E 285 F5
Naselle U.S.A. 46°22N 123°49W 306 D3
Naser, Buheirat en Egypt 23°0N 32°30E 256 C3
Nashik = Nasik India 19°58N 73°50E 244 E1
Nashua Iowa, U.S.A. 42°57N 92°32W 310 B4
Nashua Mont., U.S.A. 48°8N 106°22W 306 B10
Nashua N.H., U.S.A. 42°45N 71°28W 313 D13
Nashville Ark., U.S.A. 33°57N 93°51W 314 E8
Nashville Ga., U.S.A. 31°12N 83°15W 316 D6
Nashville Ill., U.S.A. 38°21N 89°23W 310 F7
Nashville Ind., U.S.A. 39°12N 86°15W 311 E10
Nashville Mich., U.S.A. 42°36N 85°5W 311 D11
Nashville Tenn., U.S.A. 36°10N 86°47W 315 C11
Našice Croatia 45°32N 18°4E 182 E3
Nasielsk Poland 52°35N 20°50E 185 F7
Nasik India 19°58N 73°50E 244 E1
Nasipit Phil. 8°57N 125°19E 233 G6
Nasir South Sudan 8°36N 33°4E 257 F3
Nasirabad = Mymensingh
  Bangla. 24°45N 90°24E 241 C3
Nasirabad India 26°15N 74°45E 242 F6
Nasirabad Pakistan 28°23N 68°24E 242 E3
Nasiri = Ahvāz Iran 31°20N 48°40E 247 D6
Nasiriyah = An Nāşirīyah
  Iraq 31°0N 46°15E 246 D5
Naskaupi → Canada 53°47N 60°51W 299 B7
Naso Italy 38°7N 14°47E 201 D7
Naso Pt. Phil. 10°25N 121°57E 233 F3
Nasrābād Iran 34°8N 51°26E 247 C6
Nasrīān-e Pa'īn Iran 32°52N 46°52E 246 C5
Nass → Canada 55°0N 129°40W 296 B3
Nassarawa Nigeria 8°32N 7°41E 263 D6
Nassarawa □ Nigeria 8°30N 8°20E 263 D6
Nassau Bahamas 25°5N 77°20W 153 b
Nassau N.Y., U.S.A. 42°31N 73°37W 313 D11
Nassau, B. Chile 55°20S 68°0W 336 H3
Nassau Int. ✈ (NAS)
  Bahamas 25°3N 77°28W 153 b
Nasser, L. = Naser, Buheirat en
  Egypt 23°0N 32°30E 256 C3
Nasser City = Kôm Ombo
  Egypt 24°25N 32°52E 256 C3
Nassian Ivory C. 8°28N 3°28E 262 B4
Nässjö Sweden 57°39N 14°42E 163 G8
Nastapoka → Canada 56°55N 76°33W 298 A4
Nastapoka, Is. Canada 56°55N 76°50W 298 A4
Nasugbu Phil. 14°5N 120°38E 232 D3
Nāsum Sweden 56°10N 14°29E 163 H8
Näsviken Sweden 61°46N 16°52E 162 C10
Nata Botswana 20°12S 26°12E 270 D4
Nata → Botswana 20°14S 26°10E 270 D4
Natagaima Colombia 3°37N 75°6W 328 C2
Natal Brazil 5°47S 35°13W 332 D6
Natal Indonesia 0°35N 99°7E 234 B1
Natal Drakensberg △
  S. Africa 29°27S 29°30E 271 C4
Natalinci Serbia 44°15N 20°49E 182 B5
Naţanz Iran 33°30N 51°55E 247 C6
Natashquan Canada 50°14N 61°46W 299 B7
Natashquan → Canada 50°7N 61°50W 299 B7
Natchez U.S.A. 31°34N 91°24W 314 F9
Natchitoches U.S.A. 31°46N 93°5W 314 F8
Natewa B. Fiji 16°35S 179°40E 287 A2
Nathalia Australia 36°1S 145°13E 283 D6
Nathan Philips Square Toronto, Canada 141 b2
Nathan Road Hong Kong, China 122 a2
Nathdwara India 24°55N 73°50E 242 G5
Nathu La China 27°24N 88°49E 241 G5
Nati, Pta. Spain 40°3N 3°59E 206 A4
Natimuk Australia 36°42S 141°59E 282 D4
Nation → Canada 55°30N 123°32W 296 B4
National Arboretum
  U.S.A. 38°54N 76°59W 143 B3
National Art Gallery Beijing, China 114 b2
National Capital District □
  Papua N. G. 9°25S 147°10E 286 E4
National City U.S.A. 32°40N 117°5W 307 N9
National Grand Theatre Beijing, China 114 c2
National Place Washington, D.C., U.S.A. 143 b2
National Zoological Park
  U.S.A. 38°55N 77°4W 143 B3
Nationals Park U.S.A. 38°53N 77°1W 143 B3
Natitingou Benin 10°20N 1°26E 263 C5
Natividad, I. Mexico 27°50N 115°10E 318 B1
Natividade Brazil 11°43S 47°47W 333 D2
Nativity, Basilica of
  West Bank 31°42N 33°12E 123 B2
Natkyizin Burma 14°57N 97°59E 236 E1
Natmauk Burma 20°20N 95°4E 241 G5
Natogyi Burma 21°25N 95°39E 241 G5
Natolin Poland 52°8N 21°4E 142 C2
Natron, L. Tanzania 2°20S 36°0E 268 C4
Natrona Heights U.S.A. 40°37N 79°44W 312 F5
Natrûn, W. el → Egypt 30°25N 30°13E 256 H7
Nattai △ Australia 34°12S 150°22E 283 C9
Nättraby Sweden 56°13N 15°31E 163 H9
Natuashish Canada 55°54N 61°10W 299 B7
Natukanaaka Pan
  Namibia 18°40S 15°45E 270 A2
Natuna Besar, Kepulauan
  Indonesia 4°0N 108°15E 235 B3
Natuna Is. = Natuna Besar,
  Kepulauan Indonesia 4°0N 108°15E 235 B3
Natuna Selatan, Kepulauan
  Indonesia 2°45N 109°0E 235 B3
Natural Bridge U.S.A. 44°5N 75°30W 313 B9
Natural Bridges △ U.S.A. 37°36N 110°0W 305 H8
Naturaliste, C. Tas.,
  Australia 40°50S 148°15E 281 G4
Naturaliste, C. W. Austral.,
  Australia 33°32S 115°0E 279 F2
Naturaliste Plateau Ind. Oc. 34°0S 112°0E 276 G1
Nau Qala Afghan. 34°5N 69°5E 242 B3
Naucalpan de Juárez
  Mexico 19°28N 99°14W 128 B1
Nauders Austria 46°54N 10°30E 180 E3
Nauen Germany 52°36N 12°52E 180 C8
Naugard = Nowogard
  Poland 53°41N 15°10E 184 G2
Naugatuck U.S.A. 41°30N 73°3W 313 E11
Naujaat = Repulse Bay
  Canada 66°30N 86°30W 295 D14
Naujan Phil. 13°20N 121°18E 232 D3
Naujan Lake △ Phil. 13°4N 121°18E 232 D3
Naujoji Akmenė Lithuania 56°19N 22°54E 184 B9
Naukluft Namibia 24°13S 16°19E 270 C2
Naumburg Germany 51°9N 11°47E 178 D7
Naumburg am Queis =
  Nowogrodziec Poland 51°12N 15°24E 185 G2
Naupada Andhra Pradesh,
  India 18°34N 84°18E 244 E7
Naupada Maharashtra, India 19°3N 72°50E 130 A2

Nā'ūr Jordan 31°53N 35°50E 251 G6
Naushahra = Nowshera
  Pakistan 34°0N 72°0E 240 B4
Naushahro Pakistan 26°50N 68°7E 242 F3
Naushon I. U.S.A. 41°29N 70°45W 313 E14
Nausori Fiji 18°2S 178°32E 287 B2
Nauta Peru 4°31S 73°35W 328 D3
Nautanwa India 27°20N 83°25E 243 F10
Nautla Mexico 26°55S 17°57E 270 C2
Nautla Mexico 20°13N 96°47W 319 C5
Nava del Rey Spain 43°21N 5°31W 194 B5
Nava Spain 41°22N 5°6W 194 D5
Navadwip India 23°34N 88°20E 243 H13
Navahermosa Spain 39°41N 4°28W 195 C6
Navahrudak Belarus 53°40N 25°50E 177 B13
Navai Fiji 17°36S 177°57E 287 A1
Navajo Res. U.S.A. 36°48N 107°36W 305 H10
Naval Phil. 11°34N 124°23E 233 F6
Navalcarnero Spain 40°17N 4°5W 194 E6
Navalmoral de la Mata
  Spain 39°52N 5°33W 194 F5
Navalvillar de Pela Spain 39°9N 5°24W 195 F5
Navan = An Uaimh
  Ireland 53°39N 6°41W 166 C5
Navanagar = Jamnagar
  India 22°30N 70°6E 242 H4
Navapolatsk Belarus 55°32N 28°37E 188 E5
Navarin, Mys Russia 62°15N 179°5E 215 C18
Navarino, I. Chile 55°0S 67°40W 336 H3
Navarra □ Spain 42°40N 1°40W 196 C3
Navarre Fla., U.S.A. 30°24N 86°52W 317 E23
Navarre Ohio, U.S.A. 40°43N 81°31W 312 F3
Navarro → U.S.A. 39°11N 123°45W 306 F3
Navas de San Juan Spain 38°30N 3°19W 195 G7
Navasota U.S.A. 30°23N 96°5W 314 F6
Navassa I. W. Indies 18°30N 75°0W 321 C5
Nävekvarn Sweden 58°38N 16°49E 163 F10
Naver → U.K. 58°32N 4°14W 167 C4
Navet Trin. & Tob. 10°21N 61°10W 323 t
Navet → Trin. & Tob. 10°24N 61°15W 323 t
Navet Res. Trin. & Tob. 10°24N 61°15W 323 t
Navi Mumbai India 19°5N 73°0E 130 A2
Navia Spain 43°35N 6°42W 194 B4
Navia → Spain 43°35N 6°42W 194 B4
Navia de Suarna = A Pobre
  Spain 42°58N 7°3W 194 C3
Navibandar India 21°26N 69°48E 242 J3
Navidad Chile 33°57S 71°50W 334 C1
Navidad Bank W. Indies 20°0N 68°58W 321 B6
Navíglio di Pavia Italy 45°24N 9°9E 129 B1
Navíglio Grande Italy 45°25N 9°5E 129 B1
Naviraí Brazil 23°8S 54°13W 335 A5
Naviti Fiji 17°7S 177°15E 287 A1
Navlakhi India 22°58N 70°28E 242 H4
Navlya Russia 52°53N 34°30E 189 F8
Năvodari Romania 44°19N 28°36E 183 F13
Navoi Uzbekistan 40°9N 65°22E 217 D7
Navojoa Mexico 27°6N 109°26W 318 B3
Navolato Mexico 24°47N 107°42W 318 C3
Navona, Piazza Rome, Italy 136 b2
Navotas Phil. 14°39N 120°56E 127 B1
Navrongo Ghana 10°51N 1°3W 263 C4
Navsari India 20°57N 72°59E 244 D1
Navua Fiji 18°12S 178°11E 287 B2
Navy Pier Chicago, U.S.A. 119 b3
Nawa Kot Pakistan 28°21N 71°24E 242 E4
Nawab Khan Pakistan 30°17N 69°12E 242 D3
Nawabganj Bangla. 24°35N 88°14E 241 C2
Nawabganj Ut. P., India 26°56N 81°14E 243 F9
Nawabganj Ut. P., India 28°32N 79°40E 243 E8
Nawabshah Pakistan 26°15N 68°25E 242 F3
Nawada India 24°50N 85°33E 243 G11
Nawah Afghan. 32°19N 67°50E 242 C2
Nawakot Nepal 27°55N 85°10E 243 F11
Nawalgarh India 27°50N 75°15E 242 F6
Nawanshahr India 32°33N 74°48E 243 C6
Nawapara India 20°46N 82°33E 244 D6
Nawar, Dasht-i- Afghan. 33°52N 68°0E 242 C2
Nawāsīf, Ḥarrat Si. Arabia 21°20N 42°10E 248 B3
Nawi Sudan 18°32N 30°50E 256 D3
Nawng Hpa Burma 22°30N 98°30E 241 D7
Nawoiy, Ra's Oman 17°15N 55°16E 249 C6
Naxçıvan Azerbaijan 39°12N 45°15E 213 C11
Naxçıvan □ Azerbaijan 39°25N 45°26E 213 C11
Naxos Greece 37°8N 25°25E 205 D7
Naxxar Malta 35°55N 14°27E 204 D2
Nay France 43°10N 0°18W 174 E3
Nay, Mui Vietnam 12°55N 109°23E 236 F7
Nãy Band Büshehr, Iran 27°20N 52°40E 247 E7
Nāy Band Khorāsān, Iran 32°20N 57°34E 247 C8
Naya → Colombia 3°13N 77°22W 328 C2
Nayagarh India 20°7N 85°15E 244 D7
Nayakhan Russia 61°56N 159°0E 215 C16
Nayarit □ Mexico 22°0N 105°0W 318 C4
Nayé Senegal 14°28N 12°12W 262 C2
Nayong China 26°50N 105°20E 228 D5
Nayoro Japan 44°21N 142°28E 220 B11
Naypyidaw Burma 19°44N 96°12E 236 C1
Nayudupeta India 13°58N 79°50E 245 G4
Nayyāl, W. → Si. Arabia 28°35N 39°4E 246 D3
Nazar Hikmat Beg Iraq 32°33N 44°25E 113 A2
Nazaré Bahia, Brazil 13°2S 39°0W 333 D4
Nazaré Pará, Brazil 6°25S 52°29W 331 B7
Nazaré Tocantins, Brazil 6°23S 47°40W 332 D2
Nazaré Portugal 39°36N 9°4W 195 F1
Nazareth = Nazerat Israel 32°42N 35°17E 250 F6
Nazareth U.S.A. 40°44N 75°19W 313 F9
Nazarovo Russia 56°2N 90°40E 215 D10
Nazas Mexico 25°14N 104°8W 318 B4
Nazas → Mexico 25°14N 104°6W 318 B4
Nazca = Nasca Peru 14°50S 74°57W 330 G4
Naze Japan 28°22N 129°27E 221 K4
Naze, The U.K. 51°53N 1°18E 169 F9
Nazerat Israel 32°42N 35°17E 250 F6
Nazilli Turkey 37°55N 28°15E 205 D10
Nāzīk Iran 39°1N 45°4E 213 C11
Nazilli Turkey 37°55N 28°15E 205 D10
Nazimabad Pakistan 24°54N 67°1E 123 A2
Nazinon = Red Volta →
  Africa 10°34N 0°30W 263 C4
Nazir Hat Bangla. 22°35N 91°49E 241 D3
Nazko Canada 53°1N 123°37W 296 C4
Nazko → Canada 53°7N 123°34W 296 C4
Nazlet el Simmân Egypt 29°59N 31°9E 117 B1
Nazlu → Iran 37°41N 45°0E 213 D11
Nazret Ethiopia 8°32N 39°22E 257 F4
Ncama Eq. Guin. 1°55N 10°56E 264 D2
Nchanga Zambia 12°30S 27°49E 269 E2
Ncheu Malawi 14°50S 34°47E 269 E3
Ncue Eq. Guin. 2°1N 10°28E 264 D2
Ndala Tanzania 4°45S 33°15E 268 C3
Ndalatando Angola 9°12S 14°48E 268 F2
Ndali Benin 9°50N 2°46E 263 D5
Ndareda Tanzania 4°12S 35°30E 268 C4
Ndélé C.A.R. 8°25N 20°36E 264 C4
Ndendé Gabon 2°22S 11°23E 264 E2
Ndiael △ Senegal 16°15N 16°0W 262 B1
Ndikinimeki Cameroon 4°46N 10°50E 263 E7
Ndim C.A.R. 5°10N 10°41E 264 A2

Ndindi Gabon 3°4S 11°9E 264 C2
Ndjamena Chad 12°10N 15°0E 259 F7
Ndjolé Gabon 0°10S 10°45E 264 C2
Ndogo, Lagune Gabon 2°35S 10°0E 264 C2
Ndok Cameroon 7°57N 14°42E 264 A2
Ndola Zambia 13°0S 28°34E 269 E2
Ndomo → S. Africa 26°55S 32°15E 271 C5
Ndoto Mts. Kenya 2°0N 37°0E 268 B4
Ndoua, C. N. Cal. 22°24S 166°56E 288 d
Ndouba Congo 2°23S 14°47E 264 E3
Nduguti Tanzania 4°18S 34°41E 268 C3
Nea → Norway 63°15N 11°0E 164 A8
Nea Alexandria Greece 37°52S 23°46E 112 B2
Nea Alikarnassos Greece 35°18N 25°13E 205 F7
Nea Anchialos Greece 39°16N 22°4E 204 D4
Nea Epidavros Greece 37°40N 23°7E 204 D5
Nea Ionia Athina, Greece 38°2N 23°46E 112 A2
Nea Ionia Magnisia, Greece 39°21N 22°56E 204 B4
Nea Kalikratia Greece 40°21N 23°3E 202 F7
Nea Liosia Greece 38°3N 23°43E 112 A2
Nea Makri Greece 38°5N 23°59E 204 C5
Nea Moudania Greece 40°15N 23°17E 202 F7
Nea Peramos Attiki, Greece 38°0N 23°26E 112 A1
Nea Peramos Kavala,
  Greece 40°50N 24°18E 203 F8
Nea Samsounda Greece 39°5N 20°6E 207 A2
Nea Smirni Greece 37°54N 23°43E 112 B2
Nea Visa Greece 41°34N 26°33E 203 E10
Nea Zichni Greece 41°2N 23°49E 202 E7
Neagari Japan 36°26N 136°25E 223 A8
Neagh, Lough U.K. 54°37N 6°25W 166 B5
Neah Bay U.S.A. 48°22N 124°37W 306 B2
Neale, L. Australia 24°15S 130°0E 278 D5
Neales → Australia 28°8S 136°47E 282 A2
Neamaţi Indo. 26°50N 94°20E 241 B5
Neamţ □ Romania 47°0N 26°20E 183 C11
Neapoli Athens, Greece 112 a3
Neapoli Kozani, Greece 40°20N 21°24E 202 F5
Neapoli Kriti, Greece 35°15N 25°37E 207 E6
Neapoli Lakonia, Greece 36°27N 23°8E 204 E5
Near Is. U.S.A. 52°30N 174°0E 303 K1
Near North Chicago, U.S.A. 119 b1
Neath U.K. 51°39N 3°48W 169 F4
Neath Port Talbot □ U.K. 51°42N 3°45W 169 F4
Nebbi Uganda 2°28N 31°6E 268 B3
Nebbiou Burkina Faso 11°9N 1°51W 263 C4
Nebelat el Hagana Sudan 13°13N 29°2E 257 E2
Nebine Cr. → Australia 29°27S 146°56E 281 D4
Nebitdag = Balkanabat
  Turkmenistan 39°30N 54°22E 247 B7
Nebka Algeria 27°28N 3°12W 260 C4
Neblina, Pico da Brazil 0°48N 66°0W 328 C6
Nebo Australia 21°42S 148°42E 280 C4
Nebolchy Russia 59°8N 33°18E 188 C7
Nebraska □ U.S.A. 41°30N 99°30W 308 E4
Nebraska City U.S.A. 40°41N 95°52W 308 E6
Nébrodi, Monti Italy 37°54N 14°35E 201 E7
Nebušice Czech Rep. 50°6N 14°19E 135 B1
Necedah U.S.A. 44°2N 90°4W 308 D8
Nechako → Canada 53°55N 122°42W 296 C4
Neches → U.S.A. 29°58N 93°51W 314 G8
Nechisar △ Ethiopia 5°58N 37°55E 257 F4
Neckar → Germany 49°27N 8°29E 179 F4
Neckartal-Odenwald
  Germany 49°30N 9°5E 179 F5
Necker I. U.S.A. 23°35N 164°42W 302 G11
Necochea Argentina 38°30S 58°50W 334 D4
Nectar Brook Australia 32°43S 137°57E 282 B2
Neda Spain 43°30N 8°9W 194 B2
Neda → Greece 37°25N 21°45E 204 D3
Nedalshyttan Norway 62°59N 12°3E 164 B9
Nedelino Bulgaria 41°27N 25°3E 203 E9
Nedelišće Croatia 46°23N 16°22E 199 B13
Nederhorst Neths. 52°16N 5°3E 112 B3
Nederland → Netherlands ■
  Europe 52°25N 5°30E 170 C5
Nedlitz Germany 52°25N 13°3E 115 B1
Nedoboyivtsi Ukraine 48°26N 26°21E 183 B11
Nedroboya Russia 60°59N 111°41E 164 D8
Nedroma Algeria 35°1N 1°45W 261 A4
Nedstrand Norway 59°21N 5°49E 162 C2
Nee Soon Singapore 1°24N 103°49E 138 A2
Needham U.S.A. 42°17N 71°14W 116 B1
Needham Heights U.S.A. 42°17N 71°14W 116 B1
Needles B.C., U.S.A. 34°51N 114°37W 307 L12
Needles Calif., U.S.A. 34°51N 114°37W 307 L12
Needles, The U.K. 50°39N 1°35W 169 G6
Needles Pt. N.Z. 36°5S 175°25E 284 C4
Neembucú □ Paraguay 27°0S 58°0W 334 B4
Neemuch = Nimach India 24°30N 74°56E 242 G6
Neenah U.S.A. 44°11N 88°28W 308 D9
Neepawa Canada 50°15N 99°30W 297 C9
Neeses U.S.A. 33°33N 81°7W 316 B8
Nefta Tunisia 33°53N 7°50E 258 B1
Neftçala Azerbaijan 39°19N 49°12E 213 C13
Neftegorsk Krasnodar,
  Russia 44°25N 39°45E 191 H4
Neftekamsk Russia 56°5N 54°0E 190 B10
Neftekumsk Russia 44°46N 44°50E 191 H7
Nefteyugansk Russia 61°5N 72°42E 214 C8
Nefyn U.K. 52°56N 4°31W 168 E3
Négala Mali 12°51N 8°30W 262 C3
Negapatam = Nagappattinam
  India 10°46N 79°51E 245 J4
Negaunee U.S.A. 46°30N 87°36W 308 B10
Negele Oromiya, Ethiopia 5°20N 39°36E 257 F4
Negele Oromiya, Ethiopia 7°21N 38°42E 266 C4
Negeri Sembilan □
  Malaysia 2°45N 102°10E 237 L4
Negev Desert = Hanegev
  Israel 30°50N 35°0E 251 H6
Negoiul, Vf. Romania 45°38N 24°35E 183 E9
Negombo Sri Lanka 7°12N 79°50E 245 L4
Negotin Serbia 44°16N 22°37E 182 B6
Negotino Macedonia 41°29N 22°7E 202 F7
Negra, Pta. Mauritania 22°54N 16°18W 260 D1
Negra, Pta. Peru 6°6S 81°10W 328 E2
Negrais, C. = Maudin Sun
  Burma 16°0N 94°30E 241 L10
Nègres, Pte. des Martinique 14°35N 61°5W 322 j
Negreşti Romania 46°50N 27°30E 183 D11
Negreşti-Oaş Romania 47°52N 23°27E 183 C8
Negril Jamaica 18°22N 78°20W 320 a
Négrine Algeria 34°30N 7°30E 261 B6
Negro → Argentina 41°2S 62°47W 336 B3
Negro → Bolivia 14°11S 63°7W 331 G5
Negro → Brazil 3°0S 60°0W 328 D7
Negro → Uruguay 33°24S 58°22W 334 C4
Negro, C. Tarf, Ras
  Morocco 35°40N 5°11W 260 A3
Negros Phil. 9°30N 122°40E 233 G5
Negros Occidental □ Phil. 10°0N 123°0E 233 G5
Negros Oriental □ Phil. 9°45S 123°0E 233 G6
Negru Vodă Romania 43°47N 28°21E 183 G13
Neguac Canada 47°15N 65°5W 299 C6

Nes Iceland 65°53N 17°24W 155 B9
Nes Buskerud, Norway 60°34N 9°59E 164 D6
Nesbyen Norway 60°34N 9°8E 164 D6
Nescopeck U.S.A. 41°3N 76°12W 313 E8
Nesebŭr Bulgaria 42°41N 27°46E 203 G11
Neset Norway 61°53N 10°7E 164 C7
Nesflaten Norway 59°38N 6°48E 164 D3
Neiafu Tonga 18°39S 173°59W 287 P14
Nesland Norway 59°31N 8°12E 164 D5
Neskantaga Canada 52°14N 87°53W 298 B2
Neskaupstaður Iceland 65°9N 13°42W 155 B13
Nesland Norway 59°31N 7°59E 164 E4
Neslandsvatn Norway 58°57N 9°10E 164 E6
Nesodden Norway 59°48N 10°41E 133 B3
Nesoddtangen Norway 59°48N 10°40E 133 B3
Nesøya Norway 59°52N 10°31E 133 B3
Ness, L. U.K. 57°15N 4°32W 167 D4
Ness City U.S.A. 38°27N 99°54W 308 F4
Nesterov = Zhovkva
  Ukraine 50°4N 23°58E 177 C12
Nesterov Russia 54°38N 22°41E 184 D7
Nestório Greece 40°24N 21°5E 202 F5
Nestos → Europe 40°54N 24°49E 203 E8
Nesttun Norway 60°19N 5°20E 164 D2
Nesvizh = Nyasvizh
  Belarus 53°14N 26°38E 177 B14
Netanya Israel 32°20N 34°51E 251 F5
Netarhat India 23°29N 84°16E 243 H11
Nete → Belgium 51°7N 4°14E 170 C4
Netherdale Australia 21°10S 148°33E 280 b
Netherlands ■ Europe 52°0N 5°30E 170 C5
Netherlands Antilles = ABC Islands
  W. Indies 12°15N 69°0W 321 D6
Netherlands East Indies =
  Indonesia ■ Asia 5°0S 115°0E 235 C4
Netherlands Guiana = Suriname ■
  S. Amer. 4°0N 56°0W 329 C6
Neto → Italy 39°12N 17°9E 201 C10
Netrakona Bangla. 24°53N 90°47E 241 C3
Netrang India 21°39N 73°21E 242 J5
Netzahualcóyotl, Presa
  Mexico 17°8N 93°35W 319 D6
Neu Aubing Germany 48°9N 11°27E 115 A2
Neu Buch Germany 52°37N 13°31E 115 A4
Neu Buchhorst Germany 52°24N 13°44E 115 B5
Neu Fahrland Germany 52°26N 13°3E 115 B1
Neu-Isenburg Germany 50°3N 8°42E 179 F4
Neu-Langenburg = Tukuyu
  Tanzania 9°17S 33°35E 269 D3
Neu Lindenberg Germany 52°36N 13°35E 115 A4
Neu-Mecklenburg = New Ireland
  Papua N. G. 3°20S 151°50E 286 B6
Neu Pommern = New Britain
  Papua N. G. 5°50S 150°20E 286 C6
Neu-Sandec = Nowy Sącz
  Poland 49°40N 20°41E 185 J7
Neu Sandez = Nowy Sącz
  Poland 49°40N 20°41E 185 J7
Neu-Ulm Germany 48°22N 10°0E 179 G6
Neubiberg Germany 48°4N 11°40E 131 B3
Neubrandenburg
  Germany 53°33N 13°15E 178 B9
Neubukow Germany 54°1N 11°40E 178 A7
Neuburg Germany 48°44N 11°11E 179 G7
Neuchâtel Switz. 47°0N 6°55E 179 J2
Neuchâtel □ Switz. 47°0N 6°55E 179 J2
Neuchâtel, Lac de Switz. 46°53N 6°50E 179 J2
Neudau Austria 47°11N 16°6E 180 D9
Neuenburg an der Elbe = Nymburk
  Czech Rep. 50°10N 15°1E 180 A8
Neuenhagen Germany 52°32N 13°38E 115 A4
Neuenhofen Germany 52°33N 13°6E 115 B1
Neuesslingen Austria 48°15N 16°12E 142 A3
Neuf-Brisach France 48°1N 7°30E 173 D14
Neufahrn Bayern,
  Germany 48°11N 11°40E 131 A3
Neufahrn Bayern,
  Germany 48°43N 12°11E 179 G8
Neufchâteau Belgium 49°50N 5°25E 170 E5
Neufchâteau Vosges,
  France 48°21N 5°40E 173 D12
Neufchâtel-en-Bray France 49°44N 1°26E 172 C8
Neufchâtel-sur-Aisne
  France 49°26N 4°1E 173 C11
Neuhaus = Jindřichův Hradec
  Czech Rep. 49°10N 15°2E 180 B8
Neuhaus Germany 53°17N 10°56E 178 B6
Neuhofen = Nové Zámky
  Slovak Rep. 48°2N 18°8E 181 C11
Neuherberg Germany 48°13N 11°35E 131 A2
Neuilly-Plaisance France 48°52N 2°30E 133 A4
Neuillé-Pont-Pierre France 47°33N 0°33E 172 E7
Neuilly-St-Front France 49°10N 3°15E 173 C10
Neuilly-sur-Marne France 48°51N 2°31E 133 A4
Neuilly-sur-Seine France 48°53N 2°15E 133 A3
Neukalen Germany 53°49N 12°48E 178 B7
Neukieritzsch Germany 51°9N 12°25E 179 D9
Neukenhof Austria 48°7N 16°18E 142 B3
Neukölln Germany 52°28N 13°25E 115 B3
Neumarkt = Nowy Targ
  Poland 49°29N 20°2E 185 J7
Neumarkt = Środa Śląska
  Poland 51°10N 16°36E 185 G3
Neumarkt Germany 49°16N 11°27E 179 F7
Neumarkt = Tržič
  Slovenia 46°22N 14°18E 199 B11
Neumayer Antarctica 71°0S 68°30W 151 D17
Neumittelwalde = Międzybórz
  Poland 51°25N 17°34E 185 G4
Neumünster Germany 54°4N 9°58E 178 A5
Neung-sur-Beuvron France 47°30N 1°50E 172 E8
Neunkirchen Austria 47°43N 16°4E 180 D9
Neunkirchen Saarland,
  Germany 49°20N 7°9E 179 F3
Neuötting Germany 48°14N 12°41E 179 G8
Neuperlach Germany 48°5N 11°37E 131 B3
Neuquén Argentina 38°55S 68°0W 336 B3
Neuquén □ Argentina 38°0S 69°50W 336 B2
Neuried Germany 48°5N 11°29E 131 B2
Neuruppin Germany 52°55N 12°48E 178 B8
Neusalz an der Oder = Nowa Sól
  Poland 51°48N 15°44E 185 G3
Neusatz = Novi Sad Serbia 45°18N 19°52E 182 B4
Neusiedl Austria 47°57N 16°50E 180 D9
Neusiedler See Austria 47°50N 16°47E 180 D9
Neusiedler See-Seewinkel △
  Austria 47°50N 16°52E 180 D9
Neusohl = Banská Bystrica
  Slovak Rep. 48°46N 19°14E 181 C12
Neuss Germany 51°11N 6°42E 178 D2
Neussargues-Moissac France 45°9N 3°1E 174 C7
Neustadt = Lwówek
  Poland 52°28N 16°10E 185 F3
Neustadt = Prudnik
  Poland 50°20N 17°38E 185 H4

Neustadt = Wejherowo
Poland 54°35N 18°12E 184 D5
Neustadt Bayern, Germany 49°44N 12°10E 179 F8
Neustadt Bayern, Germany 48°48N 11°46E 179 G7
Neustadt Bayern, Germany 49°34N 10°37E 179 F6
Neustadt Bayern, Germany 50°19N 11°7E 179 E7
Neustadt Brandenburg, Germany 52°50N 12°27E 178 C8
Neustadt Hessen, Germany 50°51N 9°9E 178 E5
Neustadt Niedersachsen, Germany 52°30N 9°28E 178 C5
Neustadt Rhld-Pfz., Germany 49°21N 8°10E 179 F4
Neustadt Sachsen, Germany 51°2N 14°12E 178 D10
Neustadt Schleswig-Holstein, Germany 54°6N 10°49E 178 A6
Neustadt Thüringen, Germany 50°45N 11°43E 178 E7
Neustädtel = Nowe Miasteczko
Poland 51°42N 15°42E 185 G2
Neustädtl = Novo Mesto
Slovenia 45°47N 15°12E 199 C12
Neustettin = Szczecinek
Poland 53°43N 16°41E 184 E3
Neustift am Walde Austria 48°14N 16°17E 142 A1
Neustrelitz Germany 53°21N 13°4E 178 B9
Neusüssenbrunn Austria 48°16N 16°29E 142 A2
Neutitschein = Nový Jičín
Czech Rep. 49°30N 18°2E 181 B11
Neuvic France 45°23N 2°16E 174 C6
Neuville-sur-Saône France 45°52N 4°51E 175 C8
Neuvy-le-Roi France 47°36N 0°36E 172 E7
Neuvy-St-Sépulchre France 46°35N 1°48E 173 F8
Neuvy-sur-Barangeon
France 47°20N 2°15E 173 E9
Neuwaldegg Austria 48°14N 16°17E 142 A1
Neuwedell = Drawno
Poland 53°13N 15°46E 185 E2
Neuwerk Germany 53°55N 8°30E 178 B4
Neuwied Germany 50°26N 7°29E 178 E3
Neva → Russia 59°56N 30°20E 188 C6
Nevada Iowa, U.S.A. 42°1N 93°27W 310 B3
Nevada Mo., U.S.A. 37°51N 94°22W 310 G2
Nevada □ U.S.A. 39°0N 117°0W 304 G5
Nevada City U.S.A. 39°16N 121°1W 306 F6
Nevado, Cerro Argentina 35°30S 68°32W 334 D2
Nevado de Colima = Volcán de
Colima △ Mexico 19°30N 103°40W 318 D4
Nevado de Tres Cruces △
Chile 27°13S 69°5W 334 B2
Nevado del Huila △
Colombia 3°5N 75°58W 328 C2
Nevasa India 19°34N 75°0E 244 E2
Neve, Sa. da Angola 13°43S 13°10E 265 E2
Neve Ya'akov West Bank 31°50N 35°14E 123 A2
Nevel Russia 56°0N 29°55E 188 D5
Nevelsk Russia 46°40N 141°51E 215 E15
Nevers France 47°0N 3°9E 173 F10
Nevertire Australia 31°50S 147°44E 283 A7
Neves Brazil 22°51S 43°5W 135 B2
Nevesinje Bos.-H. 43°14N 18°6E 202 C2
Neville Canada 49°58N 107°39W 297 D7
Nevinnomyssk Russia 44°40N 42°0E 191 H6
Nevis St. Kitts & Nevis 17°0N 62°30W 322 d
Nevis Pk. St. Kitts & Nevis 17°9N 62°34W 322 d
Nevlunghavn Norway 58°58N 9°53E 164 F6
Nevoso, Mte. = Snežnik
Slovenia 45°36N 14°35E 199 C11
Nevrokop = Gotse Delchev
Bulgaria 41°36N 23°46E 202 E7
Nevşehir Turkey 38°33N 34°40E 212 C6
Nevşehir □ Turkey 38°50N 34°40E 212 C6
Nevskoye Russia 54°32N 22°39E 184 D9
Nevyansk Russia 57°30N 60°13E 186 C11
New → Guyana 3°20N 57°37W 329 C6
New → W. Va., U.S.A. 38°10N 81°12W 309 F13
New Aiyansh Canada 55°12N 129°4W 296 B3
New Albany Ind., U.S.A. 38°18N 85°49W 311 F11
New Albany Miss., U.S.A. 34°29N 89°0W 315 D10
New Albany Pa., U.S.A. 41°36N 76°27W 313 E8
New Amsterdam Guyana 6°15N 57°36W 329 B6
New Athens U.S.A. 38°19N 89°53W 310 F7
New Baghdad Iraq 33°18N 44°28E 113 B2
New Baltimore U.S.A. 42°41N 82°44W 312 D2
New Barakpur India 22°40N 88°26E 124 A2
New Barbadoes = Hackensack
U.S.A. 40°52N 74°4W 132 A1
New Bedford U.S.A. 41°38N 70°56W 313 E14
New Berlin = North Canton
U.S.A. 40°53N 81°24W 312 F3
New Berlin Ill., U.S.A. 39°44N 89°55W 310 E7
New Berlin N.Y., U.S.A. 42°37N 75°20W 313 D9
New Berlin Pa., U.S.A. 40°50N 76°57W 312 F8
New Berlin Wis., U.S.A. 42°59N 88°6W 311 B8
New Bern U.S.A. 35°7N 77°3W 315 D16
New Bethlehem U.S.A. 41°0N 79°20W 312 F5
New Bight Bahamas 24°19N 75°24W 321 B4
New Bloomfield U.S.A. 40°25N 77°11W 312 F7
New Boston U.S.A. 33°28N 94°25W 314 E7
New Braunfels U.S.A. 29°42N 98°8W 314 G5
New Brighton N.Z. 43°29S 172°43E 285 D7
New Brighton N.Y., U.S.A. 40°38N 74°5W 132 C1
New Brighton Pa., U.S.A. 40°42N 80°19W 312 F4
New Britain Papua N. G. 5°50S 150°20E 286 C6
New Britain Conn.,
U.S.A. 41°40N 72°47W 313 E12
New Britain Trench Pac. Oc. 6°0S 153°0E 276 J3
New Brockton U.S.A. 31°23N 85°56W 316 D4
New Brookland = West Columbia
U.S.A. 33°59N 81°4W 316 B8
New Brunswick U.S.A. 40°30N 74°27W 313 F10
New Brunswick □
Canada 46°50N 66°30W 299 C6
New Buffalo U.S.A. 41°47N 86°45W 311 C10
New Bussa Nigeria 9°53N 4°31E 263 D5
New Caledonia ☑ Pac. Oc. 21°0S 165°0E 288 d
New Caledonia Trough
Pac. Oc. 30°0S 165°0E 288 L8
New Canada S. Africa 26°12S 27°56E 123 B1
New Canada Dam
S. Africa 26°12S 27°56E 123 B1
New Carlisle Ind., U.S.A. 41°45N 86°32W 311 C10
New Carlisle Ohio, U.S.A. 39°56N 84°2W 311 E12
New Carrollton U.S.A. 38°58N 76°53W 143 B4
New Castile = Castilla-La Mancha □
Spain 39°30N 3°30W 195 F7
New Castle Ind., U.S.A. 39°55N 85°22W 311 E11
New Castle Ky., U.S.A. 38°26N 85°10W 311 F11
New Castle Pa., U.S.A. 41°0N 80°21W 312 F4
New City U.S.A. 41°9N 73°59W 313 E11
New Concord U.S.A. 39°59N 81°54W 312 G3
New Cross U.K. 51°28N 0°1W 125 B3
New Cumberland U.S.A. 40°30N 80°36W 312 F4
New Cuyama U.S.A. 34°57N 119°38W 307 L7
New Delhi India 28°36N 77°11E 120 B2
New Denver Canada 50°0N 117°25W 296 D5
New Don Pedro Res.
U.S.A. 37°43N 120°24W 306 H6
New Dorp U.S.A. 40°34N 74°7W 132 C1
New Dorp Beach U.S.A. 40°33N 74°6W 132 C1
New Ellenton U.S.A. 33°28N 81°41W 316 B8
New England U.S.A. 43°0N 71°0W 301 G25
New England N. Dak.,
U.S.A. 46°32N 102°52W 308 B2
New England △
Australia 30°25S 152°30E 283 A10
New England Aquarium Boston, U.S.A. 116 b3
New England Ra.
Australia 30°20S 151°45E 281 E5
New England Seamounts
Atl. Oc. 38°0N 63°0W 152 C5
New Forest △ U.K. 50°53N 1°34W 169 G6
New Franklin U.S.A. 39°1N 92°44W 310 E4
New Galloway U.K. 55°5N 4°9W 167 F4
New Georgia Is.
Solomon Is. 8°15S 157°30E 287 M9
New Georgia Sound
Solomon Is. 8°0S 158°20E 287 L9
New Glarus U.S.A. 42°49N 89°38W 310 B7
New Glasgow Canada 45°35N 62°36W 299 C7
New Grant Trin. & Tob. 10°17N 61°19W 323 t
New Guinea Oceania 4°0S 136°0E 275 B7
New Halfa = Halfa al Jadidah
Sudan 15°20N 35°35E 266 A4
New Hamburg Canada 43°23N 80°42W 312 C4
New Hampshire □
U.S.A. 44°0N 71°30W 313 C13
New Hampton U.S.A. 43°3N 92°19W 310 A4
New Hanover Papua N. G. 2°30S 150°10E 286 B6
New Hanover KwaZulu Natal,
S. Africa 29°22S 30°31E 271 C5
New Harmony U.S.A. 38°8N 87°56W 311 F9
New Hartford U.S.A. 43°4N 75°18W 313 C9
New Haven Conn.,
U.S.A. 41°18N 72°55W 313 E12
New Haven Ill., U.S.A. 37°55N 88°8W 311 G8
New Haven Ind., U.S.A. 41°4N 85°1W 311 C11
New Haven Mich., U.S.A. 42°44N 82°48W 312 D2
New Haven Mo., U.S.A. 38°37N 91°13W 310 F5
New Haven N.Y., U.S.A. 43°28N 76°18W 313 C8
New Hazelton Canada 55°20N 127°30W 296 B3
New Hebrides = Vanuatu ■
Pac. Oc. 15°0S 168°0E 287 E6
New Holland U.S.A. 40°6N 76°5W 313 F8
New Iberia U.S.A. 30°1N 91°49W 314 F9
New Ireland Papua N. G. 3°20S 151°50E 286 B6
New Ireland □ Papua N. G. 3°0S 151°30E 286 B6
New Jersey □ U.S.A. 40°0N 74°30W 309 F16
New Kensington U.S.A. 40°34N 79°46W 312 F5
New Lexington U.S.A. 39°43N 82°13W 309 F12
New Liskeard Canada 47°31N 79°41W 298 C4
New London Conn.,
U.S.A. 41°22N 72°6W 313 E12
New London Iowa, U.S.A. 40°55N 91°24W 310 D5
New London Mo., U.S.A. 39°35N 91°24W 310 E5
New London Ohio, U.S.A. 41°5N 82°24W 312 E2
New London Wis., U.S.A. 44°23N 88°45W 308 C9
New Madrid U.S.A. 36°36N 89°32W 308 G9
New Malden U.K. 51°24N 0°15W 125 B2
New Martinsville U.S.A. 39°39N 80°52W 309 F13
New Meadows U.S.A. 44°58N 116°18W 304 D5
New Melones L. U.S.A. 37°57N 120°31W 306 H6
New Mexico □ U.S.A. 34°30N 106°0W 305 J11
New Miami U.S.A. 39°26N 84°32W 311 E12
New Milford Conn.,
U.S.A. 41°35N 73°25W 313 E11
New Milford N.Y., U.S.A. 40°56N 74°0W 132 A1
New Milford Pa., U.S.A. 41°52N 75°44W 313 E9
New Moore I. Ind. Oc. 21°37N 89°10E 241 E2
New Mumbai = Navi Mumbai
India 19°5N 73°0E 130 A2
New Norcia Australia 30°57S 116°13E 279 F2
New Norfolk Australia 42°46S 147°2E 281 G4
New Orleans U.S.A. 29°57N 90°4W 131 B2
New Orleans Int. ✈ (MSY)
U.S.A. 30°0N 90°15W 131 A1
New Palestine U.S.A. 39°45N 85°52W 311 E11
New Paris U.S.A. 39°51N 84°48W 311 E12
New Pekin U.S.A. 38°30N 86°0W 311 F10
New Philadelphia U.S.A. 40°30N 81°27W 312 F3
New Plymouth N.Z. 39°4S 174°5E 284 F3
New Plymouth Idaho,
U.S.A. 43°58N 116°49W 304 E5
New Pomerania = New Britain
Papua N. G. 5°50S 150°20E 286 C6
New Port Richey U.S.A. 28°16N 82°43W 317 G7
New Providence Bahamas 25°25N 78°35W 153 b
New Quay U.K. 52°13N 4°21W 169 E3
New Radnor U.K. 52°15N 3°9W 169 E4
New Richmond Qué.,
Canada 48°15N 65°45W 299 C6
New Richmond Ohio,
U.S.A. 38°57N 84°17W 311 F12
New Richmond Wis.,
U.S.A. 45°7N 92°32W 308 C7
New River Gorge ⌂
U.S.A. 37°53N 81°5W 309 G13
New Roads U.S.A. 30°42N 91°26W 314 F9
New Rochelle U.S.A. 40°55N 73°46W 313 F11
New Rockford U.S.A. 47°41N 99°8W 308 B4
New Romney U.K. 50°59N 0°57E 169 G8
New Ross Ireland 52°23N 6°57W 166 D5
New Salem U.S.A. 46°51N 101°25W 308 B3
New Scone = Scone U.K. 56°25N 3°24W 167 E5
New Sharon U.S.A. 41°28N 92°39W 310 C4
New Siberian I. = Novaya Sibir,
Ostrov Russia 75°10N 150°0E 215 B16
New Siberian Is. = Novosibirskiye
Ostrova Russia 75°0N 142°0E 215 B15
New Smyrna Beach U.S.A. 29°1N 80°56W 317 F9
New South Wales □
Australia 33°0S 146°0E 283 B7
New Stuyahok U.S.A. 59°29N 157°20W 303 G8
New Tecumseth = Alliston
Canada 44°9N 79°52W 312 B5
New Territories China 22°23N 114°10E 122 A1
New Toronto Canada 43°35N 79°30W 141 B1
New Town = Nowe Miasto
Warsaw, Poland 142 a2
New Town Edinburgh, U.K. 121 a2
New Town N. Dak.,
U.S.A. 47°59N 102°30W 308 B2
New Tredegar U.K. 51°44N 3°16W 169 F4
New Ulm U.S.A. 44°19N 94°28W 308 C6
New Utrecht U.S.A. 40°36N 73°59W 132 C2
New Vienna U.S.A. 39°19N 83°42W 311 E13
New Washington Phil. 11°39N 122°26E 233 F4
New Waterford Canada 46°13N 60°4W 299 C7
New Westminster
Canada 49°13N 122°55W 306 A4
New York U.S.A. 40°43N 74°0W 132 B3
New York □ U.S.A. 43°0N 75°0W 313 D9
New York Avenue
Washington, D.C., U.S.A. 143 a2
New York J.F. Kennedy Int. ✈ (JFK)
U.S.A. 40°38N 73°47W 313 F11
New York La Guardia ✈ (LGA)
U.S.A. 40°46N 73°52W 132 B2
New York University New York, U.S.A. 132 d2
New Zealand ■ Oceania 40°0S 176°0E 284 G5
Newaj → India 24°24N 76°49E 242 G7
Newala Tanzania 10°58S 39°18E 269 E4
Newark Del., U.S.A. 39°41N 75°46W 309 F16
Newark N.J., U.S.A. 40°44N 74°10W 313 F10
Newark N.Y., U.S.A. 43°3N 77°6W 312 C7
Newark Ohio, U.S.A. 40°3N 82°24W 312 F2
Newark B. U.S.A. 40°40N 74°8W 132 B1
Newark Liberty Int. ✈ (EWR)
U.S.A. 40°42N 74°10W 313 F10
Newark-on-Trent U.K. 53°5N 0°48W 168 D7
Newark Valley U.S.A. 42°14N 76°11W 313 D8
Newbattle U.K. 55°53N 3°4W 121 B3
Newberg U.S.A. 45°18N 122°58W 304 D2
Newberry Fla., U.S.A. 29°39N 82°37W 317 F7
Newberry Mich., U.S.A. 46°21N 85°30W 309 B11
Newberry S.C., U.S.A. 34°17N 81°37W 315 D14
Newberry Springs
U.S.A. 34°50N 116°41W 307 L10
Newboro L. Canada 44°38N 76°20W 313 B8
Newbridge = Droichead Nua
Ireland 53°11N 6°48W 166 C5
Newburg U.S.A. 37°55N 91°54W 310 G5
Newburgh Ont., Canada 44°19N 76°52W 312 B8
Newburgh Ind., U.S.A. 37°57N 87°24W 311 G9
Newburgh N.Y., U.S.A. 41°30N 74°1W 313 E10
Newbury W. Berkshire,
U.K. 51°24N 1°20W 169 F6
Newbury N.H., U.S.A. 43°19N 72°3W 313 B12
Newbury Vt., U.S.A. 44°5N 72°4W 313 B12
Newbury Park U.K. 51°34N 0°5E 125 A4
Newburyport U.S.A. 42°49N 70°53W 313 D14
Newcastle N.S.W.,
Australia 33°0S 151°46E 283 B9
Newcastle N.B., Canada 47°1N 65°38W 299 C6
Newcastle Ont., Canada 43°55N 78°35W 298 D4
Newcastle St. Kitts & Nevis 17°14N 62°42W 322 d
Newcastle KwaZulu Natal,
S. Africa 27°45S 29°58E 271 C4
Newcastle Down, U.K. 54°13N 5°54W 166 B6
Newcastle Calif., U.S.A. 38°53N 121°8W 306 G5
Newcastle Wyo., U.S.A. 43°50N 104°11W 304 E11
Newcastle Emlyn U.K. 52°2N 4°28W 169 E3
Newcastle Ra. Australia 15°45S 130°15E 278 C5
Newcastle-under-Lyme
U.K. 53°1N 2°14W 168 D5
Newcastle-upon-Tyne
U.K. 54°58N 1°35W 168 C6
Newcastle Waters
Australia 17°30S 133°28E 280 B1
Newcastle West Ireland 52°27N 9°3W 166 D2
Newcomb U.S.A. 43°58N 74°10W 313 C10
Newcomerstown U.S.A. 40°16N 81°36W 312 F3
Newcraighall U.K. 55°56N 3°5W 121 B3
Newdegate Australia 33°6S 119°0E 279 F2
Newell Queens., Australia 16°20S 145°16E 280 B4
Newell Iowa, U.S.A. 42°36N 95°0W 310 B1
Newell S. Dak., U.S.A. 44°43N 103°25W 308 C2
Newenham, C. U.S.A. 58°39N 162°11W 303 G7
Newfane U.S.A. 43°17N 78°43W 312 C6
Newfield U.S.A. 42°18N 76°33W 313 D8
Newfound L. U.S.A. 43°40N 71°47W 313 C13
Newfoundland Canada 49°0N 55°0W 299 C8
Newfoundland Pa.,
U.S.A. 41°18N 75°19W 313 E9
Newfoundland & Labrador □
Canada 53°0N 58°0W 299 B8
Newhalen U.S.A. 59°43N 154°54W 303 G9
Newham □ U.K. 51°31N 0°3E 125 A4
Newhaven E. Sussex, U.K. 50°47N 0°3E 169 G8
Newhaven Edinburgh, U.K. 55°59N 3°11W 121 B2
Newington Edinburgh, U.K. 55°56N 3°10W 121 B2
Newington London, U.K. 125 c5
Newington Ga., U.S.A. 32°35N 81°30W 316 C8
Newkirk U.S.A. 36°53N 97°3W 314 C6
Newlands Wellington,
N.Z. 41°13S 174°49E 143 B1
Newlands Gauteng,
S. Africa 26°10S 27°57E 123 B1
Newlyn U.K. 50°6N 5°34W 169 G2
Newman W. Austral.,
Australia 23°18S 119°45E 278 D2
Newman Calif., U.S.A. 37°19N 121°1W 306 H5
Newman Ill., U.S.A. 39°48N 87°59W 311 E9
Newmarket Ont., Canada 44°3N 79°28W 312 B5
Newmarket Cork, Ireland 52°13N 9°0W 166 D2
Newmarket Jamaica 18°9N 77°55W 320 a
Newmarket Suffolk, U.K. 52°15N 0°25E 169 E8
Newmarket N.H., U.S.A. 43°5N 70°56W 313 C14
Newnan U.S.A. 33°23N 84°48W 316 B5
Newport = Nieuwpoort
Curaçao 12°3N 68°49W 322 g
Newport Vic., Australia 37°50S 144°51E 128 B1
Newport Mayo, Ireland 53°53N 9°33W 166 C2
Newport I. of W., U.K. 50°42N 1°17W 169 G6
Newport Newport, U.K. 51°35N 3°0W 169 F5
Newport Ark., U.S.A. 35°37N 91°16W 314 D9
Newport Fla., U.S.A. 30°11N 84°10W 316 E5
Newport Ind., U.S.A. 39°53N 87°25W 311 E9
Newport Ky., U.S.A. 39°5N 84°29W 311 E12
Newport N.H., U.S.A. 43°22N 72°10W 313 C12
Newport N.Y., U.S.A. 43°11N 75°1W 313 C9
Newport Oreg., U.S.A. 44°39N 124°3W 304 D1
Newport Pa., U.S.A. 40°29N 77°8W 312 F7
Newport R.I., U.S.A. 41°29N 71°19W 313 E13
Newport Tenn., U.S.A. 35°58N 83°11W 315 D13
Newport Vt., U.S.A. 44°56N 72°13W 313 B12
Newport Wash., U.S.A. 48°11N 117°3W 304 B5
Newport □ U.K. 51°33N 3°1W 169 F4
Newport Beach U.S.A. 33°37N 117°56W 307 M9
Newport News U.S.A. 36°58N 76°25W 309 G15
Newport Pagnell U.K. 52°5N 0°43W 169 E7
Newquay U.K. 50°25N 5°6W 169 G2
Newry U.K. 54°11N 6°21W 166 B5
Newry Islands △ Australia 20°51S 148°56E 280 b
Newtok U.S.A. 60°56N 164°38W 303 F6
Newton Ga., U.S.A. 31°19N 84°20W 316 D5
Newton Ill., U.S.A. 38°59N 88°10W 311 F8
Newton Iowa, U.S.A. 41°42N 93°3W 310 C3
Newton Kans., U.S.A. 38°3N 97°21W 308 F5
Newton Mass., U.S.A. 42°21N 71°12W 116 B1
Newton Miss., U.S.A. 32°19N 89°10W 315 E10
Newton N.C., U.S.A. 35°40N 81°13W 315 D14
Newton N.J., U.S.A. 41°3N 74°45W 313 E10
Newton Tex., U.S.A. 30°51N 93°46W 314 F8
Newton Abbot U.K. 50°32N 3°37W 169 G4
Newton Aycliffe U.K. 54°37N 1°34W 168 C6
Newton Falls N.Y.,
U.S.A. 44°12N 74°59W 313 B10
Newton Falls Ohio, U.S.A. 41°11N 80°59W 312 E4
Newton L. U.S.A. 38°55N 88°15W 311 F8
Newton Stewart U.K. 54°57N 4°30W 167 G4
Newton Terrace Barbados 13°4N 59°32W 323 r
Newtonbrook Canada 43°47N 79°24W 141 A2
Newtongrange U.K. 55°53N 3°3W 121 B3
Newtonmore U.K. 57°4N 4°8W 167 D4
Newtontoppen Svalbard 79°0N 17°30E 154 B12
Newtonville U.S.A. 42°20N 71°11W 116 A1
Newtown N.S.W.,
Australia 33°54S 151°11E 139 B2
Newtown Powys, U.K. 52°31N 3°19W 169 E4
Newtown Ind., U.S.A. 40°13N 87°9W 311 D9
Newtown Mo., U.S.A. 40°22N 93°20W 310 D3
Newtownabbey U.K. 54°40N 5°56W 166 B6
Newtownards U.K. 54°36N 5°42W 166 B6
Newtownbarry = Bunclody
Ireland 52°39N 6°40W 166 D5
Newtownstewart U.K. 54°43N 7°23W 166 B4
Newville U.S.A. 40°10N 77°24W 312 F7
Nexon France 45°41N 1°11E 174 C5
Neya Russia 58°21N 43°49E 190 A6
Neyriz Iran 29°15N 54°19E 247 D7
Neyshābūr Iran 36°10N 58°50E 247 B8
Neyveli India 11°32N 79°29E 245 J4
Neyyattinkara India 8°26N 77°5E 245 K3
Nezametny = Aldan
Russia 58°40N 125°30E 215 D13
Nezhin = Nizhyn Ukraine 51°5N 31°55E 189 G6
Nezperce U.S.A. 46°14N 116°14W 304 C5
Nezvysko Ukraine 48°46N 25°15E 183 B10
Ngaanyatjarra ✪
Australia 22°40S 127°0E 278 D4
Ngabang Indonesia 0°23N 109°55E 235 B3
Ngabe Congo 3°12S 16°12E 264 C3
Ngabordamlu, Tanjung
Indonesia 6°56S 134°11E 231 F8
N'Gage Angola 7°46S 15°15E 265 D3
Ngaio N.Z. 41°15S 174°46E 143 B1
Ngaiphaipi Burma 22°14N 93°15E 241 D4
Ngala Nigeria 12°20N 14°11E 263 C7
Ngaliwurru Nungali ✪
Australia 15°42S 130°4E 278 C5
Ngalurrtju ✪ Australia 22°44S 132°5E 278 D5
Ngama Chad 11°45N 17°6E 259 F3
Ngambé Centre, Cameroon 5°48N 11°29E 263 D7
Ngambé Littoral, Cameroon 4°21N 10°40E 263 E7
Ngami Depression
Botswana 20°30S 22°46E 270 B3
Ngamo Zimbabwe 19°3S 27°32E 269 F2
Ngamring China 29°14N 87°10E 218 F6
Nganbéto, L. de Togo 7°25N 1°25E 263 D5
Ngangala South Sudan 4°42N 31°55E 257 G3
Nganglong Kangri China 33°0N 81°0E 243 C9
Ngao Thailand 18°46N 99°59E 236 C2
Ngaoundéré Cameroon 7°15N 13°35E 264 A2
Ngapali Burma 18°26N 94°19E 241 F5
Ngapara N.Z. 44°57S 170°46E 285 E5
Ngape Burma 20°2N 94°28E 241 E5
Ngara Tanzania 2°29S 30°40E 268 C3
Ngardmau Palau 7°37N 134°34E 288 c
Ngardmau B. Palau 7°38N 134°34E 288 c
Ngardololok Palau 7°0N 134°14E 288 c
Ngaregur Palau 7°45N 134°37E 288 c
Ngarluma ✪ Australia 21°30S 118°30E 278 D2
Ngaruawahia N.Z. 37°42S 175°11E 284 D4
Ngaruroro → N.Z. 39°34S 176°55E 284 F5
Ngatangiia Cook Is. 21°14S 159°43W 289 h
Ngatapa N.Z. 38°32S 177°45E 284 E6
Ngathainggyaung Burma 17°24N 95°5E 241 G5
Ngau Chi Wan China 22°20N 114°12E 122 A2
Ngau Tau Kok China 22°19N 114°12E 122 B2
Ngauranga N.Z. 41°15S 174°49E 143 B1
Ngauruhoe, Mt. N.Z. 39°13S 175°45E 284 F4
Ngawi Indonesia 7°24S 111°26E 235 D4
Ngcobo S. Africa 31°37S 28°0E 271 D4
Ngele Dem. Rep. of the Congo 0°30S 20°22E 264 C4
Ngelebok Cameroon 4°13N 14°3E 264 B2
Ngeregong Palau 7°6N 134°21E 288 c
Ngergoi Palau 7°5N 134°15E 288 c
Ngeru Uganda 0°27N 33°10E 268 B3
Ngesebus I. Palau 7°3N 134°15E 288 c
Nggatokae Solomon Is. 8°45S 158°15E 287 M10
Nggela Pile Solomon Is. 9°5S 160°20E 287 M11
Nggela Sule Solomon Is. 9°2S 160°12E 287 M11
Nghia Lo Vietnam 21°33N 104°28E 228 G5
Ngidinga
Dem. Rep. of the Congo 5°37S 15°17E 265 D3
Ngo Congo 2°29S 15°45E 264 C3
Ngoap Cameroon 4°9N 12°51E 264 B2
Ngobasangel Palau 7°16N 134°19E 288 c
Ngoboli South Sudan 4°57N 32°37E 257 G3
Ngol = Raqaba ez Zarqa →
South Sudan 9°14N 29°44E 257 F2
N'Gola Angola 14°10S 14°30E 265 E2
Ngoma Malawi 13°8S 33°45E 269 E3
Ngomahura Zimbabwe 20°26S 30°43E 269 G3
Ngomba Tanzania 8°20S 32°53E 269 D3
Ngomeni, Ras Kenya 2°59S 40°14E 268 C5
Ngong Kenya 1°22S 36°39E 268 C4
Ngong Shuen Chau China 22°19N 114°8E 122 B1
Ngongotaha N.Z. 38°5S 176°12E 284 E5
Ngonye Falls Zambia 16°40S 23°25E 265 F4
Ngop South Sudan 6°17N 30°9E 257 F3
Ngoring Hu China 34°55N 97°5E 218 E8
Ngorkou Mali 15°40N 3°41W 262 B4
Ngorongoro Tanzania 3°11S 35°32E 268 C4
Ngorongoro ⌂ Tanzania 2°40S 35°30E 268 C4
Ngoto C.A.R. 3°59N 17°19E 264 B3
Ngouo, Dj. C.A.R. 7°55N 24°38E 264 A4
Ngoura Chad 12°44N 16°21E 259 F3
Ngouri Chad 13°38N 15°22E 259 F3
Ngourti Niger 15°19N 13°12E 259 E2
Ngoussou Gabon 3°0S 11°7E 264 C2
Ngozi Burundi 2°54S 29°50E 268 C2
Ngua Kok Wan China 22°21N 114°5E 122 A1
Ngudu Tanzania 2°58S 33°25E 268 C3
Nguigmi Niger 14°20N 13°20E 259 F2
Nguila Cameroon 4°41N 11°43E 263 E7
Nguiu Australia 11°46S 130°38E 278 B5
Ngukurr Australia 14°44S 134°44E 280 A1
Ngum → Laos 18°31N 102°32E 236 C4
Nguna Vanuatu 17°26S 168°22E 287 G6
Ngundu Zimbabwe 18°11S 31°15E 269 F3
Ngunga Tanzania 3°37S 33°37E 268 C3
Nguru Nigeria 12°56N 10°29E 263 C7
Nguru Mts. Tanzania 6°0S 37°30E 268 D4
Ngusi Malawi 14°0S 34°50E 269 E3
Nguyen Binh Vietnam 22°39N 105°56E 228 F5
Ngwedaung Burma 19°31N 97°9E 241 F6
Nha Bang Vietnam 10°37N 105°0E 237 G5
Nha Trang Vietnam 12°16N 109°10E 237 F7
Nhacoongo Mozam. 24°18S 35°14E 271 B6
Nhamaabué Mozam. 17°25S 35°5E 269 F4
Nhambiquara Brazil 12°53S 59°49W 331 C6
Nhamundá Brazil 2°14S 56°43W 329 D6
Nhamundá → Brazil 2°12S 56°41W 329 D6
Nhangulaze, L. Mozam. 24°0S 34°30E 271 B5
Nharêa Angola 11°38S 16°58E 265 E3
Nharnuwangga, Wajarri and
Ngarlawangga ✪
Australia 24°50S 118°0E 279 D2
Nhava Sheva India 18°58N 72°55E 130 B2
Nhecolândia Brazil 19°17S 56°58W 331 D6
Nhill Australia 36°18S 141°40E 282 D4
Nho Quan Vietnam 20°18N 105°45E 228 G5
Nhulunbuy Australia 12°10S 137°20E 280 A2
Nhundo Angola 14°25S 21°23E 265 E4
Nia-nia
Dem. Rep. of the Congo 1°30N 27°40E 268 B2
Niafounké Mali 16°0N 4°5W 262 B4
Niagara Falls Ont., Canada 43°7N 79°5W 312 C5
Niagara Falls N.Y., U.S.A. 43°5N 79°4W 312 C6
Niagara-on-the-Lake
Canada 43°15N 79°4W 312 C5
Niah Malaysia 3°58N 113°46E 235 B4
Nialaha'u Pt. Solomon Is. 9°47S 161°34E 287 M11
Niamey Niger 13°27N 2°6E 263 C5
Niamtougou Togo 9°46N 1°6E 263 D5
Niandan-Koro Guinea 11°5N 9°15W 262 C3
Nianforando Guinea 9°37N 10°36W 262 D2
Niangara
Dem. Rep. of the Congo 3°42N 27°50E 268 B2
Niangay, L. Mali 15°50N 3°0W 262 B4
Niangbo Ivory C. 8°49N 5°10W 262 D3
Niangoloko Burkina Faso 10°15N 4°55W 262 C4
Niangua → U.S.A. 38°58N 92°48W 310 G4
Niantic U.S.A. 41°20N 72°11W 313 E12
Niari Congo 4°0S 14°9E 264 C2
Niaro Sudan 10°38N 31°31E 257 E3
Nias Indonesia 1°0N 97°30E 234 B1
Niassa □ Mozam. 13°30S 36°0E 269 E4
Niassa ⌂ Mozam. 12°4S 36°57E 269 E4
Nīāvarān Iran 35°47N 51°29E 141 A2
Nībāk Si. Arabia 24°25N 50°50E 247 E7
Nibe Denmark 56°59N 9°38E 163 H3
Nibra India 22°36N 88°15E 124 B1
Nicaragua ■ Cent. Amer. 11°40N 85°30W 320 D2
Nicaragua, L. de Nic. 12°0N 85°30W 320 D2
Nicastro Italy 38°59N 16°19E 201 D9
Nice France 43°42N 7°14E 175 E11
Nice-Côte-d'Azur ✈ (NCE)
France 43°41N 7°12E 175 E11
Niceville U.S.A. 30°31N 86°30W 317 E3
Nichicun, L. Canada 53°5N 71°0W 299 B5
Nichinan Japan 31°38N 131°23E 222 F3
Nicholás, Canal W. Indies 23°30N 80°5W 320 B3
Nicholasville U.S.A. 37°53N 84°34W 311 G12
Nicholls U.S.A. 31°31N 82°38W 316 D7
Nichols U.S.A. 42°1N 76°22W 313 D8
Nicholson W. Austral.,
Australia 18°2S 128°54E 278 C4
Nicholson Pa., U.S.A. 41°37N 75°47W 313 E9
Nicholson → Australia 17°31S 139°36E 280 B2
Nicholson L. Canada 62°40N 102°40W 297 A8
Nicholson Ra. Australia 27°15S 116°45E 279 E2
Nicholville U.S.A. 44°41N 74°39W 313 B10
Nickerie → Suriname 5°58N 57°0W 329 B6
Nico Pérez = José Batlle y Ordóñez
Uruguay 33°20S 55°10W 335 C4
Nicobar Is. Ind. Oc. 8°0N 93°30E 245 L11
Nicola Canada 50°12N 120°40W 296 C4
Nicolls Town Bahamas 25°8N 78°0W 320 A4
Nicosia Cyprus 35°10N 33°25E 207 E9
Nicosia Italy 37°45N 14°24E 201 E7
Nicótera Italy 38°33N 15°56E 201 D8
Nicoya Costa Rica 10°9N 85°27W 320 D2
Nicoya, G. de Costa Rica 10°0N 85°0W 320 E3
Nicoya, Pen. de Costa Rica 9°45N 85°40W 320 E2
Nictheroy = Niterói Brazil 22°53S 43°7W 135 B2
Nida Lithuania 55°20N 21°4E 184 C8
Nidāl Iraq 33°19N 44°25E 113 B2
Nidaros = Trondheim
Norway 63°36N 10°25E 164 A7
Nidd → U.K. 53°59N 1°23W 168 D6
Nidda Germany 50°23N 9°1E 179 E5
Nidda → Germany 50°17N 8°48E 179 E4
Niddrie Vic., Australia 37°44S 144°51E 128 A1
Niddrie Edinburgh, U.K. 55°56N 3°7W 121 B3
Nidri Greece 38°43N 20°42E 207 B2
Nidwalden □ Switz. 46°50N 8°25E 179 J4
Nidzica Poland 53°25N 20°28E 185 E7
Niebüll Germany 54°46N 8°48E 178 A4
Nied → Germany 49°23N 6°40E 173 C13
Nieder Neuendorf
Germany 52°36N 13°12E 115 A2
Niederaula Germany 50°47N 9°36E 178 E5
Niederbayern □ Germany 48°40N 12°50E 179 G8
Niederbronn-les-Bains
France 48°57N 7°39E 173 D14
Niedere Tauern Austria 47°20N 14°0E 180 D7
Niederlausitz Germany 51°42N 13°59E 178 D9
Niederösterreich □
Austria 48°25N 15°40E 180 C8
Niedersachsen □ Germany 52°50N 9°0E 178 C4
Niedersächsisches Wattenmeer △
Germany 53°45N 7°30E 178 B3
Niederschöneweide
Germany 52°27N 13°30E 115 B3
Niederschönhausen
Germany 52°35N 13°25E 115 A3
Niefang Eq. Guin. 1°50N 10°14E 264 B2
Niekerkshoop S. Africa 29°19S 22°51E 270 C3
Niellé Ivory C. 10°5N 5°38W 262 C3
Niellim Chad 9°42N 17°49E 259 G3
Niem C.A.R. 6°12N 15°14E 264 A3
Niemba
Dem. Rep. of the Congo 5°58S 28°24E 268 D2
Niemen = Nemunas →
Lithuania 55°25N 21°10E 184 C8
Niemeyer Brazil 22°59S 43°16W 135 B1
Niemodlin Poland 50°38N 17°38E 185 H4
Niemur Australia 35°17S 144°9E 282 C6
Nienburg Germany 52°39N 9°13E 178 C5
Niepołomice Poland 50°3N 20°13E 185 H7
Niers → Germany 51°43N 5°57E 178 D1
Niesky Germany 51°17N 14°49E 178 D10
Nieszawa Poland 52°52N 18°50E 185 F5
Nieu Bethesda S. Africa 31°51S 24°34E 270 D3
Nieuw Amsterdam
Suriname 5°53N 55°5W 329 B6
Nieuw Nickerie Suriname 6°0N 56°59W 329 B6
Nieuwe Kerk Amsterdam, Neths. 112 a2
Nieuwendam Neths. 52°23N 4°57E 112 A2
Nieuwoudtville S. Africa 31°23S 19°7E 270 D2
Nieuwpoort Belgium 51°8N 2°45E 170 C2
Nieuwpoort Curaçao 12°3N 68°49W 322 g
Nieves, Pico de las
Canary Is. 27°57N 15°35W 153 e1
Nièvre □ France 47°10N 3°40E 173 E10
Nif Micronesia 9°28N 138°4E 287 S16
Niğa Mali 13°38N 5°27W 262 C3
Niğde Turkey 37°58N 34°40E 212 D6
Niğde □ Turkey 38°0N 34°30E 212 D6
Nigel S. Africa 26°27S 28°25E 271 C4
Niger ■ W. Afr. 17°30N 10°0E 259 E2
Niger → W. Afr. 5°33N 6°33E 263 D6
Niger Delta Africa 5°0N 6°0E 263 E6
Nigeria ■ W. Afr. 8°30N 8°0E 263 D6
Nighasin India 28°14N 80°52E 243 E9
Nightcaps N.Z. 45°57S 168°2E 285 F3
Nightmute U.S.A. 60°29N 164°44W 303 F6
Nigrita Greece 40°56N 23°29E 202 F7
Nihoa U.S.A. 23°6N 161°58W 302 G11
Nihon = Japan ■ Asia 36°0N 136°0E 221 G8
Nihonbashi Tokyo, Japan 140 b5
Nii-Jima Japan 34°20N 139°15E 223 C11
Niigata Japan 37°58N 139°0E 220 F9
Niigata □ Japan 37°15N 138°45E 221 F9
Niihama Japan 33°55N 133°16E 222 D5
Ni'ihau U.S.A. 21°54N 160°9W 302 B1
Niimi Japan 34°59N 133°28E 222 C5
Niipperi Finland 60°18N 24°45E 121 B1
Niislel Khureheh = Ulaanbaatar
Mongolia 47°55N 106°53E 218 B10
Niitsu Japan 37°48N 139°7E 220 F9
Nij Laluk India 27°7N 93°56E 241 B4
Nijar Spain 36°53N 2°15W 197 J2
Nijil Jordan 30°32N 35°33E 251 H6
Nijkerk Neths. 52°13N 5°30E 170 B5
Nijmegen Neths. 51°50N 5°52E 170 C5
Nijverdal Neths. 52°22N 6°28E 170 B6
Nīk Pey Iran 36°50N 48°10E 213 D13
Nikao Cook Is. 21°12S 159°48W 289 h
Nikaweratiya Sri Lanka 7°45N 80°7E 245 L5
Nike Nigeria 6°26N 7°29E 263 D6
Nikea Greece 37°57N 23°38E 112 B1
Nikel Russia 69°24N 30°13E 160 B24
Nikiboko Bonaire 12°9N 68°16W 322 h
Nikiniki Indonesia 9°49S 124°30E 278 A3
Nikisiani Greece 40°57N 24°9E 203 F8
Nikiski U.S.A. 61°41N 151°18W 303 F10
Nikiti Greece 40°13N 23°43E 202 F7
Nikitinskiye promysly = Kirovskiy
Russia 45°51N 48°11E 191 H9
Nikki Benin 9°58N 3°12E 263 D5
Nikkō Japan 36°45N 139°35E 223 A11
Nikkō △ Japan 36°56N 139°37E 221 F9
Nikolai U.S.A. 62°58N 154°10W 303 E9
Nikolainkaupunki = Vaasa
Finland 63°6N 21°38E 160 E19
Nikolaistad = Vaasa
Finland 63°6N 21°38E 160 E19
Nikolassee Germany 52°25N 13°12E 115 B2
Nikolayev = Mykolayiv
Ukraine 46°58N 32°0E 189 J7
Nikolayevsk Russia 50°0N 45°35E 190 E7
Nikolayevsk-na-Amur
Russia 53°8N 140°44E 215 D15
Nikolsburg = Mikulov
Czech Rep. 48°48N 16°39E 181 C9
Nikolsk Russia 53°49N 46°4E 190 D8
Nikolsk-Ussuriyskiy = Ussuriysk
Russia 43°48N 131°59E 220 C5
Nikolskaya Pestravka = Nikolsk
Russia 53°49N 46°4E 190 D8
Nikolski U.S.A. 52°56N 168°52W 303 K5
Nikolskiy Russia 55°49N 37°29E 129 B2
Nikolskoye = Ussuriysk
Russia 43°48N 131°59E 220 C5
Nikolskoye Russia 55°12N 166°0E 215 D17
Nikolsky Khutor = Sursk
Russia 53°3N 45°40E 190 D7
Nikolyskoye Russia 55°46N 37°53E 129 B5
Nikopol Bulgaria 43°43N 24°54E 203 C8
Nikopol Ukraine 47°35N 34°25E 189 J8
Nikopolis Greece 39°5N 20°43E 207 A2
Niksar Turkey 40°31N 37°2E 212 B7
Nīkshahr Iran 26°15N 60°10E 247 E9
Nikšić Montenegro 42°50N 18°57E 202 D2
Nikulino Russia 55°40N 37°25E 129 B2
Nikumaroro Kiribati 4°40S 174°32W 277 A16
Nikunau Kiribati 1°22S 176°28E 277 A14
Nîl, Nahr en → Africa 30°10N 31°6E 256 H7
Nîl el Abyad → Sudan 15°38N 32°31E 257 D3
Nîl el Azraq → Sudan 15°38N 32°31E 257 D3
Nila Indonesia 6°44S 129°31E 231 F7
Nilakkottai India 10°10N 77°52E 245 J3
Niland U.S.A. 33°14N 115°31W 307 M11
Nilanga India 18°6N 76°46E 244 E3
Nile = Nîl, Nahr en →
Africa 30°10N 31°6E 256 H7
Nile Delta Egypt 31°40N 31°0E 256 H7
Niles Ill., U.S.A. 42°1N 87°48W 119 A2
Niles Mich., U.S.A. 41°50N 86°15W 311 C10
Niles Ohio, U.S.A. 41°11N 80°46W 312 E4
Niles Center = Skokie
U.S.A. 42°2N 87°43W 119 A2
Nileshwar India 12°15N 75°6E 245 H2
Nilgiri Hills India 11°30N 76°30E 245 J3
Nilo Peçanha Brazil 13°37S 39°6W 333 D4
Nilsebu Norway 59°11N 6°39E 164 E2
Nilüfer → Turkey 40°18N 28°27E 203 F12
Nim Ka Thana India 27°44N 75°48E 242 F6
Nimach India 24°30N 74°56E 242 G6
Nimba, Mts. Africa 7°37N 8°25W 262 D3
Nimbahera India 24°37N 74°45E 242 G6
Nîmes France 43°50N 4°23E 175 E8
Nimfaíon, Ákra = Pines, Akra
Greece 40°5N 24°20E 203 F8
Nimmitabel Australia 36°29S 149°15E 283 D8
Nīmrūz □ Afghan. 30°0N 62°0E 240 C1
Nimta India 22°40N 88°24E 124 A2
Nimule South Sudan 3°32N 32°3E 257 G3
Nimule △ South Sudan 3°38N 32°2E 257 G3
Nin Croatia 44°16N 15°12E 199 D12
Nīnawá Iraq 36°25N 43°10E 213 D10
Nīnawá □ Iraq 36°15N 43°0E 246 B4
Ninda Angola 14°47S 21°24E 265 E4
Nindigully Australia 28°21S 148°50E 281 D4
Nine Degree Channel India 9°0N 73°0E 245 K1
Ninepin Group China 22°16N 114°21E 219 a
Ninety Mile Beach N.Z. 34°48S 173°0E 284 A2
Ninety Mile Beach, The
Australia 38°15S 147°24E 283 E7
Ninety Six U.S.A. 34°11N 82°1W 316 A7
Ninetyeast Ridge Ind. Oc. 1°0S 90°0E 273 E7
Nineveh = Nīnawá Iraq 36°25N 43°10E 213 D10
Ning Xian China 35°30N 107°58E 226 G4
Ningaloo Marine ⌂
Australia 22°23S 113°32E 278 D1
Ning'an China 44°22N 129°20E 227 B15
Ningbo China 29°51N 121°28E 229 C13
Ningcheng China 41°32N 119°53E 227 D10
Ningde China 26°38N 119°23E 229 D12
Ningdu China 26°25N 115°59E 229 D10
Ningerum Papua N. G. 5°41S 141°8E 286 C1
Ninggang China 26°42N 113°55E 229 D9
Ningguo China 30°35N 119°0E 229 B12
Ninghai China 29°15N 121°27E 229 C13
Ninghua China 26°14N 116°45E 229 D11
Ningi Nigeria 10°55N 9°30E 263 C6
Ningjin China 37°35N 114°57E 226 F8
Ningjing Shan China 31°0N 98°20E 228 C2
Ninglang China 27°20N 100°55E 228 D3
Ningling China 34°25N 115°22E 226 G8
Ningming China 22°8N 107°4E 228 F6
Ningnan China 27°5N 102°36E 228 D4
Ningpo = Ningbo China 29°51N 121°28E 229 C13
Ningqiang China 32°47N 106°15E 226 H4
Ningshan China 33°21N 108°21E 228 A7
Ningsia Hui A.R. = Ningxia Huizu
Zizhiqu □ China 38°0N 106°0E 226 F4
Ningwu China 39°0N 112°18E 226 E7
Ningxia Huizu Zizhiqu □
China 38°0N 106°0E 226 F4
Ningxiang China 28°15N 112°30E 229 C9
Ningyang China 35°47N 116°45E 226 G9
Ningyuan China 25°37N 111°57E 229 E8
Ninh Binh Vietnam 20°15N 105°55E 228 G5
Ninh Giang Vietnam 20°44N 106°24E 236 B6
Ninh Hoa Vietnam 12°30N 109°7E 236 F7
Ninh Ma Vietnam 12°48N 109°21E 236 F7
Nini-Suhien △ Ghana 5°20N 2°34W 262 D4
Ninigo Group Papua N. G. 1°22S 144°17E 286 A3
Ninove Belgium 50°51N 4°2E 170 D4
Ninoy Aquino Int. ✈ (MNL)
Phil. 14°31N 121°0E 127 B2
Nioaque Brazil 21°5S 55°50W 335 A4
Niobrara U.S.A. 42°45N 98°2W 308 D4
Niobrara → U.S.A. 42°46N 98°3W 308 D4
Nioki Dem. Rep. of the Congo 2°47S 17°40E 264 C3
Niokolo-Koba △ Senegal 13°3N 13°2W 262 C2
Niono Mali 14°15N 6°0W 262 C3
Nionsamoridougou Guinea 8°45N 8°50W 262 D3
Nioro du Rip Senegal 13°40N 15°50W 262 C1
Nioro du Sahel Mali 15°15N 9°30W 262 B3
Niort France 46°19N 0°29W 174 B3
Niou Comoros Is. 12°21S 43°42E 272 a
Nipa Papua N. G. 6°9S 143°29E 286 D2
Nipani India 16°20N 74°25E 245 F2
Nipawin Canada 53°20N 104°0W 297 C8
Nipfjället Sweden 61°59N 12°50E 162 C6
Nipigon Canada 49°0N 88°17W 298 C2
Nipigon, L. Canada 49°50N 88°30W 298 C2
Nipishish L. Canada 54°12N 63°45W 299 B7
Nipissing, L. Canada 46°20N 80°0W 298 C4
Nipomo U.S.A. 35°3N 120°29W 307 K6
Nippa Japan 35°31N 139°36E 140 B2
Nippon = Japan ■ Asia 36°0N 136°0E 221 G8
Nipponri Japan 35°43N 139°45E 140 A3
Nipton U.S.A. 35°28N 115°16W 307 K11

Niquelândia Brazil 14°33S 48°27W 333 D2
Nīr Iran 38°2N 47°59E 213 C12
Nira → India 17°58N 75°9E 244 F2
Nirasaki Japan 35°42N 138°27E 223 B10
Nirayama Japan 35°2N 138°55E 223 B10
Nirmal India 19°3N 78°20E 244 E4
Nirmali India 26°20N 86°35E 243 F11
Niš Serbia 43°19N 21°58E 202 C5
Nisa = Nysa → Europe 52°4N 14°46E 178 C10
Nisa Portugal 39°30N 7°41W 195 F3
Nişāb Si. Arabia 29°11N 44°43E 246 D5
Nişāb Yemen 14°25N 46°29E 248 H4
Niscemi Italy 37°9N 14°23E 201 E7
Nishi Japan 34°40N 135°28E 133 A1
Nishi-Sonogi-Hantō Japan 32°55N 129°45E 222 E1
Nishi-Tosa Japan 33°13N 132°46E 222 D4
Nishinari Japan 34°37N 135°28E 133 B1
Nishinomiya Japan 34°45N 135°20E 133 A1
Nishino'omote Japan 30°43N 130°59E 221 J5
Nishio Japan 34°52N 137°3E 223 B9
Nishiwaki Japan 34°59N 134°58E 222 C6
Nishiyodogawa Japan 34°40N 135°24E 133 A1
Nisibin = Nusaybin Turkey 37°3N 41°10E 213 D9
Niška Banja Serbia 43°18N 22°1E 202 C6
Niskibi → Canada 56°29N 88°9W 298 A2
Nisko Poland 50°35N 22°7E 185 H9
Nisporeni Moldova 47°4N 28°10E 183 C13
Nisqually → U.S.A. 47°7N 122°42W 306 C4
Nissaki Greece 39°43N 19°52E 206 B9
Nissan → Sweden 56°40N 12°51E 163 H6
Nissedal Norway 59°10N 8°30E 164 E5
Nisser Norway 59°7N 8°28E 164 E5
Nissiros Greece 36°35N 27°12E 205 E9
Nissum Bredning Denmark 56°40N 8°20E 163 H2
Nissum Fjord Denmark 56°20N 8°11E 163 H2
Nistru = Dnister →
Europe 46°18N 30°17E 177 E16
Nisutlin → Canada 60°14N 132°34W 296 A2
Nitchequon Canada 53°10N 70°58W 299 B5
Niterói Brazil 22°53S 43°7W 135 B2
Nith → Ont., Canada 43°12N 80°23W 312 C4
Nith → Dumf. & Gall., U.K. 55°14N 3°33W 167 F5
Nitmiluk ∆ Australia 14°6S 132°15E 278 B5
Nitra Slovak Rep. 48°19N 18°4E 181 C11
Nitra → Slovak Rep. 47°46N 18°10E 181 D11
Nitriansky □ Slovak Rep. 48°10N 18°30E 181 C11
Nittenau Germany 49°12N 12°16E 179 F8
Niu Valley U.S.A. 21°19N 157°44W 302 K14
Niua Group Tonga 15°57S 173°45W 287 D16
Niuafo'ou Tonga 15°30S 175°58W 287 D15
Niuatoputapu Tonga 15°57S 173°45W 287 D16
Niue ☑ Pac. Oc. 19°2S 169°54W 289 g
Niulakita Pac. Oc. 10°45S 179°30E 277 C14
Niulan Jiang → China 27°30N 103°5E 228 D4
Niulantsun Taiwan 25°1N 121°2E 225 A3
Niut Indonesia 0°26S 103°30E 234 C2
Niutao Pac. Oc. 6°7S 177°18E 277 B14
Niutou Shan China 29°5N 121°59E 229 C13
Niuzhuang China 40°58N 122°28E 224 E5
Nivala Finland 63°56N 24°57E 160 E21
Nivelles Belgium 50°35N 4°20E 170 D4
Nivernais France 47°15N 3°30E 173 E10
Niverville Canada 49°36N 97°3W 297 D9
Niwas India 23°3N 80°26E 243 H9
Nixa U.S.A. 37°3N 93°18W 308 G7
Nixon U.S.A. 29°16N 97°46W 314 G6
Nizam Sagar India 18°10N 77°58E 244 E3
Nizamabad India 18°45N 78°7E 244 E4
Nizamghat India 28°20N 95°45E 241 A5
Nizhne Kolymsk Russia 68°34N 160°55E 215 C17
Nizhnegorskiy = Nyzhnohirskyy
Ukraine 45°27N 34°38E 189 K8
Nizhnekamsk Russia 55°38N 51°49E 190 C10
Nizhneudinsk Russia 54°54N 99°3E 215 D10
Nizhnevartovsk Russia 60°56N 76°38E 214 C8
Nizhniy Bestyakh
Russia 61°57N 129°54E 215 C13
Nizhniy Chir Russia 48°22N 43°5E 191 F6
Nizhniy Lomov Russia 53°34N 43°38E 190 D6
Nizhniy Novgorod Russia 56°20N 44°0E 190 B7
Nizhniy Novgorod □
Russia 56°30N 44°20E 190 B7
Nizhniy Tagil Russia 57°55N 59°57E 186 C10
Nizhniye Kresty = Cherskiy
Russia 68°45N 161°18E 215 C17
Nizhyn Ukraine 51°5N 31°55E 189 G6
Nizina Mazowiecka Poland 52°30N 21°0E 185 F8
Nizip Turkey 37°5N 37°50E 212 D7
Nízké Tatry Slovak Rep. 48°55N 19°30E 181 C12
Nízké Tatry ∆
Slovak Rep. 48°55N 19°37E 181 C12
Nízký Jeseník Czech Rep. 49°50N 17°33E 181 B10
Nizwá Oman 22°56N 57°32E 249 B7
Nizza Monferrato Italy 44°46N 8°21E 198 D5
Njakwa Malawi 11°1S 33°56E 269 E3
Njarðvík Iceland 63°59N 22°32W 155 D4
Njazidja = Grande Comore
Comoros Is. 11°35S 43°20E 272 a
Njegoš Montenegro 42°53N 18°45E 202 D2
Njinjo Tanzania 8°48S 38°54E 269 D4
Njoko → Zambia 17°8S 24°4E 265 F4
Njombe Tanzania 9°20S 34°50E 269 D3
Njombe → Tanzania 6°56S 35°6E 268 D4
Njurundabommen
Sweden 62°15N 17°25E 162 B11
Nkambe Cameroon 6°35N 10°40E 263 D7
Nkana Zambia 12°50S 28°8E 269 E2
Nkandla S. Africa 28°37S 31°5E 271 C5
Nkawkaw Ghana 6°36N 0°49W 263 D4
Nkayi Congo 4°9S 13°17E 264 C2
Nkayi Zimbabwe 19°41S 29°20E 269 F2
Nkhotakota Malawi 12°56S 34°15E 269 E3
Nkhotakota ∆ Malawi 12°50S 34°0E 269 E3
Nkolabona Gabon 1°14N 11°43E 264 C2
Nkomi, Lagune Gabon 1°35S 9°17E 264 C1
Nkondwe Tanzania 5°15S 30°51E 268 D3
Nkone Dem. Rep. of the Congo 1°2S 22°29E 268 C4
Nkongsamba Cameroon 4°55N 9°55E 263 D6
Nkoteng Cameroon 4°31N 12°2E 264 B2
Nkunga
Dem. Rep. of the Congo 4°4S 18°34E 265 C3
Nkurenkuru Namibia 17°42S 18°32E 270 A2
Nkwanta Ghana 6°10N 2°10W 262 D4
Nmai → Burma 25°30N 97°25E 228 F2
Noakhali Bangla. 22°48N 91°10E 241 D7
Noatak U.S.A. 67°34N 162°58W 303 C7
Noatak → U.S.A. 68°10N 160°0W 303 B8
Nob Hill San Francisco, U.S.A. 136 B1
Nobel Canada 45°25N 80°6W 312 A4
Nobeoka Japan 32°36N 131°41E 222 D3
Nobleford Canada 49°54N 112°56W 296 D6
Noblejas Spain 39°58N 3°26W 194 F7
Noblesville U.S.A. 40°3N 86°1W 311 D11
Nocatee U.S.A. 27°10N 81°53W 317 H14
Noccundra Australia 27°50S 142°36E 281 D3
Noce → Italy 46°9N 11°4E 198 B8
Nocera Inferiore Italy 40°44N 14°38E 201 B7
Nocera Umbra Italy 43°8N 12°47E 199 E9
Noci Italy 40°48N 17°7E 201 B10
Nockeby Sweden 59°19N 17°54E 162 n21
Nocona U.S.A. 33°47N 97°44W 314 E6

Nocrich Romania 45°55N 24°26E 183 E9
Noda Japan 35°56N 139°52E 223 B11
Nodeland Norway 58°8N 7°51E 164 F4
Noel Kempff Mercado ∆
Bolivia 14°9S 60°49W 331 C5
Noel Park U.K. 51°35N 0°5W 125 A3
Nogal Valley = Nugaaleed, Dooxo
Somali Rep. 8°35N 48°35E 267 C6
Nogales Sonora, Mexico 31°19N 110°56W 318 A2
Nogales Ariz., U.S.A. 31°21N 110°56W 305 L8
Nogaro France 43°45N 0°2W 174 E3
Nogat → Poland 54°17N 19°17E 184 D6
Nōgata Japan 33°48N 130°44E 222 D2
Nogatino Russia 55°41N 37°41E 129 c8
Nogaysk = Prymorske
Ukraine 46°48N 36°20E 189 J9
Nogent France 48°1N 5°20E 173 D12
Nogent-le-Rotrou France 48°20N 0°50E 172 D6
Nogent-sur-Marne France 48°50N 2°28E 134 A3
Nogent-sur-Seine France 48°30N 3°30E 173 D10
Noggara Ethiopia 13°54N 36°35E 257 E4
Noggerup Australia 33°32N 116°5E 279 F2
Noginsk Moskva, Russia 55°50N 38°25E 188 E10
Noginsk Tunguska, Russia 64°30N 90°50E 215 C10
Nogliki Russia 51°50N 143°10E 215 D15
Nogoa → Australia 23°40S 147°55E 280 C4
Nogoyá Argentina 32°24S 59°48W 334 C4
Nógrád □ Hungary 48°0N 19°30E 182 C4
Noguera Pallaresa →
Spain 41°55N 0°55E 196 D5
Noguera Ribagorçana →
Spain 41°40N 0°43E 196 D5
Nohar India 29°11N 74°49E 242 E6
Nohfelden Germany 49°35N 7°7E 179 F3
Nohili Pt. U.S.A. 22°4N 159°47W 302 A2
Nohta India 23°40N 79°34E 243 H8
Nohwa S. Korea 34°10N 126°34E 224 E3
Nohwado S. Korea 34°12N 126°35E 224 E3
Noia Spain 42°48N 8°53W 194 C2
Noichi Japan 33°33N 133°42E 222 D5
Noida India 28°36N 77°19E 242 E7
Noipuos Papua N. G. 2°25S 150°7E 286 B6
Noire, Montagne France 43°28N 2°18E 174 E6
Noires, Mts. France 48°11N 3°40W 172 D3
Noirétable France 45°48N 3°46E 173 G10
Noirmoutier, Î. de France 46°58N 2°10W 172 F4
Noirmoutier-en-l'Île France 47°0N 2°14W 172 F4
Noiseau France 48°51N 2°32E 134 A4
Noisiel France 48°51N 2°37E 134 A4
Noisy-le-Grand France 48°50N 2°33E 134 A4
Noisy-le-Roi France 48°50N 2°3E 134 A1
Noisy-le-Sec France 48°53N 2°27E 134 A3
Nojane Botswana 23°15S 20°14E 270 B3
Nojima-Zaki Japan 34°54N 139°53E 223 C11
Nok Kundi Pakistan 28°50N 62°45E 240 C1
Nok Ta Phao, Ko Thailand 9°23N 99°40E 237 b
Nokaneng Botswana 19°40S 22°17E 270 A3
Nokia Finland 61°30N 23°30E 188 B2
Nokkala Finland 60°8N 24°45E 121 C1
Nokkeushi = Kitami
Japan 43°48N 143°54E 220 C11
Nokomis Sask., Canada 51°35N 105°0W 297 C8
Nokomis Fla., U.S.A. 27°7N 82°27W 317 H7
Nokomis Ill., U.S.A. 39°18N 89°18W 310 F7
Nokomis L. Canada 57°0N 103°0W 297 B8
Nokou Chad 14°35N 14°47E 265 C2
Nokuku Vanuatu 14°54S 166°35E 287 D4
Nola C.A.R. 3°35N 16°4E 264 D3
Nola Italy 40°55N 14°33E 201 B7
Nolay France 46°58N 4°35E 173 F11
Noli, C. di Italy 44°12N 8°25E 198 D5
Nolinsk Russia 57°28N 49°57E 190 C9
Noma U.S.A. 30°59N 85°37W 316 E4
Noma Omuramba →
Namibia 18°52S 20°53E 270 A3
Noma-Saki Japan 31°25N 130°7E 222 E2
Nomad Papua N. G. 6°19S 142°13E 286 D2
Nombre de Dios Panama 9°34N 79°28W 320 E4
Nome U.S.A. 64°30N 165°25W 303 D6
Nomentano Italy 41°55N 12°30E 132 A2
Nomgon Mongolia 42°50N 105°8E 226 C3
Nomo-Zaki Japan 32°35N 129°44E 222 E1
Nomoneas Micronesia 7°24N 151°53E 287 T18
Nomuka Tonga 20°17S 174°48W 287 Q13
Nomuka Group Tonga 20°20S 174°48W 287 Q13
Nonacho L. Canada 61°42N 109°40W 297 A7
Nonakashinden Japan 35°44N 139°30E 140 A2
Nonancourt France 48°47N 1°11E 172 D8
Nonda Australia 20°40S 142°28E 280 C3
Nondalton U.S.A. 60°0N 154°51W 303 F9
None Italy 44°56N 7°32E 198 D4
Nong Chang Thailand 15°23N 99°51E 236 E2
Nong Han Res. Thailand 17°11N 104°9E 236 D5
Nong Khai Thailand 17°50N 102°46E 236 D4
Nong'an China 44°25N 125°5E 227 B13
Nongjrong India 25°29N 92°6E 241 C4
Nongminyundong Jiangxisuo
China 23°7N 113°15E 121 B2
Nongoma S. Africa 27°58S 31°35E 271 C5
Nongsa Indonesia 1°11N 104°8E 237 d
Nongstoin India 25°31N 91°16E 241 C3
Nonhyeon S. Korea 37°9N 126°51E 294 D6
Nono Ethiopia 8°32N 37°26E 266 C4
Nonoava Mexico 27°28N 106°44W 318 B3
Nonoc I. Phil. 9°51N 125°33E 233 G5
Nonoichi Japan 36°35N 136°23E 223 A8
Nonsan S. Korea 36°12N 127°5E 224 D3
Nonsuch Antigua & B. 17°3N 61°42W 322 b
Nonthaburi Thailand 13°50N 100°29E 113 A1
Nontron France 45°31N 0°40E 174 C4
Nonza France 42°47N 9°21E 175 F13
Noon Gun Cape Town, S. Africa 178 b1
Noonamah Australia 12°40S 131°4E 278 B5
Noondie, L. Australia 28°30S 119°30E 279 E2
Noonkanbah ◉ Australia 18°30S 124°50E 278 C3
Noord Aruba 12°34N 70°1W 322 f
Noord Brabant □ Neths. 51°40N 5°0E 170 C5
Noord Holland □ Neths. 52°30N 4°45E 170 B5
Noord Salina Bonaire 12°11N 68°16W 322 f
Noordbeveland Neths. 51°35N 3°50E 170 C3
Noorderkerk Amsterdam, Neths. 112 a1
Noordoostpolder Neths. 52°45N 5°45E 170 B5
Noordkaap Aruba 12°34N 70°1W 322 f
Noordpunt Curaçao 12°24N 69°10W 322 g
Noordwijk Neths. 52°14N 4°26E 170 B4
Noordzeekanaal Neths. 52°28N 4°37E 112 A1
Noorvik U.S.A. 66°50N 161°3W 303 C7
Noosa Heads Australia 26°25S 153°6E 281 D5
Nootka I. Canada 49°32N 126°42W 296 D3
Nopiming △ Canada 50°30N 95°37W 297 C9
Nóqui Angola 5°55S 13°30E 264 F2
Nor-Bayzzet = Kamo
Armenia 40°21N 45°7E 191 K7
Nora Eritrea 16°6N 40°4E 257 D5
Nora Sweden 59°32N 15°2E 163 G8
Nora Springs U.S.A. 43°9N 93°0W 310 A4
Norala Phil. 6°32N 124°43E 233 H5
Noralee Canada 53°59N 126°26W 296 C3
Noranda = Rouyn-Noranda
Canada 48°20N 79°0W 298 C4
Norberg Sweden 60°4N 15°56E 162 D9
Norborne U.S.A. 39°18N 93°40W 310 E3

Nocrich Romania 45°55N 24°26E 183 E9
Nórcia Italy 42°48N 13°5E 199 F10
Norco U.S.A. 33°56N 117°33W 307 M9
Norcross U.S.A. 33°56N 84°13W 316 B5
Nord □ Cameroon 8°30N 14°0E 263 D7
Nord France 50°15N 3°30E 173 B10
Nord, Gare du Paris, France 134 a4
Nord, Pt. Comoros Is. 11°22S 43°19E 272 a
Norte de Santander □
Colombia 8°0N 73°0W 328 B3
Norte Grande Azores 38°40N 28°4W 153 c
Nordelândia Brazil 14°25S 56°48W 331 C6
North U.S.A. 33°37N 81°6W 316 B6
North, C. Canada 47°2N 60°20W 299 C7
North Adams U.S.A. 42°42N 73°7W 313 D11
North America 40°0N 100°0W 292 F10
North Andaman I. India 13°15N 92°55E 245 H11
North Arlington U.S.A. 40°47N 74°7W 132 B1
North Arm Canada 62°0N 114°30W 296 A5
North Augusta U.S.A. 33°30N 81°59W 316 B6
North Australian Basin
Ind. Oc. 14°30S 116°30E 276 C2
North Ayrshire □ U.K. 55°45N 4°44W 167 F4
North Balabac Str. Phil. 8°8N 117°4E 233 G1
North Baltimore U.S.A. 41°11N 83°41W 311 C13
North Bass I. U.S.A. 41°40N 82°56W 312 E2
North Battleford Canada 52°50N 108°17W 297 C7
North Bay Canada 46°20N 79°30W 298 C4
North Bay Village N. Francisco, U.S.A. 136 a2
North Beach San Francisco, U.S.A. 25°50N 80°9W 128 A2
North Belcher Is. Canada 56°50N 79°50W 298 A4
North Bend Oreg., Canada 43°24N 124°14W 304 E1
North Bend Pa., U.S.A. 41°20N 77°42W 312 E7
North Bend Wash., U.S.A. 47°30N 121°47W 306 C5
North Bennington U.S.A. 42°56N 73°15W 313 D11
North Bergen U.S.A. 40°48N 74°0W 132 B1
North Berwick E. Loth., U.K. 56°4N 2°42W 167 E6
North Borneo = Sabah □
Malaysia 6°0N 117°0E 235 A5
North Breakers Midway Is. 28°13N 177°24W 302 c
North Brother I. India 10°59N 92°40E 245 J11
North Bruce Canada 44°22N 81°26W 312 B3
North Bull I. Ireland 53°22N 6°9W 120 A3
North C. N.B., Canada 47°2N 60°20W 299 C7
North C. N.Z. 34°23S 173°4E 284 A2
North C. Papua N. G. 2°32S 150°50E 286 B6
North Canadian →
U.S.A. 35°22N 95°37W 314 D7
North Canton U.S.A. 40°53N 81°24W 312 F3
North Cape = Nordkapp
Norway 71°10N 25°50E 160 A21
North Caribou L. Canada 52°50N 90°40W 298 B1
North Carolina □ U.S.A. 35°30N 80°0W 309 H6
North Cascades △
U.S.A. 48°45N 121°10W 304 B3
North Cay Bahamas 25°6N 77°26W 153 b
North Channel Ont., Canada 46°0N 83°0W 298 C3
North Channel U.K. 55°13N 5°52W 167 F3
North Charleston U.S.A. 32°53N 79°58W 316 C10
North Cheam U.K. 51°20N 0°11W 125 B2
North Chicago U.S.A. 42°19N 87°51W 311 B9
North College Hill
U.S.A. 39°13N 84°33W 311 E12
North Collins U.S.A. 42°35N 78°56W 312 D6
North Comino Channel
Malta 36°1N 14°20E 206 E7
North Cotabato □ Phil. 7°10N 125°0E 233 H5
North Cray U.K. 51°25N 0°8E 125 B4
North Creek U.S.A. 43°42N 73°59W 313 C11
North Dakota □ U.S.A. 47°30N 100°15W 308 B3
North Decatur U.S.A. 33°48N 84°17W 113 B3
North Downs U.K. 51°19N 0°21E 169 F8
North Druid Hills U.S.A. 33°49N 84°17W 113 B3
North East B. Ascension I. 7°55S 14°21W 153 g
North East Frontier Agency =
Arunachal Pradesh □
India 28°0N 95°0E 241 B5
North East Lincolnshire □
U.K. 53°34N 0°2W 168 D7
North Eastern □ Kenya 1°30N 40°0E 268 B5
North End Boston, U.S.A. 116 a3
North Esk → Angus, U.K. 56°46N 2°24W 167 E6
North Esk → Midloth., U.K. 55°54N 3°4W 121 B2
North European Plain
Europe 55°0N 25°0E 158 D10
North Fabius → U.S.A. 39°54N 91°30W 310 E2
North Foreland U.K. 51°22N 1°28E 169 F9
North Fork → U.S.A. 37°14N 119°21W 306 H7
North Fork, Salt →
U.S.A. 39°26N 91°53W 310 E5
North Fork American →
U.S.A. 38°57N 120°59W 306 G5
North Fork Edisto →
U.S.A. 33°16N 80°54W 316 B8
North Fork Feather →
U.S.A. 38°33N 121°30W 306 F5
North Fork Grand →
U.S.A. 45°47N 102°16W 308 C2
North Fork Red →
U.S.A. 34°24N 99°14W 314 D5
North Fort Myers U.S.A. 26°41N 81°53W 317 J8
North Frisian Is. = Nordfriesische
Inseln Germany 54°40N 8°20E 178 A4
North Gower Canada 45°8N 75°43W 313 A9
North Greenfield = West Allis
U.S.A. 43°1N 88°0W 311 B8
North Gyle U.K. 55°57N 3°19W 121 B2
North Hackensack U.S.A. 40°54N 74°2W 132 A1
North Harbor Phil. 14°37N 120°57E 127 B1
North Hd. N.S.W.,
Australia 33°49S 151°18E 139 A2
North Hd. W. Austral.,
Australia 30°14S 114°59E 279 F1
North Henik L. Canada 61°45N 97°40W 297 A9
North Highlands U.S.A. 38°40N 121°23W 306 G5
North Hollywood U.S.A. 34°9N 118°22W 126 B2
North Horr Kenya 3°20N 37°8E 268 B4
North I. India 10°8N 72°20E 245 J11
North I., Rift Valley, Kenya 4°5N 36°5E 268 B4
North I. □ Seychelles 4°25S 55°13E 273 a2
North Judson U.S.A. 41°13N 86°46W 311 C10
North Kitui □ Kenya 0°15S 38°29E 268 C4
North Knife → Canada 58°53N 94°45W 297 B10
North Koel → India 24°45N 83°50E 243 G10
North Korea ■ Asia 40°0N 127°0E 227 E14
North L. Australia 32°30S 143°5E 282 E5
North Lakhimpur India 27°14N 94°7E 241 B5
North Lanarkshire □ U.K. 55°52N 3°56W 167 F5
North Las Vegas
U.S.A. 36°11N 115°7W 307 J11
North Las Vegas ✈ (VGT)
U.S.A. 36°12N 115°11W 124 A1
North Lexington U.S.A. 42°27N 71°14W 116 A1
North Liberty U.S.A. 41°32N 86°26W 311 C10
North Lincolnshire □
U.K. 53°36N 0°30W 168 D7
North Little Rock U.S.A. 34°45N 92°16W 314 D8
North Loup → U.S.A. 41°17N 98°24W 308 E4
North Luangwa △ Zambia 11°49S 32°9E 269 E3

North Magnetic Pole
Arctic 82°42N 114°24W 150 A1
North Malé Atoll
Maldives 4°25N 73°30E 272 d
North Malosmadulu Atoll
Maldives 5°37N 72°55E 272 d
North Manchester U.S.A. 41°0N 85°46W 311 D11
North Mankato U.S.A. 44°10N 94°2W 308 C6
North Miami U.S.A. 25°53N 80°11W 128 A2
North Miami Beach
U.S.A. 25°55N 80°9W 128 A2
North Minch U.K. 58°5N 5°55W 167 C3
North Moose L. Canada 54°4N 100°12W 297 C8
North Myrtle Beach
U.S.A. 33°48N 78°42W 315 E15
North Nahanni →
Canada 62°15N 123°20W 296 A4
North Naples U.S.A. 26°12N 81°48W 317 J8
North Nazimabad Pakistan 24°55N 67°3E 123 A2
North New River Canal
U.S.A. 26°17N 80°25W 128 B2
North Nilandu Atoll
Maldives 3°14N 72°56E 272 d
North Olmsted U.S.A. 41°25N 81°56W 312 E3
North Ossetia □ Russia 43°30N 44°30E 191 J7
North Pagai, I. = Pagai Utara, Pulau
Indonesia 2°35S 100°0E 234 D2
North Palisade U.S.A. 37°6N 118°31W 306 H8
North Platte U.S.A. 41°8N 100°46W 308 E3
North Platte → U.S.A. 41°7N 100°42W 308 E3
North Point Park Boston, U.S.A. 116 a1
North Pole Arctic 90°0N 0°0 150 A
North Pole Alaska,
U.S.A. 64°45N 147°21W 303 D11
North Portal Canada 49°0N 102°33W 297 D8
North Powder U.S.A. 45°2N 117°55W 304 D5
North Pt. Ascension I. 7°53S 14°23W 153 g
North Pt. Barbados 13°20N 59°37W 323 r
North Pt. Hong Kong,
China 22°17N 114°12E 122 B2
North Pt. Mich., U.S.A. 45°2N 83°16W 312 A1
North Pt. Vanuatu 14°56S 168°6E 287 D6
North Queensferry U.K. 56°1N 3°24W 121 A2
North Quincy U.S.A. 42°16N 71°1W 116 A2
North Reef I. India 13°5N 92°43E 245 H11
Northumberland, C.
Australia 38°5S 140°40E 282 E4
Northumberland Heath
U.K. 51°28N 0°10E 125 B3
Northumberland Is.
Australia 21°30S 149°50E 280 C4
Northumberland Str.
Canada 46°20N 64°0W 299 C7
Northville Ont., Canada 43°10N 81°56W 312 C3
Northville N.Y., U.S.A. 43°13N 74°11W 313 C10
Northway U.S.A. 62°58N 141°56W 303 E12
Northwest Atlantic Mid-Ocean
Canyon Atl. Oc. 54°0N 48°0W 152 A7
Northwest Pacific Basin
Pac. Oc. 32°0N 165°0E 288 D7
Northwest Providence Channel
W. Indies 26°0N 78°0W 320 A4
Northwest Pt. Bahamas 25°4N 77°31W 153 b
Northwest Territories □
Canada 63°0N 118°0W 294 E8
Northwestern Hawaiian Is. Marine
Nat. Monument =
Papahānaumokuākea Marine
Nat. Monument
U.S.A. 25°25N 170°35W 302 F9
Northwestern Station
U.S.A. 41°52N 87°38W 119 B3
Northwestern Univ.
U.S.A. 42°3N 87°40W 119 A2
Northwich U.K. 53°15N 2°31W 168 D5
Northwood Iowa, U.S.A. 43°27N 93°13W 308 D7
Northwood N. Dak.,
U.S.A. 47°44N 97°34W 308 B5
Northwood London, U.K. 51°37N 0°25W 125 A1
Northwood Park Canada 43°45N 79°30W 141 A4
Norton Kans., U.S.A. 39°50N 99°53W 308 F4
Norton Zimbabwe 17°52S 30°40E 269 B5
Norton B. U.S.A. 64°45N 161°15W 303 D7
Norton Sd. U.S.A. 63°50N 164°0W 303 D7
Norton Shores U.S.A. 43°10N 86°16W 311 A10
Nortorf Germany 54°10N 9°58E 178 A5
Norwalk Calif., U.S.A. 33°54N 118°4W 307 M8
Norwalk Conn., U.S.A. 41°7N 73°22W 313 E11
Norwalk Iowa, U.S.A. 41°29N 93°41W 310 C3
Norwalk Ohio, U.S.A. 41°15N 82°37W 312 E2
Norwalk → U.S.A. 41°5N 73°22W 309 E11
Norway Maine, U.S.A. 44°13N 70°32W 309 D18
Norway Mich., U.S.A. 45°47N 87°55W 308 C10
Norway ■ Europe 63°0N 11°0E 160 E14
Norway House Canada 53°59N 97°50W 295 D14
Norwegian B. Canada 77°30N 90°0W 295 B14
Norwegian Sea Atl. Oc. 66°0N 1°0E 158 B6
Norwich U.K. 52°38N 1°18E 169 E9
Norwich Conn., U.S.A. 41°31N 72°5W 313 E12
Norwich N.Y., U.S.A. 42°32N 75°32W 313 D9
Norwood Gauteng, S. Africa 26°9S 28°4E 123 A2
Norwood Canada 44°23N 77°59W 312 B7
Norwood Ohio, U.S.A. 39°9N 84°27W 311 E12
Norwood Park U.S.A. 41°59N 87°48W 119 A2
Noryangin S. Korea 37°30N 126°56E 137 B1
Nosappu-Misaki Japan 45°26N 141°39E 220 C12
Noshaq Pakistan 36°50N 71°49E 240 A3
Noshiro Japan 40°12N 140°0E 220 D10
Nosivka Ukraine 50°50N 31°37E 189 G6
Nossa Senhora da Glória
Brazil 10°14S 37°25W 332 D4
Nossa Senhora das Dores
Brazil 10°29S 37°13W 332 D4
Nossa Senhora de Candelária
Rio de J., Brazil 135 a2
Nossa Senhora do Livramento
Brazil 15°48S 56°22W 331 D6
Nossa Senhora do Ó
Brazil 23°35S 46°41W 137 B1
Nossa Senhora do Socorro
Brazil 10°52S 37°7W 332 D4
Nossebro Sweden 58°12N 12°43E 163 F6
Nossegem Belgium 50°53N 4°30E 116 A3
Nossob → S. Africa 26°55S 20°45E 270 C3
Nossombougou Mali 13°5N 7°55W 262 C3
Nosy Barren Madag. 18°25S 43°40E 272 B2
Nosy Boraha Madag. 16°50S 49°55E 272 B2
Nosy Lava Madag. 14°33S 47°36E 272 A2
Nosy Mitsio Madag. 12°54S 48°36E 272 A2
Nosy Varika Madag. 20°35S 48°32E 272 C2
Notasulga U.S.A. 32°34N 85°41W 316 D4
Noté C Sudan 7°12N 29°36E -- 263 G12
Notikewin → Canada 57°2N 117°38W 296 B5
Notios Aiyaíon = Notio
Greece 38°20N 24°0E 204 C5
Notios Evvoïkos Kolpos
Greece 38°20N 24°0E 205 C6
Noto Italy 36°53N 15°4E 201 F8
Noto, G. di Italy 36°15N 15°12E 201 F8
Noto-Hantō Japan 37°15N 136°40E 221 F8

Notodden *Norway* 59°35N 9°17E **164** E6
Notre-Dame *Paris, France* **134** c4
Notre-Dame, Basilique
Montréal, Canada **130** c3
Notre-Dame, Bois *France* 48°45N 2°34E **134** B4
Notre Dame B. *Canada* 49°45N 55°30W **299** C8
Notre-Dame-de-Grace
Canada 45°28N 73°38W **130** B2
Notre-Dame-de-Koartac = Quaqtaq
Canada 60°55N 69°40W **295** E18
Notre-Dame-des-Bois
Canada 45°24N 71°4W **313** A13
Notre-Dame-d'Ivugivic = Ivujivik
Canada 62°24N 77°55W **295** E16
Notre-Dame-du-Nord
Canada 47°36N 79°30W **298** C4
Notsé *Togo* 7°0N 1°17E **263** D5
Nottawasaga B. *Canada* 44°35N 80°15W **312** B4
Nottaway = Senneterre
Canada 48°25N 77°15W **298** C4
Nottaway → *Canada* 51°22N 78°55W **298** B4
Notting Hill *London, U.K.* **125** b1
Nottingham *U.K.* 52°58N 1°10W **168** E6
Nottingham, City of □
U.K. 52°58N 1°10W **168** E6
Nottingham I. *Canada* 63°20N 77°55W **295** E16
Nottinghamshire □ *U.K.* 53°10N 1°3W **168** D6
Nottoway → *U.S.A.* 36°33N 76°55W **309** G15
Notwane → *Botswana* 23°35S 26°58E **270** B4
Nouâdhibou *Mauritania* 20°54N 17°0W **260** D1
Nouâdhibou, Dakhlet
Mauritania 20°55N 16°52W **260** D1
Nouâdhibou, Râs
Mauritania 20°50N 17°0W **260** D1
Nouakchott *Mauritania* 18°9N 15°58W **262** B1
Nouâmghâr *Mauritania* 19°20N 16°20W **262** B1
Nouméa *N. Cal.* 22°17S 166°30E **288** d
Nouna *Burkina Faso* 12°45N 3°52W **262** C4
Noupoort *S. Africa* 31°10S 24°57E **270** D3
Nouveau Comptoir = Wemindji
Canada 53°0N 78°49W **298** B4
Nouvelle Amsterdam, Î.
Ind. Oc. 38°30S 77°30E **273** H6
Nouvelle-Calédonie = New
Caledonia ☑ *Pac. Oc.* 21°0S 165°0E **288** d
Nouvelle France *Mauritius* 20°22S 57°33E **272** e
Nouzonville *France* 49°48N 4°44E **173** C11
Nová Baňa *Slovak Rep.* 48°28N 18°39E **181** C11
Nová Bystřice *Czech Rep.* 49°2N 15°8E **180** B8
Nova Cruz *Brazil* 6°28S 35°25W **332** C4
Nova Era *Brazil* 19°45S 43°3W **333** E3
Nova Esperança *Brazil* 23°8S 52°24W **335** A5
Nova Fontesvila = Vila Machado
Mozam. 19°15S 34°14E **269** F3
Nova-Freixo = Cuamba
Mozam. 14°45S 36°22E **269** E4
Nova Friburgo *Brazil* 22°16S 42°30W **333** F3
Nova Gaia = Cambundi-Catembo
Angola 10°10S 17°35E **265** E3
Nova Gorica *Slovenia* 45°57N 13°39E **199** C10
Nova Gradiška *Croatia* 45°17N 17°28E **182** E2
Nova Granada *Brazil* 20°30S 49°20W **333** F2
Nova Iguaçu *Brazil* 22°45S 43°28W **333** F3
Nova Iorque *Brazil* 7°0S 44°5W **332** C3
Nova Kakhovka *Ukraine* 46°42N 33°27E **189** J7
Nova Lamego
Guinea-Biss. 12°19N 14°11W **262** C2
Nova Lisboa = Huambo
Angola 12°42S 15°54E **265** E3
Nova Lusitânia *Mozam.* 19°50S 34°34E **269** F3
Nova Mambone *Mozam.* 21°0S 35°3E **271** B6
Nova Milanese *Italy* 45°35N 9°12E **129** A2
Nova Odesa *Ukraine* 47°19N 31°47E **189** J6
Nova Olinda do Norte
Brazil 3°45S 59°3W **329** D6
Nová Paka *Czech Rep.* 50°29N 15°30E **180** A8
Nova Pavova *Serbia* 44°56N 20°14E **182** F5
Nova Ponte *Brazil* 19°8S 47°41W **333** E2
Nova Russas *Brazil* 4°42S 40°34W **332** B3
Nova Scotia □ *Canada* 45°10N 63°0W **299** C7
Nova Siri *Italy* 40°10N 16°35E **201** B9
Nova Sofala *Mozam.* 20°7S 34°42E **271** B5
Nova Ushytsya *Ukraine* 48°50N 27°17E **183** B12
Nova Varoš *Serbia* 43°29N 19°48E **202** C3
Nova Venécia *Brazil* 18°45S 40°24W **333** E3
Nova Vida *Brazil* 10°11S 62°47W **331** C5
Nova Zagora *Bulgaria* 42°32N 26°1E **203** D10
Novaci *Macedonia* 41°5N 21°29E **202** E5
Novaci *Romania* 45°10N 23°42E **183** E8
Novafeltria *Italy* 43°53N 12°17E **199** E9
Novannenskiy = Novoannenskiy
Russia 50°32N 42°39E **190** E6
Novar *Canada* 45°27N 79°15W **312** A5
Novara *Italy* 45°28N 8°38E **198** C5
Novate Milanese *Italy* 45°30N 9°8E **129** A1
Novato *U.S.A.* 38°6N 122°35W **306** G4
Novaya Aleksandriya = Puławy
Poland 51°23N 21°59E **185** G8
Novaya Bukhara = Kogon
Uzbekistan 39°43N 64°33E **216** E6
Novaya Derevnya *Russia* 60°0N 30°19E **137** A1
Novaya Kakhovka = Nova
Kakhovka *Ukraine* 46°42N 33°27E **189** J7
Novaya Kazanka = Zhangaqala
Kazakhstan 48°56N 49°36E **191** F9
Novaya Ladoga *Russia* 60°7N 32°16E **188** B7
Novaya Lyalya *Russia* 59°4N 60°45E **186** C11
Novaya Pismyanka = Leninogorsk
Kazakhstan 50°20N 83°30E **217** B10
Novaya Sibir, Ostrov
Russia 75°10N 150°0E **215** B16
Novaya Zemlya *Russia* 75°0N 56°0E **214** B6
Nové Město *Praha, Czech Rep.* 50°4N 14°25E **135** B2
Nové Město *Slovak Rep.* 48°45N 17°50E **181** C10
Nové Město na Moravě
Czech Rep. 49°34N 16°5E **180** B9
Nové Město nad Metují
Czech Rep. 50°20N 16°10E **181** A9
Nové Zámky *Slovak Rep.* 48°2N 18°8E **181** C11
Novelda *Spain* 38°24N 0°45W **197** G4
Novellara *Italy* 44°51N 10°44E **198** D7
Novelty *U.S.A.* 40°1N 92°12W **310** D4
Noventa Vicentina *Italy* 45°17N 11°32E **199** C8
Novgorod *Russia* 58°30N 31°25E **188** C6
Novgorod □ *Russia* 58°50N 32°30E **188** C7
Novgorod-Severskiy = Novhorod-
Siverskyy *Ukraine* 52°2N 33°10E **189** G7
Novgradets = Suvorovo
Bulgaria 43°20N 27°35E **203** C11
Novhorod-Siverskyy
Ukraine 52°2N 33°10E **189** G7
Novi Bečej *Serbia* 45°36N 20°10E **182** E5
Novi Iskar *Bulgaria* 42°48N 23°21E **202** D7
Novi Kneževac *Serbia* 46°4N 20°8E **182** D5
Novi Ligure *Italy* 44°46N 8°47E **198** D5
Novi Pazar *Bulgaria* 43°25N 27°15E **203** C11
Novi Pazar *Serbia* 43°12N 20°28E **202** C4
Novi Sad *Serbia* 45°18N 19°52E **182** E4
Novi Slankamen *Serbia* 45°8N 20°15E **182** E5
Novi Travnik *Bos.-H.* 44°10N 17°40E **182** F2
Novi Vinodolski *Croatia* 45°10N 14°48E **199** C11
Novigrad *Istra, Croatia* 45°19N 13°33E **199** C10
Novigrad *Zadar, Croatia* 44°10N 15°32E **199** D12
Novigradsko More
Croatia 44°12N 15°33E **199** D12
Novinger *U.S.A.* 40°14N 92°43W **310** D4
Novo Acôrdo *Brazil* 10°10S 46°48W **332** D2
Novo Airão *Brazil* 2°40S 60°59W **329** D5
Novo Aripuanã *Brazil* 5°8S 60°22W **329** E5
Novo Cruzeiro *Brazil* 17°29S 41°53W **333** E3
Novo Hamburgo *Brazil* 29°37S 51°7W **335** B5
Novo Horizonte *Brazil* 21°25S 49°10W **333** F2
Novo Ivanivka *Ukraine* 45°55N 29°56E **183** E14
Novo-Mariinsk = Anadyr
Russia 64°35N 177°20E **215** C18
Novo Mesto *Slovenia* 45°47N 15°12E **199** C12
Novo Miloševo *Serbia* 45°42N 20°20E **182** E5
Novo Nikolaevsk = Novosibirsk
Russia 55°0N 83°5E **217** B10
Novo Paraiso *Brazil* 1°17N 60°28W **329** C5
Novo-Starobinsk = Salihorsk
Belarus 52°51N 27°27E **177** B14
Novo Urgench = Urganch
Uzbekistan 41°40N 60°41E **216** D6
Novoaleksandrovsk = Zarasai
Lithuania 55°40N 26°20E **188** E4
Novoaleksandrovsk
Russia 45°29N 41°17E **191** H5
Novoaleksandrovskaya =
Novoaleksandrovsk
Russia 45°29N 41°17E **191** H5
Novoaleksandrovskoye
Russia 59°50N 30°31E **137** B2
Novoaltaysk *Russia* 53°30N 84°0E **217** B10
Novoannenskiy *Russia* 50°32N 42°39E **190** E6
Novoazovsk *Ukraine* 47°15N 38°4E **189** J10
Novocheboksarsk *Russia* 56°5N 47°27E **190** B8
Novocherkassk *Russia* 47°27N 40°15E **191** G5
Novodevichye *Russia* 53°37N 48°50E **190** D9
Novodvinsk *Russia* 64°25N 40°42E **186** B7
Novogireyevo *Russia* 55°45N 37°46E **129** B4
Novogrudok = Navahrudak
Belarus 53°40N 25°50E **177** B13
Novohrad-Volynskyy
Ukraine 50°34N 27°35E **177** C14
Novoivanovskoye *Russia* 55°42N 37°21E **129** B1
Novokachalinsk *Russia* 45°5N 132°0E **220** B5
Novokazalinsk = Zhangaqazaly
Kazakhstan 45°48N 62°6E **216** C6
Novokhopersk *Russia* 51°5N 41°39E **190** E5
Novokiyevskoye = Kraskino
Russia 42°44N 130°48E **220** C5
Novokuybyshevsk *Russia* 53°7N 49°58E **190** D9
Novokuznetsk *Russia* 53°45N 87°10E **217** B11
Novolazarevskaya
Antarctica 71°0S 12°0E **151** D3
Novolyalinsky = Novaya Lyalya
Russia 59°4N 60°45E **186** C11
Novomoskovsk *Russia* 54°5N 38°15E **188** E10
Novomoskovsk *Ukraine* 48°33N 35°17E **139** H8
Novomyrhorod *Ukraine* 48°45N 31°33E **189** H6
Novonikolayevka = Novoazovsk
Ukraine 47°15N 38°4E **189** J10
Novonikolskoye *Russia* 55°50N 37°14E **129** A1
Novopolotsk = Navapolatsk
Belarus 55°32N 28°37E **188** E5
Novorossiysk *Russia* 44°43N 37°46E **189** K9
Novorybnoye *Russia* 72°50N 105°50E **215** B11
Novorzhev *Russia* 57°3N 29°25E **138** D5
Novosaratovka *Russia* 59°50N 30°32E **137** B3
Novosej *Albania* 41°56N 20°35E **202** E4
Novoselytsya *Ukraine* 48°14N 26°15E **183** B11
Novoshakhtinsk *Russia* 47°46N 39°58E **189** J10
Novosibirsk *Russia* 55°0N 83°5E **217** B10
Novosibirskiye Ostrova
Russia 75°0N 142°0E **215** B15
Novosibirskoye Vdkhr.
Russia 54°35N 82°35E **217** B10
Novosil *Russia* 52°59N 37°2E **189** F9
Novosokolniki *Russia* 56°20N 30°2E **188** D6
Novotitarovskaya *Russia* 45°17N 39°2E **191** H4
Novotroitsk *Russia* 51°10N 58°15E **186** D10
Novotroitskoye = Töle Bī
Kazakhstan 43°42N 73°46E **217** D8
Novoukrayinka *Ukraine* 48°25N 31°30E **139** H6
Novoulyanovsk *Russia* 54°8N 48°24E **190** C9
Novouzensk *Russia* 50°32N 48°17E **190** E9
Novovolynsk *Ukraine* 50°45N 24°4E **185** H11
Novovoronezhskiy
Russia 51°19N 39°13E **189** G10
Novoyavoriske *Ukraine* 49°53N 23°33E **185** J10
Novozybkov *Russia* 52°30N 32°0E **139** F6
Novska *Croatia* 45°19N 17°0E **199** C14
Nový Bor *Czech Rep.* 50°46N 14°35E **180** A7
Novy Bug = Novyy Buh
Ukraine 47°34N 32°29E **139** J7
Nový Bydžov *Czech Rep.* 50°14N 15°29E **180** A8
Novy Dvor *Belarus* 52°50N 24°21E **185** F11
Novy Dwór Mazowiecki
Poland 52°26N 20°44E **135** F7
Nový Jičín *Czech Rep.* 49°30N 18°2E **181** B11
Novy Margelan = Farghona
Uzbekistan 40°23N 71°19E **217** D8
Novyy Afon *Georgia* 43°7N 40°50E **191** J5
Novyy Bor *Russia* 66°43N 52°19E **186** A9
Novyy Buh *Ukraine* 47°34N 32°29E **139** J7
Novyy Oskol *Russia* 50°44N 37°55E **189** G9
Novyy Port *Russia* 67°40N 72°30E **214** C8
Novyy Urengoy *Russia* 65°48N 76°52E **214** C8
Nowa Deba *Poland* 50°26N 21°41E **185** H8
Nowa Nowa *Australia* 37°44S 148°3E **283** D8
Nowa Ruda *Poland* 50°35N 16°30E **185** H3
Nowa Sarzyna *Poland* 50°21N 22°21E **185** H9
Nowa Sól *Poland* 51°48N 15°44E **185** G2
Nowata *U.S.A.* 36°42N 95°38W **314** C7
Nowbarān *Iran* 35°8N 49°42E **247** C6
Nowe *Poland* 53°41N 18°44E **184** E5
Nowe-Babice *Poland* 52°15N 20°51E **142** B1
Nowe Miasteczko *Poland* 51°42N 15°42E **185** G2
Nowe Miasto *Mazowieckie, Poland* 51°38N 20°34E **185** G7
Nowe Miasto *Warsaw, Poland* **142** a2
Nowe Miasto Lubawskie
Poland 53°27N 19°33E **184** E6
Nowe Skalmierzyce *Poland* 51°43N 18°0E **185** G4
Nowe Warpno *Poland* 53°42N 14°18E **184** E1
Nowendoc *Australia* 31°32S 151°44E **283** A9
Nowendoc △ *Australia* 31°33S 151°45E **283** A9
Nowghāb *Iran* 33°53N 59°4E **247** C8
Nowgong *Assam, India* 26°20N 92°50E **241** B4
Nowgong *Mad. P., India* 25°4N 79°27E **243** G8
Nowitna Nat. Wildlife Refuge △
U.S.A. 64°40N 154°16W **303** D9
Nowogard *Poland* 53°41N 15°10E **184** E2
Nowogród *Poland* 53°14N 21°53E **185** E8
Nowogród Bobrzanski
Poland 51°48N 15°15E **185** G2
Nowogrodziec *Poland* 51°12N 15°24E **185** G2
Noworadomsk = Radomsko
Poland 51°5N 19°28E **185** G6
Nowra *Australia* 34°53S 150°35E **283** C9
Nowrangapur *India* 19°14N 82°33E **244** E6
Nowshāk = Noshaq
Pakistan 36°24N 71°49E **240** A3
Nowshera *Pakistan* 34°0N 72°0E **240** B4
Nowy Dwór Gdański
Poland 54°13N 19°7E **184** D6
Nowy Sącz *Poland* 49°40N 20°41E **185** J7
Nowy Staw *Poland* 54°13N 19°2E **184** D6
Nowy Targ *Poland* 49°29N 20°2E **185** J7
Nowy Tomyśl *Poland* 52°19N 16°10E **185** F3
Nowy Wiśnicz *Poland* 49°55N 20°28E **185** J7
Noxen *U.S.A.* 41°25N 76°4W **313** E8
Noyabr'sk *Russia* 64°34N 76°21E **214** C8
Noyant *France* 47°30N 0°6E **172** E7
Noyers *France* 47°40N 4°0E **173** E10
Nöykkiö *Finland* 60°10N 24°42E **121** B1
Noyon *Oise, France* 49°34N 2°59E **173** C9
Noyon *Mongolia* 43°2N 102°4E **226** C2
Nozay *France* 47°34N 1°38W **172** E5
Nqutu *S. Africa* 28°13S 30°32E **271** C5
Nsa *Congo* 2°22S 15°19E **264** C3
Nsa, O. en → *Algeria* 32°28N 5°24E **261** B6
Nsa, Plateau de *Congo* 2°26S 15°20E **264** C3
Nsanje *Malawi* 16°55S 35°12E **269** F4
Nsawam *Ghana* 5°50N 0°24W **263** D4
Nseluka *Zambia* 9°58S 31°16E **269** D3
Nsok *Eq. Guin.* 1°10N 11°19E **264** B2
Nsomba *Zambia* 10°45S 29°51E **269** E2
Nsontin
Dem. Rep. of the Congo 3°7S 17°56E **264** C3
Nsopzup *Burma* 25°51N 97°30E **241** C6
Nsukka *Nigeria* 6°51N 7°29E **263** D6
Ntaria ✪ *Australia* 24°0S 132°41E **278** D5
Ntem → *Cameroon* 2°21N 9°49E **264** B2
Ntingui, Mt. *Comoros Is.* 12°12S 44°25E **272** a
Ntoum *Gabon* 0°22N 9°47E **264** B1
N'Tsama *Congo* 0°53S 14°44E **264** C2
Ntsaouéni *Comoros Is.* 11°27S 43°15E **272** a
Ntsoudjini *Comoros Is.* 11°39S 43°15E **272** a
Ntui *Cameroon* 4°27N 11°38E **263** E7
Ntungamo *Uganda* 0°56S 30°17E **268** C3
Nu Jiang → *China* 29°58N 97°25E **228** E2
Nu Shan *China* 26°0N 99°20E **228** E2
Nuakata I. *Papua N. G.* 10°17S 151°2E **286** F6
Nuba Mts. = Nubah, Jibalan
Sudan 12°0N 31°0E **257** E3
Nubah, Jibalan *Sudan* 12°0N 31°0E **257** E3
Nubia *Africa* 21°0N 32°0E **254** D7
Nubian Desert = Nûbîya, Es Sahrâ
en *Sudan* 21°30N 33°30E **256** C3
Nûbîya, Es Sahrâ en
Sudan 21°30N 33°30E **256** C3
Nubl *Syria* 36°22N 36°59E **250** B7
Nubledo *Spain* 43°31N 5°52W **194** B5
Nuboai *Indonesia* 2°10S 136°30E **231** E9
Nubra → *India* 34°35N 77°35E **243** B7
Nucet *Romania* 46°28N 22°35E **182** D7
Nueces → *U.S.A.* 27°51N 97°30W **314** H6
Nueltin L. *Canada* 60°30N 99°30W **297** A9
Nuestra Señora del Rosario de
Caá-Catí *Argentina* 27°45S 57°36W **334** B4
Nueva, I. *Chile* 55°13S 66°30W **336** E3
Nueva Antioquia *Colombia* 6°5N 69°26W **328** B4
Nueva Atzacoalco *Mexico* 19°29N 99°4W **128** B2
Nueva Carteya *Spain* 37°35N 4°28W **196** H6
Nueva Ciudad Guerrero
Mexico 26°34N 99°12W **319** B5
Nueva Ecija □ *Phil.* 15°35N 121°0E **232** D3
Nueva Esparta □ *Venezuela* 11°0N 64°0W **329** A5
Nueva Gerona *Cuba* 21°53N 82°49W **320** B3
Nueva Imperial *Chile* 38°45S 72°58W **336** A2
Nueva Loja = Lago Agrio
Ecuador 0°5N 76°52W **328** C2
Nueva Palmira *Uruguay* 33°52S 58°20W **334** C4
Nueva Pompeya
Argentina 34°40S 58°25W **117** C2
Nueva Rosita *Mexico* 27°57N 101°13W **318** B4
Nueva San Salvador
El Salv. 13°40N 89°18W **320** D2
Nueva Tabarca *Spain* 38°17N 0°30W **197** G4
Nueva Tenochtitlán
Mexico 19°27N 99°5W **128** B2
Nueva Vizcaya □ *Phil.* 16°20N 121°20E **232** C3
Nuéve de Julio *Argentina* 35°30S 61°0W **334** D3
Nuevitas *Cuba* 21°30N 77°20W **320** B4
Nuevo, G. *Argentina* 43°0S 64°30W **336** B4
Nuevo Casas Grandes
Mexico 30°25N 107°55W **318** A3
Nuevo Laredo *Mexico* 27°30N 99°31W **319** B5
Nuevo León □ *Mexico* 25°20N 100°0W **318** C5
Nuevo Mundo, Cerro
Bolivia 21°55S 66°53W **330** E4
Nuevo Rocafuerte *Ecuador* 0°55S 75°27W **328** D2
Nugaal □ *Somali Rep.* 8°10N 49°0E **267** C6
Nugaal → *Somali Rep.* 8°0N 49°47E **267** C6
Nugaaleed, Dooxo
Somali Rep. 8°35N 48°35E **267** C6
Nugget Pt. *N.Z.* 46°27S 169°50E **285** G4
Nugrus, Gebel *Egypt* 24°47N 34°35E **256** C3
Nuguria Is. *Papua N. G.* 3°20S 154°45E **286** B8
Nuhaka *N.Z.* 39°3S 177°45E **284** F6
Nui *Pac. Oc.* 7°15S 177°10E **277** B14
Nuijala *Finland* 60°12N 24°46E **121** B1
Nuits-St-Georges *France* 47°10N 4°56E **173** E11
Nukey Bluff *Australia* 32°26S 135°29E **281** E2
Nukha = Şaki *Azerbaijan* 41°10N 47°5E **191** K8
Nukhayb *Iraq* 32°4N 42°3E **213** F10
Nukheila *Sudan* 19°1N 26°21E **256** D2
Nukiki *Solomon Is.* 6°46S 156°35E **287** L9
Nuku *Papua N. G.* 3°41S 142°28E **286** B2
Nuku Hiva *French Polynesia* 8°54S 140°6W **289** f
Nuku'alofa *Tonga* 21°10S 175°12W **287** Q13
Nukuhu *Papua N. G.* 5°34S 149°22E **286** C5
Nukulaelae *Tuvalu* 9°23S 179°52E **277** B14
Nukunonu *Pac. Oc.* 9°12S 171°54W **277** B16
Nukus *Uzbekistan* 42°27N 59°41E **216** D5
Nulato *U.S.A.* 64°43N 158°6W **303** D8
Nules *Spain* 39°51N 0°9W **196** F4
Nullagine *Australia* 21°53S 120°7E **278** D3
Nullagine → *Australia* 21°20S 120°20E **278** D3
Nullarbor *Australia* 31°28S 130°55E **279** F5
Nullarbor △ *Australia* 32°39S 130°0E **279** F4
Nullarbor Plain *Australia* 31°10S 129°0E **279** F4
Numabukuro *Japan* 35°43N 139°39E **140** A2
Numalla, L. *Australia* 28°43S 144°20E **281** D3
Numan *Nigeria* 9°29N 12°3E **263** D7
Numanuma *Papua N. G.* 9°41S 150°55E **286** E5
Numata *Japan* 36°45N 139°4E **223** A11
Numatinna → *South Sudan* 7°38N 27°20E **257** F2
Numaykoos Lake △
Canada 57°52N 95°58W **297** B9
Numazu *Japan* 35°7N 138°51E **223** B10
Numbulwar *Australia* 14°15S 135°45E **280** A2
Numedal *Norway* 60°40N 9°15E **164** D6
Numfoor *Indonesia* 1°0S 134°50E **231** E8
Numurkah *Australia* 36°5S 145°26E **283** D6
Nunaksaluk I. *Canada* 55°49N 60°20W **299** A7
Nunap Isua *Greenland* 59°48N 43°55W **154** F6
Nunavik *Greenland* 71°50N 54°25W **154** C5
Nunavut □ *Canada* 66°0N 85°0W **295** D15
Nunda *U.S.A.* 42°35N 77°56W **312** D7
Nuneaton *U.K.* 52°32N 1°27W **169** E6
Nuñez *Argentina* 34°32S 58°27W **117** B2
Nungarin *Australia* 31°12S 118°6E **279** F2
Nungo *Mozam.* 13°23S 37°43E **269** E4
Nungwe *Tanzania* 2°48S 32°2E **268** C3
Nunhead *U.K.* 51°27N 0°3W **125** B3
Nunivak I. *U.S.A.* 60°10N 166°30W **303** F6
Nunkun *India* 33°57N 76°2E **243** C7
Ñuñoa *Chile* 33°27S 70°35W **137** B2
Nunukan *Indonesia* 4°4N 117°40E **235** B5
Nùoro *Italy* 40°20N 9°20E **200** B2
Nupur *Iceland* 65°56N 23°36W **155** B3
Nuqayy, Jabal *Libya* 23°11N 19°30E **258** D3
Nuqūb *Yemen* 14°59N 45°48E **248** D4
Nuquí *Colombia* 5°42N 77°17W **328** B2
Nūr *Iran* 36°33N 52°1E **247** B7
Nur Dağı *Turkey* 36°54N 35°39E **250** B6
Nur Dağları *Turkey* 36°50N 36°23E **250** B7
Nura → *Kazakhstan* 50°30N 69°59E **217** B7
Nūrābād *Hormozgān, Iran* 27°47N 57°12E **247** E8
Nūrābād *Lorestān, Iran* 34°4N 47°58E **213** E12
Nurabad *Uzbekistan* 39°36N 66°17E **217** E7
Nure → *Italy* 45°3N 9°49E **198** C6
Nuremberg = Nürnberg
Germany 49°27N 11°3E **179** F7
Nuri *Sonora, Mexico* 28°5N 109°22W **318** B3
Nuri *Sudan* 18°29N 31°59E **256** D3
Nuriootpa *Australia* 34°27S 139°0E **282** C3
Nuristān □ *Afghan.* 35°20N 71°0E **217** E8
Nurlat *Russia* 54°29N 50°45E **190** C10
Nurmes *Finland* 63°33N 29°10E **160** E23
Nürnberg *Germany* 49°27N 11°3E **179** F7
Nurpur *Pakistan* 31°53N 71°54E **242** D4
Nurra, La *Italy* 40°45N 8°15E **200** B1
Nurran, L. = Terewah, L.
Australia 29°52S 147°35E **281** D4
Nurrari Lakes *Australia* 29°1S 130°5E **279** E5
Nurri *Italy* 39°43N 9°14E **200** C2
Nürtingen *Germany* 48°37N 9°19E **179** G5
Nurzec → *Poland* 52°37N 22°25E **185** F9
Nus *Italy* 45°45N 7°28E **198** C4
Nusa Dua *Indonesia* 8°48S 115°14E **231** K18
Nusa Tenggara Barat □
Indonesia 8°50S 117°30E **235** D5
Nusa Tenggara Timur □
Indonesia 9°30S 122°0E **231** F6
Nusaybin *Turkey* 37°3N 41°10E **213** D9
Nuşayrīyah, J. an *Syria* 35°20N 36°13E **250** C7
Nushki *Pakistan* 29°35N 66°0E **242** E2
Nusle *Czech Rep.* 50°3N 14°26E **135** B2
Nussdorf *Austria* 48°15N 16°21E **142** A2
Nuuk *Greenland* 64°10N 51°35W **154** E5
Nuupere, Pte. *Moorea* 17°36S 149°47W **289** e
Nuusuaq *Greenland* 74°8N 57°3W **154** C5
Nu'uli *Amer. Samoa* 14°19S 170°42W **302** f
Nuwakot *Nepal* 28°10N 83°55E **243** E10
Nuwara Eliya *Sri Lanka* 6°58N 80°48E **245** L5
Nuwaybi' W. an →
Si. Arabia 29°18N 34°57E **251** J5
Nuweiba' *Egypt* 28°59N 34°39E **251** K5
Nuwerus *S. Africa* 31°8S 18°24E **270** D2
Nuweveldberge *S. Africa* 32°10S 21°45E **270** D3
Nuyts, Pt. *Australia* 35°4S 116°38E **279** G2
Nuyts Arch. *Australia* 32°35S 133°20E **281** E1
N'Vinda *Angola* 15°8S 19°2E **265** E3
Nxai Pan △ *Botswana* 19°50S 24°46E **270** A3
Nxaunxau *Botswana* 18°57S 21°4E **270** A3
Nyaake *Liberia* 4°52N 7°37W **262** E3
Nyabessan *Cameroon* 2°29N 10°24E **264** B2
Nyabing *Australia* 33°33S 118°9E **279** F2
Nyack *U.S.A.* 41°5N 73°55W **313** E11
Nyagan *Russia* 62°30N 65°38E **214** C7
Nyah West *Australia* 35°16S 143°21E **282** C5
Nyahanga *Tanzania* 2°20S 33°37E **268** C3
Nyahua *Tanzania* 5°25S 33°23E **268** D3
Nyahururu *Kenya* 0°2N 36°27E **268** B4
Nyaingêntanglha Shan
China 30°0N 90°0E **218** F7
Nyakanazi *Tanzania* 3°2S 31°10E **268** C3
Nyakrom *Ghana* 5°40N 0°50W **263** D4
Nyâlâ *Sudan* 12°2N 24°58E **257** E2
Nyalam *China* 28°32N 86°4E **218** F6
Nyamandhlovu *Zimbabwe* 19°55S 28°16E **269** F2
Nyambiti *Tanzania* 2°48S 33°27E **268** C3
Nyamira *Kenya* 0°36S 34°52E **268** B4
Nyamlell *South Sudan* 9°7N 26°59E **257** F2
Nyamwaga *Tanzania* 1°27S 34°33E **268** C3
Nyandekwa *Tanzania* 3°57S 32°32E **268** C3
Nyanding → *South Sudan* 8°40N 32°41E **257** F3
Nyandoma *Russia* 61°40N 40°12E **188** B11
Nyanga *Congo* 2°58S 11°57E **264** C2
Nyanga *Western Cape, S. Africa* 33°59S 18°35E **118** A2
Nyanga → *Gabon* 2°58S 10°15E **264** C2
Nyanga △ *Zimbabwe* 18°17S 32°46E **269** F3
Nyangana *Namibia* 18°0S 20°40E **270** A3
Nyanguge *Tanzania* 2°30S 33°12E **268** C3
Nyanji *Zambia* 14°25S 31°46E **269** E3
Nyankpala *Ghana* 9°21N 0°58W **263** D4
Nyanza *Rwanda* 2°20S 29°42E **268** C2
Nyanza □ *Kenya* 0°10S 34°15E **268** C3
Nyanza-Lac *Burundi* 4°21S 29°36E **268** C2
Nyaponges *South Sudan* 8°5N 33°45E **257** F3
Nyasa, L. = Malawi, L.
Africa 12°30S 34°30E **269** E3
Nyasaland = Malawi ■
Africa 11°55S 34°0E **269** E3
Nyasvizh *Belarus* 53°14N 26°38E **177** B14
Nyaunglebin *Burma* 17°52N 96°42E **241** G6
Nyazepetrovsk *Russia* 56°3N 59°36E **186** C10
Nyazura *Zimbabwe* 18°40S 32°16E **269** F3
Nyazwidzi → *Zimbabwe* 20°0S 31°17E **269** G3
Nybergsund *Norway* 61°15N 12°19E **164** C9
Nyborg *Denmark* 55°18N 10°47E **163** J4
Nybro *Sweden* 56°44N 15°55E **163** H9
Nyda *Russia* 66°40N 72°58E **214** C8
Nyeboe Land *Greenland* 82°0N 57°0W **154** A5
Nyengo Swamp *Zambia* 14°51S 22°7E **265** E4
Nyeri *Kenya* 0°23S 36°56E **268** C4
Nyerol *South Sudan* 8°41N 32°1E **257** F3
Nyhammar *Sweden* 60°17N 14°58E **162** D8
Nyika △ *Malawi* 10°30S 33°53E **269** E3
Nyimba *Zambia* 14°33S 30°50E **269** E3
Nyinahin *Ghana* 6°43N 2°3W **262** D4
Nyingchi *China* 29°32N 94°25E **218** F7
Nyíradony *Hungary* 47°41N 21°55E **182** C6
Nyírbátor *Hungary* 47°49N 22°9E **182** C7
Nyíregyháza *Hungary* 47°58N 21°47E **182** C6
Nyiru, Mt. *Kenya* 2°8N 36°50E **268** B4
Nykarleby = Uusikaarlepyy
Finland 63°32N 22°31E **160** E20
Nykirke *Norway* 60°54N 10°19E **164** D7
Nykøbing *Nordjylland, Denmark* 56°48N 8°51E **163** H2
Nykøbing *Sjælland, Denmark* 54°56N 11°52E **163** K5
Nykøbing *Sjælland, Denmark* 55°55N 11°40E **163** J5
Nyköping *Sweden* 58°45N 17°1E **163** F11
Nykroppa *Sweden* 59°37N 14°18E **162** E8
Nykvarn *Sweden* 59°11N 17°25E **162** E11
Nyland *Sweden* 63°1N 17°45E **162** A11
Nylstroom = Modimolle
S. Africa 24°42S 28°22E **271** B4
Nymagee *Australia* 32°7S 146°20E **283** B7
Nymboida △ *Australia* 29°38S 152°26E **281** D5
Nymburk *Czech Rep.* 50°10N 15°1E **180** A8
Nymphenburg *Germany* 48°9N 11°30E **131** B2
Nymphenburg, Schloss
Germany 48°9N 11°30E **131** B2
Nynäshamn *Sweden* 58°54N 17°57E **163** F11
Nyngan *Australia* 31°30S 147°8E **283** A7
Nyoma Rap *India* 33°10N 78°40E **243** C8
Nyoman = Nemunas →
Lithuania 55°25N 21°10E **184** C8
Nyon *Switz.* 46°23N 6°14E **179** J2
Nyong → *Cameroon* 3°17N 9°54E **263** E6
Nyons *France* 44°22N 5°10E **175** D9
Nyou *Burkina Faso* 12°42N 2°1W **263** C4
Nýrsko *Czech Rep.* 49°18N 13°9E **180** B6
Nysa *Poland* 50°30N 17°22E **185** H4
Nysa → *Europe* 52°4N 14°46E **178** C10
Nysa Kłodzka → *Poland* 50°49N 17°40E **185** H4
Nysætre *Norway* 62°2N 8°20E **164** B5
Nysäter *Sweden* 59°17N 12°47E **162** E6
Nyslott = Savonlinna
Finland 61°52N 28°53E **188** B5
Nyssa *U.S.A.* 43°53N 117°0W **304** E5
Nystad = Uusikaupunki
Finland 60°47N 21°25E **188** B1
Nysted *Denmark* 54°40N 11°44E **163** K5
Nyunzu
Dem. Rep. of the Congo 5°57S 27°58E **268** D2
Nyurba *Russia* 63°17N 118°28E **215** C12
Nyzhankovychi *Ukraine* 49°40N 22°49E **185** J9
Nyzhnohirskyy *Ukraine* 45°27N 34°38E **189** K8
Nyzhny Vorota *Ukraine* 48°46N 23°6E **182** B8
Nzébéla *Guinea* 8°9N 9°7W **262** D3
Nzega *Tanzania* 4°10S 33°12E **268** C3
Nzérékoré *Guinea* 7°49N 8°48W **262** D3
Nzeto *Angola* 7°10S 12°52E **265** D2
Nzilo, Chutes de
Dem. Rep. of the Congo 10°18S 25°27E **265** E5
Nzilo, L.
Dem. Rep. of the Congo 10°35S 25°39E **265** E5
N'zo → *Ivory C.* 6°15N 7°30W **262** D3
N'zo △ *Ivory C.* 6°15N 7°15W **262** D3
Nzubuka *Tanzania* 4°45S 32°50E **268** C3
Nzwani = Anjouan
Comoros Is. 12°15S 44°20E **272** a

O

O Barco *Spain* 42°23N 6°58W **194** C4
O Carballiño *Spain* 42°26N 8°5W **194** C2
O Corgo *Spain* 42°56N 7°25W **194** C3
O Le Pupū Pu'e △
Samoa 13°59S 171°43W **287** V20
O Pino *Spain* 42°56N 8°20W **194** C2
O Porriño *Spain* 42°10N 8°38W **194** C2
Ō-Shima *Hokkaidō, Japan* 41°30N 139°22E **220** D9
Ō-Shima *Nagasaki, Japan* 33°29N 129°33E **222** D1
Ō-Shima *Shizuoka, Japan* 34°44N 139°24E **223** C11
O.R. Tambo Int. ✕ (JNB)
S. Africa 27°7S 29°16E **123** A2
Oa, Mull of *U.K.* 55°35N 6°20W **167** F2
Oacoma *U.S.A.* 43°48N 99°24W **308** D4
Oahe, L. *U.S.A.* 44°27N 100°24W **308** C3
Oahe Dam *U.S.A.* 44°27N 100°24W **308** C3
O'ahu *U.S.A.* 21°28N 157°58W **302** K14
Oak Creek *U.S.A.* 42°52N 87°55W **311** B9
Oak Grove *U.S.A.* 33°50N 84°18W **113** A3
Oak Harbor *U.S.A.* 48°18N 122°39W **306** B4
Oak Hill *Fla., U.S.A.* 28°52N 80°51W **317** G9
Oak Hill *Mass., U.S.A.* 42°18N 71°10W **116** B1
Oak Hill *W. Va., U.S.A.* 37°59N 81°9W **309** G13
Oak Island *U.S.A.* 33°55N 78°10W **315** E15
Oak Lawn *U.S.A.* 41°42N 87°45W **119** C2
Oak Park *Ga., U.S.A.* 32°22N 82°19W **316** C7
Oak Park *Ill., U.S.A.* 41°52N 87°47W **119** B2
Oak Ridge *U.S.A.* 36°1N 84°16W **315** C12
Oak Street Beach *Chicago, U.S.A.* **119** a2
Oak View *Calif., U.S.A.* 34°24N 119°18W **307** L7
Oak View *Md., U.S.A.* 39°1N 76°58W **143** A4
Oakan-Dake *Japan* 43°27N 144°10E **220** C12
Oakbank *Australia* 33°4S 140°33E **282** B4
Oakdale *Calif., U.S.A.* 37°46N 120°51W **306** H6
Oakdale *Georgia, U.S.A.* 33°51N 84°30W **113** A2
Oakdale *La., U.S.A.* 30°49N 92°40W **314** F8
Oakes *U.S.A.* 46°8N 98°6W **308** B4
Oakesdale *U.S.A.* 47°8N 117°15W **304** C5
Oakey *Australia* 27°25S 151°43E **281** D5
Oakfield *Ga., U.S.A.* 31°47N 83°58W **316** D6
Oakfield *N.Y., U.S.A.* 43°4N 78°16W **312** C6
Oakford *U.S.A.* 40°6N 89°58W **310** D7
Oakham *U.K.* 52°40N 0°43W **169** E7
Oakhurst *U.S.A.* 37°19N 119°40W **306** H7
Oakland *Calif., U.S.A.* 37°48N 122°18W **136** B3
Oakland *Ill., U.S.A.* 39°39N 88°2W **311** E8
Oakland *Md., U.S.A.* 38°53N 76°54W **143** B4
Oakland *Pa., U.S.A.* 41°57N 75°36W **313** E9
Oakland City *U.S.A.* 38°20N 87°21W **311** F9
Oakland Park *U.S.A.* 26°10N 80°7W **317** J9
Oaklands *Australia* 35°34S 146°10E **283** C7
Oaklawn *U.S.A.* 38°46N 76°56W **143** C4
Oakleigh *Australia* 37°54S 145°5E **128** B2
Oakley *Idaho, U.S.A.* 42°15N 113°53W **304** E7
Oakley *Kans., U.S.A.* 39°8N 100°51W **308** F3
Oakover → *Australia* 21°0S 120°40E **278** D3
Oakridge *U.S.A.* 43°45N 122°28W **304** E2
Oaks, The *Australia* 34°3S 150°34E **283** C9
Oakton *U.S.A.* 38°52N 77°18W **143** B2
Oaktown *U.S.A.* 38°52N 87°27W **311** F9
Oakville *Ont., Canada* 43°27N 79°41W **312** C5
Oakville *Wash., U.S.A.* 46°51N 123°14W **306** D3
Oakwood *U.S.A.* 41°6N 84°23W **311** C11
Oakwood Beach *U.S.A.* 40°33N 74°7W **132** C1
Oamaru *N.Z.* 45°5S 170°59E **285** F5
Ōamishirasato *Japan* 35°31N 140°18E **223** B12
Oancea *Romania* 45°21N 27°42E **183** E12
Oarai *Japan* 36°21N 140°34E **223** A12
Oasi Faunistica di Vendicari △
Italy 36°49N 15°6E **201** F8
Oasis *Calif., U.S.A.* 37°29N 117°55W **306** H9
Oasis *Calif., U.S.A.* 33°28N 116°6W **307** M10
Oates Land *Antarctica* 69°0S 160°0E **151** C11
Oatley *Australia* 33°59S 151°4E **139** B1
Oatman *U.S.A.* 35°1N 114°19W **307** K12
Oaxaca *Mexico* 17°3N 96°43W **319** D5
Oaxaca □ *Mexico* 17°0N 96°30W **319** D5
Ob → *Russia* 66°45N 69°30E **214** C7
Oba *Canada* 49°4N 84°7W **298** C3
Obala *Cameroon* 4°9N 11°32E **263** E7
Obalende *Nigeria* 6°26N 3°25E **124** B2
Obama *Fukui, Japan* 35°30N 135°45E **223** B7
Obama *Nagasaki, Japan* 32°43N 130°13E **222** E2
Oban *Nigeria* 5°17N 8°33E **263** D6
Oban *Argyll & Bute, U.K.* 56°25N 5°29W **167** E3
Oba's Palace *Nigeria* 6°26N 3°22E **124** B2
Obbia = Hobyo *Somali Rep.* 5°25N 48°30E **267** C6
Obdorsk = Salekhard
Russia 66°30N 66°35E **214** C7
Oberá *Argentina* 27°21S 55°2W **335** B4
Oberammergau *Germany* 47°36N 11°4E **179** H7
Oberasbach *Germany* 49°25N 10°57E **179** F6
Oberbayern □ *Germany* 48°5N 11°50E **179** G7
Oberburg = Gornji Grad
Slovenia 46°20N 14°52E **199** B11
Oberdonau = Oberösterreich □
Austria 48°10N 14°0E **180** C7
Oberdrauburg *Austria* 46°44N 12°58E **180** E5
Obere Donau △ *Germany* 48°5N 9°0E **179** G5
Oberer Bayerischer Wald △
Germany 49°15N 12°40E **179** F8
Oberföhring *Germany* 48°10N 11°37E **131** B2
Oberfranken □ *Germany* 50°10N 11°20E **179** E7
Oberglogau = Głogówek
Poland 50°21N 17°53E **185** H4
Oberhaching *Germany* 48°1N 11°35E **131** B2
Oberhausen *Germany* 51°28N 6°51E **178** D2
Oberkirch *Germany* 48°31N 8°4E **179** G4
Oberlaa *Austria* 48°8N 16°24E **142** B2
Oberlaibach = Vrhnika
Slovenia 45°58N 14°15E **199** C11
Oberlausitz *Germany* 51°16N 14°18E **178** D10
Oberlin *Kans., U.S.A.* 39°49N 100°32W **308** F3
Oberlin *La., U.S.A.* 30°37N 92°46W **314** F8
Oberlin *Ohio, U.S.A.* 41°18N 82°13W **312** E2
Oberlisse *Austria* 48°17N 16°26E **142** A2
Obermenzing *Germany* 48°10N 11°28E **131** A1
Obermoos Schwaige
Germany 48°14N 11°27E **131** A1
Obernai *France* 48°28N 7°30E **173** D14
Oberndorf *Germany* 48°17N 8°34E **179** G4
Obernigk = Oborniki Śląskie
Poland 51°17N 16°53E **185** G3
Oberon *Australia* 33°45S 149°52E **283** B8
Oberösterreich □ *Austria* 48°10N 14°0E **180** C7
Oberpfalz □ *Germany* 49°20N 12°10E **179** F8
Oberpfälzer Wald
Germany 49°30N 12°30E **179** F8
Oberpfälzer Wald △
Germany 49°40N 12°20E **179** F8
Oberschleissheim
Germany 48°15N 11°33E **131** A2
Oberschöneweide
Germany 52°27N 13°31E **115** B4
Oberstdorf *Germany* 47°24N 10°15E **179** H6
Oberting *Gabon* 0°22S 9°46E **264** C1
Obertyn *Ukraine* 48°42N 25°10E **183** B10
Oberursel *Germany* 50°11N 8°35E **179** E4
Oberwart *Austria* 47°17N 16°12E **181** D9
Obi, Kepulauan *Indonesia* 1°23S 127°45E **231** E7
Obiaruku *Nigeria* 5°51N 6°9E **263** D6
Óbidos *Brazil* 1°50S 55°30W **329** D6
Óbidos *Portugal* 39°19N 9°10W **195** F1
Obihiro *Japan* 42°56N 143°12E **220** C11
Obilatu *Indonesia* 1°25S 127°20E **231** E7
Obilnoye *Russia* 47°32N 44°30E **191** G7
Obing *Germany* 48°0N 12°24E **179** G8
Objat *France* 45°16N 1°24E **174** C5
Oblong *U.S.A.* 39°0N 87°55W **311** F9
Obluchye *Russia* 49°1N 131°4E **215** E14
Obninsk *Russia* 55°8N 36°37E **188** E9
Obo *C.A.R.* 5°20N 26°32E **264** A5
Obock *Djibouti* 12°0N 43°20E **257** E5
Obodivka *Ukraine* 48°24N 29°15E **183** B14
Oborniki *Poland* 52°39N 16°50E **185** F3
Oborniki Śląskie *Poland* 51°17N 16°53E **185** G3
Obouya *Congo* 0°56S 15°43E **264** C3
Oboyan *Russia* 51°15N 36°21E **189** G9
Obozerskaya = Obozerskiy
Russia 63°34N 40°21E **186** B7
Obozerskiy *Russia* 63°34N 40°21E **186** B7
Obrenovac *Serbia* 44°40N 20°11E **202** B4
O'Brien *U.S.A.* 30°2N 82°57W **316** E7
Obrovac *Croatia* 44°11N 15°41E **199** D12
Obruk *Turkey* 38°7N 33°12E **212** C5
Obrzycko *Poland* 52°42N 16°32E **185** F3
Observatory *Sydney, Australia* **139** a1
Observatory *Gauteng, S. Africa* 26°10S 28°4E **123** B2
Observatory Inlet
Canada 55°10N 129°54W **296** B3
Obshchi Syrt *Russia* 52°0N 53°0E **158** E16
Obskaya Guba *Russia* 69°0N 73°0E **214** C8
Obu *Japan* 35°0N 136°58E **223** B8
Obuasi *Ghana* 6°17N 1°40W **263** D4
Obubra *Nigeria* 6°8N 8°20E **263** D6
Óbuda *Hungary* 47°33N 19°2E **117** A2
Obudu *Nigeria* 6°33N 9°5E **263** D6
Obukhovo *Russia* 59°53N 30°22E **137** B2
Obura *Papua N. G.* 6°33S 145°58E **286** D3
Obvodnyy Kanal *Russia* 59°54N 30°20E **137** B2
Obwalden □ *Switz.* 46°55N 8°15E **179** J4
Obzor *Bulgaria* 42°50N 27°52E **203** D11
Ocala *U.S.A.* 29°11N 82°8W **317** F7
Ocamo → *Venezuela* 2°48N 65°14W **329** C4
Ocampo *Chihuahua, Mexico* 28°11N 108°23W **318** B3
Ocampo *Tamaulipas, Mexico* 22°50N 99°20W **319** C5
Ocaña *Colombia* 8°15N 73°20W **328** B3
Ocaña *Spain* 39°55N 3°30W **194** F7
Occidental, Cordillera
Colombia 5°0N 76°0W **328** C2
Occidental, Cordillera *Peru* 14°0S 74°0W **330** C3
Occidental, Grand Erg
Algeria 30°20N 1°0E **261** B5
Ocean City *Md., U.S.A.* 38°20N 75°5W **309** F16
Ocean City *N.J., U.S.A.* 39°17N 74°35W **309** F16
Ocean City *Wash., U.S.A.* 47°4N 124°10W **306** C2
Ocean Falls *Canada* 52°18N 127°48W **296** C3
Ocean I. = Banaba
Kiribati 0°45S 169°50E **288** H8
Ocean Park *Hong Kong, China* 22°13N 114°10E **122** B2
Ocean Park *Wash., U.S.A.* 46°30N 124°3W **306** D2
Oceano *U.S.A.* 35°6N 120°37W **307** K6
Oceanport *U.S.A.* 40°19N 74°3W **313** F10
Oceanside *U.S.A.* 33°12N 117°23W **307** M9
Ochagavía *Spain* 42°55N 1°5W **196** C3
Ochakiv *Ukraine* 46°37N 31°33E **189** J6
Ochakovo *Russia* 55°41N 37°26E **129** B2
Ochamchira *Georgia* 42°46N 41°32E **191** J5
Ochi, Oros *Greece* 38°5N 24°25E **204** C6
Ochiai *Japan* 35°1N 133°45E **222** B5
Ochil Hills *U.K.* 56°14N 3°40W **167** E5
Ochlocknee *U.S.A.* 30°58N 84°3W **316** E5
Ochlockonee → *U.S.A.* 29°59N 84°26W **316** F5
Ocho Rios *Jamaica* 18°24N 77°6W **320** a
Ochopee *U.S.A.* 25°54N 81°18W **317** K8
Ochota *Poland* 52°13N 20°58E **142** B1
Ochsenfurt *Germany* 49°40N 10°4E **179** F6
Ochsenhausen *Germany* 48°4N 9°57E **179** G5
Ocilla *U.S.A.* 31°36N 83°15W **316** D6
Ockelbo *Sweden* 60°54N 16°45E **162** D10
Ocmulgee → *U.S.A.* 31°58N 82°33W **316** D7
Ocmulgee △ *U.S.A.* 32°49N 83°37W **316** C6
Ocna Mureş *Romania* 46°23N 23°55E **183** D8
Ocna Sibiului *Romania* 45°52N 24°2E **183** E9
Ocnele Mari *Romania* 45°8N 24°18E **183** E9
Ocniţa *Moldova* 48°25N 27°30E **183** B12
Ocoee *U.S.A.* 28°34N 81°32W **133** A1
Ocoña *Peru* 16°26S 73°8W **330** D3
Ocoña → *Peru* 16°28S 73°8W **330** D3
Oconee → *U.S.A.* 31°58N 82°33W **316** D7
Oconee, L. *U.S.A.* 33°28N 83°15W **316** B6
O'Connell Street *Dublin, Ireland* **120** b2
Oconomowoc *U.S.A.* 43°7N 88°30W **311** A8
Oconto *U.S.A.* 44°53N 87°52W **308** C10
Oconto Falls *U.S.A.* 44°52N 88°9W **308** C9
Ocosingo *Mexico* 16°53N 92°6W **319** D6
Ocotal *Nic.* 13°41N 86°31W **320** D2
Ocotlán *Jalisco, Mexico* 20°21N 102°46W **318** C4
Ocotlán *Oaxaca, Mexico* 16°48N 96°40W **319** D5
Ocreza → *Portugal* 39°32N 7°50W **195** F3
Öcsa *Hungary* 47°17N 19°15E **182** C4
Octeville *France* 49°38N 1°40W **172** C5
Ocumare del Tuy
Venezuela 10°7N 66°46W **328** A4
Ocurí *Bolivia* 18°45S 65°50W **331** D4
Ocussi = Pante Macassar
E. Timor 9°30S 123°58E **231** F6
Oda *Ghana* 5°50N 0°51W **263** D4
Ōda *Shimane, Japan* 35°11N 132°30E **222** B4

Oda, J. Sudan 20°21N 36°39E 256 C4
Ódáðahraun Iceland 65°5N 17°0W 155 B9
Ōdaejin N. Korea 41°34N 129°40E 224 B4
Odaesan △ S. Korea 37°40N 128°30E 224 D4
Ödåkra Sweden 56°7N 12°45E 163 H6
Ōdana Japan 35°33N 139°35E 140 B2
Odate Japan 40°16N 140°34E 220 D10
Odawara Japan 35°20N 139°6E 223 B11
Odda Norway 60°3N 6°35E 164 D3
Odder = Xuddur
Somali Rep. 4°11N 43°52E 267 D5
Odder Denmark 55°58N 10°10E 163 J4
Odei → Canada 56°6N 96°54W 297 B9
Odell U.S.A. 41°0N 88°31W 311 C8
Odemira Portugal 37°35N 8°40W 195 H2
Ödemiş Turkey 38°15N 28°0E 205 C9
Öden-Stockach Germany 48°5N 11°41E 131 B3
Ödenburg = Sopron
Hungary 47°45N 16°32E 182 C1
Odendaalsrus S. Africa 27°48S 26°45E 270 C4
Odensbacken Sweden 59°10N 15°32E 162 E9
Odense Denmark 55°22N 10°23E 163 J4
Odenwald = Neckartal-Odenwald △
Germany 49°30N 9°5E 179 F5
Odenwald Germany 49°35N 9°0E 179 F5
Oder → Europe 53°33N 14°38E 178 B10
Oder-Havel Kanal
Germany 52°52N 14°2E 178 C10
Oderzo Italy 45°47N 12°29E 199 C9
Odesa Ukraine 46°30N 30°45E 189 J6
Odesa □ Ukraine 47°20N 29°55E 189 J5
Ödeshög Sweden 58°14N 14°39E 163 F8
Odessa = Odesa Ukraine 46°30N 30°45E 189 J6
Odessa Ont., Canada 44°17N 76°43W 313 B8
Odessa Mo., U.S.A. 39°0N 93°57W 310 F3
Odessa Tex., U.S.A. 31°52N 102°23W 314 F3
Odessa Wash., U.S.A. 47°20N 118°41W 304 C4
Odiakwe Botswana 20°12S 25°17E 270 B4
Odiel → Spain 37°10N 6°55W 195 H4
Odienné Ivory C. 9°30N 7°34W 262 D3
Odilampi Finland 60°18N 24°45E 121 B1
Odimba Gabon 2°2S 9°33E 264 C2
Odintsovo Russia 55°40N 37°16E 129 B1
Odiongan Phil. 12°24N 121°59E 232 E3
Odivelas Portugal 38°47N 9°10W 126 A1
Odobeşti Romania 45°43N 27°4E 183 E12
Odolanów Poland 51°34N 17°40E 185 G4
Odolany Poland 52°13N 20°55E 142 B1
O'Donnell U.S.A. 32°58N 101°50W 314 E4
O'Donnell Pt. Canada 45°5N 80°5W 312 A4
Odorheiu Secuiesc
Romania 46°21N 25°21E 183 D10
Odoyevo Russia 53°56N 36°42E 188 F9
Odra = Oder → Europe 53°33N 14°38E 178 B10
Odra → Spain 42°14N 4°17W 194 C6
Odum U.S.A. 31°40N 82°2W 316 D7
Odžaci Serbia 45°30N 19°17E 182 E4
Odžak Bos.-H. 45°3N 18°18E 182 E3
Odzala Congo 0°37N 14°37E 264 B2
Odzala △ Congo 0°55N 14°55E 264 B2
Odzi Zimbabwe 19°0S 32°20E 271 A5
Odzi → Zimbabwe 19°45S 32°23E 271 A5
Oebisfelde Germany 52°27N 10°57E 178 C6
Oedong S. Korea 35°42N 129°14E 224 E4
Oeiras Brazil 7°0S 42°8W 332 C3
Oeiras Portugal 38°41N 9°18W 126 A1
Oeiras do Para Brazil 1°58S 49°51W 329 D8
Oelrichs U.S.A. 43°11N 103°14W 308 D2
Oels in Schlesien = Oleśnica
Poland 51°13N 17°22E 185 G4
Oelsnitz Germany 50°24N 12°10E 179 E8
Oelwein U.S.A. 42°41N 91°55W 310 B5
Oenarodo S. Korea 34°26N 127°30E 224 E3
Oeno I. Pac. Oc. 24°0S 131°0W 289 K14
Oenpelli = Gunbalanya
Australia 12°20S 133°4E 278 B5
Oetz Austria 47°13N 10°53E 180 D3
Of Turkey 40°59N 40°23E 213 B9
O'Fallon U.S.A. 38°49N 90°42W 310 F6
Ofanto → Italy 41°22N 16°13E 201 A9
Offa Nigeria 8°13N 4°42E 263 D5
Offaly □ Ireland 53°15N 7°30W 166 C4
Offenbach Germany 50°6N 8°44E 179 E4
Offenburg Germany 48°28N 7°56E 179 G3
Officer Cr. → Australia 27°46S 132°30E 279 E5
Offida Italy 42°56N 13°41E 199 F10
Offoué → Gabon 0°4S 11°44E 264 C2
Ofidousa Greece 36°33N 26°8E 205 E8
Ofin Nigeria 6°32N 3°30E 124 A3
Ofolanga Tonga 19°38S 174°27W 287 P13
Ofotfjorden Norway 68°27N 17°0E 160 B17
Ofte Norway 59°30N 8°12E 164 E5
Ofu Amer. Samoa 14°11S 169°41W 302 g
Ōfunato Japan 39°4N 141°43E 220 E10
Oga Japan 39°55N 139°50E 220 E9
Oga-Hantō Japan 39°58N 139°47E 220 E9
Ogaden Ethiopia 7°30N 45°30E 267 C6
Ōgaki Japan 35°21N 136°37E 223 B8
Ogallala U.S.A. 41°8N 101°43W 308 E3
Ogan → Indonesia 3°1S 104°44E 234 C2
Ogasawara Gunto
Pac. Oc. 27°0N 142°0E 211 F16
Ogawa Japan 35°44N 139°28E 140 A1
Ogbomosho Nigeria 8°1N 4°11E 263 D5
Ogden Iowa, U.S.A. 42°2N 94°2W 310 B2
Ogden Utah, U.S.A. 41°13N 111°58W 304 F8
Ogden Park U.S.A. 41°46N 87°39W 119 C2
Ogden Slip Chicago, U.S.A. 119 b3
Ogdensburg U.S.A. 44°42N 75°30W 313 B9
Ogea Driki Fiji 19°12S 178°27W 287 B3
Ogea Levu Fiji 19°8S 178°24W 287 B3
Ogeechee → U.S.A. 31°50N 81°3W 316 D8
Ogi Japan 33°20N 130°15E 222 D2
Ogikubo Japan 35°42N 139°37E 140 A2
Ogilby U.S.A. 32°49N 114°50W 307 N12
Oglat Beraber Algeria 30°15N 3°34W 260 B4
Oglat el Khnâchich Mali 21°51N 3°58W 260 D4
Oglesby U.S.A. 41°18N 89°4W 310 C7
Oglethorpe U.S.A. 32°18N 84°4W 316 C5
Óglio → Italy 45°2N 10°39E 198 C7
Óglio Nord △ Italy 45°22N 9°54E 198 C6
Óglio Sud △ Italy 45°7N 10°24E 198 C7
Ogmore Australia 22°37S 149°35E 280 C4
Ognon → France 47°16N 5°28E 173 E12
Ogogoro Nigeria 6°25N 3°24E 124 B2
Ogoja Nigeria 6°38N 8°39E 263 D6
Ogoki Canada 51°38N 85°58W 298 B2
Ogoki → Canada 51°38N 85°57W 298 B2
Ogoki L. Canada 50°50N 87°10W 298 B2
Ogoki Res. Canada 50°45N 88°15W 298 B2
Ogooué → Gabon 1°0S 9°0E 264 C1
Ogōri Japan 34°6N 131°24E 222 C3
Ogōri Japan 33°25N 130°30E 222 D2
Ogosta → Bulgaria 43°48N 23°55E 202 C7
Ogou → Togo 7°50N 1°19E 263 D5
Ogoueïleten Nmâdi
Mauritania 19°46N 11°1W 260 E2
Ogowe = Ogooué → Gabon 1°0S 9°0E 264 C1
Ogoyo Nigeria 6°25N 3°29E 124 B2
Ogr = Sharafa Sudan 11°59N 27°7E 257 E2
Ogražden Macedonia 41°30N 22°50E 202 E6
Ogre Latvia 56°49N 24°36E 188 D3
Ogrein Sudan 17°55N 34°50E 256 D3
Ogudu Nigeria 6°34N 3°24E 124 A2
Ogulin Croatia 45°16N 15°16E 199 C12
Ogun □ Nigeria 7°0N 3°0E 263 D5
Oguni Japan 33°11N 131°8E 222 D3
Ögur Iceland 66°2N 22°44W 155 A4
Ogurja Ada Turkmenistan 38°55N 53°2E 247 B7
Oguta Nigeria 5°44N 6°44E 263 D6
Oğuzeli Turkey 36°57N 37°30E 250 B8
Ogwashi-Uku Nigeria 6°15N 6°30E 263 D6
Ogwe Nigeria 5°0N 7°14E 263 E6
Ohai N.Z. 45°55S 168°0E 285 F3
Ohakune N.Z. 39°24S 175°24E 284 F4
Ohanet Algeria 28°44N 8°46E 261 C6
Ōhara Japan 35°15N 140°23E 223 B12
O'Hare Int., Chicago ✕ (ORD)
U.S.A. 41°59N 87°54W 119 B1
Ohariu Stream → N.Z. 41°12S 174°47E 143 B1
Ohata Japan 41°24N 141°10E 220 D10
Ohatchee U.S.A. 33°47N 86°0W 316 B4
Ohau, L. N.Z. 44°15S 169°53E 285 E4
Ohaupo N.Z. 37°56S 175°20E 284 D4
O'Higgins, C. Chile 27°5S 109°15W 330 b
O'Higgins, Parque Chile 33°27S 70°40W 137 B2
O'Higgins, Pta. Chile 33°41S 79°0W 330 c
Ohio □ U.S.A. 40°15N 82°45W 312 F2
Ohio → U.S.A. 36°59N 89°8W 311 G8
Ohio City U.S.A. 40°46N 84°37W 311 D12
Ohiwa Harbour N.Z. 37°59S 177°10E 284 D6
Ohlau = Oława Poland 50°57N 17°20E 185 H4
Ohře → Czech Rep. 50°30N 14°10E 180 A7
Ohre → Sachsen-Anhalt,
Germany 52°18N 11°46E 178 C7
Ohrid Macedonia 41°8N 20°52E 202 E4
Ohridsko Jezero Macedonia 41°8N 20°52E 202 E4
Ohrigstad S. Africa 24°39S 30°36E 271 B5
Öhringen Germany 49°12N 9°31E 179 F5
Ohura N.Z. 38°51S 174°59E 284 E3
Oi Qu → China 28°37N 98°16E 228 C2
Oiapoque Brazil 3°50N 51°50W 329 C7
Oiapoque → S. Amer. 4°8N 51°40W 329 C7
Oikou China 38°35N 117°42E 227 E9
Oil City U.S.A. 41°26N 79°42W 312 E5
Oil Springs Canada 42°47N 82°7W 312 D2
Oildale U.S.A. 35°25N 119°1W 307 K7
Ōimachi Japan 35°35N 139°44E 140 B3
Oinousa = Inousses
Greece 38°33N 26°14E 205 C8
Oise □ France 49°28N 2°30E 173 C9
Oise → France 49°0N 2°4E 173 C9
Oistins Barbados 13°4N 59°33W 323 r
Ōita Japan 33°14N 131°36E 222 D3
Ōita □ Japan 33°15N 131°30E 222 D3
Ojai U.S.A. 34°27N 119°15W 307 L7
Ojcowski △ Poland 50°15N 19°50E 185 H6
Ojhar India 20°6N 73°56E 244 D1
Ojinaga Mexico 29°34N 104°25W 318 B4
Ojiya Japan 37°18N 138°48E 221 F9
Ojo Caliente Mexico 21°53N 102°15W 318 C4
Ojo de Liebre, L. Mexico 27°45N 114°15W 318 B2
Ojos del Salado, Cerro
Argentina 27°0S 68°40W 334 B2
Ojota Nigeria 6°35N 3°23E 124 A2
Oka Nigeria 7°9N 3°38E 263 D5
Oka → Russia 56°20N 43°59E 190 B7
Okaba Indonesia 8°6S 139°42E 231 F9
Okahandja Namibia 22°0S 16°59E 270 B2
Okahukura N.Z. 38°48S 175°14E 284 E4
Okaihau N.Z. 35°19S 173°47E 284 B3
Okalataka Congo 0°18S 14°54E 264 C2
Okanagan L. Canada 50°0N 119°30W 296 D5
Okandja Gabon 0°35S 13°45E 264 C2
Okano → Gabon 0°5S 10°57E 264 C2
Okanogan U.S.A. 48°22N 119°35W 304 B4
Okanogan → U.S.A. 48°6N 119°44W 304 B4
Okanogan Range
N. Amer. 49°0N 119°55W 296 D5
Okány Hungary 46°52N 21°21E 182 D6
Okapa Papua N. G. 6°38S 145°39E 286 D3
Okapi △
Dem. Rep. of the Congo 2°30N 27°20E 268 B2
Okaputa Namibia 20°5S 17°0E 270 B2
Okara Pakistan 30°50N 73°31E 242 D5
Okarito N.Z. 43°15S 170°9E 285 D5
Okato N.Z. 39°12S 173°53E 284 F2
Okau Micronesia 9°32N 138°6E 287 R16
Okaukuejo Namibia 19°10S 16°0E 270 A2
Okavango Delta Botswana 18°45S 22°45E 270 A3
Okavango Swamp = Okavango
Delta Botswana 18°45S 22°45E 270 A3
Ōkawa Japan 33°9N 130°21E 222 D2
Okawville U.S.A. 38°26N 89°33W 310 F7
Okaya Japan 36°5N 138°10E 223 A10
Okayama Japan 34°40N 133°54E 222 C5
Okayama □ Japan 35°0N 133°50E 222 C5
Okazaki Japan 34°57N 137°10E 223 C9
Oke-Iho Nigeria 8°1N 3°18E 263 D5
Oke-Ira Nigeria 6°29N 3°22E 124 B2
Okęcie Poland 52°11N 20°56E 142 B1
Okęcie, Warszawa ✕ (WAW)
Poland 52°9N 20°59E 142 B1
Okeechobee U.S.A. 27°15N 80°50W 317 H9
Okeechobee, L. U.S.A. 27°0N 80°50W 317 J9
Okefenokee △ U.S.A. 30°45N 82°18W 316 E7
Okefenokee Swamp
U.S.A. 30°40N 82°20W 316 E7
Okehampton U.K. 50°44N 4°0W 169 G4
Okemos U.S.A. 42°43N 84°26W 311 B12
Okene Nigeria 7°32N 6°11E 263 D6
Okeogbe Nigeria 6°24N 3°23E 124 B2
Oker → Germany 52°32N 10°22E 178 C6
Okha Gujarat, India 22°27N 69°4E 242 H3
Okha Russia 53°40N 143°0E 215 D15
Okhla India 28°33N 77°16E 120 B2
Okhotsk Russia 59°20N 143°10E 215 D15
Okhotsk, Sea of Asia 55°0N 145°0E 215 D15
Okhotskiy Perevoz
Russia 61°52N 135°35E 215 C14
Okhta → Russia 59°56N 30°25E 137 B2
Okhtyrka Ukraine 50°25N 35°0E 189 G8
Oki-no-Shima Japan 32°44N 132°33E 222 E4
Oki-Shotō Japan 36°5N 133°15E 222 A5
Okiep S. Africa 29°39S 17°53E 270 C2
Okigwi Nigeria 5°52N 7°20E 263 D6
Okija Nigeria 5°54N 6°55E 263 D6
Okinawa Japan 26°19N 127°46E 288 a
Okinawa □ Japan 26°40N 128°0E 288 a
Okinawa-Guntō Japan 26°40N 128°0E 221 L4
Okinawa-Jima Japan 26°32N 128°0E 221 L4
Okino-erabu-Shima
Japan 27°21N 128°33E 221 L4
Okitipupa Nigeria 6°31N 4°50E 263 D5
Okkervil → Russia 59°56N 30°30E 137 B2
Oklahoma □ U.S.A. 35°20N 97°30W 314 D6
Oklahoma City U.S.A. 35°30N 97°30W 314 D6
Oklawaha → U.S.A. 29°28N 81°41W 317 F8
Okmulgee U.S.A. 35°37N 95°58W 314 D7
Oknitsa = Ocniţa
Moldova 48°25N 27°30E 183 B12
Oko, W. → Sudan 21°15N 35°56E 256 C4
Okolo Uganda 2°37N 31°8E 268 B3
Okolona Ky., U.S.A. 38°8N 85°41W 311 F11
Okolona Miss., U.S.A. 34°0N 88°45W 315 E10
Okombahe Namibia 21°23S 15°22E 270 B2
Okonek Poland 53°32N 16°51E 184 E3
Okotoks Canada 50°43N 113°58W 296 C6
Okoyo Congo 1°28S 15°0E 264 C2
Okrika Nigeria 4°40N 7°10E 263 E6
Okrzeszyn Poland 52°8N 21°8E 142 C2
Oksapmin Papua N. G. 5°17S 142°15E 286 C2
Øksendalsøra Norway 62°42N 8°27E 164 B5
Oksovskiy Russia 62°33N 39°57E 186 B6
Oksval Norway 59°51N 10°40E 133 A3
Oktwin Burma 18°49N 96°26E 241 F6
Oktyabrsk = Qandyaghash
Kazakhstan 49°28N 57°25E 187 E10
Oktyabrsk Russia 53°11N 48°40E 190 D9
Oktyabrskiy = Aktsyabrski
Belarus 52°38N 28°53E 177 B15
Oktyabrskiy Bashkortostan,
Russia 54°28N 53°28E 186 D9
Oktyabrskiy Kamchatka,
Russia 52°39N 156°14E 215 D16
Oktyabrskiy Moskva,
Russia 55°41N 37°35E 129 B3
Oktyabrskiy Rostov, Russia 47°30N 40°4E 191 G5
Oktyabrskoy Revolyutsii, Ostrov
Russia 79°30N 97°0E 215 B10
Oktyabrskoye = Zhovtneve
Ukraine 46°54N 32°3E 189 J7
Okubo Tokyo, Japan 140 a2
Okuchi Japan 32°4N 130°37E 222 E2
Okulovka Russia 58°25N 33°19E 188 C7
Okura Japan 35°35N 139°27E 140 B1
Okuru N.Z. 43°55S 168°55E 285 D3
Okushiri-Tō Japan 42°15N 139°30E 220 C9
Okuta Nigeria 9°14N 3°12E 263 D5
Okwa → Botswana 22°30S 23°0E 270 B3
Ola Russia 59°35N 151°17E 215 D16
Ola Ark., U.S.A. 35°2N 93°13W 314 D8
Ólafsfjörður Iceland 66°4N 18°39W 155 A8
Ólafsvík Iceland 64°53N 23°43W 155 C3
Olaine Latvia 56°48N 23°59E 184 B10
Olancha U.S.A. 36°17N 118°1W 307 J8
Olancha Pk. U.S.A. 36°16N 118°7W 307 J8
Olanchito Honduras 15°30N 86°30W 320 C2
Öland Sweden 56°45N 16°38E 163 H10
Ölands norra udde
Sweden 57°22N 17°5E 163 G11
Ölands södra udde
Sweden 56°12N 16°23E 163 H10
Olanta U.S.A. 33°56N 79°56W 316 B10
Olar U.S.A. 33°11N 81°11W 316 B8
Olargues France 43°34N 2°53E 174 E6
Olari Finland 60°10N 24°44E 121 B1
Olaria Brazil 22°50S 43°16W 135 B1
Olary Australia 32°18S 140°19E 282 B4
Olascoaga Argentina 35°15S 60°39W 334 D3
Olathe U.S.A. 38°53N 94°49W 308 F6
Olavarría Argentina 36°55S 60°20W 334 D3
Oława Poland 50°57N 17°20E 185 H4
Olbernhau Germany 50°40N 13°19E 178 E9
Ólbia Italy 40°55N 9°31E 200 B2
Ólbia, G. di Italy 40°55N 9°39E 200 B2
Olching Germany 48°12N 11°21E 179 G7
Olcott U.S.A. 43°20N 78°42W 312 C6
Old Admiralty Russia 59°55N 30°20E 137 B1
Old Bahama Chan. = Bahama,
Canal Viejo de
W. Indies 22°10N 77°30W 320 B4
Old Baldy Pk. = San Antonio, Mt.
U.S.A. 34°17N 117°38W 307 L9
Old Bar Australia 31°58S 152°35E 283 A10
Old Bridge U.S.A. 40°25N 74°22W 313 F10
Old Castile = Castilla y Leon □
Spain 42°0N 5°0W 194 D6
Old City Shanghai, China 31°13N 121°29E 138 B1
Old City Delhi, India 120 a3
Old City Jerusalem 123 b3
Old Crow Canada 67°30N 139°55W 294 D4
Old Dale U.S.A. 34°8N 115°47W 307 L11
Old Forge N.Y., U.S.A. 43°43N 74°58W 313 C10
Old Forge Pa., U.S.A. 41°22N 75°45W 313 E9
Old Fort = Purana Qila Delhi, India 120 c3
Old Fort B. Bahamas 25°3N 77°32W 153 b
Old Fort Pt. Montserrat 16°40N 62°11W 323 p
Old Fort York Canada 43°39N 79°24W 141 B2
Old Harbor Alaska,
U.S.A. 57°12N 153°18W 303 H9
Old Harbor Mass., U.S.A. 42°19N 71°1W 116 B2
Old Harbour Jamaica 17°56N 77°6W 320 a
Old Harbour Bay Jamaica 17°54N 77°6W 320 a
Old Ironside Boston, U.S.A. 116 a3
Old Mapoon ◎ Australia 11°5S 142°22E 280 A3
Old Panamao Phil. 5°59N 121°13E 233 J3
Old Perlican Canada 48°5N 53°1W 299 C9
Old Road Bluff
Antigua & B. 16°59N 61°50W 322 b
Old Road Town
St. Kitts & Nevis 17°17N 62°47W 322 d
Old Roundhouse Toronto, Canada 141 c2
Old Shinyanga Tanzania 3°33S 33°27E 268 C3
Old Speck Mt. U.S.A. 44°34N 70°57W 313 B14
Old Town = Stare Miasto
Warsaw, Poland 142 a2
Old Town Edinburgh, U.K. 121 a2
Old Town Fla., U.S.A. 29°36N 82°59W 317 F7
Old Town Ill., U.S.A. 41°54N 87°37W 119 B3
Old Town Maine, U.S.A. 44°56N 68°39W 309 C19
Old Town Hall = Altes Rathaus
Munich, Germany 131 b3
Old Town Square Warsaw, Poland 142 a2
Old Washington U.S.A. 40°2N 81°27W 312 F3
Old Wives L. Canada 50°5N 106°0W 297 C7
Oldbawn Ireland 53°17N 6°21W 120 B1
Oldbury U.K. 51°38N 2°33W 169 F5
Oldcastle Ireland 53°46N 7°10W 166 C4
Oldeani Tanzania 3°22S 35°35E 268 C4
Olden Norway 61°49N 6°49E 164 C3
Oldenburg Niedersachsen,
Germany 53°9N 8°13E 178 B4
Oldenburg Schleswig-Holstein,
Germany 54°17N 10°52E 178 A6
Oldenzaal Neths. 52°19N 6°53E 170 B6
Oldham U.K. 53°33N 2°7W 168 D5
Oldman → Canada 49°57N 111°42W 296 D6
Oldmeldrum U.K. 57°20N 2°19W 167 D6
Olds Canada 51°50N 114°10W 296 C6
Oldsmar U.S.A. 28°2N 82°39W 317 G7
Olduvai Gorge Tanzania 2°57S 35°23E 268 C4
Öldziyt Mongolia 44°40N 109°1E 226 B5
Ole Rømer Land
Greenland 74°10N 24°30W 154 C8
Olean U.S.A. 42°5N 78°26W 312 D6
Oleby Sweden 60°8N 13°2E 162 D7
Olecko Poland 54°2N 22°31E 184 D9
Oleggio Italy 45°36N 8°38E 198 C5
Oleiros Portugal 39°56N 7°56W 194 F3
Oleiros Spain 43°20N 8°19W 194 B2
Olekma → Russia 60°22N 120°42E 215 C13
Olekminsk Russia 60°25N 120°30E 215 C13
Oleksandriya Ukraine 48°55N 32°20E 189 H7
Oleksandriya Kirovohrad,
Ukraine 48°42N 33°3E 189 H7
Oleksandriya Rivne,
Ukraine 50°37N 26°19E 177 C14
Olema U.S.A. 38°3N 122°47W 306 G4
Ølen Norway 59°36N 5°48E 164 E2
Olenegorsk Russia 68°9N 33°18E 160 B25
Olenek Russia 68°28N 112°18E 215 C12
Olenek → Russia 73°0N 120°10E 215 B13
Olenino Russia 56°15N 33°30E 188 D7
Olenya = Olenegorsk
Russia 68°9N 33°18E 160 B25
Oléron, Î. d' France 45°55N 1°15W 174 C2
Olesk Ukraine 51°6N 24°11E 185 G11
Oleśnica Poland 51°13N 17°22E 185 G4
Olesno Poland 50°51N 18°26E 185 H5
Olevsk Ukraine 51°12N 27°39E 177 C14
Olga, L. Canada 49°47N 77°15W 298 C4
Olgas, The = Kata Tjuta
Australia 25°20S 130°50E 279 E5
Olgino Russia 60°0N 30°10E 137 A1
Ölgiy Mongolia 48°56N 89°57E 217 C11
Ølgod Denmark 55°49N 8°36E 163 J2
Olhão Portugal 37°3N 7°48W 195 H3
Olhopil Ukraine 48°12N 29°30E 183 B14
Olhovatka Russia 54°30N 22°18E 184 D9
Olib Croatia 44°23N 14°44E 199 D11
Oliena Italy 40°16N 9°24E 200 B2
Oliete Spain 41°1N 0°41W 196 D4
Olifants = Elefantes →
Africa 24°10S 32°40E 271 B5
Olifants → Namibia 25°30S 19°30E 270 B2
Olifantshoek S. Africa 27°57S 22°42E 270 C3
Ólimbos Greece 35°44N 27°11E 205 F9
Ólimbos, Óros = Olymbos Oros
Greece 40°6N 22°23E 202 F6
Olímpia Brazil 20°44S 48°54W 335 A6
Olimpico, Estadio Mexico 19°20N 99°11W 128 C1
Olimpos-Beydaglari △
Turkey 36°36N 30°30E 205 E12
Olin U.S.A. 42°0N 91°9W 310 B5
Olinda Brazil 8°1S 34°51W 332 C5
Olite Spain 42°29N 1°40W 196 C3
Oliva Argentina 32°0S 63°38W 334 C3
Oliva Spain 38°58N 0°9W 197 G4
Oliva, Punta del Spain 43°37N 5°28W 194 B5
Oliva de la Frontera Spain 38°17N 6°54W 195 G4
Olivais Portugal 38°45N 9°7W 126 A2
Olivar de los Padres
Mexico 19°21N 99°14W 128 B1
Olivar del Conde Mexico 19°22N 99°12W 128 B1
Olivares, Cerro los
Argentina 30°18S 69°55W 334 C2
Olivares de Júcar Spain 39°46N 2°20W 196 F2
Olive Branch U.S.A. 34°57N 89°49W 315 D10
Olive Hill U.S.A. 38°18N 83°13W 311 F13
Olive Park Chicago, U.S.A. 119 b3
Olivehurst U.S.A. 39°6N 121°34W 306 F5
Oliveira Brazil 20°39S 44°50W 333 F3
Oliveira de Azeméis
Portugal 40°49N 8°29W 194 E2
Oliveira do Douro Portugal 41°5N 8°2W 194 D2
Oliveira dos Brejinhos
Brazil 12°19S 42°54W 333 D3
Olivenza Spain 38°41N 7°9W 195 G3
Oliver Canada 49°13N 119°37W 296 D5
Oliver L. Canada 56°56N 103°22W 297 B8
Olives, Mt. of West Bank 31°46N 35°15E 123 B2
Olivet Loiret, France 47°51N 1°55E 173 E8
Olivet Mich., U.S.A. 42°27N 84°56W 311 B12
Olivia, L. U.S.A. 28°31N 81°31W 133 A1
Olivine Ra. N.Z. 44°15S 168°30E 285 E3
Olivos Argentina 34°30S 58°28W 117 B2
Olkhovka Russia 49°48N 44°32E 190 F7
Olkusz Poland 50°18N 19°33E 185 H6
Ollachea Peru 13°49S 70°29W 330 C3
Ollagüe Chile 21°15S 68°10W 334 A2
Ollombo Congo 1°18S 15°53E 264 C3
Olloua Congo 0°54S 14°34E 264 C2
Olmaliq Uzbekistan 40°50N 69°35E 217 D7
Olmedo Spain 41°20N 4°43W 194 D6
Olmeto France 41°43N 8°55E 175 G12
Olmos Peru 5°59S 79°46W 330 B2
Olmütz = Olomouc
Czech Rep. 49°38N 17°12E 181 B10
Olney Ill., U.S.A. 38°44N 88°5W 311 F8
Olney Tex., U.S.A. 33°22N 98°45W 314 E5
Olofström Sweden 56°17N 14°32E 163 H8
Oloitokitok Kenya 2°56S 37°30E 268 C4
Ololi Congo 0°15S 14°36E 264 C2
Oloma Cameroon 3°29N 11°19E 263 E7
Olomane → Canada 50°14N 60°37W 299 B7
Olomouc Czech Rep. 49°38N 17°12E 181 B10
Olomoucký □ Czech Rep. 49°45N 17°5E 181 B10
Olona → Italy 45°29N 9°6E 129 B1
Olonets Russia 61°0N 32°54E 188 B7
Olongapo Phil. 14°50N 120°18E 232 D3
Olonne-sur-Mer France 46°32N 1°47W 174 B2
Oloron, Gave d' → France 43°33N 1°5W 174 E2
Oloron-Ste-Marie France 43°11N 0°38W 174 E3
Olosega Amer. Samoa 14°10S 169°37W 302 g
Olosenga = Swains I.
Amer. Samoa 11°11S 171°4W 289 J11
Olot Spain 42°11N 2°30E 196 C7
Olovo Bos.-H. 44°8N 18°35E 182 F3
Olovyannaya Russia 50°58N 115°35E 215 D12
Oloy → Russia 66°29N 159°29E 215 C16
Olsberg Germany 51°21N 8°31E 178 D4
Olshammar Sweden 58°45N 14°48E 163 F8
Olshanka Ukraine 48°16N 30°58E 189 H6
Olshany Ukraine 50°3N 35°53E 189 G8
Olsztyn Poland 53°48N 20°29E 184 E7
Olsztynek Poland 53°34N 20°19E 184 E7
Olt □ Romania 44°20N 24°30E 183 F9
Olt → Romania 43°43N 24°51E 183 G9
Oltedal Norway 58°49N 6°2E 164 F3
Olten Switz. 47°21N 7°53E 179 H3
Olteniţa Romania 44°7N 26°42E 183 F11
Olton U.S.A. 34°11N 102°8W 314 D3
Oltu Turkey 40°35N 41°58E 213 B9
Oluan Pi Taiwan 21°53N 120°51E 225 E2
Oluanpi Taiwan 21°54N 120°51E 225 E2
Olula del Río Spain 37°21N 2°18W 197 H2
Olur Turkey 40°49N 42°8E 213 B10
Olustee U.S.A. 30°12N 82°26W 316 E7
Olutanga Phil. 7°26N 122°54E 233 H4
Olutanga I. Phil. 7°22N 122°52E 233 H4
Olvega Spain 41°47N 2°0W 196 D2
Olvera Spain 36°55N 5°18W 195 J5
Olymbos Cyprus 35°21N 33°45E 207 E9
Olymbos Oros Greece 40°6N 22°23E 202 F6
Olympia Greece 37°39N 21°39E 204 D3
Olympia London, U.K. 125 c1
Olympia Wash., U.S.A. 47°3N 122°53W 306 D4
Olympia, L. U.S.A. 28°34N 81°31W 133 A1
Olympic △ U.S.A. 47°45N 123°43W 306 C3
Olympic Dam Australia 30°30S 136°55E 282 A2
Olympic Green China 39°59N 116°23E 114 B2
Olympic Mts. U.S.A. 47°55N 123°45W 306 C3
Olympic Stadium = Turner Field
U.S.A. 33°44N 84°23W 113 B2
Olympic Stadium Beijing,
China 39°59N 116°23E 114 B2
Olympic Stadium Helsinki,
Finland 60°11N 24°55E 121 B2
Olympique, Stade Canada 45°33N 73°33W 130 A2
Olympus Cyprus 34°56N 32°52E 207 F8
Olympus, Mt. = Olymbos Oros
Greece 40°6N 22°23E 202 F6
Olympus, Mt. = Uludağ
Turkey 40°4N 29°13E 203 F13
Olympus, Mt. U.S.A. 47°48N 123°43W 306 C3
Olyphant U.S.A. 41°27N 75°36W 313 E9
Olyutorskiy, Mys
Russia 59°55N 170°27E 215 D18
Om → Russia 54°59N 73°22E 217 B8
Om Hajer Eritrea 14°20N 36°41E 257 E4
Om Koi Thailand 17°48N 98°22E 236 D2
Ōma Japan 41°45N 141°5E 220 D10
Ōmachi Japan 36°30N 137°50E 223 A9
Omae-Zaki Japan 34°36N 138°14E 223 C10
Ōmagari Japan 39°27N 140°29E 220 E10
Omagh U.K. 54°36N 7°19W 166 B4
Omagh □ U.K. 54°35N 7°15W 166 B4
Omaha U.S.A. 41°17N 95°58W 308 E6
Omak U.S.A. 48°25N 119°31W 304 B4
Omalos Greece 35°19N 23°55E 207 E4
Omalur India 11°44N 78°4E 245 J4
Oman ■ Asia 23°0N 58°0E 249 B7
Oman, G. of Asia 24°30N 58°30E 247 E8
Omapere N.Z. 35°37S 173°25E 284 B2
Omar Combon Somali Rep. 3°10N 45°47E 267 D6
Omaruru Namibia 21°26S 16°0E 270 B2
Omaruru → Namibia 22°7S 14°15E 270 B1
Omate Peru 16°45S 71°0W 330 D3
Ombai, Selat Indonesia 8°30S 124°50E 231 F6
Omboué Gabon 1°35S 9°15E 264 C1
Ombrone → Italy 42°42N 11°5E 198 F8
Omchi Chad 21°22N 17°53E 259 D3
Omdurmân Sudan 15°40N 32°28E 257 D3
Ōme Japan 35°47N 139°15E 223 B11
Omega U.S.A. 31°21N 83°36W 316 D6
Omegna Italy 45°53N 8°24E 198 C5
Omemee Canada 44°18N 78°33W 312 B6
Omeo Australia 37°6S 147°36E 283 D7
Omeonga
Dem. Rep. of the Congo 3°40S 24°22E 264 C4
Ometepe, I. de Nic. 11°32N 85°35W 320 D2
Ometepec Mexico 16°41N 98°25W 319 D5
Ōmi-Shima Ehime, Japan 34°15N 133°0E 222 C5
Ōmi-Shima Yamaguchi,
Japan 34°25N 131°9E 222 C3
Omihachiman Japan 35°7N 136°3E 223 B8
Omin Micronesia 9°36N 138°9E 287 R16
Ominato Japan 41°17N 141°10E 220 D10
Omineca → Canada 56°3N 124°16W 296 B4
Omineca Mts. Canada 56°30N 125°30W 296 B3
Omiš Croatia 43°28N 16°40E 199 E13
Omišalj Croatia 45°13N 14°32E 199 C11
Omitara Namibia 22°16S 18°2E 270 B2
Ōmiya = Saitama Japan 35°54N 139°38E 223 B11
Ommaney, C. U.S.A. 56°10N 134°40W 303 H14
Omme Å → Denmark 55°56N 8°32E 163 J2
Ommen Neths. 52°31N 6°26E 170 B6
Ömnögovĭ □ Mongolia 43°15N 104°0E 226 C3
Omo → Ethiopia 6°25N 36°10E 257 F4
Omo △ Ethiopia 5°54N 35°55E 257 F4
Omo Valley Ethiopia 5°7N 36°0E 257 F4
Omodeo, L. Italy 40°8N 8°56E 200 B1
Omodhos Cyprus 34°51N 32°48E 207 F8
Omoï Congo 2°56S 13°13E 264 C2
Omoko Nigeria 5°19N 6°40E 263 D6
Omolon → Russia 68°42N 158°36E 215 C16
Omona Solomon Is. 7°30S 158°43E 287 L10
Omonia Square Athens, Greece 112 b1
Omono-Gawa → Japan 39°46N 140°3E 220 E10
Ōmori Japan 35°34N 139°43E 140 B3
Ompha Canada 45°0N 76°50W 313 B8
Omsk Russia 55°0N 73°12E 217 B8
Omsukchan Russia 62°32N 155°48E 215 C16
Ōmu Japan 44°34N 142°58E 220 B11
Omul, Vf. Romania 45°27N 25°29E 183 E10
Omulew → Poland 53°5N 21°33E 185 E8
Ōmura Japan 32°56N 129°57E 222 E1
Ōmura-Wan Japan 32°57N 129°52E 222 E1
Omuramba Omatako →
Namibia 17°45S 20°25E 270 A2
Omuramba Ovambo →
Namibia 18°45S 16°59E 270 A2
Omurtag Bulgaria 43°8N 26°26E 203 C10
Ōmuta Japan 33°5N 130°26E 222 D2
On-ma-thi Burma 22°17N 96°41E 241 D6
On-Take Japan 31°35N 130°39E 222 F2
Oña Spain 42°43N 3°25W 194 C7
Ona Fla., U.S.A. 27°29N 81°55W 317 H8
Ona Dikonde
Dem. Rep. of the Congo 3°51S 24°11E 264 C4
Onaga U.S.A. 39°29N 96°10W 308 F5
Onalaska U.S.A. 43°53N 91°14W 308 D8
Onancock U.S.A. 37°43N 75°45W 309 G16
Onang Indonesia 3°2S 118°49E 235 C5
Onangue, L. Gabon 0°57S 10°4E 264 C1
Onaping L. Canada 47°3N 81°30W 298 C3
Onarga U.S.A. 40°43N 88°1W 311 D8
Oñati Spain 43°3N 2°25W 196 B2
Onavas Mexico 28°31N 109°35W 318 B3
Onawa U.S.A. 42°2N 96°6W 308 D5
Oncócua Angola 16°30S 13°25E 265 F2
Onda Spain 39°55N 0°17W 196 F4
Ondangwa Namibia 17°57S 16°4E 270 A2
Ondarroa Spain 43°19N 2°25W 196 B2
Ondas → Brazil 12°8S 44°55W 333 D3
Ondava → Slovak Rep. 48°27N 21°48E 181 C14
Ondjiva Angola 16°48S 15°50E 265 F3
Ondo Japan 34°11N 132°32E 222 C4
Ondo Nigeria 7°4N 4°47E 263 D5
Ondo □ Nigeria 6°45N 5°0E 263 D6
Öndörhaan Mongolia 47°19N 110°39E 219 B11
Öndverðarnes Iceland 64°52N 24°0W 155 C2
One and a Half Degree Channel
Maldives 1°30N 73°20E 272 d
One Arm Point Australia 16°26S 123°3E 278 C3
One Arm Point ◎
Australia 16°31S 122°53E 278 C3
One Tree Australia 34°11S 144°43E 281 E3
Oneata Fiji 18°26S 178°25W 287 B3
Oneco U.S.A. 27°25N 82°31W 317 H7
Onega Russia 64°0N 38°10E 186 B6
Onega → Russia 63°58N 38°2E 186 B6
Onega, G. of = Onezhskaya Guba
Russia 64°24N 36°38E 186 B6
Onega, L. = Onezhskoye Ozero
Russia 61°44N 35°22E 188 B8
Onehunga N.Z. 36°55S 174°48E 284 C3
Oneida Ill., U.S.A. 41°4N 90°13W 310 C6
Oneida N.Y., U.S.A. 43°6N 75°39W 313 C9
Oneida L. U.S.A. 43°12N 75°54W 313 C9
O'Neill U.S.A. 42°27N 98°39W 308 D4
Onekotan, Ostrov
Russia 49°25N 154°45E 215 E16
Onema
Dem. Rep. of the Congo 4°35S 24°30E 265 C4
Oneonta U.S.A. 42°27N 75°4W 313 D9
Onerahi N.Z. 35°45S 174°22E 284 B3
Oneroa Cook Is. 21°15S 159°43W 289 h
Oneşti Romania 46°17N 26°47E 183 D11
Onezhskaya Guba Russia 64°24N 36°38E 186 B6
Onezhskoye Ozero Russia 61°44N 35°22E 188 B8
Ongarue N.Z. 38°42S 175°19E 284 E4
Ongea Levu = Ogea Levu
Fiji 19°8S 178°24W 287 B3
Ongers → S. Africa 31°4S 23°13E 270 D3
Ongerup Australia 33°58S 118°28E 279 F2
Ongi Mongolia 45°27N 103°54E 226 B2
Ongjin N. Korea 37°56N 125°21E 224 D2
Ongkharak Thailand 14°8N 101°1E 236 E3
Ongniud Qi China 43°0N 118°38E 227 C10
Ongoka
Dem. Rep. of the Congo 1°20S 26°0E 268 C2
Ongole India 15°33N 80°2E 245 G5
Ongon = Havirga
Mongolia 45°41N 113°5E 226 B7
Ongouendjo Gabon 1°23S 9°5E 264 C1
Onguojou Comoros Is. 12°18S 44°30E 272 a
Ongtüstik Qazaqstan □
Kazakhstan 43°0N 68°0E 217 D7
Oni Georgia 42°33N 43°26E 191 J6
Onida U.S.A. 44°42N 100°4W 308 C3
Onilahy → Madag. 23°34S 43°45E 272 C1
Onima Bonaire 12°15N 68°19W 322 h
Onisigun Nigeria 6°35N 3°24E 124 A2
Onitsha Nigeria 6°6N 6°42E 263 D6
Onna Japan 26°29N 127°51E 288 a
Ono Fiji 18°55S 178°29E 287 B2
Ono Fukui, Japan 35°59N 136°29E 223 B8
Ono Hyōgo, Japan 34°51N 134°56E 222 C6
Onoda Japan 33°59N 131°11E 222 C3
Onohara Japan 34°5N 133°40E 222 C5
Onoke, L. N.Z. 41°22S 175°8E 284 H4
Onomichi Japan 34°25N 133°12E 222 C5
Onotoa Kiribati 1°52S 175°34E 277 A14
Ons, I. de Spain 42°23N 8°55W 194 C2
Onsala Sweden 57°26N 12°0E 163 G6
Onslow Australia 21°40S 115°12E 278 D2
Onslow B. U.S.A. 34°20N 77°15W 315 D16
Ontake-San Japan 35°53N 137°29E 223 B9
Ontar Vanuatu 14°17S 167°27E 287 D5
Ontario Calif., U.S.A. 34°4N 117°39W 307 L9
Ontario Oreg., U.S.A. 44°2N 116°58W 304 D5
Ontario □ Canada 48°0N 83°0W 298 B2
Ontario, L. N. Amer. 43°20N 78°0W 312 C7
Ontario Science Centre
Canada 43°43N 79°20W 141 A2
Ontinyent Spain 38°50N 0°35W 197 G4
Ontonagon U.S.A. 46°52N 89°19W 308 B9
Ontong Java Plateau
Pac. Oc. 1°0N 157°0E 277 A10
Ontur Spain 38°38N 1°29W 197 G3
Onverwacht Suriname 5°35N 55°11W 329 B6
Onyx U.S.A. 35°41N 118°14W 307 K8
Oodaaq Greenland 83°40N 30°40W 154 A8
Oodnadatta Australia 27°33S 135°30E 281 D2
Oodweyne Somali Rep. 9°25N 45°4E 267 C6
'Ō'ōkala U.S.A. 20°1N 155°17W 302 C6
Ōokayama Japan 35°36N 139°40E 140 B3
Ooku = Ōma Japan 41°45N 141°5E 220 D10
Ooldea Australia 30°27S 131°50E 279 F5
Oombulgurri Australia 15°15S 127°45E 278 C4
Oombulgurri ◎ Australia 15°10S 127°50E 278 C4
Oorindi Australia 20°40S 141°1E 280 C3
Oost-Vlaanderen □ Belgium 51°5N 3°50E 170 C3
Oostende Belgium 51°15N 2°54E 170 C2
Oosterhout Neths. 51°39N 4°47E 170 C4
Oosterschelde → Neths. 51°33N 4°0E 170 C4
Oosterwolde Neths. 53°0N 6°17E 170 B6
Oostpunt Curaçao 12°2N 68°44W 322 g
Oostzaan Tuindorp Neths. 52°25N 4°54E 112 A2
Ootacamund = Udagamandalam
India 11°30N 76°44E 245 J3
Ootha Australia 33°6S 147°29E 283 B7
Ootsa L. Canada 53°50N 126°2W 296 C3
Ooty = Udagamandalam
India 11°30N 76°44E 245 J3
Op Luang △ Thailand 18°12N 98°32E 236 C2
Opa-Locka U.S.A. 25°54N 80°15W 128 A1
Opa-Locka ✕ (OPF)
U.S.A. 25°54N 80°16W 128 A1
Opacz Poland 52°10N 20°53E 142 B1
Opaka Bulgaria 43°28N 26°10E 203 C10
Opala Dem. Rep. of the Congo 0°40S 24°20E 264 C4
Opalenica Poland 52°18N 16°24E 185 F3
Opan Bulgaria 42°13N 25°41E 203 D9
Opanake Sri Lanka 6°35N 80°40E 245 L5
Opapa N.Z. 39°47S 176°42E 284 F5
Opasatika Canada 49°30N 82°50W 298 C3
Opasquia △ Canada 53°33N 93°5W 298 B1
Opatija Croatia 45°21N 14°17E 199 C11
Opatów Poland 50°50N 21°27E 185 H8
Opava Czech Rep. 49°57N 17°58E 181 B10
Opelika U.S.A. 32°39N 85°23W 316 C4
Opelousas U.S.A. 30°32N 92°5W 314 F8
Opémisca, L. Canada 49°56N 74°52W 298 C5
Opheim U.S.A. 48°51N 106°24W 304 B10
Ophir U.S.A. 63°10N 156°31W 303 E8
Ophirton S. Africa 26°13S 28°1E 123 B2
Ophthalmia Ra.
Australia 23°15S 119°30E 278 D2
Opi Nigeria 6°36N 7°28E 263 D6
Opihikao U.S.A. 19°26N 154°53W 302 D7
Opinaca → Canada 52°15N 78°2W 298 B4
Opinaca, Rés. Canada 52°39N 76°20W 298 B4
Opinnagau → Canada 54°12N 82°25W 298 B3
Opiscotéo, L. Canada 53°10N 68°10W 299 B6
Opobo Nigeria 4°35N 7°34E 263 E6
Opochka Russia 56°42N 28°45E 188 D5
Opoczno Poland 51°22N 20°18E 185 G7
Opol Phil. 8°31N 124°34E 233 G5
Opole Poland 50°42N 17°58E 185 H4
Opole Lubelskie Poland 51°9N 21°58E 185 G8
Opolskie □ Poland 50°30N 18°0E 185 H5
Opon = Lapu-Lapu Phil. 10°20N 123°55E 233 F4
Opononо L. Namibia 18°8S 15°45E 270 A2
Opornyy Kazakhstan 46°11N 54°25E 216 C4
Oporto = Porto Portugal 41°8N 8°40W 194 D2
Opotiki N.Z. 38°1S 177°19E 284 E6
Opp U.S.A. 31°17N 86°16W 316 D3
Oppdal Norway 62°35N 9°41E 164 B6
Oppegård Norway 59°45N 10°49E 133 B3
Oppeln = Opole Poland 50°42N 17°58E 185 H4
Oppem Belgium 50°56N 4°18E 116 A1
Óppido Mamertina Italy 38°16N 15°59E 201 D8
Oppland □ Norway 61°15N 9°40E 164 C6
Opportunity U.S.A. 47°39N 117°15W 304 C5
Oppsal Norway 59°53N 10°50E 133 A4
Oprişor Romania 44°17N 23°5E 182 F8
Oprtalj Croatia 45°23N 13°50E 199 C10
Opua N.Z. 35°19S 174°9E 284 B3
Opunake N.Z. 39°26S 173°52E 284 F2
Opuwo Namibia 18°3S 13°45E 270 A1
Opuzen Croatia 43°1N 17°34E 199 E14
Oquawka U.S.A. 40°56N 90°57W 310 D6
Or → Kazakhstan 51°11N 58°32E 216 B5
Ora Cyprus 34°51N 33°12E 207 F9
Ora Israel 31°45N 35°9E 123 B1
Oracabessa Jamaica 18°24N 76°57W 320 a
Oracle U.S.A. 32°37N 110°46W 305 K8
Oracuzar Peru 4°42S 78°6W 328 D2
Oradea Romania 47°2N 21°58E 182 C6
Oradell U.S.A. 40°57N 74°2W 132 A1
Oradell Res. U.S.A. 40°57N 74°1W 132 A1
Öræfajökull Iceland 64°2N 16°39W 155 C10
Orahovac Kosovo 42°24N 20°40E 202 D4
Orahovica Croatia 45°35N 17°52E 182 E2
Orai India 25°58N 79°30E 243 G8
Oraison France 43°55N 5°55E 175 E9
Oral = Zhayyq →
Kazakhstan 47°0N 51°48E 187 E9
Oral Kazakhstan 51°20N 51°20E 190 E10
Oran Algeria 35°45N 0°39W 261 A4
Oran □ Algeria 35°0N 0°45W 261 B4
Orange N.S.W., Australia 33°15S 149°7E 283 B8
Orange Vaucluse, France 44°8N 4°47E 175 D8
Orange Calif., U.S.A. 33°47N 117°51W 307 M9
Orange Mass., U.S.A. 42°35N 72°19W 313 D12
Orange Tex., U.S.A. 30°6N 93°44W 314 F8
Orange Va., U.S.A. 38°15N 78°7W 309 F14
Orange → S. Africa 28°41S 16°28E 270 C2

Orange, C. Brazil 4°20N 51°30W 329 C7
Orange Bowl Stadium U.S.A. 25°46N 80°14W 128 B2
Orange City U.S.A. 28°57N 81°18W 317 G8
Orange Cove U.S.A. 36°38N 119°19W 306 J7
Orange Free State = Free State □ S. Africa 28°30S 27°0E 270 C4
Orange Grove U.S.A. 27°58N 97°56W 314 H6
Orange Hill Barbados 13°12N 59°36W 323 r
Orange Hill Jamaica 18°16N 77°59W 320 a
Orange Hill St. Vincent 13°19N 61°7W 323 n
Orange L. U.S.A. 29°25N 82°13W 317 F7
Orange Park U.S.A. 30°10N 81°42W 316 E8
Orange River Colony = Free State □ S. Africa 28°30S 27°0E 270 C4
Orange Walk Belize 18°6N 88°33W 319 D7
Orangeburg U.S.A. 33°30N 80°52W 316 B9
Orangeville Ont., Canada 43°55N 80°5W 312 C4
Orangeville Ill., U.S.A. 42°28N 89°39W 310 B7
Orangi Pakistan 24°54N 67°0E 123 A2
Orango Guinea-Biss. 11°5N 16°0W 262 C1
Orani Phil. 14°49N 120°32E 232 D3
Oranienburg Germany 52°45N 13°14E 178 C9
Oranje = Orange → S. Africa 28°41S 16°28E 270 C2
Oranjemund Namibia 28°38S 16°29E 270 C2
Oranjerivier S. Africa 29°40S 24°12E 270 C3
Oranjestad Aruba 12°32N 70°2W 322 f
Oranjestad St. Eustatius 17°28N 62°59W 322 a
Orap Vanuatu 15°58S 167°20E 287 E5
Oras Phil. 12°9N 125°28E 232 E5
Orašje Bos.-H. 45°1N 18°42E 182 E3
Orăştie Romania 45°50N 23°10E 183 E8
Orava → Slovak Rep. 49°9N 19°8E 181 B12
Orava, Vodna nádriž Slovak Rep. 49°25N 19°35E 181 B12
Oravița Romania 45°2N 21°43E 182 E6
Orawia N.Z. 46°1S 167°50E 285 G2
Orb → France 43°15N 3°18E 174 E7
Orba → Italy 44°53N 8°37E 198 D5
Ørbæk Denmark 55°17N 10°39E 163 J4
Orbe Switz. 46°43N 6°32E 179 J2
Orbec France 49°1N 0°23E 172 C7
Orbetello Italy 42°27N 11°13E 199 F8
Órbigo → Spain 42°5N 5°42W 194 C5
Orbisonia U.S.A. 40°15N 77°54W 312 F7
Orbost Australia 37°40S 148°29E 283 D8
Örbyhus Sweden 60°15N 17°43E 162 D11
Orcadas Antarctica 60°44S 44°37W 151 C18
Orcas I. U.S.A. 48°42N 122°56W 306 B4
Orce Spain 37°44N 2°28W 197 H2
Orce → Spain 37°44N 2°28W 197 H2
Orchard City U.S.A. 38°50N 107°58W 304 G10
Orchard Homes U.S.A. 46°55N 114°4W 304 C6
Orchard Road Singapore 138 a1
Orchid I. = Lan Yü Taiwan 22°4N 121°25E 225 D3
Orchies France 50°28N 3°14E 173 B10
Orchila, I. Venezuela 11°48N 66°10W 321 D6
Orchilla, Pta. Canary Is. 27°42N 18°10W 153 e1
Orcia → Italy 42°58N 11°21E 199 F8
Orco → Italy 45°10N 7°52E 198 C4
Orcopampa Peru 15°20S 72°23W 330 D3
Orcutt U.S.A. 34°52N 120°27W 307 L6
Ord U.S.A. 41°36N 98°56W 308 E4
Ord → Australia 15°33S 128°15E 278 C4
Ord, Mt. Australia 17°20S 125°34E 278 C4
Ord Mts. U.S.A. 34°39N 116°45W 307 L10
Ordenes = Ordes Spain 43°5N 8°29W 194 B2
Orderville U.S.A. 37°17N 112°38W 305 H7
Ordes Spain 43°5N 8°29W 194 B2
Ordesa y Monte Perido △ Spain 42°40N 0°10W 196 C4
Ording = St-Peter-Ording Germany 54°20N 8°36E 178 A4
Ordos = Mu Us Shamo China 39°0N 109°0E 226 E5
Ordrup Denmark 55°45N 12°34E 118 A3
Ordu Turkey 40°55N 37°53E 212 B7
Ordu □ Turkey 41°0N 37°50E 212 B7
Ordubad Azerbaijan 38°54N 46°1E 213 C12
Orduña Álava, Spain 42°58N 2°58W 196 C2
Orduña Granada, Spain 37°20N 3°30W 195 H7
Ordway U.S.A. 38°13N 103°46W 304 G12
Ordzhonikidze = Denisovka Kazakhstan 52°27N 61°39E 216 B6
Ordzhonikidze = Vladikavkaz Russia 43°0N 44°35E 191 J7
Ordzhonikidze = Yenakiyeve Ukraine 48°15N 38°15E 189 H10
Ordzhonikidze Ukraine 47°39N 34°3E 189 J8
Ore Dem. Rep. of the Congo 3°17N 29°30E 268 B2
Ore Mts. = Erzgebirge Germany 50°27N 12°55E 178 E8
Orealla Guyana 5°15N 57°23W 329 B6
Orebić Croatia 43°0N 17°11E 199 F14
Örebro Sweden 59°20N 15°18E 162 E9
Örebro län □ Sweden 59°27N 15°0E 162 E8
Orecchiella ⌓ Italy 44°16N 10°22E 198 D7
Orech Czech Rep. 50°1N 14°17E 135 B1
Oregon Ill., U.S.A. 42°1N 89°20W 310 B7
Oregon Ohio, U.S.A. 41°38N 83°25W 311 C13
Oregon Wis., U.S.A. 42°56N 89°23W 310 B7
Oregon □ U.S.A. 44°0N 121°0W 304 E3
Oregon City U.S.A. 45°21N 122°36W 306 E4
Oregon Dunes ⌓ U.S.A. 43°40N 124°10W 304 E1
Öregrund Sweden 60°21N 18°30E 162 D12
Öregrundsgrepen Sweden 60°25N 18°15E 162 D12
Oregun Nigeria 6°35N 3°22E 124 A2
Orekhov = Orikhiv Ukraine 47°30N 35°48E 189 J8
Orekhovo-Zuyevo Russia 55°50N 38°55E 188 E10
Orel Russia 52°57N 36°3E 189 F9
Orel □ Russia 52°30N 36°40E 189 F9
Orellana □ Ecuador 0°45S 76°25W 328 D2
Orellana, Canal de Spain 39°2N 6°0W 195 F5
Orellana, Embalse de Spain 39°5N 5°10W 195 F5
Orellana la Vieja Spain 39°1N 5°32W 195 F5
Orem U.S.A. 40°19N 111°42W 304 F8
Ören Turkey 37°3N 27°57E 205 D9
Orenburg Russia 51°45N 55°6E 186 D10
Örencik Turkey 39°16N 29°33E 205 B11
Orense = Ourense Spain 42°19N 7°55W 194 C3
Orepuki N.Z. 46°19S 167°46E 285 G2
Ørestad Denmark 55°38N 12°35E 118 B3
Orestes Pereyra Mexico 26°30N 105°39W 318 B3
Orestiada Greece 41°30N 26°33E 203 E10
Øresund Europe 55°45N 12°40E 163 J6
Oretana, Cordillera = Toledo, Montes de Spain 39°33N 4°20W 195 F6
Oreti → N.Z. 46°28S 168°14E 285 G3
Orfanos Kolpos Greece 40°33N 24°0E 202 F7
Orford Ness U.K. 52°5N 1°35E 169 E9
Organ Pipe Cactus ⌓ U.S.A. 32°0N 112°52W 305 K7
Organos, Pta. de los Canary Is. 28°12N 17°17W 153 e1
Organyà Spain 42°13N 1°20E 196 C6
Orgaz Spain 39°39N 3°53W 195 F7
Ørgenvika Norway 60°17N 9°42E 164 D6
Orgeyev = Orhei Moldova 47°24N 28°50E 183 C13
Orgūn Afghan. 32°55N 69°12E 240 B3
Orhaneli Turkey 39°54N 28°59E 203 G12
Orhaneli → Turkey 39°50N 28°55E 203 G12
Orhangazi Turkey 40°29N 29°18E 203 F13
Orhei Moldova 47°24N 28°50E 183 C13
Orhon Gol → Mongolia 50°21N 106°0E 218 A10
Ória Italy 40°30N 17°38E 201 B10
Orida Niger 21°20N 12°15E 261 D7
Orient Heights U.S.A. 42°23N 70°59W 116 A3
Oriental, Cordillera Bolivia 17°0S 66°0W 331 D4
Oriental, Cordillera Colombia 6°0N 73°0W 328 B3
Oriental, Grand Erg Algeria 30°0N 6°30E 261 C6
Orientale □ Dem. Rep. of the Congo 2°20N 26°0E 268 B2
Oriente Argentina 38°44S 60°37W 334 D3
Orihuela Spain 38°7N 0°55W 197 G4
Orihuela del Tremedal Spain 40°33N 1°39W 196 E3
Orikhiv Ukraine 47°30N 35°48E 189 J8
Orikum Albania 40°20N 19°26E 202 F3
Oril → Ukraine 48°40N 34°39E 189 H8
Orillia Canada 44°40N 79°24W 312 B5
Orinduik Guyana 4°40N 60°3W 329 C5
Orinoco → Venezuela 9°15N 61°30W 329 B5
Orinoco, Delta del Venezuela 9°0N 61°30W 329 B5
Orion Canada 49°27N 110°49W 297 D6
Orion Ala., U.S.A. 31°58N 86°0W 316 D4
Orion Ill., U.S.A. 41°21N 90°23W 310 C6
Oriskany U.S.A. 43°10N 75°20W 313 C9
Orissa □ India 20°0N 84°0E 244 E7
Orissaare Estonia 58°34N 23°5E 188 C2
Oristano Italy 39°54N 8°36E 200 C1
Oristano, G. di Italy 39°50N 8°29E 200 C1
Orituco → Venezuela 8°45N 67°27W 328 B4
Oriximina Brazil 1°45S 55°52W 329 D6
Orizaba Mexico 18°51N 97°6W 319 D5
Orizaba, Pico de Mexico 18°58N 97°15W 319 D5
Orizare Bulgaria 42°44N 27°39E 203 D11
Orizona Brazil 17°3S 48°18W 333 E2
Ørje Norway 59°29N 11°39E 164 E8
Orjen Bos.-H. 42°35N 18°34E 202 D2
Orjiva Spain 36°53N 3°24W 195 J7
Orkanger Norway 63°18N 9°52E 164 A6
Örkelljunga Sweden 56°17N 13°17E 163 H7
Örken Sweden 57°6N 15°1E 163 G9
Örkény Hungary 47°9N 19°26E 182 C4
Orkhaniye = Botevgrad Bulgaria 42°55N 23°47E 202 D7
Orkla → Norway 63°18N 9°51E 164 A6
Orkney S. Africa 26°58S 26°40E 270 C4
Orkney □ U.K. 59°2N 3°13W 167 B5
Orkney Is. U.K. 59°0N 3°0W 167 B6
Orland Calif., U.S.A. 39°45N 122°12W 306 F4
Orland Ind., U.S.A. 41°47N 85°12W 311 C11
Orland Park U.S.A. 41°38N 87°52W 311 C8
Orlando U.S.A. 28°32N 81°22W 133 A2
Orlando, C. d' Italy 38°10N 14°43E 201 D7
Orlando Dam S. Africa 26°15S 27°55E 123 B1
Orlando East S. Africa 26°14S 27°55E 123 B1
Orlando Executive ✈ (ORL) U.S.A. 28°32N 81°20W 133 A2
Orlando Int. ✈ (MCO) U.S.A. 28°26N 81°19W 133 B3
Orléanais France 48°0N 2°0E 173 E9
Orléans Loiret, France 47°54N 1°52E 173 E8
Orleans Ind., U.S.A. 38°40N 86°27W 311 F10
Orleans Vt., U.S.A. 44°49N 72°12W 313 B12
Orléans, Î. d' Canada 46°54N 70°58W 299 C5
Orléansville = Ech Chéliff Algeria 36°10N 1°20E 261 A5
Orlice → Czech Rep. 50°13N 15°50E 180 A8
Orlivka Ukraine 45°19N 28°27E 183 E13
Orlov = Khalturin Russia 58°40N 48°50E 186 C8
Orlov Slovak Rep. 49°17N 20°51E 181 B13
Orlov Gay Russia 50°56N 48°19E 190 E9
Orlová Czech Rep. 49°51N 18°26E 181 B11
Orlovat Serbia 45°14N 20°33E 182 E5
Orlovista U.S.A. 28°32N 81°27W 133 A2
Orlovo Russia 55°38N 37°22E 129 C2
Orly France 48°45N 2°23E 134 B3
Orly, Paris ✈ (ORY) France 48°44N 2°23E 134 B3
Ormara Pakistan 25°16N 64°33E 240 D2
Ormea Italy 44°9N 7°54E 198 D4
Ormesson-sur-Marne France 48°47N 2°32E 134 B4
Ormilia Greece 40°16N 23°39E 202 F7
Ormoc Phil. 11°0N 124°37E 233 F5
Ormond Vic., Australia 37°54S 145°1E 128 B2
Ormond N.Z. 38°33S 177°56E 284 E6
Ormond Beach U.S.A. 29°17N 81°3W 317 F8
Ormond-by-the-Sea U.S.A. 29°21N 81°4W 317 F8
Ormondville N.Z. 40°5S 176°19E 284 G5
Ormøya Norway 59°52N 10°45E 133 A3
Ormož Slovenia 46°25N 16°10E 199 B13
Ormskirk U.K. 53°35N 2°54W 168 D5
Ormstown Canada 45°8N 74°0W 313 A11
Ormtjernkampen △ Norway 61°12N 9°48E 164 C6
Ornans France 47°7N 6°10E 173 E13
Orne □ France 48°40N 0°5E 172 D7
Orne → France 49°18N 0°15W 172 C6
Orneta Poland 54°8N 20°9E 184 D7
Ornö Sweden 59°4N 18°24E 162 E12
Örnsköldsvik Sweden 63°17N 18°40E 162 A12
Oro N. Korea 40°1N 127°27E 224 B3
Oro → Mexico 25°35N 105°2W 318 B3
Oro Grande U.S.A. 34°36N 117°20W 307 L9
Oro Valley U.S.A. 32°26N 110°58W 305 K8
Orobie, Alpi Italy 46°7N 10°0E 198 B6
Orobie Bergamasche ⌓ Italy 46°0N 9°45E 198 C6
Orobie Valtellinesi ⌓ Italy 46°5N 9°45E 198 B6
Orocué Colombia 4°48N 71°20W 328 C3
Orodara Burkina Faso 11°0N 4°55W 262 C4
Orodo Nigeria 5°34N 7°4E 263 D6
Orofino U.S.A. 46°29N 116°15W 304 C5
Orohena, Mt. Tahiti 17°37S 149°28W 289 e
Orol Dengizi = Aral Sea Asia 44°30N 60°0E 216 C5
Oromiya □ Ethiopia 7°0N 40°0E 257 F5
Oromocto Canada 45°54N 66°29W 299 C6
Oron Nigeria 4°48N 8°14E 263 E6
Orona Kiribati 4°31S 172°11W 277 A16
Orongo Chile 27°11S 109°27W 330 b
Orono Ont., Canada 43°59N 78°37W 312 C6
Orono Maine, U.S.A. 44°53N 68°40W 309 C19
Oronsay U.K. 56°1N 6°15W 167 E2
Oropesa Spain 39°57N 5°10W 194 F5
Oropuche → Trin. & Tob. 10°36N 61°6W 323 t
Oropuche Lagoon Trin. & Tob. 10°14N 61°31W 323 t
Oroquieta Phil. 8°32N 123°44E 233 G4
Orós Brazil 6°15S 38°55W 332 C4
Orosei Italy 40°23N 9°42E 200 B2
Orosei, G. di Italy 40°15N 9°44E 200 B2
Orosháza Hungary 46°32N 20°42E 182 D5
Oroszlány Hungary 47°29N 18°19E 182 C3
Orote Pen. Guam 13°26N 144°38E 302 d
Orotukan Russia 62°16N 151°42E 215 C16
Oroville Calif., U.S.A. 39°31N 121°33W 306 F5
Oroville Wash., U.S.A. 48°56N 119°26W 304 B4
Oroville, L. U.S.A. 39°33N 121°29W 306 F5
Orpington U.K. 51°22N 0°6E 125 B4
Orrefors Sweden 56°50N 15°45E 163 H9
Orrick U.S.A. 39°13N 94°7W 310 E2
Orroroo Australia 32°43S 138°38E 282 B3
Orrviken Sweden 63°6N 14°26E 162 A8
Orrville U.S.A. 40°50N 81°46W 312 F3
Orsa Sweden 61°7N 14°37E 162 C8
Orsara di Púglia Italy 41°17N 15°16E 201 A8
Orsasjön Sweden 61°7N 14°37E 162 C8
Orsay, Musée d' Paris, France 134 b3
Orsha Belarus 54°30N 30°25E 188 E6
Örsjö Sweden 56°42N 15°45E 163 H9
Orsk Russia 51°12N 58°34E 216 B5
Orşova Romania 44°41N 22°25E 182 F7
Ørsta Norway 62°13N 6°8E 164 B3
Ørsted Denmark 56°30N 10°20E 163 H4
Örsundsbro Sweden 59°44N 17°18E 162 E11
Országos Levétár Budapest, Hungary 117 b1
Orta Turkey 40°38N 33°6E 212 B5
Orta, L. d' Italy 45°49N 8°24E 198 C5
Orta Nova Italy 41°19N 15°42E 201 A8
Ortaca Turkey 36°49N 28°45E 205 E10
Ortakent Turkey 37°5N 27°21E 205 D9
Ortaklar Turkey 37°53N 27°30E 205 D9
Ortaköy Çorum, Turkey 40°16N 35°15E 212 B6
Ortaköy İstanbul, Turkey 41°3N 29°1E 122 B2
Ortaköy Niğde, Turkey 38°44N 34°3E 212 C6
Orte Italy 42°27N 12°23E 199 F9
Ortegal, C. Spain 43°43N 7°52W 194 B3
Orteguaza → Colombia 0°43N 75°16W 328 C2
Ortelsburg = Szczytno Poland 53°33N 21°0E 184 E7
Orthez France 43°29N 0°48W 174 E3
Ortica Italy 45°28N 9°16E 129 B2
Ortigueira Spain 43°40N 7°50W 194 B3
Orting U.S.A. 47°6N 122°12W 306 C4
Ortisei Italy 46°34N 11°40E 199 B8
Ortles Italy 46°31N 10°33E 198 B7
Ortnevik Norway 61°6N 6°7E 164 C3
Ortoire → Trin. & Tob. 10°20N 61°0W 323 t
Ortón → Bolivia 10°50S 67°0W 330 C4
Ortona Italy 42°21N 14°24E 199 F11
Ortonville U.S.A. 45°19N 96°27W 308 C5
Oruba Nigeria 6°34N 3°24E 124 A2
Orukuizui Palau 7°10N 134°15E 288 c
Orūmīyeh Iran 37°40N 45°0E 213 D11
Orūmīyeh, Daryācheh-ye Iran 37°50N 45°30E 213 D11
Orune Italy 40°24N 9°22E 200 B2
Oruro Bolivia 18°0S 67°9W 330 D4
Oruro □ Bolivia 18°40S 67°30W 330 D4
Orust Sweden 58°10N 11°40E 163 F5
Oruzgān □ Afghan. 33°0N 66°0E 240 B2
Orvault France 47°17N 1°38W 172 E5
Orvieto Italy 42°43N 12°7E 199 F9
Orwell N.Y., U.S.A. 43°35N 75°50W 313 C9
Orwell Ohio, U.S.A. 41°32N 80°52W 312 E4
Orwell → U.K. 51°59N 1°18E 169 F9
Orwigsburg U.S.A. 40°38N 76°6W 313 F8
Oryakhovo Bulgaria 43°40N 23°57E 202 C7
Orynyn Ukraine 48°46N 26°24E 183 B11
Oryol = Orel Russia 52°57N 36°3E 189 F9
Orzinuovi Italy 45°24N 9°55E 198 C6
Orzyc → Poland 52°46N 21°14E 185 F8
Orzysz Poland 53°50N 21°58E 184 E8
Os Norway 62°30N 11°14E 164 B8
Osa Russia 57°17N 55°25E 186 C10
Osa → Poland 53°33N 18°46E 184 E5
Osa, Pen. de Costa Rica 8°0N 84°0W 320 E3
Osage U.S.A. 43°17N 92°49W 308 D7
Osage → U.S.A. 38°36N 91°57W 310 F5
Osage City U.S.A. 38°38N 95°50W 308 F6
Ōsaka Japan 34°42N 135°30E 133 B2
Ōsaka □ Japan 34°30N 135°30E 223 C7
Ōsaka Castle Japan 34°41N 135°30E 133 A2
Ōsaka Harbour Japan 34°38N 135°25E 133 B1
Ōsaka Itami Int. ✈ (ITM) Japan 34°46N 135°26E 133 A1
Ōsaka Kansai Int. ✈ (KIX) Japan 34°27N 135°12E 133 B2
Ōsaka-Wan Japan 34°30N 135°18E 223 C7
Osakarovka Kazakhstan 50°33N 72°34E 217 B8
Ōsaki Kagoshima, Japan 31°25N 131°2E 222 F3
Ōsaki Tōkyō, Japan 35°36N 139°42E 140 B3
Osan S. Korea 37°11N 127°4E 224 D3
Osasco Brazil 23°31S 46°46W 137 B1
Osawatomie U.S.A. 38°31N 94°57W 308 F6
Osborn Plateau Ind. Oc. 14°45S 87°0E 273 F7
Osborne U.S.A. 39°26N 98°42W 308 F4
Osby Sweden 56°23N 13°59E 163 H7
Osceola Ark., U.S.A. 35°42N 89°58W 315 D10
Osceola Iowa, U.S.A. 41°2N 93°46W 310 C3
Osceola Mo., U.S.A. 38°3N 93°42W 310 F3
Oschatz Germany 51°17N 13°6E 178 D9
Oschersleben Germany 52°2N 11°14E 178 C7
Óschiri Italy 40°43N 9°6E 200 B2
Oscoda U.S.A. 44°26N 83°20W 312 B1
Osdorf Germany 52°24N 13°20E 115 B3
Osdorp Neths. 52°22N 4°47E 112 A1
Osečina Serbia 44°23N 19°34E 202 B3
Ösel = Saaremaa Estonia 58°30N 22°30E 188 C2
Osensjøen Norway 61°13N 11°50E 164 C8
Osery Russia 54°52N 38°28E 188 E10
Osgood U.S.A. 39°8N 85°18W 311 E11
Osgoode Canada 45°8N 75°36W 313 A9
Osgoode Hall Toronto, Canada 141 b2
Osh Kyrgyzstan 40°37N 72°49E 217 D8
Osh □ Kyrgyzstan 40°0N 73°0E 217 E8
Oshawa Canada 43°50N 78°50W 312 C6
Oshigambo Namibia 17°45S 16°5E 270 A2
Oshika-Hantō Japan 38°20N 141°30E 220 E10
Oshivelo Namibia 18°37S 17°10E 270 A2
Oshkosh Nebr., U.S.A. 41°24N 102°21W 308 E2
Oshkosh Wis., U.S.A. 44°1N 88°33W 308 C9
Oshmyany = Ashmyany Belarus 54°26N 25°52E 177 A13
Oshnovīyeh Iran 37°2N 45°6E 213 D11
Oshodi Nigeria 6°33N 3°21E 124 A2
Oshogbo Nigeria 7°48N 4°37E 263 D5
Oshtorīnān Iran 34°1N 48°38E 213 E13
Oshwe Dem. Rep. of the Congo 3°25S 19°28E 264 C3
Osi Nigeria 8°8N 5°14E 263 D6
Osieczna Poland 51°55N 16°40E 185 G3
Osijek Croatia 45°34N 18°41E 182 E3
Ósilo Italy 40°45N 8°40E 200 B1
Ósimo Italy 43°28N 13°30E 199 E10
Osintorf Belarus 54°40N 30°39E 188 E6
Osipenko = Berdyansk Ukraine 46°45N 36°50E 189 J9
Osipovichi = Asipovichy Belarus 53°19N 28°33E 177 B15
Osiyan India 26°43N 72°55E 242 F5
Osizweni S. Africa 27°49S 30°7E 271 C5
Oskaloosa U.S.A. 41°18N 92°39W 310 C4
Oskarshamn Sweden 57°15N 16°27E 163 G10
Oskarström Sweden 56°48N 12°58E 163 H6
Oskélanéo Canada 48°5N 75°15W 298 C4
Öskemen Kazakhstan 50°0N 82°36E 217 C10
Oskol → Ukraine 49°6N 37°25E 189 H9
Osku Iran 37°54N 46°8E 213 D12
Oslo Norway 59°54N 10°43E 133 A3
Oslo □ Norway 59°54N 10°43E 164 D7
Oslo ✈ (OSL) Norway 60°11N 11°6E 133 A4
Oslob Phil. 9°31N 123°25E 233 G4
Oslofjorden Norway 59°20N 10°35E 164 E7
Osmanabad India 18°5N 76°10E 244 E3
Osmancık Turkey 40°58N 34°47E 212 B6
Osmaniye Turkey 37°5N 36°10E 250 A7
Osmanlı Turkey 41°35N 26°51E 203 E10
Osmannagar India 18°32N 79°20E 244 E4
Ösmo Sweden 58°58N 17°55E 162 F11
Osnabrück Germany 52°17N 8°3E 178 C4
Ośno Lubuskie Poland 52°28N 14°51E 185 F1
Osoblaha Czech Rep. 50°17N 17°44E 181 A10
Osogovska Planina Macedonia 42°10N 22°30E 202 D6
Ōsone Japan 35°31N 139°37E 140 B2
Osor Italy 44°42N 14°24E 199 D11
Osório Brazil 29°53S 50°17W 335 B5
Osório da Fonseca Brazil 3°52S 58°14W 329 D6
Osorno Chile 40°25S 73°0W 336 B2
Osorno Spain 42°24N 4°22W 194 C6
Osorno □ Chile 40°34S 73°9W 336 B2
Osorno, Vol. Chile 41°0S 72°30W 336 B2
Osorun Nigeria 6°33N 3°29E 124 A2
Osoyoos Canada 49°0N 119°30W 296 D5
Osøyro Norway 60°9N 5°30E 164 D2
Óspakseyri Iceland 65°27N 21°26W 155 B5
Ospiate Italy 45°32N 9°6E 129 A1
Ospika → Canada 56°20N 124°0W 296 B4
Osprey U.S.A. 27°12N 82°29W 317 H7
Osprey Reef Australia 13°52S 146°36E 280 A4
Oss Neths. 51°46N 5°32E 170 C5
Ossa, Mt. Australia 41°52S 146°3E 281 G4
Ossa, Oros Greece 39°47N 22°42E 204 B4
Ossa de Montiel Spain 38°58N 2°45W 197 G2
Ossabaw I. U.S.A. 31°50N 81°5W 316 D8
Ossabaw Sd. U.S.A. 31°50N 81°6W 316 D8
Osse → Lot-et-Garonne, France 44°7N 0°17E 174 D4
Osse → Nigeria 6°10N 5°20E 263 D6
Ossersee = Zarasai Lithuania 55°40N 26°20E 188 E4
Ossi Italy 40°40N 8°35E 200 B1
Ossining U.S.A. 41°10N 73°55W 313 E11
Ossipee U.S.A. 43°41N 71°7W 313 C13
Ossokmanuan L. Canada 53°25N 65°0W 299 B7
Ossora Russia 59°20N 163°13E 215 D17
Ostankino Russia 55°49N 37°37E 129 B3
Ostashkov Russia 57°4N 33°2E 188 D7
Östavall Sweden 62°26N 15°29E 162 B9
Østby Norway 61°15N 12°33E 164 C9
Oste → Germany 53°49N 9°2E 178 B5
Ostenburg = Pułtusk Poland 52°43N 21°6E 185 F8
Ostend = Oostende Belgium 51°15N 2°54E 170 C2
Ostend N.Z. 36°48S 175°2E 284 C4
Oster Ukraine 50°57N 30°53E 177 C16
Österbotten = Pohjanmaa Finland 62°58N 22°50E 160 E20
Østerbro Copenhagen, Denmark 118 a1
Osterburg Sachsen-Anhalt, Germany 52°47N 11°45E 178 C7
Osterburg Pa., U.S.A. 40°16N 78°31W 312 F6
Osterburken Germany 49°25N 9°26E 179 F5
Österbybruk Sweden 60°13N 17°55E 162 D11
Österbymo Sweden 57°49N 15°15E 163 G9
Österdalälven → Sweden 60°30N 15°7E 162 C7
Østerdalen Norway 61°40N 10°50E 162 C4
Österfärnebo Sweden 60°19N 16°48E 162 D10
Österforse Sweden 63°9N 17°3E 162 A11
Östergötlands län □ Sweden 58°35N 15°45E 163 F9
Osterholz-Scharmbeck Germany 53°13N 8°47E 178 B4
Østerild Denmark 57°2N 8°51E 163 G2
Osterley U.K. 51°28N 0°21W 125 B1
Osterley Park U.K. 51°29N 0°21W 125 B1
Östermalm Stockholm, Sweden 139 a3
Östermyra = Seinäjoki Finland 62°40N 22°51E 160 E20
Osterode Germany 51°43N 10°15E 178 D6
Osterode in Ostpreussen = Ostróda Poland 53°42N 19°58E 184 E6
Österreich = Austria ■ Europe 47°0N 14°0E 180 E7
Österreich ober der Enns = Oberösterreich □ Austria 48°10N 14°0E 180 C7
Österskär Sweden 59°26N 18°16E 139 A3
Östersund Sweden 63°10N 14°38E 162 A8
Östervåla Sweden 60°11N 17°11E 162 D11
Østfold □ Norway 59°25N 11°25E 164 E8
Ostfriesische Inseln Germany 53°42N 7°0E 178 B3
Ostfriesland Germany 53°20N 7°30E 178 B3
Østgrønland = Tunu □ Greenland 75°0N 30°0W 154 C7
Östhammar Sweden 60°16N 18°22E 162 D12
Óstia, Lido di Italy 41°43N 12°17E 199 G9
Óstia Malpasso Italy 41°47N 12°26E 136 C1
Ostiense Italy 41°51N 12°29E 136 B1
Ostíglia Italy 45°4N 11°8E 199 C8
Östmark Sweden 60°17N 12°45E 162 D6
Østmarkkapellet Norway 59°52N 10°51E 133 A4
Østøya Norway 59°52N 10°34E 133 A2
Östra Husby Sweden 58°35N 16°33E 163 F10
Ostrava Czech Rep. 49°51N 18°18E 181 B11
Ostravský □ Czech Rep. 49°55N 17°58E 181 B10
Østre Aker Norway 59°54N 10°49E 133 A3
Ostróda Poland 53°42N 19°58E 184 E6
Ostrogozhsk Russia 50°55N 39°7E 189 G10
Ostroh Ukraine 50°20N 26°30E 177 C14
Ostrołęka Poland 53°4N 21°32E 185 E8
Ostrov Bulgaria 43°40N 24°9E 203 C8
Ostrov Czech Rep. 50°18N 12°57E 180 A5
Ostrov Romania 44°6N 27°24E 183 F12
Ostrov Russia 57°25N 28°20E 188 D5
Ostrów Lubelski Poland 51°29N 22°51E 185 G9
Ostrów Mazowiecka Poland 52°50N 21°51E 185 F8
Ostrów Wielkopolski Poland 51°36N 17°44E 185 G4
Ostrowiec-Świętokrzyski Poland 50°55N 21°22E 185 H8
Ostrowo = Ostrów Wielkopolski Poland 51°36N 17°44E 185 G4
Ostrožac Bos.-H. 43°43N 17°49E 182 G2
Ostrzeszów Poland 51°25N 17°52E 185 G4
Ostseebad Kühlungsborn Germany 54°8N 11°44E 178 A7
Osttirol □ Austria 46°50N 12°30E 180 E5
Ostuni Italy 40°44N 17°35E 201 B10
Ostyako-Vogulsk = Khanty-Mansiysk Russia 61°0N 69°0E 214 C7
Osum → Albania 40°40N 20°10E 202 F4
Osŭm → Bulgaria 43°40N 24°50E 203 C8
Ōsumi-Hantō Japan 31°20N 130°55E 222 F2
Ōsumi-Kaikyō Japan 30°55N 131°0E 221 J5
Ōsumi-Shotō Japan 30°30N 130°0E 221 J5
Osun □ Nigeria 7°30N 4°30E 263 D5
Osuna Spain 37°14N 5°8W 195 H5
Oswegatchie → U.S.A. 44°42N 75°30W 313 B9
Oswego U.S.A. 43°27N 76°31W 313 C8
Oswego → U.S.A. 43°27N 76°30W 313 C8
Oswestry U.K. 52°52N 3°3W 168 E4
Oświęcim Poland 50°2N 19°11E 185 H6
Ōta Fukui, Japan 35°57N 136°3E 223 B8
Ōta Gumma, Japan 36°18N 139°22E 223 A11
Ōta Tōkyō, Japan 35°34N 139°41E 140 B3
Ōta-Gawa → Japan 34°21N 132°18E 222 C4
Otaci Moldova 48°27N 27°47E 183 B12
Otago □ N.Z. 45°15S 170°0E 285 E4
Otago Harbour N.Z. 45°47S 170°42E 285 F5
Otago Pen. N.Z. 45°48S 170°39E 285 F5
Otaheite B. Trin. & Tob. 10°15N 61°30W 323 t
Otahuhu N.Z. 36°56S 174°51E 284 C3
Ōtake Japan 34°12N 132°13E 222 C4
Ōtaki Japan 35°17N 140°15E 223 B12
Otaki N.Z. 40°45S 175°10E 284 G4
Otane N.Z. 39°54S 176°39E 284 F5
Otaniemi Finland 60°11N 24°49E 121 B1
Otari Open Air Museum N.Z. 41°16S 174°46E 143 B1
Otaru Japan 43°10N 141°0E 220 C10
Otaru-Wan = Ishikari-Wan Japan 43°25N 141°1E 220 C10
Otautau N.Z. 46°9S 168°1E 285 G3
Otava → Czech Rep. 49°26N 14°12E 180 B7
Otavalo Ecuador 0°13N 78°20W 328 C2
Otavi Namibia 19°40S 17°24E 270 A2
Otawara Japan 36°50N 140°5E 221 F10
Otchinjau Angola 16°30S 13°56E 265 F2
Otego U.S.A. 42°23N 75°10W 313 D9
Oteiza = Marihatag Phil. 8°48N 126°18E 233 G6
Otelec Romania 45°36N 20°50E 182 E5
Otelnuk, L. Canada 56°9N 68°12W 299 A6
Oțelu Roșu Romania 45°32N 22°22E 182 E7
Otero de Rey = Outeiro de Rei Spain 43°6N 7°36W 194 B3
Othello U.S.A. 46°50N 119°10W 304 C4
Othoni Greece 39°52N 19°22E 206 B9
Othris, Oros Greece 39°2N 22°37E 204 B4
Oti → Africa 7°48N 0°8E 263 D5
Oti ⌓ Togo 10°40N 0°35E 263 C5
Otira N.Z. 42°49S 171°35E 285 C6
Otira Gorge N.Z. 42°53S 171°33E 285 C6
Otish, Mts. Canada 52°22N 70°30W 299 B5
Otjiwarongo Namibia 20°30S 16°33E 270 B2
Otmuchów Poland 50°28N 17°10E 185 H4
Oto Tolu Group Tonga 20°21S 174°32W 287 Q13
Otočac Croatia 44°53N 15°12E 199 D12
Otoineppu Japan 44°44N 142°16E 220 B11
Otok Croatia 43°42N 16°44E 199 E13
Otomavi = Korsakov Russia 46°36N 142°42E 215 E15
Oton Phil. 10°42N 122°29E 233 F4
Otopeni, București ✈ (OTP) Romania 44°30N 26°11E 183 F11
Otorohanga N.Z. 38°12S 175°14E 284 E4
Otoskwin → Canada 52°13N 88°6W 298 B2
Ōtoyo Japan 33°43N 133°45E 222 D5
Otpor = Zabaykalsk Russia 49°40N 117°25E 215 E12
Otra → Norway 58°9N 8°1E 164 F5
Otradnyy Russia 53°22N 51°21E 190 D10
Otranto Italy 40°9N 18°28E 201 B11
Otranto, C. d' Italy 40°7N 18°30E 201 B11
Otranto, Str. of Italy 40°15N 18°40E 201 B11
Otrobanda Curaçao 12°7N 68°57W 322 g
Otrokovice Czech Rep. 49°12N 17°32E 181 B10
Otse S. Africa 25°2S 25°45E 270 C4
Otsego U.S.A. 42°27N 85°42W 311 B11
Otsego L. U.S.A. 42°45N 74°53W 313 D10
Ōtsu Japan 35°0N 135°50E 223 C7
Otsuka Japan 35°43N 139°44E 140 A3
Ōtsuki Japan 35°36N 138°57E 223 B10
Otta Norway 61°46N 9°32E 164 C6
Otta → Norway 61°46N 9°31E 164 C6
Ottakring Austria 48°12N 16°18E 142 A1
Ottapalam India 10°46N 76°23E 245 J3
Ottávia Italy 41°57N 12°24E 136 B1
Ottawa = Outaouais → Canada 45°27N 74°8W 298 C5
Ottawa Ont., Canada 45°26N 75°42W 313 A9
Ottawa Ill., U.S.A. 41°21N 88°51W 311 C8
Ottawa Kans., U.S.A. 38°37N 95°16W 308 F6
Ottawa Ohio, U.S.A. 41°1N 84°3W 311 C12
Ottawa Is. Canada 59°35N 80°10W 295 F15
Ottélé Cameroon 3°38N 11°19E 263 E7
Ottensheim Austria 48°21N 14°12E 180 C7
Otter Cr. → U.S.A. 44°13N 73°17W 313 B11
Otter Creek U.S.A. 29°19N 82°46W 317 F7
Otter Lake Canada 45°17N 79°56W 312 A5
Otterbäcken Sweden 58°57N 14°3E 163 F8
Otterbein U.S.A. 40°29N 87°6W 311 D9
Otterndorf Germany 53°48N 8°53E 178 B4
Otterøya Norway 62°45N 6°50E 164 B3
Otterup Denmark 55°30N 10°22E 163 J4
Otterville Ont., Canada 42°55N 80°36W 312 D4
Otterville Mo., U.S.A. 38°42N 93°0W 310 F4
Ottery S. Africa 34°1S 18°32E 118 B2
Ottery St. Mary U.K. 50°44N 3°17W 169 G4
Ottilien Reef Papua N. G. 4°33S 148°49E 286 C5
Ottmachau = Otmuchów Poland 50°28N 17°10E 185 H4
Otto Beit Bridge Zimbabwe 15°59S 28°56E 269 F2
Ottobrunn Germany 48°3N 11°40E 131 B3
Ottosdal S. Africa 26°46S 25°59E 270 C4
Ottoville U.S.A. 40°57N 84°22W 311 D12
Ottumwa U.S.A. 41°1N 92°25W 310 D4
Otukpa Nigeria 7°9N 7°41E 263 D6
Otuquis △ Bolivia 19°45S 58°44W 331 D6
Oturkpo Nigeria 7°16N 8°8E 263 D6
Otvazhnoye = Zhigulevsk Russia 53°28N 49°30E 190 D9
Otvazhny = Zhigulevsk Russia 53°28N 49°30E 190 D9
Otway, B. Chile 53°30S 74°0W 336 D2
Otway, C. Australia 38°52S 143°30E 282 E5
Otway, Seno de Chile 53°0S 71°30W 336 D2
Otway △ Australia 38°47S 143°34E 282 E5
Otwock Poland 52°5N 21°20E 185 F8
Otyniya Ukraine 48°44N 24°51E 183 B9
Ötztaler Ache → Austria 47°14N 10°50E 180 D3
Ötztaler Alpen Austria 46°56N 11°0E 180 E3
Ou → Laos 20°4N 102°13E 236 B4
Ou-Sammyaku Japan 39°20N 140°35E 220 E10
Ouachita → U.S.A. 31°38N 91°49W 314 F9
Ouachita, L. U.S.A. 34°34N 93°12W 314 D8
Ouachita Mts. U.S.A. 34°30N 94°30W 314 D7
Ouadâne Mauritania 20°50N 11°40W 260 D2
Ouadda C.A.R. 8°15N 22°20E 264 A4
Ouaddaï □ Chad 13°0N 21°0E 259 F4
Ouagadougou Burkina Faso 12°25N 1°30W 263 C4
Ouahigouya Burkina Faso 13°31N 2°25W 262 C4
Ouahran = Oran Algeria 35°45N 0°39W 261 A4
Oualâta Mauritania 17°20N 6°55W 262 B3
Ouallah Comoros Is. 12°19S 43°39E 272 a
Ouallam Niger 14°23N 2°10E 263 C5
Ouallene Algeria 24°41N 1°11E 261 D5
Ouanary Fr. Guiana 4°13N 51°40W 329 C7
Ouanda Djallé C.A.R. 8°55N 22°53E 264 A4
Ouandago C.A.R. 7°13N 18°50E 264 A3
Ouandja C.A.R. 8°28N 23°17E 264 A4
Ouandjia, Bahr → C.A.R. 9°35N 21°43E 264 A4
Ouandjia-Vakaga ⌓ C.A.R. 9°2N 22°18E 264 A4
Ouangani Mayotte 12°50S 45°8E 272 b
Ouango C.A.R. 4°19N 22°30E 264 B4
Ouani Comoros Is. 12°9S 44°18E 272 a
Ouantonou C.A.R. 7°19N 15°18E 264 A3
Ouarâne Mauritania 21°0N 10°30W 260 D2
Ouargaye Burkina Faso 11°40N 0°5E 263 C5
Ouargla Algeria 31°59N 5°16E 261 B6
Ouargla □ Algeria 30°30N 6°10E 261 B6
Ouarkoye Burkina Faso 12°5N 3°40W 262 C4
Ouarkziz, Jebel Algeria 28°50N 8°0W 260 C3
Ouarra → C.A.R. 5°5N 24°26E 264 A4
Ouarzazate Morocco 30°55N 6°50W 260 B3
Ouarzazate □ Morocco 30°45N 6°30W 260 B3
Ouassouas Mali 16°10N 1°23E 263 B5
Ouatagouna Mali 15°11N 0°43E 263 B5
Ouatere C.A.R. 5°30N 19°8E 264 A3
Oubangi → Dem. Rep. of the Congo 0°30S 17°50E 264 C3
Oubarakai, O. → Algeria 27°20N 9°0E 261 C6
Ouche → France 47°6N 5°16E 173 E12
Oud Zuid Amsterdam, Neths. 112 c1
Ouddorp Neths. 51°50N 3°57E 170 C3
Oude Kerk Amsterdam, Neths. 112 a2
Oude Rijn → Neths. 52°12N 4°24E 170 B4
Oudeïka Mali 17°30N 1°40W 263 B4
Oudenaarde Belgium 50°50N 3°37E 170 D3
Ouderkerk Neths. 52°18N 4°55E 112 B2
Oudon → France 47°41N 0°53W 172 E6
Oudtshoorn S. Africa 33°35S 22°14E 270 D3
Oued Zem Morocco 32°52N 6°34W 260 B3
Ouégoa N. Cal. 20°20S 164°26E 288 d
Oueita Chad 17°47N 20°39E 259 E4
Ouella Niger 14°48N 3°38E 263 C5
Ouellé Ivory C. 7°26N 4°1W 262 D4
Ouémé → Benin 6°30N 2°30E 263 D5
Ouenza Algeria 35°57N 8°4E 261 A6
Ouessa Burkina Faso 11°4N 2°47W 262 C4
Ouessant, Î. d' France 48°28N 5°6W 172 D1
Ouesso Congo 1°37N 16°5E 264 B3
Ouest □ Cameroon 5°30N 10°30E 263 D7
Ouest, Pte. de l' Canada 49°52N 64°40W 299 C7
Ouezzane Morocco 34°51N 5°35W 260 B3
Ougarou Burkina Faso 12°10N 0°58E 263 C5
Oughter, L. Ireland 54°1N 7°28W 166 B4
Oughterard Ireland 53°26N 9°18W 166 C2
Ouham → C.A.R. 6°35N 15°12E 264 A3
Ouhan → Chad 9°18N 18°14E 259 G3
Ouidah Benin 6°25N 2°0E 263 D5
Ouidi Niger 14°10N 13°0E 259 F2
Ouissongo Angola 7°40S 15°41E 265 E3
Ouistreham France 49°17N 0°18W 172 C6
Oujda Morocco 34°41N 1°55W 261 B4
Oujda □ Morocco 33°18N 2°24W 260 B4
Oujeft Mauritania 20°2N 13°0W 260 D2
Oulad-Teïma Morocco 30°24N 9°12W 260 B3
Oulainen Finland 64°17N 24°47E 160 D21
Ould Yenjé Mauritania 15°38N 12°16W 262 B2
Ouled Djellal Algeria 34°28N 5°2E 261 B6
Ouled Naïl, Mts. des Algeria 34°30N 3°30E 261 B5
Ouli Cameroon 5°12N 14°33E 264 A2
Oullins France 45°43N 4°49E 175 C8
Oulmès Morocco 33°17N 6°0W 260 B3
Oulou, Bahr → C.A.R. 9°48N 21°32E 264 A4
Oulu Finland 65°1N 25°29E 160 D21
Oulujärvi Finland 64°25N 27°15E 160 D22
Oulujoki → Finland 65°1N 25°30E 160 D21
Oulunkylä Finland 60°13N 24°58E 121 B2
Oulx Italy 45°2N 6°50E 198 C3
Oum Chalouba Chad 15°48N 20°46E 259 E4
Oum-el-Bouaghi Algeria 35°55N 7°6E 261 A6
Oum-el-Bouaghi □ Algeria 35°50N 7°5E 261 A6
Oum el Ksi Algeria 29°4N 6°59W 260 C3
Oum-er-Rbia, O. → Morocco 33°19N 8°21W 260 B3
Oum Hadjer Chad 13°18N 19°41E 259 F3
Oum Hadjer, O. → Chad 16°38N 20°14E 259 E4
Oumé Ivory C. 6°21N 5°27W 262 D3
Oumm ed Droûs Guebli, Sebkhet Mauritania 24°3N 11°45W 260 D2
Oumm ed Droûs Telli, Sebkhet Mauritania 24°20N 11°30W 260 D2
Ounane, Dj. Algeria 25°4N 7°19E 261 C6
Ounasjoki → Finland 66°31N 25°40E 160 C21
Ounguati Namibia 22°0S 15°46E 270 B2
Ounianga Kébir Chad 19°4N 20°29E 259 E4
Ounianga Sérir Chad 18°54N 20°51E 259 E4
Ounissoui Niger 17°34N 12°13E 259 E2
Our → Lux. 49°55N 6°5E 170 E6
Oura, Akra Greece 38°10N 26°2E 205 C8
Oura-wan Japan 26°32N 128°4E 288 a
Ouranoupoli Greece 40°20N 23°59E 202 F7
Ourârene Niger 19°30N 7°10E 263 B6
Ourari, Tarso Chad 21°27N 17°27E 259 D3
Ouray U.S.A. 38°1N 107°40W 305 G10
Ourcq → France 49°1N 3°1E 173 C10
Ourcq, Canal de l' France 48°54N 2°28E 134 A3
Ourém Brazil 1°33S 47°6W 332 B2
Ourense Spain 42°19N 7°55W 194 C3
Ourense □ Spain 42°15N 7°51W 194 C3
Ouricuri Brazil 7°53S 40°5W 332 C3
Ourinhos Brazil 23°0S 49°54W 335 A6
Ourique Portugal 37°38N 8°16W 195 H2
Ouro Fino Brazil 22°16S 46°25W 335 A6
Ouro-Ndia Mali 15°8N 4°35W 262 B4
Ouro Prêto Brazil 20°20S 43°30W 333 F3
Ouro Prêto do Oeste Brazil 10°40S 62°18W 331 C5
Ouro Sogui Senegal 15°36N 13°19W 262 B2
Oursi Burkina Faso 14°41N 0°27W 263 C4
Ourthe → Belgium 50°29N 5°35E 170 D5
Ouse → E. Sussex, U.K. 50°47N 0°4E 169 G8
Ouse → N. Yorks., U.K. 53°44N 0°55W 168 D7
Oust France 42°52N 1°13E 174 F5
Oust → France 47°35N 2°6W 172 E4
Outamba-Kilimi △ S. Leone 9°50N 12°40W 262 D2
Outaouais → Canada 45°27N 74°8W 298 C5
Outardes → Canada 49°24N 69°30W 299 C6
Outat Oulad el Haj Morocco 33°22N 3°42W 261 B4
Outeiro de Rei Spain 43°6N 7°36W 194 B3
Outer Hebrides U.K. 57°30N 7°40W 167 D1
Outer Mission U.S.A. 37°43N 122°26W 136 B2
Outes = A Serra de Outes Spain 42°52N 8°55W 194 C2
Outjo Namibia 20°5S 16°7E 270 B2
Outlook Canada 51°30N 107°0W 297 C7
Outokumpu Finland 62°43N 29°1E 160 E23
Outreau France 50°40N 1°36E 173 B8
Outremont Canada 45°31N 73°36W 130 A2
Ouvéa, Î. N. Cal. 20°35S 166°35E 288 d
Ouvèze → France 43°59N 4°51E 175 E8
Ouyen Australia 35°1S 142°22E 282 C5
Ouzinkie U.S.A. 57°56N 152°30W 303 H9
Ouzouer-le-Marché France 47°54N 1°32E 173 E8
Ovacık Turkey 36°11N 33°40E 250 B4
Ovada Italy 44°38N 8°38E 198 D5
Ovahe Chile 27°5S 109°19W 330 b
Ovalau Fiji 17°40S 178°48E 287 A2
Ovalle Chile 30°33S 71°18W 334 C1
Ovamboland Namibia 18°30S 16°0E 270 A2
Ovan Gabon 0°19N 12°10E 264 B2
Ovanåker Sweden 61°22N 15°53E 162 C9
Ovar Portugal 40°51N 8°40W 194 E2
Ovau Solomon Is. 6°40S 156°8E 287 L9
Overath Germany 50°56N 7°17E 178 E3
Overflakkee Neths. 51°44N 4°10E 170 C4
Overijse Belgium 50°47N 4°32E 116 B3
Overijssel □ Neths. 52°25N 6°35E 170 B6
Overland U.S.A. 38°42N 90°21W 310 F6
Overland Park U.S.A. 38°58N 94°40W 308 F6
Overlander Roadhouse Australia 26°19S 114°28E 279 E1
Overton U.S.A. 36°33N 114°27W 307 J12
Övertorneå Sweden 66°23N 23°38E 160 C20

Överum Sweden 58°0N 16°20E 163 F10
Ovid Mich., U.S.A. 43°1N 84°22W 311 A12
Ovid N.Y., U.S.A. 42°41N 76°49W 313 D8
Ovidiopol Ukraine 46°15N 30°30E 189 J6
Ovidiu Romania 44°16N 28°34E 183 F13
Oviedo Spain 43°25N 5°50W 194 B5
Oviedo Fla., U.S.A. 28°40N 81°13W 317 G8
Oviksfjällen Sweden 63°0N 13°49E 162 A7
Ovišrags Latvia 57°33N 21°44E 184 A8
Ovoot Mongolia 45°21N 113°45E 226 B7
Övör Hangay □ Mongolia 45°0N 102°30E 226 B2
Ovoro Nigeria 5°26N 7°16E 263 D6
Øvre Årdal Norway 61°19N 7°48E 164 C4
Övre Fryken Sweden 60°0N 13°7E 162 E7
Øvre Rendal Norway 61°54N 11°4E 164 C8
Øvre Rindal Norway 63°6N 9°10E 164 A6
Øvre Sirdal Norway 58°48N 6°43E 164 F3
Ovruch Ukraine 51°25N 28°45E 177 C15
Owaka N.Z. 46°27S 169°40E 285 G4
Owambo = Ovamboland Namibia 18°30S 16°0E 270 A2
Owando Congo 0°29S 15°55E 264 C3
Owariasahi Japan 35°10N 137°5E 223 B9
Owasco L. U.S.A. 42°50N 76°31W 313 D8
Owase Japan 34°7N 136°12E 223 C8
Owatonna U.S.A. 44°5N 93°14W 308 C7
Owbeh Afghan. 34°28N 63°10E 240 B1
Owego U.S.A. 42°6N 76°16W 313 D8
Owen Australia 34°15S 138°32E 282 C3
Owen, Mt. N.Z. 41°35S 172°33E 285 B7
Owen Falls Dam = Nalubaale Dam Uganda 0°30N 33°5E 268 B3
Owen Sound Canada 44°35N 80°55W 312 B4
Owen Stanley Ra. Papua N. G. 8°30S 147°0E 286 E4
Owendo Gabon 0°17N 9°30E 264 B1
Oweniny → Ireland 54°8N 9°34W 166 B2
Owens → U.S.A. 36°32N 117°59W 306 J9
Owens L. U.S.A. 36°26N 117°57W 307 J9
Owensboro U.S.A. 37°46N 87°7W 311 G9
Owensville Ind., U.S.A. 38°16N 87°41W 311 F9
Owensville Mo., U.S.A. 38°21N 91°30W 310 F5
Owenteik Guyana 4°27N 59°35W 329 C6
Owenton U.S.A. 38°32N 84°50W 311 F12
Owerri Nigeria 5°29N 7°0E 263 D6
Owhango N.Z. 39°0S 175°23E 284 F4
Owhiro Bay N.Z. 41°21S 174°45E 143 C1
Owingsville U.S.A. 38°9N 83°46W 311 F13
Owl → Canada 57°51N 92°44W 297 B10
Owo Nigeria 7°10N 5°39E 263 D6
Oworonsoki Nigeria 6°32N 3°24E 124 A2
Owosso U.S.A. 43°0N 84°10W 311 B12
Owyhee U.S.A. 41°57N 116°6W 304 F5
Owyhee → U.S.A. 43°49N 117°2W 304 E5
Owyhee, L. U.S.A. 43°38N 117°14W 304 E5
Ox Mts. = Slieve Gamph Ireland 54°6N 9°0W 166 B3
Oxapampa Peru 10°33S 75°26W 330 C2
Öxarfjörður Iceland 66°15N 16°45W 155 A10
Oxbow Canada 49°14N 102°10W 297 D8
Oxelösund Sweden 58°43N 17°5E 163 F11
Oxford N.Z. 43°18S 172°11E 285 D7
Oxford Oxon., U.K. 51°46N 1°15W 169 F6
Oxford Ala., U.S.A. 33°36N 85°51W 316 B4
Oxford Iowa, U.S.A. 41°43N 91°47W 310 C5
Oxford Mass., U.S.A. 42°7N 71°52W 313 D13
Oxford Mich., U.S.A. 42°49N 83°16W 311 B13
Oxford Miss., U.S.A. 34°22N 89°31W 315 D10
Oxford N.C., U.S.A. 36°19N 78°35W 315 C15
Oxford N.Y., U.S.A. 42°27N 75°36W 313 D9
Oxford Ohio, U.S.A. 39°31N 84°45W 311 E12
Oxford L. Canada 54°51N 95°37W 297 C9
Oxford Street London, U.K. 125 b3
Oxfordshire □ U.K. 51°48N 1°16W 169 F6
Oxgangs U.K. 55°54N 3°13W 121 B2
Oxia Greece 38°18N 21°6E 207 C3
Oxie Sweden 55°33N 13°6E 163 J7
Oxilithos Greece 38°35N 24°7E 204 C6
Oxley Australia 34°11S 144°6E 282 C6
Oxley Wild Rivers △ Australia 30°57S 152°12E 283 A10
Oxnard U.S.A. 34°12N 119°11W 307 L7
Oxon Hill U.S.A. 38°48N 76°59W 143 C4
Oxsjövålen Sweden 62°34N 13°57E 162 B7
Oxus = Amudarya → Uzbekistan 43°58N 59°34E 216 D5
Oya Malaysia 2°55N 111°55E 235 B4
Oyabe Japan 36°47N 136°56E 223 A8
Oyama Japan 36°18N 139°48E 223 A11
Oyambre ⌓ Spain 43°22N 4°21W 194 B6
Oyapock → Fr. Guiana 4°8N 51°40W 329 C7
Øye Norway 58°16N 6°49E 164 F3
Oyem Gabon 1°34N 11°31E 264 B2
Oyen Canada 51°22N 110°28W 297 C6
Øyer Norway 61°16N 10°25E 164 C7
Øyeren Norway 59°50N 11°15E 164 E8
Oykel → U.K. 57°56N 4°26W 167 D4
Oymyakon Russia 63°25N 142°44E 215 C15
Oyo Congo 0°0 15°51E 264 C3
Oyo Nigeria 7°46N 3°56E 263 D5
Oyo Sudan 21°58N 36°10E 256 C4
Oyo □ Nigeria 8°15N 3°30E 263 D5
Oyodo Japan 34°42N 135°29E 133 A1
Oyón Peru 10°37S 76°47W 330 C2
Oyonnax France 46°16N 5°40E 173 F12
Oyrot = Gorno-Altay □ Russia 51°0N 86°0E 217 B11
Oyrot-Tura = Gorno-Altaysk Russia 51°50N 86°5E 217 B11
Øyslebø Norway 58°9N 7°34E 164 F4
Oyster Bay U.S.A. 40°52N 73°32W 313 F11
Oyster Harbour = Ladysmith Canada 49°0N 123°49W 306 B3
Oyster Rock India 18°54N 72°49E 130 B1
Oyster Rocks Pakistan 24°48N 66°59E 123 B2
Øystese Norway 60°22N 6°9E 164 D3
Ōyūbari Japan 43°1N 142°5E 220 C11
Oyyl → Kazakhstan 49°4N 54°40E 216 C4
Özalp Turkey 38°39N 43°59E 213 C10
Ozamiz Phil. 8°15N 123°50E 233 G4
Ozar = Ojhar India 20°6N 73°56E 244 D1
Ozark Ala., U.S.A. 31°28N 85°39W 316 D4
Ozark Ark., U.S.A. 35°29N 93°50W 314 D8
Ozark Mo., U.S.A. 37°1N 93°12W 308 G7
Ozark Plateau U.S.A. 37°20N 91°40W 308 G8
Ozarks, L. of the U.S.A. 38°12N 92°38W 310 F4
Ożarów Poland 50°53N 21°40E 185 H8
Ózd Hungary 48°14N 20°15E 182 B5
Ozernovskiy Russia 51°30N 156°31E 215 D16
Ozernoye Russia 51°46N 51°28E 190 E10
Ozero Svityaz Ukraine 51°30N 23°50E 185 G10
Ozersk Russia 54°25N 22°0E 184 D8
Ozette, L. U.S.A. 48°6N 124°38W 306 B2
Ozieri Italy 40°35N 9°0E 200 B2
Ozimek Poland 50°41N 18°11E 185 H5
Ozinki Russia 51°12N 49°44E 190 E9
Ozoir-la-Ferrière France 48°46N 2°40E 134 B4
Ozona U.S.A. 30°43N 101°12W 314 F4
Ozone Park U.S.A. 40°40N 73°50W 132 B2
Ozorków Poland 51°57N 19°16E 185 G6
Ozren Bos.-H. 43°55N 18°29E 182 G3
Ōzu Ehime, Japan 33°30N 132°33E 222 D4
Ōzu Kumamoto, Japan 32°52N 130°52E 222 E2
Ozuluama Mexico 21°40N 97°51W 319 C5
Ozun Romania 45°47N 25°50E 183 E10
Ozurgeti Georgia 41°55N 42°0E 191 K5

P

Pa Burkina Faso 11°33N 3°19W 262 C4
Pa-an Burma 16°51N 97°40E 241 G6
Pa Mong Dam Thailand 18°0N 102°22E 236 D4
Pa Sak → Thailand 15°30N 101°0E 236 E3
Paama Vanuatu 16°28S 168°14E 287 F6
Paamiut Greenland 62°0N 49°43W 154 E6
Paar → Germany 48°46N 11°36E 179 G7
Paarl S. Africa 33°45S 18°56E 270 D2
Pa'auilo U.S.A. 20°2N 155°22W 302 C6
Pab Hills Pakistan 26°30N 66°45E 242 F2
Pabbay U.K. 57°46N 7°14W 167 D1
Pabean Indonesia 6°49S 115°19E 235 D5
Pabianice Poland 51°40N 19°20E 185 G6
Pabna Bangla. 24°1N 89°18E 241 C2
Pabo Uganda 3°1N 32°10E 268 B3
Pacaás Novos, Serra dos Brazil 10°45S 64°15W 331 C5
Pacaás Novos △ Brazil 11°0S 63°0W 331 C5
Pacaipampa Peru 5°35S 79°39W 330 B2
Pacaja → Brazil 1°56S 50°50W 332 B1
Pacajus Brazil 4°10S 38°31W 332 B4
Pacaraima, Sa. S. Amer. 4°0N 62°30W 329 C5
Pacarán Peru 12°50S 76°3W 330 C2
Pacaraos Peru 11°12S 76°42W 330 C2
Pacasmayo Peru 7°20S 79°35W 330 B2
Pace U.S.A. 30°36N 87°10W 317 E2
Paceco Italy 37°59N 12°33E 200 E5
Pachacamac Peru 12°14S 77°53W 330 C2
Pachang Hsi → Taiwan 23°20N 120°7E 225 C2
Pachao Yü Taiwan 23°22N 119°29E 225 C1
Pachia Greece 36°17N 25°50E 205 E7
Pachino Italy 36°43N 15°5E 201 F8
Pachitea → Peru 8°46S 74°33W 330 B3
Pachiza Peru 7°16S 76°46W 330 B2
Pachmarhi India 22°28N 78°26E 243 H8
Pachnai India 26°57N 92°19E 241 B4
Pachnes Greece 35°16N 24°4E 207 E5
Pacho Colombia 5°8N 74°10W 328 B3
Pachora India 20°38N 75°29E 244 D2
Pachpadra India 25°58N 72°10E 242 G5
Pachuca Mexico 20°7N 98°44W 319 C5
Pacific U.S.A. 38°29N 90°45W 310 F6
Pacific Antarctic Ridge Pac. Oc. 43°0S 115°0W 151 B13
Pacific City = Huntington Beach U.S.A. 33°40N 118°5W 307 M9
Pacific Grove U.S.A. 36°38N 121°56W 306 J5
Pacific Heights U.S.A. 37°47N 122°26W 136 B2
Pacific Manor U.S.A. 37°38N 122°27W 136 C2
Pacific Ocean 10°0N 140°0W 289 G14
Pacific Palisades Calif., U.S.A. 34°2N 118°32W 126 B1
Pacific Palisades Hawai'i, U.S.A. 21°25N 157°58W 302 K14
Pacific Rim △ Canada 48°40N 124°45W 306 B2
Pacifica U.S.A. 37°37N 122°27W 136 C2
Pacitan Indonesia 8°12S 111°7E 235 D4
Packsaddle Australia 30°36S 141°58E 282 A4
Packwood U.S.A. 46°36N 121°40W 306 D5
Paco Phil. 14°35N 120°59E 127 B1
Paco de Arcos Portugal 38°41N 9°17W 126 A1
Paço Imperial Rio de J., Brazil 135 a2
Pacov Czech Rep. 49°27N 15°0E 180 B8
Pacoval Brazil 2°40S 54°11W 329 D7
Pacuí → Brazil 16°46S 45°1W 333 E2
Pacy-sur-Eure France 49°1N 1°23E 172 C8
Padaido, Kepulauan Indonesia 1°15S 136°30E 231 E9
Padali = Amursk Russia 50°14N 136°54E 215 D14
Padampur India 20°59N 83°4E 244 D6
Padang Kalimantan Barat, Indonesia 1°39S 108°55E 235 C3
Padang Riau, Indonesia 1°30N 102°30E 237 M4
Padang Sumatera Barat, Indonesia 1°0S 100°20E 234 C2
Padang Endau Malaysia 2°40N 103°38E 237 L4
Padang Lawas Indonesia 1°40N 99°56E 234 B1
Padangpanjang Indonesia 0°40S 100°20E 234 C2
Padangsidempuan Indonesia 1°30N 99°15E 234 B1
Padangtikar Indonesia 0°44S 109°15E 235 C3
Padatchaung Burma 19°46N 94°48E 241 F5
Padauari → Brazil 0°15S 64°5W 329 D5
Padaung Burma 18°43N 95°9E 241 F5
Padborg Denmark 54°49N 9°21E 163 K3
Padcaya Bolivia 21°52S 64°48W 331 E5
Paddington N.S.W., Australia 33°53S 151°14E 139 B2
Paddington London, U.K. 125 b2
Paddle Prairie Canada 57°57N 117°29W 296 B5
Paderborn Germany 51°42N 8°45E 178 D4
Paderno Italy 45°33N 9°9E 129 A1
Paderoo India 18°5N 82°40E 244 E6
Padeş, Vf. Romania 45°40N 22°22E 182 E7
Padilla Bolivia 19°19S 64°20W 331 D5
Padina Romania 44°50N 27°8E 183 F12
Padma India 24°12N 85°22E 243 G11
Padma → Bangla. 23°22N 90°32E 241 D3
Pádova Italy 45°25N 11°53E 199 C8
Padra India 22°15N 73°7E 242 H5
Padrão, Pta. Angola 6°5S 12°20E 265 D2
Padrauna India 26°54N 83°59E 243 F10
Padre I. U.S.A. 27°10N 97°25W 314 H6
Padre Island ⌓ U.S.A. 27°0N 97°25W 314 H6
Padrón Spain 42°41N 8°39W 194 C2
Padstow U.K. 50°33N 4°58W 169 G3
Padthaway Australia 36°36S 140°31E 282 D4
Padua = Pádova Italy 45°25N 11°53E 199 C8
Paducah Ky., U.S.A. 37°5N 88°37W 308 G9
Paducah Tex., U.S.A. 34°1N 100°18W 314 D4
Padukka Sri Lanka 6°50N 80°5E 245 L5
Padul Spain 37°1N 3°38W 195 H7
Padwa India 18°27N 82°47E 244 E6
Paea Tahiti 17°41S 149°35W 289 e
Paekakariki N.Z. 40°59S 174°58E 284 G3
Paektu-san N. Korea 41°59N 128°4E 224 B4
Paengaroa N.Z. 37°49S 176°29E 284 D5
Paeroa N.Z. 37°23S 175°41E 284 D4
Paesana Italy 44°41N 7°16E 198 D4
Paete Phil. 14°23N 121°29E 232 D3
Pafúri Mozam. 22°28S 31°17E 271 B5
Pag Croatia 44°25N 15°3E 199 D12
Paga Gabon 0°45S 10°21E 264 C2
Paga Ghana 11°1N 1°8W 263 C4
Pagadian Phil. 7°55N 123°30E 233 H4
Pagai Selatan, Pulau Indonesia 3°0S 100°15E 234 C2
Pagai Utara, Pulau Indonesia 2°35S 100°0E 234 C2
Pagalu = Annobón Atl. Oc. 1°25S 5°36E 255 G4
Pagalungan Phil. 7°4N 124°41E 233 H5
Pagan Burma 21°10N 94°52E 241 E5
Pagan N. Marianas 18°7N 145°46E 302 a
Pagara India 24°22N 80°1E 243 G9
Pagaralam Indonesia 4°1S 103°16E 234 C2
Pagastikos Kolpos Greece 39°15N 23°0E 204 B5
Pagatan Indonesia 3°33S 115°59E 235 C5
Page U.S.A. 36°57N 111°27W 305 H8
Pagėgiai Lithuania 55°9N 21°54E 184 C8
Pagei Papua N. G. 3°2S 141°10E 286 B1
Pageri South Sudan 4°0N 32°0E 257 G3
Paget, Mt. S. Georgia 54°26S 36°31W 326 H6
Paget I. India 13°26N 92°50E 245 H11
Pagewood Australia 33°56S 151°14E 139 B2
Pago B. Guam 13°25N 144°47E 302 d
Pago Pago Amer. Samoa 14°16S 170°43W 302 f
Pago Pago Harbor Amer. Samoa 14°17S 170°40W 302 f
Pagosa Springs U.S.A. 37°16N 107°1W 305 H10
Pagote India 18°53N 72°59E 130 B2
Pagri China 27°45N 89°10E 218 F6
Pagsanjan Phil. 14°16N 121°27E 232 D3
Pagua B. Dominica 15°32N 61°17W 323 k
Pagudpud Phil. 18°34N 120°47E 232 B3
Pagwa River Canada 50°2N 85°14W 298 B2
Pagwi Papua N. G. 4°4S 143°2E 286 C2
Pāhala U.S.A. 19°12N 155°29W 302 D6
Pahang □ Malaysia 3°30N 102°45E 237 L4
Pahang → Malaysia 3°30N 103°9E 237 L4
Paharpur Bangla. 24°51N 88°44E 241 C2
Pahia Pt. N.Z. 46°20S 167°41E 285 G2
Pahiatua N.Z. 40°27S 175°50E 284 G4
Pāhoa U.S.A. 19°30N 154°57W 302 D7
Pahokee U.S.A. 26°50N 80°40W 317 J9
Pahrump U.S.A. 36°12N 115°59W 307 J11
Pahute Mesa U.S.A. 37°20N 116°45W 306 H10
Pai Thailand 19°19N 98°27E 236 C2
Pai, I. do Brazil 22°59S 43°5W 135 B2
Paia U.S.A. 20°54N 156°22W 302 C5
Paichuan Liehtao Taiwan 25°58N 119°57E 225 b
Paicines U.S.A. 36°44N 121°17W 306 J5
Paide Estonia 58°53N 25°33E 188 C3
Paignton U.K. 50°26N 3°35W 169 G4
Paihia N.Z. 35°17S 174°6E 284 B3
Paiho Taiwan 23°21N 120°25E 225 C2
Paiján Peru 7°42S 79°20W 330 B2
Päijänne Finland 61°30N 25°30E 188 B3
Pailani India 25°45N 80°26E 243 G9
Pailin Cambodia 12°46N 102°36E 236 F4
Pailolo Channel U.S.A. 21°0N 156°40W 302 B5
Paimpol France 48°48N 3°4W 172 D3
Painan Indonesia 1°21S 100°34E 234 C2
Paine Grande, Cerro Chile 50°59S 73°4W 336 D2
Painesville U.S.A. 41°43N 81°15W 312 E3
Paint Hills = Wemindji Canada 53°0N 78°49W 298 B4
Paint L. Canada 55°28N 97°57W 297 B9
Painted Desert U.S.A. 36°0N 111°0W 305 H8
Paintsville U.S.A. 37°49N 82°48W 309 G12
País Vasco □ Spain 42°50N 2°45W 196 C2
Paisha Taiwan 23°40N 119°35E 225 C1
Paisley Ont., Canada 44°18N 81°16W 312 B3
Paisley Renf., U.K. 55°50N 4°25W 167 F4
Paisley Oreg., U.S.A. 42°42N 120°32W 304 E3
Païta N. Cal. 22°8S 166°22E 288 d
Paita Peru 5°11S 81°9W 330 B1
Paithan India 19°29N 75°23E 244 E2
Paiva → Portugal 41°4N 8°16W 194 D2
Paizhou China 30°12N 113°55E 229 B9
Paja, Cerro Ecuador 1°17S 90°26W 330 a
Pájara Canary Is. 28°21N 14°6W 153 e2
Pajares Spain 43°1N 5°46W 194 B5
Pajares, Puerto de Spain 42°58N 5°46W 194 C5
Pajarito Colombia 5°17N 72°43W 328 B3
Pajęczno Poland 51°10N 19°0E 185 G5
Paju S. Korea 37°45N 126°46E 224 D3
Pak Kok China 22°14N 114°7E 122 B1
Pak Kong China 22°22N 114°15E 122 A2
Pak Lay Laos 18°15N 101°27E 236 C3
Pak Ou Laos 20°3N 102°12E 236 B4
Pak Phanang Thailand 8°21N 100°12E 237 H3
Pak Sane Laos 18°22N 103°39E 236 C4
Pak Song Laos 15°11N 106°14E 236 E6
Pak Suang Laos 19°58N 102°15E 228 H4
Pak Tam Chung China 22°24N 114°19E 219 a
Pak Thong Chai Thailand 14°43N 102°1E 236 E4
Pakala India 13°29N 79°8E 245 H4
Pakaraima Mts. Guyana 6°0N 60°0W 329 B6
Pakaur India 24°38N 87°51E 243 G12
Pakch'ŏn N. Korea 39°44N 125°35E 224 C2
Pakenham Vic., Australia 38°6S 145°30E 283 E6
Pakenham Ont., Canada 45°18N 76°18W 313 A8
Pakhoi = Beihai China 21°28N 109°6E 228 G7
Pakhuis S. Africa 32°9S 19°5E 270 D2
Pakila Finland 60°15N 24°55E 121 B2
Pakistan ■ Asia 30°0N 70°0E 242 E4
Pakkading Laos 18°19N 103°59E 236 C4
Paklay = Sayaboury Laos 19°15N 101°45E 236 C3
Paklenica △ Croatia 44°20N 15°39E 199 D12
Pakokku Burma 21°20N 95°0E 241 E5
Pakość Poland 52°48N 18°6E 185 F5
Pakowki L. Canada 49°20N 111°0W 297 D6
Pakpattan Pakistan 30°25N 73°27E 242 D5
Pakrac Croatia 45°27N 17°12E 182 E2
Pakruojis Lithuania 55°58N 23°52E 184 C10
Paks Hungary 46°38N 18°55E 182 D3
Paktīā □ Afghan. 33°30N 69°15E 240 B3
Paktīkā □ Afghan. 32°30N 69°0E 240 B3
Paku, Tanjung Indonesia 3°6S 106°31E 234 C3
Pakwach Uganda 2°28N 31°27E 268 B3
Pakxe Laos 15°5N 105°52E 236 E5
Pal Lahara India 21°27N 85°11E 243 J11
Pala Chad 9°25N 15°5E 259 G3
Pala Dem. Rep. of the Congo 6°45S 29°30E 268 D2
Pala Calif., U.S.A. 33°22N 117°5W 307 M9
Palabek Uganda 3°22N 32°33E 268 B3
Palacio Real Madrid, Spain 127 b1
Palacios U.S.A. 28°42N 96°13W 314 G6
Palafrugell Spain 41°55N 3°10E 196 D8
Palagiano Italy 40°35N 17°2E 201 B10
Palagonía Italy 37°19N 14°45E 201 E7
Palagruža Croatia 42°24N 16°15E 199 F13
Palais Royal Brussels, Belgium 116 b3
Palaiseau France 48°42N 2°14E 134 B2
Palakkad = Palghat India 10°46N 76°42E 245 J3
Palakol India 16°31N 81°46E 245 F5
Palalankwe India 10°52N 92°29E 245 J11
Palam India 19°0N 77°0E 244 E3
Palamas Greece 39°26N 22°4E 204 B4
Palamós Spain 41°50N 3°10E 196 D8
Palampur India 32°10N 76°30E 242 C7
Palamut Turkey 38°59N 27°41E 205 C9
Palana Tas., Australia 39°45S 147°55E 281 F4
Palana Russia 59°10N 159°59E 215 D16
Palanan Phil. 17°8N 122°29E 232 C4
Palanan B. Phil. 17°9N 122°27E 232 C4
Palanan Pt. Phil. 17°17N 122°30E 232 C4
Palandri Pakistan 33°42N 73°40E 243 C5
Palanga Lithuania 55°58N 21°3E 184 C8
Palanganene Dem. Rep. of the Congo 6°32S 18°52E 265 D3
Palangkaraya Indonesia 2°16S 113°56E 235 C4
Palani India 10°30N 77°30E 245 J3
Palani Hills India 10°14N 77°33E 245 J3
Palanpur India 24°10N 72°25E 242 G5
Palaoa Pt. U.S.A. 20°44N 156°58W 302 C5
Palapag Phil. 12°33N 125°7E 232 E5
Palapye Botswana 22°30S 27°7E 270 B4
Palar → India 12°27N 80°13E 245 H5
Palas Pakistan 35°4N 73°14E 243 B5
Palas de Rei Spain 42°52N 7°52W 194 C3
Palasan I. Phil. 14°51N 122°2E 232 D4
Palasponga India 21°47N 85°34E 243 J11
Palatine U.S.A. 42°7N 88°3W 311 B8
Palatka Russia 60°6N 150°54E 215 C16
Palatka Fla., U.S.A. 29°39N 81°38W 316 F8
Palau Italy 41°11N 9°23E 200 A2
Palau ■ Palau 7°30N 134°30E 288 c
Palaui I. Phil. 18°32N 122°8E 232 B4
Palauk Burma 13°10N 98°40E 236 F2
Palaw Burma 12°58N 98°39E 236 F2
Palawan Phil. 9°30N 118°30E 233 G2
Palawan □ Phil. 10°0N 119°0E 233 G2
Palawan Passage Phil. 10°0N 118°0E 233 G2
Palayan Phil. 15°36N 121°8E 232 D3
Palayankottai India 8°45N 77°45E 245 K3
Palazzo, Pte. France 42°28N 8°30E 175 F12
Palazzo San Gervásio Italy 40°56N 15°59E 201 B8
Palazzolo Italy 45°34N 9°9E 129 A1
Palazzolo Acréide Italy 37°4N 14°54E 201 E7
Palca Chile 19°7S 69°9W 330 D4
Paldiski Estonia 59°23N 24°9E 188 C3
Pale Bos.-H. 43°50N 18°38E 182 G3
Palekastro Greece 35°12N 26°15E 207 E7
Palel India 24°27N 94°2E 241 C5
Paleleh Indonesia 1°10N 121°50E 231 D6
Palembang Indonesia 3°0S 104°50E 234 C2
Palena → Chile 43°50S 73°50W 336 B2
Palena, L. Chile 43°55S 71°40W 336 B2
Palencia Spain 42°1N 4°34W 194 C6
Palencia □ Spain 42°31N 4°33W 194 C6
Paleng Taiwan 24°41N 121°23E 225 B3
Palenque Mexico 17°29N 92°1W 319 D6
Paleo Faliro Greece 37°53N 23°42E 112 B2
Paleochora Greece 35°16N 23°39E 207 E4
Paleokastritsa Greece 39°40N 19°41E 206 B9
Paleometokho Cyprus 35°7N 33°11E 207 E9
Paleopoli Greece 37°49N 24°50E 204 D6
Palermo B. Aires, Argentina 34°35S 58°24W 117 B2
Palermo Colombia 2°54N 75°26W 328 C2
Palermo Italy 38°7N 13°22E 200 D6
Palermo Calif., U.S.A. 39°26N 121°33W 304 G3
Palermo ✈ (PMO) Italy 38°11N 13°5E 200 D6
Paleros Greece 38°47N 20°53E 207 B2
Palestina = Jordânia Brazil 15°55S 40°11W 333 E3
Palestine Asia 32°0N 35°0E 251 G6
Palestine Ill., U.S.A. 39°0N 87°37W 311 F9
Palestine Tex., U.S.A. 31°46N 95°38W 314 F7
Palestrina Italy 41°50N 12°53E 199 G9
Paletwa Burma 21°10N 92°50E 241 E4
Palghat India 10°46N 76°42E 245 J3
Palgrave, Mt. Australia 23°22S 115°58E 278 D2
Palhais Portugal 38°37N 9°2W 126 B2
Pali India 25°50N 73°20E 242 G5
Pali Taiwan 25°8N 121°23E 225 A3
Pali-Aike △ Chile 52°6S 69°44W 336 D3
Palikea U.S.A. 21°26N 158°6W 302 K13
Palikir Micronesia 6°55N 158°9E 288 G7
Palimbang Phil. 6°12N 124°12E 233 H5
Palin, Mt. Malaysia 6°10N 117°10E 235 A5
Palinuro Italy 40°2N 15°17E 201 B8
Palinuro, C. Italy 40°2N 15°16E 201 B8
Paliouri, Akra Greece 39°57N 23°45E 202 G7
Palisades Park U.S.A. 40°50N 74°1W 132 A1
Palisades Res. U.S.A. 43°20N 111°12W 304 E8
Palisadoes, The Jamaica 17°57N 76°48W 320 a
Paliseul Belgium 49°54N 5°8E 170 E5
Palitana India 21°32N 71°49E 242 J4
Palizada Mexico 18°15N 92°5W 319 D6
Palk Bay Asia 9°30N 79°15E 245 K4
Palk Strait Asia 10°0N 79°45E 245 K4
Palkānah Iraq 35°49N 44°26E 246 C5
Palkonda India 18°36N 83°48E 244 E6
Palkonda Ra. India 13°50N 79°20E 245 H4
Palkot India 22°53N 84°39E 243 H11
Palla Road = Dinokwe Botswana 23°29S 26°37E 270 B4
Pallanza = Verbánia Italy 45°56N 8°33E 198 C5
Pallarenda Australia 19°12S 146°46E 280 B4
Pallasovka Russia 50°4N 47°0E 190 E8
Palleru → India 16°45N 80°2E 244 F5
Pallës, Bishti i Albania 41°24N 19°24E 202 E3
Pallinup → Australia 34°27S 118°50E 279 F2
Pallisa Uganda 1°12N 33°43E 268 B3
Palliser, C. N.Z. 41°37S 175°14E 284 H4
Palliser, Îs. French Polynesia 15°30S 146°30W 289 f
Palliser B. N.Z. 41°26S 175°5E 284 H4
Pallu India 28°59N 74°14E 242 E6
Palm Bay U.S.A. 28°2N 80°35W 317 G9
Palm Beach Aruba 12°34N 70°2W 322 f
Palm Beach Fla., U.S.A. 26°43N 80°2W 317 J9
Palm Coast U.S.A. 29°35N 81°12W 317 F8
Palm Desert U.S.A. 33°43N 116°22W 307 M10
Palm-Grove △ Australia 24°57S 149°21E 280 C4
Palm Harbor U.S.A. 28°5N 82°46W 317 G7
Palm Is. Australia 18°40S 146°35E 280 B4
Palm Springs U.S.A. 33°50N 116°33W 307 M10
Palm Valley U.S.A. 30°11N 81°23W 316 E8
Palma = Paraná Brazil 12°30S 47°48W 333 D2
Palma Mozam. 10°46S 40°29E 269 E5
Palma → Brazil 12°33S 47°52W 333 D2
Palma, B. de Spain 39°30N 2°39E 206 B3
Palma de Mallorca Spain 39°35N 2°39E 206 B3
Palma de Mallorca ✈ (PMI) Spain 39°34N 2°43E 197 F7
Palma del Río Spain 37°43N 5°17W 195 H5
Palma di Montechiaro Italy 37°11N 13°46E 200 E6
Palma Nova = Palmanova Spain 39°32N 2°34E 206 B3
Palma Soriano Cuba 20°15N 76°0W 320 B4
Palmaner India 13°12N 78°45E 245 H4
Palmanova Spain 39°32N 2°34E 206 B3
Palmares Brazil 8°41S 35°28W 332 C4
Palmarito Venezuela 7°37N 70°10W 328 B3
Palmarola Italy 40°56N 12°51E 200 B5
Palmas Paraná, Brazil 26°29S 52°0W 335 B5
Palmas Tocantins, Brazil 10°13S 48°16W 332 D2
Palmas, C. Liberia 4°27N 7°46W 262 E3
Pálmas, G. di Italy 39°0N 8°30E 200 D1
Palmas de Monte Alto Brazil 14°16S 43°10W 333 D3
Palmdale Calif., U.S.A. 34°35N 118°7W 307 L8
Palmdale Fla., U.S.A. 26°57N 81°19W 317 J8
Palmeira Brazil 25°25S 50°0W 333 G2
Palmeira das Missões Brazil 27°55S 53°17W 335 B5
Palmeira dos Índios Brazil 9°25S 36°37W 332 C4
Palmeirais Brazil 6°0S 43°0W 332 C3
Palmeiras Brazil 12°31S 41°34W 333 D3
Palmeiras → Brazil 12°22S 47°8W 333 D2
Palmeirinhas, Pta. das Angola 9°2S 12°57E 265 D2
Palmela Portugal 38°32N 8°57W 195 G2
Palmelo Brazil 17°20S 48°27W 333 E2
Palmer Antarctica 64°35S 65°0W 151 C17
Palmer Alaska, U.S.A. 61°36N 149°7W 303 F10
Palmer → Australia 16°0S 142°26E 280 B3
Palmer Arch. Antarctica 64°15S 65°0W 151 C17
Palmer Lake U.S.A. 39°7N 104°55W 304 G11
Palmer Land Antarctica 73°0S 63°0W 151 D18
Palmer Park U.S.A. 38°55N 76°52W 143 B4
Palmerston = Darwin Australia 12°25S 130°51E 278 B5
Palmerston N. Terr., Australia 12°31S 130°59E 278 B5
Palmerston Ont., Canada 43°50N 80°51W 312 C4
Palmerston Dublin, Ireland 53°20N 6°22W 120 A1
Palmerston N.Z. 45°29S 170°43E 285 F5
Palmerston North N.Z. 40°21S 175°39E 284 G4
Palmerton U.S.A. 40°48N 75°37W 313 F9
Palmetto Fla., U.S.A. 27°31N 82°34W 317 H7
Palmetto Ga., U.S.A. 33°31N 84°40W 316 B5
Palmetto Pt. Antigua & B. 17°37N 61°51W 322 c
Palmetto Pt. St. Kitts & Nevis 17°18N 62°46W 322 d
Palmi Italy 38°21N 15°51E 201 D8
Palmira Argentina 32°59S 68°34W 334 C2
Palmira Colombia 3°32N 76°16W 328 C2
Palms U.S.A. 34°1N 118°24W 126 B2
Palmyra = Tudmur Syria 34°36N 38°15E 213 E8
Palmyra Ill., U.S.A. 39°26N 90°0W 310 E7
Palmyra Mo., U.S.A. 39°48N 91°32W 310 E5
Palmyra N.J., U.S.A. 40°0N 75°1W 313 F9
Palmyra N.Y., U.S.A. 43°5N 77°18W 312 C7
Palmyra Pa., U.S.A. 40°18N 76°36W 313 F8
Palmyra Wis., U.S.A. 42°52N 88°36W 311 B8
Palmyra Is. Pac. Oc. 5°52N 162°5W 289 G11
Palmyras = Santos Dumont Brazil 22°55S 43°10W 333 F3
Palmyras Pt. India 20°46N 87°1E 244 D8
Palo Phil. 11°10N 124°59E 233 F5
Palo Alto U.S.A. 37°27N 122°10W 306 H4
Palo Seco Trin. & Tob. 10°4N 61°36W 323 t
Palo Verde U.S.A. 33°26N 114°44W 307 M12
Palo Verde △ Costa Rica 10°21N 85°21W 320 D2
Paloh Indonesia 1°43N 109°18E 235 B3
Paloheinä Finland 60°15N 24°56E 121 B2
Paloich South Sudan 10°28N 32°32E 257 E3
Palomar Mt. U.S.A. 33°22N 116°50W 307 M10
Palomeras Spain 40°22N 3°39W 127 B2
Palompon Phil. 11°3N 124°23E 233 F5
Palopo Indonesia 3°0S 120°16E 231 E6
Palos, C. de Spain 37°38N 0°40W 197 H4
Palos de la Frontera Spain 37°14N 6°53W 195 H4
Palos Heights U.S.A. 41°39N 87°47W 119 D2
Palos Hills U.S.A. 41°42N 87°49W 119 C2
Palos Hills Forest U.S.A. 41°40N 87°52W 119 C1
Palos Park U.S.A. 41°40N 87°50W 119 C1
Palos Verdes, Pt. U.S.A. 33°46N 118°25W 307 M8
Palos Verdes Estates U.S.A. 33°48N 118°23W 307 M8
Palpa Peru 14°30S 75°15W 330 C2
Palpara India 22°38N 88°22E 124 B2
Pålsboda Sweden 59°3N 15°22E 162 E9
Palu Indonesia 1°0S 119°52E 235 C5
Palu Turkey 38°45N 40°0E 213 C9
Paluan Phil. 13°26N 120°29E 232 E3
Paluke Liberia 5°2N 8°5W 262 D3
Paluma Ra. Australia 19°9S 146°22E 280 B4
Paluzza Italy 46°32N 13°1E 199 B10
Palwal India 28°8N 77°19E 242 E7
Pama Burkina Faso 11°19N 0°44E 263 C5
Pama → C.A.R. 4°23N 18°43E 264 B3
Pama ⌓ Burkina Faso 11°27N 0°40E 263 C5
Pamandzi Mayotte 12°47S 45°16E 272 b
Pamanukan Indonesia 6°16S 107°49E 235 D3
Pamban I. India 9°15N 79°20E 245 K4
Pamekasan Indonesia 7°10S 113°28E 235 D4
Pamenang Indonesia 8°24S 116°6E 231 J19
Pameungpeuk Indonesia 7°37S 107°43E 235 D3
Pamiers France 43°7N 1°39E 174 E5
Pamir Tajikistan 37°40N 73°0E 217 E8
Pamirsky Post = Murgap Tajikistan 38°10N 74°2E 217 E8
Pamlico → U.S.A. 35°20N 76°28W 315 D16
Pamlico Sd. U.S.A. 35°20N 76°0W 315 D17
Pampa U.S.A. 35°32N 100°58W 314 D4
Pampa de Agma Argentina 43°45S 69°40W 336 B3
Pampa de las Salinas Argentina 32°1S 66°58W 334 C2
Pampa Grande Bolivia 18°5S 64°6W 331 D5
Pampa Hermosa Peru 7°7S 75°4W 330 B2
Pampanga □ Phil. 15°4N 120°40E 232 D3
Pampanua Indonesia 4°16S 120°8E 231 E6
Pampas Argentina 35°0S 63°0W 334 D3
Pampas Peru 12°20S 74°50W 330 C3
Pampas → Peru 13°24S 73°12W 330 C3
Pamphylia Turkey 37°0N 31°20E 250 B2
Pamplemousses Mauritius 20°6S 57°34E 272 e
Pamplona Colombia 7°23N 72°39W 328 B3
Pamplona Phil. 18°31N 121°20E 232 B3
Pamplona-Iruña Spain 42°48N 1°38W 196 C3
Pampoenpoort S. Africa 31°3S 22°40E 270 D3
Pamuk → Turkey 37°2N 34°49E 250 A5
Pamukçu Turkey 39°30N 27°54E 205 B9
Pamukkale Turkey 37°55N 29°8E 205 D11
Pan de Azúcar Chile 24°5S 68°10W 334 A2
Pan de Azúcar △ Chile 26°0S 70°40W 334 B1
Pan Xian China 25°46N 104°38E 228 E5
Pana U.S.A. 39°23N 89°5W 310 E7
Panabo Phil. 7°19N 125°42E 233 H5
Panaca U.S.A. 37°47N 114°23W 305 H6
Panacea U.S.A. 30°2N 84°23W 316 E5
Panagyurishte Bulgaria 42°30N 24°15E 203 D8
Panaitan Indonesia 6°36S 105°12E 234 D3
Panajam Indonesia 1°15S 116°46E 235 C5
Panaji India 15°25N 73°50E 245 G1
Panamá Panama 9°0N 79°25W 320 c
Panama Sri Lanka 6°45N 81°48E 245 L5
Panama ■ Cent. Amer. 8°48N 79°55W 320 E4
Panamá, G. de Panama 8°4N 79°20W 320 E4
Panama, Isthmus of Cent. Amer. 9°0N 79°0W 292 J12
Panama Basin Pac. Oc. 5°0N 83°30W 289 G19
Panama Canal Panama 9°10N 79°37W 320 c
Panama City U.S.A. 30°10N 85°40W 316 E4
Panama City Beach U.S.A. 30°11N 85°48W 316 E4
Panamint Range U.S.A. 36°20N 117°20W 307 J9
Panamint Springs U.S.A. 36°20N 117°28W 307 J9
Panão Peru 9°55S 75°55W 330 B2
Panaon I. Phil. 9°50N 125°13E 233 G5
Panare Thailand 6°51N 101°30E 237 J3
Panarea Italy 38°38N 15°4E 201 D8
Panaro → Italy 44°55N 11°25E 199 D8
Panay Phil. 11°10N 122°30E 233 F4
Panay G. Phil. 11°0N 122°30E 233 F4
Pančevo Serbia 44°52N 20°41E 182 F5
Panch'iao Taiwan 25°1N 121°27E 225 A3
Panchur India 22°32N 88°16E 124 B1
Panciu Romania 45°54N 27°8E 183 E12
Pancol Phil. 10°52N 119°25E 233 F2
Pancorbo, Desfiladero Spain 42°32N 3°5W 194 C7
Pâncota Romania 46°20N 21°45E 182 D6
Panda Mozam. 24°2S 34°45E 271 B5
Pandacan Phil. 14°35N 121°0E 127 B2
Pandan Malaysia 1°32N 103°46E 237 d
Pandan Antique, Phil. 11°45N 122°10E 233 F4
Pandan Catanduanes, Phil. 14°3N 124°10E 232 D5
Pandan, Selat Singapore 1°15N 103°44E 138 B2
Pandan B. Phil. 11°43N 122°0E 233 F4
Pandan Res. Singapore 1°18N 103°44E 138 B2
Pandan Tampoi = Tampoi Malaysia 1°30N 103°39E 237 d
Pandanan I. Phil. 8°17N 117°13E 233 G1
Pandegelang Indonesia 6°25S 106°5E 234 D3
Pandhana India 21°42N 76°13E 242 J7
Pandharkawada India 20°1N 78°32E 244 D4
Pandharpur India 17°41N 75°20E 244 F2
Pandhurna India 21°36N 78°35E 244 D4
Pando Uruguay 34°44S 56°0W 335 C4
Pando □ Bolivia 11°20S 67°40W 330 C4
Pando, L. = Hope, L. Australia 28°24S 139°18E 281 D2
Pandokratoras Greece 39°45N 19°50E 206 B9
Pandora Costa Rica 9°43N 83°3W 320 E3
Pandrup Denmark 57°14N 9°40E 163 G3
Pandu Dem. Rep. of the Congo 4°59N 19°16E 264 B3
Panepistimio Athens, Greece 112 b2
Panevéggio-Pale di San Martino ⌓ Italy 46°14N 11°46E 199 B8
Panevėžys Lithuania 55°42N 24°25E 188 E3
Panfilov = Zharkent Kazakhstan 44°10N 80°0E 217 D10
Panfilovo Russia 50°25N 42°46E 190 E6
Pang Sida △ Thailand 14°5N 102°17E 236 E4
Panga Dem. Rep. of the Congo 1°52N 26°18E 268 B2
Pangaíon Óros Greece 40°50N 24°0E 203 F8
Pangala Congo 3°16S 14°34E 264 C2
Pangalanes, Canal des = Ampangalana, Lakandranon' Madag. 22°48S 47°50E 272 C2
Pangandaran Indonesia 7°40S 108°39E 235 D3
Pangandaran △ Indonesia 7°43S 108°42E 235 D3
Pangani Tanzania 5°25S 38°58E 268 D4
Pangani → Tanzania 5°26S 38°58E 268 D4
Pangantocan Phil. 7°50N 124°49E 233 H5
Pangar Djeréme ⌓ Cameroon 5°50N 13°10E 263 D7
Pangasinan □ Phil. 15°55N 120°20E 232 D3
Pangfou = Bengbu China 32°58N 117°20E 227 H9
Pangga, Tanjung Indonesia 8°54S 116°2E 231 K19
Pangil Dem. Rep. of the Congo 3°10S 26°35E 268 C2
Pangjiabu China 40°38N 115°26E 226 D8
Pangkah, Tanjung Indonesia 6°51S 112°33E 235 D4
Pangkai Burma 22°49N 98°39E 228 F2
Pangkajene Indonesia 4°46S 119°34E 235 C5
Pangkalanbrandan Indonesia 4°1N 98°20E 234 B1
Pangkalanbuun Indonesia 2°41S 111°37E 235 C4
Pangkalansusu Indonesia 4°2N 98°13E 234 B1
Pangkalpinang Indonesia 2°10S 106°10E 234 C3
Pangkoh Indonesia 3°5S 114°8E 235 C4
Pangkor, Pulau Malaysia 4°13N 100°34E 237 K3
Panglao Phil. 9°35N 123°45E 233 G4
Panglao I. Phil. 9°35N 123°48E 233 G4
Pangniqtuuq = Pangnirtung Canada 66°8N 65°43W 295 D18
Pangnirtung Canada 66°8N 65°43W 295 D18
Pango Alucuem Angola 8°43S 14°33E 265 D2
Pangody Russia 65°52N 74°27E 214 C8
Pangong Tso = Bangong Co China 33°45N 78°43E 243 C8
Pangrati Greece 37°56N 23°45E 112 B2
Pangsau Pass Burma 27°15N 96°10E 241 B6
Pangsua, Sungei → Singapore 1°25N 103°45E 138 A2
Pangtara Burma 20°57N 96°40E 241 E6
Panguipulli Chile 39°38S 72°20W 336 A2
Panguitch U.S.A. 37°50N 112°26W 305 H7
Panguna Papua N. G. 6°21S 155°25E 286 D8
Pangururan Indonesia 2°37N 98°42E 234 B1
Pangutaran Phil. 6°18N 120°35E 233 H3
Pangutaran Group Phil. 6°18N 120°34E 233 H3
Panhala India 16°49N 74°7E 244 F2
Panhandle U.S.A. 35°21N 101°23W 314 D4
Pani Mines India 22°29N 73°50E 242 H5
Pania-Mutombo Dem. Rep. of the Congo 5°11S 23°51E 265 D4
Pänï'au U.S.A. 21°56N 160°5W 302 B1
Panié, Mt. N. Cal. 20°36S 164°46E 288 d
Panihati India 22°41N 88°22E 124 A2
Panikota I. India 20°46N 71°21E 242 J4
Panipat India 29°25N 77°2E 242 E7
Paniqui Phil. 15°40N 120°34E 232 D3
Panitan Phil. 11°28N 122°46E 233 F4
Panj = Pyandzh → Asia 37°6N 68°20E 240 A2
Panjab Afghan. 34°23N 67°1E 240 B2
Panjakent = Pendzhikent Tajikistan 39°29N 67°37E 217 E7
Panjal Range = Pir Panjal Range India 32°30N 76°50E 242 C7
Panjang Kepulauan Riau, Indonesia 4°15N 108°12E 235 B3
Panjang Lampung, Indonesia 5°25S 105°20E 234 D3
Panjang, Bukit Singapore 1°22N 103°45E 138 A2
Panjgur Pakistan 27°0N 64°5E 240 D2
Panjhra → India 21°13N 74°57E 244 D2
Panjim = Panaji India 15°25N 73°50E 245 G1
Panjin China 41°3N 122°2E 227 D12
Panjnad → Pakistan 28°57N 70°30E 242 E4
Panjnad Barrage Pakistan 29°22N 71°15E 242 E4
Panjsher □ Afghan. 35°50N 69°45E 240 B3
Panjwai Afghan. 31°26N 65°27E 242 D1
Panke → Germany 52°31N 13°22E 115 A3
Pankow Germany 52°34N 13°23E 115 A3
Pankshin Nigeria 9°16N 9°25E 263 D6
Panmunjŏm N. Korea 37°59N 126°38E 224 D3
Panna India 24°40N 80°15E 243 G9
Panna △ India 24°40N 80°0E 243 G8
Panna Hills India 24°40N 81°15E 243 G9
Pannawonica Australia 21°39S 116°19E 278 D2
Panngi Vanuatu 15°58S 168°12E 287 E6
Pano Akil Pakistan 27°51N 69°7E 242 F3
Pano Lefkara Cyprus 34°53N 33°20E 207 F9
Pano Panayia Cyprus 34°55N 32°38E 207 F8
Panopah Indonesia 1°55S 111°10E 235 C4
Panora U.S.A. 41°42N 94°22W 310 C2
Panorama Brazil 21°21S 51°51W 335 A5
Panormos Greece 35°25N 24°41E 207 E5
Panruti India 11°46N 79°35E 245 J4
Pansemal India 21°39N 74°42E 242 J6
Panshan = Panjin China 41°3N 122°2E 227 D12
Panshi China 42°58N 126°5E 227 C14
Pantabangan L. Phil. 15°50N 121°9E 232 D3
Pantanal Matogrossense △ Brazil 17°35S 57°27W 331 D6
Pantanaw Burma 16°59N 95°28E 241 G5
Pantanos de Centla ⌓ Mexico 18°25N 92°25W 319 D6
Pantar Indonesia 8°28S 124°10E 231 F6
Pante Macassar E. Timor 9°30S 123°58E 231 F6
Pantelleria Italy 36°50N 11°57E 200 F4
Panthéon Paris, France 134 c4
Pantheon Rome, Italy 136 b2
Panthersville U.S.A. 33°43N 84°16W 113 B3
Panti Indonesia 0°22N 100°3E 234 B2
Pantin France 48°53N 2°24E 134 A3
Pantin Sakan Burma 18°38N 97°33E 241 F6
Pantitlán Mexico 19°24N 99°4W 128 B2
Pantoja Peru 0°58S 75°10W 328 D2
Pantón Spain 42°31N 7°37W 194 C3
Pantukan Phil. 7°9N 125°54E 233 H5
Panu Dem. Rep. of the Congo 3°50S 19°10E 264 C3
Pánuco Mexico 22°3N 98°10W 319 C5
Panuitan I. Phil. 19°26N 121°30E 232 B3
Panukulan Phil. 14°56N 121°49E 232 D3
Panvel India 18°59N 73°4E 244 E1

Panyabungan Indonesia 0°51N 99°33E 234 B1
Panyam Nigeria 9°27N 9°8E 263 D6
Panyu = Guangzhou China 23°6N 113°13E 121 B2
Panyu China 22°51N 113°20E 229 F9
Panzhihua China 26°33N 101°44E 228 D3
Panzi Dem. Rep. of the Congo 7°17S 18°1E 265 D3
Pao → Anzoátegui, Venezuela 8°6N 64°17W 329 B5
Pao → Apure, Venezuela 8°33N 68°1W 328 B4
Paoay Phil. 18°3N 120°30E 232 B3
Paochi = Baoji China 34°20N 107°5E 226 G4
Paoki = Baoji China 34°20N 107°5E 226 G4
Páola Italy 39°21N 16°2E 201 C9
Paola Malta 35°52N 14°30E 206 F8
Paola Kans., U.S.A. 38°35N 94°53W 308 F6
Paoli U.S.A. 38°33N 86°28W 311 F10
Paonia U.S.A. 38°52N 107°36W 304 G10
Paopao Moorea 17°30S 149°49W 289 e
Paoting = Baoding China 38°50N 115°28E 226 E8
Paot'ou = Baotou China 40°32N 110°2E 226 D6
Paoua C.A.R. 7°9N 16°20E 264 A3
Pápa Hungary 47°22N 17°30E 182 C2
Päpä Hawai'i, U.S.A. 19°13N 155°52W 302 D6
Papa Stour U.K. 60°20N 1°42W 167 A7
Papa Westray U.K. 59°20N 2°55W 167 B6
Päpa'aloa U.S.A. 19°59N 155°13W 302 D6
Papagayo → Mexico 16°46N 99°43W 319 D5
Papagayo, G. de Costa Rica 10°30N 85°50W 320 D2
Papagni → India 15°35N 77°45E 245 G3
Papahänaumokuäkea Marine Nat. Monument U.S.A. 25°25N 170°35W 302 F9
Papaïchton Fr. Guiana 3°48N 54°10W 329 C7
Päpa'ikou U.S.A. 19°47N 155°6W 302 D6
Papakura N.Z. 37°4S 174°59E 284 D3
Papantla Mexico 20°27N 97°19W 319 C5
Papar Malaysia 5°45N 116°0E 235 A5
Papara Tahiti 17°43S 149°31W 289 e
Paparangi N.Z. 41°12S 174°48E 143 B1
Paparoa N.Z. 36°6S 174°16E 284 C3
Paparoa △ N.Z. 42°7S 171°26E 285 C6
Paparoa Ra. N.Z. 42°5S 171°35E 285 C6
Papas, Akra Greece 38°13N 21°20E 204 C3
Papatoetoe N.Z. 36°59S 174°51E 284 C3
Papatura Solomon Is. 7°32S 158°47E 287 L10
Papeete Tahiti 17°32S 149°34W 289 e
Papenburg Germany 53°5N 7°23E 178 B3
Papenoo Tahiti 17°30S 149°25W 289 e
Papenoo → Tahiti 17°30S 149°25W 289 e
Papetoai Moorea 17°29S 149°52W 289 e
Paphlagonia Turkey 41°30N 33°0E 212 B5
Paphos Cyprus 34°46N 32°25E 207 F8
Paphos ✕ (PFO) Cyprus 34°43N 32°30E 207 F8
Papien Chiang = Da → Vietnam 21°15N 105°20E 228 G5
Papikio Oros Greece 41°15N 25°13E 203 E9
Papiol Spain 41°25N 2°0E 114 A1
Paposo Chile 25°0S 70°30W 334 B1
Papoutsa Cyprus 34°54N 33°4E 207 F9
Papua □ Indonesia 4°0S 137°0E 231 E9
Papua, G. of Papua N. G. 9°0S 144°50E 286 E3
Papua New Guinea ■ Oceania 8°0S 145°0E 286 E3
Papudo Chile 32°29S 71°27W 334 C1
Papuk Croatia 45°30N 17°30E 182 E2
Papun Burma 18°2N 97°30E 241 F6
Papunya Australia 23°15S 131°54E 278 D5
Pará = Belém Brazil 1°20S 48°30W 332 B2
Pará □ Brazil 3°20S 52°0W 331 A7
Paraburdoo Australia 23°14S 117°32E 278 D2
Paracale Phil. 14°17N 122°48E 232 D4
Paracas, Pen. de Peru 13°53S 76°20W 330 C2
Paracatu Brazil 17°10S 46°50W 333 E2
Paracatu → Brazil 16°30S 45°4W 333 E2
Paracel Is. S. China Sea 15°50N 112°0E 230 A4
Parachilna Australia 31°10S 138°21E 282 A3
Parachinar Pakistan 33°55N 70°5E 242 C4
Paraćin Serbia 43°54N 21°27E 202 C5
Paracuru Brazil 3°24S 39°4W 332 B4
Parada, Punta Peru 15°22S 75°11W 330 D2
Paradas Spain 37°18N 5°29W 195 H5
Paradela Spain 42°44N 7°37W 194 C3
Paradera Aruba 12°32N 70°0W 322 f
Paradip India 20°15N 86°35E 244 D8
Paradise Calif., U.S.A. 39°46N 121°37W 306 F5
Paradise Nev., U.S.A. 36°5N 115°8W 124 B2
Paradise → Canada 53°27N 57°19W 299 B8
Paradise Hill Canada 53°32N 109°28W 297 C7
Paradise I. Bahamas 25°6N 77°19W 153 b
Paradise River Canada 53°27N 57°17W 299 B8
Paradise Valley U.S.A. 41°30N 117°32W 304 F5
Paradisi Greece 36°18N 28°7E 206 E12
Parado Indonesia 8°42S 118°30E 231 F5
Paragould U.S.A. 36°3N 90°29W 315 C9
Paragua = Palawan Phil. 9°30N 118°30E 233 G2
Paraguá → Bolivia 13°34S 61°53W 331 C5
Paragua → Venezuela 6°55N 62°55W 329 B5
Paraguaçu = Paraguaçu Paulista Brazil 22°22S 50°35W 335 A5
Paraguaçú → Brazil 12°45S 38°54W 333 D4
Paraguaçu Paulista Brazil 22°22S 50°35W 335 A5
Paraguaipoa Venezuela 11°21N 71°57W 328 A3
Paraguaná, Pen. de Venezuela 12°0N 70°0W 328 A4
Paraguarí Paraguay 25°36S 57°0W 334 B4
Paraguarí □ Paraguay 26°0S 57°10W 334 B4
Paraguay ■ S. Amer. 23°0S 57°0W 334 A4
Paraguay → Paraguay 27°18S 58°38W 334 B4
Paraíba = João Pessoa Brazil 7°10S 34°52W 332 C5
Paraíba □ Brazil 7°0S 36°0W 332 C4
Paraíba do Sul → Brazil 21°37S 41°3W 333 F3
Paraíso Brazil 19°3S 52°59W 331 D7
Paraíso Tabasco, Mexico 18°24N 93°14W 319 D6
Paraiso Panama 9°3N 79°38W 320 c
Parak Iran 27°38N 52°25E 247 E7
Parakhino Paddubye Russia 58°26N 33°10E 188 C7
Parakou Benin 9°25N 2°40E 263 D5
Parakylia Australia 30°24S 136°25E 282 A2
Paralimni Cyprus 35°2N 33°58E 207 E9
Paralio Astros Greece 37°25N 22°45E 204 D4
Paralkote India 19°47N 80°41E 244 E5
Param I. Micronesia 7°21N 151°47E 287 T18
Parama I. Papua N. G. 9°0S 143°25E 286 E2
Paramaribo Suriname 5°50N 55°10W 329 B6
Parambu Brazil 6°13S 40°43W 332 C3
Paramillo, Cerro Colombia 7°4N 75°55W 328 B2
Paramillo △ Colombia 7°37N 76°13W 328 B2
Paramirim Brazil 13°26S 42°15W 333 D3
Paramirim → Brazil 11°34S 43°18W 333 D3
Paramithia Greece 39°30N 20°35E 204 B2
Paramonga Peru 10°40S 77°50W 330 C2
Paramount Studios U.S.A. 34°5N 118°19W 126 B3
Paramus U.S.A. 40°56N 74°2W 132 A1
Paramushir, Ostrov Russia 50°24N 156°0E 215 D16
Paran → Israel 30°20N 35°10E 251 H6
Paraná Argentina 31°45S 60°30W 334 C3
Paraná Brazil 12°30S 47°48W 333 D2
Paraná □ Brazil 24°30S 51°0W 335 A5
Paraná → Argentina 33°43S 59°15W 334 C4
Paraná → Brazil 12°30S 48°14W 333 D2
Paranaguá Brazil 25°30S 48°30W 335 B6
Paranaíba Brazil 19°40S 51°11W 331 D7
Paranaíba → Brazil 20°6S 51°4W 333 F1
Paranapanema → Brazil 22°40S 53°9W 335 A5
Paranapiacaba, Serra do Brazil 24°31S 48°35W 335 A6
Paranaque Phil. 14°30N 120°59E 127 B1
Paranas Phil. 11°42N 125°2E 233 F5
Paranavaí Brazil 23°4S 52°56W 335 A5
Parang Maguindanao, Phil. 7°23N 124°16E 233 H5
Parang Sulu, Phil. 5°55N 120°54E 233 J3
Parangippettai India 11°30N 79°38E 245 J4
Parângul Mare, Vf. Romania 45°20N 23°37E 183 E8
Paranthan Sri Lanka 9°26N 80°24E 245 K5
Paraoa French Polynesia 19°9S 140°43W 289 f
Paraparaumu N.Z. 40°57S 175°3E 284 G4
Parapetí → Bolivia 18°58S 62°21W 331 D5
Paraspori, Akra Greece 35°55N 27°15E 205 F9
Paratinga Brazil 12°40S 43°10W 333 D3
Paratoo Australia 32°42S 139°20E 282 B3
Paraúna Brazil 16°55S 50°26W 333 E1
Paray-le-Monial France 46°27N 4°7E 173 F11
Paray-Vieille-Poste France 48°42N 2°20E 134 B3
Parbati → Mad. P., India 25°50N 76°30E 242 G7
Parbati → Raj., India 26°54N 77°53E 242 F7
Parbatipur Bangla. 25°39N 88°55E 241 C2
Parbhani India 19°8N 76°52E 244 E3
Parchim Germany 53°26N 11°52E 178 B7
Parchwitz = Prochowice Poland 51°17N 16°20E 185 G3
Parco = Sinclair U.S.A. 41°47N 107°7W 304 F10
Parczew Poland 51°40N 22°52E 185 G9
Pardes Hanna-Karkur Israel 32°28N 34°57E 251 F5
Pardilla Spain 41°33N 3°43W 194 D7
Pardisān Nature Park Iran 35°44N 51°22E 141 A2
Pardo → Bahia, Brazil 15°40S 39°0W 333 E4
Pardo → Mato Grosso, Brazil 21°46S 52°9W 335 A5
Pardo → Minas Gerais, Brazil 15°48S 44°48W 333 E3
Pardo → São Paulo, Brazil 20°10S 48°38W 333 F2
Pardoo Roadhouse Australia 20°6S 119°3E 278 D2
Pardubice Czech Rep. 50°3N 15°45E 180 A8
Pardubický □ Czech Rep. 49°50N 16°0E 180 B8
Pardubitz = Pardubice Czech Rep. 50°3N 15°45E 180 A8
Pare Indonesia 7°43S 112°12E 231 G15
Pare Mts. Tanzania 4°0S 37°45E 268 C4
Parecis, Serra dos Brazil 13°0S 60°0W 331 C6
Paredes de Nava Spain 42°9N 4°42W 194 C6
Parel India 18°59N 72°49E 130 B1
Parelhas Brazil 6°41S 36°39W 332 C4
Paren Russia 62°30N 163°15E 215 C17
Parenda India 18°16N 75°28E 244 E2
Parengarenga Harbour N.Z. 34°31S 173°0E 284 A2
Parent Canada 47°55N 74°35W 298 C5
Parent, L. Canada 48°31N 77°1W 298 C4
Parentis-en-Born France 44°21N 1°4W 174 D2
Parepare Indonesia 4°0S 119°40E 235 C5
Parfino Russia 57°59N 31°34E 188 D6
Parga Greece 39°15N 20°29E 204 B2
Pargas = Länsi-Turunmaa Finland 60°18N 22°18E 188 B2
Pargi India 17°11N 77°53E 244 E3
Pargo, Pta. do Madeira 32°49N 17°17W 153 c
Parguera Puerto Rico 17°59N 67°3W 321 b
Parham Canada 44°39N 76°43W 313 B8
Pari Brazil 23°32S 46°36W 137 B2
Paria → U.S.A. 36°52N 111°36W 305 H8
Paria, G. de Venezuela 10°20N 62°0W 323 t
Paria, Pen. de Venezuela 10°50N 62°30W 329 A5
Pariaguán Venezuela 8°51N 64°34W 329 B5
Pariaman Indonesia 0°47S 100°11E 234 C2
Paricatuba Brazil 4°26S 61°53W 329 D5
Paricutín, Cerro Mexico 19°28N 102°15W 318 D4
Parigi Indonesia 0°50S 120°5E 231 E6
Parika Guyana 6°50N 58°20W 329 B6
Parikia Greece 37°6N 25°11E 205 D7
Parikkala Finland 61°33N 29°31E 188 B5
Parima, Serra Brazil 2°30N 64°0W 329 C5
Parinari Peru 4°35S 74°25W 330 A3
Pariñas, Pta. Peru 4°30S 82°0W 330 A1
Parincea Romania 46°27N 27°9E 183 D12
Paringa Australia 34°10S 140°46E 282 C4
Parintins Brazil 2°40S 56°50W 329 D6
Parioli Italy 41°55N 12°29E 136 B1
Pariparit Kyun Burma 14°52N 93°41E 245 G11
Paris Ont., Canada 43°12N 80°25W 312 C4
Paris Paris, France 48°53N 2°20E 134 A3
Paris Idaho, U.S.A. 42°14N 111°24W 304 E8
Paris Ill., U.S.A. 39°36N 87°42W 311 E9
Paris Ky., U.S.A. 38°13N 84°15W 311 F12
Paris Mo., U.S.A. 39°29N 92°0W 310 E5
Paris Tenn., U.S.A. 36°18N 88°19W 315 C10
Paris Tex., U.S.A. 33°40N 95°33W 314 E7
Paris, Ville de □ France 48°50N 2°20E 173 D9
Paris Charles de Gaulle ✕ (CDG) France 49°0N 2°32E 173 D9
Paris Orly ✕ (ORY) France 48°44N 2°23E 134 B3
Parish U.S.A. 43°25N 76°8W 313 C8
Parishville U.S.A. 44°38N 74°49W 313 B10
Pariti Indonesia 10°1S 123°45E 278 B3
Parje India 18°54N 72°57E 130 B2
Park U.S.A. 48°45N 122°18W 306 B4
Park City U.S.A. 37°48N 97°20W 308 G5
Pārk-e Āzādegān Iran 35°37N 51°28E 141 B2
Pārk-e Mellat Iran 35°47N 51°24E 141 A2
Park Falls U.S.A. 45°56N 90°27W 308 C8
Park Forest U.S.A. 41°29N 87°40W 311 C9
Park Head Canada 44°36N 81°9W 312 B3
Park Hills U.S.A. 37°51N 90°51W 310 G6
Park Range U.S.A. 40°41N 106°41W 304 F10
Park Rapids U.S.A. 46°55N 95°4W 308 B6
Park Ridge U.S.A. 42°2N 87°51W 119 A1
Park River U.S.A. 48°24N 97°45W 308 A5
Park Royal U.K. 51°31N 0°16W 125 A2
Park Rynie S. Africa 30°25S 30°45E 271 D5
Parkā Bandar Iran 25°55N 59°35E 247 E8
Parkal India 18°12N 79°43E 244 E4
Parkán = Štúrovo Slovak Rep. 47°48N 18°41E 181 D11
Parkano Finland 62°1N 23°0E 188 A2
Parkchester U.S.A. 40°49N 73°50W 132 B2
Parkdale Canada 43°38N 79°25W 141 B2
Parkent Uzbekistan 41°18N 69°40E 217 D7
Parker Ariz., U.S.A. 34°9N 114°17W 307 L12
Parker Pa., U.S.A. 41°5N 79°41W 312 E5
Parker Center Los Angeles, U.S.A. 127 b2
Parker Dam U.S.A. 34°18N 114°8W 307 L12
Parkersburg Iowa, U.S.A. 42°35N 92°47W 310 B4
Parkersburg W. Va., U.S.A. 39°16N 81°34W 309 F13
Parkes Australia 33°9S 148°11E 283 B8
Parkfield U.S.A. 35°54N 120°26W 306 K6
Parkhill Canada 43°15N 81°38W 312 C3
Parkhurst S. Africa 26°8S 28°1E 123 A2
Parkland U.S.A. 47°9N 122°26W 306 C4
Parklawn U.S.A. 38°50N 77°7W 143 B3
Parkmore S. Africa 26°5S 28°2E 123 A2
Parkside U.S.A. 37°44N 122°29W 136 B2
Parkston U.S.A. 43°24N 97°59W 308 D5
Parksville Canada 49°20N 124°21W 296 D4
Parktown S. Africa 26°10S 28°2E 123 B2
Parkview S. Africa 26°9S 28°1E 123 A2
Parkville U.S.A. 40°38N 73°57W 132 C2
Parkway U.S.A. 38°32N 121°25W 306 G5
Parkwood Gauteng, S. Africa 26°9S 28°2E 123 A2
Parkwood Western Cape, S. Africa 34°2S 18°30E 118 B1
Parla Spain 40°14N 3°46W 194 E7
Parlakimidi India 18°45N 84°5E 244 E7
Parlatuvier Trin. & Tob. 11°18N 60°39W 323 s
Parli India 18°50N 76°35E 244 E3
Parliament Budapest, Hungary 117 b2
Pârliţa Moldova 47°19N 27°52E 183 C12
Parma Italy 44°48N 10°20E 198 D7
Parma Idaho, U.S.A. 43°47N 116°57W 304 E5
Parma Ohio, U.S.A. 41°24N 81°43W 312 E3
Parma → Italy 44°56N 10°26E 198 D7
Parnaguá Brazil 10°10S 44°38W 332 D3
Parnaíba Brazil 2°54S 41°47W 332 B3
Parnaíba → Brazil 3°0S 41°50W 332 B3
Parnamirim Pernambuco, Brazil 8°5S 39°34W 332 C4
Parnamirim Rio Grande do N., Brazil 5°55S 35°15W 332 C4
Parnarama Brazil 5°31S 43°6W 332 C3
Parnassos Greece 38°35N 22°30E 204 C4
Parnassus N.Z. 42°42S 173°23E 285 C8
Parndana Australia 35°48S 137°12E 282 C2
Parner India 19°0N 74°26E 244 E2
Parnitha Greece 38°14N 23°45E 204 C5
Parnitha △ Greece 38°12N 23°44E 204 C5
Parnonas Oros Greece 37°15N 22°45E 204 D4
Pärnu Estonia 58°28N 24°33E 188 C3
Paro Dzong Bhutan 27°32N 89°53E 241 B2
Parola India 20°47N 75°7E 244 D2
Paroo → Australia 31°28S 143°32E 282 A5
Paros Greece 37°5N 25°12E 205 D7
Parow S. Africa 33°53S 18°37E 118 A2
Parowan U.S.A. 37°51N 112°50W 305 H7
Parpaillon France 44°30N 6°40E 175 D10
Parque Chacabuco Argentina 34°39S 58°26W 117 B2
Parque Patricios Argentina 34°39S 58°23W 117 B2
Parral Chile 36°10S 71°52W 334 D1
Parramatta Australia 33°48S 151°1E 283 B9
Parramatta → Australia 33°49S 151°3E 139 A1
Parras Mexico 25°25N 102°11W 318 B4
Parrett → U.K. 51°12N 3°1W 169 F4
Parris I. U.S.A. 32°20N 80°41W 316 C9
Parrish U.S.A. 27°35N 82°26W 317 H7
Parrott U.S.A. 31°54N 84°31W 316 D5
Parrsboro Canada 45°30N 64°25W 299 C7
Parry Channel Canada 74°15N 94°0W 295 C13
Parry I. Canada 45°18N 80°10W 312 A4
Parry Is. Canada 77°0N 110°0W 295 B10
Parry Sound Canada 45°20N 80°0W 312 A5
Parsābād Iran 39°39N 47°50E 213 C12
Parsaloi Kenya 1°16N 36°51E 268 B4
Parsberg Germany 49°10N 11°43E 179 F7
Parsęta → Poland 54°11N 15°34E 184 D2
Parsnip → Canada 55°10N 123°2W 296 B4
Parsons U.S.A. 37°20N 95°16W 308 G6
Parsons Ra. Australia 13°30S 135°15E 280 A2
Partabpur India 20°0N 80°42E 244 E5
Partanna Italy 37°43N 12°53E 200 E5
Partenio ⌂ Italy 40°56N 14°33E 201 B7
Parthenay France 46°38N 0°16W 172 F6
Parthenon Athens, Greece 112 c2
Partinico Italy 38°3N 13°7E 200 D6
Partizansk Russia 43°8N 133°9E 215 E14
Partizánske Slovak Rep. 48°38N 18°23E 181 C11
Partridge I. Canada 55°59N 87°37W 298 A2
Partry Mts. Ireland 53°40N 9°28W 166 C2
Partur India 19°40N 76°14E 244 E3
Paru → Brazil 1°33S 52°38W 329 D7
Parú → Venezuela 4°20N 66°27W 328 C4
Paru de Oeste → Brazil 1°30N 56°0W 329 C6
Parucito → Venezuela 5°18N 65°59W 328 B4
Parur India 10°13N 76°14E 245 J3
Paruro Peru 13°45S 71°50W 330 C3
Parvān □ Afghan. 35°0N 69°0E 240 B3
Parvatipuram India 18°50N 83°25E 244 E6
Parvatsar India 26°52N 74°49E 242 F6
Påryd Sweden 56°34N 15°55E 163 H9
Parys S. Africa 26°52S 27°29E 270 C4
Pas, Pta. des Spain 38°46N 1°26E 206 D1
Pas, The Canada 53°45N 101°15W 297 C8
Pas-de-Calais □ France 50°30N 2°10E 173 B9
Paşabahçe Turkey 41°6N 29°5E 122 B2
Pasada Spain 43°23N 5°40W 194 B5
Pasadena Nfld. & L., Canada 49°1N 57°36W 299 C8
Pasadena Calif., U.S.A. 34°9N 118°8W 126 B4
Pasadena Tex., U.S.A. 29°43N 95°13W 314 G7
Pasaje Ecuador 3°23S 79°50W 328 D2
Pasaje → Argentina 25°39S 63°56W 334 B3
Paşalimanı Turkey 40°29N 27°36E 203 F11
Pasar Indonesia 8°27S 114°54E 231 J17
Pasar Minggu Indonesia 6°16S 106°49E 122 B1
Pasarkuok Indonesia 1°27S 100°36E 234 C2
Pasarsibuhuan Indonesia 1°3N 99°43E 234 B1
Pasay Phil. 14°32N 120°59E 127 B1
Pascagoula U.S.A. 30°21N 88°33W 315 F10
Pascagoula → U.S.A. 30°23N 88°37W 315 F10
Paşcani Romania 47°14N 26°45E 183 C11
Pasco U.S.A. 46°14N 119°6W 304 C4
Pasco □ Peru 10°40S 75°0W 330 C3
Pasco I. Australia 20°57S 115°20E 278 D2
Pascoag U.S.A. 41°57N 71°42W 313 E13
Pascoe Vale Australia 37°43S 144°55E 128 A1
Pascua, I. de Chile 27°7S 109°23W 330 b
Paseo de la Reforma Mexico City, Mexico 128 b2
Pasewalk Germany 53°30N 13°58E 178 B9
Pasfield L. Canada 58°24N 105°20W 297 B7
Pasha → Russia 60°29N 32°55E 188 B7
Pashmakli = Smolyan Bulgaria 41°36N 24°38E 203 E8
Pasig Phil. 14°33N 121°4E 127 B2
Pasig → Phil. 14°31N 121°6E 127 B2
Pasighat India 28°4N 95°21E 241 A5
Pasila Finland 60°12N 24°56E 121 B2
Pasing Germany 48°8N 11°28E 131 B1
Pasinler Turkey 39°59N 41°41E 213 C9
Pasir Mas Malaysia 6°2N 102°8E 237 J4
Pasir Panjang Singapore 1°18N 103°46E 138 B2
Pasir Putih Malaysia 5°50N 102°24E 237 K4
Pasir Ris Singapore 1°22N 103°56E 138 A3
Pasirian Indonesia 8°13S 113°8E 235 D4
Pasirkuning = Dabo Indonesia 0°30S 104°33E 234 C2
Pasirpengarayan Indonesia 0°51N 100°16E 234 B2
Påskallavik Sweden 57°10N 16°26E 163 G10
Paskūh Iran 27°34N 61°39E 247 E9
Pasłęk Poland 54°3N 19°41E 184 D6
Pasłęka → Poland 54°26N 19°46E 184 D6
Pasley, C. Australia 33°52S 123°35E 279 F3
Pašman Croatia 43°58N 15°20E 199 E12
Pasmore → Australia 31°5S 139°49E 282 A3
Pasni Pakistan 25°15N 63°27E 240 D1
Paso Bravo △ Paraguay 22°32S 57°5W 334 A4
Paso Cantinela Mexico 32°33N 115°47W 307 N11
Paso de Indios Argentina 43°55S 69°0W 336 B3
Paso de los Indios Argentina 38°32S 69°25W 336 A3
Paso de los Libres Argentina 29°44S 57°10W 334 B4
Paso de los Toros Uruguay 32°45S 56°30W 334 C4
Paso Flores Argentina 40°35S 70°38W 336 B2
Paso Robles U.S.A. 35°38N 120°41W 306 K6
Pasorapa Bolivia 18°16S 64°37W 331 D5
Paspébiac Canada 48°3N 65°17W 299 C6
Pasrur Pakistan 32°16N 74°43E 242 C6
Passage East Ireland 52°14N 7°0W 166 D5
Passage West Ireland 51°52N 8°21W 166 E3
Passaic U.S.A. 40°51N 74°7W 132 A1
Passaic → U.S.A. 40°42N 74°10W 132 B1
Passam Papua N. G. 3°41S 143°38E 286 B2
Passau Germany 48°34N 13°28E 179 G9
Passenheim = Pasym Poland 53°48N 20°49E 184 E7
Passero, C. Italy 36°41N 15°10E 201 F8
Passi Phil. 11°6N 122°38E 233 F4
Passirana Italy 45°32N 9°2E 129 A1
Passo Fundo Brazil 28°10S 52°20W 335 B5
Passos Brazil 20°45S 46°37W 333 F2
Passow Germany 53°8N 14°6E 178 B10
Passy France 45°55N 6°41E 175 C10
Pastavy Belarus 55°4N 26°50E 188 E4
Pastaza □ Ecuador 2°0S 77°0W 328 D2
Pastaza → Peru 4°50S 76°52W 328 D2
Pasto Colombia 1°13N 77°17W 328 C2
Pastol B. U.S.A. 63°7N 163°15W 303 E7
Pastos Bons Brazil 6°36S 44°5W 332 C3
Pastrana Spain 40°27N 2°53W 196 E2
Pasuquin Phil. 18°20N 120°37E 232 B3
Pasuruan Indonesia 7°40S 112°44E 235 D4
Pasym Poland 53°48N 20°49E 184 E7
Pásztó Hungary 47°52N 19°43E 182 C4
Pata Phil. 5°51N 121°10E 233 J3
Pata I. Phil. 5°49N 121°10E 233 J3
Patagonia Argentina 45°0S 69°0W 336 C3
Patagonia Ariz., U.S.A. 31°33N 110°45W 305 L8
Patambar Iran 29°45N 60°17E 247 D9
Patan = Lalitapur Nepal 27°40N 85°20E 243 F11
Patan = Somnath India 20°53N 70°22E 242 J4
Patan Gujarat, India 23°54N 72°14E 242 H5
Patan Maharashtra, India 17°22N 73°57E 244 F1
Patani Indonesia 0°20N 128°50E 231 D7
Pătârlagele Romania 45°19N 26°21E 183 E11
Pataudi India 28°18N 76°48E 242 E7
Patchewollock Australia 35°22S 142°12E 282 C5
Patchogue U.S.A. 40°46N 73°1W 313 F11
Pate Coast, Kenya 2°10S 41°0E 268 C5
Pate Taiwan 24°56N 121°17E 225 B3
Patea N.Z. 39°45S 174°30E 284 F3
Pategi Nigeria 8°50N 5°45E 263 D6
Patel Nagar India 28°39N 77°10E 120 B1
Patensie S. Africa 33°46S 24°49E 270 D3
Paterna Spain 39°30N 0°26W 197 F4
Paternion Austria 46°43N 13°38E 180 E6
Paternò Italy 37°34N 14°54E 201 E7
Pateros Manila, Phil. 14°32N 121°3E 127 B2
Pateros Wash., U.S.A. 48°3N 119°54W 304 B4
Paterson N.S.W., Australia 32°35S 151°36E 283 B9
Paterson N.J., U.S.A. 40°54N 74°9W 313 F10
Paterson Inlet N.Z. 46°56S 168°12E 285 G3
Paterson Ra. Australia 21°45S 122°10E 278 D3
Pathankot India 32°18N 75°45E 242 C6
Pathardi India 19°10N 75°11E 244 E2
Patharghata Bangla. 22°2N 89°58E 241 D2
Pathein = Bassein Burma 16°45N 94°30E 241 G5
Pathfinder Res. U.S.A. 42°28N 106°51W 304 E10
Pathiu Thailand 10°42N 99°19E 237 G2
Pathri India 19°15N 76°27E 244 E3
Pathum Thani Thailand 14°1N 100°32E 236 E3
Pathumwan Thailand 13°44N 100°31E 113 B2
Pati Indonesia 6°45S 111°1E 235 D4
Pati Pt. Guam 13°35N 144°57E 302 d
Patía Colombia 2°4N 77°4W 328 C2
Patía → Colombia 2°13N 78°40W 328 C2
Patiala Punjab, India 30°23N 76°26E 242 D7
Patiala Ut. P., India 27°43N 79°1E 243 F8
Patine Kouka Senegal 12°45N 13°45W 262 C2
Patipukur India 22°36N 88°24E 124 B2
Patisia Greece 38°2N 23°45E 112 A2
Patitiri Greece 39°8N 23°50E 204 B5
Patkai Bum India 27°0N 95°30E 241 B5
Patmos Greece 37°21N 26°36E 205 D8
Patna India 25°35N 85°12E 243 G11
Patnagarh India 20°43N 83°9E 244 D6
Patnanongan I. Phil. 14°48N 122°11E 232 D4
Patnongon Phil. 10°55N 122°0E 233 F4
Patnos Turkey 39°13N 42°51E 213 C10
Pato Branco Brazil 26°13S 52°40W 335 B5
Patoka L. U.S.A. 38°20N 86°40W 311 F10
Patong, Ao Thailand 7°54N 98°17E 237 a
Patonga Uganda 2°45N 33°15E 268 B3
Patos Albania 40°42N 19°38E 202 F3
Patos Brazil 6°55S 37°16W 332 C4
Patos, L. dos Brazil 31°20S 51°0W 335 C5
Patos, Río de los → Argentina 31°18S 69°25W 334 C2
Patos de Minas Brazil 18°35S 46°32W 333 E2
Patquía Argentina 30°2S 66°55W 334 C2
Patra Greece 38°14N 21°47E 204 C3
Patraikos Kolpos Greece 38°17N 21°30E 204 C3
Patras = Patra Greece 38°14N 21°47E 204 C3
Patreksfjörður Iceland 65°35N 24°0W 155 B2
Patriarsheye = Donskoy Russia 53°55N 38°15E 188 F10
Patricio Lynch, I. Chile 48°35S 75°30W 336 C1
Patriot Hills Antarctica 82°20S 81°25W 151 E16
Patrocínio Brazil 18°57S 47°0W 333 E2
Pattada Italy 40°35N 9°6E 200 B2
Pattallassang Indonesia 5°26S 119°26E 235 D5
Pattani Thailand 6°48N 101°15E 237 J3
Pattaya Thailand 12°52N 100°55E 236 F3
Patten U.S.A. 46°0N 68°38W 309 B19
Patterson Calif., U.S.A. 37°28N 121°8W 306 H5
Patterson Ga., U.S.A. 31°23N 82°8W 316 D7
Patterson La., U.S.A. 29°42N 91°18W 314 G9
Patterson, Mt. U.S.A. 38°29N 119°20W 306 G7
Patteson, Passage Vanuatu 15°26S 168°12E 287 E6
Patti Punjab, India 31°17N 74°54E 242 D6
Patti Ut. P., India 25°55N 82°12E 243 G10
Patti Italy 38°8N 14°58E 201 D7
Pattoki Pakistan 31°5N 73°52E 242 D5
Patton = Monroeville U.S.A. 40°26N 79°45W 312 F5
Patton U.S.A. 40°38N 78°39W 312 F6
Pattonsburg U.S.A. 40°3N 94°8W 310 D2
Pattukkattai India 10°25N 79°20E 245 J4
Patu Brazil 6°6S 37°38W 332 C4
Patuakhali Bangla. 22°20N 90°25E 241 D3
Patuanak Canada 55°55N 107°43W 297 B7
Patuca → Honduras 15°50N 84°18W 320 C3
Patuca, Punta Honduras 15°49N 84°14W 320 C3
Patuca △ Honduras 14°30N 85°30W 320 D2
Pătulele Romania 44°21N 22°47E 182 F7
Patur India 20°27N 76°56E 244 D3
Patvinsuo △ Finland 63°7N 30°45E 160 E24
Pátzcuaro Mexico 19°31N 101°38W 318 D4
Pau France 43°19N 0°25W 174 E3
Pau, Gave de → France 43°33N 1°12W 174 E2
Pau d' Arco Brazil 7°30S 49°22W 332 C2
Pau dos Ferros Brazil 6°7S 38°10W 332 C4
Pauanui N.Z. 37°1S 175°52E 284 D4
Paucartambo Peru 13°19S 71°35W 330 C3
Paudash Canada 44°59N 77°58W 312 B7
Pauillac France 45°11N 0°46W 174 C3
Pauini Brazil 7°40S 66°58W 330 B4
Pauini → Brazil 1°42S 62°50W 329 D5
Pauk Burma 21°27N 94°30E 241 E5
Paukkaung Burma 18°54N 95°33E 241 F5
Pauktaw Burma 20°11N 93°4E 241 E4
Paul I. Canada 56°30N 61°20W 299 A7
Paul Isnard Fr. Guiana 4°47N 54°1W 329 C7
Paul Revere Park Boston, U.S.A. 116 a2
Paul Smiths U.S.A. 44°26N 74°15W 313 B10
Paulatuk Canada 69°25N 124°0W 294 D7
Paulding U.S.A. 41°8N 84°35W 311 C12
Paulding Bay S. Ocean 66°0S 118°0E 151 C8
Paulhan France 43°33N 3°28E 174 E7
Paulis = Isiro Dem. Rep. of the Congo 2°53N 27°40E 268 B2
Paulista = Paulistana Brazil 8°9S 41°9W 332 C3
Paulista Brazil 7°57S 34°53W 332 C5
Paulistana Brazil 8°9S 41°9W 332 C3
Paulistrröm Sweden 57°28N 15°31E 163 G9
Paulo Afonso Brazil 9°21S 38°15W 332 C4
Paulo de Faria Brazil 20°2S 49°24W 333 F2
Paulo E. Virginia, Gruta Brazil 22°56S 43°16W 135 B1
Paulpietersburg S. Africa 27°23S 30°50E 271 C5
Pauls Valley U.S.A. 34°44N 97°13W 314 D6
Paulshof Germany 52°34N 13°42E 115 A5
Pauma Valley U.S.A. 33°16N 116°58W 307 M10
Paung Burma 16°37N 94°28E 241 G5
Paungde Burma 18°29N 95°30E 241 F5
Pauni India 20°48N 79°40E 244 D4
Pauri India 30°9N 78°47E 243 D8
Pausa Peru 15°16S 73°22W 330 D3
Pauto → Colombia 5°9N 70°55W 328 B3
Pavagada India 14°6N 77°16E 245 G3
Pāveh Iran 35°3N 46°22E 213 E12
Pavelets Russia 53°49N 39°14E 188 F10
Pavia Italy 45°7N 9°8E 198 C6
Pavilion U.S.A. 42°52N 78°1W 312 D6
Pavilly France 49°34N 0°57E 172 C7
Pāvilosta Latvia 56°53N 21°14E 184 B8
Pavlikeni Bulgaria 43°14N 25°20E 203 C9
Pavlodar Kazakhstan 52°33N 77°0E 217 B9
Pavlograd = Pavlohrad Ukraine 48°30N 35°52E 189 H8
Pavlohrad Ukraine 48°30N 35°52E 189 H8
Pavlovo Russia 55°58N 43°5E 190 C6
Pavlovsk Russia 50°26N 40°5E 190 E5
Pavlovskaya Russia 46°17N 39°47E 191 G4
Pavlovskiy-Posad Russia 55°47N 38°42E 188 E10
Pavo U.S.A. 30°58N 83°45W 316 E6
Pavshino Russia 55°49N 37°20E 129 B1
Pavullo nel Frignano Italy 44°20N 10°50E 198 D7
Pavuvu Solomon Is. 9°4S 159°8E 287 M10
Paw Paw Ill., U.S.A. 41°41N 88°59W 310 C8
Paw Paw Mich., U.S.A. 42°13N 85°53W 311 B11
Pawahku Burma 26°11N 98°40E 241 B7
Pawai, Pulau Singapore 1°11N 103°44E 237 d
Pawan → Indonesia 1°55S 110°0E 235 C4
Pawayan India 28°4N 80°6E 243 E9
Pawhuska U.S.A. 36°40N 96°20W 314 C6
Pawling U.S.A. 41°34N 73°36W 313 E11
Pawnee Ill., U.S.A. 39°36N 89°35W 310 E7
Pawnee Okla., U.S.A. 36°20N 96°48W 314 C6
Pawnee City U.S.A. 40°7N 96°9W 308 E5
Pawtucket U.S.A. 41°53N 71°23W 313 E13
Paxi Greece 39°14N 20°12E 206 C10
Paximadia Greece 35°0N 24°35E 207 F5
Paxson U.S.A. 63°2N 145°30W 303 E11
Paxton U.S.A. 40°27N 88°6W 311 D8
Paya Lebar Singapore 1°21N 103°52E 138 A3
Payagyi Burma 17°29N 96°32E 241 G6
Payakumbuh Indonesia 0°20S 100°35E 234 C2
Payapa = General Tinio Phil. 15°39N 121°10E 232 D3
Payas = Yakacık Turkey 36°46N 36°11E 250 B7
Payerne Switz. 46°49N 6°56E 179 J2
Payette U.S.A. 44°5N 116°56W 304 D5
Paymogo Spain 37°44N 7°21W 195 H3
Payne U.S.A. 41°5N 84°44W 311 C12
Payne Bay = Kangirsuk Canada 60°0N 70°0W 295 F18
Payne L. Canada 59°30N 74°30W 295 F17
Payne Pt. Ascension I. 7°57S 14°25W 153 g
Paynes Find Australia 29°15S 117°42E 279 E2
Paynesville Liberia 6°20N 10°45W 262 D2
Paynesville Minn., U.S.A. 45°23N 94°43W 308 C6
Payo Obispo = Chetumal Mexico 18°30N 88°20W 319 D7
Pays de la Loire □ France 47°45N 0°25W 172 E6
Paysandú Uruguay 32°19S 58°8W 334 C4
Payson Ariz., U.S.A. 34°14N 111°20W 305 J8
Payson Utah, U.S.A. 40°3N 111°44W 304 F8
Paz → Guatemala 13°44N 90°10W 320 D1
Paz, B. de la Mexico 24°9N 110°25W 318 C2
Pāzanān Iran 30°35N 49°59E 247 D6
Pazar Turkey 41°10N 40°50E 213 B9
Pazarcık Turkey 37°30N 37°17E 212 D7
Pazardzhik Bulgaria 42°12N 24°20E 203 D8
Pazardzhik □ Bulgaria 42°12N 24°20E 203 D8
Pazarköy Turkey 39°51N 27°24E 205 B9
Pazarlar Turkey 39°0N 29°7E 205 C11
Pazaryeri Turkey 40°0N 29°56E 205 B11
Pazaryolu Turkey 40°21N 40°47E 213 B9
Pazin Croatia 45°14N 13°56E 199 C10
Pazña Bolivia 18°36S 66°55W 330 D4
Pčinja → Macedonia 41°50N 21°45E 202 E5
Pe Ell U.S.A. 46°34N 123°18W 306 D3
Pea → U.S.A. 31°1N 85°51W 316 D4
Peabody U.S.A. 42°31N 70°56W 313 D14
Peace → Alta., Canada 59°0N 111°25W 296 B6
Peace → Fla., U.S.A. 26°56N 82°6W 317 J7
Peace Point Canada 59°7N 112°27W 296 B6
Peace River Canada 56°15N 117°18W 296 B5
Peach Springs U.S.A. 35°32N 113°25W 305 J7
Peachland Canada 49°47N 119°45W 296 D5
Peachtree City U.S.A. 33°25N 84°35W 316 B5
Peacock Pt. Wake I. 19°16N 166°37E 302 b
Peak, The = Kinder Scout U.K. 53°24N 1°52W 168 D6
Peak, The Ascension I. 7°57S 14°20W 153 g
Peak Charles △ Australia 32°42S 121°10E 279 F3
Peak District △ U.K. 53°24N 1°46W 168 D6
Peak Hill Australia 32°47S 148°11E 283 B8
Peak Ra. Australia 22°50S 148°20E 280 C4
Peake Australia 35°25S 139°55E 282 C3
Peake Cr. → Australia 28°2S 136°7E 281 D2
Peakhurst Australia 33°57S 151°3E 139 B1
Peal de Becerro Spain 37°55N 3°7W 195 H7
Peale, Mt. U.S.A. 38°26N 109°14W 304 G9
Peale I. Wake I. 19°18N 166°37E 302 b
Peania Greece 37°56N 23°50E 112 B3
Pearblossom U.S.A. 34°30N 117°55W 307 L9
Pearl U.S.A. 39°28N 90°38W 310 E6
Pearl → U.S.A. 30°11N 89°32W 315 F10
Pearl and Hermes Reef U.S.A. 27°55N 175°45W 302 F8
Pearl Banks Sri Lanka 8°45N 79°45E 245 K4
Pearl City U.S.A. 21°24N 157°59W 302 K14
Pearl Harbor U.S.A. 21°21N 157°57W 302 K14
Pearl Harbor Nat. Wildlife Refuge ⌂ U.S.A. 21°23N 157°59W 302 K14
Pearl River = Zhu Jiang → China 22°45N 113°37E 229 F9
Pearl River U.S.A. 41°4N 74°2W 313 E10
Pearl River Bridge China 22°15N 113°48E 219 a
Pearls Grenada 12°9N 61°37W 323 q
Pearls Rock Grenada 12°9N 61°36W 323 q
Pearsall U.S.A. 28°54N 99°6W 314 G5
Pearson U.S.A. 31°18N 82°51W 316 D7
Pearson Int. Toronto ✕ (YYZ) Canada 43°46N 79°35W 141 A1
Peary Land Greenland 82°40N 33°0W 154 A7
Pease → U.S.A. 34°12N 99°2W 314 D5
Peawanuck Canada 55°15N 85°12W 298 A2
Pebane Mozam. 17°10S 38°8E 269 F4
Pebas Peru 3°10S 71°46W 328 D3
Pebble, I. Falk. Is. 51°20S 59°40W 153 f
Pebble Beach U.S.A. 36°34N 121°57W 306 J5
Peć Kosovo 42°40N 20°17E 202 D4
Peçanha Brazil 18°33S 42°34W 333 E3
Pecatonica U.S.A. 42°19N 89°22W 310 B7
Pecatonica → U.S.A. 42°26N 89°12W 310 B7
Péccioli Italy 43°33N 10°43E 198 E7
Pechea Romania 45°36N 27°49E 183 E12
Pechenga Russia 69°29N 31°4E 160 B24
Pechenizhyn Ukraine 48°30N 24°48E 183 B9
Pechiguera, Pta. Canary Is. 28°51N 13°53W 153 e2
Pechnezhskoye Vdkhr. Ukraine 50°5N 36°54E 189 G9
Pechora Russia 65°10N 57°11E 186 A10
Pechora → Russia 68°13N 54°15E 186 A9
Pechorskaya Guba Russia 68°40N 54°0E 186 A9
Pechory Russia 57°48N 27°40E 188 D4
Pecica Romania 46°10N 21°3E 182 D6
Pecka Serbia 44°18N 19°33E 202 B3
Peckham U.K. 51°28N 0°3W 125 B3
Pécora, C. Italy 39°27N 8°23E 200 C1
Pecos N. Mex., U.S.A. 35°35N 105°41W 305 J11
Pecos Tex., U.S.A. 31°26N 103°30W 314 F3
Pecos → U.S.A. 29°42N 101°22W 314 G4
Pécs Hungary 46°5N 18°15E 182 D3
Pedasí Panama 7°32N 80°2W 320 E3
Pedda Bellala India 19°4N 78°49E 244 E4
Peddapalli India 18°40N 79°24E 244 E4
Peddapuram India 17°6N 82°8E 244 F6
Pedder, L. Australia 42°55S 146°10E 281 G4
Peddie S. Africa 33°14S 27°7E 271 D4
Pedernales Dom. Rep. 18°2N 71°44W 321 C5
Pedernales Ecuador 0°5N 80°3W 328 C1
Pederstrup Denmark 55°44N 12°20E 118 A2
Pedieos → Cyprus 35°10N 33°54E 207 E9
Pedirka Desert Australia 26°47S 134°11E 281 A1
Pedra Azul Brazil 16°2S 41°17W 333 E3
Pedra Branca Brazil 0°51N 51°58W 329 C7
Pedra Grande, Recifes de Brazil 17°45S 38°58W 333 E4
Pedra Lume C. Verde Is. 16°40N 22°52W 153 j
Pedralbes Spain 41°23N 2°7E 114 A1
Pedras Negras Brazil 12°51S 62°54W 331 C5
Pedras Tinhosas, I. São Tomé & Príncipe 1°22N 7°17E 265 a
Pedregal de San Angel, Jardines del Mexico 19°19N 99°12W 128 C1
Pedreguer Spain 38°48N 0°3E 197 G5
Pedreiras Brazil 4°32S 44°40W 332 B3
Pedro Afonso Brazil 9°0S 48°10W 332 C2
Pedro Bank W. Indies 17°5N 78°20W 320 C4
Pedro Bay U.S.A. 59°47N 154°7W 303 G9
Pedro Cays Jamaica 17°5N 77°48W 320 C4
Pedro Chico Colombia 1°4N 70°25W 328 C3
Pedro de Valdivia Chile 22°55S 69°38W 334 A2
Pedro Dorado Colombia 1°0N 70°14W 328 C3
Pedro Juan Caballero Paraguay 22°30S 55°40W 335 A4
Pedro Miguel Locks Panama 9°1N 79°36W 320 c
Pedro Muñoz Spain 39°25N 2°56W 195 F8
Pedro Pt. = North West Pt. Jamaica 18°27N 78°13W 320 a
Pedrógão Grande Portugal 39°55N 8°9W 194 F2
Pee Dee = Great Pee Dee → U.S.A. 33°21N 79°10W 315 E15
Peebinga Australia 34°52S 140°57E 282 C4
Peebles Borders, U.K. 55°40N 3°11W 167 F5
Peebles Ohio, U.S.A. 38°57N 83°24W 311 F13
Peekskill U.S.A. 41°17N 73°55W 313 E11
Peel I. of Man 54°13N 4°40W 168 C3
Peel → N.S.W., Australia 30°50S 150°29E 283 A9
Peel → N.W.T., Canada 67°0N 135°0W 294 D5
Peel Sd. Canada 73°0N 96°0W 294 C12
Peene → Germany 54°9N 13°46E 178 A9
Peera Peera Poolanna L. Australia 26°30S 138°0E 281 D2
Peerless Lake Canada 56°37N 114°40W 296 B6
Peers Canada 53°40N 116°0W 296 C5
Peery L. Australia 30°45S 143°35E 282 A5
Pegasus Bay N.Z. 43°20S 173°10E 285 D8
Peggau Austria 47°12N 15°21E 180 D8
Pegnitz Germany 49°44N 11°31E 179 F7
Pegnitz → Germany 49°30N 10°59E 179 F6
Pego Spain 38°51N 0°8W 197 G4
Pegu Burma 17°20N 96°29E 241 G6
Pegu □ Burma 17°30N 96°30E 241 G6
Pegu Yoma Burma 19°0N 96°0E 241 F6
Peguera Spain 39°32N 2°26E 206 B3
Pehčevo Macedonia 41°41N 22°55E 202 E6
Pehlıvanköy Turkey 41°20N 26°55E 203 E10
Pehuajó Argentina 35°45S 62°0W 334 D3
Pei Xian China 34°44N 116°55E 226 G9
Peian = Bei'an China 48°10N 126°20E 219 B14
Peihai = Beihai China 21°28N 109°6E 228 G7
Peikang Taiwan 23°34N 120°18E 225 C2
Peikang Hsi → Taiwan 24°2N 120°50E 225 B2
Peikant'ang Taiwan 26°13N 120°0E 225 b
Peimen Taiwan 23°16N 120°7E 225 C2
Peinan Taiwan 22°47N 121°7E 225 D3
Peinan Hsi → Taiwan 22°46N 121°10E 225 D3
Peinanchu Shan Taiwan 23°3N 120°52E 225 C2
Peine Chile 23°45S 68°8W 334 A2
Peine Niedersachsen, Germany 52°19N 10°14E 178 C6
Peip'ing = Beijing China 39°53N 116°21E 114 B1
Peipu Taiwan 24°2N 121°36E 225 B3
Peipus, L. = Chudskoye, Ozero Russia 58°13N 27°30E 188 C4
Peissenberg Germany 47°48N 11°4E 179 H7
Peitawu Shan Taiwan 22°38N 120°46E 225 D2
Peitou Changhua, Taiwan 23°52N 120°30E 225 C2
Peitou T'aipei, Taiwan 25°11N 121°27E 225 A3
Peitun Taiwan 24°10N 120°41E 225 B2
Peitz Germany 51°51N 14°24E 178 D10
Peixe Brazil 12°0S 48°40W 333 D2
Peixe → Brazil 21°31S 51°58W 333 F1
Peixoto de Azeredo → Brazil 10°6S 55°31W 331 C6
Pejantan, Pulau Indonesia 0°7N 107°13E 234 B3
Peje = Peć Kosovo 42°40N 20°17E 202 D4
Pek → Serbia 44°45N 21°29E 202 B5
Pekalongan Indonesia 6°53S 109°40E 235 D3
Pekan Malaysia 3°30N 103°25E 237 L4
Pekan Nenas Malaysia 1°31N 103°31E 237 d

Pekanbaru *Indonesia* 0°30N 101°15E **234** B2
Pekhorka → *Russia* 55°37N 38°2E **129** C6
Pekhra-Pokrovskoye *Russia* 55°50N 37°56E **129** A5
Pekhra-Yakovievskaya *Russia* 55°47N 37°57E **129** B5
Pekin *U.S.A.* 40°35N 89°40W **310** D7
Peking = Beijing *China* 39°53N 116°21E **114** B1
Pekutatan *Indonesia* 8°25S 114°49E **231** J17
Pela *Greece* 40°46N 22°23E **202** F6
Pelabuhan Ratu, Teluk *Indonesia* 7°5S 106°30E **234** D3
Pelabuhanratu *Indonesia* 7°0S 106°32E **234** D3
Pélagos = Kira Panagia *Greece* 39°17N 24°4E **204** B6
Pelaihari *Indonesia* 3°55S 114°45E **235** C4
Pelat, Mt. *France* 44°16N 6°42E **175** D10
Pelcowizna *Poland* 52°17N 21°0E **142** B2
Pelczyce *Poland* 53°3N 15°16E **185** E2
Peleaga, Vf. *Romania* 45°22N 22°55E **182** E7
Pelechuco *Bolivia* 14°48S 69°4W **330** C4
Pelée, Mt. *Martinique* 14°48N 61°10W **322** j
Pelee, Pt. *Canada* 41°54N 82°31W **298** D3
Pelee I. *Canada* 41°47N 82°40W **312** E2
Pelejo *Peru* 6°10S 75°49W **330** B2
Pelekech *Kenya* 3°52N 35°8E **268** B4
Peleliu I. *Palau* 7°1N 134°15E **288** c
Peleng *Indonesia* 1°20S 123°30E **231** E6
Pelenge *Dem. Rep. of the Congo* 2°44S 22°39E **264** C4
Pelentong *Malaysia* 1°32N 103°49E **237** d
Pélézi *Ivory C.* 7°17N 6°54W **262** D3
Pelham *U.S.A.* 31°8N 84°9W **316** D5
Pelhřimov *Czech Rep.* 49°24N 15°12E **180** B8
Pelican *U.S.A.* 57°58N 136°14W **296** B1
Pelican L. *Canada* 52°28N 100°20W **297** C8
Pelican Narrows *Canada* 55°10N 102°56W **297** B8
Pelion *U.S.A.* 33°46N 81°15W **316** B8
Pelister △ *Macedonia* 41°0N 21°10E **202** F5
Pelješac *Croatia* 42°55N 17°25E **199** F14
Pelkosenniemi *Finland* 67°6N 27°28E **160** C22
Pell City *U.S.A.* 33°35N 86°17W **316** B3
Pella *Northern Cape, S. Africa* 29°1S 19°6E **270** C2
Pella *Iowa, U.S.A.* 41°25N 92°55W **310** C4
Pella □ *Greece* 40°52N 22°0E **202** F6
Pello *Finland* 66°47N 23°59E **160** C20
Pellworm *Germany* 54°31N 8°39E **178** A4
Pelly → *Canada* 62°47N 137°19W **296** A1
Pelly Bay *Canada* 68°38N 89°50W **295** D14
Peloponnesos □ *Greece* 37°10N 22°0E **204** D4
Peloponnisos Station *Athens, Greece* **112** a1
Peloritani, Monti *Italy* 38°3N 15°20E **201** D8
Pelorus → *N.Z.* 41°16S 173°45E **285** B8
Pelorus Sd. *N.Z.* 40°59S 173°59E **285** A8
Pelotas *Brazil* 31°42S 52°23W **335** B5
Pelotas → *Brazil* 27°28S 51°55W **335** B5
Pelovo *Bulgaria* 43°26N 24°17E **203** C8
Pelplin *Poland* 53°55N 18°42E **184** E5
Pelvoux, Massif du *France* 44°52N 6°20E **175** D10
Pemalang *Indonesia* 6°53S 109°23E **235** D3
Pemanggil, Pulau *Malaysia* 2°37N 104°21E **237** L5
Pematangsiantar *Indonesia* 2°57N 99°5E **234** B1
Pemba *Mozam.* 12°58S 40°30E **269** E5
Pemba *Zambia* 16°30S 27°28E **269** F2
Pemba Channel *Tanzania* 5°0S 39°37E **268** D4
Pemba I. *Tanzania* 5°0S 39°45E **268** D4
Pemberton *W. Austral., Australia* 34°30S 116°0E **279** F2
Pemberton *B.C., Canada* 50°25N 122°50W **296** C4
Pembina → *Canada* 54°45N 114°17W **296** C6
Pembroke *Ont., Canada* 45°50N 77°7W **298** C4
Pembroke *Trin. & Tob.* 11°13N 60°37W **323** s
Pembroke *Pembs., U.K.* 51°41N 4°55W **169** F3
Pembroke *Ga., U.S.A.* 32°8N 81°37W **316** C8
Pembroke Pines *U.S.A.* 26°0N 80°13W **317** J9
Pembrokeshire □ *U.K.* 51°52N 4°56W **169** F3
Pembrokeshire Coast △ *U.K.* 51°50N 5°2W **169** F2
Pembuang → *Indonesia* 3°24S 112°33E **235** C4
Pen *India* 18°45N 73°5E **244** E1
Pen-y-Ghent *U.K.* 54°10N 2°14W **168** C5
Peña, Sierra de la *Spain* 42°32N 0°45W **196** C4
Peña de Francia, Sierra de la *Spain* 40°32N 6°10W **194** E4
Penafiel *Portugal* 41°12N 8°17W **194** D2
Peñafiel *Spain* 41°35N 4°7W **194** D6
Peñaflor *Spain* 37°43N 5°21W **195** H5
Penal *Trin. & Tob.* 10°9N 61°29W **323** t
Peñalara *Spain* 40°51N 3°57W **194** E7
Peñalolén *Chile* 33°28S 70°32W **137** B2
Penalva *Brazil* 3°18S 45°10W **332** B2
Penamacôr *Portugal* 40°10N 7°10W **194** E3
Penang = Pinang *Malaysia* 5°25N 100°15E **237** c
Penápolis *Brazil* 21°30S 50°0W **335** A6
Peñaranda de Bracamonte *Spain* 40°53N 5°13W **194** E5
Peñarroya *Spain* 40°25N 0°40W **196** E4
Peñarroya-Pueblonuevo *Spain* 38°19N 5°16W **195** G5
Penarth *U.K.* 51°26N 3°11W **169** F4
Peñas, C. de *Spain* 43°42N 5°52W **194** B5
Penas, G. de *Chile* 47°0S 75°0W **336** C2
Peñas, Pta. *Venezuela* 11°17N 62°0W **329** A5
Peñas de San Pedro *Spain* 38°44N 2°0W **197** G3
Peñas del Chache *Canary Is.* 29°6N 13°33W **153** e2
Peñausende *Spain* 41°17N 5°52W **194** D5
Pencarrow Hd. *N.Z.* 41°22S 174°51E **143** C2
Pench → *India* 21°17N 79°10E **244** D4
Pench △ *India* 21°45N 79°20E **243** J8
Pench'i = Benxi *China* 41°20N 123°48E **224** B1
Pend Oreille → *U.S.A.* 49°4N 117°37W **304** B5
Pend Oreille, L. *U.S.A.* 48°10N 116°21W **304** B5
Pendalofos *Greece* 40°14N 21°12E **202** F5
Pendé → *C.A.R.* 7°55N 16°36E **264** A3
Pendembu *Eastern, S. Leone* 8°10N 10°42W **262** D2
Pendembu *Northern, S. Leone* 9°7N 11°14W **262** D2
Pendências *Brazil* 5°15S 36°43W **332** C4
Pender B. *Australia* 16°45S 122°42E **278** C3
Pendik *Turkey* 40°53N 29°13E **203** F13
Pendjari → *Benin* 10°55N 0°50E **263** C5
Pendjari △ *Benin* 11°15N 1°32E **263** C5
Pendleton *Ind., U.S.A.* 40°0N 85°45W **311** E11
Pendleton *Oreg., U.S.A.* 45°40N 118°47W **304** D4
Pendopo *Indonesia* 3°16S 103°52E **234** C2
Pendra *India* 22°46N 81°57E **243** H9
Pendzhikent *Tajikistan* 39°29N 67°37E **217** E7
Penebangan *Indonesia* 1°13S 109°15E **235** C3
Peneda-Gerês △ *Portugal* 41°57N 8°15W **194** D2
Penedo *Brazil* 10°15S 36°36W **332** D4
Penelokan *Indonesia* 8°17S 115°22E **231** J18
Penetanguishene *Canada* 44°50N 79°55W **312** B5
Penfield *U.S.A.* 41°13N 78°35W **312** E6
Peng Chau *China* 22°17N 114°2E **219** a
Peng Siang → *Singapore* 1°24N 103°43E **138** A2
Peng'an *China* 31°2N 106°22E **228** B6
Penganga → *India* 19°53N 79°9E **244** E4
Penge *Kasai-Or., Dem. Rep. of the Congo* 5°30S 24°33E **265** D4
Penge *Sud-Kivu, Dem. Rep. of the Congo* 4°27S 28°25E **268** C2
Penge *London, U.K.* 51°24N 0°3W **125** B3
P'enghu □ *Taiwan* 23°30N 119°30E **225** C1
P'enghu Ch'üntou *Taiwan* 23°34N 119°30E **225** C1
P'enghu Tao *Taiwan* 23°34N 119°37E **225** C1
Penglai *China* 37°48N 120°42E **227** F11
Pengshan *China* 30°14N 103°58E **228** B4
Pengshui *China* 29°17N 108°12E **228** C7
Penguin *Australia* 41°8S 146°6E **281** G4
Pengxi *China* 30°44N 105°45E **228** B5
Pengze *China* 29°52N 116°32E **229** C11
Pengzhou *China* 31°4N 103°32E **228** B4
Penha *Brazil* 22°49S 43°17W **135** A1
Penhalonga *Zimbabwe* 18°52S 32°40E **269** F3
Peniche *Portugal* 39°19N 9°22W **195** F1
Penicuik *U.K.* 55°50N 3°13W **121** B2
Penida, Nusa *Indonesia* 8°45S 115°30E **231** K18
Peninnes, Alpes = Pennine, Alpi *Alps* 46°4N 7°30E **179** J3
Peninsular Malaysia □ *Malaysia* 4°0N 102°0E **237** L4
Peñíscola *Spain* 40°22N 0°24E **196** E5
Penitente, Serra do *Brazil* 8°45S 46°20W **332** C2
Penjaringan *Indonesia* 6°7S 106°48E **122** A1
Pēnjwīn *Iraq* 35°37N 45°56E **213** E11
Penki = Benxi *China* 41°20N 123°48E **224** B1
Penkridge *U.K.* 52°44N 2°6W **168** E5
Penmarch *France* 47°49N 4°21W **172** E2
Penmarch, Pte. de *France* 47°48N 4°22W **172** E2
Penn = Penn Hills *U.S.A.* 40°28N 79°52W **312** F5
Penn Hills *U.S.A.* 40°28N 79°52W **312** F5
Penn Station *New York, U.S.A.* **132** c2
Penn Yan *U.S.A.* 42°40N 77°3W **312** D7
Penna, Punta della *Italy* 42°10N 14°43E **199** F11
Pennant *Canada* 50°32N 108°14W **297** C7
Penne *Italy* 42°27N 13°55E **199** F10
Penner → *India* 14°35N 80°10E **245** G5
Penneshaw *Australia* 35°44S 137°56E **282** C2
Pennine, Alpi *Alps* 46°4N 7°30E **179** J3
Pennines *U.K.* 54°45N 2°27W **168** C5
Pennington *U.S.A.* 39°15N 121°47W **306** F5
Pennington → *Nigeria* 4°45N 5°35E **263** E6
Pennino, Mte. *Italy* 43°6N 12°53E **199** E9
Pennsburg *U.S.A.* 40°23N 75°29W **313** F9
Pennsylvania □ *U.S.A.* 40°45N 77°30W **309** E15
Pennsylvania Avenue *Washington, D.C., U.S.A.* **143** b2
Penville *U.S.A.* 40°30N 85°9W **311** D11
Penny *Canada* 53°51N 121°20W **296** C4
Peno *Russia* 57°2N 32°49E **188** D7
Penobscot → *U.S.A.* 44°30N 68°48W **309** C19
Penobscot B. *U.S.A.* 44°35N 68°50W **309** C19
Penola *Australia* 37°25S 140°48E **282** D4
Penong *Australia* 31°56S 133°1E **279** F5
Penonomé *Panama* 8°31N 80°21W **320** E3
Penot, Mt. *Vanuatu* 16°20S 167°31E **287** F5
Penrhyn *Cook Is.* 9°0S 158°0W **289** H12
Penrith *N.S.W., Australia* 33°43S 150°38E **283** B9
Penrith *Cumb., U.K.* 54°40N 2°45W **168** C5
Penryn *U.K.* 50°9N 5°7W **169** G2
Pensacola *U.S.A.* 30°25N 87°13W **317** E2
Pensacola B. *U.S.A.* 30°25N 87°5W **317** E2
Pensacola Mts. *Antarctica* 84°0S 40°0W **151** E1
Pense *Canada* 50°25N 104°59W **297** C8
Penshurst *Australia* 37°49S 142°20E **282** D5
Pensiangan *Malaysia* 4°33N 116°19E **235** B5
Pentagon *U.S.A.* 38°53N 77°3W **143** B3
Pentecost = Pentecôte *Vanuatu* 15°42S 168°10E **287** E6
Pentecostes *Brazil* 3°48S 39°17W **332** B4
Pentecôte *Vanuatu* 15°42S 168°10E **287** E6
Penticton *Canada* 49°30N 119°38W **296** D5
Pentland *Australia* 20°32S 145°25E **280** C4
Pentland Firth *U.K.* 58°43N 3°10W **167** C5
Pentland Hills *U.K.* 55°48N 3°25W **167** F5
Pentland Hills ⌓ *U.K.* 55°50N 3°20W **167** F5
Penukonda *India* 14°5N 77°38E **245** G3
Penyagino *Russia* 55°50N 37°20E **129** A2
Penza *Russia* 53°15N 45°5E **190** D7
Penza □ *Russia* 52°50N 44°50E **190** D7
Penzance *U.K.* 50°7N 5°33W **169** G2
Penzberg *Germany* 47°45N 11°22E **179** H7
Penzhino *Russia* 63°30N 167°55E **215** C17
Penzhinskaya Guba *Russia* 61°30N 163°0E **215** C17
Penzing *Austria* 48°11N 16°18E **142** A1
Penzlin *Germany* 53°30N 13°5E **178** B9
People's Park *China* 31°13N 121°28E **138** B1
People's Square *China* 31°13N 121°28E **138** B1
Peoria *Ariz., U.S.A.* 33°43N 112°14W **305** K7
Peoria *Ill., U.S.A.* 40°42N 89°36W **310** D7
Peoria Heights *U.S.A.* 40°45N 89°35W **310** D7
Peotone *U.S.A.* 41°20N 87°48W **311** C9
Pepacton Res. *U.S.A.* 42°5N 74°58W **313** D10
Pepani → *S. Africa* 25°49S 22°47E **270** C3
Pepeekeo *U.S.A.* 19°51N 155°6W **302** D6
Pepel *S. Leone* 8°40N 13°5W **262** D2
Peqin *Albania* 41°3N 19°44E **202** E3
Pera Hd. *Australia* 12°55S 141°37E **280** A3
Perabumulih *Indonesia* 3°27S 104°15E **234** C2
Perachora *Greece* 38°2N 22°56E **204** C4
Perachori *Greece* 38°21N 20°43E **207** C2
Perak □ *Malaysia* 5°0N 101°0E **237** K3
Perak → *Malaysia* 4°0N 100°50E **237** K3
Perales del Alfambra *Spain* 40°38N 1°0W **196** E4
Perales del Puerto *Spain* 40°10N 6°40W **194** E4
Perales del Rio *Spain* 40°18N 3°38W **127** C2
Perama *Kerkyra, Greece* 39°34N 19°54E **206** B9
Perama *Kriti, Greece* 35°20N 24°40E **207** E5
Perancak *Indonesia* 8°24S 114°37E **231** J17
Peräpohjola *Finland* 66°16N 26°10E **160** C22
Perast *Montenegro* 42°31N 18°47E **202** D2
Peratia *Greece* 38°49N 20°45E **207** B2
Peravillo *Mexico City, Mexico* **128** a3
Percé *Canada* 48°31N 64°13W **299** C7
Perche *France* 48°31N 1°1E **172** D8
Perche, Collines du *France* 48°30N 0°40E **171** B4
Perche ⌓ *France* 48°24N 0°46E **172** D7
Perchtoldsdorf *Austria* 48°7N 16°17E **142** B1
Percival Lakes *Australia* 21°25S 125°0E **278** D4
Percy *Manche, France* 48°55N 1°11W **172** D5
Percy *Ill., U.S.A.* 38°5N 89°41W **310** F7
Percy Is. *Australia* 21°39S 150°16E **280** C5
Perdido → *Argentina* 42°55S 67°0W **336** B3
Perdido, Mte. *Spain* 42°40N 0°5E **196** C5
Perdizes *Brazil* 23°32S 46°39W **137** B2
Perdu, Mt. = Perdido, Mte. *Spain* 42°40N 0°5E **196** C5
Perechyn *Ukraine* 48°44N 22°28E **182** B7
Perehinske *Ukraine* 48°49N 24°11E **183** B9
Pereira *Colombia* 4°49N 75°43W **328** C2
Perelazovskiy *Russia* 49°8N 42°35E **191** F6
Peremul Par *India* 11°10N 72°4E **245** J1
Peremyshl = Przemyśl *Poland* 49°50N 22°45E **185** J9
Perené → *Peru* 11°9S 74°14W **330** C3
Peresecina *Moldova* 47°16N 28°46E **183** C13
Pereslavl-Zalesskiy *Russia* 56°45N 38°50E **188** D10
Peretu *Romania* 44°3N 25°5E **183** F10
Pereyaslav-Khmelnytskyy *Ukraine* 50°3N 31°28E **189** G6
Pereyma *Ukraine* 48°4N 29°30E **183** B14
Pérez, I. *Mexico* 22°24N 89°42W **319** C7
Perg *Austria* 48°15N 14°38E **180** C7
Pergamino *Argentina* 33°52S 60°30W **334** C3
Pergamon Museum *Berlin, Germany* **115** a4
Pergau → *Malaysia* 5°23N 102°2E **237** K3
Perge *Turkey* 37°3N 30°56E **250** A1
Pergine Valsugana *Italy* 46°4N 11°14E **199** B8
Pérgola *Italy* 43°34N 12°50E **199** E9
Perham *U.S.A.* 46°36N 95°34W **308** B6
Perhentian, Kepulauan *Malaysia* 5°54N 102°42E **237** K4
Peri → *Turkey* 38°53N 39°52E **213** C8
Periam *Romania* 46°2N 20°52E **182** D5
Péribonka → *Canada* 48°45N 72°5W **299** C5
Péribonka, L. *Canada* 50°1N 71°10W **299** B5
Péribonka, La Centrale de *Canada* 49°30N 71°10W **299** C5
Perico *Argentina* 24°20S 65°5W **334** A2
Pericos *Mexico* 25°3N 107°42W **318** B3
Périers *France* 49°11N 1°25W **172** C5
Périgord *France* 45°0N 0°40E **174** D4
Périgord-Limousin ⌓ *France* 45°40N 0°50E **174** C4
Périgueux *France* 45°10N 0°42E **174** C4
Perijá, Sierra de *Colombia* 9°30N 73°3W **328** B3
Perijá △ *Venezuela* 9°30N 72°55W **328** B3
Peringat *Malaysia* 6°2N 102°17E **237** J4
Perisher Valley *Australia* 36°27S 148°25E **283** D8
Peristera *Greece* 39°15N 23°58E **204** B5
Peristeri *Greece* 38°1N 23°42E **112** A2
Peristerona → *Cyprus* 35°8N 33°5E **207** E9
Perito Moreno *Argentina* 46°36S 70°56W **336** C2
Perito Moreno △ *Argentina* 47°49S 72°17W **336** C2
Peritoró *Brazil* 4°20S 44°18W **332** B3
Perivale *U.K.* 51°31N 0°18W **125** A2
Perivol = Dragovishtitsa *Bulgaria* 42°22N 22°39E **202** D6
Periyakulam *India* 10°5N 77°30E **245** J3
Periyar → *India* 10°15N 76°10E **245** J3
Periyar, L. *India* 9°25N 77°10E **245** K3
Periyar △ *India* 9°25N 77°10E **245** K3
Perk *Belgium* 50°56N 4°30E **116** A2
Perkasie *U.S.A.* 40°22N 75°18W **313** F9
Perković *Croatia* 43°41N 16°10E **199** E13
Perlach *Germany* 48°5N 11°37E **131** B2
Perlacher Forst *Germany* 48°4N 11°34E **131** B2
Perlas, Arch. de las *Panama* 8°41N 79°7W **320** E4
Perlas, Punta de *Nic.* 12°30N 83°30W **320** D3
Perleberg *Germany* 53°5N 11°52E **178** B7
Perlez *Serbia* 45°11N 20°22E **182** E5
Perlis □ *Malaysia* 6°30N 100°15E **237** J2
Perm *Russia* 58°0N 56°10E **186** C10
Përmet *Albania* 40°15N 20°21E **202** F4
Permskoye = Komsomolsk-na-Amur *Russia* 50°30N 137°0E **219** A16
Pernambuco = Recife *Brazil* 8°0S 35°0W **332** C5
Pernambuco □ *Brazil* 8°0S 37°0W **332** C4
Pernambuco Abyssal Plain *Atl. Oc.* 5°0S 24°0W **152** G9
Pernatty Lagoon *Australia* 31°30S 137°12E **282** A2
Pernik *Bulgaria* 42°35N 23°2E **202** D7
Pernik □ *Bulgaria* 42°35N 23°2E **202** D7
Pernov = Pärnu *Estonia* 58°28N 24°33E **188** C3
Peron Is. *Australia* 13°9S 130°4E **278** B5
Peron Pen. *Australia* 26°0S 113°10E **279** E1
Péronne *France* 49°55N 2°57E **173** C9
Peropok, Bukit *Singapore* 1°19N 103°42E **138** B2
Perosa Argentina *Italy* 44°58N 7°10E **198** D4
Perow *Canada* 54°35N 126°10W **296** C3
Perpendicular Pt. *Australia* 31°37S 152°52E **283** A10
Perpignan *France* 42°42N 2°53E **174** F6
Perrégaux = Mohammadia *Algeria* 35°33N 0°3E **261** A5
Perris *U.S.A.* 33°47N 117°14W **307** M9
Perros-Guirec *France* 48°49N 3°28W **172** D3
Perry *Fla., U.S.A.* 30°7N 83°35W **316** E6
Perry *Ga., U.S.A.* 32°28N 83°44W **316** C6
Perry *Iowa, U.S.A.* 41°51N 94°6W **310** C2
Perry *Mich., U.S.A.* 42°50N 84°13W **311** B12
Perry *Mo., U.S.A.* 39°26N 91°40W **310** E5
Perry *N.Y., U.S.A.* 42°42N 78°0W **312** D7
Perry *Okla., U.S.A.* 36°17N 97°14W **314** C6
Perrysburg *U.S.A.* 41°34N 83°38W **311** C13
Perryton *U.S.A.* 36°24N 100°48W **314** C4
Perryville *Alaska, U.S.A.* 55°55N 159°9W **303** J8
Perryville *Mo., U.S.A.* 37°43N 89°52W **310** G7
Persan *France* 49°9N 2°16E **173** C9
Persberg *Sweden* 59°47N 14°15E **162** E8
Perşembe *Turkey* 41°5N 37°46E **212** B7
Persepolis *Iran* 29°55N 52°50E **247** D7
Perseverancia *Bolivia* 14°44S 62°48W **331** C5
Pershing Square *Los Angeles, U.S.A.* **127** c1
Pershotravensk *Ukraine* 50°13N 27°40E **177** C14
Pershotravnevoye = Pershotravensk *Ukraine* 50°13N 27°40E **177** C14
Persia = Iran ■ *Asia* 33°0N 53°0E **247** C7
Persian Gulf *Asia* 27°0N 50°0E **247** E6
Perstorp *Sweden* 56°10N 13°25E **163** H7
Pertek *Turkey* 38°51N 39°19E **213** C8
Perth *W. Austral., Australia* 31°57S 115°52E **279** F2
Perth *Ont., Canada* 44°55N 76°15W **313** B8
Perth *Perth & Kinr., U.K.* 56°24N 3°26W **167** E5
Perth & Kinross □ *U.K.* 56°45N 3°55W **167** E5
Perth Amboy *U.S.A.* 40°30N 74°15W **313** F10
Perth-Andover *Canada* 46°44N 67°42W **299** C6
Pertuis *France* 43°42N 5°30E **175** E9
Pertusato, C. *France* 41°21N 9°11E **175** G13
Pertusella *Italy* 45°35N 9°3E **129** A1
Peru *Ill., U.S.A.* 41°20N 89°8W **310** C7
Peru *Ind., U.S.A.* 40°45N 86°4W **311** D10
Peru *N.Y., U.S.A.* 44°35N 73°32W **313** B11
Peru ■ *S. Amer.* 4°0S 75°0W **328** D3
Peru Basin *Pac. Oc.* 20°0S 95°0W **289** J18
Peru-Chile Trench *Pac. Oc.* 20°0S 72°0W **326** E3
Perúgia *Italy* 43°7N 12°23E **199** E9
Perušić *Croatia* 44°40N 15°22E **199** D12
Peruvian Vale *St. Vincent* 13°13N 61°12W **323** n
Pervomaysk *Russia* 54°56N 43°58E **190** C6
Pervomaysk *Ukraine* 48°10N 30°46E **189** H6
Pervomayskiy *Kazakhstan* 50°16N 82°0E **217** B10
Pervouralsk *Russia* 56°59N 59°59E **186** C10
Pervouralskiy = Pervouralsk *Russia* 56°59N 59°59E **186** C10
Pesada *Greece* 38°7N 20°35E **207** C2
Pesagot *West Bank* 31°54N 35°13E **123** A2
Pesanggrahag, Kali → *Indonesia* 6°10S 106°44E **122** B1
Pesaro *Italy* 43°54N 12°55E **199** E9
Pescadores = P'enghu Ch'üntou *Taiwan* 23°34N 119°30E **225** C1
Pescara *Italy* 42°28N 14°13E **199** F11
Pescara → *Italy* 42°28N 14°13E **199** F11
Peschanokopskoye *Russia* 46°14N 41°4E **191** G5
Peschanoye = Yashkul *Russia* 46°11N 45°21E **191** G7
Peschiera Borromeo *Italy* 45°26N 9°19E **129** B2
Péscia *Italy* 43°54N 10°41E **198** E7
Pescina *Italy* 42°2N 13°39E **199** F10
Pesek, Pulau *Singapore* 1°17N 103°41E **138** B2
Peshawar *Pakistan* 34°2N 71°37E **242** B4
Peshkopi *Albania* 41°41N 20°25E **202** E4
Peshtera *Bulgaria* 42°2N 24°18E **203** D8
Peshtigo *U.S.A.* 45°3N 87°45W **308** C10
Peski *Russia* 51°14N 42°29E **190** E6
Peski *Turkmenistan* 38°11N 62°59E **216** E6
Pêso da Régua *Portugal* 41°10N 7°47W **194** D3
Pesochnya = Kirov *Russia* 54°3N 34°20E **188** E8
Pesqueira *Brazil* 8°20S 36°42W **332** C4
Pessac *France* 44°48N 0°37W **174** D3
Pest *Hungary* 47°29N 19°5E **117** B2
Pest □ *Hungary* 47°29N 19°5E **182** C4
Pesterzsébet *Hungary* 47°26N 19°6E **117** B2
Pesthidegkút *Hungary* 47°33N 18°57E **117** A1
Pestimre *Hungary* 47°24N 19°11E **117** B3
Pestlőrinc *Hungary* 47°26N 19°11E **117** B3
Pestovo = Zavolzhye *Russia* 56°37N 43°26E **190** B6
Pestovo *Russia* 58°33N 35°42E **188** C8
Pestravka *Russia* 52°28N 49°57E **190** D9
Pestújhely *Hungary* 47°32N 19°7E **117** A2
Petah Tiqwa *Israel* 32°6N 34°53E **251** F5
Petalas *Greece* 38°25N 21°5E **207** C3
Petalidi *Greece* 36°57N 21°55E **204** E3
Petaling Jaya *Malaysia* 3°4N 101°42E **237** L3
Petaloudes *Greece* 36°18N 28°5E **206** E12
Petaluma *U.S.A.* 38°14N 122°39W **306** G4
Pétange *Lux.* 49°33N 5°55E **170** E5
Petaro *Pakistan* 25°31N 68°18E **242** G3
Petas *Helsinki, Finland* 60°15N 24°50E **121** B2
Petas *Greece* 39°10N 21°2E **204** B3
Petatlán *Mexico* 17°31N 101°16W **318** D4
Petauke *Zambia* 14°14S 31°20E **269** E3
Petawawa *Canada* 45°54N 77°17W **298** C4
Petén Itzá, L. *Guatemala* 16°58N 89°50W **320** C2
Peter I. *Br. Virgin Is.* 18°22N 64°35W **321** b
Peter I. Øy *Antarctica* 69°0S 91°0W **151** C16
Peter Pond L. *Canada* 55°55N 108°44W **297** B7
Peterbell *Canada* 48°36N 83°21W **298** C3
Peterborough *S. Austral., Australia* 32°58S 138°51E **282** B3
Peterborough *Ont., Canada* 44°20N 78°20W **312** B6
Peterborough *Peterborough, U.K.* 52°35N 0°15W **169** E7
Peterborough *N.H., U.S.A.* 42°53N 71°57W **313** D13
Peterborough □ *U.K.* 52°35N 0°15W **169** E7
Peterculter *U.K.* 57°6N 2°16W **167** D6
Peterhead *U.K.* 57°31N 1°48W **167** D7
Peterhof = Petrodvorets *Russia* 59°52N 29°54E **188** C5
Peterlee *U.K.* 54°47N 1°20W **168** C6
Petermann ⊙ *Australia* 24°58S 130°0E **279** E4
Petermann Bjerg *Greenland* 73°7N 28°25W **154** C8
Petermann Gletscher *Greenland* 80°30N 60°0W **154** A4
Petermann Ranges *Australia* 26°0S 130°30E **279** E5
Peter's Mine *Guyana* 6°14N 59°20W **329** B6
Petersburg = Peterborough *Australia* 32°58S 138°51E **282** B3
Petersburg *Alaska, U.S.A.* 56°48N 132°58W **303** H14
Petersburg *Ill., U.S.A.* 40°1N 89°51W **310** D7
Petersburg *Ind., U.S.A.* 38°30N 87°17W **311** F9
Petersburg *Mich., U.S.A.* 41°54N 83°43W **311** C13
Petersburg *Pa., U.S.A.* 40°34N 78°3W **312** F6
Petersburg *Va., U.S.A.* 37°14N 77°24W **309** G15
Petersburg *W. Va., U.S.A.* 39°1N 79°5W **309** F14
Petersfield *U.K.* 51°1N 0°56W **169** F7
Petershagen *Germany* 52°23N 8°58E **178** C4
Petilia Policastro *Italy* 39°7N 16°48E **201** C9
Petit Batanga *Cameroon* 3°15N 9°54E **264** B1
Petit-Bourg *Guadeloupe* 16°11N 61°37W **322** e
Petit-Canal *Guadeloupe* 16°25N 61°31W **322** e
Petit Cul-de-Sac Marin *Guadeloupe* 16°12N 61°33W **322** e
Petit Dominique *Grenada* 12°30N 61°24W **323** q
Petit Goâve *Haiti* 18°27N 72°51W **321** C5
Petit Lac Manicouagan *Canada* 51°25N 67°40W **299** B6
Petit Loango ⌓ *Gabon* 2°20S 9°40E **264** C1
Petit-Mécatina → *Canada* 50°40N 59°30W **299** B8
Petit-Mécatina, Î. du *Canada* 50°30N 59°25W **299** B8
Petit Piton *St. Lucia* 13°51N 61°5W **323** m
Petit Raffray *Mauritius* 20°0S 57°36E **272** e
Petit-Saguenay *Canada* 48°15N 70°4W **299** C5
Petit Saint Bernard, Col du *Italy* 45°40N 6°52E **175** C10
Petit Saut, Barrage de *Fr. Guiana* 5°0N 53°10W **248** B7
Petit Soufrière B. *Dominica* 15°23N 61°15W **323** k
Petitcodiac *Canada* 45°57N 65°11W **299** C6
Petite Anse *Martinique* 14°28N 61°4W **322** j
Petite-Île *Réunion* 21°20S 55°35E **272** f
Petite Martinique *Grenada* 12°31N 61°23W **323** q
Petite Rivière *Mauritius* 20°11S 57°26E **272** e
Petite Savane *Dominica* 15°15N 61°17W **323** k
Petite Terre = Pamandzi *Mayotte* 12°47S 45°16E **272** b
Petite Terre, Îles de la *Guadeloupe* 16°13N 61°9W **322** e
Petites-Anses *Guadeloupe* 15°51N 61°38W **322** e
Petitjean = Sidi Kacem *Morocco* 34°12N 5°42W **260** B3
Petitot → *Canada* 60°14N 123°29W **296** A4
Petitsikapau L. *Canada* 54°37N 66°25W **299** B6
Petlad *India* 22°30N 72°45E **242** H5
Peto *Mexico* 20°8N 88°55W **319** C7
Petone *N.Z.* 41°13S 174°53E **143** B2
Petorca *Chile* 32°15S 70°56W **334** C1
Petoskey *U.S.A.* 45°22N 84°57W **309** C11
Petra *Jordan* 30°20N 35°22E **251** H6
Petra *Spain* 39°37N 3°6E **206** B4
Petra, Ostrov *Russia* 76°15N 118°30E **215** B12
Petra Velikogo, Zaliv *Russia* 42°40N 132°0E **220** C6
Petre, Pt. *Canada* 43°50N 77°9W **312** C7
Petrel = Petrer *Spain* 38°30N 0°46W **197** G4
Petrella, Monte *Italy* 41°18N 13°40E **200** A6
Petrer *Spain* 38°30N 0°46W **197** G4
Petreto-Bicchisano *France* 41°47N 8°58E **175** G12
Petrich *Bulgaria* 41°24N 23°13E **202** E7
Petrified Forest △ *U.S.A.* 35°0N 109°30W **305** J9
Petrijanec *Croatia* 46°23N 16°17E **199** B13
Petrikov = Pyetrikaw *Belarus* 52°11N 28°29E **177** B15
Petrila *Romania* 45°29N 23°29E **183** E8
Petrinja *Croatia* 45°28N 16°18E **199** C13
Petrodvorets *Russia* 59°52N 29°54E **188** C5
Petrograd = Sankt-Peterburg *Russia* 59°55N 30°20E **137** B1
Petrogradskaya Storona *Russia* 59°56N 30°20E **137** B2
Petrolândia *Brazil* 9°5S 38°20W **332** C4
Petrolia *Canada* 42°54N 82°9W **312** D2
Petrolina *Brazil* 9°24S 40°30W **332** C3
Petromaryevka = Pervomaysk *Ukraine* 48°10N 30°46E **189** H6
Petropavl *Kazakhstan* 54°53N 69°13E **217** B7
Petropavlovsk = Petropavl *Kazakhstan* 54°53N 69°13E **217** B7
Petropavlovsk-Kamchatskiy *Russia* 53°3N 158°43E **215** D16
Petropavlovskiy = Akhtubinsk *Russia* 48°13N 46°7E **191** F8
Petropavlovsky = Severouralsk *Russia* 60°9N 59°57E **186** B10
Petrópolis *Brazil* 22°33S 43°9W **333** F3
Petroşani *Romania* 45°28N 23°20E **183** E8
Petroupoli *Greece* 38°3N 23°40E **112** A2
Petrova Gora *Croatia* 45°15N 15°45E **199** C12
Petrovac *Montenegro* 42°13N 18°57E **202** D2
Petrovac *Serbia* 44°22N 21°26E **202** B5
Petrovaradin *Serbia* 45°16N 19°55E **182** E4
Petrovgrad = Zrenjanin *Serbia* 45°22N 20°23E **182** E5
Petrovice *Czech Rep.* 50°2N 14°33E **135** B3
Petrovsk *Russia* 52°22N 45°19E **190** D7
Petrovsk-Port = Makhachkala *Russia* 43°0N 47°30E **191** J8
Petrovsk-Zabaykalskiy *Russia* 51°20N 108°55E **215** D11
Petrovskaya *Russia* 45°25N 37°58E **189** K9
Petrovskiy Park *Russia* 55°47N 37°34E **129** B3
Petrovsko-Razumovskoye *Russia* 55°49N 37°34E **129** B3
Petrovskoye = Svetlograd *Russia* 45°25N 42°58E **191** H6
Petrovsky Zavod = Petrovsk-Zabaykalskiy *Russia* 51°20N 108°55E **215** D11
Petrozavodsk *Russia* 61°41N 34°20E **188** B8
Petrus Steyn *S. Africa* 27°38S 28°8E **271** C4
Petrusburg *S. Africa* 29°4S 25°26E **270** C4
Petsamo = Pechenga *Russia* 69°29N 31°4E **160** B24
Pettycur *U.K.* 56°4N 3°10W **121** A2
Petukhovo *Russia* 55°6N 67°58E **217** A7
Petuna = Fuyu *China* 45°12N 124°43E **227** B13
Petzeck *Austria* 46°57N 12°48E **180** E5
Peumo *Chile* 34°21S 71°12W **334** C1
Peureulak *Indonesia* 4°48N 97°45E **234** B1
Peusangan → *Indonesia* 5°16N 96°51E **234** A1
Peutie *Belgium* 50°56N 4°27E **116** A2
Pevek *Russia* 69°41N 171°19E **215** C18
Pevely *U.S.A.* 38°17N 90°24W **310** F6
Peveragno *Italy* 44°20N 7°37E **198** D4
Peyrehorade *France* 43°34N 1°7W **174** E2
Peyruis *France* 44°1N 5°56E **175** D9
Pézenas *France* 43°28N 3°24E **174** E7
Pezinok *Slovak Rep.* 48°17N 17°17E **181** C10
Pfaffenhofen *Germany* 48°31N 11°31E **179** G7
Pfälzerwald ⌓ *Germany* 49°18N 9°55E **179** F5
Pfarrkirchen *Germany* 48°25N 12°56E **179** G8
Pfaueninsel *Germany* 52°26N 13°7E **115** B1
Pfeffenhausen *Germany* 48°39N 11°58E **179** G7
Pforzheim *Germany* 48°52N 8°41E **179** G4
Pfullendorf *Germany* 47°55N 9°15E **179** H5
Pfungstadt *Germany* 49°48N 8°35E **179** F4
Pha Taem △ *Thailand* 15°32N 105°30E **236** E5
Phaestos *Greece* 35°2N 24°50E **207** E5
Phagwara *India* 31°10N 75°40E **242** D6
Phala *Botswana* 23°45S 26°50E **270** B4
Phalaborwa *S. Africa* 23°57S 31°7E **271** B5
Phalera = Phulera *India* 26°52N 75°16E **242** F6
Phalodi *India* 27°12N 72°24E **242** F5
Phalsbourg *France* 48°46N 7°15E **173** D14
Phaltan *India* 17°59N 74°26E **244** F2
Phaluai, Ko *Thailand* 9°32N 99°41E **237** b
Phan *Thailand* 19°28N 99°43E **236** C2
Phan Rang-Thap Cham *Vietnam* 11°34N 109°0E **237** G7
Phan Ri Cua *Vietnam* 11°16N 108°40E **237** G7
Phan Si Pan *Vietnam* 22°18N 103°46E **236** A4
Phan Thiet *Vietnam* 11°1N 108°9E **237** G7
Phan Thiet, Vinh *Vietnam* 10°53N 108°5E **237** G7
Phanae *Greece* 38°8N 25°57E **205** C7
Phanat Nikhom *Thailand* 13°27N 101°11E **236** F3
Phangan, Ko *Thailand* 9°45N 100°0E **237** H3
Phangnga *Thailand* 8°28N 98°30E **237** H2
Phangnga, Ao *Thailand* 8°16N 98°33E **237** a
Phanom Sarakham *Thailand* 13°45N 101°21E **236** F3
Phaphund *India* 26°36N 79°28E **243** F8
Pharenda *India* 27°5N 83°17E **243** F10
Pharr *U.S.A.* 26°12N 98°11W **314** H5
Phatthalung *Thailand* 7°39N 100°6E **237** J3
Phaya Thai *Thailand* 13°45N 100°37E **113** B2
Phayam, Ko *Thailand* 9°44N 98°25E **237** H2
Phayao *Thailand* 19°11N 99°55E **236** C2
Phelps *U.S.A.* 42°58N 77°3W **312** D7
Phelps L. *Canada* 59°15N 103°15W **297** B8
Phenix City *U.S.A.* 32°28N 85°0W **315** E12
Phet Buri = Phetchaburi *Thailand* 13°1N 99°55E **236** F2
Phetchabun *Thailand* 16°25N 101°8E **236** D3
Phetchabun, Thiu Khao *Thailand* 16°0N 101°20E **236** E3
Phetchaburi *Thailand* 13°1N 99°55E **236** F2
Phi Phi, Ko *Thailand* 7°45N 98°46E **237** J2
Phiafay *Laos* 14°48N 106°0E **236** E6
Phibun Mangsahan *Thailand* 15°14N 105°14E **236** E5
Phichai *Thailand* 17°22N 100°10E **236** D3
Phichit *Thailand* 16°26N 100°22E **236** D3
Phihai *Pakistan* 24°50N 67°8E **123** A2
Philadelphia *Miss., U.S.A.* 32°46N 89°7W **315** E10
Philadelphia *N.Y., U.S.A.* 44°9N 75°43W **313** B9
Philadelphia *Pa., U.S.A.* 39°57N 75°9W **313** G9
Philip *U.S.A.* 44°2N 101°40W **308** C3
Philip Smith Mts. *U.S.A.* 68°0N 148°0W **303** C10
Philipi *Greece* 41°1N 24°16E **203** E8
Philippeville = Skikda *Algeria* 36°50N 6°58E **261** A6
Philippeville *Belgium* 50°12N 4°33E **170** D4
Philippi *U.S.A.* 39°9N 80°3W **309** F13
Philippi L. *Australia* 24°20S 138°55E **280** C2
Philippine Basin *Pac. Oc.* 17°0N 132°0E **288** F5
Philippine Sea *Pac. Oc.* 18°0N 125°0E **288** F4
Philippine Trench = Mindanao Trench *Pac. Oc.* 12°0N 126°6E **232** E5
Philippines ■ *Asia* 12°0N 123°0E **232** E4
Philippolis *S. Africa* 30°15S 25°16E **270** D4
Philippopolis = Plovdiv *Bulgaria* 42°8N 24°44E **203** D8
Philipsburg *Qué., Canada* 45°2N 73°5W **313** A11
Philipsburg *St.-Maarten* 18°3N 63°5W **322** a
Philipsburg *Mont., U.S.A.* 46°20N 113°18W **304** C7
Philipsburg *Pa., U.S.A.* 40°54N 78°13W **312** F6
Philipstown = Daingean *Ireland* 53°18N 7°17W **166** C4
Philipstown *S. Africa* 30°28S 24°30E **270** D3
Phillip B. *Australia* 33°58S 151°14E **139** B2
Phillip I. *Australia* 38°30S 145°12E **283** E6
Phillips *U.S.A.* 45°42N 90°24W **308** C8
Phillipsburg *Ga., U.S.A.* 31°25N 83°30W **316** D6
Phillipsburg *Kans., U.S.A.* 39°45N 99°19W **308** F4
Phillipsburg *N.J., U.S.A.* 40°42N 75°12W **313** F9
Philmont *U.S.A.* 42°15N 73°39W **313** D11
Philomath *Ga., U.S.A.* 33°44N 82°59W **316** B7
Philomath *Oreg., U.S.A.* 44°32N 123°22W **304** D2
Phimai *Thailand* 15°13N 102°30E **236** E4
Phitsanulok *Thailand* 16°50N 100°12E **236** D3
Phnom Kulen △ *Cambodia* 13°38N 104°15E **236** F5
Phnom Penh *Cambodia* 11°33N 104°55E **237** G5
Phnum Penh = Phnom Penh *Cambodia* 11°33N 104°55E **237** G5
Phoenicia *U.S.A.* 42°5N 74°14W **313** D10
Phoenix *Mauritius* 20°17S 57°30E **272** e
Phoenix *Ariz., U.S.A.* 33°26N 112°4W **305** K7
Phoenix *N.Y., U.S.A.* 43°14N 76°18W **313** C8
Phoenix Is. *Kiribati* 3°30S 172°0W **277** A16
Phoenix Park *Ireland* 53°21N 6°20W **120** A2
Phoenixville *U.S.A.* 40°8N 75°31W **313** F9
Phon *Thailand* 15°49N 102°36E **236** E4
Phong → *Thailand* 16°23N 102°56E **236** D4
Phong Nha -Ke Bang △ *Vietnam* 17°30N 106°10E **236** D6
Phong Saly *Laos* 21°42N 102°9E **228** G4
Phong Tho *Vietnam* 22°32N 103°21E **236** A4
Phonhong *Laos* 18°30N 102°25E **236** C4
Phonsavan *Laos* 19°27N 103°10E **236** C4
Phonum *Thailand* 8°49N 98°48E **237** H2
Phosphate Hill *Australia* 21°53S 139°58E **280** C2
Photharam *Thailand* 13°41N 99°51E **236** F2
Phra Kaeo *Bangkok, Thailand* **113** b1
Phra Khanong *Thailand* 13°40N 100°36E **113** B2
Phra Nakhon *Thailand* 13°45N 100°30E **113** B2
Phra Nakhon Si Ayutthaya *Thailand* 14°25N 100°30E **236** E3
Phra Pradaeng *Thailand* 13°39N 100°33E **113** C2
Phra Thong, Ko *Thailand* 9°5N 98°17E **237** H2
Phrae *Thailand* 18°7N 100°9E **236** C3
Phranakhon *Thailand* 13°44N 100°29E **113** B1
Phrom Phiram *Thailand* 17°2N 100°12E **236** D3
Phrygia *Turkey* 38°40N 30°0E **212** C4
Phu Bia *Laos* 19°10N 103°0E **236** C4
Phu Chong-Na Yoi △ *Thailand* 14°25N 105°30E **236** E5
Phu Hin Rong Kla △ *Thailand* 17°0N 100°59E **236** D3
Phu Kao -Phu Phan Kham △ *Thailand* 16°53N 102°31E **236** D4
Phu Kradung △ *Thailand* 17°2N 101°44E **236** D3
Phu Loi *Laos* 20°14N 103°14E **236** B4
Phu Luang △ *Thailand* 17°15N 101°29E **236** D3
Phu Ly *Vietnam* 20°35N 105°50E **228** G5
Phu My *Vietnam* 14°15N 109°5E **236** E7
Phu Pha Man △ *Thailand* 16°44N 101°50E **236** D3
Phu Phan △ *Thailand* 17°0N 103°56E **236** D4
Phu Quoc, Dao *Vietnam* 10°20N 104°0E **237** G4
Phu Sa Dok Bua △ *Thailand* 16°11N 104°45E **236** D5
Phu Sang △ *Thailand* 19°35N 100°19E **236** C3
Phu Tho *Vietnam* 21°24N 105°13E **228** G5
Phu Wiang △ *Thailand* 16°39N 102°23E **236** D4
Phuc Yen *Vietnam* 21°16N 105°45E **228** G5
Phuket *Thailand* 7°53N 98°24E **237** a
Phuket, Ko *Thailand* 8°0N 98°22E **237** a
Phul *India* 30°19N 75°14E **242** D6
Phulad *India* 25°38N 73°49E **242** G5
Phulbani *India* 20°28N 84°14E **244** D7
Phulbari *India* 25°55N 90°2E **241** C3
Phulchari *Bangla.* 25°11N 89°37E **241** C2
Phulera *India* 26°52N 75°16E **242** F6
Phulpur *India* 25°31N 82°49E **243** G10
Phunphin *Thailand* 9°7N 99°12E **237** H2
Phuntsholing *Bhutan* 26°51N 89°23E **243** F13
Phuphrabat *Thailand* 17°40N 102°45E **236** D4
Phuthaditjhaba *S. Africa* 28°29S 28°48E **271** C4
Pia ⊙ *Australia* 27°7S 116°23E **279** E2
Piaçabuçu *Brazil* 10°24S 36°25W **332** D4
Piacenza *Italy* 45°1N 9°40E **198** C6
Piai, Tanjung *Malaysia* 1°17N 103°30E **237** d
Piako → *N.Z.* 37°12S 175°30E **284** D4
Pian Cr. → *Australia* 30°2S 148°12E **281** E4
Pian-Upe ⌓ *Uganda* 1°44N 34°20E **268** B3
Piana *France* 42°15N 8°34E **175** F12
Pianella *Italy* 42°24N 14°2E **199** F11
Piangil *Australia* 35°5S 143°20E **282** C5
Pianosa *Puglia, Italy* 42°12N 15°44E **199** F12
Pianosa *Toscana, Italy* 42°35N 10°5E **198** F7
Piao'ertun *China* 41°50N 123°47E **227** D12
Piapot *Canada* 49°59N 109°8W **297** D7
Piarco *Trin. & Tob.* 10°35N 61°20W **323** t
Piarco Int. ✈ (POS) *Trin. & Tob.* 10°36N 61°20W **323** t
Pias *Portugal* 38°1N 7°29W **195** G3
Piaseczno *Poland* 52°5N 21°2E **185** F8
Piaski *Poland* 51°8N 22°52E **185** G9
Piastów *Poland* 52°12N 20°48E **185** F7
Piatã *Brazil* 13°9S 41°48W **333** D3
Piatra *Romania* 43°51N 25°9E **183** G10
Piatra Craiului ⌓ *Romania* 45°30N 25°12E **183** E10
Piatra Neamţ *Romania* 46°56N 26°21E **183** D11
Piatra Olt *Romania* 44°22N 24°16E **183** F9
Piauí □ *Brazil* 7°0S 43°0W **332** C3
Piauí → *Brazil* 6°38S 42°42W **332** C3
Piave → *Italy* 45°32N 12°44E **199** C9
Piazza Ármerina *Italy* 37°21N 14°20E **201** E7
Pibor → *South Sudan* 7°35N 33°0E **257** F3
Pibor Post *South Sudan* 6°47N 33°3E **257** F3
Pica *Chile* 20°35S 69°25W **330** E4
Picardie □ *France* 49°50N 3°0E **173** C10
Picardie, Plaine de *France* 50°0N 2°0E **173** C9
Picardy = Picardie □ *France* 49°50N 3°0E **173** C10
Picasso, Museu *Barcelona, Spain* **114** c2
Picayune *U.S.A.* 30°32N 89°41W **315** F10
Piccadilly *London, U.K.* **125** b3
Picerno *Italy* 40°38N 15°38E **201** B8
Pichhor *India* 25°58N 78°20E **243** G8
Pichilemu *Chile* 34°22S 72°0W **334** C1
Pichincha, □ *Ecuador* 0°10S 78°40W **328** D2
Pichor *India* 25°11N 78°11E **242** G8
Pickerel L. *Canada* 48°40N 91°25W **298** C1
Pickering *U.K.* 54°15N 0°46W **168** C7
Pickering, Vale of *U.K.* 54°14N 0°45W **168** C7
Pickle Lake *Canada* 51°30N 90°12W **298** B1
Pickwick L. *U.S.A.* 35°4N 88°15W **315** D10
Pico *Azores* 38°28N 28°20W **153** d1
Pico, Ponta do *Azores* 38°28N 28°25W **153** d1
Pico Bonito △ *Honduras* 15°34N 86°48W **320** C2
Pico da Neblina △ *Brazil* 0°19N 66°28W **328** C4
Pico Rivera *U.S.A.* 33°59N 118°5W **126** C4
Pico Truncado *Argentina* 46°40S 68°0W **336** C3
Picos = Colinas *Brazil* 6°0S 44°10W **332** C3
Picos *Brazil* 7°5S 41°28W **332** C3
Picos de Europa △ *Spain* 43°14N 4°59W **194** B6
Picota *Peru* 6°54S 76°24W **330** B2
Picton *N.S.W., Australia* 34°12S 150°34E **283** C9
Picton *Ont., Canada* 44°1N 77°9W **312** B7
Picton *N.Z.* 41°18S 174°3E **285** B9
Picton, I. *Chile* 55°2S 66°57W **336** E3
Pictou *Canada* 45°41N 62°42W **299** C7
Picture Butte *Canada* 49°55N 112°45W **296** D6
Pictured Rocks ⌓ *U.S.A.* 46°30N 86°30W **308** B10
Picuí *Brazil* 6°31S 36°21W **332** C4
Picún Leufú *Argentina* 39°30S 69°5W **336** A3
Pidbuzh *Ukraine* 49°19N 23°14E **185** J10
Pidurutalagala *Sri Lanka* 7°10N 80°50E **245** L5
Piechowice *Poland* 50°51N 15°36E **185** H2
Piedade *Rio de J., Brazil* 22°52S 43°18W **135** B1
Piedade *Lisboa, Portugal* 38°40N 9°16W **126** A1
Piedade, Cova da *Portugal* 38°40N 9°8W **126** A2

Piedecuesta Colombia 6°59N 73°3W 328 B3
Piedimonte Matese Italy 41°22N 14°22E 201 A7
Piedmont = Piemonte □ Italy 45°0N 8°0E 198 D5
Piedmont Ala., U.S.A. 33°55N 85°37W 316 B4
Piedmont S.C., U.S.A. 34°42N 82°28W 292 F11
Piedmont Park U.S.A. 33°47N 84°22W 113 B2
Piedra → Spain 41°18N 1°47W 196 D3
Piedra del Águila Argentina 40°2S 70°4W 336 B2
Piedra del Águila, Embalse Argentina 40°15S 70°4W 336 B2
Piedra Lais Venezuela 3°10N 65°50W 328 C4
Piedrabuena Spain 39°0N 4°10W 195 G6
Piedrahita Spain 40°28N 5°23W 194 E5
Piedralaves Spain 40°19N 4°42W 194 E6
Piedras, R. de las → Peru 12°30S 69°15W 330 C4
Piedras Blancas Spain 43°33N 5°58W 194 B5
Piedras Negras Mexico 28°42N 100°31W 318 B4
Piedras Pt. Phil. 10°11N 118°48E 233 F2
Piekar = Piekary Śląskie Poland 50°24N 18°57E 185 H5
Piekary Śląskie Poland 50°24N 18°57E 185 H5
Pieksämäki Finland 62°18N 27°10E 188 A4
Pielinen Finland 63°15N 29°40E 160 E23
Piemonte □ Italy 45°0N 8°0E 198 D5
Pienaarsrivier S. Africa 25°15S 28°18E 271 C4
Pieniężno Poland 54°14N 20°8E 184 D7
Pieninský △ Europe 49°25N 20°28E 181 B13
Pieńsk Poland 51°16N 15°2E 185 G2
Piercefield U.S.A. 44°13N 74°35W 313 B10
Pierceland Canada 54°20N 109°46W 297 C7
Pieria □ Greece 40°13N 22°25E 202 F6
Pierpont U.S.A. 41°45N 80°34W 312 E4
Pierre U.S.A. 44°22N 100°21W 308 C3
Pierre-Buffière France 45°41N 1°22E 174 C5
Pierre-de-Bresse France 46°54N 5°13E 173 F12
Pierre Elliott Trudeau ✈ (YUL) Canada 45°28N 73°44W 130 B1
Pierrefonds Canada 45°29N 73°51W 313 A11
Pierrefontaine-les-Varans France 47°14N 6°32E 173 E13
Pierrefort France 44°55N 2°50E 174 D6
Pierrelatte France 44°23N 4°43E 175 D8
Pierson U.S.A. 29°14N 81°28W 317 F8
Piešťany Slovak Rep. 48°38N 17°55E 181 C10
Piesting → Austria 48°6N 16°40E 181 C9
Pieszyce Poland 50°43N 16°33E 185 H3
Piet Retief S. Africa 27°1S 30°50E 271 C5
Pietarsaari Finland 63°40N 22°43E 160 E20
Pieter Both Mauritius 20°11S 57°32E 272 e
Pietermaritzburg S. Africa 29°35S 30°25E 271 C5
Pietersburg = Polokwane S. Africa 23°54S 29°25E 271 B4
Pietragalla Italy 40°45N 15°53E 201 B8
Pietralata Italy 41°55N 12°33E 136 B2
Pietrasanta Italy 43°57N 10°14E 198 E7
Pietroșița Romania 45°11N 25°26E 183 E10
Pietrosul, Vf. Maramureș, Romania 47°35N 24°43E 183 C9
Pietrosul, Vf. Suceava, Romania 47°12N 25°18E 183 C10
Pieve di Cadore Italy 46°26N 12°22E 199 B9
Pieve di Teco Italy 44°3N 7°56E 198 D4
Pievepélago Italy 44°12N 10°37E 198 D7
Pigaditsa Greece 39°59N 21°23E 202 G5
Pigeon Guadeloupe 16°9N 61°46W 322 e
Pigeon I. India 14°2N 74°20E 245 G2
Pigeon I. St. Lucia 14°6N 60°58W 323 m
Pigeon L. Canada 44°27N 78°30W 312 B6
Piges Greece 39°17N 21°25E 204 B3
Piggott U.S.A. 36°23N 90°11W 315 C9
Pigna Italy 43°56N 7°40E 198 E4
Pigüe Argentina 37°36S 62°25W 334 D3
Piha N.Z. 36°57S 174°28E 284 C3
Pihani India 27°36N 80°15E 243 F9
Pihlajamäki Finland 60°14N 24°58E 121 B2
Pihlajasaari Finland 60°8N 24°55E 121 C2
Pihlajavesi Finland 61°45N 28°45E 188 B5
Pijijiapan Mexico 15°42N 93°14W 319 D6
Pikalevo Russia 59°37N 34°9E 188 C8
Pikangikum Canada 51°49N 94°0W 297 C10
Pikes Peak U.S.A. 38°50N 105°3W 304 G11
Piketberg S. Africa 32°55S 18°40E 270 D2
Pikeville U.S.A. 37°29N 82°31W 309 G12
Pikit Phil. 7°4N 124°41E 233 H5
Pikou China 39°18N 122°22E 227 E12
Pikounda Congo 0°30N 16°44E 264 B3
Pikwitonei Canada 55°35N 97°9W 297 B9
Piła Poland 53°10N 16°48E 185 E3
Pila Spain 38°16N 1°11W 197 G3
Pilanesberg △ S. Africa 25°15S 27°4E 270 C4
Pilani India 28°22N 75°33E 242 E6
Pilar Brazil 9°36S 35°56W 332 C4
Pilar Paraguay 26°50S 58°20W 334 B4
Pilar Capiz, Phil. 11°29N 123°0E 233 F4
Pilar Sorsogon, Phil. 12°56N 123°40E 232 E4
Pilar de la Horadada Spain 37°52N 0°47W 197 H4
Pilares Brazil 22°52S 43°18W 135 B1
Pilas Group Phil. 6°45N 121°35E 233 H3
Pilat ⌂ France 45°20N 4°30E 175 C8
Pilawa Poland 51°57N 21°32E 185 G8
Pilaya → Bolivia 20°55S 64°4W 331 E5
Pilbara Australia 21°15S 118°16E 278 D2
Pilcomaya → Paraguay 25°21S 57°42W 334 B4
Pilea Greece 40°32N 22°59E 202 F6
Pilgrim's Rest S. Africa 24°55S 30°44E 271 B5
Pilgrimstad Sweden 62°57N 15°2E 162 B9
Pili Greece 36°50N 27°15E 205 E9
Pili Phil. 13°33N 123°19E 232 E4
Pilibhit India 28°40N 79°50E 243 E8
Pilica → Poland 51°52N 21°17E 185 G8
Pilio, Oros Greece 39°27N 23°3E 204 B5
Pilipinas = Philippines ■ Asia 12°0N 123°0E 232 E4
Pilis Hungary 47°17N 19°35E 182 C4
Pilisvörösvár Hungary 47°38N 18°56E 182 C3
Pilkhawa India 28°43N 77°42E 242 E7
Pillar B. Ascension I. 7°59S 14°21W 153 g
Pillaro Ecuador 1°10S 78°32W 328 D2
Pillau = Baltiysk Russia 54°41N 19°58E 184 D6
Pilliga Australia 30°21S 148°54E 281 E4
Pilos Greece 36°55N 21°42E 204 E3
Pilot Grove U.S.A. 38°53N 92°55W 310 F4
Pilot Mound Canada 49°15N 98°54W 297 D9
Pilot Point Alaska, U.S.A. 57°34N 157°35W 303 H8
Pilot Point Tex., U.S.A. 33°24N 96°58W 314 E6
Pilot Rock U.S.A. 45°29N 118°50W 304 D4
Pilot Station U.S.A. 61°56N 162°53W 303 F7
Pilote → Martinique 14°28N 60°55W 322 j
Pilsen = Pilzno Poland 49°58N 21°16E 185 J8
Pilsen = Plzeň Czech Rep. 49°45N 13°22E 180 B6
Pilštanj Slovenia 46°8N 15°39E 199 B12
Piltene Latvia 57°13N 21°40E 184 A8
Pilton U.K. 55°58N 3°13W 121 B2
Pilzno Poland 49°58N 21°16E 185 J8
Pima U.S.A. 32°54N 109°50W 305 K9
Pimba Australia 31°18S 136°46E 282 A2
Pimenta Bueno Brazil 11°35S 61°10W 331 C5
Pimenteiras Brazil 13°40S 60°58W 331 C5
Pimentel Peru 6°45S 79°55W 330 B2
Pimlico London, U.K. 125 c3
Pimmit Hills U.S.A. 38°54N 77°12W 143 B2
Pimpri Chinchwad India 18°37N 73°47E 244 E1
Pimu Dem. Rep. of the Congo 1°42N 20°58E 264 B4
Pin Valley △ India 31°50N 77°50E 242 D7
Pina de Ebro Spain 41°29N 0°33W 196 D4
Pinamalayan Phil. 13°2N 121°29E 232 E3
Pinang Malaysia 5°25N 100°15E 237 c
Pinang □ Malaysia 5°20N 100°20E 237 K3
Pinar, C. des Spain 39°53N 3°12E 206 B4
Pinar del Río Cuba 22°26N 83°40W 320 B3
Pınarbaşı Çanakkale, Turkey 39°53N 26°15E 205 B8
Pınarbaşı Kayseri, Turkey 38°43N 36°23E 212 C7
Pınarhisar Turkey 41°37N 27°30E 203 E11
Pinatubo, Mt. Phil. 15°8N 120°21E 232 D3
Pinawa Canada 50°9N 95°50W 297 C9
Pincehely Hungary 46°41N 18°27E 182 D3
Pinchang China 31°36N 107°3E 228 B6
Pincher Creek Canada 49°30N 113°57W 296 D6
Pinchi L. Canada 54°38N 124°30W 296 C4
Pinckard U.S.A. 31°19N 85°33W 316 D4
Pinckneyville U.S.A. 38°5N 89°23W 310 F7
Pińczów Poland 50°32N 20°32E 185 H7
Pind Dadan Khan Pakistan 32°36N 73°7E 217 F8
Pindar Australia 28°30S 115°47E 279 E2
Pindaré → Brazil 3°17S 44°47W 332 B3
Pindaré-Mirim Brazil 3°37S 45°21W 332 B2
Pindera Downs ✪ Australia 29°24S 142°37E 281 A3
Pindi Gheb Pakistan 33°14N 72°21E 242 C5
Pindiga Nigeria 9°58N 10°53E 263 D7
Pindobal Brazil 3°16S 48°25W 332 B2
Pindos △ Greece 39°52N 21°11E 204 B3
Pindos Oros Greece 40°0N 21°0E 204 B3
Pindus Mts. = Pindos Oros Greece 40°0N 21°0E 204 B3
Pine → B.C., Canada 56°8N 120°43W 296 B4
Pine → Sask., Canada 58°50N 105°38W 297 B7
Pine Bluff U.S.A. 34°13N 92°1W 314 D8
Pine Bluffs U.S.A. 41°11N 104°4W 304 F11
Pine Castle U.S.A. 28°28N 81°22W 133 B2
Pine City U.S.A. 45°50N 92°59W 308 C7
Pine Cr. → U.S.A. 41°10N 77°16W 312 E7
Pine Creek Australia 13°50S 131°50E 278 B5
Pine Falls Canada 50°34N 96°11W 297 C9
Pine Flat L. U.S.A. 36°50N 119°20W 306 J7
Pine Grove Ont., Canada 43°47N 79°34W 141 A1
Pine Grove Pa., U.S.A. 40°33N 76°23W 313 F8
Pine Hill Australia 23°38S 146°57E 280 C4
Pine Hills U.S.A. 28°33N 81°27W 133 A2
Pine I. U.S.A. 26°36N 82°7W 317 J7
Pine Island Glacier Antarctica 76°0S 100°0W 151 D15
Pine Level U.S.A. 32°4N 86°4W 316 C3
Pine Mountain U.S.A. 32°49N 84°51W 316 C5
Pine Pass Canada 55°25N 122°42W 296 B4
Pine Point Canada 60°50N 114°28W 296 A6
Pine Ridge N.S.W., Australia 31°30S 150°28E 283 A9
Pine Ridge S. Dak., U.S.A. 43°2N 102°33W 308 D2
Pine River Man., Canada 51°45N 100°30W 297 C8
Pine River Minn., U.S.A. 46°43N 94°24W 308 B6
Pine Valley U.S.A. 32°50N 116°32W 307 N10
Pinecrest U.S.A. 38°12N 120°1W 306 G6
Pineda de Mar Spain 41°37N 2°42E 196 D7
Pinedale Calif., U.S.A. 36°50N 119°48W 306 J7
Pinedale Wyo., U.S.A. 42°52N 109°52W 304 E9
Pinega → Russia 64°30N 44°19E 186 B8
Pinehouse L. Canada 55°32N 106°35W 297 B7
Pineimuta → Canada 52°8N 88°33W 298 B1
Pinellas Park U.S.A. 27°50N 82°41W 317 H7
Pinerolo Italy 44°53N 7°21E 198 D4
Pines, Akra Greece 40°5N 24°20E 203 F8
Pineto Italy 42°36N 14°4E 199 F11
Pinetop-Lakeside U.S.A. 34°9N 109°58W 305 J9
Pinetown S. Africa 29°48S 30°54E 271 C5
Pinetta U.S.A. 30°36N 83°21W 316 E6
Pineview U.S.A. 32°7N 83°30W 316 C6
Pineville La., U.S.A. 31°19N 92°26W 314 F8
Pineville S.C., U.S.A. 33°26N 80°1W 316 B9
Pinewood U.S.A. 33°44N 80°27W 316 B9
Pinewood Park U.S.A. 25°52N 80°13W 128 A2
Piney France 48°22N 4°21E 173 D11
Piney Run → U.S.A. 38°58N 77°14W 143 B2
Ping → Thailand 15°42N 100°9E 236 E3
Pingaring Australia 32°40S 118°32E 279 F2
Pingba China 26°23N 106°12E 228 D6
Pingbian China 23°0N 103°45E 228 F4
Pingchuan China 27°35N 101°55E 228 D3
Pingding China 37°47N 113°38E 226 F7
Pingdingshan China 33°43N 113°27E 226 H7
Pingdu China 36°42N 119°59E 227 F10
Pingelly Australia 32°32S 117°5E 279 F2
Pingguo China 23°19N 107°36E 228 F6
Pinghe China 24°17N 117°21E 229 E11
Pinghu China 30°40N 121°2E 229 B13
Pingjiang China 28°45N 113°36E 229 C9
Pingle China 24°40N 110°40E 229 E8
Pingli China 32°27N 109°22E 228 A7
Pingliang China 35°35N 106°31E 226 G4
Pinglin Taiwan 24°56N 121°42E 225 B3
Pinglu China 39°31N 112°30E 226 E7
Pingluo China 38°52N 106°30E 226 E4
Pingnan Fujian, China 26°55N 119°0E 229 D12
Pingnan Guangxi Zhuangzu, China 23°33N 110°22E 229 F8
Pingo Gabon 1°19S 10°55E 264 C2
Pingquan China 41°1N 118°37E 227 D10
Pingrup Australia 33°32S 118°29E 279 F2
Pingshan China 28°39N 104°3E 228 C5
Pingtan China 25°31N 119°47E 229 E12
Pingtang China 25°49N 107°17E 228 E6
P'ingtung Taiwan 22°38N 120°30E 225 D2
P'ingtung □ Taiwan 22°30N 120°40E 225 D2
Pingwu China 32°25N 104°30E 226 H3
Pingxiang Guangxi Zhuangzu, China 22°6N 106°46E 228 F6
Pingxiang Jiangxi, China 27°43N 113°48E 229 D9
Pingyao China 37°12N 112°10E 226 F7
Pingyi China 35°30N 117°35E 227 G9
Pingyin China 36°20N 116°25E 226 F9
Pingyuan Guangdong, China 24°37N 115°57E 229 E10
Pingyuan Shandong, China 37°10N 116°22E 226 F9
Pingyuanjie China 23°45N 103°48E 228 F4
Pingzhou China 23°1N 113°11E 121 B2
Pinhal Novo Portugal 38°38N 8°55W 195 G2
Pinheiro = Icoraci Brazil 1°18S 48°28W 332 B2
Pinheiro Brazil 2°31S 45°5W 332 B2
Pinheiro Machado Brazil 31°34S 53°23W 335 C5
Pinheiros → Brazil 23°37S 46°44W 137 B1
Pinhel Portugal 40°50N 7°1W 194 E3
Pinhuá → Brazil 6°21S 65°0W 331 B5
Pini Indonesia 0°10N 98°40E 234 B1
Pinios → Ilia, Greece 37°48N 21°20E 204 D3
Pinios → Trikala, Greece 39°55N 22°41E 204 B4
Pinjarra Australia 32°37S 115°52E 279 F2
Pinjrapur Pakistan 24°53N 67°4E 123 A2
Pink Beach Bonaire 12°5N 68°17W 322 h
Pink Mountain Canada 57°3N 122°52W 296 B4
Pinkafeld Austria 47°22N 16°9E 181 D9
Pinlaung Burma 20°8N 96°47E 241 E6
Pinlebu Burma 24°5N 95°22E 241 C5
Pinnacle Is. = Senkaku-Shotō E. China Sea 25°45N 123°30E 221 M1
Pinnacles ⌂ U.S.A. 36°25N 121°12W 306 J5
Pinnaroo Australia 35°17S 140°53E 282 C4
Pinneberg Germany 53°40N 9°48E 178 B5
Pinner U.K. 51°35N 0°22W 125 A1
Pinner Green U.K. 51°35N 0°23W 125 A1
Pino Hachado, Paso S. Amer. 38°39S 70°54W 336 A2
Pinon Hills U.S.A. 34°26N 117°39W 307 L9
Pinos Mexico 22°18N 101°34W 318 C4
Pinos, Mt. U.S.A. 34°49N 119°8W 307 L7
Pinos Pt. U.S.A. 36°38N 121°57W 305 H3
Pinos Puente Spain 37°15N 3°45W 195 H7
Pinrang Indonesia 3°46S 119°41E 235 C5
Pins, Î. des N. Cal. 22°37S 167°30E 288 d
Pins, Pte. aux Canada 42°15N 81°51W 312 D3
Pinsk Belarus 52°10N 26°1E 177 B14
Pinta, Canal de Ecuador 0°27N 90°38W 330 a
Pinta, I. Ecuador 0°35N 90°44W 330 a
Pintados Chile 20°35S 69°40W 330 E4
Pintuyan Phil. 9°57N 125°15E 233 G5
Pinukpuk Phil. 17°35N 121°22E 232 C3
Pinyang China 27°42N 120°31E 229 D13
Pinyug Russia 60°5N 48°0E 186 B8
Pio Duran Phil. 13°2N 123°25E 232 E4
Pio V. Corpuz Phil. 11°55N 124°2E 233 F5
Pio XII Brazil 3°53S 45°17W 332 B2
Pioche U.S.A. 37°56N 114°27W 305 H6
Pioltello Italy 45°30N 9°19E 129 A2
Piombino Italy 42°55N 10°32E 198 F7
Piombino, Canale di Italy 42°53N 10°30E 198 F7
Pioner, Ostrov Russia 79°50N 92°0E 215 B10
Pionerskiy Russia 54°56N 20°14E 184 D7
Pionki Poland 51°29N 21°28E 185 G8
Piopiotaki = Milford Sd. N.Z. 44°41S 167°47E 285 E2
Piorini → Brazil 3°23S 63°30W 329 D5
Piorini, L. Brazil 3°15S 62°35W 329 D5
Piotrków Trybunalski Poland 51°23N 19°43E 185 G6
Piove di Sacco Italy 45°18N 12°2E 199 C9
Pīp Iran 26°45N 60°10E 247 E9
Pipar India 26°25N 73°31E 242 F5
Pipar Road India 26°27N 73°27E 242 F5
Piparia Mad. P., India 22°45N 78°23E 242 H8
Piparia Mad. P., India 21°49N 77°37E 242 J7
Piparo Trin. & Tob. 10°20N 61°20W 323 t
Pipas Angola 14°57S 12°11E 265 E2
Piperi Greece 39°20N 24°19E 204 B6
Piperno = Priverno Italy 41°28N 13°11E 200 A6
Pipestone U.S.A. 44°0N 96°19W 308 D5
Pipestone → Canada 52°53N 89°23W 298 B2
Pipestone Cr. → Canada 49°38N 100°15W 297 D8
Pipinui Pt. N.Z. 41°10S 174°44E 143 A1
Pipiriki N.Z. 39°28S 175°5E 284 F4
Piplan Pakistan 32°17N 71°21E 242 C4
Piploda India 23°37N 74°56E 242 H6
Pipmuacan, Rés. Canada 49°45N 70°30W 299 C5
Pippingarra Australia 20°27S 118°42E 278 D2
Pipriac France 47°59N 1°58W 172 E5
Piqua U.S.A. 40°9N 84°15W 311 D12
Piquet Carneiro Brazil 5°48S 39°25W 332 C4
Piquiri → Brazil 24°3S 54°14W 335 A5
Pir Panjal Range India 32°30N 76°50E 242 C7
Pīr Sohrāb Iran 25°44N 60°54E 247 E9
Pira Benin 8°28N 1°48E 263 D5
Piracanjuba Brazil 17°18S 49°1W 333 E2
Piracicaba Brazil 22°45S 47°40W 335 A6
Piracuruca Brazil 3°50S 41°50W 332 B3
Pirae Tahiti 17°31S 149°32W 289 e
Piræus = Pireas Greece 37°57N 23°42E 112 B1
Piraiévs = Pireas Greece 37°57N 23°42E 112 B1
Pirajuçara → Brazil 23°33S 46°42W 137 B1
Pirajuí Brazil 21°59S 49°29W 335 A6
Piram I. India 21°36N 72°21E 242 J5
Piran Slovenia 45°31N 13°33E 199 C10
Pirané Argentina 25°42S 59°6W 334 B4
Piranhas Brazil 9°27S 37°46W 332 C4
Pirano = Piran Slovenia 45°31N 13°33E 199 C10
Pīrānshahr Iran 36°41N 45°8E 213 D11
Pirapemas Brazil 3°43S 44°14W 332 B3
Pirapora Brazil 17°20S 44°56W 333 E3
Pirara Guyana 3°37N 59°40W 329 C6
Pirawa India 24°10N 76°2E 242 G7
Piray → Bolivia 16°32S 63°45W 331 D5
Pirdop Bulgaria 42°40N 24°10E 203 D8
Pireas Greece 37°57N 23°42E 112 B1
Pires do Rio Brazil 17°18S 48°17W 333 E2
Pirganj Bangla. 25°51N 88°24E 241 C2
Pirgi Greece 38°13N 25°59E 205 C7
Pirgos Ilia, Greece 37°40N 21°27E 204 D3
Pirgos Kriti, Greece 35°0N 25°9E 207 E6
Pirgovo Bulgaria 43°44N 25°43E 203 C9
Piribebuy Paraguay 25°26S 57°2W 334 B4
Pirimapun Indonesia 6°20S 138°24E 231 F9
Pirin △ Bulgaria 41°48N 23°22E 202 E7
Pirin Planina Bulgaria 41°40N 23°30E 202 E7
Pirinçci Turkey 41°10N 28°52E 122 B1
Pírineos = Pyrénées Europe 42°45N 0°18E 174 F4
Piripiri Brazil 4°15S 41°46W 332 B3
Piritu Venezuela 9°23N 69°12W 328 B4
Pirituba Brazil 23°29S 46°44W 137 A1
Pirkkola Finland 60°14N 24°55E 121 B2
Pirlangimpi Australia 11°24S 130°26E 278 B5
Pirmasens Germany 49°12N 7°36E 179 F3
Pirna Germany 50°57N 13°56E 178 E9
Pirojpur Bangla. 22°35N 90°1E 241 D3
Pirot Serbia 43°9N 22°33E 202 C6
Piru Indonesia 3°4S 128°12E 231 E7
Piru Calif., U.S.A. 34°25N 118°48W 307 L8
Piryatin = Pyryatyn Ukraine 50°15N 32°25E 189 G7
Pisa Italy 43°43N 10°23E 198 E7
Pisa → Poland 53°14N 21°52E 185 E8
Pisa, Firenze ✈ (PSA) Italy 43°40N 10°22E 198 E7
Pisa Ra. N.Z. 44°52S 169°12E 285 E4
Pisac Peru 13°25S 71°50W 330 C3
Pisagne Italy 45°45N 10°10E 198 C7
Pisagua Chile 19°40S 70°15W 330 D3
Pisarovina Croatia 45°35N 15°50E 199 C12
Pisau, Tanjong Malaysia 6°4N 117°59E 235 A5
Pisba △ Colombia 10°39N 74°30W 328 A3
Pisco Peru 13°50S 76°12W 330 C2
Piscu Romania 45°30N 27°43E 183 E12
Písek Czech Rep. 49°19N 14°10E 180 B7
Pisgat O'mer West Bank 31°49N 35°14E 123 B2
Pisgat Ze'ev West Bank 31°49N 35°14E 123 B2
Pishan China 37°30N 78°33E 217 E9
Pishcha Ukraine 51°35N 23°50E 185 G10
Pishchanka Ukraine 48°12N 28°54E 183 B13
Pīshīn Iran 26°6N 61°47E 247 E9
Pishin Pakistan 30°35N 67°0E 242 D2
Pishin Lora → Pakistan 29°9N 64°5E 242 E1
Pishpek = Bishkek Kyrgyzstan 42°54N 74°46E 218 C3
Pisidia Turkey 37°30N 31°40E 212 D4
Pising Indonesia 5°8S 121°53E 231 F6
Pisiou, Pte. Guadeloupe 15°59N 61°13W 322 e
Pismo Beach U.S.A. 35°9N 120°38W 307 K6
Písnice Czech Rep. 49°59N 14°28E 135 C2
Piso, L. Liberia 6°50N 11°15W 262 D2
Pissila Burkina Faso 13°7N 0°50W 263 C4
Pissis, Cerro Argentina 27°45S 68°48W 334 B2
Pissos France 44°19N 0°49W 174 D3
Pissouri Cyprus 34°40N 32°42E 207 F8
Pisticci Italy 40°23N 16°33E 201 B9
Pistóia Italy 43°55N 10°54E 198 E7
Pistol B. Canada 62°25N 92°37W 297 A10
Pisuerga → Spain 41°33N 4°52W 194 D6
Pisz Poland 53°38N 21°49E 184 E8
Pit → U.S.A. 40°47N 122°6W 304 F2
Pita Guinea 11°5N 12°15W 262 C2
Pitalito Colombia 1°51N 76°2W 328 C2
Pitampura India 28°41N 77°7E 120 A1
Pitanga Brazil 24°46S 51°44W 333 F1
Pitangui Brazil 19°40S 44°54W 333 E3
Pitarpunga L. Australia 34°24S 143°30E 282 C5
Pitcairn I. Pac. Oc. 25°5S 130°5W 289 K14
Pitch Pt. Trin. & Tob. 10°15N 61°37W 323 t
Piteå Sweden 65°20N 21°25E 160 D19
Piteälven → Sweden 65°20N 21°25E 160 D19
Piterka Russia 50°41N 47°29E 190 E8
Pitești Romania 44°52N 24°54E 183 F9
Pithapuram India 17°10N 82°15E 244 F6
Pithara Australia 30°20S 116°35E 279 F2
Pithio Greece 41°24N 26°40E 203 E10
Pithiviers France 48°10N 2°13E 173 D9
Pithora India 21°16N 82°31E 244 D6
Pithoragarh India 29°35N 80°13E 243 E9
Pithoro Pakistan 25°31N 69°23E 242 G3
Piti Guam 13°28N 144°41E 302 d
Pitigliano Italy 42°38N 11°40E 199 F8
Pitkäjärvi Finland 60°15N 24°45E 121 B1
Pitkyaranta Russia 61°34N 31°37E 188 B6
Pitlochry U.K. 56°42N 3°44W 167 E5
Pitnak = Drujba Uzbekistan 41°13N 61°18E 216 D6
Pitoa Cameroon 9°23N 13°32E 264 A2
Pitogo Phil. 13°47N 122°5E 232 E4
Piton, Pte. du Guadeloupe 16°30N 61°26W 322 e
Piton de la Petite Rivière Noire Mauritius 20°24S 57°23E 272 e
Pitons, Anses des St. Lucia 13°49N 61°4W 323 m
Pitou Taiwan 23°53N 120°27E 225 C2
Pitou Chiao Taiwan 25°6N 121°55E 225 A3
Pitrufquén Chile 38°59S 72°39W 336 A2
Pitschen = Byczyna Poland 51°7N 18°12E 185 G5
Pitsilia Cyprus 34°55N 33°0E 207 F9
Pitt, Pta. Ecuador 0°43S 89°14W 330 a
Pitt I. B.C., Canada 53°30N 129°50W 296 C3
Pitt I. N.Z. 44°15S 176°15W 285 a
Pitti I. India 10°50N 72°38E 245 J1
Pittsburg Calif., U.S.A. 38°2N 121°53W 306 G5
Pittsburg Kans., U.S.A. 37°25N 94°42W 308 G6
Pittsburg Tex., U.S.A. 33°0N 94°59W 314 E7
Pittsburgh U.S.A. 40°26N 79°58W 312 F5
Pittsfield Ill., U.S.A. 39°36N 90°49W 310 E6
Pittsfield Maine, U.S.A. 44°47N 69°23W 309 C19
Pittsfield Mass., U.S.A. 42°27N 73°15W 313 D11
Pittsfield N.H., U.S.A. 43°18N 71°20W 313 C13
Pittston U.S.A. 41°19N 75°47W 313 E9
Pittsview U.S.A. 32°11N 85°10W 316 C4
Pittsworth Australia 27°41S 151°37E 281 D5
Pituri → Australia 22°35S 138°30E 280 C2
Pium Brazil 10°27S 49°11W 332 D2
Piumafua Mt. Amer. Samoa 14°11S 169°37W 302 f
Piumhi Brazil 20°28S 45°58W 333 F2
Piura Peru 5°15S 80°38W 330 B1
Piura □ Peru 5°10S 80°0W 330 B2
Piva → Montenegro 43°20N 18°50E 202 C2
Pivijay Colombia 10°28N 74°37W 328 A3
Piwniczna Poland 49°27N 20°42E 185 J7
Pixian China 30°48N 103°52E 228 B4
Pixley U.S.A. 35°58N 119°18W 306 K7
Pizarra Spain 36°36N 4°42W 195 J6
Pizarro Colombia 4°58N 77°22W 328 C2
Pizhou = Pei Xian China 34°44N 116°55E 226 G9
Pizhou China 34°18N 117°57E 227 G9
Pizzo Italy 38°44N 16°10E 201 D9
Placentia Canada 47°20N 54°0W 299 C9
Placentia B. Canada 47°0N 54°40W 299 C9
Placer Masbate, Phil. 11°52N 123°55E 233 F4
Placer Surigao N., Phil. 9°36N 125°38E 233 G5
Placerville U.S.A. 38°44N 120°48W 306 G6
Placetas Cuba 22°15N 79°44W 320 B4
Plácido de Castro Brazil 10°20S 67°11W 330 C4
Plačkovica Macedonia 41°45N 22°30E 202 E6
Plaine des Jarres Laos 19°27N 103°10E 236 C4
Plaine Magnien Mauritius 20°25S 57°39E 272 e
Plaines des Papayes Mauritius 20°3S 57°34E 272 e
Plainfield Ill., U.S.A. 41°37N 88°12W 311 C8
Plainfield Ind., U.S.A. 39°42N 86°24W 311 E10
Plainfield N.J., U.S.A. 40°37N 74°25W 313 F10
Plainfield Ohio, U.S.A. 40°13N 81°43W 312 F3
Plainfield Vt., U.S.A. 44°17N 72°26W 313 B12
Plains Ga., U.S.A. 32°2N 84°24W 316 C5
Plains Mont., U.S.A. 47°28N 114°53W 304 C6
Plains Tex., U.S.A. 33°11N 102°50W 314 E3
Plainview Nebr., U.S.A. 42°21N 97°47W 308 D5
Plainview Tex., U.S.A. 34°11N 101°43W 314 D4
Plainwell U.S.A. 42°27N 85°38W 311 B11
Plaisance France 43°36N 0°3E 174 E4
Plaistow U.S.A. 42°50N 71°6W 313 D13
Plaju Indonesia 2°58S 104°49E 234 C2
Plaka Greece 40°0N 25°24E 205 B7
Plaka, Akra Greece 35°11N 26°19E 207 E7
Plakenska Planina Macedonia 41°14N 21°2E 202 E5
Plampang Indonesia 8°47S 117°46E 235 D5
Planá Czech Rep. 49°50N 12°44E 180 B5
Plana Cays Bahamas 22°38N 73°30W 321 B5
Planada U.S.A. 37°16N 120°19W 306 H6
Planchón Peru 12°14S 69°11W 330 C4
Plancoët France 48°32N 2°13W 172 D4
Plandište Serbia 45°16N 21°10E 182 E6
Planegg Germany 48°6N 11°25E 131 B1
Planeta Rica Colombia 8°25N 75°36W 328 B2
Plano U.S.A. 33°1N 96°42W 314 E6
Plant City U.S.A. 28°1N 82°7W 317 G7
Plantation U.S.A. 26°7N 80°14W 317 J9
Plaquemine U.S.A. 30°17N 91°14W 314 F9
Plaridel Phil. 8°37N 123°43E 233 G4
Plasencia Spain 40°3N 6°8W 194 E4
Plaški Croatia 45°4N 15°22E 199 C12
Plassen Norway 61°9N 12°30E 164 C9
Plast Russia 54°22N 60°50E 216 B6
Plaster City U.S.A. 32°47N 115°51W 307 N11
Plaster Rock Canada 46°53N 67°22W 299 C6
Plastun Russia 44°45N 136°19E 220 B8
Plasy Czech Rep. 49°56N 13°24E 180 B6
Plata, Río de la → S. Amer. 34°45S 57°30W 334 C4
Plátani → Italy 37°23N 13°16E 200 E6
Platanos Greece 35°28N 23°33E 207 E4
Plataria Greece 39°27N 20°16E 206 C10
Plateau □ Nigeria 8°30N 9°0E 263 D6
Plateau d'Ipassa ⌂ Gabon 0°26N 12°40E 264 B2
Plathe = Płoty Poland 53°48N 15°18E 184 E2
Platinum U.S.A. 59°1N 161°49W 303 G7
Plato Colombia 9°47N 74°47W 328 B3
Platte U.S.A. 43°23N 98°51W 308 D4
Platte → Mo., U.S.A. 39°16N 94°50W 310 E2
Platte → Nebr., U.S.A. 41°4N 95°53W 308 E6
Platte City U.S.A. 39°22N 94°47W 310 E2
Platteville U.S.A. 42°44N 90°29W 310 B6
Plattling Germany 48°46N 12°53E 179 G8
Plattsburg U.S.A. 39°34N 94°27W 310 E2
Plattsburgh U.S.A. 44°42N 73°28W 313 B11
Plattsmouth U.S.A. 41°1N 95°53W 308 E6
Plau Germany 53°27N 12°15E 178 B8
Plauen Germany 50°30N 12°8E 178 E8
Plauer See Germany 53°28N 12°17E 178 B8
Plav Montenegro 42°38N 19°57E 202 D3
Plavinas Latvia 56°35N 25°46E 188 D3
Plavnica Montenegro 42°20N 19°13E 202 D3
Plavno Croatia 44°9N 16°10E 199 D13
Plavsk Russia 53°40N 37°18E 188 F9
Playa Blanca Sur Canary Is. 28°51N 13°50W 153 e2
Playa de las Americas Canary Is. 28°5N 16°43W 153 e1
Playa de Mogán Canary Is. 27°48N 15°47W 153 e1
Playa del Carmen Mexico 20°37N 87°4W 319 C7
Playa del Inglés Canary Is. 27°45N 15°33W 153 e1
Playa Esmerelda Canary Is. 28°8N 14°16W 153 e2
Playas Ecuador 2°38S 80°23W 328 D1
Playgreen L. Canada 54°0N 98°15W 297 C9
Plaza Mayor Madrid, Spain 127 b2
Pleasant Bay Canada 46°51N 60°48W 299 C7
Pleasant Hill Calif., U.S.A. 37°57N 122°4W 306 H4
Pleasant Hill Ill., U.S.A. 39°27N 90°52W 310 E6
Pleasant Hill Mo., U.S.A. 38°47N 94°16W 310 F2
Pleasant Mount U.S.A. 41°44N 75°26W 313 E9
Pleasant Point N.Z. 44°16S 171°9E 285 E6
Pleasant Prairie U.S.A. 42°33N 87°56W 311 B9
Pleasanton Calif., U.S.A. 37°39N 121°52W 306 H5
Pleasanton Tex., U.S.A. 28°58N 98°29W 314 G5
Pleasantville Iowa, U.S.A. 41°23N 93°18W 310 C3
Pleasantville N.J., U.S.A. 39°24N 74°32W 309 F16
Pleasantville Pa., U.S.A. 41°35N 79°34W 312 E5
Pleasure Island U.S.A. 28°21N 81°31W 133 B1
Pleasure Ridge Park U.S.A. 38°9N 85°50W 311 F11
Pléaux France 45°8N 2°13E 174 C6
Plei Ku Vietnam 13°57N 108°0E 236 F7
Plélan-le-Grand France 48°0N 2°7W 172 D4
Pléneuf-Val-André France 48°35N 2°32W 172 D4
Plenița Romania 44°14N 23°10E 183 F8
Plenty → Australia 23°25S 136°31E 280 C2
Plenty, B. of N.Z. 37°45S 177°0E 284 D6
Plentywood U.S.A. 48°47N 104°34W 304 B11
Plérin France 48°32N 2°46W 172 D4
Plesetsk Russia 62°43N 40°20E 186 B7
Pleskau = Pskov Russia 57°50N 28°25E 188 D5
Plessisville Canada 46°14N 71°47W 299 C5
Plestin-les-Grèves France 48°40N 3°39W 172 D3
Pleszew Poland 51°53N 17°47E 185 G4
Pleternica Croatia 45°17N 17°48E 182 E2
Plétipi, L. Canada 51°44N 70°6W 299 B5
Pleven Bulgaria 43°26N 24°37E 203 C8
Pleven □ Bulgaria 43°26N 24°37E 203 C8
Plevlja Montenegro 43°21N 19°21E 202 C3
Plevna Canada 44°58N 76°59W 312 B8
Plitvička Jezera △ Croatia 44°54N 15°35E 199 D12
Plješevica Croatia 44°45N 15°45E 199 D12
Ploaghe Italy 40°40N 8°45E 200 B1
Ploče Croatia 43°4N 17°26E 199 E14
Płock Poland 52°32N 19°40E 185 F6
Plöckenpass Italy 46°37N 12°57E 199 B9
Plöckenstein Germany 48°46N 13°51E 179 G9
Ploemeur France 47°44N 3°26W 172 E3
Ploërmel France 47°55N 2°26W 172 E4
Plöhnen = Płońsk Poland 52°37N 20°21E 185 F7
Ploiești Romania 44°57N 26°5E 183 F11
Plomari Greece 38°59N 26°22E 205 C8
Plombières-les-Bains France 47°58N 6°27E 173 E13
Plomin Croatia 45°8N 14°10E 199 C11
Plön Germany 54°9N 10°24E 178 A6
Plonge, Lac la Canada 55°8N 107°20W 297 B7
Płońsk Poland 52°37N 20°21E 185 F7
Plopeni Romania 45°4N 25°59E 183 E10
Plopișului, Munții Romania 47°5N 22°30E 182 C7
Plotsk = Płock Poland 52°32N 19°40E 185 F6
Płoty Poland 53°48N 15°18E 184 E2
Plouaret France 48°37N 3°28W 172 D3
Plouay France 47°55N 3°21W 172 E3
Ploučnice → Czech Rep. 50°46N 14°13E 180 A7
Ploudalmézeau France 48°34N 4°41W 172 D2
Plouescat France 48°39N 4°10W 172 D2
Plougasnou France 48°42N 3°49W 172 D3
Plougastel-Daoulas France 48°22N 4°17W 172 D2
Plouguerneau France 48°36N 4°30W 172 D2
Plouha France 48°41N 2°57W 172 D4
Plouhinec France 48°0N 4°29W 172 E2
Plovdiv Bulgaria 42°8N 24°44E 203 D8
Plovdiv □ Bulgaria 42°15N 24°30E 203 D8
Plover Cove Res. China 22°28N 114°15E 219 a
Pluies, R. des → Réunion 20°52S 55°31E 272 f
Plum U.S.A. 40°29N 79°47W 312 F5
Plum I. U.S.A. 41°11N 72°12W 313 E12
Plumas U.S.A. 39°45N 120°4W 306 F6
Plummer U.S.A. 47°20N 116°53W 304 C5
Plumridge Lakes Australia 29°26S 125°16E 279 E4
Plumstead Western Cape, S. Africa 34°1S 18°28E 118 B1
Plumstead London, U.K. 51°29N 0°5E 125 B4
Plumtree Zimbabwe 20°27S 27°55E 269 G2
Plungė Lithuania 55°53N 21°59E 184 C8
Pluvigner France 47°46N 3°1W 172 E3
Plužine Montenegro 43°8N 18°51E 202 C2
Plymouth Montserrat 16°41N 62°12W 323 p
Plymouth Trin. & Tob. 11°14N 60°48W 323 s
Plymouth Plymouth, U.K. 50°22N 4°10W 169 G3
Plymouth Calif., U.S.A. 38°29N 120°51W 306 G6
Plymouth Ill., U.S.A. 40°18N 90°58W 310 D6
Plymouth Ind., U.S.A. 41°21N 86°19W 311 C10
Plymouth Mass., U.S.A. 41°57N 70°40W 313 E14
Plymouth N.C., U.S.A. 35°52N 76°43W 315 D16
Plymouth N.H., U.S.A. 43°46N 71°41W 313 C13
Plymouth Pa., U.S.A. 41°14N 75°57W 313 E9
Plymouth Wis., U.S.A. 43°45N 87°59W 308 D10
Plympton-Wyoming = Wyoming Canada 42°57N 82°7W 312 D2
Plynlimon = Pumlumon Fawr U.K. 52°28N 3°46W 169 E4
Plyusa Russia 58°28N 29°27E 188 C5
Plyusa → Russia 59°4N 28°6E 188 C5
Plyushchevo Russia 55°44N 37°45E 129 B4
Plzeň Czech Rep. 49°45N 13°22E 180 B6
Plzeňský □ Czech Rep. 49°35N 13°0E 180 B6
Pmere Nyente ✪ Australia 24°15S 136°10E 280 C2
Pniewy Poland 52°31N 16°16E 185 F3
Pnika Athens, Greece 112 c1
Pô Burkina Faso 11°14N 1°5W 263 C4
Po → Italy 44°57N 12°4E 199 D9
Po, Foci del Italy 44°55N 12°30E 199 D9
Pô △ Burkina Faso 11°25N 1°5W 263 C4
Po Hai = Bo Hai China 39°0N 119°0E 227 E10
Po Toi China 22°10N 114°16E 122 B2
Po Toi O China 22°16N 114°17E 122 B2
Poasco Italy 45°24N 9°16E 129 B2
Pobé Benin 7°0N 2°56E 263 D5
Pobé Burkina Faso 13°53N 1°42W 263 C4
Pobeda Russia 65°12N 146°12E 215 C15
Pobedy, Pik Kyrgyzstan 42°0N 79°58E 217 D9
Pobiedziska Poland 52°29N 17°11E 185 F4
Pobladura del Valle Spain 42°6N 5°44W 194 C5
Pobra de Trives Spain 42°20N 7°10W 194 C3
Pocahontas Ark., U.S.A. 36°16N 90°58W 315 C9
Pocahontas Ill., U.S.A. 38°50N 89°33W 310 F7
Pocahontas Iowa, U.S.A. 42°44N 94°40W 310 B2
Pocatello U.S.A. 42°52N 112°27W 304 E7
Počátky Czech Rep. 49°15N 15°14E 180 B8
Pocheon S. Korea 37°53N 127°13E 224 D3
Pochep Russia 52°58N 33°29E 189 F7
Pochinki Russia 54°41N 44°59E 190 C7
Pochinok Russia 54°28N 32°29E 188 E7
Pöchlarn Austria 48°12N 15°12E 180 C8
Poci Venezuela 5°57N 61°29W 329 B5
Pocinhos Brazil 7°4S 36°3W 332 C4
Pocking Germany 48°23N 13°19E 179 G9
Pocklington Reef Papua N. G. 10°51S 155°44E 286 F8
Poções Brazil 14°31S 40°21W 333 D3
Pocomoke City U.S.A. 38°5N 75°34W 309 F16
Poconé Brazil 16°15S 56°37W 331 D6
Poços de Caldas Brazil 21°50S 46°33W 335 A6
Podbaba Czech Rep. 50°7N 14°22E 135 B2
Podbořany Czech Rep. 50°14N 13°25E 180 A6
Poddębice Poland 51°54N 18°58E 185 G5
Poděbrady Czech Rep. 50°9N 15°8E 180 A8
Podensac France 44°40N 0°22W 174 D3
Podenzano Italy 44°57N 9°41E 198 D6
Podgorač Croatia 45°27N 18°13E 182 E3
Podgorica Montenegro 42°30N 19°19E 202 D3
Podgorie Albania 40°49N 20°48E 202 F4
Podile India 15°37N 79°37E 245 G4
Podilska Vysochyna Ukraine 49°0N 28°0E 183 B13
Podkarpackie □ Poland 50°0N 22°10E 185 H9
Podkova Bulgaria 41°24N 25°24E 203 E9
Podlapača Croatia 44°37N 15°47E 199 D12
Podlaskie □ Poland 53°10N 23°0E 185 E10
Podocarpus △ Ecuador 4°13S 79°2W 328 D2
Podoleni Romania 46°46N 26°39E 183 D11
Podoli Czech Rep. 50°2N 14°25E 135 B2
Podolínec Slovak Rep. 49°16N 20°31E 181 B13
Podolsk Russia 55°25N 37°30E 188 E9
Podor Senegal 16°40N 15°2W 262 B1
Podporozhye Russia 60°55N 34°2E 188 B8
Podu Iloaiei Romania 47°13N 27°16E 183 C12
Podu Turcului Romania 46°11N 27°25E 183 D12
Podujevo Kosovo 42°54N 21°10E 202 D5
Poduskino Russia 55°43N 37°15E 129 B1
Podyji △ Czech Rep. 48°51N 15°57E 180 C8
Poechos Peru 4°41S 80°34W 328 D1
Poel Germany 54°0N 11°25E 178 B6
Pofadder S. Africa 29°10S 19°22E 270 C2
Poggiardo Italy 40°3N 18°23E 201 B11
Poggibonsi Italy 43°28N 11°9E 198 E8
Póggio Mirteto Italy 42°16N 12°41E 199 F9
Pogoanele Romania 44°55N 27°0E 183 F12
Pogorzela Poland 51°50N 17°12E 185 G4
Pogoso Dem. Rep. of the Congo 6°46S 17°12E 265 D3
Pogradec Albania 40°54N 20°37E 202 F4
Pogranichnyy Russia 44°25N 131°24E 220 B5
Poh Indonesia 0°46S 122°51E 231 E6
Pohang S. Korea 36°1N 129°23E 224 D4
Pohick Creek → U.S.A. 38°48N 77°15W 143 C2
Pohjanmaa Finland 62°58N 22°50E 160 E20
Pohjois-Pirkkala = Nokia Finland 61°30N 23°30E 188 B2
Pohnpei Micronesia 6°55N 158°10E 288 G7
Pohorelá Slovak Rep. 48°50N 20°2E 181 C13
Pohořelice Czech Rep. 48°59N 16°31E 181 C9
Pohorje Slovenia 46°30N 15°20E 199 B12
Pohri India 25°32N 77°22E 242 G6
Pöhue B. U.S.A. 19°0N 155°48W 302 E6
Poi Solomon Is. 10°9S 161°42E 287 N11
Poiana Mare Romania 43°57N 23°5E 182 G8
Poiana Ruscăi, Munții Romania 45°45N 22°25E 182 E7
Poiana Stampei Romania 47°19N 25°8E 183 C10
Poie Dem. Rep. of the Congo 2°50S 23°14E 264 C4
Poike, Península Chile 27°6S 109°15W 330 b
Poindimié N. Cal. 20°56S 165°20E 288 d
Poinsett, C. Antarctica 65°42S 113°18E 151 C8
Point Arena U.S.A. 38°55N 123°41W 306 G3
Point Baker U.S.A. 56°21N 133°37W 296 B2
Point Calimere India 10°17N 79°49E 245 J4
Point Fortin Trin. & Tob. 10°10N 61°42W 323 t
Point Hope U.S.A. 68°21N 166°47W 303 B6
Point L. Canada 65°15N 113°4W 294 D9
Point Lay U.S.A. 69°46N 163°3W 303 B7
Point Lisas Trin. & Tob. 10°24N 61°29W 323 t
Point Pedro Sri Lanka 9°50N 80°15E 245 K5
Point Pelee △ Canada 41°57N 82°31W 312 E2
Point Pleasant N.J., U.S.A. 40°5N 74°4W 313 F10
Point Pleasant W. Va., U.S.A. 38°51N 82°8W 309 F12
Point Reyes ⌂ U.S.A. 38°10N 122°55W 306 G2
Point Salines Int. ✈ (GND) Grenada 12°0N 61°46W 323 q
Pointe-à-Pierre Trin. & Tob. 10°19N 61°28W 323 t
Pointe-à-Pitre Guadeloupe 16°10N 61°32W 322 e
Pointe-au-Pic = La Malbaie Canada 47°40N 70°10W 299 C5
Pointe-Aux-Trembles Canada 45°38N 73°30W 130 A2
Pointe-Claire Canada 45°26N 73°50W 313 A11
Pointe-Gatineau Canada 45°27N 75°41W 313 A9
Pointe Michel Dominica 15°15N 61°23W 323 k
Pointe-Noire Congo 4°48S 11°53E 265 C2
Pointe-Noire Guadeloupe 16°14N 61°47W 322 e
Poio Spain 42°28N 8°41W 194 C2
Poipet Cambodia 13°39N 102°33E 236 F4
Poirino Italy 44°56N 7°48E 198 D4
Poisonbush Ra. Australia 22°30S 121°30E 278 D3
Poissonnier Pt. Australia 19°57S 119°10E 278 C2
Poissy France 48°55N 2°2E 134 A1
Poitiers France 46°35N 0°20E 172 F7
Poitou France 46°40N 0°10W 174 B3
Poitou-Charentes □ France 46°10N 0°15E 174 B4
Poix-de-Picardie France 49°47N 1°58E 173 C8
Poix-Terron France 49°38N 4°38E 173 C11
Pojoaque U.S.A. 35°54N 106°1W 305 J10
Pok Fu Lam China 22°16N 114°7E 122 B1
Pōka'ī B. U.S.A. 21°27N 158°12W 302 K13
Pokaran India 27°0N 71°50E 242 F4
Pokataroo Australia 29°30S 148°36E 281 D4
Pokcheong S. Korea 37°28N 127°8E 137 C2
Pokhara Nepal 28°14N 83°58E 243 E10
Pokhvistnevo Russia 53°36N 52°0E 190 D11
Pokigron Suriname 4°30N 55°22W 329 C6
Poko Dem. Rep. of the Congo 3°7N 26°52E 268 B2
Poko South Sudan 5°41N 31°55E 257 F3
Pokrov Russia 55°55N 39°7E 188 E10
Pokrovka = Kyzyl-Suu Kyrgyzstan 42°20N 78°0E 217 D9
Pokrovsk = Engels Russia 51°28N 46°6E 190 E8
Pokrovsk Russia 61°29N 129°0E 215 C13
Pokrovsko-Sresnevo Russia 55°48N 37°27E 129 B2
Pokrovskoy = Priazovskoye Ukraine 46°44N 35°40E 189 J8
Pokrovskoye Russia 47°25N 38°54E 189 J10
Pol-e Dokhtar Iran 33°9N 47°42E 213 F12
Pol-e Khomri Afghan. 35°56N 68°42E 240 B3
Pol-e Zahāb Iran 34°27N 45°51E 213 E11
Pola = Istra Croatia 45°10N 14°0E 199 C10
Pola = Pula Croatia 44°54N 13°57E 199 D10
Pola Russia 57°55N 32°0E 188 D7
Pola de Allande Spain 43°16N 6°37W 194 B4
Pola de Lena Spain 43°10N 5°49W 194 B5

Pola de Siero Spain 43°24N 5°39W 194 B5
Pola de Somiedo Spain 43°5N 6°15W 194 B4
Pola I. Amer. Samoa 14°14S 170°40W 302 f
Polacca U.S.A. 35°50N 110°23W 305 J8
Polan Iran 25°30N 61°10E 247 E9
Pol'ana Slovak Rep. 48°38N 19°29E 181 C12
Poland U.S.A. 43°13N 75°3W 313 C9
Poland ■ Europe 52°0N 20°0E 185 G3
Polanica-Zdrój Poland 50°24N 16°32E 185 H3
Połaniec Poland 50°26N 21°17E 185 H8
Polanów Poland 54°7N 16°41E 184 D3
Polar Bear △ Canada 55°0N 83°45W 298 A2
Polatlı Turkey 39°36N 32°9E 212 C5
Polatsk Belarus 55°30N 28°50E 188 E5
Polavaram India 17°15N 81°38E 244 F5
Polcura Chile 37°17S 71°43W 334 D1
Połczyn-Zdrój Poland 53°47N 16°5E 184 E3
Poldasht Iran 39°20N 45°4E 213 C11
Poleski △ Poland 51°29N 23°5E 185 G10
Polessk Russia 54°50N 21°8E 184 D8
Polesye = Pripet Marshes Europe 52°10N 27°10E 177 B15
Polevskoy Russia 56°26N 60°11E 186 C11
Polewali Indonesia 3°25S 119°20E 235 C5
Polgar Hungary 47°54N 21°6E 182 C6
Poli Cameroon 8°34N 13°15E 263 C7
Policastro, G. di Italy 40°0N 15°35E 201 C8
Police Poland 53°33N 14°33E 184 E1
Police, Pte. Seychelles 4°51S 55°32E 272 c
Polichnitos Greece 39°6N 26°10E 205 B8
Polička Czech Rep. 49°43N 16°15E 181 B9
Policoro Italy 40°13N 16°41E 201 B9
Poliegos Greece 36°45N 24°38E 204 E6
Poligiros Greece 40°23N 23°25E 202 F7
Polignano a Mare Italy 41°0N 17°13E 201 A9
Poligny France 46°50N 5°42E 173 F12
Polillo Phil. 14°43N 121°56E 232 D3
Polillo Is. Phil. 14°56N 122°0E 232 D4
Polillo Str. Phil. 14°44N 121°51E 232 D3
Polis Cyprus 35°2N 32°26E 207 E8
Polistena Italy 38°24N 16°4E 201 D9
Pölitz = Police Poland 53°33N 14°33E 184 E1
Polk U.S.A. 41°22N 79°56W 312 E5
Polkowice Poland 51°29N 16°3E 185 G3
Polkwitz = Polkowice Poland 51°29N 16°3E 185 G3
Polla Italy 40°31N 15°29E 201 B8
Pollachi India 10°35N 77°0E 245 J3
Pollença Spain 39°54N 3°1E 206 B4
Pollença, B. de Spain 39°53N 3°8E 206 B4
Pollfoss Norway 61°58N 7°54E 164 C4
Póllica Italy 40°11N 15°3E 201 B8
Pollino, Mte. Italy 39°55N 16°11E 201 C9
Pollino △ Italy 40°0N 16°12E 201 C9
Polna Russia 58°31N 28°5E 188 C5
Polnovat Russia 63°50N 65°54E 214 C7
Polo Ill., U.S.A. 41°59N 89°35W 310 C7
Polo Mo., U.S.A. 39°33N 94°3W 310 E2
Pology Ukraine 47°29N 36°15E 189 J9
Polokwane S. Africa 23°54S 29°25E 271 B4
Polokwane → S. Africa 22°25S 30°5E 271 B5
Polomolok Phil. 6°13N 125°3E 233 H5
Polonnaruwa Sri Lanka 7°56N 81°0E 245 L5
Polonne Ukraine 50°6N 27°30E 177 C14
Polonnoye = Polonne Ukraine 50°6N 27°30E 177 C14
Polski Trŭmbesh Bulgaria 43°20N 25°38E 203 C9
Polsko Kosovo Bulgaria 43°23N 25°38E 203 C9
Polson U.S.A. 47°41N 114°9W 304 C6
Poltár Slovak Rep. 48°26N 19°48E 181 C12
Poltava Ukraine 49°35N 34°35E 189 H8
Poltava □ Ukraine 50°15N 33°15E 189 G7
Polton U.K. 55°52N 3°7W 121 B3
Poltoratsk = Ashgabat Turkmenistan 38°0N 57°50E 247 B8
Põltsamaa Estonia 58°39N 25°58E 188 C3
Polunochnoye Russia 60°52N 60°25E 214 C7
Polur India 12°32N 79°11E 245 H4
Põlva Estonia 58°3N 27°3E 188 C4
Polvoranca, Parque de Spain 40°19N 3°48W 127 C1
Polyana Ukraine 48°38N 22°58E 182 B7
Polyarny Russia 69°8N 33°20E 160 B25
Polyarnyye Zori Russia 67°22N 32°30E 160 C25
Polynesia Pac. Oc. 10°0S 162°0W 289 F11
Polynesian Cultural Center U.S.A. 21°38N 157°55W 302 J14
Polynésie française = French Polynesia ☑ Pac. Oc. 20°0S 145°0W 289 f
Polyustrovo Russia 59°57N 30°25E 137 B2
Pomabamba = Azurduy Bolivia 19°59S 64°29W 331 D5
Pomabamba Peru 8°50S 77°28W 330 B2
Pomarance Italy 43°18N 10°52E 198 E7
Pombal Brazil 6°45S 37°50W 332 C4
Pombal Portugal 39°55N 8°40W 194 F2
Pombia Greece 35°0N 24°51E 207 F5
Pombos, B. dos Angola 11°40S 13°47E 265 E2
Pomene Mozam. 22°53S 35°33E 271 B6
Pomeroy Ohio, U.S.A. 39°2N 82°2W 309 F12
Pomeroy Wash., U.S.A. 46°28N 117°36W 304 C5
Pomézia Italy 41°40N 12°30E 200 A5
Pomichna Ukraine 48°13N 31°36E 189 H6
Pomio Papua N. G. 5°32S 151°33E 286 C6
Pomme de Terre L. U.S.A. 37°54N 93°19W 310 G3
Pomme Rose Grenada 12°3N 61°39W 323 q
Pomona Queens., Australia 26°22S 152°52E 281 D5
Pomona Calif., U.S.A. 34°4N 117°45W 307 L9
Pomona Park U.S.A. 29°30N 81°36W 317 F8
Pomorie Bulgaria 42°32N 27°41E 203 D11
Pomorskie □ Poland 54°30N 18°0E 184 D5
Pomorskie, Pojezierze Poland 53°40N 16°37E 184 E3
Pomos Cyprus 35°9N 32°33E 207 E8
Pomos, C. Cyprus 35°10N 32°33E 207 D8
Pompano Beach U.S.A. 26°14N 80°7W 317 J9
Pompei Italy 40°45N 14°30E 201 B7
Pompey France 48°46N 6°6E 173 D13
Pompeys Pillar U.S.A. 45°59N 107°57W 304 D10
Pompeys Pillar △ U.S.A. 46°0N 108°0W 304 D10
Pompidou, Centre Paris, France 134 b4
Pomprap Thailand 13°44N 100°30E 113 B2
Pompton Lakes U.S.A. 41°0N 74°17W 313 F10
Ponape = Pohnpei Micronesia 6°55N 158°10E 288 G7
Ponask L. Canada 54°0N 92°41W 298 B1
Ponca U.S.A. 42°34N 96°43W 308 D5
Ponca City U.S.A. 36°42N 97°5W 314 C6
Ponce Puerto Rico 18°1N 66°37W 321 C6
Ponce de Leon U.S.A. 30°44N 85°56W 316 E4
Ponce de Leon B. U.S.A. 25°15N 81°10W 317 K8
Ponchatoula U.S.A. 30°26N 90°26W 315 F9
Poncheville, L. Canada 50°10N 76°55W 298 B4
Pond U.S.A. 35°43N 119°20W 307 K7
Pond Inlet Canada 72°40N 77°0W 295 C16
Pondicherry = Puducherry India 11°59N 79°50E 245 J4
Pondo Papua N. G. 4°33S 151°38E 286 C6
Pondok Gede Indonesia 6°20S 106°55E 122 A2
Pondok Indah Indonesia 6°16S 106°46E 122 B1
Ponds, I. of Canada 53°27N 55°52W 299 B8
Ponérihouen N. Cal. 21°5S 165°24E 288 d
Ponferrada Spain 42°32N 6°35W 194 C4
Pongo, Wadi → South Sudan 8°42N 27°40E 257 F2
Poniatowa Poland 51°11N 22°3E 185 G9
Poniec Poland 51°48N 16°50E 185 G3
Ponikva Slovenia 46°16N 15°26E 199 B12
Ponizovkino = Krasnyy Profintern Russia 57°45N 40°27E 188 D11
Ponnaiyar → India 11°50N 79°45E 245 J4
Ponnani India 10°45N 75°59E 245 J2
Ponneri India 13°20N 80°15E 245 H5
Ponnuru India 16°5N 80°34E 245 F5
Ponoka Canada 52°42N 113°40W 296 C6
Ponorogo Indonesia 7°52S 111°27E 235 D4
Ponot Phil. 8°25N 123°0E 233 G4
Ponoy Russia 67°0N 41°13E 186 A7
Ponoy → Russia 66°59N 41°17E 186 A7
Pons = Ponts Spain 41°55N 1°12E 196 D6
Pons France 45°35N 0°34W 174 C3
Ponsul → Portugal 39°40N 7°31W 194 F3
Pont-à-Mousson France 48°54N 6°1E 173 D13
Pont-Audemer France 49°21N 0°30E 172 C7
Pont-Aven France 47°51N 3°47W 172 E3
Pont Canavese Italy 45°25N 7°36E 198 C4
Pont Casse Dominica 15°22N 61°21W 323 k
Pont-d'Ain France 46°3N 5°21E 173 F12
Pont-de-Roide France 47°23N 6°45E 173 E13
Pont-de-Salars France 44°18N 2°44E 174 D6
Pont-de-Vaux France 46°26N 4°56E 173 F11
Pont-de-Veyle France 46°17N 4°53E 173 F11
Pont-du-Château France 45°47N 3°15E 173 G10
Pont-l'Abbé France 47°52N 4°15W 172 E2
Pont-l'Évêque France 49°18N 0°11E 172 C7
Pont-St-Esprit France 44°16N 4°40E 175 D8
Pont-St-Martin Italy 45°36N 7°48E 198 C4
Pont-Ste-Maxence France 49°18N 2°36E 173 C9
Pont-sur-Yonne France 48°18N 3°10E 173 D10
Pont-Viau Canada 45°35N 73°41W 130 A1
Ponta de Pedras Brazil 1°23S 48°52W 332 B2
Ponta Delgada Flores, Azores 39°31N 31°13W 153 d2
Ponta Delgada São Miguel, Azores 37°44N 25°40W 153 d3
Ponta Delgada ✈ (PDL) Azores 37°44N 25°41W 153 d3
Ponta do Sol Madeira 32°42N 17°7W 153 c
Ponta Grossa Brazil 25°7S 50°10W 335 B5
Ponta Porã Brazil 22°20S 55°35W 335 A4
Pontacq France 43°11N 0°8W 174 E3
Pontailler-sur-Saône France 47°13N 5°25E 173 E12
Pontal → Brazil 9°8S 40°12W 332 C3
Pontalina Brazil 17°31S 49°27W 333 E2
Pontarlier France 46°54N 6°20E 173 F13
Pontassieve Italy 43°46N 11°26E 199 E8
Pontault-Combault France 48°47N 2°36E 134 B4
Pontaumur France 45°52N 2°40E 174 C6
Pontcharra France 45°26N 6°1E 175 C10
Pontchartrain, L. U.S.A. 30°5N 90°5W 315 F9
Pontchâteau France 47°25N 2°5W 172 E4
Ponte Alta, Serra do Brazil 19°42S 47°40W 333 E2
Ponte Alta do Norte Brazil 10°45S 47°34W 332 D2
Ponte Branca Brazil 16°27S 52°40W 331 D7
Ponte da Barca Portugal 41°48N 8°25W 194 D2
Ponte de Sor Portugal 39°17N 8°1W 195 F2
Ponte dell'Ólio Italy 44°52N 9°39E 198 D6
Ponte di Legno Italy 46°16N 10°31E 198 B7
Ponte do Lima Portugal 41°46N 8°35W 194 D2
Ponte do Pungué Mozam. 19°30S 34°33E 269 F3
Ponte-Leccia France 42°28N 9°13E 175 F13
Ponte nelle Alpi Italy 46°11N 12°16E 199 B9
Ponte Nova Brazil 20°25S 42°54W 333 F3
Ponte Vedra Beach U.S.A. 30°15N 81°23W 316 E8
Ponteareas Spain 42°10N 8°28W 194 C2
Pontebba Italy 46°30N 13°18E 199 B10
Ponteceso Spain 43°15N 8°54W 194 B2
Pontecorvo Italy 41°27N 13°40E 200 A6
Pontedeume Spain 43°24N 8°10W 194 B2
Ponteix Canada 49°46N 107°29W 297 D7
Pontes e Lacerda Brazil 15°12S 59°22W 331 D6
Pontevedra Capiz, Phil. 11°29N 122°50E 233 F4
Pontevedra Neg. Occ., Phil. 10°22N 122°52E 233 F4
Pontevedra Spain 42°26N 8°40W 194 C2
Pontevedra □ Spain 42°25N 8°39W 194 C2
Pontevedra, R. de → Spain 42°22N 8°45W 194 C2
Pontevico Italy 45°16N 10°5E 198 C7
Pontiac Ill., U.S.A. 40°53N 88°38W 311 D8
Pontiac Mich., U.S.A. 42°38N 83°18W 311 B13
Pontian Kechil Malaysia 1°29N 103°23E 237 d
Pontianak Indonesia 0°3S 109°15E 235 C3
Pontine Is. = Ponziane, Ísole Italy 40°55N 12°57E 200 B5
Pontine Mts. = Kuzey Anadolu Dağları Turkey 41°0N 36°45E 212 B7
Pontinha Portugal 38°45N 9°11W 126 A1
Pontínia Italy 41°25N 13°2E 200 A6
Pontivy France 48°5N 2°58W 172 D4
Pontoise France 49°3N 2°5E 173 C9
Ponton → Canada 58°27N 116°11W 296 B5
Pontorson France 48°34N 1°30W 172 D5
Pontrémoli Italy 44°22N 9°53E 198 D6
Pontrieux France 48°42N 3°10W 172 D3
Ponts Spain 41°55N 1°12E 196 D6
Pontypool Ont., Canada 44°6N 78°38W 312 B6
Pontypool Torf., U.K. 51°42N 3°2W 169 F4
Ponza Italy 40°54N 12°58E 200 B5
Ponziane, Ísole Italy 40°55N 12°57E 200 B5
Poochera Australia 32°43S 134°51E 281 E1
Poole Trin. & Tob. 10°17N 61°14W 323 t
Poole Poole, U.K. 50°43N 1°59W 169 G6
Poole □ U.K. 50°43N 1°59W 169 G6
Poole → Trin. & Tob. 10°15N 61°5W 323 t
Pooler U.S.A. 32°7N 81°15W 316 C8
Poona = Pune India 18°29N 73°57E 244 E1
Poonamallee India 13°3N 80°10E 245 H5
Pooncarie Australia 33°22S 142°31E 282 B5
Poopelloe L. Australia 31°40S 144°0E 282 A6
Poopó Bolivia 18°23S 66°59W 330 D4
Poopó, L. de Bolivia 18°30S 67°35W 330 D4
Poor Knights Is. N.Z. 35°29S 174°43E 284 B3
Poorman U.S.A. 64°5N 155°33W 303 D9
Popa Gabon 1°35S 12°32E 264 C2
Popa, Mt. Burma 20°55N 95°15E 241 E5
Popayán Colombia 2°27N 76°36W 328 C2
Poperinge Belgium 50°51N 2°42E 170 D2
Popiltah L. Australia 33°10S 141°42E 282 B4
Popina Bulgaria 44°7N 26°57E 203 B10
Popio L. Australia 33°10S 141°52E 282 B4
Poplar London, U.K. 51°30N 0°0 125 A3
Poplar Mont., U.S.A. 48°7N 105°12W 304 B11
Poplar → Canada 53°0N 97°19W 296 C9
Poplar Bluff U.S.A. 36°46N 90°24W 308 G8
Poplar Head = Dothan U.S.A. 31°13N 85°24W 316 D4
Poplarville U.S.A. 30°51N 89°32W 315 F10
Popocatépetl, Volcán Mexico 19°2N 98°38W 319 D5
Popokabaka Dem. Rep. of the Congo 5°41S 16°40E 265 D3
Pópoli Italy 42°10N 13°50E 199 F10
Popolo Dem. Rep. of the Congo 2°22N 21°8E 264 B4
Popolo, Porta del Rome, Italy 136 a2
Popomanaseu, Mt. Solomon Is. 9°40S 160°1E 287 M11
Popondetta Papua N. G. 8°48S 148°17E 286 E5
Popovača Croatia 45°30N 16°41E 199 C13
Popovo Bulgaria 43°21N 26°18E 203 C10
Poppberg Germany 49°26N 11°37E 179 F7
Poppi Italy 43°43N 11°46E 199 E8
Poppintree Ireland 53°23N 6°17W 120 A2
Poprad Slovak Rep. 49°3N 20°18E 181 B13
Poprad → Slovak Rep. 49°38N 20°42E 181 B13
Poradaha Bangla. 23°51N 89°1E 241 D2
Porali → Pakistan 25°58N 66°26E 242 G2
Porangaba Brazil 8°48S 70°36W 330 B3
Porangahau N.Z. 40°17S 176°37E 284 G5
Porangatu Brazil 13°26S 49°10W 333 D2
Porbandar India 21°44N 69°43E 242 J3
Porce → Colombia 7°28N 74°53W 328 B3
Porcher I. Canada 53°50N 130°30W 296 C2
Porco Bolivia 19°50S 65°59W 331 D4
Porcos → Brazil 12°42S 45°7W 333 D2
Porcuna Spain 37°52N 4°11W 195 H6
Porcupine → Sask., Canada 59°11N 104°46W 297 B8
Porcupine → Alaska, U.S.A. 66°34N 145°19W 303 C11
Porcupine Abyssal Plain Atl. Oc. 48°0N 8°0W 152 B10
Porcupine Gorge △ Australia 20°22S 144°26E 280 C3
Pordenone Italy 45°57N 12°39E 199 C9
Pordim Bulgaria 43°23N 24°51E 203 C8
Pore Colombia 5°43N 72°0W 328 B3
Poreč Croatia 45°14N 13°36E 199 C10
Porecatu Brazil 22°43S 51°24W 333 F1
Porechye = Demidov Russia 55°16N 31°30E 188 E6
Poretskoye Russia 55°9N 46°21E 190 C8
Porgera Papua N. G. 5°28S 143°12E 286 C2
Pori Finland 61°29N 21°48E 188 B1
Pori Greece 35°58N 23°13E 204 F5
Porirua N.Z. 41°8S 174°52E 143 A2
Porirua East N.Z. 41°8S 174°52E 143 A2
Porkhov Russia 57°45N 29°38E 188 D5
Porlamar Venezuela 10°57N 63°51W 329 A5
Porlezza Italy 46°2N 9°7E 198 B6
Porma → Spain 42°49N 5°28W 194 C5
Pormpuraaw Australia 14°59S 141°26E 280 A3
Pormpuraaw ✪ Australia 14°55S 141°47E 280 A3
Pornic France 47°7N 2°5W 172 E4
Poronaysk Russia 49°13N 143°0E 219 B17
Poros Attiki, Greece 37°30N 23°30E 204 D5
Poros Kefalonia, Greece 38°9N 20°47E 207 C2
Poros Lefkada, Greece 38°38N 20°43E 207 B2
Poroshiri-Dake Japan 42°41N 142°52E 220 C11
Poroszló Hungary 47°39N 20°40E 182 C5
Poroto Mts. Tanzania 9°0S 33°30E 269 D3
Porpoise B. Antarctica 66°0S 127°0E 151 C9
Porpoise Pt. Ascension I. 7°54S 14°21W 153 g
Porquerolles, Î. de France 43°0N 6°13E 175 F10
Porrentruy Switz. 47°25N 7°6E 180 B3
Porreres Spain 39°31N 3°2E 206 B4
Porsangerfjorden Norway 70°40N 25°40E 160 A21
Porsgrunn Norway 59°10N 9°40E 164 E6
Port Adelaide Australia 34°50S 138°30E 282 C3
Port Alberni Canada 49°14N 124°50W 296 D4
Port Albert Australia 38°42S 146°42E 283 E7
Port Alexander U.S.A. 56°15N 134°38W 303 H14
Port Alfred S. Africa 33°36S 26°55E 270 D4
Port Alice Canada 50°20N 127°25W 296 C3
Port Allegany U.S.A. 41°48N 78°17W 312 E6
Port Allen U.S.A. 30°27N 91°12W 314 F9
Port Alma Queens., Australia 23°38S 150°53E 280 C5
Port Alma Ont., Canada 42°10N 82°14W 312 D2
Port Angeles U.S.A. 48°7N 123°27W 306 B3
Port Antonio Jamaica 18°10N 76°26W 320 a
Port Aransas U.S.A. 27°50N 97°4W 314 H6
Port Arthur Tas., Australia 43°7S 147°50E 281 G4
Port Arthur Tex., U.S.A. 29°54N 93°56W 314 G8
Port au Choix Canada 50°43N 57°22W 299 B8
Port au Port B. Canada 48°40N 58°50W 299 C8
Port-au-Prince Haiti 18°40N 72°20W 321 C5
Port Augusta Australia 32°30S 137°50E 282 B2
Port Austin U.S.A. 44°3N 83°1W 312 B2
Port Authority Bus Terminal New York, U.S.A. 132 c2
Port-aux-Français Kerguelen 49°21S 70°13E 273 J6
Port Bell Uganda 0°18N 32°35E 268 B3
Port Bergé Vaovao Madag. 15°33S 47°40E 272 B2
Port Blair India 11°40N 92°45E 245 J11
Port Blandford Canada 48°20N 54°10W 299 C9
Port Botany Australia 33°58S 151°13E 139 B2
Port-Bouët Ivory C. 5°16N 3°57W 262 D4
Port Bradshaw Australia 12°30S 137°20E 280 A2
Port Broughton Australia 33°37S 137°56E 282 B2
Port Bruce Canada 42°39N 81°0W 312 D4
Port Burwell Canada 42°40N 80°48W 312 D4
Port Byron U.S.A. 41°36N 90°20W 310 C6
Port Campbell Vic., Australia 38°37S 143°1E 282 E5
Port Campbell India 11°56N 92°37E 245 J11
Port Campbell △ Australia 38°38S 143°6E 282 E5
Port Canning India 22°23N 88°40E 243 H13
Port Carling Canada 45°7N 79°35W 312 A5
Port-Cartier Canada 50°2N 66°50W 299 B6
Port Chalmers N.Z. 45°49S 170°30E 285 F5
Port Charles N.Z. 36°33S 175°30E 284 C4
Port Charlotte U.S.A. 26°59N 82°6W 317 J7
Port Chester U.S.A. 41°0N 73°40W 313 F11
Port Clements Canada 53°40N 132°10W 296 C2
Port Clinton U.S.A. 41°31N 82°56W 311 C14
Port Colborne Canada 42°50N 79°10W 312 D5
Port Coquitlam Canada 49°15N 122°45W 306 A4
Port Cornwallis India 13°17N 93°5E 245 H11
Port Credit Canada 43°33N 79°35W 312 C5
Port-Cros △ France 43°0N 6°24E 175 F10
Port Curtis Australia 23°57S 151°20E 280 C5
Port d'Alcúdia Spain 39°50N 3°7E 206 B4
Port Dalhousie Canada 43°13N 79°16W 312 C5
Port d'Andratx Spain 39°32N 2°23E 206 B3
Port Darwin N. Terr., Australia 12°24S 130°45E 278 B5
Port Darwin Falk. Is. 51°50S 59°0W 153 f
Port Davey Australia 43°16S 145°55E 281 G4
Port-de-Bouc France 43°24N 4°59E 175 E8
Port-de-Paix Haiti 19°50N 72°50W 321 C5
Port de Pollença Spain 39°54N 3°4E 206 B4
Port de Sóller Spain 39°48N 2°42E 206 B3
Port Dickson Malaysia 2°30N 101°49E 237 L3
Port Douglas Australia 16°30S 145°30E 280 B4
Port Dover Canada 42°47N 80°12W 312 D4
Port Edward Canada 54°12N 130°10W 296 C2
Port Elgin Canada 44°25N 81°25W 312 B3
Port Elizabeth S. Africa 33°58S 25°40E 270 D4
Port Ellen U.K. 55°38N 6°11W 167 F2
Port Elliot Australia 35°32S 138°41E 282 C3
Port-en-Bessin-Huppain France 49°21N 0°45W 172 C6
Port Erin I. of Man 54°5N 4°45W 168 C3
Port Essington Australia 11°15S 132°10E 278 B5
Port Etienne = Nouâdhibou Mauritania 20°54N 17°0W 260 D1
Port Ewen U.S.A. 41°54N 73°59W 313 E11
Port Fairy Australia 38°22S 142°12E 282 E5
Port Fitzroy N.Z. 36°8S 175°20E 284 C4
Port Florence = Kisumu Kenya 0°3S 34°45E 268 C3
Port Fouâd = Bûr Fuad Egypt 31°15N 32°20E 256 H8
Port Francqui = Ilebo Dem. Rep. of the Congo 4°17S 20°55E 265 C4
Port Gamble U.S.A. 47°51N 122°34W 306 C4
Port-Gentil Gabon 0°40S 8°50E 264 C1
Port Germein Australia 33°1S 138°1E 281 E2
Port Ghalib Egypt 25°20N 34°50E 246 E2
Port Gibson U.S.A. 31°58N 90°59W 314 F9
Port Glasgow U.K. 55°56N 4°41W 167 F4
Port-Gueydon = Azeffoun Algeria 36°51N 4°26E 261 A5
Port Harcourt Nigeria 4°40N 7°10E 263 E6
Port Hardy Canada 50°41N 127°30W 296 C3
Port Harrison = Inukjuak Canada 58°25N 78°15W 295 F16
Port Hawkesbury Canada 45°36N 61°22W 299 C7
Port Hedland Australia 20°25S 118°35E 278 D2
Port Heiden U.S.A. 56°55N 158°41W 303 H8
Port Henry U.S.A. 44°3N 73°28W 313 B11
Port Herald = Nsanje Malawi 16°55S 35°12E 269 F4
Port Hood Canada 46°0N 61°32W 299 C7
Port Hope Ont., Canada 43°56N 78°20W 312 C6
Port Hope Mich., U.S.A. 43°57N 82°43W 312 C2
Port Hope Simpson Canada 52°33N 56°18W 299 B8
Port Hueneme U.S.A. 34°7N 119°12W 307 L7
Port Huron U.S.A. 42°58N 82°26W 312 D2
Port Iliç Azerbaijan 38°53N 48°47E 213 C13
Port Jefferson U.S.A. 40°57N 73°3W 313 F11
Port Jervis U.S.A. 41°22N 74°41W 313 E10
Port-Joinville France 46°45N 2°23W 172 F4
Port Katon Russia 46°52N 38°46E 189 J10
Port Kembla Australia 34°52S 150°49E 283 C9
Port Kenny Australia 33°10S 134°41E 281 E1
Port-la-Nouvelle France 43°1N 3°3E 174 E7
Port Lairge = Waterford Ireland 52°15N 7°8W 166 D4
Port Laoise Ireland 53°2N 7°18W 166 C4
Port Lavaca U.S.A. 28°37N 96°38W 314 G6
Port Leyden U.S.A. 43°35N 75°21W 313 C9
Port Lincoln Australia 34°42S 135°52E 282 C1
Port Lions U.S.A. 57°52N 152°53W 303 H9
Port Loko S. Leone 8°48N 12°46W 262 D2
Port Louis Morbihan, France 47°42N 3°22W 172 E3
Port-Louis Guadeloupe 16°28N 61°32W 322 e
Port Louis Mauritius 20°10S 57°30E 272 e
Port Lyautey = Kenitra Morocco 34°15N 6°40W 260 B3
Port MacDonnell Australia 38°5S 140°48E 282 E4
Port McNeill Canada 50°35N 127°6W 296 C3
Port Macquarie Australia 31°25S 152°25E 283 A10
Port Maria Jamaica 18°22N 76°54W 320 a
Port Mathurin Rodrigues 19°41S 63°25E 273 F5
Port Matilda U.S.A. 40°48N 78°3W 312 F6
Port Mayaca U.S.A. 26°59N 80°36W 317 J9
Port McNicoll Canada 44°44N 79°48W 312 B5
Port Mearnóg = Portmarnock Ireland 53°26N 6°8W 120 A3
Port Melbourne Australia 37°50S 144°54E 128 B1
Port Mellon Canada 49°32N 123°31W 296 D4
Port-Menier Canada 49°51N 64°15W 299 C7
Port Moller U.S.A. 55°59N 160°34W 303 J7
Port Moody Canada 49°17N 122°51W 306 A4
Port Morant Jamaica 17°54N 76°19W 320 a
Port Moresby Papua N. G. 9°24S 147°8E 286 E4
Port Mourant Guyana 6°15N 57°20W 329 B6
Port Musgrave Australia 11°55S 141°50E 280 A3
Port Narevin Vanuatu 18°45S 169°10E 287 H7
Port-Navalo France 47°34N 2°54W 172 E4
Port Neches U.S.A. 30°0N 93°59W 314 G8
Port Nicholson N.Z. 41°20S 174°52E 143 B2
Port Nolloth S. Africa 29°17S 16°52E 270 C2
Port Nouveau-Québec = Kangiqsualujjuaq Canada 58°30N 65°59W 295 F18
Port of Climax Canada 49°10N 108°20W 297 D7
Port of Coronach Canada 49°7N 105°31W 297 D7
Port of Spain Trin. & Tob. 10°40N 61°31W 323 t
Port Olry Vanuatu 15°1S 167°4E 287 E5
Port Orange U.S.A. 29°9N 80°59W 317 F9
Port Orchard U.S.A. 47°32N 122°38W 306 C4
Port Orford U.S.A. 42°45N 124°30W 304 E1
Port Pegasus N.Z. 47°12S 167°41E 285 H2
Port Perry Canada 44°6N 78°56W 312 B6
Port Phillip B. Australia 38°10S 144°50E 283 E6
Port Pirie Australia 33°10S 138°1E 282 B3
Port Renfrew Canada 48°30N 124°20W 306 B2
Port Richmond U.S.A. 40°38N 74°7W 132 C1
Port Roper Australia 14°45S 135°25E 280 A2
Port Rowan Canada 42°40N 80°30W 312 D4
Port Royal Jamaica 17°56N 76°51W 320 a
Port Royal Sd. U.S.A. 32°15N 80°40W 316 C9
Port Safâga = Bûr Safâga Egypt 26°43N 33°57E 246 E2
Port Said = Bûr Sa'îd Egypt 31°16N 32°18E 256 H8
Port St. Joe U.S.A. 29°49N 85°18W 316 F4
Port St. John U.S.A. 28°29N 80°47W 317 G9
Port St. Johns = Umzimvubu S. Africa 31°38S 29°33E 271 D4
Port-St-Louis-du-Rhône France 43°23N 4°49E 175 E8
Port St. Lucie U.S.A. 27°18N 80°21W 317 H9
Port-Ste-Marie France 44°15N 0°25E 174 D4
Port Salerno U.S.A. 27°9N 80°12W 317 H9
Port Sanilac U.S.A. 43°26N 82°33W 312 C2
Port Severn Canada 44°48N 79°43W 312 B5
Port Shelter China 22°20N 114°17E 122 A2
Port Shepstone S. Africa 30°44S 30°28E 271 D5
Port Simpson Canada 54°30N 130°20W 296 C2
Port Stanley = Stanley Falk. Is. 51°40S 59°51W 153 f
Port Stanley Canada 42°40N 81°10W 312 D4
Port Sudan = Bûr Sûdân Sudan 19°32N 37°9E 256 D4
Port Sulphur U.S.A. 29°29N 89°42W 315 G10
Port-sur-Saône France 47°42N 6°2E 173 E13
Port Talbot U.K. 51°35N 3°47W 169 F4
Port Taufiq = Bûr Taufiq Egypt 29°54N 32°32E 256 J8
Port Townsend U.S.A. 48°7N 122°45W 306 B4
Port Union Canada 43°47N 79°7W 141 A4
Port-Vato Vanuatu 16°20S 168°1E 287 F6
Port-Vendres France 42°32N 3°8E 174 F7
Port Victoria Australia 34°30S 137°29E 282 C2
Port Vila Vanuatu 17°45S 168°18E 287 G6
Port Vladimir Russia 69°25N 33°6E 160 B25
Port Wakefield Australia 34°12S 138°10E 282 C3
Port Washington U.S.A. 43°23N 87°53W 308 D10
Port Weld = Kuala Sepetang Malaysia 4°49N 100°28E 237 K3
Port Wentworth U.S.A. 32°9N 81°10W 316 C8
Porta Orientalis Romania 45°6N 22°18E 177 F12
Portachuelo Bolivia 17°10S 63°20W 331 D5
Portacloy Ireland 54°20N 9°46W 166 B2
Portadown U.K. 54°25N 6°27W 166 B5
Portaferry U.K. 54°23N 5°33W 166 B6
Portage Ind., U.S.A. 41°34N 87°11W 311 C10
Portage Mich., U.S.A. 42°12N 85°35W 311 B11
Portage Pa., U.S.A. 40°23N 78°41W 312 F6
Portage Wis., U.S.A. 43°33N 89°28W 308 D9
Portage → U.S.A. 41°31N 83°5W 311 C14
Portage la Prairie Canada 49°58N 98°18W 297 D9
Portage Park U.S.A. 41°56N 87°45W 119 B2
Portageville U.S.A. 36°26N 89°42W 308 G9
Portal U.S.A. 32°33N 81°56W 316 C8
Portal de la Pau, Plaza Barcelona, Spain 114 c2
Portalegre Portugal 39°19N 7°25W 195 F3
Portalegre □ Portugal 39°20N 7°40W 195 F3
Portales U.S.A. 34°11N 103°20W 305 J12
Portarlington Ireland 53°9N 7°14W 166 C4
Portbou Spain 42°25N 3°9E 196 C8
Porteira Brazil 1°5S 57°4W 329 D6
Porteirinha Brazil 15°44S 43°2W 333 E3
Portel Brazil 1°57S 50°49W 332 B1
Portel Portugal 38°19N 7°41W 195 G3
Portela, Lisboa ✈ (LIS) Portugal 38°46N 9°8W 126 A2
Porter U.S.A. 41°36N 87°4W 311 C9
Porter, L. U.S.A. 28°30N 81°19W 133 A3
Porter L. N.W.T., Canada 61°41N 108°5W 297 A7
Porter L. Sask., Canada 56°20N 107°20W 297 B7
Porterville Western Cape, S. Africa 33°0S 19°0E 270 D2
Porterville Calif., U.S.A. 36°4N 119°1W 306 J8
Portes-lès-Valence France 44°52N 4°54E 175 D8
Porthcawl U.K. 51°29N 3°42W 169 F4
Porthill U.S.A. 48°59N 116°30W 304 B5
Porthmadog U.K. 52°55N 4°8W 168 E3
Portile de Fier Europe 44°44N 22°30E 182 F7
Portimão Portugal 37°8N 8°32W 195 H2
Portishead U.K. 51°29N 2°46W 169 F5
Portiţei, Gura Romania 44°41N 29°0E 183 F14
Portknockie U.K. 57°42N 2°51W 167 D6
Portland N.S.W., Australia 33°20S 150°0E 283 B9
Portland Vic., Australia 38°20S 141°35E 282 E4
Portland Ont., Canada 44°42N 76°12W 313 B8
Portland Conn., U.S.A. 41°34N 72°38W 313 E12
Portland Fla., U.S.A. 30°31N 86°12W 316 E3
Portland Ind., U.S.A. 40°26N 84°59W 311 D12
Portland Maine, U.S.A. 43°39N 70°16W 309 D18
Portland Mich., U.S.A. 42°52N 84°54W 311 B12
Portland Oreg., U.S.A. 45°32N 122°37W 306 E4
Portland Pa., U.S.A. 40°55N 75°6W 313 F9
Portland Tex., U.S.A. 27°53N 97°20W 314 H6
Portland, I. of U.K. 50°33N 2°26W 169 G5
Portland, Récif French Polynesia 23°42S 134°30W 289 f
Portland B. Australia 38°15S 141°45E 282 E4
Portland Bight Jamaica 17°52N 77°5W 320 a
Portland Bill U.K. 50°31N 2°28W 169 G5
Portland Canal U.S.A. 55°56N 130°0W 296 B2
Portland I. N.Z. 39°20S 177°51E 284 F6
Portland Int. ✈ (PDX) U.S.A. 45°35N 122°36W 306 E4
Portland Pt. Ascension I. 7°59S 14°25W 153 g
Portland Pt. Jamaica 17°42N 77°11W 320 a
Portmadoc = Porthmadog U.K. 52°55N 4°8W 168 E3
Portmarnock Ireland 53°26N 6°8W 120 A3
Portmore Jamaica 17°53N 76°53W 320 a
Porto Brazil 3°54S 42°42W 332 B3
Porto Corse-du-Sud, France 42°16N 8°42E 175 F12
Porto Portugal 41°8N 8°40W 194 D2
Porto □ Portugal 41°8N 8°20W 194 D2
Porto, G. de France 42°17N 8°34E 175 F12
Porto Acre Brazil 9°34S 67°31W 330 B4
Pôrto Alegre = Luzilândia Brazil 3°28S 42°22W 332 B3
Pôrto Alegre Pará, Brazil 4°22S 52°44W 329 D7
Pôrto Alegre Rio Grande do S., Brazil 30°5S 51°10W 335 C5
Porto Alegre São Tomé & Príncipe 0°2N 6°32E 265 a
Porto Amboim = Gunza Angola 10°50S 13°50E 265 E2
Porto Amélia = Pemba Mozam. 12°58S 40°30E 269 E5
Porto Azzurro Italy 42°46N 10°24E 198 F7
Porto Brandão Portugal 38°40N 9°12W 126 A1
Pôrto Cajueiro Brazil 11°3S 55°53W 331 C6
Porto Colom Spain 39°26N 3°15E 206 B4
Porto Cristo Spain 39°33N 3°20E 206 B4
Pôrto da Fôlha Brazil 9°55S 37°17W 332 C4
Pôrto de Moz Brazil 1°41S 52°13W 329 D7
Pôrto de Pedras Brazil 9°10S 35°17W 332 C4
Pôrto des Meinacos Brazil 12°33S 53°7W 331 C7
Pôrto dos Gaúchos Brazil 11°32S 57°16W 331 C6
Porto Empédocle Italy 37°17N 13°32E 200 E6
Pôrto Esperança Brazil 19°37S 57°29W 331 D6
Pôrto Espiridião Brazil 15°51S 58°28W 331 D6
Porto Formoso Azores 37°49N 25°25W 153 d3
Pôrto Franco Brazil 6°20S 47°24W 332 C2
Porto Grande Brazil 0°42N 51°24W 329 C7
Porto Inglês C. Verde Is. 15°21N 23°10W 153 j
Pôrto Jofre Brazil 17°20S 56°48W 331 D6
Porto Lengone = Porto Azzurro Italy 42°46N 10°24E 198 F7
Porto Maurizio = Impéria Italy 43°53N 8°3E 198 E5
Pôrto Mendes Brazil 24°30S 54°15W 335 A5
Porto Moniz Madeira 32°52N 17°11W 153 c
Pôrto Murtinho Brazil 21°45S 57°55W 331 E6
Pôrto Nacional Brazil 10°40S 48°30W 332 D2
Porto-Novo Benin 6°23N 2°42E 263 D5
Pôrto Novo Rio de J., Brazil 22°5S 43°7W 135 A2
Porto Novo Cr. → Nigeria 6°25N 3°22E 124 B2
Porto Primavera, Represa Brazil 22°10S 52°45W 335 A5
Porto San Giórgio Italy 43°11N 13°48E 199 E10
Porto Sant' Elpídio Italy 43°15N 13°43E 199 E10
Porto Santana Brazil 0°3S 51°11W 329 D7
Porto Santo, I. de Madeira 33°45N 16°25W 260 B1
Porto Santo Stéfano Italy 42°26N 11°7E 198 F8
Pôrto São José Brazil 22°43S 53°10W 335 A5
Porto Seguro = Guadalupe Brazil 6°44S 43°47W 332 C3
Porto Seguro Brazil 16°26S 39°5W 333 E4
Porto Tolle Italy 44°56N 12°22E 199 D9
Porto Tórres Italy 40°50N 8°24E 200 B1
Pôrto União Brazil 26°10S 51°10W 335 B5
Porto-Vecchio France 41°35N 9°16E 175 G13
Pôrto Velho Brazil 8°46S 63°54W 331 B5
Porto Walter Brazil 8°15S 72°40W 330 B3
Portobello U.K. 55°57N 3°7W 121 B3
Portobelo Panama 9°35N 79°42W 320 E4
Portoferráio Italy 42°48N 10°20E 198 F7
Portogruaro Italy 45°47N 12°50E 199 C9
Portola U.S.A. 39°49N 120°28W 306 F6
Portomaggiore Italy 44°42N 11°48E 199 D8
Portopetro Spain 39°22N 3°13E 206 B4
Portoscuso Italy 39°12N 8°24E 200 C1
Portovénere Italy 44°3N 9°51E 198 D6
Portoviejo Ecuador 1°7S 80°28W 328 D1
Portpatrick U.K. 54°51N 5°7W 167 G3
Portree U.K. 57°25N 6°12W 167 D2
Portrero U.S.A. 37°46N 122°25W 136 B3
Portrush U.K. 55°12N 6°40W 166 A5
Portsmouth Dominica 15°34N 61°27W 323 k
Portsmouth Portsmouth, U.K. 50°48N 1°6W 169 G6
Portsmouth N.H., U.S.A. 43°5N 70°45W 313 C14
Portsmouth Ohio, U.S.A. 38°44N 82°57W 309 F12
Portsmouth R.I., U.S.A. 41°36N 71°15W 313 E13
Portsmouth Va., U.S.A. 36°58N 76°23W 309 G15
Portsmouth □ U.K. 50°48N 1°6W 169 G6
Portsoy U.K. 57°41N 2°41W 167 D6
Portstewart U.K. 55°11N 6°43W 166 A5
Porttipahdan tekojärvi Finland 68°5N 26°40E 160 B22
Portugal ■ Europe 40°0N 8°0W 194 F3
Portugalete Spain 43°19N 3°4W 196 B1
Portuguesa □ Venezuela 9°10N 69°15W 328 B4
Portuguese East Africa = Mozambique ■ Africa 19°0S 35°0E 269 F4
Portuguese Guinea = Guinea-Bissau ■ Africa 12°0N 15°0W 262 C2
Portuguese Timor = East Timor ■ Asia 8°50S 126°0E 231 F7
Portuguese West Africa = Angola ■ Africa 12°0S 18°0E 265 E3
Portumna Ireland 53°6N 8°14W 166 C3
Portville U.S.A. 42°3N 78°20W 312 D6
Poruma Australia 10°2S 143°4E 280 a
Porus Jamaica 18°2N 77°25W 320 a
Porvenir Bolivia 11°10S 68°50W 330 C4
Porvenir Chile 53°10S 70°16W 336 D2
Porvoo Finland 60°24N 25°40E 188 B3
Porzuna Spain 39°9N 4°9W 195 F6
Pos Chiquito Aruba 12°27N 69°57W 322 f
Posada Italy 40°38N 9°43E 200 B2
Posada → Italy 40°39N 9°45E 200 B2
Posadas Argentina 27°30S 55°50W 335 B4
Posadas Spain 37°47N 5°11W 195 H5
Poschiavo Switz. 46°19N 10°4E 179 J6
Posen = Poznań Poland 52°25N 16°55E 185 F3
Posets Spain 42°39N 0°25E 196 C5
Poseyville U.S.A. 38°10N 87°47W 311 F9
Poshan = Boshan China 36°28N 117°49E 227 F9
Posht-e Badam Iran 33°2N 55°23E 247 C7
Posidium Greece 35°30N 27°10E 205 F9
Poso Indonesia 1°20S 120°55E 231 E6
Poso, Danau Indonesia 1°52S 120°35E 231 E6
Posoegroenoe Suriname 4°23N 55°43W 329 C6
Posof Turkey 41°30N 42°43E 213 B10
Pospelikha Russia 51°57N 81°46E 217 B10
Posse Brazil 14°4S 46°18W 333 D2
Possedimenti Italiani dell'Egeo = Dodecanese Greece 36°35N 27°0E 205 E8
Possel C.A.R. 5°5N 19°10E 264 A3
Possession I. Antarctica 72°4S 172°0E 151 D11
Pössneck Germany 50°42N 11°35E 178 E7
Possum Kingdom L. U.S.A. 32°52N 98°26W 314 E5
Post U.S.A. 33°12N 101°23W 314 E4
Post Falls U.S.A. 47°43N 116°57W 304 C5
Postavy = Pastavy Belarus 55°4N 26°50E 188 E4
Poste, R. du Mauritius 20°29S 57°36E 272 e
Poste de Flacq Mauritius 20°9S 57°43E 272 e
Poste de Flacq → Mauritius 20°9S 57°44E 272 e
Poste-de-la-Baleine = Kuujjuarapik Canada 55°20N 77°35W 298 A4
Postmasburg S. Africa 28°18S 23°5E 270 C3
Postojna Slovenia 45°46N 14°12E 199 C11
Poston U.S.A. 34°0N 114°24W 307 M12
Postumia = Postojna Slovenia 45°46N 14°12E 199 C11
Postville Nfld. & L., Canada 54°54N 59°47W 299 B8
Postville Iowa, U.S.A. 43°5N 91°34W 310 A5
Posyet Russia 42°39N 130°48E 220 C5
Potamos Antikythira, Greece 35°52N 23°15E 204 F5
Potamos Kythira, Greece 36°15N 22°58E 204 E4
Potchefstroom S. Africa 26°41S 27°7E 270 C4
Potcoava Romania 44°30N 24°39E 183 F9
Poté Brazil 17°49S 41°49W 333 E3
Poteau U.S.A. 35°3N 94°37W 314 D7
Poteet U.S.A. 29°2N 98°35W 314 G5
Potenza Italy 40°38N 15°48E 201 B8
Potenza → Italy 43°25N 13°40E 199 E10
Potenza Picena Italy 43°22N 13°37E 199 E10
Poteriteri, L. N.Z. 46°5S 167°10E 285 G2
Potgietersrus = Mokopane S. Africa 24°10S 28°55E 271 B4
Poti Georgia 42°10N 41°38E 191 J5
Potiraguá Brazil 15°36S 39°53W 333 E4
Potiskum Nigeria 11°39N 11°2E 263 C7
Potlogi Romania 44°34N 25°34E 183 F10
Potomac U.S.A. 38°59N 77°13W 143 A2
Potomac → U.S.A. 38°0N 76°23W 309 F14
Potomac Park Washington, D.C., U.S.A. 143 c1
Potosí Bolivia 19°38S 65°50W 331 D4
Potosi Mo., U.S.A. 37°56N 90°47W 310 G6
Potosí □ Bolivia 20°31S 67°0W 330 E4
Potosi Mt. U.S.A. 35°57N 115°29W 307 K11
Pototan Phil. 10°54N 122°38E 233 F4
Potrerillos Chile 26°30S 69°30W 334 B2
Potrero Pt. U.S.A. 37°45N 122°22W 136 B2
Potsdam Brandenburg, Germany 52°23N 13°3E 115 B1
Potsdam N.Y., U.S.A. 44°40N 74°59W 313 B10
Potsdamer Platz Berlin, Germany 115 b3
Pottangi India 18°34N 82°58E 244 E6
Pottenstein Germany 49°46N 11°24E 179 F7
Potters Village Antigua & B. 17°5N 61°49W 322 b
Pottersville U.S.A. 43°43N 73°50W 313 C11
Pottery Hill = Abû Ballas Egypt 24°26N 27°36E 256 C2
Pottstown U.S.A. 40°15N 75°39W 313 F9
Pottsville U.S.A. 40°41N 76°12W 313 F8
Pottuvil Sri Lanka 6°55N 81°50E 245 L5
Potzham Germany 48°1N 11°36E 131 B2
Pötzleinsdorf Austria 48°14N 16°17E 142 A1
P'otzu Taiwan 23°28N 120°15E 225 C2
Pouancé France 47°44N 1°10W 172 E5
Pouce Coupé Canada 55°40N 120°10W 296 B4
Pouébo N. Cal. 20°24S 164°36E 288 d
Poughkeepsie U.S.A. 41°42N 73°56W 313 E11
Pouilly-sur-Loire France 47°17N 2°57E 173 E9
Poulan U.S.A. 31°31N 83°47W 316 D6
Poulaphouca Res. Ireland 53°8N 6°30W 166 C5
Poulata Greece 38°14N 20°36E 207 C2
Poulsbo U.S.A. 47°44N 122°38W 306 C4
Poultney U.S.A. 43°31N 73°14W 313 C11
Poulton-le-Fylde U.K. 53°51N 2°58W 168 D5
Poum N. Cal. 20°14S 164°2E 288 d
Pounga-Nganga Gabon 2°58S 10°51E 264 C2
Pouso Alegre Mato Grosso, Brazil 11°46S 57°16W 331 C6
Pouso Alegre Minas Gerais, Brazil 22°14S 45°57W 335 A6
Pouso Alto = Piracanjuba Brazil 17°18S 49°1W 333 E2
Pout Senegal 14°45N 17°0W 262 C1
Pouthisat Cambodia 12°34N 103°50E 236 F4
Pouytenga Burkina Faso 12°15N 0°25W 263 C4
Pouzauges France 46°47N 0°50W 172 F6
Povoa de Santa Iria Portugal 38°51N 9°4W 195 G1
Považská Bystrica Slovak Rep. 49°8N 18°27E 181 B11
Povenets Russia 62°50N 34°50E 186 B5
Poverty B. N.Z. 38°43S 178°2E 284 E7
Povlen Serbia 44°9N 19°44E 202 B3
Póvoa de Lanhosa Portugal 41°33N 8°15W 194 D2

Póvoa de Santo Adriao Portugal 38°47N 9°9W 126 A2
Póvoa de Varzim Portugal 41°25N 8°46W 194 D2
Povoação Azores 37°45N 25°15W 153 d3
Povorino Russia 51°12N 42°5E 190 E6
Povorotnyy, Mys Russia 42°40N 133°2E 220 C6
Povungnituk = Puvirnituq Canada 60°2N 77°10W 295 E16
Powassan Canada 46°5N 79°25W 298 C4
Poway U.S.A. 32°58N 117°2W 307 N9
Powązki Poland 52°15N 20°58E 142 B1
Powder → U.S.A. 46°45N 105°26W 304 C11
Powder River U.S.A. 43°2N 106°59W 304 E10
Powder Springs U.S.A. 33°52N 84°41W 316 B5
Powell U.S.A. 44°45N 108°46W 304 D9
Powell, L. U.S.A. 36°57N 111°29W 305 H8
Powell River Canada 49°50N 124°35W 296 D4
Powelton U.S.A. 33°26N 82°52W 316 B7
Power House = Drayton Valley Canada 53°12N 114°58W 296 C6
Powers U.S.A. 45°41N 87°32W 308 C10
Powiśle Poland 52°14N 21°1E 142 B2
Pownal U.S.A. 42°45N 73°14W 313 D11
Powsin Poland 52°8N 21°6E 142 C2
Powsinek Poland 52°9N 21°6E 142 C2
Powys □ U.K. 52°20N 3°20W 169 E4
Poxoréo Brazil 15°50S 54°23W 331 D7
Poya N. Cal. 21°19S 165°7E 288 d
Poyan Res. Singapore 1°22N 103°40E 138 A2
Poyang Hu China 29°5N 116°20E 229 C11
Poyarkovo Russia 49°36N 128°41E 215 E13
Poysdorf Austria 48°40N 16°37E 181 C9
Poza de la Sal Spain 42°35N 3°31W 194 C7
Poza Rica Mexico 20°33N 97°27W 319 C5
Pozantı Turkey 37°25N 34°50E 212 D6
Požarevac Serbia 44°35N 21°18E 202 B5
Pozazal, Puerto Spain 42°56N 4°10W 194 C6
Požega Croatia 45°20N 17°40E 182 E2
Požega Serbia 43°53N 20°2E 202 C4
Poznań Poland 52°25N 16°55E 185 F3
Poznań ✈ (POZ) Poland 52°26N 16°45E 185 F3
Pozo U.S.A. 35°20N 120°24W 307 K6
Pozo Alcón Spain 37°42N 2°56W 195 H8
Pozo Almonte Chile 20°10S 69°50W 330 E4
Pozo Colorado Paraguay 23°30S 58°45W 334 A4
Pozoblanco Spain 38°23N 4°51W 195 G6
Pozorrubio Phil. 16°7N 120°33E 232 C3
Pozuelo de Alarcón Spain 40°24N 3°53W 127 B1
Pozuzo Peru 10°5S 75°35W 330 C2
Pozzallo Italy 36°43N 14°51E 201 F7
Pozzomaggiore Italy 40°24N 8°39E 200 B1
Pozzuoli Italy 40°49N 14°7E 201 B7
Pra → Ghana 5°1N 1°37W 263 D4
Prabuty Poland 53°47N 19°15E 184 E6
Prača Bos.-H. 43°47N 18°43E 182 G3
Prachatice Czech Rep. 49°1N 14°0E 180 B6
Prachin Buri Thailand 14°0N 101°25E 236 F3
Prachuap Khirikhan Thailand 11°49N 99°48E 237 G2
Pradelles France 44°46N 3°52E 174 D7
Pradera Colombia 3°25N 76°15W 328 C2
Prades France 42°38N 2°23E 174 F6
Prado Brazil 17°20S 39°13W 333 E4
Prado, Museo del Madrid, Spain 127 b3
Prado Churubusco Mexico 19°20N 99°8W 128 B2
Prado del Rey Spain 36°48N 5°33W 195 J5
Præstø Denmark 55°8N 12°2E 163 J6
Praga Poland 52°15N 21°2E 142 B2
Pragersko Slovenia 46°27N 15°42E 199 B12
Prague = Praha Czech Rep. 50°4N 14°25E 135 B2
Praha Czech Rep. 50°4N 14°25E 135 B2
Praha ✈ (PRG) Czech Rep. 50°6N 14°16E 135 B1
Prahecq France 46°19N 0°26W 174 B3
Prahita → India 19°0N 79°55E 244 E4
Prahova □ Romania 45°10N 26°0E 183 E10
Prahova → Romania 44°50N 25°50E 183 F10
Prahovo Serbia 44°18N 22°39E 202 B6
Praia Azores 39°3N 27°58W 153 d1
Praia C. Verde Is. 15°2N 23°34W 153 j
Praia a Mare Italy 39°50N 15°45E 201 C8
Praia da Vitória Azores 38°44N 27°4W 153 d1
Praia do Norte Azores 38°36N 28°46W 153 d1
Praia Grande Brazil 24°0S 46°24W 333 F2
Praid Romania 46°32N 25°10E 183 D10
Prainha Azores 38°27N 28°12W 153 d1
Prainha Pará, Brazil 1°45S 53°30W 329 D7
Prainha Nova Brazil 7°10S 60°30W 331 B5
Praires, R. des → Canada 45°38N 73°36W 130 A2
Prairie Australia 20°50S 144°35E 280 C3
Prairie City U.S.A. 44°28N 118°43W 304 D4
Prairie Dog Town Fork Red → U.S.A. 34°34N 99°58W 314 D5
Prairie du Chien U.S.A. 43°3N 91°9W 310 A5
Prairie du Rocher U.S.A. 38°5N 90°6W 310 F6
Prairie Village U.S.A. 38°58N 94°38W 310 F2
Prairies, L. of the Canada 51°16N 101°32W 297 C8
Pramanda Greece 39°32N 21°8E 204 B3
Prambanan △ Indonesia 7°45S 110°28E 231 G14
Prampram Ghana 5°43N 0°8E 263 D5
Pran Buri Thailand 12°23N 99°55E 236 F2
Pranbanan Indonesia 7°48S 110°15E 235 D4
Prándarjökull Iceland 64°40N 14°55W 155 C12
Prang Ghana 8°1N 0°56W 263 D4
Prapat Indonesia 2°41N 98°58E 234 B1
Praslin St. Lucia 13°52N 60°54W 323 m
Praslin Seychelles 4°18S 55°45E 272 c
Prasonisi, Akra Greece 35°42N 27°46E 206 F11
Prassberg = Mozirje Slovenia 46°22N 14°58E 199 B11
Praszka Poland 51°5N 18°31E 185 G5
Prata Brazil 19°25S 48°54W 333 E2
Pratabpur India 23°28N 83°15E 243 H10
Pratapgarh Raj., India 24°2N 74°40E 242 G6
Pratapgarh Ut. P., India 25°56N 81°59E 243 G9
Pratas I. = Dongsha Dao S. China Sea 20°45N 116°43E 229 G11
Prater Austria 48°12N 16°25E 142 A2
Prato Italy 43°53N 11°6E 198 E8
Prátola Peligna Italy 42°6N 13°52E 199 F10
Prats-de-Mollo-la-Preste France 42°25N 2°27E 174 F6
Pratt U.S.A. 37°39N 98°44W 308 G4
Prattville U.S.A. 32°28N 86°29W 315 E11
Praust = Pruszcz Gdański Poland 54°17N 18°40E 184 D5
Pravara → India 19°35N 74°45E 244 E2
Pravdinsk Kaliningrad, Russia 54°27N 21°1E 184 D8
Pravdinsk Nizhniy Novgorod, Russia 56°29N 43°28E 190 B6
Pravets Bulgaria 42°53N 23°55E 202 D7
Pravia Spain 43°30N 6°12W 194 B4
Praya Indonesia 8°39S 116°17E 235 D5
Prayag = Allahabad India 25°25N 81°58E 243 G9
Pré-en-Pail France 48°28N 0°12W 172 D6
Preah Vihear Cambodia 14°23N 104°41E 236 E5
Preau Trin. & Tob. 10°12N 61°19W 323 t
Preble U.S.A. 42°44N 76°8W 313 D8
Prêcheur Martinique 14°48N 61°13W 322 j
Precipice △ Australia 25°18S 150°5E 281 D5
Precordillera Argentina 30°0S 69°1W 334 C2
Precotto Italy 45°30N 9°13E 129 A2
Predáppio Italy 44°6N 11°59E 199 D8
Predazzo Italy 46°19N 11°36E 199 B8
Predeal Romania 45°30N 25°34E 183 E10
Predejane Serbia 42°51N 22°9E 202 D6
Preeceville Canada 51°57N 102°40W 297 C8
Preetz Germany 54°14N 10°18E 178 A6
Pregolya → Russia 54°41N 20°22E 184 D7
Pregrada Croatia 46°11N 15°45E 199 B12
Preiļi Latvia 56°18N 26°43E 188 D4
Preko Croatia 44°7N 15°10E 199 D12
Prelog Croatia 46°18N 16°32E 199 B13
Premer Australia 31°29S 149°56E 283 A8
Prémery France 47°10N 3°18E 173 E10
Premià de Mar Spain 41°29N 2°22E 196 D7
Premont U.S.A. 27°22N 98°7W 314 H5
Premuda Croatia 44°20N 14°36E 199 D11
Prenestino Labicano Italy 41°53N 12°33E 136 B2
Prentice U.S.A. 45°33N 90°17W 308 C8
Prenzlau Germany 53°19N 13°50E 178 B9
Prenzlauerberg Germany 52°32N 13°24E 115 A3
Preobrazheniye Russia 42°54N 133°54E 220 C6
Preparis I. = Pariparit Kyun Burma 14°52N 93°41E 245 G11
Preparis North Channel Ind. Oc. 15°27N 94°5E 245 G11
Preparis South Channel Ind. Oc. 14°33N 93°30E 245 G11
Přerov Czech Rep. 49°28N 17°27E 181 B10
Prescott Ont., Canada 44°45N 75°30W 313 B9
Prescott Ariz., U.S.A. 34°33N 112°28W 305 J7
Prescott Ark., U.S.A. 33°48N 93°23W 314 E8
Prescott Valley U.S.A. 34°40N 112°18W 305 J7
Preservation Inlet N.Z. 46°8S 166°35E 285 G1
Preševo Serbia 42°19N 21°39E 202 D5
Presho U.S.A. 43°54N 100°3W 308 D3
Presicce Italy 39°54N 18°16E 201 C11
Presidencia de la Plaza Argentina 27°0S 59°50W 334 B4
Presidencia Roque Saenz Peña Argentina 26°45S 60°30W 334 B3
Président-Thiers, Récif French Polynesia 24°30S 146°0W 289 f
Presidente Dutra Brazil 5°15S 44°30W 332 C3
Presidente Epitácio Brazil 21°56S 52°6W 333 F1
Presidente Figueiredo Brazil 1°57S 60°2W 329 D5
Presidente Hayes □ Paraguay 24°0S 59°0W 334 A4
Presidente Juán Perón = Chaco □ Argentina 26°30S 61°0W 334 B3
Presidente Médici Brazil 11°17S 61°55W 331 C5
Presidente Prudente Brazil 22°5S 51°25W 335 A5
Presidente Vargas = Nova Era Brazil 19°45S 43°3W 333 E3
Presidio Mexico 29°29N 104°23W 318 B4
Presidio Tex., U.S.A. 29°34N 104°22W 314 G2
Preslav Bulgaria 43°10N 26°52E 203 C10
Preslavska Planina Bulgaria 43°10N 26°45E 203 C10
Prešov Slovak Rep. 49°0N 21°15E 181 B14
Prešovský □ Slovak Rep. 49°10N 21°0E 181 B13
Prespa Bulgaria 41°44N 24°55E 203 E8
Prespa, L. = Prespansko Jezero Macedonia 40°55N 21°0E 202 F5
Prespa △ Greece 40°48N 21°4E 202 F5
Prespansko Jezero Macedonia 40°55N 21°0E 202 F5
Presque I. U.S.A. 42°10N 80°6W 312 D4
Presque Isle U.S.A. 46°41N 68°1W 309 B19
Pressburg = Bratislava Slovak Rep. 48°10N 17°7E 181 C10
Prestatyn U.K. 53°20N 3°24W 168 D4
Prestea Ghana 5°22N 2°7W 262 D4
Presteigne U.K. 52°17N 3°0W 169 E5
Přeštice Czech Rep. 49°34N 13°20E 180 B6
Presto Bolivia 18°55S 64°56W 331 D5
Preston Vic., Australia 37°44S 145°0E 128 A1
Preston Ont., Canada 43°23N 80°21W 312 C4
Preston Lancs., U.K. 53°46N 2°42W 168 D5
Preston Ga., U.S.A. 32°4N 84°32W 316 C5
Preston Idaho, U.S.A. 42°6N 111°53W 304 E8
Preston Iowa, U.S.A. 42°3N 90°24W 310 B6
Preston Minn., U.S.A. 43°40N 92°5W 308 D7
Preston Mo., U.S.A. 37°56N 93°13W 310 G3
Preston, C. Australia 20°51S 116°12E 278 D2
Prestonsburg U.S.A. 37°40N 82°47W 309 G12
Prestranda Norway 59°6N 9°4E 162 E3
Prestwick U.K. 55°29N 4°37W 167 F4
Prêto → Amazonas, Brazil 0°8S 64°6W 329 D5
Prêto → Bahia, Brazil 11°21S 43°52W 332 D3
Prêto do Igapó-Açu → Brazil 4°26S 59°48W 329 D6
Pretoria S. Africa 25°44S 28°12E 271 C4
Pretos Forros, Sa. dos Brazil 22°54S 43°17W 135 B1
Preuilly-sur-Claise France 46°51N 0°56E 172 F7
Preussisch-Eylau = Bagrationovsk Russia 54°23N 20°39E 184 D7
Preussisch Friedland = Debrzno Poland 53°31N 17°14E 184 E4
Preussisch Holland = Pasłęk Poland 54°3N 19°41E 184 D6
Preussisch-Stargard = Starogard Gdański Poland 53°59N 18°30E 184 E5
Preveza Greece 38°57N 20°45E 207 B2
Preveza □ Greece 39°10N 20°40E 204 B2
Preveza-Lefkada ✈ (PVK) Greece 38°57N 20°45E 207 B2
Préville Canada 45°28N 73°29W 130 B3
Prey Veng Cambodia 11°35N 105°29E 237 G5
Přezletice Czech Rep. 50°9N 14°34E 135 B3
Priazovskoye Ukraine 46°44N 35°40E 189 J8
Pribalkhash = Balqash Kazakhstan 46°50N 74°50E 214 E8
Pribilof Is. U.S.A. 57°0N 170°0W 303 H5
Priboj Serbia 43°35N 19°32E 202 C3
Příbram Czech Rep. 49°41N 14°2E 180 B7
Price U.S.A. 39°36N 110°49W 304 G8
Price, C. India 13°34N 93°3E 245 H11
Price I. Canada 52°23N 128°41W 296 C3
Prichard U.S.A. 30°44N 88°5W 315 F10
Prickly Pear Cays Anguilla 18°16N 63°11W 322 a
Prickly Pt. Grenada 11°59N 61°45W 323 q
Priego Spain 40°26N 2°21W 196 E2
Priego de Córdoba Spain 37°27N 4°12W 195 H6
Priekule Latvia 56°26N 21°35E 184 B8
Priekule Lithuania 55°33N 21°19E 184 C8
Prien Germany 47°51N 12°20E 179 H8
Prienai Lithuania 54°38N 23°57E 184 D10
Prieska S. Africa 29°40S 22°42E 270 C3
Priest L. U.S.A. 48°35N 116°52W 304 B5
Priest River U.S.A. 48°11N 116°55W 304 B5
Priest Valley U.S.A. 36°10N 120°39W 306 J6
Prieto Diaz Phil. 13°2N 124°12E 232 E5
Prievidza Slovak Rep. 48°46N 18°36E 181 C11
Prignitz Germany 53°6N 11°45E 178 B7
Prijedor Bos.-H. 44°58N 16°41E 199 D13
Prijepolje Serbia 43°27N 19°40E 202 C3
Prikaspiyskaya Nizmennost = Caspian Depression Eurasia 47°0N 48°0E 191 G9
Prikro Ivory C. 7°40N 3°59W 262 D4
Prikubanskaya Nizmennost Russia 45°39N 38°33E 191 H4
Prilep Macedonia 41°21N 21°32E 202 E5
Priluki = Pryluky Ukraine 50°30N 32°24E 189 G7
Prima Porta Italy 42°0N 12°30E 136 B1
Primavalle Italy 41°55N 12°25E 136 B1
Prime Seal I. Australia 40°3S 147°43E 281 G4
Primeira Cruz Brazil 2°30S 43°26W 332 B3
Primkenau = Przemków Poland 51°31N 15°48E 185 G2
Primo Tapia Mexico 32°16N 116°54W 307 N10
Primorsk Kaliningrad, Russia 54°44N 20°0E 184 D6
Primorsk St. Petersburg, Russia 60°22N 28°37E 188 B5
Primorskiy Kray □ Russia 45°0N 135°0E 220 B7
Primorsko Bulgaria 42°15N 27°44E 203 D11
Primorsko-Akhtarsk Russia 46°2N 38°10E 189 J10
Primrose S. Africa 26°11S 28°9E 123 B2
Primrose L. Canada 54°55N 109°45W 297 C7
Prince Albert Sask., Canada 53°15N 105°50W 297 C7
Prince Albert Western Cape, S. Africa 33°12S 22°2E 270 D3
Prince Albert △ Canada 54°0N 106°25W 297 C7
Prince Albert Mts. Antarctica 76°0S 161°30E 151 D11
Prince Albert Pen. Canada 72°30N 116°0W 294 C8
Prince Albert Sd. Canada 70°25N 115°0W 294 C9
Prince Alfred, C. Canada 74°20N 124°40W 150 B1
Prince Charles I. Canada 67°47N 76°12W 295 D16
Prince Charles Mts. Antarctica 72°0S 67°0E 151 D6
Prince Edward Fracture Zone Ind. Oc. 46°0S 35°0E 151 A4
Prince Edward I. □ Canada 46°20N 63°20W 299 C7
Prince Edward Is. Ind. Oc. 46°35S 38°0E 273 J2
Prince George Canada 53°55N 122°50W 296 C4
Prince of Wales, C. U.S.A. 65°36N 168°5W 303 D5
Prince of Wales I. Queens., Australia 10°40S 142°10E 286 F2
Prince of Wales I. Nunavut, Canada 73°0N 99°0W 294 C12
Prince of Wales I. Alaska, U.S.A. 55°47N 132°50W 303 J14
Prince of Wales Icefield Canada 78°15N 79°0W 295 B16
Prince of Wales Str. Canada 73°0N 117°0W 294 C8
Prince Patrick I. Canada 77°0N 120°0W 295 B8
Prince Regent Inlet Canada 73°0N 90°0W 295 C14
Prince Rupert Canada 54°20N 130°20W 296 C2
Prince Rupert B. Dominica 15°34N 61°29W 323 k
Prince Rupert Bluff Pt. Dominica 15°35N 61°29W 323 k
Prince William Sd. U.S.A. 60°40N 147°0W 303 F11
Princes Street Edinburgh, U.K. 121 b2
Princes Town Trin. & Tob. 10°16N 61°23W 323 t
Princesa Isabel Brazil 7°44S 38°0W 332 C4
Princess Charlotte B. Australia 14°25S 144°0E 280 A3
Princess Elizabeth Trough S. Ocean 64°10S 83°0E 151 C7
Princess May Ranges Australia 15°30S 125°30E 278 C4
Princess Royal I. Canada 53°0N 128°40W 296 C3
Princeton B.C., Canada 49°27N 120°30W 296 D4
Princeton Calif., U.S.A. 39°24N 122°1W 306 F4
Princeton Ill., U.S.A. 41°23N 89°23W 310 C7
Princeton Ind., U.S.A. 38°21N 87°34W 311 F9
Princeton Ky., U.S.A. 37°7N 87°53W 308 G10
Princeton Mo., U.S.A. 40°24N 93°35W 310 D3
Princeton N.J., U.S.A. 40°21N 74°39W 313 F10
Princeton W. Va., U.S.A. 37°22N 81°6W 309 G13
Princeville Hawai'i, U.S.A. 22°13N 159°29W 302 A2
Princeville Ill., U.S.A. 40°56N 89°46W 310 D7
Príncipe São Tomé & Príncipe 1°37N 7°25E 265 a
Principe da Beira Brazil 12°20S 64°30W 331 C5
Prineville U.S.A. 44°18N 120°51W 304 D3
Pringles Bay Dominica 15°21N 61°25W 323 k
Pringsewu Indonesia 5°24S 104°55E 234 D2
Prins Christian Sund Greenland 60°4N 43°10W 154 E6
Prins Harald Kyst Antarctica 70°0S 35°1E 151 D4
Prins Karls Forland Svalbard 78°30N 11°0E 154 B12
Prinsesse Astrid Kyst Antarctica 70°45S 12°30E 151 D3
Prinsesse Ragnhild Kyst Antarctica 70°15S 27°30E 151 D4
Printer's Row Chicago, U.S.A. 119 d2
Prinzapolca Nic. 13°20N 83°35W 320 D3
Prior, C. Spain 43°34N 8°17W 194 B2
Priozersk Russia 61°2N 30°7E 188 B6
Pripet = Prypyat → Europe 51°20N 30°15E 177 C16
Pripet Marshes Europe 52°10N 27°10E 177 B15
Pripyat Marshes = Pripet Marshes Europe 52°10N 27°10E 177 B15
Pripyats = Prypyat → Europe 51°20N 30°15E 177 C16
Prishib = Leninsk Russia 48°40N 45°15E 191 F7
Prishtine = Priština Kosovo 42°40N 21°13E 202 D5
Prislop, Pasul Romania 47°37N 24°48E 183 C9
Pristen Russia 51°15N 36°44E 189 G9
Priština Kosovo 42°40N 21°13E 202 D5
Pritzwalk Germany 53°9N 12°10E 178 B8
Privas France 44°45N 4°37E 175 D8
Priverno Italy 41°28N 13°11E 200 A6
Privolzhsk Russia 57°23N 41°16E 190 B5
Privolzhskaya Vozvyshennost Russia 51°0N 46°0E 190 E7
Privolzhskiy Russia 51°25N 46°3E 190 E8
Privolzhskiy □ Russia 56°0N 50°0E 190 D9
Privolzhye Russia 52°52N 48°33E 190 D9
Priyutnoye Russia 46°12N 43°40E 191 G6
Prizren Kosovo 42°13N 20°45E 202 D4
Prizzi Italy 37°43N 13°26E 200 E6
Prnjavor Bos.-H. 44°52N 17°43E 182 F2
Probolinggo Indonesia 7°46S 113°13E 235 D4
Prochowice Poland 51°17N 16°20E 185 G3
Proctor U.S.A. 43°40N 73°2W 313 C11
Proddatur India 14°45N 78°30E 245 G4
Prodhromos Cyprus 34°57N 32°50E 207 F8
Proença-a-Nova Portugal 39°45N 7°54W 194 F3
Profilia Greece 36°5N 27°51E 206 E11
Profondeville Belgium 50°23N 4°52E 170 D4
Progreso Coahuila, Mexico 27°28N 100°59W 318 B4
Progreso Yucatán, Mexico 21°20N 89°40W 319 C7
Progreso Nacional Mexico 19°30N 99°9W 128 A2
Progress Antarctica 66°22S 76°22E 151 C12
Progress Russia 49°45N 129°37E 215 E13
Prokhladnyy Russia 43°50N 44°2E 191 J7
Prokletije Albania 42°30N 19°45E 202 D3
Prokopyevsk Russia 54°0N 86°45E 217 B11
Prokuplje Serbia 43°16N 21°36E 202 C5
Proletarsk Russia 46°42N 41°50E 191 G5
Proletarskaya = Proletarsk Russia 46°42N 41°50E 191 G5
Prome Burma 18°49N 95°13E 241 F5
Promise City U.S.A. 40°45N 93°9W 310 D3
Promzino = Surskoye Russia 54°30N 46°44E 190 C8
Prophet → Canada 58°48N 122°40W 296 B4
Prophet River Canada 58°6N 122°43W 296 B4
Prophetstown U.S.A. 41°40N 89°56W 310 C7
Propriá Brazil 10°13S 36°51W 332 D4
Propriano France 41°41N 8°52E 175 G12
Prosek Czech Rep. 50°7N 14°30E 135 B3
Proserpine Australia 20°21S 148°36E 280 b
Proskurov = Khmelnytskyy Ukraine 49°23N 27°0E 177 D14
Prosna → Poland 52°6N 17°44E 185 F4
Prospect N.Y., U.S.A. 43°18N 75°9W 313 C9
Prospect Ohio, U.S.A. 40°27N 83°11W 311 D13
Prospect Hill Park U.S.A. 42°23N 71°13W 116 A1
Prosperidad Phil. 8°34N 125°52E 233 G5
Prosperity U.S.A. 30°51N 85°56W 316 E4
Prosperous B. St. Helena 15°56S 5°39W 153 h
Prosser U.S.A. 46°12N 119°46W 304 C4
Prossnitz = Prostějov Czech Rep. 49°30N 17°9E 181 B10
Prostějov Czech Rep. 49°30N 17°9E 181 B10
Prostki Poland 53°42N 22°25E 184 E9
Proston Australia 26°8S 151°32E 281 D5
Proszowice Poland 50°13N 20°16E 185 H7
Proti Greece 37°5N 21°32E 204 D3
Provadiya Bulgaria 43°12N 27°30E 203 C11
Provence France 43°40N 5°46E 175 E9
Provence-Alpes-Côte d'Azur □ France 44°0N 6°15E 175 D10
Providence Seychelles 9°14S 51°2E 273 E4
Providence Ky., U.S.A. 37°24N 87°46W 308 G10
Providence R.I., U.S.A. 41°49N 71°24W 313 E13
Providence, C. N.Z. 45°59S 166°29E 285 F1
Providence Bay Canada 45°41N 82°15W 298 C3
Providence Mts. U.S.A. 35°10N 115°15W 307 K11
Providencia Chile 33°25S 70°36W 137 B2
Providencia, I. de Colombia 13°25N 81°26W 320 D3
Provideniya Russia 64°23N 173°18W 215 C19
Provincetown U.S.A. 42°3N 70°11W 309 D18
Provins France 48°33N 3°15E 173 D10
Provo U.S.A. 40°14N 111°39W 304 F8
Provost Canada 52°25N 110°20W 297 C6
Prozor Bos.-H. 43°50N 17°34E 182 G2
Prrenjas Albania 41°4N 20°32E 202 E4
Prudential Building Chicago, U.S.A. 119 c2
Prudentópolis Brazil 25°12S 50°57W 333 G1
Prudhoe Bay U.S.A. 70°18N 148°22W 303 A10
Prudhoe I. Australia 21°19S 149°41E 280 C4
Prud'homme Canada 52°20N 105°54W 297 C7
Prudnik Poland 50°20N 17°38E 185 H4
Průhonice Czech Rep. 50°0N 14°33E 135 C3
Prüm Germany 50°12N 6°25E 179 E2
Prundu Romania 44°6N 26°14E 183 F11
Pruszcz Gdański Poland 54°17N 18°40E 184 D5
Pruszków Poland 52°9N 20°49E 185 F7
Prut → Romania 45°28N 28°10E 183 E13
Pruzhany Belarus 52°33N 24°28E 177 B13
Prvič Croatia 44°55N 14°47E 199 D11
Prydz B. Antarctica 69°0S 74°0E 151 C6
Pryluky Ukraine 50°30N 32°24E 189 G7
Prymorske Ukraine 46°48N 36°20E 189 J9
Pryor U.S.A. 36°19N 95°19W 314 C7
Prypyat → Europe 51°20N 30°15E 177 C16
Przasnysz Poland 53°2N 20°54E 185 E7
Przedbórz Poland 51°6N 19°53E 185 G6
Przedecz Poland 52°20N 18°53E 185 F5
Przemków Poland 51°31N 15°48E 185 G2
Przemyśl Poland 49°50N 22°45E 185 J9
Przeworsk Poland 50°6N 22°32E 185 H9
Przewóz Poland 51°28N 14°57E 185 G1
Przhevalsk = Karakol Kyrgyzstan 42°30N 78°20E 217 D9
Przysucha Poland 51°22N 20°38E 185 G7
Psachna Greece 38°34N 23°35E 204 C5
Psara Greece 38°37N 25°38E 205 C7
Psathoura Greece 39°30N 24°12E 204 B6
Pserimos Greece 36°56N 27°8E 205 E9
Psichiko Greece 38°1N 23°46E 112 A2
Psiloritis, Oros Greece 35°15N 24°45E 207 E5
Psira Greece 35°12N 25°52E 207 E6
Pskov Russia 57°50N 28°25E 188 D5
Pskov □ Russia 57°20N 29°0E 188 D5
Pskovskoye, Ozero Russia 58°0N 27°58E 188 D5
Psol → Ukraine 49°10N 33°37E 189 H7
Psunj Croatia 45°25N 17°19E 182 E2
Pteleos Greece 39°3N 22°57E 204 B4
Ptich = Ptsich → Belarus 52°9N 28°52E 177 B15
Ptichia = Vidos Greece 39°38N 19°55E 206 B9
Ptolemaida Greece 40°30N 21°43E 202 F5
Ptsich → Belarus 52°9N 28°52E 177 B15
Ptuj Slovenia 46°28N 15°50E 199 B12
Ptujska Gora Slovenia 46°23N 15°47E 199 B12
Pu Xian China 36°24N 111°6E 226 F6
Pua Thailand 19°11N 100°55E 236 C3
Pua'ena Pt. U.S.A. 21°36N 158°6W 302 J13
Puán Argentina 37°30S 62°45W 334 D3
Pu'an Guizhou, China 25°46N 104°57E 228 E5
Pu'apu'a Samoa 13°34S 172°9W 287 V19
Pubei China 22°16N 109°31E 228 F7
Pucacuro → Peru 3°20S 74°58W 328 D3
Pucallpa Peru 8°25S 74°30W 330 B3
Pucará Bolivia 18°43S 64°11W 331 D5
Pucará Cajamarca, Peru 6°0S 79°7W 330 B2
Pucará Puno, Peru 15°5S 70°24W 330 D3
Pucarani Bolivia 16°23S 68°30W 330 D4
Pucheng China 27°59N 118°31E 229 D12
Pucheni Romania 45°12N 25°17E 183 E10
Puchheim Germany 48°9N 11°21E 179 G7
Puch'on = Bucheon S. Korea 37°28N 126°45E 224 D3
Púchov Slovak Rep. 49°8N 18°20E 181 B11
Pucio Pt. Phil. 11°46N 121°51E 233 F3
Pucioasa Romania 45°5N 25°25E 183 E10
Pučišća Croatia 43°22N 16°43E 199 E13
Puck Poland 54°45N 18°23E 184 D5
Pucka, Zatoka Poland 54°30N 18°40E 184 D5
Puçol Spain 39°37N 0°18W 197 F4
Pudasjärvi Finland 65°23N 26°53E 160 D22
Puding China 26°18N 105°44E 228 D5
Pudong New Area China 31°13N 121°30E 138 B2
Pudozh Russia 61°48N 36°32E 188 B9
Pudu = Suizhou China 31°42N 113°24E 229 B9
Puducherry India 11°59N 79°50E 245 J4
Pudukkottai India 10°28N 78°47E 245 J4
Pue Cook Is. 21°12S 159°45W 289 h
Puebla Mexico 19°3N 98°12W 319 D5
Puebla □ Mexico 18°50N 98°0W 319 D5
Puebla de Alcocer Spain 38°59N 5°14W 195 G5
Puebla de Don Fadrique Spain 37°58N 2°25W 197 H2
Puebla de Don Rodrigo Spain 39°5N 4°37W 195 F6
Puebla de Guzmán Spain 37°37N 7°15W 195 H3
Puebla de la Calzada Spain 38°54N 6°37W 195 G4
Puebla de Sanabria Spain 42°4N 6°38W 194 C4
Puebla de Trives = Pobra de Trives Spain 42°20N 7°10W 194 C3
Pueblo U.S.A. 38°16N 104°37W 304 G11
Pueblo Libre Peru 12°5S 77°4W 124 B2
Pueblo Nuevo Barcelona, Spain 41°23N 2°11E 114 A2
Pueblo Nuevo Madrid, Spain 40°25N 3°37W 127 B2
Puelches Argentina 38°5S 65°51W 334 D2
Puelén Argentina 37°32S 67°38W 334 D2
Puente Alto Chile 33°32S 70°35W 334 C1
Puente-Genil Spain 37°22N 4°47W 195 H6
Puente la Reina Spain 42°40N 1°49W 196 C3
Puente San Miguel Spain 43°21N 4°5W 194 B6
Puenteareas = Ponteareas Spain 42°10N 8°28W 194 C2
Puentedeume = Pontedeume Spain 43°24N 8°10W 194 B2
Puentes de Garcia Rodriguez = As Pontes de García Rodríguez Spain 43°27N 7°50W 194 B3
Pu'er China 23°0N 101°15E 228 F3
Puerca, Pta. Puerto Rico 18°13N 65°36W 321 b
Puerco → U.S.A. 34°22N 107°50W 305 J10
Puerta del Sol, Plaza Madrid, Spain 127 b2
Puerto Acosta Bolivia 15°32S 69°15W 330 D4
Puerto Aisén Chile 45°27S 73°0W 336 C2
Puerto Ángel Mexico 15°40N 96°29W 319 D5
Puerto Arista Mexico 15°56N 93°48W 319 D6
Puerto Armuelles Panama 8°20N 82°51W 320 E3
Puerto Asis Colombia 0°30N 76°30W 328 C2
Puerto Ayacucho Venezuela 5°40N 67°35W 328 B4
Puerto Ayora Ecuador 0°45S 90°19W 330 a
Puerto Baquerizo Moreno Ecuador 0°54S 89°36W 330 a
Puerto Barrios Guatemala 15°40N 88°32W 320 C2
Puerto Bermejo Argentina 26°55S 58°34W 334 B4
Puerto Bermúdez Peru 10°20S 74°58W 330 C3
Puerto Bolívar Ecuador 3°19S 79°55W 328 D2
Puerto Cabello Venezuela 10°28N 68°1W 328 A4
Puerto Cabezas Nic. 14°0N 83°30W 320 D3
Puerto Cabo Gracias á Dios Nic. 15°0N 83°10W 320 D3
Puerto Capaz = El Jebha Morocco 35°11N 4°43W 260 A4
Puerto Carreño Colombia 6°12N 67°22W 328 B4
Puerto Castilla Honduras 16°0N 86°0W 320 C2
Puerto Chicama Peru 7°45S 79°20W 330 B2
Puerto Cisnes Chile 44°45S 72°42W 336 B2
Puerto Coig Argentina 50°54S 69°15W 336 D3
Puerto Cortés Honduras 15°51N 88°0W 320 C2
Puerto Cumarebo Venezuela 11°29N 69°30W 328 A4
Puerto de Alcudia = Port d'Alcúdia Spain 39°50N 3°7E 206 B4
Puerto de Cabras = Puerto del Rosario Canary Is. 28°30N 13°52W 153 e2
Puerto de Cabrera Spain 39°8N 2°56E 206 B3
Puerto de Gran Tarajal Canary Is. 28°13N 14°1W 153 e2
Puerto de la Cruz Canary Is. 28°24N 16°32W 153 e1
Puerto de los Angeles ⌂ Mexico 23°39N 105°45W 318 C3
Puerto de Mazarrón Spain 37°34N 1°15W 197 H3
Puerto de Pozo Negro Canary Is. 28°19N 13°55W 153 e2
Puerto de Sóller = Port de Sóller Spain 39°48N 2°42E 206 B3
Puerto de Somosierra Spain 41°9N 3°35W 194 D7
Puerto del Carmen Canary Is. 28°55N 13°38W 153 e2
Puerto del Rosario Canary Is. 28°30N 13°52W 153 e2
Puerto Deseado Argentina 47°55S 66°0W 336 C3
Puerto Escondido Mexico 15°50N 97°3W 319 D5
Puerto Gaitán Colombia 4°19N 72°4W 328 C3
Puerto Galera Phil. 13°30N 120°57E 232 E3
Puerto Guaraní Paraguay 21°18S 57°55W 331 E6
Puerto Heath Bolivia 12°34S 68°39W 330 C4
Puerto Huitoto Colombia 0°18N 74°3W 328 C3
Puerto Inca Peru 9°22S 74°54W 330 B3
Puerto Inírida Colombia 3°53N 67°52W 328 C4
Puerto Juárez Mexico 21°11N 86°49W 319 C7
Puerto La Cruz Venezuela 10°13N 64°38W 329 A5
Puerto Leguízamo Colombia 0°12S 74°46W 328 D3
Puerto Lempira Honduras 15°16N 83°46W 320 C3
Puerto Libertad Mexico 29°55N 112°43W 318 B2
Puerto Limón Colombia 3°23N 73°30W 328 C3
Puerto Lobos Argentina 42°0S 65°3W 336 B3
Puerto López Colombia 4°5N 72°58W 328 C3
Puerto Lumbreras Spain 37°34N 1°48W 197 H3
Puerto Madero Argentina 34°37S 58°21W 117 B2
Puerto Madryn Argentina 42°48S 65°4W 336 B3
Puerto Maldonado Peru 12°30S 69°10W 330 C4
Puerto Manatí Cuba 21°22N 76°50W 320 B4
Puerto Mariti Colombia 1°10S 69°59W 328 D4
Puerto Mercedes Colombia 1°11N 72°53W 328 C3
Puerto Mexico = Coatzacoalcos Mexico 18°7N 94°25W 319 D6
Puerto Miraña Colombia 1°20S 70°19W 328 D3
Puerto Montt Chile 41°28S 73°0W 336 B2
Puerto Morazán Nic. 12°51N 87°11W 320 D2
Puerto Morelos Mexico 20°50N 86°52W 319 C7
Puerto Nariño Colombia 4°56N 67°48W 328 C4
Puerto Natales Chile 51°45S 72°15W 336 D2
Puerto Nuevo Colombia 5°53N 69°56W 328 B4
Puerto Ordaz Venezuela 8°16N 62°44W 329 B5
Puerto Oscuro Chile 31°24S 71°35W 334 C1
Puerto Padre Cuba 21°13N 76°35W 320 B4
Puerto Páez Venezuela 6°13N 67°28W 328 B4
Puerto Peñasco Mexico 31°20N 113°33W 318 A2
Puerto Pinasco Paraguay 22°36S 57°50W 334 A4
Puerto Pirámides Argentina 42°35S 64°20W 336 B4
Puerto Piritu Venezuela 10°4N 65°3W 329 A4
Puerto Plata Dom. Rep. 19°48N 70°45W 321 C5
Puerto Pollensa = Port de Pollença Spain 39°54N 3°4E 206 B4
Puerto Portillo Peru 9°45S 72°42W 330 B3
Puerto Princesa Phil. 9°46N 118°45E 233 G2
Puerto Princesa Subterranean River △ Phil. 10°10N 118°55E 233 F2
Puerto Quepos Costa Rica 9°29N 84°6W 320 E3
Puerto Real Spain 36°33N 6°12W 195 J4
Puerto Rico Bolivia 11°5S 67°38W 330 C4
Puerto Rico Canary Is. 27°47N 15°42W 153 e1
Puerto Rico ⧄ W. Indies 18°15N 66°45W 321 C6
Puerto Rico Trench Atl. Oc. 19°50N 66°0W 321 C6
Puerto Rondón Colombia 6°17N 71°6W 328 B3
Puerto Saavedra Chile 38°47S 73°24W 336 A2
Puerto San Julián Argentina 49°15S 67°45W 336 C3
Puerto Santa Cruz Argentina 50°0S 68°32W 336 D3
Puerto Sastre Paraguay 22°2S 57°55W 334 A4
Puerto Serrano Spain 36°56N 5°33W 195 J5
Puerto Siles Bolivia 12°48S 65°5W 331 C4
Puerto Suárez Bolivia 18°58S 57°52W 331 D6
Puerto Supe Peru 11°0S 77°30W 330 C2
Puerto Tejada Colombia 3°14N 76°24W 328 C2
Puerto Umbría Colombia 0°52N 76°33W 328 C2
Puerto Vallarta Mexico 20°37N 105°15W 318 C3
Puerto Varas Chile 41°19S 72°59W 336 B2
Puerto Velasco Ibarra Ecuador 1°17S 90°29W 330 a
Puerto Villamil Ecuador 0°56S 91°1W 330 a
Puerto Villazón Bolivia 13°32S 61°57W 331 C5
Puerto Wilches Colombia 7°21N 73°54W 328 B3
Puerto Williams Chile 54°56S 67°37W 336 D3
Puertollano Spain 38°43N 4°7W 195 G6
Puesto Cunambo Peru 2°10S 76°0W 328 D2
Pueu Tahiti 17°44S 149°13W 289 e
Pueyrredón, L. Argentina 47°20S 72°0W 336 C2
Púez Odle ⌂ Italy 46°37N 11°48E 199 B8
Puffin I. Ireland 51°50N 10°24W 166 E1
Pugachev Russia 52°0N 48°49E 190 D9
Pugal India 28°30N 72°48E 242 E5
Puge Sichuan, China 27°20N 102°31E 228 D4
Puge Tanzania 4°45S 33°11E 268 C3
Puget Sound U.S.A. 47°50N 122°30W 304 C2
Puget-Théniers France 43°58N 6°53E 175 E10
Púglia □ Italy 41°15N 16°15E 201 A9
Pugŏdong N. Korea 42°5N 130°0E 224 A5
Pugu Tanzania 6°55S 39°4E 268 D4
Pūgūnzī Iran 25°49N 59°10E 247 E8
Puha N.Z. 38°30S 177°50E 284 E6
Puhuangyu China 39°50N 116°22E 114 B2
Pui Romania 45°30N 23°4E 182 E8
Puica Peru 15°0S 72°33W 330 D3
Puieşti Romania 46°25N 27°33E 183 D12
Puig Major Spain 39°48N 2°47E 206 B3
Puigcerdà Spain 42°24N 1°50E 196 C6
Puigmal Spain 42°23N 2°7E 196 C7
Puigpunyent Spain 39°38N 2°32E 206 B3
Puijiang China 30°14N 103°30E 228 B4
Puisaye, Collines de la France 47°37N 3°20E 173 E10
Puiseaux France 48°11N 2°30E 173 D9
Puistola Finland 60°16N 25°2E 121 B3
Pujehun S. Leone 7°23N 11°45W 262 D2
Pujiang China 29°29N 119°54E 229 C12
Pujilí Ecuador 0°57S 78°41W 328 D2
Pujols France 44°48N 0°2W 174 D3
Pujon Indonesia 1°19S 114°19E 235 C4
Pujon-ho N. Korea 40°35N 127°35E 224 B3
Puka Puka French Polynesia 14°49S 138°48W 289 f
Puka Ruha French Polynesia 18°20S 137°2W 289 f
Pukaki, L. N.Z. 44°4S 170°1E 285 E5
Pukalani U.S.A. 20°51N 156°20W 302 C5
Pukapuka Cook Is. 10°53S 165°49W 289 J11
Pukaskwa △ Canada 48°20N 86°0W 298 C2
Pukatawagan Canada 55°45N 101°20W 297 B8
Pukchin N. Korea 40°12N 125°45E 224 B2
Pukch'ŏng N. Korea 40°14N 128°10E 224 B4
Pukë Albania 42°2N 19°53E 202 D3
Pukearuhe N.Z. 38°55S 174°31E 284 E3
Pukekohe N.Z. 37°12S 174°55E 284 D3
Puketeraki Ra. N.Z. 42°58S 172°13E 285 C7
Puketoi Ra. N.Z. 40°30S 176°5E 284 G5
Pukeuri N.Z. 45°4S 171°2E 285 F6
Pukhrayan India 26°14N 79°51E 243 F8
Pukinmäki Finland 60°15N 24°57E 121 B2
Puksubaek-san N. Korea 40°42N 127°45E 224 B3
Pula Croatia 44°54N 13°57E 199 D10
Pula Italy 39°1N 9°0E 200 C1
Pulacayo Bolivia 20°25S 66°41W 330 E4
Pulandian China 39°25N 121°58E 227 E11
Pulanduta Pt. Phil. 11°54N 123°9E 233 F4
Pulangpisau Indonesia 2°46S 114°13E 235 C4
Pulaski N.Y., U.S.A. 43°34N 76°8W 313 C8
Pulaski Tenn., U.S.A. 35°12N 87°2W 315 D11
Pulaski Va., U.S.A. 37°3N 80°47W 309 G13
Pulau → Indonesia 5°50S 138°15E 231 F9
Pulau Gili Indonesia 8°21S 116°1E 231 J19
Pulau Miangas Indonesia 5°35N 126°34E 233 J6
Puławy Poland 51°23N 21°59E 185 G8
Pulga U.S.A. 39°48N 121°29W 306 F5
Pulgaon India 20°44N 78°21E 244 D4
Puli Taiwan 23°58N 120°57E 225 C2
Pulicat India 13°25N 80°19E 245 H5
Pulicat L. India 13°40N 80°15E 245 H5
Pulivendla India 14°25N 78°14E 245 G4
Puliyangudi India 9°11N 77°24E 245 K3
Pulkovo Int. ✈ (LED) Russia 59°48N 30°18E 137 C1
Pullach Germany 48°3N 11°31E 131 B1
Pullman U.S.A. 46°44N 117°10W 304 C5
Pullman Historic District U.S.A. 41°41N 87°36W 119 C3
Pulo Gadung Indonesia 6°11S 106°54E 122 B2
Pulog, Mt. Phil. 16°40N 120°50E 232 C3
Pułtusk Poland 52°43N 21°6E 185 F8
Pülümür Turkey 39°30N 39°51E 213 C8
Pumlumon Fawr U.K. 52°28N 3°46W 169 E4
Puna Bolivia 19°45S 65°28W 331 D4
Puná, I. Ecuador 2°55S 80°5W 328 D1
Punaauia Tahiti 17°37S 149°34W 289 e
Pūnak Iran 35°46N 51°20E 141 A2
Punakha Dzong Bhutan 27°42N 89°52E 241 B2
Punalur India 9°0N 76°56E 245 K3
Punalu'u U.S.A. 21°35N 157°53W 302 J14
Punasar India 27°6N 73°6E 242 F5
Punata Bolivia 17°32S 65°50W 331 D4
Punch India 33°48N 74°4E 243 C6
Punch → Pakistan 33°12N 73°40E 242 C5
Punchbowl Australia 33°55S 151°3E 139 B1
Punda Curaçao 12°6N 68°55W 322 g
Punda Maria S. Africa 22°40S 31°5E 271 B5
Punde India 18°53N 72°57E 130 B2
Pune India 18°29N 73°57E 244 E1
Punggol Singapore 1°23N 103°54E 138 A3
Punggol, Sungei → Singapore 1°24N 103°54E 138 A3
Punggol Pt. Singapore 1°24N 103°54E 138 A3
Pungo Andongo Angola 9°44S 15°35E 265 D3
P'ungsan N. Korea 40°50N 128°9E 224 B4
Pungsan S. Korea 36°34N 128°34E 224 D4
Pungue, Ponte de Mozam. 19°0S 34°0E 269 F3
Puning China 23°20N 116°12E 229 F11
Punjab □ India 31°0N 76°0E 242 D7
Punjab □ Pakistan 32°0N 72°30E 242 E6
Punjabi Bagh India 28°40N 77°6E 120 A1
Puno Peru 15°55S 70°3W 330 D3
Puno □ Peru 15°0S 70°0W 330 C3
Punpun → India 25°31N 85°18E 243 G11
Punta, Cerro de Puerto Rico 18°10N 66°37W 321 b
Punta Alta Argentina 38°53S 62°4W 336 A4
Punta Arenas Chile 53°10S 71°0W 336 D2
Punta Cardón Venezuela 11°38N 70°14W 328 A3
Punta Coles Peru 17°43S 71°23W 330 D3
Punta de Bombón Peru 17°10S 71°48W 330 D3
Punta del Díaz Chile 28°0S 70°45W 334 B1
Punta del Hidalgo Canary Is. 28°33N 16°19W 153 e1
Punta Delgado Argentina 42°43S 63°38W 336 B4
Punta Gorda Belize 16°10N 88°45W 320 C2
Punta Gorda Fla., U.S.A. 26°56N 82°3W 317 J7
Punta Prieta Mexico 28°58N 114°17W 318 B2
Punta Prima Spain 39°48N 4°16E 206 B5
Punta Umbría Spain 37°10N 6°56W 195 H4
Puntarenas Costa Rica 10°0N 84°50W 320 E3
Puntland Somali Rep. 8°0N 49°0E 267 C6
Punto Fijo Venezuela 11°50N 70°13W 328 A3
Punxsutawney U.S.A. 40°57N 78°59W 312 F6
Punyu = Guangzhou China 23°6N 113°13E 121 B2
Puotila Finland 60°13N 25°6E 121 B3
Pupuan Indonesia 8°19S 115°0E 231 J18
Pūpūkea U.S.A. 21°40N 158°3W 302 J13
Puqi China 29°40N 113°50E 229 C9
Puquio Peru 14°45S 74°10W 330 C3
Pur → Russia 67°31N 77°55E 214 C8
Puracé, Vol. Colombia 2°21N 76°23W 328 C2

Puracé △ *Colombia* 2°10N 76°21W **328** C2
Puračić *Bos.-H.* 44°33N 18°28E **182** F3
Puralia = Puruliya *India* 23°17N 86°24E **243** H12
Purana Qila *Delhi, India* **120** c3
Puranpur *India* 28°31N 80°9E **243** E9
Purari → *Papua N. G.* 7°49S 145°0E **286** D3
Purbalingga *Indonesia* 7°23S 109°21E **235** D3
Purbeck, Isle of *U.K.* 50°39N 1°59W **169** G5
Purcell *U.S.A.* 35°1N 97°22W **314** D6
Purcell Mts. *Canada* 49°55N 116°15W **296** D5
Purdy *Canada* 45°19N 77°44W **312** A7
Puri *India* 19°50N 85°58E **244** E7
Purificación *Colombia* 3°51N 74°55W **328** C3
Purmerend *Neths.* 52°32N 4°58E **170** B4
Purna → *India* 19°6N 77°2E **244** E3
Purnia *India* 25°45N 87°31E **243** G12
Purnululu △ *Australia* 17°20S 128°20E **278** C4
Pursat = Pouthisat *Cambodia* 12°34N 103°50E **236** F4
Purukcahu *Indonesia* 0°35S 114°35E **235** C4
Puruliya *India* 23°17N 86°24E **243** H12
Purus → *Brazil* 3°42S 61°28W **329** D5
Purutu I. *Papua N. G.* 8°24S 143°27E **286** E2
Puruvesi *Finland* 61°50N 29°30E **188** B5
Purvis *U.S.A.* 31°9N 89°25W **315** F10
Pŭrvomay *Bulgaria* 42°8N 25°17E **203** D9
Purwa *India* 26°28N 80°47E **243** F9
Purwakarta *Indonesia* 6°35S 107°29E **235** D3
Purwo, Tanjung *Indonesia* 8°44S 114°21E **231** K18
Purwodadi *Indonesia* 7°7S 110°55E **235** D4
Purwokerto *Indonesia* 7°25S 109°14E **235** D3
Purworejo *Indonesia* 7°43S 110°2E **235** D4
Puryŏng *N. Korea* 42°5N 129°43E **224** A4
Pus → *India* 19°55N 77°55E **244** E3
Pusa *India* 25°59N 85°41E **243** G11
Pusad *India* 19°56N 77°36E **244** E3
Pusan = Busan *S. Korea* 35°5N 129°0E **224** E4
Pushkin *Russia* 59°45N 30°25E **188** C6
Pushkino *Moskva, Russia* 56°2N 37°49E **188** D9
Pushkino *Saratov, Russia* 51°16N 47°0E **190** E8
Püspökladány *Hungary* 47°19N 21°6E **182** C6
Pustoshka *Russia* 56°20N 29°30E **188** D5
Puszczykowo *Poland* 52°18N 16°49E **185** F3
Put-in-Bay *U.S.A.* 41°39N 82°49W **312** E2
Putahow L. *Canada* 59°54N 100°40W **297** B8
Putai *Taiwan* 23°23N 120°9E **225** C2
Putao *Burma* 27°28N 97°30E **241** B6
Putaruru *N.Z.* 38°2S 175°50E **284** E4
Putatan *Malaysia* 5°53N 116°3E **235** A5
Putbus *Germany* 54°22N 13°28E **178** A9
Puteaux *France* 48°53N 2°14E **134** A2
Puteran *Indonesia* 7°5S 114°0E **235** D4
Putian *China* 25°23N 119°0E **229** E12
Putignano *Italy* 40°51N 17°7E **201** B10
Putilkovo *Russia* 55°51N 37°22E **129** A2
Putina *Peru* 14°55S 69°55W **330** C4
Puting, Tanjung *Indonesia* 3°31S 111°46E **235** C4
Putlitz *Germany* 53°15N 12°2E **178** B8
Putna *Romania* 47°50N 25°33E **183** C10
Putna → *Romania* 45°42N 27°26E **183** E12
Putnam *U.S.A.* 41°55N 71°55W **313** E13
Putney *London, U.K.* 51°27N 0°13W **125** B2
Putney *Ga., U.S.A.* 31°29N 84°8W **316** D5
Putnok *Hungary* 48°18N 20°26E **182** B5
Putorana, Gory *Russia* 69°0N 95°0E **215** C10
Putorino *N.Z.* 39°4S 176°58E **284** F5
Putrajaya *Malaysia* 2°55N 101°40E **237** L3
Putre *Chile* 18°12S 69°35W **330** D4
Puttalam *Sri Lanka* 8°1N 79°55E **245** K5
Puttalam Lagoon *Sri Lanka* 8°15N 79°45E **245** K4
Puttegga *Norway* 62°13N 7°42E **164** B4
Puttgarden *Germany* 54°30N 11°10E **178** A7
Püttlingen *Germany* 49°17N 6°53E **179** F2
Puttur *Andhra Pradesh, India* 13°27N 79°33E **245** H4
Puttur *Karnataka, India* 12°46N 75°12E **245** H2
Putty *Australia* 32°57S 150°42E **283** B9
Putumayo → *S. Amer.* 3°7S 67°58W **328** D4
Putuo *Shanghai, China* 31°15N 121°24E **138** B1
Putuo *Zhejiang, China* 29°56N 122°20E **229** C14
Putussibau *Indonesia* 0°50N 112°56E **235** B4
Pututahi *N.Z.* 38°39S 177°53E **284** E6
Putxet *Spain* 41°24N 2°8E **114** A1
Putyla *Ukraine* 48°0N 25°5E **183** B10
Pu'uanahulu *U.S.A.* 19°49N 155°51W **302** D6
Pu'uhonua o Hōnaunau ⌓ *U.S.A.* 19°25N 155°54W **302** D6
Pu'uka'aumakua *U.S.A.* 21°30N 157°54W **302** J14
Pu'ukeahiakahoe *U.S.A.* 21°23N 157°49W **302** K14
Pu'ukoholā Heiau ⌓ *U.S.A.* 20°1N 155°49W **302** C6
P'u'ula'ula *U.S.A.* 20°42N 156°15W **302** C5
Pu'u'oke'oke'o *U.S.A.* 19°13N 155°44W **302** D6
Pu'uwai *U.S.A.* 21°54N 160°12W **302** B1
Puvirnituq *Canada* 60°2N 77°10W **295** E16
Puxi *China* 31°12N 121°30E **138** B1
Puy-de-Dôme *France* 45°46N 2°57E **174** C6
Puy-de-Dôme □ *France* 45°40N 3°5E **174** C7
Puy-l'Évêque *France* 44°31N 1°9E **174** D5
Puyallup *U.S.A.* 47°12N 122°18W **306** C4
Puyang *China* 35°40N 115°1E **226** G8
Puyehue *Chile* 40°40S 72°37W **336** B2
Puyehue △ *Chile* 40°27S 72°6W **336** B2
Puylaurens *France* 43°35N 2°0E **174** E6
Puyo *Ecuador* 1°28S 77°59W **328** D2
Puysegur Pt. *N.Z.* 46°9S 166°37E **285** G1
Pūzeh Rīg *Iran* 27°20N 58°40E **247** E8
Puzhaykove *Ukraine* 48°7N 29°50E **183** B14
Pwani □ *Tanzania* 7°0S 39°0E **268** D4
Pweto *Dem. Rep. of the Congo* 8°25S 28°51E **269** D2
Pwinbyu *Burma* 20°23N 94°40E **241** E5
Pwllheli *U.K.* 52°53N 4°25W **168** E3
Pyana → *Russia* 55°43N 46°1E **190** C8
Pyandzh = Dusti *Tajikistan* 37°20N 68°40E **217** E7
Pyandzh → *Asia* 37°6N 68°20E **240** A2
Pyaozero, Ozero *Russia* 66°5N 30°58E **160** C24
Pyapon *Burma* 16°20N 95°40E **241** G5
Pyasina → *Russia* 73°30N 87°0E **215** B9
Pyatigorsk *Russia* 44°2N 43°6E **191** H6
Pyatykhatky *Ukraine* 48°28N 33°38E **189** H7
Pyawbwe *Burma* 20°35N 96°4E **241** E6
Pyaye *Burma* 19°12N 95°10E **241** F5
Pydhuni *Mumbai, India* **130** b2
Pydna *Greece* 40°20N 22°34E **202** F6
Pyè = Prome *Burma* 18°49N 95°13E **241** F5
Pyeonghae *S. Korea* 36°43N 129°26E **224** D4
Pyeongtaek *S. Korea* 37°1N 127°4E **224** D3
Pyetrikaw *Belarus* 52°11N 28°29E **177** B15
Pyhäjoki *Finland* 64°28N 24°14E **160** D21
Pyinbauk *Burma* 19°10N 95°12E **241** F5
Pyingaing *Burma* 23°9N 94°50E **241** D5
Pyinkayaing *Burma* 15°58N 94°24E **241** H5
Pyinmana *Burma* 19°45N 96°12E **241** F6
Pyinyaung *Burma* 20°49N 96°25E **241** E6
Pyla *Cyprus* 35°1N 33°41E **250** C4
Pyla, C. *Cyprus* 34°56N 33°51E **207** F9
Pymatuning Res. *U.S.A.* 41°30N 80°28W **312** E4
Pyŏktong *N. Korea* 40°50N 125°50E **224** B2
P'yŏnganbuk-do □ *N. Korea* 40°0N 125°15E **224** C2
P'yŏngannam-do □ *N. Korea* 39°30N 126°24E **224** C3
Pyŏnggang *N. Korea* 38°24N 127°17E **224** C3
P'yŏngsong *N. Korea* 39°14N 125°52E **224** C2
P'yŏngyang *N. Korea* 39°0N 125°30E **224** C2
P'yŏngyang □ *N. Korea* 39°4N 125°50E **224** C2
Pyote *U.S.A.* 31°32N 103°8W **314** F3
Pyramid L. *U.S.A.* 40°1N 119°35W **304** F4
Pyramid Pk. *U.S.A.* 36°25N 116°37W **307** J10
Pyramid Pt. *Ascension I.* 7°55S 14°24W **153** g
Pyramids *Egypt* 29°58N 31°9E **117** B1
Pyrénées *Europe* 42°45N 0°18E **174** F4
Pyrénées △ *France* 42°52N 0°10W **174** F3
Pyrénées-Atlantiques □ *France* 43°10N 0°50W **174** E3
Pyrénées-Orientales □ *France* 42°35N 2°26E **174** F6
Pyry *Poland* 52°8N 21°0E **142** C1
Pyryatyn *Ukraine* 50°15N 32°25E **189** G7
Pyrzyce *Poland* 53°10N 14°55E **185** E1
Pyskowice *Poland* 50°24N 18°38E **185** H5
Pytalovo *Russia* 57°5N 27°55E **188** D4
Pyttegga = Puttegga *Norway* 62°13N 7°42E **164** B4
Pyu *Burma* 18°30N 96°28E **241** F6
Pyzdry *Poland* 52°11N 17°42E **185** F4

Q

Qaanaaq *Greenland* 77°30N 69°10W **154** B4
Qabanbay *Kazakhstan* 45°50N 80°37E **217** C10
Qabirri → *Azerbaijan* 41°3N 46°17E **191** K8
Qabr Hūd *Yemen* 16°9N 49°34E **249** C5
Qachasnek *S. Africa* 30°6S 28°42E **271** D4
Qādisiyah, Buhayrat al *Iraq* 34°20N 42°12E **213** E10
Qādub *Yemen* 12°37N 53°57E **249** D6
Qa'el Jafr *Jordan* 30°20N 36°25E **251** H7
Qa'emābād *Iran* 31°44N 60°2E **247** D9
Qā'emshahr *Iran* 36°30N 52°53E **247** B7
Qagan Nur *Jilin, China* 45°15N 124°18E **227** B13
Qagan Nur *Nei Monggol Zizhiqu, China* 43°30N 114°55E **226** C8
Qahar Youyi Zhongqi *China* 41°12N 112°40E **226** D7
Qahremānshahr = Kermānshāh *Iran* 34°23N 47°0E **213** E12
Qaidam Pendi *China* 37°0N 95°0E **218** D8
Qaiyara *Iraq* 35°48N 43°17E **213** E10
Qajarīyeh *Iran* 31°1N 48°22E **247** D6
Qala *Malta* 36°2N 14°19E **206** E7
Qala, Ras il *Malta* 36°2N 14°20E **206** E7
Qala-i-Jadid = Spīn Būldak *Afghan.* 31°1N 66°25E **242** D2
Qala Point = Qala, Ras il *Malta* 36°2N 14°20E **206** E7
Qala Viala *Pakistan* 30°49N 67°17E **242** D2
Qala Yangi *Afghan.* 34°20N 66°30E **242** B2
Qalācheh *Afghan.* 35°30N 67°43E **240** B2
Qalaikhum = Kalaikhum *Tajikistan* 38°28N 70°46E **217** E8
Qalandiya *West Bank* 31°52N 35°12E **123** A2
Qalansīyah *Yemen* 12°41N 53°29E **249** D6
Qal'at al Akhḍar *Si. Arabia* 28°4N 37°9E **251** K8
Qal'at Bīshah *Si. Arabia* 20°0N 42°36E **248** C3
Qal'at Dīzah *Iraq* 36°11N 45°7E **213** D11
Qalāt-i-Ghilzai *Afghan.* 32°15N 66°58E **240** B2
Qal'at Ṣāliḥ *Iraq* 31°31N 47°16E **246** D5
Qal'at Sukkar *Iraq* 31°51N 46°5E **213** G12
Qal'eh Morghī *Iran* 35°38N 51°22E **141** B2
Qal'eh-ye Bost *Afghan.* 31°30N 64°21E **240** C2
Qal'eh-ye Now *Afghan.* 35°0N 63°5E **240** B1
Qal'eh-ye Panjeh *Afghan.* 37°0N 72°35E **240** A4
Qal'eh-ye Sarkari *Afghan.* 35°54N 67°17E **240** B2
Qal'eh-ye Valī *Afghan.* 35°46N 63°45E **240** B1
Qalyûb *Egypt* 30°12N 31°11E **251** H2
Qalyûbîya □ *Egypt* 30°18N 31°18E **251** H2
Qamani'tuaq = Baker Lake *Canada* 64°20N 96°3W **294** E12
Qamar, Ghubbat al *Yemen* 16°20N 52°30E **249** C6
Qamar, Jabal al *Oman* 16°48N 53°15E **249** C6
Qamdo *China* 31°15N 97°6E **228** B1
Qamea *Fiji* 16°45S 179°45W **287** A3
Qamīnis *Libya* 31°40N 20°1E **258** B4
Qammieh Point *Malta* 35°58N 14°19E **206** F7
Qamruddin Karez *Pakistan* 31°45N 68°20E **242** D3
Qanâ el Ismâ'ilîya *Egypt* 30°7N 31°17E **117** A2
Qandahār = Kandahār *Afghan.* 31°32N 65°43E **240** C2
Qandahār = Kandahār □ *Afghan.* 31°0N 65°0E **240** C2
Qandala *Somali Rep.* 11°30N 49°58E **267** B6
Qandyaghash *Kazakhstan* 49°28N 57°25E **187** E10
Qapān *Iran* 37°40N 55°47E **247** B7
Qapqal *China* 43°48N 81°5E **217** D10
Qapshaghay *Kazakhstan* 43°51N 77°14E **217** D9
Qapshaghay Bögeni *Kazakhstan* 43°45N 77°50E **217** D9
Qaqortoq *Greenland* 60°43N 46°0W **154** E6
Qâra *Egypt* 29°38N 26°30E **256** B2
Qarā', Jabal al *Oman* 17°15N 54°15E **249** C6
Qara Dāgh *Iraq* 35°18N 45°18E **213** E11
Qara Qash → *China* 35°0N 78°30E **243** B8
Qarabalyq *Kazakhstan* 53°45N 62°2E **216** B6
Qarabutaq *Kazakhstan* 50°0N 60°14E **216** C6
Qaraçala *Azerbaijan* 39°45N 48°53E **191** L9
Qaraghandy *Kazakhstan* 49°50N 73°10E **217** C8
Qaraghayly *Kazakhstan* 49°26N 76°0E **214** E8
Qārah *Si. Arabia* 29°55N 40°3E **246** D4
Qarah Āghāj *Iran* 37°8N 46°58E **213** D12
Qarakol *Uzbekistan* 39°32N 63°50E **216** E6
Qaraoba *Kazakhstan* 47°6N 56°15E **216** C5
Qaraqīya Oyysy *Kazakhstan* 43°27N 51°45E **216** D4
Qaraqosh *Iraq* 36°16N 43°22E **213** D10
Qarataū *Ongtüstik Qazaqstan, Kazakhstan* 43°30N 69°30E **217** D7
Qarataū *Zhambyl, Kazakhstan* 43°10N 70°28E **217** D8
Qarāvol *Afghan.* 37°14N 68°46E **240** A3
Qarazhal *Kazakhstan* 48°2N 70°49E **214** E8
Qardho *Somali Rep.* 9°30N 49°6E **267** C6
Qardud *Sudan* 10°20N 29°56E **257** E2
Qareh → *Iran* 39°25N 47°22E **213** C12
Qareh Tekān *Iran* 36°38N 49°29E **247** B6
Qarnein *U.A.E.* 24°56N 52°52E **247** E7
Qarqan He → *China* 39°30N 88°30E **217** E11
Qarqaraly *Kazakhstan* 49°26N 75°30E **217** C9
Qarqin *Afghan.* 37°24N 66°4E **240** A2
Qarrasa *Sudan* 14°38N 32°5E **257** E3
Qarshi *Uzbekistan* 38°53N 65°48E **217** E7
Qartabā *Lebanon* 34°4N 35°50E **250** D6
Qārūh *Kuwait* 28°49N 48°46E **247** D6
Qaryat al Gharab *Iraq* 31°27N 44°48E **246** D5
Qaryat al 'Ulyā *Si. Arabia* 27°33N 47°42E **246** E5
Qarynzharyq Oyysy *Kazakhstan* 42°55N 54°25E **216** D4
Qaşbah, Râs al *Si. Arabia* 28°2N 34°38E **251** K5
Qāsemābād *Iran* 35°46N 51°30E **141** A3
Qashqadaryo □ *Uzbekistan* 38°35N 66°0E **217** E7
Qasigiannguit *Greenland* 68°50N 51°18W **154** D5
Qasr 'Amra *Jordan* 31°48N 36°35E **246** D3
Qaşr Bū Hadi *Libya* 31°1N 16°45E **258** B3
Qasr-e Firūzeh *Iran* 35°29N 51°31E **141** B3
Qaşr-e Qand *Iran* 26°15N 60°45E **247** E9
Qaşr-e Shīrīn *Iran* 34°31N 45°35E **213** E11
Qasr Farâfra *Egypt* 27°0N 28°1E **256** B2
Qaşr Larocu *Libya* 26°32N 13°19E **258** C2
Qasuittuq = Resolute *Canada* 74°42N 94°54W **295** C13
Qa'ṭabah *Yemen* 13°51N 44°42E **248** D4
Qatanā *Syria* 33°26N 36°4E **250** E7
Qaṭānan, Ra's *Yemen* 12°21N 53°33E **249** D6
Qatane *West Bank* 31°50N 35°6E **123** B1
Qatar ■ *Asia* 25°30N 51°15E **247** E6
Qatlīsh *Iran* 37°50N 57°19E **247** B8
Qattâra *Egypt* 30°12N 27°3E **256** A2
Qattâra, Munkhafed el *Egypt* 29°30N 27°30E **256** B2
Qattâra Depression = Qattâra, Munkhafed el *Egypt* 29°30N 27°30E **256** B2
Qawām al Ḩamzah = Al Ḩamzah *Iraq* 31°43N 44°58E **246** D5
Qawra Point *Malta* 35°58N 14°26E **206** F7
Qāyen *Iran* 33°40N 59°10E **247** C8
Qaynar *Kazakhstan* 49°12N 77°22E **217** C9
Qazaly *Kazakhstan* 45°45N 62°6E **216** C6
Qazaqstan = Kazakhstan ■ *Asia* 50°0N 70°0E **217** C8
Qazaqtyng Usaqshogylyghy *Kazakhstan* 50°0N 72°0E **217** C8
Qazax *Azerbaijan* 41°5N 45°21E **191** K7
Qazımämmäd *Azerbaijan* 40°3N 49°0E **191** K9
Qazvīn *Iran* 36°15N 50°0E **247** B6
Qazvīn □ *Iran* 36°20N 50°0E **247** B6
Qazyghurt *Kazakhstan* 41°45N 69°23E **217** D7
Qeisari = Caesarea *Israel* 32°30N 34°53E **251** F5
Qeissan *Sudan* 11°4N 34°40E **257** E3
Qena *Egypt* 26°10N 32°43E **256** B3
Qena, W. → *Egypt* 26°12N 32°44E **256** B3
Qeqertarsuaq *Greenland* 69°45N 53°30W **154** D5
Qeqertarsuaq *Greenland* 69°15N 53°38W **154** D5
Qeqertarsuatsiaat *Greenland* 63°5N 50°45W **154** E5
Qeshlāq *Iran* 34°55N 46°28E **213** E12
Qeshm *Iran* 26°55N 56°10E **247** E8
Qeydār *Iran* 36°6N 48°35E **213** D13
Qeys *Iran* 26°32N 53°58E **249** A6
Qezel Owzen → *Iran* 36°45N 49°22E **247** B6
Qezi'ot *Israel* 30°52N 34°26E **251** H5
Qi Xian *China* 34°40N 114°48E **226** G8
Qian Gorlos *China* 45°5N 124°42E **227** B13
Qian Hai *China* 22°32N 113°54E **219** a
Qian Xian *China* 34°31N 108°15E **226** G5
Qian'an *China* 40°0N 118°41E **227** E10
Qiancheng *China* 27°12N 109°50E **228** D7
Qianjiang *Guangxi Zhuangzu, China* 23°38N 108°58E **228** F7
Qianjiang *Hubei, China* 30°24N 112°55E **229** B9
Qianjiang *Sichuan, China* 29°33N 108°47E **228** C7
Qianjin *China* 47°34N 133°4E **219** B15
Qianmen *China* 39°51N 116°21E **114** B2
Qianshan *Anhui, China* 30°37N 116°35E **229** B11
Qianshan *Guangdong, China* 22°15N 113°31E **219** a
Qianwei *China* 29°13N 103°56E **228** C4
Qianxi *China* 27°3N 106°3E **228** D6
Qianyang *Hunan, China* 27°18N 110°10E **229** D8
Qianyang *Shaanxi, China* 34°40N 107°8E **226** G4
Qianyang *Zhejiang, China* 30°11N 119°25E **229** B12
Qi'ao *China* 22°25N 113°39E **219** a
Qi'ao Dao *China* 22°25N 113°38E **219** a
Qiaocun *China* 39°56N 112°55E **226** E7
Qiaojia *China* 26°56N 102°58E **228** D4
Qichun *China* 30°18N 115°25E **229** B10
Qidong *Hunan, China* 26°49N 112°7E **229** D9
Qidong *Jiangsu, China* 31°48N 121°38E **229** B13
Qiemo *China* 38°8N 85°32E **217** E11
Qijiang *China* 28°57N 106°35E **228** C6
Qijiaojing *China* 43°28N 91°36E **217** D12
Qikiqtarjuaq *Canada* 67°33N 63°0W **295** D19
Qila Saifullāh *Pakistan* 30°45N 68°17E **242** D3
Qilian Shan *China* 38°30N 96°0E **218** D8
Qimen *China* 29°50N 117°42E **229** C11
Qin He → *China* 35°1N 113°22E **226** G7
Qin Jiang → *Guangxi Zhuangzu, China* 21°53N 108°35E **228** F7
Qin Jiang → *Jiangxi, China* 26°15N 115°55E **229** D10
Qin Ling = Qinling Shandi *China* 33°50N 108°10E **226** H5
Qināb, W. → *Yemen* 17°55N 49°59E **249** C5
Qin'an *China* 34°48N 105°40E **226** G3
Qing Xian *China* 38°35N 116°45E **226** E9
Qingcheng *China* 37°15N 117°40E **227** F9
Qingcheng Shan *China* 30°58N 103°31E **228** B4
Qingchuan *China* 32°36N 105°9E **226** H3
Qingdao *China* 36°5N 120°20E **227** F11
Qingfeng *China* 35°52N 115°8E **226** G8
Qinghai □ *China* 36°0N 98°0E **218** D8
Qinghai Hu *China* 36°40N 100°10E **218** D9
Qinghe *China* 46°37N 90°25E **217** C12
Qinghecheng *China* 41°28N 124°15E **224** B2
Qinghemen *China* 41°48N 121°25E **227** D11
Qinghuayuan *China* 39°59N 116°19E **114** B1
Qingjian *China* 37°8N 110°8E **226** F6
Qingjiang = Huaiyin *China* 33°30N 119°2E **227** H10
Qingliu *China* 26°11N 116°48E **229** D11
Qinglong *China* 25°49N 105°12E **228** E5
Qingningsi *China* 31°16N 121°33E **138** B2
Qingping *China* 26°39N 107°47E **228** D6
Qingpu *China* 31°10N 121°6E **229** B13
Qingshui *China* 34°48N 106°8E **226** G4
Qingshuihe *China* 39°55N 111°35E **226** E6
Qingtian *China* 28°12N 120°15E **229** C13
Qingtongxia *China* 38°2N 106°3E **226** E4
Qingtongxia Shuiku *China* 37°50N 105°58E **226** F3
Qingxi *China* 27°8N 108°43E **228** D7
Qingxu *China* 37°34N 112°22E **226** F7
Qingyang *Anhui, China* 30°38N 117°50E **229** B11
Qingyang *Gansu, China* 36°2N 107°55E **226** F4
Qingyi Jiang → *China* 29°32N 103°44E **228** C4
Qingyuan *Guangdong, China* 23°40N 112°59E **229** F9
Qingyuan *Liaoning, China* 42°10N 124°55E **224** A2
Qingyuan *Zhejiang, China* 27°36N 119°3E **229** D12
Qingyun *China* 37°45N 117°20E **227** F9
Qingzhen *China* 26°31N 106°25E **228** D6
Qinhuangdao *China* 39°56N 119°30E **227** E10
Qinling Shandi *China* 33°50N 108°10E **226** H5
Qinshui *China* 35°40N 112°8E **226** G7
Qinyang = Jiyuan *China* 35°7N 112°57E **226** G7
Qinyang *China* 35°5N 112°56E **226** G7
Qinyuan *China* 36°29N 112°20E **226** F7
Qinzhou *China* 21°58N 108°38E **228** G7
Qionghai *China* 19°15N 110°26E **236** C8
Qionglai *China* 30°25N 103°31E **228** B4
Qionglai Shan *China* 31°0N 102°30E **228** B4
Qiongshan *China* 19°51N 110°26E **236** C8
Qiongzhou Haixia *China* 20°10N 110°15E **236** B8
Qiqihar *China* 47°26N 124°0E **219** B13
Qira *China* 37°0N 80°48E **217** E10
Qiraîya, W. → *Egypt* 30°27N 34°0E **251** H5
Qiryat Ata *Israel* 32°47N 35°6E **250** F6
Qiryat Gat *Israel* 31°32N 34°46E **251** G5
Qiryat Mal'akhi *Israel* 31°44N 34°44E **251** G5
Qiryat Shemona *Israel* 33°13N 35°35E **250** E6
Qiryat Yam *Israel* 32°51N 35°4E **250** F6
Qirzah, W. → *Libya* 30°56N 14°31E **258** B2
Qishan *China* 34°25N 107°38E **226** G4
Qishn *Yemen* 15°26N 51°40E **249** D5
Qitai *China* 44°2N 89°35E **217** D11
Qitaihe *China* 45°48N 130°51E **220** B5
Qitbīt, W. → *Oman* 19°15N 54°23E **249** C6
Qiubei *China* 24°2N 104°12E **228** E5
Qixia *China* 37°17N 120°52E **227** F11
Qiyang *China* 26°35N 111°50E **229** D8
Qızılağac Körfäzi *Azerbaijan* 39°9N 49°0E **213** C13
Qobda *Kazakhstan* 50°55N 54°31E **216** B4
Qojūr *Iran* 36°12N 47°55E **246** B5
Qolhak *Iran* 35°45N 51°26E **141** A2
Qom *Iran* 34°40N 51°0E **247** C6
Qom □ *Iran* 34°40N 51°0E **247** C6
Qomolangma Feng = Everest, Mt. *Nepal* 28°5N 86°58E **243** E12
Qomsheh *Iran* 32°0N 51°55E **247** D6
Qondūz = Kondūz *Afghan.* 36°50N 68°50E **240** A3
Qondūz → *Afghan.* 37°0N 68°16E **240** A3
Qong Muztag *China* 35°42N 82°22E **217** E10
Qoqek = Tacheng *China* 46°40N 82°58E **217** C10
Qoqon = Qŭqon *Uzbekistan* 40°31N 70°56E **217** D8
Qoraqalpoghistan □ *Uzbekistan* 43°0N 58°0E **216** D5
Qormi *Malta* 35°53N 14°28E **206** F7
Qorveh *Iran* 35°10N 47°48E **213** E12
Qosshaghyl *Kazakhstan* 46°40N 54°0E **187** E9
Qostanay *Kazakhstan* 53°10N 63°35E **216** B6
Qotanqaraghay *Kazakhstan* 49°10N 85°36E **217** C11
Qoṭūr *Iran* 38°28N 44°25E **213** C11
Qoz Salsilgo *C.A.R.* 10°45N 22°54E **264** A4
Qrejten Point *Malta* 35°57N 14°27E **206** F7
Qu Jiang → *China* 30°1N 106°24E **228** B6
Qu Xian *China* 30°48N 106°58E **228** B6
Quabbin Res. *U.S.A.* 42°20N 72°20W **313** D12
Quadraro *Italy* 41°51N 12°33E **136** B2
Quaid-i-Azam *Pakistan* 24°50N 66°59E **123** A1
Quairading *Australia* 32°0S 117°21E **279** F2
Quakenbrück *Germany* 52°41N 7°57E **178** C3
Quakertown *U.S.A.* 40°26N 75°21W **313** F9
Qualicum Beach *Canada* 49°22N 124°26W **296** D4
Quambatook *Australia* 35°49S 143°34E **282** C5
Quambone *Australia* 30°57S 147°53E **283** A7
Quamby *Australia* 20°22S 140°17E **280** C3
Quan Long = Ca Mau *Vietnam* 9°7N 105°8E **237** H5
Quanah *U.S.A.* 34°18N 99°44W **314** D5
Quandialla *Australia* 34°1S 147°47E **283** C7
Quang Ngai *Vietnam* 15°13N 108°58E **236** E7
Quang Tri *Vietnam* 16°45N 107°13E **236** D6
Quang Yen *Vietnam* 20°56N 106°52E **228** G6
Quannan *China* 24°45N 114°33E **229** E10
Quantock Hills *U.K.* 51°8N 3°10W **169** F4
Quanyang *China* 42°21N 127°32E **227** C14
Quanzhou *Fujian, China* 24°55N 118°34E **229** E12
Quanzhou *Guangxi Zhuangzu, China* 25°57N 111°5E **229** E8
Qu'Appelle → *Canada* 50°33N 103°53W **297** C8
Quaqtaq *Canada* 60°55N 69°40W **295** E18
Quaraí *Brazil* 30°15S 56°20W **334** C4
Quarré-les-Tombes *France* 47°21N 4°0E **173** E11
Quarteira *Portugal* 37°4N 8°6W **195** H2
Quarter, The *Anguilla* 18°13N 63°3W **322** a
Quartier D'Orléans *St.-Martin* 18°5N 63°2W **322** a
Quartier Militaire *Mauritius* 20°14S 57°35E **272** e
Quartiere Zingone *Italy* 45°25N 9°3E **129** B1
Quartu Sant'Élena *Italy* 39°15N 9°10E **200** C2
Quartzsite *U.S.A.* 33°40N 114°13W **307** M12
Quatre, I. à *St. Vincent* 12°59N 61°15W **323** n
Quatre Bornes *Mauritius* 20°15S 57°28E **272** e
Quatsino Sd. *Canada* 50°25N 127°58W **296** C3
Quba *Azerbaijan* 41°21N 48°32E **191** K9
Qubeiba *West Bank* 31°50N 35°8E **123** A1
Qūchān *Iran* 37°10N 58°27E **247** B8
Quds *Iraq* 33°23N 44°24E **113** A2
Queanbeyan *Australia* 35°17S 149°14E **283** C8
Québec *Canada* 46°52N 71°13W **299** C5
Québec □ *Canada* 48°0N 74°0W **299** C6
Quebo *Guinea-Biss.* 11°20N 14°56W **262** C2
Quebrada del Condorito △ *Argentina* 31°49S 64°40W **334** C3
Quebradillas *Puerto Rico* 18°29N 66°56W **321** b
Quedlinburg *Germany* 51°47N 11°8E **178** D7
Queen Alexandra Ra. *Antarctica* 85°0S 170°0E **151** E11
Queen Charlotte B. *Falk. Is.* 51°50S 60°40W **153** f
Queen Charlotte City *Canada* 53°15N 132°2W **296** C2
Queen Charlotte Is. *Canada* 53°20N 132°10W **296** C2
Queen Charlotte Sd. *B.C., Canada* 51°0N 128°0W **296** C3
Queen Charlotte Sd. *N.Z.* 41°10S 174°15E **285** B9
Queen Charlotte Strait *Canada* 50°45N 127°10W **296** C3
Queen City *U.S.A.* 40°25N 92°34W **310** D4
Queen Elizabeth △ *Uganda* 0°0 30°0E **268** C3
Queen Elizabeth ⌓ *U.K.* 56°7N 4°30W **167** E4
Queen Elizabeth Is. *Canada* 76°0N 95°0W **295** B13
Queen Elizabeth Nat. Park = Ruwenzori △ *Uganda* 0°20N 30°0E **268** B2
Queen Mary Land *Antarctica* 70°0S 95°0E **151** D7
Queen Mary Res. *U.K.* 51°24N 0°27W **125** B1
Queen Maud G. *Canada* 68°15N 102°30W **294** D11
Queen Maud Land = Dronning Maud Land *Antarctica* 72°30S 12°0E **151** D3
Queen Maud Mts. *Antarctica* 86°0S 160°0W **151** E13
Queen Street *Edinburgh, U.K.* **121** a1
Queen Victoria Market *Australia* 37°47S 144°57W **128** A1
Queens Channel *Australia* 15°0S 129°30E **278** C4
Queens-Midtown Tunnel *New York, U.S.A.* **132** d2
Queen's Quay Terminal *Toronto, Canada* **141** c2
Queensboro Bridge *New York, U.S.A.* **132** c3
Queensbury *U.K.* 51°35N 0°16W **125** A2
Queenscliff *Australia* 38°16S 144°39E **282** E6
Queenscliffe *Australia* 33°47S 151°17E **139** A2
Queensferry *U.K.* 55°59N 3°23W **121** B1
Queensland *U.S.A.* 31°46N 83°14W **316** D6
Queensland □ *Australia* 22°0S 142°0E **280** C3
Queensland Plateau *Pac. Oc.* 17°0S 150°0E **276** D8
Queenstown = Cóbh *Ireland* 51°51N 8°17W **166** E3
Queenstown *Tas., Australia* 42°4S 145°35E **281** G4
Queenstown *N.Z.* 45°1S 168°40E **285** F3
Queenstown *Singapore* 1°18N 103°48E **138** B2
Queenstown *Eastern Cape, S. Africa* 31°52S 26°52E **270** D4
Queets *U.S.A.* 47°32N 124°19W **306** C2
Queguay Grande → *Uruguay* 32°9S 58°9W **334** C4
Queimada, Pta. da *Azores* 38°23N 28°14W **153** d1
Queimadas *Brazil* 11°0S 39°38W **332** D4
Queiros, C. *Vanuatu* 14°55S 167°1E **287** D5
Quela *Angola* 9°10S 16°56E **265** D3
Quelimane *Mozam.* 17°53S 36°58E **269** F4
Quellerina *S. Africa* 26°9S 27°56E **123** A1
Quellón *Chile* 43°7S 73°37W **336** B2
Quelo *Angola* 6°29S 12°36E **265** D2
Quelpart = Jeju-do *S. Korea* 33°29N 126°34E **224** a
Queluz *Portugal* 38°45N 9°14W **126** A1
Quemado *N. Mex., U.S.A.* 34°20N 108°30W **305** J9
Quemado *Tex., U.S.A.* 28°56N 100°37W **314** G4
Quemoy = Chinmen *Taiwan* 24°26N 118°19E **225** a
Quemú-Quemú *Argentina* 36°3S 63°36W **334** D3
Quepem *India* 15°13N 74°3E **245** G2
Quequén *Argentina* 38°30S 58°30W **334** D4
Querco *Peru* 13°50S 74°52W **330** C3
Querétaro *Mexico* 20°36N 100°23W **318** C4
Querétaro □ *Mexico* 21°0N 99°55W **318** C5
Querfurt *Germany* 51°23N 11°35E **178** D7
Quérigut *France* 42°42N 2°6E **174** F6
Querqueville *France* 49°40N 1°42W **172** C5
Quesada *Spain* 37°51N 3°4W **195** H7
Queshan *China* 32°55N 114°2E **229** A10
Quesnel *Canada* 53°0N 122°30W **296** C4
Quesnel → *Canada* 52°58N 122°29W **296** C4
Quesnel L. *Canada* 52°30N 121°20W **296** C4
Questa *U.S.A.* 36°42N 105°36W **305** H11
Questembert *France* 47°40N 2°28W **172** E4
Quetena *Bolivia* 22°10S 67°25W **330** E4
Quetico ⌓ *Canada* 48°30N 91°45W **298** C1
Quetrequile *Argentina* 41°33S 69°22W **336** B3
Quetta *Pakistan* 30°15N 66°55E **242** D2
Quetzaltenango *Guatemala* 14°50N 91°30W **320** D1
Queulat △ *Chile* 44°29S 72°24W **336** B2
Quevedo *Ecuador* 1°2S 79°29W **328** D2
Queyras ⌓ *France* 44°45N 6°50E **175** D10
Quezon *Phil.* 9°15N 117°59E **233** G1
Quezon □ *Phil.* 14°40N 121°30E **232** D3
Quezon △ *Phil.* 14°0N 121°55E **232** D3
Quezon City *Phil.* 14°37N 121°2E **127** B2
Qufār *Si. Arabia* 27°26N 41°37E **246** E4
Qufu *China* 35°35N 116°59E **226** G9
Qui Nhon *Vietnam* 13°40N 109°13E **236** F7
Quibala *Angola* 10°46S 14°59E **265** E2
Quibaxe *Angola* 8°24S 14°27E **265** D2
Quibdó *Colombia* 5°42N 76°40W **328** B2
Quiberon *France* 47°29N 3°9W **172** E3
Quiberon, Presqu'île de *France* 47°30N 3°8W **172** E3
Quiçama △ *Angola* 9°41S 13°35E **265** D2
Quickborn *Germany* 53°42N 9°52E **178** B5
Quiet L. *Canada* 61°5N 133°5W **296** A2
Quiindy *Paraguay* 25°58S 57°14W **334** B4
Quilá *Mexico* 24°23N 107°13W **318** C3
Quilán, C. *Chile* 43°15S 74°30W **336** B2
Quilcene *U.S.A.* 47°49N 122°53W **306** C4
Quilenda *Angola* 10°39S 14°23E **265** E2
Quilengues *Angola* 14°12S 14°12E **265** E2
Quilicura *Chile* 33°22S 70°43W **137** B1
Quilimarí *Chile* 32°5S 71°30W **334** C1
Quilino *Argentina* 30°14S 64°29W **334** C3
Quill, The *St. Eustatius* 17°28N 62°57W **322** a
Quillabamba *Peru* 12°50S 72°50W **330** C3
Quillacollo *Bolivia* 17°26S 66°17W **330** D4
Quillagua *Chile* 21°40S 69°40W **334** A2
Quillan *France* 42°53N 2°10E **174** F6
Quillota *Chile* 32°54S 71°16W **334** C1
Quilmes *Argentina* 34°43S 58°15W **334** C4
Quilon *India* 8°50N 76°38E **245** K3
Quilpie *Australia* 26°35S 144°11E **281** D3
Quilpué *Chile* 33°5S 71°33W **334** C1
Quilua *Mozam.* 16°17S 39°54E **269** F4
Quimbele *Angola* 6°17S 16°41E **265** D3
Quimbo *Angola* 14°4S 16°11E **265** E3
Quimbonge *Angola* 8°36S 18°30E **265** D3
Quime *Bolivia* 17°2S 67°15W **330** D4
Quimilí *Argentina* 27°40S 62°30W **334** B3
Quimper *France* 48°0N 4°9W **172** E2
Quimperlé *France* 47°53N 3°33W **172** E3
Quinam B. *Trin. & Tob.* 10°4N 61°30W **323** t
Quinault → *U.S.A.* 47°21N 124°18W **306** C2
Quince Mil *Peru* 13°15S 70°40W **330** C3
Quincy *Calif., U.S.A.* 39°56N 120°57W **306** F6
Quincy *Fla., U.S.A.* 30°35N 84°34W **316** E5
Quincy *Ill., U.S.A.* 39°56N 91°23W **310** E5
Quincy *Mass., U.S.A.* 42°14N 71°0W **116** B2
Quincy *Mich., U.S.A.* 41°57N 84°53W **311** C12
Quincy *Wash., U.S.A.* 47°14N 119°51W **304** C4
Quincy B. *U.S.A.* 42°16N 70°59W **116** B3
Quines *Argentina* 32°13S 65°48W **334** C2
Quinga *Mozam.* 15°49S 40°15E **269** F5
Quingey *France* 47°7N 5°52E **173** E12
Quingombe *Angola* 6°38S 13°1E **265** D2
Quinhagak *U.S.A.* 59°45N 161°54W **303** G7
Quinhámel *Guinea-Biss.* 11°53N 15°51W **262** C1
Quiniluban Group *Phil.* 11°27N 120°48E **233** F3
Quinta Normal *Chile* 33°26S 70°42W **137** B1
Quintana de la Serena *Spain* 38°45N 5°40W **195** G5
Quintana Roo □ *Mexico* 19°40N 88°30W **319** D7
Quintanar de la Orden *Spain* 39°36N 3°5W **195** F7
Quintanar de la Sierra *Spain* 41°57N 2°55W **196** D2
Quintanar del Rey *Spain* 39°21N 1°56W **197** F3
Quintero *Chile* 32°45S 71°30W **334** C1
Quintin *France* 48°26N 2°56W **172** D4
Quinto *Spain* 41°25N 0°32W **196** D4
Quinto de Stampi *Italy* 45°24N 9°10E **129** B2
Quinto Romano *Italy* 45°28N 9°7E **129** B1
Quinzáu *Angola* 6°51S 12°44E **265** D2
Quípar → *Spain* 38°15N 1°40W **197** G3
Quipeio *Angola* 12°27S 15°30E **265** E3
Quirihue *Chile* 36°15S 72°35W **334** D1
Quirima *Angola* 10°47S 18°6E **265** E3
Quirimbas △ *Mozam.* 12°30S 40°15E **269** E5
Quirimbo *Angola* 10°36S 14°12E **265** E2
Quirinale *Italy* 41°53N 12°29E **136** B1
Quirinale, Palazzo dei *Rome, Italy* **136** b3
Quirindi *Australia* 31°28S 150°40E **283** A9
Quirino □ *Phil.* 16°15N 121°40E **232** C3
Quirinópolis *Brazil* 18°32S 50°30W **333** E1
Quiroga *Spain* 42°28N 7°18W **194** C3
Quiruvilca *Peru* 8°1S 78°19W **330** B2
Quissac *France* 43°55N 4°0E **175** E8
Quissanga *Mozam.* 12°24S 40°28E **269** E5
Quissico *Mozam.* 24°42S 34°44E **271** B5
Quitapa *Angola* 10°20S 18°19E **265** E3
Quitilipi *Argentina* 26°50S 60°13W **334** B3
Quitman *U.S.A.* 30°47N 83°34W **316** E6
Quito *Ecuador* 0°15S 78°35W **328** D2
Quitralco △ *Chile* 45°43S 73°25W **336** C2
Quixadá *Brazil* 4°55S 39°0W **332** B4
Quixaxe *Mozam.* 15°17S 40°4E **269** F5
Quixeramobim *Brazil* 5°12S 39°17W **332** C4
Quixico *Angola* 7°59S 14°25E **265** D2
Quixinge *Angola* 9°52S 14°23E **265** D2
Quizenga *Angola* 9°21S 15°28E **265** D3
Qujing *China* 25°32N 103°41E **228** E4
Qulan *Kazakhstan* 42°55N 72°43E **214** E8
Qul'ân, Jazâ'ir *Egypt* 24°22N 35°31E **246** E2
Qulsary *Kazakhstan* 46°59N 54°1E **187** E9
Qumbu *S. Africa* 31°10S 28°48E **271** D4
Qunayyin, Sabkhat al *Libya* 30°10N 21°0E **258** B4
Qŭnghirot *Uzbekistan* 43°2N 58°50E **216** D5
Qu'nyido *China* 31°15N 98°6E **228** B2
Quoin I. *Australia* 14°54S 129°32E **278** B4
Quoin Pt. *S. Africa* 34°46S 19°37E **270** D2
Quorn *Australia* 32°25S 138°5E **282** B3
Qŭqon *Uzbekistan* 40°31N 70°56E **217** D8
Qurein *Sudan* 13°30N 34°50E **257** E3
Qŭrghonteppa *Tajikistan* 37°50N 68°47E **217** E7
Qurimbas *Mozam.* 12°20S 40°10E **269** E5
Qurnat as Sawdā' *Lebanon* 34°18N 36°6E **250** D7
Quryq *Kazakhstan* 43°12N 51°39E **216** D4
Qûs *Egypt* 25°55N 32°50E **256** B3
Qusar *Azerbaijan* 41°25N 48°26E **191** K9
Quşaybā' *Si. Arabia* 26°53N 43°35E **246** E4
Qusaybah *Iraq* 34°24N 40°59E **213** E9
Quşay'ir *Yemen* 14°55N 50°20E **249** D5
Quseir *Egypt* 26°7N 34°16E **246** E2
Qūshchī *Iran* 37°59N 45°3E **213** D11
Qusmuryn *Kazakhstan* 52°27N 64°36E **216** B6
Qusmuryn Köli *Kazakhstan* 52°41N 64°48E **216** B6
Qutang Gorge = Qutang Xia *China* 31°0N 109°40E **228** B7
Qutang Xia *China* 31°0N 109°40E **228** B7
Quthing *Lesotho* 30°25S 27°36E **271** D4
Qūţīābād *Iran* 35°47N 48°30E **213** E13
Quttinirpaaq △ *Canada* 82°13N 72°13W **295** A17
Quwayq → *Syria* 36°20N 37°10E **250** B8
Quweisna *Egypt* 30°34N 31°9E **251** H2
Quwo *China* 35°38N 111°25E **226** G6
Quyang *China* 38°35N 114°40E **226** E8
Quynh Nhai *Vietnam* 21°49N 103°33E **236** B4
Quyon *Canada* 45°31N 76°14W **313** A8
Quzhou *China* 28°57N 118°54E **229** C12
Quzi *China* 36°20N 107°20E **226** F4
Qvareli *Georgia* 41°57N 45°47E **191** K7
Qytet Stalin = Kuçovë *Albania* 40°47N 19°57E **202** F3
Qyzylorda *Kazakhstan* 44°48N 65°28E **217** D7
Qyzylorda □ *Kazakhstan* 45°0N 65°0E **216** D6
Qyzylzhar *Kazakhstan* 48°17N 69°38E **217** C7

R

R.F.K. Memorial Stadium *U.S.A.* 38°52N 76°58W **143** B4
Ra, Ko *Thailand* 9°13N 98°16E **237** H2
Raab *Austria* 48°21N 13°39E **180** C6
Raahe *Finland* 64°40N 24°28E **160** D21
Raalte *Neths.* 52°23N 6°16E **170** B6
Ra'ananna *Israel* 32°10N 34°52E **251** F5
Raas *Indonesia* 7°8S 114°33E **235** D4
Raasay *U.K.* 57°25N 6°4W **167** D2
Raasay, Sd. of *U.K.* 57°30N 6°8W **167** D2
Raasdorf *Austria* 48°14N 16°33E **142** A3
Raasepori *Finland* 60°0N 23°26E **188** B2
Rab *Croatia* 44°45N 14°45E **199** D11
Raba *Indonesia* 8°36S 118°55E **235** D5
Rába → *Hungary* 47°38N 17°38E **182** C2
Raba → *Poland* 50°8N 20°30E **185** H7
Rabaçal → *Portugal* 41°30N 7°12W **194** D3
Rabah *Nigeria* 13°5N 5°30E **263** C6
Rabai *Kenya* 3°50S 39°31E **268** C4
Rabak *Sudan* 13°9N 32°44E **257** E3
Rabaraba *Papua N. G.* 9°58S 149°49E **286** E5
Rabastens *France* 43°50N 1°43E **174** E5
Rabastens-de-Bigorre *France* 43°23N 0°9E **174** E4
Rabat = Victoria *Malta* 36°3N 14°14E **206** E6
Rabat *Malta* 35°53N 14°24E **206** F7
Rabat *Morocco* 34°2N 6°48W **260** B3
Rabat □ *Morocco* 34°10N 6°45W **260** B3
Rabaul *Papua N. G.* 4°24S 152°18E **286** C7
Rabbit Flat *Australia* 20°11S 130°1E **278** D5
Rabbit Lake Mine *Canada* 58°4N 104°5W **297** B8
Rabi *Fiji* 16°30S 179°59W **287** A3
Rābigh *Si. Arabia* 22°50N 39°5E **248** B2
Rabka *Poland* 49°37N 19°59E **185** J6
Râbniţa *Moldova* 47°45N 29°0E **183** C14
Rābor *Iran* 29°17N 56°55E **247** D8
Rabwah = Chenab Nagar *Pakistan* 31°45N 72°55E **242** D5
Rabyānah *Libya* 24°15N 22°0E **258** D4
Rača *Serbia* 44°14N 21°0E **202** B4
Răcăciuni *Romania* 46°20N 26°59E **183** D11
Răcăşdia *Romania* 44°59N 21°36E **182** F6
Racconigi *Italy* 44°46N 7°46E **198** D4
Raccoon → *U.S.A.* 41°35N 93°37W **310** C3
Raccoon Cr. → *U.S.A.* 39°47N 87°23W **311** E9
Race, C. *Canada* 46°40N 53°5W **299** C9
Race Course *Jamaica* 17°51N 77°20W **320** a
Race Pond *U.S.A.* 31°1N 82°8W **316** D7
Rach Gia *Vietnam* 10°5N 105°5E **237** G5
Rach Soi *Vietnam* 9°57N 105°7E **237** H5
Racha Noi, Ko *Thailand* 7°30N 98°19E **237** J2
Racha Yai, Ko *Thailand* 7°36N 98°21E **237** J2
Rachid *Mauritania* 18°45N 11°35W **262** B2
Raciąż *Poland* 52°46N 20°10E **185** F7
Racibórz *Poland* 50°7N 18°18E **185** H5
Racichy *Belarus* 53°44N 23°42E **184** E10
Racine *U.S.A.* 42°44N 87°47W **311** B9
Račisdorf = Rača *Serbia* 44°14N 21°0E **202** B4
Rackerby *U.S.A.* 39°26N 121°22W **306** F5
Råda *Sweden* 60°0N 13°36E **162** E7
Radama, Nosy *Madag.* 14°0S 47°47E **272** A2
Radama, Saikanosy *Madag.* 14°16S 47°53E **272** A2
Radan *Serbia* 42°59N 21°29E **202** D5
Rădăuţi *Romania* 47°50N 25°59E **183** C10
Rădăuţi-Prut *Romania* 48°14N 26°48E **183** B11
Radbuza → *Czech Rep.* 49°45N 13°22E **180** B6
Radcliff *U.S.A.* 37°51N 85°57W **311** G11
Radcliffe College *U.S.A.* 42°22N 71°7W **116** A2
Radeberg *Germany* 51°7N 13°53E **178** D9
Radebeul *Germany* 51°6N 13°39E **178** D9
Radeče *Slovenia* 46°5N 15°14E **199** B12
Radekhiv *Ukraine* 50°25N 24°32E **177** C13
Radekhov = Radekhiv *Ukraine* 50°25N 24°32E **177** C13
Radenthein *Austria* 46°48N 13°43E **180** E6
Radew → *Poland* 54°2N 15°52E **184** D2
Radford *U.S.A.* 37°8N 80°34W **309** G13
Radhanpur *India* 23°50N 71°38E **242** H4
Rådhus *Oslo, Norway* **133** b1
Radhwa, Jabal *Si. Arabia* 24°34N 38°18E **246** E3
Radika → *Macedonia* 41°38N 20°37E **202** E4
Radisson *Qué., Canada* 53°47N 77°37W **298** B4
Radisson *Sask., Canada* 52°30N 107°20W **297** C7
Radium Hot Springs *Canada* 50°35N 116°2W **296** C5
Radlice *Czech Rep.* 50°3N 14°23E **135** B2
Radlje ob Dravi *Slovenia* 46°38N 15°13E **199** B12
Radmannsdorf = Radovljica *Slovenia* 46°22N 14°12E **199** B11
Radnevo *Bulgaria* 42°17N 25°58E **203** D9
Radnice *Czech Rep.* 49°51N 13°35E **180** B6
Radnor Forest *U.K.* 52°17N 3°10W **169** E4
Radolfzell *Germany* 47°39N 8°59E **179** H4
Radom *Poland* 51°23N 21°12E **185** G8
Radom △ *Sudan* 9°20N 23°50E **264** A4

Radomir Bulgaria 42°37N 22°59E 202 D6
Radomka → Poland 51°43N 21°28E 185 G8
Radomsko Poland 51°5N 19°28E 185 G6
Radomyshl Ukraine 50°30N 29°12E 177 C15
Radomyśl Wielki Poland 50°14N 21°15E 185 H8
Radošć Poland 52°11N 21°11E 142 B3
Radoszyce Poland 51°4N 20°15E 185 G7
Radotín Czech Rep. 49°59N 14°21E 135 C2
Radoviš Macedonia 41°38N 22°28E 202 E6
Radovljica Slovenia 46°22N 14°12E 199 B11
Radstadt Austria 47°24N 13°28E 180 D6
Radstock, C. Australia 33°12S 134°20E 281 E1
Răducăneni Romania 46°58N 27°54E 183 D12
Raduša Macedonia 42°7N 21°15E 202 D5
Raduzhnyy Russia 62°5N 77°28E 214 C8
Radvanichy Belarus 52°1N 24°0E 185 F11
Radviliškis Lithuania 55°49N 23°33E 184 C10
Radville Canada 49°30N 104°15W 297 D8
Raḍwá, J. Si. Arabia 24°34N 38°18E 256 C4
Radymno Poland 49°59N 22°52E 185 J9
Radzanów Poland 52°56N 20°8E 185 F7
Radziejów Poland 52°40N 18°30E 185 F5
Radzyń Chełmiński Poland 53°23N 18°55E 184 E5
Radzyń Podlaski Poland 51°47N 22°37E 185 G9
Rae Canada 62°50N 116°3W 296 A5
Rae Bareli India 26°18N 81°20E 243 F9
Rae Isthmus Canada 66°40N 87°30W 295 D14
Raeren Belgium 50°41N 6°7E 170 D6
Raeside, L. Australia 29°20S 122°0E 279 E3
Raetihi N.Z. 39°25S 175°17E 284 F4
Rafaela Argentina 31°10S 61°30W 334 C3
Rafah Gaza Strip 31°18N 34°14E 251 G5
Rafai C.A.R. 4°59N 23°58E 264 B4
Rafat West Bank 31°52N 35°11E 123 A2
Raffadali Italy 37°24N 13°32E 200 E6
Raffili South Sudan 6°50N 28°0E 257 F2
Raffles Hotel Singapore 138 b3
Raffles Park Singapore 1°19N 103°48E 138 B2
Rafḥā Si. Arabia 29°35N 43°35E 246 D4
Rafina Greece 38°2N 24°0E 204 C6
Rafsanjān Iran 30°30N 56°5E 247 D8
Raft Pt. Australia 16°4S 124°26E 278 C3
Râgâ South Sudan 8°28N 25°41E 257 F2
Râgâ → South Sudan 8°41N 25°52E 257 F2
Ragachow Belarus 53°8N 30°5E 177 B16
Ragag Sudan 10°59N 24°40E 257 E1
Ragang, Mt. Phil. 7°43N 124°32E 233 H5
Ragay Phil. 13°49N 122°47E 232 E4
Ragay G. Phil. 13°30N 122°45E 232 E4
Ragged, Mt. Australia 33°27S 123°25E 279 F3
Rāgh Afghan. 37°32N 70°27E 240 A3
Raghunathpalli India 22°14N 84°48E 243 H11
Raghunathpur India 23°33N 86°40E 243 H12
Raglan N.Z. 37°55S 174°55E 284 D3
Raglan Harbour N.Z. 37°47S 174°50E 284 D3
Ragland U.S.A. 33°45N 86°9W 316 B3
Ragnit = Neman Russia 55°2N 22°2E 184 C9
Raguda, Ghubbet Somali Rep. 10°43N 46°22E 267 B6
Ragusa = Dubrovnik Croatia 42°39N 18°6E 202 D2
Ragusa Italy 36°55N 14°44E 201 F7
Raha Indonesia 4°55S 123°0E 231 E6
Rahad, Nahr ed → Sudan 14°28N 33°31E 257 E3
Rahad al Bardī Sudan 11°20N 23°40E 259 F4
Rahaeng = Tak Thailand 16°52N 99°8E 236 D2
Rahat, Ḥarrat Si. Arabia 23°0N 40°5E 256 C5
Rahatgarh India 23°47N 78°22E 243 H8
Rahden Germany 52°26N 8°36E 178 C4
Raheb, Ras ir- Malta 35°54N 14°20E 206 F7
Raheita Eritrea 12°46N 43°4E 257 E5
Raheng = Tak Thailand 16°52N 99°8E 236 D2
Raheny Ireland 53°22N 6°10W 120 A3
Rahimyar Khan Pakistan 28°30N 70°25E 242 E4
Rāhjerd Iran 34°22N 50°22E 247 C6
Rahnsdorf Germany 52°25N 13°41E 115 B5
Rahole △ Kenya 0°5N 38°57E 268 B4
Råholt Norway 60°16N 11°11E 164 D8
Rahon India 31°3N 76°7E 242 D7
Rahotu N.Z. 39°20S 173°49E 284 F2
Rahovec = Orahovac Kosovo 42°24N 20°40E 202 D4
Rahuri India 19°23N 74°39E 244 E2
Rai, Hon Vietnam 9°48N 104°38E 237 H5
Raiatéa, Î. French Polynesia 16°50S 151°25W 289 f
Raichur India 16°10N 77°20E 245 F3
Raiford U.S.A. 30°4N 82°14W 316 E7
Raiganj India 25°37N 88°10E 243 G13
Raigarh India 21°56N 83°25E 244 D6
Raighar India 19°51N 82°6E 244 E6
Raijua Indonesia 10°37S 121°36E 231 F6
Raikot India 30°41N 75°42E 242 D6
Railton Australia 41°25S 146°28E 281 G4
Rainbow Bridge △ U.S.A. 37°5N 110°58W 305 H8
Rainbow City U.S.A. 33°57N 86°5W 316 B3
Rainbow Lake Canada 58°30N 119°23W 296 B5
Rainier U.S.A. 46°53N 122°41W 306 D4
Rainier, Mt. U.S.A. 46°52N 121°46W 306 D5
Rainy L. Canada 48°42N 93°10W 297 D10
Rainy River Canada 48°43N 94°29W 297 D10
Raippaluoto Finland 63°13N 21°14E 160 E19
Raipur India 21°17N 81°45E 244 D5
Rairakhol India 21°4N 84°21E 244 D7
Ra'is Si. Arabia 23°33N 38°43E 256 C4
Raisen India 23°20N 77°48E 242 H8
Raisio Finland 60°28N 22°11E 188 B2
Raivavae French Polynesia 23°52S 147°40W 289 f
Raj Ghat Delhi, India 120 b3
Raj Nandgaon India 21°5N 81°5E 244 D5
Raj Nilgiri India 21°28N 86°46E 243 J12
Raja, Ujung Indonesia 3°40N 96°25E 234 B1
Raja Ampat, Kepulauan Indonesia 0°30S 130°0E 231 E8
Rajah Sikatuna △ Phil. 9°40N 124°20E 233 G5
Rajahmundry India 17°1N 81°48E 244 F5
Rajaji △ India 30°10N 78°20E 242 D8
Rajakylä Finland 60°15N 25°5E 121 B3
Rajampet India 14°11N 79°10E 245 G4
Rajang → Malaysia 2°30N 112°0E 235 B4
Rajang Mangroves △ Malaysia 2°6N 111°16E 235 B4
Rajanpur Pakistan 29°6N 70°19E 242 E4
Rajapalaiyam India 9°25N 77°35E 245 K3
Rajapur India 16°40N 73°31E 244 F1
Rajasthan □ India 26°45N 73°30E 242 F5
Rajasthan Canal = Indira Gandhi Canal India 28°0N 72°0E 242 F5
Rajauri India 33°25N 74°21E 243 C6
Rajbari Bangla. 23°47N 89°41E 241 D2
Rajendranagar India 17°18N 78°27E 244 F4
Rajgarh Mad. P., India 24°2N 76°45E 242 G7
Rajgarh Raj., India 27°14N 76°38E 242 F7
Rajgarh Raj., India 28°40N 75°25E 242 E6
Rajghat Dam India 24°45N 78°20E 244 B4
Rajgir India 25°2N 85°25E 243 G11
Rajgród Poland 53°42N 22°42E 184 E9
Rajim India 20°58N 81°53E 244 D5
Rajkot India 22°15N 70°56E 242 H4
Rajmahal Hills India 24°30N 87°30E 243 G12
Rajpath Delhi, India 120 c2
Rajpipla India 21°50N 73°30E 244 D1
Rajpur India 22°18N 74°21E 242 H6
Rajpura Delhi, India 28°41N 77°12E 120 A2
Rajpura Punjab, India 30°25N 76°32E 242 D7
Rajputana = Rajasthan □ India 26°45N 73°30E 242 F5
Rajsamand = Kankroli India 25°4N 73°53E 242 G5
Rajshahi Bangla. 24°22N 88°39E 241 C2
Rajshahi □ Bangla. 25°0N 89°0E 241 C2
Rājū Syria 36°40N 36°40E 250 B7
Rajula India 21°3N 71°26E 242 J4
Rajur India 20°7N 78°55E 244 D4
Rajura India 19°47N 79°22E 244 E4
Raka N.Z. 43°45S 172°1E 285 D7
Rakaia → N.Z. 43°36S 172°15E 285 D7
Rakan, Ra's Qatar 26°10N 51°20E 247 E6
Rakaposhi Pakistan 36°10N 74°25E 243 A6
Rakata, Pulau Indonesia 6°10S 105°20E 234 D3
Rakbah, Sahl Si. Arabia 22°15N 41°0E 256 C5
Rakhiv Ukraine 48°3N 24°12E 183 B9
Rakhni Pakistan 30°4N 69°56E 242 D3
Rakhni → Pakistan 29°31N 69°36E 242 E3
Rakhny-Lisovi Ukraine 48°47N 28°29E 183 B13
Rakhyût Oman 16°44N 53°20E 249 C6
Rakiraki Fiji 17°22S 178°11E 287 A2
Rakitnoye Russia 45°36N 134°17E 220 B7
Rakitovo Bulgaria 41°59N 24°5E 203 E8
Rakiura = Stewart I. N.Z. 46°58S 167°54E 285 G2
Rakkestad Norway 59°25N 11°21E 164 E8
Rakoniewice Poland 52°10N 16°16E 185 F3
Rakops Botswana 21°1S 24°28E 270 B3
Rákos-patak → Hungary 47°29N 19°12E 117 B3
Rákoshegy Hungary 47°27N 19°14E 117 B3
Rákoskeresztúr Hungary 47°29N 19°15E 117 B3
Rákoskert Hungary 47°27N 19°18E 117 B3
Rákosliget Hungary 47°29N 19°16E 117 B3
Rákospalota Hungary 47°34N 19°7E 117 A2
Rákosszentmihály Hungary 47°31N 19°8E 117 A2
Rakovica Croatia 44°59N 15°38E 199 D12
Rakovník Czech Rep. 50°6N 13°42E 180 A6
Rakovski Bulgaria 42°21N 24°57E 203 D8
Raków Poland 52°11N 20°56E 142 B1
Rakvere Estonia 59°20N 26°25E 188 C4
Raleigh Fla., U.S.A. 29°25N 82°32W 317 F7
Raleigh N.C., U.S.A. 35°47N 78°39W 315 D15
Ralik Chain Pac. Oc. 8°0N 168°0E 288 G8
Ralja Serbia 44°33N 20°34E 202 B4
Rälla Sweden 56°40N 16°30E 163 H10
Ralls U.S.A. 33°41N 101°24W 314 E4
Ralston U.S.A. 41°30N 76°57W 312 E8
Ram West Bank 31°51N 35°14E 123 A2
Ram → Canada 62°1N 123°41W 296 A4
Rām Allāh West Bank 31°55N 35°10E 123 A2
Rama Nic. 12°9N 84°15W 320 D3
Ramacca Italy 37°23N 14°42E 201 E7
Ramachandrapuram India 16°50N 82°4E 244 F6
Ramadān Iraq 33°19N 44°20E 113 B2
Ramagiri Udayagiri India 19°5N 84°18E 244 E7
Ramagundam India 18°55N 79°15E 244 E4
Ramakona India 21°43N 78°50E 243 J8
Ramakrishna Puram India 28°32N 77°10E 120 B1
Ramales de la Victoria Spain 43°15N 3°28W 194 B7
Ramalho, Serra do Brazil 13°45S 44°0W 333 D3
Rāmallāh = Rām Allāh West Bank 31°55N 35°10E 123 A2
Raman Thailand 6°29N 101°18E 237 J3
Ramanathapuram India 9°25N 78°55E 245 K4
Ramanathpur India 22°41N 88°14E 124 A1
Ramanujganj India 23°48N 83°42E 243 H10
Ramas C. India 15°5N 73°55E 245 G1
Ramat Allon West Bank 31°49N 35°12E 123 B2
Ramat Eshkol West Bank 31°48N 35°13E 123 B2
Ramat Gan Israel 32°4N 34°48E 251 F5
Ramat Razi'el Israel 31°46N 35°4E 123 B1
Ramat Shafet West Bank 31°48N 35°12E 123 B2
Ramatlhabama S. Africa 25°37S 25°33E 270 C4
Ramban India 33°14N 75°12E 243 C6
Rambervillers France 48°20N 6°38E 173 D13
Rambi = Rabi Fiji 16°30S 179°59W 287 A3
Rambipuji Indonesia 8°12S 113°37E 235 D4
Rambla, La Barcelona, Spain 114 b2
Rambler Channel China 22°21N 114°6E 122 A1
Rambouillet France 48°39N 1°50E 173 D8
Rambrai India 25°40N 91°19E 241 C3
Rambutyo I. Papua N. G. 2°18S 147°49E 286 B4
Ramdurg India 15°58N 75°22E 245 G2
Rame Hd. Australia 37°47S 149°30E 283 D8
Ramechhap Nepal 27°25N 86°10E 243 F12
Ramenki Russia 55°41N 37°28E 129 B2
Ramenskoye Russia 55°32N 38°15E 188 E10
Ramer U.S.A. 32°3N 86°13W 316 C3
Ramersdorf Germany 48°6N 11°35E 131 B2
Rameses Station Egypt 30°3N 31°15E 117 A2
Rameswaram India 9°17N 79°18E 245 K4
Ramganga → India 27°5N 79°58E 243 F8
Ramgarh Bangla. 22°59N 91°44E 241 D3
Ramgarh Jharkhand, India 23°40N 85°35E 243 H11
Ramgarh Raj., India 27°16N 75°14E 242 F6
Ramgarh Raj., India 27°30N 70°36E 242 F4
Rāmhormoz Iran 31°15N 49°35E 247 D6
Ramīān Iran 37°3N 55°16E 247 B7
Ramingining Australia 12°19S 135°3E 280 A2
Ramla Israel 31°55N 34°52E 251 G5
Ramlat Zalṭan Libya 28°30N 19°30E 258 C3
Ramlu Eritrea 13°32N 41°40E 257 E5
Ramm = Rum Jordan 29°39N 35°26E 251 J6
Râmna → Romania 45°36N 27°3E 183 E12
Ramnad = Ramanathapuram India 9°25N 78°55E 245 K4
Ramnagar Jammu & Kashmir, India 32°47N 75°18E 243 C6
Ramnagar Uttarakhand, India 29°24N 79°7E 243 E8
Ramnäs Sweden 59°46N 16°12E 162 E10
Râmnicu Sărat Romania 45°26N 27°3E 183 E12
Râmnicu Vâlcea Romania 45°9N 24°21E 183 E9
Ramnous Greece 38°12N 24°3E 204 C6
Ramon Isabela, Phil. 16°50N 121°31E 232 C3
Ramon Russia 51°55N 39°21E 189 G10
Ramona U.S.A. 33°2N 116°52W 307 M10
Ramonville-St-Agne France 43°33N 1°28E 174 E5
Ramore Canada 48°30N 80°25W 298 C3
Ramos Brazil 22°50S 43°14W 135 B1
Ramos → Nigeria 5°8N 5°22E 263 D6
Ramos I. Phil. 8°6N 117°1E 233 G1
Ramos Mejía Argentina 34°39S 58°33W 117 B1
Ramot West Bank 31°48N 35°13E 123 B2
Ramotswa Botswana 24°50S 25°52E 270 B4
Rampanalgas Trin. & Tob. 10°44N 60°59W 323 t
Rampart U.S.A. 65°30N 150°10W 303 D10
Rampur H.P., India 31°26N 77°43E 242 D7
Rampur Mad. P., India 23°25N 73°53E 242 H5
Rampur Orissa, India 21°48N 83°58E 244 D6
Rampur Ut. P., India 28°44N 77°18E 120 A2
Rampur Ut. P., India 28°50N 79°5E 243 E8
Rampur Hat India 24°10N 87°50E 243 G12
Rampura India 24°30N 75°27E 242 G6
Rampura Tola India 21°52N 79°55E 243 J8
Ramree I. Burma 19°0N 93°40E 241 F5
Rāmsar Iran 36°53N 50°41E 247 B6
Ramsey I. of Man 54°20N 4°22W 168 C3
Ramsey Ill., U.S.A. 39°8N 89°7W 310 E7
Ramsey N.J., U.S.A. 41°4N 74°9W 313 E10
Ramsey L. Canada 47°13N 82°15W 298 C3
Ramsgate N.S.W., Australia 33°58S 151°8E 139 B1
Ramsgate Kent, U.K. 51°20N 1°25E 169 F9
Ramshai India 26°44N 88°51E 241 B2
Ramsjö Sweden 62°11N 15°37E 162 B9
Ramstein Germany 49°27N 7°32E 179 F3
Ramtek India 21°20N 79°15E 244 D4
Ramu Kenya 3°55N 41°10E 268 B5
Ramu → Papua N. G. 4°0S 144°41E 286 C3
Ramvik Sweden 62°49N 17°51E 162 B11
Ramville, Î. = Chancel, Î. Martinique 14°41N 60°53W 322 j
Rana Pratap Sagar Dam India 24°58N 75°38E 242 G6
Ranaghat India 23°15N 88°35E 243 H13
Ranahu Pakistan 25°55N 69°45E 242 G3
Ranai Indonesia 3°55N 108°22E 235 B3
Ranau Malaysia 6°2N 116°40E 235 A5
Ranau, Danau Indonesia 4°49S 103°55E 234 C2
Rancagua Chile 34°10S 70°50W 334 C1
Rance → France 48°34N 1°59W 172 D5
Rancharia Brazil 22°15S 50°55W 333 F1
Rancheria → Canada 60°13N 129°7W 296 A3
Ranchester U.S.A. 44°54N 107°10W 304 D10
Ranchi India 23°19N 85°27E 243 H11
Rancho Cordova U.S.A. 38°36N 121°18W 306 G5
Rancho Cucamonga U.S.A. 34°10N 117°30W 307 L9
Rancho Park U.S.A. 34°3N 118°26W 126 B2
Ranco, L. Chile 40°15S 72°25W 336 B2
Rand Australia 35°33S 146°32E 283 C7
Rand ✈ (QRA) S. Africa 26°14S 28°8E 123 B2
Randaberg Norway 59°1N 5°36E 164 E2
Randabygda Norway 61°51N 6°20E 164 C3
Randalls I. U.S.A. 40°47N 73°55W 132 B3
Randalstown U.K. 54°45N 6°19W 166 B5
Randan France 46°2N 3°21E 173 F10
Randazzo Italy 37°53N 14°57E 201 E7
Randburg S. Africa 26°5S 27°57E 123 A1
Rander India 21°14N 72°47E 244 D1
Randers Denmark 56°29N 10°1E 163 H4
Randers Fjord Denmark 56°37N 10°20E 163 H4
Randfontein S. Africa 26°8S 27°45E 271 C4
Randhart S. Africa 26°16S 28°7E 123 B2
Randle U.S.A. 46°32N 121°57W 306 D5
Randolph Mass., U.S.A. 42°10N 71°2W 313 D13
Randolph N.Y., U.S.A. 42°10N 78°59W 312 D6
Randolph Utah, U.S.A. 41°40N 111°11W 304 F8
Randolph Vt., U.S.A. 43°55N 72°40W 313 C12
Randpark Ridge S. Africa 26°6S 27°58E 123 A1
Randsburg U.S.A. 35°22N 117°39W 307 K9
Randsfjorden Norway 60°25N 10°24E 164 D7
Randsverk Norway 61°44N 9°3E 164 C6
Randwick Australia 33°54S 151°14E 139 B2
Råneälven → Sweden 65°50N 22°20E 160 D20
Ranelagh Ireland 53°20N 6°15W 120 A2
Ranenburg = Chaplygin Russia 53°15N 40°0E 188 F11
Ranfurly N.Z. 45°7S 170°6E 285 F5
Rangae Thailand 6°19N 101°44E 237 J3
Rangamati Bangla. 22°38N 92°12E 241 D4
Rangapara India 26°49N 92°39E 241 B4
Rangárvallasýsla □ Iceland 63°55N 20°0W 155 D7
Rangataua N.Z. 39°26S 175°28E 284 F4
Rangaunu B. N.Z. 34°51S 173°15E 284 A2
Range, The Zimbabwe 19°2S 31°2E 269 F3
Rangeley U.S.A. 44°58N 70°39W 313 B14
Rangeley L. U.S.A. 44°55N 70°43W 313 B14
Rangely U.S.A. 40°5N 108°48W 304 F9
Ranger U.S.A. 32°28N 98°41W 314 E5
Rangia India 26°28N 91°38E 241 B3
Rangiora N.Z. 43°19S 172°36E 285 D7
Rangiroa French Polynesia 15°10S 147°35W 289 f
Rangitaiki N.Z. 38°52S 176°24E 284 E5
Rangitaiki → N.Z. 37°54S 176°49E 284 D5
Rangitata → N.Z. 43°45S 171°15E 285 D6
Rangitikei → N.Z. 40°17S 175°15E 284 G4
Rangitoto ke te tonga = D'Urville I. N.Z. 40°50S 173°55E 285 A8
Rangitoto Ra. N.Z. 38°25S 175°35E 284 E4
Rangkasbitung Indonesia 6°21S 106°15E 234 D3
Rangoon Burma 16°45N 96°20E 241 G6
Rangoon □ Burma 17°0N 96°10E 241 G6
Rangpur Bangla. 25°42N 89°22E 241 C2
Rangpuri India 28°32N 77°8E 120 B1
Rangsang Indonesia 1°20N 103°5E 237 M4
Rangwe Kenya 0°36S 34°35E 266 E3
Ranibennur India 14°35N 75°30E 245 G2
Raniganj India 27°3N 82°13E 243 F9
Ranikhet India 29°39N 79°25E 243 E8
Ranippettai India 12°56N 79°23E 245 H4
Raniwara India 24°50N 72°10E 242 G5
Rāniyah Iraq 36°15N 44°53E 213 D11
Ranka India 23°59N 83°47E 243 H10
Ranken → Australia 20°31S 137°36E 280 C2
Rankin Ill., U.S.A. 40°28N 87°54W 311 D9
Rankin Tex., U.S.A. 31°13N 101°56W 314 F4
Rankin Inlet Canada 62°30N 93°0W 294 E13
Rankins Springs Australia 33°49S 146°14E 283 B7
Rankovicevo = Kraljevo Serbia 43°44N 20°41E 202 C4
Rankweil Austria 47°17N 9°39E 180 D2
Rannersdorf Austria 48°7N 16°27E 142 B2
Rannoch, L. U.K. 56°41N 4°20W 167 E4
Rannoch Moor U.K. 56°38N 4°48W 167 E4
Rano Kau Chile 27°11S 109°26W 330 b
Rano Raraku, Volcán Chile 27°7S 109°17W 330 b
Ranobe Madag. 17°10S 44°8E 272 B1
Ranobe, Helodranon' i Madag. 23°3S 43°33E 272 C1
Ranohira Madag. 22°29S 45°24E 272 C2
Ranomafana Toamasina, Madag. 18°57S 48°50E 272 B2
Ranomafana Toliara, Madag. 24°34S 47°0E 272 C2
Ranomafana △ Madag. 21°16S 47°25E 272 C2
Ranomena Madag. 23°25S 47°17E 272 C2
Ranon Vanuatu 16°8S 168°7E 287 F6
Ranong Thailand 9°56N 98°40E 237 H2
Ranongga Solomon Is. 8°5S 156°35E 287 M9
Ranotsara Nord Madag. 22°48S 46°36E 272 C2
Ranpur India 20°5N 85°20E 244 D7
Rānsa Iran 33°39N 48°18E 247 C6
Ransbèche Belgium 50°56N 4°27E 116 B2
Ransdorp Neths. 52°24N 5°0E 112 A2
Ransiki Indonesia 1°30S 134°10E 231 E8
Ransom U.S.A. 41°9N 88°39W 311 C8
Rantabe Madag. 15°42S 49°39E 272 B2
Rantau Indonesia 2°56S 115°9E 235 C5
Rantau Abang Malaysia 4°52N 103°24E 237 K4
Rantaupanjang Kalimantan Tengah, Indonesia 1°22S 112°4E 235 C4
Rantaupanjang Kalimantan Timur, Indonesia 2°9N 117°25E 235 B5
Rantauprapat Indonesia 2°15N 99°50E 234 B1
Rantaupulut Indonesia 1°55S 112°12E 235 C4
Rantemario Indonesia 3°15S 119°57E 231 E5
Ranthambore △ India 26°10N 76°30E 242 F7
Rantoul U.S.A. 40°19N 88°9W 311 D8
Ranum Denmark 56°54N 9°14E 163 H3
Ranvad India 18°53N 72°55E 130 B2
Ranyah, W. → Si. Arabia 21°18N 43°20E 248 B3
Raohe China 46°47N 134°0E 220 A7
Raon l'Étape France 48°24N 6°50E 173 D13
Raoping China 23°42N 117°1E 229 F11
Raoui, Erg er Algeria 29°0N 2°0W 261 C4
Raoul I. Pac. Oc. 29°16S 177°54W 277 F15
Raoyang China 38°15N 115°45E 226 E8
Rap, Ko Thailand 9°19N 99°58E 237 b
Rapa French Polynesia 27°35S 144°20W 289 f
Rapa Nui = Pascua, I. de Chile 27°7S 109°23W 330 b
Rapallo Italy 44°21N 9°14E 198 D6
Rapar India 23°34N 70°38E 242 H4
Rāpch Iran 25°40N 59°15E 247 E8
Rapel, Lago Chile 34°20S 71°14W 334 C1
Raper, C. Canada 69°44N 67°6W 295 D18
Rapid City U.S.A. 44°5N 103°14W 308 C2
Rapid River U.S.A. 45°55N 86°58W 308 C10
Rapla Estonia 59°1N 24°52E 188 C3
Raposo Portugal 38°40N 9°11W 126 A1
Rapti → India 26°18N 83°41E 243 F10
Rapu Rapu I. Phil. 13°12N 124°9E 232 E5
Raqaba ez Zarqa → South Sudan 9°14N 29°44E 257 F2
Raqūbah Libya 28°59N 19°2E 258 C3
Raquette → U.S.A. 45°0N 74°42W 313 B10
Raquette Lake U.S.A. 43°49N 74°40W 313 C10
Rara △ Nepal 29°30N 82°10E 243 E10
Raraka French Polynesia 16°10S 144°54W 289 f
Raroia French Polynesia 16°1S 142°27W 289 f
Rarotonga Cook Is. 21°30S 160°0W 289 h
Ras Abu Soma Egypt 26°51N 33°58E 256 B3
Ra's al 'Ayn Syria 36°45N 40°12E 213 D9
Ras al Hadd Oman 22°30N 59°50E 249 B7
Ra's al Khaymah U.A.E. 25°50N 55°59E 247 E7
Ra's aţ Tib Tunisia 37°1N 11°2E 258 A2
Ras el Ma Algeria 34°26N 0°50W 261 B4
Ras el Mâ Mali 16°35N 4°30W 262 B4
Râs el Oued Algeria 35°57N 5°2E 261 A6
Râs Ghârib Egypt 28°6N 33°18E 256 B3
Râs Kōh Pakistan 28°43N 64°55E 240 C2
Ras Lānūf Libya 30°46N 18°11E 258 B3
Râs Muhammad △ Egypt 27°45N 34°16E 256 B3
Ra's Shamrah Syria 35°35N 35°45E 250 C6
Râs Sudr Egypt 29°40N 32°42E 256 B3
Rasa, Pta. Argentina 36°20S 56°41W 334 D4
Rasa, Punta Argentina 40°50S 62°15W 336 B4
Rasa I. Phil. 9°13N 118°26E 233 G2
Rasca, Pta. de la Canary Is. 27°59N 16°41W 153 e1
Rășcani Moldova 47°58N 27°33E 183 C12
Rasdhoo Maldives 4°17N 72°58E 272 d
Rasdu Atoll Maldives 4°13N 72°58E 272 d
Raseiniai Lithuania 55°25N 23°5E 184 C10
Rashad Sudan 11°55N 31°0E 257 E3
Rashîd Egypt 31°21N 30°22E 256 H7
Rashîd, Masabb Egypt 31°22N 30°17E 256 H7
Rashin = Najin N. Korea 42°12N 130°15E 224 A5
Rashmi India 25°4N 74°22E 242 G6
Rasht Iran 37°20N 49°40E 213 D13
Rashtrapati Bhawan Delhi, India 120 c1
Rasi Salai Thailand 15°20N 104°9E 236 E5
Rasipuram India 11°30N 78°15E 245 J4
Raška Serbia 43°19N 20°39E 202 C4
Râsnov Romania 45°35N 25°27E 183 E10
Rason L. Australia 28°45S 124°25E 279 E3
Rașova Romania 44°15N 27°55E 183 F12
Rasovo Bulgaria 43°42N 23°17E 202 C7
Rasra India 25°50N 83°50E 243 G10
Rasskazovka Russia 55°38N 37°20E 129 C2
Rasskazovo Russia 52°35N 41°50E 190 D5
Rast Romania 43°53N 23°16E 183 G8
Rastaala Finland 60°15N 24°47E 121 B1
Rastatt Germany 48°50N 8°11E 179 G4
Rastede Germany 53°15N 8°12E 178 B4
Rastenburg = Kętrzyn Poland 54°7N 21°22E 184 D8
Rastila Finland 60°12N 25°7E 121 B3
Răstolița Romania 46°59N 24°58E 183 D9
Rastyapino = Dzerzhinsk Russia 56°14N 43°30E 190 B6
Rasul Pakistan 32°42N 73°34E 242 C5
Raszków Poland 51°43N 17°40E 185 G4
Raszyn Poland 52°9N 20°54E 142 C1
Rat → Canada 49°35N 97°10W 297 D9
Rat Buri = Ratchaburi Thailand 13°30N 99°54E 236 F2
Rat I. St. Lucia 14°2N 60°58W 323 m
Rat I. Alaska, U.S.A. 51°48N 178°15E 303 L2
Rat Islands U.S.A. 52°0N 178°0E 303 L2
Rat L. Canada 56°10N 99°40W 297 B9
Ratak Chain Pac. Oc. 1°0N 170°0E 288 G8
Rätan Sweden 62°29N 14°33E 162 B8
Ratangarh India 28°5N 74°35E 242 E6
Rațāwī Iraq 30°38N 47°13E 246 D5
Ratcatchers L. Australia 32°30S 143°12E 282 B5
Ratchaburi Thailand 13°30N 99°54E 236 F2
Rath India 25°36N 79°37E 243 G8
Rath Luirc Ireland 52°21N 8°40W 166 D3
Rathangan Ireland 53°13N 7°1W 166 C4
Rathbun L. U.S.A. 40°54N 93°5W 310 D4
Rathdrum Ireland 52°56N 6°14W 166 D5
Rathedaung Burma 20°29N 92°45E 241 E4
Rathenow Germany 52°37N 12°19E 178 C8
Rathfarnham Ireland 53°18N 6°16W 120 B2
Rathkeale Ireland 52°32N 8°56W 166 D3
Rathlin I. U.K. 55°18N 6°14W 166 A5
Rathmelton Ireland 55°2N 7°38W 166 A4
Ratho U.K. 55°55N 3°23W 121 B1
Ratho Station U.K. 55°56N 3°23W 121 B1
Ratibor = Racibórz Poland 50°7N 18°18E 185 H5
Rätikon Austria 47°0N 9°55E 180 D2
Ratingen Germany 51°18N 6°52E 178 D2
Ratlam India 23°20N 75°0E 242 H6
Ratmanova Ostrov Russia 65°46N 169°6W 300 B6
Ratnagiri India 16°57N 73°18E 244 F1
Ratnapura Sri Lanka 6°40N 80°20E 245 L5
Rato Portugal 38°43N 9°8W 126 A2
Ratodero Pakistan 27°48N 68°18E 242 F3
Raton U.S.A. 36°54N 104°24W 305 H11
Ratschach = Radeče Slovenia 46°5N 15°14E 199 B12
Rattaphum Thailand 7°8N 100°16E 237 J3
Ratten Austria 47°28N 15°44E 180 D8
Rattray Hd. U.K. 57°38N 1°50W 167 D7
Rättvik Sweden 60°52N 15°7E 162 D9
Ratz, Mt. Canada 57°23N 132°12W 296 B2
Ratzebuhr = Okonek Poland 53°32N 16°51E 184 E3
Ratzeburg Germany 53°40N 10°46E 178 B6
Rau Indonesia 0°34N 100°2E 234 B2
Raub Malaysia 3°47N 101°52E 237 L3
Rauch Argentina 36°45S 59°5W 334 D4
Raudales Mexico 17°27N 93°39W 319 D6
Raudeberg Norway 61°59N 5°7E 164 C2
Raufarhöfn Iceland 66°27N 15°57W 155 A11
Raufoss Norway 60°44N 10°37E 164 D7
Rauhellern Norway 60°15N 7°50E 164 D4
Raukumara Ra. N.Z. 38°5S 177°55E 284 E6
Raul Soares Brazil 20°5S 42°22W 333 F3
Rauma Finland 61°10N 21°30E 188 B1
Rauma → Norway 62°34N 7°43E 164 B4
Raumo = Rauma Finland 61°10N 21°30E 188 B1
Raung, Gunung Indonesia 8°8S 114°3E 231 J17
Raurkela India 22°14N 84°50E 243 H11
Rausu-Dake Japan 44°4N 145°7E 220 B12
Răut → Moldova 47°15N 29°9E 183 C14
Rava-Ruska Ukraine 50°15N 23°42E 185 H10
Rava Russkaya = Rava-Ruska Ukraine 50°15N 23°42E 185 H10
Ravahere French Polynesia 18°14S 142°9W 289 f
Ravalli U.S.A. 47°17N 114°11W 304 C6
Ravānsar Iran 34°43N 46°40E 213 E12
Ravanusa Italy 37°16N 13°58E 200 E6
Rāvar Iran 31°20N 56°51E 247 D8
Ravelston U.K. 55°57N 3°14W 121 B2
Ravena U.S.A. 42°28N 73°49W 313 D11
Ravenel U.S.A. 32°46N 80°15W 316 C9
Ravenna Italy 44°25N 12°12E 199 D9
Ravenna Ky., U.S.A. 37°41N 83°57W 311 G13
Ravenna Nebr., U.S.A. 41°1N 98°55W 308 E4
Ravenna Ohio, U.S.A. 41°9N 81°15W 312 E3
Ravensburg Germany 47°46N 9°36E 179 H5
Ravenshoe Australia 17°37S 145°29E 280 B4
Ravensthorpe Australia 33°35S 120°2E 279 F3
Ravenswood Queens., Australia 20°6S 146°54E 280 C4
Ravenswood W. Va., U.S.A. 38°57N 81°46W 309 F13
Ravensworth Australia 32°26S 151°4E 283 B9
Ravenwood U.S.A. 40°22N 94°41W 310 D2
Raver India 21°15N 76°2E 244 D3
Ravi → Pakistan 30°35N 71°49E 242 D4
Ravine Chaude Guadeloupe 16°14N 61°40W 322 e
Ravna Gora Croatia 45°24N 14°50E 199 C11
Ravna Reka Serbia 44°1N 21°35E 202 B5
Ravne na Koroškem Slovenia 46°36N 14°59E 199 B11
Rawa Mazowiecka Poland 51°46N 20°12E 185 G7
Rawaki Kiribati 3°43S 170°43W 277 A16
Rawalpindi Pakistan 33°38N 73°8E 242 C5
Rawamangun Indonesia 6°11S 106°52E 122 B2
Rawang Malaysia 3°20N 101°35E 237 L3
Rawene N.Z. 35°25S 173°32E 284 B2
Rawi, Ko Thailand 6°33N 99°14E 237 J2
Rawicz Poland 51°36N 16°52E 185 G3
Rawitsch = Rawicz Poland 51°36N 16°52E 185 G3
Rawka → Poland 52°9N 20°8E 185 F7
Rawlinna Australia 30°58S 125°28E 279 F4
Rawlins U.S.A. 41°47N 107°14W 304 F10
Rawlinson Ra. Australia 24°40S 128°30E 279 D4
Rawson Argentina 43°15S 65°5W 336 B3
Raxaul India 26°59N 84°51E 243 F11
Ray U.S.A. 48°21N 103°10W 308 A2
Ray, C. Canada 47°33N 59°15W 299 C8
Ray City U.S.A. 31°5N 83°11W 316 D6
Ray Mts. U.S.A. 66°0N 152°0W 303 D10
Raya Ring, Ko Thailand 8°18N 98°29E 237 a
Rayachoti India 14°4N 78°50E 245 G4
Rayadurg India 14°40N 76°50E 245 G3
Rayagada India 19°15N 83°20E 244 E6
Raychikhinsk Russia 49°46N 129°25E 215 E13
Rāyen Iran 29°34N 57°26E 247 D8
Rayle U.S.A. 33°48N 82°54W 316 B7
Rayleigh U.K. 51°36N 0°37E 169 F8
Raymond Alta., Canada 49°30N 112°35W 296 D6
Raymond Calif., U.S.A. 37°13N 119°54W 306 H7
Raymond Ill., U.S.A. 39°19N 89°34W 310 E7
Raymond N.H., U.S.A. 43°2N 71°11W 313 C13
Raymond Wash., U.S.A. 46°41N 123°44W 306 D3
Raymond Terrace Australia 32°45S 151°44E 283 B9
Raymondville U.S.A. 26°29N 97°47W 314 H6
Raymore Canada 51°25N 104°31W 297 C8
Rayners Lane U.K. 51°34N 0°23W 125 A1
Raynes Park U.K. 51°24N 0°12W 125 B2
Rayón Mexico 29°43N 110°35W 318 B2
Rayong Thailand 12°40N 101°20E 236 F3
Raypur India 22°28N 88°22E 124 C2
Raystown L. U.S.A. 40°25N 78°5W 312 F6
Raytown U.S.A. 39°1N 94°28W 310 E2
Rayville U.S.A. 32°29N 91°46W 314 E9
Raz, Pte. du France 48°2N 4°47W 172 D2
Razan Iran 35°23N 49°2E 213 E13
Răžana Serbia 44°6N 19°55E 202 B3
Ražanj Serbia 43°40N 21°31E 202 C5
Razāzah, Buḥayrat ar Iraq 32°40N 43°35E 213 F10
Razazah, L. = Razāzah, Buḥayrat ar Iraq 32°40N 43°35E 213 F10
Razdelna Bulgaria 43°13N 27°41E 203 C11
Razdel'naya = Rozdilna Ukraine 46°50N 30°2E 183 D15
Razdolnoye Russia 43°30N 131°52E 220 C5
Razdolnoye Ukraine 45°46N 33°29E 189 K7
Razdory Russia 55°44N 37°17E 129 B1
Razeh Iran 32°47N 48°9E 247 C6
Razgrad Bulgaria 43°33N 26°34E 203 C10
Razgrad □ Bulgaria 43°33N 26°34E 203 C10
Razim, Lacul Romania 44°50N 29°0E 183 F14
Razlog Bulgaria 41°53N 23°28E 202 E7
Razmak Pakistan 32°45N 69°50E 242 C3
Ré, Cu Lao Vietnam 15°22N 109°8E 236 E7
Ré, Î. de France 46°12N 1°30W 174 B2
Reach Falls Jamaica 18°2N 76°18W 320 a
Reading U.K. 51°27N 0°58W 169 F7
Reading Mich., U.S.A. 41°50N 84°45W 311 C12
Reading Ohio, U.S.A. 39°13N 84°26W 311 E11
Reading Pa., U.S.A. 40°20N 75°56W 313 F9
Reading □ U.K. 51°27N 0°58W 169 F7
Real, Cordillera Bolivia 17°0S 67°10W 330 D4
Real Felipe, Fuerte Peru 12°4S 77°9W 124 B2
Realejo Alto Canary Is. 28°22N 16°34W 153 e1
Realicó Argentina 35°0S 64°15W 334 D3
Réalmont France 43°48N 2°10E 174 E6
Ream Cambodia 10°34N 103°39E 237 G4
Ream △ Cambodia 10°30N 103°45E 237 G4
Reams, L. U.S.A. 28°26N 81°34W 133 C1
Réao French Polynesia 18°31S 136°23W 289 f
Reay Forest U.K. 58°22N 4°55W 167 C4
Rebais France 48°50N 3°10E 173 D10
Rebecca, L. Australia 30°0S 122°15E 279 F3
Rebi Indonesia 6°23S 134°7E 231 F8
Rebiana Libya 24°12N 22°10E 258 D4
Rebiana, Sahrâ' Libya 24°30N 21°0E 258 D3
Reboly Russia 63°49N 30°47E 160 E24
Rebun-Tō Japan 45°23N 141°2E 220 B10
Recanati Italy 43°24N 13°32E 199 E10
Recaș Romania 45°46N 21°30E 182 E6
Recco Italy 44°22N 9°9E 198 D6
Recherche, Arch. of the Australia 34°15S 122°50E 279 F3
Rechna Doab Pakistan 31°35N 73°30E 242 D5
Rechytsa Belarus 52°21N 30°24E 177 B16
Recife Brazil 8°0S 35°0W 332 C5
Recife Seychelles 4°36S 55°42E 272 c
Recklinghausen Germany 51°37N 7°12E 170 C7
Reclining Buddha = Wat Pho Bangkok, Thailand 113 b1
Recoleta B. Aires, Argentina 34°36S 58°24W 117 B2
Recoleta Santiago, Chile 33°25S 70°40W 137 B2
Reconquista Argentina 29°10S 59°45W 334 B4
Recreio Brazil 8°0S 58°25W 331 B6
Recreo Argentina 29°25S 65°10W 334 B2
Recuay Peru 9°43S 77°28W 330 B2
Recz Poland 53°16N 15°31E 185 E2
Red = Hong → Vietnam 20°16N 106°34E 236 B5
Red → U.S.A. 31°1N 91°45W 314 F9
Red Bank U.S.A. 40°21N 74°5W 313 F10
Red Bay Canada 51°44N 56°25W 299 B8
Red Bluff U.S.A. 40°11N 122°15W 304 F2
Red Bluff Res. U.S.A. 31°54N 103°55W 305 L12
Red Bud U.S.A. 38°13N 89°59W 310 F7
Red Cliffs Australia 34°19S 142°11E 282 C5
Red Cloud U.S.A. 40°5N 98°32W 308 E4
Red Creek U.S.A. 43°14N 76°45W 313 C8
Red Deer Canada 52°20N 113°50W 296 C6
Red Deer → Alta., Canada 50°58N 110°0W 297 C7
Red Deer → Man., Canada 52°53N 101°1W 297 C8
Red Deer L. Canada 52°55N 101°20W 297 C8
Red Devil U.S.A. 61°46N 157°19W 303 F8
Red Fort = Lal Qila Delhi, India 120 a3
Red Hook U.S.A. 41°55N 73°53W 313 E11
Red Indian L. Canada 48°35N 57°0W 299 C8
Red L. Canada 51°3N 93°49W 297 C10
Red Lake Canada 51°3N 93°49W 297 C10
Red Lake Falls U.S.A. 47°53N 96°16W 308 B5
Red Lake Road Canada 49°59N 93°25W 297 C10
Red Lodge U.S.A. 45°11N 109°15W 304 D9
Red Mountain U.S.A. 35°37N 117°38W 307 K9
Red Oak U.S.A. 41°1N 95°14W 308 E6
Red River of the North → N. Amer. 49°0N 97°15W 308 A5
Red Rock Canada 48°55N 88°15W 298 C2
Red Rock, L. U.S.A. 41°22N 92°59W 310 C3
Red Rocks Pt. Australia 32°13S 127°32E 279 F4
Red Sea Asia 25°0N 36°0E 238 E3
Red Slate Mt. U.S.A. 37°31N 118°52W 306 H8
Red Square Moscow, Russia 129 b2
Red Sucker L. Canada 54°9N 93°40W 298 B1
Red Tower Pass = Turnu Roşu, P. Romania 45°33N 24°17E 183 E9
Red Volta → Africa 10°34N 0°30W 263 C4
Red Wing U.S.A. 44°34N 92°31W 308 C7
Reda Poland 54°40N 18°19E 184 D5
Redang, Pulau Malaysia 5°49N 103°2E 237 K4
Redange Lux. 49°46N 5°52E 170 E5
Redbridge □ U.K. 51°35N 0°7E 125 A4
Redcar U.K. 54°37N 1°4W 168 C6
Redcar & Cleveland □ U.K. 54°29N 1°0W 168 C7
Redcliff Canada 50°10N 110°50W 304 A8
Redcliffe Australia 27°12S 153°6E 281 D5
Redcliffe, Mt. Australia 28°30S 121°30E 279 E3
Reddersburg S. Africa 29°41S 26°10E 270 C4
Reddick Fla., U.S.A. 29°22N 82°12W 317 F7
Reddick Ill., U.S.A. 41°6N 88°15W 311 C8
Redding Calif., U.S.A. 40°35N 122°24W 304 F2
Redding Iowa, U.S.A. 40°36N 94°23W 310 D2
Redditch U.K. 52°18N 1°55W 169 E6
Redenção Brazil 4°13S 38°43W 332 B4
Redfern Australia 33°54S 151°12E 139 B2
Redfield U.S.A. 44°53N 98°31W 308 C4
Redford U.S.A. 44°38N 73°48W 313 B11
Redhead Trin. & Tob. 10°44N 60°58W 323 t
Redkey U.S.A. 40°21N 85°9W 311 D11
Redkino Russia 56°39N 36°16E 188 D9
Redlands U.S.A. 34°4N 117°11W 307 M9
Redmond Oreg., U.S.A. 44°17N 121°11W 304 D3
Redmond Wash., U.S.A. 47°40N 122°7W 306 C4
Redon France 47°40N 2°6W 172 E4
Redonda Antigua & B. 16°58N 62°19W 321 C7
Redondela Spain 42°15N 8°38W 194 C2
Redondo Portugal 38°39N 7°37W 195 G3
Redondo Beach U.S.A. 33°50N 118°23W 307 M8
Redoubt Volcano U.S.A. 60°29N 152°45W 303 F9
Redpath Sugar Museum Toronto, Canada 141 c3
Redruth U.K. 50°14N 5°14W 169 G2
Redvers Canada 49°35N 101°40W 297 D8
Redwater Canada 53°55N 113°6W 296 C6
Redwood Wellington, N.Z. 41°11S 174°49E 143 B1
Redwood N.Y., U.S.A. 44°18N 75°48W 313 B9
Redwood △ U.S.A. 41°40N 124°5W 304 F1
Redwood City U.S.A. 37°30N 122°15W 306 H4
Redwood Falls U.S.A. 44°32N 95°7W 308 C6
Ree, L. Ireland 53°35N 8°0W 166 C3
Reed City U.S.A. 43°53N 85°31W 309 D11
Reed L. Canada 54°38N 100°30W 297 C8
Reedley U.S.A. 36°36N 119°27W 306 J7
Reedsburg U.S.A. 43°32N 90°0W 308 D8
Reedsport U.S.A. 43°42N 124°6W 304 E1
Reedsville U.S.A. 40°39N 77°35W 312 F7
Reedy Creek Australia 36°58S 140°2E 282 D4
Reef Is. Pac. Oc. 10°15S 166°10E 277 C12
Reefton N.Z. 42°6S 171°51E 285 C6
Rees Germany 51°46N 6°24E 178 D2
Reese → U.S.A. 40°48N 117°4W 304 F5
Reetz = Recz Poland 53°16N 15°31E 185 E2
Refahiye Turkey 39°54N 38°47E 213 C8
Reflecting Pool Washington, D.C., U.S.A. 143 b1
Refshaleøen Denmark 55°41N 12°36E 118 A3
Reftele Sweden 57°11N 13°35E 163 G7
Refugio U.S.A. 28°18N 97°17W 314 G6
Rega → Poland 54°10N 15°18E 184 D2
Regalbuto Italy 37°39N 14°38E 201 E7
Regana, C. de Spain 39°25N 2°43E 206 B3
Regen Germany 48°58N 13°8E 179 G9
Regen → Germany 49°1N 12°6E 179 F8
Regeneração Brazil 6°15S 42°41W 332 C3
Regensburg Germany 49°1N 12°6E 179 F8
Regenstauf Germany 49°7N 12°8E 179 F8
Regents Park Gauteng, S. Africa 26°14S 28°3E 123 B2
Regent's Park London, U.K. 125 a2
Regenwalde = Resko Poland 53°47N 15°25E 184 E2
Reggâne = Zaouiet Reggâne Algeria 26°32N 0°3E 261 C5
Reggello Italy 43°41N 11°32E 199 E8
Réggio di Calábria Italy 38°6N 15°39E 201 D8
Réggio nell'Emília Italy 44°43N 10°36E 198 D7
Reghin Romania 46°46N 24°42E 183 D9
Regina Sask., Canada 50°27N 104°35W 297 C8
Régina Fr. Guiana 4°19N 52°8W 329 C7
Regina Beach Canada 50°47N 105°0W 297 C8
Register U.S.A. 32°22N 81°53W 316 C8
Registro Brazil 24°29S 47°49W 335 A6
Rego Park U.S.A. 40°43N 73°51W 132 B2
Reguengos de Monsaraz Portugal 38°25N 7°32W 195 G3
Rehar → India 23°55N 82°40E 243 H10
Rehli India 23°38N 79°5E 243 H8
Rehoboth Namibia 23°15S 17°4E 270 B2
Rehovot Israel 31°54N 34°48E 251 G5
Reibell = Ksar Chellala Algeria 35°13N 2°19E 261 A5
Reichenau = Rychnov nad Kněžnou Czech Rep. 50°10N 16°17E 181 A9
Reichenbach = Dzierżoniów Poland 50°45N 16°39E 185 H3
Reichenbach Germany 50°37N 12°17E 178 E8
Reichenberg = Liberec Czech Rep. 50°47N 15°7E 180 A8
Reichshof = Rzeszów Poland 50°5N 21°58E 185 H8
Reichstag Berlin, Germany 115 a3
Reid Australia 30°49S 128°26E 279 F4
Reidsville Ga., U.S.A. 32°6N 82°7W 316 C7

Reidsville N.C., U.S.A. 36°21N 79°40W 315 C15
Reifnig = Ribnica Slovenia 45°45N 14°45E 199 C11
Reigate U.K. 51°14N 0°12W 169 F7
Reillo Spain 39°54N 1°53W 196 F3
Reims France 49°15N 4°1E 173 C11
Reina Adelaida, Arch. Chile 52°20S 74°0W 336 D2
Reina Beatrix Int. ✈ (AUA) Aruba 12°30N 70°1W 322 f
Reina Sofía, Centro de Arte Madrid, Spain 127 c3
Reina Sofía, Tenerife ✈ (TFS) Canary Is. 28°3N 16°33W 153 e1
Reinbeck U.S.A. 42°19N 92°36W 310 B4
Reinbek Germany 53°30N 10°16E 178 B6
Reindeer → Canada 55°36N 103°11W 297 B8
Reindeer I. Canada 52°30N 98°0W 297 C9
Reindeer L. Canada 57°15N 102°15W 297 B8
Reinga, C. N.Z. 34°25S 172°43E 284 A1
Reinheimen △ Norway 62°10N 7°45E 164 B4
Reinickendorf Germany 52°34N 13°22E 115 A3
Reinosa Spain 43°2N 4°15W 194 B6
Reinsvoll Norway 60°40N 10°38E 164 D7
Reitan Norway 62°49N 11°22E 164 B8
Reitz S. Africa 27°48S 28°29E 271 C4
Reivilo S. Africa 27°36S 24°8E 270 C3
Rejaf South Sudan 4°45N 31°35E 257 G3
Rejmyre Sweden 58°50N 15°55E 163 F9
Rejowiec Fabryczny Poland 51°5N 23°17E 185 G10
Reka → Slovenia 45°40N 14°0E 199 C11
Rekohu = Chatham I. N.Z. 43°50S 176°20W 285 a
Rekola Finland 60°19N 25°4E 121 B3
Rekovac Serbia 43°51N 21°3E 202 C5
Reliance Canada 63°0N 109°20W 297 A7
Relizane Algeria 35°44N 0°31E 261 A5
Relizane □ Algeria 35°45N 0°55E 261 A5
Remad, Oued → Algeria 33°28N 1°20W 261 B4
Rémalard France 48°26N 0°47E 172 D7
Remanso Brazil 9°41S 42°4W 332 C3
Remarkable, Mt. Australia 32°48S 138°10E 282 B3
Remarkables, The N.Z. 45°10S 168°50E 285 F3
Rembang Indonesia 6°42S 111°21E 235 D4
Rembau Malaysia 2°35N 102°6E 234 B2
Rembert U.S.A. 34°6N 80°32W 316 A9
Rembertów Poland 52°15N 21°9E 142 B2
Rembrandthuis Amsterdam, Neths. 112 b3
Rembrandtpark Neths. 52°22N 4°51E 112 A2
Rembrandtplein Amsterdam, Neths. 112 b2
Remchi Algeria 35°2N 1°26W 261 A4
Remedios Colombia 7°2N 74°41W 328 B3
Remedios Panama 8°15N 81°50W 320 E3
Remedios de Escalada Argentina 34°43S 58°24W 117 C2
Remeshk Iran 26°55N 58°50E 247 E8
Remetea Romania 46°45N 25°29E 183 D10
Remich Lux. 49°32N 6°22E 170 E6
Remington U.S.A. 40°46N 87°9W 311 D9
Rémire Fr. Guiana 4°53N 52°17W 329 C7
Remiremont France 48°2N 6°36E 173 D13
Remo Ethiopia 6°48N 41°20E 257 F5
Rémola, Estany del Spain 41°16N 2°4E 114 B1
Remontnoye Russia 46°34N 43°37E 191 G6
Remoulins France 43°55N 4°35E 175 E8
Rempang Indonesia 0°51N 104°10E 234 B2
Rempart → Mauritius 20°19S 57°22E 272 e
Remparts → Réunion 21°22S 55°37E 272 f
Remscheid Germany 51°11N 7°12E 170 C7
Ren Xian China 37°8N 114°40E 226 F8
Rena Norway 61°8N 11°20E 164 C8
Rena → Norway 61°8N 11°23E 164 C8
Renascença Brazil 3°50S 66°21W 328 D4
Renca Chile 33°24S 70°42W 137 B1
Rend Lake U.S.A. 38°2N 88°58W 310 F8
Rendang Indonesia 8°26S 115°25E 231 J18
Rende Italy 39°20N 16°11E 201 C9
Rendezvous Barbados 13°4N 59°33W 323 r
Rendina Greece 39°4N 21°58E 204 B3
Rendova Solomon Is. 8°33S 157°17E 287 M9
Rendsburg Germany 54°17N 9°39E 178 A5
Renfrew Canada 45°30N 76°40W 313 A8
Renfrewshire □ U.K. 55°49N 4°38W 167 F4
Renfroe U.S.A. 32°14N 84°43W 316 C5
Rengat Indonesia 0°30S 102°45E 234 C2
Rengo Chile 34°24S 70°50W 334 C1
Renhua China 25°5N 113°40E 229 E9
Renhuai China 27°48N 106°24E 228 D6
Reni = Taranagar India 28°43N 74°50E 242 E6
Reni Ukraine 45°28N 28°15E 183 E13
Renigunta India 13°38N 79°30E 245 H4
Renk South Sudan 11°50N 32°50E 257 E3
Renland Greenland 71°10N 26°30W 154 C8
Renmark Australia 34°11S 140°43E 282 C4
Rennebu Norway 62°52N 9°49E 164 B6
Rennell Solomon Is. 11°40S 160°10E 287 N11
Rennell Sd. Canada 53°23N 132°35W 296 C2
Rennemoulin France 48°50N 2°2E 134 A1
Renner Springs Australia 18°20S 133°47E 280 B1
Rennes France 48°7N 1°41W 172 D5
Rennick Glacier Antarctica 70°30S 161°45E 151 D11
Rennie L. Canada 61°32N 105°35W 297 A7
Reno U.S.A. 39°31N 119°48W 306 F7
Reno → Italy 44°38N 12°16E 199 D9
Renovo U.S.A. 41°20N 77°45W 312 E7
Renqiu China 38°43N 116°5E 226 E9
Rens Denmark 54°54N 9°5E 163 K3
Renshou China 29°59N 104°9E 228 C5
Rensselaer Ind., U.S.A. 40°57N 87°9W 311 D9
Rensselaer N.Y., U.S.A. 42°38N 73°45W 313 D11
Renton U.S.A. 47°28N 122°12W 306 C4
Renukoot India 24°12N 83°2E 243 G10
Renwick N.Z. 41°30S 173°51E 285 B8
Renwick Gallery Washington, D.C., U.S.A. 143 a1
Réo Burkina Faso 12°28N 2°35W 262 C4
Reocín = Puente San Miguel Spain 43°21N 4°5W 194 B6
Reotipur India 25°33N 83°45E 243 G10
Repalle India 16°2N 80°45E 245 F5
Répcelak Hungary 47°24N 17°1E 182 C2
Řeporyje Czech Rep. 50°1N 14°18E 135 B1
Reppen = Rzepin Poland 52°20N 14°49E 185 F1
Republic Mo., U.S.A. 37°7N 93°29W 308 G7
Republic Wash., U.S.A. 48°39N 118°44W 304 B4
Republican → U.S.A. 39°4N 96°48W 308 F5
Republiek Suriname 5°30N 55°13W 329 B6
République, Place de la Paris, France 134 b5
Repulse B. Australia 20°35S 148°46E 280 b
Repulse Bay Nunavut, Canada 66°30N 86°30W 295 D14
Repulse Bay Hong Kong, China 22°13N 114°10E 122 B2
Repy Czech Rep. 50°4N 14°17E 135 B1
Requena Peru 5°5S 73°52W 330 B3
Requena Spain 39°30N 1°4W 197 F3
Requin Bay Grenada 12°2N 61°39W 323 q
Réquista France 44°1N 2°32E 174 D6
Reşadiye Muğla, Turkey 36°45N 27°39E 205 E9
Reşadiye Tokat, Turkey 40°23N 37°20E 212 B7
Reşadiye Yarımadası Turkey 36°40N 27°45E 205 E9
Resavica Serbia 44°4N 21°31E 202 B5
Resen Macedonia 41°5N 21°0E 202 E5
Reserve U.S.A. 33°43N 108°45W 305 K9
Resht = Rasht Iran 37°20N 49°40E 213 D13
Residenz Germany 48°8N 11°34E 131 B2
Residenzmuseum Munich, Germany 131 b3
Resistencia Argentina 27°30S 59°0W 334 B4
Reşiţa Romania 45°18N 21°53E 182 E6
Resko Poland 53°47N 15°25E 184 E2
Reso = Raisio Finland 60°28N 22°11E 188 B2
Resolute Canada 74°42N 94°54W 295 C13
Resolution I. Nunavut, Canada 61°30N 65°0W 295 E19
Resolution I. N.Z. 45°40S 166°40E 285 F1
Resplandes Brazil 6°17S 45°13W 332 C2
Resplendor Brazil 19°20S 41°15W 333 E3
Ressano Garcia Mozam. 25°25S 32°0E 271 C5
Restinga de Jurubatiba △ Brazil 22°5S 41°20W 333 F3
Reston Man., Canada 49°33N 101°6W 297 D8
Reston Va., U.S.A. 38°57N 77°20W 143 B2
Resulayn = Ceylanpınar Turkey 36°50N 40°2E 213 D9
Reszel Poland 54°4N 21°10E 184 D8
Retalhuleu Guatemala 14°33N 91°46W 320 D1
Retenue, L. de Dem. Rep. of the Congo 11°0S 27°0E 269 E2
Retezat, Munţii Romania 45°25N 23°0E 182 E8
Retezat △ Romania 45°23N 22°56E 182 E7
Retford U.K. 53°19N 0°56W 168 D7
Rethel France 49°30N 4°20E 173 C11
Rethem Germany 52°47N 9°22E 178 C5
Rethimno Greece 35°18N 24°30E 207 E5
Rethimno □ Greece 35°23N 24°28E 207 E5
Reti Pakistan 28°5N 69°48E 242 E3
Retiche, Alpi Switz. 46°30N 10°0E 179 J6
Retiers France 47°55N 1°23W 172 E5
Retiro B. Aires, Argentina 34°35S 58°23W 117 B2
Retiro Madrid, Spain 40°24N 3°40W 127 B1
Retiro, Puerto Argentina 34°36S 58°21W 117 B2
Retortillo Spain 40°48N 6°21W 194 E4
Retournac France 45°12N 4°2E 175 C8
Retreat S. Africa 34°4S 18°28E 118 B1
Rétság Hungary 47°58N 19°10E 182 C4
Réunion ☑ Ind. Oc. 21°0S 56°0E 272 f
Reus Spain 41°10N 1°5E 196 D6
Reusam Indonesia 2°11N 96°38E 234 B1
Reuterstadt Stavenhagen Germany 53°42N 12°54E 178 B8
Reutlingen Germany 48°29N 9°12E 179 G5
Reutov Russia 55°45N 37°50E 129 B5
Reutte Austria 47°29N 10°42E 180 D3
Reval = Tallinn Estonia 59°22N 24°48E 188 C3
Revda Russia 56°48N 59°57E 186 C10
Réveillon → France 48°42N 2°30E 134 B3
Revel = Tallinn Estonia 59°22N 24°48E 188 C3
Revel France 43°28N 2°1E 174 E6
Revelganj India 25°50N 84°40E 243 G11
Revelstoke Canada 51°0N 118°10W 296 C5
Reventazón Peru 6°10S 80°58W 330 B1
Revere U.S.A. 42°25N 71°0W 116 A2
Revere House Boston, U.S.A. 116 b3
Revigny-sur-Ornain France 48°49N 4°59E 173 D11
Revillagigedo, Is. de Pac. Oc. 18°40N 112°0W 318 D2
Revin France 49°55N 4°39E 173 C11
Revúca Slovak Rep. 48°41N 20°7E 181 C13
Revuè → Mozam. 19°50S 34°0E 269 F3
Rewa India 24°33N 81°25E 243 G9
Rewa → Guyana 3°19N 58°42W 329 C6
Rewari India 28°15N 76°40E 242 E7
Rexburg U.S.A. 43°49N 111°47W 304 E8
Rexdale Canada 43°43N 79°35W 141 A1
Rey Iran 35°35N 51°25E 247 C6
Rey, I. del Panama 8°20N 78°30W 320 E4
Rey, L. del Mexico 27°1N 103°26W 318 B4
Rey, Mayo → Cameroon 8°47N 14°1E 264 B2
Rey, Rio-del- → Cameroon 4°31N 8°45E 264 B1
Rey Bouba Cameroon 8°40N 14°15E 264 A2
Rey Malabo Eq. Guin. 3°45N 8°50E 263 E6
Reyðarfjörður Iceland 65°2N 14°13W 155 B12
Reyes Bolivia 14°19S 67°23W 330 C4
Reyes, Pt. U.S.A. 38°0N 123°0W 306 H3
Reyhanlı Turkey 36°16N 36°35E 250 B7
Reykhólar Iceland 65°27N 22°12W 155 B4
Reykholt Árnessýsla, Iceland 64°20N 21°18W 155 C5
Reykholt Borgarfjarðarsýsla, Iceland 64°10N 20°25W 155 C6
Reykjahlíð Iceland 65°40N 16°55W 155 B10
Reykjanes Iceland 63°48N 22°40W 155 D4
Reykjanes Ridge Atl. Oc. 59°0N 31°0W 152 A8
Reykjavík Iceland 64°10N 21°57W 155 C5
Reykjavík Keflavík ✈ (KEF) Iceland 64°0N 22°14W 155 C4
Reynolds Ga., U.S.A. 32°33N 84°6W 316 C5
Reynolds Ill., U.S.A. 41°20N 90°40W 310 C6
Reynolds Ra. Australia 22°30S 133°0E 278 D5
Reynoldsville Ga., U.S.A. 30°51N 84°47W 316 E5
Reynoldsville Pa., U.S.A. 41°6N 78°53W 312 E6
Reynosa Mexico 26°7N 98°18W 319 B5
Reynosa Tamaulipas Mexico 19°30N 99°10W 128 A1
Reza'iyeh = Orūmīyeh Iran 37°40N 45°0E 213 D11
Reza'iyeh, L. = Orūmīyeh, Daryācheh-ye Iran 37°50N 45°30E 213 D11
Rēzekne Latvia 56°30N 27°17E 188 D4
Rezhitsa = Rēzekne Latvia 56°30N 27°17E 188 D4
Rezina Moldova 47°45N 28°58E 183 C13
Rezovo Bulgaria 42°0N 28°0E 203 D12
Rezvān Iran 27°34N 56°6E 247 E8
Rezvānshahr Iran 37°32N 49°7E 213 D13
Rgotina Serbia 44°1N 22°17E 202 B6
Rharbi, Zahrez Algeria 34°50N 2°55E 261 B5
Rharis, O. → Algeria 26°0N 5°4E 261 C6
Rhayader U.K. 52°18N 3°29W 169 E4
Rheda-Wiedenbrück Germany 51°50N 8°20E 178 D4
Rhede Germany 51°50N 6°42E 178 D2
Rhein → Europe 51°52N 6°2E 170 C6
Rhein-Main-Donau-Kanal Germany 49°1N 11°27E 179 F7
Rhein-Ruhr, Düsseldorf ✈ (DUS) Germany 51°17N 6°46E 178 D2
Rhein-Taunus △ Germany 50°10N 8°10E 179 E4
Rhein-Westerwald △ Germany 50°32N 7°20E 178 E3
Rheinbach Germany 50°38N 6°57E 178 E2
Rheine Germany 52°17N 7°26E 178 C3
Rheinfelden Germany 47°33N 7°47E 179 H3
Rheinhessen-Pfalz □ Germany 49°20N 8°0E 179 F3
Rheinland-Pfalz □ Germany 50°0N 7°0E 179 E2
Rheinsberg Germany 53°6N 12°54E 178 B8
Rheris, Oued → Morocco 30°50N 4°34W 260 B4
Rhin = Rhein → Europe 51°52N 6°2E 170 C6
Rhine = Rhein → Europe 51°52N 6°2E 170 C6
Rhine U.S.A. 31°59N 83°12W 316 D6
Rhinebeck U.S.A. 41°56N 73°55W 313 E11
Rhineland-Palatinate = Rheinland-Pfalz □ Germany 50°0N 7°0E 179 E2
Rhinelander U.S.A. 45°38N 89°25W 308 C9
Rhinns Pt. U.K. 55°40N 6°29W 167 F2
Rhino Camp Uganda 3°0N 31°22E 268 B3
Rhir, Cap Morocco 30°38N 9°54W 260 B3
Rho Italy 45°31N 9°2E 129 A1
Rhode Island □ U.S.A. 41°40N 71°30W 313 E13
Rhodes N.S.W., Australia 33°49S 151°6E 139 A1
Rhodes Greece 36°15N 28°10E 206 E12
Rhodes ✈ (RHO) Greece 36°23N 28°12E 205 E10
Rhodesia = Zimbabwe ■ Africa 19°0S 30°0E 269 F3
Rhodon France 48°42N 2°3E 134 B1
Rhodon → France 48°42N 2°4E 134 B1
Rhodope Mts. = Rhodopi Planina Bulgaria 41°40N 24°20E 203 E8
Rhodopi Planina Bulgaria 41°40N 24°20E 203 E8
Rhön Germany 50°24N 9°58E 178 E5
Rhondda U.K. 51°39N 3°31W 169 F4
Rhondda Cynon Taff □ U.K. 51°42N 3°27W 169 F4
Rhône □ France 45°54N 4°35E 175 C8
Rhône → France 43°28N 4°42E 175 E8
Rhône-Alpes □ France 45°40N 6°0E 175 C9
Rhum U.K. 57°0N 6°20W 167 E2
Rhyl U.K. 53°20N 3°29W 168 D4
Ri-Aba Eq. Guin. 3°28N 8°40E 263 E6
Ria Formosa ⌂ Portugal 37°1N 7°48W 195 H3
Riachão Brazil 7°20S 46°37W 332 C2
Riacho de Santana Brazil 13°37S 42°57W 333 D3
Rialma Brazil 15°18S 49°34W 333 E2
Rialto Towers Australia 37°49S 144°57W 128 A1
Riam Indonesia 1°49S 111°54E 235 C4
Riang India 27°31N 92°56E 241 B4
Riangnom South Sudan 9°55N 30°1E 257 F3
Riaño Spain 42°59N 4°59W 194 C6
Rians France 43°37N 5°44E 175 E9
Riansáres → Spain 39°32N 3°18W 195 F7
Riasi India 33°10N 74°50E 243 C6
Riau □ Indonesia 0°0 102°35E 234 B2
Riau, Kepulauan □ Indonesia 0°30N 104°20E 234 B2
Riau Arch. = Riau, Kepulauan □ Indonesia 0°30N 104°20E 234 B2
Riaza Spain 41°18N 3°30W 194 D7
Riaza → Spain 41°42N 3°55W 194 D7
Riba de Saelices Spain 40°55N 2°17W 196 E2
Riba-roja de Túria Spain 39°33N 0°34W 197 F4
Ribadavia Spain 42°17N 8°8W 194 C2
Ribadeo Spain 43°35N 7°5W 194 B3
Ribadesella Spain 43°30N 5°7W 194 B5
Ribado Nigeria 9°16N 12°47E 263 D7
Ribao Cameroon 6°32N 11°30E 263 D7
Ribas = Ribes de Freser Spain 42°19N 2°15E 196 C7
Ribas do Rio Pardo Brazil 20°27S 53°46W 331 E7
Ribauè Mozam. 14°57S 38°17E 269 E4
Ribble → U.K. 53°52N 2°25W 168 D5
Ribe Denmark 55°19N 8°44E 163 J2
Ribeauvillé France 48°10N 7°20E 173 D14
Ribécourt-Dreslincourt France 49°30N 2°55E 173 C9
Ribeira = Santa Uxía de Ribeira Spain 42°36N 8°58W 194 C2
Ribeira Brazil 22°49S 43°10W 135 A1
Ribeira Brava Madeira 32°41N 17°4W 153 c
Ribeira do Pombal Brazil 10°50S 38°32W 332 D4
Ribeira Grande Azores 37°49N 25°31W 153 d3
Ribeira Grande C. Verde Is. 17°0N 25°4W 153 j
Ribeirão Brazil 8°31S 35°23W 332 C4
Ribeirão Prêto Brazil 21°10S 47°50W 335 A6
Ribeiro Gonçalves Brazil 7°32S 45°14W 332 C2
Ribemont France 49°47N 3°27E 173 C10
Ribera Italy 37°30N 13°16E 200 E6
Ribérac France 45°15N 0°20E 174 C4
Riberalta Bolivia 11°0S 66°0W 331 C4
Ribes de Freser Spain 42°19N 2°15E 196 C7
Ribnica Slovenia 45°45N 14°45E 199 C11
Ribnitz-Damgarten Germany 54°15N 12°27E 178 A8
Říčany Czech Rep. 50°0N 14°40E 180 B7
Ricarda, Estany de la Spain 41°17N 2°6E 114 B1
Riccarton N.Z. 43°32S 172°37E 285 D7
Riccia Italy 41°30N 14°50E 201 A7
Riccione Italy 43°59N 12°39E 199 E9
Rice U.S.A. 34°5N 114°51W 307 L12
Rice L. Canada 44°12N 78°10W 312 B6
Rice Lake U.S.A. 45°30N 91°44W 308 C8
Riceboro U.S.A. 31°44N 81°26W 316 D8
Rich Morocco 32°16N 4°30W 260 B4
Rich, C. Canada 44°43N 80°38W 312 B4
Richard Toll Senegal 16°25N 15°42W 262 B1
Richards Bay S. Africa 28°48S 32°6E 271 C5
Richardson → Canada 58°25N 111°14W 297 B6
Richardson Lakes U.S.A. 44°46N 70°58W 309 C18
Richardson Mts. N.Z. 44°49S 168°34E 285 E3
Richardson Springs U.S.A. 39°51N 121°46W 306 F5
Riche, C. Australia 34°36S 118°47E 279 F2
Richelieu France 47°1N 0°20E 172 E7
Richey U.S.A. 47°39N 105°4W 304 C11
Richfield U.S.A. 38°46N 112°5W 304 G7
Richfield Springs U.S.A. 42°51N 74°59W 313 D10
Richford U.S.A. 45°0N 72°40W 313 B12
Richibucto Canada 46°42N 64°54W 299 C7
Richland Ga., U.S.A. 32°5N 84°40W 316 C5
Richland Iowa, U.S.A. 41°13N 92°0W 310 C5
Richland Mo., U.S.A. 37°51N 92°26W 310 G4
Richland Wash., U.S.A. 46°17N 119°18W 304 C4
Richland Center U.S.A. 43°21N 90°23W 308 D8
Richlands U.S.A. 37°6N 81°48W 309 G13
Richmond N.S.W., Australia 33°35S 150°42E 283 B9
Richmond Queens., Australia 20°43S 143°8E 280 C3
Richmond Vic., Australia 37°48S 145°0E 128 A2
Richmond Nelson-Marlborough, N.Z. 41°20S 173°12E 285 B8
Richmond N. Yorks., U.K. 54°25N 1°43W 168 C6
Richmond Calif., U.S.A. 37°46N 122°27W 136 B2
Richmond Calif., U.S.A. 37°56N 122°21W 306 H4
Richmond Ind., U.S.A. 39°50N 84°53W 311 E12
Richmond Ky., U.S.A. 37°45N 84°18W 311 G12
Richmond Mich., U.S.A. 42°49N 82°45W 312 D2
Richmond Mo., U.S.A. 39°17N 93°58W 310 E3
Richmond Tex., U.S.A. 29°35N 95°46W 314 G7
Richmond Utah, U.S.A. 41°56N 111°48W 304 F8
Richmond Va., U.S.A. 37°33N 77°27W 309 G15
Richmond Vt., U.S.A. 44°24N 72°59W 313 B12
Richmond, Mt. N.Z. 41°32S 173°22E 285 B8
Richmond Hill Ont., Canada 43°52N 79°27W 312 C5
Richmond Hill Ga., U.S.A. 31°56N 81°18W 316 D8
Richmond Hill N.Y., U.S.A. 40°41N 73°51W 132 B2
Richmond Park U.K. 51°26N 0°16W 125 B2
Richmond Peak St. Vincent 13°18N 61°13W 323 n
Richmond Ra. N.S.W., Australia 29°0S 152°45E 281 D5
Richmond Ra. N.Z. 41°32S 173°22E 285 B8
Richmond-upon-Thames □ U.K. 51°27N 0°17W 125 B2
Richmondville U.S.A. 42°38N 74°33W 313 D10
Richtersveld △ S. Africa 28°15S 17°10E 270 C2
Richville U.S.A. 44°25N 75°23W 313 B9
Richwood Ohio, U.S.A. 40°26N 83°18W 311 D13
Richwood W. Va., U.S.A. 38°14N 80°32W 309 F13
Ricla Spain 41°31N 1°24W 196 D3
Ricupe Angola 14°37S 21°25E 265 E4
Ridā' Yemen 14°25N 44°50E 248 D4
Riddarholmen Stockholm, Sweden 139 c1
Riddarhuset Stockholm, Sweden 139 c2
Ridder = Leninogorsk Kazakhstan 50°20N 83°30E 217 B10
Riddlesburg U.S.A. 40°9N 78°15W 312 F6
Ridge, The India 28°37N 77°10E 120 B2
Ridge Farm U.S.A. 39°54N 87°39W 311 E9
Ridge Spring U.S.A. 33°51N 81°40W 316 B8
Ridgecrest U.S.A. 35°38N 117°40W 307 K9
Ridgefield Conn., U.S.A. 41°17N 73°30W 313 E11
Ridgefield N.J., U.S.A. 40°49N 74°0W 132 B1
Ridgefield Wash., U.S.A. 45°49N 122°45W 306 E4
Ridgefield Park U.S.A. 40°52N 74°1W 132 A1
Ridgeland Miss., U.S.A. 32°26N 90°8W 315 E9
Ridgeland S.C., U.S.A. 32°29N 80°59W 316 C9
Ridgetown Canada 42°26N 81°52W 312 D3
Ridgeville Ind., U.S.A. 40°18N 85°2W 311 D11
Ridgeville S.C., U.S.A. 33°6N 80°19W 316 B9
Ridgewood N.J., U.S.A. 40°59N 74°7W 313 F10
Ridgewood N.Y., U.S.A. 40°42N 73°53W 132 B2
Ridgway Ill., U.S.A. 37°48N 88°16W 311 G8
Ridgway Pa., U.S.A. 41°25N 78°44W 312 E6
Riding Mountain △ Canada 50°50N 100°0W 297 C9
Ridley, Mt. Australia 33°12S 122°7E 279 F3
Riebeek-Oos S. Africa 33°10S 26°10E 270 D4
Ried Austria 48°14N 13°30E 180 C6
Riedlingen Germany 48°9N 9°28E 179 G5
Riedstadt Germany 49°45N 8°30E 179 F4
Riem Germany 48°8N 11°41E 131 B3
Rienza → Italy 46°49N 11°47E 199 B8
Riesa Germany 51°17N 13°17E 178 D9
Riesco, I. Chile 52°55S 72°40W 336 D2
Riesenburg = Prabuty Poland 53°47N 19°15E 184 E6
Riesenrad Austria 48°14N 16°23E 142 A2
Riesi Italy 37°17N 14°5E 201 E7
Riet → S. Africa 29°0S 23°54E 270 C3
Rietavas Lithuania 55°44N 21°56E 184 C8
Rietbron S. Africa 32°54S 23°10E 270 D3
Rietfontein Namibia 21°58S 20°58E 270 B3
Rieti Italy 42°24N 12°51E 199 F9
Rieupeyroux France 44°19N 2°12E 174 D6
Riez France 43°49N 6°6E 175 E10
Rif = Er Rif Morocco 35°1N 4°1W 261 A4
Rif Iceland 64°56N 23°49W 155 C3
Riffe L. U.S.A. 46°32N 122°26W 306 D4
Rifle U.S.A. 39°32N 107°47W 304 G10
Rifstangi Iceland 66°32N 16°12W 155 A10
Rift Valley Africa 7°0N 30°0E 254 G7
Rift Valley □ Kenya 0°20N 36°0E 268 B4
Rig Rig Chad 14°13N 14°25E 259 F2
Riga India 28°26N 95°2E 241 A5
Rīga Latvia 56°53N 24°8E 184 B11
Rīga ✈ (RIX) Latvia 56°54N 23°59E 184 B10
Riga, G. of Latvia 57°40N 23°45E 184 A10
Rigacikun Nigeria 10°40N 7°28E 263 C6
Rīgān Iran 28°37N 58°58E 247 D8
Rīgas Jūras Līcis = Riga, G. of Latvia 57°40N 23°45E 184 A10
Rigaud Canada 45°29N 74°18W 313 A10
Rigby U.S.A. 43°40N 111°55W 304 E8
Rīgestān Afghan. 30°15N 65°0E 240 C2
Riggins U.S.A. 45°25N 116°19W 304 D5
Rignac France 44°25N 2°16E 174 D6
Rigolet Canada 54°10N 58°23W 299 B8
Rigu Ghana 9°59N 0°48W 263 D4
Rihand Dam India 24°9N 83°2E 243 G10
Riihimäki Finland 60°45N 24°48E 188 B3
Riiser-Larsen-halvøya Antarctica 68°0S 35°0E 151 C4
Riiser-Larsen Ice Shelf S. Ocean 74°0S 19°0W 151 D2
Riiser-Larsen Sea S. Ocean 67°30S 22°0E 151 C4
Rijau Nigeria 11°8N 5°17E 263 C6
Rijeka Croatia 45°20N 14°21E 199 C11
Rijeka Crnojevića Montenegro 42°24N 19°1E 202 D3
Rijksmuseum Amsterdam, Neths. 112 c1
Rijssen Neths. 52°19N 6°31E 170 B6
Rika → Ukraine 48°11N 23°16E 183 B8
Rikā', W. ar → Si. Arabia 22°25N 44°50E 248 B4
Rike Ethiopia 10°50N 39°53E 257 E4
Rikers I. U.S.A. 40°47N 73°53W 132 B2
Riksdagshuset Stockholm, Sweden 139 b2
Rikuchū-Kaigan △ Japan 39°20N 142°0E 220 E11
Rikuzentakada Japan 39°0N 141°40E 220 E10
Rila Bulgaria 42°7N 23°7E 202 D7
Rila Planina Bulgaria 42°10N 23°20E 202 D7
Riley U.S.A. 43°32N 119°28W 304 E4
Rima → Nigeria 13°4N 5°10E 263 C6
Rimac Peru 12°2S 77°2W 124 B2
Rimah, Wadi ar → Si. Arabia 26°5N 41°30E 246 E4
Rimatara French Polynesia 22°38S 152°51W 289 f
Rimau, Pulau Malaysia 5°15N 100°16E 237 c
Rimavská Sobota Slovak Rep. 48°22N 20°2E 181 C13
Rimbey Canada 52°35N 114°15W 296 C6
Rimbo Sweden 59°44N 18°21E 162 E12
Rimé, O. → Chad 14°2N 18°3E 259 F3
Rimersburg U.S.A. 41°3N 79°30W 312 E5
Rimforsa Sweden 58°6N 15°43E 163 F9
Rímini Italy 44°3N 12°33E 199 D9
Rimouski Canada 48°27N 68°30W 299 C6
Rimrock U.S.A. 46°40N 121°7W 306 D5
Rinca Indonesia 8°45S 119°35E 235 D5
Rincon Bonaire 12°14N 68°20W 322 h
Rincon Puerto Rico 18°20N 67°15W 321 b
Rincon Ga., U.S.A. 32°18N 81°14W 316 C8
Rincón de la Victoria Spain 36°43N 4°18W 195 J6
Rincón de Romos Mexico 22°14N 102°18W 318 C4
Rincon Falls Trin. & Tob. 10°46N 61°24W 323 t
Rinconada Argentina 22°26S 66°10W 334 A2
Rind → India 25°53N 80°33E 243 G9
Rindal Norway 63°3N 9°13E 164 A6
Ringarum Sweden 58°21N 16°26E 163 F10
Ringas India 27°21N 75°34E 242 F6
Ringdove Vanuatu 16°40S 168°10E 287 F6
Ringe Denmark 55°13N 10°28E 163 J4
Ringebu Norway 61°32N 10°7E 164 C7
Ringgi Solomon Is. 8°5S 157°10E 287 M9
Ringgold Is. Fiji 16°15S 179°25W 287 A3
Ringim Nigeria 12°13N 9°10E 263 C6
Ringkøbing Denmark 56°5N 8°15E 163 H2
Ringkøbing Fjord Denmark 56°0N 8°15E 163 H2
Ringoma Angola 12°25S 17°32E 265 E3
Ringsaker Norway 60°54N 10°45E 164 D7
Ringsend Ireland 53°20N 6°12W 120 A2
Ringsjön Sweden 55°55N 13°30E 163 J7
Ringsted Denmark 55°25N 11°46E 163 J5
Ringvassøya Norway 69°56N 19°15E 160 B18
Ringwood U.S.A. 41°7N 74°15W 313 E10
Rinia Greece 37°23N 25°13E 205 D7
Rinjani, Gunung Indonesia 8°24S 116°28E 235 D5
Rinjani △ Indonesia 8°26S 116°23E 235 D5
Rinkeby Sweden 59°23N 17°55E 139 A1
Rinteln Germany 52°10N 9°8E 178 C5
Río, Punta del Spain 36°49N 2°24W 197 J2
Rio Bonito = Caiapônia Brazil 16°57S 51°49W 331 D7
Rio Branco = Arcoverde Brazil 8°25S 37°4W 332 C4
Rio Branco = Paratinga Brazil 12°40S 43°10W 333 D3
Rio Branco = Roraima □ Brazil 2°0N 61°30W 329 C5
Rio Branco Brazil 9°58S 67°49W 330 B4
Río Branco Uruguay 32°40S 53°40W 335 C5
Río Bravo Mexico 25°59N 98°6W 319 B5
Río Bravo ⌂ N. Amer. 29°2N 102°45W 318 B4
Río Bravo del Norte → Mexico 25°57N 97°9W 319 B5
Rio Brilhante Brazil 21°48S 54°33W 335 A5
Río Bueno Chile 40°19S 72°58W 336 B2
Rio Bueno Jamaica 18°28N 77°28W 320 a
Río Caribe Venezuela 10°42N 63°7W 329 A5
Río Chico Venezuela 10°19N 65°59W 328 A4
Rio Claro Brazil 22°19S 47°35W 335 A6
Rio Claro Trin. & Tob. 10°20N 61°25W 323 t
Rio Cobre → Jamaica 17°59N 76°52W 320 a
Río Colorado Argentina 39°0S 64°0W 336 A4
Rio Comprido Brazil 22°55S 43°13W 135 B1
Río Cuarto Argentina 33°10S 64°25W 334 C3
Rio das Pedras Mozam. 23°8S 35°28E 271 B6
Rio de Contas Brazil 13°36S 41°48W 333 D3
Rio de Janeiro Brazil 22°54S 43°12W 135 B1
Rio de Janeiro □ Brazil 22°50S 43°0W 333 F3
Rio de Janeiro Galeão ✈ (GIG) Brazil 22°49S 43°15W 135 A1
Rio de Mouro Portugal 38°46N 9°15W 126 A1
Río de Oro, B. de W. Sahara 23°45N 15°50W 260 D1
Rio do Prado Brazil 16°35S 40°34W 333 E3
Rio do Sul Brazil 27°13S 49°37W 335 B6
Río Dulce △ Guatemala 15°43N 88°50W 320 C2
Río Gallegos Argentina 51°35S 69°15W 336 D3
Río Grande Argentina 53°50S 67°45W 336 D3
Río Grande Bolivia 20°51S 67°17W 330 E4
Rio Grande Brazil 32°0S 52°20W 335 C5
Río Grande Zacatecas, Mexico 23°50N 103°2W 318 C4
Río Grande Puerto Rico 18°23N 65°50W 321 b
Rio Grande → N. Amer. 25°58N 97°9W 314 J6
Rio Grande City U.S.A. 26°23N 98°49W 314 H5
Río Grande de Santiago → Mexico 21°36N 105°26W 318 C3
Rio Grande do Norte □ Brazil 5°40S 36°0W 332 C4
Rio Grande do Sul □ Brazil 30°0S 53°0W 335 C5
Rio Grande Rise Atl. Oc. 31°0S 35°0W 152 K8
Río Hato Panama 8°22N 80°10W 320 E3
Río Lagartos Mexico 21°36N 88°10W 319 C7
Rio Largo Brazil 9°28S 35°50W 332 C4
Rio Maior Portugal 39°19N 8°57W 195 F2
Rio Marina Italy 42°49N 10°25E 198 F7
Río Mayo Argentina 45°40S 70°15W 336 C2
Río Mulatos Bolivia 19°40S 66°50W 330 D4
Río Muni □ Eq. Guin. 1°30N 10°0E 264 B2
Rio Negro Brazil 26°0S 49°55W 335 B6
Río Negro Chile 40°47S 73°14W 336 B2
Rio Negro, Pantanal do Brazil 19°0S 56°0W 331 D6
Rio Novo = Ipiaú Brazil 14°8S 39°44W 333 D4
Rio Pardo = Ribas do Rio Pardo Brazil 20°27S 53°46W 331 E7
Rio Pardo Brazil 30°0S 52°30W 335 C5
Río Pico Argentina 44°0S 70°22W 336 B2
Río Pilcomayo △ Argentina 25°5S 58°5W 334 B4
Río Platano ⌂ Honduras 15°45N 85°0W 320 C2
Rio Prêto = Santa Rita de Cássia Brazil 11°0S 44°32W 332 D3
Rio Preto da Eva Brazil 2°46S 59°41W 329 D6
Rio Rancho U.S.A. 35°14N 106°41W 305 J10
Rio Real Brazil 11°28S 37°56W 333 D4
Río Seco = Villa de María Argentina 29°55S 63°43W 334 B3
Río Segundo Argentina 31°40S 63°59W 334 C3
Río Simpson △ Chile 45°27S 73°30W 336 C2
Río Tercero Argentina 32°15S 64°8W 334 C3
Rio Tinto Brazil 6°48S 35°5W 332 C4
Rio Tinto Portugal 41°11N 8°34W 194 D2
Rio Tuba Phil. 8°31N 117°26E 233 G1
Río Turbio Argentina 51°32S 72°18W 336 D2
Rio Verde Brazil 17°50S 51°0W 333 E1
Río Verde San Luis Potosí, Mexico 21°56N 99°59W 319 C5
Rio Verde de Mato Grosso Brazil 18°56S 54°52W 331 D7
Río Viejo △ Venezuela 7°15N 71°20W 328 B3
Rio Vista U.S.A. 38°10N 121°42W 306 G5
Ríobamba Ecuador 1°50S 78°45W 328 D2
Ríohacha Colombia 11°33N 72°55W 328 A3
Rioja Peru 6°11S 77°5W 330 B2
Riom France 45°54N 3°7E 174 C7
Riom-ès-Montagnes France 45°17N 2°39E 174 C6
Rion-des-Landes France 43°55N 0°56W 174 E3
Rionegro Antioquía, Colombia 6°9N 75°22W 328 B2
Rionegro Santander, Colombia 7°15N 73°9W 328 B3
Rionero in Vúlture Italy 40°55N 15°40E 201 B8
Rioni → Georgia 42°14N 41°44E 191 J5
Riós Spain 41°58N 7°16W 194 D3
Riosinho → Brazil 7°7S 51°39W 331 B7
Ríosucio Caldas, Colombia 5°30N 75°40W 328 B2
Ríosucio Choco, Colombia 7°27N 77°7W 328 B2
Riou L. Canada 59°7N 106°25W 297 B7
Rioz France 47°26N 6°5E 173 E13
Riozinho → Brazil 2°55S 67°7W 328 D4
Ripatransone Italy 42°59N 13°46E 199 F10
Ripley Ont., Canada 44°4N 81°35W 312 B3
Ripley Calif., U.S.A. 33°32N 114°39W 307 M12
Ripley N.Y., U.S.A. 42°16N 79°43W 312 D5
Ripley Ohio, U.S.A. 38°45N 83°51W 311 F13
Ripley Tenn., U.S.A. 35°45N 89°32W 315 D10
Ripley W. Va., U.S.A. 38°49N 81°43W 309 F13
Ripoll Spain 42°15N 2°13E 196 C7
Ripollet Spain 41°26N 2°10E 114 A1
Ripon N. Yorks., U.K. 54°9N 1°31W 168 C6
Ripon Calif., U.S.A. 37°44N 121°7W 306 H5
Ripon Wis., U.S.A. 43°51N 88°50W 308 D9
Riposto Italy 37°44N 15°12E 201 E8
Rippin = Rypin Poland 53°3N 19°25E 185 E6
Ris Norway 59°56N 10°41E 133 A3
Risan Montenegro 42°32N 18°42E 202 D2
Risaralda □ Colombia 5°0N 76°10W 328 C2
Risby Denmark 55°41N 12°19E 118 A1
Riscle France 43°39N 0°5W 174 E3
Rishā', W. ar → Si. Arabia 25°33N 44°5E 246 E5
Rishiri-Rebun-Sarobetsu △ Japan 45°26N 141°30E 220 B10
Rishiri-Tō Japan 45°11N 141°15E 220 B10
Rishon le Ziyyon Israel 31°58N 34°48E 251 G5
Rishra India 22°42N 88°20E 124 A2
Rising Sun U.S.A. 38°57N 84°51W 311 F12
Risle → France 49°26N 0°23E 172 C7
Risnjak △ Croatia 45°25N 14°36E 199 C11
Rison U.S.A. 33°58N 92°11W 314 E8
Risør Norway 58°43N 9°13E 164 F6
Rissani Morocco 31°18N 4°12W 260 B4
Rita Blanca Cr. → U.S.A. 35°40N 102°29W 314 D3
Ritchie U.S.A. 38°52N 76°51W 143 B4
Ritchie's Arch. India 12°14N 93°10E 245 H11
Rithala India 28°43N 77°6E 120 A1
Riti Nigeria 7°57N 9°41E 263 D6
Ritidian Pt. Guam 13°39N 144°51E 302 d
Ritter, Mt. U.S.A. 37°41N 119°12W 306 H7
Rittman U.S.A. 40°58N 81°47W 312 F3
Ritzville U.S.A. 47°8N 118°23W 304 C4
Riu India 28°19N 95°3E 241 A5
Riva del Garda Italy 45°53N 10°50E 198 C7
Riva Lígure Italy 43°50N 7°50E 198 E4
Rivadavia B. Aires, Argentina 35°29S 62°59W 334 D3
Rivadavia Mendoza, Argentina 33°13S 68°30W 334 C2
Rivadavia Salta, Argentina 24°5S 62°54W 334 A3
Rivadavia Chile 29°57S 70°35W 334 B1
Rivarolo Canavese Italy 45°19N 7°43E 198 C4
Rivas Nic. 11°30N 85°50W 320 D2
Rivash Iran 35°28N 58°26E 247 C8
Rive-de-Gier France 45°32N 4°37E 175 C8
Rive Sud, Canal de la Canada 45°24N 73°31W 130 B2
River Cess Liberia 5°30N 9°32W 262 D3
River Edge U.S.A. 40°56N 74°1W 132 A1
River Estate & Waterwheel Trin. & Tob. 10°41N 61°33W 323 t
River Forest U.S.A. 41°53N 87°49W 119 B2
River Grove U.S.A. 41°55N 87°50W 119 B1
River Jordan Canada 48°26N 124°3W 306 B2
River North Chicago, U.S.A. 119 b1
River Ridge U.S.A. 29°57N 90°12W 131 B1
Rivera Argentina 37°12S 63°14W 334 D3
Rivera Uruguay 31°0S 55°50W 335 C4
Riverbank U.S.A. 37°44N 120°56W 306 H6
Riverdale Calif., U.S.A. 36°26N 119°52W 306 J7
Riverdale Ga., U.S.A. 33°34N 84°25W 316 B5
Riverdale Md., U.S.A. 38°57N 76°54W 143 B4
Riverdale N.Y., U.S.A. 40°59N 74°17W 132 A2
Riverdale Park Canada 43°40N 79°21W 141 A2
Riverhead U.S.A. 40°55N 72°40W 313 F12
Riverhurst Canada 50°55N 106°50W 297 C7
Riverlea S. Africa 26°12S 27°58E 123 B1
Rivers Canada 50°2N 100°14W 297 C8
Rivers □ Nigeria 4°30N 7°10E 263 E6
Rivers Inlet Canada 51°42N 127°15W 296 C3
Riversdale Ont., Canada 44°5N 81°20W 312 B3
Riversdale N.Z. 45°54S 168°44E 285 F3
Riversdale Western Cape, S. Africa 34°7S 21°15E 270 D3
Riverside Calif., U.S.A. 33°59N 117°22W 307 M9
Riverside Ill., U.S.A. 41°49N 87°49W 119 C2
Riverton S. Austral., Australia 34°10S 138°46E 282 C3
Riverton Man., Canada 51°1N 97°0W 297 C9
Riverton N.Z. 46°21S 168°0E 285 G3
Riverton Ill., U.S.A. 39°51N 89°33W 310 E7
Riverton Wyo., U.S.A. 43°2N 108°23W 304 E9
Riverview Fla., U.S.A. 27°52N 82°20W 317 H7
Riverview Fla., U.S.A. 30°32N 87°12W 317 E2
Riverwood Australia 33°57S 151°3E 139 B1
Rives France 45°21N 5°31E 175 C9
Rivesaltes France 42°47N 2°50E 174 F6
Riviera U.S.A. 35°4N 114°35W 307 K12
Riviera Beach U.S.A. 26°47N 80°3W 317 J9
Riviera di Levante Italy 44°15N 9°30E 198 D6
Riviera di Ponente Italy 44°10N 8°20E 198 D5
Rivière à Goyave, Pte. de la Guadeloupe 16°8N 61°33W 322 e
Rivière-au-Renard Canada 48°59N 64°23W 299 C7
Rivière des Anguilles Mauritius 20°29S 57°33E 272 e
Rivière-des-Praires Canada 45°38N 73°34W 130 A2
Rivière-du-Loup Canada 47°50N 69°30W 299 C6
Rivière du Rempart Mauritius 20°6S 57°41E 272 e
Rivière-Pentecôte Canada 49°57N 67°1W 299 C6
Rivière-Pilote Martinique 14°26N 60°53W 322 j
Rivière St-Paul Canada 51°28N 57°45W 299 B8
Rivière-Salée Martinique 14°31N 61°0W 322 j
Rivne Odesa, Ukraine 46°1N 29°10E 183 D14
Rivne Rivne, Ukraine 50°40N 26°10E 177 C14
Rivne □ Ukraine 51°15N 26°30E 177 C14
Rívoli Italy 45°3N 7°31E 198 C4
Rivoli B. Australia 37°32S 140°3E 282 D4
Riwaka N.Z. 41°5S 172°59E 285 B7
Rixensart Belgium 50°43N 4°32E 116 B3
Rixheim France 47°40N 7°24E 173 E14
Riyad Iraq 33°18N 44°27E 113 B2
Riyadh = Ar Riyāḑ Si. Arabia 24°41N 46°42E 246 E5
Riyadh al Khabrā' Si. Arabia 26°2N 43°33E 246 E4
Riza Greece 40°31N 23°15E 202 F7
Rizal Cagayan, Phil. 17°51N 121°21E 232 C3
Rizal Nueva Ecija, Phil. 15°43N 121°6E 232 D3
Rizal Zamboanga del N., Phil. 8°35N 123°26E 233 G4
Rizal Park Phil. 14°35N 120°58E 127 B1
Rizal Stadium Phil. 14°34N 120°59E 127 B1
Rize Turkey 41°0N 40°30E 213 B9
Rize □ Turkey 41°0N 40°30E 213 B9
Rizhao China 35°25N 119°30E 227 G10
Rizokarpaso Cyprus 35°36N 34°23E 207 E10
Rizzuto, C. Italy 38°53N 17°5E 201 D10
Rjukan Norway 59°54N 8°33E 164 E5
Rjuven Norway 59°9N 7°8E 164 E4
Rkîz, L. Mauritania 16°50N 15°23W 262 B1
Ro Greece 36°9N 29°33E 205 E11
Roa Dem. Rep. of the Congo 3°49N 24°56E 264 B4
Roa Oppland, Norway 60°17N 10°37E 164 D7
Røa Oslo, Norway 59°57N 10°39E 133 A2
Roa Spain 41°41N 3°56W 194 D7
Roachdale U.S.A. 39°51N 86°48W 311 E10
Road Town Br. Virgin Is. 18°27N 64°37W 321 C7
Roan Plateau U.S.A. 39°20N 109°20W 304 G9
Roanne France 46°3N 4°4E 173 F11
Roanoke Ala., U.S.A. 33°9N 85°22W 316 B4
Roanoke Ind., U.S.A. 40°58N 85°22W 311 D11
Roanoke Va., U.S.A. 37°16N 79°56W 309 G14
Roanoke → U.S.A. 35°57N 76°42W 315 D16
Roanoke I. U.S.A. 35°53N 75°39W 315 D17
Roanoke Rapids U.S.A. 36°28N 77°40W 315 C16
Roatán Honduras 16°18N 86°35W 320 C2
Rob Roy Solomon Is. 7°23S 157°36E 287 L9
Robāt Iran 34°16N 46°47E 213 E12
Robāt Sang Iran 35°35N 59°10E 247 C8
Robāţkarīm Iran 35°25N 50°59E 247 C6
Robben I. S. Africa 33°46S 18°22E 270 D2
Robbins U.S.A. 41°38N 87°42W 119 D2
Robbins I. Australia 40°42S 145°0E 281 G4
Róbbio Italy 45°17N 8°35E 198 C5
Robe Australia 37°11S 139°45E 282 D3
Robe → Australia 21°42S 116°15E 278 D2
Röbel Germany 53°22N 12°35E 178 B8
Robert, Havre du Martinique 14°40N 60°55W 322 j
Robert Bourassa, Rés. Canada 53°40N 76°55W 298 B4
Robert Lee U.S.A. 31°54N 100°29W 314 F4
Roberta U.S.A. 32°43N 84°1W 316 C5
Roberts U.S.A. 40°37N 88°11W 311 D8
Roberts, Mt. Trin. & Tob. 10°47N 61°10W 323 t

Roberts, Mt. Alaska, U.S.A. 60°2N 166°16W 303 F6
Robertsdale U.S.A. 40°11N 78°6W 312 F6
Robertsganj India 24°44N 83°4E 243 G10
Robertsham S. Africa 26°15S 28°1E 123 B2
Robertson S. Africa 33°46S 19°50E 270 D2
Robertson I. Antarctica 65°15S 59°30W 151 C18
Robertson Ra. Australia 23°15S 121°0E 278 D3
Robertsport Liberia 6°45N 11°26W 262 D2
Robertstown Australia 33°58S 139°5E 282 B3
Roberval Canada 48°32N 72°15W 299 C5
Robeson Chan. N. Amer. 82°0N 61°30W 154 A4
Robesonia U.S.A. 40°21N 76°8W 313 F8
Robi Ethiopia 7°52N 39°38E 257 F4
Robinson U.S.A. 39°0N 87°44W 311 F9
Robinson → Australia 16°3S 137°16E 280 B2
Robinson Crusoe I. Pac. Oc. 33°38S 78°52W 330 c
Robinson Ra. Australia 25°40S 119°0E 279 E2
Robinvale Australia 34°40S 142°45E 282 C5
Robledo Spain 38°46N 2°26W 197 G2
Roblin Canada 51°14N 101°21W 297 C8
Roboré Bolivia 18°10S 59°45W 331 D6
Robson, Mt. Canada 53°10N 119°10W 296 C5
Robstown U.S.A. 27°47N 97°40W 314 H6
Roca, C. da Portugal 38°40N 9°31W 195 G1
Roca Partida, I. Mexico 19°1N 112°2W 318 D2
Rocamadour France 44°48N 1°37E 174 D5
Rocca San Casciano Italy 44°3N 11°51E 199 D8
Roccadaspide Italy 40°27N 15°10E 201 B8
Roccastrada Italy 43°0N 11°10E 199 F8
Roccella Iónica Italy 38°19N 16°24E 201 D9
Rocciamelone, Monte = Roche Melon Italy 45°12N 7°5E 175 C11
Rocha Uruguay 34°30S 54°25W 335 C5
Rochdale U.K. 53°38N 2°9W 168 D5
Roche Melon Italy 45°12N 7°5E 175 C11
Rochechouart France 45°50N 0°49E 174 C4
Rochedo Brazil 19°57S 54°52W 331 D7
Rochefort Belgium 50°9N 5°12E 170 D5
Rochefort Charente-Maritime, France 45°56N 0°57W 174 C3
Rochefort-en-Terre France 47°42N 2°22W 172 E4
Rochelle Ga., U.S.A. 31°57N 83°27W 316 D6
Rochelle Ill., U.S.A. 41°56N 89°4W 310 C7
Rochelle Park U.S.A. 40°54N 74°4W 132 A1
Rocher River Canada 61°23N 112°44W 296 A6
Roches, R. des → Réunion 21°0S 55°42E 272 f
Roches's Bluff Montserrat 16°42N 62°9W 323 p
Roches Noires Mauritius 20°6S 57°42E 272 e
Rocheservière France 46°57N 1°30W 172 F5
Rochester Vic., Australia 36°22S 144°41E 282 D6
Rochester Medway, U.K. 51°23N 0°31E 169 F8
Rochester Ind., U.S.A. 41°4N 86°13W 311 C10
Rochester Minn., U.S.A. 44°1N 92°28W 308 C7
Rochester N.H., U.S.A. 43°18N 70°59W 313 C14
Rochester N.Y., U.S.A. 43°10N 77°37W 312 C7
Rochester Hills U.S.A. 42°41N 83°8W 311 B13
Rociu Romania 44°43N 25°2E 183 F10
Rock → Yukon, Canada 60°7N 127°7W 296 A3
Rock → Ill., U.S.A. 41°29N 90°37W 310 C6
Rock, The Australia 35°15S 147°2E 283 C7
Rock Cr. → U.S.A. 38°54N 77°3W 143 B3
Rock Creek U.S.A. 41°40N 80°52W 312 E4
Rock Creek Park U.S.A. 38°56N 77°2W 143 B3
Rock Falls U.S.A. 41°47N 89°41W 310 C7
Rock Flat Australia 36°21S 149°13E 283 D8
Rock Hall Barbados 13°11N 59°36W 323 r
Rock Hill U.S.A. 34°56N 81°1W 315 D14
Rock Island U.S.A. 41°30N 90°34W 310 C6
Rock Port U.S.A. 40°25N 95°31W 308 E6
Rock Pt. N.Z. 41°8S 174°47E 143 A1
Rock Rapids U.S.A. 43°26N 96°10W 308 D5
Rock Sound Bahamas 24°54N 76°12W 320 B4
Rock Springs Mont., U.S.A. 46°49N 106°15W 304 C10
Rock Springs Wyo., U.S.A. 41°35N 109°14W 304 F9
Rock Valley U.S.A. 43°12N 96°18W 308 D5
Rockall Atl. Oc. 57°37N 13°42W 158 D3
Rockall Trough Atl. Oc. 57°0N 12°0W 152 A10
Rockaway Beach U.S.A. 40°34N 73°49W 132 C3
Rockaway Pt. U.S.A. 40°33N 73°54W 132 C2
Rockdale N.S.W., Australia 33°57S 151°8E 139 B1
Rockdale Tex., U.S.A. 30°39N 97°0W 314 F6
Rockdale Wash., U.S.A. 47°22N 121°28W 306 C5
Rockeby = Mungkan Kandju △ Australia 13°35S 142°52E 280 A3
Rockefeller Center New York, U.S.A. 132 c2
Rockefeller Plateau Antarctica 76°0S 130°0W 151 E14
Rockford Ala., U.S.A. 32°53N 86°13W 316 C3
Rockford Ill., U.S.A. 42°16N 89°6W 310 B7
Rockford Iowa, U.S.A. 43°3N 92°57W 310 A4
Rockford Mich., U.S.A. 43°7N 85°34W 311 A11
Rockford Ohio, U.S.A. 40°41N 84°39W 311 D12
Rockglen Canada 49°11N 105°57W 297 D7
Rockhampton Australia 23°22S 150°32E 280 C5
Rockingham W. Austral., Australia 32°15S 115°38E 279 F2
Rockingham N.C., U.S.A. 34°57N 79°46W 315 D15
Rockingham Vt., U.S.A. 43°11N 72°29W 313 C12
Rockingham B. Australia 18°5S 146°10E 280 B4
Rocklake U.S.A. 48°47N 99°15W 308 A4
Rockland Ont., Canada 45°33N 75°17W 313 A9
Rockland Idaho, U.S.A. 42°34N 112°53W 304 E7
Rockland Maine, U.S.A. 44°6N 69°7W 309 C19
Rockland Mich., U.S.A. 46°44N 89°11W 308 B9
Rocklands Bird Sanctuary Jamaica 18°24N 77°55W 320 a
Rocklands Reservoir Australia 37°15S 142°5E 282 D5
Rockledge U.S.A. 28°20N 80°43W 317 G9
Rocklin U.S.A. 38°48N 121°14W 306 G5
Rockly B. Trin. & Tob. 11°9N 60°46W 323 s
Rockmart U.S.A. 34°0N 85°3W 315 D12
Rockport Ind., U.S.A. 37°53N 87°3W 311 G9
Rockport Mass., U.S.A. 42°39N 70°37W 313 D14
Rockport Tex., U.S.A. 28°2N 97°3W 314 G6
Rocksprings U.S.A. 30°1N 100°13W 314 F4
Rockstone Guyana 5°59N 58°33W 329 B6
Rockville Conn., U.S.A. 41°52N 72°28W 313 E12
Rockville Ind., U.S.A. 39°46N 87°14W 311 E9
Rockville Md., U.S.A. 39°5N 77°9W 309 F15
Rockwall U.S.A. 32°56N 96°28W 314 E6
Rockwell City U.S.A. 42°24N 94°38W 310 B2
Rockwood Ont., Canada 43°37N 80°8W 312 C4
Rockwood Maine, U.S.A. 45°41N 69°45W 309 C19
Rockwood Tenn., U.S.A. 35°52N 84°41W 315 D12
Rocky Ford U.S.A. 38°3N 103°43W 304 G12
Rocky Fork L. U.S.A. 39°11N 83°26W 311 E13
Rocky Gully Australia 34°30S 116°57E 279 F2
Rocky Harbour Canada 49°36N 57°55W 299 C8
Rocky Island L. Canada 46°55N 83°0W 298 C3
Rocky Lane Canada 58°31N 116°22W 296 B5
Rocky Mount U.S.A. 35°57N 77°48W 315 D16
Rocky Mountain △ U.S.A. 40°25N 105°45W 304 F11
Rocky Mountain House Canada 52°22N 114°55W 296 C6
Rocky Mts. N. Amer. 49°0N 115°0W 304 B6
Rocky Point Namibia 19°3S 12°30E 270 A2
Rocky Run → U.S.A. 38°58N 77°14W 143 B2
Rocroi France 49°55N 4°30E 173 C11
Rod Pakistan 28°10N 63°5E 240 C1
Roda = Stadtroda Germany 50°52N 11°44E 178 E7
Roda Greece 39°48N 19°46E 206 B9
Roda, Gezîret el Egypt 30°1N 31°13E 117 A2
Roda I. = Roda, Gezîret el Egypt 30°1N 31°13E 117 A2
Rodaun Austria 48°8N 16°16E 142 B1
Rødberg Norway 60°17N 8°56E 164 D5
Rødby Denmark 54°41N 11°23E 163 K5
Rødbyhavn Denmark 54°39N 11°22E 163 K5
Roddickton Canada 50°51N 56°8W 299 B8
Rødding Denmark 55°23N 9°3E 163 J3
Rödeby Sweden 56°15N 15°37E 163 H9
Rødekro Denmark 55°4N 9°20E 163 J3
Rodenkirchen Germany 53°23N 8°26E 178 B4
Rodez France 44°21N 2°33E 174 D6
Ródhos = Rhodes Greece 36°15N 28°10E 206 E12
Rodi Gargánico Italy 41°55N 15°53E 199 G12
Rodia Greece 35°22N 25°1E 207 E6
Rodīna Kazakhstan 50°16N 66°53E 217 B7
Rodna Romania 47°25N 24°50E 183 C9
Rodna ✪ Australia 23°45S 132°4E 278 D5
Rodnei, Munţii Romania 47°35N 24°35E 183 C9
Rodney Canada 42°34N 81°41W 312 D3
Rodney, C. N.Z. 36°17S 174°50E 234 C3
Rodney B. St. Lucia 14°5N 60°58W 323 m
Rodniki Russia 57°7N 41°47E 190 B5
Rodolivos Greece 40°55N 24°0E 202 F7
Rodonit, Kepi i Albania 41°35N 19°27E 202 E3
Rodopi ☐ Greece 41°5N 25°30E 203 E9
Rodopos Greece 35°34N 23°45E 207 E4
Rødovre Denmark 55°40N 12°26E 118 A2
Rodrigo de Freitas, L. Brazil 22°58S 43°12W 135 B1
Rodrigues Ind. Oc. 19°45S 63°20E 273 F5
Roe → U.K. 55°6N 6°59W 166 A5
Roebling U.S.A. 40°7N 74°47W 313 F10
Roebourne Australia 20°44S 117°9E 278 D2
Roebuck B. Australia 18°5S 122°20E 278 C3
Roebuck Roadhouse Australia 17°59S 122°36E 278 C3
Roehampton U.K. 51°27N 0°15W 125 B2
Roermond Neths. 51°12N 6°0E 170 C6
Roes Welcome Sd. Canada 65°0N 87°0W 295 E14
Roeselare Belgium 50°57N 3°7E 170 D3
Rogachev = Ragachow Belarus 53°8N 30°5E 177 B16
Rogačica Serbia 44°4N 19°40E 202 B3
Rogagua, L. Bolivia 13°43S 66°50W 330 C4
Rogaland ☐ Norway 59°12N 6°20E 164 E3
Rogaška Slatina Slovenia 46°15N 15°42E 199 B12
Rogatec Slovenia 46°15N 15°46E 199 B12
Rogatica Bos.-H. 43°47N 19°0E 182 G4
Rogatyn Ukraine 49°24N 24°36E 177 D13
Rogen Sweden 62°20N 12°20E 162 B6
Rogers U.S.A. 36°20N 94°7W 314 C7
Rogers Centre Toronto, Canada 141 c1
Rogers City U.S.A. 45°25N 83°49W 309 C12
Rogers Park U.S.A. 42°0N 87°40W 119 A3
Rogersville Canada 46°44N 65°26W 299 C6
Roggan → Canada 54°24N 79°25W 298 B4
Roggan L. Canada 54°8N 77°50W 298 B4
Roggeveen Basin Pac. Oc. 31°30S 95°30W 289 L18
Roggeveldberge S. Africa 32°10S 20°10E 270 D3
Rogliano Gravina Italy 39°37N 16°9E 201 C9
Rogliano Haute-Corse, France 42°57N 9°30E 175 F13
Rogliano Italy 39°10N 16°19E 201 C9
Rogoaguado, L. Bolivia 13°0S 65°30W 331 C4
Rogojampi Indonesia 8°19S 114°17E 231 J17
Rogoźno Poland 52°45N 16°59E 185 F3
Rogue → U.S.A. 42°26N 124°26W 304 E1
Roha India 18°26N 73°7E 244 E1
Rohan France 48°4N 2°45W 172 D4
Rohnert Park U.S.A. 38°16N 122°40W 306 G4
Rohri Pakistan 27°45N 68°51E 242 F3
Rohri Canal Pakistan 26°15N 68°27E 242 F3
Rohtak India 28°55N 76°43E 242 E7
Rohtisch-Sauerbrunn = Rogaška Slatina Slovenia 46°15N 15°42E 199 B12
Roi Et Thailand 16°4N 103°40E 236 D4
Roi-Georges, Îs. du French Polynesia 14°32S 145°8W 289 f
Roihuvuori Finland 60°11N 25°2E 121 B3
Roissy-en-Brie France 48°48N 2°39E 134 B4
Roja Latvia 57°29N 22°43E 184 A9
Rojas Argentina 34°10S 60°45W 334 C3
Rojiște Romania 44°4N 23°56E 183 F8
Rojo, C. Mexico 21°33N 97°20W 319 C5
Rokan → Indonesia 2°0N 100°50E 234 B2
Rokel → S. Leone 8°30N 12°48W 262 D2
Rokin Amsterdam, Neths. 112 b2
Rokiškis Lithuania 55°55N 25°35E 188 E3
Rokitno Russia 50°57N 35°56E 189 G8
Rokycany Czech Rep. 49°43N 13°35E 180 B6
Rokytka → Czech Rep. 50°6N 14°27E 135 B3
Rolândia Brazil 23°18S 51°23W 335 A5
Røldal Norway 59°47N 6°50E 164 E3
Rolfe U.S.A. 42°49N 94°31W 310 B2
Rolla Mo., U.S.A. 37°57N 91°46W 310 G5
Rolla N. Dak., U.S.A. 48°52N 99°37W 308 A4
Rolleston Queens., Australia 24°28S 148°35E 280 C4
Rolleston N.Z. 43°35S 172°24E 285 D7
Rolling Fork → U.S.A. 37°55N 85°50W 311 G11
Rollingstone Australia 19°2S 146°24E 280 B4
Rom Vest-Agder, Norway 58°8N 7°56E 164 F4
Rom South Sudan 9°54N 32°16E 257 F3
Roma Queens., Australia 26°32S 148°49E 281 D4
Roma Italy 41°54N 12°28E 136 B1
Roma Sweden 57°32N 18°26E 163 G12
Roma Fiumicino ✕ (FCO) Italy 41°48N 12°15E 199 G9
Roma-Los Saenz U.S.A. 26°24N 99°1W 314 H5
Roma Urbe ✕ Italy 41°57N 12°30E 136 B2
Római-Fürdö Hungary 47°34N 19°4E 117 A2
Romain, C. U.S.A. 33°0N 79°22W 315 E15
Romaine → Canada 50°18N 63°47W 299 B7
Romainville France 48°52N 2°26E 134 A3
Roman Bulgaria 43°8N 23°57E 202 C7
Roman Romania 46°57N 26°55E 183 D11
Roman Forum = Foro Romano Rome, Italy 136 c3
Roman-Kosh, Gora Ukraine 44°37N 34°15E 189 K8
Romanche → France 45°5N 5°43E 175 C9
Romang Indonesia 7°30S 127°20E 231 F7
Români Egypt 30°59N 32°38E 251 H3
Romania ■ Europe 46°0N 25°0E 183 D10
Romanija Bos.-H. 43°50N 18°45E 182 G3
Romano, C. U.S.A. 25°51N 81°41W 317 K8
Romano, Cayo Cuba 22°0N 77°30W 320 B4
Romano Banco Italy 45°25N 9°6E 129 B1
Romanov-Borisoglebsk = Tutayev Russia 57°53N 39°32E 188 D10
Romanovka = Basarabeasca Moldova 46°21N 28°58E 183 D13
Romanovna-Murmane = Murmansk Russia 68°57N 33°10E 160 B25
Romanovsk = Kropotkin Russia 45°28N 40°28E 191 H5
Romanovskiy Khutor = Kropotkin Russia 45°28N 40°28E 191 H5
Romans-sur-Isère France 45°3N 5°3E 175 C9
Romanshorn Switz. 47°33N 9°22E 179 H5
Romanzof C. U.S.A. 61°49N 166°6W 303 F6
Romashkovo Russia 55°43N 37°19E 129 B1
Rombari South Sudan 4°33N 31°2E 257 G3
Romblon Phil. 12°33N 122°17E 232 E4
Romblon ☐ Phil. 12°30N 122°15E 232 E4
Romblon Pass. Phil. 12°27N 122°12E 232 E4
Rome = Roma Italy 41°54N 12°28E 136 B1
Rome Ga., U.S.A. 34°15N 85°10W 315 D12
Rome N.Y., U.S.A. 43°13N 75°27W 313 C9
Rome Pa., U.S.A. 41°51N 76°21W 313 E8
Romema Israel 31°48N 35°12E 123 B2
Romeoville U.S.A. 41°39N 88°3W 311 C8
Rometta Italy 38°10N 15°25E 201 D8
Romford U.K. 51°34N 0°11E 125 A5
Romilly-sur-Seine France 48°31N 3°44E 173 D10
Romiton Uzbekistan 39°56N 64°23E 216 E6
Rommani Morocco 33°31N 6°40W 260 B3
Romney U.S.A. 39°21N 78°45W 309 F14
Romney Marsh U.K. 51°2N 0°54E 169 F8
Romny Ukraine 50°48N 33°28E 189 G7
Rømø Denmark 55°10N 8°30E 163 J2
Romodan Ukraine 49°55N 33°15E 189 G7
Romodanovo Russia 54°26N 45°23E 190 C7
Romont Switz. 46°42N 6°54E 179 J2
Romorantin-Lanthenay France 47°21N 1°45E 173 E8
Rompin → Malaysia 2°49N 103°29E 237 L4
Romsdalen Norway 62°25N 7°52E 164 B4
Romsdalsfjorden Norway 62°38N 7°20E 164 B4
Romsey U.K. 51°0N 1°29W 169 G6
Ron India 15°40N 75°44E 245 G2
Ron Vietnam 17°53N 106°27E 236 D6
Rona U.K. 57°34N 5°59W 167 D3
Ronald Reagan Nat. Washington ✕ (DCA) U.S.A. 38°51N 77°2W 143 B3
Ronan U.S.A. 47°32N 114°6W 304 C6
Roncador, Cayos Colombia 13°32N 80°4W 320 D3
Roncador, Serra do Brazil 12°30S 52°30W 333 D1
Ronciglione Italy 42°17N 12°13E 199 F9
Ronco → Italy 44°24N 12°12E 199 D9
Ronda Spain 36°46N 5°12W 195 J5
Ronda, Serranía de Spain 36°44N 5°3W 195 J5
Rondane Norway 61°57N 9°50E 164 C6
Rondane △ Norway 61°55N 9°44E 164 C6
Ronde, Pt. Dominica 15°33N 61°29W 323 k
Ronde I. Grenada 12°29N 61°36W 323 q
Rondebosch S. Africa 33°58S 18°28E 118 A1
Rondón Colombia 6°17N 71°6W 328 B3
Rondônia Brazil 10°52S 61°57W 331 C5
Rondônia ☐ Brazil 11°0S 63°0W 331 C5
Rondonópolis Brazil 16°28S 54°38W 331 D7
Rondslottet Norway 61°55N 9°45E 164 C6
Rondu Pakistan 35°32N 75°10E 243 B6
Rong, Koh Cambodia 10°45N 103°15E 237 G4
Rong Jiang → China 24°35N 109°20E 228 E7
Rong Xian China 22°50N 110°31E 229 F8
Rong'an China 25°14N 109°22E 228 E7
Rongchang China 29°20N 105°32E 228 C5
Rongcheng China 37°9N 122°23E 227 F12
Ronge, L. la Canada 55°6N 105°17W 297 B7
Rongjiang China 25°57N 108°28E 228 E7
Rongotea N.Z. 40°19S 175°25E 284 G4
Rongshui China 25°5N 109°12E 228 E7
Rongxian China 29°23N 104°22E 228 C5
Rønne Denmark 55°6N 14°43E 163 J8
Ronne Ice Shelf Antarctica 77°30S 60°0W 151 D18
Ronneby Sweden 56°12N 15°17E 163 H9
Ronnebyån → Sweden 56°11N 15°18E 163 H9
Rönneshytta Sweden 58°56N 15°2E 163 F9
Ronsard, C. Australia 24°46S 113°10E 279 D1
Ronse Belgium 50°45N 3°35E 170 D3
Ronuro → Brazil 11°56S 53°33W 331 C7
Roodepoort S. Africa 26°11S 27°54E 271 C4
Roodhouse U.S.A. 39°29N 90°24W 310 E6
Roof Butte U.S.A. 36°28N 109°5W 305 H9
Rooiboklaagte → Namibia 20°50S 21°0E 270 B3
Rooniu, Mt. Tahiti 17°49S 149°12W 289 e
Roopville U.S.A. 33°27N 85°8W 316 B4
Roorkee India 29°52N 77°59E 242 E7
Roosendaal Neths. 51°32N 4°29E 170 C4
Roosevelt U.S.A. 40°18N 109°59W 304 F9
Roosevelt → Brazil 7°35S 60°20W 331 B5
Roosevelt, Mt. Canada 58°26N 125°20W 296 B3
Roosevelt I. Antarctica 79°30S 162°0W 151 D12
Roosevelt Island New York, U.S.A. 132 c3
Ropczyce Poland 50°4N 21°38E 185 H8
Roper → Australia 14°43S 135°27E 280 A2
Roper Bar Australia 14°44S 134°44E 280 A1
Roper River = St. Vidgeon's ✪ Australia 14°47S 134°53E 280 A1
Roppongi Tokyo, Japan 140 c3
Roque Pérez Argentina 35°25S 59°24W 334 D4
Roquefort France 44°2N 0°20W 174 D3
Roquemaure France 44°3N 4°48E 175 D8
Roquetas de Mar Spain 36°46N 2°36W 197 J2
Roquetes Spain 40°50N 0°30E 196 E5
Roquevaire France 43°20N 5°36E 175 E9
Roraima ☐ Brazil 2°0N 61°30W 329 C5
Roraima, Mt. Venezuela 5°10N 60°40W 329 B5
Røros Norway 62°35N 11°23E 164 B8
Rorschach Switz. 47°28N 9°28E 179 H5
Ros Comáin = Roscommon Ireland 53°38N 8°11W 166 C3
Rosa Zambia 9°33S 31°15E 269 D3
Rosa, C. Algeria 37°0N 8°16E 261 A6
Rosa, C. Galápagos Is., Ecuador 1°4S 91°10W 330 a
Rosa, Monte Europe 45°57N 7°53E 198 C4
Rosais, Pta. dos Azores 38°45N 28°19W 153 d1
Rosal de la Frontera Spain 37°59N 7°13W 195 H3
Rosales Phil. 15°54N 120°38E 232 D3
Rosalia U.S.A. 47°14N 117°22W 304 C5
Rosalie Dominica 15°22N 61°16W 323 k
Rosalie → Dominica 15°22N 61°15W 323 k
Rosalind Bank W. Indies 16°30N 80°30W 320 C3
Rosamond U.S.A. 34°52N 118°10W 307 L8
Rosans France 44°24N 5°29E 175 D9
Rosario Argentina 33°0S 60°40W 334 C3
Rosário Maranhão, Brazil 3°0S 44°15W 332 B3
Rosario Baja Calif., Mexico 30°0N 115°50W 318 B1
Rosario Sinaloa, Mexico 22°58N 105°53W 318 C3
Rosario Paraguay 24°30S 57°35W 334 A4
Rosario Agusan del S., Phil. 8°24N 125°59E 233 G5
Rosario Batangas, Phil. 13°50N 121°12E 232 E3
Rosario, Villa del Venezuela 10°19N 72°19W 328 A3
Rosario de la Frontera Argentina 25°50S 65°0W 334 B3
Rosario de Lerma Argentina 24°59S 65°35W 334 A2
Rosario del Tala Argentina 32°20S 59°10W 334 C4
Rosário do Sul Brazil 30°15S 54°55W 335 C5
Rosário Oeste Brazil 14°50S 56°25W 331 C6
Rosarito Mexico 32°20N 117°2W 307 N9
Rosarno Italy 38°29N 15°58E 201 D8
Rosas = Roses Spain 42°19N 3°10E 196 C8
Roscoe Mo., U.S.A. 37°58N 93°48W 310 G3
Roscoe N.Y., U.S.A. 41°56N 74°55W 313 E10
Roscoff France 48°44N 3°56W 172 D3
Roscommon Ireland 53°38N 8°11W 166 C3
Roscommon ☐ Ireland 53°49N 8°23W 166 C3
Roscrea Ireland 52°57N 7°49W 166 D4
Rose → Australia 14°16S 135°45E 280 A2
Rose, L. Bahamas 21°0N 73°30W 321 B5
Rose, L. Fla., U.S.A. 28°32N 81°30W 133 A1
Rose Belle Mauritius 20°24S 57°36E 272 e
Rose Blanche Canada 47°38N 58°45W 299 C8
Rose Bowl U.S.A. 34°9N 118°10W 126 B4
Rose Hall Great House Jamaica 18°31N 77°49W 320 a
Rose Hill = Port Mourant Guyana 6°15N 57°20W 329 B6
Rose Hill Mauritius 20°14S 57°27E 272 e
Rose Hill Va., U.S.A. 38°47N 77°6W 143 C3
Rose Pt. Canada 54°11N 131°39W 296 C2
Rose Rock Grenada 12°24N 61°28W 323 q
Rose Valley Canada 52°19N 103°49W 297 C8
Roseau Dominica 15°17N 61°24W 323 k
Roseau Minn., U.S.A. 48°51N 95°46W 308 A6
Rosebank Gauteng, S. Africa 26°8S 28°2E 123 A2
Rosebank N.Y., U.S.A. 40°36N 74°4W 132 C1
Rosebery N.S.W., Australia 33°55S 151°12E 139 B2
Rosebery Tas., Australia 41°46S 145°33E 281 G4
Rosebud Vic., Australia 38°21S 144°54E 282 E6
Rosebud S. Dak., U.S.A. 43°14N 100°51W 308 D3
Rosebud Tex., U.S.A. 31°4N 96°59W 314 F6
Roseburg U.S.A. 43°13N 123°20W 304 E2
Rosedal La Candelaria Mexico 19°20N 99°10W 128 B2
Rosedale U.S.A. 33°51N 91°2W 315 E9
Rosehearty U.K. 57°42N 2°7W 167 D6
Roseires Res. Sudan 11°51N 34°23E 266 B3
Roseland Calif., U.S.A. 38°25N 122°43W 306 G4
Roseland Ill., U.S.A. 41°42N 87°37W 119 C3
Rosemary Canada 50°46N 112°5W 296 C6
Rosemead U.S.A. 34°4N 118°4W 126 B4
Rosemont Qué., Canada 45°34N 73°33W 130 A2
Rosemont Ill., U.S.A. 41°59N 87°53W 119 B1
Rosenberg = Olesno Poland 50°51N 18°26E 185 H5
Rosenberg = Susz Poland 53°44N 19°20E 184 E6
Rosenberg U.S.A. 29°34N 95°49W 314 G7
Rosenborg Slot Copenhagen, Denmark 118 b2
Rosendaël France 51°3N 2°24E 173 A9
Rosendal Norway 59°59N 6°0E 164 E3
Rosendale U.S.A. 40°4N 94°51W 310 D2
Rosenheim Germany 47°51N 12°7E 179 H8
Rosenthal Germany 52°35N 13°22E 115 A3
Roses Spain 42°19N 3°10E 196 C8
Roses, G. de Spain 42°10N 3°15E 196 C8
Roseto degli Abruzzi Italy 42°41N 14°1E 199 F11
Rosetown Canada 51°35N 107°59W 297 C7
Rosetta = Rashîd Egypt 31°21N 30°22E 256 H7
Rosettenville S. Africa 26°15S 28°3E 123 B2
Roseville Calif., U.S.A. 38°45N 121°17W 306 G5
Roseville Ill., U.S.A. 40°44N 90°40W 310 D6
Roseville Mich., U.S.A. 42°30N 82°56W 312 D2
Roseville Pa., U.S.A. 41°51N 76°57W 313 E8
Rosewell U.K. 55°51N 3°8W 121 B3
Rosewood Australia 27°38S 152°36E 281 D5
Rosherville Dam S. Africa 26°13S 28°6E 123 B2
Roshkhvār Iran 34°58N 59°37E 247 C8
Rosières-en-Santerre France 49°49N 2°42E 173 C9
Rosignano Marittimo Italy 43°24N 10°28E 198 E7
Rosignol Guyana 6°15N 57°30W 329 B6
Roşiori de Vede Romania 44°9N 25°0E 183 F10
Rositsa Bulgaria 43°57N 27°57E 203 C11
Rositsa → Bulgaria 43°10N 25°30E 203 C9
Rösjön Sweden 59°26N 18°0E 139 A2
Roskilde Denmark 55°38N 12°3E 163 J6
Roskovec Albania 40°44N 19°43E 202 F3
Roslags-Näsby Sweden 59°25N 18°2E 139 A2
Roslavl Russia 53°57N 32°55E 188 F7
Roslin U.K. 55°51N 3°11W 121 B3
Roslindale U.S.A. 42°17N 71°7W 116 B2
Rosmaninhal Portugal 39°44N 7°5W 194 F3
Rosmead S. Africa 31°29S 25°8E 270 D4
Røsnæs Denmark 55°44N 10°55E 163 J4
Rosny-sous-Bois France 48°52N 2°30E 134 A4
Rosolini Italy 36°49N 14°57E 201 F7
Rosporden France 47°57N 3°50W 172 E3
Ross Tas., Australia 42°2S 147°30E 281 G4
Ross N.Z. 42°53S 170°49E 285 C5
Ross Béthio Mauritania 16°15N 16°8W 262 B1
Ross Dependency Antarctica 76°0S 170°0W 151 D12
Ross I. Antarctica 77°30S 168°0E 151 D11
Ross Ice Shelf Antarctica 80°0S 180°0E 151 E12
Ross L. U.S.A. 48°44N 121°4W 304 B3
Ross Mhic Thriúin = New Ross Ireland 52°23N 6°57W 166 D5
Ross-on-Wye U.K. 51°54N 2°34W 169 F5
Ross River N. Terr., Australia 23°44S 134°30E 280 C1
Ross River Yukon, Canada 62°30N 131°30W 296 A2
Ross Sea Antarctica 74°0S 178°0E 151 D11
Rossall Pt. U.K. 53°55N 3°3W 168 D4
Rossan Pt. Ireland 54°42N 8°47W 166 B3
Rossano Italy 39°36N 16°39E 201 C9
Rossburn Canada 50°40N 100°49W 297 C8
Rosseau Canada 45°16N 79°39W 312 A5
Rosseau, L. Canada 45°10N 79°35W 312 A5
Rössel = Reszel Poland 54°4N 21°10E 184 D8
Rossel I. Papua N. G. 11°21S 154°9E 286 F8
Rosses, The Ireland 55°2N 8°20W 166 A3
Rossford U.S.A. 41°36N 83°34W 311 C13
Rossignol, L. Canada 52°43N 73°40W 298 B5
Rossignol L. Canada 44°12N 65°10W 299 D6
Rossiya = Russia ■ Eurasia 62°0N 105°0E 215 C11
Rosskreppfjorden Norway 59°4N 7°10E 164 E4
Rossland Canada 49°6N 117°50W 296 D5
Rosslare Ireland 52°17N 6°24W 166 D5
Rosslare Harbour Ireland 52°15N 6°20W 166 D5
Rosslau Germany 51°52N 12°15E 178 D8
Rosslyn U.S.A. 38°53N 77°4W 143 B3
Rossmore Canada 44°8N 77°23W 312 B7
Rosso Mauritania 16°40N 15°45W 262 B1
Rosso, C. France 42°13N 8°32E 175 F12
Rossosh Russia 50°15N 39°28E 189 G10
Rossvatnet Norway 65°45N 14°5E 160 D16
Rossville Ill., U.S.A. 40°23N 87°40W 311 D9
Rossville Ind., U.S.A. 40°25N 86°36W 311 D10
Røst Norway 67°32N 12°10E 160 C15
Rostāq Afghan. 37°7N 69°49E 240 A3
Rosthern Canada 52°40N 106°20W 297 C7
Rostock Germany 54°5N 12°8E 178 A8
Rostov Don, Russia 47°15N 39°45E 189 J10
Rostov Yaroslavl, Russia 57°14N 39°25E 188 D10
Rostov ☐ Russia 48°50N 41°10E 191 F5
Rostrenen France 48°14N 3°21W 172 D3
Roswell Ga., U.S.A. 34°2N 84°22W 316 A5
Roswell N. Mex., U.S.A. 33°24N 104°32W 305 K11
Rosyth U.K. 56°2N 3°25W 121 A1
Rot-Front = Dobropole Ukraine 48°25N 37°2E 189 H9
Rota N. Marianas 14°9N 145°12E 302 a
Rota Spain 36°37N 6°20W 195 J4
Rotan U.S.A. 32°51N 100°28W 314 E4
Rotenburg Hessen, Germany 50°59N 9°44E 178 E5
Rotenburg Niedersachsen, Germany 53°6N 9°25E 178 B5
Roth Germany 49°15N 11°5E 179 F7
Rothaargebirge Germany 51°2N 8°13E 178 D4
Rothaargebirge △ Germany 51°0N 8°15E 178 E4
Rothenburg ob der Tauber Germany 49°23N 10°11E 179 F6
Rother → U.K. 50°59N 0°45E 169 G8
Rothera Antarctica 67°34S 68°8W 151 C17
Rotherham U.K. 53°26N 1°20W 168 D6
Rotherhithe U.K. 51°29N 0°2W 125 B3
Rothes U.K. 57°32N 3°13W 167 D5
Rothesay N.B., Canada 45°23N 66°0W 299 C6
Rothesay Argyll & Bute, U.K. 55°50N 5°3W 167 F3
Rothneusiedl Austria 48°8N 16°23E 142 B2
Rothschmaige Germany 48°14N 11°27E 131 A1
Roti Indonesia 10°50S 123°0E 231 F6
Rotja, Pta. Spain 38°38N 1°35E 206 D2
Rotnes Norway 60°3N 10°51E 164 D7
Roto Australia 33°0S 145°30E 283 B6
Rotoaira, L. N.Z. 39°3S 175°45E 284 F4
Rotoehu, L. N.Z. 38°1S 176°32E 284 E5
Rotoiti, L. Bay of Plenty, N.Z. 38°2S 176°26E 284 E5
Rotoiti, L. W. Coast, N.Z. 41°51S 172°49E 285 B7
Rotoma, L. N.Z. 38°2S 176°35E 284 E5
Rotondo, Mte. France 42°14N 9°8E 175 F13
Rotoroa, L. N.Z. 41°55S 172°39E 285 B7
Rotorua N.Z. 38°9S 176°16E 284 E5
Rotorua, L. N.Z. 38°5S 176°18E 284 E5
Rott → Germany 48°27N 13°25E 179 G9
Rottenburg Germany 48°28N 8°55E 179 G4
Rottenmann Austria 47°31N 14°22E 180 D7
Rotterdam Neths. 51°55N 4°30E 170 C4
Rotterdam N.Y., U.S.A. 42°48N 74°1W 313 D10
Rottne Sweden 57°1N 14°54E 163 G8
Rottnest I. Australia 32°0S 115°27E 279 F2
Rottumeroog Neths. 53°33N 6°34E 170 A6
Rottweil Germany 48°9N 8°37E 179 G4
Rotuma Fiji 12°25S 177°5E 277 C14
Roubaix France 50°40N 3°10E 173 B10
Rouche Island St. Lucia 13°57N 60°52W 323 m
Roudnice nad Labem Czech Rep. 50°25N 14°15E 180 A7
Rouen France 49°27N 1°4E 172 C8
Rouergue France 44°15N 2°0E 174 D5
Rouge Hill Canada 43°48N 79°6W 141 A3
Rough Ridge N.Z. 45°10S 169°55E 285 F4
Rouillac France 45°47N 0°4W 174 C3
Rouissat Algeria 31°55N 5°20E 261 B6
Rouleau Canada 50°10N 104°56W 297 C8
Roulers = Roeselare Belgium 50°57N 3°7E 170 D3
Roulpmaulpma ✪ Australia 23°52S 133°0E 278 D5
Round Hill Jamaica 17°50N 77°23W 320 a
Round Hill St. Kitts & Nevis 17°11N 62°36W 322 d
Round I. China 22°13N 114°11E 122 B2
Round Mountain U.S.A. 38°43N 117°4W 304 G5
Round Mt. Australia 30°26S 152°16E 283 A10
Round Rock U.S.A. 30°31N 97°41W 314 F6
Roundhouse Park Toronto, Canada 141 c2
Roundup U.S.A. 46°27N 108°33W 304 C9
Roura Fr. Guiana 4°44N 52°20W 329 C7
Rousay U.K. 59°10N 3°2W 167 B5
Rouses Point U.S.A. 44°59N 73°22W 313 B11
Rouseville U.S.A. 41°28N 79°42W 312 E5
Rousse = Ruse Bulgaria 43°48N 25°59E 203 C9
Roussenski Lom △ Bulgaria 43°40N 26°10E 203 C10
Roussillac Swamp Trin. & Tob. 10°14N 61°35W 323 t
Roussillon Isère, France 45°24N 4°49E 175 C8
Roussillon Pyrénées-Or., France 42°30N 2°35E 174 F6
Rouxville S. Africa 30°25S 26°50E 270 D4
Rouyn-Noranda Canada 48°20N 79°0W 298 C4
Rovaniemi Finland 66°29N 25°41E 160 C21
Rovato Italy 45°34N 10°0E 198 C7
Rovenki Ukraine 48°5N 39°21E 189 H10
Rovereto Italy 45°53N 11°3E 198 C8
Roverud Norway 60°15N 12°3E 164 D9
Rovigno = Rovinj Croatia 45°5N 13°40E 199 C10
Rovigo Italy 45°4N 11°47E 199 C8
Rovinj Croatia 45°5N 13°40E 199 C10
Rovira Colombia 4°15N 75°20W 328 C2
Rovno = Rivne Ukraine 50°40N 26°10E 177 C14
Rovnoye Russia 50°52N 46°3E 190 E8
Rovuma = Ruvuma → Tanzania 10°29S 40°28E 269 E5
Row'ān Iran 35°8N 48°51E 247 C6
Rowena Australia 29°48S 148°55E 281 D4
Rowley I. Canada 69°6N 77°52W 295 D16
Rowley Shoals Australia 17°30S 119°0E 278 C2
Roxa Guinea-Biss. 11°15N 15°45W 262 C1
Roxas Capiz, Phil. 11°36N 122°49E 233 F4
Roxas Isabela, Phil. 17°8N 121°36E 232 C3
Roxas Mind. Or., Phil. 12°35N 121°31E 232 E3
Roxas Palawan, Phil. 10°20N 119°21E 233 F2
Roxboro U.S.A. 36°24N 78°59W 315 C15
Roxborough Trin. & Tob. 11°15N 60°35W 323 J
Roxburgh N.Z. 45°33S 169°19E 285 F4
Roxbury Mass., U.S.A. 42°19N 71°5W 116 B2
Roxbury N.Y., U.S.A. 42°17N 74°33W 313 D10
Roxbury Pa., U.S.A. 40°6N 77°39W 312 F7
Roxby Downs Australia 30°43S 136°46E 281 E2
Roxen Sweden 58°30N 15°40E 163 F9
Roxeth U.K. 51°33N 0°20W 125 A1
Roy Mont., U.S.A. 47°20N 108°58W 304 C9
Roy N. Mex., U.S.A. 35°57N 104°12W 305 J11
Roy Utah, U.S.A. 41°10N 112°2W 304 F7
Roy Thomson Hall Toronto, Canada 141 b2
Royal △ Australia 34°5S 151°5E 283 C9
Royal Bardia △ Nepal 28°20N 81°20E 243 E9
Royal Botanic Gardens Sydney, Australia 139 b2
Royal Botanic Gardens Edinburgh, U.K. 55°58N 3°12W 121 B2
Royal Canal Ireland 53°30N 7°13W 166 C4
Royal Center U.S.A. 40°52N 86°30W 311 D10
Royal Chitawan △ Nepal 26°30N 84°30E 243 F11
Royal Geographical Society Is. Canada 68°56N 100°15W 294 D11
Royal Leamington Spa U.K. 52°18N 1°31W 169 E6
Royal Manas △ Bhutan 26°45N 90°50E 241 B3
Royal Natal △ S. Africa 28°43S 28°51E 271 C4
Royal Oak U.S.A. 42°30N 83°9W 311 B13
Royal Observatory U.K. 55°55N 3°12W 121 B2
Royal Palace = Koninklijk Paleis Amsterdam, Neths. 112 a2
Royal Palace = Kungliga Slottet Stockholm, Sweden 139 b2
Royal Palace = Palacio Real Madrid, Spain 127 b1
Royal Palace = Palais Royal Brussels, Belgium 116 b3
Royal Palace = Slottet Oslo, Norway 133 a1
Royal Palm Beach U.S.A. 26°42N 80°14W 317 J9
Royal Park Australia 37°46S 144°57E 128 A1
Royal Tunbridge Wells U.K. 51°7N 0°16E 169 F8
Royal Turf Club Bangkok, Thailand 113 b2
Royale, Isle U.S.A. 48°0N 88°54W 308 B9
Royalla Australia 35°30S 149°9E 283 C8
Royan France 45°37N 1°2W 174 C2
Roye France 49°42N 2°48E 173 C9
Röylä Finland 60°18N 24°42E 121 B1
Royston U.K. 52°3N 0°0 169 E7
Rožaj Montenegro 42°50N 20°11E 202 D4
Różan Poland 52°52N 21°25E 185 F8
Rozas, Portilleros de las Spain 40°29N 3°49W 127 B1
Rozay-en-Brie France 48°41N 2°58E 173 D9
Rozdilna Ukraine 46°50N 30°2E 183 D15
Rozhnyativ Ukraine 48°56N 24°9E 183 B9
Rozhyshche Ukraine 50°54N 25°15E 177 C13
Rožmitál pod Třemšínem Czech Rep. 49°36N 13°53E 180 B6
Rožňava Slovak Rep. 48°37N 20°35E 181 C13
Rozogi Poland 53°28N 21°19E 184 E8
Rozoy-sur-Serre France 49°40N 4°8E 173 C11
Roztoczański △ Poland 50°37N 23°0E 185 H10
Roztoky Czech Rep. 50°9N 14°23E 135 B2
Rozzano Italy 45°22N 9°10E 129 B1
Rrëshen Albania 41°47N 19°49E 202 E3
Rrogozhine Albania 41°4N 19°50E 202 E3
Rtanj Serbia 43°45N 21°50E 202 C5
Rtem, O. er → Algeria 33°29N 5°38E 261 B6
Rtishchevo Russia 52°18N 43°46E 190 D6
Rúa = A Rúa Spain 42°24N 7°6W 194 C3
Ruacaná Namibia 17°27S 14°21E 265 F2
Ruaha △ Tanzania 7°41S 34°30E 268 D3
Ruahine Ra. N.Z. 39°55S 176°2E 284 F5
Ruamahanga → N.Z. 41°24S 175°8E 284 H4
Ruapehu N.Z. 39°17S 175°35E 284 F4
Ruapuke I. N.Z. 46°46S 168°31E 285 G3
Ruâq, W. → Egypt 30°0N 33°49E 251 J4
Ruatoria N.Z. 37°55S 178°20E 284 D7
Ruavatu Solomon Is. 9°26S 160°26E 287 M11
Ruawai N.Z. 36°8S 173°59E 284 C2
Rub' al Khālī Si. Arabia 19°0N 48°0E 249 C5
Rubeho Mts. Tanzania 6°50S 36°25E 268 D4
Rubezhnoye = Rubizhne Ukraine 49°6N 38°25E 189 H10
Rubh a' Mhail U.K. 55°56N 6°8W 167 F2
Rubha Hunish U.K. 57°42N 6°20W 167 D2
Rubha Robhanais = Lewis, Butt of U.K. 58°31N 6°16W 167 C2
Rubí Spain 41°29N 2°2E 196 D7
Rubi → Dem. Rep. of the Congo 2°48N 23°54E 264 B4
Rubí → Barcelona, Spain 41°25N 2°0E 114 A1
Rubiataba Brazil 15°8S 49°48W 333 E2
Rubicon → U.S.A. 38°53N 121°4W 306 G5
Rubicone → Italy 44°8N 12°28E 199 D9
Rubik Albania 41°46N 19°47E 202 E3
Rubinéia Brazil 20°13S 51°2W 333 F1
Rubino Ivory C. 6°4N 4°18W 262 D4
Rubio Venezuela 7°43N 72°22W 328 B3
Rubizhne Ukraine 49°6N 38°25E 189 H10
Rublovo Russia 55°47N 37°21E 129 B2
Rubondo △ Tanzania 2°18S 31°58E 268 C3
Rubtsovsk Russia 51°30N 81°10E 217 B10
Ruby U.S.A. 64°45N 155°30W 303 D9
Ruby Beach = Jacksonville Beach U.S.A. 30°17N 81°24W 316 E8
Ruby L. U.S.A. 40°10N 115°28W 304 F6
Ruby Mts. U.S.A. 40°30N 115°20W 304 F6
Rubyvale Australia 23°25S 147°42E 280 C4
Rucheng China 25°33N 113°38E 229 E9
Ruciane-Nida Poland 53°40N 21°32E 184 E8
Rūd Sar Iran 37°8N 50°18E 247 B6
Ruda Sweden 57°6N 16°7E 163 G10
Ruda Śląska Poland 50°16N 18°50E 185 H5
Rudall Australia 33°43S 136°17E 282 B2
Rudall → Australia 22°34S 122°13E 278 D3
Rudall River △ Australia 22°38S 122°30E 278 D3
Rūdbār Afghan. 30°9N 62°36E 240 C1
Rudbar Iran 36°48N 49°23E 247 B6
Rüdersdorf Germany 52°27N 13°47E 178 C9
Rudewa Tanzania 10°7S 34°40E 269 E3
Rudkøbing Denmark 54°56N 10°41E 163 K4
Rudky Ukraine 49°38N 23°29E 185 J10
Rudna Poland 51°30N 16°17E 185 G3
Rudnevka → Russia 55°43N 37°56E 129 B3
Rudnik Bulgaria 42°36N 27°30E 203 D11
Rudnik Poland 50°26N 22°15E 185 H9
Rudnik Serbia 44°7N 20°35E 202 B4
Rudnya Russia 54°55N 31°7E 188 E6
Rudnytsa Ukraine 48°16N 29°54E 183 B13
Rudnyy Kazakhstan 52°57N 63°7E 216 B6
Rudo Bos.-H. 43°41N 19°23E 182 G4
Rudolfa, Ostrov Russia 81°45N 58°30E 214 A6
Rudolfsheim Austria 48°12N 16°20E 142 A2
Rudolfshöhe Germany 52°37N 13°44E 115 A5
Rudolstadt Germany 50°44N 11°19E 178 E7
Rudong China 32°20N 121°12E 229 A13
Rudow Germany 52°24N 13°29E 115 B3
Rudozem Bulgaria 41°29N 24°51E 203 E8
Rudyard U.S.A. 46°14N 84°36W 309 B11
Rue France 50°15N 1°40E 173 B8
Rueil-Malmaison France 48°52N 2°11E 134 A2
Ruenya → Africa 16°24S 33°48E 269 F3
Rufa'a Sudan 14°44N 33°22E 257 E3
Rufflin U.S.A. 33°0N 80°49W 316 B9
Ruffling Pt. Br. Virgin Is. 18°44N 64°27W 321 b
Rufiji → Tanzania 7°50S 39°15E 268 D4
Rufino Argentina 34°20S 62°50W 334 C3
Rufisque Senegal 14°40N 17°15W 262 C1
Rufunsa Zambia 15°4S 29°34E 269 F2
Rugao China 32°23N 120°31E 229 A13
Rugby Warks., U.K. 52°23N 1°16W 169 E6
Rugby N. Dak., U.S.A. 48°22N 100°0W 308 A4
Rügen Germany 54°22N 13°24E 178 A9
Rügen △ Germany 54°25N 13°25E 178 A9
Rugles France 48°50N 0°40E 172 D7
Ruhea Bangla. 26°10N 88°25E 241 B2
Ruhengeri Rwanda 1°30S 29°36E 268 C2
Ruhla Germany 50°54N 10°23E 178 E6
Ruhland Germany 51°27N 13°51E 178 D9
Ruhnu Estonia 57°48N 23°15E 184 A10
Ruhr → Germany 51°27N 6°43E 178 D2
Ruhuhu → Tanzania 10°31S 34°34E 269 E3
Rui Barbosa Brazil 12°18S 40°27W 333 D3
Rui'an China 27°47N 120°40E 229 D13
Ruichang China 29°40N 115°39E 229 C10
Ruidoso U.S.A. 33°20N 105°41W 305 K11
Ruijin China 25°48N 116°0E 229 E10
Ruili China 24°1N 97°43E 228 E1
Ruisbroek Belgium 50°47N 4°18E 116 B1
Ruislip U.K. 51°34N 0°24W 125 A1
Ruivo, Pico Madeira 32°45N 16°56W 153 c
Ruj Bulgaria 42°52N 22°34E 202 D6
Rujen Macedonia 42°9N 22°30E 202 D6
Rujm Tal'at al Jamā'ah Jordan 30°24N 35°30E 251 H6
Ruk Pakistan 27°50N 68°42E 242 F3
Rukan-sho Japan 26°6N 127°32E 288 a
Rukhla Pakistan 32°27N 71°57E 242 C4
Rukwa ☐ Tanzania 7°0S 31°30E 268 D3
Rukwa, L. Tanzania 8°0S 32°20E 268 D3
Rulenge Burundi 2°43S 30°37E 268 C3
Rulhieres, C. Australia 13°56S 127°22E 278 B4
Rum = Rhum U.K. 57°0N 6°20W 167 E2
Rum Jordan 29°39N 35°26E 251 J6
Rum Cay Bahamas 23°40N 74°58W 321 B5
Rum Jungle Australia 13°0S 130°59E 278 B5
Ruma Serbia 45°0N 19°50E 182 E4
Ruma △ Kenya 0°39S 34°18E 268 C3
Rumāḥ Si. Arabia 25°29N 47°10E 246 E5
Rumah Kulit Malaysia 2°9N 114°14E 235 B4
Rumania = Romania ■ Europe 46°0N 25°0E 183 D10

Rumaylah *Iraq* 30°47N 47°37E **246** D5
Rumaylah, 'Urūq ar *Si. Arabia* 22°0N 48°30E **249** B5
Rumbêk *South Sudan* 6°54N 29°37E **257** F2
Rumburk *Czech Rep.* 50°57N 14°32E **180** A7
Rumelihisarı *Turkey* 41°4N 29°2E **122** B2
Rumford *U.S.A.* 44°33N 70°33W **313** B14
Rumia *Poland* 54°37N 18°25E **184** D5
Rumilly *France* 45°53N 5°56E **175** C9
Rummelsburg = Miastko *Poland* 54°0N 16°58E **184** E3
Rumoi *Japan* 43°56N 141°39E **220** C10
Rumonge *Burundi* 3°59S 29°26E **268** C2
Rumphi *Malaysia* 11°1S 33°52E **269** E3
Rumson *U.S.A.* 40°23N 74°0W **313** F11
Rumung *Micronesia* 9°37N 138°9E **287** R16
Rumuruti *Kenya* 0°17N 36°32E **268** B4
Rumyantsevo *Russia* 55°38N 37°25E **129** C2
Runan *China* 33°0N 114°30E **226** H8
Runanga *N.Z.* 42°25S 171°15E **285** C6
Runaway, C. *N.Z.* 37°32S 177°59E **284** D6
Runaway B. *Antigua & B.* 17°9N 61°51W **322** b
Runaway Bay *Jamaica* 18°27N 77°20W **320** a
Runcorn *U.K.* 53°21N 2°44W **168** D5
Rundu *Namibia* 17°52S 19°43E **270** A2
Rungis *France* 48°44N 2°20E **134** B3
Rungwa *Tanzania* 6°55S 33°32E **268** D3
Rungwa → *Tanzania* 7°36S 31°50E **268** D3
Rungwa △ *Tanzania* 6°53S 34°2E **268** D3
Rungwe *Tanzania* 9°11S 33°32E **269** D3
Runka *Nigeria* 12°28N 7°20E **263** C6
Runn *Sweden* 60°30N 15°40E **162** D9
Runton Ra. *Australia* 23°31S 123°6E **278** D3
Runu *Micronesia* 9°35N 138°8E **287** R16
Ruo Shui → *China* 41°0N 100°16E **218** C9
Ruokolahti *Finland* 61°17N 28°50E **188** B5
Ruoqiang *China* 38°55N 88°10E **217** E11
Rupa *India* 27°15N 92°21E **241** B4
Rupar *India* 31°2N 76°38E **242** D7
Rupat *Indonesia* 1°45N 101°40E **234** B2
Rupea *Romania* 46°2N 25°13E **183** D10
Rupen → *India* 23°28N 71°31E **242** H4
Rupert *U.S.A.* 42°37N 113°41W **304** E7
Rupert → *Canada* 51°29N 78°45W **298** B4
Rupert B. *Canada* 51°35N 79°0W **298** B4
Rupert House = Waskaganish *Canada* 51°30N 78°40W **298** B4
Rupsa *India* 21°37N 87°1E **243** J12
Rupununi → *Guyana* 4°3N 58°35W **329** C6
Rur → *Germany* 51°11N 5°59E **178** D1
Rurópolis *Brazil* 4°3S 54°59W **329** D7
Rurrenabaque *Bolivia* 14°30S 67°32W **330** C4
Rurutu *French Polynesia* 22°26S 151°20W **289** f
Rus → *Spain* 39°30N 2°30W **197** F2
Rusāfa *Iraq* 33°21N 44°23E **113** A2
Rusambo *Zimbabwe* 16°30S 32°4E **269** F3
Rusape *Zimbabwe* 18°35S 32°8E **269** F3
Ruschuk = Ruse *Bulgaria* 43°48N 25°59E **203** C9
Ruse *Bulgaria* 43°48N 25°59E **203** C9
Ruse □ *Bulgaria* 43°35N 25°40E **203** C9
Ruşeţu *Romania* 44°57N 27°14E **183** F12
Rush *Ireland* 53°31N 6°6W **166** C5
Rush Green *U.K.* 51°33N 0°10E **125** A5
Rushan *China* 36°56N 121°30E **227** F11
Rushden *U.K.* 52°18N 0°35W **169** E7
Rushikulya → *India* 19°23N 85°5E **244** E7
Rushmore, Mt. *U.S.A.* 43°53N 103°28W **308** D2
Rushville *Ill., U.S.A.* 40°7N 90°34W **310** D6
Rushville *Ind., U.S.A.* 39°37N 85°27W **311** E11
Rushville *Nebr., U.S.A.* 42°43N 102°28W **308** D2
Rushworth *Australia* 36°32S 145°1E **283** D6
Ruskin *U.S.A.* 27°43N 82°26W **317** H7
Russa *India* 22°29N 88°21E **124** C2
Russas *Brazil* 4°55S 37°50W **332** B4
Russell *Man., Canada* 50°50N 101°20W **297** C8
Russell *N.Z.* 35°16S 174°10E **284** B3
Russell *Fla., U.S.A.* 30°3N 81°45W **316** E8
Russell *Kans., U.S.A.* 38°54N 98°52W **308** F4
Russell *N.Y., U.S.A.* 44°27N 75°9W **313** B9
Russell *Pa., U.S.A.* 41°56N 79°8W **312** E5
Russell Cave △ *U.S.A.* 34°59N 85°49W **315** D12
Russell Is. *Solomon Is.* 9°4S 159°12E **287** M10
Russell L. *Man., Canada* 56°15N 101°30W **297** B8
Russell L. *N.W.T., Canada* 63°5N 115°44W **296** A5
Russellkonda *India* 19°57N 84°42E **244** E7
Russells Point *U.S.A.* 40°28N 83°54W **311** D13
Russellville *Ala., U.S.A.* 34°30N 87°44W **315** D11
Russellville *Ark., U.S.A.* 35°17N 93°8W **314** D8
Russellville *Ky., U.S.A.* 36°51N 86°53W **308** G10
Rüsselsheim *Germany* 49°59N 8°23E **179** F4
Russi *Italy* 44°22N 12°2E **199** D9
Russia ■ *Eurasia* 62°0N 105°0E **215** C11
Russian → *U.S.A.* 38°27N 123°8W **306** G3
Russian Hill *San Francisco, U.S.A.* **136** a1
Russian Mission *U.S.A.* 61°47N 161°19W **303** F7
Russiaville *U.S.A.* 40°25N 86°16W **311** D10
Rust *Austria* 47°49N 16°42E **181** D9
Rustam Shahr *Pakistan* 26°58N 66°6E **242** F2
Rustavi *Georgia* 41°30N 45°0E **191** K7
Rustenburg *S. Africa* 25°41S 27°14E **270** C4
Ruston *U.S.A.* 32°32N 92°38W **314** E8
Rutana *Burundi* 3°55S 30°0E **268** C3
Rute *Spain* 37°19N 4°23W **195** H6
Ruteng *Indonesia* 8°35S 120°30E **231** F6
Rutenga *Zimbabwe* 21°15S 30°44E **269** G3
Ruth *U.S.A.* 43°42N 82°45W **312** C2
Rutherford *Calif., U.S.A.* 38°26N 122°24W **306** G4
Rutherford *N.J., U.S.A.* 40°49N 74°6W **132** B1
Rutherglen *Australia* 36°5S 146°29E **283** D7
Rutland *U.S.A.* 43°37N 72°58W **313** C12
Rutland □ *U.K.* 52°38N 0°40W **169** E7
Rutland I. *India* 11°25N 92°10E **245** J11
Rutland Water *U.K.* 52°39N 0°38W **169** E7
Rutledalen *Norway* 61°4N 5°10E **164** C2
Rutledge *U.S.A.* 33°38N 83°37W **316** B6
Rutledge → *Canada* 61°4N 112°0W **297** A6
Rutledge L. *Canada* 61°33N 110°47W **297** A6
Rutog *China* 33°27N 79°42E **217** F9
Rutqa, W. → *Syria* 34°30N 41°3E **213** E9
Rutshuru *Dem. Rep. of the Congo* 1°13S 29°25E **268** C2
Ruvo di Púglia *Italy* 41°7N 16°29E **201** A9
Ruvu *Tanzania* 6°49S 38°43E **268** D4
Ruvu → *Tanzania* 6°23S 38°52E **268** D4
Ruvuba △ *Burundi* 3°3S 29°33E **268** C2
Ruvuma □ *Tanzania* 10°20S 36°0E **269** E4
Ruvuma → *Tanzania* 10°29S 40°28E **269** E5
Ruwais *U.A.E.* 24°5N 52°50E **247** E7
Ruwenzori *Africa* 0°30N 29°55E **268** B2
Ruwenzori △ *Uganda* 0°20N 30°0E **268** B2
Ruya → *Zimbabwe* 16°27S 32°5E **271** A5
Ruyang *China* 34°9N 112°27E **226** G7
Ruyigi *Burundi* 3°29S 30°15E **268** C3
Ruyuan *China* 24°46N 113°16E **229** E9
Rŭzaevka *Kazakhstan* 52°49N 66°56E **217** B7
Ruzayevka *Russia* 54°4N 45°0E **190** C7
Rŭzhevo Konare *Bulgaria* 42°23N 24°46E **203** D8
Ruzhou *China* 34°11N 112°52E **226** G7
Ružomberok *Slovak Rep.* 49°3N 19°17E **181** B12
Ruzyně *Czech Rep.* 50°5N 14°17E **135** B1
Ruzyne, Praha ✈ (PRG) *Czech Rep.* 50°6N 14°16E **135** B1
Rwanda ■ *Africa* 2°0S 30°0E **268** C3
Ryakhovo *Bulgaria* 43°58N 26°18E **203** C10
Ryan, L. *U.K.* 55°0N 5°2W **167** G3
Ryazan *Russia* 54°40N 39°40E **188** E10
Ryazan □ *Russia* 54°5N 39°30E **190** C4
Ryazhsk *Russia* 53°45N 40°3E **188** F11
Rybachiy *Russia* 55°10N 20°50E **184** C7
Rybachiy Poluostrov *Russia* 69°43N 32°0E **160** B25
Rybachye = Balykchy *Kyrgyzstan* 42°26N 76°12E **217** D9
Rybatskaya *Russia* 59°50N 30°29E **137** B2
Rybinsk *Russia* 58°5N 38°50E **188** C10
Rybinskoye Vdkhr. *Russia* 58°30N 38°25E **188** C10
Rybnik *Poland* 50°6N 18°32E **185** H5
Rybnitsa = Râbniţa *Moldova* 47°45N 29°0E **183** C14
Rybnoye *Russia* 54°45N 39°30E **188** E10
Rychnov nad Kněžnou *Czech Rep.* 50°10N 16°17E **181** A9
Rychwał *Poland* 52°4N 18°10E **185** F5
Rycroft *Canada* 55°45N 118°40W **296** B5
Ryd *Sweden* 56°27N 14°42E **163** H8
Rydaholm *Sweden* 56°59N 14°18E **163** H8
Rydboholm *Sweden* 59°26N 18°12E **139** A3
Ryde *N.S.W., Australia* 33°48S 151°6E **139** A1
Ryde *I. of W., U.K.* 50°43N 1°9W **169** G6
Ryderwood *U.S.A.* 46°23N 123°3W **306** D3
Rydzyna *Poland* 51°47N 16°39E **185** G3
Rye *U.K.* 50°57N 0°45E **169** G8
Rye → *U.K.* 54°11N 0°44W **168** C7
Rye Bay *U.K.* 50°52N 0°49E **169** G8
Rye Patch Res. *U.S.A.* 40°28N 118°19W **304** F4
Ryegate *U.S.A.* 46°18N 109°15W **304** C9
Ryerson University *Toronto, Canada* **141** a3
Ryfylke *Norway* 59°25N 6°25E **164** E3
Rykene *Norway* 58°24N 8°37E **164** F5
Ryki *Poland* 51°38N 21°56E **185** G8
Rykovo = Yenakiyeve *Ukraine* 48°15N 38°15E **189** H10
Ryley *Canada* 53°17N 112°26W **296** C6
Rylsk *Russia* 51°36N 34°43E **189** G8
Rylstone *Australia* 32°46S 149°58E **283** B8
Rymanów *Poland* 49°35N 21°51E **185** J8
Ryn *Poland* 53°57N 21°34E **184** E8
Ryn Peski = Naryn Qum *Kazakhstan* 47°30N 49°0E **191** G9
Ryogoku *Japan* 35°40N 139°48E **140** A3
Ryōhaku-Sanchi *Japan* 36°9N 136°49E **223** A8
Ryojun = Lüshun *China* 38°45N 121°15E **227** E11
Ryōtsu *Japan* 38°5N 138°26E **220** E9
Rypin *Poland* 53°3N 19°25E **185** E6
Ryssby *Sweden* 56°52N 14°10E **163** H8
Rysy *Europe* 49°10N 20°4E **181** B13
Ryūgasaki *Japan* 35°54N 140°11E **223** B12
Ryukyu Is. = Ryūkyū-Rettō *Japan* 26°0N 126°0E **221** M3
Ryūkyū-Rettō *Japan* 26°0N 126°0E **221** M3
Ryūō *Japan* 35°42N 138°30E **223** B10
Rzepin *Poland* 52°20N 14°49E **185** F1
Rzeszów *Poland* 50°5N 21°58E **185** H8
Rzhev *Russia* 56°20N 34°20E **188** D8
Rzhevka *Russia* 59°59N 30°31E **137** B3

S

Sa Cabaneta *Spain* 39°37N 2°45E **206** B3
Sa Canal *Spain* 38°51N 1°23E **206** D1
Sa Conillera *Spain* 38°59N 1°13E **206** D1
Sa Dec *Vietnam* 10°20N 105°46E **237** G5
Sa Dragonera *Spain* 39°35N 2°19E **206** B3
Sa Kaeo *Thailand* 13°49N 102°4E **236** F4
Sa-koi *Burma* 19°54N 97°3E **241** F6
Sa Mesquida *Spain* 39°55N 4°16E **206** B5
Sa Pa *Vietnam* 22°20N 103°47E **236** A4
Sa Pobla *Spain* 39°46N 3°1E **206** B4
Sa Savina *Spain* 38°44N 1°25E **206** D1
Sa'a *Solomon Is.* 9°43S 161°35E **287** M11
Sa'ādatābād *Fārs, Iran* 30°10N 53°5E **247** D7
Sa'ādatābād *Hormozgān, Iran* 28°3N 55°53E **247** D7
Sa'ādatābād *Kermān, Iran* 29°40N 55°51E **247** D7
Sa'ādatābād *Tehrān, Iran* 35°47N 51°22E **141** A2
Saadūn *Iraq* 33°19N 44°25E **113** B2
Saale → *Germany* 51°56N 11°54E **178** D7
Saaler Bodden *Germany* 54°20N 12°27E **178** A8
Saalfeld *Germany* 50°38N 11°21E **178** E7
Saalfelden *Austria* 47°25N 12°51E **180** D5
Saane → *Switz.* 47°8N 7°10E **179** H3
Saanich *Canada* 48°29N 123°26W **306** B3
Saar → *Europe* 49°41N 6°32E **170** E6
Saar-Hunsrück △ *Germany* 49°30N 6°50E **179** F2
Saar in Mähren = Žďár nad Sázavou *Czech Rep.* 49°34N 15°57E **180** B8
Saarbrücken *Germany* 49°14N 6°59E **179** F2
Saarburg *Germany* 49°36N 6°32E **179** F2
Saaremaa *Estonia* 58°30N 22°30E **188** C2
Saarijärvi *Finland* 62°43N 25°16E **160** E21
Saarland □ *Germany* 49°20N 7°0E **179** F2
Saarlautern = Saarlouis *Germany* 49°18N 6°45E **179** F2
Saarlouis *Germany* 49°18N 6°45E **179** F2
Saatlı *Azerbaijan* 39°55N 48°22E **213** C13
Saavedra *Argentina* 34°33S 58°29W **117** B2
Saaz = Žatec *Czech Rep.* 50°20N 13°32E **180** A6
Sab 'Ābar *Syria* 33°46N 37°41E **212** F7
Saba *W. Indies* 17°38N 63°14W **322** a
Šabac *Serbia* 44°48N 19°42E **202** B3
Sabadell *Spain* 41°28N 2°7E **196** D7
Sabae *Japan* 35°57N 136°11E **223** B8
Sabah □ *Malaysia* 6°0N 117°0E **235** A5
Şabāḩ, Wadi → *Si. Arabia* 23°50N 48°30E **249** B5
Sabak Bernam *Malaysia* 3°46N 100°58E **237** L3
Sabalān, Kūhhā-ye *Iran* 38°15N 47°45E **213** C12
Sabalana, Kepulauan *Indonesia* 6°45S 118°50E **231** F5
Sabalana, Kepulauan *Indonesia* 6°45S 118°49E **235** D5
Sabana, Arch. de *Cuba* 23°0N 80°0W **320** B3
Sábana de la Mar *Dom. Rep.* 19°7N 69°24W **321** C6
Sabana Grande *Puerto Rico* 18°5N 66°58W **321** b
Sabana Westpunt = Westpunt *Curaçao* 12°22N 69°10W **322** g
Sabanalarga *Colombia* 10°38N 74°55W **328** A3
Sabaneta Pt. *N. Marianas* 15°17N 145°49E **302** e
Sabang *Indonesia* 5°50N 95°15E **234** A1
Şabanözü *Turkey* 40°28N 33°16E **212** B5
Săbăoani *Romania* 47°1N 26°51E **183** C11
Sabari → *India* 17°35N 81°16E **244** F5
Sabarmati → *India* 22°18N 72°22E **242** H5
Sab'atayn, Ramlat as *Yemen* 15°30N 46°10E **248** D4
Sabattis *U.S.A.* 44°6N 74°40W **313** B10
Sabáudia *Italy* 41°18N 13°1E **200** A6
Sabaya *Bolivia* 19°1S 68°23W **330** D4
Şābīyā, Jaza'ir *Si. Arabia* 18°35N 41°3E **248** C3
Saberania *Indonesia* 2°5S 138°18E **231** E9
Sabhā *Libya* 27°9N 14°29E **258** C2
Sabi → *India* 28°29N 76°44E **242** E7
Sabi Game Reserve = Kruger △ *S. Africa* 24°50S 26°10E **271** B4
Sabidana, J. *Sudan* 18°4N 36°50E **256** D4
Sabie *S. Africa* 25°10S 30°48E **271** C5
Sabina *U.S.A.* 39°29N 83°38W **311** E13
Sabinal *Chihuahua, Mexico* 30°57N 107°30W **318** A3
Sabinal *Tex., U.S.A.* 29°19N 99°28W **314** G5
Sabiñánigo *Spain* 42°31N 0°22W **196** C4
Sabinar, Punta del *Spain* 36°43N 2°44W **197** J2
Sabinas *Mexico* 27°51N 101°7W **318** B4
Sabinas → *Mexico* 27°37N 100°42W **318** B4
Sabinas Hidalgo *Mexico* 26°30N 100°10W **318** B4
Sabine → *U.S.A.* 29°59N 93°47W **314** G8
Sabine L. *U.S.A.* 29°53N 93°51W **314** G8
Sabine Pass *U.S.A.* 29°44N 93°54W **314** G8
Sabinópolis *Brazil* 18°40S 43°6W **333** E3
Sabinov *Slovak Rep.* 49°6N 21°5E **181** B14
Sabirabad *Azerbaijan* 40°5N 48°30E **191** K9
Sabka *Chad* 19°15N 16°35E **259** E3
Sablayan *Phil.* 12°50N 120°50E **232** E3
Sable *Canada* 55°30N 68°21W **299** A6
Sable, C. *N.S., Canada* 43°29N 65°38W **299** D6
Sable, C. *Fla., U.S.A.* 25°9N 81°8W **317** K8
Sable I. *N.S., Canada* 44°0N 60°0W **299** D8
Sable I. *Papua N. G.* 3°38S 154°42E **286** B8
Sablé-sur-Sarthe *France* 47°50N 0°20W **172** E6
Saboeiro *Brazil* 6°32S 39°54W **332** C4
Saboli *India* 28°42N 77°18E **120** A2
Sabonkafi *Niger* 14°40N 8°45E **259** F1
Sabor → *Portugal* 41°10N 7°7W **194** D3
Sabou *Burkina Faso* 12°1N 2°15W **262** C4
Şabrātah *Libya* 32°47N 12°29E **258** B2
Sabres *France* 44°9N 0°43W **174** D3
Sabrina Coast *Antarctica* 68°0S 120°0E **151** C9
Sabtang I. *Phil.* 20°19N 121°52E **232** A3
Sabugal *Portugal* 40°20N 7°5W **194** E3
Sabugo *Portugal* 38°49N 9°17W **126** A1
Sabula *U.S.A.* 42°4N 90°10W **310** B6
Sabulubek *Indonesia* 1°36S 98°40E **234** C1
Sabuncu *Turkey* 39°33N 30°12E **205** B12
Şabyā *Si. Arabia* 17°9N 42°37E **248** C3
Sabzevār *Iran* 36°15N 57°40E **247** B8
Sabzi Mand *India* 28°40N 77°12E **120** A2
Sabzvārān = Jīroft *Iran* 28°45N 57°50E **247** D8
Sac City *U.S.A.* 42°25N 95°0W **310** B2
Sacaolo *Angola* 12°58S 22°28E **265** E4
Sacandica *Angola* 6°0S 15°57E **265** D3
Sacatengo *Angola* 13°16S 21°20E **265** E4
Sacavém *Portugal* 38°47N 9°5W **126** A2
Sacedón *Spain* 40°29N 2°41W **196** E2
Săcele *Romania* 45°37N 25°41E **183** E10
Sacheon *S. Korea* 35°0N 128°6E **224** E4
Sachigo → *Canada* 55°6N 88°58W **298** A2
Sachigo, L. *Canada* 53°50N 92°12W **298** B1
Sachimbo *Angola* 9°14S 20°16E **265** D4
Sachin *India* 21°5N 72°53E **244** D1
Sachkhere *Georgia* 42°25N 43°28E **191** J6
Sachsen □ *Germany* 50°55N 13°10E **178** E9
Sachsen-Anhalt □ *Germany* 52°0N 12°0E **178** D7
Sächsische Schweiz △ *Germany* 50°55N 14°10E **178** E10
Sacile *Italy* 45°57N 12°30E **199** C9
Sackets Harbor *U.S.A.* 43°57N 76°7W **313** C8
Sackville *Canada* 45°54N 64°22W **299** C7
Saclay *France* 48°43N 2°10E **134** B2
Saclay, Étang de *France* 48°44N 2°9E **134** B1
Saco *Maine, U.S.A.* 43°30N 70°27W **313** C14
Saco *Mont., U.S.A.* 48°28N 107°21W **304** B10
Sacol I. *Phil.* 6°58N 122°13E **233** H4
Sacomã *Brazil* 23°36S 46°35W **137** B2
Sacramento = Itatupã *Brazil* 0°37S 51°12W **329** D7
Sacramento *Brazil* 19°53S 47°27W **333** E2
Sacramento *Calif., U.S.A.* 38°35N 121°29W **306** G5
Sacramento → *U.S.A.* 38°3N 121°56W **306** G5
Sacramento Mts. *U.S.A.* 32°30N 105°30W **305** K11
Sacramento Valley *U.S.A.* 39°30N 122°0W **306** G5
Sacratif, C. *Spain* 36°42N 3°28W **195** J7
Sacré Cœur *Paris, France* **134** a4
Sacrow *Germany* 52°25N 13°6E **115** B1
Sacrower See *Germany* 52°26N 13°6E **115** B1
Săcueni *Romania* 47°20N 22°5E **182** C7
Sada *Mayotte* 12°51S 45°6E **272** b
Sada *Spain* 43°22N 8°15W **194** B2
Sada-Misaki *Japan* 33°20N 132°5E **222** D4
Sada-Misaki-Hantō *Japan* 33°22N 132°1E **222** D4
Sádaba *Spain* 42°19N 1°12W **196** C3
Sadabad *India* 27°27N 78°3E **242** F8
Şa'dah *Yemen* 16°15N 43°37E **248** C3
Sadang *S. Korea* 37°29N 126°58E **137** C1
Sadani *Tanzania* 5°58S 38°35E **268** D4
Sadani △ *Tanzania* 6°3S 38°47E **268** D4
Sadao *Thailand* 6°38N 100°26E **237** J3
Sadar Bazar *Delhi, India* **120** a1
Sadaseopet *India* 17°38N 77°59E **244** F3
Sadd el Aali *Egypt* 23°54N 32°54E **256** C3
Saddle → *U.S.A.* 40°51N 74°6W **132** A1
Saddle Brook *U.S.A.* 40°54N 74°5W **132** A1
Saddle Hill *St. Kitts & Nevis* 17°7N 62°33W **322** d
Saddle Mt. *U.S.A.* 45°58N 123°41W **306** E3
Saddle Pk. *India* 13°9N 93°1E **245** H11
Saddle Pt. *St. Helena* 15°57S 5°38W **153** h
Sade *Nigeria* 11°22N 10°45E **263** C7
Şadh *Oman* 17°3N 55°4E **249** C6
Sadhoowa *Trin. & Tob.* 10°8N 61°27W **323** t
Sadimi *Dem. Rep. of the Congo* 9°25S 23°32E **265** D4
Sadiola *Mali* 13°50N 11°40W **262** C2
Sadiya *India* 27°50N 95°40E **241** B5
Sa'dīyah, Hawr as *Iraq* 32°15N 46°30E **213** F12
Sadlers *St. Kitts & Nevis* 17°24N 62°47W **322** d
Sado *Japan* 38°0N 138°25E **220** F9
Sado → *Portugal* 38°29N 8°55W **195** G2
Sadon *Russia* 42°52N 43°58E **191** J6
Sadovoye *Russia* 47°47N 44°31E **191** G7
Sadowara *Japan* 32°2N 131°26E **222** E3
Sadr *Pakistan* 24°51N 67°2E **123** A2
Sadr City *Iraq* 33°23N 44°27E **113** A2
Sadra *India* 23°21N 72°43E **242** H5
Sadri *India* 25°11N 73°26E **242** G5
Sadyba *Poland* 52°11N 21°3E **142** B2
Sæbøvik *Norway* 59°47N 5°40E **164** E2
Sæby *Denmark* 57°21N 10°30E **163** G4
Saegertown *U.S.A.* 41°43N 80°9W **312** E4
Saelices *Spain* 39°55N 2°49W **196** F2
Sætre *Norway* 59°41N 10°33E **164** E7
Sævareid *Norway* 60°11N 5°46E **164** D2
Safaalan *Turkey* 41°26N 28°6E **203** E12
Şafājah *Si. Arabia* 26°25N 39°0E **246** E3
Šafárikovo = Tornal'a *Slovak Rep.* 48°25N 20°20E **181** C13
Safata B. *Samoa* 14°0S 171°50W **287** W20
Safdar Jang's Tomb *India* 28°35N 77°12E **120** B2
Safed Koh *Afghan.* 34°0N 70°0E **240** B3
Säffle *Sweden* 59°8N 12°55E **162** E6
Safford *U.S.A.* 32°50N 109°43W **305** K9
Saffron Walden *U.K.* 52°1N 0°16E **169** E8
Safi *Morocco* 32°18N 9°20W **260** B3
Safi □ *Morocco* 32°10N 8°50W **260** B3
Safia *Papua N. G.* 9°35S 148°38E **286** E5
Safia, Hamada *Mali* 23°10N 4°15W **260** D4
Şafīābād *Iran* 36°45N 57°58E **247** B8
Safid Dasht *Iran* 33°27N 48°11E **247** C6
Safid Kūh *Afghan.* 34°45N 63°0E **240** B1
Safid Rūd → *Iran* 37°23N 50°11E **247** B6
Safipur *India* 26°44N 80°21E **243** F9
Şāfītā *Syria* 34°48N 36°7E **250** D7
Safonovo *Russia* 55°4N 33°16E **188** E7
Safranbolu *Turkey* 41°15N 32°41E **212** B5
Saft el Laban *Egypt* 30°1N 31°10E **117** A2
Saft Rashîn *Egypt* 28°58N 30°55E **256** J7
Safune *Samoa* 13°25S 172°21W **287** V19
Şafwān *Iraq* 30°7N 47°43E **246** D5
Sag Harbor *U.S.A.* 41°0N 72°18W **313** F12
Sag Sag *Papua N. G.* 5°32S 148°23E **286** C5
Saga *Kōchi, Japan* 33°5N 133°6E **222** D5
Saga *Saga, Japan* 33°15N 130°16E **222** D2
Saga □ *Japan* 33°15N 130°20E **222** D2
Sagae *Japan* 38°22N 140°17E **220** E10
Sagaing *Burma* 21°52N 95°59E **241** E5
Sagaing □ *Burma* 23°55N 95°56E **241** D5
Sagala *Mali* 14°9N 6°38W **262** C3
Sagami-Nada *Japan* 34°58N 139°30E **223** C11
Sagami-Wan *Japan* 35°15N 139°25E **223** B11
Sagamihara *Japan* 35°33N 139°25E **223** B11
Sagamore *U.S.A.* 40°46N 79°14W **312** F5
Sagan = Żagań *Poland* 51°39N 15°22E **185** G2
Saganaga L. *Canada* 48°14N 90°52W **308** A8
Saganashkee Slough *U.S.A.* 41°41N 87°53W **119** C1
Saganoseki *Japan* 33°15N 131°53E **222** D3
Saganthit Kyun *Burma* 11°56N 98°29E **237** G2
Sagar *Karnataka, India* 16°38N 76°48E **244** F3
Sagar *Karnataka, India* 14°14N 75°6E **245** G2
Sagar *Mad. P., India* 23°50N 78°44E **243** H8
Sagara *Japan* 34°41N 138°12E **223** C10
Sagara, L. *Tanzania* 5°20S 31°0E **268** D3
Sagarejo *Georgia* 41°44N 45°19E **191** K7
Sagarmatha = Everest, Mt. *Nepal* 28°5N 86°58E **243** E12
Sagarmatha △ *Nepal* 27°55N 86°45E **243** F12
Sagavanirktok → *U.S.A.* 70°19N 147°53W **303** A11
Sagay *Phil.* 10°57N 123°25E **233** F4
Sagene *Norway* 59°55N 10°46E **133** A3
Saghîr, El Bahr el → *Egypt* 31°8N 31°54E **251** G2
Sagiada *Greece* 39°38N 20°12E **206** B10
Saginaw *U.S.A.* 43°26N 83°56W **309** D12
Saginaw B. *U.S.A.* 43°50N 83°40W **309** D12
Sagleipie *Liberia* 7°0N 8°52W **262** D3
Saglouc = Salluit *Canada* 62°14N 75°38W **295** E16
Sagone *France* 42°7N 8°42E **175** F12
Sagone, G. de *France* 42°4N 8°40E **175** F12
Sagrada Família, Templo de *Barcelona, Spain* **114** a2
Sagres *Portugal* 37°0N 8°58W **195** J2
Sagu *Burma* 20°13N 94°46E **241** E5
Sagua la Grande *Cuba* 22°50N 80°10W **320** B3
Saguache *U.S.A.* 38°5N 106°8W **304** G10
Saguaro △ *U.S.A.* 32°12N 110°38W **305** K8
Saguenay → *Canada* 48°22N 71°0W **299** C5
Saguia el Hamra → *W. Sahara* 27°24N 13°43W **260** C2
Sagunt *Spain* 39°42N 0°18W **196** F4
Sagunto = Sagunt *Spain* 39°42N 0°18W **196** F4
Sagvåg *Norway* 59°46N 5°25E **164** E2
Sagwara *India* 23°41N 74°1E **242** H6
Sahaba *Sudan* 18°57N 30°25E **256** D3
Sahagún *Colombia* 8°57N 75°27W **328** B2
Sahagún *Spain* 42°18N 5°2W **194** C5
Şaḩam al Jawlān *Syria* 32°45N 35°55E **250** F6
Sahamandrevo *Madag.* 23°15S 45°35E **272** C2
Sahand, Kūh-e *Iran* 37°44N 46°27E **213** D12
Sahar, Mumbai ✈ (BOM) *India* 19°5N 72°51E **130** A2
Sahara *Africa* 23°0N 5°0E **254** D4
Saḩara, G. *Egypt* 28°2N 34°8E **251** K5
Saharan Atlas = Saharien, Atlas *Algeria* 33°30N 1°0E **261** B5
Saharan Seamounts *Atl. Oc.* 25°30N 19°50W **152** D10
Saharanpur *India* 29°58N 77°33E **242** E7
Saharien, Atlas *Algeria* 33°30N 1°0E **261** B5
Saharsa *India* 25°53N 86°36E **243** G12
Sahasinaka *Madag.* 21°49S 47°49E **272** C2
Sahaswan *India* 28°5N 78°45E **243** E8
Saheira, W. el → *Egypt* 30°5N 33°25E **251** F3
Sahel *Africa* 16°0N 5°0E **254** E3
Sahel, Canal du *Mali* 14°20N 6°0W **262** C3
Sahibganj *India* 25°12N 87°40E **243** G12
Şāḩilīyah *Iraq* 33°43N 42°42E **213** F10
Sahiwal *Pakistan* 30°45N 73°8E **242** D5
Şahneh *Iran* 34°29N 47°41E **213** E12
Sahrawi = Western Sahara ■ *Africa* 25°0N 13°0W **260** D2
Sahuaripa *Mexico* 29°3N 109°14W **318** B3
Sahuarita *U.S.A.* 31°57N 110°58W **305** L8
Sahuayo de Diaz *Mexico* 20°4N 102°43W **318** C4
Šahy *Slovak Rep.* 48°4N 18°55E **181** C11
Sai → *India* 25°39N 82°47E **243** G10
Sai Buri *Thailand* 6°43N 101°45E **237** J3
Sai-Cinza *Brazil* 6°17S 57°42W **331** B6
Sai Kung *China* 22°23N 114°16E **122** A2
Sai Thong △ *Thailand* 15°56N 101°10E **236** E3
Sai Wan Ho *China* 22°17N 114°12E **122** B2
Sai Ying Pun *China* 22°17N 114°8E **122** B1
Sai Yok △ *Thailand* 14°25N 98°40E **236** E2
Saibai I. *Australia* 9°25S 142°40E **280** a
Sa'id Bundâs *South Sudan* 8°24N 24°48E **259** G4
Saïda *Algeria* 34°50N 0°11E **261** B5
Saïda □ *Algeria* 34°40N 0°20E **261** B5
Sa'īdābād = Sīrjān *Iran* 29°30N 55°45E **247** D7
Sa'īdābād *Iran* 36°8N 54°11E **247** B7
Saidaiji *Japan* 34°39N 134°2E **222** C6
Saïdia *Morocco* 35°5N 2°14W **261** A4
Sa'īdīyeh *Iran* 36°20N 48°55E **247** B6
Saidor *Papua N. G.* 5°40S 146°29E **286** C4
Saidpur *Bangla.* 25°48N 89°0E **241** C2
Saidpur *India* 25°33N 83°11E **243** G10
Saidu Sharif *Pakistan* 34°43N 72°24E **243** B5
Saignes *France* 45°20N 2°31E **174** C6
Saigō *Japan* 36°12N 133°20E **222** A5
Saigon = Thanh Pho Ho Chi Minh *Vietnam* 10°58N 106°40E **237** G6
Saijō *Japan* 33°55N 133°11E **222** D5
Saikai △ *Japan* 33°12N 129°36E **222** D1
Saikanosy Masoala *Madag.* 15°45S 50°10E **272** B3
Saikhoa Ghat *India* 27°50N 95°40E **241** B5
Saiki *Japan* 32°58N 131°51E **222** E3
Sailana *India* 23°28N 74°55E **242** H6
Saillans *France* 44°42N 5°12E **175** D9
Sailolof *Indonesia* 1°15S 130°46E **231** E8
Sailu *India* 19°28N 76°28E **244** E3
Saimaa *Finland* 61°15N 28°15E **188** B5
Saimbeyli *Turkey* 37°59N 36°6E **212** D7
Saimen = Saimaa *Finland* 61°15N 28°15E **188** B5
Şa'in Dezh *Iran* 36°40N 46°25E **213** D12
St. Abb's Head *U.K.* 55°55N 2°8W **167** F6
St-Affrique *France* 43°57N 2°53E **174** E6
St-Agrève *France* 45°0N 4°23E **175** C8
St-Aignan *France* 47°16N 1°22E **172** E8
St. Alban's *Nfld. & L., Canada* 47°51N 55°50W **299** C8
St. Albans *Herts., U.K.* 51°45N 0°19W **169** F7
St. Albans *Vt., U.S.A.* 44°49N 73°5W **313** B11
St. Albans *W. Va., U.S.A.* 38°23N 81°50W **309** F13
St. Alban's Head *U.K.* 50°34N 2°4W **169** G5
St. Albert *Canada* 53°37N 113°32W **296** C6
St-Amand-en-Puisaye *France* 47°32N 3°5E **173** E10
St-Amand-les-Eaux *France* 50°27N 3°25E **173** B10
St-Amand-Montrond *France* 46°43N 2°30E **173** F9
St-Amarin *France* 47°54N 7°2E **173** E14
St-Amour *France* 46°26N 5°21E **173** F12
St-André *Montréal, Canada* **130** c1
St-André *Réunion* 20°57S 55°39E **272** f
St-André-de-Cubzac *France* 44°59N 0°26W **174** D3
St-André-les-Alpes *France* 43°58N 6°30E **175** E10
St. Andrew □ *Trin. & Tob.* 10°35N 61°10W **323** t
St. Andrew Sd. *U.S.A.* 30°58N 81°25W **316** E8
St. Andrew's *Nfld. & L., Canada* 47°45N 59°15W **299** C8
St. Andrews *N.Z.* 44°33S 171°10E **285** E6
St. Andrews *Fife, U.K.* 56°20N 2°47W **167** E6
St. Andrews *S.C., U.S.A.* 32°47N 80°0W **316** C9
St-Anicet *Canada* 45°8N 74°22W **313** A10
St. Anne *U.S.A.* 41°1N 87°43W **311** C9
St. Annes *Canada* 49°40N 96°39W **297** D9
St. Anns B. *Canada* 46°22N 60°25W **299** C7
St. Ann's Bay *Jamaica* 18°26N 77°12W **320** a
St. Anthony *Nfld. & L., Canada* 51°22N 55°35W **299** B8
St. Anthony *Idaho, U.S.A.* 43°58N 111°41W **304** E8
St-Antoine *Canada* 46°22N 64°45W **299** C7
St-Antonin-Noble-Val *France* 44°10N 1°45E **174** D5
St. Arnaud = El Eulma *Algeria* 36°9N 5°42E **261** A6
St. Arnaud *Australia* 36°40S 143°16E **282** D5
St. Arnaud Ra. *N.Z.* 42°1S 172°53E **285** C7
St-Astier *France* 45°8N 0°31E **174** C4
St-Aubin *France* 48°44N 2°8E **134** B1
St-Aubin-du-Cormier *France* 48°15N 1°26W **172** D5
St-Augustin *Canada* 51°13N 58°38W **299** B8
St-Augustin → *Canada* 51°16N 58°40W **299** B8
St. Augustine *U.S.A.* 29°54N 81°19W **316** F8
St. Augustine Beach *U.S.A.* 29°51N 81°16W **316** F8
St-Aulaye *France* 45°12N 0°9E **174** C4
St. Austell *U.K.* 50°20N 4°47W **169** G3
St-Avold *France* 49°6N 6°43E **173** C13
St. Barbe *Canada* 51°12N 56°46W **299** B8
St-Barthélemy *W. Indies* 17°50N 62°50W **322** a
St-Barthélemy Channel *St.-Martin* 18°0N 63°0W **322** a
St. Basil's Cathedral *Moscow, Russia* **129** b3
St. Bathans *N.Z.* 44°53S 169°50E **285** E4
St. Bathan's, Mt. *N.Z.* 44°45S 169°45E **285** E4
St-Béat *France* 42°55N 0°41E **174** F4
St. Bees Hd. *U.K.* 54°31N 3°38W **168** C4
St. Bees I. *Australia* 20°56S 149°26E **280** b
St-Benoît *Réunion* 21°2S 55°43E **272** f
St-Benoît-du-Sault *France* 46°26N 1°24E **174** B5
St-Bonnet-en-Champsaur *France* 44°40N 6°5E **175** D10
St-Brevin-les-Pins *France* 47°14N 2°10W **172** E4
St-Brice-en-Coglès *France* 48°25N 1°22W **172** D5
St. Bride's *Canada* 46°56N 54°10W **299** C9
St. Brides B. *U.K.* 51°49N 5°9W **169** F2
St-Brieuc *France* 48°30N 2°46W **172** D4
St-Calais *France* 47°55N 0°45E **172** E7
St-Cast-le-Guildo *France* 48°37N 2°18W **172** D4
St. Catharines *Canada* 43°10N 79°15W **312** C5
St. Catherine, Mt. *Grenada* 12°10N 61°40W **323** q
St. Catherine Pt. *Bermuda* 32°23N 64°40W **153** a
St. Catherines I. *U.S.A.* 31°40N 81°10W **316** D8
St. Catherine's Monastery *Egypt* 28°34N 33°58E **251** K4
St. Catherine's Pt. *U.K.* 50°34N 1°18W **169** G6
St-Céré *France* 44°51N 1°54E **174** D5
St-Cergue *Switz.* 46°27N 6°10E **179** J2
St-Cernin *France* 45°5N 2°25E **174** C6
St-Chamond *France* 45°28N 4°31E **175** C8
St. Charles *Ill., U.S.A.* 41°54N 88°19W **310** C8
St. Charles *Md., U.S.A.* 38°36N 76°56W **309** F15
St. Charles *Mo., U.S.A.* 38°47N 90°29W **310** F6
St. Charles *Va., U.S.A.* 36°48N 83°4W **309** G12
St-Chély-d'Apcher *France* 44°48N 3°17E **174** D7
St-Chinian *France* 43°25N 2°56E **174** E6
St. Christopher = St. Kitts *W. Indies* 17°20N 62°40W **322** d
St. Christopher-Nevis = St. Kitts & Nevis ■ *W. Indies* 17°20N 62°40W **322** d
St-Ciers-sur-Gironde *France* 45°17N 0°37W **174** C3
St. Clair *Ga., U.S.A.* 33°9N 82°13W **316** B7
St. Clair *Mich., U.S.A.* 42°50N 82°30W **312** D2
St. Clair *Mo., U.S.A.* 38°21N 90°59W **310** F6
St. Clair *Pa., U.S.A.* 40°43N 76°12W **313** F8
St. Clair → *U.S.A.* 42°38N 82°31W **312** D2
St. Clair, L. *S. Austral., Australia* 37°20S 139°55E **282** D3
St. Clair, L. *N. Amer.* 42°27N 82°39W **312** D2
St. Clair Shores *U.S.A.* 42°30N 82°53W **311** B14
St. Clairsville *U.S.A.* 40°5N 80°54W **312** F4
St-Claud *France* 45°54N 0°28E **174** C4
St. Claude *Canada* 49°40N 98°20W **297** D9
St-Claude *Jura, France* 46°22N 5°52E **173** F12
St-Claude *Guadeloupe* 16°3N 61°42W **322** e
St. Clears *U.K.* 51°49N 4°31W **169** F3
St-Clet *Canada* 45°21N 74°13W **313** A10
St. Cloud *France* 48°50N 2°12E **134** A2
St. Cloud *Fla., U.S.A.* 28°15N 81°17W **317** G8
St. Cloud *Minn., U.S.A.* 45°34N 94°10W **308** C6
St. Cricq, C. *Australia* 25°17S 113°6E **279** E1
St. Croix *U.S. Virgin Is.* 17°45N 64°45W **321** C7
St. Croix → *U.S.A.* 44°45N 92°48W **308** C7
St. Croix Falls *U.S.A.* 45°24N 92°38W **308** C7
St-Cyprien *France* 42°37N 3°2E **174** F7
St-Cyr-l'École *France* 48°47N 2°4E **134** B1
St-Cyr-l'École ✈ *France* 48°48N 2°4E **134** B1
St-Cyr-sur-Mer *France* 43°11N 5°43E **175** E9
St. David *U.S.A.* 40°30N 90°3W **310** D6
St. David □ *Trin. & Tob.* 10°47N 61°3W **323** t
St. David's *Nfld. & L., Canada* 48°12N 58°52W **299** C8
St. David's *Grenada* 12°2N 61°40W **323** q
St. David's *Pembs., U.K.* 51°53N 5°16W **169** F2
St. David's Head *U.K.* 51°54N 5°19W **169** F2
St. David's I. *Bermuda* 32°21N 64°39W **153** a
St-Denis = Sig *Algeria* 35°32N 0°12W **261** A4
St-Denis *Seine-St-Denis, France* 48°56N 2°20E **134** A3
St-Denis *Réunion* 20°52S 55°27E **272** f
St-Denis → *Réunion* 20°52S 55°27E **272** f
St-Denis ✈ (RUN) *Réunion* 20°53S 55°32E **272** f
St-Dié *France* 48°17N 6°56E **173** D13
St-Dizier *France* 48°38N 4°58E **173** D11
St-Égrève *France* 45°14N 5°41E **175** C9
St. Elias, Mt. *U.S.A.* 60°18N 140°56W **303** F12
St. Elias Mts. *N. Amer.* 60°33N 139°28W **296** A1
St-Élie *Fr. Guiana* 4°49N 53°17W **329** C7
St. Elmo *U.S.A.* 39°2N 88°51W **311** E8
St-Eloy-les-Mines *France* 46°10N 2°51E **173** F9
St-Émilion *France* 44°53N 0°9W **174** D3
St-Étienne *France* 45°27N 4°22E **175** C8
St-Étienne → *Réunion* 21°17S 55°25E **272** f
St-Étienne-de-Tinée *France* 44°16N 6°56E **175** D10
St-Étienne-du-Rouvray *France* 49°23N 1°6E **172** C8
St. Eugène *Canada* 45°30N 74°28W **313** A10
St. Eustatius *W. Indies* 17°20N 63°0W **322** a
St-Exupery, Lyon ✈ (LYS) *France* 45°44N 5°2E **175** C9
St-Fargeau *France* 47°39N 3°4E **173** E10
St-Félicien *Canada* 48°40N 72°25W **298** C5
St. Ferdinand = Florissant *U.S.A.* 38°47N 90°19W **310** F6
St-Florent *France* 42°41N 9°18E **175** F13
St-Florent, G. de *France* 42°47N 9°12E **175** F13
St-Florent-sur-Cher *France* 46°59N 2°15E **173** F9
St-Florentin *France* 48°0N 3°45E **173** E10
St-Flour *France* 45°2N 3°6E **174** C7
St. Francis *U.S.A.* 39°47N 101°48W **308** F3
St. Francis → *U.S.A.* 34°38N 90°36W **315** D9
St. Francis, C. *S. Africa* 34°14S 24°49E **270** D3
St. Francisville *Ill., U.S.A.* 38°36N 87°39W **311** F9
St. Francisville *La., U.S.A.* 30°47N 91°23W **314** F9
St-François *Guadeloupe* 16°16N 61°18W **322** e
St-François, L. *Canada* 45°10N 74°22W **313** A10
St-Fulgent *France* 46°50N 1°10W **172** F5
St-Gabriel *Canada* 46°17N 73°24W **298** C5
St. Gallen = Sankt Gallen *Switz.* 47°26N 9°22E **179** H5
St-Galmier *France* 45°35N 4°19E **173** G11
St-Gaudens *France* 43°6N 0°44E **174** E4
St-Gaultier *France* 46°39N 1°26E **172** F8
St-Gengoux-le-National *France* 46°37N 4°40E **173** F11
St-Geniez-d'Olt *France* 44°27N 2°58E **174** D6
St. George *Queens., Australia* 28°1S 148°30E **281** D4
St. George *Bermuda* 32°22N 64°40W **153** a
St. George *N.B., Canada* 45°11N 66°50W **299** C6
St. George *Ont., Canada* 43°15N 80°15W **312** C4
St. George *Ga., U.S.A.* 30°31N 82°2W **316** E7
St. George *S.C., U.S.A.* 33°11N 80°35W **316** B9
St. George *Utah, U.S.A.* 37°6N 113°35W **305** H7
St. George □ *Trin. & Tob.* 10°40N 61°25W **323** t
St. George, C. *Nfld. & L., Canada* 48°30N 59°16W **299** C8
St. George, C. *Papua N. G.* 4°49S 152°53E **286** C7
St. George, C. *Fla., U.S.A.* 29°40N 85°5W **316** F4
St. George I. *Alaska, U.S.A.* 56°35N 169°35W **303** H5
St. George I. *Fla., U.S.A.* 29°35N 84°55W **316** F5
St. George Ra. *Australia* 18°40S 125°0E **278** C4
St. George's *Canada* 48°26N 58°31W **299** C8
St-Georges *Qué., Canada* 46°8N 70°40W **299** C5
St-Georges *Fr. Guiana* 3°53N 51°50W **329** C7
St. George's *Grenada* 12°5N 61°43W **323** q
St. George's B. *Canada* 48°24N 58°53W **299** C8
St. Georges Basin *N.S.W., Australia* 35°7S 150°36E **283** C9
St. Georges Basin *W. Austral., Australia* 15°23S 125°2E **278** C4
St. George's Channel *Europe* 52°0N 6°0W **166** E6
St. George's Channel *India* 7°15N 93°43E **245** L11
St. George's Channel *Papua N. G.* 4°10S 152°20E **286** C7
St. Georges Harbour *Bermuda* 32°33N 64°42W **153** a
St. Georges Hd. *Australia* 35°12S 150°42E **283** C9
St. Georges I. *Bermuda* 32°23N 64°40W **153** a
St-Georges-lès-Baillargeaux *France* 46°41N 0°22E **174** B4
St-Germain, Forêt de *France* 48°57N 2°5E **134** A1
St-Germain-de-Calberte *France* 44°13N 3°48E **174** D7
St-Germain-en-Laye *France* 48°53N 2°4E **134** A1
St-Germain-Lembron *France* 45°27N 3°14E **174** C7
St-Gervais-d'Auvergne *France* 46°4N 2°50E **173** F9
St-Gervais-les-Bains *France* 45°53N 6°42E **175** C10
St-Gildas, Pte. de *France* 47°8N 2°14W **172** E4
St. Giles Cathedral *Edinburgh, U.K.* **121** b2
St-Gilles *Brussels, Belgium* 50°49N 4°20E **116** B2
St-Gilles *Gard, France* 43°40N 4°26E **175** E8
St-Gilles-les-Bains *Réunion* 21°2S 55°14E **272** f
St-Gilles-les-Hauts *Réunion* 21°2S 55°15E **272** f
St-Girons *Ariège, France* 42°59N 1°8E **174** F5
St-Girons *Landes, France* 43°56N 1°18W **174** E2
St. Gotthard P. = San Gottardo, P. del *Switz.* 46°33N 8°33E **179** J4
St. Helena *Atl. Oc.* 15°58S 5°42W **153** h
St. Helena *Calif., U.S.A.* 38°30N 122°28W **304** G2
St. Helena, Mt. *U.S.A.* 38°40N 122°36W **306** G4
St. Helena B. *S. Africa* 32°40S 18°10E **270** D2
St. Helena Sd. *U.S.A.* 32°15N 80°25W **316** C9
St. Helens *Tas., Australia* 41°20S 148°15E **281** G4
St. Helens *Mersey., U.K.* 53°27N 2°44W **168** D5
St. Helens *Oreg., U.S.A.* 45°52N 122°48W **306** E4
St. Helens, Mt. *U.S.A.* 46°12N 122°12W **306** D4
St. Helier *Chan. Is., U.K.* 49°10N 2°7W **169** H5
St. Helier *London, U.K.* 51°23N 0°11W **125** B2
St-Herblain *France* 47°13N 1°40W **172** E5
St-Hilaire-du-Harcouët *France* 48°35N 1°5W **172** D5
St-Hippolyte *France* 47°19N 6°50E **173** E13
St-Hippolyte-du-Fort *France* 43°58N 3°52E **174** E7
St-Honoré-les-Bains *France* 46°54N 3°50E **173** F10
St-Hubert *Belgium* 50°2N 5°23E **170** D5
St-Hubert *Qué., Canada* 45°29N 73°25W **130** B3
St. Hubert, Galeries Royales *Brussels, Belgium* **116** b2
St-Hyacinthe *Canada* 45°40N 72°58W **298** C5
St. Ignace *U.S.A.* 45°52N 84°44W **309** C11
St. Ignace I. *Canada* 48°45N 88°0W **298** C2
St. Ignatius *U.S.A.* 47°19N 114°6W **304** C6
St-Imier *Switz.* 47°9N 6°58E **179** H2
St. Isaac's Cathedral *Russia* 59°55N 30°19E **137** B1
St. Ives *Cambs., U.K.* 52°20N 0°4W **169** E7
St. Ives *Corn., U.K.* 50°12N 5°30W **169** G2
St-Jacques *Montréal, Canada* **130** a2
St-Jacques → *Canada* 45°26N 73°29W **130** B3
St-James *France* 48°31N 1°20W **172** D5
St. James *Minn., U.S.A.* 43°59N 94°38W **308** D6
St. James *Mo., U.S.A.* 38°0N 91°37W **310** G5
St. James Cathedral *Toronto, Canada* **141** b3
St. James's *London, U.K.* **125** b3
St-Jean *St.-Martin* 17°53N 62°50W **322** a
St-Jean → *Canada* 50°17N 64°20W **299** B7
St-Jean, L. *Canada* 48°40N 72°0W **299** C5
St-Jean Baptiste *Montréal, Canada* **130** a1
St-Jean-d'Angély *France* 45°57N 0°31W **174** C3
St-Jean-de-Braye *France* 47°53N 1°58E **173** E8
St-Jean-de-Luz *France* 43°23N 1°39W **174** E2
St-Jean-de-Maurienne *France* 45°16N 6°21E **175** C10
St-Jean-de-Monts *France* 46°47N 2°4W **172** F4
St-Jean-du-Gard *France* 44°7N 3°52E **174** D7
St-Jean-en-Royans *France* 45°1N 5°18E **175** C9
St-Jean-Pied-de-Port *France* 43°10N 1°14W **174** E2
St-Jean-Port-Joli *Canada* 47°15N 70°13W **299** C5
St-Jean-sur-Richelieu *Canada* 45°20N 73°20W **313** A11
St-Jérôme *Canada* 45°47N 74°0W **298** C5
St. Joe *U.S.A.* 41°19N 84°54W **311** C12
St. John *N.B., Canada* 45°20N 66°8W **299** C6
St. John *Kans., U.S.A.* 38°0N 98°46W **308** F4
St. John → *Liberia* 6°40N 9°10W **262** D2
St. John → *N. Amer.* 45°12N 66°5W **309** C20
St. John, C. *Canada* 50°0N 55°32W **299** C8

St. John I. *U.S. Virgin Is.* 18°20N 64°42W **321** b
St. John's *Antigua & B.* 17°6N 61°51W **322** b
St. John's *Nfld. & L., Canada* 47°35N 52°40W **299** C9
St. Johns *Montserrat* 16°48N 62°11W **323** p
St. Johns *Ariz., U.S.A.* 34°30N 109°22W **305** J9
St. Johns *Mich., U.S.A.* 43°0N 84°33W **311** B12
St. Johns → *U.S.A.* 30°24N 81°24W **316** E8
St. John's Cathedral *Hong Kong, China* **122** c1
St. John's Pt. *Ireland* 54°34N 8°27W **166** B3
St. Johnsbury *U.S.A.* 44°25N 72°1W **313** B12
St. Johnston Village *Antigua & B.* 17°7N 61°50W **322** b
St. Johnsville *U.S.A.* 43°0N 74°43W **313** C10
St-Joost-Ten-Node *Belgium* 50°51N 4°21E **116** A2
St. Joseph *Ont., Canada* 43°24N 81°42W **312** C3
St. Joseph *Dominica* 15°24N 61°26W **323** k
St-Joseph *Martinique* 14°39N 61°4W **322** j
St-Joseph *Réunion* 21°22S 55°37E **272** f
St. Joseph *Mayaro, Trin. & Tob.* 10°18N 60°59W **323** t
St. Joseph *St. George, Trin. & Tob.* 10°40N 61°25W **323** t
St. Joseph *Ill., U.S.A.* 40°7N 88°2W **311** D8
St. Joseph *La., U.S.A.* 31°55N 91°14W **314** F9
St. Joseph *Mich., U.S.A.* 42°6N 86°29W **311** B10
St. Joseph *Mo., U.S.A.* 39°46N 94°50W **310** E2
St. Joseph → *U.S.A.* 42°7N 86°29W **311** B10
St. Joseph, I. *Canada* 46°12N 83°58W **298** C3
St. Joseph, L. *Canada* 51°10N 90°35W **298** B1
St. Joseph Pt. *U.S.A.* 29°52N 85°24W **316** F4
St-Juéry *France* 43°57N 2°12E **174** E6
St. Julian's *Malta* 35°55N 14°29E **206** F7
St-Julien-Chapteuil *France* 45°2N 4°4E **175** C8
St-Julien-de-Vouvantes *France* 47°38N 1°13W **172** E5
St-Julien-en-Genevois *France* 46°9N 6°5E **173** F13
St-Junien *France* 45°53N 0°55E **174** C4
St-Just-en-Chaussée *France* 49°30N 2°25E **173** C9
St-Just-en-Chevalet *France* 45°55N 3°50E **174** C7
St. Kilda *Vic., Australia* 37°51S 144°58E **128** B1
St. Kilda *N.Z.* 45°53S 170°31E **285** F5
St. Kilda *W. Isles, U.K.* 57°49N 8°34W **165** C2
St. Kitts *W. Indies* 17°20N 62°40W **322** d
St. Kitts & Nevis ■ *W. Indies* 17°20N 62°40W **322** d
St-Lambert *Qué., Canada* 45°30N 73°29W **130** A3
St-Lambert *Yvelines, France* 48°43N 2°1E **134** B1
St. Laurent *Canada* 50°25N 97°58W **297** C9
St-Laurent *Canada* 45°30N 73°43W **130** A1
St-Laurent-de-la-Salanque *France* 42°46N 2°59E **174** F6
St-Laurent du Maroni *Fr. Guiana* 5°29N 54°3W **329** B7
St-Laurent-du-Pont *France* 45°23N 5°45E **175** C9
St-Laurent-en-Grandvaux *France* 46°35N 5°58E **173** F12
St-Laurent-Médoc *France* 45°8N 0°49W **174** C3
St. Lawrence *Queens., Australia* 22°16S 149°31E **280** C4
St. Lawrence *Nfld. & L., Canada* 46°54N 55°23W **299** C8
St. Lawrence → *Canada* 49°30N 66°0W **299** C6
St. Lawrence, Gulf of *Canada* 48°25N 62°0W **299** C7
St. Lawrence I. *U.S.A.* 63°30N 170°30W **303** E5
St. Lawrence Islands △ *Canada* 44°27N 75°52W **313** B9
St. Lawrence Market *Toronto, Canada* **141** b3
St-Lazare, Gare *Paris, France* **134** a3
St. Léonard *Canada* 47°12N 67°58W **299** C6
St-Léonard *Canada* 45°35N 73°34W **130** A2
St-Léonard-de-Noblat *France* 45°49N 1°29E **174** C5
St-Leu *Réunion* 21°9S 55°18E **272** f
St. Lewis → *Canada* 52°26N 56°11W **299** B8
St-Lô *France* 49°7N 1°5W **172** C5
St-Louis *Montréal, Canada* **130** b2
St-Louis *Haut-Rhin, France* 47°30N 7°34E **173** E14
St-Louis *Guadeloupe* 15°56N 61°19W **322** e
St-Louis *Réunion* 21°16S 55°25E **272** f
St. Louis *Senegal* 16°8N 16°27W **262** B1
St. Louis *Mo., U.S.A.* 38°37N 90°11W **310** F6
St. Louis □ *Senegal* 16°20N 15°0W **262** B2
St. Louis → *U.S.A.* 46°44N 92°9W **308** B7
St. Louis Lambert Int. ✕ (STL) *U.S.A.* 38°45N 90°22W **310** F6
St-Loup-sur-Semouse *France* 47°53N 6°16E **173** E13
St-Luc *Canada* 45°22N 73°18W **313** A11
St. Lucia ■ *W. Indies* 14°0N 60°57W **323** m
St. Lucia, L. *S. Africa* 28°5S 32°30E **271** C5
St. Lucia Channel *W. Indies* 14°15N 61°0W **321** D7
St. Lucie *U.S.A.* 27°29N 80°20W **317** H9
St. Lucie Canal *U.S.A.* 27°10N 80°18W **317** H9
St. Maarten ☑ *W. Indies* 18°0N 63°5W **322** a
St. Magnus B. *U.K.* 60°25N 1°35W **167** A7
St-Maixent-l'École *France* 46°24N 0°12W **174** B3
St-Malo *France* 48°39N 2°1W **172** D4
St-Malo, G. de *France* 48°50N 2°30W **172** D4
St-Mandé *France* 48°50N 2°24E **134** A3
St-Mandrier-sur-Mer *France* 43°4N 5°57E **175** E9
St-Marc *Haiti* 19°10N 72°41W **321** C5
St-Marcellin *France* 45°9N 5°20E **175** C9
St-Marcouf, Îs. *France* 49°30N 1°10W **172** C5
St. Margaret's *Ireland* 53°25N 6°18W **120** A2
St. Maries *U.S.A.* 47°19N 116°35W **304** C5
St. Mark B. *Grenada* 12°11N 61°42W **323** q
St. Marks *U.S.A.* 30°9N 84°12W **316** E5
St-Martin ☑ *W. Indies* 18°0N 63°0W **322** a
St-Martin, Bois *France* 48°48N 2°35E **134** B4
St-Martin, C. *Martinique* 14°52N 61°14W **322** j
St. Martin, L. *Canada* 51°40N 98°30W **297** C9
St-Martin-de-Crau *France* 43°38N 4°48E **175** E8
St-Martin-de-Ré *France* 46°12N 1°21W **174** B2
St-Martin-d'Hères *France* 45°9N 5°45E **175** C9
St-Martin-Vésubie *France* 44°4N 7°15E **175** D11
St. Martin's I. *Bangla.* 20°36N 92°20E **241** E4
St-Martory *France* 43°9N 0°56E **174** E4
St. Mary *U.S.A.* 37°53N 89°57W **310** G7
St. Mary, Mt. *Papua N. G.* 8°8S 147°2E **286** E4
St. Mary Cray *U.K.* 51°23N 0°7E **125** B4
St. Mary Is. *India* 13°20N 74°35E **245** H2
St. Mary Pk. *Australia* 31°32S 138°34E **282** A3
St. Marys *Tas., Australia* 41°35S 148°11E **281** G4
St. Marys *Ont., Canada* 43°20N 81°10W **312** C3
St. Mary's *Trin. & Tob.* 10°14N 61°33W **323** t
St. Mary's *Corn., U.K.* 49°55N 6°18W **169** H1
St. Mary's *Orkney, U.K.* 58°54N 2°54W **167** C6
St. Mary's *Alaska, U.S.A.* 62°4N 163°10W **303** E7
St. Marys *Ga., U.S.A.* 30°44N 81°33W **316** E8
St. Marys *Ohio, U.S.A.* 40°33N 84°24W **311** D12
St. Marys *Pa., U.S.A.* 41°26N 78°34W **312** E6
St. Marys → *U.S.A.* 30°43N 81°27W **316** E8
St. Mary's, C. *Canada* 46°50N 54°12W **299** C9
St. Mary's B. *Canada* 46°50N 53°50W **299** C9
St. Mary's Bay *Canada* 44°25N 66°10W **299** D6
St. Mary's Cathedral *San Francisco, U.S.A.* **136** c2
St-Mathieu, Pte. *France* 48°20N 4°45W **172** D2
St. Matthew I. *U.S.A.* 60°24N 172°42W **303** F4
St. Matthews *Ky., U.S.A.* 38°15N 85°39W **311** F11
St. Matthews *S.C., U.S.A.* 33°40N 80°46W **316** B9
St. Matthews, I. = Zadetkyi Kyun *Burma* 10°0N 98°25E **237** G2
St. Matthias Group *Papua N. G.* 1°30S 150°0E **286** A6
St-Maur-des-Fossés *France* 48°48N 2°29E **134** B3
St-Maurice *France* 48°49N 2°24E **134** B3
St-Maurice → *Canada* 46°21N 72°31W **298** C5
St. Mawes *U.K.* 50°10N 5°2W **169** G2
St-Maximin-la-Ste-Baume *France* 43°27N 5°52E **175** E9
St-Médard-en-Jalles *France* 44°53N 0°43W **174** D3
St-Méen-le-Grand *France* 48°11N 2°12W **172** D4
St. Meinrad *U.S.A.* 38°10N 86°49W **311** F10
St. Michael *U.S.A.* 63°29N 162°2W **303** E7
St. Michael's Cathedral *Toronto, Canada* **141** a3
St-Michel *Canada* 45°34N 73°37W **130** A2
St-Mihiel *France* 48°54N 5°32E **173** D12
St-Nazaire *France* 47°17N 2°12W **172** E4
St. Neots *U.K.* 52°14N 0°15W **169** E7
St-Nicolas-de-Port *France* 48°38N 6°18E **173** D13
St-Niklaas *Belgium* 51°10N 4°8E **170** C4
St. Nikolaus-Kirken *Czech Rep.* 50°5N 14°23E **135** B2
St-Omer *France* 50°45N 2°15E **173** B9
St-Ouen *France* 48°56N 2°20E **134** A3
St-Palais-sur-Mer *France* 45°38N 1°5W **174** C2
St-Pamphile *Canada* 46°58N 69°48W **299** C6
St. Pancras International *London, U.K.* **125** a4
St-Pardoux-la-Rivière *France* 45°29N 0°45E **174** C4
St. Paris *U.S.A.* 40°8N 83°58W **311** D13
St-Pascal *Canada* 47°32N 69°48W **299** C6
St. Patrick □ *Trin. & Tob.* 10°10N 61°35W **323** t
St. Patricks *Barbados* 13°6N 59°30W **323** r
St. Patrick's Cathedral *Dublin, Ireland* **120** c1
St. Patrick's Cathedral *New York, U.S.A.* **132** c2
St. Patrick's Church *Toronto, Canada* **141** a1
St. Paul *Canada* 54°0N 111°17W **296** C6
St-Paul *Alpes-de-Haute-Provence, France* 44°31N 6°45E **175** D10
St-Paul *Réunion* 20°59S 55°17E **272** f
St. Paul *Alaska, U.S.A.* 57°7N 170°17W **303** H5
St. Paul *Ind., U.S.A.* 39°26N 85°38W **311** E11
St. Paul *Minn., U.S.A.* 44°56N 93°5W **308** C7
St. Paul *Nebr., U.S.A.* 41°13N 98°27W **308** E4
St-Paul → *Canada* 51°27N 57°42W **299** B8
St. Paul → *Liberia* 6°25N 10°48W **252** D2
St-Paul, Î. *Ind. Oc.* 38°55S 77°34E **273** H6
St-Paul-de-Fenouillet *France* 42°48N 2°30E **174** F6
St. Paul I. *N.S., Canada* 47°12N 60°9W **299** C7
St. Paul I. *Alaska, U.S.A.* 57°10N 170°15W **303** H5
St-Paul-lès-Dax *France* 43°44N 1°3W **174** E2
St. Paul's Bay *Malta* 35°57N 14°24E **206** F7
St. Paul's Cathedral *London, U.K.* **125** b4
St. Paul's Cray *U.K.* 51°23N 0°6E **125** B4
St-Péray *France* 44°57N 4°50E **175** D8
St. Pete Beach *U.S.A.* 27°43N 82°44W **317** H7
St. Peter *U.S.A.* 44°20N 93°57W **308** C7
St. Peter & St. Paul *San Francisco, U.S.A.* **136** a2
St-Peter-Ording *Germany* 54°20N 8°36E **178** A4
St. Peter Port *U.K.* 49°26N 2°33W **169** H5
St. Peters *N.S.W., Australia* 33°55S 151°11E **139** B2
St. Peters *N.S., Canada* 45°40N 60°53W **299** C7
St. Peters *P.E.I., Canada* 46°25N 62°35W **299** C7
St. Peters *Montserrat* 16°43N 62°13W **323** p
St. Peters *Mo., U.S.A.* 38°48N 90°37W **310** F6
St. Peter's Square = San Pietro, Piazza *Rome, Italy* **136** b1
St. Petersburg = Sankt-Peterburg *Russia* 59°55N 30°20E **137** B1
St. Petersburg *U.S.A.* 27°46N 82°40W **317** H7
St. Petersburg Pulkovo Int. ✕ (LED) *Russia* 59°48N 30°18E **137** C1
St-Philbert-de-Grand-Lieu *France* 47°2N 1°39W **172** E5
St-Phillippe *Réunion* 21°21S 55°44E **272** f
St-Pie *Canada* 45°30N 72°54W **313** A12
St-Pierre *Qué., Canada* 45°27N 73°38W **130** B2
St-Pierre *Martinique* 14°45N 61°10W **322** j
St-Pierre *Mauritius* 20°13S 57°31E **272** e
St-Pierre *Réunion* 21°19S 55°28E **272** f
St-Pierre *St-P. & M.* 46°46N 56°12W **299** C8
St-Pierre *Seychelles* 9°20S 46°0E **273** E3
St-Pierre, L. *Canada* 46°12N 72°52W **298** C5
St-Pierre, Rade de *Martinique* 14°44N 61°11W **322** j
St-Pierre-de-la-Pointe-aux-Esquimaux = Havre-St.-Pierre *Canada* 50°18N 63°33W **299** B7
St-Pierre-d'Oléron *France* 45°57N 1°19W **174** C2
St-Pierre-en-Port *France* 49°48N 0°30E **172** C7
St-Pierre-et-Miquelon ☑ *N. Amer.* 46°55N 56°10W **299** C8
St-Pierre-le-Moûtier *France* 46°47N 3°7E **173** F10
St-Pierre-sur-Dives *France* 49°2N 0°1W **172** C6
St-Pieters Leew *Belgium* 50°47N 4°16E **116** B1
St-Pol-de-Léon *France* 48°41N 4°0W **172** D3
St-Pol-sur-Mer *France* 51°1N 2°20E **173** A9
St-Pol-sur-Ternoise *France* 50°23N 2°20E **173** B9
St-Pons *France* 43°30N 2°45E **174** E6
St-Pourçain-sur-Sioule *France* 46°18N 3°18E **173** F10
St-Priest *France* 45°42N 4°57E **175** C8
St-Quay-Portrieux *France* 48°39N 2°51W **172** D4
St-Quentin *N.B., Canada* 47°30N 67°23W **299** C6
St-Quentin *Aisne, France* 49°50N 3°16E **173** C10
St-Quentin, Étang de *France* 48°47N 2°0E **134** B1
St-Rambert-d'Albon *France* 45°17N 4°49E **175** C8
St-Raphaël *France* 43°25N 6°46E **175** E10
St. Regis *U.S.A.* 47°18N 115°6W **304** C6
St. Regis Falls *U.S.A.* 44°40N 74°32W **313** B10
St-Renan *France* 48°26N 4°37W **172** D2
St. Robert *U.S.A.* 37°50N 92°11W **310** G4
St-Saëns *France* 49°41N 1°16E **172** C8
St-Savin *France* 46°34N 0°53E **174** B4
St-Savinien *France* 45°53N 0°42W **174** C3
St. Sebastien, Tanjon' i *Madag.* 12°26S 48°44E **272** A2
St-Seine-l'Abbaye *France* 47°26N 4°47E **173** E11
St-Sernin-sur-Rance *France* 43°54N 2°35E **174** E6
St-Sever *France* 43°45N 0°35W **174** E3
St-Siméon *Canada* 47°51N 69°54W **299** C6
St. Simons I. *U.S.A.* 31°12N 81°15W **316** D8
St. Simons Island *U.S.A.* 31°9N 81°22W **315** F14
St. Stephen *N.B., Canada* 45°16N 67°17W **299** C6
St. Stephen *S.C., U.S.A.* 33°24N 79°55W **316** B10
St. Stephen's Basilica *Budapest, Hungary* **117** b2
St. Stephens Cathedral = Stephansdom *Vienna, Austria* **142** b2
St. Stephen's Green *Dublin, Ireland* **120** c3
St-Stevens-Woluwe *Belgium* 50°52N 4°26E **116** A2
St-Sulpice *France* 43°46N 1°41E **174** E5
St-Sulpice-Laurière *France* 46°3N 1°29E **174** B5
St-Sulpice-les-Feuilles *France* 46°19N 1°21E **174** B5
St-Syprien = St-Cyprien *France* 42°37N 3°2E **174** F7
St. Teresa *U.S.A.* 29°55N 84°27W **316** F5
St-Thégonnec *France* 48°31N 3°57W **172** D3
St. Thomas = Charlotte Amalie *U.S. Virgin Is.* 18°21N 64°56W **321** C7
St. Thomas *Canada* 42°45N 81°10W **312** D3
St. Thomas Bay *Malta* 35°51N 14°34E **206** F8
St. Thomas I. *U.S. Virgin Is.* 18°20N 64°55W **321** C7
St-Tite *Canada* 46°45N 72°34W **298** C5
St-Tropez *France* 43°17N 6°38E **175** E10
St-Troud = St. Truiden *Belgium* 50°48N 5°10E **170** D5
St. Truiden *Belgium* 50°48N 5°10E **170** D5
St-Vaast-la-Hougue *France* 49°35N 1°17W **172** C5
St-Valery-en-Caux *France* 49°52N 0°43E **172** C7
St-Valéry-sur-Somme *France* 50°11N 1°38E **173** B8
St-Vallier *France* 46°38N 4°22E **173** F11
St-Vallier-de-Thiey *France* 43°42N 6°51E **175** E10
St-Varent *France* 46°53N 0°13W **172** F6
St-Vaury *France* 46°12N 1°46E **174** B5
St. Vidgeon's ✪ *Australia* 14°47S 134°53E **280** A1
St. Vincent = São Vicente *C. Verde Is.* 17°0N 25°0W **153** j
St. Vincent *Italy* 45°45N 7°39E **198** C4
St. Vincent *W. Indies* 13°10N 61°10W **323** n
St. Vincent, G. *Australia* 35°0S 138°0E **282** C3
St. Vincent & the Grenadines ■ *W. Indies* 13°0N 61°10W **323** n
St-Vincent-de-Paul *Canada* 45°36N 73°39W **130** A2
St-Vincent-de-Tyrosse *France* 43°39N 1°19W **174** E2
St. Vincent I. *U.S.A.* 29°42N 85°3W **317** F4
St. Vincent Passage *W. Indies* 13°30N 61°0W **321** D7
St-Vith *Belgium* 50°17N 5°9E **170** D6
St-Vivien-de-Médoc *France* 45°25N 1°2W **174** C2
St. Walburg *Canada* 53°39N 109°12W **297** C7
St. Xavier Univ. *U.S.A.* 41°42N 87°42W **119** C2
St-Yrieix-la-Perche *France* 45°31N 1°12E **174** C5
Saintala *India* 20°26N 83°20E **244** D6
Ste-Adresse *France* 49°31N 0°5E **172** C7
Ste-Agathe-des-Monts *Canada* 46°3N 74°17W **298** C5
Ste-Anne *Guadeloupe* 16°13N 61°24W **322** e
Ste-Anne *Martinique* 14°25N 60°54W **322** j
Ste-Anne *Réunion* 21°4S 55°45E **272** f
Ste-Anne *Seychelles* 4°36S 55°31E **272** c
Ste-Anne, L. *Canada* 50°0N 67°42W **299** B6
Ste-Anne-des-Monts *Canada* 49°8N 66°30W **299** C6
Ste-Catherine *Canada* 45°24N 73°34W **130** B2
Ste-Croix *Switz.* 46°49N 6°34E **179** J2
Ste-Enimie *France* 44°22N 3°26E **174** D7
Ste-Foy-la-Grande *France* 44°50N 0°13E **174** D4
Ste. Genevieve *U.S.A.* 37°59N 90°2W **310** G6
Ste-Hélène, Î. *Canada* 45°31N 73°32W **130** A2
Ste-Hermine *France* 46°32N 1°4W **174** B2
Ste-Livrade-sur-Lot *France* 44°24N 0°36E **174** D4
Ste-Luce *Martinique* 14°28N 60°55W **322** j
Ste. Madeleine *Trin. & Tob.* 10°16N 61°26W **323** t
Ste-Marguerite *Guadeloupe* 16°23N 61°24W **322** e
Ste-Marguerite → *Canada* 50°9N 66°36W **299** B6
Ste-Marie *Canada* 46°26N 71°0W **299** C5
Ste. Marie *Gabon* 3°48S 11°3E **264** C2
Ste-Marie *Guadeloupe* 16°6N 61°33W **322** e
Ste-Marie *Martinique* 14°48N 61°1W **322** j
Ste-Marie *Réunion* 20°53S 55°33E **272** f
Ste-Marie, Ile = Nosy Boraha *Madag.* 16°50S 49°55E **272** B2
Ste-Marie-aux-Mines *France* 48°15N 7°12E **173** D14
Ste-Marthe *Guadeloupe* 16°15N 61°15W **322** e
Ste-Maure-de-Touraine *France* 47°7N 0°37E **172** E7
Ste-Maxime *France* 43°19N 6°39E **175** E10
Ste-Menehould *France* 49°5N 4°54E **173** C11
Ste-Mère-Église *France* 49°24N 1°19W **172** C5
Ste-Rose *Guadeloupe* 16°20N 61°45W **322** e
Ste-Rose *Réunion* 21°8S 55°45E **272** f
Ste. Rose du Lac *Canada* 51°4N 99°30W **297** C9
Ste-Savine *France* 48°18N 4°3E **173** D11
Ste-Sigolène *France* 45°15N 4°14E **175** C8
Ste-Suzanne *Réunion* 20°54S 55°36E **272** f
Saintes *France* 45°45N 0°37W **174** C3
Saintes, Canal des *Guadeloupe* 15°55N 61°40W **322** e
Saintes, Îs. des *Guadeloupe* 15°50N 61°35W **322** e
Stes-Maries-de-la-Mer *France* 43°26N 4°26E **175** E8
Saintfield *U.K.* 54°28N 5°49W **166** B6
Saintonge *France* 45°40N 0°50W **174** C3
Saipan *N. Marianas* 15°12N 145°45E **302** e
Saipan Channel *N. Marianas* 15°5N 145°41E **302** e
Sairang *India* 23°50N 92°45E **241** D4
Sairecábur, Cerro *Bolivia* 22°43S 67°54W **334** A2
Saitama *Japan* 35°54N 139°38E **223** B11
Saitama □ *Japan* 36°25N 139°30E **223** A11
Saiteli = Kadınhanı *Turkey* 38°14N 32°13E **212** C5
Saiți *Moldova* 46°30N 29°24E **183** D14
Saito *Japan* 32°3N 131°24E **222** E3
Saiwai *Japan* 35°32N 139°41E **140** B3
Saiyid *Pakistan* 33°7N 73°2E **242** C5
Saja-Besaya ⌂ *Spain* 43°10N 4°9W **194** B6
Sajama *Bolivia* 18°7S 69°0W **330** D4
Sajama, Nevado *Bolivia* 18°6S 68°54W **330** D4
Sajan *Serbia* 45°50N 20°20E **182** E5
Sajó → *Hungary* 47°56N 21°7E **182** C6
Sajókazinc = Kazincbarcika *Hungary* 48°17N 20°36E **182** B5
Sajószentpéter *Hungary* 48°12N 20°44E **182** B5
Sajum *India* 33°20N 79°0E **243** C8
Sak → *S. Africa* 30°52S 20°25E **270** D3
Saka *Kenya* 0°9S 39°20E **268** B4
Saka Kalat *Pakistan* 27°3N 65°3E **240** D2
Sakaba *Nigeria* 11°4N 5°35E **263** C6
Sakai *Japan* 34°34N 135°27E **133** B1
Sakai Harbour *Japan* 34°36N 135°26E **133** B1
Sakaide *Japan* 34°19N 133°50E **222** C5
Sakaiminato *Japan* 35°38N 133°11E **222** B5
Sakākah *Si. Arabia* 30°0N 40°8E **246** D4
Sakakawea, L. *U.S.A.* 47°30N 101°25W **308** B3
Sakami → *Canada* 53°40N 76°40W **298** B4
Sakami, L. *Canada* 53°15N 77°0W **298** B4
Sakâne, 'Erg i-n *Mali* 20°30N 1°30W **260** D4
Sakania *Dem. Rep. of the Congo* 12°43S 28°30E **269** E2
Sakar I. *Papua N. G.* 5°25S 148°6E **286** C5
Sakaraha *Madag.* 22°55S 44°32E **272** C1
Sakartvelo = Georgia ■ *Asia* 42°0N 43°0E **191** J6
Sakarya *Turkey* 40°48N 30°25E **212** B4
Sakarya □ *Turkey* 40°45N 30°25E **212** B4
Sakarya → *Turkey* 41°7N 30°39E **212** B4
Sakashima-Guntō *Japan* 24°46N 124°0E **221** M2
Sakassou *Ivory C.* 7°29N 5°19W **262** D3
Sakata *Japan* 38°55N 139°50E **220** E9
Sakawa *Japan* 33°28N 133°11E **222** D5
Sakchu *N. Korea* 40°23N 125°2E **224** B2
Sakeny → *Madag.* 20°0S 45°25E **272** C2
Sakété *Benin* 6°40N 2°45E **263** D5
Sakha □ *Russia* 66°0N 130°0E **215** C14
Sakhalin *Russia* 51°0N 143°0E **215** D15
Sakhalinskiy Zaliv *Russia* 54°0N 141°0E **215** D15
Sakhi Gopal *India* 19°58N 85°50E **244** E7
Şaki *Azerbaijan* 41°10N 47°5E **191** K8
Šakiai *Lithuania* 54°59N 23°2E **184** D10
Sakiz-Adasi = Chios *Greece* 38°27N 26°9E **205** C8
Sakmara → *Russia* 51°46N 55°1E **216** B5
Sakoli *India* 21°5N 79°59E **244** D4
Sakon Nakhon *Thailand* 17°10N 104°9E **236** D5
Sakra, Pulau *Singapore* 1°15N 103°41E **138** B2
Sakrand *Pakistan* 26°10N 68°15E **242** F3
Sakri *Maharashtra, India* 26°13N 86°5E **243** F12
Sakri *Maharashtra, India* 21°2N 74°20E **244** D2
Sakrivier *S. Africa* 30°54S 20°28E **270** D3
Sakskøbing *Denmark* 54°49N 11°39E **163** K5
Sakti *India* 22°2N 82°58E **243** H10
Saku *Japan* 36°17N 138°31E **223** A10
Sakuma *Japan* 35°3N 137°49E **223** B9
Sakura *Japan* 35°43N 140°14E **223** B12
Sakurai *Japan* 34°30N 135°51E **223** C7
Sakurajima = On-Take *Japan* 31°35N 130°39E **222** F2
Saky *Ukraine* 45°9N 33°34E **189** K7
Sal → *Russia* 47°31N 40°45E **191** G5
Sal Rei *C. Verde Is.* 16°11N 22°53W **153** j
Sala *Eritrea* 16°53N 37°36E **257** D4
Šal'a *Slovak Rep.* 48°10N 17°50E **181** C10
Sala *Sweden* 59°58N 16°35E **162** E10
Sala → *Eritrea* 16°53N 37°36E **257** D4
Sala, O. → *Chad* 17°0N 20°53E **259** E4
Sala Consilina *Italy* 40°23N 15°36E **201** B8
Sala-y-Gómez *Pac. Oc.* 26°28S 105°28W **289** K17
Sala y Gómez Ridge *Pac. Oc.* 25°0S 98°0W **289** K18
Salaberry-de-Valleyfield *Canada* 45°15N 74°8W **313** A10
Salacgrīva *Latvia* 57°45N 24°21E **184** A11
Salada, L. *Mexico* 32°20N 115°40W **305** K6
Saladas *Argentina* 28°15S 58°40W **334** B4
Saladillo *Argentina* 35°40S 59°55W **334** D4
Salado → *B. Aires, Argentina* 35°44S 57°22W **334** D4
Salado → *La Pampa, Argentina* 37°30S 67°0W **336** A3
Salado → *Rio Negro, Argentina* 41°34S 65°3W **336** B3
Salado → *Santa Fe, Argentina* 31°40S 60°41W **334** C3
Salado → *Tamaulipas, Mexico* 26°52N 99°19W **314** H5
Salaga *Ghana* 8°31N 0°31W **263** D4
Salah *Syria* 32°40N 36°45E **250** F7
Şalāḥ ad Dīn □ *Iraq* 34°35N 43°35E **246** C4
Sălaj □ *Romania* 47°15N 23°0E **182** C8
Salakos *Greece* 36°17N 27°57E **206** E11
Salal *Chad* 14°48N 17°12E **259** F3
Salala *Liberia* 6°42N 10°7W **262** D2
Salala *Sudan* 21°17N 36°16E **256** C4
Salālah *Oman* 16°56N 53°59E **249** C6
Salam *Iraq* 33°20N 44°20E **113** A2
Salamanca *Chile* 31°46S 70°59W **334** C1
Salamanca *Madrid, Spain* 40°25N 3°41W **127** B1
Salamanca *Salamanca, Spain* 40°58N 5°39W **194** E5
Salamanca *N.Y., U.S.A.* 42°10N 78°43W **312** D6
Salamanca □ *Spain* 40°57N 5°40W **194** E5
Salamat □ *Chad* 11°0N 20°30E **259** F4
Salamat, Bahr → *Chad* 9°20N 18°0E **259** G3
Salamatābād *Iran* 35°39N 47°50E **246** C5
Salamina *Colombia* 5°25N 75°29W **328** B2
Salamina *Greece* 37°56N 23°30E **204** D5
Salamis *Cyprus* 35°11N 33°54E **207** E9
Salamonie L. *U.S.A.* 40°46N 85°37W **311** D11
Salar de Atacama *Chile* 23°30S 68°25W **334** A2
Salar de Uyuni *Bolivia* 20°30S 67°45W **330** E4
Sălard *Romania* 47°12N 22°3E **182** C7
Salas *Spain* 43°25N 6°15W **194** B4
Salas de los Infantes *Spain* 42°2N 3°17W **194** C7
Salatiga *Indonesia* 7°19S 110°30E **235** D4
Salavat *Russia* 53°21N 55°55E **186** D10
Salaverry *Peru* 8°15S 79°0W **330** B2
Salawati *Indonesia* 1°7S 130°52E **231** E8
Salawin △ *Thailand* 18°18N 97°40E **236** C1
Salay *Phil.* 8°52N 124°47E **233** G5
Salayar *Indonesia* 6°7S 120°30E **231** F6
Salazar → *Spain* 42°40N 1°20W **196** C3
Salazie *Réunion* 21°2S 55°33E **272** f
Salazie, Cirque de *Réunion* 21°3S 55°30E **272** f
Salbris *France* 47°25N 2°3E **173** E9
S'Albufera *Spain* 39°47N 3°7E **206** B4
S'albufera d'es Grau *Spain* 39°56N 4°16E **206** B5
Salcantay, Nevado *Peru* 13°19S 72°33W **330** C3
Salcedo *Phil.* 11°9N 125°40E **233** F5
Salcia *Romania* 43°53N 24°55E **183** G9
Sălciua *Romania* 46°24N 23°26E **183** D8
Salcombe *U.K.* 50°14N 3°47W **169** G4
Saldaña *Spain* 42°32N 4°48W **194** C6
Saldanha *S. Africa* 33°0S 17°58E **270** D2
Saldanha B. *S. Africa* 33°6S 18°0E **270** D2
Saldus *Latvia* 56°38N 22°30E **184** B9
Saldus □ *Latvia* 56°35N 22°30E **184** B9
Sale *Vic., Australia* 38°6S 147°6E **283** E7
Sale *Burma* 20°50N 94°45E **241** E5
Sale *Italy* 44°59N 8°48E **198** D5
Salé *Morocco* 34°3N 6°48W **260** B3
Sale *U.K.* 53°26N 2°19W **168** D5
Sale City *U.S.A.* 31°16N 84°1W **316** D5
Salée, Rivière *Guadeloupe* 16°17N 61°33W **322** e
Salegard = Salekhard *Russia* 66°30N 66°35E **214** C7
Saleh, Teluk *Indonesia* 8°34S 117°57E **235** D5
Salekhard *Russia* 66°30N 66°35E **214** C7
Salelologa *Samoa* 13°41S 172°11W **287** V19
Salem *India* 11°40N 78°11E **245** J4
Salem *Montserrat* 16°45N 62°13W **323** p
Salem *Fla., U.S.A.* 29°53N 83°25W **316** F6
Salem *Ill., U.S.A.* 38°38N 88°57W **310** F8
Salem *Ind., U.S.A.* 38°36N 86°6W **311** F10
Salem *Mass., U.S.A.* 42°31N 70°53W **313** D14
Salem *Mo., U.S.A.* 37°39N 91°32W **308** G8
Salem *N.H., U.S.A.* 42°45N 71°12W **313** D13
Salem *N.J., U.S.A.* 39°34N 75°28W **309** F16
Salem *N.Y., U.S.A.* 43°10N 73°20W **313** C11
Salem *Ohio, U.S.A.* 40°54N 80°52W **312** F4
Salem *Oreg., U.S.A.* 44°56N 123°2W **304** D2
Salem *S. Dak., U.S.A.* 43°44N 97°23W **308** D5
Salem *Va., U.S.A.* 37°18N 80°3W **309** G13
Salemi *Italy* 37°49N 12°48E **200** E5
Salen *Sweden* 61°20N 13°10E **162** C7
Salernes *France* 43°34N 6°15E **175** E10
Salerno *Italy* 40°41N 14°47E **201** B7
Salerno, G. di *Italy* 40°32N 14°42E **201** B7
Sales *Brazil* 4°2S 63°40W **329** D5
Salford *U.K.* 53°30N 2°18W **168** D5
Salgótarján *Hungary* 48°5N 19°47E **182** B4
Salgueiro *Brazil* 8°4S 39°6W **333** C4
Salher *India* 20°40N 73°55E **244** D1
Salhus *Norway* 60°30N 5°15E **164** D2
Salhyr → *Ukraine* 45°38N 35°1E **189** K8
Salibabu *Indonesia* 3°51N 126°40E **231** D7
Salibea = Salybia *Trin. & Tob.* 10°43N 61°2W **323** t
Salibia *Dominica* 15°30N 61°16W **323** k
Salida *U.S.A.* 38°32N 106°0W **301** H18
Salies-de-Béarn *France* 43°28N 0°56W **174** E3
Şalif *Yemen* 15°18N 42°41E **248** D3
Salihli *Turkey* 38°28N 28°8E **212** C3
Salihorsk *Belarus* 52°51N 27°27E **177** B14
Salin *Burma* 20°35N 94°40E **241** E5
Salina *Italy* 38°34N 14°50E **201** D7
Salina *Kans., U.S.A.* 38°50N 97°37W **308** F5
Salina *Utah, U.S.A.* 38°58N 111°51W **304** G8
Salina Cruz *Mexico* 16°10N 95°12W **319** D5
Salina di Margherita di Savoia ⌂ *Italy* 41°23N 16°4E **201** A9
Salinas = Salinópolis *Brazil* 0°40S 47°20W **332** B2
Salinas *Brazil* 16°10S 42°10W **333** E3
Salinas *Ecuador* 2°10S 80°58W **328** D1
Salinas *Calif., U.S.A.* 36°40N 121°39W **306** J5
Salinas → *Guatemala* 16°28N 90°31W **319** D6
Salinas → *Calif., U.S.A.* 36°45N 121°48W **306** J5
Salinas, B. das *Angola* 14°11S 12°21E **265** E2
Salinas, B. de *Nic.* 11°4N 85°45W **320** D2
Salinas, Pampa de las *Argentina* 31°58S 66°42W **334** C2
Salinas Ambargasta *Argentina* 29°0S 65°0W **334** B3
Salinas de Hidalgo *Mexico* 22°38N 101°43W **318** C4
Salinas Grandes *Argentina* 30°0S 65°0W **334** C3
Salinas Pueblo Missions ⌂ *U.S.A.* 34°6N 106°4W **305** J10
Salinas Valley *U.S.A.* 36°15N 121°15W **306** J5
Saline *U.S.A.* 42°10N 83°47W **311** B13
Saline → *Ark., U.S.A.* 33°10N 92°8W **314** E8
Saline → *Kans., U.S.A.* 38°52N 97°30W **308** F5
Saline B. *Trin. & Tob.* 10°42N 61°2W **323** t
Saline di Trapani e Paceco ⌂ *Italy* 37°59N 12°28E **200** E5
Saline I. *Grenada* 12°26N 61°28W **323** q
Salines, C. de ses *Spain* 39°16N 3°4E **206** B4
Salines, Étang des *Martinique* 14°24N 60°52W **322** j
Salines, Pt. *Grenada* 12°0N 61°48W **323** q
Salines, Pte. de *Martinique* 14°23N 60°53W **322** j
Salinópolis *Brazil* 0°40S 47°20W **332** B2
Salins-les-Bains *France* 46°58N 5°52E **173** F12
Salir *Portugal* 37°14N 8°2W **195** H2
Salisbury = Harare *Zimbabwe* 17°43S 31°2E **269** F3
Salisbury *S. Austral., Australia* 34°46S 138°38E **282** C3
Salisbury *Dominica* 15°26N 61°27W **323** k
Salisbury *Wilts., U.K.* 51°4N 1°47W **169** F6
Salisbury *Md., U.S.A.* 38°22N 75°36W **309** F16
Salisbury *Mo., U.S.A.* 39°25N 92°48W **310** E4
Salisbury *N.C., U.S.A.* 35°40N 80°29W **315** D14
Salisbury I. *Canada* 63°30N 77°0W **297** A12
Salisbury Plain *U.K.* 51°14N 1°55W **169** F6
Săliște *Romania* 45°45N 23°56E **183** E8
Salitre → *Brazil* 9°29S 40°39W **332** C3
Salkehatchie → *U.S.A.* 32°37N 80°53W **316** C9
Şalkhad *Syria* 32°29N 36°43E **251** F7
Salkove *Ukraine* 48°15N 29°59E **183** B14
Salla *Finland* 66°50N 28°49E **160** C23
Sallanches *France* 45°55N 6°38E **175** C10
Sallent *Spain* 41°49N 1°54E **196** D6
Salles *France* 44°33N 0°52W **174** D3
Salles-Curan *France* 44°11N 2°48E **174** D6
Salling *Denmark* 56°40N 8°55E **163** H2
Salliq = Coral Harbour *Canada* 64°8N 83°10W **295** E15
Sallisaw *U.S.A.* 35°28N 94°47W **314** D7
Sallom *Sudan* 19°17N 37°6E **256** D4
Salluit *Canada* 62°14N 75°38W **295** E16
Sallynoggin *Ireland* 53°17N 6°8W **120** B3
Salmān Pak *Iraq* 33°6N 44°34E **213** G11
Salmannsdorf *Austria* 48°14N 16°14E **142** A1
Salmās *Iran* 38°11N 44°47E **213** C11
Salmedina *Spain* 40°18N 3°35W **127** C2
Salmerón *Spain* 40°33N 2°29W **196** E2
Salmo *Canada* 49°10N 117°20W **296** D5
Salmon *U.S.A.* 45°11N 113°54W **304** D7
Salmon → *B.C., Canada* 54°3N 122°40W **296** C4
Salmon → *Idaho, U.S.A.* 45°51N 116°47W **304** D5
Salmon Arm *Canada* 50°40N 119°15W **296** C5
Salmon Gums *Australia* 32°59S 121°38E **279** F3
Salmon Pt. *Canada* 43°52N 77°15W **312** C7
Salmon River Mts. *U.S.A.* 44°50N 115°30W **304** D6
Salmon River Res. *U.S.A.* 43°32N 75°55W **313** C9
Salo *C.A.R.* 3°10N 16°8E **264** B3
Salo *Finland* 60°22N 23°10E **188** D2
Salò *Italy* 45°36N 10°31E **198** C7
Salobreña *Spain* 36°44N 3°35W **195** J7
Salome *U.S.A.* 33°47N 113°37W **307** M13
Salomea *Poland* 52°11N 20°55E **142** B1
Salomon, C. *Martinique* 14°30N 61°6W **322** j
Salon *India* 26°2N 81°27E **243** F9
Salon-de-Provence *France* 43°39N 5°6E **175** E9
Salonga → *Dem. Rep. of the Congo* 0°10S 19°50E **264** C4
Salonga-Nord △ *Dem. Rep. of the Congo* 1°55S 21°45E **264** C4
Salonga-Sud △ *Dem. Rep. of the Congo* 2°25S 21°0E **264** C4
Salonica = Thessaloniki *Greece* 40°38N 22°58E **202** F6
Salonta *Romania* 46°49N 21°42E **182** D6
Salop = Shropshire □ *U.K.* 52°36N 2°45W **169** E5
Salor → *Spain* 39°39N 7°3W **195** F3
Salou *Spain* 41°4N 1°8E **196** D6
Salou, C. de *Spain* 41°3N 1°10E **196** D6
Saloum → *Senegal* 13°50N 16°45W **262** C1
Salpausselkä *Finland* 61°3N 26°15E **188** B4
Salsacate *Argentina* 31°20S 65°5W **334** C2
Salses *France* 42°50N 2°55E **174** F6
Salsette I. *India* 19°12N 72°53E **130** A2
Salsk *Russia* 46°28N 41°30E **191** G5
Salso → *Italy* 37°6N 13°57E **200** E6
Salsomaggiore Terme *Italy* 44°49N 9°59E **198** D6
Salt *Spain* 41°59N 2°47E **196** D7
Salt → *Alta., Canada* 60°0N 112°25W **296** B6
Salt → *Ariz., U.S.A.* 33°23N 112°19W **305** K7
Salt → *Mo., U.S.A.* 39°28N 91°4W **310** E5
Salt Cay *Bahamas* 25°6N 77°18W **153** b
Salt Flats = Witte Pan *Bonaire* 12°3N 68°17W **322** h
Salt Fork Red → *U.S.A.* 34°27N 99°21W **314** D5
Salt L. *N.S.W., Australia* 30°6S 142°8E **281** E3
Salt L. *Hawai'i, U.S.A.* 21°21N 157°55W **302** K14
Salt Lake City = Bidhan Nagar *India* 22°35N 88°25E **124** B2
Salt Lake City *U.S.A.* 40°45N 111°53W **304** F8
Salt Range *Pakistan* 32°30N 72°25E **242** C5
Salt River *S. Africa* 34°6S 18°28E **118** A1
Salt Springs *U.S.A.* 29°21N 81°44W **317** F8
Salt Water L. *India* 22°33N 88°26E **124** B2
Salta *Argentina* 24°57S 65°25W **334** A2
Salta □ *Argentina* 24°48S 65°30W **334** A2
Saltara *Italy* 43°45N 12°50E **199** E9
Saltash *U.K.* 50°24N 4°14W **169** G3
Saltburn by the Sea *U.K.* 54°35N 0°58W **168** C7
Saltcoats *U.K.* 55°38N 4°47W **167** F4
Saltee Is. *Ireland* 52°7N 6°37W **166** D5
Salters *U.S.A.* 33°36N 79°51W **316** B10
Saltfjellet *Norway* 66°40N 15°15E **160** C16
Saltfjorden *Norway* 67°15N 14°10E **160** C16
Saltholm *Denmark* 55°38N 12°43E **163** J6
Salthólmavík *Iceland* 65°24N 21°57W **155** B5
Saltillo *Mexico* 25°25N 101°0W **318** B4
Salto *Argentina* 34°20S 60°15W **334** C3
Salto *Uruguay* 31°27S 57°50W **334** C4
Salto da Divisa *Brazil* 16°0S 39°57W **333** E4
Salto del Guaíra *Paraguay* 24°3S 54°17W **335** A5
Salton City *U.S.A.* 33°18N 115°57W **307** M11
Salton Sea *U.S.A.* 33°15N 115°45W **307** M11
Saltpond *Ghana* 5°15N 1°3W **263** D4
Saltrød *Norway* 58°30N 8°49E **164** F5
Saltsburg *U.S.A.* 40°29N 79°27W **312** F5
Saltsjö-Duvnäs *Sweden* 59°18N 18°12E **139** B3
Saltsjöbaden *Sweden* 59°15N 18°20E **162** E12
Saltykovka *Russia* 55°45N 37°54E **129** B5
Saluda *U.S.A.* 34°0N 81°46W **316** A8
Saluda → *U.S.A.* 34°1N 81°4W **315** D14
Salug *Phil.* 8°7N 122°47E **233** G4
Salûm *Egypt* 31°31N 25°7E **256** A2
Salûm, Khâlig el *Egypt* 31°35N 25°24E **256** A2
Salur *India* 18°27N 83°18E **244** E6
Salut, Is. du *Fr. Guiana* 5°15N 52°35W **329** B7
Saluzzo *Italy* 44°39N 7°29E **198** D4
Salvación, B. *Chile* 50°50S 75°10W **336** D1
Salvador *Brazil* 13°0S 38°30W **333** D4
Salvador *Sask., Canada* 52°10N 109°32W **297** C7
Salvador, El ■ *Cent. Amer.* 13°50N 89°0W **320** D2
Salvador, L. *U.S.A.* 29°43N 90°15W **315** G9
Salvaterra *Brazil* 0°46S 48°31W **332** B2
Salvaterra de Magos *Portugal* 39°1N 8°47W **195** F2
Salvisa *U.S.A.* 37°54N 84°51W **311** G12
Sálvora, I. de *Spain* 42°30N 8°58W **194** C2
Salween → *Burma* 16°31N 97°37E **241** G6
Salyan *Azerbaijan* 39°33N 48°59E **213** C13
Salybia *Trin. & Tob.* 10°43N 61°2W **323** t
Salza → *Austria* 47°40N 14°43E **180** D7
Salzach → *Austria* 48°12N 12°56E **180** C5
Salzburg *Austria* 47°48N 13°2E **180** D6
Salzburg □ *Austria* 47°15N 13°0E **180** D6
Salzburgen = Château-Salins *France* 48°50N 6°30E **173** D13
Salzgitter *Germany* 52°9N 10°19E **178** C6
Salzkotten *Germany* 51°40N 8°37E **178** D4
Salzwedel *Germany* 52°52N 11°10E **178** C7
Sam *Gabon* 0°58N 11°16E **264** B2
Sam *India* 26°50N 70°31E **242** F4
Sam Neua *Laos* 20°29N 104°5E **228** G5
Sam Ngao *Thailand* 17°18N 99°0E **236** D2
Sam Rayburn Res. *U.S.A.* 31°4N 94°5W **314** F7
Sam Son *Vietnam* 19°44N 105°54E **236** C5
Sama de Langreo = Langreo *Spain* 43°18N 5°40W **194** B5
Samacimbo *Angola* 13°33S 16°59E **265** E3
Şamad *Oman* 22°48N 58°9E **249** B7
Samagaltay *Russia* 50°36N 95°3E **217** B13
Samaipata *Bolivia* 18°9S 63°52W **331** D5
Samal *Phil.* 7°5N 125°42E **233** H5
Samal I. *Phil.* 7°3N 125°44E **233** H5
Samales Group *Phil.* 6°0N 122°0E **233** J3
Samalkot *India* 17°3N 82°13E **244** F6
Samâlût *Egypt* 28°20N 30°42E **256** B3
Samana *India* 30°10N 76°13E **242** D7
Samana Cay *Bahamas* 23°3N 73°45W **321** B5
Samandağ *Turkey* 36°5N 35°59E **250** B6
Samandıra *Turkey* 40°59N 29°13E **203** F13
Samanga *Tanzania* 8°20S 39°13E **269** D4
Samangān □ *Afghan.* 36°15N 68°3E **240** A3
Samangwa *Dem. Rep. of the Congo* 4°23S 24°10E **265** C4
Samani *Japan* 42°7N 142°56E **220** C11
Samanlı Dağları *Turkey* 40°32N 29°10E **203** F13
Samannûd *Egypt* 30°57N 31°14E **251** H2
Samar *Phil.* 12°0N 125°0E **233** F5
Samar □ *Phil.* 11°50N 125°0E **233** F5
Samar Sea *Phil.* 12°0N 124°15E **232** E5
Samara *Russia* 53°8N 50°6E **190** D10
Samara → *Russia* 53°10N 50°4E **190** D10
Samara → *Ukraine* 48°26N 35°7E **189** H8
Samarai *Papua N. G.* 10°39S 150°41E **286** F6
Samaria = Shōmrōn *West Bank* 32°15N 35°13E **251** F6
Samaria *West Bank* 32°17N 35°12E **251** F6
Samariá △ *Greece* 35°17N 23°58E **207** E4
Samariapo *Venezuela* 5°15N 67°48W **328** B4
Samarinda *Indonesia* 0°30S 117°9E **235** C5
Samarkand = Samarqand *Uzbekistan* 39°40N 66°55E **217** E7
Samarkandsky = Temirtau *Kazakhstan* 50°5N 72°56E **217** B8
Samarqand *Uzbekistan* 39°40N 66°55E **217** E7
Samarqand □ *Uzbekistan* 39°35N 66°35E **217** E7
Sāmarrā' *Iraq* 34°12N 43°52E **213** E10
Samastipur *India* 25°50N 85°50E **243** G11
Samatya *Turkey* 40°59N 28°55E **122** C1
Samaúma *Brazil* 7°50S 60°2W **331** B5
Şamaxı *Azerbaijan* 40°38N 48°37E **191** K9
Samba *Équateur, Dem. Rep. of the Congo* 0°13N 21°25E **264** B4
Samba *Maniema, Dem. Rep. of the Congo* 4°38S 26°22E **265** C5
Samba *Jammu & Kashmir, India* 32°32N 75°10E **243** C6
Samba Caju *Angola* 8°46S 15°24E **265** D3
Sambaíba *Brazil* 7°8S 45°21W **332** C2
Sambalpur *India* 21°28N 84°4E **244** D7
Sambar, Tanjung *Indonesia* 2°59S 110°19E **235** C4
Sambas *Indonesia* 1°20N 109°20E **235** B3
Sambava *Madag.* 14°16S 50°10E **272** A3
Sambawizi *Zimbabwe* 18°24S 26°13E **269** F2
Sambhajinagar = Aurangabad *India* 19°50N 75°23E **244** E2
Sambhal *India* 28°35N 78°37E **243** E8
Sambhar *India* 26°52N 75°6E **242** F6
Sambhar L. *India* 26°55N 75°12E **242** F6
Sambiase *Italy* 38°58N 16°17E **201** D9
Sambir *Ukraine* 49°30N 23°10E **185** J10
Sambo *Angola* 13°3S 16°8E **265** E3
Sambo *Indonesia* 3°22S 118°52E **235** C5
Samboja *Indonesia* 1°1S 117°1E **235** C5
Sambor *Cambodia* 12°46N 106°0E **236** F6
Sambor Prei Kuk *Cambodia* 12°46N 105°58E **236** F5
Samborombón, B. *Argentina* 36°5S 57°20W **334** D4
Sambuca di Sicilia *Italy* 37°39N 13°7E **200** E6
Samburu ⌂ *Kenya* 0°37N 37°31E **268** B4
Samcheok *S. Korea* 37°30N 129°10E **224** C4
Same *Tanzania* 4°2S 37°38E **268** C4
Samer *France* 50°38N 1°44E **173** B8
Samet, Ko *Thailand* 12°34N 101°27E **236** F3
Samfya *Zambia* 11°22S 29°31E **269** E2
Samḥān, Jabal *Oman* 17°12N 54°55E **249** C6
Sami *Greece* 38°15N 20°39E **207** C2
Samka *Burma* 20°9N 96°57E **241** E6
Şämkir *Azerbaijan* 40°50N 46°0E **191** K8
Şamlı *Turkey* 39°48N 27°51E **205** B9
Sammanturai *Sri Lanka* 7°36N 81°39E **245** L5
Samnah *Si. Arabia* 25°10N 37°15E **246** E3
Samnū *Libya* 27°15N 14°55E **258** C2
Samo Alto *Chile* 30°22S 71°0W **334** C1
Samoa ■ *Pac. Oc.* 14°0S 172°0W **287** V20
Samoan Is. *Pac. Oc.* 14°0S 171°0W **287** V20
Samobor *Croatia* 45°47N 15°44E **199** C12

Samoëns France 46°5N 6°45E 173 F13
Samokov Bulgaria 42°18N 23°35E 202 D7
Šamorín Slovak Rep. 48°2N 17°19E 181 C10
Samorogouan Burkina Faso 11°21N 4°57W 262 C4
Samos Greece 37°45N 26°50E 205 D8
Samoš Serbia 45°13N 20°46E 182 E5
Samos Spain 42°44N 7°20W 194 C3
Samos □ Greece 37°45N 26°50E 205 D8
Samoset U.S.A. 27°28N 82°33W 317 H7
Samosir Indonesia 2°55N 98°50E 234 B1
Samothráki = Mathraki Greece 39°48N 19°31E 206 B9
Samothraki Greece 40°28N 25°28E 203 F9
Samoylovka Russia 51°12N 43°43E 190 E6
Sampa Angola 10°38S 18°56E 265 E3
Sampa Ghana 8°0N 2°36W 262 D4
Sampacho Argentina 33°20S 64°50W 334 C3
Sampalan Indonesia 8°41S 115°34E 231 K18
Sampaloc Phil. 14°36N 120°59E 127 B1
Sampang Indonesia 7°11S 113°13E 235 D4
Samper de Calanda Spain 41°11N 0°28W 196 D4
Sampéyre Italy 44°34N 7°11E 198 D4
Samphan Thawong Thailand 13°44N 100°31E 113 B2
Sampit Indonesia 2°34S 113°0E 235 C4
Sampit → Indonesia 2°44S 112°54E 235 C4
Sampit, Teluk Indonesia 3°5S 113°3E 235 C4
Sampun Papua N. G. 5°21S 152°8E 286 C7
Samrong Cambodia 14°15N 103°30E 236 E4
Samseon S. Korea 37°34N 127°0E 137 B2
Samsø Denmark 55°50N 10°35E 163 J4
Samsø Bælt Denmark 55°45N 10°45E 163 J4
Samson U.S.A. 31°7N 86°3W 316 D3
Samsun Turkey 41°15N 36°22E 212 B7
Samsun □ Turkey 41°10N 36°10E 212 B7
Samtah Si. Arabia 16°36N 42°56E 248 C3
Samtredia Georgia 42°7N 42°24E 191 J6
Samuel Smith Park Canada 43°35N 79°30W 141 B1
Samui, Ko Thailand 9°30N 100°0E 237 b
Samur → Russia 41°53N 48°32E 191 K9
Samurskiy Khrebet Russia 41°55N 47°11E 191 K8
Samusole Dem. Rep. of the Congo 10°2S 24°0E 265 E4
Samut Prakan Thailand 13°40N 100°36E 113 B2
Samut Sakhon Thailand 13°32N 100°17E 236 F3
Samut Songkhram Thailand 13°24N 100°1E 236 F3
Samwari Pakistan 28°30N 66°46E 242 E2
San Mali 13°15N 4°57W 262 C4
San → Cambodia 13°32N 105°57E 236 F5
San → Poland 50°45N 21°51E 185 H8
San Adrián Spain 42°20N 1°56W 196 C3
San Adrián, C. de Spain 43°21N 8°50W 194 B2
San Agustín Colombia 1°53N 76°16W 328 C2
San Agustin Romblon, Phil. 12°34N 122°6E 232 E4
San Agustin, C. Phil. 6°20N 126°13E 233 H6
San Agustín de Valle Fértil Argentina 30°35S 67°30W 334 C2
San Ambrosio Pac. Oc. 26°28S 79°53W 326 F3
San Andreas U.S.A. 38°12N 120°41W 306 G6
San Andres Catanduanes, Phil. 13°36N 124°6E 232 E5
San Andres Romblon, Phil. 13°19N 122°41E 232 E4
San Andres Romblon, Phil. 12°31N 122°2E 232 E4
San Andrés Barcelona, Spain 41°26N 2°11E 114 A2
San Andrés, I. de Caribbean 12°42N 81°46W 320 D3
San Andrês del Rabanedo Spain 42°37N 5°36W 194 C5
San Andres Mts. U.S.A. 33°0N 106°30W 305 K10
San Andres Pt. Phil. 13°34N 121°52E 232 E3
San Andrés Tuxtla Mexico 18°27N 95°13W 319 D5
San Angel Mexico 19°20N 99°11W 128 B1
San Angelo U.S.A. 31°28N 100°26W 314 F4
San Anselmo U.S.A. 37°59N 122°34W 306 H4
San Antonio Belize 16°15N 89°2W 320 C2
San Antonio Chile 33°40S 71°40W 334 C1
San Antonio Phil. 14°57N 120°5E 232 D3
San Antonio N. Mex., U.S.A. 33°55N 106°52W 305 K10
San Antonio Tex., U.S.A. 29°25N 98°29W 314 G5
San Antonio Venezuela 3°30N 66°44W 328 C4
San Antonio → U.S.A. 28°30N 96°54W 314 G6
San Antonio, C. Argentina 36°15S 56°40W 334 D4
San Antonio, C. de Cuba 21°50N 84°57W 320 B3
San Antonio, C. de Spain 38°48N 0°12E 197 G5
San Antonio, Mt. U.S.A. 34°17N 117°38W 307 L9
San Antonio B. Phil. 8°38N 117°35E 233 G1
San Antonio de los Baños Cuba 22°54N 82°31W 320 B3
San Antonio de los Cobres Argentina 24°10S 66°17W 334 A2
San Antonio Oeste Argentina 40°40S 65°0W 336 B4
San Arcángelo Italy 40°14N 16°14E 201 B9
San Ardo U.S.A. 36°1N 120°54W 306 J6
San Augustín Canary Is. 27°47N 15°32W 153 e1
San Augustine U.S.A. 31°32N 94°7W 314 F7
San Bartolomé Canary Is. 28°59N 13°37W 153 e2
San Bartolomé de Tirajana Canary Is. 27°54N 15°34W 153 e1
San Bartolomeo in Galdo Italy 41°24N 15°1E 201 A8
San Basilio Italy 41°56N 12°35E 136 B2
San Benedetto del Tronto Italy 42°57N 13°53E 199 F10
San Benedetto Po Italy 45°2N 10°55E 198 C7
San Benedicto, I. Mexico 19°18N 110°49W 318 D2
San Benito U.S.A. 26°8N 97°38W 314 H6
San Benito → U.S.A. 36°53N 121°34W 306 J5
San Benito Mt. U.S.A. 36°22N 120°37W 306 J6
San Bernardino U.S.A. 34°7N 117°19W 307 L9
San Bernardino Mts. U.S.A. 34°10N 116°45W 307 L10
San Bernardino Str. Phil. 12°30N 124°10E 232 E5
San Bernardo Chile 33°40S 70°50W 334 C1
San Bernardo, I. de Colombia 9°45N 75°50W 328 B2
San-Beyse = Choybalsan Mongolia 48°4N 114°30E 219 B11
San Blas Mexico 26°5N 108°46W 318 B3
San Blas, Arch. de Panama 9°50N 78°31W 320 E4
San Blas, C. U.S.A. 29°40N 85°21W 316 F4
San Bonifacio Italy 45°24N 11°16E 199 C8
San Borja Bolivia 14°50S 66°52W 330 C4
San Borja Lima, Peru 12°6S 76°59W 124 B3
San Bóvio Italy 45°27N 9°18E 129 B2
San Bruno, Pt. U.S.A. 37°39N 122°22W 136 C2
San Bruno Mountain State Park ⌂ U.S.A. 37°41N 122°26W 136 B2
San Buenaventura = Ventura U.S.A. 34°17N 119°18W 307 L7
San Buenaventura Bolivia 14°28S 67°35W 330 C4
San Buenaventura Coahuila, Mexico 27°5N 101°32W 318 B4
San Carlos = Butuku-Luba Eq. Guin. 3°29N 8°33E 263 E6
San Carlos = Sant Carles Spain 39°3N 1°34E 206 C2
San Carlos Argentina 33°50S 69°0W 334 C2
San Carlos Bolivia 17°24S 63°45W 331 D5
San Carlos Chile 36°10S 72°0W 334 D1
San Carlos Baja Calif. S., Mexico 24°47N 112°7W 318 C2
San Carlos Coahuila, Mexico 29°1N 100°51W 318 B4
San Carlos Nic. 11°12N 84°50W 320 D3
San Carlos Neg. Occ., Phil. 10°29N 123°25E 233 F4
San Carlos Pangasinan, Phil. 15°55N 120°20E 232 D3
San Carlos Uruguay 34°46S 54°58W 335 C5
San Carlos Ariz., U.S.A. 33°21N 110°27W 305 K8
San Carlos Amazonas, Venezuela 1°55N 67°4W 328 C4
San Carlos Cojedes, Venezuela 9°40N 68°36W 328 B4
San Carlos de Bariloche Argentina 41°10S 71°25W 336 B2
San Carlos de Bolívar Argentina 36°15S 61°6W 334 D3
San Carlos de la Rápita = Sant Carles de la Ràpita Spain 40°37N 0°35E 196 E5
San Carlos de Río Negro Venezuela 1°55N 67°4W 328 C4
San Carlos del Zulia Venezuela 9°1N 71°55W 328 B3
San Carlos L. U.S.A. 33°11N 110°32W 305 K8
San Carlos Park U.S.A. 26°28N 81°49W 317 J8
San Cataldo Italy 37°29N 13°59E 200 E6
San Celoni = Sant Celoni Spain 41°42N 2°30E 196 D7
San Clemente Chile 35°30S 71°29W 334 D1
San Clemente Spain 39°24N 2°25W 197 F2
San Clemente Calif., U.S.A. 33°26N 117°37W 307 M9
San Clemente I. U.S.A. 32°53N 118°29W 307 N8
San Cristóbal = Es Migjorn Gran Spain 39°57N 4°3E 206 B5
San Cristóbal B. Aires, Argentina 34°38S 58°23W 117 B2
San Cristóbal Santa Fe, Argentina 30°20S 61°10W 334 C3
San Cristóbal Colombia 2°18S 73°2W 328 D3
San Cristóbal Dom. Rep. 18°25N 70°6W 321 C5
San Cristóbal Solomon Is. 10°30S 161°0E 287 N11
San Cristobal Madrid, Spain 40°25N 3°35W 127 B2
San Cristóbal Venezuela 7°46N 72°14W 328 B3
San Cristóbal, Cerro Chile 33°25S 70°38W 137 B2
San Cristóbal, I. Ecuador 0°50S 89°26W 330 a
San Cristóbal, Virgen del Chile 33°25S 70°38W 137 B2
San Cristóbal de las Casas Mexico 16°45N 92°38W 319 D6
San Cristoforo Italy 45°26N 9°9E 129 B1
San Damiano d'Asti Italy 44°50N 8°4E 198 D5
San Daniele del Friuli Italy 46°9N 13°1E 199 B10
San Diego Calif., U.S.A. 32°42N 117°9W 307 N9
San Diego Tex., U.S.A. 27°46N 98°14W 314 H5
San Diego, C. Argentina 54°40S 65°10W 336 D3
San Diego de la Unión Mexico 21°28N 100°52W 318 C4
San Diego Int. ✈ (SAN) U.S.A. 32°44N 117°11W 307 N9
San Dimitri, Ras Malta 36°4N 14°11E 206 E6
San Dimitri Point = San Dimitri, Ras Malta 36°4N 14°11E 206 E6
San Donà di Piave Italy 45°38N 12°34E 199 C9
San Donato Milanese Italy 45°24N 9°16E 129 B2
Sân el Hagar Egypt 30°58N 31°52E 251 H2
San Estanislao Paraguay 24°39S 56°26W 334 A4
San Esteban △ Venezuela 10°24N 67°58W 328 A4
San Esteban de Gormaz Spain 41°34N 3°13W 196 D1
San Eugenio = Artigas Uruguay 30°20S 56°30W 334 C4
San Felice Circeo Italy 41°14N 13°5E 200 A6
San Felice sul Panaro Italy 44°50N 11°8E 199 D8
San Felipe Chile 32°43S 70°42W 334 C1
San Felipe Colombia 1°55N 67°6W 328 C4
San Felipe Baja Calif., Mexico 31°1N 114°52W 318 A2
San Felipe Phil. 15°4N 120°4E 232 D3
San Felipe Venezuela 10°20N 68°44W 328 A4
San Felipe → U.S.A. 33°10N 115°49W 307 M11
San Félix Chile 28°56S 70°28W 334 B1
San Félix Pac. Oc. 26°23S 80°0W 326 F2
San Fernando = Sant Ferran Spain 38°42N 1°28E 206 D1
San Fernando Chile 34°30S 71°0W 334 C1
San Fernando Tamaulipas, Mexico 24°51N 98°10W 319 C5
San Fernando Cebu, Phil. 10°10N 123°42E 233 F4
San Fernando La Union, Phil. 16°40N 120°23E 232 C3
San Fernando Pampanga, Phil. 15°5N 120°37E 232 D3
San Fernando Romblon, Phil. 12°18N 122°36E 232 E4
San Fernando Cádiz, Spain 36°28N 6°17W 195 J4
San Fernando Trin. & Tob. 10°16N 61°28W 323 t
San Fernando Calif., U.S.A. 34°17N 118°26W 307 L8
San Fernando de Apure Venezuela 7°54N 67°15W 328 B4
San Fernando de Atabapo Venezuela 4°3N 67°42W 328 C4
San Fernando di Púglia Italy 41°18N 16°5E 201 A9
San Francique = Erin Trin. & Tob. 10°5N 61°39W 323 t
San Francisco Córdoba, Argentina 31°30S 62°5W 334 C3
San Francisco Bolivia 15°16S 65°31W 331 D4
San Francisco Peru 12°36S 73°49W 330 C3
San Francisco Agusan del S., Phil. 8°30N 125°56E 233 G5
San Francisco Cebu, Phil. 10°39N 124°23E 233 F5
San Francisco Quezon, Phil. 13°21N 122°31E 232 E4
San Francisco S. Leyte, Phil. 10°4N 125°9E 233 F5
San Francisco Calif., U.S.A. 37°46N 122°23W 136 B2
San Francisco → U.S.A. 32°59N 109°22W 305 K9
San Francisco, C. de Colombia 6°18N 77°29W 328 B2
San Francisco, Paso de S. Amer. 27°0S 68°0W 334 B2
San Francisco B. U.S.A. 37°39N 122°14W 136 B3
San Francisco Culhuacán Mexico 19°19N 99°8W 128 C2
San Francisco de Macorís Dom. Rep. 19°19N 70°15W 321 C5
San Francisco del Monte de Oro Argentina 32°36S 66°8W 334 C2
San Francisco del Oro Mexico 26°52N 105°51W 318 B3
San Francisco Int. ✈ (SFO) U.S.A. 37°37N 122°22W 306 H4
San Francisco Javier = Sant Francesc de Formentera Spain 38°42N 1°26E 206 D1
San Fratello Italy 38°1N 14°36E 201 D7
San Fruttuoso Italy 45°34N 9°14E 129 A2
San Gabriel Chile 33°47S 70°15W 334 C1
San Gabriel Ecuador 0°36N 77°49W 328 C2
San Gabriel Calif., U.S.A. 34°5N 118°5W 126 B4
San Gabriel → U.S.A. 33°58N 118°5W 126 C4
San Gabriel Chilac Mexico 18°19N 97°21W 319 D5
San Gabriel Mts. U.S.A. 34°17N 117°38W 307 L9
San Gavino Monreale Italy 39°33N 8°47E 200 C1
San German Puerto Rico 18°4N 67°4W 321 b
San Gil Colombia 6°33N 73°8W 328 B3
San Giljan = St. Julian's Malta 35°55N 14°29E 206 F7
San Gimignano Italy 43°28N 11°2E 198 E8
San Giórgio di Nogaro Italy 45°50N 13°13E 199 C10
San Giórgio Iónico Italy 40°27N 17°23E 201 B10
San Giovanni Bianco Italy 45°52N 9°39E 198 C6
San Giovanni in Fiore Italy 39°15N 16°42E 201 C9
San Giovanni in Persiceto Italy 44°38N 11°11E 199 D8
San Giovanni Rotondo Italy 41°42N 15°44E 199 G12
San Giovanni Valdarno Italy 43°34N 11°32E 199 E8
San Giuliano Milanese Italy 45°24N 9°17E 129 B2
San Giuliano Terme Italy 43°46N 10°26E 198 E7
San Gorgonio Mt. U.S.A. 34°6N 116°50W 307 L10
San Gottardo, P. del Switz. 46°33N 8°33E 179 J4
San Gregorio Uruguay 32°37S 55°40W 335 C4
San Gregorio Calif., U.S.A. 37°20N 122°23W 306 H4
San Guillermo △ Argentina 27°50S 69°45W 334 B2
San Guiseppe Jato Italy 37°57N 13°11E 200 E6
San Ignacio Belize 17°10N 89°5W 320 C2
San Ignacio Beni, Bolivia 14°53S 65°36W 331 C4
San Ignacio Santa Cruz, Bolivia 16°20S 60°55W 331 D5
San Ignacio Baja Calif. S., Mexico 27°27N 112°51W 318 B2
San Ignacio Paraguay 26°52S 57°3W 334 B4
San Ignacio Peru 5°8S 78°59W 330 B2
San Ignacio, L. Mexico 26°54N 113°13W 318 B2
San Ildefonso Phil. 15°4N 120°56E 232 D3
San Ildefonso, C. Phil. 16°0N 122°1E 232 C4
San Ildefonso Pen. Phil. 16°9N 122°5E 232 C4
San Isidro Argentina 34°29S 58°31W 334 C4
San Isidro Lima, Peru 12°5S 77°2W 124 B2
San Isidro Phil. 6°50N 126°5E 233 H6
San Isidro de Potot = Burgos Phil. 16°4N 119°52E 232 C2
San Jacinto Colombia 9°50N 75°8W 328 B2
San Jacinto Phil. 12°34N 123°44E 232 E4
San Jacinto Calif., U.S.A. 33°47N 116°57W 307 M10
San Jaime = Sant Jaume Spain 39°54N 4°4E 206 B5
San Javier Misiones, Argentina 27°55S 55°5W 335 B4
San Javier Santa Fe, Argentina 30°40S 59°55W 334 C4
San Javier Beni, Bolivia 14°34S 64°42W 331 C5
San Javier Santa Cruz, Bolivia 16°18S 62°30W 331 D5
San Javier Chile 35°40S 71°45W 334 D1
San Javier Spain 37°49N 0°50W 197 H4
San Jerónimo Lidice Mexico 19°19N 99°14W 128 C1
San Jerónimo Taviche Mexico 16°44N 96°35W 319 D5
San Joaquín Bolivia 13°4S 64°49W 331 C5
San Joaquín Santiago, Chile 33°29S 70°35W 137 B2
San Joaquin Phil. 10°35N 122°8E 233 F4
San Joaquin Calif., U.S.A. 36°36N 120°11W 306 J6
San Joaquín → Bolivia 13°8S 63°41W 331 C5
San Joaquin → Calif., U.S.A. 38°4N 121°51W 306 G5
San Joaquín, Cerro Ecuador 0°53S 89°30W 330 a
San Joaquin Valley U.S.A. 37°20N 121°0W 306 J6
San Jon U.S.A. 35°6N 103°20W 305 J12
San Jordi = Sant Jordi Spain 39°33N 2°46E 206 B3
San Jorge Argentina 31°54S 61°50W 334 C3
San Jorge Solomon Is. 8°28S 159°38E 287 M10
San Jorge, B. Mexico 31°20N 113°20W 318 A2
San Jorge, G. Argentina 46°0S 66°0W 336 C3
San José = San Josep Spain 38°55N 1°18E 206 D1
San José Argentina 32°12S 58°15W 334 C4
San José Costa Rica 9°55N 84°2W 320 E3
San José Guatemala 14°0N 90°50W 320 D1
San Jose N. Marianas 14°58N 145°37E 302 e
San Jose Mind. Occ., Phil. 12°27N 121°4E 232 E3
San Jose Nueva Ecija, Phil. 15°45N 120°55E 232 D3
San Jose Calif., U.S.A. 37°20N 121°53W 306 H5
San Jose Ill., U.S.A. 40°18N 89°36W 310 D7
San Jose → U.S.A. 34°25N 106°45W 305 J10
San José, Golfo Argentina 42°20S 64°18W 336 B4
San José, I. Mexico 25°0N 110°38W 318 C2
San Jose de Buenavista Phil. 10°45N 121°56E 233 F3
San José de Chiquitos Bolivia 17°53S 60°50W 331 D5
San José de Feliciano Argentina 30°26S 58°46W 334 C4
San José de Guanipa Venezuela 8°53N 64°9W 329 B5
San José de Jáchal Argentina 30°15S 68°46W 334 C2
San José de Mayo Uruguay 34°27S 56°40W 334 C4
San José de Ocuné Colombia 4°15N 70°20W 328 C3
San José de Uchapiamonas Bolivia 14°13S 68°5W 330 C4
San José del Cabo Mexico 23°3N 109°41W 318 C3
San José del Guaviare Colombia 2°35N 72°38W 328 C3
San Jose del Monte Phil. 14°49N 121°3E 232 D3
San José do Anauá Brazil 0°58N 61°22W 329 C5
San José Río Hondo Mexico 19°26N 99°14W 128 B1
San Josep Spain 38°55N 1°18E 206 D1
San Juan Argentina 31°30S 68°30W 334 C2
San Juan Antioquía, Colombia 8°46N 76°32W 328 B2
San Juan Curaçao 12°15N 69°6W 322 g
San Juan Ica, Peru 15°22S 75°7W 330 D2
San Juan Batangas, Phil. 13°50N 121°24E 232 E3
San Juan S. Leyte, Phil. 10°16N 125°10E 233 F5
San Juan Puerto Rico 18°28N 66°7W 321 C6
San Juan Trin. & Tob. 10°39N 61°29W 323 t
San Juan □ Argentina 31°9S 69°0W 334 C2
San Juan → Argentina 32°20S 67°25W 334 C2
San Juan → Bolivia 21°2S 65°19W 331 E4
San Juan → Colombia 4°3N 77°27W 328 C2
San Juan → Nic. 10°56N 83°42W 320 D3
San Juan → Manila, Phil. 14°35N 121°0E 127 B2
San Juan → Utah, U.S.A. 37°16N 110°26W 305 H8
San Juan → Venezuela 10°14N 62°38W 329 A5
San Juan, C. Argentina 54°44S 63°44W 336 D4
San Juan, C. Eq. Guin. 1°5N 9°20E 264 B1
San Juan Bautista = Sant Joan de Labritja Spain 39°5N 1°31E 206 C2
San Juan Bautista = Villahermosa Mexico 17°59N 92°55W 319 D6
San Juan Bautista Chile 33°37S 78°50W 330 c
San Juan Bautista Paraguay 26°37S 57°6W 334 B4
San Juan Bautista Calif., U.S.A. 36°51N 121°32W 306 J5
San Juan Capistrano U.S.A. 33°30N 117°40W 307 M9
San Juan Cr. → U.S.A. 35°40N 120°22W 306 J5
San Juan de Aragón Mexico 19°28N 99°4W 128 B2
San Juan de Aragón, Parque Mexico 19°27N 99°4W 128 B2
San Juan de Guadelupe Mexico 24°38N 102°44W 318 C4
San Juan de Guía, Cabo de Colombia 11°21N 73°59W 328 A3
San Juan de la Costa Mexico 24°20N 110°41W 318 C2
San Juan de los Lagos Mexico 21°15N 102°18W 318 C4
San Juan de los Morros Venezuela 9°55N 67°21W 328 B4
San Juan de Lurigancho Peru 11°59S 77°0W 124 A2
San Juan de Manapiare Venezuela 5°15N 66°5W 328 B4
San Juan de Villa Hermosa = Villahermosa Mexico 17°59N 92°55W 319 D6
San Juan del César Colombia 10°46N 73°1W 328 A3
San Juan del Monte Phil. 14°36N 121°1E 127 B2
San Juan del Norte Nic. 10°58N 83°40W 320 D3
San Juan del Norte, B. de Nic. 11°0N 83°40W 320 D3
San Juan del Río Mexico 20°23N 100°0W 319 C5
San Juan del Sur Nic. 11°20N 85°51W 320 D2
San Juan I. U.S.A. 48°32N 123°5W 306 B3
San Juan Island ⌂ U.S.A. 48°35N 123°8W 306 B4
San Juan Ixtacala Mexico 19°31N 99°10W 128 A1
San Juan Mts. U.S.A. 37°30N 107°0W 305 H10
San Julian Phil. 11°45N 125°27E 233 F5
San Just, Sierra de Spain 40°45N 0°49W 196 E4
San Just Desvern Spain 41°22N 2°4E 114 A1
San Justo B. Aires, Argentina 34°40S 58°33W 117 C1
San Justo Santa Fe, Argentina 30°47S 60°30W 334 C3
San Kamphaeng Thailand 18°45N 99°8E 236 C2
San Lázaro, C. Mexico 24°50N 112°18W 318 C2
San Leandro U.S.A. 37°42N 122°9W 306 H4
San Leonardo de Yagüe Spain 41°51N 3°5W 196 D1
San Lorenzo = Sant Llorenç des Cardassar Spain 39°37N 3°17E 206 B4
San Lorenzo Argentina 32°45S 60°45W 334 C3
San Lorenzo Beni, Bolivia 15°22S 65°48W 331 D4
San Lorenzo Tarija, Bolivia 21°26S 64°47W 331 E5
San Lorenzo Ecuador 1°15N 78°50W 328 C2
San Lorenzo Paraguay 25°20S 57°32W 334 B4
San Lorenzo → Mexico 24°15N 107°24W 318 C3
San Lorenzo, I. Baja Calif., Mexico 28°38N 112°51W 318 B2
San Lorenzo, I. Peru 12°7S 77°15W 330 C2
San Lorenzo, Mte. Argentina 47°40S 72°20W 336 C2
San Lorenzo de la Parrilla Spain 39°51N 2°22W 196 F2
San Lorenzo de Morunys = Sant Llorenç de Morunys Spain 42°8N 1°35E 196 C6
San Lorenzo Tezonco Mexico 19°19N 99°3W 128 C2
San Lucas = Cabo San Lucas Mexico 22°53N 109°54W 318 C3
San Lucas Bolivia 20°5S 65°7W 331 E4
San Lucas Baja Calif. S., Mexico 27°10N 112°14W 318 B2
San Lucas Calif., U.S.A. 36°8N 121°1W 306 J5
San Lucas, C. Mexico 22°52N 109°53W 318 C3
San Lúcido Italy 39°18N 16°3E 201 C9
San Luis = Entre Ríos Bolivia 21°30S 64°25W 334 A3
San Luis = Sevilla Colombia 4°16N 75°57W 328 C2
San Luis Argentina 33°20S 66°20W 334 C2
San Luis Pinar del Rio, Cuba 22°17N 83°46W 320 B3
San Luis Guatemala 16°14N 89°27W 320 C2
San Luis Lima, Peru 12°4S 77°0W 124 B2
San Luis Ariz., U.S.A. 32°29N 114°47W 305 K6
San Luis Colo., U.S.A. 37°12N 105°25W 305 H11
San Luis □ Argentina 34°0S 66°0W 334 C2
San Luis, I. Mexico 29°58N 114°26W 318 B2
San Luis, L. de Bolivia 13°45S 64°0W 331 C5
San Luis, Sierra de Argentina 32°30S 66°10W 334 C2
San Luis de la Paz Mexico 21°18N 100°31W 318 C4
San Luis Obispo U.S.A. 35°17N 120°40W 307 K6
San Luis Potosí Mexico 22°9N 100°59W 318 C4
San Luis Potosí □ Mexico 23°0N 101°0W 318 C4
San Luis Res. U.S.A. 37°4N 121°5W 306 H5
San Luis Río Colorado Mexico 32°29N 114°58W 318 A2
San Manuel Phil. 16°4N 120°40E 232 C3
San Manuel Ariz., U.S.A. 32°36N 110°38W 305 K8
San Marco, C. Italy 39°51N 8°26E 200 C1
San Marco Argentano Italy 39°33N 16°7E 201 C9
San Marco in Lámis Italy 41°43N 15°38E 199 G12
San Marcos Colombia 8°39N 75°8W 328 B2
San Marcos Guatemala 14°59N 91°52W 320 D1
San Marcos Calif., U.S.A. 33°9N 117°10W 307 M9
San Marcos Tex., U.S.A. 29°53N 97°56W 314 G6
San Marcos, I. Mexico 27°13N 112°6W 318 B2
San Mariano Phil. 17°0N 122°2E 232 C4
San Marino San Marino 43°55N 12°30E 199 E9
San Marino Calif., U.S.A. 34°7N 118°5W 126 B4
San Marino ■ Europe 43°56N 12°25E 199 E9
San Martín = Tarapoto Peru 6°30S 76°20W 330 B2
San Martín Antarctica 68°11S 67°0W 151 C17
San Martín Argentina 33°5S 68°28W 334 C2
San Martín Colombia 3°42N 73°42W 328 C3
San Martín Barcelona, Spain 41°24N 2°11E 114 A2
San Martín □ Peru 7°0S 76°50W 330 B2
San Martín → Bolivia 13°8S 63°43W 331 C5
San Martín, L. Argentina 48°50S 72°50W 336 C2
San Martín de la Vega Spain 40°13N 3°34W 194 E7
San Martin de los Andes Argentina 40°10S 71°20W 336 B2
San Martín de Porras Peru 12°1S 77°5W 124 B2
San Martín de Valdeiglesias Spain 40°21N 4°24W 194 E6
San Mateo = Sant Mateu Baleares, Spain 39°3N 1°23E 206 C1
San Mateo = Sant Mateu Valencia, Spain 40°28N 0°10E 196 E5
San Mateo Isabela, Phil. 16°54N 121°33E 232 C3
San Mateo Calif., U.S.A. 37°34N 122°19W 306 H4
San Mateo Tlaltenango Mexico 19°20N 99°16W 128 B1
San Matías Bolivia 16°25S 58°20W 331 D6
San Matías, G. Argentina 41°30S 64°0W 336 B4
San Miguel = Linapacan Phil. 11°30N 119°52E 233 F2
San Miguel = Sant Miquel Spain 39°3N 1°26E 206 C1
San Miguel = Sarrat Phil. 18°9N 120°39E 232 B3
San Miguel Bolivia 16°42S 61°1W 331 C5
San Miguel Santiago, Chile 33°29S 70°39W 137 B2
San Miguel El Salv. 13°30N 88°12W 320 D2
San Miguel Panama 8°27N 78°55W 320 E4
San Miguel Lima, Peru 12°5S 77°6W 124 B2
San Miguel Bulacan, Phil. 15°9N 120°59E 232 D3
San Miguel Palawan, Phil. 11°30N 119°51E 233 F2
San Miguel Surigao S., Phil. 9°3N 125°59E 233 G5
San Miguel Calif., U.S.A. 35°45N 120°42W 306 K6
San Miguel → Bolivia 13°52S 63°56W 331 C5
San Miguel → Ecuador 0°25N 76°30W 328 C2
San Miguel, Golfo de Panama 8°22N 78°17W 328 B2
San Miguel B. Phil. 13°51N 123°11E 232 E4
San Miguel de Huachi Bolivia 15°40S 67°15W 330 D4
San Miguel de Tucumán Argentina 26°50S 65°20W 334 B2
San Miguel del Monte Argentina 35°23S 58°50W 334 D4
San Miguel I. U.S.A. 34°2N 120°23W 307 L6
San Miguel Is. Phil. 7°45N 118°28E 233 H2
San Miniato Italy 43°41N 10°51E 198 E7
San Narciso Phil. 13°34N 122°34E 232 E4
San Nicolas = Sint Nicolaas Curaçao 12°17N 69°8W 322 g
San Nicolás B. Aires, Argentina 34°36S 58°22W 117 B2
San Nicolás Canary Is. 27°58N 15°47W 153 e1
San Nicolas Phil. 18°10N 120°36E 232 B3
San Nicolás de los Arroyos Argentina 33°25S 60°10W 334 C3
San Nicolas I. U.S.A. 33°15N 119°30W 307 M7
San Onofre Colombia 9°44N 75°32W 328 B2
San Onofre Calif., U.S.A. 33°22N 117°34W 307 M9
San Onófrio Italy 41°57N 12°25E 136 B1
San Pablo Bolivia 21°43S 66°38W 334 A2
San Pablo Isabela, Phil. 17°27N 121°48E 232 C3
San Pablo Laguna, Phil. 14°11N 121°31E 232 D3
San Pablo Calif., U.S.A. 37°58N 122°21W 306 H4
San Pablo de Manta = Manta Ecuador 1°0S 80°40W 328 D1
San Páolo di Civitate Italy 41°44N 15°15E 199 G12
San Pascual Phil. 13°8N 122°59E 232 E4
San Pedro B. Aires, Argentina 33°40S 59°40W 334 C4
San Pedro Misiones, Argentina 26°30S 54°10W 335 B5
San Pedro Chile 33°54S 71°28W 334 C1
San Pedro Colombia 4°56N 71°53W 328 C3
San Pedro Ivory C. 4°50N 6°33W 262 E3
San Pedro Baja Calif. S., Mexico 23°55N 110°17W 318 C2
San Pedro Peru 14°49S 74°5W 330 C3
San Pedro □ Paraguay 24°0S 57°0W 334 A4
San Pedro → Chihuahua, Mexico 28°20N 106°10W 318 B3
San Pedro → Nayarit, Mexico 21°45N 105°30W 318 C3
San Pedro → Ariz., U.S.A. 32°59N 110°47W 305 K8
San Pedro, Pta. Chile 25°30S 70°38W 334 B1
San Pedro, Sierra de Spain 39°18N 6°40W 195 F4
San Pedro B. Phil. 11°10N 125°6E 233 F5
San Pedro Channel U.S.A. 33°30N 118°25W 307 M8
San Pedro de Arimena Colombia 4°37N 71°42W 328 C3
San Pedro de Atacama Chile 22°55S 68°15W 334 A2
San Pedro de Jujuy Argentina 24°12S 64°55W 334 A3
San Pedro de las Colonias Mexico 25°45N 102°59W 318 B4
San Pedro de Lloc Peru 7°15S 79°28W 330 B2
San Pedro de Macorís Dom. Rep. 18°30N 69°18W 321 C6
San Pedro del Norte Nic. 13°4N 84°33W 320 D3
San Pedro del Paraná Paraguay 26°43S 56°13W 334 B4
San Pedro del Pinatar Spain 37°50N 0°50W 197 H4
San Pedro Mártir Spain 41°23N 2°6E 114 A1
San Pedro Mártir, Sierra Mexico 31°0N 115°30W 318 A1
San Pedro Mártir △ Mexico 31°0N 115°21W 318 A1
San Pedro Ocampo = Melchor Ocampo Mexico 24°51N 101°39W 318 C4
San Pedro Pochutla Mexico 15°44N 96°28W 319 D5
San Pedro Sula Honduras 15°30N 88°0W 320 C2
San Pedro Tututepec Mexico 16°9N 97°38W 319 D5
San Pedro Zacatenco Mexico 19°30N 99°6W 128 A2
San Pietro Italy 39°8N 8°17E 200 C1
San Pietro, Piazza Rome, Italy 136 b1
San Pietro Vernótico Italy 40°29N 18°0E 201 B11
San Po Kong China 22°20N 114°11E 122 A2
San Rafael Argentina 34°40S 68°21W 334 C2
San Rafael Bolivia 16°45S 60°34W 331 D5
San Rafael Trin. & Tob. 10°34N 61°16W 323 t
San Rafael Calif., U.S.A. 37°58N 122°32W 306 H4
San Rafael N. Mex., U.S.A. 35°7N 107°53W 305 J10
San Rafael Venezuela 10°58N 71°46W 328 A3
San Rafael Chamapa Mexico 19°27N 99°15W 128 B1
San Rafael Hills U.S.A. 34°10N 118°12W 126 A3
San Rafael Mt. U.S.A. 34°41N 119°52W 307 L7
San Rafael Mts. U.S.A. 34°40N 119°50W 307 L7
San Ramón Bolivia 13°17S 64°43W 331 C5
San Ramón de la Nueva Orán Argentina 23°10S 64°20W 334 A3
San Remo Italy 43°49N 7°46E 198 E4
San Román, C. Venezuela 12°12N 70°0W 328 A4
San Roque Argentina 28°25S 58°45W 334 B4
San Roque Manila, Phil. 14°37N 121°5E 127 B2
San Roque N. Samar, Phil. 12°37N 124°52E 232 E5
San Roque Spain 36°17N 5°21W 195 J5
San Rosendo Chile 37°16S 72°43W 334 D1
San Saba U.S.A. 31°12N 98°43W 314 F5
San Salvador El Salv. 13°40N 89°10W 320 D2
San Salvador, Canal de Ecuador 0°25S 90°30W 330 a
San Salvador, I. Ecuador 0°16S 90°42W 330 a
San Salvador de Jujuy Argentina 24°10S 64°48W 334 A3
San Salvador I. Bahamas 24°0N 74°40W 321 B5
San Salvo Italy 42°3N 14°44E 199 F11
San Sebastián = Donostia-San Sebastián Spain 43°17N 1°58W 196 B3
San Sebastián Argentina 53°10S 68°30W 336 D3
San Sebastián Puerto Rico 18°20N 66°59W 321 b
San Sebastián de la Gomera Canary Is. 28°5N 17°7W 153 e1
San Serra = Son Serra Spain 39°43N 3°13E 206 B4
San Serverino Marche Italy 43°13N 13°10E 199 E10
San Severo Italy 41°41N 15°23E 199 G12
San Simeon U.S.A. 35°39N 121°11W 306 K5
San Simon U.S.A. 32°16N 109°14W 305 K9
San Siro Italy 45°28N 9°7E 129 B1
San Souci Australia 33°59S 151°8E 139 B1
San Stéfano di Cadore Italy 46°34N 12°33E 199 B9
San Stino di Livenza Italy 45°44N 12°41E 199 C9
San Telmo = Sant Elm Spain 39°35N 2°21E 206 B3
San Telmo B. Aires, Argentina 34°37S 58°23W 117 B2
San Telmo Baja Calif., Mexico 30°58N 116°6W 318 A1
San Teodoro Phil. 13°26N 121°1E 232 E3
San Tiburcio Mexico 24°8N 101°32W 318 C4
San Valentin, Mte. Chile 46°30S 73°30W 336 C2
San Vicenç dels Horts Spain 41°23N 2°0E 114 A1
San Vicente de Alcántara Spain 39°22N 7°8W 195 F3
San Vicente de Cañete Peru 13°8S 76°30W 330 C2
San Vicente de la Barquera Spain 43°23N 4°29W 194 B6
San Vicente del Caguán Colombia 2°7N 74°46W 328 C3
San Vincenzo Italy 43°6N 10°32E 198 E7
San Vito Costa Rica 8°50N 82°58W 320 E3
San Vito Italy 39°26N 9°32E 200 C2
San Vito, C. Italy 38°11N 12°41E 200 D5
San Vito al Tagliamento Italy 45°54N 12°52E 199 C9
San Vito Chietino Italy 42°18N 14°27E 199 F11
San Vito dei Normanni Italy 40°39N 17°42E 201 B10
San Yanaro Colombia 2°47N 69°42W 328 C4
Saña Peru 6°54S 79°36W 330 B2
Sana' Yemen 15°27N 44°12E 248 D4
Sana → Bos.-H. 45°3N 16°23E 199 C13
Sanaag □ Somali Rep. 10°30N 48°0E 267 B6
Sanaba Burkina Faso 12°25N 3°47W 262 C4
Sanae IV Antarctica 70°20S 9°0W 151 D2
Şanāfir Si. Arabia 27°56N 34°42E 251 L5
Sanaga → Cameroon 3°35N 9°38E 263 E6
Sanak I. U.S.A. 54°25N 162°40W 303 J7
Sanaloa, Presa Mexico 24°50N 107°20W 318 C3
Sanām Si. Arabia 23°40N 44°45E 248 B4
Sanana Indonesia 2°4S 125°58E 231 E7
Sanand India 22°59N 72°25E 242 H5
Sanandaj Iran 35°18N 47°1E 213 E12
Sanandita Bolivia 21°40S 63°45W 334 A3
Sanaroa I. Papua N. G. 9°37S 151°0E 286 E6
Sanary-sur-Mer France 43°7N 5°49E 175 E9
Sanāw Yemen 17°50N 51°5E 249 C5
Sanawad India 22°11N 76°5E 242 H7
Sanbancho Tokyo, Japan 140 a3
Sanbe-San Japan 35°6N 132°38E 222 B4
Sancellas = Sencelles Spain 39°39N 2°54E 206 B3
Sancergues France 47°10N 2°54E 173 E9
Sancerre France 47°20N 2°50E 173 E9
Sancerrois, Collines du France 47°20N 2°40E 173 E9
Sancha He → China 26°48N 106°7E 228 D6
Sanchahe China 44°50N 126°2E 227 B14
Sánchez Dom. Rep. 19°15N 69°36W 321 C6
Sanchez Mira Phil. 18°34N 121°14E 232 B3
Sanchih Taiwan 25°15N 121°30E 225 A3
Sanchor India 24°45N 71°55E 242 G4
Sanch'ung Taiwan 25°4N 121°30E 225 A3
Sanco Pt. Phil. 8°15N 126°27E 233 G6
Sancoins France 46°47N 2°55E 173 F9
Sancti Spíritus Cuba 21°52N 79°33W 320 B4
Sancy, Puy de France 45°32N 2°50E 174 C6
Sand = Polokwane → S. Africa 22°25S 30°5E 271 B5
Sand Norway 59°29N 6°16E 164 E3
Sand Bank B. St. Kitts & Nevis 17°15N 62°38W 322 d
Sand Cr. → U.S.A. 39°3N 85°51W 311 E11
Sand Hills Guyana 6°27N 58°19W 329 B6
Sand Hills Nebr., U.S.A. 42°10N 101°30W 308 D3
Sand I. Midway Is. 28°12N 177°23W 302 c
Sand I. Hawai'i, U.S.A. 21°19N 157°53W 302 K14
Sand Islet Midway Is. 28°16N 177°22W 302 c
Sand Lakes ⌂ Canada 57°51N 98°32W 297 B9
Sand Point U.S.A. 55°20N 160°30W 303 J7
Sand Springs U.S.A. 36°9N 96°7W 314 C6
Sanda Japan 34°53N 135°14E 223 C7
Sandai Indonesia 1°15S 110°31E 235 C4
Sandakan Malaysia 5°53N 118°4E 235 A5
Sandalwood Australia 34°55S 140°9E 282 C4
Sandan = Sambor Cambodia 12°46N 106°0E 236 F6
Sandane Norway 61°46N 6°13E 164 C3
Sandanski Bulgaria 41°35N 23°16E 202 E7
Sandaré Mali 14°40N 10°15W 262 C2
Sandared Sweden 57°43N 12°47E 163 G6
Sandarne Sweden 61°16N 17°9E 162 C11
Sanday U.K. 59°16N 2°31W 167 B6
Sande Møre og Romsdal, Norway 62°15N 5°27E 164 B2
Sande Sogn og Fjordane, Norway 61°20N 5°47E 164 C2
Sande Vestfold, Norway 59°36N 10°12E 162 E4
Sandefjord Norway 59°10N 10°15E 164 E7
Sandeid Norway 59°33N 5°52E 164 E2
Sanders Ariz., U.S.A. 35°13N 109°20W 305 J9
Sanders Ky., U.S.A. 38°40N 84°56W 311 F12
Sanderson Fla., U.S.A. 30°15N 82°16W 316 E7
Sanderson Tex., U.S.A. 30°9N 102°24W 314 F3
Sandersville U.S.A. 32°59N 82°48W 316 C7
Sandfire Roadhouse Australia 19°45S 121°15E 278 C3
Sandfloegga Norway 59°58N 7°10E 164 E4
Sandfly L. Canada 55°43N 106°6W 297 B7
Sandfontein Namibia 23°48S 19°1E 270 B2
Sandhammaren Sweden 55°23N 14°14E 163 J8
Sandheads, The India 21°10N 88°20E 241 E2
Sanðgerði Iceland 64°3N 22°42W 155 C4
Sandía Peru 14°10S 69°30W 330 C4
Sandıklı Turkey 38°28N 30°17E 205 C12
Sandila India 27°5N 80°31E 243 F9
Sandilands Bahamas 25°3N 77°19W 153 b
Sanding Indonesia 3°28S 100°40E 234 C2
Sanding, Selat Indonesia 3°24S 100°34E 234 C2
Sandnes Aust-Agder, Norway 58°53N 7°45E 164 F4
Sandnes Rogaland, Norway 58°50N 5°45E 164 F2
Sandnessjøen Norway 66°2N 12°38E 160 C15
Sandoa Dem. Rep. of the Congo 9°41S 23°0E 265 D4
Sandomierz Poland 50°40N 21°43E 185 H8
Sândominic Romania 46°35N 25°47E 183 D10
Sandona Colombia 1°17N 77°28W 328 C2
Sandongo Angola 15°30S 21°28E 265 F4
Sandoval U.S.A. 38°37N 89°7W 310 F7
Sandover → Australia 21°43S 136°32E 280 C2
Sandoway = Thandwe Burma 18°20N 94°30E 241 F5
Sandown S. Africa 26°5S 28°4E 123 A2
Sandown Park Races U.K. 51°22N 0°21W 125 B1

Sandoy Færoe Is. 61°52N 6°46W 160 F9
Sandpoint U.S.A. 48°17N 116°33W 304 B5
Sandray U.K. 56°53N 7°31W 167 E1
Sandringham U.K. 52°51N 0°31E 168 E8
Sandstone Australia 27°59S 119°16E 279 E2
Sandton S. Africa 26°5S 28°4E 123 A2
Sandu China 26°0N 107°52E 228 E6
Sandumba Angola 13°45S 17°34E 265 E3
Sandur India 15°6N 76°33E 245 F3
Sandusky Mich., U.S.A. 43°25N 82°50W 312 C2
Sandusky Ohio, U.S.A. 41°27N 82°42W 312 E2
Sandusky → U.S.A. 41°27N 83°0W 311 C14
Sandveld Namibia 21°25S 20°0E 270 B3
Sandvig Denmark 55°18N 14°47E 163 J8
Sandvika Norway 59°54N 10°31E 133 A2
Sandviken Sweden 60°38N 16°46E 162 D10
Sandwich U.S.A. 41°39N 88°37W 311 C8
Sandwich, C. Australia 18°14S 146°18E 280 B4
Sandwich B. Nfld. & L., Canada 53°40N 57°15W 299 B8
Sandwich B. Namibia 23°25S 14°20E 270 B1
Sandwip I. Bangla. 22°30N 91°25E 241 D3
Sandy Oreg., U.S.A. 45°24N 122°16W 306 E4
Sandy Pa., U.S.A. 41°6N 78°46W 312 E6
Sandy Utah, U.S.A. 40°32N 111°50W 304 F8
Sandy B. St. Helena 16°0S 5°43W 153 h
Sandy Bay Canada 55°31N 102°19W 297 B8
Sandy Bight Australia 33°50S 123°20E 279 F3
Sandy C. Queens., Australia 24°42S 153°15E 280 C5
Sandy C. Tas., Australia 41°25S 144°45E 281 G3
Sandy Cay Bahamas 23°13N 75°18W 321 B4
Sandy Cr. → N.S.W., Australia 31°54S 145°18E 281 B4
Sandy Cr. → Wyo., U.S.A. 41°51N 109°47W 304 F9
Sandy Creek U.S.A. 43°38N 76°5W 313 C8
Sandy Ground Village Anguilla 18°12N 63°6W 322 a
Sandy Hill Bay Anguilla 18°13N 63°1W 322 a
Sandy I. Anguilla 18°13N 63°7W 322 a
Sandy I. Grenada 12°29N 61°29W 323 q
Sandy I. Grenada 12°13N 61°35W 323 q
Sandy L. Canada 53°2N 93°0W 298 B1
Sandy Lake Canada 53°0N 93°15W 298 B1
Sandy Point India 10°32N 92°22E 245 J11
Sandy Point Town St. Kitts & Nevis 17°22N 62°51W 322 d
Sandy Springs U.S.A. 33°56N 84°23W 316 B5
Sandy Valley U.S.A. 35°49N 115°38W 307 K11
Sandyford Ireland 53°17N 6°13W 120 B2
Sandymount Ireland 53°20N 6°13W 120 B2
Sånfjället △ Sweden 62°17N 13°35E 162 B7
Sanford Fla., U.S.A. 28°48N 81°16W 317 G8
Sanford Maine, U.S.A. 43°27N 70°47W 313 C14
Sanford N.C., U.S.A. 35°29N 79°10W 315 D15
Sanford → Australia 27°22S 115°53E 279 E2
Sanford, Mt. U.S.A. 62°13N 144°8W 303 E11
Sang-i-Masha Afghan. 33°8N 67°27E 242 C2
Sanga Angola 11°9S 15°21E 265 E3
Sanga Mozam. 12°22S 35°21E 269 E4
Sanga → Congo 1°5S 17°0E 264 C3
Sangaie Dem. Rep. of the Congo 6°48S 22°46E 265 D4
Sangamner India 19°37N 74°15E 244 E2
Sangamon → U.S.A. 40°1N 90°26W 310 D6
Sangān Iran 34°23N 60°15E 247 C9
Sanganeb Atoll △ Sudan 19°33N 37°11E 256 D4
Sangar Afghan. 32°56N 65°30E 242 C1
Sangar Russia 64°2N 127°31E 215 C13
Sangar Sarai Afghan. 34°27N 70°35E 242 B4
Sangareddi India 17°38N 78°7E 244 F4
Sangaredi Guinea 11°7N 13°52W 262 C2
Sangarh → Pakistan 30°43N 70°44E 242 D4
Sangasanga Indonesia 0°36S 117°13E 235 C5
Sangasso Mali 12°5N 5°35W 262 C3
Sangatte France 50°56N 1°44E 173 B8
Sangāw Iraq 35°17N 45°10E 213 E11
Sangay Ecuador 2°0S 78°20W 328 D2
Sangay △ Ecuador 2°15S 78°26W 328 D2
Sangbé Cameroon 6°3N 12°28E 264 A2
Sangchris L. U.S.A. 39°39N 89°29W 310 E7
Sangdong S. Korea 37°7N 128°49E 224 D4
Sange Dem. Rep. of the Congo 6°58S 28°21E 268 D2
Sangeang Indonesia 8°12S 119°6E 235 D5
Sangenjaya Japan 35°37N 139°39E 140 B2
Sângeorz-Băi Romania 47°22N 24°41E 183 C9
Sanger U.S.A. 36°42N 119°33W 306 J7
Sângera Moldova 46°55N 28°58E 183 D13
Sangerhausen Germany 51°28N 11°18E 178 D7
Sanggan He → China 38°12N 117°15E 226 E9
Sanggau Kalimantan Barat, Indonesia 0°5N 110°30E 235 B4
Sanggau Kalimantan Barat, Indonesia 1°7N 109°36E 235 B3
Sanggye S. Korea 37°38N 127°3E 137 B2
Sanghar Pakistan 26°2N 68°57E 242 F3
Sangihe, Kepulauan Indonesia 3°0N 125°30E 231 D7
Sangihe, Pulau Indonesia 3°35N 125°30E 231 D7
Sangiran Indonesia 7°25S 110°55E 235 D4
Sangiran △ Indonesia 7°27S 110°50E 231 G14
Sangju S. Korea 36°25N 128°10E 224 D4
Sangkapura Indonesia 5°52S 112°40E 235 D4
Sangkha Thailand 14°37N 103°52E 236 E4
Sangkhla Buri Thailand 14°57N 98°28E 236 E2
Sangkulirang Indonesia 0°59N 117°58E 235 B5
Sangla Pakistan 31°43N 73°23E 242 D5
Sangley Pt. Phil. 14°29N 120°54E 127 C1
Sangli India 16°55N 74°33E 244 F2
Sangmélima Cameroon 2°57N 12°1E 263 E7
Sango Angola 9°51S 15°44E 265 D2
Sango Zimbabwe 18°44S 31°44E 269 F3
Sangod India 24°55N 76°17E 242 G7
Sangole India 17°26N 75°12E 244 F2
Sangorodok = Ust-Vorkuta Russia 67°24N 64°0E 186 A11
Sangpang Bum Burma 26°30N 95°50E 241 B5
Sangre de Cristo Mts. U.S.A. 37°30N 105°20W 305 H11
Sangre Grande Trin. & Tob. 10°35N 61°8W 323 t
Sangro → Italy 42°14N 14°32E 199 F11
Sangrur India 30°14N 75°50E 242 D6
Sangudo Canada 53°50N 114°54W 296 C6
Sangue → Brazil 11°1S 58°39W 331 C6
Sangüesa Spain 42°37N 1°17W 196 C3
Sanguinaires, Îs. France 41°51N 8°36E 175 G12
Sangzhi China 29°25N 110°12E 229 B8
Sanhala Ivory C. 10°3N 6°51W 262 C3
Sanhsia Taiwan 24°56N 121°22E 225 B3
Sanhsien Hualien, Taiwan 23°8N 121°25E 225 C3
Sanhsien T'aitung, Taiwan 23°24N 121°19E 225 C3
Sanhsing Taiwan 24°40N 121°36E 225 B3
Sani Taiwan 24°24N 120°46E 225 B2
Sanibel U.S.A. 26°27N 82°1W 317 J7
Sanibel I. U.S.A. 26°26N 82°6W 317 J7
Sanikluaq Canada 56°32N 79°14W 298 A4
Sanin-Kaigan △ Japan 35°39N 134°37E 222 B6
Sanirajak = Hall Beach Canada 68°46N 81°12W 295 D15
Sanjawi Pakistan 30°17N 68°21E 242 D3
Sanje Uganda 0°49S 31°30E 268 C3
Sanjiang China 25°48N 109°37E 228 E7
Sanjo Japan 37°37N 138°57E 220 F9
Sankarankovil India 9°10N 77°35E 245 K3
Sankeshwar India 16°23N 74°32E 245 F2
Sankh → India 22°15N 84°48E 243 H11
Sankosh → India 26°24N 89°47E 241 B2
Sankrail India 22°33N 88°13E 124 B1
Sankt Andrä Austria 46°46N 14°50E 180 E7
Sankt Anton Austria 47°8N 10°16E 179 H6
Sankt Augustin Germany 50°45N 7°10E 178 E3
Sankt Blasien Germany 47°47N 8°7E 179 H4
Sankt Gallen Switz. 47°26N 9°22E 179 H5
Sankt Gallen □ Switz. 47°25N 9°22E 179 H5
Sankt Goar Germany 50°12N 7°43E 179 E3
Sankt Ingbert Germany 49°16N 7°6E 179 F3
Sankt Johann im Pongau Austria 47°22N 13°12E 180 D6
Sankt Johann in Tirol Austria 47°30N 12°25E 180 D5
Sankt Marein = Smarje Slovenia 46°15N 15°34E 199 B12
Sankt Michel = Mikkeli Finland 61°43N 27°15E 188 B4
Sankt Moritz Switz. 46°30N 9°51E 179 J5
Sankt-Peterburg Russia 59°55N 30°20E 137 B1
Sankt Pölten Austria 48°12N 15°38E 180 C8
Sankt Ulrich = Ortisei Italy 46°34N 11°40E 199 B8
Sankt Valentin Austria 48°11N 14°33E 180 C7
Sankt Veit Austria 48°11N 16°16E 142 A1
Sankt Veit an der Glan Austria 46°47N 14°22E 180 E7
Sankt Wendel Germany 49°27N 7°9E 179 F3
Sankt Wolfgang Austria 47°43N 13°27E 180 D6
Sankuru → Dem. Rep. of the Congo 4°17S 20°25E 265 C4
Sanlihe China 39°53N 116°18E 114 B1
Sanlintang China 31°9N 121°29E 138 C1
Sanliurfa Turkey 37°12N 38°50E 213 D8
Sanliurfa □ Turkey 37°0N 39°0E 213 D8
Sanlúcar de Barrameda Spain 36°46N 6°21W 195 J4
Sanluri Italy 39°34N 8°54E 200 C1
Sânmartin Romania 46°19N 25°58E 183 D10
Sanmen China 29°5N 121°35E 229 C13
Sanmenxia China 34°47N 111°12E 226 G6
Sanming China 26°15N 117°40E 229 D11
Sannan Japan 35°2N 135°1E 223 B7
Sannat Malta 36°1N 14°15E 206 E6
Sannicandro Garganico Italy 41°50N 15°34E 199 G12
Sânnicolau Mare Romania 46°5N 20°39E 182 D5
Sannieshof S. Africa 26°30S 25°47E 270 C4
Sannīn, J. Lebanon 33°57N 35°52E 250 E6
Sanniquellie Liberia 7°19N 8°38W 262 D3
Sannûr Egypt 28°58N 31°3E 251 K2
Sannûr, W. → Egypt 28°59N 31°3E 251 K2
Sano Japan 36°19N 139°35E 223 A11
Sanok Poland 49°35N 22°10E 185 J9
Sanqingshan △ China 28°50N 118°5E 229 C12
Sanquhar U.K. 55°22N 3°54W 167 F5
Sanquianga △ Colombia 2°33N 78°14W 329 C2
Sans Spain 41°22N 2°7E 114 A1
Sans Souci St. Vincent 13°13N 61°7W 323 n
Sans Souci Trin. & Tob. 10°50N 61°0W 323 t
Sansanding Mali 13°48N 6°0W 262 C3
Sansané Niger 13°50N 1°36E 263 C5
Sansepolcro Italy 43°34N 12°8E 199 E9
Sansha China 26°58N 120°12E 229 D13
Sanshui China 23°10N 112°56E 229 F9
Sanski Most Bos.-H. 44°46N 16°40E 199 D13
Sanssouci Germany 52°23N 13°2E 115 B1
Sansui China 26°58N 108°39E 228 D7
Sant Agusti Barcelona, Spain 114 c2
Sant Ambrogio, Basilica di Italy 45°27N 9°10E 129 B2
Sant Antoni de Portmany Spain 38°59N 1°19E 206 D1
Sant Boi de Llobregat Spain 41°20N 2°2E 114 A1
Sant Carles Spain 39°3N 1°34E 206 C2
Sant Carles de la Ràpita Spain 40°37N 0°35E 196 E5
Sant Celoni Spain 41°42N 2°30E 196 D7
Sant Cugat Spain 41°28N 2°5E 114 A1
Sant Elm Spain 39°35N 2°21E 206 B3
Sant Feliu de Guíxols Spain 41°45N 3°1E 196 D8
Sant Feliu de Llobregat Spain 41°22N 2°2E 114 A1
Sant Ferran Spain 38°42N 1°28E 206 D1
Sant Francesc de Formentera Spain 38°42N 1°26E 206 D1
Sant Jaume Spain 39°54N 4°4E 206 B5
Sant Joan Spain 39°36N 3°4E 206 B4
Sant Joan d'Alacant Spain 38°24N 0°26W 197 G4
Sant Joan de Labritja Spain 39°5N 1°31E 206 C2
Sant Joan Despi Spain 41°22N 2°2E 114 A1
Sant Jordi Ibiza, Spain 38°53N 1°24E 206 D1
Sant Jordi Mallorca, Spain 39°33N 2°46E 206 B3
Sant Jordi, G. de Spain 40°53N 1°2E 196 E6
Sant Llorenç de Morunys Spain 42°8N 1°35E 196 C6
Sant Llorenç del Munt y l'Obac △ Spain 41°39N 1°55W 196 D3
Sant Llorenç des Cardassar Spain 39°37N 3°17E 206 B4
Sant Marià del Mar Barcelona, Spain 114 b3
Sant Mateu Baleares, Spain 39°3N 1°23E 206 C1
Sant Mateu Valencia, Spain 40°28N 0°10E 196 E5
Sant Miquel Spain 39°3N 1°26E 206 C1
Sant Pau del Camp Barcelona, Spain 114 c2
Sant Salvador Spain 39°27N 3°11E 206 B4
Sant Vicent del Raspeig Spain 38°24N 0°31W 197 G4
Santa Peru 8°59S 78°40W 330 B2
Sant' Ágata Militello Italy 38°2N 14°8E 201 D7
Santa Agnés Spain 39°3N 1°21E 206 C1
Santa Ana Beni, Bolivia 13°50S 65°40W 331 C4
Santa Ana La Paz, Bolivia 15°31S 67°30W 330 D4
Santa Ana Santa Cruz, Bolivia 18°43S 58°44W 331 D6
Santa Ana Santa Cruz, Bolivia 16°37S 60°43W 331 D5
Santa Ana Ecuador 1°16S 80°20W 328 D1
Santa Ana El Salv. 14°0N 89°31W 320 D2
Santa Ana Guam 13°32N 145°46E 302 d
Santa Ana Sonora, Mexico 30°33N 111°7W 318 A2
Santa Ana Cagayan, Phil. 18°28N 122°20E 232 B4
Santa Ana Manila, Phil. 14°34N 121°0E 127 B2
Santa Ana Solomon Is. 10°50S 162°30E 287 N12
Santa Ana Calif., U.S.A. 33°46N 117°52W 307 M9
Santa Ana → Venezuela 9°30N 71°57W 328 B3
Sant' Ángelo Lodigiano Italy 45°14N 9°25E 198 C6
Santa Anita Park U.S.A. 34°8N 118°5W 126 B4
Sant' Antioco Italy 39°4N 8°27E 200 C1
Santa Bárbara Santa Maria, Azores 36°59N 25°4W 153 d4
Santa Bárbara Terceira, Azores 38°41N 27°20W 153 d1
Santa Bárbara Chile 37°40S 72°1W 334 D1
Santa Bárbara Colombia 5°53N 75°35W 328 B2
Santa Bárbara Curaçao 12°5N 68°51W 322 g
Santa Bárbara Honduras 14°53N 88°14W 320 D2
Santa Bárbara Chihuahua, Mexico 26°48N 105°49W 318 B3
Santa Barbara Phil. 10°50N 122°32E 233 F4
Santa Bárbara Spain 40°42N 0°29E 196 E5
Santa Barbara Calif., U.S.A. 34°25N 119°42W 307 L7
Santa Bárbara Amazonas, Venezuela 3°57N 67°6W 328 C4
Santa Bárbara Barinas, Venezuela 7°47N 71°10W 328 B3
Santa Bárbara, Mt. Spain 37°23N 2°50W 197 H2
Santa Bárbara, Serra de Azores 38°44N 27°19W 153 d1
Santa Barbara Channel U.S.A. 34°15N 120°0W 307 L7
Santa Barbara I. U.S.A. 33°29N 119°2W 307 M7
Santa Catalina Colombia 10°36N 75°17W 328 A2
Santa Catalina Neg. Or., Phil. 9°20N 122°52E 233 G4
Santa Catalina Solomon Is. 10°53S 162°23E 287 N12
Santa Catalina, Gulf of U.S.A. 33°10N 117°50W 307 N9
Santa Catalina, I. Mexico 25°40N 110°47W 318 B2
Santa Catalina I. U.S.A. 33°23N 118°25W 307 M8
Santa Catarina □ Brazil 27°25S 48°30W 335 B6
Santa Catarina, I. de Brazil 27°30S 48°40W 335 B6
Santa Caterina di Pittinuri Italy 40°6N 8°27E 200 B1
Santa Caterina Villarmosa Italy 37°35N 14°2E 201 E7
Santa Cecília Brazil 26°56S 50°18W 335 B5
Santa Clara Cuba 22°20N 80°0W 320 B4
Santa Clara Calif., U.S.A. 37°21N 121°57W 306 H5
Santa Clara N.Y., U.S.A. 44°38N 74°27W 313 B10
Santa Clara Utah, U.S.A. 37°8N 113°39W 305 H7
Santa Clara, I. Chile 33°42S 79°0W 330 c
Santa Clara de Olimar Uruguay 32°50S 54°54W 335 C5
Santa Clara Valley U.S.A. 36°50N 121°30W 306 J5
Santa Clarita U.S.A. 34°24N 118°33W 307 L8
Santa Clotilde Peru 2°33S 73°45W 328 D3
Santa Coloma de Farners Spain 41°50N 2°39E 196 D7
Santa Coloma de Gramenet Spain 41°27N 2°13E 114 A2
Santa Comba Spain 43°2N 8°49W 194 B2
Santa Croce Camerina Italy 36°50N 14°31E 201 F7
Santa Croce di Magliano Italy 41°42N 14°59E 199 G11
Santa Cruz Aruba 12°30N 69°59W 322 f
Santa Cruz Bolivia 17°43S 63°10W 331 D5
Santa Cruz Brazil 6°13S 36°1W 332 C4
Santa Cruz Chile 34°38S 71°27W 334 C1
Santa Cruz Costa Rica 10°15N 85°35W 320 D2
Santa Cruz Curaçao 12°18N 69°7W 322 g
Santa Cruz Maharashtra, India 19°4N 72°51E 130 A1
Santa Cruz Jamaica 18°3N 77°43W 320 a
Santa Cruz Madeira 32°42N 16°46W 153 c
Santa Cruz Peru 5°40S 75°56W 330 B2
Santa Cruz Davao del S., Phil. 6°50N 125°25E 233 H5
Santa Cruz Laguna, Phil. 14°20N 121°24E 232 D3
Santa Cruz Manila, Phil. 14°36N 120°58E 127 B1
Santa Cruz Marinduque, Phil. 13°28N 122°2E 232 E4
Santa Cruz Mind. Occ., Phil. 13°4N 120°43E 232 E3
Santa Cruz Zambales, Phil. 15°46N 119°55E 232 D2
Santa Cruz Calif., U.S.A. 36°58N 122°1W 306 J4
Santa Cruz Venezuela 8°3N 64°27W 329 B5
Santa Cruz □ Argentina 49°0S 70°0W 336 C3
Santa Cruz □ Bolivia 17°43S 63°10W 331 D5
Santa Cruz → Argentina 50°10S 68°20W 336 D3
Santa Cruz, B. Curaçao 12°18N 69°10W 322 g
Santa Cruz, I. Ecuador 0°38S 90°23W 330 a
Santa Cruz, I. de Brazil 22°51S 43°7W 135 B2
Santa Cruz Cabrália Brazil 16°17S 39°2W 333 E4
Santa Cruz da Graciosa Azores 39°5N 28°1W 153 d1
Santa Cruz das Flores Azores 39°27N 31°7W 153 d2
Santa Cruz de Bravo = Felipe Carrillo Puerto Mexico 19°38N 88°3W 319 D7
Santa Cruz de la Palma Canary Is. 28°41N 17°46W 153 e1
Santa Cruz de la Palma ✕ (SPC) Canary Is. 28°40N 17°45W 153 e1
Santa Cruz de Mudela Spain 38°39N 3°28W 195 G7
Santa Cruz de Olorde Spain 41°25N 2°3E 114 A1
Santa Cruz de Tenerife Canary Is. 28°28N 16°15W 153 e1
Santa Cruz del Norte Cuba 23°9N 81°55W 320 B3
Santa Cruz del Retamar Spain 40°8N 4°14W 194 E6
Santa Cruz del Sur Cuba 20°44N 78°0W 320 B4
Santa Cruz do Rio Pardo Brazil 22°54S 49°37W 335 A6
Santa Cruz do Sul Brazil 29°42S 52°25W 335 B5
Santa Cruz I. U.S.A. 34°1N 119°43W 307 M7
Santa Cruz Is. Solomon Is. 10°30S 166°0E 277 C12
Santa Cruz la Vieja △ Bolivia 17°55S 60°50W 331 D5
Santa Cruz Mts. Jamaica 17°58N 77°43W 320 a
Santa Domingo, Cay Bahamas 21°25N 75°15W 320 B4
Santa Efigênia Brazil 23°32S 46°33W 137 B2
Sant' Egidio alla Vibrata Italy 42°49N 13°42E 199 F10
Santa Elena Argentina 30°58S 59°47W 334 C4
Santa Elena Ecuador 2°16S 80°52W 328 D1
Santa Elena Camarines N., Phil. 14°12N 122°24E 232 D4
Santa Elena Manila, Phil. 14°38N 121°5E 127 B2
Santa Elena, C. Costa Rica 10°54N 85°56W 320 D2
Santa Elena del Gomero Chile 33°28S 70°45W 137 B1
Sant' Eufêmia, G. di Italy 38°51N 16°4E 201 D9
Santa Eulalia Spain 41°25N 2°10E 114 A2
Santa Eulària des Riu Spain 38°59N 1°32E 206 D2
Santa Fé Argentina 31°35S 60°41W 334 C3
Santa Fe Nueva Vizcaya, Phil. 16°10N 120°57E 232 C3
Santa Fe Romblon, Phil. 12°10N 122°0E 232 E4
Santa Fé Spain 37°11N 3°43W 195 H7
Santa Fe N. Mex., U.S.A. 35°41N 105°57W 305 J11
Santa Fé □ Argentina 31°50S 60°55W 334 C3
Santa Fé, Canal de Ecuador 0°48S 89°55W 330 a
Santa Fé, I. Ecuador 0°49S 90°5W 330 a
Santa Fé do Sul Brazil 20°13S 50°56W 333 F1
Santa Fe Springs U.S.A. 33°56N 118°3W 126 C4
Santa Filomena Brazil 9°6S 45°50W 332 C2
Santa Fiora Italy 42°50N 11°35E 199 F8
Santa Gertrudis Spain 39°0N 1°26E 206 C1
Santa Giustina Italy 46°10N 12°5E 199 B9
Santa Helena Brazil 2°14S 45°18W 332 B2
Santa Helena de Goiás Brazil 17°53S 50°35W 333 E1
Santa Inês Bahia, Brazil 13°17S 39°48W 333 D4
Santa Inês Maranhão, Brazil 3°39S 45°20W 332 B2
Santa Inés Extremadura, Spain 38°32N 5°37W 195 G5
Santa Inés, I. Chile 54°0S 73°0W 336 D2
Santa Iria da Azóia Portugal 38°49N 9°5W 126 A2
Santa Isabel = Rey Malabo Eq. Guin. 3°45N 8°50E 263 E6
Santa Isabel Argentina 36°10S 66°54W 334 D2
Santa Isabel Puerto Rico 17°58N 66°24W 321 b
Santa Isabel Solomon Is. 8°0S 159°0E 287 M10
Santa Isabel do Araguaia Brazil 6°7S 48°19W 332 C2
Santa Isabel do Morro Brazil 11°34S 50°40W 333 D1
Santa Isabel do Río Negro Brazil 0°24S 65°2W 329 D4
Santa Julia Chile 33°30S 70°35W 137 C2
Santa Lucía Corrientes, Argentina 28°58S 59°5W 334 B4
Santa Lucía San Juan, Argentina 31°30S 68°30W 334 C2
Santa Lucía Canary Is. 27°55N 15°32W 153 e1
Santa Lucia Phil. 17°7N 120°27E 232 C3
Santa Lucía Spain 37°35N 0°58W 197 H4
Santa Lucía Uruguay 34°27S 56°24W 334 C4
Santa Lucia Range U.S.A. 36°0N 121°20W 306 K5
Santa Luzia = Luziânia Brazil 16°20S 48°0W 333 E2
Santa Luzia Brazil 19°47S 43°52W 333 E3
Santa Luzia C. Verde Is. 16°50N 24°35W 153 j
Santa Magdalena Spain 39°42N 3°6E 206 B4
Santa Margarita Argentina 38°28S 61°35W 334 D3
Santa Margarita Calif., U.S.A. 35°23N 120°37W 306 K6
Santa Margarita → U.S.A. 33°13N 117°23W 307 M9
Santa Margarita, I. Mexico 24°27N 111°50W 318 C2
Santa Margherita Italy 38°58N 8°58E 200 D1
Santa Margherita Ligure Italy 44°20N 9°11E 198 D6
Santa María Argentina 26°40S 66°0W 334 B2
Santa Maria Azores 36°58N 25°6W 153 d4
Santa Maria Brazil 29°40S 53°48W 335 B5
Santa Maria C. Verde Is. 16°31N 22°53W 153 j
Santa María Mexico City, Mexico 128 a1
Santa Maria Ilocos S., Phil. 17°22N 120°29E 232 C3
Santa Maria Isabela, Phil. 17°28N 121°45E 232 C3
Santa Maria Calif., U.S.A. 34°57N 120°26W 307 L6
Santa María → Mexico 31°0N 107°14W 318 A3
Santa María, B. de Mexico 25°4N 108°6W 318 B3
Santa Maria, C. de Portugal 36°58N 7°53W 195 J3
Santa María, I. Ecuador 1°17S 90°26W 330 a
Santa Maria Cápua Vétere Italy 41°5N 14°15E 201 A7
Santa Maria da Feira Portugal 40°55N 8°35W 194 E2
Santa Maria da Vitória Brazil 13°24S 44°12W 333 D3
Santa María de Ipire Venezuela 8°49N 65°19W 329 B4
Santa Maria del Camí Spain 39°38N 2°47E 206 B3
Santa Maria di Léuca, C. Italy 39°47N 18°22E 201 C11
Santa Maria do Boiaçu Brazil 0°25S 61°48W 329 D5
Santa Maria do Suaçuí Brazil 18°12S 42°25W 333 E3
Santa Maria dos Marmelos Brazil 6°7S 61°51W 331 B5
Santa María la Real de Nieva Spain 41°4N 4°24W 194 D6
Santa Marinella Italy 42°2N 11°52E 199 F8
Santa Marta Colombia 11°15N 74°13W 328 A3
Santa Marta, Sierra Nevada de Colombia 10°55N 73°50W 328 A3
Santa Marta de Tormes Spain 40°57N 5°38W 194 E5
Santa Marta Grande, C. Brazil 28°43S 48°50W 335 B6
Santa Marta Ortigueira, Ría de Spain 43°44N 7°45W 194 B3
Santa Martabaai = Sint Marthabaai Curaçao 12°17N 69°8W 322 g
Santa Maura = Lefkada Greece 38°40N 20°43E 207 B2
Santa Monica U.S.A. 34°1N 118°29W 126 B2
Santa Monica Mts. U.S.A. 34°6N 118°29W 126 B2
Santa Monica Mts. △ U.S.A. 34°4N 118°44W 307 L8
Santa Olalla Spain 40°2N 4°25W 194 E6
Santa Olalla del Cala Spain 37°54N 6°14W 195 H4
Santa Paula U.S.A. 34°21N 119°4W 307 L7
Santa Pola Spain 38°13N 0°35W 197 G4
Santa Ponça Spain 39°30N 2°28E 206 B3
Santa Quitéria Brazil 4°20S 40°10W 332 B3
Santa Rita = Itumbiara Brazil 18°20S 49°10W 333 E2
Santa Rita Amazonas, Brazil 3°29S 69°19W 328 D4
Santa Rita Paraíba, Brazil 7°8S 34°58W 332 C5
Santa Rita Colombia 4°53N 68°24W 328 C4
Santa Rita Guam 13°23N 144°40E 302 d
Santa Rita Samar, Phil. 11°27N 124°56E 233 F5
Santa Rita Zulia, Venezuela 10°32N 71°32W 328 A3
Santa Rita de Cássia Brazil 11°0S 44°32W 332 D3
Santa Rita do Araguaia = Guiratinga Brazil 16°21S 53°45W 331 D7
Santa Rita do Araguaia Brazil 17°20S 53°12W 331 D7
Santa Rosa = Bella Unión Uruguay 30°15S 57°40W 334 C4
Santa Rosa La Pampa, Argentina 36°40S 64°17W 334 D3
Santa Rosa San Luis, Argentina 32°21S 65°10W 334 C2
Santa Rosa Beni, Bolivia 14°10S 66°53W 330 C4
Santa Rosa Pando, Bolivia 10°36S 67°20W 330 C4
Santa Rosa Santa Cruz, Bolivia 17°7S 63°35W 331 D5
Santa Rosa Brazil 27°52S 54°29W 335 B5
Santa Rosa Colombia 3°32N 69°48W 328 C4
Santa Rosa Curaçao 12°8N 68°53W 322 g
Santa Rosa El Oro, Ecuador 3°27S 79°58W 328 D2
Santa Rosa Galápagos Is., Ecuador 0°4S 90°25W 330 a
Santa Rosa Puno, Peru 14°30S 70°50W 330 C3
Santa Rosa San Martín, Peru 6°41S 76°37W 330 B2
Santa Rosa Phil. 15°25N 120°57E 232 D3
Santa Rosa Calif., U.S.A. 38°26N 122°43W 306 G4
Santa Rosa N. Mex., U.S.A. 34°57N 104°41W 305 J11
Santa Rosa Amazonas, Venezuela 1°29N 66°55W 328 C4
Santa Rosa, Mt. Guam 13°32N 144°55E 302 d
Santa Rosa and San Jacinto Mts. △ U.S.A. 33°28N 116°20W 307 M10
Santa Rosa Beach U.S.A. 30°22N 86°14W 316 E3
Santa Rosa de Amanadona Venezuela 1°29N 66°55W 328 C4
Santa Rosa de Cabal Colombia 4°52N 75°38W 328 C2
Santa Rosa de Copán Honduras 14°47N 88°46W 320 D2
Santa Rosa de la Roca Bolivia 16°3S 61°34W 331 D5
Santa Rosa de Locobe Chile 33°25S 70°33W 137 B2
Santa Rosa de Osos Colombia 6°39N 75°28W 328 B2
Santa Rosa de Río Primero Argentina 31°8S 63°20W 334 C3
Santa Rosa de Viterbo Colombia 5°53N 72°59W 328 B3
Santa Rosa del Palmar Bolivia 16°54S 62°24W 331 D5
Santa Rosa I. Calif., U.S.A. 33°58N 120°6W 307 M6
Santa Rosa I. Fla., U.S.A. 30°20N 86°50W 317 E3
Santa Rosa Range U.S.A. 41°45N 117°40W 304 F5
Santa Rosalía Mexico 27°19N 112°17W 318 B2
Santa Sylvina Argentina 27°50S 61°10W 334 B3
Santa Tecla = Nueva San Salvador El Salv. 13°40N 89°18W 320 D2
Santa Teresa Argentina 33°25S 60°47W 334 C3
Santa Teresa N. Terr., Australia 24°8S 134°22E 280 C1
Santa Teresa Brazil 19°55S 40°36W 333 E3
Santa Teresa Tamaulipas, Mexico 25°17N 97°51W 319 B5
Santa Teresa Venezuela 4°43N 61°4W 329 C5
Santa Teresa △ Uruguay 33°57S 53°31W 335 C5
Santa Teresa de la Ovalle Chile 33°22S 70°44W 137 B1
Santa Teresa di Riva Italy 37°57N 15°22E 201 E8
Santa Teresa Gallura Italy 41°14N 9°11E 200 A2
Santa Teresinha Brazil 10°28S 50°31W 332 D1
Santa Teresita Argentina 36°32S 56°41W 334 D4
Santa Uxía de Ribeira Spain 42°36N 8°58W 194 C2
Santa Vitória Brazil 18°50S 50°8W 333 E1
Santa Vitória do Palmar Brazil 33°32S 53°25W 335 C5
Santa Ynez → U.S.A. 34°41N 120°36W 307 L6
Santa Ynez Mts. U.S.A. 34°30N 120°0W 307 L6
Santa Ysabel U.S.A. 33°7N 116°40W 307 M10
Santadi Italy 39°5N 8°43E 200 C1
Santaella Spain 37°34N 4°51W 195 H6
Santahamina Finland 60°8N 25°2E 121 C3
Santai China 31°5N 104°58E 228 B5
Santaluz Brazil 11°15S 39°22W 332 D4
Santan Indonesia 0°3S 117°28E 235 C5
Santana = Uruaçu Brazil 14°30S 49°10W 333 D2
Santana Bahia, Brazil 13°2S 44°5W 333 D3
Santana São Paulo, Brazil 23°29S 46°36W 137 A2
Santana Madeira 32°48N 16°52W 153 c
Sântana Romania 46°20N 21°30E 182 D6
Santana, Coxilha de Brazil 30°50S 55°35W 335 C4
Santana do Ipanema Brazil 9°22S 37°14W 332 C4
Santana do Livramento Brazil 30°55S 55°30W 335 C4
Santana do Paranaíba = Paranaíba Brazil 19°40S 51°11W 331 D7
Santander Colombia 3°1N 76°28W 328 C2
Santander Phil. 9°25N 123°20E 233 G4
Santander Spain 43°27N 3°51W 194 B7
Santander □ Colombia 7°0N 73°15W 328 B3
Santander Jiménez Mexico 24°13N 98°28W 319 C5
Sant'Angelo, Castel Rome, Italy 136 b1
Santanilla, Is. Honduras 17°22N 83°57W 320 C3
Santanyí Spain 39°20N 3°5E 206 B4
Santaquin U.S.A. 39°59N 111°47W 304 G8
Santarcángelo di Romagna Italy 44°4N 12°26E 199 D9
Santarém Brazil 2°25S 54°42W 329 D7
Santarém Portugal 39°12N 8°42W 195 F2
Santarém □ Portugal 39°10N 8°40W 195 F2
Santaren Channel W. Indies 24°0N 79°30W 320 B4
Santee U.S.A. 32°50N 116°58W 307 N10
Santee → U.S.A. 33°7N 79°17W 315 E15
Santeny France 48°43N 2°34E 134 B4
Santéramo in Colle Italy 40°49N 16°45E 201 B9
Santerno → Italy 44°34N 11°58E 199 D8
Santhià Italy 45°22N 8°10E 198 C5
Santi Taiwan 22°43N 120°39E 225 D2
Santi-Quaranta = Sarandë Albania 39°52N 19°55E 206 B9
Santiago = Río Grande de Santiago → Mexico 21°36N 105°26W 318 C3
Santiago = São Tiago C. Verde Is. 15°0N 23°40W 153 j
Santiago Brazil 29°11S 54°52W 335 B5
Santiago Canary Is. 28°2N 17°12W 153 e1
Santiago Chile 33°26S 70°40W 137 B2
Santiago Panama 8°0N 81°0W 320 E3
Santiago Peru 14°11S 75°43W 330 C2
Santiago Ilocos S., Phil. 17°18N 120°27E 232 C3
Santiago Isabela, Phil. 16°41N 121°33E 232 C3
Santiago → Peru 4°27S 77°38W 328 D2
Santiago, C. Chile 50°46S 75°27W 336 D1
Santiago, I. = San Salvador, I. Ecuador 0°16S 90°42W 330 a
Santiago, Punta de Eq. Guin. 3°12N 8°40E 263 E6
Santiago, Sierra de Bolivia 18°25S 59°25W 331 D6
Santiago Benítez ✕ (SCL) Chile 33°33S 70°42W 137 B1
Santiago de Chiquitos Bolivia 18°19S 59°34W 331 D6
Santiago de Chuco Peru 8°9S 78°11W 330 B2
Santiago de Compostela Spain 42°52N 8°37W 194 C2
Santiago de Cuba Cuba 20°0N 75°49W 320 C4
Santiago de los Caballeros Dom. Rep. 19°30N 70°40W 321 C5
Santiago de Surco Peru 12°9S 77°0W 124 B2
Santiago del Estero Argentina 27°50S 64°15W 334 B3
Santiago del Estero □ Argentina 27°40S 63°15W 334 B3
Santiago del Teide Canary Is. 28°17N 16°48W 153 e1
Santiago do Boqueirão = Santiago Brazil 29°11S 54°52W 335 B5
Santiago do Cacém Portugal 38°1N 8°42W 195 G2
Santiago I. Phil. 16°23N 119°56E 232 C2
Santiago Ixcuintla Mexico 21°49N 105°13W 318 C3
Santiago Jamiltepec Mexico 16°17N 97°49W 319 D5
Santiago Papasquiaro Mexico 25°3N 105°25W 318 C3
Santiago Pinotepa Nacional Mexico 16°19N 98°1W 319 D5
Santiaguillo, L. de Mexico 24°48N 104°48W 318 C4
Santialing Taiwan 25°5N 121°51E 225 A3
Santiao Chiao Taiwan 25°1N 122°0E 225 A3
Santiaolun Taiwan 23°39N 120°9E 225 C2
Santiguila Mali 12°42N 7°25W 262 C3
Santillana del Mar Spain 43°24N 4°6W 194 B6
Santisteban del Puerto Spain 38°17N 3°15W 195 G7
Santo → Peru 8°56S 78°37W 330 B2
Santo Amaro Bahia, Brazil 12°30S 38°43W 333 D4
Santo Amaro São Paulo, Brazil 23°39S 46°42W 137 B1
Santo Amaro Lisboa, Portugal 38°42N 9°11W 126 A1
Santo Anastácio Brazil 21°58S 51°39W 335 A5
Santo André Brazil 23°39S 46°29W 335 A6
Santo André Lisboa, Portugal 38°38N 9°3W 126 B2
Santo Ângelo Brazil 28°15S 54°15W 335 B5
Santo Antão C. Verde Is. 16°52N 25°10W 153 j
Santo Antão do Tojal Portugal 38°49N 9°9W 126 A2
Santo Antônio São Tomé & Príncipe 1°37N 7°27E 265 a
Santo Antônio Brazil 2°24S 60°58W 329 D5
Santo Antônio, Qta. de Portugal 38°39N 9°15W 126 B1
Santo Antônio da Cachoeira = Itaguatins Brazil 5°47S 47°29W 332 C2
Santo Antônio de Jesus Brazil 12°58S 39°16W 333 D4
Santo Antônio do Abaixo = Santo Antônio do Leverger Brazil 15°52S 56°5W 331 D6
Santo Antônio do Içá Brazil 3°5S 67°57W 328 D4
Santo Antônio do Leverger Brazil 15°52S 56°5W 331 D6
Santo Corazón Bolivia 18°0S 58°45W 331 D6
Santo Domingo Dom. Rep. 18°30N 69°59W 321 C6
Santo Domingo Baja Calif., Mexico 30°43N 116°2W 318 A1
Santo Domingo Baja Calif. S., Mexico 25°29N 111°55W 318 B2
Santo Domingo Nic. 12°14N 84°59W 320 D3
Santo Domingo de la Calzada Spain 42°26N 2°57W 196 C2
Santo Domingo de los Colorados Ecuador 0°15S 79°9W 328 D2
Santo Domingo Pueblo U.S.A. 35°31N 106°22W 305 J10
Santo Nino I. Phil. 11°54N 124°26E 233 F5
Santo Stéfano di Camastro Italy 38°1N 14°22E 201 D7
Santo Tirso Portugal 41°21N 8°28W 194 D2
Santo Tomás Galápagos Is., Ecuador 0°51S 91°2W 330 a
Santo Tomás Baja Calif., Mexico 31°33N 116°24W 318 A1
Santo Tomás Peru 14°26S 72°8W 330 C3
Santo Tomas Phil. 7°32N 125°37E 233 H5
Santo Tomas, Univ. of Phil. 14°36N 120°59E 127 B1
Santo Tomás, Volcán Ecuador 0°48S 91°7W 330 a
Santo Tomé Argentina 28°40S 56°5W 335 B4
Santo Tomé de Guayana = Ciudad Guayana Venezuela 8°0N 62°30W 329 B5
Santomera Spain 38°4N 1°3W 197 G3
Santoña Spain 43°29N 3°27W 194 B7
Santorini Greece 36°23N 25°27E 205 E7
Santos Brazil 24°0S 46°20W 335 A6
Santos, Sierra de los Spain 38°7N 5°12W 195 G5
Santos Dumont Brazil 22°55S 43°10W 333 F3
Santos Dumont ✕ (SDU) Brazil 22°54S 43°9W 135 B2
Santoshpur India 22°31N 88°16E 124 B1
Santragachi India 22°35N 88°17E 124 B1
Santry Ireland 53°24N 6°15W 120 A2
Santuario de Aves Laguna Colorada △ Bolivia 22°10S 67°45W 334 A2
Sanur Indonesia 8°41S 115°15E 231 K18
Sanwan Taiwan 24°39N 120°57E 225 B2
Sanwer India 22°59N 75°50E 242 H6
Sanxenxo Spain 42°24N 8°49W 194 C2
Sanxia Shuiku China 30°3N 107°58E 228 B6
Sanxiang China 22°21N 113°25E 219 a
Sanya China 18°14N 109°29E 236 C7
San'yō Japan 34°2N 131°5E 222 C3
Sanyuan China 34°35N 108°58E 226 G5
Sanyuanli China 23°8N 113°14E 121 B2
Sanyuki-Sammyaku Japan 34°5N 134°0E 222 C6
Sanza Pombo Angola 7°18S 15°56E 265 D3
São Bartolomeu de Messines Portugal 37°15N 8°17W 195 H2
São Benedito = Beneditinos Brazil 5°27S 42°22W 332 C3
São Benedito Brazil 4°3S 40°53W 332 B3
São Benedito → Brazil 9°11S 57°2W 331 B6
São Bento Brazil 2°42S 44°50W 332 B3
São Bento do Norte Brazil 5°4S 36°2W 332 C4
São Bernardo do Campo Brazil 23°45S 46°34W 333 F2
São Borja Brazil 28°39S 56°0W 335 B4
São Brás de Alportel Portugal 37°8N 7°37W 195 H3
São Braz, C. de Angola 9°58S 13°19E 265 D2
São Caetano do Sul Brazil 23°37S 46°34W 137 B2
São Caitano Brazil 8°21S 36°6W 332 C4
São Carlos Brazil 22°0S 47°50W 335 A6
São Conrado Brazil 23°5S 43°17W 135 B1
São Cristóvão Rio de J., Brazil 22°53S 43°13W 135 B1
São Cristóvão Sergipe, Brazil 11°1S 37°15W 332 D4
São Domingo do Capim Brazil 1°41S 47°47W 332 B2
São Domingos Brazil 13°25S 43°19W 333 D2
São Domingos Guinea-Biss. 12°19N 15°13W 262 C1
São Domingos da Boa Vista = São Domingo do Capim Brazil 1°41S 47°47W 332 B2
São Domingos do Maranhão Brazil 5°42S 44°22W 332 C3
São Felipe = Içana Brazil 0°21N 67°19W 328 C4
São Felipe = Eirunepé Brazil 6°35S 69°53W 330 B4
São Félix Brazil 11°36S 50°39W 333 D1
São Félix do Xingu Brazil 6°38S 51°59W 331 B7
São Filipe C. Verde Is. 15°2N 24°30W 153 j
São Francisco = Itapagé Brazil 3°41S 39°34W 332 B4
São Francisco Brazil 16°0S 44°50W 333 E3
São Francisco → Brazil 10°30S 36°24W 332 D4
São Francisco do Maranhão Brazil 6°15S 42°52W 332 C3
São Francisco do Sul Brazil 26°15S 48°36W 335 B6
São Francisco Penitência Rio de J., Brazil 135 b1
São Gabriel Brazil 30°20S 54°20W 335 C5
São Gabriel da Cachoeira Brazil 0°8S 67°5W 328 D4
São Gabriel da Palha Brazil 18°47S 40°39W 333 E3
São Gonçalo = Araripina Brazil 7°33S 40°34W 332 C3
São Gonçalo Brazil 22°48S 43°5W 333 F3

São Gotardo Brazil 19°19S 46°3W 333 E2
Sao Hill Tanzania 8°20S 35°12E 269 D4
São João Guinea-Biss. 11°32N 15°25W 262 C1
São João da Baliza Brazil 0°52N 59°52W 329 C6
São João da Barra Brazil 21°38S 41°3W 333 F3
São João da Boa Vista Brazil 22°0S 46°52W 335 A6
São João da Madeira Portugal 40°54N 8°30W 194 E2
São João da Pesqueira Portugal 41°8N 7°24W 194 D3
São João da Ponte Brazil 15°56S 44°1W 333 E3
São João de Meriti Brazil 22°48S 43°21W 333 F3
São João de Montenegro = Montenegro Brazil 29°39S 51°29W 335 B5
São João del Rei Brazil 21°8S 44°15W 333 F3
São João do Araguaia Brazil 5°23S 48°46W 332 C2
São João do Paraíso Brazil 15°19S 42°1W 333 E3
São João do Piauí Brazil 8°21S 42°15W 332 C3
São João do Sul Angola 15°46S 12°0E 265 F2
São João dos Patos Brazil 6°30S 43°42W 332 C3
São Joaquim Amazonas, Brazil 0°1S 67°16W 328 D4
São Joaquim Sta. Catarina, Brazil 28°18S 49°56W 335 B6
São Joaquim △ Brazil 28°12S 49°37W 335 B6
São Joaquim da Barra Brazil 20°35S 47°53W 333 F2
São Jorge Azores 38°38N 28°3W 153 d1
São Jorge, Canal de Azores 38°30N 28°0W 153 d1
São Jorge, Castelo de Portugal 38°42N 9°8W 126 A2
São Jorge, Pta. de Azores 38°42N 27°3W 153 d1
São Jorge, Pta. de Madeira 32°50N 16°53W 153 c
São José Brazil 27°38S 48°39W 335 B5
São José, B. de Brazil 2°38S 44°4W 332 B3
São José da Lagoa = Nova Era Brazil 19°45S 43°3W 333 E3
São José da Laje Brazil 9°1S 36°3W 332 C4
São José de Mipibu Brazil 6°5S 35°15W 332 C4
São José de Ribamar Brazil 2°33S 44°3W 332 B3
São José de Tocantins = Niquelândia Brazil 14°33S 48°23W 333 D2
São José do Norte Brazil 32°1S 52°3W 335 C5
São José do Peixe Brazil 7°24S 42°34W 332 C3
São José do Rio Preto Brazil 20°50S 49°20W 335 A6
São José dos Campos Brazil 23°7S 45°52W 335 A6
São José dos Cocais = Nossa Senhora do Livramento Brazil 15°48S 56°22W 331 D6
São José dos Matões = Parnarama Brazil 5°31S 43°6W 332 C3
São Juliao do Tojal Portugal 38°49N 9°8W 126 A2
São Leopoldo Brazil 29°50S 51°10W 335 B5
São Lourenço Brazil 22°7S 45°3W 333 F2
São Lourenço → Brazil 17°53S 57°27W 331 D6
São Lourenço, Pantanal do Brazil 17°30S 56°20W 331 D6
São Lourenço, Pta. de Madeira 32°44N 16°39W 153 c
São Lourenço do Sul Brazil 31°22S 51°58W 335 C5
São Luís Brazil 2°39S 44°15W 332 B3
São Luís do Curu Brazil 3°40S 39°14W 332 B4
São Luís do Tapajós Brazil 4°25S 56°12W 329 D6
São Luís Gonzaga = Ipixuna Brazil 7°0S 71°40W 330 B3
São Luís Gonzaga Brazil 28°25S 55°0W 335 B5
São Marcos → Brazil 18°15S 47°37W 333 E2
São Marcos, B. de Brazil 2°0S 44°0W 332 B3
São Martinho da Cortiça Portugal 40°18N 8°8W 194 E2
São Mateus Azores 38°26N 28°27W 153 d1
São Mateus Brazil 18°44S 39°50W 333 E4
São Mateus → Brazil 18°35S 39°44W 333 E4
São Mateus do Sul Brazil 25°52S 50°23W 335 B5
São Miguel Azores 37°47N 25°30W 153 d3
São Miguel do Araguaia Brazil 13°19S 50°13W 333 D1
São Miguel do Guamá Brazil 1°37S 47°29W 332 B2
São Miguel do Oeste Brazil 26°45S 53°34W 335 B5
São Miguel dos Campos Brazil 9°47S 36°5W 332 C4
São Nicolau C. Verde Is. 16°20N 24°20W 153 j
São Nicolau → Angola 14°16S 12°22E 265 E2
São Nicolau → Brazil 5°45S 42°2W 332 C3
São Paulo Atl. Oc. 0°56N 29°22W 152 F9
São Paulo Brazil 23°32S 46°38W 137 B2
São Paulo □ Brazil 22°0S 49°0W 335 A6
São Paulo Congonhas ✈ (CGH) Brazil 23°38S 46°39W 137 B2
São Paulo de Olivença Brazil 3°27S 68°48W 328 D4
São Pedro Atl. Oc. 0°56N 29°22W 152 F9
São Pedro do Sul Portugal 40°46N 8°4W 194 E2
São Rafael Brazil 5°47S 36°55W 332 C4
São Raimundo das Mangabeiras Brazil 7°1S 45°29W 332 C2
São Raimundo Nonato Brazil 9°1S 42°42W 332 C3
São Romão Brazil 16°22S 45°4W 333 E2
São Roque Madeira 32°46N 16°48W 153 c
São Roque, C. de Brazil 5°30S 35°16W 332 C4
São Roque do Pico Azores 38°31N 28°19W 153 d1
São Salvador do Congo = Mbanza Congo Angola 6°18S 14°16E 265 D2
São Sebastião Azores 38°39N 27°6W 153 d1
São Sebastião, I. de Brazil 23°50S 45°18W 335 A6
São Sebastião do Paraíso Brazil 20°54S 46°59W 335 A6
São Simão Brazil 18°56S 50°30W 333 E1
São Teotónio Portugal 37°30N 8°42W 195 H2
São Tiago C. Verde Is. 15°0N 23°40W 153 j
São Tomé Brazil 5°58S 36°4W 332 C4
São Tomé São Tomé & Príncipe 0°10N 6°39E 265 a
São Tomé, C. de Brazil 22°0S 40°59W 333 F3
São Tomé, Pico de São Tomé & Príncipe 0°16N 6°33E 265 a
São Tomé & Príncipe ■ Africa 0°12N 6°39E 265 a
São Vicente = Araguatins Brazil 5°38S 48°7W 332 C2
São Vicente Brazil 23°57S 46°23W 335 A6
São Vicente C. Verde Is. 17°0N 25°0W 153 j
São Vicente Madeira 32°48N 17°3W 153 c
São Vicente, C. de Portugal 37°0N 9°0W 195 H1
Saona, I. Dom. Rep. 18°10N 68°40W 321 C6
Saône → France 45°44N 4°50E 173 G11
Saône-et-Loire □ France 46°30N 4°50E 173 F11
Saonek Indonesia 0°22S 130°55E 231 E8
Saoura, O. → Algeria 29°0N 0°55W 261 C4
Sapa India 22°30N 88°15E 124 B1
Sapam, Ao Thailand 8°0N 98°26E 237 a
Sapanca Turkey 40°41N 30°16E 212 B4
Sapanjang Indonesia 7°10S 115°50E 235 D5
Sapão → Brazil 11°1S 45°32W 332 D2
Saparua Indonesia 3°33S 128°40E 231 E7
Sapateiro, Cor. do → Brazil 23°35S 46°41W 137 B1
Sapé Brazil 7°6S 35°13W 332 C4
Sape Indonesia 8°34S 118°59E 235 D5
Sape, Teluk Indonesia 8°32S 119°4E 235 D5
Sapele Nigeria 5°50N 5°40E 263 D6
Sapelo I. U.S.A. 31°25N 81°12W 316 D8
Sapelo Sound U.S.A. 31°30N 81°10W 316 D8
Sapes Greece 41°2N 25°43E 203 E9
Şaphane Turkey 39°1N 29°13E 205 B11
Sapi ◠ Zimbabwe 15°48S 29°42E 269 F2
Sapienza Greece 36°45N 21°43E 204 E3
Sapindji Dem. Rep. of the Congo 9°39S 23°12E 265 D4
Sapo △ Liberia 5°15N 8°30W 262 D3
Sapone Burkina Faso 12°3N 1°35W 263 C4
Saposoa Peru 6°55S 76°45W 330 B2
Sapotskina Belarus 53°49N 23°40E 184 E10
Sapouy Burkina Faso 11°34N 1°44W 263 C4
Sapozhok Russia 53°59N 40°41E 190 D5
Sapphire Australia 23°28S 147°43E 280 C4
Sappho U.S.A. 48°4N 124°16W 306 B2
Sapporo Japan 43°0N 141°21E 220 C10
Sapri Italy 40°4N 15°38E 201 B8
Sapu Angola 12°28S 19°26E 265 E3
Sapudi Indonesia 7°6S 114°20E 235 D4
Sapulpa U.S.A. 35°59N 96°5W 314 D6
Sapulut Malaysia 4°42N 116°28E 235 B5
Saqqez Iran 36°15N 46°20E 213 D12
Sar Dasht Āżarbāyjān-e Gharbī, Iran 36°9N 45°28E 213 D11
Sar Dasht Khuzestān, Iran 32°32N 48°52E 247 C6
Sar-e Pol Afghan. 36°10N 66°0E 240 A2
Sar-e Pol □ Afghan. 36°20N 65°50E 240 A2
Sar Gachīneh = Yāsūj Iran 30°31N 51°31E 247 D6
Sar Passage Palau 7°12N 134°22E 288 c
Sar Planina Macedonia 42°0N 21°0E 202 E4
Sara Burkina Faso 11°40N 3°53W 262 C4
Sara Niger 20°46N 12°35E 259 D2
Sara Phil. 11°16N 123°1E 233 F4
Šara △ Serbia 42°12N 21°0E 202 D5
Sara Buri = Saraburi Thailand 14°30N 100°55E 236 E3
Sarāb Iran 37°55N 47°40E 213 D12
Sarābādī Iraq 33°1N 44°48E 246 C5
Sarabît el Khâdim Egypt 29°2N 33°25E 251 J4
Sarābleh Iran 33°44N 46°34E 213 F12
Saraburi Thailand 14°30N 100°55E 236 E3
Saradiya India 21°34N 70°2E 242 J4
Saraféré Mali 15°50N 3°40W 262 B4
Saragossa = Zaragoza Spain 41°39N 0°53W 196 D4
Saraguro Ecuador 3°35S 79°16W 328 D2
Sarahs Turkmenistan 36°32N 61°13E 247 B9
Sarai Naurang Pakistan 32°50N 70°47E 242 C4
Saraikela India 22°42N 85°56E 243 H11
Saraipali India 21°20N 82°59E 244 D6
Saraiu Romania 44°43N 28°10E 183 F13
Sarajevo Bos.-H. 43°52N 18°26E 182 G3
Sarakhs = Sarahs Turkmenistan 36°32N 61°13E 247 B9
Sarakhs Iran 36°32N 61°9E 216 E6
Saramacca → Suriname 5°50N 55°55W 329 B6
Saramati Burma 25°44N 95°2E 241 C5
Saran, Gunung Indonesia 0°30S 111°25E 235 C4
Saranac U.S.A. 42°56N 85°13W 311 B11
Saranac Lake U.S.A. 44°20N 74°10W 313 B10
Saranac Lakes U.S.A. 44°20N 74°28W 313 B10
Saranda Tanzania 5°45S 34°59E 268 D3
Sarandë Albania 39°52N 19°55E 206 B9
Sarandi Argentina 34°40S 58°20W 117 C2
Sarandí del Yí Uruguay 33°18S 55°38W 335 C4
Sarandí Grande Uruguay 33°44S 56°20W 334 C4
Sarangani □ Phil. 5°45N 125°20E 233 J5
Sarangani B. Phil. 6°0N 125°13E 233 J5
Sarangani I. Phil. 5°26N 125°28E 233 J5
Sarangani Is. Phil. 5°25N 125°25E 233 J5
Sarangarh India 21°30N 83°5E 244 D6
Saranovo = Septemvri Bulgaria 42°13N 24°6E 203 D8
Saransk Russia 54°10N 45°10E 190 C7
Sarapul Russia 56°28N 53°48E 186 C9
Sarāqib Syria 35°52N 36°47E 250 C7
Sarar Plain = Bannaanka Saraar Somali Rep. 9°25N 46°17E 267 C6
Sarasota U.S.A. 27°20N 82°32W 317 H7
Saraswati → India 22°46N 88°15E 124 A1
Sarata Ukraine 46°1N 29°40E 183 D14
Sarata → Ukraine 45°51N 29°41E 183 E14
Saratoga Calif., U.S.A. 37°16N 122°2W 306 H4
Saratoga Wyo., U.S.A. 41°27N 106°49W 304 F10
Saratoga ◠ U.S.A. 43°0N 73°38W 313 D11
Saratoga L. U.S.A. 43°1N 73°44W 313 C11
Saratoga Springs U.S.A. 43°5N 73°47W 313 C11
Saratok Malaysia 1°55N 111°17E 235 B4
Saratov Russia 51°30N 46°2E 190 E7
Saratov □ Russia 51°50N 46°20E 190 E8
Sarāvān Iran 27°25N 62°15E 247 E9
Saravane Laos 15°43N 106°25E 236 E6
Sarawak □ Malaysia 2°0N 113°0E 235 B4
Saray Tekirdağ, Turkey 41°26N 27°55E 203 E11
Saray Van, Turkey 38°38N 44°9E 213 C11
Saraya Senegal 12°50N 11°45W 262 C2
Saraycık Turkey 39°1N 29°49E 205 B11
Sarayköy Turkey 37°55N 28°54E 205 D10
Saraylar Turkey 40°39N 27°40E 203 F11
Sarayönü Turkey 38°16N 32°24E 212 C5
Sarbāz Iran 26°38N 61°19E 247 E9
Sarbīsheh Iran 32°30N 59°40E 247 C8
Sárbogárd Hungary 46°50N 18°40E 182 D3
Sarca → Italy 45°52N 10°52E 198 C7
Sarcelles France 49°1N 2°23E 173 D9
Sarda → India 27°21N 81°23E 243 F9
Sardalas Libya 25°50N 10°34E 258 C2
Sardar Sarovar Dam India 21°50N 73°50E 244 D1
Sardarshahr India 28°30N 74°29E 242 E6
Sardegna □ Italy 40°0N 9°0E 200 B1
Sardhana India 29°9N 77°39E 242 E7
Sardina, Pta. Canary Is. 28°9N 15°44W 153 e1
Sardinata Colombia 8°5N 72°48W 328 B3
Sardinia = Sardegna □ Italy 40°0N 9°0E 200 B1
Sardinia U.S.A. 39°0N 83°49W 311 F13
Sardis Turkey 38°28N 27°58E 205 C10
Sardis Ga., U.S.A. 32°58N 81°46W 316 C8
Sārdūīyeh = Dar Mazār Iran 29°14N 57°20E 247 D8
Sarecky potok → Czech Rep. 50°7N 14°23E 135 B2
Saren Indonesia 8°26S 115°34E 231 J18
S'Arenal Spain 39°30N 2°45E 206 B3
Sarentino Italy 46°38N 11°21E 199 B8
Saréyamou Mali 16°7N 3°10W 262 B4
Sargasso Sea Atl. Oc. 27°0N 72°0W 292 G13
Sargent U.S.A. 33°26N 84°52W 316 B5
Sargodha Pakistan 32°10N 72°40E 242 C5
Sarh Chad 9°5N 18°23E 259 G3
Sarhala Ivory C. 8°22N 6°8W 262 D3
Sarhro, Jebel Morocco 31°6N 5°0W 260 B4
Sārī Iran 36°30N 53°4E 247 B7
Sari d'Orcino France 42°3N 8°49E 175 F12
Saria Greece 35°54N 27°17E 205 F9
Saria India 21°38N 83°22E 243 J10
Sariab Pakistan 30°6N 66°59E 242 D2
Sarıbeyler Turkey 39°24N 27°35E 205 B9
Saricumbe Angola 12°12S 19°46E 265 E3
Sarigan N. Marianas 16°43N 145°47E 302 a
Sarıgöl Turkey 38°14N 28°41E 212 C3
Sarıkamiş Turkey 40°22N 42°35E 213 B10
Sarıkaya Turkey 39°29N 35°22E 212 C6
Sarikei Malaysia 2°8N 111°30E 235 B4
Sarıköy Turkey 40°12N 27°37E 203 F11
Sarila India 25°46N 79°41E 243 G8
Sarimbun Singapore 1°24N 103°40E 138 A2
Sarimbun Res. Singapore 1°25N 103°41E 138 A2
Sarina Australia 21°22S 149°13E 280 C4
Sariñena Spain 41°47N 0°10W 196 D4
Sarinleey Somali Rep. 2°22N 42°17E 267 D5
Sarıoğlan Turkey 39°5N 35°59E 212 C6
Sariri Papua N. G. 9°11S 148°35E 286 E5
Sarita U.S.A. 27°13N 97°47W 314 H6
Sarıveliler Turkey 36°41N 32°37E 250 B3
Sariwŏn N. Korea 38°31N 125°46E 224 C2
Sariyar Barajı Turkey 40°2N 31°33E 212 B4
Sarıyer Turkey 41°10N 29°3E 122 A2
Sarız Turkey 38°28N 36°30E 212 C7
Sarju → India 27°21N 81°23E 243 F9
Sark U.K. 49°25N 2°22W 169 H5
Sarkad Hungary 46°47N 21°23E 182 D6
Sarkari Tala India 27°39N 70°52E 242 F4
Şarkışla Turkey 39°21N 36°25E 212 C7
Şarköy Turkey 40°36N 27°6E 203 F11
Sarlat-la-Canéda France 44°54N 1°13E 174 D5
Sărmăşag Romania 47°21N 22°50E 182 C7
Sărmaşu Romania 46°45N 24°13E 183 D9
Sarmi Indonesia 1°49S 138°44E 231 E9
Sarmiento Argentina 45°35S 69°5W 336 C3
Sarmizegetusa Romania 45°31N 22°47E 182 E7
Särna Sweden 61°41N 13°8E 162 C7
Sarnano Italy 43°2N 13°18E 199 E10
Sarnen Switz. 46°53N 8°13E 179 J4
Sarnia Canada 42°58N 82°23W 312 D2
Sarno Italy 40°49N 14°37E 201 B7
Sarnthein = Sarentino Italy 46°38N 11°21E 199 B8
Särö Sweden 57°31N 11°57E 163 G5
Sarolangun Indonesia 2°19S 102°42E 234 C2
Saronikos Kolpos Greece 37°45N 23°45E 204 D5
Saronno Italy 45°38N 9°2E 198 C6
Saros Körfezi Turkey 40°30N 26°15E 203 F10
Sárospatak Hungary 48°18N 21°33E 182 B6
Sarowbī Afghan. 34°36N 69°44E 240 B3
Sarpsborg Norway 59°16N 11°7E 164 E8
Sarqan Kazakhstan 45°24N 79°55E 217 C9
Sarracín Spain 42°15N 3°45W 194 C7
Sarralbe France 49°0N 7°1E 173 D14
Sarrat Phil. 18°9N 120°39E 232 B3
Sarre = Saar → Europe 49°41N 6°32E 170 E6
Sarre Italy 45°40N 7°15E 198 C4
Sarre-Union France 48°57N 7°4E 173 D14
Sarrebourg France 48°43N 7°3E 173 D14
Sarreguemines France 49°5N 7°4E 173 C14
Sarriá Barcelona, Spain 41°22N 2°8E 114 A1
Sarria Galicia, Spain 42°49N 7°29W 194 C3
Sarrión Spain 40°9N 0°49W 196 E4
Sarro Mali 13°40N 5°15W 262 C3
Sarsing Iraq 37°2N 43°20E 213 D10
Sarstedt Germany 52°14N 9°52E 178 C5
Sarsuna India 22°28N 88°17E 124 C1
Sartène France 41°38N 8°58E 175 G12
Sarthe □ France 48°10N 0°10E 172 D7
Sarthe → France 47°33N 0°31W 172 E6
Sartilly France 48°45N 1°28W 172 D5
Sartrouville France 48°56N 2°10E 134 A2
Saruhanlı Turkey 38°44N 27°36E 205 C9
Săruleşti Romania 44°25N 26°39E 183 F11
Saruna → Pakistan 26°31N 67°7E 242 F2
Sarupeta India 26°30N 91°5E 241 B3
Särur Azerbaijan 39°22N 45°5E 213 C11
Saruwaged Ra. Papua N. G. 6°13S 146°45E 286 D4
Sárvár Hungary 47°15N 16°56E 182 C1
Sarvar India 26°4N 75°0E 242 F6
Sarvestān Iran 29°20N 53°10E 247 D7
Särvfjället Sweden 62°42N 13°30E 162 B7
Sárviz → Hungary 46°24N 18°41E 182 D3
Sary-Tash Kyrgyzstan 39°44N 73°15E 217 E8
Sarych, Mys Ukraine 44°25N 33°45E 189 K7
Saryesik-Atyraū Qumy Kazakhstan 45°30N 76°0E 217 C9
Sarykamyshskoye, Ozero = Saryqamysh Köli Turkmenistan 41°56N 57°25E 216 D5
Sarykemer Kazakhstan 43°0N 71°30E 217 D8
Sarykenggir → Kazakhstan 48°22N 67°59E 217 C7
Saryköl Kazakhstan 53°20N 65°12E 216 B7
Sarykolskiy Khrebet Tajikistan 38°30N 74°30E 217 E8
Saryözek Kazakhstan 44°22N 77°59E 217 D9
Saryqamysh Köli Turkmenistan 41°56N 57°25E 216 D5
Saryshaghan Kazakhstan 46°12N 73°38E 217 C8
Sarysū → Kazakhstan 45°12N 66°36E 217 C7
Sarzana Italy 44°7N 9°58E 198 D6
Sarzeau France 47°31N 2°48W 172 E4
Sasabeneh Ethiopia 7°59N 44°43E 267 C5
Sasad Hungary 47°28N 19°0E 117 B2
Sasamungga Solomon Is. 7°0S 156°50E 287 L9
Sasan Gir India 21°10N 70°36E 242 J4
Sasaram India 24°57N 84°5E 243 G11
Sasari, Mt. Solomon Is. 8°10S 159°30E 287 M10
Sasayama Japan 35°4N 135°13E 223 B7
Sasebo Japan 33°10N 129°43E 222 D1
Saser Kangri India 34°50N 77°50E 243 B7
Sashalom Hungary 47°30N 19°10E 117 A3
Saska Poland 52°14N 21°3E 142 B2
Saskatchewan □ Canada 54°40N 106°0W 297 C7
Saskatchewan → Canada 53°37N 100°40W 297 C8
Saskatoon Canada 52°10N 106°38W 297 C7
Saskylakh Russia 71°55N 114°1E 215 B12
Sasolburg S. Africa 26°46S 27°49E 271 C4
Sason Turkey 38°19N 41°24E 213 C9
Sasovo Russia 54°25N 41°55E 190 C5
Sassandra Ivory C. 4°55N 6°8W 262 E3
Sassandra → Ivory C. 4°58N 6°5W 262 E3
Sássari Italy 40°43N 8°34E 200 B1
Sassie Australia 10°2S 142°51E 280 a
Sassnitz Germany 54°29N 13°39E 178 A9
Sasso Marconi Italy 44°24N 11°15E 199 D8
Sassocorvaro Italy 43°47N 12°30E 199 E9
Sassoferrato Italy 43°26N 12°51E 199 E9
Sassuolo Italy 44°33N 10°47E 198 D7
Sástago Spain 41°19N 0°21W 196 D4
Sastamala Finland 61°20N 22°54E 188 B2
Sastown Liberia 4°45N 8°27W 262 E3
Sasvad India 18°20N 74°2E 244 E2
Sasyk, Ozero Ukraine 45°45N 29°40E 183 E14
Sasyqköl Kazakhstan 46°35N 81°0E 217 C10
Sata-Misaki Japan 31°0N 130°40E 222 F2
Satadougou Mali 12°25N 11°25W 262 C2
Satakunda = Satakunta Finland 61°45N 23°0E 160 F20
Satakunta Finland 61°45N 23°0E 160 F20
Satalice Czech Rep. 50°7N 14°34E 135 B3
Satama-Soukoura Ivory C. 7°55N 4°27W 262 D4
Satara India 17°44N 73°58E 244 F1
Satara S. Africa 24°29S 31°47E 271 B5
Sätbaev Kazakhstan 48°10N 67°31E 217 C7
Satbarwa India 23°55N 84°16E 243 H11
Satellite Beach U.S.A. 28°10N 80°36W 317 G9
Säter Sweden 60°21N 15°45E 162 D9
Satevó Mexico 27°57N 106°7W 318 B3
Satgachi India 22°37N 88°25E 124 B2
Satilla → U.S.A. 30°59N 81°29W 316 E8
Satipo Peru 11°15S 74°25W 330 C3
Satka Russia 55°3N 59°1E 186 C10
Satkania Bangla. 22°4N 92°3E 241 D4
Satkhira Bangla. 22°43N 89°8E 241 D2
Satmala Hills Andhra Pradesh, India 19°45N 78°45E 244 E4
Satmala Hills Maharashtra, India 20°15N 74°40E 244 D2
Satna India 24°35N 80°50E 243 G9
Šator Bos.-H. 44°11N 16°37E 199 D13
Sátoraljaújhely Hungary 48°25N 21°41E 182 B6
Satpukur India 22°37N 88°24E 124 B2
Satpura △ India 22°40N 78°15E 242 H8
Satpura Ra. India 21°25N 76°10E 244 D3
Sätra Sweden 59°17N 17°54E 139 B1
Satrup Germany 54°41N 9°36E 178 A5
Satsuma-Hantō Japan 31°25N 130°25E 222 F2
Satsuna-Shotō Japan 30°0N 130°0E 221 K5
Sattahip Thailand 12°41N 100°54E 236 F3
Sattenapalle India 16°25N 80°6E 245 F5
Sattru Phai Bangkok, Thailand 113 b2
Satu Mare Romania 47°46N 22°55E 182 C7
Satu Mare □ Romania 47°45N 23°0E 182 C8
Satui Indonesia 3°50S 115°27E 235 C5
Satun Thailand 6°43N 100°2E 237 J3
Satupa'itea Samoa 13°45S 172°18W 287 V19
Saturnina → Brazil 12°15S 58°10W 331 C6
Sauce = Juan L. Lacaze Uruguay 34°26S 57°25W 334 C4
Sauce Argentina 30°5S 58°46W 334 C4
Sauceda Mexico 25°46N 101°19W 318 B4
Saucillo Mexico 28°1N 105°17W 318 B3
Sauda Norway 59°40N 6°20E 164 E3
Saudasjøen Norway 59°38N 6°17E 164 E3
Saúde Bahia, Brazil 10°56S 40°24W 332 D3
Saúde São Paulo, Brazil 23°36S 46°37W 137 B2
Sauðarkrókur Iceland 65°45N 19°40W 155 B7
Saudi Arabia ■ Asia 26°0N 44°0E 246 B3
Sauerland Germany 51°12N 7°59E 176 C4
Saugatuck U.S.A. 42°40N 86°12W 311 B10
Saugeen → Canada 44°30N 81°22W 312 B3
Saugerties U.S.A. 42°5N 73°57W 313 D11
Saugues France 44°58N 3°32E 174 D7
Saugus Calif., U.S.A. 34°25N 118°32W 307 L8
Saugus Mass., U.S.A. 42°28N 71°0W 116 A2
Saugus → U.S.A. 42°27N 70°58W 116 A2
Saujbulagh = Mahābād Iran 36°50N 45°45E 213 D11
Saujon France 45°41N 0°55W 174 C3
Sauk Centre U.S.A. 45°44N 94°57W 308 C6
Sauk City U.S.A. 43°17N 89°43W 310 A7
Sauk Rapids U.S.A. 45°35N 94°10W 308 C6
Saül Fr. Guiana 3°37N 53°12W 329 C7
Sauland Norway 59°37N 8°56E 164 E5
Saulgau Germany 48°1N 9°29E 179 G5
Saulieu France 47°17N 4°14E 173 E11
Sault France 44°6N 5°24E 175 D9
Sault-au-Récollet Canada 45°35N 73°39W 130 A2
Sault Ste. Marie Ont., Canada 46°30N 84°20W 298 C3
Sault Ste. Marie Mich., U.S.A. 46°30N 84°21W 309 B11
Saūmalkol Kazakhstan 53°17N 68°6E 217 B7
Saumlaki Indonesia 7°55S 131°20E 231 F8
Saumur France 47°15N 0°5W 172 E6
Saundatti India 15°47N 75°7E 245 G2
Saunders, C. N.Z. 45°53S 170°45E 285 F5
Saunders I. Antarctica 57°48S 26°28W 151 B1
Saunders Pt. Australia 27°52S 125°38E 279 E4
Saunemin U.S.A. 40°54N 88°24W 311 D8
Saupite Angola 13°54S 17°43E 265 E3
Saurbær Borgarfjarðarsýsla, Iceland 64°24N 21°35W 155 C5
Saurbær Eyjafjarðarsýsla, Iceland 65°27N 18°13W 155 B8
Sauri Nigeria 11°42N 6°44E 263 C6
Saurimo Angola 9°40S 20°12E 265 D4
Sausalito U.S.A. 37°51N 122°29W 136 A2
Sautatá Colombia 7°50N 77°4W 328 B2
Sauteurs Grenada 12°14N 61°38W 323 q
Sauveterre-de-Béarn France 43°24N 0°57W 174 E3
Sauzé-Vaussais France 46°8N 0°8E 174 B4
Savá Honduras 15°32N 86°15W 320 C2
Sava Italy 40°24N 17°33E 201 B10
Sava → Serbia 44°50N 20°26E 182 F5
Savage U.S.A. 47°27N 104°21W 304 C11
Savage I. = Niue ☒ Pac. Oc. 19°2S 169°54W 289 g
Savage River Australia 41°31S 145°14E 281 G4
Savai'i Samoa 13°28S 172°24W 287 V19
Savalou Benin 7°57N 1°58E 263 D5
Savane Mozam. 19°37S 35°8E 269 F4
Savaneta Aruba 12°27N 69°56W 322 f
Savanna U.S.A. 42°5N 90°8W 310 B6
Savanna-la-Mar Jamaica 18°10N 78°10W 320 a
Savannah Ga., U.S.A. 32°5N 81°6W 316 C8
Savannah Mo., U.S.A. 39°56N 94°50W 310 E2
Savannah Tenn., U.S.A. 35°14N 88°15W 315 D10
Savannah → U.S.A. 32°2N 80°53W 316 C9
Savannah Beach = Tybee Island U.S.A. 32°1N 80°51W 316 C9
Savannakhet Laos 16°30N 104°49E 236 D5
Savanne, Piton Mauritius 20°26S 57°29E 272 e
Savannes B. St. Lucia 13°45N 60°56W 323 m
Savant L. Canada 50°16N 90°44W 298 B1
Savant Lake Canada 50°14N 90°40W 298 B1
Savantvadi India 15°55N 73°54E 245 G1
Savanur India 14°59N 75°21E 245 G2
Savarkundla = Kundla India 21°21N 71°25E 242 J4
Săvârşin Romania 46°1N 22°14E 182 D7
Savaştepe Turkey 39°22N 27°42E 205 B9
Savda India 21°9N 75°56E 244 D2
Savé Benin 8°2N 2°29E 263 D5
Save → Haute-Garonne, France 43°47N 1°17E 174 E5
Save → Mozam. 21°16S 34°0E 271 B5
Sāveh Iran 35°2N 50°20E 247 C6
Savelugu Ghana 9°38N 0°54W 263 D4
Savenay France 47°20N 1°55W 172 E5
Săveni Romania 47°57N 26°52E 183 C11
Saverdun France 43°14N 1°34E 174 E5
Saverne France 48°43N 7°20E 173 D14
Savigliano Italy 44°38N 7°40E 198 D4
Savigny-sur-Braye France 47°53N 0°49E 172 E7
Sávio → Italy 44°19N 12°20E 199 D9
Šavnik Montenegro 42°59N 19°10E 202 D3
Savo Finland 62°45N 27°30E 160 E22
Savo Solomon Is. 9°8S 159°48E 287 M10
Savoie □ France 45°26N 6°25E 175 C10
Savolax = Savo Finland 62°45N 27°30E 160 E22
Savona Italy 44°17N 8°30E 198 D5
Savona N.Y., U.S.A. 42°17N 77°13W 312 D7
Savonet Curaçao 12°21N 69°7W 322 g
Savonlinna Finland 61°52N 28°53E 188 B5
Savoonga U.S.A. 63°42N 170°29W 303 E5
Savoy = Savoie □ France 45°26N 6°25E 175 C10
Şavşat Turkey 41°15N 42°20E 213 B10
Sävsjö Sweden 57°20N 14°40E 163 G8
Savur Turkey 37°34N 40°53E 246 B4
Savusavu Fiji 16°34S 179°15E 287 A2
Savusavu B. Fiji 16°45S 179°15E 287 A2
Sawah Besar Indonesia 6°8S 106°49E 122 A1
Sawahlunto Indonesia 0°40S 100°52E 234 C2
Sawai Indonesia 3°0S 129°5E 231 E7
Sawai Madhopur India 26°0N 76°25E 242 G7
Sawaleke Fiji 17°59S 179°18E 287 A2
Sawang Daen Din Thailand 17°28N 103°28E 236 D4
Sawankhalok Thailand 17°19N 99°50E 236 D2
Sawara Japan 35°55N 140°30E 223 B12
Sawatch Range U.S.A. 39°0N 106°30W 304 G10
Sawdā', Jabal as Libya 28°51N 15°12E 258 C3
Sawel Mt. U.K. 54°50N 7°2W 166 B4
Sawfajjin, W. → Libya 31°41N 14°44E 258 B2
Sawi Thailand 10°14N 99°5E 237 G2
Sawla Ghana 9°17N 2°25W 262 D4
Sawmills Zimbabwe 19°30S 28°2E 269 F2
Şawqirah Oman 18°7N 56°32E 249 C7
Şawqirah, Ghubbat Oman 18°35N 57°0E 249 C7
Sawtell Australia 30°19S 153°6E 283 A10
Sawtelle U.S.A. 34°2N 118°27W 126 B2
Sawtooth ◠ U.S.A. 44°0N 114°50W 304 D6
Sawtooth Range U.S.A. 44°3N 114°58W 304 D6
Sawu Indonesia 10°35S 121°50E 231 F6
Sawu Sea Indonesia 9°30S 121°50E 231 F6
Saxby → Australia 18°25S 140°53E 280 B3
Saxmundham U.K. 52°13N 1°30E 169 E9
Saxony = Sachsen □ Germany 50°55N 13°10E 178 E9
Saxony, Lower = Niedersachsen □ Germany 52°50N 9°0E 178 C4
Saxton U.S.A. 40°13N 78°15W 312 F6
Say Mali 13°50N 4°57W 262 C4
Say Niger 13°8N 2°22E 263 C5
Saya Nigeria 9°30N 3°18E 263 D5
Sayabec Canada 48°35N 67°41W 299 C6
Sayaboury Laos 19°15N 101°45E 236 C3
Sayán Peru 11°8S 77°12W 330 C2
Sayan, Vostochnyy Russia 54°0N 96°0E 215 D10
Sayan, Zapadnyy Russia 52°30N 94°0E 217 B12
Sayanogorsk Russia 53°5N 91°23E 215 D10
Saydā Lebanon 33°35N 35°25E 250 E6
Sayghān Afghan. 35°10N 67°55E 240 B2
Sayhandulaan = Öldziyt Mongolia 44°40N 109°1E 226 B5
Sayḩūt Yemen 15°12N 51°10E 249 D5
Saykhin Kazakhstan 48°50N 46°47E 191 F8
Saylac Somali Rep. 11°21N 43°30E 267 B5
Saylorville L. U.S.A. 41°48N 93°46W 310 C3
Saynshand = Buyant-Uhaa Mongolia 44°55N 110°11E 226 B6
Sayō Japan 34°59N 134°22E 222 C6
Sayre Okla., U.S.A. 35°18N 99°38W 314 D5
Sayre Pa., U.S.A. 41°59N 76°32W 313 E8
Sayreville U.S.A. 40°28N 74°22W 313 F10
Sayula Mexico 19°52N 103°36W 318 D4
Sayward Canada 50°21N 125°55W 296 C3
Saywūn Yemen 15°56N 48°47E 249 D5
Saza Japan 33°14N 129°39E 222 D1
Sazanit Albania 40°30N 19°20E 202 F3
Sázava → Czech Rep. 49°53N 14°24E 180 B7
Sazin Pakistan 35°35N 73°30E 243 B5
Sazlika → Bulgaria 41°59N 25°50E 203 E9
Sbeïtla Tunisia 35°12N 9°7E 258 A1
Scaër France 48°2N 3°42W 172 D3
Scafell Pike U.K. 54°27N 3°14W 168 C4
Scald Law U.K. 55°50N 3°17W 121 B2
Scalea Italy 39°49N 15°47E 201 C8
Scalloway U.K. 60°9N 1°17W 167 A7
Scalpay U.K. 57°18N 6°0W 167 D3
Scammon Bay U.S.A. 61°51N 165°35W 303 F6
Scandia Canada 50°20N 112°2W 296 C6
Scandiano Italy 44°36N 10°43E 198 D7
Scandicci Italy 43°45N 11°11E 199 E8
Scandinavia Europe 64°0N 12°0E 160 E15
Scansano Italy 42°41N 11°20E 199 F8
Scapa Flow U.K. 58°53N 3°3W 167 C5
Scappoose U.S.A. 45°45N 122°53W 306 E4
Scarámia, Capo Italy 36°47N 14°29E 201 F7
Scarba U.K. 56°11N 5°43W 167 E3
Scarborough Ont., Canada 43°44N 79°14W 141 A3
Scarborough Trin. & Tob. 11°11N 60°42W 323 s
Scarborough N. Yorks., U.K. 54°17N 0°24W 168 C7
Scarborough Bluffs Canada 43°42N 79°14W 141 A3
Scarborough Shoal S. China Sea 15°0N 117°50E 232 D1
Scargill N.Z. 42°56S 172°58E 285 C7
Scariff I. Ireland 51°44N 10°15W 166 E1
Scarp U.K. 58°1N 7°8W 167 C1
Scarpanto = Karpathos Greece 35°37N 27°10E 205 F9
Scarpe-Escaut ◠ France 50°26N 3°23E 173 B10
Scarsdale Australia 37°41S 143°39E 282 D5
Sceaux France 48°46N 2°17E 134 B2
Scebeli = Shabeelle → Somali Rep. 2°0N 44°0E 267 D5
Šćedro Croatia 43°6N 16°43E 199 E13
Scenery, Mt. Saba 17°38N 63°14W 322 a
Schaal See Germany 53°36N 10°55E 178 B6
Schaalsee ◠ Germany 53°40N 10°59E 178 B6
Schaerbeek Belgium 50°52N 4°22E 116 A2
Schaffhausen Switz. 47°42N 8°39E 179 H4
Schagen Neths. 52°49N 4°48E 170 B4
Schaghticoke U.S.A. 42°54N 73°35W 313 D11
Schärding Austria 48°27N 13°27E 180 C6
Scharfenberg Germany 52°35N 13°15E 115 A2
Scharfenwiese = Ostrołęka Poland 53°4N 21°32E 185 E8
Scharhörn Germany 53°57N 8°24E 178 B4
Schässburg = Sighişoara Romania 46°12N 24°50E 183 D9
Scheessel Germany 53°10N 9°29E 178 B5
Schefferville Canada 54°48N 66°50W 299 B6
Scheibbs Austria 48°1N 15°9E 180 C8
Scheidt = Schelde → Belgium 51°15N 4°16E 170 C4
Schelde → Belgium 51°15N 4°16E 170 C4
Schell City U.S.A. 38°1N 94°7W 310 F2
Schell Creek Ra. U.S.A. 39°25N 114°40W 304 G6
Schellsburg U.S.A. 40°3N 78°39W 312 F6
Schemnitz = Banská Štiavnica Slovak Rep. 48°25N 18°55E 181 C11
Schenectady U.S.A. 42°49N 73°57W 313 D11
Schenevus U.S.A. 42°33N 74°50W 313 D10
Scherfede Germany 51°32N 9°2E 178 D5
Schesslitz Germany 49°58N 11°1E 179 F7
Schiedam Neths. 51°55N 4°25E 170 C4
Schieratz = Sieradz Poland 51°37N 18°41E 185 G5
Schiermonnikoog Neths. 53°30N 6°15E 170 A6
Schiller Park U.S.A. 41°56N 87°52W 119 B1
Schiller Woods U.S.A. 41°57N 87°51W 119 B1
Schiltigheim France 48°35N 7°45E 173 D14
Schinousa Greece 36°53N 25°31E 205 E7
Schio Italy 45°43N 11°21E 199 C8
Schiphol, Amsterdam ✈ (AMS) Neths. 52°18N 4°45E 112 B1
Schippenbeil = Sępopol Poland 54°16N 21°2E 184 D8
Schivelbein = Świdwin Poland 53°47N 15°49E 184 E2
Schlachtensee Germany 52°26N 13°13E 115 B2
Schladming Austria 47°23N 13°41E 180 D6
Schlanders = Silandro Italy 46°38N 10°46E 198 B7
Schlawa = Sława Poland 51°52N 16°2E 185 G3
Schlei → Germany 54°40N 10°0E 178 A5
Schleiden Germany 50°31N 6°28E 178 E2
Schleinitz Ra. Papua N. G. 3°0S 151°30E 286 B6
Schleiz Germany 50°35N 11°49E 178 E7
Schlesiersee = Sława Poland 51°52N 16°2E 185 G3
Schleswig Germany 54°31N 9°34E 178 A5
Schleswig-Holstein □ Germany 54°30N 9°30E 178 A5
Schlettstadt = Sélestat France 48°16N 7°26E 173 D14
Schlichtingsheim = Szlichtyngowa Poland 51°42N 16°15E 185 G3
Schlochau = Człuchów Poland 53°41N 17°22E 184 E4
Schloppe = Człopa Poland 53°6N 16°6E 185 E3
Schlossgarten Germany 52°31N 13°18E 115 A2
Schlüchtern Germany 50°20N 9°32E 179 E5
Schmalkalden Germany 50°44N 10°26E 178 E6
Schmargendorf Germany 52°28N 13°17E 115 B2
Schmölln Germany 50°54N 12°19E 178 E8
Schneeberg Austria 47°47N 15°48E 180 D8
Schneeberg Sachsen, Germany 50°35N 12°38E 178 E8
Schneidemühl = Piła Poland 53°10N 16°48E 185 E3
Schneider U.S.A. 41°13N 87°28W 311 C9
Schneverdingen Germany 53°7N 9°48E 178 B5
Schœlcher Martinique 14°36N 61°7W 322 j
Schofield Barracks U.S.A. 21°29N 158°7W 302 K13
Schoharie U.S.A. 42°40N 74°19W 313 D10
Schoharie Cr. → U.S.A. 42°57N 74°18W 313 D10
Scholls U.S.A. 45°24N 122°56W 306 E4
Schönau = Swierzawa Poland 51°1N 15°54E 185 G2
Schönberg Mecklenburg-Vorpommern, Germany 53°52N 10°56E 178 B6
Schönberg Schleswig-Holstein, Germany 54°23N 10°21E 178 A6
Schönblick Germany 52°27N 13°43E 115 B5
Schönbrunn Austria 48°10N 16°19E 142 A1
Schönbuch ◠ Germany 48°35N 9°2E 179 G5
Schönebeck Germany 52°2N 11°44E 178 C7
Schöneberg Germany 52°28N 13°20E 115 B3
Schönefeld Germany 52°22N 13°33E 115 B4
Schöneiche Germany 52°28N 13°41E 115 B5
Schöngau Germany 47°47N 10°53E 179 H6
Schöningen Germany 52°8N 10°56E 178 C6
Schönlanke = Trzcianka Poland 53°3N 16°25E 185 E3
Schönstein = Šoštanj Slovenia 46°23N 15°4E 199 B12
Schönwalde Germany 52°37N 13°7E 115 A1
Schoolcraft U.S.A. 42°7N 85°38W 311 B11
Schopfheim Germany 47°38N 7°50E 179 H3
Schorndorf Germany 48°47N 9°32E 179 G5
Schortens Germany 53°31N 7°56E 178 B3
Schotschekloof Cape Town, S. Africa 118 b1
Schottegat Curaçao 12°7N 68°55W 322 g
Schouten I. Australia 42°20S 148°20E 281 G4
Schouten Is. = Supiori Indonesia 1°0S 136°0E 231 E9
Schouten Is. Papua N. G. 3°30S 144°30E 286 B3
Schouwen Neths. 51°43N 3°45E 170 C3
Schramberg Germany 48°13N 8°22E 179 G4
Schrankogel Austria 47°3N 11°7E 180 D4
Schreiber Canada 48°45N 87°20W 298 C2
Schrems Austria 48°47N 15°4E 180 C8
Schrobenhausen Germany 48°34N 11°16E 179 G7
Schroffenstein Namibia 27°11S 18°42E 270 C2
Schroon Lake U.S.A. 43°50N 73°46W 313 C11
Schröttersberg = Płock Poland 52°32N 19°40E 185 F6
Schruns Austria 47°5N 9°56E 180 D2
Schuchye = Shchūchīnsk Kazakhstan 52°56N 70°12E 217 B8
Schuler Canada 50°20N 110°6W 297 C6
Schulzendorf Germany 52°36N 13°16E 115 A2
Schumacher Canada 48°30N 81°16W 298 C3
Schurz U.S.A. 38°57N 118°49W 304 G4
Schuyler U.S.A. 41°27N 97°4W 308 E5
Schuylerville U.S.A. 43°6N 73°35W 313 C11
Schuylkill → U.S.A. 39°53N 75°12W 313 G9
Schuylkill Haven U.S.A. 40°37N 76°11W 313 F8
Schwabach Germany 49°19N 11°2E 179 F7
Schwaben □ Germany 48°15N 10°30E 179 G6
Schwabing Germany 48°10N 11°35E 131 B2
Schwäbisch-Fränkischer Wald ◠ Germany 49°0N 9°30E 179 G5
Schwäbisch Gmünd Germany 48°48N 9°47E 179 G5
Schwäbisch Hall Germany 49°6N 9°44E 179 F5
Schwäbische Alb Germany 48°20N 9°30E 179 G5
Schwabmünchen Germany 48°10N 10°46E 179 G6
Schwalmstadt Germany 50°55N 9°10E 178 E5
Schwandorf Germany 49°20N 12°7E 179 F8
Schwanebeck Germany 52°37N 13°32E 115 A4
Schwanenwerder Germany 52°26N 13°10E 115 B2
Schwaner, Pegunungan Indonesia 1°0S 112°30E 235 C4
Schwanewede Germany 53°14N 8°35E 178 B4
Schwarmstedt Germany 52°39N 9°38E 178 C5
Schwarze Elster → Germany 51°48N 12°50E 178 D8
Schwarzenberg Germany 50°32N 12°47E 178 E8
Schwarzlackenau Austria 48°16N 16°23E 142 A2
Schwarzrand Namibia 25°37S 16°50E 270 C2
Schwarzwald Germany 48°30N 8°20E 179 G4
Schwatka Mts. U.S.A. 67°20N 156°30W 303 C8
Schwaz Austria 47°20N 11°44E 180 D4
Schwechat Austria 48°8N 16°28E 142 B2
Schwechat, Wien ✈ (VIE) Austria 48°7N 16°35E 142 B3
Schwedt Germany 53°3N 14°16E 178 B10
Schweidnitz = Świdnica Poland 50°50N 16°30E 185 H3
Schweinfurt Germany 50°3N 10°14E 179 E6
Schweiz = Switzerland ■ Europe 46°30N 8°0E 179 J4
Schweizer-Reneke S. Africa 27°11S 25°18E 270 C4
Schwenningen = Villingen-Schwenningen Germany 48°3N 8°26E 179 G4
Schwerin = Skwierzyna Poland 52°33N 15°30E 185 F2
Schwerin Germany 53°36N 11°22E 178 B7
Schweriner See Germany 53°43N 11°28E 178 B7
Schwetzingen Germany 49°23N 8°35E 179 F4
Schwiebus = Świebodzin Poland 52°15N 15°31E 185 F2
Schwyz Switz. 47°2N 8°39E 179 H4
Schwyz □ Switz. 47°2N 8°39E 179 H4
Sciacca Italy 37°31N 13°3E 200 E6
Scicli Italy 36°47N 14°42E 201 F7
Science and Industry, Museum of U.S.A. 41°47N 87°34W 119 C3
Sciliar ◠ Italy 46°28N 11°35E 199 B8
Scilla Italy 38°15N 15°43E 201 D8
Scilly, Isles of U.K. 49°56N 6°22W 169 H1
Ścinawa Poland 51°25N 16°26E 185 G3
Scione Greece 39°57N 23°36E 202 G7
Scioto → U.S.A. 38°44N 83°1W 311 D13
Scitrek Museum U.S.A. 33°46N 84°22W 113 B2
Scituate U.S.A. 42°12N 70°44W 313 D14
Scobey U.S.A. 48°47N 105°25W 304 B11

Scone *N.S.W., Australia* 32°55S 150°52E **283** B9
Scone *Perth & Kinr., U.K.* 56°25N 3°24W **167** E5
Scopus, Mt. *West Bank* 31°48N 35°14E **123** B2
Scordia *Italy* 37°18N 14°51E **201** E7
Scoresby Sund *Greenland* 70°28N 21°46W **154** C8
Scoresbysund = Ittoqqortoormiit
  Greenland 70°28N 23°00W **154** C8
Scorniceşti *Romania* 44°34N 24°33E **183** F9
Scotia *Calif., U.S.A.* 40°29N 124°6W **304** F1
Scotia *N.Y., U.S.A.* 42°50N 73°58W **311** D11
Scotia Sea *Antarctica* 56°5S 56°0W **151** B18
Scotland *Canada* 43°1N 80°22W **312** C4
Scotland □ *U.K.* 57°0N 4°0W **167** E5
Scott *Antarctica* 77°0S 166°45E **151** C8
Scott, C *Australia* 13°30S 129°49E **278** B4
Scott Circle *Washington, D.C., U.S.A.* 143 a1
Scott City *U.S.A.* 38°29N 100°54W **308** F3
Scott Glacier *Antarctica* 66°15S 100°5E **151** C8
Scott I. *Antarctica* 67°0S 179°0E **151** C11
Scott Is. *Canada* 50°48N 128°40W **296** C3
Scott L. *Canada* 59°55N 106°18W **297** B7
Scott Monument *Edinburgh, U.K.* 121 b2
Scott Reef *Australia* 14°0S 121°50E **278** B3
Scottburgh *S. Africa* 30°15S 30°47E **271** D5
Scottdale *Georgia, U.S.A.* 33°47N 84°16W **113** B3
Scottdale *Pa., U.S.A.* 40°6N 79°35W **312** F5
Scottish Borders □ *U.K.* 55°35N 2°50W **167** F6
Scotts Head *N.S.W.,
  Australia* 30°45S 153°0E **283** A10
Scotts Head *Dominica* 15°13N 61°23W **323** k
Scotts Head Village
  Dominica 15°12N 61°22W **323** k
Scottsbluff *U.S.A.* 41°52N 103°40W **308** E2
Scottsboro *U.S.A.* 34°40N 86°2W **315** D11
Scottsburg *U.S.A.* 38°41N 85°47W **311** F11
Scottsdale *Tas., Australia* 41°9S 147°31E **281** G4
Scottsdale *Ariz., U.S.A.* 33°40N 111°53W **305** K8
Scottsville *Ky., U.S.A.* 36°45N 86°11W **306** G10
Scottsville *N.Y., U.S.A.* 43°2N 77°47W **312** C7
Scottville *U.S.A.* 43°58N 86°17W **308** D10
Scranton *U.S.A.* 41°25N 75°40W **313** E9
Screven *U.S.A.* 31°29N 82°1W **316** D7
Scrub I. *Anguilla* 18°19N 62°55W **322** a
Scugog, L. *Canada* 44°10N 78°55W **312** B6
Sculeni *Moldova* 47°20N 27°37E **183** C12
Scunthorpe *U.K.* 53°36N 0°39W **168** D7
Scuol Schuls *Switz.* 46°48N 10°17E **179** J6
Scutari = Shkodër *Albania* 42°4N 19°32E **202** C6
Scutari = Üsküdar *Turkey* 41°1N 29°0E **122** B2
Sea Is. *U.S.A.* 31°30N 81°7W **315** F14
Sea Lake *Australia* 35°28S 142°55E **282** C5
Sea Point *S. Africa* 33°54S 18°23E **118** A1
Seabra *Tarauacá Brazil* 8°6S 70°48W **330** B3
Seabra *Brazil* 12°25S 41°46W **333** D3
Seabrook *E. Sussex, U.K.* 53°58N 76°49W **143** B5
Seabrook, L. *Australia* 30°55S 119°40E **279** F2
Seacliff *Australia* 34°77N 122°28W **136** B2
Seaford *E. Sussex, U.K.* 50°47N 0°7E **169** G8
Seaford *Del., U.S.A.* 38°39N 75°37W **309** F16
Seaforth *N.S.W., Australia* 33°48S 151°15E **139** A4
Seaforth *Queens., Australia* 20°55S 148°57E **280** b
Seaforth *Ont., Canada* 43°35N 81°25W **312** C3
Seaforth, L. *U.K.* 57°52N 6°36W **167** D2
Seagate *U.S.A.* 40°34N 74°0W **132** C1
Seagraves *U.S.A.* 32°57N 102°34W **314** C3
Seaham *U.K.* 54°50N 1°20W **168** C6
Seagull *Seget Indonesia* 1°24S 130°58E **231** E8
Seagora *Russia* 63°44N 34°19E **188** B5
Seaguer, O. → *Algeria* 32°41N 1°48E **261** B5
Seghe *Solomon Is.* 8°32S 157°54E **287** M9
Segmon *Sweden* 59°17N 13°3E **162** E7
Segonzac *France* 45°36N 0°14W **174** C3
Segorbe *Spain* 39°50N 0°30W **195** F4
Ségou *Mali* 13°30N 6°16W **262** C3
Ségou □ *Mali* 14°0N 6°0W **262** C3
Segovia *Colombia* 7°7N 74°42W **323** B3
Segovia *Spain* 40°57N 4°10W **194** E6
Segovia □ *Spain* 40°55N 4°10W **194** E6
Segrate *Italy* 45°29N 9°17E **123** B2
Segré *France* 47°40N 0°52W **172** E6
Segre → *Spain* 41°40N 0°43E **196** D5
Seguam I. *U.S.A.* 52°19N 172°30W **303** E4
Seguam Pass *U.S.A.* 52°0N 172°30W **303** K4
Séguédine *Niger* 20°9N 12°52E **259** D2
Séguéla *Ivory C.* 7°55N 6°40W **262** D3
Séguénéga *Burkina Faso* 13°25N 1°58W **263** C4
Segundo → *Argentina* 30°53S 62°44W **334** C3
Segura → *Argentina* 38°3N 0°44W **195** G4
Segura, Sierra de *Spain* 38°5N 2°45W **197** G2
Seh Konj, Küh-e *Iran* 30°6N 57°30E **247** D8
Seh Qal'eh *Iran* 33°40N 58°24E **247** C8
Sehitwa *Botswana* 20°30S 22°30E **270** B3
Sehlabathebe △ *Lesotho* 29°53S 29°7E **271** C4
Sehore *India* 23°10N 77°5E **242** H7
Sehwan *Pakistan* 26°28N 67°53E **242** F2
Şeica Mare *Romania* 46°1N 24°7E **183** E9
Seikan Tunnel *Japan* 41°28N 140°10E **220** D10
Seikpyu *Burma* 20°54N 94°48E **241** E5
Seil *U.K.* 56°18N 5°38W **167** E3
Seiland *Norway* 70°25N 23°15E **160** A20
Seilhac *France* 45°22N 1°41E **174** C5
Seim → *Moselle, France* 49°7N 6°11E **173** C13
Seim → *Saône-et-Loire,
  France* 46°31N 4°57E **173** F11
Sein, Î. de *France* 48°2N 4°52W **172** D2
Seinäjoki *Finland* 62°40N 22°51E **160** E20
Seine → *France* 49°26N 0°26E **172** C7
Seine, B. de la *France* 49°40N 0°40W **172** C6
Seine-et-Marne □ *France* 48°45N 3°0E **173** D10
Seine-Inférieure =
  Seine-Maritime □ *France* 49°40N 1°0E **172** C7
Seine-Maritime □ *France* 49°40N 1°0E **172** C7
Seine-St-Denis □ *France* 48°58N 2°24E **173** D9
Seini *Romania* 47°44N 23°21E **183** C8
Seirijai *Lithuania* 54°14N 23°49E **184** D10
Seis de Septiembre = Moron
  Argentina 34°39S 58°37W **334** C4
Seistan = Sīstān *Asia* 30°50N 61°0E **247** D9
Seistan, Daryācheh-ye = Sīstan,
  Daryācheh-ye *Iran* 31°0N 61°0E **247** D9
Seitler = Nyzhnohirskyy
  Ukraine 45°27N 34°38E **189** K8
Seixal *Portugal* 38°38N 9°5W **196** D2
Seixe → *Denmark* 55°54N 11°9E **163** J5
Sejerø Bugt *Denmark* 55°53N 11°15E **163** J5
Seka *Ethiopia* 8°10N 36°52E **257** F4
Sekayu *Indonesia* 2°51S 103°51E **234** E2
Seke-Banza
  Dem. Rep. of the Congo 5°25S 13°16E **268** D2
Sekenke *Tanzania* 4°18S 34°11E **266** C3
Sekhira *Tunisia* 34°20N 10°8E **261** B7
Seki *Japan* 35°29N 136°55E **223** B8
Seki *Turkey* 36°48N 29°33E **205** E11
Sekigahara *Japan* 35°22N 136°28E **223** B8

Sedan *Ardennes, France* 49°43N 4°57E **173** C11
Sedan *Kans., U.S.A.* 37°8N 96°11W **308** G6
Sedano *Spain* 42°43N 3°49W **194** C7
Sedan *Burma* 22°19N 96°19E **241** D6
Seddinsee *Germany* 52°23N 13°41E **115** B5
Seddon *N.Z.* 41°40S 174°7E **285** E9
Seddonville *N.Z.* 41°33S 172°1E **285** D7
Sedé Boqér *Israel* 30°52N 34°47E **251** H5
Sedeh *Fārs, Iran* 30°45N 52°11E **247** D7
Sedeh *Khorāsān, Iran* 33°20N 59°14E **247** C8
Séderon *France* 44°12N 5°32E **175** D9
Sederot *Israel* 31°32N 34°37E **251** G5
Sédhiou *Senegal* 12°44N 15°30W **262** C1
Sedico *Italy* 46°8N 12°6E **199** B9
Sedlčany *Czech Rep.* 49°40N 14°25E **180** F7
Sedley *Canada* 50°10N 104°0W **297** C8
Sedom *Israel* 31°5N 35°20E **251** G4
Sedona *U.S.A.* 34°52N 111°46W **305** J8
Sedova, Pik *Russia* 73°29N 54°58E **214** B6
Sedro-Woolley *U.S.A.* 48°30N 122°14W **306** B4
Šeduva *Lithuania* 55°45N 23°45E **184** C10
Sędziejów *Poland* 50°35N 20°4E **185** H7
Sędziszów Małopolski
  Poland 50°5N 21°45E **185** H8
Seebergen *Germany* 52°33N 13°41E **115** A5
Seeburg = Jeziorany
  Poland 53°58N 20°46E **184** E7
Seeburg *Germany* 52°30N 13°7E **115** A1
Seefeld in Tirol *Austria* 47°19N 11°13E **180** D4
Seefeld *Germany* 52°33N 13°5E **115** A1
Seegefeld *Germany* 52°33N 13°5E **115** A1
Seehausen *Germany* 52°54N 11°45E **178** C7
Seeheim *Namibia* 26°50S 17°45E **270** C2
Seeheim-Jugenheim
  Germany 49°49N 8°40E **179** F4
Seelengbach *Germany* 52°24N 13°17E **115** B2
Seeis *Namibia* 22°29S 17°39E **270** B2
Seekoei → *S. Africa* 30°18S 25°1E **270** D4
Seeley's Bay *Canada* 44°29N 76°14W **313** B8
Seelow *Germany* 52°32N 14°22E **178** C10
Sées *France* 48°38N 0°10E **172** D7
Seevetal *Germany* 53°26N 10°1E **178** B6
Seewinkel = Neusiedler See-
  Seewinkel △ *Austria* 50°N 16°45E **181** D9
Şefaatli *Turkey* 39°30N 34°45E **212** C6
Seferihisar *Turkey* 38°10N 26°50E **205** C8
Séféto *Mali* 14°8N 9°49W **262** C3
Sefophe *Botswana* 22°11S 27°58E **271** B4
Sefrou *Morocco* 33°52N 4°52W **260** B4
Sefrou □ *Morocco* 33°49N 4°49W **260** B4
Sefton *U.K.* 43°15S 172°41E **285** E7
Sêrt Bekwai *Ghana* 6°10N 2°25W **262** D4
Seg-ozero *Russia* 63°20N 33°46E **186** B5
Segag *Ethiopia* 7°39N 42°50E **267** C5
Segamat *Malaysia* 2°30N 102°50E **237** L4
Ségbana *Benin* 10°55N 3°42E **263** C5
Segbwema *S. Leone* 8°0N 11°0W **262** D2
Segeltorp *Sweden* 59°16N 17°56E **139** B1
Segerstad *Sweden* 61°16N 16°39E **162** C10
Segesta *Italy* 37°56N 12°50E **200** E5
Seget *Indonesia* 1°24S 130°58E **231** E8

Sekondi-Takoradi *Ghana* 4°58N 1°45W **262** E4
Sekota *Ethiopia* 12°40N 39°2E **257** F4
Sekseūil *Kazakhstan* 47°5N 6 °9E **216** D6
Seksna *Russia* 59°13N 38°0E **188** C10
Sekudai *Malaysia* 1°32N 103°39E **237** d
Sekuma *Botswana* 24°36S 23°50E **270** B3
Selah *U.S.A.* 46°39N 120°32W **304** C3
Selama *Malaysia* 5°12N 100°42E **237** K3
Selangor □ *Malaysia* 3°10N 101°30E **237** L3
Selárgius *Italy* 39°16N 9°10E **200** C2
Selaru *Indonesia* 8°9S 131°0E **231** F8
Selatan, Selat *Malaysia* 5°15N 100°20E **237** c
Selatpanjang *Indonesia* 1°0N 102°43E **234** B2
Selawik *U.S.A.* 66°36N 160°0W **303** B8
Selawik L. *U.S.A.* 66°30N 160°45W **303** C7
Selawik Nat. Wildlife Refuge △
  U.S.A. 66°35N 159°0W **303** C8
Selb *Germany* 50°10N 12°7E **178** E8
Selbusjøen *Norway* 63°15N 10°50E **164** A7
Selby *Gauteng, S. Africa* 26°12S 26°2E **123** B2
Selby *N. Yorks., U.K.* 53°47N 1°5W **168** D6
Selby *S. Dak., U.S.A.* 45°31N 100°2W **308** C4
Selca *Croatia* 43°20N 16°50E **199** E13
Selçuk *Turkey* 37°56N 27°22E **205** D8
Selden *U.S.A.* 39°33N 100°34W **308** F3
Seldovia *U.S.A.* 59°26N 151°43W **303** G10
Sele → *Italy* 40°29N 14°56E **201** B7
Selebi-Phikwe *Botswana* 21°58S 27°48E **271** B4
Selemdzha → *Russia* 51°42N 128°53E **215** D13
Selendi *Manisa, Turkey* 38°43N 28°50E **205** C10
Selendi *Manisa, Turkey* 38°46N 27°53E **205** C9
Selenga = Selenge Mörön →
  Asia 52°16N 106°16E **218** A10
Selenge
  Dem. Rep. of the Congo 1°58S 18°11E **264** C3
Selenge Mörön → *Asia* 52°16N 106°16E **218** A10
Selenicë *Albania* 40°33N 19°39E **202** F3
Selenter See *Germany* 54°18N 10°26E **178** A6
Sélestat *France* 48°16N 7°26E **173** D14
Seletan, Tanjung
  Indonesia 4°10S 114°40E **235** C4
Seletar, Pulau *Singapore* 1°26N 103°51E **138** A3
Seletar Hills *Singapore* 1°23N 103°52E **138** A3
Seletar Res. *Singapore* 1°24N 103°48E **138** A2
Selevac *Serbia* 44°28N 20°52E **202** B4
Selfoss *Iceland* 63°56N 21°0W **155** D6
Selhurst *U.K.* 51°23N 0°5W **125** B3
Sélibabi *Mauritania* 15°10N 12°15W **262** B2
Seliger, Ozero *Russia* 57°15N 33°0E **188** C7
Seligman *U.S.A.* 35°20N 112°53W **305** J7
Şelim *Turkey* 40°30N 42°43E **213** B10
Selima *Sudan* 21°22N 29°19E **256** C2
Selimiye *Turkey* 37°24N 27°40E **205** D9
Selinda Spillway →
  Botswana 18°35S 23°10E **270** A3
Sélingué, L. de *Mali* 11°37N 8°14W **262** C3
Selinsgrove *U.S.A.* 40°48N 76°52W **313** F8
Selizharovo *Russia* 56°51N 33°27E **188** D7
Selje *Norway* 62°3N 5°22E **161** E10
Seljord *Norway* 59°30N 8°40E **164** E5
Selkirk *Man., Canada* 50°10N 96°55W **297** C9
Selkirk *Ont., Canada* 42°49N 79°56W **312** D5
Selkirk *U.K.* 55°33N 2°50W **167** F6
Selkirk I. = Horse I.
  Canada 53°20N 99°6W **297** C9
Selkirk Mts. *Canada* 51°15N 117°40W **294** G8
Sellafield *U.K.* 54°25N 3°29W **168** C4
Sellama *Sudan* 12°51N 29°46E **257** E2
Sellia *Greece* 35°12N 24°23E **207** E5
Sellières *France* 46°50N 5°32E **173** F12
Sells *U.S.A.* 31°55N 111°53W **305** L8
Sellye *Hungary* 45°52N 17°51E **182** E2
Selma *Ala., U.S.A.* 32°25N 87°1W **315** E11
Selma *Calif., U.S.A.* 36°34N 119°37W **306** J7
Selma *N.C., U.S.A.* 35°32N 78°17W **315** D15
Selmer *U.S.A.* 35°10N 88°36W **315** D10
Selong *Indonesia* 8°39S 116°32E **235** D5
Selongey *France* 47°36N 5°11E **173** E12
Selouane *Morocco* 35°7N 2°57E **264** A4
Selous △ *Tanzania* 8°37S 37°42E **269** D4
Selowandoma Falls
  Zimbabwe 21°15S 31°50E **269** G3
Selpele *Indonesia* 0°1S 130°5E **231** E8
Selsey Bill *U.K.* 50°43N 0°47W **169** G7
Seltso *Russia* 53°22N 34°4E **188** F8
Seltz *France* 48°54N 8°4E **173** D15
Selu *Indonesia* 7°32S 130°55E **231** F8
Sélune → *France* 48°38N 1°22W **172** D5
Selva = La Selva del Camp
  Spain 41°13N 1°8E **196** D6
Selva *Argentina* 29°50S 62°0W **334** B3
Selva *Mallorca, Spain* 39°46N 2°54E **208** B9
Selva Lancandona = Montes
  Azules △ *Mexico* 16°21N 91°3W **319** D6
Selvagens, Ilhas *Madeira* 30°0N 16°0W **260** B1
Selwyn △ *S. Africa* 6°30S 67°0W **330** B4
Selwyn L. *Canada* 60°0N 104°30W **297** B8
Selwyn Mts. *Canada* 63°0N 130°0W **292** C6
Selwyn Passage *Vanuatu* 16°35S 168°12E **287** F5
Selwyn Ra. *Australia* 21°10S 140°0E **280** C3
Selyatyn *Ukraine* 47°50N 25°12E **183** C10
Sem *Norway* 59°14N 10°17E **164** E7
Sem Kolodezy = Lenine
  Ukraine 45°17N 35°46E **189** K8
Semadrek = Samothraki
  Greece 40°28N 25°28E **203** F9
Sentosa *Singapore* 1°16N 103°50E **138** B2
Seman → *Albania* 40°47N 19°30E **202** F3
Semangka, Teluk
  Indonesia 5°35S 104°42E **234** D2
Semarang *Indonesia* 7°0S 110°26E **235** D4
Semarapura = Klungkung
  Indonesia 8°32S 115°24E **231** K18
Sematan *Malaysia* 1°48N 109°46E **235** B3
Semayang, Danau
  Indonesia 0°14S 116°28E **235** C5
Sembabule *Uganda* 0°4S 31°25E **268** C3
Sembawang *Singapore* 1°27N 103°50E **138** A2
Sembé *Congo* 1°39N 14°36E **268** B2
Sembilang △ *Indonesia* 1°59S 104°44E **234** C2
Sembung *Indonesia* 8°28S 115°1E **231** J18
Şemdinli *Turkey* 37°18N 44°33E **213** D11
Sémé *Senegal* 15°4N 13°41W **262** B2
Semeih *Sudan* 12°43N 33°55E **257** E3
Semendua
  Dem. Rep. of the Congo 3°10S 18°6E **264** C3
Semenivka *Chernihiv,
  Ukraine* 52°8N 32°36E **189** F7
Semenivka *Kremenchuk,
  Ukraine* 49°37N 33°10E **189** H7
Semenov *Russia* 56°45N 44°25E **188** C16
Semeru *Indonesia* 8°4S 112°55E **235** D4
Semey *Kazakhstan* 50°30N 80°10E **217** B10
Semichi Is. *U.S.A.* 52°42N 174°0E **303** K1
Semikarakorskiy *Russia* 47°31N 40°48E **191** G5
Semiluki *Russia* 51°41N 39°2E **190** E10
Seminoe Res. *U.S.A.* 42°9N 106°55W **304** E10
Seminole *Fla., U.S.A.* 27°50N 82°47W **317** H7
Seminole *Okla., U.S.A.* 35°14N 96°41W **314** B6
Seminole *Tex., U.S.A.* 32°43N 102°39W **314** C3
Seminole, L. *U.S.A.* 30°54N 84°45W **316** F5
Seminole Draw →
  U.S.A. 32°27N 102°20W **314** C3
Semipalatinsk = Semey
  Kazakhstan 50°30N 80°10E **217** B10
Semirara Is. *Phil.* 12°0N 121°20E **239** F5

Semisopochnoi I. *U.S.A.* 51°55N 179°36E **303** L2
Semitau *Indonesia* 0°29N 111°57E **235** B4
Semliki △ *Uganda* 0°49N 30°4E **268** B3
Semlin = Zemun *Serbia* 44°51N 20°25E **202** B4
Semmelweis Museum
  Budapest, Hungary 117 c2
Semmering P. *Austria* 47°41'N 15°45E **180** D8
Semnān *Iran* 35°40N 53°23E **247** C7
Semnān □ *Iran* 36°0N 54°0E **247** C7
Sempang Mengayo, Tanjong
  Malaysia 1°0N 116°40E **235** A5
Semporna *Malaysia* 4°48N 118°33E **235** B5
Semuda *Indonesia* 2°51S 112°58E **235** C4
Semur-en-Auxois *France* 47°30N 4°20E **173** E11
Semuy → *Indonesia* 2°30S 112°35E **231** E7
Sen → *Cambodia* 12°32N 104°28E **236** F5
Sen Bolivia 11°32S 67°11W **330** C4
Senā *Iran* 28°27N 51°36E **247** D6
Sena *Mozam.* 17°25S 35°0E **269** B6
Sena → *Bolivia* 11°31S 67°11W **330** C4
Sena Madureira *Brazil* 9°5S 68°45W **330** B4
Senachwine L. *U.S.A.* 41°1'0 89°18W **310** C7
Senador José Porfírio
  Brazil 2°35S 51°55W **329** D7
Senador Pompeu *Brazil* 5°40S 39°20W **332** C4
Senago *Italy* 45°34N 9°7E **129** A1
Senaja *Malaysia* 6°45N 117°3E **235** A5
Senanga, Pulau *Singapore* 1°16N 103°43E **138** B2
Senanga *Zambia* 16°7S 23°16E **265** F4
Senatobia *U.S.A.* 34°37N 89°58W **315** D10
Sencelles *Spain* 39°39N 2°54E **206** B3
Sendafa *Ethiopia* 9° 1N 39°3E **257** F4
Sendai *Kagoshima, Japan* 31°50N 130°20E **222** F2
Sendai *Miyagi, Japan* 38°15N 140°53E **220** E10
Sendai-Wan *Japan* 38°15N 141°0E **220** E10
Senden *Bayern, Germany* 48°19N 10°4E **179** G6
Senden *Nordrhein-Westfalen,
  Germany* 51°52N 7°22E **178** D3
Sendhwa *India* 21°41N 75°6E **242** J6
Sendling *Germany* 48°7N 11°33E **131** B2
Sendlinger Tor Platz *Munich, Germany* 131 c1
Sendurjana *India* 21°32N 78°17E **244** D4
Sene → *Ghana* 7°30N 0°33E **263** D4
Senec *Slovak Rep.* 48°12N 17°23E **181** C10
Seneca *Ill., U.S.A.* 41°19N 88°37W **314** B8
Seneca S.C. *U.S.A.* 34°41N 82°57W **315** D13
Seneca Falls *U.S.A.* 42°55N 76°48W **313** D8
Senecaville L. *U.S.A.* 39°55N 81°25W **312** G3
Senegal ■ *W. Afr.* 14°30N 14°30W **262** C2
Sénégal → *W. Afr.* 15°48N 16°32W **262** B1
Senegambia *Africa* 12°45N 12°0W **254** E2
Senegambia & Niger = Mali ■
  Africa 17°0N 3°0W **262** B4
Senekal *S. Africa* 28°20S 27°36E **271** C4
Senftenberg *Germany* 51°32N 14°0E **178** D10
Senga Hill *Zambia* 9°19S 31°11E **269** D3
Senge Khambab = Indus →
  Pakistan 24°20N 67°47E **242** G2
Sengerema *Tanzania* 2°42S 32°35E **268** C3
Sengiley *Russia* 53°58N 48°46E **190** D9
Sengua → *Zimbabwe* 17°7S 28°5E **269** F2
Senhor-do-Bonfim *Brazil* 10°30S 40°10W **332** D3
Senica *Slovak Rep.* 48°41N 17°25E **181** C10
Senigállia *Italy* 43°43N 13°13E **199** C10
Senio → *Italy* 44°35N 12°15E **199** D9
Senirkent *Turkey* 38°6N 30°33E **205** C12
Senise *Italy* 40°9N 16°17E **201** B9
Senj *Croatia* 45°0N 14°58E **199** D11
Senja *Norway* 69°25N 17°30E **160** B17
Senju *Japan* 35°44N 139°48E **140** A3
Senkaku-Shoto
  E. China Sea 25°45N 123°30E **221** M1
Senlis *France* 49°13N 2°35E **173** C9
Senmonorom *Cambodia* 12°27N 107°12E **236** F6
Sennori *Italy* 40°47N 8°35E **200** B1
Seno *Laos* 16°35N 104°50E **236** D5
Senoia *U.S.A.* 33°18N 84°33W **316** B5
Senonches *France* 48°34N 1°2E **172** D8
Senorbì *Italy* 39°32N 9°8E **200** C2
Senožeče *Slovenia* 45°43N 14°3E **199** C11
Senqu → = Orange → *S. Africa* 28°41S 16°28E **270** D2
Senriyama *Japan* 34°47N 135°30E **133** A2
Sens *France* 48°11N 3°15E **173** D10
Senta *Serbia* 45°55N 20°3E **182** E5
Sentani, Danau
  Indonesia 0°51N 112°6E **235** B4
Sentinel *U.S.A.* 32°52N 113°13W **305** K7
Şentjur *Slovenia* 46°14N 15°24E **199** B12
Sentosa *Singapore* 1°16N 103°50E **138** B2
Sentry Hill *St.-Maarten* 18°2N 63°4W **322** a
Senwabarwana *S. Africa* 23°17S 29°7E **271** B4
Senya Beraku *Ghana* 5°28N 0°31W **263** D4
Seo de Urgel = La Seu d'Urgell
  Spain 42°22N 1°23E **196** C6
Seobi-ri *S. Korea* 35°31N 126°58E **137** B1
Seocho *S. Korea* 37°29N 126°0E **137** B1
Seodaemun *S. Korea* 37°34N 126°56E **137** C1
Seogwipo *S. Korea* 33° 3N 126°34E **224** a
Seohara *India* 29°1'N 78°48E **243** B8
Seokguram Grotto
  S. Korea 35°45N 129°18E **224** E4
Seokkwan *S. Korea* 37°31N 126°59E **137** B3
Seonath → *India* 21°44N 82°28E **243** J10
Seonath *India* 29° 1N 78°48E **243** B8
Seongbuk *S. Korea* 37°36N 127°0E **137** B3
Seongdong *S. Korea* 37°33N 127°2E **137** B3
Seongdong-gu *S. Korea* 37°33N 127°2E **137** B3
Seongmodo *S. Korea* 37°41N 126°19E **137** C1
Seonggu *S. Korea* 37° 1N 126°44E **137** B2
Seoni *India* 22°5N 79°30E **244** D4
Seoni Malwa *India* 22°27N 77°28E **244** D3
Seoraksan △ *S. Korea* 38°7N 128°27E **137** B6
Seoraksan △ *S. Korea* 38°10N 128°25E **224** D4
Seoriuarayan *India* 21°45N 82°34E **243** J10
Seosan *S. Korea* 36°47N 126°27E **224** E3
Seoul = Sŏul *S. Korea* 37°31N 126°58E **137** C1
Seoul Nat. Univ. *S. Korea* 37°31N 126°57E **137** C2
Seoul Tower *S. Korea* 37°33N 126°59E **137** C2
Separation Pt. *N.Z.* 40°47S 172°58E **285** D7
Sepang *Malaysia* 2°37S 101°46E **237** L3
Sepi *Solomon Is.* 8°31S 159°52E **287** M10
Sepídān *Iran* 30°20N 52°5E **247** D7
Sepik → *Papua N. G.* 3°46S 144°30E **286** B6
Sepo-ri *N. Korea* 38°57N 127°25E **137** B2
Sępólno Krajeńskie
  Poland 53°26N 17°30E **184** E4

Sepone *Laos* 16°45N 106°13E **236** D6
Sępopol *Poland* 54°16N 21°2E **184** D8
Sept-Îles *Canada* 50°13N 66°22W **299** B6
Sertã *Portugal* 39°48N 8°6W **194** F2
Sertânia *Brazil* 8°5S 37°20W **332** C4
Sertanópolis *Brazil* 23°4S 51°2W **335** A5
Sértar *China* 32°20N 100°41E **228** A3
Serua *Indonesia* 6°18S 130°1E **231** F8
Serui *Indonesia* 1°53S 136°10E **231** E9
Serule *Botswana* 21°57S 27°20E **270** B4
Serutu *Indonesia* 1°42S 108°45E **235** C3
Servia *Greece* 40°11N 22°0E **202** F6
Serzedelo *Portugal* 41°24N 8°14W **194** D2
Ses Salines *Spain* 39°21N 3°3E **206** B4
Sesayap → *Indonesia* 3°36N 117°15E **235** B5
Sese Is. *Uganda* 0°20S 32°20E **268** C3
Seseko-shima *Japan* 26°39N 127°52E **288** a
Sesepe *Indonesia* 1°30S 127°59E **231** E7
Sesfontein *Namibia* 19°7S 13°39E **271** A1
Sesheke *Zambia* 17°29S 24°13E **270** B3
Sésia → *Italy* 45°5N 8°37E **198** C5
Sesimbra *Portugal* 38°28N 9°6W **195** G1
S'Espalmador *Spain* 38°47N 1°26E **206** D1
S'Espardell *Spain* 38°48N 1°29E **206** D1
Sessa *Angola* 13°56S 20°38E **265** E4
Sessa Aurunca *Italy* 41°14N 13°56E **200** A6
S'Estanyol *Spain* 39°22N 2°54E **206** B3
Sestao *Spain* 43°18N 3°0W **198** A1
Sesto Calende *Italy* 45°44N 8°37E **198** C5
Sesto San Giovanni *Italy* 45°31N 9°13E **129** A2
Sesto Ulteriano *Italy* 45°24N 9°16E **129** B2
Sestri Levante *Italy* 44°17N 9°24E **196** C7
Sestriere *Italy* 44°57N 6°53E **198** D3
Sestroretsk *Russia* 60°5N 29°58E **188** B6
Sestrunj *Croatia* 44°10N 15°0E **199** D11
Sestu *Italy* 39°18N 9°6E **200** C2
Setagaya *Japan* 35°37N 139°36E **140** B2
Setaka *Japan* 33°9N 130°28E **222** D2
Setana *Japan* 42°26N 139°51E **220** C10
Sète *France* 43°25N 3°42E **174** E7
Sete Lagoas *Brazil* 19°27S 44°16W **333** E3
Setesdalsheiene = Suldalsheiene
  Norway 59°28N 7°10E **164** E3
Setia Budi *Indonesia* 6°12S 106°49E **122** B1
Sétif *Algeria* 36°9N 5°26E **261** A6
Sétif □ *Algeria* 36°10N 5°0E **261** A6
Setit → *Sudan* 14°20N 35°50E **257** E4
Seto *Japan* 35°14N 137°6E **223** B9
Setonaikai *Japan* 34°20N 133°30E **222** C5
Setonaikai △ *Japan* 34°15N 133°15E **222** C5
Setsan *Burma* 16°30N 95°8E **241** d1
Settat *Morocco* 33°0N 7°40W **260** B3
Settat □ *Morocco* 33°5N 7°25W **260** B3
Setté-Cama *Gabon* 2°32S 9°45E **264** C1
Settebagni *Italy* 42°0N 12°31E **136** A2
Settecamini *Italy* 41°57N 12°38E **136** B2
Séttimo Milanese *Italy* 45°28N 9°3E **129** A1
Séttimo Torinese *Italy* 45°9N 7°46E **198** C4
Setting L. *Canada* 55°0N 98°38W **297** C9
Settle *U.K.* 54°5N 2°16W **168** C5
Settlement *Wake I.* 19°18N 166°38E **302** b
Settlement, The
  Br. Virgin Is. 18°43N 64°22W **321** b
Settlers *S. Africa* 25°2S 28°30E **271** C4
Settsu *Japan* 34°47N 135°33E **133** A2
Setúbal *Portugal* 38°30N 8°58W **195** G2
Setúbal □ *Portugal* 38°30N 8°35W **195** G2
Setúbal, B. de *Portugal* 38°40N 8°56W **195** G2
Setuny → *France* 55°43N 37°21E **132** D3
Seugne → *France* 45°42N 0°32W **174** C3
Seul, Lac *Canada* 50°20N 92°30W **298** B1
Seulimeum *Indonesia* 5°27N 95°15E **234** A1
Seurre *France* 47°0N 5°8E **173** F12
Seutula *Finland* 60°20N 24°52E **121** A2
Sevan *Armenia* 40°33N 44°56E **191** K7
Sevan, Ozero = Sevana Lich
  Armenia 40°30N 45°20E **191** K7
Sevana Lich *Armenia* 40°30N 45°20E **191** K7
Sevastopol *Ukraine* 44°35N 33°30E **189** F7
Seven Corners *U.S.A.* 38°53N 77°9W **143** B3
Seven Islands = Sept-Îles
  Canada 50°13N 66°22W **299** B6
Seven Kings *U.K.* 51°33N 0°5E **125** A4
Seven Sisters *Canada* 50°10N 109°20W **126** B5
Seventeen Street Canal
  U.S.A. 30°3N 90°7W **131** A2
Sever → *Spain* 39°40N 7°32W **195** F3
Sévérac-le-Château *France* 44°20N 3°5E **174** D7
Severn → *Ont., Canada* 56°2N 87°36W **298** A2
Severn → *U.K.* 51°35N 2°40W **169** F5
Severnaya Zemlya *Russia* 79°0N 100°0E **215** B11
Severnyye Uvaly *Russia* 60°0N 50°0E **186** C9
Severo-Kurilsk *Russia* 50°40N 156°8E **215** D16
Severo-Yeniseyskiy
  Russia 60°22N 93°1E **215** C10
Severo-Zapadnyy □ *Russia* 65°0N 40°0E **214** C4
Severočeský □
  Czech Rep. 49°30N 13°40E **180** B7
Severodonetsk = Syeverodonetsk
  Ukraine 48°58N 38°35E **189** H10
Severodvinsk *Russia* 64°27N 39°58E **186** B6
Severomoravský □
  Czech Rep. 49°38N 17°40E **181** B10
Severomorsk *Russia* 69°5N 33°27E **160** B25
Severouralsk *Russia* 60°9N 59°57E **186** B11
Seversk *Russia* 56°36N 84°49E **214** D9
Sévesco *Italy* 45°39N 9°9E **129** A1
Sevier → *U.S.A.* 39°4N 113°6W **304** G7
Sevier Desert *U.S.A.* 39°40N 112°45W **304** G7
Sevier L. *U.S.A.* 38°54N 113°9W **304** G6
Sevilla *Colombia* 4°16N 75°57W **328** C2
Sevilla *Spain* 37°23N 5°58W **195** H5
Sevilla □ *Spain* 37°25N 5°58W **195** H5
Seville = Sevilla *Spain* 37°23N 5°58W **195** H5
Seville *Fla., U.S.A.* 29°19N 81°30W **317** F8
Seville *Ga., U.S.A.* 31°58N 83°36W **316** D6
Sevlievo *Bulgaria* 43°2N 25°6E **203** D9
Sevnica *Slovenia* 46°2N 15°19E **199** B12
Sevran *France* 48°56N 2°31E **134** A4
Sèvre-Niortaise → *France* 46°28N 1°33W **172** F5
Sèvre-Niortaise → *France* 47°12N 1°33W **172** E5
Sevsk *Russia* 52°10N 34°30E **188** F8
Sewa → *S. Leone* 7°12N 12°10W **262** D2
Seward *Alaska, U.S.A.* 60°7N 149°27W **303** F10
Seward *Nebr., U.S.A.* 40°55N 97°6W **308** E6
Seward *Pa., U.S.A.* 40°25N 79°1W **312** F5
Seward Peninsula *U.S.A.* 65°0N 164°0W **303** B7
Sewell *Chile* 34°10S 70°23W **334** C1
Sewer *Indonesia* 5°53S 134°40E **231** F8
Sewickley *U.S.A.* 40°32N 80°12W **312** F4
Sewri *India* 18°59N 72°50E **138** e
Sexsmith *Canada* 55°21N 118°47W **296** B5
Seychelles ■ *Ind. Oc.* 5°0S 56°0E **272** c
Seyðisfjörður *Iceland* 65°16N 13°57W **155** D7
Seydişehir *Turkey* 37°25N 31°51E **212** D4
Seydvān *Iran* 38°34N 44°45E **246** B5
Seyhan → *Turkey* 36°43N 34°53E **250** B5
Seyhan Barajı *Turkey* 37°20N 35°18E **250** B6
Seyitgazi *Turkey* 39°26N 30°42E **205** B12
Seyitömer *Turkey* 39°37N 29°56E **205** B11
Seym → *Ukraine* 51°27N 32°34E **189** G7
Seymour *Vic., Australia* 37°2S 145°10E **283** D6

428 Seymour INDEX

Seymour *Eastern Cape, S. Africa* 32°33S 26°46E **271** D4
Seymour *Conn., U.S.A.* 41°24N 73°4W **313** E11
Seymour *Ind., U.S.A.* 38°58N 85°53W **311** F11
Seymour *Tex., U.S.A.* 33°35N 99°16W **314** E5
Seyne *France* 44°21N 6°22E **175** D10
Seyssel *France* 45°57N 5°50E **175** C9
Sežana *Slovenia* 45°43N 13°41E **199** C10
Sézanne *France* 48°40N 3°40E **173** D10
Sezze *Italy* 41°30N 13°3E **200** A6
Sfântu Gheorghe *Covasna, Romania* 45°52N 25°48E **183** E10
Sfântu Gheorghe *Tulcea, Romania* 44°53N 29°36E **183** F14
Sfântu Gheorghe, Braţul → *Romania* 44°51N 29°36E **183** F14
Sfax *Tunisia* 34°49N 10°48E **258** B2
Sfax □ *Tunisia* 34°40N 10°20E **261** B7
Sforzesco, Castello *Italy* 45°28N 9°10E **129** B2
Sha Kok Mei *China* 22°23N 114°16E **122** A2
Sha Tau Kok *China* 22°33N 114°13E **219** a
Sha Tin *China* 22°23N 114°12E **122** A2
Sha Xi → *China* 26°35N 118°0E **229** D12
Sha Xian *China* 26°23N 117°45E **229** D11
Shaanxi □ *China* 35°0N 109°0E **226** G5
Sha'ar Binyamin *West Bank* 31°52N 35°16E **123** A2
Shaba = Katanga □ *Dem. Rep. of the Congo* 8°0S 25°0E **268** D2
Shaba △ *Kenya* 0°38N 37°48E **268** B4
Shabeellaha Dhexe □ *Somali Rep.* 3°0N 46°0E **267** D6
Shabeellaha Hoose □ *Somali Rep.* 1°0N 44°0E **267** D5
Shabeelle → *Somali Rep.* 2°0N 44°0E **267** D5
Shabestar *Iran* 38°11N 45°41E **213** C11
Shabla *Bulgaria* 43°31N 28°32E **203** C12
Shabogamo L. *Canada* 53°15N 66°30W **299** B6
Shabrâmant *Egypt* 29°56N 31°11E **117** B2
Shabunda *Dem. Rep. of the Congo* 2°40S 27°16E **268** C2
Shabwah *Yemen* 15°22N 47°1E **248** D4
Shache *China* 38°20N 77°10E **217** E9
Shackleton Fracture Zone *S. Ocean* 60°0S 60°0W **151** B18
Shackleton Ice Shelf *Antarctica* 66°0S 100°0E **151** C8
Shackleton Inlet *Antarctica* 83°0S 160°0E **151** E11
Shādegān *Iran* 30°40N 48°38E **247** D6
Shadi *Jiangxi, China* 26°7N 114°47E **229** D10
Shadi *Jammu & Kashmir, India* 33°24N 77°14E **243** C7
Shadrinsk *Russia* 56°5N 63°32E **214** D7
Shady Dale *U.S.A.* 33°24N 83°36W **316** B6
Shady Grove *U.S.A.* 30°17N 83°38W **316** E6
Shadyside *U.S.A.* 39°58N 80°45W **312** G4
Shafer, L. *U.S.A.* 40°46N 86°46W **311** D10
Shaffa *Nigeria* 10°30N 12°6E **263** C7
Shafter *U.S.A.* 35°30N 119°16W **307** K7
Shaftesbury *U.K.* 51°0N 2°11W **169** F5
Shaftsbury *U.S.A.* 43°0N 73°11W **313** D11
Shag Pt. *N.Z.* 45°29S 170°52E **285** F5
Shag Rocks *Atl. Oc.* 53°0S 41°0W **152** M7
Shagamu *Nigeria* 6°51N 3°39E **263** D5
Shageluk *U.S.A.* 62°41N 159°34W **303** E8
Shagram *Pakistan* 36°24N 72°20E **243** A5
Shah Alam *Malaysia* 3°5N 101°32E **237** L3
Shah Alizai *Pakistan* 29°25N 66°33E **242** E2
Shah Bunder *Pakistan* 24°13N 67°56E **242** G2
Shāh Jūy *Afghan.* 32°31N 67°25E **240** B2
Shah Mosque *Iran* 35°41N 51°25E **141** A2
Shahabad *Karnataka, India* 17°10N 76°54E **244** F3
Shahabad *Punjab, India* 30°10N 76°55E **242** D7
Shahabad *Raj., India* 25°15N 77°11E **242** G7
Shahabad *Ut. P., India* 27°36N 79°56E **243** F8
Shahada *India* 21°33N 74°30E **244** D2
Shahadpur *Pakistan* 25°55N 68°35E **242** G3
Shahapur *India* 15°50N 74°34E **245** G2
Shahbā' *Syria* 32°52N 36°38E **250** F7
Shahbazpur I. *Bangla.* 22°30N 90°45E **241** D3
Shahdād *Iran* 30°30N 57°40E **247** D8
Shahdād, Namakzār-e *Iran* 30°20N 58°20E **247** D8
Shahdadkot *Pakistan* 27°50N 67°55E **242** F2
Shahdara *India* 28°40N 77°18E **120** A2
Shahdol *India* 23°19N 81°26E **243** H9
Shahe *Guangdong, China* 23°9N 113°19E **121** B2
Shahe *Hebei, China* 37°0N 114°32E **226** F8
Shahganj *India* 26°3N 82°44E **243** F10
Shahgarh *India* 27°15N 69°50E **242** F3
Shahḥāt *Libya* 32°48N 21°54E **258** B4
Shahīdān *Afghan.* 36°42N 67°49E **240** A2
Shahjahanpur *India* 27°54N 79°57E **243** F8
Shahpur = Salmās *Iran* 38°11N 44°47E **213** C11
Shahpur *Karnataka, India* 16°40N 76°48E **244** F3
Shahpur *Mad. P., India* 22°12N 77°58E **242** H7
Shahpur *Baluchistan, Pakistan* 28°46N 68°27E **242** E3
Shahpur *Punjab, Pakistan* 32°17N 72°26E **242** C5
Shahpur Chakar *Pakistan* 26°9N 68°39E **242** F3
Shahpura *Mad. P., India* 23°10N 80°45E **243** H9
Shahpura *Raj., India* 25°38N 74°56E **242** G6
Shahr-e Bābak *Iran* 30°7N 55°9E **247** D7
Shahr-e Kord *Iran* 32°15N 50°55E **247** C6
Shahr-e Rey *Iran* 35°36N 51°25E **141** B2
Shahrak-e Golshahr *Iran* 35°37N 51°18E **141** B1
Shahrak-e Qods *Iran* 35°47N 51°22E **141** A2
Shāhrakht *Iran* 33°38N 60°16E **247** C9
Shahreză = Qomsheh *Iran* 32°0N 51°55E **247** D6
Shahrig *Pakistan* 30°15N 67°40E **242** D2
Shahrisabz *Uzbekistan* 39°3N 66°50E **217** E7
Shāhrud = Emāmrūd *Iran* 36°30N 55°0E **247** B7
Shahukou *China* 40°20N 112°18E **226** D7
Shaikh Aomar *Iraq* 33°20N 44°23E **113** A2
Shaikhabad *Afghan.* 34°2N 68°45E **242** B3
Shajapur *India* 23°27N 76°21E **242** H7
Shajing *China* 22°44N 113°48E **219** a
Shajuwan *Taiwan* 23°13N 121°23E **225** C3
Shakargarh *Pakistan* 32°17N 75°10E **242** C6
Shakawe *Botswana* 18°28S 21°49E **270** A3
Shakenge *Dem. Rep. of the Congo* 6°14S 18°41E **265** D3
Shaker Heights *U.S.A.* 41°28N 81°32W **312** E3
Shakhtersk *Russia* 49°10N 142°8E **215** E15
Shakhtinsk *Kazakhstan* 49°42N 72°35E **217** C8
Shakhty *Russia* 47°40N 40°16E **191** G5
Shakhtyorskoye = Pershotravensk *Ukraine* 50°13N 27°40E **177** C14
Shakhunya *Russia* 57°40N 46°46E **190** B8
Shaki *Nigeria* 8°41N 3°21E **263** D5
Shākir *Egypt* 27°30N 33°59E **256** B3
Shakotan-Hantō *Japan* 43°10N 140°30E **220** C10
Shaksam Valley *Asia* 36°0N 76°20E **243** A7
Shaktoolik *U.S.A.* 64°20N 161°9W **303** D7
Shakurbasti *India* 28°41N 77°6E **120** A1
Shala, L. *Ethiopia* 7°30N 38°30E **257** F4
Shali *Russia* 43°9N 45°55E **191** J7
Shalkar Köli *Kazakhstan* 50°35N 51°47E **190** E10
Shalkiya *India* 22°36N 88°21E **124** B2
Shallow Lake *Canada* 44°36N 81°5W **312** B3
Shalqar *Kazakhstan* 47°48N 59°39E **216** C5
Shalqar Köli *Kazakhstan* 50°33N 51°40E **216** B4
Shalskiy *Russia* 61°48N 35°58E **188** B8
Shalu *Taiwan* 24°14N 120°34E **225** B2
Shaluli Shan *China* 30°40N 99°55E **228** B2
Shām *Iran* 26°39N 57°21E **247** E8
Shām, Bādiyat ash *Asia* 32°0N 40°0E **246** C3
Shām, J. ash *Oman* 23°10N 57°5E **249** B7
Sham Shui Po *China* 22°19N 114°9E **122** B1
Shamâl Bahr el Ghazal = Northern Bahr el Ghazal □ *South Sudan* 8°0N 27°30E **257** F2
Shamâl Dârfûr □ *Sudan* 15°0N 25°0E **257** E2
Shamâl Kordofân □ *Sudan* 15°0N 30°0E **257** E3
Shamâl Sînî □ *Egypt* 30°30N 33°30E **251** H4
Shamapur *India* 28°44N 77°8E **120** A1
Shamattawa *Canada* 55°51N 92°5W **298** A1
Shamattawa → *Canada* 55°1N 85°23W **298** A2
Shambe *South Sudan* 7°8N 30°46E **257** F3
Shambe △ *South Sudan* 6°57N 30°50E **257** F3
Shambu *Ethiopia* 9°32N 37°3E **257** F4
Shamgong Dzong *Bhutan* 27°13N 90°35E **241** B3
Shamian *China* 23°6N 113°13E **121** B2
Shamīl *Iran* 27°30N 56°55E **247** E8
Shamkhor = Şämkir *Azerbaijan* 40°50N 46°0E **191** K8
Shāmkūh *Iran* 35°47N 57°50E **247** C8
Shamli *India* 29°32N 77°18E **242** E7
Shammar, Jabal *Si. Arabia* 27°40N 41°0E **246** E4
Shamo = Gobi *Asia* 44°0N 110°0E **226** C6
Shamo, L. *Ethiopia* 5°45N 37°30E **257** F4
Shamokin *U.S.A.* 40°47N 76°34W **313** F8
Shamrock *Ont., Canada* 45°23N 76°50W **313** A8
Shamrock *Tex., U.S.A.* 35°13N 100°15W **314** D4
Shamva *Zimbabwe* 17°20S 31°32E **269** F3
Shan □ *Burma* 21°30N 98°30E **241** E7
Shan Mei *China* 22°24N 114°10E **122** A2
Shan Shan *China* 42°52N 90°10E **217** D12
Shan Xian *China* 34°50N 116°5E **226** G9
Shana = Kurilsk *Russia* 45°14N 147°53E **215** E15
Shanan → *Ethiopia* 8°0N 40°20E **257** F5
Shanchengzhen *China* 42°20N 125°20E **224** A2
Shāndak *Iran* 28°28N 60°27E **247** D9
Shandan *China* 38°45N 101°15E **218** D9
Shandon *U.S.A.* 35°39N 120°23W **306** K6
Shandong □ *China* 36°0N 118°0E **227** G10
Shandong Bandao *China* 37°0N 121°0E **227** F11
Shandur Pass *Pakistan* 36°4N 72°31E **243** A5
Shang Xian = Shangzhou *China* 33°50N 109°58E **226** H5
Shangalowe *Dem. Rep. of the Congo* 10°50S 26°30E **269** E2
Shangani *Zimbabwe* 19°41S 29°20E **271** A4
Shangani → *Zimbabwe* 18°41S 27°10E **269** F2
Shangbancheng *China* 40°50N 118°1E **227** D10
Shangcheng *China* 31°47N 115°26E **229** B10
Shangchuan Dao *China* 21°40N 112°50E **229** G9
Shangdu *China* 41°30N 113°30E **226** D7
Shanggao *China* 28°17N 114°55E **229** C10
Shanghai *China* 31°15N 121°26E **138** B2
Shanghai Hongqiao ✈ (SHA) *China* 31°12N 121°20E **138** B1
Shanghai Pudong ✈ (PVG) *China* 31°9N 121°47E **138** B2
Shanghai Shi □ *China* 31°0N 121°30E **229** B13
Shanghang *China* 25°2N 116°23E **229** E11
Shanghe *China* 37°20N 117°10E **227** F9
Shangjao = Shangrao *China* 28°25N 117°59E **229** C11
Shanglin *China* 23°27N 108°33E **228** F7
Shangnan *China* 33°32N 110°50E **226** H6
Shangqiu *China* 34°26N 115°36E **226** G8
Shangrao *China* 28°25N 117°59E **229** C11
Shangri-La = Zhongdian *China* 27°48N 99°42E **228** D2
Shangshui *China* 33°32N 114°35E **226** H8
Shangsi *China* 22°8N 107°58E **228** F6
Shangyi *China* 41°4N 113°57E **226** D7
Shangyou *China* 25°48N 114°32E **229** E10
Shangyu *China* 30°3N 120°52E **229** B13
Shangzhi *China* 45°22N 127°56E **227** B14
Shangzhou *China* 33°50N 109°58E **226** H5
Shanhetun *China* 44°33N 127°15E **227** B14
Shanhu Tan *Taiwan* 23°12N 120°23E **225** C2
Shanhua *Taiwan* 23°8N 120°17E **225** C2
Shani *Nigeria* 10°14N 12°2E **263** C7
Shānidar *Iraq* 36°48N 44°14E **213** D11
Shankill *Ireland* 53°14N 6°7W **120** B3
Shanklin *U.K.* 50°38N 1°11W **169** G6
Shanlin *Taiwan* 23°0N 120°32E **225** C2
Shannon *N.Z.* 40°33S 175°25E **284** G4
Shannon → *Ireland* 52°35N 9°30W **166** D2
Shannon ✈ (SNN) *Ireland* 52°42N 8°57W **166** D3
Shannon, Mouth of the *Ireland* 52°30N 9°55W **166** D2
Shannon △ *Australia* 34°35S 116°25E **279** F2
Shannon Ø *Greenland* 75°10N 18°30W **154** B9
Shannonbridge *Ireland* 53°17N 8°3W **166** C3
Shannontown *U.S.A.* 33°53N 80°21W **316** B9
Shanshang *Taiwan* 23°6N 120°21E **225** C2
Shansi = Shanxi □ *China* 37°0N 112°0E **226** F7
Shantar, Ostrov Bolshoy *Russia* 55°9N 137°40E **215** D14
Shantipur *India* 23°17N 88°25E **243** H13
Shantou *China* 23°18N 116°40E **229** F11
Shantung = Shandong □ *China* 36°0N 118°0E **227** G10
Shanwei *China* 22°48N 115°22E **229** F10
Shanxi □ *China* 37°0N 112°0E **226** F7
Shanyang *China* 33°31N 109°55E **226** H5
Shanyin *China* 39°25N 112°56E **226** E7
Shaodong *China* 27°15N 111°43E **229** D8
Shaoguan *China* 24°48N 113°35E **229** E9
Shaohing = Shaoxing *China* 30°0N 120°35E **229** C13
Shaoshan *China* 27°55N 112°33E **229** D9
Shaowu *China* 27°22N 117°28E **229** D11
Shaoxing *China* 30°0N 120°35E **229** C13
Shaoyang *Hunan, China* 26°59N 111°20E **229** D8
Shaoyang *Hunan, China* 27°14N 111°25E **229** D8
Shap *U.K.* 54°32N 2°40W **168** C5
Shapinsay *U.K.* 59°3N 2°51W **167** B6
Shaqlāwah *Iraq* 36°23N 44°20E **213** D11
Shaqq el Gi'eifer → *Sudan* 15°16N 26°0E **257** D2
Shaqra' *Si. Arabia* 25°15N 45°16E **246** E5
Shaqrā' *Yemen* 13°22N 45°44E **248** D4
Shar *Kazakhstan* 49°35N 81°2E **217** C10
Sharafa *Sudan* 11°59N 27°7E **257** E2
Sharafkhāneh *Iran* 38°11N 45°29E **213** C11
Sharashova *Belarus* 52°34N 24°12E **185** F11
Sharavati → *India* 14°20N 74°25E **245** G2
Sharbaqty *Kazakhstan* 51°23N 78°17E **217** B9
Sharbatāt, Ra's ash *Oman* 17°56N 56°21E **249** C7
Sharbot Lake *Canada* 44°46N 76°41W **313** B8
Shardara, Step *Kazakhstan* 42°20N 68°0E **217** D7
Sharhorod *Ukraine* 48°45N 28°5E **183** B13
Shari *Japan* 43°55N 144°40E **220** C12
Shariff Aguak = Maganoy *Phil.* 6°51N 124°31E **233** H5
Shariff Kabunsuan □ *Phil.* 7°5N 124°5E **233** H5
Sharjah = Ash Shāriqah *U.A.E.* 25°23N 55°26E **247** E7
Shark B. *Australia* 25°30S 113°32E **279** E1
Shark Bay △ *Australia* 25°30S 113°30E **279** E1
Sharm el Sheikh *Egypt* 27°53N 34°18E **251** L5
Sharon *Ont., Canada* 44°6N 79°26W **312** B5
Sharon *Mass., U.S.A.* 42°7N 71°11W **313** D13
Sharon *Pa., U.S.A.* 41°14N 80°31W **312** E4
Sharon *Wis., U.S.A.* 42°30N 88°44W **311** B8
Sharon Springs *Kans., U.S.A.* 38°54N 101°45W **308** F3
Sharon Springs *N.Y., U.S.A.* 42°48N 74°37W **313** D10
Sharonville *U.S.A.* 39°16N 84°25W **311** E12
Sharp I. *China* 22°21N 114°17E **122** A2
Sharp Pk. *Phil.* 5°58N 125°31E **233** J5
Sharp Pt. *Australia* 10°58S 142°43E **286** F2
Sharpe L. *Canada* 54°24N 93°40W **298** B1
Sharpes *U.S.A.* 28°26N 80°46W **317** G9
Sharpsville *U.S.A.* 41°15N 80°29W **312** E4
Sharq el Istiwa'iya = Eastern Equatoria □ *South Sudan* 5°0N 33°0E **257** G3
Sharqi, Al Jabal ash *Lebanon* 33°40N 36°10E **250** E7
Sharqîya □ *Egypt* 30°48N 31°48E **251** H2
Sharya *Russia* 58°22N 45°20E **190** A7
Shasha *Ethiopia* 6°29N 35°59E **257** F4
Shashemene *Ethiopia* 7°13N 38°33E **257** F4
Shashi *Botswana* 21°15S 27°27E **271** B4
Shashi → *Africa* 21°14S 29°20E **269** G2
Shasta, Mt. *U.S.A.* 41°25N 122°12W **304** F2
Shasta L. *U.S.A.* 40°43N 122°25W **304** F2
Shastrinagar *India* 28°40N 77°10E **120** A2
Shatawi *Sudan* 14°39N 32°6E **257** E3
Shāṭi', Wādī ash → *Libya* 27°30N 15°0E **258** C3
Shatilki = Svyetlahorsk *Belarus* 52°38N 29°46E **177** B15
Shatsk *Russia* 54°5N 41°45E **190** C5
Shatsk *Ukraine* 51°29N 23°55E **185** G10
Shatsky Rise *Pac. Oc.* 34°0N 157°0E **288** D7
Shatskyi △ *Ukraine* 51°30N 23°52E **185** G10
Shatt al Arab *Asia* 29°57N 48°34E **247** D6
Shatura *Russia* 55°33N 39°21E **188** E10
Shaturtof = Shatura *Russia* 55°33N 39°21E **188** E10
Shau Kei Wan *China* 22°16N 114°13E **122** B2
Shaumyani = Shulaveri *Georgia* 41°22N 44°45E **191** K7
Shaunavon *Canada* 49°35N 108°25W **297** D7
Shaver L. *U.S.A.* 37°9N 119°18W **306** H7
Shavli = Šiauliai *Lithuania* 55°56N 23°15E **184** C10
Shaw → *Australia* 20°21S 119°17E **278** D2
Shaw I. *Australia* 20°30S 149°2E **280** b
Shawanaga *Canada* 45°31N 80°17W **312** A4
Shawangunk Mts. *U.S.A.* 41°35N 74°30W **313** E10
Shawano *U.S.A.* 44°47N 88°36W **308** C9
Shawinigan *Canada* 46°35N 72°50W **298** C5
Shawmari, J. ash *Jordan* 30°35N 36°35E **251** H7
Shawnee *Ga., U.S.A.* 32°29N 81°25W **316** C8
Shawnee *Kans., U.S.A.* 39°1N 94°43W **310** E2
Shawnee *Okla., U.S.A.* 35°20N 96°55W **314** D6
Shawocun *China* 39°53N 116°13E **114** B1
Shay Gap *Australia* 20°30S 120°10E **278** D3
Shayang *China* 30°42N 112°29E **229** B9
Shaybārā *Si. Arabia* 25°26N 36°47E **246** E3
Shayib el Banat, Gebel *Egypt* 26°59N 33°29E **256** B3
Shaykh, J. ash *Lebanon* 33°25N 35°50E **250** E6
Shaykh Miskīn *Syria* 32°49N 36°9E **250** F7
Shaykh Sa'd *Iraq* 32°34N 46°17E **213** F12
Shaykh 'Uthmān *Yemen* 12°52N 44°59E **248** D4
Shaytansky Zavod = Pervouralsk *Russia* 56°59N 59°59E **186** C10
Shayuan *China* 23°5N 113°15E **121** B2
Shāzand *Iran* 33°56N 49°24E **247** C6
Shazud *Tajikistan* 37°45N 72°25E **217** E8
Shcheglovo = Kemerovo *Russia* 55°20N 86°5E **214** D9
Shchekino *Russia* 54°1N 37°34E **188** E9
Shcherbakov = Rybinsk *Russia* 58°5N 38°50E **188** C10
Shchigry *Russia* 51°55N 36°58E **189** G9
Shchors *Ukraine* 51°48N 31°56E **189** G6
Shchūchīnsk *Kazakhstan* 52°56N 70°12E **217** B8
She Xian *Anhui, China* 29°50N 118°25E **229** C12
She Xian *Hebei, China* 36°30N 113°40E **226** F7
Shea *Guyana* 2°48N 59°4W **329** C6
Shebekino *Russia* 50°28N 36°54E **189** G9
Shebela → *Ethiopia* 7°32N 45°43E **267** C6
Shebele = Shabeelle → *Somali Rep.* 2°0N 44°0E **267** D5
Shebele *Ethiopia* 8°8N 42°40E **267** C5
Sheberghān *Afghan.* 36°40N 65°45E **240** A2
Sheboygan *U.S.A.* 43°46N 87°45W **308** D10
Shebshi Mts. *Nigeria* 8°30N 12°0E **263** D7
Shedd Aquarium *Chicago, U.S.A.* **119** e3
Shediac *Canada* 46°14N 64°32W **299** C7
Sheelin, L. *Ireland* 53°48N 7°20W **166** C4
Sheen, L. *U.S.A.* 28°25N 81°31W **133** B1
Sheenjek → *U.S.A.* 66°45N 144°33W **303** C11
Sheep Haven *Ireland* 55°11N 7°52W **166** A4
Sheep Range *U.S.A.* 36°35N 115°15W **307** J11
Sheepshead Bay *U.S.A.* 40°35N 73°55W **132** C2
Sheerness *U.K.* 51°26N 0°47E **169** F8
Sheet Harbour *Canada* 44°56N 62°31W **299** D7
Sheffield *N.Z.* 43°23S 172°1E **285** D7
Sheffield *S. Yorks., U.K.* 53°23N 1°28W **168** D6
Sheffield *Ala., U.S.A.* 34°46N 87°41W **315** D11
Sheffield *Ill., U.S.A.* 41°21N 89°44W **310** C7
Sheffield *Iowa, U.S.A.* 42°54N 93°13W **310** B3
Sheffield *Mass., U.S.A.* 42°5N 73°21W **313** D11
Sheffield *Pa., U.S.A.* 41°42N 79°3W **312** E5
Shegaon *India* 20°48N 76°47E **244** D3
Shehojele *Ethiopia* 10°40N 35°9E **257** E4
Shehong *China* 30°54N 105°18E **228** B5
Shehuen → *Argentina* 49°35S 69°34W **336** C3
Shei-Pa △ *Taiwan* 24°36N 121°22E **225** B3
Shei Shan *Taiwan* 24°22N 121°15E **225** B3
Sheikh, W. el → *Egypt* 28°41N 33°41E **251** K4
Sheikh Zayed Canal *Egypt* 23°30N 30°15E **256** C3
Sheikhpura *India* 25°9N 85°53E **243** G11
Shek Hasan *Ethiopia* 12°5N 35°58E **257** E4
Shek O *China* 22°13N 114°15E **122** B2
Shekhupura *Pakistan* 31°42N 73°58E **242** D5
Shekki = Şaki *Azerbaijan* 41°10N 47°5E **191** K8
Shekki = Zhongshan *China* 22°26N 113°20E **229** F9
Shekou *China* 22°30N 113°55E **219** a
Shelbina *U.S.A.* 39°47N 92°2W **310** E4
Shelburn *U.S.A.* 39°11N 87°24W **311** E9
Shelburne *N.S., Canada* 43°47N 65°20W **299** D6
Shelburne *Ont., Canada* 44°4N 80°15W **312** B4
Shelburne *Vt., U.S.A.* 44°23N 73°14W **313** B11
Shelburne B. *Australia* 11°50S 142°50E **286** F2
Shelburne Falls *U.S.A.* 42°36N 72°45W **313** D12
Shelby *Mich., U.S.A.* 43°37N 86°22W **308** D10
Shelby *Miss., U.S.A.* 33°57N 90°46W **315** E9
Shelby *Mont., U.S.A.* 48°30N 111°51W **304** B8
Shelby *N.C., U.S.A.* 35°17N 81°32W **315** D14
Shelby *Ohio, U.S.A.* 40°53N 82°40W **312** F2
Shelbyville *Ill., U.S.A.* 39°24N 88°48W **311** E8
Shelbyville *Ind., U.S.A.* 39°31N 85°47W **311** E11
Shelbyville *Ky., U.S.A.* 38°13N 85°14W **311** F11
Shelbyville *Mo., U.S.A.* 39°48N 92°2W **310** E4
Shelbyville *Tenn., U.S.A.* 35°29N 86°28W **315** D11
Shelbyville, L. *U.S.A.* 39°26N 88°46W **311** E8
Sheldon *Ill., U.S.A.* 40°46N 87°34W **311** D9
Sheldon *Iowa, U.S.A.* 43°11N 95°51W **308** D6
Sheldon *Mo., U.S.A.* 37°40N 94°18W **310** G2
Sheldon *S.C., U.S.A.* 32°36N 80°48W **316** C9
Sheldon Point *U.S.A.* 62°32N 164°52W **303** E6
Sheldrake *Canada* 50°20N 64°51W **299** B7
Shelek *Kazakhstan* 43°33N 78°17E **217** D9
Shelengo, Khawr → *Sudan* 10°33N 28°40E **257** E2
Shelikhova, Zaliv *Russia* 59°30N 157°0E **215** D16
Shelikof Strait *U.S.A.* 57°30N 155°0W **303** H9
Shell Beach = Huntington Beach *U.S.A.* 33°40N 118°5W **307** M9
Shell Lakes *Australia* 29°20S 127°30E **279** E4
Shellbrook *Canada* 53°13N 106°24W **297** C7
Shellharbour *Australia* 34°31S 150°51E **283** C9
Shellman *U.S.A.* 31°46N 84°37W **316** D5
Shellsburg *U.S.A.* 42°6N 91°52W **310** B5
Shelon → *Russia* 58°13N 30°47E **188** C6
Shelter Bay = Port-Cartier *Canada* 50°2N 66°50W **299** B6
Shelter I. *Hong Kong, China* 22°19N 114°17E **122** B2
Shelter I. *N.Y., U.S.A.* 41°4N 72°20W **313** E12
Shelton *Conn., U.S.A.* 41°19N 73°5W **313** E11
Shelton *Wash., U.S.A.* 47°13N 123°6W **306** C3
Shemakha = Şamaxı *Azerbaijan* 40°38N 48°37E **191** K9
Shemonaīkha *Kazakhstan* 50°37N 81°54E **217** B10
Shëmri *Albania* 42°7N 20°13E **202** D4
Shemsi *Sudan* 19°2N 29°57E **256** D2
Shen Xian *China* 36°15N 115°40E **226** F8
Shenandoah *Iowa, U.S.A.* 40°46N 95°22W **308** E6
Shenandoah *Pa., U.S.A.* 40°49N 76°12W **313** F8
Shenandoah *Va., U.S.A.* 38°29N 78°37W **309** F14
Shenandoah → *U.S.A.* 39°19N 77°44W **309** F15
Shenandoah △ *U.S.A.* 38°35N 78°22W **309** F14
Shenchi *China* 39°8N 112°10E **226** E7
Shencottah *India* 8°59N 77°18E **245** K3
Shendam *Nigeria* 8°49N 9°30E **263** D6
Shendî *Sudan* 16°46N 33°22E **257** D3
Shendurni *India* 20°39N 75°36E **244** D2
Shenge *S. Leone* 7°54N 12°55W **262** D2
Shengfang *China* 39°3N 116°42E **226** E9
Shëngjergj *Albania* 41°17N 20°10E **202** E4
Shëngjin *Albania* 41°50N 19°35E **202** E3
Shengzhou *China* 29°35N 120°50E **229** C13
Shenjingzi *China* 44°40N 124°30E **227** B13
Shenkang *Taiwan* 24°9N 120°39E **225** B2
Shenmu *China* 38°50N 110°29E **226** E6
Shennongjia *China* 31°43N 110°44E **229** B8
Shenqiu *China* 33°25N 115°5E **226** H8
Shensi = Shaanxi □ *China* 35°0N 109°0E **226** G5
Shenyang *China* 41°48N 123°27E **224** B1
Shenzhen *China* 22°32N 114°5E **229** F10
Shenzhen ✈ (SZX) *China* 22°41N 113°49E **219** a
Shenzhen Shuiku *China* 22°34N 114°8E **219** a
Shenzhen Wan *China* 22°27N 113°55E **219** a
Sheo *India* 26°11N 71°15E **242** F4
Sheopur Kalan *India* 25°40N 76°40E **242** G7
Shepetivka *Ukraine* 50°10N 27°10E **177** C14
Shepherd Is. *Vanuatu* 16°55S 168°36E **287** F6
Shepherds Bush *U.K.* 51°30N 0°13W **125** A2
Shepherdsville *U.S.A.* 37°59N 85°43W **311** G11
Shepparton *Australia* 36°23S 145°26E **283** D6
Shepperton *U.K.* 51°23N 0°26W **125** B1
Sheppey, I. of *U.K.* 51°25N 0°48E **169** F8
Shepton Mallet *U.K.* 51°11N 2°33W **169** F5
Sheqi *China* 33°12N 112°57E **226** H7
Sher Khan Qala *Afghan.* 29°53N 66°13E **240** C2
Sher Qila *Pakistan* 36°7N 74°2E **243** A6
Sherab *Sudan* 10°44N 24°41E **257** E1
Sherabad *Uzbekistan* 37°40N 67°1E **217** E7
Sherborne *U.K.* 50°57N 2°31W **169** G5
Sherbro → *S. Leone* 7°45N 12°55W **262** D2
Sherbro I. *S. Leone* 7°30N 12°40W **262** D2
Sherbrooke *N.S., Canada* 45°8N 61°59W **299** C7
Sherbrooke *Qué., Canada* 45°28N 71°57W **313** A13
Sherburne *U.S.A.* 42°41N 75°30W **313** D9
Sherburne Reef *Papua N. G.* 3°20S 148°0E **286** B5
Sherda *Chad* 20°7N 16°46E **259** D3
Shereik *Sudan* 18°44N 33°47E **256** D3
Shergaon *India* 27°7N 92°16E **241** B4
Shergarh *India* 26°20N 72°18E **242** F5
Sherghati *India* 24°34N 84°47E **243** G11
Sheridan *Ark., U.S.A.* 34°19N 92°24W **314** D8
Sheridan *Ill., U.S.A.* 41°32N 88°41W **311** C8
Sheridan *Ind., U.S.A.* 40°8N 86°13W **311** D10
Sheridan *Wyo., U.S.A.* 44°48N 106°58W **304** D10
Sheringham *U.K.* 52°56N 1°13E **168** E9
Sherkin I. *Ireland* 51°28N 9°26W **166** E2
Sherkot *India* 29°22N 78°35E **243** E8
Sherlovaya Gora *Russia* 50°34N 116°15E **215** D12
Sherman *N.Y., U.S.A.* 42°9N 79°35W **312** D5
Sherman *Tex., U.S.A.* 33°38N 96°36W **314** E6
Sherman Oaks *U.S.A.* 34°8N 118°29W **126** B2
Sherman Park *U.S.A.* 41°47N 87°39W **119** C2
Sherpur *Bangla.* 25°0N 90°0E **241** C3
Sherpur *India* 25°34N 83°47E **243** G10
Sherridon *Canada* 55°8N 101°5W **297** B8
Sherriffs *St. Kitts & Nevis* 17°10N 62°32W **322** d
Shertallai *India* 9°42N 76°20E **245** K3
Sherwood *U.S.A.* 41°17N 84°33W **311** C12
Sherwood, L. *U.S.A.* 28°33N 81°29W **133** A2
Sherwood Forest *U.K.* 53°6N 1°7W **168** D6
Sherwood Park *Canada* 53°31N 113°19W **296** C6
Sheslay → *Canada* 58°48N 132°5W **296** B2
Shet Bandar *India* 18°57N 72°55E **130** B2
Shethanei L. *Canada* 58°48N 97°50W **297** B9
Shetland □ *U.K.* 60°30N 1°30W **167** A7
Shetland Is. *U.K.* 60°30N 1°30W **167** A7
Shetou *Taiwan* 23°53N 120°35E **225** B2
Shetpe *Kazakhstan* 44°10N 52°7E **216** D4
Shetrunji → *India* 21°19N 72°7E **242** J5
Sheung Fa Shan *China* 22°23N 114°5E **122** A1
Sheung Lau Wan *China* 22°16N 114°16E **122** B2
Sheung Shui *China* 22°31N 114°7E **219** a
Sheung Wan *China* 22°16N 114°9E **122** B1
Sheva *India* 18°56N 72°57E **130** B2
Sheva Nhava *India* 18°57N 72°57E **130** B2
Shevaroy Hills *India* 11°58N 78°12E **245** J4
Shevchenkovo = Dolynska *Ukraine* 48°6N 32°46E **189** H7
Shevchenkovo *Ukraine* 45°33N 29°20E **183** E14
Shevgaon *India* 19°21N 75°14E **244** E2
Shevisheh *Iran* 35°21N 46°40E **213** E12
Shewa *Ethiopia* 9°33N 38°10E **257** F4
Shewa Gimira *Ethiopia* 7°4N 35°51E **257** F4
Shey-Phoksundo △ *Nepal* 29°30N 82°45E **243** E10
Sheyang *China* 33°48N 120°29E **227** H11
Sheyenne → *U.S.A.* 47°2N 96°50W **308** B5
Shiashkotan, Ostrov *Russia* 48°49N 154°6E **215** E16
Shiba *Tokyo, Japan* **140** c4
Shibām *Yemen* 15°59N 48°36E **249** D5
Shibata *Japan* 37°57N 139°20E **220** F9
Shibecha *Japan* 43°17N 144°36E **220** C12
Shibetsu *Japan* 43°30N 145°10E **220** C12
Shibetsu *Japan* 44°10N 142°23E **220** B11
Shibîn el Kôm *Egypt* 30°31N 30°55E **256** H7
Shibîn el Qanâtir *Egypt* 30°19N 31°19E **256** H7
Shibing *China* 27°2N 108°7E **228** D7
Shibogama L. *Canada* 53°35N 88°15W **298** B2
Shibpur *India* 22°34N 88°19E **124** B1
Shibukawa *Japan* 36°29N 139°0E **223** A11
Shibushi *Japan* 31°25N 131°8E **222** F3
Shibushi-Wan *Japan* 31°24N 131°8E **222** F3
Shibuya *Tokyo, Japan* **140** c1
Shicheng *China* 26°22N 116°20E **229** D11
Shicheng Dao *China* 39°31N 122°59E **224** C1
Shickshinny *U.S.A.* 41°9N 76°9W **313** E8
Shickshock Mts. = Chic-Chocs, Mts. *Canada* 48°55N 66°0W **299** C6
Shidād *Si. Arabia* 21°19N 40°3E **248** B3
Shidao *China* 36°50N 122°25E **227** F12
Shiderti → *Kazakhstan* 52°32N 74°50E **217** B8
Shidian *China* 24°40N 99°5E **228** E2
Shido *Japan* 34°19N 134°10E **222** C6
Shiel, L. *U.K.* 56°48N 5°34W **167** E3
Shield, C. *Australia* 13°20S 136°20E **280** A2
Shīeli *Kazakhstan* 44°20N 66°15E **217** D7
Shifang *China* 31°8N 104°10E **228** B5
Shiga □ *Japan* 35°20N 136°0E **223** B8
Shigaib *Sudan* 15°5N 23°35E **259** E4
Shigu *China* 26°51N 99°56E **228** D2
Shiguaigou *China* 40°52N 110°15E **226** D6
Shihan, W. → *Yemen* 17°24N 51°26E **249** C5
Shihchiachuangi = Shijiazhuang *China* 38°2N 114°28E **226** E8
Shihezi *China* 44°15N 86°2E **217** D11
Shihiu *Taiwan* 24°38N 121°10E **225** B3
Shihkangkeng *Taiwan* 24°1N 120°57E **225** B2
Shihmen *Taiwan* 25°17N 121°33E **225** A3
Shihmen Shuiku *Taiwan* 24°49N 121°21E **225** B3
Shihtan *Taiwan* 24°32N 120°55E **225** B2
Shiiba *Japan* 32°29N 131°4E **222** E3
Shiikh *Somali Rep.* 9°56N 45°13E **267** C6
Shijak *Albania* 41°21N 19°33E **202** E3
Shijiazhuang *China* 38°2N 114°28E **226** E8
Shijiu Hu *China* 31°25N 118°50E **229** B12
Shikarpur *India* 28°17N 78°7E **242** E8
Shikarpur *Pakistan* 27°57N 68°39E **242** F3
Shikhrany = Kanash *Russia* 55°30N 47°32E **190** C8
Shikine-Jima *Japan* 34°19N 139°13E **223** C11
Shikohabad *India* 27°6N 78°36E **243** F8
Shikoku *Japan* 33°30N 133°30E **222** D5
Shikoku □ *Japan* 33°30N 133°30E **222** D5
Shikoku-Sanchi *Japan* 33°30N 133°30E **222** D5
Shikotan, Ostrov *Asia* 43°47N 146°44E **215** E15
Shikotsu-Ko *Japan* 42°45N 141°25E **220** C10
Shikotsu-Tōya △ *Japan* 44°4N 145°8E **220** C10
Shikuka = Poronaysk *Russia* 49°13N 143°0E **219** B17
Shilabo *Ethiopia* 6°5N 44°46E **267** C5
Shiliguri *India* 26°45N 88°25E **241** B2
Shilihe *China* 39°50N 116°25E **114** B2
Shiliu = Changjiang *China* 19°20N 108°55E **236** C7
Shilka *Russia* 52°0N 115°55E **215** D12
Shilka → *Russia* 53°20N 121°26E **215** D13
Shillelagh *Ireland* 52°45N 6°32W **166** D5
Shillington *U.S.A.* 40°18N 75°58W **313** F9
Shillong *India* 25°35N 91°53E **241** C3
Shilo *West Bank* 32°4N 35°18E **251** F6
Shilong *China* 23°5N 113°52E **229** F9
Shilou *China* 37°0N 110°48E **226** F6
Shilovo *Russia* 54°25N 40°57E **190** C5
Shima-Hantō *Japan* 34°22N 136°45E **223** C8
Shimabara *Japan* 32°48N 130°20E **222** E2
Shimada *Japan* 34°49N 138°10E **223** C10
Shimane □ *Japan* 35°0N 132°30E **222** C4
Shimane-Hantō *Japan* 35°30N 133°0E **222** B5
Shimanovsk *Russia* 52°15N 127°30E **215** D13
Shimba Hills △ *Kenya* 4°14S 39°25E **268** C4
Shimbiris *Somali Rep.* 10°44N 47°14E **267** B6
Shimen *China* 29°35N 111°20E **229** C8
Shimenjie *China* 29°29N 116°48E **229** C11
Shimian *China* 29°17N 102°23E **228** C4
Shimizu *Japan* 35°0N 138°30E **223** C10
Shimla *India* 31°2N 77°9E **242** D7
Shimo-Jima *Japan* 32°15N 130°7E **222** E2
Shimo-Koshiki-Jima *Japan* 31°40N 129°43E **222** F1
Shimoda *Japan* 34°40N 138°57E **223** C10
Shimodate *Japan* 36°20N 139°55E **223** A11
Shimoga *India* 13°57N 75°32E **245** H2
Shimogawara *Japan* 35°39N 139°27E **140** B1
Shimokita-Hantō *Japan* 41°20N 141°0E **220** D10
Shimoni *Kenya* 4°38S 39°20E **268** C4
Shimonita *Japan* 36°13N 138°47E **223** A10
Shimonoseki *Japan* 33°58N 130°55E **222** D2
Shimosalo *Japan* 35°45N 139°31E **140** A2
Shimoshakujii *Japan* 35°43N 139°35E **140** A2
Shimotsuma *Japan* 36°11N 139°58E **223** A11
Shimpuru Rapids *Namibia* 17°45S 19°55E **265** F3
Shimsha → *India* 13°15N 77°10E **245** H3
Shimsk *Russia* 58°15N 30°50E **188** C6
Shin, L. *U.K.* 58°5N 4°30W **167** C4
Shin-Nan'yō *Japan* 34°3N 131°49E **222** C3
Shin-Tone-Gawa → *Japan* 35°44N 140°51E **223** B12
Shinagawa *Japan* 35°36N 139°44E **140** B3
Shinan *China* 22°44N 109°53E **228** F7
Shinano-Gawa → *Japan* 36°50N 138°30E **221** F9
Shināş *Oman* 24°46N 56°28E **247** E8
Shīndand *Afghan.* 33°12N 62°8E **240** B1
Shing Mun Res. *China* 22°23N 114°8E **122** A1
Shingbwiyang *Burma* 26°41N 96°13E **241** B6
Shinglehouse *U.S.A.* 41°58N 78°12W **312** E6
Shingū *Japan* 33°40N 135°55E **223** D7
Shingwidzi *S. Africa* 23°5S 31°25E **271** B5
Shinji *Japan* 35°24N 132°54E **222** B4
Shinji-Ko *Japan* 35°26N 132°57E **222** B4
Shinjō *Japan* 38°46N 140°18E **220** E10
Shinjuku *Tokyo, Japan* **140** a1
Shinjuku Nat. Garden *Tokyo, Japan* **140** a2
Shinkafe *Nigeria* 13°8N 6°29E **263** C6
Shinkoiwa *Japan* 35°43N 139°51E **140** A4
Shinminato *Japan* 36°47N 137°4E **223** A9
Shinnakano *Japan* 35°41N 139°40E **140** A3
Shinshār *Syria* 34°36N 36°43E **250** D7
Shinshiro *Japan* 34°54N 137°30E **223** C9
Shintuya *Peru* 12°41S 71°15W **330** C3
Shinyanga *Tanzania* 3°45S 33°27E **268** C3
Shinyanga □ *Tanzania* 3°50S 34°0E **268** C3
Shio-no-Misaki *Japan* 33°25N 135°45E **223** D7
Shiogama *Japan* 38°19N 141°1E **220** E10
Shiojiri *Japan* 36°6N 137°58E **223** A9
Shipai *China* 23°8N 113°20E **121** B3
Shipchenski Prokhod *Bulgaria* 42°45N 25°15E **203** D9
Shiping *China* 23°45N 102°23E **228** F4
Shippagan *Canada* 47°45N 64°45W **299** C7
Shippensburg *U.S.A.* 40°3N 77°31W **312** F7
Shippenville *U.S.A.* 41°15N 79°28W **312** E5
Shiprock *U.S.A.* 36°47N 108°41W **305** H9
Shiqian *China* 27°32N 108°13E **228** D7
Shiqma, N. → *Israel* 31°37N 34°30E **251** G5
Shiquan *China* 33°5N 108°15E **228** A7
Shiquan He = Indus → *Pakistan* 24°20N 67°47E **242** G2
Shīr Khān *Afghan.* 37°11N 68°36E **240** A3
Shīr Kūh *Iran* 31°39N 54°3E **247** D7
Shirabad = Sherabad *Uzbekistan* 37°40N 67°1E **217** E7
Shiragami-Misaki *Japan* 41°24N 140°12E **220** D10
Shirahama *Japan* 33°41N 135°20E **223** D7
Shirakawa *Fukushima, Japan* 37°7N 140°13E **221** F10
Shirakawa *Gifu, Japan* 36°17N 136°56E **223** A8
Shirane-San *Gumma, Japan* 36°48N 139°22E **223** A11
Shirane-San *Yamanashi, Japan* 35°42N 138°9E **223** B10
Shiraoi *Japan* 42°33N 141°21E **220** C10
Shirati *Tanzania* 1°8S 33°59E **266** E3
Shīrāz *Iran* 29°42N 52°30E **247** D7
Shirbīn *Egypt* 31°11N 31°32E **256** H7
Shire → *Africa* 17°42S 35°19E **269** F4
Shiren *China* 41°57N 126°34E **227** D14
Shiretoko △ *Japan* 44°15N 145°15E **220** B12
Shiretoko-Misaki *Japan* 44°21N 145°20E **220** B12
Shirinab → *Pakistan* 30°15N 66°28E **242** D2
Shirinashi → *Japan* 34°38N 135°27E **133** B1
Shiriya-Zaki *Japan* 41°25N 141°30E **220** D10
Shirley *U.S.A.* 39°53N 85°35W **311** E11
Shirogane *Japan* 35°37N 139°44E **140** B3
Shiroishi *Japan* 38°0N 140°37E **220** F10
Shirol *India* 16°47N 74°41E **244** F2
Shiroro Res. *Nigeria* 9°56N 6°54E **263** D6
Shirpur *India* 21°21N 74°57E **244** D2
Shirshov Ridge *Pac. Oc.* 58°0N 170°0E **288** B8
Shīrvān *Iran* 37°30N 57°50E **247** B8
Shirwa, L. = Chilwa, L. *Malawi* 15°15S 35°40E **269** F4
Shishaldin Volcano *U.S.A.* 54°45N 163°58W **303** J7
Shishi *China* 24°44N 118°37E **229** E12
Shishmaref *U.S.A.* 66°15N 166°4W **303** C6
Shishou *China* 29°38N 112°22E **229** C9
Shitai *China* 30°12N 117°25E **229** B11
Shitata *South Sudan* 4°30N 30°10E **257** G3
Shitennoji Temple *Japan* 34°39N 135°31E **133** B2
Shithāthah *Iraq* 32°34N 43°28E **213** G10
Shivamogga = Shimoga *India* 13°57N 75°32E **245** H2
Shively *U.S.A.* 38°12N 85°49W **311** F11
Shivpuri *India* 25°26N 77°42E **242** G7
Shiweitang *China* 23°6N 113°12E **121** B2
Shixian *China* 43°5N 129°50E **227** C15
Shixing *China* 24°46N 114°5E **229** E10
Shiyan *Guangdong, China* 22°42N 113°56E **219** a
Shiyan *Hubei, China* 32°35N 110°45E **229** A8
Shiyan Shuiku *China* 22°42N 113°54E **219** a
Shiyata *Egypt* 29°25N 25°7E **256** B2
Shizhu *China* 29°58N 108°7E **228** C7
Shizong *China* 24°50N 104°0E **228** E5
Shizuishan *China* 39°15N 106°50E **226** E4
Shizuoka *Japan* 34°57N 138°24E **223** C10
Shizuoka □ *Japan* 35°15N 138°40E **223** B10
Shkhara *Georgia* 43°0N 43°8E **213** A10
Shklov = Shklow *Belarus* 54°16N 30°15E **177** A16
Shklow *Belarus* 54°16N 30°15E **177** A16
Shkodër *Albania* 42°4N 19°32E **202** D3
Shkodra = Shkodër *Albania* 42°4N 19°32E **202** D3
Shkumbini → *Albania* 41°2N 19°31E **202** E3
Shmidta, Ostrov *Russia* 81°0N 91°0E **215** A10
Shō-Gawa → *Japan* 36°47N 137°4E **223** A9
Shoal Cr. → *U.S.A.* 39°44N 93°32W **310** E3
Shoal L. *Canada* 49°33N 95°1W **297** D9
Shoal Lake *Canada* 50°30N 100°35W **297** C8
Shoalhaven → *Australia* 34°54S 150°42E **283** C9
Shoals *U.S.A.* 38°40N 86°47W **311** F10
Shōbara *Japan* 34°51N 133°1E **222** C5
Shōdo-Shima *Japan* 34°30N 134°15E **222** C6
Shogunle *Nigeria* 6°34N 3°20E **124** A2
Sholapur = Solapur *India* 17°43N 75°56E **244** F2
Shomolu *Nigeria* 6°32N 3°22E **124** A2
Shōmrōn *West Bank* 32°15N 35°13E **251** F6
Shonian Harb. *Palau* 7°10N 134°23E **288** c
Shonzhy *Kazakhstan* 43°32N 79°28E **217** D9
Shooters Hill *U.K.* 51°28N 0°4E **125** B4
Shoranur *India* 10°46N 76°19E **245** J3
Shorapur *India* 16°31N 76°48E **245** F3
Shoreditch *London, U.K.* **125** a5
Shoreham *U.S.A.* 43°53N 73°18W **313** C11
Shoreham by Sea *U.K.* 50°50N 0°16W **169** G7
Shorewood *U.S.A.* 43°5N 87°53W **311** A9
Shori → *Pakistan* 28°29N 69°44E **242** E3
Shorkot *Pakistan* 30°50N 72°0E **242** D4
Shorkot Road *Pakistan* 30°47N 72°15E **242** D5
Shorter *U.S.A.* 32°24N 85°57W **316** C4
Shorterville *U.S.A.* 31°34N 85°6W **316** D4
Shortland I. *Solomon Is.* 7°0S 155°45E **287** L8
Shortland Is. *Solomon Is.* 7°0S 156°0E **287** L8
Shortlands *U.K.* 51°23N 0°0 **125** B4
Shortt's I. *India* 20°47N 87°4E **244** D8
Shoshone *Calif., U.S.A.* 35°58N 116°16W **307** K10
Shoshone *Idaho, U.S.A.* 42°56N 114°25W **304** E6
Shoshone L. *U.S.A.* 44°22N 110°43W **304** D8
Shoshone Mts. *U.S.A.* 39°20N 117°25W **304** G5
Shoshong *Botswana* 22°56S 26°31E **270** B4
Shoshoni *U.S.A.* 43°14N 108°7W **304** E9
Shostka *Ukraine* 51°57N 33°32E **189** G7
Shot *Iran* 39°12N 44°49E **213** C11
Shotor Khūn *Afghan.* 34°19N 64°56E **240** B2
Shotover → *N.Z.* 44°59S 168°41E **285** E3
Shou Xian *China* 32°37N 116°42E **229** A11
Shouchang *China* 29°18N 119°12E **229** C12
Shouchia *Taiwan* 22°14N 120°50E **225** D2
Shoufeng *Taiwan* 23°52N 121°30E **225** C3
Shouguang *China* 37°52N 118°45E **227** F10
Shouning *China* 27°27N 119°31E **229** D12
Shouyang *China* 37°54N 113°8E **226** F7
Show Low *U.S.A.* 34°15N 110°2W **305** J8
Showa *Japan* 35°36N 138°29E **223** B10
Showak *Sudan* 14°23N 35°52E **257** E4
Shpola *Ukraine* 49°1N 31°30E **189** H6
Shpykiv *Ukraine* 48°47N 28°34E **183** B13
Shqipëria = Albania ■ *Europe* 41°0N 20°0E **202** E4
Shreveport *U.S.A.* 32°31N 93°45W **314** E8
Shrewsbury *U.K.* 52°43N 2°45W **169** E5
Shri Mohangarh *India* 27°17N 71°18E **242** F4
Shrigonda *India* 18°37N 74°41E **244** E2
Shrirampur *India* 22°44N 88°21E **243** H13
Shropshire □ *U.K.* 52°36N 2°45W **169** E5
Shterpce = Štrpce *Kosovo* 42°14N 21°1E **202** D5
Shū *Kazakhstan* 43°36N 73°42E **217** D8
Shū → *Kazakhstan* 45°0N 67°44E **217** D7
Shu'afat *West Bank* 31°49N 35°14E **123** B2
Shuangbai *China* 24°42N 101°38E **228** E3
Shuangcheng *China* 45°20N 126°15E **227** B14
Shuangfeng *China* 27°29N 112°11E **229** D9
Shuanggou *China* 34°2N 117°30E **227** G9
Shuangjiang *China* 23°26N 99°58E **228** F2
Shuangliao *China* 43°29N 123°30E **227** C12
Shuangshanzi *China* 40°20N 119°8E **227** D10
Shuangyang *China* 43°28N 125°40E **227** C13
Shuangyashan *China* 46°28N 131°5E **219** B15
Shu'b, Ra's *Yemen* 12°30N 53°25E **249** D6
Shubarqudyq *Kazakhstan* 49°13N 56°34E **216** C5
Shubarshī *Kazakhstan* 48°39N 57°11E **216** C5
Shubrâ *Egypt* 30°5N 31°14E **117** A2
Shubrâ el Kheima *Egypt* 30°4N 31°14E **117** A2
Shubrâ Khit *Egypt* 31°2N 30°42E **256** H7
Shucheng *China* 31°28N 116°57E **229** B11
Shugozero *Russia* 59°54N 34°10E **188** C8
Shuguri Falls *Tanzania* 8°33S 37°22E **269** D4
Shuḥayr *Yemen* 14°41N 49°23E **249** D5
Shuiding = Huocheng *China* 44°0N 80°48E **217** D10
Shuiji *China* 27°13N 118°20E **229** D12
Shuikuo *China* 23°10N 113°10E **121** A2
Shuili *Taiwan* 23°49N 120°51E **225** C2
Shuilien *Taiwan* 23°47N 121°34E **225** C3
Shuishang *Taiwan* 23°25N 120°23E **225** C2
Shuitiliao *Taiwan* 22°23N 120°35E **225** D2
Shujalpur *India* 23°18N 76°46E **242** H7
Shukpa Kunzang *India* 34°22N 78°22E **243** B8
Shulan *China* 44°28N 127°0E **227** B14
Shulaveri *Georgia* 41°22N 44°45E **191** K7

Shule *Caina* 39°25'N 76°3'E 217 E9
Shule He → *China* 40°20'N 92°50'E 218 C7
Shullsburg *U.S.A.* 42°35'N 90°13'W 310 B6
Shumagin Is. *U.S.A.* 55°7'N 160°30'W 303 J7
Shumanay *Uzbekistan* 42°38'N 58°55'E 216 D5
Shumen *Bulgaria* 43°18'N 26°55'E 203 C10
Shumerlya *Russia* 55°30'N 46°25'E 190 C8
Shumikha *Russia* 55°10'N 63°15'E 214 D7
Shūna, W. el → *Egypt* 32°39'N 32°6'E 251 J3
Shunayn, Sabkhat *Libya* 30°10'N 21°0'E 258 B4
Shunchang *China* 26°54'N 117°48'E 229 D11
Shunde *China* 22°42'N 113°14'E 229 F9
Shungay *Kazakhstan* 48°30'N 46°45'E 191 F8
Shungnak *U.S.A.* 66°52'N 157°9'W 303 C8
Shuo Xian = Shuozhou
  China 39°20'N 112°33'E 226 E7
Shuozhou *China* 39°20'N 112°33'E 226 E7
Shūr → *Fārs, Iran* 28°30'N 55°0'E 247 D7
Shūr → *Kermān, Iran* 30°52'N 57°37'E 247 D8
Shūr → *Yazd, Iran* 31°45'N 55°15'E 247 D7
Shūr Āb *Iran* 34°23'N 51°11'E 247 C6
Shūr Gaz *Iran* 29°10'N 59°20'E 247 D8
Shūrāb *Iran* 33°43'N 56°29'E 247 C8
Shuri *Japan* 26°13'N 127°43'E 288 a
Shūrjestān *Iran* 31°24'N 52°25'E 247 D7
Shurkhna *Russia* 22°15'N 93°38'E 241 D4
Shurugwi *Zimbabwe* 19°40'S 30°0'E 269 F3
Shūsf *Iran* 31°50'N 60°5'E 247 D9
Shūsh *Iran* 32°11'N 48°15'E 213 F13
Shusherskoye *Russia* 53°19'N 91°56'E 217 B12
Shūshtar *Iran* 32°0'N 48°50'E 247 D6
Shuswap L. *Canada* 50°55'N 119°3'W 296 C5
Shute Harbour △
  Australia 20°17'S 148°47'E 280 b
Shuya *Russia* 56°50'N 41°28'E 190 B5
Shuyak I. *U.S.A.* 58°31'N 152°30'W 303 G9
Shuyang *China* 34°10'N 118°42'E 227 G10
Shuzenji *Japan* 34°58'N 138°56'E 223 C10
Shūzū *Iran* 29°52'N 54°30'E 247 D7
Shwangliao = Liaoyuan
  China 42°58'N 125°2'E 227 C13
Shwebo *Burma* 22°30'N 95°45'E 241 D5
Shwegu *Burma* 24°15'N 96°26'E 241 C6
Shwegun *Burma* 17°9'N 97°39'E 241 G6
Shwegyin *Burma* 17°55'N 96°53'E 241 G6
Shweli → *Burma* 23°45'N 96°45'E 241 C6
Shwenyaung *Burma* 20°46'N 96°57'E 241 E6
Shyamnagar *India* 13°21'N 92°57'E 245 H11
Shygharaq *Kazakhstan* 45°6'N 73°59'E 217 C8
Shyghys Qazaqstan □
  Kazakhstan 48°30'N 82°0'E 217 D10
Shymkent *Kazakhstan* 42°18'N 69°36'E 217 D7
Shyok *India* 34°13'N 78°12'E 243 B8
Shyroke *Odesa, Ukraine* 45°59'N 30°5'E 183 E15
Shyroke *Ternopil, Ukraine* 48°13'N 23°6'E 182 B8
Si Kiang = Xi Jiang →
  China 22°5'N 113°20'E 229 F9
Si Lanna △ *Thailand* 19°17'N 99°12'E 236 C2
Si Nakarin Res. *Thailand* 14°35'N 99°0'E 236 E2
Si-ngan = Xi'an *China* 34°15'N 109°0'E 226 G5
Si Phangnga *Thailand* 9°8'N 98°29'E 237 H2
Si Prachan *Thailand* 13°10'N 100°48'E 236 E3
Si Sa Ket *Thailand* 15°8'N 104°23'E 236 E5
Siachen Glacier *Asia* 35°20'N 77°30'E 243 B7
Sīāh Chashmeh *Iran* 39°3'N 44°25'E 213 C11
Siahaf → *Pakistan* 29°3'N 68°57'E 242 E3
Siahan Range *Pakistan* 27°30'N 64°40'E 240 D2
Siak → *Indonesia* 1°13'N 102°0'E 234 B2
Siak Sri Indrapura
  Indonesia 0°51'N 102°0'E 234 B2
Sialkot *Pakistan* 32°32'N 74°30'E 242 C6
Sialsuk *India* 23°24'N 92°45'E 241 D4
Sialum *Papua N. G.* 6°5'S 147°36'E 286 D4
Siam = Thailand ■ *Asia* 16°0'N 102°0'E 236 E4
Sian = Xi'an *China* 34°15'N 109°0'E 226 G5
Sian Ka'an → *Mexico* 19°35'N 87°40'W 319 D7
Siangtan = Xiangtan
  China 27°51'N 112°54'E 229 D9
Sianów *Poland* 54°13'N 16°18'E 184 D3
Siantan *Indonesia* 3°10'N 106°15'E 234 B3
Siàpo → *Venezuela* 2°7'N 66°28'W 328 C4
Siäreh *Iran* 28°5'N 60°14'E 247 D9
Siargao I. *Phil.* 9°52'N 126°3'E 233 G6
Siasi *Phil.* 5°34'N 120°50'E 233 J3
Siasi I. *Phil.* 5°33'N 120°51'E 233 J3
Siassi *Papua N. G.* 5°40'S 147°51'E 286 C4
Siatista *Greece* 40°15'N 21°33'E 202 F5
Siaton *Phil.* 9°4'N 123°3'E 233 G6
Siau *Indonesia* 2°50'N 125°25'E 231 D7
Šiauliai *Lithuania* 55°56'N 23°15'E 184 C10
Šiauliai □ *Lithuania* 55°56'N 23°19'E 184 C10
Siavonga *Zambia* 16°33'S 28°42'E 271 A4
Siazan = Siyäzän
  Azerbaijan 41°3'N 49°10'E 191 K9
Sībāī, Gebel el *Egypt* 25°45'N 34°10'E 246 E2
Sibang *Gabon* 0°25'N 9°31'E 261 A4
Sibang *Beli, Indonesia* 8°34'S 115°13'E 231 K18
Sibay *Russia* 52°42'N 58°39'E 186 D10
Sibay I. *Phil.* 11°51'N 121°29'E 233 F3
Sibayi, L. *S. Africa* 27°20'S 32°45'E 271 C5
Sibdu *Sudan* 10°57'N 26°17'E 257 E2
Šibenik *Croatia* 43°48'N 15°54'E 199 E12
Siberia = Sibirskiy □
  Russia 60°0'N 100°0'E 150 D13
Siberia *Russia* 58°0'N 90°0'E 150 D13
Sibérie *Curaçao* 12°14'N 69°3'W 322 g
Siberut *Indonesia* 1°30'S 99°0'E 234 C1
Siberut, Selat *Indonesia* 0°42'S 98°35'E 234 C1
Siberut △ *Indonesia* 1°17'S 98°45'E 234 C1
Sibi *Pakistan* 29°30'N 67°54'E 242 E2
Sibigo *Indonesia* 2°50'N 95°54'E 234 B1
Sibiloi △ *Kenya* 4°0'N 36°20'E 268 B4
Sibirskiy □ *Russia* 58°0'N 90°0'E 215 D10
Sibirtsevo *Russia* 44°12'N 132°26'E 220 B5
Sibiti *Congo* 3°38'S 13°19'E 264 C2
Sibiu *Romania* 45°45'N 24°9'E 183 E9
Sibiu □ *Romania* 45°50'N 24°15'E 183 E9
Sibium Mts. *Papua N. G.* 9°19'S 148°25'E 286 E5
Sibley *U.S.A.* 43°24'N 95°45'W 308 D6
Sibley Iowa, *U.S.A.* 43°24'N 95°45'W 308 D6
Sibo *Sweden* 61°13'N 16°37'E 162 C10
Sibolga *Indonesia* 1°42'N 98°45'E 234 B1
Siborongborong *Indonesia* 2°13'N 98°58'E 237 L2
Sibsagar *India* 27°0'N 94°36'E 241 C10
Sibu *Malaysia* 2°18'N 111°49'E 235 B4
Sibuco *Phil.* 7°20'N 122°10'E 233 H5
Sibuguey B. *Phil.* 7°50'N 122°45'E 233 H4
Sibut *C.A.R.* 5°46'N 19°10'E 264 A3
Sibutu *Phil.* 4°45'N 119°30'E 233 B5
Sibutu Group *Phil.* 4°45'N 119°30'E 233 J2
Sibutu Passage *E. Indies* 4°50'N 120°0'E 233 J2
Sibuyan *Phil.* 12°25'N 122°40'E 233 F4
Sibuyan Sea *Phil.* 12°30'N 122°20'E 233 E4
Sic *Romania* 46°56'N 23°53'E 183 D8
Sicamous *Canada* 50°49'N 119°0'W 296 C5
Sicapoo, Mt. *Phil.* 17°7'N 120°58'E 233 A4
Sicasica *Bolivia* 17°22'S 67°45'W 330 D4
Siccus → *Australia* 31°55'S 139°17'E 282 A3
Sichelberg = Sierpc *Poland* 52°30'N 19°22'E 185 F6
Sichon *Thailand* 9°0'N 99°54'E 237 H2
Sichuan □ *China* 30°30'N 103°0'E 228 B5
Sichuan Pendi *China* 30°30'N 105°0'E 228 B5
Sicilia *Italy* 37°30'N 14°30'E 201 F7

Sicily = Sicilia *Italy* 37°30'N 14°30'E 201 E7
Sicily, Str. of *Medit. S.* 37°35'N 11°56'E 200 E4
Sico → *Honduras* 15°58'N 84°58'W 320 C3
Sicuani *Peru* 14°21'S 71°10'W 330 C3
Šid *Serbia* 45°8'N 19°14'E 182 E4
Sidari *Greece* 39°47'N 19°41'E 205 B9
Sidcup *U.K.* 51°25'N 0°6'E 125 B4
Siddhapur *India* 23°56'N 72°25'E 242 H5
Siddipet *India* 18°5'N 78°51'E 244 G4
Side *Turkey* 36°45'N 31°23'E 250 B2
Sidensjö *Sweden* 63°18'N 18°17'E 162 A12
Sidéradougou *Burkina Faso* 10°42'N 4°12'W 262 C4
Siderno *Italy* 38°16'N 16°18'E 201 D9
Sideros, Akra *Greece* 35°19'N 26°19'E 207 E7
Sidhi *India* 24°25'N 81°53'E 243 G9
Sidi Abd el Rahmân *Egypt* 30°55'N 29°44'E 256 A2
Sidi-bel-Abbès *Algeria* 35°13'N 0°39'W 261 A4
Sidi-bel-Abbès □ *Algeria* 34°50'N 0°30'W 261 B4
Sidi Barrâni *Egypt* 31°38'N 25°58'E 256 A2
Sidi Bennour *Morocco* 32°40'N 8°25'W 260 B3
Sidi Bou Zid *Tunisia* 35°1'N 9°16'E 253 B1
Sidi Boubekeur *Algeria* 35°1'N 0°4'E 261 A5
Sidi Haneish *Egypt* 31°10'N 27°35'E 256 A2
Sidi Ifni *Morocco* 29°29'N 10°12'W 260 C2
Sidi Kacem *Morocco* 34°11'N 5°49'W 260 B3
Sidi Omar *Egypt* 31°24'N 24°57'E 256 A1
Sidi Slimane *Morocco* 34°16'N 5°56'W 260 B3
Sidi Smaïl *Morocco* 32°50'N 8°31'W 260 B3
Sidi 'Uzayz *Libya* 31°41'N 24°55'E 258 B4
Sidikalang *Indonesia* 2°45'N 98°19'E 237 L2
Siding No 14 = Ponoka
  Canada 52°42'N 113°40'W 296 C6
Sidirokastro *Greece* 41°13'N 23°24'E 202 E7
Sidlaw Hills *U.K.* 56°32'N 3°2'W 127 E5
Sidley, Mt. *Antarctica* 77°2'S 126°2'W 151 D14
Sidmouth *U.K.* 50°40'N 3°15'W 169 G4
Sidmouth, C. *Australia* 13°25'S 143°36'E 280 A3
Sidney *B.C., Canada* 48°39'N 123°24'W 306 B3
Sidney *Mont., U.S.A.* 47°43'N 104°9'W 304 C11
Sidney *N.Y., U.S.A.* 42°19'N 75°24'W 313 D9
Sidney *Nebr., U.S.A.* 41°8'N 102°59'W 308 E2
Sidney *Ohio, U.S.A.* 40°17'N 84°9'W 311 D12
Sidney Lanier, L. *U.S.A.* 34°10'N 84°4'W 316 A5
Sido *Mali* 11°37'N 7°29'W 262 C3
Sidoarjo *Indonesia* 7°27'S 112°43'E 235 D4
Sidoktaya *Burma* 20°27'N 94°15'E 241 E5
Sidon = Saydā *Lebanon* 33°35'N 35°25'E 250 B6
Sidra, G. of = Surt, Khalīj
  Libya 31°40'N 18°30'E 258 B3
Siebenhirten *Austria* 48°8'N 16°17'E 142 B1
Siedlce *Poland* 52°10'N 22°20'E 185 F9
Siedlung *Germany* 52°35'N 13°7'E 115 A1
Sieg → *Germany* 50°46'N 7°6'E 178 E3
Siegburg *Germany* 50°47'N 7°12'E 178 E3
Siegen *Germany* 50°51'N 8°0'E 178 E4
Siekierki *Poland* 52°12'N 21°4'E 142 B2
Siem Pang *Cambodia* 14°7'N 106°23'E 236 E6
Siem Reap = Siemreab
  Cambodia 13°20'N 103°52'E 236 F4
Siemiensstadt *Germany* 52°32'N 13°16'E 115 A2
Siemiatycze *Poland* 52°27'N 22°53'E 185 F9
Siemreab *Cambodia* 13°20'N 103°52'E 236 F4
Siena *Italy* 43°19'N 11°21'E 199 C8
Sieniawa *Poland* 50°11'N 22°38'E 185 H9
Sienyang = Xianyang
  China 34°20'N 108°40'E 226 G5
Sieradz *Poland* 51°37'N 18°41'E 185 G5
Sieraków *Poland* 52°39'N 16°2'E 185 F3
Sierck-les-Bains *France* 49°26'N 6°20'E 173 C13
Sierning *Austria* 48°2'N 14°18'E 180 C7
Sierpc *Poland* 52°55'N 19°43'E 185 F6
Sierpe, Bocas de la
  Venezuela 10°0'N 61°30'W 323 K15
Sierra Blanca *U.S.A.* 31°11'N 105°22'W 314 F2
Sierra Blanca Peak
  U.S.A. 33°23'N 105°49'W 305 K11
Sierra City *U.S.A.* 39°34'N 120°38'W 306 F6
Sierra Colorada *Argentina* 40°35'N 67°50'W 332 C3
Sierra de Agalta △
  Honduras 15°1'N 85°48'W 320 C2
Sierra de Aracena y Picas de
  Aroche △ *Spain* 37°53'N 6°41'W 195 H4
Sierra de Bahoruco △
  Dom. Rep. 18°10'N 71°25'W 321 C5
Sierra de Baza △ *Spain* 37°15'N 2°48'W 197 H2
Sierra de Castril △ *Spain* 37°54'N 2°50'W 197 H2
Sierra de España △ *Spain* 37°50'N 1°17'W 197 H3
Sierra de Grazalema △
  Spain 36°31'N 5°28'W 195 J5
Sierra de Gredos △ *Spain* 40°17'N 5°17'W 194 E5
Sierra de Hornachuelos △
  Spain 37°56'N 5°14'W 195 H5
Sierra de Huétor △ *Spain* 37°14'N 3°30'W 195 H7
Sierra de la Culata △
  Venezuela 8°48'N 70°56'W 328 B3
Sierra de la Macarena △
  Colombia 11°19'N 74°1'W 328 A3
Sierra de las Nieves △ *Spain* 36°42'N 5°0'W 195 J5
Sierra de las Quijadas △
  Argentina 32°29'S 67°5'W 334 C2
Sierra de María-Los Vélez △
  Spain 37°42'N 2°10'W 197 H2
Sierra de San Luis △
  Venezuela 11°11'N 69°33'W 328 A4
Sierra de San Pedro Mártir △
  Mexico 31°10'N 115°30'W 318 A1
Sierra de Yeguas *Spain* 37°7'N 4°52'W 195 H5
Sierra del São Mamede △
  Portugal 39°17'N 7°18'W 195 F3
Sierra Gorda *Chile* 22°50'S 69°15'W 334 A2
Sierra Grande *Argentina* 41°36'S 65°3'W 332 C3
Sierra Leone ■ *W. Afr.* 9°0'N 12°0'W 262 D2
Sierra Leone Basin *Atl. Oc.* 5°0'N 17°0'W 152 F10
Sierra Leone Rise *Atl. Oc.* 7°0'N 20°0'W 152 F10
Sierra Madre *Mexico* 16°0'N 93°0'W 319 D6
Sierra Madre *India* 24°34'N 118°3'W 316 J4
Sierra Madre Occidental
  Mexico 27°0'N 107°0'W 318 B3
Sierra Madre Oriental
  Mexico 25°0'N 100°0'W 318 C5
Sierra Mágina △ *Spain* 37°44'N 3°28'W 195 H7
Sierra Mojada *Mexico* 27°18'N 103°41'W 318 B4
Sierra Nevada *Spain* 37°3'N 3°15'W 195 H7
Sierra Nevada *Calif.,*
  U.S.A. 39°0'N 120°30'W 306 H8
Sierra Nevada △ *Spain* 37°4'N 3°7'W 195 H7
Sierra Norte de Sevilla △
  Spain 37°55'N 5°46'W 195 H5
Sierra Subbéticas △ *Spain* 37°26'N 4°18'W 195 H6
Sierra Vista *U.S.A.* 31°33'N 110°18'W 305 L8
Sierras de Cardeña y Montoro △
  Spain 38°13'N 4°15'W 195 G6
Sierras de Cazorla, Segura y las
  Villas △ *Spain* 38°2'N 2°45'W 197 H2
Sierraville *U.S.A.* 39°36'N 120°22'W 306 F6
Sièrre *Switz.* 46°17'N 7°31'E 179 J3
Sievering *Austria* 48°15'N 16°20'E 142 A2
Sifani *Ethiopia* 12°18'N 40°19'E 257 E5

Sifié *Ivory C.* 8°0'N 7°5'W 262 D3
Sifnos *Greece* 37°0'N 24°45'E 204 E6
Sifton *Canada* 51°21'N 100°8'W 297 C8
Sifton Pass *Canada* 57°52'N 126°15'W 296 B3
Sig *Algeria* 35°32'N 0°12'W 261 A4
Sigaboy = Governor Generoso
  Phil. 6°39'N 126°5'E 233 H6
Sigatoka *Fiji* 18°8'S 177°32'E 287 B1
Sigdal *Norway* 60°3'N 9°38'E 164 D6
Sigean *France* 43°2'N 2°58'E 174 E6
Siggiewi *Malta* 35°51'N 14°26'E 206 F7
Sighetu-Marmaţiei
  Romania 47°57'N 23°52'E 183 C8
Sighişoara *Romania* 46°12'N 24°58'E 183 D9
Sighthill *U.K.* 55°56'N 3°17'W 121 B2
Sigira *Yemen* 12°37'N 54°0'E 249 E6
Sigiriya *Sri Lanka* 7°57'N 80°45'E 245 L5
Sigli *Indonesia* 5°25'N 96°0'E 234 A1
Siglufjörður *Iceland* 66°12'N 18°55'W 155 A4
Siglunes *Canada* 66°12'N 98°50'W 328 D2
Sigmaringen *Germany* 48°5'N 9°12'E 179 G5
Signa *Italy* 43°47'N 11°5'E 199 B8
Signakhi = Tsnori *Georgia* 41°40'N 45°57'E 191 K7
Signal de Botrang *Belgium* 50°29'N 6°4'E 176 D6
Signal Hill △ *S. Africa* 34°5'S 18°24'E 118 A1
Signal Pk. *U.S.A.* 33°20'N 114°2'W 307 M12
Signy I. *Antarctica* 60°43'S 45°36'W 151 C18
Signy-l'Abbaye *France* 49°40'N 4°25'E 173 C11
Sigourney *U.S.A.* 41°20'N 92°12'W 310 C4
Sigsbee *U.S.A.* 31°16'N 83°52'W 316 E5
Sigsbee Deep *Caribbean* 25°0'N 92°0'W 152 D1
Sigsig *Ecuador* 3°0'S 78°50'W 328 D2
Sigtuna *Sweden* 59°36'N 17°44'E 162 E11
Sigüenza *Spain* 41°3'N 2°40'W 194 D2
Siguiri *Guinea* 11°31'N 9°10'W 262 C3
Sigulda *Latvia* 57°10'N 24°55'E 188 B4
Siguniangshan *China* 31°15'N 103°0'E 228 B4
Sihanoukville = Kampong Saom
  Cambodia 10°38'N 103°30'E 237 G4
Sihawa *India* 20°19'N 81°55'E 244 D5
Siheung *Gyeonggi-do,*
  S. Korea 37°25'N 126°47'E 224 D3
Siheung *Seoul, S. Korea* 37°28'N 126°54'E 137 C1
Sihong *China* 33°27'N 118°16'E 227 H10
Sihora *India* 23°29'N 80°6'E 243 H9
Sihuas *Peru* 8°40'S 77°40'W 330 B2
Sihui *China* 23°20'N 112°40'E 229 F9
Siikajoki → *Finland* 64°50'N 24°43'E 160 D21
Siilinjärvi *Finland* 63°4'N 27°39'E 160 E22
Siirt *Turkey* 37°57'N 41°55'E 213 D9
Siirt □ *Turkey* 37°55'N 41°55'E 213 D9
Sijarira Ra. = Chizarira
  Zimbabwe 17°36'S 27°45'E 269 F2
Sijunjung *Indonesia* 0°42'S 100°58'E 234 C2
Sika *India* 22°26'N 69°47'E 242 H3
Sikanni Chief → *Canada* 57°47'N 122°15'W 296 B4
Sikao *Thailand* 7°34'N 99°21'E 237 J2
Sikar *India* 27°33'N 75°10'E 242 F6
Sikasso *Mali* 11°18'N 5°35'W 262 C3
Sikasso □ *Mali* 10°55'N 7°0'W 262 C3
Sikátorpuszta *Hungary* 47°34'N 19°16'E 117 A3
Sikelenge *Zambia* 14°53'S 24°14'E 265 E4
Sikeston *U.S.A.* 36°53'N 89°35'W 308 G9
Sikhote Alin, Khrebet
  Russia 45°0'N 136°0'E 220 B8
Sikhote Alin Ra. = Sikhote Alin,
  Khrebet *Russia* 45°0'N 136°0'E 220 B8
Sikia *Greece* 40°2'N 23°56'E 202 F7
Sikinos *Greece* 36°40'N 25°8'E 205 F7
Sikkim □ *India* 27°50'N 88°30'E 241 B7
Siklós *Hungary* 45°50'N 18°19'E 182 E3
Sil → *Spain* 42°27'N 7°43'W 194 C3
Silacayoapan *Mexico* 17°30'N 98°9'W 319 D5
Šilalė *Lithuania* 55°28'N 22°12'E 184 C9
Silampur *India* 28°39'N 77°15'E 242 H7
Silandro *Italy* 46°38'N 10°46'E 198 B7
Silang *Phil.* 14°14'N 120°58'E 222 D2
Silawad *India* 21°54'N 74°54'E 242 J6
Silay *Phil.* 10°47'N 122°58'E 233 F5
Silba *Croatia* 44°24'N 14°41'E 199 D11
Silchar *India* 24°49'N 92°43'E 241 C4
Sildegapet *Norway* 62°5'N 5°6'E 164 B2
Şile *Turkey* 41°10'N 29°37'E 203 E13
Silent Valley △ *India* 11°10'N 76°20'E 245 J3
Siler City *U.S.A.* 35°44'N 79°28'W 315 D5
Sileru → *India* 17°49'N 81°24'E 244 F5
Silesia = Śląsk *Poland* 51°0'N 16°30'E 176 C9
Silet *Algeria* 22°44'N 4°37'E 261 D6
Siletitengiz Köli
  Kazakhstan 53°20'N 73°10'E 217 B8
Silgarhi Doti *Nepal* 29°15'N 81°0'E 243 E9
Silghat *India* 26°35'N 93°0'E 241 C4
Silhouette *Seychelles* 4°29'S 55°12'E 272 c
Sili *Burkina Faso* 11°37'N 2°30'W 262 C4
Siliana *Tunisia* 36°20'N 9°22'E 261 A6
Siliana □ *Tunisia* 35°55'N 9°20'E 253 B1
Silifke *Turkey* 36°22'N 33°58'E 250 B4
Siliguri = Shiliguri *India* 26°45'N 88°25'E 241 B7
Silil *Somali Rep.* 11°0'N 43°26'E 267 E5
Siling Co *China* 31°50'N 89°20'E 230 C3
Silistea Nouă *Romania* 44°23'N 25°11'E 183 F10
Silistra *Bulgaria* 44°6'N 27°19'E 203 B11
Silistra □ *Bulgaria* 44°0'N 27°0'E 203 B11
Silivri *Turkey* 41°4'N 28°14'E 203 E12
Siljan *Sweden* 60°55'N 14°45'E 164 C9
Siljan, L. *Sweden* 60°55'N 14°45'E 162 D8
Siljansnäs *Sweden* 60°40'N 14°50'E 162 D8
Silkeborg *Denmark* 56°10'N 9°32'E 163 H3
Silkwood *Australia* 17°45'S 146°2'E 280 B4
Silla *Spain* 39°22'N 0°25'W 197 F4
Sillajhuay, Cordillera
  Chile 19°46'S 68°40'W 330 D4
Sillamäe *Estonia* 59°24'N 27°45'E 188 C4
Sillé-le-Guillaume *France* 48°10'N 0°8'W 172 D6
Silleda *Spain* 42°42'N 8°14'W 194 C2
Sillein = Žilina
  Slovak Rep. 49°12'N 18°42'E 181 B11
Sillim *S. Korea* 37°52'N 120°27'E 232 C5
Sillod *India* 20°18'N 75°39'E 244 D2
Sillotth *U.K.* 54°52'N 3°23'W 169 C4
Sillustani *Peru* 15°50'S 70°7'W 330 D3
Silo *Greece* 37°36'N 25°33'E 202 F7
Siloam Springs *U.S.A.* 36°11'N 94°32'W 314 C7
Silopi *Turkey* 37°15'N 42°27'E 213 D10
Silsbee *U.S.A.* 30°21'N 94°11'W 314 F7
Siltou *Chad* 16°57'N 17°11'E 257 E3
Siluko *Nigeria* 6°35'N 5°10'E 263 D6
Šilutė *Lithuania* 55°21'N 21°33'E 184 C8
Silva Porto = Kuito
  Angola 12°22'S 16°55'E 265 E3
Silvan *Turkey* 38°13'N 41°2'E 213 C9
Silvani *India* 23°18'N 78°25'E 243 H8
Silvassa *India* 20°16'N 73°1'E 244 D1
Silver, L. *U.S.A.* 28°35'N 81°23'W 317 G14
Silver Bank *W. Indies* 20°44'N 69°45'W 321 B6
Silver Bank Passage
  W. Indies 20°0'N 70°0'W 321 B5
Silver City *U.S.A.* 32°46'N 108°17'W 305 K9
Silver Cr. → *U.S.A.* 43°16'N 119°13'W 304 E4
Silver Creek *U.S.A.* 42°33'N 79°10'W 312 D6
Silver Grove *U.S.A.* 39°1'N 84°23'W 311 F12
Silver Hill *Montserrat* 16°49'N 62°11'W 322 a
Silver L. *U.S.A.* 43°8'N 121°3'W 304 E3
Silver Lake *Calif., U.S.A.* 35°21'N 116°7'W 307 K10

Silver Lake *Ind., U.S.A.* 41°4'N 85°53'W 311 C11
Silver Lake *Oreg., U.S.A.* 43°8'N 121°3'W 304 E3
Silver Lake *Wis., U.S.A.* 42°33'N 88°13'W 311 B8
Silver Spring *U.S.A.* 38°59'N 77°2'W 313 F7
Silver Springs *U.S.A.* 29°13'N 82°3'W 317 F7
Silverdalen *Sweden* 57°32'N 15°45'E 163 G9
Silvermine Mts. *Ireland* 52°47'N 8°15'W 166 D3
Silvermine Nature Reserve
  S. Africa 34°6'S 18°27'E 118 B1
Silverton *N.S.W.,*
  Australia 31°52'S 141°10'E 282 A4
Silverton *Colo., U.S.A.* 37°49'N 107°40'W 305 H10
Silverton *Tex., U.S.A.* 34°28'N 101°19'W 314 D4
Silves *Brazil* 2°54'S 58°27'W 329 D6
Silves *Portugal* 37°11'N 8°26'W 195 H2
Silvi Marina *Italy* 42°34'N 14°5'E 199 F11
Silvia *Colombia* 2°37'N 76°21'W 328 C2
Silvies → *U.S.A.* 43°34'N 119°2'W 304 E4
Silvolantekojärvi *Finland* 60°17'N 24°42'E 121 B2
Silvrettahorn *Switz.* 46°50'N 10°6'E 198 B7
Silwa Bahari *Egypt* 24°45'N 32°55'E 256 C3
Silz *Austria* 47°6'N 10°56'E 180 D3
Sim, C. *Morocco* 31°26'N 9°51'W 260 B3
Simakomba *Zambia* 14°12'S 23°16'E 265 E4
Simaltala *India* 24°43'N 86°33'E 243 G12
Simanggang = Bandar Sri Aman
  Malaysia 1°15'N 111°32'E 235 B4
Simao *China* 22°47'N 101°5'E 228 D3
Simão Dias *Brazil* 10°44'S 37°49'W 332 D4
Simar *Iran* 33°9'N 47°41'E 213 F12
Simard, L. *Canada* 47°40'N 78°40'W 298 C4
Şimareh → *Iran* 33°9'N 47°41'E 213 F12
Simav *Turkey* 39°4'N 28°58'E 205 B10
Simav → *Turkey* 40°23'N 28°31'E 203 F12
Simav Dağları *Turkey* 39°10'N 28°30'E 205 B10
Simba *Dem. Rep. of the Congo* 0°3'N 22°59'E 264 B4
Simba *Tanzania* 2°10'S 37°36'E 268 C4
Simbach *Germany* 48°16'N 13°2'E 179 G9
Simberi I. *Papua N. G.* 2°38'S 152°0'E 286 B7
Simeto → *Italy* 37°24'N 15°6'E 201 E8
Simeulue → *Indonesia* 2°45'N 95°45'E 234 B1
Simferopol *Ukraine* 44°55'N 34°3'E 189 K8
Simi *Greece* 36°35'N 27°50'E 205 F9
Simi Valley *U.S.A.* 34°16'N 118°47'W 307 L8
Simikot *Nepal* 30°0'N 81°50'E 243 E9
Similajau △ *Malaysia* 3°27'N 113°15'E 235 B4
Simineh → *Iran* 36°59'N 45°54'E 213 D11
Simití *Colombia* 7°58'N 73°57'W 328 B3
Simitli *Bulgaria* 41°52'N 23°7'E 202 E7
Simla = Shimla *India* 31°2'N 77°9'E 242 D7
Simla *India* 22°35'N 88°22'E 124 B2
Šimlângsdalen *Sweden* 56°40'N 13°6'E 163 H7
Şimleu-Silvaniei *Romania* 47°17'N 22°50'E 183 C7
Simla *India* 21°45'N 86°30'E 243 J12
Simmering *Austria* 48°10'N 16°26'E 142 A2
Simmering Heide *Austria* 48°10'N 16°26'E 142 A2
Simmern *Germany* 49°59'N 7°30'E 179 F3
Simmie *Canada* 49°56'N 109°6'W 297 D7
Simmler *U.S.A.* 35°21'N 119°59'W 307 K7
Simnas *Lithuania* 54°24'N 23°39'E 184 D10
Simo älv = Simojoki →
  Finland 65°35'N 25°1'E 160 D21
Simojärvi *Finland* 66°35'N 25°1'E 160 D21
Simojovel *Mexico* 17°12'N 92°38'W 319 D6
Simonette → *Canada* 55°9'N 118°15'W 296 B5
Simonière, Plaine de la
  Guadeloupe 16°16'N 61°19'W 322 a
Simonkylä *Finland* 60°18'N 25°1'E 121 B3
Simonovany = Partizánske
  Slovak Rep. 48°38'N 18°23'E 181 C11
Simonstown *S. Africa* 34°14'S 18°26'E 270 D2
Simontornya *Hungary* 46°45'N 18°33'E 182 D3
Simpang *Indonesia* 1°16'S 104°4'E 234 C2
Simpang Empat *Malaysia* 5°27'N 100°29'E 237 c
Simpangkiri → *Indonesia* 5°20'N 97°40'E 234 B1
Simplicio Mendes *Brazil* 7°51'S 41°54'W 332 D3
Simplonpass *Switz.* 46°15'N 8°3'E 179 J4
Simplontunnel *Switz.* 46°15'N 8°7'E 179 J4
Simpson Bay Lagoon
  St.-Martin 18°3'N 63°6'W 322 a
Simpson Desert *Australia* 25°0'S 137°0'E 280 D2
Simpson Desert △
  Australia 24°59'S 138°21'E 280 C2
Simpson Pen. *Canada* 68°34'N 88°45'W 295 D14
Simrishamn *Sweden* 55°33'N 14°22'E 163 J8
Simsbury *U.S.A.* 41°53'N 72°48'W 313 E12
Simsonbaai St.-Maarten *Sint Maarten* 18°2'N 63°7'W 322 a
Simunjan *Indonesia* 1°25'N 110°45'E 235 B4
Simunul *Phil.* 4°54'N 119°51'E 233 J2
Simushir, Ostrov *Russia* 46°50'N 152°30'E 215 E16
Sin Cowe I. *S. China Sea* 9°53'N 114°19'E 230 D4
Sin-do *N. Korea* 39°52'N 124°14'E 224 C2
Sina → *India* 17°30'N 75°55'E 244 F2
Sina Dhaqo *Somali Rep.* 5°50'N 46°0'E 267 G4
Sinabang *Indonesia* 2°30'N 96°24'E 234 B1
Sinai = Es Sînâ' *Egypt* 29°0'N 34°0'E 256 B3
Sinai, Mt. = Mûsa, Gebel
  Egypt 28°33'N 33°59'E 251 K4
Sinai Peninsula *Egypt* 29°30'N 34°0'E 256 B3
Sinaia *Romania* 45°21'N 25°38'E 183 E10
Sinaloa *Mexico* 17°52'N 120°27'E 232 C5
Sinaloa, Mt. *Phil.* 7°30'N 125°17'E 233 G6
Sinaloa □ *Mexico* 25°0'N 107°30'W 318 C3
Sinaloa de Leyva *Mexico* 25°50'N 108°14'W 318 B3
Sinalunga *Italy* 43°12'N 11°44'E 199 C8
Sinan *China* 27°56'N 108°13'E 229 D7
Sinandrei *Romania* 45°52'N 21°13'E 182 E6
Sinarades *Greece* 39°35'N 19°48'E 205 B8
Sinawān *Libya* 31°0'N 10°37'E 258 B2
Sinbo *Burma* 24°40'N 97°3'E 241 C6
Sincan *Turkey* 40°0'N 32°30'E 212 B5
Sincanlı *Turkey* 38°45'N 30°15'E 205 C12
Sincé *Colombia* 9°15'N 75°9'W 328 B2
Sincelejo *Colombia* 9°18'N 75°24'W 328 B2
Sinch'ang *N. Korea* 40°7'N 128°28'E 224 D3
Sincheorwon *S. Korea* 38°15'N 127°13'E 137 B1
Sinch'ŏn *N. Korea* 38°17'N 125°21'E 224 E2
Sinchon *Seoul, S. Korea* 37°34'N 126°56'E 137 C1
Sinclair *U.S.A.* 41°47'N 107°7'W 304 F10
Sinclair, L. *U.S.A.* 33°5'N 83°12'W 316 B6
Sinclair Mills *Canada* 54°5'N 121°40'W 296 C4
Sinclair's B. *U.K.* 58°31'N 3°5'W 127 C5
Sinclairville *U.S.A.* 42°16'N 79°16'W 312 D5
Sind = Sindh □ *Pakistan* 26°0'N 69°0'E 242 G3
Sind → *Jammu & Kashmir,*
  India 34°18'N 74°45'E 243 B6
Sind → *Mad. P., India* 26°26'N 79°13'E 243 F8
Sind Sagar Doab *Pakistan* 32°0'N 71°30'E 242 D4

Sindal *Denmark* 57°28'N 10°10'E 163 G4
Sindang *S. Korea* 37°35'N 127°2'E 137 B2
Sindangan *Phil.* 8°10'N 123°5'E 233 G4
Sindangan B. *Phil.* 8°11'N 122°50'E 233 G4
Sindangbarang *Indonesia* 7°27'S 107°1'E 234 D3
Sinde *Zambia* 17°28'S 25°51'E 269 F2
Sindelfingen *Germany* 48°42'N 9°0'E 179 G4
Sindewahi *India* 20°17'N 79°39'E 244 D4
Sindgi *India* 16°55'N 76°14'E 244 F3
Sindh = Indus →
  Pakistan 24°20'N 67°47'E 242 G2
Sindh □ *Pakistan* 26°0'N 69°0'E 242 G3
Sindhnur *India* 15°47'N 76°46'E 245 G3
Sindi *India* 20°48'N 78°52'E 244 D4
Sındırgı *Turkey* 39°13'N 28°10'E 205 B10
Sindou *Burkina Faso* 10°35'N 5°4'W 262 C3
Sinekli *Turkey* 41°14'N 28°12'E 203 E12
Sines *Portugal* 37°56'N 8°51'W 195 H2
Sines, C. de *Portugal* 37°58'N 8°53'W 195 H2
Sineu *Spain* 39°38'N 3°1'E 206 B4
Sinewit, Mt. *Papua N. G.* 4°44'S 152°2'E 286 C7
Sinfra *Ivory C.* 6°35'N 5°56'W 262 D3
Sing Buri *Thailand* 14°53'N 100°25'E 236 E3
Sing Sing = Ossining
  U.S.A. 41°10'N 73°55'W 313 E11
Singa *Sudan* 13°10'N 33°57'E 257 E3
Singako *Chad* 9°50'N 19°24'E 259 G3
Singalila △ *India* 27°10'N 88°5'E 241 B7
Singanallur *India* 11°2'N 77°1'E 245 J3
Singapore ■ *Asia* 1°17'N 103°51'E 138 B3
Singapore, Straits of *Asia* 1°15'N 104°0'E 237 d
Singapore, Univ. of
  Singapore 1°19'N 103°49'E 138 B2
Singapore Changi ✈ (SIN)
  Singapore 1°23'N 103°59'E 138 A3
Singaraja *Indonesia* 8°7'S 115°6'E 231 J18
Singatoka = Sigatoka *Fiji* 18°8'S 177°32'E 287 B1
Singen *Germany* 47°45'N 8°58'E 179 H4
Singida *Tanzania* 4°49'S 34°48'E 268 C3
Singida □ *Tanzania* 6°0'S 34°30'E 268 D3
Singkaling Hkamti *Burma* 26°0'N 95°39'E 241 C5
Singkang *Indonesia* 4°8'S 120°1'E 231 E6
Singkarak, Danau
  Indonesia 0°36'S 100°32'E 234 C2
Singkawang *Indonesia* 1°0'N 108°57'E 235 B3
Singkep *Indonesia* 0°30'S 104°25'E 234 C2
Singkil *Indonesia* 2°17'N 97°49'E 237 L1
Singkuang *Indonesia* 1°3'N 98°55'E 237 L2
Sirjän *Iran* 29°30'N 55°45'E 247 D7
Sirkali = Sirkazhi *India* 11°15'N 79°41'E 245 J4
Sirkazhi *India* 11°15'N 79°41'E 245 J4
Sirmans *U.S.A.* 30°21'N 83°39'W 316 E6
Sirmaur *India* 24°51'N 81°23'E 243 G9
Sirmilik △ *Canada* 72°50'N 80°35'W 295 C15
Sirna *Greece* 36°22'N 26°42'E 205 E8
Şırnak *Turkey* 37°32'N 42°28'E 213 D10
Sirohi *India* 24°52'N 72°53'E 242 G5
Sironj *India* 24°5'N 77°39'E 242 G7
Siros = Ermoupoli *Greece* 37°28'N 24°57'E 204 D6
Siroz = Serres *Greece* 41°5'N 23°31'E 202 E7
Sirpur *India* 19°29'N 79°36'E 244 E4
Sirr, Nafud as *Si. Arabia* 25°33'N 44°35'E 246 E5
Sirrayn *Si. Arabia* 18°55'N 39°56'E 246 E2
Sirretta Pk. *U.S.A.* 35°56'N 118°19'W 307 K8
Sírri *Iran* 25°55'N 54°32'E 247 E7
Sirsa *India* 29°33'N 75°4'E 242 E6
Sirsa → *India* 14°40'N 74°49'E 245 G2
Sirsilla *India* 18°23'N 78°50'E 244 E4
Siruela *Spain* 38°58'N 5°3'W 195 G5
Siruguppa *India* 15°38'N 76°54'E 245 F3
Sirur *India* 18°50'N 74°23'E 244 E2
Sirván → *Iran* 35°24'N 46°5'E 213 C11
Sisak *Croatia* 45°30'N 16°21'E 199 C13
Sisante *Spain* 39°25'N 2°12'W 197 F2
Sisargas, Is. *Spain* 43°21'N 8°50'W 194 B2
Sishen *S. Africa* 27°47'S 22°59'E 270 C3
Sisian *Armenia* 39°31'N 46°2'E 213 C12
Sisiga *Solomon Is.* 7°54'S 159°10'E 287 L10
Sisimiut *Greenland* 66°40'N 53°30'W 154 D5
Sisipuk L. *Canada* 55°45'N 101°50'W 297 B8
Sismak *N. Korea* 38°25'N 126°41'E 224 C3
Sisophon *Cambodia* 13°38'N 102°59'E 236 F4
Sissano *Papua N. G.* 3°0'S 142°3'E 286 B2
Sisseton *U.S.A.* 45°40'N 97°3'W 308 C6
Sisson = Mount Shasta
  U.S.A. 41°19'N 122°19'W 304 F2
Sissonne *France* 49°34'N 3°51'E 173 C10
Sistän *Asia* 30°50'N 61°0'E 247 D9
Sistän, Daryächeh-ye *Iran* 31°0'N 61°0'E 247 D9
Sistän va Balūchestän □
  Iran 27°0'N 62°0'E 247 E9
Sisteron *France* 44°12'N 5°57'E 175 D9
Sisters *U.S.A.* 44°18'N 121°33'W 304 D3
Sisters, The *Grenada* 12°18'N 61°36'W 323 a
Sisters, The *Seychelles* 4°16'S 55°52'E 272 c
Sisters Pk. Ascension I.
  Ascension 7°54'S 14°22'W 153 g
Sisters Rocks Trin. & Tob.
  Trin. & Tob. 11°20'N 60°39'W 323 a
Siswa Bazar *India* 27°9'N 83°46'E 243 F10
Sitakili *Mali* 13°7'N 11°14'W 262 C2
Sitamarhi *India* 26°37'N 85°30'E 243 F11
Sitamau *India* 24°0'N 75°38'E 242 G6
Sitangkai *Phil.* 4°40'N 119°23'E 233 J2
Sitapur *India* 27°38'N 80°45'E 243 F9
Siteki *Swaziland* 26°32'S 31°58'E 271 C5
Sitges *Spain* 41°17'N 1°47'E 196 D6
Sithonia *Greece* 40°14'N 24°0'E 202 F7
Sitía *Greece* 35°13'N 26°6'E 207 D8
Sítio da Abadia *Brazil* 14°48'S 46°16'E 332 D2
Sitito-Ozima Ridge *Pac. Oc.* 23°0'N 143°0'E 288 E6
Sitka *U.S.A.* 57°3'N 135°20'W 303 H14
Sitkinak I. *U.S.A.* 56°33'N 154°10'W 303 H9
Sitoti *Botswana* 23°15'S 23°40'E 270 B3
Sitra *Egypt* 28°40'N 26°53'E 256 C2
Sittang Myit → *Burma* 17°20'N 96°45'E 241 G6
Sittard *Neths.* 51°0'N 5°52'E 176 C6
Sittaung *Burma* 24°10'N 94°35'E 241 C5
Sittensen *Germany* 53°17'N 9°31'E 178 B5
Sittingbourne *U.K.* 51°21'N 0°45'E 125 B4
Sittona *Eritrea* 14°25'N 37°23'E 257 E4
Sittoung = Sittang Myit →
  Burma 17°20'N 96°45'E 241 G6
Sittwe *Burma* 20°18'N 92°45'E 241 E4
Siubondo *Indonesia* 7°42'S 114°12'E 235 D5
Siufalaele Pt. Amer. Samoa *Amer. Samoa* 14°17'S 169°29'W 302 f
Siulagi Pt. Amer. Samoa *Amer. Samoa* 14°16'S 169°38'W 302 f
Si'umu *Samoa* 14°1'S 171°49'W 287 W20
Siuna *Nic.* 13°37'N 84°45'W 320 D3
Siuri *India* 23°50'N 87°34'E 243 H12
Siutghiol, Lacul *Romania* 44°15'N 28°38'E 183 F11
Sivágiri *India* 9°5'N 77°38'E 245 K3
Sivakási *India* 9°24'N 77°45'E 245 K3
Sīvand *Iran* 30°5'N 52°55'E 247 D7
Sivas *Turkey* 39°43'N 36°58'E 212 C7
Sivas □ *Turkey* 39°45'N 37°0'E 212 C7

Sivasamudram India 12°16N 77°10E 245 H3
Sivaslı Turkey 38°31N 29°42E 205 C11
Siverek Turkey 37°50N 39°19E 213 D8
Sivomaskinskiy Russia 66°40N 62°35E 186 A11
Sivota Greece 39°24N 20°13E 206 C10
Sivrihisar Turkey 39°30N 31°35E 212 C4
Sivros Greece 38°40N 20°39E 207 B2
Sîwa Egypt 29°11N 25°31E 256 B2
Sîwa, El Wâhât es Egypt 29°10N 25°30E 256 B2
Siwa Oasis = Sîwa, El Wâhât es Egypt 29°10N 25°30E 256 B2
Siwalik Range Nepal 28°0N 83°0E 243 F10
Siwan India 26°13N 84°21E 243 F11
Siwana India 25°38N 72°25E 242 G5
Six Cross Roads Barbados 13°7N 59°28W 323 r
Sixian China 33°30N 117°50E 227 H9
Sixmilebridge Ireland 52°44N 8°46W 166 D3
Sixth Cataract Sudan 16°20N 32°42E 257 D3
Siyabuswa S. Africa 25°7S 29°3E 271 C4
Siyah Kuh, Kavīr-e Iran 32°55N 53°55E 247 C7
Siyâl, Jazâ'ir Egypt 22°49N 36°12E 256 C4
Siyang China 33°42N 118°40E 227 H10
Siyäzän Azerbaijan 41°3N 49°10E 191 K9
Siziwang Qi China 41°25N 111°40E 226 D6
Sjælland Denmark 55°30N 11°30E 163 J5
Sjælland □ Denmark 55°30N 11°30E 163 J5
Sjællands Odde Denmark 55°58N 11°24E 163 J5
Sjenica Serbia 43°16N 20°0E 202 C3
Sjoa Norway 61°41N 9°33E 164 C6
Sjöbo Sweden 55°37N 13°45E 163 J7
Sjøholt Norway 62°27N 6°52E 164 B3
Sjølisand Norway 61°29N 11°18E 164 C8
Sjötofta Sweden 57°22N 13°17E 163 G7
Sjötorp Sweden 58°50N 14°0E 163 F8
Sjumen = Shumen Bulgaria 43°18N 26°55E 203 C10
Sjuntorp Sweden 58°12N 12°13E 163 F6
Skåbu Norway 61°32N 9°24E 164 C6
Skadarsko Jezero Europe 42°10N 19°20E 202 D3
Skadarsko Jezero △ Montenegro 42°10N 19°20E 202 D3
Skadovsk Ukraine 46°17N 32°52E 189 J7
Skælskør Denmark 55°15N 11°18E 163 J5
Skærbæk Denmark 55°9N 8°45E 163 J2
Skaftafell Iceland 64°1N 17°0W 155 C9
Skaftafell △ Iceland 64°9N 16°50W 155 C9
Skagafjarðarsýsla □ Iceland 65°30N 19°0W 155 B7
Skagafjörður Iceland 65°54N 19°35W 155 B7
Skagastølstindane Norway 61°28N 7°52E 164 C4
Skagaströnd Iceland 65°50N 20°19W 155 B6
Skagatá Iceland 66°7N 20°6W 155 A6
Skagen Denmark 57°43N 10°35E 163 G4
Skagern Sweden 59°0N 14°20E 162 E8
Skagerrak Denmark 57°30N 9°0E 163 G2
Skagit → U.S.A. 48°23N 122°22W 306 B4
Skagway U.S.A. 59°28N 135°19W 303 G14
Skala Greece 38°5N 20°47E 207 C2
Skala nad Zbruczem = Skala-Podilska Ukraine 48°50N 26°15E 183 B11
Skala-Podilska Ukraine 48°50N 26°15E 183 B11
Skalat Ukraine 49°23N 25°55E 177 D13
Skálavík Iceland 66°11N 23°29W 155 A3
Skalbmierz Poland 50°20N 20°25E 185 H7
Skälderviken Sweden 56°22N 12°30E 163 H6
Skålevik Norway 58°5N 8°1E 164 F5
Skalica Slovak Rep. 48°50N 17°15E 181 C10
Skallingen Denmark 55°32N 8°13E 163 J2
Skalni Dol = Kamenyak Bulgaria 43°24N 26°57E 203 C10
Skanderborg Denmark 56°2N 9°55E 163 H3
Skåne Sweden 55°59N 13°30E 163 J7
Skåne län □ Sweden 56°15N 14°0E 163 H7
Skaneateles U.S.A. 42°57N 76°26W 313 D8
Skaneateles L. U.S.A. 42°51N 76°22W 313 D8
Skånevik Norway 59°43N 5°53E 164 E2
Skänninge Sweden 58°24N 15°5E 163 F9
Skanör med Falsterbo Sweden 55°24N 12°50E 163 J6
Skansen Sweden 59°19N 18°7E 139 B2
Skantzoura Greece 39°5N 24°6E 204 B6
Skara Sweden 58°25N 13°30E 163 F7
Skärblacka Sweden 58°35N 15°54E 163 F9
Skarð Iceland 65°17N 22°19W 155 B4
Skardu Pakistan 35°20N 75°44E 243 B6
Skare Hordaland, Norway 59°55N 6°36E 164 E3
Skåre Sweden 59°26N 13°26E 162 E7
Skärhamn Sweden 57°59N 11°34E 163 G5
Skärholmen Sweden 59°16N 17°53E 139 B1
Skarnes Norway 60°15N 11°41E 164 D8
Skarpäng Sweden 59°26N 18°0E 139 A2
Skarpnäck Sweden 59°16N 18°7E 139 B2
Skarszewy Poland 54°4N 18°25E 184 D5
Skaryszew Poland 51°19N 21°15E 185 G8
Skaryszewski, Park Poland 52°15N 21°3E 142 B2
Skarżysko-Kamienna Poland 51°7N 20°52E 185 G7
Skattkärr Sweden 59°25N 13°40E 162 E7
Skattungbyn Sweden 61°10N 14°56E 162 C8
Skawina Poland 49°59N 19°50E 185 J6
Skebobruk Sweden 59°58N 18°36E 162 E12
Skee Sweden 58°56N 11°19E 163 F5
Skeena → Canada 54°9N 130°5W 296 C2
Skeena Mts. Canada 56°40N 128°30W 296 B3
Skegness U.K. 53°9N 0°20E 168 D8
Skei Norway 61°34N 6°28E 164 C3
Skeiðarársandur Iceland 63°54N 17°14W 155 D9
Skeiðflötur Iceland 63°26N 19°11W 155 D7
Skeldon = Corriverton Guyana 5°55N 57°20W 329 B6
Skeleton Coast ⌓ Namibia 20°0S 13°20E 270 B1
Skellefteå Sweden 64°45N 20°50E 160 D19
Skellefteälven → Sweden 64°45N 21°10E 160 D19
Skelleftehamn Sweden 64°40N 21°9E 160 D19
Skellig Michael = Great Skellig Ireland 51°47N 10°33W 166 E1
Skender Vakuf Bos.-H. 44°29N 17°22E 182 F2
Skenderaj = Srbica Kosovo 42°45N 20°47E 202 D4
Skeppsholmen Stockholm, Sweden 139 c3
Skerries, The U.K. 53°25N 4°36W 168 D3
Skhidnytsya Ukraine 49°13N 23°20E 185 J10
Skhiza Greece 36°41N 21°40E 204 E3
Ski Norway 59°43N 10°52E 164 E7
Skiathos Greece 39°12N 23°30E 204 B5
Skibbereen Ireland 51°33N 9°16W 166 E2
Skiddaw U.K. 54°39N 3°9W 168 C4
Skidegate Canada 53°15N 132°1W 296 C2
Skidra Greece 40°46N 22°10E 202 F6
Skien Norway 59°12N 9°35E 164 E6
Skierniewice Poland 51°58N 20°10E 185 G7
Skihist, Mt. Canada 50°12N 121°54W 296 C4
Skikda Algeria 36°50N 6°58E 261 A6
Skikda □ Algeria 36°45N 6°50E 261 A6
Skillet Fork → U.S.A. 38°5N 88°5W 311 F8
Skillingaryd Sweden 57°27N 14°5E 163 G8
Skillinge Sweden 55°30N 14°16E 163 J8
Skilloura Cyprus 35°14N 33°10E 207 E9
Skinari, Akra Greece 37°56N 20°42E 207 D2
Skinnastaður Iceland 66°4N 16°27W 155 A10
Skinnskatteberg Sweden 59°50N 15°42E 162 E9
Skipton Vic., Australia 37°39S 143°40E 282 D5
Skipton N. Yorks., U.K. 53°58N 2°3W 168 D5
Skiptvet Norway 59°28N 11°11E 164 E8
Skiring, C. Senegal 12°26N 16°46W 262 C1
Skirmish Pt. Australia 11°59S 134°17E 280 A1
Skiropoula Greece 38°50N 24°21E 204 C6
Skiros Greece 38°55N 24°34E 204 C6
Skivarp Sweden 55°26N 13°34E 163 J7
Skive Denmark 56°33N 9°2E 163 H3
Skjærhalden Norway 59°2N 11°2E 164 E8
Skjálfandafljót → Iceland 65°59N 17°25W 155 B9
Skjálfandi Iceland 66°5N 17°30W 155 A9
Skjeberg Norway 59°12N 11°12E 164 E8
Skjern Denmark 55°57N 8°30E 163 J2
Skjold Norway 59°31N 5°34E 164 E2
Skjolden Norway 61°29N 7°36E 164 C4
Skjöldólfsstaðir Iceland 65°19N 15°7W 155 B11
Skjønhaug Norway 59°39N 11°19E 164 E8
Skobelev = Farghona Uzbekistan 40°23N 71°19E 217 D8
Skoczów Poland 49°49N 18°45E 185 J5
Skodje Norway 62°30N 6°43E 164 B3
Škofja Loka Slovenia 46°9N 14°19E 199 B11
Skógar Iceland 63°32N 19°28W 155 D7
Skógarnes Iceland 64°46N 22°34W 155 C4
Skoghall Sweden 59°20N 13°30E 162 E7
Skogstorp Sweden 59°19N 16°29E 162 E10
Skoki Poland 52°40N 17°11E 185 F4
Skokie U.S.A. 42°2N 87°43W 119 A2
Skokie → U.S.A. 42°3N 87°46W 119 A2
Skokie Heritage Museum U.S.A. 42°2N 87°44W 119 A2
Skoklefall Norway 59°50N 10°40E 133 A3
Skole Ukraine 49°3N 23°30E 177 D12
Skollenborg Norway 59°38N 9°43E 164 E6
Sköndal Sweden 59°15N 18°6E 139 B2
Skopelos Greece 39°9N 23°47E 204 B5
Skopi Greece 35°11N 26°2E 207 E7
Skopin Russia 53°55N 39°32E 188 F10
Skopje Macedonia 42°1N 21°26E 202 D5
Skopje ✈ (SKP) Macedonia 41°59N 21°29E 202 E5
Skoppum Norway 59°23N 10°26E 164 E7
Skórcz Poland 53°47N 18°30E 184 E5
Skørping Denmark 56°50N 9°53E 163 H3
Skotfoss Norway 59°12N 9°30E 164 E6
Skotterud Norway 60°0N 12°7E 164 D9
Skövde Sweden 58°24N 13°50E 163 F7
Skovlunde Denmark 55°42N 12°25E 118 A2
Skovorodino Russia 54°0N 124°0E 215 D13
Skovshoved Denmark 55°45N 12°35E 118 A3
Skowhegan U.S.A. 44°46N 69°43W 309 C19
Skradin Croatia 43°52N 15°53E 199 E12
Skrea Sweden 56°53N 12°34E 163 H6
Skreia Norway 60°40N 10°56E 164 D7
Skrim Norway 59°31N 9°38E 164 E6
Skrunda Latvia 56°41N 22°1E 184 B9
Skrwa → Poland 52°35N 19°32E 185 F6
Skudeneshavn Norway 59°10N 5°10E 164 E2
Skuleskogen △ Sweden 63°6N 18°30E 162 A12
Skull Ireland 51°32N 9°34W 166 E2
Skultorp Sweden 58°24N 13°51E 163 F7
Skultuna Sweden 59°43N 16°25E 162 E10
Skunk → U.S.A. 40°42N 91°7W 310 D5
Skuodas Lithuania 56°16N 21°33E 184 B8
Skuru Sweden 59°18N 18°12E 139 B3
Skurup Sweden 55°28N 13°30E 163 J7
Skutskär Sweden 60°37N 17°25E 162 D11
Skútustaðir Iceland 65°34N 17°2W 155 B9
Skvyra Ukraine 49°44N 29°40E 177 D15
Skwierzyna Poland 52°33N 15°30E 185 F2
Sky Dome = Rogers Centre Toronto, Canada 141 c1
Sky Lake U.S.A. 28°27N 81°23W 133 B2
Skye U.K. 57°15N 6°10W 167 D2
Skykomish U.S.A. 47°42N 121°22W 304 C3
Skyland U.S.A. 33°53N 84°19W 113 A3
Skyring, Seno Chile 52°35S 72°0W 336 D3
Skyros = Skiros Greece 38°55N 24°34E 204 C6
Skyttorp Sweden 60°5N 17°44E 162 D11
Slade Green U.K. 51°27N 0°11E 125 B5
Slade Point Australia 21°4S 149°13E 280 b
Slade Pt. Australia 21°5S 149°13E 280 b
Slættaratindur Færoe Is. 62°18N 7°1W 160 E9
Slagelse Denmark 55°23N 11°19E 163 J5
Slamet Indonesia 7°16S 109°8E 235 D3
Slane Ireland 53°42N 6°33W 166 C5
Slaney → Ireland 52°26N 6°33W 166 D5
Slangberge S. Africa 31°32S 20°48E 270 D3
Slănic Romania 45°14N 25°58E 183 E10
Slano Croatia 42°48N 17°53E 202 D1
Slantsy Russia 59°7N 28°5E 188 C5
Slaný Czech Rep. 50°13N 14°6E 180 A7
Śląsk Poland 51°0N 16°30E 176 C9
Śląskie □ Poland 50°30N 19°0E 185 H6
Slätbaken Sweden 58°25N 16°45E 163 F10
Slate Is. Canada 48°40N 87°0W 298 C2
Slater U.S.A. 39°13N 93°4W 310 E3
Slatina Croatia 45°42N 17°45E 182 E2
Slatina Romania 44°28N 24°22E 183 F9
Slatina Timiş Romania 45°15N 22°17E 182 E7
Slatington U.S.A. 40°45N 75°37W 313 F9
Slaton U.S.A. 33°26N 101°39W 314 E4
Slave → Canada 61°18N 113°39W 296 A6
Slave Coast W. Afr. 6°0N 2°30E 263 D5
Slave Lake Canada 55°17N 114°43W 296 B6
Slave Pt. Canada 61°11N 115°56W 296 A5
Slavgorod Russia 53°1N 78°37E 217 B9
Slavinja Serbia 43°9N 22°50E 202 C6
Slavkov u Brna Czech Rep. 49°10N 16°52E 181 B9
Slavkovský Les ⌓ Czech Rep. 50°5N 12°44E 180 A5
Slavonija Europe 45°20N 17°40E 182 E2
Slavonski Brod Croatia 45°11N 18°1E 182 E3
Slavsk Russia 55°3N 21°41E 184 C8
Slavske Ukraine 48°51N 23°27E 183 B8
Slavskoye Russia 54°30N 20°27E 184 D7
Slavuta Ukraine 50°15N 27°2E 177 C14
Slavyanka Russia 42°53N 131°21E 220 C5
Slavyanovo Bulgaria 43°28N 24°52E 203 C8
Slavyansk = Slovyansk Ukraine 48°55N 37°36E 189 H9
Slavyansk-na-Kubani Russia 45°15N 38°11E 189 K10
Sława Poland 51°52N 16°2E 185 G3
Slawharad Belarus 53°27N 31°0E 177 B16
Sławno Poland 54°20N 16°41E 184 D3
Sławoborze Poland 53°55N 15°42E 184 E2
Sleaford U.K. 53°0N 0°24W 168 D7
Sleaford B. Australia 34°55S 135°45E 281 E2
Sleat, Sd. of U.K. 57°5N 5°47W 167 D3
Sleðbrjótur Iceland 65°34N 14°30W 155 B12
Sleeper Is. Canada 58°30N 81°0W 295 F15
Sleeping Bear Dunes ⌓ U.S.A. 44°50N 86°5W 308 C10
Sleepy Eye U.S.A. 44°18N 94°43W 308 C6
Sleetmute U.S.A. 61°42N 157°10W 303 F8
Slemon L. Canada 63°13N 116°4W 296 A5
Slependen Norway 59°52N 10°30E 133 A2
Ślesin Poland 52°22N 18°14E 185 F5
Slide Mt. U.S.A. 42°0N 74°25W 313 E10
Slidell U.S.A. 30°17N 89°47W 315 F10
Slidre Norway 61°5N 8°58E 164 C5
Sliema Malta 35°55N 14°30E 206 F8
Slieve Aughty Ireland 53°4N 8°30W 166 C3
Slieve Bloom Ireland 53°4N 7°40W 166 C4
Slieve Donard U.K. 54°11N 5°55W 166 B6
Slieve Gamph Ireland 54°6N 9°0W 166 B3
Slieve Gullion U.K. 54°7N 6°26W 166 B5
Slieve League Ireland 54°40N 8°42W 166 B3
Slieve Mish Ireland 52°12N 9°50W 166 D2
Slievenamon Ireland 52°25N 7°34W 166 D4
Sligeach = Sligo Ireland 54°16N 8°28W 166 B3
Sligo Sligo, Ireland 54°16N 8°28W 166 B3
Sligo Pa., U.S.A. 41°6N 79°29W 312 E5
Sligo □ Ireland 54°8N 8°42W 166 B3
Sligo B. Ireland 54°18N 8°40W 166 B3
Slipi Indonesia 6°11S 106°47E 122 B1
Slippery Rock U.S.A. 41°4N 80°3W 312 E4
Slite Sweden 57°42N 18°48E 163 G12
Slīteres ⌓ Latvia 57°41N 22°21E 184 A9
Sliven Bulgaria 42°42N 26°19E 203 D10
Sliven □ Bulgaria 42°42N 26°19E 203 D10
Slivenec Czech Rep. 50°1N 14°21E 135 B2
Slivnitsa Bulgaria 42°50N 23°2E 202 D7
Sljeme Croatia 45°57N 15°58E 199 C12
Sloan U.S.A. 35°57N 115°13W 307 K11
Sloansville U.S.A. 42°45N 74°22W 313 D10
Slobidka Ukraine 47°54N 29°21E 183 C14
Slobodskoy Russia 58°40N 50°6E 186 C9
Slobozia Moldova 46°45N 29°42E 183 D14
Slobozia Argeş, Romania 44°30N 25°14E 183 F10
Slobozia Ialomiţa, Romania 44°34N 27°23E 183 F12
Slocan Canada 49°48N 117°28W 296 D5
Slocomb U.S.A. 31°7N 85°36W 316 D4
Slomikhino = Zhalpaqtal Kazakhstan 49°42N 49°25E 190 F9
Słomniki Poland 50°16N 20°4E 185 H7
Slonim Belarus 53°4N 25°19E 177 B13
Slot, The = New Georgia Sound Solomon Is. 8°0S 158°20E 287 L9
Sloten Neths. 52°21N 4°48E 112 A1
Sloterdijk Neths. 52°23N 4°51E 112 A1
Sloterpark Neths. 52°22N 4°49E 112 A1
Slottet Oslo, Norway 133 a1
Slough U.K. 51°30N 0°36W 169 F7
Slough □ U.K. 51°30N 0°36W 169 F7
Sloughhouse U.S.A. 38°26N 121°12W 306 G5
Slovak Rep. ■ Europe 48°30N 20°0E 181 C13
Slovakia = Slovak Rep. ■ Europe 48°30N 20°0E 181 C13
Slovakian Ore Mts. = Slovenské Rudohorie Slovak Rep. 48°45N 20°0E 181 C12
Slovenia ■ Europe 45°58N 14°30E 199 C11
Slovenija = Slovenia ■ Europe 45°58N 14°30E 199 C11
Slovenj Gradec Slovenia 46°31N 15°5E 199 B12
Slovenska = Slovak Rep. ■ Europe 48°30N 20°0E 181 C13
Slovenska Bistrica Slovenia 46°24N 15°35E 199 B12
Slovenské Konjice Slovenia 46°20N 15°28E 199 B12
Slovenské Rudohorie Slovak Rep. 48°45N 20°0E 181 C12
Slovenský Raj △ Slovak Rep. 48°53N 20°25E 181 C13
Slovyansk Ukraine 48°55N 37°36E 189 H9
Słowiński △ Poland 54°43N 17°26E 184 D4
Słubice Poland 52°22N 14°35E 185 F1
Sluch → Ukraine 51°37N 26°38E 177 C14
Sluhy Czech Rep. 50°11N 14°33E 135 A3
Sluis Neths. 51°18N 3°23E 170 C3
Slŭnchev Bryag Bulgaria 42°40N 27°41E 203 D11
Slunj Croatia 45°6N 15°33E 199 C12
Słupca Poland 52°15N 17°52E 185 F4
Słupia → Poland 54°35N 16°51E 184 D3
Słupsk Poland 54°30N 17°3E 184 D4
Slurry S. Africa 25°49S 25°42E 270 C4
Slutsk = Pavlovsk Russia 50°26N 40°5E 190 E5
Slutsk Belarus 53°2N 27°31E 177 B14
Służew Poland 52°10N 21°1E 142 B2
Służewiec Poland 52°10N 21°0E 142 B2
Slyne Hd. Ireland 53°25N 10°10W 166 C1
Slyudyanka Russia 51°40N 103°40E 215 D11
Smaalenene = Østfold □ Norway 59°25N 11°25E 164 E8
Småland Sweden 57°15N 15°25E 163 G9
Smålandsfarvandet Denmark 55°10N 11°20E 163 J5
Smålandsstenar Sweden 57°10N 13°25E 163 G7
Smaldeel = Theunissen S. Africa 28°26S 26°43E 270 C4
Smalltree L. Canada 61°0N 105°0W 297 A8
Smallwood Res. Canada 54°5N 64°30W 299 B7
Smara W. Sahara 26°48N 11°41W 260 C2
Smarhon Belarus 54°20N 26°24E 177 A14
Smarje Slovenia 46°15N 15°34E 199 B12
Smartt Syndicate Dam S. Africa 30°45S 23°10E 270 D3
Smartville U.S.A. 39°13N 121°18W 306 F5
Smeaton Canada 53°30N 104°49W 297 C8
Smedby Sweden 56°41N 16°13E 163 H10
Smederevo Serbia 44°40N 20°57E 202 B4
Smederevska Palanka Serbia 44°22N 20°58E 202 B4
Smedjebacken Sweden 60°8N 15°25E 162 D9
Smela = Smila Ukraine 49°15N 31°58E 189 H6
Smerwick Harbour Ireland 52°12N 10°23W 166 D1
Smethport U.S.A. 41°49N 78°27W 312 E6
Smíchov Czech Rep. 50°4N 14°23E 135 B2
Smidovich Russia 48°36N 133°49E 215 E14
Śmigiel Poland 52°1N 16°32E 185 F3
Smila Ukraine 49°15N 31°58E 189 H6
Smilyan Bulgaria 41°29N 24°46E 203 E8
Smith Canada 55°10N 114°0W 296 B6
Smith B. U.S.A. 70°30N 154°20W 303 A9
Smith Center U.S.A. 39°47N 98°47W 308 F4
Smith Forest Preserve U.S.A. 41°59N 87°45W 119 B2
Smith I. Nunavut, Canada 60°45N 78°25W 295 E16
Smith I. India 13°20N 93°4E 245 H11
Smith Islands △ Australia 20°40S 149°9E 280 b
Smith River ⌓ U.S.A. 41°55N 124°0W 304 F2
Smith Sd. N. Amer. 78°25N 74°0W 154 B3
Smithburne → Australia 17°3S 140°57E 280 B3
Smithers Canada 54°45N 127°10W 296 C3
Smithfield Free State, S. Africa 30°9S 26°30E 271 D4
Smithfield N.C., U.S.A. 35°31N 78°21W 315 D15
Smithfield Utah, U.S.A. 41°50N 111°50W 304 F8
Smiths U.S.A. 32°32N 85°6W 316 C4
Smiths Falls Canada 44°55N 76°0W 313 B9
Smithsonian Institution Washington, D.C., U.S.A. 143 b2
Smithton Australia 40°53S 145°6E 281 G4
Smithville Ont., Canada 43°6N 79°33W 312 C5
Smithville Ga., U.S.A. 31°54N 84°15W 316 D5
Smithville Mo., U.S.A. 39°23N 94°35W 310 E2
Smithville Tex., U.S.A. 30°1N 97°10W 314 F6
Smoke Creek Desert U.S.A. 40°30N 119°40W 304 F4
Smoky → Canada 56°10N 117°21W 296 B5
Smoky Bay Australia 32°22S 134°13E 281 E1
Smoky Hill → U.S.A. 39°4N 96°48W 308 F5
Smoky Hills U.S.A. 39°15N 99°30W 308 F4
Smoky Lake Canada 54°10N 112°30W 296 C6
Smøla Norway 63°23N 8°3E 164 A5
Smolensk Russia 54°45N 32°5E 188 E7
Smolensk □ Russia 55°20N 33°0E 188 E7
Smolikas, Oros Greece 40°9N 20°58E 202 F4
Smolník Slovak Rep. 48°43N 20°44E 181 C13
Smolny Russia 59°56N 30°25E 137 B2
Smolny Cathedral Russia 59°56N 30°24E 137 B2
Smolyan Bulgaria 41°36N 24°38E 203 E8
Smolyan □ Bulgaria 41°36N 24°38E 203 E8
Smooth Rock Falls Canada 49°17N 81°37W 298 C3
Smoothstone L. Canada 54°40N 106°50W 297 C7
Smorgon = Smarhon Belarus 54°20N 26°24E 177 A14
Smotrych Ukraine 48°57N 26°33E 183 B11
Smotrych → 48°34N 26°39E 183 B11
Smulţi Romania 45°57N 27°44E 183 E12
Smyadovo Bulgaria 43°2N 27°1E 203 C11
Smygehamn Sweden 55°21N 13°22E 163 J7
Smygehuk Sweden 55°20N 13°20E 163 J7
Smyrna = İzmir Turkey 38°25N 27°8E 205 C9
Smyrna Del., U.S.A. 39°18N 75°36W 309 F16
Smyrna Ga., U.S.A. 33°53N 84°31W 316 B5
Snæfell Iceland 64°48N 15°34W 155 C11
Snaefell I. of Man 54°16N 4°27W 168 C3
Snæfellsjökull Iceland 64°49N 23°46W 155 C3
Snæfellsnessýsla □ Iceland 65°0N 23°0W 155 C3
Snake → U.S.A. 46°12N 119°2W 304 C4
Snake Creek Canal U.S.A. 25°57N 80°19W 128 A2
Snake I. Australia 38°47S 146°33E 283 E7
Snake Pt. Anguilla 18°17N 62°58W 322 a
Snake Range U.S.A. 39°0N 114°20W 304 G6
Snake River Plain U.S.A. 42°50N 114°0W 304 E7
Snakeden Branch → U.S.A. 38°55N 77°18W 143 B1
Snarøya Norway 59°52N 10°33E 133 A2
Snasahögarna Sweden 63°13N 12°21E 162 A6
Snåsavatnet Norway 64°12N 12°0E 160 D15
Snättringe Sweden 59°15N 17°58E 139 B1
Snedsted Denmark 56°55N 8°32E 163 H2
Sneek Neths. 53°2N 5°40E 170 A5
Sneem Ireland 51°50N 9°54W 166 E2
Sneeuberge S. Africa 31°46S 24°20E 270 D3
Snegurovka = Tetiyev Ukraine 49°22N 29°38E 177 D15
Snejbjerg Denmark 56°8N 8°54E 163 H2
Snelling Calif., U.S.A. 37°31N 120°26W 306 H6
Snelling S.C., U.S.A. 33°15N 81°27W 316 B8
Snells Beach N.Z. 36°25S 174°44E 284 C3
Snezhnoye Ukraine 48°0N 38°58E 189 J10
Sněžka Europe 50°41N 15°50E 185 A8
Snežnik Slovenia 45°36N 14°35E 199 C11
Śniadowo Poland 53°2N 22°0E 185 E8
Sniardwy, Jezioro Poland 53°48N 21°50E 184 E8
Śnieżka Europe 50°44N 15°44E 180 A8
Snigirevka = Snihurivka Ukraine 47°2N 32°49E 189 J7
Snihurivka Ukraine 47°2N 32°49E 189 J7
Snillfjord Norway 63°24N 9°30E 164 A6
Snina Slovak Rep. 48°58N 22°9E 181 C15
Snizort, L. U.K. 57°33N 6°28W 167 D2
Snøhetta Norway 62°19N 9°16E 164 B6
Snohomish U.S.A. 47°55N 122°6W 306 C4
Snønuten Norway 59°31N 6°52E 164 E3
Snoqualmie Pass U.S.A. 47°25N 121°25W 306 C5
Snoul Cambodia 12°4N 106°26E 237 F6
Snover U.S.A. 43°27N 82°58W 312 C2
Snovsk = Shchors Ukraine 51°48N 31°56E 189 G6
Snow Hill U.S.A. 38°11N 75°24W 309 F16
Snow Lake Canada 54°52N 100°3W 297 C8
Snow Mt. Calif., U.S.A. 39°23N 122°45W 306 F4
Snow Mt. Maine, U.S.A. 45°18N 70°48W 313 A14
Snow Shoe U.S.A. 41°2N 77°57W 312 E7
Snowbird L. Canada 60°45N 103°0W 297 A8
Snowdon U.K. 53°4N 4°5W 168 D3
Snowdonia △ U.K. 53°7N 3°59W 168 D4
Snowdoun U.S.A. 32°15N 86°18W 316 C3
Snowdrift = Łutsel K'e Canada 62°24N 110°44W 297 A6
Snowdrift → Canada 62°24N 110°44W 297 A6
Snowflake U.S.A. 34°30N 110°5W 305 J8
Snowshoe Pk. U.S.A. 48°13N 115°41W 304 B6
Snowtown Australia 33°46S 138°14E 282 B3
Snowville U.S.A. 41°58N 112°43W 304 F7
Snowy → Australia 37°46S 148°30E 283 D8
Snowy Mt. U.S.A. 43°42N 74°23W 313 C10
Snowy Mts. Australia 36°30S 148°20E 283 D8
Snowy River △ Australia 37°15S 147°29E 283 D7
Snug Corner Bahamas 22°33N 73°52W 321 B5
Snug Harbour Canada 45°22N 80°17W 312 A4
Snyatyn Ukraine 48°27N 25°38E 183 B10
Snyder Okla., U.S.A. 34°40N 98°57W 314 D5
Snyder Tex., U.S.A. 32°44N 100°55W 314 E4
Soacha Colombia 4°35N 74°13W 328 C3
Soahanina Madag. 18°42S 44°13E 272 B1
Soalala Madag. 16°6S 45°20E 272 B2
Soaloka Madag. 18°32S 45°15E 272 B2
Soamanonga Madag. 23°52S 44°47E 272 C1
Soan → Pakistan 33°1N 71°44E 242 C4
Soanierana-Ivongo Madag. 16°55S 49°35E 272 B2
Soanindraniny Madag. 19°54S 47°14E 272 B2
Şoarş Romania 45°56N 24°55E 183 E9
Soavina Madag. 20°23S 46°56E 272 C2
Soavinandriana Madag. 19°9S 46°45E 272 B2
Soba Nigeria 10°58N 8°4E 263 C6
Sobaeksan △ S. Korea 36°50N 128°25E 224 D4
Sobat, Nahr → South Sudan 9°22N 31°33E 257 F3
Soběslav Czech Rep. 49°16N 14°45E 180 B7
Sobhapur India 22°47N 78°17E 242 H8
Sobinka Russia 56°0N 40°0E 188 E11
Sobo-Yama Japan 32°51N 131°22E 222 E3
Søborg Denmark 55°43N 12°29E 118 A2
Sobótka Poland 50°54N 16°44E 185 H3
Sobra Croatia 42°44N 17°34E 199 F14
Sobradinho, Represa de Brazil 9°30S 42°0W 332 C3
Sobral Brazil 3°50S 40°20W 332 B3
Sobrance Slovak Rep. 48°45N 22°11E 181 C15
Sobreda Portugal 38°39N 9°11W 126 B1
Sobreira Formosa Portugal 39°46N 7°51W 194 F3
Soc Giang Vietnam 22°54N 106°1E 228 F6
Soc Trang Vietnam 9°37N 105°50E 237 H5
Soča → Europe 46°20N 13°40E 180 E6
Socastee U.S.A. 33°41N 78°59W 315 E15
Soccsksargen □ Phil. 6°30N 125°0E 233 J5
Sochaczew Poland 52°15N 20°13E 185 F7
Soch'e = Shache China 38°20N 77°10E 217 E9
Sochi Russia 43°35N 39°40E 191 J4
Sochos Greece 40°48N 23°22E 202 F7
Social Circle U.S.A. 33°39N 83°43W 316 B6
Société, Îs. de la French Polynesia 17°0S 151°0W 289 f
Society Hill U.S.A. 32°26N 85°27W 316 C4
Society Is. = Société, Îs. de la French Polynesia 17°0S 151°0W 289 f
Socompa, Portezuelo de Chile 24°27S 68°18W 334 A2
Socorro = Fronteiras Brazil 7°5S 40°37W 332 C3
Socorro Colombia 6°29N 73°16W 328 B3
Socorro Phil. 9°37N 125°58E 233 G5
Socorro N. Mex., U.S.A. 34°4N 106°54W 305 J10
Socorro Tex., U.S.A. 31°39N 106°18W 314 F1
Socorro, I. Mexico 18°45N 110°58W 318 D2
Socotra Yemen 12°30N 54°0E 249 D6
Socovos Spain 38°20N 1°58W 197 G3
Socuéllamos Spain 39°16N 2°47W 197 F2
Soda L. U.S.A. 35°10N 116°4W 305 J5
Soda Plains India 35°30N 79°0E 243 B8
Soda Springs U.S.A. 42°39N 111°36W 304 E8
Sodankylä Finland 67°29N 26°40E 160 C22
Soddy-Daisy U.S.A. 35°17N 85°10W 315 D12
Söderala Sweden 61°17N 16°55E 162 C10
Söderåsen △ Sweden 56°2N 13°13E 163 H7
Söderbärke Sweden 60°5N 15°33E 162 D9
Söderby Sweden 59°24N 18°12E 139 A3
Söderfors Sweden 60°23N 17°25E 162 D11
Söderhamn Sweden 61°18N 17°10E 162 C11
Söderköping Sweden 58°31N 16°20E 163 F10
Södermalm Sweden 59°18N 18°4E 139 B2
Södermanland Sweden 58°56N 16°55E 161 G17
Södermanlands län □ Sweden 59°10N 16°30E 162 E10
Södertälje Sweden 59°12N 17°39E 162 E11
Sodiri Sudan 14°27N 29°0E 257 E2
Sodo Ethiopia 7°0N 37°41E 257 F4
Sodpur India 22°42N 88°24E 124 A2
Södra Finnskoga Sweden 60°42N 12°34E 162 D6
Södra Sandby Sweden 55°43N 13°21E 163 J7
Södra Ulvön Sweden 62°59N 18°38E 162 B12
Södra Vi Sweden 57°45N 15°45E 163 G9
Sodražica Slovenia 45°45N 14°39E 199 C11
Sodus U.S.A. 43°14N 77°4W 312 C7
Sodwana Bay △ S. Africa 27°35S 32°43E 271 C5
Soe Indonesia 9°52S 124°17E 278 A3
Soekmekaar = Morebeng S. Africa 23°30S 29°55E 271 B4
Soest Nordrhein-Westfalen, Germany 51°34N 8°7E 178 D4
Soest Neths. 52°9N 5°19E 170 B5
Soeurs, Î. des Canada 45°27N 73°32W 130 B2
Sofades Greece 39°20N 22°4E 204 B4
Sofaïa Guadeloupe 16°17N 61°43W 322 e
Sofala □ Mozam. 19°30S 34°30E 271 A5
Sofara Mali 13°59N 4°9W 262 C4
Sofia = Sofiya Bulgaria 42°45N 23°20E 202 D7
Sofia → Madag. 15°27S 47°23E 272 B2
Sofievka Ukraine 48°6N 33°55E 189 H7
Sofiko Greece 37°47N 23°3E 204 D5
Sofiya Bulgaria 42°45N 23°20E 202 D7
Sofiya □ Bulgaria 42°15N 23°20E 202 D7
Sofiya ✈ (SOF) Bulgaria 42°46N 23°28E 202 D7
Sofrana Greece 36°5N 26°24E 205 E8
Sōfu-Gan Japan 29°49N 140°21E 221 K10
Sogakofe Ghana 6°2N 0°39E 263 D5
Sogamoso Colombia 5°43N 72°56W 328 B3
Sogār Iran 25°53N 58°6E 247 E8
Sögel Germany 52°50N 7°31E 178 C3
Sogeri Papua N. G. 9°26S 147°35E 286 E4
Sogn og Fjordane □ Norway 61°40N 6°45E 164 C3
Sogndalsfjøra Norway 61°14N 7°5E 164 C4
Søgne Norway 58°5N 7°48E 164 F4
Sognefjorden Norway 61°10N 5°50E 164 C2
Sognsvatn Norway 59°58N 10°43E 133 A3
Sogod Phil. 10°28N 124°59E 233 F5
Söğüt Bilecik, Turkey 40°2N 30°11E 205 A12
Söğüt Burdur, Turkey 37°2N 29°50E 205 D11
Söğüt Dağı Turkey 37°50N 29°55E 205 D11
Söğütköy Turkey 36°40N 28°8E 205 E10
Soh Iran 33°26N 51°27E 247 C6
Sohâg Egypt 26°33N 31°43E 256 B3
Sohagpur India 22°42N 78°12E 242 H8
Sohano Papua N. G. 5°22S 154°37E 286 C8
Sohela India 21°18N 83°24E 244 D6
Soheuksando S. Korea 34°4N 125°7E 224 E2
Sohm Abyssal Plain Atl. Oc. 36°0N 55°0W 152 C6
Soho London, U.K. 125 b3
Soho New York, U.S.A. 132 e1
Sohoton △ Phil. 11°22N 125°6E 233 F5
Soignes, Forêt de Belgium 50°47N 4°25E 116 B2
Soignies Belgium 50°35N 4°5E 170 D4
Soin Burkina Faso 12°47N 3°50W 262 C4
Soira Eritrea 14°45N 39°30E 257 E4
Soissons France 49°25N 3°19E 173 C10
Sōja Japan 34°40N 133°45E 222 C5
Sojat India 25°55N 73°45E 242 G5
Sok → Russia 53°24N 50°8E 190 D10
Sok Kwu Wan China 22°12N 114°7E 122 B1
Sokal Ukraine 50°31N 24°15E 177 C13
Sokcho S. Korea 38°12N 128°36E 224 C4
Söke Turkey 37°48N 27°28E 205 D9
Sokelo Dem. Rep. of the Congo 9°55S 24°36E 265 D4
Sokhumi Georgia 43°0N 41°0E 191 J5
Sokki, Oued In → Algeria 29°30N 3°42E 261 C5
Sokna Norway 60°16N 9°58E 164 D6
Soknedal Norway 62°57N 10°13E 164 B7
Soko Banja Serbia 43°40N 21°51E 202 C5
Soko Is. China 22°10N 113°54E 219 a
Sokodé Togo 9°0N 1°11E 263 D5
Sokol Russia 59°30N 40°5E 188 C11
Sokolac Bos.-H. 43°56N 18°48E 182 G3
Sokółka Poland 53°25N 23°30E 184 E10
Sokolniki Russia 55°47N 37°40E 129 B4
Sokolniki Park Russia 55°48N 37°40E 129 B4
Sokolo Ségou, Mali 14°53N 6°8W 262 C3
Sokolo Sikasso, Mali 10°52N 6°59W 262 C3
Sokolov Czech Rep. 50°12N 12°40E 180 A5
Sokołów Poland 52°9N 20°51E 142 C1
Sokołów Małpolski Poland 50°12N 22°7E 185 H9
Sokołów Podlaski Poland 52°25N 22°15E 185 F9
Sokoły Poland 52°59N 22°42E 185 F9
Sokoto Nigeria 13°2N 5°16E 263 C6
Sokoto □ Nigeria 12°30N 6°0E 263 C6
Sokoto → Nigeria 11°20N 4°10E 263 C5
Sokyrnytsya Ukraine 48°7N 23°23E 183 B8
Sokyryany Ukraine 48°27N 27°25E 183 B12
Sol Iletsk Russia 51°10N 55°0E 186 D10
Sola Rogaland, Norway 58°53N 5°36E 164 F2
Sola Vanuatu 13°51S 167°33E 287 C5
Sola → Poland 50°4N 19°15E 185 H6
Solai Kenya 0°2N 36°12E 268 B4
Solalinden Germany 48°5N 11°42E 131 B3
Solan India 30°55N 77°7E 242 D7
Solana Phil. 17°39N 121°41E 232 C3
Solana Beach U.S.A. 32°58N 117°16W 307 N9
Solander I. N.Z. 46°34S 166°54E 285 G1
Solano Phil. 16°31N 121°15E 232 C3
Solapur India 17°43N 75°56E 244 F2
Solca Romania 47°40N 25°50E 183 C10
Solda Gölü Turkey 37°33N 29°42E 205 D11
Soldăneşti Moldova 47°49N 28°48E 183 C13
Soldeu Andorra 42°35N 1°40E 196 C6
Soldier Field Chicago, U.S.A. 119 e3
Soldier Pt. Antigua & B. 17°2N 61°41W 322 b
Soldin = Myślibórz Poland 52°55N 14°50E 185 F1
Soldotna U.S.A. 60°29N 151°3W 303 F10
Soléa Cyprus 35°5N 33°4E 207 E9
Solec Kujawski Poland 53°5N 18°14E 185 E5
Soledad Colombia 10°55N 74°46W 328 A3
Soledad Calif., U.S.A. 36°26N 121°20W 306 J5
Soledad Venezuela 8°10N 63°34W 329 B5
Sølen Norway 61°53N 11°31E 164 C8
Solent, The U.K. 50°45N 1°25W 169 G6
Solenzara France 41°53N 9°23E 175 G13
Solesmes France 50°10N 3°30E 173 B10
Solfonntaggen Norway 60°2N 6°57E 164 D3
Solhan Turkey 38°57N 41°3E 213 C9
Solheim Norway 60°53N 5°27E 164 D2
Soligalich Russia 59°5N 42°10E 186 C7
Soligorsk = Salihorsk Belarus 52°51N 27°27E 177 B14
Solihull U.K. 52°26N 1°47W 169 E6
Solikamsk Russia 59°38N 56°50E 186 C10
Solila Madag. 21°25S 46°37E 272 C2
Solimões = Amazonas → S. Amer. 0°5S 50°0W 329 D8
Solin Croatia 43°33N 16°30E 199 E13
Solingen Germany 51°10N 7°5E 178 D3
Söll Austria 47°30N 12°11E 179 H8
Sollebrunn Sweden 58°8N 12°32E 163 F6
Sollefteå Sweden 63°12N 17°20E 162 A11
Sollentuna Sweden 59°25N 17°56E 139 A1
Sóller Spain 39°46N 2°43E 206 B3
Sollerön Sweden 60°55N 14°37E 162 D8
Solling Germany 51°42N 9°38E 178 D5
Solling-Vogler ⌓ Germany 51°45N 9°32E 178 D5
Solln Germany 48°4N 11°31E 131 B2
Sollsvika Norway 60°26N 4°58E 164 D1
Solna Sweden 59°21N 17°59E 139 A1
Solnechnogorsk Russia 56°10N 36°57E 188 D9
Solntsevo Russia 55°39N 37°24E 129 C2
Solo → Indonesia 6°47S 112°22E 231 G15
Solofra Italy 40°50N 14°51E 201 B7
Sologne France 47°40N 1°45E 173 E8
Solok Indonesia 0°45S 100°40E 234 C2
Sololá Guatemala 14°49N 91°10W 320 D1
Sololo Kenya 3°33N 38°39E 268 B4
Solomon, N. Fork → U.S.A. 39°29N 98°26W 308 F4
Solomon, S. Fork → U.S.A. 39°25N 99°12W 308 F4
Solomon Is. Papua N. G. 6°0S 155°0E 286 D8
Solomon Is. ■ Pac. Oc. 6°0S 155°0E 287 L8
Solomon Rise Pac. Oc. 1°0N 157°0E 288 G7
Solomon Sea Papua N. G. 7°0S 150°0E 286 D6
Solon China 46°32N 121°10E 219 B13
Solon Springs U.S.A. 46°22N 91°49W 308 B8
Solonópole Brazil 5°44S 39°1W 332 C4
Solor Indonesia 8°27S 123°0E 231 F6
Solotcha Russia 54°48N 39°53E 188 E10
Solothurn Switz. 47°13N 7°32E 179 H3
Solothurn □ Switz. 47°18N 7°40E 179 H3
Solotvyn Ukraine 48°42N 24°25E 183 B9
Solsona Phil. 18°5N 120°46E 232 B3
Solsona Spain 42°0N 1°31E 196 C6
Solt Hungary 46°45N 19°1E 182 D4
Šolta Croatia 43°24N 16°15E 199 E13
Solţānābād Khorāsān, Iran 34°13N 59°58E 247 C8
Solţānābād Khorāsān, Iran 36°29N 58°5E 247 B8
Soltau Germany 52°59N 9°50E 178 C5
Soltsy Russia 58°10N 30°30E 188 C6
Soltüstik Qazaqstan □ Kazakhstan 54°0N 70°0E 217 B8
Solund Norway 61°5N 4°50E 164 C1
Solunska Glava Macedonia 41°44N 21°31E 202 E5
Solvang U.S.A. 34°36N 120°8W 307 L6
Solvay U.S.A. 43°3N 76°13W 313 C8
Sölvesborg Sweden 56°5N 14°35E 163 H8
Solvychegodsk Russia 61°21N 46°56E 186 B8
Solway Firth U.K. 54°49N 3°35W 168 C4
Solwezi Zambia 12°11S 26°21E 269 E2
Sōma Japan 37°40N 140°50E 220 F10
Soma Turkey 39°10N 27°35E 205 B9
Somabhula Zimbabwe 19°42S 29°40E 271 A4
Somali = Sumale □ Ethiopia 7°0N 45°0E 267 C6
Somali Pen. Africa 7°0N 46°0E 254 F8
Somali Rep. ■ Africa 7°0N 47°0E 267 C6
Somalia = Somali Rep. ■ Africa 7°0N 47°0E 267 C6
Somaliland □ Somali Rep. 9°0N 46°0E 267 C6
Sombe Dzong Bhutan 27°13N 89°8E 241 B2
Sombernon France 47°20N 4°40E 173 E11
Sombo Angola 8°42S 20°59E 265 D4
Sombor Serbia 45°46N 19°9E 182 E4
Sombra Canada 42°43N 82°29W 312 D2
Sombrerete Mexico 23°38N 103°39W 318 C4
Sombrero Anguilla 18°37N 63°30W 321 C7
Sombrero Channel India 7°41N 93°35E 245 L11
Şomcuta Mare Romania 47°31N 23°28E 183 C8
Somdari India 25°47N 72°38E 242 G5
Someido ⌓ Spain 43°5N 6°11W 194 B4
Somers U.S.A. 48°5N 114°13W 304 B6
Somerset Bermuda 32°17N 64°52W 153 a
Somerset Ky., U.S.A. 37°5N 84°36W 309 G11
Somerset Mass., U.S.A. 41°47N 71°8W 313 E13
Somerset Md., U.S.A. 38°57N 77°5W 143 B3
Somerset Pa., U.S.A. 40°1N 79°5W 312 F5
Somerset □ U.K. 51°9N 3°0W 169 F5
Somerset East S. Africa 32°42S 25°35E 270 D4
Somerset I. Bermuda 32°17N 64°52W 153 a
Somerset I. Nunavut, Canada 73°30N 93°0W 294 C13
Somerset West S. Africa 34°8S 18°50E 270 D2
Somersworth U.S.A. 43°16N 70°52W 313 C14
Somerton U.S.A. 32°36N 114°43W 305 K6
Somerville Mass., U.S.A. 42°22N 71°5W 116 A2
Somerville N.J., U.S.A. 40°35N 74°38W 313 F10
Someş → Romania 47°49N 22°43E 182 C7
Somes I. N.Z. 41°15S 174°52E 143 B2
Someşul Mare → Romania 47°9N 23°55E 183 C8
Somme □ France 49°57N 2°20E 173 C9
Somme → France 50°11N 1°38E 173 B8
Somme, B. de la France 50°14N 1°33E 172 B8
Sommen Jönköping, Sweden 58°12N 14°58E 163 F8
Sommen Östergötland, Sweden 58°0N 15°15E 163 F9
Sommepy-Tahure France 49°15N 4°31E 173 C11
Sömmerda Germany 51°9N 11°7E 178 D7
Sommerfeld = Lubsko Poland 51°45N 14°57E 185 G1
Sommesous France 48°44N 4°12E 173 D11
Sommières France 43°47N 4°6E 175 E8
Somnath India 20°53N 70°22E 242 J4
Somogy □ Hungary 46°19N 17°30E 182 D2
Somogyszob Hungary 46°18N 17°20E 182 D2
Somosomo Fiji 16°47S 179°58W 287 A3
Somosomo Str. Fiji 16°0S 180°0E 287 A3
Somoto Nic. 13°28N 86°37W 320 D2
Sompolno Poland 52°26N 18°30E 185 F5
Somport, Tunnel de Spain 42°48N 0°31W 196 C4
Somuncurá, Meseta de Argentina 41°30S 67°0W 336 B3
Somvarpet India 12°36N 75°52E 245 H2
Son Norway 59°32N 10°42E 164 E7
Son → India 25°42N 84°52E 243 G11
Son Ha Vietnam 15°3N 108°34E 236 E7
Son La Vietnam 21°20N 103°50E 228 G4
Son Morrell Spain 39°44N 3°20E 206 B4
Son Rapinya Spain 39°35N 2°37E 206 B3
Son Sardina Spain 39°37N 2°40E 206 B3
Son Serra Spain 39°43N 3°13E 206 B4
Son Servera Spain 39°37N 3°21E 206 B4
Son Tay Vietnam 21°8N 105°30E 228 G5
Son Tinh Vietnam 15°10N 108°40E 236 E7
Soná Panama 8°0N 81°20W 320 E3
Sonamarg India 34°18N 75°21E 243 B6
Sonamukhi India 23°18N 87°27E 243 H12
Sonamura India 23°29N 91°15E 241 D3
Sonar → India 24°24N 79°56E 243 G8
Sonari India 18°54N 72°59E 130 B2
Sŏnch'ŏn N. Korea 39°48N 124°55E 224 C2
Sondags → S. Africa 33°44S 25°51E 270 D4
Sóndalo Italy 46°20N 10°19E 198 B7
Søndeled Norway 58°46N 9°3E 164 F6
Sønder Felding Denmark 55°57N 8°47E 163 J2
Sønder Omme Denmark 55°50N 8°54E 163 J2
Sønderborg Denmark 54°55N 9°49E 163 K3
Sondershausen Germany 51°22N 10°51E 178 D6
Søndersø Denmark 55°46N 12°21E 118 A2
Søndre Bergenhaus = Hordaland □ Norway 60°25N 6°15E 164 D3
Søndre Strømfjord = Kangerlussuaq Greenland 66°59N 50°40W 154 D5

Søndre Trøndhjem =
Sør-Trøndelag □ Norway 63°0N 11°0E 164 A7
Søndrio Italy 46°10N 9°52E 198 B6
Sondur → India 20°40N 82°1E 244 D6
Sone Mozam. 17°23S 34°55E 269 F3
Sonepur India 20°55N 83°50E 244 D6
Sonfim Brazil 6°0S 67°52W 330 B4
Song Nigeria 9°49N 12°39E 263 D7
Song Thailand 18°28N 100°11E 236 C3
Song Cau Vietnam 13°27N 109°18E 236 F7
Song-Köl Kyrgyzstan 41°50N 75°12E 217 D9
Song Ma Vietnam 20°56N 103°53E 228 G4
Song Qingling, Former Residence of
Beijing, China 114 a2
Song Xian China 34°12N 112°8E 226 G7
Songadh India 21°9N 73°33E 244 D1
Songan Indonesia 8°13S 115°24E 231 J18
Songavatnet Norway 59°52N 7°32E 164 E4
Songea Tanzania 10°40S 35°40E 269 E4
Songeons France 49°32N 1°50E 173 C8
Sŏnggan N. Korea 40°47N 126°34E 224 B3
Sŏnggang China 22°46N 113°50E 219 a
Songhua Hu China 43°35N 126°50E 227 C14
Songhua Jiang →
China 47°45N 132°30E 219 B15
Songimvelo △ S. Africa 25°50S 31°2E 271 C5
Songjiang Jilin, China 42°34N 128°20E 224 A4
Songjiang Shanghai,
China 31°1N 121°12E 229 B13
Songjianghe China 42°10N 127°29E 224 A3
Sŏngjin = Kimch'aek
N. Korea 40°40N 129°10E 224 B4
Songkan China 28°35N 106°52E 228 C6
Songkhla Thailand 7°13N 100°37E 237 J3
Songming China 25°12N 103°2E 228 E4
Songnim N. Korea 38°45N 125°39E 224 C2
Songnisan △ S. Korea 36°28N 127°45E 224 D3
Songo Angola 7°22S 14°51E 265 D2
Songo Mozam. 15°34S 32°38E 271 A5
Songololo = Mbanza Ngungu
Dem. Rep. of the Congo 5°12S 14°53E 265 D2
Songololo
Dem. Rep. of the Congo 5°42S 14°2E 265 D2
Songpa S. Korea 37°30N 127°7E 137 B2
Songpan China 32°40N 103°30E 228 A4
Songtao China 28°11N 109°10E 228 C7
Songwe
Dem. Rep. of the Congo 3°20S 26°16E 268 C2
Songwe → Africa 9°44S 33°58E 269 D3
Songxi China 27°31N 118°44E 229 D12
Songzi China 30°12N 111°45E 229 B8
Sonhat India 23°29N 82°31E 243 H10
Sonid Youqi China 42°45N 112°48E 226 C7
Sonid Zuoqi China 43°50N 113°42E 226 C7
Sonipat India 29°0N 77°5E 242 E7
Sonkach India 22°59N 76°21E 242 H7
Sonkovo Russia 57°50N 37°5E 188 D9
Sonmiani Pakistan 25°25N 66°40E 242 G2
Sonmiani B. Pakistan 25°15N 66°30E 242 G2
Sonnino Italy 41°25N 13°14E 200 A6
Sono → Minas Gerais,
Brazil 17°2S 45°32W 333 E2
Sono → Tocantins, Brazil 9°58S 48°11W 332 C2
Sonobe Japan 35°6N 135°28E 223 B7
Sonoma U.S.A. 38°18N 122°28W 306 G4
Sonora Calif., U.S.A. 37°59N 120°23W 306 H6
Sonora Tex., U.S.A. 30°34N 100°39W 314 F4
Sonora □ Mexico 29°20N 110°40W 318 B2
Sonora → Mexico 29°5N 110°55W 318 B2
Sonoran Desert U.S.A. 33°40N 113°30W 307 L12
Sonoyta Mexico 31°51N 112°50W 318 A2
Sonqor Iran 34°47N 47°36E 213 E12
Sonseca Spain 39°42N 3°57W 195 F7
Sonsón Colombia 5°43N 75°18W 328 B2
Sonsonate El Salv. 13°43N 89°44W 320 D2
Sonstorp Sweden 58°44N 15°38E 163 F9
Sonthofen Germany 47°30N 10°16E 179 H6
Sony Picture Studio
U.S.A. 34°1N 118°4W 126 B2
Soochow = Suzhou
China 31°19N 120°38E 229 B13
Sooke Canada 48°13N 123°43W 306 B3
Sool □ Somali Rep. 8°40N 47°30E 267 C6
Soomaaliya = Somali Rep. ■
Africa 7°0N 47°0E 267 C6
Sop Hao Laos 20°33N 104°27E 228 G5
Sop Prap Thailand 17°53N 99°20E 236 D2
Sopachuy Bolivia 19°29S 64°31W 331 D5
Sopchoppy U.S.A. 30°4N 84°29W 316 E5
Sopelana Spain 43°23N 2°58W 196 B2
Soperton U.S.A. 32°23N 82°35W 316 C7
Sopi Indonesia 2°34N 128°28E 231 D7
Sopo, Nahr → South Sudan 8°40N 26°30E 257 F2
Sopot Bulgaria 42°39N 24°45E 203 D8
Sopot Poland 54°27N 18°31E 184 D5
Sopot Serbia 44°29N 20°36E 202 B4
Sopotnica Macedonia 41°18N 21°13E 202 E5
Sopron Hungary 47°45N 16°32E 182 C1
Sopur India 34°18N 74°27E 243 B6
Sør-Rondane Antarctica 72°0S 25°0E 151 D4
Sør-Trøndelag □ Norway 63°0N 11°0E 164 A7
Sora Italy 41°43N 13°37E 199 G10
Sorab India 14°23N 75°6E 245 G2
Sorada India 19°45N 84°26E 244 E7
Sorah Pakistan 27°13N 68°56E 242 F3
Soråker Sweden 62°30N 17°32E 162 B11
Sorang Kazakhstan 49°46N 72°51E 217 C8
Sorano Italy 42°41N 11°43E 199 F8
Soraon India 25°37N 81°51E 243 G9
Sorata Bolivia 15°50S 68°40W 330 D4
Sorbas Spain 37°6N 2°7W 197 H2
Sörbygden Sweden 62°48N 16°12E 162 B10
Sord = Swords Ireland 53°28N 6°13W 120 A2
Sordellen Sweden 61°48N 16°43E 162 C10
Sore France 44°18N 0°35W 174 D3
Sore Osa → Norway 61°18N 11°46E 164 C8
Sorel-Tracy Canada 46°0N 73°10W 298 C5
Soresina Italy 45°17N 9°51E 198 C6
Sørfjorden Norway 60°20N 6°37E 164 D3
Sörforsa Sweden 61°43N 16°58E 162 C10
Sórgono Italy 40°1N 9°6E 200 B2
Sorgues France 44°1N 4°53E 175 D8
Sorgun Turkey 39°46N 35°11E 212 C6
Sorgun → Turkey 36°36N 34°20E 250 B5
Sori Papua N. G. 1°58S 146°42E 286 A4
Soria Spain 41°43N 2°32W 196 D2
Soria □ Spain 41°46N 2°28W 196 D2
Soriano Uruguay 33°24S 58°19W 334 C4
Soriano nel Cimino Italy 42°25N 12°14E 199 F9
Sorkh, Kuh-e Iran 35°40N 58°30E 247 C8
Sorø Denmark 55°26N 11°32E 163 J5
Soro Guinea 10°9N 9°48W 262 C3
Soroca Moldova 48°8N 28°12E 183 B13
Sorocaba Brazil 23°31S 47°27W 335 A6
Sorochinsk Russia 52°26N 53°10E 186 D9
Soroka = Belomorsk
Russia 64°35N 34°54E 186 B5
Soroki = Soroca Moldova 48°8N 28°12E 183 B13
Sorokino = Krasnodon
Ukraine 48°17N 39°44E 189 H10
Soroksár Hungary 47°24N 19°7E 117 B2
Soroksari Duna →
Hungary 47°25N 19°5E 117 B2
Sorong Indonesia 0°55S 131°15E 231 E8
Soroni Greece 36°21N 28°1E 206 E12
Soroti Uganda 1°43N 33°35E 266 B3
Sørøya Norway 70°40N 22°30E 160 A20
Sørøyane Norway 62°25N 5°32E 164 B2
Sørøysundet Norway 70°25N 23°0E 160 A20
Sorraia → Portugal 38°55N 8°53W 195 G2
Sorrell Australia 42°47S 147°34E 281 G4
Sorrento Italy 40°37N 14°22E 201 B7
Sorsele Sweden 65°31N 17°30E 160 D17
Sörsjön Sweden 61°24N 13°5E 162 C7
Sorso Italy 40°48N 8°34E 200 B1
Sorsogon Phil. 13°0N 124°0E 232 E5
Sorsogon □ Phil. 12°50N 123°55E 232 E4
Sortavala Russia 61°42N 30°41E 188 B6
Sortino Italy 37°9N 15°2E 201 E8
Sortland Norway 68°42N 15°25E 160 B16
Sortot Sudan 19°30N 30°28E 256 D3
Sørum Norway 60°30N 10°17E 164 D7
Sorvizhi Russia 57°52N 48°32E 190 B9
Sos del Rey Católico Spain 42°30N 1°13W 196 C3
Soscumica, L. Canada 50°15N 77°27W 298 B4
Sösdala Sweden 56°2N 13°41E 163 H7
Sosenka → Russia 55°46N 37°42E 129 B4
Sosna → Russia 52°42N 38°55E 189 F10
Sosnogorsk Russia 63°37N 53°51E 186 B9
Sosnovka Kirov, Russia 56°17N 51°17E 190 B10
Sosnovka St. Petersburg,
Russia 60°0N 30°22E 137 B2
Sosnovka Tambov, Russia 53°13N 41°24E 190 D5
Sosnovyy Bor Russia 59°55N 29°6E 188 C5
Sosnowiec Poland 50°20N 19°10E 185 H6
Sosnowitz = Sosnowiec
Poland 50°20N 19°10E 185 H6
Soso C.A.R. 3°55N 15°30E 264 B3
Sospel France 43°52N 7°27E 175 E11
Sossus Vlei Namibia 24°40S 15°23E 270 B2
Šoštanj Slovenia 46°23N 15°4E 199 B12
Sŏsura N. Korea 42°16N 130°36E 224 A5
Sot → India 27°27N 79°37E 243 F8
Sotasæter Norway 61°49N 7°43E 164 C4
Sotavento C. Verde Is. 15°0N 25°0W 153 j
Sotik Kenya 0°41S 35°7E 268 C4
Sotkamo Finland 64°8N 28°23E 160 D23
Soto Curaçao 12°16N 69°6W 322 g
Soto del Barco Spain 43°32N 6°4W 194 B4
Soto la Marina Mexico 23°46N 98°13W 319 C5
Soto la Marina →
Mexico 23°45N 97°45W 319 C5
Soto y Amío Spain 42°46N 5°53W 194 C5
Sotouboua Togo 8°34N 0°59E 263 D5
Sotrondio Spain 43°17N 5°36W 194 B5
Sotuf, Adrar W. Sahara 21°42N 15°36W 260 D1
Sotuta Mexico 20°36N 89°1W 319 C7
Souanké Congo 2°10N 14°3E 264 B2
Soubré Ivory C. 5°50N 6°35W 262 D3
Souda Greece 35°29N 24°4E 207 E5
Soudas, Ormos Greece 35°25N 24°10E 207 E5
Souderton U.S.A. 40°19N 75°19W 313 F9
Soufflay Congo 2°1N 14°54E 264 B2
Soufli Greece 41°12N 26°18E 203 E10
Soufrière Dominica 15°13N 61°22W 323 k
Soufrière Guadeloupe 16°5N 61°40W 322 e
Soufrière St. Lucia 13°51N 61°3W 323 m
Soufrière Bay Dominica 15°13N 61°22W 323 k
Soufrière Bay St. Lucia 13°51N 61°4W 323 m
Soufrière Hills Volcano
Montserrat 16°43N 62°10W 323 p
Souillac Lot, France 44°53N 1°29E 174 D5
Souillac Mauritius 20°31S 57°31E 272 e
Souilly France 49°3N 5°17E 173 C12
Souk-Ahras Algeria 36°23N 7°57E 261 A6
Souk-Ahras □ Algeria 36°10N 7°55E 261 A6
Souk el Arba du Rharb
Morocco 34°43N 5°59W 260 B3
Soukhouma Laos 14°38N 105°48E 236 E5
Sŏul = Seoul S. Korea 37°31N 126°58E 137 B2
Soulac-sur-Mer France 45°30N 1°7W 174 C2
Soulougou Burkina Faso 13°1N 0°25E 263 C5
Soultz-sous-Forêts France 48°57N 7°52E 173 D14
Sound, The = Øresund
Europe 55°45N 12°40E 163 J6
Sound, The U.K. 50°20N 4°10W 169 G3
Sound I. India 12°58N 92°59E 245 H11
Soundview U.S.A. 40°49N 73°53W 132 B2
Sounio, Akra Greece 37°37N 24°1E 204 D6
Sour el Ghozlane Algeria 36°10N 3°45E 261 A5
Sources, Mt. aux Lesotho 28°45S 28°50E 271 C4
Soure Brazil 0°35S 48°30W 332 B2
Soure Portugal 40°4N 8°38W 194 E2
Souris Man., Canada 49°40N 100°20W 297 D8
Souris P.E.I., Canada 46°21N 62°15W 299 C7
Souris → N. Amer. 49°40N 99°34W 308 A4
Sourou → Africa 12°45N 3°25W 262 C4
Sourpi Greece 39°6N 22°54E 204 B4
Sous, O. → Morocco 30°27N 9°31W 260 B3
Sous le Vent, Is.
French Polynesia 16°30S 155°30W 289 f
Sous le Vent, Région
Réunion 21°12S 55°20E 272 f
Sous-Massa △ Morocco 31°26N 9°35W 260 B3
Sousa Brazil 6°45S 38°10W 332 C4
Sousel Brazil 2°38S 52°29W 332 B1
Sousel Portugal 38°57N 7°40W 195 G3
Sousse Tunisia 35°50N 10°38E 258 A2
Sousse □ Tunisia 35°40N 10°30E 261 A7
Soustons France 43°45N 1°19W 174 E2
Sout → S. Africa 31°35S 18°24E 270 D2
South Africa ■ Africa 32°0S 23°0E 270 D3
South America 10°0S 60°0W 326 E5
South Andaman India 11°45N 92°10E 245 J11
South Aulatsivik I.
Canada 56°45N 61°30W 299 A7
South Australia □
Australia 32°0S 139°0E 282 B3
South Australian Basin
Ind. Oc. 38°0S 126°0E 288 L4
South Ayrshire □ U.K. 55°18N 4°41W 167 F4
South Baldy Pk. U.S.A. 34°6N 107°11W 305 J10
South Bass I. U.S.A. 41°39N 82°49W 312 E2
South Bay U.S.A. 26°40N 80°43W 317 J9
South Beach Bahamas 25°1N 77°20W 153 b
South Beach N.Y., U.S.A. 40°35N 74°4W 132 C1
South Beach Harbor
San Francisco, U.S.A. 136 c3
South Beloit U.S.A. 42°29N 89°2W 310 B7
South Bend Ind., U.S.A. 41°41N 86°15W 311 C10
South Bend Wash.,
U.S.A. 46°40N 123°48W 306 D3
South Bend Park U.S.A. 33°42N 84°23W 113 B2
South Boston Mass., U.S.A. 42°20N 71°2W 116 A2
South Boston Va., U.S.A. 36°42N 78°54W 309 G14
South Branch Canada 47°55N 59°2W 299 C8
South Branch Chicago River →
Chicago, U.S.A. 119 d1
South Brook Canada 49°26N 56°5W 299 C8
South Brother I. India 10°56N 92°37E 245 J11
South Bruny I. Australia 43°20S 147°15E 281 G4
South C. = Kalae U.S.A. 18°55N 155°41W 302 E6
South Carolina □ U.S.A. 34°0N 81°0W 315 E14
South Channel Phil. 14°18N 120°37E 232 D3
South Charleston U.S.A. 38°22N 81°44W 309 F13
South China Sea Asia 10°0N 113°0E 230 C4
South Comino Channel
Malta 36°0N 14°20E 206 F7
South Congaree U.S.A. 33°53N 81°9W 316 B8
South Cotabato □ Phil. 6°0N 125°0E 233 J5
South Cumberland Is. △
Australia 20°42S 149°11E 280 b
South Dakota □ U.S.A. 44°15N 100°0W 308 C4
South Dayton U.S.A. 42°21N 79°3W 312 D5
South Daytona U.S.A. 29°10N 81°0W 317 F8
South Decatur U.S.A. 33°44N 84°16W 113 B3
South Deerfield U.S.A. 42°29N 72°37W 313 D12
South Deering U.S.A. 41°42N 87°33W 119 C3
South Downs U.K. 50°52N 0°25W 169 G7
South Downs △ U.K. 50°50N 0°50W 169 G7
South East B. Ascension I. 7°57S 14°18W 153 g
South East C. Australia 43°40S 146°50E 281 G4
South East Forest △
Australia 37°0S 149°30E 283 D8
South East Is. Australia 34°17S 123°30E 279 F3
South El Monte U.S.A. 34°3N 118°2W 126 B4
South Elgin U.S.A. 42°0N 88°18W 311 C8
South Esk → U.K. 56°43N 2°31W 167 E6
South Fiji Basin Pac. Oc. 26°0S 175°0E 288 K9
South Foreland U.K. 51°8N 1°24E 169 F9
South Fork American →
U.S.A. 38°57N 120°59W 306 G5
South Fork Edisto →
U.S.A. 33°16N 80°54W 316 B9
South Fork Feather →
U.S.A. 39°17N 121°36W 306 F5
South Fork Grand →
U.S.A. 45°43N 102°17W 308 C2
South Fork Licking →
U.S.A. 38°40N 84°18W 311 F12
South Fork Milk →
U.S.A. 48°4N 106°19W 304 B10
South Fork Republican →
U.S.A. 40°3N 101°31W 308 E3
South Gate U.S.A. 33°56N 118°12W 126 C3
South Georgia Antarctica 54°30S 37°0W 151 B1
South Gloucestershire □
U.K. 51°32N 2°28W 169 F5
South Grand → U.S.A. 38°17N 93°25W 310 F3
South Hadley U.S.A. 42°16N 72°35W 313 D12
South Harbor Phil. 14°34N 120°58E 127 B1
South Harrow U.K. 51°33N 0°21W 125 A1
South Haven U.S.A. 42°24N 86°16W 311 B10
South Hd. Australia 33°50S 151°16E 139 B2
South Henik L. Canada 61°30N 97°20W 297 A9
South Hill Village Anguilla 18°11N 63°5W 322 a
South Hills S. Africa 26°14S 28°5E 123 B2
South Horr Kenya 2°12N 36°56E 268 B4
South I. India 10°3N 72°17E 245 J1
South I. Eastern, Kenya 2°35N 36°35E 268 B4
South I. N.Z. 44°0S 170°0E 285 E5
South Indian Lake
Canada 56°47N 98°56W 297 B9
South Invercargill N.Z. 46°26S 168°23E 285 G3
South Island △ Kenya 2°39N 36°35E 268 B4
South Kensington London, U.K. 125 c2
South Kitui △ Kenya 1°48S 38°46E 268 C4
South Knife → Canada 58°55N 94°37W 297 B10
South Koel → India 22°32N 85°14E 243 H11
South Korea ■ Asia 36°0N 128°0E 227 G15
South Lake Tahoe
U.S.A. 38°57N 119°59W 306 G6
South Lanarkshire □ U.K. 55°37N 3°53W 167 F5
South Lawn U.S.A. 38°47N 77°0W 143 C3
South Loop Chicago, U.S.A. 119 f2
South Loup → U.S.A. 41°4N 98°39W 308 E4
South Luangwa △ Zambia 13°0S 31°20E 269 E3
South Lyon U.S.A. 42°28N 83°39W 311 B13
South Magnetic Pole
Antarctica 64°8S 138°8E 151 C9
South Malé Atoll Maldives 4°0N 73°25E 272 d
South Malosmadulu Atoll
Maldives 5°12N 73°0E 272 d
South Miami U.S.A. 25°42N 80°17W 128 B1
South Milwaukee U.S.A. 42°55N 87°52W 311 B9
South Molton U.K. 51°1N 3°51W 169 F4
South Monroe U.S.A. 41°54N 83°26W 311 C13
South Moose L. Canada 53°49N 100°1W 297 C8
South Nahanni →
Canada 61°3N 123°21W 296 A4
South Nation → Canada 45°34N 75°6W 313 A9
South Natuna Is. = Natuna Selatan,
Kepulauan Indonesia 2°45N 109°0E 235 B3
South Negril Pt. Jamaica 18°16N 78°22W 320 a
South New Hebrides Trench
Pac. Oc. 22°30S 170°0E 277 E13
South Newport U.S.A. 31°38N 81°24W 316 D8
South Nilandu Atoll
Maldives 2°52N 72°57E 272 d
South Norwood U.K. 51°23N 0°3W 125 B3
South of Market San Francisco, U.S.A. 136 c2
South Orkney Is.
Antarctica 63°0S 45°0W 151 C18
South Ossetia □ Georgia 42°21N 44°2E 191 J7
South Otselic U.S.A. 42°38N 75°46W 313 D9
South Ozone Park U.S.A. 40°41N 73°49W 132 B3
South Pagai, I. = Pagai Selatan,
Pulau Indonesia 3°0S 100°15E 234 C2
South Paris U.S.A. 44°14N 70°31W 313 B14
South Pasadena U.S.A. 34°7N 118°9W 126 B3
South Pekin U.S.A. 40°30N 89°39W 310 D7
South Pittsburg U.S.A. 35°1N 85°42W 315 D12
South Platte → U.S.A. 41°7N 100°42W 308 E3
South Pole Antarctica 90°0S 0°0 151 E
South Ponte Vedra Beach
U.S.A. 30°3N 81°20W 316 E8
South Porcupine Canada 48°30N 81°12W 298 C3
South Portland U.S.A. 43°38N 70°15W 309 D18
South Pt. Ascension I. 8°0S 14°24W 153 g
South Pt. Barbados 13°2N 59°32W 323 r
South Pt. Mich., U.S.A. 44°52N 83°19W 312 B1
South Res. U.S.A. 42°26N 71°6W 116 A2
South River Ont., Canada 45°52N 79°23W 298 C4
South River N.J., U.S.A. 40°27N 74°23W 313 F10
South Ronaldsay U.K. 58°48N 2°58W 167 C6
South Ruislip U.K. 51°33N 0°24W 125 A1
South Rukuru Malaysia 10°44S 34°14E 269 E3
South San Francisco
U.S.A. 37°38N 122°26W 136 C2
South San Gabriel U.S.A. 34°3N 118°6W 126 B4
South Sandwich Is.
Antarctica 57°0S 27°0W 151 B1
South Sandwich Trench
Atl. Oc. 56°0S 24°0W 151 B1
South Saskatchewan →
Canada 53°15N 105°5W 297 C7
South Seal → Canada 58°48N 98°8W 297 B9
South Sentinel I. India 10°59N 92°14E 245 J11
South Shetland Is.
Antarctica 62°0S 59°0W 151 C18
South Shields U.K. 55°0N 1°25W 168 C6
South Shore U.S.A. 41°45N 87°34W 119 C3
South Sioux City U.S.A. 42°28N 96°24W 308 D5
South Sister U.S.A. 44°4N 121°51W 304 D3
South Solomon Trench
Pac. Oc. 11°0S 164°30E 277 C11
South Soufrière Hills
Montserrat 16°41N 62°10W 323 p
South Street Boston, U.S.A. 116 c2
South Sudan ■ Africa 8°0N 30°0E 257 F2
South Talpatti = New Moore I.
Ind. Oc. 21°37N 89°10E 241 E2
South Taranaki Bight
N.Z. 39°40S 174°5E 284 F3
South Tasman Rise
S. Ocean 48°0S 146°0E 151 A10
South Thompson →
Canada 50°40N 120°20W 296 C4
South Twin I. Canada 53°7N 79°52W 298 B4
South Tyne → U.K. 54°59N 2°8W 168 C5
South Ubian Phil. 5°11N 120°30E 233 J3
South Uist U.K. 57°20N 7°15W 167 D1
South Valley U.S.A. 35°1N 106°41W 305 J10
South Venice U.S.A. 27°3N 82°25W 317 H7
South Verde I. Phil. 10°4N 119°13E 233 F2
South Wayne U.S.A. 42°34N 89°53W 310 B7
South Wellesley Is.
Australia 16°58S 139°17E 280 B2
South West Africa = Namibia ■
Africa 22°0S 18°9E 270 B2
South West B. Ascension I. 7°58S 14°25W 153 g
South West B. Bahamas 25°0N 77°32W 153 b
South West C. Tas.,
Australia 43°34S 146°3E 281 G4
South West C. N.Z. 47°17S 167°28E 285 H2
South West Pt.
Papua N. G. 2°14S 146°34E 286 B4
South West Pt. St. Helena 15°59S 5°48W 153 h
South West Rocks
Australia 30°52S 153°3E 283 A10
South Whitley U.S.A. 41°5N 85°38W 311 C11
South Williamsport U.S.A. 41°13N 77°0W 312 E8
South Yemen = Yemen ■
Asia 15°0N 44°0E 248 D4
South Yorkshire □ U.K. 53°27N 1°36W 168 D6
Southall U.K. 51°30N 0°22W 125 A1
Southampton Ont.,
Canada 44°30N 81°25W 312 B3
Southampton Southampton,
U.K. 50°54N 1°23W 169 G6
Southampton N.Y.,
U.S.A. 40°53N 72°23W 313 F12
Southampton □ U.K. 50°54N 1°23W 169 G6
Southampton I. Canada 64°30N 84°0W 295 E15
Southaven U.S.A. 34°59N 90°0W 315 D9
Southbank Canada 54°2N 125°46W 296 C3
Southborough U.K. 51°23N 0°3E 125 B4
Southbridge N.Z. 43°48S 172°16E 285 D7
Southbridge Mass., U.S.A. 42°5N 72°2W 313 D12
Southeast C. U.S.A. 62°56N 169°39W 303 E5
Southeast Indian Ridge
Ind. Oc. 43°0S 80°0E 273 J10
Southend Sask., Canada 56°19N 103°22W 297 B8
Southend London, U.K. 51°25N 0°0 125 B3
Southend-on-Sea U.K. 51°32N 0°44E 169 F8
Southend-on-Sea □ U.K. 51°32N 0°44E 169 F8
Southern = Yedebub Biherocn
Bihereseboch na Hizboch □
Ethiopia 12°0N 36°0E 257 F4
Southern = Yuzhnyy □
Russia 44°0N 40°0E 191 H6
Southern □ Malawi 15°0S 35°0E 269 F4
Southern □ S. Leone 8°0N 12°30W 262 D2
Southern □ Zambia 16°20S 26°20E 269 F2
Southern △ South Sudan 6°50N 28°45E 257 F2
Southern Alps N.Z. 43°41S 170°11E 285 D5
Southern California, Univ. of
U.S.A. 34°1N 118°17W 126 B3
Southern Cross Australia 31°12S 119°15E 279 F2
Southern Highlands □
Papua N. G. 6°15S 143°25E 286 D2
Southern Indian L.
Canada 57°10N 98°30W 297 B9
Southern Lau Group
Fiji 18°40S 178°40W 287 B3
Southern Leyte □ Phil. 10°30N 125°10E 233 F5
Southern Ocean Antarctica 62°0S 60°0E 151 C6
Southern Pines U.S.A. 35°11N 79°24W 315 D15
Southern Rhodesia = Zimbabwe ■
Africa 19°0S 30°0E 269 F3
Southern Uplands U.K. 55°28N 3°52W 167 F5
Southfield U.S.A. 42°28N 83°15W 311 B13
Southfields U.K. 51°26N 0°11W 125 B2
Southington U.S.A. 41°36N 72°53W 313 E12
Southland □ N.Z. 45°30S 168°0E 285 F3
Southold U.S.A. 41°4N 72°26W 313 E12
Southport Queens.,
Australia 27°58S 153°25E 281 D5
Southport Mersey., U.K. 53°39N 3°0W 168 D4
Southport Fla., U.S.A. 30°17N 85°38W 316 E4
Southport La., U.S.A. 29°57N 90°8W 131 B2
Southport N.Y., U.S.A. 42°3N 76°49W 312 D8
Southwark □ U.K. 51°29N 0°6W 125 B3
Southwest △ Australia 43°8S 146°5E 281 G4
Southwest Museum
U.S.A. 34°6N 118°13W 126 B3
Southwest Pacific Basin
Pac. Oc. 40°0S 140°0W 277 G17
Southwest Pt.
U.S. Virgin Is. 17°40N 64°55W 321 b
Southwold U.K. 52°20N 1°41E 169 E9
Southwood △ Australia 27°48S 150°8E 281 D5
Soutpansberg S. Africa 23°0S 29°30E 271 B4
Souvigny France 46°33N 3°10E 173 F10
Søvang Denmark 55°34N 12°37E 118 B3
Sovata Romania 46°35N 25°3E 183 D10
Soverato Italy 38°41N 16°33E 201 D9
Sovetsk Kaliningrad, Russia 55°6N 21°50E 184 C8
Sovetsk Kirov, Russia 57°38N 48°53E 190 B9
Sovetskaya Gavan
Russia 48°58N 140°18E 215 E15
Sovetskoye = Zelenokumsk
Russia 44°24N 44°0E 191 H6
Sovicille Italy 43°17N 11°13E 199 E8
Søvik Norway 62°33N 6°17E 164 B3
Soweto S. Africa 26°14S 27°52E 123 B1
Sowhānak Iran 35°48N 51°31E 141 A3
Sowma'eh Sarā Iran 37°17N 49°18E 213 D13
Soya Japan 35°44N 139°55E 140 A4
Sōya-Kaikyō = La Perouse Str.
Asia 45°40N 142°0E 220 B11
Sōya-Misaki Japan 45°30N 141°55E 220 B10
Soyangho S. Korea 37°57N 127°54E 224 D3
Soyaux France 45°39N 0°12E 174 C4
Søyland Norway 58°41N 5°36E 164 F2
Soyo Angola 6°13S 12°20E 265 D2
Sozaq Kazakhstan 44°9N 68°28E 217 D7
Sozh → Belarus 51°57N 30°48E 177 B16
Sozopol Bulgaria 42°23N 27°42E 203 D11
Spa Belgium 50°29N 5°53E 170 D5
Spaans Lagoen Aruba 12°28N 69°58W 322 f
Spaanse Water Curaçao 12°4N 68°51W 322 g
Spaccaforno = Ispica Italy 36°47N 14°55E 201 F7
Spain ■ Europe 39°0N 4°0W 192 D3
Spalato = Split Croatia 43°31N 16°26E 199 E13
Spalding S. Austral.,
Australia 33°30S 138°37E 282 B3
Spalding Lincs., U.K. 52°48N 0°9W 168 E7
Spanaway U.S.A. 47°6N 122°26W 306 C4
Spandau Germany 52°33N 13°9E 115 A1
Spånga Sweden 59°23N 17°53E 139 A1
Spangler U.S.A. 40°39N 78°48W 312 F6
Spanische Reitschule Vienna, Austria 142 b1
Spanish Canada 46°12N 82°20W 298 C3
Spanish Fork U.S.A. 40°7N 111°39W 304 F8
Spanish Monastery
U.S.A. 25°55N 80°11W 128 A2
Spanish Pt. Antigua & B. 17°33N 61°44W 322 c
Spanish Pt. Bermuda 32°18N 64°49W 153 a
Spanish Riding School = Spanische
Reitschule Vienna, Austria 142 b1
Spanish Town
Br. Virgin Is. 17°43N 64°26W 321 b
Spanish Town Jamaica 18°0N 76°57W 320 a
Sparks Ga., U.S.A. 31°11N 83°26W 316 D6
Sparks Nev., U.S.A. 39°32N 119°45W 306 F7
Sparreholm Sweden 59°4N 16°49E 162 E10
Sparrow Bay Grenada 12°30N 61°27W 323 q
Sparta = Sparti Greece 37°5N 22°25E 204 D4
Sparta Ga., U.S.A. 33°17N 82°58W 316 B7
Sparta Ill., U.S.A. 38°8N 89°42W 310 F7
Sparta Mich., U.S.A. 43°10N 85°42W 311 A11
Sparta N.J., U.S.A. 41°2N 74°38W 313 E10
Sparta Wis., U.S.A. 43°56N 90°49W 308 D8
Spartanburg U.S.A. 34°56N 81°57W 315 D14
Spartel, C. Morocco 35°47N 5°56W 260 A3
Sparti Greece 37°5N 22°25E 204 D4
Spartivento, C. Calabria,
Italy 37°55N 16°4E 201 E9
Spartivento, C. Sard., Italy 38°53N 8°50E 200 D1
Spartochori Greece 38°40N 20°46E 207 B2
Sparwood Canada 49°44N 114°53W 296 D6
Spas-Demensk Russia 54°20N 34°0E 188 E7
Spas-Klepiki Russia 55°10N 40°10E 188 E11
Spassk = Bednodemyanovsk
Russia 53°55N 43°15E 190 D6
Spassk Dalniy Russia 44°40N 132°48E 220 B6
Spassk-Ryazanskiy
Russia 54°24N 40°25E 188 E11
Spatha, Akra Greece 35°42N 23°43E 207 E4
Spatsizi → Canada 57°42N 128°7W 296 B3
Spatsizi Plateau Wilderness △
Canada 57°40N 128°0W 296 B3
Spean → U.K. 56°55N 4°59W 167 E4
Spearfish U.S.A. 44°30N 103°52W 308 C2
Spearman U.S.A. 36°12N 101°12W 314 C4
Spectacle I. U.S.A. 42°19N 70°59W 116 A3
Speculator U.S.A. 43°30N 74°22W 313 C10
Speed Australia 35°21S 142°27E 282 C5
Speedway U.S.A. 39°48N 86°16W 311 E10
Speery I. St. Helena 16°1S 5°46W 153 h
Speia Moldova 46°59N 29°19E 183 D14
Speicher-See Germany 48°12N 11°42E 131 A3
Speightstown Barbados 13°15N 59°39W 323 r
Speising Austria 48°10N 16°17E 142 B1
Speke Gulf Tanzania 2°20S 32°50E 268 C3
Spello Italy 42°59N 12°40E 199 F9
Spence Bay = Taloyoak
Canada 69°32N 93°32W 294 D13
Spencer Idaho, U.S.A. 44°22N 112°11W 304 D7
Spencer Ind., U.S.A. 39°17N 86°46W 311 E10
Spencer Iowa, U.S.A. 43°9N 95°9W 308 D6
Spencer N.Y., U.S.A. 42°13N 76°30W 313 D8
Spencer Nebr., U.S.A. 42°53N 98°42W 308 D4
Spencer, C. Australia 35°20S 136°53E 282 C2
Spencer B. Namibia 25°30S 14°47E 270 C1
Spencer G. Australia 34°0S 137°20E 282 C2
Spencerville Ont., Canada 44°51N 75°33W 313 B9
Spencerville Ohio, U.S.A. 40°43N 84°21W 311 D12
Spences Bridge Canada 50°25N 121°20W 296 C4
Spennymoor U.K. 54°42N 1°36W 168 C6
Spenser Mts. N.Z. 42°15S 172°45E 285 C7
Spentrup Denmark 56°33N 10°2E 163 H4
Sperchios → Greece 38°57N 22°3E 204 C4
Sperillen Norway 60°28N 10°3E 164 D7
Sperrin Mts. U.K. 54°50N 7°0W 166 B5
Spessart Germany 49°56N 9°18E 179 F5
Spetalen Norway 59°18N 10°45E 164 E7
Spetses Greece 37°15N 23°10E 204 D5
Spey → U.K. 57°40N 3°6W 167 D5
Speyer Germany 49°29N 8°25E 179 F4
Speyside Trin. & Tob. 11°17N 60°32W 323 s
Spezand Pakistan 29°59N 67°0E 242 E2
Spezzano Albanese Italy 39°40N 16°19E 201 C9
Sphinx Egypt 29°58N 31°8E 117 B1
Spickard U.S.A. 40°14N 93°36W 310 D3
Spiddle Ireland 53°15N 9°18W 166 C2
Spiekeroog Germany 53°46N 7°42E 178 B3
Spiez Switz. 46°40N 7°40E 179 J3
Spili Greece 35°13N 24°31E 207 E5
Spilimbergo Italy 46°7N 12°54E 199 B9
Spīn Būldak Afghan. 31°1N 66°25E 242 D2
Spinaceto Italy 41°47N 12°27E 136 C1
Spinalonga Greece 35°18N 25°44E 207 E6
Spinazzola Italy 40°58N 16°5E 201 B9
Spineni Romania 44°43N 24°37E 183 F9
Spinifex © Australia 28°30S 128°30E 279 E4
Spirding = Śniardwy, Jezioro
Poland 53°48N 21°50E 184 E8
Spirit Lake U.S.A. 46°15N 122°9W 306 D4
Spirit River Canada 55°45N 118°50W 296 B5
Spiritwood Canada 53°24N 107°33W 297 C7
Spišská Nová Ves
Slovak Rep. 48°58N 20°34E 181 C13
Spišské Podhradie
Slovak Rep. 49°0N 20°48E 181 B13
Spit Junction Australia 33°49S 151°14E 139 A2
Spital Austria 47°42N 14°18E 180 D7
Spithead U.K. 50°45N 1°10W 169 G6
Spittal an der Drau
Austria 46°48N 13°31E 180 E6
Spitzbergen = Svalbard
Arctic 78°0N 17°0E 154 B12
Spjelkavik Norway 62°28N 6°22E 164 B3
Split Croatia 43°31N 16°26E 199 E13
Split ✕ (SPU) Croatia 43°33N 16°15E 199 E13
Split L. Canada 56°8N 96°15W 297 B9
Split Lake Canada 56°8N 96°15W 297 B9
Splitski Kanal Croatia 43°31N 16°20E 199 E13
Splügenpass Switz. 46°30N 9°20E 179 J5
Spofford U.S.A. 29°10N 100°25W 314 G4
Spokane U.S.A. 47°40N 117°24W 304 C5
Spoleto Italy 42°44N 12°44E 199 F9
Sponvika Norway 59°7N 11°15E 164 E8
Spoon → U.S.A. 40°19N 90°4W 310 D6
Spooner U.S.A. 45°50N 91°53W 308 C8
Spořilov Czech Rep. 50°2N 14°29E 135 B3
Sporyy Navolok, Mys
Russia 75°50N 68°40E 214 B7
Spot Pond U.S.A. 42°26N 71°4W 116 A2
Spotswood Australia 37°50S 144°52E 128 B1
Sprague U.S.A. 47°18N 117°59W 304 C5
Spratly I. S. China Sea 8°38N 111°55E 230 C4
Spratly Is. S. China Sea 8°20N 112°0E 230 C4
Spray U.S.A. 44°50N 119°48W 304 D4
Spreča → Bos.-H. 44°44N 18°6E 182 F3
Spree → Germany 52°32N 13°12E 178 C9
Spreewald Germany 51°58N 13°51E 178 D9
Spremberg Germany 51°34N 14°22E 178 D10
Sprengisandur Iceland 64°52N 18°7W 155 C8
Spring City U.S.A. 40°11N 75°33W 313 F9
Spring Cr. → U.S.A. 30°54N 84°45W 316 E5
Spring Creek U.S.A. 40°44N 115°35W 304 F6
Spring Garden Guyana 6°59N 58°31W 329 B6
Spring Garden Calif.,
U.S.A. 39°52N 120°47W 306 F6
Spring Green U.S.A. 43°11N 90°4W 310 A6
Spring Hill Ala., U.S.A. 31°42N 85°58W 316 D4
Spring Hill Fla., U.S.A. 28°27N 82°41W 317 G7
Spring Mts. U.S.A. 36°0N 115°45W 307 J11
Spring Valley Calif.,
U.S.A. 32°44N 116°59W 307 N10
Spring Valley Ill., U.S.A. 41°20N 89°12W 310 C7
Spring Valley Nev., U.S.A. 36°6N 115°14W 124 B1
Springbok S. Africa 29°42S 17°54E 270 C2
Springboro U.S.A. 41°48N 80°22W 312 E4
Springdale Nfld. & L.,
Canada 49°30N 56°6W 299 C8
Springdale Ark., U.S.A. 36°11N 94°8W 314 C7
Springdale Ohio, U.S.A. 39°17N 84°29W 311 E12
Springe Germany 52°13N 9°33E 178 C5
Springeberg Germany 52°26N 13°43E 115 B5
Springer U.S.A. 36°22N 104°36W 305 H11
Springerville U.S.A. 34°8N 109°17W 305 J9
Springfield Ont., Canada 42°50N 80°56W 312 D4
Springfield Dominica 15°21N 61°23W 323 k
Springfield N.Z. 43°19S 171°56E 285 D6
Springfield Colo., U.S.A. 37°24N 102°37W 305 H12
Springfield Fla., U.S.A. 30°10N 85°37W 316 E4
Springfield Ga., U.S.A. 32°22N 81°18W 316 C8
Springfield Ill., U.S.A. 39°48N 89°39W 310 E7
Springfield Ky., U.S.A. 37°41N 85°13W 311 G11
Springfield Mass., U.S.A. 42°6N 72°35W 313 D12
Springfield Mo., U.S.A. 37°13N 93°17W 308 G7
Springfield Ohio, U.S.A. 39°55N 83°49W 311 E13
Springfield Oreg., U.S.A. 44°3N 123°1W 304 D2
Springfield S.C., U.S.A. 33°30N 81°17W 316 B8
Springfield Tenn., U.S.A. 36°31N 86°53W 315 C11
Springfield Va., U.S.A. 38°46N 77°10W 143 C2
Springfield Vt., U.S.A. 43°18N 72°29W 313 C12
Springfield, L. U.S.A. 39°46N 89°36W 310 E7
Springfontein S. Africa 30°15S 25°40E 270 D4
Springhill Canada 45°40N 64°4W 299 C7
Springhill La., U.S.A. 33°0N 93°28W 314 E8
Springhouse Canada 51°56N 122°7W 296 C4
Springs S. Africa 26°13S 28°25E 271 C4
Springsure Australia 24°8S 148°6E 280 C4
Springvale Ga., U.S.A. 31°50N 84°53W 316 D5
Springvale Maine, U.S.A. 43°28N 70°48W 313 C14
Springville Calif., U.S.A. 36°8N 118°49W 306 J8
Springville Iowa, U.S.A. 42°3N 91°27W 310 B5
Springville N.Y., U.S.A. 42°31N 78°40W 312 D6
Springville Utah, U.S.A. 40°10N 111°37W 304 F8
Springwater U.S.A. 42°38N 77°35W 312 D7
Sprottau = Szprotawa
Poland 51°33N 15°35E 185 G2
Spruce-Creek U.S.A. 40°36N 78°9W 312 F6
Spruce Knob-Seneca Rocks △
U.S.A. 38°50N 79°30W 309 F14
Spruce Mt. U.S.A. 44°12N 72°19W 313 B12
Sprucedale Canada 45°29N 79°28W 312 A5
Spur U.S.A. 33°28N 100°52W 314 E4
Spurn Hd. U.K. 53°35N 0°8E 168 D8
Spuž Montenegro 42°32N 19°10E 202 D3
Spuzzum Canada 49°37N 121°23W 296 D4
Spydeberg Norway 59°36N 11°5E 164 E8
Squam L. U.S.A. 43°45N 71°32W 313 C13
Squamish Canada 49°45N 123°10W 296 D4
Squantum U.S.A. 42°17N 71°0W 116 B2
Square Islands Canada 52°47N 55°47W 299 B8
Squillace, G. di Italy 38°45N 16°50E 201 D9
Squinzano Italy 40°26N 18°2E 201 B11
Squires, Mt. Australia 26°14S 127°28E 279 E4
Sragen Indonesia 7°26S 111°2E 235 D4
Srbac Bos.-H. 45°7N 17°30E 182 E2
Srbica Kosovo 42°45N 20°47E 202 D4
Srbija = Serbia ■ Europe 43°20N 20°0E 202 C4
Srbobran Serbia 45°32N 19°48E 182 E4
Sre Ambel Cambodia 11°8N 103°46E 237 G4
Sre Khtum Cambodia 12°10N 106°52E 237 F6
Sre Umbell = Sre Ambel
Cambodia 11°8N 103°46E 237 G4
Srebrenica Bos.-H. 44°6N 19°18E 182 F4
Sredinnyy Khrebet Russia 57°0N 160°0E 215 D17
Sredinnyy Ra. = Sredinnyy Khrebet
Russia 57°0N 160°0E 215 D17
Središče Slovenia 46°24N 16°17E 199 B13
Sredna Gora Bulgaria 42°40N 24°20E 203 D8
Srednaya Rogatka Russia 59°49N 30°22E 137 C2
Srednekolymsk Russia 67°27N 153°40E 215 C16
Sredni Rodopi Bulgaria 41°40N 24°45E 203 E8
Srednogorie Bulgaria 42°43N 24°10E 203 D8
Śrem Poland 52°6N 17°2E 185 F4
Sremska Mitrovica Serbia 44°59N 19°38E 182 F4
Sremski Karlovci Serbia 45°12N 19°56E 182 E4
Srepok → Cambodia 13°33N 106°16E 236 F6
Sretensk Russia 52°10N 117°40E 215 D12
Sri Aman = Bandar Sri Aman
Malaysia 1°15N 111°32E 235 B4
Sri Kalahasti India 13°45N 79°44E 245 H4
Sri Lanka ■ Asia 7°30N 80°50E 245 L5
Sriharikota I. India 13°40N 80°20E 245 H5
Srikakulam India 18°14N 83°58E 244 E6
Srinagar India 34°5N 74°50E 243 B6
Sripur Bangla. 24°14N 90°30E 241 C3
Srivardhan India 18°4N 73°3E 244 E1
Srivilliputtur India 9°31N 77°40E 245 K3
Środa Śląska Poland 51°10N 16°36E 185 G3
Środa Wielkopolski
Poland 52°15N 17°19E 185 F4
Śródmieście Poland 52°13N 21°0E 142 B2
Srono Indonesia 8°24S 114°16E 231 J17
Srpska Crnja Serbia 45°38N 20°44E 182 E5
Srpski Itebej Serbia 45°35N 20°44E 182 E5
Srungavarapukota India 18°7N 83°10E 244 E6
Ssese Is. = Sese Is. Uganda 0°20S 32°20E 268 C3
Ssuhu Taiwan 23°38N 120°13E 225 C2
Staaken Germany 52°31N 13°8E 115 A1
Staaten → Australia 16°24S 141°17E 280 B3
Staaten River △ Australia 16°15S 142°40E 280 B3
Stabekk Norway 59°54N 10°36E 133 A2
Staberhuk Germany 54°23N 11°18E 178 A7
Stade Germany 53°35N 9°29E 178 B5
Staðarfell Iceland 65°7N 22°12W 155 B4
Staðarhólskirkja Iceland 65°23N 21°58W 155 B5
Staðastaður Iceland 64°49N 23°1W 155 C3
Stadhavet Norway 62°13N 5°0E 164 B2
Stadhiou Athens, Greece 112 c3
Stadhuis Amsterdam, Neths. 112 b3
Staður Húnavatnssýsla,
Iceland 65°9N 21°3W 155 B5
Staður Ísafjarðarsýsla,
Iceland 66°15N 22°50W 155 A4
Stadlandet Norway 62°10N 5°10E 164 B2
Stadlau Austria 48°13N 16°27E 142 A2
Stadshuset Stockholm, Sweden 139 b1
Stadskanaal Neths. 53°4N 6°55E 170 A6
Stadsschouwburg Amsterdam, Neths. 112 c1
Stadtallendorf Germany 50°48N 9°1E 178 E5
Stadthagen Germany 52°19N 9°13E 178 C5
Stadtlohn Germany 51°59N 6°55E 178 D2
Stadtroda Germany 50°52N 11°44E 178 E7
Stafafell Iceland 64°25N 14°52W 155 C12
Staffa U.K. 56°27N 6°21W 167 E2
Staffanstorp Sweden 55°39N 13°13E 163 J7
Stafford Staffs., U.K. 52°49N 2°7W 168 E5
Stafford Kans., U.S.A. 37°58N 98°36W 308 G4
Stafford, L. U.S.A. 29°20N 82°29W 317 F7
Stafford Springs U.S.A. 41°57N 72°18W 313 E12
Staffordshire □ U.K. 52°53N 2°10W 168 E5
Stagnone Italy 37°53N 12°26E 200 E5
Stagnone di Marsala △
Italy 37°52N 12°26E 200 E5
Staines U.K. 51°26N 0°29W 169 F7
Stains France 48°57N 2°22E 134 A3
Stainz Austria 46°53N 15°17E 180 E8
Stakhanov Ukraine 48°35N 38°40E 189 H10
Stalać Serbia 43°43N 21°28E 202 C5
Stalin = Kuçovë Albania 40°47N 19°57E 202 F3
Stalin = Varna Bulgaria 43°13N 27°56E 203 C11
Stalin Pk. = Gerlachovský štít
Slovak Rep. 49°11N 20°7E 181 B13
Stalin Pk. = imeni Ismail Samani,
Pik Tajikistan 39°0N 72°2E 217 E8
Stalin Pk. = Musala
Bulgaria 42°13N 23°37E 202 D7

Stalinabad = Dushanbe Tajikistan 38°33N 68°48E 217 E7
Stalingrad = Volgograd Russia 48°40N 44°25E 191 F7
Staliniri = Tskhinvali Georgia 42°14N 44°1E 191 J7
Stalinogorsk = Novomoskovsk Russia 54°5N 38°15E 188 E10
Stalinogrod = Katowice Poland 50°17N 19°5E 185 H6
Stalinsk = Novokuznetsk Russia 53°45N 87°10E 217 B11
Stalinstadt = Eisenhüttenstadt Germany 52°9N 14°38E 178 C10
Stallarholmen Sweden 59°22N 17°12E 162 E11
Ställdalen Sweden 59°56N 14°56E 162 E8
Stalowa Wola Poland 50°34N 22°3E 185 H9
Stalybridge U.K. 53°28N 2°3W 168 D5
Stamford Queens., Australia 21°15S 143°46E 280 C3
Stamford Lincs., U.K. 52°39N 0°29W 169 E7
Stamford Conn., U.S.A. 41°3N 73°32W 313 E11
Stamford N.Y., U.S.A. 42°25N 74°38W 313 D10
Stamford Tex., U.S.A. 32°57N 99°48W 314 E5
Stamford Hill U.K. 51°34N 0°4W 125 A3
Stammersdorf Austria 48°18N 16°24E 142 A2
Stamnes Norway 60°40N 5°45E 164 D2
Stamping Ground U.S.A. 38°16N 84°41W 311 F12
Stampriet Namibia 24°20S 18°28E 270 B2
Stamps U.S.A. 33°22N 93°30W 314 E8
Stanberry U.S.A. 40°13N 94°35W 310 D2
Stančevo = Kalipetrovo Bulgaria 44°5N 27°14E 203 B11
Standerton S. Africa 26°55S 29°7E 271 C4
Standish U.S.A. 43°59N 83°57W 309 D12
Stanford S. Africa 34°26S 19°29E 270 D2
Stanford Mont., U.S.A. 47°9N 110°13W 304 C8
Stånga Sweden 57°17N 18°29E 163 G12
Stange Norway 60°43N 11°5E 164 D8
Stanger S. Africa 29°27S 31°14E 271 C5
Stängselåsen = Salpausselkä Finland 61°3N 26°15E 188 B4
Stangvik Norway 62°55N 8°28E 164 B5
Stanhope Vic., Australia 36°27S 144°59E 283 D6
Stanhope Iowa, U.S.A. 42°17N 93°48W 310 B3
Stanimaka = Asenovgrad Bulgaria 42°1N 24°51E 203 D8
Stanišić Serbia 45°56N 19°10E 182 E4
Stanislaus → U.S.A. 37°40N 121°14W 306 H5
Stanislav = Ivano-Frankivsk Ukraine 48°40N 24°40E 183 B9
Stanisławów = Ivano-Frankivsk Ukraine 48°40N 24°40E 183 B9
Stanisławów Poland 52°18N 21°33E 185 F8
Stanley Tas., Australia 40°46S 145°19E 281 G4
Stanley Hong Kong, China 22°13N 114°12E 122 B2
Stanley Falk. Is. 51°40S 59°51W 153 f
Stanley Durham, U.K. 54°53N 1°41W 168 C6
Stanley Idaho, U.S.A. 44°13N 114°56W 304 D6
Stanley N. Dak., U.S.A. 48°19N 102°23W 308 A2
Stanley N.Y., U.S.A. 42°48N 77°6W 312 D7
Stanley Falls = Boyoma, Chutes Dem. Rep. of the Congo 0°35N 25°23E 264 B5
Stanley Mission Canada 55°25N 104°33W 297 B8
Stanley Pen. China 22°12N 114°12E 122 B2
Stanley Pool = Malebo, Pool Africa 4°17S 15°20E 265 C3
Stanley Res. India 11°50N 77°40E 245 J3
Stanleyville = Kisangani Dem. Rep. of the Congo 0°35N 25°15E 268 B2
Stanmore U.K. 51°37N 0°18W 125 A2
Stannards U.S.A. 42°5N 77°55W 312 D7
Stanovoy Khrebet Russia 55°0N 130°0E 215 D14
Stanovoy Ra. = Stanovoy Khrebet Russia 55°0N 130°0E 215 D14
Stansmore Ra. Australia 21°23S 128°33E 278 D4
Stansted, London ✕ (STN) U.K. 51°54N 0°14E 169 F8
Stanthorpe Australia 28°36S 151°59E 281 D5
Stanton Ky., U.S.A. 37°54N 83°52W 311 G13
Stanton Tex., U.S.A. 32°8N 101°48W 314 E4
Stanwood U.S.A. 48°15N 122°23W 306 B4
Staples Ont., Canada 42°10N 82°35W 312 D2
Staples Minn., U.S.A. 46°21N 94°48W 308 B6
Stapleton N.Y., U.S.A. 40°36N 74°5W 132 C1
Stapleton Nebr., U.S.A. 41°29N 100°31W 308 E3
Stąporków Poland 51°9N 20°31E 185 G7
Star City Canada 52°50N 104°20W 297 C8
Star Ferry Hong Kong, China 122 a2
Star Harbour Solomon Is. 10°47S 162°19E 287 N12
Star Lake U.S.A. 44°10N 75°2W 313 B9
Stará Ďala = Hurbanovo Slovak Rep. 47°51N 18°11E 181 D11
Stará L'ubovňa Slovak Rep. 49°18N 20°42E 181 B13
Stara Moravica Serbia 45°50N 19°30E 182 E4
Stara Pazova Serbia 44°58N 20°10E 182 F5
Stara Planina Bulgaria 43°15N 23°0E 202 C7
Stara Sil Ukraine 49°29N 22°58E 185 J9
Stará Turá Slovak Rep. 48°47N 17°42E 181 C10
Stara Ushytsya Ukraine 48°35N 27°8E 183 B12
Stara Zagora Bulgaria 42°26N 25°39E 203 D9
Stara Zagora □ Bulgaria 42°26N 25°39E 203 D9
Starachowice Poland 51°3N 21°2E 185 G8
Staraya Derevnya Russia 59°58N 30°15E 137 B1
Staraya Russa Russia 57°58N 31°23E 188 D6
Starbuck I. Kiribati 5°37S 155°55W 289 H12
Starchiojd Romania 45°19N 26°11E 183 E11
Starcke △ Australia 14°56S 145°2E 280 A4
Staré Město Czech Rep. 50°5N 14°25E 135 B2
Stare Miasto Warsaw, Poland 142 a2
Stargard in Pommern = Stargard Szczeciński Poland 53°20N 15°0E 184 E2
Stargard Szczeciński Poland 53°20N 15°0E 184 E2
Stårheim Norway 61°56N 5°40E 164 C2
Stari Bar Montenegro 42°7N 19°10E 202 D3
Stari Bečej = Bečej Serbia 45°36N 20°3E 182 E5
Stari Trg Slovenia 45°29N 15°7E 199 C12
Staritsa Russia 56°33N 34°55E 188 D8
Starke U.S.A. 29°57N 82°7W 316 F7
Starke, L. U.S.A. 28°34N 81°32W 133 A1
Starkville U.S.A. 33°28N 88°49W 315 E10
Starnberg Germany 48°0N 11°21E 179 H7
Starnberger See Germany 47°54N 11°19E 179 H7
Starobilsk Ukraine 49°16N 39°0E 189 H10
Starodub Russia 52°30N 32°50E 189 F7
Starogard Gdański Poland 53°59N 18°30E 184 E5
Starokonstantinov = Starokonstyantyniv Ukraine 49°48N 27°10E 177 D14
Starokonstyantyniv Ukraine 49°48N 27°10E 177 D14
Starokozache Ukraine 46°20N 29°59E 183 D14
Starominskaya Russia 46°33N 39°0E 191 G4
Staroshcherbinovskaya Russia 46°40N 38°53E 191 G4
Starrs Mill U.S.A. 33°19N 84°31W 316 B5
Start Pt. U.K. 50°13N 3°39W 169 G4
Stary Sącz Poland 49°33N 20°35E 185 J7
Staryy Biryuzyak Russia 44°46N 46°50E 191 H8
Staryy Chartoriysk Ukraine 51°15N 25°54E 177 C13
Staryy Krym Ukraine 45°3N 35°8E 189 K8
Staryy Margilan = Marghilon Uzbekistan 40°27N 71°42E 217 D8
Staryy Oskol Russia 51°19N 37°55E 189 G9
Staryy Sambir Ukraine 49°27N 22°59E 185 J9
Stassfurt Germany 51°51N 11°35E 178 D7
Staszów Poland 50°33N 21°10E 185 H8
State Center U.S.A. 42°1N 93°10W 310 B3
State College U.S.A. 40°48N 77°52W 312 F7
Stateline U.S.A. 38°57N 119°56W 306 G7
Staten, I. = Estados, I. de Los Argentina 54°40S 64°30W 336 D4
Staten I. U.S.A. 40°35N 74°9W 313 F10
Staten Island Zoo U.S.A. 40°38N 74°6W 132 C1
Staten Islands Ferry Terminal U.S.A. 40°38N 74°4W 132 C1
Statenice Czech Rep. 50°9N 14°19E 135 B1
Statenville U.S.A. 30°42N 83°2W 316 E6
Statesboro U.S.A. 32°27N 81°47W 316 C8
Statesville U.S.A. 35°47N 80°53W 315 D14
Statham U.S.A. 33°58N 83°35W 316 B6
Stathelle Norway 59°3N 9°41E 164 E6
Statia = St. Eustatius W. Indies 17°20N 63°0W 322 a
Statue Square Hong Kong, China 122 c1
Stauffer U.S.A. 34°45N 119°3W 307 L7
Staunton Ill., U.S.A. 39°1N 89°47W 310 E2
Staunton Va., U.S.A. 38°9N 79°4W 309 F14
Stavanger = Rogaland □ Norway 59°12N 6°20E 164 E3
Stavanger Norway 58°57N 5°40E 164 F2
Stavelot Belgium 50°23N 5°55E 170 D5
Stavern Norway 59°0N 10°1E 164 F7
Stavoren Neths. 52°53N 5°22E 170 B5
Stavropol Russia 45°5N 42°0E 191 H6
Stavropol □ Russia 47°20N 42°50E 191 G6
Stavros Cyprus 35°1N 32°38E 207 E8
Stavros Ithaki, Greece 38°27N 20°39E 207 C2
Stavros Kriti, Greece 35°12N 24°45E 207 E5
Stavros Thessaloniki, Greece 40°39N 23°43E 202 F7
Stavros, Akra Greece 35°26N 24°58E 207 E5
Stavroupoli Greece 41°12N 24°45E 203 E8
Stawell Australia 37°5S 142°47E 282 D5
Stawell → Australia 20°20S 142°55E 280 C3
Stawiski Poland 53°22N 22°9E 184 E9
Stawiszyn Poland 51°56N 18°4E 185 G5
Stayner Canada 44°25N 80°5W 312 B4
Stayton U.S.A. 44°48N 122°48W 304 D2
Steamboat Springs U.S.A. 40°29N 106°50W 304 F10
Stean Norway 59°16N 8°33E 164 E5
Stebbins U.S.A. 63°31N 162°17W 303 E7
Steblevë Albania 41°23N 20°33E 202 E4
Stedelijk Museum Neths. 52°21N 4°52E 112 A2
Steele Ala., U.S.A. 33°56N 86°12W 316 B3
Steele N. Dak., U.S.A. 46°51N 99°55W 308 B4
Steele Creek Australia 37°44S 144°52E 128 A1
Steelton U.S.A. 40°14N 76°50W 312 F8
Steelville U.S.A. 37°58N 91°22W 310 G5
Steen River Canada 59°40N 117°12W 296 B5
Steenkool = Bintuni Indonesia 2°7S 133°32E 231 E8
Steenokkerzeel Belgium 50°55N 4°31E 116 A2
Steens Mt. U.S.A. 42°35N 118°40W 304 E4
Steenstrup Gletscher Greenland 75°15N 57°0W 154 B5
Steenwijk Neths. 52°47N 6°7E 170 B6
Steep Pt. Australia 26°8S 113°8E 279 E1
Steep Rock Canada 51°30N 98°48W 297 C9
Steer, L. U.S.A. 28°31N 81°30W 133 A2
Ştefan Vodă Moldova 46°27N 29°42E 183 D14
Ştefăneşti Romania 47°44N 27°15E 183 C12
Stefanie △ Ethiopia 4°55N 36°55E 257 G4
Stefanie L. = Chew Bahir Ethiopia 4°40N 36°50E 257 G4
Stefansson Bay Antarctica 67°20S 59°8E 151 C5
Stefansson I. Canada 73°20N 105°45W 295 C10
Stege Denmark 54°59N 12°18E 163 K6
Stegi = Siteki Swaziland 26°32S 31°58E 271 C5
Steglitz Germany 52°27N 13°19E 115 B2
Stegman = Artesia U.S.A. 32°51N 104°24W 305 K11
Ştei Romania 46°32N 22°27E 182 D7
Steiermark □ Austria 47°26N 15°0E 180 D8
Steigerwald Germany 49°44N 10°26E 179 F6
Steigerwald ⌂ Germany 49°50N 10°30E 179 F6
Steilacoom U.S.A. 47°10N 122°36W 306 C4
Steilrandberge Namibia 17°45S 13°20E 270 A1
Stein = Kamnik Slovenia 46°14N 14°37E 199 B11
Steinbach Canada 49°32N 96°40W 297 D9
Steinfurt Germany 52°9N 7°20E 178 C3
Steinhatchee U.S.A. 29°40N 83°23W 316 F6
Steinhausen Namibia 21°49S 18°20E 270 B2
Steinheim Germany 51°51N 9°5E 178 D5
Steinhuder Meer Germany 52°29N 9°21E 178 C5
Steinhuder Meer ⌂ Germany 52°30N 9°16E 178 C5
Steinkjer Norway 64°1N 11°31E 160 D14
Steinkopf S. Africa 29°18S 17°43E 270 C2
Steinshamn Norway 62°47N 6°28E 164 B3
Steinwald ⌂ Germany 49°55N 12°8E 179 F8
Stellarton Canada 45°32N 62°30W 299 C7
Stellenbosch S. Africa 33°58S 18°50E 270 D2
Stelvio, Paso dello Italy 46°32N 10°27E 198 B7
Stenay France 49°29N 5°12E 173 C12
Stendal Germany 52°36N 11°53E 178 C7
Stende Latvia 57°11N 22°33E 184 A9
Stenen Koraal Curaçao 12°10N 68°56W 322 g
Stenhamra Sweden 59°20N 17°41E 162 E11
Stenshuvud △ Sweden 55°39N 14°15E 163 J8
Stenstorp Sweden 58°17N 13°45E 163 F7
Stenungsund Sweden 58°6N 11°50E 163 F5
Steornabhaigh = Stornoway U.K. 58°13N 6°23W 167 C2
Stepanakert = Xankändi Azerbaijan 39°52N 46°49E 213 C12
Stepanavan Armenia 41°1N 44°23E 191 K7
Stepaside Ireland 53°15N 6°12W 120 B2
Stephansdom Vienna, Austria 142 b2
Stephens, C. N.Z. 40°42S 173°58E 285 A8
Stephens Creek Australia 31°50S 141°30E 282 A4
Stephens I. B.C., Canada 54°10N 130°45W 296 C2
Stephens I. N.Z. 40°40S 174°1E 285 A9
Stephens L. Canada 56°32N 95°0W 297 B9
Stephenville Nfld. & L., Canada 48°31N 58°35W 299 C8
Stephenville Tex., U.S.A. 32°13N 98°12W 314 E5
Stepney U.K. 51°30N 0°3W 125 A3
Stepnica Poland 53°38N 14°36E 184 E1
Stepnogorsk Kazakhstan 52°21N 71°53E 217 B8
Stepnoi = Elista Russia 46°16N 44°14E 191 G7
Steppe Asia 50°0N 50°0E 210 C7
Steps Pt. Amer. Samoa 14°23S 170°45W 302 f
Sterea Ellas □ Greece 38°50N 23°0E 204 C4
Sterkstroom S. Africa 31°32S 26°32E 270 D4
Sterling Alaska, U.S.A. 60°32N 150°46W 303 F10
Sterling Colo., U.S.A. 40°37N 103°13W 304 F12
Sterling Ga., U.S.A. 31°16N 81°34W 316 D8
Sterling Ill., U.S.A. 41°48N 89°42W 310 C7
Sterling Kans., U.S.A. 38°13N 98°12W 308 F4
Sterling City U.S.A. 31°51N 101°0W 314 F4
Sterling Heights U.S.A. 42°35N 83°2W 311 B13
Sterling Park U.S.A. 37°41N 122°27W 136 B2
Sterling Run U.S.A. 41°25N 78°12W 312 E6
Sterlitamak Russia 53°40N 56°0E 186 D10
Sternberg Germany 53°42N 11°50E 178 B7
Šternberk Czech Rep. 49°45N 17°15E 181 B10
Sternes Greece 35°30N 24°9E 207 E5
Sterzing = Vipiteno Italy 46°54N 11°26E 199 B8
Stettin = Szczecin Poland 53°27N 14°27E 184 E1
Stettiner Haff Germany 53°47N 14°15E 178 B10
Stettler Canada 52°19N 112°40W 296 C6
Steubenville U.S.A. 40°22N 80°37W 312 F4
Stevenage U.K. 51°55N 0°13W 169 F7
Stevens Point U.S.A. 44°31N 89°34W 308 C9
Stevens Pottery U.S.A. 32°57N 83°17W 316 C6
Stevens Village U.S.A. 66°1N 149°6W 303 C10
Stevenson U.S.A. 45°42N 121°53W 306 E5
Stevenson → Australia 27°6S 135°33E 281 D2
Stevenson L. Canada 53°55N 96°0W 297 C9
Stevensville U.S.A. 46°30N 114°5W 304 C6
Stevns Klint Denmark 55°17N 12°28E 163 J6
Steward U.S.A. 41°51N 89°1W 310 C7
Stewardson U.S.A. 39°16N 88°38W 311 E8
Stewart B.C., Canada 55°56N 129°57W 296 B3
Stewart Ga., U.S.A. 33°25N 83°52W 316 B6
Stewart Nev., U.S.A. 39°5N 119°46W 306 F7
Stewart → Canada 63°19N 139°26W 294 E4
Stewart, C. Australia 11°57S 134°56E 280 A1
Stewart, I. Chile 54°50S 71°15W 336 D2
Stewart I. N.Z. 46°58S 167°54E 285 G2
Stewarts Point U.S.A. 38°39N 123°24W 306 G3
Stewartsville U.S.A. 39°45N 94°30W 310 E2
Stewartville U.S.A. 43°51N 92°29W 308 D7
Stewiacke Canada 45°9N 63°22W 299 C7
Steynsburg S. Africa 31°15S 25°49E 270 D4
Steyr Austria 48°3N 14°25E 180 C7
Steyr → Austria 48°3N 14°25E 180 C7
Steytlerville S. Africa 33°17S 24°19E 270 D3
Stia Italy 43°48N 11°42E 199 E8
Stickloinge udde Sweden 59°23N 18°6E 139 A2
Stickney U.S.A. 41°49N 87°46W 119 C2
Stigler U.S.A. 35°15N 95°8W 314 D7
Stigliano Italy 40°24N 16°14E 201 B9
Stigtomta Sweden 58°47N 16°48E 163 F10
Stikine → Canada 56°40N 132°30W 296 B2
Stilfontein S. Africa 26°51S 26°50E 270 C4
Stilida Greece 38°55N 22°47E 204 C4
Stillmore U.S.A. 32°27N 82°13W 316 C7
Stillorgan Ireland 53°17N 6°11W 120 B2
Stillwater N.Y., U.S.A. 42°55N 73°41W 313 D11
Stillwater Okla., U.S.A. 36°7N 97°4W 314 C6
Stillwater Range U.S.A. 39°50N 118°5W 304 G4
Stillwater Res. U.S.A. 43°54N 75°3W 313 C9
Stilo, Pta. Italy 38°25N 16°35E 201 D9
Stilwell U.S.A. 35°49N 94°38W 314 D7
Stînga Nistrului □ Moldova 47°20N 29°15E 183 C14
Štip Macedonia 41°42N 22°10E 202 E6
Stira Greece 38°9N 24°14E 204 C6
Stirling Ont., Canada 44°18N 77°33W 312 B7
Stirling N.Z. 46°14S 169°49E 285 G4
Stirling Stirling, U.K. 56°8N 3°57W 167 E5
Stirling □ U.K. 56°12N 4°18W 167 E4
Stirling Ra. Australia 34°23S 118°0E 279 F2
Stirling Range △ Australia 34°26S 118°20E 279 F2
Stittsville Canada 45°15N 75°55W 313 A9
Stjernøya Norway 70°20N 22°40E 160 A20
Stjørdalshalsen Norway 63°29N 10°51E 164 A7
Stock Island U.S.A. 24°32N 81°34W 317 L8
Stocka Sweden 61°53N 17°20E 162 C11
Stockach Germany 47°50N 9°1E 179 H5
Stockaryd Sweden 57°19N 14°36E 163 G8
Stockbridge Ga., U.S.A. 33°33N 84°14W 316 B5
Stockbridge Mich., U.S.A. 42°27N 84°11W 311 B12
Stockerau Austria 48°24N 16°12E 181 C9
Stockholm Sweden 59°19N 18°4E 139 B2
Stockholm Arlanda ✕ (ARN) Sweden 59°41N 17°56E 139 A1
Stockholms län □ Sweden 59°30N 18°20E 162 E12
Stockport U.K. 53°25N 2°9W 168 D5
Stocksbridge U.K. 53°29N 1°35W 168 D6
Stocksund Sweden 59°23N 18°3E 139 A2
Stockton Calif., U.S.A. 37°58N 121°17W 306 H5
Stockton Ill., U.S.A. 42°21N 90°1W 310 B6
Stockton Kans., U.S.A. 39°26N 99°16W 308 F4
Stockton Mo., U.S.A. 37°42N 93°48W 310 G3
Stockton-on-Tees U.K. 54°35N 1°19W 168 C6
Stockton-on-Tees □ U.K. 54°35N 1°19W 168 C6
Stockton Plateau U.S.A. 30°30N 102°30W 314 F3
Stoczek Łukowski Poland 51°58N 21°58E 185 G8
Stöde Sweden 62°28N 16°35E 162 B10
Stöðvarfjörður Iceland 64°49N 13°52W 155 C13
Stodůlky Czech Rep. 50°3N 14°19E 135 B1
Stoeng Treng Cambodia 13°31N 105°58E 236 F5
Stoer, Pt. of U.K. 58°16N 5°23W 167 C3
Stogovo Macedonia 41°31N 20°38E 202 E4
Stoholm Denmark 56°30N 9°8E 163 H3
Stoke N.Z. 41°19S 173°14E 285 B8
Stoke Newington U.K. 51°33N 0°4W 125 A3
Stoke-on-Trent U.K. 53°1N 2°11W 168 D5
Stoke-on-Trent □ U.K. 53°1N 2°11W 168 D5
Stokes △ Australia 33°45S 121°11E 279 F3
Stokes Bay Canada 45°0N 81°28W 312 B3
Stokes Pt. Australia 40°10S 143°56E 281 G3
Stokes Ra. Australia 15°50S 130°50E 278 C5
Stokes Valley N.Z. 41°10S 174°59E 124 B3
Stokkseyri Iceland 63°50N 21°2W 155 D5
Stokksnes Iceland 64°14N 14°58W 155 C12
Stokmarknes Norway 68°34N 14°54E 160 B16
Stolac Bos.-H. 43°5N 17°59E 202 C1
Stolberg Germany 50°47N 6°13E 178 E2
Stolbovoy, Ostrov Russia 74°44N 135°14E 215 B14
Stolbtsy = Stowbtsy Belarus 53°30N 26°43E 177 B14
Stolin Belarus 51°53N 26°50E 177 C14
Stöllet Sweden 60°26N 13°15E 162 D7
Stolnici Romania 44°31N 24°48E 183 F9
Stolp = Słupsk Poland 54°30N 17°3E 184 D4
Stolpmünde = Ustka Poland 54°35N 16°55E 184 D3
Stomio Greece 35°21N 23°32E 207 E4
Ston Croatia 42°51N 17°43E 199 F14
Stone U.K. 52°55N 2°9W 168 E5
Stone Canyon Res. U.S.A. 34°6N 118°27W 126 B2
Stone Mountain U.S.A. 33°49N 84°10W 316 B5
Stone Park U.S.A. 41°53N 87°52W 119 B1
Stoneboro U.S.A. 41°20N 80°7W 312 E4
Stonebridge U.K. 51°32N 0°16W 125 A2
Stoneham U.S.A. 42°29N 71°5W 116 A2
Stonehaven U.K. 56°59N 2°12W 167 E6
Stonehenge Queens., Australia 24°22S 143°17E 280 C3
Stonehenge Wilts., U.K. 51°9N 1°45W 169 F6
Stonewall Canada 50°10N 97°19W 297 C9
Stongfjorden Norway 61°26N 5°10E 164 C2
Stonington U.S.A. 39°44N 89°12W 310 E7
Stony Brook Res. U.S.A. 42°15N 71°19W 116 B2
Stony Creek → U.S.A. 41°38N 87°41W 119 C2
Stony Hill Jamaica 18°5N 76°48W 320 a
Stony I. U.S.A. 43°53N 76°19W 313 C8
Stony L. Man., Canada 58°51N 98°40W 297 B9
Stony L. Ont., Canada 44°30N 78°5W 312 B6
Stony Point U.S.A. 41°14N 73°59W 313 E11
Stony Pt. U.S.A. 43°50N 76°18W 313 C8
Stony Rapids Canada 59°16N 105°50W 297 B7
Stony River U.S.A. 61°47N 156°35W 303 F8
Stony Tunguska = Tunguska, Podkamennaya → Russia 61°50N 90°13E 215 C10
Stonyford U.S.A. 39°23N 122°33W 306 F4
Stopnica Poland 50°27N 20°57E 185 H7
Storå Sweden 59°42N 15°6E 162 E9
Storå → Denmark 56°20N 8°19E 163 H2
Stora Gla Sweden 59°30N 12°30E 162 E6
Stora Le Sweden 59°5N 11°55E 162 E5
Stora Lulevatten Sweden 67°10N 19°30E 160 C18
Stora Sjöfallet △ Sweden 67°29N 18°40E 160 C18
Stora Värtan Sweden 59°25N 18°7E 139 A2
Stóra-Vatnshorn Iceland 65°4N 21°33W 155 B5
Storavan Sweden 65°45N 18°10E 160 D18
Stord Norway 59°52N 5°23E 164 E2
Stordalen Norway 62°23N 7°0E 164 B4
Store Bælt Denmark 55°20N 11°0E 163 J4
Store Hareskov Denmark 55°46N 12°23E 118 A2
Store Heddinge Denmark 55°18N 12°23E 163 J6
Store Jukleggi = Høgeloft Norway 61°3N 8°12E 164 C5
Store Koldewey Greenland 76°30N 19°0W 154 B9
Store Magleby Denmark 55°35N 12°35E 118 B3
Store Mosse △ Sweden 57°18N 13°55E 163 G7
Store Sotra Norway 60°18N 5°4E 164 D1
Storebro Sweden 57°35N 15°52E 163 G9
Støren Norway 63°3N 10°18E 164 A7
Storerikvollen Norway 63°7N 11°58E 164 A8
Storfjellsætra Norway 61°40N 10°30E 164 C7
Storfjorden Norway 62°28N 6°35E 164 B3
Storfors Sweden 59°32N 14°17E 162 E8
Storholmen Sweden 59°23N 18°8E 139 A2
Stóridalur Iceland 63°38N 19°57W 155 D7
Stórinúpur Iceland 64°3N 20°10W 155 C6
Storkerson Pen. Canada 72°30N 106°30W 294 C10
Storkyrkan Stockholm, Sweden 139 c2
Storli Norway 62°42N 9°5E 164 B6
Storlien Sweden 63°19N 12°6E 162 A6
Storm B. Australia 43°10S 147°30E 281 G4
Storm Lake U.S.A. 42°39N 95°13W 308 D6
Stormberge S. Africa 31°16S 26°17E 270 D4
Stormsrivier S. Africa 33°59S 23°52E 270 D3
Stornoway U.K. 58°13N 6°23W 167 C2
Storo Italy 45°51N 10°35E 198 C7
Storozhinets = Storozhynets Ukraine 48°14N 25°45E 183 B10
Storozhynets Ukraine 48°14N 25°45E 183 B10
Storrs U.S.A. 41°49N 72°15W 313 E12
Storsjøen Hedmark, Norway 60°20N 11°40E 164 D8
Storsjøen Hedmark, Norway 61°30N 11°14E 164 C8
Storsjön Gävleborg, Sweden 60°35N 16°45E 162 D10
Storsjön Jämtland, Sweden 62°48N 13°7E 162 B7
Storsjön Jämtland, Sweden 63°9N 14°30E 162 A8
Storsølnkletten Norway 61°59N 10°16E 164 C7
Storstrømmen Greenland 76°17N 22°25W 154 B8
Storuman Sweden 65°5N 17°10E 160 D17
Storuman, L. Sweden 65°13N 16°50E 160 D17
Storuvellir Iceland 65°30N 17°29W 155 B9
Storvätteshågna Sweden 62°6N 12°30E 162 B6
Storvigelen Norway 62°32N 12°2E 164 B9
Storvik Sweden 60°35N 16°33E 162 D10
Storvreta Sweden 59°58N 17°44E 162 E11
Story City U.S.A. 42°11N 93°36W 310 B3
Stouffville Canada 43°58N 79°15W 312 C5
Stoughton Sask., Canada 49°40N 103°0W 297 D8
Stoughton Wis., U.S.A. 42°55N 89°13W 310 B8
Stour → Dorset, U.K. 50°43N 1°47W 169 G6
Stour → Kent, U.K. 51°18N 1°22E 169 F9
Stour → Suffolk, U.K. 51°57N 1°4E 169 F9
Stourbridge U.K. 52°28N 2°8W 169 E5
Stout L. Canada 52°0N 94°40W 297 C10
Stove Pipe Wells Village U.S.A. 36°35N 117°11W 307 J9
Støvring Denmark 56°54N 9°50E 163 H3
Stow U.S.A. 41°10N 81°27W 312 E3
Stowbtsy Belarus 53°30N 26°43E 177 B14
Stowmarket U.K. 52°12N 1°0E 169 E9
Stoyka Russia 59°57N 30°25E 137 B2
Strabane U.K. 54°50N 7°27W 166 B4
Stracin Macedonia 42°13N 22°2E 202 D6
Stradella Italy 45°5N 9°18E 198 C6
Strahan Australia 42°9S 145°20E 281 G4
Straiton U.K. 55°53N 3°9W 121 B3
Strajitsa Bulgaria 43°14N 25°58E 203 C9
Strakonice Czech Rep. 49°15N 13°53E 180 B6
Straldzha Bulgaria 42°35N 26°40E 203 D10
Stralsund Germany 54°18N 13°4E 178 A9
Strand Hedmark, Norway 61°17N 11°17E 164 C8
Strand Western Cape, S. Africa 34°9S 18°48E 270 D2
Strand London, U.K. 125 b4
Stranda Møre og Romsdal, Norway 62°19N 6°58E 164 B3
Stranda Nord-Trøndelag, Norway 63°33N 10°14E 160 E14
Strandasýsla □ Iceland 65°45N 21°45W 155 B5
Strandby Denmark 57°30N 10°29E 163 G4
Strandfontein S. Africa 34°4S 18°34E 118 B2
Strangford L. U.K. 54°30N 5°37W 166 B6
Strängnäs Sweden 59°23N 17°2E 162 E11
Stranorlar Ireland 54°48N 7°46W 166 B4
Stranraer U.K. 54°54N 5°1W 167 G3
Strasbourg Sask., Canada 51°4N 104°55W 297 C8
Strasbourg Bas-Rhin, France 48°35N 7°42E 173 D14
Strasburg Germany 53°30N 13°43E 178 B9
Străşeni Moldova 47°8N 28°36E 183 C13
Strašnice Czech Rep. 50°4N 14°28E 135 B2
Strässa Sweden 59°44N 15°12E 162 E9
Strassburg = Aiud Romania 46°19N 23°44E 183 D8
Strasstrudering Germany 48°6N 11°41E 131 B3
Stratford N.S.W., Australia 32°7S 151°55E 283 B9
Stratford Vic., Australia 37°59S 147°7E 283 D7
Stratford Ont., Canada 43°23N 81°0W 312 C4
Stratford N.Z. 39°20S 174°19E 284 F3
Stratford London, U.K. 51°33N 0°0 125 A4
Stratford Calif., U.S.A. 36°11N 119°49W 306 J7
Stratford Conn., U.S.A. 41°12N 73°8W 313 E11
Stratford Tex., U.S.A. 36°20N 102°4W 314 C3
Stratford-upon-Avon U.K. 52°12N 1°42W 169 E6
Strath Spey U.K. 57°9N 3°49W 167 D5
Strathalbyn Australia 35°13S 138°53E 282 C3
Strathaven U.K. 55°40N 4°5W 167 F4
Strathcona ⌂ Canada 49°38N 125°40W 296 D3
Strathfield Australia 33°52S 151°5E 139 B1
Strathmore Alta., Canada 51°5N 113°18W 296 C6
Strathmore Angus, U.K. 56°37N 3°7W 167 E5
Strathmore Calif., U.S.A. 36°9N 119°4W 306 J7
Strathnaver Canada 53°20N 122°33W 296 C4
Strathpeffer U.K. 57°35N 4°32W 167 D4
Strathroy Canada 42°58N 81°38W 312 D3
Strathy Pt. U.K. 58°36N 4°1W 167 C4
Strattanville U.S.A. 41°12N 79°19W 312 E5
Stratton U.S.A. 45°8N 70°26W 313 A14
Stratton Mt. U.S.A. 43°4N 72°55W 313 C12
Straubing Germany 48°52N 12°34E 179 G8
Straumnes Iceland 66°26N 23°8W 155 A3
Strausberg Germany 52°35N 13°54E 178 C9
Strawberry → U.S.A. 40°10N 110°24W 304 F8
Strawberry Point U.S.A. 42°41N 91°32W 310 B5
Strážnice Czech Rep. 48°54N 17°19E 181 C10
Streaky B. Australia 32°48S 134°13E 281 E1
Streaky Bay Australia 32°51S 134°18E 281 E1
Streatham U.K. 51°25N 0°7W 125 B3
Streatham Vale U.K. 51°24N 0°8W 125 B3
Streator U.S.A. 41°8N 88°50W 311 C8
Strebersdorf Austria 48°17N 16°23E 142 A2
Středočeský □ Czech Rep. 49°55N 14°30E 180 B7
Streetsboro U.S.A. 41°14N 81°21W 312 E3
Streetsville Canada 43°35N 79°42W 312 C5
Strehaia Romania 44°37N 23°10E 183 F8
Strehlen = Strzelin Poland 50°46N 17°2E 185 H4
Strelcha Bulgaria 42°25N 24°19E 203 D8
Streng → Cambodia 13°12N 103°37E 236 F4
Stresa Italy 45°52N 8°28E 198 C5
Strešovice Czech Rep. 50°5N 14°23E 135 B2
Streymoy Færoe Is. 62°8N 7°5W 160 E9
Strezhevoy Russia 60°42N 77°34E 214 C8
Stříbro Czech Rep. 49°44N 13°0E 180 A6
Strickland → Papua N. G. 7°35S 141°36E 286 D1
Striegau = Strzegom Poland 50°58N 16°20E 185 H3
Strilky Ukraine 49°20N 22°59E 185 J9
Strimonas → Greece 40°46N 23°51E 202 F7
Strip, The U.S.A. 36°7N 115°10W 124 B2
Střížkov Czech Rep. 50°7N 14°28E 135 B2
Stroeder Argentina 40°12S 62°37W 336 B4
Strofades Greece 37°15N 21°0E 204 D3
Strogino Russia 55°48N 37°24E 129 B2
Strokestown Ireland 53°46N 8°7W 166 C3
Stroma U.K. 58°41N 3°7W 167 C5
Strombeek-Bever Belgium 50°54N 4°21E 116 A2
Stromberg-Heuchelberg ⌂ Germany 49°2N 8°50E 179 F4
Strómboli Italy 38°47N 15°13E 201 D8
Stromeferry U.K. 57°21N 5°33W 167 D3
Strommen Norway 59°57N 11°0E 164 E7
Stromness U.K. 58°58N 3°17W 167 C5
Stromovka Czech Rep. 50°6N 14°25E 135 B2
Strömsbruk Sweden 61°52N 17°18E 162 C11
Stromsburg U.S.A. 41°7N 97°36W 308 E5
Strömsnäsbruk Sweden 56°35N 13°45E 163 H7
Strömstad Sweden 58°56N 11°10E 163 F5
Strömsund Sweden 63°51N 15°33E 160 E16
Stronghurst U.S.A. 40°45N 90°55W 310 D6
Strongili Greece 36°6N 29°42E 205 E11
Strongoli Italy 39°16N 17°3E 201 C10
Strongsville U.S.A. 41°19N 81°50W 312 E3
Stronie Śląskie Poland 50°18N 16°53E 185 H3
Stronsay U.K. 59°7N 2°35W 167 B6
Stropkov Slovak Rep. 49°13N 21°39E 181 B14
Stroud U.K. 51°45N 2°13W 169 F5
Stroud Road Australia 32°18S 151°57E 283 B9
Stroudsburg U.S.A. 40°59N 75°12W 313 F9
Stroumbi Cyprus 34°53N 32°29E 207 E8
Štrpce Kosovo 42°14N 21°1E 202 D5
Struer Denmark 56°30N 8°35E 163 H2
Struga Macedonia 41°11N 20°44E 202 E4
Strugi Krasnyye Russia 58°21N 29°1E 188 C5
Strumica Macedonia 41°28N 22°41E 202 E6
Strumica → Europe 41°20N 23°22E 202 E7
Strumok Ukraine 45°43N 29°27E 183 E14
Struthers U.S.A. 41°4N 80°39W 312 E4
Stryama Bulgaria 42°16N 24°54E 203 D8
Stryker U.S.A. 48°41N 114°46W 304 B6
Stryków Poland 51°55N 19°33E 185 G6
Stryn Norway 61°54N 6°43E 164 C3
Stryy Ukraine 49°16N 23°48E 177 D12
Strzegom Poland 50°58N 16°20E 185 H3
Strzelce Krajeńskie Poland 52°52N 15°33E 185 F2
Strzelce Opolskie Poland 50°31N 18°18E 185 H5
Strzelecki Cr. → Australia 29°37S 139°59E 281 D2
Strzelecki Desert Australia 29°30S 140°0E 281 D3
Strzelin Poland 50°46N 17°2E 185 H4
Strzelno Poland 52°35N 18°9E 185 F5
Strzybnica Poland 50°28N 18°48E 185 H5
Strzyżów Poland 49°52N 21°47E 185 J8
Stuart Fla., U.S.A. 27°12N 80°15W 317 H9
Stuart Iowa, U.S.A. 41°30N 94°19W 310 C2
Stuart Nebr., U.S.A. 42°36N 99°8W 308 D4
Stuart → Canada 54°0N 123°35W 296 C4
Stuart Bluff Ra. Australia 22°50S 131°52E 278 D5
Stuart I. U.S.A. 63°35N 162°30W 303 E7
Stuart L. Canada 54°30N 124°30W 296 C4
Stuart Mts. N.Z. 45°2S 167°39E 285 F2
Stuart Ra. Australia 29°10S 134°56E 281 D1
Stubbekøbing Denmark 54°53N 12°9E 163 K6
Stubbs St. Vincent 13°7N 61°9W 323 n
Stuben Austria 47°10N 10°8E 180 D3
Štubnianske Teplice = Turčianske Teplice Slovak Rep. 48°52N 18°52E 181 C11
Studen Kladenets, Yazovir Bulgaria 41°37N 25°30E 203 E9
Studenka Czech Rep. 49°44N 18°5E 181 B11
Studholme N.Z. 44°42S 171°9E 285 E6
Studio City U.S.A. 34°8N 118°24W 126 B2
Studley Park Trin. & Tob. 11°11N 60°40W 323 s
Stugudalen Norway 62°53N 11°53E 164 B8
Stugun Sweden 63°10N 15°40E 162 A9
Stuhlweissenberg = Székesfehérvár Hungary 47°15N 18°25E 182 C3
Stuhm = Sztum Poland 53°55N 19°1E 184 E6
Stuhr Germany 53°5N 8°44E 178 B4
Stull L. Canada 54°24N 92°34W 298 B1
Stung Treng = Stoeng Treng Cambodia 13°31N 105°58E 236 F5
Stupart → Canada 56°0N 93°25W 298 A1
Stupava Slovak Rep. 48°17N 17°2E 181 C10
Stupino Russia 54°57N 38°2E 188 E10
Stureby Sweden 59°15N 18°4E 139 B2
Sturge I. Antarctica 67°26S 164°47E 151 C11
Sturgeon B. Canada 52°0N 97°50W 297 C9
Sturgeon Bay U.S.A. 44°50N 87°23W 308 C10
Sturgeon Falls Canada 46°25N 79°57W 298 C4
Sturgeon L. Alta., Canada 55°6N 117°32W 296 B5
Sturgeon L. Ont., Canada 50°0N 90°45W 298 C1
Sturgeon L. Ont., Canada 44°28N 78°43W 312 B6
Sturgis Sask., Canada 51°56N 102°36W 297 C8
Sturgis Mich., U.S.A. 41°48N 85°25W 311 C11
Sturgis S. Dak., U.S.A. 44°25N 103°31W 308 C2
Sturkö Sweden 56°5N 15°42E 163 H9
Štúrovo Slovak Rep. 47°48N 18°41E 181 D11
Sturt △ Australia 27°17S 141°37E 281 D3
Sturt Cr. → Australia 19°8S 127°50E 278 C4
Sturt Stony Desert Australia 28°30S 141°0E 281 D3
Sturts Meadows Australia 31°18S 141°42E 282 A4
Stutterheim S. Africa 32°33S 27°28E 270 D4
Stuttgart Baden-W., Germany 48°48N 9°11E 179 G5
Stuttgart Ark., U.S.A. 34°30N 91°33W 314 D9
Stuttgart Echterdingen ✕ (STR) Germany 48°42N 9°11E 179 G5
Stutthof = Sztutowo Poland 54°20N 19°15E 184 D6
Stuvsta Sweden 59°15N 18°0E 139 B2
Stuyvesant U.S.A. 42°23N 73°45W 313 D11
Stykkishólmur Iceland 65°2N 22°40W 155 B4
Styria = Steiermark □ Austria 47°26N 15°0E 180 D8
Styrsö Sweden 57°37N 11°46E 163 G5
Su-no-Saki Japan 34°58N 139°45E 223 C11
Su Xian = Suzhou China 33°41N 116°59E 226 H9
Suakin Sudan 19°8N 37°20E 256 D4
Suakin Archipelago Sudan 18°42N 38°30E 256 D4
Suan N. Korea 38°42N 126°22E 224 C3
Suana Indonesia 8°44S 115°36E 231 K18
Süanhwa = Xuanhua China 40°40N 115°2E 226 D8
Suao Taiwan 24°36N 121°51E 225 E13
Suapure → Venezuela 6°48N 67°1W 328 B4
Suar India 29°2N 79°3E 243 E8
Suau Papua N. G. 10°37S 150°22E 286 F6
Suavanao Solomon Is. 7°35S 158°47E 287 L10
Şubā St. Arabia 27°10N 35°40E 246 E2
Subang Indonesia 6°34S 107°45E 235 D3
Subankhata India 26°48N 91°25E 241 B3
Subansiri → India 26°48N 93°50E 241 B4
Subarnagiri India 19°50N 83°51E 244 E6
Subarnarekha → India 22°34N 87°24E 243 H12
Subay', Urūq St. Arabia 22°15N 43°5E 256 C5
Şubayhah St. Arabia 30°2N 38°50E 246 D3
Subcetate Romania 45°36N 23°0E 182 E8
Subhepur India 28°44N 77°15E 120 A2
Subi Indonesia 2°58N 108°50E 235 B3
Subiaco Italy 41°56N 13°5E 199 G10
Subic B. Phil. 14°44N 120°12E 232 D3
Subotica Serbia 46°6N 19°39E 182 D4
Suburban Canal U.S.A. 30°2N 90°11W 131 B1
Suca Ethiopia 6°31N 39°14E 257 F4
Sucat Phil. 14°27N 121°2E 127 C2
Suceava Romania 47°38N 26°16E 183 C11
Suceava □ Romania 47°37N 25°40E 183 C10
Suceava → Romania 47°32N 26°32E 183 C11
Sucha-Beskidzka Poland 49°44N 19°35E 185 J6
Suchan = Partizansk Russia 43°8N 133°9E 215 E14
Suchań Poland 53°18N 15°18E 185 E2
Suchdol Czech Rep. 50°8N 14°22E 135 B2
Suchedniów Poland 51°3N 20°49E 185 G7
Suchil Mexico 23°39N 103°54W 318 C4
Suchou = Suzhou China 31°19N 120°38E 229 B13
Süchow = Xuzhou China 34°18N 117°10E 227 G9
Suchowola Poland 53°33N 23°3E 184 E10
Sucio → Colombia 7°27N 77°7W 328 B2
Suck → Ireland 53°17N 8°3W 166 C3
Suckling, Mt. Papua N. G. 9°49S 148°53E 286 E5
Sucre Bolivia 19°0S 65°15W 331 D4
Sucre Colombia 8°49N 74°44W 328 B3
Sucre □ Colombia 8°50N 75°40W 328 B2
Sucre □ Venezuela 10°25N 63°30W 329 A5
Sucuaro Colombia 4°34N 68°50W 328 C4
Sucumbíos □ Ecuador 0°6S 76°52W 328 D2
Sućuraj Croatia 43°10N 17°8E 199 E14
Sucuriju Brazil 1°39N 49°57W 332 A2
Sucuriú → Brazil 20°47S 51°38W 331 E7
Sucy-en-Brie France 48°46N 2°31E 134 B4
Sud □ Cameroon 2°30N 11°45E 263 E7
Sud, Pte. Comoros Is. 11°53S 43°29E 272 a
Sud, Pte. du Canada 49°3N 62°14W 299 C7
Sud-Kivu □ Dem. Rep. of the Congo 3°0S 28°30E 268 C2
Sud-Ouest □ Cameroon 5°25N 9°20E 263 D6
Sud-Ouest, Pte. Qué., Canada 49°23N 63°36W 299 C7
Sud Ouest, Pte. Mauritius 20°28S 57°18E 272 e
Suda → Russia 59°0N 37°40E 188 C9
Sudak Ukraine 44°51N 34°57E 189 K8
Sudan U.S.A. 34°4N 102°31W 314 D3
Sudan ■ Africa 15°0N 30°0E 257 E3
Sudan, South ■ Africa 8°0N 30°0E 257 F2
Sudauen = Suwałki Poland 54°8N 22°59E 184 D9
Sudbury Ont., Canada 46°30N 81°0W 298 C3
Sudbury Suffolk, U.K. 52°2N 0°45E 169 E8
Sudd South Sudan 8°20N 30°0E 257 F3
Sudie Guyana 7°8N 58°29W 329 B6
Sudeifel = Deutsch-Luxemburgischer ⌂ Germany 49°58N 6°12E 179 F2
Süderbrarup Germany 54°38N 9°45E 178 A5
Süderlügum Germany 54°52N 8°54E 178 A4
Süderoogsand Germany 54°27N 8°28E 178 A4
Sudeten Mts. = Sudety Europe 50°20N 16°45E 181 A9
Sudety Europe 50°20N 16°45E 181 A9
Suðavík Iceland 66°2N 23°0W 155 A3
Südheide ⌂ Germany 52°46N 10°10E 178 C6
Suður-múlasýsla □ Iceland 65°0N 14°30W 155 C12
Suður-þingeyjarsýsla □ Iceland 65°30N 17°0W 155 B9
Suðureyri Iceland 66°7N 23°32W 155 A3
Suðuroy Færoe Is. 61°32N 6°50W 160 F9
Sudi Tanzania 10°11S 39°57E 269 E4
Sudirman, Pegunungan Indonesia 4°30S 137°0E 231 E9
Sudiți Romania 44°35N 27°38E 183 F12
Sudogda Russia 55°55N 40°50E 190 C5
Sudong, Pulau Singapore 1°13N 103°44E 127 D1
Sudostroy = Severodvinsk Russia 64°27N 39°58E 186 B6
Sudova Vyshnya Ukraine 49°46N 23°22E 185 J10
Sudzha Russia 51°14N 35°17E 189 G8
Sue → South Sudan 7°41N 28°3E 257 F2
Sue, L. U.S.A. 28°34N 81°21W 133 A2
Sueca Spain 39°12N 0°21W 197 F4
Süedinenie Bulgaria 42°16N 24°33E 203 D8
Suemez I. U.S.A. 55°15N 133°20W 296 B2
Sueyoshi Japan 31°40N 131°5E 222 F3
Suez = El Suweis Egypt 29°58N 32°31E 256 B3
Suez, G. of = Suweis, Khalîg el Egypt 28°40N 33°0E 256 J8
Suez Canal = Suweis, Qanâ es Egypt 31°0N 32°20E 256 H8
Suffield Canada 50°12N 111°10W 296 C6
Suffolk U.S.A. 36°44N 76°35W 309 G15
Suffolk □ U.K. 52°16N 1°0E 169 E9
Şufiān Iran 38°16N 45°58E 213 C11
Sugag-no-Sen Japan 35°25N 134°25E 222 B6
Şugag Romania 45°47N 23°37E 183 E8
Sugamo Japan 35°44N 139°43E 140 A3
Sugar → U.S.A. 42°26N 89°12W 310 B7
Sugar Cr. → Ill., U.S.A. 40°9N 89°38W 310 D7
Sugar Cr. → Ind., U.S.A. 39°51N 87°21W 311 E9
Sugar Grove U.S.A. 41°59N 79°20W 312 E5
Sugar Hill U.S.A. 34°6N 84°2W 316 A5
Sugar Loaf Grenada 12°13N 61°36W 323 q
Sugar Loaf Mt. = Açúcar, Pão de Brazil 22°56S 43°9W 135 B2
Sugar Loaf Pt. St. Helena 15°54S 5°42W 153 h
Sugarcreek U.S.A. 41°25N 79°52W 312 E5
Sugarive → India 26°16N 86°24E 243 F12
Sugbai Passage Phil. 5°22N 120°33E 233 J3
Suge Japan 35°37N 139°32E 140 B2
Sughd □ Tajikistan 40°0N 69°0E 217 E7
Sugihwaras Indonesia 4°1S 103°46E 234 C2
Suginami Japan 35°41N 139°37E 140 A2
Suğla Gölü Turkey 37°20N 32°0E 212 D5
Sugluk = Salluit Canada 62°14N 75°38W 295 E16
Sugun Japan 35°34N 139°35E 140 B2
Sugun China 39°53N 76°47E 217 E9
Suha Reke = Suva Reka Kosovo 42°21N 20°50E 202 D4
Suhaia, Lacul Romania 43°45N 25°15E 183 G10
Şuḩār Oman 24°20N 56°40E 247 E8
Sühbaatar Mongolia 50°17N 106°10E 218 A10
Sühbaatar □ Mongolia 45°30N 114°0E 226 B8
Suheli Par India 10°5N 72°17E 245 J1
Suhl Germany 50°36N 10°42E 178 E6
Şuhut Turkey 38°31N 30°32E 205 C12
Sui Pakistan 28°37N 69°19E 242 E3

Sui Sai Wan *China* 22°16N 114°14E **122** B1
Sui Xian *China* 34°25N 115°2E **226** G8
Suiá Missu → *Brazil* 11°13S 53°15W **331** C7
Šuica *Bos.-H.* 43°52N 17°11E **182** G2
Suichang *China* 28°29N 119°15E **229** C12
Suichuan *China* 26°20N 114°32E **229** D10
Suide *China* 37°30N 110°12E **226** F6
Suifenhe *China* 44°25N 131°10E **227** B16
Suihua *China* 46°32N 126°55E **219** B14
Suijiang *China* 28°40N 103°59E **228** C4
Suining *Hunan, China* 26°35N 110°10E **229** D8
Suining *Jiangsu, China* 33°56N 117°58E **227** H9
Suining *Sichuan, China* 30°26N 105°35E **228** B5
Suiping *China* 33°10N 113°59E **226** H7
Suippes *France* 49°8N 4°30E **173** C11
Suir → *Ireland* 52°16N 7°9W **166** D4
Suisse = Switzerland ■ *Europe* 46°30N 8°0E **179** J4
Suisun City *U.S.A.* 38°15N 122°2W **306** G4
Suita *Japan* 34°45N 135°30E **133** A2
Suitland *U.S.A.* 38°50N 76°55W **143** B4
Suixi *China* 21°19N 110°18E **229** G8
Suiyang *Guizhou, China* 27°58N 107°18E **228** D6
Suiyang *Heilongjiang, China* 44°30N 130°56E **227** B16
Suizhong *China* 40°21N 120°20E **227** D11
Suizhou *China* 31°42N 113°24E **229** B9
Sujangarh *India* 27°42N 74°31E **242** F6
Sujiatun *China* 41°39N 123°20E **227** D12
Sukabumi *Indonesia* 6°56S 106°50E **234** D3
Sukadana *Kalimantan Barat, Indonesia* 1°10S 110°0E **235** C4
Sukadana *Lampung, Indonesia* 5°5S 105°33E **234** D3
Sukadana, Teluk *Indonesia* 1°24S 109°50E **235** C3
Sukagawa *Japan* 37°17N 140°23E **221** F10
Sukamade *Indonesia* 8°30S 113°52E **235** D4
Sukamara *Indonesia* 2°43S 111°10E **235** C4
Sukaraja *Indonesia* 2°28S 110°25E **235** C4
Sukarnapura = Jayapura *Indonesia* 2°28S 140°38E **231** E10
Sukarno, Puntjak = Jaya, Puncak *Indonesia* 3°57S 137°17E **231** E9
Sukau *Malaysia* 5°32N 118°17E **235** A5
Sukawati *Indonesia* 8°35S 115°17E **231** K18
Sukchar *India* 22°42N 88°22E **124** A2
Sukch'ŏn *N. Korea* 39°22N 125°35E **224** C2
Sukhindol *Bulgaria* 43°11N 25°10E **203** C9
Sukhinichi *Russia* 54°8N 35°10E **188** E8
Sukhona → *Russia* 61°15N 46°39E **186** C6
Sukhothai *Thailand* 17°1N 99°49E **236** D2
Sukhumi = Sokhumi *Georgia* 43°0N 41°0E **191** J5
Sukkertoppen = Maniitsoq *Greenland* 65°26N 52°55W **154** D5
Sukkur *Pakistan* 27°42N 68°54E **242** F3
Sukkur Barrage *Pakistan* 27°40N 68°50E **242** F3
Sukma *India* 18°24N 81°45E **244** E5
Sukovo *Serbia* 43°4N 22°37E **202** C6
Sukri → *India* 25°4N 71°43E **242** G4
Sukumo *Japan* 32°56N 132°44E **222** E4
Sukunka → *Canada* 55°45N 121°15W **296** B4
Sul, Canal do *Brazil* 0°10S 48°30W **332** B2
Sula *Norway* 61°7N 4°54E **164** C1
Sula → *Ukraine* 49°40N 32°41E **189** H7
Sula, Kepulauan *Indonesia* 1°45S 125°0E **231** E7
Sulaco → *Honduras* 15°2N 87°44W **320** C2
Sulaiman Range *Pakistan* 30°30N 69°50E **242** D3
Sulak → *Russia* 43°20N 47°34E **191** J8
Sulakyurt *Turkey* 40°9N 33°43E **212** B5
Sūlār *Iran* 31°53N 51°54E **247** D6
Sulawesi *Indonesia* 2°0S 120°0E **235** C5
Sulawesi Barat □ *Indonesia* 3°0S 119°0E **235** C5
Sulawesi Sea = Celebes Sea *Indonesia* 3°0N 123°0E **231** D6
Sulawesi Selatan □ *Indonesia* 2°30S 120°0E **231** E6
Sulawesi Tengah □ *Indonesia* 1°30S 121°0E **231** E6
Sulawesi Tenggara □ *Indonesia* 3°50S 122°0E **231** E6
Sulawesi Utara □ *Indonesia* 1°0N 124°0E **231** D6
Suldalsheiene *Norway* 59°28N 7°10E **164** E3
Suldalsosen *Norway* 59°29N 6°29E **164** E3
Sulechów *Poland* 52°5N 15°40E **185** F2
Sulęcin *Poland* 52°26N 15°10E **185** F2
Sulei *Solomon Is.* 8°3S 159°34E **287** M10
Suleja *Nigeria* 9°10N 7°10E **263** D6
Sulejów *Poland* 51°26N 19°53E **185** G6
Sulejówek *Poland* 52°13N 21°17E **185** F8
Süleymanlı *Turkey* 38°58N 27°47E **205** C9
Sulima *S. Leone* 6°58N 11°32W **262** D2
Sulina *Romania* 45°10N 29°40E **183** E14
Sulina, Braţul → *Romania* 45°10N 29°40E **183** E14
Sulingen *Germany* 52°41N 8°48E **178** C4
Suliţa *Romania* 47°39N 26°59E **183** C11
Sulitjelma *Norway* 67°9N 16°3E **160** C17
Sulkowice *Poland* 49°50N 19°49E **185** J6
Sullana *Peru* 4°52S 80°39W **330** A1
Süller *Turkey* 38°9N 29°29E **205** C11
Sullivan *Ill., U.S.A.* 39°36N 88°37W **311** E8
Sullivan *Ind., U.S.A.* 39°6N 87°24W **311** E9
Sullivan *Mo., U.S.A.* 38°13N 91°10W **310** F5
Sullivan Bay *Canada* 50°55N 126°50W **296** C3
Sullivan I. = Lanbi Kyun *Burma* 10°50N 98°20E **237** G2
Sullom Voe *U.K.* 60°27N 1°20W **167** A7
Sullorsuaq *Greenland* 70°5N 53°0W **154** C5
Sully *U.S.A.* 41°34N 92°50W **310** C4
Sully-sur-Loire *France* 47°45N 2°20E **173** E9
Sulmierzyce *Poland* 51°37N 17°32E **185** G4
Sulmona *Italy* 42°3N 13°55E **199** F10
Süloğlu *Turkey* 41°44N 26°53E **203** E10
Sulphur *La., U.S.A.* 30°14N 93°23W **314** F8
Sulphur *Okla., U.S.A.* 34°31N 96°58W **314** D6
Sulphur Ft. *Canada* 60°56N 114°48W **296** A6
Sulphur Springs *U.S.A.* 33°8N 95°36W **314** E7
Sulsul *Ethiopia* 5°5N 44°50E **267** C5
Sultan *Ont., Canada* 47°36N 82°47W **298** C3
Sultan *Wash., U.S.A.* 47°52N 121°49W **306** C5
Sultan Dağları *Turkey* 38°20N 31°20E **212** C4
Sultan Hamud *Kenya* 2°1S 37°22E **268** C4
Sultan Kudarat *Phil.* 7°16N 124°18E **233** H5
Sultan Kudarat □ *Phil.* 6°30N 124°10E **233** H5
Sultan Naga Dimaporo *Phil.* 7°55N 123°44E **233** H4
Sultan sa Barongis *Phil.* 6°45N 124°35E **233** H5
Sultanābād = Arāk *Iran* 34°0N 49°40E **247** C6
Sultanahme Camil *Turkey* 41°0N 28°58E **122** B1
Sultanhisar *Turkey* 37°53N 28°9E **205** D10
Sultaniça *Turkey* 40°37N 26°8E **203** F10
Sultaniye *Turkey* 40°11N 28°12E **203** F12
Sultanpur *Mad. P., India* 23°9N 77°56E **242** H8
Sultanpur *Punjab, India* 31°13N 75°11E **242** D6
Sultanpur *Ut. P., India* 26°18N 82°4E **243** F10
Sulu □ *Phil.* 5°30N 120°30E **233** J3
Sulu Arch. *Phil.* 6°0N 121°0E **233** J3
Sulu Sea *E. Indies* 8°0N 120°0E **233** G3
Sülüklü *Turkey* 38°53N 32°20E **212** C5
Suluḷta *Ethiopia* 9°10N 38°43E **257** F4
Suluova *Turkey* 40°46N 35°32E **212** B6
Sulūq *Libya* 31°44N 20°14E **258** B4
Sulurú *India* 13°42N 80°1E **245** H5
Sulzbach *Germany* 49°18N 7°3E **179** F3
Sulzbach-Rosenberg *Germany* 49°30N 11°44E **179** F7
Sulzberger Ice Shelf *Antarctica* 78°0S 150°0W **151** E13
Sumaco -Napo Galeras △ *Ecuador* 0°34S 77°38W **328** D2
Sumalata *Indonesia* 1°0N 122°31E **231** D6
Sumale □ *Ethiopia* 7°0N 45°0E **257** G6
Sumampa *Argentina* 29°25S 63°29W **334** B3
Sumapaz △ *Colombia* 3°49N 74°13W **328** C3
Sumaré *Brazil* 22°48S 47°17W **333** F2
Sumatera *Indonesia* 0°40N 100°20E **234** B2
Sumatera Barat □ *Indonesia* 1°0S 101°0E **234** B1
Sumatera Selatan □ *Indonesia* 3°0S 104°0E **234** C2
Sumatera Utara □ *Indonesia* 2°30N 98°0E **234** B1
Sumatra = Sumatera *Indonesia* 0°40N 100°20E **234** B2
Sumatra *U.S.A.* 30°1N 84°59W **316** E5
Sumava △ *Czech Rep.* 49°0N 13°49E **180** C6
Sumba *Angola* 6°15S 12°38E **265** D2
Sumba *Indonesia* 9°45S 119°35E **231** F5
Sumba, Selat *Indonesia* 9°0S 118°40E **231** F5
Sumbawa *Indonesia* 8°26S 117°30E **235** D5
Sumbawa Besar *Indonesia* 8°30S 117°26E **235** D5
Sumbe *Angola* 11°10S 13°48E **265** E2
Sumbu △ *Zambia* 8°43S 30°22E **269** D3
Sumburgh Hd. *U.K.* 59°52N 1°17W **167** B7
Sumdeo *India* 31°26N 78°44E **243** D8
Sumdo *China* 35°6N 78°41E **243** B8
Sumé *Brazil* 7°39S 36°55W **332** C4
Sumedang *Indonesia* 6°52S 107°55E **235** D3
Sümeg *Hungary* 46°59N 17°20E **182** D2
Sumeih *Sudan* 9°50N 27°39E **257** F2
Šumen = Shumen *Bulgaria* 43°18N 26°55E **203** C10
Sumenep *Indonesia* 7°1S 113°52E **235** D4
Sumgait = Sumqayıt *Azerbaijan* 40°34N 49°38E **191** K9
Sumida *Japan* 35°42N 139°49E **140** A3
Sumida → *Japan* 35°39N 139°45E **140** A3
Sumisu-Jima *Japan* 31°27N 140°3E **223** F12
Sumiyoshi *Japan* 34°36N 135°30E **133** B2
Sumiyoshi Shrine *Japan* 34°36N 135°30E **133** B1
Summer L. *U.S.A.* 42°50N 120°45W **304** E3
Summerland *Canada* 49°32N 119°41W **296** D5
Summerland Key *U.S.A.* 24°40N 81°27W **317** L8
Summerside *Canada* 46°24N 63°47W **299** C7
Summersville *U.S.A.* 38°17N 80°51W **309** F13
Summerton *U.S.A.* 33°36N 80°20W **316** B9
Summertown *U.S.A.* 32°45N 82°16W **316** C7
Summerville *Ont., Canada* 43°37N 79°33W **141** B1
Summerville *Ga., U.S.A.* 34°29N 85°21W **315** D12
Summerville *S.C., U.S.A.* 33°1N 80°11W **316** B9
Summit *Alaska, U.S.A.* 63°20N 149°7W **303** E10
Summit *Ill., U.S.A.* 41°47N 87°47W **119** C2
Summit Lake *Canada* 54°20N 122°40W **296** C4
Summit Peak *U.S.A.* 37°21N 106°42W **305** H10
Sumner *N.Z.* 43°35S 172°48E **285** D7
Sumner *Ill., U.S.A.* 38°42N 87°53W **311** F9
Sumner *Iowa, U.S.A.* 42°51N 92°6W **310** B4
Sumner *Wash., U.S.A.* 47°12N 122°14W **306** C4
Sumner, L. *N.Z.* 42°42S 172°15E **285** C7
Sumner Tunnel *Boston, U.S.A.* **118** a3
Sumoto *Japan* 34°21N 134°54E **222** C6
Šumpangbinangae *Indonesia* 4°24S 119°36E **235** C5
Šumperk *Czech Rep.* 49°59N 16°59E **181** B9
Sumprabum *Burma* 26°33N 97°36E **241** B6
Sumqayıt *Azerbaijan* 40°34N 49°38E **191** K9
Sumter *U.S.A.* 33°55N 80°21W **316** B9
Sumxi *China* 34°35N 80°22E **217** F10
Sumy *Ukraine* 50°57N 34°50E **189** G8
Sumy □ *Ukraine* 50°50N 33°50E **189** G7
Sun City *North West, S. Africa* 25°17S 27°3E **270** C4
Sun City *Ariz., U.S.A.* 33°35N 112°16W **305** K7
Sun City *Calif., U.S.A.* 33°42N 117°11W **307** M9
Sun City Center *U.S.A.* 27°43N 82°21W **317** H7
Sun Lakes *U.S.A.* 33°10N 111°52W **305** K8
Sun Prairie *U.S.A.* 43°11N 89°13W **310** A7
Sun Valley *U.S.A.* 43°42N 114°21W **304** E6
Sunagawa *Japan* 43°29N 141°55E **220** C10
Sunamachi *Japan* 35°40N 139°50E **140** A4
Sunan *N. Korea* 39°15N 125°40E **224** C2
Sunart, L. *U.K.* 56°42N 5°43W **167** E3
Sunburst *U.S.A.* 48°53N 111°55W **304** B8
Sunbury *Vic., Australia* 37°35S 144°44E **283** D6
Sunbury *Pa., U.S.A.* 40°52N 76°48W **313** F8
Sunbury-on-Thames *U.K.* 51°25N 0°26W **125** B1
Sunchales *Argentina* 30°58S 61°35W **334** C3
Suncheon *S. Korea* 34°52N 127°31E **224** E3
Suncho Corral *Argentina* 27°55S 63°27W **334** B3
Sunch'ŏn *N. Korea* 39°25N 125°56E **224** C2
Suncook *U.S.A.* 43°8N 71°27W **313** C13
Sunda, Selat *Indonesia* 6°20S 105°30E **234** D3
Sunda Is. *Indonesia* 5°0S 105°0E **288** H2
Sunda Str. = Sunda, Selat *Indonesia* 6°20S 105°30E **234** D3
Sunda Trench = Java Trench *Ind. Oc.* 9°0S 105°0E **234** D2
Sundance *Man., Canada* 56°32N 94°4W **297** E10
Sundance *Wyo., U.S.A.* 44°24N 104°23W **304** E11
Sundar Nagar *India* 31°32N 76°53E **242** D7
Sundarbans *Asia* 22°0N 89°0E **241** E2
Sundarbans △ *India* 22°0N 88°45E **241** E2
Sundargarh *India* 22°4N 84°5E **244** C7
Sundays = Sondags → *S. Africa* 33°44S 25°51E **270** D4
Sundbyberg *Sweden* 59°22N 17°57E **139** A1
Sundbyerne *Denmark* 55°39N 12°36E **118** B3
Sunderland *Canada* 44°16N 79°4W **312** B5
Sunderland *Tyne & W., U.K.* 54°55N 1°23W **168** C6
Sundi Lutete *Dem. Rep. of the Congo* 4°34S 14°14E **265** C2
Sundown △ *Australia* 28°49S 151°38E **281** D5
Sundre *Canada* 51°49N 114°38W **296** C6
Sunds *Denmark* 56°13N 9°1E **163** H3
Sundsvall *Sweden* 62°23N 17°17E **162** B11
Sundsvallsbukten *Sweden* 62°21N 17°25E **162** B11
Sung Kong *China* 22°11N 114°17E **122** B2
Sungai Acheh *Malaysia* 5°8N 100°30E **237** c
Sungai Kolok *Thailand* 6°2N 101°58E **237** J3
Sungai Lembing *Malaysia* 3°55N 103°3E **237** L4
Sungai Petani *Malaysia* 5°37N 100°30E **237** K3
Sungai Siput *Malaysia* 4°49N 101°4E **234** B2
Sungaidurian *Indonesia* 0°6S 109°21E **235** C3
Sungaigerong *Indonesia* 2°59S 104°52E **234** C2
Sungailiat *Indonesia* 1°51S 106°8E **234** C3
Sungaipakning *Indonesia* 1°19N 102°8E **234** B2
Sungaipenuh *Indonesia* 2°1S 101°20E **234** C2
Sungari = Songhua Jiang → *China* 47°45N 132°30E **219** B15
Sungei Kadut Industrial Estate *Singapore* 1°24N 103°44E **138** A2
Sungei Selatar Res. *Singapore* 1°24N 103°51E **138** A3
Sungguminasa *Indonesia* 5°17S 119°30E **235** D5
Sunghua Chiang = Songhua Jiang → *China* 47°45N 132°30E **219** B15
Sungikai *Sudan* 12°20N 29°51E **257** E2
Sungsang *Indonesia* 2°22S 104°55E **234** C2
Sungu *Dem. Rep. of the Congo* 1°15S 17°21E **264** C3
Sungurlu *Turkey* 40°12N 34°21E **212** B6
Sunja *Croatia* 45°21N 16°35E **199** C13
Sunland Park *U.S.A.* 31°50N 106°40W **305** L10
Sunnansjö *Sweden* 60°13N 14°58E **162** D8
Sunndalsøra *Norway* 62°40N 8°33E **164** B5
Sunne *Sweden* 59°52N 13°5E **162** E7
Sunnemo *Sweden* 59°53N 13°44E **162** E7
Sunnfjord *Norway* 61°35N 5°45E **164** C2
Sunnmøre *Norway* 62°35N 6°30E **164** B3
Sunnyside *U.S.A.* 46°20N 120°0W **304** C4
Sunnyvale *U.S.A.* 37°23N 122°2W **306** H4
Sunrise *U.S.A.* 26°8N 80°14W **317** J9
Sunrise Manor *U.S.A.* 36°12N 115°4W **124** A2
Sunrise Mountain Natural Area *U.S.A.* 36°12N 114°58W **124** A2
Sunset Beach *U.S.A.* 21°40N 158°3W **302** J13
Sunset Park *N.Y., U.S.A.* 40°38N 73°59W **132** C2
Sunset Park *Nev., U.S.A.* 36°3N 115°6W **124** B2
Sunshine Coast *Australia* 26°30S 153°0E **276** F9
Suntar *Russia* 62°15N 117°30E **215** C12
Sunter *Indonesia* 6°7S 106°51E **122** A2
Sunter, Kali → *Indonesia* 6°10S 106°53E **122** B2
Suntrana *U.S.A.* 63°52N 148°51W **303** E10
Sunwi-do *N. Korea* 37°43N 125°16E **224** D2
Sunyani *Ghana* 7°21N 2°22W **262** D4
Suō-Nada *Japan* 33°50N 131°30E **222** D3
Suomenlinna *Finland* 60°9N 24°59E **121** C2
Suomenselkä *Finland* 62°52N 24°0E **160** E21
Suomi = Finland ■ *Europe* 63°0N 27°0E **160** E22
Suomussalmi *Finland* 64°54N 29°10E **160** D23
Suoyarvi *Russia* 62°3N 32°20E **188** A7
Supai *U.S.A.* 36°15N 112°41W **305** H7
Supamo → *Venezuela* 6°48N 61°50W **329** B5
Supaul *India* 26°10N 86°40E **243** F12
Superagüi △ *Brazil* 25°6S 48°18W **333** G2
Superior *Ariz., U.S.A.* 33°18N 111°6W **305** K8
Superior *Mont., U.S.A.* 47°12N 114°53W **304** C6
Superior *Nebr., U.S.A.* 40°1N 98°4W **308** E4
Superior *Wis., U.S.A.* 46°44N 92°6W **308** B7
Superior, L. *N. Amer.* 47°0N 87°0W **298** C2
Supetar *Croatia* 43°25N 16°32E **199** E13
Suphan Buri *Thailand* 14°14N 100°10E **236** E3
Suphan Dağı *Turkey* 38°54N 42°48E **213** C10
Supiori *Indonesia* 1°0S 136°0E **231** E9
Supraśl *Poland* 53°13N 23°19E **185** E10
Supraśl → *Poland* 53°11N 22°57E **185** E9
Supreme Court *Washington, D.C., U.S.A.* **143** b3
Supung *N. Korea* 40°27N 124°54E **224** B2
Supung Shuiku *China* 40°35N 124°50E **224** B2
Sūq' Abs *Yemen* 16°0N 43°12E **248** D3
Sūq ash Shuyūkh *Iraq* 30°53N 46°28E **246** D5
Sūq Suwayq *Si. Arabia* 24°23N 38°27E **246** E3
Şuqaylabīyah *Syria* 35°23N 36°23E **250** C7
Suqian *China* 33°54N 118°8E **227** H10
Suqutra = Socotra *Yemen* 12°30N 54°0E **249** D6
Şūr *Lebanon* 33°19N 35°16E **250** E6
Şūr *Oman* 22°34N 59°32E **249** B7
Sur, C. *Chile* 27°12S 109°26W **330** b
Sur, Pt. *U.S.A.* 36°18N 121°54W **306** J5
Sur Bahr *West Bank* 31°44N 35°13E **123** B2
Sura *India* 22°33N 88°24E **124** B2
Sura → *Russia* 56°6N 46°0E **190** C8
Surab *Pakistan* 28°25N 66°15E **242** E2
Surabaja = Surabaya *Indonesia* 7°17S 112°45E **235** D4
Surabaya *Indonesia* 7°17S 112°45E **235** D4
Surahammar *Sweden* 59°43N 16°13E **162** E10
Suraia *Romania* 45°40N 27°25E **183** E12
Surakarta *Indonesia* 7°35S 110°48E **235** D4
Suraksan *S. Korea* 37°40N 127°4E **137** A2
Surallah *Phil.* 6°22N 124°44E **233** H5
Šurany *Slovak Rep.* 48°6N 18°10E **181** C11
Surat *Queens., Australia* 27°10S 149°6E **281** D4
Surat *India* 21°12N 72°55E **244** D1
Surat Thani *Thailand* 9°6N 99°20E **237** H2
Suratgarh *India* 29°18N 73°55E **242** E5
Surathkal *India* 12°58N 74°46E **245** H2
Suraxanı *Azerbaijan* 40°25N 50°1E **191** K10
Şuraymilā *Si. Arabia* 25°7N 46°7E **246** E5
Suraż *Poland* 52°57N 22°57E **185** F9
Surazh *Belarus* 55°25N 30°44E **188** E6
Surazh *Russia* 53°5N 32°27E **189** F7
Surbiton *U.K.* 51°23N 0°17W **125** B2
Surduc *Romania* 47°15N 23°25E **183** C8
Surduc Pasul *Romania* 45°21N 23°23E **183** E8
Surdulica *Serbia* 42°41N 22°11E **202** D6
Surendranagar *India* 22°45N 71°40E **242** H4
Suresnes *France* 48°52N 2°13E **134** A2
Surf *U.S.A.* 34°41N 120°36W **307** L6
Surfers Paradise *Australia* 28°0S 153°25E **281** D5
Surfside *U.S.A.* 25°52N 80°7W **128** A2
Surgana *India* 20°34N 73°37E **244** D1
Surgères *France* 46°7N 0°47W **174** B3
Surgut *Russia* 61°14N 73°20E **214** C8
Sùria *Spain* 41°50N 1°45E **196** D6
Suriapet *India* 17°10N 79°40E **244** F4
Suribachi Yama *Iwo Jima* 24°45N 141°17E **288** b
Surigao *Phil.* 9°47N 125°29E **233** G5
Surigao del Norte □ *Phil.* 9°40N 125°40E **233** G5
Surigao del Sur □ *Phil.* 8°45N 126°0E **233** G6
Surigao Str. *Phil.* 10°15N 125°23E **233** F5
Surin *Thailand* 14°50N 103°34E **236** E4
Surinam = Suriname ■ *S. Amer.* 4°0N 56°0W **329** C6
Surinam *Mauritius* 20°30S 57°30E **272** d
Suriname ■ *S. Amer.* 4°0N 56°0W **329** C6
Suriname → *Suriname* 5°50N 55°15W **329** B6
Surjagarh *India* 19°36N 80°25E **244** E5
Surkhet → *Bangla.* 24°34N 91°14E **241** C3
Sūrmaq *Iran* 31°3N 52°48E **247** D7
Sürmene *Turkey* 41°0N 40°1E **213** B9
Surna → *Norway* 62°59N 8°40E **164** B5
Surnadalsøra *Norway* 62°58N 8°44E **164** B5
Surovikino *Russia* 48°32N 42°55E **191** F6
Surquillo *Peru* 12°6S 77°1W **126** B2
Surrency *U.S.A.* 31°44N 82°12W **316** D7
Surrey *Canada* 49°7N 122°45W **306** A4
Surrey □ *Jamaica* 18°5N 76°34W **320** a
Surrey □ *U.K.* 51°15N 0°31W **169** F7
Surrey Hills *Australia* 33°53S 151°13E **139** B2
Sursand *India* 26°39N 85°43E **243** F11
Sursar → *India* 26°14N 87°3E **243** F12
Sursee *Switz.* 47°11N 8°6E **179** H4
Sursk *Russia* 53°3N 45°40E **190** D7
Surskoye *Russia* 54°30N 46°44E **190** C8
Surt *Libya* 31°11N 16°39E **258** B3
Surt □ *Libya* 30°0N 17°30E **258** B3
Surt, Al Ḩamādah al *Libya* 30°0N 17°50E **258** C3
Surt, Khalīj *Libya* 31°40N 18°30E **258** B3
Surtanahu *Pakistan* 26°22N 70°0E **242** F4
Surte *Sweden* 57°50N 12°1E **163** G6
Surtsey *Iceland* 63°20N 20°30W **155** D3
Surubim *Brazil* 7°50S 35°45W **332** C4
Sürüç *Turkey* 36°58N 38°25E **213** D8
Surud, Ras *Somali Rep.* 11°10N 47°30E **267** B6
Surud Ad *Somali Rep.* 10°42N 47°9E **267** B6
Suruga-Wan *Japan* 34°45N 138°30E **223** C10
Surulangun *Indonesia* 2°37S 102°45E **234** C2
Surumu → *Brazil* 3°22N 60°19W **329** C5
Surxondaryo □ *Uzbekistan* 38°0N 67°30E **217** E7
Susa = Sousse *Tunisia* 35°50N 10°38E **258** A2
Susa *Italy* 45°8N 7°3E **198** C4
Suså → *Denmark* 55°12N 11°42E **163** J5
Sušac *Croatia* 42°46N 16°30E **199** F13
Susaek *S. Korea* 37°34N 126°54E **137** B1
Susak *Croatia* 44°30N 14°18E **199** D11
Susaki *Japan* 33°22N 133°17E **222** D5
Susam-Adasi = Samos *Europe* 37°45N 26°50E **205** D8
Süsangerd *Iran* 31°35N 48°6E **213** G13
Susanville *U.S.A.* 40°25N 120°39W **304** F3
Susch *Switz.* 46°46N 10°5E **179** J6
Suşehri *Turkey* 40°10N 38°6E **213** B8
Sušice *Czech Rep.* 49°17N 13°30E **180** B6
Susleni *Moldova* 47°25N 28°59E **183** C13
Susner *India* 23°57N 76°5E **242** H7
Susong *China* 30°10N 116°5E **229** B11
Susono *Japan* 35°10N 138°55E **223** B10
Susquehanna *U.S.A.* 41°57N 75°36W **313** E9
Susquehanna → *U.S.A.* 39°33N 76°5W **313** G8
Susques *Argentina* 23°35S 66°25W **334** A2
Süssenbrunn *Austria* 48°15N 16°29E **142** A2
Sussex *N.B., Canada* 45°45N 65°37W **299** C6
Sussex *N.J., U.S.A.* 41°13N 74°37W **313** E10
Sussex, E. □ *U.K.* 51°0N 0°20E **169** G8
Sussex, W. □ *U.K.* 51°0N 0°30W **169** G7
Sussex Inlet *Australia* 35°10S 150°36E **283** C9
Sustut → *Canada* 56°20N 127°30W **296** B3
Susuman *Russia* 62°47N 148°10E **215** C15
Susunu *Indonesia* 3°7S 133°39E **231** E8
Susurluk *Turkey* 39°54N 28°8E **205** B10
Susuz *Turkey* 40°46N 43°8E **213** B10
Susz *Poland* 53°44N 19°20E **184** E6
Sutay Uul *Asia* 46°35N 93°38E **218** B7
Sütçüler *Turkey* 37°29N 30°57E **212** D4
Şuteşti *Romania* 45°13N 27°27E **183** E12
Sutherland *N.S.W., Australia* 34°2S 151°4E **283** C9
Sutherland *Northern Cape, S. Africa* 32°24S 20°40E **270** D3
Sutherland *Highl., U.K.* 58°12N 4°50W **167** C4
Sutherland *Nebr., U.S.A.* 41°10N 101°8W **308** E3
Sutherland Falls *N.Z.* 44°48S 167°46E **285** E2
Sutherland Road *Barbados* 13°16N 59°39W **323** r
Sutherlin *U.S.A.* 43°23N 123°19W **304** E2
Suthri *India* 23°3N 68°55E **242** H3
Sutjeska △ *Bos.-H.* 43°30N 18°32E **182** G3
Sutlej → *Pakistan* 29°23N 71°3E **242** E4
Sutter *U.S.A.* 39°10N 121°45W **306** F5
Sutter Buttes *U.S.A.* 39°12N 121°49W **306** F5
Sutter Creek *U.S.A.* 38°24N 120°48W **306** G6
Sutton *Qué., Canada* 45°6N 72°37W **313** A12
Sutton *Dublin, Ireland* 53°23N 6°7W **120** A3
Sutton *N.Z.* 45°34S 170°8E **285** F5
Sutton *London, U.K.* 51°21N 0°11W **125** B2
Sutton *Nebr., U.S.A.* 40°36N 97°52W **308** E5
Sutton *W. Va., U.S.A.* 38°40N 80°43W **309** F13
Sutton → *Canada* 55°15N 83°45W **298** A3
Sutton Coldfield *U.K.* 52°35N 1°49W **169** E6
Sutton in Ashfield *U.K.* 53°8N 1°16W **168** D6
Sutton L. *Canada* 54°15N 84°42W **298** B3
Suttor → *Australia* 21°36S 147°2E **280** C4
Suttsu *Japan* 42°48N 140°14E **220** C10
Sutwik I. *U.S.A.* 56°34N 157°12W **303** H8
Suva *Fiji* 18°6S 178°30E **287** B2
Suva Gora *Macedonia* 41°45N 21°3E **202** E5
Suva Planina *Serbia* 43°10N 22°5E **202** C6
Suva Reka *Kosovo* 42°21N 20°50E **202** D4
Suvorov Russia 54°7N 36°30E **188** E9
Suvorov Is. = Suwarrow Is. *Cook Is.* 13°15S 163°5W **289** J11
Suvorove *Ukraine* 45°35N 28°59E **183** E13
Suvorovo *Bulgaria* 43°20N 27°35E **203** C11
Suwa *Japan* 36°2N 138°8E **223** A10
Suwa-Ko *Japan* 36°3N 138°5E **223** A10
Suwałki *Poland* 54°8N 22°59E **184** D9
Suwanee *U.S.A.* 34°3N 84°4W **316** A5
Suwannaphum *Thailand* 15°33N 103°47E **236** E4
Suwannee *U.S.A.* 29°20N 83°9W **317** F6
Suwannee → *U.S.A.* 29°17N 83°10W **317** F6
Suwannee Sd. *U.S.A.* 29°20N 83°15W **317** F6
Suwanose-Jima *Japan* 29°38N 129°43E **221** K4
Suwarrow Is. *Cook Is.* 13°15S 163°5W **289** J11
Suwayqiyah, Hawr as *Iraq* 32°40N 46°3E **213** G12
Suweis, Khalîg el *Egypt* 28°40N 33°0E **256** J8
Suweis, Qanâ es *Egypt* 31°0N 32°20E **256** H8
Suwon *S. Korea* 37°17N 127°1E **224** D3
Suyu *S. Korea* 37°37N 127°0E **137** B2
Suzaka *Japan* 36°39N 138°19E **223** A10
Suzdal *Russia* 56°29N 40°26E **188** D11
Suzhou *Anhui, China* 33°41N 116°59E **226** H9
Suzhou *Jiangsu, China* 31°19N 120°38E **229** B13
Suzu *Japan* 37°25N 137°17E **221** F8
Suzu-Misaki *Japan* 37°31N 137°21E **221** F8
Suzuka *Japan* 34°55N 136°36E **223** C8
Suzuka-Sammyaku *Japan* 35°5N 136°30E **223** B8
Suzukishinden *Japan* 35°43N 139°31E **140** A2
Suzun *Russia* 53°47N 82°18E **217** B10
Suzzara *Italy* 44°59N 10°45E **198** D7
Svalbard *Arctic* 78°0N 17°0E **154** B12
Svalbard Radio = Longyearbyen *Svalbard* 78°13N 15°40E **150** B8
Svalbarð *Iceland* 66°12N 15°43W **155** A11
Svalbarðseyri *Iceland* 65°45N 18°5W **155** B8
Svalöv *Sweden* 55°57N 13°8E **163** J7
Svalyava *Ukraine* 48°33N 22°59E **182** B7
Svaneke *Denmark* 55°8N 15°8E **163** J9
Svanemøllen *Denmark* 55°43N 12°34E **118** A3
Svängsta *Sweden* 56°16N 14°47E **163** H8
Svanskog *Sweden* 59°11N 12°33E **162** E6
Svappavaara *Sweden* 67°40N 21°3E **160** C19
Svärdsjö *Sweden* 60°45N 15°54E **162** D9
Svarstad *Norway* 59°27N 9°56E **164** E6
Svartå *Sweden* 59°8N 14°32E **162** E8
Svartárkot *Iceland* 65°20N 17°15W **155** B9
Svartevatn *Norway* 59°10N 6°56E **164** E3
Svartisen *Norway* 66°40N 13°59E **160** C15
Svartvik *Sweden* 62°19N 17°24E **162** B11
Svatove *Ukraine* 49°22N 38°15E **189** H10
Svatovo = Svatove *Ukraine* 49°22N 38°15E **189** H10
Svatsum *Norway* 61°20N 9°50E **164** D6
Svay Chek *Cambodia* 13°48N 102°58E **236** F4
Svay Rieng *Cambodia* 11°9N 105°45E **237** G5
Sveaborg = Suomenlinna *Finland* 60°9N 24°59E **121** C2
Svealand *Sweden* 60°20N 15°0E **162** D9
Svedala *Sweden* 55°30N 13°15E **163** J7
Sveg *Sweden* 62°2N 14°21E **162** B8
Sveindal *Norway* 58°29N 7°30E **164** F4
Sveinseyri *Iceland* 65°38N 23°51W **155** B3
Sveio *Norway* 59°33N 5°23E **164** E2
Svelgen *Norway* 61°45N 5°17E **164** C2
Svelvik *Norway* 59°37N 10°24E **164** E7
Svendborg *Denmark* 55°4N 10°35E **163** J4
Svene *Norway* 59°45N 9°31E **164** E6
Svenljunga *Sweden* 57°29N 13°5E **163** G7
Svenstavik *Sweden* 62°45N 14°26E **162** B8
Svenstrup *Denmark* 56°58N 9°50E **163** H3
Svenyhorodka *Ukraine* 49°4N 30°56E **189** H6
Sverdlov *Russia* 55°46N 37°36E **129** b
Sverdlovsk = Yekaterinburg *Russia* 56°50N 60°30E **214** D7
Sverdlovsk *Ukraine* 48°5N 39°47E **189** H10
Sverdrup Chan. *Canada* 79°56N 96°25W **295** B12
Sverdrup Is. *Canada* 79°0N 97°0W **292** B10
Sverige = Sweden ■ *Europe* 57°0N 15°0E **161** H16
Svestad *Norway* 59°46N 10°36E **133** B2
Svetac *Croatia* 43°3N 15°43E **199** E12
Sveti Ivan = Zelina *Croatia* 45°57N 16°16E **199** C13
Sveti Nikola, Prokhad *Europe* 43°27N 22°6E **202** C6
Sveti Nikole *Macedonia* 41°51N 21°56E **202** E5
Sveti Rok *Croatia* 44°22N 15°43E **199** D12
Sveti Vrach = Sandanski *Bulgaria* 41°35N 23°16E **202** E7
Svetlaya *Russia* 46°33N 138°18E **220** A9
Svetlogorsk = Svyetlahorsk *Belarus* 52°38N 29°46E **177** B15
Svetlogorsk *Russia* 54°56N 20°10E **184** D7
Svetlograd *Russia* 45°25N 42°58E **191** H6
Svetlovodsk = Svitlovodsk *Ukraine* 49°2N 33°13E **189** H7
Svetlyy *Kaliningrad, Russia* 54°41N 20°8E **184** D7
Svetlyy *Orenburg, Russia* 50°48N 60°51E **216** B6
Svidník *Slovak Rep.* 49°20N 21°37E **181** B14
Svignaskarð *Iceland* 64°40N 21°42W **155** C5
Svilaja Planina *Croatia* 43°49N 16°31E **199** E13
Svilajnac *Serbia* 44°15N 21°11E **202** B5
Svilengrad *Bulgaria* 41°49N 26°12E **203** E10
Svínafell *Iceland* 63°59N 16°51W **155** D10
Svinö *Finland* 60°7N 24°44E **121** C1
Svir → *Russia* 60°30N 32°48E **188** B7
Sviritsa *Russia* 60°29N 32°51E **188** B7
Svishtov *Bulgaria* 43°36N 25°23E **203** C9
Svislach *Belarus* 53°3N 24°2E **185** E11
Svitava → *Czech Rep.* 49°11N 16°37E **181** B9
Svitavy *Czech Rep.* 49°47N 16°28E **181** B9
Svitlovodsk *Ukraine* 49°2N 33°13E **189** H7
Svizzera = Switzerland ■ *Europe* 46°30N 8°0E **179** J4
Svobodnyy *Russia* 51°20N 128°0E **215** D13
Svoge *Bulgaria* 42°59N 23°23E **202** D7
Svolvær *Norway* 68°15N 14°34E **160** B16
Svorkmo *Norway* 63°10N 9°46E **164** A6
Svoronata *Greece* 38°7N 20°31E **207** C2
Svratka → *Czech Rep.* 49°11N 16°38E **181** B9
Svrljig *Serbia* 43°25N 22°6E **202** C6
Svullrya *Norway* 60°25N 12°23E **164** D9
Svyatogorovsky Rudnik = Dobropole *Ukraine* 48°25N 37°2E **189** H9
Svyetlahorsk *Belarus* 52°38N 29°46E **177** B15
Swa *Burma* 19°15N 96°17E **241** F6
Swa Tende *Dem. Rep. of the Congo* 7°9S 17°7E **265** D3
Swabian Alps = Schwäbische Alb *Germany* 48°20N 9°30E **179** G5
Swaffham *U.K.* 52°39N 0°42E **169** E8
Swains I. *Amer. Samoa* 11°11S 171°4W **289** J11
Swainsboro *U.S.A.* 32°36N 82°20W **316** C7
Swakop → *Namibia* 22°38S 14°36E **270** B2
Swakopmund *Namibia* 22°37S 14°30E **270** B1
Swale → *U.K.* 54°5N 1°20W **168** C6
Swamihalli *India* 14°52N 76°38E **245** G3
Swan → *W. Austral., Australia* 32°3S 115°45E **279** F2
Swan → *Man., Canada* 52°30N 100°45W **297** C8
Swan Hill *Australia* 35°20S 143°33E **282** C5
Swan Hills *Canada* 54°43N 115°24W **296** C5
Swan Is. = Santanilla, Is. *Honduras* 17°22N 83°57W **320** C3
Swan L. *Man., Canada* 52°30N 100°40W **297** C8
Swan L. *Ont., Canada* 54°16N 91°11W **298** B1
Swan Ra. *U.S.A.* 48°0N 113°45W **304** C7
Swan Reach *Australia* 34°35S 139°37E **282** C3
Swan River *Canada* 52°10N 101°16W **297** C8
Swanage *U.K.* 50°36N 1°58W **169** G6
Swanley *U.K.* 51°23N 0°11E **125** B4
Swansea *N.S.W., Australia* 33°3S 151°35E **283** B9
Swansea *Tas., Australia* 42°8S 148°4E **281** G4
Swansea *Ont., Canada* 43°38N 79°28W **141** B2
Swansea *Swansea, U.K.* 51°37N 3°57W **169** F4
Swansea *S.C., U.S.A.* 33°44N 81°6W **316** B8
Swansea □ *U.K.* 51°38N 4°3W **169** F3
Swanton *U.S.A.* 41°35N 83°53W **311** C13
Swartberge *S. Africa* 33°20S 22°0E **270** D3
Swartmodder *S. Africa* 28°1S 20°32E **270** C3
Swartnossob → *Namibia* 23°8S 18°42E **270** B2
Swartruggens *S. Africa* 25°39S 26°42E **270** C4
Swarzędz *Poland* 52°25N 17°4E **185** F4
Swastika *Canada* 48°7N 80°6W **298** C3
Swat → *Pakistan* 34°40N 72°5E **243** B5
Swatow = Shantou *China* 23°18N 116°40E **229** F11
Swaziland ■ *Africa* 26°30S 31°30E **271** C5
Sweden ■ *Europe* 57°0N 15°0E **161** H16
Swedru *Ghana* 5°32N 0°41W **263** D4
Sweet Grass *U.S.A.* 48°59N 111°58W **304** B8
Sweet Home *U.S.A.* 44°24N 122°44W **304** D2
Sweet Springs *U.S.A.* 38°58N 93°25W **310** F3
Sweetwater *Nev., U.S.A.* 38°27N 119°9W **306** G7
Sweetwater *Tenn., U.S.A.* 35°36N 84°28W **315** D12
Sweetwater *Tex., U.S.A.* 32°28N 100°25W **314** E4
Sweetwater → *U.S.A.* 42°31N 107°2W **304** E10
Swellendam *S. Africa* 34°1S 20°26E **270** D3
Swider → *Poland* 52°6N 21°14E **185** F8
Świdnica *Poland* 50°50N 16°30E **185** H3
Świdnik *Poland* 51°13N 22°39E **185** G9
Świdwin *Poland* 53°47N 15°49E **184** E2
Świebodzice *Poland* 50°51N 16°20E **185** H3
Świebodzin *Poland* 52°15N 15°31E **185** F2
Świecie *Poland* 53°25N 18°30E **184** E5
Świerzawa *Poland* 51°1N 15°54E **185** G2
Świętokrzyski △ *Poland* 50°53N 20°59E **185** H7
Świętokrzyskie □ *Poland* 50°45N 20°45E **185** H7
Świętokrzyskie, Góry *Poland* 51°0N 20°30E **185** H7
Swift Current *Canada* 50°20N 107°45W **297** C7
Swift Current → *Canada* 50°38N 107°44W **297** C7
Swifts Creek *Australia* 37°17S 147°44E **283** D7
Swilly, L. *Ireland* 55°12N 7°33W **166** A4
Swinburne I. *U.S.A.* 40°33N 74°3W **132** C2
Swindon *U.K.* 51°34N 1°46W **169** F6
Swindon □ *U.K.* 51°34N 1°46W **169** F6
Swinemünde = Świnoujście *Poland* 53°54N 14°16E **184** E1
Swinford *Ireland* 53°57N 8°58W **166** C3
Świnoujście *Poland* 53°54N 14°16E **184** E1
Switzerland ■ *Europe* 46°30N 8°0E **179** J4
Swords *Ireland* 53°28N 6°13W **120** A2
Swoyerville *U.S.A.* 41°18N 75°53W **313** E9
Syasstroy *Russia* 60°9N 32°33E **188** B7
Sycamore *Ill., U.S.A.* 41°59N 88°41W **310** C8
Sycamore *Ohio, U.S.A.* 40°57N 83°10W **311** D13
Sychevka *Russia* 55°59N 34°16E **188** E8
Syców *Poland* 51°19N 17°40E **185** G4
Sydamark □ *Denmark* 55°30N 9°0E **163** J3
Sydenham *S. Africa* 26°9S 28°5E **123** A2
Sydenham → *Canada* 42°33N 82°25W **312** D2
Sydney *N.S.W., Australia* 33°52S 151°12E **139** B2
Sydney *N.S., Canada* 46°7N 60°7W **299** C7
Sydney, Univ. of *Australia* 33°54S 151°11E **139** B2
Sydney Harbour △ *Australia* 33°50S 151°14E **139** B2
Sydney Harbour Bridge *Australia* 33°51S 151°12E **139** B2
Sydney Kingsford Smith ✕ (SYD) *Australia* 33°57S 151°11E **139** B2
Sydney L. *Canada* 50°41N 94°25W **297** C10
Sydney Mines *Canada* 46°18N 60°15W **299** C7
Sydney Opera House *Sydney, Australia* **139** a2
Sydprøven = Alluitsup Paa *Greenland* 60°30N 45°35W **154** E6
Sydra, G. of = Surt, Khalīj *Libya* 31°40N 18°30E **258** B3
Sydstranden *Denmark* 55°34N 12°38E **118** B3
Syeverodonetsk *Ukraine* 48°58N 38°35E **189** H10
Syfteland *Norway* 60°14N 5°27E **164** D2
Syke *Germany* 52°55N 8°50E **178** C4
Sykesville *U.S.A.* 41°3N 78°50W **312** E6
Sykkylven *Norway* 62°23N 6°35E **164** B3
Syktyvkar *Russia* 61°45N 50°40E **186** B9
Sylacauga *U.S.A.* 33°10N 86°15W **316** B3
Sylarna *Sweden* 63°2N 12°13E **164** A9
Sylhet *Bangla.* 24°54N 91°52E **241** C3
Sylhet □ *Bangla.* 24°50N 91°50E **241** C3
Sylt *Germany* 54°54N 8°22E **178** A4
Sylte *Norway* 62°18N 7°17E **164** B4
Sylvan Beach *U.S.A.* 43°12N 75°44W **313** C9
Sylvan Lake *Canada* 52°20N 114°3W **296** C6
Sylvania *N.S.W., Australia* 34°0S 151°7E **139** C1
Sylvania *Ga., U.S.A.* 32°45N 81°38W **316** C8
Sylvania *Ohio, U.S.A.* 41°43N 83°42W **311** C13
Sylvester *U.S.A.* 31°32N 83°50W **316** D6
Sym *Russia* 60°20N 88°18E **214** C9
Symphony Hall *San Francisco, U.S.A.* **136** c1
Synelnykove *Ukraine* 48°25N 35°30E **189** H8
Synevyr △ *Ukraine* 48°30N 23°40E **183** B8
Synevyrska Polyana *Ukraine* 48°35N 23°41E **183** B8
Synnervika *Norway* 62°25N 11°54E **164** B8
Synnfjell *Norway* 61°5N 9°46E **164** C6
Synnot Ra. *Australia* 16°30S 125°20E **278** C4
Syntagma Square *Athens, Greece* **112** b2
Synyak *Ukraine* 48°35N 22°51E **182** B7
Syon Park *U.K.* 51°28N 0°18W **125** B2
Syowa *Antarctica* 68°50S 12°0E **151** C5
Syracuse = Siracusa *Italy* 37°4N 15°17E **201** E8
Syracuse *Ind., U.S.A.* 41°26N 85°45W **311** C11
Syracuse *Kans., U.S.A.* 37°59N 101°45W **308** G3
Syracuse *N.Y., U.S.A.* 43°3N 76°9W **313** C8
Syracuse *Nebr., U.S.A.* 40°39N 96°11W **308** E5
Syrdarya → *Kazakhstan* 46°3N 61°0E **216** C6
Syria ■ *Asia* 35°0N 38°0E **213** E8
Syriam *Burma* 16°44N 96°19E **241** G6
Syrian Desert = Shām, Bādiyat ash *Asia* 32°0N 40°0E **246** C3
Syros = Ermoupoli *Greece* 37°28N 24°57E **204** D6
Syssleback *Sweden* 60°44N 12°52E **162** D6
Syvden *Norway* 62°5N 5°44E **164** B2
Syzran *Russia* 53°12N 48°30E **190** D9
Szabolcs-Szatmár-Bereg □ *Hungary* 48°2N 21°45E **182** B6
Szadek *Poland* 51°41N 18°59E **185** G5
Szamocin *Poland* 53°2N 17°7E **185** E4
Szamos → *Hungary* 48°7N 22°20E **182** B7
Szamotuły *Poland* 52°37N 16°33E **185** F3
Száraz → *Hungary* 46°10N 21°15E **182** D6
Szarvas *Hungary* 46°50N 20°38E **182** D5
Százhalombatta *Hungary* 47°20N 18°58E **182** C3
Szczawnica *Poland* 49°26N 20°30E **185** J7
Szczebrzeszyn *Poland* 50°42N 22°59E **185** H9
Szczecin *Poland* 53°27N 14°27E **184** E1
Szczecinek *Poland* 53°43N 16°41E **184** E3
Szczeciński, Zalew = Stettiner Haff *Germany* 53°47N 14°15E **178** B10
Szczekociny *Poland* 50°38N 19°48E **185** H6
Szczęśliwice *Poland* 52°12N 20°57E **142** B1
Szczucin *Poland* 50°18N 21°4E **185** H8
Szczuczyn *Poland* 53°36N 22°19E **184** E9
Szczyrk *Poland* 49°43N 19°2E **185** J6
Szczytna *Poland* 50°25N 16°28E **185** H3
Szczytno *Poland* 53°33N 21°0E **184** E7
Széchenyi-hegy *Hungary* 47°29N 18°57E **117** B1
Szechuan Basin = Sichuan Pendi *China* 31°0N 105°0E **228** B5
Szechwan = Sichuan □ *China* 30°30N 103°0E **228** B5
Szécsény *Hungary* 48°7N 19°30E **182** B4
Szeged *Hungary* 46°16N 20°10E **182** D5
Szeghalom *Hungary* 47°1N 21°10E **182** C6
Székesfehérvár *Hungary* 47°15N 18°25E **182** C3
Szekszárd *Hungary* 46°22N 18°42E **182** D3
Szendrő *Hungary* 48°24N 20°41E **182** B5
Szentendre *Hungary* 47°39N 19°4E **182** C4
Szentes *Hungary* 46°39N 20°21E **182** D5
Szentgotthárd *Hungary* 46°58N 16°19E **182** D1
Szentlőrinc *Hungary* 46°3N 18°1E **182** D3
Széphalom *Hungary* 47°34N 13°57E **117** A1
Szeping = Siping *China* 43°8N 124°21E **227** C13
Szerencs *Hungary* 48°10N 21°12E **182** B6
Szigetszentmiklós *Hungary* 47°21N 19°3E **182** C4
Szigetvár *Hungary* 46°3N 17°46E **182** D2
Szikszó *Hungary* 48°12N 20°56E **182** B5
Szklarska Poreba *Poland* 50°50N 15°33E **185** H2
Szkwa → *Poland* 53°11N 21°43E **185** E8
Szlichtyngowa *Poland* 51°42N 16°15E **185** G3
Szob *Hungary* 47°48N 18°53E **182** C3
Szolnok *Hungary* 47°10N 20°15E **182** C5
Szombathely *Hungary* 47°14N 16°38E **182** C1
Szprotawa *Poland* 51°33N 15°35E **185** G2
Sztálinváros = Dunaújváros *Hungary* 46°58N 18°57E **182** D3
Sztum *Poland* 53°55N 19°1E **184** E6
Sztutowo *Poland* 54°20N 19°15E **184** D6
Szubin *Poland* 53°1N 17°45E **185** E4
Szydłowiec *Poland* 51°15N 20°51E **185** G7
Szypliszki *Poland* 54°17N 23°2E **184** D10

T

Ta Khli *Thailand* 15°15N 100°21E **236** E3
Ta Lai *Vietnam* 11°24N 107°23E **237** G6
Ta Phraya △ *Thailand* 14°11N 102°49E **236** E4
Ta Pieh Shan = Dabie Shan *China* 31°20N 115°20E **229** B10
Taakoka *Cook Is.* 21°15S 159°43W **289** h
Taal, L. *Phil.* 13°56N 121°0E **232** E3
Taal Volcano △ *Phil.* 14°1N 120°59E **232** D3
Taan *Taiwan* 24°22N 120°35E **225** B2
Taastrup *Denmark* 55°39N 12°18E **118** B1
Tab *Hungary* 46°44N 15°2E **182** D3
Tabacal *Argentina* 23°15S 64°15W **334** A3
Tabaco *Phil.* 13°22N 123°44E **232** E4
Tabagné *Ivory C.* 7°59N 3°4W **262** D4
Ţābah *Si. Arabia* 26°55N 42°38E **246** E4
Tabajara *Brazil* 8°56S 62°8W **331** B5
Tabalo *Papua N. G.* 1°24S 149°40E **286** A5
Tabalos *Peru* 6°26S 76°37W **330** B2
Tabanan *Indonesia* 8°32S 115°8E **231** K18
Tabang *Indonesia* 0°34N 115°1E **235** B5
Tabankort *Niger* 17°44N 0°20E **263** B5
Tabaquite *Trin. & Tob.* 10°23N 61°18W **323** K7
Tabar I. *Papua N. G.* 2°50S 152°0E **286** B7
Tabar Is. *Papua N. G.* 2°50S 152°0E **286** B7
Tabarka *Tunisia* 36°56N 8°46E **258** A1
Ţabas *Khorāsān, Iran* 32°48N 60°12E **247** C9
Ţabas *Yazd, Iran* 33°35N 56°55E **247** C8
Tabasará, Serranía de *Panama* 8°35N 81°40W **320** E3
Tabasco □ *Mexico* 18°0N 92°40W **319** D6
Tabāsīn *Iran* 31°12N 57°54E **247** D8
Tabata *Japan* 35°44N 139°46E **140** A3
Tabatinga *Brazil* 4°16S 69°56W **330** A4
Tabatinga, Serra da *Brazil* 10°30S 44°0W **332** D3
Tabayin *Burma* 22°42N 95°20E **241** D5
Tabelbala *Algeria* 29°24N 3°15W **260** C4
Tabelbala, Kahal de *Algeria* 28°47N 2°0W **261** C4

Tabelembila Algeria 24°43N 4°16E 261 D5
Taber Canada 49°47N 112°8W 296 D6
Taberg Sweden 57°40N 14°6E 163 G8
Tabernacle St. Kitts & Nevis 17°23N 62°46W 322 d
Tabi Angola 8°10S 13°18E 265 D2
Tabina Phil. 7°28N 123°24E 233 H4
Tabira Brazil 7°35S 37°33W 332 C4
Tabiteuea Kiribati 1°25S 174°50E 277 A13
Tabla Niger 13°46N 3°1E 263 C5
Tablada Argentina 34°41S 58°32W 117 C1
Tablas de Daimiel △ Spain 39°9N 3°40W 195 F7
Tablas I. Phil. 12°25N 122°2E 232 E4
Tablas Str. Phil. 12°40N 121°48E 232 E3
Table, Pte. de la Réunion 21°14S 55°48E 272 f
Table B. Nfld. & L., Canada 53°40N 56°25W 299 B8
Table B. Western Cape, S. Africa 33°35S 18°25E 118 A1
Table C. N.Z. 39°6S 178°0E 284 F7
Table Grove U.S.A. 40°20N 90°27W 310 D6
Table I. Burma 14°12N 93°22E 245 G11
Table Mountain △ S. Africa 34°20S 18°28E 118 A1
Table Mt. S. Africa 33°58S 18°26E 118 A1
Table Rock L. U.S.A. 36°36N 93°19W 308 G7
Tableland Trin. & Tob. 10°16N 61°16W 323 t
Tabletop, Mt. Australia 23°24S 147°11E 280 C4
Taboão da Serra Brazil 23°36S 46°45W 137 B1
Tabocal Brazil 2°42S 57°40W 329 D6
Tabon Cave Complex Phil. 9°17N 118°5E 233 G2
Tábor Czech Rep. 49°25N 14°39E 180 B7
Tabora Tanzania 5°2S 32°50E 268 D3
Tabora □ Tanzania 5°0S 33°0E 268 D3
Tabou Ivory C. 4°30N 7°20W 262 E3
Tabrīz Iran 38°7N 46°20E 213 C12
Tabuaeran Kiribati 3°51N 159°22W 289 G12
Tabubil Papua N. G. 5°20S 141°15E 286 C1
Tabuenca Spain 41°42N 1°33W 196 D3
Tabuk Phil. 17°24N 121°25E 232 C3
Tabūk Si. Arabia 28°23N 36°36E 251 K7
Tabūk □ Si. Arabia 27°40N 36°50E 246 E3
Tabunifi Micronesia 9°28N 138°4E 287 S16
Taburno-Camposauro ⌓ Italy 41°8N 14°37E 201 A7
Tabwemasana, Mt. Vanuatu 15°20S 166°44E 287 E4
Täby Sweden 59°26N 18°2E 139 A2
Tacámbaro de Codallos Mexico 19°14N 101°28W 318 D4
Tacarigua Trin. & Tob. 10°38N 61°22W 323 t
Tacariqua, Laguna de Venezuela 10°15N 65°50W 328 A4
Tacheng Xinjiang Uygur, China 46°40N 82°58E 217 C10
Tacheng Taiwan 23°51N 120°19E 225 C2
Tach'i Taiwan 24°53N 121°17E 225 B3
Tachia Taiwan 24°25N 120°28E 225 B2
Tachia Hsi → Taiwan 24°20N 120°33E 225 B3
Tachibana-Wan Japan 32°45N 130°7E 222 E2
Tachikawa Japan 35°42N 139°25E 223 B11
Tachilek Burma 20°26N 99°52E 236 B2
Tach'ing Shan = Daqing Shan China 40°40N 111°0E 226 D6
Táchira □ Venezuela 8°7N 72°15W 328 B3
Tachiumet Libya 26°19N 10°3E 261 C7
Tachoshui Taiwan 24°20N 121°44E 225 B3
Tachov Czech Rep. 49°47N 12°39E 180 B5
Tácina → Italy 38°57N 16°55E 201 D9
Tacloban Phil. 11°15N 124°58E 233 F5
Tacna Peru 18°0S 70°20W 330 D3
Tacna □ Peru 17°40S 70°20W 330 D3
Tacoma U.S.A. 47°14N 122°26W 306 C4
Tacopaya = Zudañez Bolivia 19°6S 64°44W 331 D5
Tacuarembó Uruguay 31°45S 56°0W 335 C4
Tacuba Mexico 19°26N 99°11W 128 B1
Tacubaya Mexico 19°24N 99°10W 128 B1
Tacurong Phil. 6°40N 124°41E 233 H5
Tada-u Burma 21°49N 95°58E 241 E5
Tadahadi Solomon Is. 10°18S 161°35E 287 N11
Tademaït, Plateau du Algeria 28°30N 2°30E 261 C5
Tādepallegudem India 16°50N 81°30E 244 F5
Tadéra Niger 20°29N 8°18E 261 D6
Tadine N. Cal. 21°33S 167°52E 288 d
Tadio, L. Ivory C. 5°10N 5°15W 262 D3
Tadjerdjeri, O. → Algeria 26°0N 8°0E 261 C6
Tadjerouna Algeria 33°31N 2°3E 261 B5
Tadjettaret, O. → Algeria 21°20N 7°22E 261 D6
Tadjmout Laghouat, Algeria 33°52N 2°30E 261 B5
Tadjmout Saoura, Algeria 25°37N 3°48E 261 C5
Tadjoura Djibouti 11°50N 42°55E 257 E5
Tadjoura, Golfe de Djibouti 11°50N 43°0E 257 E5
Tadmor N.Z. 41°27S 172°45E 285 B7
Tadoba △ India 20°30N 78°20E 244 D4
Tadotsu Japan 34°16N 133°45E 222 C5
Tadoule L. Canada 58°36N 98°20W 297 B9
Tadoussac Canada 48°11N 69°42W 299 C6
Tadpatri India 14°55N 78°1E 245 G4
Tadrés ⌓ Niger 16°0N 7°10E 263 B6
Tadzhikistan = Tajikistan ■ Asia 38°30N 70°0E 217 E8
Tae-an S. Korea 36°45N 126°17E 224 D3
Tae-an Seashore Nat. Park △ S. Korea 36°40N 126°0E 224 D3
Taebaek S. Korea 37°10N 128°59E 224 D4
Taebaeksan S. Korea 37°5N 128°54E 224 D4
T'aebaeksanmaek S. Korea 37°40N 128°50E 224 D4
Taedong-gang → N. Korea 38°41N 125°15E 224 C2
Taedong-man N. Korea 38°4N 125°7E 224 C2
Taegu = Daegu S. Korea 35°50N 128°37E 224 E4
Taegwan N. Korea 40°13N 125°12E 224 B2
Taehung N. Korea 40°5N 126°56E 224 B3
Taehwa-do N. Korea 39°26N 124°36E 224 C2
Taejŏn = Daejeon S. Korea 36°20N 127°28E 224 D3
Tælavåg Norway 60°15N 4°58E 164 D1
Taen, Ko Thailand 9°22N 99°57E 237 b
Tafalla Spain 42°30N 1°41W 196 C3
Tafar South Sudan 6°52N 28°15E 257 F2
Tafassasset, O. → Algeria 22°0N 9°57E 261 D6
Tafelbaai = Table B. S. Africa 33°35S 18°25E 118 A1
Tafelberg Curaçao 12°4N 68°50W 322 g
Tafelney, C. Morocco 31°3N 9°51W 260 B3
Tafermaar Indonesia 6°47S 134°10E 231 F8
Taffermit Morocco 29°37N 9°15W 260 C3
Tafí Viejo Argentina 26°43S 65°17W 334 B2
Tafihān Iran 29°25N 52°39E 247 D7
Tafilalet Morocco 31°20N 4°45W 260 B4
Tafiré Ivory C. 9°4N 5°4W 262 D3
Tafjord Norway 62°14N 7°24E 164 B4
Tafnidilt Morocco 28°47N 10°58W 260 C2
Tafo Ghana 6°15N 0°20W 263 D4
Tafraoute Morocco 29°50N 8°58W 260 C3
Tafresh Iran 34°45N 49°57E 247 C6
Taft Iran 31°45N 54°14E 247 D7
Taft Phil. 11°57N 125°30E 233 F5
Taft Calif., U.S.A. 35°8N 119°28W 307 K7
Taft Fla., U.S.A. 28°25N 81°21W 133 B2
Taftan Pakistan 29°0N 61°30E 240 C1
Taftān, Kūh-e Iran 28°40N 61°0E 247 D9
Tafu Taiwan 23°37N 121°23E 225 C3
Tafwap India 7°23N 93°43E 245 L11
Taga Samoa 13°46S 172°28W 287 V19
Taga Dzong Bhutan 27°5N 89°55E 241 B2
Tagana-an Phil. 9°42N 125°35E 233 G5
Taganrog Russia 47°12N 38°50E 189 J10
Taganrogskiy Zaliv Russia 47°0N 38°30E 189 J10
Tagânt □ Mauritania 19°0N 10°0W 260 E3
Tagap Ga Burma 26°56N 96°13E 241 B6
Tagauayan I. Phil. 10°58N 121°13E 233 F3
Tagaung Burma 23°30N 96°2E 241 D6
Tagawa Japan 33°38N 130°51E 222 D2
Tagaytay Phil. 14°6N 120°56E 232 D3
Tagbilaran Phil. 9°39N 123°51E 233 G4
Tagdempt = Tiaret Algeria 35°20N 1°21E 261 A5
Tage Papua N. G. 6°19S 143°20E 286 D2
Tageren Canal Micronesia 9°33N 138°8E 287 R16
Tággia Italy 43°52N 7°51E 198 E4
Taghit Algeria 30°58N 2°0W 261 B4
Tagig → Phil. 14°31N 121°5E 127 B2
Tagish Canada 60°19N 134°16W 296 A2
Tagish L. Canada 60°10N 134°20W 296 A2
Tagkawayan Phil. 13°58N 122°32E 232 E4
Tagliacozzo Italy 42°4N 13°14E 199 F10
Tagliamento → Italy 45°38N 13°6E 199 C10
Táglio di Po Italy 45°0N 12°12E 199 D9
Tagna Colombia 2°24S 70°37W 328 D3
Tago Phil. 9°2N 126°13E 233 G6
Tago, Mt. Phil. 8°23N 125°5E 233 G5
Tagomago Spain 39°2N 1°39E 206 C2
Tagourâret Mauritania 17°45N 7°45W 262 B3
Tagpochau, Mt. N. Marianas 15°11N 145°44E 302 e
Taguatinga Distrito Federal, Brazil 16°12S 44°35W 333 E2
Taguatinga Tocantins, Brazil 12°27S 46°22W 333 D2
Tagudin Phil. 16°56N 120°27E 232 C3
Taguenout Chagueret Mali 21°14N 0°48W 261 D4
Taguig Phil. 14°31N 121°4E 127 B2
Tagula Papua N. G. 11°22S 153°15E 286 F7
Tagula I. Papua N. G. 11°30S 153°30E 286 F7
Tagum Phil. 7°33N 125°53E 233 H5
Tagus = Tejo → Europe 38°40N 9°24W 195 F2
Tahakopa N.Z. 46°30S 169°23E 285 G4
Tahala Morocco 34°0N 4°28W 260 B4
Tahan, Gunung Malaysia 4°34N 102°17E 237 K4
Tahānah-ye sūr Gol Afghan. 31°43N 67°53E 240 C2
Tahara Japan 34°40N 137°16E 223 C9
Tahat Algeria 23°18N 5°33E 261 D6
Tāherī Iran 27°43N 52°20E 247 E7
Tahgong Pt. N. Marianas 15°6N 145°39E 302 e
Tahifet Algeria 22°58N 6°0E 261 D6
Tahiti French Polynesia 17°37S 149°27W 289 e
Tahlab → Pakistan 28°9N 62°45E 240 C1
Tahlequah U.S.A. 35°55N 94°58W 314 D7
Tahoe, L. U.S.A. 39°6N 120°2W 306 G6
Tahoe City U.S.A. 39°10N 120°9W 306 F6
Tahoka U.S.A. 33°10N 101°48W 314 E4
Taholah U.S.A. 47°21N 124°17W 306 C2
Tahora N.Z. 39°2S 174°49E 284 F3
Tahoua Niger 14°57N 5°16E 263 C6
Tahrūd Iran 29°26N 57°49E 247 D8
Tahsis Canada 49°55N 126°40W 296 D3
Tahta Egypt 26°44N 31°32E 256 B3
Tahtaköprü Turkey 39°57N 29°39E 203 G13
Tahtalı Dağları Turkey 38°20N 36°0E 212 C7
Tahu Taiwan 24°26N 120°52E 225 B2
Tahuamanú → Bolivia 11°6S 67°36W 330 C4
Tahuata, I. French Polynesia 9°57S 139°5W 289 f
Tahulandang Indonesia 2°27N 125°23E 231 D7
Tahuna Indonesia 3°38N 125°30E 231 D7
Taï Ivory C. 5°55N 7°30W 262 D3
Taï △ Ivory C. 5°25N 7°5W 262 D3
Tai Hu China 31°5N 120°10E 229 B12
Tai Lo Shan China 22°21N 114°13E 122 A2
Tai Mo Shan China 22°25N 114°7E 219 a
Tai O China 22°15N 113°52E 219 a
Tai Pang Wan China 22°33N 114°24E 219 a
Tai Po China 22°27N 114°10E 219 a
Tai Po Tsai China 22°20N 114°15E 122 A2
Tai Rom Yen △ Thailand 8°45N 99°30E 237 H2
Tai Seng Singapore 1°20N 103°53E 138 A3
Tai Shan China 36°25N 117°20E 227 F9
Tai Shui Hang China 22°24N 114°13E 122 A2
Tai Tam B. China 22°12N 114°13E 122 B2
Tai Tam Tuk Res. China 22°14N 114°13E 122 B2
Tai Wai China 22°22N 114°10E 122 A2
Tai Wan Tau China 22°17N 114°17E 122 B2
Tai Wo Hau China 22°21N 114°7E 122 A1
Tai Yue Shan = Lantau I. China 22°15N 113°56E 219 a
Tai'an China 36°12N 117°8E 227 F9
Taiarapu, Presqu'île de Tahiti 17°47S 149°14W 289 e
Taibai Shan China 33°57N 107°45E 226 H4
Taibei = T'aipei Taiwan 25°4N 121°29E 225 A3
Taibique Canary Is. 27°42N 17°58W 153 e1
Taibus Qi China 41°54N 115°22E 226 D8
Taichow = Taizhou China 32°28N 119°55E 229 A12
T'aichung Taiwan 24°9N 120°37E 225 B2
Taieri → N.Z. 46°3S 170°12E 285 G5
Taigu China 37°28N 112°30E 226 F7
Taihang Shan China 36°0N 113°30E 226 G7
Taihape N.Z. 39°41S 175°48E 284 F4
Taihe Anhui, China 33°20N 115°42E 226 H8
Taihe Jiangxi, China 26°47N 114°52E 229 D10
Taihoku = T'aipei Taiwan 25°4N 121°29E 225 A3
Taihsi Taiwan 23°51N 120°16E 225 C2
Taihu China 30°22N 116°20E 229 B11
Taijiang China 26°39N 108°21E 228 D7
Taikang China 34°5N 114°50E 226 G8
Taikkyi Burma 17°20N 96°0E 241 G6
Tailem Bend Australia 35°12S 139°29E 282 C3
Tailfingen Germany 48°15N 9°1E 179 G5
T'ailuko Taiwan 24°9N 121°37E 225 B3
T'aimali Taiwan 22°36N 121°0E 225 D2
Taimyr Peninsula = Taymyr, Poluostrov Russia 75°0N 100°0E 215 B11
Tain U.K. 57°49N 4°4W 167 D4
Tainaka Japan 34°36N 135°35E 133 B2
T'ainan Taiwan 23°0N 120°10E 225 D2
T'ainan □ Taiwan 23°15N 120°20E 225 C2
Tainggyo Burma 17°49N 94°29E 241 G5
Taining China 26°54N 117°9E 229 D11
Taiobeiras Brazil 15°49S 42°14W 333 E3
Taipa China 22°10N 113°35E 219 a
T'aipei Taiwan 25°4N 121°29E 225 A3
T'aipei □ Taiwan 24°50N 121°35E 225 B3
Taiping Anhui, China 30°15N 118°6E 229 B12
Taiping Malaysia 4°51N 100°44E 237 K3
Taipingchuan China 44°23N 123°11E 227 B12
Taipingzhen China 33°35N 111°42E 226 H6
Taipu Brazil 5°37S 35°36W 332 C4
Tairbeart = Tarbert U.K. 57°54N 6°49W 167 D2
Tairenpokpi India 24°39N 93°40E 241 C4
Tairua N.Z. 37°0S 175°51E 284 D4
Tais Indonesia 4°6S 102°34E 234 C2
Taisha Japan 35°24N 132°40E 222 B4
Taishan China 22°14N 112°41E 229 F9
Taishō Japan 34°38N 135°27E 133 B1
Taishun China 27°30N 119°42E 229 D12
Taita N.Z. 41°12S 174°57E 143 B2
Taita Hills Kenya 3°25S 38°15E 268 C4
Taitao, C. Chile 45°53S 75°5W 336 C1
Taitao, Pen. de Chile 46°30S 75°0W 336 C2
T'aitung Taiwan 22°43N 121°4E 225 D3
T'aitung □ Taiwan 23°0N 121°0E 225 D3
Taivalkoski Finland 65°33N 28°12E 160 D23
Taiwan ■ Asia 23°30N 121°0E 225 C3
Taiwan Strait Asia 24°40N 120°0E 229 E12
Taixing China 32°11N 120°0E 229 A13
Taiyara Sudan 13°12N 30°47E 257 E3
Taiyiba Israel 32°36N 35°27E 250 F6
Taiyuan China 37°52N 112°33E 226 F7
Taizhong = T'aichung Taiwan 24°9N 120°37E 225 B2
Taizhou Jiangsu, China 32°28N 119°55E 229 A12
Taizhou Zhejiang, China 28°40N 121°24E 229 C13
Taizhou Liedao China 28°30N 121°55E 229 C13
Ta'izz Yemen 13°35N 44°2E 248 D4
Tājābād Iran 30°2N 54°24E 247 D7
Tajapuru, Furo do Brazil 1°50S 50°25W 332 B1
Tajarḥī Libya 24°21N 14°28E 258 D2
Tajen Taiwan 22°17N 120°53E 225 D2
Tajikistan ■ Asia 38°30N 70°0E 217 E8
Tajima Japan 37°12N 139°46E 221 F9
Tajimi Japan 35°19N 137°8E 223 B9
Tajo = Tejo → Europe 38°40N 9°24W 195 F2
Tajrīsh Iran 35°48N 51°25E 141 A2
Tajumulco, Vol. Guatemala 15°2N 91°55W 320 C1
Tājūrā Libya 32°51N 13°21E 258 B2
Tak Thailand 16°52N 99°8E 236 D2
Takāb Iran 36°24N 47°7E 213 D12
Takabanare-shima Japan 26°22N 127°59E 288 a
Takabba Kenya 3°21N 40°13E 267 D5
Takachiho Japan 32°42N 131°18E 222 E3
Takachu Botswana 22°37S 21°58E 270 B3
Takada Japan 37°7N 138°15E 221 F9
Takahagi Japan 36°43N 140°45E 221 F10
Takahashi Japan 34°51N 133°39E 222 C5
Takaido Japan 35°40N 139°37E 140 A2
Takaishi Japan 35°36N 139°31E 140 B2
Takaka N.Z. 40°51S 172°50E 285 A7
Takaki = Yamato Japan 35°27N 139°25E 223 B11
Takalar Indonesia 5°28S 119°24E 235 D5
Takalous, O. → Algeria 22°36N 7°21E 261 D6
Takamaka Seychelles 4°50S 55°30E 272 c
Takamatsu Japan 34°20N 134°5E 222 C6
Takanabe Japan 32°8N 131°30E 222 E3
Takangkou Taiwan 23°28N 121°29E 225 C3
Takaoka Japan 36°47N 137°0E 223 A9
Takapau N.Z. 40°2S 176°21E 284 G5
Takapuna N.Z. 36°47S 174°47E 284 C3
Takarazuka Japan 34°47N 135°20E 133 A1
Takaroa French Polynesia 14°28S 144°58W 289 f
Takasago Japan 34°45N 134°48E 140 A4
Takasaki Japan 36°20N 139°0E 223 A11
Takashima Japan 35°24N 136°2E 223 B8
Takatsu Japan 35°36N 139°37E 140 B2
Takatsuki Japan 34°51N 135°37E 223 C7
Takaungu Kenya 3°38S 39°52E 268 C4
Takayama Japan 36°18N 137°11E 223 A9
Takayama-Bonchi Japan 36°0N 137°18E 223 B9
Take-Shima Japan 30°49N 130°26E 221 J5
Takefu Japan 35°50N 136°10E 223 B8
Takehara Japan 34°21N 132°55E 222 C4
Takengon Indonesia 4°45N 96°50E 234 B1
Takeo Cambodia 10°59N 104°47E 237 G5
Takeo Japan 33°12N 130°1E 222 D2
Tåkern Sweden 58°22N 14°45E 163 F8
Takeshima = Tokdo Asia 37°15N 131°52E 221 F5
Takeshita Japan 35°33N 139°32E 140 B2
Tākestān Iran 36°0N 49°40E 247 C6
Taketa Japan 32°58N 131°24E 222 E3
Takh India 33°6N 77°32E 243 C7
Takhār □ Afghan. 36°40N 70°0E 240 A3
Takhiatash Uzbekistan 42°20N 59°33E 216 D5
Takhmau Cambodia 11°29N 104°57E 237 G5
Takht-Sulaiman Pakistan 31°40N 69°58E 242 D3
Taki Papua N. G. 6°29S 155°52E 286 D8
Takiéta Niger 13°41N 8°32E 263 C6
Takikawa Japan 43°33N 141°54E 220 C10
Takinegawa Japan 35°45N 139°44E 140 A3
Takla L. Canada 55°15N 125°45W 296 B3
Takla Landing Canada 55°30N 125°50W 296 B3
Takla Makan China 38°0N 83°0E 217 E10
Taklamakan Shamo = Takla Makan China 38°0N 83°0E 217 E10
Takoma Park U.S.A. 38°58N 77°0W 143 B3
Takotna U.S.A. 62°59N 156°4W 303 E8
Taksim Turkey 41°2N 28°58E 122 B1
Taksimo Russia 56°20N 114°52E 215 D12
Taku Japan 33°18N 130°3E 222 D2
Taku → Canada 58°30N 133°50W 296 B2
Takua Thung Thailand 8°24N 98°27E 237 a
Takum India 27°47N 93°37E 241 B4
Takum Nigeria 7°18N 9°36E 263 D6
Takume French Polynesia 15°49S 142°12W 289 f
Takundi Dem. Rep. of the Congo 4°45S 16°34E 265 C3
Takutu → Brazil 3°1N 60°29W 329 C5
Takutu → Guyana 3°1N 60°29W 329 C5
Tal Halāl Iran 28°54N 55°1E 247 D7
Tala Uruguay 34°21S 55°46W 335 C4
Talachyn Belarus 54°25N 29°42E 188 E5
Talacogon Phil. 8°32N 125°39E 233 G5
Talagang Pakistan 32°55N 72°25E 242 C5
Talagante Chile 33°40S 70°50W 334 C1
Talahouhait Algeria 24°52N 1°5E 261 D5
Talaide Portugal 38°44N 9°18W 126 A1
Talaimannar Sri Lanka 9°6N 79°43E 245 K4
Talaïnt Morocco 29°41N 9°40W 260 C3
Talak Niger 18°0N 5°0E 263 B6
Talakag Phil. 8°16N 124°37E 233 G5
Talamanca, Cordillera de Cent. Amer. 9°20N 83°20W 320 E3
Talampaya △ Argentina 29°43S 67°42W 334 B2
Talangbetutu Indonesia 2°53S 104°41E 234 C2
Talant France 47°19N 4°58E 173 E11
Talara Peru 4°38S 81°18W 330 A1
Talas Kyrgyzstan 42°30N 72°13E 217 D8
Talas Turkey 38°41N 35°33E 212 C6
Talas □ Kyrgyzstan 42°20N 72°0E 217 D8
Talas → Kazakhstan 44°0N 70°20E 217 D8
Talas Ala Too Kyrgyzstan 42°15N 72°0E 217 D8
Talasea Papua N. G. 5°20S 150°2E 286 C6
Talasskiy Alatau = Talas Ala Too Kyrgyzstan 42°15N 72°0E 217 D8
Talâta Egypt 30°36N 32°20E 251 H3
Talata Mafara Nigeria 12°38N 6°4E 263 C6
Talaud, Kepulauan Indonesia 4°30N 126°50E 231 D7
Talaud Is. = Talaud, Kepulauan Indonesia 4°30N 126°50E 231 D7
Talavera de la Reina Spain 39°55N 4°46W 194 F6
Talavera la Real Spain 38°53N 6°46W 195 G4
Talawgyi Burma 25°4N 97°19E 241 C6
Talayan Phil. 6°52N 124°24E 233 H5
Talayuela Spain 39°59N 5°36W 194 F5
Talbandh India 22°3N 86°20E 243 H12
Talbert, Sillon de France 48°53N 3°5W 172 D3
Talbot Australia 37°10S 143°44E 282 D5
Talbot, C. Australia 13°48S 126°43E 278 B4
Talbotton U.S.A. 32°41N 84°32W 316 C5
Talbragar → Australia 32°12S 148°37E 283 B8
Talca Chile 35°28S 71°40W 334 D1
Talcahuano Chile 36°40S 73°10W 334 D1
Talcher India 21°0N 85°18E 244 D7
Talcho Niger 14°44N 3°28E 263 C5
Taldy Kurgan = Taldyqorghan Kazakhstan 45°10N 78°45E 217 C9
Taldyqorghan Kazakhstan 45°10N 78°45E 217 C9
Tālesh Iran 37°58N 48°58E 213 D13
Tālesh, Kūhhā-ye Iran 37°42N 48°55E 213 D13
Talgar = Talghar Kazakhstan 43°19N 77°15E 217 D9
Talghar Kazakhstan 43°19N 77°15E 217 D9
Talguharai Sudan 18°19N 35°56E 256 D4
Talguppa India 14°13N 74°56E 245 G2
Tali Post South Sudan 5°55N 30°44E 257 F3
Taliabu Indonesia 1°50S 125°0E 231 E6
Taliao Taiwan 22°36N 120°23E 225 D2
Talibon Phil. 10°9N 124°20E 233 F5
Talichien Taiwan 24°58N 121°55E 225 B3
Taliganga India 22°30N 88°22E 124 B2
Talihina U.S.A. 34°45N 95°3W 314 D7
Talikota India 16°29N 76°17E 245 F3
Talikud I. Phil. 6°56N 125°41E 233 H5
Talin Taiwan 23°36N 120°27E 225 C2
Talipapa Phil. 14°41N 121°1E 127 A2
Talipaw Phil. 5°59N 121°7E 233 J3
Talipparamba India 12°3N 75°21E 245 H2
Talisay Phil. 10°44N 122°58E 233 F4
Talisayan Phil. 9°0N 124°55E 233 G5
Taliwang Indonesia 8°50S 116°55E 235 D5
Talkeetna U.S.A. 62°20N 150°6W 303 E10
Talkha Egypt 31°3N 31°22E 251 G2
Tálknafjörður Iceland 65°34N 24°0W 155 B2
Tall 'Afar Iraq 36°22N 42°27E 213 D10
Tall Kalakh Syria 34°41N 36°15E 250 D7
Tall Kayf Iraq 36°29N 43°7E 213 D10
Talla Egypt 28°5N 30°43E 256 B3
Talladega U.S.A. 33°26N 86°6W 316 B3
Tallaganda △ Australia 35°29S 149°37E 283 C8
Tallaght Ireland 53°17N 6°22W 120 B1
Tallahassee U.S.A. 30°27N 84°17W 316 E5
Tallangatta Australia 36°15S 147°19E 283 D7
Tallapoosa U.S.A. 33°45N 85°17W 316 B4
Tallapoosa → U.S.A. 32°30N 86°16W 316 C3
Tallard France 44°28N 6°3E 175 D10
Tallarook Australia 37°5S 145°6E 283 D6
Tallassee U.S.A. 32°32N 85°54W 316 C4
Tällberg Sweden 60°51N 15°2E 162 D9
Tallering Pk. Australia 28°6S 115°37E 279 E2
Talli Pakistan 29°32N 68°8E 242 E3
Tallinn Estonia 59°22N 24°48E 188 C3
Tallkrogen Sweden 59°16N 18°4E 139 B2
Tallmadge U.S.A. 41°6N 81°27W 312 E3
Tallulah U.S.A. 32°25N 91°11W 314 E9
Tălmaciu Romania 45°38N 24°19E 183 E9
Talmest Morocco 31°48N 9°21W 260 B3
Talmont-St-Hilaire France 46°27N 1°37W 174 B2
Talnakh Russia 69°29N 88°22E 215 C9
Talne Ukraine 48°50N 30°44E 189 H6
Talnoye = Talne Ukraine 48°50N 30°44E 189 H6
Taloda India 21°34N 74°11E 244 D2
Talodi Sudan 10°35N 30°22E 257 E3
Talofofo Guam 13°21N 144°45E 302 d
Tāloqān Afghan. 36°44N 69°33E 240 A3
Talovaya Russia 51°6N 40°45E 190 E5
Taloyoak Canada 69°32N 93°32W 294 D13
Talpa de Allende Mexico 20°23N 104°51W 318 C4
Talparo Trin. & Tob. 10°30N 61°17W 323 t
Talparo → Trin. & Tob. 10°34N 61°17W 323 t
Talquin, L. U.S.A. 30°23N 84°39W 316 E5
Talsi Latvia 57°10N 22°30E 184 A9
Talsi □ Latvia 57°20N 22°40E 184 A9
Talsinnt Morocco 32°33N 3°27W 261 B4
Taltal Chile 25°23S 70°33W 334 B1
Taltson → Canada 61°24N 112°46W 296 A6
Talu Indonesia 0°13N 99°58E 234 B1
Taluk Indonesia 0°31S 101°34E 234 C2
Talwood Australia 28°29S 149°29E 281 D4
Talyawalka Cr. → Australia 32°28S 142°22E 282 B5
Tam Dao △ Vietnam 21°45N 105°45E 236 B5
Tam Ky Vietnam 15°34N 108°29E 236 E7
Tam Quan Vietnam 14°35N 109°3E 236 E7
Tama Tōkyō, Japan 35°38N 139°26E 140 B1
Tama Iowa, U.S.A. 41°58N 92°35W 310 C4
Tama → Japan 35°32N 139°39E 140 B2
Tama ⌓ Ethiopia 5°55N 36°5E 257 F4
Tama Abu, Banjaran Malaysia 3°50N 115°5E 235 B5
Tama Kyūryō Japan 35°34N 139°30E 140 B2
Tamada Algeria 21°34N 3°20E 261 D5
Tamaden Japan 35°39N 139°38E 140 B2
Tamagawa-josui → Japan 35°41N 139°47E 140 A1
Tamakautoga Cook Is. 19°5S 169°55W 289 g
Tamalameque Colombia 8°52N 73°49W 328 B3
Tamale Ghana 9°22N 0°50W 263 D4
Taman Russia 45°14N 36°41E 189 K9
Taman Negara △ Malaysia 4°38N 102°26E 237 K4
Taman Sari Indonesia 6°8S 106°48E 122 A1
T'aman Shan Taiwan 24°42N 121°27E 225 B3
Tamana Japan 32°58N 130°32E 222 E2
Tamana Kiribati 2°30S 175°59E 277 A14
Tamana, Mt. Trin. & Tob. 10°28N 61°12W 323 t
Tamanar Morocco 31°1N 9°46W 260 B3
Tamanduateí → Brazil 23°37S 46°38W 137 B2
Tamanhint Libya 27°13N 14°37E 258 C2
Tamani Mali 13°20N 6°50W 262 C3
Tamano Japan 34°29N 133°59E 222 C5
Tamanrasset Algeria 22°50N 5°30E 261 D6
Tamanrasset □ Algeria 23°45N 4°40E 261 D5
Tamanrasset, O. → Algeria 22°0N 2°0E 261 D5
Tamanthi Burma 25°19N 95°17E 241 C5
Tamaqua U.S.A. 40°48N 75°58W 313 F9
Tamar → U.K. 50°27N 4°15W 169 G3
Támara Colombia 5°50N 72°10W 328 B3
Tamarac U.S.A. 26°12N 80°15W 317 J9
Tamarin Mauritius 20°19S 57°20E 272 e
Tamarinda Spain 39°55N 3°49E 206 B4
Tamarite de Litera Spain 41°52N 0°25E 196 D5
Tamaroa U.S.A. 38°8N 89°14W 310 F7
Tamashima Japan 34°32N 133°40E 221 G6
Tamási Hungary 46°40N 18°18E 182 D3
Tamaské Niger 14°49N 5°43E 263 C6
Tamatave = Toamasina Madag. 18°10S 49°25E 272 B2
Tamaulipas □ Mexico 24°0N 98°45W 319 C5
Tamaulipas, Sierra de Mexico 23°30N 98°20W 319 C5
Tamazula Mexico 24°57N 106°57W 318 C3
Tamazunchale Mexico 21°16N 98°47W 319 C5
Tamba-Dabatou Guinea 11°50N 10°40W 262 C2
Tambach Kenya 0°36N 35°31E 268 B4
Tambacounda Senegal 13°45N 13°40W 262 C2
Tambacounda □ Senegal 14°0N 13°0W 262 C2
Tambaram India 12°55N 80°7E 245 H5
Tambea Solomon Is. 9°16S 159°41E 287 M10
Tambelan, Kepulauan Indonesia 1°0N 107°30E 235 B3
Tambellup Australia 34°4S 117°37E 279 F2
Tambo Queens., Australia 24°54S 146°14E 280 C4
Tambo Peru 12°57S 74°1W 330 C3
Tambo → Peru 10°42S 73°47W 330 C3
Tambo de Mora Peru 13°30S 76°8W 330 C2
Tambobamba Peru 13°54S 72°8W 330 C3
Tamboerskloof S. Africa 33°56S 18°25E 118 A1
Tambohorano Madag. 17°30S 43°58E 272 B1
Tambopata → Peru 13°21S 69°36W 330 C4
Tambora Jakarta, Indonesia 6°8S 106°47E 122 A1
Tambora Nusa Tenggara Barat, Indonesia 8°12S 118°5E 235 D5
Tamboritha, Mt. Australia 37°31S 146°40E 283 D7
Tamboura C.A.R. 5°10N 25°12E 264 A5
Tambov Russia 52°45N 41°28E 190 D5
Tambov □ Russia 52°50N 41°20E 190 D5
Tambre → Spain 42°49N 8°53W 194 C2
Tambuku Indonesia 7°8S 113°40E 235 D4
Tambul Papua N. G. 5°54S 143°54E 286 C2
Tambunar Malaysia 5°43N 116°24E 235 A5
Tamburâ South Sudan 5°40N 27°25E 257 F2
Tambuyukan, Gunong Malaysia 6°13N 116°39E 235 A5
Tâmchekket Mauritania 17°25N 10°40W 262 B2
Tame Colombia 6°28N 71°44W 328 B3
Tâmega → Portugal 41°5N 8°21W 194 D2
Tamegroute Morocco 30°15N 5°39W 260 B3
Tamelelt Morocco 31°50N 7°32W 260 B3
Tamenglong India 25°0N 93°35E 241 C4
Tamerza Tunisia 34°23N 7°58E 258 B1
Tamgak, Adrar Niger 19°12N 8°35E 259 E1
Tamgué, Massif du Guinea 12°0N 12°18W 262 C2
Tami Is. Papua N. G. 6°46S 147°55E 286 D4
Tamiahua, L. de Mexico 21°35N 97°35W 319 C5
Tamiami Canal U.S.A. 25°50N 81°0W 317 K8
Tamianglayang Indonesia 2°7S 115°10E 235 C5
Tamil Nadu □ India 11°0N 77°0E 245 J3
Tamis → Serbia 44°51N 20°39E 182 F5
Tamiya Egypt 29°29N 30°58E 256 J7
Tamlelt, Plaine de Morocco 32°30N 2°20W 261 B4
Tamluk India 22°18N 87°58E 243 H12
Tammerfors = Tampere Finland 61°30N 23°50E 188 B2
Tammisalo Finland 60°11N 25°5E 121 B3
Tammûh Egypt 29°55N 31°15E 117 B2
Tämnaren Sweden 60°10N 17°25E 162 D11
Tampa Angola 15°30S 13°27E 265 F2
Tampa Fla., U.S.A. 27°56N 82°27W 317 H7
Tampa, Tanjung Indonesia 8°55S 116°12E 231 K19
Tampa B. U.S.A. 27°50N 82°30W 317 H7
Tampa Int. ✈ (TPA) U.S.A. 27°59N 82°32W 317 H7
Tamparan Phil. 7°53N 124°20E 233 H5
Tampere Finland 61°30N 23°50E 188 B2
Tampico Tamaulipas, Mexico 22°13N 97°51W 319 C5
Tampico Ill., U.S.A. 41°38N 89°47W 310 C7
Tampin Malaysia 2°28N 102°13E 237 L4
Tampines Singapore 1°21N 103°56E 138 A3
Tampoi Malaysia 1°30N 103°39E 237 d
Tamrah Si. Arabia 20°24N 45°25E 248 B4
Tamri Morocco 30°49N 9°50W 260 B3
Tamrida = Qādub Yemen 12°37N 53°57E 249 D6
Tamsagbulag Mongolia 47°14N 117°21E 219 B12
Tamsweg Austria 47°7N 13°49E 180 D6
Tamu Burma 24°13N 94°12E 241 C5
Tamuja → Spain 39°38N 6°29W 195 F4
Tamuning Guam 13°29N 144°47E 302 d
Tamworth N.S.W., Australia 31°7S 150°58E 283 A9
Tamworth Ont., Canada 44°29N 77°0W 312 B8
Tamworth Staffs., U.K. 52°39N 1°41W 169 E6
Tan An Vietnam 10°32N 106°25E 237 G6
Tan Chau Vietnam 10°48N 105°12E 237 G5
T'an-do N. Korea 39°30N 124°41E 224 C2
Tan Hiep Vietnam 10°27N 106°21E 237 G6
Tan Iddah Algeria 26°33N 9°42E 261 C6
Tan-Tan Morocco 28°29N 11°1W 260 C2
Tan Yen Vietnam 22°4N 105°3E 236 A5
Tana → Coast, Kenya 2°32S 40°31E 268 C5
Tana → Finnmark, Norway 70°30N 28°14E 160 A23
Tana, L. Ethiopia 13°5N 37°30E 257 E4
Tana River Primate ⌓ Kenya 1°55S 40°7E 268 C5
Tanabe Japan 33°44N 135°22E 223 D7
Tanabi Brazil 20°37S 49°37W 333 F2
Tanacross U.S.A. 63°23N 143°21W 303 E12
Tanafjorden Norway 70°45N 28°25E 160 A23
Tanaga I. U.S.A. 51°48N 177°53W 303 L3
Tanaga Volcano U.S.A. 51°53N 178°8W 303 L3
Tanah Abang Indonesia 6°12S 106°48E 122 B1
Tanah Kusir Indonesia 6°15S 106°46E 122 B1
Tanah Merah Malaysia 5°48N 102°9E 237 K4
Tanahbala Indonesia 0°30S 98°30E 234 C1
Tanahgrogot Indonesia 1°55S 116°15E 235 C5
Tanahjampea Indonesia 7°10S 120°35E 231 F6
Tanahmasa Indonesia 0°12S 98°39E 234 C1
Tanahmerah Indonesia 6°5S 140°16E 231 F10
Tanahputih Indonesia 1°40N 101°3E 234 B2
Tanakpur India 29°5N 80°7E 243 E9
Tanakura Japan 37°10N 140°20E 221 F10
Tanamalwila Sri Lanka 6°26N 81°8E 245 L5
Tanami Desert Australia 18°50S 132°0E 278 C5
Tanana U.S.A. 65°10N 152°4W 303 D9
Tanana → U.S.A. 65°10N 151°58W 303 D10
Tananarive = Antananarivo Madag. 18°55S 47°31E 272 B2
Tananger Norway 58°57N 5°37E 164 F2
Tanannt Morocco 31°54N 6°56W 260 B3
Tanapag N. Marianas 15°14N 145°45E 302 e
Tánaro → Italy 44°55N 8°40E 198 D5
Tanauan Phil. 14°5N 121°10E 232 D3
Tanay Phil. 14°30N 121°17E 232 D3
Tanba-Sanchi Japan 35°7N 135°48E 223 B7
Tancheng China 34°25N 118°20E 227 G10
Tanch'ŏn N. Korea 40°27N 128°54E 224 B4
Tanda Ut. P., India 26°33N 82°35E 243 F10
Tanda Ut. P., India 28°57N 78°56E 243 E8
Tanda Ivory C. 7°48N 3°10W 262 D4
Tandag Phil. 9°4N 126°9E 233 G6
Tandaia Tanzania 9°25S 34°15E 269 D3
Tăndărei Romania 44°39N 27°40E 183 F12
Tandaué Angola 16°58S 18°5E 265 F3
Tandil Argentina 37°15S 59°6W 334 D4
Tandil, Sa. del Argentina 37°30S 59°0W 334 D4
Tandin Burma 19°33N 93°58E 241 F4
Tandjilé □ Chad 9°30N 16°30E 259 G3
Tandjilé → Chad 9°45N 15°50E 259 G3
Tandlianwala Pakistan 31°3N 73°9E 242 D5
Tando Adam Pakistan 25°45N 68°40E 242 G3
Tando Allahyar Pakistan 25°28N 68°43E 242 G3
Tando Bago Pakistan 24°47N 68°58E 242 G3
Tando Mohommed Khan Pakistan 25°8N 68°32E 242 G3
Tando-Zinze Angola 5°22S 12°30E 265 D2
Tandou-Bengou Congo 3°50S 11°44E 264 C2
Tandou L. Australia 32°40S 142°5E 282 B5
Tandoureh △ Iran 37°50N 59°0E 247 B8
Tandragee U.K. 54°21N 6°24W 166 B5
Tandsjöborg Sweden 61°42N 14°43E 162 C8
Tandubas Phil. 5°8N 120°20E 233 J3
Tandula → India 21°6N 81°14E 244 D5
Tandula Tank India 20°40N 81°12E 244 D5
Tandur Andhra Pradesh, India 19°11N 79°30E 244 E4
Tandur Andhra Pradesh, India 17°14N 77°35E 244 F3
Tane-ga-Shima Japan 30°30N 131°0E 221 J5
Taneatua N.Z. 38°4S 177°1E 284 E6
Tanen Tong Dan = Dawna Ra. Burma 16°30N 98°30E 236 D2
Tanew → Poland 50°29N 22°16E 185 H9
Tanezrouft Algeria 23°9N 0°11E 261 D5
Tanezzuft, W. → Libya 25°51N 10°19E 258 C2
Tang, Koh Cambodia 10°16N 103°7E 237 G4
Tang, Ra's-e Iran 25°21N 59°52E 247 E8
Tang Krasang Cambodia 12°34N 105°3E 236 F5
Tanga Tanzania 5°5S 39°2E 268 D4
Tanga □ Tanzania 5°20S 38°0E 268 D4
Tanga Is. Papua N. G. 3°20S 153°15E 286 B7
Tanga Langua Grenada 12°14N 61°39W 323 q
Tangail Bangla. 24°15N 89°55E 241 C2
Tangalla Sri Lanka 6°1N 80°48E 245 L5
Tanganyika = Tanzania ■ Africa 6°0S 34°0E 268 D3
Tanganyika, L. Africa 6°40S 30°0E 268 D3
Tangará da Serra Brazil 14°50S 57°47W 331 C6
Tangarare Solomon Is. 9°36S 159°41E 287 M10
Tangasseri India 8°53N 76°35E 245 K3
Tangaza Nigeria 13°19N 4°55E 263 C5
Tangelo Park U.S.A. 28°27N 81°26W 133 B2
Tangen Norway 60°37N 11°15E 164 D8
Tanger Morocco 35°50N 5°49W 260 A3
Tanger □ Morocco 35°43N 5°50W 260 A3
Tangerang Indonesia 6°11S 106°37E 234 D3
Tangerhütte Germany 52°26N 11°48E 178 C7
Tangermünde Germany 52°33N 11°58E 178 C7
Tanggu China 39°2N 117°40E 227 E9
Tanggula Shan China 32°40N 92°10E 218 E7
Tanggula Shankou China 32°42N 92°27E 218 E7
Tanghe China 32°47N 112°50E 226 H7
Tanghla Range = Tanggula Shan China 32°40N 92°10E 218 E7
Tangi India 19°56N 85°24E 244 E7
Tangier = Tanger Morocco 35°50N 5°49W 260 A3
Tangjia China 22°22N 113°35E 219 a
Tangjia Wan China 22°21N 113°36E 219 a
Tango-Hantō Japan 35°45N 135°10E 223 B7
Tangorin Australia 21°47S 144°12E 280 C3
Tangorombohitr'i Makay Madag. 21°0S 45°15E 272 C2
Tangra Yumco China 31°0N 86°38E 218 E6
Tangshan China 39°38N 118°10E 227 E10
Tangtou China 35°28N 118°30E 227 G10
Tangub Phil. 8°3N 123°44E 233 G4
Tanguen-Dassouri Burkina Faso 12°16N 1°42W 263 C4
Tanguiéta Benin 10°35N 1°21E 263 C5
Tangxi China 29°3N 119°25E 229 C12
Tangyan He → China 28°54N 108°19E 228 C7
Tangyin China 35°54N 114°21E 226 G8
Taniantaweng Shan China 31°20N 98°0E 228 B2
Taniao Taiwan 22°23N 120°53E 225 D2
Tanimbar, Kepulauan Indonesia 7°30S 131°30E 231 F8
Tanimbar Is. = Tanimbar, Kepulauan Indonesia 7°30S 131°30E 231 F8
Taninthari = Tenasserim Burma 12°6N 99°3E 237 F2
Tanis Egypt 31°0N 31°54E 251 H2
Tanjay Phil. 9°30N 123°5E 233 G4
Tanjong Pelepas Malaysia 1°21N 103°33E 237 d
Tanjong Po Malaysia 1°45N 110°30E 235 B4
Tanjore = Thanjavur India 10°48N 79°12E 245 J4
Tanjung Kalimantan Selatan, Indonesia 2°10S 115°25E 235 C5
Tanjung Nusa Tenggara Barat, Indonesia 8°21S 116°9E 231 J19
Tanjung Datu △ Malaysia 2°13N 109°3E 235 B3
Tanjung Duren Indonesia 6°10S 106°46E 122 B1
Tanjung Malim Malaysia 3°42N 101°31E 237 L3
Tanjung Priok Indonesia 6°6S 106°52E 122 A2
Tanjung Putung △ Indonesia 2°54S 111°59E 235 C4
Tanjung Tokong Malaysia 5°28N 100°18E 237 c
Tanjungbalai Kepulauan Riau, Indonesia 1°0N 103°25E 234 B2
Tanjungbalai Sumatera Utara, Indonesia 2°55N 99°44E 234 B1
Tanjungbatu Kalimantan Selatan, Indonesia 3°0S 116°13E 235 C5
Tanjungbatu Kalimantan Timur, Indonesia 2°23N 118°3E 235 B5
Tanjungbatu Kepulauan Riau, Indonesia 0°37N 103°25E 234 B2
Tanjungisui Indonesia 0°30S 116°8E 235 C5
Tanjungkarang Telukbetung = Bandar Lampung Indonesia 5°20S 105°10E 234 D3
Tanjungpandan Indonesia 2°43S 107°38E 235 C3
Tanjungpinang Indonesia 1°5N 104°30E 234 B2
Tanjungpriok Indonesia 6°8S 106°55E 234 D3
Tanjungraja Indonesia 3°21S 104°46E 234 C2
Tanjungredeb Indonesia 2°9N 117°29E 235 B5
Tanjungselor Indonesia 2°55N 117°25E 235 B5
Tank Pakistan 32°14N 70°25E 242 C4
Tankhala India 21°58N 73°47E 242 J5
Tankwa-Karoo △ S. Africa 32°14S 19°50E 270 D2
Tanlu Taiwan 22°12N 120°44E 225 D2
Tanna Vanuatu 19°30S 169°20E 287 J7
Tännäs Sweden 62°26N 12°42E 162 B6
Tannersville U.S.A. 41°3N 75°18W 313 E9
Tannis Bugt Denmark 57°40N 10°15E 163 G4
Tannu Ola Asia 51°0N 94°0E 217 B12
Tannum Sands Australia 23°57S 151°22E 280 C5
Tano → Ghana 5°7N 2°56W 262 D4
Tanombella Algeria 25°30N 5°49E 261 C6
Tanon Str. Phil. 10°20N 123°30E 233 F4
Tanout Niger 14°50N 8°55E 259 F1
Tanquinho Brazil 11°58S 39°6W 333 D4
Tanshui Taiwan 25°10N 121°28E 225 A3
Tanshui Kang → Taiwan 25°10N 121°25E 225 A3
Tansilla Burkina Faso 12°25N 4°23W 262 C4
Tanta Egypt 30°45N 30°57E 256 H7
Tantabin Burma 17°1N 95°59E 241 G5
Tantoyuca Mexico 21°21N 98°14W 319 C5
Tantung = Dandong China 40°10N 124°20E 224 B2
T'antzu Taiwan 24°13N 120°42E 225 B2
Tanuku India 16°45N 81°44E 244 F5
Tanum Norway 59°53N 10°28E 133 A1
Tanūmah Si. Arabia 18°58N 42°10E 248 C3
Tanumshede Sweden 58°42N 11°20E 163 F5
Tanunda Australia 34°30S 139°0E 282 C3
Tanur India 11°1N 75°52E 245 J2
Tanus France 44°8N 2°19E 174 D6
Tanzania ■ Africa 6°0S 34°0E 268 D3
Tanzawa-Sanchi Japan 35°27N 139°0E 223 B11
Tanzhou China 22°16N 113°28E 219 a
Tanzilla → Canada 58°8N 130°43W 296 B2
Tao, Ko Thailand 10°5N 99°52E 237 G2
Tao'an = Taonan China 45°22N 122°40E 227 B12
Tao'er He → China 45°45N 124°5E 227 B13
Taohua Dao China 29°50N 122°20E 229 C14
Taolanaro Madag. 25°2S 47°0E 272 D2
Taole China 38°48N 106°40E 226 E4
Taonan China 45°22N 122°40E 227 B12
Taora Solomon Is. 7°21S 157°30E 287 L9
Taormina Italy 37°51N 15°17E 201 E8
Taos U.S.A. 36°24N 105°35W 305 H11
Taoudenni Mali 22°40N 3°55W 260 D4
Taoudrart, Adrar Algeria 24°25N 2°24E 261 D5
Taounate Morocco 34°25N 4°41W 260 B4
Taounate □ Morocco 34°30N 4°50W 260 B4
Taourirt Algeria 26°37N 0°20E 261 C5
Taourirt Morocco 34°25N 2°53W 261 B4

Taouz Morocco 30°53N 4°0W 260 B4
Taoyuan Hunan, China 28°55N 111°16E 229 C8
T'aoyüan Kaohsiung, Taiwan 23°9N 120°46E 225 C2
T'aoyüan Yünlin, Taiwan 25°0N 121°4E 225 B3
T'aoyüan □ Taiwan 24°55N 121°15E 225 B3
Tapa Estonia 59°15N 25°50E 161 G21
Tapa Shan = Daba Shan China 32°0N 109°0E 228 B7
Tapachula Mexico 14°54N 92°17W 319 E6
Tapada Portugal 38°49N 9°16W 126 A1
Tapah Malaysia 4°12N 101°15E 237 K3
Tapajós → Brazil 2°24S 54°41W 329 D7
Tapaktuan Indonesia 3°15N 97°10E 234 B1
Tapanahoni → Suriname 4°20N 54°25W 329 C7
Tapanila Finland 60°15N 25°2E 121 B3
Tapanui N.Z. 45°56S 169°18E 285 F4
Taparo Pt. Trin. & Tob. 10°3N 61°38W 323 t
Tapauá Brazil 5°40S 64°20W 331 B5
Tapauá → Brazil 5°40S 64°21W 331 B5
Tapaz Phil. 11°16N 122°32E 233 F4
Tapes Brazil 30°40S 51°23W 335 C5
Tapeta Liberia 6°29N 8°52W 262 D3
Taphan Hin Thailand 16°13N 100°26E 236 D3
Tapia de Casariego Spain 43°34N 6°56W 194 B4
Tapiales Argentina 34°42S 58°30W 117 C1
Tapiantana Channel Phil. 6°22N 122°1E 233 H4
Tapiantana Group Phil. 6°20N 122°0E 233 H4
Tapiau = Gvardeysk Russia 54°39N 21°5E 184 D8
Tapilon = Daanbantayan Phil. 11°17N 124°2E 233 F5
Taping Taiwan 24°6N 120°53E 225 B2
Tapini Papua N. G. 8°19S 147°0E 286 E4
Tapiola Finland 60°10N 24°48E 121 B1
Tapiraí Brazil 19°52S 46°1W 333 E2
Tapirapé → Brazil 10°41S 50°38W 332 D1
Tapirapecó, Serra Venezuela 1°10N 65°0W 329 C5
Taplan Australia 34°33S 140°52E 282 C4
Tapo-Capara △ Venezuela 7°55N 71°15W 328 B3
Tapoeripa Suriname 5°22N 56°34W 329 B6
Tapolca Hungary 46°53N 17°29E 182 D2
Tapsia India 22°32N 88°23E 124 B2
Tapti → India 21°8N 72°41E 244 D1
Tapu Taiwan 23°18N 120°35E 225 C2
Tapuae-o-Uenuku N.Z. 42°0S 173°39E 285 C8
Tapul Phil. 5°42N 120°55E 233 J3
Tapul Group Phil. 5°35N 120°50E 233 J3
Tapul I. Phil. 5°43N 120°55E 233 J3
Tapun India 27°35N 96°22E 241 B6
Tapurucuará Brazil 0°24S 65°2W 329 D5
Taputapu, C. Amer. Samoa 14°20S 170°51W 302 f
Taputimu Amer. Samoa 14°21S 170°46W 302 f
Ţaqţaq Iraq 35°53N 44°35E 213 E11
Taquara Brazil 29°36S 50°46W 335 B5
Taquari → Brazil 19°15S 57°17W 331 D6
Taquaritinga Brazil 21°24S 48°30W 333 F2
Tara Queens., Australia 27°17S 150°31E 281 D5
Tara Ont., Canada 44°28N 81°9W 312 B3
Tara Maharashtra, India 19°5N 72°49E 130 A1
Tara Japan 33°2N 130°11E 222 D2
Tara Russia 56°55N 74°24E 214 D8
Tara Zambia 16°58S 26°45E 269 F2
Tara → Montenegro 43°21N 18°51E 202 C2
Tara △ Serbia 43°55N 19°30E 202 C3
Tara-Dake Japan 32°58N 130°6E 222 E2
Taraba □ Nigeria 8°0N 10°30E 263 D7
Taraba → Nigeria 8°30N 10°15E 263 D7
Tarabuco Bolivia 19°10S 64°57W 331 D5
Tarābulus Lebanon 34°31N 35°50E 250 D6
Tarābulus Libya 32°49N 13°7E 258 B2
Tarābulus N. Afr. 31°0N 13°0E 258 B2
Tarābulus □ Libya 32°53N 13°11E 261 B7
Tarabya Turkey 41°8N 29°3E 122 B2
Taraclia Taraclia, Moldova 45°54N 28°40E 183 E13
Taraclia Tighina, Moldova 46°34N 29°7E 183 D14
Taradale N.Z. 39°33S 176°53E 284 F5
Taradehi India 23°18N 79°21E 243 H8
Tarāghin Libya 26°0N 14°30E 258 C2
Taragi Japan 32°16N 130°56E 222 E2
Tarahouahout Algeria 22°41N 5°59E 261 D6
Tarajalejo Canary Is. 28°12N 14°7W 153 e2
Tarakan Indonesia 3°20N 117°35E 235 B5
Tarakit, Mt. Kenya 2°2N 35°10E 268 B4
Taralga Australia 34°26S 149°52E 283 C8
Tarama-Jima Japan 24°39N 124°42E 221 M2
Taramakau → N.Z. 42°34S 171°8E 285 C6
Taran, Mys Russia 54°56N 19°59E 184 D6
Taranagar India 28°43N 74°50E 242 E6
Taranaki □ N.Z. 39°25S 174°30E 284 F3
Taranaki, Mt. N.Z. 39°17S 174°5E 284 F3
Tarancón Spain 40°1N 3°1W 196 E1
Tarangire △ Tanzania 4°21S 36°7E 268 C4
Taransay U.K. 57°54N 7°0W 167 D1
Táranto Italy 40°28N 17°14E 201 B10
Táranto, G. di Italy 40°8N 17°20E 201 B10
Tarapacá Colombia 2°56S 69°46W 328 D4
Tarapacá □ Chile 20°45S 69°30W 334 A2
Tarapoto Peru 6°30S 76°20W 330 B2
Taraquá Brazil 0°6N 68°28W 328 C4
Tarare France 45°54N 4°26E 175 C8
Tararua Ra. N.Z. 40°45S 175°25E 284 G4
Tarasag Vanuatu 14°12S 167°36E 287 D5
Tarascon France 43°48N 4°39E 175 E8
Tarascon-sur-Ariège France 42°50N 1°36E 174 F5
Tarashcha Ukraine 49°30N 30°31E 177 D16
Tarata Peru 17°27S 70°2W 330 D3
Tarauacá Brazil 8°6S 70°48W 330 B3
Tarauacá → Brazil 6°42S 69°48W 330 B4
Taravao Tahiti 17°43S 149°18W 289 e
Taravao, Isthme de Tahiti 17°43S 149°19W 289 e
Taravo → France 41°42N 8°49E 175 G12
Tarawa Kiribati 1°30N 173°0E 288 G9
Tarawai I. Papua N. G. 3°13S 143°15E 286 B2
Tarawera N.Z. 39°2S 176°36E 284 F5
Tarawera, L. N.Z. 38°13S 176°27E 284 E5
Tarawera, Mt. N.Z. 38°14S 176°32E 284 E5
Taraz Kazakhstan 42°54N 71°22E 217 D8
Tarazona Spain 41°55N 1°43W 196 D3
Tarazona de la Mancha Spain 39°16N 1°55W 197 F3
Tårbæk Denmark 55°46N 12°35E 118 A3
Tarbagatay, Khrebet Kazakhstan 48°0N 83°0E 217 C10
Tarbaj Kenya 2°12N 40°8E 267 D5
Tarbat Ness U.K. 57°52N 3°47W 167 D5
Tarbela Dam Pakistan 34°8N 72°52E 242 B5
Tarbert Kerry, Ireland 52°34N 9°22W 166 D2
Tarbert Argyll & Bute, U.K. 55°52N 5°25W 167 F3
Tarbert W. Isles, U.K. 57°54N 6°49W 167 D2
Tarbes France 43°15N 0°3E 174 E4
Tarboro U.S.A. 35°54N 77°32W 315 D16
Tarbū Libya 26°0N 15°5E 258 C3
Tărcău, Munţii Romania 46°39N 26°7E 183 D11
Tarcento Italy 46°13N 13°13E 199 B10
Tarchomin Poland 52°19N 20°58E 142 B1
Tarcoola Australia 30°44S 134°36E 281 E1
Tarcoon Australia 30°15S 146°43E 281 E4
Tarcutta Australia 35°16S 147°44E 283 C7
Tardeo India 18°57N 72°48E 130 B1
Tardets-Sorholus France 43°8N 0°52W 174 E3
Tardoire → France 45°52N 0°14E 174 C4
Taredjerdja Algeria 25°12N 2°32E 261 C5
Taree Australia 31°50S 152°30E 283 A10
Tarella Australia 31°2S 143°2E 282 A5
Tarf, Ras Morocco 35°40N 5°11W 260 A3
Ţarfā, Ra's aţ Si. Arabia 17°2N 42°22E 248 D3
Ţarfā, W. el → Egypt 28°25N 30°50E 256 B3
Tarfaya Morocco 27°55N 12°55W 260 C2
Târgovişte Romania 44°55N 25°27E 183 F10
Targówek Poland 52°16N 21°3E 142 B2
Târgu Bujor Romania 45°52N 27°54E 183 E12
Târgu Cărbuneşti Romania 44°57N 23°31E 183 F8
Târgu Frumos Romania 47°12N 27°2E 183 C12
Târgu Jiu Romania 45°5N 23°19E 183 E8
Târgu Lăpuş Romania 47°27N 23°52E 183 C8
Târgu Mureş Romania 46°31N 24°38E 183 D9
Târgu Neamţ Romania 47°12N 26°25E 183 C11
Târgu Ocna Romania 46°16N 26°39E 183 D11
Târgu Secuiesc Romania 46°0N 26°10E 183 E11
Targuist Morocco 34°59N 4°14W 260 B4
Tărguşor Romania 44°27N 28°25E 183 F13
Tarhăus, Vf. Romania 46°40N 26°8E 183 D11
Tarhbalt Morocco 30°39N 5°20W 260 B3
Tarhūnah Libya 32°27N 13°36E 258 B2
Tari Papua N. G. 5°54S 142°59E 286 C2
Táriba Venezuela 7°49N 72°13W 328 B3
Ţarīf U.A.E. 24°3N 53°46E 247 E7
Tarifa Spain 36°1N 5°36W 195 J5
Tarigtig Pt. Phil. 16°25N 122°14E 232 C4
Tarija Bolivia 21°30S 64°40W 334 A3
Tarija □ Bolivia 21°30S 63°30W 334 A3
Tarik I. Micronesia 7°20N 151°46E 287 T18
Tariku → Indonesia 2°55S 138°26E 231 E9
Tarīm Yemen 16°3N 49°0E 249 C5
Tarim Basin = Tarim Pendi China 40°0N 84°0E 217 E10
Tarim He → China 39°30N 88°30E 217 E11
Tarim Pendi China 40°0N 84°0E 217 E10
Tarime Tanzania 1°21S 34°22E 266 E3
Taritatu → Indonesia 2°54S 138°27E 231 E9
Tarka → S. Africa 32°10S 26°0E 270 D4
Tarka La Bhutan 27°12N 89°44E 243 F13
Tarkastad S. Africa 32°0S 26°16E 270 D4
Tarkhankut, Mys Ukraine 45°25N 32°30E 189 K7
Tarko Sale Russia 64°55N 77°50E 214 C8
Tarkwa Ghana 5°20N 2°0W 262 D4
Tarlac Phil. 15°29N 120°35E 232 D3
Tarlac □ Phil. 15°30N 120°30E 232 D3
Tarm Denmark 55°56N 8°31E 163 J2
Tarma Peru 11°25S 75°45W 330 C2
Tarmiya Iraq 33°40N 44°23E 213 G11
Tarn □ France 43°49N 2°8E 174 E6
Tarn → France 44°5N 1°6E 174 D5
Tarn-et-Garonne □ France 44°8N 1°20E 174 D5
Tarna → Hungary 47°31N 19°59E 182 C4
Târnava Mare → Romania 46°10N 23°43E 183 D8
Târnava Mică → Romania 46°9N 23°55E 183 D8
Târnăveni Romania 46°19N 24°13E 183 D9
Tårnby Denmark 55°37N 12°35E 118 B3
Tarnica Poland 49°4N 22°44E 135 J9
Tarnobrzeg Poland 50°35N 21°41E 185 H8
Tarnogród Poland 50°22N 22°45E 185 H9
Tarnopol = Ternopil Ukraine 49°30N 25°40E 177 D13
Tarnos France 43°32N 1°28W 174 E2
Târnova Moldova 48°10N 27°40E 183 B12
Târnova Romania 45°23N 21°59E 182 E6
Tarnów Poland 50°3N 21°0E 185 H8
Tarnowitz = Tarnowskie Góry Poland 50°27N 18°54E 185 H5
Tarnowskie Góry Poland 50°27N 18°54E 185 H5
Tärnsjö Sweden 60°9N 16°56E 162 D10
Táro → Italy 45°2N 10°15E 198 C7
Taroko △ Taiwan 24°10N 121°33E 225 B3
Ţārom Iran 28°11N 55°46E 247 D7
Taroom Australia 25°36S 149°48E 281 D4
Taroudannt Morocco 30°30N 8°52W 260 B3
Taroudannt □ Morocco 30°30N 8°25W 260 B3
Taroume Cook Is. 21°15S 159°45W 289 h
Tarp Germany 54°39N 9°24E 178 A5
Tarpeena Australia 37°37S 140°47E 282 D4
Tarpon Springs U.S.A. 28°9N 82°45W 317 G7
Tarqua Bay Nigeria 6°24N 3°23E 124 B2
Tarquínia Italy 42°15N 11°45E 199 F8
Tarra Bulga △ Australia 38°27S 146°31E 283 E7
Tarrafal C. Verde Is. 15°18N 23°39W 153 j
Tarragona Spain 41°5N 1°17E 196 D6
Tarragona □ Spain 41°5N 1°0E 196 D6
Tarraleah Australia 42°17S 146°26E 281 G4
Tarrasa = Terrassa Spain 41°34N 2°1E 196 D7
Tàrrega Spain 41°39N 1°9E 196 D6
Tarrytown Ga., U.S.A. 32°19N 82°34W 316 C7
Tarrytown N.Y., U.S.A. 41°4N 73°52W 313 E11
Târs Denmark 57°23N 10°7E 163 G4
Tarshiha = Me'ona Israel 33°1N 35°15E 250 E6
Tarsus Turkey 36°58N 34°55E 250 B5
Tarsus → Turkey 36°46N 34°52E 250 B5
Tartagal Argentina 22°30S 63°50W 334 A3
Tartane Martinique 14°45N 60°55W 322 j
Tärtär Azerbaijan 40°20N 46°58E 191 K8
Tärtär → Azerbaijan 40°26N 47°20E 191 K8
Tartas France 43°50N 0°49W 174 E3
Tartu Estonia 58°20N 26°44E 188 C4
Ţarţūs Syria 34°55N 35°55E 250 D6
Ţarţūs □ Syria 35°0N 36°0E 250 D7
Tarumirim Brazil 19°16S 41°59W 333 E3
Tarumizu Japan 31°29N 130°42E 222 F2
Tarussa Russia 54°44N 37°10E 188 E9
Tarutao = Ko Tarutao △ Thailand 6°31N 99°26E 237 J2
Tarutao, Ko Thailand 6°33N 99°40E 237 J2
Tarutung Indonesia 2°0N 98°54E 234 B1
Tarutyne Ukraine 46°12N 29°9E 183 D14
Tarvísio Italy 46°30N 13°35E 199 B10
Tarxien Malta 35°52N 14°31E 206 F8
Taşağıl Turkey 36°55N 31°14E 250 B2
Tasahku Burma 27°33N 97°52E 241 B6
Tasaret, O. → Algeria 26°25N 1°59E 261 C5
Tasāwah Libya 26°0N 13°30E 258 C2
Tasböget Kazakhstan 44°46N 65°33E 217 D7
Tasek Merimbun △ Brunei 4°31N 114°41E 235 B4
Taseko → Canada 52°8N 123°45W 296 C4
Tasgaon India 17°2N 74°39E 244 F2
Tash-Kömür Kyrgyzstan 41°40N 72°10E 217 D8
Tash-Kumyr = Tash-Kömür Kyrgyzstan 41°40N 72°10E 217 D8
Tashauz = Dashoguz Turkmenistan 41°49N 59°58E 216 D5
Tashi Chho Dzong = Thimphu Bhutan 27°31N 89°45E 241 B2
Tashino = Pervomaysk Russia 54°56N 43°58E 190 C6
Ţashk, Daryācheh-ye Iran 29°45N 53°35E 247 D7
Tashkent = Toshkent Uzbekistan 41°20N 69°10E 217 D7
Tashtagol Russia 52°47N 87°53E 217 B11
Tashu Taiwan 22°41N 120°25E 225 D2
Tasiilaq Greenland 65°40N 37°20W 154 D7
Tasik Bera Malaysia 3°5N 102°38E 234 B2
Tasik Kenyir Malaysia 5°5N 102°45E 234 A2
Tasikmalaya Indonesia 7°18S 108°12E 235 D3
Tåsinge Denmark 55°0N 10°35E 163 J4
Tåsjön Sweden 64°15N 15°40E 160 D16
Task Niger 14°56N 10°46E 259 F2
Taskan Russia 62°59N 150°20E 215 C16
Taşkent Turkey 36°55N 32°29E 250 B3
Taşköprü Turkey 41°30N 34°15E 212 B6
Taskul Papua N. G. 2°32S 150°27E 286 B6
Taşlâc Moldova 47°4N 29°24E 183 C14
Taşlıçay Turkey 39°38N 43°22E 213 C10
Tasman □ N.Z. 41°30S 172°40E 285 B7
Tasman → N.Z. 43°48S 170°8E 285 D5
Tasman, Mt. N.Z. 43°34S 170°12E 285 D5
Tasman Abyssal Plain Pac. Oc. 34°30S 153°15E 276 G9
Tasman B. N.Z. 40°59S 173°25E 285 A8
Tasman Basin Pac. Oc. 46°0S 158°0E 288 M7
Tasman Glacier N.Z. 43°37S 170°12E 285 D5
Tasman Mts. N.Z. 41°3S 172°25E 285 B7
Tasman Pen. Australia 43°10S 148°0E 281 G4
Tasman Sea Pac. Oc. 36°0S 160°0E 277 H10
Tasmania □ Australia 42°0S 146°30E 281 G4
Tasmanian Wilderness World Heritage Area △ Australia 43°0S 146°0E 281 G4
Tăşnad Romania 47°30N 22°33E 182 C7
Taşova Turkey 40°45N 36°19E 212 B7
Tassili n'Ajjer Algeria 25°47N 8°1E 261 C6
Tassili n'Ajjer △ Algeria 26°5N 6°0E 258 C1
Tassili-Oua-n-Ahaggar Algeria 20°41N 5°30E 261 D6
Tassili Tin-Rerhoh Algeria 20°5N 3°55E 261 D5
Taşucu Turkey 36°19N 33°52E 250 B4
Taşucu Körfezi Turkey 36°16N 33°56E 250 B4
Tasuj Iran 38°18N 45°23E 213 C11
Tat Ton △ Thailand 15°57N 102°2E 236 E4
Tata Hungary 47°37N 18°19E 182 C3
Tata Morocco 29°46N 7°56W 260 C3
Tatabánya Hungary 47°32N 18°25E 182 C3
Tatakoto French Polynesia 17°20S 138°23W 289 f
Tatamá △ Colombia 5°5N 76°9W 328 B2
Tatamba Solomon Is. 8°21S 159°51E 287 M10
Tataouine Tunisia 32°57N 10°29E 258 B2
Tataouine □ Tunisia 32°0N 10°0E 261 B7
Tatar-Pazardzhik = Pazardzhik Bulgaria 42°12N 24°20E 203 D8
Tatar Republic = Tatarstan □ Russia 55°30N 51°30E 190 C10
Tatarbunary Ukraine 45°50N 29°39E 183 E14
Tatarovo Russia 55°45N 37°24E 129 B2
Tatarsk Russia 55°14N 76°0E 214 D8
Tatarskiy Proliv Russia 50°0N 141°0E 215 E15
Tatarstan □ Russia 55°30N 51°30E 190 C10
Tatatóváros = Tata Hungary 47°37N 18°19E 182 C3
Tatatua, Pte. Tahiti 17°44S 149°8W 289 e
Tatau Malaysia 2°53N 112°51E 235 B4
Tatau I. Papua N. G. 2°48S 151°57E 286 B6
Tatebayashi Japan 36°15N 139°32E 223 A11
Tateshina-Yama Japan 36°8N 138°11E 223 A10
Tateyama Japan 35°0N 139°50E 223 C11
Tateyama Japan 36°40N 137°35E 223 A9
Tathlina L. Canada 60°33N 117°39W 296 A5
Tathlīth Si. Arabia 19°32N 43°30E 248 C3
Tathlīth, W. → Si. Arabia 20°35N 44°20E 248 B4
Tathong Channel China 22°15N 114°16E 122 B2
Tathong Pt. China 22°14N 114°17E 122 B2
Tathra Australia 36°44S 149°59E 283 D8
Tatinnai L. Canada 60°55N 97°40W 297 A9
Tatitlek U.S.A. 60°52N 146°41W 303 F11
Tatkon Burma 20°7N 96°13E 241 E6
Tatla Lake Canada 52°0N 124°20W 296 C4
Tatlisu Turkey 40°24N 27°55E 203 F11
Tatnam, C. Canada 57°16N 91°0W 297 B10
Tatra = Tatry Slovak Rep. 49°20N 20°0E 181 B13
Tatranský △ Slovak Rep. 49°10N 20°0E 181 B13
Tatry Slovak Rep. 49°20N 20°0E 181 B13
Tatshenshini → Canada 59°28N 137°45W 296 B1
Tatsuno Hyōgo, Japan 34°52N 134°33E 222 C6
Tatsuno Nagano, Japan 35°58N 138°0E 223 B10
Tatta Pakistan 24°42N 67°55E 242 G2
Tatuapé Brazil 23°31S 46°33W 137 B2
Tatuí Brazil 23°25S 47°53W 335 A6
Tatum U.S.A. 33°16N 103°19W 305 K12
Tat'ung = Datong China 40°6N 113°18E 226 D7
Tatura Australia 36°29S 145°16E 283 D6
Tatvan Turkey 38°31N 42°15E 213 C10
Ta'ū Amer. Samoa 14°15S 169°30W 302 g
Tau Rogaland, Norway 59°3N 5°55E 164 E2
Tauá Brazil 6°1S 40°26W 332 C3
Taubaté Brazil 23°0S 45°36W 335 A6
Tauberbischofsheim Germany 49°37N 9°39E 179 F5
Taucha Germany 51°23N 12°29E 178 D8
Tauern Austria 47°15N 12°40E 176 E7
Tauern-tunnel Austria 47°0N 13°12E 180 D6
Taufikia South Sudan 9°24N 31°37E 257 F3
Taufkirchen Germany 48°2N 11°36E 131 B2
Taulé France 48°37N 3°55W 172 D3
Taumarunui N.Z. 38°53S 175°15E 284 E4
Taumaturgo Brazil 8°54S 72°51W 330 B3
Taung S. Africa 27°33S 24°47E 270 C3
Taungdwingyi Burma 20°1N 95°40E 241 E5
Taunggyi Burma 20°50N 97°0E 241 E6
Taungtha Burma 21°12N 95°25E 241 E5
Taungup Burma 18°51N 94°14E 241 F5
Taungup Pass Burma 18°40N 94°45E 241 F5
Taunsa Pakistan 30°42N 70°39E 242 D4
Taunsa Barrage Pakistan 30°42N 70°50E 242 D4
Taunton Somst., U.K. 51°1N 3°5W 169 F4
Taunton Mass., U.S.A. 41°54N 71°6W 313 E13
Taunus Germany 50°13N 8°34E 179 E4
Taupo N.Z. 38°41S 176°7E 284 E5
Taupo, L. N.Z. 38°46S 175°55E 284 E4
Tauragė Lithuania 55°14N 22°16E 184 C9
Tauragė □ Lithuania 55°15N 22°17E 184 C9
Tauranga N.Z. 37°42S 176°11E 284 D5
Tauranga Harb. N.Z. 37°30S 176°5E 284 D5
Taureau, Rés. Canada 46°46N 73°50W 298 C5
Tauri → Papua N. G. 8°8S 146°8E 286 E4
Taurianova Italy 38°21N 16°1E 201 D9
Taurus Mts. = Toros Dağları Turkey 37°0N 32°30E 250 B3
Taus = Domažlice Czech Rep. 49°28N 12°58E 180 B5
Tauste Spain 41°58N 1°18W 196 D3
Tautira Tahiti 17°44S 149°9W 289 e
Tauyskaya Guba Russia 59°20N 150°20E 215 D16
Tauz = Tovuz Azerbaijan 41°0N 45°40E 191 K7
Tavan Bogd Uul Mongolia 49°10N 87°49E 217 C11
Tavares U.S.A. 28°48N 81°44W 317 G8
Tavares, I. dos Brazil 22°49S 43°6W 135 A2
Tavas Turkey 37°34N 29°4E 205 D11
Tavastehus = Hämeenlinna Finland 61°0N 24°28E 188 B3
Tavda Russia 58°7N 65°8E 214 D7
Tavda → Russia 57°47N 67°18E 214 D7
Taverner B. Canada 67°12N 72°25W 295 D17
Tavernes de la Valldigna Spain 39°5N 0°13W 197 F4
Tavernier U.S.A. 25°1N 80°31W 317 K9
Taveta Kenya 3°23S 37°37E 268 C4
Taveuni Fiji 16°51S 179°58W 287 A3
Taviano Italy 39°59N 18°5E 201 C11
Tavignano → France 42°7N 9°33E 175 F13
Tavira Portugal 37°8N 7°40W 195 H3
Tavistock Ont., Canada 43°19N 80°50W 312 C4
Tavistock Devon, U.K. 50°33N 4°9W 169 G3
Tavolara Italy 40°54N 9°42E 200 B2
Távora → Portugal 41°8N 7°35W 194 D3
Tavoy Burma 14°2N 98°12E 236 E2
Tavoy Pt. Burma 13°32N 98°10E 236 F2
Tavrichanka Russia 43°18N 131°59E 220 C5
Tavropos → Greece 39°10N 21°45E 204 B3
Tavros Greece 37°57N 23°43E 112 B2
Tavşanlı Turkey 39°32N 29°30E 205 B11
Tavua Fiji 17°37S 177°5E 287 A1
Tavuki Fiji 19°7S 178°8E 287 B2
Taw → U.K. 51°4N 4°4W 169 F3
Tawa N.Z. 41°10S 174°49E 143 A1
Tawa → India 22°48N 77°48E 242 H8
Tawa Res. India 22°35N 78°5E 244 C4
Tawa Tawa Mal Reef Papua N. G. 11°3S 152°55E 286 F7
Tawai India 27°48N 96°47E 241 B6
Tawas City U.S.A. 44°16N 83°31W 309 C12
Tawau Malaysia 4°20N 117°55E 235 B5
Tawau Hills △ Malaysia 4°20N 117°54E 235 B5
Taweisha Sudan 12°19N 26°40E 257 E2
Tawi-tawi □ Phil. 5°0N 120°0E 233 J3
Tawi-tawi I. Phil. 5°10N 120°15E 233 J3
Tawngche Burma 26°34N 95°38E 241 B5
Tawu Taiwan 22°22N 120°54E 225 D2
Tāwūq Iraq 35°8N 44°26E 213 E11
Tāwurghā' Libya 32°1N 15°2E 258 B3
Tāwurghā', Sabkhat Libya 31°21N 15°15E 258 B3
Taxco Mexico 18°33N 99°36W 319 D5
Taxila Pakistan 33°42N 72°52E 242 C5
Taxkorgan Tajik Zizhixian China 37°49N 75°14E 217 E9
Tay → U.K. 56°37N 3°38W 167 E5
Tay, Firth of U.K. 56°25N 3°8W 167 E5
Tay, L. W. Austral., Australia 32°55S 120°48E 279 F3
Tay, L. Perth & Kinr., U.K. 56°32N 4°8W 167 E4
Tay △ U.K. 56°43N 3°59W 167 E5
Tay Ninh Vietnam 11°20N 106°5E 237 G6
Tayabamba Peru 8°15S 77°16W 330 B2
Tayabas = Quezon Phil. 9°15N 117°59E 233 G1
Tayabas Phil. 14°1N 121°35E 232 D3
Tayabas B. Phil. 13°45N 121°45E 232 E3
Tayan Indonesia 0°1S 110°7E 235 C4
Taygetos Oros Greece 37°0N 22°23E 204 D4
Taylakova Russia 59°13N 74°0E 214 D8
Taylor B.C., Canada 56°13N 120°40W 296 B4
Taylor Fla., U.S.A. 30°26N 82°18W 316 E7
Taylor Mich., U.S.A. 42°14N 83°16W 311 B13
Taylor Nebr., U.S.A. 41°46N 99°23W 308 E4
Taylor Pa., U.S.A. 41°23N 75°43W 313 E9
Taylor Tex., U.S.A. 30°34N 97°25W 314 F6
Taylor, Mt. N.Z. 43°30S 171°20E 285 D6
Taylor, Mt. N. Mex., U.S.A. 35°14N 107°37W 305 J10
Taylorsville U.S.A. 38°2N 85°21W 311 F11
Taylorsville L. U.S.A. 38°0N 85°15W 311 G11
Taylorville U.S.A. 39°33N 89°18W 310 E7
Taymā Si. Arabia 27°35N 38°45E 246 E3
Taymyr, Oz. Russia 74°20N 102°0E 215 B11
Taymyr, Poluostrov Russia 75°0N 100°0E 215 B11
Taypaq Kazakhstan 49°0N 51°47E 187 E9
Tayport U.K. 56°27N 2°52W 167 E6
Tayrona △ Colombia 11°20N 74°2W 328 A3
Tayshet Russia 55°58N 98°1E 215 D10
Taytay Phil. 10°45N 119°30E 233 F2
Taytay B. Phil. 10°55N 119°35E 233 F2
Tayuan Taiwan 25°3N 121°1E 225 A3
Tayug Phil. 16°2N 120°45E 232 C3
Tayüling Taiwan 24°11N 121°18E 225 B3
Tāyyebād Iran 34°45N 60°45E 247 C9
Tāyyebād □ Iran 34°44N 60°44E 247 C9
Tayynsha Kazakhstan 53°50N 69°45E 217 B7
Taz → Russia 67°32N 78°40E 214 C8
Taza Morocco 34°16N 4°6W 260 B4
Taza □ Morocco 34°15N 3°45W 260 B4
Tāza Khurmātū Iraq 35°18N 44°20E 213 E11
Tazawa-Ko Japan 39°43N 140°40E 220 E10
Taze Burma 22°57N 95°24E 241 D5
Tazenakht Morocco 30°35N 7°12W 260 B3
Tazerbo Libya 25°45N 21°0E 258 C4
Tazin → Canada 59°48N 109°55W 297 B7
Tazin L. Canada 59°44N 108°42W 297 B7
Tazlina U.S.A. 62°4N 146°27W 303 E11
Tazouikert Mali 21°2N 1°16W 261 D4
Tazoult Algeria 35°29N 6°11E 261 A6
Tazovskiy Russia 67°30N 78°44E 214 C8
Tazrouk Algeria 23°24N 6°15E 261 D6
Tbilisi Georgia 41°43N 44°50E 191 K7
Tchad = Chad ■ Africa 15°0N 17°15E 259 F3
Tchad, L. Chad 13°30N 14°30E 259 F2
Tchaourou Benin 8°58N 2°40E 263 D5
Tch'eng-tou = Chengdu China 30°38N 104°2E 228 B5
Tchentlo L. Canada 55°15N 125°0W 296 B4
Tchetti Benin 7°50N 1°40E 263 D5
Tchibanga Gabon 2°45S 11°0E 264 C2
Tchien Liberia 5°59N 8°15W 262 D3
Tchin Tabaraden Niger 15°58N 5°56E 263 B6
Tcholliré Cameroon 8°24N 14°10E 264 A2
Tch'ong-k'ing = Chongqing China 29°35N 106°25E 228 C6
Tchoupitoulas Street New Orleans, U.S.A. 131 b2
Tczew Poland 54°8N 18°50E 184 D5
Te Anau N.Z. 45°25S 167°43E 285 F2
Te Anau, L. N.Z. 45°15S 167°45E 285 F2
Te Araroa N.Z. 37°39S 178°25E 284 D7
Te Aroha N.Z. 37°32S 175°44E 284 D4
Te Awamutu N.Z. 38°1S 175°20E 284 E4
Te Ika a Maui = North I. N.Z. 38°0S 175°0E 284 E4
Te Kaha N.Z. 37°44S 177°52E 284 D6
Te Karaka N.Z. 38°26S 177°53E 284 E6
Te Kauwhata N.Z. 37°25S 175°9E 284 D4
Te Kopuru N.Z. 36°2S 173°56E 284 C2
Te Kou Cook Is. 21°14S 159°46W 289 h
Te Kuiti N.Z. 38°20S 175°11E 284 E4
Te Manga Cook Is. 21°14S 159°45W 289 h
Te-n-Dghâmcha, Sebkhet Mauritania 18°30N 15°55W 262 B1
Te Papa Museum N.Z. 41°18S 174°47E 143 B1
Te Puke N.Z. 37°46S 176°22E 284 D5
Te Teko N.Z. 38°2S 176°48E 284 E5
Te Waewae B. N.Z. 46°13S 167°33E 285 G2
Te Wai Pounamu = South I. N.Z. 44°0S 170°0E 285 E5
Tea → Brazil 0°30S 65°9W 328 D4
Teaca Romania 46°55N 24°30E 183 D9
Teague U.S.A. 31°38N 96°17W 314 F6
Teahupoo Tahiti 17°50S 149°16W 289 e
Teaneck U.S.A. 40°53N 74°1W 132 A1
Teano Italy 41°15N 14°4E 201 A7
Teapa Mexico 17°33N 92°57W 319 D6
Teba Spain 36°59N 4°55W 195 J6
Tebakang Malaysia 1°6N 110°30E 235 B4
Tébarat Niger 14°49N 4°27E 263 C5
Teberau → Malaysia 1°30N 103°42E 237 d
Teberda Russia 43°30N 41°46E 191 J5
Tébessa Algeria 35°22N 8°8E 261 A6
Tébessa □ Algeria 35°0N 7°50E 261 B6
Tebet Indonesia 6°14S 106°50E 122 B2
Tebicuary → Paraguay 26°36S 58°16W 334 B4
Tebingtinggi Riau, Indonesia 1°0N 102°45E 234 B2
Tebingtinggi Sumatera Selatan, Indonesia 3°36S 103°4E 234 C2
Tebingtinggi Sumatera Utara, Indonesia 3°20N 99°9E 234 B1
Tébourba Tunisia 36°49N 9°51E 258 A1
Téboursouk Tunisia 36°29N 9°10E 258 A1
Tebulos Georgia 42°36N 45°17E 191 J7
Tecamachalco Mexico 19°25N 99°14W 128 B1
Tecate Mexico 32°34N 116°38W 307 N10
Tecer Dağları Turkey 39°27N 37°27E 212 C7
Tech → France 42°36N 3°3E 174 F7
Techiman Ghana 7°35N 1°58W 262 D4
Techirghiol Romania 44°4N 28°32E 183 F13
Techou = Dezhou China 37°26N 116°18E 226 F9
Tecka Argentina 43°29S 70°48W 336 B2
Tecomán Mexico 18°55N 103°53W 318 D4
Tecopa U.S.A. 35°51N 116°13W 307 K10
Tecoripa Mexico 28°37N 109°57W 318 B3
Tecuala Mexico 22°23N 105°27W 318 C3
Tecuci Romania 45°51N 27°27E 183 E12
Tecumseh Ont., Canada 42°19N 82°54W 312 D2
Tecumseh Mich., U.S.A. 42°0N 83°57W 311 B13
Tecumseh Okla., U.S.A. 35°15N 96°56W 314 D6
Ted Somali Rep. 4°24N 43°55E 267 D5
Ted Williams Tunnel U.S.A. 42°21N 71°1W 116 A2
Teddington U.K. 51°25N 0°20W 125 B1
Tedjert Algeria 21°23N 6°25E 261 D6
Tedzhen = Tejen Turkmenistan 37°23N 60°31E 216 E6
Tees → U.K. 54°37N 1°10W 168 C6
Tees B. U.K. 54°40N 1°9W 168 C6
Teeswater Canada 43°59N 81°17W 312 C3
Tefé Brazil 3°25S 64°50W 329 D5
Tefé → Brazil 3°35S 64°47W 329 D5
Tefenni Turkey 37°18N 29°45E 205 D11
Tegal Indonesia 6°52S 109°8E 235 D3
Tegallalang Indonesia 8°27S 115°17E 231 J18
Tegalsari Indonesia 8°25S 114°8E 231 J17
Tegel Germany 52°34N 13°16E 115 A2
Tegel, Berlin ✕ (TXL) Germany 52°35N 13°14E 115 A2
Tegeler See Germany 52°34N 13°15E 115 A2
Tegelort Germany 52°34N 13°13E 115 A2
Tegernsee Germany 47°43N 11°46E 179 H7
Teggiano Italy 40°23N 15°32E 201 B8
Tegid, L. = Bala, L. U.K. 52°53N 3°37W 168 E4
Tegina Nigeria 10°5N 6°11E 263 C6
Tegua Vanuatu 13°15S 166°37E 287 C4
Tegucigalpa Honduras 14°5N 87°14W 320 D2
Teguidda i-n-Tessoum Niger 17°25N 6°37E 263 B6
Teguise Canary Is. 29°3N 13°33W 153 e2
Tehachapi U.S.A. 35°8N 118°27W 307 K8
Tehachapi Mts. U.S.A. 35°0N 118°30W 307 L8
Tehamiyam Sudan 18°20N 36°32E 256 D4
Teheran = Tehrān Iran 35°41N 51°25E 141 A2
Tehilla Sudan 17°42N 36°6E 256 D4
Téhini Ivory C. 9°39N 3°40W 262 D4
Tehoru Indonesia 3°23S 129°30E 231 E7
Tehrān Iran 35°41N 51°25E 141 A2
Tehrān □ Iran 35°30N 51°30E 247 C6
Tehrān Mehrābād ✕ (THR) Iran 35°41N 51°18E 141 A1
Tehrān Pārs Iran 35°44N 51°32E 141 A3
Tehri India 30°23N 78°29E 243 D8
Tehuacán Mexico 18°27N 97°23W 319 D5
Tehuantepec Mexico 16°21N 95°13W 319 D5
Tehuantepec, G. de Mexico 15°50N 95°12W 319 D5
Tehuantepec, Istmo de Mexico 17°15N 94°30W 319 D6
Tehuantepec Fracture Zone Pac. Oc. 13°0N 97°0W 289 F18
Tei Tong Tsui China 22°16N 114°17E 122 B2
Teide, Pico de Canary Is. 28°15N 16°38W 153 e1
Teifi → U.K. 52°5N 4°41W 169 E3
Teigebyen Norway 60°12N 11°0E 162 D5
Teign → U.K. 50°32N 3°32W 169 G4
Teignmouth U.K. 50°33N 3°31W 169 G4
Teiuş Romania 46°12N 23°40E 183 D8
Teixeira Brazil 7°13S 37°15W 332 C4
Teixeira Pinto Guinea-Biss. 12°3N 16°0W 262 C1
Tejakula Indonesia 8°8S 115°20E 231 J18
Tejam India 29°57N 80°11E 243 E9
Tejen Turkmenistan 37°23N 60°31E 216 E6
Tejen → Turkmenistan 37°24N 60°38E 247 B9
Tejo → Europe 38°40N 9°24W 195 F2
Tejo, Rio → Portugal 38°45N 9°3W 126 A2
Tejon Pass U.S.A. 34°49N 118°53W 307 L8
Tekamah U.S.A. 41°47N 96°13W 308 E5
Tekapo → N.Z. 44°13S 170°21E 285 E5
Tekapo, L. N.Z. 43°53S 170°33E 285 D5
Tekax Mexico 20°12N 89°17W 319 C7
Teke Turkey 41°4N 29°39E 203 E13
Tekeli Kazakhstan 44°50N 79°0E 217 D9
Tekeze → Ethiopia 14°20N 35°50E 257 E4
Tekeze Dam Ethiopia 13°10N 38°45E 257 E4
Tekija Serbia 44°42N 22°26E 202 B6
Tekirdağ Turkey 40°58N 27°30E 203 F11
Tekirdağ □ Turkey 41°0N 27°0E 203 E11
Tekirova Turkey 36°30N 30°32E 205 E12
Tekkali India 18°37N 84°15E 244 E7
Tekke Turkey 40°42N 36°12E 212 B7
Tekman Turkey 39°38N 41°29E 213 C9
Teknaf Bangla. 20°52N 92°18E 241 E4
Tekoa U.S.A. 47°14N 117°4W 304 C5
Tekokota French Polynesia 17°18S 142°34W 289 f
Tekong Besar, Pulau Singapore 1°25N 104°3E 237 d
Tekouiât, O. → Algeria 22°25N 2°35E 261 D5
Tékro Chad 19°32N 20°56E 259 E4
Tekstilyshchik Russia 55°42N 37°41E 129 B4
Tel → India 20°50N 83°54E 244 D6
Tel Aviv-Yafo Israel 32°4N 34°48E 251 F5
Tel Lakhish Israel 31°34N 34°51E 251 G5
Tel Megiddo Israel 32°35N 35°11E 250 F6
Tela Honduras 15°40N 87°28W 320 C2
Télagh Algeria 34°51N 0°32W 261 B4
Telanaipura = Jambi Indonesia 1°38S 103°30E 234 C2
Telašćica △ Croatia 43°55N 15°10E 199 E12
Telavi Georgia 42°0N 45°30E 191 J7
Telč Czech Rep. 49°11N 15°28E 180 B8
Telciu Romania 47°25N 24°24E 183 C9
Telde Canary Is. 27°59N 15°25W 153 e1
Tele → Dem. Rep. of the Congo 2°48N 23°54E 264 B4
Telefomin Papua N. G. 5°10S 141°31E 286 C1
Telegraph Creek Canada 58°0N 131°10W 296 B2
Telegraph Hill San Francisco, U.S.A. 136 b2
Telekhany = Tsyelyakhany Belarus 52°30N 25°46E 177 B13
Telemark Norway 59°15N 7°40E 161 G12
Telemark □ Norway 59°25N 8°30E 164 E5
Télemsès Niger 15°37N 4°44E 263 B5
Telén Argentina 36°15S 65°31W 334 D3
Telen → Indonesia 0°10S 117°20E 235 C5
Teleneşti Moldova 47°30N 28°22E 183 C13
Teleng Iran 25°47N 61°3E 247 E9
Teleño Spain 42°23N 6°22W 194 C4
Teleorman □ Romania 44°0N 25°0E 183 G10
Teleorman → Romania 43°52N 25°26E 183 G10
Telerhteba, Djebel Algeria 24°10N 6°51E 261 D6
Teles Pires → Brazil 7°21S 58°3W 331 B6
Telescope Pk. U.S.A. 36°10N 117°5W 307 J9
Telescope Pt. Grenada 12°7N 61°36W 323 q
Teletaye Mali 16°31N 1°30E 263 B5
Telford U.K. 52°40N 2°27W 169 E5
Telford and Wrekin □ U.K. 52°45N 2°27W 168 E5
Telfs Austria 47°19N 11°4E 180 D4
Telhal Portugal 38°48N 9°18W 126 A1
Telida U.S.A. 63°23N 153°16W 303 E9
Télimélé Guinea 10°54N 13°2W 262 C2
Teljo, J. Sudan 14°42N 25°26E 257 E2
Telkwa Canada 54°41N 127°5W 296 C3
Tell City U.S.A. 37°57N 86°46W 311 G10
Teller U.S.A. 65°16N 166°22W 303 D6
Tellicherry India 11°45N 75°30E 245 J2
Telluride U.S.A. 37°56N 107°49W 305 H10
Telok Blangah Singapore 1°17N 103°49E 138 B2
Teloloapán Mexico 18°21N 99°51W 319 D5
Telpos Iz Russia 63°16N 59°13E 186 B10
Telsen Argentina 42°30S 66°50W 336 B3
Telšiai Lithuania 55°59N 22°14E 184 C9
Telšiai □ Lithuania 55°59N 22°15E 184 C9
Teltow Germany 52°23N 13°17E 115 B2
Teltow kanal Germany 52°26N 13°29E 115 B3
Teluk Anson = Teluk Intan Malaysia 4°3N 101°0E 237 K3
Teluk Bahang Malaysia 5°28N 100°13E 237 c
Teluk Betung = Bandar Lampung Indonesia 5°20S 105°10E 234 D3
Teluk Intan Malaysia 4°3N 101°0E 237 K3
Teluk Kumbar Malaysia 5°18N 100°14E 237 c
Telukbatang Indonesia 1°10S 109°46E 235 C3
Telukbayur Kalimantan Timur, Indonesia 2°9N 117°24E 235 B5
Telukbayur Sumatera Barat, Indonesia 0°59S 100°23E 234 C2
Telukbutun Indonesia 4°13N 108°12E 235 B3
Telukdalam Indonesia 0°33N 97°50E 234 B1
Tema Ghana 5°41N 0°0E 263 D5
Temagami, L. Canada 47°0N 80°10W 298 C3
Temasint Algeria 23°18N 7°40E 261 D6
Tematangi French Polynesia 21°41S 140°40W 289 f
Temax Mexico 21°9N 88°56W 319 C7
Temba S. Africa 25°20S 28°17E 271 C4
Tembagapura Indonesia 4°20S 137°0E 231 E9
Tembe Dem. Rep. of the Congo 0°16S 28°14E 268 C2
Tembe △ S. Africa 26°51S 32°24E 271 C5
Tembesi → Indonesia 1°43S 103°6E 234 C2
Tembilahan Indonesia 0°19S 103°9E 234 C2
Temblador Venezuela 8°59N 62°44W 329 B5
Tembleque Spain 39°41N 3°30W 194 F7
Temblor Range U.S.A. 35°20N 119°50W 307 K7
Tembo Aluma Angola 7°42S 17°17E 265 D3
Teme → U.K. 52°11N 2°13W 169 E5
Temecula U.S.A. 33°30N 117°9W 307 M9
Temengor, Tasik Malaysia 5°24N 101°18E 237 K3
Temerloh Malaysia 3°27N 102°25E 237 L4
Temiang Indonesia 0°19N 104°23E 234 B2
Teminabuan Indonesia 1°26S 132°1E 231 E8
Temir Kazakhstan 49°1N 57°14E 187 E10
Temir-Khan-Shura = Buynaksk Russia 42°48N 47°7E 191 J8
Temirtau Kazakhstan 50°5N 72°56E 217 B8
Temirtau Russia 53°10N 87°30E 217 B11
Témiscamie → Canada 50°59N 73°5W 299 B5
Témiscaming Canada 46°44N 79°5W 298 C4
Témiscamingue, L. Canada 47°10N 79°25W 298 C4
Temnikov Russia 54°40N 43°11E 190 C6
Temnikovo Russia 55°43N 38°1E 129 B6
Temo → Italy 40°17N 8°28E 200 B1
Temora Australia 34°30S 147°30E 283 C7
Temosachic Mexico 28°57N 107°51W 318 B3
Tempe U.S.A. 33°24N 111°54W 305 K8
Tempelburg = Czaplinek Poland 53°34N 16°14E 184 E3
Tempelhof Germany 52°27N 13°23E 115 B3
Temperance U.S.A. 41°47N 83°34W 311 C13
Tempino Indonesia 1°46S 103°30E 234 C2
Témpio Pausánia Italy 40°54N 9°6E 200 B2
Tempiute U.S.A. 37°39N 115°38W 306 H11
Temple Bank S. China Sea 9°0N 117°30E 233 F1
Temple U.S.A. 31°6N 97°21W 314 F6
Temple B. Australia 12°15S 143°3E 286 G2
Temple City U.S.A. 34°6N 118°3W 126 B4
Temple Hills U.S.A. 38°48N 76°56W 143 C4
Temple Mount Jerusalem 123 b3
Temple of Heaven China 39°52N 116°23E 114 B2
Temple of the Dawn = Arun Bangkok, Thailand 113 b1
Temple Terrace U.S.A. 28°2N 82°23W 317 G7
Templemore Ireland 52°47N 7°51W 166 D4
Templeogue Ireland 53°18N 6°18W 120 B2
Templeton U.S.A. 35°33N 120°42W 306 K6
Templeton → Australia 21°0S 138°40E 280 C2
Templin Germany 53°7N 13°28E 178 B9
Templo Mayor Mexico City, Mexico 128 b3
Tempoal de Sánchez Mexico 21°31N 98°23W 319 C5
Temppeliaukio Church Finland 60°10N 24°56E 121 B2
Tempué Angola 13°27S 18°49E 265 E3
Temryuk Russia 45°15N 37°24E 189 K9
Temska → Serbia 43°17N 22°33E 202 C6
Temuco Chile 38°45S 72°40W 336 A2
Temuka N.Z. 44°14S 171°17E 285 E6
Ten Degree Channel India 10°0N 92°30E 245 K11
Ten Thousand Is. U.S.A. 25°55N 81°45W 317 K8
Tena Ecuador 0°59S 77°49W 328 D2
Tenabo Mexico 20°3N 90°14W 319 C6
Tenafly U.S.A. 40°54N 73°58W 132 A2
Tenaha U.S.A. 31°57N 94°15W 314 F7
Tenakee Springs U.S.A. 57°47N 135°13W 296 B1
Tenali India 16°15N 80°35E 245 F5
Tenancingo de Degollado Mexico 18°58N 99°36W 319 D5
Tenango del Valle Mexico 19°7N 99°33W 319 D5
Tenaro, Akra Greece 36°22N 22°27E 204 E4
Tenasserim Burma 12°6N 99°3E 237 F2
Tenasserim □ Burma 14°0N 98°30E 236 F2
Tenasserim → Burma 12°24N 98°37E 236 F2
Tenayuca, Piramide de Mexico 19°31N 99°10W 128 A1
Tenby U.K. 51°40N 4°42W 169 F3
Tenda, Colle di France 44°7N 7°36E 175 D11
Tendaho Ethiopia 11°48N 40°54E 257 E5
Tende France 44°5N 7°35E 175 D11
Tendelti Sudan 13°1N 31°55E 257 E3
Tendjedi, Adrar Algeria 23°41N 7°32E 261 D6
Tendō Japan 38°20N 140°30E 220 E10
Tendrara Morocco 33°3N 1°58W 261 B4
Tendrovskaya Kosa Ukraine 46°16N 31°35E 189 J6
Tendukhera India 23°24N 79°33E 243 H8
Teneguía, Volcanes de Canary Is. 28°28N 17°51W 153 e1
Teneida Egypt 25°30N 29°19E 256 B2
Tenenkou Mali 14°28N 4°55W 262 C4
Tenente Marques → Brazil 11°10S 59°56W 331 C6
Ténéré Niger 19°0N 10°30E 259 E2
Ténéré, Erg du Niger 17°35N 10°55E 259 E2
Tenerife Canary Is. 28°15N 16°35W 153 e1
Tenerife, Pico Canary Is. 27°43N 18°1W 153 e1

Tenerife Norte ✕ (TFN)
  Canary Is.   28°28N 16°17W 153 e1
Tenerife Sur ✕ (TFS)
  Canary Is.   28°3N 16°33W 153 e1
Ténès Algeria   36°31N 1°14E 261 K5
Teng Xian Guangxi Zhuangzu,
  China   23°21N 110°56E 229 F8
Teng Xian Shandong, China 35°5N 117°10E 227 G9
Tengah → Singapore   1°23N 103°43E 138 A2
Tengah, Kepulauan
  Indonesia   7°5S 118°15E 235 D5
Tengchong China   25°0N 98°28E 228 C2
Tengchowfu = Penglai
  China   37°48N 120°42E 227 F11
Tengger Feng China   43°12N 86°48E 217 D11
Tengger Shamo China   38°0N 104°10E 226 F3
Tenggol, Pulau Malaysia 4°48N 103°41E 237 K4
Tengiz Köli Kazakhstan 50°30N 69°0E 217 B7
Tengzhou China   35°4N 117°9E 227 G9
Tenhult Sweden   57°41N 14°20E 163 G8
Teniente Enciso △ Paraguay 21°5S 61°8W 334 A3
Teniente Rodolfo Marsh
  Antarctica   62°30S 58°0W 151 C18
Tenille U.S.A.   29°46N 83°19W 316 F6
Tenino U.S.A.   46°51N 122°51W 306 D4
Tenkasi India   8°55N 77°20E 245 K3
Tenke
  Dem. Rep. of the Congo   11°22S 26°40E 269 G2
Tenke Katanga,
  Dem. Rep. of the Congo   10°32S 26°7E 269 G2
Tenkodogo Burkina Faso   11°54N 0°19W 263 C4
Tenna → India   19°14N 13°47E 199 D12
Tennant Creek Australia 19°30S 134°15E 280 B1
Tennessee □ U.S.A.   36°0N 86°30W 315 D11
Tennessee → U.S.A. 37°4N 88°34W 315 C10
Tennille U.S.A.   32°56N 82°48W 316 C7
Tennoji Japan   34°39N 135°30E 133 B2
Teno, Pta. de Canary Is.   28°21N 16°55W 153 e1
Tenojoki → Tana →
  Norway   70°30N 28°14E 160 A23
Tenom Malaysia   5°4N 115°57E 235 K5
Tenosique Mexico   17°29N 91°26W 319 D6
Tenri Japan   34°39N 135°49E 223 C7
Tenryū Japan   34°52N 137°49E 223 C9
Tenryū-Gawa → Japan 35°39N 137°48E 223 B9
Tensift, Oued → Morocco 32°50N 9°50W 260 B3
Tente Indonesia   8°35S 118°41E 235 D5
Tenterden U.K.   51°4N 0°42E 169 F8
Tenterfield Australia   29°0S 152°0E 281 D5
Tenuajuir, Uad →
  W. Sahara   21°36N 16°0W 260 D1
Teo → A Ramallosa Spain 42°45N 8°30W 194 C2
Teófilo Otoni Brazil   17°50S 41°30W 333 E3
Tepa Indonesia   7°52S 129°31E 231 F7
Tepalcatepec → Mexico 18°35N 101°59W 318 D4
Tepalcates Mexico   19°23N 99°3W 128 B2
Tepecik Bursa, Turkey 40°7N 28°25E 203 F12
Tepecik Kütahya, Turkey 39°32N 29°28E 205 B11
Tepehuanes Mexico   25°21N 105°44W 318 B3
Tepelenë Albania   40°17N 20°2E 202 F4
Tepequem, Serra Brazil 3°41N 61°45W 329 C5
Tepetongo Mexico   22°28N 103°9W 318 C4
Tepeyac △ Mexico   19°30N 99°7W 128 B2
Tepic = Nayarit □ Mexico 22°0N 105°0W 318 C4
Tepic Mexico   21°30N 104°54W 318 C4
Teplá Czech Rep.   49°59N 12°52E 180 B5
Teplice Czech Rep.   50°40N 13°48E 180 A6
Teplitz = Teplice
  Czech Rep.   50°40N 13°48E 180 A6
Teplyk Ukraine   48°40N 29°44E 183 B14
Tepoca, C. Mexico   30°20N 112°25W 318 A2
Tequila Mexico   20°54N 103°47W 318 C4
Ter → Spain   42°2N 3°12E 196 C8
Ter Apel Neths.   52°53N 7°5E 170 B7
Têra Niger   14°0N 0°45E 263 C5
Tera → Spain   41°54N 5°44W 194 D5
Tera Kora Bonaire   12°11N 68°16W 322 h
Teraina Kiribati   4°43N 160°25W 289 G12
Terakeka South Sudan   5°26N 31°45E 257 F3
Téramo Italy   42°39N 13°42E 199 F10
Terang Australia   38°15S 142°55E 282 E5
Terang, Teluk Indonesia 8°39S 116°0E 231 K19
Terawhiti, C. N.Z.   41°16S 174°38E 284 H3
Terazit, Massif de Niger 20°2N 8°30E 259 D1
Tercan Turkey   39°47N 40°23E 213 C9
Terceira Azores   38°43N 27°13W 153 d1
Tercero → Argentina   32°58S 61°47W 334 C3
Terdal India   16°33N 75°3E 244 F2
Terebovlya Ukraine   49°18N 25°44E 177 D13
Teregova Romania   45°10N 22°16E 182 E7
Tereida Sudan   10°35N 31°17E 257 E3
Terek → Russia   44°0N 47°30E 191 J8
Terek □ Malaysia   4°55N 103°0E 237 K4
Terenos Brazil   20°26S 54°50W 331 E7
Terepaima △ Venezuela   9°58N 69°17W 328 B4
Tereshka → Russia   51°48N 46°26E 190 B5
Teresina Brazil   5°9S 42°45W 332 C3
Teresinha Brazil   0°58N 52°2W 329 C7
Terespol Poland   52°5N 23°37E 185 F10
Teressa India   8°15N 93°10E 245 K11
Tereswa Ukraine   48°0N 23°42E 188 B8
Terewah, L. Australia   29°52S 147°35E 281 D4
Terges → Portugal   37°49N 7°41W 195 H3
Tergnier France   49°40N 3°17E 173 C10
Terhazza Mali   23°38N 5°22W 260 D3
Teridgerie Cr. →
  Australia   30°25S 148°50E 283 A8
Terijoki = Zelenogorsk
  Russia   60°12N 29°43E 188 B5
Terlizzi Italy   41°8N 16°32E 201 A9
Termas de Rio Hondo
  Argentina   27°29S 64°52W 334 B3
Terme Turkey   41°11N 37°0E 212 B7
Termez = Termiz
  Uzbekistan   37°15N 67°15E 217 F7
Términi Imerese Italy   37°59N 13°42E 200 E6
Términos, L. de Mexico 18°37N 91°33W 319 D6
Termit, Massif de Niger 16°2N 11°20E 259 E2
Termiz Uzbekistan   37°15N 67°15E 217 F7
Térmoli Italy   42°0N 15°0E 199 F12
Ternate Indonesia   0°45N 127°25E 231 D7
Terneuzen Neths.   51°20N 3°50E 170 C3
Terney Russia   45°3N 136°37E 222 B8
Terni Italy   42°34N 12°37E 199 F9
Ternitz Austria   47°43N 16°2E 180 D9
Ternopil Ukraine   49°30N 25°40E 177 D13
Ternopil □ Ukraine   49°30N 25°40E 177 D13
Ternopol = Ternopil
  Ukraine   49°30N 25°40E 177 D13
Terowie Australia   33°8S 138°55E 282 B3
Terpni Greece   40°55N 23°26E 202 F7
Terra Bella U.S.A.   35°58N 119°3W 307 K7
Terra Nova △ Canada 48°33N 53°55W 298 C2
Terrace Canada   54°30N 128°35W 296 C3
Terrace Bay Canada   48°47N 87°5W 298 C2
Terracina Italy   41°17N 13°15E 200 A6
Terralba Italy   39°43N 8°39E 200 C1
Terranova di Sicília = Gela
  Italy   37°4N 14°15E 201 F7
Terranova Pausania = Ólbia
  Italy   40°55N 9°31E 200 B2
Terrasini Italy   38°9N 13°5E 200 D6
Terrassa Spain   41°34N 2°1E 196 D7

Terrasson-la-Villedieu
  France   45°8N 1°18E 174 C5
Terrazzano Italy   45°32N 9°4E 129 A1
Terre-de-Bas Guadeloupe 15°51N 61°38W 322 e
Terre-de-Bas Guadeloupe 16°10N 61°7W 322 g
Terre-de-Haut Guadeloupe 15°52N 61°34W 322 e
Terre des Hommes
  Canada   45°31N 73°32W 130 A2
Terre Haute U.S.A.   39°28N 87°25W 311 E9
Terre Rouge Mauritius 20°7S 57°31E 272 e
Terrebonne B. U.S.A. 29°5N 90°35W 315 G9
Terrecht Mali   19°35N 0°22E 261 D5
Terrell U.S.A.   32°44N 96°17W 314 E6
Terrenceville Canada   47°40N 54°44W 299 C9
Terrick Terrick △
  Australia   36°8S 144°13E 282 D6
Terrugem Portugal   38°41N 9°17W 126 A1
Terry U.S.A.   46°47N 105°19W 304 C11
Terrytown U.S.A.   29°54N 90°1W 131 B2
Terryville U.S.A.   41°41N 73°3E 311 E11
Terschelling Neths.   53°25N 5°20E 170 A5
Tersko-Kumskiy Kanal
  Russia   44°32N 44°38E 191 H7
Tertenía Italy   39°42N 9°34E 200 C2
Terter = Tärtär →
  Azerbaijan   40°26N 47°20E 191 K8
Teruel Spain   40°22N 1°8W 196 E3
Teruel □ Spain   40°48N 1°0W 196 E4
Tervel Bulgaria   43°45N 27°28E 203 C11
Tervola Finland   66°6N 24°49E 160 C21
Tervuren Belgium   50°49N 4°31E 116 B3
Teryaweynya L.
  Australia   32°18S 143°22E 282 B5
Tešanj Bos.-H.   44°38N 18°1E 182 F3
Teschen = Cieszyn Poland 49°45N 18°35E 185 D5
Teseney Eritrea   15°5N 36°42E 257 D4
Tesha → Russia   55°38N 42°9E 190 C6
Teshekpuk L. U.S.A. 70°35N 153°26W 303 A9
Teshio Japan   44°53N 141°44E 220 B10
Teshio-Gawa → Japan 44°53N 141°45E 220 B10
Tešica Serbia   43°27N 21°45E 202 C5
Tesiyn Gol → Mongolia 50°40N 93°20E 218 A7
Teslić Bos.-H.   44°37N 17°54E 182 F2
Teslin Canada   60°10N 132°43W 296 A2
Teslin → Canada   61°34N 134°35W 296 A2
Teslin L. Canada   60°15N 132°57W 296 A2
Tesouro Brazil   16°4S 53°34W 331 D7
Tessalit Mali   20°12N 1°0E 261 D5
Tessaoua Niger   13°47N 7°56E 259 F1
Tessin Germany   54°2N 12°26E 172 A7
Tessit Mali   15°13N 0°18E 263 B5
Tessounfat Mali   22°53N 0°32E 261 D5
Test → U.K.   50°56N 1°29W 169 G6
Testa del Gargano Italy 41°50N 16°10E 199 G13
Testigos, Is. Los Venezuela 11°23N 63°7W 321 D7
Tét Hungary   47°30N 17°33E 182 C2
Têt → France   42°44N 3°2E 174 F7
Tetachuck L. Canada 53°18N 125°55W 296 C3
Tetas, Pta. Chile   23°31S 70°38W 334 A1
Tete Mozam.   16°13S 33°33E 269 F3
Tete □ Mozam.   15°15S 32°40E 269 F3
Tetenga, Caleta Chile 27°9S 109°19W 330 b
Tetepare Solomon Is. 8°45S 157°35E 287 M9
Teterev → Ukraine   51°1N 30°5E 177 C16
Teterow Germany   53°46N 12°34E 178 B8
Teteven Bulgaria   42°58N 24°17E 203 D8
Tethul → Canada   60°35N 112°12W 296 A6
Tetiyev Ukraine   49°22N 29°38E 177 D15
Tetlin U.S.A.   63°8N 142°31W 303 E12
Tetlin Junction U.S.A. 63°19N 142°36W 303 E12
Tetlin Nat. Wildlife Refuge △
  U.S.A.   62°40N 141°50W 303 E12
Tetlit Zheh = Fort McPherson
  Canada   67°30N 134°55W 294 D5
Teton → U.S.A.   47°56N 110°31W 304 C8
Tétouan Morocco   35°35N 5°21W 260 A4
Tetovo Macedonia   42°1N 20°59E 202 F5
Tetschen = Děčín
  Czech Rep.   50°47N 14°12E 180 A7
Tetuán Spain   40°27N 3°42W 127 B1
Tetufera, Mt. Tahiti 17°40S 149°29W 289 d
Tetyukhe = Dalnegorsk
  Russia   44°32N 135°33E 220 B7
Tetyushi Russia   54°55N 48°49E 190 C9
Teuco → Argentina   25°35S 60°11W 334 B3
Teufelsberg Germany 52°29N 13°14E 115 B2
Teulada Australia   38°58N 8°46E 200 D1
Teulon Canada   50°23N 97°16W 297 C9
Teun Indonesia   6°59S 129°8E 231 F7
Teutoburger Wald Germany 52°5N 8°22E 178 C4
Teutopolis U.S.A.   39°8N 88°29W 311 E8
Tevere → Italy   41°44N 12°14E 199 F9
Teverya Israel   32°47N 35°32E 250 F6
Teviot → U.K.   55°29N 2°38W 167 F6
Tewantin Australia   26°27S 153°3E 281 D5
Teweh → Indonesia   0°58N 114°54E 235 C5
Tewkesbury U.K.   51°59N 2°9W 169 F5
Texada I. Canada   49°40N 124°25W 296 D4
Texarkana Ark., U.S.A. 33°26N 94°2W 314 E7
Texarkana Tex., U.S.A. 33°26N 94°3W 314 E7
Texas Australia   28°49S 151°9E 281 D5
Texas □ U.S.A.   31°40N 98°30W 314 F5
Texas City U.S.A.   29°24N 94°54W 314 G7
Texel Neths.   53°5N 4°50E 170 A4
Texline U.S.A.   36°23N 103°2W 314 C3
Texoma, L. U.S.A.   33°50N 96°34W 314 E6
Teykovo Russia   56°55N 40°30E 188 D11
Teyvareh Afghan.   33°30N 64°24E 240 B2
Teza → Russia   56°32N 41°53E 190 B5
Tezin Afghan.   34°24N 69°30E 242 B3
Teziutlán Mexico   19°49N 97°21W 319 D5
Tezpur India   26°40N 92°45E 241 B4
Tezu India   27°55N 96°10E 241 B6
Tezzeron L. Canada   54°43N 124°30W 296 C4
Tha-anne → Canada 60°31N 94°37W 297 A10
Tha Deua Laos   17°57N 102°53E 236 D4
Tha Deua Laos   19°26N 101°50E 236 C3
Tha Li Thailand   17°37N 101°25E 236 D3
Tha Pla Thailand   17°48N 100°32E 236 D3
Tha Rua Thailand   14°34N 100°44E 236 E3
Tha Sala Thailand   8°40N 99°56E 237 H2
Tha Song Yang Thailand 17°34N 97°55E 237 D1
Thaba Putsoa Lesotho 29°45S 28°0E 271 C4
Thaba-Tseka Lesotho 29°34S 28°46E 271 C4
Thabana Ntlenyana
  Lesotho   29°30S 29°16E 271 C4
Thabazimbi S. Africa 24°40S 27°21E 271 B4
Thabeikkyin Burma   22°53N 95°59E 241 D5
Thabt, G.el Saudi Arabia 28°17N 34°1E 251 K5
Thādiq St. Arabia   25°18N 45°52E 246 E5
Thai Binh Vietnam   20°35N 106°1E 236 B6
Thai Muang Thailand 8°24N 98°16E 237 H2
Thai Nguyen Vietnam 21°35N 105°55E 236 B5
Thailand ■ Asia   16°0N 102°0E 236 E4
Thailand, G. of Thailand 11°30N 101°0E 237 G3
Thakhek Laos   17°25N 104°45E 236 D5
Thakurgaon Bangla. 26°2N 88°34E 241 D2
Thal Pakistan   33°28N 70°33E 242 C4
Thal Desert Pakistan 31°10N 71°30E 242 D4
Thala Tunisia   35°35N 8°40E 258 A1

Thala La = Hkakabo Razi
  Burma   28°25N 97°23E 228 C1
Thalabarivat Cambodia 13°33N 105°57E 236 F5
Thalang = Amphoe Thalang
  Thailand   8°1N 98°20E 237 a
Thalang Thailand   8°2N 98°20E 237 H2
Thalassery = Tellicherry
  India   11°45N 75°30E 245 J2
Thale Sap Songkhla
  Thailand   7°12N 100°28E 237 J3
Thalkirchen Germany 48°6N 11°32E 131 B2
Thallon Australia   28°39S 148°49E 281 D4
Thalu, Ko Thailand   9°26N 99°54E 237 b
Thalwil Switz.   47°17N 8°35E 179 H4
Thamarit Oman   17°39N 54°2E 249 C6
Thames → Ont., Canada 42°20N 82°25W 312 D2
Thames → U.K.   51°29N 0°34E 169 F8
Thames → Conn., U.S.A. 41°18N 72°5W 313 E12
Thames, Firth of N.Z. 37°0S 175°25E 284 D4
Thames Ditton U.K. 51°23N 0°20W 125 B1
Thamesford Canada   43°4N 81°0W 312 C4
Thamesmead U.K.   51°30N 0°7E 125 A4
Thamesville Canada   42°33N 81°59W 312 D3
Thámit, W. Libya   31°11N 16°9E 258 B3
Thandi Yemen   17°18N 49°55E 249 C5
Than India   22°34N 71°11E 242 H4
Than Kyun Burma   9°49N 98°4E 237 H1
Than Uyen Vietnam   22°0N 103°54E 236 B4
Thana Cr. → India   19°4N 72°54E 130 A2
Thanbyuzayat Burma 15°58N 97°44E 241 G6
Thandaung Burma   19°4N 96°41E 241 H6
Thandla India   23°0N 74°34E 242 H6
Thandwe Burma   18°20N 94°30E 241 H5
Thane India   19°12N 72°59E 244 E1
Thanet, I. of U.K.   51°21N 1°20E 169 F9
Thangool Australia   24°38S 150°42E 280 C5
Thanh Hoa Vietnam   19°48N 105°46E 236 C5
Thanh Pho Ho Chi Minh
  Vietnam   10°58N 106°40E 237 G6
Thanh Thuy Vietnam 22°55N 104°51E 236 A5
Thanjavur India   10°48N 79°12E 245 J4
Thanlwin = Salween →
  Burma   16°31N 97°37E 241 G6
Thann France   47°48N 7°5E 173 E14
Thano Bula Khan
  Pakistan   25°22N 67°50E 242 G2
Thanya Buri Thailand 14°1N 100°45E 236 E3
Thaoge → Botswana 20°27S 22°36E 270 B3
Thaolintoa L. Canada 61°30N 96°25W 297 A9
Thaon-les-Vosges France 48°15N 6°24E 173 D13
Thap Lan △ Thailand 14°15N 102°16E 236 E4
Thap Sakae Thailand 11°30N 99°37E 237 G2
Thap Than Thailand 15°27N 99°54E 237 E2
Thar Desert India   28°0N 72°0E 242 F5
Tharad India   24°30N 71°44E 242 G4
Thargomindah Australia 27°58S 143°46E 281 D3
Tharp Fracture Zone
  S. Ocean   54°0S 135°0W 151 B14
Tharrawaddy Burma 17°38N 95°48E 241 G5
Tharrawaw Burma   17°41N 95°28E 241 G5
Tharthār, Buḩayrat ath
  Iraq   34°0N 43°15E 213 E10
Tharthar, L. = Tharthār, Buḩayrat
  ath Iraq   34°0N 43°15E 213 E10
Tharthār, W. ath → Iraq 34°32N 43°4E 213 E10
Thasopoula Greece   40°49N 24°45E 203 F8
Thasos Greece   40°40N 24°40E 203 F8
That Khe Vietnam   22°16N 106°28E 236 A6
Thatcher Ariz., U.S.A. 32°51N 109°46W 305 K9
Thatcher Colo., U.S.A. 37°33N 104°7W 305 H11
Thaton Burma   16°55N 97°22E 241 G6
Thau, Bassin de France 43°23N 3°36E 174 E7
Thaungdut Burma   24°30N 94°40E 241 C5
Thawatti Burma   19°32N 96°1E 241 H6
Thayawthadangy Kyun
  Burma   12°19N 98°0E 238 F1
Thayer U.S.A.   36°31N 91°33W 308 G8
Thayetmyo Burma   19°20N 95°10E 241 H5
Thazi Magwe, Burma 19°59N 95°3E 241 H5
Thazi Mandalay, Burma 21°0N 96°5E 241 G6
Thbeng Meanchey
  Cambodia   13°49N 104°58E 236 F5
The Broads U.K.   52°45N 1°30E 168 E9
The Everglades U.S.A. 25°50N 81°0W 317 K9
The Gulf = Persian Gulf
  Asia   27°0N 50°0E 247 E6
The Hague = 's-Gravenhage
  Neths.   52°7N 4°17E 170 B4
The Pas Canada   53°45N 101°15W 297 C8
The Wash U.K.   52°58N 0°20E 168 E8
The Weald U.K.   51°4N 0°20E 169 F8
Thebes = Thíva Greece 38°19N 23°19E 205 C4
Thebes Egypt   25°40N 32°35E 256 B3
Thedaw Burma   20°50N 96°13E 241 G6
Thedford U.S.A.   41°59N 100°35W 308 E3
Theebine Australia   25°57S 152°34E 281 D5
Thègon Burma   18°13N 95°35E 241 H5
Thekulthili L. Canada 61°3N 110°0W 297 A7
Thelon → Canada   64°16N 96°4W 297 A8
Thénezay France   46°44N 0°2W 172 F6
Thenon France   45°9N 1°4E 174 C5
Theodore Queens.,
  Australia   24°55S 150°3E 280 C5
Theodore Sask., Canada 51°26N 102°55W 297 C8
Theodore Ala., U.S.A. 30°33N 88°10W 315 F10
Theodore Roosevelt △
  U.S.A.   47°0N 103°25W 308 B2
Theodore Roosevelt L.
  U.S.A.   33°40N 111°10W 305 K8
Thepha Thailand   6°52N 100°58E 237 J3
Thérain → France   49°15N 2°27E 173 C9
Theresa U.S.A.   44°13N 75°48W 313 B9
Theressa U.S.A.   29°50N 82°4W 316 F7
Therma = Eagle Nest
  U.S.A.   36°33N 105°16W 305 H11
Thermopolis U.S.A. 43°39N 108°13W 304 E9
Thermopylæ Greece 38°48N 22°35E 205 C4
Thesprotia □ Greece 39°27N 20°22E 204 B2
Thessalon Canada   46°20N 83°30W 312 B3
Thessalonica, Gulf of = Thessaloniki
  Kolpos Greece   40°15N 22°45E 202 F6
Thessaloniki Greece 40°38N 22°58E 202 F6
Thessaloniki ✕ (SKG)
  Greece   40°30N 23°0E 202 F6
Thessaloniki Kolpos
  Greece   40°15N 22°45E 202 F6
Thessaly □ Greece   39°25N 22°0E 204 B4
Thetford U.K.   52°25N 0°45E 168 E8
Thetford Mines Canada 46°8N 71°18W 299 C5
Theun → Laos   18°19N 104°0E 236 D5
Theunissen S. Africa 28°26S 26°43E 270 D4
Thevenard Australia   32°9S 133°38E 281 E1
Thiais France   48°46N 2°23E 134 B3
Thiamis → Greece   39°27N 20°22E 204 B2
Thiaucourt-Regniéville
  France   48°57N 5°52E 173 C12
Thibaud Dominica   15°36N 61°24W 323 b
Thibodaux U.S.A.   29°48N 90°49W 315 G9
Thicket Portage Canada 55°19N 97°42W 297 B9
Thief River Falls U.S.A. 48°7N 96°10W 308 A5

Thiel Mts. Antarctica 85°15S 91°0W 151 E16
Thiene Italy   45°42N 11°29E 199 C8
Thiérache France   49°51N 3°45E 173 C10
Thiers France   45°52N 3°33E 174 C7
Thiès Senegal   14°50N 16°51W 262 C1
Thiesi Italy   40°31N 8°43E 200 B1
Thika Kenya   1°1S 37°5E 268 C4
Thikombia Fiji   15°44N 179°55W 287 a
Thimân, W. → Egypt 28°4N 33°45E 251 K4
Thimphu Bhutan   27°31N 89°45E 241 B2
Thina → S. Africa   31°18S 29°13E 271 D4
Thínadhoo Maldives 0°32N 72°56E 272 d
Thinyung Burma   19°46N 96°12E 241 G6
Thio N. Cal.   21°37S 166°14E 288 d
Thíonville France   49°20N 6°10E 173 C13
Thíra = Santorini Greece 36°23N 25°27E 205 E7
Thirasía Greece   36°26N 25°21E 205 E7
Third Cataract Sudan 19°42N 30°20E 256 D3
Thirsk U.K.   54°14N 1°19W 168 C6
Thiruvananthapuram =
  Trivandrum India   8°41N 77°0E 245 K3
Thiruvarur India   10°46N 79°38E 245 J4
Thisio Athens, Greece 112 c1
Thisted Denmark   56°58N 8°40E 163 H2
Þistilfjörður Iceland 66°18N 15°24W 155 A11
Thistle I. Australia   35°0S 136°8E 282 C2
Thistletown Canada   43°44N 79°34W 141 A1
Thítsi Burma   18°15N 96°13E 241 F6
Thíthia = Cicia Fiji   17°45S 179°18W 287 A3
Thitpokpin Burma   19°24N 95°58E 241 F5
Thíva Greece   38°19N 23°19E 205 C5
Thíviers France   45°25N 0°54E 174 C4
Thízy France   46°2N 4°18E 173 F11
Þjórsá → Iceland   63°47N 20°48W 155 D6
Thlewiaza → Canada 60°29N 94°40W 297 A10
Thmar Puok Cambodia 13°57N 103°4E 236 F4
Tho Chu, Dao Vietnam 9°20N 103°28E 237 H4
Tho Vinh Vietnam   19°16N 105°42E 236 C5
Thoa → Canada   60°31N 109°47W 297 A7
Thoen Thailand   17°43N 99°12E 236 D2
Thoeng Thailand   19°41N 100°12E 236 C3
Thomas U.S.A.   35°45N 98°45W 314 D5
Thomas, L. Australia 26°4S 137°58E 281 D2
Thomas Circle Washington, D.C., U.S.A. 143 a1
Thomas Hill Res. U.S.A. 39°34N 92°39W 308 E4
Thomas Hubbard, C.
  Canada   82°0N 94°25W 295 A13
Thomaston U.S.A.   32°53N 84°20W 316 D5
Thomastown Australia 37°40S 145°2E 128 A2
Thomasville Ala., U.S.A. 31°55N 87°44W 315 F11
Thomasville Ga., U.S.A. 30°50N 83°59W 316 F6
Thomasville N.C., U.S.A. 35°53N 80°5W 315 D14
Thompson Man., Canada 55°45N 97°52W 297 B9
Thompson Pa., U.S.A. 41°52N 75°31W 313 E9
Thompson →
  Canada   50°15N 121°24W 296 C4
Thompson → Mo., U.S.A. 39°46N 93°37W 308 F4
Thompson Falls U.S.A. 47°36N 115°21W 304 C6
Thompson I. U.S.A. 42°19N 70°59W 116 B3
Thompson Pk. U.S.A. 41°0N 123°2W 304 F2
Thompson Sd. N.Z. 45°8S 166°46E 285 F1
Thompson Springs
  U.S.A.   38°58N 109°43W 304 G9
Thompsontown U.S.A. 40°33N 77°14W 312 F7
Thomson Greece   33°28N 82°30W 316 D6
Thomson Ill., U.S.A. 41°58N 90°6W 310 C8
Thomson → Australia 25°11S 142°53E 280 C3
Thomson's Falls = Nyahururu
  Kenya   0°2N 36°27E 268 B4
Thon Buri Thailand   13°45N 100°29E 113 B1
Thônes France   45°54N 6°18E 173 F13
Thong Yang Thailand 9°28N 99°56E 237 b
Thongwa Burma   16°45N 96°33E 241 G6
Thonon-les-Bains France 46°22N 6°29E 173 F13
Thonze Burma   17°38N 95°47E 241 G5
Thoothukudi = Tuticorin
  India   8°50N 78°12E 245 K4
Thorez Ukraine   48°4N 38°34E 189 H10
Þórisvatn Iceland   64°20N 20°43W 155 C6
Þórisvatn Iceland   64°20N 18°55W 155 C8
Þórkötlustaðir Iceland 63°50N 22°24W 155 E3
Þorlákshöfn Iceland   63°51N 21°22W 155 E4
Thorn = Toruń Poland 53°2N 18°39E 185 E5
Thornaby on Tees U.K. 54°33N 1°18W 168 C6
Thornbury Vic., Australia 37°45S 145°1E 128 A2
Thornbury Ont., Canada 44°34N 80°26W 312 B4
Thornbury N.Z.   46°17S 168°9E 285 G3
Thorncliffe Canada   43°42N 79°20W 141 A2
Thorne U.K.   53°37N 0°57W 168 D7
Thornhill Canada   43°48N 79°25W 141 A2
Thornton Canada   44°13N 79°42W 141 A2
Thornton Western Cape,
  S. Africa   33°55N 18°32E 118 A2
Thornton Colo., U.S.A. 39°52N 104°58W 304 G11
Thornton Iowa, U.S.A. 42°57N 93°23W 310 B3
Thornton Heath U.K. 51°23N 0°6W 125 B3
Thorntown U.S.A. 40°8N 86°36W 311 D10
Thorold Canada   43°7N 79°12W 312 C5
Thorpe Barbados   13°9N 59°37W 323 r
Þórshöfn Iceland   66°12N 15°20W 155 A11
Þorshöfn Iceland   62°12N 6°59E 162 A2
Thouars France   46°58N 0°15W 172 F6
Thouet → France   47°0N 0°15W 172 F6
Thoune = Thun Switz. 46°45N 7°38E 179 H3
Thousand Islands U.S.A. 44°20N 76°0W 313 B9
Thousand Oaks U.S.A. 34°10N 118°50W 307 L8
Thrace Turkey   41°0N 27°0E 203 F10
Thrace, Sea of Greece 40°30N 25°0E 203 F8
Thrakikon Pelagos = Thrace, Sea of
  Greece   40°30N 25°0E 203 F8
Three Forks U.S.A. 45°54N 111°33W 304 D8
Three Gorges Dam China 30°45N 111°15E 229 B8
Three Gorges Res. = Sanxia Shuiku
  China   30°30N 107°58E 229 B6
Three Hills Canada   51°43N 113°15W 296 C6
Three Hummock I.
  Australia   40°25S 144°55E 281 G3
Three Oaks U.S.A.   41°48N 86°36W 311 C10
Three Pagodas Pass Asia 15°18N 98°30E 236 E2
Three Points, C. Ghana 4°42N 2°6W 262 E4
Three Rivers Mich.,
  U.S.A.   41°57N 85°38W 311 C11
Three Rivers Tex., U.S.A. 28°28N 98°11W 314 G5
Three Sisters Is.
  Solomon Is.   10°10S 161°57E 287 N11
Three Springs Australia 29°32S 115°45E 279 F2
Threipmuir Res. U.K. 55°51N 3°19W 121 B2
Thrissur = Trichur India 10°30N 76°18E 245 J3
Throgs Neck U.S.A. 40°48N 73°49W 132 E3
Throssell, L. Australia 27°33S 124°10E 279 E3
Throssell Ra. Australia 22°3S 121°43E 278 D3
Thrumshing △ Bhutan 27°25N 91°15E 241 B3
Thu Dau Mot Vietnam 10°58N 106°39E 237 G6
Thua → Kenya   1°31S 39°50E 268 C5
Thuamal Rampur India 19°23N 82°56E 244 H6
Thuan Hoa Vietnam   9°58N 105°30E 237 J5
Thubun Lakes Canada 61°30N 112°0W 297 A6

Thueyts France   44°41N 4°9E 175 D8
Thuin Belgium   50°20N 4°17E 170 D4
Thuir France   42°38N 2°45E 174 F6
Thule = Qaanaaq
  Greenland   77°30N 69°10W 154 B4
Thule Air Base = Uummannaq
  Greenland   77°33N 68°52W 154 B4
Thun Switz.   46°45N 7°38E 179 H3
Thunder B. U.S.A.   45°0N 83°20W 312 B1
Thunder Bay Canada 48°20N 89°15W 298 C2
Thunderbolt U.S.A. 32°3N 81°4W 316 D7
Thunersee Switz.   46°43N 7°39E 179 H3
Thung Salaeng Luang △
  Thailand   16°43N 100°50E 236 D3
Thung Song Thailand 8°10N 99°40E 237 H2
Thungyai △ Thailand 15°30N 98°40E 236 E2
Thunkar Bhutan   27°55N 91°0E 241 B3
Thuong Tra Vietnam 16°2N 107°42E 236 D6
Thur → Switz.   47°32N 9°10E 179 H5
Thurgau □ Switz.   47°34N 9°10E 179 H5
Thüringen □ Germany 51°0N 11°0E 178 D6
Thüringer Wald Germany 50°35N 11°0E 178 D6
Thurinowa □ Australia 19°18S 146°43E 280 B4
Thurles Ireland   52°41N 7°49W 166 D5
Thurn P. Austria   47°20N 12°25E 180 D5
Thurrock □ U.K.   51°31N 0°23E 169 F8
Thursday I. Australia 10°30S 142°3E 280 A3
Thurso Qué., Canada 45°36N 75°15W 298 C4
Thurso U.K.   58°36N 3°32W 167 C5
Thurso → U.K.   58°36N 3°32W 167 C5
Thurston I. Antarctica 72°0S 100°0W 151 D16
Thury-Harcourt France 48°59N 0°30W 172 D6
Thutade L. Canada   57°0N 126°55W 296 B3
Thy Denmark   56°52N 8°25E 163 H2
Thyborøn Denmark   56°42N 8°12E 163 H2
Þykkvabæjarklaustur
  Iceland   63°30N 18°22W 155 D8
Þykkviber Iceland   63°45N 20°37W 155 D6
Tiga, Ì. N. Cal.   21°7S 167°49E 288 d
Tiga Res. Nigeria   11°35N 8°30E 263 C6
Tigalda I. U.S.A.   54°6N 165°5W 303 J6
Tigaon Phil.   13°38N 123°30E 232 E4
Tigbauan Phil.   10°41N 122°27E 233 F4
Tiger Leaping Gorge = Hutiao Xia
  China   27°13N 100°9E 228 D3
Tighina Moldova   46°50N 29°30E 183 D14
Tigil Russia   57°49N 158°40E 215 D16
Tignall U.S.A.   33°52N 82°44W 316 D6
Tignish Canada   46°58N 64°2W 299 C7
Tigray □ Ethiopia   13°35N 39°15E 257 E4
Tigre → Peru   4°30S 74°10W 328 D3
Tigre → Venezuela   9°20N 62°30W 329 B5
Tigris = Dijlah, Nahr →
  Asia   31°0N 47°25E 246 D5
Tiguentourine Algeria 27°52N 9°8E 261 C6
Tigveni Romania   45°10N 24°31E 183 E9
Tigyaing Burma   23°45N 96°10E 241 D6
Tigzerte, O. → Morocco 28°10N 9°37W 260 C3
Tîh, Gebel el Egypt 29°32N 33°26E 256 B3
Tihodaine, Erg de Algeria 25°15N 7°15E 261 C6
Tihwa = Ürümqi China 43°45N 87°45E 217 D11
Tijara India   27°56N 76°31E 242 F7
Tijgerhof S. Africa   33°53S 18°30E 118 A2
Tiji Libya   32°0N 11°18E 258 B2
Tijuana Mexico   32°32N 117°1W 307 N9
Tijuca Brazil   22°56S 43°13W 135 B1
Tijuca, Pico da Brazil 22°56S 43°15W 135 B1
Tijuca → Brazil   22°56S 43°14W 135 B1
Tikahau French Polynesia 15°0S 148°10W 289 f
Tikal Guatemala   17°13N 89°24W 320 C2
Tikamgarh India   24°44N 78°50E 243 G8
Tikaré Burkina Faso   13°15N 1°43W 263 C4
Tîkha Lakes U.S.A.   60°0N 159°0W 303 G8
Tikei French Polynesia 14°58S 144°32W 289 f
Tikhonkaya = Birobidzhan
  Russia   48°50N 132°50E 219 B15
Tikhoretsk Russia   45°56N 40°5E 191 H5
Tikhvin Russia   59°35N 33°30E 188 C7
Tikiraqjuaq = Whale Cove
  Canada   62°10N 92°34W 297 A10
Tikkadouine, Adrar
  Algeria   24°28N 1°30E 261 D5
Tikkurila Finland   60°17N 25°2E 121 B3
Tikmehdāsh Iran   37°16N 46°54E 213 D12
Tiko Cameroon   4°4N 9°20E 263 E6
Tikopia Pac. Oc.   12°19S 168°49E 277 C12
Tikrīt Iraq   34°35N 43°37E 213 E10
Tiksi Russia   71°40N 128°45E 215 B13
Tiladummati Atoll Maldives 7°0N 73°20E 272 d
Tilak Nagar India   28°38N 77°5E 138 B1
Tilamuta Indonesia 0°32N 122°23E 231 D6
Tilangiao China   31°15N 121°29E 138 B1
Tilburg Neths.   51°31N 5°6E 170 C5
Tilbury Ont., Canada 42°17N 82°23W 312 D2
Tilbury U.K.   51°27N 0°22E 169 F8
Tilbury Essex, U.K. 51°27N 0°22E 169 F8
Tilcara Argentina   23°36S 65°23W 334 A2
Tilden U.S.A.   42°3N 97°50W 308 D5
Tilhar India   28°0N 79°45E 243 F8
Tilia, O. → Algeria 28°27N 8°11W 261 C5
Tilichiki Russia   60°27N 166°5E 215 C17
Tililane Algeria   27°15N 1°31E 261 C4
Tilin Burma   21°41N 94°6E 241 E5
Tilissos Greece   35°20N 25°1E 207 E6
Till → U.K.   55°41N 2°13W 168 B5
Tillabéri Niger   14°28N 1°28E 263 C5
Tillamook U.S.A.   45°27N 123°51W 304 D2
Tillanchong I. India 8°30N 93°30E 245 K11
Tillberga Sweden   59°40N 16°39E 162 E10
Tillia Niger   16°8N 4°47E 263 B5
Tillman U.S.A.   32°28N 81°36W 316 D7
Tillsonburg Canada 42°53N 80°44W 312 D4
Tillyeria Cyprus   35°6N 32°40E 207 E8
Tilogne Senegal   16°0N 13°40W 262 B2
Tilos Greece   36°27N 27°27E 205 E9
Tilpa Australia   30°57S 144°24E 282 A4
Tilrhemt Algeria   33°9N 3°22E 261 B5
Tilsit = Sovetsk Russia 55°6N 21°50E 163 J10
Tilt → U.K.   56°46N 3°51W 167 E5
Tilton U.S.A.   43°27N 71°36W 313 C13
Tiltonsville U.S.A. 40°10N 80°41W 312 F4
Tim Denmark   56°12N 8°19E 163 H2
Timah, Bukit Singapore 1°21N 103°46E 138 A2
Timanskiy Kryazh Russia 65°58N 50°5E 186 A9
Timaru N.Z.   44°23S 171°14E 285 E6
Timashevsk Russia   45°35N 39°0E 191 H4
Timau Italy   46°32N 12°58E 199 D9
Timbaki Greece   35°4N 24°45E 207 E6
Timbaúba Brazil   7°31S 35°19W 332 D6
Timbedgha Mauritania 16°17N 8°16W 262 B3
Timber Creek Australia 15°40S 130°29E 278 C5
Timber Lake U.S.A. 45°26N 101°5W 308 C3
Timber Mt. U.S.A.   37°6N 116°28W 306 H11
Timbo Guinea   10°30N 11°25W 262 C2
Timbó Brazil   26°49S 49°16W 335 B6
Timbouctou = Tombouctou
  Mali   16°50N 3°0W 262 B4
Timbiqui Colombia   2°46N 77°42W 328 C2
Timboon Australia   38°30S 142°58E 282 E5
Timbuktu = Tombouctou
  Mali   16°50N 3°0W 262 B4
Timdjaouine Algeria 21°37N 4°30E 261 D5

Timelaouine Algeria 20°27N 1°50E 261 D5
Timellouline Algeria 29°22N 8°55E 261 C6
Times Square New York, U.S.A. 132 c2
Timétrin Mali 19°19N 0°34W 263 B4
Timétrine, Mts. Mali 19°25N 1°0W 263 B4
Timfi Oros Greece 39°59N 20°45E 204 B2
Timfristos, Oros Greece 38°57N 21°50E 204 C3
Timgad Algeria 35°29N 6°28E 261 A6
Timhadit Morocco 33°15N 5°4W 260 B3
Timi Cyprus 34°44N 32°31E 207 F8
Timia Niger 18°4N 8°40E 259 E1
Timika Indonesia 4°47S 136°32E 231 E9
Timimoun Algeria 29°14N 0°16E 261 C5
Timimoun, Sebkha de Algeria 28°50N 0°46E 261 C5
Timiris, Râs Mauritania 19°21N 16°30W 262 B1
Timiryazev Park Russia 55°49N 37°33E 129 B3
Timiş = Tamis → Serbia 44°51N 20°39E 182 F5
Timiş □ Romania 45°40N 21°30E 182 E6
Timiskaming, L. = Témiscamingue, L. Canada 47°10N 79°25W 298 C4
Timişoara Romania 45°43N 21°15E 182 E6
Timmersdala Sweden 58°32N 13°46E 163 F7
Timmins Canada 48°28N 81°25W 298 C3
Timmonsville U.S.A. 34°8N 79°57W 316 A10
Timok → Serbia 44°10N 22°40E 202 B6
Timoleague Ireland 51°39N 8°46W 166 E3
Timon Brazil 5°8S 42°52W 332 C3
Timor Asia 9°0S 125°0E 231 F7
Timor Leste = East Timor ■ Asia 8°50S 126°0E 231 F7
Timor Sea Ind. Oc. 12°0S 127°0E 278 B4
Timrå Sweden 62°29N 17°18E 162 B11
Timucuan ⌂ U.S.A. 30°28N 81°27W 316 E8
Tīn, Ra's at Libya 32°37N 23°8E 258 B4
Tin Alkoum Algeria 24°42N 10°17E 261 D7
Tin Amzi, O. → Algeria 18°20N 4°32E 261 D6
Tin Atanai Algeria 25°52N 1°37E 261 C5
Tin Can Bay Australia 25°56S 153°0E 281 D5
Tin Can I. Nigeria 6°26N 3°21E 124 B2
Tin Ethisane Mali 19°3N 0°52W 263 B4
Tin Gornai Mali 16°38N 0°38W 263 B4
Tin Mt. U.S.A. 36°50N 117°10W 306 J9
Tina = Thina → S. Africa 31°18S 29°13E 271 D4
Tîna, Khalîg el Egypt 31°10N 32°40E 251 G3
Tinaca Pt. Phil. 5°30N 125°25E 233 J5
Tinaco Venezuela 9°42N 68°26W 328 B4
Tinajo Canary Is. 29°4N 13°42W 153 e2
Tinca Romania 46°46N 21°58E 182 D6
Tindal Australia 14°31S 132°22E 278 B5
Tindivanam India 12°15N 79°41E 245 H4
Tindouf Algeria 27°42N 8°10W 260 C3
Tindouf □ Algeria 27°25N 5°50W 260 C3
Tinée → France 43°55N 7°11E 175 E11
Tineo Spain 43°21N 6°27W 194 B4
Tinerhir Morocco 31°29N 5°31W 260 B3
Tinfouchi Algeria 28°52N 5°49W 260 C3
Tinfunque △ Paraguay 23°55S 60°17W 334 A3
Ting Jiang → China 24°45N 116°35E 229 E11
Ting Kau China 22°22N 114°4E 122 A1
Tinggi, Pulau Malaysia 2°18N 104°7E 237 L5
Tinghert, Ḥamādat Libya 29°0N 9°0E 258 C1
Tingi Mts. S. Leone 8°55N 10°47W 262 D2
Tingkan Taiwan 23°48N 120°52E 225 C2
Tingkawk Sakan Burma 26°4N 96°44E 241 B6
Tinglayan Phil. 17°15N 121°9E 232 C3
Tinglev Denmark 54°57N 9°13E 163 K3
Tingmerkpuk Mt. U.S.A. 68°34N 162°28W 303 B7
Tingo María Peru 9°10S 75°54W 330 B2
Tingrela Ivory C. 10°27N 6°25W 262 C3
Tingri China 28°34N 86°38E 218 F6
Tingsryd Sweden 56°31N 15°0E 163 H9
Tingstäde Sweden 57°44N 18°37E 163 G12
Tingvoll Norway 62°55N 8°12E 164 B5
Tingwon Group Papua N. G. 2°37S 149°42E 286 B5
Tinh Bien Vietnam 10°36N 104°57E 237 G5
Tinharé, I. de Brazil 13°30S 38°58W 333 D4
Tinian N. Marianas 15°0N 145°38E 302 e
Tinian Channel N. Marianas 14°54N 145°36E 302 e
Tinigua △ Colombia 2°30N 74°8W 328 C3
Tiniguiban Phil. 11°22N 119°30E 233 F2
Tinjar → Malaysia 4°4N 114°18E 235 B4
Tinkisso → Guinea 11°21N 9°10W 262 C3
Tinn = Atrå Norway 59°59N 8°45E 164 E5
Tinnevelly = Tirunelveli India 8°45N 77°45E 245 K3
Tinnoset Norway 59°43N 9°3E 164 E6
Tinnsjå Norway 59°55N 8°54E 164 E5
Tinogasta Argentina 28°5S 67°32W 334 B2
Tinos Greece 37°33N 25°8E 205 D7
Tiñoso, C. Spain 37°32N 1°6W 197 H3
Tinpahar India 24°59N 87°44E 243 G12
Tinputz Papua N. G. 5°33S 155°0E 286 C8
Tinrhert, Plateau du Algeria 29°30N 9°0E 258 C1
Tinsukia India 27°29N 95°20E 241 B5
Tinta Peru 14°3S 71°20W 330 C3
Tintamarre, Île St-Martin 18°8N 63°2W 322 a
Tintâne Mauritania 16°18N 10°10W 262 B2
Tintina Argentina 27°2S 62°45W 334 B3
Tintinara Australia 35°48S 140°2E 282 C4
Tintioulé Guinea 10°13N 9°12W 262 C3
Tinto → Spain 37°12N 6°55W 195 H4
Tinui N.Z. 40°52S 176°5E 284 G5
Tinwald N.Z. 43°55S 171°43E 285 D6
Tiobraid Árann = Tipperary Ireland 52°28N 8°10W 166 D3
Tioga N. Dak., U.S.A. 48°24N 102°56W 308 A2
Tioga Pa., U.S.A. 41°55N 77°8W 312 E7
Tioman, Pulau Malaysia 2°50N 104°10E 237 L5
Tione di Trento Italy 46°2N 10°43E 198 B7
Tionesta U.S.A. 41°30N 79°28W 312 E5
Tior South Sudan 6°26N 31°11E 257 F3
Tiouliline Algeria 27°1N 0°2W 261 C4
Tipaza Algeria 36°35N 2°26E 261 A5
Tipaza □ Algeria 36°35N 2°25E 261 A5
Tipitapa Nic. 12°12N 86°5W 320 D2
Tipp City U.S.A. 39°58N 84°11W 311 E12
Tippecanoe → U.S.A. 40°30N 86°45W 311 D10
Tipperary Ireland 52°28N 8°10W 166 D3
Tipperary □ Ireland 52°37N 7°55W 166 D4
Tipton Calif., U.S.A. 36°4N 119°19W 306 J7
Tipton Ind., U.S.A. 40°17N 86°2W 311 D10
Tipton Iowa, U.S.A. 41°46N 91°8W 310 C5
Tipton Mo., U.S.A. 38°39N 92°47W 310 F4
Tipton Mt. U.S.A. 35°32N 114°12W 307 K12
Tiptonville U.S.A. 36°23N 89°29W 315 C10
Tiptur India 13°15N 76°26E 245 H3
Tiquié → Brazil 0°5N 68°25W 328 C4
Tiquina Bolivia 16°13S 68°50W 330 D4
Tira West Bank 31°52N 35°7E 123 A1
Tiracambu, Serra do Brazil 3°15S 46°30W 332 B2
Tirad Pass △ Phil. 17°3N 120°38E 232 C3
Tirahart, O. → Algeria 23°45N 3°10E 261 D5
Tirān Iran 32°45N 51°8E 247 C6
Tīrān Si. Arabia 27°57N 34°32E 251 L5
Tiranë Albania 41°18N 19°49E 202 E3
Tiranë ✕ (TIA) Albania 41°57N 19°42E 202 E3
Tirano Italy 46°13N 10°10E 198 B7
Tirari Desert Australia 28°22S 138°7E 282 A3
Tiraspol Moldova 46°55N 29°35E 183 D14
Tiratimine Algeria 25°56N 3°37E 261 C5
Tirau N.Z. 37°58S 175°46E 284 D4
Tirdout Mali 16°7N 1°5W 263 B4
Tire Turkey 38°5N 27°45E 205 C9
Tirebolu Turkey 40°58N 38°45E 213 B8
Tiree U.K. 56°31N 6°55W 167 E2
Tiree, Passage of U.K. 56°30N 6°30W 167 E2
Tîrgovişte = Târgovişte Romania 44°55N 25°27E 183 F10
Tîrgu Jiu = Târgu Jiu Romania 45°5N 23°19E 183 E8
Tîrgu Mureş = Târgu Mureş Romania 46°31N 24°38E 183 D9
Tirgua △ Venezuela 10°5N 68°48W 328 A4
Tirich Mir Pakistan 36°15N 71°55E 240 A3
Tiriolo Italy 38°57N 16°30E 201 D9
Tiririca, Serra da Brazil 17°6S 47°6W 333 E2
Tiriro Guinea 10°27N 8°40W 262 C3
Tiris Zemmour □ Mauritania 24°0N 9°0W 260 D3
Tiritiri o te Moana = Southern Alps N.Z. 43°41S 170°11E 285 D5
Tirna → India 18°4N 76°57E 244 E3
Tîrnavos Greece 39°45N 22°18E 204 B4
Tirodi India 21°40N 79°44E 244 D4
Tirol □ Austria 47°3N 10°43E 180 D3
Tiros Brazil 19°0S 45°58W 333 E2
Tirrukkovil Sri Lanka 7°7N 81°51E 245 L5
Tirsa Egypt 29°57N 31°12E 117 B2
Tirschenreuth Germany 49°53N 12°19E 179 F8
Tirschtiegel = Trzciel Poland 52°23N 15°50E 185 F2
Tirso → Italy 39°53N 8°32E 200 C1
Tirstrup Denmark 56°18N 10°42E 163 H4
Tirtagangga Indonesia 8°24S 115°35E 231 J18
Tirthahalli India 13°42N 75°14E 245 H2
Tirua Pt. N.Z. 38°25S 174°40E 284 E3
Tiruchchendur India 8°30N 78°11E 245 K4
Tiruchchirappalli India 10°45N 78°45E 245 J4
Tirukkoyilur India 11°57N 79°12E 245 J4
Tirumangalam India 9°49N 77°58E 245 K3
Tirumayam India 10°14N 78°45E 245 J4
Tirunelveli India 8°45N 77°45E 245 K3
Tirupati India 13°39N 79°25E 245 H4
Tiruppattur Tamil Nadu, India 10°8N 78°37E 245 J4
Tiruppattur Tamil Nadu, India 12°30N 78°30E 245 H4
Tiruppur India 11°5N 77°22E 245 J3
Tirur India 10°54N 75°55E 245 J2
Tiruttani India 13°11N 79°58E 245 H4
Tirutturaippundi India 10°32N 79°41E 245 J4
Tiruvadaimarudur India 11°2N 79°27E 245 J4
Tiruvalla India 9°23N 76°34E 245 K3
Tiruvallar India 13°9N 79°57E 245 H4
Tiruvannamalai India 12°15N 79°5E 245 H4
Tiruvettipuram India 12°39N 79°33E 245 H4
Tiruvottiyur India 13°10N 80°22E 245 H5
Tis Issat Ethiopia 11°25N 37°45E 257 E4
Tisa India 32°50N 76°9E 242 C7
Tisa → Serbia 45°15N 20°17E 182 E5
Tisdale Canada 52°50N 104°0W 297 C8
Tishomingo U.S.A. 34°14N 96°41W 314 D6
Tishrīyaa Iraq 33°18N 44°24E 113 B2
Tisjön Sweden 60°56N 13°0E 162 D7
Tisnaren Sweden 58°58N 15°56E 163 F9
Tišnov Czech Rep. 49°21N 16°25E 181 B9
Tisovec Slovak Rep. 48°41N 19°56E 181 C12
Tissamaharama Sri Lanka 6°17N 81°17E 245 L5
Tissān, Ḥasy Libya 28°14N 12°26E 261 C7
Tissemsilt Algeria 35°35N 1°50E 261 A5
Tissemsilt □ Algeria 35°45N 1°45E 261 A5
Tissint Morocco 29°57N 7°16W 260 C3
Tista → India 25°23N 89°43E 241 C2
Tistedal Norway 59°8N 11°27E 164 E8
Tisza = Tisa → Serbia 45°15N 20°17E 182 E5
Tiszaföldvár Hungary 46°58N 20°14E 182 D5
Tiszafüred Hungary 47°38N 20°50E 182 C5
Tiszalök Hungary 48°1N 21°20E 182 B6
Tiszavasvári Hungary 47°58N 21°18E 182 C6
Tit Ahaggar, Algeria 23°0N 5°10E 261 D6
Tit Tademait, Algeria 27°0N 1°29E 261 C5
Tit-Ary Russia 71°55N 127°2E 215 B13
Titabar India 26°36N 94°12E 241 B5
Titaguas Spain 39°53N 1°6W 196 F3
Titao Burkina Faso 13°45N 2°5W 263 C4
Titel Serbia 45°10N 20°18E 182 E5
Tithwal Pakistan 34°21N 73°50E 243 B5
Titicaca, L. S. Amer. 15°30S 69°30W 330 D4
Titikaveka Cook Is. 21°16S 159°45W 239 h
Titisee Germany 47°54N 8°10E 179 H4
Tititira Hd. N.Z. 43°36S 169°25E 285 D4
Tititut Burma 18°54N 95°16E 241 F5
Titiwa Nigeria 12°14N 12°53E 263 C7
Titlagarh India 20°15N 83°11E 244 D6
Tito Italy 40°35N 15°40E 201 B8
Titograd = Podgorica Montenegro 42°30N 19°19E 202 D3
Titova Korenica Croatia 44°45N 15°41E 199 D12
Titu Romania 44°39N 25°32E 183 F10
Titule Dem. Rep. of the Congo 3°15N 25°31E 268 B2
Titusville Fla., U.S.A. 28°37N 80°49W 317 G9
Titusville Pa., U.S.A. 41°38N 79°41W 312 E5
Tiu Keng Leng China 22°18N 114°15E 122 B2
Tivaouane Senegal 14°56N 16°45W 262 C1
Tivat Montenegro 42°28N 18°43E 202 D2
Tivedens △ Sweden 58°45N 14°35E 163 F8
Tiverton Ont., Canada 44°16N 81°32W 312 B3
Tiverton Devon, U.K. 50°54N 3°29W 169 G4
Tivoli Grenada 12°10N 61°37W 323 q
Tivoli Italy 41°58N 12°45E 199 G9
Tiwī Oman 22°45N 59°12E 249 B7
Tiwi ✪ Australia 11°33S 130°42E 278 B5
Tiyo Eritrea 14°41N 40°15E 257 E5
Tizapán Mexico 19°19N 99°13W 128 C1
Tizga Morocco 32°1N 5°9W 260 B3
Ti'zi N'Isli Morocco 32°28N 5°47W 260 B3
Tizi-Ouzou Algeria 36°42N 4°3E 261 A5
Tizi-Ouzou □ Algeria 36°35N 4°5E 261 A5
Tizimín Mexico 21°9N 88°9W 319 C7
Tiznados → Venezuela 8°16N 67°47W 328 B4
Tiznap He → China 38°21N 77°26E 217 E9
Tiznit Morocco 29°48N 9°45W 260 C3
Tiznit □ Morocco 29°35N 9°30W 260 C3
Tjæreborg Denmark 55°28N 8°36E 163 J2
Tjällmo Sweden 58°43N 15°21E 163 F9
Tjeggelvas Sweden 66°37N 17°45E 160 C17
Tjieggelvas = Tjeggelvas Sweden 66°37N 17°45E 160 C17
Tjirebon = Cirebon Indonesia 6°45S 108°32E 235 D3
Tjirrkarli ✪ Australia 26°0S 125°28E 279 E4
Tjluring Indonesia 8°25S 114°13E 231 J17
Tjøme Norway 59°8N 10°26E 164 E7
Tjörn Sweden 58°0N 11°35E 163 F5
Tjukayirla Roadhouse Australia 27°9S 124°34E 279 E3
Tjurabalan ✪ Australia 19°50S 128°0E 278 C4
Tkibuli = Tqibuli Georgia 42°26N 43°0E 191 J6
Tkvarcheli = Tqvarcheli Georgia 42°47N 41°42E 191 J5
Tlacotalpan Mexico 18°37N 95°40W 319 D5
Tlahualilo de Zaragoza Mexico 26°7N 103°27W 318 B4
Tlalnepantla → Mexico 19°30N 99°18W 128 A1
Tlalpan Mexico 19°18N 99°10W 128 C2
Tlaquepaque Mexico 20°39N 103°19W 318 C4
Tlaxcala Mexico 19°19N 98°14W 319 D5
Tlaxcala □ Mexico 19°25N 98°10W 319 D5
Tlaxiaco Mexico 17°25N 97°35W 319 D5
Tlemcen Algeria 34°52N 1°21W 261 B4
Tlemcen □ Algeria 34°38N 1°30W 261 B4
Tleta Sidi Bouguedra Morocco 32°16N 9°59W 260 B3
Tlokweng Botswana 24°40S 25°58E 270 B4
Tlumach Ukraine 48°51N 25°0E 183 B10
Tłuszcz Poland 52°25N 21°25E 185 F8
Tlyarata Russia 42°9N 46°26E 191 J8
Tmassah Libya 26°19N 15°51E 258 C3
To Bong Vietnam 12°45N 109°16E 236 F7
To Kwai Wan China 22°18N 114°11E 122 B2
To-Shima Japan 34°31N 139°17E 223 C11
Toa Payoh Singapore 1°20N 103°51E 138 A3
Toad → Canada 59°25N 124°57W 296 B4
Toad River Canada 58°51N 125°14W 296 B3
Toamasina Madag. 18°10S 49°25E 272 B2
Toamasina □ Madag. 18°0S 49°0E 272 B2
Toay Argentina 36°43S 64°38W 334 D3
Toba China 31°19N 97°42E 228 B1
Toba Japan 34°30N 136°51E 223 C8
Toba, Danau Indonesia 2°30N 98°30E 234 B1
Toba Kakar Pakistan 31°30N 69°0E 242 D3
Toba Tek Singh Pakistan 30°55N 72°25E 242 D5
Tobago Trin. & Tob. 11°10N 60°30W 323 s
Tobarra Spain 38°37N 1°44W 197 G3
Tobelo Indonesia 1°45N 127°56E 231 D7
Tobermory Ont., Canada 45°12N 81°40W 312 A3
Tobermory Argyll & Bute, U.K. 56°38N 6°5W 167 E2
Tobi Palau 2°40N 131°10E 231 D8
Tobi-Shima Japan 41°12N 139°34E 220 D9
Tobias Fornier = Dao Phil. 10°30N 121°57E 233 F3
Tobishi Hana Iwo Jima 24°45N 141°17E 288 b
Tobin, L. Australia 21°45S 125°49E 278 D4
Tobin L. Canada 53°35N 103°30W 297 C8
Toblach = Dobbiaco Italy 46°44N 12°14E 199 B9
Toboali Indonesia 3°0S 106°25E 234 C3
Tobol → Russia 58°10N 68°12E 214 D7
Toboli Indonesia 0°38S 120°5E 231 E6
Tobolsk Russia 58°15N 68°10E 214 D7
Tobor Senegal 12°40N 16°15W 262 C1
Toboso Phil. 10°43N 123°31E 233 F4
Tobruk = Tubruq Libya 32°7N 23°55E 258 B4
Tobyhanna U.S.A. 41°11N 75°25W 313 E9
Tobyl = Tobol → Russia 58°10N 68°12E 214 D7
Tobyl Kazakhstan 52°41N 62°34E 216 B6
Tocache Nuevo Peru 8°9S 76°26W 330 B2
Tocantinia Brazil 9°33S 48°22W 332 C2
Tocantinópolis Brazil 6°20S 47°25W 332 C2
Tocantins □ Brazil 10°0S 48°0W 332 D2
Tocantins → Brazil 1°45S 49°10W 332 B2
Toccoa U.S.A. 34°35N 83°19W 315 D13
Toce → Italy 45°56N 8°29E 198 C5
Tochi → Pakistan 32°49N 70°41E 242 C4
Tochigi Japan 36°25N 139°45E 223 A11
Tochigi □ Japan 36°45N 139°45E 223 A11
Tocina Spain 37°37N 5°44W 195 H5
Töcksfors Sweden 59°31N 11°52E 162 E5
Točná Czech Rep. 49°58N 14°25E 135 C2
Toco Chile 22°5S 69°35W 330 E4
Toco Trin. & Tob. 10°49N 60°57W 323 t
Toco Hills U.S.A. 33°49N 84°20W 113 B2
Toconao Chile 23°11S 68°1W 334 A2
Tocopilla Chile 22°5S 70°10W 334 A1
Tocqueville = Râs el Oued Algeria 35°57N 5°2E 261 A6
Tocumwal Australia 35°51S 145°31E 283 C6
Tocuyo → Venezuela 11°3N 68°23W 328 A4
Tocuyo de la Costa Venezuela 11°2N 68°23W 328 A4
Todalen Norway 62°49N 8°44E 164 B5
Todd → Australia 24°52S 135°48E 280 C2
Todds Road Trin. & Tob. 10°28N 61°20W 323 t
Toddu Atoll Maldives 4°25N 72°57E 272 d
Todeli Indonesia 1°40S 124°29E 231 E6
Todenyang Kenya 4°35N 35°56E 268 B4
Todgarh India 25°42N 73°58E 242 G5
Todi Italy 42°47N 12°24E 199 F9
Todos os Santos, B. de Brazil 12°48S 38°38W 333 D4
Todos Santos Mexico 23°26N 110°13W 318 C2
Todt Hill U.S.A. 40°36N 74°5W 132 C1
Todtnau Germany 47°49N 7°56E 179 H3
Toe Hd. U.K. 57°50N 7°8W 167 D1
Toecé Burkina Faso 11°50N 1°15W 263 C4
Toekornstig Stuwmeer Suriname 4°45N 57°30W 329 C6
Toetoes B. N.Z. 46°42S 168°41E 285 G3
Tofield Canada 53°25N 112°40W 296 C6
Tofino Canada 49°11N 125°55W 296 D3
Töfsingdalen △ Sweden 62°10N 12°28E 162 B6
Tofte Norway 59°33N 10°34E 164 E7
Tofua Tonga 19°45S 175°5W 287 P13
Toga Vanuatu 13°26S 166°42E 287 C4
Tōgane Japan 35°33N 140°22E 223 B12
Togba Mauritania 17°26N 10°12W 262 B2
Togbo C.A.R. 6°0N 17°27E 264 A3
Togdheer □ Somali Rep. 9°20N 45°25E 267 C6
Togdheer → Somali Rep. 6°26N 48°39E 267 C6
Togiak U.S.A. 59°4N 160°24W 303 G7
Togiak Nat. Wildlife Refuge ⌂ U.S.A. 59°20N 160°15W 303 G7
Togian, Kepulauan Indonesia 0°20S 121°50E 231 E6
Togliatti Russia 53°32N 49°24E 190 D9
Togo ■ W. Afr. 8°30N 1°35E 263 D5
Togo Wichale Somali Rep. 9°22N 43°47E 267 C5
Tögrög Mongolia 47°25N 92°13E 217 C12
Togtoh China 40°15N 111°10E 226 D6
Tohiea, Mt. Moorea 17°33S 149°49W 289 e
Tohma → Turkey 38°29N 38°23E 212 C8
Tōhoku □ Japan 39°50N 141°45E 220 E10
Töhöm Mongolia 44°27N 108°2E 226 B5
Tohopekaliga, East L. U.S.A. 28°18N 81°15W 317 G8
Tohopekaliga, L. U.S.A. 28°12N 81°24W 317 G8
Toi Cook Is. 18°57S 169°51W 289 g
Toi Japan 34°54N 138°47E 223 C10
Toibalewe India 10°32N 92°30E 245 J11
Toinya South Sudan 6°17N 29°46E 257 F2
Toiyabe Range U.S.A. 39°30N 117°0W 304 G5
Tojikiston = Tajikistan ■ Asia 38°30N 70°0E 217 E8
Tojo Indonesia 1°20S 121°15E 231 E6
Tōjō Japan 34°53N 133°16E 222 C5
Tok U.S.A. 63°20N 142°59W 303 E12
Toka Guyana 3°58N 59°17W 329 C6
Tokaanu N.Z. 38°58S 175°46E 284 E4
Tokachi-Dake Japan 43°17N 142°5E 220 C11
Tokachi-Gawa → Japan 42°44N 143°42E 220 C11
Tokagi Japan 35°42N 139°55E 140 A4
Tokai Japan 35°2N 136°55E 223 B8
Tokai Plantation S. Africa 34°3S 18°24E 118 B1
Tokaichiba Japan 35°31N 139°30E 140 B2
Tokaj Hungary 48°8N 21°27E 182 B6
Tokala Indonesia 1°30S 121°40E 231 E6
Tōkamachi Japan 37°8N 138°43E 221 F9
Tokanui N.Z. 46°34S 168°56E 285 G3
Tokar Sudan 18°27N 37°56E 256 D4
Tokara-Rettō Japan 29°37N 129°43E 221 K4
Tokarahi N.Z. 44°56S 170°39E 285 E5
Tokarevo Russia 55°38N 37°54E 129 C5
Tokashiki-Shima Japan 26°11N 127°21E 221 L3
Tokat Turkey 40°22N 36°35E 212 B7
Tokat □ Turkey 40°15N 36°30E 212 B7
Tŏkch'ŏn N. Korea 39°45N 126°18E 224 C3
Tokdo Asia 37°15N 131°52E 221 F5
Tokeland U.S.A. 46°42N 123°59W 306 D3
Tokelau Is. ☒ Pac. Oc. 9°0S 171°45W 277 B16
Toki Japan 35°18N 137°8E 223 B9
Toki Pt. Wake I. 19°19N 166°35E 302 b
Tokmak Kyrgyzstan 42°49N 75°15E 217 D9
Tokmak Ukraine 47°16N 35°42E 189 J8
Toko Ra. Australia 23°5S 138°20E 280 C2
Tokomaru Bay N.Z. 38°8S 178°22E 284 E7
Tokoname Japan 34°53N 136°51E 223 C8
Tokoro-Gawa → Japan 44°7N 144°5E 220 B12
Tokoroa N.Z. 38°13S 175°50E 284 E4
Tokorozawa Japan 35°47N 139°28E 223 B11
Toksook Bay U.S.A. 60°32N 165°0W 303 F6
Toksun China 42°47N 88°38E 217 D11
Toktogul Kyrgyzstan 41°50N 72°50E 217 D8
Toku Tonga 18°10S 174°11W 287 P13
Tokuji Japan 34°11N 131°42E 222 C3
Tokuno-Shima Japan 27°56N 128°55E 221 L4
Tokushima Japan 34°4N 134°34E 222 C6
Tokushima □ Japan 33°55N 134°0E 222 D6
Tokuyama Japan 34°3N 131°50E 222 C3
Tōkyō Japan 35°43N 139°45E 140 B3
Tōkyō □ Japan 35°40N 139°30E 223 B11
Tōkyō B. = Tōkyō-Wan Japan 35°25N 139°50E 140 B4
Tōkyō Disneyland Japan 35°37N 139°53E 140 B4
Tōkyō Haneda ✕ (HND) Japan 35°33N 139°46E 140 B3
Tōkyō Harbour Japan 35°38N 139°46E 140 B3
Tōkyō Narita ✕ (NRT) Japan 35°45N 140°25E 223 B12
Tōkyō-Wan Japan 35°25N 139°50E 140 B4
Tokzār Afghan. 35°52N 66°26E 240 B2
Tol I. Micronesia 7°20N 151°37E 287 U17
Tolaga Bay N.Z. 38°21S 178°20E 284 E7
Tolageak U.S.A. 70°3N 162°27W 303 A7
Tolbo Mongolia 48°25N 90°17E 217 C12
Tolbukhin = Dobrich Bulgaria 43°37N 27°49E 203 C11
Tolé C.A.R. 6°34N 16°1E 264 A3
Töle Bī Kazakhstan 43°42N 73°46E 217 D8
Toledo Brazil 24°44S 53°45W 335 A5
Toledo Phil. 10°23N 123°38E 233 F4
Toledo Spain 39°50N 4°2W 194 F6
Toledo Ill., U.S.A. 39°16N 88°15W 311 E8
Toledo Iowa, U.S.A. 42°0N 92°35W 310 C4
Toledo Ohio, U.S.A. 41°39N 83°33W 311 C13
Toledo Oreg., U.S.A. 44°37N 123°56W 304 D2
Toledo Wash., U.S.A. 46°26N 122°51W 304 C2
Toledo, Montes de Spain 39°33N 4°20W 195 F6
Toledo Bend Res. U.S.A. 31°11N 93°34W 314 F8
Tolentino Italy 43°12N 13°17E 199 E10
Tolfa Italy 42°9N 11°56E 199 F8
Tolga Algeria 34°40N 5°22E 261 B6
Tolga Queens., Australia 17°15S 145°29E 280 B4
Tolga Hedmark, Norway 62°26N 11°1E 164 B8
Tolhuaca △ Chile 38°15S 71°50W 336 A2
Toli China 45°57N 83°37E 217 C10
Toliara Madag. 23°21S 43°40E 272 C1
Toliara □ Madag. 21°0S 45°0E 272 C2
Tolima Colombia 4°40N 75°19W 328 C2
Tolima □ Colombia 3°45N 75°15W 328 C2
Tolitoli Indonesia 1°5N 120°50E 231 D6
Tolka → Ireland 53°21N 6°14W 120 A1
Tolkmicko Poland 54°19N 19°31E 184 D6
Tollarp Sweden 55°55N 13°58E 163 J7
Tollensesee Germany 53°30N 13°13E 178 B9
Tollhouse U.S.A. 37°1N 119°24W 306 H7
Tollygunge = Taliganga India 22°30N 88°22E 124 B2
Tolmachevo Russia 58°56N 29°51E 188 C5
Tolmezzo Italy 46°24N 13°1E 199 B10
Tolmin Slovenia 46°11N 13°45E 199 B10
Tolna Hungary 46°25N 18°48E 182 D3
Tolna □ Hungary 46°30N 18°30E 182 D3
Tolo Dem. Rep. of the Congo 2°55S 18°34E 264 C3
Tolo, Teluk Indonesia 2°20S 122°10E 231 E6
Tolo Harbour China 22°27N 114°12E 219 a
Tolochin = Talachyn Belarus 54°25N 29°42E 188 E5
Tolokiwa I. Papua N. G. 5°15S 147°37E 286 C4
Tolong B. Phil. 9°20N 122°49E 233 G4
Tolono U.S.A. 39°59N 88°16W 311 E8
Tolosa Spain 43°8N 2°5W 196 B2
Tolox Spain 36°41N 4°54W 195 J6
Toltén Chile 39°13S 74°14W 336 A2
Toluca México, Mexico 19°17N 99°40W 319 D5
Toluca Ill., U.S.A. 41°0N 89°8W 310 C7
Tolworth U.K. 51°22N 0°17W 125 B2
Tolyatti = Togliatti Russia 53°32N 49°24E 190 D9
Tom Burke S. Africa 23°5S 28°0E 271 B4
Tom Price Australia 22°40S 117°48E 278 D2
Toma Burkina Faso 12°45N 2°53W 262 C4
Tomah U.S.A. 43°59N 90°30W 308 D8
Tomahawk U.S.A. 45°28N 89°44W 308 C9
Tomai Moldova 46°34N 28°19E 183 D13
Tomakomai Japan 42°38N 141°36E 220 C10
Tomales U.S.A. 38°15N 122°53W 306 G4
Tomales B. U.S.A. 38°15N 123°58W 306 G3
Tomanivi Fiji 17°37S 178°1E 287 A2
Tomar Portugal 39°36N 8°25W 195 F2
Tomaros, Oros Greece 39°29N 20°48E 204 B2
Tomarza Turkey 38°27N 35°48E 212 C6
Tomás Barrón Bolivia 17°35S 67°31W 330 D4
Tomashevka Belarus 51°33N 23°36E 185 G10
Tomashpil Ukraine 48°32N 28°31E 183 B13
Tomaszów Lubelski Poland 50°27N 23°25E 185 H10
Tomaszów Mazowiecki Poland 51°30N 20°2E 185 G7
Tomatlán Mexico 19°56N 105°15W 318 D3
Tomb of the Kings Jerusalem 123 a2
Tomba di Nerone Italy 41°58N 12°26E 136 B1
Tombador, Serra do Brazil 12°0S 58°0W 331 C6
Tombadonkéa Guinea 11°0N 14°25W 262 C2
Tombe South Sudan 5°53N 31°40E 257 F3
Tombeau Bay Mauritius 20°6S 57°30E 272 e
Tombel Cameroon 4°45N 9°40E 264 B1
Tombigbee → U.S.A. 31°8N 87°57W 315 F11
Tombouctou Mali 16°50N 3°0W 262 B4
Tombouctou □ Mali 20°0N 3°0W 262 B4
Tombstone U.S.A. 31°43N 110°4W 305 L8
Tombua Angola 15°55S 11°55E 265 F2
Tomé Chile 36°36S 72°57W 334 D1
Tome Japan 38°40N 141°20E 220 E10
Tomé-Açu Brazil 2°25S 48°9W 332 B2
Tomelilla Sweden 55°33N 13°58E 163 J7
Tomelloso Spain 39°10N 3°2W 195 F7
Tomil Micronesia 9°31N 138°9E 287 R16
Tomil Harbor Pac. Oc. 9°30N 138°10E 287 R16
Tomilino Russia 55°39N 37°55E 129 C5
Tomingley Australia 32°26S 148°16E 283 B8
Tomini Indonesia 0°30N 120°30E 231 D6
Tomini, Teluk Indonesia 0°10S 121°0E 231 E6
Tominian Mali 13°17N 4°35W 262 C4
Tomiño Spain 41°59N 8°46W 194 D2
Tomintoul U.K. 57°15N 3°23W 167 D5
Tomioka Japan 36°15N 138°54E 223 A10
Tomislavgrad Bos.-H. 43°42N 17°13E 182 G2
Tomkinson Ranges Australia 26°11S 129°5E 279 E4
Tommot Russia 59°4N 126°20E 215 D13
Tommy Thompson Park Canada 43°38N 79°20W 141 B3
Tomnop Ta Suos Cambodia 11°20N 104°15E 237 G5
Tomo Colombia 2°38N 67°32W 328 C4
Tomo → Colombia 5°20N 67°48W 328 B4
Tomobe Japan 36°20N 140°20E 223 A12
Tomra Norway 62°34N 6°56E 164 B3
Toms Place U.S.A. 37°34N 118°41W 306 H8
Toms River U.S.A. 39°58N 74°12W 313 G10
Tomsk Russia 56°30N 85°5E 214 D9
Tomtabacken Sweden 57°30N 14°30E 163 G8
Tömük Turkey 36°42N 34°23E 250 B5
Tona Spain 41°51N 2°14E 196 D7
Tonalá Chiapas, Mexico 16°4N 93°45W 319 D6
Tonalá Jalisco, Mexico 20°37N 103°14W 318 C4
Tonale, Passo del Italy 46°16N 10°35E 198 B7
Tonami Japan 36°40N 136°58E 223 A8
Tonantins Brazil 2°45S 67°45W 328 D4
Tonasket U.S.A. 48°42N 119°26W 304 B4
Tonate Fr. Guiana 5°0N 52°28W 329 C7
Tonawanda U.S.A. 43°1N 78°53W 312 D6
Tonb Iran 26°15N 55°15E 247 E7
Tonbo Burma 18°31N 95°5E 241 F5
Tonbridge U.K. 51°11N 0°17E 169 F8
Tonda Papua N. G. 8°55S 141°34E 286 E1
Tondabayashi Japan 34°30N 135°36E 223 C7
Tondano Indonesia 1°35N 124°54E 231 D6
Tondela Portugal 40°31N 8°5W 194 E2
Tønder Denmark 54°58N 8°50E 163 K2
Tondern = Tønder Denmark 54°58N 8°50E 163 K2
Tondi India 9°45N 79°4E 245 K4
Tondi Kiwindi Niger 14°28N 2°2E 263 C5
Tondibi Mali 16°39N 0°14W 263 B4
Tondo Phil. 14°36N 120°57E 127 B1
Tondoro Namibia 17°45S 18°50E 270 A2
Tone → Australia 34°25S 116°25E 279 F2
Tone-Gawa → Japan 35°44N 140°51E 223 B12
Tonekābon Iran 36°45N 51°12E 247 B6
Tong I. Papua N. G. 2°2S 147°47E 286 B4
Tong Xian China 39°55N 116°35E 226 E9
Tong-yeong S. Korea 34°50N 128°20E 224 E4
Tonga Cameroon 4°58N 10°42E 264 B2
Tonga South Sudan 9°28N 31°3E 257 F3
Tonga ■ Pac. Oc. 19°50S 174°30W 287 P13
Tonga Trench Pac. Oc. 18°0S 173°0W 277 D16
Tongaat S. Africa 29°33S 31°9E 271 C5
Tongala Australia 36°14S 144°56E 283 D6
Tong'an China 24°37N 118°8E 229 E12
Tongareva = Penrhyn Cook Is. 9°0S 158°0W 289 H12
Tongariro, Mt. N.Z. 39°8S 175°38E 284 F4
Tongariro △ N.Z. 39°8S 175°33E 284 F4
Tongass Nat. Forest U.S.A. 54°45N 133°0W 303 J14
Tongatapu Tonga 21°10S 175°10W 287 Q13
Tongatapu Group Tonga 21°0S 175°0W 287 Q13
Tongbai China 32°20N 113°23E 229 A9
Tongbinggo S. Korea 37°31N 126°58E 137 B1
Tongcheng Anhui, China 31°4N 116°56E 229 B11
Tongcheng Hubei, China 29°15N 113°50E 229 C9
Tongchuan China 35°6N 109°3E 226 G5
Tongdao China 26°10N 109°42E 228 D7
Tongeren Belgium 50°47N 5°28E 170 D5
Tonggu China 28°31N 114°20E 229 C10
Tonggu Jiao China 22°22N 113°37E 219 a
Tongguan China 34°40N 110°25E 226 G6
Tonghai China 24°10N 102°53E 228 E4
Tonghua China 41°42N 125°58E 224 B2
Tongi = Tungi Bangla. 23°53N 90°24E 241 D3
Tongjiang Heilongjiang, China 47°40N 132°27E 219 B15
Tongjiang Sichuan, China 31°58N 107°11E 228 B6
Tongjosŏn Man N. Korea 39°30N 128°0E 224 C4
Tongking, G. of = Tonkin, G. of Asia 20°0N 108°0E 236 C7
Tongliang China 29°50N 106°3E 228 C6
Tongliao China 43°38N 122°18E 227 C12
Tongling China 30°55N 117°48E 229 B11
Tonglu China 29°45N 119°37E 229 C12
Tongnae = Anyue China 30°9N 105°50E 228 B5
Tongoa Vanuatu 16°54S 168°34E 287 F6
Tongobory Madag. 23°32S 44°20E 272 C1
Tongoy Chile 30°16S 71°31W 334 C1
Tongqiao China 31°21N 121°22E 138 A1
Tongquil I. Phil. 6°2N 121°51E 233 H3
Tongren China 27°43N 109°11E 228 D7
Tongres = Tongeren Belgium 50°47N 5°28E 170 D5
Tongsa Dzong Bhutan 27°31N 90°31E 241 B3
Tongsha Tao Taiwan 26°12N 128°28E 225 b
Tongshi China 18°30N 109°20E 236 C7
Tongue U.K. 58°29N 4°25W 167 C4
Tongue → U.S.A. 46°25N 105°52W 304 C11
Tongwei China 35°0N 105°5E 226 G3
Tongxiang China 30°39N 120°34E 229 B13
Tongxin China 36°59N 105°58E 226 F3
Tongyang N. Korea 39°9N 126°53E 224 C3
Tongyu China 44°45N 123°4E 227 B12
Tongzhou China 32°12N 121°2E 229 A13
Tonica U.S.A. 41°13N 89°4W 310 C7
Tonj South Sudan 7°20N 28°44E 257 F2
Tonj → South Sudan 7°31N 28°55E 257 F2
Tonk India 26°6N 75°54E 242 F6
Tonkawa U.S.A. 36°41N 97°18W 314 C6
Tonkin = Bac Phan Vietnam 22°0N 105°0E 228 G5
Tonkin, G. of Asia 20°0N 108°0E 236 C7
Tonlé Sap Cambodia 13°0N 104°0E 236 F5
Tonnay-Charente France 45°56N 0°55W 174 C3
Tonneins France 44°23N 0°19E 174 D4
Tonnerre France 47°51N 3°59E 173 E10
Tönning Germany 54°19N 8°56E 178 A4
Tono Japan 39°19N 141°32E 220 E10
Tonoas I. Micronesia 7°22N 151°52E 287 T18
Tonopah U.S.A. 38°4N 117°14W 305 G5
Tonoshō Japan 34°29N 134°11E 222 C6
Tonosí Panama 7°20N 80°20W 320 E3
Tons → Haryana, India 30°30N 77°39E 242 D7
Tons → Ut. P., India 26°1N 83°33E 243 F10
Tønsberg Norway 59°19N 10°25E 164 E7
Tonsina U.S.A. 61°39N 145°11W 303 F11
Tonstad Norway 58°40N 6°45E 164 F3
Tonto △ U.S.A. 33°39N 111°7W 305 K8
Tonumea Tonga 20°30S 174°30W 287 Q13
Tonya Turkey 40°53N 39°16E 213 B8
Tonzang Burma 23°36N 93°42E 241 D4
Tonzi Burma 24°39N 94°57E 241 C5
Toobanna Australia 18°42S 146°9E 280 B4
Toodyay Australia 31°34S 116°28E 279 F2
Tooele U.S.A. 40°32N 112°18W 304 F7
Toompine Australia 27°15S 144°19E 281 D3
Toomsboro U.S.A. 32°50N 83°5W 316 C6
Toora Australia 38°39S 146°23E 283 E7
Toora-Khem Russia 52°28N 96°17E 217 B13
Toorak Australia 37°50S 145°1E 128 B2
Tootias Somali Rep. 3°57N 43°57E 267 D5
Toowoomba Australia 27°32S 151°56E 281 D5
Top Springs Australia 16°37S 131°51E 278 C5
Topalu Romania 44°31N 28°3E 183 F13
Topanga State Park ⌂ U.S.A. 34°7N 118°31W 126 B1
Topaz U.S.A. 38°41N 119°30W 306 G7
Topeka U.S.A. 39°3N 95°40W 308 F6
Topkapı Turkey 41°1N 28°55E 122 B1
Topkapı Palaca Turkey 41°1N 28°58E 122 B1
Topl'a → Slovak Rep. 48°45N 21°45E 181 C14
Topley Canada 54°49N 126°18W 296 C3
Toplica → Serbia 43°15N 21°49E 202 C5
Toplița Romania 46°55N 25°20E 183 D10
Topo Azores 38°33N 27°45W 153 d1
Topo, Pta. do Azores 38°33N 27°46W 153 d1
Topocalma, Pta. Chile 34°10S 72°2W 334 C1
Topock U.S.A. 34°46N 114°29W 307 L12
Topola Serbia 44°17N 20°41E 202 B4
Topolčani Macedonia 41°14N 21°25E 202 E5
Topol'čany Slovak Rep. 48°35N 18°12E 181 C11
Topolnitsa → Bulgaria 42°11N 24°18E 203 D8
Topolobampo Mexico 25°36N 109°3W 318 B3
Topoloveni Romania 44°49N 25°5E 183 F10
Topolovgrad Bulgaria 42°5N 26°20E 203 D10
Topolvățu Mare Romania 45°46N 21°41E 182 E6
Topozero, Ozero Russia 65°35N 32°0E 160 D25
Toppenish U.S.A. 46°23N 120°19W 304 C3
Topraisar Romania 44°1N 28°27E 183 F13
Toprakkale Turkey 37°5N 36°8E 250 A7
Topusko Croatia 45°18N 15°59E 199 C12
Toquepala Peru 17°24S 70°25W 330 D3
Toqyraūyn → Kazakhstan 46°48N 75°24E 217 C9
Tor di Quinto Italy 41°56N 12°27E 136 B1
Tor Pignattara Italy 41°53N 12°31E 136 B2
Tor Sapienza Italy 41°53N 12°35E 136 B2
Torà Spain 41°49N 1°25E 196 D6
Tora Kit South Sudan 11°2N 32°36E 257 E3
Toraka Vestale Madag. 16°20S 43°58E 272 B1
Toranomon Tokyo, Japan 140 c3
Torata Peru 17°23S 70°1W 330 D3
Torbalı Turkey 38°10N 27°21E 205 C9
Torbat-e Heydārīyeh Iran 35°15N 59°12E 247 C8
Torbat-e Jām Iran 35°16N 60°35E 247 C9
Torbay Canada 47°40N 52°42W 299 C9
Torbay □ U.K. 50°26N 3°31W 169 G4
Torberget Norway 61°8N 12°7E 164 C9
Torbjörntorp Sweden 58°12N 13°36E 163 F7
Torcy France 48°51N 2°39E 134 A4
Tordesillas Spain 41°30N 5°0W 194 D6
Töreboda Sweden 58°41N 14°7E 163 F8
Torekov Sweden 56°26N 12°37E 163 H6
Torellò Spain 42°3N 2°16E 196 C7
Toreno Spain 42°42N 6°30W 194 C4
Torfaen □ U.K. 51°43N 3°3W 169 F4
Torfajökull Iceland 63°54N 19°0W 155 D7
Torgau Germany 51°34N 13°0E 178 D8
Torgelow Germany 53°37N 14°1E 178 B10
Torghay Kazakhstan 49°38N 63°29E 216 C6
Torghay → Kazakhstan 48°1N 62°45E 216 C6
Torghay Ustirti Asia 51°0N 63°0E 216 B6
Torghay Zhylghasy Kazakhstan 52°0N 64°30E 216 B6
Torgovaya = Salsk Russia 46°28N 41°30E 191 G5
Torhamn Sweden 56°6N 15°50E 163 H9
Torhout Belgium 51°5N 3°7E 170 C3
Torhovytsya Ukraine 48°36N 25°26E 183 B10
Tori Ethiopia 7°53N 33°35E 257 F3
Tori-Shima Japan 30°29N 140°19E 221 J10
Torigni-sur-Vire France 49°3N 0°58W 172 C6
Torija Spain 40°44N 3°2W 196 E1
Torilla Pen. Australia 22°29S 150°5E 280 C5
Torino Italy 45°3N 7°40E 198 C4
Torit South Sudan 4°27N 32°31E 257 G3
Torkamān Iran 37°35N 47°23E 213 D12
Torkovichi Russia 58°51N 30°21E 188 C6
Tormac Romania 45°30N 21°30E 182 E6
Tormes → Spain 41°18N 6°29W 194 D4
Tornado Mt. Canada 49°55N 114°40W 296 D6
Tornal'a Slovak Rep. 48°25N 20°20E 181 C13
Torneå = Tornio Finland 65°50N 24°12E 160 D21
Torneälven → Europe 65°50N 24°12E 160 D21
Torneträsk Sweden 68°24N 19°15E 160 B18
Torngat Mts. Canada 59°0N 63°40W 295 F19
Tornio Finland 65°50N 24°12E 160 D21
Tornionjoki = Torneälven → Europe 65°50N 24°12E 160 D21
Tornquist Argentina 38°8S 62°15W 334 D3
Toro Baleares, Spain 39°59N 4°8E 206 B5
Toro Zamora, Spain 41°35N 5°24W 194 D5
Torö Sweden 58°48N 17°50E 163 F11
Toro, Cerro del Chile 29°10S 69°50W 334 B2
Toro ⌂ Uganda 1°5N 30°22E 268 C3
Toro Pk. U.S.A. 33°34N 116°24W 307 M10
Torodi Niger 13°7N 1°47E 263 C5
Torokina Papua N. G. 6°14S 155°3E 286 D8
Törökszentmiklós Hungary 47°11N 20°27E 182 C5
Toronto N.S.W., Australia 33°0S 151°30E 283 B9
Toronto Ont., Canada 43°39N 79°20W 141 B2
Toronto Ohio, U.S.A. 40°28N 80°36W 312 F4
Toronto, Univ. of Canada 43°39N 79°23W 141 B2
Toronto City Centre ✕ (YTZ) Canada 43°38N 79°24W 141 B2
Toronto Harbour Canada 43°38N 79°21W 141 B2
Toronto I. Canada 43°37N 79°23W 141 B2
Toronto Lester B. Pearson Int. ✕ (YYZ) Canada 43°46N 79°35W 141 A1
Toropets Russia 56°30N 31°40E 188 D6
Tororo Uganda 0°45N 34°12E 268 B3
Toros Dağları Turkey 37°0N 32°30E 250 B3
Toros Monumental, Templo de Barcelona, Spain 114 a3
Torotoro Bolivia 18°7S 65°46W 331 D4
Torotoro △ Bolivia 18°8S 65°46W 331 D4
Torpa India 22°57N 85°6E 243 H11
Torpo Norway 60°40N 8°43E 164 D5
Torquay Vic., Australia 38°20S 144°19E 282 E6
Torquay Torbay, U.K. 50°27N 3°32W 169 G4
Torquemada Spain 42°2N 4°19W 194 C6
Torrais, Pta. Azores 39°43N 31°7W 153 d2
Torrance U.S.A. 33°50N 118°20W 307 M8
Torrão Portugal 38°16N 8°11W 195 G2
Torre Annunziata Italy 40°45N 14°27E 201 B7
Torre de Moncorvo Portugal 41°12N 7°8W 194 D3
Torre del Campo Spain 37°46N 3°53W 195 H7
Torre del Greco Italy 40°47N 14°22E 201 B7
Torre del Mar Spain 36°44N 4°6W 195 J6
Torre Latino-americana Mexico City, Mexico 128 b2
Torre Lupara Italy 41°59N 12°39E 136 B2
Torre Nova Italy 41°51N 12°36E 136 B2
Torre-Pacheco Spain 37°44N 0°57W 197 H4
Torre Pellice Italy 44°49N 7°13E 198 D4
Torreblanca Spain 40°14N 0°12E 196 E5
Torrecampo Spain 38°29N 4°41W 195 G6
Torrecilla en Cameros Spain 42°15N 2°38W 196 C2
Torredembarra Spain 41°9N 1°24E 196 D6
Torredonjimeno Spain 37°46N 3°57W 195 H7
Torrejón de Ardoz Spain 40°27N 3°29W 194 E7
Torrejoncillo Spain 39°54N 6°28W 194 F4
Torrelaguna Spain 40°50N 3°38W 194 E7
Torrelavega Spain 43°20N 4°5W 194 B6
Torrellas → Spain 41°23N 2°1E 114 A1
Torremaggiore Italy 41°41N 15°17E 199 G12
Torremolinos Spain 36°38N 4°30W 195 J6
Torrens, L. Australia 31°0S 137°50E 282 A2
Torrens Cr. → Australia 22°23S 145°9E 280 C4

Torrens Creek *Australia* 20°48S 145°3E **280** C4
Torrent *Spain* 39°27N 0°28W **197** F4
Torrenueva *Spain* 38°38N 3°22W **195** G7
Torreón *Mexico* 25°33N 103°26W **318** B4
Torreperogil *Spain* 38°2N 3°17W **195** G7
Torres *Brazil* 29°21S 49°44W **335** B5
Torres *Mexico* 28°46N 110°47W **318** B2
Torres, Is. *Vanuatu* 13°15S 166°37E **287** C4
Torres del Paine △ *Chile* 51°3S 72°58W **336** D2
Torres Novas *Portugal* 39°27N 8°33W **195** F2
Torres Strait *Australia* 9°50S 142°20E **280** a
Torres Vedras *Portugal* 39°5N 9°15W **195** F1
Torrevécchia *Italy* 41°55N 12°25E **136** B1
Torrevieja *Spain* 37°59N 0°42W **197** H4
Torrey *U.S.A.* 38°18N 111°25W **304** G8
Torricelli Mts. *Papua N. G.* 3°23S 142°15E **286** B2
Torridge → *U.K.* 51°0N 4°13W **169** G3
Torridon, L. *U.K.* 57°35N 5°50W **167** D3
Torrijos *Phil.* 13°19N 122°5E **232** E4
Torrijos *Spain* 39°59N 4°18W **194** F6
Tørring *Denmark* 55°52N 9°29E **163** J3
Torrington *Conn., U.S.A.* 41°48N 73°7W **313** E11
Torrington *Wyo., U.S.A.* 42°4N 104°11W **304** E11
Torroella de Montgrí *Spain* 42°2N 3°8E **196** C8
Torrox *Spain* 36°46N 3°57W **195** J7
Torsås *Sweden* 56°24N 16°0E **163** H9
Torsby *Sweden* 60°7N 13°0E **162** D6
Torshälla *Sweden* 59°25N 16°28E **162** E10
Tórshavn *Færoe Is.* 62°5N 6°56W **160** E9
Torslanda *Sweden* 57°44N 11°45E **163** G5
Torsö *Sweden* 58°48N 13°45E **163** F7
Tortola *Br. Virgin Is.* 18°19N 64°45W **321** C7
Tórtoles de Esgueva *Spain* 41°49N 4°2W **194** D6
Tortolì *Italy* 39°55N 9°39E **200** C2
Tortona *Italy* 44°54N 8°52E **198** D5
Tortorici *Italy* 38°2N 14°49E **201** D7
Tortosa *Spain* 40°49N 0°31E **196** E5
Tortosa, C. *Spain* 40°41N 0°52E **196** E5
Tortosendo *Portugal* 40°15N 7°31W **194** E3
Tortue, Î. de la *Haiti* 20°5N 72°57W **321** B5
Tortuga *Trin. & Tob.* 10°22N 61°24W **323** t
Tortuguero △ *Costa Rica* 10°31N 83°29W **320** D3
Tortum *Turkey* 40°19N 41°35E **213** B9
Ţorūd *Iran* 35°25N 55°5E **247** C7
Torul *Turkey* 40°34N 39°18E **213** B8
Toruń *Poland* 53°2N 18°39E **185** E5
Torun *Ukraine* 48°40N 23°34E **183** B8
Tory Hill *Canada* 44°58N 78°16W **312** B6
Tory I. *Ireland* 55°16N 8°14W **166** A3
Torysa → *Slovak Rep.* 48°39N 21°21E **181** C14
Torzhok *Russia* 57°5N 34°55E **188** D8
Torzym *Poland* 52°19N 15°5E **185** F2
Tosa *Japan* 33°24N 133°23E **222** D5
Tosa-Shimizu *Japan* 32°52N 132°58E **222** E4
Tosa-Wan *Japan* 33°15N 133°30E **222** D5
Tosa-Yamada *Japan* 33°36N 133°38E **222** D5
Toscana □ *Italy* 43°25N 11°0E **198** E8
Toscanella = Tuscánia *Italy* 42°25N 11°52E **199** F8
Toscano, Arcipelago *Italy* 42°30N 10°30E **198** F7
Toshima *Japan* 35°43N 139°43E **140** A3
Toshimaen *Japan* 35°43N 139°38E **140** A2
Toshka *Egypt* 22°30N 31°53E **256** C3
Toshka Lakes *Egypt* 22°50N 31°0E **256** C3
Toshkent *Uzbekistan* 41°20N 69°10E **217** D7
Toshkent □ *Uzbekistan* 41°0N 69°40E **217** D7
Tosno *Russia* 59°38N 30°46E **188** C6
Tossa de Mar *Spain* 41°43N 2°56E **196** D7
Tösse *Sweden* 58°58N 12°39E **163** F6
Tostado *Argentina* 29°15S 61°50W **334** B3
Tostedt *Germany* 53°17N 9°42E **178** B5
Tostón, Pta. de *Canary Is.* 28°42N 14°2W **153** e2
Tosu *Japan* 33°22N 130°31E **222** D2
Tosya *Turkey* 41°1N 34°2E **212** B6
Toszek *Poland* 50°27N 18°32E **185** H5
Totak *Norway* 59°40N 8°0E **164** E5
Totana *Spain* 37°45N 1°30W **197** H3
Totebo *Sweden* 57°38N 16°12E **163** G10
Toteng *Botswana* 20°22S 22°58E **270** B3
Tôtes *France* 49°41N 1°2E **172** C8
Tótkomlós *Hungary* 46°24N 20°45E **182** D5
Totland *Norway* 61°56N 5°23E **164** C2
Totma *Russia* 60°0N 42°40E **186** C7
Totnes *U.K.* 50°26N 3°42W **169** G4
Totness *Suriname* 5°53N 56°19W **329** B6
Toto *Angola* 7°9S 14°16E **265** D2
Toto *Nigeria* 8°26N 7°5E **263** D6
Totonicapán *Guatemala* 14°58N 91°12W **320** D1
Totora *Bolivia* 17°42S 65°9W **331** D4
Totoya, I. *Fiji* 18°57S 179°50W **287** B3
Totten Glacier *Antarctica* 66°45S 116°10E **151** C8
Tottenham *N.S.W., Australia* 32°14S 147°21E **283** B7
Tottenham *Vic., Australia* 37°48S 144°51E **128** A1
Tottenham *Ont., Canada* 44°1N 79°49W **312** B5
Tottenham *London, U.K.* 51°35N 0°4W **125** A3
Tottori *Japan* 35°30N 134°15E **222** B6
Tottori □ *Japan* 35°30N 134°12E **222** B6
Touáret *Niger* 20°17N 7°8E **261** D6
Touat *Algeria* 27°27N 0°30E **261** C5
Touba *Ivory C.* 8°22N 7°40W **262** D3
Touba *Senegal* 14°50N 15°55W **262** C1
Toubkal, Djebel *Morocco* 31°0N 8°0W **260** B3
Toubkal △ *Morocco* 31°0N 8°2W **260** B3
Touboro *Cameroon* 7°47N 15°22E **264** A3
T'ouch'eng *Taiwan* 24°52N 121°49E **225** B3
Toucy *France* 47°44N 3°15E **173** E10
T'oufen *Taiwan* 24°41N 120°54E **225** B2
Tougan *Burkina Faso* 13°11N 2°58W **262** C4
Touggourt *Algeria* 33°6N 6°4E **261** B6
Tougouri *Burkina Faso* 13°20N 0°30W **263** C4
Tougué *Guinea* 11°25N 11°50W **262** C2
Toukoto *Mali* 13°27N 9°52W **262** C3
Toul *France* 48°40N 5°53E **173** D12
Toulepleu *Ivory C.* 6°32N 8°24W **262** D3
Touliu *Taiwan* 23°42N 120°31E **225** C2
Toulon *Var, France* 43°10N 5°55E **175** E9
Toulon *Ill., U.S.A.* 41°6N 89°52W **310** C7
Toulouse *France* 43°37N 1°27E **174** E5
Toulouse Blagnac ✈ (TLS) *France* 43°37N 1°22E **174** E5
Toulouse Street *New Orleans, U.S.A.* **131** b2
Toummo *Niger* 22°45N 14°8E **258** D2
Toummo, Mts. de *Africa* 22°43N 14°12E **258** D2
Toumodi *Ivory C.* 6°32N 5°4W **262** D3
Tounan *Taiwan* 23°41N 120°28E **225** C2
Tounassine, Hamada *Algeria* 28°48N 5°0W **260** C4
Toungo *Nigeria* 8°20N 12°3E **263** D7
Toungoo *Burma* 19°0N 96°30E **241** F6
Touques → *France* 49°22N 0°8E **172** C7
Touraine *France* 47°20N 0°30E **172** E7
Tourane = Da Nang *Vietnam* 16°4N 108°13E **236** D7
Tourcoing *France* 50°42N 3°10E **173** B10
Touriñán, C. *Spain* 43°3N 9°18W **194** B1
Tourîne *Mauritania* 22°23N 11°50W **260** D2
Tournai *Belgium* 50°35N 3°25E **170** D3
Tournan-en-Brie *France* 48°44N 2°46E **173** D9
Tournay *France* 43°13N 0°13E **174** E4
Tournon-St-Martin *France* 46°45N 0°58E **172** F7
Tournon-sur-Rhône *France* 45°4N 4°50E **175** C8
Tournus *France* 46°35N 4°54E **173** F11
Touros *Brazil* 5°12S 35°28W **332** C4
Tours *France* 47°22N 0°40E **172** E7
Tousidé, Pic *Chad* 21°1N 16°29E **259** D3
Toussoro, Mt. *C.A.R.* 9°7N 23°14E **264** A4
Toussus-le-Noble *France* 48°44N 2°6E **134** B1
Toussus-le-Noble ✈ (TNF) *France* 48°44N 2°6E **134** B1
Touws → *S. Africa* 33°45S 21°11E **270** D3
Touwsrivier *S. Africa* 33°20S 20°2E **270** D3
Tovar *Venezuela* 8°20N 71°46W **328** B3
Tovarkovskiy *Russia* 53°40N 38°14E **188** F10
Tovdal *Norway* 58°47N 8°10E **164** F5
Tovdalselva → *Norway* 58°11N 8°7E **164** F5
Tovste *Ukraine* 48°50N 25°44E **183** B10
Tovuz *Azerbaijan* 41°0N 45°40E **191** K7
Towada *Japan* 40°37N 141°13E **220** D10
Towada-Hachimantai △ *Japan* 40°20N 140°55E **220** D10
Towada-Ko *Japan* 40°28N 140°55E **220** D10
Towanda *Ill., U.S.A.* 40°36N 88°53W **311** D8
Towanda *Pa., U.S.A.* 41°46N 76°27W **313** E8
Towarri △ *Australia* 31°50S 150°37E **283** A9
Towchāl Cable Car *Iran* 35°49N 51°24E **141** A2
Tower *U.S.A.* 47°48N 92°17W **308** B7
Tower, I. = Genovesa, I. *Ecuador* 0°20N 89°58W **330** a
Tower Bridge *London, U.K.* **125** b5
Tower Hamlets □ *U.K.* 51°32N 0°2W **125** A3
Tower of London *U.K.* 51°30N 0°4W **125** A3
Towerhill Cr. → *Australia* 22°28S 144°35E **280** C3
Towner *U.S.A.* 48°21N 100°25W **308** A3
Townsend *Ga., U.S.A.* 31°33N 81°31W **316** D8
Townsend *Mont., U.S.A.* 46°19N 111°31W **304** C8
Townshend I. *Australia* 22°10S 150°31E **280** C5
Townsville *Australia* 19°15S 146°45E **280** B4
Towot *South Sudan* 6°12N 34°25E **257** F3
Towra Pt. *Australia* 34°0S 151°10E **139** C2
Towraghondī *Afghan.* 35°13N 62°16E **240** B1
Towson *U.S.A.* 39°24N 76°36W **309** F15
Towuti, Danau *Indonesia* 2°45S 121°32E **231** E6
Toxkan He → *China* 41°8N 80°11E **217** D10
Tōya-Ko *Japan* 42°35N 140°51E **220** C10
Toyama *Japan* 36°40N 137°15E **223** A9
Toyama □ *Japan* 36°45N 137°30E **223** A9
Toyama-Wan *Japan* 37°0N 137°30E **221** F8
Toyapakeh *Indonesia* 8°41S 115°29E **231** K18
Tøyen *Norway* 59°55N 10°47E **133** A3
Tōyō *Ehime, Japan* 33°56N 133°5E **222** D5
Tōyō *Kōchi, Japan* 33°26N 134°16E **222** D6
Toyohara = Yuzhno-Sakhalinsk *Russia* 46°58N 142°45E **219** B17
Toyohashi *Japan* 34°45N 137°25E **223** C9
Toyokawa *Japan* 34°48N 137°27E **223** C9
Toyonaka *Japan* 34°46N 135°28E **133** A1
Toyooka *Japan* 35°35N 134°48E **222** B6
Toyota *Japan* 35°3N 137°7E **223** B9
Toyoura *Japan* 34°6N 130°57E **222** C2
Tozeur *Tunisia* 33°56N 8°8E **258** B1
Tozeur □ *Tunisia* 34°0N 8°5E **261** B6
Tqibuli *Georgia* 42°26N 43°0E **191** J6
Tqvarcheli *Georgia* 42°47N 41°42E **191** J5
Trá Lí = Tralee *Ireland* 52°16N 9°42W **166** D2
Trá Mhór = Tramore *Ireland* 52°10N 7°10W **166** D4
Tra On *Vietnam* 9°58N 105°55E **237** H5
Tra Vinh *Vietnam* 9°50N 106°15E **237** H6
Trabancos → *Spain* 41°36N 5°15W **194** D5
Traben-Trarbach *Germany* 49°57N 7°7E **179** F3
Trabzon *Turkey* 41°0N 39°45E **213** B8
Trabzon □ *Turkey* 41°10N 39°45E **213** B8
Tracadie *Canada* 47°30N 64°55W **299** C7
Trachenburg = Żmigród *Poland* 51°28N 16°53E **185** G3
Tracy *Qué., Canada* 46°1N 73°9W **298** C5
Tracy *Calif., U.S.A.* 37°44N 121°26W **306** H5
Tracy *Minn., U.S.A.* 44°14N 95°37W **308** C6
Tradate *Italy* 45°43N 8°54E **198** C5
Trade Town *Liberia* 5°40N 9°50W **262** D3
Traer *U.S.A.* 42°12N 92°28W **310** B4
Trafalgar *Vic., Australia* 38°14S 146°12E **283** E7
Trafalgar *Dominica* 15°19N 61°21W **323** k
Trafalgar, C. *Spain* 36°10N 6°2W **195** J4
Trafalgar Square *London, U.K.* **125** b3
Trafaria *Portugal* 38°40N 9°13W **126** A1
Tragonhsi *Greece* 37°27N 25°29E **205** D7
Traian *Brăila, Romania* 45°11N 27°44E **183** E12
Traian *Tulcea, Romania* 45°2N 28°15E **183** E13
Traição, Cor. → *Brazil* 23°35S 46°41W **137** B2
Traiguén *Chile* 38°15S 72°41W **336** A2
Trail *Canada* 49°5N 117°40W **296** D5
Traill Ø *Greenland* 72°30N 23°0W **154** C8
Traimit *Bangkok, Thailand* **113** c2
Trainor L. *Canada* 60°24N 120°17W **296** A4
Traíra → *Brazil* 1°4S 69°26W **328** D4
Trakai △ *Lithuania* 54°30N 25°10E **161** J21
Trákhonas *Cyprus* 35°12N 33°21E **207** E9
Tralee *Ireland* 52°16N 9°42W **166** D2
Tralee B. *Ireland* 52°17N 9°55W **166** D2
Tram Chim △ *Vietnam* 10°43N 105°31E **237** G5
Tramore *Ireland* 52°10N 7°10W **166** D4
Tramore B. *Ireland* 52°9N 7°10W **166** D4
Tramuntana, Serra de *Spain* 39°48N 2°54E **206** B3
Tran Ninh, Cao Nguyen *Laos* 19°30N 103°10E **236** C4
Tranås *Sweden* 58°3N 14°59E **163** F8
Tranbjerg *Denmark* 56°6N 10°9E **163** H4
Tranby *Norway* 59°49N 10°15E **164** E7
Trancas *Argentina* 26°11S 65°20W **334** B2
Trancoso *Portugal* 40°49N 7°21W **194** E3
Tranebjerg *Denmark* 55°51N 10°36E **163** J4
Tranegilde *Denmark* 55°37N 12°20E **118** B2
Tranemo *Sweden* 57°30N 13°20E **163** G7
Trang *Thailand* 7°33N 99°38E **237** J2
Trangahy *Madag.* 19°7S 44°31E **272** B1
Trangan *Indonesia* 6°40S 134°20E **231** F8
Trangie *Australia* 32°4S 148°0E **283** B8
Trångsund *Sweden* 59°13N 18°8E **139** B2
Trångsviken *Sweden* 63°19N 13°59E **162** A7
Trani *Italy* 41°17N 16°25E **201** A9
Tranoroa *Madag.* 24°42S 45°4E **272** C2
Tranqueras *Uruguay* 31°13S 55°45W **335** C4
Trans-Alaska Pipeline *U.S.A.* 70°11N 148°27W **303** A10
Transamerica Pyramid *San Francisco, U.S.A.* **136** b2
Transantarctic Mts. *Antarctica* 85°0S 170°0W **151** E12
Transbay Terminal *San Francisco, U.S.A.* **136** b3
Transcarpathia = Zakarpattya □ *Ukraine* 48°20N 23°20E **183** B8
Transilvania *Romania* 46°30N 24°0E **183** D9
Transilvanian Alps = Carpaţii Meridionali *Romania* 45°30N 25°0E **183** E9
Transjordan = Jordan ■ *Asia* 31°0N 36°0E **251** H7
Transnistria = Stînga Nistrului □ *Moldova* 47°20N 29°15E **183** C14
Transtrand *Sweden* 61°6N 13°20E **162** C7
Transtrandsfjällen *Sweden* 61°8N 13°0E **162** C6
Transylvania = Transilvania *Romania* 46°30N 24°0E **183** D9
Trants Bay *Montserrat* 16°46N 62°9W **323** p
Trápani *Italy* 38°1N 12°29E **200** D5
Trappenfelde *Germany* 52°34N 13°39E **115** A4
Trapper Pk. *U.S.A.* 45°54N 114°18W **304** D6
Traralgon *Australia* 38°12S 146°34E **283** E7
Traryd *Sweden* 56°35N 13°45E **163** H7
Trarza □ *Mauritania* 18°0N 15°0W **260** E2
Trás-os-Montes = Cucumbi *Angola* 10°17S 19°5E **265** E3
Trasacco *Italy* 41°57N 13°32E **199** G10
Trăscău, Munţii *Romania* 46°14N 23°14E **183** D8
Trasimeno, L. *Italy* 43°8N 12°6E **199** E9
Träslövsläge *Sweden* 57°4N 12°16E **163** G6
Trastévere *Italy* 41°53N 12°28E **136** B1
Trasvase Tajo-Segura, Canal de *Spain* 40°15N 2°55W **196** E2
Trat *Thailand* 12°14N 102°33E **237** F4
Tratani → *Pakistan* 29°19N 68°20E **242** E3
Traun *Austria* 48°14N 14°15E **180** C7
Traunreut *Germany* 47°57N 12°36E **179** H8
Traunsee *Austria* 47°55N 13°50E **180** D6
Traunstein *Germany* 47°52N 12°37E **179** H8
Travellers L. *Australia* 33°20S 142°0E **282** B5
Travemünde *Germany* 53°57N 10°52E **178** B6
Travers, Mt. *N.Z.* 42°1S 172°45E **285** C7
Traverse City *U.S.A.* 44°46N 85°38W **309** C11
Travis, L. *U.S.A.* 30°24N 97°55W **314** F6
Travnik *Bos.-H.* 44°17N 17°39E **182** F2
Trawbreaga B. *Ireland* 55°20N 7°25W **166** A4
Trbovlje *Slovenia* 46°12N 15°5E **199** B12
Treasure I. *U.S.A.* 37°49N 122°22W **136** B2
Treasure Island *U.S.A.* 27°46N 82°46W **317** H7
Treasury Is. *Solomon Is.* 7°22S 155°37E **287** L8
Trébbia → *Italy* 45°4N 9°41E **198** C6
Trebel → *Germany* 53°54N 13°2E **178** B9
Trébeurden *France* 48°46N 3°35W **172** D3
Trebević △ *Bos.-H.* 43°20N 18°45E **182** G3
Třebíč *Czech Rep.* 49°14N 15°55E **180** B8
Trebinje *Bos.-H.* 42°44N 18°22E **202** D2
Trebisacce *Italy* 39°52N 16°32E **201** C9
Trebišnjica → *Bos.-H.* 42°47N 18°8E **202** D2
Trebišov *Slovak Rep.* 48°38N 21°41E **181** C14
Trebitsch = Třebíč *Czech Rep.* 49°14N 15°55E **180** B8
Trebižat → *Bos.-H.* 43°15N 17°30E **199** E14
Trebnitz = Trzebnica *Poland* 51°20N 17°1E **185** G4
Trebnje *Slovenia* 45°54N 15°1E **199** C12
Třeboň *Czech Rep.* 49°1N 14°48E **180** B7
Trebonne *Australia* 18°37S 146°5E **280** B4
Třeboňsko ⌓ *Czech Rep.* 49°1N 14°49E **180** B7
Třeboradice *Czech Rep.* 50°9N 14°31E **135** B3
Třebotov *Czech Rep.* 49°58N 14°17E **135** C1
Trebujena *Spain* 36°52N 6°11W **195** J4
Trecate *Italy* 45°26N 8°44E **198** C5
Tregaron *U.K.* 52°14N 3°56W **169** E4
Tregnago *Italy* 45°31N 11°10E **199** C8
Tregrosse Is. *Australia* 17°41S 150°43E **280** B5
Tréguier *France* 48°47N 3°16W **172** D3
Trégunc *France* 47°51N 3°51W **172** E3
Treherne *Canada* 49°38N 98°42W **297** D9
Tréia *Italy* 43°19N 13°19E **199** E10
Treignac *France* 45°32N 1°48E **174** C5
Treinta y Tres *Uruguay* 33°16S 54°17W **335** C5
Treis-karden *Germany* 50°10N 7°18E **179** E3
Treklyano *Bulgaria* 42°33N 22°36E **202** D6
Trelawney *Zimbabwe* 17°30S 30°30E **271** A5
Trélazé *France* 47°26N 0°30W **172** E6
Trelew *Argentina* 43°10S 65°20W **336** B3
Trélissac *France* 45°11N 0°47E **174** C4
Trelleborg *Sweden* 55°20N 13°10E **163** J7
Tremadog Bay *U.K.* 52°51N 4°18W **168** E3
Tremblay-en-France *France* 48°56N 2°35E **134** A4
Tremblet *Réunion* 21°17S 55°48E **272** f
Trembowla = Terebovlya *Ukraine* 49°18N 25°44E **177** D13
Tremedal = Monte Azul *Brazil* 15°9S 42°53W **333** E3
Tremembe → *Brazil* 23°27S 46°34W **137** A2
Trémiti *Italy* 42°8N 15°30E **199** F12
Tremont *U.S.A.* 40°50N 73°52W **132** A2
Tremonton *U.S.A.* 41°43N 112°10W **304** F7
Tremp *Spain* 42°10N 0°52E **196** C5
Trenche → *Canada* 47°46N 72°53W **298** C5
Trenčiansky □ *Slovak Rep.* 48°45N 18°20E **181** C11
Trenčín *Slovak Rep.* 48°52N 18°4E **181** C11
Trengereid *Norway* 60°26N 5°37E **164** D2
Trenggalek *Indonesia* 8°3S 111°43E **235** D4
Trenno *Italy* 45°29N 9°6E **129** B1
Trenque Lauquen *Argentina* 36°5S 62°45W **334** D3
Trent → *Ont., Canada* 44°6N 77°34W **312** B7
Trent → *England, U.K.* 53°41N 0°42W **168** D7
Trentino-Alto Adige □ *Italy* 46°30N 11°20E **199** B8
Trento *Italy* 46°4N 11°8E **198** B8
Trento *Agusan del S., Phil.* 8°3N 126°2E **233** G6
Trenton *Ont., Canada* 44°10N 77°34W **312** B7
Trenton *Fla., U.S.A.* 29°37N 82°49W **317** F7
Trenton *Mich., U.S.A.* 42°8N 83°11W **311** B13
Trenton *Mo., U.S.A.* 40°5N 93°37W **310** D3
Trenton *N.J., U.S.A.* 40°14N 74°46W **313** F10
Trenton *Nebr., U.S.A.* 40°11N 101°1W **308** E3
Trenton *Ohio, U.S.A.* 39°29N 84°28W **311** E12
Trenton *S.C., U.S.A.* 33°45N 81°51W **316** B8
Trepassey *Canada* 46°43N 53°25W **299** C9
Treptow *Germany* 52°29N 13°27E **115** B3
Treptow an der Rega = Trzebiatów *Poland* 54°3N 15°18E **184** D2
Trepuzzi *Italy* 40°24N 18°4E **201** B11
Tres Arroyos *Argentina* 38°26S 60°20W **334** D3
Três Casas *Brazil* 6°59S 62°41W **331** B5
Três Corações *Brazil* 21°44S 45°15W **333** F2
Tres Equinas *Colombia* 0°43N 75°16W **328** C2
Três Lagoas *Brazil* 20°50S 51°43W **333** F1
Tres Lagos *Argentina* 49°35S 71°25W **336** C2
Tres Lomas *Argentina* 36°27S 62°51W **334** D3
Três Marias, Represa *Brazil* 18°12S 45°15W **333** E2
Tres Montes, C. *Chile* 46°50S 75°30W **336** C1
Tres Pinos *U.S.A.* 36°48N 121°19W **306** J5
Três Pontas *Brazil* 21°23S 45°29W **333** F2
Três Pontas, C. das *Angola* 10°28S 13°32E **265** E2
Tres Puentes *Chile* 27°50S 70°15W **334** B1
Tres Puntas, C. *Argentina* 47°0S 66°0W **336** C3
Três Rios *Brazil* 22°6S 43°15W **333** F3
Três Rios, Sa. dos *Brazil* 22°56S 43°17W **135** B1
Tres Valles *Mexico* 18°15N 96°8W **319** D5
Tresco *U.K.* 49°57N 6°20W **169** H1
Tresfjord *Norway* 62°31N 7°7E **164** B4
Treska → *Macedonia* 42°0N 21°20E **202** E5
Treskavica *Bos.-H.* 43°40N 18°20E **182** G3
Trespaderne *Spain* 42°47N 3°24W **194** C7
Tresticklan △ *Sweden* 59°0N 11°42E **163** F5
Trets *France* 43°27N 5°41E **175** E9
Treuburg = Olecko *Poland* 54°2N 22°31E **184** D9
Treuchtlingen *Germany* 48°58N 10°54E **179** G6
Treuenbrietzen *Germany* 52°5N 12°52E **178** C8
Treungen *Norway* 59°1N 8°31E **164** E5
Trèves = Trier *Germany* 49°45N 6°38E **179** F2
Trevi *Italy* 42°52N 12°45E **199** F9
Trevi, Fontana di *Rome, Italy* **136** b3
Trevíglio *Italy* 45°31N 9°35E **198** C6
Trevínca, Peña *Spain* 42°15N 6°46W **194** C4
Treviso *Italy* 45°40N 12°15E **199** C9
Trévoux *France* 45°57N 4°47E **175** C8
Trezzano sul Navíglio *Italy* 45°24N 9°4E **129** B1
Trgovište *Serbia* 42°20N 22°10E **202** D6
Triabunna *Australia* 42°30S 147°55E **281** G4
Trianda = Ialissos *Greece* 36°24N 28°10E **206** E12
Trianda *Greece* 36°25N 28°10E **206** E12
Triangle *Zimbabwe* 21°2S 31°28E **271** B5
Triaucourt-en-Argonne *France* 48°59N 5°2E **173** D12
Tribal Areas □ *Pakistan* 33°0N 70°0E **242** C4
Tribsees *Germany* 54°5N 12°44E **178** A8
Tribugá, G. de *Colombia* 5°45N 77°20W **328** B2
Tribulation, C. *Australia* 16°5S 145°29E **280** B4
Tribune *U.S.A.* 38°28N 101°45W **308** F3
Tribune Tower *Chicago, U.S.A.* **119** b2
Tricárico *Italy* 40°37N 16°9E **201** B9
Tricase *Italy* 39°56N 18°22E **201** C11
Trichinopoly = Tiruchchirappalli *India* 10°45N 78°45E **245** J4
Trichonida, L. *Greece* 38°34N 21°30E **204** C3
Trichur *India* 10°30N 76°18E **245** J3
Trichy = Tiruchchirappalli *India* 10°45N 78°45E **245** J4
Trida *Australia* 33°1S 145°1E **283** B6
Trier *Germany* 49°45N 6°38E **179** F2
Trieste *Lazio, Italy* 41°55N 12°30E **136** B2
Trieste *Trieste, Italy* 45°40N 13°46E **199** C10
Trieste, G. di *Italy* 45°40N 13°35E **199** C10
Trieux → *France* 48°43N 3°9W **172** D3
Triggiano *Italy* 41°4N 16°55E **201** A9
Triglav *Slovenia* 46°21N 13°50E **199** B10
Triglavski △ *Slovenia* 46°20N 13°50E **199** B10
Trigno → *Italy* 42°4N 14°48E **199** F11
Trigo de Morais = Guijá *Mozam.* 24°27S 33°0E **271** B5
Trigueros *Spain* 37°24N 6°50W **195** H4
Trikala *Greece* 39°34N 21°47E **204** B3
Trikala □ *Greece* 39°41N 21°30E **204** B3
Trikeri *Greece* 39°6N 23°5E **204** B5
Trikomo *Cyprus* 35°17N 33°52E **207** E9
Trikora, Puncak *Indonesia* 4°15S 138°45E **231** E9
Trilby *U.S.A.* 28°28N 82°12W **317** G7
Trilj *Croatia* 43°38N 16°42E **199** E13
Trillo *Spain* 40°42N 2°35W **196** E2
Trim *Ireland* 53°33N 6°48W **166** C5
Trimbak *India* 19°56N 73°33E **244** E1
Trimmu Dam *Pakistan* 31°10N 72°8E **242** D5
Trincomalee *Sri Lanka* 8°38N 81°15E **245** K5
Trindade *Atl. Oc.* 20°20S 29°50W **152** J9
Trindade *Brazil* 16°40S 49°30W **333** E2
Třinec *Czech Rep.* 49°41N 18°39E **181** B11
Trinidad = Jose Abad Santos *Phil.* 5°55N 125°39E **233** J5
Trinidad *Bolivia* 14°46S 64°50W **331** C5
Trinidad *Colombia* 5°25N 71°40W **328** B3
Trinidad *Cuba* 21°48N 80°0W **320** B4
Trinidad *Trin. & Tob.* 10°30N 61°15W **323** t
Trinidad *Uruguay* 33°30S 56°50W **334** C4
Trinidad *Colo., U.S.A.* 37°10N 104°31W **305** H11
Trinidad *D.C., U.S.A.* 38°54N 76°59W **143** B4
Trinidad → *Mexico* 17°49N 95°9W **319** D5
Trinidad, G. *Chile* 49°55S 75°25W **336** C1
Trinidad, I. *Argentina* 39°10S 62°0W **336** A4
Trinidad & Tobago ■ *W. Indies* 10°30N 61°20W **323** t
Trinitápoli *Italy* 41°21N 16°5E **201** A9
Trinité, Havre de *Martinique* 14°44N 60°58W **322** j
Trinity *Nfld. & L., Canada* 48°59N 53°55W **299** C9
Trinity *Edinburgh, U.K.* 55°58N 3°12W **121** B2
Trinity *Tex., U.S.A.* 30°57N 95°22W **314** F7
Trinity → *Calif., U.S.A.* 41°11N 123°42W **304** F2
Trinity → *Tex., U.S.A.* 29°45N 94°43W **314** G7
Trinity B. *Canada* 48°20N 53°10W **299** C9
Trinity Church *New York, U.S.A.* **132** f1
Trinity College *Dublin, Ireland* **120** c3
Trinity Hills *Trin. & Tob.* 10°7N 61°7W **323** t
Trinity Is. *U.S.A.* 56°33N 154°25W **303** H9
Trinity Range *U.S.A.* 40°10N 118°40W **304** F4
Trinkat *India* 8°5N 93°30E **245** K11
Trinkitat *Sudan* 18°45N 37°51E **256** D4
Trino *Italy* 45°12N 8°18E **198** C5
Trinway *U.S.A.* 40°9N 82°1W **312** F2
Triolet *Mauritius* 20°4S 57°32E **272** e
Trionfale *Italy* 41°54N 12°26E **136** B1
Trionto, C. *Italy* 39°37N 16°43E **201** C9
Triora *Italy* 44°1N 7°46E **198** D4
Tripoli = Tarābulus *Lebanon* 34°31N 35°50E **250** D6
Tripoli = Tarābulus *Libya* 32°49N 13°7E **258** B2
Tripoli *Greece* 37°31N 22°25E **204** D4
Tripoli *Iowa, U.S.A.* 42°49N 92°16W **310** B4
Tripolitania = Tarābulus *N. Afr.* 31°0N 13°0E **258** B2
Tripura □ *India* 24°0N 92°0E **241** D4
Tripylos *Cyprus* 34°59N 32°41E **207** F8
Trischen *Germany* 54°4N 8°40E **178** A4
Tristan da Cunha *Atl. Oc.* 37°6S 12°20W **255** K2
Trisul *India* 30°19N 79°47E **243** D8
Triulzo *Italy* 45°25N 9°16E **129** B2
Trivandrum *India* 8°41N 77°0E **245** K3
Trivento *Italy* 41°47N 14°33E **199** G11
Trizin *Greece* 37°25N 23°15E **204** D5
Trnava *Slovak Rep.* 48°23N 17°35E **181** C10
Trnavský □ *Slovak Rep.* 48°30N 17°45E **181** C10
Troarn *France* 49°11N 0°11W **172** C6
Trobriand Is. *Papua N. G.* 8°30S 151°0E **286** E6
Trocadero *Paris, France* **134** b1
Trochu *Canada* 51°50N 113°13W **296** C6
Trodely I. *Canada* 52°15N 79°26W **298** B4
Troebratskīy *Kazakhstan* 54°25N 66°4E **217** B7
Trogir *Croatia* 43°32N 16°15E **199** E13
Troglav *Croatia* 43°56N 16°36E **199** E13
Tróia *Italy* 41°22N 15°18E **201** A8
Troilus, L. *Canada* 50°50N 74°35W **298** B5
Troina *Italy* 37°47N 14°36E **201** E7
Trois Boutiques *Mauritius* 20°26S 57°38E **272** e
Trois Fourches, Cap des *Morocco* 35°26N 2°58W **261** A4
Trois-Pistoles *Canada* 48°5N 69°10W **299** C6
Trois Pitons, Morne *Dominica* 15°22N 61°20W **323** k
Trois-Rivières *Qué., Canada* 46°25N 72°34W **298** C5
Trois-Rivières *Guadeloupe* 15°57N 61°40W **322** e
Trois Rivières *Martinique* 14°28N 60°58W **322** j
Troisdorf *Germany* 50°48N 7°11E **178** E3
Troitse-Lykovo *Russia* 55°47N 37°23E **129** B2
Troitsk *Russia* 54°10N 61°35E **216** B6
Troitsko Pechorsk *Russia* 62°40N 56°10E **186** B10
Troitskosavsk = Kyakhta *Russia* 50°30N 106°25E **215** D11
Troitskoye *Russia* 46°26N 44°15E **191** G7
Troitsky = Troitsk *Russia* 54°10N 61°35E **216** B6
Troja *Czech Rep.* 50°7N 14°25E **135** B2
Trölladyngja *Iceland* 64°54N 17°16W **155** C9
Trollbäcken *Sweden* 59°14N 18°12E **139** B3
Trollhättan *Sweden* 58°17N 12°20E **163** F6
Trollheimen *Norway* 62°46N 9°1E **164** B6
Trombay *India* 19°2N 72°56E **130** A2
Trombetas → *Brazil* 1°55S 55°35W **329** D6
Tromelin I. *Ind. Oc.* 15°52S 54°25E **273** F4
Tromøy *Norway* 58°27N 8°51E **164** F5
Tromsø *Norway* 69°40N 18°56E **160** B18
Tron *Thailand* 17°28N 100°7E **236** D3
Trona *U.S.A.* 35°46N 117°23W **307** K9
Tronador, Mte. *Argentina* 41°10S 71°50W **336** B2
Trøndelag *Norway* 64°17N 11°50E **160** D14
Trondheim *Norway* 63°36N 10°25E **164** A7
Trondheimsfjorden *Norway* 63°35N 10°30E **160** E14
Trondheimsleia *Norway* 63°25N 8°30E **164** A5
Trondhjem = Trondheim *Norway* 63°36N 10°25E **164** A7
Trönninge *Sweden* 56°37N 12°51E **163** H6
Tronto → *Italy* 42°54N 13°55E **199** F10
Troodos *Cyprus* 34°55N 32°52E **207** F8
Troon *U.K.* 55°33N 4°39W **167** F4
Troparevo *Russia* 55°39N 37°29E **129** C2
Tropea *Italy* 38°41N 15°54E **201** D8
Tropic *U.S.A.* 37°37N 112°5W **305** H7
Tropojë *Albania* 42°23N 20°10E **202** D4
Troppau = Opava *Czech Rep.* 49°57N 17°58E **181** B10
Trosa *Sweden* 58°54N 17°33E **163** F11
Trostan *U.K.* 55°3N 6°10W **166** A5
Trostberg *Germany* 48°1N 12°33E **179** G8
Trostyanets *Sumy, Ukraine* 50°33N 34°59E **189** G8
Trostyanets *Vinnyts'ka, Ukraine* 48°31N 29°11E **183** B14
Trotsk = Chapayevsk *Russia* 53°0N 49°40E **190** D9
Trotsk = Gatchina *Russia* 59°35N 30°9E **188** C6
Trou Gras Pt. *St. Lucia* 13°51N 60°53W **323** m
Troumaka *St. Vincent* 13°18N 61°17W **323** n
Trout → *Canada* 61°19N 119°51W **296** A5
Trout L. *N.W.T., Canada* 60°40N 121°14W **296** A4
Trout L. *Ont., Canada* 51°20N 93°15W **297** C10
Trout Lake *N.W.T., Canada* 56°30N 114°32W **296** B6
Trout Lake *Wash., U.S.A.* 46°0N 121°32W **306** E5
Trout River *Canada* 49°29N 58°8W **299** C8
Trout Run *U.S.A.* 41°23N 77°3W **312** E7
Trouville-sur-Mer *France* 49°21N 0°5E **172** C7
Trowbridge *U.K.* 51°18N 2°12W **169** F5
Troy *Turkey* 39°57N 26°12E **205** B8
Troy *Ala., U.S.A.* 31°48N 85°58W **316** D4
Troy *Ill., U.S.A.* 38°44N 89°54W **310** F7
Troy *Ind., U.S.A.* 37°59N 86°55W **311** G10
Troy *Kans., U.S.A.* 39°47N 95°5W **308** F6
Troy *Mich., U.S.A.* 42°37N 83°9W **311** B13
Troy *Mo., U.S.A.* 38°59N 90°59W **310** F6
Troy *Mont., U.S.A.* 48°28N 115°53W **304** B6
Troy *N.Y., U.S.A.* 42°44N 73°41W **313** D11
Troy *Ohio, U.S.A.* 40°2N 84°12W **311** D12
Troy *Pa., U.S.A.* 41°47N 76°47W **313** E8
Troyan *Bulgaria* 42°57N 24°43E **203** D8
Troyes *France* 48°19N 4°3E **173** D11
Trpanj *Croatia* 43°1N 17°15E **199** E14
Trstenik *Serbia* 43°36N 21°0E **202** C5
Trubchevsk *Russia* 52°33N 33°47E **189** F7
Truchas Pk. *U.S.A.* 35°58N 105°39W **305** J11
Trucial States = United Arab Emirates ■ *Asia* 23°50N 54°0E **247** F7
Truckee *U.S.A.* 39°20N 120°11W **306** F6
Trudeau, Montréal ✈ (YUL) *Canada* 45°28N 73°44W **130** B1
Trudfront *Russia* 45°56N 47°40E **191** H8
Trudovoye *Russia* 43°17N 132°5E **220** C6
Trudyashchikhsya, Ostrov *Russia* 59°58N 30°18E **137** B1
Trujillo *Colombia* 4°10N 76°19W **328** C2
Trujillo *Honduras* 16°0N 86°0W **320** C2
Trujillo *Peru* 8°6S 79°0W **330** B2
Trujillo *Spain* 39°28N 5°55W **195** F5
Trujillo *N. Mex., U.S.A.* 35°32N 104°42W **305** J11
Trujillo *Venezuela* 9°22N 70°38W **328** B3
Trujillo □ *Venezuela* 9°25N 70°30W **328** B3
Trujillo, Mte. = Duarte, Pico *Dom. Rep.* 19°2N 70°59W **321** C5
Trujillo Alto *Puerto Rico* 18°21N 66°1W **321** b
Truk *Micronesia* 7°25N 151°46E **287** T17
Trumann *U.S.A.* 35°41N 90°31W **315** D9
Trumansburg *U.S.A.* 42°33N 76°40W **313** D8
Trumbull, Mt. *U.S.A.* 36°25N 113°19W **305** H7
Trŭn *Bulgaria* 42°51N 22°38E **202** D6
Trun *Orne, France* 48°50N 0°2E **172** D7
Trundle *Australia* 32°53S 147°35E **283** B7
Trung Lon, Hon *Vietnam* 8°36N 106°8E **237** H6
Trung-Phan *Vietnam* 17°0N 109°0E **236** D6
Truro *S. Austral., Australia* 34°24S 139°9E **282** C3
Truro *N.S., Canada* 45°21N 63°14W **299** C7
Truro *Corn., U.K.* 50°16N 5°4W **169** G2
Trus Madi, Gunung *Malaysia* 5°33N 116°31E **235** A5
Truskavets *Ukraine* 49°17N 23°30E **177** D12
Trŭstenik *Bulgaria* 43°31N 24°28E **203** C8
Trustrup *Denmark* 56°20N 10°46E **163** H4
Trutch *Canada* 57°44N 122°57W **296** B4
Truth or Consequences *U.S.A.* 33°8N 107°15W **305** K10
Trutnov *Czech Rep.* 50°37N 15°54E **180** A8
Truyère → *France* 44°38N 2°34E **174** D6
Tryavna *Bulgaria* 42°54N 25°25E **203** D9
Tryonville *U.S.A.* 41°42N 79°48W **312** E5
Tryphena *N.Z.* 36°18S 175°28E **284** C4
Trysilelva → *Norway* 61°2N 12°35E **164** C9
Tryvasshøgda *Norway* 59°59N 10°40E **133** A3
Trzcianka *Poland* 53°3N 16°25E **185** E3
Trzciel *Poland* 52°23N 15°50E **185** F2
Trzcińsko Zdrój *Poland* 52°58N 14°35E **185** F1
Trzebiatów *Poland* 54°3N 15°18E **184** D2
Trzebiez *Poland* 53°38N 14°31E **184** E1
Trzebnica *Poland* 51°20N 17°1E **185** G4
Trzemeszno *Poland* 52°33N 17°48E **185** F4
Tržič *Slovenia* 46°22N 14°18E **199** B11
Tsagaannur *Mongolia* 49°32N 89°42E **217** C11
Tsagan Aman *Russia* 47°34N 46°43E **191** G8
Tsala Apopka L. *U.S.A.* 28°53N 82°19W **317** G7
Tsamandas *Greece* 39°46N 20°21E **204** B2
Tsamkong = Zhanjiang *China* 21°15N 110°20E **229** G8
Tsandi *Namibia* 17°42S 14°50E **270** A1
Tsangpo = Brahmaputra → *Asia* 23°40N 90°35E **241** D3
Tsaochiao *Taiwan* 24°39N 120°51E **225** B2
Ts'aot'un *Taiwan* 23°58N 120°41E **225** C2
Tsaratanana *Madag.* 16°47S 47°39E **272** B2
Tsaratanana, Mt. de = Maromokotro *Madag.* 14°0S 49°0E **272** A2
Tsaratanana ⌓ *Madag.* 13°57S 48°52E **272** A2
Tsarekonstantinovka = Kuybyshevo *Ukraine* 47°25N 36°40E **189** J9
Tsarevo = Michurin *Bulgaria* 42°9N 27°51E **203** D11
Tsarevo *Bulgaria* 42°28N 25°52E **203** D9
Tsaribrod = Dimitrovgrad *Serbia* 43°2N 22°48E **202** C6
Tsaritsani *Greece* 39°53N 22°14E **204** B4
Tsarkasianos *Greece* 38°10N 20°40E **207** C2
Tsarskoye Selo = Pushkin *Russia* 59°45N 30°25E **188** C6
Tsaryovokokshaysk = Yoshkar Ola *Russia* 56°38N 47°55E **190** B8
Tsau *Botswana* 20°8S 22°22E **270** B3
Tsavo *Kenya* 2°59S 38°28E **268** C4
Tsavo East △ *Kenya* 2°44S 38°47E **268** C4
Tsavo West △ *Kenya* 3°19S 37°57E **268** C4
Tselinograd = Astana *Kazakhstan* 51°10N 71°30E **217** B8
Tsementny = Fokino *Russia* 53°30N 34°22E **188** F8
Tseng Lan Shue *China* 22°20N 114°14E **122** A2
Tsengwen Hsi → *Taiwan* 23°8N 120°19E **225** C2
Tsengwen Shuiku *Taiwan* 23°16N 120°34E **225** C2
Tsentralnyy □ *Russia* 52°0N 40°0E **190** D3
Tses *Namibia* 25°58S 18°8E **270** C2
Tsetserleg *Mongolia* 47°36N 101°32E **218** B9
Tseung Kwan *China* 22°20N 114°15E **122** B2
Tsévié *Togo* 6°25N 1°20E **263** D5
Tshabong *Botswana* 26°2S 22°29E **270** C3
Tshabuta *Dem. Rep. of the Congo* 7°42S 23°7E **265** D4
Tshane *Botswana* 24°5S 21°54E **270** B3
Tshela *Dem. Rep. of the Congo* 4°57S 13°4E **265** C2
Tshesebe *Botswana* 21°51S 27°32E **271** B4
Tshibeke *Dem. Rep. of the Congo* 2°40S 28°35E **268** C2
Tshibinda *Dem. Rep. of the Congo* 2°23S 28°43E **268** C2
Tshikapa *Dem. Rep. of the Congo* 6°28S 20°48E **265** D4
Tshilenge *Dem. Rep. of the Congo* 6°17S 23°48E **265** D4
Tshindjambo *Dem. Rep. of the Congo* 10°52S 22°43E **265** E4
Tshinota *Dem. Rep. of the Congo* 7°2S 20°58E **265** D4
Tshinsenda *Dem. Rep. of the Congo* 12°20S 28°0E **269** E2
Tshitadi *Dem. Rep. of the Congo* 6°46S 21°43E **265** D4
Tshofa *Dem. Rep. of the Congo* 5°13S 25°16E **265** D5
Tshuapa → *Dem. Rep. of the Congo* 0°14S 20°42E **264** C4
Tshumbiri *Dem. Rep. of the Congo* 2°38S 16°18E **264** C3
Tshwane = Pretoria *S. Africa* 25°44S 28°12E **271** C4
Tshwane *Botswana* 22°24S 22°1E **270** B3
Tsiaotso = Jiaozuo *China* 35°16N 113°12E **226** G7
Tsibirihina → *Madag.* 19°42S 44°31E **272** B1
Tsigara *Botswana* 20°22S 25°54E **270** B4
Tsihombe *Madag.* 25°10S 45°41E **272** D2
Tsiigehtchic *Canada* 67°15N 134°0W **294** D5
Ts'il-os ⌓ *Canada* 51°9N 123°59W **296** C4
Tsim Sha Tsui *China* 22°18N 114°10E **122** B2
Tsimlyansk *Russia* 47°40N 42°6E **191** G6
Tsimlyansk Res. = Tsimlyanskoye Vdkhr. *Russia* 48°0N 43°0E **191** F6
Tsimlyanskoye Vdkhr. *Russia* 48°0N 43°0E **191** F6
Tsinan = Jinan *China* 36°38N 117°1E **226** F9
Tsineng *S. Africa* 27°5S 23°5E **270** C3
Tsing Yi *China* 22°21N 114°6E **122** A1
Tsinghai = Qinghai □ *China* 36°0N 98°0E **218** D8
Tsingshih = Jinshi *China* 29°40N 111°50E **229** C8
Tsingtao = Qingdao *China* 36°5N 120°20E **227** F11
Tsingy de Bemaraha ⌓ *Madag.* 18°35S 44°55E **272** B2
Tsingy de Namoraka ⌓ *Madag.* 16°29S 45°25E **272** B2
Tsining = Jining *China* 35°22N 116°34E **226** G9
Tsinjoarivo *Madag.* 19°37S 47°40E **272** B2
Tsinjomitondraka *Madag.* 15°40S 47°8E **272** B2
Tsinling Shan = Qinling Shandi *China* 33°50N 108°10E **226** H5
Tsirigo = Kythira *Greece* 36°8N 23°0E **204** E5
Tsiroanomandidy *Madag.* 18°46S 46°2E **272** B2
Tsis I. *Micronesia* 7°17N 151°49E **287** U18
Tsiteli-Tsqaro *Georgia* 41°33N 46°0E **191** K8
Tsitondroina *Madag.* 21°19S 46°0E **272** C2
Tsitsihar = Qiqihar *China* 47°26N 124°0E **219** B13
Tsitsikamma △ *S. Africa* 34°3S 23°40E **270** D3
Tsivilsk *Russia* 55°50N 47°25E **190** C8
Tsivory *Madag.* 24°4S 46°5E **272** C2
Tskhinvali *Georgia* 42°14N 44°1E **191** J7
Tsna → *Russia* 54°55N 41°58E **190** C6
Tsnori *Georgia* 41°40N 45°57E **191** K7
Tso Moriri, L. *India* 32°50N 78°20E **243** C8
Tsobis *Namibia* 19°27S 17°30E **270** A2
Tsodilo Hill *Botswana* 18°49S 21°43E **270** A3
Tsogni *Gabon* 2°48S 10°10E **264** C2
Tsogttsetsiy = Baruunsuu *Mongolia* 43°43N 105°35E **226** C3
Tsolo *S. Africa* 31°18S 28°37E **271** D4
Tsomo *S. Africa* 32°0S 27°42E **271** D4
Tsoukalades *Greece* 38°41N 20°47E **207** B2
Tsova *West Bank* 31°47N 35°6E **123** B1
Tsoying *Taiwan* 22°41N 120°17E **225** D2
Tsu *Japan* 34°45N 136°25E **223** C8
Tsu L. *Canada* 60°40N 111°52W **296** A6
Tsubata *Japan* 36°40N 136°44E **223** A8
Tsuchiura *Japan* 36°5N 140°15E **223** A12
Tsuen Wan *China* 22°22N 114°6E **122** A1
Tsugaru-Hantō *Japan* 41°0N 140°30E **220** D10
Tsugaru-Kaikyō *Japan* 41°35N 141°0E **220** D10
Tsuken-jima *Japan* 26°15N 127°56E **288** a
Tsukiji *Tokyo, Japan* **140** c5
Tsukuba *Japan* 36°2N 140°4E **223** A12
Tsukumi *Japan* 33°4N 131°52E **222** D3
Tsukushi-Sanchi *Japan* 33°25N 130°30E **222** D2
Tsumeb *Namibia* 19°9S 17°44E **270** A2
Tsumis *Namibia* 23°39S 17°29E **270** B2
Tsuna *Japan* 34°28N 134°56E **222** C6
Tsuno-Shima *Japan* 34°21N 130°52E **222** C2
Tsur Hadassa *Israel* 31°43N 35°6E **123** B1
Tsuru *Japan* 35°31N 138°57E **223** B10
Tsuruga *Japan* 35°45N 136°2E **223** B8
Tsuruga-Wan *Japan* 35°50N 136°3E **223** B8
Tsurugi *Japan* 36°29N 136°37E **223** A8
Tsurugi-San *Japan* 33°51N 134°6E **222** D6
Tsurumi → *Japan* 35°32N 139°40E **140** B3
Tsurumi-Saki *Japan* 32°56N 132°5E **222** E4
Tsuruoka *Japan* 38°44N 139°50E **220** E9
Tsurusaki *Japan* 33°14N 131°41E **222** D3
Tsushima *Ehime, Japan* 33°7N 132°32E **222** D4
Tsushima *Gifu, Japan* 35°10N 136°43E **223** B8
Tsushima *Nagasaki, Japan* 34°20N 129°20E **222** C1
Tsuyama *Japan* 35°3N 134°0E **222** B6
Tsvetkovo *Ukraine* 49°8N 31°33E **189** H6
Tsyelyakhany *Belarus* 52°30N 25°46E **177** B13
Tsz Wan Shan *China* 22°20N 114°11E **122** A2
Tu → *Burma* 21°50N 96°15E **241** E6
Tua *Dem. Rep. of the Congo* 3°38S 16°38E **264** C3
Tua → *Papua N. G.* 6°30S 144°28E **286** D3
Tua → *Portugal* 41°13N 7°26W **194** D3
Tuaheni Pt. *N.Z.* 38°43S 178°4E **284** E7
Tuai *N.Z.* 38°47S 177°10E **284** E6
Tuaim = Tuam *Ireland* 53°31N 8°51W **166** C3
Tuakau *N.Z.* 37°16S 174°59E **284** D3
Tual *Indonesia* 5°38S 132°44E **231** F8
Tualatin *U.S.A.* 45°23N 122°45W **306** E4
Tuam *Ireland* 53°31N 8°51W **166** C3
Tuamarina *N.Z.* 41°25S 173°59E **285** B8
Tuamotu, Îs. *French Polynesia* 17°0S 144°0W **289** f
Tuamotu Arch. = Tuamotu, Îs. *French Polynesia* 17°0S 144°0W **289** f
Tuamotu Ridge *Pac. Oc.* 20°0S 138°0W **289** K14
Tuan Giao *Vietnam* 21°35N 103°25E **236** B4
Tuanfeng *China* 30°38N 114°52E **229** B10
Tuangku *Indonesia* 2°10N 97°16E **234** B1
Tuanxi *China* 27°28N 107°8E **228** D6
Tuao *Phil.* 17°45N 121°22E **232** C3

Tuapa Cook Is. 18°57S 159°54W 289 g
Tuapse Russia 44°5N 39°10E 191 H4
Tuaran Malaysia 6°10N 116°13E 235 A5
Tuas Singapore 1°19N 103°39E 138 B1
Tuatapere N.Z. 46°8S 167°41E 285 G2
Tuba City U.S.A. 36°8N 111°14W 305 H8
Tuban Indonesia 6°54S 112°3E 235 D4
Tubani Botswana 24°46S 24°18E 270 B3
Tubarão Brazil 28°30S 49°0W 335 B6
Tūbās West Bank 32°20N 35°22E 251 F6
Tubas → Namibia 22°54S 14°35E 270 B2
Tubau Malaysia 3°10N 113°40E 235 B4
Tubbataha Reefs △ Phil. 8°53N 119°53E 233 G2
Tubigon Phil. 9°57N 123°58E 233 G4
Tübingen Germany 48°31N 9°4E 179 G5
Tubod Phil. 8°3N 123°48E 233 G4
Tubou Fiji 18°13S 178°48W 287 B3
Tubruq Libya 32°7N 23°55E 258 B4
Tubuaï French Polynesia 23°18S 149°30W 289 f
Tubuaï, Îs. French Polynesia 25°0S 150°0W 289 f
Tuburan Basilan, Phil. 6°39N 122°16E 233 H4
Tuburan Cebu, Phil. 10°44N 123°49E 233 F4
Tuc Trung Vietnam 11°1N 107°12E 237 G6
Tucacas Venezuela 10°48N 68°19W 328 A4
Tucano Brazil 10°58S 38°48W 332 D4
T'uch'ang Taiwan 24°35N 121°29E 225 B3
Tuchitua Canada 60°55N 129°13W 296 A3
Tuchodi → Canada 58°17N 123°42W 296 B4
Tuchola Poland 53°33N 17°52E 184 E4
Tuchoměřice Czech Rep. 50°7N 14°16E 135 B1
Tuchów Poland 49°54N 21°1E 185 J8
Tuckahoe U.S.A. 40°56N 73°49W 132 A3
Tuckanarra Australia 27°7S 118°5E 279 E2
Tucker U.S.A. 33°51N 84°13W 316 B5
Tuckers Town Bermuda 32°20N 64°42W 153 a
Tucson U.S.A. 32°13N 110°58W 305 K8
Tucumán □ Argentina 26°48S 66°2W 334 B2
Tucumcari U.S.A. 35°10N 103°44W 305 J12
Tucunaré Brazil 5°18S 55°51W 331 B6
Tucupido Venezuela 9°17N 65°47W 328 B4
Tucupita Venezuela 9°2N 62°3W 329 B5
Tucuruí Brazil 3°42S 49°44W 332 B2
Tucuruí, Represa de Brazil 4°0S 49°30W 332 B2
Tucuruvi Brazil 23°28S 46°35W 137 A2
Tuczno Poland 53°13N 16°10E 185 E3
Tuddal Norway 59°46N 8°49E 164 E5
Tudela Spain 42°4N 1°39W 196 C3
Tudmur Syria 34°36N 38°15E 213 E8
Tudor, L. Canada 55°50N 65°25W 299 A6
Tudora Romania 47°31N 26°45E 183 C11
Tuella → Portugal 41°30N 7°12W 194 D3
Tuen Mun China 22°24N 113°59E 219 a
Tueré → Brazil 2°48S 50°59W 332 B1
Tufanbeyli Turkey 38°15N 36°13E 212 C7
Tufello Italy 41°56N 12°32E 136 B2
Tüffer = Laško Slovenia 46°10N 15°16E 199 B12
Tufi Papua N. G. 9°8S 149°19E 286 E5
Tufnell Park U.K. 51°33N 0°8W 125 A3
Tufsingdal Norway 62°18N 11°44E 164 B8
Tufts Abyssal Plain Pac. Oc. 47°0N 140°0W 289 C14
Tufts Univ. U.S.A. 42°24N 71°7W 116 A2
Tufu Pt. Amer. Samoa 14°13S 169°30W 302 g
Tugaya Phil. 7°53N 124°10E 233 H5
Tugela → S. Africa 29°14S 31°30E 271 C5
Tughlakabad India 28°30N 77°16E 120 B2
Tugidak I. U.S.A. 56°30N 154°40W 303 H9
Tuguegarao Phil. 17°35N 121°42E 232 C3
Tugur Russia 53°44N 136°45E 215 D14
Tui Spain 42°3N 8°39W 194 C2
Tuileries, Jardin des Paris, France 134 b3
Tuineje Canary Is. 28°19N 14°3W 153 e2
Tukangbesi, Kepulauan Indonesia 6°0S 124°0E 231 F6
Tukarak I. Canada 56°15N 78°45W 298 A4
Tukayyid Iraq 29°47N 45°36E 246 D5
Tûkh Egypt 30°21N 31°12E 256 H7
Tukhlya Ukraine 48°55N 23°28E 183 B8
Tukituki → N.Z. 39°36S 176°56E 284 F5
Tukobo Ghana 5°1N 2°47W 262 D4
Tūkrah Libya 32°30N 20°37E 258 B4
Tuktoyaktuk Canada 69°27N 133°2W 294 D5
Tuktuk Indonesia 2°37N 98°54E 234 B1
Tuktut Nogait △ Canada 69°15N 122°0W 294 D7
Tuku Taiwan 23°41N 120°23E 225 C2
Tukums Latvia 56°58N 23°10E 184 B10
Tukums □ Latvia 56°55N 23°0E 184 B10
Tukuran Phil. 7°51N 123°34E 233 H4
Tukuyu Tanzania 9°17S 33°35E 269 D3
Tula Amer. Samoa 14°15S 170°34W 302 f
Tula Hidalgo, Mexico 20°3N 99°21W 319 C5
Tula Tamaulipas, Mexico 23°0N 99°43W 319 C5
Tula Nigeria 9°51N 11°27E 263 D7
Tula Russia 54°13N 37°38E 188 E9
Tula □ Russia 53°45N 37°30E 188 F9
Tulach Mhór = Tullamore Ireland 53°16N 7°31W 166 C4
Tulagi Solomon Is. 9°5S 160°10E 287 M11
Tūlak Afghan. 33°55N 63°40E 240 B1
Tulan Taiwan 22°53N 121°13E 225 D3
Tulancingo Mexico 20°5N 98°22W 319 C5
Tulangbawang → Indonesia 4°24S 105°52E 234 C3
Tulare Serbia 42°48N 21°28E 202 D5
Tulare Calif., U.S.A. 36°13N 119°21W 306 J7
Tulare Lake Bed U.S.A. 36°0N 119°48W 306 K7
Tularosa U.S.A. 33°5N 106°1W 305 K10
Tulbagh S. Africa 33°16S 19°6E 270 D2
Tulcán Ecuador 0°48N 77°43W 328 C2
Tulcea Romania 45°13N 28°46E 183 E13
Tulcea □ Romania 45°0N 28°30E 183 E13
Tulchyn Ukraine 48°41N 28°49E 183 B13
Tüledi Araldary Kazakhstan 45°2N 50°16E 191 H10
Tūleh Iran 34°35N 52°33E 247 C7
Tulemalu L. Canada 62°58N 99°25W 297 A9
Tulgheş Romania 46°58N 25°45E 183 D10
Tuli Zimbabwe 21°58S 29°13E 269 G2
Tulia U.S.A. 34°32N 101°46W 314 D4
Tuliszków Poland 52°5N 18°18E 185 F5
Tulita Canada 64°57N 125°30W 294 E6
Ţūlkarm West Bank 32°19N 35°2E 251 F6
Tulla Ireland 52°53N 8°46W 166 D3
Tullahoma U.S.A. 35°22N 86°13W 315 D11
Tullamarine Australia 37°41S 144°50E 128 A1
Tullamore N.S.W., Australia 32°39S 147°36E 283 B7
Tullamore Offaly, Ireland 53°16N 7°31W 166 C4
Tulle France 45°16N 1°46E 174 C5
Tulln Austria 48°20N 16°4E 180 C9
Tullow Ireland 52°49N 6°45W 166 D5
Tullus Sudan 11°7N 24°31E 257 E1
Tully Queens., Australia 17°56S 145°55E 280 B4
Tully N.Y., U.S.A. 42°48N 76°7W 313 D8
Tulmaythah Libya 32°40N 20°55E 258 B4
Tulnici Romania 45°51N 26°38E 183 E11
Tulovo Bulgaria 42°33N 25°32E 203 D9
Tulsa U.S.A. 36°10N 95°55W 314 C7
Tulse Hill U.K. 51°26N 0°6W 125 B3
Tulsequah Canada 58°39N 133°35W 296 B2
Tulu Milki Ethiopia 9°55N 38°20E 257 F4
Tulu Welel Ethiopia 8°56N 34°47E 257 F3
Tuluá Colombia 4°6N 76°11W 328 C2
Tuluceşti Romania 45°34N 28°2E 183 E13
Tuluksak U.S.A. 61°6N 160°58W 303 F7
Tulun Russia 54°32N 100°35E 215 D11
Tulungagung Indonesia 8°5S 111°54E 235 D4
Tuluran I. Phil. 10°58N 119°16E 233 F2
Tuma Russia 55°10N 40°30E 188 E11
Tuma → Nic. 13°6N 84°35W 320 D3
Tumacacori ⌂ U.S.A. 31°35N 111°6W 305 L8
Tumaco Colombia 1°50N 78°45W 328 C2
Tumaco, Ensenada Colombia 1°55N 78°45W 328 C2
Tumakuru = Tumkur India 13°18N 77°6E 245 H3
Tumatumari Guyana 5°20N 58°55W 329 B6
Tumauini Phil. 17°17N 121°49E 232 C3
Tumba Dem. Rep. of the Congo 3°10S 23°36E 264 C4
Tumba Sweden 59°12N 17°48E 162 E11
Tumba, L. Dem. Rep. of the Congo 0°50S 18°0E 264 C3
Tumbangsamba Indonesia 1°27S 113°7E 235 C4
Tumbarumba Australia 35°44S 148°0E 283 C8
Tumbaya Argentina 23°50S 65°26W 334 A2
Tumbes Peru 3°37S 80°27W 330 A1
Tumbes □ Peru 3°50S 80°30W 330 A1
Tumbler Ridge Canada 55°8N 121°0W 296 B4
Tumbur South Sudan 4°20N 31°34E 257 G3
Tumbwe Dem. Rep. of the Congo 11°25S 27°15E 269 E2
Tumby Bay Australia 34°21S 136°8E 282 C2
Tumd Youqi China 40°30N 110°30E 226 D6
Tumen China 43°0N 129°50E 224 A4
Tumen Jiang → China 42°20N 130°35E 224 A5
Tumeremo Venezuela 7°18N 61°30W 329 B5
Tumindao I. Phil. 4°41N 119°24E 233 J2
Tumiritinga Brazil 18°58S 41°38W 333 E3
Tumkur India 13°18N 77°6E 245 H3
Tumon B. Guam 13°31N 144°48E 302 d
Tump Pakistan 26°7N 62°16E 240 D1
Tumpat Malaysia 6°11N 102°10E 237 J4
Tumsar India 21°26N 79°45E 244 D4
Tumu Ghana 10°56N 1°56W 262 C4
Tumucumaque, Serra Brazil 2°0N 55°0W 329 C7
Tumupasa Bolivia 14°9S 67°55W 330 C4
Tumut Australia 35°16S 148°13E 283 C8
Tumwater U.S.A. 47°1N 122°54W 306 C4
Tun Sweden 58°26N 12°43E 163 F6
Tuna India 22°59N 70°5E 242 H4
Tunapuna Trin. & Tob. 10°38N 61°24W 323 f
Tunas de Zaza Cuba 21°39N 79°34W 320 B4
Tunbridge Wells = Royal Tunbridge Wells U.K. 51°7N 0°16E 169 F8
Tunçbilek Turkey 39°37N 29°29E 205 B11
Tunceli Turkey 39°6N 39°31E 213 C8
Tunceli □ Turkey 39°5N 39°35E 213 C8
Tunchang China 19°21N 110°5E 236 C8
Tuncurry Australia 32°17S 152°29E 283 B10
Tundla India 27°12N 78°17E 242 F8
Tundubai Sudan 18°36N 28°35E 256 D2
Tunduru Tanzania 11°8S 37°25E 269 E4
Tundzha → Bulgaria 41°40N 26°35E 203 E10
Tung Chung China 22°17N 113°57E 219 a
Tung Lung Chau China 22°15N 114°17E 122 B2
Tung O China 22°11N 114°8E 122 B1
Tunga → India 15°0N 75°50E 245 G2
Tunga Pass India 29°0N 94°14E 241 A5
Tungabhadra → India 15°57N 78°15E 245 G4
Tungabhadra Dam India 15°0N 75°50E 245 G2
Tungao Taiwan 24°31N 121°50E 225 B3
Tungaru Sudan 10°9N 30°52E 257 E3
Tungawan Phil. 7°30N 122°20E 233 H4
Tungchi Yü Taiwan 23°15N 119°40E 225 C1
Tungch'uan = Dongchuan China 26°3N 103°1E 228 D4
Tungho Taiwan 22°58N 121°18E 225 D3
T'unghsiao Taiwan 24°29N 120°40E 225 B2
Tunghwa = Tonghua China 41°42N 125°58E 224 B2
Tungi Bangla. 23°53N 90°24E 241 D3
Tungkang Taiwan 22°27N 120°26E 225 D2
Tungku Malaysia 5°1N 118°53E 235 A5
Tungla Nic. 13°24N 84°21W 320 D3
T'unglo Taiwan 24°30N 120°47E 225 B2
Tungnafellsjökull Iceland 64°45N 17°55W 155 D6
Tungsha Tao = Dongsha Dao S. China Sea 20°45N 116°43E 229 G11
Tungshan Taiwan 24°38N 121°47E 225 B3
Tungshih Changhua, Taiwan 24°12N 120°43E 225 B2
Tungshih Chiai, Taiwan 23°27N 120°8E 225 C2
Tungsten Canada 61°57N 128°16W 296 A3
Tungufell Iceland 64°17N 20°10W 155 C6
Tunguráhua □ Ecuador 1°15S 78°35W 328 D2
Tunguska, Nizhnyaya → Russia 65°48N 88°4E 215 C9
Tunguska, Podkamennaya → Russia 61°50N 90°13E 215 C10
Tungyin Tao Taiwan 26°22N 120°29E 225 b
Tuni India 17°22N 82°36E 244 F6
Tunia Colombia 2°41N 76°31W 328 C2
Tunica U.S.A. 34°41N 90°23W 315 D9
Tunis Baghdad, Iraq 33°23N 44°21E 113 A2
Tunis Tunisia 36°50N 10°11E 258 A2
Tunis □ Tunisia 36°46N 10°10E 261 A7
Tunis ✕ (TUN) Tunisia 36°52N 10°14E 200 F3
Tunis, Golfe de Tunisia 37°0N 10°30E 258 A2
Tunisia ■ Africa 33°30N 9°10E 258 B1
Tunja Colombia 5°33N 73°25W 328 B3
Tunkhannock U.S.A. 41°32N 75°57W 313 E9
Tunliu China 36°13N 112°52E 226 F7
Tunnel Creek △ Australia 17°41S 125°18E 278 C4
Tunnsjøen Norway 64°45N 13°25E 160 D15
Tunø Denmark 55°57N 10°27E 163 J4
Tuntutuliak U.S.A. 60°22N 162°38W 303 F7
Tunu □ Greenland 75°0N 30°0W 154 C7
Tununak U.S.A. 60°37N 165°15W 303 F6
Tunungayualok I. Canada 56°0N 61°0W 299 A7
Tunuyán Argentina 33°35S 69°0W 334 C2
Tunuyán → Argentina 33°33S 67°30W 334 C2
Tunxi = Huangshan China 30°8N 118°9E 229 B12
Tuo Jiang → China 28°50N 105°35E 228 C5
Tuolumne U.S.A. 37°58N 120°15W 306 H6
Tuolumne → U.S.A. 37°36N 121°13W 306 H5
Tuomaria Finland 60°11N 24°41E 121 B1
Tüp Kyrgyzstan 42°45N 78°20E 217 D9
Tūp Āghāj Iran 36°3N 47°50E 213 D12
Tupã Brazil 21°57S 50°28W 335 A5
Tupaciguara Brazil 18°35S 48°42W 333 E2
Tupelo U.S.A. 34°16N 88°43W 315 D10
Tupik Russia 55°42N 33°22E 188 E7
Tupinambarana, I. Brazil 3°0S 58°0W 329 D6
Tupirama Brazil 8°58S 48°12W 332 C2
Tupiratins Brazil 8°23S 48°8W 332 C2
Tupiza Bolivia 21°30S 65°40W 334 A2
Tupižnica Serbia 43°43N 22°10E 202 C6
Tupman U.S.A. 35°18N 119°21W 307 K7
Tupper Canada 55°32N 120°1W 296 B4
Tupper L. U.S.A. 44°10N 74°32W 313 B10
Tupper Lake U.S.A. 44°14N 74°28W 313 B10
Tüpqaraghan Muyis Kazakhstan 44°40N 50°19E 191 H10
Tupungato, Cerro S. Amer. 33°15S 69°50W 334 C2
Tuquan China 45°18N 121°38E 227 B11
Túquerres Colombia 1°5N 77°37W 328 C2
Tura India 25°30N 90°16E 241 C3
Tura Russia 64°20N 100°17E 215 C11
Turabah Ḥā'il, Si. Arabia 28°20N 43°15E 246 D4
Turabah Makkah, Si. Arabia 21°15N 41°34E 248 B3
Turagua, Serranía Venezuela 7°20N 64°35W 329 B5
Turakina N.Z. 40°3S 175°16E 284 G4
Turakina → N.Z. 40°5S 175°8E 284 G4
Turakirae Hd. N.Z. 41°26S 174°56E 284 H3
Turama → Papua N. G. 7°40S 143°50E 286 D2
Tūrān Iran 35°39N 56°42E 247 C8
Turan Russia 51°55N 94°0E 217 B12
Turan Lowland Asia 43°30N 62°0E 216 D8
Turangi N.Z. 38°59S 175°48E 284 E4
Ţurayf Si. Arabia 31°41N 38°39E 246 D3
Turbaco Colombia 10°20N 75°25W 328 A2
Turbacz Poland 49°30N 20°8E 185 J7
Turbat Pakistan 25°59N 63°4E 240 D1
Turbe Bos.-H. 44°15N 17°35E 182 F2
Turbeville U.S.A. 33°54N 80°1W 316 B9
Turbo Colombia 8°6N 76°43W 328 B2
Turčianske Teplice Slovak Rep. 48°52N 18°52E 181 C11
Turco Bolivia 18°10S 68°11W 330 D4
Turcoaia Romania 45°7N 28°11E 183 E13
Turda Romania 46°34N 23°47E 183 D8
Tureberg Sweden 59°25N 17°55E 139 A1
Turéia French Polynesia 20°50S 138°32W 289 f
Turek Poland 52°3N 18°30E 185 F5
Turfan = Turpan China 43°58N 89°10E 217 D11
Turfan Basin = Turpan Pendi China 42°40N 89°25E 217 D11
Turfan Depression = Turpan Pendi China 42°40N 89°25E 217 D11
Turffontein S. Africa 26°14S 28°2E 123 B2
Turgayskaya Stolovaya Strana = Torghay Ustirti Asia 51°0N 63°0E 216 B6
Turgeon → Canada 50°0N 78°56W 298 C4
Tŭrgovishte Bulgaria 43°17N 26°38E 203 C10
Tŭrgovishte □ Bulgaria 43°17N 26°38E 203 C10
Turgut Turkey 37°22N 28°4E 205 D10
Turgutlu Turkey 38°30N 27°43E 205 C9
Turhal Turkey 40°24N 36°5E 212 B7
Turia → Spain 39°27N 0°19W 197 F4
Turiaçu Brazil 1°40S 45°19W 332 B2
Turiaçu → Brazil 1°36S 45°19W 332 B2
Turiec → Slovak Rep. 49°7N 18°55E 181 B11
Turin = Torino Italy 45°3N 7°40E 198 C4
Turinskaya Kultbaza = Tura Russia 64°20N 100°17E 215 C11
Turka Ukraine 49°10N 23°2E 185 J10
Turkana, L. Africa 3°30N 36°5E 268 B4
Turkayel Ethiopia 8°7N 45°21E 267 C6
Türkeli Turkey 40°30N 27°30E 203 F11
Turkestan = Türkistan Kazakhstan 43°17N 68°16E 217 D7
Turkestan Range Asia 39°35N 69°0E 217 E7
Túrkeve Hungary 47°6N 20°44E 182 C5
Turkey ■ Eurasia 39°0N 36°0E 212 C7
Turkey → U.S.A. 42°43N 91°2W 310 B5
Turkey Creek = Warmun Australia 17°2S 128°12E 278 C4
Turkey L. U.S.A. 28°30N 81°28W 133 A2
Turkey Lake Park U.S.A. 28°30N 81°28W 133 A2
Turki Russia 52°0N 43°15E 190 D6
Türkistan Kazakhstan 43°17N 68°16E 217 D7
Türkmenabat Turkmenistan 39°6N 63°34E 247 B9
Türkmenbashi Turkmenistan 40°5N 53°5E 247 A7
Turkmenistan ■ Asia 39°0N 59°0E 216 E5
Türkmenli Turkey 39°45N 26°30E 205 B8
Türkoğlu Turkey 37°23N 36°50E 212 D7
Turks & Caicos Is. ☑ W. Indies 21°20N 71°20W 321 B5
Turks Island Passage W. Indies 21°30N 71°30W 321 B5
Turku Finland 60°30N 22°19E 188 B2
Turkwel → Kenya 3°6N 36°6E 268 B4
Turlock U.S.A. 37°30N 120°51W 306 H6
Turnagain Australia 9°34S 142°17E 280 a
Turnagain → Canada 59°12N 127°35W 296 B3
Turnagain, C. N.Z. 40°28S 176°38E 284 G5
Turneffe Is. Belize 17°20N 87°50W 320 C2
Turner U.S.A. 48°51N 108°24W 304 B9
Turner Field U.S.A. 33°44N 84°23W 113 B2
Turner Pt. Australia 11°47S 133°32E 280 A1
Turner Valley Canada 50°40N 114°17W 296 C6
Turners Falls U.S.A. 42°36N 72°33W 313 D12
Turner's Pen. S. Leone 7°22N 12°24W 262 D2
Turnham Green U.K. 51°29N 0°16W 125 B2
Turnhout Belgium 51°19N 4°57E 170 C4
Turnhouse U.K. 55°57N 3°20W 121 B1
Türnitz Austria 47°55N 15°29E 180 D8
Turnor L. Canada 56°35N 108°35W 297 B7
Turnov Czech Rep. 50°34N 15°10E 180 A8
Tŭrnovo = Veliko Tŭrnovo Bulgaria 43°5N 25°41E 203 C9
Turnu Măgurele Romania 43°46N 24°56E 183 G9
Turnu Roşu, P. Romania 45°33N 24°17E 183 E9
Turobin Poland 50°50N 22°44E 185 H9
Tuross Head Australia 36°3S 150°8E 283 D9
Turpan China 43°58N 89°10E 217 D11
Turpan Pendi China 42°40N 89°25E 217 D11
Turrawan Australia 30°28S 149°53E 283 A8
Turrës, Kala e Albania 41°10N 19°28E 202 E3
Turriff U.K. 57°32N 2°27W 167 D6
Tursāq Iraq 33°27N 45°47E 213 F11
Tursi Italy 40°15N 16°28E 201 B9
Tursunzoda Tajikistan 38°30N 68°13E 217 E7
Turtle Head I. Australia 10°56S 142°37E 286 F2
Turtle Is. Phil. 6°7N 118°14E 233 H2
Turtle Is. S. Leone 7°40N 13°0W 262 D2
Turtle Islands Phil. 6°13N 118°6E 235 A5
Turtle L. Canada 53°36N 108°38W 297 C7
Turtle Lake U.S.A. 47°31N 100°53W 308 B3
Turtleford Canada 53°23N 108°57W 297 C7
Turtucaia = Tutrakan Bulgaria 44°2N 26°40E 203 B10
Turua N.Z. 37°14S 175°35E 284 D4
Turukhansk Russia 65°21N 88°5E 215 C10
Turyinskiye Rudniki = Krasnoturinsk Russia 59°46N 60°12E 186 C11
Turzovka Slovak Rep. 49°25N 18°35E 181 B11
Tuscaloosa U.S.A. 33°12N 87°34W 315 E11
Tuscánia Italy 42°25N 11°52E 199 F8
Tuscany = Toscana □ Italy 43°25N 11°0E 198 E8
Tuscarawas → U.S.A. 40°24N 81°25W 312 F3
Tuscarora Mt. U.S.A. 40°55N 77°55W 312 F7
Tuscola Ill., U.S.A. 39°48N 88°17W 311 E9
Tuscola Tex., U.S.A. 32°12N 99°48W 314 E5
Tuscolano, Via Italy 41°52N 12°31E 136 B2
Tuscumbia Ala., U.S.A. 34°44N 87°42W 315 D11
Tuscumbia Mo., U.S.A. 38°14N 92°28W 310 F3
Tushino Russia 55°50N 37°24E 129 A2
Tuskegee U.S.A. 32°25N 85°42W 316 C4
Tusket Wedge = Wedgeport Canada 43°44N 65°59W 299 D6
Tustna Norway 63°10N 8°5E 164 A5
Tuszyn Poland 51°36N 19°33E 185 G6
Tutak Turkey 39°31N 42°46E 213 C10
Tutayev Russia 57°53N 39°32E 188 D10
Tuticorin India 8°50N 78°12E 245 K4
Tutin Serbia 42°58N 20°20E 202 D4
Tutóia Brazil 2°45S 42°20W 332 B3
Tutong Brunei 4°47N 114°40E 235 B4
Tutova → Romania 46°7N 27°30E 183 D12
Tutrakan Bulgaria 44°2N 26°40E 203 B10
Tuttle Creek L. U.S.A. 39°15N 96°36W 308 F5
Tuttlingen Germany 47°58N 8°48E 179 H4
Tutuala E. Timor 8°25S 127°15E 231 F7
Tutuba Vanuatu 15°33S 167°16E 287 E5
Tutubeia Papua N. G. 9°34S 150°40E 286 E6
Tutuila Amer. Samoa 14°19S 170°50W 302 f
Tutuko, Mt. N.Z. 44°35S 168°1E 285 E3
Tutun Egypt 29°9N 30°46E 256 J7
Tütz = Tuczno Poland 53°13N 16°10E 185 E3
Tuul Gol → Mongolia 48°30N 104°25E 218 B9
Tuva □ Russia 51°30N 95°0E 217 B12
Tuvalu ■ Pac. Oc. 8°0S 178°0E 277 B14
Tuvuca Fiji 17°40S 178°48W 287 A3
Tuwal Si. Arabia 22°17N 39°6E 248 B2
Tuxer Alpen Austria 47°10N 11°45E 180 D4
Tuxpan Mexico 20°57N 97°24W 319 C5
Tuxtla Gutiérrez Mexico 16°45N 93°7W 319 D6
Tuy = Tui Spain 42°3N 8°39W 194 C2
Tuy Duc Vietnam 12°15N 107°27E 237 F6
Tuy Phong Vietnam 11°14N 108°43E 237 G7
Tuya L. Canada 59°7N 130°35W 296 B2
Tuyen Hoa Vietnam 17°50N 106°10E 236 D6
Tuyen Quang Vietnam 21°50N 105°10E 228 G5
Tuymazy Russia 54°36N 53°42E 216 B4
Tūysarkān Iran 34°33N 48°27E 213 E13
Tuyūn = Duyun China 26°18N 107°29E 228 D6
Tuz Gölü Turkey 38°42N 33°18E 212 C5
Ţūz Khurmātū Iraq 34°56N 44°38E 213 E11
Tuzi Montenegro 42°22N 19°20E 202 D3
Tuzigoot ⌂ U.S.A. 34°46N 112°2W 305 J7
Tuzla Bos.-H. 44°34N 18°41E 182 F3
Tuzla Turkey 36°42N 35°6E 250 B6
Tuzlov → Russia 47°17N 39°57E 189 J10
Tuzluca Turkey 40°3N 43°39E 213 B10
Tuzly Ukraine 45°54N 30°6E 183 E15
Tvååker Sweden 57°4N 12°25E 163 G6
Tvardița Moldova 46°9N 28°58E 183 D13
Tvedestrand Norway 58°38N 8°58E 164 F5
Tver Russia 56°55N 35°59E 188 D8
Tver □ Russia 56°50N 35°0E 188 D8
Tvrdošín Slovak Rep. 49°21N 19°36E 181 B12
Tvrdošovce Slovak Rep. 48°6N 18°4E 181 C11
Tvŭrditsa Bulgaria 42°42N 25°53E 203 D9
Twain U.S.A. 40°1N 121°3W 306 E5
Twain Harte U.S.A. 38°2N 120°14W 306 G6
Twardogóra Poland 51°23N 17°28E 185 G4
Twee Rivier Namibia 25°27S 19°27E 270 C2
Tweed Canada 44°29N 77°19W 312 B7
Tweed → U.K. 55°45N 2°0W 167 F6
Tweed Heads Australia 28°10S 153°31E 281 D5
Tweedsmuir ⌂ Canada 53°0N 126°20W 296 C3
Twelve Apostles S. Africa 33°58S 18°23E 118 A1
Twentieth Century Fox Studios U.S.A. 34°4N 118°25W 126 B2
Twentynine Palms U.S.A. 34°8N 116°3W 307 L10
Tweya Dem. Rep. of the Congo 0°54S 18°58E 264 C3
Twickenham U.K. 51°26N 0°20W 125 B1
Twickenham Rugby Ground U.K. 51°27N 0°20W 125 B1
Twillingate Canada 49°42N 54°45W 299 C9
Twin Bridges U.S.A. 45°33N 112°20W 304 D7
Twin City U.S.A. 32°35N 82°10W 316 C7
Twin Falls Canada 53°30N 64°32W 299 B7
Twin Falls Idaho, U.S.A. 42°34N 114°28W 304 E6
Twin Hills U.S.A. 59°23N 160°58W 303 G8
Twin Lakes U.S.A. 30°43N 83°13W 316 E6
Twin Peaks U.S.A. 37°45N 122°26W 136 B2
Twin Valley U.S.A. 47°16N 96°16W 308 B5
Twinnge Burma 23°10N 96°2E 241 D6
Twinsburg U.S.A. 41°19N 81°26W 312 E3
Twistringen Germany 52°48N 8°37E 178 C4
Twitchell Res. U.S.A. 34°59N 120°19W 307 L6
Two Boats Village Ascension I. 7°56S 14°22W 153 g
Two Harbors U.S.A. 47°2N 91°40W 308 B8
Two Hills Canada 53°43N 111°52W 296 C6
Two Rivers U.S.A. 44°9N 87°34W 308 C10
Two Rock Mt. Ireland 53°15N 6°14W 120 B2
Two Rocks Australia 31°30S 115°35E 279 F2
Two Thumb Ra. N.Z. 43°45S 170°44E 285 E3
Twofold B. Australia 37°8S 149°59E 283 D8
Twyfelfontein Namibia 20°34S 14°22E 270 B1
Ty Ty U.S.A. 31°29N 83°39W 316 D6
Tyachiv Ukraine 48°1N 23°35E 177 D12
Tybee Island U.S.A. 32°1N 80°51W 316 C9
Tychy Poland 50°9N 18°59E 185 H5
Tyczyn Poland 49°58N 22°2E 185 J9
Tydal Norway 63°4N 11°34E 164 A8
Tyin Norway 61°13N 8°15E 164 C5
Tykocin Poland 53°13N 22°46E 185 E9
Tyler Minn., U.S.A. 44°17N 96°8W 308 C5
Tyler Tex., U.S.A. 32°21N 95°18W 314 E7
Tyligul → Ukraine 47°4N 30°57E 189 J6
Tylldal Norway 62°8N 10°48E 164 B7
Tymanivka Ukraine 48°34N 28°50E 183 B13
Tymon North Ireland 53°18N 6°20W 120 B1
Týn nad Vltavou Czech Rep. 49°13N 14°26E 180 B7
Tynda Russia 55°10N 124°43E 215 D13
Tyndall U.S.A. 43°0N 97°50W 308 D5
Tyndinsky = Tynda Russia 55°10N 124°43E 215 D13
Tyne → U.K. 54°59N 1°32W 168 C6
Tyne & Wear □ U.K. 55°6N 1°17W 168 B6
Týnec nad Sázavou Czech Rep. 49°50N 14°36E 180 B7
Tynemouth U.K. 55°1N 1°26W 168 B6
Tynset Norway 62°17N 10°47E 164 B7
Tyonek U.S.A. 61°4N 151°8W 303 F10
Tyre = Sūr Lebanon 33°19N 35°16E 250 B4
Tyresta △ Sweden 59°12N 18°14E 162 E12
Tyrifjorden Norway 60°2N 10°8E 164 D7
Tyringe Sweden 56°9N 13°35E 163 H7
Tyristrand Norway 60°5N 10°5E 164 D7
Tyrnyauz Russia 43°21N 42°45E 191 J6
Tyrol = Tirol □ Austria 47°3N 10°43E 180 D3
Tyrone U.S.A. 40°40N 78°14W 312 F6
Tyrone □ U.K. 54°38N 7°11W 166 B4
Tyrrell Bay Grenada 12°27N 61°29W 323 q
Tyrrell → Australia 35°26S 142°51E 282 C5
Tyrrell, L. Australia 35°20S 142°50E 282 C5
Tyrrell L. Canada 63°7N 105°27W 297 A7
Tyrrhenian Sea Medit. S. 40°0N 12°30E 192 D6
Tysfjorden Norway 68°7N 16°25E 160 B17
Tysmenytsya Ukraine 48°58N 24°51E 183 B9
Tysnes Norway 60°1N 5°30E 164 D2
Tysnesøya Norway 60°0N 5°35E 164 D2
Tysons Corner U.S.A. 38°55N 77°14W 132 B1
Tysse Norway 60°23N 5°45E 164 D2
Tyssedal Norway 60°7N 6°35E 164 D3
Tystberga Sweden 58°51N 17°15E 163 F11
Tytuvėnai Lithuania 55°36N 23°12E 184 C10
Tyub Karagan, Mys = Tüpqaraghan Muyis Kazakhstan 44°40N 50°19E 191 H10
Tyuleni, Ostrova = Tüledi Araldary Kazakhstan 45°2N 50°16E 191 H10
Tyuleniy Russia 44°28N 47°30E 191 H8
Tyuleniy, Mys Azerbaijan 40°12N 50°22E 191 K10
Tyulgan Russia 52°22N 56°12E 186 D10
Tyumen Russia 57°11N 65°29E 214 D7
Tyup = Tüp Kyrgyzstan 42°45N 78°20E 217 D9
Tywi → U.K. 51°48N 4°21W 169 F3
Tywyn U.K. 52°35N 4°5W 169 E3
Tzaneen S. Africa 23°47S 30°9E 271 B5
Tzermiado Greece 35°12N 25°29E 207 E6
Tzia = Kea Greece 37°35N 24°22E 204 D6
Tzoumérka, Óros = Athamanon Oros Greece 39°30N 21°26E 204 B3
Tzukong = Zigong China 29°15N 104°48E 228 C5
Tzukuan Taiwan 22°46N 120°16E 225 D2
Tzupo = Boshan China 36°28N 117°49E 227 F9
Tzutung Taiwan 23°45N 120°30E 225 C2

U

U.S.A. = United States of America ■ N. Amer. 37°0N 96°0W 301 H20
U.S. Capitol Washington, D.C., U.S.A. 143 b3
U.S. Cellular Field U.S.A. 41°50N 87°37W 119 C3
U.S.S. Arizona ⌂ U.S.A. 21°22N 157°57W 302 K14
U.S.S. Constitution = Old Ironside Boston, U.S.A. 116 a3
U.S. Virgin Is. ☑ W. Indies 18°20N 65°0W 321 C7
Ua Huka French Polynesia 8°55S 139°32W 289 f
Ua Pu French Polynesia 9°25S 140°0W 289 f
Uachadi, Sierra = Uasadi-jidi Venezuela 4°54N 65°18W 329 C4
Uad Atui → W. Sahara 20°4N 15°59W 260 D2
Uad el Jat → W. Sahara 26°47N 13°3W 260 C2
Uainambi Colombia 1°43N 69°51W 328 C4
Uamba Angola 7°21S 16°10E 265 D3
Uanle Uen = Wanleweyne Somali Rep. 2°37N 44°54E 267 D5
Uasadi-jidi Venezuela 4°54N 65°18W 329 C4
Uati-Paranã → Brazil 1°51S 65°37W 328 D4
Uatumã → Brazil 2°26S 57°37W 329 D6
Uauá Brazil 9°50S 39°28W 332 C4
Uaupés Brazil 0°8S 67°5W 328 D4
Uaupés → Brazil 0°2N 67°16W 328 C4
Uaxactún Guatemala 17°25N 89°29W 320 C2
Ub Serbia 44°28N 20°6E 202 B4
Ubá Brazil 21°8S 43°0W 333 F3
Uba Nigeria 10°29N 13°13E 263 C7
Ubai Papua N. G. 5°39S 150°38E 286 C6
Ubaitaba Brazil 14°18S 39°20W 333 D4
Ubajara △ Brazil 3°55S 40°50W 332 B3
Ubangi = Oubangi → Dem. Rep. of the Congo 0°30S 17°50E 264 C3
Ubaté Colombia 5°19N 73°49W 328 B3
Ubauro Pakistan 28°15N 69°45E 242 E3
Ubay Phil. 10°3N 124°28E 233 F5
Ubaye → France 44°28N 6°18E 175 D10
Ubayyiḍ, W. al → Iraq 32°34N 43°48E 213 F10
Ube Japan 33°56N 131°15E 222 D3
Úbeda Spain 38°3N 3°23W 195 G7
Ubeidiya West Bank 31°43N 35°17E 123 B2
Uberaba Brazil 19°50S 47°55W 333 E2
Uberaba → Brazil 23°35S 46°41W 137 B2
Uberaba, L. Brazil 17°30S 57°50W 331 D6
Uberlândia Minas Gerais, Brazil 19°0S 48°20W 333 E2
Uberlândia Roraima, Brazil 0°48N 59°20W 329 C6
Überlingen Germany 47°46N 9°10E 179 H5
Ubiaja Nigeria 6°41N 6°22E 263 D6
Ubin, Pulau Singapore 1°24N 103°57E 138 A3
Ubly U.S.A. 43°42N 82°55W 312 C2
Ubolratna Res. Thailand 16°45N 102°30E 236 D4
Ubombo S. Africa 27°31S 32°4E 271 C5
Ubon Ratchathani Thailand 15°15N 104°50E 236 E5
Ubondo Dem. Rep. of the Congo 0°55S 25°42E 268 C2
Ubort → Belarus 52°6N 28°30E 177 B15
Ubrique Spain 36°41N 5°27W 195 J5
Ubud Indonesia 8°30S 115°16E 231 J18
Ubuna Solomon Is. 10°11S 161°24E 287 N11
Ubundu Dem. Rep. of the Congo 0°22S 25°30E 264 C5
Ucar Azerbaijan 40°31N 47°39E 191 K8
Ucayali → Peru 4°30S 73°30W 328 D3
Uccle Belgium 50°48N 4°22E 116 B2
Uchab Namibia 19°47S 17°42E 270 A2
Uchiko Japan 33°33N 132°39E 222 D4
Uchiura-Wan Japan 42°25N 140°40E 220 C10
Uchiza Peru 8°25S 76°20W 330 B2
Uchquduq Uzbekistan 41°50N 62°50E 216 D6
Uchte Germany 52°30N 8°54E 178 C4
Uchur → Russia 58°48N 130°35E 215 D14
Uckermark Germany 53°5N 13°30E 178 B9
Ucluelet Canada 48°57N 125°32W 296 D3
Úcua Angola 8°43S 14°8E 265 D2
Uda → Russia 54°42N 135°14E 215 D14
Uda Walawe △ Sri Lanka 6°20N 81°0E 245 L5
Udachnyy Russia 66°25N 112°24E 215 C12
Udagamandalam India 11°30N 76°44E 245 J3
Udainagar India 22°33N 76°13E 242 H7
Udaipur Raj., India 24°36N 73°44E 242 G5
Udaipur Tripura, India 23°32N 91°30E 241 D3
Udaipur Garhi Nepal 27°0N 86°35E 243 F12
Udala India 21°35N 86°34E 243 J12
Udalguri India 26°46N 92°8E 241 B4
Udayagiri Andhra Pradesh, India 14°52N 79°19E 245 G4
Udayagiri Orissa, India 20°8N 84°23E 244 D7
Udbina Croatia 44°31N 15°47E 199 D12
Uddeholm Sweden 60°1N 13°38E 162 D7
Uddevalla Sweden 58°21N 11°55E 163 F5
Uddheden Sweden 59°57N 12°54E 162 E6
Uddjaure Sweden 65°56N 17°49E 160 D17
Udelnaya Russia 60°0N 30°21E 137 A2
Udelnoe Russia 59°58N 30°20E 137 B1
Uden Neths. 51°40N 5°37E 170 C5
Udgir India 18°25N 77°5E 244 E3
Udhampur India 33°0N 75°5E 243 C6
Udi Nigeria 6°17N 7°21E 263 D6
Údine Italy 46°3N 13°14E 199 B10
Udintsev Fracture Zone S. Ocean 57°0S 145°0W 151 B13
Udlding Germany 48°15N 11°25E 131 A1
Udmurtia □ Russia 57°30N 52°30E 186 C9
Udon Thani Thailand 17°29N 102°46E 236 D4
Udong Cambodia 11°48N 104°45E 237 G5
Udot I. Micronesia 7°22N 151°42E 287 T17
Udskaya Guba Russia 54°50N 135°45E 215 D14
Udu Pt. Fiji 16°9S 179°57W 287 A3
Udumalaippettai India 10°35N 77°15E 245 J3
Udupi India 13°25N 74°42E 245 H2
Udva India 20°5N 73°0E 244 D1
Udvoy Balkan Bulgaria 42°50N 26°50E 203 D10
Udzungwa △ Tanzania 7°52S 36°35E 268 D4
Udzungwa Range Tanzania 9°30S 35°10E 269 D4
Ueckermünde Germany 53°44N 14°1E 178 B10
Ueda Japan 36°24N 138°16E 223 A10
Uedineniya, Os. Russia 78°0N 85°0E 150 B12
Uele → Dem. Rep. of the Congo 3°45N 24°45E 264 B4
Uelen Russia 66°10N 170°0W 215 C19
Uelzen Germany 52°57N 10°32E 178 C6
Ueno Mie, Japan 34°45N 136°8E 223 C8
Ueno Tōkyō, Japan 35°42N 139°46E 140 A3
Uetersen Germany 53°40N 9°40E 178 B5
Uetze Germany 52°28N 10°11E 178 C6
Ufa Russia 54°45N 55°55E 186 D10
Ufa → Russia 54°40N 56°0E 186 D10
Uffenheim Germany 49°33N 10°14E 179 F6
Ugab → Namibia 20°55S 13°30E 270 B1
Ugalla → Tanzania 5°8S 30°42E 268 D3
Ugalla River ⌂ Tanzania 5°50S 31°54E 268 D3
Uganda ■ Africa 2°0N 32°0E 268 B3
Ugento Italy 39°56N 18°10E 201 C11
Ugep Nigeria 5°53N 8°2E 263 D6
Ughelli Nigeria 5°33N 6°0E 263 D6
Ugie S. Africa 31°10S 28°13E 271 D4
Ugíjar Spain 36°58N 3°7W 195 J7
Ugine France 45°45N 6°25E 175 C10
Uglegorsk Russia 49°5N 142°2E 215 E15
Uglich Russia 57°33N 38°20E 188 D10
Ugljan Croatia 44°12N 15°10E 199 D12
Ugljane Croatia 43°35N 16°46E 199 E13
Ugolny = Beringovskiy Russia 63°3N 179°19E 215 C18
Ugolnyy = Karpinsk Russia 59°45N 60°1E 186 C11
Ugolnyye Kopi Russia 64°44N 177°42E 215 C18
Ugolnyye Kopi = Kopeysk Russia 55°7N 61°37E 216 A6
Ugoofaaru Maldives 5°40N 73°0E 272 d
Ugra → Russia 54°30N 36°7E 188 E9
Ugŭrchin Bulgaria 43°6N 24°26E 203 C8
Uh → Slovak Rep. 48°37N 22°0E 181 C15
Uherské Hradiště Czech Rep. 49°4N 17°30E 181 B10
Uherský Brod Czech Rep. 49°1N 17°40E 181 B10
Úhlava → Czech Rep. 49°45N 13°24E 180 B6
Uhlenhorst Namibia 23°45S 17°55E 270 B2
Uhniv Ukraine 50°22N 23°45E 185 H10
Úholičky Czech Rep. 50°9N 14°19E 135 B1
Uhrichsville U.S.A. 40°24N 81°21W 312 F3
Uhříněves Czech Rep. 50°2N 14°35E 135 B3
Uibhist a Deas = South Uist U.K. 57°20N 7°15W 167 D1
Uibhist a Tuath = North Uist U.K. 57°40N 7°15W 167 D1
Uiche Angola 12°2S 20°51E 265 E4
Uido S. Korea 34°36N 125°50E 224 E2
Uig U.K. 57°35N 6°21W 167 D2
Uíge Angola 7°30S 14°40E 265 D2
Uíge □ Angola 7°0S 16°0E 265 D3
Uiha Tonga 19°54S 174°25W 287 P13
Uijeongbu S. Korea 37°44N 127°2E 224 D3
Ŭiju N. Korea 40°15N 124°35E 224 B2
Uinta Mts. U.S.A. 40°45N 110°30W 304 F8
Uiryeong S. Korea 35°19N 128°15E 224 E4
Uis Namibia 21°8S 14°49E 270 B1
Uiseong S. Korea 36°21N 128°45E 224 D4
Uitenhage S. Africa 33°40S 25°28E 270 D4
Uithoorn Neths. 52°14N 4°50E 112 B1
Uithuizen Neths. 53°24N 6°41E 170 A6
Ujazd Poland 50°23N 18°21E 185 H5
Ujazdów Poland 52°13N 21°1E 142 B2
Ujazdowski Castle Warsaw, Poland 142 c3
Újfehértó Hungary 47°49N 21°41E 182 C6
Ujh → India 32°10N 75°18E 242 C6
Ujhani India 28°0N 79°6E 243 F8
Uji Japan 34°53N 135°48E 223 C7
Uji-guntō Japan 31°15N 129°25E 221 J4
Ujiyamada = Ise Japan 34°25N 136°45E 223 C8
Ujjain India 23°9N 75°43E 242 H6
Újpalota Hungary 47°32N 19°8E 117 A2
Újpest Hungary 47°35N 19°4E 117 A2
Ujście Poland 53°3N 16°45E 185 E3
Újszász Hungary 47°19N 20°7E 182 C5
Ujung Kulon △ Indonesia 6°46S 105°19E 234 D3
Ujung Pandang = Makassar Indonesia 5°10S 119°20E 235 D5
Uka Russia 57°50N 162°0E 215 D17
Ukai Sagar India 21°20N 73°43E 244 D1
Ukara I. Tanzania 1°50S 33°0E 268 C3
Uke-Shima Japan 28°2N 129°14E 221 K4
Ukerewe I. Tanzania 2°0S 33°0E 268 C3
Ukholovo Russia 53°47N 40°30E 190 D5
Ukhrul India 25°10N 94°25E 241 C5
Ukhta Russia 63°34N 53°41E 186 B9
Uki Ni Masi Solomon Is. 10°15S 161°47E 287 N11
Ukiah U.S.A. 39°9N 123°13W 306 F3
Ukita Japan 35°40N 139°51E 140 A4
Ukmergė Lithuania 55°15N 24°45E 188 E3
Ukraine ■ Europe 49°0N 32°0E 189 H7
Uku Angola 11°24S 14°22E 265 E2
Ukwi Botswana 23°29S 20°30E 270 B3
Ula Turkey 37°6N 28°25E 212 D3
Ulaan Nuur Mongolia 44°30N 103°40E 226 B2
Ulaan-Uul Mongolia 46°4N 100°49E 226 B6
Ulaanbaatar Mongolia 47°55N 106°53E 218 B10
Ulaangom Mongolia 50°5N 92°10E 217 B12
Ulaanjirem Mongolia 45°5N 105°30E 226 B3
Ulak I. U.S.A. 51°22N 178°57W 303 L3
Ulala = Gorno-Altaysk Russia 51°50N 86°5E 217 B11
Ulalu I. Micronesia 7°23N 151°41E 287 T17
Ulamambri Australia 31°19S 149°23E 283 A8
Ulamba Dem. Rep. of the Congo 9°3S 23°38E 265 D4
Ulamona Papua N. G. 5°0S 151°15E 286 C6
Ulan Bator = Ulaanbaatar Mongolia 47°55N 106°53E 218 B10
Ulan Erge Russia 46°19N 44°53E 191 G7
Ulan Khol Russia 45°18N 47°4E 191 H8
Ulan Ude Russia 51°45N 107°40E 219 A10
Ulanhad = Chifeng China 42°18N 118°58E 227 C10
Ulanhot = Horqin Youyi Qianqi China 46°5N 122°3E 227 A12
Ulanów Poland 50°30N 22°16E 185 H9
Ulansuhai Nur China 40°53N 108°51E 226 D5
Ulaş Sivas, Turkey 39°26N 37°2E 212 C7
Ulaş Tekirdağ, Turkey 41°14N 27°42E 203 E11
Ulawa Solomon Is. 9°46S 161°57E 287 M11
Ulaya Morogoro, Tanzania 7°3S 36°55E 268 D4
Ulaya Tabora, Tanzania 4°25S 33°30E 268 C3
Ulcinj Montenegro 41°58N 19°10E 202 E3
Ulco S. Africa 28°21S 24°15E 270 C3
Ule älv = Oulujoki → Finland 65°1N 25°30E 160 D21
Ule träsk = Oulujärvi Finland 64°25N 27°15E 160 D22
Uleåborg = Oulu Finland 65°1N 25°29E 160 D21
Ulefoss Norway 59°17N 9°16E 164 E6
Ulëz Albania 41°46N 19°57E 202 E3
Ulfborg Denmark 56°16N 8°20E 163 H2
Ulhasnagar India 19°15N 73°10E 244 E1
Uliastay Mongolia 47°56N 97°28E 218 B8
Uljin S. Korea 36°59N 129°24E 224 D4
Uljma Serbia 45°2N 21°10E 182 E6
Ülken Kazakhstan 45°12N 73°58E 217 C8
Ülken Borsyq Qumy Kazakhstan 47°0N 59°11E 216 C5
Ulla → Spain 42°39N 8°44W 194 C2
Ulladulla Australia 35°21S 150°29E 283 C9
Ullal India 12°48N 74°51E 245 H2
Ullapool U.K. 57°54N 5°9W 167 D3
Ullared Sweden 57°8N 12°42E 163 G6
Ulldecona Spain 40°36N 0°20E 196 E5
Ullerup Denmark 55°34N 12°36E 118 B3
Ulleungdo S. Korea 37°30N 130°30E 224 C6
Ullevål Norway 59°56N 10°46E 133 A3
Ullswater Ont., Canada 45°12N 79°29W 312 A5
Ullswater Cumb., U.K. 54°34N 2°52W 168 C5
Ulm Germany 48°23N 9°58E 179 G5
Ulmarra Australia 29°37S 153°4E 281 D5
Ulmeni Buzău, Romania 45°4N 26°40E 183 E11
Ulmeni Maramureş, Romania 47°28N 23°18E 183 C8
Ulonguè Mozam. 14°37S 34°19E 269 E3

Ulricehamn Sweden 57°46N 13°26E 163 G7
Ulrika Sweden 58°5N 15°23E 163 F9
Ulriksdal Sweden 59°23N 17°59E 139 A1
Ulsan S. Korea 35°20N 129°15E 224 E4
Ulsberg Norway 62°45N 10°0E 164 B6
Ulsta U.K. 60°30N 1°9W 167 A7
Ulsteinvik Norway 62°21N 5°53E 164 B2
Ulster □ U.K. 54°35N 6°30W 166 B5
Ulstrem Bulgaria 42°1N 26°27E 203 D10
Ultima Australia 35°30S 143°18E 282 C5
Ulu Temburong △ Brunei 4°27N 115°15E 235 B5
Uluçat Gölü Turkey 40°9N 28°35E 203 F12
Uluborlu Turkey 38°4N 30°28E 205 C12
Uluçinar Turkey 36°24N 35°53E 250 B6
Uludağ Turkey 40°4N 29°13E 203 F13
Uludağ △ Turkey 40°5N 29°12E 203 F13
Uludere Turkey 37°28N 42°42E 250 B10
Uluguru Mts. Tanzania 7°15S 37°40E 268 D4
Ulukışla Turkey 37°33N 34°28E 212 D6
Ulundi S. Africa 28°20S 31°25E 271 C6
Ulungur He → China 47°1N 87°24E 217 C11
Ulungur Hu China 47°20N 87°10E 217 C11
Ulupalakua U.S.A. 20°39N 156°24W 302 C5
Uluru Australia 25°23S 131°5E 279 E5
Uluru-Kata Tjuta △
Australia 25°19S 131°1E 279 E5
Ulutau Kazakhstan 48°39N 67°1E 217 C7
Uluwatu Indonesia 8°50S 115°5E 231 K18
Ulva U.K. 56°29N 6°13W 167 E2
Ulverston U.K. 54°13N 3°5W 168 C4
Ulverstone Australia 41°11S 146°11E 281 G4
Ulvik Norway 60°35N 6°52E 164 C2
Ulya Russia 59°10N 142°0E 215 D15
Ulyanka Russia 59°50N 30°14E 137 B1
Ulyanovo Russia 54°50N 22°6E 184 D9
Ulyanovsk Russia 54°20N 48°25E 190 C9
Ulyanovsk □ Russia 54°5N 48°5E 190 C9
Ulyasutay = Uliastay
Mongolia 47°56N 97°28E 218 B8
Ulysses Kans., U.S.A. 37°35N 101°22W 308 G3
Ulysses Pa., U.S.A. 41°54N 77°46E 312 E7
Ulysses, Mt. Canada 57°20N 124°5W 296 B4
Ulysses S. Grant Nat. Historic Site □
U.S.A. 38°33N 90°28W 310 F6
Ulyzhylanshyq →
Kazakhstan 48°51N 63°46E 216 C6
Um Al-Khanazir Island
Iraq 33°17N 44°22E 113 E2
Umag Croatia 45°26N 13°31E 199 C10
Umala Bolivia 17°25S 68°5W 330 D4
'Umān = Oman ■ Asia 23°0N 58°0E 249 B7
Uman Ukraine 48°40N 30°12E 177 D16
Uman I. Micronesia 7°17N 151°52E 287 U18
Umaria India 23°35N 80°50E 243 H9
Umarkhed India 19°37N 77°46E 244 E3
Umarkot Pakistan 25°15N 69°40E 242 G3
Umarpada India 21°27N 73°30E 242 J5
Umatac Guam 13°18N 144°39E 302 d
Umatilla U.S.A. 45°55N 119°21W 304 D4
Umba Russia 66°42N 34°11E 186 A5
Umbagog L. U.S.A. 44°46N 71°3W 313 B13
Umbakumba Australia 13°47S 136°50E 280 A2
Umbértide Italy 43°18N 12°20E 199 E9
Umboi I. Papua N. G. 5°40S 148°0E 286 C5
Umbrella Mts. N.Z. 45°35S 169°5E 285 F4
Umbria □ Italy 42°53N 12°30E 199 F9
Umeå Sweden 63°45N 20°20E 160 E19
Umeälven → Sweden 63°45N 20°20E 160 E19
Umeda Japan 34°41N 135°29E 133 A1
Umera Indonesia 0°12S 129°37E 231 E7
Umerkhadi Mumbai, India 130 b2
Umfuli → Zimbabwe 17°30S 29°23E 269 F2
Umfurudzi → Zimbabwe 16°15S 31°40E 269 F3
Umgusa Zimbabwe 19°29S 27°52E 269 F2
Umgwenya → Mozam. 25°14S 32°18E 271 C5
Umiat U.S.A. 69°22N 152°8W 303 B9
Umiray Phil. 15°13N 121°25E 232 D3
Umjuujaq Canada 56°33N 76°33W 298 A4
Umka Serbia 44°40N 20°19E 202 B4
Umkomaas S. Africa 30°13S 30°48E 271 D5
Umm ad Daraj, J. Jordan 32°18N 35°48E 251 F6
Umm al Aränib Libya 26°10N 14°43E 258 C2
Umm al Khashab
Si. Arabia 17°23N 42°32E 256 D5
Umm al Qaywayn U.A.E. 25°30N 55°35E 247 E7
Umm al Qittayn Jordan 32°18N 36°40E 251 F7
Umm al' Abīd Libya 27°31N 15°2E 258 C3
Umm Arda Sudan 15°17N 32°31E 257 D3
Umm Bäb Qatar 25°12N 50°48E 247 E6
Umm Badr Sudan 14°13N 27°58E 257 E2
Umm Bel Sudan 13°35N 28°0E 257 E2
Umm Birkah Si. Arabia 27°44N 36°31E 256 B4
Umm Bom Sudan 11°43N 25°27E 257 E2
Umm Dam Sudan 13°45N 30°59E 257 E3
Umm Debi Sudan 14°37N 30°23E 257 E3
Umm Dubban Sudan 15°23N 32°52E 257 D3
Umm Durman = Omdurmân
Sudan 15°40N 32°28E 257 D3
Umm el Fahm Israel 32°31N 35°9E 251 F6
Umm Gafala Sudan 13°22N 27°15E 257 E2
Umm Gimala Sudan 11°27N 28°12E 257 E2
Umm Inderaba Sudan 17°30N 33°13E 256 D3
Umm Isheirât, G. Egypt 24°18N 33°18E 251 K5
Umm Keddada Sudan 13°33N 26°35E 257 E2
Umm Koweika Sudan 13°10N 32°16E 257 E3
Umm Merwa Sudan 18°4N 32°30E 256 D3
Umm Qantur Sudan 9°58N 28°55E 257 F2
Umm Qasr Iraq 30°1N 47°58E 246 D5
Umm Ruwaba Sudan 12°50N 31°20E 257 E3
Umm Saiyala Sudan 14°25N 31°10E 257 E3
Umm Shanqa Sudan 13°14N 27°14E 257 E2
Umm Shugeira Sudan 13°34N 29°37E 266 E6
Umm Shutur South Sudan 7°17N 33°14E 257 F3
Umm Sidr Sudan 14°25N 25°10E 257 E2
Umm Tais □ Qatar 26°7N 51°15E 249 A5
Umm Urūmah Si. Arabia 25°43N 36°35E 256 B4
Umm Zehetir Egypt 28°48N 32°31E 166 b4
Umnak I. U.S.A. 53°15N 168°20W 303 K5
Umniati → Zimbabwe 16°49N 28°45E 269 F2
Umpqua → U.S.A. 43°40N 124°12W 304 E1
Umpulo Angola 12°38S 17°42E 266 G3
Umraniye Turkey 41°1N 29°4E 122 B2
Umred India 20°51N 79°18E 244 E4
Umreth India 22°41N 73°4E 242 H5
Umri India 19°2N 77°39E 244 E3
Umtata = Mthatha
S. Africa 31°36S 28°49E 271 D4
Umuahia Nigeria 5°31N 7°26E 263 D6
Umuarama Brazil 23°45S 53°20W 336 A5
Umuda I. Papua N. G. 8°29S 143°46E 286 E2
Umurbey Turkey 40°13N 26°36E 203 F10
Umuzimvubu S. Africa 31°38S 29°33E 271 D4
Umzingwane →
Zimbabwe 22°12S 29°56E 269 G2
Umzinto = eMuziwezinto
S. Africa 30°15S 30°45E 271 D5
Una India 20°46N 71°8E 242 J4
Una → Bos.-H. 45°0N 16°20E 199 D13
Unac → Bos.-H. 44°30N 16°9E 199 D13
Unaðsdalur Iceland 66°7N 22°36W 155 A4

Unadilla Ga., U.S.A. 32°16N 83°44W 316 C6
Unadilla N.Y., U.S.A. 42°20N 75°19W 313 D9
Unai Brazil 16°23S 46°53W 333 E2
Unalakleet U.S.A. 63°52N 160°47W 303 E7
Unalaska U.S.A. 53°53N 166°32W 303 K6
Unalaska I. U.S.A. 53°35N 166°50W 303 K6
'Unayzah Si. Arabia 26°6N 43°58E 246 E4
'Unayzah, J. Asia 32°12N 39°18E 213 F8
Uncastillo Spain 42°21N 1°8W 196 C3
Uncía Bolivia 18°25S 66°40W 330 D4
Uncompahgre Peak
U.S.A. 38°4N 107°28W 304 G10
Uncompahgre Plateau
U.S.A. 38°20N 108°15W 304 G9
Undara Volcanic △
Australia 18°14S 144°41E 280 B3
Unden Sweden 58°45N 14°25E 163 F8
Underbool Australia 35°10S 141°51E 282 C4
Underground Atlanta
U.S.A. 33°45N 84°24W 118 B2
Underhill, L. U.S.A. 28°32N 81°20W 133 A3
Undersaker Sweden 63°19N 13°21E 162 A7
Underwood Canada 44°18N 81°29W 312 B3
Unedral Norway 60°57N 7°6E 164 D4
Unea I. Papua N. G. 4°53S 149°9E 286 C5
Unecha Russia 52°50N 32°37E 189 F7
Ueneixui → Brazil 0°37S 65°34W 328 D4
Unětický potok →
Czech Rep. 50°9N 14°24E 135 B2
Unga I. U.S.A. 55°15N 160°40W 303 J7
Ungarie Australia 33°38S 146°56E 283 B7
Ungarisch-Hradisch = Uherské
Hradiště Czech Rep. 49°4N 17°30E 181 B10
Ungarisch-Ostra = Uherský Brod
Czech Rep. 49°1N 17°40E 181 B10
Ungarra Australia 34°12S 136°2E 282 C2
Ungat Papua N. G. 2°40S 150°15E 286 B6
Ungava B. Canada 59°30N 67°30W 299 F13
Ungava, Pén. d' Canada 60°0N 74°0W 295 F17
Ungeny = Ungheni
Moldova 47°11N 27°51E 183 C12
Unggi N. Korea 42°16N 130°28E 224 A5
Ungheni Moldova 47°11N 27°51E 183 C12
Unguala → Ethiopia 8°6N 41°9E 257 F5
Ungvár = Uzhhorod
Ukraine 48°36N 22°18E 182 B7
Ungwana B. Kenya 2°45S 40°20E 268 C5
Ungwatiri Sudan 16°52N 36°10E 257 D4
Unhos Portugal 38°49N 9°7E 126 A2
Uni Russia 57°46N 51°31E 190 B10
União Brazil 4°35S 42°52W 332 B3
União da Vitória Brazil 26°13S 51°5W 335 B5
União dos Palmares Brazil 9°10S 36°2W 332 C4
Uničov Czech Rep. 49°48N 17°9E 181 B10
Unidad Santa Fe Mexico 22°9N 99°13W 128 B1
Uniejów Poland 51°59N 18°46E 185 G5
Unije Croatia 44°40N 14°15E 199 D11
Unimak I. U.S.A. 54°45N 164°0W 303 J7
Unimak Pass. U.S.A. 54°15N 164°30W 303 J6
Unini → Brazil 1°41S 61°31W 329 D5
Union Miss., U.S.A. 32°34N 89°7W 315 E10
Union Mo., U.S.A. 38°27N 91°0W 310 F6
Union Ohio, U.S.A. 39°55N 84°21W 314 F3
Union S.C., U.S.A. 34°43N 81°37W 315 D14
Union City Calif., U.S.A. 37°36N 122°1W 306 H4
Union City Ga., U.S.A. 33°35N 84°33W 118 B5
Union City New York, U.S.A. 132 b1
Union City Ohio, U.S.A. 40°12N 84°49W 311 D12
Union City Pa., U.S.A. 41°54N 79°51W 312 E5
Union City Tenn., U.S.A. 36°26N 89°3W 315 C10
Union Dale U.S.A. 41°43N 75°29W 313 E9
Union Gap U.S.A. 46°33N 120°28W 304 C5
Union Grove U.S.A. 42°41N 88°3W 311 B8
Union I. St. Vincent 12°36N 61°26W 323 n
Union Park U.S.A. 28°34N 81°17W 317 C8
Union Point U.S.A. 33°37N 83°4W 316 B6
Union Port U.S.A. 40°48N 73°51W 132 B2
Union Springs Ala., U.S.A. 32°9N 85°43W 316 C4
Union Springs N.Y.,
U.S.A. 42°50N 76°41W 313 D8
Union Square San Francisco, U.S.A. 136 b2
Union Star U.S.A. 39°59N 94°36W 310 E2
Union Station Toronto, Canada 141 c2
Union Station Chicago, U.S.A. 119 c1
Union Station Washington, D.C., U.S.A. 143 b3
Union Station Los Angeles, U.S.A. 127 b3
Union Station New Orleans, U.S.A. 131 b1
Union Plaza
Washington, D.C., U.S.A. 143 b3
Uniondale S. Africa 33°39S 23°7E 270 D3
Uniontown Ky., U.S.A. 37°47N 87°56W 311 G9
Uniontown Pa., U.S.A. 39°54N 79°44W 309 F14
Unionville Ga., U.S.A. 31°26N 83°30W 316 D5
Unionville Mo., U.S.A. 40°29N 93°1W 310 D3
Unirea Romania 44°15N 27°35E 183 F12
United Arab Emirates ■
Asia 23°50N 54°0E 247 F7
United Arab Republic = Egypt ■
Africa 28°0N 31°0E 256 B3
United Center U.S.A. 41°53N 87°41W 119 B2
United Kingdom ■ Europe 53°0N 2°0W 165 E6
United Nations Headquarters
New York, U.S.A. 132 c3
United Provinces = Uttar Pradesh □
India 27°0N 80°0E 243 F9
United States of America ■
N. Amer. 37°0N 96°0W 301 H20
Unity Canada 52°30N 109°5W 297 C7
Unity □ South Sudan 8°30N 30°0E 257 F3
Universal Studios Calif.,
U.S.A. 34°9N 118°21W 126 B2
Universal Studios Fla.,
U.S.A. 28°29N 81°29W 133 A2
Universales, Mtes. Spain 40°18N 1°33W 196 E3
Universidad Spain 40°27N 3°44W 127 B1
University City U.S.A. 38°39N 90°18W 310 F6
University Park Md.,
U.S.A. 38°58N 76°56W 143 B4
University Park N. Mex.,
U.S.A. 32°17N 106°45W 305 K10
University Place U.S.A. 47°14N 122°33W 128 C3
Unjha India 23°46N 72°24E 242 H5
Unmet Vanuatu 16°8S 167°15E 287 F5
Unna Germany 51°32N 7°42E 178 D3
Uno, Ilha Guinea-Biss. 11°15N 16°13W 262 C1
Unnao India 26°35N 80°30E 243 F9
Unpongkor Vanuatu 18°50S 169°0E 287 H6
Unruhstadt = Kargowa
Poland 52°5N 15°51E 185 F2
Unsan N. Korea 40°6N 125°51E 224 E3
Unsengedsi → Zimbabwe 15°43S 31°14E 269 F3
Unst U.K. 60°44N 0°53W 167 A8
Unstrut → Germany 51°32N 7°42E 178 D3
Unter den Linden Berlin, Germany 115 a4
Unterberg Germany 48°41N 11°38E 131 b2
Unterdrauburg = Dravograd
Slovenia 46°36N 15°5E 199 D11
Unterföhring Germany 48°11N 11°38E 131 A3
Unterfranken □ Germany 50°0N 10°0E 179 A5
Unterhaching Germany 48°3N 11°37E 131 B2
Unterlaa Austria 48°8N 16°24E 136 E10
Untermenzing Germany 48°10N 11°28E 131 A1
Unterschleissheim
Germany 48°17N 11°34E 179 G7
Unterwalden □ Switz. 46°53N 8°20E 179 J4
Unuk → Canada 56°5N 131°3W 296 B2

Ünye Turkey 41°5N 37°15E 212 B7
Unzen-Amakusa △
Japan 32°15N 130°10E 222 E2
Unzen-Dake Japan 32°45N 130°17E 222 E2
Unzha Russia 58°0N 44°0E 190 A7
Unzha → Russia 57°49N 43°47E 190 A6
Uong Bi Vietnam 21°2N 106°47E 236 B6
Uozu Japan 36°48N 137°24E 223 A9
Upata Venezuela 8°1N 62°24W 329 B5
Upemba, L.
Dem. Rep. of the Congo 8°30S 26°20E 269 D2
Upemba □
Dem. Rep. of the Congo 9°0S 26°35E 269 D2
Upernavik Greenland 72°49N 56°20W 154 C5
Upington S. Africa 28°25S 21°15E 270 C3
Upleta India 21°46N 70°16E 242 J4
'Upolu Samoa 13°58S 172°0W 287 V20
Upolu Pt. U.S.A. 20°16N 155°52W 302 C6
Upper □ Ghana 10°30N 1°30W 263 C4
Upper Alkali L. U.S.A. 41°47N 120°8W 304 F3
Upper Arlington U.S.A. 40°0N 83°4W 311 E13
Upper Arrow L. Canada 50°30N 117°50W 296 C5
Upper Austria = Oberösterreich □
Austria 48°10N 14°0E 180 C7
Upper B. U.S.A. 40°40N 74°3W 132 c1
Upper Daly □ Australia 14°26S 131°3E 278 B5
Upper Darby U.S.A. 39°55N 75°16W 309 F16
Upper East Side New York, U.S.A. 132 b3
Upper Elmers End U.K. 51°23N 0°1W 125 B3
Upper Foster L. Canada 56°47N 105°20W 297 B7
Upper Hutt N.Z. 41°8S 175°5E 284 H4
Upper Klamath L.
U.S.A. 42°25N 121°55W 304 E4
Upper Lake U.S.A. 39°10N 122°54W 306 F4
Upper Liard Canada 60°3N 128°54W 296 A3
Upper Manilla Australia 30°38S 150°40E 283 A9
Upper Manzanilla
Trin. & Tob. 10°31N 61°4W 323 t
Upper Missouri Breaks △
U.S.A. 47°50N 109°55W 304 C9
Upper Musquodoboit
Canada 45°10N 62°58W 299 C7
Upper New York B. = Upper B.
U.S.A. 40°40N 74°3W 132 c1
Upper Nile □ South Sudan 9°30N 33°0E 257 F3
Upper Norwood U.K. 51°24N 0°6W 125 B3
Upper Peirce Res.
Singapore 1°22N 103°47E 138 A2
Upper Red L. U.S.A. 48°8N 94°45W 308 A6
Upper Sandusky U.S.A. 40°50N 83°17W 311 D13
Upper Senegal & Niger = Mali ■
Africa 17°0N 3°0W 262 B4
Upper Sydenham U.K. 51°26N 0°4W 125 B3
Upper Tooting U.K. 51°26N 0°10W 125 B3
Upper Volta = Burkina Faso ■
Africa 12°0N 1°0W 262 C4
Upper West Side New York, U.S.A. 132 a2
Uppháaräd Sweden 58°9N 12°19E 163 F6
Uppland Sweden 59°59N 17°48E 162 D12
Upplands-Väsby Sweden 59°31N 17°54E 162 E11
Uppsala Sweden 59°53N 17°38E 162 E11
Uppsala län □ Sweden 60°0N 17°30E 162 D11
Upshi India 33°48N 77°52E 243 C7
Upton London, U.K. 52°36N 2°17E 125 A4
Upton Wyo., U.S.A. 44°6N 104°38W 304 D11
Uptown U.S.A. 41°58N 87°40W 119 B2
Uqsuqtuuq = Gjoa Haven
Canada 68°38N 95°53W 294 D12
Ur Iraq 30°55N 46°25E 246 D5
Ur Kut Somali Rep. 3°31N 42°47E 267 D5
Ura-Tyube = Üroteppa
Tajikistan 39°55N 69°1E 217 E7
Urabá, G. de Colombia 8°25N 76°53W 328 B2
Urad Qianqi China 40°20N 108°30E 226 D5
Uraga-Suidō Japan 35°13N 139°43E 133 B3
Urahoro Japan 42°50N 143°40E 220 C11
Urakawa Japan 42°9N 142°47E 220 C11
Ural = Uralskiy □ Russia 64°0N 70°0E 214 C7
Ural → Zhayyq
Kazakhstan 47°0N 51°48E 187 E9
Ural Mts. = Uralskie Gory
Eurasia 60°0N 59°0E 186 C10
Uralla Australia 30°37S 151°29E 283 A9
Uralmedstroy = Krasnouralsk
Russia 58°21N 60°3E 186 C11
Uralsk = Oral Kazakhstan 51°20N 51°20E 190 E10
Uralskie Gory Eurasia 60°0N 59°0E 186 C10
Uralskiy □ Russia 64°0N 70°0E 214 C7
Urambo Tanzania 5°4S 32°0E 268 D3
Uran India 18°54N 72°52E 130 b1
Urana Australia 35°15S 146°21E 283 C7
Urana, L. Australia 35°16S 146°10E 283 C7
Urandangi Australia 21°32S 138°14E 280 C2
Uranga Australia 30°31S 153°1E 283 A10
Uranium City Canada 59°34N 108°37W 297 B7
Urapuntja = Utopia
Australia 22°14S 134°33E 280 C1
Uraricaá → Brazil 3°20N 61°56W 329 C5
Uraricoera Brazil 3°27N 60°59W 329 C5
Uraricoera → Brazil 3°2N 60°30W 329 C5
Urasoe Japan 26°15N 127°43E 288 a
Uravakonda India 14°57N 77°12E 245 G3
Urawa = Saitama Japan 35°54N 139°38E 223 B11
Uray Russia 60°5N 65°15E 214 C7
Urayasu Japan 35°39N 139°55E 140 B4
'Uray'irah Si. Arabia 25°57N 48°53E 247 E6
Urbakh = Pushkino Russia 51°16N 47°0E 190 D8
Urbana Ill., U.S.A. 40°7N 88°12W 311 D8
Urbana Ohio, U.S.A. 40°7N 83°45W 311 D13
Urbandale U.S.A. 41°38N 93°43W 310 E3
Urbánia Italy 43°40N 12°31E 199 E9
Urbano Santos Brazil 3°12S 43°23W 332 B3
Urbe □ Italy 44°29N 8°38W 198 D5
Urbel → Spain 42°21N 3°40W 194 C7
Urbino Italy 43°43N 12°38E 199 E9
Urbión, Picos de Spain 42°1N 2°52N 196 C2
Urca Brazil 22°56S 43°9W 135 B2
Urdaneta Phil. 15°57N 120°34E 232 D3
Urdinarrain Argentina 32°37S 58°52W 334 C4
Urdos France 42°51N 0°35W 174 E6
Ure → U.K. 54°5N 1°20W 168 C6
Uren Russia 57°35N 45°55E 190 B7
Urengoy Russia 65°58N 78°22E 214 C8
Ureparapara Vanuatu 13°32S 167°20E 287 E5
Ures Mexico 29°26N 110°24W 318 B2
Ureshino Japan 33°6N 129°59E 222 E2
Urewera △ N.Z. 38°29S 177°7E 284 F6
Urfa = Sanliurfa Turkey 37°12N 38°50E 213 D8
Urga = Ulaanbaatar
Mongolia 47°55N 106°53E 218 B10
Urgench Uzbekistan 41°40N 60°41E 216 E6
Ürgench = Urganch
Uzbekistan 41°40N 60°41E 216 E6
Ürgüp Turkey 38°38N 34°56E 212 C6
Uri India 34°8N 74°2E 243 B6
Uri □ Switz. 46°43N 8°35E 179 J4
Uribante → Venezuela 7°25N 71°50N 328 B3
Uribe Colombia 3°13N 74°24W 328 C3
Uribia Colombia 11°43N 72°16W 328 A3
Uricani Romania 45°21N 23°12E 183 E8
Uriimba Angola 10°30S 17°30E 266 F3
Uriondo Bolivia 21°41S 64°41W 334 A3

Ust-Zhuya = Chara
Russia 56°54N 118°20E 215 D12
Ustaoset Norway 60°30N 8°2E 164 C5
Ustaritz France 43°24N 1°27W 174 E2
Ustecký □ Czech Rep. 50°30N 14°0E 181 A7
Uster Switz. 47°22N 8°43E 179 H4
Ústí nad Labem Czech Rep. 50°41N 14°3E 180 A7
Ústí nad Orlicí Czech Rep. 49°58N 16°24E 181 B9
Ústica Italy 38°42N 13°11E 200 D6
Ustinov = Izhevsk Russia 56°51N 53°14E 186 D9
Ustka Poland 54°35N 16°55E 184 D3
Ustroń Poland 49°43N 18°48E 185 D5
Ustroppa Tajikistan 39°55N 69°1E 217 E7
Ustyluh Ukraine 50°51N 24°10E 185 H11
Ustyurt Plateau Asia 44°0N 55°0E 216 D5
Ustyuzhna Russia 58°50N 36°32E 188 C9
Usu China 44°27N 84°40E 217 C10
Usuki Japan 33°8N 131°49E 222 E4
Usulután El Salv. 13°25N 88°28W 328 D2
Usumacinta → Mexico 18°24N 92°38W 319 D6
Usumbura = Bujumbura
Burundi 3°16S 29°18E 268 C2
Usure Tanzania 4°40S 34°22E 268 C3
Usutuo → Mozam. 26°48S 32°7E 271 C5
Uta Indonesia 4°33S 136°0E 231 E9
Utah □ U.S.A. 39°20N 111°30W 304 G8
Utah L. U.S.A. 40°12N 111°48W 304 F8
Utansjö Sweden 62°46N 17°55E 162 B11
Utara, Selat Malaysia 5°28N 100°2E 237 c
Utarni India 26°5N 71°58E 242 F4
Utatlan Guatemala 15°2N 91°11W 320 C1
Ute Creek → U.S.A. 35°21N 103°50W 305 J12
Utebo Spain 41°43N 1°0W 196 D3
Utegi Tanzania 1°19S 34°13E 266 E3
Uteke Sweden 59°24N 18°15E 139 A3
Utena Lithuania 55°27N 25°40E 188 E5
Utete Tanzania 8°0S 38°45E 268 D4
Uthai Thani Thailand 15°22N 100°3E 236 E3
Uthal Pakistan 25°44N 66°40E 242 G2
Utiariti Brazil 13°0S 58°10W 331 C6
Utica N.Y., U.S.A. 43°6N 75°14W 313 D9
Utica Ohio, U.S.A. 40°14N 82°27W 312 F2
Utiel Spain 39°37N 1°11W 197 F3
Utikuma L. Canada 55°50N 115°30W 296 B5
Utila Honduras 16°6N 86°56W 320 C2
Utinga Brazil 12°6S 41°5W 333 D3
Utkela India 20°6N 83°10E 244 D6
Utlängen Sweden 56°2N 15°48E 163 H9
Utne Norway 60°25N 6°37E 164 D3
Utnur India 19°22N 78°46E 244 E4
Uto Japan 32°41N 130°40E 222 E2
Utö Sweden 58°56N 18°16E 162 F12
Utopia Australia 22°14S 134°33E 280 C1
Utraula India 27°19N 82°25E 243 F10
Utrecht Neths. 52°5N 5°8E 170 B5
Utrecht KwaZulu Natal,
S. Africa 27°38S 30°20E 271 C5
Utrecht □ Neths. 52°6N 5°7E 170 B5
Utrera Spain 37°12N 5°48W 195 H5
Utría □ Colombia 5°57N 77°21W 328 B2
Utsira Norway 59°19N 4°53E 164 E1
Utsjoki → Finland 69°51N 26°59E 160 B22
Utsunomiya Japan 36°30N 139°50E 223 A11
Uttar Pradesh □ India 27°0N 80°0E 243 F9
Uttaradit Thailand 17°36N 100°5E 236 D3
Uttaranchal = Uttarakhand □
India 30°0N 79°30E 243 D8
Uttarpara India 22°39N 88°21E 124 B1
Utterslev Mose Denmark 55°42N 12°29E 138 d1
Utterson U.K. 52°54N 1°52W 168 E6
Uttoxeter U.K. 52°54N 1°52W 168 E6
Utuado Puerto Rico 18°16N 66°42W 321 b
Uummannaq Avannaarsua,
Greenland 77°33N 68°52W 154 B4
Uummannaq Kitaa,
Greenland 70°58N 52°17W 150 B5
Uummannarsuaq = Nunap Isua
Greenland 59°48N 43°55W 154 F5
Uummannaq Qeqertaq
Greenland 71°33N 21°47W 154 C8
Uusikaarlepyy Finland 63°32N 22°31E 160 E20
Uusikaupunki Finland 60°47N 21°25E 160 F19
Uva → Colombia 3°41N 70°3W 328 C3
Uvac → Serbia 43°35N 19°30E 202 C3
Uvalde U.S.A. 29°13N 99°47W 314 G5
Uvarovo Russia 51°59N 42°14E 190 D6
Uvat Russia 59°5N 68°50E 186 C7
Uvéa, I. Wall. & F. Is. 13°18S 176°10W 287 C15
Uvinza Tanzania 5°5S 30°24E 268 D3
Uvira Dem. Rep. of the Congo 3°22S 29°3E 268 C2
Uvs Nuur Mongolia 50°20N 92°30E 217 D12
Uvuno Uganda 1°4S 33°40E 268 C3
Uwajima Japan 33°10N 132°35E 222 E4
Uwanda □ Tanzania 7°46S 32°0E 268 D3
Uweinat, Jebel Sudan 21°54N 24°58E 256 C1
Uxbridge Canada 44°6N 79°7W 312 B5
Uxin Qi China 38°50N 109°5E 226 D5
Uxmal Mexico 20°22N 89°46W 319 C7
Uyak U.S.A. 57°38N 154°0W 303 H9
Uyo Nigeria 5°1N 7°53E 263 D6
Uyu → Burma 24°51N 94°57E 241 C5
Üyüklü Tepe Turkey 36°56N 32°40E 205 D5
Uyun Müsa Egypt 29°53N 32°40E 251 J3
Uyuni Bolivia 20°28S 66°47W 330 E4
Uzbekistan ■ Asia 41°30N 65°0E 216 E7
Uzboy → Turkmenistan 39°30N 55°0E 247 B7
Uzen, Pen. Argentina 42°30S 63°45W 336 D4
Uzerche France 45°25N 1°34E 174 C5
Uzès France 44°1N 4°26E 175 D8
Uzh → Ukraine 51°15N 30°12E 177 C16
Uzhgorod = Uzhhorod
Ukraine 48°36N 22°18E 182 B7
Uzhhorod Ukraine 48°36N 22°18E 182 B7
Uzhok Ukraine 48°59N 22°52E 182 B7
Užice Serbia 43°55N 19°50E 202 C3
Uzlovaya Russia 54°0N 38°5E 188 D10
Üzümlü Turkey 36°33N 57°5E 250 B4
Üzüncaburç Turkey 36°35N 33°56E 205 D6
Üzünköprü Turkey 41°16N 26°43E 203 F10
Uzunkuyu Turkey 38°17N 26°33E 205 C10

Vaccarès, Étang de France 43°32N 4°34E 175 E8
Vach = Vakh → Russia 60°45N 76°45E 214 C8
Vache, Î. à Haiti 18°2N 73°35W 321 C5
Väckelsång Sweden 56°37N 14°58E 163 H8
Vaclavské náměstí Prague, Czech Rep. 135 b2
Vacoas Mauritius 20°18S 57°29E 272 e
Vada India 19°39N 73°8E 244 E1
Vadakara = Badagara
India 11°35N 75°40E 245 J2
Vadaul India 19°2N 72°55E 130 A2
Väddö Sweden 60°0N 18°50E 162 D12
Väderstad Sweden 58°19N 14°58E 163 F8
Vadheim Norway 61°13N 5°49E 164 C2
Vadnagar Norway 23°47N 72°40E 242 H5
Vado Ligure Italy 44°17N 8°26E 198 D5
Vadodara India 22°20N 73°10E 242 H5
Vadsø Norway 70°3N 29°50E 160 A23
Vadstena Sweden 58°28N 14°54E 163 F8
Værlandet Norway 61°18N 4°44E 164 C1
Værøy Norway 67°40N 12°40E 160 C15
Vagalat Albania 39°44N 20°8E 206 B10
Vágámo Norway 61°52N 9°6E 164 C6
Vágar Faroe Is. 62°5N 7°15W 160 E9
Vagarshapat = Yejmiadzin
Armenia 40°12N 44°19E 191 K7
Vaggeryd Sweden 57°30N 14°10E 163 G8
Vaghena Solomon Is. 7°25S 157°45E 287 L9
Vaghia Greece 38°19N 23°11E 204 C5
Vagia, Akra Greece 36°15N 28°11E 206 E12
Vagnhärad Sweden 58°57N 17°33E 162 F11
Vagos Portugal 40°33N 8°42W 194 E2
Vágsfjorden Norway 68°50N 16°50E 160 B17
Váh → Slovak Rep. 47°43N 18°7E 181 D11
Vahitahi French Polynesia 18°44S 138°52W 289 f
Vahsel B. Antarctica 75°0S 35°0W 151 D1
Váhtjer = Gällivare
Sweden 67°9N 20°40E 160 C19
Vai Greece 35°15N 26°18E 207 E7
Vaieia Cook Is. 19°6S 169°54W 289 g
Vaigai → India 9°15N 79°10E 245 K4
Vaiges France 48°2N 0°30W 172 D6
Vaihingen Germany 48°54N 8°57E 179 G4
Vaihiria, L. Tahiti 17°40S 149°25W 289 e
Vaijapur India 19°58N 74°45E 244 E2
Vaikam India 9°45N 76°25E 245 K3
Vail U.S.A. 39°40N 106°20W 301 H18
Vailala → Papua N. G. 7°57S 145°25E 286 D3
Vailhau, Récif Comoros Is. 11°48S 43°4E 272 a
Vailly-sur-Aisne France 49°24N 3°31E 173 C10
Vailoatai Amer. Samoa 14°21S 170°46W 302 f
Vaippar → India 9°0N 78°25E 245 K4
Vairaatea French Polynesia 19°19S 139°20W 289 f
Vairao Tahiti 17°47S 149°17W 289 e
Vaires-sur-Marne France 48°52N 2°38E 144 A4
Vaisali → India 26°28N 78°53E 243 F8
Vaison-la-Romaine France 44°14N 5°4E 175 D9
Vaitogi Amer. Samoa 14°24S 170°44W 302 f
Vaitupu Pac. Oc. 7°28S 178°41E 277 B14
Vajpur India 21°24N 73°17E 244 D1
Vakarai Sri Lanka 8°8N 81°26E 245 K5
Vakarel Bulgaria 42°35N 23°40E 202 D7
Vakfikebir Turkey 41°2N 39°17E 213 B8
Vakh → Russia 60°45N 76°45E 214 C8
Vakhan Russia 57°53N 46°47E 190 B8
Vaksdal Norway 60°29N 5°45E 164 D2
Vakuta I. Papua N. G. 8°51S 151°10E 286 E6
Vál Hungary 47°22N 18°40E 182 C3
Val-de-Marne □ France 48°45N 2°28E 173 D9
Val-d'Isère France 45°27N 6°59E 175 C10
Val-d'Oise □ France 49°5N 2°0E 173 C9
Val-d'Or Canada 48°7N 77°47W 298 C4
Val Grande △ Italy 46°4N 8°30E 198 C5
Val Marie Canada 49°15N 107°45W 297 D7
Val Thorens France 45°20N 6°33E 175 C10
Valaam Russia 61°22N 30°57E 188 B6
Valadares Portugal 41°5N 8°38W 194 D2
Valahia Romania 44°35N 25°0E 183 F9
Valaichenai Sri Lanka 7°54N 81°32E 245 L5
Valais □ Switz. 46°12N 7°45E 179 J3
Valais, Alpes du Switz. 46°0N 7°30E 179 J3
Valandovo Macedonia 41°19N 22°34E 202 E6
Valašské Meziříčí
Czech Rep. 49°29N 17°59E 181 B10
Valatie U.S.A. 42°24N 73°40W 313 D11
Valaxa Greece 38°50N 24°29E 204 C6
Vålberg Sweden 59°23N 13°11E 162 E7
Valbo Sweden 60°40N 17°2E 162 D11
Valbondione Italy 46°1N 10°0E 198 C6
Valby Denmark 55°39N 12°29E 138 B2
Vâlcani Romania 46°0N 20°26E 182 G6
Vâlcea □ Romania 45°0N 24°0E 183 E8
Vâlcea → Romania 44°52N 24°12E 183 E8
Valcheta Argentina 40°40S 66°8W 336 D3
Valdagno Italy 45°39N 11°18E 199 C8
Valdahon France 47°8N 6°21E 173 E13
Valdai Hills = Valdayskaya
Vozvyshennost Russia 57°0N 33°30E 188 D7
Valday Russia 57°58N 33°9E 188 D7
Valdayskaya Vozvyshennost
Russia 57°0N 33°30E 188 D7
Valdeazogues → Spain 38°45N 4°55W 195 G6
Valdecañas, Embalse de
Spain 39°45N 5°25W 194 F5
Valdelatas Spain 40°33N 3°42W 127 A1
Valdemarsvik Sweden 58°14N 16°40E 163 F10
Valdemoro Spain 40°12N 3°40W 194 F7
Valdepeñas Spain 38°43N 3°25W 195 G7
Valderaduey → Spain 41°31N 5°42W 194 D5
Valdérice Italy 38°4N 12°37E 200 D5
Valderrobres Spain 40°53N 0°9E 196 D5
Valdés, Pen. Argentina 42°30S 63°45W 336 D4
Valdez Ecuador 1°15N 79°0W 328 C2
Valdez Alaska, U.S.A. 61°7N 146°16W 303 F11
Valdgeym = Dobrolege
Ukraine
Valdivia Chile 39°50S 73°14W 336 D2
Valdivia Colombia 7°11N 75°27W 328 B2
Valdivia Abyssal Plain
S. Ocean 62°30S 70°0E 151 C8
Valdobbiádene Italy 45°53N 11°59E 199 C8
Valdosta U.S.A. 30°50N 83°17W 316 F6
Valdoviño Spain 43°36N 8°8W 194 B2
Vale Georgia 41°30N 42°58E 191 K6
Vale U.S.A. 43°59N 117°15W 304 E5
Vale Va., U.S.A. 38°55N 77°20W 143 B1
Vale of Glamorgan □ U.K. 51°28N 3°25W 169 F4
Valea lui Mihai Romania 47°32N 22°11E 182 C7
Valea Mârului Romania 45°49N 27°42E 183 E12
Valemount Canada 52°50N 119°15W 296 C5
Valença Brazil 13°20S 39°5W 333 D4
Valença Portugal 42°1N 8°34W 194 C2
Valença do Piauí
Brazil 6°20S 41°45W 332 C3
Valença Brazil 13°20S 39°5W 333 D4
Valença do Piauí Brazil 6°20S 41°45W 332 C3
Valençay France 47°9N 1°34E 172 E8
Valence France 44°57N 4°54E 175 D8
Valence d'Agen France 44°6N 0°53E 174 D4
Valencia Spain 39°27N 0°23W 196 F4
Valencia Phil. 7°57N 125°3E 233 H5
Valencia Trin. & Tob. 10°39N 61°11W 323 t

Valencia N. Mex., U.S.A. 34°48N 106°43W 305 J10
Valencia Venezuela 10°11N 68°0W 328 A4
Valencia □ Spain 39°20N 0°40W 197 F4
Valencia ✕ (VLC) Spain 39°20N 0°26W 197 F4
Valencia, G. de Spain 39°30N 0°20E 197 F5
Valencia de Alcántara Spain 39°25N 7°14W 195 F3
Valencia de Don Juan Spain 42°17N 5°31W 194 C5
Valencia I. Ireland 51°54N 10°22W 166 E1
Valenciennes France 50°20N 3°34E 173 B10
Văleni Romania 44°15N 24°45E 183 F9
Vălenii de Munte Romania 45°11N 26°2E 183 E11
Valensole France 43°50N 5°59E 175 E9
Valentigney France 47°27N 6°51E 173 E13
Valentim, Sa. do Brazil 6°0S 43°30W 332 C3
Valentin Russia 43°8N 134°17E 220 C7
Valentine Nebr., U.S.A. 42°52N 100°33W 308 D3
Valentine Tex., U.S.A. 30°35N 104°30W 314 F2
Valenton France 48°44N 2°27E 134 B3
Valenza Italy 45°1N 8°38E 198 C5
Våler Hedmark, Norway 60°41N 11°50E 164 D8
Våler Østfold, Norway 59°29N 10°51E 164 E7
Valera Piemonte, Italy 45°33N 9°3E 129 A1
Valera Venezuela 9°19N 70°37W 328 B3
Valesdir Vanuatu 16°47S 168°10E 287 F6
Valestrand Norway 59°40N 5°26E 164 E2
Valga Estonia 57°47N 26°2E 188 D4
Valguarnera Caropepe Italy 37°30N 14°23E 201 E7
Valier U.S.A. 48°18N 112°16W 304 B7
Valinco, G. de France 41°40N 8°52E 175 G12
Valjevo Serbia 44°18N 19°53E 202 B3
Valka Latvia 57°46N 26°3E 188 D3
Valkeakoski Finland 61°16N 24°2E 188 B2
Valkenswaard Neths. 51°21N 5°29E 170 C5
Vall de Uxó = La Vall d'Uixó Spain 39°49N 0°15W 196 F4
Valla Sweden 59°2N 16°20E 162 E10
Valladolid Yucatán, Mexico 20°41N 88°12W 319 C7
Valladolid Spain 41°38N 4°43W 194 D6
Valladolid □ Spain 41°38N 4°43W 194 D6
Vallata Italy 41°2N 15°15E 201 A8
Vallcarca Spain 41°25N 2°9E 114 A1
Valldemossa Spain 39°43N 2°37E 206 B3
Valldoreix Spain 41°27N 2°3E 114 A1
Valle Norway 59°13N 7°33E 164 E4
Valle d'Aosta □ Italy 45°45N 7°15E 198 C4
Valle de Aran Spain 42°50N 0°55E 196 C5
Valle de la Pascua Venezuela 9°13N 66°0W 328 B4
Valle de las Palmas Mexico 32°20N 116°43W 307 N10
Valle de Santiago Mexico 20°23N 101°12W 318 C4
Valle de Zaragoza Mexico 27°25N 105°50W 318 B3
Valle del Cauca □ Colombia 3°45N 76°30W 328 C2
Valle del Ticino △ Italy 45°22N 9°0E 198 C6
Valle Fértil, Sierra del Argentina 30°20S 68°0W 334 C2
Valle Gran Rey Canary Is. 28°5N 17°20W 153 e1
Valle Hermoso Mexico 25°35N 97°40W 319 B5
Valle Nacional Mexico 17°47N 96°18W 319 D5
Vallecas Spain 40°22N 3°37W 127 B2
Vallecas, Cumbres de Spain 40°20N 3°33W 127 B2
Valledupar Colombia 10°29N 73°15W 328 A3
Vallegrande Bolivia 18°30S 64°10W 331 D5
Vallehermoso Canary Is. 28°10N 17°15W 153 e1
Vallejo U.S.A. 38°7N 122°14W 306 G4
Vallenar Chile 28°30S 70°50W 334 B1
Vallensbæk Denmark 55°38N 12°21E 118 B2
Vallensbæk Strand Denmark 55°36N 12°23E 118 B2
Vallentuna Sweden 59°32N 18°5E 162 E12
Vallentunasjön Sweden 59°27N 18°1E 139 A2
Vallerano Italy 41°46N 12°29E 136 C1
Valleraugue France 44°6N 3°39E 174 D7
Vallet France 47°10N 1°15W 172 E5
Valletta Malta 35°54N 14°31E 206 F8
Valley, The Anguilla 18°13N 63°4W 322 a
Valley Center U.S.A. 33°13N 117°2W 307 M9
Valley City U.S.A. 46°55N 98°0W 308 B5
Valley Falls Oreg., U.S.A. 42°29N 120°17W 304 E3
Valley Falls R.I., U.S.A. 41°54N 71°24W 313 E13
Valley Junction = West Des Moines U.S.A. 41°35N 93°43W 310 C3
Valley of Flowers △ India 30°50N 79°40E 243 D8
Valley of the Kings Egypt 25°41N 32°34E 256 B3
Valley Springs U.S.A. 38°12N 120°50W 306 G6
Valley Station U.S.A. 38°6N 85°52W 311 F11
Valley View U.S.A. 40°39N 76°33W 313 F8
Valley Wells U.S.A. 35°27N 115°46W 307 K11
Valleyview Canada 55°5N 117°17W 296 B5
Valli di Comácchio Italy 44°40N 12°15E 199 D9
Vallimanca, Arroyo Argentina 35°40S 59°10W 334 D4
Vallisaari Finland 60°7N 25°0E 121 C3
Vallo della Lucánia Italy 40°14N 15°16E 201 B8
Vallon-Pont-d'Arc France 44°24N 4°24E 175 D8
Vallorbe Switz. 46°42N 6°20E 179 J2
Valls Spain 41°18N 1°15E 196 D6
Vallvidrera Spain 41°24N 2°6E 114 A1
Vallvik Sweden 61°11N 17°10E 162 C11
Valmaseda = Balmaseda Spain 43°11N 3°12W 196 B1
Valmeyer U.S.A. 38°18N 90°19W 310 F6
Valmiera Latvia 57°37N 25°29E 188 D3
Valnera Spain 43°9N 3°40W 194 B7
Valognes France 49°30N 1°28W 172 C5
Valona = Vlorë Albania 40°32N 19°28E 202 F3
Valongo Portugal 41°8N 8°30W 194 D2
Valozhyn Belarus 54°3N 26°30E 177 A14
Valpaços Portugal 41°36N 7°17W 194 D3
Valparai India 10°22N 76°58E 245 J3
Valparaíso Chile 33°2S 71°40W 334 C1
Valparaíso Zacatecas, Mexico 22°46N 103°34W 318 C4
Valparaiso Fla., U.S.A. 30°29N 86°30W 317 E3
Valparaiso Ind., U.S.A. 41°28N 87°4W 311 C9
Valparaíso □ Chile 33°2S 71°40W 334 C1
Valpovo Croatia 45°39N 18°25E 182 E3
Valpoy India 15°32N 74°8E 245 G2
Valréas France 44°24N 5°0E 175 D9
Vals Switz. 46°39N 9°11E 179 J5
Vals → S. Africa 27°23S 26°30E 270 C4
Vals, Tanjung Indonesia 8°26S 137°25E 231 F9
Vals-les-Bains France 44°42N 4°24E 175 D8
Valsad India 20°40N 72°58E 244 D1
Valsamata Greece 38°10N 20°36E 207 C2
Valtellina Italy 46°11N 9°55E 198 B6
Valþjófsstaður Iceland 65°1N 14°59W 155 B12
Valti Greece 38°27N 21°7E 207 C3
Valuyki Russia 50°10N 38°5E 189 G10
Valverde Canary Is. 27°48N 17°55W 153 e1
Valverde del Camino Spain 37°35N 6°47W 195 H4
Valverde del Fresno Spain 40°15N 6°51W 194 E4
Valvidrera → Spain 41°25N 2°0E 114 A1
Vama Romania 47°34N 25°42E 183 C10
Vambori India 19°17N 74°44E 244 E2
Vamdrup Denmark 55°25N 9°17E 163 J3
Våmhus Sweden 61°7N 14°29E 162 C8
Vamizi, I. Mozam. 11°2S 40°40E 269 E5
Vammala = Sastamala Finland 61°20N 22°54E 188 B2
Vamos Greece 35°24N 24°13E 207 E5
Vamsadhara → India 18°21N 84°8E 244 E7
Van Turkey 38°30N 43°20E 213 C10
Van □ Turkey 38°30N 43°20E 213 C10
Van, L. = Van Gölü Turkey 38°30N 43°0E 213 C10
Van Alstyne U.S.A. 33°25N 96°35W 314 E6
Van Blommestein Meer Suriname 4°45N 55°5W 329 C6
Van Buren = Kettering U.S.A. 39°41N 84°10W 311 E12
Van Buren N.B., Canada 47°10N 67°55W 299 C6
Van Buren Ark., U.S.A. 35°26N 94°21W 314 D7
Van Buren Maine, U.S.A. 47°10N 67°58W 309 B20
Van Buren Mo., U.S.A. 37°0N 91°1W 308 G8
Van Canh Vietnam 13°37N 109°0E 236 F7
Van Diemen, C. N. Terr., Australia 11°9S 130°24E 278 B5
Van Diemen, C. Queens., Australia 16°30S 139°46E 280 B2
Van Diemen G. Australia 11°45S 132°0E 278 B5
Van Gogh Museum Amsterdam, Neths. 112 c1
Van Gölü Turkey 38°30N 43°0E 213 C10
Van Horn U.S.A. 31°3N 104°50W 314 F2
Van Horne U.S.A. 42°1N 92°5W 310 B4
Van Meter U.S.A. 41°32N 93°57W 310 C3
Van Ninh Vietnam 12°42N 109°14E 236 F7
Van Rees, Pegunungan Indonesia 2°35S 138°15E 231 E9
Van Tivu India 8°51N 78°15E 245 K4
Van Wert U.S.A. 40°52N 84°35W 311 D12
Van Yen Vietnam 21°4N 104°42E 228 G5
Van Zylsrus S. Africa 26°52S 22°4E 270 C3
Vanadzor Armenia 40°48N 44°30E 191 K7
Vanak Iran 35°45N 51°23E 141 A2
Vanavana French Polynesia 20°47S 139°9W 289 f
Vanavara Russia 60°22N 102°16E 215 C11
Vanceburg U.S.A. 38°36N 83°19W 311 F13
Vancouver B.C., Canada 49°15N 123°7W 306 A3
Vancouver Wash., U.S.A. 45°38N 122°40W 306 E4
Vancouver, C. Australia 35°2S 118°11E 279 G2
Vancouver, Mt. U.S.A. 60°20N 139°41W 303 F13
Vancouver I. Canada 49°50N 126°0W 306 B2
Vancouver Int. ✕ (YVR) Canada 49°10N 123°10W 306 A3
Vanda = Vantaa Finland 60°18N 24°56E 121 B2
Vandalia Ill., U.S.A. 38°58N 89°6W 310 F7
Vandalia Mo., U.S.A. 39°19N 91°29W 310 E5
Vandalia Ohio, U.S.A. 39°54N 84°12W 311 E12
Vandavasi India 12°30N 79°30E 245 H4
Vandeloos B. Sri Lanka 8°0N 81°45E 245 L5
Vandenberg Village U.S.A. 34°43N 120°28W 307 L6
Vandergrift U.S.A. 40°36N 79°34W 312 F5
Vanderhoof Canada 54°0N 124°0W 296 C4
Vanderkloof Dam S. Africa 30°4S 24°40E 270 D3
Vanderlin I. Australia 15°44S 137°2E 280 B2
Vänern Sweden 58°47N 13°30E 163 F7
Vänersborg Sweden 58°26N 12°19E 163 F6
Vang Norway 61°7N 8°34E 164 C5
Vang Vieng Laos 18°58N 102°32E 236 C4
Vanga Kenya 4°35S 39°12E 268 C4
Vangaindrano Madag. 23°21S 47°36E 272 C2
Vänge Sweden 59°50N 17°20E 162 E11
Vangede Denmark 55°45N 12°30E 118 A3
Vangsnes Norway 61°9N 6°39E 164 C3
Vanguard Canada 49°55N 107°20W 297 D7
Vangunu Solomon Is. 8°40S 158°5E 287 M10
Vanikoro Pac. Oc. 11°39S 166°54E 277 C12
Vaniköy Turkey 41°3N 29°3E 122 B2
Vanimo Papua N. G. 2°42S 141°21E 286 B1
Vanino Russia 48°50N 140°5E 215 E15
Vanivilasa Sagara India 13°45N 76°30E 245 H3
Vaniyambadi India 12°46N 78°44E 245 H4
Vânju Mare Romania 44°25N 22°52E 182 F7
Vankleek Hill Canada 45°32N 74°40W 313 A10
Vanløse Denmark 55°41N 12°28E 118 A2
Vännäs Sweden 63°58N 19°48E 160 E18
Vannes France 47°40N 2°47W 172 E4
Vannøya Norway 70°6N 19°50E 160 A18
Vanoise, Massif de la France 45°25N 6°40E 175 C10
Vanrhynsdorp S. Africa 31°36S 18°44E 270 D2
Vansada India 20°47N 73°25E 244 D1
Vansbro Sweden 60°32N 14°15E 162 D8
Vanse Norway 58°6N 6°41E 164 F3
Vansittart B. Australia 14°3S 126°17E 278 B4
Vansittart I. Canada 65°50N 84°0W 295 D15
Vantaa Finland 60°18N 24°56E 121 B2
Vantaankoski Finland 60°18N 24°50E 121 B2
Vantaanjoki Finland 60°18N 24°58E 121 B2
Vanua Balavu Fiji 17°12S 178°55W 287 A3
Vanua Lava Vanuatu 13°50S 167°30E 287 C5
Vanua Levu Fiji 16°33S 179°15E 287 A2
Vanua Vatu Fiji 18°22S 179°15W 287 B3
Vanuatu ■ Pac. Oc. 15°0S 168°0E 287 E6
Vanves France 48°49N 2°17E 134 B2
Vanwyksvlei S. Africa 30°18S 21°49E 270 D3
Vao N. Cal. 22°39S 167°32E 288 d
Vapnyarka Ukraine 48°32N 28°45E 183 B13
Var □ France 43°27N 6°18E 175 E10
Var → France 43°39N 7°12E 175 E11
Vara Sweden 58°16N 12°55E 163 F6
Vara, Pico da Azores 37°48N 25°13W 153 d3
Varada → India 15°0N 75°40E 245 G2
Varades France 47°25N 1°1W 172 E5
Varáita → Italy 44°9N 7°53E 198 D4
Varaldsøy Norway 60°6N 5°59E 164 D2
Varalé Ivory C. 9°40N 3°17W 262 D4
Varallo Italy 45°49N 8°15E 198 C5
Varāmīn Iran 35°20N 51°39E 247 C6
Varāmīn □ Iran 35°18N 51°35E 247 B6
Varanasi India 25°22N 83°0E 243 G10
Varangerfjorden Norway 70°3N 29°25E 160 A23
Varangerhalvøya Norway 70°25N 29°30E 160 A23
Varano, Lago di Italy 41°53N 15°45E 199 G12
Varaždin Croatia 46°20N 16°20E 199 B13
Varazze Italy 44°22N 8°34E 198 D5
Varberg Sweden 57°6N 12°20E 163 G6
Varcar Vakuf = Mrkonjić Grad Bos.-H. 44°26N 17°4E 182 F2
Vardak □ Afghan. 34°0N 68°0E 240 B3
Vardar = Axios → Greece 40°57N 22°35E 202 F6
Varde Denmark 55°38N 8°29E 163 J2
Varde Å → Denmark 55°35N 8°19E 163 J2
Vardenis Armenia 40°10N 45°43E 191 K7
Vardø Norway 70°23N 31°5E 160 A24
Varedo Italy 45°35N 9°8E 129 A1
Varel Germany 53°23N 8°8E 178 B4
Varella, Mui = Nay, Mui Vietnam 12°54N 109°26E 236 F7
Varėna Lithuania 54°12N 24°30E 188 E3
Varennes-sur-Allier France 46°19N 3°24E 173 F10
Varennes-Vauzelles France 47°3N 3°9E 173 E10
Vareš Bos.-H. 44°12N 18°23E 182 F3
Varese Italy 45°48N 8°50E 198 C5
Vârfurile Romania 46°19N 22°31E 182 D7
Vårgårda Sweden 58°2N 12°49E 163 F6
Vargem Bonita Brazil 20°20S 46°22W 333 F2
Vargem Grande Brazil 3°33S 43°56W 332 B3
Varginha Brazil 21°33S 45°25W 335 A6
Vargön Sweden 58°22N 12°20E 163 F6
Varhaug Norway 58°37N 5°41E 164 F2
Vari Greece 38°24N 20°35E 207 C2
Varillas Chile 24°0S 70°10W 334 A1
Varkaus Finland 62°19N 27°50E 188 A4
Varkiza Greece 37°50N 23°49E 112 C2
Värmdölandet Sweden 59°20N 18°33E 162 E12
Värmeln Sweden 59°35N 12°54E 162 E6
Värmlands län □ Sweden 60°0N 13°20E 162 E6
Värmlandsbro Sweden 59°11N 13°0E 162 E7
Varna Bulgaria 43°13N 27°56E 203 C11
Varna □ Bulgaria 43°20N 27°30E 203 C11
Varna → India 16°48N 74°32E 244 F2
Värnamo Sweden 57°10N 14°3E 163 G8
Varnjárga = Varangerhalvøya Norway 70°25N 29°30E 160 A23
Varnsdorf Czech Rep. 50°55N 14°35E 180 A7
Varnville U.S.A. 32°51N 81°5W 316 C8
Várpalota Hungary 47°12N 18°8E 182 C3
Vars Ont., Canada 45°21N 75°21W 313 A9
Vars Hautes-Alpes, France 44°37N 6°42E 175 D10
Vartdal Norway 62°20N 6°8E 164 B3
Vartiokylä Finland 60°13N 25°6E 121 B3
Vartiosaari Finland 60°11N 25°5E 121 B3
Varto Turkey 39°10N 41°27E 213 C9
Varvarin Serbia 43°43N 21°20E 202 C5
Varysburg U.S.A. 42°46N 78°19W 312 D6
Varzaneh Iran 32°25N 52°40E 247 C7
Varzaqān Iran 38°29N 46°40E 213 C12
Várzea Alegre Brazil 6°47S 39°17W 332 C4
Várzea da Palma Brazil 17°36S 44°44W 333 E3
Várzea Grande Brazil 15°39S 56°8W 331 D6
Varzi Italy 44°49N 9°12E 198 D6
Varzo Italy 46°12N 8°15E 198 B5
Varzy France 47°22N 3°20E 173 E10
Vas □ Hungary 47°10N 16°55E 182 C1
Vasa = Vaasa Finland 63°6N 21°38E 160 E19
Vasa Barris → Brazil 11°10S 37°10W 332 D4
Vasamuseet Stockholm, Sweden 139 b3
Vásárosnamény Hungary 48°9N 22°19E 182 B7
Vascão → Portugal 37°31N 7°31W 195 H3
Vașcău Romania 46°28N 22°30E 182 D7
Vasco S. Africa 33°54S 18°34E 118 A2
Vascongadas = País Vasco □ Spain 42°50N 2°45W 196 C2
Vasfanārd Iran 35°38N 51°20E 141 B2
Vashi India 19°4N 72°59E 130 A2
Vāshīr Afghan. 32°16N 63°51E 240 B1
Vashkivtsi Ukraine 48°23N 25°31E 183 B10
Vasht = Khāsh Iran 28°15N 61°15E 240 C1
Vasilevichi Belarus 52°15N 29°50E 177 B16
Vasiliki Greece 38°37N 20°36E 207 B2
Vasiliko = Michurin Bulgaria 42°9N 27°51E 203 D11
Vasiliko Greece 38°25N 23°40E 204 C5
Vasilikos Greece 37°43N 20°59E 207 D2
Vasilkov = Vasylkiv Ukraine 50°7N 30°15E 177 C16
Vasilyevskiy, Ostrov Russia 59°55N 30°16E 137 B1
Vasilyova Sloboda = Chkolovsk Russia 56°50N 43°10E 190 B6
Vasilyovo = Chkolovsk Russia 56°50N 43°10E 190 B6
Väskinde Sweden 57°40N 18°20E 163 G10
Vaslui Romania 46°38N 27°42E 183 D12
Vaslui □ Romania 46°30N 27°45E 183 D12
Väsman Sweden 60°9N 15°5E 162 D9
Vassar Man., Canada 49°10N 95°55W 297 D9
Vassar Mich., U.S.A. 43°22N 83°35W 309 D12
Vassfaret Norway 60°38N 9°28E 164 D6
Västerås Sweden 59°37N 16°38E 162 E10
Västerbotten Sweden 64°36N 20°4E 160 D19
Västerdalälven → Sweden 60°30N 15°7E 162 D9
Västergötland Sweden 58°0N 13°10E 163 F7
Västerhaninge Sweden 59°7N 18°6E 162 E12
Västervik Sweden 57°43N 16°33E 163 G10
Västmanland Sweden 59°45N 16°20E 161 G17
Västmanlands län □ Sweden 59°45N 16°20E 162 E10
Vasto Italy 42°8N 14°40E 199 F11
Västra Götalands Län □ Sweden 58°0N 13°0E 163 F6
Vasvár Hungary 47°3N 16°47E 182 C1
Vasylivka Ukraine 45°38N 28°50E 183 E13
Vasylkiv Ukraine 50°7N 30°15E 177 C16
Vat Phou Laos 14°51N 105°49E 236 E5
Vatan France 47°4N 1°50E 173 E8
Vaté = Efate, I. Vanuatu 17°40S 168°25E 287 G6
Vatersay U.K. 56°55N 7°32W 167 E1
Vathi Greece 38°41N 20°47E 207 B2
Vathia Greece 36°29N 22°29E 204 E4
Vati Greece 36°3N 27°53E 206 E11
Vatia Amer. Samoa 14°15S 170°40W 302 f
Vatican City ■ Europe 41°54N 12°27E 136 B1
Vaticano, C. Italy 38°37N 15°50E 201 D8
Vatili Cyprus 35°6N 33°40E 207 D12
Vatin Serbia 45°12N 21°20E 182 E6
Vatiu = Atiu Cook Is. 20°0S 158°10W 289 J12
Vatnajökull Iceland 64°30N 16°48W 155 C10
Vatnajökull △ Iceland 64°24N 16°48W 155 C10
Vatnås Norway 59°58N 9°37E 164 E6
Vatnsfjörður Iceland 65°56N 22°30W 155 B4
Vato Sweden 59°50N 19°0E 162 E12
Vatolakkos Greece 35°27N 23°53E 207 E4
Vatoloha Madag. 17°52S 47°48E 272 B2
Vatomandry Madag. 19°20S 48°59E 272 B2
Vatra-Dornei Romania 47°22N 25°22E 183 C10
Vatrak → India 23°9N 73°2E 242 H5
Vättern Sweden 58°25N 14°30E 163 F8
Vatu Vara Fiji 17°26S 179°31W 287 A3
Vatulele Fiji 18°33S 177°37E 287 B1
Vauclin, Mt. du Martinique 14°33N 60°53W 322 j
Vauclin, Pte. de Martinique 14°34N 60°49W 322 j
Vaucluse Australia 33°51S 151°15E 139 B2
Vaucluse □ France 43°50N 5°20E 175 E9
Vaucluse House Australia 33°51S 151°15E 139 B2
Vaucouleurs France 48°37N 5°40E 173 D12
Vaucresson France 48°50N 2°9E 134 A1
Vaud □ Switz. 46°35N 6°30E 179 J2
Vaudreuil-Dorion Canada 45°23N 74°3W 313 A10
Vaughan Canada 43°50N 79°32W 312 C5
Vaughn Mont., U.S.A. 47°33N 111°33W 304 C8
Vaughn N. Mex., U.S.A. 34°36N 105°13W 305 J11
Vauhallan France 48°44N 2°12E 134 B2
Vaujours France 48°56N 2°34E 134 A4
Vaujours L. Canada 55°27N 74°15W 298 A5
Vaupés = Uaupés → Brazil 0°2N 67°16W 328 C4
Vaupés □ Colombia 1°0N 71°0W 328 C3
Vauvert France 43°42N 4°17E 175 E8
Vauxhall Alta., Canada 50°5N 112°9W 296 C6
Vauxhall London, U.K. 125 c4
Vav India 24°22N 71°31E 242 G4
Vavatenina Madag. 17°28S 49°12E 272 B2
Vava'u Tonga 18°36S 174°0W 287 D4
Vava'u Group Tonga 18°40S 174°0W 287 D4
Vavoua Ivory C. 7°23N 6°29W 262 D3
Vavuniya Sri Lanka 8°45N 80°30E 245 K5
Vawkavysk Belarus 53°9N 24°30E 177 B13
Vaxholm Sweden 59°25N 18°20E 162 E12
Växjö Sweden 56°52N 14°50E 163 H8
Växtorp Sweden 56°25N 13°8E 163 H7
Vayalpad India 13°39N 78°38E 245 H4
Vayenga = Severomorsk Russia 69°5N 33°27E 160 B25
Vaygach, Ostrov Russia 70°0N 60°0E 214 C7
Veadeiros Brazil 14°7S 47°31W 333 D2
Veaikevárri = Svappavaara Sweden 67°40N 21°3E 160 C19
Vechelde Germany 52°16N 10°22E 178 C6
Vechta Germany 52°44N 8°17E 178 C4
Vechte → Neths. 52°34N 6°6E 170 B6
Vecsés Hungary 47°26N 19°19E 117 B3
Vedaranniyam India 10°25N 79°50E 245 J4
Vedavågen Norway 59°17N 5°12E 164 E2
Veddige Sweden 57°17N 12°20E 163 G6
Vedea → Romania 43°42N 25°41E 183 G10
Vedi Armenia 39°54N 44°43E 213 C11
Vedia Argentina 34°30S 61°31W 334 C3
Vedrette di Ries-Aurina △ Italy 46°54N 12°5E 199 B9
Vedum Sweden 58°11N 12°58E 163 F7
Veedersburg U.S.A. 40°7N 87°16W 311 D9
Veendam Neths. 53°5N 6°52E 170 A6
Veenendaal Neths. 52°2N 5°34E 170 B5
Vefsna → Norway 65°48N 13°10E 160 D15
Vega Nordland, Norway 65°40N 11°55E 160 D14
Vega Tex., U.S.A. 35°15N 102°26W 314 D3
Vega Alta Puerto Rico 18°25N 66°20W 321 b
Vega Baja Puerto Rico 18°27N 66°23W 321 b
Vega de Ribadeo = Vegadeo Spain 43°27N 7°4W 194 B3
Vegadeo Spain 43°27N 7°4W 194 B3
Vegårshei Norway 58°44N 8°51E 164 F5
Vegas Verde = North Las Vegas U.S.A. 36°11N 115°7W 124 A1
Veggli Norway 60°3N 9°9E 164 D6
Veglia = Krk Croatia 45°8N 14°40E 199 C11
Vegoritida, L. Greece 40°45N 21°45E 202 F5
Vegreville Canada 53°30N 112°5W 296 C6
Veiholmen Norway 63°26N 7°58E 164 A4
Veimandu Channel Maldives 2°10N 73°20E 272 d
Veinge Sweden 56°33N 13°4E 163 H7
Veisiejai Lithuania 54°6N 23°42E 184 D10
Vejbystrand Sweden 56°19N 12°45E 163 H6
Vejen Denmark 55°30N 9°9E 163 J3
Vejer de la Frontera Spain 36°15N 5°59W 195 J5
Vejle Denmark 55°43N 9°30E 163 J3
Vejle Fjord Denmark 55°40N 9°50E 163 J3
Vela Luka Croatia 42°59N 16°44E 199 F13
Velachha India 21°23N 73°1E 244 D1
Velanai I. Sri Lanka 9°45N 79°45E 245 K4
Velas Azores 38°41N 28°13W 153 d1
Velas, C. Costa Rica 10°21N 85°52W 320 D2
Velasco, Sierra de Argentina 29°20S 67°10W 334 B2
Velay, Mts. du France 45°0N 3°40E 174 D7
Velbert Germany 51°20N 7°3E 178 D3
Velddrif S. Africa 32°42S 18°11E 270 D2
Velebit △ Croatia 44°30N 15°15E 199 D12
Velebit Planina Croatia 44°50N 15°20E 199 D12
Velebitski Kanal Croatia 44°45N 14°55E 199 D11
Veleka → Bulgaria 42°4N 27°58E 203 D11
Veleň Czech Rep. 50°10N 14°33E 135 A3
Velencei-tó Hungary 47°13N 18°36E 182 C3
Velenje Slovenia 46°23N 15°8E 199 B12
Veles Macedonia 41°46N 21°47E 202 E5
Veleslavín Czech Rep. 50°5N 14°21E 135 B2
Velestino Greece 39°23N 22°43E 204 B4
Vélez Colombia 6°1N 73°41W 328 B3
Vélez-Málaga Spain 36°48N 4°5W 195 J6
Vélez Rubio Spain 37°41N 2°5W 197 H2
Velhas → Brazil 17°13S 44°49W 333 E3
Velika Croatia 45°27N 17°40E 182 E2
Velika Gorica Croatia 45°44N 16°5E 199 C13
Velika Kapela Croatia 45°10N 15°5E 199 C12
Velika Kikinda = Kikinda Serbia 45°50N 20°30E 182 E5
Velika Kladuša Bos.-H. 45°11N 15°48E 199 C12
Velika Kruša Kosovo 42°19N 20°39E 202 D4
Velika Morava → Serbia 44°43N 21°3E 202 B5
Velika Plana Serbia 44°20N 21°4E 202 B5
Velikaya → Russia 57°48N 28°10E 188 D5
Velikaya Kema Russia 45°30N 137°12E 220 B8
Velikaya Lepetikha Ukraine 47°2N 33°58E 189 J7
Veliké Kapušany Slovak Rep. 48°34N 22°5E 181 C15
Velike Lašče Slovenia 45°49N 14°45E 199 C11
Veliki Jastrebac Serbia 43°25N 21°30E 202 C5
Veliki Kanal Serbia 45°45N 19°15E 182 E4
Veliki Popović Serbia 44°8N 21°18E 202 B5
Veliki Ustyug Russia 60°47N 46°20E 186 B8
Velikiye Luki Russia 56°25N 30°32E 188 D6
Veliko Gradište Serbia 44°46N 21°29E 202 B5
Veliko Tŭrnovo Bulgaria 43°5N 25°41E 203 C9
Veliko Tŭrnovo □ Bulgaria 43°5N 25°41E 203 C9
Velikonda Range India 14°45N 79°10E 245 G4
Vélingara Kolda, Senegal 13°12N 14°5W 252 C2
Vélingara Louga, Senegal 15°0N 14°40W 252 B2
Velingrad Bulgaria 42°4N 23°58E 202 D7
Velino, Mte. Italy 42°9N 13°23E 199 F10
Velizh Russia 55°36N 31°11E 188 E6
Vélizy-Villacoublay France 48°47N 2°11E 134 B2
Velká Chuchle Czech Rep. 50°0N 14°23E 135 B2
Velké Karlovice Czech Rep. 49°20N 18°17E 181 B11
Velké Meziříčí Czech Rep. 49°21N 16°1E 180 B9
Velké Přílepy Czech Rep. 50°9N 14°19E 135 B1
Veľký Javorník Slovak Rep. 49°19N 18°22E 181 B11
Veľký Krtíš Slovak Rep. 48°12N 19°21E 181 C12
Veľký Meder Slovak Rep. 47°52N 17°46E 181 D10
Veľký Tribeč Slovak Rep. 48°28N 18°15E 181 C11
Vella Gulf Solomon Is. 8°0S 156°50E 287 M9
Vella Lavella Solomon Is. 7°45S 156°40E 287 L9
Vellar → India 11°30N 79°36E 245 J4
Velletri Italy 41°41N 12°47E 200 A5
Vellinge Sweden 55°29N 13°2E 163 J6
Vellmar Germany 51°22N 9°28E 178 D5
Vellore India 12°57N 79°10E 245 H4
Velopoula Greece 36°55N 23°27E 204 E5
Velsk Russia 61°10N 42°5E 186 B11
Velten Germany 52°42N 13°10E 178 C9
Veluwezoom △ Neths. 52°5N 6°0E 170 B6
Velva U.S.A. 48°4N 100°56W 308 A3
Velvendos Greece 40°15N 22°6E 202 F6
Velyka Mykhaylivka Ukraine 47°4N 29°52E 183 C14
Velyki Luchky Ukraine 48°25N 22°34E 182 B7
Velykyy Bereznyy Ukraine 48°54N 22°28E 182 B7
Velykyy Bychkiv Ukraine 47°58N 24°1E 183 C9
Vemb Denmark 56°21N 8°21E 163 H2
Vembanad L. India 9°36N 76°15E 245 K3
Vemdalen Sweden 62°27N 13°51E 162 B7
Ven Sweden 55°55N 12°45E 163 J6
Venaco France 42°14N 9°11E 175 F13
Venado Mexico 22°56N 101°6W 318 C4
Venado Tuerto Argentina 33°50S 62°0W 334 C3
Venafro Italy 41°29N 14°2E 201 A7
Venarey-les-Laumes France 47°32N 4°26E 173 E11
Venaria Italy 45°8N 7°38E 198 C4
Venčane Serbia 44°24N 20°28E 202 B4
Vence France 43°43N 7°6E 175 E11
Venda Seca Portugal 38°46N 9°15W 126 A1
Vendas Novas Portugal 38°39N 8°27W 195 G2
Vendée □ France 46°50N 1°35W 172 F5
Vendée → France 46°20N 1°10W 172 F5
Vendéen, Bocage France 46°40N 1°20W 174 B2
Vendeuvre-sur-Barse France 48°14N 4°28E 173 D11
Vendôme France 47°47N 1°3E 172 E8
Vendrell = El Vendrell Spain 41°10N 1°30E 196 D6
Vendsyssel Denmark 57°22N 10°0E 163 G4
Vendychany Ukraine 48°38N 27°48E 183 B12
Venelles France 43°35N 5°28E 175 E9
Véneta, L. Italy 45°23N 12°25E 199 C9
Venetian Islands U.S.A. 25°47N 80°9W 128 B2
Venetie U.S.A. 67°1N 146°25W 303 C11
Véneto □ Italy 45°30N 12°0E 199 C9
Venev Russia 54°22N 38°17E 188 E10
Venézia Italy 45°27N 12°21E 199 C9
Venézia, G. di Italy 45°15N 13°0E 199 C10
Venézia, Palazzo Rome, Italy 136 c2
Venézia Tridentina = Trentino-Alto Adige □ Italy 46°30N 11°20E 199 B8
Venezuela ■ S. Amer. 8°0N 66°0W 328 B4
Venezuela, G. de Venezuela 11°30N 71°0W 328 A3
Venezuelan Basin Cent. Amer. 14°0N 68°0W 321 C6
Vengurla India 15°53N 73°45E 245 G1
Vengurla Rocks India 15°55N 73°22E 245 G1
Venice = Venézia Italy 45°27N 12°21E 199 C9
Venice Calif., U.S.A. 33°59N 118°27W 126 C2
Venice Fla., U.S.A. 27°6N 82°27W 317 F7
Vénissieux France 45°42N 4°53E 175 C8
Venjan Sweden 60°57N 13°55E 162 D7
Venjansjön Sweden 60°54N 14°0E 162 D8
Venkatagiri India 14°0N 79°35E 245 H4
Venkatapuram India 18°20N 80°30E 244 E5
Venlo Neths. 51°22N 6°11E 170 C6
Vennachar Junction Canada 45°5N 77°14W 312 A7
Vennesla Norway 58°15N 7°59E 164 F4
Venosa Italy 40°58N 15°49E 201 B8
Venray Neths. 51°31N 6°0E 170 C6
Vent, Îs. du French Polynesia 17°30S 149°30W 289 f
Venta Lithuania 56°12N 22°42E 184 B9
Venta → Latvia 57°24N 21°33E 184 A8
Venta de Baños Spain 41°55N 4°30W 194 D6
Venta de Cardeña = Cardeña Spain 38°16N 4°20W 195 G6
Ventana, Punta de la Mexico 24°4N 109°48W 318 C3
Ventana, Sa. de la Argentina 38°0S 62°30W 334 D3
Ventas Spain 40°26N 3°40W 127 B2
Ventersburg S. Africa 28°7S 27°9E 270 C4
Ventersburgweg = Hennenman S. Africa 27°59S 27°1E 270 C4
Venterstad S. Africa 30°47S 25°48E 270 D4
Ventimiglia Italy 43°47N 7°36E 198 E4
Ventnor U.K. 50°36N 1°12W 169 G6
Ventorro del Cano Spain 40°23N 3°49W 127 B1
Ventotène Italy 40°47N 13°25E 200 B6
Ventoux, Mt. France 44°10N 5°17E 175 D9
Ventspils Latvia 57°25N 21°32E 184 A8
Ventspils □ Latvia 57°20N 21°50E 184 A8
Ventuarí → Venezuela 3°58N 67°2W 328 C4
Ventucopa U.S.A. 34°50N 119°29W 307 L7
Ventura U.S.A. 34°17N 119°18W 307 L7
Venus U.S.A. 27°4N 81°22W 317 H8
Vénus, Pte. Tahiti 17°29S 149°29W 289 e
Venus B. Australia 38°40S 145°42E 283 E6
Venustiano Carranza Baja Calif., Mexico 30°25N 115°53W 318 A1
Venustiano Carranza Distrito Federal, Mexico 19°25N 99°5W 128 B2
Vera Argentina 29°30S 60°20W 334 B3
Vera Spain 37°15N 1°51W 197 H3
Veracruz Mexico 19°11N 96°8W 319 D5
Veracruz □ Mexico 19°0N 96°15W 319 D5
Veraval India 20°53N 70°27E 242 J4
Verbánia Italy 45°56N 8°33E 198 C5
Verbicaro Italy 39°45N 15°55E 201 C8
Verbier Switz. 46°6N 7°13E 179 J3
Vercelli Italy 45°19N 8°25E 198 C5
Verchovchevo Ukraine 48°32N 34°10E 189 H8
Vercors △ France 45°0N 5°25E 175 D9
Verdalsøra Norway 63°48N 11°30E 160 E14
Verde → Argentina 41°56S 65°5W 336 B3
Verde → Goiás, Brazil 19°11S 50°44W 333 E1
Verde → Goiás, Brazil 18°1S 50°14W 333 E1
Verde → Mato Grosso, Brazil 11°54S 55°48W 331 C6
Verde → Mato Grosso do Sul, Brazil 21°25S 52°20W 331 E7
Verde → São Paulo, Brazil 23°29S 46°27W 137 A1
Verde → Chihuahua, Mexico 26°29N 107°58W 318 B3
Verde → Oaxaca, Mexico 15°59N 97°50W 319 D5
Verde → Veracruz, Mexico 21°10N 102°50W 318 C4
Verde → Paraguay 23°9S 57°37W 334 A4
Verde → Ariz., U.S.A. 33°33N 111°40W 300 J17
Verde, Cay Bahamas 23°0N 75°5W 321 B4
Verde Grande → Brazil 16°13S 43°49W 333 E3
Verde I. Phil. 13°33N 121°5E 232 E3
Verde Island Pass. Phil. 13°34N 120°51E 232 E3
Verde Pequeno → Brazil 14°48S 43°31W 333 D3
Verden Germany 52°55N 9°14E 178 C5
Verdi Athina, Greece 38°2N 23°40E 112 A2
Verdi Nev., U.S.A. 39°31N 119°59W 306 F7
Verdikoussa Greece 39°47N 21°59E 204 B3
Verdon → France 43°43N 5°46E 175 E9
Verdon △ France 43°50N 6°5E 175 E10
Verdugo Mts. U.S.A. 34°10N 118°16W 126 A2
Verdun Qué., Canada 45°27N 73°35W 130 B2
Verdun Meuse, France 49°9N 5°24E 173 C12
Verdun-sur-le-Doubs France 46°54N 5°2E 173 F12
Vereeniging S. Africa 26°38S 27°57E 271 C4
Verga, C. Guinea 10°30N 14°10W 262 C2
Vergara Uruguay 32°56S 53°57W 335 C5
Vergato Italy 44°17N 11°7E 199 D8
Vergemont Cr. → Australia 24°16S 143°16E 280 C3
Vergennes U.S.A. 44°10N 73°15W 313 B11
Vergt France 45°2N 0°43E 174 C4
Verhalom Hungary 47°31N 19°1E 117 A2
Veria Greece 40°34N 22°12E 202 F6
Verín Spain 41°57N 7°27W 194 D3
Verkhnedvinsk = Vyerkhnyadzvinsk Belarus 55°45N 27°58E 188 E4
Verkhnetulomskoye Vdkhr. Russia 68°36N 31°12E 160 B24
Verkhnevilyuysk Russia 63°27N 120°18E 215 C13
Verkhniy Baskunchak Russia 48°14N 46°44E 191 F8
Verkhovye Russia 52°55N 37°15E 189 F9
Verkhovyna Ukraine 48°9N 24°47E 183 B9
Verkhoyansk Russia 67°35N 133°25E 215 C14
Verkhoyansk Ra. = Verkhoyanskiy Khrebet Russia 66°0N 129°0E 215 C13
Verkhoyanskiy Khrebet Russia 66°0N 129°0E 215 C13
Verma Norway 62°21N 8°3E 164 B5
Vermelho → Brazil 23°30S 46°46W 137 B1
Vermenton France 47°40N 3°42E 173 E10
Vermilion Alta., Canada 53°20N 110°50W 297 C6
Vermilion Ohio, U.S.A. 41°25N 82°22W 312 E2
Vermilion → Alta., Canada 53°22N 110°51W 297 C6
Vermilion → Ill., U.S.A. 41°19N 89°4W 310 C7
Vermilion B. U.S.A. 29°42N 92°0W 314 G9
Vermilion Bay Canada 49°51N 93°34W 297 D10
Vermilion L. U.S.A. 47°53N 92°26W 308 B7
Vermillion U.S.A. 42°47N 96°56W 308 D5
Vermillion → Canada 47°38N 72°56W 298 C5
Vermont U.S.A. 40°18N 90°26W 310 D6
Vermont □ U.S.A. 44°0N 73°0W 313 C12
Vermont Knolls U.S.A. 33°57N 118°17W 126 C3
Vermosh Albania 42°35N 19°42E 202 D3
Verna U.S.A. 27°23N 82°16W 317 H7
Vernadsky Antarctica 65°0S 64°0W 151 C17
Vernal U.S.A. 40°27N 109°32W 304 F9
Vernalis U.S.A. 37°36N 121°17W 306 H5
Vernazza Italy 44°10N 9°45E 198 D6
Verner Canada 46°25N 80°8W 298 C3
Verneuil-sur-Avre France 48°45N 0°55E 172 D7
Verneukpan S. Africa 30°0S 21°0E 270 D3
Vernier Switz. 46°11N 6°12E 179 J2
Vérnio Italy 44°3N 11°9E 198 D8
Vernon B.C., Canada 50°20N 119°15W 296 C5
Vernon Eure, France 49°5N 1°30E 172 C8
Vernon Calif., U.S.A. 34°0N 118°13W 126 B3
Vernon Ill., U.S.A. 38°48N 89°5W 310 F7
Vernon Ind., U.S.A. 38°59N 85°36W 311 F11
Vernon Tex., U.S.A. 34°9N 99°17W 314 D5
Vernonia U.S.A. 45°52N 123°11W 306 E3
Vernou Guadeloupe 16°11N 61°39W 322 e
Verny = Almaty Kazakhstan 43°15N 76°57E 217 D9
Vero Beach U.S.A. 27°38N 80°24W 317 H9
Véroia = Veria Greece 40°34N 22°12E 202 F6
Véroli Italy 41°41N 13°25E 199 G10
Verona Ont., Canada 44°29N 76°42W 313 B8
Verona Italy 45°27N 10°59E 198 C7
Verona Wis., U.S.A. 42°59N 89°32W 310 B7
Verrès Italy 45°40N 7°42E 198 C4
Verrières-le-Buisson France 48°44N 2°16E 134 B2
Verron Ra. Papua N. G. 4°21S 152°46E 286 C7
Versailles B. Aires, Argentina 34°38S 58°31W 117 B1
Versailles Yvelines, France 48°48N 2°7E 134 B1
Versailles Ill., U.S.A. 39°53N 90°39W 310 E6
Versailles Ind., U.S.A. 39°4N 85°15W 311 E11
Versailles Ky., U.S.A. 38°3N 84°44W 311 F12
Versailles Mo., U.S.A. 38°26N 92°51W 310 F4
Versailles Ohio, U.S.A. 40°13N 84°29W 311 D12
Versalles Bolivia 12°44S 63°18W 331 C5
Versmold Germany 52°2N 8°9E 178 C4
Vert, C. Senegal 14°45N 17°30W 262 C1
Vertou France 47°10N 1°28W 172 E5
Vertus France 48°54N 4°2E 173 D11
Verulam S. Africa 29°38S 31°2E 271 C5
Verviers Belgium 50°37N 5°52E 170 D5
Vervins France 49°50N 3°53E 173 C10
Veržej Slovenia 46°34N 16°13E 199 B13
Verzy France 49°9N 4°10E 173 C11
Vescovato France 42°30N 9°27E 175 F13
Veselí nad Lužnicí Czech Rep. 49°12N 14°43E 180 B7
Veselie Bulgaria 42°18N 27°38E 203 D11
Veselovskoye Vdkhr. Russia 46°58N 41°25E 191 G5
Veshenskaya Russia 49°35N 41°44E 190 F5
Veshnyaki Russia 55°43N 37°48E 129 B4
Vesle → France 49°23N 3°28E 173 C10
Vesolyy Posolok Russia 59°53N 30°28E 137 B2
Vesoul France 47°40N 6°11E 173 E13
Vessigebro Sweden 56°58N 12°40E 163 H6
Vest-Agder □ Norway 58°30N 7°15E 164 F4
Vestbygd Norway 58°6N 6°34E 164 F3
Vesterålen Norway 68°45N 15°0E 160 B16
Vestfjorden Norway 67°55N 14°0E 160 C16
Vestfold □ Norway 59°15N 10°0E 164 E7
Vestfossen Norway 59°44N 9°52E 164 E6
Vestgrønland = Kitaa □ Greenland 70°0N 47°0W 154 C6
Vestmannaeyjar Iceland 63°27N 20°15W 155 D6
Vestnes Norway 62°36N 7°5E 164 B4
Vestra Finland 60°19N 24°46E 121 B1
Vestre Gausdal Norway 61°12N 10°8E 164 C7
Vestskoven Denmark 55°41N 12°23E 118 A2
Vestspitsbergen Svalbard 78°40N 17°0E 150 B8
Vestur-skaftafellssýsla □ Iceland 63°50N 18°30W 155 D8
Vestvågøya Norway 68°18N 13°50E 160 B15
Vesuvio Italy 40°49N 14°26E 201 B7
Vesuvius, Mt. = Vesuvio Italy 40°49N 14°26E 201 B7
Vesyegonsk Russia 58°40N 37°16E 188 C9
Veszprém Hungary 47°8N 17°57E 182 C2
Veszprém □ Hungary 47°5N 17°55E 182 C2
Vésztő Hungary 46°55N 21°16E 182 D6
Vetapalem India 15°47N 80°18E 245 G5
Vetlanda Sweden 57°24N 15°3E 163 G9
Vetluga Russia 57°53N 45°45E 190 B7
Vetluga → Russia 56°36N 46°4E 190 B8
Vetluzhskiy Kostroma, Russia 58°23N 45°26E 190 A7
Vetluzhskiy Nizhniy Novgorod, Russia 57°17N 45°12E 190 B7
Vetovo Bulgaria 43°42N 26°16E 203 C10
Vetralla Italy 42°20N 12°2E 199 F9
Vetren Bulgaria 42°15N 24°3E 203 D8
Vettore, Mte. Italy 42°49N 13°16E 199 F10
Veurne Belgium 51°5N 2°40E 170 C2
Vevay U.S.A. 38°45N 85°4W 311 F11
Veveno → South Sudan 6°40N 32°58E 257 F3
Vevey Switz. 46°28N 6°51E 179 J2
Vevi Greece 40°47N 21°38E 202 F5
Veynes France 44°32N 5°49E 175 D9
Veys Iran 31°30N 49°0E 247 D6
Vézelay France 47°27N 3°45E 173 E10
Vézelise France 48°30N 6°5E 173 D13
Vézère → France 44°53N 0°53E 174 D4
Vezhen Bulgaria 42°50N 24°20E 203 D8
Vezirköprü Turkey 41°8N 35°27E 212 B6
Vezzani France 42°10N 9°15E 175 F13
Vi Thanh Vietnam 9°42N 105°26E 237 H5
Viacha Bolivia 16°39S 68°18W 330 D4
Viadana Italy 44°56N 10°31E 198 D7
Vialar = Tissemsilt Algeria 35°35N 1°50E 261 A5
Viamão Brazil 30°5S 51°0W 335 C5
Viana Brazil 3°13S 44°55W 332 B3
Viana Spain 42°31N 2°22W 196 C2
Viana do Alentejo Portugal 38°17N 7°59W 195 G3
Viana do Bolo Spain 42°11N 7°6W 194 C3
Viana do Castelo Portugal 41°42N 8°50W 194 D2
Viana do Castelo □ Portugal 41°50N 8°30W 194 D2
Vianden Lux. 49°56N 6°12E 170 E6
Viangchan = Vientiane Laos 17°58N 102°36E 236 D4
Vianópolis Brazil 16°40S 48°35W 333 E2
Vianos Greece 35°2N 25°21E 207 F5
Viar → Spain 37°36N 5°50W 195 H5

Viaréggio *Italy* 43°52N 10°14E **198** E7
Viaur → *France* 44°8N 1°58E **174** D5
Vibble *Sweden* 57°37N 18°16E **163** G12
Vibo Valéntia *Italy* 38°40N 16°6E **201** D9
Viborg *Denmark* 56°27N 9°23E **163** H3
Vibraye *France* 48°3N 0°44E **172** D7
Vic *Spain* 41°58N 2°19E **196** D7
Vic, Étang de *France* 43°29N 3°50E **174** E7
Vic-en-Bigorre *France* 43°24N 0°3E **174** E4
Vic-Fezensac *France* 43°47N 0°19E **174** E4
Vic-le-Comte *France* 45°39N 3°14E **173** G10
Vic-sur-Cère *France* 44°59N 2°38E **174** D6
Vicálvaro *Spain* 40°24N 3°36W **127** B2
Vícar *Spain* 36°50N 2°38W **197** J2
Vicente Lopez *Argentina* 34°31S 58°30W **117** B2
Vicente Pérez Rosales △ *Chile* 41°11S 72°12W **336** B2
Vicenza *Italy* 45°33N 11°33E **199** C8
Vich = Vic *Spain* 41°58N 2°19E **196** D7
Vichada □ *Colombia* 5°0N 69°30W **328** C4
Vichada → *Colombia* 4°55N 67°50W **328** C4
Vichuga *Russia* 57°12N 41°55E **190** B5
Vichy *France* 46°9N 3°26E **173** F10
Vickan *Sweden* 57°25N 6°10E **164** G3
Vicksburg *Ariz., U.S.A.* 33°45N 113°45W **307** M13
Vicksburg *Mich., U.S.A.* 42°7N 85°32W **311** B11
Vicksburg *Miss., U.S.A.* 32°21N 90°53W **315** E9
Vico *France* 42°10N 8°49E **175** F12
Vico, L. di *Italy* 42°19N 12°10E **199** F9
Vico del Gargano *Italy* 41°54N 15°57E **199** G12
Viçosa *Brazil* 9°28S 36°14W **332** C4
Viçosa do Ceará *Brazil* 3°34S 41°5W **332** B3
Vicovu de Sus *Romania* 47°56N 25°41E **183** C10
Victor *India* 21°0N 71°30E **242** J4
Victor Emanuel Ra. *Papua N. G.* 5°20S 142°15E **286** C2
Victor Harbor *Australia* 35°30S 138°37E **282** C3
Victor Hugo = Hamadia *Algeria* 35°28N 1°57E **261** A5
Victoria = Bandar Labuan *Malaysia* 5°20N 115°14E **235** A5
Victoria *Argentina* 32°40S 60°10W **334** C3
Victoria *B.C., Canada* 48°30N 123°25W **306** B3
Victoria *Chile* 38°13S 72°20W **336** A2
Victoria *Hong Kong, China* 22°17N 114°9E **122** B2
Victoria *Grenada* 12°12N 61°42W **323** q
Victoria *Guinea* 10°50N 14°32W **262** C2
Victoria *Gozo, Malta* 36°3N 14°14E **206** E6
Victoria *Mind. Or., Phil.* 13°12N 121°12E **232** E3
Victoria *Tarlac, Phil.* 15°35N 120°41E **232** D3
Victoria *Romania* 45°44N 24°41E **183** E9
Victoria *Seychelles* 4°38S 55°28E **272** c
Victoria *London, U.K.* **125** c3
Victoria *Kans., U.S.A.* 38°52N 99°9W **308** F4
Victoria *Tex., U.S.A.* 28°48N 97°0W **314** G6
Victoria □ *Australia* 37°0S 144°0E **282** D6
Victoria □ *Trin. & Tob.* 10°15N 61°27W **323** t
Victoria → *Australia* 15°10S 129°40E **278** C4
Victoria, Grand L. *Canada* 47°31N 77°30W **298** C4
Victoria, L. *Africa* 1°0S 33°0E **268** C3
Victoria, L. *N.S.W., Australia* 33°57S 141°15E **282** B4
Victoria, Mt. = Tomanivi *Fiji* 17°37S 178°1E **287** A2
Victoria, Mt. *Burma* 21°14N 93°55E **241** E4
Victoria, Mt. *Wellington, N.Z.* 41°18S 174°48E **143** B1
Victoria, Mt. *Papua N. G.* 8°55S 147°32E **286** E4
Victoria, Pont *Canada* 45°29N 73°32W **130** B2
Victoria and Alfred Waterfront *Cape Town, S. Africa* **118** a1
Victoria Beach *Canada* 50°40N 96°35W **297** C9
Victoria de Durango = Durango *Mexico* 24°3N 104°39W **318** C4
Victoria de las Tunas = Las Tunas *Cuba* 20°58N 76°59W **320** B4
Victoria Falls *Zimbabwe* 17°58S 25°52E **269** F2
Victoria Fjord *Greenland* 82°10N 46°0W **154** A6
Victoria Gardens *India* 18°58N 72°50E **130** B2
Victoria Harbour *Ont., Canada* 44°45N 79°45W **312** B5
Victoria Harbour *Hong Kong, China* 22°17N 114°10E **122** B1
Victoria I. *Canada* 71°0N 111°0W **294** C9
Victoria Island *Nigeria* 6°25N 3°25E **124** B2
Victoria L. *Nfld. & L., Canada* 48°20N 57°27W **299** C8
Victoria L. *Gauteng, S. Africa* 26°13S 28°9E **123** B2
Victoria Lawn Tennis Courts *Australia* 37°50S 145°1E **128** B2
Victoria Ld. *Antarctica* 75°0S 160°0E **151** D11
Victoria Nile → *Uganda* 2°14N 31°26E **268** B3
Victoria Park *Singapore* 1°19N 103°49E **138** B2
Victoria Peak *China* 22°16N 114°8E **122** B1
Victoria Peaks *Phil.* 9°22N 118°20E **233** G2
Victoria Pk. *Belize* 16°48N 88°37W **319** D7
Victoria Ra. *N.Z.* 42°12S 172°7E **285** C7
Victoria River *Australia* 16°25S 131°0E **278** C5
Victoria Str. *Canada* 69°31N 100°30W **294** D11
Victoria West *S. Africa* 31°25S 23°4E **270** D3
Victoria Wharf *Cape Town, S. Africa* **118** a2
Victorias *Phil.* 10°54N 123°5E **233** F4
Victoriaville *Canada* 46°4N 71°56W **299** C5
Victorica *Argentina* 36°20S 65°30W **334** D2
Victorville *U.S.A.* 34°32N 117°18W **307** L9
Vicuña *Chile* 30°0S 70°50W **334** C1
Vicuña Mackenna *Argentina* 33°53S 64°25W **334** C3
Vidal *U.S.A.* 34°7N 114°31W **307** L12
Vidalia *U.S.A.* 32°13N 82°25W **316** C7
Vidamlya *Belarus* 52°19N 23°47E **185** F10
Vidauban *France* 43°25N 6°27E **175** E10
Viddolatno = Vindelälven → *Sweden* 63°55N 19°50E **160** E18
Videbæk *Denmark* 56°6N 8°38E **163** H2
Videle *Romania* 44°17N 25°31E **183** F10
Videsæter *Norway* 61°57N 7°14E **164** C4
Vidette *U.S.A.* 33°2N 82°15W **316** B7
Vidigueira *Portugal* 38°12N 7°48W **195** G3
Vidin *Bulgaria* 43°59N 22°50E **202** C6
Vidin □ *Bulgaria* 43°59N 22°50E **202** C6
Vidio, C. *Spain* 43°35N 6°14W **194** B4
Vidisha *India* 23°28N 77°53E **242** H7
Vidos *Greece* 39°38N 19°55E **206** B9
Vidra *Romania* 45°56N 26°55E **183** E11
Viduša *Bos.-H.* 42°55N 18°21E **202** D2
Vidzy *Belarus* 55°23N 26°37E **188** E4
Viechtach *Germany* 49°4N 12°53E **179** F8
Viedma *Argentina* 40°50S 63°0W **336** B4
Viedma, L. *Argentina* 49°30S 72°30W **336** C2
Vieille Case *Dominica* 15°36N 61°24W **323** k
Vieira do Minho *Portugal* 41°38N 8°8W **194** D2
Vielha *Spain* 42°43N 0°44E **196** C5
Viella = Vielha *Spain* 42°43N 0°44E **196** C5
Vielsalm *Belgium* 50°17N 5°54E **170** D5
Vienenburg *Germany* 51°57N 10°34E **178** D6
Vieng Pou Kha *Laos* 20°41N 101°4E **228** G3
Vienna = Wien *Austria* 48°12N 16°22E **142** A2
Vienna *Ont., Canada* 42°41N 80°48W **312** D4
Vienna *Ga., U.S.A.* 32°6N 83°47W **316** C6
Vienna *Ill., U.S.A.* 37°25N 88°54W **308** G9
Vienna *Mo., U.S.A.* 38°11N 91°57W **310** F5
Vienna *Va., U.S.A.* 38°54N 77°16W **143** B2
Vienne *France* 45°31N 4°53E **175** C8
Vienne □ *France* 46°30N 0°42E **174** B4
Vienne → *France* 47°13N 0°5E **172** E7
Vientiane *Laos* 17°58N 102°36E **236** D4
Vientos, Paso de los *Caribbean* 20°0N 74°0W **321** C5
Vieques *Puerto Rico* 18°8N 65°25W **321** b
Vierge Pt. *St. Lucia* 13°49N 60°53W **323** m
Vierkant Pt. *Bonaire* 12°7N 68°17W **322** h
Viernheim *Germany* 49°31N 8°35E **179** F4
Viersen *Germany* 51°15N 6°23E **178** D2
Vierwaldstättersee *Switz.* 47°0N 8°30E **179** J4
Vierzon *France* 47°13N 2°5E **173** E9
Vieste *Italy* 41°53N 16°10E **199** G13
Viet Quang *Vietnam* 22°30N 104°48E **228** F5
Viet Tri *Vietnam* 21°18N 105°25E **236** B5
Vietnam ■ *Asia* 19°0N 106°0E **236** C6
Vietnam Veterans Memorial *U.S.A.* 38°53N 77°2W **143** B3
Vietnam War Museum *U.S.A.* 41°58N 87°39W **119** B3
Vietz = Witnica *Poland* 52°40N 14°54E **185** F1
Vieux-Boucau-les-Bains *France* 43°48N 1°23W **174** E2
Vieux Bourg *Guadeloupe* 16°20N 61°36W **322** e
Vieux Carré = French Quarter *New Orleans, U.S.A.* **131** a2
Vieux Fort *Guadeloupe* 15°57N 61°41W **322** e
Vieux Fort *Marie-Galante, Guadeloupe* 15°59N 61°17W **322** e
Vieux Fort *St. Lucia* 13°46N 60°58W **323** m
Vieux Fort, Pte. du *Guadeloupe* 15°57N 61°42W **322** e
Vieux Fort, R. du → *Guadeloupe* 15°59N 61°17W **322** e
Vieux Grand Port *Mauritius* 20°22S 57°42E **272** e
Vieux-Habitants *Guadeloupe* 16°4N 61°46W **322** e
Vieux-Habitants, Rivière des → *Guadeloupe* 16°3N 61°46W **322** e
Vieux-Montréal *Montréal, Canada* **130** b3
View Park *U.S.A.* 34°0N 118°20W **126** B3
Vif *France* 45°5N 5°41E **175** C9
Viga *Phil.* 13°52N 124°18E **232** E5
Vigan *Phil.* 17°35N 120°28E **232** C3
Vigário Geral *Brazil* 22°48S 43°18W **135** A1
Vigeland *Norway* 58°5N 7°18E **164** F4
Vigentino *Italy* 45°26N 9°13E **129** B2
Vigévano *Italy* 45°19N 8°51E **198** C5
Viggbyholm *Sweden* 59°26N 18°7E **129** A2
Vighignolo *Italy* 45°29N 9°2E **129** B1
Vigia = Almenara *Brazil* 16°11S 40°42W **333** E3
Vigia *Brazil* 0°50S 48°5W **332** B2
Vigla *Greece* 39°7N 20°50E **207** A2
Viglas, Akra *Greece* 35°54N 27°51E **206** F11
Vignemale *France* 42°47N 0°10W **174** F3
Vigneulles-lès-Hattonchâtel *France* 48°59N 5°43E **173** D12
Vignola *Italy* 44°29N 11°1E **198** D8
Vigo *Spain* 42°12N 8°41W **194** C2
Vigo, Ría de *Spain* 42°15N 8°45W **194** C2
Vigrestad *Norway* 58°34N 5°42E **164** F2
Vigsø Bugt *Denmark* 57°8N 8°47E **163** G2
Vihiers *France* 47°10N 0°30W **172** E6
Vihowa *Pakistan* 31°8N 70°30E **242** D4
Vihowa → *Pakistan* 31°8N 70°41E **242** D4
Viikki *Finland* 60°13N 25°1E **121** B3
Viipuri = Vyborg *Russia* 60°43N 28°47E **188** B5
Vijayadurg *India* 16°30N 73°25E **244** F1
Vijayawada *India* 16°31N 80°39E **244** F5
Vijosë → *Albania* 40°37N 19°24E **202** F3
Vík *Iceland* 63°25N 19°1W **155** D7
Vik *Sogn og Fjordane, Norway* 61°21N 6°6E **164** C3
Vika *Sweden* 60°57N 14°28E **162** D8
Vikarabad *India* 17°20N 77°54E **244** E3
Vikarbyn *Sweden* 60°55N 15°1E **162** D9
Vikeland *Norway* 60°42N 5°35E **164** D2
Vikedal *Norway* 59°30N 5°55E **164** E2
Vikeke = Viqueque *E. Timor* 8°52S 126°23E **231** F7
Vikeland = Vigeland *Norway* 58°5N 7°18E **164** F4
Viken *Skåne, Sweden* 56°9N 12°34E **163** H6
Viken *Västra Götaland, Sweden* 58°39N 14°20E **163** F8
Vikersund *Norway* 59°58N 9°59E **164** E6
Vikeså *Norway* 58°38N 6°3E **164** F3
Vikevåg *Norway* 59°5N 5°41E **164** E2
Vikhammer *Norway* 63°26N 10°37E **164** A7
Vikhroli *India* 19°6N 72°55E **130** A2
Viking *Canada* 53°7N 111°50W **296** C6
Vikmanshyttan *Sweden* 60°18N 15°50E **162** D9
Vikna *Norway* 64°55N 10°58E **160** D14
Vikos-Aoos △ *Greece* 40°0N 20°45E **204** B2
Vikøyri *Norway* 61°4N 6°34E **164** C3
Vila Alferes Chamusca = Guijá *Mozam.* 24°27S 33°0E **271** B5
Vila António Enes = Angoche *Mozam.* 16°8S 39°55E **269** F4
Vila Baleira *Madeira* 33°4N 16°20W **260** B1
Vila Bela da Santissima Trindade *Brazil* 15°0S 59°57W **331** C6
Vila Cabral = Lichinga *Mozam.* 13°13S 35°11E **269** E4
Vila Cabral = Niassa □ *Mozam.* 13°30S 36°0E **269** E4
Vila da Maganja *Mozam.* 17°18S 37°30E **269** F4
Vila da Ribeira Brava *C. Verde Is.* 16°32N 24°25W **153** j
Vila de Rei *Portugal* 39°41N 8°9W **194** F2
Vila do Bispo *Portugal* 37°5N 8°53W **195** H2
Vila do Conde *Portugal* 41°21N 8°45W **194** D2
Vila do Porto *Azores* 36°56N 25°9W **153** d4
Vila Franca de Xira *Portugal* 38°57N 8°59W **195** G2
Vila Franca do Campo *Azores* 37°43N 25°26W **153** d3
Vila Gamito *Mozam.* 14°12S 33°0E **269** E3
Vila Gomes da Costa *Mozam.* 24°20S 33°37E **271** B5
Vila Guilherme *Brazil* 23°30S 46°38W **137** B2
Vila Isabel *Brazil* 22°54S 43°15W **135** B1
Vila Jaguára *Brazil* 23°30S 46°45W **137** B1
Vila Machado *Mozam.* 19°15S 34°14E **269** F3
Vila Madalena *Brazil* 23°32S 46°41W **137** B1
Vila Maria *Brazil* 23°31S 46°36W **137** B2
Vila Mariana *Brazil* 23°34S 46°36W **137** B2
Vila Mouzinho *Mozam.* 14°48S 34°25E **269** E3
Vila Nova de Famalicão *Portugal* 41°25N 8°32W **194** D2
Vila Nova de Fos Côa *Portugal* 41°5N 7°9W **194** D3
Vila Nova de Gaia *Portugal* 41°8N 8°37W **194** D2
Vila Nova de Gaza = Xai-Xai *Mozam.* 25°6S 33°31E **271** C5
Vila Nova de Ourém *Portugal* 39°40N 8°35W **194** F2
Vila Nova do Corvo *Azores* 39°40N 31°8W **153** d2
Vila Pereira de Eça = Ondjiva *Angola* 16°48S 15°50E **265** F3
Vila Pery = Manica *Mozam.* 18°58S 32°59E **271** A5
Vila Pouca de Aguiar *Portugal* 41°30N 7°38W **194** D3
Vila Prudente *Brazil* 23°35S 46°33W **137** B2
Vila Real *Portugal* 41°17N 7°48W **194** D3
Vila-Real *Spain* 39°55N 0°3W **196** F4
Vila Real □ *Portugal* 41°36N 7°35W **194** D3
Vila Real de Santo António *Portugal* 37°10N 7°28W **195** H3
Vila-seca *Spain* 41°7N 1°9E **196** D6
Vila Texeira da Silva = Luau *Angola* 10°40S 22°10E **265** E4
Vila Vasco da Gama *Mozam.* 14°54S 32°14E **269** E3
Vila Velha *Amapá, Brazil* 3°13N 51°13W **329** C7
Vila Velha *Espírito Santo, Brazil* 20°20S 40°17W **333** F3
Vila Velha *Sergipe, Brazil* 11°20S 38°9W **332** D4
Vila Viçosa *Portugal* 38°45N 7°27W **195** G3
Viladecans *Spain* 41°18N 2°1E **114** B1
Vilafranca del Maestrat *Spain* 40°26N 0°16W **196** E4
Vilafranca del Penedès *Spain* 41°21N 1°40E **196** D6
Vilagarcía de Arousa *Spain* 42°34N 8°46W **194** C2
Vilaine → *France* 47°30N 2°27W **172** E4
Vilakalaka *Vanuatu* 15°25S 167°42E **287** E5
Vilanandro, Tanjona *Madag.* 16°11S 44°27E **272** B1
Vilanculos *Mozam.* 22°1S 35°17E **271** B6
Vilanova i la Geltrú *Spain* 41°13N 1°40E **196** D6
Vilar Formoso *Portugal* 40°38N 6°45W **194** E4
Vilaseca-Salou = Vila-seca *Spain* 41°7N 1°9E **196** D6
Vilbjerg *Denmark* 56°12N 8°46E **163** H2
Vilcabamba, Cordillera *Peru* 13°0S 73°0W **330** C3
Vilcanchos *Peru* 13°40S 74°25W **330** C3
Vilcheka, Ostrov *Russia* 80°0N 58°31E **214** B6
Vilcheka, Zemlya *Russia* 80°30N 60°30E **150** A11
Vilches *Spain* 38°12N 3°30W **195** G7
Vile Parle *India* 19°6N 72°51E **130** A2
Vileyka *Belarus* 54°30N 26°53E **177** A14
Vilhelmina *Sweden* 64°35N 16°39E **160** D17
Vilhena *Brazil* 12°40S 60°5W **331** C5
Viliya → = Neris → *Lithuania* 55°8N 24°16E **188** E3
Viljandi *Estonia* 58°28N 25°30E **188** C3
Viljoensdorp = Newcastle *S. Africa* 27°45S 29°58E **271** C4
Vilkaviškis *Lithuania* 54°39N 23°2E **184** D10
Vilkija *Lithuania* 55°3N 23°35E **184** C10
Vil'kitskogo, Proliv *Russia* 78°0N 103°0E **215** B11
Vilkomir = Ukmergė *Lithuania* 55°15N 24°45E **188** E3
Vilkovo = Vylkove *Ukraine* 45°28N 29°32E **183** E14
Villa Abecia *Bolivia* 21°0S 68°18W **334** A2
Villa Adelina *Argentina* 34°31S 58°33W **117** B1
Villa Ana *Argentina* 28°28S 59°40W **334** B4
Villa Angela *Argentina* 27°34S 60°45W **334** B3
Villa Ballester *Argentina* 34°33S 58°33W **117** B1
Villa Barilari *Argentina* 34°42S 58°20W **117** C2
Villa Bella = Serra Talhada *Brazil* 7°59S 38°18W **332** C4
Villa Bella *Bolivia* 10°25S 65°22W **331** C4
Villa Borghese *Rome, Italy* **136** a3
Villa Bosch *Argentina* 34°35S 58°33W **117** B1
Villa Bruzual *Venezuela* 9°20N 69°6W **328** C4
Villa C. Colon *Argentina* 34°41S 58°21W **117** C2
Villa Cañás *Argentina* 34°0S 61°35W **334** C3
Villa Cecilia = Ciudad Madero *Mexico* 22°19N 97°50W **319** C5
Villa Cisneros = Dakhla *W. Sahara* 23°50N 15°53W **260** D1
Villa Ciudadela *Argentina* 34°38S 58°33W **117** B1
Villa Constitución *Argentina* 33°15S 60°20W **334** C3
Villa de Arriaga *Mexico* 21°56N 101°20W **318** C4
Villa de Cura *Venezuela* 10°2N 67°29W **328** A4
Villa de Guadalupe *Mexico* 19°29N 99°6W **128** B2
Villa de María *Argentina* 29°55S 63°43W **334** B3
Villa de Méndez *Mexico* 25°7N 98°34W **319** B5
Villa del Nevoso = Ilirska-Bistrica *Slovenia* 45°34N 14°14E **199** C11
Villa del Rio *Spain* 37°59N 4°17W **195** H6
Villa del Rosario *Venezuela* 10°19N 72°19W **328** A3
Villa Devoto *Argentina* 34°36S 58°31W **117** B1
Villa Diamante *Argentina* 34°41S 58°25W **117** C2
Villa Dolores *Argentina* 31°58S 65°15W **334** C2
Villa Dominico *Argentina* 34°41S 58°19W **117** C3
Villa Frontera *Mexico* 26°56N 101°27W **318** B4
Villa Gesell *Argentina* 37°15S 56°55W **334** D4
Villa Grove *U.S.A.* 39°52N 88°10W **311** E8
Villa Guillermina *Argentina* 28°15S 59°29W **334** B4
Villa Hayes *Paraguay* 25°5S 57°20W **334** B4
Villa Hidalgo *Mexico* 24°15N 99°26W **319** C5
Villa Iris *Argentina* 38°12S 63°12W **334** D3
Villa Lugano *Argentina* 34°41S 58°27W **117** C2
Villa Lynch *Argentina* 34°35S 58°31W **117** B1
Villa Madero *Argentina* 34°41S 58°30W **117** C1
Villa María *Argentina* 32°20S 63°10W **334** C3
Villa Mazán *Argentina* 28°40S 66°30W **334** B2
Villa Minozzo *Italy* 44°22N 10°28E **198** D7
Villa Montes *Bolivia* 21°10S 63°30W **334** A3
Villa Ocampo *Argentina* 28°30S 59°20W **334** B4
Villa Ocampo *Durango, Mexico* 26°27N 105°31W **318** B3
Villa Ojo de Agua *Argentina* 29°30S 63°44W **334** B3
Villa Regina *Argentina* 39°6S 67°4W **336** A3
Villa Rica *U.S.A.* 33°44N 84°55W **316** B5
Villa Sáenz Pena *Argentina* 34°37S 58°32W **117** B1
Villa San Giovanni *Italy* 38°13N 15°38E **201** D8
Villa San Martín *Argentina* 28°15S 64°9W **334** B3
Villa Sanjurjo = Al Hoceïma *Morocco* 35°8N 3°58W **261** A4
Villa Santina *Italy* 46°24N 12°55E **199** B9
Villa Unión *Mexico* 23°12N 106°14W **318** C3
Villa Urquiza *Argentina* 34°34S 58°28W **117** B2
Villaba *Phil.* 11°13N 124°24E **233** F5
Villablino *Spain* 42°57N 6°19W **194** C4
Villacarlos *Spain* 39°53N 4°17E **206** B5
Villacarriedo *Spain* 43°14N 3°48W **194** B7
Villacarrillo *Spain* 38°7N 3°3W **195** G7
Villacastín *Spain* 40°46N 4°25W **194** E6
Villach *Austria* 46°37N 13°51E **180** E6
Villacidro *Italy* 39°27N 8°44E **200** C1
Villada *Spain* 42°15N 4°59W **194** C6
Villadiego *Spain* 42°31N 4°1W **194** C6
Villadóssola *Italy* 46°4N 8°16E **198** B5
Villafeliche *Spain* 41°10N 1°30W **196** D3
Villafranca *Spain* 42°17N 1°46W **196** C3
Villafranca de los Barros *Spain* 38°35N 6°18W **195** G4
Villafranca de los Caballeros *Spain* 39°26N 3°21W **195** F7
Villafranca del Cid = Vilafranca del Maestrat *Spain* 40°26N 0°16W **196** E4
Villafranca del Panadés = Vilafranca del Penedès *Spain* 41°21N 1°40E **196** D6
Villafranca di Verona *Italy* 45°21N 10°50E **198** C7
Villafranca Tirrena *Italy* 38°20N 15°25E **201** D8
Villagio Mussolini = Arborèa *Italy* 39°46N 8°35E **200** C1
Villagrán *Mexico* 24°29N 99°29W **319** C5
Villaguay *Argentina* 32°0S 59°0W **334** C4
Villaharta *Spain* 38°9N 4°54W **195** G6
Villahermosa *Tabasco, Mexico* 17°59N 92°55W **319** D6
Villahermosa *Spain* 38°46N 2°52W **197** G2
Villaines-la-Juhel *France* 48°21N 0°20W **172** D6
Villajoyosa *Spain* 38°30N 0°12W **197** G4
Villalba *Puerto Rico* 18°8N 66°30W **321** b
Villalba *Spain* 43°26N 7°40W **194** B3
Villalba de Guardo *Spain* 42°42N 4°49W **194** C6
Villalón de Campos *Spain* 42°5N 5°4W **194** C5
Villalpando *Spain* 41°51N 5°25W **194** D5
Villaluenga de la Sagra *Spain* 40°2N 3°54W **194** E7
Villamanán *Spain* 42°19N 5°35W **194** C5
Villamartín *Spain* 36°52N 5°38W **195** J5
Villamayor de Santiago *Spain* 39°50N 2°59W **196** F2
Villamblard *France* 45°2N 0°32E **174** C4
Villanova Monteleone *Italy* 40°30N 8°28E **200** B1
Villanueva *Colombia* 10°37N 72°59W **328** A3
Villanueva *N. Mex., U.S.A.* 35°16N 105°22W **305** J11
Villanueva de Castellón *Spain* 39°5N 0°31W **197** F4
Villanueva de Córdoba *Spain* 38°20N 4°38W **195** G6
Villanueva de la Fuente *Spain* 38°42N 2°42W **197** G2
Villanueva de la Serena *Spain* 38°59N 5°50W **195** G5
Villanueva de la Sierra *Spain* 40°12N 6°24W **194** E4
Villanueva de los Castillejos *Spain* 37°30N 7°15W **195** H3
Villanueva de los Infantes *Spain* 38°43N 3°1W **195** G7
Villanueva del Arzobispo *Spain* 38°10N 3°0W **197** G2
Villanueva del Fresno *Spain* 38°23N 7°10W **195** G3
Villanueva y Geltrú = Vilanova i la Geltrú *Spain* 41°13N 1°40E **196** D6
Villaputzu *Italy* 39°26N 9°34E **200** C2
Villaquilambre *Spain* 42°39N 5°33W **194** C5
Villar del Arzobispo *Spain* 39°44N 0°50W **196** F4
Villar del Rey *Spain* 39°7N 6°50W **195** F4
Villard-de-Lans *France* 45°3N 5°33E **175** C9
Villarramiel *Spain* 42°2N 4°55W **194** C6
Villarreal = Vila-Real *Spain* 39°55N 0°3W **196** F4
Villarrica *Chile* 39°15S 72°15W **336** A2
Villarrica *Paraguay* 25°40S 56°30W **334** B4
Villarrica △ *Chile* 39°24S 71°46W **336** A2
Villarrobledo *Spain* 39°18N 2°36W **197** F2
Villarroya de la Sierra *Spain* 41°27N 1°46W **196** D3
Villarrubia de los Ojos *Spain* 39°14N 3°36W **195** F7
Villars-les-Dombes *France* 46°0N 5°3E **173** F12
Villasayas *Spain* 41°24N 2°39W **196** D2
Villaseco de los Gamitos *Spain* 41°2N 6°7W **194** D4
Villasimíus *Italy* 39°8N 9°31E **200** C2
Villastar *Spain* 40°17N 1°9W **196** E3
Villatobas *Spain* 39°54N 3°20W **194** F7
Villaverde *Spain* 40°21N 3°42W **127** B1
Villaverde Bajo *Spain* 40°20N 3°40W **127** B1
Villavicencio *Argentina* 32°28S 69°0W **334** C2
Villavicencio *Colombia* 4°9N 73°37W **328** C3
Villaviciosa *Spain* 43°32N 5°27W **194** B5
Villazón *Bolivia* 22°0S 65°35W **334** A2
Ville-d'Avray *France* 48°49N 2°11E **134** B2
Ville-Marie *Canada* 47°20N 79°30W **298** C4
Ville Platte *U.S.A.* 30°41N 92°17W **314** F8
Villecresnes *France* 48°43N 2°31E **134** B4
Villedieu-les-Poêles *France* 48°50N 1°13W **172** D5
Villefort *France* 44°28N 3°56E **174** D7
Villefranche-de-Lauragais *France* 43°25N 1°44E **174** E5
Villefranche-de-Rouergue *France* 44°21N 2°2E **174** D6
Villefranche-du-Périgord *France* 44°38N 1°5E **174** D5
Villefranche-sur-Saône *France* 45°59N 4°43E **175** C8
Villejuif *France* 48°47N 2°21E **134** B3
Villel *Spain* 40°14N 1°12W **196** E3
Villemomble *France* 48°52N 2°30E **134** A4
Villemur-sur-Tarn *France* 43°51N 1°31E **174** E5
Villena *Spain* 38°39N 0°52W **197** G4
Villenauxe-la-Grande *France* 48°35N 3°33E **173** D10
Villenave-d'Ornon *France* 44°46N 0°33W **174** D3
Villeneuve-d'Ascq *France* 50°38N 3°9E **173** B10
Villeneuve-la-Garenne *France* 48°56N 2°19E **134** A3
Villeneuve-l'Archevêque *France* 48°14N 3°32E **173** D10
Villeneuve-le-Roi *France* 48°43N 2°24E **134** B3
Villeneuve-lès-Avignon *France* 43°58N 4°49E **175** E8
Villeneuve-St-Georges *France* 48°43N 2°27E **134** B3
Villeneuve-sur-Allier *France* 46°40N 3°13E **173** F10
Villeneuve-sur-Lot *France* 44°24N 0°42E **174** D4
Villeneuve-sur-Yonne *France* 48°5N 3°18E **173** D10
Villeparisis *France* 48°56N 2°36E **134** A4
Villeréal *France* 44°38N 0°45E **174** D4
Villers-Bocage *France* 49°3N 0°40W **172** C6
Villers-Cotterêts *France* 49°15N 3°4E **173** C10
Villers-sur-Mer *France* 49°21N 0°2W **172** C6
Villersexel *France* 47°33N 6°26E **173** E13
Villerupt *France* 49°28N 5°55E **173** C12
Villeurbanne *France* 45°46N 4°55E **175** C8
Villevaudé *France* 48°55N 2°39E **134** A4
Villiers *S. Africa* 27°2S 28°36E **271** C4
Villiers-le-Bâcle *France* 48°44N 2°8E **134** B1
Villiers-sur-Marne *France* 48°49N 2°32E **134** B4
Villingen-Schwenningen *Germany* 48°3N 8°26E **179** G4
Villinki *Finland* 60°9N 25°6E **121** C3
Villisca *U.S.A.* 40°56N 94°59W **310** D2
Villmanstrand = Lappeenranta *Finland* 61°3N 28°12E **188** B5
Villoresi, Canale *Italy* 45°33N 8°59E **129** A1
Villupuram *India* 11°59N 79°31E **245** J4
Vilna = Vilnius *Lithuania* 54°38N 25°19E **188** E3
Vilna *Canada* 54°7N 111°55W **296** C6
Vilnius *Lithuania* 54°38N 25°19E **188** E3
Vils *Austria* 47°33N 10°38E **180** D3
Vils → *Bayern, Germany* 48°37N 13°11E **179** G9
Vils → *Bayern, Germany* 49°10N 11°57E **179** F7
Vilsbiburg *Germany* 48°26N 12°22E **179** G8
Vilshofen *Germany* 48°37N 13°11E **179** G9
Vilusi *Montenegro* 42°44N 18°34E **202** D2
Vilvoorde *Belgium* 50°56N 4°26E **116** A2
Vilyuchinsk *Russia* 52°55N 158°24E **215** D16
Vilyuy → *Russia* 64°24N 126°26E **215** C13
Vilyuysk *Russia* 63°40N 121°35E **215** C13
Vimianzo *Spain* 43°7N 9°2W **194** B1
Vimioso *Portugal* 41°35N 6°31W **194** D4
Vimmerby *Sweden* 57°40N 15°55E **163** G9
Vimodrone *Italy* 45°30N 9°16E **129** A2
Vimont *Canada* 45°36N 73°43W **130** A1
Vimoutiers *France* 48°57N 0°10E **172** D7
Vimperk *Czech Rep.* 49°3N 13°46E **180** B6
Vina → *Cameroon* 7°45N 15°36E **264** A3
Viña del Mar *Chile* 33°0S 71°30W **334** C1
Vinanmek Mansion *Bangkok, Thailand* **113** a2
Vinarós *Spain* 40°30N 0°27E **196** E5
Vincendo *Réunion* 21°21S 55°41E **272** f
Vincennes *Val-de-Marne, France* 48°51N 2°26E **134** A3
Vincennes *Ind., U.S.A.* 38°41N 87°32W **311** F9
Vincennes, Bois de *France* 48°49N 2°26E **134** B3
Vincennes Bay *S. Ocean* 66°0S 109°0E **151** C8
Vincent *U.S.A.* 34°33N 118°11W **307** L8
Vinces *Ecuador* 1°32S 79°45W **328** D2
Vinchina *Argentina* 28°45S 68°15W **334** B2
Vindava = Ventspils *Latvia* 57°25N 21°32E **184** A8
Vindelälven → *Sweden* 63°55N 19°50E **160** E18
Vindeln *Sweden* 64°12N 19°43E **160** D18
Vinderup *Denmark* 56°29N 8°45E **163** H2
Vindhya Ra. *India* 22°50N 77°0E **242** H7
Vine Grove *U.S.A.* 37°49N 85°59W **311** G11
Vineland *Fla., U.S.A.* 28°23N 81°30W **133** B1
Vineland *N.J., U.S.A.* 39°29N 75°2W **309** F16
Vineuil *France* 47°35N 1°22E **172** E8
Vinga *Romania* 46°1N 21°14E **182** D6
Vingåker *Sweden* 59°2N 15°52E **162** E9
Vingelen *Norway* 62°25N 10°52E **164** B7
Vingnes *Norway* 61°7N 10°26E **164** C7
Vinh *Vietnam* 18°45N 105°38E **236** C5
Vinh Loi = Bac Lieu *Vietnam* 9°17N 105°43E **237** H5
Vinh Long *Vietnam* 10°16N 105°57E **237** G5
Vinh Moc *Vietnam* 21°18N 105°1E **236** B5
Vinh Yen *Vietnam* 21°21N 105°35E **228** G5
Vinhais *Portugal* 41°50N 7°5W **194** D3
Vinica *Croatia* 46°20N 16°9E **199** B13
Vinica *Macedonia* 41°53N 22°30E **202** E6
Vinica *Slovenia* 45°28N 15°16E **199** C12
Vinings *U.S.A.* 33°53N 84°29W **113** A2
Vinita *U.S.A.* 36°39N 95°9W **314** C7
Vinje *Sør-Trøndelag, Norway* 63°12N 9°0E **164** B6
Vinje *Telemark, Norway* 59°37N 7°51E **164** E4
Vinjo *Norway* 60°48N 6°30E **164** D3
Vinkovci *Croatia* 45°19N 18°48E **182** E3
Vinnitsa = Vinnytsya *Ukraine* 49°15N 28°30E **177** D15
Vinnytsya *Ukraine* 49°15N 28°30E **177** D15
Vinnytsya □ *Ukraine* 49°20N 28°15E **177** D15
Vinodelnoye = Ipatovo *Russia* 45°45N 42°50E **191** H6
Vinohrady *Prague, Czech Rep.* **135** c3
Vinoř *Czech Rep.* 50°8N 14°34E **135** B3
Vinslöv *Sweden* 56°7N 13°55E **163** H7
Vinson Massif *Antarctica* 78°35S 85°25W **151** D16
Vinstra *Norway* 61°37N 9°44E **164** C6
Vinstra → *Norway* 61°37N 9°44E **164** C6
Vintar *Phil.* 18°14N 120°39E **232** B3
Vintjärn *Sweden* 60°50N 16°4E **162** D10
Vinton *Calif., U.S.A.* 39°48N 120°10W **306** F6
Vinton *Iowa, U.S.A.* 42°10N 92°1W **310** B4
Vinton *La., U.S.A.* 30°11N 93°35W **314** F8
Vințu de Jos *Romania* 46°0N 23°30E **183** D8
Vinukonda *India* 16°4N 79°45E **244** F4
Viöl *Germany* 54°34N 9°11E **178** A5
Viola *U.S.A.* 41°12N 90°35W **310** C6
Violet Hill *China* 22°15N 114°11E **122** B2
Violet Town *Australia* 36°38S 145°42E **283** D6
Violet Valley ◎ *Australia* 17°10S 127°55E **278** C4
Vioolsdrif *S. Africa* 28°46S 17°39E **270** C2
Viotía □ *Greece* 38°20N 23°0E **204** C5
Vipacco = Vipava *Slovenia* 45°51N 13°58E **199** C10
Vipava *Slovenia* 45°51N 13°58E **199** C10
Vipiteno *Italy* 46°54N 11°26E **199** B8
Viqueque *E. Timor* 8°52S 126°23E **231** F7
Vir *Croatia* 44°17N 15°3E **199** D12
Virac *Phil.* 13°30N 124°20E **232** E5
Virachey *Cambodia* 13°59N 106°49E **236** F6
Virachey △ *Cambodia* 14°14N 106°55E **236** E6
Virago Sd. *Canada* 54°0N 132°30W **296** C2
Virajpet = Virarajendrapet *India* 12°10N 75°50E **245** H2
Viramgam *India* 23°5N 72°0E **242** H5
Viranşehir *Turkey* 37°13N 39°45E **213** D8
Virányos *Hungary* 47°31N 18°59E **117** A1
Virarajendrapet *India* 12°10N 75°50E **245** H2
Virawah *Pakistan* 24°31N 70°46E **242** G4
Virbalis *Lithuania* 54°39N 22°49E **184** D9
Virden *Man., Canada* 49°50N 100°56W **297** D8
Virden *Ill., U.S.A.* 39°30N 89°46W **310** E7
Vire *France* 48°50N 0°53W **172** D6
Vire → *France* 49°20N 1°7W **172** C5
Virei *Angola* 15°43S 12°52E **265** F2
Virgem da Lapa *Brazil* 16°49S 42°21W **333** E3
Vírgenes, C. *Argentina* 52°19S 68°21W **336** D3
Virgin → *U.S.A.* 36°28N 114°21W **305** H6
Virgin Gorda *Br. Virgin Is.* 18°30N 64°26W **321** C7
Virgin Is. (British) ☑ *W. Indies* 18°30N 64°30W **321** C7
Virgin Is. (U.S.) ☑ *W. Indies* 18°20N 65°0W **321** C7
Virgin Islands △ *U.S. Virgin Is.* 18°21N 64°43W **321** b
Virginia *Free State, S. Africa* 28°8S 26°55E **270** C4
Virginia *Ill., U.S.A.* 39°57N 90°13W **310** E6
Virginia *Minn., U.S.A.* 47°31N 92°32W **308** B7
Virginia □ *U.S.A.* 37°30N 78°45W **309** G14
Virginia, L. *U.S.A.* 28°35N 81°20W **133** A2
Virginia Beach *U.S.A.* 36°49N 76°9W **309** F16
Virginia City *Mont., U.S.A.* 45°18N 111°56W **304** D8
Virginia City *Nev., U.S.A.* 39°19N 119°39W **306** F7
Virginia Falls *Canada* 61°38N 125°42W **296** A3
Virginia Gardens *U.S.A.* 25°48N 80°18W **128** B1
Virginia Key *U.S.A.* 25°44N 80°9W **128** B2
Virginiatown *Canada* 48°9N 79°36W **298** C4
Virje *Croatia* 46°4N 16°59E **199** B13
Viroflay *France* 48°48N 2°10E **134** B2
Vironas *Greece* 37°55N 23°46E **112** B2
Viroqua *U.S.A.* 43°34N 90°53W **308** D8
Virovitica *Croatia* 45°51N 17°21E **182** E2
Virpazar *Montenegro* 42°14N 19°6E **202** D3
Virpur *India* 21°51N 70°42E **242** J4
Virsbo *Sweden* 59°52N 16°2E **162** E10
Virserum *Sweden* 57°20N 15°35E **163** G9
Virton *Belgium* 49°35N 5°32E **170** E5
Virú *Peru* 8°25S 78°45W **330** B2
Virudunagar *India* 9°30N 77°58E **245** K3
Virum *Denmark* 55°47N 12°27E **118** B2
Virunga △ *Dem. Rep. of the Congo* 0°5N 29°38E **268** B2
Vis *Croatia* 43°4N 16°10E **199** E13
Visalia *U.S.A.* 36°20N 119°18W **306** J7
Visayan Sea *Phil.* 11°30N 123°30E **233** F4
Visayas □ *Phil.* 9°30N 122°45E **233** G4
Visby *Sweden* 57°37N 18°18E **163** G12
Viscount Melville Sd. *Canada* 74°10N 108°0W **295** C10
Visé *Belgium* 50°44N 5°41E **170** D5
Vise, Ostrov *Russia* 79°33N 76°50E **214** B8
Višegrad *Bos.-H.* 43°47N 19°17E **182** G4
Viseu *Brazil* 1°10S 46°5W **332** B2
Viseu *Portugal* 40°40N 7°55W **194** E3
Viseu □ *Portugal* 40°40N 7°55W **194** E3
Vișeu de Sus *Romania* 47°45N 24°25E **183** C9
Vishakhapatnam *India* 17°45N 83°20E **244** F6
Vishnyaki *Russia* 55°46N 37°53E **129** B5
Višina *Romania* 43°52N 24°27E **183** G9
Vișinești *Moldova* 46°20N 28°27E **183** D13
Visingsö *Sweden* 58°2N 14°20E **163** F8
Visitacion Valley *U.S.A.* 37°42N 122°23W **136** B2
Viskafors *Sweden* 57°37N 12°50E **163** G6
Viskan → *Sweden* 57°14N 12°12E **163** G6
Viški Kanal *Croatia* 43°4N 16°5E **199** E13
Vislanda *Sweden* 56°46N 14°30E **163** H8
Visnagar *India* 23°45N 72°32E **242** H5
Višnja Gora *Slovenia* 45°58N 14°45E **199** C11
Viso, Mte. *Italy* 44°38N 7°5E **198** D4
Viso del Marqués *Spain* 38°32N 3°34W **195** G7
Visoko *Bos.-H.* 43°58N 18°10E **182** G3
Visokoi I. *Antarctica* 56°43S 27°15W **151** B1
Visp *Switz.* 46°17N 7°52E **179** J3
Vissefjärda *Sweden* 56°32N 15°35E **163** H9
Visselhövede *Germany* 52°59N 9°34E **178** C5
Vissenbjerg *Denmark* 55°23N 10°7E **163** J4
Vista *U.S.A.* 33°12N 117°14W **307** M9
Vista Alegre *Santiago, Chile* 33°30S 70°43W **137** C1
Vista Alegre *Lima, Peru* 12°9S 76°59W **124** B3
Vista Bella *Trin. & Tob.* 10°17N 61°27W **323** t
Vista Grove *U.S.A.* 33°51N 84°16W **113** A3
Vistonida, L. *Greece* 41°0N 25°7E **203** E9
Vistonikos, Ormos = Vistonida, L. *Greece* 41°0N 25°7E **203** E9
Vistula = Wisła → *Poland* 54°22N 18°55E **184** D5
Vistula Lagoon = Zalew Wiślany *Poland* 54°20N 19°50E **184** D6
Vit → *Bulgaria* 43°30N 24°30E **203** C8
Vita *India* 17°17N 74°33E **244** F2
Vitacura *Chile* 33°23S 70°35W **137** B2
Vitanje *Slovenia* 46°25N 15°18E **199** B12
Vitebsk = Vitsyebsk *Belarus* 55°10N 30°15E **188** E6
Viterbo *Italy* 42°25N 12°6E **199** F9
Vitez *Bos.-H.* 44°10N 17°48E **182** F2
Viti Levu *Fiji* 17°30S 177°30E **287** A1
Vitiaz Str. *Papua N. G.* 5°40S 147°10E **286** C4
Vitiaz Trench *Pac. Oc.* 10°0S 170°0E **277** C13
Vitigudino *Spain* 41°1N 6°26W **194** D4
Vitim *Russia* 59°28N 112°35E **215** D12
Vitim → *Russia* 59°26N 112°34E **215** D12
Vitina *Bos.-H.* 43°17N 17°29E **199** E14
Vitina *Greece* 37°40N 22°10E **204** D4
Vitínia *Italy* 41°47N 12°24E **136** C1
Vitkov *Czech Rep.* 49°46N 17°45E **181** B10
Vitória = Vitória de Santo Antão *Brazil* 8°10S 35°20W **332** C4
Vitória *Espírito Santo, Brazil* 20°20S 40°22W **333** F3
Vitória *Pará, Brazil* 2°54S 52°1W **329** D7
Vitória da Conquista *Brazil* 14°51S 40°51W **333** D3
Vitória de Santo Antão *Brazil* 8°10S 35°20W **332** C4
Vitoria-Gasteiz *Spain* 42°50N 2°41W **196** C2
Vitoria Seamount *Atl. Oc.* 20°0S 44°0W **152** J8
Vitorino Freire *Brazil* 4°4S 45°10W **332** B2
Vitosha △ *Bulgaria* 42°36N 23°18E **202** D7
Vitré *France* 48°8N 1°12W **172** D5
Vitry-le-François *France* 48°43N 4°33E **173** D11
Vitry-sur-Seine *France* 48°47N 2°23E **134** B3
Vitsand *Sweden* 60°20N 13°0E **162** D7
Vitsi, Oros *Greece* 40°40N 21°25E **202** F5
Vitsyebsk *Belarus* 55°10N 30°15E **188** E6
Vitsyebsk □ *Belarus* 55°10N 28°50E **188** E5
Vittaryd *Sweden* 56°58N 13°57E **163** H7
Vitteaux *France* 47°24N 4°30E **173** E11
Vittel *France* 48°12N 5°57E **173** D12
Vittória *Italy* 36°57N 14°32E **201** F7
Vittório = Vittório Véneto *Italy* 45°59N 12°18E **199** C9
Vittório Véneto *Italy* 45°59N 12°18E **199** C9
Vittoriosa *Malta* 35°54N 14°31E **206** F8
Vittsjö *Sweden* 56°20N 13°40E **163** H7
Viveiro *Spain* 43°39N 7°38W **194** B3
Vivian *U.S.A.* 32°53N 93°59W **314** E8
Viviers *France* 44°30N 4°40E **175** D8
Vivonne *S. Austral., Australia* 35°59S 137°9E **282** C2
Vivonne *Vienne, France* 46°25N 0°15E **174** B4
Vivonne B. *Australia* 35°59S 137°9E **282** C2
Viwa *Fiji* 17°10S 177°58E **287** A1
Vizagapatam = Vishakhapatnam *India* 17°45N 83°20E **244** F6
Vizandino, Moussio *Athens, Greece* **112** b3
Vizcaíno, Desierto de *Mexico* 27°30N 113°45W **318** B2
Vizcaíno, Sierra *Mexico* 27°30N 114°0W **318** B2
Vizcaya □ *Spain* 43°15N 2°45W **196** B2
Vizcaya Museum and Gardens *U.S.A.* 25°44N 80°13W **128** B2
Vize *Turkey* 41°34N 27°45E **203** E11
Vizianagaram *India* 18°6N 83°30E **244** E6
Vizille *France* 45°5N 5°46E **175** C9
Viziñada *Croatia* 45°20N 13°46E **199** C10
Viziru *Romania* 45°0N 27°43E **183** E12
Vizlinsky Zaliv = Zalew Wiślany *Poland* 54°20N 19°50E **184** D6
Vizzini *Italy* 37°10N 14°45E **201** E7
Vlaardingen *Neths.* 51°55N 4°21E **170** C4
Vlachiotis *Greece* 36°52N 22°42E **204** E4
Vlădeasa, Vf. *Romania* 46°47N 22°50E **182** D7
Vladičin Han *Serbia* 42°42N 22°1E **202** D6
Vladikavkaz *Russia* 43°0N 44°35E **191** J7
Vladimir *Russia* 56°15N 40°30E **188** D11
Vladimir □ *Russia* 56°5N 40°10E **190** B5
Vladimir Volynskiy = Volodymyr-Volynskyy *Ukraine* 50°50N 24°18E **177** C13
Vladimirci *Serbia* 44°36N 19°50E **202** B3
Vladimirovac *Serbia* 45°1N 20°53E **182** E5
Vladimirovka = Yuzhno-Sakhalinsk *Russia* 46°58N 142°45E **219** B17
Vladimirovka *Russia* 48°27N 46°10E **191** F8
Vladimirovo *Bulgaria* 43°32N 23°22E **202** C7
Vladislavovka *Ukraine* 45°12N 35°29E **189** K8
Vladivostok *Russia* 43°10N 131°53E **220** C5
Vladykino *Russia* 55°51N 37°35E **129** A3
Vlăhița *Romania* 46°21N 25°31E **183** D10
Vlasenica *Bos.-H.* 44°11N 18°59E **182** F3
Vlašić *Bos.-H.* 44°19N 17°37E **182** F2
Vlašim *Czech Rep.* 49°40N 14°53E **180** B7
Vlasinsko Jezero *Serbia* 42°44N 22°22E **202** D6
Vlasotince *Serbia* 42°59N 22°7E **202** D6
Vlieland *Neths.* 53°16N 4°55E **170** A4
Vlissingen *Neths.* 51°26N 3°34E **170** C3
Vlorë *Albania* 40°32N 19°28E **202** F3
Vlorës, Gjiri i *Albania* 40°29N 19°27E **202** F3
Vltava → *Czech Rep.* 50°21N 14°30E **180** A7
Vnukovo *Russia* 55°37N 37°17E **129** C1
Vo Dat *Vietnam* 11°9N 107°31E **237** G6
Vobarno *Italy* 45°39N 10°30E **198** C7
Voćin *Croatia* 45°37N 17°33E **182** E2
Vöcklabruck *Austria* 48°1N 13°39E **180** C6
Vodice *Croatia* 43°47N 15°47E **199** E12
Vodňany *Czech Rep.* 49°9N 14°11E **180** B7
Vodnjan *Croatia* 44°59N 13°52E **199** D10
Vodopyanovo = Donskoy *Russia* 53°55N 38°15E **188** F10

Voe U.K. 60°21N 1°16W 167 A7
Vogan Togo 6°23N 1°30E 263 D5
Vogar Iceland 63°58N 22°22W 155 D4
Vogel Pk. Nigeria 8°24N 11°47E 263 D7
Vogelkop = Doberai, Jazirah Indonesia 1°25S 133°0E 231 E8
Vogelsberg Germany 50°31N 9°12E 178 E5
Voghera Italy 44°59N 9°1E 198 D6
Voh N. Cal. 20°58S 164°42E 288 d
Vohibinany Madag. 18°49S 49°4E 272 B2
Vohilava Madag. 21°4S 48°0E 272 C2
Vohimarina = Iharana Madag. 13°25S 50°0E 272 A3
Vohimena, Tanjon' i Madag. 25°36S 45°8E 272 D2
Vohipeno Madag. 22°22S 47°51E 272 C2
Voi Kenya 3°25S 38°32E 268 C4
Void-Vacon France 48°40N 5°36E 173 D12
Voineşti Iaşi, Romania 47°5N 27°27E 183 C12
Voineşti Prahova, Romania 45°5N 25°14E 183 E10
Voinjama Liberia 8°25N 9°44W 262 D3
Voiron France 45°22N 5°35E 175 C9
Voisey B. Canada 56°15N 61°50W 299 A7
Voitsberg Austria 47°3N 15°9E 180 D8
Vojens Denmark 55°16N 9°18E 163 J3
Vojmsjön Sweden 65°0N 16°24E 160 D17
Vojnić Croatia 45°19N 15°43E 199 C12
Vojnik Italy 46°18N 15°19E 199 B12
Vojvodina ☐ Serbia 45°20N 20°0E 182 E5
Vokeo I. Papua N. G. 3°14S 144°2E 286 B3
Vokhtoga Russia 58°46N 41°8E 188 C11
Vokovice Czech Rep. 50°5N 14°21E 135 B2
Volary Czech Rep. 48°54N 13°52E 180 C6
Volborg U.S.A. 45°51N 105°41W 304 D11
Volcán de Colima △ Mexico 19°30N 103°40W 318 D4
Volcano U.S.A. 19°26N 155°14W 302 D6
Volcano Is. = Kazan-Rettō Pac. Oc. 25°0N 141°0E 288 E6
Volcans △ Rwanda 1°30S 29°26E 268 C2
Volcans d'Auvergne ⌓ France 45°20N 2°40E 174 C6
Volchansk = Vovchansk Ukraine 50°17N 36°58E 189 G9
Volchikha Russia 52°2N 80°23E 217 B10
Volchya → Ukraine 48°32N 36°0E 189 H8
Volda Norway 62°9N 6°5E 164 B3
Volga = Privolzhskiy ☐ Russia 56°0N 50°0E 190 D9
Volga Russia 57°58N 38°16E 188 C10
Volga → Russia 46°0N 48°30E 191 G9
Volga Hts. = Privolzhskaya Vozvyshennost Russia 51°0N 46°0E 190 E7
Volgelsdorf Germany 52°30N 13°44E 115 B5
Volgo-Baltiyskiy Kanal Russia 60°0N 38°0E 188 B9
Volgo-Donskoy Kanal Russia 48°40N 43°37E 191 F7
Volgodonsk Russia 47°33N 42°5E 191 G6
Volgograd Russia 48°40N 44°25E 191 F7
Volgograd ☐ Russia 49°40N 44°30E 190 F7
Volgogradskoye Vdkhr. Russia 50°0N 45°20E 190 E8
Volgorechensk Russia 57°28N 41°14E 190 B5
Volimes Greece 37°52N 20°39E 207 D2
Volintiri Moldova 46°26N 29°37E 183 D14
Volissos Greece 38°29N 25°54E 205 C7
Volkach Germany 49°52N 10°14E 179 F6
Völkermarkt Austria 46°39N 14°39E 180 E7
Volkhonka-Zil Russia 55°39N 37°37E 129 C3
Volkhov Russia 59°55N 32°15E 188 C7
Volkhov → Russia 60°8N 32°20E 188 B7
Volkhovstroy = Volkhov Russia 59°55N 32°15E 188 C7
Völklingen Germany 49°15N 6°50E 179 F2
Volkovysk = Vawkavysk Belarus 53°9N 24°30E 177 B13
Volksrust S. Africa 27°24S 29°53E 271 C4
Voll Norway 62°31N 7°27E 164 B4
Vollen Norway 59°48N 10°27E 133 B1
Volnovakha Ukraine 47°35N 37°30E 189 J9
Volochanka Russia 71°0N 94°28E 215 B10
Volodarsk Russia 56°12N 43°15E 190 B6
Volodarskoye Russia 59°54N 30°23E 137 B2
Volodymyr-Volynskyy Ukraine 50°50N 24°18E 177 C13
Vologda Russia 59°10N 39°45E 188 C10
Vologda ☐ Russia 60°15N 39°0E 188 B10
Volokolamsk Russia 56°5N 35°57E 188 D8
Volokonovka Russia 50°33N 37°52E 189 G9
Volos Greece 39°24N 22°59E 204 B4
Vološinovo = Novi Bečej Serbia 45°36N 20°10E 182 E5
Volosovo Russia 59°27N 29°32E 188 C5
Volovets Ukraine 48°43N 23°11E 183 B8
Volovo Russia 53°35N 38°1E 188 F10
Volozhin = Valozhyn Belarus 54°3N 26°30E 177 A14
Volsk Russia 52°5N 47°22E 190 D8
Volta ☐ Ghana 7°0N 0°30E 263 D5
Volta → Ghana 5°46N 0°41E 263 D5
Volta, L. Ghana 7°30N 0°0 263 D5
Volta Blanche = White Volta → Ghana 9°10N 1°15W 263 D4
Volta Redonda Brazil 22°31S 44°5W 333 F3
Voltaire, C. Australia 14°16S 125°35E 278 B4
Volterra Italy 43°24N 10°51E 198 E7
Voltri Italy 44°26N 8°45E 198 D5
Volturno → Italy 41°1N 13°55E 200 A6
Volubilis Morocco 34°2N 5°33W 260 B3
Volvi, L. Greece 40°40N 23°34E 202 F7
Volyn ☐ Ukraine 51°15N 24°30E 177 C13
Volyně Czech Rep. 49°10N 13°53E 180 B6
Volynkina-Derevnya Russia 59°53N 30°18E 137 B1
Volzhsk Russia 55°57N 48°23E 190 C9
Volzhskiy Russia 48°56N 44°46E 191 F7
Vomo Fiji 17°30S 177°15E 287 A1
Vonavona Solomon Is. 8°15S 157°5E 287 M9
Vondelpark Neths. 52°21N 4°52E 112 A2
Vondrozo Madag. 22°49S 47°20E 272 C2
Vonitsa Greece 38°55N 20°53E 207 B2
Vopnafjörður Iceland 65°45N 14°50W 155 B12
Vorarlberg ☐ Austria 47°20N 10°0E 180 D2
Voras Oros Greece 40°57N 21°45E 202 F5
Vorbasse Denmark 55°39N 9°6E 163 J3
Vorchdorf Austria 48°0N 13°55E 180 C6
Vorderrhein → Switz. 46°49N 9°25E 179 J5
Vordingborg Denmark 55°0N 11°54E 163 J5
Vorë Albania 41°23N 19°40E 202 E3
Voreio Aigaio ☐ Greece 38°50N 25°30E 205 C7
Voreppe France 45°18N 5°39E 175 C9
Vori Greece 35°4N 24°49E 207 E5
Vorios Evoikos Kolpos Greece 38°45N 23°15E 204 C5
Vorkuta Russia 67°48N 64°20E 186 A11
Vorma → Norway 60°9N 11°29E 164 D8
Vormsi Estonia 59°1N 23°13E 188 C2
Vorona → Russia 51°22N 42°3E 190 E6
Voronezh Russia 51°40N 39°10E 189 G10
Voronezh Ukraine 51°47N 33°28E 189 G7
Voronezh ☐ Russia 51°30N 39°30E 190 E4
Voronezh → Russia 51°32N 39°10E 189 G10
Vorontsovo-Aleksandrovskoye = Zelenokumsk Russia 44°24N 44°0E 191 H6
Voroshilov = Ussuriysk Russia 43°48N 131°59E 220 C5
Voroshilovgrad = Luhansk Ukraine 48°38N 39°15E 189 H10
Voroshilovsk = Alchevsk Ukraine 48°30N 38°45E 189 H10
Voroshilovsk = Stavropol Russia 45°5N 42°0E 191 H6
Vorpommersche Boddenlandschaft △ Germany 54°25N 12°32E 178 A8
Vorskla → Ukraine 48°50N 34°10E 189 H8
Võrts järv Estonia 58°16N 26°3E 188 C4
Võru Estonia 57°48N 26°54E 188 D4
Vösendorf Austria 48°7N 16°20E 142 B2
Vosges France 48°20N 7°10E 173 D14
Vosges ☐ France 48°12N 6°20E 173 D13
Vosges du Nord ⌓ France 49°0N 7°30E 173 D14
Voskopojë Albania 40°35N 20°33E 202 F4
Voskresensk Russia 55°19N 38°43E 188 E10
Voskresenskoye Russia 56°51N 45°30E 190 B7
Voss Norway 60°38N 6°26E 164 D3
Vostochnyy Russia 55°49N 37°51E 129 B5
Vostok = Neftegorsk Russia 44°25N 39°45E 191 H4
Vostok Antarctica 78°30S 106°50E 151 D8
Vostok I. Kiribati 10°5S 152°23W 289 J12
Votice Czech Rep. 49°38N 14°39E 180 B7
Votkinsk Russia 57°0N 53°55E 186 C9
Votkinskoye Vdkhr. Russia 57°22N 55°12E 186 C10
Votsuri-Shima Japan 25°45N 123°29E 221 M1
Votuporanga Brazil 20°24S 49°59W 333 F2
Vouga → Portugal 40°41N 8°40W 194 E2
Vouillé France 46°38N 0°10E 172 F7
Voula Greece 37°49N 23°45E 112 C2
Vouliagmeni Greece 37°50N 23°46E 112 C2
Voulkaria, L. Greece 38°52N 20°50E 207 B2
Voulou C.A.R. 8°33N 22°36E 264 A4
Vouxa, Akra Greece 35°37N 23°32E 207 E4
Vouzela Portugal 40°43N 8°7W 194 E2
Vouziers France 49°22N 4°40E 173 C11
Vovchansk Ukraine 50°17N 36°58E 189 G9
Vovodo → C.A.R. 5°40N 24°21E 264 A4
Vowchyn Belarus 52°18N 23°18E 185 F10
Voyageurs △ U.S.A. 48°32N 93°0W 308 A7
Voynitsa Russia 65°10N 30°20E 160 D24
Voyvozh Russia 62°56N 54°56E 214 C6
Vozhe, Ozero Russia 60°45N 39°0E 188 B10
Vozhega Russia 60°29N 40°12E 188 B11
Voznesensk Ukraine 47°35N 31°21E 189 J6
Voznesenye Russia 61°0N 35°28E 188 B8
Vrå Denmark 57°21N 9°56E 163 G3
Vráble Slovak Rep. 48°15N 18°16E 181 C11
Vraćevšnica Serbia 44°2N 20°34E 202 B4
Vrachneika Greece 38°10N 21°40E 204 C3
Vrådal Norway 59°20N 8°25E 164 E5
Vrancea ☐ Romania 45°50N 26°45E 183 E11
Vrancei, Munţii Romania 46°0N 26°30E 183 E11
Vrangel Russia 42°43N 133°5E 220 C6
Vrangelya, Ostrov Russia 71°0N 180°0E 215 B18
Vranica Bos.-H. 43°55N 17°50E 182 G2
Vranje Serbia 42°34N 21°54E 202 D5
Vranjska Banja Serbia 42°34N 22°1E 202 D6
Vranov nad Topl'ou Slovak Rep. 48°53N 21°40E 181 C14
Vransko Slovenia 46°17N 14°58E 199 B11
Vransko Jezero Croatia 43°53N 15°34E 199 E12
Vrapčište Macedonia 41°50N 20°53E 202 E4
Vratsa Bulgaria 43°15N 23°30E 202 C7
Vratsa ☐ Bulgaria 43°15N 23°30E 202 C7
Vråvatn Norway 59°20N 8°8E 164 E5
Vrbas Serbia 45°40N 19°40E 182 E4
Vrbas → Bos.-H. 45°8N 17°29E 182 E2
Vrbnik Croatia 45°4N 14°40E 199 C11
Vrbovec Croatia 45°53N 16°28E 199 C13
Vrbovsko Croatia 45°24N 15°5E 199 C12
Vrchlabí Czech Rep. 50°38N 15°37E 180 A8
Vrede S. Africa 27°24S 29°6E 271 C4
Vredefort S. Africa 27°0S 27°22E 270 C4
Vredehoek S. Africa 33°57S 18°25E 118 A1
Vreden Germany 52°2N 6°50E 178 C2
Vredenburg S. Africa 32°56S 18°0E 270 D2
Vredendal S. Africa 31°41S 18°35E 270 D2
Vretstorp Sweden 59°1N 14°53E 162 E8
Vrgorac Croatia 43°12N 17°20E 199 E14
Vrhnika Slovenia 45°58N 14°15E 199 C11
Vriddhachalam India 11°30N 79°20E 245 J4
Vridi Ivory C. 5°15N 4°3W 262 D4
Vrigstad Sweden 57°22N 14°28E 163 G8
Vrindavan India 27°37N 77°40E 242 F7
Vrisses Greece 35°23N 24°13E 207 E5
Vrnograč Bos.-H. 45°10N 15°57E 199 C12
Vrondados Greece 38°25N 26°7E 205 C8
Vrpolje Croatia 45°13N 18°24E 182 E3
Vršac Serbia 45°8N 21°20E 182 E6
Vrsacki Kanal Serbia 45°15N 21°0E 182 E5
Vršovice Czech Rep. 50°4N 14°28E 135 B2
Vrútky Slovak Rep. 49°7N 18°55E 181 B11
Vryburg S. Africa 26°55S 24°45E 270 C3
Vryheid S. Africa 27°45S 30°47E 271 C5
Vsetín Czech Rep. 49°20N 18°0E 181 B11
Vu Liet Vietnam 18°43N 105°23E 236 C5
Vŭcha → Bulgaria 42°10N 24°26E 203 D8
Vučitrn Kosovo 42°49N 20°59E 202 D4
Vuga South Sudan 5°21N 29°40E 257 F2
Vukovar Croatia 45°21N 18°59E 182 E3
Vuktyl Russia 63°52N 57°20E 214 C6
Vulcan Alta., Canada 50°25N 113°15W 296 C6
Vulcan Romania 45°23N 23°17E 183 E8
Vulcaneşti Moldova 45°41N 28°18E 183 E13
Vulcano Italy 38°24N 14°58E 201 D7
Vŭlchedruma Bulgaria 43°42N 23°27E 202 C7
Vulkaneshty = Vulcaneşti Moldova 45°41N 28°18E 183 E13
Vunduzi → Mozam. 18°56S 34°1E 269 F3
Vung Tau Vietnam 10°21N 107°4E 237 G6
Vunidawa Fiji 17°50S 178°21E 287 A2
Vunisea Fiji 19°3S 178°10E 287 B2
Vuranggo Solomon Is. 6°39S 156°38E 287 L9
Vŭrbitsa Bulgaria 42°59N 26°40E 203 D10
Vurshets Bulgaria 43°13N 23°23E 202 C7
Vushtrri = Vučitrn Kosovo 42°49N 20°59E 202 D4
Vutcani Romania 46°26N 27°59E 183 D12
Vuzlove Ukraine 48°22N 22°24E 182 B7
Vwaza ⌓ Malawi 10°58S 33°25E 269 E3
Vyara India 21°8N 73°28E 244 D1
Vyartsilya Russia 62°8N 30°45E 188 A6
Vyatka = Kirov Russia 58°35N 49°40E 186 C8
Vyatka → Russia 55°37N 51°28E 190 C10
Vyatskiye Polyany Russia 56°14N 51°5E 190 B10
Vyazemskiy Russia 47°32N 134°45E 215 E14
Vyazma Russia 55°10N 34°15E 188 E8
Vyazniki Russia 56°10N 42°10E 190 B6
Vyborg Russia 60°43N 28°47E 188 B5
Vyborgskaya Storona Russia 59°57N 30°22E 137 B2
Vychegda → Russia 61°18N 46°36E 186 B8
Vychodné Beskydy Europe 49°20N 22°0E 181 B15
Vyerkhnyadzvinsk Belarus 55°45N 27°58E 188 E4
Vyg-ozero Russia 63°47N 34°29E 186 B5
Vyhoda Ukraine 48°56N 23°55E 183 B8
Vykhino Russia 55°42N 37°48E 129 B4
Vyksa Russia 55°19N 42°11E 190 C6
Vylkove Ukraine 45°28N 29°32E 183 E14
Vylok Ukraine 48°6N 22°50E 182 B7
Vynohradiv Ukraine 48°9N 23°2E 182 B8
Vypin India 10°10N 76°15E 245 J3
Vyrnwy, L. U.K. 52°48N 3°31W 168 E4
Vyšehrad Czech Rep. 50°3N 14°25E 135 B2
Vyshkiv Ukraine 48°44N 23°39E 183 B8
Vyshkove Ukraine 48°3N 23°25E 183 B8
Vyshniy Volochek Russia 57°30N 34°30E 188 D8
Vyshzha = imeni 26 Bakinskikh Komissarov Turkmenistan 39°22N 54°10E 247 B7
Vyškov Czech Rep. 49°17N 17°0E 181 B9
Vysokaye Belarus 52°22N 23°22E 185 F10
Vysoké Mýto Czech Rep. 49°58N 16°10E 181 B9
Vysokovsk Russia 56°22N 36°30E 188 D9
Vyšší Brod Czech Rep. 48°37N 14°19E 180 C7
Vytegra Russia 61°0N 36°27E 188 B9
Vyzhnytsya Ukraine 48°15N 25°11E 183 B10
Vyzhnytsya ⌓ Ukraine 48°7N 25°15E 183 B10

W

W du Benin △ Benin 11°57N 2°43E 263 C5
W du Burkina Faso △ Burkina Faso 11°52N 2°50E 263 C5
W du Niger △ Niger 13°31N 2°28E 263 C5
W.A.C. Bennett Dam Canada 56°2N 122°6W 296 B4
Wa Ghana 10°7N 2°25W 262 C4
Waag Amsterdam, Neths. 112 b3
Waal → Neths. 51°37N 5°0E 170 C5
Waalwijk Neths. 51°42N 5°4E 170 C5
Waanyi-Garawa ✪ Australia 18°2S 137°33E 280 B2
Waat South Sudan 8°10N 32°7E 257 F3
Wabag Papua N. G. 5°32S 143°40E 286 C2
Wabakimi △ Canada 50°43N 89°29W 298 B2
Wabana Canada 47°40N 53°0W 299 C9
Wabasca → Canada 58°22N 115°20W 296 B5
Wabasca-Desmarais Canada 55°57N 113°56W 296 B6
Wabash U.S.A. 40°48N 85°49W 311 D11
Wabash → U.S.A. 37°48N 88°2W 311 G8
Wabasso U.S.A. 27°45N 80°26W 317 H9
Wabawng Burma 26°20N 97°25E 241 B6
Wabi → Ethiopia 7°45N 40°50E 257 F5
Wabigoon L. Canada 49°44N 92°44W 297 D10
Wabowden Canada 54°55N 98°38W 297 C9
Wąbrzeźno Poland 53°16N 18°57E 185 E5
Wabu Hu China 32°20N 116°50E 229 A11
Wabuda I. Papua N. G. 8°23S 143°37E 286 E2
Wabuk Pt. Canada 55°20N 85°5W 298 A2
Wabush Canada 52°55N 66°52W 299 B6
Waccasassa B. U.S.A. 29°10N 82°50W 317 F7
Wąchock Poland 51°4N 21°1E 185 G8
Wachterhof Germany 48°2N 11°42E 131 B3
Wächtersbach Germany 50°14N 9°17E 179 E5
Wacissa U.S.A. 30°22N 83°59W 316 E6
Waco U.S.A. 31°33N 97°9W 314 F6
Waconichi, L. Canada 50°8N 74°0W 298 B5
Wad Ban Naqa Sudan 16°32N 33°9E 257 D3
Wad Banda Sudan 13°10N 27°56E 257 E2
Wad el Haddad Sudan 13°50N 33°30E 257 E3
Wad en Nau Sudan 14°10N 33°34E 257 E3
Wad Hamid Sudan 16°30N 32°45E 257 D3
Wad Medanî Sudan 14°28N 33°30E 257 E3
Wad Thana Pakistan 27°22N 66°23E 242 F2
Wadai Africa 12°0N 19°0E 254 E5
Wadala India 19°1N 72°51E 130 A2
Wadayama Japan 35°19N 134°52E 222 B6
Wadbilliga △ Australia 36°25S 149°35E 283 D8
Waddān Libya 29°9N 16°10E 258 C3
Waddeneilanden Neths. 53°25N 5°10E 170 A5
Waddenzee Neths. 53°6N 5°10E 170 A5
Waddi, Chappal Nigeria 7°2N 11°43E 263 D7
Waddington U.S.A. 44°52N 75°12W 313 B9
Waddington, Mt. Canada 51°23N 125°15W 296 C3
Waddy Pt. Australia 24°58S 153°21E 281 C5
Wadebridge U.K. 50°31N 4°51W 169 G3
Wadena Sask., Canada 51°57N 103°47W 297 C8
Wadena Minn., U.S.A. 46°26N 95°8W 308 B6
Wädenswil Switz. 47°14N 8°40E 179 H4
Wadern Germany 49°32N 6°53E 179 F2
Wadestown N.Z. 41°16S 174°46E 143 B1
Wadeye Australia 14°28S 129°52E 278 B4
Wadgaon India 18°44N 73°39E 244 E1
Wadhams Canada 51°30N 127°30W 296 C3
Wadhwan = Surendranagar India 22°45N 71°40E 242 H4
Wadhwan India 22°42N 71°41E 242 H4
Wadi India 17°4N 76°59E 244 F3
Wadi al-Arayis West Bank 31°43N 35°15E 123 B2
Wādī Al Ḩayāt ☐ Libya 26°26N 12°30E 258 C2
Wādī as Sīr Jordan 31°56N 35°49E 251 G6
Wādī Ash Shāţi ☐ Libya 27°27N 13°37E 258 C2
Wâdi Feirân Egypt 28°42N 33°19E 251 K4
Wadi Fira ☐ Chad 15°0N 21°0E 259 F4
Wadi Fukin West Bank 31°42N 35°6E 123 B1
Wâdi Gemâl, J. Egypt 24°35N 35°10E 256 C4
Wadi Halfa Sudan 21°53N 31°19E 256 C3
Wādī Mūsá Jordan 30°19N 35°29E 251 H6
Wadi Rum △ Jordan 29°30N 35°20E 251 J6
Wadian China 32°42N 112°29E 229 A9
Wadlew Poland 51°31N 19°23E 185 G6
Wadley Ala., U.S.A. 33°7N 85°34W 316 B4
Wadley Ga., U.S.A. 32°52N 82°24W 316 C7
Wadowice Poland 49°52N 19°30E 185 J6
Wadsworth Nev., U.S.A. 39°38N 119°17W 304 G4
Wadsworth Ohio, U.S.A. 41°2N 81°44W 312 E3
Waduk Pluit Indonesia 6°5S 106°46E 122 A1
Waegwan S. Korea 35°59N 128°23E 224 E4
Wafangdian China 39°38N 121°58E 227 E11
Wafania Dem. Rep. of the Congo 1°23S 20°22E 264 C4
Wafrah Kuwait 28°33N 47°56E 246 D5
Wagadugu = Ouagadougou Burkina Faso 12°25N 1°30W 263 C4
Wagait ✪ Australia 13°1S 130°5E 278 B5
Wagener U.S.A. 33°39N 81°22W 316 B8
Wageningen Neths. 51°58N 5°40E 170 C5
Wageningen Suriname 5°50N 56°50W 329 B6
Wager B. Canada 65°26N 88°40W 295 D14
Wagga Wagga Australia 35°7S 147°24E 283 C7
Waggaman U.S.A. 29°55N 90°12W 131 B1
Waghai India 20°46N 73°29E 244 D1
Waghete Indonesia 4°10S 135°50E 231 E9
Wagin Australia 33°17S 117°25E 279 F2
Wagner U.S.A. 43°5N 98°18W 308 D4
Wagon Mound U.S.A. 36°1N 104°42W 305 H11
Wagoner U.S.A. 35°58N 95°22W 314 D7
Wągrowiec Poland 52°48N 17°11E 185 F4
Wah Pakistan 33°45N 72°40E 242 C5
Wah Fu China 22°15N 114°8E 122 B1
Wahai Indonesia 2°48S 129°35E 231 E7
Waharoa N.Z. 37°46S 175°45E 284 D4
Wahda = Unity ☐ South Sudan 8°30N 30°0E 257 F3
Wahda Iraq 33°18N 44°26E 113 B2
Wahiawā U.S.A. 21°30N 158°2W 302 K13
Wahiawā District U.S.A. 21°31N 157°58W 302 J14
Wahiawā Res. U.S.A. 21°30N 158°3W 302 K13
Wâḩid Egypt 30°48N 32°21E 251 H3
Wahnai Afghan. 32°40N 65°50E 242 C1
Wahni Ethiopia 12°40N 36°39E 257 E4
Wahoo U.S.A. 41°13N 96°37W 308 E5
Wahpeton U.S.A. 46°16N 96°36W 308 B5
Währing Austria 48°14N 16°20E 142 A2
Wahx, Ras il- Malta 35°56N 14°20E 206 F7
Wai India 17°56N 73°57E 244 F1
Wai'ale'ale U.S.A. 22°4N 159°30W 302 A2
Waiale'e U.S.A. 21°41N 158°1W 302 J13
Waialua U.S.A. 21°34N 158°8W 302 J13
Waialua B. U.S.A. 21°35N 158°5W 302 J13
Waialua District U.S.A. 21°35N 158°5W 302 J13
Wai'anae U.S.A. 21°27N 158°11W 302 K13
Wai'anae Coast U.S.A. 21°26N 158°11W 302 K13
Wai'anae District U.S.A. 21°28N 158°10W 302 K13
Wai'anae Range U.S.A. 21°30N 158°10W 302 K13
Waiao Taiwan 24°54N 121°51E 225 B3
Waiapu → N.Z. 37°47S 178°29E 284 D7
Waiau N.Z. 42°39S 173°5E 285 C8
Waiau → Canterbury, N.Z. 42°47S 173°22E 285 C8
Waiau → Southland, N.Z. 46°12S 167°38E 285 G2
Waiawa → U.S.A. 21°23N 157°59W 302 K14
Waiawe Ganga → Sri Lanka 6°15N 81°0E 245 L5
Waibeem Indonesia 0°30S 132°59E 231 E8
Waiblingen Germany 48°49N 9°18E 179 G5
Waidhofen an der Thaya Austria 48°49N 15°17E 180 C8
Waidhofen an der Ybbs Austria 47°57N 14°46E 180 D7
Waidmannslust Germany 52°36N 13°20E 115 A3
Waigeo Indonesia 0°20S 130°40E 231 E8
Waihao → N.Z. 44°47S 171°10E 285 E6
Waihao Downs N.Z. 44°48S 170°55E 285 E5
Waiheke I. N.Z. 36°48S 175°6E 284 C4
Waihi N.Z. 37°23S 175°52E 284 D4
Waihi Beach N.Z. 37°25S 175°57E 284 D7
Waihola N.Z. 46°1S 170°8E 285 G5
Waihola L. N.Z. 45°59S 170°8E 285 F5
Waihou → N.Z. 37°15S 175°40E 284 D4
Waika Dem. Rep. of the Congo 2°22S 25°42E 264 C5
Waikabubak Indonesia 9°45S 119°25E 231 F5
Waikaia N.Z. 45°44S 168°51E 285 F3
Waikaka N.Z. 45°55S 169°1E 285 F4
Waikane U.S.A. 21°30N 157°51W 302 J14
Waikare, L. N.Z. 37°26S 175°13E 284 D4
Waikareiti, L. N.Z. 38°43S 177°10E 284 E6
Waikaremoana N.Z. 38°42S 177°12E 284 E6
Waikaremoana, L. N.Z. 38°49S 177°9E 284 E6
Waikari N.Z. 42°58S 172°41E 285 C7
Waikato → N.Z. 37°23S 174°43E 284 D3
Waikelo Indonesia 9°24S 119°19E 278 A2
Waikerie Australia 34°9S 140°0E 282 C4
Waikiekie N.Z. 35°57S 174°16E 284 B3
Waikīkī U.S.A. 21°17N 157°50W 302 K14
Waikokopu N.Z. 39°3S 177°52E 284 F6
Waikoloa Village U.S.A. 19°55N 155°49W 302 D6
Waikouaiti N.Z. 45°36S 170°41E 285 F5
Waikouaiti Downs N.Z. 45°30S 170°30E 285 F5
Wailea-Makena U.S.A. 20°40N 156°27W 302 C5
Wailing Wall = Western Wall Jerusalem 123 b3
Wailua U.S.A. 22°3N 159°20W 302 A2
Wailuku U.S.A. 20°53N 156°30W 302 C5
Waimakariri → N.Z. 43°24S 172°42E 285 D7
Waimalu U.S.A. 21°24N 157°57W 302 K14
Waimānalo U.S.A. 21°21N 157°43W 302 K14
Waimānalo B. U.S.A. 21°20N 157°40W 302 K14
Waimānalo Beach U.S.A. 21°21N 157°42W 302 K14
Waimangaroa N.Z. 41°43S 171°46E 285 B6
Waimano → U.S.A. 21°25N 157°58W 302 K14
Waimarie N.Z. 41°35S 171°58E 285 B6
Waimate N.Z. 44°45S 171°3E 285 E6
Waimea Hawai'i, U.S.A. 21°58N 159°40W 302 B2
Waimea Hawai'i, U.S.A. 21°39N 158°3W 302 J13
Waimea B. U.S.A. 21°40N 158°5W 302 J13
Waimea Plain N.Z. 45°55S 168°35E 285 F3
Wainganga → India 18°50N 79°55E 244 E4
Waingapu Indonesia 9°35S 120°11E 231 F6
Waingmaw Burma 25°21N 97°26E 241 C6
Waini → Guyana 8°20N 59°50W 329 B6
Wainuiomata N.Z. 41°17S 174°56E 143 B2
Wainuiomata → N.Z. 41°20S 174°55E 143 B2
Wainwright Alta., Canada 52°50N 110°50W 297 C6
Wainwright Alaska, U.S.A. 70°38N 160°2W 303 A7
Waiotapu N.Z. 38°21S 176°25E 284 E5
Waiouru N.Z. 39°28S 175°41E 284 F4
Waipa → N.Z. 38°16S 175°21E 284 E4
Waipahi N.Z. 46°6S 169°15E 285 G4
Waipahu U.S.A. 21°23N 158°1W 302 K13
Waipapa Pt. N.Z. 46°40S 168°51E 285 G3
Waipara N.Z. 43°3S 172°46E 285 D7
Waipawa N.Z. 39°56S 176°38E 284 F5
Waipi'o U.S.A. 21°25N 158°0W 302 K14
Waipi'o Acres U.S.A. 21°28N 158°1W 302 K13
Waipi'o Peninsula U.S.A. 21°20N 158°0W 302 K14
Waipiro N.Z. 38°2S 178°22E 284 E7
Waipiro Bay N.Z. 38°1S 178°21E 284 E7
Waipoua Forest N.Z. 35°39S 173°33E 284 B2
Waipu N.Z. 35°59S 174°29E 284 B3
Waipukurau N.Z. 40°1S 176°33E 284 G5
Wairakei N.Z. 38°37S 176°6E 284 E5
Wairarapa, L. N.Z. 41°14S 175°15E 284 H4
Wairau → N.Z. 41°32S 174°7E 285 B9
Wairio N.Z. 45°59S 168°3E 285 F3
Wairoa N.Z. 39°3S 177°25E 284 F6
Wairoa → Hawke's Bay, N.Z. 39°4S 177°25E 284 F6
Wairoa → Northland, N.Z. 36°5S 173°59E 284 C2
Waisantiang Taiwan 23°29N 120°1E 225 C2
Waïsisi Vanuatu 19°32S 169°22E 287 J7
Waitaki → N.Z. 44°56S 171°7E 285 E6
Waitaki Plains N.Z. 44°22S 170°0E 285 E5
Waitangi N.Z. 35°16S 174°5E 284 B3
Waitara N.Z. 38°59S 174°15E 284 E3
Waitara → N.Z. 38°59S 174°14E 284 E3
Waitiki Landing N.Z. 34°31S 172°50E 284 A1
Waitoa N.Z. 37°37S 175°35E 284 D4
Waitomo Caves N.Z. 38°16S 175°7E 284 E4
Waitotara N.Z. 39°49S 174°44E 284 F3
Waitotara → N.Z. 39°51S 174°41E 284 F3
Waitsburg U.S.A. 46°16N 118°9W 304 C4
Waitzen = Vác Hungary 47°49N 19°10E 182 C4
Waiuku N.Z. 37°15S 174°45E 284 D3
Wajima Japan 37°30N 137°0E 221 F8
Wajir Kenya 1°42N 40°5E 268 B5
Waka Dem. Rep. of the Congo 1°1N 20°13E 264 B4
Waka Ethiopia 7°2N 37°20E 257 F4
Waka-Kungo Angola 11°21S 15°7E 265 E3
Wakarusa U.S.A. 41°32N 86°1W 311 C10
Wakasa Japan 35°20N 134°24E 222 B6
Wakasa-Wan Japan 35°40N 135°30E 223 B7
Wakatipu, L. N.Z. 45°5S 168°33E 285 F3
Wakaw Canada 52°39N 105°44W 297 C7
Wakaya Fiji 17°37S 179°0E 287 A2
Wakayama Japan 34°15N 135°15E 223 C7
Wakayama ☐ Japan 33°50N 135°30E 223 D7
Wake Japan 34°48N 134°8E 222 C6
Wake Forest U.S.A. 35°59N 78°30W 315 D15
Wake I. Pac. Oc. 19°18N 166°36E 302 b
WaKeeney U.S.A. 39°1N 99°53W 308 F4
Wakefield Jamaica 18°26N 77°42W 320 a
Wakefield N.Z. 41°24S 173°5E 285 B8
Wakefield W. Yorks., U.K. 53°41N 1°29W 168 D6
Wakefield Mass., U.S.A. 42°30N 71°5W 116 A2
Wakefield Mich., U.S.A. 46°29N 89°56W 308 B9
Wakema Burma 16°30N 95°11E 241 G5
Wākhān Afghan. 37°8N 73°4E 240 A4
Waki Japan 34°4N 134°9E 222 C6
Wakkanai Japan 45°28N 141°35E 220 B10
Wakkerstroom S. Africa 27°24S 30°10E 271 C5
Wakool Australia 35°28S 144°23E 282 C6
Wakool → Australia 35°5S 143°33E 282 C5
Wakre Indonesia 0°19S 131°5E 231 E8
Waku Papua N. G. 6°5S 149°9E 286 D5
Wakuach, L. Canada 55°34N 67°32W 299 A6
Wakulla U.S.A. 30°14N 84°14W 316 E5
Wakunai Papua N. G. 5°52S 155°13E 286 C8
Walagunya ✪ Australia 23°10S 120°50E 278 D3
Walamba Zambia 13°30S 28°42E 269 E2
Wałbrzych Poland 50°45N 16°18E 185 H3
Walbury Hill U.K. 51°21N 1°28W 169 F6
Walcha Australia 30°55S 151°31E 283 A9
Walcheren Neths. 51°30N 3°35E 170 C3
Walcott U.S.A. 41°46N 106°51W 304 F10
Wałcz Poland 53°17N 16°27E 185 E3
Waldbröl Germany 50°52N 7°37E 178 E3
Waldburg Ra. Australia 24°40S 117°35E 279 D2
Waldeck Germany 51°12N 9°4E 178 D5
Walden Colo., U.S.A. 40°44N 106°17W 304 F10
Walden N.Y., U.S.A. 41°34N 74°11W 313 E10
Waldenberg = Wałbrzych Poland 50°45N 16°18E 185 H3
Waldesruh Germany 52°28N 13°37E 115 B4
Waldkirch Germany 48°5N 7°58E 179 G3
Waldkirchen Germany 48°43N 13°36E 179 G9
Waldkraiburg Germany 48°11N 12°24E 179 G8
Waldo U.S.A. 29°48N 82°10W 316 F7
Waldperlach Germany 48°4N 11°40E 131 B3
Waldport U.S.A. 44°26N 124°4W 304 D1
Waldron U.S.A. 34°54N 94°5W 314 D7
Waldtrudering Germany 48°6N 11°42E 131 B3
Waldviertel Austria 48°30N 15°30E 180 C8
Walebing Australia 30°41S 116°13E 279 F2
Walembele Ghana 10°30N 1°58W 262 C4
Walensee Switz. 47°7N 9°13E 179 H5
Wales U.S.A. 65°37N 168°5W 303 D5
Wales ☐ U.K. 52°19N 4°43W 169 E3
Wales I. Canada 68°1N 86°40W 295 D14
Walewale Ghana 10°21N 0°50W 263 C4
Walgett Australia 30°0S 148°5E 281 E4
Walgreen Coast Antarctica 75°15S 105°0W 151 D15
Walhalla Australia 37°56S 146°29E 283 D7
Walis I. Papua N. G. 3°14S 143°18E 286 B2
Walker Mich., U.S.A. 42°58N 85°46W 311 B11
Walker Minn., U.S.A. 47°6N 94°35W 308 B6
Walker, L. Canada 50°20N 67°11W 299 B6
Walker L. Man., Canada 54°42N 95°57W 297 C9
Walker L. Nev., U.S.A. 38°42N 118°43W 304 G4
Walkerston Australia 21°11S 149°8E 280 b
Walkerton Ont., Canada 44°10N 81°10W 312 B3
Walkerton Ind., U.S.A. 41°28N 86°29W 311 C10
Walkinstown Ireland 53°19N 6°20W 120 B1
Wall U.S.A. 44°0N 102°8W 308 C2
Wall Street New York, U.S.A. 132 f1
Walla Walla N.S.W., Australia 35°45S 146°54E 283 C7
Walla Walla Wash., U.S.A. 46°4N 118°20W 304 C4
Wallabout Bay New York, U.S.A. 132 f2
Wallace Idaho, U.S.A. 47°28N 115°56W 304 C6
Wallace N.C., U.S.A. 34°44N 77°59W 315 D16
Wallaceburg Canada 42°34N 82°23W 312 D2
Wallacetown N.Z. 46°21S 168°19E 285 G3
Wallachia = Valahia Romania 44°35N 25°0E 183 F9
Wallal Australia 26°32S 146°7E 281 D4
Wallam Cr. → Australia 28°40S 147°20E 281 D4
Wallambin, L. Australia 30°57S 117°35E 279 F2
Wallan Australia 37°26S 144°59E 283 D6
Wallangarra Australia 28°56S 151°58E 281 D5
Wallaroo Australia 33°56S 137°39E 282 B2
Walldürn Germany 49°34N 9°22E 179 F5
Wallenhorst Germany 52°21N 8°1E 178 C4
Wallenpaupack, L. U.S.A. 41°25N 75°15W 313 E9
Wallerawang Australia 33°25S 150°4E 283 B9
Wallingat △ Australia 32°14S 152°25E 283 B10
Wallingford Conn., U.S.A. 41°27N 72°50W 313 E12
Wallingford Vt., U.S.A. 43°28N 72°58W 313 C12
Wallis & Futuna, Is. ☒ Pac. Oc. 13°18S 176°10W 277 C15
Wallowa U.S.A. 45°34N 117°32W 304 D5
Wallowa Mts. U.S.A. 45°20N 117°30W 304 D5
Walls U.K. 60°14N 1°33W 167 A7
Walls of Jerusalem △ Australia 41°56S 146°15E 281 G4
Wallsend Australia 32°55S 151°40E 283 B9
Wallula U.S.A. 46°5N 118°54W 304 C4
Wallumbilla Australia 26°33S 149°9E 281 D4
Walmsley L. Canada 63°25N 108°36W 297 A7
Walney, I. of U.K. 54°6N 3°15W 168 C4
Walnut U.S.A. 41°33N 89°36W 310 C7
Walnut Canyon ⌓ U.S.A. 35°15N 111°20W 305 J8
Walnut Creek U.S.A. 37°54N 122°4W 306 H4
Walnut Grove U.S.A. 34°4N 86°18W 316 A3
Walnut Hill U.S.A. 30°53N 87°30W 317 E2
Walnut Ridge U.S.A. 36°4N 90°57W 315 C9
Walpeup Australia 35°7S 142°2E 282 C5
Walpole W. Austral., Australia 34°58S 116°44E 279 F2
Walpole Mass., U.S.A. 42°9N 71°15W 313 D13
Walpole-Nornalup △ Australia 35°0S 116°45E 279 G2
Wals Austria 47°47N 12°58E 180 D5
Walsall U.K. 52°35N 1°58W 169 E6
Walsenburg U.S.A. 37°38N 104°47W 305 H11
Walsh U.S.A. 37°23N 102°17W 305 H12
Walsh → Australia 16°31S 143°42E 280 B3
Walsingham Canada 42°40N 80°31W 312 D4
Walsrode Germany 52°51N 9°35E 178 C5
Walt Disney Concert Hall Los Angeles, U.S.A. 127 b1
Walt Disney World U.S.A. 28°22N 81°33W 133 B1
Waltair India 17°44N 83°23E 244 F6
Walter D. Stone Memorial Zoo U.S.A. 42°28N 71°6W 116 A2
Walter F. George Res. U.S.A. 31°38N 85°4W 316 D4
Walterboro U.S.A. 32°55N 80°40W 316 C9
Walters U.S.A. 34°22N 98°19W 314 D5
Waltershausen Germany 50°54N 10°33E 178 E6
Waltershausen Gletscher Greenland 73°54N 24°25W 154 C8
Waltham U.S.A. 42°23N 71°14W 116 A1
Waltham Forest ☐ U.K. 51°35N 0°0 125 A3
Walthamstow U.K. 51°34N 0°1W 125 A3
Waltman U.S.A. 43°4N 107°12W 304 E10
Walton Ky., U.S.A. 38°52N 84°37W 311 F12
Walton N.Y., U.S.A. 42°10N 75°8W 313 D9
Walton-on-Thames U.K. 51°23N 0°24W 125 B1
Walton-on-the-Naze U.K. 51°51N 1°17E 169 F9
Waltonville U.S.A. 38°13N 89°2W 310 F7
Walu Burma 26°28N 98°2E 241 B7
Walvis Bay Namibia 23°0S 14°28E 270 B1
Walvis Ridge Atl. Oc. 26°0S 5°0E 152 J12
Walvisbaai = Walvis Bay Namibia 23°0S 14°28E 270 B1
Walwa Australia 35°59S 147°44E 283 C7
Wamba Équateur, Dem. Rep. of the Congo 1°37S 22°30E 264 C4
Wamba Orientale, Dem. Rep. of the Congo 2°10N 27°57E 268 B2
Wamba Rift Valley, Kenya 0°58N 37°19E 268 B4
Wamba Nigeria 8°57N 8°42E 263 D6
Wamba → Dem. Rep. of the Congo 3°56S 17°12E 265 C3
Wambardi ✪ Australia 16°2S 130°55E 278 C5
Wambeek Belgium 50°55N 4°30E 116 A3
Wamego U.S.A. 39°12N 96°18W 308 F5
Wamena Indonesia 4°4S 138°57E 231 E9
Wampana Karlantijpa ✪ Australia 17°45S 132°10E 278 C5
Wampaya ✪ Australia 17°20S 135°0E 280 B2
Wampsville U.S.A. 43°4N 75°42W 313 C9
Wamsutter U.S.A. 41°40N 107°58W 304 F10
Wamulan Indonesia 3°27S 126°7E 231 E7
Wan Chai China 22°16N 114°10E 122 B2
Wan Chai Lanes Hong Kong, China 122 c2
Wan Hat Burma 20°14N 97°53E 241 E6
Wan Kinghao Burma 21°34N 98°17E 241 E7
Wan Lai-kam Burma 21°21N 98°22E 241 E7
Wan Tup Burma 21°13N 98°42E 228 G2
Wan Xian China 38°47N 115°7E 226 E8
Wana Pakistan 32°20N 69°32E 242 C3
Wanaaring Australia 29°38S 144°9E 281 D3
Wanaka N.Z. 44°42S 169°9E 285 E4
Wanaka, L. N.Z. 44°33S 169°7E 285 E4
Wan'an China 26°26N 114°49E 229 D10
Wanani Comoros Is. 12°20S 43°47E 272 a
Wanapa Bonaire 12°7N 68°14W 322 h
Wanapitei L. Canada 46°45N 80°40W 298 C3
Wanbi Australia 34°46S 140°17E 282 C4
Wandaik Guyana 4°27N 59°35W 329 C6
Wandel Sea = McKinley Sea Arctic 82°0N 0°0 154 A11
Wandérama Ivory C. 8°37N 4°25W 262 D4
Wandhari Pakistan 27°42N 66°48E 242 F2
Wanding China 24°5N 98°4E 228 E2
Wandle → U.K. 51°27N 0°12W 125 B2
Wando S. Korea 34°21N 126°41E 224 E3
Wandoan Australia 26°5S 149°55E 281 D4
Wandsworth ☐ U.K. 51°27N 0°11W 125 B2
Wandur Marine △ India 11°30N 92°30E 245 J11
Wanfu China 40°8N 122°38E 224 B1
Wang → Thailand 17°8N 99°2E 236 D2
Wang Center, The Boston, U.S.A. 116 c2
Wang Kai South Sudan 9°3N 29°23E 257 F2
Wang Noi Thailand 14°13N 100°44E 236 E3
Wang Saphung Thailand 17°18N 101°46E 236 D3
Wang Thong Thailand 16°50N 100°26E 236 D3
Wanga Dem. Rep. of the Congo 2°58N 29°12E 268 B2
Wangal Indonesia 6°8S 134°9E 231 F8
Wangan Taiwan 23°21N 119°29E 225 C1
Wanganella Australia 35°6S 144°49E 283 C6
Wanganui N.Z. 39°56S 175°3E 284 F4
Wanganui → W. Coast, N.Z. 43°3S 170°26E 285 D5
Wanganui → Wanganui-Manawatu, N.Z. 39°55S 175°4E 284 F4
Wangaratta Australia 36°21S 146°19E 283 D7
Wangary Australia 34°35S 135°29E 281 E2
Wangcang China 32°18N 106°20E 228 A6
Wangcheng China 28°22N 112°49E 229 C9
Wangcun China 36°41N 117°41E 227 F9
Wangdu China 38°40N 115°7E 226 E8
Wangdu Phodrang Bhutan 27°28N 89°54E 241 B2
Wangen Germany 47°41N 9°50E 179 H5
Wangerin = Węgorzyno Poland 53°32N 15°33E 184 E2
Wangerooge Germany 53°47N 7°54E 178 B3
Wangiwangi Indonesia 5°22S 123°37E 231 F6
Wangjiang China 30°10N 116°42E 229 B11
Wangjing China 40°0N 116°28E 114 B2
Wangkung Taiwan 23°57N 120°20E 225 C2
Wangmo China 25°11N 106°5E 228 E6
Wangolodougou Ivory C. 9°55N 5°10W 262 D3
Wangqing China 43°12N 129°42E 227 C15
Wani India 20°5N 78°55E 244 D4
Wanigela Papua N. G. 9°21S 149°9E 286 E5
Wanimiyn ✪ Australia 15°55S 130°49E 278 C5
Wanjina Wunggurr Wilinggin ✪ Australia 16°0S 127°0E 278 C4
Wanjung Taiwan 23°43N 121°25E 225 C3
Wankaner India 22°35N 71°0E 242 H4
Wankhede Stadium Mumbai, India 130 c2
Wanless Canada 54°11N 101°21W 297 C8
Wanleweyne Somali Rep. 2°37N 44°54E 267 D5
Wanli Taiwan 25°10N 121°41E 225 A3
Wanluan Taiwan 22°34N 120°34E 225 D2
Wanneroo Australia 31°42S 115°46E 279 F2
Wannian China 28°42N 117°4E 229 C11
Wanning China 18°48N 110°22E 236 C8
Wannoo Billabong Roadhouse Australia 27°25S 115°49E 279 E2
Wannsee Germany 52°25N 13°9E 115 B1
Wanon Niwat Thailand 17°38N 103°46E 236 D4
Wanqinsha China 22°43N 113°33E 219 a
Wanquan China 40°50N 114°40E 226 D8
Wanrong China 35°25N 110°50E 226 G6
Wansdorf Germany 52°38N 13°5E 115 A1
Wansen = Wiązów Poland 50°50N 17°10E 185 H4
Wanshan China 27°30N 109°12E 228 D7
Wanshan Qundao China 21°57N 113°45E 219 a
Wansheng China 28°57N 106°53E 228 C6
Wanstead N.Z. 40°8S 176°30E 284 G5
Wanstead London, U.K. 51°34N 0°1E 125 A4
Wantage U.K. 51°35N 1°25W 169 F6
Wantan Taiwan 22°35N 120°29E 225 D2
Wantouliu Taiwan 24°1N 120°41E 225 B2
Wanxian China 30°42N 108°20E 228 B7
Wanyin Burma 20°23N 97°15E 241 E6
Wanyuan China 32°4N 108°3E 228 A7
Wanzai Guangdong, China 22°12N 113°31E 219 a
Wanzai Jiangxi, China 28°7N 114°30E 229 C10
Wapakoneta U.S.A. 40°34N 84°12W 311 D12
Wapato U.S.A. 46°27N 120°25W 304 C3
Wapawekka L. Canada 54°55N 104°40W 297 C8
Wapello U.S.A. 41°11N 91°11W 310 C5
Wapikopa L. Canada 52°56N 87°53W 298 B2
Wapinda Dem. Rep. of the Congo 3°41N 22°48E 264 B4
Wapiti → Canada 55°5N 118°18W 296 B5
Wapping U.K. 51°30N 0°3W 125 A3
Wappingers Falls U.S.A. 41°36N 73°55W 313 E11
Wapsipinicon → U.S.A. 41°44N 90°19W 310 C6
Wapusk △ Canada 57°46N 93°22W 297 B10
War Galoh Somali Rep. 6°17N 47°31E 267 C6
War in the Pacific Nat. Hist. Park △ Guam 13°24N 144°39E 302 d

Warab *South Sudan* 8°8N 28°37E 257 F2
Warab □ *South Sudan* 7°30N 28°30E 257 F2
Warabi *Japan* 35°49N 139°41E 223 B11
Warakurna *Australia* 24°59S 128°17E 279 D4
Warangal *India* 17°58N 79°35E 244 F4
Waraseoni *India* 21°45N 80°2E 243 J9
Waratah *Australia* 41°30S 145°30E 281 G4
Waratah B. *Australia* 38°54S 146°5E 283 E7
Warburg *Germany* 51°28N 9°11E 178 D5
Warburton *Vic., Australia* 37°47S 145°42E 283 D6
Warburton *W. Austral., Australia* 26°8S 126°35E 279 E4
Warburton ✪ *Australia* 26°7S 126°34E 279 E4
Warburton → *Australia* 28°4S 137°28E 281 D2
Warburton Groove *Australia* 28°18S 137°8E 281 A2
Warburton Ra. *Australia* 25°55S 126°28E 279 E4
Ward *N.Z.* 41°49S 174°11E 285 B9
Ward → *Australia* 26°28S 146°6E 281 D4
Ward Hunt, C. *Papua N. G.* 8°2S 148°10E 286 E5
Ward Hunt Str. *Papua N. G.* 9°30S 150°0E 286 E6
Ward I. *N.Z.* 41°18S 174°54E 143 B2
Ward Mt. *U.S.A.* 37°12N 118°54W 306 H8
Wardang I. *Australia* 34°30S 137°20E 282 C2
Warden *S. Africa* 27°50S 29°0E 271 C4
Wardha *India* 20°45N 78°39E 244 D4
Wardha → *India* 19°57N 79°11E 244 E4
Wardija Point *Malta* 36°2N 14°11E 206 E6
Wards I. *U.S.A.* 40°47N 73°55W 132 B2
Wardsville *Canada* 42°39N 81°45W 312 D3
Ware *Herts., U.K.* 51°49N 0°0 169 F8
Ware *Mass., U.S.A.* 42°16N 72°14W 313 D12
Waregem *Belgium* 50°53N 3°27E 170 D3
Wareham *U.S.A.* 41°46N 70°43W 313 E14
Waremme *Belgium* 50°43N 5°15E 170 D5
Waren *Germany* 53°31N 12°40E 178 B8
Warendorf *Germany* 51°57N 8°1E 178 D4
Waresboro *U.S.A.* 31°15N 82°29W 316 D7
Waria → *Papua N. G.* 7°49S 147°41E 286 D4
Warialda *Australia* 29°29S 150°33E 281 D5
Wariap *Indonesia* 1°30S 134°5E 231 E8
Warin Chamrap *Thailand* 15°12N 104°53E 236 E5
Warka *Poland* 51°47N 21°12E 185 G8
Warkopi *Indonesia* 1°12S 134°9E 231 E8
Warkworth *N.Z.* 36°24S 174°41E 284 C3
Warm Baths = Bela Bela *S. Africa* 24°51S 28°19E 271 B4
Warm Springs *Ga., U.S.A.* 32°53N 84°41W 316 C5
Warm Springs *Nev., U.S.A.* 38°10N 116°20W 305 G5
Warman *Canada* 52°19N 106°30W 297 C7
Warmbad = Bela Bela *S. Africa* 24°51S 28°19E 271 B4
Warmbad *Namibia* 28°25S 18°42E 270 C2
Warming I. = Uunartoq Qeqertoq *Greenland* 71°33N 21°47W 154 C8
Warmińsko-Mazurskie □ *Poland* 54°0N 21°0E 184 D8
Warminster *Wilts., U.K.* 51°12N 2°10W 169 F5
Warminster *Pa., U.S.A.* 40°12N 75°6W 313 F9
Warmun *Australia* 17°2S 128°12E 278 C4
Warnberg *Germany* 48°4N 11°31E 131 B2
Warnemünde *Germany* 54°10N 12°4E 178 A8
Warner Brothers Studios *U.S.A.* 34°9N 118°20W 126 B2
Warner Mts. *U.S.A.* 41°40N 120°15W 304 F3
Warner Robins *U.S.A.* 32°37N 83°36W 316 C6
Warnes *Bolivia* 17°30S 63°10W 331 D5
Warnow → *Germany* 54°6N 12°9E 178 A8
Waroona *Australia* 32°50S 115°58E 279 F2
Warora *India* 20°14N 79°1E 244 D4
Warrabah △ *Australia* 30°31S 150°56E 283 A10
Warrabri ✪ *Australia* 21°1S 134°19E 280 C1
Warracknabeal *Australia* 36°9S 142°26E 282 D5
Warragul *Australia* 38°10S 145°58E 283 E6
Warrâq el 'Arab *Egypt* 30°4N 31°11E 117 A2
Warrego → *Australia* 30°24S 145°21E 281 E4
Warrego Ra. *Australia* 24°58S 146°0E 280 C4
Warren *N.S.W., Australia* 31°42S 147°51E 283 A7
Warren *Ark., U.S.A.* 33°37N 92°4W 314 E8
Warren *Ill., U.S.A.* 42°29N 90°0W 310 B7
Warren *Ind., U.S.A.* 40°41N 85°26W 311 D11
Warren *Mich., U.S.A.* 42°28N 83°1W 311 B13
Warren *Minn., U.S.A.* 48°12N 96°46W 308 A5
Warren *Ohio, U.S.A.* 41°14N 80°49W 312 E4
Warren *Pa., U.S.A.* 41°51N 79°9W 312 E5
Warrenpoint *U.K.* 54°6N 6°15W 166 B5
Warrensburg *Ill., U.S.A.* 39°56N 89°4W 310 E7
Warrensburg *Mo., U.S.A.* 38°46N 93°44W 310 F3
Warrensburg *N.Y., U.S.A.* 43°29N 73°46W 313 C11
Warrenton *Northern Cape, S. Africa* 28°9S 24°47E 270 C3
Warrenton *Ga., U.S.A.* 33°24N 82°40W 316 B7
Warrenton *Mo., U.S.A.* 38°49N 91°9W 310 F5
Warrenton *Oreg., U.S.A.* 46°10N 123°56W 306 D3
Warrenville *U.S.A.* 33°33N 81°48W 316 B8
Warri *Nigeria* 5°30N 5°41E 263 D6
Warringal Park *Australia* 37°45S 145°4E 128 A2
Warrington *N.Z.* 45°43S 170°35E 285 F5
Warrington *Warrington, U.K.* 53°24N 2°35W 168 D5
Warrington *Fla., U.S.A.* 30°23N 87°17W 317 E2
Warrington □ *U.K.* 53°24N 2°35W 168 D5
Warriston *U.K.* 55°58N 3°11W 121 B2
Warrnambool *Australia* 38°25S 142°30E 282 E5
Warroad *U.S.A.* 48°54N 95°19W 308 A6
Warrumbungle △ *Australia* 31°18S 149°1E 283 A8
Warruwi *Australia* 11°36S 133°20E 280 A1
Warsa *Indonesia* 0°47S 135°55E 231 E9
Warsak Dam *Pakistan* 34°11N 71°19E 242 B4
Warsaw = Warszawa *Poland* 52°14N 21°0E 142 B2
Warsaw *Ill., U.S.A.* 40°22N 91°26W 310 D5
Warsaw *Ind., U.S.A.* 41°14N 85°51W 311 C11
Warsaw *Ky., U.S.A.* 38°47N 84°54W 311 F12
Warsaw *Mo., U.S.A.* 38°15N 93°23W 310 F3
Warsaw *N.Y., U.S.A.* 42°45N 78°8W 312 D6
Warsaw *Ohio, U.S.A.* 40°20N 82°0W 312 F3
Warshiikh *Somali Rep.* 2°28N 45°55E 267 D6
Warstein *Germany* 51°26N 8°22E 178 D4
Warszawa *Poland* 52°14N 21°0E 142 B2
Warszawa ✈ (WAW) *Poland* 52°9N 20°59E 142 B1
Warta *Poland* 51°43N 18°38E 185 G5
Warta → *Poland* 52°35N 14°39E 185 F1
Wartenberg *Germany* 52°34N 13°31E 115 A4
Wartenburg = Barczewo *Poland* 53°50N 20°42E 184 E7
Warthbrücken = Koło *Poland* 52°14N 18°40E 185 F5
Warthe = Warta → *Poland* 52°35N 14°39E 185 F1
Warthen *U.S.A.* 33°6N 82°48W 316 B7
Warthenau = Zawiercie *Poland* 50°30N 19°24E 185 H6
Waru *Indonesia* 3°30S 130°36E 231 E8
Warud *India* 21°30N 78°16E 244 D4
Warumungu ✪ *Australia* 19°15S 134°44E 280 B1
Warwick *Queens., Australia* 28°10S 152°1E 281 D5
Warwick *Warks., U.K* 52°18N 1°35W 169 E6
Warwick *Ga., U.S.A.* 31°50N 83°57W 316 D6
Warwick *N.Y., U.S.A.* 41°16N 74°22W 313 E10
Warwick *R.I., U.S.A.* 41°42N 71°28W 313 E13
Warwickshire □ *U.K.* 52°14N 1°38W 169 E6
Wasaga Beach *Canada* 44°31N 80°1W 312 B4
Wasagaming *Canada* 50°39N 99°58W 297 C9
Wasatch Ra. *U.S.A.* 40°0N 111°30W 304 F8
Wasbank *S. Africa* 28°15S 30°9E 271 C5
Wasco *Calif., U.S.A.* 35°36N 119°20W 307 K7
Wasco *Oreg., U.S.A.* 45°36N 120°42W 304 D3
Wase *Nigeria* 9°4N 9°54E 263 D6
Waseca *U.S.A.* 44°5N 93°30W 308 C7
Wasekamio L. *Canada* 56°45N 108°45W 297 B7
Wasgomura △ *Sri Lanka* 7°45N 81°0E 245 L5
Wash, The *U.K.* 52°58N 0°20E 168 E8
Washago *Canada* 44°45N 79°20W 312 B5
Washburn *Ill., U.S.A.* 40°55N 89°17W 310 D7
Washburn *N. Dak., U.S.A.* 47°17N 101°2W 308 B3
Washburn *Wis., U.S.A.* 46°40N 90°54W 308 B8
Washim *India* 20°3N 77°0E 244 D3
Washington *Bonaire* 12°17N 68°23W 322 h
Washington *Tyne & W., U.K.* 54°55N 1°30W 168 C6
Washington *D.C., U.S.A.* 38°53N 77°2W 143 B3
Washington *Ga., U.S.A.* 33°44N 82°44W 316 B7
Washington *Ill., U.S.A.* 40°42N 89°24W 310 D7
Washington *Ind., U.S.A.* 38°40N 87°10W 311 F9
Washington *Iowa, U.S.A.* 41°18N 91°42W 310 C5
Washington *Mo., U.S.A.* 38°33N 91°1W 310 F5
Washington *N.C., U.S.A.* 35°33N 77°3W 315 D16
Washington *N.J., U.S.A.* 40°46N 74°59W 313 F10
Washington *Pa., U.S.A.* 40°10N 80°15W 312 F4
Washington *Utah, U.S.A.* 37°8N 113°31W 305 H7
Washington □ *U.S.A.* 47°30N 120°30W 304 C3
Washington, Mt. *U.S.A.* 44°16N 71°18W 313 B13
Washington Court House *U.S.A.* 39°32N 83°26W 311 E13
Washington Dulles Int. ✈ (IAD) *U.S.A.* 38°57N 77°27W 143 B1
Washington Heights *U.S.A.* 40°51N 73°56W 132 A2
Washington I. *U.S.A.* 45°23N 86°54W 308 C10
Washington Land *Greenland* 80°30N 66°0W 154 A4
Washington Monument *Washington, D.C., U.S.A.* 143 b1
Washington Park *U.S.A.* 41°47N 87°36W 119 C3
Washington Ronald Reagan Nat. ✈ (DCA) *U.S.A.* 38°51N 77°2W 143 B3
Washington Slagbaai △ *Bonaire* 12°16N 68°23W 322 h
Washougal *U.S.A.* 45°35N 122°21W 306 E4
Washpool △ *Australia* 29°22S 152°20E 281 D5
Washuk *Pakistan* 27°42N 64°45E 240 D2
Wasian *Indonesia* 1°47S 133°19E 231 E8
Wasilków *Poland* 53°12N 23°13E 185 E10
Wasilla *U.S.A.* 61°35N 149°26W 303 F10
Wasini Marine ⌓ *Kenya* 4°33S 39°14E 268 C4
Wasior *Indonesia* 2°43S 134°30E 231 E8
Wāsiţ □ *Iraq* 32°50N 45°50E 213 F11
Wasjabo *Suriname* 5°13N 57°11W 329 B6
Waskaganish *Canada* 51°30N 78°40W 298 B4
Waskaiowaka L. *Canada* 56°33N 96°23W 297 B9
Waskesiu Lake *Canada* 53°55N 106°5W 297 C7
Wassaw I. *U.S.A.* 31°53N 80°58W 316 D9
Wassaw Sd. *U.S.A.* 31°55N 80°55W 316 D9
Wasserburg *Germany* 48°3N 12°14E 179 G8
Wasserkuppe *Germany* 50°29N 9°55E 178 E5
Wassy *France* 48°30N 4°58E 173 D11
Wasu *Papua N. G.* 5°58S 147°12E 286 C4
Wasua *Papua N. G.* 8°18S 142°52E 286 E2
Waswanipi *Canada* 49°40N 76°29W 298 C4
Waswanipi, L. *Canada* 49°35N 76°40W 298 C4
Wat Pho *Bangkok, Thailand* 113 b1
Watagans △ *Australia* 33°0S 151°28E 283 B9
Watam *Papua N. G.* 3°55S 144°33E 286 B3
Watampone *Indonesia* 4°29S 120°25E 231 E6
Watamu *Kenya* 3°23S 40°0E 268 C5
Watansoppeng *Indonesia* 4°10S 119°56E 235 C5
Watarrka △ *Australia* 24°20S 131°30E 278 D5
Watee *Solomon Is.* 10°30S 162°2E 287 N12
Watenstadt-Salzgitter = Salzgitter *Germany* 52°9N 10°19E 178 C6
Water of Leith → *U.K.* 55°59N 3°10W 121 B1
Water Park Pt. *Australia* 22°56S 150°47E 280 C5
Water Tower Place *Chicago, U.S.A.* 119 a2
Water Valley *U.S.A.* 34°10N 89°38W 315 D10
Waterberg Plateau ⌓ *Namibia* 20°25S 17°18E 270 B2
Waterberge *S. Africa* 24°10S 28°0E 271 B4
Waterbury *Conn., U.S.A.* 41°33N 73°3W 313 E11
Waterbury *Vt., U.S.A.* 44°20N 72°46W 313 B12
Waterbury L. *Canada* 58°10N 104°22W 297 B8
Waterdown *Canada* 43°20N 79°53W 312 C5
Wateree → *U.S.A.* 33°45N 80°37W 316 B9
Waterford *Ont., Canada* 42°56N 80°17W 312 D4
Waterford *Waterford, Ireland* 52°15N 7°8W 166 D4
Waterford *Calif., U.S.A.* 37°38N 120°46W 306 H6
Waterford *Mich., U.S.A.* 42°45N 83°32W 311 B13
Waterford *Pa., U.S.A.* 41°57N 79°59W 312 E5
Waterford *Wis., U.S.A.* 42°46N 88°13W 311 B8
Waterford □ *Ireland* 52°10N 7°40W 166 D4
Waterford Harbour *Ireland* 52°8N 6°58W 166 D5
Watergraafsmeer *Neths.* 52°21N 4°56E 112 A2
Waterhen L. *Canada* 52°10N 99°40W 297 C9
Waterland *Neths.* 52°26N 4°58E 112 A2
Waterloo *Belgium* 50°43N 4°25E 116 B2
Waterloo *Ont., Canada* 43°30N 80°32W 312 C4
Waterloo *Qué., Canada* 45°22N 72°32W 313 A12
Waterloo *Wellington, N.Z.* 41°13S 174°56E 143 B2
Waterloo *S. Leone* 8°26N 13°8W 262 D2
Waterloo *Trin. & Tob.* 10°28N 61°28W 323 t
Waterloo *London, U.K.* 125 b4
Waterloo *Ill., U.S.A.* 38°20N 90°9W 310 F6
Waterloo *Ind., U.S.A.* 41°26N 85°1W 311 C11
Waterloo *Iowa, U.S.A.* 42°30N 92°21W 310 B4
Waterloo *N.Y., U.S.A.* 42°54N 76°52W 312 D8
Waterloo *Wis., U.S.A.* 43°11N 88°59W 310 A8
Waterman *U.S.A.* 41°46N 88°47W 311 C8
Watermeal-Boitsfort *Belgium* 50°48N 4°25E 116 B2
Watersmeet *U.S.A.* 46°16N 89°11W 308 B9
Waterton Lakes △ *Canada* 48°45N 115°0W 296 D6
Watertown *Conn., U.S.A.* 41°36N 73°7W 313 E11
Watertown *Fla., U.S.A.* 30°11N 82°36W 316 E7
Watertown *Mass., U.S.A.* 42°22N 71°10W 116 A1
Watertown *N.Y., U.S.A.* 43°59N 75°55W 313 C9
Watertown *S. Dak., U.S.A.* 44°54N 97°7W 308 C5
Watertown *Wis., U.S.A.* 43°12N 88°43W 311 A8
Waterval-Boven *S. Africa* 25°40S 30°18E 271 C5
Waterville *Qué., Canada* 45°16N 71°54W 313 A13
Waterville *Maine, U.S.A.* 44°33N 69°38W 309 C19
Waterville *N.Y., U.S.A.* 42°56N 75°23W 313 D9
Waterville *Pa., U.S.A.* 41°19N 77°21W 312 E7
Waterville *Wash., U.S.A.* 47°39N 120°4W 304 C3
Watervliet *Mich., U.S.A.* 42°11N 86°18W 311 B10
Watervliet *N.Y., U.S.A.* 42°44N 73°42W 313 D11
Wates *Indonesia* 7°51S 110°10E 235 D4
Watford *Ont., Canada* 42°57N 81°53W 312 D3
Watford *Herts., U.K.* 51°40N 0°24W 169 F7
Watford City *U.S.A.* 47°48N 103°17W 308 B2
Wathaman → *Canada* 57°16N 102°59W 297 B8
Wathaman L. *Canada* 56°58N 103°44W 297 B8
Watheroo *Australia* 30°15S 116°5E 279 F2
Watheroo △ *Australia* 30°19S 115°48E 279 F2
Wating *China* 35°40N 106°38E 226 G4
Watîr, W. → *Egypt* 29°0N 34°40E 251 K5
Watkins Glen *U.S.A.* 42°23N 76°52W 312 D8
Watkinsville *U.S.A.* 33°52N 83°25W 316 B6
Watling I. = San Salvador I. *Bahamas* 24°0N 74°40W 321 B5
Watom I. *Papua N. G.* 4°7S 152°4E 286 C7
Watonga *U.S.A.* 35°51N 98°25W 314 D5
Watrous *Sask., Canada* 51°40N 105°25W 297 C7
Watrous *N. Mex., U.S.A.* 35°48N 104°59W 305 J11
Watsa *Dem. Rep. of the Congo* 3°4N 29°30E 268 B2
Watseka *U.S.A.* 40°47N 87°44W 311 D9
Watsi Kenga *Dem. Rep. of the Congo* 0°49S 20°34E 264 C4
Watson *Canada* 52°10N 104°30W 297 C8
Watson Lake *Canada* 60°6N 128°49W 296 A3
Watsonia *Australia* 37°43S 145°6E 128 A2
Watsontown *U.S.A.* 41°5N 76°52W 312 E8
Watsonville *U.S.A.* 36°55N 121°45W 306 J5
Watt Mt. *Dominica* 15°19N 61°19W 323 k
Wattiwarriganna Cr. → *Australia* 28°57S 136°10E 281 D2
Wattwil *Switz.* 47°18N 9°6E 179 H5
Watu *Dem. Rep. of the Congo* 3°18S 20°3E 264 C4
Watuata = Batuata *Indonesia* 6°12S 122°42E 231 F6
Watubela, Kepulauan *Indonesia* 4°28S 131°35E 231 E8
Watubela Is. = Watubela, Kepulauan *Indonesia* 4°28S 131°35E 231 E8
Wau *Papua N. G.* 7°21S 146°47E 286 D4
Wau *South Sudan* 7°45N 28°1E 257 F2
Waubamik *Canada* 45°27N 80°1W 312 A4
Waubay *U.S.A.* 45°20N 97°18W 308 C5
Waubra *Australia* 37°21S 143°39E 282 D5
Wauchope *N.S.W., Australia* 31°28S 152°45E 283 A10
Wauchope *N. Terr., Australia* 20°36S 134°15E 280 C1
Wauchula *U.S.A.* 27°33N 81°49W 317 H8
Waukarlycarly, L. *Australia* 21°18S 121°56E 278 D3
Waukeenah *U.S.A.* 30°25N 83°57W 316 E6
Waukegan *U.S.A.* 42°22N 87°50W 311 B9
Waukesha *U.S.A.* 43°1N 88°14W 311 B8
Waukon *U.S.A.* 43°16N 91°29W 308 D8
Waupaca *U.S.A.* 44°21N 89°5W 308 C9
Waupun *U.S.A.* 43°38N 88°44W 308 D9
Waurika *U.S.A.* 34°10N 98°0W 314 D6
Wausau *Fla., U.S.A.* 30°38N 85°35W 316 E4
Wausau *Wis., U.S.A.* 44°58N 89°38W 308 C9
Wauseon *U.S.A.* 41°33N 84°8W 311 C12
Wautoma *U.S.A.* 44°4N 89°18W 308 C9
Wauwatosa *U.S.A.* 43°2N 88°0W 311 A9
Wave Hill = Kalkarindji *Australia* 17°30S 130°47E 278 C5
Wave Rock ⌓ *Australia* 32°26S 118°53E 279 F2
Waveland *U.S.A.* 39°53N 87°3W 311 E9
Waveney → *U.K.* 52°35N 1°39E 169 E9
Waverley *N.S.W., Australia* 33°53S 151°15E 139 B2
Waverley *N.Z.* 39°46S 174°37E 284 F3
Waverley *Gauteng, S. Africa* 26°7S 28°4E 123 A2
Waverley *Mass., U.S.A.* 42°23N 71°10W 116 A1
Waverley Station *Edinburgh, U.K.* 121 b3
Waverly *Ala., U.S.A.* 32°44N 85°35W 316 C4
Waverly *Fla., U.S.A.* 27°59N 81°37W 317 H8
Waverly *Ga., U.S.A.* 31°6N 81°43W 316 D8
Waverly *Ill., U.S.A.* 39°36N 89°57W 310 E7
Waverly *Iowa, U.S.A.* 42°44N 92°29W 310 B4
Waverly *Mo., U.S.A.* 39°13N 93°31W 310 E3
Waverly *N.Y., U.S.A.* 42°1N 76°32W 313 E8
Waverly Hall *U.S.A.* 32°41N 84°44W 316 C5
Wavre *Belgium* 50°43N 4°38E 170 D4
Wâw = Wau *South Sudan* 7°45N 28°1E 257 F2
Waw *Burma* 17°28N 96°41E 241 G6
Wāw al Kabīr *Libya* 25°20N 16°43E 258 C3
Wāw an Nāmūs *Libya* 24°55N 17°46E 258 D3
Wawa *Ont., Canada* 47°59N 84°47W 298 C3
Wawa *Nigeria* 9°54N 4°27E 263 D5
Wawa *Sudan* 20°30N 30°22E 256 C3
Wawanesa *Canada* 49°36N 99°40W 297 D9
Wawasee, L. *U.S.A.* 41°24N 85°42W 311 C11
Wawer *Poland* 52°13N 21°8E 142 B2
Wawoi → *Papua N. G.* 7°48S 143°16E 286 D2
Wawona *U.S.A.* 37°32N 119°39W 306 H7
Wawrzyszew *Poland* 52°17N 20°53E 142 B1
Waxahachie *U.S.A.* 32°24N 96°51W 314 E6
Waxxari *China* 38°42N 87°19E 217 E11
Way, L. *Australia* 26°45S 120°16E 279 E3
Way Kambas △ *Indonesia* 4°54S 105°43E 234 C3
Waya *Fiji* 17°19S 177°10E 287 A1
Waycross *U.S.A.* 31°13N 82°21W 316 D7
Wayi *South Sudan* 5°8N 30°10E 257 F3
Wayland *Mich., U.S.A.* 42°40N 85°39W 311 B11
Wayland *N.Y., U.S.A.* 42°34N 77°35W 312 D7
Wayne *Nebr., U.S.A.* 42°14N 97°1W 308 D5
Wayne *W. Va., U.S.A.* 38°13N 82°27W 309 F12
Wayne City *U.S.A.* 38°21N 88°35W 311 F8
Wayne County, Detroit ✈ (DTW) *U.S.A.* 42°13N 83°21W 311 B13
Wayne Lakes *U.S.A.* 40°1N 84°40W 311 D12
Waynesboro *Ga., U.S.A.* 33°6N 82°1W 316 B7
Waynesboro *Miss., U.S.A.* 31°40N 88°39W 315 F10
Waynesboro *Pa., U.S.A.* 39°45N 77°35W 309 F15
Waynesboro *Va., U.S.A.* 38°4N 78°53W 309 F14
Waynesburg *U.S.A.* 39°54N 80°11W 309 F13
Waynesville *Mo., U.S.A.* 37°50N 92°12W 310 G4
Waynesville *N.C., U.S.A.* 35°28N 82°58W 315 D13
Waynesville *Ohio, U.S.A.* 39°32N 84°5W 311 E12
Waynoka *U.S.A.* 36°35N 98°53W 314 C5
Wayside *U.S.A.* 33°4N 83°37W 316 B6
Waza *Afghan.* 33°22N 69°26E 240 B3
Waza △ *Cameroon* 11°15N 14°38E 259 F2
Wazikhwah *Afghan.* 32°11N 68°21E 240 B3
Wāzin *Libya* 31°58N 10°40E 258 B2
Wazirabad *Delhi, India* 28°43N 77°13E 120 A2
Wazirabad *Pakistan* 32°30N 74°8E 242 C6
Waziristan *Pakistan* 33°0N 70°0E 242 C4
Wazīrīya *Iraq* 33°22N 44°23E 113 A2
Wazirpur *India* 28°41N 77°10E 120 A2
Wda → *Poland* 53°25N 18°29E 184 E5
We *Indonesia* 5°51N 95°18E 234 A1
Wé *N. Cal.* 20°55S 167°16E 288 d
Weald, The *U.K.* 51°4N 0°20E 169 F8
Wealdstone *U.K.* 51°35N 0°17W 125 A1
Weam *Papua N. G.* 8°37S 141°8E 286 E1
Wear → *U.K.* 54°55N 1°23W 168 C6
Weatherford *Okla., U.S.A.* 35°32N 98°43W 314 D5
Weatherford *Tex., U.S.A.* 32°46N 97°48W 314 E6
Weaubleau *U.S.A.* 37°54N 93°32W 310 G3
Weaverville *U.S.A.* 40°44N 122°56W 304 F2
Webb City *U.S.A.* 37°9N 94°28W 308 G6
Webequie *Canada* 52°59N 87°21W 298 B2
Weber *N.Z.* 40°24S 176°20E 284 G5
Weber Basin *Pac. Oc.* 6°0S 131°0E 276 B5
Webo = Nyaake *Liberia* 4°52N 7°37W 262 E3
Webster *Mass., U.S.A.* 42°3N 71°53W 313 D13
Webster *N.Y., U.S.A.* 43°13N 77°26W 312 C7
Webster *S. Dak., U.S.A.* 45°20N 97°31W 308 C5
Webster City *U.S.A.* 42°28N 93°49W 310 B3
Webster Springs *U.S.A.* 38°29N 80°25W 309 F13
Webuye *Kenya* 0°37N 34°46E 268 B3
Weda *Indonesia* 0°21N 127°50E 231 D7
Weda, Teluk *Indonesia* 0°20N 128°0E 231 D7
Weddell Abyssal Plain *S. Ocean* 65°0S 20°0W 151 C2
Weddell I. *Falk. Is.* 51°50S 61°0W 153 f
Weddell Sea *Antarctica* 72°30S 40°0W 151 D1
Wedderburn *Australia* 36°26S 143°33E 282 D5
Weddin Mts. △ *Australia* 33°59S 148°0E 283 C8
Wedding *Germany* 52°32N 13°21E 115 A3
Wedel *Germany* 53°34N 9°42E 178 B5
Wedemark *Germany* 52°32N 9°43E 178 C5
Wedgeport *Canada* 43°44N 65°59W 299 D6
Wednesday I. *Australia* 10°31S 142°16E 286 F2
Wedowee *U.S.A.* 33°19N 85°29W 316 B4
Wedza *Zimbabwe* 18°40S 31°33E 269 F3
Wee Waa *Australia* 30°11S 149°26E 281 E4
Weed *U.S.A.* 41°25N 122°23W 304 F2
Weed Heights *U.S.A.* 38°59N 119°13W 306 G7
Weedsport *U.S.A.* 43°2N 76°33W 313 C8
Weedville *U.S.A.* 41°17N 78°30W 312 E6
Weehawken *New York, U.S.A.* 132 b1
Weeki Wachee *U.S.A.* 28°32N 82°35W 317 G7
Weel Shimbirro *Somali Rep.* 2°23N 44°14E 267 D5
Weenen *S. Africa* 28°48S 30°7E 271 C5
Weener *Germany* 53°9N 7°20E 178 B3
Weert *Neths.* 51°15N 5°43E 170 C5
Weesp *Neths.* 52°18N 5°2E 112 B3
Węgierska-Górka *Poland* 49°36N 19°7E 185 J6
Węgliniec *Poland* 51°18N 15°10E 185 G2
Węgorzewo *Poland* 54°13N 21°43E 184 D8
Węgorzyno *Poland* 53°32N 15°33E 184 E2
Węgrów *Poland* 52°24N 22°0E 185 F9
Wei He → *Hebei, China* 36°10N 115°45E 226 F8
Wei He → *Shaanxi, China* 34°38N 110°15E 226 G6
Weichang *China* 41°58N 117°49E 227 D9
Weichuan *China* 34°20N 113°59E 226 G7
Weida *Germany* 50°46N 12°2E 178 E8
Weiden *Germany* 49°41N 12°10E 179 F8
Weidling *Austria* 48°17N 16°18E 142 A1
Weidlingbach *Austria* 48°16N 16°15E 142 A1
Weifang *China* 36°44N 119°7E 227 F10
Weihai *China* 37°30N 122°6E 227 F12
Weihui *China* 35°25N 114°3E 226 G8
Weil *Germany* 47°35N 7°37E 179 H3
Weilburg *Germany* 50°28N 8°17E 178 E4
Weilheim *Germany* 47°50N 11°9E 179 H7
Weimar *Germany* 50°58N 11°19E 178 E7
Weinan *China* 34°31N 109°29E 226 G5
Weingarten *Germany* 49°3N 8°31E 179 F4
Weinheim *Germany* 49°32N 8°39E 179 F4
Weining *China* 26°50N 104°17E 228 D5
Weipa *Australia* 12°40S 141°50E 280 A3
Weir → *Queens., Australia* 28°20S 149°50E 281 D4
Weir → *Man., Canada* 56°54N 93°21W 297 B10
Weir, L. *U.S.A.* 29°0N 81°57W 317 F8
Weir River *Canada* 56°49N 94°6W 297 B10
Weirsdale *U.S.A.* 28°59N 81°55W 317 G8
Weirton *U.S.A.* 40°24N 80°35W 312 F4
Weiser *U.S.A.* 44°15N 116°58W 304 D5
Weishan *Shandong, China* 34°47N 117°5E 227 G9
Weishan *Yunnan, China* 25°12N 100°20E 228 E3
Weishan Hu *China* 34°35N 117°14E 227 G9
Weissenburg *Germany* 49°2N 10°58E 179 F6
Weissenfels *Germany* 51°11N 12°0E 178 D7
Weissensee *Germany* 52°33N 13°27E 115 A3
Weisskirchen = Hranice *Czech Rep.* 49°34N 17°45E 181 B10
Weisswasser *Germany* 51°30N 14°36E 178 D10
Weistritz = Bystrzyca → *Dolnośląskie, Poland* 51°12N 16°55E 185 G3
Weistritz = Bystrzyca → *Lubelskie, Poland* 51°21N 22°46E 185 G9
Wéitra *Austria* 48°41N 14°54E 180 C7
Weixi *China* 27°10N 99°10E 228 D2
Weixin *China* 27°48N 105°3E 228 D5
Weiyuan *Gansu, China* 35°7N 104°10E 226 G3
Weiyuan *Sichuan, China* 29°35N 104°36E 228 C5
Weiz *Austria* 47°13N 15°39E 180 D8
Weizhou Dao *China* 21°0N 109°5E 228 G7
Wejherowo *Poland* 54°35N 18°12E 184 D5
Wekoewa Pt. *Bonaire* 12°13N 68°24W 322 h
Wekusko L. *Canada* 54°40N 99°50W 297 C9
Welch *U.S.A.* 37°26N 81°35W 309 G13
Welchman Hall *Barbados* 13°11N 59°34W 323 r
Weldya *Ethiopia* 11°50N 39°34E 257 E4
Welega *Ethiopia* 9°25N 34°20E 257 F3
Welford △ *Australia* 25°5S 143°16E 280 D3
Weligama *Sri Lanka* 5°58N 80°25E 245 M5
Welkite *Ethiopia* 8°15N 37°42E 257 F4
Welkom *S. Africa* 28°0S 26°46E 270 C4
Welland *Canada* 43°0N 79°15W 312 D5
Welland → *U.K.* 52°51N 0°5W 169 E7
Wellawaya *Sri Lanka* 6°44N 81°6E 245 L5
Welles Harbor *Midway Is.* 28°13N 177°25W 302 c
Wellesley Hills *U.S.A.* 42°18N 71°16W 116 B1
Wellesley Is. *Australia* 16°42S 139°30E 280 B2
Wellesley Islands ✪ *Australia* 16°32S 139°23E 280 B2
Welling *U.K.* 51°27N 0°6E 125 B4
Wellingborough *U.K.* 52°19N 0°41W 169 E7
Wellington *N.S.W., Australia* 32°35S 148°59E 283 B8
Wellington *Ont., Canada* 43°57N 77°20W 312 C7
Wellington *N.Z.* 41°19S 174°46E 143 B1
Wellington *Western Cape, S. Africa* 33°38S 19°1E 270 D2
Wellington *Somst., U.K.* 50°58N 3°13W 169 G4
Wellington *Telford & Wrekin, U.K.* 52°42N 2°30W 169 E5
Wellington *Colo., U.S.A.* 40°42N 105°0W 304 F11
Wellington *Kans., U.S.A.* 37°16N 97°24W 308 G5
Wellington *Mass., U.S.A.* 42°24N 71°5W 116 A2
Wellington *Mo., U.S.A.* 39°8N 93°59W 310 E3
Wellington *Nev., U.S.A.* 38°45N 119°23W 306 G7
Wellington *Ohio, U.S.A.* 41°10N 82°13W 312 E2
Wellington *Tex., U.S.A.* 34°51N 100°13W 314 D4
Wellington □ *N.Z.* 41°0S 175°30E 284 G4
Wellington, I. *Chile* 49°30S 75°0W 336 C2
Wellington, L. *Australia* 38°6S 147°20E 283 E7
Wellington Chan. *Canada* 75°0N 93°0W 295 C13
Wellington Int. ✈ (WLE) *N.Z.* 41°20S 174°50E 143 B1
Wellman *U.S.A.* 41°28N 91°50W 310 C5
Wells *Somst., U.K.* 51°13N 2°39W 169 F5
Wells *Maine, U.S.A.* 43°20N 70°35W 313 C14
Wells *N.Y., U.S.A.* 43°24N 74°17W 313 C10
Wells *Nev., U.S.A.* 41°7N 114°58W 304 F6
Wells, L. *Australia* 26°44S 123°15E 279 E3
Wells, Mt. *Australia* 17°25S 127°8E 278 C4
Wells Fargo Center *Los Angeles, U.S.A.* 127 b1
Wells Gray ⌓ *Canada* 52°30N 120°15W 296 C4
Wells-next-the-Sea *U.K.* 52°57N 0°51E 168 E8
Wells River *U.S.A.* 44°9N 72°4W 313 B12
Wellsboro *U.S.A.* 41°45N 77°18W 312 E7
Wellsburg *U.S.A.* 40°16N 80°37W 312 F4
Wellsford *N.Z.* 36°16S 174°32E 284 C3
Wellston = Warner Robins *U.S.A.* 32°37N 83°36W 316 C6
Wellsville *Mo., U.S.A.* 39°4N 91°34W 310 E5
Wellsville *N.Y., U.S.A.* 42°7N 77°57W 312 D7
Wellsville *Ohio, U.S.A.* 40°36N 80°39W 312 F4
Wellsville *Utah, U.S.A.* 41°38N 111°56W 304 F8
Wellton *U.S.A.* 32°40N 114°8W 305 K6
Welmel, Wabi → *Ethiopia* 5°38N 40°47E 257 F5
Welo *Ethiopia* 11°50N 39°48E 257 E4
Welo *Somali Rep.* 9°25N 48°55E 267 C6
Wels *Austria* 48°9N 14°1E 180 C7
Welshpool *Vic., Australia* 38°42S 146°26E 283 E7
Welshpool *Powys, U.K.* 52°39N 3°8W 169 E4
Weltevreden Park *S. Africa* 26°7S 27°56E 123 A1
Welungen = Wieluń *Poland* 51°15N 18°34E 185 G5
Welwitschia = Khorixas *Namibia* 20°16S 14°59E 270 B1
Welwyn Garden City *U.K.* 51°48N 0°12W 169 F7
Wem *U.K.* 52°52N 2°44W 168 E5
Wembere → *Tanzania* 4°10S 34°15E 268 C3
Wembley *U.K.* 51°33N 0°17W 125 A2
Wemindji *Canada* 53°0N 78°49W 298 B4
Wemmel *Belgium* 50°55N 4°18E 116 A1
Wemmer Pan *S. Africa* 26°13S 28°3E 123 B2
Wemyss *Canada* 44°52N 76°23W 313 B8
Wen Xian *Gansu, China* 32°43N 104°36E 226 H3
Wen Xian *Henan, China* 34°55N 113°5E 226 G7
Wenatchee *U.S.A.* 47°25N 120°19W 304 C3
Wenceslas Square = Vaclavské náměstí *Prague, Czech Rep.* 135 b2
Wenchang *China* 19°38N 110°42E 236 C8
Wencheng *China* 27°46N 120°4E 229 D13
Wenchi *Ghana* 7°46N 2°8W 262 D4
Wenchow = Wenzhou *China* 28°0N 120°38E 229 D13
Wenchuan *China* 31°22N 103°35E 228 B4
Wenden *U.S.A.* 33°49N 113°33W 307 M13
Wendeng *China* 37°15N 122°5E 227 F12
Wendenschloss *Germany* 52°24N 13°35E 115 B4
Wendesi *Indonesia* 2°30S 134°17E 231 E8
Wendo *Ethiopia* 6°40N 38°27E 257 F4
Wendover *U.S.A.* 40°44N 114°2W 304 F6
Weng'an *China* 27°5N 107°25E 228 D6
Wengcheng *China* 24°22N 113°50E 229 E9
Wengen *Switz.* 46°37N 7°55E 173 F14
Wengyuan *China* 24°20N 114°9E 229 E10
Wenling *China* 28°21N 121°20E 229 C13
Wenlock → *Australia* 12°2S 141°55E 286 G1
Wennington *U.K.* 51°30N 0°12E 125 A5
Weno *Pac. Oc.* 7°27N 151°52E 287 T18
Wenona *U.S.A.* 41°3N 89°3W 310 C7
Wenshan *China* 23°20N 104°18E 228 F5
Wenshang *China* 35°45N 116°30E 226 G9
Wenshui *China* 37°26N 112°1E 226 F7
Wensleydale *U.K.* 54°17N 2°0W 168 C6
Wensu *China* 41°15N 80°10E 217 D10
Wensum → *U.K.* 52°40N 1°15E 168 E8
Wentworth *Australia* 34°2S 141°54E 282 C4
Wentzel L. *Canada* 59°2N 114°28W 296 B6
Wentzville *U.S.A.* 38°49N 90°51W 310 F6
Wenut *Indonesia* 3°11S 133°19E 231 E8
Wenxi *China* 35°20N 111°10E 226 G6
Wenzhou *China* 28°0N 120°38E 229 D13
Weott *U.S.A.* 40°20N 123°55W 304 F2
Wepener *S. Africa* 29°42S 27°3E 270 C4
Werda *Botswana* 25°24S 23°15E 270 C3
Werdau *Germany* 50°44N 12°22E 178 E8
Werder *Ethiopia* 6°58N 45°1E 267 C6
Werder *Brandenburg, Germany* 52°23N 12°55E 178 C8
Werdohl *Germany* 51°15N 7°46E 178 D3
Wereilu *Ethiopia* 10°40N 39°28E 257 E4
Weri *Indonesia* 3°10S 132°38E 231 E8
Werneck *Germany* 49°58N 10°5E 179 F6
Werneuchen *Germany* 52°38N 13°44E 115 A5
Wernigerode *Germany* 51°50N 10°47E 178 D6
Werra → *Germany* 51°24N 9°39E 178 D5
Werribee *Australia* 37°54S 144°40E 282 D6
Werrikimbe △ *Australia* 31°11S 152°15E 283 A10
Werrimull *Australia* 34°25S 141°38E 282 C4
Werris Creek *Australia* 31°18S 150°38E 283 A9
Werschetz = Vršac *Serbia* 45°8N 21°20E 182 E6
Wertach → *Germany* 48°22N 10°54E 179 G6
Wertheim *Germany* 49°45N 9°32E 179 F5
Wertingen *Germany* 48°33N 10°41E 179 G6
Wesel *Germany* 51°39N 6°37E 178 D2
Weser → *Germany* 53°36N 8°28E 178 B4
Weser-Ems □ *Germany* 53°0N 7°30E 178 C3
Weserbergland *Germany* 52°12N 9°7E 178 C5
Weserbergland Schaumburg Hameln ⌓ *Germany* 52°8N 9°20E 178 C5
Wesermünde = Bremerhaven *Germany* 53°33N 8°36E 178 B4
Wesiri *Indonesia* 7°30S 126°30E 231 F7
Weslaco *U.S.A.* 26°10N 97°58W 314 H6
Weslemkoon L. *Canada* 45°2N 77°25W 312 A7
Wesley *Dominica* 15°33N 61°18W 323 k
Wesleyville *Nfld. & L., Canada* 49°9N 53°33W 299 C9
Wesleyville *Pa., U.S.A.* 42°9N 80°1W 312 D4
Wessel, C. *Australia* 10°59S 136°46E 280 A2
Wessel Is. *Australia* 11°10S 136°45E 280 A2
Wesselburen *Germany* 54°13N 8°54E 178 A4
Wessington Springs *U.S.A.* 44°5N 98°34W 308 C4
West *U.S.A.* 31°48N 97°6W 314 F6
West → *U.S.A.* 42°52N 72°33W 313 D12
West Allis *U.S.A.* 43°1N 88°0W 311 B8
West Antarctica *Antarctica* 80°0S 90°0W 151 D15
West Baines → *Australia* 15°38S 129°59E 278 C4
West Bank ■ *Asia* 32°6N 35°13E 251 F6
West Bend *U.S.A.* 43°25N 88°11W 308 D9
West Bengal □ *India* 23°0N 88°0E 243 H13
West Berkshire □ *U.K.* 51°25N 1°17W 169 F6
West Beskids = Západné Beskydy *Europe* 49°30N 19°0E 181 B12
West Branch *U.S.A.* 44°17N 84°14W 309 C11
West Branch Susquehanna → *U.S.A.* 40°53N 76°48W 313 F8
West Bromwich *U.K.* 52°32N 1°59W 169 E6
West Burra *U.K.* 60°5N 1°21W 167 A7
West Canada Cr. → *U.S.A.* 43°1N 74°58W 313 C10
West Caroline Basin *Pac. Oc.* 4°0N 138°0E 288 G5
West Carrollton *U.S.A.* 39°40N 84°17W 311 E12
West Chazy *U.S.A.* 44°49N 73°28W 313 B11
West Chester *U.S.A.* 39°58N 75°36W 313 G9
West Chicago *U.S.A.* 41°53N 88°12W 311 C8
West Coast □ *N.Z.* 43°15S 170°30E 285 D5
West Coast ⌓ *Namibia* 21°53S 14°14E 270 B1
West Coast △ *S. Africa* 33°13S 18°0E 270 D2
West Columbia *S.C., U.S.A.* 33°59N 81°4W 316 B8
West Columbia *Tex., U.S.A.* 29°9N 95°39W 314 G7
West Covina *U.S.A.* 34°4N 117°54W 307 L9
West Des Moines *U.S.A.* 41°35N 93°43W 310 C3
West Don → *Canada* 43°44N 79°24W 141 A2
West Drayton *U.K.* 51°30N 0°28W 125 A1
West Dunbartonshire □ *U.K.* 55°59N 4°30W 167 F4
West End *Bahamas* 26°41N 78°58W 320 A4
West End *Boston, U.S.A.* 116 b1
West End Village *Anguilla* 18°10N 63°10W 322 a
West Falkland *Falk. Is.* 51°40S 60°0W 153 f
West Fargo *U.S.A.* 46°52N 96°54W 308 B5
West Fiji Basin *Pac. Oc.* 17°0S 173°0E 288 J9
West Fjord = Vestfjorden *Norway* 67°55N 14°0E 160 C16
West Fork Trinity → *U.S.A.* 32°48N 96°54W 314 E6
West Frankfort *U.S.A.* 37°54N 88°55W 310 G8
West Grand L. *U.S.A.* 45°14N 67°51W 309 C20
West Green *U.S.A.* 31°37N 82°44W 316 D7
West Ham *U.K.* 51°31N 0°1E 125 A4
West Harrow *U.K.* 51°34N 0°21W 125 A1
West Hartford *U.S.A.* 41°45N 72°44W 313 E12
West Haven *U.S.A.* 41°17N 72°57W 313 E12
West Hazleton *U.S.A.* 40°58N 76°0W 313 F9
West Heath *U.K.* 51°29N 0°7E 125 B4
West Helena *U.S.A.* 34°33N 90°38W 315 D9
West Hill *Canada* 43°46N 79°10W 141 A3
West Hollywood *U.S.A.* 34°5N 118°21W 126 B2
West Hurley *U.S.A.* 41°59N 74°7W 313 E10
West I. *India* 13°35N 92°54E 245 H11
West Ice Shelf *Antarctica* 67°0S 85°0E 151 C7
West Indies *Cent. Amer.* 15°0N 65°0W 321 D7
West Jefferson *U.S.A.* 39°57N 83°17W 311 E13
West Jordan *U.S.A.* 40°36N 111°56W 304 F8
West Kensington *London, U.K.* 125 c1
West Kilburn *London, U.K.* 125 a1
West Lafayette *U.S.A.* 40°27N 86°55W 311 D10
West Lamma Channel *China* 22°14N 114°4E 122 B1
West Liberty *Iowa, U.S.A.* 41°34N 91°16W 310 C5
West Liberty *Ky., U.S.A.* 37°55N 83°16W 311 G13
West Liberty *Ohio, U.S.A.* 40°15N 83°45W 311 D13
West Linn *U.S.A.* 45°21N 122°36W 306 E4
West Lorne *Canada* 42°36N 81°36W 312 D3
West Los Angeles, Univ. of *U.S.A.* 34°7N 118°23W 126 C2
West Lothian □ *U.K.* 55°54N 3°36W 167 F5
West Lunga → *Zambia* 13°6S 24°39E 265 E4
West Lunga △ *Zambia* 12°49S 24°47E 265 E4
West MacDonnell △ *Australia* 23°38S 132°59E 278 D5
West Mariana Basin *Pac. Oc.* 15°0N 137°0E 288 F5
West Medford *U.S.A.* 42°25N 71°7W 116 A2
West Memphis *U.S.A.* 35°8N 90°10W 315 D9
West Miami *U.S.A.* 25°45N 80°17W 128 B1
West Midlands □ *U.K.* 52°26N 2°0W 169 E6
West Mifflin *U.S.A.* 40°21N 79°52W 312 F5
West Milford *U.S.A.* 41°8N 74°22W 313 E10
West Milton *Ohio, U.S.A.* 39°58N 84°20W 311 E12
West Milton *Pa., U.S.A.* 41°1N 76°50W 312 E8
West Molesey *U.K.* 51°24N 0°22W 125 B1
West Monroe *U.S.A.* 32°31N 92°9W 314 E8
West New Britain □ *Papua N. G.* 5°0S 149°30E 286 C5
West New York *New York, U.S.A.* 132 a1
West Newton *U.S.A.* 40°14N 79°46W 312 F5
West Nicholson *Zimbabwe* 21°2S 29°20E 269 G2
West Odessa *U.S.A.* 31°50N 102°30W 314 F3
West of Twin Peaks *U.S.A.* 37°43N 122°27W 136 B2
West Palm Beach *U.S.A.* 26°43N 80°3W 317 J9
West Palm Beach Canal *U.S.A.* 26°40N 80°15W 317 J9
West Park *S. Africa* 26°9S 27°59E 123 A1
West Pensacola *U.S.A.* 30°25N 87°16W 317 E2
West Plains *U.S.A.* 36°44N 91°51W 308 G8
West Point *Ga., U.S.A.* 32°53N 85°11W 316 C4
West Point *Iowa, U.S.A.* 40°43N 91°27W 310 D5
West Point *Ky., U.S.A.* 37°59N 85°57W 311 G11
West Point *Miss., U.S.A.* 33°36N 88°39W 315 E10
West Point *N.Y., U.S.A.* 41°24N 73°58W 313 E11
West Point *Nebr., U.S.A.* 41°51N 96°43W 308 E5
West Point *Va., U.S.A.* 37°32N 76°48W 309 G15
West Point L. *U.S.A.* 33°8N 85°0W 316 B4
West Pt. = Ouest, Pte. de l' *Canada* 49°52N 64°40W 299 C7
West Pt. *Australia* 35°1S 135°56E 282 C1
West Ra. *Papua N. G.* 4°15S 141°30E 286 C1
West Road → *Canada* 53°18N 122°53W 296 C4
West Rouge *Canada* 43°48N 79°7W 141 A4
West Roxbury *U.S.A.* 42°16N 71°9W 116 B2
West Rutland *U.S.A.* 43°36N 73°3W 313 C11
West Salem *U.S.A.* 38°31N 88°1W 311 F8
West Schelde = Westerschelde → *Neths.* 51°25N 3°25E 170 C3
West Seneca *U.S.A.* 42°51N 78°48W 312 D6
West Sepik □ *Papua N. G.* 3°30S 142°0E 286 B2
West Siberian Plain *Russia* 62°0N 75°0E 210 B9
West Springfield *U.S.A.* 38°47N 77°13W 143 C2
West Sussex □ *U.K.* 50°55N 0°30W 169 G7
West Terre Haute *U.S.A.* 39°28N 87°27W 311 E9
West-Terschelling *Neths.* 53°22N 5°13E 170 A5
West Town *U.S.A.* 41°53N 87°42W 119 B2
West Union *Iowa, U.S.A.* 42°57N 91°49W 310 B5
West Union *Ohio, U.S.A.* 38°48N 83°33W 311 F13
West Unity *U.S.A.* 41°35N 84°26W 311 C12
West Valley City *U.S.A.* 40°42N 111°58W 304 F8
West Virginia □ *U.S.A.* 38°45N 80°30W 309 F13
West-Vlaanderen □ *Belgium* 51°0N 3°0E 170 D2
West Walker → *U.S.A.* 38°54N 119°9W 306 G7
West Wharf *Pakistan* 24°49N 66°58E 123 B1
West Wyalong *Australia* 33°56S 147°10E 283 B7
West Yellowstone *U.S.A.* 44°40N 111°6W 304 D8
West Yorkshire □ *U.K.* 53°45N 1°40W 168 D6
Westall, Pt. *Australia* 32°55S 134°4E 281 E1
Westbay *U.S.A.* 30°18N 85°52W 316 E4
Westbourne Green *London, U.K.* 125 a1
Westbrook *U.S.A.* 43°41N 70°22W 309 D18
Westbury *Australia* 41°30S 146°51E 281 G4
Westby *U.S.A.* 48°52N 104°3W 304 B11
Westchester *Calif., U.S.A.* 33°57N 118°23W 126 C2
Westchester *Ill., U.S.A.* 41°51N 87°53W 119 B1
Westchester *N.Y., U.S.A.* 40°51N 73°51W 132 A2
Westcliff *S. Africa* 26°10S 28°1E 123 B2
Westdene *S. Africa* 26°10S 27°59E 123 B1
Westend *Helsinki, Finland* 60°9N 24°48E 121 C1
Westend *Calif., U.S.A.* 35°42N 117°24W 307 K9
Wester Hailes *U.K.* 55°55N 3°16W 121 B2
Westerham *Germany* 48°3N 11°36E 131 B2
Westerland *Germany* 54°54N 8°17E 178 A4
Westerly *U.S.A.* 41°22N 71°50W 313 E13
Western □ *Ghana* 5°30N 2°30W 262 D4
Western □ *Kenya* 0°30N 34°30E 268 B3
Western □ *Papua N. G.* 7°30S 142°0E 286 D2
Western □ *S. Leone* 8°30N 13°20W 262 D2
Western □ *Zambia* 15°0S 24°4E 265 F4
Western Addition *U.S.A.* 37°47N 122°25W 136 B2
Western Australia □ *Australia* 25°0S 118°0E 279 E2
Western Bahr el Ghazâl □ *South Sudan* 7°30N 25°30E 257 F2
Western Cape □ *S. Africa* 34°0S 20°0E 270 D3
Western Dvina = Daugava → *Latvia* 57°4N 24°3E 188 D3
Western Equatoria □ *South Sudan* 5°0N 30°0E 257 G3
Western Ghats *India* 14°0N 75°0E 245 H2
Western Highlands □ *Papua N. G.* 5°45S 144°30E 286 C3
Western Isles □ *U.K.* 57°30N 7°10W 167 D1
Western Sahara ■ *Africa* 25°0N 13°0W 260 D2
Western Samoa = Samoa ■ *Pac. Oc.* 14°0S 172°0W 287 V20
Western Sierra Madre = Madre Occidental, Sierra *Mexico* 27°0N 107°0W 318 B3
Western Wall *Jerusalem* 123 b3
Westernport *U.S.A.* 39°29N 79°3W 309 F14

Westerschelde → Neths. 51°25N 3°25E 170 C3
Westerstede Germany 53°15N 7°55E 178 B3
Westerwald Germany 50°38N 7°56E 178 E3
Westfield Ill., U.S.A. 39°27N 88°0W 311 E8
Westfield Ind., U.S.A. 40°2N 86°8W 311 D10
Westfield Mass., U.S.A. 42°7N 72°45W 313 D12
Westfield N.Y., U.S.A. 42°20N 79°35W 312 D5
Westfield Pa., U.S.A. 41°55N 77°32W 312 E7
Westgate La., U.S.A. 30°0N 90°13W 131 A1
Westgate Md. U.S.A. 38°57N 77°6W 143 B3
Westhill U.K. 57°9N 2°19W 167 D6
Westhope U.S.A. 48°55N 101°1W 308 A3
Westlake Western Cape, S. Africa 34°4S 18°26E 118 B1
Westlake Calif., U.S.A. 34°4N 118°15W 126 B3
Westlake Calif., U.S.A. 37°42N 122°29W 136 B2
Westland U.S.A. 42°15N 83°20W 311 B13
Westland △ N.Z. 43°16S 170°16E 285 D5
Westland Bight N.Z. 42°55S 170°5E 285 C5
Westlock Canada 54°9N 113°55W 296 C6
Westmar Australia 27°55S 149°44E 281 D4
Westmeath □ Ireland 53°33N 7°34W 166 C4
Westminster London, U.K. 51°30N 0°7W 125 A3
Westminster Calif., U.S.A. 33°45N 118°0W 307 M8
Westminster Colo., U.S.A. 39°50N 105°2W 304 G11
Westminster Md., U.S.A. 39°34N 76°59W 309 F15
Westmont U.S.A. 40°19N 78°58W 312 F6
Westmorland U.S.A. 33°2N 115°37W 307 M11
Westmount Canada 45°29N 73°35W 130 B2
Weston Ont., Canada 43°42N 79°30W 141 A1
Weston Ohio, U.S.A. 41°21N 83°47W 311 C13
Weston Oreg., U.S.A. 45°49N 118°26W 304 D4
Weston W. Va., U.S.A. 39°2N 80°28W 309 F13
Weston I. Canada 52°33N 79°36W 298 B4
Weston-super-Mare U.K. 51°21N 2°58W 169 F5
Westover U.S.A. 40°45N 78°40W 312 F6
Westphalia U.S.A. 38°26N 92°0W 310 F5
Westport Ont., Canada 44°40N 76°25W 313 B8
Westport Mayo, Ireland 53°48N 9°31W 166 C2
Westport N.Z. 41°46S 171°37E 285 B6
Westport Ind., U.S.A. 39°11N 85°34W 311 E11
Westport N.Y., U.S.A. 44°11N 73°26W 313 B11
Westport Oreg., U.S.A. 46°8N 123°23W 306 D3
Westport Wash., U.S.A. 46°53N 124°6W 306 D2
Westpunt Curaçao 12°22N 69°10W 322 g
Westray Man., Canada 53°36N 101°24W 297 C8
Westray Orkney, U.K. 59°18N 3°0W 167 B5
Westree Canada 47°26N 81°34W 298 C3
Westville Calif., U.S.A. 39°8N 120°42W 306 F6
Westville Fla., U.S.A. 30°46N 85°51W 316 E4
Westville Ill., U.S.A. 40°2N 87°38W 311 D9
Westville Ind., U.S.A. 41°32N 86°54W 311 C10
Westwego U.S.A. 29°54N 90°8W 131 B2
Westwood U.S.A. 40°18N 121°0W 304 F3
Westwood Lake U.S.A. 25°44N 80°23W 317 K9
Westwood Village U.S.A. 34°3N 118°26W 126 B2
Westzaan Neths. 52°28N 4°46E 112 A1
Wetar Indonesia 7°48S 126°30E 231 F7
Wetaskiwin Canada 52°55N 113°24W 296 C6
Wetherby U.K. 53°56N 1°23W 168 D6
Wethersfield U.S.A. 41°42N 72°40W 313 E12
Wetlet Burma 22°20N 95°53E 241 D5
Wetteren Belgium 51°0N 3°53E 170 D3
Wetton S. Africa 34°0S 18°31E 118 B2
Wetumpka U.S.A. 32°32N 86°13W 316 C3
Wetzlar Germany 50°32N 8°31E 178 E4
Wevok U.S.A. 68°53N 166°13W 303 B6
Wewahitchka U.S.A. 30°7N 85°12W 316 E4
Wewak Papua N. G. 3°38S 143°41E 286 B2
Wewoka U.S.A. 35°9N 96°30W 314 D6
Wexford Ont., Canada 43°45N 79°18W 141 A3
Wexford Wexford, Ireland 52°20N 6°28W 166 D5
Wexford □ Ireland 52°20N 6°25W 166 D5
Wexford Harbour Ireland 52°20N 6°25W 166 D5
Weybridge U.K. 51°22N 0°27W 125 B1
Weyburn Canada 49°40N 103°50W 297 D8
Weyer Markt Austria 47°51N 14°40E 180 D7
Weyhe Germany 52°58N 8°49E 178 C4
Weyib → Ethiopia 7°15N 40°15E 257 F5
Weymouth N.S., Canada 44°30N 66°1W 299 D6
Weymouth Dorset, U.K. 50°37N 2°28W 169 G5
Weymouth Mass., U.S.A. 42°13N 70°58W 313 D14
Weymouth, C. Australia 12°37S 143°27E 280 A3
Wezembeek-Oppem Belgium 50°51N 4°29E 116 A2
Wha Ti Canada 63°8N 117°16W 294 E8
Whakaari N.Z. 37°30S 177°13E 284 D6
Whakamaru N.Z. 38°23S 175°50E 284 E4
Whakatane N.Z. 37°57S 177°1E 284 D6
Whakatane → N.Z. 37°57S 177°1E 284 D6
Whale = Baleine → Canada 58°15N 67°40W 299 A6
Whale B. Burma 11°37N 98°38E 237 G2
Whale Cove Canada 62°10N 92°34W 297 A10
Whale Pt. Ascension I. 7°57S 14°18W 153 g
Whales, B. of Antarctica 78°0S 160°0W 151 D12
Whalsay U.K. 60°22N 0°59W 167 A8
Whangaehu → N.Z. 40°3S 175°6E 284 G4
Whangamata N.Z. 37°12S 175°53E 284 D4
Whangamomona N.Z. 39°8S 174°44E 284 F3
Whanganui △ N.Z. 39°17S 174°53E 284 F3
Whangaparaoa Pen. N.Z. 36°40S 174°45E 284 C4
Whangarei N.Z. 35°43S 174°21E 284 B3
Whangarei Harb. N.Z. 35°45S 174°28E 284 B3
Whangaroa Harb. N.Z. 35°4S 173°46E 284 B2
Whangaruru Harb. N.Z. 35°24S 174°23E 284 B3
Wharanui N.Z. 41°55S 174°6E 285 B9
Wharekauri = Chatham Is. Pac. Oc. 44°0S 176°40W 285 a
Wharfe → U.K. 53°51N 1°9W 168 D6
Wharfedale U.K. 54°6N 2°1W 168 C5
Wharton N.J., U.S.A. 40°54N 74°35W 313 F10
Wharton Pa., U.S.A. 41°31N 78°1W 312 E6
Wharton Tex., U.S.A. 29°19N 96°6W 314 G6
Wharton Basin Ind. Oc. 22°0S 92°0E 273 F8
Whataroa N.Z. 43°18S 170°24E 285 D5
Whataroa → N.Z. 43°7S 170°16E 285 D5
Whatcom = Bellingham U.S.A. 48°46N 122°29W 306 B4
Wheatfield U.S.A. 41°13N 87°4W 311 C9
Wheatland Calif., U.S.A. 39°1N 121°25W 306 F5
Wheatland Ind., U.S.A. 38°40N 87°19W 311 F9
Wheatland Wyo. U.S.A. 42°3N 104°58W 304 E11
Wheatley Canada 42°6N 82°27W 312 D2
Wheaton Ill., U.S.A. 41°52N 88°6W 311 C8
Wheaton Md., U.S.A. 39°3N 77°3W 309 F15
Wheaton Minn., U.S.A. 45°48N 96°30W 308 C5
Wheelbarrow Pk. U.S.A. 37°26N 116°5W 306 H10
Wheeler Oreg., U.S.A. 45°41N 123°53W 304 D2
Wheeler Tex., U.S.A. 35°27N 100°16W 314 D4
Wheeler → Canada 57°2N 67°13W 299 A6
Wheeler L. U.S.A. 34°48N 87°23W 315 D11
Wheeler Pk. N. Mex., U.S.A. 36°34N 105°25W 305 H11
Wheeler Pk. Nev., U.S.A. 38°57N 114°15W 306 G6
Wheeler Ridge U.S.A. 35°0N 118°57W 307 L8
Wheelersburg U.S.A. 38°44N 82°51W 309 F12
Wheeling U.S.A. 40°4N 80°43W 312 F4
Whernside U.K. 54°14N 2°24W 168 C5
Whiddy I. Ireland 51°41N 9°31W 166 E2
Whim Creek Australia 20°50S 117°49E 278 D2
Whirlwind Reef Papua N. G. 4°42S 148°16E 286 C5
Whiskey Jack L. Canada 58°23N 101°55W 297 B8
Whiskeytown-Shasta-Trinity △ U.S.A. 40°45N 122°15W 304 F2
Whistleduck Cr. → Australia 20°15S 135°18E 280 C2
Whistler Canada 50°7N 122°58W 296 C4
Whitby Ont., Canada 43°52N 78°56W 312 C6
Whitby N. Yorks., U.K. 54°29N 0°37W 168 C7
Whitcombe Pass N.Z. 43°13S 170°55E 285 D5
White → Ark., U.S.A. 33°57N 91°5W 314 E9
White → Ind., U.S.A. 38°25N 87°45W 311 F9
White → S. Dak., U.S.A. 43°42N 99°27W 308 D4
White → Tex., U.S.A. 33°14N 100°56W 314 E4
White → Utah, U.S.A. 40°4N 109°41W 304 F9
White → Vt., U.S.A. 43°37N 72°20W 313 C12
White → Wash., U.S.A. 47°12N 122°15W 306 C4
White, L. Australia 21°9S 128°56E 278 D4
White B. Canada 50°0N 56°35W 299 C8
White Bird U.S.A. 45°46N 116°18W 304 D5
White Butte U.S.A. 46°23N 103°18W 308 B2
White City Fla., U.S.A. 29°53N 85°13W 316 F4
White City Oreg., U.S.A. 42°26N 122°51W 304 E2
White Cliffs Australia 30°50S 143°10E 282 A5
White Cloud Hill = Baiyun Hill China 23°8N 113°15E 121 B2
White Desert = Es Sahrâ al Beida Egypt 27°50N 28°45E 256 B2
White Hall U.S.A. 39°26N 90°24W 310 E6
White Haven U.S.A. 41°4N 75°47W 313 E9
White Horse, Vale of U.K. 51°37N 1°30W 169 F6
White House, The Washington, D.C., U.S.A. 143 b1
White I. = Whakaari N.Z. 37°30S 177°13E 284 D6
White I. Grenada 12°26N 61°28W 323 q
White L. Ont., Canada 45°18N 76°31W 313 A8
White L. La., U.S.A. 29°44N 92°30W 314 G8
White Lake Canada 45°21N 76°29W 313 A8
White Mountain U.S.A. 64°41N 163°24W 303 D7
White Mountain Peak U.S.A. 37°38N 118°15W 305 H4
White Mountains Nat. Recr. Area △ U.S.A. 65°30N 147°40W 303 D11
White Mts. Alaska, U.S.A. 65°30N 146°30W 303 D11
White Mts. Calif., U.S.A. 37°30N 118°15W 306 H8
White Mts. N.H., U.S.A. 44°15N 71°15W 313 B13
White Mts. △ Australia 20°43S 145°12E 280 C4
White Nile = Nîl el Abyad → Sudan 15°38N 32°31E 257 D3
White Nile Dam = Khazzân Jabal al Awliyâ Sudan 15°24N 32°30E 257 D3
White Oak U.S.A. 31°2N 81°43W 316 D8
White Otter L. Canada 49°5N 91°55W 298 C1
White Pass U.S.A. 46°38N 121°24W 306 D5
White Pigeon U.S.A. 41°48N 85°39W 311 C11
White Plains Ga., U.S.A. 33°28N 83°1W 316 B6
White Plains N.Y., U.S.A. 41°2N 73°46W 313 E11
White River Ont., Canada 48°35N 85°20W 298 C2
White River S. Dak., U.S.A. 43°34N 100°45W 308 D3
White Rock B.C., Canada 49°2N 122°48W 306 A4
White Rock N. Mex., U.S.A. 35°50N 106°12W 305 J10
White Russia = Belarus ■ Europe 53°30N 27°0E 177 B14
White Sands △ U.S.A. 32°46N 106°20W 305 K10
White Sea = Beloye More Russia 66°30N 38°0E 186 A6
White Springs U.S.A. 30°20N 82°45W 316 E7
White Sulphur Springs Mont., U.S.A. 46°33N 110°54W 304 C8
White Sulphur Springs W. Va., U.S.A. 37°48N 80°18W 309 G13
White Swan U.S.A. 46°23N 120°44W 306 D6
White Volta → Ghana 9°10N 1°15W 263 D4
Whitechapel U.K. 51°31N 0°3W 125 A3
Whitecliffs N.Z. 43°26S 171°55E 285 D6
Whitecourt Canada 54°10N 115°45W 296 C5
Whiteface Mt. U.S.A. 44°22N 73°54W 313 B11
Whitefield U.S.A. 44°23N 71°37W 313 B13
Whitefish U.S.A. 48°25N 114°20W 304 B6
Whitefish B. U.S.A. 46°40N 84°55W 298 C3
Whitefish Bay U.S.A. 43°6N 87°54W 311 A9
Whitefish L. Canada 62°41N 106°48W 297 A7
Whitefish Pt. U.S.A. 46°45N 84°59W 309 B11
Whitegull, L. = Goélands, L. aux Canada 55°27N 64°17W 299 A7
Whitehall Dublin, Ireland 53°22N 6°16W 120 A2
Whitehall London, U.K. 125 b3
Whitehall Mich., U.S.A. 43°24N 86°21W 308 D10
Whitehall Mont., U.S.A. 45°52N 112°6W 304 D7
Whitehall N.Y., U.S.A. 43°33N 73°24W 313 C11
Whitehall Wis., U.S.A. 44°22N 91°19W 308 C8
Whitehaven U.K. 54°33N 3°35W 168 C4
Whitehorse Canada 60°43N 135°3W 296 A1
Whiteman Ra. Papua N. G. 5°55S 150°0E 286 C6
Whitemark Australia 40°7S 148°3E 281 G4
Whiteplains Liberia 6°28N 10°40W 262 D2
Whiteriver U.S.A. 33°50N 109°58W 305 K9
Whitesand → Canada 60°9N 115°45W 296 A5
Whitesands S. Africa 34°23S 20°50E 270 D3
Whitesboro N.Y., U.S.A. 43°7N 75°18W 313 C9
Whitesboro Tex., U.S.A. 33°39N 96°54W 314 E6
Whiteshell △ Canada 50°0N 95°40W 297 D9
Whiteside, Canal Chile 53°55S 70°15W 336 D2
Whiteville U.S.A. 34°20N 78°42W 315 D15
Whitewater U.S.A. 42°50N 88°44W 311 B8
Whitewater B. U.S.A. 25°15N 81°0W 317 K9
Whitewater Baldy U.S.A. 33°20N 108°39W 305 K9
Whitewater L. Canada 50°50N 89°10W 298 B2
Whitewood Queens., Australia 21°28S 143°30E 280 C3
Whitewood Sask., Canada 50°20N 102°20W 297 C8
Whitfield Australia 36°42S 146°24E 283 D7
Whithorn U.K. 54°44N 4°26W 167 G4
Whitianga N.Z. 36°47S 175°41E 284 C4
Whiting U.S.A. 41°41N 87°30W 311 C9
Whitman U.S.A. 42°5N 70°56W 313 D14
Whitmore Village U.S.A. 21°31N 158°1W 302 J13
Whitney Ont., Canada 45°31N 78°14W 312 A6
Whitney Nev., U.S.A. 36°4N 115°5W 124 B2
Whitney, Mt. U.S.A. 36°35N 118°18W 306 J8
Whitney Point U.S.A. 42°20N 75°58W 313 D9
Whitstable U.K. 51°21N 1°3E 169 F9
Whitsunday I. Australia 20°15S 149°4E 280 b
Whitsunday Islands △ Australia 20°15S 149°0E 280 b
Whittemore U.S.A. 43°4N 94°26W 310 A2
Whittier Alaska, U.S.A. 60°47N 148°41W 303 F10
Whittier Calif., U.S.A. 33°58N 118°2W 126 C4
Whittlesea Australia 37°27S 145°9E 283 D6
Whitton U.K. 51°27N 0°21W 125 B1
Wholdaia L. Canada 60°43N 104°20W 297 A8
Whyalla Australia 33°2S 137°30E 282 B2
Wiang Kosai △ Thailand 17°54N 99°29E 236 D2
Wiang Sa Thailand 18°34N 100°45E 236 C3
Wiarton Canada 44°40N 81°10W 312 B3
Wiasso Ghana 6°10N 2°25W 262 D4
Wiay U.K. 57°24N 7°13W 167 D1
Wiązów Poland 50°50N 17°10E 185 H4
Wibaux U.S.A. 46°59N 104°11W 304 C11
Wichabai Guyana 2°57N 59°35W 329 C6
Wichian Buri Thailand 15°39N 101°7E 236 E3
Wichita U.S.A. 37°42N 97°20W 308 G5
Wichita Falls U.S.A. 33°54N 98°30W 314 E5
Wick U.K. 58°26N 3°5W 167 C5
Wickenburg U.S.A. 33°58N 112°44W 305 K7
Wickepin Australia 32°50S 117°30E 279 F2
Wickham Australia 20°42S 117°11E 278 D2
Wickham, C. Australia 39°35S 143°57E 281 F3
Wickliffe U.S.A. 41°36N 81°28W 312 E3
Wicklow Ireland 52°59N 6°3W 166 D5
Wicklow □ Ireland 52°57N 6°25W 166 D5
Wicklow Hd. Ireland 52°58N 6°0W 166 D6
Wicklow Mts. Ireland 52°58N 6°26W 166 C5
Wicklow Mts. △ Ireland 53°6N 6°21W 166 C5
Widawa Poland 51°27N 18°51E 185 G5
Widawka → Poland 51°27N 18°52E 185 G5
Wide B. Papua N. G. 5°5S 152°5E 286 C7
Widgeegoara Cr. → Australia 28°51S 146°34E 281 D4
Widgiemooltha Australia 31°30S 121°34E 279 F3
Widnes U.K. 53°23N 2°45W 168 D5
Wido S. Korea 35°35N 126°17E 224 E3
Więcbork Poland 53°21N 17°30E 185 E4
Wieden Austria 48°11N 16°22E 142 A2
Wiehengebirge = Nördlicher Teutoburger Wald-Wiehengebirge △ Germany 52°18N 8°10E 178 C4
Wiehl Germany 50°56N 7°34E 178 E3
Wiek Germany 54°37N 13°17E 178 A9
Wielbark Poland 53°24N 20°55E 184 E7
Wieleń Poland 52°53N 16°9E 185 F3
Wielichowo Poland 52°7N 16°22E 185 F3
Wieliczka Poland 50°0N 20°5E 185 J7
Wielkopolski △ Poland 52°18N 16°45E 185 F3
Wielkopolskie □ Poland 52°10N 17°30E 185 F4
Wieluń Poland 51°15N 18°34E 185 G5
Wien Austria 48°12N 16°22E 142 A2
Wien-Schwechat ✕ (VIE) Austria 48°7N 16°35E 142 B3
Wiener Neustadt Austria 47°49N 16°16E 181 D9
Wienerberg Austria 48°9N 16°21E 142 B2
Wieprz → Poland 51°34N 21°49E 185 G8
Wieprza → Poland 54°26N 16°25E 184 D3
Wieruszów Poland 51°19N 18°9E 185 G5
Wierzbno Poland 52°11N 21°1E 142 B2
Wiesbaden Germany 50°4N 8°14E 179 E4
Wiesental Germany 49°13N 8°31E 179 F4
Wiesloch Germany 49°18N 8°41E 179 F4
Wiesmoor Germany 53°24N 7°47E 178 B3
Wieżyca Poland 54°14N 18°8E 184 D5
Wigan U.K. 53°33N 2°38W 168 D5
Wiggins Colo., U.S.A. 40°14N 104°4W 304 F11
Wiggins Miss., U.S.A. 30°51N 89°8W 315 F10
Wight, I. of U.K. 50°41N 1°17W 169 G6
Wigierski △ Poland 54°5N 23°5E 184 D10
Wigry, Jezioro Poland 54°2N 23°8E 184 D10
Wigston U.K. 52°35N 1°6W 169 E6
Wigton U.K. 54°50N 3°10W 168 C4
Wigtown U.K. 54°53N 4°27W 167 G4
Wigtown B. U.K. 54°46N 4°15W 167 G4
Wijde Wormer Neths. 52°28N 4°52E 112 A2
Wik and Wikway People ✪ Australia 13°55S 142°28E 280 A3
Wil Switz. 47°28N 9°3E 179 H5
Wilamowice Poland 49°55N 19°9E 185 J6
Wilanów Poland 52°10N 21°4E 142 B2
Wilanówka → Poland 52°13N 21°6E 142 C2
Wilber U.S.A. 40°29N 96°58W 308 E5
Wilberforce Canada 45°2N 78°13W 312 A6
Wilberforce, C. Australia 11°54S 136°35E 280 A2
Wilburton U.S.A. 34°55N 95°19W 314 D7
Wilcannia Australia 31°30S 143°26E 282 A5
Wilcox U.S.A. 41°35N 78°41W 312 E6
Wildbad Germany 48°44N 8°33E 179 G4
Wildcat Cr. → U.S.A. 40°28N 86°52W 311 D10
Wildenschwert = Ústí nad Orlicí Czech Rep. 49°58N 16°24E 181 B9
Wildeshausen Germany 52°54N 8°27E 178 C4
Wildeshauser Geest △ Germany 52°54N 8°30E 178 C4
Wildon Austria 46°52N 15°31E 180 E8
Wildrose U.S.A. 36°14N 117°11W 307 J9
Wilds, The S. Africa 26°10S 28°2E 123 B2
Wildspitze Austria 46°53N 10°53E 180 E3
Wildwood U.S.A. 28°52N 82°2W 317 G7
Wilga → Poland 51°52N 21°18E 185 G8
Wilge → S. Africa 27°3S 28°20E 271 C4
Wilhelm, Mt. Papua N. G. 5°50S 145°1E 286 C3
Wilhelm II Coast Antarctica 68°0S 90°0E 151 C7
Wilhelmina Geb. Suriname 3°50N 56°30W 329 C6
Wilhelmina Top = Trikora, Puncak Indonesia 4°15S 138°45E 231 E9
Wilhelmsburg Austria 48°6N 15°36E 180 C8
Wilhelmshagen Germany 52°26N 13°42E 115 B5
Wilhelmshaven Germany 53°31N 8°7E 178 B4
Wilhelmstal Namibia 21°58S 16°21E 270 B2
Wilis Indonesia 7°51S 111°48E 235 D4
Wilkes-Barre U.S.A. 41°15N 75°53W 313 E9
Wilkes I. Wake I. 19°18N 166°34E 302 b
Wilkes Land Antarctica 69°0S 120°0E 151 D9
Wilket Creek Park Canada 43°43N 79°21W 141 A2
Wilkie Canada 52°27N 108°42W 297 C7
Wilkieston U.K. 55°54N 3°24W 121 B1
Wilkinsburg U.S.A. 40°26N 79°52W 312 F5
Wilkinson Lakes Australia 29°40S 132°39E 279 E5
Will Rogers State Historical Park △ U.S.A. 34°2N 118°30W 126 B1
Willacoochee U.S.A. 31°20N 83°3W 316 D6
Willandra △ Australia 33°12S 145°0E 283 B6
Willandra Creek → Australia 33°22S 145°52E 282 B6
Willapa B. U.S.A. 46°40N 124°0W 304 C1
Willapa Hills U.S.A. 46°35N 123°25W 306 D3
Willard U.S.A. 41°3N 82°44W 312 E2
Willare Bridge Roadhouse Australia 17°43S 123°38E 278 C3
Willaumez Pen. Papua N. G. 5°15S 150°2E 286 C6
Willbriggie Australia 34°28S 146°2E 283 C7
Willbrook Ireland 53°17N 6°16W 120 B2
Willcox U.S.A. 32°15N 109°50W 305 K9
Willemstad Curaçao 12°5N 68°55W 322 g
Willenberg = Wielbark Poland 53°24N 20°55E 184 E7
Willesden U.K. 51°32N 0°15W 125 A2
Willesden Green U.K. 51°32N 0°13W 125 A2
Willi Willi △ Australia 30°57S 152°27E 283 A10
William → Canada 59°8N 109°19W 297 B7
William, Mt. Australia 37°17S 142°35E 282 D5
William 'Bill' Dannelly Res. U.S.A. 32°6N 87°24W 315 E11
William Creek Australia 28°58S 136°22E 281 D2
Williams W. Austral., Australia 33°2S 116°52E 279 F2
Williams Ariz., U.S.A. 35°15N 112°11W 305 J7
Williams Calif., U.S.A. 39°9N 122°9W 306 F4
Williams Harbour Canada 52°33N 55°47W 299 B8
Williams Lake Canada 52°10N 122°10W 296 C4
Williamsbridge U.S.A. 40°52N 73°51W 132 A2
Williamsburg Fla., U.S.A. 28°24N 81°26W 133 B2
Williamsburg Iowa, U.S.A. 41°40N 92°1W 310 C4
Williamsburg Ky., U.S.A. 36°44N 84°10W 309 G11
Williamsburg New York, U.S.A. 132 f3
Williamsburg Pa., U.S.A. 40°28N 78°12W 312 F6
Williamsburg Va., U.S.A. 37°16N 76°43W 309 G15
Williamsburg Bridge New York, U.S.A. 132 e2
Williamsfield U.S.A. 40°55N 90°1W 310 D6
Williamson N.Y., U.S.A. 43°14N 77°11W 312 C7
Williamson W. Va., U.S.A. 37°41N 82°17W 309 G12
Williamsport Ind., U.S.A. 40°17N 87°17W 311 D9
Williamsport Pa., U.S.A. 41°15N 77°1W 312 E7
Williamston Mich., U.S.A. 42°41N 84°17W 311 B12
Williamston N.C., U.S.A. 35°51N 77°4W 315 D16
Williamstown Vic., Australia 37°51S 144°52E 128 B1
Williamstown Ky., U.S.A. 38°38N 84°34W 311 F12
Williamstown Mass., U.S.A. 42°43N 73°12W 313 D11
Williamstown N.Y., U.S.A. 43°26N 75°53W 313 C9
Williamsville U.S.A. 39°57N 89°33W 310 E7
Willikies Antigua & B. 17°3N 61°42W 322 b
Willimantic U.S.A. 41°43N 72°13W 313 E12
Willingboro U.S.A. 40°3N 74°54W 309 E16
Willis, L. U.S.A. 28°23N 81°28W 133 B2
Willisburg U.S.A. 37°49N 85°8W 311 G11
Williston Northern Cape, S. Africa 31°20S 20°53E 270 D3
Williston Fla., U.S.A. 29°23N 82°27W 317 F7
Williston N. Dak., U.S.A. 48°9N 103°37W 308 A2
Williston S.C., U.S.A. 33°24N 81°25W 316 B8
Williston L. Canada 56°0N 124°0W 296 B4
Willits U.S.A. 39°25N 123°21W 304 G2
Willmar U.S.A. 45°7N 95°3W 308 C6
Willmore Wilderness △ Canada 53°45N 119°30W 296 C5
Willoughby N.S.W., Australia 33°48S 151°12E 139 A2
Willoughby Ohio, U.S.A. 41°39N 81°24W 312 E3
Willoughby B. Antigua & B. 17°2N 61°44W 322 b
Willow U.S.A. 61°45N 150°3W 303 F10
Willow Bunch Canada 49°20N 105°35W 297 D7
Willow L. Canada 62°10N 119°8W 296 A5
Willow Springs U.S.A. 41°44N 87°51W 119 C1
Willow Tree Australia 31°40S 150°45E 283 A9
Willow Wall, The China 42°10N 122°0E 227 C12
Willowdale Ont., Canada 43°46N 79°25W 141 A2
Willowdale La., U.S.A. 30°0N 90°12W 131 A1
Willowick U.S.A. 41°38N 81°28W 312 E3
Willowlake → Canada 62°42N 123°8W 296 A4
Willowmore S. Africa 33°15S 23°30E 270 D3
Willows U.S.A. 39°31N 122°12W 306 F4
Willowvale = Gatyana S. Africa 32°16S 28°31E 271 D4
Wills, L. Australia 21°25S 128°51E 278 D4
Wills Cr. → Australia 22°43S 140°2E 280 C3
Willsboro U.S.A. 44°21N 73°24W 313 B11
Willunga Australia 35°15S 138°30E 282 C3
Wilma U.S.A. 30°9N 84°58W 316 E5
Wilmersdorf Berlin, Germany 115 c1
Wilmette U.S.A. 42°4N 87°42W 119 A2
Wilmington S. Austral., Australia 32°39S 138°7E 282 B3
Wilmington Kent, U.K. 51°25N 0°12E 125 B5
Wilmington Del., U.S.A. 39°45N 75°33W 309 F16
Wilmington Ill., U.S.A. 41°18N 88°9W 311 C8
Wilmington N.C., U.S.A. 34°14N 77°55W 315 D16
Wilmington Ohio, U.S.A. 39°27N 83°50W 311 E13
Wilmington Vt., U.S.A. 42°52N 72°52W 313 D12
Wilmslow U.K. 53°19N 2°13W 168 D5
Wilna = Vilnius Lithuania 54°38N 25°19E 188 E3
Wilpattu △ Sri Lanka 8°20N 79°50E 245 K4
Wilpena Australia 31°3S 138°37E 282 A3
Wilpena Cr. → Australia 31°25S 139°29E 282 A3
Wilsall U.S.A. 45°59N 110°38W 304 D8
Wilson N.C., U.S.A. 35°44N 77°55W 315 D16
Wilson N.Y., U.S.A. 43°19N 78°50W 312 C6
Wilson Pa., U.S.A. 40°41N 75°15W 313 F9
Wilson → Australia 16°48S 128°16E 278 C4
Wilson Bluff Australia 31°41S 129°0E 279 F4
Wilson Inlet Australia 35°0S 117°22E 279 G2
Wilson Str. Solomon Is. 8°0S 156°39E 287 M9
Wilsons Promontory Australia 38°59S 146°23E 283 E7
Wilsons Promontory △ Australia 38°59S 146°23E 283 D7
Wilster Germany 53°55N 9°23E 178 B5
Wilton Iowa, U.S.A. 41°35N 91°1W 310 C5
Wilton N. Dak., U.S.A. 47°10N 100°47W 308 B3
Wilton → Australia 14°45S 134°33E 280 A1
Wiltshire □ U.K. 51°18N 1°53W 169 F6
Wiltz Lux. 49°57N 5°55E 170 E5
Wiluna Australia 26°36S 120°14E 279 E3
Wimbledon U.K. 51°25N 0°13W 125 B2
Wimbledon Common U.K. 51°26N 0°14W 125 B2
Wimbledon Park U.K. 51°25N 0°11W 125 B2
Wimbledon Tennis Ground U.K. 51°25N 0°12W 125 B2
Wimborne Minster U.K. 50°48N 1°59W 169 G6
Wimereux France 50°45N 1°37E 173 B8
Wimmera → Australia 36°8S 141°56E 282 D4
Winam G. Kenya 0°20S 34°15E 266 C3
Winamac U.S.A. 41°3N 86°36W 311 C10
Winburg S. Africa 28°30S 27°2E 270 C4
Winchelsea Australia 38°10S 144°1E 282 E6
Winchendon U.S.A. 42°41N 72°3W 313 D12
Winchester N.Z. 44°11S 171°17E 285 E6
Winchester Hants., U.K. 51°4N 1°18W 169 F6
Winchester Conn., U.S.A. 41°53N 73°9W 313 E11
Winchester Idaho, U.S.A. 46°14N 116°38W 304 C5
Winchester Ill., U.S.A. 39°38N 90°27W 310 E6
Winchester Ind., U.S.A. 40°10N 84°59W 311 D12
Winchester Ky., U.S.A. 37°59N 84°11W 311 G12
Winchester Mass., U.S.A. 42°26N 71°8W 116 A2
Winchester N.H., U.S.A. 42°46N 72°23W 313 D12
Winchester Nev., U.S.A. 36°7N 115°7W 124 B2
Winchester Ohio, U.S.A. 38°56N 83°39W 311 F13
Winchester Tenn., U.S.A. 35°11N 86°7W 315 D11
Winchester Va., U.S.A. 39°11N 78°10W 309 F14
Wind → U.S.A. 43°12N 108°12W 304 E9
Wind Cave △ U.S.A. 43°32N 103°17W 308 D2
Wind Point U.S.A. 42°47N 87°46W 311 B9
Wind River Range U.S.A. 43°0N 109°30W 304 E9
Windamere, L. Australia 32°48S 149°51E 283 B8
Windau = Ventspils Latvia 57°25N 21°32E 184 A8
Windber U.S.A. 40°14N 78°50W 312 F6
Winder U.S.A. 34°0N 83°45W 316 A6
Windermere Western Cape, S. Africa 33°55S 18°30E 118 A2
Windermere Cumb., U.K. 54°23N 2°55W 168 C5
Windermere Fla., U.S.A. 28°29N 81°32W 133 B1
Windfall U.S.A. 40°22N 85°57W 311 D11
Windhoek Namibia 22°35S 17°4E 270 B2
Windidda ✪ Australia 26°23S 122°12E 279 E3
Windisch-Feistritz = Slovenska Bistrica Slovenia 46°24N 15°35E 199 B12
Windischgarsten Austria 47°42N 14°21E 180 D7
Windischgratz = Slovenj Gradec Slovenia 46°31N 15°5E 199 B12
Windjana Gorge △ Australia 17°51S 125°0E 278 C3
Windom U.S.A. 43°52N 95°7W 308 D6
Windorah Australia 25°24S 142°36E 280 D3
Window Rock U.S.A. 35°41N 109°3W 305 J9
Windrush → U.K. 51°43N 1°24W 169 F6
Windsor N.S.W., Australia 33°37S 150°50E 283 B9
Windsor N.S., Canada 44°59N 64°5W 299 D7
Windsor Ont., Canada 42°18N 83°0W 312 D2
Windsor N.Z. 44°59S 170°49E 285 E5
Windsor Gauteng, S. Africa 26°7S 27°59E 123 A1
Windsor Windsor & Maidenhead, U.K. 51°29N 0°36W 169 F7
Windsor Calif., U.S.A. 38°33N 122°49W 304 G2
Windsor Colo., U.S.A. 40°29N 104°54W 304 F11
Windsor Conn., U.S.A. 41°50N 72°39W 313 E12
Windsor Ill., U.S.A. 39°26N 88°36W 311 E8
Windsor Mo., U.S.A. 38°32N 93°31W 310 F3
Windsor N.Y., U.S.A. 42°5N 75°37W 313 D9
Windsor Vt., U.S.A. 43°29N 72°24W 313 C12
Windsor, Gare Montréal, Canada 130 c2
Windsor & Maidenhead □ U.K. 51°29N 0°40W 169 F7
Windsor Caves Jamaica 18°21N 77°39W 320 a
Windsor Hills U.S.A. 33°59N 118°22W 126 C2
Windsorton S. Africa 28°16S 24°44E 270 C3
Windward Grenada 12°31N 61°26W 323 q
Windward Is. W. Indies 13°0N 61°0W 321 D7
Windward Passage = Vientos, Paso de los Caribbean 20°0N 74°0W 321 C5
Windward Side Saba 17°38N 63°14W 322 a
Windy Arbour Ireland 53°18N 6°14W 120 B2
Winefred L. Canada 55°30N 110°30W 297 B6
Winejok South Sudan 9°1N 27°30E 257 F2
Winfield Iowa, U.S.A. 41°7N 91°26W 310 C5
Winfield Kans., U.S.A. 37°15N 96°59W 308 G5
Winfield Mo., U.S.A. 39°0N 90°44W 310 F6
Wingate Mts. Australia 14°25S 130°40E 278 B5
Wingellina = Irrunytju Australia 26°3S 128°56E 279 E4
Wingham N.S.W., Australia 31°48S 152°22E 283 A10
Wingham Ont., Canada 43°55N 81°20W 312 C3
Winisk Canada 55°17N 85°5W 298 A2
Winisk → Canada 55°17N 85°5W 298 A2
Winisk L. Canada 52°55N 87°22W 298 B2
Wink U.S.A. 31°45N 103°9W 314 F3
Winkler Canada 49°10N 97°56W 297 D9
Winklern Austria 46°52N 12°52E 180 E5
Winlock U.S.A. 46°30N 122°56W 306 D4
Winneba Ghana 5°25N 0°36W 263 D4
Winnebago U.S.A. 42°16N 89°15W 310 B7
Winnebago, L. U.S.A. 44°0N 88°26W 308 D9
Winnecke Cr. → Australia 18°35S 131°34E 278 C5
Winnemucca U.S.A. 40°58N 117°44W 304 F5
Winnemucca L. U.S.A. 40°7N 119°21W 304 F4
Winner U.S.A. 43°22N 99°52W 308 D4
Winnett U.S.A. 47°0N 108°21W 304 C9
Winnfield U.S.A. 31°56N 92°38W 314 F8
Winnibigoshish, L. U.S.A. 47°27N 94°13W 308 B6
Winning Germany 48°2N 11°37E 131 B2
Winnipeg Canada 49°54N 97°9W 297 D9
Winnipeg → Canada 50°38N 96°19W 297 C9
Winnipeg, L. Canada 52°0N 97°0W 297 C9
Winnipeg Beach Canada 50°30N 96°58W 297 C9
Winnipegosis Canada 51°39N 99°55W 297 C9
Winnipegosis L. Canada 52°30N 100°0W 297 C9
Winnipesaukee, L. U.S.A. 43°38N 71°21W 313 C13
Winnisquam L. U.S.A. 43°33N 71°31W 313 C13
Winnsboro La., U.S.A. 32°10N 91°43W 314 E9
Winnsboro S.C., U.S.A. 34°23N 81°5W 315 D14
Winnsboro Tex., U.S.A. 32°58N 95°17W 314 E7
Winokapau, L. Canada 53°15N 62°50W 299 B7
Winona Minn., U.S.A. 44°3N 91°39W 308 C8
Winona Miss., U.S.A. 33°29N 89°44W 315 E10
Winooski U.S.A. 44°29N 73°11W 313 B11
Winooski → U.S.A. 44°32N 73°17W 313 B11
Winschoten Neths. 53°9N 7°3E 170 A7
Winsen Germany 53°22N 10°13E 178 B6
Winsford U.K. 53°12N 2°31W 168 D5
Winslow = Bainbridge Island U.S.A. 47°38N 122°32W 306 C4
Winslow Ariz., U.S.A. 35°2N 110°42W 305 J8
Winslow Ind., U.S.A. 38°23N 87°13W 311 F9
Winslow Reef Kiribati 1°36S 174°57W 277 A16
Winsted U.S.A. 41°55N 73°4W 313 E11
Winston-Salem U.S.A. 36°6N 80°15W 315 C14
Winter Garden U.S.A. 28°34N 81°35W 317 G8
Winter Haven U.S.A. 28°1N 81°44W 317 G8
Winter Park U.S.A. 28°36N 81°20W 317 G8
Winterberg Germany 51°11N 8°33E 178 D4
Winterhaven U.S.A. 32°44N 114°38W 307 N12
Winters U.S.A. 38°32N 121°58W 306 G5
Winterset U.S.A. 41°20N 94°1W 310 C2
Wintersville U.S.A. 40°23N 80°42W 312 F4
Winterswijk Neths. 51°58N 6°43E 170 C6
Winterthur Switz. 47°30N 8°44E 179 H4
Winthrop U.S.A. 48°28N 120°10W 304 B3
Winton Queens., Australia 22°24S 143°3E 280 C3
Winton N.Z. 46°8S 168°20E 285 G3
Wintua Vanuatu 16°30S 167°26E 287 F5
Wipper → Germany 51°16N 11°12E 178 D7
Wirlyajarrayi ✪ Australia 21°45S 132°35E 278 D5
Wirraminna Australia 31°12S 136°13E 282 A2
Wirrulla Australia 32°24S 134°31E 281 E1
Wisbech U.K. 52°41N 0°9E 169 E8
Wisconsin □ U.S.A. 44°45N 89°30W 310 B7
Wisconsin → U.S.A. 43°0N 91°15W 310 A5
Wisconsin Rapids U.S.A. 44°23N 89°49W 308 C9
Wisdom U.S.A. 45°37N 113°27W 304 D7
Wiseman U.S.A. 67°25N 150°6W 303 C10
Wishaw U.K. 55°46N 3°54W 167 F5
Wishek U.S.A. 46°16N 99°33W 308 B4
Wisła Poland 49°38N 18°53E 185 J5
Wisła → Poland 54°22N 18°55E 184 D5
Wisłok → Poland 50°13N 22°32E 185 H9
Wisłoka → Poland 50°27N 21°23E 185 H8
Wismar Mecklenburg-Vorpommern, Germany 53°54N 11°29E 178 B7
Wismar Guyana 5°59N 58°18W 329 B6
Wisner U.S.A. 41°59N 96°55W 308 E5
Wissant France 50°52N 1°40E 173 B8
Wissembourg France 49°2N 7°57E 173 C14
Wissous France 48°44N 2°19E 134 B2
Wisznice Poland 51°48N 23°13E 185 G10
Witbank = eMalahleni S. Africa 25°51S 29°14E 271 C4
Witches Gorge = Wu Xia China 31°2N 110°10E 229 B8
Witdraai S. Africa 26°58S 20°48E 270 C3
Witham U.K. 51°48N 0°40E 169 F8
Witham → U.K. 52°59N 0°2W 168 E7
Withernsea U.K. 53°44N 0°1E 168 D8
Withlacoochee → Fla., U.S.A. 30°24N 83°10W 316 E6
Withlacoochee → Fla., U.S.A. 29°0N 82°45W 317 G7
Witjira △ Australia 26°22S 135°37E 281 D2
Witkowo Poland 52°26N 17°45E 185 F4
Witless Bay Canada 47°17N 52°50W 299 C9
Witney U.K. 51°48N 1°28W 169 F6
Witnica Poland 52°40N 14°54E 185 F1
Witnossob → Namibia 23°55S 18°45E 270 C3
Witriver S. Africa 25°20S 31°0E 271 C5
Wittdün Germany 54°38N 8°23E 178 A4
Witte Pan Bonaire 12°3N 68°17W 322 h
Witten Germany 51°26N 7°20E 178 D3
Wittenau Germany 52°35N 13°19E 115 A2
Wittenberge Germany 53°0N 11°45E 178 B7
Wittenburg Germany 53°31N 11°4E 178 B7
Wittenheim France 47°44N 7°20E 173 E14
Wittenoom Australia 22°15S 118°20E 278 D2
Witti, Banjaran Malaysia 5°11N 116°29E 235 A5
Wittingau = Třeboň Czech Rep. 49°1N 14°48E 180 B7
Wittingen Germany 52°44N 10°44E 178 C6
Wittlich Germany 49°59N 6°53E 179 F2
Wittmund Germany 53°34N 7°46E 178 B3
Wittow Germany 54°38N 13°20E 178 A9
Wittstock Germany 53°10N 12°28E 178 B8
Witu Kenya 2°23S 40°26E 268 C5
Witu Is. Papua N. G. 4°50S 149°25E 286 C5
Witvlei Namibia 22°23S 18°32E 270 B2
Witwatersrand, Univ. of S. Africa 26°11S 28°1E 123 B2
Witzenhausen Germany 51°20N 9°51E 178 D5
Wiwon N. Korea 40°54N 126°3E 224 B3
Wixom U.S.A. 42°32N 83°32W 311 B13
Wkra → Poland 52°27N 20°44E 185 F7
Władysławowo Poland 54°48N 18°25E 184 D5
Wleń Poland 51°2N 15°39E 185 G2
Wlingi Indonesia 8°5S 112°25E 235 D4
Włochy Poland 52°12N 20°54E 142 B1
Włocławek Poland 52°40N 19°3E 185 F6
Włodawa Poland 51°33N 23°31E 185 G10
Włoszczowa Poland 50°50N 19°55E 185 H6
Wo Mei China 22°21N 114°15E 122 A2
Wo Yi Hop China 22°23N 114°8E 122 A1
Woburn Ont., Canada 43°46N 79°12W 141 A3
Woburn Mass., U.S.A. 42°29N 71°9W 116 A2
Wodian China 32°50N 112°35E 226 H7
Wodonga Australia 36°5S 146°50E 283 D7
Wodzisław Śląski Poland 50°1N 18°26E 185 H5
Wœrth France 48°57N 7°45E 173 D14
Wohlau = Wołów Poland 51°20N 16°38E 185 G3
Woinbogoin China 32°51N 98°39E 228 A2
Woippy France 49°10N 6°8E 173 C13
Woitape Papua N. G. 8°33S 147°15E 286 E4
Wojcieszow Poland 50°58N 15°55E 185 H2
Wokam Indonesia 5°45S 134°28E 231 F8
Wokha India 26°6N 94°16E 241 B5
Woking U.K. 51°19N 0°34W 169 F7
Wokingham U.K. 51°24N 0°49W 169 F7
Wokingham □ U.K. 51°25N 0°51W 169 F7
Woko △ Australia 31°46S 151°49E 283 A9
Wola Poland 52°14N 20°57E 142 B1
Wolbrom Poland 50°24N 19°45E 185 H6
Wolcottville U.S.A. 41°32N 85°22W 311 C11
Wolczyn Poland 51°1N 18°3E 185 G5
Woldegk Germany 53°27N 13°34E 178 B9
Woldenberg = Dobiegniew Poland 52°59N 15°45E 185 F2
Woldenberg Park New Orleans, U.S.A. 131 b3
Wolf → Canada 60°17N 132°33W 296 A2
Wolf, Volcán Ecuador 0°2N 91°20W 330 a
Wolf Creek U.S.A. 47°0N 112°4W 304 C7
Wolf L. Canada 60°24N 131°40W 296 A2
Wolf Point U.S.A. 48°5N 105°39W 304 B11
Wolf Trap Farm Park U.S.A. 38°56N 77°17W 143 B2
Wolfe Creek Crater △ Australia 19°10S 127°47E 278 C4
Wolfe I. Canada 44°7N 76°20W 313 B8
Wolfeboro U.S.A. 43°35N 71°13W 313 C13
Wolfen Germany 51°39N 12°15E 178 D8
Wolfenbüttel Germany 52°10N 10°33E 178 C6
Wolfratshausen Germany 47°54N 11°24E 179 H7
Wolfsberg Austria 46°50N 14°52E 180 E7
Wolfsburg Germany 52°25N 10°48E 178 C6
Wolgast Germany 54°3N 13°44E 178 A9
Wolgok S. Korea 37°35N 127°1E 137 B2
Wolhusen Switz. 47°4N 8°4E 179 H4
Wolica Warszawa, Poland 52°9N 21°3E 142 C2
Wolica Warszawa, Poland 52°7N 20°51E 142 C1
Wolin Poland 53°50N 14°37E 184 E1
Woliński △ Poland 53°57N 14°28E 184 E1
Wollaston U.S.A. 42°15N 71°2W 116 B2
Wollaston, Is. Chile 55°40S 67°30W 336 E3
Wollaston Forland Greenland 74°25N 19°40W 154 C9
Wollaston L. Canada 58°7N 103°10W 297 B8
Wollaston Lake Canada 58°3N 103°33W 297 B8
Wollaston Pen. Canada 69°30N 115°0W 294 D9
Wollemi △ Australia 33°0S 150°30E 283 B9
Wollongong Australia 34°25S 150°54E 283 C9
Wolmar = Valmiera Latvia 57°37N 25°29E 188 D3
Wolmaransstad S. Africa 27°12S 25°59E 270 C4
Wolmirstedt Germany 52°14N 11°37E 178 C7
Wolomin Poland 52°19N 21°15E 185 F8
Wołów Poland 51°20N 13°38E 185 G3
Wolseley S. Austral., Australia 36°23S 140°54E 282 D4
Wolseley Western Cape, S. Africa 33°26S 19°7E 270 D2
Wolsey U.S.A. 44°25N 98°28W 308 C4
Wolstenholme, C. Canada 62°35N 77°30W 292 C12
Wolsztyn Poland 52°8N 16°5E 185 F3
Woltersdorf Germany 52°27N 13°44E 115 B5
Woluwe-St-Lambert Belgium 50°50N 4°24E 116 A2
Woluwe-St-Pierre Belgium 50°50N 4°25E 116 A2
Wolvega Neths. 52°52N 6°0E 170 B6
Wolverhampton U.K. 52°35N 2°7W 169 E5
Wondai Australia 26°20S 151°49E 281 D5
Wonenara Papua N. G. 6°48S 145°53E 286 D3
Wong Chuk Hang China 22°15N 114°10E 122 B2
Wong Chuk Wan China 22°23N 114°17E 122 A2
Wong Chuk Yeung China 22°24N 114°15E 122 A2
Wonga Wongué △ Gabon 0°29S 9°25E 254 C1
Wongalarroo L. Australia 31°32S 144°0E 282 A6
Wongan Hills Australia 30°51S 116°37E 279 F2
Wonju S. Korea 37°22N 127°58E 224 D3
Wonosari Indonesia 7°58S 110°36E 231 G14
Wonosobo Indonesia 7°22S 109°54E 235 D3
Wonowon Canada 56°44N 121°48W 296 B4
Wŏnsan N. Korea 39°11N 127°27E 224 C3
Wonthaggi Australia 38°37S 145°37E 283 E6
Wood Buffalo △ Canada 59°0N 113°41W 296 B6
Wood Green U.K. 51°35N 0°6W 125 A3
Wood Is. Australia 16°24S 123°19E 278 C3
Wood L. Canada 55°17N 103°17W 297 B8
Wood Ridge U.S.A. 40°50N 74°4W 132 A1
Wood River U.S.A. 38°52N 90°5W 310 F6
Woodah, I. Australia 13°27S 136°10E 280 A2
Woodbine U.S.A. 30°58N 81°44W 316 E8
Woodbine Race Track Canada 43°43N 79°36W 141 A1
Woodbourne U.S.A. 41°46N 74°36W 313 E10
Woodbridge Ont., Canada 43°47N 79°36W 141 A1
Woodbridge Suffolk, U.K. 52°6N 1°20E 169 E9
Woodbridge B. Dominica 15°19N 61°25W 323 k
Woodburn N.S.W., Australia 29°6S 153°23E 281 A5

Woodburn Oreg., U.S.A. 45°9N 122°51W 304 D2
Woodbury U.S.A. 32°59N 84°35W 316 C5
Woodenbong Australia 28°24S 152°39E 281 D5
Woodend Australia 37°20S 144°33E 282 D6
Woodford Queens., Australia 26°58S 152°47E 281 D5
Woodford London, U.K. 51°36N 0°1E 125 A4
Woodford Bridge U.K. 51°36N 0°3E 125 A4
Woodford Green U.K. 51°36N 0°1E 125 A4
Woodfords U.S.A. 38°47N 119°50W 306 G7
Woodhaven U.S.A. 40°41N 73°51W 132 B2
Woodhouselee U.K. 55°52N 3°13W 121 B2
Woodlake U.S.A. 36°25N 119°6W 306 J7
Woodland Calif., U.S.A. 38°41N 121°46W 306 G5
Woodland Maine, U.S.A. 45°9N 67°25W 309 C20
Woodland Pa., U.S.A. 41°0N 78°21W 312 F6
Woodland Wash., U.S.A. 45°54N 122°45W 306 E4
Woodland Caribou ⌂ Canada 51°0N 94°45W 297 C10
Woodlands Singapore 1°26N 103°46E 138 A2
Woodlands, The U.S.A. 30°9N 95°29W 314 F7
Woodlark I. Papua N. G. 9°10S 152°50E 286 E7
Woodmont U.S.A. 38°59N 77°5W 143 B3
Woodonga Australia 36°10S 146°50E 281 F4
Woodridge Canada 49°20N 96°9W 297 D9
Woodroffe, Mt. Australia 26°20S 131°45E 279 E5
Woods, L. Australia 17°50S 133°30E 280 B1
Woods, L. of the N. Amer. 49°15N 94°45W 297 D10
Woods Bay Canada 45°8N 79°59W 312 A5
Woodside S. Austral., Australia 34°58S 138°52E 282 C3
Woodside Vic., Australia 38°31S 146°52E 283 E7
Woodside London, U.K. 51°23N 0°4W 125 B3
Woodside N.Y., U.S.A. 40°44N 73°54W 132 B2
Woodson U.S.A. 39°37N 90°14W 310 E6
Woodstock N.S.W., Australia 33°45S 148°53E 283 B8
Woodstock Queens., Australia 19°35S 146°50E 280 B4
Woodstock N.B., Canada 46°11N 67°37W 299 C6
Woodstock Ont., Canada 43°10N 80°45W 312 C4
Woodstock Western Cape, S. Africa 33°55S 18°27E 118 A1
Woodstock Oxon., U.K. 51°51N 1°20W 169 F6
Woodstock Ga., U.S.A. 34°6N 84°31W 316 A5
Woodstock Ill., U.S.A. 42°19N 88°27W 311 B8
Woodstock N.Y., U.S.A. 42°2N 74°7W 313 D10
Woodstock Vt., U.S.A. 43°37N 72°31W 313 C12
Woodsville U.S.A. 44°9N 72°2W 313 B13
Woodview Canada 44°35N 78°8W 312 B6
Woodville N.Z. 40°20S 175°53E 284 G4
Woodville Fla., U.S.A. 30°19N 84°15W 316 E5
Woodville Ga., U.S.A. 33°40N 83°7W 316 B6
Woodville Miss., U.S.A. 31°6N 91°18W 314 F9
Woodville Ohio, U.S.A. 41°27N 83°22W 311 C13
Woodville Tex., U.S.A. 30°47N 94°25W 314 F7
Woodward U.S.A. 36°26N 99°24W 314 C5
Woody U.S.A. 35°42N 118°50W 307 K8
Woody → Canada 52°31N 100°51W 297 C8
Woolacombe U.K. 51°10N 4°13W 169 F3
Woolamai, C. Australia 38°30S 145°23E 283 E6
Woolbrook Australia 30°56S 151°25E 283 A9
Wooler U.K. 55°33N 2°1W 168 B5
Woolgoolga Australia 30°6S 153°11E 281 E5
Woollahra Australia 33°53S 151°15E 139 B2
Woolloomooloo Sydney, Australia 139 b2
Woolooware B. Australia 34°1S 151°8E 139 C1
Woolwich U.K. 51°29N 0°4E 125 B4
Woolworth Building New York, U.S.A. 132 e1
Woomargama △ Australia 35°50S 147°15E 283 C7
Woomera Australia 31°5S 136°50E 282 A2
Woonsocket R.I., U.S.A. 42°0N 71°31W 313 E13
Woonsocket S. Dak., U.S.A. 44°3N 98°17W 308 C4
Wooramel → Australia 25°47S 114°10E 279 E1
Wooramel Roadhouse Australia 25°45S 114°17E 279 E1
Wooroonooran △ Australia 16°25S 146°1E 280 B4
Wooster U.S.A. 40°48N 81°56W 312 F3
Woqooyi Galbeed ☐ Somali Rep. 10°0N 44°30E 267 C5
Woraksan △ S. Korea 36°50N 128°5E 224 D4
Worcester Western Cape, S. Africa 33°39S 19°27E 270 D2
Worcester Worcs., U.K. 52°11N 2°12W 169 E5
Worcester Mass., U.S.A. 42°16N 71°48W 313 D13
Worcester N.Y., U.S.A. 42°36N 74°45W 313 D10
Worcestershire ☐ U.K. 52°13N 2°10W 169 E5
Worden U.S.A. 38°56N 89°50W 310 F7
Wörgl Austria 47°29N 12°3E 180 D5
Worker's Stadium China 39°55N 116°25E 114 B2
Workington U.K. 54°39N 3°33W 168 C4
Worksop U.K. 53°18N 1°7W 168 D6
Workum Neths. 52°59N 5°26E 170 B5
Worland U.S.A. 44°1N 107°57W 304 D10
World Bank Washington, D.C., U.S.A. 143 b1
World Financial Center New York, U.S.A. 132 e1
World Financial Centre China 31°14N 121°30E 138 B2
World Trade Center, Site of former = Ground Zero New York, U.S.A. 132 e1
World War Two Memorial Washington, D.C., U.S.A. 143 b1
Worli India 19°1N 72°49E 130 A1
Wormhout France 50°52N 2°28E 173 B9
Worms Germany 49°37N 8°21E 179 F4
Worsley Canada 56°31N 119°8W 296 B5
Wörth Bayern, Germany 49°1N 12°24E 179 F8
Worth Ill., U.S.A. 41°41N 87°47W 119 C2
Wortham U.S.A. 31°47N 96°28W 314 F6
Wörther See Austria 46°37N 14°10E 180 E7
Worthing U.K. 50°49N 0°21W 169 G7
Worthington Ind., U.S.A. 39°7N 86°59W 311 E10
Worthington Minn., U.S.A. 43°37N 95°36W 308 D6
Worthington Ohio, U.S.A. 40°5N 83°1W 311 D13
Worthington Pa., U.S.A. 40°50N 79°38W 312 F5
Wosi Indonesia 0°15S 128°0E 231 E7
Wote Kenya 1°47S 37°38E 268 C4
Wotjalum ✪ Australia 16°30S 123°45E 278 C3
Wotjobaluk ✪ Australia 37°0S 142°0E 281 C3
Wou-han = Wuhan China 30°31N 114°18E 229 B10
Wour Chad 21°14N 16°0E 259 D3
Wousi = Wuxi China 31°33N 120°18E 229 B13
Wowoni Indonesia 4°5S 123°5E 231 E6
Woy Woy Australia 33°30S 151°19E 283 B9
Wrangel I. = Vrangelya, Ostrov Russia 71°0N 180°0E 215 B18
Wrangell U.S.A. 56°28N 132°23W 296 B2
Wrangell Mts. U.S.A. 61°30N 142°0W 303 F12
Wrangell-St. Elias △ U.S.A. 61°0N 142°0W 303 F12
Wrath, C. U.K. 58°38N 5°1W 167 C3
Wray U.S.A. 40°5N 102°13W 304 F12
Wrekin, The U.K. 52°41N 2°32W 169 E5
Wrens U.S.A. 33°12N 82°23W 316 B7
Wren's Nest U.S.A. 33°44N 84°25W 113 B2
Wrexham U.K. 53°3N 3°0W 168 D4
Wrexham ☐ U.K. 53°1N 2°58W 168 D5
Wriezen Germany 52°42N 14°7E 178 C10
Wright = Paranas Phil. 11°42N 125°2E 233 F5
Wright Fla., U.S.A. 30°27N 86°38W 317 E3
Wright Wyo., U.S.A. 43°45N 105°28W 304 E11
Wright Pt. Canada 43°48N 81°44W 312 C3
Wrightmyo India 11°47N 92°43E 245 J11
Wrightson, Mt. U.S.A. 31°42N 110°51W 305 L8
Wrightsville U.S.A. 32°44N 82°43W 316 C7
Wrightwood U.S.A. 34°22N 117°38W 307 L9
Wrigley Canada 63°16N 123°37W 294 E7
Wrigley Building Chicago, U.S.A. 119 b2
Wrigley Field U.S.A. 41°56N 87°39W 119 B3
Wrocław Poland 51°5N 17°5E 185 G4
Wronki Poland 52°41N 16°21E 185 F3
Września Poland 52°21N 17°36E 185 F4
Wschowa Poland 51°48N 16°20E 185 G3
Wu Hsi → Taiwan 24°9N 120°31E 225 B2
Wu Jiang → China 29°40N 107°20E 228 C6
Wu Kau Tang China 22°30N 114°14E 219 a
Wu Xia China 31°2N 110°10E 229 B8
Wu'an China 36°40N 114°15E 226 F8
Wubalawun ✪ Australia 15°28S 133°1E 278 C5
Wubin Australia 30°6S 116°37E 279 F2
Wubu China 37°28N 110°42E 226 F6
Wuchang China 44°55N 127°5E 227 B14
Wucheng China 37°12N 116°20E 226 F9
Wuch'i Taiwan 24°16N 120°31E 225 B2
Wuchieh Taiwan 24°41N 121°47E 225 B3
Wuchow = Wuzhou China 23°30N 111°18E 229 F8
Wuchuan Guangdong, China 21°33N 110°43E 229 G8
Wuchuan Guizhou, China 28°25N 108°3E 228 C7
Wuchuan Nei Monggol Zizhiqu, China 41°5N 111°28E 226 D6
Wuda China 39°29N 106°42E 226 E4
Wudang Shan China 32°23N 111°2E 229 A8
Wuday'ah Si. Arabia 17°2N 47°7E 248 C4
Wudi China 37°40N 117°35E 227 F9
Wuding China 25°24N 102°21E 228 E4
Wuding He → China 37°2N 110°23E 226 F6
Wudinna Australia 33°0S 135°22E 281 E2
Wudongde Dam China 26°20N 102°15E 228 D4
Wudu China 33°22N 104°54E 226 H3
Wufeng Henan, China 30°12N 110°42E 229 B8
Wufeng Taiwan 24°4N 120°42E 225 B2
Wugang China 26°44N 110°35E 229 D8
Wugong Shan China 27°30N 114°0E 229 D9
Wuguishan China 22°25N 113°25E 219 a
Wugullar = Beswick Australia 14°34S 132°53E 278 B5
Wuhai China 39°39N 106°48E 226 E4
Wuhan China 30°31N 114°18E 229 B10
Wuhe China 33°10N 117°50E 227 H9
Wuhlgarten Germany 52°31N 13°34E 115 A4
Wuhsi = Wuxi China 31°33N 120°18E 229 B13
Wuhu China 31°22N 118°21E 229 B12
Wujiang China 31°10N 120°38E 229 B13
Wujiaochang China 31°18N 121°31E 138 B2
Wujih Taiwan 24°6N 120°38E 225 B2
Wukari Nigeria 7°51N 9°42E 263 D6
Wulai Taiwan 24°52N 121°33E 225 B3
Wulajie China 44°6N 126°33E 227 B14
Wulanbulang China 41°5N 110°55E 226 D6
Wular L. India 34°20N 74°30E 243 B6
Wulehe Ghana 8°39N 0°0 263 D5
Wulff Land Greenland 82°0N 49°0W 154 A6
Wulian China 35°40N 119°12E 227 G10
Wulian Feng China 27°48N 103°36E 228 D4
Wuliang Shan China 24°30N 100°40E 228 E3
Wuliaru Indonesia 7°27S 131°0E 231 F8
Wulicheng Taiwan 23°47N 121°0E 225 C3
Wuling Shan China 30°0N 110°0E 228 C7
Wulingyuan △ China 29°20N 110°32E 229 C8
Wulong China 29°22N 107°43E 228 C6
Wulong △ China 31°8N 103°5E 228 B4
Wulu Taiwan 23°10N 121°2E 225 C3
Wulumuchi = Ürümqi China 43°45N 87°45E 217 D11
Wum Cameroon 6°24N 10°2E 263 D7
Wumeng Shan China 26°48N 104°0E 228 D5
Wuming China 23°12N 108°18E 228 F7
Wun Rog South Sudan 9°0N 28°20E 257 F2
Wundanyi Kenya 3°24S 38°22E 268 C4
Wuning China 29°17N 115°5E 229 C10
Wunna → India 20°18N 78°48E 244 D4
Wunnummin L. Canada 52°55N 89°10W 298 B2
Wunsiedel Germany 50°2N 12°0E 179 E8
Wunstorf Germany 52°25N 9°26E 178 C5
Wuntho Burma 23°55N 95°45E 241 D5
Wupatki ⌂ U.S.A. 35°35N 111°20W 305 J8
Wuping China 25°5N 116°5E 229 E11
Wuppertal Nordrhein-Westfalen, Germany 51°16N 7°12E 178 D3
Wuppertal Western Cape, S. Africa 32°13S 19°12E 270 D2
Wuqia China 39°40N 75°7E 217 E9
Wuqing China 39°23N 117°4E 227 E9
Würm → Germany 48°8N 11°27E 131 B1
Würm-kanal Germany 48°13N 11°29E 131 A1
Wurralibi ✪ Australia 15°43S 137°1E 280 B2
Wurtsboro U.S.A. 41°35N 74°29W 313 E10
Würzburg Germany 49°46N 9°55E 179 F5
Wurzen Germany 51°22N 12°44E 178 D8
Wushan China 34°43N 104°53E 226 G3
Wushi China 41°9N 79°13E 217 D9
Wushishi Nigeria 9°46N 6°7E 263 D6
Wusi Vanuatu 15°21S 166°40E 287 E4
Wusih = Wuxi China 31°33N 120°18E 229 B13
Wusong China 31°22N 121°29E 138 A1
Wutach → Germany 47°37N 8°15E 179 H4
Wutai China 38°40N 113°12E 226 E7
Wutai Shan China 39°3N 113°32E 226 E7
Wuting = Huimin China 37°27N 117°28E 227 F9
Wutong China 25°24N 110°4E 229 E8
Wutonghaolai China 42°50N 120°5E 227 C11
Wutongqiao China 29°22N 103°50E 228 C4
Wutung Papua N. G. 2°37S 141°1E 286 B1
Wuwei Anhui, China 31°18N 117°54E 229 B11
Wuwei Gansu, China 37°57N 102°34E 218 D9
Wuxi Jiangsu, China 31°33N 120°18E 229 B13
Wuxi Sichuan, China 31°23N 109°35E 228 B7
Wuxiang China 36°49N 112°50E 226 F7
Wuxuan China 23°34N 109°38E 228 F7
Wuxue China 29°52N 115°30E 229 C10
Wuyang China 33°25N 113°35E 226 H7
Wuyi Hebei, China 37°46N 115°56E 226 F8
Wuyi Zhejiang, China 28°52N 119°50E 229 C12
Wuyi Shan China 27°0N 117°0E 229 D11
Wuyishan China 27°45N 118°0E 229 D12
Wuyishan △ China 27°55N 117°54E 229 D11
Wuyo Nigeria 10°23N 11°50E 263 C7
Wuyuan Jiangxi, China 29°15N 117°50E 229 C11
Wuyuan Nei Monggol Zizhiqu, China 41°2N 108°20E 226 D5
Wuzhai China 38°54N 111°48E 226 E6
Wuzhi Shan China 18°45N 109°45E 236 C7
Wuzhong China 38°2N 106°12E 226 E4
Wuzhou China 23°30N 111°18E 229 F8
Wuzishan = Tongshi China 18°30N 109°20E 236 C7
Wyaaba Cr. → Australia 16°27S 141°35E 280 B3
Wyalkatchem Australia 31°8S 117°22E 279 F2
Wyalusing U.S.A. 41°40N 76°16W 313 E8
Wyandotte U.S.A. 42°12N 83°9W 311 B13
Wyandra Australia 27°12S 145°56E 281 D4
Wyangala, L. Australia 33°54S 149°0E 283 B8
Wyara, L. Australia 28°42S 144°14E 281 D3
Wycheproof Australia 36°5S 143°17E 282 D5
Wycliffe Well Australia 20°48S 134°14E 280 C1
Wyczółki Poland 52°9N 20°59E 142 C1
Wye → U.K. 51°38N 2°40W 169 F5
Wyemandoo Australia 28°28S 118°29E 279 E2
Wygoda Poland 52°15N 21°7E 142 B2
Wyk Germany 54°41N 8°33E 178 A4
Wymondham U.K. 52°35N 1°7E 169 E9
Wymore U.S.A. 40°7N 96°40W 308 E5
Wynberg S. Africa 34°2S 18°28E 118 B1
Wyndham W. Austral., Australia 15°33S 128°3E 278 C4
Wyndham N.Z. 46°20S 168°51E 285 G3
Wynne U.S.A. 35°14N 90°47W 315 D9
Wynyard Tas., Australia 41°5S 145°44E 281 G4
Wynyard Sask., Canada 51°45N 104°10W 297 C8
Wyola L. Australia 29°8S 130°17E 279 E5
Wyoming Ont., Canada 42°57N 82°7W 312 D2
Wyoming Ill., U.S.A. 41°4N 89°47W 310 C7
Wyoming Iowa, U.S.A. 42°4N 91°0W 310 B6
Wyoming Mich., U.S.A. 42°54N 85°42W 311 B11
Wyoming ☐ U.S.A. 43°0N 107°30W 304 E10
Wyomissing U.S.A. 40°20N 75°59W 313 F9
Wyong Australia 33°14S 151°24E 283 B9
Wyperfeld △ Australia 35°35S 141°42E 282 C4
Wyrzysk Poland 53°10N 17°17E 185 E4
Wyśmierzyce Poland 51°37N 20°50E 185 G7
Wysoka Poland 53°13N 17°2E 185 E4
Wysokie Poland 50°55N 22°40E 185 H9
Wysokie Mazowieckie Poland 52°55N 22°30E 185 F9
Wyszków Poland 52°36N 21°25E 185 F8
Wyszogród Poland 52°23N 20°9E 185 F7
Wytheville U.S.A. 36°57N 81°5W 309 G13
Wyżyna Małopolska Poland 50°45N 20°0E 185 H7

X

Xa-Cassau Angola 9°5S 20°15E 265 D4
Xa-Muteba Angola 9°34S 17°50E 265 D3
Xaafuun Somali Rep. 10°25N 51°16E 267 B7
Xaafuun, Ras Somali Rep. 10°27N 51°24E 267 B7
Xabregas Portugal 38°43N 9°6W 126 A2
Xaçmaz Azerbaijan 41°31N 48°42E 191 K9
Xaghra Malta 36°3N 14°16E 206 E7
Xai-Xai Mozam. 25°6S 33°31E 271 C5
Xaidulla China 36°28N 77°59E 217 E9
Xaignabouri = Sayaboury Laos 19°15N 101°45E 236 C3
Xainza China 30°58N 88°35E 218 E6
Xalapa Mexico 19°32N 96°55W 319 D5
Xalin Somali Rep. 9°6N 48°37E 267 C6
Xallas → Spain 42°54N 9°8W 194 C1
Xambioá Brazil 6°25S 48°40W 332 C2
Xangongo Angola 16°45S 15°5E 265 F3
Xankändi Azerbaijan 39°52N 46°49E 213 C12
Xanlar Azerbaijan 40°37N 46°12E 191 K8
Xanten Germany 51°39N 6°26E 178 D2
Xanthi Greece 41°10N 24°58E 203 E8
Xanthi ☐ Greece 41°10N 24°58E 203 E8
Xanthos Turkey 36°19N 29°18E 205 E11
Xanxerê Brazil 26°53S 52°23W 335 B5
Xapuri Brazil 10°35S 68°35W 330 C4
Xar Moron He → China 43°25N 120°35E 227 C11
Xarardheere Somali Rep. 4°33N 47°38E 267 D6
Xarrë Albania 39°44N 20°3E 206 B10
Xátiva Spain 38°59N 0°32W 197 G4
Xau, L. Botswana 21°15S 24°44E 270 B3
Xavantina Brazil 21°15S 52°48W 335 A5
Xayar China 41°13N 82°48E 217 D10
Xebert China 44°2N 122°0E 227 B12
Xenia U.S.A. 39°41N 83°56W 311 E13
Xeropotamos → Cyprus 34°42N 32°33E 207 F8
Xertigny France 48°3N 6°24E 173 D13
Xewkija Malta 36°2N 14°15E 206 E7
Xhora S. Africa 31°55S 28°38E 271 D4
Xhumo Botswana 21°7S 24°35E 270 B3
Xi Jiang → China 22°5N 113°20E 229 F9
Xi Ujimqin Qi China 44°32N 117°40E 227 B9
Xi Xian Henan, China 32°20N 114°43E 229 A10
Xi Xian Shanxi, China 36°41N 110°58E 226 F6
Xia Xian China 35°8N 111°12E 226 G6
Xiachengzi China 44°40N 130°18E 227 B16
Xiachuan Dao China 21°40N 112°40E 229 G9
Xiajiang China 27°30N 115°10E 229 D10
Xiajin China 36°56N 116°0E 226 F9
Xiamen China 24°25N 118°4E 229 E12
Xi'an China 34°15N 109°0E 226 G5
Xian Xian China 38°12N 116°6E 226 E9
Xianfeng China 29°40N 109°8E 228 C7
Xiang Jiang → China 28°55N 112°50E 229 C9
Xiang Khouang Laos 19°17N 103°25E 236 C4
Xiangcheng Henan, China 33°50N 113°27E 226 H7
Xiangcheng Sichuan, China 28°53N 99°47E 228 C2
Xiangdu China 23°13N 106°58E 228 F6
Xiangfan China 32°2N 112°8E 229 A9
Xianggang = Hong Kong ☐ China 22°11N 114°14E 229 F10
Xianghuang Qi China 42°2N 113°50E 226 C7
Xiangjiaba Dam China 28°37N 104°17E 228 C5
Xiangning China 35°58N 110°50E 226 G6
Xiangquan China 36°30N 113°1E 226 F7
Xiangquan He = Sutlej → Pakistan 29°23N 71°3E 242 E4
Xiangshan China 29°29N 121°51E 229 C13
Xiangshui China 34°12N 119°33E 227 G10
Xiangtan China 27°51N 112°54E 229 D9
Xiangxiang China 27°43N 112°28E 229 D9
Xiangyin China 28°38N 112°54E 229 C9
Xiangyun China 25°34N 100°35E 228 E3
Xiangzhou China 23°58N 109°40E 228 F7
Xianju China 28°51N 120°44E 229 C13
Xianning China 29°51N 114°16E 229 C10
Xianshui He → China 30°10N 100°59E 228 B3
Xiantao China 30°25N 113°25E 229 B9
Xianyang China 34°20N 108°40E 226 G5
Xianyou China 25°22N 118°38E 229 E12
Xiao Hinggan Ling China 49°0N 127°0E 219 B14
Xiao Xian China 34°15N 116°55E 226 G9
Xiaofeng China 30°35N 119°32E 229 B12
Xiaogan China 30°52N 113°55E 229 B9
Xiaogang Park China 23°6N 113°16E 121 B2
Xiaojin China 30°59N 102°21E 228 B4
Xiaolan China 22°38N 113°13E 229 F9
Xiaoping China 23°12N 113°13E 121 A2
Xiaoshan China 30°12N 120°18E 229 B13
Xiaowutai Shan China 39°51N 114°59E 226 E8
Xiaoyi China 37°8N 111°48E 226 F6
Xiapu China 26°54N 119°59E 229 D12
Xiasha chong China 23°8N 113°9E 121 B1
Xiashan = Zhanjiang China 21°15N 110°20E 229 G8
Xiawa China 42°35N 120°38E 227 C11
Xiayi China 34°15N 116°10E 226 G9
Xichang Guangdong, China 23°9N 113°13E 121 B2
Xichang Sichuan, China 27°51N 102°19E 228 D4
Xicheng Beijing, China 114 b1
Xichong China 30°57N 105°54E 228 B5
Xichou China 23°25N 104°42E 228 E5
Xichuan China 33°0N 111°30E 226 H6
Xidan China 39°52N 116°20E 114 B2
Xide China 28°8N 102°19E 228 C4
Xiemahe China 31°38N 111°12E 229 B8
Xifei He → China 32°45N 116°40E 226 H9
Xifeng Gansu, China 35°40N 107°40E 226 G4
Xifeng Guizhou, China 27°7N 106°42E 228 D6
Xifeng Liaoning, China 42°42N 124°45E 227 C13
Xifengzhen = Xifeng China 35°40N 107°40E 226 G4
Xigazê China 29°5N 88°45E 218 F6
Xihe China 34°2N 105°20E 226 G3
Xihua China 33°45N 114°30E 226 H8
Xilagani Greece 40°58N 25°28E 203 F9
Xili Shuiku China 22°36N 113°57E 219 a
Xiliao He → China 43°32N 123°35E 227 C12
Xilin China 24°30N 105°6E 228 E5
Xiling Gorge = Xiling Xia China 30°54N 110°48E 229 B8
Xiling Xia China 30°54N 110°48E 229 B8
Xilinhot China 43°52N 116°2E 226 C9
Xilokastro Greece 38°5N 22°38E 204 C4
Xiluodu Dam China 28°12N 103°34E 228 C4
Ximana Mozam. 19°24S 33°58E 269 F3
Xime Guinea-Biss. 11°59N 14°57W 262 C2
Ximeng China 22°50N 99°27E 228 F2
Ximiao China 40°59N 100°12E 218 C9
Xin Jiang → China 28°45N 116°35E 229 C11
Xin Xian = Xinzhou China 38°22N 112°46E 226 E7
Xin'anjiang Shuiku China 29°33N 118°56E 229 C12
Xinavane Mozam. 25°2S 32°47E 271 C5
Xinbin China 41°40N 125°2E 224 B2
Xincai China 32°43N 114°58E 229 A10
Xinchang China 29°28N 120°52E 229 C13
Xincheng Guangxi Zhuangzu, China 24°5N 108°39E 228 E7
Xincheng Jiangxi, China 26°48N 114°6E 229 D10
Xinchengzi China 42°2N 123°30E 224 A1
Xinfeng Guangdong, China 24°5N 114°16E 229 E10
Xinfeng Jiangxi, China 27°7N 116°11E 229 D11
Xinfeng Jiangxi, China 25°27N 114°58E 229 E10
Xinfengjiang Shuiku China 23°52N 114°30E 229 F10
Xing Xian China 38°27N 111°7E 226 E6
Xing'an Guangxi Zhuangzu, China 25°38N 110°40E 229 E8
Xingan Jiangxi, China 27°46N 115°20E 229 D10
Xingcheng China 40°40N 120°45E 227 D11
Xingguo China 26°21N 115°21E 229 D10
Xinghe China 40°55N 113°55E 226 D7
Xinghua China 32°58N 119°48E 227 H10
Xinghua Wan China 25°15N 119°20E 229 E12
Xinglong China 40°25N 117°30E 227 D9
Xingning China 24°3N 115°42E 229 E10
Xingping China 34°20N 108°28E 226 G5
Xingren China 25°24N 105°11E 228 E5
Xingshan China 31°15N 110°45E 229 B8
Xingtai China 37°3N 114°32E 226 F8
Xingu → Brazil 1°30S 51°53W 329 D7
Xingwen China 28°22N 104°50E 228 C5
Xingxingxia China 41°47N 95°0E 218 C8
Xingyang China 34°45N 112°52E 226 G7
Xingyi China 25°3N 104°59E 228 E5
Xinhe Hebei, China 37°30N 115°15E 226 F8
Xinhe Xinjiang Uygur, China 41°33N 82°37E 217 D10
Xinhua China 27°42N 111°13E 229 D8
Xinhuang China 27°21N 109°12E 228 D7
Xinhui China 22°25N 113°0E 229 F9
Xining China 36°34N 101°40E 218 D9
Xinjian China 28°37N 115°46E 229 C10
Xinjiang China 35°34N 111°11E 226 G6
Xinjiang Uygur Zizhiqu ☐ China 42°0N 86°0E 217 D11
Xinjin = Pulandian China 39°25N 121°58E 227 E11
Xinjin China 30°24N 103°47E 228 B4
Xinkai He → China 43°32N 123°35E 227 C12
Xinken China 22°39N 113°36E 219 a
Xinle China 38°25N 114°40E 226 E8
Xinlitun China 42°0N 122°8E 227 D12
Xinlong China 30°57N 100°12E 228 B3
Xinmin China 41°59N 122°50E 224 B1
Xinning China 26°28N 110°50E 229 D8
Xinping China 24°5N 101°59E 228 E3
Xinshao China 27°21N 111°26E 229 D8
Xintai China 35°55N 117°45E 227 G9
Xintian China 25°55N 112°13E 229 E9
Xinwan China 22°47N 113°40E 219 a
Xinxiang China 35°18N 113°50E 226 G7
Xinxing China 22°35N 112°15E 229 F9
Xinyang China 32°6N 114°3E 229 A10
Xinye China 32°30N 112°21E 229 A9
Xinyi Guangdong, China 22°25N 111°0E 229 F8
Xinyi Nei Monggol Zizhiqu, China 34°23N 118°21E 227 G10
Xinyu China 27°49N 114°58E 229 D10
Xinzhan China 43°50N 127°18E 227 C14
Xinzheng China 34°20N 113°45E 226 G7
Xinzhou Hainan, China 19°43N 109°17E 236 C7
Xinzhou Hubei, China 30°50N 114°48E 229 B10
Xinzhou Shanxi, China 38°22N 112°46E 226 E7
Xinzo de Limia Spain 42°3N 7°47W 194 C3
Xiongyuecheng China 40°12N 122°5E 227 D12
Xiping Henan, China 33°22N 114°5E 226 H8
Xiping Henan, China 33°25N 111°8E 226 H6
Xiping Zhejiang, China 28°16N 119°29E 229 C12
Xique-Xique Brazil 10°50S 42°40W 332 D3
Xiruá → Brazil 6°3S 67°50W 330 B4
Xisha Qundao = Paracel Is. S. China Sea 15°50N 112°0E 230 A4
Xishuangbanna China 22°5N 101°1E 228 F3
Xishui Guizhou, China 28°19N 106°9E 228 C6
Xishui Hubei, China 30°30N 115°15E 229 B10
Xitole Guinea-Biss. 11°43N 14°50W 262 C2
Xiu Shui → China 29°13N 116°0E 229 C10
Xiuning China 29°45N 118°10E 229 C12
Xiuren China 24°27N 110°12E 229 E8
Xiushan China 28°25N 108°57E 228 C7
Xiushui China 29°2N 114°33E 229 C10
Xiuwen China 26°49N 106°32E 228 D6
Xiuyan China 40°18N 123°11E 224 B1
Xixabangma Feng China 28°20N 85°40E 243 E11
Xixia China 33°25N 111°29E 226 H6
Xixiang Guangdong, China 22°34N 113°52E 219 a
Xixiang Shaanxi, China 33°0N 107°44E 226 H4
Xixón = Gijón Spain 43°32N 5°42W 194 B5
Xiyang China 37°38N 113°38E 226 F7
Xizang Zizhiqu ☐ China 32°0N 88°0E 217 F11
Xizhimen China 39°55N 116°19E 114 B1
Xlendi Malta 36°1N 14°12E 206 E6
Xochimilco, Parque Ecológico Mexico 19°18N 99°5W 128 C2
Xochob Mexico 19°21N 89°48W 319 D7
Xojayli = Khojayli Uzbekistan 42°29N 59°31E 216 D5
Xorazm ☐ Uzbekistan 43°0N 60°0E 216 D6
Xu Beihong Memorial Hall Beijing, China 114 a2
Xu Jiang → China 28°0N 116°25E 229 D11
Xuan Loc Vietnam 10°56N 107°14E 237 G6
Xuan'en China 30°0N 109°30E 228 C7
Xuanhan China 31°18N 107°38E 228 B6
Xuanhua China 40°40N 115°2E 226 D8
Xuanwei China 26°15N 103°59E 228 C5
Xuanwu Beijing, China 114 c1
Xuanzhou China 30°56N 118°43E 229 B12
Xuchang China 34°2N 113°48E 226 G7
Xudat Azerbaijan 41°38N 48°41E 191 K9
Xuddur Somali Rep. 4°11N 43°52E 267 D5
Xuefeng Shan China 27°5N 110°35E 229 D8
Xuejiaping China 31°39N 110°16E 229 B8
Xuhui China 31°11N 121°26E 138 B1
Xun Jiang → China 23°35N 111°30E 229 F8
Xun Xian China 35°42N 114°33E 226 G8
Xundian China 25°36N 103°15E 228 E4
Xunwu China 24°54N 115°37E 229 E10
Xunyang China 32°48N 109°22E 226 H5
Xunyi China 35°8N 108°20E 226 G5
Xupu China 27°53N 110°32E 229 D8
Xúquer → Spain 39°5N 0°10W 197 F4
Xushui China 39°2N 115°40E 226 E8
Xuwen China 20°20N 110°10E 229 G8
Xuyi China 32°55N 118°32E 229 A12
Xuyong China 28°10N 105°22E 228 C5
Xuzhou China 34°18N 117°10E 227 G9
Xylophagou Cyprus 34°54N 33°51E 207 F9

Y

Y.S. Falls Jamaica 18°9N 77°49W 320 a
Ya Xian = Sanya China 18°14N 109°29E 236 C7
Yaamba Australia 23°8S 150°22E 280 C5
Ya'an China 29°58N 103°5E 228 C4
Yaapeet Australia 35°45S 142°3E 282 C5
Yaba Nigeria 6°30N 3°22E 124 A2
Yabassi Cameroon 4°30N 9°57E 263 E6
Yabayo Ivory C. 5°56N 6°36W 262 D3
Yabelo Ethiopia 4°50N 38°8E 257 G4
Yabelo ⌂ Ethiopia 6°0N 37°50E 257 F4
Yablanitsa Bulgaria 43°2N 24°5E 203 C8
Yablonovyy Khrebet Russia 53°0N 114°0E 215 D12
Yablonovyy Ra. = Yablonovyy Khrebet Russia 53°0N 114°0E 215 D12
Yabluniv Ukraine 48°24N 24°57E 183 B9
Yablunytsya Ukraine 48°19N 24°29E 183 B9
Yabrai Shan China 39°40N 103°0E 226 E2
Yabrūd Syria 33°58N 36°39E 250 E7
Yabucoa Puerto Rico 18°3N 65°53W 321 b
Yacambú △ Venezuela 9°42N 69°27W 328 B4
Yacheng China 18°22N 109°6E 236 C7
Yackandandah Australia 36°18S 146°52E 283 D7
Yacuiba Bolivia 22°0S 63°43W 334 A3
Yacuma → Bolivia 13°38S 65°23W 331 C4
Yadgir India 16°45N 77°5E 244 F3
Yadkin → U.S.A. 35°23N 80°4W 315 D14
Yadong China 27°26N 88°56E 241 B2
Yadrin Russia 55°57N 46°12E 190 C8
Yadua Fiji 16°49S 178°18E 287 A2
Yaeyama-Rettō Japan 24°30N 123°40E 221 M1
Yafran Libya 32°4N 12°31E 258 B2
Yafran ☐ Libya 32°0N 12°20E 258 B2
Yaftābād Iran 35°37N 51°17E 141 B1
Yagaba Ghana 10°14N 1°20W 263 C4
Yagaji-shima Japan 26°39N 128°0E 288 a
Yagasa Cluster Fiji 18°57S 178°28W 287 B3
Yağcılar Turkey 39°25N 28°23E 205 B10
Yagodnoye Russia 62°33N 149°40E 215 C15
Yagoua Cameroon 10°20N 15°13E 259 F3
Yaguas → Peru 2°45S 70°10W 328 D3
Yahara Japan 35°44N 139°37E 140 A2
Yahila Orientale, Dem. Rep. of the Congo 0°13N 24°28E 264 B4
Yahila Orientale, Dem. Rep. of the Congo 1°48N 23°37E 264 B4
Yahk Canada 49°6N 116°10W 296 D5
Yaho Japan 35°40N 139°26E 140 A1
Yahotyn Ukraine 50°17N 31°46E 189 G6
Yahuma Dem. Rep. of the Congo 1°0N 23°10E 264 B4
Yahyalı Turkey 38°5N 35°2E 212 C6
Yaita Japan 36°48N 139°56E 221 F9
Yaiza Canary Is. 28°57N 13°46W 153 e2
Yaizu Japan 34°52N 138°20E 223 C10
Yajiang China 30°2N 100°57E 228 B3
Yajua Nigeria 11°27N 12°49E 263 C7
Yakacık Turkey 36°46N 36°11E 250 B7
Yakage Japan 34°37N 133°35E 222 C5
Yakamba Dem. Rep. of the Congo 2°42N 19°38E 264 B3
Yakapınar Turkey 36°57N 35°36E 250 B6
Yakeshi China 49°17N 120°44E 219 B13
Yakima U.S.A. 46°36N 120°31W 304 C3
Yakima → U.S.A. 46°15N 119°14W 304 C4
Yakire Japan 35°45N 139°54E 140 A4
Yakishiri-Jima Japan 44°26N 141°25E 220 B10
Yako Burkina Faso 12°59N 2°15W 262 C4
Yakobi I. U.S.A. 58°0N 136°30W 296 B1
Yakoma Dem. Rep. of the Congo 4°5N 22°27E 264 B4
Yakoruda Bulgaria 42°1N 23°39E 202 D7
Yakossi C.A.R. 5°37N 23°19E 264 A4
Yakovlevka Russia 44°26N 133°28E 220 B6
Yakovlevskoye = Privolzhsk Russia 57°23N 41°16E 190 B5
Yaksu S. Korea 37°34N 127°1E 137 B2
Yaku-Shima Japan 30°20N 130°30E 221 J5
Yakumo Japan 42°15N 140°16E 220 C10
Yakutat U.S.A. 59°33N 139°44W 303 G13
Yakutat B. U.S.A. 59°45N 140°45W 303 G12
Yakutia = Sakha ☐ Russia 66°0N 130°0E 215 C14
Yakutsk Russia 62°5N 129°50E 215 C13
Yakymivka Ukraine 46°44N 35°0E 189 J8
Yala Thailand 6°33N 101°18E 237 J3
Yala △ Sri Lanka 6°20N 81°30E 245 L5
Yalata Australia 31°59S 132°26E 279 F5
Yalata ✪ Australia 31°35S 132°7E 279 F5
Yalboroo Australia 20°50S 148°40E 280 b
Yale U.S.A. 43°8N 82°48W 312 C2
Yalgorup △ Australia 32°39S 115°38E 279 F2
Yali Dem. Rep. of the Congo 0°4N 21°3E 264 B4
Yaligimba Dem. Rep. of the Congo 2°13N 22°56E 264 B4
Yalikanda Dem. Rep. of the Congo 0°23N 24°47E 264 B4
Yalinga C.A.R. 6°33N 23°10E 264 A4
Yalkabul, Pta. Mexico 21°32N 88°37W 319 C7
Yallahs Jamaica 17°53N 76°35W 320 a
Yallahs Hill Jamaica 17°54N 76°30W 320 a
Yalleroi Australia 24°3S 145°42E 280 C4
Yalobusha → U.S.A. 33°33N 90°10W 315 E9
Yaloké C.A.R. 5°19N 17°5E 264 A3
Yalong China 18°12N 109°42E 236 C7
Yalong Jiang → China 26°40N 101°55E 228 D3
Yalova Turkey 40°41N 29°15E 203 F13
Yalpirakinu ✪ Australia 22°24S 132°15E 278 D5
Yalpuh, Ozero Ukraine 45°30N 28°41E 183 E13
Yalta Ukraine 44°30N 34°10E 189 K8
Yalu Jiang → China 39°55N 124°19E 224 C2
Yalvaç Turkey 38°17N 31°10E 212 C4
Yam Australia 9°54S 142°46E 280 a
Yam Ha Melah = Dead Sea Asia 31°30N 35°30E 251 G6
Yam Kinneret Israel 32°45N 35°35E 250 F6
Yamada Fukuoka, Japan 33°33N 130°49E 222 D2
Yamada Kanagawa, Japan 35°33N 139°37E 140 B2
Yamada Ōsaka, Japan 34°47N 135°32E 133 A2
Yamaga Japan 33°1N 130°41E 222 D2
Yamagata Japan 38°15N 140°15E 220 E10
Yamagata ☐ Japan 38°30N 140°0E 220 E10
Yamagawa Japan 31°12N 130°39E 222 F2
Yamaguchi Japan 34°10N 131°32E 222 C3
Yamaguchi ☐ Japan 34°20N 131°40E 222 C3
Yamal, Poluostrov Russia 71°0N 70°0E 214 B8
Yamal Pen. = Yamal, Poluostrov Russia 71°0N 70°0E 214 B8
Yamanaka Japan 36°15N 136°22E 223 A8
Yamanashi Japan 35°41N 138°40E 223 B10
Yamanashi ☐ Japan 35°40N 138°40E 223 B10
Yamantau, Gora Russia 54°15N 58°6E 186 D10
Yamasaki Japan 35°0N 134°32E 222 C6
Yamato Japan 35°27N 139°25E 223 B11
Yamato → Japan 34°36N 135°26E 133 B1
Yamato Ridge Sea of Japan 39°20N 135°0E 220 E7
Yamatotakada Japan 34°31N 135°45E 223 C7
Yamba Australia 29°26S 153°23E 281 D5
Yambarran Ra. Australia 15°10S 130°25E 278 C5
Yambata Dem. Rep. of the Congo 2°26N 21°58E 264 B4
Yambéring Guinea 11°50N 12°18W 262 C2
Yâmbiô South Sudan 4°35N 28°16E 257 G2
Yambol Bulgaria 42°30N 26°30E 203 D10
Yambol ☐ Bulgaria 42°30N 26°30E 203 D10
Yamboyo Dem. Rep. of the Congo 0°40N 22°18E 264 B4
Yamburg Russia 68°21N 77°8E 214 C8
Yambuya Dem. Rep. of the Congo 1°17N 24°34E 264 B4
Yamdena Indonesia 7°45S 131°20E 231 F8
Yame Japan 33°13N 130°35E 222 D2
Yamethin Burma 20°29N 96°18E 241 E6
Y'Ami I. Phil. 21°6N 121°57E 232 A3
Yamma Yamma, L. Australia 26°16S 141°20E 281 D3
Yamoussoukro Ivory C. 6°49N 5°17W 262 D3
Yampa → U.S.A. 40°32N 108°59W 304 F9
Yampi Sd. Australia 16°8S 123°38E 278 C3
Yampil Moldova 48°15N 28°15E 177 D15
Yampol = Yampil Moldova 48°15N 28°15E 177 D15
Yamrat Nigeria 10°11N 9°55E 263 C6
Yamrukchal = Botev Bulgaria 42°44N 24°52E 203 D8
Yamuna → India 25°30N 81°53E 243 G9
Yamunanagar India 30°7N 77°17E 242 D7
Yamzho Yumco China 28°48N 90°35E 218 F7
Yan Nigeria 10°5N 12°11E 263 C7
Yan Kit Singapore 1°21N 103°58E 138 A3
Yan Oya → Sri Lanka 9°0N 81°10E 245 K5
Yana → Russia 71°30N 136°0E 215 B14
Yanagawa Japan 33°10N 130°24E 222 D2
Yanahara Japan 34°58N 134°2E 222 C6
Yanai Japan 33°58N 132°7E 222 D4
Yan'an China 36°35N 109°26E 226 F5
Yanaul Russia 56°25N 55°0E 186 C10
Yanbian China 26°47N 101°31E 228 D3
Yanbu China 23°5N 113°9E 121 B1
Yanbu 'al Baḩr Si. Arabia 24°0N 38°5E 246 F3
Yanchang China 36°43N 110°1E 226 F6
Yancheng Henan, China 33°35N 114°0E 226 H8
Yancheng Jiangsu, China 33°23N 120°8E 227 H11
Yanchep Australia 31°33S 115°37E 279 F2
Yanchi China 37°48N 107°20E 226 F4
Yanchuan China 36°51N 110°10E 226 F6
Yanco Australia 34°38S 146°27E 283 C7
Yanco Cr. → Australia 35°14S 145°35E 283 C6
Yandang Shan China 28°0N 120°25E 229 D13
Yandeyarra ✪ Australia 21°17S 118°24E 278 D2
Yandicoogina Australia 22°49S 119°12E 278 D2
Yandina Solomon Is. 9°7S 159°13E 287 M10
Yandja Dem. Rep. of the Congo 1°41S 17°43E 264 C3
Yandongi Dem. Rep. of the Congo 2°51N 22°16E 264 B4
Yandoon Burma 17°0N 95°40E 241 G5
Yanfeng China 25°52N 101°8E 228 E3
Yanfolila Mali 11°11N 8°9W 262 C3
Yang Xian China 33°15N 107°30E 228 A6
Yang-yang S. Korea 38°4N 128°38E 224 C4
Yang-Yang Senegal 15°30N 15°20W 262 B1
Yangambi Dem. Rep. of the Congo 0°47N 24°24E 264 B4
Yangbi China 25°41N 99°58E 228 E2
Yangcheng China 35°28N 112°22E 226 G7
Yangcheon S. Korea 37°30N 126°51E 137 B1
Yangchow = Yangzhou China 32°21N 119°26E 229 A12
Yangch'ü = Taiyuan China 37°52N 112°33E 226 F7
Yangchüan = Yangquan China 37°58N 113°31E 226 F7
Yangchun China 22°11N 111°48E 229 F8
Yangdok N. Korea 39°13N 126°38E 224 C3
Yanggang-do ☐ N. Korea 41°15N 128°0E 224 B4
Yanggao China 40°21N 113°55E 226 D7
Yanggu China 36°8N 115°43E 226 F8
Yanghuayuan China 39°49N 116°18E 114 C1
Yangiyul Uzbekistan 41°0N 69°3E 217 D7
Yangjae S. Korea 37°29N 127°2E 137 C2
Yangjiang China 21°50N 111°59E 229 G8
Yangjiazhuang China 31°22N 121°25E 138 A1
Yangjing China 31°15N 121°32E 138 B2
Yangju S. Korea 37°47N 127°7E 224 D3
Yangliuqing China 39°2N 117°5E 227 E9
Yangmei Taiwan 24°55N 121°8E 225 B3
Yangmingshan △ Taiwan 25°9N 121°32E 225 A3
Yangon = Rangoon Burma 16°45N 96°20E 241 G6
Yangonde Dem. Rep. of the Congo 0°3N 22°43E 264 B4
Yangping China 31°12N 111°25E 229 B8
Yangpingguan China 32°58N 106°5E 228 A6
Yangpu China 31°16N 121°32E 138 B2
Yangpu Park China 31°17N 121°31E 138 B2
Yangquan China 37°58N 113°31E 226 F7
Yangsan S. Korea 35°20N 129°2E 224 E4
Yangshan China 24°30N 112°40E 229 E9
Yangshuo China 24°48N 110°29E 229 E8
Yangtse = Chang Jiang → China 31°48N 121°10E 229 B13
Yangtze Kiang = Chang Jiang → China 31°48N 121°10E 229 B13
Yangudi Rassa △ Ethiopia 10°50N 40°42E 257 E5
Yangxin China 29°50N 115°12E 229 C10
Yangyuan China 40°1N 114°10E 226 D8
Yangzhong China 32°22N 119°22E 229 A12
Yangzhou China 32°21N 119°26E 229 A12
Yanhe China 28°31N 108°29E 228 C7
Yanji China 42°59N 129°30E 227 C15
Yanjin China 28°5N 104°18E 228 C5
Yanjing China 29°7N 98°33E 228 C2
Yankari △ Nigeria 9°50N 10°28E 259 G2
Yankton U.S.A. 42°53N 97°23W 308 D5
Yankunytjatjara-Antakirinja ✪ Australia 27°20S 134°30E 281 A1
Yannawa Thailand 13°43N 100°32E 113 B2
Yanonge Dem. Rep. of the Congo 0°35N 24°38E 264 B4
Yanov = Ivanava Belarus 52°7N 25°29E 177 B13
Yanqi China 42°5N 86°35E 217 D11
Yanqing China 40°30N 115°58E 226 D8

Yanshan Hebei, China 38°4N 117°22E 227 E9
Yanshan Jiangxi, China 28°15N 117°41E 229 C11
Yanshan Yunnan, China 23°35N 104°20E 228 F5
Yanshou China 45°28N 128°22E 227 B15
Yantabulla Australia 29°21S 145°0E 281 D4
Yantai China 37°34N 121°22E 227 F11
Yantarnyy Russia 54°52N 19°57E 184 D6
Yantian China 22°35N 114°16E 219 a
Yanting China 31°11N 105°24E 228 B5
Yantongshan China 43°17N 126°0E 227 C14
Yantra → Bulgaria 43°40N 25°37E 203 C9
Yanuca Fiji 18°24S 178°0E 287 B1
Yanununbeyan △ Australia 35°29S 149°24E 283 C8
Yanwa China 27°35N 98°55E 228 D2
Yanyuan China 27°25N 101°30E 228 D3
Yanzhou China 35°35N 116°49E 226 G9
Yao Chad 12°56N 17°33E 259 F3
Yao Japan 34°37N 135°36E 223 C7
Yao Noi, Ko Thailand 8°7N 98°37E 237 a
Yao Xian China 34°55N 108°59E 226 G5
Yao Yai, Ko Thailand 8°0N 98°35E 237 a
Yao'an China 25°31N 101°18E 228 E3
Yaoundé Cameroon 3°50N 11°35E 263 E7
Yaowan China 34°15N 118°3E 227 G10
Yap Pac. Oc. 9°30N 138°10E 287 R16
Yapacana △ Venezuela 3°49N 66°44W 328 C4
Yapehe Dem. Rep. of the Congo 0°13S 24°28E 264 C4
Yapei Ghana 9°10N 1°10W 263 D4
Yapen Indonesia 1°50S 136°0E 231 E9
Yapen, Selat Indonesia 1°20S 136°10E 231 E9
Yapero Indonesia 4°59S 137°11E 231 E9
Yappar → Australia 18°22S 141°16E 280 B3
Yapuparra ✪ Australia 27°15S 126°20E 279 E4
Yaqaga Fiji 16°35S 178°36E 287 A2
Yaqui → Mexico 27°37N 110°39W 318 B2
Yar-Sale Russia 66°50N 70°50E 214 C8
Yaracuy □ Venezuela 10°20N 68°45W 328 A4
Yaracuy → Venezuela 10°33N 68°15W 328 A4
Yaraka Australia 24°53S 144°3E 280 C3
Yaransk Russia 57°22N 47°49E 190 B8
Yarbasan Turkey 38°59N 28°49E 205 C10
Yardımcı Burnu Turkey 36°13N 30°25E 205 E12
Yare → U.K. 52°35N 1°38E 169 E9
Yaremcha Ukraine 48°27N 24°33E 183 B9
Yaren Nauru 0°33S 166°55E 288 H8
Yarensk Russia 62°11N 49°15E 186 B8
Yarfa Si. Arabia 24°37N 38°35E 256 C4
Yarí → Colombia 0°20S 72°20W 328 D3
Yarīm Yemen 14°20N 44°22E 248 D4
Yaritagua Venezuela 10°5N 69°8W 328 A4
Yarkand = Shache China 38°20N 77°10E 217 E9
Yarkant He → China 40°26N 80°59E 217 D10
Yarker Canada 44°23N 76°46W 313 B8
Yarkhun → Pakistan 36°17N 72°30E 243 A5
Yarlung Ziangbo Jiang = Brahmaputra → Asia 23°40N 90°35E 241 D3
Yarmouth Canada 43°50N 66°7W 299 D6
Yarmūk Iraq 33°18N 44°19E 113 B1
Yarmūk → Syria 32°42N 35°40E 250 F6
Yaroslavl Russia 57°35N 39°55E 188 D10
Yaroslavl □ Russia 59°20N 38°50E 188 C10
Yarra → Trin. & Tob. 10°48N 61°21W 323 t
Yarra Bend Park Australia 37°47S 145°0E 128 A2
Yarra Ranges △ Australia 37°40S 146°3E 283 D7
Yarra Yarra Lakes Australia 29°40S 115°45E 279 E2
Yarram Australia 38°29S 146°39E 283 E7
Yarraman Australia 26°50S 152°0E 281 D5
Yarras Australia 31°25S 152°20E 283 A10
Yarraville Australia 37°48S 144°53E 128 A1
Yarrawonga Australia 36°0S 146°0E 283 D7
Yarrie Australia 20°40S 120°12E 278 D3
Yartsevo Sib., Russia 60°20N 90°0E 215 C10
Yartsevo Smolensk, Russia 55°6N 32°43E 188 E7
Yarumal Colombia 6°58N 75°24W 328 B2
Yasa Dem. Rep. of the Congo 3°50S 21°25E 264 C4
Yasawa Fiji 16°47S 177°31E 287 A1
Yasawa Group Fiji 17°0S 177°23E 287 A1
Yaselda Belarus 52°7N 26°28E 177 B14
Yasen Ukraine 48°45N 24°10E 183 B9
Yashbum Yemen 14°19N 46°56E 248 D4
Yashi Nigeria 12°23N 7°54E 263 C6
Yashikera Nigeria 9°44N 3°29E 263 D5
Yashiro-Jima Japan 33°55N 132°15E 222 D4
Yashkul Russia 46°11N 45°21E 191 G7
Yasin Pakistan 36°24N 73°23E 243 A5
Yasinovataya Ukraine 48°7N 37°57E 189 H9
Yasinski, L. Canada 53°16N 77°35W 298 B4
Yasinya Ukraine 48°16N 24°21E 183 B9
Yasnyy Russia 51°1N 59°58E 216 B5
Yasothon Thailand 15°50N 104°10E 236 E5
Yass Australia 34°49S 148°54E 283 C8
Yasugi Japan 35°26N 133°15E 222 B5
Yāsūj Iran 30°31N 51°31E 247 D6
Yasuní △ Ecuador 1°19S 76°3W 328 D2
Yat Niger 20°28N 13°27E 259 D2
Yata → Bolivia 10°29S 65°26W 331 C4
Yata → C.A.R. 10°23N 22°45E 264 A4
Yata-Ngaya ⌂ C.A.R. 9°15N 23°25E 264 A4
Yatağan Turkey 37°20N 28°10E 205 D10
Yatakala Niger 14°50N 0°22E 263 C5
Yaté N. Cal. 22°9S 166°57E 288 d
Yates Center U.S.A. 37°53N 95°44W 308 G6
Yates Pt. N.Z. 44°29S 167°49E 285 E2
Yathkyed L. Canada 62°40N 98°0W 297 A9
Yathong Australia 32°37S 145°33E 283 B6
Yatolemu Dem. Rep. of the Congo 0°25N 24°35E 264 B4
Yatsuo Japan 36°34N 137°8E 223 A9
Yatsushiro Japan 32°30N 130°40E 222 E2
Yatsushiro-Kai Japan 32°30N 130°25E 222 E2
Yatta Plateau Kenya 2°0S 38°0E 268 C4
Yatua → Venezuela 1°30N 66°30W 328 C4
Yauca Peru 15°39S 74°35W 330 D3
Yauco Puerto Rico 18°2N 66°51W 321 b
Yauri Peru 14°47S 71°25W 330 C3
Yauya Peru 8°59S 77°17W 330 B2
Yauyos Peru 12°19S 75°50W 330 C2
Yauza → Russia 55°54N 37°43E 129 B4
Yaval India 21°10N 75°42E 244 D2
Yavarí → Peru 4°21S 70°2W 330 A3
Yávaros Mexico 26°42N 109°31W 318 B3
Yavatmal India 20°20N 78°15E 244 D4
Yavero → Peru 12°6S 72°57W 330 C3
Yavne Israel 31°52N 34°45E 251 G5
Yavoriv Ukraine 49°55N 23°20E 177 D12
Yavorov = Yavoriv Ukraine 49°55N 23°20E 177 D12
Yavuzeli Turkey 37°18N 37°24E 212 D7
Yawatahama Japan 33°27N 132°24E 222 D4
Yawnghwe Burma 20°39N 96°56E 241 E6
Yawri B. S. Leone 8°22N 13°0W 262 D2
Yaxi China 27°33N 106°41E 228 D6
Yaxian = Sanya China 18°14N 109°29E 236 C7
Yayama Dem. Rep. of the Congo 1°16S 23°7E 264 C4
Yayladağı Turkey 35°54N 36°3E 250 C7
Yazagyo Burma 23°30N 94°6E 241 D5
Yazd Iran 31°55N 54°27E 247 D7
Yazd □ Iran 32°0N 55°0E 247 D7
Yazd-e Khvāst Iran 31°31N 52°7E 247 D7
Yazdān Iran 33°30N 60°50E 240 B1
Yazıköy Turkey 36°40N 27°20E 205 E9
Yazman Pakistan 29°8N 71°45E 242 E4
Yazoo → U.S.A. 32°22N 90°54W 315 E9
Yazoo City U.S.A. 32°51N 90°25W 315 E9
Ybbs Austria 48°12N 15°4E 180 C8
Ybycuí △ Paraguay 26°5S 56°46W 334 B4
Ybytyruzú △ Paraguay 25°51S 56°11W 335 B4
Ye Burma 15°15N 97°15E 236 E1
Ye-ngan Burma 21°9N 96°27E 241 E6
Ye-u Burma 22°46N 95°26E 241 D5
Ye Xian = Laizhou China 37°8N 119°57E 227 F10
Ye Xian China 33°35N 113°25E 226 H7
Yea Australia 37°14S 145°26E 283 D6
Yeading U.K. 51°31N 0°23W 125 A1
Yebawmi Burma 25°15N 95°45E 241 C5
Yebbi-Souma Chad 21°7N 17°54E 259 D3
Yebyu Burma 14°15N 98°13E 236 E2
Yecheng China 37°54N 77°26E 217 E9
Yecheon S. Korea 36°39N 128°27E 224 D4
Yecla Spain 38°35N 1°5W 197 G3
Yécora Mexico 28°20N 108°58W 318 B3
Yedashe Burma 19°10N 96°20E 241 F6
Yedebub Biheroch Bihereseboch na Hizboch □ Ethiopia 12°0N 36°0E 257 F4
Yedigöller △ Turkey 40°55N 31°55E 212 B4
Yedikule Turkey 40°59N 28°55E 122 C1
Yedintsy = Edineţ Moldova 48°9N 27°18E 183 B12
Yedri Chad 22°25N 17°30E 259 D3
Yedseram → Nigeria 12°30N 14°5E 263 C7
Yeed Somali Rep. 4°33N 43°2E 267 D5
Yefremov Russia 53°8N 38°3E 188 F10
Yegguéba Niger 19°59N 12°52E 259 E2
Yeghegnadzor Armenia 39°44N 45°19E 213 C11
Yegorlyk → Russia 46°35N 41°57E 191 G5
Yegorlykskaya Russia 46°35N 40°35E 191 G5
Yegoryevsk Russia 55°27N 38°55E 188 E10
Yegri-Dere = Ardino Bulgaria 41°34N 25°9E 203 E9
Yegros Paraguay 26°20S 56°25W 334 B4
Yehbuah Indonesia 8°23S 114°45E 231 J17
Yehuda, Midbar Israel 31°35N 35°15E 251 G6
Yei South Sudan 4°9N 30°40E 257 G3
Yei, Nahr → South Sudan 6°15N 30°13E 257 F3
Yeji Ghana 8°13N 0°39W 263 D4
Yejmiadzin Armenia 40°12N 44°19E 191 K7
Yekaterinburg Russia 56°50N 60°30E 214 D7
Yekaterinenshtadt = Marks Russia 51°45N 46°50E 190 E8
Yekaterinodar = Krasnodar Russia 45°5N 39°0E 191 H4
Yekumbe Dem. Rep. of the Congo 1°2S 23°27E 264 C4
Yelan Russia 50°55N 43°43E 190 E6
Yelandur India 12°6N 77°0E 245 H3
Yelarbon Australia 28°33S 150°38E 281 D5
Yelatma Russia 55°0N 41°45E 190 C5
Yelcho, L. Chile 43°18S 72°18W 336 B2
Yelenovka = Sevan Armenia 40°33N 44°56E 191 K7
Yelenovskiye Karyery = Dokuchayevsk Ukraine 47°44N 37°40E 189 J9
Yelets Russia 52°40N 38°30E 189 F10
Yélimané Mali 15°9N 10°34W 262 B2
Yelin = Lingshui China 18°27N 110°0E 236 C8
Yelizavetgrad = Kirovohrad Ukraine 48°35N 32°20E 189 H7
Yelizovo Russia 53°11N 158°23E 215 D16
Yell U.K. 60°35N 1°5W 167 A7
Yell Sd. U.K. 60°33N 1°15W 167 A7
Yellamanchilli = Elamanchili India 17°33N 82°50E 244 F6
Yellandu India 17°39N 80°23E 244 F5
Yellapur India 14°58N 74°43E 245 G2
Yellareddi India 18°12N 78°2E 244 E4
Yellow = Huang He → China 37°55N 118°50E 227 F10
Yellow → U.S.A. 30°30N 87°0W 317 E3
Yellow Sea China 35°0N 123°0E 227 G12
Yellowhead Pass Canada 52°53N 118°25W 296 C5
Yellowknife Canada 62°27N 114°29W 296 A6
Yellowknife → Canada 62°31N 114°19W 296 A6
Yellowstone → U.S.A. 47°59N 103°59W 304 C12
Yellowstone △ U.S.A. 44°40N 110°30W 304 D8
Yellowstone L. U.S.A. 44°27N 110°22W 304 D8
Yelnya Russia 54°35N 33°15E 188 E7
Yelsk Belarus 51°50N 29°10E 177 C15
Yelwa Nigeria 10°49N 4°41E 263 C5
Yemanzhelinsk Russia 54°58N 61°18E 216 B6
Yemassee U.S.A. 32°41N 80°51W 316 C9
Yembongo Dem. Rep. of the Congo 3°12N 19°2E 264 B3
Yemen ■ Asia 15°0N 44°0E 248 D4
Yemin Moshe Jerusalem 123 b2
Yemmiganur India 15°44N 77°29E 245 G3
Yen Bai Vietnam 21°42N 104°52E 228 G5
Yenagoa Nigeria 4°58N 6°16E 263 E6
Yenakiyeve Ukraine 48°15N 38°15E 189 H10
Yenakiyevo = Yenakiyeve Ukraine 48°15N 38°15E 189 H10
Yenangyat Burma 21°6N 94°48E 241 E5
Yenangyaung Burma 20°30N 95°0E 241 E5
Yenanma Burma 19°46N 94°49E 241 F5
Yenbo = Yanbu 'al Baḥr Si. Arabia 24°0N 38°5E 246 F3
Yenchao Taiwan 22°46N 120°21E 225 D2
Yenda Australia 34°13S 146°14E 283 C7
Yende Millimou Guinea 8°55N 10°10W 262 D2
Yendéré Burkina Faso 10°12N 4°59W 262 C4
Yendi Ghana 9°29N 0°1W 263 D4
Yengisar China 38°56N 76°9E 217 E9
Yengo Congo 0°22N 15°29E 264 B3
Yengo △ Australia 33°0S 150°55E 283 B9
Yéni Niger 13°30N 3°1E 263 C5
Yeni Erenköy = Yialousa Cyprus 35°32N 34°10E 207 E10
Yeni-Pazar = Novi Pazar Serbia 43°12N 20°28E 202 C4
Yenice Ankara, Turkey 39°14N 32°42E 212 C5
Yenice Aydın, Turkey 37°49N 28°35E 205 D10
Yenice Çanakkale, Turkey 39°55N 27°17E 205 B9
Yenice Edirne, Turkey 40°42N 26°9E 203 F10
Yenice Kahramanmaraş, Turkey 37°0N 35°4E 250 B6
Yenice → Turkey 37°37N 35°33E 212 D6
Yenifoça Turkey 38°44N 26°51E 205 C8
Yenihisar Turkey 37°22N 27°16E 205 D9
Yenikapı Turkey 41°0N 28°56E 122 B1
Yeniköy Bursa, Turkey 40°31N 29°22E 203 F13
Yeniköy Çanakkale, Turkey 39°55N 26°10E 205 B8
Yeniköy İstanbul, Turkey 41°6N 29°3E 122 B2
Yeniköy Kütahya, Turkey 38°52N 29°17E 205 C11
Yenipazar Turkey 37°49N 28°11E 205 D10
Yenişehir Turkey 40°16N 29°38E 203 F13
Yenisey → Russia 71°50N 82°40E 214 B9
Yeniseysk Russia 58°27N 92°13E 215 D10
Yeniseyskiy Zaliv Russia 72°20N 81°0E 214 B9
Yenki = Yanji China 42°59N 129°30E 227 C15
Yenne France 45°43N 5°44E 175 C9
Yenotayevka Russia 47°15N 47°0E 191 G8
Yenpu Taiwan 22°45N 120°35E 225 D2
Yenshui Taiwan 23°19N 120°16E 225 C2
Yenyuka Russia 57°57N 121°15E 215 D13
Yeo → U.K. 51°2N 2°49W 169 G5
Yeo, L. Australia 28°0S 124°30E 279 E3
Yeo I. Canada 45°24N 81°48W 312 A3
Yeoju S. Korea 37°20N 127°35E 224 D3
Yeola India 20°2N 74°30E 244 D2
Yeon-gi S. Korea 36°35N 127°15E 224 D3
Yeoncheon S. Korea 38°5N 127°4E 224 C3
Yeong-am S. Korea 34°47N 126°42E 224 E3
Yeong-ilman S. Korea 36°4N 129°28E 224 D4
Yeong-wol S. Korea 37°11N 128°28E 224 D4
Yeong-yang S. Korea 36°39N 129°7E 224 D4
Yeongcheon S. Korea 35°58N 128°56E 224 E4
Yeongdeok S. Korea 36°24N 129°22E 224 D4
Yeongdeungpo S. Korea 37°31N 126°54E 137 B1
Yeongdong Chungcheongbuk-do, S. Korea 36°10N 127°46E 224 D3
Yeongdong Seoul, S. Korea 37°30N 127°1E 137 B2
Yeonggwang S. Korea 35°16N 126°30E 224 E3
Yeongheungdo S. Korea 37°15N 126°27E 224 D3
Yeongju S. Korea 36°50N 128°40E 224 D4
Yeongju △ S. Korea 35°45N 129°20E 224 D4
Yeosu S. Korea 34°47N 127°45E 224 E3
Yeotmal = Yavatmal India 20°20N 78°15E 244 D4
Yeouido S. Korea 37°31N 126°55E 137 B1
Yeovil U.K. 50°57N 2°38W 169 G5
Yepes Spain 39°55N 3°39W 194 F7
Yeppoon Australia 23°5S 150°47E 280 C5
Yerba Buena I. U.S.A. 37°48N 122°21W 136 B2
Yerbent Turkmenistan 39°30N 58°50E 216 E5
Yerbogachen Russia 61°16N 108°0E 215 C11
Yerevan Armenia 40°10N 44°31E 191 K7
Yerington U.S.A. 38°59N 119°10W 304 G4
Yerkesik Turkey 37°7N 28°19E 205 D10
Yerköy Turkey 39°38N 34°28E 212 C6
Yerla → India 16°50N 74°30E 244 F2
Yermo U.S.A. 34°54N 116°50W 307 L10
Yerólakkos Cyprus 35°11N 33°15E 207 E9
Yeropol Russia 65°15N 168°40E 215 C17
Yeroskipos Cyprus 34°46N 32°28E 207 F8
Yerres France 48°43N 2°30E 134 B4
Yershov Russia 51°23N 48°27E 190 E9
Yerupajá, Cerro Peru 10°16S 76°55W 330 C2
Yerushalayim = Jerusalem Israel/West Bank 31°47N 35°10E 123 B2
Yerville France 49°40N 0°53E 172 C7
Yes Tor U.K. 50°41N 4°0W 169 G4
Yesagyo Burma 21°38N 95°14E 241 E5
Yesan S. Korea 36°41N 126°51E 224 D3
Yeshin Burma 23°43N 95°6E 241 D5
Yeşikent = Erzin Turkey 36°57N 36°11E 250 B7
Yeşil → Turkey 37°20N 33°16E 250 A4
Yeşildere Turkey 37°9N 33°31E 250 A4
Yeşilhisar Turkey 38°20N 35°5E 212 C6
Yeşilırmak → Turkey 41°22N 36°37E 212 B7
Yeşilkent Turkey 36°57N 36°12E 212 D7
Yeşilköy Turkey 40°57N 28°49E 203 F12
Yeşilova Turkey 37°31N 29°46E 205 D11
Yeşilyurt Manisa, Turkey 38°22N 28°40E 205 C10
Yeşilyurt Muğla, Turkey 37°10N 28°20E 205 D10
Yeski Dzhumaya = Târgovişte Romania 44°55N 25°27E 183 F10
Yesnogorsk Russia 54°32N 37°38E 188 E9
Yeso U.S.A. 34°26N 104°37W 305 J11
Yessentuki Russia 44°5N 42°53E 191 H6
Yessey Russia 68°29N 102°10E 215 C11
Yeste Spain 38°22N 2°19W 197 G2
Yetman Australia 28°56S 150°48E 281 D5
Yetti Mauritania 26°10N 7°50W 260 C3
Yeu, Î. d' France 46°42N 2°20W 172 F4
Yevdokimovskoye = Krasnogvardeyskoye Russia 45°52N 41°33E 191 H5
Yevlakh = Yevlax Azerbaijan 40°39N 47°7E 191 K8
Yevlax Azerbaijan 40°39N 47°7E 191 K8
Yevpatoriya Ukraine 45°15N 33°20E 189 K7
Yeya → Russia 46°40N 38°40E 191 G4
Yeysk Russia 46°40N 38°12E 189 J10
Yezd = Yazd Iran 31°55N 54°27E 247 D7
Yezerishche Belarus 55°50N 30°0E 188 E5
Ygatimi Paraguay 24°5S 55°40W 335 A4
Yhati Paraguay 25°45S 56°35W 334 B4
Yhú Paraguay 25°0S 56°0W 335 B4
Yí → Uruguay 33°7S 57°8W 334 C4
Yi 'Allaq, G. Egypt 30°21N 33°31E 251 H4
Yi He → China 34°10N 118°8E 227 G10
Yi Xian Anhui, China 29°55N 117°57E 229 C11
Yi Xian Hebei, China 39°20N 115°30E 226 E8
Yi Xian Liaoning, China 41°30N 121°22E 227 D11
Yialiás → Cyprus 35°9N 33°44E 207 E9
Yialousa Cyprus 35°32N 34°10E 207 E10
Yibin China 28°45N 104°32E 228 C5
Yichang China 30°40N 111°20E 229 B8
Yicheng Henan, China 31°41N 112°12E 229 B9
Yicheng Shanxi, China 35°42N 111°40E 226 G6
Yichuan China 36°2N 110°10E 226 F6
Yichun Heilongjiang, China 47°44N 128°52E 219 B14
Yichun Jiangxi, China 27°48N 114°22E 229 D10
Yidu China 36°43N 118°28E 227 F10
Yidun China 30°22N 99°21E 228 B2
Yifag Ethiopia 12°4N 37°46E 257 E4
Yifeng China 28°22N 114°45E 229 C10
Yigo Guam 13°32N 144°53E 302 d
Yiheyuan China 39°59N 116°15E 114 B1
Yihuang China 27°30N 116°12E 229 D11
Yijun China 35°28N 109°8E 226 G5
Yılanlıkale Turkey 36°59N 35°47E 250 B6
Yıldız Dağları Turkey 41°48N 27°36E 203 E11
Yıldız Park Turkey 41°2N 29°1E 122 B2
Yıldızeli Turkey 39°51N 36°36E 212 C7
Yilehuli Shan China 51°20N 124°20E 219 A13
Yiliang Yunnan, China 27°38N 104°2E 228 D5
Yiliang Yunnan, China 24°56N 103°11E 228 E4
Yilong China 31°34N 106°23E 228 B6
Yima China 34°44N 111°53E 226 G6
Yimen China 24°40N 102°10E 228 E4
Yimianpo China 45°7N 128°2E 227 B15
Yin Xu China 36°8N 114°10E 226 F8
Yi'nan China 35°31N 118°24E 227 G10
Yinchuan China 38°30N 106°15E 226 E4
Yindaik Burma 23°35N 95°22E 241 D5
Yindarlgooda, L. Australia 30°40S 121°52E 279 F3
Yindjibarndi ✪ Australia 22°0S 118°35E 278 D2
Ying He → China 32°30N 116°30E 226 H9
Ying Xian China 39°32N 113°10E 226 E7
Yingcheng China 30°56N 113°35E 229 B9
Yingde China 24°10N 113°25E 229 E9
Yingjiang China 24°41N 97°55E 228 E1
Yingjing China 29°41N 102°52E 228 C4
Yingkou China 40°37N 122°18E 224 B1
Yingkow = Yingkou China 40°37N 122°18E 224 B1
Yingpanshui China 37°26N 104°18E 226 F3
Yingshan Hubei, China 30°41N 115°32E 229 B10
Yingshan Sichuan, China 31°4N 106°35E 228 B6
Yingshang China 32°38N 116°12E 229 A11
Yingtan China 28°12N 117°0E 229 C11
Yingualyalya ✪ Australia 18°49S 129°12E 278 C4
Yinhangzhen China 31°20N 121°31E 138 A2
Yining China 43°58N 81°10E 217 D10
Yiningarra ✪ Australia 20°53S 129°27E 278 D4
Yinjiang China 28°1N 108°21E 228 C7
Yinmabin Burma 22°10N 94°55E 241 D5
Yioúra = Giaros Greece 37°32N 24°40E 204 D6
Yipinglang China 25°10N 101°52E 228 E3
Yirba Muda Ethiopia 6°12N 38°42E 257 F4
Yirga Alem Ethiopia 6°48N 38°22E 257 F4
Yirol South Sudan 6°33N 30°30E 257 F3
Yirrkala Australia 12°14S 136°56E 280 A2
Yishan China 24°28N 108°38E 228 E7
Yishui China 35°47N 118°30E 227 G10
Yishun Singapore 1°26N 103°51E 138 A3
Yitong China 43°13N 125°20E 227 C13
Yiwu China 29°20N 120°3E 229 C13
Yixing China 31°21N 119°48E 229 B12
Yiyang Henan, China 34°27N 112°10E 226 G7
Yiyang Hunan, China 28°35N 112°18E 229 C9
Yiyang Jiangxi, China 28°22N 117°20E 229 C11
Yizhang China 25°27N 112°57E 229 E9
Yizheng China 32°18N 119°10E 229 A12
Ylästö Finland 60°17N 24°54E 121 B2
Yli-Kitka Finland 66°8N 28°30E 160 C23
Yliki, L. Greece 38°24N 23°15E 204 C5
Ylitornio Finland 66°19N 23°39E 160 C20
Ylivieska Finland 64°4N 24°28E 160 D21
Ymer Ø Greenland 73°9N 24°20W 154 C8
Yngaren Sweden 58°50N 16°35E 163 F10
Yoakum U.S.A. 29°17N 97°9W 314 G6
Yob ⌂ Eritrea 17°15N 37°50E 257 D4
Yobe □ Nigeria 12°0N 11°30E 263 C7
Yoboki Djibouti 11°30N 42°6E 267 B5
Yobuko Japan 33°32N 129°54E 222 D1
Yodo → Japan 34°45N 135°35E 133 A2
Yog Pt. Phil. 14°6N 124°12E 232 D5
Yoğuntaş Turkey 41°50N 27°4E 203 E11
Yogyakarta Indonesia 7°49S 110°22E 235 D4
Yogyakarta □ Indonesia 7°48S 110°22E 235 D4
Yoho △ Canada 51°25N 116°30W 296 C5
Yojoa, L. de Honduras 14°53N 88°0W 320 D2
Yok Don △ Vietnam 12°50N 107°40E 236 F6
Yokadouma Cameroon 3°26N 14°55E 264 B2
Yōkaichi Japan 35°6N 136°12E 223 B8
Yōkaichiba Japan 35°42N 140°33E 223 B12
Yokkaichi Japan 34°55N 136°38E 223 C8
Yoko Cameroon 5°32N 12°20E 263 D7
Yokohama Japan 35°27N 139°28E 223 B11
Yokosuka Japan 35°20N 139°40E 223 B11
Yokote Japan 39°20N 140°30E 220 E10
Yola Nigeria 9°10N 12°29E 263 D7
Yolaina, Cordillera de Nic. 11°30N 84°0W 320 D3
Yolombo Dem. Rep. of the Congo 1°36S 23°12E 264 C4
Yólöten Turkmenistan 37°18N 62°21E 247 B9
Yom → Thailand 15°35N 100°1E 236 E3
Yombi Gabon 1°26S 10°37E 264 C2
Yona Guam 13°25N 144°46E 302 d
Yonago Japan 35°25N 133°19E 222 B5
Yonaguni-Jima Japan 24°27N 123°0E 221 M1
Yonaha-Dake Japan 26°43N 128°13E 288 a
Yŏnan N. Korea 37°55N 126°11E 224 D3
Yonezawa Japan 37°57N 140°4E 220 F10
Yong-in S. Korea 37°14N 127°12E 224 D3
Yong Peng Malaysia 2°0N 103°3E 237 M4
Yong Sata Thailand 7°8N 99°41E 237 J2
Yongama Dem. Rep. of the Congo 0°2N 24°35E 264 B4
Yongamp'o N. Korea 39°56N 124°23E 224 C2
Yong'an China 25°59N 117°25E 229 E11
Yongchang China 38°17N 102°7E 218 D9
Yongcheng China 33°55N 116°20E 226 H9
Yongchuan China 29°17N 105°55E 228 C5
Yongchun China 25°16N 118°20E 229 E12
Yongde China 24°5N 99°25E 228 E2
Yongdeng China 36°38N 103°25E 226 F2
Yongding China 24°43N 116°45E 229 E11
Yongdingman China 39°50N 116°20E 114 B2
Yonge Street Toronto Canada 141 b3
Yongfeng China 27°20N 115°22E 229 D10
Yongfu China 24°59N 109°59E 228 E7
Yongfucun China 23°8N 113°17E 121 B2
Yonggyap Pass India 29°17N 95°37E 241 A5
Yonghe China 36°46N 110°38E 226 F6
Yonghong India 26°28N 94°58E 241 B5
Yŏnghŭng N. Korea 39°31N 127°18E 224 C3
Yŏnghŭng-man N. Korea 39°14N 127°30E 224 C3
Yongji Jilin, China 43°33N 126°13E 227 C14
Yongji Shanxi, China 34°52N 110°28E 226 G6
Yongjia China 28°10N 120°45E 229 C13
Yongkang Yunnan, China 24°9N 99°20E 228 E2
Yongkang Zhejiang, China 28°55N 120°2E 229 C13
Yongnian China 36°47N 114°29E 226 F8
Yongning Guangxi Zhuangzu, China 22°44N 108°28E 228 F7
Yongning Ningxia Huizu, China 38°15N 106°14E 226 E4
Yongping China 25°27N 99°38E 228 E2
Yongren China 26°4N 101°40E 228 D3
Yongsan S. Korea 37°32N 126°58E 137 B1
Yongshan China 28°11N 103°35E 228 C4
Yongsheng China 26°38N 100°46E 228 D3
Yongshun China 29°2N 109°51E 228 C7
Yongtai China 25°49N 118°58E 229 E12
Yongxin = Jinggangshan China 26°58N 114°15E 229 D10
Yongxing China 26°9N 113°8E 229 D9
Yongxiu China 29°2N 115°42E 229 C10
Yongzhou China 26°17N 111°37E 229 D8
Yonibana S. Leone 8°30N 12°19W 262 D2
Yonkers U.S.A. 40°56N 73°52W 132 A2
Yonne □ France 47°50N 3°40E 173 E10
Yonne → France 48°23N 2°58E 173 D9
Yopal Colombia 5°21N 72°23W 328 B3
York W. Austral., Australia 31°52S 116°47E 279 F2
York Ont., Canada 43°40N 79°26W 141 A2
York York, U.K. 53°58N 1°6W 168 D6
York Ala., U.S.A. 32°29N 88°18W 315 E10
York Nebr., U.S.A. 40°52N 97°36W 308 E5
York Pa., U.S.A. 39°58N 76°44W 309 F15
York, C. Australia 10°42S 142°31E 286 F2
York, City of □ U.K. 53°58N 1°6W 168 D6
York, Kap Greenland 75°55N 66°25W 154 B4
York, Vale of U.K. 54°15N 1°25W 168 C6
York I. Antigua & B. 17°2N 61°40W 322 b
York Mills Canada 43°45N 79°22W 141 A2
York Sd. Australia 15°0S 125°5E 278 C4
York Univ. Canada 43°43N 79°22W 141 A1
Yorke Pen. Australia 34°50S 137°40E 282 C2
Yorketown Australia 35°2S 137°33E 282 C2
Yorkshire Dales △ U.K. 54°12N 2°10W 168 C5
Yorkshire Wolds U.K. 54°8N 0°31W 168 C7
Yorkton Canada 51°11N 102°28W 297 C8
Yorkville Calif., U.S.A. 38°52N 123°13W 306 G3
Yorkville Ga., U.S.A. 33°55N 84°58W 316 B5
Yorkville Ill., U.S.A. 41°38N 88°27W 311 C8
Yoro Honduras 15°9N 87°7W 320 C2
Yoron-Jima Japan 27°2N 128°26E 221 L4
Yorosso Mali 12°17N 4°55W 262 C4
Yos Sudarso, Pulau = Dolak, Pulau Indonesia 8°0S 138°30E 231 F9
Yosemite △ U.S.A. 37°45N 119°40W 306 H7
Yosemite Village U.S.A. 37°45N 119°35W 306 H7
Yoshida Japan 34°40N 132°42E 222 C4
Yoshimatsu Japan 32°0N 130°47E 222 F2
Yoshino-Kumano △ Japan 34°12N 135°55E 223 C7
Yoshkar Ola Russia 56°38N 47°55E 190 B8
Yotala Bolivia 19°10S 65°17W 331 D4
Yotsuya Tokyo, Japan 140 a2
Yotvata Israel 29°55N 35°2E 251 J6
You Jiang → China 22°50N 108°6E 228 F6
You Xian China 27°1N 113°17E 229 D9
You'anmen China 39°51N 116°19E 114 B1
Youbou Canada 48°53N 124°13W 306 B2
Youghal Ireland 51°56N 7°52W 166 E4
Youghal B. Ireland 51°55N 7°49W 166 E4
Youkounkoun Guinea 12°35N 13°11W 262 C2
Young N.S.W., Australia 34°19S 148°18E 283 C8
Young Sask., Canada 51°47N 105°45W 297 C7
Young Uruguay 32°44S 57°36W 334 C4
Young I. Antarctica 66°25S 162°24E 151 C11
Young Ra. N.Z. 44°10S 169°30E 285 E4
Younghusband, L. Australia 30°50S 136°5E 282 A2
Younghusband Pen. Australia 36°0S 139°25E 282 D3
Youngsfield S. Africa 34°0S 18°30E 118 B1
Youngstown Alta., Canada 51°35N 111°10W 297 C6
Youngstown Fla., U.S.A. 30°22N 85°26W 316 E4
Youngstown N.Y., U.S.A. 43°15N 79°3W 312 C5
Youngstown Ohio, U.S.A. 41°6N 80°39W 312 E4
Youngsville U.S.A. 41°51N 79°19W 312 E5
Youngwood U.S.A. 40°14N 79°34W 312 F5
Youssoufia Morocco 32°16N 8°31W 260 B3
Youxi China 26°10N 118°13E 229 D12
Youyang China 28°47N 108°42E 228 C7
Youyu China 40°10N 112°20E 226 D7
Yozgat Turkey 39°51N 34°47E 212 C6
Yozgat □ Turkey 39°30N 35°0E 212 C6
Ypacaraí △ Paraguay 25°18S 57°19W 334 B4
Ypané → Paraguay 23°29S 57°19W 334 A4
Yport France 49°45N 0°15E 172 C7
Ypres = Ieper Belgium 50°51N 2°53E 170 D2
Ypsilanti U.S.A. 42°14N 83°37W 311 B13
Yreka U.S.A. 41°44N 122°38W 304 F2
Yrghyz Kazakhstan 48°37N 61°16E 216 C6
Yrghyz → Kazakhstan 48°6N 62°30E 216 C6
Ysabel Chan. Papua N. G. 2°0S 150°0E 286 B6
Yssingeaux France 45°9N 4°8E 175 C8
Ystabøhamn Norway 59°3N 5°23E 164 E2
Ystad Sweden 55°26N 13°50E 163 J7
Ysyk-Köl = Balykchy Kyrgyzstan 42°26N 76°12E 217 D9
Ysyk-Köl Kyrgyzstan 42°25N 77°15E 217 D9
Ysyk-Köl □ Kyrgyzstan 42°0N 78°0E 217 D9
Ythan → U.K. 57°19N 1°59W 167 D7
Ytre Arna Norway 60°27N 5°25E 164 D2
Ytre Enebakk Norway 59°44N 11°0E 164 E8
Ytre Rendal Norway 61°46N 11°8E 164 C8
Ytteran Sweden 63°16N 14°7E 162 A8
Ytterhogdal Sweden 62°12N 14°56E 162 B8
Yttermalung Sweden 60°35N 13°51E 162 D7
Ytyk-Kyuyel Russia 62°30N 133°45E 215 C14
Yu Jiang → China 23°22N 110°3E 228 F7
Yü Shan Taiwan 23°25N 120°52E 225 C2
Yü Shan △ Taiwan 24°45N 121°12E 225 C3
Yu Xian = Yuzhou China 34°10N 113°28E 226 G7
Yu Xian Hebei, China 39°50N 114°35E 226 E8
Yu Xian Shanxi, China 38°5N 113°20E 226 E7
Yuan Jiang → Hunan, China 28°55N 111°50E 229 C8
Yuan Jiang → Yunnan, China 22°20N 103°59E 228 F4
Yuan'an China 31°3N 111°34E 229 B8
Yüanch'ang Taiwan 23°39N 120°18E 225 C2
Yuanjiang Hunan, China 28°47N 112°21E 229 C9
Yuanjiang Yunnan, China 23°32N 102°0E 228 F4
Yüanli Taiwan 24°27N 120°39E 225 B2
Yüanlin Taiwan 23°58N 120°30E 225 C2
Yuanling China 28°29N 110°22E 229 C8
Yuanmingyuan Park China 40°0N 116°17E 114 A1
Yuanmou China 25°42N 101°53E 228 E3
Yuanping China 38°42N 112°46E 226 E7
Yuanqu China 35°18N 111°40E 226 G6
Yuanshan Taiwan 24°45N 121°43E 225 B3
Yuanxiatian China 23°12N 113°17E 121 A2
Yuanyang Henan, China 35°3N 113°58E 226 G7
Yuanyang Yunnan, China 23°10N 102°43E 228 F4
Yuat → Papua N. G. 4°10S 143°52E 286 C2
Yuba → U.S.A. 39°8N 121°36W 306 F5
Yuba City U.S.A. 39°8N 121°37W 306 F5
Yūbari Japan 43°4N 141°59E 220 C10
Yubdo Ethiopia 8°58N 35°24E 257 F4
Yūbetsu Japan 44°13N 143°50E 220 B11
Yucatán □ Mexico 20°50N 89°0W 319 C7
Yucatán, Canal de Caribbean 22°0N 86°30W 320 B2
Yucatán, Península de Mexico 19°30N 89°0W 292 H11
Yucatan Basin Cent. Amer. 19°0N 86°0W 320 C3
Yucatan Channel = Yucatán, Canal de Caribbean 22°0N 86°30W 320 B2
Yucca U.S.A. 34°52N 114°9W 307 L12
Yucca Valley U.S.A. 34°8N 116°27W 307 L10
Yucheng China 36°55N 116°32E 226 F9
Yüch'ih Taiwan 23°54N 120°56E 225 C2
Yuching Taiwan 23°7N 120°27E 225 C2
Yuci = Jinzhong China 37°42N 112°46E 226 F7
Yudu China 25°59N 115°30E 229 E10
Yuechi China 30°34N 106°25E 228 B6
Yuen Long China 22°26N 114°2E 219 a
Yuendumu Australia 22°16S 131°49E 278 D5
Yuendumu ✪ Australia 22°21S 131°40E 278 D5
Yueqing China 28°9N 120°59E 229 C13
Yueqing Wan China 28°5N 121°20E 229 D13
Yuexi Anhui, China 30°50N 116°20E 229 B11
Yuexi Sichuan, China 28°37N 102°26E 228 C4
Yuexiu China 23°8N 113°16E 121 B2
Yuexiu Park China 23°8N 113°16E 121 B2
Yueyang China 29°21N 113°5E 229 C9
Yufu-Dake Japan 33°17N 131°33E 222 D3
Yugan China 28°43N 116°37E 229 C11
Yuğluk Dağı Turkey 36°59N 33°50E 250 B4
Yugo-Zarad Russia 55°40N 37°30E 129 B3
Yugorenok Russia 59°47N 137°40E 215 D14
Yuhalixqui, Volcan Mexico 19°19N 99°4W 128 C2
Yuhuan China 28°9N 121°12E 229 C13
Yühuan Dao China 28°5N 121°15E 229 C13
Yujiang China 28°10N 116°43E 229 C11
Yukhnov Russia 54°44N 35°15E 188 E8
Yūki Japan 36°18N 139°53E 223 A11
Yukon U.S.A. 35°31N 97°45W 314 D6
Yukon → U.S.A. 62°32N 163°54W 303 E7
Yukon-Charley Rivers ⌂ U.S.A. 65°15N 144°0W 303 D12
Yukon Delta Nat. Wildlife Refuge ⌂ U.S.A. 61°0N 163°0W 303 F7
Yukon Flats U.S.A. 66°40N 145°45W 303 C11
Yukon Territory □ Canada 63°0N 135°0W 294 E5
Yüksekova Turkey 37°34N 44°16E 213 D11
Yukta Russia 63°26N 105°42E 215 C11
Yukuhashi Japan 33°44N 130°59E 222 D2
Yulara Australia 25°10S 130°55E 279 E5
Yule → Australia 20°41S 118°17E 278 D2
Yuleba Australia 26°37S 149°24E 281 D4
Yulee U.S.A. 30°38N 81°36W 316 E8
Yuli China 41°19N 86°15E 217 D11
Yuli Nigeria 9°44N 10°12E 263 D7
Yüli Taiwan 23°20N 121°18E 225 C3
Yulin Guangxi Zhuangzu, China 22°40N 110°8E 229 F8
Yulin Hainan, China 18°10N 109°31E 236 C7
Yulin Shaanxi, China 38°20N 109°30E 226 E5
Yulong Xueshan China 27°6N 100°10E 228 D3
Yuma Ariz., U.S.A. 32°43N 114°37W 307 N12
Yuma Colo., U.S.A. 40°8N 102°43W 304 F12
Yuma, B. de Dom. Rep. 18°20N 68°35W 321 C6
Yumali Australia 35°32S 139°45E 282 C3
Yumbe Uganda 3°28N 31°15E 268 B3
Yumbi Équateur, Dem. Rep. of the Congo 1°53S 16°34E 264 C3
Yumbi Maniema, Dem. Rep. of the Congo 1°12S 26°15E 268 C2
Yumbo Colombia 3°35N 76°28W 328 C2
Yumen China 39°50N 97°30E 218 D8
Yumurtalık Turkey 36°45N 35°48E 250 B6
Yun Gui Gaoyuan China 26°0N 104°0E 228 E3
Yun Ling Shan China 27°0N 99°20E 228 D2
Yun Xian Hubei, China 32°50N 110°46E 226 H6
Yun Xian Yunnan, China 24°27N 100°8E 228 E3
Yuna Australia 28°20S 115°0E 279 E2
Yunak Turkey 38°49N 31°43E 212 C4
Yunan China 23°12N 111°30E 229 F8
Yunaska I. U.S.A. 52°38N 170°40W 303 K5
Yuncheng Henan, China 35°36N 115°57E 226 G8
Yuncheng Shanxi, China 35°2N 111°0E 226 G6
Yunfu China 22°50N 112°5E 229 F9
Yung Shue Wan China 22°13N 114°6E 122 B1
Yungan Taiwan 22°49N 120°12E 225 D2
Yungang Shiku China 40°5N 113°0E 226 D7
Yungas Bolivia 17°0S 66°0W 331 D4
Yungay Chile 37°10S 72°5W 334 D1
Yungay Peru 9°2S 77°45W 330 B2
Yungk'ang Taiwan 23°2N 120°15E 225 C2
Yungki = Jilin China 43°44N 126°30E 227 C14
Yungning = Nanning China 22°48N 108°20E 228 F7
Yunhe China 28°8N 119°33E 229 C12
Yunkai Dashan China 22°30N 111°0E 229 F8
Yunkanjini ✪ Australia 22°33S 131°6E 278 D5
Yünlin □ Taiwan 23°40N 120°20E 225 C2
Yunling Shan China 28°30N 98°50E 218 F8
Yunlong China 25°57N 99°13E 228 E2
Yunmeng China 31°2N 113°43E 229 B9
Yunnan □ China 25°0N 102°0E 228 E4
Yunotsu Japan 35°5N 132°21E 222 B4
Yunquera de Henares Spain 40°47N 3°11W 196 E1
Yunshui Taiwan 23°23N 120°31E 225 C2
Yunt Dağı Turkey 38°56N 27°13E 205 C9
Yunta Australia 32°34S 139°36E 281 E2
Yunxi China 33°0N 110°22E 226 H6
Yunxiao China 23°59N 117°18E 229 F11
Yunyang Chongqing, China 31°2N 108°51E 228 B7
Yunyang Henan, China 33°26N 112°42E 229 A9
Yupanqui Basin Pac. Oc. 19°0S 101°0W 289 J17
Yuping China 27°13N 108°56E 228 D7
Yupukarri Guyana 3°45N 59°20W 329 C6
Yuqing China 27°13N 107°53E 228 D6
Yuraygir △ Australia 29°45S 153°15E 281 D5
Yurga Russia 55°42N 84°51E 214 D9
Yurimaguas Peru 5°55S 76°7W 330 B2
Yurkiyka Ukraine 48°42N 28°35E 183 B13
Yurungkax He → China 38°5N 80°34E 217 E10
Yuryev = Tartu Estonia 58°20N 26°44E 188 C4
Yuryev-Polskiy Russia 56°30N 39°40E 188 D10
Yuryevets Russia 57°25N 43°2E 190 B6
Yuscarán Honduras 13°58N 86°45W 320 D2
Yûsef, Bahr → Egypt 28°25N 30°35E 256 B3
Yushan China 28°42N 118°10E 229 C12
Yushanzhen China 29°28N 108°22E 228 C7
Yushe China 37°4N 112°58E 226 F7
Yushu Jilin, China 44°43N 126°38E 227 B14
Yushu Qinghai, China 33°5N 96°55E 218 E8
Yūsofābād Iran 35°43N 51°24E 141 A2
Yusufeli Turkey 40°50N 41°33E 213 B9
Yutai China 35°0N 116°45E 226 G9
Yutian Hebei, China 39°53N 117°45E 227 E9
Yutian Sinkiang-Uigur, China 36°52N 81°42E 217 E10
Yütze = Jinzhong China 37°42N 112°46E 226 F7
Yüweng Tao Taiwan 23°36N 119°30E 225 C1
Yuxarı Qarabağ = Nagorno-Karabakh □ Azerbaijan 39°55N 46°45E 213 C12
Yuxi China 24°30N 102°35E 228 E4
Yuyao China 30°3N 121°10E 229 B13
Yuzawa Japan 39°10N 140°30E 220 E10
Yuzha Russia 56°34N 42°1E 190 B6
Yuzhno-Kurilsk Russia 44°1N 145°51E 215 E15
Yuzhno-Sakhalinsk Russia 46°58N 142°45E 219 B17
Yuzhno-Sukhokumsk Russia 44°40N 45°35E 191 H7
Yuzhnouralsk Russia 54°26N 61°15E 216 B6
Yuzhnyy □ Russia 44°0N 40°0E 191 H6
Yuzhou China 34°10N 113°28E 226 G7
Yuzovka = Donetsk Ukraine 48°0N 37°45E 189 J9
Yvelines □ France 48°40N 1°45E 173 D8
Yverdon-les-Bains Switz. 46°47N 6°39E 179 J2
Yvetot France 49°37N 0°44E 172 C7
Yzeure France 46°33N 3°22E 173 F10

Z

Zaandam Neths. 52°26N 4°49E 112 A1
Zaandijk Neths. 52°28N 4°49E 112 A1
Zaanstad Neths. 52°27N 4°50E 112 A1
Zab, Monts du Algeria 34°55N 5°0E 261 B6
Zāb al Kabīr → Iraq 36°1N 43°24E 213 D10
Zāb aş Şaghīr → Iraq 35°17N 43°29E 213 E10
Žabalj Serbia 45°21N 20°5E 182 E5
Žabari Serbia 44°22N 21°15E 202 B5
Zabarjad Egypt 23°40N 36°12E 256 C4
Zabaykalsk Russia 49°40N 117°25E 215 E12
Zabbar Malta 35°53N 14°32E 206 F8
Záběhlice Czech Rep. 50°3N 14°29E 135 B2
Zabīd Yemen 14°0N 43°10E 248 D3
Zabīd, W. → Yemen 14°7N 43°6E 248 D3
Zabki Poland 52°17N 21°6E 142 B2
Ząbkowice Śląskie Poland 50°35N 16°50E 185 H3
Žabljak Montenegro 43°18N 19°5E 202 C3
Zabłudów Poland 53°0N 23°19E 185 F9
Żabno Poland 50°9N 20°53E 185 H7
Zabol Iran 31°0N 61°32E 247 D9
Zābol □ Afghan. 32°0N 67°0E 240 C2
Zābolī Iran 27°10N 61°35E 247 E9
Zabolotiv Ukraine 48°28N 25°18E 183 B10
Zabolottya Ukraine 51°38N 24°16E 185 G11
Zabré Burkina Faso 11°12N 0°36W 263 C4
Zábřeh Czech Rep. 49°53N 16°52E 181 B9
Zabrze Poland 50°18N 18°50E 185 H5
Zabuzhzhya Ukraine 51°21N 23°42E 185 G10
Zabzuga Ghana 9°20N 0°30E 263 D5
Zacapa Guatemala 14°59N 89°31W 320 D2
Zacapu Mexico 19°50N 101°43W 318 D4
Zacatecas Mexico 22°47N 102°35W 318 C4
Zacatecas □ Mexico 23°0N 103°0W 318 C4
Zacatecoluca El Salv. 13°29N 88°51W 320 D2
Zacharo Greece 37°30N 21°39E 204 D3
Zachary U.S.A. 30°39N 91°9W 314 F9
Zachodnio-Pomorskie □ Poland 53°40N 15°50E 184 E2
Żacisze Poland 52°17N 21°4E 142 B2
Zacoalco de Torres Mexico 20°14N 103°35W 318 C4

Zacualtipán *Mexico* 20°39N 98°36W 319 C5
Zadar *Croatia* 44°8N 15°14E 199 D12
Zadawa *Nigeria* 11°33N 10°19E 263 C7
Zadetkyi Kyun *Burma* 10°0N 98°25E 237 G2
Zadonsk *Russia* 52°25N 38°56E 189 F10
Zafarqand *Iran* 33°11N 52°29E 247 C7
Zafra *Spain* 38°26N 6°30W 195 G4
Żagań *Poland* 51°39N 15°22E 185 G2
Zagaoua *Chad* 16°0N 21°10E 259 E4
Žagarė *Lithuania* 56°21N 23°15E 184 B10
Zagazig *Egypt* 30°40N 31°30E 256 H7
Zāgheh *Iran* 33°30N 48°42E 247 C6
Zaghouan *Tunisia* 36°23N 10°10E 258 A2
Zaghouan □ *Tunisia* 36°20N 10°0E 261 A7
Zaglou *Algeria* 27°17N 0°3W 261 C4
Zagnanado *Benin* 7°18N 2°28E 263 D5
Zagora *Greece* 39°27N 23°6E 204 B5
Zagora *Morocco* 30°22N 5°51W 260 B3
Zagorje *Slovenia* 46°8N 15°0E 199 B11
Zagórów *Poland* 52°10N 17°54E 185 F4
Zagorsk = Sergiyev Posad *Russia* 56°20N 38°10E 188 D10
Zagorsky = Krasnozavodsk *Russia* 56°27N 38°25E 188 D10
Zagórz *Poland* 49°30N 22°14E 185 J9
Zagreb *Croatia* 45°50N 15°58E 199 C12
Zagreb ✈ (ZAG) *Croatia* 45°45N 16°4E 199 C13
Zāgros, Kūhhā-ye *Iran* 33°45N 48°5E 247 C6
Zagros Mts. = Zāgros, Kūhhā-ye *Iran* 33°45N 48°5E 247 C6
Žagubica *Serbia* 44°15N 21°47E 202 B5
Zaguinaso *Ivory C.* 10°1N 6°14W 262 C3
Zagyva → *Hungary* 47°5N 20°4E 182 C5
Zahamena ⌓ *Madag.* 17°37S 48°49E 272 B2
Zāhedān *Fārs, Iran* 28°46N 53°52E 247 D7
Zāhedān *Sīstān va Balūchestān, Iran* 29°30N 60°50E 247 D9
Zahirabad *India* 17°43N 77°37E 244 F3
Zahlah *Lebanon* 33°52N 35°50E 250 E6
Zahna *Germany* 51°55N 12°49E 178 D8
Záhony *Hungary* 48°25N 22°11E 182 B7
Zahrā *Iraq* 33°22N 44°19E 113 A1
Ẓahrān *Si. Arabia* 17°40N 43°30E 248 C3
Zainsk *Russia* 55°18N 52°4E 190 C11
Zaïre = Congo → *Africa* 6°4S 12°24E 265 D2
Zaïre = Congo, Dem. Rep. of the ■ *Africa* 3°0S 23°0E 265 C4
Zaire □ *Angola* 7°0S 14°0E 265 D2
Zaječar *Serbia* 43°53N 22°18E 202 C6
Zaka *Zimbabwe* 20°20S 31°29E 271 B5
Zakamensk *Russia* 50°23N 103°17E 215 D11
Zakani *Dem. Rep. of the Congo* 2°33N 23°16E 264 B4
Zakarpattya □ *Ukraine* 48°20N 23°20E 183 B8
Zakataly = Zaqatala *Azerbaijan* 41°38N 46°35E 191 K8
Zakbayemé *Cameroon* 4°2N 10°34E 264 B2
Zakharkovo *Russia* 55°46N 37°18E 129 B1
Zakhodnaya Dzvina = Daugava → *Latvia* 57°4N 24°3E 188 D3
Zākhū *Iraq* 37°10N 42°50E 213 D10
Zakinthos = Zakynthos *Greece* 37°47N 20°54E 207 D2
Zakinthos, Diavlos *Greece* 37°50N 21°0E 207 D2
Zakopane *Poland* 49°18N 19°57E 185 J6
Zakouma *Chad* 10°54N 19°49E 259 F3
Zakouma △ *Chad* 10°52N 19°45E 259 F3
Zakroczym *Poland* 52°26N 20°38E 185 F7
Zakros *Greece* 35°6N 26°10E 207 E7
Zakynthos *Greece* 37°47N 20°54E 207 D2
Zakynthos □ *Greece* 37°47N 20°57E 204 D2
Zakynthos ✈ (ZTH) *Greece* 37°45N 20°50E 207 D2
Zala *Angola* 7°52S 13°42E 265 D2
Zala *Ethiopia* 6°28N 37°13E 257 F4
Zala □ *Hungary* 46°42N 16°50E 182 D1
Zala → *Hungary* 46°43N 17°16E 182 D2
Zalaegerszeg *Hungary* 46°53N 16°47E 182 D1
Zalakomár *Hungary* 46°33N 17°10E 182 D2
Zalalövő *Hungary* 46°51N 16°35E 182 D1
Zalamea de la Serena *Spain* 38°40N 5°38W 195 G5
Zalamea la Real *Spain* 37°41N 6°38W 195 H4
Zalantun *China* 48°0N 122°43E 219 B13
Zalari *Russia* 53°33N 102°30E 215 D11
Zalău *Romania* 47°12N 23°3E 182 C8
Žalec *Slovenia* 46°16N 15°10E 199 B12
Zaleshchiki = Zalishchyky *Ukraine* 48°45N 25°45E 183 B10
Zalesye *Russia* 54°50N 21°31E 184 D8
Zalew Wiślany *Poland* 54°20N 19°50E 184 D6
Zalewo *Poland* 53°50N 19°41E 184 E6
Ẓalīm *Si. Arabia* 22°43N 42°10E 248 B3
Zalingei *Sudan* 12°51N 23°29E 259 F4
Zalishchyky *Ukraine* 48°45N 25°45E 183 B10
Zalmah, J. az *Libya* 25°30N 24°40E 258 C4
Žalov *Czech Rep.* 50°10N 14°22E 135 A2
Zalṭan *Ajdābiyā, Libya* 28°51N 19°52E 258 C3
Zalṭan *Zuwārah, Libya* 32°57N 11°52E 258 B2
Zalṭan, Jabal *Libya* 28°46N 19°45E 258 C3
Zalun *Burma* 17°29N 95°34E 241 G5
Załuski *Poland* 52°9N 20°55E 142 C1
Zama L. *Canada* 58°45N 119°5W 296 B5
Zambales □ *Phil.* 15°20N 120°10E 232 D3
Zambales Mts. *Phil.* 15°45N 120°5E 232 D3
Zambeke *Dem. Rep. of the Congo* 2°8N 25°17E 268 B2
Zambeze → *Africa* 18°35S 36°20E 269 F4
Zambezi = Zambeze → *Africa* 18°35S 36°20E 269 F4
Zambezi *Zambia* 13°30S 23°15E 265 E4
Zambezi △ *Zimbabwe* 17°54S 25°41E 269 F2
Zambezia □ *Mozam.* 16°15S 37°30E 269 F4
Zambia ■ *Africa* 15°0S 28°0E 269 F2
Zamboanga *Phil.* 6°59N 122°3E 233 H4
Zamboanga del Norte □ *Phil.* 8°0N 123°0E 233 G4
Zamboanga del Sur □ *Phil.* 7°40N 123°0E 233 H4
Zamboanga Pen. *Phil.* 7°32N 122°16E 233 H4
Zamboanguita *Phil.* 9°6N 123°11E 233 G4
Zambrano *Colombia* 9°45N 74°49W 328 B3
Zambrów *Poland* 52°59N 22°14E 185 F9
Zamdorf *Germany* 48°8N 11°35E 131 B2
Zametchino *Russia* 53°30N 42°30E 190 D6
Zamfara □ *Nigeria* 12°10N 6°0E 263 C6
Zamfara → *Nigeria* 12°5N 4°2E 263 C5
Zamora *Ecuador* 4°4S 78°58W 328 D2
Zamora *Michoacan, Mexico* 19°59N 102°16W 318 D4
Zamora *Spain* 41°30N 5°45W 194 D5
Zamora □ *Spain* 41°30N 5°46W 194 D5
Zamora → *Ecuador* 2°59S 78°13W 328 D2
Zamora-Chinchipe □ *Ecuador* 4°15S 78°50W 328 D2
Zamość *Poland* 50°43N 23°15E 185 H10
Zamtang *China* 32°26N 101°6E 228 A3
Zamuro, Sierra del *Venezuela* 4°0N 62°30W 329 C5
Zamzam, W. → *Libya* 30°58N 14°48E 258 B2
Zan *Ghana* 9°26N 0°17W 263 D4
Zanaga *Congo* 2°48S 13°48E 264 C2
Záncara → *Spain* 39°18N 3°18W 197 F1
Zanda *China* 31°32N 79°50E 218 E4
Zanderij *Suriname* 5°20N 55°16W 329 B6
Zandu *Dem. Rep. of the Congo* 5°11S 18°16E 265 D3
Zandvoort *Neths.* 52°22N 4°32E 170 B4
Zanesville *U.S.A.* 39°56N 82°1W 312 G2
Zanevka *Russia* 59°55N 30°31E 137 B3
Zangābād *Iran* 38°26N 46°44E 246 B5
Zangliveri *Greece* 40°36N 23°15E 202 F7
Zangoza = Sangüesa *Spain* 42°37N 1°17W 196 C3
Zangue → *Mozam.* 17°50S 35°21E 269 F4
Zanjān *Iran* 36°40N 48°35E 213 D13
Zanjān □ *Iran* 37°20N 49°30E 247 B6
Zanjān → *Iran* 37°8N 47°47E 247 B6
Zannone *Italy* 40°58N 13°3E 200 B6
Zanow = Sianów *Poland* 54°13N 16°18E 184 D3
Zante = Zakynthos *Greece* 37°47N 20°54E 207 D2
Zanthus *Australia* 31°2S 123°34E 279 F3
Zanzibar *Tanzania* 6°12S 39°12E 268 D4
Zanzūr *Libya* 32°55N 13°1E 258 B2
Zaouatallaz *Algeria* 24°52N 8°30E 261 D6
Zaouiet El-Kala = Bordj Omar Driss *Algeria* 28°10N 6°40E 261 C6
Zaouiet Reggâne *Algeria* 26°32N 0°3E 261 C5
Zaoyang *China* 32°10N 112°45E 229 A9
Zaozernyy *Kazakhstan* 53°6N 71°9E 217 B8
Zaozhuang *China* 34°50N 117°35E 227 G9
Zap Suyu = Zāb al Kabīr → *Iraq* 36°1N 43°24E 213 D10
Zapadna Morava → *Serbia* 43°38N 21°30E 202 C5
Zapadnaya Dvina = Daugava → *Latvia* 57°4N 24°3E 188 D3
Zapadnaya Dvina *Russia* 56°15N 32°3E 188 D7
Západné Beskydy *Europe* 49°30N 19°0E 181 B12
Zapadni Rodopi *Bulgaria* 41°50N 24°0E 202 E7
Západočeský □ *Czech Rep.* 49°35N 13°0E 180 B6
Zapala *Argentina* 39°0S 70°5W 336 A2
Zapaleri, Cerro *Bolivia* 22°49S 67°11W 334 A2
Zapata *U.S.A.* 26°55N 99°16W 314 H5
Zapatón → *Spain* 39°0N 6°49W 195 F4
Zapiga *Chile* 19°40S 69°55W 330 D4
Zapolyarnyy *Russia* 69°26N 30°51E 160 B24
Zapopán *Mexico* 20°43N 103°24W 318 C4
Zaporizhzhya *Ukraine* 47°50N 35°10E 189 J8
Zaporizhzhya □ *Ukraine* 46°55N 35°50E 189 J8
Zaporozhye = Zaporizhzhya *Ukraine* 47°50N 35°10E 189 J8
Zapote *Phil.* 14°27N 120°56E 127 C1
Zappeion *Athens, Greece* 112 c2
Zaqatala *Azerbaijan* 41°38N 46°35E 191 K8
Zara *Turkey* 39°58N 37°43E 212 C7
Zarafshon *Uzbekistan* 41°34N 64°12E 216 D6
Zaragoza *Colombia* 7°30N 74°52W 328 B3
Zaragoza *Coahuila, Mexico* 28°29N 100°55W 318 B4
Zaragoza *Nuevo León, Mexico* 23°58N 99°46W 319 C5
Zaragoza *Spain* 41°39N 0°53W 196 D4
Zaragoza □ *Spain* 41°35N 1°0W 196 D4
Zarand *Kermān, Iran* 30°46N 56°34E 247 D8
Zarand *Markazī, Iran* 35°18N 50°25E 247 C6
Zărandului, Munţii *Romania* 46°14N 22°7E 182 D7
Zaranj *Afghan.* 30°55N 61°55E 240 C1
Zarasai *Lithuania* 55°40N 26°20E 188 E4
Zárate *Argentina* 34°7S 59°0W 334 C4
Zarautz *Spain* 43°17N 2°10W 196 B2
Zaraysk *Russia* 54°48N 38°53E 188 E10
Zaraza *Venezuela* 9°21N 65°19W 329 B4
Zard, Kūh-e *Iran* 32°22N 50°4E 247 C6
Zarechye *Russia* 55°41N 37°22E 129 B2
Zāreh *Iran* 35°7N 49°9E 247 C6
Zari *Nigeria* 13°4N 12°45E 263 C7
Zaria *Nigeria* 11°0N 7°40E 263 C6
Zarineh → *Iran* 36°17N 46°26E 213 D12
Zarinsk *Russia* 53°43N 84°55E 217 B10
Żarki *Poland* 50°38N 19°23E 185 H6
Zarko *Greece* 39°38N 22°6E 204 B4
Zarneh *Iran* 33°55N 46°10E 246 C5
Zărneşti *Romania* 45°33N 25°18E 183 E10
Zaros *Greece* 35°8N 24°54E 207 E5
Żarów *Poland* 50°56N 16°29E 185 H3
Zarqā', Nahr az → *Jordan* 32°10N 35°37E 251 F6
Zarrīn *Iran* 32°46N 54°37E 247 C7
Zarrinābād *Iran* 36°25N 48°17E 213 D13
Zaruma *Ecuador* 3°40S 79°38W 328 D2
Żary *Poland* 51°37N 15°10E 185 G2
Zarza de Granadilla *Spain* 40°14N 6°3W 194 E4
Zarzaïtine *Algeria* 28°15N 9°34E 261 C6
Zarzal *Colombia* 4°24N 76°4W 328 C2
Zarzis *Tunisia* 33°31N 11°2E 258 B2
Zas *Spain* 43°4N 8°53W 194 B2
Zashaghan *Kazakhstan* 51°11N 51°20E 216 B4
Zaskar → *India* 34°13N 77°20E 243 B7
Zaskar Mts. *India* 33°15N 77°30E 243 C7
Zastavna *Ukraine* 48°31N 25°51E 183 B10
Zastron *S. Africa* 30°18S 27°7E 270 D4
Žatec *Czech Rep.* 50°20N 13°32E 180 A6
Zaterechnyy *Russia* 44°48N 45°11E 191 H7
Zatishye = Elektrostal *Russia* 55°41N 38°32E 188 E10
Zator *Poland* 49°59N 19°28E 185 J6
Zatyshshya *Ukraine* 47°20N 29°51E 183 C14
Zavala *Bos.-H.* 42°50N 17°59E 202 D1
Zavāreh *Iran* 33°29N 52°28E 247 C7
Zave *Zimbabwe* 17°6S 30°1E 271 A5
Zaventem *Belgium* 50°53N 4°28E 116 A2
Zavetnoye *Russia* 47°13N 43°50E 191 G6
Zavidovići *Bos.-H.* 44°27N 18°10E 182 F3
Zavitaya = Zavitinsk *Russia* 50°10N 129°20E 215 D13
Zavitinsk *Russia* 50°10N 129°20E 215 D13
Zavodovski I. *Antarctica* 56°0S 27°45W 151 B1
Zavodskoy = Komsomolskiy *Russia* 54°27N 45°33E 190 C7
Zavolzhsk *Russia* 57°30N 42°3E 190 B6
Zavolzhye = Zavolzhsk *Russia* 57°30N 42°3E 190 B6
Zavolzhye *Russia* 56°37N 43°26E 190 B6
Zawady *Poland* 52°10N 21°6E 142 B2
Zawadzkie *Poland* 50°37N 18°28E 185 H5
Zawichost *Poland* 50°48N 21°51E 185 H8
Zawidów *Poland* 51°1N 15°1E 185 G2
Zawiercie *Poland* 50°30N 19°24E 185 H6
Zāwīyah, J. az *Syria* 35°45N 36°35E 250 C7
Zāwiyat al Bayḍā = Al Bayḍā *Libya* 32°50N 21°44E 258 B4
Zāwiyat Masūs *Libya* 31°35N 21°1E 258 B4
Zâwiyet Abû Musallam *Egypt* 29°56N 31°9E 117 B1
Zawrā' Park *Iraq* 33°18N 44°23E 113 B2
Zâwyet Shammas *Egypt* 31°30N 26°37E 256 A2
Zâwyet Um el Rakham *Egypt* 31°18N 27°1E 256 A2
Zâwyet Ungeîla *Egypt* 31°23N 26°42E 256 A2
Zāyā *Iraq* 33°33N 44°13E 246 C5
Zāyandeh → *Iran* 32°35N 52°0E 247 C7
Zaymah *Si. Arabia* 21°37N 40°6E 248 B3
Zaysan *Kazakhstan* 47°28N 84°52E 217 C10
Zaysan Köli *Kazakhstan* 48°0N 83°0E 217 C10
Zayü *China* 28°48N 97°27E 228 C1
Zazafotsy *Madag.* 21°11S 46°21E 272 C2
Zāzamt, W. → *Libya* 30°29N 14°30E 258 B2
Zazir, O. → *Algeria* 22°0N 5°40E 261 D6
Zázrivá *Slovak Rep.* 49°16N 19°7E 181 B12
Zbarazh *Ukraine* 49°43N 25°44E 177 D13
Zbąszyń *Poland* 52°14N 15°56E 185 F2
Zbąszynek *Poland* 52°16N 15°51E 185 F2
Zblewo *Poland* 53°56N 18°19E 184 E5
Zbraslav *Czech Rep.* 49°58N 14°23E 135 C2
Zbruch → 48°32N 26°27E 183 B11
Zbuzany *Czech Rep.* 50°1N 14°17E 135 B1
Žďár nad Sázavov *Czech Rep.* 49°34N 15°57E 180 B8
Zdiby *Czech Rep.* 50°9N 14°27E 135 B2
Zdolbuniv *Ukraine* 50°30N 26°15E 177 C14
Ždrelo *Serbia* 44°16N 21°28E 202 B5
Zduńska Wola *Poland* 51°37N 18°59E 185 G5
Zduny *Poland* 51°39N 17°21E 185 G4
Zearing *U.S.A.* 42°10N 93°18W 310 B3
Zeballos *Canada* 49°59N 126°50W 296 D3
Zebbug *Malta* 35°52N 14°26E 206 F7
Zebbug *Gozo, Malta* 36°4N 14°14E 206 E6
Zebediela *S. Africa* 24°20S 29°17E 271 B4
Zebila *Ghana* 10°55N 0°30W 263 C4
Zebulon *U.S.A.* 33°6N 84°21W 316 B5
Zeebrugge *Belgium* 51°19N 3°12E 170 C3
Zeehan *Australia* 41°52S 145°25E 281 G4
Zeekoevlei *S. Africa* 34°4S 18°31E 118 B2
Zeeland *U.S.A.* 42°49N 86°1W 311 B10
Zeeland □ *Neths.* 51°30N 3°50E 170 C3
Zeelandia *St. Eustatius* 17°30N 62°59W 322 a
Zeerust *S. Africa* 25°31S 26°4E 270 C4
Ẕefat *Israel* 32°58N 35°29E 250 F6
Zegdou *Algeria* 29°51N 4°45W 260 C4
Zege *Ethiopia* 11°43N 37°18E 257 E4
Zeggerene, Iracher *Mali* 16°49N 2°16E 263 B5
Zégoua *Mali* 10°32N 5°35W 262 C3
Zehak *Iran* 30°53N 61°42E 247 D9
Zehden = Cedynia *Poland* 52°53N 14°12E 185 F1
Zehdenick *Germany* 52°58N 13°20E 178 C9
Zehlendorf *Germany* 52°26N 13°16E 115 B2
Zeigler *U.S.A.* 37°54N 89°3W 310 G7
Zeil, Mt. *Australia* 23°30S 132°23E 278 D5
Zeila = Saylac *Somali Rep.* 11°21N 43°30E 267 B5
Zeist *Neths.* 52°5N 5°15E 170 B5
Zeitz *Germany* 51°2N 12°7E 178 D8
Zejtun *Malta* 35°51N 14°32E 206 F8
Żelechów *Poland* 51°49N 21°54E 185 G8
Zelena *Ukraine* 48°3N 24°45E 183 B9
Zelengora *Bos.-H.* 43°22N 18°30E 202 C2
Zelenodolsk *Russia* 55°55N 48°30E 190 C9
Zelenogorsk *Russia* 60°12N 29°43E 188 B5
Zelenograd *Russia* 56°1N 37°12E 188 D9
Zelenogradsk *Russia* 54°53N 20°29E 184 D7
Zelenokumsk *Russia* 44°24N 44°0E 191 H6
Zeleqa, W. → *Egypt* 29°7N 34°31E 251 J5
Železná Ruda *Czech Rep.* 49°8N 13°15E 180 B6
Železnik *Serbia* 44°43N 20°23E 202 B4
Zelfana *Algeria* 32°27N 4°15E 261 B5
Zelienople *U.S.A.* 40°48N 80°8W 312 F4
Želiezovce *Slovak Rep.* 48°3N 18°40E 181 C11
Zelina *Croatia* 45°57N 16°16E 199 C13
Zell *Baden-W., Germany* 47°42N 7°52E 179 H3
Zell *Rhld-Pfz., Germany* 50°1N 7°10E 179 E3
Zell am See *Austria* 47°19N 12°47E 180 D5
Zella-Mehlis *Germany* 50°39N 10°40E 178 E6
Zelmen = Rovnoye *Russia* 50°52N 46°3E 190 E8
Zelów *Poland* 51°28N 19°14E 185 G6
Zeltweg *Austria* 47°11N 14°45E 180 D7
Zelyony Dol = Zelenodolsk *Russia* 55°55N 48°30E 190 C9
Žemaitijos △ *Lithuania* 56°2N 21°55E 184 B8
Zembra, I. *Tunisia* 37°5N 10°56E 258 A2
Zemgale = Jelgava *Latvia* 56°41N 23°49E 184 B10
Zémio *C.A.R.* 5°2N 25°5E 264 A5
Zemlya Imperatora Nikolaya II = Severnaya Zemlya *Russia* 79°0N 100°0E 215 B11
Zemmora *Algeria* 35°44N 0°51E 261 A5
Zemmur *W. Sahara* 25°5N 12°0W 260 C2
Zemongo ⌓ *C.A.R.* 6°45N 25°5E 264 A5
Zemoul, O. → *Algeria* 29°15N 7°0W 260 C3
Zempelburg = Sępólno Krajeńskie *Poland* 53°26N 17°30E 184 E4
Zempléni-hegység *Hungary* 48°25N 21°25E 182 B6
Zemplínska šírava *Slovak Rep.* 48°48N 22°0E 181 C15
Zempoala *Mexico* 19°27N 96°23W 319 D5
Zemun *Serbia* 44°51N 20°25E 202 B4
Zendeh Jān *Afghan.* 34°21N 61°45E 240 B1
Zengbé *Cameroon* 5°46N 13°4E 263 D7
Zengcheng *China* 23°13N 113°52E 229 F9
Zenica *Bos.-H.* 44°10N 17°57E 182 F2
Zenne → *Belgium* 51°4N 4°26E 116 A2
Zentsūji *Japan* 34°14N 133°47E 222 C5
Zenza → *Angola* 8°45S 13°24E 265 D2
Zenza do Itombe *Angola* 9°16S 14°13E 265 D2
Žepče *Bos.-H.* 44°28N 18°2E 182 F3
Zephyr Field *U.S.A.* 30°1N 90°5W 131 B1
Zephyrhills *U.S.A.* 28°14N 82°11W 317 G7
Zepu *China* 38°11N 77°16E 217 E9
Zeraf, Bahr ez → *South Sudan* 9°42N 30°52E 257 F3
Żerań *Poland* 52°18N 20°58E 142 B1
Zerbst *Germany* 51°58N 12°5E 178 D8
Zerhamra *Algeria* 29°58N 2°30W 261 C4
Żerków *Poland* 52°4N 17°32E 185 F4
Zermatt *Switz.* 46°2N 7°46E 179 J3
Zernez *Switz.* 46°42N 10°7E 179 J6
Zernograd *Russia* 46°52N 40°19E 191 G5
Zernovoy = Zernograd *Russia* 46°52N 40°19E 191 G5
Zero Milestone *Washington, D.C., U.S.A.* 143 b1
Zerqan *Albania* 41°27N 20°20E 202 E4
Zerzeń *Poland* 52°12N 21°7E 142 B2
Zestaponi *Georgia* 42°6N 43°0E 191 J6
Zetel *Germany* 53°25N 7°58E 178 B3
Zetland = Shetland □ *U.K.* 60°30N 1°30W 167 A7
Zeulenroda *Germany* 50°39N 11°59E 178 E7
Zévallos *Guadeloupe* 16°18N 61°17W 322 e
Zeven *Germany* 53°17N 9°16E 178 B5
Zevenaar *Neths.* 51°56N 6°5E 170 C6
Zévio *Italy* 45°22N 11°8E 198 C8
Zeya *Russia* 53°48N 127°14E 215 D13
Zeya → *Russia* 51°42N 128°53E 215 D13
Zeyne *Turkey* 36°25N 33°31E 250 B4
Zeytinbaği *Turkey* 40°24N 28°47E 203 F12
Zeytinburnu *Turkey* 40°58N 28°53E 122 C1
Zeytindağ *Turkey* 38°58N 27°4E 205 C9
Zghartā *Lebanon* 34°21N 35°53E 250 D6
Zgierz *Poland* 51°50N 19°27E 185 G6
Zgorzelec *Poland* 51°10N 15°0E 185 G2
Zguriţa *Moldova* 48°8N 28°1E 183 B13
Zhabei *China* 31°16N 121°26E 138 B1
Zhabinka *Belarus* 52°13N 24°2E 185 F11
Zhabokrych *Ukraine* 48°23N 28°59E 183 B13
Zhalaghash *Kazakhstan* 45°5N 64°40E 216 C6
Zhalpaqtal *Kazakhstan* 49°42N 49°25E 190 F9
Zhaltyr *Kazakhstan* 51°37N 69°49E 217 B7
Zhambyl = Taraz *Kazakhstan* 42°54N 71°22E 217 D8
Zhambyl □ *Kazakhstan* 44°0N 72°0E 217 D8
Zhanatas *Kazakhstan* 43°35N 69°35E 217 D7
Zhangaly *Kazakhstan* 47°1N 50°37E 191 G10
Zhangaözen *Kazakhstan* 43°18N 52°48E 187 F9
Zhangaqala *Kazakhstan* 48°56N 49°36E 191 F9
Zhangaqazaly *Kazakhstan* 45°48N 62°6E 216 C6
Zhangatas = Zhanatas *Kazakhstan* 43°35N 69°35E 217 D7
Zhangbei *China* 41°10N 114°45E 226 D8
Zhangguangcai Ling *China* 45°0N 129°0E 227 B15
Zhangjiabian *China* 22°33N 113°28E 219 a
Zhangjiagang *China* 31°55N 120°30E 229 B13
Zhangjiakou *China* 40°48N 114°55E 226 D8
Zhangping *China* 25°17N 117°23E 229 E11
Zhangpu *China* 24°8N 117°35E 229 E11
Zhangshu *China* 28°4N 115°29E 229 C10
Zhangye *China* 38°50N 100°23E 218 D9
Zhangzhou *China* 24°30N 117°35E 229 E11
Zhanhua *China* 37°40N 118°8E 227 F10
Zhänibek *Kazakhstan* 49°25N 46°50E 190 F8
Zhanjiang *China* 21°15N 110°20E 229 G8
Zhannetty, Ostrov *Russia* 76°43N 158°0E 215 B16
Zhanyi *China* 25°38N 103°48E 228 E4
Zhanyu *China* 44°30N 122°30E 227 B12
Zhao Xian *China* 37°43N 114°45E 226 F8
Zhao'an *China* 23°41N 117°10E 229 F11
Zhaocheng *China* 36°22N 111°38E 226 F6
Zhaojue *China* 28°1N 102°49E 228 C4
Zhaoping *China* 24°11N 110°48E 229 E8
Zhaoqing *China* 23°0N 112°20E 229 F9
Zhaotong *China* 27°20N 103°44E 228 D4
Zhaoyang Hu *China* 35°4N 116°47E 226 G9
Zhaoyuan *Heilongjiang, China* 45°27N 125°0E 227 B13
Zhaoyuan *Shandong, China* 37°20N 120°23E 227 F11
Zhari Namco *China* 31°6N 85°36E 218 E6
Zharkent *Kazakhstan* 44°10N 80°0E 217 D10
Zharkovskiy *Russia* 55°56N 32°19E 188 E7
Zhashkiv *Ukraine* 49°15N 30°5E 177 D16
Zhashui *China* 33°40N 109°8E 226 H5
Zhaslyk *Uzbekistan* 43°58N 57°10E 216 D5
Zhayrang *Kazakhstan* 48°20N 70°10E 217 C8
Zhayylma *Kazakhstan* 51°37N 61°33E 216 B6
Zhayyq → *Kazakhstan* 47°0N 51°48E 187 E9
Zhdanov = Mariupol *Ukraine* 47°5N 37°31E 189 J9
Zhdanov *Russia* 55°44N 37°41E 129 B4
Zhecheng *China* 34°7N 115°20E 226 G8
Zhegao *China* 31°46N 117°45E 229 B11
Zhejiang □ *China* 29°0N 120°0E 229 C13
Zheleznodorozhnyy = Qŭnghirot *Uzbekistan* 43°2N 58°50E 216 D5
Zheleznodorozhnyy *Kaliningrad, Russia* 54°22N 21°19E 184 D8
Zheleznodorozhnyy *Komi, Russia* 62°35N 50°55E 186 B9
Zheleznodorozhnyy *Moskva, Russia* 55°45N 38°0E 129 B6
Zheleznogorsk *Russia* 52°22N 35°23E 189 F8
Zheleznogorsk-Ilimskiy *Russia* 56°34N 104°8E 215 D11
Zheltyye Vody = Zhovti Vody *Ukraine* 48°21N 33°31E 189 H7
Zhen'an *China* 33°27N 109°9E 228 A7
Zhenba *China* 32°34N 107°58E 228 A6
Zhenfeng *China* 25°22N 105°40E 228 E5
Zheng'an *China* 28°32N 107°27E 228 C6
Zhengding *China* 38°8N 114°32E 226 E8
Zhenghe *China* 27°20N 118°50E 229 D12
Zhengyang *China* 32°37N 114°22E 229 A10
Zhengyangguan *China* 32°30N 116°29E 229 A11
Zhengzhou *China* 34°45N 113°34E 226 G7
Zhenhai *China* 29°59N 121°42E 229 C13
Zhenjiang *China* 32°11N 119°26E 229 A12
Zhenkang *China* 23°58N 99°0E 228 F2
Zhenlai *China* 45°50N 123°5E 227 B12
Zhenning *China* 26°4N 105°45E 228 D5
Zhenping *Henan, China* 33°10N 112°16E 226 H7
Zhenping *Shaanxi, China* 31°59N 109°31E 228 B7
Zhenru *China* 31°16N 121°22E 138 B1
Zhenxiong *China* 27°27N 104°50E 228 D5
Zhenyuan *Gansu, China* 35°35N 107°30E 226 G4
Zhenyuan *Guizhou, China* 27°4N 108°21E 228 D7
Zhenyuan *Yunnan, China* 23°51N 100°59E 228 F3
Zherdevka *Russia* 51°56N 41°29E 190 E5
Zherebkove *Ukraine* 47°50N 29°52E 183 C14
Zhernovka *Russia* 59°56N 30°30E 137 B2
Zherong *China* 27°15N 119°52E 229 D12
Zhetiqara *Kazakhstan* 52°11N 61°12E 216 B6
Zhezdi *Kazakhstan* 48°3N 67°3E 217 C7
Zhezqazghan *Kazakhstan* 47°44N 67°40E 217 C7
Zhicheng *China* 30°25N 111°27E 229 B8
Zhicun *China* 23°0N 113°18E 121 B2
Zhidan *China* 36°48N 108°48E 226 F5
Zhigansk *Russia* 66°48N 123°27E 215 C13
Zhigulevsk *Russia* 53°28N 49°30E 190 D9
Zhijiang *Hubei, China* 30°28N 111°45E 229 B8
Zhijiang *Hunan, China* 27°27N 109°42E 228 D7
Zhijin *China* 26°37N 105°45E 228 D5
Zhilinda *Russia* 70°0N 114°20E 215 C12
Zhilino *Russia* 54°54N 21°54E 184 D8
Zhirnovsk *Russia* 50°57N 44°49E 190 E7
Zhirnovsky = Zhirnovsk *Russia* 50°57N 44°49E 190 E7
Zhirnoye = Zhirnovsk *Russia* 50°57N 44°49E 190 E7
Zhitomir = Zhytomyr *Ukraine* 50°20N 28°40E 177 C15
Zhizdra *Russia* 53°45N 34°40E 188 F8
Zhlobin *Belarus* 52°55N 30°0E 177 B16
Zhmerynka *Ukraine* 49°2N 28°2E 177 D15
Zhob *Pakistan* 31°20N 69°31E 242 D3
Zhob → *Pakistan* 32°4N 69°50E 242 C3
Zhodzina *Belarus* 54°5N 28°17E 177 A15
Zhokhova, Ostrov *Russia* 76°4N 152°40E 215 B16
Zholkev = Zhovkva *Ukraine* 50°4N 23°58E 177 C12
Zholkva = Zhovkva *Ukraine* 50°4N 23°58E 177 C12
Zhongba *China* 29°39N 84°10E 218 F5
Zhongdian *China* 27°48N 99°42E 228 D2
Zhongdong *China* 22°48N 107°47E 228 F6
Zhongdu *China* 24°40N 109°40E 228 E7
Zhongguancun *China* 39°59N 116°18E 114 B1
Zhongjiang *China* 30°53N 104°46E 228 B5
Zhongning *China* 37°29N 105°40E 226 F3
Zhongshan *Antarctica* 69°0S 39°50E 151 C6
Zhongshan *Guangdong, China* 22°26N 113°20E 229 F9
Zhongshan *Guangxi Zhuangzu, China* 24°29N 111°18E 229 E8
Zhongshan Park *Beijing, China* 114 c3
Zhongshan Park *Shanghai, China* 31°13N 121°24E 138 B1
Zhongshankong *China* 22°35N 113°29E 219 a
Zhongtiao Shan *China* 35°0N 111°10E 226 G6
Zhongwei *China* 37°30N 105°12E 226 F3
Zhongxian *China* 30°18N 107°58E 228 B6
Zhongxiang *China* 31°12N 112°34E 229 B9
Zhongyang *China* 37°20N 111°11E 226 F6
Zhorany *Ukraine* 51°19N 23°58E 185 G10
Zhosaly *Kazakhstan* 45°29N 64°4E 216 C6
Zhoucun *Guangdong, China* 23°11N 113°11E 121 A2
Zhoucun *Shandong, China* 36°47N 117°48E 227 F9
Zhoujiadu *China* 31°11N 121°29E 138 B1
Zhoujiazhen *China* 31°16N 121°33E 138 B2
Zhoukou *China* 33°38N 114°38E 226 H8
Zhoukoudian *China* 39°41N 115°56E 226 E8
Zhouning *China* 27°12N 119°20E 229 D12
Zhoushan *China* 30°1N 122°6E 229 B14
Zhoushan Dao *China* 30°5N 122°10E 229 C14
Zhouzhi *China* 34°10N 108°12E 226 G5
Zhouzhuangzi *China* 39°51N 116°16E 114 B1
Zhovkva *Ukraine* 50°4N 23°58E 177 C12
Zhovti Vody *Ukraine* 48°21N 33°31E 189 H7
Zhovtneve *Lubelskie, Ukraine* 50°42N 24°12E 185 H11
Zhovtneve *Mykolayiv, Ukraine* 46°54N 32°3E 189 J7
Zhu Jiang → *China* 22°45N 113°37E 229 F9
Zhuanghe *China* 39°40N 123°0E 224 C1
Zhucheng *China* 36°0N 119°27E 227 G10
Zhugqu *China* 33°40N 104°30E 226 H3
Zhuhai *China* 22°17N 113°34E 229 F9
Zhuji *China* 29°40N 120°10E 229 C13
Zhujiang Kou *China* 22°20N 113°45E 219 a
Zhukovka *Russia* 53°35N 33°50E 188 F7
Zhulebino *Russia* 55°42N 37°50E 129 B5
Zhumadian *China* 32°59N 114°2E 229 A10
Zhuo Xian = Zhuozhou *China* 39°28N 115°58E 226 E8
Zhuolu *China* 40°20N 115°12E 226 D8
Zhuozhou *China* 39°28N 115°58E 226 E8
Zhuozi *China* 41°0N 112°25E 226 D7
Zhushadi *China* 23°11N 113°22E 121 A3
Zhushan *China* 32°15N 110°13E 229 A8
Zhuxi *China* 32°25N 109°40E 228 A7
Zhuzhou *China* 27°49N 113°12E 229 D9
Zhvanets *Ukraine* 48°33N 26°30E 183 B11
Zhympīty *Kazakhstan* 50°16N 52°35E 216 B4
Zhytomyr *Ukraine* 50°20N 28°40E 177 C15
Zhytomyr □ *Ukraine* 50°50N 28°10E 177 C14
Zi Shui → *China* 28°40N 112°40E 229 C9
Žiar nad Hronom *Slovak Rep.* 48°35N 18°53E 181 C11
Ziarat *Pakistan* 30°25N 67°49E 242 D2
Zibo *China* 36°47N 118°3E 227 F10
Zichang *China* 37°18N 109°40E 226 F5
Zidarovo *Bulgaria* 42°20N 27°24E 203 D11
Zidi = Wandhari *Pakistan* 27°42N 66°48E 242 F2
Ziębice *Poland* 50°37N 17°2E 185 H4
Ziebingen = Cybinka *Poland* 52°12N 14°46E 185 F1
Ziegenhals = Głuchołazy *Poland* 50°19N 17°24E 185 H4
Zielenzig = Sulęcin *Poland* 52°26N 15°10E 185 F2
Zielona *Poland* 52°14N 21°11E 142 B3
Zielona Góra *Poland* 51°57N 15°31E 185 G2
Zielonka *Poland* 52°18N 21°9E 142 B2
Zierikzee *Neths.* 51°40N 3°55E 170 C3
Ziesar *Germany* 52°16N 12°17E 178 C8
Zifta *Egypt* 30°43N 31°14E 256 H7
Zīghan *Libya* 25°29N 22°8E 258 C4
Zigon *Burma* 18°20N 95°37E 241 F5
Zigong *China* 29°15N 104°48E 228 C5
Ziguéy *Chad* 14°43N 15°50E 259 F3
Ziguinchor *Senegal* 12°35N 16°20W 262 C1
Ziguinchor □ *Senegal* 12°45N 16°20W 262 C1
Zihuatanejo *Mexico* 17°39N 101°33W 318 D4
Zijin *China* 23°33N 115°8E 229 F10
Zile *Turkey* 40°15N 35°52E 212 B6
Žilina *Slovak Rep.* 49°12N 18°42E 181 B11
Žilinský □ *Slovak Rep.* 49°10N 19°0E 181 B12
Zillah *Libya* 28°30N 17°33E 258 C3
Zillertaler Alpen *Austria* 47°6N 11°45E 180 D4
Zima *Russia* 54°0N 102°5E 215 D11
Zimapán *Mexico* 20°45N 99°21W 319 C5
Zimba *Zambia* 17°20S 26°11E 269 F2
Zimbabwe *Zimbabwe* 20°16S 30°54E 269 G3
Zimbabwe ■ *Africa* 19°0S 30°0E 269 F3
Zimmi *S. Leone* 7°20N 11°20W 262 D2
Zimnicea *Romania* 43°40N 25°22E 183 G10
Zimovniki *Russia* 47°10N 42°25E 191 G6
Zina *Cameroon* 11°19N 14°54E 259 F2
Zinave △ *Mozam.* 21°35S 33°40E 271 B5
Zinder *Niger* 13°48N 9°0E 259 F1
Zinder □ *Niger* 15°0N 10°30E 263 C7
Zinga *C.A.R.* 3°49N 18°34E 264 B3
Zinga *Tanzania* 9°16S 38°49E 269 D4
Zingaro ⌓ *Italy* 38°6N 12°53E 200 D5
Zingst *Germany* 54°26N 12°39E 178 A8
Ziniaré *Burkina Faso* 12°35N 1°18W 263 C4
Zinnowitz *Germany* 54°4N 13°54E 178 A9
Zinovyevsk = Kirovohrad *Ukraine* 48°35N 32°20E 189 H7
Zion *St. Kitts & Nevis* 17°8N 62°33W 322 d
Zion *Ill., U.S.A.* 42°27N 87°50W 311 B9
Zion △ *U.S.A.* 37°15N 113°5W 305 H7
Zionsville *U.S.A.* 39°57N 86°16W 311 E10
Zipaquirá *Colombia* 5°0N 74°0W 328 C3
Zirbitzkogel *Austria* 47°4N 14°34E 180 D7
Zirc *Hungary* 47°17N 17°52E 182 C2
Žiri *Slovenia* 46°5N 14°5E 199 B11
Žirje *Croatia* 43°39N 15°42E 199 E12
Zirke = Sieraków *Poland* 52°39N 16°2E 185 F3
Zirl *Austria* 47°17N 11°14E 180 D4
Zirndorf *Germany* 49°27N 10°57E 179 F6
Ziros *Greece* 35°5N 26°8E 207 E7
Zirreh, Gowd-e *Afghan.* 29°45N 62°0E 240 C1
Zisterdorf *Austria* 48°33N 16°45E 181 C9
Zitácuaro *Mexico* 19°24N 100°22W 318 D4
Žitava → *Slovak Rep.* 48°14N 18°21E 181 C11
Žitište *Serbia* 45°30N 20°32E 182 E5
Zitong *China* 31°37N 105°10E 228 B5
Zitsa *Greece* 39°47N 20°40E 204 B2
Zittau *Germany* 50°53N 14°48E 178 E10
Zitundo *Mozam.* 26°48S 32°47E 271 C5
Živinice *Bos.-H.* 44°27N 18°36E 182 F3
Ziwa Magharibа = Kagera □ *Tanzania* 2°0S 31°30E 268 C3
Ziway *Ethiopia* 7°56N 38°43E 266 C4
Ziway, L. *Ethiopia* 8°0N 38°50E 257 F4
Zixi *China* 27°45N 117°4E 229 D11
Zixing *China* 25°59N 113°21E 229 E9
Ziyang *Shaanxi, China* 32°32N 108°31E 226 H5
Ziyang *Sichuan, China* 30°6N 104°40E 228 B5
Ziyuan *China* 26°2N 110°40E 229 D8
Ziyun *China* 25°45N 106°5E 228 E6
Ziz, Oued → *Morocco* 31°40N 4°15W 260 B4
Zizhong *China* 29°48N 104°47E 228 C5
Zizhuyuan Park *China* 39°54N 116°18E 114 B1
Žižkov *Czech Rep.* 50°5N 14°28E 135 B2
Zizur Mayor *Spain* 42°47N 1°41W 196 C3
Zlarin *Croatia* 43°42N 15°49E 199 E12
Zlatar *Croatia* 46°5N 16°3E 199 B13
Zlatar *Serbia* 43°25N 19°47E 202 C3
Zlataritsa *Bulgaria* 43°2N 25°55E 203 C9
Zlaté Moravce *Slovak Rep.* 48°23N 18°24E 181 C11
Zlatibor *Serbia* 43°45N 19°43E 202 C3
Zlatitsa *Bulgaria* 42°41N 24°7E 203 D8
Zlatna *Romania* 46°8N 23°11E 183 D8
Zlatna Panega *Bulgaria* 43°5N 24°9E 203 C8
Zlatni Pyasŭtsi *Bulgaria* 43°17N 28°3E 203 C12
Zlatograd *Bulgaria* 41°22N 25°7E 203 E9
Zlatoust *Russia* 55°10N 59°40E 186 C10
Zletovo *Macedonia* 41°59N 22°17E 202 E6
Zličín *Czech Rep.* 50°3N 14°17E 135 B1
Zlín *Czech Rep.* 49°14N 17°40E 181 B10
Zlínský □ *Czech Rep.* 49°20N 17°40E 181 B10
Ẓlīṭan *Libya* 32°32N 14°35E 258 B2
Złocieniec *Poland* 53°30N 16°1E 184 E3
Złoczew *Poland* 51°24N 18°35E 185 G5
Zlot *Serbia* 44°1N 21°58E 202 B5
Złotoryja *Poland* 51°8N 15°55E 185 G2
Złotów *Poland* 53°22N 17°2E 184 E4
Zmeinogorsk *Kazakhstan* 51°10N 82°13E 217 B10
Żmigród *Poland* 51°28N 16°53E 185 G3
Zmiyev *Ukraine* 49°39N 36°27E 189 H9
Znamenka = Znamyanka *Ukraine* 48°45N 32°30E 189 H7
Znamensk *Russia* 54°36N 21°16E 184 D8
Znamyanka *Ukraine* 48°45N 32°30E 189 H7
Żnin *Poland* 52°51N 17°44E 185 F4
Znojmo *Czech Rep.* 48°50N 16°2E 180 C9
Zobeyrī *Iran* 34°10N 46°40E 246 C5
Zobia *Dem. Rep. of the Congo* 3°0N 25°59E 268 B2
Zobten = Sobótka *Poland* 50°54N 16°44E 185 H3
Zócalo *Mexico City, Mexico* 128 b3
Zoetermeer *Neths.* 52°3N 4°30E 170 B4
Zogang *China* 29°55N 97°42E 228 C1
Zogno *Italy* 45°48N 9°40E 198 C6
Zografou *Greece* 37°58N 23°47E 112 B2
Zohreh → *Iran* 30°16N 51°15E 247 D6
Zolfo Springs *U.S.A.* 27°30N 81°48W 317 H8
Żoliborz *Poland* 52°16N 20°57E 142 B1
Zolochiv *Ukraine* 49°45N 24°51E 177 D13
Zolotonosha *Ukraine* 49°39N 32°5E 189 H7
Zolotyy Potik *Ukraine* 48°54N 25°20E 183 B10
Zomba *Malawi* 15°22S 35°19E 269 F4
Zongo *Dem. Rep. of the Congo* 4°20N 18°35E 264 B3
Zonguldak *Turkey* 41°28N 31°50E 212 B4
Zonguldak □ *Turkey* 41°20N 31°45E 212 B4
Zongyang *China* 30°42N 117°12E 229 B11
Zonnebloem *S. Africa* 33°56S 18°26E 118 A1
Zonqor Pt. *Malta* 35°52N 14°34E 206 F8
Zonza *France* 41°45N 9°11E 175 G13
Zoo Baba *Niger* 18°13N 13°2E 259 E2
Zorgo *Burkina Faso* 12°15N 0°35W 263 C4
Zorita *Spain* 39°17N 5°39W 195 F5
Zorleni *Romania* 46°14N 27°44E 183 D12
Zornitsa *Bulgaria* 42°23N 26°58E 203 D10
Zorritos *Peru* 3°43S 80°40W 330 A1
Żory *Poland* 50°3N 18°44E 185 H5
Zorzor *Liberia* 7°46N 9°28W 262 D3
Zossen *Germany* 52°13N 13°27E 178 C9
Zou Xiang *China* 35°30N 116°58E 226 G9
Zouan-Hounien *Ivory C.* 6°55N 8°15W 262 D3
Zouar *Chad* 20°30N 16°32E 259 D3
Zouérate = Zouîrât *Mauritania* 22°44N 12°21W 260 D2
Zouîrât *Mauritania* 22°44N 12°21W 260 D2
Zouri *Gabon* 1°1S 8°53E 264 C1
Zourika *Niger* 19°16N 7°52E 259 E1
Zourma *Burkina Faso* 11°20N 0°50W 263 C4
Zousfana, O. → *Algeria* 31°28N 2°17W 261 B4
Zoutkamp *Neths.* 53°20N 6°18E 170 A6
Zrenjanin *Serbia* 45°22N 20°23E 182 E5
Zuarungu *Ghana* 10°49N 0°46W 263 C4
Zuatá → *Venezuela* 7°52N 65°22W 329 B4
Zuba *Nigeria* 9°11N 7°12E 263 D6
Zubayr *Yemen* 15°3N 42°10E 248 D3
Zubin Potok *Kosovo* 42°54N 20°41E 202 D4
Zubtsov *Russia* 56°10N 34°34E 188 D8
Zudañez *Bolivia* 19°6S 64°44W 331 D5
Zuénoula *Ivory C.* 7°34N 6°3W 262 D3
Zuera *Spain* 41°51N 0°49W 196 D4
Zuetina = Az Zuwaytīnah *Libya* 30°58N 20°7E 258 B4
Ẓufār *Oman* 17°40N 54°0E 249 C6
Zug *Switz.* 47°10N 8°31E 179 H4
Zug *W. Sahara* 21°36N 14°9W 260 D2
Zugdidi *Georgia* 42°30N 41°55E 191 J5
Zugersee *Switz.* 47°7N 8°35E 179 H4
Zugliget *Hungary* 47°30N 18°59E 117 B1
Zugló *Hungary* 47°31N 19°8E 117 A2
Zugspitze *Germany* 47°25N 10°59E 179 H6
Zuhd, J. az *Si. Arabia* 28°20N 35°17E 251 K6
Zuid-Holland □ *Neths.* 52°0N 4°35E 170 C4
Zuidbeveland *Neths.* 51°30N 3°50E 170 C3
Zuiderwoude *Neths.* 52°26N 5°2E 112 A3
Zuidhorn *Neths.* 53°15N 6°23E 170 A6
Zújar *Spain* 37°34N 2°50W 195 H8
Zújar → *Spain* 39°1N 5°47W 195 G5
Żukowo *Poland* 54°21N 18°22E 184 D5
Zula *Eritrea* 15°17N 39°40E 257 D4
Zulia □ *Venezuela* 10°0N 72°10W 328 B3
Züllichau = Sulechów *Poland* 52°5N 15°40E 185 F2
Zülpich *Germany* 50°41N 6°39E 178 E2
Zülz = Biała *Poland* 50°24N 17°40E 185 H4
Zumaia *Spain* 43°19N 2°15W 196 B2
Zumárraga *Spain* 43°5N 2°19W 196 B2
Zumbi *Brazil* 22°49S 43°10W 135 A1
Zumbo *Mozam.* 15°35S 30°26E 269 F3
Zummo *Nigeria* 9°51N 12°59E 263 D7
Zumpango *Mexico* 19°48N 99°6W 319 D5
Zunderdorp *Neths.* 52°24N 4°58E 112 A2
Zundi *Angola* 10°28S 16°48E 265 E3
Zungeru *Nigeria* 9°48N 6°8E 263 D6
Zunhua *China* 40°18N 117°58E 227 D9
Zuni Pueblo *U.S.A.* 35°4N 108°51W 305 J9
Zunyi *China* 27°42N 106°53E 228 D6
Zuo Jiang → *China* 22°50N 108°6E 228 F6
Zuoquan *China* 37°1N 113°27E 226 F7
Zuozhou *China* 22°42N 107°27E 228 F6
Županja *Croatia* 45°4N 18°43E 182 E3
Žur *Kosovo* 42°13N 20°34E 202 D4
Zurbātīyah *Iraq* 33°9N 46°3E 213 F12
Zürich *Switz.* 47°22N 8°32E 179 H4
Zürich □ *Switz.* 47°26N 8°40E 179 H4
Zürichsee *Switz.* 47°18N 8°40E 179 H4
Żuromin *Poland* 53°4N 19°51E 185 E6
Zurrieq *Malta* 35°50N 14°28E 206 F7
Žut *Croatia* 43°52N 15°17E 199 E12
Zutphen *Neths.* 52°9N 6°12E 170 B6
Zuurberg △ *S. Africa* 33°12S 25°32E 270 D4
Zuvuvu → *Brazil* 23°40S 46°42W 137 C1
Zuwārah *Libya* 32°58N 12°1E 258 B2
Zūzan *Iran* 34°22N 59°53E 247 C8
Žužemberk *Slovenia* 45°52N 14°56E 199 C11
Zvanka = Volkhov *Russia* 59°55N 32°15E 188 C7
Zvečan *Kosovo* 42°54N 20°50E 202 D4
Zvenigorodka = Svenyhorodka *Ukraine* 49°4N 30°56E 189 H6
Zvezdets *Bulgaria* 42°6N 27°26E 203 D11
Zvishavane *Zimbabwe* 20°17S 30°2E 269 G3
Zvolen *Slovak Rep.* 48°33N 19°10E 181 C12
Zvonce *Serbia* 42°57N 22°34E 202 D6
Zvornik *Bos.-H.* 44°26N 19°5E 182 F4
Zwanenburg *Neths.* 52°23N 4°45E 112 A1
Zwedru = Tchien *Liberia* 5°59N 8°15W 262 D3
Zweibrücken *Germany* 49°15N 7°21E 179 F3
Zwenkau *Germany* 51°13N 12°20E 178 D8
Zwettl *Austria* 48°35N 15°9E 180 C8
Zwickau *Germany* 50°44N 12°30E 178 E8
Zwierzyniec *Poland* 50°36N 22°58E 185 H9
Zwiesel *Germany* 49°1N 13°13E 179 F9
Zwittau = Svitavy *Czech Rep.* 49°47N 16°28E 181 B9
Zwoleń *Poland* 51°21N 21°36E 185 G8
Zwölfaxing *Austria* 48°6N 16°28E 142 B2
Zwolle *Neths.* 52°31N 6°6E 170 B6
Zwolle *La., U.S.A.* 31°38N 93°39W 314 F8
Żychlin *Poland* 52°15N 19°37E 185 F6
Żyrardów *Poland* 52°3N 20°28E 185 F7
Zyryan *Kazakhstan* 49°43N 84°20E 217 C10
Zyryanka *Russia* 65°45N 150°51E 215 C16
Zyryanovsk = Zyryan *Kazakhstan* 49°43N 84°20E 217 C10
Zyuzino *Russia* 55°39N 37°34E 129 C3
Żywiec *Poland* 49°42N 19°10E 185 J6

KEY TO EUROPEAN MAP PAGES

■ Large scale maps
(>1:3 900 000)

■ Medium scale maps
(1:4 000 000 – 1:7 900 000)

■ Small scale maps
(<1:8 000 000)

● Paris p134   City maps

155 ICELAND

160 Færoe Is.

165

167 Shetland Is.

167 Orkney Is.

166

168 Edinburgh p121

176

170

UNITED KINGDOM

Dublin p120

IRELAND

192

171 London p125

172

174 FRAN

194

196

ANDORRA

Barcelona p114

PORTUGAL

SPAIN

Madrid p127

206

Lisbon p126

Balear

Arctic Circle

MOROCCO   AL

WORLD COUNTRY INDEX

Afghanistan	240
Albania	202
Algeria	260–261
Angola	265
Argentina	334, 336
Armenia	213
Australia	278–283
Austria	180–181
Azerbaijan	213
Azores	153
Bahamas	320–321
Bahrain	249
Bangladesh	241
Barbados	322
Belarus	188–189
Belgium	170
Belize	320
Benin	263
Bhutan	241
Bolivia	330–331
Bosnia-Herzegovina	198, 202
Botswana	270
Brazil	328–335
Brunei	235
Bulgaria	202–203
Burkina Faso	262–263
Burma (Myanmar)	236–237, 241
Burundi	268
Cambodia	236–237
Canary Is.	153
Cameroon	259, 264
Canada	294–299
Cape Verde Is.	153
Central African Republic	264
Chad	259
Chile	330, 334, 336
China	218–219, 226–229
Colombia	328
Comoros	272
Congo	264–265
Congo, Dem. Rep. of the	264–265, 268–269
Costa Rica	320
Croatia	182, 199
Cuba	320–321
Cyprus	207
Czech Republic	180–181
Denmark	163
Djibouti	267
Dominican Republic	321
Ecuador	328
Egypt	256
El Salvador	320
England	168–169
Equatorial Guinea	264
Eritrea	266–267
Estonia	188
Ethiopia	266–267
Fiji	287
Finland	160–161
France	172–175
French Guiana	329
Gabon	264
Gambia	262
Georgia	213

Germany	178–179
Ghana	262–263
Greece	202–205
Greenland	154
Guadeloupe	322
Guatemala	320
Guinea	262
Guinea-Bissau	262
Guyana	329
Haiti	321
Honduras	320
Hungary	182
Iceland	155
India	241, 242–245
Indonesia	230–231, 234–235
Iran	246–247
Iraq	246–247
Irish Republic	166
Israel	250–251
Italy	198–201
Ivory Coast	262
Jamaica	320
Japan	220–223
Jordan	251
Kazakhstan	216–217
Kenya	268
Korea, North	224
Korea, South	224
Kosovo	202
Kuwait	246–247
Kyrgyzstan	217
Laos	236
Latvia	188
Lebanon	250
Lesotho	271
Liberia	262
Libya	258
Lithuania	188
Luxembourg	170
Macedonia	202
Madagascar	272
Malawi	269
Malaysia	234–235
Mali	260–263
Malta	206
Martinique	322
Mauritania	260, 262
Mauritius	272
Mexico	318–319
Moldova	183
Mongolia	218–219
Montenegro	202
Morocco	260–261
Mozambique	269, 271
Namibia	270
Nepal	243
Netherlands	170
New Zealand	284–285
Nicaragua	320
Niger	259, 263
Nigeria	263
Northern Ireland	166
Norway	160–161, 164

Oman	249
Pakistan	240
Panama	320
Papua New Guinea	286
Paraguay	334–335
Peru	328, 330
Philippines	232–233
Poland	184–185
Portugal	194–195
Puerto Rico	321
Qatar	249
Réunion	272
Romania	182–183
Russia	186–191, 214–215
Rwanda	268
Samoa	287
Saudi Arabia	246–249
Scotland	167
Senegal	262
Serbia	182, 202
Seychelles	272
Sierra Leone	262
Singapore	237
Slovak Republic	181
Slovenia	199
Solomon Is.	287
Somali Republic	267
South Africa	270–271
Spain	194–197
Sri Lanka	245
Sudan	256–257
Sudan, South	257
Suriname	329
Swaziland	271
Sweden	160–163
Switzerland	179
Syria	212–213
Taiwan	225
Tajikistan	217
Tanzania	268–269
Thailand	236–237
Togo	263
Tonga	287
Trinidad and Tobago	323
Tunisia	261
Turkey	212–213
Turkmenistan	216–217
Uganda	268
Ukraine	189
United Arab Emirates	249
United Kingdom	166–169
USA	300–317
Uruguay	334–335
Uzbekistan	216–217
Vanuatu	287
Venezuela	328–329
Vietnam	236–237
Wales	168–169
Yemen	248–249
Zambia	265, 269
Zimbabwe	269